CONCORDANCE
to the
Good News Bible

CONCORDANCE

to the Good News Bible

Editor David Robinson

Assistant Editor L. Jane Rowley

The Bible Societies

Bible Text from the Good News Bible (Today's English Version),
British usage edition first published 1976

BFBS/1983/TEV733

ISBN 0 564 07202 8

Text set by computer by C.R. Barber and Partners, Wrotham, Kent

Printed in Great Britain by
St Edmundsbury Press, Bury St Edmunds, Suffolk

Published by The British and Foreign Bible Society (Publishing Division), Stonehill Green,
Westlea, SWINDON SN5 7DG

CONTENTS

PREFACE vii

HOW TO USE THE CONCORDANCE ix

CONCORDANCE TO THE GOOD NEWS BIBLE C1–C1333

NUMERICS C1334–C1347

CONCORDANCE OF BIBLICAL NAMES N1–N23

THEMATIC INDEX T1–T25

DEDICATION

To the greater glory of God
and in tribute to Robert Young,
whose concordance of 1879
sets our standard today.

ACKNOWLEDGEMENTS

The editors wish to thank all who have contributed in various ways to the production of this volume, and in particular Gwen Anderson, Ian Crookston, John Elwolde, Hazel Medcalf, David Mowbray, Brynmor Price, David Rooke, Joanna Stringer and Elsa Turceninoff.

Special praise is due to C.R. Barber and Partners for their computing and typesetting skills. The main responsibility for computer processing has lain with Peter Bush, for whose patience and dedication we are most grateful.

D.W.C.R.
L.J.R.

PREFACE

It used to take decades to compile a concordance to the Bible. Diligent, scholarly men laboured for years to list every reference by hand. The *Concordance to the Good News Bible* has been produced with the help of a computer. This preface tells you something of the way in which this modern tool has made it possible to produce a concordance quickly and comprehensively. Scholarship and diligence remain essential, but they have been joined by imaginative use of new technology.

The *Good News Bible* text was fed into a computer which was programmed to identify each unique word and group of words within the text, and to count and list how each one occurred within the whole Bible. This provided a basis from which the editors could work. The computer listing of unique words and phrases was then reduced by the elimination of such words as "the", "and", "of" and so on. The editing process which followed, with its application of discretion and judgement, was the most crucial, and longest, part of the production process.

The list of unique words and groups of words was next fed back into the computer. Then the computer was programmed to print twelve words of context around each unique word or phrase, for each of its occurrences within the Bible. This was the basic file from which all the Concordance material in this book was produced. Further editing was needed, however, to distinguish homonyms, such as the noun "cross" and the verb "cross", so that these would appear under separate headings within the Concordance. References containing different tenses of verbs, or singular and plural forms of nouns, were merged together, as were derivatives of words (e.g. re-, un-). Again the edited details were fed back into the computer and the revised file printed to allow yet more editing. This time, major Authorized (King James) Version words were cross-referenced to their GNB equivalents. These AV words were then merged into their appropriate alphabetical locations within the main Concordance file. Short descriptions of people, places and unusual words were compiled and inserted in the appropriate entries. Biblical names of infrequent occurrence were extracted from the main Concordance file and prepared as a separate *Concordance of Biblical Names* containing names and their biblical references. Numbers were also collected in a separate listing.

A *Thematic Index* was developed from the Concordance files to group words of similar meanings or referring to similar concepts. Links between these meaning groups were identified, and the list fed back into the computer, coded and sorted into alphabetical order.

The whole Concordance then existed on several magnetic tapes. These were merged into a single file, appropriate page format and typesetting codes were inserted and the magnetic file was used to enable the photocomposition and printing of the book as you now have it.

This is only the first product which has been developed from the computerized reference system. From the beginning the needs of other countries have been kept in view, and the computer processes used for the Concordance and other products in English are capable of adaptation to produce Bible reference materials in other languages. The *Concordance to the Good News Bible* is the first stage of a process which puts new technology to work in providing reference and study tools for new Bible translations world-wide.

Gwen Anderson
Translations Department
B.F.B.S.

HOW TO USE THE CONCORDANCE

You may have been a regular user of concordances for many years. On the other hand, you may never have used a Bible concordance before. In either case we recommend that you read the following notes as they will explain not only when and how to use this book, but how the *Concordance to the Good News Bible* is different from other concordances.

This Concordance is based upon the British usage edition of the *Good News Bible* but it includes important American usage GNB vocabulary differences, and significant Authorized (King James) Version words. These are indicated by the letters *Am* and *AV* in the margin. The provision of a *Thematic Index* also makes it usable with other translations.

The *Good News Bible* is a thorough, scholarly, modern translation of the Bible, based upon the best manuscripts of the Old and New Testaments in the original languages. It preserves every element of the biblical text but avoids both archaic vocabulary and technical terms. It is therefore a reliable translation for the ordinary reader and the serious student.

The *Concordance to the Good News Bible* takes all meaningful words in the text of the GNB and lists their occurrences in context with Bible references. It also links words that are connected in meaning, and distinguishes individual people and places.

The format of this Concordance differs from many others so it will help if, before you look up an entry, you ask yourself what sort of information you are looking for.

Are you looking for a word?

If you are sure which word you want, simply turn to the alphabetical lists in the main Concordance.

If the word has more than one meaning (e.g. cross) you will find a different list for each meaning. These are marked with numbers after the word, e.g. **CROSS (1)**, **CROSS (2)**. A glance at the page will tell you which entries have the meaning you are looking for.

You will find all the different forms of a word (e.g. sang, sing, singing, sung) listed together, with the most obvious form of the word as the heading (in this case **SING**). There are also cross-references to words of similar meaning (e.g. **RIGHT (1)**, see also **RIGHT WITH GOD, RIGHTEOUS**).

The key word(s) in each entry are highlighted in bold type in the lists. So under **ETERNAL** you will be able to pick out easily the references to **eternal life**. Sometimes the same meaning is conveyed by a different phrase and thus under **UNLEAVENED** are highlighted references to **without yeast** and **Unleavened Bread**. Significantly different words and phrases which are highlighted in a list are printed in square brackets under the heading.

Remember that if you are looking for a particular phrase, it is always quicker to look up the least common word (e.g. for **the Lord is my shepherd** it is easier to look under **SHEPHERD** than under **LORD**).

CROSS (1)

Mt	10.38	does not take up his **cross** and follow in my steps is
	16.24	he must forget self, carry his **cross,** and follow me.
	27.32	named Simon, and the soldiers forced him to carry Jesus' **cross.**
	27.40	Come on down from the **cross!"**

CROSS (2)
[RIVER CROSSING]

Gen	12.11	When he was about to **cross** the border into Egypt, he
	12.14	When he **crossed** the border into Egypt, the Egyptians did
	31.21	He **crossed** the River Euphrates
	32.10	I **crossed** the Jordan with nothing but a walking-stick, and
	32.22	and his eleven children, and **crossed** the River Jabbok.

SING
[SANG, SUNG]

Gen	31.27	your way with rejoicing and **singing** to the music of
Ex	15. 1	Then Moses and the Israelites **sang** this song to the Lord:
	15. 1	"I will **sing** to the Lord, because he has won a glorious
	15. 2	him, my father's God, and I will **sing** about his greatness.

RIGHT (1)
see also **RIGHT WITH GOD, RIGHTEOUS**

Gen	4. 7	If you had done the **right** thing, you would be smiling;
	7. 1	the only one in all the world who does what is **right.**

ETERNAL
[LIFE ETERNAL]

1 Cor	13. 8	Love is **eternal.**
2 Cor	4.17	a tremendous and **eternal** glory, much greater than the trouble.
Gal	6. 8	from the Spirit he will gather the harvest of **eternal life.**
Eph	3.11	according to his **eternal** purpose, which he achieved through

UNLEAVENED
[WITHOUT YEAST]
The Israelite festival of Unleavened Bread lasted seven days after Passover; it also celebrated the deliverance of the ancient Hebrews from Egypt. The name came from the practice of not using leaven (yeast) in making bread during that week. It was held from the 15th to the 22nd day of the month Nisan (about the first week of April).
see also **LEAVEN, YEAST**

Ex	12. 8	eaten with bitter herbs and with bread made **without yeast.**
	12.15	not eat any bread made with yeast—eat only **unleavened** bread.
	12.34	baking-pans with **unleavened** dough, wrapped them in clothing,
	12.39	They baked **unleavened** bread from the dough that they had
	13. 6	seven days you must eat **unleavened** bread and on the seventh
	23.15	Egypt, celebrate the Festival of **Unleavened Bread** in the way

It may be that the word you look up is not used by the GNB in the passage you want. If it is a key technical word used in the Authorized (King James) Version you will find an entry in the main Concordance referring you to equivalent GNB words. For example, the AV word **PROPITIATION** will direct you to the GNB equivalent, **FORGIVE**. In many cases, you will also find a list of examples of how the GNB translates the AV word. If you still cannot find your word consult the *Thematic Index* (see below).

AV **PROPITIATION** see **FORGIVE**

If you are looking for a number, you will find numbers **ONE** to **TWELVE** and **HUNDRED, THOUSAND** and **MILLION** in words in the main Concordance. All other numbers, including decimal figures and fractions, are to be found at the end of the main Concordance. For ease of reference, numbers appear according to their first digit, so that all numbers beginning with 1 (including 1.5, $\frac{1}{60}$ etc.) are followed by all numbers beginning with 2. Please note that GNB uses metric measurements.

187

Gen 5.25 When Methuselah was **187,** he had a son, Lamech,

188

Neh 7.26 Bethlehem and Netophah - **188**

19

Josh 19.38 **nineteen** cities, along with the towns round them.
Jer 52.12 of the **nineteenth** year of King Nebuchadnezzar of Babylonia,
also 1 Chr 24.7 1 Chr 25.9

2.2

Ex 27. 1 It is to be square, **2.2** metres long and 2.2 metres wide,
27.18 to be 44 metres long, 22 metres wide, and **2.2** metres high.
38. 1 It was square, **2.2** metres long and 2.2 metres wide, and it

Are you looking for an idea or theme?

Suppose, for example, that you wish to find out what the Scriptures say about obey. There are several English (as well as Hebrew and Greek) words which convey this idea. So turn to the tinted section at the back of the book which contains the *Thematic Index*. The entry **Obey** directs you to a theme heading – **ALLEGIANCE.** (The theme headings have been chosen because they are words with broad, general meanings, not because they are the most important words in a group.) If you now turn to **ALLEGIANCE** in the *Thematic Index* you will find a list of words with related meaning. Words in capitals in this list refer you to other theme headings. You can now choose which word(s) to look up in the main Concordance, and decide how detailed you want your study to be. The *Thematic Index* also helps you to find the major festivals of the Christian Year, well-known Bible passages (e.g. Beatitudes, Lord's Prayer), and lists all the parables and miracles with their references.

Oasis *see* WATER
Oath *see* PROMISE
Obey *see* ALLEGIANCE
Object *see* COMPLAIN
Obligation *see* NECESSARY

ALLEGIANCE
faithful
FOLLOW
footstool
kneel
loyal
obey
subject
tribute

BEATITUDES: Mt 5.3f. Lk 6.20f.

PARABLES
(a) reason and use
Mt 13.1-17,34-35; Mk 4.10-12; Lk 8.9-10,16-18
(b) told by Jesus:
children playing
Mt 11.16-19; Lk 7.31-35;
faithful servant
Mt 24.45-51; Lk 12.42-46;

Are you looking for a name?

If it is a very common name (e.g. Abraham, David, Peter), you will find it in the main Concordance. If it is uncommon, you will find it in the *Concordance of Biblical Names* just before the tinted section of the book. It is best to start with the *Concordance of Biblical Names*, which lists all names in the Bible. Names printed in bold capitals are those which appear in the main Concordance.

PERSIA		
Persis	Rom	16.12
Peruda	Ezra	2.55
PETER		
Pethahiah (1)	1 Chr	24. 7
Pethahiah (2)	Ezra	10.23
	Neh	9. 5
Pethahiah (3)	Neh	11.24
Pethor	Num	22. 5
	Deut	23. 4
Pethuel	Joel	1. 1

For some names which occur very frequently, the main Concordance gives references in bold type for incidents in the person's life based on the section headings in the GNB. All other references (mainly to related people or the person after his death) are listed below the section heading entries, in the usual format. So in looking for David's battle with Goliath you may first turn in the main Concordance to the section heading entries under **DAVID**. You do not need to know any specific Bible text – simply look for the relevant heading **David defeats Goliath**. If you wish to find a particular phrase or verse in the passage (e.g. **David . . . killed Goliath**) you may follow one of two routes. We recommend that you read the passage in a Bible, since in this way you will find the full context of the phrase. If you need a quicker route, remember the book (1 Samuel), chapter (17) and verse (41) at which the passage starts, then turn to **KILL** in the main Concordance and look for the entries immediately following that verse.

DAVID
[DESCENDANT OF DAVID]
Son of Jesse chosen to succeed Saul as king of Israel.
see also **SON OF DAVID**

Ruth	4.13-22	**Boaz and his descendants**
1 Sam	16.1-13	**David is anointed king**
	14-23	**David in Saul's court**
	17.12-40	**David in Saul's camp**
	41-54	**David defeats Goliath**
	17.55–18.5	**David is presented to Saul**

1 Sam	17.26	will the man get who **kills** this Philistine and frees Israel
	17.27	told him what would be done for the man who **killed** Goliath.
	17.36	I have **killed** lions and bears, and I will do the same
	17.50	David defeated and **killed** Goliath with a catapult
	17.51	out of its sheath, and cut off his head and **killed** him.
	17.57	David returned to camp after **killing** Goliath,

It is of course always quicker to look up the least common name in the phrase (in this case Goliath) because you will come to the reference you want more quickly.

If you can remember only part of a compound name (e.g. that it ends with **Maacah**) simply look up that part in the *Concordance of Biblical Names*. You will then be prompted by a list of names ending with that form.

Maacah
see also Abel Beth Maacah

Maacah (1)	Deut	3.14
	Josh	12. 5
		13.11
		13.13
	2 Sam	10. 6

Some people and many places in the Bible are known by more than one name. In such cases, when you look up one name you will be directed to the alternatives, e.g. **MATTANIAH (1)** refers you to **ZEDEKIAH (1)**.

Mattan (2)	Jer	38. 1
Mattanah	Num	21.18
Mattaniah (1) *see also* Zedekiah (1)		
	2 Kgs	24.17
Mattaniah (2)	1 Chr	9.14
Mattaniah (3)	1 Chr	25. 4
		25. 9

Some names refer to more than one person or place. This is shown by a number after the name, e.g. **NOAH (1)** refers to the hero of the flood story, and **NOAH (2)** refers to Zelophehad's daughter. The brief description of names in the main Concordance will help you decide which person or place you want.

NOAH (1)

Noah (2)	Num	26.33
		27. 1
		36.10
	Josh	17. 3

NOAH (1)
Head of the family which survived the Flood.

Gen	5.29	so he named him **Noah.**
	5.32	After **Noah** was 500 years old, he had three sons, Shem,
	6. 8	But the Lord was pleased with **Noah.**

Some names in the Authorized Version, the Revised Version or the Revised Standard Version appear in a different form in the Good News Bible. For example the AV uses **Elijah** in the Old Testament and **Elias** in the New Testament: GNB uses Elijah for both. In such cases the *Concordance of Biblical Names* will direct you to the appropriate GNB form. The AV, RV and RSV names are all identified by the letters *AV* in front of the name.

Eliam (1) *see also* Ammiel (4)		
	2 Sam	11. 3
Eliam (2)	2 Sam	23.24
AV Elias *see* Elijah (1)		
Eliasaph (1)	Num	1. 5
		2.10
		7.12
		10.20

In the Greek and Hebrew volume of the Concordance (to be published later) you will be able to link this information about the GNB text with the original languages of the Bible.

CONCORDANCE TO THE GOOD NEWS BIBLE

AARON

Moses' elder brother, responsible for making the gold bull-calf, but also the ancestor of the Israelite priesthood.

Ex 4.1-17 **God gives Moses miraculous power**
18-31 **Moses returns to Egypt**
5.1-21 **Moses and Aaron before the King of Egypt**
6.2-13 **God calls Moses**
14-27 **The family record of Moses and Aaron**
6.28–7.7 **The LORD's command to Moses and Aaron**
7.8-13 **Aaron's stick**
7.14–10.29 **Disasters strike Egypt**
11.1-10 **Moses announces the death of the first-born**
12.1-14 **The Passover**
21-28 **The first Passover**
29-36 **The death of the first-born**
43-51 **Regulations about Passover**
16.1-36 **The manna and the quails**
17.8-16 **War with the Amalekites**
18.1-12 **Jethro visits Moses**
19.1-25 **The Israelites at Mount Sinai**
24.1-11 **The Covenant is sealed**
12-18 **Moses on Mount Sinai**
27.20-21 **Taking care of the lamp**
28.1-14 **Garments for the priests**
15-30 **The breast-piece**
31-43 **The other priestly garments**
29.1-37 **Instructions for ordaining Aaron and his sons as priests**
38-46 **The daily offering**
30.1-10 **The altar for burning incense**
17-21 **The bronze basin**
22-33 **The anointing oil**
31.1-11 **Craftsmen for the Tent of the LORD's presence**
32.1-35 **The gold bull-calf**
34.29-35 **Moses goes down from Mount Sinai**
35.10-19 **Articles for the Tent of the LORD's presence**
39.1-7 **Making the garments for the priests**
22-31 **Making the other priestly garments**
32-43 **The completion of the work**
40.1-33 **Setting up and dedicating the Tent of the LORD's presence**
Lev 6.8-13 **Sacrifices burnt whole**
24-30 **Sin-offerings**
7.11-38 **Fellowship-offerings**
8.1-36 **The ordination of Aaron and his sons**
9.1-24 **Aaron offers sacrifices**
10.1-7 **The sin of Nadab and Abihu**
8-20 **Rules for priests**
11.1-47 **Animals that may be eaten**
13.1-46 **Laws concerning skin-diseases**
14.33-57 **Mildew in houses**
15.1-33 **Unclean bodily discharges**
16.1-19 **The Day of Atonement**
20-28 **The scapegoat**
17.1-16 **The sacredness of blood**
21.1-24 **The holiness of the priests**
22.1-33 **The holiness of the offerings**
24.1-4 **Taking care of the lamps**
5-9 **The bread offered to God**
Num 1.1-54 **The first census of Israel**
2.1-34 **The arrangement of the tribes in camp**
3.1-4 **Aaron's sons**
5-13 **The Levites are appointed to serve the priests**
14-39 **The census of the Levites**
40-51 **The Levites take the place of the first-born sons**
4.1-20 **The duties of the Levite clan of Kohath**
21-28 **The duties of the Levite clan of Gershon**
34-49 **The census of the Levites**
6.22-27 **The priestly blessing**
8.1-4 **Placing the lamps**
5-26 **The purification and dedication of the Levites**
9.1-14 **The second Passover**
12.1-16 **Miriam is punished**
13.1-33 **The spies**
14.1-10 **The people complain**
Num 26-38 **The LORD punishes the people for complaining**
15.32-36 **The man who broke the Sabbath**
16.1-35 **The rebellion of Korah, Dathan, and Abiram**
41-50 **Aaron saves the people**
17.1-13 **Aaron's stick**
18.1-7 **Duties of priests and Levites**
8-20 **The share of the priests**
25-32 **The Levites' tithe**
19.1-10 **Ashes of the red cow**
20.1-13 **Events at Kadesh**
22-29 **The death of Aaron**
Deut 9.1-29 **The people's disobedience**
10.1-11 **Moses receives the Commandments again**
1 Chr 6.1-15 **The family line of the High Priests**
49-53 **The descendants of Aaron**

Ex 6.25 Eleazar, **Aaron's** son, married one of Putiel's daughters, who bore him Phinehas.
15.20 The prophet Miriam, **Aaron's** sister, took her tambourine,
28.40 shirts, sashes, and caps for **Aaron's** sons, to provide them
29.30 The son of **Aaron** who succeeds him as priest and who goes
38.21 under the direction of Ithamar son of **Aaron** the priest.
Lev 1. 5 and the **Aaronite** priests shall present the blood
2. 2 incense on it [2] and bring it to the **Aaronite** priests.
3. 2 The **Aaronite** priests shall throw the blood against all four
6.14 An **Aaronite** priest shall present the grain-offering to the Lord
6.18 of the male descendants of **Aaron** may eat it as their
6.20 following regulations [20] for the ordination of an **Aaronite** priest.
6.22 by every descendant of **Aaron** who is serving as High Priest.
7.10 belong to all the **Aaronite** priests and must be shared
8.13 Moses brought the sons of **Aaron** forward and put shirts on them,
8.24 Then he brought **Aaron's** sons forward and put some of the
10. 1 **Aaron's** sons Nadab and Abihu, each took his fire-pan, put
10. 4 Elzaphan, the sons of Uzziel, **Aaron's** uncle, and said to them,
13. 2 skin-disease, he shall be brought to the **Aaronite** priest.
16. 1 of the two sons of **Aaron** who were killed when they offered
21. 1 Moses to say to the **Aaronite** priests, "No priest is to make
21.21 No descendant of **Aaron** the priest who has any physical
22. 4 "None of the descendants of **Aaron** who has a dreaded
Num 3.32 The chief of the Levites was Eleazar son of **Aaron** the priest.
4.16 Eleazar son of **Aaron** the priest shall be responsible for
4.28 out under the direction of Ithamar son of **Aaron** the priest.
4.33 out under the direction of Ithamar son of **Aaron** the priest.
7. 8 was to be done under the direction of Ithamar son of **Aaron.**
10. 8 The trumpets are to be blown by **Aaron's** sons, the
16.37 Moses, [37] "Tell Eleazar son of **Aaron** the priest to remove
16.40 was not a descendant of **Aaron** should come to the altar to
25. 7 of Eleazar and grandson of **Aaron** the priest, saw this, he
26. 1 Moses and Eleazar son of **Aaron,** [2] "Take a census by
26. 9 They defied Moses and **Aaron** and joined the followers of
26.59 She bore Amram two sons, **Aaron** and Moses, and a daughter,
26.60 **Aaron** had four sons, Nadab, Abihu, Eleazar, and Ithamar.
26.64 among those whom Moses and **Aaron** had listed in the first
27.13 will die, as your brother **Aaron** did, [14] because both of you
33. 1 Egypt in their tribes under the leadership of Moses and **Aaron.**
33.38 At the command of the Lord, **Aaron** the priest climbed Mount Hor.
Deut 32.50 that mountain as your brother **Aaron** died on Mount Hor,
Josh 21. 4 families who were descended from **Aaron** the priest were
21.10 given [10] to the descendants of **Aaron** who were of the clan
21.13 cities were assigned to the descendants of **Aaron** the priest:
21.19 lands, were given to the priests, the descendants of **Aaron.**
24. 5 Later I sent Moses and **Aaron,** and I brought great trouble
24.33 Eleazar son of **Aaron** died and was buried at Gibeah, the
Judg 20.27 son of Eleazar and grandson of **Aaron,** was in charge of it.
1 Sam 2.27 "When your ancestor **Aaron** and his family were slaves
2.27 slaves of the king of Egypt, I revealed myself to **Aaron.**
12. 6 one who chose Moses and **Aaron** and who brought your ancestors
12. 8 and he sent Moses and **Aaron,** who brought them out of Egypt
1 Chr 6.54 assigned to the descendants of **Aaron** of the clan of Kohath.
6.57 The following towns were assigned to **Aaron's** descendants:
12.23 Followers of Jehoiada, descendant of **Aaron:**
15. 4 Next he sent for the descendants of **Aaron** and for the Levites.
23.13 His eldest son, Amram, was the father of **Aaron** and Moses.
23.13 (**Aaron** and his descendants were set apart to be in charge of

1 Chr 23.28 the priests descended from **Aaron** with the temple worship,
23.32 the priests descended from **Aaron,** in the temple worship.
24. 1 These are the groups to which the descendants of **Aaron** belong.
24. 1 **Aaron** had four sons:
24. 3 David organized the descendants of **Aaron** into groups according to their duties.
24.19 duties established by their ancestor **Aaron** in obedience to
24.31 just as their relatives, the priests descended from **Aaron,**
27.16 **Aaron** Zadok
2 Chr 13. 9 Lord's priests, the descendants of **Aaron,** and you drove out the Levites.
13.10 Priests descended from **Aaron** perform their duties, and Levites assist them.
26.18 are descended from **Aaron** have been consecrated to do this.
29.21 priests, who were descendants of **Aaron,** to offer the animals
31.19 in the cities assigned to **Aaron's** descendants, or in the
35.14 for the priests descended from **Aaron,** for the priests were
Ezra 7. 1 He traced his ancestors back to **Aaron,** the High Priest, as
7. 5 son of Abishua, son of Phinehas, son of Eleazar, son of **Aaron.**
Neh 10.38 Priests who are descended from **Aaron** are to be with the
Ps 77.20 people like a shepherd, with Moses and **Aaron** in charge.
99. 6 Moses and **Aaron** were his priests, and Samuel was one who
105.26 Then he sent his servant Moses, and **Aaron,** whom he had chosen.
106.16 jealous of Moses and of **Aaron,** the Lord's holy servant.
133. 2 anointing oil running down from **Aaron's** head and beard, down
Mic 6. 4 I sent Moses, **Aaron,** and Miriam to lead you.
Acts 7.40 So they said to **Aaron,** 'Make us some gods who will lead
Heb 5. 4 that a man is made a high priest—just as **Aaron** was.
7.11 who is in the priestly order of Melchizedek, not of **Aaron.**
9. 4 with the manna in it, **Aaron's** stick that had sprouted leaves,

ABANDON

Lev 19. 4 "Do not **abandon** me and worship idols;
26.34 it will lie **abandoned** and get its rest while you are in
26.44 I will not completely **abandon** or destroy them.
Num 32.15 he will once again **abandon** all these people in the wilderness,
Deut 4.31 He will not **abandon** you or destroy you,
31. 6 He will not fail you or **abandon** you."
31. 8 will not fail you or **abandon** you, so do not lose courage
31.16 They will **abandon** me and worship the pagan gods of the land
31.17 I will **abandon** them, and they will be destroyed.
32.15 They **abandoned** God their Creator
32.30 The Lord, their God, had **abandoned** them;
Josh 1. 5 I will never **abandon** you.
10. 6 "Do not **abandon** us, sir!
Judg 5. 7 The towns of Israel stood **abandoned,** Deborah;
6.13 The Lord has **abandoned** us and left us to the mercy of
8.27 All the Israelites **abandoned** God
10. 6 They **abandoned** the Lord and stopped worshipping him.
1 Sam 12.22 promise, and he will not **abandon** you, for he has decided to
18.12 David because the Lord was with David but had **abandoned** him.
28.15 The Philistines are at war with me, and God has **abandoned** me.
28.16 me when the Lord has **abandoned** you and become your enemy?
31. 7 they **abandoned** their towns and fled.
2 Sam 1.27 "The brave soldiers have fallen, their weapons **abandoned**
1 Kgs 6.13 Temple that you are building, and I will never **abandon** them."
8.57 may he never leave us, or **abandon** us;
9. 7 I will also **abandon** this Temple which I have consecrated as
9. 9 answer, 'It is because they **abandoned** the Lord their God,
14.16 The Lord will **abandon** Israel because Jeroboam sinned
2 Kgs 7. 7 had fled for their lives, **abandoning** their tents,
7.15 equipment that the Syrians had **abandoned** as they fled.
17.13 "**Abandon** your evil ways and obey my commands,
17.21 Jeroboam made them **abandon** the Lord
21.14 I will **abandon** the people who survive,
1 Chr 10. 7 they **abandoned** their towns and ran off.
28. 9 if you turn away from him, he will **abandon** you for ever.
28.20 He will not **abandon** you, but he will stay with you until
2 Chr 7.20 and I will **abandon** this Temple that I have consecrated
7.22 'It is because they **abandoned** the Lord their God,
11.14 The Levites **abandoned** their pastures and other land
12. 1 king, he and all his people **abandoned** the Law of the Lord.
12. 5 'You have **abandoned** me, so now I have abandoned you to Shishak.' "
13.10 we still serve the Lord our God and have not **abandoned** him.
13.11 We do what the Lord has commanded, but you have **abandoned** him.
15. 2 you find him, but if you turn away, he will **abandon** you.
16. 5 he stopped fortifying Ramah and **abandoned** the work.
21.10 also revolted, because Jehoram had **abandoned** the Lord,
24.20 You **abandoned** him, so he has abandoned you!"
24.24 army because the people had **abandoned** him, the Lord
28. 5 because the people of Judah had **abandoned** him.
29. 6 They **abandoned** him and turned their backs on the place
Neh 9.19 But you did not **abandon** them there in the desert,
Job 8.20 But God will never **abandon** the faithful
Ps 9.10 you do not **abandon** anyone who comes to you.
16.10 and you will not **abandon** me
22. 1 My God, my God, why have you **abandoned** me?
27. 9 don't leave me, don't **abandon** me, O God, my saviour.
27.10 My father and mother may **abandon** me, but the Lord
27.12 Don't **abandon** me to my enemies, who attack me with lies
37.25 never seen a good man **abandoned** by the Lord or his children
37.28 Lord loves what is right and does not **abandon** his faithful people.
37.33 but the Lord will not **abandon** him to his enemy's power
38.21 Do not **abandon** me, O Lord;
41. 2 he will not **abandon** them to the power of their enemies.
43. 2 why have you **abandoned** me?
44.19 you **abandoned** us in deepest darkness.
71. 9 do not **abandon** me now that I am feeble.
Ps 71.11 They say, "God has **abandoned** him;
71.18 old and my hair is grey, do not **abandon** me, O God!
73.27 Those who **abandon** you will certainly perish;
74. 1 Why have you **abandoned** us like this, O God?
74.19 Don't **abandon** your helpless people to their cruel enemies;
78.60 He **abandoned** his tent in Shiloh,
88. 5 I am **abandoned** among the dead;
88. 8 You have caused my friends to **abandon** me;
88.18 made even my closest friends **abandon** me,
94.14 The Lord will not **abandon** his people;
102. 6 a wild bird in the desert, like an owl in **abandoned** ruins.
106.41 He **abandoned** them to the power of the heathen,
119. 8 never **abandon** me!
119.121 don't **abandon** me to my enemies!
125. 5 punish also those who **abandon** your ways.
Prov 2.13 men who have **abandoned** a righteous life
4. 6 Do not **abandon** wisdom, and she will protect you;
Is 2.20 idols they have made, and **abandon** them to the moles
17. 9 the Amorites **abandoned** as they fled from the people
31. 9 so frightened that they will **abandon** their battle flags."
32.14 Even the palace will be **abandoned**
41.17 I, the God of Israel, will never **abandon** them.
49.14 "The Lord has **abandoned** us!
57.17 sin and greed, and so I punished them and **abandoned** them.
64. 7 and have **abandoned** us because of our sins.
Jer 1.16 they have **abandoned** me, have offered sacrifices to other gods,
2.15 and his towns lie in ruins, completely **abandoned.**
2.19 and wrong it is to **abandon** me, the Lord your God, and
5. 7 They have **abandoned** me and have worshipped gods that are not
6. 8 troubles be a warning to you, or else I will **abandon** you;
9.13 because my people have **abandoned** the teaching
12. 7 "I have **abandoned** Israel;
14. 5 the mother deer **abandons** her new-born fawn
14. 9 do not **abandon** us.' "
16.11 They **abandoned** me and did not obey my teachings.
17.13 all who **abandon** you will be put to shame.
17.13 because they have **abandoned** you, the Lord,
19. 4 because the people have **abandoned** me and defiled this place
22. 9 it is because you have **abandoned** your covenant with me,
25.38 The Lord has **abandoned** his people
51. 5 Lord God Almighty, have not **abandoned** Israel and Judah,
Lam 1.13 Then he **abandoned** me and left me in constant pain.
2. 1 On the day of his anger he **abandoned** even his Temple.
5.20 Why have you **abandoned** us so long?
Ezek 8.12 He has **abandoned** the country.' "
9. 9 that I, the Lord, have **abandoned** their country
39. 9 will go out and collect the **abandoned** weapons for firewood.
39.10 because they will have the **abandoned** weapons to burn.
Dan 11.30 the advice of those who have **abandoned** that religion.
11.32 those who have already **abandoned** their religion,
Hos 5.15 "I will **abandon** my people until they have suffered
9.12 When I **abandon** these people, terrible things will happen to them."
11. 8 How can I **abandon** you?
Amos 5. 2 She lies **abandoned** on the ground, And no one helps her up.
Jon 2. 8 Those who worship worthless idols have **abandoned** their loyalty
Mic 5. 3 So the Lord will **abandon** his people to their enemies
Zech 11.17 He has **abandoned** his flock.
Mal 1. 3 I have devastated Esau's hill-country and **abandoned** the land
Mt 23.38 And so your Temple will be **abandoned** and empty.
27.46 which means, "My God, my God, why did you **abandon** me?"
Mk 15.34 which means, "My God, my God, why did you **abandon** me?"
Lk 13.35 And so your Temple will be **abandoned.**
Acts 2.27 because you will not **abandon** me in the world of the
2.31 he said, 'He was not **abandoned** in the world of the dead;
21.21 live in Gentile countries to **abandon** the Law of Moses,
Rom 11.23 And if the Jews **abandon** their unbelief, they will be put
2 Cor 11. 3 corrupted and that you will **abandon** your full and pure devotion
1 Tim 4. 1 clearly that some people will **abandon** the faith in later times;
Heb 6. 4 For how can those who **abandon** their faith be brought back
6. 6 And then they **abandoned** their faith!
13. 5 I will never **abandon** you."
2 Pet 1.10 if you do so, you will never **abandon** your faith.
Jude 6 their proper authority, but **abandoned** their own dwelling place:
Rev 2.13 and you did not **abandon** your faith in me even during

ABEDNEGO

One of Daniel's three companions.
see also AZARIAH (25)

Dan 1. 7 Belteshazzar, Shadrach, Meshach, and **Abednego.**
2.49 king put Shadrach, Meshach, and **Abednego** in charge
3.12 Shadrach, Meshach, and **Abednego**—who are disobeying Your Majesty's orders.
3.14 "Shadrach, Meshach, and **Abednego,** is it true that you refuse
3.16 Shadrach, Meshach, and **Abednego** answered, "Your Majesty,
3.19 his face turned red with anger at Shadrach, Meshach, and **Abednego.**
3.23 Then Shadrach, Meshach, and **Abednego,** still tied up, fell
3.26 **Abednego!**
3.28 The king said, "Praise the God of Shadrach, Meshach, and **Abednego!**
3.29 God of Shadrach, Meshach, and **Abednego,** he is to be torn
3.30 king promoted Shadrach, Meshach, and **Abednego** to higher positions

ABEL (1)

Adam's second son, murdered by his brother Cain.

Gen 4. 2 Later she gave birth to another son, **Abel.**
4. 2 **Abel** became a shepherd, but Cain was a farmer.
4. 4 Then **Abel** brought the first lamb born to one of his sheep,

Gen 4. 4 The Lord was pleased with **Abel** and his offering,
4. 8 Cain said to his brother **Abel,** "Let's go out in the fields."
4. 9 The Lord asked Cain, "Where is your brother **Abel?"**
4.25 "God has given me a son to replace **Abel,** whom Cain killed."
Mt 23.35 from the murder of innocent **Abel** to the murder of Zachariah
Lk 11.51 from the murder of **Abel** to the murder of Zechariah,
Heb 11. 4 It was faith that made **Abel** offer to God a better
11. 4 By means of his faith **Abel** still speaks, even though he is
12.24 that promises much better things than does the blood of **Abel.**
1 Jn 3.12 belonged to the Evil One and murdered his own brother **Abel.**

ABIATHAR
Priest in the time of David, who supported Adonijah as David's successor.

1 Sam 22.1-23 **The slaughter of the priests**
23.1-13 **David saves the town of Keilah**
30.1-31 **The war against the Amalekites**
2 Sam 15.13-37 **David flees from Jerusalem**
17.15-29 **David is warned and escapes**
19.8b-18a **David starts back to Jerusalem**
20.23-26 **David's officials**
1 Kgs 1.5-10 **Adonijah claims the throne**
11-53 **Solomon is made king**
2.13-25 **The death of Adonijah**
26-35 **Abiathar's banishment and Joab's death**
4.1-19 **Solomon's officials**

2 Sam 8.17 Zadok son of Ahitub and Ahimelech son of **Abiathar** were priests;
1 Chr 15.11 the priests Zadok and **Abiathar** and the six Levites,
18.16 Zadok son of Ahitub and Ahimelech son of **Abiathar** were priests;
24. 6 Ahimelech son of **Abiathar,** and the heads of the priestly
27.34 **Abiathar** and Jehoiada son of Benaiah became advisers.
Mk 2.26 This happened when **Abiathar** was the High Priest.

ABIB
First month of the Hebrew calendar, also known as Nisan.
see also TEL ABIB

Ex 13. 4 Egypt on this day in the first month, the month of **Abib.**
23.15 In the month of **Abib,** the month in which you left Egypt,
34.18 days in the month of **Abib,** because it was in that month
Deut 16. 1 Lord your God by celebrating Passover in the month of **Abib;**

ABIGAIL (1)
Nabal's wife, who subsequently married David.

1 Sam 25. 2 His wife **Abigail** was beautiful and intelligent,
25.14 One of Nabal's servants said to Nabal's wife **Abigail,**
25.18 **Abigail** quickly collected two hundred loaves of bread,
25.23 When **Abigail** saw David, she quickly dismounted
25.36 **Abigail** went back to Nabal, who was at home having a
25.39 Then David sent a proposal of marriage to **Abigail.**
25.41 **Abigail** bowed down to the ground and said, "I am his servant,
25.43 and now **Abigail** also became his wife.
27. 3 Ahinoam from Jezreel, and **Abigail,** Nabal's widow, from Carmel.
30. 5 David's two wives, Ahinoam and **Abigail,** had been taken away.
2 Sam 2. 2 **Abigail,** Nabal's widow, who was from Carmel.
3. 3 Chileab, whose mother was **Abigail,** Nabal's widow, from
1 Chr 3. 1 Daniel, whose mother was **Abigail** from Carmel

ABIJAH (1)
Rehoboam's son and his successor as king of Judah.

1 Kgs 14.31 and his son **Abijah** succeeded him as king.
15. 1 **Abijah** became king of Judah,
15. 4 the Lord his God gave **Abijah** a son to rule after him
15. 6 Rehoboam and Jeroboam continued throughout **Abijah's** lifetime.
15. 7 everything else that **Abijah** did is recorded in The History
15. 8 **Abijah** died and was buried in David's City,
1 Chr 3.10 Solomon, Rehoboam, **Abijah,** Asa, Jehoshaphat,
2 Chr 11.20 **Abijah,** Attai, Ziza, and Shelomith.
11.22 and he favoured her son **Abijah** over all his other children,
12.16 and his son **Abijah** succeeded him as king.
13. 1 **Abijah** became king of Judah,
13. 2 War broke out between **Abijah** and Jeroboam.
13. 3 **Abijah** raised an army of 400,000 soldiers,
13. 4 King **Abijah** went up Mount Zemaraim and called out to Jeroboam
13.15 Judaeans gave a loud shout, and led by **Abijah,** they attacked;
13.17 **Abijah** and his army dealt the Israelites a crushing defeat—
13.19 **Abijah** pursued Jeroboam's army and occupied some of his cities:
13.20 Jeroboam never regained his power during **Abijah's** reign.
13.21 **Abijah,** however, grew more powerful.
13.22 rest of the history of **Abijah,** what he said and what he
14. 1 King **Abijah** died and was buried in the royal tombs
15.18 all the objects his father **Abijah** had dedicated to God, as
Mt 1. 6 Rehoboam, **Abijah,** Asa, Jehoshaphat, Jehoram,

ABILITY see ABLE

ABIMELECH (1)
King of Gerar in the time of Abraham.

Gen 20.1-18 **Abraham and Abimelech**
21.22-34 **The agreement between Abraham and Abimelech**
26.1-25 **Isaac lives at Gerar**
26-33 **The agreement between Isaac and Abimelech**

ABIMELECH (2)
Gideon's son, who killed 70 of his brothers.

Judg. 8.29-35 **The death of Gideon**
9.1-57 **Abimelech**

Judg 10. 1 After **Abimelech's** death Tola, the son of Puah
2 Sam 11.21 Don't you remember how **Abimelech** son of Gideon was killed?

ABIRAM (1)
Dathan's fellow-conspirator in rebelling against Moses.

Num 16. 1 tribe of Reuben—Dathan and **Abiram,** the sons of Eliab,
16.12 Moses sent for Dathan and **Abiram,** but they said, 'We will
16.24 to move away from the tents of Korah, Dathan, and **Abiram."**
16.25 accompanied by the leaders of Israel, went to Dathan and **Abiram.**
16.27 So they moved away from the tents of Korah, Dathan, and **Abiram.**
16.27 Dathan and **Abiram** had come out
16.31 the ground under Dathan and **Abiram** split open
26. 9 Eliab [9] and his sons Nemuel, Dathan, and **Abiram.**
26. 9 (These are the Dathan and **Abiram** who were chosen by the community.
Deut 11. 6 he did to Dathan and **Abiram,** the sons of Eliab
Ps 106.17 earth opened up and swallowed Dathan and buried **Abiram**

ABISHAI
Joab's brother, and one of David's famous soldiers.

1 Sam 26. 6 asked Ahimelech the Hittite, and **Abishai** the brother of Joab
26. 6 "I will," **Abishai** answered.
26. 7 So that night David and **Abishai** entered Saul's camp
26. 8 **Abishai** said to David, "God has put your enemy in your
26.12 jar from just beside Saul's head, and he and **Abishai** left.
2 Sam 2.18 Joab, **Abishai,** and Asahel.
2.24 But Joab and **Abishai** started out after Abner,
3.30 So Joab and his brother **Abishai** took revenge on Abner
10.10 the command of his brother **Abishai,** who put them in position
10.14 they fled from **Abishai** and retreated into the city.
16. 9 **Abishai,** whose mother was Zeruiah, said to the king,
16.10 business," the king said to **Abishai** and his brother Joab.
16.11 And David said to **Abishai** and to all his officials,
18. 2 with Joab and Joab's brother **Abishai** and Ittai from Gath,
18. 5 He gave orders to Joab, **Abishai,** and Ittai:
18.12 the king command you and **Abishai** and Ittai, 'For my sake
19.21 **Abishai** son of Zeruiah spoke up:
19.22 But David said to **Abishai** and his brother Joab,
20. 6 So the king said to **Abishai,** "Sheba will give us more
20. 7 the other soldiers left Jerusalem with **Abishai** to go after Sheba.
20.10 Then Joab and his brother **Abishai** went on after Sheba.
21.17 But **Abishai** son of Zeruiah came to David's help,
23.18 Joab's brother **Abishai** (their mother was Zeruiah)
1 Chr 2.16 **Abishai,** Joab, and Asahel.
11.20 Joab's brother **Abishai** was the leader of "The Famous Thirty."
18.12 **Abishai,** whose mother was Zeruiah, defeated the Edomites
18.15 **Abishai's** brother Joab was commander of the army;
19.11 the command of his brother **Abishai,** who put them in position
19.15 they fled from **Abishai** and retreated into the city.

ABLE
[ABILITY, ENABLE, UNABLE]

Gen 31.35 sir, but I am not **able** to stand up in your presence;
40. 8 "It is God who gives the **ability** to interpret dreams,"
45. 1 Joseph was no longer **able** to control his feelings
Ex 7.24 because they were not **able** to drink water from the river.
9.11 The magicians were not **able** to appear before Moses,
28. 3 to whom I have given **ability,** and tell them to make Aaron's
31. 3 given him understanding, skill, and **ability** for every kind
31. 6 I have also given great **ability** to all the other skilful craftsmen,
35.31 power and given him skill, **ability,** and understanding for
35.34 tribe of Dan, the **ability** to teach their crafts to others.
36. 2 the Lord had given **ability** and who were willing to help,
Lev 26.37 you, and you will be **unable** to fight against any enemy.
27. 8 a lower price, according to the **ability** of the man to pay.
Num 9. 6 and they were not **able** to keep the Passover
14.16 because you were not **able** to bring them into the land
22.37 Did you think I wasn't **able** to reward you enough?"
Deut 7.24 No one will be **able** to stop you;
9.28 will say that you were **unable** to take your people into the
11. 8 Then you will be **able** to cross the river
11.25 and no one will be **able** to stop you.
16.17 a gift [17] as he is **able,** in proportion to the blessings
31. 2 twenty years old and am no longer **able** to be your leader.
Josh 1. 5 Joshua, no one will be **able** to defeat you
15.63 people of Judah were not **able** to drive out the Jebusites,
17.12 Manasseh, however, were not **able** to drive out the people
23. 9 advanced and no one has ever been **able** to stand against you.
24.19 "But you may not be **able** to serve the Lord.
Judg 1.18 so the people of Judah were not **able** to drive them out.
1 Sam 16.18 brave and handsome man, a good soldier, and an **able** speaker.
2 Sam 5. 6 that David would not be **able** to conquer the city,
1 Kgs 3. 9 how would I ever be **able** to rule this great people
11.28 Jeroboam was an **able** young man,
2 Kgs 24.16 all of them **able-bodied** men fit for military duty.
1 Chr 12.23 Relatives of Zadok, an **able** young fighter:
21.30 but David was not **able** to go there to worship God,
26. 6 They were important men in their clan because of their great **ability;**
2 Chr 1.10 how would I ever be **able** to rule this great people
14.13 Sudanese were killed that the army was **unable** to rally and fight.
26.21 **Unable** to enter the Temple again, he lived in his own house,
30. 1 The people had not been **able** to celebrate the Passover

2 Chr	32.15	any nation has ever been **able** to save his people from any
Ezra	2.61	Since they were **unable** to prove who their ancestors were,
	8.18	they sent us Sherebiah, an **able** man, a Levite
Neh	5. 8	far as we have been **able,** we have been buying back our
	6.10	grandson of Mehetabel, who was **unable** to leave his house.
	7.63	Since they were **unable** to prove who their ancestors were,
Ps	30. 9	Are dead people **able** to praise you?
	36.12	There they lie, **unable** to rise.
	119.43	**Enable** me to speak the truth at all times, because my
Prov	22.27	If you should be **unable** to pay, they will take away even
Ecc	8.17	and never be **able** to understand what God is doing.
Is	5.18	You are **unable** to break free from your sins.
	7. 1	Israel, attacked Jerusalem, but were **unable** to capture it.
	46. 7	and there it stands, **unable** to move from where it is.
Dan	2.47	I know this because you have been **able** to explain this mystery."
	3.17	God whom we serve is **able** to save us
	5.12	He has unusual **ability** and is wise and skilful in interpreting dreams,
	6.20	God you serve so loyally **able** to save you from the lions?"
Hos	9.14	Make them **unable** to nurse their babies!
Mt	8. 6	in bed at home, **unable** to move and suffering terribly."
	22.46	No one was **able** to give Jesus any answer, and from that
	25.15	He gave to each one according to his **ability:**
	26.40	that you three were not **able** to keep watch with me even
	26.61	"This man said, 'I am **able** to tear down God's Temple and
Mk	6. 5	He was not **able** to perform any miracles there, except that
	9.39	in my name will be **able** soon afterwards to say evil things
	14.37	Weren't you **able** to stay awake even for one hour?"
Lk	1.20	Because you have not believed, you will be **unable** to speak;
	1.22	**Unable** to say a word, he made signs to them with his
	8.19	came to him, but were **unable** to join him because of the
	8.43	had on doctors, but no one had been **able** to cure her.
	13.24	people will surely try to go in but will not be **able.**
	14. 6	But they were not **able** to answer him about this.
	14.14	will be blessed, because they are not **able** to pay you back.
	14.29	he will not be **able** to finish the tower after laying
	21.15	of your enemies will be **able** to refute or contradict what
Jn	9.33	came from God, he would not be **able** to do a thing."
	12.39	so they were not **able** to believe, because Isaiah also said,
Acts	2. 4	talk in other languages, as the Spirit **enabled** them to speak.
	15.10	which neither our ancestors nor we ourselves were **able** to carry?
	16.16	had an evil spirit that **enabled** her to predict the future.
	19.40	and we would not be **able** to give a good reason for
	20.32	of his grace, which is **able** to build you up and give
	24. 8	you yourself will be **able** to learn from him all the
	25. 7	charges against him, which they were not **able** to prove.
Rom	4.21	sure that God would be **able** to do what he had promised.
	8.39	creation that will ever be **able** to separate us from the love
	11.23	for God is **able** to do that.
	14. 4	will succeed, because the Lord is **able** to make him succeed.
	15. 5	of patience and encouragement, **enable** you to have the same point
	15. 9	and to **enable** even the Gentiles to praise God
	15.14	all knowledge, and that you are **able** to teach one another.
	16.25	He is **able** to make you stand firm in your faith,
1 Cor	12. 6	There are different **abilities** to perform service, but
	12. 6	the same God gives **ability** to all for their particular service.
	12.10	and to yet another, the **ability** to tell the difference between
	12.10	one person he gives the **ability** to speak in strange tongues,
	12.10	and to another he gives the **ability** to explain what is said.
2 Cor	1. 4	troubles, so that we are **able** to help others who have all
	5.12	so that you will be **able** to answer those who boast about
	9. 8	And God is **able** to give you more than you need,
Eph	3.20	power working in us is **able** to do so much more than
	6.11	so that you will be **able** to stand up against the Devil's
	6.13	day comes, you will be **able** to resist the enemy's attacks;
	6.16	with it you will be **able** to put out all the burning
Phil	3.21	power by which he is **able** to bring all things under his
Col	1.11	so that you may be **able** to endure everything with patience.
2 Tim	1.12	am sure that he is **able** to keep safe until that Day
	2. 2	to reliable people, who will be **able** to teach others also.
	2. 7	saying, because the Lord will **enable** you to understand it all.
	3.15	the Holy Scriptures, which are **able** to give you the wisdom
Tit	1. 9	this way he will be **able** to encourage others with the true
Heb	3.19	that they were not **able** to enter the land, because they
	5. 2	in many ways, he is **able** to be gentle with those who
	7.25	And so he is **able,** now and always, to save those who
	11.11	was faith that made Abraham **able** to become a father, even
	11.19	Abraham reckoned that God was **able** to raise Isaac from death—
Jas	1. 3	in facing such trials, the result is the **ability** to endure.
	1. 7	A person like that, **unable** to make up his mind and
	1.21	that he plants in your hearts, which is **able** to save you.
	3. 2	he is perfect and is also **able** to control his whole being.
	3. 8	But no one has ever been **able** to tame the tongue.
Jude	24	To him who is **able** to keep you from falling, and to

ABNER

Saul's cousin and army commander.

1 Sam	14.47-52	**Saul's reign and family**
	17.55–18.5	**David is presented to Saul**
	20.1-42	**Jonathan helps David**
	26.1-25	**David spares Saul's life again**
2 Sam	2.8-11	**Ishbosheth is made king of Israel**
	2.12–3.1	**War between Israel and Judah**
	3.6-21	**Abner joins David**
	22-30	**Abner is murdered**
	31-39	**Abner is buried**
	4.1-12	**Ishbosheth is murdered**

1 Sam	14.51	Saul's father Kish and **Abner's** father Ner were sons of Abiel.
1 Kgs	2. 5	two commanders of Israel's armies, **Abner** son of Ner and Amasa
1 Kgs	2.32	**Abner,** commander of the army of Israel, and Amasa,
1 Chr	26.28	Samuel, by King Saul, by **Abner** son of Ner, and by Joab
	27.16	Benjamin Jaasiel son of **Abner**

ABNORMAL

1 Cor	15. 8	me—even though I am like someone whose birth was **abnormal.**

ABOARD

Jon	1. 3	paid his fare and went **aboard** with the crew to sail to
Jn	21.11	Simon Peter went **aboard** and dragged the net ashore
Acts	20.13	off to Assos, where we were going to take Paul **aboard.**
	20.14	we took him **aboard** and went on to Mitylene.
	21. 2	was going to Phoenicia, so we went **aboard** and sailed away.
	27. 2	went **aboard** a ship from Adramyttium, which was ready to leave
	27. 6	that was going to sail for Italy, so he put us **aboard.**
	27.17	They pulled it **aboard** and then fastened some ropes tight

ABOLISH

2 Chr	14. 5	Because he **abolished** the pagan places of worship
Is	28.18	made with death will be **abolished,** and your agreement with the
Eph	2.15	He **abolished** the Jewish Law with its commandments and rules,

AV ABOMINATION

see also **DISGUST**

Gen	43.32	they considered it beneath their **dignity** to eat with Hebrews.
	46.34	Egyptians will have **nothing** to do with shepherds.
Ex	8.26	"because the Egyptians would be **offended** by our sacrificing
	8.26	we use these animals and **offend** the Egyptians by sacrificing
Lev	7.18	credit but will be considered **unclean,** and whoever eats it
	11.10	water that does not have fins and scales must not be **eaten.**
	11.11	Such creatures must be considered **unclean.**
	11.11	You must not **eat** them or even touch their dead bodies.
	11.12	You must not **eat** anything that lives in the water and
	11.13	You must not **eat** any of the following birds:
	11.20	All winged insects are **unclean,** [21] except those that hop.
	11.23	that have wings and also crawl must be considered **unclean.**
	11.41	You must not **eat** any of the small animals that move on
	18.22	God **hates** that.
Deut	7.25	If you do, that will be fatal, because the Lord **hates** idolatry.
	7.26	not bring any of these **idols** into your homes, or the same
	13.14	it is true that this **evil** thing did happen, [15] then kill
	17. 1	the Lord **hates** this.
	17. 4	it is true that this **evil** thing has happened in Israel,
	18.12	Lord your God **hates** people who do these disgusting things,
	22. 5	the Lord your God **hates** people who do such things.
	23.18	The Lord **hates** temple prostitutes.
	24. 4	If he married her again, it would be **offensive** to the Lord.
	25.16	The Lord **hates** people who cheat.
	27.15	the Lord **hates** idolatry.'
	32.16	the **evil** they did made him angry.
1 Sam	13. 4	and that the Philistines **hated** them.
1 Kgs	14.24	of Judah practised all the **shameful** things done by the
2 Kgs	23.24	gods, idols, and all other **pagan** objects of worship.
2 Chr	36.14	nations round them in worshipping **idols,** and so they defiled
Ezra	9.14	commandments again and intermarry with these **wicked** people?
Ps	88. 8	you have made me **repulsive** to them.
Prov	3.32	they do, [32] because the Lord **hates** people who do evil, but
	6.16	There are seven things that the Lord hates and cannot **tolerate:**
	8. 7	lies are **hateful** to me.
	11. 1	The Lord **hates** people who use dishonest scales.
	11.20	Lord **hates** evil-minded people, but loves those who do right.
	12.22	The Lord **hates** liars, but is pleased with those who keep
	13.19	Stupid people **refuse** to turn away from evil.
	15. 8	when good men pray, but **hates** the sacrifices that wicked men
	15. 9	The Lord **hates** the ways of evil people, but loves those
	15.26	Lord **hates** evil thoughts, but he is pleased with friendly words.
	16. 5	The Lord **hates** everyone who is arrogant;
	16.12	Kings cannot **tolerate** evil, because justice is what makes
	17.15	or letting the wicked go—both are **hateful** to the Lord.
	20.10	The Lord **hates** people who use dishonest weights and measures.
	20.23	The Lord **hates** people who use dishonest scales and weights.
	21.27	The Lord **hates** it when wicked men offer him sacrifices,
	24. 9	People **hate** a person who has nothing but scorn for others.
	26.25	him, because his heart is filled to the brim with **hate.**
	28. 9	the law, God will find your prayers too **hateful** to hear.
	29.27	The righteous **hate** the wicked, and the wicked hate the righteous.
Is	44.19	And the rest of the wood I made into an **idol.**
Jer	2. 7	they **defiled** the country I had given them.
	4. 1	to me and remove the **idols** I hate, [2] it will be right
	7.10	You do these things I **hate,** and then you come and stand
	7.30	They have placed their **idols,** which I hate, in my Temple and
	13.27	has seen you go after **pagan** gods on the hills and in
	44.22	Lord could no longer endure your **wicked** and evil practices.
Ezek	5. 9	things you do that I **hate,** I will punish Jerusalem as I
	6. 9	because of the **evil** and degrading things they have done.
	8. 6	You will see even more **disgraceful** things than this."
	16.50	did the things that I **hate,** so I destroyed them, as you
	20.30	same sins your fathers did and go running after their **idols?**
	22.11	Some commit **adultery,** and others seduce
	33.29	the people for their **sins** and make the country a waste,
	36.31	with yourselves because of your **sins** and your iniquities.
Dan	9.27	The **Awful Horror** will be placed on the highest point of the
	11.31	They will stop the daily sacrifices and set up The **Awful Horror.**
	12.11	is, from the time of The **Awful Horror,** 1,290 days will pass.
Zech	9. 7	longer eat meat with blood in it, or other **forbidden** food.
Mal	2.11	to God and done a **horrible** thing in Jerusalem and all over
Mt	24.15	will see 'The **Awful Horror**' of which the prophet Daniel spoke.

Mk 13.14 will see 'The **Awful Horror**' standing in the place where he
Lk 16.15 of great value by man are worth **nothing** in God's sight.
Rev 17. 4 a gold cup full of **obscene** and filthy things, the result of
17. 5 the mother of all the prostitutes and **perverts** in the world."
21.27 the city, nor anyone who does **shameful** things or tells lies.

ABOVE

Gen 49.25 With blessings of rain from **above** And of deep waters from
Josh 2.11 Lord your God is God in heaven **above** and here on earth.
2 Sam 22.17 The Lord reached down from **above** and took hold of me;
1 Kgs 8.23 is no god like you in heaven **above** or on earth below!
Ps 7. 7 all the peoples round you, and rule over them from **above.**
18.16 The Lord reached down from **above** and took hold of me;
78.23 he spoke to the sky **above** and commanded its doors to open;
104. 3 like a tent [3]and built your home on the waters **above.**
113. 5 He lives in the heights **above,** [6]but he bends down to see
138. 6 though you are so high **above,** you care for the lowly, and
144. 7 Reach down from **above,** pull me out of the deep water, and
148. 1 Praise the Lord from heaven, you that live in the heights **above.**
Is 24.21 Lord will punish the powers **above** and the rulers of the earth.
Lam 1.13 "He sent fire from **above,** a fire that burnt inside me.
Ezek 1.22 **Above** the heads of the creatures there was something
3.12 that said, "Praise the glory of the Lord in heaven **above!"**
Lk 24.49 the city until the power from **above** comes down upon you."
Jn 3.31 He who comes from **above** is greater than all.
8.23 "You belong to this world here below, but I come from **above.**
Rom 8.39 neither the world **above** nor the world below—
Phil 2. 9 him to the highest place **above** and gave him the name
3.14 which is God's call through Christ Jesus to the life **above.**
Jas 3.17 But the wisdom from **above** is pure first of all;
2 Pet 2.10 and arrogant, and show no respect for the glorious beings **above;**
Jude 8 God's authority and insult the glorious beings **above.**

ABRAHAM

(ABRAM until Gen. 17.5)
Terah's son, Isaac and Ishmael's father and Jacob's grandfather, so regarded as the ancestor of the Israelites.

Gen 11.10-26 **The descendants of Shem**
27-32 **The descendants of Terah**
12.1-9 **God's call to Abram**
10-20 **Abram in Egypt**
13.1-13 **Abram and Lot separate**
14-18 **Abram moves to Hebron**
14.1-16 **Abram rescues Lot**
17-24 **Melchizedek blesses Abram**
15.1-21 **God's covenant with Abram**
16.1-16 **Hagar and Ishmael**
17.1-27 **Circumcision, the sign of the covenant**
18.1-15 **A son is promised to Abraham**
16-33 **Abraham pleads for Sodom**
19.23-29 **The destruction of Sodom and Gomorrah**
20.1-18 **Abraham and Abimelech**
21.1-8 **The birth of Isaac**
9-21 **Hagar and Ishmael are sent away**
22-34 **The agreement between Abraham and Abimelech**
22.1-19 **God commands Abraham to offer Isaac**
20-24 **The descendants of Nahor**
23.1-20 **Sarah dies and Abraham buys a burial-ground**
24.1-67 **A wife for Isaac**
25.1-6 **Other descendants of Abraham**
7-11 **The death and burial of Abraham**

Gen 11.31 and his daughter-in-law Sarai, **Abram's** wife,
13. 7 men who took care of **Abram's** animals
14.12 Lot, **Abram's** nephew, was living in Sodom,
14.13 and his brothers Eshcol and Aner were **Abram's** allies.
16. 1 **Abram's** wife Sarai had not borne him any children.
25.12 slave of Sarah, bore to **Abraham,** [13]had the following sons,
25.18 They lived apart from the other descendants of **Abraham.**
25.19 This is the story of **Abraham's** son Isaac.
26. 1 the land besides the earlier one during the time of **Abraham.**
26. 3 I will keep the promise I made to your father **Abraham.**
26. 5 I will bless you, because **Abraham** obeyed me and kept all
26.15 of his father **Abraham** had dug while Abraham was alive.
26.18 dug during the time of **Abraham**
26.18 and which the Philistines had stopped up after **Abraham's** death.
26.24 to him and said, "I am the God of your father **Abraham.**
26.24 many descendants because of my promise to my servant **Abraham."**
28. 4 your descendants as he blessed **Abraham,**
28. 4 in which you have lived and which God gave to **Abraham!"**
28. 9 went to Ishmael son of **Abraham** and married his daughter Mahalath,
28.13 "I am the Lord, the God of **Abraham** and Isaac," he said.
31.42 my fathers, the God of **Abraham** and Isaac, had not been with
31.53 The God of **Abraham** and the God of Nahor will judge
32. 9 "God of my grandfather **Abraham** and God of my father Isaac,
35.12 land which I gave to **Abraham** and to Isaac, and I will
35.27 at Mamre, near Hebron, where **Abraham** and Isaac had lived.
48.15 God whom my fathers **Abraham** and Isaac served bless these boys!
48.16 the name of my fathers **Abraham** and Isaac live on through
49.30 **Abraham** bought this cave and field from Ephron
49.31 That is where they buried **Abraham** and his wife Sarah;
50.13 Mamre, in the field which **Abraham** had bought from Ephron
50.24 land he solemnly promised to **Abraham,** Isaac, and Jacob."
Ex 2.24 remembered his covenant with **Abraham,** Isaac, and Jacob.
3. 6 the God of your ancestors, the God of **Abraham,** Isaac, and
3.15 the God of **Abraham,** Isaac, and Jacob, have sent you
3.16 the God of **Abraham,** Isaac, and Jacob, appeared to you.
4. 5 the God of **Abraham,** Isaac, and Jacob, has appeared to
Ex 6. 3 I appeared to **Abraham,** to Isaac, and to Jacob as Almighty God,
6. 8 I solemnly promised to give to **Abraham,** Isaac, and Jacob;
32.13 Remember your servants **Abraham,** Isaac, and Jacob.
33. 1 I promised to give to **Abraham,** Isaac, and Jacob
Lev 26.42 and with Isaac and with **Abraham,** and I will renew my promise
Num 32.11 enter the land that I promised to **Abraham,** Isaac, and Jacob.'
Deut 1. 8 to give to your ancestors, **Abraham,** Isaac, and Jacob,
6.10 your God promised your ancestors, **Abraham,** Isaac, and Jacob,
9. 5 promise that he made to your ancestors, **Abraham,** Isaac, and
9.27 Remember your servants, **Abraham,** Isaac, and Jacob,
29.13 he promised you and your ancestors, **Abraham,** Isaac, and Jacob.
30.20 land that he promised to give your ancestors, **Abraham,** Isaac,
34. 4 the land that I promised **Abraham,** Isaac, and Jacob I would
Josh 24. 2 One of those ancestors was Terah, the father of **Abraham**
24. 3 Then I took **Abraham,** your ancestor, from the land
1 Kgs 18.36 "O Lord, the God of **Abraham,** Isaac, and Jacob, prove now
2 Kgs 13.23 because of his covenant with **Abraham,** Isaac, and Jacob.
1 Chr 1.24 The family line from Shem to **Abram** is as follows:
1.27 Serug, Nahor, Terah, [27]and Abram (also known as **Abraham).**
1.28 **Abraham** had two sons, Isaac and Ishmael.
1.32 **Abraham** had a concubine named Keturah,
1.34 **Abraham's** son Isaac had two sons, Esau and Jacob.
16.16 the covenant he made with **Abraham,**
29.18 Lord God of our ancestors **Abraham,** Isaac, and Jacob,
2 Chr 20. 7 land to the descendants of **Abraham,** your friend,
30. 6 the Lord, the God of **Abraham,** Isaac, and Jacob,
Neh 9. 7 You, Lord God, chose **Abram** and led him out of Ur
9. 7 you changed his name to **Abraham.**
Ps 47. 9 the nations assemble with the people of the God of **Abraham.**
105. 5 You descendants of **Abraham,** his servant;
105. 9 keep the agreement he made with **Abraham**
105.42 He remembered his sacred promise to **Abraham** his servant.
Is 29.22 God of Israel, who rescued **Abraham** from trouble,
41. 8 the people that I have chosen, the descendants of **Abraham,**
51. 2 Think of your ancestor, **Abraham,** and of Sarah,
51. 2 When I called **Abraham,** he was childless,
63.16 Our ancestors **Abraham** and Jacob do not acknowledge us,
Jer 33.26 David's descendants to rule over the descendants of **Abraham,**
Ezek 33.24 **'Abraham** was only one man, and he was given the whole land.
Mic 7.20 your people, the descendants of **Abraham** and of Jacob,
Mt 1. 1 who was a descendant of **Abraham.**
1. 2 **Abraham** to King David, the following ancestors are listed:
1. 2 **Abraham,** Isaac, Jacob, Judah and his brothers;
1.17 there were fourteen generations from **Abraham** to David,
3. 9 can escape punishment by saying that **Abraham** is your ancestor.
3. 9 God can take these stones and make descendants for **Abraham!**
8.11 and sit down with **Abraham,** Isaac, and Jacob at the feast
22.32 'I am the God of **Abraham,** the God of Isaac,
Mk 12.26 'I am the God of **Abraham,** the God of Isaac,
Lk 1.55 remembered to show mercy to **Abraham** and to all his descendants
1.73 solemn oath to our ancestor **Abraham** he promised to rescue us
3. 8 saying among yourselves that **Abraham** is your ancestor.
3. 8 God can take these stones and make descendants for **Abraham!**
3.34 the son of **Abraham,** the son of Terah,
13.16 Now here is this descendant of **Abraham** whom Satan has kept
13.28 your teeth when you see **Abraham,** Isaac, and Jacob,
16.22 to sit beside **Abraham** at the feast in heaven.
16.23 he looked up and saw **Abraham,** far away, with Lazarus
16.24 So he called out, 'Father **Abraham!**
16.25 "But **Abraham** said, 'Remember, my son, that in your lifetime
16.27 I beg you, father **Abraham,** send Lazarus to my father's house,
16.29 **"Abraham** said, 'Your brothers have Moses and the prophets
16.30 The rich man answered, 'That is not enough, father **Abraham!**
16.31 But **Abraham** said, 'If they will not listen to Moses
19. 9 for this man, also, is a descendant of **Abraham.**
20.37 Lord as 'the God of **Abraham,** the God of Isaac,
Jn 8.33 "We are the descendants of **Abraham,"** they answered,
8.37 I know you are **Abraham's** descendants.
8.39 They answered him, "Our father is **Abraham."**
8.39 "If you really were **Abraham's** children," Jesus replied,
8.40 **Abraham** did nothing like this!
8.52 **Abraham** died, and the prophets died, yet you say that whoever
8.53 Our father **Abraham** died;
8.53 you do not claim to be greater than **Abraham,** do you?
8.56 Your father **Abraham** rejoiced that he was to see the time
8.57 "You are not even fifty years old—and you have seen **Abraham?"**
8.58 "Before **Abraham** was born, 'I Am'."
Acts 3.13 God of **Abraham,** Isaac, and Jacob, the God of our ancestors,
3.25 As he said to **Abraham,** 'Through your descendants I will bless
7. 2 Before our ancestor **Abraham** had gone to live in Haran,
7. 4 After **Abraham's** father died, God made him move to this land
7. 5 God did not then give **Abraham** any part of it as his
7. 5 At the time God made this promise, **Abraham** had no children.
7. 8 Then God gave **Abraham** the ceremony of circumcision as a sign
7. 8 So **Abraham** circumcised Isaac a week after he was born;
7.16 buried in the grave which **Abraham** had bought from the clan
7.17 promise he had made to **Abraham,** the number of our people
7.32 God of your ancestors, the God of **Abraham,** Isaac, and Jacob.'
13.26 "My fellow-Israelites, descendants of **Abraham,** and all Gentiles here
Rom 4. 1 What shall we say, then, of **Abraham,** the father of our race?
4. 3 says, **"Abraham** believed God, and because of his faith God
4. 9 we have quoted the scripture, **"Abraham** believed God,
4.10 Was it before or after **Abraham** was circumcised?
4.11 And so **Abraham** is the spiritual father of all who believe
4.12 life of faith that our father **Abraham** lived before he was
4.13 When God promised **Abraham** and his descendants that the world
4.13 he did so, not because **Abraham** obeyed the Law, but because
4.16 gift to all of **Abraham's** descendants—not just to those who
4.16 but also to those who believe as **Abraham** did.

Rom 4.16 For **Abraham** is the spiritual father of us all;
4.17 sight of God, in whom **Abraham** believed—the God who brings
4.18 **Abraham** believed and hoped, even when there was no reason for
4.22 why **Abraham,** through faith, "was accepted as righteous by God."
9. 7 Nor are all **Abraham's** descendants the children of God.
9. 7 God said to **Abraham,** "It is through Isaac that you will
11. 1 myself am an Israelite, a descendant of **Abraham,** a member of
2 Cor 11.22 Are they **Abraham's** descendants?
Gal 3. 6 Consider the experience of **Abraham;**
3. 7 that the real descendants of **Abraham** are the people who
3. 8 And so the scripture announced the Good News to **Abraham:**
3. 9 **Abraham** believed and was blessed;
3.14 blessing which God promised to **Abraham** might be given to
3.16 Now, God made his promises to **Abraham** and to his descendant.
3.17 God made a covenant with **Abraham** and promised to keep it.
3.18 because of his promise that God gave that gift to **Abraham.**
3.19 the coming of **Abraham's** descendant, to whom the promise was made.
3.29 then you are the descendants of **Abraham** and will receive what
4.22 It says that **Abraham** had two sons, one by a slave-woman,
Heb 2.16 as the scripture says, "He helps the descendants of **Abraham."**
6.13 God made his promise to **Abraham,** he made a vow
6.15 **Abraham** was patient, and so he received what God had promised.
7. 1 As **Abraham** was coming back from the battle
7. 2 and **Abraham** gave him a tenth of all
7. 4 **Abraham,** our famous ancestor, gave him a tenth of all he got
7. 5 even though their countrymen are also descendants of **Abraham.**
7. 6 he collected a tenth from **Abraham** and blessed him,
7. 9 And, so to speak, when **Abraham** paid the tenth,
7.10 in the body of his ancestor **Abraham** when Melchizedek met him.
11. 8 It was faith that made **Abraham** obey when God called him
11.10 For **Abraham** was waiting for the city which God has designed
11.11 It was faith that made **Abraham** able to become a father,
11.12 **Abraham** was practically dead, from this one man came as many
11.17 It was faith that made **Abraham** offer his son Isaac
11.17 as a sacrifice when God put **Abraham** to the test.
11.17 **Abraham** was the one to whom God had made the promise,
11.19 **Abraham** reckoned that God was able to raise Isaac from death—
11.19 and, so to speak, **Abraham** did receive Isaac back from death.
Jas 2.21 How was our ancestor **Abraham** put right with God?
2.23 scripture came true that said, **"Abraham** believed God,
2.23 And so **Abraham** was called God's friend.
1 Pet 3. 6 she obeyed **Abraham** and called him her master.

ABROAD

Job 18.17 His fame is ended at home and **abroad;**

ABSALOM

David's son, who led a rebellion against his father and was killed in the fighting.

2 Sam 3.2-5 **David's sons**
13.1-22 **Amnon and Tamar**
23-39 **Absalom's revenge**
14.1-24 **Joab arranges for Absalom's return**
25-33 **Absalom is reconciled to David**
15.1-12 **Absalom plans rebellion**
13-37 **David flees from Jerusalem**
16.5-14 **David and Shimei**
15-23 **Absalom in Jerusalem**
17.1-14 **Hushai misleads Absalom**
15-29 **David is warned and escapes**
18.1-18 **Absalom is defeated and killed**
19-33 **David is told of Absalom's death**
19.1-8 **Joab reprimands David**

2 Sam 19. 9 but now he has fled from **Absalom** and left the country.
19.10 We anointed **Absalom** as our king, but he has been killed
20. 6 to Abishai, "Sheba will give us more trouble than **Absalom.**
1 Kgs 1. 5 Now that **Absalom** was dead, Adonijah, the son of David
2. 7 kind to me when I was fleeing from your brother **Absalom.**
2.28 (He had supported Adonijah, but not **Absalom.)**
15. 2 His mother was Maacah, the daughter of **Absalom.**
15.10 His grandmother was Maacah, the daughter of **Absalom.**
1 Chr 3. 1 **Absalom,** whose mother was Maacah,
2 Chr 11.20 he married Maacah, the daughter of **Absalom,**

ABSALOM'S MONUMENT

2 Sam 18.18 and to this day it is known as **Absalom's Monument.**

ABSENCE

Gen 31.19 and during his **absence** Rachel stole the household gods
1 Sam 20.18 the New Moon Festival, your **absence** will be noticed
20.19 The day after tomorrow your **absence** will be noticed
2 Sam 11.10 he asked him, "You have just returned after a long **absence;**
1 Cor 16.17 have made up for your **absence** [18]and have cheered me up,
Col 2. 5 For even though I am **absent** in body, yet I am with

ABSTAIN

Num 6. 3 dedicates himself to the Lord [3]shall **abstain** from wine and beer.
30. 2 takes an oath to **abstain** from something,
30. 3 or promises to **abstain** from something, [4]she must do everything
30. 6 or promises to **abstain** from something, and then marries,
30. 9 every vow she makes and every promise to **abstain** from something.
30.10 or promises to **abstain** from something,

AV **ABSTAIN** see **KEEP FROM**

ABUNDANT

Gen 41.47 the land produced **abundant** crops,
Num 24. 7 They will have **abundant** rainfall
Deut 28. 4 with many children, with **abundant** crops, and with many cattle
28.11 many children, many cattle, and **abundant** crops
30. 9 and your fields will produce **abundant** crops.
Job 36.31 how he feeds the people and provides an **abundance** of food.
Ps 36. 8 We feast on the **abundant** food you provide;
65.10 you send **abundant** rain on the ploughed fields
68. 9 You caused **abundant** rain to fall
107.37 planted grapevines and reaped an **abundant** harvest.
Jer 33. 6 I will show them **abundant** peace and security.
Ezek 27.12 iron, tin, and lead in payment for your **abundant** goods.
Joel 2.14 God will change his mind and bless you with **abundant** crops.
Zech 14.14 gold, silver, and clothing in great **abundance.**
Mal 3.10 and pour out on you in **abundance** all kinds of good things.
Rom 5.17 All who receive God's **abundant** grace and are freely put right
9.23 wanted to reveal his **abundant** glory, which was poured out
Eph 2. 4 But God's mercy is so **abundant,** and his love for us
Phil 4.19 And with all his **abundant** wealth through Christ Jesus,
1 Tim 1.14 our Lord poured out his **abundant** grace on me
Tit 3. 6 poured out the Holy Spirit **abundantly** on us through Jesus
2 Pet 1. 8 if you have them in **abundance,** they will make you active

ABUSE

Judg 19.25 They raped her and **abused** her all night long and didn't stop
Job 19. 3 insult me and show no shame for the way you **abuse** me.
Prov 29. 9 the fool only laughs and becomes loud and **abusive.**

ABYSS

The place in the depths of the earth where, according to ancient Jewish teaching, the demons were imprisoned until their final punishment.

Lk 8.31 The demons begged Jesus not to send them into the **abyss.**
Rev 9. 1 to the earth, and it was given the key to the **abyss.**
9. 2 The star opened the **abyss,** and smoke poured out of it,
9. 2 and the air were darkened by the smoke from the **abyss.**
9.11 who is the angel in charge of the **abyss.**
11. 7 that comes up out of the **abyss** will fight against them.
17. 8 to come up from the **abyss** and will go off
20. 1 in his hand the key of the **abyss** and a heavy chain.
20. 3 angel threw him into the **abyss,** locked it, and sealed it,

ACACIA-WOOD

A flowering tree with hard and durable wood.

Ex 25. 5 **acacia-wood;**
25.10 "Make a box out of **acacia-wood,** 110 centimetres long,
25.13 Make carrying-poles of **acacia-wood** and cover them with gold
25.23 "Make a table out of **acacia-wood,** 88 centimetres long,
25.28 Make the poles of **acacia-wood** and cover them with gold.
26.15 "Make upright frames for the Tent out of **acacia-wood.**
26.26 "Make fifteen cross-bars of **acacia-wood,**
26.32 four posts of **acacia-wood** covered with gold, fitted with hooks,
26.37 make five posts of **acacia-wood** covered with gold
27. 1 "Make an altar out of **acacia-wood.**
27. 6 Make carrying-poles of **acacia-wood,** cover them with bronze,
30. 1 "Make an altar out of **acacia-wood,** for burning incense.
30. 5 Make these poles of **acacia-wood** and cover them with gold.
35. 7 **acacia-wood;**
35.24 and all who had **acacia-wood** which could be used
36.20 They made upright frames of **acacia-wood** for the Tent.
36.31 They made fifteen cross-bars of **acacia-wood,**
36.36 They made four posts of **acacia-wood** to hold the curtain,
37. 1 the Covenant Box out of **acacia-wood,** 110 centimetres long,
37. 4 He made carrying-poles of **acacia-wood,** covered them with gold,
37.10 made the table out of **acacia-wood,** 88 centimetres long,
37.15 He made the poles of **acacia-wood** and covered them with gold.
37.25 He made an altar out of **acacia-wood,** for burning incense.
37.28 He made the poles of **acacia-wood** and covered them with gold.
38. 1 For burning offerings, he made an altar out of **acacia-wood.**
38. 6 He made carrying-poles of **acacia-wood,** covered them with bronze,
Deut 10. 3 I made a box of **acacia-wood** and cut two stone tablets
Is 41.19 make cedars grow in the desert, and **acacias** and myrtles

ACCENT

Judg 18. 3 they recognized the **accent** of the young Levite,

ACCEPT

Gen 14.24 I will **accept** only what my men have used.
15. 6 the Lord was pleased with him and **accepted** him.
18. 5 we **accept."**
21.30 Abraham answered, **"Accept** these seven lambs.
23.13 **Accept** my payment, and I will bury my wife there."
30.20 Now my husband will **accept** me, because I have borne him six
33.10 "No, please, if I have gained your favour, **accept** my gift.
33.11 Please **accept** this gift which I have brought for you;
33.11 Jacob kept on urging him until he **accepted.**
34.17 But if you will not **accept** our terms and be circumcised,
Ex 22.11 not stolen, the owner shall **accept** the loss, and the other
23. 8 Do not **accept** a bribe, for a bribe makes people blind to
28.38 the Lord, will **accept** all the offerings that the Israelites

Ex	34. 9	our evil and our sin, and **accept** us as your own people."
Lev	1. 3	Tent of the Lord's presence so that the Lord will **accept** him.
	1. 4	and it will be **accepted** as a sacrifice
	7.18	on the third day, God will not **accept** the man's offering.
	19. 5	and I will **accept** the offering.
	19. 7	and if anyone eats it, I will not **accept** the offering.
	22.19	To be **accepted,** it must be a male without any defects.
	22.20	any animal that has any defect, the Lord will not **accept** it.
	22.21	animal must be without any defect if it is to be **accepted.**
	22.23	but it is not **acceptable** in fulfilment of a vow.
	22.25	Such animals are considered defective and are not **acceptable.**
	22.26	but after that it is **acceptable** as a food-offering.
	22.29	to the Lord, follow the rules so that you will be **accepted;**
	23.11	a special offering to the Lord, so that you may be **accepted.**
	26.31	and refuse to **accept** your sacrifices.
	27. 9	an animal that is **acceptable** as an offering to the Lord,
	27.11	unclean animal, which is not **acceptable** as an offering
Num	7. 5	the Lord said to Moses, [5]"**Accept** these gifts
	16.15	"Do not **accept** any offerings these men bring.
	18.15	But you must **accept** payment to buy back every first-born child,
	18.15	and must also **accept** payment for every first-born animal that
Deut	10.17	He does not show partiality, and he does not **accept** bribes.
	16.19	they are not to **accept** bribes, for gifts blind the eyes
	17.11	**Accept** their verdict and follow their instructions
	26.18	Today the Lord has **accepted** you as his own people,
	27.25	" 'God's curse on anyone who **accepts** money to murder
	29.12	making with you and to **accept** its obligations,
Josh	9.14	The men of Israel **accepted** some food from them,
Judg	13.23	wanted to kill us, he would not have **accepted** our offerings;
1 Sam	2.15	he won't **accept** boiled meat from you, only raw meat."
	8. 3	so they **accepted** bribes and did not decide cases
	10. 4	and offer you two of the loaves, which you are to **accept.**
	11. 1	a treaty with us, and we will **accept** you as our ruler."
	12. 3	Have I **accepted** a bribe from anyone?
	25.27	Please, sir, **accept** this present I have brought you,
	25.35	Then David **accepted** what she had brought him
2 Sam	3.21	They will **accept** you as king, and then you will get what
	16.23	gave in those days was **accepted** as though it were the very
	24.23	to him, "May the Lord your God **accept** your offering."
1 Kgs	7.14	He **accepted** King Solomon's invitation to be in charge
	13.16	"I can't go home with you or **accept** your hospitality.
2 Kgs	5.15	so please, sir, **accept** a gift from me."
	5.16	whom I serve, I swear that I will not **accept** a gift."
	5.16	Naaman insisted that he **accept** it, but he would not.
	5.17	Naaman said, "If you won't **accept** my gift,
	5.20	He should have **accepted** what that Syrian offered him.
	5.26	This is no time to **accept** money and clothes,
1 Chr	28. 9	If you go to him, he will **accept** you;
2 Chr	7.12	heard your prayer, and I **accept** this Temple as the place
	15.15	and he **accepted** them and gave them peace
	30. 9	merciful, and if you return to him, he will **accept** you."
	30.27	In his home in heaven God heard their prayers and **accepted** them.
	33.13	God **accepted** Manasseh's prayer and answered it
Ezra	2.61	they were not **accepted** as priests.
	6.10	can offer sacrifices that are **acceptable** to the God of Heaven
	10.16	The returned exiles **accepted** the plan,
Neh	7.63	they were not **accepted** as priests.
Esth	4. 4	on instead of the sackcloth, but he would not **accept** them.
Job	5.27	It is true, so now **accept** it.
	17. 3	**Accept** my word.
	21.16	own strength, but their way of thinking I can't **accept.**
	22.22	**Accept** the teaching he gives;
Ps	19.14	words and my thoughts be **acceptable** to you, O Lord, my
	20. 3	May he **accept** all your offerings
	119.108	**Accept** my prayer of thanks, O Lord,
	141. 5	but I will never **accept** honour from evil men,
Prov	6.35	He will not **accept** any payment;
	10. 8	Sensible people **accept** good advice.
	15. 5	it is wise to **accept** his correction.
	15.32	If you **accept** correction, you will become wiser.
	17.23	Corrupt judges **accept** secret bribes,
	18.21	so you must **accept** the consequences of your words.
	21.28	but the word of someone who thinks matters through is **accepted.**
Is	1.23	they are always **accepting** gifts and bribes.
	33.15	Don't use your power to cheat the poor and don't **accept** bribes.
	56. 7	and **accept** the sacrifices you offer
Jer	3.19	"Israel, I wanted to **accept** you as my son
	6.20	I will not **accept** their offerings
	12.16	they will **accept** the religion of my people
Lam	3.30	Though beaten and insulted, we should **accept** it all.
Ezek	20.41	I will **accept** the sacrifices that you burn,
Dan	11.39	great honour to those who **accept** him as ruler,
Hos	14. 2	"Forgive all our sins and **accept** our prayer,
Amos	5.22	burnt-offerings and grain-offerings, I will not **accept** them;
	5.22	I will not **accept** the animals you have fattened
Zeph	3. 2	It has not listened to the Lord or **accepted** his discipline.
	3. 7	have reverence for me and **accept** my discipline,
Mal	1.10	I will not **accept** the offerings you bring me.
	1.11	they burn incense to me and offer **acceptable** sacrifices.
	1.13	Do you think I will **accept** that from you?
	2.13	because he no longer **accepts** the offerings you bring him.
	2.14	You ask why he no longer **accepts** them.
Mt	19.12	Let him who can **accept** this teaching do so."
Mk	4.20	They hear the message, **accept** it, and bear fruit:
Lk	7.35	wisdom, however, is shown to be true by all who **accept** it."
	14.18	please **accept** my apologies.'
	14.19	please **accept** my apologies.'
Jn	3.11	yet none of you is willing to **accept** our message.
	3.32	what he has seen and heard, yet no one **accepts** his message.
	3.33	whoever **accepts** his message confirms by this that God is truthful.
Jn	5.31	what I say is not to be **accepted** as real proof.
	8.37	trying to kill me, because you will not **accept** my teaching.
	12.48	rejects me and does not **accept** my message has one who will
	13.30	Judas **accepted** the bread and went out at once.
	14.21	"Whoever **accepts** my commandments and obeys them is the one
Acts	6. 7	and a great number of priests **accepted** the faith.
	10.35	does what is right is **acceptable** to him, no matter what race
	16.21	are Roman citizens, and we cannot **accept** these customs
	22.18	because the people here will not **accept** your witness about me.'
Rom	4. 3	and because of his faith God **accepted** him as righteous."
	4. 6	the person whom God **accepts** as righteous, apart from anything
	4. 9	and because of his faith God **accepted** him as righteous."
	4.11	his faith God had **accepted** him as righteous before he had
	4.11	believe in God and are **accepted** as righteous by him,
	4.13	but because he believed and was **accepted** as righteous by God.
	4.22	why Abraham, through faith, "was **accepted** as righteous by God."
	4.23	words "he was **accepted** as righteous" were not written for him
	4.24	us who are to be **accepted** as righteous, who believe in him
	10.16	But not all have **accepted** the Good News.
	11.15	What will it be, then, when they are **accepted?**
	12.16	Do not be proud, but **accept** humble duties.
	14. 3	for God has **accepted** him.
	15. 7	**Accept** one another, then, for the glory of God,
	15. 7	as Christ has **accepted** you.
	15.16	Gentiles may be an offering **acceptable** to God, dedicated to him
	15.31	my service in Jerusalem may be **acceptable** to God's people there.
1 Cor	7.14	unbelieving husband is made **acceptable** to God by being united
	7.14	the unbelieving wife is made **acceptable** to God by being united
	7.14	but as it is, they are **acceptable** to God.
	7.18	If a circumcised man has **accepted** God's call, he should not
	7.18	if an uncircumcised man has **accepted** God's call, he should not
	7.20	Everyone should remain as he was when he **accepted** God's call.
	9. 2	Even if others do not **accept** me as an apostle, surely you
2 Cor	6.17	nothing to do with what is unclean, and I will **accept** you.
	8.12	God will **accept** your gift on the basis of
	11. 4	and you **accept** a spirit and a gospel completely different from
	11.16	if you do, at least **accept** me as a fool,
Gal	1. 6	you by the grace of Christ, and are **accepting** another gospel.
	1. 9	from the one you **accepted,** may he be condemned to hell!
	3. 6	and because of his faith God **accepted** him as righteous."
Eph	6.17	And **accept** salvation as a helmet, and the word of God
Phil	4.18	to God, a sacrifice which is **acceptable** and pleasing to him.
Col	2. 6	Since you have **accepted** Christ Jesus as Lord,
1 Thes	2.13	message, you heard it and **accepted** it, not as man's message
2 Thes	3. 8	We did not **accept** anyone's support without paying for it.
1 Tim	1.15	This is a true saying, to be completely **accepted** and believed:
	4. 5	the word of God and the prayer make it **acceptable** to God.
	4. 9	This is a true saying, to be completely **accepted** and believed.
Heb	4. 2	when they heard it, they did not **accept** it with faith.
	11.35	Others, refusing to **accept** freedom, died under torture
	12. 6	everyone he loves, and punishes everyone he **accepts** as a son."
Jas	1.21	Submit to God and **accept** the word that he plants in your
	2.23	and because of his faith God **accepted** him as righteous."
1 Pet	2. 5	offer spiritual and **acceptable** sacrifices to God through Jesus
1 Jn	2.23	whoever **accepts** the Son has the Father also.
3 Jn	7	service of Christ without **accepting** any help from unbelievers.
Rev	22.17	**accept** the water of life as a gift, whoever wants it.

AV ACCEPT

Gen	19.21	He answered, "All right, I **agree.**
Lev	10.19	"If I had eaten the sin-offering today, would the Lord have **approved?**
1 Sam	18. 5	This **pleased** all of Saul's officers and men.
Esth	10. 3	He was honoured and **well-liked** by his fellow-Jews.
Job	34.19	the side of rulers nor **favour** the rich against the poor, for
	42. 9	Lord had told them to do, and the Lord **answered** Job's prayer.
Hos	8.13	I, the Lord, am not **pleased** with them, and now I will

ACCIDENT

Ex	21.13	But if it was an **accident** and he did not mean to
Num	35. 6	to which a man can escape if he kills someone **accidentally.**
	35.11	to which a man can escape if he kills someone **accidentally.**
	35.15	Anyone who kills someone **accidentally** can escape to one of them.
	35.22	"But suppose a man **accidentally** kills someone
Deut	4.42	be safe if he had **accidentally** killed someone
	19. 4	If a man **accidentally** kills someone who is not his enemy,
	19. 6	After all, it was by **accident** that he killed a man
Josh	20. 3	A person who kills someone **accidentally** can go there
	20. 5	he killed the person **accidentally** and not out of anger.
	20. 9	Anyone who killed a person **accidentally** could find protection
1 Kgs	3.19	Then one night she **accidentally** rolled over on her baby

ACCOMPANY

Num	15.12	the **accompanying** offering is to be increased proportionately.
	16.25	Then Moses, **accompanied** by the leaders of Israel,
	22.22	riding along on his donkey, **accompanied** by his two servants,
1 Sam	2.19	when she **accompanied** her husband to offer the yearly
	25.42	**Accompanied** by her five maids, she went with David's servants
2 Sam	15.16	So the king left, **accompanied** by all his family
1 Kgs	20.20	Benhadad escaped on horseback, **accompanied** by some of the cavalry.
2 Kgs	5.18	will forgive me when I **accompany** my king to the temple
	23. 2	they went to the Temple, **accompanied** by the priests
1 Chr	15.28	So all the Israelites **accompanied** the Covenant Box
	25. 1	to proclaim God's messages, **accompanied** by the music of harps
	25. 3	proclaimed God's message, **accompanied** by the music of harps,
	25. 6	under their father's direction, to **accompany** the temple worship.
2 Chr	5.11	The singers were **accompanied** in perfect harmony by trumpets,

2 Chr 17. 8 They were **accompanied** by nine Levites and two priests.
22. 8 Ahaziah's nephews that had **accompanied** Ahaziah on his visit.
26.17 Azariah the priest, **accompanied** by eighty strong and
34.30 they went to the Temple, **accompanied** by the priests
Lk 7.11 to a town called Nain, **accompanied** by his disciples
Acts 11.12 These six fellow-believers from Joppa **accompanied** me to Caesarea,

ACCOMPLISH

1 Kgs 16.27 Omri did and all his **accomplishments** are recorded in The History
Neh 1. 1 This is the account of what Nehemiah son of Hacaliah **accomplished.**
Ecc 2. 4 I **accomplished** great things.
Is 26.18 we have **accomplished** nothing.
46.11 swoop down like a hawk and **accomplish** what I have planned.
49. 4 I have used up my strength, but have **accomplished** nothing."
1 Cor 15.29 What do they hope to **accomplish?**
2 Cor 8. 1 what God's grace has **accomplished** in the churches in Macedonia.
Heb 9.14 how much more is **accomplished** by the blood of Christ!
Rev 10. 7 then God will **accomplish** his secret plan,

ACCORD

Jn 11.51 Actually, he did not say this of his own **accord;**

ACCOUNT

Ex 17.14 said to Moses, "Write an **account** of this victory,
Num 33. 1 The following **account** gives the names of the places
Josh 14. 1 What follows is an **account** of how the land of Canaan west
1 Kgs 16.20 that Zimri did, including the **account** of his conspiracy,
22.39 King Ahab did, including an **account** of his palace
2 Kgs 12.15 there was no need to require them to **account** for the funds.
15.15 that Shallum did, including an **account** of his conspiracy,
20.20 his brave deeds, and an **account** of how he built a reservoir
22. 7 is no need to require them to **account** for the funds."
2 Chr 33.19 answer to it, and an **account** of the sins he committed
Neh 1. 1 the **account** of what Nehemiah son of Hacaliah accomplished.
Esth 2.23 The king ordered an **account** of this to be written down
6. 2 included the **account** of how Mordecai had uncovered
Jer 1. 1 This book is the **account** of what was said by Jeremiah son
51.60 wrote in a book an **account** of all the destruction
Dan 4. 2 Listen to my **account** of the wonders and miracles
7.28 This is the end of the **account.**
Nah 1. 1 about Nineveh, the **account** of a vision seen by Nahum,
Mt 12.36 everyone will have to give **account** of every useless word he
18.23 was a king who decided to check on his servants' **accounts.**
25.19 master of those servants came back and settled **accounts** with
27.19 in a dream last night I suffered much on **account** of him."
Mk 16. 9 and gave them a brief **account** of all they had been told.
Lk 1. 3 it would be good to write an orderly **account** for you.
16. 2 Hand in a complete **account** of your handling of my property,
16. 6 'Here is your **account,'** the manager told him;
16. 7 'Here is your **account,'** the manager told him;
Jn 12.11 because on his **account** many Jews were rejecting them
Acts 11. 4 Peter gave them a complete **account** of what had happened
24. 4 I beg you to be kind and listen to our brief **account.**
28. 3 a snake came out on **account** of the heat and fastened itself
Rom 4. 5 faith that God takes into **account** in order to put him right
4. 8 the person whose sins the Lord will not keep **account** of!"
5.13 but where there is no law, no **account** is kept of sins.
9.28 the Lord will quickly settle his full **account** with the world."
14.12 us, then, will have to give an **account** of himself to God.
1 Cor 11.10 On **account** of the angels, then, a woman should have a
2 Cor 5.19 God did not keep an **account** of their sins,
Phil 4.17 rather, I want to see profit added to your **account.**
Phlm 18 you any wrong or owes you anything, charge it to my **account.**
Heb 4.13 is to him that we must all give an **account** of ourselves.
13.17 since they must give God an **account** of their service.
1 Pet 4. 5 will have to give an **account** of themselves to God, who is
Rev 16.21 people, who cursed God on **account** of the plague of hail,

ACCUMULATE

1 Chr 22.14 by my efforts I have **accumulated** more than 3,400 metric tons

ACCURATE

Acts 23.15 pretending that you want to get more **accurate** information
23.20 the Council wants to get more **accurate** information about him.

ACCUSE

Gen 18.20 "There are terrible **accusations** against Sodom and Gomorrah,
18.21 whether or not the **accusations** which I have heard are true."
19.13 Lord has heard the terrible **accusations** against these people
42.30 **accused** us of spying against his country.
Ex 20.16 "Do not **accuse** anyone falsely.
23. 7 Do not make false **accusations,**
Num 35.12 A man **accused** of manslaughter is not to be put to death
35.30 "A man **accused** of murder may be found guilty
35.30 one witness is not sufficient to support an **accusation** of murder.
Deut 5.20 " 'Do not **accuse** anyone falsely.
19.16 to harm another by falsely **accusing** him of a crime,
19.18 man has made a false **accusation** against his fellow-Israelite,
19.19 the punishment the **accused** man would have received.
22.14 false charges against her, **accusing** her of not being a virgin
1 Sam 12. 3 I have done anything wrong, **accuse** me now
12. 7 and I will **accuse** you before the Lord
1 Sam 22.15 Your Majesty must not **accuse** me or anyone else
2 Sam 3. 7 Ishbosheth son of Saul **accused** Abner of sleeping with Saul's concubine
1 Kgs 8.31 "When a person is **accused** of wronging another
21.10 a couple of scoundrels to **accuse** him to his face of cursing
21.13 The two scoundrels publicly **accused** him of cursing God
2 Chr 6.22 "When a person is **accused** of wronging another
Job 13.19 Are you coming to **accuse** me, God?
21.31 There is no one to **accuse** a wicked man
33.13 Why do you **accuse** God of never answering a man's complaints?
36.23 can tell God what to do or **accuse** him of doing evil.
Ps 32. 2 whom the Lord does not **accuse** of doing wrong
35.11 men testify against me and **accuse** me of crimes
35.21 They **accuse** me, shouting, "We saw what you did!"
50.20 You are ready to **accuse** your own brothers
109. 6 and let one of his own enemies **accuse** him.
119.78 May the proud be ashamed for falsely **accusing** me;
140.11 May those who **accuse** others falsely not succeed;
Prov 25.18 A false **accusation** is as deadly as a sword, a club,
Is 3.14 He makes this **accusation:**
43.26 bring your **accusation!**
50. 8 Let him bring his **accusation!**
50. 9 All my **accusers** will disappear;
54.17 you will have an answer for all who **accuse** you.
57.16 I will not continue to **accuse** them or be angry with them
59.12 Our sins **accuse** us.
Jer 2. 5 "What **accusation** did your ancestors bring against me?
14. 7 'Even though our sins **accuse** us, help us, Lord,
32. 3 imprisoned me there and had **accused** me of announcing that
Ezek 23.36 **Accuse** them of the disgusting things they have done.
Dan 6. 5 find anything of which to **accuse** Daniel unless it is something
6.12 all of them went together to the king to **accuse** Daniel.
6.24 all the men who had **accused** Daniel, and they were thrown,
Hos 4. 1 The Lord has an **accusation** to bring against the people
4. 4 Lord says, "Let no one **accuse** the people or reprimand them—
12. 2 The Lord has an **accusation** to bring against the people of Judah;
12. 8 And no one can **accuse** us of getting rich dishonestly.'
Mic 6. 2 He is going to bring an **accusation** against Israel.
Zeph 3. 8 "Wait for the day when I rise to **accuse** the nations.
Zech 3. 1 beside Joshua stood Satan, ready to bring an **accusation**
Mt 12.10 were there who wanted to **accuse** Jesus of doing wrong,
12.41 Nineveh will stand up and **accuse** you, because they turned
12.42 Sheba will stand up and **accuse** you, because she travelled
18.16 so that 'every **accusation** may be upheld by the testimony
19.18 do not **accuse** anyone falsely;
26.62 "Have you no answer to give to this **accusation** against you?"
27.12 nothing in response to the **accusations** of the chief priests
27.13 "Don't you hear all these things they **accuse** you of?"
27.37 they put the written notice of the **accusation** against him:
Mk 3. 2 people were there who wanted to **accuse** Jesus of doing wrong;
10.19 do not **accuse** anyone falsely;
14.60 "Have you no answer to the **accusation** they bring against you?"
14.70 little while later the bystanders **accused** Peter again,
15. 3 The chief priests were **accusing** Jesus of many things,
15. 4 Listen to all their **accusations!"**
15.26 The notice of the **accusation** against him said:
Lk 3.14 "Don't take money from anyone by force or **accuse** anyone falsely.
6. 7 Pharisees wanted a reason to **accuse** Jesus of doing wrong,
11.31 Sheba will stand up and **accuse** the people of today,
11.32 Nineveh will stand up and **accuse** you, because they turned
18.20 do not **accuse** anyone falsely;
23. 2 took Jesus before Pilate, [2] where they began to **accuse** him:
23.10 stepped forward and made strong **accusations** against Jesus.
23.14 found him guilty of any of the crimes you **accuse** him of.
Jn 5.45 I am the one who will **accuse** you to my Father.
5.45 have put your hope, is the very one who will **accuse** you.
8. 6 They said this to trap Jesus, so that they could **accuse** him.
18.29 to them and asked, "What do you **accuse** this man of?"
Acts 19.38 and his workers have an **accusation** against anyone,
19.40 there is the danger that we will be **accused** of a riot.
22.30 to find out for certain what the Jews were **accusing** Paul of;
23.28 to know what they were **accusing** him of, so I took him
23.29 the **accusation** against him had to do with questions about their
23.30 I have told his **accusers** to make their charges against him
23.35 he said, "I will hear you when your **accusers** arrive."
24. 2 and Tertullus began to make his **accusation,** as follows:
24. 8 learn from him all the things that we are **accusing** him of."
24. 9 The Jews joined in the **accusation** and said that all this
24.13 give you proof of the **accusations** they now bring against me.
24.19 and make their **accusations** if they have anything against me.
25. 5 to Caesarea with me and **accuse** the man if he has done
25.16 of handing over any man **accused** of a crime
25.16 before he has met his **accusers** face to face and has had
25.16 the chance of defending himself against the **accusation.**
25.18 but they did not **accuse** him of any of the evil
26. 2 the things the Jews **accuse** me of, [3] particularly since you know
26. 7 hope, Your Majesty, that I am being **accused** by the Jews!
28.19 though I had no **accusation** to make against my own people.
Rom 2.15 their thoughts sometimes **accuse** them and sometimes defend them.
3. 8 have insulted me by **accusing** me of saying this very thing!
8.33 Who will **accuse** God's chosen people?
2 Cor 13. 1 "Any **accusation** must be upheld by the evidence of two or
1 Tim 5.19 Do not listen to an **accusation** against an elder unless
1 Pet 2.12 so good that when they **accuse** you of being evildoers, they
2 Pet 2.11 false teachers, do not **accuse** them with insults in the presence
Rev 12.10 stood before our God and **accused** our brothers day and night

ACHAIA
Roman province corresponding to s. modern Greece.

Acts 18.12 made the Roman governor of **Achaia,** the Jews got together,
18.27 decided to go to **Achaia,** so the believers in Ephesus helped
18.27 writing to the believers in **Achaia,** urging them to welcome him.
19.21 to travel through Macedonia and **Achaia** and go on to Jerusalem.
20. 2 Then he came to **Achaia,** [3] where he stayed three months.
Rom 15.26 churches in Macedonia and **Achaia** have freely decided to give
1 Cor 16.15 first Christian converts in **Achaia** and have given themselves
2 Cor 1. 1 of God in Corinth, and to all God's people throughout **Achaia:**
9. 2 "The brothers in **Achaia,"** I said, "have been ready to help
11.10 boast of mine will not be silenced anywhere in all **Achaia.**
1 Thes 1. 7 you became an example to all believers in Macedonia and **Achaia.**
1. 8 throughout Macedonia and **Achaia,** but the news about your faith

ACHAN
Member of the tribe of Judah who was put to death for keeping for himself part of the treasure taken when Jericho was captured.

Josh 7. 1 A man named **Achan** disobeyed that order,
7. 1 **(Achan** was the son of Carmi and grandson of Zabdi,
7.18 forward, man by man, and **Achan,** the son of Carmi and
7.20 "It's true," **Achan** answered.
7.24 the people of Israel, seized **Achan,** the silver, the cloak,
7.24 together with **Achan's** sons and daughters, his cattle,
7.25 All the people then stoned **Achan** to death;
22.20 Remember how **Achan** son of Zerah refused to obey the command
22.20 **Achan** was not the only one who died because of his sin."
1 Chr 2. 7 **Achan** son of Carmi, one of Zerah's descendants,

ACHE
[HEARTACHE]

Job 30.17 At night my bones all **ache;**
Ps 69. 3 am worn out from calling for help, and my throat is **aching.**
119.20 My heart **aches** with longing;
Ecc 2.23 everything you do brings nothing but worry and **heartache.**

ACHIEVE

Is 26.12 everything that we **achieve** is the result of what you do.
Eph 3.11 his eternal purpose, which he **achieved** through Christ Jesus
Heb 1. 3 After **achieving** forgiveness for the sins of mankind, he sat down
Jas 1.20 Man's anger does not **achieve** God's righteous purpose.

ACHISH (1)
King of Gath with whom David took refuge when escaping from Saul.

1 Sam 21.10 David left, fleeing from Saul, and went to King **Achish** of Gath.
21.11 The king's officials said to **Achish,** "Isn't this David,
21.12 David, and he became very much afraid of King **Achish.**
21.14 So **Achish** said to his officials, "Look!
27. 2 went over at once to **Achish** son of Maoch, king of Gath.
27. 5 David said to **Achish,** "If you are my friend,
27. 6 So **Achish** gave him the town of Ziklag,
27. 9 he would come back to **Achish,** [10] who would ask him,
27.12 But **Achish** trusted David
28. 1 troops to fight Israel, and **Achish** said to David,
28. 2 **Achish** said, "Good!
29. 2 David and his men marched in the rear with King **Achish.**
29. 3 **Achish** answered, "This is David, an official of King Saul
29. 4 Philistine commanders were angry with **Achish** and said to him,
29. 6 **Achish** called David and said to him, "I swear
29. 9 "I agree," **Achish** replied.

ACHISH (2)
A later king of Gath, or possibly the same king.

1 Kgs 2.39 slaves ran away to the king of Gath, **Achish** son of Maacah.
2.40 and went to King **Achish** in Gath, to find his slaves.

ACKNOWLEDGE

Lev 22.32 all the people of Israel must **acknowledge** me to be holy.
Num 20.12 not have enough faith to **acknowledge** my holy power
27.14 you refused to **acknowledge** my holy power before them."
32.22 Then the Lord will **acknowledge** that this land east of the
Deut 21.17 A man must **acknowledge** his first son
26. 3 say to him, 'I now **acknowledge** to the Lord my God
26.17 Today you have **acknowledged** the Lord as your God;
1 Chr 28. 9 I charge you to **acknowledge** your father's God
Ps 83.16 with shame, O Lord, and make them **acknowledge** your power.
91.14 will protect those who **acknowledge** me as Lord.
100. 3 **Acknowledge** that the Lord is God.
Is 19.21 and then they will **acknowledge** and worship him,
29.23 then you will **acknowledge** that I am the holy God
33.13 and far hear what I have done and **acknowledge** my power."
46. 9 **acknowledge** that I alone am God
52. 6 time to come you will **acknowledge** that I am God
63.16 Abraham and Jacob do not **acknowledge** us,
Jer 9. 3 and do not **acknowledge** me as their God."
Ezek 6. 7 those who survive will **acknowledge** that I am the Lord.
12.16 and will **acknowledge** that I am the Lord."
Dan 4.26 when you **acknowledge** that God rules all the world.
4.32 Then you will **acknowledge** that the Supreme God has power
Hos 2. 8 She would never **acknowledge** that I am the one who gave
2.20 and you will **acknowledge** me as Lord.
4. 1 and the people do not **acknowledge** me as God.
4. 6 My people are doomed because they do not **acknowledge** me.
4. 6 You priests have refused to **acknowledge** me
4. 6 I reject you and will not **acknowledge** your sons as my priests.
5. 4 and they do not **acknowledge** the Lord.
11. 3 but they did not **acknowledge** that I took care of them.
Mic 5. 4 all over the earth will **acknowledge** his greatness,
Zech 1. 6 Then they repented and **acknowledged** that I, the Lord Almighty,
1 Jn 4. 2 anyone who **acknowledges** that Jesus Christ came as a human
2 Jn 7 people who do not **acknowledge** that Jesus Christ came as

AV **ACKNOWLEDGE** see **RECOGNIZE**

ACQUIRE

Gen 4. 1 "By the Lord's help I have **acquired** a son."
12. 5 all the slaves they had **acquired** in Haran, and they started
31.17 with everything that he had **acquired** in Mesopotamia.
36. 6 all the possessions he had **acquired** in the land of Canaan,
46. 6 and the possessions they had **acquired** in Canaan
Neh 5.16 rebuilding the wall and did not **acquire** any property.
Ezek 28. 7 all the beautiful things you have **acquired** by your skill
Mic 1. 7 Samaria **acquired** these things for its fertility rites,

ACQUIT

1 Kgs 8.32 one as he deserves, and **acquit** the one who is innocent.
2 Chr 6.23 one as he deserves and **acquit** the one who is innocent.
Ps 35.27 who want to see me **acquitted** shout for joy and say again
75. 7 God who is the judge, condemning some and **acquitting** others.

ACT

Gen 18.25 The judge of all the earth has to **act** justly."
38.24 "Your daughter-in-law Tamar has been **acting** like a whore,
42. 7 he recognized them, but he **acted** as if he did not know
Ex 2. 7 I go and call a Hebrew woman to **act** as a wet-nurse?"
15.11 Who can work miracles and mighty **acts** like yours?
18.12 with him to eat the sacred meal as an **act** of worship.
22.25 who are poor, do not **act** like a money-lender and require him
Lev 18.24 unclean by any of these **acts,** for that is how the pagans
Num 5.12 there was no witness, and she was not caught in the **act.**
11.12 should you ask me to **act** like a nurse and carry them
35.27 finds him and kills him, this **act** of revenge is not murder.
Deut 17.13 and no one else will dare to **act** in such a way.
Josh 8.14 When the king of Ai saw Joshua's men, he **acted** quickly.
Judg 15. 7 Samson told them, "So this is how you **act!**
20. 6 These people have committed an evil and immoral **act** among us.
20.10 punish Gibeah for this immoral **act** that they have committed
1 Sam 21.13 pretended to be insane and **acted** like a madman when they
2 Sam 14. 2 **Act** like a woman who has been in mourning for a long
24.10 I have **acted** foolishly."
1 Chr 21. 8 I have **acted** foolishly."
2 Chr 6.32 you are always ready to **act,** and then he comes to pray
12.15 Rehoboam's **acts** from beginning to end
16. 9 You have **acted** foolishly, and so from now on you will always
17. 4 God's commands, and did not **act** in the way the kings of
19. 6 you are not **acting** on human authority,
19. 7 Honour the Lord and **act** carefully,
24. 5 He told them to **act** promptly, but the Levites delayed,
Ezra 10. 4 It is your responsibility to **act.**
Neh 1. 7 We have **acted** wickedly against you and have not done what
5. 7 I was angry [7] and decided to **act.**
5.15 But I **acted** differently, because I honoured God.
Job 12.12 God has insight and power to **act.**
12.17 makes leaders **act** like fools.
24.22 God **acts**—and the wicked man dies.
29.14 I have always **acted** justly and fairly.
31. 5 I swear I have never **acted** wickedly and never tried to
39.16 She **acts** as if the eggs were not hers,
Ps 24. 4 Those who are pure in **act** and in thought,
37. 7 Be patient and wait for the Lord to **act;**
66. 5 Come and see what God has done, his wonderful **acts** among men.
71.17 since I was young, and I still tell of your wonderful **acts.**
73.15 such things, I would not be **acting** as one of your people.
77.12 I will meditate on all your mighty **acts.**
78.43 and performed his mighty **acts** and miracles
105.27 They did God's mighty **acts** and performed miracles in Egypt.
106. 7 Our ancestors in Egypt did not understand God's wonderful **acts;**
106.13 what he had done and **acted** without waiting for his advice.
106.21 the God who had saved them by his mighty **acts** in Egypt.
107.24 saw what the Lord can do, his wonderful **acts** on the seas.
119.126 time for you to **act,** because people are disobeying your law.
145. 4 they will proclaim your mighty **acts.**
145.13 to his promises, and he is merciful in all his **acts.**
145.17 Lord is righteous in all he does, merciful in all his **acts.**
Prov 3.31 or decide to **act** as they do, [32] because the Lord
13.16 people always think before they **act,** but stupid people
14.16 but stupid people are careless and **act** too quickly.
14.31 but kindness shown to the poor is an **act** of worship.
21. 5 if you **act** too quickly, you will never have enough.
30.20 This is how an unfaithful wife **acts:**
Ecc 7. 7 When a wise man cheats someone, he is **acting** like a fool.
8. 4 The king **acts** with authority, and no one can challenge
Is 31. 3 When the Lord **acts,** the strong nation will crumble,
32. 4 but they will **act** with understanding
32. 8 But an honourable person **acts** honestly and stands firm
33.10 The Lord says to the nations, "Now I will **act.**
42.14 But now the time to **act** has come;
57.18 "I have seen how they **acted,** but I will heal them.
Jer 3. 2 Is there any place where you have not **acted** like a prostitute?

Jer	3. 6	and under every green tree she has **acted** like a prostitute.
	6.14	They **act** as if my people's wounds were only scratches.
	8.11	They **act** as if my people's wounds were only scratches.
	9. 5	and one deceitful **act** follows another.
	50.29	has treated others, because it **acted** with pride against me,
Ezek	16.51	You have **acted** more disgustingly than she ever did.
	16.61	will remember how you have **acted,** and be ashamed of it when
	20.44	When I **act** to protect my honour, you Israelites will know
	23.19	of a prostitute than ever, **acting** just as she did as a
	24.14	The time has come for me to **act.**
	24.19	The people asked me, "Why are you **acting** like this?"
	28.17	of being handsome, and your fame made you **act** like a fool.
	30. 3	day when the Lord will **act,** A day of clouds and trouble
	32. 2	You **act** like a lion among the nations, but you are more
	36.17	their land, they defiled it by the way they lived and **acted.**
	36.19	the way they lived and **acted,** and I scattered them
Dan	4.37	and he can humble anyone who **acts** proudly."
	5.23	You **acted** against the Lord of heaven and brought in the
	9. 8	our ancestors have **acted** shamefully and sinned against you,
	9.19	Lord, listen to us, and **act!**
Hos	12. 1	Treachery and **acts** of violence increase among them.
	12. 2	is also going to punish Israel for the way her people **act.**
	12. 6	Be loyal and just, and wait patiently for your God to **act.**
Zech	11. 4	my God said to me, **"Act** the part of the shepherd of
	11.15	said to me, "Once again **act** the part of a shepherd, this
	13. 4	proud of his visions, or **act** like a prophet, or wear a
Mal	3.17	"On the day when I **act,** they will be my very own.
	4. 3	On the day when I **act,** you will overcome the wicked, and
Lk	10.36	which one of these three **acted** like a neighbour towards the
	18. 4	time the judge refused to **act,** but at last he said
	22.53	is your hour to **act,** when the power of darkness rules."
	24.28	they were going, Jesus **acted** as if he were going farther;
Jn	8. 4	"this woman was caught in the very **act** of committing adultery.
Acts	1.18	Judas got for his evil **act** he bought a field,
Rom	1.26	pervert the natural use of their sex by unnatural **acts.**
	5.18	same way the one righteous **act** sets all mankind free and
	14.15	something you eat, then you are no longer **acting** from love.
1 Cor	3. 4	"I follow Apollos"—aren't you **acting** like worldly people?
	7.15	the Christian partner, whether husband or wife, is free to **act.**
	7.36	feels that he is not **acting** properly towards the girl
	10.29	"why should my freedom to **act** be limited by another person's
2 Cor	4. 2	we do not **act** with deceit, nor do we falsify the word
	8.10	not only to act, but also to be willing to **act.**
	10. 2	harshly with those who say that we **act** from worldly motives.
	10. 6	we will be ready to punish any **act** of disloyalty.
	12. 7	physical ailment, which **acts** as Satan's messenger to beat me
	12.11	I am **acting** like a fool—but you have made me do
	12.18	Do he and I not **act** from the very same motives
Gal	2.13	Jewish brothers also started **acting** like cowards along with
	3.19	handed down by angels, with a man **acting** as a go-between.
	5.15	if you **act** like wild animals, hurting and harming each other,
Col	4. 5	wise in the way you **act** towards those who are not believers,
Jas	2.12	Speak and **act** as people who will be judged by the law
1 Pet	2. 9	chosen to proclaim the wonderful **acts** of God, who called you
2 Pet	2.12	But these men **act** by instinct, like wild animals born to
Jude	7	the nearby towns, whose people **acted** as those angels did and
Rev	17.17	carry out his purpose by **acting** together and giving the beast

ACTION

Lev	18.25	Their **actions** made the land unclean,
Judg	9.16	treat his family properly, as his **actions** deserved?
1 Sam	12. 7	you of all the mighty **actions** the Lord did to save you
	21.15	me with his daft **actions** right here in my own house?"
	24.12	he punish you for your **action** against me, for I will not
2 Kgs	21.21	he imitated his father's **actions,**
2 Chr	23. 1	Jehoiada the priest decided that it was time to take **action.**
	28.12	Amasa son of Hadlai also opposed the **actions** of the army.
Ezra	5. 5	decided to take no **action** until they could write to Darius
	9.11	from one end to the other with disgusting, filthy **actions.**
Ps	92. 5	How great are your **actions,** Lord!
	101. 3	I hate the **actions** of those who turn away from God;
	106.29	the Lord's anger by their **actions,** and a terrible disease
	106.39	They made themselves impure by their **actions**
	111. 4	The Lord does not let us forget his wonderful **actions;**
	139. 3	you know all my **actions.**
Prov	1.31	what you deserve, and your own **actions** will make you sick.
	16. 9	You may make your plans, but God directs your **actions.**
	17.24	intelligent person aims at wise **action,** but a fool starts off
	19. 3	by their own stupid **actions** and then blame the Lord.
Ecc	3.17	because every thing, every **action,** will happen at its own set
	9. 1	saw that God controls the **actions** of wise and righteous men,
	9.10	there will be no **action,** no thought, no knowledge, no wisdom
Is	1.25	I will take **action** against you.
	28.21	do what he intends to do—strange as his **actions** may seem.
	45.13	myself have stirred Cyrus to **action** to fulfil my purpose
	64. 6	even our best **actions** are filthy through and through.
Jer	32.19	and you reward them according to their **actions.**
Ezek	12.16	will realize how disgusting their **actions** have been
	16.27	who hate you and are disgusted with your immoral **actions.**
	16.47	to follow in their footsteps and copy their disgusting **actions?**
	20.44	I do not deal with you as your wicked, evil **actions** deserve."
	21.24	You show your sins in your every **action.**
	22.15	country and nation and will put an end to your evil **actions.**
	24.13	Jerusalem, your immoral **actions** have defiled you.
	33.26	Your **actions** are disgusting.
	43.10	Make them ashamed of their sinful **actions.**
Jon	3. 8	God and must give up his wicked behaviour and his evil **actions.**
Mt	23. 3	do not, however, imitate their **actions,** because they don't
Lk	12.35	for whatever comes, dressed for **action** and with your lamps lit,
	23.50	he had not agreed with their decision and **action.**
Jn	11.48	the Roman authorities will take **action** and destroy our Temple
Acts	5.17	so they decided to take **action.**
	5.38	I tell you, do not take any **action** against these men.
Rom	8.13	the Spirit you put to death your sinful **actions,** you will
	14.23	when he eats it, because his **action** is not based on faith.
1 Cor	8. 9	let your freedom of **action** make those who are weak in
2 Cor	11.15	In the end they will get exactly what their **actions** deserve.
Gal	2.13	and even Barnabas was swept along by their cowardly **action.**
	5.19	It shows itself in immoral, filthy, and indecent **actions;**
Phil	4. 9	received from me, both from my words and from my **actions.**
Tit	1.16	They claim that they know God, but their **actions** deny it.
Jas	2.14	say that he has faith if his **actions** do not prove it?
	2.17	if it is alone and includes no **actions,** then it is dead.
	2.18	someone will say, "One person has faith, another has **actions."**
	2.18	My answer is, "Show me how anyone can have faith without **actions.**
	2.18	I will show you my faith by my **actions."**
	2.20	Do you want to be shown that faith without **actions** is useless?
	2.21	It was through his **actions,** when he offered his son Isaac
	2.22	His faith and his **actions** worked together;
	2.22	his faith was made perfect through his **actions.**
	2.24	that it is by his **actions** that a person is put right
	2.25	right with God through her **actions,** by welcoming the Israelite
	2.26	spirit is dead, so also faith without **actions** is dead.
1 Pet	1.13	So then, have your minds ready for **action.**
	4.19	should by their good **actions** trust themselves completely to
2 Pet	2. 8	he suffered agony as he saw and heard their evil **actions.**
	2.16	spoke with a human voice and stopped the prophet's insane **action.**
1 Jn	1. 6	we are lying both in our words and in our **actions.**
	3.18	it must be true love, which shows itself in **action.**
Rev	15. 4	and worship you, because your just **actions** are seen by all."

ACTIVE

2 Cor	3. 8	is the glory that belongs to the **activity** of the Spirit!
	3. 9	much more glorious is the **activity** which brings salvation!
Col	2.12	through your faith in the **active** power of God, who raised
2 Tim	2. 4	soldier on **active** service wants to please his commanding officer
Heb	4.12	word of God is alive and **active,** sharper than any double-edged
2 Pet	1. 8	they will make you **active** and effective in your knowledge

ADAM (1)

The first man.

Gen	3.20	**Adam** named his wife Eve, because she was the mother of
	3.21	out of animal skins for **Adam** and his wife, and he clothed
	4. 1	**Adam** had intercourse with his wife, and she became pregnant.
	4.25	**Adam** and his wife had another son.
	5. 1	This is the list of the descendants of **Adam.**
	5. 3	When **Adam** was 130 years old, he had a son
	5. 4	After that, **Adam** lived another 800 years.
1 Chr	1. 1	**Adam** was the father of Seth, Seth was the father of Enosh,
Lk	3.38	the son of Seth, the son of **Adam,** the son of God.
Rom	5.14	But from the time of **Adam** to the time of Moses death
	5.14	the same way that **Adam** did when he disobeyed God's command.
	5.14	**Adam** was a figure of the one who was to come.
	5.15	the same, because God's free gift is not like **Adam's** sin.
1 Cor	15.22	because of their union with **Adam,** in the same way all will
	15.45	says, "The first man, **Adam,** was created a living being";
	15.45	but the last **Adam** is the life-giving Spirit.
	15.47	The first **Adam,** made of earth, came from the earth;
	15.47	the second **Adam** came from heaven.
1 Tim	2.13	For **Adam** was created first, and then Eve.
	2.14	And it was not **Adam** who was deceived;
Jude	14	sixth direct descendant from **Adam,** who long ago prophesied this

ADAR

Ezra	6.15	third day of the month **Adar** in the sixth year of the
Esth	3. 7	of the twelfth month, the month of **Adar,** was decided on.
	3.13	day, the thirteenth day of **Adar,** all Jews—young and old,
	8.12	of the Jews, the thirteenth of **Adar,** the twelfth month.
	9. 1	The thirteenth day of **Adar** came, the day on which the
	9.15	On the fourteenth day of **Adar** the Jews of Susa got
	9.17	This was on the thirteenth day of **Adar.**
	9.19	day of the month of **Adar** as a joyous holiday, a time
	9.21	and fifteenth days of **Adar** as holidays every year.

ADD

Ex	30.24	**Add** four litres of olive-oil, [25] and make a sacred anointing oil,
	30.35	**Add** salt to keep it pure and holy.
Lev	2.15	**Add** olive-oil and put incense on it.
	10. 1	put live coals in it, **added** incense, and presented it
Num	19.17	shall be taken and put in a pot, and fresh water **added.**
	36. 4	Zelophehad's daughters will be permanently **added** to the tribe
Deut	4. 2	Do not **add** anything to what I command you,
	12.32	do not **add** anything to it or take anything from it.
2 Kgs	12.18	had dedicated to the Lord, **added** to them his own offerings
Job	34.37	To his sins he **adds** rebellion;
Ps	61. 6	**Add** many years to the king's life;
Prov	1. 5	These proverbs can even **add** to the knowledge of wise men
	3.35	but stupid men will only **add** to their own disgrace.
	9. 9	Whatever you tell a righteous man will **add** to his knowledge.
	9.11	Wisdom will **add** years to your life.
Ecc	3.14	You can't **add** anything to it or take anything away from it.
Is	5. 8	buy more houses and fields to **add** to those you already have.
Jer	45. 3	The Lord has **added** sorrow to my troubles.
Ezek	16.43	Why did you **add** sexual immorality to all the other disgusting
Mt	6.34	There is no need to **add** to the troubles each day brings.
Acts	1.26	was Matthias, who was **added** to the group of eleven apostles.

Acts 2.41 about three thousand people were **added** to the group that day.
2.47 And every day the Lord **added** to their group those who were
5.14 more and more people were **added** to the group—a crowd
19.19 They **added** up the price of the books, and the total came
Gal 3.15 an agreement, no one can break it or **add** anything to it.
3.19 It was **added** in order to show what wrongdoing is,
Eph 6. 2 and mother" is the first commandment that has a promise **added:**
Phil 1.25 on with you all, to **add** to your progress and joy
4.17 rather, I want to see profit **added** to your account.
Col 3.14 to all these qualities **add** love, which binds all things together
1 Tim 5. 9 Do not **add** any widow to the list of widows unless she
Heb 2. 4 At the same time God **added** his witness to theirs by
6.17 so he **added** his vow to the promise.
2 Pet 1. 5 do your best to **add** goodness to your faith;
1. 5 to your goodness **add** knowledge;
1. 6 to your knowledge **add** self-control;
1. 6 to your self-control **add** endurance;
1. 6 to your endurance **add** godliness;
1. 7 to your godliness **add** brotherly affection;
1. 7 and to your brotherly affection **add** love.
3 Jn 12 And we **add** our testimony, and you know that what we say
Rev 8. 3 a lot of incense to **add** to the prayers of all God's
22.18 if anyone **adds** anything to them, God will add to his punishment

ADDRESS

Deut 20. 5 "Then the officers will **address** the men and say,
1 Chr 28. 2 David stood before them and **addressed** them:
2 Chr 20.20 Jehoshaphat **addressed** them with these words:
Esth 9.30 The letter was **addressed** to all the Jews,

ADMINISTER

1 Chr 23. 4 twenty-four thousand to **administer** the work of the Temple,
26.29 Chenaniah and his sons were assigned **administrative** duties:
26.30 in charge of the **administration** of all religious and civil matters
26.32 in charge of **administering** all religious and civil matters
27. 1 their officials who **administered** the work of the kingdom.
27.16 the list of the **administrators** of the tribes of Israel:
27.25 the list of those who **administered** the royal property:
28. 1 the officials who **administered** the work of the kingdom,
29. 6 the **administrators** of the royal property volunteered
29. 8 the temple treasury, which was **administered** by Jehiel
2 Chr 28. 7 the palace **administrator** Azrikam,
Ezra 7.25 are to appoint **administrators** and judges to govern
Esth 1. 3 he gave a banquet for all his officials and **administrators.**
2.18 and invited all his officials and **administrators.**
2.19 Mordecai had been appointed by the king to an **administrative** position.
3. 9 into the royal treasury for the **administration** of the empire."
8. 9 Jews and to the governors, **administrators,** and officials
9. 3 all the provincial officials—governors, **administrators,**
Dan 6. 4 wrong with the way Daniel **administered** the empire,
6. 7 All of us who **administer** your empire—

ADMIRE

Esth 2.15 Esther—**admired** by everyone who saw her.
Prov 20.29 We **admire** the strength of youth and respect the grey hair

ADMIT (1)

Gen 21.30 By doing this, you **admit** that I am the one who dug
26. 7 He would not **admit** that she was his wife, because he was
Num 14.40 We **admit** that we have sinned."
2 Sam 1.16 You condemned yourself when you **admitted** that you killed
2 Chr 12. 6 The king and the leaders **admitted** that they had sinned,
12. 7 said to him, "Because they **admit** their sin, I will not
Job 28.22 Even death and destruction **Admit** they have heard only rumours.
33.32 I would gladly **admit** you are in the right.
40.14 to praise you and **admit** that you won the victory yourself.
Ps 141. 6 cliffs, the people will **admit** that my words were true.
Prov 10.17 but those who will not **admit** that they are wrong are in
13. 1 but an arrogant person never **admits** he is wrong.
Is 44.20 He won't **admit** to himself that the idol he holds in his
48. 6 you have to **admit** my predictions were right.
Jer 3.13 Only **admit** that you are guilty and that you have rebelled
Dan 4.25 Then you will **admit** that the Supreme God controls all
5.21 he **admitted** that the Supreme God controls all human kingdoms
Amos 6. 3 You refuse to **admit** that a day of disaster is coming,
Mt 23.31 So you actually **admit** that you are the descendants of those
Lk 11.48 yourselves **admit,** then, that you approve of what your ancestors
Acts 19.18 believers came, publicly **admitting** and revealing what they had
24.14 I do **admit** this to you:
2 Cor 11.21 I am ashamed to **admit** that we were too timid to do
Heb 11.13 welcomed them, and **admitted** openly that they were foreigners

ADMIT (2)

Gen 43. 3 that we would not be **admitted** to his presence unless we had
43. 5 us we would not be **admitted** to his presence unless our
44.23 'You will not be **admitted** to my presence again unless your
44.26 we will not be **admitted** to the man's presence unless our

ADONIJAH (1)

David's son, who tried unsuccessfully to establish himself as David's successor.

2 Sam 3. 4 **Adonijah,** whose mother was Haggith;
1 Kgs 1. 5 Now that Absalom was dead, **Adonijah,** the son of David
1. 8 Rei, and David's bodyguard were not on **Adonijah's** side.
1. 9 One day **Adonijah** offered a sacrifice of sheep, bulls,
1.11 Haggith's son **Adonijah** has made himself king?
1.13 How is it, then, that **Adonijah** has become king?' "
1.18 But **Adonijah** has already become king,
1.24 have you announced that **Adonijah** would succeed you as king?
1.25 feasting with him and shouting, 'Long live King **Adonijah!'**
1.41 As **Adonijah** and all his guests were finishing the feast,
1.42 "Come in," **Adonijah** said.
1.49 Then **Adonijah's** guests were afraid, and they all got up
1.50 **Adonijah,** in great fear of Solomon, went to the Tent
1.51 King Solomon was told that **Adonijah** was afraid of him
1.53 King Solomon then sent for **Adonijah** and had him brought
1.53 **Adonijah** went to the king and bowed low before him,
2.13 Then **Adonijah,** whose mother was Haggith, went to Bathsheba,
2.19 went to the king to speak to him on behalf of **Adonijah.**
2.21 She answered, "Let your brother **Adonijah** have Abishag
2.23 dead if I don't make **Adonijah** pay with his life for asking
2.24 by the living Lord that **Adonijah** will die this very day!"
2.25 gave orders to Benaiah, who went out and killed **Adonijah.**
2.28 (He had supported **Adonijah,** but not Absalom.)
1 Chr 3. 1 **Adonijah,** whose mother was Haggith

ADOPT

Ex 2.10 him to the king's daughter, who **adopted** him as her own son.
23.24 and do not **adopt** their religious practices.
Lev 20.23 Do not **adopt** the customs of people who live there;
2 Kgs 17. 8 and **adopted** customs introduced by the kings
17.19 they imitated the customs **adopted** by the people of Israel.
Esth 2. 7 Mordecai had **adopted** her and brought her up
2.15 Mordecai, who had **adopted** her as his daughter;
9.31 just as they had **adopted** rules for the observance of fasts
Ps 106.35 they intermarried with them and **adopted** their pagan ways.
Acts 7.21 the king's daughter **adopted** him and brought him up

ADORN

2 Sam 1.24 rich scarlet dresses and **adorned** you with jewels and gold.
Ps 144.12 like stately pillars which **adorn** the corners of a palace.
Rev 21.19 city wall were **adorned** with all kinds of precious stones.

ADULLAM

City in s. Judah near which David lived in a cave as an outlaw.

Gen 38. 1 with a man named Hirah, who was from the town of **Adullam.**
38.12 and his friend Hirah of **Adullam** went to Timnah, where his
Josh 12.15 Libnah, **Adullam,** [16] Makkedah, Bethel,
15.35 Jarmuth, **Adullam,** Socoh, Azekah, [36] Shaaraim,
1 Sam 22. 1 and went to a cave near the town of **Adullam.**
2 Sam 23.13 down to the cave of **Adullam,** where David was,
1 Chr 11.15 staying near the cave of **Adullam,**
2 Chr 11. 7 Bethzur, Soco, **Adullam,** [8] Gath, Mareshah, Ziph,
Neh 11.30 in Zanoah, in **Adullam,** and in the villages near
Mic 1.15 leaders of Israel will go and hide in the cave at **Adullam.**

ADULT

Lev 27. 3 **adult** male, twenty to sixty years old:
27. 3 —**adult** female:
Heb 5.14 the other hand, is for **adults,** who through practice are able

ADULTERY

Ex 20.14 "Do not commit **adultery.**
Lev 20.10 If a man commits **adultery** with the wife of a fellow-Israelite,
Num 5.19 "If you have not committed **adultery,** you will not be harmed
5.20 But if you have committed **adultery,**
5.27 If she has committed **adultery,** the water will cause bitter pain;
5.29 suspicious that his wife has committed **adultery.**
Deut 5.18 " 'Do not commit **adultery.**
Job 24.15 The **adulterer** waits for twilight to come;
Ps 50.18 of every thief you see and you associate with **adulterers.**
Prov 6.26 but **adultery** will cost him all he has.
6.32 But a man who commits **adultery** hasn't any sense.
22.14 **Adultery** is a trap—
30.20 she commits **adultery,** has a bath,
Is 57. 3 You are no better than sorcerers, **adulterers,** and prostitutes.
Jer 3. 9 she committed **adultery** by worshipping stones and trees.
5. 7 they committed **adultery** and spent their time with prostitutes.
7. 9 You steal, murder, commit **adultery,** tell lies under oath,
23.14 they commit **adultery** and tell lies;
29.23 they have committed **adultery** and have told lies
Ezek 16.17 used it to make male images, and committed **adultery** with them.
16.32 like a woman who commits **adultery** with strangers
16.38 I will condemn you for **adultery** and murder,
22.11 Some commit **adultery,** and others seduce
23.37 They have committed **adultery** and murder—adultery with idols
23.43 were using as a prostitute a woman worn out by **adultery.**
23.45 them on the charge of **adultery** and murder,
23.45 because they practise **adultery** and their hands are stained with
23.48 a warning to every woman not to commit **adultery** as they did.
33.26 Everyone commits **adultery.**
Hos 2. 2 Plead with her to stop her **adultery** and prostitution.
3. 1 love for a woman who is committing **adultery** with a lover.
3. 3 wait for me without being a prostitute or committing **adultery;**
4. 2 they lie, murder, steal, and commit **adultery.**
4.13 and your daughters-in-law commit **adultery.**
Mal 3. 5 against **adulterers,** against those who give false testimony,
Mt 5.27 "You have heard that it was said, 'Do not commit **adultery.'**
5.28 is guilty of committing **adultery** with her in his heart.
5.32 guilty of making her commit **adultery** if she marries again;

Mt	5.32	and the man who marries her commits **adultery** also.
	15.19	lead him to kill, commit **adultery,** and do other immoral things;
	19. 9	unfaithfulness commits **adultery** if he marries some other woman."
	19.18	do not commit **adultery;**
Mk	7.22	to rob, kill, [22] commit **adultery,** be greedy, and do all sorts
	10.11	divorces his wife and marries another woman commits **adultery**
	10.12	who divorces her husband and marries another man commits **adultery."**
	10.19	do not commit **adultery;**
Lk	16.18	who divorces his wife and marries another woman commits **adultery;**
	16.18	and the man who marries a divorced woman commits **adultery.**
	18.11	am not greedy, dishonest, or an **adulterer,** like everybody else.
	18.20	'Do not commit **adultery;**
Jn	8. 3	who had been caught committing **adultery,** and they made her stand
	8. 4	"this woman was caught in the very act of committing **adultery.**
Rom	2.22	You say, "Do not commit **adultery"**—but do you commit adultery?
	7. 3	her husband is alive, she will be called an **adulteress;**
	7. 3	free woman and does not commit **adultery** if she marries another
	13. 9	The commandments, "Do not commit **adultery;**
1 Cor	6. 9	who worship idols or are **adulterers** or homosexual perverts
Heb	13. 4	will judge those who are immoral and those who commit **adultery.**
Jas	2.11	who said, "Do not commit **adultery,"** also said, "Do not commit
	2.11	if you do not commit **adultery,** you have become a law-breaker
Rev	2.22	where she and those who committed **adultery** with her will suffer

ADVANCE

Ex	23.28	the Canaanites, and the Hittites as you **advance.**
	23.31	and you will drive them out as you **advance.**
	34.11	the Perizzites, the Hivites, and the Jebusites, as you **advance.**
Deut	4.38	As you **advanced,** he drove out nations
	7. 1	As you **advance,** he will drive out seven nations larger
	7.22	he will drive out these nations as you **advance.**
	8.20	those nations that he is going to destroy as you **advance.**
	9. 3	will defeat them as you **advance,**
	11.23	all those nations as you **advance,** and you will occupy the
	18.12	he is driving those nations out of the land as you **advance.**
	33.27	out your enemies as you **advanced,** and told you to destroy
Josh	3.10	As you **advance,** he will surely drive out the Canaanites,
	6. 7	round the city, with an **advance** guard going on ahead
	6. 8	as Joshua had ordered, an **advance** guard started out ahead of
	6.12	first, the **advance** guard;
	9.24	and to kill the people living in it as you **advanced.**
	13. 6	drive all these peoples out as the people of Israel **advance.**
	23. 5	from you, and he will drive them away as you **advance.**
	23. 9	powerful nations out as you **advanced**
	23.13	God will no longer drive these nations out as you **advance.**
	24. 8	You took their land, and I destroyed them as you **advanced.**
	24.12	As you **advanced,** I threw them into panic
	24.18	As we **advanced** into this land, the Lord drove out all
Judg	2. 3	now that I will not drive these people out as you **advance.**
	6. 9	drove them out as you **advanced,** and I gave you their land.
2 Sam	7. 9	and I have defeated all your enemies as you **advanced.**
	7.23	their gods as your people **advanced,** the people whom you set
	10.13	Joab and his men **advanced** to attack, and the Syrians fled.
1 Kgs	14.24	driven out of the land as the Israelites **advanced**
	20.17	The young soldiers **advanced** first.
	21.26	driven out of the land as the people of Israel **advanced.)**
2 Kgs	7. 6	hear what sounded like the **advance** of a large army,
	14.13	Jehoash took Amaziah prisoner, **advanced** on Jerusalem,
	16. 3	Lord had driven out of the land as the Israelites **advanced.**
	17. 8	driven out as his people **advanced,** and adopted customs
	21. 2	as his people **advanced,** Manasseh sinned against the Lord.
	21. 9	the Lord had driven out of the land as his people **advanced.**
1 Chr	17. 8	and I have defeated all your enemies as you **advanced.**
	17.21	drove out other nations as your people **advanced.**
	19.14	Joab and his men **advanced** to attack, and the Syrians fled.
2 Chr	12. 4	fortified cities of Judah and **advanced** as far as Jerusalem.
	14. 9	three hundred chariots and **advanced** as far as Mareshah.
	28. 3	Lord had driven out of the land as the Israelites **advanced.**
	33. 2	as his people **advanced,** Manasseh sinned against the Lord.
	33. 9	the Lord had driven out of the land as his people **advanced.**
Ps	78.55	He drove out the inhabitants as his people **advanced;**
Is	8. 7	They will **advance** like the flood waters of the River Euphrates,
	17.13	The nations **advance** like rushing waves,
Joel	2. 2	The great army of locusts **advances** like darkness spreading
	2.10	The earth shakes as they **advance;**
Hab	1. 9	"Their armies **advance** in violent conquest,
Acts	7.45	land from the nations that God drove out as they **advanced.**

ADVANTAGE

Lev	19.13	"Do not take **advantage** of anyone or rob him.
Job	21.15	no need to serve God nor any **advantage** in praying to him.
Prov	22.22	Don't take **advantage** of the poor just because you can;
	22.22	don't take **advantage** of those who stand helpless in court.
	28. 8	and taking **advantage** of people, your wealth will go
	30.14	There are people who take cruel **advantage** of the poor
Ecc	7.12	Wisdom keeps you safe—this is the **advantage** of knowledge.
Is	3. 5	Everyone will take **advantage** of everyone else.
	3.15	no right to crush my people and take **advantage** of the poor.
	56.11	one of them does as he pleases and seeks his own **advantage.**
Jer	7. 6	Stop taking **advantage** of aliens, orphans, and widows.
Ezek	16.15	"But you took **advantage** of your beauty and fame
	22. 7	You cheat foreigners and take **advantage** of widows and orphans.
	22.12	and get rich by taking **advantage** of them.
	22.29	They ill-treat the poor and take **advantage** of foreigners.
Zeph	3. 4	is sacred, and twist the law of God to their own **advantage.**
Mal	3. 5	those who take **advantage** of widows, orphans, and foreigners—
Mk	12.40	They take **advantage** of widows and rob them of their homes,
Lk	20.47	who take **advantage** of widows and rob them of their homes,
Rom	3. 1	Have the Jews then any **advantage** over the Gentiles?
2 Cor	7. 2	have ruined no one, nor tried to take **advantage** of anyone.
	11.20	orders you about or takes **advantage** of you or traps you
	12.17	Did I take **advantage** of you through any of the messengers
	12.18	Would you say that Titus took **advantage** of you?
1 Thes	4. 6	do wrong to his fellow-Christian or take **advantage** of him.

AV **ADVERSARY** see **DEVIL, SATAN**

ADVERTISE

Prov	12.23	but stupid people **advertise** their ignorance.
	13.16	but stupid people **advertise** their ignorance.

ADVICE

Ex	18.19	me give you some good **advice,** and God will be with you.
	18.24	Moses took Jethro's **advice** [25] and chose capable men
Lev	19.31	"Do not go for **advice** to people who consult the spirits
	20. 6	"If anyone goes for **advice** to people who consult the spirits
Deut	18.14	people follow the **advice** of those who practise divination
Ruth	2. 8	Then Boaz said to Ruth, "Let me give you some **advice.**
2 Sam	15.31	"Please, Lord, turn Ahithophel's **advice** into nonsense!"
	15.34	And do all you can to oppose any **advice** that Ahithophel gives.
	16.20	"Now that we are here, what do you **advise** us to do?"
	16.23	Any **advice** that Ahithophel gave in those days was accepted
	17. 4	This seemed like good **advice** to Absalom
	17. 6	"This is the **advice** that Ahithophel has given us;
	17. 7	"The **advice** Ahithophel gave you this time is no good.
	17.11	My **advice** is that you bring all the Israelites together
	17.14	"Hushai's **advice** is better than Ahithophel's."
	17.14	Ahithophel's good **advice** would not be followed,
	17.15	priests Zadok and Abiathar what **advice** he had given to Absalom
	17.15	and the Israelite leaders and what **advice** Ahithophel had given.
	17.23	When Ahithophel saw that his **advice** had not been followed,
1 Kgs	1.12	your son Solomon, I would **advise** you [13] to go at once to
	12. 6	"What answer do you **advise** me to give these people?"
	12. 8	But he ignored the **advice** of the older men
	12. 9	"What do you **advise** me to do?"
	12.13	The king ignored the **advice** of the older men
	12.14	harshly to the people, [14] as the younger men had **advised.**
	20.25	King Benhadad agreed and followed their **advice.**
1 Chr	26.14	Zechariah, a man who always gave good **advice,**
2 Chr	10. 6	"What answer do you **advise** me to give these people?"
	10. 8	But he ignored the **advice** of the older men
	10. 9	"What do you **advise** me to do?"
	10.13	The king ignored the **advice** of the older men
	10.14	harshly to the people, [14] as the younger men had **advised.**
	22. 2	gave him **advice** that led him into evil.
	22. 5	Following their **advice,** he joined King Joram of Israel
	25.16	you have done all this and have ignored my **advice."**
	25.19	defeated the Edomites, but I **advise** you to stay at home.
Ezra	10. 3	and the others who honour God's commands **advise** us to do.
Esth	1.14	most often turned to for **advice** were Carshena, Shethar,
	2. 4	The king thought this was good **advice,** so he followed it.
	2.10	Now, on the **advice** of Mordecai, Esther had kept it secret
	2.15	Hegai, the eunuch in charge of the harem, **advised** her to wear.
Job	16. 5	I could strengthen you with **advice**
	18. 7	he falls—a victim of his own **advice.**
	26. 3	You give such good **advice** and share your knowledge with a
	29.21	When I gave **advice,** people were silent and listened
Ps	1. 1	those who reject the **advice** of evil men,
	32. 8	I will instruct you and **advise** you.
	106.13	what he had done and acted without waiting for his **advice.**
Prov	1. 2	to recognize wisdom and good **advice,**
	1.23	I will give you good **advice** and share my knowledge with you.
	1.25	You have ignored all my **advice**
	1.30	You have never wanted my **advice** or paid any attention
	6.22	travel, protect you at night, and **advise** you during the day.
	10. 8	Sensible people accept good **advice.**
	12.15	Wise people listen to **advice.**
	13.10	It is wiser to ask for **advice.**
	13.13	If you refuse good **advice,** you are asking for trouble;
	15.12	they never ask for **advice** from those who are wiser.
	15.22	Get all the **advice** you can, and you will succeed;
	19.20	If you listen to **advice** and are willing to learn,
	20.18	Get good **advice** and you will succeed;
	22.20	They contain knowledge and good **advice,**
	24. 6	and the more good **advice** you get, the more likely you
Ecc	4.13	is too foolish to take **advice,** he is not as well off
Is	19. 3	consult mediums and ask the spirits of the dead for **advice.**
	19.11	Egypt's wisest men give stupid **advice!**
	19.14	The Lord has made them give confusing **advice.**
	30. 2	They go to Egypt for help without asking for my **advice.**
	40.13	Who can teach him or give him **advice?**
	47.13	You are powerless in spite of the **advice** you get.
Jer	38.15	and if I give you **advice,** you won't pay any attention."
Ezek	7.26	the people, and the elders will have no **advice** to give.
	11. 2	these men make evil plans and give bad **advice** in this city.
Dan	4.27	So then, Your Majesty, follow my **advice.**
	11.30	He will follow the **advice** of those who have abandoned that religion.
Hos	10. 6	put to shame because of the **advice** she followed.
Jn	18.14	It was Caiaphas who had **advised** the Jewish authorities that
Acts	5.39	The Council followed Gamaliel's **advice.**
	27. 9	So Paul gave them this **advice:**
Rom	11.34	Who is able to give him **advice?**

1 Cor 2.16 Who is able to give him **advice?"**
Gal 1.16 not go to anyone for **advice,** [17] nor did I go to Jerusalem
Rev 3.18 I **advise** you, then, to buy gold from me, pure gold,

ADVISER

Gen 26.26 with Ahuzzath his **adviser** and Phicol the commander
Judg 17.10 Be my **adviser** and priest, and I will give you ten pieces
18.19 Come with us and be our priest and **adviser.**
2 Sam 15.12 Gilo for Ahithophel, who was one of King David's **advisers.**
1 Kgs 4. 5 Royal **adviser:** the priest Zabud
12. 6 the older men who had served as his father Solomon's **advisers.**
12. 8 who had grown up with him and who were now his **advisers.**
2 Kgs 25. 8 Nebuzaradan, **adviser** to the king
25.19 of the king's personal **advisers** who were still in the city,
1 Chr 27.32 Jonathan, King David's uncle, was a skilful **adviser**
27.33 Ahithophel was **adviser** to the king,
27.34 Abiathar and Jehoiada son of Benaiah became **advisers.**
2 Chr 10. 6 the older men who had served as his father Solomon's **advisers.**
10. 8 who had grown up with him and who were now his **advisers.**
22. 4 King Ahab's family became his **advisers,**
25.16 Amaziah interrupted, "have we made you **adviser** to the king?
25.17 Amaziah of Judah and his **advisers** plotted against Israel.
26. 5 long as Zechariah, his religious **adviser,** was living,
Ezra 8.25 utensils which the emperor, his **advisers** and officials,
Esth 1.13 so he called for his **advisers,**
2. 2 So some of the king's **advisers** who were close to him suggested,
4.11 everyone, from the king's **advisers** to the people in the provinces,
Ps 105.22 the king's officials and authority to instruct his **advisers.**
119.24 they are my **advisers.**
Prov 11.14 Many **advisers** mean security.
25. 5 Keep evil **advisers** away from the king
Is 1.26 give you rulers and **advisers** like those you had long ago.
19.12 King of Egypt, where are those clever **advisers** of yours?
Jer 49. 7 Can their **advisers** no longer tell them what to do?
52.12 Nebuzaradan, **adviser** to the king
52.25 of the king's personal **advisers** who were still in the city,
Ezek 12.14 his **advisers** and bodyguard, and people will search
Dan 2.10 The **advisers** replied, "There is no one
2.12 ordered the execution of all the royal **advisers** in Babylon.
2.18 would not be killed along with the other **advisers** in Babylon.
2.24 Arioch, whom the king had commanded to execute the royal **advisers.**
2.48 and made him the head of all the royal **advisers.**
4. 6 I ordered all the royal **advisers** in Babylon to be brought
4.18 None of my royal **advisers** could tell me, but you can,
5. 8 The royal **advisers** came forward, but none of them could read
5.15 The **advisers** and magicians were brought in to read this
11.26 His closest **advisers** will ruin him.
Acts 25.12 Festus, after conferring with his **advisers,** answered,

AV ADVOCATE see PLEAD

AFFAIRS

Num 27.21 Joshua and the whole community of Israel in all their **affairs."**
2 Sam 17.23 After putting his **affairs** in order, he hanged himself.
Dan 2.49 Abednego in charge of the **affairs** of the province of Babylon;
Lk 16. 8 more shrewd in handling their **affairs** than the people who belong
Gal 4. 2 of him and manage his **affairs** until the time set by his
Phil 2.21 concerned only with his own **affairs,** not with the cause of
2 Tim 2. 4 so does not get mixed up in the **affairs** of civilian life.
1 Pet 4.15 a thief or a criminal or a meddler in other people's **affairs.**

AFFECT

Lev 14.34 regulations about houses **affected** by spreading mildew.
Job 35. 3 or to ask God, "How does my sin **affect** you?
35. 6 If you do wrong many times, does that **affect** him?
1 Cor 6.18 Any other sin a man commits does not **affect** his body;

AFFECTION

Gen 34. 3 he fell in love with her and tried to win her **affection.**
1 Sam 18. 3 friendship with David because of his deep **affection** for him.
Esth 2.17 than any of the others she won his favour and **affection.**
Hos 11. 4 I drew them to me with **affection** and love.
2 Cor 9.14 And so with deep **affection** they will pray for you
2 Pet 1. 7 to your godliness add brotherly **affection;**
1. 7 and to your brotherly **affection** add love.

AFFIRM

Num 30.13 husband has the right to **affirm** or to annul any vow
30.14 He has **affirmed** the vow by not objecting on the day
Ps 25.14 those who obey him and he **affirms** his covenant with them.

AFFORD

Lev 5. 7 If a man cannot **afford** a sheep or a goat,
5.11 If a man cannot **afford** two doves or two pigeons,
12. 8 If the woman cannot **afford** a lamb, she shall bring two
14.21 man is poor and cannot **afford** any more, he shall bring
14.32 dreaded skin-disease but who cannot **afford** the normal offerings
Is 40.20 The man who cannot **afford** silver or gold chooses wood
Zech 8.10 that time no one could **afford** to hire either men or animals,

AFRAID
[UNAFRAID]

Gen 3.10 I was **afraid** and hid from you, because I was naked."
15. 1 and heard the Lord say to him, "Do not be **afraid,** Abram.
18.15 Because Sarah was **afraid,** she denied it.
19.30 Because Lot was **afraid** to stay in Zoar, he and his two
21.17 Don't be **afraid.**
26. 7 his wife, because he was **afraid** that the men there would
26.24 Do not be **afraid;**
28.17 He was **afraid** and said, "What a terrifying place this is!
31.31 Jacob answered, "I was **afraid,**
32.11 I am **afraid**—afraid that he is coming to attack us and
35.17 the midwife said to her, "Don't be **afraid,** Rachel;
38.11 said this because he was **afraid** that Shelah would be killed,
42. 4 because he was **afraid** that something might happen to him.
42.35 they saw the money, they and their father Jacob were **afraid.**
43.18 they were **afraid** and thought, "We are being brought
43.23 Don't be **afraid.**
46. 3 "Do not be **afraid** to go to Egypt;
50.19 But Joseph said to them, "Don't be **afraid;**
Ex 2.14 Then Moses was **afraid** and said to himself,
3. 6 Moses covered his face, because he was **afraid** to look at God.
9.20 the king's officials were **afraid** because of what the Lord
14.13 Moses answered, "Don't be **afraid!**
20.19 but we are **afraid** that if God speaks to us,
20.20 Moses replied, "Don't be **afraid;**
23.27 "I will make the people who oppose you **afraid** of me;
34.30 his face was shining, and they were **afraid** to go near him.
Lev 26. 6 and you will sleep without being **afraid** of anyone.
Num 14. 9 and don't be **afraid** of the people who live there.
14. 9 so don't be **afraid."**
21.34 The Lord said to Moses, "Do not be **afraid** of him.
Deut 1.17 Do not be **afraid** of anyone, for the decisions you make
1.20 Do not hesitate or be **afraid.'**
1.28 We are **afraid.**
1.29 "But I said, 'Don't be **afraid** of those people.
2. 4 They will be **afraid** of you, [5] but you must not start
2.25 From today on I will make people everywhere **afraid** of you.
3. 2 But the Lord said to me, 'Don't be **afraid** of him.
3.22 Don't be **afraid** of them, for the Lord your God will
5. 5 because you were **afraid** of the fire
7.18 Do not be **afraid** of them;
7.21 So do not be **afraid** of these people.
9.19 I was **afraid** of the Lord's fierce anger,
13.11 they will be **afraid,** and no one will ever again do such
17.13 hear of it and be **afraid,** and no one else will dare
18.16 presence any more, because you were **afraid** you would die.
19.20 they will be **afraid,** and no one will ever again do such
20. 1 and an army that outnumbers yours, do not be **afraid** of them.
20. 3 Do not be **afraid** of your enemies, or lose courage, or panic.
20. 8 there any man here who has lost his nerve and is **afraid?**
21.21 Everyone in Israel will hear what has happened and be **afraid.**
28.10 to be his own people, and they will be **afraid** of you.
31. 6 Do not be **afraid** of them.
31. 8 you or abandon you, so do not lose courage or be **afraid."**
Josh 1. 9 Don't be **afraid** or discouraged, for I, the Lord your God, am
2.11 We were **afraid** as soon as we heard about it;
5. 1 They became **afraid** and lost their courage
7. 5 Then the Israelites lost their courage and were **afraid.**
8. 1 Don't be **afraid** or discouraged.
10. 8 The Lord said to Joshua, "Do not be **afraid** of them.
10.25 Then Joshua said to his officers, "Don't be **afraid**
11. 6 The Lord said to Joshua, "Do not be **afraid** of them.
14. 8 The men who went with me, however, made our people **afraid.**
22.24 because we were **afraid** that in the future your descendants
Judg 4.18 Don't be **afraid."**
6.23 Don't be **afraid.**
6.27 He was too **afraid** of his family and the people of the
7. 3 'Anyone who is **afraid** should go back home,
7.10 But if you are **afraid** to attack, go down to the camp
9.21 Then because he was **afraid** of his brother Abimelech,
1 Sam 3.15 He was **afraid** to tell Eli about the vision.
4. 7 they were **afraid,** and said, "A god has come
7. 7 and were **afraid,** [8] and said to Samuel, "Keep praying
11. 7 The people of Israel were **afraid** of what the Lord might do,
12.18 Then all the people became **afraid** of the Lord and of Samuel,
12.20 "Don't be **afraid,"** Samuel answered.
14.26 ate any of it because they were all **afraid** of Saul's curse.
15.24 I was **afraid** of my men and did what they wanted.
17.32 "Your Majesty, no one should be **afraid** of this Philistine!
18.12 Saul was **afraid** of David because the Lord was with David
18.15 Saul noticed David's success and became even more **afraid**
18.29 So he became even more **afraid** of David and was his enemy
21.12 David, and he became very much **afraid** of King Achish.
22.23 Stay with me and don't be **afraid.**
23. 3 to him, "We have enough to be **afraid** of here in Judah;
23.17 assurances of God's protection, [17] saying to him, "Don't be **afraid.**
28.13 "Don't be **afraid!"**
2 Sam 3.11 Ishbosheth was so **afraid** of Abner that he could not say
4. 1 killed in Hebron, he was **afraid,** and all the people of
6. 9 Then David was **afraid** of the Lord and said, "How can I
9. 7 "Don't be **afraid,"** David replied.
10.19 And the Syrians were **afraid** to help the Ammonites any more.
12.18 child died, and David's officials were **afraid** to tell him
13.28 Don't be **afraid.**
17.10 fearless as lions, will be **afraid** because everyone in Israel
1 Kgs 1.43 "I'm **afraid** not," Jonathan answered.
1.49 Then Adonijah's guests were **afraid,** and they all got up
1.51 was told that Adonijah was **afraid** of him and that he was
2.29 he had fled to the Lord because he was **afraid** of Solomon.

1 Kgs	19. 3	Elijah was **afraid,** and fled for his life;
	20.13	said, "The Lord says, 'Don't be **afraid** of that huge army!
2 Kgs	1.15	Lord said to Elijah, "Go down with him, and don't be **afraid."**
	6.16	"Don't be **afraid,"** Elisha answered.
	25.24	is no need for you to be **afraid** of the Babylonian officials.
	25.26	went to Egypt, because they were **afraid** of the Babylonians.
1 Chr	12.19	for their kings were **afraid** that he would betray them
	13.12	Then David was **afraid** of God and said, "How can I take
	14.17	and the Lord made every nation **afraid** of him.
	21.30	worship God, because he was **afraid** of the sword of the
	22.13	Be determined and confident, and don't let anything make you **afraid.**
2 Chr	17.10	made all the surrounding kingdoms **afraid** to go to war against
	20.15	not be discouraged or be **afraid** to face this large army.
	20.17	People of Judah and Jerusalem, do not hesitate or be **afraid.**
	32. 7	and confident, and don't be **afraid** of the Assyrian emperor
Ezra	3. 3	though the returning exiles were **afraid** of the people
Neh	4.14	leaders and officials, "Don't be **afraid** of our enemies.
Esth	8.17	other people became Jews, because they were **afraid** of them now.
	9. 2	People everywhere were **afraid** of them,
	9. 3	helped the Jews because they were all **afraid** of Mordecai.
Job	5.22	at violence and hunger and not be **afraid** of wild animals.
	9.35	I am not **afraid.**
	11.19	You won't be **afraid** of your enemies;
	19.29	But now, be **afraid** of the sword— the sword that brings
	23.16	the dark, that makes me **afraid**— even though the darkness
	32. 6	are old, so I was **afraid** to tell you what I think.
	40.23	He is not **afraid** of a rushing river;
Ps	3. 6	I am not **afraid** of the thousands of enemies who surround
	9.20	Make them **afraid,** O Lord;
	23. 4	darkness, I will not be **afraid,** Lord, for you are with me.
	27. 1	I will never be **afraid.**
	27. 3	Even if a whole army surrounds me, I will not be **afraid;**
	30. 7	But then you hid yourself from me, and I was **afraid.**
	31.11	those who know me are **afraid** of me;
	31.22	I was **afraid** and thought that he had driven me out
	46. 2	So we will not be **afraid,** even if the earth is shaken
	48. 5	they were **afraid** and ran away.
	49. 5	I am not **afraid** in times of danger when I am surrounded
	52. 6	Righteous people will see this and be **afraid;**
	56. 3	When I am **afraid,** O Lord Almighty, I put my trust
	56. 4	I trust in God and am not **afraid;**
	56.11	In him I trust, and I will not be **afraid.**
	64. 1	I am **afraid** of my enemies—save my life!
	64. 9	They will all be **afraid;**
	76. 8	the world was **afraid** and kept silent, [9]when you rose up
	77.16	you, O God, they were **afraid,** and the depths of the sea
	78.53	He led them safely, and they were not **afraid;**
	104.29	When you turn away, they are **afraid;**
	105.38	Egyptians were **afraid** of them and were glad when they left.
	112. 7	He is not **afraid** of receiving bad news;
	112. 8	He is not worried or **afraid;**
	116.11	crushed," [11]even when I was **afraid** and said, "No one can
	118. 6	The Lord is with me, I will not be **afraid;**
	119.120	Because of you I am **afraid;**
Prov	1.33	He will be safe, with no reason to be **afraid."**
	3.24	You will not be **afraid** when you go to bed,
	26.13	What is he **afraid** of?
	30.30	lions, strongest of all animals and **afraid** of none;
	31.25	She is strong and respected and not **afraid** of the future.
Ecc	12. 5	You will be **afraid** of high places,
Is	8. 9	Get ready to fight, but be **afraid!**
	8. 9	Yes, get ready, but be **afraid!**
	8.12	people and do not be **afraid** of the things that they fear.
	10.24	in Zion, "Do not be **afraid** of the Assyrians,
	12. 2	I will trust him and not be **afraid.**
	35. 4	Tell everyone who is discouraged, "Be strong and don't be **afraid!**
	40. 9	Speak out and do not be **afraid.**
	41.10	Do not be **afraid**—I am with you!
	41.13	I strengthen you and say, 'Do not be **afraid;**
	41.14	"Small and weak as you are, Israel, don't be **afraid;**
	43. 1	"Do not be **afraid**—I will save you.
	43. 5	Do not be **afraid**—I am with you!
	44. 2	Do not be **afraid;**
	44. 8	Do not be **afraid,** my people!
	51. 7	Do not be **afraid** when people taunt and insult you;
	54. 4	Do not be **afraid**—you will not be disgraced again;
	57.11	these gods that make you **afraid,** so that you tell me lies
	66. 4	the very things they are **afraid** of—because no one answered
Jer	1. 8	Do not be **afraid** of them, for I will be with you
	1.17	Do not be **afraid** of them now, or
	1.17	I will make you even more **afraid** when you are with them.
	3. 8	But Judah, Israel's unfaithful sister, was not **afraid.**
	10. 5	Do not be **afraid** of them:
	17. 8	It is not **afraid** when hot weather comes, because its leaves
	22.25	you to people you are **afraid** of, people who want to kill
	23. 4	people will no longer be **afraid** or terrified, and I will not
	30.10	"My people, do not be **afraid;**
	30.10	you will be secure, and no one will make you **afraid.**
	36.24	who heard all this was **afraid** or showed any sign of sorrow.
	38.19	the king answered, "I am **afraid** of our countrymen
	39.17	will not be handed over to the men you are **afraid** of.
	40. 9	need for you to be **afraid** to surrender to the Babylonians.
	41.17	They were **afraid** of the Babylonians
	42.11	Stop being **afraid** of the king of Babylonia.
	46.27	"My people, do not be **afraid,** people of Israel,
	46.27	you will be secure, and no one will make you **afraid.**
	49.37	make the people of Elam **afraid** of their enemies,
	50.16	foreigner living there will be **afraid** of the attacking army
	51.46	lose courage or be **afraid** because of the rumours you hear.
Lam	3.57	You answered me and told me not to be **afraid.**
Ezek	2. 6	mortal man, must not be **afraid** of them
	2. 6	Still, don't be **afraid** of those rebels or of anything they say.
	3. 9	don't be **afraid** of those rebels."
	11. 8	Are you **afraid** of swords?
	27.36	terrified, **afraid** that they will share your fate."
	28.19	terrified, **afraid** that they will share your fate."
Dan	1.10	Ashpenaz, however, was **afraid** of the king,
	5.19	all nations, races, and languages were **afraid** of him
	10.12	Then he said, "Daniel, don't be **afraid.**
Hos	10. 5	city of Samaria will be **afraid** and will mourn
	13. 1	of Ephraim spoke, the other tribes of Israel were **afraid;**
Joel	2.21	"Fields, don't be **afraid,** but be joyful and glad
	2.22	Animals, don't be **afraid.**
Amos	3. 6	trumpet sound in a city without making the people **afraid?**
	3. 8	When a lion roars, who can avoid being **afraid?**
Jon	1.16	This made the sailors so **afraid** of the Lord that they
Mic	4. 4	vineyards and fig-trees, and no one will make him **afraid.**
	7.17	they will come from their fortresses, trembling and **afraid.**
Hab	3. 7	people of Cushan **afraid** and the people of Midian tremble.
Zeph	3.13	They will be prosperous and secure, **afraid** of no one."
	3.15	there is no reason now to be **afraid.**
	3.16	they will say to Jerusalem, "Do not be **afraid,** city of
Hag	1.12	They were **afraid** and obeyed the prophet Haggai,
	2. 5	I am still with you, so do not be **afraid.**
Zech	8.13	So have courage and don't be **afraid."**
	8.15	So don't be **afraid.**
	9. 5	The city of Ashkelon will see this and be **afraid.**
	14.13	so confused and **afraid** that everyone will seize the man
Mt	1.20	of David, do not be **afraid** to take Mary to be your
	2.22	father Herod as king of Judaea, he was **afraid** to go there.
	9. 8	people saw it, they were **afraid,** and praised God for giving
	10.26	"So do not be **afraid** of people.
	10.28	Do not be **afraid** of those who kill the body but cannot
	10.28	rather be **afraid** of God, who can destroy both body and soul
	10.31	So do not be **afraid;**
	14. 5	kill him, but he was **afraid** of the Jewish people, because
	14.27	Don't be **afraid!"**
	14.30	the strong wind, he was **afraid** and started to sink down
	17. 7	"Don't be **afraid!"**
	21.26	say, 'From man,' we are **afraid** of what the people might do,
	21.46	But they were **afraid** of the crowds, who considered Jesus to
	25.25	I was **afraid,** so I went off and hid your money
	28. 4	guards were so **afraid** that they trembled and became like dead
	28. 5	"You must not be **afraid,"** he said.
	28. 8	the tomb in a hurry, **afraid** and yet filled with joy,
	28.10	"Do not be **afraid,"** Jesus said to them.
Mk	4.41	But they were terribly **afraid** and said to one another,
	5.15	and they were all **afraid.**
	5.36	but told him, "Don't be **afraid,** only believe."
	6.20	Herod was **afraid** of John because he knew that John was
	6.50	Don't be **afraid!"**
	9.32	understand what this teaching meant, and they were **afraid** to ask
	10.32	the people who followed behind were **afraid.**
	11.18	They were **afraid** of him, because the whole crowd was amazed
	11.32	(They were **afraid** of the people, because everyone was convinced
	12.12	But they were **afraid** of the crowd, so they left him
	16. 8	They said nothing to anyone, because they were **afraid.**
Lk	1.12	When Zechariah saw him, he was alarmed and felt **afraid.**
	1.13	But the angel said to him, "Don't be **afraid,** Zechariah!
	1.30	The angel said to her, "Don't be **afraid,** Mary;
	2. 9	They were terribly **afraid,**
	2.10	but the angel said to them, "Don't be **afraid!**
	5.10	Jesus said to Simon, "Don't be **afraid;**
	8.25	But they were amazed and **afraid,** and said to one another,
	8.35	and they were all **afraid.**
	8.37	asked Jesus to go away, because they were terribly **afraid.**
	8.50	But Jesus heard it and said to Jairus, "Don't be **afraid;**
	9.34	and the disciples were **afraid** as the cloud came over them.
	9.45	it, and they were **afraid** to ask him about the matter.
	12. 4	my friends, do not be **afraid** of those who kill the body
	12. 7	So do not be **afraid.**
	12.32	"Do not be **afraid,** little flock, for your Father is pleased
	19.21	I was **afraid** of you, because you are a hard man.
	20.19	but they were **afraid** of the people.
	21. 9	Don't be **afraid** when you hear of wars and revolutions;
	21.25	countries will be in despair, **afraid** of the roar of the sea
	22. 2	teachers of the Law were **afraid** of the people,
Jn	6.20	"Don't be **afraid,"** Jesus told them, "it is I!"
	7.13	talked about him openly, because they were **afraid** of the Jewish
	9.22	said this because they were **afraid** of the Jewish authorities,
	12.15	as the scripture says, [15]"Do not be **afraid,** city of Zion!
	14.27	do not be **afraid.**
	19. 8	When Pilate heard this, he was even more **afraid.**
	19.38	but in secret, because he was **afraid** of the Jewish authorities.)
	20.19	behind locked doors, because they were **afraid** of the Jewish
Acts	5.26	because they were **afraid** that the people might stone them.
	9.26	that he was a disciple, and they were all **afraid** of him.
	16.38	heard that Paul and Silas were Roman citizens, they were **afraid.**
	18. 9	"Do not be **afraid,** but keep on speaking and do
	23.10	violent that the commander was **afraid** that Paul would be torn
	23.11	That night the Lord stood by Paul and said, "Don't be **afraid!**
	24.25	Felix was **afraid** and said, "You may leave now.
	27.17	They were **afraid** that they might run into the sandbanks
	27.24	whom I worship came to me [24]and said, 'Don't be **afraid,**
	27.29	They were **afraid** that the ship would go on the rocks,
Rom	8.15	does not make you slaves and cause you to be **afraid;**
	11.20	instead, be **afraid.**
	13. 3	Would you like to be **unafraid** of the man in authority?
	13. 4	you do evil, then be **afraid** of him, because his power
2 Cor	11. 3	I am **afraid** that your minds will be corrupted and that you
	12.20	I am **afraid** that when I get there I will find you

2 Cor 12.20 I am **afraid** that I will find quarrelling and jealousy,
12.21 I am **afraid** that the next time I come my God will
Gal 2.12 the Gentiles, because he was **afraid** of those who were in
Phil 1.28 Don't be **afraid** of your enemies;
1 Tim 5.20 all those who commit sins, so that the rest may be **afraid.**
Heb 11.23 beautiful child, and they were not **afraid** to disobey the king's
11.27 made Moses leave Egypt without being **afraid** of the king's anger.
12.21 was so terrifying that Moses said, "I am trembling and **afraid!**"
13. 6 and say, "The Lord is my helper, I will not be **afraid.**
1 Pet 3. 6 daughters if you do good and are not **afraid** of anything.
3.14 Do not be **afraid** of anyone, and do not worry.
1 Jn 4.18 perfect in anyone who is **afraid,** because fear has to do with
Rev 1.17 He placed his right hand on me and said, "Don't be **afraid!**
2.10 Don't be **afraid** of anything you are about to suffer.
18.10 because they are **afraid** of sharing in her suffering.
18.15 because they are **afraid** of sharing in her suffering.

AFTER ME

Mt 3.11 the one who will come **after me** will baptize you with the
Mk 1. 7 "The man who will come **after me** is much greater than I
Jn 1.15 when I said, 'He comes **after me,** but he is greater than
1.27 He is coming **after me,** but I am not good enough even
1.30 said, 'A man is coming **after me,** but he is greater than
Acts 13.25 He is coming **after me,** and I am not good enough to

AFTERBIRTH

Deut 28.56 eat her newborn child and the **afterbirth** as well.

AFTERNOON

Gen 24.11 It was late **afternoon,** the time when women came out
2 Sam 11. 2 One day, late in the **afternoon,** David got up from his nap
1 Kgs 18.29 ranting and raving until the middle of the **afternoon;**
18.36 At the hour of the **afternoon** sacrifice the prophet Elijah
Jn 1.39 (It was then about four o'clock in the **afternoon.)**
4.52 was one o'clock yesterday **afternoon** when the fever left him."
Acts 3. 1 Temple at three o'clock in the **afternoon,** the hour for prayer.
10. 3 was about three o'clock one **afternoon** when he had a vision,
10.30 I was praying in my house at three o'clock in the **afternoon.**

AGAG

King of Amalek, defeated by Saul and put to death by Samuel.

Num 24. 7 king shall be greater than **Agag,** And his rule shall be
1 Sam 15. 8 he captured King **Agag** of Amalek alive
15. 9 Saul and his men spared **Agag's** life
15.20 brought back King **Agag,** and killed all the Amalekites.
15.32 "Bring King **Agag** here to me," Samuel ordered.
15.32 **Agag** came to him, trembling with fear,
15.33 And he cut **Agag** to pieces in front of the altar
Esth 3. 1 Haman was the son of Hammedatha, a descendant of **Agag.**
3.10 Haman son of Hammedatha, the descendant of **Agag.**
8. 3 plot that Haman, the descendant of **Agag,** had made
8. 5 of Hammedatha the descendant of **Agag** gave for the destruction
9.24 of Hammedatha—the descendant of **Agag** and the enemy of the

AGAINST

Gen 13.13 Sodom, [13] whose people were wicked and sinned **against the Lord.**
39. 9 then could I do such an immoral thing and sin **against God?"**
Ex 10.16 "I have sinned **against the Lord** your God and against you.
16. 8 complain against us, you are really complaining **against the Lord."**
Lev 5.19 a repayment-offering for the sin he committed **against the Lord.**
6. 2 if any one sins **against the Lord** by refusing to return what
Num 14. 9 Do not rebel **against the Lord** and don't be afraid of the
14.36 false report which caused the people to complain **against the Lord.**
16.11 it is really **against the Lord** that you and your followers
20.13 people of Israel complained **against the Lord** and where he showed
21. 5 people lost their patience [5] and spoke **against God** and Moses.
21. 7 "We sinned when we spoke **against the Lord** and against you.
26. 9 joined the followers of Korah when they rebelled **against the Lord.**
27. 3 not among the followers of Korah, who rebelled **against the Lord;**
32.23 I warn you that you will be sinning **against the Lord.**
Deut 1.41 "You replied, 'Moses, we have sinned **against the Lord.**
9.18 you had sinned **against the Lord** and had made him angry.
9.24 Ever since I have known you, you have rebelled **against the Lord.**
13. 5 you to rebel **against the Lord,** who rescued you from Egypt,
17. 2 or woman has sinned **against the Lord** and broken his covenant
20.18 not make you sin **against the Lord** by teaching you to do
31.27 They have rebelled **against the Lord** during my lifetime,
Josh 7.20 "I have sinned **against the Lord,** Israel's God, and this is
22.16 "Why have you done this evil thing **against the God** of Israel?
22.16 You have rebelled **against the Lord** by building this altar for
22.18 If you rebel **against the Lord** today, he will be angry with
22.19 But don't rebel **against the Lord** or make rebels out of us
22.29 would certainly not rebel **against the Lord** or stop following
24.27 witness against you, to keep you from rebelling **against your God."**
Judg 2.11 people of Israel sinned **against the Lord** and began to serve
3.12 The people of Israel sinned **against the Lord** again.
4. 1 After Ehud died, the people of Israel sinned **against the Lord**
6. 1 people of Israel sinned **against the Lord,** so he let the
10. 6 the Israelites sinned **against the Lord** by worshipping the Baals
13. 1 The Israelites sinned **against the Lord** again, and he let the
1 Sam 2.25 but who can defend a man who sins **against the Lord?"**
7. 6 They said, "We have sinned **against the Lord."**
12.17 committed a great sin **against the Lord** when you asked him
1 Sam 14.33 the people are sinning **against the Lord** by eating meat with
14.34 they must not sin **against the Lord** by eating meat with blood
2 Sam 12.13 "I have sinned **against the Lord,"** David said.
1 Kgs 11. 6 He sinned **against the Lord** and was not true to him as
14.22 people of Judah sinned **against the Lord** and did more to
15.26 him, he sinned **against the Lord** and led Israel into sin.
15.34 him, he sinned **against the Lord** and led Israel into sin.
16. 7 because of the sins that Baasha committed **against the Lord.**
16.19 This happened because of his sins **against the Lord.**
16.25 Omri sinned **against the Lord** more than any of his predecessors.
16.30 He sinned **against the Lord** more than any of his predecessors.
22.52 He sinned **against the Lord,** following the wicked example of
2 Kgs 3. 2 He sinned **against the Lord,** but he was not as bad as
8.18 He sinned **against the Lord,** [19] but the Lord was not willing
8.27 he sinned **against the Lord,** just as Ahab's family did.
13. 2 him he sinned **against the Lord** and led Israel into sin;
13.11 He too sinned **against the Lord** and followed the evil example
14.24 He sinned **against the Lord,** following the wicked example of
15. 9 He, like his predecessors, sinned **against the Lord.**
15.18 He sinned **against the Lord,** for until the day of his
15.24 He sinned **against the Lord,** following the wicked example of
15.28 He sinned **against the Lord,** following the wicked example of
17. 2 He sinned **against the Lord,** but not as much as the kings
17. 7 Israelites sinned **against the Lord** their God, who had rescued
21. 2 the land as his people advanced, Manasseh sinned **against the Lord.**
21. 6 He sinned greatly **against the Lord** and stirred up his anger.
21.16 of Judah into idolatry, causing them to sin **against the Lord.**
21.20 Like his father Manasseh, he sinned **against the Lord;**
23.32 the example of his ancestors, he sinned **against the Lord.**
23.37 the example of his ancestors, Jehoiakim sinned **against the Lord.**
24. 9 the example of his father, Jehoiachin sinned **against the Lord.**
24.19 King Zedekiah sinned **against the Lord,** just as King
2 Chr 13.12 Israel, don't fight **against the Lord,** the God of your ancestors!
19.10 that they do not become guilty of sinning **against the Lord.**
21. 6 He sinned **against the Lord,** [7] but the Lord was not willing
21.11 the people of Judah and Jerusalem to sin **against the Lord.**
22. 4 He sinned **against the Lord,** because after his father's death
25.27 time when he rebelled **against the Lord,** there had been a
28.10 that you also have committed sins **against the Lord** your God?
28.13 We have already sinned **against the Lord** and made him angry
28.22 that man Ahaz sinned **against the Lord** more than ever.
33. 2 the land as his people advanced, Manasseh sinned **against the Lord.**
33. 6 He sinned greatly **against the Lord** and stirred up his anger.
33.22 father Manasseh, he sinned **against the Lord,** and he worshipped
36. 5 He sinned **against the Lord** his God.
36. 9 He too sinned **against the Lord.**
36.12 He sinned **against the Lord** and did not listen humbly to
Job 2.10 In spite of everything he suffered, Job said nothing **against God.**
8. 4 Your children must have sinned **against God,** and so he
9. 1 But how can a man win his case **against God?**
15.26 stubbornly holds up his shield and rushes to fight **against God.**
23. 1 I still rebel and complain **against God;**
Ps 2. 2 their rulers plot together **against the Lord** and against the king
78.17 But they continued to sin **against God,** and in the desert
78.19 They spoke **against God** and said, "Can God supply food in
106.23 servant, Moses, stood up **against God** and prevented his anger
Is 3. 8 Everything they say and do is **against the Lord;**
30. 9 They are always rebelling **against God,** always lying,
Jer 3.13 guilty and that you have rebelled **against the Lord,** your God.
3.25 and our ancestors have always sinned **against the Lord** our God;
4.17 guarding a field, because her people have rebelled **against the Lord.**
16.10 and what sin they have committed **against the Lord** their God.
28.16 you have told the people to rebel **against the Lord."**
29.23 This was **against the Lord's** will;
40. 3 this happened because your people sinned **against the Lord**
44.23 other gods and sinned **against the Lord** by not obeying all
50. 7 enemies say, 'They sinned **against the Lord,** and so what we
52. 2 King Zedekiah sinned **against the Lord,** just as King Jehoiakim
Dan 5.23 You acted **against the Lord** of heaven and brought in the
Hos 12. 3 Jacob grew up, he fought **against God—** [4] he fought against
Mic 1. 5 because the people of Israel have sinned and rebelled **against God.**
7. 9 We have sinned **against the Lord,** so now we must endure his
Nah 1. 9 What are you plotting **against the Lord?**
1.11 a man full of wicked schemes, who plotted **against the Lord.**
Mt 5.11 kinds of evil lies **against** you because you are my followers.
5.23 that your brother has something **against** you, [24] leave your gift
5.25 someone brings a lawsuit **against** you and takes you to court,
7.15 "Be on your guard **against** false prophets;
7.25 rivers overflowed, and the wind blew hard **against** that house.
7.27 the wind blew hard **against** that house, and it fell.
10.21 children will turn **against** their parents and have them put to
10.35 I came to set sons **against** their fathers,
10.35 daughters **against** their mothers,
10.35 daughters-in-law **against** their mothers-in-law;
12. 2 Jesus, "Look, it is **against our Law** for your disciples to
12. 4 even though it was **against the Law** for them to eat it
12.10 asked him, "Is it **against our Law** to heal on the Sabbath?"
12.15 Jesus heard about the plot **against** him, he went away from
12.30 "Anyone who is not for me is really **against** me;
12.31 whoever says evil things **against** the Holy Spirit will not be
12.32 who says something **against** the Son of Man can be forgiven;
12.32 but whoever says something **against** the Holy Spirit will not be
14.24 about by the waves, because the wind was blowing **against** it.
16. 6 guard **against** the yeast of the Pharisees and Sadducees."
18.15 "If your brother sins **against** you, go to him and show
18.21 my brother keeps on sinning **against** me, how many times do I
20.11 took their money and started grumbling **against** the employer.
22.17 Is it **against our Law** to pay taxes to the Roman Emperor,

Mt 26.59 find some false evidence **against** Jesus to put him to death;
26.62 "Have you no answer to give to this accusation **against** you?"
27. 1 elders made their plans **against** Jesus to put him to death.
27. 6 money, and it is **against our Law** to put it in the
27.37 head they put the written notice of the accusation **against** him:
Mk 2.24 Jesus, "Look, it is **against our Law** for your disciples to
3.29 But whoever says evil things **against** the Holy Spirit will
6.19 So Herodias held a grudge **against** John and wanted to kill him,
6.48 straining at the oars, because they were rowing **against** the wind;
8.15 "and be on your guard **against** the yeast of the Pharisees
9.40 For whoever is not **against** us is for us.
10.11 and marries another woman commits adultery **against** his wife.
11.25 forgive anything you may have **against** anyone, so that your Father
12.12 because they knew that he had told this parable **against** them.
12.14 Tell us, is it **against our Law** to pay taxes to the
13.12 will turn **against** their parents and have them put to death.
14.55 tried to find some evidence **against** Jesus in order to put
14.56 Many witnesses told lies **against** Jesus, but their stories
14.57 Then some men stood up and told this lie **against** Jesus:
14.60 "Have you no answer to the accusation they bring **against** you?"
14.64 They all voted **against** him:
15.26 The notice of the accusation **against** him said:
Lk 2.34 which many people will speak **against** [35] and so reveal their
6. 4 Yet it is **against our Law** for anyone except the priests to
9.50 "because whoever is not **against** you is for you."
10.11 your town that sticks to our feet we wipe off **against** you.
11.17 a family divided **against** itself falls apart.
11.23 "Anyone who is not for me is really **against** me;
12. 1 his disciples, "Be on guard **against** the yeast of the Pharisees—
12.10 "Anyone who says a word **against** the Son of Man can be
12.10 but whoever says evil things **against** the Holy Spirit will not
12.52 five will be divided, three **against** two and two against three.
12.53 Fathers will be **against** their sons,
12.53 and sons **against** their fathers;
12.53 mothers will be **against** their daughters,
12.53 and daughters **against** their mothers;
12.53 mothers-in-law will be **against** their daughters-in-law,
12.53 and daughters-in-law **against** their mothers-in-law."
12.58 someone brings a lawsuit **against** you and takes you to court,
14.31 another king who comes **against** him with twenty thousand men,
15.18 and say, Father, I have sinned **against God** and against you.
15.21 the son said, 'I have sinned **against God** and against you.
17. 4 If he sins **against** you seven times in one day, and each
18. 3 pleading for her rights, saying, 'Help me **against** my opponent!'
20.19 because they knew that he had told this parable **against** them;
20.22 Tell us, is it **against our Law** for us to pay taxes
20.46 "Be on your guard **against** the teachers of the Law, who
23.10 Law stepped forward and made strong accusations **against** Jesus.
Jn 5.10 Sabbath, and it is **against our Law** for you to carry your
7.26 He is talking in public, and they say nothing **against** him!
13.18 that says, 'The man who shared my food turned **against** me.'
19.12 who claims to be a king is a rebel **against** the Emperor!"
Acts 4.26 and the rulers met together **against the Lord** and his Messiah.'
4.27 and the people of Israel **against** Jesus, your holy Servant,
5.38 I tell you, do not take any action **against** these men.
5.39 You could find yourselves fighting **against God!"**
6.11 to say, "We heard him speaking against Moses and **against God!"**
6.13 "is always talking **against** our sacred Temple and the Law
7.60 Do not remember this sin **against** them!"
9. 1 his violent threats of murder **against** the followers of the Lord.
13.50 They started a persecution **against** Paul and Barnabas and threw
13.51 their feet in protest **against** them and went on to Iconium.
14. 2 stirred up the Gentiles and turned them **against** the believers.
16.21 They are teaching customs that are **against our law;**
16.22 And the crowd joined in the attack **against** Paul and Silas.
18.13 people to worship God in a way that is **against the law!"**
19.38 have an accusation **against** anyone, we have the authorities and
20. 3 when he discovered that the Jews were plotting **against** him;
21.28 goes everywhere teaching everyone **against** the people of Israel,
22.24 find out why the Jews were screaming like this **against** him.
23.29 the accusation **against** him had to do with questions about their
23.30 that there was a plot **against** him, at once I decided to
23.30 told his accusers to make their charges **against** him before you."
24. 1 They appeared before Felix and made their charges **against** Paul.
24.13 give you proof of the accusations they now bring **against** me.
24.19 and make their accusations if they have anything **against** me.
25. 2 and the Jewish leaders brought their charges **against** Paul.
25. 7 many serious charges **against** him, which they were not able
25. 8 have done nothing wrong **against the Law** of the Jews or
25. 8 or against the Temple or **against** the Roman Emperor."
25.11 in the charges they bring **against** me, no one can hand me
25.15 and elders brought charges **against** him and asked me to condemn
25.16 has had the chance of defending himself **against** the accusation.
25.24 You see this man **against** whom all the Jewish people, both
25.27 a prisoner without clearly indicating the charges **against** him."
26. 9 do everything I could **against** the cause of Jesus of Nazareth.
26.10 when they were sentenced to death, I also voted **against** them.
26.14 by hitting back, like an ox kicking **against** its owner's stick.'
27. 4 the winds were blowing **against** us, we sailed on the sheltered
28.17 though I did nothing **against** our people or the customs that
28.19 though I had no accusation to make **against** my own people.
28.22 everywhere people speak **against** this party to which you belong."
Rom 1.18 anger is revealed from heaven **against** all the sin and evil
7.23 a law that fights **against** the law which my mind approves
8.31 If God is for us, who can be **against** us?
11. 2 says in the passage where Elijah pleads with God **against** Israel:
16.17 upset people's faith and go **against** the teaching which you have
1 Cor 6. 6 Christian goes to court **against** another and lets unbelievers
6.18 who is guilty of sexual immorality sins **against** his own body.
8.12 way you will be sinning **against** Christ
1 Cor 8.12 by sinning **against** your Christian brothers and wounding their
11.27 he is guilty of sin **against** the Lord's body and blood.
2 Cor 10. 5 proud obstacle that is raised **against** the knowledge of God;
13. 8 we cannot do a thing **against** the truth, but only for it.
Gal 3.21 Does this mean that the Law is **against** God's promises?
5.23 There is no law **against** such things as these.
Eph 6.11 will be able to stand up **against** the Devil's evil tricks.
6.12 For we are not fighting **against** human beings
6.12 but **against** the wicked spiritual forces in the
Col 3.13 whenever any of you has a complaint **against** someone else.
1 Tim 5.19 not listen to an accusation **against** an elder unless it is
2 Tim 4.15 guard **against** him yourself, because he was violently opposed
4.16 May God not count it **against** them!
Heb 3. 8 ancestors were when they rebelled **against God,**
3.15 stubborn, as your ancestors were when they rebelled **against God."**
3.16 were the people who heard God's voice and rebelled **against** him?
12. 4 For in your struggle **against** sin you have not yet had to
12.15 Guard **against** turning back from the grace of God.
Jas 3.14 bitter, and selfish, don't sin **against** the truth by boasting of
5. 3 rust will be a witness **against** you and will eat up your
5. 9 Do not complain **against** one another, my brothers, so that God
1 Pet 2.11 bodily passions, which are always at war **against** the soul.
1 Jn 3.17 yet closes his heart **against** his brother, how can he claim
Jude 8 have visions which make them sin **against** their own bodies;
15 terrible words that godless sinners have spoken **against** him!"
Rev 2. 4 But this is what I have **against** you:
2. 9 know the evil things said **against** you by those who claim to
2.14 But there are a few things I have **against** you:
2.16 to you soon and fight **against** those people with the sword
2.20 But this is what I have **against** you:
6.17 day of their anger is here, and who can stand **against** it?"
7. 1 should blow on the earth or the sea or **against** any tree.
11. 7 that comes up out of the abyss will fight **against** them.
12. 7 Michael and his angels fought **against** the dragon, who fought
12.17 and went off to fight **against** the rest of her descendants,
13. 4 Who can fight **against** it?"
13. 7 It was allowed to fight **against** God's people and to defeat them,
17.14 They will fight **against** the Lamb;
19.19 against the one who was riding the horse and **against** his army.

AGATE

A semi-precious stone of different colours, but usually white and brown.

Ex 28.19 in the third row, a turquoise, an **agate,** and an amethyst;
39.12 in the third row, a turquoise, an **agate,** and an amethyst;
Rev 21.19 the second sapphire, the third **agate,** the fourth emerald,

AGE (1)

[NEW AGE]

Ps 72. 5 shines, as long as the moon gives light, for **ages** to come.
119.90 Your faithfulness endures through all the **ages;**
Is 34.10 The land will lie waste **age after age,** and no one will
34.17 will live in the land **age after age,** and it will belong
Ezek 25.15 taken cruel revenge on their **age-long** enemies and destroyed them
Mt 13.39 is the end of the **age,** and the harvest workers are angels.
13.40 so the same thing will happen at the end of the **age:**
13.49 It will be like this at the end of the **age:**
19.28 glorious throne in the **New Age,** then you twelve followers
24. 3 is the time for your coming and the end of the **age."**
28.20 I will be with you always, to the end of the **age."**
Mk 10.30 for the gospel, [30] will receive much more in this present **age.**
10.30 and in the **age** to come he will receive eternal life.
Lk 18.30 much more in this present **age**
18.30 and eternal life in the **age** to come."
20.34 men and women of this **age** marry, [35] but the men and women
20.35 death and live in the **age** to come will not then marry.
Rom 16.25 the secret truth which was hidden for long **ages** in the past.
Gal 1. 4 from this present evil **age,** Christ gave himself for our sins,
Eph 3. 9 hidden through all the past **ages,** [10] in order that at the
6.12 the rulers, authorities, and cosmic powers of this dark **age.**
Col 1.26 he hid through all past **ages** from all mankind but has now
Heb 6. 5 is good, and they had felt the powers of the coming **age.**
9.26 Instead, now when all **ages** of time are nearing the end, he
Jude 25 might, and authority, from all **ages** past, and now, and for

AGE (2)

[OLD AGE]

Gen 5. 5 He had other children [5] and died at the **age** of 930.
5. 8 He had other children [8] and died at the **age** of 912.
5.11 He had other children [11] and died at the **age** of 905.
5.14 He had other children [14] and died at the **age** of 910.
5.17 He had other children [17] and died at the **age** of 895.
5.20 He had other children [20] and died at the **age** of 962.
5.27 He had other children [27] and died at the **age** of 969.
5.31 He had other children [31] and died at the **age** of 777.
9.29 Noah lived for 350 years [29] and died at the **age** of 950.
11.32 Terah died there at the **age** of two hundred and five.
15.15 will live to a ripe **old age,** die in peace, and be
21. 7 Yet I have borne him a son in his **old age."**
25. 7 Abraham died at the ripe **old age** of a hundred and seventy-five.
35.29 hundred and eighty years old [29] and died at a ripe **old age;**
43.33 in the order of their **age** from the eldest to the youngest.
44.20 old and a younger brother, born to him in his **old age.**
48.10 was failing because of his **age,** and he could not see very
50.26 Joseph died in Egypt at the **age** of a hundred and ten.
Lev 27. 3 3 pieces of silver —male above sixty years of **age:**

Num	4. 3	all the men between the **ages** of thirty and fifty who were
	4.23	all the men between the **ages** of thirty and fifty who were
	4.30	all the men between the **ages** of thirty and fifty who were
	4.34	all the men between the **ages** of thirty and fifty who were
	8.24	"From the **age** of twenty-five each Levite shall perform
	8.25	of my presence, [25] and at the **age** of fifty he shall retire.
	14.29	none of you over twenty years of **age** will enter that land.
	18.16	be bought back at the **age** of one month for the fixed
	26. 3	Eleazar obeyed, and called together all the men of that **age** group.
	33.38	At the **age** of 123 he died there on the first day
Josh	5. 4	men who were of fighting **age** when they left Egypt had died
	24.29	son of Nun died at the **age** of a hundred and ten.
Judg	2. 8	son of Nun died at the **age** of a hundred and ten.
	8.32	Joash died at a ripe **old age** and was buried in the
Ruth	4.15	new life to you and give you security in your **old age."**
1 Sam	2.32	no one in your family will ever again live to **old age.**
1 Kgs	14. 4	**Old age** had made Ahijah blind.
	15.23	But in his **old age** he was crippled by a foot disease.
	22.42	king of Judah [42] at the **age** of thirty-five, and he ruled in
2 Kgs	8.17	king of Judah [17] at the **age** of thirty-two, and he ruled in
	8.26	king of Judah [26] at the **age** of twenty-two, and he ruled in
	11.21	Joash became king of Judah at the **age** of seven.
	14. 2	king of Judah [2] at the **age** of twenty-five, and he ruled in
	15. 2	king of Judah [2] at the **age** of sixteen, and he ruled in
	15.33	king of Judah [33] at the **age** of twenty-five, and he ruled in
	16. 2	king of Judah [2] at the **age** of twenty, and he ruled in
	18. 2	king of Judah [2] at the **age** of twenty-five, and he ruled in
1 Chr	2.13	In order of **age** they were:
	3. 1	following, in order of **age,** are David's sons who were born
	8. 1	In order of **age** they were Bela, Ashbel, Aharah, [2] Nohah,
	23. 3	took a census of all the male Levites **aged** thirty or older.
	23.10	Jahath, Zina, Jeush, and Beriah, in order of **age.**
	23.24	his descendants, twenty years of **age** or older, had a share
	23.27	service when they reached the **age** of twenty,
	24.23	Amariah, Jehaziel, and Jekameam, sons of Hebron, in order of **age;**
	26. 2	He had seven sons, listed in order of **age:**
	26. 4	God blessed by giving him eight sons, listed in order of **age:**
	27.23	people who were under the **age** of twenty, because of the
	29.28	He died at a ripe **old age,** wealthy and respected, and
2 Chr	20.31	king of Judah at the **age** of thirty-five and had ruled in
	21. 5	Jehoram became king at the **age** of thirty-two, and he ruled
	21.20	had become king at the **age** of thirty-two and had ruled in
	22. 2	Ahaziah became king at the **age** of twenty-two, and he ruled
	24. 1	king of Judah at the **age** of seven, and he ruled in
	24.15	After reaching the very **old age** of a hundred and thirty,
	25. 1	Amaziah became king at the **age** of twenty-five, and he ruled
	25. 5	all men twenty years of **age** or older, 300,000 in all.
	26. 3	Uzziah became king at the **age** of sixteen, and he ruled in
	27. 1	Jotham became king at the **age** of twenty-five, and he ruled
	28. 1	Ahaz became king at the **age** of twenty, and he ruled in
	29. 1	king of Judah at the **age** of twenty-five, and he ruled in
	31.16	males thirty years of **age** or older who had daily responsibilities
	31.17	the Levites twenty years of **age** or older were assigned theirs
Ezra	3. 8	the Levites twenty years of **age** or older were put in charge
Job	5.26	ripens till harvest time, you will live to a ripe **old age.**
	42.17	And then he died at a very great **age.**
Ps	92.14	that still bear fruit in **old age** and are always green
Prov	20.29	the strength of youth and respect the grey hair of **age.**
	30.17	despises his mother in her **old age** ought to be eaten by
Ecc	4.13	throne, but if in his **old age** he is too foolish to
Is	47. 6	even the **aged** you treated harshly.
Gal	1.14	of most fellow-Jews of my **age** in my practice of the Jewish
1 Tim	5. 9	the list of widows unless she is over sixty years of **age.**
1 Pet	3. 4	your true inner self, the **ageless** beauty of a gentle and

AGENT

1 Kgs	10.28	The king's **agents** controlled the export of horses from
2 Chr	1.16	The king's **agents** controlled the export of horses from
Ezek	17.15	of Judah rebelled and sent **agents** to Egypt to get horses

AGGRESSIVE

Prov	11.16	will never have money, but an **aggressive** man will get rich.

AGONY

2 Chr	21.19	it grew steadily worse until finally the king died in **agony.**
Is	26.18	We were in pain and **agony,** but we gave birth to nothing.
Lam	1. 4	The city gates stand empty, and Zion is in **agony.**
	1.20	"Look, O Lord, at my **agony,** at the anguish of my soul!
Ezek	30.16	I will set fire to Egypt, and Pelusium will be in **agony.**
2 Pet	2. 8	day after day he suffered **agony** as he saw and heard their

AGREE
[DISAGREE]

Gen	16. 2	Abram **agreed** with what Sarai said.
	17. 9	Abraham, "You also must **agree** to keep the covenant with me,
	17.10	and your descendants must all **agree** to circumcise every male
	19.21	He answered, "All right, I **agree.**
	21.27	cattle to Abimelech, and the two of them made an **agreement.**
	21.32	they had made this **agreement** at Beersheba, Abimelech and Phicol
	23.16	Abraham **agreed** and weighed out the amount that Ephron had
	24.44	If she **agrees** and also offers to bring water for my camels,
	26.28	we think that there should be a solemn **agreement** between us.
	29.28	Jacob **agreed,** and when the week of marriage celebrations
	30.31	to take care of your flocks if you **agree** to this suggestion:
	30.34	Laban answered, **"Agreed.**
	31.44	their children, [44] I am ready to make an **agreement** with you.
Gen	31.44	us make a pile of stones to remind us of our **agreement."**
	34. 9	Let us make an **agreement** that there will be intermarriage
	34.15	We can **agree** only on the condition that you become like
	34.16	Then we will **agree** to intermarriage.
	34.22	But these men will **agree** to live among us and be one
	34.23	So let us **agree** that they can live among us."
	34.24	citizens of the city **agreed** with what Hamor and Shechem proposed,
	37.27	His brothers **agreed,** [28] and when some Midianite traders came by,
	42.20	They **agreed** to this [21] and said to one another, "Yes, now
	44.10	He said, "I **agree;**
Ex	2.21	Moses **agreed** to live there, and Jethro gave him his daughter
	4.18	Jethro **agreed** and said good-bye to him.
	22. 7	a man **agrees** to keep another man's money or other valuables
	22.10	"If a man **agrees** to keep another man's donkey, cow, sheep,
	23.32	Do not make any **agreement** with them or with their gods.
Num	5.19	priest shall make the woman **agree** to this oath spoken by the
	5.22	The woman shall respond, "I **agree;**
Deut	1.14	And you **agreed** that this was a good thing to do.
	10.10	Lord listened to me once more and **agreed** not to destroy you.
Josh	2.21	She **agreed** and sent them away.
	7.11	They have broken the **agreement** with me that I ordered them
Judg	11.10	They replied, "We **agree.**
	17.11	The young Levite **agreed** to stay with Micah and became like
1 Sam	20.35	Jonathan went to the fields to meet David, as they had **agreed.**
	29. 9	"I **agree,"** Achish replied.
	30.24	No one can **agree** with what you say!
2 Sam	3.12	Make an **agreement** with me, and I will help you win all
	3.13	"I will make an **agreement** with you on one condition:
	3.19	what the people of Benjamin and of Israel had **agreed** to do.
	23. 5	eternal covenant with me, an **agreement** that will not be broken,
1 Kgs	1. 7	with Abiathar the priest, and they **agreed** to support his cause.
	2.42	Did you not **agree** to it and say that you would obey
	15.20	King Benhadad **agreed** to Asa's proposal and sent his
	18. 6	They **agreed** on which part of the land each one would explore,
	20. 4	"Tell my lord, King Benhadad, that I **agree;**
	20. 7	my wives and children, my silver and gold, and I **agreed."**
	20. 9	lord the king that I **agreed** to his first demand,
	20. 9	but I cannot **agree** to the second."
	20.25	King Benhadad **agreed** and followed their advice.
2 Kgs	6. 3	he **agreed,** [4] and they set out together.
	11. 4	where he made them **agree** under oath to what he planned
	12. 8	The priests **agreed** to this
	12. 8	and also **agreed** not to make the repairs in
1 Chr	13. 4	The people were pleased with the suggestion and **agreed** to it.
2 Chr	15.12	a covenant in which they **agreed** to worship the Lord, the God
	16. 4	Benhadad **agreed** to Asa's proposal and sent his
	30. 1	the people of Jerusalem **agreed** to celebrate it in the second
Neh	9.38	hereby make a solemn written **agreement,** and our leaders,
Job	13.20	**agree** to them, and I will not try to hide from you;
	34.32	you your faults, and have you **agreed** to stop doing evil?
	34.34	Any sensible person will surely **agree;**
	41. 4	Will he make an **agreement** with you and promise to serve
Ps	83. 5	They **agree** on their plan and form an alliance against you:
	105. 9	He will keep the **agreement** he made with Abraham and his
Prov	18. 1	they will **disagree** with what everyone else knows is right.
Is	28.15	death and reached an **agreement** with the world of the dead.
	28.18	be abolished, and your **agreement** with the world of the dead
	33. 8	Treaties are broken and **agreements** are violated.
Jer	34. 8	Jerusalem had made an **agreement** to set free [9] their Hebrew slaves,
	34.10	the people and their leaders **agreed** to free their slaves
	34.15	All of you **agreed** to set your fellow-Israelites free,
Ezek	20.12	Sabbath a sign of the **agreement** between us, to remind them
Dan	1.14	He **agreed** to let them try it for ten days.
	2. 9	You have **agreed** among yourselves to go on telling me lies
	6. 7	the other officials—have **agreed** that Your Majesty should issue
	9.27	ruler will have a firm **agreement** with many people for seven
Mt	3.15	So John **agreed.**
	18.19	two of you on earth **agree** about anything you pray for,
	20. 2	He **agreed** to pay them the regular wage, a silver coin
	20.13	After all, you **agreed** to do a day's work for one silver
	27. 7	After reaching an **agreement** about it, they used the money
	27. 9	the people of Israel had **agreed** to pay for him,
Mk	14.56	witnesses told lies against Jesus, but their stories did not **agree.**
	14.59	Not even they, however, could make their stories **agree.**
Lk	22. 6	Judas **agreed** to it and started looking for a good chance
	23.50	he had not **agreed** with their decision and action.
Jn	8.17	Law that when two witnesses **agree,** what they say is true.
	9.22	Jewish authorities, who had already **agreed** that anyone who said
Acts	5. 2	But with his wife's **agreement** he kept part of the money
	15.15	The words of the prophets **agree** completely with this.
	15.25	met together and have all **agreed** to choose some messengers
	15.28	Holy Spirit and we have **agreed** not to put any other burden
	23.20	"The Jewish authorities have **agreed** to ask you tomorrow to take
	28.25	they left, **disagreeing** among themselves, after Paul had said
Rom	7.16	this shows that I **agree** that the Law is right.
1 Cor	1.10	of you, my brothers, to **agree** in what you say,
	7. 5	each other, unless you first **agree** to do so for a while
	7.12	is an unbeliever and she **agrees** to go on living with him,
	7.13	is an unbeliever and he **agrees** to go on living with her,
2 Cor	6.15	How can Christ and the Devil **agree?**
	12.16	You will **agree,** then, that I was not a burden to you.
	13.11	**agree** with one another;
Gal	2. 9	We **agreed** that Barnabas and I would work among the Gentiles
	3.15	when two people **agree** on a matter and sign an agreement,
Phil	4. 2	please, I beg you, try to **agree** as sisters in the Lord.
1 Tim	6. 3	different doctrine and does not **agree** with the true words of
Tit	1. 9	message which can be trusted and which **agrees** with the doctrine.
	2. 1	But you must teach what **agrees** with sound doctrine.
Phlm	14	So I will not do anything unless you **agree.**

AGRIPPA
Herod Agrippa II, king of territories in the n. of Palestine.

Acts 25.13 Some time later King **Agrippa** and Bernice came to Caesarea
25.22 **Agrippa** said to Festus, "I would like to hear this man myself."
25.23 The next day **Agrippa** and Bernice came with great pomp
25.24 Festus said, "King **Agrippa** and all who are here with us:
25.26 here before you—and especially before you, King **Agrippa!**
26. 1 **Agrippa** said to Paul, "You have permission to speak on
26. 2 "King **Agrippa!**
26.19 "And so, King **Agrippa,** I did not disobey the vision I
26.26 King **Agrippa!**
26.27 King **Agrippa,** do you believe the prophets?
26.28 **Agrippa** said to Paul, "In this short time do you think
26.32 **Agrippa** said to Festus, "This man could have been released

AGROUND

Acts 27.39 decided that, if possible, they would run the ship **aground** there.
27.41 But the ship hit a sandbank and went **aground;**

AHAB (1)
King of Israel, vigorously opposed by the prophet Elijah.

1 Kgs 16.29-34 **King Ahab of Israel**
17.1-7 **Elijah and the drought**
18.1-40 **Elijah and the prophets of Baal**
41-46 **The end of the drought**
19.1-18 **Elijah on Mount Sinai**
20.1-22 **War with Syria**
23-34 **The second Syrian attack**
35-43 **A prophet condemns Ahab**
21.1-29 **Naboth's vineyard**
22.1-28 **The prophet Micaiah warns Ahab**
29-40 **The death of Ahab**
2 Chr 18.1-27 **The prophet Micaiah warns Ahab**
28-34 **The death of Ahab**

1 Kgs 16.28 buried in Samaria, and his son **Ahab** succeeded him as king.
22.41 of the reign of King **Ahab** of Israel, Jehoshaphat son of Asa
22.51 of Judah, Ahaziah son of **Ahab** became king of Israel,
22.52 wicked example of his father **Ahab,** his mother Jezebel,
2 Kgs 1. 1 After the death of King **Ahab** of Israel, the country of
3. 1 of Judah, Joram son of **Ahab** became king of Israel,
3. 5 when King **Ahab** of Israel died, Mesha rebelled against Israel.
8.16 reign of Joram son of **Ahab** as king of Israel, Jehoram son
8.18 His wife was **Ahab's** daughter,
8.18 and like the family of **Ahab** he followed the evil ways of
8.25 reign of Joram son of **Ahab** as king of Israel, Ahaziah son
8.26 Athaliah, the daughter of King **Ahab** and granddaughter of King
8.27 Ahaziah was related to King **Ahab** by marriage,
8.27 he sinned against the Lord, just as **Ahab's** family did.
9. 7 the king, that son of **Ahab,** so that I may punish Jezebel
9. 8 All **Ahab's** family and descendants are to die;
9.25 together behind King Joram's father **Ahab,**
9.25 the Lord spoke these words against **Ahab:**
9.29 eleventh year that Joram son of **Ahab** was king of Israel.
10. 1 seventy descendants of King **Ahab** living in the city of Samaria.
10. 1 leading citizens, and to the guardians of **Ahab's** descendants.
10. 6 bring the heads of King **Ahab's** descendants to me at Jezreel
10. 6 The seventy descendants of King **Ahab** were under the care of
10. 7 killed all seventy of **Ahab's** descendants, put their heads in
10. 8 told that the heads of **Ahab's** descendants had been brought,
10.10 the Lord said about the descendants of **Ahab** will come true.
10.11 all the other relatives of **Ahab** living in Jezreel, and all
10.17 Jehu killed all of **Ahab's** relatives, not sparing even one.
10.18 together and said, "King **Ahab** served the god Baal a little,
10.30 Jehu, "You have done to **Ahab's** descendants everything I wanted
21. 3 of the goddess Asherah, as King **Ahab** of Israel had done.
21.13 Samaria, as I did King **Ahab** of Israel and his descendants.
2 Chr 21. 6 wicked example of King **Ahab** and the other kings of Israel,
21. 6 because he had married one of **Ahab's** daughters.
21.13 unfaithful to God, just as **Ahab** and his successors led Israel
22. 2 followed the example of King **Ahab's** family, since his mother
22. 2 Athaliah—the daughter of King **Ahab** and granddaughter of King
22. 4 other members of King **Ahab's** family became his advisers,
22. 7 Nimshi, whom the Lord had chosen to destroy the dynasty of **Ahab.**
Mic 6.16 the evil practices of King Omri and of his son, King **Ahab.**

AHAZ (1)
King of Judah, a contemporary of Isaiah.

2 Kgs 15.38 in David's City, and his son **Ahaz** succeeded him as king.
16. 1 Remaliah as king of Israel, **Ahaz** son of Jotham became king
16. 4 hills, and under every shady tree, **Ahaz** offered sacrifices
16. 5 attacked Jerusalem and besieged it, but could not defeat **Ahaz.**
16. 7 **Ahaz** sent men to Tiglath Pileser, the emperor of Assyria,
16. 8 **Ahaz** took the silver and gold from the Temple and the
16. 9 Tiglath Pileser, in answer to **Ahaz'** plea, marched out with
16.10 King **Ahaz** went to Damascus to meet Emperor Tiglath Pileser,
16.11 an altar just like it, and finished it before **Ahaz** returned.
16.12 his return from Damascus, **Ahaz** saw that the altar was finished,
16.14 altar and the Temple, so **Ahaz** moved it to the north side
16.17 King **Ahaz** took apart the bronze carts used in the Temple
16.18 please the Assyrian emperor, **Ahaz** also removed from the Temple
16.19 Everything else that King **Ahaz** did is recorded in
16.20 **Ahaz** died and was buried in the royal tombs in David's City,
17. 1 of the reign of King **Ahaz** of Judah, Hoshea son of Elah
18. 1 of Israel, Hezekiah son of **Ahaz** became king of Judah
20.11 go back ten steps on the stairway set up by King **Ahaz.**
23.12 palace roof above King **Ahaz'** quarters, King Josiah tore down,
1 Chr 3.13 Amaziah, Uzziah, Jotham, [13] **Ahaz,** Hezekiah, Manasseh,
2 Chr 27. 9 in David's City and his son **Ahaz** succeeded him as king.
28. 1 **Ahaz** became king at the age of twenty, and he ruled in
28. 4 hills, and under every shady tree **Ahaz** offered sacrifices
28. 5 Because King **Ahaz** sinned, the Lord his God let the king
28. 5 Pekah son of Remaliah, defeat **Ahaz** and kill 120,000 of the
28. 7 soldier named Zichri killed King **Ahaz'** son Maaseiah,
28.16 captured many prisoners, so King **Ahaz** asked Tiglath Pileser,
28.19 King **Ahaz** of Judah had violated the rights of his people
28.20 Assyrian emperor, instead of helping **Ahaz,** opposed him
28.21 So **Ahaz** took the gold from the Temple, the palace,
28.22 at their worst, that man **Ahaz** sinned against the Lord more
28.27 King **Ahaz** died and was buried in Jerusalem, but not in
29.19 all the equipment which King **Ahaz** took away during those years
Is 1. 1 when Uzziah, Jotham, **Ahaz,** and Hezekiah were kings of Judah.
7. 1 King **Ahaz,** the son of Jotham and grandson of Uzziah, ruled
7. 3 Isaiah, "Take your son Shear Jashub, and go to meet King **Ahaz.**
7.10 The Lord sent another message to **Ahaz:**
7.12 **Ahaz** answered, "I will not ask for a sign.
14.28 that was proclaimed in the year that King **Ahaz** died.
38. 8 the stairway built by King **Ahaz,** the Lord will make the
Hos 1. 1 time that Uzziah, Jotham, **Ahaz,** and Hezekiah were kings of Judah,
Mic 1. 1 the time that Jotham, **Ahaz,** and Hezekiah were kings of Judah,
Mt 1. 6 Jehoram, Uzziah, Jotham, **Ahaz,** Hezekiah, Manasseh, Amon, Josiah,

AHAZIAH (1)
King of Israel.

1 Kgs 22.40 At his death his son **Ahaziah** succeeded him as king.
22.49 Then King **Ahaziah** of Israel offered to let his men sail
22.51 of King Jehoshaphat of Judah, **Ahaziah** son of Ahab became king
2 Kgs 1. 2 King **Ahaziah** of Israel fell off the balcony on the roof
1. 3 meet the messengers of King **Ahaziah** and ask them, "Why are
1.17 **Ahaziah** died, as the Lord had said through Elijah.
1.17 **Ahaziah** had no sons, so his brother Joram succeeded him as
1.18 Everything else that King **Ahaziah** did is recorded in
2 Chr 20.35 an alliance with King **Ahaziah** of Israel, who did many wicked
20.37 made an alliance with **Ahaziah,** the Lord will destroy what you

AHAZIAH (2)
King of Judah.

2 Kgs 8.24 in David's City, and his son **Ahaziah** succeeded him as king.
8.25 Ahab as king of Israel, **Ahaziah** son of Jehoram became king
8.27 Since **Ahaziah** was related to King Ahab by marriage,
8.28 King **Ahaziah** joined King Joram of Israel in a war against
8.29 from his wounds, and **Ahaziah** went there to visit him.
9.16 not recovered, and King **Ahaziah** of Judah was there, visiting him.
9.21 done, and he and King **Ahaziah** rode out, each in his own
9.23 "It's treason, **Ahaziah!"**
9.27 King **Ahaziah** saw what happened, so he fled in his chariot
9.29 **Ahaziah** had become king of Judah in the eleventh year that
10. 4 they said, "when neither King Joram nor King **Ahaziah** could?"
10.13 relatives of the late King **Ahaziah** of Judah and asked them,
10.13 **"Ahaziah's** relatives," they answered.
11. 1 King **Ahaziah's** mother Athaliah learnt of her son's murder,
11. 2 Only **Ahaziah's** son Joash escaped.
11. 2 Jehosheba, who was King Jehoram's daughter and **Ahaziah's** half-sister.
11. 4 He showed them King **Ahaziah's** son Joash
12.18 predecessors Jehoshaphat, Jehoram, and **Ahaziah** had dedicated to
13. 1 reign of Joash son of **Ahaziah** as king of Judah, Jehoahaz
1 Chr 3.11 Rehoboam, Abijah, Asa, Jehoshaphat, [11] Jehoram, **Ahaziah,** Joash,
2 Chr 21.17 all the king's wives and sons except **Ahaziah,** his youngest son.
22. 1 and killed all King Jehoram's sons except **Ahaziah,** the youngest.
22. 1 people of Jerusalem made **Ahaziah** king as his father's successor.
22. 2 **Ahaziah** became king at the age of twenty-two,
22. 2 **Ahaziah** also followed the example of King Ahab's family,
22. 6 from his wounds, and **Ahaziah** went there to visit him.
22. 7 God used this visit to Joram to bring about **Ahaziah's** downfall.
22. 7 While **Ahaziah** was there, he and Joram were confronted by a
22. 8 of Ahaziah's nephews that had accompanied **Ahaziah** on his visit.
22. 9 A search was made for **Ahaziah,** and he was found hiding in
22. 9 No member of **Ahaziah's** family was left who could rule the kingdom.
22.10 King **Ahaziah's** mother Athaliah learnt of her son's murder,
22.11 **Ahaziah** had a half-sister, Jehosheba, who was married to
22.11 secretly rescued one of **Ahaziah's** sons, Joash, took him away

AHEAD OF YOU

Mt 11.10 will send my messenger **ahead of you** to open the way
21. 2 to the village there **ahead of you,** and at once you will
21.31 prostitutes are going into the Kingdom of God **ahead of you.**
26.32 am raised to life, I will go to Galilee **ahead of you."**
28. 7 from death, and now he is going to Galilee **ahead of you;**
Mk 1. 2 will send my messenger **ahead of you** to clear the way
11. 2 "Go to the village there **ahead of you.**
14.28 am raised to life, I will go to Galilee **ahead of you."**
16. 7 'He is going to Galilee **ahead of you;**
Lk 7.27 will send my messenger **ahead of you** to open the way
19.30 "Go to the village there **ahead of you;**

AHIJAH (1)
Prophet who encouraged Jeroboam to rebel against the s. kingdom (Judah).

1 Kgs	11.29	from Jerusalem, the prophet **Ahijah,** from Shiloh, met him alone
	11.30	**Ahijah** took off the new robe he was wearing, tore it
	12.15	spoken to Jeroboam son of Nebat through the prophet **Ahijah**
	14. 2	to Shiloh, where the prophet **Ahijah** lives, the one who said
	14. 4	So she went to **Ahijah's** home in Shiloh.
	14. 4	Old age had made **Ahijah** blind.
	14. 5	And the Lord told **Ahijah** what to say.
	14. 6	But when **Ahijah** heard her coming in the door, he said,
	14.12	And **Ahijah** went on to say to Jeroboam's wife, "Now go
	14.18	as the Lord had said through his servant, the prophet **Ahijah.**
	15.29	his servant, the prophet **Ahijah** from Shiloh, all Jeroboam's
2 Chr	9.29	in The Prophecy of **Ahijah** of Shiloh, and in The Visions
	10.15	spoken to Jeroboam son of Nebat through the prophet **Ahijah**

AHIMAAZ (1)
Son of Zadok the priest.

2 Sam	15.27	"Look, take your son **Ahimaaz** and Abiathar's son Jonathan and go
	15.36	They have their sons **Ahimaaz** and Jonathan with them,
	17.17	son Jonathan and Zadok's son **Ahimaaz** were waiting at the spring
	17.20	and asked the woman, "Where are **Ahimaaz** and Jonathan?"
	17.21	they left, **Ahimaaz** and Jonathan came up out of the well
	18.19	Then **Ahimaaz** son of Zadok said to Joab, "Let me run to
	18.22	**Ahimaaz** insisted, "I don't care what happens;
	18.23	"Whatever happens," **Ahimaaz** said again, "I want to go."
	18.23	So **Ahimaaz** ran off down the road through the Jordan Valley,
	18.27	said, "I can see that the first man runs like **Ahimaaz."**
	18.28	**Ahimaaz** called out a greeting to the king, threw himself
	18.29	**Ahimaaz** answered, "Sir, when your officer Joab sent me, I saw
1 Chr	6. 8	Zerahiah, Meraioth, [7] Amariah, Ahitub, [8] Zadok, **Ahimaaz,**
	6.53	Meraioth, Amariah, Ahitub, [53] Zadok, **Ahimaaz.**

AHIMELECH (1)
Priest who helped David escape from Saul.

1 Sam	21. 1	David went to the priest **Ahimelech** in Nob.
	21. 1	**Ahimelech** came out trembling to meet him and asked, "Why did
	21. 8	David said to **Ahimelech,** "Have you got a spear or a
	21. 9	**Ahimelech** answered, "I have the sword of Goliath
	22. 9	saw David when he went to **Ahimelech** son of Ahitub in Nob.
	22.10	**Ahimelech** asked the Lord what David should do, and then he
	22.11	Saul sent [illegible] priest **Ahimelech** and all his relatives,
	22.12	Saul said to **Ahimelech,** "Listen, Ahimelech!"
	22.14	**Ahimelech** answered, "David is the most faithful officer
	22.16	king said, **"Ahimelech,** you and all your relatives must die."
	22.20	But Abiathar, one of **Ahimelech's** sons, escaped, and went
	23. 6	Abiathar son of **Ahimelech** escaped and joined David in Keilah,
	30. 7	the priest Abiathar son of **Ahimelech,** "Bring me the ephod,"
2 Sam	8.17	son of Ahitub and **Ahimelech** son of Abiathar were priests;
1 Chr	18.16	son of Ahitub and **Ahimelech** son of Abiathar were priests;
	24. 3	of Eleazar, and by **Ahimelech,** a descendant of Ithamar.
	24. 6	his officials, the priest Zadok, **Ahimelech** son of Abiathar,
	24.31	King David, Zadok, **Ahimelech,** and the heads of families of the

AHITHOPHEL
One of David's chief advisers, who supported Absalom against David.

2 Sam	15.12	the town of Gilo for **Ahithophel,** who was one of King David's
	15.31	David was told that **Ahithophel** had joined Absalom's rebellion,
	15.31	he prayed, "Please, Lord, turn **Ahithophel's** advice into nonsense!"
	15.34	And do all you can to oppose any advice that **Ahithophel** gives.
	16.15	Israelites with him entered Jerusalem, and **Ahithophel** was with
	16.20	Absalom turned to **Ahithophel** and said, "Now that we are here,
	16.21	**Ahithophel** answered, "Go and have intercourse with your
	16.23	Any advice that **Ahithophel** gave in those days was accepted
	17. 1	after that, **Ahithophel** said to Absalom, "Let me choose twelve
	17. 6	to him, "This is the advice that **Ahithophel** has given us;
	17. 7	answered, "The advice **Ahithophel** gave you this time is no good.
	17.14	Israelites said, "Hushai's advice is better than **Ahithophel's."**
	17.14	decided that **Ahithophel's** good advice would not be followed,
	17.15	and the Israelite leaders and what advice **Ahithophel** had given.
	17.21	They told him what **Ahithophel** had planned against him and said,
	17.23	When **Ahithophel** saw that his advice had not been followed,
	23.24	Eliam son of **Ahithophel** from Gilo
1 Chr	27.33	**Ahithophel** was adviser to the king, and Hushai the
	27.34	After **Ahithophel** died, Abiathar and Jehoiada son of Benaiah became advisers.

AI (1)
City near Bethel, captured by Joshua.

Gen	12. 8	his camp between Bethel on the west and **Ai** on the east.
	13. 3	the place between Bethel and **Ai** where he had camped before
Josh	7. 2	some men from Jericho to **Ai,** a city east of Bethel, near
	7. 3	"There is no need for everyone to attack **Ai.**
	7. 5	The men of **Ai** chased them from the city gate as far
	8. 1	"Take all the soldiers with you and go on up to **Ai.**
	8. 1	I will give you victory over the king of **Ai;**
	8. 2	You are to do to **Ai** and its king what you did
	8. 3	So Joshua got ready to go to **Ai** with all his soldiers.
	8. 5	When the men of **Ai** come out against us, we will turn
	8. 9	place and waited there, west of **Ai,** between **Ai** and Bethel.
	8.10	Then he and the leaders of Israel led them to **Ai.**
	8.11	on the north side, with a valley between themselves and **Ai.**
	8.12	put them in hiding west of the city, between **Ai** and Bethel.
	8.14	When the king of **Ai** saw Joshua's men, he acted quickly.
Josh	8.17	Every man in **Ai** went after the Israelites, and the city
	8.18	Then the Lord said to Joshua, "Point your spear at **Ai;**
	8.20	When the men of **Ai** looked back, they saw the smoke
	8.21	on fire, they turned round and began killing the men of **Ai.**
	8.22	men of **Ai** found themselves completely surrounded by Israelites,
	8.23	away, and no one lived through it [23] except the king of **Ai.**
	8.24	Then they went back to **Ai** and killed everyone there.
	8.25	kept his spear pointed at **Ai** and did not put it down
	8.25	The whole population of **Ai** was killed that day—twelve thousand
	8.28	Joshua burnt **Ai** and left it in ruins.
	8.29	He hanged the king of **Ai** from a tree and left his
	9. 3	done to Jericho and **Ai,** [4] and they decided to deceive him.
	10. 1	had captured and totally destroyed **Ai** and had killed its king,
	10. 2	it was larger than **Ai,** and its men were good fighters.
	12. 9	Jericho, **Ai** (near Bethel), [10] Jerusalem, Hebron,
Ezra	2.21	Bethel and **Ai** - 223
Neh	7.26	Bethel and **Ai** - 123
	11.31	Benjamin lived in Geba, Michmash, **Ai,** Bethel and the nearby
Jer	49. 3	**Ai** is destroyed!

AID

Deut	33.26	the sky, riding through the clouds to come to your **aid.**
Josh	10.33	of Gezer came to the **aid** of Lachish, but Joshua defeated him
Job	33.23	angel may come to his **aid**— one of God's thousands of
Ps	20. 2	you help from his Temple and give you **aid** from Mount Zion.
	39.12	come to my **aid** when I weep.
	40.17	You are my saviour and my God— hurry to my **aid!**
	44.26	Come to our **aid!**
	46. 5	at early dawn he will come to its **aid.**
	59. 5	Rise, Lord God Almighty, and come to my **aid;**
	70. 5	You are my saviour, O Lord— hurry to my **aid!**
	71.12	my God, hurry to my **aid!**
	78.35	God was their protector, that the Almighty came to their **aid.**
Is	43.12	I predicted what would happen, and then I came to your **aid.**
1 Pet	3. 3	You should not use outward **aids** to make yourselves beautiful,

AIDE

2 Kgs	9.25	and Jehu said to his **aide** Bidkar, "Get his body and
	9.26	Joram's body," Jehu ordered his **aide,** "and throw it in the

AILMENT

2 Cor	12. 7	a painful physical **ailment,** which acts as Satan's messenger

AIM

Ps	7.13	takes up his deadly weapons and **aims** his burning arrows.
	11. 2	have drawn their bows and **aimed** their arrows to shoot from
	64. 3	their tongues like swords and **aim** cruel words like arrows.
Prov	17.24	An intelligent person **aims** at wise action, but a fool
Is	16. 2	River Arnon and move **aimlessly** to and fro, like birds driven
Lam	2. 4	He **aimed** his arrows at us like an enemy;
Amos	5.14	Make it your **aim** to do what is right, not what is
Rom	14.19	So then, we must always **aim** at those things that bring
1 Thes	4.11	Make it your **aim** to live a quiet life, to mind your
	5.15	all times make it your **aim** to do good to one another

AIR
[MIDAIR]

Gen	1.20	of living beings, and let the **air** be filled with birds."
Ex	9. 8	Moses shall throw them into the **air** in front of the king.
	9.10	Moses threw them into the **air,** and they produced boils that
2 Sam	18. 9	The mule ran on and Absalom was left hanging in **mid air.**
1 Chr	21.16	angel standing in mid **air,** holding his sword in his hand,
Neh	8. 6	the people raised their arms in the **air** and answered, "Amen!
Job	2.12	in grief and throwing dust into the **air** and on their heads.
Ps	107.26	lifted high in the **air** and plunged down into the depths.
Song	1.12	on his couch, and my perfume filled the **air** with fragrance.
	2.13	the **air** is fragrant with blossoming vines.
	4.16	fill the **air** with fragrance.
Is	3.16	They walk along with their noses in the **air.**
	41.16	You will toss them in the **air;**
Ezek	1.21	or rose in the **air,** the wheels did exactly the same.
	3.13	creatures beating together in the **air,** and the noise of the
	8. 3	spirit lifted me high in the **air** and took me to Jerusalem.
	10.15	the creatures rose in the **air** [16] and moved, the wheels went
Dan	4.25	and sleep in the open **air,** where the dew will fall on
	5.21	and slept in the open **air** with nothing to protect him from
Zech	5. 1	again, and this time I saw a scroll flying through the **air.**
	5. 2	I answered, "A scroll flying through the **air;**
Acts	22.23	waving their clothes, and throwing dust up in the **air.**
1 Cor	14. 9	Your words will vanish in the **air!**
1 Thes	4.17	with them in the clouds to meet the Lord in the **air.**
Rev	8.13	flying high in the **air** say in a loud voice,
	9. 2	the sunlight and the **air** were darkened by the smoke
	14. 6	angel flying high in the **air,** with an eternal message of
	16.17	Then the seventh angel poured out his bowl in the **air.**
	19.17	shouted in a loud voice to all the birds flying in **midair:**

ALABASTER
A soft stone, usually of light creamy colour, from which vases and jars were made.

Song	5.15	His thighs are columns of **alabaster** set in sockets of gold.
Mt	26. 7	with an **alabaster jar** filled with an expensive perfume,
Mk	14. 3	woman came in with an **alabaster jar** full of a very expensive
Lk	7.37	so she brought an **alabaster jar** full of perfume

ALARM

Josh 10. 2 people of Jerusalem were greatly **alarmed** at this because Gibeon
2 Sam 4. 1 Hebron, he was afraid, and all the people of Israel were **alarmed.**
Neh 4.18 who was to sound the **alarm** on the bugle stayed with me.
Jer 20.16 the morning and the battle **alarm** at noon, [17]because he didn't
36.16 turned to one another in **alarm,** and said to Baruch, "We
49.21 shake, and the cries of **alarm** will be heard as far away
50.46 shake, and the cries of **alarm** will be heard by the other
Ezek 33. 3 the enemy approaching, he sounds the **alarm** to warn everyone.
33. 6 and does not sound the **alarm,** the enemy will come and kill
Dan 4.19 Belteshazzar, was so **alarmed** that he could not say anything.
4.19 "Belteshazzar, don't let the dream and its message **alarm** you."
7.15 The visions I saw **alarmed** me, and I was deeply disturbed.
Hos 5. 8 Sound the **alarm** in Ramah!
8. 1 The Lord says, "Sound the **alarm!**
Joel 2. 1 sound the **alarm** on Zion, God's sacred hill.
Mk 10.32 Jesus was going ahead of the disciples, who were filled with **alarm;**
16. 5 on the right, wearing a white robe—and they were **alarmed.**
16. 6 "Don't be **alarmed,**" he said.
Lk 1.12 When Zechariah saw him, he was **alarmed** and felt afraid.
24.38 But he said to them, "Why are you **alarmed?**
2 Cor 7.11 Such indignation, such **alarm,** such feelings, such devotion,

ALCOHOL

Prov 31. 4 Kings should not drink wine or have a craving for **alcohol.**
31. 6 **Alcohol** is for people who are dying, for those who are in

ALERT

Is 7. 4 Tell him to keep **alert,** to stay calm, and not to be
Dan 4.13 I saw coming down from heaven an angel, **alert** and watchful.
4.17 This is the decision of the **alert** and watchful angels.
Mk 13.33 Be on watch, be **alert,** for you do not know when the
Lk 21.36 Be on the **alert** and pray always that you will have the
1 Cor 16.13 Be **alert,** stand firm in the faith, be brave, be strong.
Eph 6.18 For this reason keep **alert** and never give up;
Col 4. 2 persistent in prayer, and keep **alert** as you pray, giving
1 Pet 1.13 Keep **alert** and set your hope completely on the blessing
4. 7 You must be self-controlled and **alert,** to be able to pray.
5. 8 Be **alert,** be on the watch!

ALIEN see FOREIGNER

ALIEN

Jer 7. 6 Stop taking advantage of **aliens,** orphans, and widows.

ALIGHT

Gen 8. 9 all the land, the dove did not find a place to **alight.**
Mt 3.16 Spirit of God coming down like a dove and **alighting** on him.

ALIVE

Gen 6.19 and of every kind of bird, in order to keep them **alive.**
7. 3 and bird will be kept **alive** to reproduce again on the earth.
25. 6 but while he was still **alive,** he gave presents to the sons
26.15 of his father Abraham had dug while Abraham was **alive.**
32.30 "I have seen God face to face, and I am still **alive**";
43.27 Is he still **alive** and well?"
43.28 "Your humble servant, our father, is still **alive** and well."
44.20 and he is the only one of his mother's children still **alive;**
45. 3 Is my father still **alive?**"
45.26 "Joseph is still **alive!**"
45.28 "My son Joseph is still **alive!**"
46.30 that I have seen you and know that you are still **alive.**"
47.19 us corn to keep us **alive** and seed to sow in our
50.20 of many people who are **alive** today because of what happened.
Ex 4.18 to my relatives in Egypt to see if they are still **alive.**"
22. 2 or a sheep, is found **alive** in his possession, he shall pay
33.20 can see me and stay **alive,** [21] but here is a place beside
Lev 16.10 for Azazel shall be presented **alive** to the Lord and sent off
Num 16.30 so that they go down **alive** to the world of the dead,
16.33 So they went down **alive** to the world of the dead, with
31.15 He asked them, "Why have you kept all the women **alive?**
31.18 but keep **alive** for yourselves all the girls and
Deut 4. 4 were faithful to the Lord your God are still **alive** today.
24. 6 away the family's means of preparing food to keep **alive.**
Josh 10.28 no one was left **alive.**
10.33 Joshua defeated him and his army and left none of them **alive.**
10.37 No one in it was left **alive.**
11. 8 The fight continued until none of the enemy was left **alive.**
11.11 no one was left **alive,** and the city was burnt.
11.14 no one was left **alive.**
14.10 and the Lord, as he promised, has kept me **alive** ever since.
24.31 long as those leaders were **alive** who had seen for themselves
Judg 2. 7 long as the leaders were **alive** who had seen for themselves
1 Sam 2.33 keep one of your descendants **alive,** and he will serve me as
15. 8 captured King Agag of Amalek **alive** and killed all the people.
20.14 And if I remain **alive,** please keep your sacred promise
20.31 as long as David is **alive,** you will never be king of
2 Sam 12.21 "While the child was **alive,** you wept for him and would not
12.22 David answered, "I did fast and weep while he was still **alive.**
14. 7 leave my husband without a son to keep his name **alive.**"
18.14 into Absalom's chest while he was still **alive,** hanging in the
18.18 King's Valley, because he had no son to keep his name **alive.**
19. 6 quite happy if Absalom were **alive** today and all of us were
21. 5 to destroy us and leave none of us **alive** anywhere in Israel.
1 Kgs 17.23 to his mother and said to her, "Look, your son is **alive!**"
18. 5 we can find enough grass to keep the horses and mules **alive.**
19.18 will leave seven thousand people **alive** in Israel—all those who
20.18 He ordered, "Take them **alive,** no matter whether they are
20.32 Ahab answered, "Is he still **alive?**
2 Kgs 7.12 and then they will take us **alive** and capture the city."
10.11 not one of them was left **alive.**
10.14 Jehu ordered his men, "Take them **alive!**"
10.14 people in all, and not one of them was left **alive.**
2 Chr 24. 2 to the Lord as long as Jehoiada the priest was **alive.**
24.14 long as Jehoiada was **alive,** sacrifices were offered regularly
Neh 5. 2 "We have large families, we need corn to keep us **alive.**"
Job 2. 4 "A man will give up everything in order to stay **alive.**
4.20 A man may be **alive** in the morning, but die unnoticed
5.20 comes, he will keep you **alive,** and in war protect you from
10.12 me life and constant love, and your care has kept me **alive.**
33.28 going to the world of the dead, and I am still **alive.**"
Ps 33.19 he keeps them **alive** in times of famine.
45.17 will keep your fame **alive** for ever, and everyone will praise
55.15 may they go down **alive** into the world of the dead!
66. 9 He has kept us **alive** and has not allowed us to fall.
69.25 may no one be left **alive** in their tents.
80.18 keep us **alive,** and we will praise you.
119.93 your instructions, because by them you have kept me **alive.**
119.107 keep me **alive,** as you have promised.
124. 3 they would have swallowed us **alive** in their furious anger
Prov 1.12 They may be **alive** and well when we find them, but
26.21 keeps the fire burning, and troublemakers keep arguments **alive.**
Ecc 3.12 happy and do the best we can while we are still **alive.**
4. 2 they are better off than those who are still **alive.**
9. 4 But anyone who is **alive** in the world of the living has
Is 14.30 on you Philistines, and it will not leave any of you **alive.**
24. 6 Fewer and fewer remain **alive.**
Jer 15. 9 let your enemies kill those of you who are still **alive.**
29.22 like Zedekiah and Ahab, whom the king of Babylonia roasted **alive!**'
Lam 1.11 They exchange their treasures for food to keep themselves **alive.**
1.19 in the city streets, Looking for food to keep themselves **alive.**
3.53 They threw me **alive** into a pit and closed the opening
4. 9 starved slowly to death, with no food to keep them **alive.**
5. 6 get food enough to stay **alive,** we went begging to Egypt and
Ezek 3.21 doesn't sin, he will stay **alive,** and your life will also be
5.10 you and scatter in every direction any who are left **alive.**
13.19 to die, and you keep people **alive** who don't deserve to live.
23.25 take your sons and daughters from you and burn them **alive.**
Dan 5.19 if he wanted to keep someone **alive,** he did.
Hos 9.12 up children, I would take them away and not leave one **alive.**
14. 6 will be **alive** with new growth, and beautiful like olive-trees.
Amos 5.15 to the people of this nation who are still left **alive.**
Jon 2. 6 you, O Lord my God, brought me back from the depths **alive.**
4. 3 I am better off dead than **alive.**"
4. 8 "I am better off dead than **alive,**" he said.
Mic 3. 2 You skin my people **alive** and tear the flesh off their bones.
Zech 1. 5 Your ancestors and those prophets are no longer **alive.**
14.12 Their flesh will rot away while they are still **alive;**
Mt 6.25 need in order to stay **alive,** or about clothes for your body.
27.63 while that liar was still **alive** he said, 'I will be raised
Mk 16.11 her say that Jesus was **alive** and that she had seen him,
16.14 were too stubborn to believe those who had seen him **alive.**
Lk 12.22 food you need to stay **alive** or about the clothes you need
15.24 For this son of mine was dead, but now he is **alive;**
15.32 happy, because your brother was dead, but now he is **alive;**
20.38 the living, not of the dead, for to him all are **alive.**"
24. 5 "Why are you looking among the dead for one who is **alive?**
24.23 seen a vision of angels who told them that he is **alive.**
Acts 1. 3 times in ways that proved beyond doubt that he was **alive.**
9.39 shirts and coats that Dorcas had made while she was **alive.**
9.41 including the widows, and presented her **alive** to them.
20.10 "Don't worry," he said, "he is still **alive!**"
20.12 They took the young man home **alive** and were greatly comforted.
25.19 but Paul claims that he is **alive.**
Rom 7. 3 while her husband is **alive,** she will be called an adulteress;
7. 9 I myself was once **alive** apart from law;
1 Cor 15. 6 most of whom are still **alive,** although some have died.
2 Cor 1. 8 and so heavy that we gave up all hope of staying **alive.**
Phil 1.24 for your sake it is much more important that I remain **alive.**
1 Thes 4.15 we who are **alive** on the day the Lord comes will not
5.10 with him, whether we are **alive** or dead when he comes.
2 Tim 1. 6 I remind you to keep **alive** the gift that God gave you
Heb 4.12 The word of God is **alive** and active,
9.17 a will means nothing while the person who made it is **alive;**
1 Pet 3.18 to death physically, but made **alive** spiritually,
2 Pet 1.13 your memory of these matters as long as I am still **alive.**
Rev 1.18 I was dead, but now I am **alive** for ever and ever.
3. 1 the reputation of being **alive,** even though you are dead!
17. 8 That beast was once **alive,** but lives no longer;
17. 8 It was once **alive;**
17.11 the beast that was once **alive,** but lives no longer,
19.20 false prophet were both thrown **alive** into the lake of fire

ALL

Mt 5.18 will be done away with—not until the end of **all things.**
11.27 "My Father has given me **all things.**
11.28 "Come to me, **all of you** who are tired from carrying
12.21 to triumph, [21]and in him **all peoples** will put their hope."
18.18 "And so I tell **all of you:**
24.14 will be preached through **all the world** for a witness to all
26.27 "Drink it, **all of you,**" he said;
26.31 "This very night **all of you** will run away and leave
26.64 But I tell **all of you:**

Mt 28.19 then, to **all peoples** everywhere and make them my disciples:
Mk 7.14 said to them, "Listen to me, **all of you,** and understand.
13.10 the end comes, the gospel must be preached to **all peoples.**
14.27 Jesus said to them, **"All of you** will run away and leave
14.36 **All things** are possible for you.
Lk 1.48 From now on **all people** will call me happy, [49] because of
2.31 which you have prepared in the presence of **all peoples:**
6.26 "How terrible when **all people** speak well of you;
10.22 "My Father has given me **all things.**
21.35 For it will come upon **all people** everywhere on earth.
22.31 received permission to test **all of you,** to separate the good
Jn 1. 3 Through him God made **all things;**
13.10 **All of you** are clean—all except one."
13.11 that is why he said, **"All of you,** except one, are clean.")
13.18 "I am not talking about **all of you;**
16.32 is already here, when **all of you** will be scattered, each one
Acts 2. 8 is it, then, that **all of us** hear them speaking in our
2.11 Crete and Arabia—yet **all of us** hear them speaking in our
2.14 "Fellow-Jews and **all of you** who live in Jerusalem, listen
3.21 until the time comes for **all things** to be made new,
4.12 in **all the world** there is no one else whom God has
13.47 for the Gentiles, so that **all the world** may be saved.' "
14.16 In the past he allowed **all people** to go their own way.
19.27 worshipped by everyone in Asia and in **all the world!"**
20.25 gone about among **all of you,** preaching the Kingdom of God.
20.35 I have shown you in **all things** that by working hard in
22. 3 dedicated to God as are **all of you** who are here today.
24.15 themselves have, namely, that **all people,** both the good and the
26.14 **All of us** fell to the ground, and I heard a voice
Rom 1. 7 so I write to **all of you** in Rome whom God loves
1. 8 through Jesus Christ for **all of you,** because the whole world
1.14 I have an obligation to **all peoples,** to the civilized and to
5.19 And just as **all people** were made sinners as the result
7. 1 to say, my brothers, because **all of you** know about law.
8.28 We know that in **all things** God works for good with those
8.32 us his Son—will he not also freely give us **all things?**
10.18 "The sound of their voice went out to **all the world;**
11.32 For God has made **all people** prisoners of disobedience,
11.36 For **all things** were created by him,
11.36 and **all things** exist through him
14.10 **All of us** will stand before God to be judged by him.
15. 6 Christ Jesus, [6] so that **all of you** together may praise with
15.11 praise him, **all peoples!"**
15.33 May God, our source of peace, be with **all of you.**
1 Cor 1. 2 together with **all people** everywhere who worship our Lord
1. 5 you have become rich in **all things,** including all speech and
1.10 Christ I appeal to **all of you,** my brothers, to agree in
7. 7 Actually I would prefer that **all of you** were as I am;
8. 1 true, of course, that **"all of us** have knowledge," as they
8. 6 who is the Creator of **all things** and for whom we live;
8. 6 Jesus Christ, through whom **all things** were created and through
9.22 So I become **all things** to all men, that I may save
10.17 one loaf of bread, **all of us,** though many, are one body,
12.13 In the same way, **all of us,** whether Jews or Gentiles,
12.27 **All of you** are Christ's body, and each one is a part
14. 5 I would like **all of you** to speak in strange tongues;
14.31 **All of you** may proclaim God's message, one by one, so
15.19 we deserve more pity than anyone else in **all the world.**
15.22 For just as **all people** die because of their union with Adam,
15.27 For the scripture says, "God put **all things** under his feet."
15.27 that the words **"all things"** do not include God himself,
15.27 who puts **all things** under Christ.
15.28 But when **all things** have been placed under Christ's rule,
15.28 will place himself under God, who placed **all things** under him;
2 Cor 2. 3 that when I am happy, then **all of you** are happy too.
2. 5 to me but to **all of you**—in part at least.
3.18 **All of us,** then, reflect the glory of the Lord with
5.10 For **all of us** must appear before Christ, to be judged by
7.13 the way in which **all of you** helped to cheer him up!
7.15 as he remembers how **all of you** were ready to obey his
Gal 3.26 is through faith that **all of you** are God's sons in union
Eph 1.11 **All things** are done according to God's plan and decision;
1.22 God put **all things** under Christ's feet
1.22 and gave him to the church as supreme Lord over **all things.**
1.23 completion of him who himself completes **all things** everywhere.
2. 3 Actually **all of us** were like them and lived according to
2.18 is through Christ that **all of us,** Jews and Gentiles, are
3. 9 of Christ, [9] and of making **all people** see how God's secret
3. 9 who is the Creator of **all things,** kept his secret hidden
5.13 And when **all things** are brought out to the light, then
6.22 to tell you how **all of us** are getting on, and to
Phil 3.15 **All of us** who are spiritually mature should have this same
3.21 by which he is able to bring **all things** under his rule.
Col 1.17 Christ existed before **all things,**
1.17 and in union with him **all things** have their proper place.
1.18 that he alone might have the first place in **all things.**
1.20 so brought back to himself **all things,** both on earth and in
1.27 this rich and glorious secret which he has for **all peoples.**
3.14 add love, which binds **all things** together in perfect unity.
3.22 obey your human masters in **all things,** not only when they
4. 8 you up by telling you how **all of us** are getting on.
1 Thes 3.12 for one another and for **all people** grow more and more and
5. 5 **All of you** are people who belong to the light, who belong
5.15 your aim to do good to one another and to **all people.**
5.21 Put **all things** to the test:
1 Tim 2. 1 requests, and thanksgivings be offered to God for **all people;**
6.13 God, who gives life to **all things,** and before Christ Jesus,
Tit 2. 7 In **all things** you yourself must be an example of good
2. 9 to submit to their masters and please them in **all things.**
Phlm 22 answer the prayers of **all of you** and give me back to
Heb 1. 2 one whom God has chosen to possess **all things** at the end.
Heb 2. 8 glory and honour, [8] and made him ruler over **all things."**
2. 8 It says that God made man "ruler over **all things";**
2. 8 We do not, however, see man ruling over **all things** now.
2.10 God, who creates and preserves **all things,** should make Jesus
3. 4 by someone—and God is the one who has built **all things.**
Jas 3. 2 **All of us** often make mistakes.
1 Pet 1.17 pray to God, who judges **all people** by the same standard,
4. 7 The end of **all things** is near.
4.11 gives him, so that in **all things** praise may be given to
5. 5 And **all of you** must put on the apron of humility,
5. 9 fellow-believers in **all the world** are going through the same
5.14 May peace be with **all of you** who belong to Christ.
1 Jn 2.20 on you by Christ, and so **all of you** know the truth.
Rev 1. 7 **All peoples** on earth will mourn over him.
4.11 For you created **all things,** and by your will they were given
13. 8 **All people** living on earth will worship it, except those whose
14. 8 She made **all peoples** drink her wine—the strong wine of her
18.23 the most powerful in **all the world,** and with your false
19. 5 God, all his servants and **all people,** both great and small,
19.18 the flesh of **all people,** slave and free, great and
21. 5 sits on the throne said, "And now I make **all things** new!"

ALL-POWERFUL see POWER

ALL-WISE see WISE

ALLEGIANCE

1 Kgs 9. 9 They gave their **allegiance** to other gods and worshipped them.
12.26 they will transfer their **allegiance** to King Rehoboam of Judah
2 Chr 7.22 They gave their **allegiance** to other gods and worshipped them.

ALLEY

Song 3. 2 I went wandering through the city, through its streets and **alleys.**
Lk 14.21 out to the streets and **alleys** of the town, and bring back

ALLIANCE see ALLY

ALLOT

Num 36. 3 to that tribe, and the total **allotted** to us will be reduced.
1 Chr 26.15 Obed Edom was **allotted** the south gate,
26.15 and his sons were **allotted** to guard the storerooms.
26.16 Shuppim and Hosah were **allotted** the west gate
Ps 139.16 The days **allotted** to me had all been recorded in your book,
Ezek 45. 7 length of one of the areas **allotted** to the tribes of Israel.

ALLOW

Gen 3.22 He must not be **allowed** to take fruit from the tree that
6. 3 the Lord said, "I will not **allow** people to live for ever;
19.29 kept Abraham in mind and **allowed** Lot to escape to safety.
44.18 Joseph and said, "Please, sir, **allow** me to speak with you freely.
Ex 3.18 Now **allow** us to travel for three days into the desert to
5. 3 **Allow** us to travel for three days into the desert to offer
21.30 However, if the owner is **allowed** to pay a fine to save
Lev 6.12 the altar must be kept burning and never **allowed** to go out.
6.13 be kept burning on the altar and never **allowed** to go out.
10. 6 But all your fellow-Israelites are **allowed** to mourn this death
25.23 you are like foreigners who are **allowed** to make use of it.
Num 32.16 approached Moses and said, "First, **allow** us to build
35.32 city of refuge, do not **allow** him to make a payment in
Deut 2.29 Moabites, who live in Ar, **allowed** us to pass through
18.14 but the Lord your God does not **allow** you to do this.
Josh 5. 4 had sworn, they were not **allowed** to see the rich and fertile
9.15 with the people of Gibeon and **allowed** them to live.
9.26 protected them and did not **allow** the people of Israel to
Judg 2.23 So the Lord **allowed** those nations to remain in the land;
3.28 they did not **allow** a single man to cross.
21. 1 "None of us will **allow** a Benjaminite to marry a daughter of
21.18 but we cannot **allow** them to marry our daughters,
21.18 on anyone of us who **allows** a Benjaminite to marry one of
1 Sam 2.36 food, and beg to be **allowed** to help the priests, in order
2 Sam 4. 8 Today the Lord has **allowed** Your Majesty to take revenge on
14.13 You have not **allowed** your own son to return from exile, and
1 Kgs 20.42 'Because you **allowed** the man to escape whom I had ordered to
2 Kgs 13. 3 angry with Israel, and he **allowed** King Hazael of Syria and
18.31 You will all be **allowed** to eat grapes from your own vines,
21. 8 them, then I will not **allow** them to be driven out of
23. 9 Those priests were not **allowed** to serve in the Temple, but
2 Chr 20.10 of Egypt, you did not **allow** them to enter those lands, so
25.13 soldiers that Amaziah had not **allowed** to go into battle with
33. 8 them, then I will not **allow** them to be driven out of
34.11 the buildings that the kings of Judah had **allowed** to decay.
Ezra 9.13 us less than we deserve and have **allowed** us to survive.
Neh 13. 5 He **allowed** Tobiah to use a large room that was intended
13. 7 to find that Eliashib had **allowed** Tobiah to use a room in
Esth 4. 2 go in because no one wearing sackcloth was **allowed** inside.
8. 1 from then on Mordecai was **allowed** to enter the king's presence.
8.11 explained that the king would **allow** the Jews in every city
9.13 Susa do again tomorrow what they were **allowed** to do today.
Job 36. 7 he **allows** them to rule like kings and lets them be
Ps 5. 4 you **allow** no evil in your presence.
44.11 You **allowed** us to be slaughtered like sheep;
66. 9 He has kept us alive and has not **allowed** us to fall.
78.61 He **allowed** our enemies to capture the Covenant Box, the
78.64 and their widows were not **allowed** to mourn.

Ps 101. 6 Those who are completely honest will be **allowed** to serve me.
Ecc 5.20 Since God has **allowed** him to be happy, he will not worry
Is 36.16 You will all be **allowed** to eat grapes from your own vines
Jer 8.13 Therefore, I have **allowed** outsiders to take over the land."
27.18 the Lord Almighty, not to **allow** the treasures that remain in
29. 4 all those people whom he **allowed** Nebuchadnezzar to take away
36. 5 "I am no longer **allowed** to go into the Temple.
40.11 the king of Babylonia had **allowed** some Israelites to stay on
40.15 Why should he be **allowed** to murder you?
Lam 2. 7 He **allowed** the enemy to tear down its walls.
5. 5 donkeys or camels, we are tired, but are **allowed** no rest.
Ezek 4.10 You will be **allowed** 230 grammes of bread a day, and it
44. 2 No human being is **allowed** to use it, because I, the Lord
44. 5 Note carefully which persons are **allowed** to go in and out of
Zech 9. 8 I will not **allow** tyrants to oppress my people any more.
Mt 12. 4 to eat it—only the priests were **allowed** to eat that bread.
12.12 So then, our Law does **allow** us to help someone on the
19. 3 by asking, "Does our Law **allow** a man to divorce his wife
23.13 go in, nor do you **allow** in those who are trying
Mk 3. 4 "What does our Law **allow** us to do on the Sabbath?
10. 2 asked, "does our Law **allow** a man to divorce his wife?"
Lk 1.73 us from our enemies and **allow** us to serve him without fear,
6. 9 What does our Law **allow** us to do on the Sabbath?
14. 3 "Does our Law **allow** healing on the Sabbath or not?"
Jn 18.31 They replied, "We are not **allowed** to put anyone to death."
19.31 Jewish authorities asked Pilate to **allow** them to break the legs
Acts 2.27 you will not **allow** your faithful servant to rot in the grave.
4.29 threats they have made, and **allow** us, your servants, to speak
7.46 favour and asked God to **allow** him to provide a dwelling
10.28 that a Jew is not **allowed** by his religion to visit
13.35 'You will not **allow** your devoted servant to rot in
14.16 In the past he **allowed** all people to go their own way.
16. 7 of Bithynia, but the Spirit of Jesus did not **allow** them.
24.23 give him some freedom and **allow** his friends to provide for
27. 3 was kind to Paul and **allowed** him to go and see his
28.16 arrived in Rome, Paul was **allowed** to live by himself
Rom 14. 2 One person's faith **allows** him to eat anything, but the person
1 Cor 6.12 Someone will say, "I am **allowed** to do anything."
6.12 could say that I am **allowed** to do anything, but I am
10.13 and he will not **allow** you to be tested beyond your
10.23 "We are **allowed** to do anything," so they say.
10.23 "We are **allowed** to do anything"—but not everything is helpful.
14.34 They are not **allowed** to speak;
16. 7 to spend quite a long time with you, if the Lord **allows.**
2 Cor 3. 5 is nothing in us that **allows** us to claim that we are
Gal 5. 1 free people, and do not **allow** yourselves to become slaves again.
5. 2 that if you **allow** yourselves to be circumcised, it means
5. 3 I warn any man who **allows** himself to be circumcised that he
Col 1.23 and must not **allow** yourselves to be shaken from the
2.18 Do not **allow** yourselves to be condemned by anyone who claims
2 Thes 3.10 "Whoever refuses to work is not **allowed** to eat."
1 Tim 2.12 I do not **allow** them to teach or to have authority
Heb 4. 6 There are, then, others who are **allowed** to receive it.
6. 3 And this is what we will do, if God **allows.**
1 Pet 1.14 and do not **allow** your lives to be shaped by
Rev 9. 5 The locusts were not **allowed** to kill these people, but only
11. 9 and a half days and will not **allow** them to be buried.
12. 8 his angels were not **allowed** to stay in heaven any longer.
13. 5 beast was **allowed** to make proud claims which were insulting
13. 7 It was **allowed** to fight against God's people and to defeat them,
13.14 the miracles which it was **allowed** to perform in the presence
13.15 The second beast was **allowed** to breathe life into the image
16. 8 and it was **allowed** to burn people with its fiery

ALLOWANCE

Gen 47.22 lands, because the king gave them an **allowance** to live on.
2 Kgs 25.30 he lived, he was given a regular **allowance** for his needs.
Neh 5.18 I did not claim the **allowance** that the governor is entitled to.
Jer 52.34 he lived, he was given a regular **allowance** for his needs.

ALLY

[ALLIANCE]

Gen 14. 3 five kings had formed an **alliance** and joined forces in the
14. 5 Chedorlaomer and his **allies** came with their armies and defeated
14.13 Mamre and his brothers Eshcol and Aner were Abram's **allies.**
14.24 But let my **allies,** Aner, Eshcol, and Mamre, take their share."
Deut 7. 2 Do not make an **alliance** with them or show them any mercy.
1 Sam 22. 8 told me that my own son had made an **alliance** with David.
2 Sam 5. 3 He made a sacred **alliance** with them, they anointed him, and
1 Kgs 3. 1 Solomon made an **alliance** with the king of Egypt by
11.24 David had defeated Hadadezer and had slaughtered his Syrian **allies.)**
15.19 "Let us be **allies,** as our fathers were.
15.19 Now break your **alliance** with King Baasha of Israel, so that
20.12 answer as he and his **allies,** the other rulers, were drinking
20.16 as Benhadad and his thirty-two **allies** were getting drunk
2 Kgs 3.14 you if I didn't respect your **ally** King Jehoshaphat of Judah.
1 Chr 5.20 and made them victorious over the Hagrites and their **allies.**
11. 3 He made a sacred **alliance** with them, they anointed him, and
2 Chr 16. 3 "Let us be **allies,** as our fathers were.
16. 3 Now break your **alliance** with King Baasha of Israel so that
20. 1 of Moab and Ammon, together with their **allies,** the Meunites,
20.35 Jehoshaphat of Judah made an **alliance** with King Ahaziah of Israel,
20.37 you have made an **alliance** with Ahaziah, the Lord will destroy
Ps 83. 5 They agree on their plan and form an **alliance** against you:
83. 8 joined them as a strong **ally** of the Ammonites and Moabites,
Jer 22.20 because all your **allies** have been defeated.
22.22 away by the wind, your **allies** taken as prisoners of war,
Lam 1. 2 Her **allies** have betrayed her and all are now against her.
1.19 "I called to my **allies,** but they refused to help me.
Ezek 39. 4 and his army and his **allies** will fall dead on the mountains
Dan 11. 6 of Egypt will make an **alliance** with the king of Syria and
11. 6 But the **alliance** will not last, and she, her husband, her
11.17 kingdom, he will make an **alliance** with him and offer him his
Obad 7 Your **allies** have deceived you;
Nah 3. 9 Libya was her **ally.**

ALMIGHTY

Gen 17. 1 the Lord appeared to him and said, "I am the **Almighty** God.
28. 3 May **Almighty** God bless your marriage and give you many children,
35.11 And God said to him, "I am **Almighty** God.
43.14 May **Almighty** God cause the man to have pity on you, so
48. 3 Jacob said to Joseph, **"Almighty** God appeared to me at Luz
49.25 God who helps you, The **Almighty** God who blesses you
Ex 6. 3 Isaac, and to Jacob as **Almighty** God, but I did not make
Num 24. 4 staring eyes I see in a trance A vision from **Almighty** God.
24.16 staring eyes I see in a trance A vision from **Almighty** God.
Ruth 1.20 "call me Marah, because **Almighty** God has made my life bitter.
1.21 me Naomi when the Lord **Almighty** has condemned me and sent me
1 Sam 1. 3 offer sacrifices to the Lord **Almighty** at Shiloh,
1.11 **"Almighty** Lord, look at me, your servant!
4. 4 Shiloh and fetched the Covenant Box of the Lord **Almighty;**
15. 1 Now listen to what the Lord **Almighty** says.
17.45 name of the Lord **Almighty,** the God of the Israelite armies,
2 Sam 5.10 all the time, because the Lord God **Almighty** was with him.
6. 2 the name of the Lord **Almighty,** who is enthroned above the
6.18 the name of the Lord **Almighty** [19] and distributed food to them
7. 8 David that I, the Lord **Almighty,** say to him, 'I took you
7.26 will for ever say, 'The Lord **Almighty** is God over Israel.'
7.27 **Almighty** Lord, God of Israel!
22.14 from the sky, and the voice of **Almighty** God was heard.
1 Kgs 19.10 He answered, "Lord God **Almighty,** I have always served you—
19.14 He answered, "Lord God **Almighty,** I have always served you—
2 Kgs 20.16 to the king, "The Lord **Almighty** says that [17] a time is
1 Chr 11. 9 stronger and stronger, because the Lord **Almighty** was with him.
17. 7 David that I, the Lord **Almighty,** say to him, 'I took you
17.24 will for ever say, 'The Lord **Almighty** is God over Israel.'
Job 6. 4 **Almighty** God has pierced me with arrows, and their poison spreads
8. 5 But turn now and plead with **Almighty** God;
15.25 the man who shakes his fist at God and defies the **Almighty.**
21.20 let them feel the wrath of **Almighty** God.
22.25 Let **Almighty** God be your gold, and let him be silver,
23.16 **Almighty** God has destroyed my courage.
27. 1 I swear by the living **Almighty** God, who refuses me justice
27.11 and explain what **Almighty** God has planned.
27.13 This is how **Almighty** God punishes wicked, violent men.
29. 5 **Almighty** God was with me then, and I was surrounded by all
31. 2 What does **Almighty** God do to us?
31.28 it denies **Almighty** God.
31.35 Let **Almighty** God answer me.
32. 8 it is the spirit of **Almighty** God that comes to men and
34.10 Will **Almighty** God do what is wrong?
34.12 **Almighty** God does not do evil;
35.13 **Almighty** God does not see or hear them.
40. 1 Job, you challenged **Almighty** God;
Ps 9. 2 I will sing praise to you, **Almighty** God.
21. 7 The king trusts in the Lord **Almighty;**
46. 7 The Lord **Almighty** is with us;
46.11 The Lord **Almighty** is with us;
48. 8 have seen it in the city of our God, the Lord **Almighty;**
50. 1 The **Almighty** God, the Lord, speaks;
50.14 and give the **Almighty** all that you promised.
56. 3 I am afraid, O Lord **Almighty,** I put my trust in you.
59. 5 Rise, Lord God **Almighty,** and come to my aid;
68.14 When **Almighty** God scattered the kings on Mount Zalmon,
69. 6 shame on those who trust in you, Sovereign Lord **Almighty!**
78.35 God was their protector, that the **Almighty** came to their aid.
78.56 But they rebelled against **Almighty** God and put him to the test.
80. 4 How much longer, Lord God **Almighty,** will you be angry with
80. 7 Bring us back, **Almighty** God!
80.14 Turn to us, **Almighty** God!
80.19 Bring us back, Lord God **Almighty.**
84. 1 How I love your Temple, Lord **Almighty!**
84. 3 young near your altars, Lord **Almighty,** my king and my God.
84. 8 Hear my prayer, Lord God **Almighty.**
84.12 Lord **Almighty,** how happy are those who trust in you!
87. 5 and that the **Almighty** will make her strong.
89. 8 Lord God **Almighty,** none is as mighty as you;
91. 1 under the protection of the **Almighty,** [2] can say to him,
97. 9 Lord **Almighty,** you are ruler of all the earth;
106. 7 and they rebelled against the **Almighty** at the Red Sea.
107.11 rebelled against the commands of **Almighty** God
Is 1. 9 If the Lord **Almighty** had not let some of the people survive,
1.24 listen to what the Lord **Almighty,** Israel's powerful God, is saying:
2.12 On that day the Lord **Almighty** will humble everyone who is powerful,
3. 1 Now the Lord, the **Almighty** Lord, is about to take away
3.15 I, the Sovereign Lord **Almighty,** have spoken."
5. 7 Israel is the vineyard of the Lord **Almighty;**
5. 9 I have heard the Lord **Almighty** say, "All these big, fine
5.16 But the Lord **Almighty** shows his greatness by doing what is right,
5.24 rejected what the Lord **Almighty,** Israel's holy God, has taught
6. 3 The Lord **Almighty** is holy!
6. 5 my own eyes, I have seen the King, the Lord **Almighty!"**
8.13 Remember that I, the Lord **Almighty,** am holy;

Is 8.18 The Lord **Almighty,** whose throne is on Mount Zion, has sent
9. 7 The Lord **Almighty** is determined to do all this.
9.13 even though the Lord **Almighty** has punished them,
9.19 Because the Lord **Almighty** is angry,
10.16 The Lord **Almighty** is going to send disease to punish
10.23 the Sovereign Lord **Almighty** will bring destruction,
10.24 The Sovereign Lord **Almighty** says to his people who live in Zion,
10.26 I, the Lord **Almighty,** will beat them with my whip
10.33 The Lord **Almighty** will bring them crashing down like branches
13. 6 Lord is near, the day when the **Almighty** brings destruction.
13.13 place on that day when I, the Lord **Almighty,** show my anger.
14.14 climb to the tops of the clouds and be like the **Almighty.**
14.22 The Lord **Almighty** says, "I will attack Babylon
14.23 I, the Lord **Almighty,** have spoken."
14.24 The Lord **Almighty** has sworn an oath:
14.27 The Lord **Almighty** is determined to do this;
17. 3 I, the Lord **Almighty,** have spoken."
18. 7 when the Lord **Almighty** will receive offerings from this land
18. 7 will come to Mount Zion, where the Lord **Almighty** is worshipped.
19. 4 I, the Lord **Almighty,** have spoken."
19.12 can tell you what plans the Lord **Almighty** has for Egypt.
19.16 they see that the Lord **Almighty** has stretched out his hand
19.17 of the fate that the Lord **Almighty** has prepared for them.
19.18 will take their oaths in the name of the Lord **Almighty.**
19.20 They will be symbols of the Lord **Almighty's** presence in Egypt.
19.25 The Lord **Almighty** will bless them and say, "I will bless you,
21.10 I have heard from the Lord **Almighty,** the God of Israel.
22. 5 Vision, and the Sovereign Lord **Almighty** has sent it on us.
22.12 The Sovereign Lord **Almighty** was calling you then to weep
22.14 The Sovereign Lord **Almighty** himself spoke to me and said,
22.14 I, the Sovereign Lord **Almighty,** have spoken."
22.15 The Sovereign Lord **Almighty** told me to go to Shebna,
23. 9 The Lord **Almighty** planned it.
24.23 will no longer shine, for the Lord **Almighty** will be king.
25. 6 on Mount Zion the Lord **Almighty** will prepare a banquet for
28. 5 when the Lord **Almighty** will be like a glorious crown
28.22 I have heard the Lord **Almighty's** decision to destroy the whole
28.29 All this wisdom comes from the Lord **Almighty.**
29. 6 Suddenly and unexpectedly [6]the Lord **Almighty** will rescue you
31. 4 that can keep me, the Lord **Almighty,** from protecting Mount Zion.
31. 5 so I, the Lord **Almighty,** will protect Jerusalem and defend it."
37.16 "**Almighty** Lord, God of Israel, enthroned above
37.32 because the Lord **Almighty** is determined to make this happen.
39. 5 told the king, "The Lord **Almighty** says that [6]a time is
44. 6 and protects Israel, the Lord **Almighty,** has this to say:
45.13 The Lord **Almighty** has spoken.
47. 4 of Israel sets us free— his name is the Lord **Almighty.**
48. 2 depend on Israel's God, whose name is the Lord **Almighty.**
51.15 My name is the Lord **Almighty!**
54. 5 like a husband to you— the Lord **Almighty** is his name.
Jer 2.19 I, the Sovereign Lord **Almighty,** have spoken."
5.13 The Lord God **Almighty** said to me, "Jeremiah,
6. 6 The Lord **Almighty** has ordered these kings to cut down trees
6. 9 The Lord **Almighty** said to me, "Israel will be stripped clean
7. 1 and announce what the Lord **Almighty,** the God of Israel, had
8. 3 I, the Lord **Almighty,** have spoken."
9. 7 Because of this the Lord **Almighty** says, "I will refine my
9.15 to what I, the Lord **Almighty,** the God of Israel, will do:
9.17 The Lord **Almighty** said,
10.16 The Lord **Almighty** is his name.
11.17 "I, the Lord **Almighty,** planted Israel and Judah;
11.20 Then I prayed, "**Almighty** Lord, you are a just judge;
11.22 So the Lord **Almighty** said, "I will punish them!
15.16 belong to you, Lord God **Almighty,** and so your words filled
16. 9 to what I, the Lord **Almighty,** the God of Israel, have to
19. 3 to what I, the Lord **Almighty,** the God of Israel, have to
19.11 tell them that the Lord **Almighty** had said, "I will break
19.15 that the Lord **Almighty,** the God of Israel, had said,
20.12 But, **Almighty** Lord, you test men justly;
23.15 what I, the Lord **Almighty,** say about the prophets of Jerusalem:
23.16 The Lord **Almighty** said to the people of Jerusalem,
23.36 the words of their God, the living God, the Lord **Almighty.**
25. 8 listen to him, the Lord **Almighty** says, [9]'I am going to send
25.27 that I, the Lord **Almighty,** the God of Israel, am commanding
25.28 tell them that the Lord **Almighty** has said that they will
25.29 I, the Lord **Almighty,** have spoken.
25.32 The Lord **Almighty** says that disaster is coming on one nation
26.18 Moresheth told all the people that the Lord **Almighty** had said,
27. 4 The Lord **Almighty,** the God of Israel, told me to command
27.18 them ask me, the Lord **Almighty,** not to allow the treasures
27.21 to what I, the Lord **Almighty,** the God of Israel, say about
28. 2 told me [2]that the Lord **Almighty,** the God of Israel, had
28.14 The Lord **Almighty,** the God of Israel, has said that he
29. 4 "The Lord **Almighty,** the God of Israel, says to all those
29. 9 I, the Lord **Almighty,** have spoken.'
29.17 The Lord **Almighty** says, 'I am bringing war, starvation,
29.21 "The Lord **Almighty,** the God of Israel, has spoken about Ahab
29.24 The Lord **Almighty,** the God of Israel, gave me a
30. 8 The Lord **Almighty** says:
31.23 The Lord **Almighty,** the God of Israel, says, "When I restore
31.35 his name is the Lord **Almighty.**
32.14 said to Baruch, [14]"The Lord **Almighty,** the God of Israel,
32.15 The Lord **Almighty,** the God of Israel, has said that houses,
32.18 you are the Lord **Almighty.**
33.11 'Give thanks to the Lord **Almighty,** because he is good and
33.12 The Lord **Almighty** said, "In this land that is like a
35.12 Then the Lord **Almighty,** the God of Israel, told me
35.17 So now, I, the Lord **Almighty,** the God of Israel, will
35.18 clan that the Lord **Almighty,** the God of Israel, had said,
35.19 So I, the Lord **Almighty,** the God of Israel, promise that
38.17 told Zedekiah that the Lord **Almighty,** the God of Israel, had
Jer 39.16 the Sudanese that the Lord **Almighty,** the God of Israel, had
42.13 say this, then the Lord **Almighty,** the God of Israel, says,
43.10 them that I, the Lord **Almighty,** the God of Israel, am going
44. 2 The Lord **Almighty,** the God of Israel, said,
44. 7 "And so I, the Lord **Almighty,** the God of Israel, now ask
44.11 "So then, I, the Lord **Almighty,** the God of Israel, will
44.24 the women, what the Lord **Almighty,** the God of Israel, was
46.10 This is the day of the Sovereign Lord **Almighty:**
46.10 Today the **Almighty** sacrifices his victims in the north,
46.18 I, the Lord **Almighty,** am king.
46.25 The Lord **Almighty,** the God of Israel, says, "I am going
48. 1 This is what the Lord **Almighty** said about Moab:
48.15 I am the king, the Lord **Almighty,** and I have spoken.
49. 7 This is what the Lord **Almighty** said about Edom:
49.27 I, the Lord **Almighty,** have spoken."
49.34 king of Judah, the Lord **Almighty** spoke to me about the
50.18 I, the Lord **Almighty,** the God of Israel, will punish
50.25 I, the Sovereign Lord **Almighty,** have work to do in Babylonia.
50.31 so I, the Sovereign Lord **Almighty,** am against you!
50.33 The Lord **Almighty** says, "The people of Israel and of Judah
50.34 will rescue them is strong—his name is the Lord **Almighty.**
51. 5 I, the Lord God **Almighty,** have not abandoned Israel and Judah,
51.14 The Lord **Almighty** has sworn by his own life that he will
51.19 The Lord **Almighty** is his name.
51.33 I, the Lord **Almighty,** the God of Israel, have spoken."
51.57 I, the king, have spoken, I am the Lord **Almighty.**
51.58 I, the Lord **Almighty,** have spoken."
Ezek 1.24 the noise of a huge army, like the voice of **Almighty** God.
10. 5 It sounded like the voice of **Almighty** God.
Hos 12. 5 This was the Lord God **Almighty**—the Lord is the name by
Joel 1.15 the day when the **Almighty** brings destruction.
Amos 3.13 warn the descendants of Jacob," says the Sovereign Lord **Almighty.**
4.13 the Lord God **Almighty!**
5.14 Then the Lord God **Almighty** really will be with you, as you
5.16 so the Sovereign Lord **Almighty** says, "There will be wailing
5.27 beyond Damascus," says the Lord, whose name is **Almighty** God.
6. 8 The Sovereign Lord **Almighty** has given this solemn warning:
6.14 The Lord God **Almighty** himself says, "People of Israel,
9. 5 The Sovereign Lord **Almighty** touches the earth, and it quakes;
Mic 4. 4 The Lord **Almighty** has promised this.
Nah 2.13 says the Lord **Almighty.**
3. 5 The Lord **Almighty** says,
Hab 2.13 The Lord **Almighty** has done this.
Zeph 2. 8 The Lord **Almighty** says, "I have heard the people of Moab
2.10 and for insulting the people of the Lord **Almighty.**
Hag 1. 2 The Lord **Almighty** said to Haggai, "These people say
1.14 the Temple of the Lord **Almighty,** their God,
2. 9 The Lord **Almighty** has spoken.
2.10 the Lord **Almighty** spoke again to the prophet Haggai.
2.23 The Lord **Almighty** has spoken.
Zech 1. 2 The Lord **Almighty** told Zechariah to say to the people,
1. 6 acknowledged that I, the Lord **Almighty,** had punished them
1.12 "**Almighty** Lord, you have been angry with Jerusalem
1.14 angel told me to proclaim what the Lord **Almighty** had said:
1.17 "The Lord **Almighty** says that his cities will be prosperous again
2. 8 So the Lord **Almighty** sent me with this message for the
2. 9 everyone will know that the Lord **Almighty** sent me.
3. 7 Then the angel told Joshua that [7]the Lord **Almighty** had said:
5. 4 The Lord **Almighty** says that he will send this curse out,
6.12 Tell him that the Lord **Almighty** says, 'The man who is
6.15 you will know that the Lord **Almighty** sent me to you.
7. 2 the Temple of the Lord **Almighty** to pray for the Lord's
8. 1 The Lord **Almighty** gave this message to Zechariah:
8. 3 hill of the Lord **Almighty** will be called the sacred hill.
8.14 The Lord **Almighty** says, "When your ancestors made me angry,
8.18 The Lord **Almighty** gave this message to Zechariah:
8.20 The Lord **Almighty** says, "The time is coming
8.21 to worship the Lord **Almighty** and pray for his blessing.
8.22 to worship the Lord **Almighty,** and to pray for his blessing.
9.15 The Lord **Almighty** will protect his people,
10. 3 are mine, and I, the Lord **Almighty,** will take care of them.
12. 5 'The Lord God **Almighty** gives strength to his people
13. 1 'says the Lord **Almighty,** "a fountain will be opened
13. 7 The Lord **Almighty** says, "Wake up, sword, and attack
14.16 year to worship the Lord **Almighty** as king, and to celebrate
14.17 go and worship the Lord **Almighty** as king, then rain will not
14.21 be set apart for use in the worship of the Lord **Almighty.**
14.21 longer be any merchant in the Temple of the Lord **Almighty.**
Mal 1. 6 The Lord **Almighty** says to the priests, "A son honours his father,
1.10 The Lord **Almighty** says, "I wish one of you would close
2. 1 The Lord **Almighty** says to the priests, "This command is for you:
2. 7 will, because they are the messengers of the Lord **Almighty.**
2.12 participate in the offerings our nation brings to the Lord **Almighty.**
2.17 By saying, "The Lord **Almighty** thinks all evildoers are good;
3. 1 The Lord **Almighty** answers, "I will send my messenger
3. 5 The Lord **Almighty** says, "I will appear among you to judge,
3.14 trying to show the Lord **Almighty** that we are sorry for what
3.17 "They will be my people," says the Lord **Almighty.**
4. 1 The Lord **Almighty** says, "The day is coming when all proud
Mt 26.64 on the right of the **Almighty** and coming on the clouds of
Mk 14.62 on the right of the **Almighty** and coming with the clouds of
Lk 22.69 Son of Man will be seated on the right of **Almighty** God."
Rom 9.29 "If the Lord **Almighty** had not left us some descendants,
2 Cor 6.18 shall be my sons and daughters, says the Lord **Almighty.**"
Jas 5. 4 your crops have reached the ears of God, the Lord **Almighty.**
Rev 1. 8 says the Lord God **Almighty,** who is, who was, and who
4. 8 holy, is the Lord God **Almighty,** who was, who is, and who
6.10 They shouted in a loud voice, "**Almighty** Lord, holy and
11.17 "Lord God **Almighty,** the one who is and who was!
15. 3 "Lord God **Almighty,** how great and wonderful are your deeds!

Rev 16. 7 Then I heard a voice from the altar saying, "Lord God **Almighty!**
16.14 together for the battle on the great Day of **Almighty** God.
19. 6 For the Lord, our **Almighty** God, is King!
19.15 in the winepress of the furious anger of the **Almighty** God.
21.22 because its temple is the Lord God **Almighty** and the Lamb.

ALMOND

Gen 30.37 got green branches of poplar, **almond,** and plane trees
43.11 resin, a little honey, spices, pistachio nuts, and **almonds.**
Ex 25.33 have three decorative flowers shaped like **almond** blossoms
25.34 have four decorative flowers shaped like **almond** blossoms
37.19 had three decorative flowers shaped like **almond** blossoms
37.20 had four decorative flowers shaped like **almond** blossoms
Num 17. 8 It had budded, blossomed, and produced ripe **almonds!**
Song 6.11 have come down among the **almond-trees** to see the young plants
Jer 1.11 I answered, "A branch of an **almond-tree.**"

ALOES

A sweet-smelling liquid, produced from a plant. It was used as medicine and as a perfume.

Num 24. 6 gardens beside a river, Like **aloes** planted by the Lord Or
Ps 45. 8 The perfume of myrrh and **aloes** is on your clothes;
Prov 7.17 I've perfumed it with myrrh, **aloes,** and cinnamon.
Song 4.14 Myrrh and **aloes** grow there with all the most fragrant perfumes.
Jn 19.39 about thirty kilogrammes of spices, a mixture of myrrh and **aloes.**

ALONE

Gen 2.18 God said, "It is not good for the man to live **alone.**
3.14 you **alone** of all the animals must bear this curse:
32.24 across all that he owned, [24]but he stayed behind, **alone.**
Ex 14.12 told you to leave us **alone** and let us go on being
18.14 are you doing this all **alone,** with people standing here
18.18 This is too much for you to do **alone.**
19. 6 a people dedicated to me **alone,** and you will serve me as
24. 2 You **alone,** and none of the others, are to come near me.
Lev 20.26 the other nations so that you would belong to me **alone.**
Num 8.16 sons of the Israelites, and they belong to me **alone.**
11.17 for these people, and you will not have to bear it **alone.**
18. 5 You and your sons **alone** must fulfil the responsibilities
18. 7 you and your sons **alone** shall fulfil all the responsibilities
23. 3 So he went **alone** to the top of a hill, [4]and God
23. 9 They are a nation that lives **alone;**
Deut 1. 9 I can't do it **alone.**
1.12 But how can I **alone** bear the heavy responsibility
4.35 prove to you that he **alone** is God and that there is
6. 4 The Lord—and the Lord **alone**—is our God.
6.13 God, worship only him, and make your promises in his name **alone.**
8. 3 must not depend on bread **alone** to sustain him, but on
10.20 Be faithful to him and make your promises in his name **alone.**
32.12 The Lord **alone** led his people without the help of a
32.39 'I, and I **alone,** am God;
Judg 3.19 So the king ordered his servants, "Leave us **alone!**"
3.20 the king was sitting there **alone** in his cool room on the
11.37 Leave me **alone** for two months, so that I can go with
Ruth 1. 3 died, and Naomi was left **alone** with her two sons, [4]who
1. 5 and Naomi was left all **alone,** without husband or sons.
2 Sam 7.22 we have always known that you **alone** are God.
16.11 so leave him **alone** and let him do it.
18.24 he looked out and saw a man running **alone.**
18.25 the king said, "If he is **alone,** he is bringing good news."
18.26 watchman saw another man running **alone,** and he called down
22.32 The Lord **alone** is God;
22.32 God **alone** is our defence.
1 Kgs 8.39 You **alone** know the thoughts of the human heart.
8.60 will know that the Lord **alone** is God—there is no other.
11.29 Ahijah, from Shiloh, met him **alone** on the road in the open
18.39 the Lord **alone** is God!"
19.10 "Lord God Almighty, I have always served you—you **alone.**
19.14 "Lord God Almighty, I have always served you—you **alone.**
2 Kgs 4.27 about to push her away, but Elisha said, "Leave her **alone.**
4.32 When Elisha arrived, he went **alone** into the room and
19.15 you **alone** are God, ruling all the kingdoms
1 Chr 17.20 we have always known that you **alone** are God.
2 Chr 6.30 You **alone** know the thoughts of the human heart.
Neh 9. 6 "You, Lord, you **alone** are Lord;
Esth 3. 6 was a Jew, he decided to do more than punish Mordecai **alone.**
9.12 "In Susa **alone** the Jews have killed five hundred
Job 7.16 Leave me **alone.**
10.20 Leave me **alone!**
14. 6 Look away from him and leave him **alone;**
15. 8 Does human wisdom belong to you **alone?**
21.14 The wicked tell God to leave them **alone;**
28.23 God **alone** knows the way, Knows the place where wisdom is found,
Ps 4. 8 you **alone,** O Lord, keep me perfectly safe.
18.31 The Lord **alone** is God;
18.31 God **alone** is our defence.
39.13 Leave me **alone** so that I may have some happiness before
62. 1 I depend on him **alone.**
62. 2 He **alone** protects and saves me;
62. 5 I depend on God **alone;**
62. 6 He **alone** protects and saves me;
71.16 I will proclaim your goodness, yours **alone.**
72.18 He **alone** does these wonderful things.
83.18 May they know that you **alone** are the Lord, supreme ruler
86.10 you **alone** are God.
115. 1 To you **alone,** O Lord, to you alone, and not to us,
Ps 115.16 Heaven belongs to the Lord **alone,** but he gave the earth
136. 4 He **alone** performs great miracles;
139.19 How I wish violent men would leave me **alone!**
Prov 5.15 faithful to your own wife and give your love to her **alone.**
Ecc 4. 8 Here is a man who lives **alone.**
4.10 But if someone is **alone** and falls, it's just too bad,
4.12 Two men can resist an attack that would defeat one man **alone.**
Is 1. 8 Jerusalem **alone** is left, a city under siege—as defenceless
2.11 Then the Lord **alone** will be exalted.
2.17 and the Lord **alone** will be exalted on that day.
5. 8 anyone else to live, and you **alone** will live in the land.
22. 4 Now leave me **alone** to weep bitterly over all those of my
26.13 we have been ruled by others, but you **alone** are our Lord.
37.16 you **alone** are God, ruling all the kingdoms
37.20 nations of the world will know that you **alone** are God."
38.16 Lord, I will live for you, for you **alone;**
42. 8 "I **alone** am the Lord your God.
43.11 "I **alone** am the Lord, the only one who can save you.
44.24 I **alone** stretched out the heavens;
45.14 to you and confess, 'God is with you—he **alone** is God.
46. 9 acknowledge that I **alone** am God and that there is no one
48.11 else share the glory that should be mine and mine **alone.**"
49.21 I was left all **alone**— where did these children come from?' "
Jer 2. 3 Israel, you belonged to me **alone;**
29.11 I **alone** know the plans I have for you, plans to bring
Lam 3.28 When we suffer, we should sit **alone** in silent patience;
3.37 The will of the Lord **alone** is always carried out.
Ezek 9. 8 While the killing was going on, I was there **alone.**
44.16 They **alone** will enter my Temple, serve at my altar,
Dan 10. 8 I was left there **alone,** watching this amazing vision.
10.13 to help me, because I had been left there **alone** in Persia.
Hos 13. 4 I **alone** am your saviour.
Zeph 3. 9 and they will pray to me **alone** and not to other gods.
Mt 4. 4 'Man cannot live on bread **alone,** but needs every word that
14.23 When evening came, Jesus was there **alone;**
17. 1 and led them up a high mountain where they were **alone.**
24.36 the Father **alone** knows.
Mk 4.10 When Jesus was **alone,** some of those who had heard him
4.34 but when he was **alone** with his disciples, he would explain
6.31 place where we will be **alone** and you can rest
6.47 in the middle of the lake, while Jesus was **alone** on land.
7.33 So Jesus took him off **alone,** away from the crowd,
9. 2 and led them up a high mountain, where they were **alone.**
10.18 "No one is good except God **alone.**
14. 6 But Jesus said, "Leave her **alone!**
Lk 4. 4 answered, "The scripture says, 'Man cannot live on bread **alone.**' "
9.18 day when Jesus was praying **alone,** the disciples came to him.
9.36 When the voice stopped, there was Jesus all **alone.**
13. 8 the gardener answered, 'Leave it **alone,** sir, just one more year;
18.19 "No one is good except God **alone.**
Jn 5.44 not try to win praise from the one who **alone** is God;
8. 9 Jesus was left **alone,** with the woman still standing there.
8.16 my judgement would be true, because I am not **alone** in this;
8.29 he has not left me **alone,** because I always do what pleases
12. 7 But Jesus said, "Leave her **alone!**
14.18 "When I go, you will not be left all **alone;**
16.32 one to his own home, and I will be left all **alone.**
16.32 But I am not really **alone,** because the Father is with me.
Acts 4.12 Salvation is to be found through him **alone;**
5.38 Leave them **alone!**
Rom 4.23 "he was accepted as righteous" were not written for him **alone.**
8.23 But it is not just creation **alone** which groans;
16.27 To the only God, who **alone** is all-wise, be glory through
1 Cor 7. 8 be better for you to continue to live **alone** as I do.
Col 1.18 in order that he **alone** might have the first place
1 Thes 3. 1 decided to stay on **alone** in Athens [2]while we sent Timothy,
1 Tim 5. 3 Show respect for widows who really are all **alone.**
5. 5 A widow who is all **alone,** with no one to take care
5.16 it may take care of the widows who are all **alone.**
6.16 He **alone** is immortal;
Tit 2.14 people who belong to him **alone** and are eager to do good.
Jas 2.17 if it is **alone** and includes no actions, then it is dead.
2.24 person is put right with God, and not by his faith **alone.**
4.12 He **alone** can save and destroy.
Rev 15. 4 You **alone** are holy.

ALOUD

Ex 24. 7 Lord's commands were written, and read it **aloud** to the people.
Deut 31.10 read this **aloud** at the Festival of Shelters.
Josh 8.34 Joshua then read **aloud** the whole Law,
2 Sam 3.32 Hebron, and the king wept **aloud** at the grave, and so did
1 Kgs 17.20 Then he prayed **aloud,** "O Lord my God, why have you done
2 Kgs 22.10 And he read it **aloud** to the king.
23. 2 them all, the king read **aloud** the whole book of the covenant
2 Chr 20. 6 and prayed **aloud,** "O Lord God of our ancestors,
34.18 And he read it **aloud** to the king.
34.30 all, the king read **aloud** the whole book of the covenant,
36.22 out in writing to be read **aloud** everywhere in his empire:
Ezra 1. 1 out in writing to be read **aloud** everywhere in his empire:
Neh 9. 4 They prayed **aloud** to the Lord their God.
13. 1 of Moses was being read **aloud** to the people, they came to
Ps 32. 7 I sing **aloud** of your salvation, because you protect me.
59.16 every morning I will sing **aloud** of your constant love.
77. 1 I cry **aloud** to God;
77. 1 I cry **aloud,** and he hears me.
102. 5 I groan **aloud;**
119.13 I will repeat **aloud** all the laws you have given.
149. 6 Let them shout **aloud** as they praise God,
Is 29.18 hear a book being read **aloud,** and the blind, who have been
Jer 36. 6 are to read the scroll **aloud,** so that they will hear

Jer 51.61 Babylon, be sure to read **aloud** to the people everything that
Lam 3. 8 I cry **aloud** for help, but God refuses to listen;

ALTAR
[GOD'S ALTAR, INCENSE-ALTAR]

Gen 8.20 Noah built an **altar** to the Lord;
8.20 and bird, and burnt them whole as a sacrifice on the **altar.**
12. 7 Then Abram built an **altar** there to the Lord, who had
12. 8 There also he built an **altar** and worshipped the Lord.
13. 4 and Ai where he had camped before [4] and had built an **altar.**
13.18 Mamre at Hebron, and there he built an **altar** to the Lord.
22. 9 about, Abraham built an **altar** and arranged the wood on it.
22. 9 son and placed him on the **altar,** on top of the wood.
26.25 Isaac built an **altar** there and worshipped the Lord.
33.20 He put up an **altar** there and named it after El, the
35. 1 Build an **altar** there to me, the God who appeared to you
35. 3 where I will build an **altar** to the God who helped me
35. 7 He built an **altar** there and named the place after the God
Ex 17.15 Moses built an **altar** and named it "The Lord is my Banner."
20.24 Make an **altar** of earth for me, and on it sacrifice your
20.25 If you make an **altar** of stone for me, do not build
20.26 Do not build an **altar** for me with steps leading up to
21.14 to death, even if he has run to my **altar** for safety.
24. 4 next morning he built an **altar** at the foot of the mountain
24. 6 and the other half he threw against the **altar.**
27. 1 "Make an **altar** out of acacia-wood.
27. 2 form one piece with the **altar,** and the whole is to be
27. 5 under the rim of the **altar,**
27. 5 so that it reaches half-way up the **altar.**
27. 7 the rings on each side of the **altar** when it is carried.
27. 8 Make the **altar** out of boards and leave it hollow,
28.43 my presence or approach the **altar** to serve as priests in the
29.12 and with your finger put it on the projections of the **altar.**
29.12 out the rest of the blood at the base of the **altar.**
29.13 them and burn them on the **altar** as an offering to me.
29.16 its blood and throw it against all four sides of the **altar.**
29.18 Burn the whole ram on the **altar** as a food offering.
29.20 the rest of the blood against all four sides of the **altar.**
29.21 blood that is on the **altar** and some of the anointing oil,
29.25 and burn it on the **altar,** on top of the burnt-offering, as
29.36 This will purify the **altar.**
29.37 Then the **altar** will be completely holy,
29.38 sacrifice on the **altar** two one-year-old lambs.
29.44 make the Tent and the **altar** holy, and I will set Aaron
30. 1 "Make an **altar** out of acacia-wood, for burning incense.
30. 6 Put this **altar** outside the curtain which hangs in front of
30. 9 Do not offer on this **altar** any forbidden
30.10 for purifying the **altar** by putting on its four projections
30.10 This **altar** is to be completely holy, dedicated to me, the
30.18 it between the Tent and the **altar,** and put water in it.
30.20 the Tent or approach the **altar** to offer the food offering.
30.27 the **altar** for burning incense,
30.28 the **altar** for burning offerings,
31. 8 the **altar** for burning incense,
31. 9 the **altar** for burnt-offerings and all its equipment,
32. 5 Then Aaron built an **altar** in front of the gold bull and
34.13 Instead, tear down their **altars,** destroy their sacred pillars,
35.15 the **altar** for burning incense and its poles;
35.16 the **altar** on which to burn offerings, with its bronze grating
37.25 He made an **altar** out of acacia-wood, for burning incense.
38. 1 For burning offerings, he made an **altar** out of acacia-wood.
38. 2 four corners, so that they formed one piece with the **altar.**
38. 3 He also made all the equipment for the **altar:**
38. 4 under the rim of the **altar,**
38. 4 so that it reached half-way up the **altar.**
38. 7 and put them in the rings on each side of the **altar.**
38. 7 The **altar** was made of boards and was hollow.
38.30 the Lord's presence, the bronze **altar** with its bronze grating,
38.30 all the equipment for the **altar,**
39.38 the gold **altar;**
39.39 the bronze **altar** with its bronze grating, its poles,
40. 5 Put the gold **altar** for burning incense in front of the
40. 6 Put in front of the Tent the **altar** for burning offerings.
40. 7 between the Tent and the **altar** and fill it with water.
40.10 Next, dedicate the **altar** and all its equipment by anointing it,
40.26 He put the gold **altar** in the Tent, in front of the
40.29 of the curtain he placed the **altar** for burning offerings.
40.30 between the Tent and the **altar** and filled it with water.
40.32 the Tent or to the **altar,** just as the Lord had commanded.
40.33 round the Tent and the **altar** and hung the curtain at the
Lev 1. 5 all four sides of the **altar** which is at the entrance of
1. 7 the priests shall arrange fire-wood on the **altar** and light it.
1. 9 the officiating priest will burn the whole sacrifice on the **altar.**
1.11 the north side of the **altar,** and the priests
1.11 shall throw its blood on all four sides of the **altar.**
1.13 sacrifice to the Lord and burn all of it on the **altar.**
1.15 shall present it at the **altar,** wring its neck,
1.15 and burn its head on the **altar.**
1.15 Its blood shall be drained out against the side of the **altar.**
1.16 on the east side of the **altar** where the ashes are put.
1.17 tearing the wings off, and then burn it whole on the **altar.**
2. 2 and burn it on the **altar** as a token that it has
2. 8 present it to the priest, who will take it to the **altar.**
2. 9 offered to the Lord, and he will burn it on the **altar.**
2.12 the Lord, but it is not to be burnt on the **altar.**
3. 2 all four sides of the **altar** [3] and present the following
3. 5 priests shall burn all this on the **altar**
3. 8 all four sides of the **altar** [9] and present the following
3.11 burn all this on the **altar** as a food-offering to the Lord.
3.13 all four sides of the **altar** [14] and present the following parts
Lev 3.16 burn all this on the **altar** as a food-offering pleasing to
4. 7 projections at the corners of the **incense-altar** in the Tent.
4. 7 at the base of the **altar** used for burning sacrifices, which
4.10 and burn it on the **altar** used for the burnt-offerings, just
4.18 the corners of the **incense-altar** inside the Tent and pour out
4.18 at the base of the **altar** used for burning sacrifices, which
4.19 he shall take all its fat and burn it on the **altar.**
4.24 the north side of the **altar,** where the animals
4.25 at the corners of the **altar,** and
4.25 pour out the rest of it at the base of the **altar.**
4.26 all its fat on the **altar,** just as he burns the fat
4.29 the north side of the **altar,** where the animals
4.30 at the corners of the **altar,** and
4.30 pour out the rest of it at the base of the **altar.**
4.31 shall burn it on the **altar** so that the smell pleases the
4.33 the north side of the **altar,** where the animals
4.34 at the corners of the **altar,** and pour out
4.34 the rest of it at the base of the **altar.**
4.35 shall burn it on the **altar** along with the food-offerings
5. 9 and sprinkle some of its blood against the side of the **altar.**
5. 9 the blood will be drained out at the base of the **altar.**
5.12 Lord, and he will burn it on the **altar** as a food-offering.
6. 9 to be left on the **altar** all night long, and the fire
6.10 greasy ashes left on the **altar**
6.10 and put them at the side of the **altar.**
6.12 The fire on the **altar** must be kept burning and never
6.13 be kept burning on the **altar** and never allowed to go out.
6.14 the grain-offering to the Lord in front of the **altar.**
6.15 and burn it on the **altar** as a token that all of
6.25 the north side of the **altar,** where the animals
7. 2 the north side of the **altar,** where the animals
7. 2 blood is to be thrown against all four sides of the **altar.**
7. 3 All its fat shall be removed and offered on the **altar:**
7. 5 all the fat on the **altar** as a food-offering to the Lord.
7.14 the blood of the animal and throws it against the **altar.**
7.31 burn the fat on the **altar,** but the breast shall belong to
8.11 it seven times on the **altar** and its equipment and on the
8.15 at the corners of the **altar,** in order to dedicate it.
8.15 out the rest of the blood at the base of the **altar.**
8.16 with the fat on them, and burnt it all on the **altar.**
8.19 it and threw the blood on all four sides of the **altar.**
8.20 of the ram on the **altar,** just as the Lord had commanded.
8.24 the rest of the blood on all four sides of the **altar.**
8.28 and burnt it on the **altar,** on top of the burnt-offering, as
8.30 blood that was on the **altar** and sprinkled them on Aaron and
9. 7 to Aaron, "Go to the **altar** and offer the sin-offering and
9. 8 Aaron went to the **altar** and killed the young bull which
9. 9 at the corners of the **altar,** and poured out
9. 9 the rest of it at the base of the **altar.**
9.10 Then he burnt on the **altar** the fat, the kidneys, and the
9.12 blood, and he threw it on all four sides of the **altar.**
9.13 other pieces of the animal, and he burnt them on the **altar.**
9.14 and burnt them on the **altar** on top of the rest of
9.17 and took a handful of flour and burnt it on the **altar.**
9.18 blood, and he threw it on all four sides of the **altar.**
9.20 the breasts of the animals and carried it all to the **altar.**
9.20 burnt the fat on the **altar** [21] and presented the breasts and
9.24 consumed the burnt-offering and the fat parts on the **altar.**
10.12 eat it beside the **altar,** because this offering is very holy.
14.20 and offer it with the grain-offering on the **altar.**
16.12 of burning coals from the **altar** and two handfuls of fine
16.18 then go out to the **altar** for burnt-offerings and purify it.
16.18 put it all over the projections at the corners of the **altar.**
16.19 he must sprinkle some of the blood on the **altar** seven times.
16.20 the Lord's presence, and the **altar,** he shall present to the
16.25 He shall burn on the **altar** the fat of the animal for
16.33 the **altar,** the priests, and all the people
17. 6 against the sides of the **altar** at the entrance of the Tent
17.11 be poured out on the **altar** to take away the people's sins.
21.23 not come near the sacred curtain or approach the **altar.**
22. 3 have dedicated to me, he can never again serve at the **altar.**
22.22 Do not offer any such animals on the **altar** as a food-offering.
26.30 tear down your **incense-altars,** and throw your dead bodies on
Num 3.26 round the Tent and the **altar,** and the curtain for the
3.31 the lamp-stand, the **altars,** the utensils the priests use
4.11 blue cloth over the gold **altar,** put a fine leather cover
4.13 the greasy ashes from the **altar** and spread a purple cloth
4.14 on it all the equipment used in the service at the **altar:**
4.26 round the Tent and the **altar,** the curtains for the entrance
5.16 the woman forward and make her stand in front of the **altar.**
5.25 out in dedication to the Lord, and present it on the **altar.**
5.26 of it as a token offering and burn it on the **altar.**
5.29 stand in front of the **altar,** and the priest shall perform
7. 1 Tent and all its equipment, and the **altar** and all its equipment.
7.10 offerings to celebrate the dedication of the **altar.**
7.10 present their gifts at the **altar,**
7.11 is to present his gifts for the dedication of the **altar."**
7.84 the twelve leaders for the dedication of the **altar** were
15.28 At the **altar** the priest shall perform the ritual of purification
16. 5 that is, the one he has chosen, approach him at the **altar.**
16. 6 live coals and incense on them, and take them to the **altar.**
16.17 put incense on it, and then present it at the **altar."**
16.38 They became holy when they were presented at the Lord's **altar.**
16.38 them into thin plates, and make a covering for the **altar.**
16.39 beaten into thin plates to make a covering for the **altar.**
16.40 Aaron should come to the **altar** to burn incense for the Lord.
16.46 put live coals from the **altar** in it, and put some incense
18. 3 with sacred objects in the Holy Place or with the **altar.**
18. 5 the Holy Place and the **altar,** so that my anger will not
18. 7 the priesthood that concern the **altar** and what is in the
18. 9 sacred offerings not burnt on the **altar,**

Num	18.17	Throw their blood against the **altar** and burn their fat as a
	23. 1	said to Balak, "Build seven **altars** here for me, and bring
	23. 2	he and Balaam offered a bull and a ram on each **altar.**
	23. 4	"I have built the seven **altars** and offered a bull and a
	23.14	There also he built seven **altars** and offered a bull and a
	23.29	said to him, "Build seven **altars** for me here and bring me
	23.30	was told, and offered a bull and a ram on each **altar.**
	28. 7	the first lamb, pour out at the **altar** one litre of wine.
Deut	7. 5	tear down their **altars,** break their sacred stone pillars
	12. 3	Tear down their **altars** and smash their sacred stone pillars
	12.27	which are to be completely burnt on the Lord's **altar.**
	12.27	you eat the meat and pour the blood out on the **altar.**
	12.31	They even sacrifice their children in the fires on their **altars.**
	16.21	"When you make an **altar** for the Lord your God, do not
	18.10	Don't sacrifice your children in the fires on your **altars;**
	26. 4	you and place it before the **altar** of the Lord your God.
	27. 5	Build an **altar** there made of stones that have had no iron
	27. 6	used on them, [6]because any **altar** you build for the Lord
	33.10	They will offer sacrifices on your **altar.**
Josh	8.30	built on Mount Ebal an **altar** to the Lord, the God of
	8.31	"an **altar** made of stones which have not been cut with iron
	9.27	water for the people of Israel and for the Lord's **altar.**
	13.14	sacrifices burnt on the **altar** to the Lord God of Israel.
	22.10	Jordan, they built a large, impressive **altar** there by the river.
	22.11	East Manasseh have built an **altar** at Geliloth, on our side
	22.16	You have rebelled against the Lord by building this **altar**
	22.19	an altar in addition to the **altar** of the Lord our God.
	22.23	Lord and built our own **altar** to burn sacrifices on or to
	22.26	So we built an **altar,** not to burn sacrifices or make offerings,
	22.28	Our ancestors made an **altar** just like the Lord's altar.
	22.29	him now by building an **altar** to burn offerings on or for
	22.29	would not build any other **altar** than the altar of the Lord
	22.34	Reuben and Gad said, "This **altar** is a witness to all of
Judg	2. 2	You must tear down their **altars.'**
	6.24	Gideon built an **altar** to the Lord there and named it
	6.25	old, tear down your father's **altar** to Baal, and cut down the
	6.26	Build a well-constructed **altar** to the Lord your God on
	6.28	morning, they found that the **altar** to Baal and the symbol of
	6.28	bull had been burnt on the **altar** that had been built there.
	6.30	He tore down the **altar** to Baal and cut down the symbol
	6.31	It is his **altar** that was torn down."
	6.32	it is his **altar** that was torn down."
	13.19	them on the rock **altar** to the Lord who works wonders.
	13.20	were going up from the **altar,** Manoah and his wife saw the
	21. 4	people built an **altar** there, offered fellowship sacrifices
1 Sam	2.28	priests, to serve at the **altar,** to burn the incense, and to
	2.28	right to keep a share of the sacrifices burnt on the **altar.**
	7.17	In Ramah he built an **altar** to the Lord.
	9.12	are going to offer a sacrifice on the **altar** on the hill.
	10. 5	prophets coming down from the **altar** on the hill, playing harps,
	10.13	dancing and shouting, he went to the **altar** on the hill.
	14.35	Saul built an **altar** to the Lord, the first one that he
	15.33	he cut Agag to pieces in front of the **altar** in Gilgal.
2 Sam	24.18	"Go up to Araunah's threshing-place and build an **altar** to the Lord."
	24.21	your threshing-place and build an **altar** for the Lord, in
	24.22	Here are these oxen to burn as an offering on the **altar;**
	24.25	Then he built an **altar** to the Lord and offered burnt-offerings
1 Kgs	1.50	Lord's presence and took hold of the corners of the **altar.**
	1.51	to the corners of the **altar** and had said, "First, I want
	1.53	sent for Adonijah and had him brought down from the **altar.**
	2.28	Lord's presence and took hold of the corners of the **altar.**
	2.29	Tent and was by the **altar,** Solomon sent a messenger
	2.29	to Joab to ask him why he had fled to the **altar.**
	3. 2	people were still offering sacrifices at many different **altars.**
	3. 3	animals and offered them as sacrifices on various **altars.**
	3. 4	because that was where the most famous **altar** was.
	6.20	The **altar** was covered with cedar panels.
	6.22	with gold, as well as the **altar** in the Most Holy Place.
	7.48	the **altar,** the table for the bread offered to God, [49]the
	8.22	stood in front of the **altar,** where he raised his arms
	8.31	and is brought to your **altar** in this Temple to take an
	8.54	up in front of the **altar,** where he had been kneeling with
	8.64	did this because the bronze **altar** was too small for all
	9.25	fellowship-offerings on the **altar** he had built to the Lord.
	12.32	On the **altar** in Bethel he offered sacrifices
	12.33	offered a sacrifice on the **altar** in celebration of the festival
	13. 1	as Jeroboam stood at the **altar** to offer the sacrifice.
	13. 2	Following the Lord's command, the prophet denounced the **altar:**
	13. 2	"O **altar,** altar, this is what the Lord says:
	13. 2	priests serving at the pagan **altars** who offer sacrifices on you,
	13. 3	went on to say, "This **altar** will fall apart, and the ashes
	13. 5	The **altar** suddenly fell apart and the ashes spilt to the ground,
	13.32	the Lord's command against the **altar** in Bethel
	13.33	from ordinary families to serve at the **altars** he had built.
	16.32	Baal in Samaria, made an **altar** for him, and put it in
	18.26	and kept dancing round the **altar** they had built.
	18.30	He set about repairing the **altar** of the Lord which had been
	18.32	stones he rebuilt the **altar** for the worship of the Lord.
	18.33	placed the wood on the **altar,** cut the bull in pieces, and
	18.35	The water ran down round the **altar** and filled the trench.
	18.36	the prophet Elijah approached the **altar** and prayed, "O Lord,
	19.10	torn down your **altars,** and killed all your prophets.
	19.14	torn down your **altars,** and killed all your prophets.
	22.46	prostitutes serving at the pagan **altars** who were still left
2 Kgs	11.18	they smashed the **altars** and the idols,
	11.18	killed Mattan, the priest of Baal, in front of the **altars.**
	12. 9	placed the box by the **altar,** on the right side as one
	16.10	Tiglath Pileser, he saw the **altar** there and sent back to
	16.11	So Uriah built an **altar** just like it, and finished it
	16.12	Ahaz saw that the **altar** was finished, [13]so he burnt animal
2 Kgs	16.14	The bronze **altar** dedicated to the Lord
	16.14	was between the new **altar** and the Temple,
	16.14	so Ahaz moved it to the north side of his new **altar.**
	16.15	"Use this large **altar** of mine for the morning burnt-offerings
	16.15	But keep the bronze **altar** for me to use for divination."
	17.11	on all the pagan **altars,** following the practice of the people
	18.22	the Lord's shrines and **altars** that Hezekiah destroyed,
	18.22	Judah and Jerusalem to worship only at the **altar** in Jerusalem.
	21. 3	he built **altars** for the worship of Baal and made an image
	21. 4	He built pagan **altars** in the Temple, the place that the
	21. 5	of the Temple he built **altars** for the worship of the stars.
	23. 5	offer sacrifices on the pagan **altars** in the cities of Judah
	23. 8	he desecrated the **altars** where they had offered sacrifices.
	23. 8	He also tore down the **altars** dedicated to the goat-demons
	23.12	The **altars** which the kings of Judah had built on the
	23.12	tore down, along with the **altars** put up by King Manasseh in
	23.12	he smashed the **altars** to bits and threw them into the valley
	23.13	Josiah desecrated the **altars** that King Solomon had built
	23.15	Josiah pulled down the **altar,** broke its stones into pieces,
	23.16	had the bones taken out of them and burnt on the **altar.**
	23.16	he desecrated the **altar,** doing what the prophet had predicted
	23.16	during the festival as King Jeroboam was standing by the **altar.**
	23.17	Judah and predicted these things that you have done to this **altar."**
	23.19	He did to all those **altars** what he had done in Bethel.
	23.20	the pagan priests on the **altars** where they served,
	23.20	and he burnt human bones on every **altar.**
	25.14	containers used in cleaning the **altar,** the tools used in tending
1 Chr	6.49	and offered the sacrifices that were burnt on the **altar.**
	16.40	whole on the **altar** in accordance with what was written
	21.18	and build an **altar** to the Lord at Araunah's threshing-place.
	21.22	that I can build an **altar** to the Lord, to stop the
	21.23	as an offering on the **altar,** and here are the
	21.26	He built an **altar** to the Lord there and offered burnt-offerings
	21.26	fire from heaven to burn the sacrifices on the **altar.**
	21.28	he offered sacrifices on the **altar** at Araunah's threshing-place.
	21.29	in the wilderness, and the **altar** on which sacrifices were burnt
	22. 1	Here is the **altar** where the people of Israel are to offer
	28.18	pure gold in making the **altar** on which incense was burnt and
	29.21	and a thousand lambs, which they burnt whole on the **altar.**
2 Chr	1. 5	The bronze **altar** which had been made by Bezalel, the son
	1. 6	worshipped the Lord by offering sacrifices on the bronze **altar;**
	4. 1	Solomon had a bronze **altar** made, which was nine metres square
	4.19	the **altar** and the tables for the bread offered to God;
	5.11	the east side of the **altar** with cymbals and harps, and with
	6.12	stood in front of the **altar** and raised his arms in prayer.
	6.22	and is brought to your **altar** in this Temple to take an
	7. 7	did this because the bronze **altar** which he had made was too
	7. 9	for the dedication of the **altar** and then seven more days for
	8.12	to the Lord on the **altar** which he had built in front
	14. 3	He removed the foreign **altars** and the pagan places of worship,
	14. 5	places of worship and the **incense-altars** from all the cities
	15. 8	He also repaired the **altar** of the Lord that stood in the
	23.17	They smashed the **altars** and idols there
	23.17	and killed Mattan, the priest of Baal, in front of the **altars.**
	26.16	into the Temple to burn incense on the **altar of incense.**
	26.19	in the Temple beside the **incense altar** and was holding
	28.24	the Temple and set up **altars** in every part of Jerusalem.
	29.18	the whole Temple, including the **altar** for burnt-offerings,
	29.19	It is all in front of the Lord's **altar."**
	29.21	to offer the animals as sacrifices on the **altar.**
	29.22	and sprinkled the blood of each sacrifice on the **altar.**
	29.24	poured their blood on the **altar** as a sacrifice to take away
	30.14	They took all the **altars** that had been used in Jerusalem
	30.16	sacrifices to the priests, who sprinkled it on the **altar.**
	31. 1	and destroyed the **altars** and the pagan places of worship.
	32.12	destroyed the Lord's shrines and **altars** and then told the people
	32.12	Judah and Jerusalem to worship and burn incense at one **altar** only.
	33. 3	He built **altars** for the worship of Baal, made images of the
	33. 4	He built pagan **altars** in the Temple, the place that the
	33. 5	of the Temple he built **altars** for the worship of the stars.
	33.15	placed there, and the pagan **altars** that were on the hill
	33.16	He also repaired the **altar** where the Lord was worshipped,
	34. 4	his men smashed the **altars** where Baal was worshipped
	34. 4	and tore down the **incense-altars** near them.
	34. 5	of the pagan priests on the **altars** where they had worshipped.
	34. 7	he smashed the **altars** and the symbols of Asherah,
	34. 7	the idols to dust, and broke in pieces all the **incense-altars.**
	35.11	and the priests sprinkled the blood on the **altar.**
	35.16	and the offering of burnt-offerings on the **altar.**
Ezra	3. 2	with his relatives, rebuilt the **altar** of the God of Israel,
	3. 3	the land, they rebuilt the **altar** where it had stood before.
	7.17	wine and offer them on the **altar** of the Temple in Jerusalem.
Ps	26. 6	that I am innocent and march in worship round your **altar.**
	40. 6	animals burnt whole on the **altar** or for sacrifices to take
	43. 4	Then I will go to your **altar,** O God;
	51.19	and bulls will be sacrificed on your **altar.**
	66.15	I will offer sheep to be burnt on the **altar;**
	84. 3	keep their young near your **altars,** Lord Almighty, my king
	118.27	your hands, start the festival and march round the **altar.**
Is	6. 6	that he had taken from the **altar** with a pair of tongs.
	17. 8	no longer rely on the **altars** they made with their own hands,
	17. 8	symbols of the goddess Asherah and **altars** for burning incense.
	19.19	comes, there will be an **altar** to the Lord in the land
	27. 9	when the stones of pagan **altars** are ground up like chalk,
	27. 9	and no more **incense-altars** or symbols of the goddess Asherah
	29. 1	**God's altar,** Jerusalem itself, is doomed!
	29. 2	God will bring disaster on the city that is called **"God's altar."**
	29. 2	and the whole city will be like an **altar** covered with blood.
	29. 7	attacking the city of **God's altar,** all their weapons
	36. 7	was the Lord's shrines and **altars** that Hezekiah destroyed

Is	36. 7	people of Judah and Jerusalem to worship at one **altar** only.
	56. 7	of prayer, and accept the sacrifices you offer on my **altar.**
	60. 7	as sacrifices And offered on the **altar** to please the Lord.
	65. 3	pagan sacrifices in sacred gardens and burn incense on pagan **altars.**
Jer	7.21	you burn completely on the **altar,** and some you are permitted
	7.31	Hinnom they have built an **altar** called Topheth, so that they
	11.13	have set up as many **altars** for sacrifices to that disgusting
	17. 1	a diamond point and carved on the corners of your **altars.**
	17. 2	Your people worship at the **altars** and the symbols that
	19. 5	people, [5]and they have built **altars** for Baal in order to
	32.35	They have built **altars** to Baal in the Valley of Hinnom,
	52.18	containers used in cleaning the **altar,** the tools used in tending
Lam	2. 7	The Lord rejected his **altar** and deserted his holy Temple;
Ezek	6. 4	The altars will be torn down and the **incense-altars** broken.
	6. 5	I will scatter their bones all round the **altars.**
	6. 6	so that all their **altars** and their idols will be smashed
	6. 6	be smashed to pieces, their **incense-altars** will be shattered,
	6.13	idols and round the **altars,** scattered on every high hill,
	8. 5	looked, and there near the **altar** by the entrance of the
	8.16	of the sanctuary, between the **altar** and the passage,
	9. 2	They all came and stood by the bronze **altar.**
	40.46	faced north was for the priests who served at the **altar.**
	40.47	on the west side, and in front of it was an **altar.**
	41.22	there was something that looked like [22]a wooden **altar.**
	43.13	the measurements of the **altar,** using the same unit of measurement
	43.13	round the base of the **altar** there was a gutter fifty
	43.14	The lowest section of the **altar,** from the top of the base,
	43.16	The top of the **altar** was a square, six metres on each
	43.17	The steps going up the **altar** were on the east side.
	43.18	When the **altar** is built, you are to dedicate it by burning
	43.20	the top corners of the **altar,** and on the corners
	43.20	of the middle section of the **altar,** and all round its edges.
	43.20	In this way you will purify the **altar** and consecrate it.
	43.22	Purify the **altar** with its blood in the same way as you
	43.26	are to consecrate the **altar** and make it ready for use.
	43.27	to begin offerings on the **altar** the burnt-offerings
	44.16	serve at my **altar,** and conduct the temple worship.
	45.19	the four corners of the **altar,** and on the posts of the
	47. 1	south part of the temple past the south side of the **altar.**
Hos	8.11	"The more **altars** the people of Israel build for removing sin,
	10. 1	The more prosperous they were, the more **altars** they built.
	10. 2	God will break down their **altars** and destroy their sacred pillars.
	10. 8	Thorns and weeds will grow up over their **altars.**
	12.11	and the **altars** there will become piles of stone
Joel	1.13	Put on sackcloth and weep, you priests who serve at the **altar!**
	2.17	the Lord between the **altar** and the entrance of the Temple,
Amos	3.14	Israel for their sins, I will destroy the **altars** of Bethel.
	3.14	The corners of every **altar** will be broken off and will fall
	9. 1	I saw the Lord standing by the **altar.**
Hag	2.14	and so everything they offer on the **altar** is defiled."
Zech	9.15	the blood of a sacrifice poured on the **altar** from a bowl.
	14.20	the Temple will be as sacred as the bowls before the **altar.**
Mal	1. 7	This is how—by offering worthless food on my **altar.**
	1. 7	I will tell you—by showing contempt for my **altar.**
	1.10	as to prevent you from lighting useless fires on my **altar.**
	1.12	when you say that my **altar** is worthless and when you offer
	2.13	You drown the Lord's **altar** with tears, weeping and wailing
Mt	5.23	gift to God at the **altar** and there you remember that your
	5.24	there in front of the **altar,** go at once and make peace
	23.18	'If someone swears by the **altar,** he isn't bound by his vow;
	23.18	if he swears by the gift on the **altar,** he is bound.'
	23.19	important, the gift or the **altar** which makes the gift holy?
	23.20	a person swears by the **altar,** he is swearing by it and
	23.35	whom you murdered between the Temple and the **altar.**
Lk	1. 9	he was chosen by lot to burn incense on the **altar.**
	1.11	on the right of the **altar** where the incense was burnt.
	11.51	Zechariah, who was killed between the **altar** and the Holy Place.
Acts	17.23	you worship, I found an **altar** on which is written,
Rom	11. 3	"Lord, they have killed your prophets and torn down your **altars;**
1 Cor	9.13	the sacrifices on the **altar** get a share of the sacrifices.
	10.18	is offered in sacrifice share in the **altar's** service to God.
	10.20	what is sacrificed on pagan **altars** is offered to demons,
Heb	9. 4	In it were the gold **altar** for the burning of incense
	10. 6	animals burnt whole on the **altar** or with sacrifices to take
	10. 8	with animals burnt on the **altar** and the sacrifices to take
	13.10	have no right to eat any of the sacrifice on our **altar.**
Jas	2.21	his actions, when he offered his son Isaac on the **altar.**
Rev	6. 9	I saw underneath the **altar** the souls of those who had been
	8. 3	who had a gold incense-burner, came and stood at the **altar.**
	8. 3	to offer it on the gold **altar** that stands before the throne.
	8. 5	it with fire from the **altar,** and threw it on the earth.
	9.13	from the four corners of the gold **altar** standing before God.
	11. 1	temple of God and the **altar,** and count those who are
	14.18	angel, who is in charge of the fire, came from the **altar.**
	16. 7	Then I heard a voice from the **altar** saying, "Lord God Almighty!

ALWAYS

Gen	3.15	her offspring and yours will **always** be enemies.
	8.22	There will **always** be cold and heat, summer and winter, day
	17. 1	Obey me and **always** do what is right.
	24.40	'The Lord, whom I have **always** obeyed, will send his angel
	31.39	was killed by wild animals, I **always** bore the loss myself.
	43. 9	back to you safe and sound, I will **always** bear the blame.
	49.10	And his descendants will **always** rule.
Ex	13.22	The pillar of cloud was **always** in front of the people
	16.29	the sixth day I will **always** give you enough food for two
	25.30	on the table there is **always** to be the sacred bread offered
	28.12	so that I, the Lord, will **always** remember my people.
Ex	28.29	Israel, so that I, the Lord, will **always** remember my people.
	28.30	At such times he must **always** wear this breast-piece, so that
	28.43	Aaron and his sons must **always** wear them when they go
Lev	6.13	The fire must **always** be kept burning on the altar and
Num	4. 7	There shall **always** be bread on the table.
	10.33	The Lord's Covenant Box **always** went ahead of them to find a
Deut	1.33	the Lord, [33]even though he **always** went ahead of you to
	5.29	If only they would **always** feel like this!
	5.29	If only they would **always** honour me and obey all my commands,
	6.24	If we do, he will **always** watch over our nation and keep
	11. 1	"Love the Lord your God and **always** obey all his laws.
	14.23	so that you may learn to honour the Lord your God **always.**
	15.11	There will **always** be some Israelites who are poor and in need,
	16.20	**Always** be fair and just, so that you will occupy the
	28.13	you will **always** prosper and never fail if you obey
	28.66	Your life will **always** be in danger.
	33.25	protected with iron gates, And may he **always** live secure."
	33.27	God has **always** been your defence;
Josh	1. 5	I will **always** be with you;
	1. 8	that the book of the Law is **always** read in your worship.
	1.17	obey you, just as we **always** obeyed Moses, and may the Lord
	4. 7	These stones will **always** remind the people of Israel
	9.23	Your people will **always** be slaves, cutting wood and carrying
Judg	16.20	up and thought, "I'll get loose and go free, as **always."**
Ruth	2.20	"The Lord **always** keeps his promises to the living and the dead."
1 Sam	1. 8	Why are you **always** so sad?
	1.18	"May you **always** think kindly of me," she replied.
	2.35	give him descendants, who will **always** serve in the presence
	8. 8	they are doing to you what they have **always** done to me.
	21. 5	"My men **always** keep themselves ritually pure even when we
	23.14	Saul was **always** trying to find him, but God did not hand
2 Sam	1.21	may its fields be **always** barren!
	7.16	You will **always** have descendants,
	7.22	we have **always** known that you alone are God.
	7.28	you **always** keep your promises,
	8.15	made sure that his people were **always** treated fairly and justly.
	9. 7	and you will **always** be welcome at my table."
	9.10	But Mephibosheth himself will **always** be a guest at my table."
	15.21	Lord's name that I will **always** go with you wherever you go,
	16. 4	"May I **always** please Your Majesty!"
1 Kgs	2.33	But the Lord will **always** give success to David's descendants
	3. 6	"You **always** showed great love for my father David,
	4.27	they **always** supplied everything needed.
	5. 1	King Hiram of Tyre had **always** been a friend of David's,
	8.25	told him that there would **always** be one of his descendants
	8.52	"Sovereign Lord, may you **always** look with favour on your people
	8.58	him, so that we will **always** live as he wants us to
	8.59	May he **always** be merciful to the people of Israel and to
	8.61	May you, his people, **always** be faithful to the Lord our God,
	9. 5	I told him that Israel would **always** be ruled by his descendants.
	10. 8	fortunate your servants, who are **always** in your presence
	11.36	tribe, so that I will **always** have a descendant of my servant
	11.38	command, as my servant David did, I will **always** be with you.
	12. 7	answer to their request, and they will **always** serve you loyally."
	19.10	He answered, "Lord God Almighty, I have **always** served you—
	19.14	He answered, "Lord God Almighty, I have **always** served you—
	22. 8	it's **always** something bad."
	22.18	It's **always** something bad!"
2 Kgs	8.19	that his descendants would **always** continue to rule.
	17.37	You shall **always** obey the laws and commands that I wrote
	20. 3	loyally, and that I have **always** tried to do what you wanted
1 Chr	17. 5	I have **always** lived in tents and moved from place to place.
	17.20	we have **always** known that you alone are God.
	18.14	made sure that his people were **always** treated fairly and justly.
	26.14	son Zechariah, a man who **always** gave good advice, drew the
	29.18	in your people's hearts and keep them **always** faithful to you.
2 Chr	1. 8	Solomon answered, "You **always** showed great love for my father
	6.16	told him that there would **always** be one of his descendants
	6.32	are and how you are **always** ready to act, and then he
	7.18	I told him that Israel would **always** be ruled by his descendants.
	9. 7	who serve you, who are **always** in your presence and serve you
	10. 7	by giving a considerate answer, they will **always** serve you
	16. 9	foolishly, and so from now on you will **always** be at war."
	18. 7	it's **always** something bad."
	18.17	it's **always** something bad!"
	21. 7	promised that his descendants would **always** continue to rule.
Ezra	4.15	discover that this city has **always** been rebellious
	4.15	Its people have **always** been hard to govern.
Job	1. 4	and they **always** invited their three sisters to join
	1. 5	He **always** did this because he thought that one of them might
	1.10	You have **always** protected him and his family and everything
	10.17	You **always** have some witness against me;
	10.17	you **always** plan some new attack.
	12.16	God is strong and **always** victorious;
	15.35	their hearts are **always** full of deceit.
	16. 3	Do you **always** have to have the last word?
	21.30	and punishes, it is the wicked man who is **always** spared.
	22.15	to walk in the paths that evil men have **always** followed?
	22.26	Then you will **always** trust in God and find that he is
	23.12	I **always** do what God commands;
	29. 3	God was **always** with me then and gave me light as I
	29.14	I have **always** acted justly and fairly.
	29.18	I **always** expected to live a long life and to die at
	29.19	like a tree whose roots **always** have water and whose branches
	29.20	Everyone was **always** praising me, and my strength never failed
	30. 1	Their fathers have **always** been so worthless
	31.31	who work for me know that I have **always** welcomed strangers.
	36. 6	live on, and he **always** treats the poor with justice.
	36.24	He has **always** been praised for what he does;
Ps	3. 3	But you, O Lord, are **always** my shield from danger;
	5.11	they can **always** sing for joy.

Ps 7.11 God is a righteous judge and **always** condemns the wicked.
9.18 The needy will not **always** be neglected;
10.14 of trouble and suffering and are **always** ready to help.
10.14 you have **always** helped the needy.
12. 7 Keep us **always** safe, O Lord, and preserve us from such people.
15. 2 obeys God in everything and **always** does what is right,
15. 4 He **always** does what he promises, no matter how much it may
15. 5 Whoever does these things will **always** be secure.
16. 8 I am **always** aware of the Lord's presence;
17. 5 I have **always** walked in your way and have never strayed
19. 9 they are **always** fair.
21. 7 because of the Lord's constant love he will **always** be secure.
22.10 the day I was born, and you have **always** been my God.
25. 5 I **always** trust in you.
25.13 They will **always** be prosperous, and their children will possess
26. 3 your faithfulness **always** leads me.
26.10 do evil all the time and are **always** ready to take bribes.
31.15 I am **always** in your care;
34. 1 I will **always** thank the Lord;
37.27 do good, and your descendants will **always** live in the land;
37.30 A good man's words are wise, and he is **always** fair.
40.10 I have **always** spoken of your faithfulness and help.
40.11 Your love and loyalty will **always** keep me safe.
40.16 thankful for your salvation **always** say, "How great is the Lord!"
44. 8 We will **always** praise you and give thanks to you for ever.
44.15 I am **always** in disgrace;
45. 2 God has **always** blessed you.
46. 1 is our shelter and strength, **always** ready to help in times
50. 8 and the burnt-offerings you **always** bring me.
50.19 "You are **always** ready to speak evil;
51. 3 I am **always** conscious of my sins.
52. 2 You are **always** inventing lies.
52. 9 I will **always** thank you, God, for what you have done;
56. 5 they are **always** planning how to hurt me!
61. 8 So I will **always** sing praises to you, as I offer you
63. 7 I think of you, [7] because you have **always** been my help.
69.23 Make their backs **always** weak!
70. 4 thankful for your salvation **always** say, "How great is God!"
71. 6 I will **always** praise you.
71.14 I will **always** put my hope in you;
72.15 may God's blessings be on him **always!**
73.12 They have plenty and are **always** getting more.
73.23 Yet I **always** stay close to you, and you hold me by
77. 7 "Will the Lord **always** reject us?
78. 7 not forget what he has done, but **always** obey his commandments.
84. 4 who live in your Temple, **always** singing praise to you.
86.15 a merciful and loving God, **always** patient, always kind
89. 1 O Lord, I will **always** sing of your constant love;
89. 4 'A descendant of yours will **always** be king;
89.21 My strength will **always** be with him, my power will make
89.24 I will make him **always** victorious.
89.28 I will **always** keep my promise to him, and my covenant
89.29 a descendant of his will **always** be king.
89.36 He will **always** have descendants, and I will watch
90. 1 O Lord, you have **always** been our home.
92.14 bear fruit in old age and are **always** green and strong.
102.27 But you are **always** the same, and your life never ends.
106. 3 those who obey his commands, who **always** do what is right.
109.15 May the Lord **always** remember their sins,
109.19 cover him like clothes and **always** be round him like a belt!
112. 6 he will **always** be remembered.
119.44 I will **always** obey your law, for ever and ever.
119.51 The proud are **always** scornful of me, but I have not
119.109 I am **always** ready to risk my life;
119.117 be safe, and I will **always** pay attention to your commands.
119.142 and your law is **always** true.
119.144 Your instructions are **always** just;
119.171 I will **always** praise you, because you teach me your laws.
119.173 **Always** be ready to help me, because I follow your commands.
121. 3 your protector is **always** awake.
125. 3 The wicked will not **always** rule over the land of the righteous;
130. 7 his love is constant and he is **always** willing to save.
132. 9 May your priests do **always** what is right;
135.13 Lord, you will **always** be proclaimed as God;
140. 2 They are **always** plotting evil, always stirring up quarrels.
141. 5 because I am **always** praying against their evil deeds.
145.21 I will **always** praise the Lord;
146. 6 He **always** keeps his promises;
Prov 1.16 They're **always** ready to kill.
1.19 Robbery **always** claims the life of the robber—
1.29 use for knowledge and have **always** refused to obey the Lord.
3. 1 **Always** remember what I tell you to do.
4.13 **Always** remember what you have learnt.
6.21 Keep their words with you **always,** locked in your heart.
7.11 bold and shameless woman who **always** walked the streets
8.30 his daily source of joy, **always** happy in his presence—
10.25 wicked are blown away, but honest people are **always** safe.
10.30 Righteous people will **always** have security,
10.32 to say, but the wicked are **always** saying things that hurt.
11.23 What good people want **always** results in good;
11.29 Foolish men will **always** be servants to the wise.
12.15 Stupid people **always** think they are right.
13.16 Sensible people **always** think before they act,
13.25 but the wicked are **always** hungry.
14. 5 A reliable witness **always** tells the truth,
14.13 When happiness is gone, sorrow is **always** there.
15.15 but happy people **always** enjoy life.
16.10 his decisions are **always** right.
17.11 to wicked people who are **always** stirring up trouble.
17.17 Friends **always** show their love.
18.15 Intelligent people are **always** eager and ready to learn.
Prov 18.17 to speak in court **always** seems right until his opponent begins
19. 4 Rich people are **always** finding new friends,
20.14 The customer **always** complains that the price is too high,
21.10 Wicked people are **always** hungry for evil;
23.29 sorry for himself, **always** causing trouble and always complaining.
24. 8 If you are **always** planning evil, you will earn a
24.16 how often an honest man falls, he **always** gets up again;
27.20 like the world of the dead—there is **always** room for more.
28.11 Rich people **always** think they are wise, but a poor
28.14 **Always** obey the Lord and you will be happy.
28.19 People who waste time will **always** be poor.
29.17 Discipline your son and you can **always** be proud of him.
31.27 She is **always** busy and looks after her family's needs.
Ecc 4. 8 yet he is **always** working, never satisfied with the wealth
6. 9 satisfied with what you have than to be **always** wanting something
7. 2 the living should **always** remind themselves that death is waiting
7. 4 Someone who is **always** thinking about happiness is a fool.
9. 8 **Always** look happy and cheerful.
9.11 fast runners do not **always** win the race,
9.11 and the brave do not **always** win the battle.
9.11 Wise men do not **always** earn a living,
9.11 intelligent men do not **always** get rich,
9.11 and capable men do not **always** rise to high positions.
9.16 I have **always** said that wisdom is better than strength,
Is 1.23 they are **always** accepting gifts and bribes.
3.16 They are **always** flirting.
9. 7 his kingdom will **always** be at peace.
26. 4 he will **always** protect us.
28.29 The plans God makes are wise, and they **always** succeed!
29.24 understand, and those who are **always** grumbling will be glad
30. 9 They are **always** rebelling against God, always lying,
30. 9 **always** refusing to listen to the Lord's
30.18 to take pity on you because he **always** does what is right.
33. 6 He **always** protects his people and gives them wisdom and knowledge.
38. 3 loyally, and that I have **always** tried to do what you wanted
43.13 I am God and **always** will be.
47. 7 You thought you would **always** be a queen, and did not take
48. 8 be trusted, that you have **always** been known as a rebel.
48.16 I have spoken openly, and have **always** made my words come true."
56. 2 I will bless those who **always** observe the Sabbath and do
58. 8 I will **always** be with you to save you;
58.11 And I will **always** guide you and satisfy you with good things.
59. 7 You are **always** planning something evil, and you can hardly wait
63. 9 He had **always** taken care of them in the past, [10] but they
63.16 Lord, are our father, the one who has **always** rescued us.
63.17 you, for the sake of the people who have **always** been yours.
65. 1 me, even though I was **always** ready to answer, 'Here I am;
65. 2 I have **always** been ready to welcome my people,
Jer 2.24 she is **always** available at mating time.
3. 5 You won't **always** be angry;
3.25 We and our ancestors have **always** sinned against the Lord our God;
9. 3 They are **always** ready to tell lies;
9. 8 they **always** tell lies.
12. 2 They **always** speak well of you, yet they do not really care
17.25 and the city of Jerusalem will **always** be filled with people.
18.18 There will **always** be priests to instruct us, wise men to
22.15 He was **always** just and fair, and he prospered in
31. 3 People of Israel, I have **always** loved you, so I continue to
33.17 Lord, promise that there will **always** be a descendant of
33.18 and that there will **always** be priests from the tribe of
33.20 the night, so that they **always** come at their proper times;
33.21 David that he would **always** have a descendant to be king,
33.21 from the tribe of Levi that they would **always** serve me;
35. 7 He commanded us **always** to live in tents, so that we might
35.19 Jonadab son of Rechab will **always** have a male descendant to
48.11 The Lord said, "Moab has **always** lived secure
Lam 3.37 The will of the Lord alone is **always** carried out.
Ezek 16.13 gold and silver, and you **always** wore clothes of embroidered linen
17. 5 fertile field, where there was **always** water to make it grow.
18.18 cheated and robbed, and **always** did evil to everyone.
20.49 Everyone is already complaining that I **always** speak in riddles."
22. 9 Some are **always** satisfying their lusts.
Dan 6.10 There, just as he had **always** done, he knelt down at the
9. 7 You, Lord, **always** do what is right,
9. 7 but we have **always** brought disgrace on ourselves.
9.14 and you did, because you **always** do what is right, and we
Joel 2.13 he is **always** ready to forgive and not punish.
Obad 5 When people gather grapes, they **always** leave a few.
Jon 4. 2 a loving and merciful God, **always** patient, always kind,
4. 2 and **always** ready to change your mind and
Hag 2. 5 out of Egypt, I promised that I would **always** be with you.
Zech 14. 7 There will **always** be daylight, even at night-time.
Mal 1. 2 The Lord says to his people, "I have **always** loved you."
Mt 1.19 Joseph was a man who **always** did what was right,
6.21 For your heart will **always** be where your riches are.
6.32 (These are the things the pagans are **always** concerned about.)
18. 7 Such things will **always** happen—but how terrible for the one
18.10 heaven, I tell you, are **always** in the presence of my Father
24.44 So then, you also must **always** be ready, because the Son
26.11 You will **always** have poor people with you,
26.11 but you will not **always** have me.
28.20 I will be with you **always,** to the end of the age."
Mk 10. 1 to him again, and he taught them, as he **always** did.
14. 7 You will **always** have poor people with you, and any time
14. 7 But you will not **always** have me.
Lk 12.29 don't be all upset, **always** concerned about what you will eat
12.30 the pagans of this world are **always** concerned about all these
12.34 For your heart will **always** be where your riches are.

Lk	15.31	father answered, 'you are **always** here with me, and everything
	18. 1	that they should **always** pray and never become discouraged.
	21.36	on the alert and pray **always** that you will have the strength
Jn	5.17	"My Father is **always** working, and I too must work."
	6.34	"Sir," they asked him, "give us this bread **always.**"
	8.29	not left me alone, because I **always** do what pleases him."
	11.42	I know that you **always** listen to me, but I say this
	12. 8	You will **always** have poor people with you,
	12. 8	but you will not **always** have me."
	13. 1	He had **always** loved those in the world who were his own,
	18.20	Jesus answered, "I have **always** spoken publicly to everyone;
	18.39	the custom you have, I **always** set free a prisoner for you
Acts	6.13	man," they said, "is **always** talking against our sacred Temple
	7.51	you too have **always** resisted the Holy Spirit!
	13.10	and you **always** keep trying to turn the Lord's
	14.17	But he has **always** given evidence of his existence by the
	24.16	so I do my best **always** to have a clear conscience
	26. 5	They have **always** known, if they are willing to testify,
Rom	1.13	visit you, but something has **always** kept me from doing so.
	14.19	So then, we must **always** aim at those things that bring
	15.20	My ambition has **always** been to proclaim the Good News
	16.13	and to his mother, who has **always** treated me like a son.
1 Cor	1. 4	I **always** give thanks to my God for you because of the
	11. 2	I praise you because you **always** remember me and follow the
	15.58	Keep busy **always** in your work for the Lord, since you know
2 Cor	2. 9	and whether you are **always** ready to obey my instructions.
	2.14	union with Christ we are **always** led by God as prisoners in
	4.11	Throughout our lives we are **always** in danger of death for
	5. 6	So we are **always** full of courage.
	6.10	although saddened, we are **always** glad;
	7. 3	that we are **always** together, whether we live or die.
	7.14	We have **always** spoken the truth to you, and in the same
	8.22	him many times and found him **always** very eager to help.
	9. 8	so that you will **always** have all you need for yourselves
	9.11	He will **always** make you rich enough to be generous at
	10.15	greater work among you, **always** within the limits that God has
Gal	3.10	"Whoever does not **always** obey everything that is written in
	4.18	is good—this is true **always,** and not merely when I am
Eph	4. 2	Be **always** humble, gentle, and patient.
	5.20	our Lord Jesus Christ, **always** give thanks for everything to God
	6.18	pray **always** for all God's people.
Phil	1. 7	You are **always** in my heart!
	1.28	**always** be courageous, and this will prove to them that they
	2. 3	towards one another, **always** considering others better than yourselves.
	2. 6	He **always** had the nature of God, but he did not think
	2.12	then, dear friends, as you **always** obeyed me when I was with
	2.13	because God is **always** at work in you to make
	4. 4	May you **always** be joyful in your union with the Lord.
	4. 6	God for what you need, **always** asking him with a thankful heart.
Col	1. 3	We **always** give thanks to God, the Father of our Lord Jesus
	1. 9	For this reason we have **always** prayed for you,
	1.10	live as the Lord wants and will **always** do what pleases him.
	3.20	to obey your parents **always,** for that is what pleases God.
	4. 6	Your speech should **always** be pleasant and interesting,
	4.12	He **always** prays fervently for you, asking God to make you
1 Thes	1. 2	We **always** thank God for you all
	1. 2	and **always** mention you in our prayers.
	2. 4	Instead, we **always** speak as God wants us to,
	2.13	And there is another reason why we **always** give thanks to God.
	2.16	brought to completion all the sins they have **always** committed.
	3. 6	has told us that you **always** think well of us and that
	4.17	And so we will **always** be with the Lord.
	5.16	Be joyful **always,** [17] pray at all times, [18] be thankful
2 Thes	1.11	That is why we **always** pray for you.
	2.17	and strengthen you to **always** do and say what is good.
2 Tim	1. 3	as I remember you **always** in my prayers night and day.
	3. 7	women who are **always** trying to learn but who can
Tit	1.12	"Cretans are **always** liars, wicked beasts, and lazy gluttons."
	2.10	must show that they are **always** good and faithful,
	3. 2	be peaceful and friendly, and **always** to show a gentle attitude
Heb	1.12	But you are **always** the same, and your life never ends."
	3.10	and said, 'They are **always** disloyal and refuse to obey
	7.25	he is able, now and **always,** to save those who come
	13.15	Let us, then, **always** offer praise to God as our sacrifice
1 Pet	2. 2	like new-born babies, **always** thirsty for the pure spiritual milk,
	2.11	bodily passions, which are **always** at war against the soul.
	4.19	completely to their Creator, who **always** keeps his promise.
2 Pet	1.12	And so I will **always** remind you of these matters,
1 Jn	2.24	then you will **always** live in union with the Son
3 Jn	3	are to the truth—just as you **always** live in the truth.
Jude	16	These people are **always** grumbling and blaming others;

AMALEK

Esau's grandson, and the desert tribe descended from him, with which Israel was often at war.

Gen	14. 7	all the land of the **Amalekites** and defeated the Amorites
	36.10	And by another wife, Timna, he had one more son, **Amalek.**
	36.16	Teman, Omar, Zepho, Kenaz, [16] Korah, Gatam, and **Amalek.**
Ex	17. 8	The **Amalekites** came and attacked the Israelites at Rephidim.
	17. 9	"Pick out some men to go and fight the **Amalekites** tomorrow.
	17.10	went out to fight the **Amalekites,** while Moses, Aaron, and Hur
	17.11	but when he put his arms down, the **Amalekites** started winning.
	17.13	In this way Joshua totally defeated the **Amalekites.**
	17.14	Tell Joshua that I will completely destroy the **Amalekites.**"
	17.16	The Lord will continue to fight against the **Amalekites** for ever!"
Num	13.29	**Amalekites** live in the southern part of the land;
	14.25	in whose valleys the **Amalekites** and the Canaanites now live.
	14.43	When you face the **Amalekites** and the Canaanites, you will die
	14.45	the **Amalekites** and the Canaanites who lived there attacked
Num	24.20	Then in his vision Balaam saw the **Amalekites** and uttered this
	24.20	"**Amalek** was the most powerful nation of all, But at the end
Deut	25.17	"Remember what the **Amalekites** did to you as you were coming
	25.19	sure to kill all the **Amalekites,** so that no one will
Judg	1.16	There they settled among the **Amalekites.**
	3.13	Eglon joined the Ammonites and the **Amalekites;**
	6. 3	Midianites would come with the **Amalekites** and the desert tribes
	6.33	Then all the Midianites, the **Amalekites,** and the desert tribes
	7.12	The Midianites, the **Amalekites,** and the desert tribesmen
	10.12	the **Amalekites,** and the Maonites oppressed you in
	12.15	in the territory of Ephraim in the hill-country of the **Amalekites.**
1 Sam	14.48	He fought heroically and defeated even the people of **Amalek.**
	15. 2	to punish the people of **Amalek**
	15. 3	Go and attack the **Amalekites** and completely destroy everything
	15. 5	went to the city of **Amalek** and waited in ambush in a
	15. 6	"Go away and leave the **Amalekites,** so that I won't kill you
	15. 7	Saul defeated the **Amalekites,** fighting all the way from Havilah
	15. 8	he captured King Agag of **Amalek** alive and killed all the people.
	15.15	Saul answered, "My men took them from the **Amalekites.**
	15.18	out with orders to destroy those wicked people of **Amalek.**
	15.20	to, brought back King Agag, and killed all the **Amalekites.**
	27. 8	people of Geshur, Girzi, and **Amalek,** who had been living in
	28.18	and did not completely destroy the **Amalekites** and all they had.
	30. 1	The **Amalekites** had raided southern Judah and attacked Ziklag.
	30.13	"I am an Egyptian, the slave of an **Amalekite,**" he
	30.18	rescued everyone and everything the **Amalekites** had taken,
	30.19	sons and daughters, and all the loot the **Amalekites** had taken.
2 Sam	1. 1	from his victory over the **Amalekites** and stayed in Ziklag
	1. 8	who I was, and I told him that I was an **Amalekite.**
	1.13	He answered, "I'm an **Amalekite,** but I live in your country."
	1.15	The man struck the **Amalekite** and mortally wounded him,
	1.16	and David said to the **Amalekite,** "You brought this on yourself.
	8.12	Edom, Moab, Ammon, Philistia, and **Amalek**—
1 Chr	1.36	Teman, Omar, Zephi, Gatam, Kenaz, Timna, and **Amalek.**
	4.43	There they killed the surviving **Amalekites,**
	18.11	the nations he conquered—Edom, Moab, Ammon, Philistia, and **Amalek.**
Ps	83. 7	the people of Gebal, Ammon, and **Amalek,** and of Philistia

AMASA (1)

Commander of Absalom's army.

2 Sam	17.25	(Absalom had put **Amasa** in command of the army in the
	17.25	**Amasa** was the son of Jether the Ishmaelite;
	19.13	David also told them to say to **Amasa,** "You are my relative.
	20. 4	The king said to **Amasa,** "Call the men of Judah together
	20. 5	**Amasa** went to call them, but he did not get back by
	20. 8	When they reached the large rock at Gibeon, **Amasa** met them.
	20. 9	Joab said to **Amasa,** "How are you, my friend?"
	20.10	**Amasa** was not on guard against the sword that Joab was
	20.11	Joab's men stood by **Amasa's** body and called out, "Everyone
	20.12	**Amasa's** body, covered with blood, was lying in the
1 Kgs	2. 5	Israel's armies, Abner son of Ner and **Amasa** son of Jether.
	2.32	army of Israel, and **Amasa,** commander of the army of Judah.
1 Chr	2.17	Jether, a descendant of Ishmael, and they had a son named **Amasa.**

AMATEUR

2 Cor	11. 6	I am an **amateur** in speaking, but certainly not in knowledge;

AMAZE

Gen	43.33	had been seated, they looked at one another in **amazement.**
	45. 7	to rescue you in this **amazing** way and to make sure that
Judg	20.40	looked behind them and were **amazed** to see the whole city
1 Kgs	9. 8	and everyone who passes by will be shocked and **amazed.**
	10. 5	It left her breathless and **amazed.**
2 Chr	7.21	passes by it will be **amazed** and will ask, 'Why did the
	9. 4	It left her breathless and **amazed.**
Neh	9.10	You worked **amazing** miracles against the king,
Job	37. 5	At God's command **amazing** things happen, wonderful things
	37.16	clouds float in the sky, the work of God's **amazing** skill?
	40.19	The most **amazing** of all my creatures!
Ps	46. 8	See what **amazing** things he has done on earth.
	48. 5	But when they saw it, they were **amazed;**
	106.22	What **amazing** things at the Red Sea!
Is	25. 1	You have done **amazing** things;
	52.15	and kings will be speechless with **amazement.**
	63. 5	I was **amazed** when I looked and saw that there was no
Jer	2.12	shake with horror, to be **amazed** and astonished,
	18.16	they will shake their heads in **amazement.**
	19. 8	city that everyone who passes by will be shocked and **amazed.**
	50.13	in ruins, and all who pass by will be shocked and **amazed.**
Dan	3.24	Suddenly Nebuchadnezzar leapt to his feet in **amazement.**
	10. 8	I was left there alone, watching this **amazing** vision.
	12. 6	will it be until these **amazing** events come to an end?"
Mt	7.28	these things, the crowd was **amazed** at the way he taught.
	8.27	Everyone was **amazed.**
	9.33	was driven out, the man started talking, and everyone was **amazed.**
	12.23	The crowds were all **amazed** at what Jesus had done.
	13.54	He taught in the synagogue, and those who heard him were **amazed.**
	15.31	The people were **amazed** as they saw the dumb speaking,
	19.25	When the disciples heard this, they were completely **amazed.**
	22.22	When they heard this, they were **amazed;**
	22.33	When the crowds heard this, they were **amazed** at his teaching.
Mk	1.22	people who heard him were **amazed** at the way he taught,
	1.27	The people were all so **amazed** that they started saying
	2.12	They were all completely **amazed** and praised God, saying,

Mk 5.20 And all who heard it were **amazed.**
5.42 When this happened, they were completely **amazed.**
6. 2 and when they heard him, they were all **amazed.**
6.51 The disciples were completely **amazed,** [52] because they had not
7.37 And all who heard were completely **amazed.**
10.26 disciples were completely **amazed** and asked one another, "Who,
11.18 of him, because the whole crowd was **amazed** at his teaching.
12.17 And they were **amazed** at Jesus.
15. 5 Again Jesus refused to say a word, and Pilate was **amazed.**
Lk 2.18 All who heard it were **amazed** at what the shepherds said.
2.33 child's father and mother were **amazed** at the things Simeon said
2.47 All who heard him were **amazed** at his intelligent answers.
4.32 They were all **amazed** at the way he taught, because he
4.36 people were all **amazed** and said to one another, "What kind
5. 9 others with him were all **amazed** at the large number of fish
5.26 They were all completely **amazed!**
8.25 But they were **amazed** and afraid, and said to one another,
9.43 All the people were **amazed** at the mighty power of God.
11.14 The crowds were **amazed,** [15] but some of the people said,
20.26 out in anything, so they kept quiet, **amazed** at his answer.
24.12 Then he went back home **amazed** at what had happened.
Jn 5.20 greater things to do than this, and you will all be **amazed.**
Acts 2. 7 In **amazement** and wonder they exclaimed, "These people who are
2.12 **Amazed** and confused, they kept asking each other, "What does
3.10 were all surprised and **amazed** at what had happened to him.
3.11 as it was called, the people were **amazed** and ran to them.
4.13 members of the Council were **amazed** to see how bold Peter and
7.31 Moses was **amazed** by what he saw, and went near the bush
9.21 All who heard him were **amazed** and asked, "Isn't he the
10.45 from Joppa with Peter were **amazed** that God had poured out
12.16 opened the door, and when they saw him, they were **amazed.**
13.12 for he was greatly **amazed** at the teaching about the Lord.
Rev 13. 3 The whole earth was **amazed** and followed the beast.
15. 1 Then I saw in the sky another mysterious sight, great and **amazing.**
17. 6 When I saw her, I was completely **amazed.**
17. 7 "Why are you **amazed?**"
17. 8 the living, will all be **amazed** as they look at the beast.

AMAZIAH (1)

King of Judah.

2 Kgs 12.20 in David's City, and his son **Amaziah** succeeded him as king.
13.12 in the war against King **Amaziah** of Judah, is recorded in The
14. 1 Jehoahaz as king of Israel, **Amaziah** son of Joash became king
14. 5 As soon as **Amaziah** was firmly in power, he executed the
14. 7 **Amaziah** killed ten thousand Edomite soldiers in Salt Valley;
14. 8 Then **Amaziah** sent messengers to King Jehoash of Israel,
14.10 Now **Amaziah,** you have defeated the Edomites,
14.11 But **Amaziah** refused to listen, so King Jehoash marched out
14.12 **Amaziah's** army was defeated, and all his soldiers fled
14.13 Jehoash took **Amaziah** prisoner, advanced on Jerusalem,
14.15 in the war against King **Amaziah** of Judah, is recorded in The
14.17 King **Amaziah** of Judah lived fifteen years after
14.18 Everything else that **Amaziah** did is recorded in The History
14.19 plot in Jerusalem to assassinate **Amaziah,** so he fled to the
14.23 year of the reign of **Amaziah** son of Joash as king of
15. 1 of Israel, Uzziah son of **Amaziah** became king of Judah [2] at
1 Chr 3.12 Jehoram, Ahaziah, Joash, [12] **Amaziah,** Uzziah, Jotham,
2 Chr 24.27 His son **Amaziah** succeeded him as king.
25. 1 **Amaziah** became king at the age of twenty-five, and he
25. 5 King **Amaziah** organized all the men of the tribes of Judah
25. 9 **Amaziah** asked the prophet, "But what about all that silver
25.10 So **Amaziah** sent the hired troops away and told them to
25.11 **Amaziah** summoned up his courage and led his army to the
25.13 the Israelite soldiers that **Amaziah** had not allowed to go
25.14 When **Amaziah** returned from defeating the Edomites,
25.15 This made the Lord angry, so he sent a prophet to **Amaziah.**
25.16 "Since when," **Amaziah** interrupted, "have we made you adviser
25.17 King **Amaziah** of Judah and his advisers plotted against Israel.
25.18 Jehoash sent this answer to **Amaziah:**
25.19 Now **Amaziah,** you boast that you have defeated the Edomites,
25.20 But **Amaziah** refused to listen.
25.20 It was God's will for **Amaziah** to be defeated, because he had
25.21 Jehoash of Israel went into battle against King **Amaziah** of Judah.
25.23 Jehoash captured **Amaziah** and took him to Jerusalem.
25.25 King **Amaziah** of Judah outlived King Jehoash of Israel
25.26 All the other things that **Amaziah** did from the beginning
26. 1 the people of Judah chose **Amaziah's** sixteen-year-old son Uzziah
26. 2 was after the death of **Amaziah** that Uzziah recaptured Elath

AMBASSADOR

1 Kgs 5. 1 his father David as king he sent **ambassadors** to him.
2 Chr 32.31 and even when the Babylonian **ambassadors** came to inquire
Ps 68.31 **Ambassadors** will come from Egypt;
Is 18. 2 From that land **ambassadors** come down the Nile in boats
30. 4 Although their **ambassadors** have already arrived
30. 6 "The **ambassadors** travel through dangerous country,
33. 7 The **ambassadors** who tried to bring about peace are crying
Jer 27. 3 through their **ambassadors** who had come to Jerusalem
Eph 6.20 this gospel I am an **ambassador,** though now I am in prison.
Phlm 9 though I am Paul, the **ambassador** of Christ Jesus, and at

AMBITION

1 Kgs 1. 5 and he was **ambitious** to be king.
Rom 15.20 My **ambition** has always been to proclaim the Good News
Gal 5.20 they become jealous, angry, and **ambitious.**
Phil 1.17 not proclaim Christ sincerely, but from a spirit of selfish **ambition;**
2. 3 Don't do anything from selfish **ambition** or from a cheap desire

AMBUSH

Judg 9.25 put men in **ambush** against Abimelech on the mountain-tops,
1 Sam 15. 5 the city of Amalek and waited in **ambush** in a dry river-bed.
2 Kgs 6. 9 because the Syrians were waiting in **ambush** there.
2 Chr 13.13 some of his troops to **ambush** the Judaean army from the rear,
Ezra 8.31 protected us from enemy attacks and from **ambush** as we travelled.
Jer 51.12 Place men in **ambush!"**
Hos 6. 9 like a gang of robbers who wait in **ambush** for a man.

AMEN

A Hebrew word which means "it is so" or "may it be so". It can also be translated "certainly", "truly", or "surely". In Revelation 3.14 it is used as a name for Christ.

Deut 27.15 Deut 27.16 Deut 27.17 Deut 27.18 Deut 27.19 Deut 27.20 Deut 27.21 Deut 27.22 Deut 27.23 Deut 27.24 Deut 27.25 Deut 27.26 1 Chr 16.36 Neh 5.13 Neh 8.6 Neh 8.6 Ps 41.13 Ps 41.13 Ps 72.19 Ps 72.19 Ps 89.52 Ps 89.52 Ps 106.48 Rom 1.25 Rom 9.5 Rom 11.36 Rom 15.33 Rom 16.27 1 Cor 14.16 2 Cor 1.20 Gal 1.5 Gal 6.18 Eph 3.21 Phil 4.20 1 Tim 1.17 1 Tim 6.16 2 Tim 4.18 Heb 13.20 1 Pet 4.11 1 Pet 5.11 2 Pet 3.18 Jude 25 Rev 1.6 Rev 3.14 Rev 5.14 Rev 7.12 Rev 7.12 Rev 19.4

AMETHYST

A semi-precious stone, usually purple or violet in colour.

Ex 28.19 in the third row, a turquoise, an agate, and an **amethyst;**
39.12 in the third row, a turquoise, an agate, and an **amethyst;**
Rev 21.20 tenth chalcedony, the eleventh turquoise, the twelfth **amethyst.**

AMMON

Country of the R. Jordan, with which Israel was often at war.

Gen 19.38 He was the ancestor of the present-day **Ammonites.**
Num 21.24 to the **Ammonites,** because the Ammonite border was strongly
Deut 2.19 be near the land of the **Ammonites,** the descendants of Lot.
2.20 the **Ammonites** called them Zamzummim.
2.21 destroyed them, so that the **Ammonites** took over their land
2.37 near the territory of the **Ammonites** or to the banks of the
3.11 It can still be seen in the **Ammonite** city of Rabbah.)
3.16 the River Jabbok, part of which formed the **Ammonite** border.
23. 3 "No **Ammonite** or Moabite—or any of their descendants,
Josh 12. 2 valley, as far as the River Jabbok, the border of **Ammon;**
13.10 far as the border of **Ammon** and included all the cities that
13.25 Gilead, half the land of **Ammon** as far as Aroer, which is
Judg 3.13 Eglon joined the **Ammonites** and the Amalekites;
10. 6 of Syria, of Sidon, of Moab, of **Ammon,** and of Philistia.
10. 7 and let the Philistines and the **Ammonites** conquer them.
10. 9 The **Ammonites** even crossed the Jordan to fight the tribes
10.11 "The Egyptians, the Amorites, the **Ammonites,** the Philistines,
10.17 Then the **Ammonite** army prepared for battle and made camp
10.18 "Who will lead the fight against the **Ammonites?**
11. 4 some time later that the **Ammonites** went to war against Israel.
11. 6 "Come and lead us, so that we can fight the **Ammonites."**
11. 8 with us and fight the **Ammonites** and lead all the people of
11. 9 home to fight the **Ammonites** and the Lord gives me victory,
11.12 messengers to the king of **Ammon** to say, "What is your
11.13 The king of **Ammon** answered Jephthah's messengers,
11.14 Jephthah sent messengers back to the king of **Ammon**
11.15 Israel took away the land of Moab or the land of **Ammon.**
11.27 He will decide today between the Israelites and the **Ammonites."**
11.28 But the king of **Ammon** paid no attention to this message
11.29 Manasseh and returned to Mizpah in Gilead and went on to **Ammon.**
11.30 give me victory over the **Ammonites,** [31] I will burn
11.32 river to fight the **Ammonites,** and the Lord gave him victory.
11.33 There was a great slaughter, and the **Ammonites** were defeated
11.36 Lord has given you revenge on your enemies, the **Ammonites."**
12. 1 the border to fight the **Ammonites** without calling us to go
12. 2 "My people and I had a serious quarrel with the **Ammonites.**
1 Sam 11. 1 month later King Nahash of **Ammon** led his army against the
11.11 they rushed into the enemy camp and attacked the **Ammonites.**
12.12 saw that King Nahash of **Ammon** was about to attack you, you
14.47 the people of Moab, of **Ammon,** and of Edom, the kings of
2 Sam 8.12 Edom, Moab, **Ammon,** Philistia, and Amalek—
10. 1 time later King Nahash of **Ammon** died, and his son Hanun
10. 2 When they arrived in **Ammon,** [3] the Ammonite leaders said
10. 6 The **Ammonites** realized that they had made David their enemy,
10. 8 The **Ammonites** marched out and took up their position
10.10 Abishai, who put them in position facing the **Ammonites.**
10.11 help me, and if the **Ammonites** are defeating you, I will go
10.14 When the **Ammonites** saw the Syrians running away, they fled
10.14 Joab turned back from fighting the **Ammonites** and went back
10.19 And the Syrians were afraid to help the **Ammonites** any more.
11. 1 they defeated the **Ammonites** and besieged the city of Rabbah.
12. 9 you let the **Ammonites** kill him, and then you took his wife!
12.26 Rabbah, the capital city of **Ammon,** and was about to capture it.
12.30 of the idol of the **Ammonite** god Molech David took a gold
12.31 the same to the people of all the other towns of **Ammon.**
17.27 the city of Rabbah in **Ammon,** and by Machir son of Ammiel,
23.24 Bani from Gad Zelek from **Ammon** Naharai from Beeroth,
1 Kgs 11. 1 he married Hittite women and women from Moab, **Ammon,** Edom,
11. 5 Astarte the goddess of Sidon, and Molech the disgusting god of **Ammon.**

1 Kgs 11. 7 Moab, and a place to worship Molech, the disgusting god of **Ammon.**
11.33 and Molech, the god of **Ammon.**
14.21 Rehoboam's mother was Naamah from **Ammon.**
2 Kgs 23.13 Sidon, Chemosh the god of Moab, and Molech the god of **Ammon.**
24. 2 Babylonians, Syrians, Moabites, and **Ammonites** against Jehoiakim
1 Chr 11.26 son of Hagri Zelek from **Ammon** Naharai, Joab's armour-bearer,
18.11 nations he conquered—Edom, Moab, **Ammon,** Philistia, and Amalek.
19. 1 later King Nahash of **Ammon** died, and his son Hanun became
19. 2 When they arrived in **Ammon** and called on King Hanun,
19. 3 called on King Hanun, [3]the **Ammonite** leaders said to the king,
19. 6 King Hanun and the **Ammonites** realized that they had made David
19. 7 The **Ammonites** too came out from all their cities and got
19. 9 The **Ammonites** marched out and took up their position
19.11 his brother Abishai, who put them in position facing the **Ammonites.**
19.12 help me, and if the **Ammonites** are defeating you, I will go
19.15 When the **Ammonites** saw the Syrians running away, they fled
19.19 The Syrians were never again willing to help the **Ammonites.**
20. 1 war, Joab led out the army and invaded the land of **Ammon;**
20. 2 The **Ammonite** idol Molech had a gold crown
20. 3 the same to the people of all the other towns of **Ammon.**
2 Chr 12.13 Rehoboam's mother was Naamah, from the land of **Ammon.**
20. 1 the armies of Moab and **Ammon,** together with their allies,
20.10 "Now the people of **Ammon,** Moab, and Edom have attacked us.
20.23 The **Ammonites** and the Moabites attacked the Edomite army
24.26 Zabad, the son of an **Ammonite** woman named Shimeath,
26. 8 The **Ammonites** paid tribute to Uzziah, and he became so powerful
27. 5 against the king of **Ammon** and his army and defeated them.
27. 5 Then he forced the **Ammonites** to pay him the following tribute
Ezra 9. 1 in the neighbouring countries of **Ammon,** Moab, and Egypt
Neh 2.10 official in the province of **Ammon,** heard that someone had come
4. 7 and the people of Arabia, **Ammon,** and Ashdod heard that we
13. 1 passage that said that no **Ammonite** or Moabite was ever to be
13. 2 was because the people of **Ammon** and Moab did not give food
13.23 of the Jewish men had married women from Ashdod, **Ammon,** and
Ps 83. 7 the people of Gebal, **Ammon,** and Amalek, and of Philistia
83. 8 ally of the **Ammonites** and Moabites, the descendants of Lot.
Is 11.14 of Edom and Moab, and the people of **Ammon** will obey them.
Jer 9.25 people of Egypt, Judah, Edom, **Ammon,** Moab, and the desert people,
25.19 all the people of Edom, Moab, and **Ammon;**
27. 3 the kings of Edom, Moab, **Ammon,** Tyre, and Sidon
40.11 Israelites who were in Moab, **Ammon,** Edom, and other countries,
40.14 that King Baalis of **Ammon** has sent Ishmael to murder you?"
41.10 and started off in the direction of the territory of **Ammon.**
41.15 men got away from Johanan and escaped to the land of **Ammon.**
49. 1 This is what the Lord said about **Ammon:**
49. 6 "But later on I will make **Ammon** prosperous again.
Ezek 21.20 king the way to the **Ammonite** city of Rabbah, and the other
21.28 saying to the **Ammonites,** who are insulting Israel.
25. 2 "Mortal man," he said, "denounce the country of **Ammon.**
25. 5 and the whole country of **Ammon** into a place to keep sheep,
25.10 conquer Moab, together with **Ammon,** so that Moab will no longer
Dan 11.41 of Edom, Moab, and what is left of **Ammon** will escape.
Amos 1.13 Lord says, "The people of **Ammon** have sinned again and again,
Zeph 2. 8 the people of Moab and **Ammon** insulting and taunting my people,
2. 9 I swear that Moab and **Ammon** are going to be destroyed like
2.10 the people of Moab and **Ammon** will be punished for their

AMNON (1)

David's eldest son.

2 Sam 3. 2 **Amnon,** whose mother was Ahinoam, from Jezreel;
13. 1 **Amnon,** another of David's sons, fell in love with her.
13. 4 Jonadab said to **Amnon,** "You are the king's son, yet day
13. 6 So **Amnon** pretended that he was ill and went to bed.
13. 6 went to see him, and **Amnon** said to him, "Please let Tamar
13. 7 "Go to **Amnon's** house and prepare some food for him."
13.15 Then **Amnon** was filled with a deep hatred for her;
13.16 But **Amnon** would not listen to her;
13.20 Absalom saw her, he asked, "Has **Amnon** molested you?
13.22 Absalom hated **Amnon** so much for having raped his sister Tamar
13.26 "Well, then, will you at least let my brother **Amnon** come?"
13.27 insisting until David finally let **Amnon** and all his other
13.28 "Notice when **Amnon** has had too much to drink, and then when
13.29 So the servants followed Absalom's instructions and killed **Amnon.**
13.32 Only **Amnon** is dead.
13.32 to do this from the time that **Amnon** raped his sister Tamar.
13.33 only **Amnon** was killed."
13.37 David mourned a long time for his son **Amnon;**
13.39 but when he got over **Amnon's** death, he was filled with
1 Chr 3. 1 **Amnon,** whose mother was Ahinoam from Jezreel

AMON (1)

King of Judah.

2 Kgs 21.18 the garden of Uzza, and his son **Amon** succeeded him as king.
21.19 **Amon** was twenty-two years old when he became king of Judah,
21.23 **Amon's** officials plotted against him and assassinated him
21.24 The people of Judah killed **Amon's** assassins
21.25 Everything else that **Amon** did is recorded in The History
21.26 **Amon** was buried in the tomb in the garden of Uzza, and
1 Chr 3.14 Ahaz, Hezekiah, Manasseh, [14]**Amon,**
2 Chr 33.20 at the palace, and his son **Amon** succeeded him as king.
33.21 **Amon** was twenty-two years old when he became king of Judah,
33.24 **Amon's** officials plotted against him and assassinated him
2 Chr 33.25 The people of Judah killed **Amon's** assassins
Jer 1. 2 year that Josiah son of **Amon** was king of Judah, [3]and he
25. 3 year that Josiah son of **Amon** was king of Judah until this
Zeph 1. 1 during the time that Josiah son of **Amon** was king of Judah.
Mt 1. 6 Manasseh, **Amon,** Josiah, and Jehoiachin and his brothers.

AMORITES

Inhabitants of Canaan before its conquest by Israel.

Gen 10.16 ancestor of the Jebusites, the **Amorites,** the Girgashites,
14. 7 and defeated the **Amorites** who lived in Hazazon Tamar.
14.13 living near the sacred trees belonging to Mamre the **Amorite.**
15.16 will not drive out the **Amorites** until they become so wicked
15.21 the Perizzites, the Rephaim, [21]the **Amorites,** the Canaanites,
48.22 which I took from the **Amorites** with my sword and my bow."
Ex 3. 8 the Canaanites, the Hittites, the **Amorites,** the Perizzites,
3.17 the Canaanites, the Hittites, the **Amorites,** the Perizzites,
13. 5 of the Canaanites, the Hittites, the **Amorites,** the Hivites,
23.23 into the land of the **Amorites,** the Hittites, the Perizzites,
33. 2 drive out the Canaanites, the **Amorites,** the Hittites,
34.11 I will drive out the **Amorites,** the Canaanites, the Hittites,
Num 13.29 Hittites, Jebusites, and **Amorites** live in the hill-country;
21.13 River Arnon, in the wilderness which extends into **Amorite** territory.
21.13 (The Arnon was the border between the Moabites and the **Amorites.)**
21.21 of Israel sent messengers to the **Amorite** king Sihon to say:
21.25 of Israel captured all the **Amorite** cities, including Heshbon
21.26 the capital city of the **Amorite** king Sihon, who had fought
21.29 And the women became captives of the **Amorite** king.
21.31 in the territory of the **Amorites,** [32]and Moses sent men to
21.32 and drove out the **Amorites** living there.
21.34 you did to Sihon, the **Amorite** king who ruled at Heshbon."
22. 2 Israelites had done to the **Amorites**
32.33 of King Sihon of the **Amorites** and King Og of Bashan,
32.39 Gilead, occupied it, and drove out the **Amorites** who were there.
Deut 1. 4 defeated King Sihon of the **Amorites,** who ruled in the town
1. 7 hill-country of the **Amorites** and to all the surrounding regions
1.19 desert on the way to the hill-country of the **Amorites.**
1.20 to the hill-country of the **Amorites,** which the Lord our God,
1.27 hand us over to these **Amorites,** so that they could kill us.
1.44 Then the **Amorites** who lived in those hills came out
2.24 in your power Sihon, the **Amorite** king of Heshbon, along with
3. 2 as you did to Sihon the **Amorite** king who ruled in Heshbon.'
3. 8 we took from those two **Amorite** kings the land east of the
3. 9 Hermon is called Sirion by the Sidonians, and Senir by the **Amorites.)**
4.45 to King Sihon of the **Amorites,** who had ruled in the town
4.47 Og of Bashan, the other **Amorite** king who lived east of the
7. 1 the Hittites, the Girgashites, the **Amorites,** the Canaanites,
20.17 the Hittites, the **Amorites,** the Canaanites, the Perizzites,
31. 4 defeated Sihon and Og, kings of the **Amorites,**
Josh 2.10 Sihon and Og, the two **Amorite** kings east of the Jordan.
3.10 the Hivites, the Perizzites, the Girgashites, the **Amorites,**
5. 1 All the **Amorite** kings west of the Jordan and all the
7. 7 To hand us over to the **Amorites?**
9. 1 kings of the Hittites, the **Amorites,** the Canaanites,
9.10 what he did to the two **Amorite** kings east of the Jordan:
10. 5 These five **Amorite** kings, the kings of Jerusalem, Hebron,
10. 6 All the **Amorite** kings in the hill-country have joined forces
10. 9 Gilgal to Gibeon, and they made a surprise attack on the **Amorites.**
10.10 The Lord made the **Amorites** panic at the sight of Israel's army.
10.11 While the **Amorites** were running down the pass
10.12 Israel victory over the **Amorites,** Joshua spoke to the Lord.
10.16 The five **Amorite** kings, however, had escaped and were hiding
11. 3 of the Jordan, to the **Amorites,** the Hittites, the Perizzites,
12. 2 One was Sihon, the **Amorite** king who ruled at Heshbon.
12. 8 home of the Hittites, the **Amorites,** the Canaanites,
13. 4 as far as Aphek, at the **Amorite** border;
13.10 had been ruled by the **Amorite** king Sihon, who had ruled at
13.21 the whole kingdom of the **Amorite** king Sihon, who had ruled
24. 8 to the land of the **Amorites,** who lived on the east side
24.11 as did the **Amorites,** the Perizzites, the Canaanites,
24.12 them into panic in order to drive out the two **Amorite** kings.
24.15 or the gods of the **Amorites,** in whose land you are now
24.18 land, the Lord drove out all the **Amorites** who lived here.
Judg 1.34 The **Amorites** forced the people of the tribe of Dan into
1.35 The **Amorites** continued to live at Aijalon, Shaalbim,
3. 5 the Canaanites, the Hittites, the **Amorites,** the Perizzites,
6.10 worship the gods of the **Amorites,** whose land you are now
10. 8 Israelites who lived in **Amorite** country east of the River Jordan
10.11 "The Egyptians, the **Amorites,** the Ammonites, the Philistines,
11.19 sent messengers to Sihon, the **Amorite** king of Heshbon, and asked
11.21 all the territory of the **Amorites** who lived in that country.
11.22 They occupied all the **Amorite** territory from the Arnon
11.23 who drove out the **Amorites** for his people, the Israelites.
2 Sam 21. 2 a small group of **Amorites** whom the Israelites had promised to
1 Kgs 4.19 by King Sihon of the **Amorites** and King Og of Bashan Besides
9.20 These included **Amorites,** Hittites, Perizzites, Hivites,
21.26 by worshipping idols, as the **Amorites** had done,
1 Chr 1.14 ancestor of the Jebusites, the **Amorites,** Girgashites,
2 Chr 8. 7 These included Hittites, **Amorites,** Perizzites, Hivites,
Ezra 9. 1 from the Canaanites, Hittites, Perizzites, Jebusites, and **Amorites.**
Neh 9. 8 of the Hittites and the **Amorites,** the land of the Perizzites,
Ps 135.11 Sihon, king of the **Amorites,** Og, king of Bashan, and all
136.19 Sihon, king of the **Amorites;**
Is 17. 9 that the Hivites and the **Amorites** abandoned as they fled
Ezek 16. 3 Your father was an **Amorite,** and your mother was a Hittite.
16.45 your sister cities had a Hittite mother and an **Amorite** father.

Amos 2. 9 that I totally destroyed the **Amorites,** men who were as tall
2.10 and gave you the land of the **Amorites** to be your own.

AMOUNT

Gen 23.16 agreed and weighed out the **amount** that Ephron had mentioned
Ex 12. 4 number of people and the **amount** that each person can eat.
21.10 his first wife the same **amount** of food and clothing and the
21.22 is to be fined whatever **amount** the woman's husband demands,
21.30 fine to save his life, he must pay the full **amount** required.
29.41 offer with it the same **amounts** of flour, olive-oil, and wine
30.13 census must pay the required **amount** of money,
30.14 man twenty years old or older, is to pay me this **amount.**
30.15 poor man less, when they pay this **amount** for their lives.
38.21 is a list of the **amounts** of the metals used in the
38.26 This **amount** equalled the total paid by all persons enrolled
38.26 each one paying the required **amount,** weighed
38.29 was dedicated to the Lord **amounted** to 2,425 kilogrammes.
Lev 6.20 kilogramme of flour (the same **amount** as the daily grain-offering),
27.16 be fixed according to the **amount** of seed it takes to sow
Deut 18. 8 is to receive the same **amount** of food as the other priests,
1 Sam 30.16 because of the enormous **amount** of loot they had captured
2 Sam 3.22 from a raid, bringing a large **amount** of loot with them.
12.30 He also took a large **amount** of loot from the city [31] and
1 Kgs 10. 2 loaded with spices, jewels, and a large **amount** of gold.
10.10 of gold and a very large **amount** of spices and jewels.
10.10 The **amount** of spices she gave him was by far the greatest
10.11 from there a large **amount** of juniper wood and jewels.
2 Kgs 12.10 Whenever there was a large **amount** of money in the box,
12.11 After recording the exact **amount,** they would hand the silver over
22. 4 get a report on the **amount** of money that the priests on
23.35 in order to raise the **amount** needed to pay the tribute
1 Chr 20. 2 He also took a large **amount** of loot from the city.
22. 3 He supplied a large **amount** of iron for making nails and
22. 5 So David got large **amounts** of the materials ready before he died.
2 Chr 9. 1 loaded with spices, jewels, and a large **amount** of gold.
9. 9 of gold and a very large **amount** of spices and jewels.
14.13 Lord and his army, and the army took large **amounts** of loot.
14.14 The army plundered all those cities and captured large **amounts**
17.11 Philistines brought Jehoshaphat a large **amount** of silver
17.13 cities, [13] where supplies were stored in huge **amounts.**
21. 3 Their father gave them large **amounts** of gold, silver,
24.23 leaders, and took large **amounts** of loot back to Damascus.
28. 8 them back to Samaria, along with large **amounts** of loot.
Prov 6.35 no **amount** of gifts will satisfy his anger.
Jer 40.12 and there they gathered in large **amounts** of wine and fruit.
48.30 Their boasts **amount** to nothing, and the things they do will
Ezek 4.11 will also have a limited **amount** of water to drink, two cups
Joel 2.23 He has given you the right **amount** of autumn rain;
Mal 3.10 Bring the full **amount** of your tithes to the Temple, so
Mt 18.32 'I forgave you the whole **amount** you owed me, just because
18.34 to be punished until he should pay back the whole **amount."**
25.21 been faithful in managing small **amounts,**
25.21 so I will put you in charge of large **amounts.**
25.23 been faithful in managing small **amounts,**
25.23 so I will put you in charge of large **amounts.**
26. 9 been sold for a large **amount** and the money given to the
27. 9 thirty silver coins, the **amount** the people of Israel had agreed
Lk 6.34 Even sinners lend to sinners, to get back the same **amount!**
Acts 5. 8 was this the full **amount** you and your husband received
5. 8 "Yes," she answered, "the full **amount."**
17. 9 the others pay the required **amount** of money to be released,
22.28 said, "I became one by paying a large **amount** of money."
Rom 12. 3 yourself according to the **amount** of faith that God has given
1 Cor 10.19 idol or the food offered to it really **amounts** to anything?

AMUSE

Job 41. 5 like a pet bird, like something to **amuse** your servant-girls?

ANAKIM

Race of giants descended from Anak, who lived in Canaan before its conquest by Israel.

Num 13.22 Talmai, the descendants of a race of giants called the **Anakim,**
13.33 and we even saw giants there, the descendants of **Anak.**
Deut 2.10 They were as tall as the **Anakim,** another race of giants.
2.11 Like the **Anakim** they were also known as Rephaim;
2.21 They were as tall as the **Anakim.**
Josh 11.21 race of giants called the **Anakim** who lived in the hill-country—
11.22 None of the **Anakim** were left in the land of Israel;
14.12 giants called the **Anakim** were there in large walled cities.
14.15 (Arba had been the greatest of the **Anakim.)**
15.13 He received Hebron, the city belonging to Arba, father of **Anak.**
15.14 Caleb drove the descendants of **Anak** out of the city—the
21.11 city of Arba (Arba was **Anak's** father), now called Hebron, in
Judg 1.20 drove out of the city the three clans descended from **Anak.**

ANANIAS (1)

Early Christian who kept part of the money obtained by selling his property.

Acts 5. 1 there was a man named **Ananias,** who with his wife Sapphira
5. 3 said to him, **"Ananias,** why did you let Satan take control
5. 5 As soon as **Ananias** heard this, he fell down dead;

ANANIAS (2)

Christian in Damascus who supported Paul at the time of his conversion.

Acts 9.10 There was a Christian in Damascus named **Ananias.**
9.10 He had a vision, in which the Lord said to him, **"Ananias!"**
9.12 has seen a man named **Ananias** come in and place his hands
9.13 **Ananias** answered, "Lord, many people have told me about this
9.17 So **Ananias** went, entered the house where Saul was, and placed
22.12 city was a man named **Ananias,** a religious man who obeyed our

ANANIAS (3)

High Priest.

Acts 23. 2 The High Priest **Ananias** ordered those who were standing close
24. 1 later the High Priest **Ananias** went to Caesarea with some elders

AV **ANATHEMA** see **CURSE**

ANCESTOR

Gen 4.20 to Jabal, who was the **ancestor** of those who raise livestock
4.21 His brother was Jubal, the **ancestor** of all musicians
9.19 sons of Noah were the **ancestors** of all the people on earth.
10. 2 Meshech, and Tiras—were the **ancestors** of the peoples
10. 5 they were the **ancestors** of the people who live along the
10. 6 Libya and Canaan—were the **ancestors** of the peoples who bear
10.15 eldest, and Heth—were the **ancestors** of the peoples who bear
10.16 Canaan was also the **ancestor** of the Jebusites, the Amorites,
10.21 brother of Japheth, was the **ancestor** of all the Hebrews.
10.22 Lud, and Aram—were the **ancestors** of the peoples who bear
17. 4 I promise that you will be the **ancestor** of many nations.
17. 5 Abraham, because I am making you the **ancestor** of many nations.
19.37 He was the **ancestor** of the present-day Moabites.
19.38 He was the **ancestor** of the present-day Ammonites.
25.16 They were the **ancestors** of twelve tribes, and their names were
35.11 descended from you, and you will be the **ancestor** of kings.
36. 9 These are the descendants of Esau, the **ancestor** of the Edomites.
36.15 Esau's first son Eliphaz was the **ancestor** of the following tribes:
36.17 Esau's son Reuel was the **ancestor** of the following tribes:
36.20 traced their **ancestry** to the following descendants of Seir,
36.22 Lotan was the **ancestor** of the clans of Hori and Heman.
36.23 Shobal was the **ancestor** of the clans of Alvan, Manahath, Ebal,
36.25 of Dishon, who was the **ancestor** of the clans of Hemdan,
36.27 Ezer was the **ancestor** of the clans of Bilhan, Zaavan,
36.28 Dishan was the **ancestor** of the clans of Uz and Aran.
36.40 Esau was the **ancestor** of the following Edomite tribes:
46.34 care of livestock all your lives, just as your **ancestors** did.
47. 3 "We are shepherds, sir, just as our **ancestors** were,"
47. 9 unlike the long years of my **ancestors** in their wanderings."
48.21 you and will take you back to the land of your **ancestors.**
Ex 3. 6 am the God of your **ancestors,** the God of Abraham, Isaac, and
3.13 them, 'The God of your **ancestors** sent me to you,' they will
3.15 Lord, the God of their **ancestors,** the God of Abraham, Isaac,
3.16 Lord, the God of their **ancestors,** the God of Abraham, Isaac,
4. 5 Lord, the God of their **ancestors,** the God of Abraham, Isaac,
6.14 they were the **ancestors** of the clans that bear their names.
6.15 they were the **ancestors** of the clans that bear their names.
6.16 they were the **ancestors** of the clans that bear their names.
6.24 were the **ancestors** of the divisions of the clan of Korah.
10. 6 They will be worse than anything your **ancestors** ever saw.' "
13. 5 The Lord solemnly promised your **ancestors** to give you the land
13.11 which he solemnly promised to you and your **ancestors.**
Lev 25.41 return to his family and to the property of his **ancestors.**
26.39 away because of your own sin and the sin of your **ancestors.**
26.40 and the sins of their **ancestors,** who resisted me and rebelled
26.45 that I made with their **ancestors** when I showed all the
Num 3.17 and Merari, who were the **ancestors** of the clans that bear
3.17 They were the **ancestors** of the families that bear their names.
11.12 all the way to the land you promised to their **ancestors?**
14.23 will never enter the land which I promised to their **ancestors.**
20.15 how our **ancestors** went to Egypt, where we lived
20.15 The Egyptians ill-treated our **ancestors** and us,
26.29 and the following clans traced their **ancestry** to Gilead:
36. 8 inherit the property of his **ancestors,**
Deut 1. 8 promised to give to your **ancestors,** Abraham, Isaac, and Jacob,
1.11 the God of your **ancestors,** make you increase a thousand times
1.20 the Lord our God, the God of our **ancestors,** is giving us.
1.35 the fertile land that I promised to give your **ancestors.**
4. 1 land which the Lord, the God of your **ancestors,** is giving
4.31 not forget the covenant that he himself made with your **ancestors.**
4.37 Because he loved your **ancestors,** he chose you,
6. 3 land, just as the Lord, the God of our **ancestors,** has
6.10 Lord your God promised your **ancestors,** Abraham, Isaac, and Jacob,
6.18 that the Lord promised your **ancestors,** [19] and you will drive out
6.23 us this land, as he had promised our **ancestors** he would.
7. 8 wanted to keep the promise that he made to your **ancestors.**
7.12 show you his constant love, as he promised your **ancestors.**
7.13 land that he promised your **ancestors** he would give to you.
8. 1 and occupy the land which the Lord promised to your **ancestors.**
8. 3 food that you and your **ancestors** had never eaten before.
8.16 you manna to eat, food that your **ancestors** had never eaten.
8.18 faithful today to the covenant that he made with your **ancestors.**
9. 5 promise that he made to your **ancestors,** Abraham, Isaac, and Jacob.
10.11 of the land that he had promised to give to your **ancestors.**
10.15 the Lord's love for your **ancestors** was so strong that he
10.22 When your **ancestors** went to Egypt, there were only seventy
11. 9 the Lord promised to give your **ancestors** and their descendants.

Deut 11.21 that the Lord your God promised to give to your **ancestors.**
12. 1 land that the Lord, the God of your **ancestors,** is giving
13. 6 gods that you and your **ancestors** have never worshipped.
13.17 as he promised your **ancestors,** [18]if you obey all his commands
19. 8 territory, as he told your **ancestors** he would, and gives you
26. 3 the land that he promised our **ancestors** to give us.'
26. 5 'My **ancestor** was a wandering Aramean, who took his family to
26. 7 cried out for help to the Lord, the God of our **ancestors.**
26.15 that you have given us, as you promised our **ancestors.'**
27. 3 Lord, the God of your **ancestors,** promised you, [4]and you are
28.11 in the land that he promised your **ancestors** to give you.
28.36 where neither you nor your **ancestors** ever lived before;
28.64 gods that neither you nor your **ancestors** have ever worshipped
29.13 as he promised you and your **ancestors,** Abraham, Isaac, and Jacob.
29.25 him, the God of their **ancestors,** when he brought them out of
30. 5 take possession of the land where your **ancestors** once lived.
30. 5 more prosperous and more numerous than your **ancestors** ever were.
30. 9 he was to make your **ancestors** prosperous,
30.20 he promised to give your **ancestors,** Abraham, Isaac, and Jacob."
31. 7 occupy the land that the Lord promised to their **ancestors.**
31.20 this rich and fertile land, as I promised their **ancestors.**
32.17 not real, new gods their **ancestors** had never known,
Josh 1. 6 as they occupy this land which I promised their **ancestors.**
5. 4 rich and fertile land that he had promised their **ancestors.**
18. 3 land that the God of your **ancestors,** has given
19.47 city from Laish to Dan, naming it after their **ancestor** Dan.
21.43 that he had solemnly promised their **ancestors** he would give them.
21.44 peace throughout the land, just as he had promised their **ancestors.**
22.28 Our **ancestors** made an altar just like the Lord's altar.
24. 2 'Long ago your **ancestors** lived on the other side of the
24. 2 One of those **ancestors** was Terah, the father of Abraham and Nahor.
24. 3 I took Abraham, your **ancestor,** from the land beyond the Euphrates
24. 4 but your **ancestor** Jacob and his children went down
24. 6 I brought your **ancestors** out of Egypt,
24. 6 But when your **ancestors** got to the Red Sea [7]they cried out
24.14 of the gods which your **ancestors** used to worship in Mesopotamia
24.15 the gods your **ancestors** worshipped in Mesopotamia
Judg 2. 1 brought you to the land that I promised to your **ancestors.**
2.12 Lord, the God of their **ancestors,** the God who had brought
2.20 the covenant that I commanded their **ancestors** to keep.
2.22 these Israelites will follow my ways, as their **ancestors** did."
3. 4 commands that the Lord had given their **ancestors** through Moses.
9.28 Be loyal to your **ancestor** Hamor, who founded your clan!
18.29 Laish to Dan, after their **ancestor** Dan, the son of Jacob.
1 Sam 2.27 "When your **ancestor** Aaron and his family were slaves of the
12. 6 Moses and Aaron and who brought your **ancestors** out of Egypt.
12. 7 mighty actions the Lord did to save you and your **ancestors.**
12. 8 **ancestors** cried to the Lord for help,
12. 9 fight against your **ancestors** and conquer them.
15. 2 because their **ancestors** opposed the Israelites when they were
15. 6 a people whose **ancestors** had been kind to the Israelites
2 Sam 7.12 and are buried with your **ancestors,** I will make one of your
1 Kgs 8.21 the Lord made with our **ancestors** when he brought them out of
8.34 them back to the land which you gave to their **ancestors.**
8.40 time they live in the land which you gave to our **ancestors.**
8.48 you gave to our **ancestors,** this city which you have chosen,
8.53 through your servant Moses when you brought our **ancestors** out
8.57 Lord our God be with us, as he was with our **ancestors;**
8.58 and keep all the laws and commands he gave our **ancestors.**
9. 9 the Lord their God, who brought their **ancestors** out of Egypt.
14.15 which he gave to their **ancestors,** and he will scatter them
14.22 arouse his anger against them than all their **ancestors** had done.
15.11 Asa did what pleased the Lord, as his **ancestor** David had done.
21. 3 "I inherited this vineyard from my **ancestors,"** Naboth replied.
2 Kgs 14. 3 to the Lord, but he was not like his **ancestor** King David;
16. 2 He did not follow the good example of his **ancestor** King David;
17.13 Law I gave to your **ancestors** and which I handed on to
17.14 they were stubborn like their **ancestors,** who had not trusted
17.15 covenant he had made with their **ancestors,**
18. 3 Following the example of his **ancestor** King David,
19.12 My **ancestors** destroyed the cities of Gozan, Haran, and Rezeph,
20. 5 Lord, the God of your **ancestor** David, have heard your prayer
20.17 everything that your **ancestors** have stored up to this day,
21. 8 be driven out of the land that I gave to their **ancestors."**
21.15 anger from the time their **ancestors** came out of Egypt to
21.22 the God of his **ancestors,** and disobeyed the Lord's commands.
22. 2 followed the example of his **ancestor** King David,
22.13 angry with us because our **ancestors** have not done what this
23.32 Following the example of his **ancestors,** he sinned
23.37 Following the example of his **ancestors,** Jehoiakim sinned
1 Chr 1. 5 Meshech, and Tiras—were the **ancestors** of the peoples
1. 8 Libya, and Canaan—were the **ancestors** of the peoples
1.13 eldest, and Heth—were the **ancestors** of the peoples who bear
1.14 Canaan was also the **ancestor** of the Jebusites, the Amorites,
1.17 Gether, and Meshek—were the **ancestors** of the peoples
1.36 Eliphaz became the **ancestor** of the following tribes:
1.37 And Reuel became the **ancestor** of the tribes of Nahath, Zerah,
1.38 Lotan, who was the **ancestor** of the clans of Hori and Homam.
1.38 Shobal, who was the **ancestor** of the clans of Alvan, Manahath,
1.38 and Dishon was the **ancestor** of the clans of Hamran, Eshban,
1.38 Ezer, who was the **ancestor** of the clans of Bilhan, Zaavan,
1.38 Dishan, who was the **ancestor** of the clans of Uz and Aran.
2.52 of Kiriath Jearim, was the **ancestor** of the people of Haroeh,
2.54 founder of Bethlehem, was the **ancestor** of the people of Netophath,
1 Chr 4. 2 of Ahumai and Lahad, the **ancestors** of the people who lived
4. 8 and the **ancestor** of the clans descended from Aharhel
5.14 Abihail son of Huri, whose **ancestors** were traced back as follows:
5.25 to the God of their **ancestors** and deserted him to worship
8.28 These were the **ancestral** heads of families
9. 4 His other **ancestors** included Imri and Bani.
9.10 whose **ancestors** included Meshullam, Zadok, Meraioth, and Ahitub
9.10 Adaiah son of Jeroham, whose **ancestors** included Pashhur
9.10 Maasai son of Adiel, whose **ancestors** included Jahzerah,
9.14 Shemaiah son of Hasshub, whose **ancestors** included Azrikam
9.14 Mattaniah son of Mica, whose **ancestors** included Zichri and Asaph
9.14 Obadiah son of Shemaiah, whose **ancestors** included Galal
9.19 Lord's presence, just as their **ancestors** had been
9.22 Samuel who had put their **ancestors** in these responsible positions.
9.34 heads of Levite families, according to their **ancestral** lines.
12.17 the God of our **ancestors** will know it and punish you."
17.11 and are buried with your **ancestors,** I will make one of your
24.19 the duties established by their **ancestor** Aaron
26.21 was the **ancestor** of several family groups,
29.10 said, "Lord God of our **ancestor** Jacob, may you be praised
29.15 through life like exiles and strangers, as our **ancestors** did.
29.18 Lord God of our **ancestors** Abraham, Isaac, and Jacob,
29.20 Lord, the God of their **ancestors,** and they bowed low and
2 Chr 6.25 to the land which you gave to them and to their **ancestors.**
6.31 time they live in the land which you gave to our **ancestors.**
6.38 you gave to our **ancestors,** this city which you have chosen,
7.22 the Lord their God, who brought their **ancestors** out of Egypt.
11.16 offer sacrifices to the Lord, the God of their **ancestors.**
13.12 Israel, don't fight against the Lord, the God of your **ancestors!**
13.18 Israel, because they relied on the Lord, the God of their **ancestors.**
14. 4 Lord, the God of their **ancestors,** and to obey his teachings
15.12 Lord, the God of their **ancestors,** with all their heart and soul.
19. 4 the people back to the Lord, the God of their **ancestors.**
20. 6 "O Lord God of our **ancestors,** you rule in heaven over all
20.10 When our **ancestors** came out of Egypt, you did not allow them
20.10 enter those lands, so our **ancestors** went round them and did
20.33 to the worship of the God of their **ancestors.**
21.10 because Jehoram had abandoned the Lord, the God of his **ancestors.**
21.12 Lord, the God of your **ancestor** David, condemns you,
21.19 in mourning for him as had been done for his **ancestors.**
24.18 Lord, the God of their **ancestors,** and began to worship idols
24.24 the people had abandoned him, the Lord God of their **ancestors.**
28. 1 He did not follow the good example of his **ancestor** King David;
28. 5 Lord, the God of their **ancestors,** permitted this to happen,
28. 9 "The Lord God of your **ancestors** was angry with Judah and
28.25 on himself the anger of the Lord, the God of his **ancestors.**
29. 2 Following the example of his **ancestor** King David,
29. 5 purify the Temple of the Lord, the God of your **ancestors.**
29. 6 Our **ancestors** were unfaithful to the Lord our God and did
30. 7 Do not be like your **ancestors** and your fellow-Israelites
30.19 Lord, the God of our **ancestors,** in your goodness forgive
30.22 Lord, the God of their **ancestors,**
32.13 Don't you know what my **ancestors** and I have done to the
33. 8 be driven out of the land that I gave to their **ancestors."**
34. 2 followed the example of his **ancestor** King David,
34. 3 he began to worship the God of his **ancestor** King David.
34.21 angry with us because our **ancestors** have not obeyed the word
34.32 the covenant they had made with the God of their **ancestors.**
34.33 the people to serve the Lord, the God of their **ancestors.**
36.15 Lord, the God of their **ancestors,** had continued to send prophets
Ezra 2.21 People whose **ancestors** had lived in the following towns
2.61 priestly clans could find no record to prove their **ancestry:**
2.61 (The **ancestor** of the priestly clan of Barzillai had married
2.61 unable to prove who their **ancestors** were, they were not accepted
2.70 Israelites settled in the towns where their **ancestors** had lived.
4.15 a search to be made in the records your **ancestors** kept.
5.12 But because our **ancestors** made the God of Heaven angry,
7. 1 He traced his **ancestors** back to Aaron, the High Priest,
7.27 Ezra said, "Praise the Lord, the God of our **ancestors!**
8. 2 (there were records of their **ancestry)**
8.20 temple workmen whose **ancestors** had been designated by King David
8.28 Lord, the God of your **ancestors,** and so are all the silver
9. 7 From the days of our **ancestors** until now, we, your people,
10.11 Lord, the God of your **ancestors,** and do what pleases him.
Neh 1. 6 My **ancestors** and I have sinned.
2. 3 when the city where my **ancestors** are buried is in ruins and
2. 5 to the city where my **ancestors** are buried, so that I can
7.26 People whose **ancestors** had lived in the following towns
7.63 priestly clans could find no record to prove their **ancestry:**
7.63 (The **ancestor** of the priestly clan of Barzillai had married
7.63 unable to prove who their **ancestors** were, they were not accepted
9. 1 to confess the sins that they and their **ancestors** had committed.
9. 9 "You saw how our **ancestors** suffered in Egypt;
9.16 But our **ancestors** grew proud and stubborn and refused to obey
9.23 land that you had promised their **ancestors** to give them.
9.32 our priests and prophets, our **ancestors,** and all our people
9.34 Our **ancestors,** our kings, leaders, and priests
11. 4 His other **ancestors** included Amariah, Shephatiah, and Mahalalel,
11. 5 His other **ancestors** included Hazaiah, Adaiah, Joiarib,
11. 7 His other **ancestors** included Pedaiah, Kolaiah, Maaseiah, Ithiel,
11.11 His **ancestors** included Zadok, Meraioth, and Ahitub,
11.12 His **ancestors** included Amzi, Zechariah, Pashhur, and
11.13 His **ancestors** included Meshillemoth and Immer.
11.15 His **ancestors** included Hashabiah and Bunni.
11.22 His **ancestors** included Mattaniah and Mica,
12.33 (His **ancestors** also included Mattaniah, Micaiah, and Zaccur,

Neh 13.18 why God punished your **ancestors** when he brought destruction
Ps 22. 4 Our **ancestors** put their trust in you;
39.12 Like all my **ancestors** I am only your guest for a little
44. 1 it, O God— our **ancestors** have told us about it, about
45.16 many sons to succeed your **ancestors** as kings, and you will
49.19 he will join all his **ancestors** in death, where the darkness
66. 6 our **ancestors** crossed the river on foot.
78. 5 He instructed our **ancestors** to teach his laws to their children,
78. 8 not be like their **ancestors,** a rebellious and disobedient people,
78.12 While their **ancestors** watched, God performed miracles
79. 8 Do not punish us for the sins of our **ancestors.**
95. 8 "Don't be stubborn, as your **ancestors** were at Meribah,
106. 6 We have sinned as our **ancestors** did;
106. 7 Our **ancestors** in Egypt did not understand God's wonderful acts;
109.14 remember the evil of his **ancestors** and never forgive
Prov 22.28 Never move an old boundary-mark that your **ancestors** established.
Is 11.16 just as there was for their **ancestors** when they left Egypt.
14.21 The sons of this king will die because of their **ancestors'**
37.12 My **ancestors** destroyed the cities of Gozan, Haran, and Rezeph,
38. 5 Lord, the God of your **ancestor** David, have heard your prayer
39. 6 everything that your **ancestors** have stored up to this day,
43.27 Your earliest **ancestor** sinned;
51. 2 Think of your **ancestor,** Abraham, and of Sarah, from whom you
58.14 and you will enjoy the land I gave to your **ancestor,** Jacob.
63.16 Our **ancestors** Abraham and Jacob do not acknowledge us,
64.11 place where our **ancestors** praised you, has been destroyed
65. 7 repay them [7]for their sins and the sins of their **ancestors.**
Jer 2. 5 "What accusation did your **ancestors** bring against me?
3.18 that I gave your **ancestors** as a permanent possession."
3.24 everything that our **ancestors** have worked for since ancient times.
3.25 We and our **ancestors** have always sinned against the Lord our God;
7. 7 land which I gave your **ancestors** as a permanent possession.
7.14 that I gave to your **ancestors** and to you, I will do
7.22 I gave your **ancestors** no commands about burnt-offerings
7.25 From the day that your **ancestors** came out of Egypt until
7.26 Instead, you became more stubborn and rebellious than your **ancestors.**
9.16 that neither they nor their **ancestors** have heard about,
11. 4 covenant I made with their **ancestors** when I brought them out
11. 5 promise I made to their **ancestors** that I would give them the
11. 7 When I brought their **ancestors** out of Egypt, I solemnly warned
11.10 to the sins of their **ancestors,** who refused to do what I
11.10 Judah have broken the covenant that I made with their **ancestors.**
14.20 we confess our own sins and the sins of our **ancestors.**
16.11 the Lord has said, 'Your **ancestors** turned away from me
16.12 But you have done even worse than your **ancestors.**
16.13 a land that neither you nor your **ancestors** have ever known.
16.15 their own country, to the land that I gave their **ancestors.**
16.19 the earth and say, "Our **ancestors** had nothing but false gods,
17.22 observe it as a sacred day, as I commanded their **ancestors.**
17.23 Their **ancestors** did not listen to me or pay any attention.
19. 4 that neither they nor their **ancestors** nor the kings of Judah
23.39 them and the city that I gave to them and their **ancestors.**
24.10 left in the land that I gave to them and their **ancestors."**
25. 5 the Lord gave you and your **ancestors** as a permanent possession.
30. 3 land that I gave their **ancestors,** and they will take possession
31.32 that I made with their **ancestors** when I took them by the
32.22 rich and fertile land, as you had promised their **ancestors.**
34. 5 when they buried your **ancestors,** who were kings before you,
34.13 a covenant with your **ancestors** when I rescued them from Egypt
34.14 But your **ancestors** would not pay any attention to me or
35. 6 Our **ancestor** Jonadab son of Rechab told us that neither we
35. 9 fully obeyed everything that our **ancestor** Jonadab commanded us.
35.15 on living in the land that I gave you and your **ancestors.**
35.16 obeyed the command that their **ancestor** gave them, but you people
35.18 "You have obeyed the command that your **ancestor** Jonadab gave you;
44. 3 gods that neither they nor you nor your **ancestors** ever worshipped.
44. 9 streets of Jerusalem by your **ancestors,** by the kings of Judah
44.10 to all the laws that I gave you and your **ancestors.**
44.17 just as we and our **ancestors,** our king and our leaders, used
44.21 which you and your **ancestors,** your kings and your leaders,
50. 7 Their **ancestors** trusted in the Lord, and they themselves should
Lam 5. 7 Our **ancestors** sinned, but now they are gone,
Ezek 2. 3 turned against me and are still rebels, just as their **ancestors**
20.18 Do not keep the laws your **ancestors** made;
20.24 and worshipped the same idols their **ancestors** had served.
20.42 I would give to your **ancestors,** then you will know that I
36.28 Then you will live in the land I gave your **ancestors.**
37.25 I gave to my servant Jacob, the land where their **ancestors** lived.
47.14 I solemnly promised your **ancestors** that I would give them
Dan 2.23 I praise you and honour you, God of my **ancestors.**
9. 6 to our kings, our rulers, our **ancestors,** and our whole nation.
9. 8 our rulers, and our **ancestors** have acted shamefully
9.16 people because of our sins and the evil our **ancestors** did.
11.24 and will do things that none of his **ancestors** ever did.
11.37 will ignore the god his **ancestors** served, and also the god
11.38 and other rich gifts to a god his **ancestors** never worshipped.
Hos 1. 4 for the murders that his **ancestor** Jehu committed at Jezreel.
9.10 When I first saw your **ancestors,** it was like seeing the
12. 3 Their **ancestor** Jacob struggled with his twin brother Esau
12. 4 Bethel God came to our **ancestor** Jacob and spoke with him.
12.12 Our **ancestor** Jacob had to flee to Mesopotamia,
Amos 2. 4 led astray by the same false gods that their **ancestors** served.
Mic 7.20 Abraham and of Jacob, as you promised our **ancestors** long ago.
Zech 1. 2 was very angry with your **ancestors,** [3]but now I say to you,
Zech 1. 4 Do not be like your **ancestors.**
1. 5 Your **ancestors** and those prophets are no longer alive.
1. 6 I gave your **ancestors** commands and warnings,
8.14 "When your **ancestors** made me angry, I planned disaster
14. 5 You will flee as your **ancestors** did when the earthquake struck
Mal 2.10 do we despise the covenant that God made with our **ancestors?**
3. 7 You, like your **ancestors** before you, have turned away
Mt 1. 1 is the list of the **ancestors** of Jesus Christ, a descendant
1. 2 Abraham to King David, the following **ancestors** are listed:
1. 6 taken into exile in Babylon, the following **ancestors** are listed:
1.12 in Babylon to the birth of Jesus, the following **ancestors** are
3. 9 can escape punishment by saying that Abraham is your **ancestor.**
15. 2 your disciples disobey the teaching handed down by our **ancestors?**
23.30 during the time of your **ancestors,** you would not have done
23.32 Go on, then, and finish what your **ancestors** started!
Mk 7. 3 the Jews, follow the teaching they received from their **ancestors:**
7. 5 teaching handed down by our **ancestors,** but instead eat with
Lk 1.32 him a king, as his **ancestor** David was,
1.54 promise he made to our **ancestors,** and has come to the help
1.72 show mercy to our **ancestors** and remember his sacred covenant.
1.73 a solemn oath to our **ancestor** Abraham he promised to rescue
3. 8 don't start saying among yourselves that Abraham is your **ancestor.**
6.23 For their **ancestors** did the very same things to the prophets.
6.26 their **ancestors** said the very same things about the false
11.47 tombs for the prophets—the very prophets your **ancestors** murdered.
11.48 admit, then, that you approve of what your **ancestors** did;
Jn 4.12 It was our **ancestor** Jacob who gave us this well;
4.20 "My Samaritan **ancestors** worshipped God on this mountain,
6.31 Our **ancestors** ate manna in the desert, just as the scripture
6.49 Your **ancestors** ate manna in the desert, but they died.
6.58 like the bread that your **ancestors** ate, but then later died.
7.22 was not Moses but your **ancestors** who started it),
Acts 2.29 must speak to you plainly about our famous **ancestor** King David.
3.13 the God of our **ancestors,** has given divine glory to his
3.25 share in the covenant which God made with your **ancestors.**
4.25 Spirit you spoke through our **ancestor** David, your servant,
5.30 The God of our **ancestors** raised Jesus from death,
7. 2 Before our **ancestor** Abraham had gone to live in Haran,
7. 8 circumcised his twelve sons, the famous **ancestors** of our race.
7.11 Our **ancestors** could not find any food, [12]and when Jacob heard
7.12 Egypt, he sent his sons, our **ancestors,** on their first visit
7.19 He tricked our **ancestors** and was cruel to them, forcing them
7.32 am the God of your **ancestors,** the God of Abraham, Isaac, and
7.38 he was there with our **ancestors** and with the angel who spoke
7.39 "But our **ancestors** refused to obey him;
7.44 "Our **ancestors** had the Tent of God's presence with them
7.45 our **ancestors** who received the tent from their fathers carried
7.51 You are just like your **ancestors:**
7.52 Was there any prophet that your **ancestors** did not persecute?
13.17 of Israel chose our **ancestors** and made the people a great
13.32 what God promised our **ancestors** he would do, he has now done
13.36 died, was buried with his **ancestors,** and his body rotted in
15.10 the believers which neither our **ancestors** nor we ourselves were
22. 3 in the Law of our **ancestors** and was just as dedicated
22.14 'The God of our **ancestors** has chosen you to know his
24.14 worship the God of our **ancestors** by following that Way which
26. 6 that God made to our **ancestors—**[7]the very thing that the
28.17 that we received from our **ancestors,** I was made a prisoner
28.25 Holy Spirit spoke through the prophet Isaiah to your **ancestors!**
Rom 9. 5 they are descended from the famous Hebrew **ancestors;**
9.10 For Rebecca's two sons had the same father, our **ancestor** Isaac.
11.28 of God's choice, they are his friends because of their **ancestors.**
15. 8 make his promises to their **ancestors** come true,
1 Cor 10. 1 my brothers, what happened to our **ancestors** who followed Moses.
Gal 1.14 and was much more devoted to the traditions of our **ancestors.**
1 Tim 1. 4 and those long lists of **ancestors,** which only produce arguments;
2 Tim 1. 3 God, whom I serve with a clear conscience, as my **ancestors** did.
Tit 3. 9 stupid arguments, long lists of **ancestors,** quarrels, and fights
Heb 1. 1 God spoke to our **ancestors** many times and in many ways
2. 2 The message given to our **ancestors** by the angels was shown
3. 8 not be stubborn, as your **ancestors** were when they rebelled
3.15 not be stubborn, as your **ancestors** were when they rebelled
7. 3 of Melchizedek's father or mother or of any of his **ancestors;**
7. 4 Abraham, our famous **ancestor,** gave him a tenth of all he got
7.10 in the body of his **ancestor** Abraham when Melchizedek met him.
8. 9 that I made with their **ancestors** on the day I took them
Jas 2.21 How was our **ancestor** Abraham put right with God?
1 Pet 1.18 from the worthless manner of life handed down by your **ancestors.**

ANCHOR

Ezek 41. 6 rooms could rest on the wall without being **anchored** into it.
Acts 27.13 so they pulled up the **anchor** and sailed as close as possible
27.29 rocks, so they lowered four **anchors** from the back of the
27.30 going to put out some **anchors** from the front of the ship.
27.40 So they cut off the **anchors** and let them sink in the
Heb 6.19 We have this hope as an **anchor** for our lives.

ANCIENT

Gen 49.26 corn and flowers, Blessings of **ancient** mountains,
Deut 33.15 May their **ancient** hills be covered with choice fruit.
1 Chr 20. 6 He was a descendant of the **ancient** giants.
Ezra 4.15 been rebellious and that from **ancient** times it has given trouble
4.19 indeed been found that from **ancient** times Jerusalem has revolted
Job 3.14 sleeping like the kings and rulers who rebuilt **ancient** palaces.
8. 8 Look for a moment at **ancient** wisdom;

Job 8.10 But let the **ancient** wise men teach you;
20. 4 Surely you know that from **ancient** times, when man was first
Ps 24. 7 wide the gates, open the **ancient** doors, and the great king
24. 9 wide the gates, open the **ancient** doors, and the great king
68.33 the Lord, [33] to him who rides in the sky, the **ancient** sky.
Is 19.11 that they are successors to the **ancient** scholars and kings?
44. 8 You know that from **ancient** times until now I have predicted
51. 9 use it as you did in **ancient** times.
64. 5 we have continued to do wrong since **ancient** times.
Jer 3.24 everything that our ancestors have worked for since **ancient** times.
5.15 It is a strong and **ancient** nation, a nation whose language
6.16 Ask for the **ancient** paths and where the best road is.
30.20 I will restore the nation's **ancient** power and establish it
Lam 1. 7 A lonely ruin now, Jerusalem recalls her **ancient** splendour.
5.21 Restore our **ancient** glory.
Ezek 26.20 of the dead to join the people who lived in **ancient** times.
32.27 burial like the heroes of **ancient** times, who went fully
36. 2 enemies gloated and said, 'Now those **ancient** hills are ours!'
Mic 5. 2 for Israel, whose family line goes back to **ancient** times."
Hab 3. 6 the hills where he walked in **ancient** times.
Heb 11. 2 by their faith that people of **ancient** times won God's approval.
2 Pet 2. 5 God did not spare the **ancient** world, but brought the flood
Rev 12. 9 dragon was thrown out—that **ancient** serpent, called the Devil,
20. 2 He seized the dragon, that **ancient** serpent—that is, the Devil,

ANDREW

One of Jesus' first disciples, and Simon Peter's brother.

Mt 4.18 (called Peter) and his brother **Andrew,** catching fish in the lake
10. 2 first, Simon (called Peter) and his brother **Andrew;**
Mk 1.16 two fishermen, Simon and his brother **Andrew,** catching fish with
1.29 synagogue and went straight to the home of Simon and **Andrew.**
3.18 **Andrew,** Philip, Bartholomew, Matthew, Thomas, James
13. 3 when Peter, James, John, and **Andrew** came to him in private.
Lk 6.14 Simon (whom he named Peter) and his brother **Andrew;**
Jn 1.40 One of them was **Andrew,** Simon Peter's brother.
1.44 was from Bethsaida, the town where **Andrew** and Peter lived.)
6. 8 Another of his disciples, **Andrew,** who was Simon Peter's brother,
12.22 Philip went and told **Andrew,** and the two of them went
Acts 1.13 Peter, John, James and **Andrew,** Philip and Thomas, Bartholomew

ANGEL

[ARCHANGEL'S, CHIEF ANGEL, GOD'S ANGEL, LORD'S ANGEL]

Gen 16. 7 The **angel of the Lord** met Hagar at a spring in the
19. 1 When the two **angels** came to Sodom that evening, Lot was
19.15 At dawn the **angels** tried to make Lot hurry.
19.17 Then one of the **angels** said, "Run for your lives!
21.17 and from heaven the **angel of God** spoke to Hagar, "What are
22.11 But the **angel of the Lord** called to him from heaven,
22.15 The **angel of the Lord** called to Abraham from heaven a
24. 7 He will send his **angel** before you, so that you can get
24.40 obeyed, will send his **angel** with you and give you success.
28.12 from earth to heaven, with **angels** going up and coming down
31.11 The **angel of God** spoke to me in the dream and said,
32. 1 As Jacob went on his way, some **angels** met him.
48.16 May the **angel,** who has rescued me from all harm, bless
Ex 3. 2 There the **angel of the Lord** appeared to him as a flame
12.23 and will not let the **Angel of Death** enter your houses and
14.19 The **angel of God,** who had been in front of the army
23.20 "I will send an **angel** ahead of you to protect you as
23.23 My **angel** will go ahead of you and take you into the
32.34 Remember that my **angel** will guide you, but the time is
33. 2 I will send an **angel** to guide you, and I will drive
Num 20.16 our cry and sent an **angel,** who led us out of Egypt.
22.22 his two servants, the **angel of the Lord** stood in the road
22.23 When the donkey saw the **angel** standing there holding a sword,
22.24 Then the **angel** stood where the road narrowed
22.25 When the donkey saw the **angel,** it moved over against the
22.26 Once more the **angel** moved ahead;
22.27 This time, when the donkey saw the **angel,** it lay down.
22.31 Lord let Balaam see the **angel** standing there with his sword;
22.32 The **angel** demanded, "Why have you beaten your donkey
22.35 But the **angel** said, "Go on with these men, but say only
Deut 33. 2 Ten thousand **angels** were with him, a flaming fire at his
Judg 2. 1 The **angel of the Lord** went from Gilgal to Bochim and said
2. 4 When the **angel** had said this, all the people of Israel
5.23 on Meroz," says the **angel of the Lord,** "a curse, a curse
6.11 Then the **Lord's angel** came to the village of Ophrah and
6.12 The **Lord's angel** appeared to him there and said, "The Lord
6.19 pot, brought them to the **Lord's angel** under the oak-tree,
6.20 The **angel** ordered him, "Put the meat and the bread on
6.21 Then the **Lord's angel** reached out and touched the meat
6.21 Then the **angel** disappeared.
6.22 realized that it was the **Lord's angel** he had seen, and he
6.22 I have seen your **angel** face to face!"
13. 3 The **Lord's angel** appeared to her and said, "You have
13. 6 to me, and he looked as frightening as the **angel of God.**
13. 9 what Manoah asked, and his **angel** came back to the woman
13.13 The **Lord's angel** answered, "Your wife must be sure to
13.15 know that it was the **Lord's angel,** so he said to him,
13.15 But the **angel** said, "If I do stay, I will not eat
13.18 The **angel** asked, "Why do you want to know my name?
13.20 and his wife saw the **Lord's angel** go up towards heaven in
13.20 the man had been the **Lord's angel,** and he and his wife
13.20 They never saw the **angel** again.
1 Sam 29. 9 "I consider you as loyal as an **angel of God.**
2 Sam 14.17 is like **God's angel** and can distinguish good from evil.
14.20 as the **angel of God** and knows everything that happens."
2 Sam 19.27 but you are like **God's angel,** so do what seems right to
24.16 When the **Lord's angel** was about to destroy Jerusalem, the Lord
24.16 the people and said to the **angel** who was killing them,
24.16 The **angel** was by the threshing-place of Araunah, a
24.17 David saw the **angel** who was killing the people, and
1 Kgs 13.18 at the Lord's command an **angel** told me to take you home
19. 5 Suddenly an **angel** touched him and said, "Wake up and eat."
19. 7 The **Lord's angel** returned and woke him up a second time,
22.19 throne in heaven, with all his **angels** standing beside him.
22.20 Some of the **angels** said one thing, and others said something else,
2 Kgs 1. 3 But an **angel of the Lord** commanded Elijah, the prophet
1.15 The **angel of the Lord** said to Elijah, "Go down with him,
19.35 That night an **angel of the Lord** went to the Assyrian
1 Chr 21.12 using his **angel** to bring death throughout Israel?
21.15 Then he sent an **angel** to destroy Jerusalem,
21.15 but he changed his mind and said to the **angel,** "Stop!
21.15 The **angel** was standing by the threshing-place of Araunah,
21.16 David saw the **angel** standing in mid air, holding his sword
21.18 The **angel of the Lord** told Gad to command David to go
21.20 wheat, and when they saw the **angel,** the sons ran and hid.
21.27 The Lord told the **angel** to put his sword away,
21.27 and the **angel** obeyed.
21.30 because he was afraid of the sword of the **Lord's angel.**
2 Chr 18.18 throne in heaven, with all his **angels** standing beside him.
18.19 Some of the **angels** said one thing, and others said something else,
32.21 The Lord sent an **angel** that killed the soldiers and officers
Job 4.18 he finds fault even with his **angels.**
5. 1 Is there any **angel** to whom you can turn?
15.15 Why, God does not trust even his **angels;**
25. 3 Can anyone count the **angels** who serve him?
33.23 Perhaps an **angel** may come to his aid— one of God's
33.23 of God's thousands of **angels,** who remind men of their duty.
33.24 In mercy the **angel** will say, "Release him!
Ps 34. 7 His **angel** guards those who honour the Lord and rescues them
35. 5 blown by the wind as the **angel of the Lord** pursues them!
35. 6 and slippery while the **angel of the Lord** strikes them down!
78.25 they ate the food of **angels,** and God gave them all they
91.11 God will put his **angels** in charge of you to protect you
103.20 you strong and mighty **angels,** who obey his commands, who listen
148. 2 Praise him, all his **angels,** all his heavenly armies.
Is 37.36 An **angel of the Lord** went to the Assyrian camp and
63. 9 It was not an **angel,** but the Lord himself who saved them.
Ezek 28.14 I put a terrifying **angel** there to guard you.
28.16 my holy mountain, and the **angel** who guarded you drove you
Dan 3.25 of being hurt—and the fourth one looks like an **angel."**
3.28 He sent his **angel** and rescued these men who serve and trust
4.13 I saw coming down from heaven an **angel,** alert and watchful.
4.17 This is the decision of the alert and watchful **angels.**
4.23 Your Majesty was watching, an **angel** came down from heaven
4.26 The **angel** ordered the stump to be left in the ground.
4.35 **angels** in heaven and people on earth are under his control.
6.22 God sent his **angel** to shut the mouths of the lions so
8.13 Then I heard one **angel** ask another, "How long
8.14 I heard the other **angel** answer, "It will continue
10.11 The **angel** said to me, "Daniel, God loves you.
10.13 The **angel** prince of the kingdom of Persia opposed me
10.13 Michael, one of the chief **angels,** came to help me, because I
10.16 Then the **angel,** who looked like a man, stretched out his
10.20 I have to go back and fight the guardian **angel** of Persia.
10.20 After that, the guardian **angel** of Greece will appear.
10.20 There is no one to help me except Michael, Israel's guardian **angel.**
11. 2 The **angel** said, "Three more kings will rule over Persia,
11.21 The **angel** went on to explain:
12. 1 The **angel** wearing linen clothes said,
12. 1 "At that time the great **angel** Michael, who guards your people,
12. 6 One of them asked the **angel** who was standing further upstream,
12. 7 The **angel** raised both hands towards the sky and made a
Hos 12. 4 he fought against God—[4] he fought against an **angel** and won.
Zech 1. 8 I saw an **angel of the Lord** riding a red horse.
1.11 They reported to the **angel:**
1.12 Then the **angel** said, "Almighty Lord, you have been angry
1.13 The Lord answered the **angel** with comforting words,
1.14 and the **angel** told me to proclaim
1.17 The **angel** also told me to proclaim:
1.19 I asked the **angel** that had been speaking to me, "What
2. 3 Then I saw the **angel** who had been speaking to me step
2. 3 step forward, and another **angel** came to meet him.
3. 1 High Priest Joshua standing before the **angel of the Lord.**
3. 2 The **angel of the Lord** said to Satan, "May the Lord
3. 4 The **angel** said to his heavenly attendants,
3. 5 new clothes on him while the **angel of the Lord** stood there.
3. 6 Then the **angel** told Joshua that [7] the Lord Almighty had said:
3. 7 I hear the prayers of the **angels** who are in my presence.
4. 1 The **angel** who had been speaking to me came again and
4. 4 Then I asked the **angel,** "What do these things stand for,
4. 6 The **angel** told me to give Zerubbabel this message from the Lord:
4.10b The **angel** said to me, "The seven lamps are the seven
5. 2 The **angel** asked me what I saw.
5. 5 The **angel** appeared again and said, "Look!
5. 8 The **angel** said, "This woman represents wickedness."
5.10 I asked the **angel,** "Where are they taking it?"
6. 4 Then I asked the **angel,** "Sir, what do these chariots mean?"
6. 7 The **angel** said, "Go and inspect the earth!"—
6. 8 Then the **angel** cried out to me, "The horses that went
12. 8 will lead them like the **angel of the Lord,** like God himself.
14. 5 The Lord my God will come, bringing all the **angels** with him.
Mt 1.20 thinking about this, an **angel of the Lord** appeared to him
1.24 married Mary, as the **angel of the Lord** had told him to
2.13 they had left, an **angel of the Lord** appeared in a dream
2.19 After Herod died, an **angel of the Lord** appeared in a

Mt	4. 6	scripture says, 'God will give orders to his **angels** about you;
	4.11	and **angels** came and helped him.
	13.39	is the end of the age, and the harvest workers are **angels.**
	13.41	Man will send out his **angels** to gather up out of his
	13.49	the **angels** will go out and gather up the evil people
	16.27	of his Father with his **angels,** and then he will reward each
	18.10	Their **angels** in heaven, I tell you, are always in the
	22.30	they will be like the **angels** in heaven and will not marry.
	24.31	he will send out his **angels** to the four corners of the
	24.36	and hour will come—neither the **angels** in heaven nor the Son;
	25.31	as King and all the **angels** with him, he will sit on
	25.41	fire which has been prepared for the Devil and his **angels!**
	26.53	at once he would send me more than twelve armies of **angels?**
	28. 2	an **angel of the Lord** came down from heaven, rolled the stone
	28. 5	The **angel** spoke to the women.
Mk	1.13	Wild animals were there also, but **angels** came and helped him.
	8.38	he comes in the glory of his Father with the holy **angels."**
	12.25	they will be like the **angels** in heaven and will not marry.
	13.27	He will send the **angels** out to the four corners of the
	13.32	or hour will come—neither the **angels** in heaven, nor the Son;
Lk	1.11	An **angel of the Lord** appeared to him, standing on the
	1.13	But the **angel** said to him, "Don't be afraid, Zechariah!
	1.18	Zechariah said to the **angel,** "How shall I know if this
	1.19	"I am Gabriel," the **angel** answered.
	1.26	God sent the **angel** Gabriel to a town in Galilee
	1.28	The **angel** came to her and said, "Peace be with you!
	1.29	deeply troubled by the **angel's** message, and she wondered what
	1.30	The **angel** said to her, "Don't be afraid, Mary;
	1.34	Mary said to the **angel,** "I am a virgin.
	1.35	The **angel** answered, "The Holy Spirit will come on
	1.38	And the **angel** left her.
	2. 9	An **angel of the Lord** appeared to them, and the glory
	2.10	but the **angel** said to them, "Don't be afraid!
	2.13	army of heaven's angels appeared with the **angel,** singing praises
	2.15	the **angels** went away from them back into heaven, the shepherds
	2.17	they told them what the **angel** had said about the child.
	2.20	it had been just as the **angel** had told them.
	2.21	Jesus, the name which the **angel** had given him before he had
	4.10	'God will order his **angels** to take good care of you.'
	9.26	and in the glory of the Father and of the holy **angels.**
	12. 8	Man will do the same for him before the **angels of God.**
	12. 9	Son of Man will also reject him before the **angels of God.**
	15.10	way, I tell you, the **angels of God** rejoice over one sinner
	16.22	and was carried by the **angels** to sit beside Abraham
	20.36	They will be like **angels** and cannot die.
	22.43	An **angel** from heaven appeared to him and strengthened him.
	24.23	had seen a vision of **angels** who told them that he is
Jn	1.51	see heaven open and **God's angels** going up and coming down
	12.29	was thunder, while others said, "An **angel** spoke to him!"
	20.12	the tomb [12]and saw two **angels** there dressed in white, sitting
Acts	5.19	But that night an **angel of the Lord** opened the prison gates,
	6.15	and saw that his face looked like the face of an **angel.**
	7.30	forty years had passed, an **angel** appeared to Moses in the
	7.35	with the help of the **angel** who appeared to him in the
	7.38	our ancestors and with the **angel** who spoke to him on Mount
	7.53	that was handed down by **angels**—yet you have not obeyed it!"
	8.26	An **angel of the Lord** said to Philip, "Get ready and go
	10. 3	which he clearly saw an **angel** of God come in and say
	10. 4	He stared at the **angel** in fear and said, "What is it,
	10. 4	The **angel** answered, "God is pleased with your prayers and works
	10. 7	Then the **angel** went away, and Cornelius called two of his
	10.22	An **angel of God** told him to invite you to his house,
	11.13	how he had seen an **angel** standing in his house, who said
	12. 7	Suddenly an **angel of the Lord** stood there, and a light
	12. 7	The **angel** shook Peter by the shoulder, woke him up, and
	12. 8	Then the **angel** said, "Fasten your belt and put on your sandals."
	12. 8	Peter did so, and the **angel** said, "Put your cloak round you
	12. 9	not knowing, however, if what the **angel** was doing was real;
	12.10	They walked down a street, and suddenly the **angel** left Peter.
	12.11	The Lord sent his **angel** to rescue me from Herod's power
	12.15	So they answered, "It is his **angel."**
	12.23	At once the **angel of the Lord** struck Herod down, because
	23. 8	not rise from death and that there are no **angels** or spirits;
	23. 9	Perhaps a spirit or an **angel** really did speak to him!"
	27.23	For last night an **angel** of the God to whom I belong
Rom	8.38	neither death nor life, neither **angels** nor other heavenly rulers
1 Cor	4. 9	as a spectacle for the whole world of **angels** and of mankind.
	6. 3	Do you not know that we shall judge the **angels?**
	10.10	and they were destroyed by the **Angel of Death.**
	11.10	On account of the **angels,** then, a woman should have a
	13. 1	of men and even of **angels,** but if I have no love,
2 Cor	11.14	Even Satan can disguise himself to look like an **angel** of light!
Gal	1. 8	even if we or an **angel** from heaven should preach to you
	3.19	Law was handed down by **angels,** with a man acting as
	4.14	Instead, you received me as you would an **angel** from heaven;
Eph	3.10	of the church, the **angelic rulers** and powers in the heavenly
Col	2.18	and who insists on false humility and the worship of **angels.**
	2.23	in their forced worship of **angels,** and false humility,
1 Thes	4.16	the shout of command, the **archangel's** voice, the sound of God's
2 Thes	1. 7	from heaven with his mighty **angels,** [8]with a flaming fire,
1 Tim	3.16	shown to be right by the Spirit, and was seen by **angels.**
	5.21	Jesus and of the holy **angels** I solemnly call upon you to
Heb	1. 4	was made greater than the **angels,** just as the name that God
	1. 5	God never said to any of his **angels,** "You are my Son;
	1. 5	did God say about any **angel,** "I will be his Father,
	1. 6	Son into the world, he said, "All **God's angels** must worship him."
	1. 7	But about the **angels** God said, "God makes his angels winds,
	1.13	God never said to any of his **angels:**
	1.14	What are the **angels,** then?
	2. 2	to our ancestors by the **angels** was shown to be true,
	2. 5	God has not placed the **angels** as rulers over the new world
Heb	2. 7	You made him for a little while lower than the **angels;**
	2. 9	was made lower than the **angels,** so that through God's grace
	2.16	it is clear that it is not the **angels** that he helps.
	11.28	the doors, so that the **Angel of Death** would not kill
	12.22	living God, the heavenly Jerusalem, with its thousands of **angels.**
	13. 2	were some who did that and welcomed **angels** without knowing it.
1 Pet	1.12	These are things which even the **angels** would like to understand.
	3.22	side of God, ruling over all **angels** and heavenly authorities
2 Pet	2. 4	God did not spare the **angels** who sinned, but threw them
	2.11	Even the **angels,** who are so much stronger and mightier
Jude	6	Remember the **angels** who did not stay within the limits of
	7	acted as those **angels** did and indulged in sexual immorality
	9	Not even the **chief angel** Michael did this.
	14	many thousands of his holy **angels** [15]to bring judgement on all,
Rev	1. 1	servant John by sending his **angel** to him, [2]and John has
	1.20	the seven stars are the **angels** of the seven churches,
	2. 1	"To the **angel** of the church in Ephesus write:
	2. 8	"To the **angel** of the church in Smyrna write:
	2.12	"To the **angel** of the church in Pergamum write:
	2.18	"To the **angel** of the church in Thyatira write:
	3. 1	"To the **angel** of the church in Sardis write:
	3. 5	my Father and of his **angels** I will declare openly that they
	3. 7	"To the **angel** of the church in Philadelphia write:
	3.14	"To the **angel** of the church in Laodicea write:
	5. 2	And I saw a mighty **angel,** who announced in a loud voice,
	5.11	I looked, and I heard **angels,** thousands and millions of them!
	7. 1	After this I saw four **angels** standing at the four corners
	7. 2	And I saw another **angel** coming up from the east
	7. 2	loud voice to the four **angels** to whom God had given the
	7. 3	The **angel** said, "Do not harm the earth, the sea, or the
	7.11	All the **angels** stood round the throne, the elders, and the
	8. 2	Then I saw the seven **angels** who stand before God,
	8. 3	Another **angel,** who had a gold incense-burner, came and stood
	8. 4	God's people from the hands of the **angel** standing before God.
	8. 5	Then the **angel** took the incense-burner, filled it with fire
	8. 6	the seven **angels** with the seven trumpets prepared to blow them.
	8. 7	The first **angel** blew his trumpet.
	8. 8	Then the second **angel** blew his trumpet.
	8.10	Then the third **angel** blew his trumpet.
	8.12	Then the fourth **angel** blew his trumpet.
	8.13	comes from the trumpets that the other three **angels** must blow!"
	9. 1	Then the fifth **angel** blew his trumpet.
	9.11	ruling over them, who is the **angel** in charge of the abyss.
	9.13	Then the sixth **angel** blew his trumpet.
	9.14	voice said to the sixth **angel,** "Release the four angels
	9.15	The four **angels** were released;
	10. 1	Then I saw another mighty **angel** coming down out of heaven.
	10. 5	Then the **angel** that I saw standing on the sea
	10. 6	The **angel** said, "There will be no more delay!
	10. 7	the seventh **angel** blows his trumpet, then God will accomplish
	10. 8	in the hand of the **angel** standing on the sea
	10. 9	I went to the **angel** and asked him to give me
	11.15	the seventh **angel** blew his trumpet, and there were loud voices
	12. 7	Michael and his **angels** fought against the dragon,
	12. 7	who fought back with his **angels;**
	12. 8	defeated, and he and his **angels** were not allowed to stay
	12. 9	He was thrown down to earth, and all his **angels** with him.
	14. 6	Then I saw another **angel** flying high in the air,
	14. 8	A second **angel** followed the first one, saying, "She has fallen!
	14. 9	A third **angel** followed the first two, saying in a loud voice,
	14.10	in fire and sulphur before the holy **angels** and the Lamb.
	14.15	Then another **angel** came out from the temple and cried out
	14.17	Then I saw another **angel** come out of the temple in heaven,
	14.18	Then another **angel,** who is in charge of the fire, came
	14.18	a loud voice to the **angel** who had the sharp sickle,
	14.19	So the **angel** swung his sickle on the earth, cut the
	15. 1	were seven **angels** with seven plagues, which are the last ones,
	15. 6	The seven **angels** who had the seven plagues came out of the
	15. 7	living creatures gave the seven **angels** seven gold bowls full of
	15. 8	plagues brought by the seven **angels** had come to an end.
	16. 1	a loud voice speaking from the temple to the seven **angels:**
	16. 2	The first **angel** went and poured out his bowl on the earth.
	16. 3	Then the second **angel** poured out his bowl on the sea.
	16. 4	Then the third **angel** poured out his bowl on the rivers
	16. 5	I heard the **angel** in charge of the waters say, "The
	16. 8	Then the fourth **angel** poured out his bowl on the sun,
	16.10	Then the fifth **angel** poured out his bowl on the throne
	16.12	Then the sixth **angel** poured out his bowl on the great
	16.17	Then the seventh **angel** poured out his bowl in the air.
	17. 1	Then one of the seven **angels** who had the seven bowls came
	17. 3	took control of me, and the **angel** carried me to a desert.
	17. 7	the **angel** asked me.
	17.15	The **angel** also said to me, "The waters you saw,
	18. 1	After this I saw another **angel** coming down out of heaven.
	18.21	Then a mighty **angel** picked up a stone the size of
	19. 9	Then the **angel** said to me, "Write this:
	19. 9	And the **angel** added, "These are the true words of God."
	19.17	Then I saw an **angel** standing on the sun.
	20. 1	Then I saw an **angel** coming down from heaven, holding in
	20. 3	The **angel** threw him into the abyss, locked it, and sealed
	21. 9	One of the seven **angels** who had the seven bowls full of
	21.10	control of me, and the **angel** carried me to the top of
	21.12	twelve gates and with twelve **angels** in charge of the gates.
	21.15	The **angel** who spoke to me had a gold measuring-rod to
	21.16	The **angel** measured the city with his measuring-rod:
	21.17	The **angel** also measured the wall, and it was sixty metres high,
	22. 1	The **angel** also showed me the river of the water of life,
	22. 6	Then the **angel** said to me, "These words are true and can
	22. 6	the prophets, has sent his **angel** to show his servants what
	22. 8	at the feet of the **angel** who had shown me these things,
	22.16	"I, Jesus, have sent my **angel** to announce these things

ANGER

[ANGRY, GOD'S ANGER, LORD'S ANGER]

Gen 4. 5 Cain became furious, and he scowled in **anger.**
4. 6 Then the Lord said to Cain, "Why are you **angry?**
18.30 Abraham said, "Please don't be **angry,** Lord, but I must speak
18.32 Abraham said, "Please don't be **angry,** Lord, and I will speak
27.44 until your brother's **anger** cools down [45] and he forgets
30. 2 Jacob became **angry** with Rachel and said, "I can't take
31.35 her father, "Do not be **angry** with me, sir, but I am
31.36 he asked **angrily.**
40. 2 He was **angry** with these two officials [3] and put them in
41.10 You were **angry** with the chief baker and me, and you put
44.18 Don't be **angry** with me;
49. 6 For they killed men in **anger** And they crippled bulls for sport.
49. 7 A curse be on their **anger,** because it is so fierce, And
Ex 4.14 At this the Lord became **angry** with Moses and said,
11. 8 Then in great **anger** Moses left the king.
15. 7 your **anger** blazes out and burns them up like straw.
16.20 of worms and smelt rotten, and Moses was **angry** with them.
21.14 But when a man gets **angry** and deliberately kills another man,
22.24 for help, [24] and I will be **angry** and kill you in war.
32.10 I am **angry** with them, and I am going to destroy them.
32.11 why should you be so **angry** with your people, whom you
32.12 Stop being **angry;**
32.22 Aaron answered, "Don't be **angry** with me;
34. 6 pity, who is not easily **angered** and who shows great love and
Lev 10. 6 die, and the Lord will be **angry** with the whole community.
10.16 This made him **angry** with Eleazar and Ithamar, and he demanded,
26.28 obey me, [28] then in my **anger** I will turn on you and
Num 1.53 near and cause my **anger** to strike the community of Israel."
11. 1 Lord heard them, he was **angry** and sent fire on the people.
11.10 distressed because the Lord was **angry** with them,
11.33 to eat, the Lord became **angry** with the people and caused an
12. 9 The Lord was **angry** with them;
14.18 the Lord, am not easily **angered,** and I show great love and
16.15 Moses was **angry** and said to the Lord, "Do not accept
16.22 When one man sins, do you get **angry** with the whole community?"
16.46 The **Lord's anger** has already broken out and an epidemic
18. 5 the altar, so that my **anger** will not again break out against
22.22 God was **angry** that Balaam was going, and as Balaam was
24.10 Balak clenched his fists in **anger** and said to Balaam,
25. 3 So the Lord was **angry** with them [4] and said to Moses, "Take
25. 4 and then I will no longer be **angry** with the people."
25.11 has done, I am no longer **angry** with the people of Israel.
25.11 and that is why I did not destroy them in my **anger.**
31.14 Moses was **angry** with the officers, the commanders of battalions
32.10 The Lord was **angry** that day and made a promise:
32.13 The Lord was **angry** with the people and made them wander
32.14 to bring down the fierce **anger of the Lord** on Israel again.
Deut 1.34 heard your complaints and became **angry,** and so he solemnly
1.37 you the Lord also became **angry** with me and said, 'Not even
3.26 you people the Lord was **angry** with me and would not listen.
4.21 the Lord your God was **angry** with me and solemnly declared
4.25 is evil in the Lord's sight, and it will make him **angry.**
6.15 worship other gods, the **Lord's anger** will come against you
7. 4 happens, the Lord will be **angry** with you and destroy you at
9. 7 forget how you made the Lord your God **angry** in the desert.
9. 8 Mount Sinai you made the Lord **angry**—angry enough to destroy you.
9.18 you had sinned against the Lord and had made him **angry.**
9.19 afraid of the **Lord's fierce anger,** because he was furious enough
9.20 The Lord was also **angry** enough with Aaron to kill him,
9.22 made the Lord your God **angry** when you were at Taberah,
11.17 If you do, the Lord will become **angry** with you.
13.17 the Lord will turn from his fierce **anger** and show you mercy.
19. 6 might catch him and in his **anger** kill an innocent man.
29.20 Instead, the **Lord's burning anger** will flame up against him,
29.23 Zeboiim, which the Lord destroyed when he was furiously **angry.**
29.24 What was the reason for his fierce **anger?'**
29.27 And so the Lord became **angry** with his people and brought
29.28 The Lord became furiously **angry,**
29.28 and in his great **anger** he uprooted them from their land
31.17 When that happens, I will become **angry** with them;
31.29 have made the Lord **angry** by doing what he has forbidden."
32.16 the evil they did made him **angry.**
32.19 Lord saw this, he was **angry** and rejected his sons and daughters.
32.21 they have made me **angry,** jealous with their so-called gods,
32.21 So I will use a so-called nation to make them **angry;**
32.22 My **anger** will flame up like fire and burn everything on earth.
Josh 20. 5 he killed the person accidentally and not out of **anger.**
22.18 he will be **angry** with everyone in Israel tomorrow.
23.16 other gods, then in his **anger** he will punish you, and soon
Judg 2.12 They bowed down to them and made the Lord **angry.**
3. 8 So the Lord became **angry** with Israel and let King Cushan
6.39 Then Gideon said to God, "Don't be **angry** with me;
8. 3 When he said this, they were no longer so **angry.**
9.30 ruler of the city, became **angry** when he heard what Gaal had
10. 7 So the Lord became **angry** with the Israelites,
18.25 else unless you want these men to get **angry** and attack you.
19. 2 his concubine, [2] but she became **angry** with him, went back to
1 Sam 15.11 Samuel was **angry,** and all night long he pleaded with the Lord.
17.28 He was **angry** with David and said, "What are you doing here?
18. 8 Saul did not like this, and he became very **angry.**
20. 7 but if he becomes **angry,** you will know that he is determined
20.10 "Who will let me know if your father answers you **angrily?"**
29. 4 But the Philistine commanders were **angry** with Achish
2 Sam 6. 7 once the Lord God became **angry** with Uzzah and killed him
6. 8 David was furious because the Lord had punished Uzzah in **anger.**
11.20 the battle, [20] he may get **angry** and ask you, 'Why did you
2 Sam 12. 5 David was very **angry** with the rich man and said, "I
19.42 So why should this make you **angry?**
22. 8 the sky rocked and quivered because God was **angry!**
22.16 the Lord rebuked his enemies and roared at them in **anger.**
24. 1 The Lord was **angry** with Israel once more, and he made
1 Kgs 8.46 not sin—and in your **anger** you let their enemies defeat them
11. 9 So the Lord was **angry** with Solomon
14. 9 me and have aroused my **anger** by making idols and metal
14.15 they have aroused his **anger** by making idols of the goddess
14.22 more to arouse his **anger** against them than all their ancestors
15.30 Jeroboam aroused the **anger of the Lord,** the God of Israel,
16. 2 Their sins have aroused my **anger,** [3] and so I will do away
16. 7 He aroused the **Lord's anger** not only because of the evil he
16.13 Elah had aroused the **anger of the Lord,** the God of Israel.
16.26 him, he aroused the **anger of the Lord,** the God of Israel,
16.33 more to arouse the **anger of the Lord,** the God of Israel,
21. 4 Ahab went home, depressed and **angry** over what Naboth had said
21.22 you have stirred up my **anger** by leading Israel into sin.'
22.53 him, he aroused the **anger of the Lord,** the God of Israel.
2 Kgs 13. 3 So the Lord was **angry** with Israel, and he allowed King
13.19 This made Elisha **angry,** and he said to the king,
17.11 They aroused the **Lord's anger** with all their wicked deeds
17.17 what is wrong in the Lord's sight, and so aroused his **anger.**
17.18 The Lord was **angry** with the Israelites and banished them
21. 6 He sinned greatly against the Lord and stirred up his **anger.**
21.15 and have stirred up my **anger** from the time their ancestors
22.13 The Lord is **angry** with us because our ancestors have not
22.17 and so have stirred up my **anger** by all they have done.
22.17 My **anger** is aroused against Jerusalem, and it will not die down.
23.19 the kings of Israel, who thereby aroused the **Lord's anger.**
23.26 But the **Lord's fierce anger** had been aroused against Judah
24.20 The Lord became so **angry** with the people of Jerusalem
1 Chr 13.10 At once the Lord became **angry** with Uzzah and killed him
13.11 David was furious because the Lord had punished Uzzah in **anger.**
2 Chr 6.36 not sin—and in your **anger** you let their enemies defeat them
12. 7 the full force of my **anger,** [8] but Shishak will conquer them,
12.12 the Lord, the **Lord's anger** did not completely destroy him,
16.10 This made Asa so **angry** with the prophet that he had him
19. 2 What you have done has brought the **Lord's anger** on you.
19.10 fellow-citizens will feel the force of the **Lord's anger.**
24.18 guilt for these sins brought the **Lord's anger** on Judah
25.10 At this they went home, bitterly **angry** with the people of Judah.
25.15 This made the Lord **angry,** so he sent a prophet to Amaziah.
26.19 He became **angry** with the priests, and immediately
28. 9 God of your ancestors was **angry** with Judah and let you
28.11 Let them go, or the Lord will punish you in his **anger."**
28.13 against the Lord and made him **angry** enough to punish us.
28.25 brought on himself the **anger of the Lord,** the God of his
29. 8 this the Lord has been **angry** with Judah and Jerusalem, and
29.10 of Israel, so that he will no longer be **angry** with us.
30. 8 worship him so that he will no longer be **angry** with you.
33. 6 He sinned greatly against the Lord and stirred up his **anger.**
34.21 The Lord is **angry** with us because our ancestors have not
34.25 and so have stirred up my **anger** by all they have done.
34.25 My **anger** is aroused against Jerusalem, and it will not die down.
36.16 until at last the **Lord's anger** against his people was so
Ezra 5.12 made the God of Heaven **angry,** he let them be conquered by
7.23 sure that he is never **angry** with me or with those who
9.14 do, you will be so **angry** that you will destroy us completely
10.14 In this way **God's anger** over this situation will be turned away."
Neh 4. 7 in the wall were being closed, and they were very **angry.**
5. 6 When I heard their complaints, I was **angry**
9.17 you are gracious and loving, slow to be **angry.**
13.18 on bringing more of **God's anger** down on Israel by profaning
Esth 1.18 and husbands will be **angry** with their wives.
2. 1 Later, even after the king's **anger** had cooled down,
7.10 Then the king's **anger** cooled down.
Job 4. 9 Like a storm, God destroys them in his **anger.**
7.11 I am **angry** and bitter.
9. 5 he moves mountains and in **anger** he destroys them.
9.13 **God's anger** is constant.
10.17 your **anger** towards me grows and grows;
14.13 me be hidden until your **anger** is over, and then set a
15.12 But you are excited and glare at us in **anger.**
15.13 You are **angry** with God and denounce him.
16. 9 In **anger** God tears me limb from limb;
18. 4 You are only hurting yourself with your **anger.**
18. 4 Will the earth be deserted because you are **angry?**
19.11 God is **angry** and rages against me;
20.23 God will punish him in fury and **anger.**
20.28 All his wealth will be destroyed in the flood of **God's anger.**
21.17 punish the wicked in **anger** [18] and blow them away like straw
21.30 On the day God is **angry** and punishes, it is the wicked
32. 2 Elihu could not control his **anger** any longer,
32. 3 He was also **angry** with Job's three friends.
32. 5 could not answer Job, he was **angry** [6] and began to speak.
36.13 godless keep on being **angry,** and even when punished,
40.11 pour out your **anger** and humble them.
42. 7 said to Eliphaz, "I am **angry** with you and your two friends,
Ps 2. 5 Then he warns them in **anger** and terrifies them with his fury.
2.12 or else his **anger** will be quickly aroused, and you will
6. 1 Lord, don't be **angry** and rebuke me!
6. 1 Don't punish me in your **anger!**
7. 6 Rise in your **anger,** O Lord!
18. 7 the mountains rocked and quivered, because God was **angry.**
18.15 rebuked your enemies, Lord, and roared at them in **anger.**
21. 9 Lord will devour them in his **anger,** and fire will consume them.
27. 9 Don't be **angry** with me;
30. 5 His **anger** lasts only a moment, his goodness for a lifetime.
37. 8 Don't give in to worry or **anger;**
38. 1 O Lord, don't punish me in your **anger!**

Ps 38. 3 Because of your **anger,** I am in great pain;
55. 3 they are **angry** with me and hate me.
56. 7 defeat those people in your **anger!**
58. 9 in his fierce **anger** God will blow them away while they are
59.13 Because they curse and lie, [13]destroy them in your **anger;**
60. 1 you have been **angry** with us—but now turn back to us.
69.24 Pour out your **anger** on them;
74. 1 Will you be **angry** with your own people for ever?
74.23 Don't forget the **angry** shouts of your enemies,
75. 8 cup in his hand, filled with the strong wine of his **anger.**
76. 7 No one can stand in your presence when you are **angry.**
76.10 Men's **anger** only results in more praise for you;
77. 9 Has **anger** taken the place of his compassion?"
78.21 And so the Lord was **angry** when he heard them;
78.21 people with fire, and his **anger** against them grew,
78.31 when God became **angry** with them and killed their strongest
78.38 Many times he held back his **anger** and restrained his fury.
78.49 distress by pouring out his **anger** and fierce rage, which
78.50 He did not restrain his **anger** or spare their lives,
78.58 They **angered** him with their heathen places of worship,
78.59 God was **angry** when he saw it, so he rejected his people
78.62 He was **angry** with his own people and let them be killed
79. 5 Lord, will you be **angry** with us for ever?
79. 5 Will your **anger** continue to burn like fire?
79. 6 Turn your **anger** on the nations that do not worship you, on
80. 4 Lord God Almighty, will you be **angry** with your people's prayers?
80.16 look at them in **anger** and destroy them!
85. 3 You stopped being **angry** with them and held back your furious rage.
85. 5 Will you be **angry** with us for ever?
85. 5 Will your **anger** never cease?
88. 7 Your **anger** lies heavy on me, and I am crushed beneath its
88.16 Your furious **anger** crushes me;
89. 9 you calm its **angry** waves.
89.38 But you are **angry** with your chosen king;
89.46 How long will your **anger** burn like fire?
90. 7 We are destroyed by your **anger;**
90. 9 Our life is cut short by your **anger;**
90.11 Who has felt the full power of your **anger?**
90.13 How much longer will your **anger** last?
94. 1 reveal your **anger!**
95.11 I was **angry** and made a solemn promise:
102. 9 Because of your **anger** and fury, ashes are my food,
103. 8 slow to become **angry** and full of constant love.
103. 9 he is not **angry** for ever.
106.23 and prevented his **anger** from destroying them.
106.29 They stirred up the **Lord's anger** by their actions,
106.32 the people made the Lord **angry,** and Moses was in trouble on
106.40 So the Lord was **angry** with his people;
110. 5 when he becomes **angry,** he will defeat kings.
112.10 The wicked see this and are **angry;**
119.53 I see the wicked breaking your law, I am filled with **anger.**
119.139 My **anger** burns in me like a fire, because my enemies
124. 3 they would have swallowed us alive in their furious **anger**
138. 7 You oppose my **angry** enemies and save me by your power.
145. 8 slow to become **angry** and full of constant love.

Prov 6.34 A husband is never **angrier** than when he is jealous;
6.35 no amount of gifts will satisfy his **anger.**
11.23 when the wicked get what they want, everyone is **angry.**
15. 1 A gentle answer quietens **anger,** but a harsh one stirs it up.
16.14 if the king becomes **angry,** someone may die.
19.12 The king's **anger** is like the roar of a lion,
20. 2 Fear an **angry** king as you would a growling lion;
20. 2 making him **angry** is suicide.
21.14 If someone is **angry** with you, a gift given secretly will
22.14 is a trap—it catches those with whom the Lord is **angry.**
25.23 Gossip brings **anger** just as surely as the north wind brings rain.
25.28 If you cannot control your **anger,** you are as helpless as
27. 4 **Anger** is cruel and destructive, but it is nothing compared to jealousy.
29.11 Stupid people express their **anger** openly,
30.33 If you stir up **anger,** you get into trouble.

Ecc 5. 6 Why make God **angry** with you?
5.17 live our lives in darkness and grief, worried, **angry,** and sick.
10. 4 If your ruler becomes **angry** with you, do not hand in your

Song 1. 6 My brothers were **angry** with me and made me work

Is 2.10 to escape from the **Lord's anger** and to hide from his power
2.19 to escape from the **Lord's anger** and to hide from his power
2.21 try to escape from his **anger** and to hide from his power
5.25 The Lord is **angry** with his people and has stretched out
5.25 Yet even then the **Lord's anger** will not be ended, but his
7. 4 The **anger** of King Rezin and his Syrians and of King Pekah
8.21 In their hunger and their **anger** they will curse their king
9.12 Yet even so the **Lord's anger** is not ended;
9.17 Yet even so the **Lord's anger** will not be ended, but his
9.19 Because the Lord Almighty is **angry,** his punishment burns
9.21 Yet even so the **Lord's anger** is not ended;
10. 4 Yet even so the **Lord's anger** will not be ended;
10. 5 Assyria like a club to punish those with whom I am **angry.**
10. 6 Assyria to attack a godless nation, people who have made me **angry.**
12. 1 You were **angry** with me,
12. 1 but now you comfort me and are **angry** no longer.
13. 3 to fight a holy war and punish those he is **angry** with.
13. 5 In his **anger** the Lord is coming to devastate the whole country.
13. 9 Lord is coming—that cruel day of his fierce **anger** and fury.
13.13 place on that day when I, the Lord Almighty, show my **anger.**
14. 6 of the evil rulers [6]who **angrily** oppressed the peoples
26.20 Hide yourselves for a little while until **God's anger** is over.
27. 4 I am no longer **angry** with the vineyard.
30.27 Fire and smoke show his **anger.**
30.30 hear his majestic voice and feel the force of his **anger.**
34. 2 The Lord is **angry** with all the nations and all their armies.
41.11 "Those who are **angry** with you will know the shame of defeat.
42.25 feel the force of his **anger** and suffer the violence of war.
42.25 Like fire his **anger** burned throughout Israel, but we never knew
47. 6 I was **angry** with my people;
48. 9 people will praise my name, I am holding my **anger** in check;
51.17 of punishment that the Lord in his **anger** gave you to drink;
51.20 They have felt the force of **God's anger.**
51.22 am taking away the cup that I gave you in my **anger.**
54. 8 I turned away **angry** for only a moment, but I will show
54. 9 Now I promise not to be **angry** with you again;
57.16 not continue to accuse them or be **angry** with them for ever.
57.17 I was **angry** with them because of their sin and greed,
60.10 In my **anger** I punished you, But now I will show you
63. 3 I trampled them in my **anger,** and their blood has stained all
63. 5 But my **anger** made me strong, and I won the victory myself.
63. 6 In my **anger** I trampled whole nations and shattered them.
64. 5 You were **angry** with us, but we went on sinning;
64. 5 in spite of your great **anger** we have continued to do wrong
64. 9 so do not be too **angry** with us or hold our sins
65. 3 They shamelessly keep on making me **angry.**
65. 5 stand people like that—my **anger** against them is like a fire
66.14 who obey me, and I show my **anger** against my enemies."
66.15 the wings of a storm to punish those he is **angry** with.

Jer 2.35 surely the Lord is no longer **angry** with me.'
3. 5 You won't always be **angry;**
3.12 I am merciful and will not be **angry;**
3.12 I will not be **angry** with you for ever.
4. 4 If you don't, my **anger** will burn like fire because of the
4. 8 wail because the fierce **anger of the Lord** has not turned
4.26 its cities were in ruins because of the **Lord's fierce anger.**
6.11 Your **anger** against them burns in me too, Lord, and I
6.11 to me, "Pour out my **anger** on the children in the streets
7.20 Sovereign Lord, will pour out my fierce **anger** on this Temple.
7.20 My **anger** will be like a fire that no one can put
7.29 because I, the Lord, am **angry,** and have rejected my people.
8.19 "Why have you made me **angry** by worshipping your idols and
10.10 When you are **angry,** the world trembles;
10.10 the nations cannot endure your **anger.**
10.24 be too hard on us or punish us when you are **angry;**
10.25 Turn your **anger** on the nations that do not worship you
11.17 they have made me **angry** by offering sacrifices to Baal."
12.13 Because of my fierce **anger** their crops have failed."
15. 6 crushed you because I was tired of controlling my **anger.**
15.14 because my **anger** is like fire,
15.17 I stayed by myself and was filled with **anger.**
17. 4 because my **anger** is like a fire,
18.20 so that you would not deal with them in **anger.**
18.23 down in defeat and deal with them while you are **angry."**
21. 5 you with all my might, my **anger,** my wrath, and my fury.
21.11 are doing will make my **anger** burn like a fire that cannot
23.19 His **anger** is a storm, a furious wind that will rage
25. 6 not to make the Lord **angry** by worshipping the idols
25. 7 Instead, you made him **angry** with your idols
25.15 said to me, "Here is a wine cup filled with my **anger.**
25.36 because the Lord in his **anger** has destroyed your nation
25.38 war and the **Lord's fierce anger** have turned the country into
30.23 The **Lord's anger** is a storm, a furious wind
32.29 where people have made me **angry** by burning incense to Baal
32.30 have displeased me and made me **angry** by what they have done.
32.31 this city have made me **angry** and furious from the day it
32.37 have scattered them in my **anger** and fury, and I am going
33. 5 whom I am going to strike down in my **anger** and fury.
36. 7 the Lord has threatened this people with his terrible **anger**
42.18 Israel, says, 'Just as my **anger** and fury were poured out on
44. 3 because their people had done evil and had made me **angry.**
44. 6 So I poured out my **anger** and fury on the towns
44. 8 Why do you make me **angry** by worshipping idols
49.37 In my great **anger** I will destroy the people of Elam
50.13 Because of my **anger** no one will live in Babylon;
50.25 are stored, and in my **anger** I have taken them out,
51.45 Run for your life from my fierce **anger.**
52. 3 The Lord became so **angry** with the people of Jerusalem

Lam 1.12 that the Lord brought on me in the time of his **anger.**
2. 1 The Lord in his **anger** has covered Zion with darkness.
2. 1 On the day of his **anger** he abandoned even his Temple.
2. 4 Here in Jerusalem we felt his burning **anger.**
2. 6 King and priest alike have felt the force of his **anger.**
2.21 You slaughtered them without mercy on the day of your **anger.**
2.22 And no one could escape on that day of your **anger.**
3.43 mercy was hidden by your **anger,** [44]By a cloud of fury
5.22 Is there no limit to your **anger?**

Ezek 3.14 and as his spirit carried me off, I felt bitter and **angry.**
5.13 all the force of my **anger** and rage until I am satisfied.
5.15 "When I am **angry** and furious with you and punish you,
6.12 They will feel all the force of my **anger.**
7. 3 You will feel my **anger,** because I am judging you
7. 8 "Very soon now you will feel all the force of my **anger.**
7.13 back what he has lost, because **God's anger** is on everyone.
7.14 off to war, for **God's anger** will fall on everyone alike.
8.17 them here in the Temple itself and make me even more **angry.**
8.18 They will feel all the force of my **anger.**
9. 8 "Sovereign Lord, are you so **angry** with Jerusalem
13.13 "In my **anger** I will send a strong wind, pouring rain,
13.15 covered it with whitewash will feel the force of my **anger.**
14.19 that country and in my **anger** take many lives, killing people
16.26 with you, and you used your prostitution to make me **angry.**
16.38 and murder, and in my **anger** and fury I will punish you
16.42 Then my **anger** will be over, and I will be calm.
16.42 I will not be **angry** or jealous any more.

Ezek 16.43 and you have made me **angry** by all the things you did.
19.12 But **angry** hands pulled it up by the roots and threw it
20. 8 let them feel the full force of my **anger** there in Egypt.
20.13 feel the force of my **anger** there in the desert
20.21 feel the force of my **anger** there in the desert
20.28 They made me **angry** by the sacrifices they burnt
20.33 warn you that in my **anger** I will rule over you
20.34 you my power and my **anger** when I gather you together
21.17 I also will clap my hands, and my **anger** will be over.
21.31 You will feel my **anger** when I turn it loose on you
22.20 My **anger** and rage will melt them just as fire melts ore.
22.21 Jerusalem, build a fire under them, and melt them with my **anger.**
22.22 will know that they are feeling the **anger of the Lord."**
22.24 land is unholy, and so I am punishing it in my **anger.**
22.30 defend the land when my **anger** is about to destroy it,
22.31 So I will turn my **anger** loose on them,
23.22 but I will make them **angry** with you
23.25 Because I am **angry** with you,
23.25 I will let them deal with you in their **anger.**
24. 8 where it cannot be hidden, where it demands **angry** revenge."
24.13 pure again until you have felt the full force of my **anger.**
25.14 Edom for me, and they will make Edom feel my furious **anger.**
25.17 They will feel my **anger.**
35.11 pay you back for your **anger,** your jealousy, and your hatred
36. 5 in the heat of my **anger** against the surrounding nations,
36. 6 Lord, am saying in jealous **anger** because of the way the
36.18 feel the force of my **anger** because of the murders they had
38.19 in the heat of my **anger** that on that day there will
43. 8 things they did, and so in my **anger** I destroyed them.
Dan 3.19 and his face turned red with **anger** at Shadrach, Meshach,
8. 7 He was so **angry** that he smashed into him and broke the
8.19 "I am showing you what the result of **God's anger** will be.
9.16 in the past, so do not be **angry** with Jerusalem any longer.
11.11 In his **anger** the king of Egypt will go to war against
Hos 5.10 The Lord says, "I am **angry** because the leaders of Judah
7. 6 All night their **anger** smouldered, and in the morning it burst
7. 7 "In the heat of their **anger** they murdered their rulers.
11. 9 I will not punish you in my **anger;**
11. 9 I will not come to you in **anger.**
12.14 The people of Israel have made the Lord bitterly **angry;**
13.11 In my **anger** I have given you kings, and in my fury
14. 4 no longer am I **angry** with them.
Amos 1.11 Their **anger** had no limits, and they never let it die.
Jon 3. 9 perhaps he will stop being **angry,** and we will not die!"
4. 1 Jonah was very unhappy about this and became **angry.**
4. 4 The Lord answered, "What right have you to be **angry?"**
4. 9 him, "What right have you to be **angry** about the plant?"
4. 9 "I have every right to be **angry—angry** enough to die!"
Mic 5.15 And in my great **anger** I will take revenge on all nations
7. 9 the Lord, so now we must endure his **anger** for a while.
7.18 You do not stay **angry** for ever, but you take pleasure in
Nah 1. 2 In his **anger** he pays them back.
1. 3 Lord does not easily become **angry,** but he is powerful and
1. 6 When he is **angry,** who can survive?
1. 6 He pours out his flaming **anger;**
Hab 3. 2 Be merciful, even when you are **angry.**
3. 8 Was it the rivers that made you **angry,** Lord?
3.12 You marched across the earth in **anger;**
Zeph 1.18 The whole earth will be destroyed by the fire of his **anger.**
2. 2 wind, before the burning **anger of the Lord** comes upon you,
2. 3 escape punishment on the day when the Lord shows his **anger.**
3. 8 kingdoms, in order to let them feel the force of my **anger.**
Zech 1. 2 "I, the Lord, was very **angry** with your ancestors, [3]but now
1.12 "Almighty Lord, you have been **angry** with Jerusalem
1.15 city, [15]and I am very **angry** with the nations that enjoy
1.15 I was holding back my **anger** against my people, those nations
6. 8 that went north to Babylonia have calmed down the **Lord's anger."**
7.12 the prophets who lived long ago, I became very **angry.**
8. 2 her people, a love which has made me **angry** with her enemies.
8.14 "When your ancestors made me **angry,** I planned disaster for them
10. 3 The Lord says, "I am **angry** with those foreigners who rule
Mal 1. 4 and 'The nation with whom the Lord is **angry** for ever.' "
Mt 5.22 whoever is **angry** with his brother will be brought to trial,
18.34 The king was very **angry,** and he sent the servant to jail
20.24 ten disciples heard about this, they became **angry** with the two
21.15 teachers of the Law became **angry** when they saw the wonderful
22. 7 The king was very **angry;**
26. 8 The disciples saw this and became **angry.**
Mk 3. 5 Jesus was **angry** as he looked round at them,
10.14 Jesus noticed this, he was **angry** and said to his disciples,
10.41 disciples heard about it, they became **angry** with James and John.
14. 4 of the people there became **angry** and said to one another,
Lk 4.28 people in the synagogue heard this, they were filled with **anger.**
13.14 official of the synagogue was **angry** that Jesus had healed on
15.28 "The elder brother was so **angry** that he would not go
Jn 6.52 This started an **angry** argument among them.
7.23 why are you **angry** with me because I made a
Acts 7.54 they became furious and ground their teeth at him in **anger.**
12.20 Herod was very **angry** with the people of Tyre and Sidon,
Rom 1.18 **God's anger** is revealed from heaven against all the sin
2. 5 Day when **God's anger** and righteous judgements will be revealed.
2. 8 on them God will pour out his **anger** and fury.
4.15 The Law brings down **God's anger;**
5. 9 much more, then, will we be saved by him from **God's anger!**
9.22 He wanted to show his **anger** and to make his power known.
9.22 were the objects of his **anger,** who were doomed to destruction.
10.19 means of a nation of fools I will make my people **angry."**
12.19 Never take revenge, my friends, but instead let **God's anger** do it.
Gal 5.20 they become jealous, **angry,** and ambitious.
Eph 2. 3 we, like everyone else, were destined to suffer **God's anger.**
Eph 4.26 If you become **angry,**
4.26 do not let your **anger** lead you into sin,
4.26 and do not stay **angry** all day.
4.31 Get rid of all bitterness, passion, and **anger.**
5. 6 these very things that **God's anger** will come upon those who
6. 4 treat your children in such a way as to make them **angry.**
Col 3. 6 Because of such things **God's anger** will come upon those
3. 8 **anger,** passion, and hateful feelings.
1 Thes 1.10 death and who rescues us from **God's anger** that is coming.
2.16 And now **God's anger** has at last come down on them!
5. 9 choose us to suffer his **anger,** but to possess salvation through
1 Tim 2. 8 can lift up their hands in prayer without **anger** or argument.
Heb 3.10 And so I was **angry** with those people and said,
3.11 I was **angry** and made a solemn promise:
3.17 With whom was God **angry** for forty years?
4. 3 just as he said, "I was **angry** and made a solemn promise:
11.27 made Moses leave Egypt without being afraid of the king's **anger.**
Jas 1.19 quick to listen, but slow to speak and slow to become **angry.**
1.20 Man's **anger** does not achieve God's righteous purpose.
Rev 6.16 who sits on the throne and from the **anger** of the Lamb!
6.17 The terrible day of their **anger** is here, and who can
11.18 because the time for your **anger** has come, the time for the
14.10 he has poured at full strength into the cup of his **anger!**
14.19 and threw them into the winepress of **God's furious anger.**
15. 1 last ones, because they are the final expression of **God's anger.**
15. 7 gold bowls full of the **anger of God,** who lives for ever
16. 1 and pour out the seven bowls of **God's anger** on the earth!"
16.19 drink the wine from his cup—the wine of his furious **anger.**
19.15 in the winepress of the furious **anger of the Almighty God.**

ANGLES

Ezek 1.16 wheel intersecting it at right **angles,**
10. 9 one had another wheel which intersected it at right **angles.**

ANGRY see ANGER

ANGUISH

Esth 4. 1 of all that had been done, he tore his clothes in **anguish.**
Ps 48. 6 were seized with fear and **anguish,** like a woman about to
Is 26.16 You punished your people, Lord, and in **anguish** they prayed
Jer 6.24 we are seized by **anguish** and pain like a woman in labour.
15. 8 I suddenly struck them with **anguish** and terror.
50.43 He is seized by **anguish,** by pain like a woman in labour.
Lam 1.20 "Look, O Lord, at my agony, at the **anguish** of my soul!
2.11 my soul is in **anguish.**
3. 5 He has shut me in a prison of misery and **anguish.**
Mt 26.37 Grief and **anguish** came over him, [38]and he said to them,
Mk 14.33 Distress and **anguish** came over him, [34]and he said to them,
Lk 22.44 In great **anguish** he prayed even more fervently;

ANIMAL
[PACK-ANIMALS]

Gen 1.24 Then God commanded, "Let the earth produce all kinds of **animal**
1.26 the birds, and all **animals,** domestic and wild, large and small."
1.28 in charge of the fish, the birds, and all the wild **animals.**
1.30 but for all the wild **animals** and for all the birds I
2.19 the ground and formed all the **animals** and all the birds.
2.20 So the man named all the birds and all the **animals;**
3. 1 was the most cunning **animal** that the Lord God had made.
3.14 you alone of all the **animals** must bear this curse:
3.21 God made clothes out of **animal** skins for Adam and his wife,
6. 7 have created, and also the **animals** and the birds, because I
6.19 female of every kind of **animal** and of every kind of bird,
7. 2 each kind of ritually clean **animal,**
7. 2 but only one pair of each kind of unclean **animal.**
7. 3 so that every kind of **animal** and bird will be kept alive
7. 8 female of every kind of **animal** and bird, whether ritually clean
7.14 went every kind of **animal,** domestic and wild, large and small,
7.21 on the earth died—every bird, every **animal,** and every person.
7.23 all living beings on the earth—human beings, **animals,** and birds.
8. 1 not forgotten Noah and all the **animals** with him in the boat;
8.17 Take all the birds and **animals** out with you, so that
8.19 All the **animals** and birds went out of the boat in groups
8.20 each kind of ritually clean **animal** and bird, and burnt them
9. 2 All the **animals,** birds, and fish will live in fear of you.
9. 5 I will punish with death any **animal** that takes a human life.
9.10 beings—all birds and all **animals**—everything that came out of
9.15 you and to all the **animals** that a flood will never again
13. 6 of them to stay together, because they had too many **animals.**
13. 7 who took care of Abram's **animals**
13. 7 and those who took care of Lot's **animals.**
15.10 Abram brought the **animals** to God, cut them in half, and
15.17 suddenly appeared and passed between the pieces of the **animals.**
24.20 emptied her jar into the **animals'** drinking-trough and ran
25.28 because he enjoyed eating the **animals** Esau killed,
27. 3 arrows, go out into the country, and kill an **animal** for me.
27. 7 say to Esau, [7]'Bring me an **animal** and cook it for me.
27.33 was it, then, who killed an **animal** and brought it to me?
30.38 there, because the **animals** mated when they came to drink.
30.40 the direction of the streaked and black **animals** of Laban's flock.
30.41 When the healthy **animals** were mating, Jacob put the branches
30.42 he did not put the branches in front of the weak **animals.**
30.42 Laban had all the weak **animals,** and Jacob all the healthy ones.
31.39 was killed by wild **animals,** I always bore the loss myself.
31.54 He killed an **animal,** which he offered as a sacrifice on
32.17 Who owns these **animals** in front of you?'
37.20 We can say that a wild **animal** killed him.

Gen	37.33	Some wild **animal** has killed him.
	43.16	eat with me at noon, so kill an **animal** and prepare it."
	44.28	torn to pieces by wild **animals,** because I have not seen him
	45.17	your brothers to load their **animals** and to return to the
Ex	2.17	Moses went to their rescue and watered their **animals** for them.
	2.19	"and he even drew water for us and watered our **animals."**
	8.17	was turned into gnats, which covered the people and the **animals.**
	8.26	offended by our sacrificing the **animals** that we offer to the
	8.26	If we use these **animals** and offend the Egyptians by sacrificing
	9. 3	terrible disease on all your **animals**—your horses, donkeys, camels,
	9. 4	make a distinction between the **animals** of the Israelites
	9. 4	and no **animal** that belongs to the Israelites will
	9. 6	and all the **animals** of the Egyptians died,
	9. 6	but not one of the **animals** of the Israelites died.
	9. 7	told that none of the **animals** of the Israelites had died.
	9. 9	that become open sores on the people and the **animals."**
	9.10	boils that became open sores on the people and the **animals.**
	9.19	fall on the people and **animals** left outside unprotected,
	9.20	and they brought their slaves and **animals** indoors for shelter.
	9.21	Lord's warning and left their slaves and **animals** out in the open.
	9.22	Egypt—on the people, the **animals,** and all the plants in the
	9.25	in the open, including all the people and all the **animals.**
	10.25	to provide us with **animals** for sacrifices and burnt-offerings
	10.26	No, we will take our **animals** with us;
	10.26	We ourselves must select the **animals** with which to worship
	10.26	there, we will not know what **animals** to sacrifice to him."
	11. 7	not even a dog will bark at the Israelites or their **animals.**
	12. 4	small to eat a whole **animal,** he and his next-door neighbour
	12. 4	share an **animal,** in proportion to the number of
	12. 6	month, the whole community of Israel will kill the **animals.**
	12. 7	doors of the houses in which the **animals** are to be eaten.
	12.12	first-born male, both human and **animal,** and punishing
	12.22	in the bowl containing the **animal's** blood, and wipe the
	12.29	all the first-born of the **animals** were also killed.
	12.46	And do not break any of the **animal's** bones.
	13. 2	every first-born male Israelite and every first-born male **animal**
	13.12	Every first-born male of your **animals** belongs to the Lord,
	13.15	first-born male in the land of Egypt, both human and **animal.**
	13.15	we sacrifice every first-born male **animal** to the Lord,
	19.13	This applies to both men and **animals;**
	20.10	your children, your slaves, your **animals,** nor the foreigners
	21.34	or a donkey falls into it, [34] he must pay for the **animal.**
	21.34	pay the money to the owner and may keep the dead **animal.**
	21.35	they shall also divide up the meat from the dead **animal.**
	21.36	other man a live bull, but he may keep the dead **animal.**
	22. 2	If the stolen **animal,** whether a cow, a donkey, or a sheep,
	22. 5	"If a man lets his **animals** graze in a field or a
	22.10	cow, sheep, or other **animal** for him, and the animal dies
	22.11	take an oath that he has not stolen the other man's **animal.**
	22.11	If the **animal** was not stolen, the owner shall accept the loss,
	22.12	but if the **animal** was stolen, the man must repay the owner.
	22.13	it was killed by wild **animals,** the man is to bring the
	22.13	he need not pay for what has been killed by wild **animals.**
	22.14	"If a man borrows an **animal** from another man and it is
	22.15	If it is a hired **animal,** the loss is covered by the
	22.19	"Put to death any man who has sexual relations with an **animal.**
	22.31	the meat of any animal that has been killed by wild **animals;**
	23.11	grows there, and the wild **animals** can have what is left.
	23.12	foreigners who work for you and even your **animals** can rest.
	23.18	bread made with yeast when you sacrifice an **animal** to me.
	23.18	The fat of **animals** sacrificed to me during these festivals
	23.29	deserted, and the wild **animals** would be too many for you.
	24. 6	took half the blood of the **animals** and put it in bowls;
	29.26	This part of the **animal** will be yours,
	29.28	breast and the thigh of the **animal** belong to the priests.
	30. 9	forbidden incense, any **animal-offering,** or any grain-offering,
	30.10	on its four projections the blood of the **animal** sacrificed
	32. 6	next morning they brought some **animals** to burn as sacrifices
	34.19	son and first-born male domestic **animal** belongs to me,
	34.25	bread made with yeast when you sacrifice an **animal** to me.
	34.25	any part of the **animal** killed at the Passover Festival.
Lev	1. 2	When anyone offers an **animal** sacrifice, it may be one of
	1. 6	Then he shall skin the **animal** and cut it up, [7] and the
	1. 8	the pieces of the **animal,** including the head and the fat.
	3. 2	on the head of the **animal** and kill it at the entrance
	3. 3	parts of the **animal** as a food-offering to the Lord:
	3. 9	parts of the **animal** as a food-offering to the Lord:
	4.10	the fat from the **animal** killed for the fellowship-offering.
	4.24	where the **animals** for the burnt-offerings are killed.
	4.25	in the blood of the **animal,** put it on the projections at
	4.26	the fat of the **animals** killed for the fellowship-offerings.
	4.29	where the **animals** for the burnt-offerings are killed.
	4.30	in the blood of the **animal,** put it on the projections at
	4.31	removed from the **animals** killed for the fellowship-offerings,
	4.33	where the **animals** for the burnt-offerings are killed.
	4.34	in the blood of the **animal,** put it on the projections at
	5. 2	unclean, such as a dead **animal,** he is unclean and guilty as
	5.16	the priest shall offer the **animal** as a sacrifice for the
	6.25	The **animal** for a sin-offering shall be killed on the north
	6.25	where the **animals** for the burnt offerings are killed.
	6.26	The priest who sacrifices the **animal** shall eat it in a
	6.27	touches the flesh of the **animal** will be harmed by the power
	6.27	clothing is spattered with the **animal's** blood, it must be washed
	6.30	the ritual to take away sin, the **animal** must not be eaten;
	7. 2	The **animal** for this offering is to be killed on the north
	7. 2	where the **animals** for the burnt-offerings are killed,
	7. 8	The skin of an **animal** offered as a burnt-offering belongs to
	7.12	shall present, together with the **animal** to be sacrificed,
	7.14	the blood of the **animal** and throws it against the altar.
	7.15	The flesh of the **animal** must be eaten on the day it
Lev	7.21	from a man or an **animal,** he shall no longer be considered
	7.24	The fat of an **animal** that has died a natural death or
	7.24	been killed by a wild **animal** must not be eaten, but it
	7.25	eats the fat of an **animal** that may be offered as a
	7.26	they must never use the blood of birds or **animals** for food.
	7.30	bring the fat of the **animal** with its breast and present it
	7.32	right hind leg of the **animal** shall be given as a special
	7.34	The breast of the **animal** is a special gift, and the
	9.12	He killed the **animal** which was for his own burnt-offering.
	9.13	the other pieces of the **animal,** and he burnt them on the
	9.16	He also brought the **animal** for the burnt-offering
	9.20	of the breasts of the **animals** and carried it all to the
	11. 2	You may eat any land **animal** [3] that has divided hoofs and
	11. 8	Do not eat these **animals** or even touch their dead bodies;
	11.24	the dead bodies of the following **animals** will be unclean
	11.24	all **animals** with hoofs, unless their hoofs are divided
	11.24	and they chew the cud, and all four-footed **animals** with paws.
	11.39	If any **animal** that may be eaten dies, anyone who touches
	11.40	eats any part of the **animal,** he must wash his clothes, but
	11.41	eat any of the small **animals** that move on the ground,
	11.46	the law about **animals** and birds, about everything that lives
	11.47	clean and unclean, between **animals** that may be eaten and those
	14.13	where the **animals** for the sin-offerings and the burnt-offerings
	14.19	he shall kill the **animal** for the burnt-offering
	16.25	on the altar the fat of the **animal** for the sin-offering.
	17. 5	bring to the Lord the **animals** which they used to kill in
	17. 7	the Lord by killing their **animals** in the fields as
	17.13	in the community hunts an **animal** or a bird which is ritually
	17.15	who eats meat from an **animal** that has died a natural death
	17.15	has been killed by wild **animals** must wash his clothes, have
	18.23	No man or woman is to have sexual relations with an **animal;**
	19. 5	"When you kill an **animal** for a fellowship-offering,
	19. 6	eaten on the day the **animal** is killed or on the next
	19.19	Do not crossbreed domestic **animals.**
	20.15	has sexual relations with an **animal,**
	20.15	he and the **animal** shall be put to death.
	20.16	have sexual relations with an **animal,**
	20.16	she and the **animal** shall be put to death.
	20.25	distinction between **animals** and birds that are ritually clean
	20.25	Do not eat unclean **animals** or birds.
	22. 5	of semen [5] or if he has touched an unclean **animal** or person.
	22. 8	eat the meat of any **animal** that has died a natural death
	22. 8	or has been killed by wild **animals;**
	22.18	a freewill offering, the **animal** must not have any defects.
	22.20	If you offer any **animal** that has any defect, the Lord
	22.21	as a freewill offering, the **animal** must be without any
	22.22	offer to the Lord any **animal** that is blind or crippled or
	22.22	Do not offer any such **animals** on the altar as a food-offering.
	22.23	offering you may offer an **animal** that is stunted or not
	22.24	offer to the Lord any **animal** whose testicles have been crushed,
	22.25	as a food-offering any **animal** obtained from a foreigner.
	22.25	Such **animals** are considered defective and are not acceptable.
	24.18	and anyone who kills an **animal** belonging to someone else
	24.21	Whoever kills an **animal** shall replace it,
	25. 7	your domestic animals, and the wild **animals** in your fields.
	26. 6	get rid of the dangerous **animals** in the land, and there will
	26.22	I will send dangerous **animals** among you, and they will kill
	27. 9	If the vow concerns an **animal** that is acceptable as an
	27.10	who made the vow may not substitute another **animal** for it.
	27.10	If he does, both **animals** belong to the Lord.
	27.11	vow concerns a ritually unclean **animal,** which is not acceptable
	27.11	to the Lord, the man shall take the **animal** to the priest.
	27.26	The first-born of an **animal** already belongs to the Lord,
	27.27	the first-born of an unclean **animal** may be bought back at
	27.28	the Lord, whether it is a human being, an **animal,** or land.
	27.32	One out of every ten domestic **animals** belongs to the Lord.
	27.32	When the **animals** are counted, every tenth one belongs to the Lord.
	27.33	owner may not arrange the **animals**
	27.33	so that the poor **animals** are chosen, and he may not
	27.33	If he does substitute one **animal** for another,
	27.33	then both **animals** will belong to the Lord
Num	3.12	son of each Israelite family and the first-born of every **animal.**
	6.14	and present to the Lord three **animals** without any defects:
	8.17	son of each Israelite family and the first-born of every **animal.**
	9.12	morning and do not break any of the **animal's** bones.
	15. 4	is to bring with each **animal** a kilogramme of flour mixed
	15.12	When more than one **animal** is offered, the accompanying offering
	18.15	"Every first-born child or **animal** that the Israelites present
	18.15	payment for every first-born **animal** that is ritually unclean.
	19. 5	The whole **animal,** including skin, meat, blood, and intestines,
	20. 4	Just so that we can die here with our **animals?**
	20. 8	rock for the people, for them and their **animals** to drink."
	20.11	of water gushed out, and all the people and **animals** drank.
	20.19	and if we or our **animals** drink any of your water, we
	31.11	including the prisoners and the **animals,**
	31.26	that has been captured, including the prisoners and the **animals.**
	31.47	every fifty prisoners and **animals,** and as the Lord had commanded,
	35. 3	land will be for their cattle and all their other **animals.**
Deut	4.17	whether man or woman, [17] **animal** or bird, [18] reptile or fish.
	5.14	your children, your slaves, your **animals,** nor the foreigners
	7.22	did, the number of wild **animals** would increase and be a
	11. 6	their families, their tents, and all their servants and **animals.**
	12.15	you are free to kill and eat your **animals** wherever you live.
	14. 4	You may eat these **animals:**
	14. 6	wild goats, or antelopes—[6] any **animals** that have divided hoofs
	14. 7	But no **animals** may be eaten unless they have divided hoofs
	14. 8	eat any of these **animals** or even touch their dead bodies.
	14.21	"Do not eat any **animal** that dies a natural death.

Deut 15.21 is anything wrong with the **animals,** if they are crippled or
15.22 You may eat such **animals** at home.
16. 4 and the meat of the **animal** killed on the evening of the
16. 5 "Slaughter the Passover **animals** at the one place of worship—
22. 4 help him to get the **animal** to its feet again.
27.21 " 'God's curse on anyone who has sexual relations with an **animal.'**
28.26 die, birds and wild **animals** will come and eat your bodies,
32.24 I will send wild **animals** to attack them, and poisonous
Judg 20.48 killed them all—men, women, and children, and **animals** as well.
1 Sam 10.16 "He told us that the **animals** had been found," Saul answered—
17.44 I will give your body to the birds and **animals** to eat."
17.46 of the Philistine soldiers to the birds and **animals** to eat.
25.11 and the **animals** I have slaughtered for my shearers,
2 Sam 12. 4 kill one of his own **animals** to prepare a meal for him;
21.10 and at night she would protect them from wild **animals.**
1 Kgs 3. 3 but he also slaughtered **animals** and offered them as sacrifices
4.28 where it was needed, for the chariot-horses and the draught **animals.**
4.33 he talked about **animals,** birds, reptiles, and fish.
8.64 and the fat of the **animals** for the fellowship-offerings.
18. 5 Maybe we won't have to kill any of our **animals."**
2 Kgs 1. 8 a cloak made of **animal** skins, tied with a leather belt,"
3. 9 and there was none left for the men or the **pack-animals.**
3.17 livestock, and your **pack-animals** will have plenty to drink.'
14. 9 A wild **animal** passed by and trampled the bush down.
16.13 so he burnt **animal** sacrifices and grain-offerings on it,
16.15 Pour on it the blood of all the **animals** that are sacrificed.
1 Chr 29.21 The following day they killed **animals** as sacrifices,
2 Chr 1. 6 he had a thousand **animals** killed and burnt whole on it.
4. 6 the parts of the **animals** that were burnt as sacrifices.
13.11 and every evening they offer him incense and **animal** sacrifices
25.18 A wild **animal** passed by and trampled the bush down.
29.21 to offer the **animals** as sacrifices on the altar.
29.31 some of them also voluntarily brought **animals** to be sacrificed
29.34 priests to kill all these **animals,** the Levites helped them
31. 3 he provided **animals** for the burnt-offerings each morning
35. 1 of the first month they killed the **animals** for the festival.
35.12 people, by family groups, the **animals** for burnt-offerings,
35.14 busy until night, burning the **animals** that were burnt whole
Ezra 1. 4 silver and gold, supplies and **pack animals,** as well as
1. 6 utensils, gold, supplies, **pack animals,** other valuables,
6.20 The Levites killed the **animals** for the Passover sacrifices
8.35 All these **animals** were burnt as sacrifices to the Lord.
Neh 2.12 The only **animal** we took was the donkey that I rode on.
10.33 the daily grain-offering, the **animals** to be burnt each day
Job 5.22 at violence and hunger and not be afraid of wild **animals.**
5.23 wild **animals** will never attack you.
12. 7 Even birds and **animals** have much they could teach you;
30. 7 they howled like **animals** and huddled together under the bushes.
35.11 to God, who makes us wise, wiser than any **animal** or bird.
37. 8 The wild **animals** go to their dens.
39.15 that a foot may crush them or a wild **animal** break them.
41.34 He looks down on even the proudest **animals;**
Ps 8. 7 sheep and cattle, and the wild **animals** too;
36. 6 Men and **animals** are in your care.
40. 6 you do not ask for **animals** burnt whole on the altar or
44.19 Yet you left us helpless among wild **animals;**
49.12 he will still die like the **animals.**
49.20 he will still die like the **animals.**
50.10 all the **animals** in the forest are mine and the cattle on
68.30 Rebuke Egypt, that wild **animal** in the reeds;
73.22 my feelings were hurt, [22] I was as stupid as an **animal;**
74.14 the monster Leviathan and fed his body to desert **animals.**
79. 2 the bodies of your servants for wild **animals** to eat.
80.13 wild pigs trample it down, and wild **animals** feed on it.
104.11 They provide water for the wild **animals;**
104.20 night, and in the darkness all the wild **animals** come out.
106.20 glory of God for the image of an **animal** that eats grass.
135. 8 In Egypt he killed all the first-born of men and **animals** alike.
147. 9 He gives **animals** their food and feeds the young ravens
148.10 all **animals,** tame and wild, reptiles and birds.
Prov 9. 2 She has had an **animal** killed for a feast, mixed spices in
12.10 man takes care of his **animals,** but wicked men are cruel to
30. 2 I am more like an **animal** than a man;
30.24 There are four **animals** in the world that are small, but
30.30 lions, strongest of all **animals** and afraid of none;
Ecc 3.18 testing us, to show us that we are no better than **animals.**
3.19 After all, the same fate awaits man and **animal** alike.
3.19 no better off than an **animal,** because life has no meaning
3.21 while an **animal's** spirit goes down into the ground?
Is 1.11 you burn as sacrifices and of the fat of your fine **animals.**
5. 5 it, and let wild **animals** eat it and trample it down.
5.29 lions that have killed an **animal** and are carrying it off
13.21 be a place where desert **animals** live and where owls build
18. 6 will be left exposed to the birds and the wild **animals.**
18. 6 the birds will feed on them, and in winter, the **animals."**
23.13 not the Assyrians, who let the wild **animals** overrun Tyre.
30. 6 This is God's message about the **animals** of the southern desert:
31. 4 can't scare away a lion from an **animal** that it has killed;
34.14 Wild **animals** will roam there, and demons will call
35. 9 no fierce **animals** will pass that way.
40.16 All the **animals** in the forests of Lebanon are not enough
43.20 Even the wild **animals** will honour me;
43.24 incense for me or satisfy me with the fat of your **animals.**
46. 1 loaded on donkeys, a burden for the backs of tired **animals.**
56. 9 nations to come like wild **animals** and devour his people.
Jer 7.20 it out on people and **animals** alike, and even on the trees
7.33 for the birds and wild **animals,** and there will be no one
9.10 birds and wild **animals** have fled and gone."
11.15 by making promises and by offering **animal** sacrifices?
Jer 12. 4 **Animals** and birds are dying because of the wickedness of our people,
12. 9 Call the wild **animals** to come and join in the feast!
15. 3 eat them, and wild **animals** will devour what is left over.
16. 4 bodies will be food for the birds and the wild **animals.**
19. 7 their corpses to the birds and the wild **animals** as food.
21. 6 people and **animals** alike will die of a terrible disease.
27. 5 world, mankind, and all the **animals** that live on the earth;
27. 6 Babylonia, and I have made even the wild **animals** serve him.
28.14 that he will make even the wild **animals** serve Nebuchadnezzar."
31.18 we were like an untamed **animal,** but you taught us to obey.
31.27 fill the land of Israel and Judah with people and **animals.**
32.43 desert where neither people nor **animals** live,
33.10 a desert, that it has no people or **animals** living in it.
33.10 no people or **animals** live there.
33.12 and where no people or **animals** live, there will once again
34.20 and their corpses will be eaten by birds and wild **animals.**
36.29 and destroy this land and kill its people and its **animals.**
50. 3 Men and **animals** will run away, and no one will live there."
51.37 country will become a pile of ruins where wild **animals** live.
51.62 in it, neither man nor **animal,** and it would be like a
Ezek 4.14 never eaten meat from any **animal** that died a natural death
4.14 or was killed by wild **animals.**
5.17 will send hunger and wild **animals** to kill your children,
8.10 of snakes and other unclean **animals,** and of the other things
14.13 I will send a famine and kill people and **animals** alike.
14.15 "Or I might send wild **animals** to kill the people,
14.17 to wipe out people and **animals** alike,
14.19 many lives, killing people and **animals,**
14.21 on Jerusalem—war, famine, wild **animals,** and disease—
14.21 to destroy people and **animals** alike.
21.21 he examines the liver of a sacrificed **animal.**
22.25 The leaders are like lions roaring over the **animals**
22.27 government officials are like wolves tearing apart the **animals**
25.13 that I will punish Edom and kill every man and **animal** there.
29. 5 I will give it to the birds and **animals** for food.
29. 8 swords, and they will kill your people and your **animals.**
29.11 No human being or **animal** will walk through it.
31. 6 The wild **animals** bore their young in its shelter;
31.13 tree, and the wild **animals** will walk over its branches.
32. 4 bring all the birds and **animals** of the world to feed on
33.27 Those living in the country will be eaten by wild **animals.**
34. 5 they were scattered, and wild **animals** killed and ate them.
34. 8 have been attacked by wild **animals** that killed and ate them
34.25 rid of all the dangerous **animals** in the land, so that my
34.28 any more, and the wild **animals** will not kill and eat them.
38.20 Every fish and bird, every **animal** large and small,
39. 4 let their bodies be food for all the birds and wild **animals.**
39.17 call all the birds and **animals** to come from all round to
39.19 like sacrifices, the birds and **animals** are to eat all the
40.38 washed the carcasses of the **animals** to be burnt whole
40.39 tables that they killed the **animals** to be offered as sacrifices,
40.41 eight tables on which the **animals** to be sacrificed were killed:
40.42 equipment used in killing the sacrificial **animals** was kept
43.18 sprinkling on it the blood of the **animals** that were sacrificed.
44.11 They may kill the **animals** which the people offer
44.31 not eat any bird or **animal** that dies a natural death
44.31 or is killed by another **animal."**
45.13 "You are to bring grain-offerings, **animals** to be burnt whole,
45.13 and **animals** for fellowship-offerings, so that your sins
45.17 his duty to provide the **animals** to be burnt whole,
47. 9 stream flows, there will be all kinds of **animals** and fish.
Dan 2.38 inhabited earth and ruler over all the **animals** and birds.
4.12 Wild **animals** rested in its shade, birds built nests
4.14 Drive the **animals** from under it and the birds out of its
4.15 this man, and let him live with the **animals** and the plants.
4.16 will not have a human mind, but the mind of an **animal.**
4.21 Wild **animals** rested under it, and birds made their nests in
4.23 and let him live there with the **animals** for seven years.'
4.25 away from human society and will live with wild **animals.**
4.32 human society, live with wild **animals,** and eat grass like an
5.21 human society, and his mind became like that of an **animal.**
8. 4 No **animal** could stop him or escape his power.
Hos 2.12 wild **animals** will destroy them.
2.18 covenant with all the wild **animals** and birds, so that they
4. 3 All the **animals** and birds, and even the fish, will die."
6. 6 I want your constant love, not your **animal** sacrifices.
13. 8 the spot, and will tear you to pieces like a wild **animal.**
Joel 1.20 Even the wild **animals** cry out to you because the streams
2.22 **Animals,** don't be afraid.
Amos 4. 4 Go ahead and bring **animals** to be sacrificed morning after morning,
5.22 I will not accept the **animals** you have fattened to bring me
Jon 3. 8 All persons and **animals** must wear sackcloth.
4.11 120,000 innocent children in it, as well as many **animals!"**
Hab 2.17 You killed its **animals;**
2.17 now **animals** will terrify you.
Zeph 1. 3 destroy everything on earth, [3] all human beings and **animals,**
2.14 where flocks, herds, and **animals** of every kind will lie down.
2.15 it will become, a place where wild **animals** will rest!
Hag 1.11 on men and **animals,** on everything you try to grow."
Zech 8.10 to hire either men or **animals,** and no one was safe from
14.15 the donkeys—on all the **animals** in the camps of the enemy.
Mal 1. 8 blind or sick or lame **animal** to sacrifice to me, do you
1. 8 Try giving an **animal** like that to the governor!
1.13 me you bring a stolen **animal** or one that is lame or
1.14 cheat who sacrifices a worthless **animal** to me, when he has
1.14 in his flock a good **animal** that he promised to give me!
2. 3 in the dung of the **animals** you sacrifice—and you will be
Mt 9.13 'It is kindness that I want, not **animal sacrifices.'**
12. 7 scripture says, 'It is kindness that I want, not **animal sacrifices.'**

Mk 1.13 Wild **animals** were there also, but angels came and helped him.
11. 7 threw their cloaks over the **animal,** and Jesus got on.
12.33 these two commandments than to offer **animals** and other sacrifices
Lk 10.34 the man on his own **animal** and took him to an inn,
19.35 threw their cloaks over the **animal** and helped Jesus get on.
Jn 2.15 cords and drove all the **animals** out of the Temple,
Acts 7.42 slaughtered and sacrificed **animals** for forty years in the desert.
10.12 In it were all kinds of **animals,** reptiles, and wild birds.
11. 6 and saw domesticated and wild **animals,** reptiles, and wild birds.
15.20 and not to eat any **animal** that has been strangled,
15.29 eat no **animal** that has been strangled;
21.25 or any blood, or any **animal** that has been strangled,
Rom 1.23 to look like mortal man or birds or **animals** or reptiles.
1 Cor 15.39 have one kind of flesh, **animals** another, birds another,
Gal 5.15 if you act like wild **animals,** hurting and harming each other,
Heb 8. 3 appointed to present offerings and **animal sacrifices** to God,
9. 9 the offerings and **animal sacrifices** presented to God cannot make
9.25 the Most Holy Place every year with the blood of an **animal.**
10. 6 You are not pleased with **animals** burnt whole on the altar
10. 8 sacrifices and offerings or with **animals** burnt on the altar
12.20 which said, "If even an **animal** touches the mountain, it
13.11 brings the blood of the **animals** into the Most Holy Place
13.11 but the bodies of the **animals** are burnt outside the camp.
Jas 3. 7 has tamed all other creatures—wild **animals** and birds, reptiles
2 Pet 2.12 instinct, like wild **animals** born to be captured and killed;
2.12 will be destroyed like wild **animals,** [13] and they will be paid
Jude 10 by instinct, like wild **animals,** are the very things that destroy
Rev 6. 8 to kill by means of war, famine, disease, and wild **animals.**

ANKLES

Is 3.16 dainty little steps, and the bracelets on their **ankles** jingle.
3.18 ornaments they wear on their **ankles,** on their heads,
Ezek 47. 3 The water came only to my **ankles.**
Acts 3. 7 At once the man's feet and **ankles** became strong;

ANNEXE

1 Kgs 6. 5 a three-storied **annexe** was built, each storey 2.2 metres
6. 8 the lowest storey of the **annexe** was on the south side of
6.10 The three-storied **annexe,** each storey 2.2 metres high,
Ezek 40.38 there was an **annexe** attached to the inner gateway
40.42 The four tables in the **annexe,** used to prepare the offerings

ANNOUNCE

Ex 32. 5 and **announced,** "Tomorrow there will be a festival
Judg 7. 3 **Announce** to the people, 'Anyone who is afraid should go back home,
2 Sam 1.20 Do not **announce** it in Gath or in the streets of Ashkelon.
1 Kgs 1.24 "Your Majesty, have you **announced** that Adonijah would succeed
2 Kgs 7.11 The guards **announced** the news, and it was reported in the palace.
1 Chr 13. 2 Then he **announced** to all the people of Israel, "If you
29. 1 King David **announced** to the whole assembly:
2 Chr 20. 2 Some messengers came and **announced** to King Jehoshaphat:
Esth 6. 9 Let the nobleman **announce** as they go:
6.11 through the city square, **announcing** to the people as they went:
Job 36.33 Thunder **announces** the approaching storm, and the cattle know
Ps 2. 7 "I will **announce,"** says the king, "what the Lord has declared.
19. 2 Each day **announces** it to the following day;
98. 2 The Lord **announced** his victory;
119.46 I will **announce** your commands to kings and I will not be
Is 21.10 wheat, but now I have **announced** to you the good news that
40. 9 **announce** the good news!
48. 5 your future long ago, **announcing** events before they took place,
52. 7 He **announces** victory and says to Zion, "Your God is king!"
61. 1 To heal the broken-hearted, To **announce** release to captives
62.11 can know [11] That the Lord is **announcing** to all the earth:
63. 1 "It is the Lord, powerful to save, coming to **announce** his victory."
Jer 4.15 of Dan and from the hills of Ephraim **announce** the bad news.
7. 1 me to stand there and **announce** what the Lord Almighty, the
17.19 "Jeremiah, go and **announce** my message at the People's Gate,
32. 3 and had accused me of **announcing** that the Lord had said, "I
48.20 **Announce** along the River Arnon that Moab is destroyed!'
50. 2 Give the signal and **announce** the news!
Ezek 3.18 If I **announce** that an evil man is going to die but
20. 9 they were living I had **announced** to Israel that I was going
21.28 **Announce** what I, the Sovereign Lord, am saying to the Ammonites,
25.13 Now I **announce** that I will punish Edom and kill every
25.16 And so I am **announcing** that I will attack the Philistines
30. 2 he said, "prophesy and **announce** what I, the Sovereign Lord, am
33. 8 If I **announce** that an evil man is going to die but
36. 3 "Prophesy, then, and **announce** what I, the Sovereign Lord,
38.17 when I **announced** through my servants, the prophets
Dan 3. 4 of the statue, [4] a herald **announced** in a loud voice,
Joel 3. 9 "Make this **announcement** among the nations:
Amos 3. 9 **Announce** to those who live in the palaces of Egypt and Ashdod:
Nah 1.15 He is on his way to **announce** the victory!
Mt 10.27 have heard in private you must **announce** from the housetops.
12.18 Spirit upon him, and he will **announce** my judgement to the nations.
Mk 1. 7 He **announced** to the people, "The man who will come after
Lk 4.19 set free the oppressed [19] and **announce** that the time has come
Acts 3.18 **announced** long ago through all the prophets that his Messiah had
3.21 made new, as God **announced** through his holy prophets who lived
3.24 after him, also **announced** what has been happening these days.
7.52 God's messengers, who long ago **announced** the coming of his
12.14 without opening the door, and **announced** that Peter was standing
14.15 We are here to **announce** the Good News, to turn you away
Acts 16.17 They **announce** to you how you can be saved!"
17. 3 Jesus whom I **announce** to you," Paul said, "is the Messiah."
20.27 have not held back from **announcing** to you the whole purpose
26.23 to rise from death, to **announce** the light of salvation to
Gal 3. 8 And so the scripture **announced** the Good News to Abraham:
Eph 6.15 your shoes the readiness to **announce** the Good News of peace.
1 Tim 1.11 was entrusted to me to **announce,** the Good News from the
Heb 2. 3 Lord himself first **announced** this salvation, and those who heard
1 Pet 1.12 from the messengers who **announced** the Good News by the power
1 Jn 1. 3 have seen and heard we **announce** to you also, so that you
1. 5 that we have heard from his Son and **announce** is this:
Rev 5. 2 saw a mighty angel, who **announced** in a loud voice,
10. 7 his secret plan, as he **announced** to his servants, the prophets."
14. 6 of Good News to **announce** to the peoples of the earth,
22.16 have sent my angel to **announce** these things to you

ANNOY

1 Sam 21.15 Why bring another one to **annoy** me with his daft actions
Job 4. 1 Job, will you be **annoyed** if I speak?
Prov 12.16 When a fool is **annoyed,** he quickly lets it be known.
Acts 4. 2 were **annoyed** because the two apostles were teaching the people

ANNUAL

Lev 23.26 is the day when the **annual** ritual is to be performed to
25.53 years left, [53] as if he had been hired on an **annual** basis.
1 Sam 20. 6 the time for the **annual** sacrifice there for my whole family.
2 Kgs 17. 4 and stopped paying the **annual** tribute to Assyria.
2 Chr 8.13 Moon Festivals, and the three **annual** festivals—
24. 5 enough money to make the **annual** repairs on the Temple.
Esth 9.23 and the celebration became an **annual** custom.
Hos 2.11 to all her festivities—her **annual** and monthly festivals

ANNUL

Num 30.13 right to affirm or to **annul** any vow or promise that she
30.15 But if he later **annuls** the vow, he must suffer the

ANOINT

To pour or rub olive-oil on someone in order to honour him or to appoint him to some special work. The Israelite kings were anointed when they took office, and so the king could be called "the anointed one". Christ, the Greek word for "The Anointed One", is the title of the one whom God chose and appointed as Saviour and Lord.

Ex 25. 6 for the **anointing** oil and for the sweet-smelling incense;
28.41 them and dedicate them by **anointing** them with olive-oil,
29. 7 Then take the **anointing** oil,
29. 7 pour it on his head, and **anoint** him.
29.21 altar and some of the **anointing** oil, and sprinkle it on
29.36 Then **anoint** it with olive-oil to make it holy.
30.25 and make a sacred **anointing** oil, mixed like perfume.
30.26 Use it to **anoint** the Tent of my presence, the Covenant Box,
30.30 Then **anoint** Aaron and his sons, and ordain them as priests
30.31 people of Israel, 'This holy **anointing** oil is to be used in
31.11 the **anointing** oil, and the sweet-smelling incense
35. 8 for the **anointing** oil and for the sweet-smelling incense;
35.15 the **anointing** oil;
35.28 for the **anointing** oil, and for the sweet-smelling incense.
37.29 the sacred **anointing** oil and the pure sweet-smelling incense,
39.38 the **anointing** oil;
40. 9 and all its equipment by **anointing** it with the sacred oil,
40.10 and all its equipment by **anointing** it, and it will be
40.13 in the priestly garments, **anoint** him, and in this way consecrate
40.15 Then **anoint** them, just as you anointed their father,
40.15 This **anointing** will make them priests for all time to come."
Lev 8. 2 bring the priestly garments, the **anointing** oil, the young bull
8.10 Then Moses took the **anointing** oil and put it on the Tent
8.12 Aaron by pouring some of the **anointing** oil on his head.
8.30 Moses took some of the **anointing** oil and some of the
10. 7 have been consecrated by the **anointing** oil of the Lord."
21.10 High Priest has had the **anointing** oil poured on his head and
Num 3. 3 They were **anointed** and ordained as priests,
4.16 the incense, the grain-offerings, the **anointing** oil,
7. 1 of the Lord's presence, he **anointed** and dedicated the Tent
1 Sam 9.16 **anoint** him as ruler of my people Israel, and he will rescue
10. 1 him, and said, "The Lord **anoints** you as ruler of his people
15. 1 whom the Lord sent to **anoint** you king of his people Israel.
15.17 The Lord **anointed** you king of Israel, [18] and he sent you
16. 3 You will **anoint** as king the man I tell you to."
16.12 The Lord said to Samuel, "This is the one—**anoint** him!"
16.13 Samuel took the olive-oil and **anointed** David
2 Sam 2. 4 Judah came to Hebron and **anointed** David as king of Judah.
2. 7 and the people of Judah have **anointed** me as their king."
5. 3 sacred alliance with them, they **anointed** him, and he became king
19.10 We **anointed** Absalom as our king, but he has been killed
1 Kgs 1.34 where Zadok and Nathan are to **anoint** him as king of Israel.
1.39 from the Tent of the Lord's presence, and **anointed** Solomon.
1.45 mule, [45] and Zadok and Nathan **anointed** him as king at the
19.15 Damascus, then enter the city and **anoint** Hazael as king of Syria;
19.16 **anoint** Jehu son of Nimshi as king of Israel,
19.16 and **anoint** Elisha son of Shaphat from Abel
2 Kgs 9. 3 'The Lord proclaims that he **anoints** you king of Israel.'
9. 6 '**I anoint** you king of my people Israel.
9.12 '**I anoint** you king of Israel.' "
11.12 Then Joash was **anointed** and proclaimed king.
23.30 The people of Judah chose Josiah's son Joahaz and **anointed** him

1 Chr 11. 3 sacred alliance with them, they **anointed** him, and he became king
29.22 name of the Lord they **anointed** him as their ruler and Zadok
2 Chr 23.11 the priest and his sons **anointed** Joash, and everyone shouted,
36. 1 of Judah chose Josiah's son Joahaz and **anointed** him king
Ps 89.20 made my servant David king by **anointing** him with holy oil.
133. 2 like the precious **anointing** oil running down from Aaron's head
Zech 4.14 whom God has chosen and **anointed** to serve him, the Lord of
Mk 16. 1 and Salome bought spices to go and **anoint** the body of Jesus.

AV **ANOINT**
see also **CONSECRATE, OIL, OLIVE-OIL**

Gen 31.13 stone as a memorial by **pouring** olive-oil on it and where you
Lev 4. 3 If it is the **High Priest** who sins and so brings guilt
6.20 On the day he is **ordained,** he shall present as an offering
8.11 some of the oil and **sprinkled** it seven times on the altar
8.12 He **ordained** Aaron by pouring some of the anointing oil
16.32 The High Priest, properly **ordained** and consecrated
Num 7.10 brought offerings to celebrate the **dedication** of the altar.
7.84 the twelve leaders for the **dedication** of the altar
35.25 there until the death of the man who is then **High Priest.**
Judg 9. 8 time the trees got together to **choose** a king for themselves.
9.15 want to make me your **king,** then come and take shelter
Ruth 3. 3 wash yourself, put on some **perfume,** and get dressed in your
2 Sam 1.21 the shield of Saul is no longer **polished** with oil.
3.39 though I am the king **chosen** by God, I feel weak today.
5.17 David had been made **king of Israel,** so their army set out
12. 7 'I made you **king of Israel** and rescued you from Saul.
12.20 floor, had a bath, **combed** his hair, and changed his clothes.
14. 2 put on your mourning clothes, and don't **comb** your hair.
23. 1 whom the God of Jacob **chose** to be king, and who was
1 Chr 14. 8 David had now been made **king** over the whole country of Israel,
Ps 45. 7 has chosen you and has **poured** out more happiness on you than
Is 61. 1 He has **chosen** me and sent me To bring good news to
Dan 9.24 will come true, and the holy Temple will be **rededicated.**
10. 3 meat, drink any wine, or **comb** my hair until the three weeks
Amos 6. 6 bowlful and use the finest **perfumes,** but you do not mourn
Mt 6.17 wash your face and **comb** your hair, [18] so that others cannot
Mk 14. 8 she poured **perfume** on my body to prepare it ahead of time
Lk 4.18 upon me, because he has **chosen** me to bring good news to
7.38 with her hair, kissed them, and **poured** the perfume on them.
7.46 You provided no **olive-oil** for my head, but she has
7.46 for my head, but she has covered my feet with **perfume.**
Jn 9. 6 he **rubbed** the mud on the man's eyes [7] and said, "Go
9.11 called Jesus made some mud, **rubbed** it on my eyes, and told
11. 2 Mary was the one who **poured** the perfume on the Lord's feet
12. 3 perfume made of pure nard, **poured** it on Jesus' feet, and
12. 3 perfume made of pure nard, **poured** it on Jesus' feet, and
Acts 4.27 of Israel against Jesus, your holy Servant, whom you made **Messiah.**
10.38 and how God **poured** out on him the Holy Spirit
Heb 1. 9 why God, your God, has **chosen** you and has given you the
Rev 3.18 Buy also some **ointment** to put on your eyes, so that you

AV **ANOINTED** see **CHRIST, KING, MESSIAH**

ANSWER

Gen 25.21 The Lord **answered** his prayer, and Rebecca became pregnant.
25.22 So she went to ask the Lord for an **answer.**
30.17 God **answered** Leah's prayer, and she became pregnant and
30.22 he **answered** her prayer and made it possible for her to have
34.13 their sister Dinah, Jacob's sons **answered** Shechem and his
43. 7 We had to **answer** his questions.
44.22 could see him, [22] and we **answered** that the boy could not
45. 3 they were so terrified that they could not **answer.**
Ex 19. 9 Lord what the people had **answered,** [10] and the Lord said to him,
19.19 Moses spoke, and God **answered** him with thunder.
22.23 do, I, the Lord, will **answer** them when they cry out to
22.27 to me for help, I will **answer** him because I am merciful.
Num 14.28 Now give them this **answer:**
Deut 4. 7 He **answers** us whenever we call for help.
29.25 And the **answer** will be, 'It is because the Lord's people
Judg 8. 8 men of Penuel gave the same **answer** as the men of Sukkoth.
10.11 The Lord gave them this **answer:**
11.15 sent messengers back to the king of Ammon [15] with this **answer:**
14.18 hadn't been ploughing with my cow, You wouldn't know the **answer**
19.28 But there was no **answer.**
20. 1 as from the land of Gilead in the east, **answered** the call.
1 Sam 1.19 with his wife Hannah, and the Lord **answered** her prayer.
4.20 But she paid no attention and did not **answer.**
7. 9 the Lord to help Israel, and the Lord **answered** his prayer.
9.19 Tomorrow morning I will **answer** all your questions and send
13. 4 So the people **answered** the call to join Saul at Gilgal.
14.37 But God did not **answer** that day.
14.41 God of Israel, "Lord, why have you not **answered** me today?
14.41 Lord, God of Israel, **answer** me by the sacred stones.
14.41 If the guilt is Jonathan's or mine, **answer** by the Urim;
14.41 it belongs to your people Israel, **answer** by the Thummim."
14.41 The **answer** indicated Jonathan and Saul;
17.30 question, and every time he asked, he got the same **answer.**
20.10 "Who will let me know if your father **answers** you angrily?"
23.11 Lord, God of Israel, I beg you to **answer** me!"
28. 6 But the Lord did not **answer** him at all, either by dreams
28.15 He doesn't **answer** me any more, either by prophets or by dreams.
2 Sam 12.18 was living, David wouldn't **answer** us when we spoke to him.
14.19 that there is no way to avoid **answering** your question.
20.18 say, 'Go and get your **answer** in the city of Abel'—and
2 Sam 21.14 And after that, God **answered** their prayers for the country.
22.42 they call to the Lord, but he does not **answer.**
24.13 over, and tell me what **answer** to take back to the Lord."
24.25 The Lord **answered** his prayer, and the epidemic in Israel was stopped.
1 Kgs 2.29 Joab **answered** that he had fled to the Lord because he was
10. 3 He **answered** them all;
12. 5 in three days and I will give you my **answer,"** he replied.
12. 6 "What **answer** do you advise me to give these people?"
12. 7 give a favourable **answer** to their request, and they will
17.22 The Lord **answered** Elijah's prayer;
18.24 Lord, and the one who **answers** by sending fire—he is God."
18.26 They shouted, **"Answer** us, Baal!"
18.26 But no **answer** came.
18.29 but no **answer** came, not a sound was heard.
18.37 **Answer** me, Lord, answer me, so that this people will know
20.12 Benhadad received Ahab's **answer** as he and his allies,
2 Kgs 4.29 meet, and if anyone greets you, don't take time to **answer.**
6.17 The Lord **answered** his prayer, and Elisha's servant looked up
6.18 The Lord **answered** his prayer and struck them blind.
6.20 The Lord **answered** his prayer;
8. 6 In **answer** to the king's question, she confirmed Gehazi's story,
13. 4 of Syria was oppressing the Israelites, **answered** his prayer.
16. 9 Tiglath Pileser, in **answer** to Ahaz' plea, marched out
18.14 The emperor's **answer** was that Hezekiah should send him
19. 6 Isaiah received King Hezekiah's message, [6] he sent back this **answer:**
19.20 telling King Hezekiah that in **answer** to the king's prayer
1 Chr 5.20 and God **answered** their prayers and made them victorious
21.12 What **answer** shall I give the Lord?"
21.26 He prayed, and the Lord **answered** him by sending fire from
21.28 the Lord had **answered** his prayer, so he offered sacrifices
2 Chr 9. 2 He **answered** them all;
10. 6 "What **answer** do you advise me to give these people?"
10. 7 by giving a considerate **answer,** they will always serve you
25.18 Jehoash sent this **answer** to Amaziah:
30.20 The Lord **answered** Hezekiah's prayer;
33.13 God accepted Manasseh's prayer and **answered** it
33.19 The king's prayer and God's **answer** to it, and an account
Ezra 4.17 The emperor sent this **answer:**
8.23 prayed for God to protect us, and he **answered** our prayers.
10.12 The people shouted in **answer,** "We will do whatever you say."
Neh 9.27 called to you for help, and you **answered** them from heaven.
Job 5. 1 See if anyone **answers.**
6. 8 Why won't he **answer** my prayer?
6.26 then why do you **answer** my words of despair?
9. 3 He can ask a thousand questions that no one could ever **answer.**
9.14 So how can I find words to **answer** God?
9.32 If God were human, I could **answer** him;
11. 1 Will no one **answer** all this nonsense?
11. 3 Job, do you think we can't **answer** you?
11. 5 How I wish God would **answer** you!
12. 4 but there was a time when God **answered** my prayers.
13.22 Speak first, O God, and I will **answer.**
13.22 Or let me speak, and you **answer** me.
14.15 will call, and I will **answer,** and you will be pleased with
19.16 call a servant, he doesn't **answer**— even when I beg him
20. 1 Now I'm impatient to **answer.**
21.34 Every **answer** you give is a lie!
22.27 When you pray, he will **answer** you, and you will keep the
23. 5 to know what he would say and how he would **answer** me.
30.20 I call to you, O God, but you never **answer;**
31.35 Let Almighty God **answer** me.
32. 1 own innocence, the three men gave up trying to **answer** him.
32. 3 could find no way to **answer** Job, and this made it appear
32. 5 the three men could not **answer** Job, he was angry [6] and began
32.13 God must **answer** Job, for you have failed.
32.14 you, not to me, but I would never **answer** as you did.
32.15 they have no **answer** for you.
32.17 I will give my own **answer** now and tell you what I
33. 5 **Answer** me if you can.
33.13 Why do you accuse God of never **answering** a man's complaints?
33.26 when he prays, God will **answer** him;
35. 4 I am going to **answer** you and your friends too.
35.12 for help, but God doesn't **answer,** for they are proud and
38. 3 up now like a man and **answer** the questions I ask you.
38. 5 Do you know all the **answers?**
38.18 **Answer** me if you know.
40. 1 will you give up now, or will you **answer?**
40. 3 What can I **answer?**
40. 7 Stand up now like a man, and **answer** my questions.
42. 1 Then Job **answered** the Lord.
42. 4 listen while you spoke and to try to **answer** your questions.
42. 8 for you, and I will **answer** his prayer and not disgrace you
42. 9 Lord had told them to do, and the Lord **answered** Job's prayer.
Ps 3. 4 the Lord for help, and from his sacred hill he **answers** me.
4. 1 **Answer** me when I pray, O God, my defender!
5. 3 at sunrise I offer my prayer and wait for your **answer.**
6. 9 he listens to my cry for help and will **answer** my prayer.
13. 3 Look at me, O Lord my God, and **answer** me.
17. 6 I pray to you, O God, because you **answer** me;
18.41 they call to the Lord, but he does not **answer.**
20. 1 May the Lord **answer** you when you are in trouble!
20. 5 May the Lord **answer** all your requests.
20. 6 he **answers** him from his holy heaven and by his power gives
20. 9 **answer** us when we call.
21. 2 you have **answered** his request.
22. 2 day I call to you, my God, but you do not **answer;**
22.24 turn away from them, but **answers** when they call for help."
27. 7 Be merciful and **answer** me!
28. 1 If you do not **answer** me, I will be among those who

Ps 34. 4 I prayed to the Lord, and he **answered** me;
34. 6 The helpless call to him, and he **answers;**
38.14 am like a man who does not **answer,** because he cannot hear.
38.15 and you, O Lord my God, will **answer** me.
55. 2 Listen to me and **answer** me;
57. 3 He will **answer** from heaven and save me;
60. 5 **answer** our prayer, so that the people you love may be rescued.
65. 2 and keep our promises to you, [2]because you **answer** prayers.
65. 5 You **answer** us by giving us victory and you do wonderful
69.13 **answer** me, God, at a time you choose.
69.13 **Answer** me because of your great love, because you keep your
69.16 **Answer** me, Lord, in the goodness of your constant love;
69.17 I am in great trouble—**answer** me now!
81. 7 From my hiding-place in the storm, I **answered** you.
86. 1 Listen to me, Lord, and **answer** me, for I am helpless and
86. 7 to you in times of trouble, because you **answer** my prayers.
91.15 When they call to me, I will **answer** them;
99. 6 they called to the Lord, and he **answered** them.
99. 8 O Lord, our God, you **answered** your people;
102. 2 Listen to me, and **answer** me quickly when I call!
108. 6 **answer** my prayer, so that the people you love may be rescued.
118. 5 he **answered** me and set me free.
119.26 I confessed all I have done, and you **answered** me;
119.42 Then I can **answer** those who insult me because I trust in
119.145 **answer** me, Lord, and I will obey your commands!
120. 1 was in trouble, I called to the Lord, and he **answered** me.
124. 1 **Answer,** O Israel!
138. 3 You **answered** me when I called to you;
143. 1 **answer** me in your faithfulness!
143. 7 **Answer** me now, Lord!
Prov 1.28 Then you will call for wisdom, but I will not **answer.**
15. 1 A gentle **answer** quietens anger, but a harsh one stirs it up.
15.28 Good people think before they **answer.**
16.33 to learn God's will, but God himself determines the **answer.**
18.13 Listen before you **answer.**
18.23 to beg politely, but when the rich man **answers,** he is rude.
22.21 sent to find it out, you will bring back the right **answer.**
24.26 An honest **answer** is a sign of true friendship.
26. 4 If you **answer** a silly question, you are just as silly as
26. 5 Give a silly **answer** to a silly question, and the one who
27.11 I will have an **answer** for anyone who criticizes me.
31. 2 "You are my own dear son, the **answer** to my prayers.
Ecc 7.25 to find wisdom and the **answers** to my questions, and to learn
7.27 this out little by little while I was looking for **answers.**
7.28 I have looked for other **answers** but have found none.
Song 5. 6 I called to him, but heard no **answer.**
Is 10.30 **Answer,** people of Anathoth!
14.32 How shall we **answer** the messengers that come to us from Philistia?
29.12 read it to you, he will **answer** that he doesn't know how.
30.19 and when you cry to him for help, he will **answer** you.
37. 6 Isaiah received King Hezekiah's message, [6]he sent back this **answer:**
37.21 telling King Hezekiah that in **answer** to the king's prayer
41.17 with thirst, then I, the Lord, will **answer** their prayer;
41.28 not one could **answer** the questions I asked.
42.14 I did not **answer** my people.
46. 7 prays to it, it cannot **answer** or save him from disaster.
49. 8 you, I will show you favour and **answer** your cries for help.
50. 2 Why did they not **answer** when I called?
54.17 you will have an **answer** for all who accuse you.
58. 9 When you pray, I will **answer** you.
65. 1 said, "I was ready to **answer** my people's prayers, but they
65.12 death, because you did not **answer** when I called you or
65.24 Even before they finish praying to me, I will **answer**
66. 4 afraid of—because no one **answered** when I called or listened
Jer 7.13 You would not **answer** when I called you.
7.27 you will call them, but they will not **answer.**
13.12 They will **answer** that they know every wine-jar should be filled
22. 9 Then they will **answer** that it is because you have
23.35 his friends and his relatives, 'What **answer** has the Lord given?
23.37 Jeremiah, ask the prophets, 'What **answer** did the Lord give
29.12 You will come and pray to me, and I will **answer** you.
33. 3 is the Lord said, [3]"Call to me, and I will **answer** you;
35.17 spoke to you, and you would not **answer** when I called you."
40. 5 When I did not **answer,** Nebuzaradan said, "Go back to Gedaliah,
44.20 and the women who had **answered** me in this way,
Lam 3.57 You **answered** me and told me not to be afraid.
Ezek 14. 3 Do they think I will give them an **answer?**
14. 4 an answer from me—the **answer** that his many idols deserve!
14. 5 from me, but by my **answer** I hope to win back their
14. 7 to consult a prophet, I, the Lord, will give him his **answer!**
14. 9 deceived into giving a false **answer,** it is because I, the
18.19 The **answer** is that the son did what was right and good.
37. 3 I replied, "Sovereign Lord, only you can **answer** that!"
Dan 2.23 you have **answered** my prayer and shown us what to tell the
9.23 When you began to plead with God, he **answered** you.
9.23 loves you, and so I have come to tell you the **answer.**
10.12 I have come in **answer** to your prayer.
Hos 2.21 At that time I will **answer** the prayers of my people Israel.
14. 8 I will **answer** their prayers and take care of them;
Jon 2. 2 my distress, O Lord, I called to you, and you **answered** me.
Mic 3. 4 will cry out to the Lord, but he will not **answer** you.
3. 7 They will all be humiliated because God does not **answer** them.
6. 3 **Answer** me.
6. 5 to do to you and how Balaam son of Beor **answered** him.
Hab 2. 1 me to say and what **answer** he will give to my complaint.
2. 2 The Lord gave me this **answer:**
Zech 1.13 The Lord **answered** the angel with comforting words,
7.13 not listen when I spoke, I did not **answer** when they prayed.
10. 2 idols and fortune-tellers, but the **answers** they get are lies
Zech 10. 6 I will **answer** their prayers.
13. 9 Then they will pray to me, and I will **answer** them.
Mal 1. 9 He will not **answer** your prayer, and it will be your fault.
Mt 21.24 if you give me an **answer,** I will tell you what right
21.25 If we **answer,** 'From God,' he will say to us, 'Why, then,
22.46 able to give Jesus any **answer,** and from that day on no
25.37 righteous will then **answer** him, 'When, Lord, did we ever see
25.44 "Then they will **answer** him, 'When, Lord, did we ever
26.62 "Have you no **answer** to give to this accusation against
27.14 Jesus refused to **answer** a single word, with the result that
Mk 7.29 "Because of that **answer,** go back home, where you will
9.12 His **answer** was, "Elijah is indeed coming first in order to
9.34 But they would not **answer** him, because on the road they
10. 4 Their **answer** was, "Moses gave permission for a man to write
11.29 if you give me an **answer,** I will tell you what right
11.31 If we **answer,** 'From God,' he will say, 'Why, then, did you
11.33 So their **answer** to Jesus was, "We don't know."
12.28 given the Sadducees a good **answer,** so he came to him
12.34 Jesus noticed how wise his **answer** was, and so he told him,
14.60 "Have you no **answer** to the accusation they bring against
15. 4 so Pilate questioned him again, "Aren't you going to **answer?**
Lk 2.47 All who heard him were amazed at his intelligent **answers.**
2.50 But they did not understand his **answer.**
11. 7 suppose your friend should **answer** from inside, 'Don't bother me!
13.17 His **answer** made his enemies ashamed of themselves,
13.25 he will **answer** you, 'I don't know where you come from!'
13.26 Then you will **answer,** 'We ate and drank with you;
14. 6 But they were not able to **answer** him about this.
17.20 His **answer** was, "The Kingdom of God does not come in such
20.26 out in anything, so they kept quiet, amazed at his **answer.**
20.39 of the teachers of the Law spoke up, "A good **answer,**
22.68 and if I ask you a question, you will not **answer.**
23. 9 So Herod asked Jesus many questions, but Jesus made no **answer.**
Jn 1.20 John did not refuse to **answer,** but spoke out openly
1.22 "We have to take an **answer** back to those who sent us.
9.21 he is old enough, and he can **answer** for himself!"
18.30 Their **answer** was, "We would not have brought him to you
19. 9 But Jesus did not **answer.**
Acts 9.22 that the Jews who lived in Damascus could not **answer** him.
10. 4 prayers and works of charity, and is ready to **answer** you.
12.13 outside door, and a servant-girl named Rhoda came to **answer** it.
Rom 9.20 But who are you, my friend, to **answer** God back?
10.19 Moses himself is the first one to **answer:**
11. 4 What **answer** did God give him?
1 Cor 4.13 when we are insulted, we **answer** with kind words.
2 Cor 5.12 you will be able to **answer** those who boast about a man's
Col 4. 6 you should know how to give the right **answer** to everyone.
Tit 2. 9 They must not **answer** them back [10]or steal from them.
Phlm 22 I hope that God will **answer** the prayers of all of you
Jas 2.18 My **answer** is, "Show me how anyone can have faith without
1 Pet 2.23 When he was insulted, he did not **answer** back with an insult;
3.15 ready at all times to **answer** anyone who asks you to explain
Rev 10. 3 After he had called out, the seven thunders **answered** with a roar.

ANTELOPE

Deut 12.15 them, just as you would eat the meat of deer or **antelope.**
12.22 meat, just as he would eat the meat of deer or **antelope.**
14. 5 wild sheep, wild goats, or **antelopes—**
15.22 or unclean, may eat them, just as you eat deer or **antelope.**

AV **ANTICHRIST** see **ENEMY (of Christ)**

ANTIOCH IN PISIDIA

A city in Asia Minor.

Acts 13.14 Perga and arrived in **Antioch in Pisidia,** and on the Sabbath
13.52 The believers in **Antioch** were full of joy and the Holy Spirit.
14.19 Some Jews came from **Antioch in Pisidia** and from Iconium;
14.21 back to Lystra, to Iconium, and on to **Antioch in Pisidia.**
2 Tim 3.11 happened to me in **Antioch,** Iconium, and Lystra, the terrible

ANTIOCH IN SYRIA

Large city in Syria and an early stronghold of Christianity, the starting point of Paul's missionary journeys.

Acts 6. 5 Nicolaus, a Gentile from **Antioch** who had earlier been converted
11.19 Phoenicia, Cyprus, and **Antioch,** telling the message to Jews only.
11.20 went to **Antioch** and proclaimed the message to Gentiles
11.22 reached the church in Jerusalem, so they sent Barnabas to **Antioch.**
11.26 he took him to **Antioch,** and for a whole year
11.26 was at **Antioch** that the believers were first called Christians.
11.27 About that time some prophets went from Jerusalem to **Antioch.**
13. 1 In the church at **Antioch** there were some prophets and teachers:
14.26 they sailed back to **Antioch,** the place where they had been
14.27 When they arrived in **Antioch,** they gathered the people
15. 1 came from Judaea to **Antioch** and started teaching the believers,
15. 2 some of the others in **Antioch** should go to Jerusalem and see
15.22 the group and send them to **Antioch** with Paul and Barnabas.
15.23 our brothers of Gentile birth who live in **Antioch,** Syria, and
15.30 sent off and went to **Antioch,** where they gathered the whole
15.35 Barnabas spent some time in **Antioch,** and together with many
18.22 to Jerusalem and greeted the church, and then went to **Antioch.**
Gal 2.11 But when Peter came to **Antioch,** I opposed him in public,

ANTS

Prov	6. 6	Lazy people should learn a lesson from the way **ants** live.
	30.25	**Ants:** they are weak,
Is	40.22	the people below look as tiny as **ants.**

ANXIOUS

Gen	31.30	left because you were so **anxious** to get back home, but why
Deut	28.65	the Lord will overwhelm you with **anxiety,** hopelessness,
1 Sam	4.13	Eli, who was very **anxious** about the Covenant Box, was sitting
Ps	38.18	they fill me with **anxiety.**
	39. 3	But my suffering only grew worse, [3]and I was overcome with **anxiety.**
	94.19	Whenever I am **anxious** and worried, you comfort me and
	116. 3	I was filled with fear and **anxiety.**
	119.143	filled with trouble and **anxiety,** but your commandments bring
Jer	49.23	**Anxiety** rolls over them like a sea, and they cannot rest.
Ezek	4.16	will be distressed and **anxious** as they measure out the food
Dan	6.20	he called out **anxiously,** "Daniel, servant of the living God!
Mic	1.12	The people of Maroth wait **anxiously** for relief,
Phil	2.26	He is **anxious** to see you all and is very upset because

APART

Gen	2. 3	seventh day and set it **apart** as a special day, because by
	16.12	He will live **apart** from all his relatives."
	25.18	They lived **apart** from the other descendants of Abraham.
	30.40	he built up his own flock and kept it **apart** from Laban's.
	49.26	Joseph, On the brow of the one set **apart** from his brothers.
Ex	29.44	will set Aaron and his sons **apart** to serve me as priests.
Lev	20.24	your God, and I have set you **apart** from the other nations.
	20.26	I have set you **apart** from the other nations so that you
	21.15	the Lord and I have set him **apart** as the High Priest."
	25.10	shall set the fiftieth year **apart** and proclaim freedom to
Num	16. 9	of Israel has set you **apart** from the rest of the community,
Josh	6.19	of silver, gold, bronze, or iron is set **apart** for the Lord.
Judg	14. 6	and he tore the lion **apart** with his bare hands, as if
2 Sam	22.10	He tore the sky **apart** and came down, with a dark cloud
1 Kgs	13. 3	say, "This altar will fall **apart,** and the ashes on it will
	13. 5	The altar suddenly fell **apart** and the ashes spilt to the ground,
2 Kgs	16.17	King Ahaz took **apart** the bronze carts used in the
1 Chr	23.13	and his descendants were set **apart** to be in charge of the
Job	30.27	I am torn **apart** by worry and pain;
	41.17	fastened so firmly together that nothing can ever pull them **apart.**
Ps	1. 5	be condemned by God and kept **apart** from God's own people.
	11. 3	There is nothing a good man can do when everything falls **apart."**
	18. 9	He tore the sky **apart** and came down with a dark cloud
	60. 2	now heal its wounds, because it is falling **apart.**
	144. 5	O Lord, tear the sky **apart** and come down;
Is	64. 1	Why don't you tear the sky **apart** and come down?
Jer	5. 6	out, they will be torn **apart** because their sins are numerous
Ezek	22.27	like wolves tearing **apart** the animals they have killed.
	44.29	to receive everything in Israel that is set **apart** for me.
	48. 8	section of the land is to be set **apart** for special use.
	48.20	the section which was set **apart** will be a square measuring
Mic	7.14	Although they live **apart** in the wilderness, there is fertile land
Zech	14.21	all Judah will be set **apart** for use in the worship of
Mt	12.25	divides itself into groups which fight each other will fall **apart.**
	12.26	it is already divided into groups and will soon fall **apart!**
	27.51	earth shook, the rocks split **apart,** [52]the graves broke open,
Mk	3.24	into groups which fight each other, that country will fall **apart.**
	3.25	into groups which fight each other, that family will fall **apart.**
	3.26	it cannot last, but will fall **apart** and come to an end.
Lk	11.17	a family divided against itself falls **apart.**
	18.11	Pharisee stood **apart** by himself and prayed, 'I thank you, God,
Acts	13. 2	Spirit said to them, "Set **apart** for me Barnabas and Saul,
Rom	2.12	they sin and are lost **apart from** the Law.
	4. 6	God accepts as righteous, **apart from** anything that person does:
	7. 8	**Apart from** law, sin is a dead thing.
	7. 9	I myself was once alive **apart from** law;
	8.29	already chosen he also set **apart** to become like his Son,
	8.30	And so those whom God set **apart,** he called;
2 Cor	1.21	himself who has set us **apart,** [22]who has placed his mark
Eph	2.12	At that time you were **apart from** Christ.
Heb	7.26	been set **apart** from sinners and raised above the heavens.

APES

1 Kgs	10.22	his fleet would return, bringing gold, silver, ivory, **apes,**
2 Chr	9.21	his fleet would return, bringing gold, silver, ivory, **apes,**

APOLLOS

Jew who was a native of Alexandria and who preached in Ephesus and Corinth.

Acts	18.24	time a Jew named **Apollos,** who had been born in Alexandria,
	18.27	**Apollos** then decided to go to Achaia, so the believers
	19. 1	**Apollos** was in Corinth, Paul travelled through the interior
1 Cor	1.12	another, "I follow **Apollos";**
	3. 4	and another, "I follow **Apollos"**—aren't you acting like worldly
	3. 5	After all, who is **Apollos?**
	3. 6	I sowed the seed, **Apollos** watered the plant, but it was
	3.22	Paul, **Apollos,** and Peter;
	4. 6	have applied all this to **Apollos** and me, using the two
	16.12	Now, about brother **Apollos.**
Tit	3.13	Zenas the lawyer and **Apollos** to get started on their travels,

APOLOGY

Lk	14.18	please accept my **apologies.'**
	14.19	please accept my **apologies.'**
Acts	16.39	So they went and **apologized** to them;

APOSTLE

Usually one of the group of twelve men whom Jesus chose to be his special followers and helpers. It is also used in the New Testament to refer to Paul and other Christian workers. The word means "messenger".

see also **ANDREW, BARNABAS, BARTHOLOMEW, JAMES, JOHN (2), JUDAS (3), JUDE, LEVI (4), MARK, MATTHEW, PAUL, PETER, PHILIP (3), SIMON (1), (2), THADDEUS, THOMAS**

Mt	10. 2	These are the names of the twelve **apostles:**
Mk	3.14	They came to him, [14]and he chose twelve, whom he named **apostles.**
	6.30	**apostles** returned and met with Jesus, and told him all they
Lk	6.13	to him and chose twelve of them, whom he named **apostles:**
	6.17	from the hill with the **apostles,** he stood on a level place
	9.10	**apostles** came back and told Jesus everything they had done.
	17. 5	The **apostles** said to the Lord, "Make our faith greater."
	22.14	Jesus took his place at the table with the **apostles.**
	24.10	the other women with them told these things to the **apostles.**
	24.11	the **apostles** thought that what the women said was nonsense,
Acts	1. 2	the Holy Spirit to the men he had chosen as his **apostles.**
	1. 6	When the **apostles** met together with Jesus, they asked him,
	1.12	the **apostles** went back to Jerusalem from the Mount of Olives,
	1.25	chosen [25]to serve as an **apostle** in the place of Judas,
	1.26	was Matthias, who was added to the group of eleven **apostles.**
	2.14	with the other eleven **apostles** and in a loud voice began
	2.37	to Peter and the other **apostles,** "What shall we do, brothers?"
	2.42	in learning from the **apostles,** taking part in the fellowship,
	2.43	done through the **apostles,** and everyone was filled with awe.
	4. 2	because the two **apostles** were teaching the people that Jesus
	4. 7	made the **apostles** stand before them and asked them, "How did
	4.33	With great power the **apostles** gave witness to the resurrection
	4.35	from the sale, [35]and hand it over to the **apostles;**
	4.36	born in Cyprus, whom the **apostles** called Barnabas
	4.37	brought the money, and handed it over to the **apostles.**
	5. 2	money for himself and handed the rest over to the **apostles.**
	5.12	and wonders were being performed among the people by the **apostles.**
	5.15	result of what the **apostles** were doing, sick people were carried
	5.17	party of the Sadducees, became extremely jealous of the **apostles;**
	5.18	They arrested the **apostles** and put them in the public jail.
	5.19	the prison gates, led the **apostles** out, and said to them,
	5.21	The **apostles** obeyed, and at dawn they entered the Temple
	5.21	orders to the prison to have the **apostles** brought before them.
	5.22	they did not find the **apostles** in prison, so they returned
	5.24	guards heard this, they wondered what had happened to the **apostles.**
	5.26	officer went off with his men and brought the **apostles** back.
	5.27	brought the **apostles** in, made them stand before the Council,
	5.29	Peter and the other **apostles** replied, "We must obey God,
	5.33	furious that they wanted to have the **apostles** put to death.
	5.34	He ordered the **apostles** to be taken out for a while,
	5.40	called the **apostles** in, had them whipped, and ordered them never
	5.41	the **apostles** left the Council, they were happy, because God had
	6. 2	the twelve **apostles** called the whole group of believers together
	6. 5	pleased with the **apostles'** proposal, so they chose Stephen,
	6. 6	presented them to the **apostles,** who prayed and placed their hands
	8. 1	All the believers, except the **apostles,** were scattered throughout
	8.14	**apostles** in Jerusalem heard that the people of Samaria had received
	8.18	given to the believers when the **apostles** placed their hands on
	9.27	Then Barnabas came to his help and took him to the **apostles.**
	11. 1	The **apostles** and the other believers throughout Judaea heard
	13.43	The **apostles** spoke to them and encouraged them to keep on
	13.51	**apostles** shook the dust off their feet in protest against them
	14. 3	**apostles** stayed there for a long time, speaking boldly about the
	14. 4	some were for the Jews, others for the **apostles.**
	14. 5	their leaders, decided to ill-treat the **apostles** and stone them.
	14. 6	When the **apostles** learnt about it, they fled to the cities
	14.13	and the crowds wanted to offer sacrifice to the **apostles.**
	14.18	Even with these words the **apostles** could hardly keep the crowd
	15. 2	to Jerusalem and see the **apostles** and elders about this matter.
	15. 4	welcomed by the church, the **apostles,** and the elders, to whom
	15. 6	**apostles** and the elders met together to consider this question.
	15.22	the **apostles** and the elders, together with the whole church, decided
	15.23	"We, the **apostles** and the elders, your brothers, send greetings
	16. 4	rules decided upon by the **apostles** and elders in Jerusalem,
Rom	1. 1	of Christ Jesus and an **apostle** chosen and called by God
	1. 5	the privilege of being an **apostle** for the sake of Christ,
	11.13	long as I am an **apostle** to the Gentiles, I will take
	16. 7	well known among the **apostles,** and they became Christians before
1 Cor	1. 1	of God to be an **apostle** of Christ Jesus, and from our
	4. 9	very last place to us **apostles,** like men condemned to die
	9. 1	Am I not an **apostle?**
	9. 2	if others do not accept me as an **apostle,** surely you do!
	9. 2	you yourselves are proof of the fact that I am an **apostle.**
	9. 5	example of the other **apostles** and the Lord's brothers and Peter,
	12.28	in the first place **apostles,** in the second place prophets,
	12.29	They are not all **apostles** or prophets or teachers.
	15. 5	that he appeared to Peter and then to all twelve **apostles.**
	15. 7	Then he appeared to James, and afterwards to all the **apostles.**

1 Cor 15. 9 the least of all the **apostles**—I do not even deserve
15. 9 to be called an **apostle,** because I persecuted God's church.
15.10 than any of the other **apostles,** although it was not really
2 Cor 1. 1 From Paul, an **apostle** of Christ Jesus by God's will,
11. 5 inferior to those very special so-called **"apostles"** of yours!
11.12 keep those other **"apostles"** from having any reason for boasting
11.13 Those men are not true **apostles**—
11.13 they are false **apostles,** who lie about their work
11.13 and disguise themselves to look like real **apostles** of Christ.
12.11 in no way inferior to those very special **"apostles"** of yours.
12.12 prove that I am an **apostle** were performed among you with
Gal 1. 1 whose call to be an **apostle** did not come from man
1.17 I go to Jerusalem to see those who were **apostles** before me.
1.19 did not see any other **apostle** except James, the Lord's brother.
2. 8 power I was made an **apostle** to the Gentiles,
2. 8 just as Peter was made an **apostle** to the Jews.
Eph 1. 1 by God's will is an **apostle** of Christ Jesus— To God's
2.20 foundation laid by the **apostles** and prophets, the cornerstone
3. 5 it now by the Spirit to his holy **apostles** and prophets.
4.11 he appointed some to be **apostles,** others to be prophets,
Col 1. 1 by God's will is an **apostle** of Christ Jesus, and from our
1 Thes 2. 7 even though as **apostles** of Christ we could have made
1 Tim 1. 1 From Paul, an **apostle** of Christ Jesus by order of God
2. 7 I was sent as an **apostle** and teacher of the Gentiles,
2 Tim 1. 1 From Paul, an **apostle** of Christ Jesus by God's will, sent
1.11 has appointed me as an **apostle** and teacher to proclaim the
Tit 1. 1 From Paul, a servant of God and an **apostle** of Jesus Christ.
1 Pet 1. 1 From Peter, **apostle** of Jesus Christ— To God's chosen people
2 Pet 1. 1 Simon Peter, a servant which and **apostle** of Jesus Christ— To those
3. 2 the Lord and Saviour which was given you by your **apostles.**
Jude 17 told in the past by the **apostles** of our Lord Jesus Christ.
Rev 2. 2 those who say they are **apostles** but are not, and have found
18.20 Be glad, God's people and the **apostles** and prophets!
21.14 were written the names of the twelve **apostles** of the Lamb.

APPEAL

2 Kgs 8. 5 person back to life, the woman made her **appeal** to the king.
Prov 8. 4 "I **appeal** to you, mankind;
Lk 23.20 wanted to set Jesus free, so he **appealed** to the crowd again.
Acts 2.40 Peter made his **appeal** to them and with many other words
25.11 I **appeal** to the Emperor."
25.12 his advisers, answered, "You have **appealed** to the Emperor,
25.21 But Paul **appealed;**
25.25 since he himself made an **appeal** to the Emperor, I have
26.32 have been released if he had not **appealed** to the Emperor."
28.19 I was forced to **appeal** to the Emperor, even though I
Rom 12. 1 because of God's great mercy to us I **appeal** to you:
1 Cor 1.10 our Lord Jesus Christ I **appeal** to all of you, my brothers,
2 Cor 5.20 as though God himself were making his **appeal** through us.
10. 1 I, Paul, make a personal **appeal** to you—I who am said
13.11 listen to my **appeals;**
1 Thes 2. 3 Our **appeal** to you is not based on error or impure motives,
1 Tim 5. 1 rebuke an older man, but **appeal** to him as if he were
1 Pet 2.11 I **appeal** to you, my friends, as strangers and refugees in
5. 1 am an elder myself, **appeal** to the church elders among you.
5. 1 I **appeal** to you [2] to be shepherds of the flock that God

APPEAR
[REAPPEAR]

Gen 1. 3 Then God commanded, "Let there be light"—and light **appeared.**
1. 9 one place, so that the land will **appear"**—and it was done.
1.14 Then God commanded, "Let lights **appear** in the sky
8. 5 day of the tenth month the tops of the mountains **appeared.**
9.14 and the rainbow **appears,** [15] I will remember my promise
9.16 When the rainbow **appears** in the clouds, I will see it
12. 7 The Lord **appeared** to Abram and said to him, "This is the
12. 7 built an altar there to the Lord, who had **appeared** to him.
15.17 a flaming torch suddenly **appeared** and passed between the pieces
17. 1 ninety-nine years old, the Lord **appeared** to him and said,
18. 1 The Lord **appeared** to Abraham at the sacred trees of Mamre.
20. 3 One night God **appeared** to him in a dream and said:
26. 2 The Lord had **appeared** to Isaac and had said, "Do not go
26.24 That night the Lord **appeared** to him and said, "I am the
31.13 I am the God who **appeared** to you at Bethel, where you
35. 1 to me, the God who **appeared** to you when you were running
35. 9 Jacob returned from Mesopotamia, God **appeared** to him again
40.10 the blossoms **appeared,** and the grapes ripened.
48. 3 said to Joseph, "Almighty God **appeared** to me at Luz in the
Ex 3. 2 the angel of the Lord **appeared** to him as a flame coming
3.16 the God of Abraham, Isaac, and Jacob, **appeared** to you.
4. 1 I do if they say that you did not **appear** to me?"
4. 5 the God of Abraham, Isaac, and Jacob, has **appeared** to you."
6. 3 I **appeared** to Abraham, to Isaac, and to Jacob as Almighty God,
8.18 to use their magic to make gnats **appear,** but they failed.
9.11 magicians were not able to **appear** before Moses,
16.10 suddenly the dazzling light of the Lord **appeared** in a cloud.
19.16 and lightning, a thick cloud **appeared** on the mountain,
23. 6 not deny justice to a poor man when he **appears** in court.
34.20 "No one is to **appear** before me without an offering.
Lev 9. 4 They must do this because the Lord will **appear** to them today."
9. 6 that the dazzling light of his presence can **appear** to you."
9.23 the dazzling light of the Lord's presence **appeared** to all
13. 3 and the sore **appears** to be deeper than the surrounding
13. 4 is white and does not **appear** to be deeper than the skin
13. 7 pronounced him clean, he must **appear** before the priest again.
13.14 But from the moment an open sore **appears,** he is unclean.
13.19 swelling or a reddish-white spot **appears** where the boil was,
13.25 turned white and it **appears** deeper than the surrounding skin,
13.31 him, the sore does not **appear** to be deeper than the
Lev 13.42 But if a reddish-white sore **appears** on the bald spot, it
13.57 Then, if the mildew **reappears,** it is spreading again,
14.37 or reddish spots that **appear** to be eating into the wall,
14.48 has not **reappeared** after the house has been
16. 2 because that is where I **appear** in a cloud above the lid
Num 14.10 the dazzling light of the Lord's presence **appear** over the tent.
16.19 light of the Lord's presence **appeared** to the whole community,
16.42 that the dazzling light of the Lord's presence had **appeared.**
20. 6 and the dazzling light of the Lord's presence **appeared** to them.
Deut 31.15 the Tent, [15] and the Lord **appeared** to them there in a
Judg 6.12 The Lord's angel **appeared** to him there and said, "The Lord
13. 3 The Lord's angel **appeared** to her and said, "You have never
13.10 who came to me the other day has **appeared** to me again."
20.40 Then the signal **appeared;**
1 Sam 3.21 at Shiloh, where he had **appeared** to Samuel and had spoken to
2 Sam 14.24 lived in his own house and did not **appear** before the king.
1 Kgs 3. 5 That night the Lord **appeared** to him in a dream and asked
9. 2 wanted to build, [2] the Lord **appeared** to him again, as he had
11. 9 the God of Israel, had **appeared** to Solomon twice
22.15 When he **appeared** before King Ahab, the king asked him,
1 Chr 16.29 Bow down before the Holy One when he **appears;**
2 Chr 1. 7 That night God **appeared** to Solomon and asked, "What would you
3. 1 Mount Moriah, where the Lord **appeared** to David,
7.12 his plans for them, [12] the Lord **appeared** to him at night.
18.14 When he **appeared** before King Ahab, the king asked him,
Esth 1.19 that Vashti may never again **appear** before the king.
Job 1. 6 for the heavenly beings to **appear** before the Lord,
2. 1 for the heavenly beings to **appear** before the Lord again,
32. 3 Job, and this made it **appear** that God was in the wrong.
Ps 9. 3 My enemies turn back when you **appear;**
21. 9 He will destroy them like a blazing fire when he **appears.**
29. 2 bow down before the Holy One when he **appears.**
33. 9 at his command everything **appeared.**
96. 9 Bow down before the Holy One when he **appears;**
Prov 23.33 Weird sights will **appear** before your eyes, and you will
Jer 31. 3 Israel longed for rest, [3] I **appeared** to them from far away.
Dan 1. 5 years of this training they were to **appear** before the king.
5. 5 Suddenly a human hand **appeared** and began writing on the plaster
7. 6 While I was watching, another beast **appeared.**
7. 7 As I was watching, a fourth beast **appeared.**
7.24 Then another king will **appear;**
10.20 After that, the guardian angel of Greece will **appear.**
11. 3 "Then a heroic king will **appear.**
12. 1 the great angel Michael, who guards your people, will **appear.**
Nah 1. 5 The earth shakes when the Lord **appears;**
Zech 5. 5 The angel **appeared** again and said, "Look!
9.14 The Lord will **appear** above his people;
Mal 3. 2 Who will be able to survive when he **appears?**
3. 5 Lord Almighty says, "I will **appear** among you to judge, and
Mt 1.20 an angel of the Lord **appeared** to him in a dream
2. 7 found out from them the exact time the star had **appeared.**
2.13 an angel of the Lord **appeared** in a dream to Joseph
2.16 from the visitors about the time when the star had **appeared.**
2.19 an angel of the Lord **appeared** in a dream to Joseph
23.28 on the outside you **appear** good to everybody, but inside you
24.11 Then many false prophets will **appear** and deceive many people.
24.24 For false Messiahs and false prophets will **appear;**
24.30 the sign of the Son of Man will **appear** in the sky;
Mk 1. 4 So John **appeared** in the desert, baptizing and preaching.
4.28 first the tender stalk **appears,** then the ear, and finally
9. 7 Then a cloud **appeared** and covered them with its shadow,
13.22 For false Messiahs and false prophets will **appear.**
13.26 the Son of Man will **appear,** coming in the clouds with great
16. 9 early on Sunday, he **appeared** first to Mary Magdalene,
16.12 After this, Jesus **appeared** in a different manner to two of
16.14 Last of all, Jesus **appeared** to the eleven disciples as they
Lk 1.11 An angel of the Lord **appeared** to him, standing on the
1.80 the day when he **appeared** publicly to the people of Israel.
2. 9 An angel of the Lord **appeared** to them, and the glory of
2.13 great army of heaven's angels **appeared** with the angel, singing
7.16 "A great prophet has **appeared** among us!"
9. 8 saying that Elijah had **appeared,** and still others that one of
9.31 Moses and Elijah, [31] who **appeared** in heavenly glory and talked
9.34 speaking, a cloud **appeared** and covered them with its shadow;
19.11 supposed that the Kingdom of God was just about to **appear.**
19.15 he ordered his servants to **appear** before him, in order to
21.27 the Son of Man will **appear,** coming in a cloud with great
21.30 their leaves beginning to **appear,** you know that summer is near.
22.43 An angel from heaven **appeared** to him and strengthened him.
24.34 He has **appeared** to Simon!"
Jn 21. 1 Jesus **appeared** once more to his disciples at Lake Tiberias.
21.14 was the third time Jesus **appeared** to the disciples after he
Acts 1. 3 days after his death he **appeared** to them many times in ways
5.36 You remember that Theudas **appeared** some time ago, claiming to
5.37 Judas the Galilean **appeared** during the time of the census;
7. 2 the God of glory **appeared** to him in Mesopotamia
7.10 When Joseph **appeared** before the king of Egypt, God gave him
7.30 years had passed, an angel **appeared** to Moses in the flames
7.35 help of the angel who **appeared** to him in the burning bush.
9.17 Jesus himself, who **appeared** to you on the road
10.40 later and caused him to **appear,** [41] not to everyone, but only
13.31 for many days he **appeared** to those who had travelled with
24. 1 They **appeared** before Felix and made their charges against Paul.
26.16 I have **appeared** to you to appoint you as my servant.
Rom 10.20 I **appeared** to those who were not asking for me."
15.12 And again, Isaiah says, "A descendant of Jesse will **appear;**
1 Cor 15. 5 that he **appeared** to Peter and then to all twelve apostles.
15. 6 Then he **appeared** to more than five hundred of his followers
15. 7 Then he **appeared** to James, and afterwards to all the apostles.

1 Cor 15. 8 Last of all he **appeared** also to me—even though I am
2 Cor 1.17 In planning this, did I **appear** fickle?
3. 7 on stone tablets, and God's glory **appeared** when it was given.
5.10 For all of us must **appear** before Christ, to be judged
10. 9 do not want it to **appear** that I am trying to frighten
Phil 2. 7 He became like man and **appeared** in human likeness.
Col 2.23 Of course such rules **appear** to be based on wisdom in
3. 4 is Christ and when he **appears**, then you too will appear
2 Thes 1. 7 when the Lord Jesus **appears** from heaven with his mighty angels,
2. 3 and the Wicked One **appears**, who is destined for hell.
2. 6 At the proper time, then, the Wicked One will **appear.**
1 Tim 3.16 He **appeared** in human form, was shown to be right
6.14 faithfully until the Day when our Lord Jesus Christ will **appear.**
6.15 His **appearing** will be brought about at the right time by God,
2 Tim 4. 8 but to all those who wait with love for him to **appear.**
Tit 2.13 glory of our great God and Saviour Jesus Christ will **appear.**
Heb 7.11 different kind of priest to **appear**, one who is in the
7.15 a different priest has **appeared**, who is like Melchizedek.
9.24 heaven itself, where he now **appears** on our behalf in the
9.26 nearing the end, he has **appeared** once and for all, to remove
9.28 He will **appear** a second time, not to deal with sin,
Jas 4.14 a puff of smoke, which **appears** for a moment and then disappears.
5. 9 The Judge is near, ready to **appear.**
1 Pet 5. 4 when the Chief Shepherd **appears**, you will receive the glorious
2 Pet 2. 1 False prophets **appeared** in the past among the people,
2. 1 and in the same way false teachers will **appear** among you.
3. 3 last days some people will **appear** whose lives are controlled by
1 Jn 2.18 enemies of Christ have already **appeared**, and so we know
2.28 so that when he **appears** we may be full of courage
3. 2 we know that when Christ **appears**, we shall be like him,
3. 5 You know that Christ **appeared** in order to take away sins,
3. 8 The Son of God **appeared** for this very reason, to destroy
Jude 18 last days come, people will **appear** who will mock you,
Rev 12. 1 Then a great and mysterious sight **appeared** in the sky.
12. 3 Another mysterious sight **appeared** in the sky.
16. 2 Terrible and painful sores **appeared** on those who had the mark
17. 8 now it no longer lives, but it will **reappear.**

APPEARANCE

1 Sam 16. 7 Man looks at the outward **appearance**, but I look at the heart."
Prov 1. 9 as a handsome turban or a necklace improves your **appearance.**
Is 11. 3 He will not judge by **appearance** or hearsay;
Mt 6.16 They neglect their **appearance** so that everyone will see that
28. 3 His **appearance** was like lightning, and his clothes were white
Lk 9.29 his face changed its **appearance**, and his clothes became dazzling
2 Cor 5.12 who boast about a man's **appearance** and not about his character.
10. 7 You are looking at the outward **appearance** of things.
Gal 2. 6 does not judge by outward **appearances**—those leaders, I say,
Jas 2. 1 people in different ways according to their outward **appearance.**
2. 9 according to their outward **appearance**, you are guilty of sin,

APPETITE

Job 6. 7 I have no **appetite** for food like that, and everything I
33.20 The sick man loses his **appetite**, and even the finest food
Prov 16.26 A labourer's **appetite** makes him work harder,
23. 2 If you have a big **appetite**, restrain yourself.
Rom 16.18 are not serving Christ our Lord, but their own **appetites.**
2 Pet 2.13 anything in broad daylight that will satisfy their bodily **appetites;**
2.14 their **appetite** for sin is never satisfied.

APPLE

Song 2. 3 Like an **apple-tree** among the trees of the forest, so is my
2. 5 Restore my strength with raisins and refresh me with **apples!**
7. 8 like the fragrance of **apples**, [9] and your mouth like the finest
8. 5 Under the **apple-tree** I woke you, in the place where you were

APPLY

Mt 7. 2 he will apply to you the same rules you **apply** to others.
13.14 So the prophecy of Isaiah **applies** to them:
19.11 "This teaching does not **apply** to everyone, but only to those
Lk 12.41 "Lord, does this parable **apply** to us, or do you mean
Rom 3.19 that everything in the Law **applies** to those who live under
1 Cor 4. 6 my brothers, I have **applied** all this to Apollos and me,
Eph 5.32 scripture, which I understand as **applying** to Christ and the
5.33 But it also **applies** to you:
Heb 3.13 long as the word "Today" in the scripture **applies** to us.
9.10 are all outward rules, which **apply** only until the time when
1 Jn 5.16 This **applies** to those whose sins do not lead to death.

APPOINT

Gen 41.34 You must also **appoint** other officials and take a fifth
41.41 I now **appoint** you governor over all Egypt."
41.43 And so Joseph was **appointed** governor over all Egypt.
Ex 13.10 Celebrate this festival at the **appointed** time each year.
18.21 some capable men and **appoint** them as leaders of the people:
18.25 He **appointed** them as leaders of thousands, hundreds, fifties,
Lev 16.21 driven off into the desert by a man **appointed** to do it.
23. 4 Proclaim the following festivals at the **appointed** times.
Num 3. 6 the tribe of Levi and **appoint** them as servants of Aaron the
3.10 You shall **appoint** Aaron and his sons to carry out the
9.13 he did not present the offering to me at the **appointed** time.
27.16 God, source of all life, **appoint**, I pray, a man who can
28. 2 present to God at the **appointed** times the required food-offerings
29.39 you are to make to the Lord at your **appointed** festivals.
Deut 1.15 I also **appointed** other officials throughout the tribes.
10. 8 At the mountain the Lord **appointed** the men of the tribe of
Deut 16.18 "**Appoint** judges and other officials in every town that the Lord
34. 9 because Moses had **appointed** him to be his successor.
Judg 17. 5 idols and an ephod, and **appointed** one of his sons as his
17.12 Micah **appointed** him as his priest, and he lived in Micah's home.
1 Sam 8. 5 So then, **appoint** a king to rule over us, so that we
2 Sam 7. 7 of the leaders that I **appointed** why they had not built me
1 Kgs 4. 7 Solomon **appointed** twelve men as district governors in
22.47 it was ruled by a deputy **appointed** by the king of Judah.
1 Chr 16. 4 David **appointed** some of the Levites to lead the worship
16. 5 Asaph was **appointed** leader, with Zechariah as his assistant.
17. 6 of the leaders that I **appointed** why they had not built me
2 Chr 2.18 stones in the mountains, and **appointed** 3,600 supervisors
11.11 had them strongly fortified and **appointed** a commander for each
11.15 Jeroboam **appointed** priests of his own to serve at the pagan
13. 9 In their place you **appointed** priests in the same way that
19. 5 He **appointed** judges in each of the fortified cities of Judah
19. 8 In Jerusalem Jehoshaphat **appointed** Levites, priests,
28.15 four men were **appointed** to provide the prisoners with clothing
Ezra 5.14 to a man named Sheshbazzar, whom he **appointed** governor of Judah.
7.25 are to **appoint** administrators and judges to govern all
10.16 plan, so Ezra the priest **appointed** men from among the heads
Neh 7. 3 I also told them to **appoint** guards from among the people who
Esth 2. 3 You can **appoint** officials in every province of the empire
2.19 Meanwhile Mordecai had been **appointed** by the king
4. 5 of the palace eunuchs **appointed** as her servant by the king,
Ps 8. 6 You **appointed** him ruler over everything you made;
Is 45. 1 He has **appointed** him to conquer nations;
45. 4 I **appoint** you to help my servant Israel, the people that I
49. 1 born, the Lord chose me and **appointed** me to be his servant.
49. 5 Before I was born, the Lord **appointed** me;
Jer 6.17 the Lord **appointed** watchmen to listen for the trumpet's warning.
23. 4 I will **appoint** rulers to take care of them.
51.27 **Appoint** an officer to lead the attack.
Dan 6. 1 Darius decided to **appoint** a hundred and twenty governors
Hos 8. 4 They **appointed** leaders, but without my approval.
9. 5 comes for the **appointed** festivals in honour of the Lord,
Hag 2.23 my servant, and I will **appoint** you to rule in my name.
Jn 15.16 I chose you and **appointed** you to go and bear much fruit,
Acts 10.42 the one whom God has **appointed** judge of the living and the
14.23 In each church they **appointed** elders, and with prayers
26.16 I have appeared to you to **appoint** you as my servant.
2 Cor 8.19 he has been chosen and **appointed** by the churches to travel
Eph 4.11 he **appointed** some to be apostles, others to be prophets,
1 Tim 1.12 for considering me worthy and **appointing** me to serve him,
2 Tim 1.11 God has **appointed** me as an apostle and teacher to proclaim
Tit 1. 5 things that still needed doing and **appoint** church elders
Heb 5. 1 from his fellow-men and **appointed** to serve God on their behalf,
7.28 The Law of Moses **appoints** men who are imperfect to be
7.28 came later than the Law, **appoints** the Son, who has been made
8. 3 Every High Priest is **appointed** to present offerings and animal
1 Pet 2.14 the governors, who have been **appointed** by him to punish the

APPRECIATE

Prov 23. 9 he can't **appreciate** it.
23.22 When your mother is old, show her your **appreciation.**
28.23 and afterwards he will **appreciate** it more than flattery.
29. 3 If you **appreciate** wisdom, your father will be proud of you.
30.11 and do not show their **appreciation** for their mothers.
31.28 Her children show their **appreciation**, and her husband praises her.

APPROACH

Gen 18.23 Abraham **approached** the Lord and asked,
33. 3 down to the ground seven times as he **approached** his brother.
Ex 28.43 Tent of my presence or **approach** the altar to serve as
30.20 go into the Tent or **approach** the altar to offer the food
Lev 21.23 not come near the sacred curtain or **approach** the altar.
Num 16. 5 that is, the one he has chosen, **approach** him at the altar.
16. 9 community, so that you can **approach** him, perform your service
18.22 other Israelites must no longer **approach** the Tent and in
32.16 They **approached** Moses and said, "First, allow us to build
Josh 8. 5 My men and I will **approach** the city.
2 Sam 15. 5 When the man **approached** Absalom to bow down before him,
1 Kgs 18.36 the prophet Elijah **approached** the altar and prayed, "O Lord,
18.41 I hear the roar of rain **approaching.**"
22.21 until a spirit stepped forward, **approached** the Lord, and said,
2 Kgs 9.17 the watch-tower at Jezreel saw Jehu and his men **approaching.**
1 Chr 21.21 Araunah saw King David **approaching**, he left the threshing-place
2 Chr 18.20 until a spirit stepped forward, **approached** the Lord, and said,
Job 36.33 Thunder announces the **approaching** storm, and the cattle know
Prov 2.18 To go there is to **approach** the world of the dead.
Jer 30.21 He will **approach** me when I invite him, for who would dare
37.11 retreated from Jerusalem because the Egyptian army was **approaching.**
46.22 runs away, hissing like a snake, as the enemy's army **approaches.**
48.16 Moab's doom **approaches;**
Ezek 33. 3 When he sees the enemy **approaching**, he sounds the alarm to
Dan 7.13 He was **approaching** me, surrounded by clouds, and he went to
Joel 2. 6 As they **approach**, everyone is terrified;
Hab 1. 9 and everyone is terrified as they **approach.**
Mt 21. 1 As Jesus and his disciples **approached** Jerusalem, they came to
Mk 11. 1 As they **approached** Jerusalem, near the towns of Bethphage and
1 Tim 6.16 he lives in the light that no one can **approach.**
Heb 4.16 have confidence, then, and **approach** God's throne,

APPROVE
[DISAPPROVED]

Gen 28. 8 that his father Isaac did not **approve** of Canaanite women.
41.37 The king and his officials **approved** this plan,
Ex 21.22 the woman's husband demands, subject to the **approval** of the judges.
Lev 10.19 "If I had eaten the sin-offering today, would the Lord have **approved?**
1 Sam 29. 6 But the other kings don't **approve** of you.
1 Kgs 1.27 Did Your Majesty **approve** all this and not even tell
11.38 my laws, and win my **approval** by doing what I command, as
14. 8 to me, obeyed my commands, and did only what I **approve** of.
18.24 The people shouted their **approval.**
2 Kgs 17. 9 Israelites did things that the Lord their God **disapproved** of.
1 Chr 13. 2 Israel, "If you give your **approval** and if it is the will
21. 6 Because Joab **disapproved** of the king's command,
Neh 2. 6 The emperor, with the empress sitting at his side, **approved**
Job 28.27 saw wisdom and tested its worth— He gave it his **approval.**
Ps 101. 6 I will **approve** of those who are faithful to God and will
Jer 44.19 our husbands **approved** of what we were doing."
Hos 8. 4 They appointed leaders, but without my **approval.**
Mt 16. 1 a miracle for them, to show that God **approved** of him.
Mk 8.11 him to perform a miracle to show that God **approved** of him.
Lk 11.16 him to perform a miracle to show that God **approved** of him.
11.48 yourselves admit, then, that you **approve** of what your ancestors
Jn 6.27 God, the Father, has put his mark of **approval** on him."
12.43 They loved the **approval** of men rather than the approval of God.
Acts 8. 1 And Saul **approved** of his murder.
15. 8 of everyone, showed his **approval** of the Gentiles by giving
22.20 I myself was there, **approving** of his murder and taking care
Rom 1.32 very things, but they even **approve** of others who do them.
5. 4 endurance brings God's approval, and his **approval** creates hope.
7.23 a law that fights against the law which my mind **approves** of.
14.18 Christ in this way, he pleases God and is **approved** by others.
1 Cor 16. 3 to the men you have **approved,** and send them to take your
2 Cor 10.18 person that he is really **approved,** and not when he thinks
12.11 You are the ones who ought to show your **approval** of me.
Gal 1.10 Does this sound as if I am trying to win man's **approval?**
1.10 What I want is God's **approval!**
Eph 6. 6 they are watching you, because you want to gain their **approval;**
Col 3.22 they are watching you because you want to gain their **approval;**
2 Tim 2.15 your best to win full **approval** in God's sight, as a worker
Heb 11. 2 by their faith that people of ancient times won God's **approval.**
11. 4 his faith he won God's **approval** as a righteous man,
11. 4 because God himself **approved** of his gifts.

APRON

1 Sam 2.18 Samuel continued to serve the Lord, wearing a sacred linen **apron.**
Lk 17. 8 ready, then put on your **apron** and wait on me while I
Acts 19.12 Even handkerchiefs and **aprons** he had used were taken to those
1 Pet 5. 5 you must put on the **apron** of humility, to serve one another;

AQABA
[GULF OF AQABA]
A northward extension of what is now known as the Red Sea.

Ex 23.31 extend from the **Gulf of Aqaba** to the Mediterranean Sea and
Num 14.25 the wilderness in the direction of the **Gulf of Aqaba."**
21. 4 leads to the **Gulf of Aqaba,** in order to go round the
Deut 1.40 back into the desert along the road to the **Gulf of Aqaba.'**
2. 1 road to the **Gulf of Aqaba,** as the Lord had commanded, and
Judg 11.16 through the desert to the **Gulf of Aqaba** and came to Kadesh.
1 Kgs 9.26 the shore of the **Gulf of Aqaba,** in the land of Edom.
2 Chr 8.17 the shore of the **Gulf of Aqaba,** in the land of Edom.
Jer 49.21 alarm will be heard as far away as the **Gulf of Aqaba.**

ARAB (1)
Inhabitant of Arabia or desert area of Palestine.

1 Kgs 10.15 and tribute paid by the **Arabian** kings and the governors of
2 Chr 9.14 The kings of **Arabia** and the governors of the Israelite districts
17.11 and other gifts, and some **Arabs** brought him 7,700 sheep and
21.16 Some Philistines and **Arabs** lived near where some Sudanese
22. 1 Some **Arabs** had led a raid and killed all King Jehoram's
26. 7 to defeat the Philistines, the **Arabs** living at Gurbaal,
Neh 2.19 When Sanballat, Tobiah, and an **Arab** named Geshem heard
4. 7 Tobiah, and the people of **Arabia,** Ammon, and Ashdod heard
Ps 72.15 May he be given gold from **Arabia;**
Is 13.20 No wandering **Arab** will ever pitch his tent there, and no
21.13 This is a message about **Arabia.**
21.13 in the barren country of **Arabia,** [14]give water to the thirsty
Jer 3. 2 the roadside, as an **Arab** waits for victims in the desert.
25.19 all the kings of **Arabia;**
Ezek 27.21 The **Arabians** and the rulers of the land of Kedar paid
30. 5 hired from Sudan, Lydia, Libya, **Arabia,** Kub,
Acts 2.11 us are from Crete and **Arabia**—yet all of us hear them
Gal 1.17 I went at once to **Arabia,** and then I returned to Damascus.
4.25 stands for Mount Sinai in **Arabia,** is a figure of the present

ARAMAIC
Language which was used throughout much of the Middle East, in which parts of Ezra and Daniel were written.

2 Kgs 18.26 Shebna, and Joah told the official, "Speak **Aramaic** to us,
Ezra 4. 7 The letter was written in **Aramaic** and was to be translated
Is 36.11 Shebna, and Joah said to the official, "Speak **Aramaic** to us.
Dan 2. 4 They answered the king in **Aramaic,** "May Your Majesty live

ARAMEAN
Another name for Syrian.

Gen 25.20 the daughter of Bethuel (an **Aramean** from Mesopotamia)
28. 5 the son of Bethuel the **Aramean** and the brother of Rebecca,
Deut 26. 5 'My ancestor was a wandering **Aramean,** who took his family to
1 Chr 7.14 By his **Aramean** concubine, Manasseh had two sons,

ARAUNAH
Jebusite, who sold his threshing-place to David for an altar.

2 Sam 24.16 The angel was by the threshing-place of **Araunah,**
24.18 to him, "Go up to **Araunah's** threshing-place and build an altar
24.20 **Araunah** looked down and saw the king and his officials coming
24.22 "Take it, Your Majesty," **Araunah** said, "and offer to the Lord
24.23 **Araunah** gave it all to the king and said to him, "May
1 Chr 21.15 standing by the threshing-place of **Araunah,** a Jebusite.
21.18 and build an altar to the Lord at **Araunah's** threshing-place.
21.20 There at the threshing-place **Araunah** and his four sons
21.21 As soon as **Araunah** saw King David approaching,
21.23 "Take it, Your Majesty," **Araunah** said,
21.25 And he paid **Araunah** six hundred gold coins
21.28 he offered sacrifices on the altar at **Araunah's** threshing-place.
2 Chr 3. 1 to David, the place which **Araunah** the Jebusite had used as a

ARCH

1 Kgs 6.31 the top of the doorway was a pointed **arch.**

ARCHANGEL see ANGEL

ARCHER

1 Chr 8.40 Ulam's sons were outstanding soldiers and **archers.**

ARCHITECT

Prov 8.30 was beside him like an **architect,** I was his daily source of

AV ARCTURUS see (Great) BEAR

AREA

Gen 36.40 The **area** where each of these tribes lived was known by the
Lev 13.33 the person shall shave the head except the **area** round the sore.
Num 21.14 the town of Waheb in the **area** of Suphah, and the valleys;
35. 5 there is a square **area** measuring 900 metres on each side,
Josh 10.41 the coast, including all the **area** of Goshen, and as far
11.16 north and south, all the **area** of Goshen and the dry country
16. 3 then went west to the **area** of the Japhletites,
16. 3 as far as the **area** of Lower Beth Horon.
19.18 Its **area** included Jezreel, Chesulloth, Shunem,
19.25 Its **area** included Helkath, Hali, Beten, Achshaph,
19.41 Its **area** included Zorah, Eshtaol, Irshemesh,
Judg 6. 4 and destroy the crops as far south as the **area** round Gaza.
11.33 from Aroer to the **area** round Minnith, twenty cities in all,
20.48 They burnt every town in the **area.**
1 Sam 14.14 about twenty men in an **area** of about a quarter of a
14.25 They all came into a wooded **area** and found honey everywhere.
1 Kgs 8.64 part of the courtyard, the **area** in front of the Temple, and
9.13 For this reason the **area** is still called Cabul.
15.20 Dan, Abel Beth Maacah, the **area** near Lake Galilee, and the
2 Kgs 11.15 Athaliah killed in the temple **area,** so he ordered the army
2 Chr 7. 7 part of the courtyard, the **area** in front of the Temple, and
14.14 destroy the cities in the **area** around Gerar, because the people
23.14 Athaliah killed in the temple **area,** so he called out the
27. 3 work on the city wall in the **area** of Jerusalem called Ophel.
31.11 prepared storerooms in the Temple **area** [12]and put all the gifts
33.14 to the Fish Gate and the **area** of the city called Ophel.
34. 6 the devastated **areas** of Manasseh, Ephraim, and Simeon,
Neh 3.22 Priests from the **area** around Jerusalem built the next section;
7. 3 and others to patrol the **area** round their own houses.
12.28 gathered from the **area** where they had settled round Jerusalem
12.40 that were giving thanks to God reached the temple **area.**
Ezek 40.17 there was an **area** paved with stones, [18]which extended round
42.14 before going out to the **area** where the people gather."
42.15 finished measuring inside the temple **area,** he took me out
42.15 the east gate and then measured the outside of the **area.**
43.12 All the **area** surrounding it on the top of the mountain is
43.21 and burn it at the specified place outside the temple **area.**
44. 1 to the outer gate at the east side of the temple **area.**
45. 1 The entire **area** will be holy.
45. 2 In this **area** there is to be a square plot of land
45. 3 Half of this **area,** a section twelve and a half kilometres
45. 5 The other half of the **area** is to be set aside as
45. 6 Next to the holy **area,** another section,
45. 7 western boundary of the holy **area** it will extend west to the
45. 7 length of one of the **areas** allotted to the tribes of Israel.
45. 8 This **area** will be the share the ruling prince will have in
47. 2 me out of the temple **area** by way of the north gate
48. 9 of this section, a special **area** twelve and a half kilometres
48.10 The priests are to have a portion of this holy **area.**
48.10 of the Lord is to be in the middle of this **area.**
48.11 This holy **area** is to be for the priests who are
48.12 special area next to the **area** belonging to the Levites,
48.13 are to have a special **area,** south of that of the priests.
48.14 The **area** dedicated to the Lord is the best part of all
48.15 The part of the special **area** that is left, twelve and a
48.18 has been built in the **area** immediately to the south of

Ezek 48.18 south of the holy **area**—five kilometres by two and a
48.20 And so the total **area** in the centre of the section which
48.20 side, and it will include the **area** occupied by the city.
48.21 to the west of this **area** which contains the Temple, the

AREOPAGUS

Hill in Athens where the city council used to meet.

Acts 17.19 before the city council, the **Areopagus**, and said, "We would

ARGUE

Gen 44.16 "How can we **argue?**
1 Kgs 3.22 And so they **argued** before the king.
Job 9. 3 How can anyone **argue** with him?
13. 3 I want to **argue** my case with him.
13. 8 Are you going to **argue** his case in court?
13.12 your **arguments** crumble like clay.
23. 4 case before him and present all the **arguments** in my favour.
33. 5 Prepare your **arguments.**
Prov 3.30 Don't **argue** with someone for no reason when he has never
15.18 Hot tempers cause **arguments**, but patience brings peace.
17.14 The start of an **argument** is like the first break in a
18. 6 When some fool starts an **argument**, he is asking for a beating.
20. 3 Any fool can start **arguments;**
22.10 will be no more **arguments**, quarrelling, or calling of names.
22.23 The Lord will **argue** their case for them and threaten the
23.11 their powerful defender, and he will **argue** their case against you.
26.17 Getting involved in an **argument** that is none of your business
26.21 wood keeps the fire burning, and troublemakers keep **arguments**
Ecc 6.10 know that a man cannot **argue** with someone who is stronger
6.11 The longer you **argue**, the more useless it is, and you
Is 41.21 Bring the best **arguments** you have!
45. 9 a clay pot dare to **argue** with its maker, a pot that
Jer 12. 1 Lord, if I **argued** my case with you, you would prove to
15.10 I have to quarrel and **argue** with everyone in the land.
Mt 12.19 He will not **argue** or shout, or make loud speeches in the
21.25 They started to **argue** among themselves, "What shall we say?
Mk 8.11 Some Pharisees came to Jesus and started to **argue** with him.
9.14 round them and some teachers of the Law **arguing** with them.
9.16 Jesus asked his disciples, "What are you **arguing** with them about?"
9.33 Jesus asked his disciples, "What were you **arguing** about on the road?"
9.34 the road they had been **arguing** among themselves about who
11.31 They started to **argue** among themselves:
Lk 9.46 An **argument** broke out among the disciples as to which
20. 5 They started to **argue** among themselves, "What shall we say?
22.24 An **argument** broke out among the disciples as to which
Jn 3.25 Some of John's disciples began **arguing** with a Jew about
6.52 This started an angry **argument** among them.
Acts 6. 9 provinces of Cilicia and Asia started **arguing** with Stephen.
15. 2 Barnabas got into a fierce **argument** with them about this,
15.39 There was a sharp **argument**, and they separated:
18.15 But since it is an **argument** about words and names
18.28 with his strong **arguments** he defeated the Jews in public debates
23.10 The **argument** became so violent that the commander was afraid
24.12 Jews did not find me **arguing** with anyone in the Temple,
25.19 All they had were some **arguments** with him about their
Rom 14. 1 but do not **argue** with him about his personal opinions.
1 Cor 11.16 But if anyone wants to **argue** about it, all I have to
2 Cor 10. 4 We destroy false **arguments;**
Phil 2.14 without complaining or **arguing**, [15] so that you may be innocent
Col 2. 4 anyone deceive you with false **arguments**, no matter how good
1 Tim 1. 4 those long lists of ancestors, which only produce **arguments;**
2. 8 can lift up their hands in prayer without anger or **argument.**
6. 4 has an unhealthy desire to **argue** and quarrel about words,
6. 5 insults, evil suspicions, [5] and constant **arguments** from
6.20 the profane talk and foolish **arguments** of what some people
2 Tim 2.23 But keep away from foolish and ignorant **arguments;**
Tit 3. 9 But avoid stupid **arguments**, long lists of ancestors,
Heb 6.16 greater than himself, and the vow settles all **arguments.**
Jude 9 with the Devil, when they **argued** about who would have the

ARISE

Num 10.35 Whenever the Covenant Box started out, Moses would say, **"Arise,**
24.17 A king, like a bright star, will **arise** in that nation.
Is 11. 1 so a new king will **arise** from among David's descendants.
60. 1 **Arise,** Jerusalem, and shine like the sun;
Ezek 44.24 When a legal dispute **arises**, the priests are to decide
Dan 7.17 "These four huge beasts are four empires which will **arise** on earth.
Mic 6. 1 **Arise,** O Lord, and present your case;
Nah 1. 3 Where the Lord walks, storms **arise;**

AV **ARK (OF NOAH)** see **BOAT**

AV **ARK (OF THE COVENANT)** see **COVENANT BOX**

ARM (1)

Gen 24.22 in her nose and put two large gold bracelets on her **arms.**
24.30 the bracelets on his sister's **arms** and had heard her say
24.47 put the ring in her nose and the bracelets on her **arms.**
27.16 of the goats on his **arms** and on the hairless part of
27.22 like Jacob's voice, but your **arms** feel like Esau's arms."
27.23 He did not recognize Jacob, because his **arms** were hairy
33. 4 ran to meet him, threw his **arms** round him, and kissed him.
38.28 While she was in labour, one of them put out an **arm;**
38.29 But he pulled his **arm** back, and his brother was born first.
38.30 with the red thread on his **arm**, and he was named Zerah.
45.14 He threw his **arms** round his brother Benjamin and began to cry;
46.29 they met, Joseph threw his **arms** round his father's neck and
49.24 bow remains steady, And his **arms** are made strong By the
Ex 6. 6 I will raise my mighty **arm** to bring terrible punishment upon them,
17.11 as Moses held up his **arms**, the Israelites won,
17.11 but when he put his **arms** down, the Amalekites started winning.
17.12 When Moses' **arms** grew tired, Aaron and Hur brought a
17.12 him and held up his **arms**, holding them steady until the sun
Num 11.12 and carry them in my **arms** like babies all the way to
Deut 6. 8 Tie them on your **arms** and wear them on your foreheads as
11.18 Tie them on your **arms** and wear them on your foreheads as
33.20 waits like a lion To tear off an **arm** or a scalp.
33.27 his eternal **arms** are your support.
Judg 15.14 broke the ropes round his **arms** and hands as if they were
16.12 But he snapped the ropes off his **arms** like thread.
1 Sam 5. 4 its head and both its **arms** were broken off and were lying
2 Sam 1.10 and the bracelet from his **arm**, and I have brought them to
1 Kgs 8.22 where he raised his **arms** [23] and prayed, "Lord God of Israel,
10.19 beside each of the two **arms** was the figure of a lion.
13. 4 At once the king's **arm** became paralysed so that he couldn't
13. 6 to the Lord your God, and ask him to heal my **arm!"**
13. 6 The prophet prayed to the Lord, and the king's **arm** was healed.
17.19 took the boy from her **arms**, carried him upstairs to the room
2 Kgs 4.16 time next year you will be holding a son in your **arms."**
2 Chr 6.12 stood in front of the altar and raised his **arms** in prayer.
9.18 There were **arms** on each side of the throne, and the figure
Neh 8. 6 All the people raised their **arms** in the air and answered,
Job 17. 7 my **arms** and legs are as thin as shadows.
18.13 spreads over his body and causes his **arms** and legs to rot.
31.22 I could win in court, [22] then may my **arms** be broken;
Ps 131. 2 lies quietly in its mother's **arms**, so my heart is quiet
136.12 with his strong hand, his powerful **arm;**
Prov 7.13 She threw her **arms** round the young man, kissed him,
7.18 We'll be happy in each other's **arms.**
27. 6 But when an enemy puts his **arm** round your shoulder—watch out!
Ecc 7.26 and her **arms** round you will hold you like a chain.
12. 3 Then your **arms**, that have protected you, will tremble,
Song 8. 5 is this coming from the desert, **arm** in arm with her lover?
8. 6 hold no one in your **arms** but me.
Is 3.20 magic charms they wear on their **arms** and at their waists;
13. 2 the soldiers and raise your **arm** as the signal for them to
14.26 for the world, and my **arm** is stretched out to punish the
14.27 he has stretched out his **arm** to punish, and no one can
40.11 he will gather the lambs together and carry them in his **arms;**
44. 5 of the Lord on his **arm** and call himself one of God's
44.12 His strong **arm** swings a hammer to pound the metal into shape.
66.12 by its mother, carried in her **arms**, and treated with love.
Jer 38.12 put the rags under my **arms**, so that the ropes wouldn't hurt
Lam 2.12 they were wounded, And slowly die in their mothers' **arms.**
Ezek 13.20 will rip them off your **arms** and set free the people that
23.42 put bracelets on the women's **arms** and beautiful crowns
29. 7 pierced their **armpits**, and made them wrench their backs.
30.21 he said, "I have broken the **arm** of the king of Egypt.
30.22 going to break both his **arms**—the good one and the one
30.24 Then I will make the **arms** of the king of Babylonia
30.24 But I will break the **arms** of the king of Egypt, and
Dan 2.32 its chest and **arms** were made of silver;
10. 6 His **arms** and legs shone like polished bronze, and his voice
Hos 11. 3 my people up in my **arms**, but they did not acknowledge that
Zech 11.17 His **arm** will wither, and his right eye will go blind."
Mt 23. 5 on their foreheads and **arms**, and notice how large they are!
23.37 I wanted to put my **arms** round all your people, just as
Mk 9.36 He put his **arms** round him and said to them, [37] "Whoever
10.16 took the children in his **arms**, placed his hands on each of
Lk 1.51 has stretched out his mighty **arm** and scattered the proud
2.28 Simeon took the child in his **arms** and gave thanks to God:
13.34 I wanted to put my **arms** round all your people, just as
14. 2 A man whose legs and **arms** were swollen came to Jesus,
15.20 and he ran, threw his **arms** round his son, and kissed him.

ARM (2)

Ex 13.18 The Israelites were **armed** for battle.
Deut 3.18 Now **arm** your fighting men and send them across the Jordan
Josh 1.14 but your soldiers, **armed** for battle, will cross over ahead
Judg 18.17 priest stayed at the gate with the six hundred **armed** men.
1 Sam 17. 5 bronze **armour** that weighed about fifty-seven kilogrammes
17. 6 protected by bronze **armour**, and he carried a bronze javelin
17.38 He gave his own **armour** to David for him to wear:
17.38 helmet, which he put on David's head, and a coat of **armour.**
17.39 strapped Saul's sword over the **armour** and tried to walk, but
18. 4 to David, together with his **armour** and also his sword, bow,
31. 9 stripped off his **armour**, and sent messengers with them
2 Sam 2.14 the young men from each side to fight an **armed** contest."
23.10 to where Eleazar was and stripped the **armour** from the dead.
23.21 killed an Egyptian, a huge man who was **armed** with a spear.
23.24 Ammon Naharai from Beeroth, Joab's **armour** bearer Ira
1 Kgs 22.34 which struck King Ahab between the joints of his **armour.**
2 Kgs 3.21 men who could bear **arms**, from the oldest to the youngest,
13. 7 Jehoahaz had no **armed** forces left except fifty horsemen,
24. 2 The Lord sent **armed** bands of Babylonians, Syrians, Moabites,
1 Chr 10. 9 stripped off his **armour**, and sent messengers with them
11.23 over two metres tall, who was **armed** with a gigantic spear.
11.26 Joab's **armour-bearer**, from Beeroth
12.23 6,800 well-equipped men, **armed** with shields and spears;
12.23 together with 37,000 men **armed** with shields and spears;

2 Chr 14. 8 300,000 men from Judah, **armed** with shields and spears,
14. 8 and 280,000 men from Benjamin, **armed** with shields and bows.
17.17 in command of 200,000 men **armed** with shields and bows.
18.33 which struck King Ahab between the joints of his **armour.**
26.14 shields, spears, helmets, coats of **armour,** bows and arrows,
Neh 3.19 section in front of the **armoury,** as far as the place where
4.13 So I **armed** the people with swords, spears, and bows,
4.16 wearing coats of **armour** and armed with spears, shields,
Esth 8.11 If **armed** men of any nationality in any province attacked
Job 41.13 can tear off his outer coat or pierce the **armour** he wears.
Ps 35. 2 Take your shield and **armour** and come to my rescue.
78. 9 The Ephraimites, **armed** with bows and arrows, ran away on
Prov 6.11 while he sleeps, poverty will attack him like an **armed** robber.
24.34 you are asleep, poverty will attack you like an **armed** robber.
Song 3. 8 Each of them is **armed** with a sword, on guard against a
Is 22. 6 came riding on horseback, **armed** with bows and arrows.
59.17 like a coat of **armour** and saving power like a helmet.
Jer 6.25 because our enemies are **armed** and terror is all round us."
46. 4 Put on your **armour!**
51. 3 time to shoot their arrows or to put on their **armour.**
Ezek 32.27 times, who went fully **armed** to the world of the dead,
38. 4 every soldier carries a shield and is **armed** with a sword.
Mic 5. 6 By force of **arms** they will conquer Assyria, the land of Nimrod,
Mt 26.47 him was a large crowd **armed** with swords and clubs and sent
Mk 14.43 With him was a crowd **armed** with swords and clubs, and sent
Jn 18. 3 they were **armed** and carried lanterns and torches.
Acts 21.38 a revolution and led four thousand **armed** terrorists out into the desert?"
Eph 6.11 Put on all the **armour** that God gives you, so that you
6.13 So put on God's **armour** now!

ARMLETS

Num 31.50 are bringing the gold ornaments, **armlets,** bracelets, rings,

ARMY

Gen 14. 5 his allies came with their **armies** and defeated the Rephaim
14. 8 and Bela drew up their **armies** for battle in the Valley of
21.22 Phicol, the commander of his **army,** and said to Abraham,
26.26 adviser and Phicol the commander of his **army** to see Isaac.
Ex 14. 4 my victory over the king and his **army** will bring me honour.
14. 6 The king got his war chariot and his **army** ready.
14. 9 The Egyptian **army,** with all the horses, chariots, and drivers,
14.10 saw the king and his **army** marching against them,
14.17 victory over the king, his **army,** his chariots, and his drivers.
14.19 been in front of the **army** of Israel, moved and went to
14.20 of Israel, and so the **armies** could not come near each other
14.24 and cloud at the Egyptian **army** and threw them into a panic.
14.28 and all the Egyptian **army** that had followed the Israelites
15. 4 "He threw Egypt's **army** and its chariots into the sea;
Num 20.20 out with a powerful **army** to attack the people of Israel.
21.23 He gathered his **army** and went out to Jahaz in the wilderness
21.28 this city of Heshbon Sihon's **army** went forth like a fire;
21.33 of Bashan marched out with his **army** to attack them at Edrei.
31.13 of the community went out of the camp to meet the **army.**
31.48 officers who had commanded the **army** went to Moses
Deut 11. 4 completely wiped out the Egyptian **army,** along with their horses
17.16 number of horses for his **army,** and he is not to send
20. 1 chariots and horses and an **army** that outnumbers yours, do
20. 2 to come forward and say to the **army,** [3]'Men of Israel,
20. 9 have finished speaking to the **army,** leaders are to be chosen
20.12 surrender, but choose to fight, surround it with your **army.**
Josh 5.14 "I am here as the commander of the Lord's **army."**
5.15 the commander of the Lord's **army** told him, "Take your sandals
6. 5 Then the whole **army** will go straight into the city."
6.20 Then all the **army** went straight up the hill into the city
7. 3 Don't send the whole **army** up there to fight;
10. 7 So Joshua and his whole **army,** including the best troops,
10. 9 All night Joshua and his **army** marched from Gilgal to Gibeon,
10.10 The Lord made the Amorites panic at the sight of Israel's **army.**
10.11 the pass from the Israelite **army,** the Lord made large hailstones
10.15 After this, Joshua and his **army** went back to the camp at
10.29 After this, Joshua and his **army** went on from Makkedah to
10.31 After this, Joshua and his **army** went on from Libnah to Lachish,
10.33 Joshua defeated him and his **army** and left none of them alive.
10.34 Next, Joshua and his **army** went on from Lachish to Eglon,
10.36 After this, Joshua and his **army** went from Eglon up into
10.38 Then Joshua and his **army** turned back to Debir and attacked it.
10.43 After this, Joshua and his **army** went back to the camp at
11. 4 with all their soldiers—an **army** with as many men as there
Judg 4. 2 The commander of his **army** was Sisera, who lived at Harosheth-of-the-Gentiles.
4. 7 Sisera, the commander of Jabin's **army,** to fight against you
4.15 When Barak attacked with his **army,** the Lord threw Sisera
4.16 pursued the chariots and the **army** to Harosheth-of-the-Gentiles,
4.16 and Sisera's whole **army** was killed.
7.14 God has given him victory over Midian and our whole **army!"**
7.15 The Lord is giving you victory over the Midianite **army!"**
7.21 round the camp, and the whole enemy **army** ran away yelling.
8. 6 of Sukkoth said, "Why should we give your **army** any food?
8.10 Zebah and Zalmunna were at Karkor with their **army.**
8.10 Of the whole **army** of desert tribesmen, only about 15,000
8.11 east of Nobah and Jogbehah, and attacked the **army** by surprise.
8.12 and captured them, and caused their whole **army** to panic.
8.15 any food to my exhausted **army** because I hadn't captured Zebah
9.29 to him, 'Reinforce your **army,** come on out and fight!' "
10.17 Then the Ammonite **army** prepared for battle and made camp
11.20 He brought his whole **army** together, made camp at Jahaz,
11.21 God of Israel, gave the Israelites victory over Sihon and his **army.**
20.10 will provide food for the **army,** and the others will go and
Judg 20.20 They went to attack the **army** of Benjamin, and placed
20.21 The **army** of Benjamin came out of the city, and before
20.22 So the Israelite **army** was encouraged, and they placed their
20.24 They marched against the **army** of Benjamin a second time.
20.30 marched against the **army** of Benjamin and placed their soldiers
20.33 So when the main **army** of the Israelites pulled back
20.35 The Lord gave Israel victory over the **army** of Benjamin.
20.36 body of the Israelite **army** had retreated from the Benjaminites
20.38 The main Israelite **army** and the men in hiding had
20.42 were caught between the main **army** and the men who were now
21. 9 the roll call of the **army** no one from Jabesh had responded.
1 Sam 11. 1 Nahash of Ammon led his **army** against the town of Jabesh in
12. 9 and Sisera, commander of the **army** of the city of Hazor,
14.50 his **army** commander was his cousin Abner, the son of his
14.52 who was strong or brave, he would enlist him in his **army.**
17.10 Here and now I challenge the Israelite **army.**
17.21 The Philistine and the Israelite **armies** took up positions
17.26 heathen Philistine to defy the **army** of the living God?"
17.36 heathen Philistine, who has defied the **army** of the living God.
17.45 the God of the Israelite **armies,** which you have defied.
17.55 Abner, the commander of his **army,** "Abner, whose son is he?"
18. 5 sent him, and so Saul made him an officer in his **army.**
18.30 The Philistine **armies** would come and fight, but in every battle
22. 7 vineyards to all of you, and make you officers in his **army?**
26. 5 where Saul and Abner son of Ner, commander of Saul's **army,**
28. 5 When Saul saw the Philistine **army,** he was terrified,
28.19 Lord will also hand the **army** of Israel over to the Philistines."
31. 7 Jordan heard that the Israelite **army** had fled and that Saul
2 Sam 1. 4 "Our **army** ran away from the battle," he replied, "and many
2. 8 The commander of Saul's **army,** Abner son of Ner, had fled
5.17 made king of Israel, so their **army** set out to capture him.
5.24 I will be marching ahead of you to defeat the Philistine **army."**
8. 5 Syrians of Damascus sent an **army** to help King Hadadezer,
8. 9 Toi of Hamath heard that David had defeated all of Hadadezer's **army,**
8.16 Joab, whose mother was Zeruiah, was the commander of the **army;**
10. 7 heard of it and sent Joab against them with the whole **army.**
10.16 Shobach, commander of the **army** of King Hadadezer of Zobah.
10.18 and the Israelites drove the Syrian **army** back.
11. 1 David sent out Joab with his officers and the Israelite **army;**
17.25 put Amasa in command of the **army** in the place of Joab.
18. 6 David's **army** went out into the countryside and fought
19.13 am putting you in charge of the **army** in place of Joab.
20.23 Joab was in command of the **army** of Israel;
24. 2 So David gave orders to Joab, the commander of his **army:**
1 Kgs 1.19 Joab the commander of your **army** to the feast, but he did
1.25 Joab the commander of your **army,** and Abiathar the priest,
2. 5 the two commanders of Israel's **armies,** Abner son of Ner and
2.32 Abner, commander of the **army** of Israel,
2.32 and Amasa, commander of the **army** of Judah.
2.35 made Benaiah commander of the **army** in Joab's place and put
4. 4 Jehoshaphat son of Ahilud [4]Commander of the **army:**
11.15 Joab the commander of his **army** had gone there to bury the
11.21 Joab the commander of the **army** was dead, Hadad said to the
15.20 his commanding officers and their **armies** to attack the cities
15.27 him as Nadab and his **army** were besieging the city of
20.13 said, "The Lord says, 'Don't be afraid of that huge **army!**
20.15 out the Israelite **army,** a total of seven thousand men.
20.19 followed by the Israelite **army,** [20]and each one killed the man
20.25 Then call up an **army** as large as the one that deserted
20.28 you victory over their huge **army,** and you and your people
20.42 and your army will be destroyed for letting his **army** escape.' "
22.17 answered, "I can see the **army** of Israel scattered over the
2 Kgs 3.23 "The three enemy **armies** must have fought and killed each other!
4.13 to the king or the **army** commander and put in a good
5. 1 the commander of the Syrian **army,** was highly respected
6.24 of Syria led his entire **army** against Israel and laid siege
7. 6 the advance of a large **army,** with horses and chariots, and
7. 6 had hired Hittite and Egyptian kings and their **armies** to attack
7.14 to go and find out what had happened to the Syrian **army.**
8.21 all his chariots for Zair, where the Edomite **army** surrounded them.
8.28 The **armies** clashed at Ramoth in Gilead, and Joram was
9. 5 to Ramoth, [5]where he found the **army** officers in a conference.
11.15 in the temple area, so he ordered the **army** officers:
12.18 to King Hazael, who then led his **army** away from Jerusalem.
14.12 Amaziah's **army** was defeated, and all his soldiers fled
16. 9 marched out with his **army** against Damascus, captured it,
18.17 Assyrian emperor sent a large **army** from Lachish to attack
18.30 he will stop our Assyrian **army** from capturing your city.
19. 9 the Assyrians that the Egyptian **army,** led by King Tirhakah
23.29 Neco of Egypt led an **army** to the River Euphrates to help
23.29 tried to stop the Egyptian **army** at Megiddo and was killed in
24. 7 king of Egypt and his **army** never marched out of Egypt again,
24.10 the Babylonian **army,** commanded by King Nebuchadnezzar's officers,
25. 1 Nebuchadnezzar came with all his **army** and attacked Jerusalem
25. 5 But the Babylonian **army** pursued King Zedekiah, captured him
25. 8 Nebuzaradan, adviser to the king and commander of his **army,**
25.26 together with the **army** officers, left and went to Egypt,
1 Chr 10. 7 of Jezreel heard that the **army** had fled and that Saul and
11. 6 man to kill a Jebusite will be commander of the **army!"**
12.18 David welcomed them and made them officers in his **army.**
12.21 Later they were officers in the Israelite **army.**
12.22 joined David's forces, so that his **army** was soon enormous.
12.23 many trained soldiers joined his **army** to help make him king
14. 8 whole country of Israel, their **army** went out to capture him.
14.11 has used me to break through the enemy **army** like a flood."
14.15 I will be marching ahead of you to defeat the Philistine **army."**
18. 5 Syrians of Damascus sent an **army** to help King Hadadezer,

1 Chr 18. 9 heard that David had defeated Hadadezer's entire **army.**
18.15 Abishai's brother Joab was commander of the **army;**
19. 7 chariots they hired and the **army** of the king of Maacah came
19. 8 what was happening, he sent out Joab and the whole **army.**
19.16 Shobach, commander of the **army** of King Hadadezer of Zobah.
19.18 and the Israelites drove the Syrian **army** back.
20. 1 war, Joab led out the **army** and invaded the land of Ammon;
21.12 Or three months of running away from the **armies** of your enemies?
26.26 heads of families, leaders of clan groups, and **army** officers.
27.34 Joab was commander of the royal **army.**
29. 6 the commanders of the **army,** and the administrators of the royal
2 Chr 12. 3 attacked Jerusalem [3] with an **army** of twelve hundred chariots,
13. 3 Abijah raised an **army** of 400,000 soldiers,
13. 3 and Jeroboam opposed him with an **army** of 800,000.
13. 4 The **armies** met in the hill-country of Ephraim.
13. 8 You have a huge **army** and have with you the gold bull-calves
13.13 troops to ambush the Judaean **army** from the rear, while the
13.15 God defeated Jeroboam and the Israelite **army.**
13.17 Abijah and his **army** dealt the Israelites a crushing defeat—
13.19 Abijah pursued Jeroboam's **army** and occupied some of his cities:
14. 8 King Asa had an **army** of 300,000 men from Judah, armed with
14. 9 Zerah invaded Judah with an **army** of a million men and three
14.11 you can help a weak **army** as easily as a powerful one.
14.11 your name we have come out to fight against this huge **army.**
14.12 The Lord defeated the Sudanese **army**
14.12 when Asa and the Judaean **army** attacked them.
14.13 Sudanese were killed that the **army** was unable to rally and fight.
14.13 by the Lord and his **army,**
14.13 and the **army** took large amounts of loot.
14.14 The **army** plundered all those cities and captured large amounts
16. 4 his commanding officers and their **armies** to attack the cities
16. 7 the Lord your God, the **army** of the king of Israel has
16. 8 Sudanese and the Libyans have large **armies** with many chariots
18. 3 replied, "I am ready when you are, and so is my **army.**
18.16 "I can see the **army** of Israel scattered over the hills
20. 1 Some time later the **armies** of Moab and Ammon, together with
20. 2 "A large **army** from Edom has come from the other side of
20.12 in the face of this large **army** that is attacking us.
20.15 not be discouraged or be afraid to face this large **army.**
20.21 wore on sacred occasions and to march ahead of the **army,**
20.22 to sing, the Lord threw the invading **armies** into a panic.
20.23 Moabites attacked the Edomite **army** and completely destroyed it,
20.24 When the Judaean **army** reached a tower that was in the desert,
21. 9 There the Edomite **army** surrounded them, but during the night
22. 5 The **armies** clashed at Ramoth in Gilead, and Joram was
23. 1 He made a pact with five **army** officers:
23.13 and surrounded by the **army** officers and the trumpeters.
23.14 so he called out the **army** officers and said, "Take her out
23.20 The **army** officers, the leading citizens, the officials,
24.23 the Syrian **army** attacked Judah and Jerusalem, killed all
24.24 The Syrian **army** was small, but the Lord let them defeat
24.24 much larger Judaean **army** because the people had abandoned him,
25. 5 of Judah and Benjamin into **army** units, according to the clans
25.11 up his courage and led his **army** to the Valley of Salt.
25.22 the Judaean **army** was defeated, and the soldiers fled
26.11 He had a large **army** ready for battle.
26.12 The **army** was commanded by 2,600 officers.
26.14 Uzziah supplied the **army** with shields, spears, helmets,
27. 5 against the king of Ammon and his **army** and defeated them.
28. 8 the Israelite **army** captured 200,000 women and children
28. 9 He met the returning Israelite **army** with its Judaean prisoners
28.12 Amasa son of Hadlai also opposed the actions of the **army.**
28.14 So then the **army** handed the prisoners and the loot over
32. 1 and gave orders for his **army** to break their way through the
32. 6 under the command of **army** officers and ordered them to assemble
32. 7 afraid of the Assyrian emperor or of the **army** he is leading.
32. 9 later, while Sennacherib and his **army** were still at Lachish,
32.21 that killed the soldiers and officers of the Assyrian **army.**
33.11 So the Lord let the commanders of the Assyrian **army** invade Judah.
33.14 He also stationed an **army** officer in command of a unit of
35.20 Neco of Egypt led an **army** to fight at Carchemish on the
Neh 2. 9 The emperor sent some **army** officers and a troop of horsemen
Esth 1. 3 The **armies** of Persia and Media were present, as well as the
Job 7. 1 Human life is like forced **army** service, like a life of
19.12 He sends his **army** to attack me;
Ps 27. 3 Even if a whole **army** surrounds me, I will not be afraid;
33.16 A king does not win because of his powerful **army;**
44. 9 you no longer march out with our **armies.**
47. 9 More powerful than all **armies** is he;
60.10 Aren't you going to march out with our **armies?**
68.12 "Kings and their **armies** are running away!"
108.11 Aren't you going to march out with our **armies?**
136.15 but he drowned the king of Egypt and his **army;**
148. 2 Praise him, all his angels, all his heavenly **armies.**
Is 7. 2 king of Judah that the **armies** of Syria were already in the
9. 4 people, just as you defeated the **army** of Midian long ago.
9. 5 The boots of the invading **army** and all their bloodstained
10.28 The enemy **army** has captured the city of Ai!
13. 4 The Lord of **Armies** is preparing his troops for battle.
14.31 the north—it is an **army** with no cowards in its ranks.
20. 1 the commander-in-chief of the Assyrian **army** attacked
21. 2 **Army** of Elam, attack!
21. 2 **Army** of Media, lay siege to the cities!
29. 5 and their terrifying **armies** will fly away like straw.
29. 7 then all the **armies** of the nations attacking the city of
30.17 will be left of your **army** except a lonely flagstaff on the
33.22 all the wealth of enemy **armies,** and there will be so much
Is 34. 2 The Lord is angry with all the nations and all their **armies.**
36.15 he will stop our Assyrian **army** from capturing your city.
37. 9 the Assyrians that the Egyptian **army,** led by King Tirhakah
40.26 leads them out like an **army,** he knows how many there are
43.14 "To save you, I will send an **army** against Babylon;
43.17 He led a mighty **army** to destruction,
43.17 an **army** of chariots and horses.
Jer 5.17 cities in which you trust will be destroyed by their **army.**
6. 3 kings will camp there with their **armies.**
9.16 and I will send **armies** against them until I have completely
10.22 its **army** will turn the cities of Judah into a desert, a
21. 2 Nebuchadnezzar of Babylonia and his **army** are besieging the city.
21. 4 am going to defeat your **army** that is fighting
21. 4 against the king of Babylonia and his **army.**
32. 2 At that time the **army** of the king of Babylonia was
32.28 city over to King Nebuchadnezzar of Babylonia and his **army;**
34. 1 Nebuchadnezzar of Babylonia and his **army,** supported by troops
34. 7 Zedekiah in Jerusalem [7] while the **army** of the king of Babylonia
34. 7 The **army** was also attacking Lachish and Azekah,
34.21 to the Babylonian **army,** which has stopped its attack
35.11 Jerusalem to get away from the Babylonian and Syrian **armies.**
37. 5 The Babylonian **army** had been besieging Jerusalem,
37. 5 heard that the Egyptian **army** had crossed the Egyptian border,
37. 7 say to Zedekiah, "The Egyptian **army** is on its way to help
37.10 you defeat the whole Babylonian **army,** so that only wounded men
37.11 The Babylonian **army** retreated from Jerusalem
37.11 because the Egyptian **army** was approaching.
38. 3 city to the Babylonian **army,** and they will capture it."
39. 1 King Nebuchadnezzar of Babylonia came with his whole **army**
39. 5 But the Babylonian **army** pursued them and captured Zedekiah
41.11 Johanan and all the **army** leaders with him heard of the
42. 1 Then all the **army** leaders, including Johanan son of Kareah
42. 8 called together Johanan, all the **army** leaders who were with him,
43. 4 Johanan nor any of the **army** officers nor any of the people
43. 5 Then Johanan and all the **army** officers took everybody left
46. 2 what he said about the **army** of King Neco of Egypt, which
46.22 hissing like a snake, as the enemy's **army** approaches.
46.26 kill them, to King Nebuchadnezzar of Babylonia and his **army.**
48. 2 **armies** will march against it.
49.14 the nations to assemble their **armies** and to get ready to
49.37 people of Elam and send **armies** against them until I have
50.16 be afraid of the attacking **army** and will go back home."
51. 3 Destroy the whole **army!**
51.28 and the **armies** of all the countries they control.
51.55 The **armies** rush in like roaring waves and attack
52. 4 Nebuchadnezzar came with all his **army** and attacked Jerusalem
52. 8 But the Babylonian **army** pursued King Zedekiah, captured him
52.12 Nebuzaradan, adviser to the king and commander of his **army,**
Lam 1.15 He sent an **army** to destroy my young men.
Ezek 1.24 the noise of a huge **army,** like the voice of Almighty God.
17.15 and sent agents to Egypt to get horses and a large **army.**
17.17 Even the powerful **army** of the king of Egypt will not be
23.24 bringing a large **army** with chariots and supply wagons.
26. 7 the north with a huge **army,** with horses and chariots and
27.10 "Soldiers from Persia, Lydia, and Libya served in your **army.**
29.18 the king nor his **army** got anything for all their trouble.
29.19 and carry off all the wealth of Egypt as his **army's** pay.
29.20 for his services, because his **army** was working for me.
30. 6 Egypt's proud **army** will be destroyed.
30.11 He and his ruthless **army** will come to devastate the land.
32.31 the king of Egypt and his **army,"** says the Sovereign Lord.
32.32 but he and all his **army** will be killed and laid to
37.10 There were enough of them to form an **army.**
38. 4 His **army,** with its horses and uniformed riders, is enormous,
38. 9 He and his **army** and the many nations with him will attack
38.13 you, 'Have you assembled your **army** and attacked in order to
38.15 leading a large, powerful **army** of soldiers from many nations,
38.22 down on him and his **army** and on the many nations that
39. 4 Gog and his **army** and his allies will fall dead on the
39.11 Gog and all his **army** will be buried there,
39.11 and the valley will be called 'The Valley of Gog's **Army.'**
39.15 can come and bury it in the Valley of Gog's **Army.**
39.16 (There will be a town near by named after the **army.)**
Dan 3.20 the strongest men in his **army** to tie the three men up
8.10 strong enough to attack the **army** of heaven, the stars themselves,
8.11 the Prince of the heavenly **army,** stopped the daily sacrifices
8.13 How long will the **army** of heaven and the Temple be trampled
9.26 Temple will be destroyed by the invading **army** of a powerful ruler.
11. 7 He will attack the **army** of the king of Syria, enter their
11.10 king of Syria will prepare for war and gather a large **army.**
11.11 to war against the king of Syria and capture his huge **army.**
11.13 will go back and gather a larger **army** than he had before.
11.13 proper time comes, he will return with a large, well-equipped **army.**
11.17 "The king of Syria will plan an expedition, using his whole **army.**
11.25 will boldly raise a large **army** to attack the king of Egypt,
11.25 will prepare to fight back with a huge and powerful **army.**
11.26 his soldiers will be killed, and his **army** will be wiped out.
Joel 1. 6 An **army** of locusts has attacked our land;
2. 2 The great **army** of locusts advances like darkness spreading
2. 5 They are lined up like a great **army** ready for battle.
2.11 The Lord thunders commands to his **army.**
2.20 I will remove the locust **army** that came from the north
2.25 It was I who sent this **army** against you.
3.11 Send down, O Lord, your **army** to attack them.
Amos 6.14 I am going to send a foreign **army** to occupy your country.
Obad 20 The **army** of exiles from northern Israel will return
Hab 1. 9 "Their **armies** advance in violent conquest, and everyone
3.14 pierced the commander of his **army** when it came like a storm
Zech 9. 8 I will guard my land and keep **armies** from passing through it.

Zech 12. 7 will give victory to the **armies** of Judah first, so that the
Mt 26.53 at once he would send me more than twelve **armies** of angels?
27.54 When the **army officer** and the soldiers with him who were
Mk 15.39 The **army officer** who was standing there in front of the
15.44 He called the **army officer** and asked him if Jesus had been
Lk 2.13 Suddenly a great **army** of heaven's angels appeared with the angel,
21.20 you see Jerusalem surrounded by **armies,** then you will know
23.47 The **army officer** saw what had happened, and he praised God,
Acts 27.11 But the **army officer** was convinced by what the captain
27.31 But Paul said to the **army officer** and soldiers, "If the
27.43 But the **army officer** wanted to save Paul, so he stopped
1 Cor 9. 7 What soldier ever has to pay his own expenses in the **army?**
Heb 11.34 were mighty in battle and defeated the **armies** of foreigners.
Rev 19.14 The **armies** of heaven followed him, riding on white
19.19 of the earth and their **armies** gathered to fight against
19.19 the one who was riding the horse and against his **army.**
19.21 Their **armies** were killed by the sword that comes out of

ARNON

River which flows westward into the Dead Sea.

Num 21.13 north side of the River **Arnon,** in the wilderness
21.13 (The **Arnon** was the border between the Moabites and the Amorites.)
21.14 the River **Arnon,** [15] and the slope of the valleys that
21.24 their land from the River **Arnon** north to the Jabbok, that
21.26 and had captured all his land as far as the River **Arnon.**
21.28 of Ar in Moab And devoured the hills of the upper **Arnon.**
22.36 Ar, a city on the River **Arnon** at the border of Moab.
Deut 2.24 Lord said to us, 'Now, start out and cross the River **Arnon.**
2.36 of the valley of the **Arnon,** and the city in the middle
3. 8 of the River Jordan, from the River **Arnon** to Mount Hermon.
3.12 of Aroer near the River **Arnon** and part of the hill-country
3.16 Gad I assigned the territory from Gilead to the River **Arnon.**
4.48 the edge of the River **Arnon,** all the way north to Mount
Josh 12. 1 of the Jordan, from the **Arnon** Valley up the Jordan Valley
12. 2 of the valley of the **Arnon)** and the city in the middle
13. 9 (on the edge of the **Arnon** Valley) and the city in the
13.16 (on the edge of the **Arnon** Valley) and the city in the
Judg 11.13 my land from the River **Arnon** to the River Jabbok and the
11.18 east side of Moab, on the other side of the River **Arnon.**
11.18 they did not cross the **Arnon** because it was the boundary of
11.22 the Amorite territory from the **Arnon** in the south to the
11.26 them, and all the cities on the banks of the River **Arnon.**
2 Kgs 10.33 Aroer on the River **Arnon**—this included the territories of Gilead
Is 16. 2 the banks of the River **Arnon** and move aimlessly to and fro,
Jer 48.20 Announce along the River **Arnon** that Moab is destroyed!'

AROER (1)

City e. of the R. Jordan, sometimes occupied by Israel and sometimes by Moab.

Deut 2.36 capture all the towns from **Aroer,** on the edge of the valley
3.12 north of the town of **Aroer** near the River Arnon and part
4.48 extended from the town of **Aroer,** on the edge of the River
Josh 12. 2 from **Aroer** (on the edge of the valley of the Arnon) and
13. 9 Their territory extended to **Aroer** (on the edge of the Arnon
13.16 Their territory extended to **Aroer** (on the edge of the Arnon
Judg 11.26 Israel has occupied Heshbon and **Aroer,** and the towns round them,
11.33 He struck at them from **Aroer** to the area round Minnith,
2 Kgs 10.33 south as the town of **Aroer** on the River Arnon—this included
1 Chr 5. 8 This clan lived in **Aroer** and in the territory from there
11.26 from **Aroer** Jediael and Joha, sons of Shimri,
Jer 48.19 You that live in **Aroer,** stand by the road and wait;

AROUSE

Gen 34.25 went into the city without **arousing** suspicion, and killed all
1 Kgs 14. 9 have rejected me and have **aroused** my anger by making idols
14.15 because they have **aroused** his anger by making idols
14.22 Lord and did more to **arouse** his anger against them than all
15.30 This happened because Jeroboam **aroused** the anger of the Lord,
16. 2 Their sins have **aroused** my anger, [3] and so I will do away
16. 7 He **aroused** the Lord's anger not only because of the evil he
16.13 and his son Elah had **aroused** the anger of the Lord, the
16.26 Like Jeroboam before him, he **aroused** the anger of the Lord,
16.33 He did more to **arouse** the anger of the Lord, the God
22.53 his father before him, he **aroused** the anger of the Lord, the
2 Kgs 17.11 They **aroused** the Lord's anger with all their wicked deeds
17.17 what is wrong in the Lord's sight, and so **aroused** his anger.
22.17 My anger is **aroused** against Jerusalem, and it will not die down.
23.19 by the kings of Israel, who thereby **aroused** the Lord's anger.
23.26 Lord's fierce anger had been **aroused** against Judah
2 Chr 34.25 My anger is **aroused** against Jerusalem, and it will not die down.
Job 41.10 When he is **aroused,** he is fierce;
Ps 2.12 anger will be quickly **aroused,** and you will suddenly die.
Ezek 30. 9 send messengers in ships to **arouse** the unsuspecting people
1 Tim 1. 5 of this order is to **arouse** the love that comes from a
2 Pet 3. 1 letters I have tried to **arouse** pure thoughts in your minds

ARRANGE

Gen 22. 9 about, Abraham built an altar and **arranged** the wood on it.
Lev 1. 7 and the priests shall **arrange** fire-wood on the altar and light
6.12 shall put firewood on it, **arrange** the burnt-offering on it,
27.33 The owner may not **arrange** the animals so that the poor
Josh 8.13 The soldiers were **arranged** for battle with the main camp north
Judg 18. 4 He answered, "I have an **arrangement** with Micah, who pays me
20.38 Israelite army and the men in hiding had **arranged** a signal.
2 Sam 14.32 on, "I want you to **arrange** for me to see the king,
2 Kgs 9.30 put on eyeshadow, **arranged** her hair, and stood looking down
1 Chr 22. 4 He **arranged** for the people of Tyre and Sidon to bring him
2 Chr 4.11 The four hundred bronze pomegranates **arranged** in two rows
18. 1 became rich and famous, he **arranged** a marriage between a member
35. 5 his son King Solomon, [5] and **arrange** yourselves so that some
35.10 When everything was **arranged** for the Passover, the priests
Neh 6. 7 and that you have **arranged** for some prophets to proclaim
13.31 I **arranged** for the wood used for burning the offerings
Ezek 43.11 its shape, the **arrangement** of everything, and all its rules
43.11 can see how everything is **arranged** and can carry out all the
Amos 3. 3 Do two men start travelling together without **arranging** to meet?
Heb 8. 6 as the covenant which he **arranged** between God and his people
9. 6 This is how those things have been **arranged.**
9. 8 clearly teaches from all these **arrangements** that the way
9.15 Christ is the one who **arranges** a new covenant, so that those
12.24 have come to Jesus, who **arranged** the new covenant, and to

ARREST

Gen 39.20 was furious [20] and had Joseph **arrested** and put in the prison
1 Sam 19.20 in Naioth in Ramah, [20] so he sent some men to **arrest** him.
1 Kgs 22.26 ordered one of his officers, "**Arrest** Micaiah and take him
2 Kgs 17. 4 Shalmaneser learnt of this, he had Hoshea **arrested**
2 Chr 18.25 ordered one of his officers, "**Arrest** Micaiah and take him
Job 11.10 If God **arrests** you and brings you to trial, who is there
Is 53. 8 He was **arrested** and sentenced and led off to die, and no
Jer 36.26 Shelemiah son of Abdeel, to **arrest** me and my secretary Baruch.
37.14 Instead, he **arrested** me and took me to the officials.
Dan 6.16 orders for Daniel to be **arrested** and he was thrown into the
6.24 the king gave orders to **arrest** all the men who had accused
Mt 10.17 will be men who will **arrest** you and take you to court,
14. 3 Herod had earlier ordered John's **arrest,** and he had him
21.46 he was talking about them, [46] so they tried to **arrest** him.
24. 9 "Then you will be **arrested** and handed over to be punished
26. 4 and made plans to **arrest** Jesus secretly and put him to
26.48 **Arrest** him!"
26.50 Then they came up, **arrested** Jesus, and held him tight.
26.55 and taught in the Temple, and you did not **arrest** me.
26.57 who had **arrested** Jesus took him to the house of Caiaphas,
Mk 6.17 had ordered John's **arrest,** and he had him chained
12.12 The Jewish leaders tried to **arrest** Jesus, because they knew
13. 9 You will be **arrested** and taken to court.
13.11 And when you are **arrested** and taken to court, do not
14. 1 looking for a way to **arrest** Jesus secretly and put him
14.44 **Arrest** him and take him away under guard."
14.46 So they **arrested** Jesus and held him tight.
14.49 with you teaching in the Temple, and you did not **arrest** me.
14.51 They tried to **arrest** him, [52] but he ran away naked,
Lk 20.19 the chief priests tried to **arrest** Jesus on the spot,
21.12 things take place, however, you will be **arrested** and persecuted;
22.53 the Temple every day, and you did not try to **arrest** me.
22.54 They **arrested** Jesus and took him away into the house of
Jn 7.32 they and the chief priests sent some guards to **arrest** him.
8.20 And no one **arrested** him, because his hour had not come.
11.57 Jesus was, he must report it, so that they could **arrest** him.
18.12 officer and the Jewish guards **arrested** Jesus, bound him,
Acts 1.16 about Judas, who was the guide for those who **arrested** Jesus.
4. 3 So they **arrested** them and put them in jail until the next
5.18 They **arrested** the apostles and put them in the public jail.
9. 2 he would be able to **arrest** them, both men and women,
9.14 authority from the chief priests to **arrest** all who worship you."
9.21 for the very purpose of **arresting** those people and taking them
12. 3 saw that this pleased the Jews, he went on to **arrest** Peter.
12. 4 After his **arrest** Peter was put in jail, where he was
21.33 commander went over to Paul, **arrested** him, and ordered him
22. 4 I **arrested** men and women and threw them into prison.
22. 5 so I went there to **arrest** these people and bring them back
22.19 went to the synagogues and **arrested** and beat those who believe
24. 6 He also tried to defile the Temple, and we **arrested** him.
2 Cor 11.32 King Aretas placed guards at the city gates to **arrest** me.

ARRIVE

Gen 12. 5 When they **arrived** in Canaan, [6] Abram travelled through the land
24.11 When he **arrived,** he made the camels kneel down at the
24.15 Rebecca **arrived** with a water-jar on her shoulder.
29. 9 While Jacob was still talking to them, Rachel **arrived**
33.18 from Mesopotamia Jacob **arrived** safely at the city of Shechem
37.14 Joseph **arrived** at Shechem [15] and was wandering about
43.25 present to Joseph when he **arrived** at noon, because they had
46.28 When they **arrived,** [29] Joseph got in his chariot
47. 5 your brothers have **arrived,** [6] the land of Egypt is theirs.
Num 10.21 By the time they **arrived** at the next camp, the Tent had
20.22 of Israel left Kadesh and **arrived** at Mount Hor, [23] on the
Deut 9. 7 until the day you **arrived** here, you have rebelled against him.
11. 5 the Lord did for you in the desert before you **arrived** here.
Josh 9.17 out and three days later **arrived** at the cities where these
22.10 Reuben, Gad, and East Manasseh **arrived** at Geliloth,
Judg 3.27 When he **arrived** there in the hill-country of Ephraim,
7.13 When Gideon **arrived,** he heard a man telling a friend
8. 5 When they **arrived** at Sukkoth, he said to the men of the
18. 2 When they **arrived** in the hill-country of Ephraim, they stayed
19.29 When he **arrived,** he went into the house and got a knife.
Ruth 1.19 When they **arrived,** the whole town got excited, and the women
1.22 The barley harvest was just beginning when they **arrived**
2. 4 Some time later Boaz himself **arrived** from Bethlehem
3.16 When she **arrived** home, her mother-in-law asked her,
1 Sam 4. 5 When the Covenant Box **arrived,** the Israelites
4. 6 the Lord's Covenant Box had **arrived** in the Hebrew camp,

1 Sam	4.12	from the battlefield to Shiloh and **arrived** there the same day.
	5. 9	But after it **arrived** there, the Lord punished that city
	5.10	but when it **arrived** there, the people cried out,
	9.12	He **arrived** in town today because the people are going to
	9.27	When they **arrived** at the edge of the town, Samuel said
	10.10	When Saul and his servant **arrived** at Gibeah, a group
	11. 4	The messengers **arrived** at Gibeah, where Saul lived,
	13.10	and just as he was finishing, Samuel **arrived.**
	16. 6	When they **arrived,** Samuel saw Jesse's son Eliab
	17.20	He **arrived** at the camp just as the Israelites were going out
	23.27	Just then a messenger **arrived** and said to Saul, "Come back
	25.25	I wasn't there when your servants **arrived,** sir.
	30. 1	Two days later David and his men **arrived** back at Ziklag.
	30. 3	When David and his men **arrived,** they found that the town
	30. 9	started out, and when they **arrived** at the brook of Besor,
2 Sam	1. 2	The next day a young man **arrived** from Saul's camp.
	2.29	and after marching all the next morning, they **arrived** back
	2.32	Then they marched all night and at dawn **arrived** back at Hebron.
	3.23	When Joab and his men **arrived,** he was told that Abner
	3.27	When Abner **arrived** in Hebron, Joab took him aside at the gate,
	4. 5	out for Ishbosheth's house and **arrived** there about noon,
	5.18	The Philistines **arrived** at the Valley of Rephaim
	9. 6	Jonathan and grandson of Saul, **arrived,** he bowed down
	10. 2	When they **arrived** in Ammon, [3] the Ammonite leaders
	11. 7	When Uriah **arrived,** David asked him if Joab and the troops
	12. 4	One day a visitor **arrived** at the rich man's home.
	14. 2	When she **arrived,** he said to her, "Pretend that you are in
	15.37	David's friend, returned to the city just as Absalom was **arriving.**
	16. 5	When King David **arrived** at Bahurim, one of Saul's relatives,
	17. 6	When Hushai **arrived,** Absalom said to him, "This is the advice
	17.27	When David **arrived** at Mahanaim, he was met by Shobi son
	18.31	Then the Sudanese slave **arrived** and said to the king,
	19.17	twenty servants, and they **arrived** at the Jordan before the king.
	19.25	When Mephibosheth **arrived** from Jerusalem to meet the king,
	20. 3	When David **arrived** at his palace in Jerusalem, he took
1 Kgs	1.22	She was still speaking, when Nathan **arrived** at the palace.
	1.42	Jonathan, the son of the priest Abiathar, **arrived.**
	12.21	When Rehoboam **arrived** in Jerusalem, he called together 180,000
	13. 1	Judah went to Bethel and **arrived** there as Jeroboam stood at
	14. 5	When Jeroboam's wife **arrived,** she pretended to be someone else.
	20.33	When Benhadad **arrived,** Ahab invited him to get in the chariot
2 Kgs	4.32	When Elisha **arrived,** he went alone into the room and
	5.22	in the hill-country of Ephraim **arrived,** and he would like
	6. 4	When they **arrived** at the Jordan, they began to work.
	6.32	Before the king's messenger **arrived,** Elisha said to the elders,
	6.33	saying this, when the king **arrived** and said, "It's the Lord
	9.30	Jehu **arrived** in Jezreel.
	10.17	When they **arrived** there, Jehu killed all of Ahab's relatives,
	18.17	When they **arrived** at Jerusalem, they occupied the road
1 Chr	14. 9	The Philistines **arrived** at the Valley of Rephaim
	19. 2	When they **arrived** in Ammon and called on King Hanun,
2 Chr	11. 1	When King Rehoboam **arrived** in Jerusalem, he called together
	31. 7	The gifts started **arriving** in the third month and continued
Ezra	2.68	When the exiles **arrived** at the Lord's Temple in Jerusalem,
	7. 8	and with God's help they **arrived** in Jerusalem on the first
Neh	1. 2	Hanani, one of my brothers, **arrived** from Judah with a
Esth	6.14	the palace eunuchs **arrived** in a hurry to take Haman
Is	30. 4	Although their ambassadors have already **arrived** at the Egyptian
Jer	41. 5	eighty men **arrived** from Shechem, Shiloh, and Samaria.
	46.21	The day of their doom had **arrived,** the time of their destruction.
Ezek	33.22	When the man **arrived** the next morning, the Lord gave me back
Dan	7.22	The time had **arrived** for God's people to receive royal power.
Mt	3.13	At that time Jesus **arrived** from Galilee and came to John
	12.46	still talking to the people when his mother and brothers **arrived.**
	25.10	and while they were gone, the bridegroom **arrived.**
	25.11	"Later the other girls **arrived.**
	26.47	still speaking when Judas, one of the twelve disciples, **arrived.**
	27.57	When it was evening, a rich man from Arimathea **arrived;**
Mk	1.30	and as soon as Jesus **arrived,** he was told about her.
	2. 3	when four men **arrived,** carrying a paralysed man to Jesus.
	3.31	Then Jesus' mother and brothers **arrived.**
	5. 1	Jesus and his disciples **arrived** on the other side of Lake
	5.22	official of the local synagogue, **arrived,** and when he saw Jesus,
	5.38	They **arrived** at Jairus' house, where Jesus saw the confusion
	6.33	ran ahead by land and **arrived** at the place ahead of Jesus
	11.15	When they **arrived** in Jerusalem, Jesus went to the Temple
	11.27	They **arrived** once again in Jerusalem.
	14.43	still speaking when Judas, one of the twelve disciples, **arrived.**
	14.45	As soon as Judas **arrived,** he went up to Jesus and said,
	15.42	It was towards evening when Joseph of Arimathea **arrived.**
Lk	2.38	That very same hour she **arrived** and gave thanks to God
	7.12	Just as he **arrived** at the gate of the town, a funeral
	8.41	Then a man named Jairus **arrived;**
	8.51	When he **arrived** at the house, he would not let anyone go
	22.40	When he **arrived** at the place, he said to them, "Pray
	22.47	still speaking when a crowd **arrived,** led by Judas, one of
Jn	4.45	When he **arrived** in Galilee, the people there welcomed him.
	11.17	When Jesus **arrived,** he found that Lazarus had been buried
	11.30	(Jesus had not yet **arrived** in the village, but was still
	11.32	Mary **arrived** where Jesus was, and as soon as she saw him,
Acts	4. 1	officer in charge of the temple guards, and some Sadducees **arrived.**
	5.22	when the officials **arrived,** they did not find the apostles
	5.23	and reported, [23] "When we **arrived** at the jail, we found it
	8.15	When they **arrived,** they prayed for the believers that they
	9.39	When he **arrived,** he was taken to the room upstairs, where
	10.24	The following day he **arrived** in Caesarea, where Cornelius was
	11.11	sent to me from Caesarea **arrived** at the house where I was
	11.23	When he **arrived** and saw how God had blessed the people,
	13. 5	When they **arrived** at Salamis, they preached the word of God
	13.14	went on from Perga and **arrived** in Antioch in Pisidia,
Acts	14.27	they **arrived** in Antioch, they gathered the people of the church
	15. 4	When they **arrived** in Jerusalem, they were welcomed by the church,
	17.10	When they **arrived,** they went to the synagogue.
	18. 5	Silas and Timothy **arrived** from Macedonia, Paul gave his whole
	18.19	They **arrived** in Ephesus, where Paul left Priscilla and Aquila.
	18.22	When he **arrived** at Caesarea, he went to Jerusalem and greeted
	18.27	When he **arrived,** he was a great help to those who through
	19. 1	through the interior of the province and **arrived** in Ephesus.
	20.15	We sailed from there and **arrived** off Chios the next day.
	20.16	was in a hurry to **arrive** in Jerusalem by the day of
	20.18	When they **arrived,** he said to them, "You know how I
	20.18	from the first day I **arrived** in the province of Asia.
	21. 8	On the following day we left and **arrived** in Caesarea.
	21.10	for several days when a prophet named Agabus **arrived** from Judaea.
	21.17	When we **arrived** in Jerusalem, the believers welcomed us warmly.
	21.22	They are sure to hear that you have **arrived.**
	23.35	he said, "I will hear you when your accusers **arrive."**
	24.22	Lysias the commander **arrives,"** he told them, "I will decide
	25. 1	Three days after Festus **arrived** in the province, he went
	25. 7	Paul **arrived,** the Jews who had come from Jerusalem stood round
	27. 3	The next day we **arrived** at Sidon.
	27. 7	with great difficulty finally **arrived** off the town of Cnidus.
	28.12	We **arrived** in the city of Syracuse and stayed there for
	28.13	From there we sailed on and **arrived** in the city of Rhegium.
	28.16	When we **arrived** in Rome, Paul was allowed to live by
2 Cor	2.12	When I **arrived** in Troas to preach the Good News about Christ,
	6. 2	when the day **arrived** for me to save you I helped you."
	7. 5	Even after we **arrived** in Macedonia, we had no rest.
	9. 5	will be ready when I **arrive,** and it will show that you
	13.10	is so that when I **arrive** I will not have to deal
Gal	2.12	had been sent by James **arrived** there, Peter had been eating
	2.12	But after these men **arrived,** he drew back and would not eat
2 Tim	1.17	but as soon as he **arrived** in Rome, he started looking
3 Jn	3	when some Christian brothers **arrived** and told me how faithful you

ARROGANT

Ex	9.17	Yet you are still **arrogant** and refuse to let my people go.
1 Sam	15.23	bad as witchcraft, and **arrogance** is as sinful as idolatry.
2 Chr	26.16	Uzziah became strong, he grew **arrogant,** and that led
Ps	31.18	all the proud and **arrogant** who speak with
	73. 9	God in heaven and give **arrogant** orders to men on earth,
	75. 4	I tell the wicked not to be **arrogant;**
	101. 5	I will not tolerate a man who is proud and **arrogant.**
	119.122	don't let **arrogant** men oppress me!
	131. 1	I have given up my pride and turned away from my **arrogance.**
Prov	8.13	I hate pride and **arrogance,** evil ways and false words.
	13. 1	but an **arrogant** person never admits he is wrong.
	13.10	**Arrogance** causes nothing but trouble.
	15.25	will destroy the homes of **arrogant** men, but he will protect
	16. 5	The Lord hates everyone who is **arrogant;**
	16.18	Pride leads to destruction, and **arrogance** to downfall.
	16.19	to be one of the **arrogant** and get a share of their
	18.12	**arrogant** people are on the way to ruin.
	19.25	**Arrogance** should be punished, so that people who don't know
	21. 4	people are controlled by their conceit and **arrogance,**
	21.24	and I will show you someone who is **arrogant,** proud,
	29.23	**Arrogance** will bring your downfall, but if you are humble,
	30.32	foolish enough to be **arrogant** and plan evil, stop and think!
Is	2.11	when human pride will be ended and human **arrogance** destroyed.
	2.17	Human pride will be ended, and human **arrogance**
	9. 9	Now they are proud and **arrogant.**
	13.11	everyone who is proud and punish everyone who is **arrogant**
	16. 6	We know that they are **arrogant** and conceited, but their boasts
	28.14	Now you **arrogant** men who rule here in Jerusalem over this people,
	33.19	will no longer see any **arrogant** foreigners who speak a language
Jer	43. 2	Kareah and all the other **arrogant** men said to me, "You are
	48.29	I have heard how proud, **arrogant,** and conceited the people are,
	48.30	I, the Lord, know of their **arrogance.**
Dan	8. 4	He did as he pleased and grew **arrogant.**
	8. 8	goat grew more and more **arrogant,** but at the height of his
	11.18	leader will defeat him and put an end to his **arrogance;**
	11.18	he will turn the **arrogance** of Syria's king back on him.
Hos	5. 5	The **arrogance** of the people of Israel cries out against them.
	7.10	The **arrogance** of the people of Israel cries out against them.
	7.16	Because their leaders talk **arrogantly,** they will die
Zeph	2.10	punished for their pride and **arrogance** and for insulting
	3.11	everyone who is proud and **arrogant,** and you will never again
Tit	1. 7	He must not be **arrogant** or quick-tempered, or a drunkard
2 Pet	2.10	false teachers are bold and **arrogant,** and show no respect for

ARROW

Gen	27. 3	Take your bow and **arrows,** go out into the country, and
	49.23	attack him fiercely And pursue him with their bows and **arrows.**
Ex	19.13	either be stoned or shot with **arrows,** without anyone touching
Num	24. 8	They devour their enemies, Crush their bones, smash their **arrows.**
Deut	32.23	bring on them endless disasters and use all my **arrows** against
	32.42	My **arrows** will drip with their blood, and my sword will
1 Sam	20.20	I will then shoot three **arrows** at it, as though it were
	20.21	I tell him, 'Look, the **arrows** are on this side of you;
	20.22	if I tell him, 'The **arrows** are on the other side of
	20.36	said to him, "Run and find the **arrows** I'm going to shoot."
	20.36	The boy ran, and Jonathan shot an **arrow** beyond him.
	20.37	reached the place where the **arrow** had fallen,
	20.37	Jonathan shouted to him, "The **arrow** is further on!

1 Sam 20.38 The boy picked up the **arrow** and returned to his master,
31. 3 Saul, and he himself was hit by enemy **arrows** and badly wounded.
2 Sam 11.20 Didn't you realize that they would shoot **arrows** from the walls?
11.24 Then they shot **arrows** at us from the wall, and some of
22.15 He shot his **arrows** and scattered his enemies;
1 Kgs 22.34 a Syrian soldier shot an **arrow** which struck King Ahab
2 Kgs 9.24 all his strength shot an **arrow** that struck Joram in the back
13.15 "Get a bow and some **arrows**," Elisha ordered him.
13.17 "Shoot the **arrow**!"
13.17 as the king shot the **arrow**, the prophet exclaimed,
13.17 "You are the Lord's **arrow**, with which he will win victory
13.18 to take the other **arrows** and strike the ground with them.
19.32 will not enter this city or shoot a single **arrow** against it.
1 Chr 10. 3 Saul, and he was hit by enemy **arrows** and badly wounded.
12. 2 They could shoot **arrows** and sling stones either right-handed
2 Chr 18.33 a Syrian soldier shot an **arrow** which struck King Ahab
26.14 spears, helmets, coats of armour, bows and **arrows**, and stones
26.15 inventors made equipment for shooting **arrows** and for throwing
35.23 During the battle King Josiah was struck by Egyptian **arrows**.
Job 6. 4 God has pierced me with **arrows**, and their poison spreads
16.13 for target-practice [13] and shoots **arrows** at me from every side—
16.13 **arrows** that pierce and wound me;
20.25 An **arrow** sticks through his body;
41.26 no spear or **arrow** or lance that can harm him.
41.28 There is no **arrow** that can make him run;
Ps 7.13 he takes up his deadly weapons and aims his burning **arrows**.
11. 2 their bows and aimed their **arrows** to shoot from the shadows
18.14 He shot his **arrows** and scattered his enemies;
21.12 He will shoot his **arrows** at them and make them turn and
38. 2 You have wounded me with your **arrows**;
45. 5 Your **arrows** are sharp, they pierce the hearts of your enemies;
57. 4 Their teeth are like spears and **arrows**;
64. 3 sharpen their tongues like swords and aim cruel words like **arrows**.
64. 7 God shoots his **arrows** at them, and suddenly they are wounded.
76. 3 There he broke the **arrows** of the enemy, their shields and swords,
78. 9 Ephraimites, armed with bows and **arrows**, ran away on the day
78.57 disloyal like their fathers, unreliable as a crooked **arrow**.
120. 4 With a soldier's sharp **arrows**, with red-hot charcoal!
127. 4 has when he is young are like **arrows** in a soldier's hand.
127. 5 Happy is the man who has many such **arrows**.
144. 6 shoot your **arrows** and send them running.
Prov 7.23 prancing into a trap [23] where an **arrow** would pierce its heart.
25.18 is as deadly as a sword, a club, or a sharp **arrow**.
Is 5.28 Their **arrows** are sharp, and their bows are ready to shoot.
7.24 People will go hunting there with bows and **arrows**.
13.18 With their bows and **arrows** they will kill the young men.
22. 3 ran away and were captured before they shot a single **arrow**.
22. 6 Elam came riding on horseback, armed with bows and **arrows**.
37.33 will not enter this city or shoot a single **arrow** against it.
41. 2 His **arrows** scatter them like straw before the wind.
49. 2 He made me like an **arrow**, sharp and ready for use.
Jer 9. 8 Their tongues are like deadly **arrows**;
50. 9 They are skilful hunters, shooting **arrows** that never miss
50.14 Shoot all your **arrows** at Babylon, because it has sinned
50.29 Send out everyone who knows how to use the bow and **arrow**.
51. 3 time to shoot their **arrows** or to put on their armour.
51.11 The attacking officers command, "Sharpen your **arrows**!
Lam 2. 4 He aimed his **arrows** at us like an enemy;
3.12 He drew his bow and made me the target for his **arrows**.
3.13 He shot his **arrows** deep into my body.
Ezek 5.16 the pains of hunger like sharp **arrows** sent to destroy you.
21.21 To discover which way to go, he shakes the **arrows**;
21.22 His right hand holds the **arrow** marked 'Jerusalem'!
39. 3 of his left hand and his **arrows** out of his right hand.
39. 9 fires with the shields, bows, **arrows**, spears, and clubs,
Hos 1. 7 swords or bows and **arrows** or with horses and horsemen."
Hab 3. 9 You got ready to use your bow, ready to shoot your **arrows**.
3.11 the flash of your speeding **arrows** and the gleam of your
3.14 Your **arrows** pierced the commander of his army when it came
Zech 9.13 use Judah like a soldier's bow and Israel like the **arrows**.
9.14 he will shoot his **arrows** like lightning.
Eph 6.16 to put out all the burning **arrows** shot by the Evil One.

ARSENAL

Is 22. 8 When that happened, you brought weapons out of the **arsenal**.

ART

Ex 31. 3 for every kind of **artistic** work—[4] for planning skilful designs
31. 5 and for every other kind of **artistic** work.
35.31 understanding for every kind of **artistic** work,
35.33 and for every other kind of **artistic** work.
Prov 25. 4 out of silver and the **artist** can produce a thing of beauty.
Song 7. 1 The curve of your thighs is like the work of an **artist**.
Jer 10. 9 Spain and with gold from Uphaz, all the work of **artists**;
Acts 17.29 or silver or stone, shaped by the **art** and skill of man.

ARTAXERXES (1)

Emperor of Persia.

Ezra 7. 1 Many years later, when **Artaxerxes** was emperor of Persia,
7. 6 year of the reign of **Artaxerxes**, Ezra set out from Babylonia
7.11 **Artaxerxes** gave the following document to Ezra, the priest
7.12 "From **Artaxerxes** the emperor to Ezra the priest,
8. 1 who returned with Ezra to Jerusalem when **Artaxerxes** was emperor:
Neh 1. 1 in the twentieth year that **Artaxerxes** was emperor of Persia,
2. 1 when Emperor **Artaxerxes** was dining, I took the wine
Neh 5.14 from the twentieth year that **Artaxerxes** was emperor
13. 6 in the thirty-second year that **Artaxerxes** was king of Babylon

ARTAXERXES (2)

Emperor of Persia, perhaps the same as (1).

Ezra 4. 7 Again, in the reign of **Artaxerxes**, emperor of Persia,
4. 8 secretary of the province, wrote the following letter to **Artaxerxes**
4.11 Emperor **Artaxerxes** from his servants, the men of West Euphrates.
4.23 soon as this letter from **Artaxerxes** was read to Rehum, Shimshai,

ARTAXERXES (3)

Emperor of Persia, perhaps the same as (1).

Ezra 6.14 and by Cyrus, Darius, and **Artaxerxes**, emperors of Persia.

ARTICLE

Gen 31.37 what household **article** have you found that belongs to
38.20 back from the woman the **articles** he had pledged, but Hirah
Lev 6.27 If any **article** of clothing is spattered with the animal's blood,
11.32 This applies to any **article** of wood, cloth, leather, or sacking,
1 Kgs 7.51 David had dedicated to the Lord—the silver, gold, and other **articles**.
10.25 brought him a gift—**articles** of silver and gold, robes, weapons,
2 Kgs 12.13 the lamps, or any other **article** of silver or of gold.
25.14 and all the other bronze **articles** used in the temple service.
2 Chr 5. 1 David had dedicated to the Lord—the silver, gold, and other **articles**.
9.24 brought Solomon gifts—**articles** of silver and gold, robes,
Ezra 1.11 and silver bowls and other **articles** which Sheshbazzar took
Jer 52.18 and all the other bronze **articles** used in the temple service.
Ezek 27.13 and traded your goods for slaves and for **articles** of bronze.
Dan 11. 8 of their gods and the **articles** of gold and silver dedicated

ASA (1)

King of Judah.

1 Kgs 15.9-24 **King Asa of Judah**
1 Chr 3.10-16 **The descendants of King Solomon**
2 Chr 14.1-15 **King Asa defeats the Sudanese**
15.1-19 **Asa's reforms**
16.1-6 **Troubles with Israel**
7-10 **The prophet Hanani**
11-14 **The end of Asa's reign**

1 Kgs 15. 8 in David's City, and his son **Asa** succeeded him as king.
15.25 of the reign of King **Asa** of Judah, King Jeroboam's son Nadab
15.28 during the third year of the reign of King **Asa** of Judah.
15.32 King **Asa** of Judah and King Baasha of Israel were
15.33 of the reign of King **Asa** of Judah, Baasha son of Ahijah
16. 8 of the reign of King **Asa** of Judah, Elah son of Baasha
16.10 the twenty-seventh year of the reign of King **Asa** of Judah.
16.15 of the reign of King **Asa** of Judah, Zimri ruled in Tirzah
16.23 of the reign of King **Asa** of Judah, Omri became king of
16.29 of the reign of King **Asa** of Judah, Ahab son of Omri
22.41 of Israel, Jehoshaphat son of **Asa** became king of Judah
22.43 Like his father **Asa** before him, he did what was right in
22.46 altars who were still left from the days of his father **Asa**.
2 Chr 17. 1 Jehoshaphat succeeded his father **Asa** as king and
17. 2 and in the cities which **Asa** had captured in the territory of
20.32 Like his father **Asa** before him, he did what was right in
21.12 King Jehoshaphat, or that of your grandfather, King **Asa**.
Jer 41. 9 the large one that King **Asa** had dug when he was being
Mt 1. 6 Rehoboam, Abijah, **Asa**, Jehoshaphat, Jehoram, Uzziah, Jotham,

ASAHEL (1)

One of David's famous soldiers.

2 Sam 2.18 Joab, Abishai, and **Asahel**.
2.18 **Asahel**, who could run as fast as a wild deer, [19] started
2.20 Abner looked back and said, "Is that you, **Asahel**?"
2.21 But **Asahel** kept on chasing him.
2.23 But **Asahel** would not give up;
2.23 **Asahel** dropped to the ground dead, and everyone who came to
2.30 that nineteen of them were missing, in addition to **Asahel**.
2.32 Joab and his men took **Asahel's** body and buried it in the
3.27 And so Abner was murdered because he had killed Joab's brother **Asahel**.
3.30 Abner for killing their brother **Asahel** in the battle at Gibeon.
23.24 **Asahel**, Joab's brother Elhanan son of Dodo from Bethlehem
1 Chr 2.16 Abishai, Joab, and **Asahel**.
11.26 **Asahel**, Joab's brother Elhanan son of Dodo from Bethlehem
27. 2 **Asahel**, brother of Joab (his son Zebadiah succeeded him)

ASAPH (1)

Levite singer in David's time.

1 Chr 6.39 **Asaph** was leader of the second choir.
6.39 **Asaph**, Berechiah, Shimea, [40] Michael, Baaseiah, Malchijah,
9.14 ancestors included Zichri and **Asaph** Obadiah son of Shemaiah,
15.17 son of Joel, his relative **Asaph** son of Berechiah, and Ethan
16. 5 **Asaph** was appointed leader, with Zechariah as his assistant.
16. 5 **Asaph** was to sound the cymbals, [6] and two priests, Benaiah and Jahaziel,
16. 7 then that David first gave **Asaph** and his fellow-Levites the
16.37 King David put **Asaph** and his fellow-Levites in permanent
25. 1 **Asaph**, Heman, and Jeduthun.
25. 2 The four sons of **Asaph**:
25. 2 were under the direction of **Asaph**, who proclaimed God's

1 Chr 25. 6 And **Asaph,** Jeduthun, and Heman were under orders from the king.
25. 9 Joseph of the family of **Asaph** 2.
2 Chr 5.11 And all the Levite musicians—**Asaph,** Heman, and Jeduthun, and
20.14 member of the clan of **Asaph** and was descended from Asaph
29.12 Jeuel From the clan of **Asaph,** Zechariah and Mattaniah From
29.30 praise that were written by David and by **Asaph** the prophet.
35.15 of the Levite clan of **Asaph** were in the places assigned to
35.15 **Asaph,** Heman, and Jeduthun, the king's prophet.
Ezra 2.40 Temple musicians (descendants of **Asaph**) - 128
3.10 the Levites of the clan of **Asaph** stood there with cymbals.
Neh 7.43 (descendants of **Asaph**) - 148
11.17 son of Mica and grandson of Zabdi, a descendant of **Asaph.**
11.22 belonged to the clan of **Asaph,** the clan that was responsible
12.33 Mattaniah, Micaiah, and Zaccur, of the clan of **Asaph.)**
12.46 King David and the musician **Asaph** long ago, the musicians

ASH

Ex 9. 8 Moses and Aaron, "Take a few handfuls of **ashes** from a furnace;
9.10 So they got some **ashes** and stood before the king;
27. 3 Make pans for the greasy **ashes,** and make shovels, bowls,
Lev 1.16 on the east side of the altar where the **ashes** are put.
4.12 ritually clean place where the **ashes** are poured out, and
6.10 shorts, shall remove the greasy **ashes** left on the altar and
6.11 his clothes and take the **ashes** outside the camp to a
Num 4.13 They shall remove the greasy **ashes** from the altar and
19. 9 clean is to collect the **ashes** of the cow and put them
19.10 The man who collected the **ashes** must wash his clothes,
19.17 To remove the uncleanness, some **ashes** from the red cow
2 Sam 13.19 She sprinkled **ashes** on her head, tore her robe, and with
1 Kgs 13. 3 will fall apart, and the **ashes** on it will be scattered.
13. 5 suddenly fell apart and the **ashes** spilt to the ground, as
2 Kgs 23. 4 of the Kidron, and then had the **ashes** taken to Bethel.
23. 6 Kidron, burnt it, pounded its **ashes** to dust, and scattered
25.14 shovels and the **ash** containers used in cleaning the altar,
Esth 4. 1 covered his head with **ashes,** and walked through the city,
4. 3 wailed, and most of them put on sackcloth and lay in **ashes.**
Job 13.12 Your proverbs are as useless as **ashes;**
42. 6 ashamed of all I have said and repent in dust and **ashes.**
Ps 102. 9 of your anger and fury, **ashes** are my food, and my tears
Is 33.12 like rocks burnt to make lime, like thorns burnt to **ashes.**
44.20 It makes as much sense as eating **ashes.**
58. 5 of grass, and spread out sackcloth and **ashes** to lie on.
Jer 6.26 Lord says to his people, "Put on sackcloth and roll in **ashes.**
51.25 of you, level you to the ground, and leave you in **ashes.**
52.18 shovels and the **ash** containers used in cleaning the altar,
52.19 from the sacrifices, the **ash** containers, the lampstands,
Ezek 27.30 for you, Throwing dust on their heads and rolling in **ashes.**
28.18 All who look at you now see you reduced to **ashes.**
Dan 9. 3 Lord God, pleading with him, fasting, wearing sackcloth, and sitting in **ashes.**
Amos 2. 1 the bones of the king of Edom by burning them to **ashes.**
Jon 3. 6 took off his robe, put on sackcloth, and sat down in **ashes.**
Mt 11.21 put on sackcloth and sprinkled **ashes** on themselves, to show that
Lk 10.13 put on sackcloth, and sprinkled **ashes** on themselves, to show that
Heb 9.13 goats and bulls and the **ashes** of a burnt calf are sprinkled

ASHAMED

2 Sam 10. 5 They were too **ashamed** to return home.
19. 3 quietly, like soldiers who are **ashamed** because they are
1 Chr 19. 5 They were too **ashamed** to return home.
2 Chr 30.15 not ritually clean were so **ashamed** that they dedicated
Ezra 8.22 I would have been **ashamed** to ask the emperor for a troop
9. 6 "O God, I am too **ashamed** to raise my head in your
Job 9.31 a pit of filth, and even my clothes are **ashamed** of me.
42. 6 So I am **ashamed** of all I have said and repent in
Ps 86.17 who hate me will be **ashamed** when they see that you have
119.46 announce your commands to kings and I will not be **ashamed.**
119.78 May the proud be **ashamed** for falsely accusing me;
Prov 29.15 has his own way, he will make his mother **ashamed** of him.
29.17 He will never give you reason to be **ashamed.**
Is 45.16 Those who make idols will all be **ashamed;**
Jer 3. 9 She too became a prostitute [9]and was not at all **ashamed.**
6.15 Were they **ashamed** because they did these disgusting things?
6.15 No, they were not at all **ashamed;**
8.12 were you **ashamed** because you did these disgusting things?
8.12 No, you were not **ashamed** at all;
31.19 We were **ashamed** and disgraced, because we sinned when we were young.'
51.51 You say, 'We've been disgraced and made **ashamed;**
Ezek 16.54 You will be **ashamed** of yourself, and your disgrace will
16.61 you have acted, and be **ashamed** of it when you get your
16.63 will remember them and be too **ashamed** to open your mouth."
43.10 Make them **ashamed** of their sinful actions.
43.11 Then if they are **ashamed** of what they have done, explain
Hos 4.19 wind, and they will be **ashamed** of their pagan sacrifices.
Mic 1.11 You people of Shaphir, go into exile, naked and **ashamed.**
Zeph 3. 5 people there keep on doing wrong and are not **ashamed.**
3.11 no longer need to be **ashamed** that you rebelled against me.
Mk 8.38 If a person is **ashamed** of me and of my teaching
8.38 Son of Man will be **ashamed** of him when he comes
Lk 9.26 If a person is **ashamed** of me and of my teaching,
9.26 Son of Man will be **ashamed** of him when he comes in
11. 8 you need because you are not **ashamed** to keep on asking.
13.17 His answer made his enemies **ashamed** of themselves,
16. 3 not strong enough to dig ditches, and I am **ashamed** to beg.
Rom 6.21 you gain from doing the things that you are now **ashamed** of?
1 Cor 4.14 want to make you feel **ashamed,** but to instruct you as my
2 Cor 9. 4 you are not ready, how **ashamed** we would be—not to speak
2 Cor 10. 8 For I am not **ashamed,** even if I have boasted somewhat too
11.21 I am **ashamed** to admit that we were too timid to do
Phil 3.19 of what they should be **ashamed** of, and they think only
2 Thes 3.14 have nothing to do with him, so that he will be **ashamed.**
2 Tim 1. 8 Do not be **ashamed,** then, of witnessing for our Lord;
1. 8 nor be **ashamed** of me, a prisoner for Christ's sake.
1.16 He was not **ashamed** that I am in prison,
2.15 a worker who is not **ashamed** of his work, one who correctly
Heb 2.11 That is why Jesus is not **ashamed** to call them his brothers.
11.16 And so God is not **ashamed** for them to call him their
1 Pet 3.16 as followers of Christ will be **ashamed** of what they say.
4.16 are a Christian, don't be **ashamed** of it, but thank God
Rev 16.15 he will not walk around naked and be **ashamed** in public!"

ASHDOD

One of the five chief cities of the Philistines.
see also AZOTUS

Josh 11.22 a few, however, were left in Gaza, Gath, and **Ashdod.**
13. 3 kings of the Philistines lived at Gaza, **Ashdod,** Ashkelon,
15.46 and towns near **Ashdod,** from Ekron to the Mediterranean Sea.
15.47 There were **Ashdod** and Gaza, with their towns and villages,
1 Sam 5. 1 Ebenezer to their city of **Ashdod,** [2]took it into the temple
5. 3 next morning the people of **Ashdod** saw that the statue of
5. 5 and all his worshippers in **Ashdod** step over that place and
5. 6 The Lord punished the people of **Ashdod** severely and terrified them.
6.17 one each for the cities of **Ashdod,** Gaza, Ashkelon, Gath, and
2 Chr 26. 6 cities of Gath, Jamnia, and **Ashdod,**
26. 6 fortified cities near **Ashdod** and in the rest of Philistia.
Neh 4. 7 people of Arabia, Ammon, and **Ashdod** heard that we were
13.23 of the Jewish men had married women from **Ashdod,** Ammon, and
13.24 children spoke the language of **Ashdod** or some other language
Is 20. 1 of the Assyrian army attacked the Philistine city of **Ashdod.**
20. 3 When **Ashdod** was captured, the Lord said, "My servant
Jer 25.19 Philistine cities of Ashkelon, Gaza, Ekron, and what remains of **Ashdod;**
Amos 1. 8 I will remove the rulers of the cities of **Ashdod** and Ashkelon.
3. 9 Announce to those who live in the palaces of Egypt and **Ashdod:**
Zeph 2. 4 The people of **Ashdod** will be driven out in half a day,
Zech 9. 6 People of mixed race will live in **Ashdod.**

ASHER (1)

Jacob's son by Zilpah, his tribe and its territory.

Gen 30.13 so she named him **Asher.**
35.26 The sons of Leah's slave Zilpah were Gad and **Asher.**
46.17 **Asher** and his sons:
49.20 **"Asher's** land will produce rich food.
Ex 1. 4 Reuben, Simeon, Levi, Judah, [3]Issachar, Zebulun, Benjamin, [4]Dan, Naphtali, Gad, and **Asher.**
Num 10.26 command of the tribe of **Asher,** [27]and Ahira son of Enan was
26.44 The tribe of **Asher:**
26.46 **Asher** had a daughter named Serah.
34.19 **Asher** Ahihud son of Shelomi
Deut 27.13 Reuben, Gad, **Asher,** Zebulun, Dan, and Naphtali.
33.24 About the tribe of **Asher** he said:
33.24 **"Asher** is blessed more than the other tribes.
Josh 17.10 **Asher** was to the north-west, and Issachar to the north-east.
17.11 Issachar and **Asher,** Manasseh possessed Beth Shan and Ibleam,
19.24 assignment made was for the families of the tribe of **Asher.**
19.31 of the tribe of **Asher** received as their possession.
19.34 touching Zebulun on the south, **Asher** on the west, and the
21. 6 of Issachar, **Asher,** Naphtali, and East Manasseh.
21.30 From the territory of **Asher** they received four cities:
Judg 1.31 The tribe of **Asher** did not drive out the people living
1.32 The people of **Asher** lived with the local Canaanites,
5.17 The tribe of **Asher** stayed by the sea-coast;
6.35 messengers to the tribes of **Asher,** Zebulun, and Naphtali,
7.23 from the tribes of Naphtali, **Asher,** and both parts of
2 Sam 2. 9 of the territories of Gilead, **Asher,** Jezreel, Ephraim, and
1 Kgs 4.16 the region of **Asher** and the town of Bealoth [17]Jehoshaphat
1 Chr 2. 2 Simeon, Levi, Judah, Issachar, Zebulun, [2]Dan, Joseph, Benjamin, Naphtali, Gad, and **Asher.**
6.62 of Issachar, **Asher,** Naphtali, and East Manasseh in Bashan.
6.74 In the territory of **Asher:**
7.30 These are the descendants of **Asher.**
7.40 All these were descendants of **Asher.**
7.40 **Asher's** descendants included 26,000 men eligible for military service.
2 Chr 30.11 some from the tribes of **Asher,** Manasseh, and Zebulun who
Ezek 48. 1 Dan **Asher** Naphtali Manasseh Ephraim Reuben Judah
48.30 those in the west wall are named after Gad, **Asher,** and
Lk 2.36 a widow named Anna, daughter of Phanuel of the tribe of **Asher.**
Rev 7. 5 Judah, Reuben, Gad, **Asher,** Naphtali, Manasseh, Simeon, Levi,
also Num 1.5 Num 1.20 Num 2.25 Num 7.12 Num 13.3 1 Chr 12.23

ASHERAH

Goddess of fertility worshipped by the Canaanites.

Ex 34.13 and cut down the symbols of their goddess **Asherah.**
Deut 7. 5 cut down the symbols of their goddess **Asherah,**
12. 3 their symbols of the goddess **Asherah** and chop down their idols,
16.21 do not put beside it a wooden symbol of the goddess **Asherah.**
Judg 3. 7 sinned against him and worshipped the idols of Baal and **Asherah.**
6.25 down the symbol of the goddess **Asherah,** which is beside it.
6.26 using for firewood the symbol of **Asherah** you have cut down."
6.28 Baal and the symbol of **Asherah** had been cut down,
6.30 to Baal and cut down the symbol of **Asherah** beside it."
1 Kgs 14.15 aroused his anger by making idols of the goddess **Asherah.**

1 Kgs 14.23 stone pillars and symbols of **Asherah** to worship on the hills
15.13 she had made an obscene idol of the fertility goddess **Asherah.**
16.33 He also put up an image of the goddess **Asherah.**
18.19 400 prophets of the goddess **Asherah** who are supported by Queen Jezebel."
2 Kgs 13. 6 and the image of the goddess **Asherah** remained in Samaria.
17.10 and images of the goddess **Asherah,** [11]and they burnt incense
17.16 an image of the goddess **Asherah,** worshipped the stars,
18. 4 pillars, and cut down the images of the goddess **Asherah.**
21. 3 an image of the goddess **Asherah,** as King Ahab of Israel had
21. 7 the symbol of the goddess **Asherah** in the Temple,
23. 4 worship of Baal, of the goddess **Asherah,** and of the stars.
23. 6 the symbol of the goddess **Asherah,** took it out of the city
23. 7 there that women wove robes used in the worship of **Asherah.)**
23.14 the symbols of the goddess **Asherah,** and the ground where they
23.15 he also burnt the image of **Asherah.**
2 Chr 14. 3 stone columns, and cut down the symbols of the goddess **Asherah.**
15.16 she had made an obscene idol of the fertility goddess **Asherah.**
17. 6 of worship and the symbols of the goddess **Asherah** in Judah.
19. 3 the symbols of the goddess **Asherah** which people worshipped,
24.18 to worship idols and the images of the goddess **Asherah.**
31. 1 the symbols of the goddess **Asherah,** and destroyed the altars
33. 3 made images of the goddess **Asherah,** and worshipped the stars.
33.19 the symbols of the goddess **Asherah** that he made and the
34. 3 the symbols of the goddess **Asherah,** and all the other idols.
34. 4 to dust the images of **Asherah** and all the other idols
34. 7 altars and the symbols of **Asherah,** ground the idols to dust,
Is 17. 8 symbols of the goddess **Asherah** and altars for burning incense.
27. 9 no more incense-altars or symbols of the goddess **Asherah** are left.
Jer 17. 2 set up for the goddess **Asherah** by every green tree,
Mic 5.14 images of the goddess **Asherah** in your land and destroy your

ASHKELON

One of the five chief cities of the Philistines.

Josh 13. 3 kings of the Philistines lived at Gaza, Ashdod, **Ashkelon,**
Judg 1.18 Gaza, **Ashkelon,** or Ekron, with their surrounding territories.
14.19 and he went down to **Ashkelon,** where he killed thirty men,
1 Sam 6.17 one each for the cities of Ashdod, Gaza, **Ashkelon,** Gath, and
2 Sam 1.20 Do not announce it in Gath or in the streets of **Ashkelon.**
Jer 25.19 of the Philistine cities of **Ashkelon,** Gaza, Ekron, and what
47. 5 to the people of Gaza, and **Ashkelon's** people are silent.
47. 7 have commanded it to attack **Ashkelon** and the people who live
Amos 1. 8 I will remove the rulers of the cities of Ashdod and **Ashkelon.**
Zeph 2. 4 **Ashkelon** will be deserted.
2. 7 their flocks there and sleep in the houses of **Ashkelon.**
Zech 9. 5 The city of **Ashkelon** will see this and be afraid.
9. 5 Gaza will lose her king, and **Ashkelon** will be left deserted.

ASHORE

Ezek 27.29 "Every ship is now deserted, And every sailor has gone **ashore.**
32. 3 catch you in my net and let them drag the net **ashore.**
Lk 8.27 As Jesus stepped **ashore,** he was met by a man from the
Jn 21. 9 they stepped **ashore,** they saw a charcoal fire there with fish
21.11 aboard and dragged the net **ashore** full of big fish, a
Acts 21. 3 We went **ashore** at Tyre, where the ship was going to unload
27.26 But we will be driven **ashore** on some island."
27.42 in order to keep them from swimming **ashore** and escaping.
27.43 men who could swim to jump overboard first and swim **ashore;**
27.44 And this was how we all got safely **ashore.**
28. 1 When we were safely **ashore,** we learnt that the island was

ASIA

Roman province, a part of what is now Asia Minor or modern Turkey.

Acts 2. 9 from Pontus and **Asia,** [10]from Phrygia and Pamphylia, from Egypt
6. 9 the provinces of Cilicia and **Asia** started arguing with Stephen.
16. 6 did not let them preach the message in the province of **Asia.**
19.10 lived in the province of **Asia,** both Jews and Gentiles, heard
19.22 Macedonia, while he spent more time in the province of **Asia.**
19.26 here in Ephesus and in nearly the whole province of **Asia.**
19.27 goddess worshipped by everyone in **Asia** and in all the world!"
20. 4 Tychicus and Trophimus, from the province of **Asia;**
20.16 so as not to lose any time in the province of **Asia.**
20.18 from the first day I arrived in the province of **Asia.**
21.27 some Jews from the province of **Asia** saw Paul in the Temple.
24.19 But some Jews from the province of **Asia** were there;
27. 2 the seaports of the province of **Asia,** and we sailed away.
Rom 16. 5 the first man in the province of **Asia** to believe in Christ.
1 Cor 16.19 The churches in the province of **Asia** send you their greetings;
2 Cor 1. 8 brothers, of the trouble we had in the province of **Asia.**
2 Tim 1.15 everyone in the province of **Asia,** including Phygelus and
1 Pet 1. 1 throughout the provinces of Pontus, Galatia, Cappadocia, **Asia,**
Rev 1. 4 From John to the seven churches in the province of **Asia:**

ASK

Gen 24. 9 his master, and made a vow to do what Abraham had **asked.**
25.22 So she went to **ask the Lord for** an answer.
34.12 will give you whatever you **ask,** if you will only let me
39.10 Although she **asked** Joseph day after day, he would not go
45.28 "This is all I could **ask for!**
Ex 3.22 in her house and will **ask for** clothing and for gold and
5. 8 that is why they keep **asking** me to let them go and
8.10 "I will do as you **ask,** and then you will know that
8.13 The Lord did as Moses **asked,** and the frogs in the houses,
8.31 and prayed to the Lord, [31]and the Lord did as Moses **asked.**
11. 2 to **ask their neighbours for** gold and silver jewellery."
Ex 12.31 go and worship the Lord, as you **asked.**
12.35 had said, and had **asked the Egyptians for** gold and silver
12.36 Egyptians respect the people and give them what they **asked for.**
13.14 the future, when your son **asks** what this observance means,
33.17 do just as you have **asked,** because I know you very well
Num 11.13 They keep whining and **asking for** meat.
14.20 The Lord answered, "I will forgive them, as you have **asked.**
14.28 I live, I will do to you just what you have **asked.**
Josh 15.18 wedding day Othniel urged her to **ask her father for** a field.
19.50 the Lord had commanded, they gave him the city he **asked for:**
Judg 1.14 wedding day Othniel urged her to **ask her father for** a field.
4.20 and if anyone comes and **asks** you if someone is here, say
5.25 Sisera **asked for** water, but she gave him milk;
8.24 he went on to say, "Let me **ask** one thing of you.
11.17 They also **asked** the king of Moab, but neither would he let
11.19 king of Heshbon, and **asked him for** permission to go through
13. 9 God did what Manoah **asked,** and his angel came back to the
16.16 She kept on **asking** him, day after day.
Ruth 3.11 I will do everything you **ask;**
1 Sam 1.17 the God of Israel give you what you have **asked him for."**
1.20 She named him Samuel, and explained, "I **asked the Lord for** him."
1.27 I **asked him for** this child,
1.27 and he gave me what I **asked for.**
2.36 to that priest and **ask him for** money and food, and beg
8.10 the people who were **asking him for** a king everything that
12. 1 people of Israel, "I have done what you **asked** me to do.
12.13 you **asked for** him, and now the Lord has given him to
12.17 great sin against the Lord when you **asked him for** a king."
12.19 all our other sins, we have sinned by **asking for** a king."
17.30 question, and every time he **asked,** he got the same answer.
25. 8 Just **ask** them, and they will tell you.
28. 6 he was terrified, [6]and so he **asked** the Lord what to do.
28.21 "Please, sir, I risked my life by doing what you **asked.**
28.22 Now please do what I **ask.**
2 Sam 1. 8 He **asked** who I was, and I told him that I was
12.20 returned to the palace, he **asked for** food and ate it as
14.15 to you in the hope that you would do what I **ask.**
16.10 him to, who has the right to **ask** why he does it?"
19.28 I have no right to **ask for** any more favours from Your
19.38 And I will do for you anything you **ask."**
1 Kgs 2.14 and then he added, "I have something to **ask** of you."
2.23 if I don't make Adonijah pay with his life for **asking** this!
3.10 was pleased that Solomon had **asked for** this, [11]and so he
3.11 him, "Because you have **asked for** the wisdom to rule justly,
3.12 death of your enemies, [12]I will do what you have **asked.**
3.13 I will also give you what you have not **asked for:**
5. 8 received your message and I am ready to do what you **ask.**
8.14 Solomon turned to face them, and he **asked** God's blessing on them.
8.43 him and do what he **asks** you to do, so that all
8.55 In a loud voice he **asked** God's blessings on all the
10.13 queen of Sheba everything she **asked for,** besides all the
20.18 whether they are coming to fight or to **ask for** peace."
2 Kgs 4. 6 had filled all the jars, she **asked** if there were any more.
4.28 woman said to him, "Sir, did I **ask you for** a son?
4.41 Elisha **asked for** some meal, threw it into the pot, and
8. 3 went to the king to **ask for** her house and her land
17. 4 to So, king of Egypt, **asking for** his help, and stopped
2 Chr 1.11 Instead of **asking for** wealth or treasure or fame or the
1.11 life for yourself, you have **asked for** wisdom and knowledge
6. 3 The king turned to face them and **asked** God's blessing on them.
6.33 him and do what he **asks** you to do, so that all
9.12 King Solomon gave the queen of Sheba everything she **asked for.**
20. 4 hurried to Jerusalem to **ask the Lord for** guidance, [5]and
30.27 The priests and the Levites **asked** the Lord's blessing on the people.
Ezra 5. 4 They also **asked for** the names of all the men who were
7. 6 Lord his God, the emperor gave him everything he **asked for.**
7.21 of Heaven, everything he **asks you for,** [22]up to a limit of
8.22 have been ashamed to **ask the emperor for** a troop of cavalry
Neh 2. 6 He **asked** me how long I would be gone and when I
2. 8 I **asked also for** a letter to Asaph, keeper of the royal
2. 8 emperor gave me all I **asked for,** because God was with me.
Esth 1.13 was the king's custom to **ask for** expert opinion on questions
2.14 again unless he liked her enough to **ask for** her by name.
5. 6 grant your request, even if you **ask for** half my empire."
Job 6. 8 Why won't God give me what I **ask?**
11.19 many people will **ask you for** help.
12. 8 **ask** the creatures of earth and sea for their wisdom.
13.20 Let me **ask for** two things;
21. 1 that is all the comfort I **ask** from you.
Ps 2. 8 **Ask,** and I will give you all the nations;
21. 4 He **asked for** life, and you gave it, a long and lasting
27. 4 I have **asked the Lord for** one thing;
27. 4 marvel there at his goodness, and to **ask for** his guidance.
39. 3 I could not keep from **asking:**
40. 6 you do not **ask for** animals burnt whole on the altar or
50.12 hungry, I would not **ask you for** food, for the world and
105.40 They **asked,** and he sent quails;
106.15 he gave them what they **asked for,** but also sent a terrible
Prov 13.10 It is wiser to **ask for** advice.
15.12 they never **ask for** advice from those who are wiser.
16. 3 **Ask** the Lord to bless your plans, and you will be
27.10 If you are in trouble, don't **ask your brother for** help;
Is 1.12 Who **asked** you to bring me all this when you come to
1.12 Who **asked** you to do all this tramping about in my Temple?
7.11 **"Ask** the Lord your God to give you a sign.
7.12 Ahaz answered, "I will not **ask for** a sign.
8.19 you to **ask for** messages from fortune-tellers and mediums,
8.19 say, "After all, people should **ask for** messages from the
19. 3 go and consult mediums and **ask** the spirits of the dead for

Is	21.12	If you want to **ask** again, come back and ask."
	30. 2	They go to Egypt for help without **asking for** my advice.
	31. 1	the Lord, the holy God of Israel, or **ask him for** help.
	43.23	demanding offerings or wear you out by **asking for** incense.
	65.16	Anyone in the land who **asks for** a blessing will ask to
Jer	6.16	**Ask for** the ancient paths and where the best road is.
	10.21	they do not **ask the Lord for** guidance.
	15. 5	Who will stop long enough to **ask** how you are?
	18.13	**"Ask** every nation if such a thing has ever happened before.
	23.37	Jeremiah, **ask** the prophets, 'What answer did the Lord give you?
	37.20	I beg you to listen to me and do what I **ask.**
	42. 2	every class [2]and said to me, "Please do what we **ask** you!
	42. 4	God, just as you have **asked,** and whatever he says, I will
	48.19	**ask** those who are running away, find out from them what
Ezek	13.12	and everyone will **ask** you what good the whitewash did."
	17. 9	"So I, the Sovereign Lord, **ask:**
	17.12	The Lord said to me, [12]**"Ask** these rebels if they know
	18.19	"But you **ask:**
	20. 3	You have come to **ask** my will, have you?
	20. 3	am the living God, I will not let you **ask** me anything.
	20.31	am the living God, I will not let you **ask** me anything.
	36.37	again let the Israelites **ask me for** help, and I will let
Dan	2.11	What Your Majesty is **asking for** is so difficult that no
Hos	4.12	They **ask for** revelations from a piece of wood!
	5.13	to Assyria to **ask the great emperor for** help, but he could
	9.14	What shall I **ask** you to do to these people?
	12. 4	He wept and **asked for** a blessing.
	13.10	You **asked for** a king and for leaders, but how can they
Joel	2.32	But all who **ask the Lord for** help will be saved.
Mic	7. 3	Officials and judges **ask for** bribes.
Zeph	3. 2	not put its trust in the Lord or **asked for** his help.
Hag	2.11	He said, **"Ask the priests for** a ruling on this question:
Zech	5. 2	The angel **asked** me what I saw.
	10. 1	**Ask the Lord for** rain in the spring of the year.
Mal	1. 9	Now, you priests, try **asking** God to be good to us.
Mt	2. 2	the east to Jerusalem [2]and **asked,** "Where is the baby born
	2. 4	teachers of the Law and **asked** them, "Where will the Messiah
	5.42	When someone **asks you for** something, give it to him;
	6. 8	Your Father already knows what you need before you **ask** him.
	7. 7	**"Ask,** and you will receive;
	7. 8	everyone who **asks** will receive, and anyone who seeks will find,
	7. 9	are fathers give your son a stone when he **asks for** bread?
	7.10	would you give him a snake when he **asks for** a fish?
	7.11	Father in heaven give good things to those who **ask** him!
	9.11	Pharisees saw this and **asked** his disciples, "Why does your
	9.14	the Baptist came to Jesus, **asking,** "Why is it that we and
	9.28	came to him, and he **asked** them, "Do you believe that I
	11. 3	"Tell us," they **asked** Jesus, "are you the one John said
	12.10	of doing wrong, so they **asked** him, "Is it against our Law
	12.39	"You **ask me for** a miracle?
	12.46	They stood outside, **asking** to speak with him.
	13.10	disciples came to Jesus and **asked** him, "Why do you use
	14. 7	"I swear that I will give you anything you **ask for!"**
	14. 8	her mother's suggestion she **asked** him, "Give me here and now
	15. 1	from Jerusalem to Jesus and **asked** him, [2]"Why is it that
	15.33	The disciples **asked** him, "Where will we find enough food
	16. 1	to trap him, so they **asked** him to perform a miracle for
	16. 4	You **ask me for** a miracle?
	16. 8	they were saying, so he **asked** them, "Why are you discussing
	16.13	Caesarea Philippi, where he **asked** his disciples, "Who do people
	17.10	the disciples **asked** Jesus, "Why do the teachers of the Law
	17.19	to Jesus in private and **asked** him, "Why couldn't we drive
	17.24	came to Peter and **asked,** "Does your teacher pay the temple-tax?"
	18. 1	the disciples came to Jesus, **asking,** "Who is the greatest in
	18.21	Peter came to Jesus and **asked,** "Lord, if my brother keeps
	18.32	the whole amount you owed me, just because you **asked** me to.
	19. 3	tried to trap him by **asking,** "Does our Law allow a man
	19. 7	Pharisees **asked** him, "Why, then, did Moses give the law for
	19.16	"Teacher," he **asked,** "what good thing must I do to receive
	19.17	"Why do you **ask** me concerning what is good?"
	20.20	her two sons, bowed before him, and **asked** him a favour.
	20.22	don't know what you are **asking for,"** Jesus answered the sons.
	21.16	So they **asked** Jesus, "Do you hear what they are saying?"
	21.22	you believe, you will receive whatever you **ask for** in prayer."
	21.23	elders came to him and **asked,** "What right have you to do
	21.24	Jesus answered them, "I will **ask** you just one question,
	22.20	him the coin, [20]and he **asked** them, "Whose face and name
	22.36	"Teacher," he **asked,** "which is the greatest commandment in
	22.41	gathered together, Jesus **asked** them, [42]"What do you think
	22.43	"Why, then," Jesus **asked,** "did the Spirit inspire David
	22.46	that day on no one dared to **ask** him any more questions.
	24. 3	all this will be," they **asked,** "and what will happen to
	26.15	to the chief priests [15]and **asked,** "What will you give me
	26.17	disciples came to Jesus and **asked** him, "Where do you want
	26.22	very upset and began to **ask** him, one after the other,
	27.15	habit of setting free any one prisoner the crowd **asked for.**
	27.17	the crowd gathered, Pilate **asked** them, "Which one do you want
	27.20	elders persuaded the crowd to **ask** Pilate to set Barabbas free
	27.21	But Pilate **asked** the crowd, "Which one of these two do
	27.22	Pilate **asked** them.
	27.23	But Pilate **asked,** "What crime has he committed?"
	27.58	into the presence of Pilate and **asked for** the body of Jesus.
Mk	2.16	tax collectors, so they **asked** his disciples, "Why does he eat
	2.18	people came to Jesus and **asked** him, "Why is it that the
	3. 4	Then he **asked** the people, "What does our Law allow us to
	3.31	outside the house and sent in a message, **asking for** him.
	4.10	with the twelve disciples and **asked** him to explain the parables.
	4.13	Then Jesus **asked** them, "Don't you understand this parable?
	5. 9	So Jesus **asked** him, "What is your name?"
	5.17	So they **asked** Jesus to leave their territory.
Mk	5.30	turned round in the crowd and **asked,** "Who touched my clothes?"
	5.31	why do you **ask** who touched you?"
	6.23	will give you anything you **ask for,** even as much as half
	6.24	went out and asked her mother, "What shall I **ask for?"**
	6.37	They **asked,** "Do you want us to go and spend two hundred
	6.38	So Jesus **asked** them, "How much bread have you got?
	7. 5	the teachers of the Law **asked** Jesus, "Why is it that your
	7.17	into the house, his disciples **asked** him to explain this saying.
	8. 4	His disciples **asked** him, "Where in this desert can anyone find
	8.11	to trap him, so they **asked** him to perform a miracle to
	8.12	said, "Why do the people of this day **ask for** a miracle?
	8.17	they were saying, so he **asked** them, "Why are you discussing
	8.20	the four thousand people," **asked** Jesus, "how many baskets full
	8.23	his hands on him and **asked** him, "Can you see anything?"
	8.27	On the way he **asked** them, "Tell me, who do people say
	9.11	And they **asked** Jesus, "Why do the teachers of the Law
	9.16	**asked** his disciples, "What are you arguing with them about?"
	9.18	I **asked** your disciples to drive the spirit out, but they
	9.21	Jesus **asked** the father.
	9.28	his disciples **asked** him privately, "Why couldn't we drive
	9.32	what this teaching meant, and they were afraid to **ask** him.
	9.33	going indoors Jesus **asked** his disciples, "What were you arguing
	10. 2	"Tell us," they **asked,** "does our Law allow a man to
	10.10	into the house, the disciples **asked** Jesus about this matter.
	10.17	knelt before him, and **asked** him, "Good Teacher, what must I
	10.26	completely amazed and **asked** one another, "Who, then, can be
	10.38	Jesus said to them, "You don't know what you are **asking for.**
	11. 3	And if someone **asks** you why you are doing that, tell him
	11. 5	some of the bystanders **asked** them, "What are you doing,
	11.24	When you pray and **ask for** something, believe that you have
	11.24	received it, and you will be given whatever you **ask for.**
	11.28	elders came to him [28]and **asked** him, "What right have you
	11.29	Jesus answered them, "I will **ask** you just one question,
	12.16	him one, and he **asked,** "Whose face and name are these?"
	12.34	After this nobody dared to **ask** Jesus any more questions.
	12.35	in the Temple, he **asked** the question, "How can the teachers
	14.12	were killed, Jesus' disciples **asked** him, "Where do you want us
	14.19	were upset and began to **ask** him, one after the other,
	15. 6	habit of setting free any one prisoner the people **asked for.**
	15. 8	crowd gathered and began to **ask** Pilate for the usual favour,
	15. 9	he **asked** them, "Do you want me to
	15.11	stirred up the crowd to **ask,** instead, for Pilate to set
	15.42	the presence of Pilate and **asked him for** the body of Jesus.
	15.44	called the army officer and **asked** him if Jesus had been dead
Lk	1.62	made signs to his father, **asking** him what name he would like
	1.63	Zechariah **asked for** a writing tablet and wrote, "His name
	1.66	thought about it and **asked,** "What is this child going to
	2.46	with the Jewish teachers, listening to them and **asking** questions.
	3.10	The people **asked** him, "What are we to do, then?"
	3.12	to be baptized, and they **asked** him, "Teacher, what are we
	3.14	Some soldiers also **asked** him, "What about us?
	5. 3	it belonged to Simon—and **asked** him to push off a little
	6. 2	Pharisees **asked,** "Why are you doing what our Law says you
	6. 9	Then Jesus said to them, "I **ask** you:
	6.30	Give to everyone who **asks you for** something,
	6.30	when someone takes what is yours, do not **ask for** it back.
	7. 3	sent some Jewish elders to **ask** him to come and heal his
	7.19	them to the Lord to **ask** him, "Are you the one John
	7.20	the Baptist sent us to **ask** if you are the one he
	8. 9	His disciples **asked** Jesus what this parable meant,
	8.30	Jesus **asked** him, "What is your name?"
	8.37	the people from that territory **asked** Jesus to go away,
	8.45	Jesus **asked,** "Who touched me?"
	9.45	it, and they were afraid to **ask** him about the matter.
	10.25	"Teacher," he **asked,** "what must I do to receive eternal life?"
	10.29	to justify himself, so he **asked** Jesus, "Who is my neighbour?"
	11. 8	you need because you are not ashamed to keep on **asking.**
	11. 9	**Ask,** and you will receive;
	11.10	everyone who **asks** will receive, and he who seeks will find,
	11.11	are fathers give your son a snake when he **asks for** fish?
	11.12	would you give him a scorpion when he **asks for** an egg?
	11.13	Father in heaven give the Holy Spirit to those who **ask** him!"
	11.16	to trap Jesus, so they **asked** him to perform a miracle to
	11.29	They **ask for** a miracle, but none will be given them except
	11.53	to criticize him bitterly and **ask** him questions about many things,
	12.37	will take off his coat, **ask** them to sit down, and will
	13.18	Jesus **asked,** "What is the Kingdom of God like?
	13.20	Jesus **asked,** "What shall I compare the Kingdom of God with?
	13.23	Someone **asked** him, "Sir, will just a few people be saved?"
	14. 3	came to Jesus, [3]and Jesus **asked** the teachers of the Law and
	14.32	meet the other king, to **ask for** terms of peace while he
	15.26	called one of the servants and **asked** him, 'What's going on?'
	16. 5	He **asked** the first one, 'How much do you owe my master?'
	16. 7	Then he **asked** another one, 'And you—how much do you owe?'
	17.20	Some Pharisees **asked** Jesus when the Kingdom of God would come.
	17.37	The disciples **asked** him, "Where, Lord?"
	18.18	Jewish leader **asked** Jesus, "Good Teacher, what must I do to
	18.26	The people who heard him **asked,** "Who, then, can be saved?"
	18.36	When he heard the crowd passing by, he **asked,** "What is this?"
	18.40	When he came near, Jesus **asked** him, [41]"What do you want
	19.31	If someone **asks** you why you are untying it, tell him
	20. 3	Jesus answered them, "Now let me **ask** you a question.
	20.17	Jesus looked at them and **asked,** "What, then, does this
	20.40	For they did not dare **ask** him any more questions.
	20.41	Jesus **asked** them, "How can it be said that the Messiah
	21. 7	"Teacher," they **asked,** "when will this be?
	22.23	Then they began to **ask** among themselves which one of
	22.35	Jesus **asked** his disciples, "When I sent you out that time
	22.49	going to happen, they **asked,** "Shall we use our swords, Lord?"
	22.64	They blindfolded him and **asked** him, "Who hit you?

Lk 22.68 and if I **ask** you a question, you will not answer.
23. 3 Pilate **asked** him, "Are you the king of the Jews?"
23. 6 When Pilate heard this, he **asked,** "Is this man a Galilean?"
23. 9 So Herod **asked** Jesus many questions, but Jesus made no answer.
23.24 Pilate passed the sentence on Jesus that they were **asking for.**
23.52 into the presence of Pilate and **asked for** the body of Jesus.
24.18 of them, named Cleopas, **asked** him, "Are you the only visitor
24.41 so he **asked** them, "Have you anything here to eat?"
Jn 1.19 priests and Levites to John, to **ask** him, "Who are you?"
1.25 sent by the Pharisees, [25] then **asked** John, "If you are not
1.38 saw them following him, and **asked,** "What are you looking for?"
1.48 Nathanael **asked** him, "How do you know me?"
4. 9 am a Samaritan—so how can you **ask me for** a drink?"
4.10 who it is that is **asking you for** a drink,
4.10 you would **ask** him, and he would give you
4.27 or **asked** him, "Why are you talking with her?"
4.33 disciples started **asking** among themselves, "Could somebody have
4.47 he went to him and **asked** him to go to Capernaum and
4.52 He **asked** them what time it was when his son got better,
5. 6 so he **asked** him, "Do you want to get well?"
5.12 They **asked** him, "Who is the man who told you to do
6. 5 coming to him, so he **asked** Philip, "Where can we buy enough
6.28 So they **asked** him, "What can we do in order to do
6.34 "Sir," they **asked** him, "give us this bread always."
6.67 he **asked** the twelve disciples, "And you—would you also like
7.45 chief priests and Pharisees **asked** them, "Why did you not bring
8. 7 they stood there **asking** him questions, he straightened himself
8.48 They **asked** Jesus, "Were we not right in saying that you
9. 2 His disciples **asked** him, "Teacher, whose sin caused him to
9. 8 seen him begging before this, **asked,** "Isn't this the man who
9.15 The Pharisees, then, **asked** the man again how he had received
9.17 So the Pharisees **asked** the man once more, "You say he
9.19 they called his parents [19] and **asked** them, "Is this your son?
9.21 **Ask** him;
9.23 **ask** him!"
9.35 he found the man and **asked** him, "Do you believe in the
9.40 heard him say this and **asked** him, "Surely you don't mean
10.24 people gathered round him and **asked,** "How long are you
11.22 that even now God will give you whatever you **ask him for."**
11.28 "The Teacher is here," she told her, "and is **asking for** you."
11.56 in the Temple, they **asked** one another, "What do you think?
13.24 to him and said, **"Ask** him whom he is talking about."
13.25 moved closer to Jesus' side and **asked,** "Who is it, Lord?"
14.13 I will do whatever you **ask for** in my name, so that
14.14 If you **ask me for** anything in my name, I will do
14.16 I will **ask** the Father, and he will give you another Helper,
15. 7 in you, then you will **ask for** anything you wish, and you
15.16 Father will give you whatever you **ask** of him in my name.
16. 5 sent me, yet none of you **asks** me where I am going.
16.17 of his disciples **asked** among themselves, "What does this mean?
16.19 Is this what you are **asking** about among yourselves?
16.23 "When that day comes, you will not **ask me for** anything.
16.23 Father will give you whatever you **ask him for** in my name.
16.24 Until now you have not **asked for** anything in my name;
16.24 **ask** and you will receive, so that your happiness may be complete.
16.26 When that day comes, you will **ask** him in my name;
16.26 not say that I will **ask** him on your behalf,
16.30 you do not need someone to **ask** you questions.
17.15 I do not **ask** you to take them out of the world,
17.15 but I do **ask** you to keep them safe from
18. 4 so he stepped forward and **asked** them, "Who is it you are
18. 7 Again Jesus **asked** them, "Who is it you are looking for?"
18.21 **Ask** them what I told them—they know what I said."
18.29 went outside to them and **asked,** "What do you accuse this
18.37 So Pilate **asked** him, "Are you a king, then?"
19. 9 into the palace and **asked** Jesus, "Where do you come from?"
19.15 Pilate **asked** them, "Do you want me to crucify your king?"
19.31 the Jewish authorities **asked** Pilate to allow them to break the
19.38 the town of Arimathea, **asked** Pilate if he could take Jesus'
21. 5 Then he **asked** them, "Young men, haven't you caught anything?"
21.12 None of the disciples dared **ask** him, "Who are you?"
21.17 Peter was sad because Jesus **asked** him the third time, "Do
21.20 at the meal and had **asked,** "Lord, who is going to betray
21.21 Peter saw him, he **asked** Jesus, "Lord, what about this man?"
Acts 1. 6 together with Jesus, they **asked** him, "Lord, will you at this
2.12 confused, they kept **asking** each other, "What does this mean?"
3.14 rejected him, and instead you **asked** Pilate to do you the
4. 7 stand before them and **asked** them, "How did you do this?
5. 8 Peter **asked** her, "Tell me, was this the full amount you
7. 1 The High Priest **asked** Stephen, "Is this true?"
7.46 He won God's favour and **asked** God to allow him to
8.30 He **asked** him, "Do you understand what you are reading?"
8.34 official **asked** Philip, "Tell me, of whom is the prophet saying
9. 2 to the High Priest [2] and **asked for** letters of introduction to
9.11 at the house of Judas **ask for** a man from Tarsus named
9.21 heard him were amazed and **asked,** "Isn't he the one who in
10.18 They called out and **asked,** "Is there a guest here by
10.29 I **ask** you, then, why did you send for me?"
10.48 Then they **asked** him to stay with them for a few days.
12.20 they went to Herod and **asked him for** peace, because their
13.21 And when they **asked for** a king, God gave them Saul
13.28 death sentence on him, they **asked** Pilate to have him put to
16.30 he led them out and **asked,** "Sirs, what must I do to
16.39 them out of the prison and **asked** them to leave the city.
17.18 Some of them **asked,** "What is this ignorant show-off trying to
18.20 people **asked** him to stay longer, but he would not consent.
19. 2 he found some disciples [2] and **asked** them, "Did you receive the
20.17 sent a message to Ephesus, **asking** the elders of the church
21.33 Then he **asked,** "Who is this man, and what has he done?"
22.10 I **asked,** 'What shall I do, Lord?'
Acts 22.26 went to the commander and **asked** him, "What are you doing?
22.27 commander went to Paul and **asked** him, "Tell me, are you a
23.18 prisoner Paul called me and **asked** me to bring this young man
23.19 him off by himself, and **asked** him, "What have you got to
23.20 Jewish authorities have agreed to **ask** you tomorrow to take Paul
23.34 read the letter and **asked** Paul what province he was from.
25. 9 with the Jews, so he **asked** Paul, "Would you be willing to
25.11 I deserve the death penalty, I do not **ask** to escape it.
25.15 elders brought charges against him and **asked** me to condemn him.
25.20 on these matters, so I **asked** Paul if he would be willing
25.21 he **asked** to be kept under guard and to let the Emperor
26. 3 I **ask** you, then, to listen to me with patience.
28.14 found some believers there who **asked** us to stay with them
28.20 That is why I **asked** to see you and talk with you.
Rom 1.10 I **ask** that God in his good will may at last make
3. 5 (This would be the natural question to **ask.)**
9.20 A clay pot does not **ask** the man who made it, "Why
10. 6 "You are not to **ask** yourself, Who will go up into heaven?"
10. 7 "Nor are you to **ask,** Who will go down into the world
10.20 I appeared to those who were not **asking for** me."
12.14 **Ask** God to bless those who persecute you—
12.14 yes, **ask** him to bless, not to curse.
1 Cor 10.25 in the meat-market, without **asking** any questions because of your
10.27 is set before you, without **asking** any questions because of your
10.29 "Well, then," someone **asks,** "why should my freedom to act be
14.35 find out about something, they should **ask** their husbands at home.
15.35 Someone will **ask,** "How can the dead be raised to life?
2 Cor 12. 8 to the Lord about this and **asked** him to take it away.
Gal 2.10 All they **asked** was that we should remember the needy in
4.21 Let me **ask** those of you who want to be subject to
Eph 1.17 you in my prayers [17] and **ask** the God of our Lord Jesus
1.18 I **ask** that your minds may be opened to see his light,
3.16 I **ask** God from the wealth of his glory to give you
3.20 much more than we can ever **ask for,** or even think of:
6.18 Do all this in prayer, **asking for** God's help.
Phil 4. 6 but in all your prayers **ask God for** what you need,
4. 6 always **asking** him with a thankful heart.
Col 1. 9 We **ask** God to fill you with the knowledge of his will,
4.12 prays fervently for you, **asking** God to make you stand firm,
1 Thes 3.10 Day and night we **ask** him with all our heart to let
2 Thes 1.11 We **ask** our God to make you worthy of the life he
1 Tim 5. 5 and continues to pray and **ask him for** his help night and
Phlm 21 you will do what I **ask**—in fact I know that you
Jas 4. 2 have what you want because you do not **ask God for** it.
4. 3 And when you **ask,** you do not receive it, because your
4. 3 you **ask for** things to use for your own pleasures.
1 Pet 3.15 times to answer anyone who **asks** you to explain the hope you
2 Pet 3. 4 will mock you [4] and will **ask,** "He promised to come, didn't
1 Jn 3.22 receive from him whatever we **ask,** because we obey his commands
5.14 he hears us if we **ask him for** anything that is according
5.15 He hears us whenever we **ask** him;
5.15 we know also that he gives us what we **ask** from him.
2 Jn 5 And so I **ask** you, dear Lady:
Rev 7.13 One of the elders **asked** me, "Who are these people
10. 9 went to the angel and **asked** him to give me the little
17. 7 the angel **asked** me.
also Mt 12.23 Mt 13.28 Mt 13.51 Mt 13.54 Mt 15.34 Mt 16.15 Mt 19.18 Mt 19.25 Mt 20.6 Mt 20.21 Mt 20.32 Mt 21.10 Mt 21.20 Mt 21.40 Mt 22.12 Mt 26.8 Mt 26.25 Mt 27.11 Mk 4.30 Mk 6.2 Mk 8.5 Mk 8.21 Mk 8.29 Mk 10.18 Mk 10.36 Mk 10.51 Mk 12.9 Mk 15.14 Lk 5.30 Lk 9.18 Lk 9.20 Lk 18.19 Lk 20.15 Lk 22.9 Lk 24.19 Jn 1.21 Jn 1.21 Jn 1.46 Jn 2.20 Jn 3.4 Jn 3.9 Jn 6.52 Jn 7.11 Jn 7.47 Jn 8.19 Jn 8.25 Jn 9.10 Jn 9.12 Jn 9.26 Jn 11.34 Jn 13.12 Jn 13.36 Jn 13.37 Jn 18.26 Jn 18.33 Jn 18.38 Jn 20.13 Jn 20.15 Acts 4.16 Acts 7.27 Acts 7.35 Acts 9.5 Acts 19.3 Acts 21.37 Acts 22.8 Acts 26.15 Rom 10.18 Rom 10.19 Rom 11.1 Rom 11.11

ASLEEP

Gen 41. 5 He fell **asleep** again and had another dream.
Judg 4.21 Sisera was so tired that he fell sound **asleep.**
Ruth 3. 4 down, and after he falls **asleep,** go and lift the covers and
1 Sam 26.12 up—they were all sound **asleep,** because the Lord had sent a
2 Sam 4. 6 and had fallen **asleep,** so Rechab and Baanah slipped in.
4. 7 Ishbosheth's bedroom, where he was sound **asleep,** and killed him.
4.11 evil men who murder an innocent man **asleep** in his own house!
1 Kgs 3.20 my side while I was **asleep,** and carried him to her bed;
19. 5 He lay down under the tree and fell **asleep.**
Job 33.15 At night when men are **asleep,** God speaks in dreams and visions.
Ps 44.23 Why are you **asleep?**
127. 2 For the Lord provides for those he loves, while they are **asleep.**
Prov 24.34 awhile, [34] but while you are **asleep,** poverty will attack
Song 3. 1 **Asleep** on my bed, night after night I dreamt of the one
Dan 2.28 you the dream, the vision you had while you were **asleep.**
4. 5 dream and saw terrifying visions while I was **asleep.**
4.10 "While I was **asleep,** I had a vision of a huge tree
Jon 1. 5 gone below and was lying in the ship's hold, sound **asleep.**
1. 6 him there and said to him, "What are you doing **asleep?**
Nah 3.18 Assyria, your governors are dead, and your noblemen are **asleep** for ever!
Mt 8.24 But Jesus was **asleep.**
13.25 One night, when everyone was **asleep,** an enemy came and sowed
25. 5 late in coming, so the girls began to nod and fall **asleep.**
26.40 Then he returned to the three disciples and found them **asleep;**
26.43 He returned once more and found the disciples **asleep;**
28.13 during the night and stole his body while you were **asleep.**
Mk 13.36 If he comes suddenly, he must not find you **asleep.**
14.37 Then he returned and found the three disciples **asleep.**
14.37 He said to Peter, "Simon, are you **asleep?**

Mk 14.40 Then he came back to the disciples and found them **asleep;**
Lk 8.23 As they were sailing, Jesus fell **asleep.**
9.32 and his companions were sound **asleep,** but they woke up and
22.45 disciples and found them **asleep,** worn out by their grief.
Jn 11.11 "Our friend Lazarus has fallen **asleep,** but I will go and
11.12 disciples answered, "If he is **asleep,** Lord, he will get well."
Acts 20. 9 he finally went sound **asleep** and fell from the third storey

ASSASSIN

1 Kgs 16.10 Zimri entered the house, **assassinated** Elah, and succeeded him as king.
16.16 plotted against the king and **assassinated** him, then and
2 Kgs 9.31 You **assassin!**
14.19 a plot in Jerusalem to **assassinate** Amaziah, so he fled to
15.10 Jabesh conspired against King Zechariah, **assassinated** him at Ibleam,
15.14 Tirzah to Samaria, **assassinated** Shallum, and succeeded him as king.
15.25 with fifty men from Gilead, **assassinated** Pekahiah in the
15.30 Elah plotted against King Pekah, **assassinated** him, and succeeded him as king.
21.23 Amon's officials plotted against him and **assassinated** him in the palace.
21.24 Judah killed Amon's **assassins** and made his son Josiah king.
2 Chr 33.24 Amon's officials plotted against him and **assassinated** him in the palace.
33.25 Judah killed Amon's **assassins** and made his son Josiah king.
Esth 2.21 hostile to King Xerxes and plotted to **assassinate** him.
6. 2 had uncovered a plot to **assassinate** the king—the plot made
Hos 7. 7 Their kings have been **assassinated** one after another, but no

ASSAULT

Job 30.12 they prepare their final **assault.**

ASSEMBLE

Lev 8. 4 and when the community had **assembled,** [5] he said to them,
9. 5 and the whole community **assembled** there to worship the Lord.
Num 8. 9 Then **assemble** the whole community of Israel and make the
11.16 The Lord said to Moses, **"Assemble** seventy respected men
11.24 He **assembled** seventy of the leaders and placed them round the Tent.
16. 3 They **assembled** before Moses and Aaron and said to them,
16.47 his firepan and ran into the middle of the **assembled** people.
20. 8 Covenant Box, and then you and Aaron **assemble** the whole community.
20.10 He and Aaron **assembled** the whole community in front of the rock,
25. 7 Aaron the priest, saw this, he got up and left the **assembly.**
26. 3 They **assembled** in the plains of Moab across the River Jordan
Deut 4.10 God at Mount Sinai, when he said to me, **'Assemble** the people.
16. 8 on the seventh day **assemble** to worship the Lord your God,
31.28 **Assemble** all your tribal leaders and officials before me,
Josh 18. 1 the entire community of Israel **assembled** at Shiloh and set
Judg 6.33 Amalekites, and the desert tribes **assembled,** crossed the River Jordan,
20.11 all the men in Israel **assembled** with one purpose—to attack
21.10 So the **assembly** sent twelve thousand of their bravest
21.13 Then the whole **assembly** sent word to the Benjaminites
1 Sam 13. 5 The Philistines **assembled** to fight the Israelites;
17. 2 Saul and the Israelites **assembled** and camped in the Valley of Elah,
28. 4 The Philistine troops **assembled** and camped near the town of Shunem;
2 Sam 20.14 the clan of Bikri **assembled** and followed him into the city.
1 Kgs 8. 2 They all **assembled** during the Festival of Shelters in the seventh month,
8. 5 all the people of Israel **assembled** in front of the Covenant
8.55 he asked God's blessings on all the people **assembled** there.
1 Chr 13. 2 Levites in their towns, and tell them to **assemble** here with us.
13. 5 So David **assembled** the people of Israel from all over the country,
22. 2 the land of Israel to **assemble,** and he put them to work.
28. 1 King David commanded all the officials of Israel to **assemble** in Jerusalem.
28. 8 God and of this **assembly** of all Israel, the Lord's people,
29. 1 King David announced to the whole **assembly:**
29.10 There in front of the whole **assembly** King David praised the Lord.
29.20 And the whole **assembly** praised the Lord, the God of their ancestors,
2 Chr 5. 2 and clans of Israel to **assemble** in Jerusalem, in order to
5. 3 They all **assembled** at the time of the Festival of Shelters.
5. 6 all the people of Israel **assembled** in front of the Covenant
15.10 They **assembled** in Jerusalem in the third month of the
20.26 On the fourth day they **assembled** in the Valley of
23. 5 All the people will **assemble** in the temple courtyard.
29. 4 He **assembled** a group of priests and Levites in the east
29.15 These men **assembled** their fellow-Levites,
29.20 Without delay King Hezekiah **assembled** the leading men of the city,
30. 1 clean and not many people had **assembled** in Jerusalem.
32. 6 officers and ordered them to **assemble** in the open square at
Ezra 3. 1 Then they all **assembled** in Jerusalem, [2] and Joshua son of Jehozadak,
3. 5 other regular **assemblies** at which the Lord is worshipped,
8.15 I **assembled** the entire group by the canal that runs to
10. 9 Judah and Benjamin came to Jerusalem and **assembled** in the temple square.
Neh 5. 7 I called a public **assembly** to deal with the problem [8] and said,
7. 5 God inspired me to **assemble** the people and their leaders
Neh 8. 1 of that month they all **assembled** in Jerusalem, in the square
9. 1 month the people of Israel **assembled** to fast in order to
12.31 I **assembled** the leaders of Judah on top of the wall and
Ps 22.22 I will praise you in their **assembly:**
22.25 In the full **assembly** I will praise you for what you have
26.12 in the **assembly** of his people I praise the Lord.
35.18 Then I will thank you in the **assembly** of your people;
40. 9 In the **assembly** of all your people, Lord, I told the good
40.10 In the **assembly** of all your people I have not been silent
47. 9 The rulers of the nations **assemble** with the people of the
82. 1 in the **assembly** of the gods he gives his decision:
107.32 proclaim his greatness in the **assembly** of the people and
109.30 will praise him in the **assembly** of the people, [31] because
111. 1 heart I will thank the Lord in the **assembly** of his people.
116.14 In the **assembly** of all his people I will give him what
116.18 In the **assembly** of all your people, in the
142. 7 then in the **assembly** of your people I will praise you
149. 1 praise him in the **assembly** of his faithful people!
Is 14.13 king on that mountain in the north where the gods **assemble.**
29. 8 All the nations that **assemble** to attack Jerusalem will be
41. 5 So they all **assemble** and come.
48.14 **"Assemble** and listen, all of you!
49.18 Your people are **assembling**—they are coming home!
Jer 26.17 who had **assembled,** [18] "When Hezekiah was king of Judah,
49.14 to tell the nations to **assemble** their armies and to get
Ezek 38.13 will ask you, 'Have you **assembled** your army and attacked in
Joel 1.14 call an **assembly!**
2.15 give orders for a fast and call an **assembly!**
Mic 6. 9 to the city, "Listen, you people who **assemble** in the city!
Acts 7.38 who was with the people of Israel **assembled** in the desert;

ASSIGN

Gen 40. 4 prison, and the captain **assigned** Joseph as their servant.
Lev 25.32 at any time their property in the cities **assigned** to them.
Num 3.36 They were **assigned** responsibility for the frames for the Tent,
4.19 sons shall go in and **assign** each man his task and tell
4.27 and carry everything that Aaron and his sons **assign** to them.
4.49 through Moses, each man was **assigned** responsibility for his
8.19 of the Israelites, [19] and I **assign** the Levites to Aaron and
18. 8 to your descendants as the part **assigned** to you for ever.
18.20 no part of the land of Israel will be **assigned** to you.
32.18 Israelites have taken possession of the land **assigned** to them.
32.33 So Moses **assigned** to the tribes of Gad and Reuben and to
34.13 land that the Lord has **assigned** to the nine and a half
34.29 the men that the Lord **assigned** to divide the property for
Deut 3.12 possession of the land, I **assigned** to the tribes of Reuben
3.13 the tribe of Manasseh I **assigned** the rest of Gilead and also
3.15 "I **assigned** Gilead to the clan of Machir of the tribe
3.16 of Reuben and Gad I **assigned** the territory from Gilead to
3.19 will remain behind in the towns that I have **assigned** to you.
3.20 you may return to this land which I have **assigned** to you.'
32. 8 The Most High **assigned** nations their lands;
32. 8 He **assigned** to each nation a god, [9] but Jacob's descendants
33.21 A leader's share was **assigned** to them.
Josh 13.33 But Moses did not **assign** any land to the tribe of Levi.
14. 3 Moses had already **assigned** the land east of the Jordan
16. 1 southern boundary of the land **assigned** to the descendants of
17. 1 west of the Jordan was **assigned** to some of the families
17. 1 Gilead and Bashan, east of the Jordan, were **assigned** to him.
17. 2 west of the Jordan was **assigned** to the rest of the families
17. 6 as well as his male descendants were **assigned** land.
17. 6 The land of Gilead was **assigned** to the rest of the
18. 2 Israel who had not yet been **assigned** their share of the land.
18.10 the Lord for them, and **assigned** each of the remaining tribes
18.11 of the tribe of Benjamin was the first to be **assigned.**
19. 1 The second **assignment** made was for the families of the
19. 1 Its territory extended into the land **assigned** to the tribe of Judah.
19. 9 Since Judah's **assignment** was larger than was needed, part
19.10 The third **assignment** made was for the families of the
19.17 The fourth **assignment** made was for the families of the
19.24 The fifth **assignment** made was for the families of the
19.32 The sixth **assignment** made was for the families of the
19.40 The seventh **assignment** made was for the families of the
19.51 of the tribes of Israel **assigned** these parts of the land by
21. 4 Levite clan of Kohath were the first to be **assigned** cities.
21. 4 from Aaron the priest were **assigned** thirteen cities from the
21. 5 the clan of Kohath was **assigned** ten cities from the
21. 6 The clan of Gershon was **assigned** thirteen cities from the
21. 7 the clan of Merari were **assigned** twelve cities from the
21. 8 lots, the people of Israel **assigned** these cities and their
21.10 Their **assignment** was the first to be made.
21.13 refuge), the following cities were **assigned** to the
21.20 Levite clan of Kohath were **assigned** some cities from the
21.40 So the clan of Merari was **assigned** a total of twelve cities.
23. 4 I have **assigned** as the possession of your tribes the land
Judg 1. 3 with us into the territory **assigned** to us, and we will fight
1. 3 Then we will go with you into the territory **assigned** to you."
1 Kgs 4.27 each one in the month **assigned** to him, supplied the food
1 Chr 6.48 Their fellow-Levites were **assigned** all the other duties
6.54 This is the territory **assigned** to the descendants of
6.54 They received the first share of the land **assigned** to the Levites.
6.56 to the city were **assigned** to Caleb son of Jephunneh.
6.57 The following towns were **assigned** to Aaron's descendants:
6.60 territory of Benjamin they were **assigned** the following towns
6.61 territory of West Manasseh were **assigned** by lot to the rest
6.62 Gershon, family by family, were **assigned** thirteen towns in
6.63 Reuben, Gad, and Zebulun were **assigned** to the clan of Merari,
6.64 way the people of Israel **assigned** towns for the Levites to
6.65 Judah, Simeon, and Benjamin, mentioned above, were also **assigned**

1 Chr 6.66 the clan of Kohath were **assigned** towns and pasture lands in
6.70 of West Manasseh they were **assigned** the towns of Aner and
6.71 the clan of Gershon were **assigned** the following towns, with
6.77 the clan of Merari were **assigned** the following towns with
15.16 leaders of the Levites to **assign** various Levites to sing and
23. 4 The king **assigned** twenty-four thousand to administer the work
23.28 age of twenty, [28]and were **assigned** the following duties:
23.31 the number of Levites **assigned** to do this work each time.
23.31 The Levites were **assigned** the duty of worshipping the Lord
24. 5 Eleazar and Ithamar, **assignments** were made by drawing lots.
24. 7 the twenty-four family groups were given their **assignments:**
24.19 were registered according to their **assignments** for going to
24.31 drew lots for their **assignments,** just as their relatives,
25. 8 To determine the **assignment** of duties they all drew lots,
26. 1 These are the **assignments** of work for the Levites who
26.12 to families, and they were **assigned** duties in the Temple,
26.16 Guard duty was divided into **assigned** periods, one after another.
26.19 This is the **assignment** of guard duty to the clan of
26.23 Duties were also **assigned** to the descendants of Amram,
26.29 Izhar, Chenaniah and his sons were **assigned** administrative duties:
28.21 Levites have been **assigned** duties to perform in the Temple.
2 Chr 2.18 He **assigned** 70,000 of them to transport materials and
7. 6 in the places that were **assigned** to them, and facing them
11.23 Rehoboam wisely **assigned** responsibilities to his sons,
23.18 to carry out the duties **assigned** to them by King David and
31.13 Ten Levites were **assigned** to work under them:
31.17 The priests were **assigned** their duties by clans,
31.17 years of age or older were **assigned** theirs by work groups.
31.19 who lived in the cities **assigned** to Aaron's descendants, or
35. 2 He **assigned** to the priests the duties they were to perform
35. 4 clans, according to the responsibilities **assigned** to you by
35.15 in the places **assigned** to them by King David's instructions:
Neh 3. 5 do the manual labour **assigned** to them by the supervisors.
7. 1 choir, and the other Levites had been **assigned** their work.
7. 3 lived in Jerusalem and to **assign** some of them to specific
11.36 the territory of Judah were **assigned** to live with the people
Esth 2. 9 place in the harem and **assigned** seven girls specially chosen
Job 20.29 the fate of wicked men, the fate that God **assigns** to them.
Ezek 44.14 I am **assigning** to them the menial work that is to be
46.18 from the land that is **assigned** to him, so that he will
Dan 8.27 work that the king had **assigned** to me, but I was puzzled
Zech 3. 7 perform the duties I have **assigned** to you, then you will

ASSIST

2 Kgs 3.11 He was Elijah's **assistant."**
23. 4 the High Priest Hilkiah, his **assistant** priests, and the
25.19 in the city, the commander's **assistant,** who was in charge of
1 Chr 9.25 These guards were **assisted** by their relatives, who lived
15.17 To **assist** them they chose the following Levites to play the
16. 5 Asaph was appointed leader, with Zechariah as his **assistant.**
16.38 Jeduthun and sixty-eight men of his clan were to **assist** them.
23.32 and the Temple, and of **assisting** their relatives, the
24. 3 He was **assisted** in this by Zadok, a descendant of Eleazar,
2 Chr 2. 8 to send my men to **assist** yours [9]in preparing large
8.14 and of the Levites who **assisted** the priests in singing hymns
13.10 perform their duties, and Levites **assist** them.
31.12 Conaniah in charge and made his brother Shimei his **assistant.**
31.15 lived, he was faithfully **assisted** in this by other Levites:
Ezra 8.20 by King David and his officials to **assist** the Levites.
Neh 11.17 Bakbukiah, who was Mattaniah's **assistant.**
13.13 Zaccur and grandson of Mattaniah, was to be their **assistant.**
Jer 52.25 in the city, the commander's **assistant,** who was in charge of

ASSOCIATE

Josh 23. 7 and then you will not **associate** with these peoples left
Ezra 4. 7 Mithredath, Tabeel, and their **associates** wrote a letter
4. 9 of the province, from their **associates,** the judges, and from
4.17 the province, and to their **associates** who live in Samaria
4.23 to Rehum, Shimshai, and their **associates,** they hurried to
8.17 to ask him and his **associates,** the temple workmen, to send
Ps 50.18 of every thief you see and you **associate** with adulterers.
Prov 23.20 Don't **associate** with people who drink too much wine or
Acts 10.28 not allowed by his religion to visit or **associate** with Gentiles.
1 Cor 5. 9 I wrote you I told you not to **associate** with immoral people.
5.11 that you should not **associate** with a person who calls himself

ASSUME

Gen 12.12 Egyptians see you, they will **assume** that you are my wife,

ASSURE

1 Sam 23.16 him with **assurances** of God's protection, [17]saying to him,
Ps 44. 3 and your strength, by the **assurance** of your presence, which
Ezek 13.16 those prophets who **assured** Jerusalem that all was well,
Mt 6. 2 I **assure** you, they have already been paid in full.
6. 5 I **assure** you, they have already been paid in full.
6.16 I **assure** you, they have already been paid in full.
8.11 I **assure** you that many will come from the east and the
10.15 I **assure** you that on the Judgement Day God will show
10.23 I **assure** you that you will not finish your work in all
11.11 I **assure** you that John the Baptist is greater than any
11.22 I **assure** you that on the Judgement Day God will show
12.42 I **assure** you that there is something here greater than Solomon!
13.17 I **assure** you that many prophets and many of God's people
16.28 I **assure** you that there are some here who will not die
17.20 "I **assure** you that if you have faith as big as
18. 3 and said, "I **assure** you that unless you change
Mt 19.23 Jesus then said to his disciples, "I **assure** you:
21.21 Jesus answered, "I **assure** you that if you believe and
26.13 Now, I **assure** you that wherever this gospel is preached
Mk 3.28 "I **assure** you that people can be forgiven all their sins
9.41 I **assure** you that anyone who gives you a drink of water
10.15 I **assure** you that whoever does not receive the Kingdom
11.23 I **assure** you that whoever tells this hill to get up and
14. 9 Now, I **assure** you that wherever the gospel is preached
Lk 2.26 was with him [26]and had **assured** him that he would not die
9.27 I **assure** you that there are some here who will not die
10.12 I **assure** you that on Judgement Day God will show more
11.32 I **assure** you that there is something here greater than Jonah!
12. 8 "I **assure** you that whoever declares publicly that he belongs
13.35 I **assure** you that you will not see me until the time
18.29 said to them, "and I **assure** you that anyone who leaves home
Acts 2.26 will rest **assured** in hope, [27]because you will not
Rom 9. 1 by the Holy Spirit, also **assures** me that I am not lying
10. 2 I can **assure** you that they are deeply devoted to God;
2 Cor 1.12 are proud that our conscience **assures** us that our lives in
8. 3 I can **assure** you that they gave as much as they could,
Eph 1.14 promised his people, and this **assures** us that God will give
Col 2. 2 have the full wealth of **assurance** which true understanding brings.

ASSYRIA

[EMPEROR OF ASSYRIA]

Powerful empire based in Mesopotamia, which conquered the n. kingdom (Israel).

Gen 2.14 Tigris, which flows east of **Assyria,** and the fourth river is
10.11 land he went to **Assyria** and built the cities of Nineveh,
25.18 and Shur, to the east of Egypt on the way to **Assyria.**
Num 24.22 you Kenites will be destroyed When **Assyria** takes you captive."
24.24 They will conquer **Assyria** and Eber, But they, in turn, will
2 Kgs 15.19 Tiglath Pileser, the **emperor of Assyria,** invaded Israel,
15.29 Tiglath Pileser, the **emperor of Assyria,** captured the cities
15.29 and took the people to **Assyria** as prisoners.
16. 7 Tiglath Pileser, the **emperor of Assyria,** with this message:
16.18 in order to please the **Assyrian emperor,** Ahaz also removed
17. 3 **Emperor Shalmaneser of Assyria** made war against him;
17. 4 his help, and stopped paying the annual tribute to **Assyria.**
17. 6 the reign of Hoshea, the **Assyrian emperor** captured Samaria,
17. 6 took the Israelites to **Assyria** as prisoners, and
17.23 Israel were taken into exile to **Assyria,** where they still live.
17.24 The **emperor of Assyria** took people from the cities of Babylon,
17.26 The **emperor of Assyria** was told that the people he had
18. 7 He rebelled against the **emperor of Assyria** and refused to
18. 9 Hoshea's reign over Israel—**Emperor Shalmaneser of Assyria**
18.11 The **Assyrian emperor** took the Israelites to Assyria as
18.13 King Hezekiah, Sennacherib, the **emperor of Assyria,** attacked
18.17 The **Assyrian emperor** sent a large army from Lachish to
18.19 One of the **Assyrian** officials told them that the emperor
18.20 Who do you think will help you rebel against **Assyria?**
18.22 The **Assyrian** official went on, "Or will you tell me
18.24 for even the lowest ranking **Assyrian** official, and yet you
18.28 "Listen to what the **emperor of Assyria** is telling you!
18.30 he will stop our **Assyrian** army from capturing your city.
18.31 The **emperor of Assyria** commands you to come out of the city
18.33 nations save their countries from the **emperor of Assyria?**
18.37 reported to the king what the **Assyrian** official had said.
19. 4 The **Assyrian emperor** has sent his chief official to insult
19. 6 you not to let the **Assyrians** frighten you with their claims
19. 8 The **Assyrian** official learnt that the emperor had left
19. 9 Word reached the **Assyrians** that the Egyptian army, led by
19.11 You have heard what an **Assyrian emperor** does to any
19.17 Lord, that the emperors of **Assyria** have destroyed many nations,
19.19 God, rescue us from the **Assyrians,** so that all the nations
19.32 "This is what the Lord has said about the **Assyrian emperor:**
19.35 Lord went to the **Assyrian** camp and killed 185,000 soldiers.
19.36 Then the **Assyrian emperor** Sennacherib withdrew and returned to Nineveh.
20. 6 you and this city of Jerusalem from the **emperor of Assyria.**
23.29 army to the River Euphrates to help the **emperor of Assyria.**
1 Chr 5. 4 The **Assyrian emperor,** Tiglath Pileser, captured Beerah,
5.26 So God made **Emperor Pul of Assyria** (also known as Tiglath Pileser)
2 Chr 28.16 King Ahaz asked Tiglath Pileser, the **emperor of Assyria,** to
28.20 The **Assyrian emperor,** instead of helping Ahaz, opposed
30. 6 "People of Israel, You have survived the **Assyrian** conquest of the land.
32. 1 Sennacherib, the **emperor of Assyria,** invaded Judah.
32. 3 in order to prevent the **Assyrians** from having any water when
32. 7 don't be afraid of the **Assyrian emperor** or of the army he
32.10 "I, Sennacherib, **Emperor of Assyria,** ask what gives you
32.13 other nation save their people from the **emperor of Assyria?**
32.15 ever been able to save his people from any **Assyrian emperor.**
32.16 The **Assyrian** officials said even worse things about the
32.21 that killed the soldiers and officers of the **Assyrian** army.
32.21 So the emperor went back to **Assyria** disgraced.
32.22 power of Sennacherib, the **emperor of Assyria,** and also from
33.11 So the Lord let the commanders of the **Assyrian** army invade Judah.
Ezra 4. 2 Esarhaddon, **emperor of Assyria,** sent us here to live."
6.22 Lord had made the **emperor of Assyria** favourable to them, so
Neh 9.32 From the time when **Assyrian** kings oppressed us, even till
Ps 83. 8 **Assyria** has also joined them as a strong ally of the
Is 7.17 from Judah—he is going to bring the king of **Assyria.**
7.18 the Nile, and for the **Assyrians** to come from their land like
7.20 a barber from across the Euphrates—the **emperor of Assyria!—**
8. 4 of Samaria will be carried off by the king of **Assyria."**
8. 7 Lord, will bring the **emperor of Assyria** and all his forces
10. 5 The Lord said, **"Assyria!**

Is 10. 5 I use **Assyria** like a club to punish those with whom I
10. 6 I sent **Assyria** to attack a godless nation, people who have
10. 7 But the **Assyrian emperor** has his own violent plans in mind.
10.12 I will punish the **emperor of Assyria** for all his boasting
10.13 The **emperor of Assyria** boasts, "I have done it all myself.
10.24 not be afraid of the **Assyrians,** even though they oppress you
10.26 I will punish **Assyria** as I punished Egypt.
10.27 you from the power of **Assyria,** and their yoke will no longer
11.11 people who are left in **Assyria** and Egypt, in the lands of
11.16 be a highway out of **Assyria** for those of his people Israel
14.25 I will destroy the **Assyrians** in my land of Israel and
14.25 free my people from the **Assyrian** yoke and from the burdens
19.23 comes, there will be a highway between Egypt and **Assyria.**
19.24 will rank with Egypt and **Assyria,** and these three nations
19.25 you, **Assyria,** whom I created;
20. 1 the orders of Sargon, **emperor of Assyria,**
20. 1 the commander-in-chief of the **Assyrian** army
20. 4 The **emperor of Assyria** will lead away naked the prisoners
20. 6 we relied on to protect us from the **emperor of Assyria!**
23.13 was the Babylonians, not the **Assyrians,** who let the wild
27.13 blown to call back from **Assyria** and Egypt all the Israelites
30.31 The **Assyrians** will be terrified when they hear the
30.32 God himself will fight against the **Assyrians.**
30.33 prepared where a huge fire will burn the **emperor of Assyria.**
31. 8 **Assyria** will be destroyed in war, but not by human power.
31. 8 The **Assyrians** will run from battle, and their young men will
36. 1 of Judah, Sennacherib, the **emperor of Assyria,** attacked the
36. 4 The **Assyrian** official told them that the emperor wanted to
36. 5 Who do you think will help you rebel against **Assyria?**
36. 7 The **Assyrian** official went on, "Or will you tell me that
36. 9 for even the lowest ranking **Assyrian** official, and yet you
36.13 "Listen to what the **emperor of Assyria** is telling you.
36.15 he will stop our **Assyrian** army from capturing your city.
36.16 The **emperor of Assyria** commands you to come out of the city
36.18 nations save their countries from the **emperor of Assyria?**
36.22 reported to the king what the **Assyrian** official had said.
37. 4 The **Assyrian emperor** has sent his chief official to insult
37. 6 you not to let the **Assyrians** frighten you by their claims
37. 8 The **Assyrian** official learnt that the emperor had left
37. 9 Word reached the **Assyrians** that the Egyptian army, led by
37.11 You have heard what an **Assyrian emperor** does to any
37.18 Lord, that the emperors of **Assyria** have destroyed many nations,
37.20 God, rescue us from the **Assyrians,** so that all the nations
37.33 "This is what the Lord has said about the **Assyrian emperor:**
37.36 Lord went to the **Assyrian** camp and killed 185,000 soldiers.
37.37 Then the **Assyrian emperor** Sennacherib withdrew and returned to Nineveh.
38. 6 of Jerusalem from the **emperor of Assyria,** and I will
52. 4 **Assyria,** however, took you away by force and paid nothing for you.
Jer 2.18 gain by going to **Assyria** to drink water from the Euphrates?
2.36 You will be disappointed by Egypt, just as you were by **Assyria.**
50.17 were attacked by the **emperor of Assyria,** and then King
50.18 just as I punished the **emperor of Assyria.**
Lam 5. 6 enough to stay alive, we went begging to Egypt and **Assyria.**
Ezek 16.28 by the others, you went running after the **Assyrians.**
23. 5 prostitute and was full of lust for her lovers from **Assyria.**
23. 7 the whore for all the **Assyrian** officers, and her lust led
23. 7 led her to defile herself by worshipping **Assyrian** idols.
23. 9 her over to her **Assyrian** lovers whom she wanted so much.
23.12 full of lust for the **Assyrian** noblemen and officers—soldiers
23.23 Chaldeans, men from Pekod, Shoa, and Koa, and all the **Assyrians.**
32.22 **"Assyria** is there, with the graves of her soldiers all around.
Hos 5.13 wounds, then Israel went to **Assyria** to ask the great emperor
7.11 people call on Egypt for help, and then they run to **Assyria!**
8. 9 off to seek help from **Assyria,** and have paid other nations
8.10 writhe in pain, when the **emperor of Assyria** oppresses them.
9. 3 to Egypt and will have to eat forbidden food in **Assyria.**
10. 6 be carried off to **Assyria** as tribute to the great emperor.
11. 5 so they must return to Egypt, and **Assyria** will rule them.
11.11 come from Egypt, as swiftly as birds, and from **Assyria,** like
12. 1 They make treaties with **Assyria** and do business with Egypt."
14. 3 **Assyria** can never save us, and war-horses cannot protect us.
Mic 5. 5 When the **Assyrians** invade our country and break through our defences,
5. 6 of arms they will conquer **Assyria,** the land of Nimrod, and
5. 6 save us from the **Assyrians** when they invade our territory.
7.12 to you from everywhere—from **Assyria** in the east, from Egypt
Nah 1.12 "Even though the **Assyrians** are strong and numerous, they
1.13 I will now end **Assyria's** power over you and break the
1.14 This is what the Lord has decreed about the **Assyrians:**
1.14 a grave for the **Assyrians**—they don't deserve to live!"
3.18 **Emperor of Assyria,** your governors are dead, and your
Zeph 2.13 The Lord will use his power to destroy **Assyria.**
Zech 10.10 From Egypt and **Assyria** I will bring them home and settle
10.11 Proud **Assyria** will be humbled, and mighty Egypt will lose her power.

ASTARTE

Goddess of fertility and war who was widely worshipped in the ancient Near East.

Judg 2.13 They stopped worshipping the Lord and served the Baals and the **Astartes.**
10. 6 worshipping the Baals and the **Astartes,** as well as the gods
1 Sam 7. 3 all the foreign gods and the images of the goddess **Astarte.**
7. 4 idols of Baal and **Astarte,** and worshipped only the Lord.
12.10 you, Lord, and worshipped the idols of Baal and **Astarte.**
31.10 the temple of the goddess **Astarte,** and they nailed his body
1 Kgs 11. 5 He worshipped **Astarte** the goddess of Sidon, and Molech the
1 Kgs 11.33 **Astarte,** the goddess of Sidon;
2 Kgs 23.13 worship of disgusting idols—**Astarte** the goddess of Sidon,

ASTONISHED

Is 59.16 He is **astonished** to see that there is no one to help
Jer 2.12 horror, to be amazed and **astonished,** [13] for my people have
4. 9 priests will be shocked and prophets will be **astonished."**
Hab 1. 5 round you, and you will be **astonished** at what you see.
Lk 2.48 parents were **astonished** when they saw him, and his mother said
Acts 8.11 for such a long time he had **astonished** them with his magic.
13.41 Be **astonished** and die!

ASTOUND

Deut 10.21 own eyes the great and **astounding** things that he has done
Mt 21.20 The disciples saw this and were **astounded.**
Lk 8.56 parents were **astounded,** but Jesus commanded them not to tell
Acts 8. 9 who for some time had **astounded** the Samaritans with his magic.
8.13 close to Philip and was **astounded** when he saw the great

ASTRAY

Job 31.27 I have not been led **astray** to honour them by kissing my
36.18 not to let bribes deceive you, or riches lead you **astray.**
Prov 12.26 his friend, but the path of the wicked leads them **astray.**
Is 47.10 and knowledge led you **astray,** and you said to yourself,
Jer 23.13 spoken in the name of Baal and have led my people **astray.**
23.32 lead my people **astray** with their lies and their boasting.
Amos 2. 4 They have been led **astray** by the same false gods that their
1 Cor 12. 2 still heathen, you were led **astray** in many ways to the

ASTROLOGER

Is 44.25 I make fools of fortune-tellers and frustrate the predictions of **astrologers.**
47.13 Let your **astrologers** come forward and save you— those people
47.15 do you— those **astrologers** you've consulted all your life.
Dan 2.27 fortune-teller, or **astrologer** who can tell you that.
4. 7 magicians, wizards, and **astrologers** were brought in,
5. 7 He shouted for someone to bring in the magicians, wizards, and **astrologers.**
5.11 of the fortune-tellers, magicians, wizards, and **astrologers.**

AT ONCE

Mt 4.20 **At once** they left their nets and went with him.
4.22 Jesus called them, [22] and **at once** they left the boat and
5.24 front of the altar, go **at once** and make peace with your
8. 3 **At once** the man was healed of his disease.
8.29 **At once** they screamed, "What do you want with us, you
13.21 comes because of the message, they give up **at once.**
14.27 Jesus spoke to them **at once.**
14.31 **At once** Jesus reached out and grabbed hold of him and said,
20.34 **at once** they were able to see, and they followed him.
21. 2 there ahead of you, and **at once** you will find a donkey
21. 3 and then he will let them go **at once."**
21.19 **At once** the fig-tree dried up.
25.16 received five thousand coins went **at once** and invested his money
26.53 my Father for help, and **at once** he would send me more
27.48 One of them ran up **at once,** took a sponge, soaked it
Mk 1.12 **At once** the Spirit made him go into the desert,
1.18 **At once** they left their nets and went with him.
1.42 **At once** the disease left the man, and he was clean.
1.43 and sent him away **at once,** [44] after saying to him, "Listen,
2. 8 **At once** Jesus knew what they were thinking, so he said
3. 6 left the synagogue and met **at once** with some members of
4.17 comes because of the message, they give up **at once.**
5.29 She touched his cloak, and her bleeding stopped **at once;**
5.30 **At once** Jesus knew that power had gone out of him,
5.42 She got up **at once** and started walking around.
6.25 The girl hurried back **at once** to the king and demanded,
6.27 he sent off a guard **at once** with orders to bring John's
6.33 however, saw them leave and knew **at once** who they were;
6.45 **At once** Jesus made his disciples get into the boat and
6.50 Jesus spoke to them **at once,** "Courage!"
6.54 As they left the boat, people recognized Jesus **at once.**
7.25 Jesus and came to him **at once** and fell at his feet.
7.35 **At once** the man was able to hear, his speech impediment
8.10 sent the people away [10] and **at once** got into a boat
9.24 The father **at once** cried out, "I do have faith, but not
10.52 **At once** he was able to see and followed Jesus
11. 3 the Master needs it and will send it back **at once."**
Lk 4.39 and she got up **at once** and began to wait on
5.13 **At once** the disease left the man.
5.25 **At once** the man got up in front of them all,
6.49 hit that house it fell **at once**—and what a terrible crash
8.44 the edge of his cloak, and her bleeding stopped **at once.**
8.47 she had touched him and how she had been healed **at once.**
8.55 returned, and she got up **at once,** and Jesus ordered them to
12.36 comes and knocks, they will open the door for him **at once.**
12.54 coming up in the west, **at once** you say that it is
13.13 his hands on her, and **at once** she straightened herself up
14. 5 would you not pull him out **at once** on the Sabbath itself?"
18.43 **At once** he was able to see, and he followed Jesus,
19.15 **At once** he ordered his servants to appear before him, in
22.60 **At once,** while he was still speaking, a cock crowed.
24.33 They got up **at once** and went back to Jerusalem,
Jn 1.41 **At once** he found his brother Simon and told him,
13.30 Judas accepted the bread and went out **at once.**
13.32 Son of Man in himself, and he will do so **at once.**

Jn 18.27 Again Peter said "No"—and **at once** a cock crowed.
19.34 into Jesus' side, and **at once** blood and water poured out.
Acts 3. 7 **At once** the man's feet and ankles became strong;
5.10 **At once** she fell down at his feet and died.
7.57 they all rushed at him **at once,** [58] threw him out of the
9.18 **At once** something like fish scales fell from Saul's eyes,
9.34 **At once** Aeneas got up.
10.33 so I sent for you **at once,** and you have been good
12. 7 **At once** the chains fell off Peter's hands.
12.23 **At once** the angel of the Lord struck Herod down,
13.11 **At once** Elymas felt a dark mist cover his eyes,
16.26 **At once** all the doors opened, and the chains fell off all
16.33 and he and all his family were baptized **at once.**
17.14 **At once** the believers sent Paul away to the coast;
21.30 **At once** the Temple doors were closed.
21.32 **At once** the commander took some officers and soldiers
22.29 **At once** the men who were going to question Paul drew
23.30 was a plot against him, **at once** I decided to send him
1 Cor 15. 6 five hundred of his followers **at once,** most of whom are
Gal 1.17 Instead, I went **at once** to Arabia, and then I returned
Jas 1.24 and then goes away and **at once** forgets what he looks like.
Jude 3 felt the need of writing **at once** to encourage you to fight
Rev 4. 2 **At once** the Spirit took control of me.

ATE see EAT

ATHALIAH (1)

Queen who usurped the throne of Judah.

2 Kgs 8.26 His mother was **Athaliah,** the daughter of King Ahab and
11. 1 King Ahaziah's mother **Athaliah** learnt of her son's murder,
11. 2 Temple and hid him from **Athaliah,** so that he was not killed.
11. 3 him hidden in the Temple, while **Athaliah** ruled as queen.
11.13 Queen **Athaliah** heard the noise being made by the guards
11.14 **Athaliah** tore her clothes in distress and shouted,
11.15 Jehoiada did not want **Athaliah** killed in the temple area,
11.20 was quiet, now that **Athaliah** had been killed in the palace.
2 Chr 22. 2 Ahab's family, since his mother **Athaliah**—the daughter of
22.10 King Ahaziah's mother **Athaliah** learnt of her son's murder,
22.11 hidden, she saved him from death at the hands of **Athaliah.**
22.12 he remained there in hiding, while **Athaliah** ruled as queen.
23.12 **Athaliah** heard the people cheering for the king, so she
23.14 Jehoiada did not want **Athaliah** killed in the temple area,
23.21 and the city was quiet, now that **Athaliah** had been killed.
24. 7 (The followers of **Athaliah,** that corrupt woman, had

ATHLETE

Ps 19. 5 a happy bridegroom, like an **athlete** eager to run a race.
1 Cor 9.25 Every **athlete** in training submits to strict discipline,
2 Tim 2. 5 An **athlete** who runs in a race cannot win the prize unless

ATONEMENT

The Day of Atonement was the most important of Israel's holy days, when the High Priest would offer sacrifice for the sins of the people of Israel. It was held on the 10th day of the seventh month of the Hebrew calendar (about October 1st). The Jewish name for this day is Yom Kippur.

Lev 25. 9 seventh month, the Day of **Atonement,** send a man to blow a
Acts 27. 9 voyage, for by now the Day of **Atonement** was already past.

AV ATONEMENT

see also **PURIFY**

Ex 29.33 what was used in the ritual of **forgiveness** at their ordination.
29.36 offer a bull as a sacrifice, so that sin may be **forgiven.**
30.10 four projections the blood of the animal **sacrificed** for sin.
30.15 when they **pay** this amount for their lives.
30.16 This tax will be the **payment** for their lives, and I will
32.30 perhaps I can obtain **forgiveness** for your sin."
Lev 1. 4 it will be accepted as a sacrifice to **take away** his sins.
4.20 way he shall make the **sacrifice** for the people's sin, and
4.26 priest shall offer the **sacrifice** for the sin of the ruler,
4.31 the priest shall offer the **sacrifice** for the man's sin, and
4.35 the priest shall offer the **sacrifice** for the man's sin, and
5. 6 The priest shall offer the **sacrifice** for the man's sin.
5.10 the priest shall offer the **sacrifice** for the man's sin, and
5.13 the priest shall offer the **sacrifice** for the man's sin, and
5.16 offer the animal as a **sacrifice** for the man's sin, and he
5.18 The priest shall offer the **sacrifice** for the sin which the
6. 7 The priest shall offer the **sacrifice** for the man's sin,
7. 7 the meat belongs to the priest who offers the **sacrifice.**
8.34 what we have done today, in order to **take away** your sin.
9. 7 sin-offering and the burnt-offering to **take away** your sins
9. 7 Present this offering to **take away** the sins of the people,
10.17 to you in order to **take away** the sin of the community.
12. 7 and perform the ritual to **take away** her impurity, and she
12. 8 shall perform the ritual to **take away** her impurity, and she
16. 6 bull as a sacrifice to **take away** his own sins and those
16.10 to Azazel, in order to **take away** the sins of the people.
16.17 When he has performed the **ritual** for himself, his family,
16.24 and offer the burnt-offering to **remove** his own sins and
16.27 the Most Holy Place to **take away** sin, shall be carried
17.11 be poured out on the altar to **take away** the people's sins.
17.11 Blood, which is life, **takes away** sins.
23.26 is to be performed to **take away** the sins of the people.
23.28 it is the day for performing the ritual to **take away** sin.
Num 25.13 to me and brought about **forgiveness** for the people's sin."
31.50 to the Lord as a **payment** for our lives, so that he
2 Sam 21. 3 to make up for the **wrong** that was done to you, so
1 Chr 6.49 and for the sacrifices by which God **forgives** Israel's sins.
2 Chr 29.24 altar as a sacrifice to **take away** the sin of all the
Neh 10.33 offerings, the offerings to **take away** the sins of Israel,
Rom 5.11 our Lord Jesus Christ, who has now made us God's **friends.**

ATTACH

Ex 25.12 of gold for it and **attach** them to its four legs, with
28. 7 which it can be fastened, are to be **attached** to the sides.
28. 8 same materials is to be **attached** to the ephod so as to
28.14 gold twisted like cords, and **attach** them to the settings.
28.23 Make two gold rings and **attach** them to the upper corners
28.25 settings, and in this way **attach** them in front to the
28.26 two rings of gold and **attach** them to the lower corners of
28.27 two more gold rings and **attach** them to the lower part of
30. 4 gold carrying-rings for it and **attach** them below the border
35.16 bronze grating **attached,** its poles, and all its equipment;
37. 3 of gold for it and **attached** them to its four feet, with
37.27 gold carrying-rings for it and **attached** them below the
39. 4 for the ephod and **attached** them to its sides,
39. 5 of the same materials, was **attached** to the ephod so as to
39.16 and two gold rings and **attached** the two rings to the upper
39.18 settings and in this way **attached** them in front to the
39.19 two rings of gold and **attached** them to the lower corners of
39.20 two more gold rings and **attached** them to the lower part of
40.18 bases, set up its frames, **attached** its cross-bars, and put
Num 36. 7 The property of every Israelite will remain **attached** to his tribe.
2 Kgs 23. 3 put into practice the demands **attached** to the covenant, as
2 Chr 9.18 and there was a footstool **attached** to it, covered with gold.
34.31 put into practice the demands **attached** to the covenant, as
Ezek 40.38 courtyard there was an annexe **attached** to the inner gateway

ATTACK

Gen 14.15 divided his men into groups, **attacked** the enemy by night,
31.52 go beyond this pile to **attack** you, and you must never
31.52 go beyond it or beyond this memorial stone to **attack** me.
32. 8 thought, "If Esau comes and **attacks** the first group, the
32.11 that he is coming to **attack** us and destroy us all, even
34.30 band together against me and **attack** me, our whole family
43.18 They will suddenly **attack** us, take our donkeys, and make us
49.19 "Gad will be **attacked** by a band of robbers, But he will
49.23 His enemies **attack** him fiercely And pursue him with
Ex 17. 8 The Amalekites came and **attacked** the Israelites at Rephidim.
21.29 been in the habit of **attacking** people and its owner had been
21.36 been in the habit of **attacking** and its owner did not keep
Num 10. 9 against an enemy who has **attacked** you, sound the signal for
13.30 Moses, and said, "We should **attack** now and take the land;
13.31 Caleb said, "No, we are not strong enough to **attack** them;
14.45 the Canaanites who lived there **attacked** and defeated them,
20.18 If you try, we will march out and **attack** you."
20.20 out with a powerful army to **attack** the people of Israel.
21. 1 way of Atharim, he **attacked** them and captured some of them.
21.23 out to Jahaz in the wilderness and **attacked** the Israelites.
21.32 men to find the best way to **attack** the city of Jazer.
21.33 of Bashan marched out with his army to **attack** them at Edrei.
25.17 The Lord commanded Moses, [17] "**Attack** the Midianites
31. 3 war, so that you can **attack** Midian and punish them for what
31. 7 They **attacked** Midian, as the Lord had commanded Moses, and
32.17 into battle and lead the **attack** until we have settled them
32.21 the Lord they are to **attack** our enemies until the Lord
32.41 of the tribe of Manasseh, **attacked** and captured some
32.42 Nobah **attacked** and captured Kenath and its villages, and
Deut 1.41 But now we will **attack,** just as the Lord our God commanded
1.42 me, 'Warn them not to **attack,** for I will not be with
2.24 **Attack** him, and begin occupying his land.
20.10 "When you go to **attack** a city, first give its people a
22.26 same as when one man **attacks** another man and murders him.
25.18 of God, and so they **attacked** you from the rear when you
28. 7 "The Lord will defeat your enemies when they **attack** you.
28. 7 They will **attack** from one direction, but they will run from
28.25 You will **attack** them from one direction, but you will run
28.52 They will **attack** every town in the land that the Lord
32.24 will send wild animals to **attack** them, and poisonous snakes
Josh 7. 3 "There is no need for everyone to **attack** Ai.
7. 4 Israelites made the **attack,** but they were forced to retreat.
8. 2 Prepare to **attack** the city by surprise from the rear."
8. 4 be ready to **attack.**
8.14 not knowing that he was about to be **attacked** from the rear.
8.20 towards the barren country now turned round to **attack** them.
10. 4 "Come and help me **attack** Gibeon, because its people have
10. 5 joined forces, surrounded Gibeon, and **attacked** it.
10. 6 Amorite kings in the hill-country have joined forces and have **attacked** us!"
10. 9 Gilgal to Gibeon, and they made a surprise **attack** on the Amorites.
10.10 Beth Horon, keeping up the **attack** as far south as Azekah and
10.19 Keep on after the enemy and **attack** them from the rear;
10.28 Joshua **attacked** and captured Makkedah and its king that day.
10.29 his army went on from Makkedah to Libnah and **attacked** it.
10.31 on from Libnah to Lachish, surrounded it and **attacked** it.
10.34 on from Lachish to Eglon, surrounded it and **attacked** it.
10.36 up into the hills to Hebron, **attacked** it [37] and captured it.
10.38 Then Joshua and his army turned back to Debir and **attacked** it.
11. 7 Joshua and all his men **attacked** them by surprise at Merom Brook.
11. 8 the Israelites **attacked** and pursued them as far north as
15.15 From there he went to **attack** the people living in Debir.
19.47 of Dan lost their land, they went to Laish and **attacked** it.
Judg 1. 1 should be the first to go and **attack** the Canaanites?"
1. 8 The men of Judah **attacked** Jerusalem and captured it.

Judg 1.22 Ephraim and Manasseh went to **attack** the city of Bethel, at
2.14 Lord became furious with Israel and let raiders **attack** and rob them.
4.15 When Barak **attacked** with his army, the Lord threw Sisera
6. 3 with the Amalekites and the desert tribes and **attack** them.
7. 9 That night the Lord commanded Gideon, "Get up and **attack** the camp;
7.10 if you are afraid to **attack,** go down to the camp with
7.11 are saying, and then you will have the courage to **attack."**
7.22 Lord made the enemy troops **attack** each other with their swords.
8.11 of Nobah and Jogbehah, and **attacked** the army by surprise.
9.33 morning at sunrise and make a sudden **attack** on the city.
9.44 gate, the other two companies **attacked** the people in the
9.52 When Abimelech came to **attack** the tower, he went up to
11.20 army together, made camp at Jahaz, and **attacked** Israel.
15. 8 He **attacked** them fiercely and killed many of them.
15. 9 came and made camp in Judah, and **attacked** the town of Lehi.
15.10 The men of Judah asked them, "Why are you **attacking** us?"
18. 9 "Let's **attack** Laish.
18.25 else unless you want these men to get angry and **attack** you.
18.27 made, they went and **attacked** Laish, that town of peaceful,
20. 5 men of Gibeah came to **attack** me and surrounded the house at
20. 9 we will draw lots and choose some men to **attack** Gibeah.
20.11 in Israel assembled with one purpose—to **attack** the town.
20.18 God, "Which tribe should **attack** the Benjaminites first?"
20.20 They went to **attack** the army of Benjamin, and placed the
20.34 of all Israel, **attacked** Gibeah, and the fighting was hard.
1 Sam 4. 2 The Philistines **attacked,** and after fierce fighting they
7. 7 Philistine kings started out with their men to **attack** them.
7.10 the Philistines moved forward to **attack;**
11.11 they rushed into the enemy camp and **attacked** the Ammonites.
12.12 of Ammon was about to **attack** you, you rejected the Lord as
13. 6 Then they launched a strong **attack** against the Israelites,
13.12 'The Philistines are going to **attack** me here in Gilgal, and
14.13 Jonathan **attacked** the Philistines and knocked them down, and
14.22 they also joined in and **attacked** the Philistines,
14.36 "Let's go down and **attack** the Philistines in the night,
14.37 So Saul asked God, "Shall I **attack** the Philistines?
14.48 He saved the Israelites from all **attacks.**
15. 3 Go and **attack** the Amalekites and completely destroy everything
17.35 a lamb, [35]I go after it, **attack** it, and rescue the lamb.
19. 8 David **attacked** them and defeated them so thoroughly that they fled.
23. 1 heard that the Philistines were **attacking** the town of Keilah
23. 2 So he asked the Lord, "Shall I go and **attack** the Philistines?"
23. 2 **"Attack** them and save Keilah."
23. 3 worse if we go to Keilah and **attack** the Philistine forces!"
23. 4 said to him, "Go and **attack** Keilah, because I will give you
23. 5 So David and his men went to Keilah and **attacked** the Philistines;
23. 9 that Saul was planning to **attack** him, he said to the priest
24. 7 So David convinced his men that they should not **attack** Saul.
25.29 If anyone should **attack** you and try to kill you, the
27. 8 David and his men would **attack** the people of Geshur, Girzi,
30. 1 The Amalekites had raided southern Judah and **attacked** Ziklag.
30.17 At dawn the next day David **attacked** them and fought until evening.
2 Sam 5. 6 when King David and his men set out to **attack** Jerusalem.
5. 8 the water tunnel and **attack** those poor blind cripples."
5.19 David asked the Lord, "Shall I **attack** the Philistines?
5.19 "Yes, **attack!"**
5.23 the Lord, who answered, "Don't **attack** them from here, but go
5.23 round and get ready to **attack** them from the other side,
5.24 marching in the tree-tops, then **attack** because I will be
7.10 this land, they have been **attacked** by violent people, but
8. 1 Some time later King David **attacked** the Philistines again,
8. 5 King Hadadezer, David **attacked** it and killed twenty-two thousand men.
10. 9 that the enemy troops would **attack** him in front and from the
10.13 Joab and his men advanced to **attack,** and the Syrians fled.
11.25 to launch a stronger **attack** on the city and capture it."
12.27 "I have **attacked** Rabbah and have captured its water supply.
12.28 rest of your forces, **attack** the city and take it yourself.
12.29 David gathered his forces, went to Rabbah, **attacked** it, and conquered it.
17. 2 I will **attack** him while he is tired and discouraged.
17. 9 As soon as David **attacks** your men, whoever hears about it
17.12 David wherever he is, and **attack** him before he knows what's happening.
21.17 Zeruiah came to David's help, **attacked** the giant, and killed him.
22.19 I was in trouble, they **attacked** me, but the Lord protected me.
22.30 You give me strength to **attack** my enemies and power to
23.21 Benaiah **attacked** him with his club, snatched the spear from
1 Kgs 5. 4 I have no enemies, and there is no danger of **attack.**
8.37 or when your people are **attacked** by their enemies, or when
9.16 (The king of Egypt had **attacked** Gezer and captured it,
12.24 "Do not **attack** your own brothers, the people of Israel.
13.26 Lord sent the lion to **attack** and kill him, just as the
13.28 The lion had not eaten the body or **attacked** the donkey.
14.25 Rehoboam's reign King Shishak of Egypt **attacked** Jerusalem.
15.20 officers and their armies to **attack** the cities of Israel.
20. 1 up, laid siege to Samaria, and launched **attacks** against it.
20.12 men to get ready to **attack** the city, so they moved into
20.14 "Who will lead the **attack?"**
20.16 The **attack** began at noon, as Benhadad and his
20.19 The young soldiers led the **attack,** followed by the Israelite army,
20.22 because the king of Syria will **attack** again next spring."
20.26 with them to the city of Aphek to **attack** the Israelites.
22. 4 And Ahab asked Jehoshaphat, "Will you go with me to **attack** Ramoth?"
22. 6 them, and asked them, "Should I go and **attack** Ramoth, or
22. 6 **"Attack** it," they answered.
1 Kgs 22.15 "Micaiah, should King Jehoshaphat and I go and **attack** Ramoth,
22.15 **"Attack!"**
22.29 Jehoshaphat of Judah went to **attack** the city of Ramoth in Gilead.
22.31 his thirty-two chariot commanders to **attack** no one else
22.32 he was the king of Israel, and they turned to **attack** him.
22.33 was not the king of Israel, and they stopped their **attack.**
2 Kgs 3. 8 What route shall we take for the **attack?"**
3.21 three kings had come to **attack** them, all the men who could
3.24 the camp, the Israelites **attacked** them and drove them back.
3.25 Kir Heres was left, and the slingers surrounded it and **attacked** it.
6.18 When the Syrians **attacked,** Elisha prayed, "O Lord,
7. 6 Hittite and Egyptian kings and their armies to **attack** them.
12.17 time King Hazael of Syria **attacked** the city of Gath and
12.17 then he decided to **attack** Jerusalem.
15.37 King Rezin of Syria and King Pekah of Israel to **attack** Judah.
16. 5 and King Pekah of Israel **attacked** Jerusalem and besieged it,
16. 7 the kings of Syria and of Israel, who are **attacking** me."
18.13 Sennacherib, the emperor of Assyria, **attacked** the fortified
18.14 stop your **attack,** and I will pay whatever you demand."
18.17 a large army from Lachish to **attack** Hezekiah at Jerusalem;
18.25 Do you think I have **attacked** your country and destroyed
18.25 The Lord himself told me to **attack** it and destroy it."
19. 9 led by King Tirhakah of Sudan, was coming to **attack** them.
25. 1 with all his army and **attacked** Jerusalem on the tenth day of
25.25 to Mizpah with ten men, **attacked** Gedaliah and killed him.
1 Chr 5.10 the tribe of Reuben **attacked** the Hagrites, killed them in battle,
11. 4 David and all the Israelites went and **attacked** the city of Jerusalem.
11. 6 Joab, whose mother was Zeruiah, led the **attack** and became commander.
11.23 Benaiah **attacked** him with a club, snatched the spear from
14.10 David asked God, "Shall I **attack** the Philistines?
14.10 The Lord answered, "Yes, **attack!**
14.11 So David **attacked** them at Baal Perazim and defeated them.
14.14 God, who answered, "Don't **attack** them from here, but go round
14.14 and get ready to **attack** them from the other side,
14.15 marching in the tree-tops, then **attack,** because I will be
17. 9 this land they have been **attacked** by violent people, but
18. 1 Some time later King David **attacked** the Philistines again and defeated them.
18. 3 Next, David **attacked** King Hadadezer of the Syrian state of Zobah,
18. 5 King Hadadezer, David **attacked** it and killed twenty-two thousand men.
19.10 that the enemy troops would **attack** him in front and from the
19.14 Joab and his men advanced to **attack,** and the Syrians fled.
20. 1 They besieged the city of Rabbah, **attacked** it, and destroyed it.
21.12 days during which the Lord **attacks** you with his sword and
2 Chr 6.28 or when your people are **attacked** by their enemies, or when
11. 4 "Do not **attack** your fellow-Israelites.
12. 2 King Shishak of Egypt **attacked** Jerusalem [3]with an army of
12. 7 But when Shishak **attacks,** they will barely survive.
13.15 The Judaeans gave a loud shout, and led by Abijah, they **attacked;**
14.12 Sudanese army when Asa and the Judaean army **attacked** them.
14.15 They also **attacked** the camps of some shepherds,
16. 4 officers and their armies to **attack** the cities of Israel.
18. 2 Jehoshaphat to join him in **attacking** the city of Ramoth in Gilead.
18. 3 He asked, "Will you go with me to **attack** Ramoth?"
18. 5 them, and asked them, "Should I go and **attack** Ramoth, or
18. 5 **"Attack** it," they answered.
18.14 "Micaiah, should King Jehoshaphat and I go and **attack** Ramoth,
18.14 **"Attack!"**
18.28 Jehoshaphat of Judah went to **attack** the city of Ramoth in Gilead.
18.30 ordered his chariot commanders to **attack** no one else except
18.31 he was the king of Israel, and they turned to **attack** him.
18.31 Lord God rescued him and turned the **attack** away from him.
20. 2 come from the other side of the Dead Sea to **attack** you.
20.10 "Now the people of Ammon, Moab, and Edom have **attacked** us.
20.12 in the face of this large army that is **attacking** us.
20.16 **Attack** them tomorrow as they come up the pass at Ziz.
20.23 The Ammonites and the Moabites **attacked** the Edomite army
24.23 that year, the Syrian army **attacked** Judah and Jerusalem,
25.13 go into battle with him **attacked** the Judaean cities between
32. 2 saw that Sennacherib intended to **attack** Jerusalem also,
36.17 So the Lord brought the king of Babylonia to **attack** them.
Ezra 8.31 us from enemy **attacks** and from ambush as we travelled.
Neh 4. 8 together to come and **attack** Jerusalem and create confusion,
Esth 8.11 any nationality in any province **attacked** the Jewish men,
8.11 women, the Jews could fight back and destroy the **attackers;**
9. 2 Jews organized themselves to **attack** anyone who tried to harm them.
9. 5 They **attacked** them with swords and slaughtered them.
Job 1.15 Suddenly the Sabeans **attacked** and stole them all.
1.17 "Three bands of Chaldean raiders **attacked** us, took away the camels,
2. 3 persuaded me to let you **attack** him for no reason at all,
5.23 wild animals will never **attack** you.
10.17 you always plan some new **attack.**
13.25 you are **attacking** a piece of dry straw.
15.21 in his ears, and robbers **attack** when he thinks he is safe.
15.24 disaster, like a powerful king, is waiting to **attack** him.
16.14 he **attacks** like a soldier gone mad with hate.
19.12 He sends his army to **attack** me;
19.28 You looked for some excuse to **attack** me.
30.12 This mob **attacks** me head-on;
30.24 Why do you **attack** a ruined man, one who can do nothing
33.10 But God finds excuses for **attacking** me and treats me
41.11 Who can **attack** him and still be safe?
Ps 17. 9 the shadow of your wings [9]from the **attacks** of the wicked.
18.18 I was in trouble, they **attacked** me, but the Lord protected me.
18.29 You give me strength to **attack** my enemies and power to

Ps 27. 2 When evil men **attack** me and try to kill me, they stumble
27. 3 even if enemies **attack** me, I will still trust God.
27.12 me to my enemies, who **attack** me with lies and threats.
31.21 showed his love for me when I was surrounded and **attacked!**
35.17 Rescue me from their **attacks;**
36.11 Do not let proud men **attack** me or wicked men make me
48. 4 The kings gathered together and came to **attack** Mount Zion.
54. 3 Proud men are coming to **attack** me;
55.20 My former companion **attacked** his friends;
56. 1 Be merciful to me, O God, because I am under **attack;**
56. 2 All day long my opponents **attack** me.
59. 1 protect me from those who **attack** me!
62. 3 longer will all of you **attack** a man who is no stronger
71.13 May those who **attack** me be defeated and destroyed.
78.21 he **attacked** his people with fire, and his anger against them grew,
81. 5 to the people of Israel when he **attacked** the land of Egypt.
88.16 your terrible **attacks** destroy me.
91. 5 dangers at night or sudden **attacks** during the day [6] or the
109. 2 Wicked men and liars have **attacked** me.
109. 3 and they say evil things about me, **attacking** me for no reason.
118.13 I was fiercely **attacked** and was being defeated, but the
119.161 Powerful men **attack** me unjustly, but I respect your law.
124. 2 our side when our enemies **attacked** us, [3] then they would
Prov 1.11 Let's **attack** some innocent people for the fun of it!
6.11 But while he sleeps, poverty will **attack** him like an armed robber.
24.34 are asleep, poverty will **attack** you like an armed robber.
25.28 are as helpless as a city without walls, open to **attack.**
Ecc 4.12 Two men can resist an **attack** that would defeat one man alone.
9.14 A powerful king **attacked** it.
Song 3. 8 is armed with a sword, on guard against a night **attack.**
Is 7. 1 of Remaliah, king of Israel, **attacked** Jerusalem, but were
8. 7 the emperor of Assyria and all his forces to **attack** Judah.
9.11 The Lord has stirred up their enemies to **attack** them.
9.21 and the people of Ephraim **attack** each other,
9.21 and together they **attack** Judah.
10. 6 I sent Assyria to **attack** a godless nation, people who have
11.14 Together they will **attack** the Philistines on the west
13. 2 the signal for them to **attack** the gates of the proud city.
13.17 The Lord says, "I am stirring up the Medes to **attack** Babylon.
14.22 Lord Almighty says, "I will **attack** Babylon and bring it to ruin.
20. 1 of the Assyrian army **attacked** the Philistine city of Ashdod.
21. 2 Army of Elam, **attack!**
25. 4 Cruel men **attack** like a winter storm, [5] like drought in a
28. 2 strong and powerful ready to **attack** them, someone who will
28. 6 and courage to those who defend the city gates from **attack.**
29. 3 God will **attack** the city, surround it, and besiege it.
29. 5 Jerusalem, all the foreigners who **attack** you will be blown
29. 7 the armies of the nations **attacking** the city of God's altar,
29. 8 the nations that assemble to **attack** Jerusalem will be like a
36. 1 Sennacherib, the emperor of Assyria, **attacked** the fortified
36.10 Do you think I have **attacked** your country and destroyed
36.10 The Lord himself told me to **attack** it and destroy it."
37. 9 led by King Tirhakah of Sudan, was coming to **attack** them.
41.25 I will bring him to **attack** from the north.
48.14 predict that the man I have chosen would **attack** Babylon;
54.15 If anyone **attacks** you, he does it without my consent;
Jer 5.15 Israel, the Lord is bringing a nation from afar to **attack** you.
6. 4 They will say, "Prepare to **attack** Jerusalem!
6. 4 We'll **attack** at noon!"
6. 5 We'll **attack** by night;
6.26 the one who comes to destroy you will suddenly **attack.**
12. 6 they join in the **attacks** against you.
12. 9 people are like a bird **attacked** from all sides by hawks.
21. 9 Babylonians, who are now **attacking** the city, will not be killed;
21.13 that no one can **attack** you or break through your defences.
30.14 I have **attacked** you like an enemy;
32. 2 the king of Babylonia was **attacking** Jerusalem, and I was
32.24 mounds round the city to capture it, and they are **attacking.**
33. 4 be torn down as a result of the siege and the **attack.**
34. 1 to him, were **attacking** Jerusalem and its nearby towns.
34. 7 while the army of the king of Babylonia was **attacking** the city.
34. 7 The army was also **attacking** Lachish and Azekah, the only
34.21 Babylonian army, which has stopped its **attack** against you.
34.22 They will **attack** it, capture it, and burn it down.
37. 8 the Babylonians will come back, **attack** the city, capture it,
37.19 the king of Babylonia would not **attack** you or the country?
39. 1 King Nebuchadnezzar of Babylonia came with his whole army and **attacked** Jerusalem.
41. 9 had dug when he was being **attacked** by King Baasha of Israel.
46.13 Nebuchadnezzar of Babylonia came to **attack** Egypt,
46.18 sea, so will be the strength of the one who **attacks** you.
46.20 is like a splendid cow, **attacked** by a stinging fly from the
46.22 They **attack** her with axes, like men cutting down trees
47. 1 Before the king of Egypt **attacked** Gaza, the Lord spoke to
47. 7 I have commanded it to **attack** Ashkelon and the people who
49. 4 in your power and say that no one would dare **attack** you?
49.14 to assemble their armies and to get ready to **attack** you.
49.22 The enemy will **attack** Bozrah like an eagle swooping down
49.28 "**Attack** the people of Kedar and destroy that tribe of eastern people!
49.31 We'll **attack** those people that feel safe and secure!
50. 3 the north has come to **attack** Babylonia and will make it a
50. 7 They are **attacked** by all who find them.
50. 9 strong nations in the north and make them **attack** Babylonia.
50.16 be afraid of the **attacking** army and will go back home."
50.17 First, they were **attacked** by the emperor of Assyria, and
50.21 The Lord says, "**Attack** the people of Merathaim and of Pekod.
50.26 **Attack** it from every side and break open the places
50.29 "Tell the bowmen to **attack** Babylon.
51. 2 of destruction comes, they will **attack** from every side and
51.11 The **attacking** officers command, "Sharpen your arrows!

Jer 51.12 Give the signal to **attack** Babylon's walls.
51.14 bring many men to **attack** Babylonia like a swarm of locusts,
51.27 "Give the signal to **attack!**
51.27 Tell the kingdoms of Ararat, Minni, and Ashkenaz to **attack.**
51.27 Appoint an officer to lead the **attack.**
51.55 The armies rush in like roaring waves and **attack** with noisy shouts.
52. 4 with all his army and **attacked** Jerusalem on the tenth day of
Ezek 11. 8 I will bring men with swords to **attack** you.
23.24 They will **attack** you from the north, bringing a large
23.47 stone them and **attack** them with swords, kill their children,
25. 9 the border of Moab be **attacked,** including even the finest
25.16 that I will **attack** the Philistines and wipe them out.
26. 3 will bring many nations to **attack** you, and they will come
26. 7 king of all—King Nebuchadnezzar of Babylonia—to **attack** Tyre.
28. 7 as a god, [7] I will bring ruthless enemies to **attack** you.
28.23 You will be **attacked** from every side, and your people will
29. 8 I will get men to **attack** you with swords, and they will
29.18 "King Nebuchadnezzar of Babylonia launched an **attack** on Tyre.
30.11 They will **attack** Egypt with swords, and the land will be
34. 8 My sheep have been **attacked** by wild animals that killed and
38. 9 many nations with him will **attack** like a storm and cover the
38.13 your army and **attacked** in order to loot and plunder?
38.16 You will **attack** my people Israel like a storm moving
38.17 in days to come I would bring someone to **attack** Israel."
Dan 1. 1 King Nebuchadnezzar of Babylonia **attacked** Jerusalem and surrounded the city.
8. 7 I watched him **attack** the ram.
8.10 It grew strong enough to **attack** the army of heaven, the
11. 7 He will **attack** the army of the king of Syria, enter their
11.10 will sweep on like a flood and **attack** an enemy fortress.
11.18 After that he will **attack** the nations by the sea and
11.24 He will make plans to **attack** fortresses, but his time will
11.25 raise a large army to **attack** the king of Egypt, who will
11.40 the king of Egypt will **attack** him, and the king of Syria
Hos 5.14 I will **attack** the people of Israel and Judah like a lion.
10.10 I will **attack** this sinful people and punish them.
13. 7 So I will **attack** you like a lion.
13. 8 I will **attack** you like a bear that has lost her cubs,
Joel 1. 6 An army of locusts has **attacked** our land;
2. 7 They **attack** like warriors;
3.11 Send down, O Lord, your army to **attack** them.
3.19 a ruined waste, because they **attacked** the land of Judah and
Obad 21 The victorious men of Jerusalem will **attack** Edom and rule over it.
Jon 4. 7 day, at God's command, a worm **attacked** the plant, and it
Mic 2. 8 The Lord replies, "You **attack** my people like enemies.
4.11 Many nations have gathered to **attack** you.
5. 1 They are **attacking** the leader of Israel!
Nah 2. 1 Nineveh, you are under **attack!**
2. 3 They are preparing to **attack!**
2. 5 The **attackers** rush to the wall and set up the shield for
Hab 1. 8 They come swooping down like eagles **attacking** their prey.
3.16 the time to come when God will punish those who **attack** us.
Zeph 1.16 of soldiers **attacking** fortified cities and high towers.
Zech 12. 3 All the nations of the world will join forces to **attack** her.
12. 9 I will destroy every nation that tries to **attack** Jerusalem.
13. 7 "Wake up, sword, and **attack** the shepherd who works for me!
13. 7 I will **attack** my people [8] and throughout the land two-thirds
14.13 that everyone will seize the man next to him and **attack** him.
14.16 from the nations that have **attacked** Jerusalem will go there
Mt 7. 6 what is holy to dogs—they will only turn and **attack** you.
11.12 heaven has suffered violent **attacks,** and violent men try to seize
24. 7 will fight each other, kingdoms will **attack** one another.
Mk 9.18 Whenever the spirit **attacks** him, it throws him to the ground,
13. 8 kingdoms will **attack** one another.
Lk 9.39 A spirit **attacks** him with a sudden shout and throws him
10.30 Jerusalem to Jericho when robbers **attacked** him, stripped him,
10.36 acted like a neighbour towards the man **attacked** by the robbers?"
11.22 But when a stronger man **attacks** him and defeats him,
21.10 kingdoms will **attack** one another.
Acts 16.22 And the crowd joined in the **attack** against Paul and Silas.
17. 5 city in an uproar and **attacked** the home of a man called
19.16 the evil spirit in him **attacked** them with such violence
2 Cor 6. 7 have righteousness as our weapon, both to **attack** and to defend
Eph 6.13 day comes, you will be able to resist the enemy's **attacks;**
2 Pet 2.12 they **attack** with insults anything they do not understand.
Jude 10 these people **attack** with insults anything they do not understand;
Rev 12.14 for three and a half years, safe from the dragon's **attack.**

ATTEMPT

Ezek 13.20 that you use in your **attempt** to control life and death.
Acts 17. 5 man called Jason, in an **attempt** to find Paul and Silas

ATTEND

Dan 3. 2 They were to **attend** the dedication of the statue which King

ATTENDANT

1 Sam 16.18 One of his **attendants** said, "Jesse, of the town of Bethlehem,
1 Kgs 10. 2 her a large group of **attendants,** as well as camels loaded
10.13 Then she and her **attendants** returned to the land of Sheba.
2 Kgs 7. 2 The personal **attendant** of the king said to Elisha, "That
7.17 the command of the officer who was his personal **attendant.**
20. 7 Then Isaiah told the king's **attendants** to put on his boil
22.12 Micaiah, to Shaphan, the court secretary, and to Asaiah, the king's **attendant:**
2 Chr 9. 1 her a large group of **attendants,** as well as camels loaded
9.12 Then she and her **attendants** returned to the land of Sheba.

2 Chr 34.20 Micaiah, to Shaphan, the court secretary, and to Asaiah, the king's **attendant:**
Jer 51.59 King Zedekiah's personal **attendant** was Seraiah, the son
Zech 3. 4 angel said to his heavenly **attendants,** "Take away the
3. 5 He commanded the **attendants** to put a clean turban on Joshua's head.
Lk 4.20 up the scroll, gave it back to the **attendant,** and sat down.
Acts 10. 7 a soldier, a religious man who was one of his personal **attendants.**

ATTENTION

Ex 7.23 to his palace without paying any **attention** even to this.
9.21 Others, however, paid no **attention** to the Lord's warning
23.21 Pay **attention** to him and obey him.
Lev 4.23 then as soon as his **attention** is called to the sin, he
4.28 then as soon as his **attention** is called to the sin, he
Deut 1.43 told you what the Lord had said, but you paid no **attention.**
1.45 he would not listen to you or pay any **attention** to you.
9.27 and do not pay any **attention** to the stubbornness,
13. 3 he promises comes true, [3]do not pay any **attention** to him.
27. 9 of Israel, "Give me your **attention,** people of Israel, and
Judg 2.17 But the Israelites paid no **attention** to their leaders.
5. 3 Pay **attention,** you rulers!
11.28 of Ammon paid no **attention** to this message from Jephthah.
14. 2 Philistine girl down at Timnah who has caught my **attention.**
20.13 But the people of Benjamin paid no **attention** to the other Israelites.
1 Sam 2.12 They paid no **attention** to the Lord [13]or to the regulations
4.20 But she paid no **attention** and did not answer.
8.19 The people paid no **attention** to Samuel, but said "No!
16. 7 said to him, "Pay no **attention** to how tall and handsome he
25.25 Please, don't pay any **attention** to Nabal, that good-for-nothing!
1 Kgs 12.15 is why the king did not pay any **attention** to the people.
20. 8 The leaders and the people answered, "Don't pay any **attention** to him;
2 Chr 10.15 is why the king did not pay any **attention** to the people.
Neh 8. 3 Law to them from dawn until noon, and they all listened **attentively.**
Job 7.17 Why pay **attention** to what he does?
30.20 and when I pray, you pay no **attention.**
32.12 I paid close **attention** and heard you fail;
33.14 again and again, no one pays **attention** to what he says.
35.15 God does not punish, that he pays little **attention** to sin.
Ps 17. 1 pay **attention** to my cry for help!
49. 4 I will turn my **attention** to proverbs and explain their
78. 1 my people, to my teaching, and pay **attention** to what I say.
86.14 trying to kill me— people who pay no **attention** to you.
119. 6 If I pay **attention** to all your commands, then I will not
119.30 I have paid **attention** to your judgements.
119.37 Keep me from paying **attention** to what is worthless;
119.117 be safe, and I will always pay **attention** to your commands.
144. 3 mere man, that you pay **attention** to him?
Prov 1. 8 Pay **attention** to what your father and mother tell you, my
1.24 You paid no **attention** to me.
1.30 wanted my advice or paid any **attention** when I corrected you.
3.11 you, my son, pay close **attention** and take it as a warning.
4. 1 Pay **attention,** and you will have understanding.
4.20 Pay **attention** to what I say, my son.
5. 1 Pay **attention,** my son, and listen to my wisdom and insight.
5.13 I paid no **attention** to them.
7.24 Pay **attention** to what I say.
13. 1 A wise son pays **attention** when his father corrects him,
15.31 If you pay **attention** when you are corrected, you are
16.20 Pay **attention** to what you are taught, and you will be successful;
23.12 Pay **attention** to your teacher and learn all you can.
23.26 Pay close **attention,** son, and let my life be your example.
29.12 If a ruler pays **attention** to false information, all his
29.19 He may understand you, but he will pay no **attention.**
Ecc 7.21 Don't pay **attention** to everything people say—you may
9.16 poor man as wise or pays any **attention** to what he says.
Is 1.10 Pay **attention** to what our God is teaching you.
22.11 But you paid no **attention** to God, who planned all this long
28.23 pay **attention** to what I am telling you.
58. 3 Why should we go without food if he pays no **attention?"**
Jer 5. 3 He struck you, but you paid no **attention;**
5.21 Pay **attention,** you foolish and stupid people, who have
7.24 But they did not obey or pay any **attention.**
7.26 Yet no one listened or paid any **attention.**
9.20 "Listen to the Lord, you women, and pay **attention** to his words.
17.23 Their ancestors did not listen to me or pay any **attention.**
23.18 message, or ever listened or paid **attention** to what he said.
25. 3 But you have paid no **attention.**
25. 4 would not listen or pay **attention,** even though the Lord has
26. 5 you, [5]and by paying **attention** to the words of my servants,
27.22 Babylonia and will remain there until I turn my **attention** to them.
29. 8 Do not pay any **attention** to their dreams.
34.14 ancestors would not pay any **attention** to me or listen to
35.15 But you would not listen to me or pay **attention** to me.
36.25 king not to burn the scroll, he paid no **attention** to them.
36.31 of Judah have paid any **attention** to my warnings, and so I
38.15 and if I give you advice, you won't pay any **attention."**
44. 5 But you would not listen or pay any **attention.**
Ezek 3.10 "Mortal man, pay close **attention** and remember everything I tell you.
3.11 saying to them, whether they pay **attention** to you or not."
33. 4 hears it but pays no **attention** and the enemy comes and kills
33. 5 his own fault, because he paid no **attention** to the warning.
33. 5 If he had paid **attention,** he could have escaped.
40. 4 Listen carefully and pay close **attention** to everything I show you,
44. 5 "Mortal man, pay **attention** to everything you see and hear.
Dan 9.23 Now pay **attention** while I explain the vision.
Hos 5. 1 Pay **attention,** people of Israel!
Joel 1. 2 Pay **attention,** you older people;
Mt 7. 3 brother's eye, and pay no **attention** to the log in your own
22. 5 invited guests paid no **attention** and went about their business:
22.16 people think, because you pay no **attention** to a man's status.
24. 1 disciples came to him to call his **attention** to its buildings.
Mk 4.24 He also said to them, "Pay **attention** to what you hear!
5.36 Jesus paid no **attention** to what they said, but told him,
12.14 You pay no **attention** to a man's status, but teach the truth
Lk 6.41 brother's eye, but pay no **attention** to the log in your own
20.21 know that you pay no **attention** to a man's status, but teach
Acts 8. 6 The crowds paid close **attention** to what Philip said,
8.10 from all classes of society, paid close **attention** to him.
8.11 They paid this **attention** to him because for such a long
16.14 Lord opened her mind to pay **attention** to what Paul was saying.
Rom 13.14 and stop paying **attention** to your sinful nature and satisfying
1 Cor 14.38 if he does not pay **attention** to this,
14.38 pay no **attention** to him.
2 Cor 4.18 For we fix our **attention,** not on things that are seen,
Gal 4.10 You pay special **attention** to certain days, months, seasons,
Phil 3.17 Pay **attention** to those who follow the right example that we
2 Tim 4. 4 from listening to the truth and give their **attention** to legends.
Heb 2. 3 we escape if we pay no **attention** to such a great salvation?
8. 9 I made with them, and so I paid no **attention** to them.
12. 5 "My son, pay **attention** when the Lord corrects you, and do
Jas 1.25 who keeps on paying **attention** to it and does not simply
2 Pet 1.19 will do well to pay **attention** to it, because it is like
3 Jn 9 be their leader, will not pay any **attention** to what I say.
10 I come, then, I will call **attention** to everything he has done:

ATTITUDE

Num 14.24 Caleb has a different **attitude** and has remained loyal to me,
1 Sam 20.12 If his **attitude** towards you is good, I will send you word.
Gal 4.20 so that I could take a different **attitude** towards you.
Phil 2. 5 The **attitude** you should have is the one that Christ Jesus had:
3.15 of us who are spiritually mature should have this same **attitude.**
3.15 of you have a different **attitude,** God will make this clear
4. 5 Show a gentle **attitude** towards everyone.
Tit 3. 2 friendly, and always to show a gentle **attitude** towards everyone.
1 Pet 3. 8 you must all have the same **attitude** and the same feelings;

ATTRACT

Gen 34. 3 he found the girl so **attractive** that he fell in love with
Judg 11. 3 There he **attracted** a group of worthless men, and they went
1 Sam 18. 1 Saul's son Jonathan was deeply **attracted** to David and came
Job 31. 7 path or let myself be **attracted** to evil, if my hands are
31. 9 If I have been **attracted** to my neighbour's wife, and
Prov 15. 2 knowledge **attractive,** but stupid people spout nonsense.
Is 53. 2 There was nothing **attractive** about him, nothing that would
Ezek 23.14 She was **attracted** by the images of high Babylonian officials
Nah 3. 4 **Attractive** and full of deadly charms, she enchanted nations and enslaved them.

AUDIENCE HALL

Acts 25.23 ceremony and entered the **audience hall** with the military chiefs

AUNT

Lev 18.12 not have intercourse with an **aunt,** whether she is your
18.14 she, too, is your **aunt.**
20.19 man has intercourse with his **aunt,** both of them must suffer
2 Kgs 11. 2 but was rescued by his **aunt** Jehosheba, who was King

AUTHORITIES

Jer 20.10 So let's report him to the **authorities!"**
Mt 27.18 very well that the Jewish **authorities** had handed Jesus over to
Jn 1.19 Jewish **authorities** in Jerusalem sent some priests and Levites
2.18 Jewish **authorities** replied with a question, "What miracle can
5.10 so the Jewish **authorities** told the man who had been
5.15 and told the Jewish **authorities** that it was Jesus who had
5.18 made the Jewish **authorities** all the more determined to kill
7. 1 because the Jewish **authorities** there were wanting to kill him.
7.11 The Jewish **authorities** were looking for him at the festival.
7.13 openly, because they were afraid of the Jewish **authorities.**
7.15 The Jewish **authorities** were greatly surprised and said,
7.25 "Isn't this the man the **authorities** are trying to kill?
7.35 Jewish **authorities** said among themselves, "Where is he about to
7.48 ever known one of the **authorities** or one Pharisee to believe
8.22 So the Jewish **authorities** said, "He says that we cannot go
9.18 The Jewish **authorities,** however, were not willing to believe
9.22 afraid of the Jewish **authorities,** who had already agreed that
11.48 and the Roman **authorities** will take action and destroy
11.53 that day on the Jewish **authorities** made plans to kill Jesus.
12.42 Even then, many of the Jewish **authorities** believed in Jesus;
13.33 what I told the Jewish **authorities,** 'You cannot go where I
18.14 had advised the Jewish **authorities** that it was better that one
18.28 The Jewish **authorities** did not go inside the palace,
18.36 to keep me from being handed over to the Jewish **authorities.**
19.31 the Jewish **authorities** asked Pilate to allow them to break
19.38 but in secret, because he was afraid of the Jewish **authorities.)**
20.19 locked doors, because they were afraid of the Jewish **authorities.**
Acts 3.13 handed him over to the **authorities,** and you rejected him
16.19 and dragged them to the **authorities** in the public square.
16.35 The next morning the Roman **authorities** sent police officers
17. 6 believers before the city **authorities** and shouted, "These men
17. 8 they threw the crowd and the city **authorities** into an uproar.
17. 9 **authorities** made Jason and the others pay the required amount

Acts 19.31 of the provincial **authorities,** who were his friends, also sent
19.38 we have the **authorities** and the regular days for court;
23.20 said, "The Jewish **authorities** have agreed to ask you tomorrow
Rom 13. 1 Everyone must obey the state **authorities,**
13. 1 and the existing **authorities** have been put there by God.
13. 5 must obey the **authorities**—not just because of God's punishment,
13. 6 you pay taxes, because the **authorities** are working for God when
1 Cor 15.24 will overcome all spiritual rulers, **authorities,** and powers,
Eph 1.21 Christ rules there above all heavenly rulers, **authorities,**
6.12 the heavenly world, the rulers, **authorities,** and cosmic powers
Col 1.16 including spiritual powers, lords, rulers, and **authorities.**
2.15 himself from the power of the spiritual rulers and **authorities;**
Tit 3. 1 to submit to rulers and **authorities,** to obey them,
1 Pet 3.22 ruling over all angels and heavenly **authorities** and powers.

AUTHORITY

Gen 39. 9 I have as much **authority** in this house as he has, and
41.35 are coming, and give them **authority** to store up corn in the
41.40 Your **authority** will be second only to mine.
Num 27.20 him some of your own **authority,** so that the whole community
Deut 18.22 has spoken on his own **authority,** and you are not to fear
Josh 1.18 Whoever questions your **authority** or disobeys any of your
2 Chr 12. 1 as Rehoboam had established his **authority** as king, he and
13. 8 to fight against the royal **authority** that the Lord gave to
19. 6 are not acting on human **authority,**
19. 6 but on the **authority** of the Lord, and he is
19.11 High Priest will have final **authority** in all religious cases,
19.11 Ishmael, governor of Judah, will have final **authority** in all civil cases.
31.13 this was done under the **authority** of King Hezekiah and
Ezra 4.19 Jerusalem has revolted against royal **authority** and that it
5. 9 us who had given them **authority** to rebuild the Temple and to
Esth 1.22 be the master of his home and speak with final **authority.**
9.29 putting her full **authority** behind the letter about Purim,
Ps 105.22 with power over the king's officials and **authority** to instruct his advisers.
Prov 16.10 The king speaks with divine **authority;**
17. 2 A shrewd servant will gain **authority** over a master's
28. 3 A man in **authority** who oppresses poor people is like a
Ecc 8. 4 The king acts with **authority,** and no one can challenge
10. 6 Stupid people are given positions of **authority** while rich men are ignored.
Is 22.21 belt on him and give him all the **authority** you have had.
22.22 I will give him complete **authority** under the king, the
Jer 1.10 Today I give you **authority** over nations and kingdoms to
2.20 "Israel, long ago you rejected my **authority;**
5. 5 have rejected the Lord's **authority** and refuse to obey him.
Dan 7. 6 It had a look of **authority** about it.
7.14 He was given **authority,** honour, and royal power, so that
7.14 His **authority** would last for ever, and his kingdom would never end.
Mt 7.29 instead, he taught with **authority.**
8. 9 am a man under the **authority** of superior officers,
9. 6 the Son of Man has **authority** on earth to forgive sins."
9. 8 were afraid, and praised God for giving such **authority** to men.
10. 1 disciples together and gave them **authority** to drive out evil
20.25 have power over them, and the leaders have complete **authority.**
28.18 "I have been given all **authority** in heaven and on earth.
Mk 1.22 instead, he taught with **authority.**
1.27 This man has **authority** to give orders to the evil spirits,
2.10 the Son of Man has **authority** on earth to forgive sins."
3.15 and you will have **authority** to drive out demons."
6. 7 He gave them **authority** over the evil spirits [8] and ordered them,
10.42 have power over them, and the leaders have complete **authority.**
Lk 4.32 at the way he taught, because he spoke with **authority.**
4.36 With **authority** and power this man gives orders to the evil
5.24 the Son of Man has **authority** on earth to forgive sins."
7. 8 a man placed under the **authority** of superior officers,
9. 1 and gave them power and **authority** to drive out all demons
10.19 I have given you **authority,** so that you can walk on snakes
12. 5 God, who, after killing, has the **authority** to throw into hell.
20.20 him over to the **authority** and power of the Roman Governor.
Jn 5.30 "I can do nothing on my own **authority;**
5.43 come with my Father's **authority,** but you have not received me;
5.43 someone comes with his own **authority,** you will receive him.
7.17 comes from God or whether I speak on my own **authority.**
7.18 who speaks on his own **authority** is trying to gain glory
7.28 I have not come on my own **authority.**
8.28 do nothing on my own **authority,** but I say only what
8.42 I did not come on my own **authority,** but he sent me.
10.25 The things I do by my Father's **authority** speak on my behalf;
12.49 not spoken on my own **authority,** but the Father who sent me
16.13 not speak on his own **authority,** but he will speak of what
17. 2 For you gave him **authority** over all mankind, so that he
19.10 Remember, I have the **authority** to set you free and also to
19.11 answered, "You have **authority** over me only because it was given
Acts 1. 7 set by my Father's own **authority,** and it is not for you
2.22 was a man whose divine **authority** was clearly proven to you
9.14 come to Damascus with **authority** from the chief priests to arrest
26.10 I received **authority** from the chief priests and put many of
26.12 went to Damascus with **authority** and orders from the chief priests.
Rom 12. 8 whoever has **authority** should work hard;
13. 1 because no **authority** exists without God's permission,
13. 2 Whoever opposes the existing **authority** opposes what God has
13. 3 Would you like to be unafraid of the man in **authority?**
1 Cor 1.10 By the **authority** of our Lord Jesus Christ I appeal to
11.10 her head to show that she is under her husband's **authority.**
2 Cor 10. 8 somewhat too much about the **authority** that the Lord has
10. 8 **authority** to build you up, not to
2 Cor 13.10 with you in using the **authority** that the Lord has given me
13.10 **authority** to build you up, not to
Eph 1.21 superior to all titles of **authority** in this world and in the
5.23 For a husband has **authority** over his wife
5.23 just as Christ has **authority** over the church;
Col 2.10 He is supreme over every spiritual ruler and **authority.**
1 Thes 4. 2 instructions we gave you by the **authority** of the Lord Jesus.
5.27 I urge you by the **authority** of the Lord to read this
1 Tim 2. 2 all others who are in **authority,** that we may live a quiet
2.12 do not allow them to teach or to have **authority** over men;
Tit 2.15 and use your full **authority** as you encourage and rebuke your
1 Pet 2.13 For the sake of the Lord submit to every human **authority:**
2.13 Emperor, who is the supreme **authority,** [14] and to the governors,
2 Pet 2.10 who follow their filthy bodily lusts and despise God's **authority.**
Jude 6 the limits of their proper **authority,** but abandoned their own
8 they despise God's **authority** and insult the glorious beings
25 be glory, majesty, might, and **authority,** from all ages past,
Rev 1.18 I have **authority** over death and the world of the dead.
2.26 I will give the same **authority** that I received from my Father:
2.26 I will give them **authority** over the nations, to rule them
6. 8 They were given **authority** over a quarter of the earth,
11. 6 They have **authority** to shut up the sky so that there will
11. 6 They have **authority** also over the springs of water,
11. 6 they have **authority** also to strike the earth with every kind
12.10 Now his Messiah has shown his **authority!**
13. 2 the beast his own power, his throne, and his vast **authority.**
13. 4 worshipped the dragon because he had given his **authority** to the
13. 5 and it was permitted to have **authority** for forty-two months.
13. 7 and it was given **authority** over every tribe, nation, language,
13.12 It used the vast **authority** of the first beast in its presence.
16. 9 cursed the name of God, who has **authority** over these plagues.
17.12 but who will be given **authority** to rule as kings for one
17.13 and they give their power and **authority** to the beast.
18. 1 He had great **authority,** and his splendour brightened the whole

AV AUTHORITY

Prov 29. 2 Show me a righteous **ruler** and I will show you a happy
Mt 21.23 to him and asked, "What **right** have you to do these things?
21.23 Who gave you this **right?"**
21.24 I will tell you what **right** I have to do these things.
21.27 will I tell you, then, by what **right** I do these things.
Mk 11.28 and asked him, "What **right** have you to do these things?
11.28 Who gave you this **right?"**
11.29 I will tell you what **right** I have to do these things.
11.33 will I tell you, then, by what **right** I do these things."
13.34 and leaves his servants in **charge,** after giving to each one
Lk 19.17 in small matters, I will put you in **charge** of ten cities.'
20. 2 to him, "Tell us, what **right** have you to do these things?
20. 2 Who gave you this **right?"**
20. 8 will I tell you, then, by what **right** I do these things."
22.25 over their people, and the **rulers** claim the title 'Friends
Jn 5.27 has given the Son the **right** to judge, because he is the
Acts 8.27 eunuch, who was an **important** official in charge of the treasury

AUTHORIZED INTERPRETERS

Mt 23. 2 and the Pharisees are the **authorized interpreters** of Moses' Law.

AUTUMN

Ex 23.16 Festival of Shelters in the **autumn,** when you gather the
34.22 Festival of Shelters in the **autumn** when you gather your fruit.
Deut 11.14 it is needed, in the **autumn** and in the spring, so that
2 Sam 21.10 from the beginning of harvest until the **autumn** rains came.
2 Chr 24.23 When **autumn** came that year, the Syrian army attacked Judah and Jerusalem,
Ps 84. 6 the **autumn** rain fills it with pools.
Prov 11.28 fall like the leaves of **autumn,** but the righteous will
Jer 5.24 even though I send the **autumn** rains and the spring rains and
Joel 2.23 He has given you the right amount of **autumn** rain;
Jas 5. 7 He waits patiently for the **autumn** and spring rains.
Jude 12 bear no fruit, even in **autumn,** trees that have been pulled

AVAILABLE

2 Chr 23. 8 Sabbath, so the commanders had **available** both those coming
35. 5 some of you will be **available** to help each family of the
Jer 2.24 she is always **available** at mating time.

AVENGE

2 Sam 14.11 relative who is responsible for **avenging** the death of my son
2 Chr 24.25 him in his bed to **avenge** the murder of the son of
Is 59.17 and to punish and **avenge** the wrongs that people suffer.
Joel 3.20 I will **avenge** those who were killed;

AVOID

Deut 23. 9 of war, you are to **avoid** anything that would make you
2 Sam 14.19 Your Majesty, that there is no way to **avoid** answering your question.
Job 13.24 Why do you **avoid** me?
24.16 into houses, but by day they hide and **avoid** the light.
Ps 26. 5 I hate the company of evil men and **avoid** the wicked.
119.101 I have **avoided** all evil conduct, because I want to
Prov 4.27 **Avoid** evil and walk straight ahead.
14.27 Do you want to **avoid** death?
16.17 Those who are good travel a road that **avoids** evil;
22. 3 will see trouble coming and **avoid** it, but an unthinking
23.29 bloodshot, and he has bruises that could have been **avoided.**

Prov	27.12	will see trouble coming and **avoid** it, but an unthinking
Ecc	7.18	**Avoid** both extremes.
Hos	7. 2	their sins surround them, and I cannot **avoid** seeing them."
Amos	3. 8	When a lion roars, who can **avoid** being afraid?
	3. 8	When the Sovereign Lord speaks, who can **avoid** proclaiming his message?
Acts	27.21	then we would have **avoided** all this damage and loss.
1 Cor	5.10	To **avoid** them you would have to get out of the world
	6.18	**Avoid** immorality.
1 Thes	5.22	keep what is good [22] and **avoid** every kind of evil.
1 Tim	6.11	But you, man of God, **avoid** all these things.
	6.20	**Avoid** the profane talk and foolish arguments of what some people
2 Tim	2.22	**Avoid** the passions of youth, and strive for righteousness,
Tit	3. 9	But **avoid** stupid arguments, long lists of ancestors, quarrels,

AWAITS see WAIT (1)

AWAKE
see also **WAKE**

Ex	12.30	his officials, and all the other Egyptians were **awakened.**
Ps	17.15	and when I **awake,** your presence will fill me with joy.
	77. 4	He keeps me **awake** all night;
	102. 7	I lie **awake;**
	119.148	All night long I lie **awake,** to meditate on your instructions.
	121. 3	your protector is always **awake.**
	139.18	When I **awake,** I am still with you.
Prov	4.16	They lie **awake** unless they have hurt someone.
Ecc	5.12	A rich man, however, has so much that he stays **awake** worrying.
	8.16	realized that you could stay **awake** night and day [17] and
Song	5. 2	While I slept, my heart was **awake.**
Mic	2. 1	terrible it will be for those who lie **awake** and plan evil!
Mt	24.43	sure that he would stay **awake** and not let the thief break
Mk	14.37	Weren't you able to stay **awake** even for one hour?"
Lk	12.37	servants whose master finds them **awake** and ready when he returns!
1 Thes	5. 6	we should be **awake** and sober.
2 Pet	2. 3	Judge has been ready, and their Destroyer has been wide **awake!**
Rev	16.15	Happy is he who stays **awake** and guards his clothes, so that

AWARE
[UNAWARE]

Job	39.15	She is **unaware** that a foot may crush them or a wild
Ps	16. 8	I am always **aware** of the Lord's presence;
Is	59.12	We are well **aware** of them all.
Jon	1. 2	I am **aware** how wicked its people are."
Mt	22.18	Jesus, however, was **aware** of their evil plan, and so he said,
Acts	12.12	**Aware** of his situation, he went to the home of Mary, the

AWE

Ex	14.31	Lord had defeated the Egyptians, they stood in **awe** of the Lord;
	15. 6	"Your right hand, Lord, is **awesome** in power;
	34.10	do, because I am going to do an **awesome** thing for you.
Deut	28.58	honour the wonderful and **awesome** name of the Lord your God,
1 Chr	29.25	the whole nation stand in **awe** of Solomon, and he made him
Job	22. 4	not because you stand in **awe** of God that he reprimands you
	25. 1	all must stand in **awe** of him;
	37.22	in the north, and the glory of God fills us with **awe.**
	37.24	then, that everyone stands in **awe** of him, and that he
Ps	65. 8	The whole world stands in **awe** of the great things that you
	68.35	How **awesome** is God as he comes from his sanctuary— the
	89. 7	and all of them stand in **awe** of you.
	130. 4	you forgive us, so that we should stand in **awe** of you.
Ecc	3.14	thing God does is to make us stand in **awe** of him.
	5. 7	how much you talk, you must still stand in **awe** of God.
Is	8.14	Because of my **awesome** holiness I am like a stone that
	29.23	You will honour me and stand in **awe** of me.
	41.23	fill us with fear and **awe!**
Hab	3. 2	heard of what you have done, and I am filled with **awe.**
Acts	2.43	being done through the apostles, and everyone was filled with **awe.**
2 Cor	7. 1	and let us be completely holy by living in **awe** of God.
Heb	12.28	God in a way that will please him, with reverence and **awe;**
Rev	15. 4	Who will not stand in **awe** of you, Lord?

AWFUL

Judg	19.24	But don't do such an **awful** thing to this man!"
1 Sam	2.24	This is an **awful** thing the people of the Lord are talking
2 Sam	13.12	That's **awful!**
Dan	8.13	How long will an **awful** sin replace the daily sacrifices?
Jon	1.10	and said to him, "That was an **awful** thing to do!"
Rev	18.10	How **awful!**
	18.16	How **awful** for the great city!
	18.19	How **awful** for the great city!

AWFUL HORROR

Dan	9.27	The **Awful Horror** will be placed on the highest point of the
	11.31	They will stop the daily sacrifices and set up The **Awful Horror.**
	12.11	is, from the time of The **Awful Horror,** 1,290 days will pass.
Mt	24.15	will see 'The **Awful Horror'** of which the prophet Daniel spoke.
Mk	13.14	will see 'The **Awful Horror'** standing in the place where he

AWNINGS

Ezek	27. 7	Your **awnings** were made of finest cloth, Of purple from the

Am AX see AXE

AXE

Deut	19. 5	tree, the head of the **axe** comes off the handle and kills
Judg	9.48	There he took an **axe,** cut a branch off a tree, and
1 Sam	13.20	Philistines to get their ploughs, hoes, **axes,** and sickles sharpened;
	13.21	small coin for sharpening **axes** and for repairing ox-goads,
2 Sam	12.31	saws, iron hoes, and iron **axes,** and forced them to work at
1 Kgs	6. 7	no noise made by hammers, **axes,** or any other iron tools as
2 Kgs	6. 5	down a tree, suddenly his iron **axe-head** fell in the water.
	6. 5	"It was a borrowed **axe!"**
	6. 6	a stick, threw it in the water, and made the **axe-head** float.
1 Chr	20. 3	city and put them to work with saws, iron hoes, and **axes.**
Ps	35. 3	Lift up your spear and your **axe** against those who pursue me.
	74. 5	They looked like woodmen cutting down trees with their **axes.**
	74. 6	They smashed all the wooden panels with their **axes** and sledge-hammers.
Ecc	10.10	If your **axe** is blunt and you don't sharpen it, you have
Is	10.15	the Lord says, "Can an **axe** claim to be greater than the
	10.34	are cut down with an **axe,** as even the finest trees of
Jer	22. 7	They will all bring their **axes,** cut down its beautiful cedar pillars,
	46.22	They attack her with **axes,** like men cutting down trees
Mt	3.10	The **axe** is ready to cut down the trees at the roots;
Lk	3. 9	The **axe** is ready to cut down the trees at the roots;

AXLE

1 Kgs	7.30	Each cart had four bronze wheels with bronze **axles.**
	7.32	under the panels, and the **axles** were of one piece with the
	7.33	their **axles,** rims, spokes, and hubs were all of bronze.

BAAL (1)
God of fertility worshipped by Canaanites.

Num	25. 3	The Israelites ate the food and worshipped the god [3] **Baal of Peor.**
	25. 5	your tribe who has become a worshipper of **Baal of Peor."**
Deut	4. 3	He destroyed everyone who worshipped **Baal** there, [4] but those
Judg	2.11	Israel sinned against the Lord and began to serve the **Baals.**
	2.13	They stopped worshipping the Lord and served the **Baals** and the Astartes.
	3. 7	against him and worshipped the idols of **Baal** and Asherah.
	6.25	down your father's altar to **Baal,** and cut down the symbol of
	6.28	found that the altar to **Baal** and the symbol of Asherah had
	6.30	tore down the altar to **Baal** and cut down the symbol of
	6.31	those who confronted him, "Are you standing up for **Baal?**
	6.31	If **Baal** is a god, let him defend himself.
	6.32	Gideon was known as Jerubbaal, because Joash said, "Let **Baal** defend himself;
	8.33	Israel were again unfaithful to God and worshipped the **Baals.**
	10. 6	the Lord by worshipping the **Baals** and the Astartes, as well
	10.10	you, for we left you, our God, and worshipped the **Baals."**
1 Sam	7. 4	rid of their idols of **Baal** and Astarte, and worshipped only
	12.10	you, Lord, and worshipped the idols of **Baal** and Astarte.
1 Kgs	16.31	Jezebel, the daughter of King Ethbaal of Sidon, and worshipped **Baal.**
	16.32	He built a temple to **Baal** in Samaria, made an altar for
	18.18	You are disobeying the Lord's commands and worshipping the idols of **Baal.**
	18.19	along the 450 prophets of **Baal** and the 400 prophets of the
	18.20	Israelites and the prophets of **Baal** to meet at Mount Carmel.
	18.21	but if **Baal** is God, worship him!"
	18.22	of the Lord still left, but there are 450 prophets of **Baal.**
	18.23	let the prophets of **Baal** take one, kill it, cut it in
	18.24	Then let the prophets of **Baal** pray to their god, and I
	18.25	said to the prophets of **Baal,** "Since there are so many of
	18.26	brought to them, prepared it, and prayed to **Baal** until noon.
	18.26	They shouted, "Answer us, **Baal!"**
	18.40	Elijah ordered, "Seize the prophets of **Baal;**
	19. 1	and how he had put all the prophets of **Baal** to death.
	19.18	to me and have not bowed to **Baal** or kissed his idol."
	22.53	He worshipped and served **Baal,** and like his father before him,
2 Kgs	3. 2	down the image his father had made for the worship of **Baal.**
	10.18	"King Ahab served the god **Baal** a little, but I will serve
	10.19	together all the prophets of **Baal,** all his worshippers, and
	10.19	offer a great sacrifice to **Baal,** and whoever is not present
	10.19	Jehu by which he meant to kill all the worshippers of **Baal.)**
	10.20	Then Jehu ordered, "Proclaim a day of worship in honour of **Baal!"**
	10.21	All who worshipped **Baal** came;
	10.21	went into the temple of **Baal,** filling it from one end to
	10.23	sure that only worshippers of **Baal** are present and that no
	10.24	Jonadab went in to offer sacrifices and burnt-offerings to **Baal.**
	10.28	That was how Jehu wiped out the worship of **Baal** in Israel.
	11.18	the people went to the temple of **Baal** and tore it down;
	11.18	killed Mattan, the priest of **Baal,** in front of the altars.
	17.16	Asherah, worshipped the stars, and served the god **Baal.**
	21. 3	altars for the worship of **Baal** and made an image of the
	23. 4	used in the worship of **Baal,** of the goddess Asherah, and of
	23. 5	priests who offered sacrifices to **Baal,** to the sun, the
2 Chr	17. 3	example of his father's early life and did not worship **Baal.**
	23.17	they all went to the temple of **Baal** and tore it down.
	23.17	killed Mattan, the priest of **Baal,** in front of the altars.
	24. 7	used many of the sacred objects in the worship of **Baal.)**
	28. 2	He had metal images of **Baal** made, [3] burnt incense in the
	33. 3	for the worship of **Baal,** made images of the goddess Asherah,
	34. 4	men smashed the altars where **Baal** was worshipped and tore
Ps	106.28	joined in the worship of **Baal,** and ate sacrifices offered to
Jer	2. 8	the prophets spoke in the name of **Baal** and worshipped useless idols.
	2.23	not defiled yourself, that you have never worshipped **Baal?**

Jer 3.24 But the worship of **Baal,** the god of shame, has made us
7. 9 under oath, offer sacrifices to **Baal,** and worship gods that
9.14 have worshipped the idols of **Baal** as their fathers taught
11.13 sacrifices to that disgusting god **Baal** as there are streets
11.17 they have made me angry by offering sacrifices to **Baal."**
12.16 my people to swear by **Baal**—then they will also be a
19. 5 they have built altars for **Baal** in order to burn their children
23.13 spoken in the name of **Baal** and have led my people astray.
23.27 me, just as their fathers forgot me and turned to **Baal.**
32.29 angry by burning incense to **Baal** on the roof-tops and by
32.35 They have built altars to **Baal** in the Valley of Hinnom,
Hos 2. 8 the silver and gold that she used in the worship of **Baal.**
2.13 when she burnt incense to **Baal** and put on her jewellery to
2.16 call me her husband—she will no longer call me her **Baal.**
2.17 I will never let her speak the name of **Baal** again.
9. 1 like prostitutes to the god **Baal** and have loved the corn you
9.10 Peor, they began to worship **Baal,** and soon became as
11. 2 My people sacrificed to **Baal;**
13. 1 sinned by worshipping **Baal,** and for this they will die.
Zeph 1. 4 trace of the worship of **Baal** there, and no one will even
Rom 11. 4 seven thousand men who have not worshipped the false god **Baal."**

BAAL-OF-THE-COVENANT

Judg 8.33 They made **Baal-of-the-Covenant** their god, [34]and no longer
9. 4 silver from the temple of **Baal-of-the-Covenant,** and with
9.46 in the stronghold of the temple of **Baal-of-the-Covenant.**

BAALZEBUB

God worshipped in Philistine city of Ekron.
see also BEELZEBUL

2 Kgs 1. 2 sent some messengers to consult **Baalzebub,** the god of the
1. 3 "Why are you going to consult **Baalzebub,** the god of Ekron?
1. 6 'Why are you sending messengers to consult **Baalzebub,** the god of Ekron?
1.16 you sent messengers to consult **Baalzebub,** the god of

BAASHA

King of the n. kingdom (Israel).

1 Kgs 15.16 Asa of Judah and King **Baasha** of Israel were constantly at
15.17 **Baasha** invaded Judah and started to fortify Ramah in
15.19 break your alliance with King **Baasha** of Israel, so that he
15.21 When King **Baasha** heard what had happened, he stopped
15.22 stones and timber that **Baasha** had been using to fortify it.
15.27 **Baasha** son of Ahijah, of the tribe of Issachar, plotted
15.28 And so **Baasha** succeeded Nadab as king of Israel.
15.32 Asa of Judah and King **Baasha** of Israel were constantly at
15.33 of King Asa of Judah, **Baasha** son of Ahijah became king of
16. 1 Jehu son of Hanani and gave him this message for **Baasha:**
16. 5 Everything else that **Baasha** did and all his brave deeds
16. 6 **Baasha** died and was buried in Tirzah, and his son Elah
16. 7 message from the Lord against **Baasha** and his family was
16. 7 Jehu because of the sins that **Baasha** committed against the Lord.
16. 8 of Judah, Elah son of **Baasha** became king of Israel, and he
16.11 Zimri became king he killed off all the members of **Baasha's** family.
16.12 the Lord had said against **Baasha** through the prophet Jehu,
16.12 Zimri killed all the family of **Baasha.**
16.13 they led Israel into sin, **Baasha** and his son Elah had
21.22 like the family of King **Baasha** son of Ahijah, because you
2 Kgs 9. 9 of King Jeroboam of Israel and of King **Baasha** of Israel.
2 Chr 16. 1 King Asa of Judah, King **Baasha** of Israel invaded Judah and
16. 3 break your alliance with King **Baasha** of Israel so that he
16. 5 When King **Baasha** heard what was happening, he stopped
16. 6 the stones and timber that **Baasha** had been using at Ramah,
Jer 41. 9 had dug when he was being attacked by King **Baasha** of Israel.

BABY

Gen 17.11 on you must circumcise every **baby** boy when he is eight days
35.16 Rachel to have her **baby,** and she was having difficult labour.
Ex 1.16 he said to them, "kill the **baby** if it is a boy;
1.19 give birth easily, and their **babies** are born before either
2. 2 she saw what a fine **baby** he was, she hid him for
2. 3 She put the **baby** in it and then placed it in the
2. 4 The **baby's** sister stood some distance away to see what
2. 6 The princess opened it and saw a **baby** boy.
2. 6 "This is one of the Hebrew **babies,"** she said.
2. 8 So the girl went and brought the **baby's** own mother.
2. 9 told the woman, "Take this **baby** and nurse him for me, and
2. 9 So she took the **baby** and nursed him.
Num 11.12 them in my arms like **babies** all the way to the land
Deut 32.25 neither **babies** nor old men will be spared.
Josh 5. 4 the desert, none of the **baby** boys had been circumcised.
1 Sam 4.19 pregnant, and it was almost time for her **baby** to be born.
15. 3 kill all the men, women, children, and **babies;**
22.19 men and women, children and **babies,** cattle, donkeys, and
1 Kgs 3.17 I gave birth to a **baby** boy at home while she was
3.18 my child was born she also gave birth to a **baby** boy.
3.19 she accidentally rolled over on her **baby** and smothered it.
3.21 was going to feed my **baby,** I saw that it was dead.
Ps 8. 2 it is sung by children and **babies.**
22. 9 through birth, and when I was a **baby,** you kept me safe.
58. 8 may they be like a **baby** born dead that never sees the
137. 9 who takes your **babies** and smashes them against a rock.
Ecc 6. 3 burial, then I say that a **baby** born dead is better off.
6. 4 It does that **baby** no good to be born;
Is 11. 8 Even a **baby** will not be harmed if it plays near a
13.16 look on helplessly, their **babies** will be battered to death,
Is 13.18 will show no mercy to **babies** and take no pity on children.
28. 9 It's only good for **babies** that have just been weaned!
49.15 a woman forget her own **baby** and not love the child she
65.20 **Babies** will no longer die in infancy, and all people
Jer 44. 7 men and women, children and **babies,** so that none of your
Lam 2.11 Children and **babies** are fainting in the streets of the city.
4. 4 They let their **babies** die of hunger and thirst;
Hos 9.14 Make them unable to nurse their **babies!**
13.16 **babies** will be dashed to the ground, and pregnant women will
Joel 2.16 gather the children and the **babies** too.
Mt 1.18 that she was going to have a **baby** by the Holy Spirit.
2. 2 and asked, "Where is the **baby** born to be the king of
21.16 'You have trained children and **babies** to offer perfect praise.'"
24.19 for women who are pregnant and for mothers with little **babies!**
Mk 13.17 for women who are pregnant and for mothers with little **babies!**
Lk 1.41 Elizabeth heard Mary's greeting, the **baby** moved within her.
1.44 I heard your greeting, the **baby** within me jumped with gladness.
1.57 for Elizabeth to have her **baby,** and she gave birth to
1.59 When the **baby** was a week old, they came to circumcise him,
2. 6 were in Bethlehem, the time came for her to have her **baby.**
2.12 you will find a **baby** wrapped in strips of cloth and lying
2.16 found Mary and Joseph and saw the **baby** lying in the manger.
2.21 the time came for the **baby** to be circumcised, he was named
18.15 people brought their **babies** to Jesus for him to place his
21.23 for women who are pregnant and for mothers with little **babies!**
23.29 never had children, who never bore **babies,** who never nursed them!'
Jn 16.21 but when the **baby** is born, she forgets her suffering, because
16.21 she is happy that a **baby** has been born into the world.
Acts 7.19 forcing them to put their **babies** out of their homes, so that
1 Pet 2. 2 like new-born **babies,** always thirsty for the pure spiritual milk,

BABYLON

[EMPEROR OF BABYLONIA, KING OF BABYLON, KING OF BABYLONIA]
Important city in s. Mesopotamia, and the empire centred round it which conquered Jerusalem beginning of 6th century BC. The name was used by early Christians to refer to Rome.

Gen 10.10 At first his kingdom included **Babylon,** Erech, and Accad,
10.10 all three of them in **Babylonia.**
11. 2 East, they came to a plain in **Babylonia** and settled there.
11. 9 The city was called **Babylon,** because there the Lord mixed
11.28 city, Ur in **Babylonia,** while his father was still living.
11.31 the city of Ur in **Babylonia** to go to the land of
14. 1 Four kings, Amraphel of **Babylonia,** Arioch of Ellasar, Chedorlaomer of Elam,
14. 9 Elam, Goiim, **Babylonia,** and Ellasar, five kings against four.
15. 7 you out of Ur in **Babylonia,** to give you this land as
Josh 7.21 I saw a beautiful **Babylonian** cloak, about two kilogrammes of silver,
2 Kgs 17.24 the cities of **Babylon,** Cuth, Ivvah, Hamath, and Sepharvaim,
17.30 The people of **Babylon** made idols of the god Succoth Benoth;
20.12 that same time the **king of Babylonia,** Merodach Baladan,
20.14 Hezekiah answered, "They came from a very distant country, from **Babylonia."**
20.17 stored up to this day, will be carried off to **Babylonia.**
20.18 eunuchs to serve in the palace of the **king of Babylonia."**
24. 1 **King Nebuchadnezzar of Babylonia** invaded Judah,
24. 2 Lord sent armed bands of **Babylonians,** Syrians, Moabites, and
24. 7 because the **king of Babylonia** now controlled all the territory
24.10 **Babylonian** army, commanded by King Nebuchadnezzar's officers,
24.12 and the palace officials, surrendered to the **Babylonians.**
24.13 prisoner [13]and carried off to **Babylon** all the treasures in
24.15 Nebuchadnezzar took Jehoiachin to **Babylon** as a prisoner, together with Jehoiachin's mother,
24.16 all the important men to **Babylonia,** seven thousand in all,
25. 1 Zedekiah rebelled against **King Nebuchadnezzar of Babylonia,**
25. 4 Although the **Babylonians** were surrounding the city, all the
25. 5 But the **Babylonian** army pursued King Zedekiah, captured
25. 7 put out, placed him in chains, and took him to **Babylon.**
25. 8 the nineteenth year of **King Nebuchadnezzar of Babylonia,**
25.11 Then Nebuzaradan took away to **Babylonia** the people who
25.11 workmen, and those who had deserted to the **Babylonians.**
25.13 The **Babylonians** broke in pieces the bronze columns and
25.13 large bronze tank, and they took all the bronze to **Babylon.**
25.20 took them to the **king of Babylonia,** who was in the city
25.22 **King Nebuchadnezzar of Babylonia** made Gedaliah, the son
25.22 of all those who had not been taken away to **Babylonia.**
25.24 is no need for you to be afraid of the **Babylonian** officials.
25.24 this land, serve the **king of Babylonia,** and all will go well
25.25 He also killed the Israelites and **Babylonians** who were there with him.
25.26 went to Egypt, because they were afraid of the **Babylonians.**
25.27 Evilmerodach became **king of Babylonia,** he showed kindness
25.28 gave the other kings who were exiles with him in **Babylonia.**
1 Chr 3.17 King Jehoiachin, who was taken prisoner by the **Babylonians.**
9. 1 Judah had been deported to **Babylon** as punishment for their sins.
2 Chr 32.31 did, [31]and even when the **Babylonian** ambassadors came to
33.11 hooks in him, put him in chains, and took him to **Babylon.**
36. 6 **King Nebuchadnezzar of Babylonia** invaded Judah,
36. 6 captured Jehoiakim, and took him to **Babylonia** in chains.
36. 7 of the Temple and put them in his palace in **Babylon.**
36.10 King Nebuchadnezzar took Jehoiachin to **Babylonia** as a prisoner,
36.17 So the Lord brought the **king of Babylonia** to attack them.
36.18 The **king of Babylonia** looted the Temple,
36.18 king and his officials, and took everything back to **Babylon.**
36.20 took all the survivors to **Babylonia,** where they served him
Ezra 1.11 he and the other exiles went from **Babylon** to Jerusalem.
2. 1 the province of **Babylon** and returned to Jerusalem and Judah,
2. 1 been living in exile in **Babylonia** ever since King
4. 9 are men originally from Erech, **Babylon,** and Susa in the land

Ezra 5.12 conquered by **King Nebuchadnezzar of Babylonia,**
5.12 Temple was destroyed, and the people were taken into exile in **Babylonia.**
5.13 of King Cyrus as **emperor of Babylonia,** Cyrus issued orders
5.14 Temple in Jerusalem and had placed in the temple in **Babylon.**
5.17 in the royal records in **Babylon** to find whether or not Cyrus
6. 1 to be made in the royal records that were kept in **Babylon.**
6. 5 which King Nebuchadnezzar brought to **Babylon** from the Temple
7. 6 Artaxerxes, Ezra set out from **Babylonia** for Jerusalem with a
7. 8 They left **Babylonia** on the first day of the first month,
7.16 collect throughout the province of **Babylon** and the offerings
8. 1 had been in exile in **Babylonia** and who returned with Ezra to
Neh 1. 2 Jerusalem and about our fellow-Jews who had returned from exile in **Babylonia.**
7. 6 the province of **Babylon** and returned to Jerusalem and Judah,
7. 6 been living in exile in **Babylonia** ever since King
9. 7 Lord God, chose Abram and led him out of Ur in **Babylonia;**
13. 6 that Artaxerxes was **king of Babylon** I had gone back to
Esth 2. 6 When **King Nebuchadnezzar of Babylon** took King Jehoiachin
Ps 87. 4 "I will include Egypt and **Babylonia** when I list the
137. 1 By the rivers of **Babylon** we sat down;
137. 8 **Babylon,** you will be destroyed.
Is 11.11 lands of Pathros, Sudan, Elam, **Babylonia,** and Hamath, and in
13. 1 This is a message about **Babylon,** which Isaiah son of Amoz
13.14 "The foreigners living in **Babylon** will run away to their own countries,
13.17 The Lord says, "I am stirring up the Medes to attack **Babylon.**
13.19 **Babylonia** is the most beautiful kingdom of all;
13.19 I, the Lord, will overthrow **Babylon** as I did Sodom and Gomorrah!
13.22 **Babylon's** time has come!
14. 4 they are to mock the **king of Babylonia** and say:
14. 9 the dead is getting ready to welcome the **king of Babylonia.**
14.12 **"King of Babylonia,** bright morning star,
14.22 Lord Almighty says, "I will attack **Babylon** and bring it to ruin.
14.23 I will turn **Babylon** into a marsh, and owls will live there.
14.23 I will sweep **Babylon** with a broom that will sweep everything away.
21. 1 This is a message about **Babylonia.**
21. 2 God will put an end to the suffering which **Babylon** has caused.
21. 9 The sentry gives the news, **"Babylon** has fallen!
23.13 (It was the **Babylonians,** not the Assyrians, who let the
23.13 It was the **Babylonians** who put up siege-towers, tore down
39. 1 the **king of Babylonia,** Merodach Baladan, son of Baladan,
39. 3 Hezekiah answered, "They came from a very distant country, from **Babylonia."**
39. 6 stored up to this day, will be carried off to **Babylonia.**
39. 7 eunuchs to serve in the palace of the **king of Babylonia."**
43.14 "To save you, I will send an army against **Babylon;**
46. 1 "This is the end for **Babylon's** gods!
46. 2 This is the end for **Babylon's** gods!
47. 1 **"Babylon,** come down from your throne, and sit in the dust
47. 5 The Lord says to **Babylon,**
48.14 predict that the man I have chosen would attack **Babylon;**
48.20 Go out from **Babylon,** go free!
52. 5 And now in **Babylonia** the same thing has happened:
52.11 Make sure you leave **Babylonia,** all you that carry the temple equipment!
55.12 "You will leave **Babylon** with joy;
Jer 20. 4 people of Judah under the power of the **king of Babylonia;**
20. 5 the kings of Judah, and carry everything off to **Babylonia.**
20. 6 family will also be captured and taken off to **Babylonia.**
21. 2 because **King Nebuchadnezzar of Babylonia** and his army are
21. 4 fighting against the **king of Babylonia** and his army.
21. 9 to the **Babylonians,** who are now attacking the city,
21.10 given over to the **king of Babylonia** and he will burn it
22.25 I will give you to **King Nebuchadnezzar of Babylonia**
24. 1 **King Nebuchadnezzar of Babylonia** had taken away Jehoiakim's son,
24. 1 Jerusalem to **Babylonia,** together with the leaders of Judah,
24. 5 who were taken away to **Babylonia** are like these good figs,
25. 1 (This was the first year that Nebuchadnezzar was **king of Babylonia.)**
25. 9 and for my servant, **King Nebuchadnezzar of Babylonia.**
25.11 the neighbouring nations will serve the **king of Babylonia**
25.12 After that I will punish **Babylonia** and its king for their sin.
25.13 I will punish **Babylonia** with all the disasters that I
25.14 I will pay the **Babylonians** back for what they have done,
25.19 Last of all, the **king of Babylonia** will drink from it.
27. 6 power of my servant, **King Nebuchadnezzar of Babylonia,**
27. 9 They all tell you not to submit to the **king of Babylonia.**
27.11 nation submits to the **king of Babylonia** and serves him,
27.12 to King Zedekiah of Judah, "Submit to the **king of Babylonia.**
27.13 to any nation that does not submit to the **king of Babylonia.**
27.16 temple treasures will soon be brought back from **Babylonia.**
27.17 Submit to the **king of Babylonia** and you will live!
27.18 Temple and in the royal palace to be taken to **Babylonia."**
27.19 King Nebuchadnezzar took away to **Babylonia** the king of Judah,
27.22 They will be taken to **Babylonia** and will remain there
28. 2 "I have broken the power of the **king of Babylonia.**
28. 3 temple treasures that King Nebuchadnezzar took to **Babylonia.**
28. 4 all the people of Judah who went into exile in **Babylonia.**
28. 4 Yes, I will break the power of the **king of Babylonia.**
28. 6 and will bring back from **Babylonia** all the temple treasures
28.14 they will serve **King Nebuchadnezzar of Babylonia.**
29. 1 Nebuchadnezzar had taken away as prisoners from Jerusalem to **Babylonia.**
29. 3 Zedekiah of Judah was sending to **King Nebuchadnezzar of Babylonia.**
29. 4 Nebuchadnezzar to take away as prisoners from Jerusalem to **Babylonia:**
29.10 "The Lord says, 'When **Babylonia's** seventy years are over,
Jer 29.15 "You say that the Lord has given you prophets in **Babylonia.**
29.20 I sent into exile in **Babylonia,** listen to what I, the Lord,
29.21 to the power of **King Nebuchadnezzar of Babylonia,**
29.22 as prisoners from Jerusalem to **Babylonia** want to bring a
29.22 Zedekiah and Ahab, whom the **king of Babylonia** roasted alive!'
29.28 he told the people in **Babylonia** that they would be prisoners
29.31 to send to all the prisoners in **Babylon** this message about Shemaiah:
32. 1 the eighteenth year of **King Nebuchadnezzar of Babylonia.**
32. 2 the army of the **king of Babylonia** was attacking Jerusalem,
32. 3 going to let the **king of Babylonia** capture this city,
32. 4 He will be handed over to the **king of Babylonia;**
32. 5 Zedekiah will be taken to **Babylonia,** and he will remain
32. 5 Even if he fights the **Babylonians,** he will not be successful.
32.24 "The **Babylonians** have built siege mounds round the city to capture it,
32.25 the city is about to be captured by the **Babylonians."**
32.28 give this city over to **King Nebuchadnezzar of Babylonia**
32.36 make this city fall into the hands of the **king of Babylonia.**
32.43 live, and that it will be given over to the **Babylonians.**
33. 5 Some will fight against the **Babylonians,** who will fill the
34. 1 spoke to me when **King Nebuchadnezzar of Babylonia** and his army,
34. 2 city over to the **king of Babylonia,** and he will burn it
34. 3 then you will go to **Babylonia.**
34. 7 the army of the **king of Babylonia** was attacking the city.
34.21 hand them over to the **Babylonian** army, which has stopped its
35.11 Jerusalem to get away from the **Babylonian** and Syrian armies.
36.29 he wrote that the **king of Babylonia** would come and destroy
37. 1 **King Nebuchadnezzar of Babylonia** made Zedekiah son of Josiah
37. 5 The **Babylonian** army had been besieging Jerusalem, but when
37. 8 Then the **Babylonians** will come back, attack the city,
37. 9 into thinking that the **Babylonians** will not come back,
37.10 if you defeat the whole **Babylonian** army, so that only
37.11 The **Babylonian** army retreated from Jerusalem because the Egyptian army was approaching.
37.13 Hananiah, stopped me and said, "You are deserting to the **Babylonians!"**
37.17 added, "You will be handed over to the **king of Babylonia."**
37.19 told you that the **king of Babylonia** would not attack you
38. 2 out and surrenders to the **Babylonians** will not be killed;
38. 3 city to the **Babylonian** army, and they will capture it."
38.17 you surrender to the **king of Babylonia's** officers,
38.18 be handed over to the **Babylonians,** who will burn it down,
38.19 "I am afraid of our countrymen who have deserted to the **Babylonians.**
38.22 being led out to the **king of Babylonia's** officers.
38.23 be taken out to the **Babylonians,** and you yourself will not
38.23 taken prisoner by the **king of Babylonia,**
39. 1 **King Nebuchadnezzar of Babylonia** came with his whole
39. 3 officials of the **king of Babylonia** came and took their places
39. 5 But the **Babylonian** army pursued them and captured Zedekiah
39. 7 out and had him placed in chains to be taken to **Babylonia.**
39. 8 Meanwhile, the **Babylonians** burnt down the royal palace and
39. 9 took away as prisoners to **Babylonia** the people who were left
39.13 other officers of the **king of Babylonia,**
40. 1 Jerusalem and Judah who were being taken away as prisoners to **Babylonia.**
40. 4 you want to go to **Babylonia** with me, you may do so,
40. 5 of Shaphan, whom the **king of Babylonia** has made governor
40. 7 heard that the **king of Babylonia** had made Gedaliah governor
40. 7 been taken away to **Babylonia**—the poorest people in the land.
40. 9 need for you to be afraid to surrender to the **Babylonians.**
40. 9 serve the **king of Babylonia,** and all will go well
40.10 Mizpah and be your representative when the **Babylonians** come here.
40.11 heard that the **king of Babylonia** had allowed some Israelites
41. 3 Gedaliah at Mizpah and the **Babylonian** soldiers who happened to be there.
41.17 They were afraid of the **Babylonians** because Ishmael had murdered Gedaliah,
41.17 Gedaliah, whom the **king of Babylonia** had made governor
41.17 out for Egypt, in order to get away from the **Babylonians.**
42.11 Stop being afraid of the **king of Babylonia.**
43. 3 against us, so that the **Babylonians** will gain power over us
43. 3 and can either kill us or take us away to **Babylonia."**
43.10 bring my servant **King Nebuchadnezzar of Babylonia** to this place,
43.12 and the **king of Babylonia** will either burn their gods
43.12 of lice, so the **king of Babylonia** will pick the land
44.30 to **King Nebuchadnezzar of Babylonia,** who was his enemy
46. 2 which **King Nebuchadnezzar of Babylonia** defeated at Carchemish
46.13 When **King Nebuchadnezzar of Babylonia** came to attack Egypt,
46.26 to **King Nebuchadnezzar of Babylonia** and his army.
49.28 which were conquered by **King Nebuchadnezzar of Babylonia:**
49.30 **King Nebuchadnezzar of Babylonia** has plotted against you,
50. 1 the Lord gave me about the city of **Babylon** and its people:
50. 2 **Babylon** has fallen!
50. 2 **Babylon's** idols are put to shame, her disgusting images are crushed!
50. 3 has come to attack **Babylonia** and will make it a desert.
50. 8 "People of Israel, run away from **Babylonia!**
50. 9 strong nations in the north and make them attack **Babylonia.**
50.10 **Babylonia** will be looted, and those who loot it will
50.11 The Lord says, "People of **Babylonia,** you plundered my nation.
50.12 **Babylonia** will be the least important nation of all;
50.13 Because of my anger no one will live in **Babylon;**
50.14 "Bowmen, line up for battle against **Babylon** and surround it.
50.14 Shoot all your arrows at **Babylon,** because it has sinned against me,

Jer 50.15 Now **Babylon** has surrendered.
50.15 I am taking my revenge on the **Babylonians.**
50.17 and then **King Nebuchadnezzar of Babylonia** gnawed their bones.
50.23 **Babylonia** hammered the whole world to pieces, and now
50.24 **Babylonia,** you fought against me, and you have been
50.25 I, the Sovereign Lord Almighty, have work to do in **Babylonia.**
50.27 The people of **Babylonia** are doomed!
50.28 (Refugees escape from **Babylonia** and come to Jerusalem,
50.28 God took revenge for what the **Babylonians** had done to his Temple.)
50.29 "Tell the bowmen to attack **Babylon.**
50.31 **"Babylonia,** you are filled with pride, so I, the Sovereign Lord Almighty,
50.34 to the earth, but trouble to the people of **Babylonia."**
50.35 "Death to **Babylonia!**
50.38 **Babylonia** is a land of terrifying idols, that have made
50.39 "And so **Babylon** will be haunted by demons and evil spirits,
50.40 will happen to **Babylon** as happened to Sodom and Gomorrah,
50.42 They are ready for battle against **Babylonia.**
50.43 The **king of Babylonia** hears the news, and his hands hang limp.
50.44 and make the **Babylonians** run away suddenly from their city.
50.45 made against the city of **Babylon** and to what I intend to
50.46 When **Babylon** falls, there will be such a noise that the
51. 1 "I am bringing a destructive wind against **Babylonia** and its people.
51. 2 will send foreigners to destroy **Babylonia** like a wind that
51. 6 Run away from **Babylonia!**
51. 6 Do not be killed because of **Babylonia's** sin.
51. 7 **Babylonia** was like a gold cup in my hand, making the whole
51. 8 **Babylonia** has suddenly fallen and is destroyed!
51. 9 said, 'We tried to help **Babylonia,** but it was too late.
51. 9 God has punished **Babylonia** with all his might and has
51.11 the kings of Media, because he intends to destroy **Babylonia.**
51.12 Give the signal to attack **Babylon's** walls.
51.12 done what he said he would do to the people of **Babylonia.**
51.14 bring many men to attack **Babylonia** like a swarm of locusts,
51.20 **"Babylonia,** you are my hammer, my weapon of war.
51.24 "You will see me repay **Babylonia** and its people for all the
51.25 **Babylonia,** you are like a mountain that destroys the whole world,
51.27 Prepare the nations for war against **Babylonia!**
51.28 Prepare the nations for war against **Babylonia.**
51.29 out his plan to make **Babylonia** a desert, where no one lives.
51.30 The **Babylonian** soldiers have stopped fighting and remain in their forts.
51.31 runs to tell the **king of Babylonia** that his city
51.32 The **Babylonian** soldiers have panicked.
51.34 The **king of Babylonia** cut Jerusalem up and ate it.
51.35 people of Zion say, "May **Babylonia** be held responsible for
51.35 people of Jerusalem say, "May **Babylonia** be held responsible
51.36 dry up the source of **Babylonia's** water and make its rivers
51.38 The **Babylonians** all roar like lions and growl like lion cubs.
51.41 The Lord says about **Babylon:**
51.41 What a horrifying sight **Babylon** has become to the nations!
51.42 The sea has rolled over **Babylon** and covered it with roaring waves.
51.44 punish Bel, the god of **Babylonia,** and make him give up his
51.44 **"Babylon's** walls have fallen.
51.47 the time is coming when I will deal with **Babylonia's** idols.
51.48 will shout for joy when **Babylonia** falls to the people who
51.49 **Babylonia** caused the death of people all over the world,
51.49 and now **Babylonia** will fall because it caused the
51.50 The Lord says to his people in **Babylonia:**
51.52 when I will deal with **Babylon's** idols, and the wounded will
51.53 Even if **Babylon** could climb to the sky and build a
51.54 the sound of crying in **Babylon,** of mourning for the
51.55 I am destroying **Babylon** and putting it to silence.
51.56 They have come to destroy **Babylon;**
51.56 God who punishes evil, and I will treat **Babylon** as it deserves.
51.58 The walls of mighty **Babylon** will be thrown to the ground,
51.59 Judah, Seraiah was going to **Babylonia** with him, and I gave
51.60 destruction that would come on **Babylonia,**
51.60 as well as all these other things about **Babylonia.**
51.61 Seraiah, "When you get to **Babylon,** be sure to read aloud to
51.64 is what will happen to **Babylonia**—it will sink and never rise
52. 3 Zedekiah rebelled against **King Nebuchadnezzar of Babylonia,**
52. 7 Although the **Babylonians** were surrounding the city, all the
52. 8 But the **Babylonian** army pursued King Zedekiah, captured
52.11 put out and had him placed in chains and taken to **Babylon.**
52.11 Zedekiah remained in prison in **Babylon** until the day he died.
52.12 the nineteenth year of **King Nebuchadnezzar of Babylonia,**
52.15 Then Nebuzaradan took away to **Babylonia** the people who
52.15 workmen, and those who had deserted to the **Babylonians.**
52.17 The **Babylonians** broke in pieces the bronze columns and
52.17 large bronze tank, and they took all the bronze to **Babylon.**
52.26 took them to the **king of Babylonia,** who was in the city
52.31 year that Evilmerodach became **king of Babylonia,**
52.32 gave the other kings who were exiles with him in **Babylonia.**
Ezek 1. 1 with the Jewish exiles by the River Chebar in **Babylonia.**
1. 3 There in **Babylonia** beside the River Chebar, I heard the
11.24 lifted me up and brought me back to the exiles in **Babylonia.**
12.13 him to the city of **Babylon,** where he will die without having
16.29 prostitute for the **Babylonians,** that nation of businessmen,
17.12 Tell them that the **king of Babylonia** came to Jerusalem
17.12 took the king and his officials back with him to **Babylonia.**
17.16 "this king will die in **Babylonia** because he broke his oath
17.16 had made with the **king of Babylonia,** who put him on the
17.17 help him fight when the **Babylonians** build earthworks and dig
17.20 I will take him to **Babylonia** and punish him there, because
19. 9 him in a cage and took him to the **king of Babylonia.**
21.19 by which the **king of Babylonia** can come with his sword.
21.21 The **king of Babylonia** stands by the signpost
Ezek 23.14 by the images of high **Babylonian** officials carved into the
23.16 filled with lust and sent messengers to them in **Babylonia.**
23.17 The **Babylonians** came to have sex with her.
23.23 I will bring all the **Babylonians** and Chaldeans, men from Pekod,
24. 2 the day that the **king of Babylonia** is beginning the siege
26. 7 the greatest king of all—**King Nebuchadnezzar of Babylonia**—
29.18 "Mortal man," he said, **"King Nebuchadnezzar of Babylonia**
30.10 "I will use **King Nebuchadnezzar of Babylonia** to put an end
30.24 the arms of the **king of Babylonia** strong
30.25 Yes, I will weaken him and strengthen the **king of Babylonia.**
32.11 "You will face the sword of the **king of Babylonia.**
Dan 1. 1 **King Nebuchadnezzar of Babylonia** attacked Jerusalem
1. 2 temple of his gods in **Babylon,** and put the captured
1. 4 Ashpenaz was to teach them to read and write the **Babylonian** language.
1.21 until Cyrus the emperor of Persia conquered **Babylonia.**
2.12 ordered the execution of all the royal advisers in **Babylon.**
2.18 not be killed along with the other advisers in **Babylon.**
2.48 charge of the province of **Babylon,** and made him the head of
2.49 Abednego in charge of the affairs of the province of **Babylon;**
3. 1 set up in the plain of Dura in the province of **Babylon.**
3. 8 It was then that some **Babylonians** took the opportunity to
3.12 charge of the province of **Babylon**—Shadrach, Meshach, and
3.30 Shadrach, Meshach, and Abednego to higher positions in the province of **Babylon.**
4. 6 all the royal advisers in **Babylon** to be brought to me so
4.29 of his royal palace in **Babylon,**
4.30 he said, "Look how great **Babylon** is!
5.30 Belshazzar, the **king of Babylonia,** was killed;
7. 1 year that Belshazzar was **king of Babylonia,** I had a dream
9. 1 was the son of Xerxes, ruled over the kingdom of **Babylonia.**
Mic 4.10 will have to go to **Babylon,** but there the Lord will save
Hab 1. 6 I am bringing the **Babylonians** to power, those fierce, restless people.
1.12 protector, you have chosen the **Babylonians** and made them
1.15 The **Babylonians** catch people with hooks, as though they were fish.
Hag 1.12 returned from the exile in **Babylonia,** did what the Lord
Zech 2. 6 But now, you exiles, escape from **Babylonia** and return to Jerusalem.
5.11 He answered, "To **Babylonia,** where they will build a temple for it.
6. 6 horses was going north to **Babylonia,** the white horses were
6. 8 north to **Babylonia** have calmed down the Lord's anger."
6.10 All these men have returned from exile in **Babylonia.**
Mt 1. 6 Israel were taken into exile in **Babylon,** the following ancestors
1.12 time after the exile in **Babylon** to the birth of Jesus,
1.17 David to the exile in **Babylon,** and fourteen from then
Acts 7.43 And so I will send you into exile beyond **Babylon.'**
1 Pet 5.13 Your sister church in **Babylon,** also chosen by God, sends you
Rev 14. 8 Great **Babylon** has fallen!
16.19 God remembered great **Babylon** and made her drink the wine
17. 5 "Great **Babylon,** the mother of all the prostitutes and perverts
18. 2 Great **Babylon** has fallen!
18.10 This great and mighty city **Babylon!**
18.21 is how the great city **Babylon** will be violently thrown down
18.24 **Babylon** was punished because the blood of prophets and of

BACK

Gen 9.23 They walked **backwards** into the tent and covered their father,
21.14 He put the child on her **back** and sent her away.
49.15 So he bends his **back** to carry the load And is forced
49.17 horse's heel, So that the rider is thrown off **backwards.**
Ex 26.12 Hang the extra half-piece over the **back** of the Tent.
26.22 For the **back** of the Tent on the west, make six frames,
26.27 and five for the frames on the west end, at the **back.**
33.23 hand away, and you will see my **back** but not my face."
36.27 For the **back** of the Tent, on the west, they made six
36.32 and five for the frames on the west end, at the **back.**
Lev 3. 9 tail cut off near the **backbone,** all the fat covering the
13.40 loses his hair at the **back** or the front of his head,
13.55 the object, whether the rot is on the front or the **back.**
Josh 8.33 the people stood with their **backs** to Mount Gerizim
8.33 and the other half with their **backs** to Mount Ebal.
23.13 painful as a whip on your **back** or thorns in your eyes.
1 Sam 4.18 Covenant Box, Eli fell **backwards** from his seat beside the gate.
2 Sam 2.23 Abner, with a **backward** thrust of his spear, struck him
2.23 through the belly so that the spear came out at his **back.**
1 Kgs 6. 5 on the sides and the **back** of the Temple, a three-storied
7.25 The tank rested on the **backs** of twelve bronze bulls
10.19 At the **back** of the throne was the figure of a bull's
20.30 the city and took refuge in the **back** room of a house.
22.25 when you go into some **back** room to hide," Micaiah replied.
2 Kgs 9.24 arrow that struck Joram in the **back** and pierced his heart.
16.17 the bronze tank from the **backs** of the twelve bronze bulls,
2 Chr 4. 4 The tank rested on the **backs** of twelve bronze bulls
18.24 when you go into some **back** room to hide," Micaiah replied.
29. 6 abandoned him and turned their **backs** on the place where he
Neh 9.26 they turned their **backs** on your Law.
Job 9. 8 God spread out the heavens or trample the sea-monster's **back.**
41.15 His **back** is made of rows of shields, fastened together
Ps 66.11 us fall into a trap and placed heavy burdens on our **backs.**
69.23 Make their **backs** always weak!
81. 6 an unknown voice saying, [6] "I took the burdens off your **backs;**
129. 3 cut deep wounds in my **back** and made it like a ploughed
Is 1. 4 the holy God of Israel, and have turned your **backs** on him.
46. 1 loaded on donkeys, a burden for the **backs** of tired animals.
50. 6 I bared my **back** to those who beat me.
Jer 15. 6 you have turned your **backs** on me.
32.33 They turned their **backs** on me;
Ezek 1.10 bull's face at the left, and an eagle's face at the **back.**

Ezek 8.16 They had turned their **backs** to the sanctuary and were bowing
10.12 bodies, **backs,** hands, wings, and wheels were covered with eyes.
23.35 forgot me and turned your **back** on me, you will suffer for
29. 7 pierced their armpits, and made them wrench their **backs.**
40.13 measured the distance from the **back** wall of one room
40.13 to the **back** wall of the room across the
41.13 And from the **back** of the Temple, across the open space to
42. 3 levels, each one set further **back** than the one below it.
42. 5 middle and lower levels because they were set further **back.**
43.14 The next section was set **back** from the edge fifty centimetres
43.14 after that was also set **back** from the edge fifty centimetres
Dan 7. 6 a leopard, but on its **back** there were four wings, like the
Mic 2. 8 there you are, waiting to steal the coats off their **backs.**
Mt 23. 4 They tie on to people's **backs** loads that are heavy and
Mk 4.38 Jesus was in the **back** of the boat, sleeping with his
Lk 11.46 You put loads on people's **backs** which are hard to carry,
Acts 15.10 laying a load on the **backs** of the believers
27.29 lowered four anchors from the **back** of the ship and prayed
27.41 could not move, while the **back** part was being broken to

BAD

Gen 2. 9 tree that gives knowledge of what is good and what is **bad.**
2.17 tree that gives knowledge of what is good and what is **bad.**
3. 5 be like God and know what is good and what is **bad."**
3.22 us and has knowledge of what is good and what is **bad.**
12.10 Canaan, and it was so **bad** that Abram went farther south to
37. 2 He brought **bad** reports to his father about what his brothers
41.21 have known it, because they looked just as **bad** as before.
Ex 7.21 died, and it smelt so **bad** that the Egyptians could not drink
Lev 27.12 according to its good or **bad** qualities, and the price will
27.14 according to its good or **bad** points, and the price will be
Num 11.11 he said to the Lord, "Why have you treated me so **badly?**
13.19 the land is good or **bad** and whether the people live in
1 Sam 15.23 Rebellion against him is as **bad** as witchcraft,
31. 3 Saul, and he himself was hit by enemy arrows and **badly** wounded.
2 Sam 1. 9 I have been **badly** wounded, and I'm about to die.'
1 Kgs 14. 6 I have **bad** news for you.
22. 8 it's always something **bad."**
22.18 It's always something **bad!"**
2 Kgs 2.19 fine city, but the water is **bad** and causes miscarriages."
3. 2 but he was not as **bad** as his father or his mother
25. 3 when the famine was so **bad** that the people had nothing left
1 Chr 10. 3 Saul, and he was hit by enemy arrows and **badly** wounded.
2 Chr 18. 7 it's always something **bad."**
18.17 it's always something **bad!"**
35.23 I'm **badly** hurt!"
Ps 14. 3 they are all equally **bad.**
37.19 They will not suffer when times are **bad;**
41. 6 they gather **bad** news about me and then go out and tell
53. 3 they are all equally **bad.**
112. 7 He is not afraid of receiving **bad** news;
119.104 gain wisdom from your laws, and so I hate all **bad** conduct.
120. 5 Living among you is as **bad** as living in Meshech or among
Prov 1.16 They can't wait to do something **bad.**
6.24 can keep you away from **bad** women, from the seductive words
12.21 Nothing **bad** happens to righteous people, but the wicked
14.14 **Bad** people will get what they deserve.
18. 9 A lazy person is as **bad** as someone who is destructive.
25.27 Too much honey is **bad** for you, and so is trying to
28.12 but when **bad** men rule, people stay in hiding.
28.28 People stay in hiding when **bad** men come to power.
Ecc 4.10 and falls, it's just too **bad,** because there is no one to
5. 3 likely you are to have **bad** dreams, and the more you talk,
9. 2 to the good and the **bad,** to those who are religious and
9.11 **Bad** luck happens to everyone.
11. 2 never know what kind of **bad** luck you are going to have
12.14 everything we do, whether good or **bad,** even things done in
Is 7.13 It's **bad** enough for you to wear out the patience of men
30.14 like a clay pot, so **badly** broken that there is no piece
Jer 4.15 of Dan and from the hills of Ephraim announce the **bad** news.
10.19 "How **badly** we are hurt!
14.17 weeping, for my people are deeply wounded and are **badly** hurt.
14.19 Why have you hurt us so **badly** that we cannot be healed?
23.14 they are all as **bad** as the people of Sodom and
24. 2 the other one contained **bad** figs, too bad to eat.
24. 3 and the bad ones are very bad, too **bad** to eat."
24. 8 them all like these figs that are too **bad** to be eaten.
49.23 Arpad are worried and troubled because they have heard **bad** news.
52. 6 when the famine was so **bad** that the people had nothing left
Ezek 7.26 another, and a steady stream of **bad** news will pour in.
11. 2 these men make evil plans and give **bad** advice in this city.
16.20 Wasn't it **bad** enough to be unfaithful to me, [21] without taking
23.13 immoral, that the second sister was as **bad** as the first.
34.17 separate the good from the **bad,** the sheep from the goats.
34.22 judge each of my sheep and separate the good from the **bad.**
Obad 11 You were as **bad** as those strangers who carried off Jerusalem's
Zeph 3. 7 But soon they were behaving as **badly** as ever.
Mt 5.45 his sun to shine on **bad** and good people alike,
7.11 **Bad** as you are, you know how to give good things
7.17 tree bears good fruit, but a poor tree bears **bad** fruit.
7.18 A healthy tree cannot bear **bad** fruit, and a poor tree
12.33 if you have a poor tree, you will have **bad** fruit.
12.35 a bad person brings **bad** things
12.35 out of his treasure of **bad** things.
22.10 gathered all the people they could find, good and **bad** alike;
24.48 But if he is a **bad** servant, he will tell himself
25.26 'You **bad** and lazy servant!'
Mk 9.26 spirit screamed, threw the boy into a **bad** fit, and came out.
Lk 6.43 healthy tree does not bear **bad** fruit, nor does a poor tree
6.45 a **bad** person brings bad out of his treasure of bad things.
11.13 **Bad** as you are, you know how to give good things
16.25 all the good things, while Lazarus got all the **bad** things.
19.22 He said to him, 'You **bad** servant!
22.31 separate the good from the **bad,** as a farmer separates the
Jn 6.27 Do not work for food that goes **bad;**
7. 7 hates me, because I keep telling it that its ways are **bad.**
11.39 dead man's sister, answered, "There will be a **bad** smell, Lord.
Acts 7. 6 be slaves and will be **badly** treated for four hundred years.
19.27 then, that this business of ours will get a **bad** name.
24.15 all people, both the good and the **bad,** will rise from death.
28.21 from there with any news or anything **bad** to say about you.
Rom 9.11 were born, before they had done anything either good or **bad;**
14.16 Do not let what you regard as good get a **bad** name.
1 Cor 15.33 **"Bad** companions ruin good character."
2 Cor 4. 9 and though **badly** hurt at times, we are not destroyed.
5.10 everything he has done, good or **bad,** in his bodily life.
2 Tim 3.13 will keep on going from **bad** to worse, deceiving others
Tit 2. 8 put to shame by not having anything **bad** to say about us.
Jas 4. 3 you do not receive it, because your motives are **bad;**
3 Jn 11 do not imitate what is **bad,** but imitate what is good.
11 whoever does what is **bad** has not seen God.

BAD-TEMPERED see TEMPER

BAG
[SADDLEBAG]

Gen 21.14 Abraham gave Hagar some food and a leather **bag** full of water.
21.19 went and filled the leather **bag** with water and gave some to
31.34 and put them in a camel's **saddlebag** and was sitting on them.
42.35 out their sacks, every one of them found his **bag** of money;
49.14 a donkey That lies stretched out between its **saddlebags.**
Judg 4.19 She opened a leather **bag** of milk, gave him a drink, and
1 Sam 1.24 ten kilogrammes of flour, and a leather **bag** full of wine.
10. 3 and the third one will have a leather **bag** full of wine.
16.20 a donkey loaded with bread, and a leather **bag** full of wine.
17.40 five smooth stones from the stream and put them in his **bag.**
17.49 put his hand into his **bag** and took out a stone, which
25.18 of bread, two leather **bags** full of wine, five roasted sheep,
2 Sam 16. 1 bunches of fresh fruit, and a leather **bag** full of wine.
2 Kgs 5.23 up the silver in two **bags,** gave them and two changes of
5.24 Gehazi took the two **bags** and carried them into the house.
Mt 10.10 do not carry a beggar's **bag** for the journey or an extra
Mk 6. 8 a stick—no bread, no beggar's **bag,** no money in your pockets.
Lk 9. 3 no stick, no beggar's **bag,** no food, no money, not even
10. 4 Don't take a purse or a beggar's **bag** or shoes;
22.35 that time without purse, **bag,** or shoes, did you lack anything?"
22.36 Jesus said, "whoever has a purse or a **bag** must take it;
Jn 12. 6 He carried the money **bag** and would help himself from it.
13.29 in charge of the money **bag,** some of the disciples thought

BAITED

Amos 3. 5 get caught in a trap if the trap has not been **baited?**

BAKE
[BAKING-PANS, HALF-BAKED]

Gen 11. 3 Let's make bricks and **bake** them hard."
18. 6 "Quick, take a sack of your best flour, and **bake** some bread."
19. 3 Lot ordered his servants to **bake** some bread and prepare a
27.17 him the tasty food, together with the bread she had **baked.**
40. 1 of Egypt's wine steward and his chief **baker** offended the king.
40. 5 wine steward and the chief **baker** each had a dream,
40.16 When the chief **baker** saw that the interpretation of the
40.20 and his chief **baker** and brought them before his officials.
40.22 to his former position, [22] but he executed the chief **baker.**
41.10 were angry with the chief **baker** and me, and you put us
41.13 restored me to my position, but you executed the **baker."**
Ex 8. 3 and your people, and even into your ovens and **baking-pans.**
12.34 the people filled their **baking-pans** with unleavened dough,
12.39 **baked** unleavened bread from the dough that they had brought out
16.23 **Bake** today what you want to bake and boil what you want
Lev 2. 4 If the offering is bread **baked** in an oven, it must be
6.16 shall be made into bread **baked** without yeast and eaten in a
7. 9 grain-offering that has been **baked** in an oven or prepared in
7.13 In addition, he shall offer loaves of bread **baked** without yeast.
23.14 corn, whether raw, roasted, or **baked** into bread, until you have
23.17 two kilogrammes of flour **baked** with yeast and shall be presented
24. 5 Take twelve kilogrammes of flour and **bake** twelve loaves
26.26 will need only one oven to **bake** all the bread they have.
Num 11. 8 It tasted like bread **baked** with olive-oil.)
15.20 When you **bake** bread, the first loaf of the first bread
15.21 is to be given to the Lord from the bread you **bake.**
1 Sam 8.13 make perfumes for him and work as his cooks and his **bakers.**
28.24 some flour, prepared it, and **baked** some bread without yeast.
2 Sam 13. 8 Then she **baked** the cakes [9] and emptied them out of the pan
1 Chr 9.31 of Korah, was responsible for preparing the **baked** offerings.
23.29 wafers made without yeast, the **baked** offerings, and the flour
Is 44.15 one part he builds a fire to warm himself and **bake** bread;
44.19 I **baked** some bread on the embers and I roasted meat and
Jer 7.18 the women mix dough to **bake** cakes for the goddess they call
37.21 loaf of bread from the **bakeries** until all the bread in the
44.19 the women added, "When we **baked** cakes shaped like the Queen
Ezek 4.12 out of dried human excrement, **bake** bread on the fire, and
4.15 cow dung instead, and you can **bake** your bread on that."
44.30 Each time the people **bake** bread, they are to give the
46.20 or as repayment-offerings, and to **bake** the offerings of flour,

Hos 7. 4 not stirred by the baker until the dough is ready to **bake.**
7. 8 "The people of Israel are like a **half-baked** loaf of bread.

BAKING-PANS see BAKE, PAN

BALAAM
Midianite prophet.
Num 22.1-21 **The king of Moab sends for Balaam**
22-35 **Balaam and his donkey**
36-40 **Balak welcomes Balaam**
22.41–23.12 **Balaam's first prophecy**
23.13-26 **Balaam's second prophecy**
23.27–24.13 **Balaam's third prophecy**
24.14-25 **Balaam's final prophecies**
Num 31. 8 They also killed **Balaam** son of Beor.
31.16 the women who followed **Balaam's** instructions and at Peor led
Deut 23. 4 of Egypt, and they hired **Balaam** son of Beor, from the city
23. 5 But the Lord your God would not listen to **Balaam;**
Josh 13.22 of Israel killed was the fortune-teller **Balaam** son of Beor.
24. 9 He sent word to **Balaam** son of Beor and asked him to
24.10 I would not listen to **Balaam,** so he blessed you, and in
Neh 13. 2 Instead, they paid money to **Balaam** to curse Israel, but our
Mic 6. 5 to do to you and how **Balaam** son of Beor answered him.
2 Pet 2.15 followed the path taken by **Balaam** son of Beor,
Jude 11 have given themselves over to the error that **Balaam** committed.
Rev 2.14 follow the teaching of **Balaam,** who taught Balak how to lead

BALAK
King of Moab who opposed Israel.
Num 22. 2 When the king of Moab, **Balak** son of Zippor, heard what the
22. 4 So King **Balak** [5]sent messengers to summon Balaam son of Beor,
22. 5 They brought him this message from **Balak:**
22. 7 for the curse, went to Balaam, and gave him **Balak's** message.
22.10 He answered, "King **Balak** of Moab has sent them to tell
22.13 Balaam went to **Balak's** messengers and said, "Go back home;
22.14 they returned to **Balak** and told him that Balaam had refused
22.15 **Balak** sent a larger number of leaders, who were more important
22.16 They went to Balaam and gave him this message from **Balak:**
22.18 But Balaam answered, "Even if **Balak** gave me all the silver
22.36 When **Balak** heard that Balaam was coming, he went to meet
22.37 **Balak** said to him, "Why didn't you come when I sent for
22.39 So Balaam went with **Balak** to the town of Huzoth,
22.40 where **Balak** slaughtered cattle and sheep and gave
22.41 Next morning **Balak** took Balaam up to Bamoth Baal,
23. 1 He said to **Balak,** "Build seven altars here for me, and
23. 2 **Balak** did as he was told, and he and Balaam offered a
23. 3 Then Balaam said to **Balak,** "Stand here by your burnt-offering,
23. 5 say and sent him back to **Balak** to give him his message.
23. 6 went back and found **Balak** still standing by his burnt-offering,
23. 7 **"Balak** king of Moab has brought me From Syria,
23.11 Then **Balak** said to Balaam, "What have you done to me?
23.13 Then **Balak** said to Balaam, "Come with me to another place
23.15 Balaam said to **Balak,** "Stand here by your burnt-offering,
23.16 say, and sent him back to **Balak** to give him his message.
23.17 went back and found **Balak** still standing by his burnt-offering,
23.17 **Balak** asked what the Lord had said, [18]and Balaam uttered this
23.18 "Come, **Balak** son of Zippor, And listen to what I have to
23.25 Then **Balak** said to Balaam, "You refuse to curse the people
23.27 **Balak** said, "Come with me, and I will take you to
23.30 **Balak** did as he was told, and offered a bull and a
24.10 **Balak** clenched his fists in anger and said to Balaam,
24.14 Balaam said to **Balak,** "Now I am going back to my own
24.25 got ready and went back home, and **Balak** went on his way.
Josh 24. 9 the king of Moab, **Balak** son of Zippor, fought against you.
24.10 he blessed you, and in this way I rescued you from **Balak.**
Judg 11.25 you are any better than **Balak** son of Zippor, king of Moab?
Mic 6. 5 My people, remember what King **Balak** of Moab planned to do
Rev 2.14 teaching of Balaam, who taught **Balak** how to lead the people

BALCONY
2 Kgs 1. 2 of Israel fell off the **balcony** on the roof of his palace

BALD
Lev 13.42 reddish-white sore appears on the **bald** spot, it is a dreaded
2 Kgs 2.23 "Get out of here, **baldy!"**
Is 3.17 punish them—I will shave their heads and leave them **bald."**
3.24 instead of having beautiful hair, they will be **bald;**
Ezek 29.18 their heads were rubbed **bald** and their shoulders were worn raw,
Mic 1.16 Make yourselves as **bald** as vultures, because your children will

BALL
Is 22.18 pick you up like a **ball** and throw you into a much

BALSAM
A tree from which sweet-smelling resin was obtained; the resin was used for perfume and medicine.
2 Sam 5.23 ready to attack them from the other side, near the **balsam-trees.**
1 Chr 14.14 ready to attack them from the other side, near the **balsam-trees.**
Esth 2.12 myrrh for six months and with oil of **balsam** for six more.
Song 6. 2 My lover has gone to his garden, where the **balsam-trees** grow.

AV BAN see CONDEMN

BAND (1)
Gen 34.30 if they all **band** together against me and attack me, our
49.19 will be attacked by a **band** of robbers, But he will turn
2 Sam 23.13 where David was, while a **band** of Philistines was camping in
2 Kgs 13.20 Every year **bands** of Moabites used to invade the land of Israel.
13.21 a funeral, one of those **bands** was seen, and the people threw
24. 2 The Lord sent armed **bands** of Babylonians, Syrians, Moabites,
1 Chr 11.15 cave of Adullam, while a **band** of Philistines was camping in
Job 1.17 came and said, "Three **bands** of Chaldean raiders attacked us,

BAND (2)
1 Kgs 7.35 There was a 22 centimetre **band** round the top of each cart;
Dan 4.15 in the ground with a **band** of iron and bronze round it.
4.23 Wrap a **band** of iron and bronze round it, and leave it

BANDAGE
1 Kgs 20.38 prophet **bandaged** his face with a cloth, to disguise himself,
Job 5.18 God **bandages** the wounds he makes;
Ps 147. 3 He heals the broken-hearted and **bandages** their wounds.
Is 1. 6 Your wounds have not been cleaned or **bandaged.**
30.26 all happen when the Lord **bandages** and heals the wounds he
Ezek 30.21 No one has **bandaged** it or put it in a sling so
34. 4 healed those that are sick, **bandaged** those that are hurt,
34.16 back those that wander off, **bandage** those that are hurt,
Hos 6. 1 he has wounded us, but he will **bandage** our wounds, won't he?
Lk 10.34 poured oil and wine on his wounds and **bandaged** them;

BANDIT
Mt 27.38 Then they crucified two **bandits** with Jesus, one on his right
27.44 Even the **bandits** who had been crucified with him insulted him
Mk 15.27 They also crucified two **bandits** with Jesus, one on his right
Jn 18.40 (Barabbas was a **bandit.)**

BANISH
2 Kgs 17.18 angry with the Israelites and **banished** them from his sight,
17.20 enemies until at last he had **banished** them from his sight.
17.23 until at last the Lord **banished** them from his sight,
23.27 I will **banish** the people of Judah from my sight,
24. 3 Lord's command, in order to **banish** the people of Judah from
24.20 of Jerusalem and Judah that he **banished** them from his sight.
Ps 51.11 Do not **banish** me from your presence;
Is 24.11 it has been **banished** from the land.
Jer 52. 3 of Jerusalem and Judah that he **banished** them from his sight.
Jon 2. 4 thought I had been **banished** from your presence and would never

BANK (1)
[RIVER-BANK, SANDBANK]
Gen 41. 3 the other cows on the **river-bank,** [4]and the thin cows ate up
41.17 I was standing on the **bank** of the Nile, [18]when seven cows,
Ex 2. 5 river to bathe, while her servants walked along the **bank.**
7.15 a snake, and wait for him on the **bank** of the river.
7.24 Egyptians dug along the **bank** of the river for drinking water,
Deut 2.37 the Ammonites or to the **banks** of the River Jabbok or to
Josh 3. 8 the river, they must wade in and stand near the **bank."**
4.18 when the priests reached the **river bank,**
4.18 the river began flowing once more and flooded its **banks** again.
Judg 11.26 them, and all the cities on the **banks** of the River Arnon.
2 Kgs 2.13 him, and went back and stood on the **bank** of the Jordan.
1 Chr 12.15 the River Jordan overflowed its **banks,** they crossed the river,
Is 8. 7 the flood waters of the River Euphrates, overflowing all its **banks.**
16. 2 They wait on the **banks** of the River Arnon and move
19. 7 the crops sown along the **banks** of the Nile will dry up
Jer 46. 7 that rises like the Nile, like a river flooding its **banks?**
46. 8 Egypt, rising like the Nile, like a river flooding its **banks.**
Ezek 47. 6 took me back to the **bank** of the river, [7]and when I
47. 7 there I saw that there were very many trees on each **bank.**
47.12 On each **bank** of the stream all kinds of trees will grow
Dan 10. 4 year, I was standing on the **bank** of the mighty River Tigris.
12. 5 I saw two men standing by a river, one on each **bank.**
Acts 27.17 they might run into the **sandbanks** off the coast of Libya,
27.41 But the ship hit a **sandbank** and went aground;

BANK (2)
Mt 25.27 deposited my money in the **bank,** and I would have received it
Lk 19.23 Well, then, why didn't you put my money in the **bank?**

BANNER
[THE LORD IS MY BANNER]
Ex 17.15 Moses built an altar and named it **"The Lord is my Banner."**
17.16 He said, "Hold high the **banner** of the Lord!
Num 1.52 each man with his own group and under his own **banner.**
2. 2 man will camp under the **banner** of his division and the flag
2. 3 those under the **banner** of the division of Judah shall
2.10 those under the **banner** of the division of Reuben shall
2.17 same order as they camp, each in position under its **banner.**
2.18 those under the **banner** of the division of Ephraim shall
2.25 those under the **banner** of the division of Dan shall
2.34 camped, each under his own **banner,** and they marched, each with
10.14 Those under the **banner** of the division led by the tribe of
10.18 those under the **banner** of the division led by the tribe
10.22 those under the **banner** of the division led by the tribe

Num 10.25 Finally, those under the **banner** of the division led by the
Song 2. 4 his banqueting hall and raised the **banner** of love over me.

BANQUET

Gen 40.20 days later the king gave a **banquet** for all his officials;
Judg 14.10 went to the girl's house, and Samson gave a **banquet** there.
2 Sam 13.27 Absalom prepared a **banquet** fit for a king [28]and instructed
Esth 1. 3 he gave a **banquet** for all his officials and administrators.
1. 5 the king gave a **banquet** for all the men in the
1. 9 royal palace Queen Vashti was giving a **banquet** for the women.
1.10 seventh day of his **banquet** the king was drinking and feeling
2.18 king gave a great **banquet** in Esther's honour and invited all
5. 4 be my guests tonight at a **banquet** I am preparing for you."
5. 5 So the king and Haman went to Esther's **banquet.**
5. 8 guests tomorrow at another **banquet** that I will prepare for you.
5. 9 When Haman left the **banquet** he was happy and in a good
5.12 on, "Queen Esther gave a **banquet** for no one but the king
5.14 hanged on it, and then you can go to the **banquet** happy."
6.14 eunuchs arrived in a hurry to take Haman to Esther's **banquet.**
Ps 23. 5 You prepare a **banquet** for me, where all my enemies can see
69.22 May their **banquets** cause their ruin;
Prov 17. 1 mind than to have a **banquet** in a house full of trouble.
Song 2. 4 He brought me to his **banqueting** hall and raised the banner
Is 21. 5 In the vision a **banquet** is ready;
25. 6 Lord Almighty will prepare a **banquet** for all the nations
25. 6 world—a **banquet** of the richest food
Dan 5. 1 a thousand noblemen to a great **banquet,** and they drank wine
5.10 made by the king and his noblemen and entered the **banqueting-hall.**
Amos 6. 7 Your feasts and **banquets** will come to an end.

BAPTIST see JOHN (1)

BAPTIZE

Mt 3. 6 They confessed their sins, and he **baptized** them in the Jordan.
3. 7 coming to him to be **baptized,** he said to them, "You snakes
3.11 I **baptize** you with water to show that you have repented,
3.11 will come after me will **baptize** you with the Holy Spirit
3.13 and came to John at the Jordan to be **baptized** by him.
3.14 "I ought to be **baptized** by you," John said,
3.16 As soon as Jesus was **baptized,** he came up out of
21.25 Where did John's right to **baptize** come from:
28.19 **baptize** them in the name of the Father, the Son, and the
Mk 1. 4 So John appeared in the desert, **baptizing** and preaching.
1. 4 from your sins and be **baptized,"** he told the people,
1. 5 confessed their sins, and he **baptized** them in the River Jordan.
1. 8 I **baptize** you with water,
1. 8 but he will **baptize** you with the Holy Spirit."
1. 9 province of Galilee, and was **baptized** by John in the Jordan.
10.38 Can you be **baptized** in the way I must be baptized?"
10.39 and be baptized in the way I must be **baptized.**
11.30 Tell me, where did John's right to **baptize** come from:
16.16 Whoever believes and is **baptized** will be saved;
Lk 3. 3 your sins and be **baptized,** and God will forgive your sins."
3. 7 Crowds of people came out to John to be **baptized** by him.
3.12 tax collectors came to be **baptized,** and they asked him,
3.16 to all of them, "I **baptize** you with water, but someone
3.16 He will **baptize** you with the Holy Spirit and fire.
3.21 After all the people had been **baptized,**
3.21 Jesus also was **baptized.**
7.29 God's righteous demands and had been **baptized** by John.
7.30 rejected God's purpose for themselves and refused to be **baptized**
12.50 I have a **baptism** to receive, and how distressed I am
20. 4 did John's right to **baptize** come from God or from man?"
Jn 1.25 Messiah nor Elijah nor the Prophet, why do you **baptize?"**
1.26 John answered, "I **baptize** with water, but among you stands
1.28 east side of the River Jordan, where John was **baptizing.**
1.31 but I came **baptizing** with water in order to make
1.33 God, who sent me to **baptize** with water, had said to me,
1.33 he is the one who **baptizes** with the Holy Spirit.'
3.22 of Judaea, where he spent some time with them and **baptized.**
3.23 John also was **baptizing** in Aenon, not far from Salim,
3.23 People were going to him, and he was **baptizing** them.
3.26 Well, he is **baptizing** now, and everyone is going to him!"
4. 1 that Jesus was winning and **baptizing** more disciples than John.
4. 2 (Actually, Jesus himself did not **baptize** anyone;
10.40 place where John had been **baptizing,** and he stayed there.
Acts 1. 5 John **baptized** with water, but in a few days
1. 5 you will be **baptized** with the Holy Spirit."
1.21 John preached his message of **baptism** until the day Jesus was
2.38 from his sins and be **baptized** in the name of Jesus Christ,
2.41 believed his message and were **baptized,** and about three thousand
8.12 and about Jesus Christ, they were **baptized,** both men and women.
8.13 and after being **baptized,** he stayed close to Philip and was
8.16 they had only been **baptized** in the name of the Lord Jesus.
8.36 What is to keep me from being **baptized?"**
8.38 the official went down into the water, and Philip **baptized** him.
9.18 He stood up and was **baptized;**
10.37 beginning in Galilee after John preached his message of **baptism.**
10.47 Can anyone, then, stop them from being **baptized** with water?"
10.48 he ordered them to be **baptized** in the name of Jesus Christ.
11.16 'John **baptized** with water,
11.16 but you will be **baptized** with the Holy Spirit.'
13.24 Israel that they should turn from their sins and be **baptized.**
16.15 of her house had been **baptized,** she invited us, "Come and
16.33 and he and all his family were **baptized** at once.
18. 8 people in Corinth heard the message, believed, and were **baptized.**
Acts 18.25 However, he knew only the **baptism** of John.
19. 3 "Well, then, what kind of **baptism** did you receive?"
19. 3 "The **baptism** of John," they answered.
19. 4 Paul said, "The **baptism** of John was for those who turned
19. 5 they heard this, they were **baptized** in the name of the Lord
22.16 Get up and be **baptized** and have your sins washed away
Rom 6. 3 know that when we were **baptized** into union with Christ Jesus,
6. 3 we were **baptized** into union with his death.
6. 4 By our **baptism,** then, we were buried with him and shared
1 Cor 1.13 Were you **baptized** as Paul's disciples?
1.14 I did not **baptize** any of you except Crispus and
1.15 No one can say, then, that you were **baptized** as my disciples.
1.16 (Oh yes, I also **baptized** Stephanas and his family;
1.16 but I can't remember whether I **baptized** anyone else.)
1.17 Christ did not send me to **baptize.**
10. 2 and in the sea they were all **baptized** as followers of Moses.
12.13 slaves or free, have been **baptized** into the one body
15.29 Now, what about those people who are **baptized** for the dead?
15.29 to life, why are those people being **baptized** for the dead?
Gal 3.27 You were **baptized** into union with Christ, and now you are
Eph 4. 5 There is one Lord, one faith, one **baptism;**
Col 2.12 For when you were **baptized,** you were buried with Christ,
2.12 and in **baptism** you were also raised with Christ
Heb 6. 2 of the teaching about **baptisms** and the laying on of hands;
1 Pet 3.21 which was a symbol pointing to **baptism,** which now saves you.
1 Jn 5. 6 with the water of his **baptism** and the blood of his death.

BAR
see also **CROSS-BAR**

BAR (1)

Num 22.22 angel of the Lord stood in the road to **bar** his way.
22.32 I have come to **bar** your way, because you should not be

BAR (2)

Num 3.36 for the Tent, its **bars,** posts, bases, and all its fittings.
4.31 for carrying the frames, **bars,** posts, and bases of the Tent,
Deut 3. 5 with high walls, gates, and **bars** to lock the gates, and
Josh 7.21 kilogrammes of silver, and a **bar** of gold weighing over half
7.24 the cloak, and the **bar** of gold, together with Achan's sons
1 Sam 17. 7 was as thick as the **bar** on a weaver's loom, and its
2 Sam 21.19 had a shaft as thick as the **bar** on a weaver's loom.
1 Kgs 4.13 with walls and with bronze **bars** on the gates
1 Chr 20. 5 had a shaft as thick as the **bar** on a weaver's loom.
2 Chr 8. 5 with gates that could be **barred),** [6]the city of Baalath, all
14. 7 walls and towers, and gates that can be shut and **barred.**
Neh 3. 3 place, and put in the bolts and **bars** for locking the gate.
3. 6 place, and put in the bolts and **bars** for locking the gate.
3.13 in the bolts and the **bars** for locking the gate, and repaired
3.14 and put in the bolts and the **bars** for locking the gate.
3.15 the gates in place, and put in the bolts and the **bars.**
7. 3 to have them closed and **barred** before the guards went off
Job 40.18 are as strong as bronze, and his legs are like iron **bars.**
Ps 107.16 He breaks down doors of bronze and smashes iron **bars.**
Is 45. 2 I will break down bronze gates and smash their iron **bars.**
Lam 2. 9 The gates lie buried in rubble, their **bars** smashed to pieces.
Ezek 26. 9 with battering-rams and tear down your towers with iron **bars.**
Nah 3.13 Fire will destroy the **bars** across your gates.

BARABBAS
Criminal released by Pilate when Jesus was condemned to death.

Mt 27.16 that time there was a well-known prisoner named Jesus **Barabbas.**
27.17 Jesus **Barabbas** or Jesus called the Messiah?"
27.20 to ask Pilate to set **Barabbas** free and have Jesus put to
27.21 **"Barabbas!"**
27.26 Then Pilate set **Barabbas** free for them;
Mk 15. 7 that time a man named **Barabbas** was in prison with the rebels
15.11 to ask, instead, for Pilate to set **Barabbas** free for them.
15.15 to please the crowd, so he set **Barabbas** free for them.
Lk 23.18 Set **Barabbas** free for us!"
23.19 **(Barabbas** had been put in prison for a riot that had
Jn 18.40 We want **Barabbas!"**
18.40 **(Barabbas** was a bandit.)

BARAK
Military leader from n. Israel in Deborah's time.

Judg 4. 6 One day she sent for **Barak** son of Abinoam from the city
4. 8 Then **Barak** replied, "I will go if you go with me, but
4. 9 So Deborah set off for Kedesh with **Barak.**
4.10 **Barak** called the tribes of Zebulun and Naphtali to Kedesh,
4.12 When Sisera learnt that **Barak** had gone up to Mount Tabor,
4.14 Then Deborah said to **Barak,** "Go!
4.14 So **Barak** went down from Mount Tabor with his ten thousand men.
4.15 **Barak** attacked with his army, the Lord threw Sisera into confusion
4.16 **Barak** pursued the chariots and the army to
4.22 **Barak** came looking for Sisera, Jael went out to meet him
5. 1 On that day Deborah and **Barak** son of Abinoam sang this song:
5.12 Forward, **Barak** son of Abinoam, lead your captives away!
5.15 yes, Issachar came and **Barak** too, and they followed him into
1 Sam 12.11 And the Lord sent Gideon, **Barak,** Jephthah, and finally me.
Heb 11.32 to speak of Gideon, **Barak,** Samson, Jephthah, David, Samuel,

BARBARIANS

Col 3.11 circumcised and uncircumcised, **barbarians,** savages, slaves, and

BARBER

Is 7.20 Lord will hire a **barber** from across the Euphrates—the emperor

BARE

Judg 14. 6 the lion apart with his **bare** hands, as if it were a
2 Sam 22.16 of the ocean was laid **bare,** and the foundations of the earth
23. 6 no one can touch them with **bare** hands.
Job 6.17 heat they disappear, and the stream beds lie **bare** and dry.
Ps 18.15 of the ocean was laid **bare,** and the foundations of the earth
Is 17. 5 field in the valley of Rephaim when it has been picked **bare.**
50. 6 I **bared** my back to those who beat me.
Jer 51. 2 they will attack from every side and leave the land **bare.**
Ezek 12.19 Their land will be stripped **bare,** because everyone who lives
13.14 to shatter it, and to leave the foundation stones **bare.**
24. 7 it was spilt on a **bare** rock.
26. 4 will sweep away all the dust and leave only a **bare** rock.
26.14 I will leave only a **bare** rock where fishermen can dry
Joel 1.10 The fields are **bare;**
Mic 1. 6 down into the valley, and will lay **bare** the city's foundations.
1 Cor 15.37 what you sow is a **bare** seed, perhaps a grain of wheat

BAREFOOT

2 Sam 15.30 he was **barefoot** and had his head covered as a sign of
Is 20. 2 He obeyed and went about naked and **barefoot.**
20. 3 Isaiah has been going about naked and **barefoot** for three years.
20. 4 they will walk **barefoot** and naked, with their buttocks exposed,
Ezek 24.17 Do not go bareheaded or **barefoot** as a sign of mourning.
24.23 You will not go bareheaded or **barefoot** or mourn or cry.
Mic 1. 8 To show my sorrow, I will walk about **barefoot** and naked.

BAREHEADED

Ezek 24.17 Do not go **bareheaded** or barefoot as a sign of mourning.
24.23 You will not go **bareheaded** or barefoot or mourn or cry.

BARGAIN

2 Kgs 18.23 I will make a **bargain** with you in the name of the
Job 41. 6 Will fishermen **bargain** over him?
Prov 20.14 but then he goes off and brags about the **bargain** he got.
Is 36. 8 I will make a **bargain** with you in the name of the

BARK (1)

Gen 30.37 stripped off some of the **bark** so that the branches had white
Joel 1. 7 They have stripped off the **bark,** till the branches are white.

BARK (2)

Ex 11. 7 not even a dog will **bark** at the Israelites or their animals.
Is 56.10 like watchdogs that don't **bark**—they only lie about and dream.

BARLEY

A cultivated grain similar to wheat, grown as a food crop.

Ex 9.31 flax and the **barley** were ruined, because the barley was ripe,
Lev 27.16 of ten pieces of silver for every twenty kilogrammes of **barley.**
Num 5.15 offering of one kilogramme of **barley** flour, but he shall not
Deut 8. 8 land that produces wheat and **barley,** grapes, figs, pomegranates,
Judg 7.13 dreamt that a loaf of **barley** bread rolled into our camp
Ruth 1.22 **barley** harvest was just beginning when they arrived in Bethlehem.
2.23 gathered corn until all the **barley** and wheat had been harvested.
3. 2 This evening he will be threshing the **barley.**
3. 7 He went to the pile of **barley** and lay down to sleep.
3.15 out nearly twenty kilogrammes of **barley** and helped her to lift
3.17 back to you empty-handed, so he gave me all this **barley."**
2 Sam 14.30 field is next to mine, and it has **barley** growing in it.
17.28 wheat, **barley,** meal, roasted grain, beans, peas, honey, cheese,
21. 9 at the beginning of the **barley** harvest, when they were put
1 Kgs 4.28 supplied his share of **barley** and straw, where it was needed,
2 Kgs 4.42 bread made from the first **barley** harvested that year,
7. 1 wheat or six kilogrammes of **barley** for one piece of silver."
7.16 wheat or six kilogrammes of **barley** were sold for one piece
7.18 wheat or six kilogrammes of **barley** would be sold in Samaria
1 Chr 11.13 was in a **barley-field** when the Israelites started to run away,
2 Chr 2.10 two thousand metric tons of **barley,** four hundred thousand
2.15 send us the wheat, **barley,** wine, and olive-oil that you promised.
27. 5 1,000 metric tons of wheat, and 1,000 metric tons of **barley.**
Job 31.40 then instead of wheat and **barley,** may weeds and thistles grow.
Is 28.25 sows rows of wheat and **barley,** and at the edges of his
Jer 41. 8 have wheat, **barley,** olive-oil, and honey hidden in the fields."
Ezek 4. 9 "Now take some wheat, **barley,** beans, peas, millet, and
13.19 get a few handfuls of **barley** and a few pieces of bread.
45.13 **Barley:** 1/60th of your harvest
Hos 3. 2 pieces of silver and 150 kilogrammes of **barley** to buy her
Joel 1.11 because the wheat, the **barley,** yes all the crops are destroyed.
Jn 6. 9 boy here who has five loaves of **barley** bread and two fish.
6.13 from the five **barley** loaves which the people had eaten.
Rev 6. 6 and three litres of **barley** for a day's wages.

BARN

Deut 28. 8 your God will bless your work and fill your **barns** with corn.
1 Sam 6. 7 them to the wagon and drive their calves back to the **barn.**
6.10 hitched them to the wagon, and shut the calves in the **barn.**
2 Chr 32.28 **barns** for his cattle;
Ps 144.13 May our **barns** be filled with crops of every kind.
Prov 3.10 If you do, your **barns** will be filled with grain, and you
14. 4 to pull the plough your **barn** will be empty, but with them
Mt 3.12 gather his wheat into his **barn,** but he will burn the chaff
6.26 do not sow seeds, gather a harvest and put it in **barns;**
13.30 then to gather in the wheat and put it in my **barn.'"**
Lk 3.17 thresh out all the grain and gather the wheat into his **barn;**
12.18 'I will tear down my **barns** and build bigger ones,
12.24 they don't have store-rooms or **barns;**

BARNABAS

Native of Cyprus, Mark's cousin and Paul's companion on his first missionary journey.
see also **JOSEPH (7)**

Acts 4.36 the apostles called **Barnabas** (which means "One who Encourages"),
9.27 Then **Barnabas** came to his help and took him to the apostles.
11.22 the church in Jerusalem, so they sent **Barnabas** to Antioch.
11.24 **Barnabas** was a good man, full of the Holy Spirit and faith,
11.25 Then **Barnabas** went to Tarsus to look for Saul.
11.30 sent the money to the church elders by **Barnabas** and Saul.
12.25 **Barnabas** and Saul finished their mission and returned from
13. 1 **Barnabas,** Simeon (called the Black), Lucius (from Cyrene), Manaen
13. 2 "Set apart for me **Barnabas** and Saul, to do the work
13. 4 sent by the Holy Spirit, **Barnabas** and Saul went to Seleucia
13. 7 governor called **Barnabas** and Saul before him because he wanted
13.42 Paul and **Barnabas** were leaving the synagogue, the people invited
13.43 left the meeting, Paul and **Barnabas** were followed by many Jews
13.46 But Paul and **Barnabas** spoke out even more boldly:
13.50 persecution against Paul and **Barnabas** and threw them out of
14. 1 Paul and **Barnabas** went to the synagogue and spoke in such
14.12 They gave **Barnabas** the name Zeus, and Paul the name Hermes,
14.14 When **Barnabas** and Paul heard what they were about to do,
14.20 The next day he and **Barnabas** went to Derbe.
14.21 Paul and **Barnabas** preached the Good News in Derbe and won
15. 2 Paul and **Barnabas** got into a fierce argument with them about
15. 2 was decided that Paul and **Barnabas** and some of the others
15.12 silent as they heard **Barnabas** and Paul report all the miracles
15.22 the group and send them to Antioch with Paul and **Barnabas.**
15.25 go with our dear friends **Barnabas** and Paul, [26] who have risked
15.35 Paul and **Barnabas** spent some time in Antioch,
15.36 later Paul said to **Barnabas,** "Let us go back and visit
15.37 **Barnabas** wanted to take John Mark with them,
15.39 **Barnabas** took Mark and sailed off for Cyprus,
1 Cor 9. 6 Or are **Barnabas** and I the only ones who have to work
Gal 2. 1 went back to Jerusalem with **Barnabas,** taking Titus along with me.
2. 9 so they shook hands with **Barnabas** and me, as a sign
2. 9 We agreed that **Barnabas** and I would work among the Gentiles
2.13 and even **Barnabas** was swept along by their cowardly action.
Col 4.10 sends you greetings, and so does Mark, the cousin of **Barnabas.**

BARRACKS

Neh 3.16 as far as David's tomb, the pool, and the **barracks.**
Ezek 27.10 They hung their shields and their helmets in your **barracks.**

BARREL

Lk 16. 6 'One hundred **barrels** of olive-oil,' he answered.

BARREN

Deut 29.23 fields will be a **barren** waste, covered with sulphur and salt;
Josh 8.15 they were retreating, and ran away towards the **barren** country.
8.20 had run towards the **barren** country now turned round to attack
8.24 the enemy in the **barren** country where they had chased them.
Judg 1.16 city of palm-trees, into the **barren** country south of Arad
2 Sam 1.21 may its fields be always **barren!**
Job 3. 7 make it a **barren,** joyless night.
Is 13. 2 On the top of a **barren** hill raise the battle flag!
21.13 whose caravans camp in the **barren** country of Arabia,
32. 2 desert, like the shadow of a giant rock in a **barren** land.
34.11 Lord will make it a **barren** waste again, as it was before
41.18 will make rivers flow among **barren** hills and springs of water
41.19 Forests will grow in **barren** land, forests of pine and juniper
Jer 4.23 I looked at the earth—it was a **barren** waste;
Hos 2. 3 her like a dry and **barren** land, and she will die of
9.14 Make their women **barren!**
Joel 2. 3 the Garden of Eden, but behind them it is a **barren** desert.

BARRICADE

Lk 19.43 enemies will surround you with **barricades,** blockade you,

BARUCH (1)

Jeremiah's companion who recorded the prophet's messages.

Jer 32.12 and gave them to **Baruch,** the son of Neriah and grandson
32.13 them all I said to **Baruch,** [14] "The Lord Almighty, the God
32.16 the deed of purchase to **Baruch,** I prayed, [17] "Sovereign Lord,
36. 4 I called **Baruch** son of Neriah and dictated to him everything
36. 4 And **Baruch** wrote it all down on a scroll.
36. 5 Then I gave **Baruch** the following instructions:
36. 8 So **Baruch** read the Lord's words in the Temple exactly as I
36.10 all the people were listening, **Baruch** read from the scroll
36.11 and grandson of Shaphan, heard **Baruch** read from the scroll what
36.13 them everything that he had heard **Baruch** read to the people.
36.14 great-grandson of Cushi) to tell **Baruch** to bring the scroll

Jer	36.14	**Baruch** brought them the scroll.
	36.15	So **Baruch** did.
	36.16	in alarm, and said to **Baruch,** "We must report this to the
	36.18	**Baruch** answered, "Jeremiah dictated every word of it to me,
	36.26	Shelemiah son of Abdeel, to arrest me and my secretary **Baruch.**
	36.27	that I had dictated to **Baruch,** the Lord told me [28] to take
	36.32	gave it to my secretary **Baruch,** and he wrote down everything
	43. 3	**Baruch** son of Neriah has stirred you up against us, so
	43. 6	had left under the care of Gedaliah, including **Baruch** and me.
	45. 1	Josiah was king of Judah, **Baruch** wrote down what I had
	45. 2	God of Israel, had said, **"Baruch,** [3] you are saying, 'I give

BASE
see also **BASIS**

Ex	25.31	Make its **base** and its shaft of hammered gold;
	26.19	south side [19] and forty silver **bases** to go under them,
	26.19	two **bases** under each frame to hold its
	26.21	of the Tent [21] and forty silver **bases,** two under each frame.
	26.25	be eight frames with their sixteen silver **bases,** two under each
	26.32	with gold, fitted with hooks, and set in four silver **bases.**
	26.37	make five bronze **bases** for these posts.
	27.10	bronze posts in twenty bronze **bases,** with hooks and rods made
	27.12	to be curtains 22 metres long, with ten posts and ten **bases.**
	27.14	be 6.6 metres of curtains, with three posts and three **bases.**
	27.16	It is to be supported by four posts in four **bases.**
	27.17	hooks are to be made of silver and their **bases** of bronze.
	27.18	are to be made of fine linen and the **bases** of bronze.
	29.12	out the rest of the blood at the **base** of the altar.
	30.18	Lord said to Moses, [18] "Make a bronze basin with a bronze **base.**
	30.28	together with all its equipment, and the wash-basin with its **base.**
	31. 9	wash-basin and its **base,** [10] the magnificent priestly garments
	35.11	hooks and its frames, its cross-bars, its posts, and its **bases;**
	35.16	the wash-basin and its **base;**
	35.17	the curtains for the enclosure, its posts and **bases;**
	36.24	south side [24] and forty silver **bases** to go under them,
	36.24	two **bases** under each frame to hold its
	36.26	of the Tent [26] and forty silver **bases,** two under each frame.
	36.30	there were eight frames and sixteen silver **bases,** two under
	36.36	Then they made four silver **bases** to hold the posts.
	36.38	rods with gold, and made five bronze **bases** for the posts.
	37.17	He made its **base** and its shaft of hammered gold;
	38. 8	bronze basin and its bronze **base** out of the mirrors
	38.10	bronze posts in twenty bronze **bases,** with hooks and rods made
	38.12	with ten posts and ten **bases** and with hooks and rods made
	38.14	were 6.6 metres of curtains, with three posts and three **bases.**
	38.17	The **bases** for the posts were made of bronze, and the
	38.19	It was supported by four posts in four bronze **bases.**
	38.27	used to make the hundred **bases** for the sacred Tent
	38.27	and for the curtain, 34 kilogrammes for each **base.**
	38.30	With it he made the **bases** for the entrance of the Tent
	38.31	for the altar, [31] the **bases** for the surrounding enclosure
	39.33	its hooks, its frames, its cross-bars, its posts, and its **bases;**
	39.39	the wash-basin and its **base;**
	39.40	the curtains for the enclosure and its posts and **bases;**
	40.11	Also dedicate the wash-basin and its **base** in the same way.
	40.18	Moses put down its **bases,** set up its frames, attached its
Lev	4. 7	of the blood at the **base** of the altar used for burning
	4.18	rest of it at the **base** of the altar used for burning
	4.25	pour out the rest of it at the **base** of the altar.
	4.30	pour out the rest of it at the **base** of the altar.
	4.34	pour out the rest of it at the **base** of the altar.
	5. 9	the blood will be drained out at the **base** of the altar.
	8.11	on the basin and its **base,** in order to dedicate them to
	8.15	out the rest of the blood at the **base** of the altar.
	9. 9	poured out the rest of it at the **base** of the altar.
Num	3.36	for the Tent, its bars, posts, **bases,** and all its fittings.
	3.37	also responsible for the posts, **bases,** pegs, and ropes for the
	4.31	the frames, bars, posts, and **bases** of the Tent,
	4.32	and the posts, **bases,** pegs, and ropes of the court
Job	28. 9	Men dig the hardest rocks, Dig mountains away at their **base.**
Is	40.19	metalworkers cover with gold and set in a **base** of silver.
Ezek	41.22	Its corner-posts, its **base,** and its sides were all made of wood.
	43.13	All round the **base** of the altar there was a gutter fifty
	43.14	the altar, from the top of the **base,** was one metre high.

BASED ON see BASIS

BASHAN
Area of Lake Galilee which belonged to the tribe of Manasseh.

Num	21.33	and took the road to **Bashan,**
	21.33	and King Og of **Bashan** marched out with his army to
	32.33	Amorites and King Og of **Bashan,** including the towns and the
Deut	1. 4	Heshbon, and King Og of **Bashan,** who ruled in the towns of
	3. 1	north towards the region of **Bashan,** and King Og came out
	3. 4	whole region of Argob, where King Og of **Bashan** ruled.
	3.10	We took all the territory of King Og of **Bashan:**
	3.10	regions of Gilead and of **Bashan,** as far east as the towns
	3.13	Gilead and also all of **Bashan,** where Og had ruled, that is,
	3.13	**(Bashan** was known as the land of the Rephaim.
	3.14	region of Argob, that is, **Bashan,** as far as the border of
	4.43	of Manasseh there was Golan, in the territory of **Bashan.**
	4.47	land of King Og of **Bashan,** the other Amorite king who lived
	29. 7	Heshbon and King Og of **Bashan** came out to fight against us.
	33.22	He leaps out from **Bashan."**
Josh	9.10	Sihon of Heshbon and King Og of **Bashan,** who lived in Ashtaroth.
	12. 4	also defeated King Og of **Bashan,** who was one of the last
	12. 5	Hermon, Salecah, and all of **Bashan** as far as the boundaries
	13.11	Maacah, all Mount Hermon, and all of **Bashan** as far as Salecah.
Josh	13.30	Mahanaim and included all of **Bashan**—the whole kingdom of Og,
	13.30	Og, the king of **Bashan,**
	13.30	as well as all sixty of the villages of Jair in **Bashan.**
	13.31	Ashtaroth and Edrei, the capital cities of Og's kingdom in **Bashan.**
	17. 1	so Gilead and **Bashan,** east of the Jordan, were assigned
	17. 5	in addition to Gilead and **Bashan** on the east side of the
	20. 8	and Golan in **Bashan,** in the territory of Manasseh.
	21.27	Golan in **Bashan** (one of the cities of refuge) and Beeshterah,
1 Kgs	4.13	the region of Argob in **Bashan,** sixty large towns in all,
	4.19	Amorites and King Og of **Bashan**
2 Kgs	10.33	the territories of Gilead and **Bashan,** where the tribes of Gad,
1 Chr	5.11	of Reuben in the land of **Bashan** as far east as Salecah.
	5.12	Janai and Shaphat were founders of other clans in **Bashan.**
	5.16	lived in the territory of **Bashan** and Gilead, in the towns
	5.23	in the territory of **Bashan** as far north as Baal Hermon,
	6.62	of Issachar, Asher, Naphtali, and East Manasseh in **Bashan.**
	6.71	Golan in **Bashan,** and Ashtaroth.
Neh	9.22	Sihon ruled, and the land of **Bashan,** where Og was king.
Ps	22.12	all round me, like fierce bulls from the land of **Bashan.**
	68.15	What a mighty mountain is **Bashan,** a mountain of many peaks!
	68.22	Lord has said, "I will bring your enemies back from **Bashan;**
	135.11	Amorites, Og, king of **Bashan,** and all the kings in Canaan.
	136.20	and Og, king of **Bashan;**
Is	2.13	cedars of Lebanon and all the oaks in the land of **Bashan.**
	33. 9	like a desert, and in **Bashan** and on Mount Carmel the leaves
Jer	22.20	to Lebanon and shout, go to the land of **Bashan** and cry;
	50.19	and in the region of **Bashan,** and they will eat all they
Ezek	27. 6	They took oak-trees from **Bashan** to make oars;
Amos	4. 1	like the well-fed cows of **Bashan,** who ill-treat the weak,
Mic	7.14	in the rich pastures of **Bashan** and Gilead, as they did long
Nah	1. 4	The fields of **Bashan** wither, Mount Carmel turns brown,
Zech	11. 2	Weep and wail, oaks of **Bashan**— the dense forest has been

BASIN
[WASH-BASIN]

Ex	30.18	said to Moses, [18] "Make a bronze **basin** with a bronze base.
	30.28	with all its equipment, and the **wash-basin** with its base.
	31. 9	and all its equipment, the **wash-basin** and its base, [10] the
	35.16	the **wash-basin** and its base;
	38. 8	He made the bronze **basin** and its bronze base out of the
	39.39	the **wash-basin** and its base;
	40. 7	Put the **wash-basin** between the Tent and the altar and fill
	40.11	Also dedicate the **wash-basin** and its base in the same way.
	40.30	He put the **wash-basin** between the Tent and the altar and
Lev	8.11	its equipment and on the **basin** and its base, in order to
Num	4.14	firepans, hooks, shovels, and **basins.**
	7.12	and one silver **basin** weighing 800 grammes, by the official
	7.84	and twelve silver **basins** weighing a total of 27.6 kilogrammes
1 Kgs	7.30	At the four corners were bronze supports for a **basin;**
	7.31	There was a circular frame on top for the **basin.**
	7.38	Huram also made ten **basins,** one for each cart.
	7.38	Each **basin** was 1.8 metres in diameter,
	7.40	The ten **basins** The tank The twelve bulls supporting
2 Kgs	16.17	used in the Temple and removed the **basins** that were on them;
2 Chr	4. 6	They also made ten **basins,** five to be placed on the south
	4.11	The ten **basins** The tank The twelve bulls supporting
Ps	60. 8	will use Moab as my **wash-basin** and I will throw my sandals
	108. 9	will use Moab as my **wash-basin** and I will throw my sandals
Jn	13. 5	some water into a **basin** and began to wash the disciples'

BASIS
[BASED ON]

Acts	10.34	that it is true that God treats everyone on the same **basis.**
Rom	3.30	right with himself on the **basis** of their faith,
	4.16	And so the promise was **based on** faith, in order that
	9.11	God's choice was **based on** his call, and not on anything
	10. 2	but their devotion is not **based on** true knowledge.
	11. 6	His choice is **based on** his grace, not on what they have
	11. 6	For if God's choice were **based on** what people do,
	14.23	when he eats it, because his action is not **based on** faith.
	14.23	And anything that is not **based on** faith is sin.
1 Cor	2.14	because their value can be judged only on a spiritual **basis.**
2 Cor	8.12	accept your gift on the **basis** of what you have to give,
Gal	3.22	which is promised on the **basis** of faith in Jesus Christ
Eph	1.11	because of his own purpose, **based on** what he had decided
	2.12	the covenants, which were **based on** God's promises to his people,
Phil	3. 9	the righteousness that comes from God and is **based on** faith.
Col	1. 5	your faith and love are **based on** what you hope for,
	2.23	such rules appear to be **based on** wisdom in their forced
1 Thes	2. 3	appeal to you is not **based on** error or impure motives,
Tit	1. 2	our religion, [2] which is **based on** the hope for eternal life.
Heb	7.11	It was on the **basis** of the levitical priesthood that the
	8. 6	one, because it is **based on** promises of better things.
Jas	2. 4	and of making judgements **based on** evil motives.

BASKET
[BREAD-BASKETS]

Gen	40.16	I was carrying three **bread-baskets** on my head.
	40.17	In the top **basket** there were all kinds of pastries for
	40.18	the three **baskets** are three days.
Ex	2. 3	any longer, she took a **basket** made of reeds and covered it
	2. 5	Suddenly she noticed the **basket** in the tall grass and sent a
	29. 3	Put them in a **basket** and offer them to me when you
	29.23	From the **basket** of bread which has been offered to me,
	29.32	are to eat it along with the bread left in the **basket.**
Lev	8. 2	sin-offering, the two rams, and the **basket** of unleavened bread.
	8.26	loaf of bread from the **basket** of unleavened bread dedicated to
	8.31	bread that is in the **basket** of ordination offerings,

Num 6.15 He shall also offer a **basket** of bread made without yeast:
6.17 as a fellowship-offering, and offer it with the **basket** of bread;
6.19 one biscuit from the **basket**, into the hands of the Nazirite.
Deut 26. 2 you must place in a **basket** the first part of each crop
26. 4 "The priest will take the **basket** from you and place it
26.10 set the **basket** down in the Lord's presence and worship there.
Judg 6.19 put the meat in a **basket** and the broth in a pot,
2 Kgs 10. 7 descendants, put their heads in **baskets**, and sent them to Jehu
Jer 24. 1 The Lord showed me two **baskets** of figs placed in front of
24. 2 The first **basket** contained good figs, those that ripen early;
Amos 8. 1 In it I saw a **basket** of fruit.
8. 1 "A **basket** of fruit," I answered.
Zech 5. 6 He replied, "It is a **basket**, and it stands for the sin
5. 7 The **basket** had a lid made of lead.
5. 7 the lid was raised, and there in the **basket** sat a woman!
5. 8 pushed her down into the **basket** and put the lid back down.
5. 9 They picked up the **basket** and flew off with it.
5.11 the temple is finished, the **basket** will be placed there to
Mt 14.20 disciples took up twelve **baskets** full of what was left over.
15.37 the disciples took up seven **baskets** full of pieces left over.
16. 9 How many **baskets** did you fill?
16.10 How many **baskets** did you fill?
Mk 6.43 the disciples took up twelve **baskets** full of what was left
8. 8 the disciples took up seven **baskets** full of pieces left over.
8.19 How many **baskets** full of leftover pieces did you take up?"
8.20 asked Jesus, "how many **baskets** full of leftover pieces did you
Lk 9.17 the disciples took up twelve **baskets** of what was left over.
Jn 6.13 all up and filled twelve **baskets** with the pieces left over
Acts 9.25 through an opening in the wall, lowering him in a **basket**.
2 Cor 11.33 was let down in a **basket** through an opening in the wall

BASTARD

Heb 12. 8 his sons are, it means you are not real sons, but **bastards**.

BAT

Lev 11.13 cormorants; hoopoes; or **bats**.
Deut 14.12 cormorants; hoopoes; and **bats**.
Is 2.20 they have made, and abandon them to the moles and the **bats**.

BATCH

Mt 13.33 litres of flour until the whole **batch of dough** rises."
Lk 13.21 litres of flour until the whole **batch of dough** rises."
1 Cor 5. 6 "A little bit of yeast makes the whole **batch of dough** rise."
5. 7 be like a new **batch of dough** without any yeast,
Gal 5. 9 yeast to make the whole **batch of dough** rise," as they say.

BATH (1)

Ex 2. 5 down to the river to **bathe**, while her servants walked along
29. 4 Tent of my presence, and tell them to take a ritual **bath**.
40.12 entrance of the Tent, and tell them to take a ritual **bath**.
Lev 8. 6 and his sons forward and told them to take a ritual **bath**.
14. 8 wash his clothes, shave off all his hair, and have a **bath**;
14. 9 clothes and have a **bath**, and then he will be ritually
15. 6 clothes and have a **bath**, and he remains unclean until evening.
15. 7 clothes and have a **bath**, and he remains unclean until evening.
15. 8 clothes and have a **bath**, and he remains unclean until evening.
15.10 clothes and have a **bath**, and he remains unclean until evening.
15.11 clothes and have a **bath**, and he remains unclean until evening.
15.13 then wash his clothes and **bathe** in fresh spring water,
15.16 emission of semen, he must **bathe** his whole body,
15.18 woman must have a **bath**, and they remain unclean until evening.
15.21 clothes and have a **bath**, and he remains unclean until evening.
15.27 them is unclean and must wash his clothes and have a **bath**;
16. 4 Place, he must have a **bath** and put on the priestly garments:
16.24 He must **bathe** in a holy place and put on his own
16.26 his clothes and have a **bath** before he comes back into camp.
16.28 wash his clothes and have a **bath** before he returns to camp.
17.15 wash his clothes, have a **bath**, and wait until evening before
22. 6 eat any of the sacred offerings until he has had a **bath**.
2 Sam 11. 2 he walked about up there, he saw a woman having a **bath**.
12.20 had a **bath**, combed his hair, and changed
Prov 30.20 commits adultery, has a **bath**, and says, "But I haven't done
Ezek 23.40 The two sisters would **bathe** and put on eye-shadow and jewellery.
Jn 13.10 "Anyone who has had a **bath** is completely clean

BATH (2)

Liquid measure equal to one ephah, about 17.5 litres.

Ezek 45.11 dry measure is to be equal to the **bath** for liquid measure.
45.11 1 homer = 10 ephahs = 10 **baths**
45.13 (Measure it by the **bath**:
45.13 10 **baths** = 1 homer = 1 kor.)

BATHSHEBA

Uriah the Hittite's wife whom David took for himself, and mother of King Solomon.

2 Sam 11. 3 and learnt that she was **Bathsheba**, the daughter of Eliam
11.26 When **Bathsheba** heard that her husband had been killed,
12.24 Then David comforted his wife **Bathsheba**.
1 Kgs 1.11 Nathan went to **Bathsheba**, Solomon's mother, and asked her,
1.15 So **Bathsheba** went to see the king in his bedroom.
1.16 **Bathsheba** bowed low before the king, and he asked,
1.28 King David said, "Ask **Bathsheba** to come back in"—
1.31 **Bathsheba** bowed low and said, "May my lord the king live
2.13 Adonijah, whose mother was Haggith, went to **Bathsheba**,
2.16 **Bathsheba** asked.
1 Kgs 2.19 So **Bathsheba** went to the king to speak to him on behalf
1 Chr 3. 5 His wife **Bathsheba**, daughter of Ammiel, bore him four sons:

BATTALION

Num 31.14 the commanders of **battalions** and companies, who had returned

BATTER

2 Kgs 8.12 their finest young men, **batter** their children to death,
Job 9.17 He sends storms to **batter** and bruise me without any reason
16.12 God took me by the throat and **battered** me and crushed me.
19.10 He **batters** me from every side.
Is 13.16 their babies will be **battered** to death, their houses will be
22. 5 of our city have been **battered** down, and cries for help have
Ezek 4. 2 put trenches, earthworks, camps, and **battering-rams** all round
21.22 to go and set up **battering-rams**, to shout the battle-cry,
21.22 to place **battering-rams** against the gates,
26. 9 pound in your walls with **battering-rams** and tear down your
Nah 2. 5 to the wall and set up the shield for the **battering-ram**.

BATTLE

Gen 14. 8 drew up their armies for **battle** in the Valley of Siddim and
14.10 tried to run away from the **battle**, they fell into the pits;
36.31 defeated the Midianites in a **battle** in the country of Moab)
Ex 13.18 The Israelites were armed for **battle**.
32.17 said to Moses, "I hear the sound of **battle** in the camp."
Lev 26.36 you were being pursued in **battle**, and you will fall when
Num 10. 9 attacked you, sound the signal for **battle** on these trumpets.
14. 3 We will be killed in **battle**, and our wives and children will
14.43 face the Amalekites and the Canaanites, you will die in **battle**;
21.14 That is why The Book of the Lord's **Battles** speaks of
21.24 many of the enemy in **battle** and occupied their land from the
27.17 and can command them in **battle**, so that your community will
31. 5 each tribe, a total of twelve thousand men ready for **battle**.
31.21 men who had returned from **battle**, "These are the regulations
32.17 go with our fellow-Israelites into **battle** and lead the attack
32.20 in the presence of the Lord get ready to go into **battle**.
32.27 of us are ready to go into **battle** under the Lord's command.
32.29 cross the Jordan ready for **battle** at the Lord's command
32.30 the Jordan and go into **battle** with you, they are to receive
32.32 of Canaan and go into **battle**, so that we can retain our
Deut 20. 3 Today you are going into **battle**.
20. 5 is killed in **battle**, someone else will dedicate his house.
20. 6 if he is killed in **battle**, someone else will enjoy the wine.
20. 7 if he is killed in **battle**, someone else will marry the woman
21.10 God gives you victory in **battle** and you take prisoners,
Josh 1.14 but your soldiers, armed for **battle**, will cross over ahead of
4.12 tribe of Manasseh, ready for **battle**, crossed ahead of the rest
8.13 soldiers were arranged for **battle** with the main camp north of
8.22 The Israelites in the city now came down to join the **battle**.
10.32 Israelites victory over Lachish on the second day of the **battle**.
11.19 All the others were conquered in **battle**.
Judg 1. 4 So the tribes of Simeon [4] and Judah went into **battle** together.
2.15 Every time they went into **battle**, the Lord was against them,
3. 2 about war, especially those who had never been in **battle** before.
3.27 he blew a trumpet to call the men of Israel to **battle**;
5.18 of Zebulun and Naphtali risked their lives on the **battlefield**.
8.13 Gideon was returning from the **battle** by way of Heres Pass,
10.17 the Ammonite army prepared for **battle** and made camp in Gilead.
12. 1 The men of Ephraim prepared for **battle**;
18.11 the tribe of Dan left Zorah and Eshtaol, ready for **battle**.
18.16 soldiers from Dan, ready for **battle**, were standing at the gate.
18.22 from the house when Micah called his neighbours out for **battle**.
20.22 go again into **battle** against our brothers the Benjaminites?"
20.30 and placed their soldiers in **battle** position facing Gibeah,
20.39 the Israelites out on the **battlefield** were to turn round.
21.22 did not take them from you in **battle** to be our wives.
1 Sam 4. 2 and killed about four thousand men on the **battlefield**.
4.12 all the way from the **battlefield** to Shiloh and arrived there
4.16 "I have escaped from the **battle** and have run all the way
8.20 and to lead us out to war and to fight our **battles**."
11. 7 follow Saul and Samuel into **battle** will have this done to
13.22 so on the day of **battle** none of the Israelite soldiers
14.20 and his men marched into **battle** against the Philistines,
17. 1 Philistines gathered for **battle** in Socoh, a town in Judah;
17. 8 the Israelites, "What are you doing there, lined up for **battle**?
17.20 the Israelites were going out to their **battle** line, shouting
17.21 and the Israelite armies took up positions for **battle**, facing
17.22 the supplies, ran to the **battle** line, went to his brothers,
17.47 He is victorious in **battle**, and he will put all of you
17.48 David ran quickly towards the Philistine **battle** line to fight
18.13 David led his men in **battle** [14] and was successful in all he
18.17 a brave and loyal soldier, and fight the Lord's **battles**."
18.30 and fight, but in every **battle** David was more successful than
25.28 and your descendants also, because you are fighting his **battles**;
26.10 comes to die a natural death or when he dies in **battle**.
29. 4 Don't let him go into **battle** with us;
29. 6 pleased to let you go with me and fight in this **battle**.
29. 9 other kings have said that you can't go with us into **battle**.
30.24 gets the same share as the one who goes into **battle**."
31. 1 The Philistines fought a **battle** against the Israelites on
31. 8 after the **battle** the Philistines went to plunder the corpses,
2 Sam 1. 4 army ran away from the **battle**," he replied, "and many of
1.12 of the Lord, because so many had been killed in **battle**.
1.25 "The brave soldiers have fallen, they were killed in **battle**.
2.17 a furious **battle** broke out, and Abner and the Israelites were
3.29 work or is killed in **battle** or hasn't enough to eat!"
3.30 Abner for killing their brother Asahel in the **battle** at Gibeon.
5. 2 the people of Israel in **battle**, and the Lord promised you

2 Sam	10.18	wounded Shobach, the enemy commander, who died on the **battlefield.**
	11.18	David telling him about the **battle,** [19]and he instructed the
	11.19	the king all about the **battle,** [20]he may get angry and ask
	11.25	be upset, since you never can tell who will die in **battle.**
	12. 9	You had Uriah killed in **battle;**
	17.11	on the sea-shore, and that you lead them personally in **battle.**
	18. 8	and more men died in the forest than were killed in **battle.**
	19. 3	soldiers who are ashamed because they are running away from **battle.**
	19.10	Absalom as our king, but he has been killed in **battle.**
	20. 8	Joab was dressed for **battle,** with a sword in its sheath
	21.15	During one of the **battles** David grew tired.
	21.17	that he would never again go out with them to **battle.**
	21.18	After this there was a **battle** with the Philistines at Gob,
	21.19	There was another **battle** with the Philistines at Gob,
	21.20	there was another **battle** at Gath, where there was a giant
	22.35	He trains me for **battle,** so that I can use the strongest
	22.40	give me strength for the **battle** and victory over my enemies.
	23. 8	eight hundred men and killed them all in one **battle.**
	23. 9	he and David challenged the Philistines who had gathered for **battle.**
1 Kgs	8.44	your people to go into **battle** against their enemies and they
	20.11	real soldier does his boasting after a **battle,** not before it."
	20.39	I was fighting in the **battle** when a soldier brought a
	22.30	Jehoshaphat, "As we go into **battle,** I will disguise myself,
	22.30	So the king of Israel went into **battle** in disguise.
	22.34	"Turn round and pull out of the **battle!"**
	22.35	While the **battle** raged on, King Ahab remained propped up
	22.45	all his bravery and his **battles,** are recorded in The History
2 Kgs	3.26	that he was losing the **battle,** he took seven hundred swordsmen
	8.28	clashed at Ramoth in Gilead, and Joram was wounded in **battle.**
	9.14	he had received in the **battle** at Ramoth against King Hazael
	14. 7	the city of Sela in **battle** and called it Joktheel, the name
	14.28	Jeroboam II did, his brave **battles,** and how he restored Damascus
	23.29	stop the Egyptian army at Megiddo and was killed in **battle.**
1 Chr	1.43	defeated the Midianites in a **battle** in the country of Moab)
	5.10	the Hagrites, killed them in **battle,** and occupied their land
	10. 1	The Philistines fought a **battle** against the Israelites on
	10. 8	after the **battle,** the Philistines went to plunder the corpses,
	11. 2	the people of Israel in **battle,** and the Lord your God
	11.11	against three hundred men and killed them all in one **battle.**
	11.13	David's side against the Philistines at the **battle** of Pas Dammim.
	12.23	40,000 men ready for **battle;**
	12.38	All these soldiers, ready for **battle,** went to Hebron,
	20. 5	There was another **battle** with the Philistines, and Elhanan
	20. 6	Another **battle** took place at Gath, where there was a giant
	26.27	the loot they captured in **battle** and dedicated it for use in
2 Chr	6.34	your people to go into **battle** against their enemies and they
	13.12	ready to blow them and call us to **battle** against you.
	17.18	command was Jehozabad with 180,000 men, well-equipped for **battle.**
	18.29	Jehoshaphat, "As we go into **battle,** I will disguise myself,
	18.29	So the king of Israel went into **battle** in disguise.
	18.33	"Turn round and pull out of the **battle!"**
	18.34	While the **battle** raged on, King Ahab remained propped up
	20.15	The **battle** depends on God, not on you.
	20.17	You will not have to fight this **battle.**
	20.17	Go out to **battle,** and the Lord will be with you!"
	22. 5	clashed at Ramoth in Gilead, and Joram was wounded in **battle.**
	25. 5	were picked troops, ready for **battle,** skilled in using spears
	25. 8	will make you stronger in **battle,** but it is God who has
	25.13	not allowed to go into **battle** with him attacked the Judaean
	25.21	King Jehoash of Israel went into **battle** against King Amaziah
	26.11	He had a large army ready for **battle.**
	29. 9	Our fathers were killed in **battle,** and our wives and children
	32. 8	the Lord our God to help us and to fight our **battles."**
	35.22	disguised himself and went into **battle** on the plain of Megiddo.
	35.23	During the **battle** King Josiah was struck by Egyptian arrows.
Job	38.23	ready for times of trouble, for days of **battle** and war.
	39.21	they rush into **battle** with all their strength.
	39.25	they can smell a **battle** before they get near, and they
Ps	18.34	He trains me for **battle,** so that I can use the strongest
	18.39	give me strength for the **battle** and victory over my enemies.
	24. 8	He is the Lord, strong and mighty, the Lord, victorious in **battle.**
	55.18	me safely back from the **battles** that I fight against so many
	63.10	will be killed in **battle,** and their bodies eaten by wolves.
	68.13	of you stay among the sheep pens on the day of **battle?)**
	78. 9	armed with bows and arrows, ran away on the day of **battle.**
	89.43	made his weapons useless and let him be defeated in **battle.**
	110. 6	judgement on the nations and fill the **battlefield** with corpses;
	118.16	His power has brought us victory— his mighty power in **battle!"**
	140. 7	Lord, my strong defender, you have protected me in **battle.**
	144. 1	He trains me for **battle** and prepares me for war.
Prov	20.18	don't go charging into **battle** without a plan.
	21.31	can get horses ready for **battle,** but it is the Lord who
	24. 6	plans before you fight a **battle,** and the more good advice
Ecc	8. 8	That is a **battle** we cannot escape;
	9.11	win the race, and the brave do not always win the **battle.**
Song	3. 8	they are **battle-hardened** veterans.
	6.12	me as eager for love as a chariot driver is for **battle.**
Is	2. 4	will never again go to war, never prepare for **battle** again.
	10. 4	You will be killed in **battle** or dragged off as prisoners.
	13. 2	On the top of a barren hill raise the **battle** flag!
	13. 4	The Lord of Armies is preparing his troops for **battle.**
	14.19	bodies of soldiers killed in **battle,** thrown with them into a
	31. 8	The Assyrians will run from **battle,** and their young men will
	31. 9	be so frightened that they will abandon their **battle** flags."
	33. 3	you fight for us, nations run away from the noise of **battle.**
	42.13	he is ready and eager for **battle.**
	42.13	He gives a war-cry, a **battle-shout;**
Jer	4.19	I hear the trumpets and the shouts of **battle.**
	4.21	long must I see the **battle** raging and hear the blasts of
	6.23	They are ready for **battle** against Jerusalem."
	8. 6	on going his own way, like a horse rushing into **battle.**
	18.21	men die of disease and the young men be killed in **battle.**
	19. 7	let their enemies triumph over them and kill them in **battle.**
	20.16	the morning and the **battle** alarm at noon, [17]because he didn't
	34. 4	You will not be killed in **battle.**
	42.13	war any more or hear the call to **battle** or go hungry.'
	46. 3	officers shout, 'Get your shields ready and march into **battle!**
	49. 2	Rabbah hear the noise of **battle,** and it will be left in
	50. 9	They will line up in **battle** against the country and conquer it.
	50.14	"Bowmen, line up for **battle** against Babylon and surround it.
	50.22	The noise of **battle** is heard in the land, and there is
	50.42	They are ready for **battle** against Babylonia.
Ezek	11.10	and you will be killed in **battle** in your own country.
	17.21	soldiers will be killed in **battle,** and the survivors will be
	21.22	shout the **battle-cry,** to place battering-rams against the gates,
	25.13	the city of Dedan, and the people will be killed in **battle.**
	30. 6	Aswan in the south, all Egypt's defenders will be killed in **battle.**
	31.18	of the dead and join the ungodly and those killed in **battle.**
	32.20	of Egypt will fall with those who are killed in **battle.**
	32.21	ungodly who were killed in **battle** have come down here,
	32.22	They were all killed in **battle,** [23]and their graves are in
	32.23	her soldiers fell in **battle,** and their graves surround her tomb.
	32.24	were all killed in **battle,** and they went down, uncircumcised,
	32.25	among those killed in **battle,** and the graves of her soldiers
	32.25	They are all uncircumcised, all killed in **battle.**
	32.25	dead and disgraced, sharing the fate of those killed in **battle.**
	32.26	They are all uncircumcised, all killed in **battle.**
	32.28	will lie crushed among the uncircumcised who were killed in **battle.**
	32.29	the dead with the uncircumcised who were killed in **battle.**
	32.30	with those killed in **battle** and are laid to rest, uncircumcised.
	32.31	these who were killed in **battle** will be a comfort to the
	32.32	laid to rest with all the uncircumcised who die in **battle."**
	35. 8	who are killed in **battle** will cover the hills and valleys.
	39.23	and let their enemies defeat them and kill them in **battle.**
Dan	11.20	king will be killed, but not publicly and not in **battle."**
	11.33	them will be killed in **battle** or be burnt to death, and
Hos	5. 8	Into **battle,** men of Benjamin!
	10.14	city of Betharbel in **battle,** and mothers and their children
	10.15	As soon as the **battle** begins, the king of Israel will die."
Joel	2. 5	They are lined up like a great army ready for **battle.**
Amos	1.14	shouts on the day of **battle,** and the fighting will rage like
	2. 2	die in the noise of **battle** while soldiers are shouting
	4.10	I killed your young men in **battle** and took your horses away.
	7.11	'Jeroboam will die in **battle,** and the people of Israel will
Mic	2. 8	Men return from **battle,** thinking they are safe at home,
	4. 3	Nations will never again go to war, never prepare for **battle** again.
Nah	2. 1	Prepare for **battle!**
	3.15	do, you will still be burnt to death or killed in **battle.**
Zeph	1.16	sound of war-trumpets and the **battle-cry** of soldiers attacking
Zech	9.10	the bows used in **battle** will be destroyed.
	9.15	They will shout in **battle** like drunken men and will shed the
Mt	24. 6	to hear the noise of **battles** close by
	24. 6	and the news of **battles** far away;
Mk	13. 7	you hear the noise of **battles** close by
	13. 7	and news of **battles** far away.
1 Cor	14. 8	does not sound a clear call, who will prepare for **battle?**
Phil	1.30	Now you can take part with me in the **battle.**
	1.30	It is the same **battle** you saw me fighting in the past,
Heb	7. 1	was coming back from the **battle** in which he defeated the
	7. 4	gave him a tenth of all he got in the **battle.**
	11.34	were mighty in **battle** and defeated the armies of foreigners.
Rev	9. 7	The locusts looked like horses ready for **battle;**
	9. 9	like the noise of many horse-drawn chariots rushing into **battle.**
	16.14	bring them together for the **battle** on the great Day of
	19.11	it is with justice that he judges and fights his **battles.**
	20. 8	bring them all together for **battle,** as many as the grains of

BAY

Acts	27.39	coast, but they noticed a **bay** with a beach and decided that,

BEACH

Jon	2.10	the fish to spew Jonah up on the **beach,** and it did.
Lk	5. 2	He saw two boats pulled up on the **beach;**
	5.11	pulled the boats up on the **beach,** left everything, and followed
Acts	21. 5	of the city to the **beach,** where we all knelt and prayed.
	27.39	noticed a bay with a **beach** and decided that, if possible,

BEAK

Gen	8.11	him in the evening with a fresh olive leaf in its **beak.**
Is	10.14	no **beak** opened to scream at me!"

BEAM

Ex	12.22	blood on the door-posts and the **beam** above the door of your
	12.23	see the blood on the **beams** and the door-posts and will not
1 Kgs	6. 6	rest on the wall without having their **beams** built into it.
	6. 9	He put in a ceiling made of **beams** and boards of cedar.
	6.10	walls of the Temple, and was joined to them by cedar **beams.**
	6.36	one layer of cedar **beams** for every three layers of stone.
	7. 2	pillars, fifteen in each row, with cedar **beams** resting on them.
	7.11	of them were other stones, cut to measure, and cedar **beams.**
	7.12	with one layer of cedar **beams** for every three layers of cut
Ezra	5. 8	large stone blocks and with wooden **beams** set in the wall.
	6.11	disobeys this order, a wooden **beam** is to be torn out of

Neh	3. 3	They put the **beams** and the gates in place, and put in
	3. 6	They put the **beams** and the gates in place, and put in
Song	1.17	the cedars will be the **beams** of our house,
Is	9.10	The **beams** of sycomore wood have been cut down, but we will

BEAN

Gen	25.29	Jacob was cooking some **bean** soup, Esau came in from hunting.
2 Sam	17.28	wheat, barley, meal, roasted grain, **beans,** peas, honey, cheese,
Ezek	4. 9	"Now take some wheat, barley, **beans,** peas, millet, and
Lk	15.16	could fill himself with the **bean pods** the pigs ate,

BEAR (1)
[BORE]

Gen	1.11	of plants, those that **bear** grain and those that bear fruit"
Lev	19.25	If you do all this, your trees will **bear** more fruit.
	26. 4	the land will produce crops and the trees will **bear** fruit.
	26.20	will not produce crops and the trees will not **bear** fruit.
Deut	32.32	Gomorrah, are like vines that **bear** bitter and poisonous grapes,
Ps	1. 3	grow beside a stream, that **bear** fruit at the right time, and
	92.14	of our God, [14]that still **bear** fruit in old age and are
Song	4.13	like an orchard of pomegranate-trees and **bear** the finest fruits.
Jer	12. 2	they grow and **bear** fruit.
	17. 8	it keeps on **bearing** fruit.
Ezek	17. 8	grow leaves and **bear** grapes and be a magnificent vine.
	17.23	will grow branches and **bear** seed and become a magnificent cedar.
	34.27	The trees will **bear** fruit, the fields will produce crops,
	36. 8	again grow leaves and **bear** fruit for you, my people Israel.
	47.12	will never wither, and they will never stop **bearing** fruit.
Hos	9.16	a plant whose roots have dried up and which **bears** no fruit.
Joel	2.22	the trees **bear** their fruit, and there are plenty of figs
Zech	8.12	Their vines will **bear** grapes, the earth will produce crops,
Mt	3.10	every tree that does not **bear** good fruit will be cut down
	7.16	Thorn bushes do not **bear** grapes,
	7.16	and briars do not **bear** figs.
	7.17	tree bears good fruit, but a poor tree **bears** bad fruit.
	7.18	A healthy tree cannot **bear** bad fruit,
	7.18	and a poor tree cannot **bear** good fruit.
	7.19	any tree that does not **bear** good fruit is cut down
	12.33	A tree is known by the kind of fruit it **bears.**
	13.22	for riches choke the message, and they don't **bear** fruit.
	13.23	they **bear** fruit, some as much as a hundred, others sixty,
	21.19	So he said to the tree, "You will never again **bear** fruit!"
Mk	4.19	crowd in and choke the message, and they don't **bear** fruit.
	4.20	They hear the message, accept it, and **bear** fruit:
	4.28	The soil itself makes the plants grow and **bear** fruit;
Lk	3. 9	every tree that does not **bear** good fruit will be cut down
	6.43	"A healthy tree does not **bear** bad fruit,
	6.43	nor does a poor tree **bear** good fruit.
	6.44	Every tree is known by the fruit it **bears;**
	8.15	good and obedient heart, and they persist until they **bear** fruit.
	12.16	was once a rich man who had land which **bore** good crops.
	13. 9	Then if the tree **bears** figs next year, so much the better;
Jn	15. 2	in me that does not **bear** fruit, and he
	15. 2	prunes every branch that does **bear** fruit,
	15. 2	so that it will be clean and **bear** more fruit.
	15. 4	A branch cannot **bear** fruit by itself;
	15. 4	the same way you cannot **bear** fruit unless you remain in me.
	15. 5	Whoever remains in me, and I in him, will **bear** much fruit;
	15. 8	My Father's glory is shown by your **bearing** much fruit;
	15.16	appointed you to go and **bear** much fruit, the kind of fruit
Jas	3.12	A fig-tree, my brothers, cannot **bear** olives;
	3.12	a grapevine cannot **bear** figs,
Jude	12	They are like trees that **bear** no fruit, even in autumn,
Rev	22. 2	the tree of life, which **bears** fruit twelve times a year,

BEAR (2)
[BORE, BORNE]

Gen	3.14	you alone of all the animals must **bear** this curse:
	4.13	to the Lord, "This punishment is too hard for me to **bear.**
	21.16	She said to herself, "I can't **bear** to see my child die."
	31.39	was killed by wild animals, I always **bore** the loss myself.
	43. 9	back to you safe and sound, I will always **bear** the blame.
	44.32	boy back to him, I would **bear** the blame all my life.
	44.34	I cannot **bear** to see this disaster come upon my father."
Lev	19.17	"Do not **bear** a grudge against anyone, but settle your
Num	11.17	they can help you to **bear** the responsibility for these people,
	11.17	and you will not have to **bear** it alone.
	12.14	face, she would have to **bear** her disgrace for seven days.
	18.23	care of the Tent and **bear** the full responsibility for it.
Deut	1.12	how can I alone **bear** the heavy responsibility for settling your
1 Kgs	2. 5	men and now I **bear** the responsibility for what he did,
Neh	5.18	burdens the people had to **bear,** so I did not claim the
Job	21.20	Let sinners **bear** their own punishment;
Ps	38. 4	they are a burden too heavy to **bear.**
Is	1.14	they are a burden that I am tired of **bearing.**
	14.25	Assyrian yoke and from the burdens they have had to **bear.**
	28.19	You will have to **bear** it day and night.
	53. 4	should have been ours, the pain that we should have **borne.**
	53.11	whom I am pleased, will **bear** the punishment of many and for
Jer	4.19	I can't **bear** the pain!
Ezek	16.52	Now blush and **bear** your shame, because you make your sisters
Jn	8.43	It is because you cannot **bear** to listen to my message.
	16.12	but now it would be too much for you to **bear.**
1 Thes	3. 1	Finally, we could not **bear** it any longer.
	3. 5	I could not **bear** it any longer, so I sent him
Heb	12.20	because they could not **bear** the order which said,

BEAR (3)
[BORE, BORNE]

Gen	4. 1	She **bore** a son and said, "By the Lord's help I have
	16. 1	Abram's wife Sarai had not **borne** him any children.
	16.15	Hagar **bore** Abram a son, and he named him Ishmael.
	17.19	Your wife Sarah will **bear** you a son and you will name
	21. 2	and she became pregnant and **bore** a son to Abraham when he
	21. 7	Yet I have **borne** him a son in his old age."
	21. 9	whom Hagar the Egyptian had **borne** to Abraham, was playing
	22.20	Abraham learnt that Milcah had **borne** eight children
	22.23	Milcah **bore** these eight sons to Nahor, Abraham's brother.
	22.24	Reumah, Nahor's concubine, **bore** Tebah, Gaham, Tahash,
	24.36	Sarah, my master's wife, **bore** him a son when she was old,
	25. 2	She **bore** him Zimran, Jokshan, Medan, Midian, Ishbak, and
	25. 6	he gave presents to the sons his other wives had **borne** him.
	25.12	Egyptian slave of Sarah, **bore** to Abraham, [13]had the following sons,
	29.34	more tightly to me, because I have **borne** him three sons";
	30. 1	But Rachel had not **borne** Jacob any children, and so she
	30. 5	Bilhah became pregnant and **bore** Jacob a son.
	30. 7	Bilhah became pregnant again and **bore** Jacob a second son.
	30.10	Then Zilpah **bore** Jacob a son.
	30.12	Zilpah **bore** Jacob another son, [13]and Leah said, "How happy I am!
	30.17	Leah's prayer, and she became pregnant and **bore** Jacob a fifth son.
	30.19	Leah became pregnant again and **bore** Jacob a sixth son.
	30.20	husband will accept me, because I have **borne** him six sons";
	30.21	Later she **bore** a daughter, whom she named Dinah.
	36. 4	Adah **bore** Eliphaz;
	36. 4	Basemath **bore** Reuel;
	36. 5	and Oholibamah **bore** Jeush, Jalam, and Korah.
	36.10	Esau's wife Adah **bore** him one son, Eliphaz,
	36.10	Esau's wife Basemath **bore** him one son, Reuel,
	36.14	Oholibamah, the daughter of Anah son of Zibeon, **bore** him three sons:
	38. 3	He married her, [3]and she **bore** him a son,
	38. 4	She became pregnant again and **bore** another son and named him Onan.
	44.27	us, 'You know that my wife Rachel **bore** me only two sons.
	46.15	the sons that Leah had **borne** to Jacob in Mesopotamia,
	46.19	Jacob's wife Rachel **bore** him two sons:
	49.21	"Naphtali is a deer that runs free, Who **bears** lovely fawns.
Ex	2. 2	a woman of his own tribe, [2]and she **bore** him a son.
	2.22	his daughter Zipporah in marriage, [22]who **bore** him a son.
	6.20	Amram married his father's sister Jochebed, who **bore** him Aaron and Moses.
	6.23	she **bore** him Nadab, Abihu, Eleazar, and Ithamar.
	6.25	Eleazar, Aaron's son, married one of Putiel's daughters, who **bore** him Phinehas.
	21. 4	him a wife and she **bore** him sons or daughters, the woman
Num	5.28	she will not be harmed and will be able to **bear** children.
	26.59	She **bore** Amram two sons, Aaron and Moses, and a daughter,
Deut	21.15	two wives and they both **bear** him sons, but the first son
Judg	8.31	she **bore** him a son, and he named him Abimelech.
Ruth	4.11	like Rachel and Leah, who **bore** many children to Jacob.
1 Sam	2. 5	The childless wife has **borne** seven children, but the mother
2 Sam	11.27	she became his wife and **bore** him a son.
	12.15	that Uriah's wife had **borne** to David to become very ill.
	12.24	with her, and she **bore** a son, whom David named Solomon.
	21. 8	two sons that Rizpah the daughter of Aiah had **borne** to Saul;
	21. 8	daughter Merab, whom she had **borne** to Adriel son of Barzillai,
1 Kgs	11.20	She **bore** him a son, Genubath, who was brought up by the
1 Chr	1.32	Abraham had a concubine named Keturah, who **bore** him six sons:
	2.48	Maacah, who **bore** him two sons, Sheber and Tirhanah.
	3. 5	His wife Bathsheba, daughter of Ammiel, **bore** him four sons:
2 Chr	24. 3	wives for King Joash, and they **bore** him sons and daughters.
Ps	48. 6	like a woman about to **bear** a child, [7]like ships tossing in
	144.13	sheep in our fields **bear** young by the tens of thousands.
Is	49.15	woman forget her own baby and not love the child she **bore?**
	49.21	will say to yourself, 'Who **bore** all these children for me?
Jer	4.31	in labour, a scream like a woman **bearing** her first child.
Ezek	16.20	and the daughters you had **borne** me and offered them as
	23. 4	I married both of them, and they **bore** me children.
	23.37	with idols and murder of the sons they **bore** me.
	31. 6	The wild animals **bore** their young in its shelter;
Lk	1.13	your prayer, and your wife Elizabeth will **bear** you a son.
	1.42	of all women, and blessed is the child you will **bear!**
	11.27	"How happy is the woman who **bore** you and nursed you!"
	23.29	never had children, who never **bore** babies, who never nursed them!'

BEAR (4)

Gen	10. 2	Tiras—were the ancestors of the peoples who **bear** their names.
	10. 6	Canaan—were the ancestors of the peoples who **bear** their names.
	10.15	Heth—were the ancestors of the peoples who **bear** their names.
	10.22	Aram—were the ancestors of the peoples who **bear** their names.
Ex	6.14	they were the ancestors of the clans that **bear** their names.
	6.15	they were the ancestors of the clans that **bear** their names.
	6.16	they were the ancestors of the clans that **bear** their names.
Num	3.17	who were the ancestors of the clans that **bear** their names.
	3.17	They were the ancestors of the families that **bear** their names.
2 Sam	6. 2	God's Covenant Box, **bearing** the name of the Lord Almighty,
1 Chr	1. 5	Tiras—were the ancestors of the peoples who **bear** their names.
	1. 8	Canaan—were the ancestors of the peoples who **bear** their names.
	1.13	Heth—were the ancestors of the peoples who **bear** their names.
	1.17	Meshek—were the ancestors of the peoples who **bear** their names.
	13. 6	Covenant Box of God, which **bears** the name of the Lord
Dan	9.18	are in and the suffering of the city that **bears** your name.
1 Pet	4.16	but thank God that you **bear** Christ's name.

BEAR (5)
[SHE-BEARS]

1 Sam 17.34 Whenever a lion or a **bear** carries off a lamb, [35] I go
17.35 And if the lion or **bear** turns on me, I grab it
17.36 I have killed lions and **bears,** and I will do the same
17.37 The Lord has saved me from lions and **bears;**
2 Sam 17. 8 they are as fierce as a mother **bear** robbed of her cubs.
2 Kgs 2.24 Then two **she-bears** came out of the woods and tore forty-two
Job 9. 9 in the sky—the Great **Bear,** Orion, the Pleiades, and the
38.32 season by season and direct the Great and the Little **Bear?**
Prov 17.12 better to meet a mother **bear** robbed of her cubs than to
28.15 he is as dangerous as a growling lion or a prowling **bear.**
Is 11. 7 Cows and **bears** will eat together, and their calves and cubs
Lam 3.10 He waited for me like a **bear;**
Dan 7. 5 second beast looked like a **bear** standing on its hind legs.
Hos 13. 8 will attack you like a **bear** that has lost her cubs,
Amos 5.19 like a man who runs from a lion and meets a **bear!**
Rev 13. 2 leopard, with feet like a **bear's** feet and a mouth like a

BEAR (6)

2 Sam 23.24 Naharai from Beeroth, Joab's armour **bearer**
2 Kgs 3.21 all the men who could **bear** arms, from the oldest to the

BEARD

Lev 14. 9 again shave his head, his **beard,** his eyebrows, and all the
19.27 your head or trim your **beard** [28] or tattoo yourselves or cut
21. 5 his head or trim his **beard** or cut gashes on his body
Num 6. 5 to the Lord, and he shall let his hair and **beard** grow.
6. 9 must wait seven days and then shave off his hair and **beard;**
1 Sam 21.13 would scribble on the city gates and dribble down his **beard.**
2 Sam 10. 4 off one side of their **beards,** cut off their clothes at the
10. 5 stay in Jericho and not return until their **beards** had grown
19.24 washed his feet, trimmed his **beard,** or washed his clothes from
20. 9 and took hold of his **beard** with his right hand in order
1 Chr 19. 4 David's messengers, shaved off their **beards,** cut off their
19. 5 stay in Jericho and not return until their **beards** had grown
Ezra 9. 3 tore my hair and my **beard,** and sat down crushed with grief.
Ps 133. 2 down from Aaron's head and **beard,** down to the collar of his
Is 7.20 he will shave off your **beards,** and the hair on your heads
15. 2 they have shaved their heads and their **beards** in grief.
50. 6 pulled out the hairs of my **beard** and spat in my face.
Jer 41. 5 They had shaved off their **beards,** torn their clothes,
48.37 All of them have shaved their heads and cut off their **beards.**
Ezek 5. 1 and use it to shave off your **beard** and all your hair.

BEAST (1)

Job 28. 8 No lion or other fierce **beast** Ever travels those lonely roads.
40.20 Grass to feed him grows on the hills where wild **beasts** play.
41.34 he is king of all wild **beasts.**
Dan 7. 3 Four huge **beasts** came up out of the ocean, each one
7. 4 The **beast** was lifted up and made to stand like a man.
7. 5 second **beast** looked like a bear standing on its hind legs.
7. 6 While I was watching, another **beast** appeared.
7. 7 As I was watching, a fourth **beast** appeared.
7. 7 Unlike the other **beasts,** it had ten horns.
7.11 As I watched, the fourth **beast** was killed, and its body was
7.12 other **beasts** had their power taken away, but they were permitted
7.17 "These four huge **beasts** are four empires which will arise
7.19 know more about the fourth **beast,** which was not like any of
7.19 of the others—the terrifying **beast** which crushed its victims
7.23 "The fourth **beast** is a fourth empire that will be on the
1 Cor 15.32 fought "wild **beasts**" here in Ephesus simply from human
Tit 1.12 "Cretans are always liars, wicked **beasts,** and lazy gluttons."

BEAST (2)

Rev 11. 7 finish proclaiming their message, the **beast** that comes up out of
13. 1 Then I saw a **beast** coming up out of the sea.
13. 2 The **beast** looked like a leopard, with feet like a bear's
13. 2 The dragon gave the **beast** his own power, his throne, and his
13. 3 the heads of the **beast** seemed to have been fatally wounded,
13. 3 The whole earth was amazed and followed the **beast.**
13. 4 the dragon because he had given his authority to the **beast.**
13. 4 They worshipped the **beast** also,
13. 4 saying, "Who is like the **beast?**
13. 5 The **beast** was allowed to make proud claims which were insulting
13.11 Then I saw another **beast,** which came up out of the earth.
13.12 It used the vast authority of the first **beast** in its presence.
13.12 on it to worship the first **beast,** whose wound had healed.
13.13 This second **beast** performed great miracles;
13.14 was allowed to perform in the presence of the first **beast.**
13.14 The **beast** told them to build an image
13.14 in honour of the **beast** that had been wounded
13.15 The second **beast** was allowed to breathe life into
13.15 the image of the first **beast,** so that the image could talk
13.16 The **beast** forced all the people, small and great, rich and
13.17 this mark, that is, the **beast's** name or the number that
13.18 the number of the **beast,** because the number stands for
14. 9 "Whoever worships the **beast** and its image and receives
14.11 for those who worship the **beast** and its image, for anyone
15. 2 won the victory over the **beast** and its image and over
16. 2 had the mark of the **beast** and on those who had worshipped
16.10 fifth angel poured out his bowl on the throne of the **beast.**
16.10 Darkness fell over the **beast's** kingdom, and people bit their
16.13 the mouth of the **beast,** and the mouth of the false
17. 3 woman sitting on a red **beast** that had names insulting to God
17. 3 the **beast** had seven heads and ten horns.
Rev 17. 7 the woman and of the **beast** that carries her,
17. 7 the **beast** with seven heads and ten horns.
17. 8 That **beast** was once alive, but lives no longer;
17. 8 the living, will all be amazed as they look at the **beast.**
17.11 And the **beast** that was once alive, but lives no longer,
17.12 authority to rule as kings for one hour with the **beast.**
17.13 and they give their power and authority to the **beast.**
17.16 ten horns you saw, and the **beast,** will hate the prostitute;
17.17 acting together and giving the **beast** their power to rule until
19.19 Then I saw the **beast** and the kings of the earth
19.20 The **beast** was taken prisoner, together with the false prophet
19.20 had the mark of the **beast**
19.20 and those who had worshipped the image of the **beast.)**
19.20 The **beast** and the false prophet were both thrown alive into
20. 4 They had not worshipped the **beast** or its image, nor had they
20. 4 the mark of the **beast** on their foreheads or their hands.
20.10 fire and sulphur, where the **beast** and the false prophet had

BEAT

Ex 2.13 in the wrong, "Why are you **beating** up a fellow-Hebrew?"
5.14 The Egyptian slave-drivers **beat** the Israelite foremen,
5.16 And now we are being **beaten.**
9.25 It **beat** down all the plants in the fields and broke all
21.20 takes a stick and **beats** his slave, whether male or female,
30.36 **Beat** part of it into a fine powder, take it into the
Num 16.38 to death for their sin, **beat** them into thin plates, and make
16.39 the firepans and had them **beaten** into thin plates to make a
22.23 Balaam **beat** the donkey and brought it back on to the road.
22.25 Again Balaam **beat** the donkey.
22.27 lost his temper and began to **beat** the donkey with his stick.
22.28 Why have you **beaten** me these three times?"
22.32 angel demanded, "Why have you **beaten** your donkey three times
24.17 the leaders of Moab And **beat** down all the people of Seth.
Deut 22.18 Then the town leaders are to take the husband and **beat** him.
25. 2 man is sentenced to be **beaten,** the judge is to make him
Judg 8. 7 over to me, I will **beat** you with thorns and briars from
19.22 surrounded the house and started **beating** on the door.
20.32 Benjaminites said, "We've **beaten** them just as we did before."
20.39 "Yes, we've **beaten** them just as we did before."
Ruth 2.17 evening, and when she had **beaten** it out, she found she had
1 Sam 17.35 me, I grab it by the throat and **beat** it to death.
1 Kgs 12.11 He **beat** you with a whip;
12.14 He **beat** you with a whip;
2 Kgs 25.21 There the king had them **beaten** and put to death.
2 Chr 9.15 about seven kilogrammes of **beaten** gold, [16] and three hundred
9.16 smaller shields, each covered with about three kilogrammes of **beaten** gold.
10.11 He **beat** you with a whip;
10.14 He **beat** you with a whip;
Neh 13.25 down curses on them, **beat** them, and pulled out their hair.
Job 37. 1 The storm makes my heart **beat** wildly.
39.13 How fast the wings of an ostrich **beat!**
Ps 35.15 strangers **beat** me and kept striking me.
68.25 in between are the girls **beating** the tambourines.
81. 2 Start the music and **beat** the tambourines;
102. 4 I am **beaten** down like dry grass;
Prov 6.33 He will be dishonoured and **beaten** up;
17.10 than a fool learns from being **beaten** a hundred times.
18. 6 When some fool starts an argument, he is asking for a **beating.**
19.29 A conceited fool is sure to get a **beating.**
23.35 "I must have been **beaten** up, but I don't remember it.
26. 3 have to bridle a donkey, and you have to **beat** a fool.
27.22 Even if you **beat** a fool until he's half dead,
27.22 you still can't **beat** his foolishness out of him.
Is 9. 4 yoke that burdened them and the rod that **beat** their shoulders.
10.26 I, the Lord Almighty, will **beat** them with my whip
10.26 as I **beat** the people of Midian at the
14.29 of Philistia, the rod that **beat** you is broken, but you have
24.13 when the olives have been **beaten** off every tree and the last
28.27 uses a heavy club to **beat** out dill seeds or cumin seeds;
32.12 **Beat** your breasts in grief because the fertile fields and
41. 7 man who **beats** the idol smooth encourages the one who nails
50. 6 I bared my back to those who **beat** me.
53. 5 our sins he was wounded, **beaten** because of the evil we did.
Jer 4.19 My heart is **beating** wildly!
20. 2 he ordered me to be **beaten** and placed in chains near the
37.15 and ordered me to be **beaten** and locked up in the house
46. 5 Their soldiers are **beaten** back;
47. 3 will hear the hoof **beats** of horses, the clatter of chariots,
52.27 There the king had them **beaten** and put to death.
Lam 3. 3 into darkness [3] And **beat** me again and again with merciless
3.30 Though **beaten** and insulted, we should accept it all.
Ezek 3.13 the wings of the creatures **beating** together in the air,
21.12 **Beat** your breast in despair!
Jon 4. 8 faint from the heat of the sun **beating** down on his head.
Nah 2. 7 her servants moan like doves and **beat** their breasts in sorrow.
3.10 At every street corner their children were **beaten** to death.
Mt 21.35 The tenants seized his slaves, **beat** one, killed another,
22. 6 while others grabbed the servants, **beat** them, and killed them.
24.49 and he will begin to **beat** his fellow-servants and to eat
26.67 Then they spat in his face and **beat** him;
Mk 12. 3 The tenants seized the slave, **beat** him, and sent him back
12. 4 tenants **beat** him over the head and treated him shamefully.
12. 5 treated many others the same way, **beating** some and killing
13. 9 You will be **beaten** in the synagogues;
15.19 They **beat** him over the head with a stick, spat on him,
Lk 10.30 stripped him, and **beat** him up, leaving him half dead.
12.45 and if he begins to **beat** the other servants, both the men
18.13 his face to heaven, but **beat** on his breast and said,
20.10 But the tenants **beat** the slave and sent him back without a

Lk 20.11 the tenants **beat** him also, treated him shamefully, and sent him
22.63 The men who were guarding Jesus mocked him and **beat** him.
23.48 they all went back home, **beating** their breasts in sorrow.
Acts 16.23 After a severe **beating,** they were thrown into jail,
18.17 leader of the synagogue, and **beat** him in front of the court.
21.32 the people saw him with the soldiers, they stopped **beating** Paul.
22.19 synagogues and arrested and **beat** those who believe in you.
1 Cor 4.11 we are **beaten;**
2 Cor 6. 5 We have been **beaten,** imprisoned, and mobbed;
12. 7 acts as Satan's messenger to **beat** me and keep me from being
1 Pet 2.20 if you endure the **beatings** you deserve for having done wrong?

BEAUTIFUL GATE

Acts 3. 2 There at the **Beautiful Gate,** as it was called, was a man
3.10 who had sat at the **Beautiful Gate,** they were all surprised

BEAUTY

Gen 2. 9 He made all kinds of **beautiful** trees grow there and produce
3. 6 The woman saw how **beautiful** the tree was and how good its
6. 2 saw that these girls were **beautiful,** so they took the ones
12.11 Egypt, he said to his wife Sarai, "You are a **beautiful** woman.
12.14 into Egypt, the Egyptians did see that his wife was **beautiful.**
12.15 officials saw her and told the king how **beautiful** she was;
24.16 She was a very **beautiful** young girl and still a virgin.
26. 7 there would kill him to get Rebecca, who was very **beautiful.**
29.17 Leah had lovely eyes, but Rachel was shapely and **beautiful.**
Ex 28. 2 for your brother Aaron, to provide him with dignity and **beauty.**
28.40 caps for Aaron's sons, to provide them with dignity and **beauty.**
Num 24. 5 The tents of Israel are **beautiful,** [6]Like long rows of palms
Deut 3.25 the **beautiful** hill-country and the Lebanon Mountains.'
21.11 may see among them a **beautiful** woman that you like and want
Josh 7.21 I saw a **beautiful** Babylonian cloak, about two kilogrammes of
Judg 5.25 she brought him cream in a **beautiful** bowl.
1 Sam 25. 2 wife Abigail was **beautiful** and intelligent, but he was a mean,
2 Sam 11. 2 She was very **beautiful.**
13. 1 David's son Absalom had a **beautiful** unmarried sister named
14.27 sons and one daughter named Tamar, a very **beautiful** woman.
23. 1 and who was the composer of **beautiful** songs for Israel.
1 Kgs 1. 3 all over Israel for a **beautiful** girl, and in Shunem they
1. 4 She was very **beautiful,** and waited on the king and took
2 Kgs 3.19 You will conquer all their **beautiful** fortified cities;
2 Chr 3. 6 king decorated the Temple with **beautiful** precious stones
Esth 1.11 The queen was a **beautiful** woman, and the king wanted
1.11 to show off her **beauty** to the officials and all his
2. 2 don't you make a search to find some **beautiful** young virgins?
2. 3 to bring all these **beautiful** young girls to your harem here
2. 3 of your women, and let them be given a **beauty** treatment.
2. 7 she was a **beautiful** girl, and had a good figure.
2. 9 in beginning her **beauty** treatment of massage and special diet.
2.12 The regular **beauty** treatment for the women lasted a year—
Job 31.26 the sun in its brightness or the moon in all its **beauty.**
42.15 other women in the whole world as **beautiful** as Job's daughters.
Ps 45. 1 **Beautiful** words fill my mind, as I compose this song for
45.11 Your **beauty** will make the king desire you;
45.13 The princess is in the palace—how **beautiful** she is!
48. 2 Zion, the mountain of God, is high and **beautiful;**
50. 2 God shines from Zion, the city perfect in its **beauty.**
96. 6 power and **beauty** fill his Temple.
122. 3 Jerusalem is a city restored in **beautiful** order and harmony.
Prov 6.25 Don't be tempted by their **beauty;**
11.22 **Beauty** in a woman without good judgement is like a gold
24. 4 the rooms are furnished with valuable, **beautiful** things.
25. 4 out of silver and the artist can produce a thing of **beauty.**
31.30 Charm is deceptive and **beauty** disappears, but a woman who
Song 1. 1 The most **beautiful** of songs, by Solomon.
1. 5 I am dark but **beautiful,** dark as the desert tents
1. 5 of Kedar, but **beautiful** as the curtains in Solomon's palace.
1.10 Your hair is **beautiful** upon your cheeks and falls along
1.15 How **beautiful** you are, my love;
4. 1 How **beautiful** you are, my love!
4. 7 How **beautiful** you are, my love;
5. 9 Most **beautiful** of women, is your lover different from
5.12 His eyes are as **beautiful** as doves by a flowing brook,
6. 1 Most **beautiful** of women, where has your lover gone?
6. 4 My love, you are as **beautiful** as Jerusalem, as lovely as
6.10 She is **beautiful** and bright, as dazzling as the sun or the
7. 1 How **beautiful** are your feet in sandals.
7. 5 its **beauty** could hold a king captive.
7. 6 How pretty you are, how **beautiful;**
Is 2.16 He will sink even the largest and most **beautiful** ships.
3.24 instead of having **beautiful** hair, they will be bald;
3.24 their **beauty** will be turned to shame!
4. 2 every plant and tree in the land grow large and **beautiful.**
13.19 Babylonia is the most **beautiful** kingdom of all;
35. 2 will be as **beautiful** as the Lebanon Mountains and as fertile
44.16 What a **beautiful** fire!"
53. 2 He had no dignity or **beauty** to make us take notice of
60.13 To make my Temple **beautiful,** To make my city glorious.
60.15 will make you great and **beautiful,** A place of joy for ever
62. 3 You will be like a **beautiful** crown for the Lord.
64.11 our Temple, the sacred and **beautiful** place where our ancestors
Jer 3.19 delightful land, the most **beautiful** land in all the world.
4.30 You are making yourself **beautiful** for nothing!
6. 2 The city of Zion is **beautiful,** but it will be destroyed;
11.16 once called them a leafy olive-tree, full of **beautiful** fruit;
13.18 because their **beautiful** crowns have fallen from their heads.
22. 6 Judah's royal palace is as **beautiful** as the land of Gilead
22. 7 cut down its **beautiful** cedar pillars, and throw them into
Ezek 7.20 they were proud of their **beautiful** jewels, but they used them
Ezek 16.12 you a nose-ring and earrings and a **beautiful** crown to wear.
16.13 Your **beauty** was dazzling, and you became a queen.
16.14 every nation for your perfect **beauty,** because I was the one
16.15 took advantage of your **beauty** and fame to sleep with everyone
16.25 You dragged your **beauty** through the mud.
17. 3 was a giant eagle with **beautiful** feathers and huge wings,
23.41 They would sit on a **beautiful** couch, and in front of
23.42 put bracelets on the women's arms and **beautiful** crowns on their
27. 3 Tyre, you boasted of your perfect **beauty.**
27. 4 Your builders made you like a **beautiful** ship;
27.11 They are the men who made you **beautiful.**
28. 7 They will destroy all the **beautiful** things you have acquired by
31. 3 a cedar in Lebanon, With **beautiful,** shady branches, A tree so
31. 7 How **beautiful** the tree was— So tall, with such long branches.
31. 8 No tree in God's own garden was so **beautiful.**
31. 9 I made it **beautiful,** with spreading branches.
32.19 "Do you think you are more **beautiful** than anyone else?
Dan 4.12 leaves were **beautiful,** and it was loaded down with fruit—
4.21 Its leaves were **beautiful,** and it had enough fruit on it
Hos 10. 1 land was, the more **beautiful** they made the sacred stone pillars
10.11 put a yoke on her **beautiful** neck and to harness her for
14. 6 will be alive with new growth, and **beautiful** like olive-trees.
Amos 5.11 you build or drink wine from the **beautiful** vineyards you plant.
Zech 4. 7 in place, the people will shout, **'Beautiful,** beautiful!' "
9.17 How good and **beautiful** the land will be!
Mt 6.29 his wealth had clothes as **beautiful** as one of these flowers.
26.10 It is a fine and **beautiful** thing that she has done
Mk 14. 6 She has done a fine and **beautiful** thing for me.
Lk 12.27 his wealth had clothes as **beautiful** as one of these flowers.
21. 5 about the Temple, how **beautiful** it looked with its fine stones
Acts 7.20 at this time that Moses was born, a very **beautiful** child.
1 Cor 11.15 a disgrace, [15]but on a woman it is a thing of **beauty.**
12.24 special modesty, [24]which the more **beautiful** parts do not need.
15.40 the **beauty** that belongs to heavenly bodies is different
15.40 from the **beauty** that belongs to earthly bodies.
15.41 The sun has its own **beauty,**
15.41 the moon another **beauty,** and the stars a different beauty;
15.41 and even among stars there are different kinds of **beauty.**
15.43 when raised, it will be **beautiful** and strong.
Eph 5.27 to himself in all its **beauty**—pure and faultless, without spot
Heb 11.23 saw that he was a **beautiful** child, and they were not afraid
Jas 1.11 its flower falls off, and its **beauty** is destroyed.
1 Pet 3. 3 outward aids to make yourselves **beautiful,** such as the way you
3. 4 Instead, your **beauty** should consist of your true inner self,
3. 4 the ageless **beauty** of a gentle and quiet spirit,
3. 5 to make themselves **beautiful** by submitting to their husbands.

BED (1)

Gen 19. 4 Before the guests went to **bed,** the men of Sodom surrounded
39. 7 to desire Joseph and asked him to go to **bed** with her.
39.10 Joseph day after day, he would not go to **bed** with her.
39.12 caught him by his robe and said, "Come to **bed** with me."
47.31 Joseph made the vow, and Jacob gave thanks there on his **bed.**
48. 2 to see him, he gathered his strength and sat up in **bed.**
49. 4 For you slept with my concubine And dishonoured your father's **bed.**
Ex 8. 3 go into your palace, your **bedroom,** your bed, the houses of
21.18 hit has to stay in **bed,** but later is able to get
Lev 15. 4 Any **bed** on which he sits or lies is unclean.
15. 5 Anyone who touches his **bed** [6]or sits on anything the man
15.21 who touches her **bed** or anything on which she has sat
15.24 for seven days, and any **bed** on which he lies is unclean.
15.26 Any **bed** on which she lies and anything on which she sits
Judg 14.18 before Samson went into the **bedroom,** the men of the city
16. 1 Gaza, where he met a prostitute and went to **bed** with her.
16. 3 But Samson stayed in **bed** only until midnight.
1 Sam 3. 5 go back to **bed."**
3. 5 So Samuel went back to **bed.**
3. 6 go back to **bed."**
3. 9 calling the boy, [9]so he said to him, "Go back to **bed;**
3. 9 So Samuel went back to **bed.**
3.15 Samuel stayed in **bed** until morning;
9.25 town, they made up a **bed** for Saul on the roof, [26]and
19.13 idol, laid it on the **bed,** put a pillow made of goats'-hair
19.15 them, "Carry him here in his **bed,** and I will kill him."
19.16 the household idol in the **bed** and the goats'-hair pillow at
28.23 gave in, got up from the ground, and sat on the **bed.**
2 Sam 4. 7 they went to Ishbosheth's **bedroom,** where he was sound asleep,
13. 5 said to him, "Pretend that you are ill and go to **bed.**
13. 6 So Amnon pretended that he was ill and went to **bed.**
13. 8 She went there and found him in **bed.**
13.10 the cakes here to my **bed** and serve them to me yourself."
13.11 to him, he grabbed her and said, "Come to **bed** with me!"
17.28 brought bowls, clay pots, and **bedding,** and also food for David
1 Kgs 1.15 So Bathsheba went to see the king in his **bedroom.**
1.47 bowed in worship on his **bed** [48]and prayed, 'Let us praise
3.20 my side while I was asleep, and carried him to her **bed;**
3.20 then she put the dead child in my **bed.**
17.19 the room where he was staying, and laid him on the **bed.**
21. 4 He lay down on his **bed,** facing the wall, and would not
21. 7 "Get out of **bed,** cheer up and eat.
2 Kgs 4.10 on the roof, put a **bed,** a table, a chair, and a
4.21 room, put him on the **bed** and left, closing the door behind
4.32 into the room and saw the boy lying dead on the **bed.**
7.12 the king got out of **bed** and said to his officials, "I'll
11. 2 and his nurse into a **bedroom** in the Temple and hid him
2 Chr 22.11 and hid him and a nurse in a **bedroom** at the Temple.
24.25 and killed him in his **bed** to avenge the murder of the
Job 31.10 cook another man's food and sleep in another man's **bed.**
Ps 4. 4 think deeply about this, when you lie in silence on your **beds.**

Ps 6. 6 every night my **bed** is damp from my weeping;
36. 4 He makes evil plans as he lies in **bed;**
41. 8 he will never leave his **bed** again."
63. 6 As I lie in **bed,** I remember you;
127. 2 hard for a living, getting up early and going to **bed** late.
132. 3 "I will not go home or go to **bed;**
Prov 3.24 afraid when you go to **bed,** and you will sleep soundly
6. 9 How long is the lazy man going to lie in **bed?**
7.16 I've covered my **bed** with sheets of coloured linen from Egypt.
22.27 should be unable to pay, they will take away even your **bed.**
26.14 The lazy man turns over in **bed.**
31.22 She makes **bedspreads** and wears clothes of fine purple linen.
Ecc 10.20 criticize the rich, even in the privacy of your **bedroom.**
Song 1.16 The green grass will be our **bed;**
3. 1 Asleep on my **bed,** night after night I dreamt of the one
Is 14.11 You lie on a **bed** of maggots and are covered with a
28.20 tries to sleep in a **bed** too short to stretch out on,
57. 8 and climb into your large **beds** with your lovers, whom you
Ezek 16.26 neighbours, the Egyptians, go to **bed** with you, and you used
Mt 8. 6 my servant is sick in **bed** at home, unable to move
8.14 there he saw Peter's mother-in-law sick in **bed** with a fever.
9. 2 some people brought to him a paralysed man, lying on a **bed.**
9. 6 the paralysed man, "Get up, pick up your **bed,** and go
Mk 1.30 Simon's mother-in-law was sick in **bed** with a fever,
4.21 a lamp and put it under a bowl or under the **bed?**
7. 4 the proper way to wash cups, pots, copper bowls, and **beds.**
7.30 She went home and found her child lying on the **bed;**
Lk 4.39 went and stood at her **bedside** and ordered the fever to leave
5.18 a paralysed man on a **bed,** and they tried to take him
5.19 let him down on his **bed** into the middle of the group
5.24 "I tell you, get up, pick up your **bed,** and go home!"
5.25 of them all, took the **bed** he had been lying on,
8.16 and covers it with a bowl or puts it under a **bed.**
11. 7 door is already locked, and my children and I are in **bed.**
17.34 there will be two people sleeping in the same **bed:**
Acts 5.15 the streets and placed on **beds** and mats so that at least
9.33 had not been able to get out of **bed** for eight years.
9.34 Get up and make your **bed."**
28. 8 Publius' father was in **bed,** sick with fever and dysentery.
Rev 2.22 throw her on to a **bed** where she and those who committed

BED (2)
[RIVER-BED, STREAM BED]

1 Sam 15. 5 the city of Amalek and waited in ambush in a dry **river-bed.**
1 Kgs 18. 5 at every spring and every **river-bed** in the land to see if
2 Kgs 3.16 'Dig ditches all over this dry **stream bed.**
3.17 rain or wind, this **stream bed** will be filled with water, and
Job 6.17 heat they disappear, and the **stream beds** lie bare and dry.
22.24 dump your finest gold in the dry **stream bed.**
Ps 126. 4 just as the rain brings water back to dry **river-beds.**
Is 57. 5 as sacrifices in the rocky caves near the **bed** of a stream.

BEEF

Deut 14.26 it on whatever you want—**beef,** lamb, wine, beer—and there, in

BEELZEBUL
Name given to the Devil.
see also **BAALZEBUB**

Mt 10.25 of the family is called **Beelzebul,** the members of the family
12.24 because their ruler **Beelzebul** gives him power to do so."
12.27 I drive out demons because **Beelzebul** gives me the power to
12.28 No, it is not **Beelzebul,** but God's Spirit, who gives me
Mk 3.22 come from Jerusalem were saying, "He has **Beelzebul** in him!
Lk 11.15 the people said, "It is **Beelzebul,** the chief of the demons,
11.18 I drive out demons because **Beelzebul** gives me the power to

BEER (1)

Lev 10. 9 enter the Tent of my presence after drinking wine or **beer;**
Num 6. 3 dedicates himself to the Lord [3] shall abstain from wine and **beer.**
Deut 14.26 you want—beef, lamb, wine, **beer**—and there, in the presence
29. 6 to eat or wine or **beer** to drink, but the Lord provided
Judg 13. 4 not to drink any wine or **beer,** or eat any forbidden food;
13. 7 to drink any wine or **beer,** or eat any forbidden food,
13.14 must not drink any wine or **beer,** or eat any forbidden food.

BEERSHEBA
An important city in s. Judah or Simeon.

Gen 21.14 She left and wandered about in the wilderness of **Beersheba.**
21.31 so the place was called **Beersheba,** because it was there that
21.32 made this agreement at **Beersheba,** Abimelech and Phicol went back
21.33 Abraham planted a tamarisk-tree in **Beersheba** and worshipped
22.19 and they went together to **Beersheba,** where Abraham settled.
26.23 Isaac left and went to **Beersheba.**
26.33 That is how the city of **Beersheba** got its name.
28.10 Jacob left **Beersheba** and started towards Haran.
46. 1 and went to **Beersheba,** where he offered sacrifices to the
46. 5 Jacob set out from **Beersheba.**
Josh 15.28 Gaddah, Heshmon, Bethpelet, [28] Hazar Shual, **Beersheba,**
19. 2 It included **Beersheba,** Sheba, Moladah, [3] Hazar Shual, Balah,
Judg 20. 1 Dan in the north to **Beersheba** in the south, as well as
1 Sam 8. 2 they were judges in **Beersheba.**
2 Sam 24. 7 and finally to **Beersheba,** in the southern part of Judah.
1 Kgs 19. 3 he took his servant and went to **Beersheba** in Judah.
2 Kgs 12. 1 His mother was Zibiah from the city of **Beersheba.**
1 Chr 4.28 **Beersheba,** Moladah, Hazarshual, [29] Bilhah, Ezem, Tolad,
2 Chr 19. 4 regularly among the people, from **Beersheba** in the south to the
24. 1 His mother was Zibiah from the city of **Beersheba.**
30. 5 Dan in the north to **Beersheba** in the south, to come together
Neh 11.27 and Hazarshual, and in **Beersheba** and the villages around it.
11.30 lived in the territory between **Beersheba** in the south and the
Amos 5. 5 Do not go to **Beersheba** to worship.
8.14 or, 'By the god of **Beersheba'**—those people will fall and not

BEES

Deut 1.44 in those hills came out against you like a swarm of **bees.**
Judg 14. 8 to find a swarm of **bees** and some honey inside the dead
Ps 118.12 swarmed round me like **bees,** but they burnt out as quickly
Is 7.18 Nile, and for the Assyrians to come from their land like **bees.**

BEFOREHAND

Mk 13.11 do not worry **beforehand** about what you are going to
Lk 21.14 Make up your minds **beforehand** not to worry about how you
Acts 17.26 He himself fixed **beforehand** the exact times and the limits
1 Thes 3. 4 we told you **beforehand** that we were going to be

BEG

Gen 19. 7 said to them, "Friends, I **beg** you, don't do such a wicked
42.21 he was in when he **begged** for help, but we would not
Ex 11. 8 before me, and they will **beg** me to take all my people
Deut 18.16 gathered at Mount Sinai, you **begged** not to hear the Lord
33.29 Your enemies will come **begging** for mercy, and you will trample
1 Sam 2.36 for money and food, and **beg** to be allowed to help the
15.25 But now I **beg** you, forgive my sin and go back with
20. 6 table, tell him that I **begged** your permission to hurry home
20.28 Jonathan answered, "He **begged** me to let him go to Bethlehem.
23.11 Lord, God of Israel, I **beg** you to answer me!"
2 Chr 33.12 turned to the Lord his God, and **begged** him for help.
Esth 4. 8 plead with the king and **beg** him to have mercy on her
7. 7 this, so he stayed behind to **beg** Queen Esther for his life.
7. 8 down on Esther's couch to **beg** for mercy, when the king came
8. 3 She **begged** him to do something to stop the evil plot that
Job 9.15 all I can do is **beg** for mercy from God my judge.
19.16 he doesn't answer— even when I **beg** him to help me.
30.24 a ruined man, one who can do nothing but **beg** for pity?
41. 3 Will he **beg** you to let him go?
Ps 30. 8 I **begged** for your help:
37.25 man abandoned by the Lord or his children **begging** for food.
116. 4 Then I called to the Lord, "I **beg** you, Lord, save me!"
Prov 2. 3 Yes, **beg** for knowledge;
6. 3 hurry to him, and **beg** him to release you.
14.19 to bow down to the righteous and humbly **beg** their favour.
18.23 man speaks, he has to **beg** politely, but when the rich man
Jer 36.25 Elnathan, Delaiah, and Gemariah **begged** the king not to burn the
37.20 And now, Your Majesty, I **beg** you to listen to me and
38.20 I **beg** you to obey the Lord's message;
38.26 Just tell them you were **begging** me not to send you back
Lam 2.19 Pour out your heart and **beg** him for mercy on your children
3.56 to you, [56] And when I **begged** you to listen to my cry,
4. 4 children are **begging** for food that no one will give them.
5. 6 enough to stay alive, we went **begging** to Egypt and Assyria.
Ezek 7.26 You will **beg** the prophets to reveal what they foresee.
Mt 8. 5 entered Capernaum, a Roman officer met him and **begged** for help:
8.31 So the demons **begged** Jesus, "If you are going to drive
8.34 they saw him, they **begged** him to leave their territory.
14.36 They **begged** him to let those who were ill at least touch
15.23 His disciples came to him and **begged** him, "Send her away!
18.26 'Be patient with me,' he **begged,** 'and I will pay you everything!'
18.29 His fellow-servant fell down and **begged** him, 'Be patient
Mk 1.40 skin-disease came to Jesus, knelt down, and **begged** him for help.
5. 7 For God's sake, I **beg** you, don't punish me!"
5.10 And he kept **begging** Jesus not to send the evil spirits
5.12 So the spirits **begged** Jesus, "Send us to the pigs,
5.18 who had had the demons **begged** him, "Let me go with you!"
5.23 and **begged** him earnestly, "My little daughter is
6.56 to the market-places and **beg** him to let them at least
7.26 She **begged** Jesus to drive the demon out of her daughter.
7.32 could hardly speak, and they **begged** Jesus to place his hands
8.22 brought a blind man to Jesus and **begged** him to touch him.
Lk 5.12 he threw himself down and **begged** him, "Sir, if you want to,
7. 4 to Jesus and **begged** him earnestly, "This man really deserves
8.28 I **beg** you, don't punish me!"
8.31 The demons **begged** Jesus not to send them into the abyss.
8.32 So the demons **begged** Jesus to let them go into the pigs,
8.38 demons had gone out **begged** Jesus, "Let me go with you."
8.41 down at Jesus' feet and **begged** him to go to his home,
9.38 I **beg** you, look at my son—my only son!
9.40 I **begged** your disciples to drive it out, but they couldn't."
15.28 so his father came out and **begged** him to come in.
16. 3 not strong enough to dig ditches, and I am ashamed to **beg.**
16.27 rich man said, 'Then I **beg** you, father Abraham, send Lazarus
18.35 Jericho, there was a blind man sitting by the road, **begging.**
Jn 4.31 disciples were **begging** Jesus, "Teacher, have something to eat!"
4.40 Samaritans came to him, they **begged** him to stay with them,
9. 8 people who had seen him **begging** before this, asked,
9. 8 "Isn't this the man who used to sit and **beg?"**
Acts 3. 2 carried to the gate to **beg** for money from the people
3. 3 Peter and John going in, he **begged** them to give him something.
16. 9 a Macedonian standing and **begging** him, "Come over to
19.31 also sent him a message **begging** him not to show himself
21.12 we and the others there **begged** Paul not to go to Jerusalem.

Acts 24. 4 so I **beg** you to be kind and listen
25. 2 They **begged** Festus [3] to do them the favour of bringing Paul
27.22 But now I **beg** you, take heart!
27.33 Just before dawn, Paul **begged** them all to eat some food:
27.34 I **beg** you, then, eat some food;
1 Cor 4.16 I **beg** you, then, to follow my example.
16.15 I **beg** you, my brothers, [16] to follow the leadership of such
2 Cor 2. 8 And so I **beg** you to let him know that you really
6. 1 together with God, then, we **beg** you who have received God's
8. 4 own free will [4] they **begged** us and pleaded for the privilege
10. 1 and kindness of Christ I **beg** you [2] not to force me to
12.18 I **begged** Titus to go, and I sent the other Christian
Gal 4.12 I **beg** you, my brothers, be like me.
Eph 3.13 I **beg** you, then, not to be discouraged because I am
Phil 4. 2 Euodia and Syntyche, please, I **beg** you, try to agree as
1 Thes 4. 1 And now we **beg** and urge you in the name of
4.10 So we **beg** you, our brothers, to do even more.
5.12 We **beg** you, our brothers, to pay proper respect to those
2 Thes 2. 1 I **beg** you, my brothers, [2] not to be so easily confused
Heb 12.19 people heard the voice, they **begged** not to hear another word,
13.19 And I **beg** you even more earnestly to pray that God will
13.22 I **beg** you, my brothers, to listen patiently to this message

BEGET

Job 10.10 You gave my father strength to **beget** me;

AV **BEGET** see **FATHER**

BEGGAR

Ps 109.10 May his children be homeless **beggars;**
Mt 10.10 do not carry a **beggar's bag** for the journey or an extra
Mk 6. 8 a stick—no bread, no **beggar's bag,** no money in your pockets.
10.46 a large crowd, a blind **beggar** named Bartimaeus son of Timaeus
Lk 9. 3 no stick, no **beggar's bag,** no food, no money, not even
10. 4 Don't take a purse or a **beggar's bag** or shoes;
Acts 3.10 they recognized him as the **beggar** who had sat at the

BEGIN
[BEGAN, BEGUN]

Gen 1. 1 In the **beginning,** when God created the universe, [2] the earth
11. 6 this is just the **beginning** of what they are going to do.
Num 28.11 a burnt-offering to the Lord at the **beginning** of each month:
Deut 3.24 shown me only the **beginning** of the great and wonderful things
1 Sam 3.12 out all my threats against Eli's family, from **beginning** to end.
2 Sam 21. 9 in the spring, at the **beginning** of the barley harvest,
21.10 she stayed there from the **beginning** of harvest until the autumn
23.13 Near the **beginning** of harvest time three of "The Thirty"
1 Chr 25. 8 drew lots, whether they were young or old, experts or **beginners.**
29.29 history of King David from **beginning** to end is recorded in
2 Chr 9.29 the history of Solomon from **beginning** to end is recorded in
12.15 Rehoboam's acts from **beginning** to end and his family records
16.11 events of Asa's reign from **beginning** to end are recorded in
20.34 Jehoshaphat did, from the **beginning** of his reign to its end,
25.26 that Amaziah did from the **beginning** to the end of his reign
28.26 events of his reign, from **beginning** to end, are recorded in
35.27 and his history from **beginning** to end—is all recorded in
Ezra 4. 6 the **beginning** of the reign of Xerxes the emperor, the enemies
Neh 13.19 to be shut at the **beginning** of every Sabbath, as soon as
Ps 74.12 But you have been our king from the **beginning,** O God;
93. 2 been firm from the **beginning,** and you existed before time began.
Prov 8.23 was made in the very **beginning,** at the first, before the
Ecc 7. 8 The end of anything is better than its **beginning.**
Is 6.13 (The stump represents a new **beginning** for God's people.)
41. 4 Lord, was there at the **beginning,** and I, the Lord, will be
44. 7 would happen from the very **beginning** to the end of time?
46.10 From the **beginning** I predicted the outcome;
48.16 From the **beginning** I have spoken openly, and have always made
Jer 17.12 glorious throne, standing on a high mountain from the **beginning.**
32.30 the very **beginning** of their history the people of Israel
Mic 4. 7 I will make a new **beginning** with those who are left,
Hab 1.12 Lord, from the very **beginning** you are God.
Mt 4.17 From that time Jesus **began** to preach his message:
12.45 person is in a worse state than he was at the **beginning.**
18.24 He had just **begun** to do so when one of them
19. 4 says that in the **beginning** the Creator made people male and
20. 9 The men who had **begun** to work at five o'clock were paid
24.21 has ever been, from the **beginning** of the world to this very
24.33 you will know that the time is near, ready to **begin.**
Mk 1. 2 It **began** as the prophet Isaiah had written:
10. 6 But in the **beginning,** at the time of creation, 'God made
13.19 ever known from the very **beginning** when God created the world
13.29 you will know that the time is near, ready to **begin.**
Lk 1. 2 who saw these things from the **beginning** and who proclaimed the
1. 3 these matters from their **beginning,** I thought it would be good
3.23 When Jesus **began** his work, he was about thirty years old.
9.12 When the sun was **beginning** to set, the twelve disciples came
11.26 person is in a worse state than he was at the **beginning."**
14.30 'This man **began** to build but can't finish the job!'
21.28 When these things **begin** to happen, stand up and raise your
21.30 you see their leaves **beginning** to appear, you know that summer
23. 5 He **began** in Galilee and now has come here."
23.54 It was Friday, and the Sabbath was about to **begin.**
24.27 himself in all the Scriptures, **beginning** with the books of Moses
24.47 of sins must be preached to all nations, **beginning** in Jerusalem.
Jn 1. 2 From the very **beginning** the Word was with God.
6.64 (Jesus knew from the very **beginning** who were the ones that
8.25 Jesus answered, "What I have told you from the very **beginning.**
8.44 From the very **beginning** he was a murderer and has never been
9.32 Since the **beginning** of the world nobody has ever heard of
15.27 because you have been with me from the very **beginning.**
16. 4 tell you these things at the **beginning,** for I was with you.
Acts 1. 1 taught from the time he **began** his work [2] until the day
1.21 travelled about with us, **beginning** from the time John preached
10.37 the land of Israel, **beginning** in Galilee after John preached
11. 4 a complete account of what had happened from the very **beginning:**
11.15 Spirit came down on them just as on us at the **beginning.**
13.24 Before Jesus **began** his work, John preached to all the people
Rom 1.17 it is through faith from **beginning** to end.
5.17 sin of one man death **began** to rule because of that one
11. 2 God has not rejected his people, whom he chose from the **beginning.**
2 Cor 8. 6 So we urged Titus, who **began** this work, to continue it and
8.10 is better for you to finish now what you **began** last year.
Gal 3. 3 You **began** by God's Spirit;
Eph 1.11 based on what he had decided from the very **beginning.**
Phil 1. 6 am sure that God, who **began** this good work in you, will
2 Tim 1. 9 of Christ Jesus before the **beginning** of time,
Tit 1. 2 us this life before the **beginning** of time,
Heb 1.10 "You, Lord, in the **beginning** created the earth, and with your
3.14 firmly to the end the confidence we had at the **beginning.**
12. 2 on Jesus, on whom our faith depends from **beginning** to end.
1 Pet 4.17 has come for judgement to **begin,** and God's own people are
2 Pet 2.18 trap those who are just **beginning** to escape from among people
2.20 a worse state at the end than they were at the **beginning.**
1 Jn 1. 1 the Word of life, which has existed from the very **beginning.**
2. 7 old command, the one you have had from the very **beginning.**
2.13 because you know him who has existed from the **beginning.**
2.14 because you know him who has existed from the **beginning.**
2.24 in your hearts the message you heard from the **beginning.**
3. 8 because the Devil has sinned from the very **beginning.**
3.11 The message you heard from the very **beginning** is this:
2 Jn 5 it is the command which we have had from the **beginning.**
6 have all heard from the **beginning,** is that you must all live
Rev 11.17 you have taken your great power and have **begun** to rule!
17.12 kings who have not yet **begun** to rule, but who will be
21. 6 I am the first and the last, the **beginning** and the end.
22.13 I am the first and the last, the **beginning** and the end."

BEHALF

Jn 5.31 I testify on my own **behalf,** what I say is not
5.32 who testifies on my **behalf,** and I know that what he
5.33 sent your messengers, and he spoke on **behalf** of the truth.
5.36 have a witness on my **behalf** which is even greater than
5.36 these speak on my **behalf** and show that the Father has
5.37 And the Father, who sent me, also testifies on my **behalf.**
8.13 Pharisees said to him, "Now you are testifying on your own **behalf;**
8.14 testify on my own **behalf,** what I say is true,
8.18 I testify on my own **behalf,**
8.18 and the Father who sent me also testifies on my **behalf."**
10.25 The things I do by my Father's authority speak on my **behalf;**
16.26 ask him on your **behalf,** [27] for the Father himself loves you.
Acts 26. 1 Paul, "You have permission to speak on your own **behalf."**
Rom 8.27 Spirit pleads with God on **behalf** of his people
15. 8 life of service was on **behalf** of the Jews, to show that
2 Cor 5.20 We plead on Christ's **behalf:**
Col 1. 7 dear fellow-servant, who is Christ's faithful worker on our **behalf.**
1.24 remains of Christ's sufferings on **behalf** of his body, the church.
Phlm 10 a request to you on **behalf** of Onesimus, who is my own
Heb 5. 1 to serve God on their **behalf,** to offer sacrifices and offerings
6.20 On our **behalf** Jesus has gone in there before us,
9. 7 he offers to God on **behalf** of himself and for the sins
9.24 where he now appears on our **behalf** in the presence of God.
1 Pet 3.18 a good man on **behalf** of sinners, in order to lead
1 Jn 2. 1 pleads with the Father on our **behalf**—Jesus Christ, the righteous

BEHAVE

2 Cor 12.18 act from the very same motives and **behave** in the same way?
Eph 6. 9 Masters, **behave** in the same way towards your slaves and stop
1 Thes 4.10 you have, in fact, **behaved** like this towards all the brothers
Tit 2. 3 instruct the older women to **behave** as women should who live
2. 7 In all things you yourself must be an example of good **behaviour.**

BEHEADED

2 Kgs 6.31 me dead if Elisha is not **beheaded** before the day is over!"
Mt 14.10 So he had John **beheaded** in prison.

BEHEMOTH
Either the hippopotamus or a legendary creature.

Job 40.15 Look at the monster **Behemoth;**

BEING

Gen 1.20 with many kinds of living **beings,** and let the air be filled
1.26 Then God said, "And now we will make human **beings;**
1.27 So God created human **beings,** making them to be like himself.
3.20 wife Eve, because she was the mother of all human **beings.**
5. 1 (When God created human **beings,** he made them like himself.
6. 2 some of the heavenly **beings** saw that these girls were beautiful,
6. 4 who were descendants of human women and the heavenly **beings.**
6.17 to send a flood on the earth to destroy every living **being.**
7. 4 order to destroy all the living **beings** that I have made."
7.15 of each kind of living **being** went into the boat with Noah,
7.21 Every living **being** on the earth died—every bird,

Gen 7.23 The Lord destroyed all living **beings** on the earth—
7.23 human **beings,** animals, and birds.
8.21 will I destroy all living **beings,** as I have done this time.
9.10 and with all living **beings**—all birds and all animals—
9.11 never again will all living **beings** be destroyed by a flood;
9.12 you and with all living **beings,** [13] I am putting my bow in
9.15 that a flood will never again destroy all living **beings.**
9.16 everlasting covenant between me and all living **beings** on earth.
9.17 of the promise which I am making to all living **beings."**
Lev 27.28 the Lord, whether it is a human **being,** an animal, or land.
27.29 even a human **being** who has been unconditionally dedicated
Deut 5.26 Has any human **being** ever lived after hearing the living God
Josh 10.14 been a day like it, when the Lord obeyed a human **being.**
Job 1. 6 day came for the heavenly **beings** to appear before the Lord,
2. 1 came for the heavenly **beings** to appear before the Lord again,
38. 7 stars sang together, and the heavenly **beings** shouted for joy.
Ps 6. 3 I am completely exhausted [3] and my whole **being** is deeply troubled.
9.20 make them know that they are only mortal **beings.**
29. 1 Praise the Lord, you heavenly **beings;**
56. 4 What can a mere human **being** do to me?
56.11 What can a mere human **being** do to me?
63. 1 My whole **being** desires you;
71.23 with my whole **being** I will sing because you have saved me.
78.39 that they were only mortal **beings,** like a wind that blows by
84. 2 With my whole **being** I sing for joy to the living God.
89. 6 none of the heavenly **beings** is your equal.
90. 2 or brought the world into **being,** you were eternally God,
103. 1 All my **being,** praise his holy name!
146. 3 no human **being** can save you.
Ecc 3.19 A human **being** is no better off than an animal, because life
Is 44.11 The people who make idols are human **beings** and nothing more.
66. 3 they kill a bull as a sacrifice or sacrifice a human **being;**
Ezek 29.11 No human **being** or animal will walk through it.
38.20 and small, and every human **being** on the face of the earth
44. 2 No human **being** is allowed to use it, because I, the Lord
Dan 2.11 except the gods, and they do not live among human **beings."**
4.12 its branches, and every kind of living **being** ate its fruit.
7.13 vision in the night, I saw what looked like a human **being.**
Zeph 1. 3 destroy everything on earth, [3] all human **beings** and animals,
Mt 16.17 to you from any human **being,** but it was given to you
Jn 1.14 The Word became a human **being** and, full of grace and truth,
Acts 14.15 We ourselves are only human **beings** like you!
Rom 4.17 and whose command brings into **being** what did not exist.
6. 6 we know that our old **being** has been put to death
6.13 and surrender your whole **being** to him to be used for
7.22 My inner **being** delights in the law of God.
8.23 God to make us his sons and set our whole **being** free.
9. 5 and Christ, as a human **being,** belongs to their race.
1 Cor 15.39 And the flesh of living **beings** is not all the same kind
15.39 human **beings** have one kind of flesh, animals another,
15.45 says, "The first man, Adam, was created a living **being";**
2 Cor 4.16 Even though our physical **being** is gradually decaying,
4.16 yet our spiritual **being** is renewed day after day.
5.17 When anyone is joined to Christ, he is a new **being;**
Gal 4. 8 and so you were slaves of **beings** who are not gods.
Eph 6.12 are not fighting against human **beings** but against the wicked
Phil 1.20 so that with my whole **being** I shall bring honour to Christ,
2.10 the name of Jesus all **beings** in heaven, on earth, and in
Col 3.10 is the new **being** which God, its Creator, is constantly renewing
1 Thes 5.23 and keep your whole **being**—spirit, soul, and body—free from
Heb 1. 3 exact likeness of God's own **being,** sustaining the universe with
Jas 1.18 he brought us into **being** through the word of truth,
3. 2 he is perfect and is also able to control his whole **being.**
3. 6 in our bodies and spreading evil through our whole **being.**
2 Pet 2.10 and arrogant, and show no respect for the glorious **beings** above;
1 Jn 4. 2 Christ came as a human **being** has the Spirit who comes from
2 Jn 7 do not acknowledge that Jesus Christ came as a human **being.**
Jude 8 despise God's authority and insult the glorious **beings** above.
Rev 1.13 what looked like a human **being,** wearing a robe that reached
5.13 in the sea—all living **beings** in the universe—
14.14 what looked like a human **being,** with a crown of gold

BELIEVE

Gen 45.26 Jacob was stunned and could not **believe** them.
Ex 4. 1 suppose the Israelites do not **believe** me and will not listen
4. 8 said, "If they will not **believe** you or be convinced by the
4. 9 miracles they still will not **believe** you, and if they refuse
4.31 They **believed,** and when they heard that the Lord had come
19. 9 me speaking with you and will **believe** you from now on."
2 Sam 13.33 So don't **believe** the news that all your sons are dead;
1 Kgs 10. 7 But I couldn't **believe** it until I had come and seen it
2 Chr 9. 6 I did not **believe** what they told me until I came and
20.20 **Believe** what his prophets tell you, and you will succeed."
32.15 Don't **believe** him!
Job 9.16 he lets me speak, I can't **believe** he would listen to me.
22.17 men who rejected God and **believed** that he could do nothing
Ps 73.10 God's people turn to them and eagerly **believe** whatever they say.
78.22 faith in him and did not **believe** that he would save them.
106.12 his people **believed** his promises and sang praises to him.
106.24 rejected the pleasant land, because they did not **believe** God's promise.
116.10 kept on **believing,** even when I said, "I am completely crushed,"
Prov 14.15 A fool will **believe** anything;
17. 8 they **believe** it can do anything.
21.28 of a liar is not **believed,** but the word of someone who
26.25 may sound fine, but don't **believe** him, because his heart is
Is 43.10 you would know me and **believe** in me and understand that I
53. 1 "Who would have **believed** what we now report?
Jer 7. 4 Stop **believing** those deceitful words, 'We are safe!
Jer 28.15 not send you, and you are making these people **believe** a lie.
29.31 as if he were a prophet, and he made you **believe** lies.
40.14 But Gedaliah did not **believe** it.
Lam 4.12 **believed** that any invader could enter Jerusalem's
Ezek 13.19 So you tell lies to my people, and they **believe** you."
21.23 people of Jerusalem won't **believe** this, because of the treaties
Jon 3. 5 The people of Nineveh **believed** God's message.
Mic 7. 5 Don't **believe** your neighbour or trust your friend.
Hab 1. 5 something that you will not **believe** when you hear about it.
Mt 8.13 "Go home, and what you **believe** will be done for you."
9.28 and he asked them, "Do you **believe** that I can heal you?"
9.29 and said, "Let it happen, then, just as you **believe!"**
11.14 if you are willing to **believe** their message, John is Elijah,
21.21 assure you that if you **believe** and do not doubt, you will
21.22 If you **believe,** you will receive whatever you ask for
21.25 he will say to us, 'Why, then, did you not **believe** John?'
21.32 you the right path to take, and you would not **believe** him;
21.32 but the tax collectors and the prostitutes **believed** him.
21.32 this, you did not later change your minds and **believe** him.
24.23 do not **believe** him.
24.26 don't **believe** it.
27.42 he comes down off the cross now, we will **believe** in him!
Mk 1.15 Turn away from your sins and **believe** the Good News!"
5.36 they said, but told him, "Don't be afraid, only **believe."**
11.23 in his heart, but **believes** that what he says will happen,
11.24 pray and ask for something, **believe** that you have received it,
11.31 'From God,' he will say, 'Why, then, did you not **believe** John?'
13.21 do not **believe** him.
15.32 come down from the cross now, and we will **believe** in him!"
16.11 and that she had seen him, they did not **believe** her.
16.13 returned and told the others, but they would not **believe** it.
16.14 were too stubborn to **believe** those who had seen him alive.
16.16 Whoever **believes** and is baptized will be saved;
16.16 whoever does not **believe** will be condemned.
Lk 1.20 But you have not **believed** my message, which will come true
1.20 Because you have not **believed,** you will be unable to speak;
1.45 How happy you are to **believe** that the Lord's message to
8.12 in order to keep them from **believing** and being saved.
8.13 they **believe** only for a while but when the time of testing
8.50 only **believe,** and she will be well."
12. 5 **Believe** me, he is the one you must fear!
20. 5 'From God,' he will say, 'Why, then, did you not **believe** John?'
22.67 He answered, "If I tell you, you will not **believe** me;
24.11 the women said was nonsense, and they did not **believe** them.
24.25 how slow you are to **believe** everything the prophets said!
24.41 They still could not **believe,** they were so full of joy
Jn 1. 7 the light, so that all should hear the message and **believe.**
1.12 Some, however, did receive him and **believed** in him;
1.50 Jesus said, "Do you **believe** just because I told you I
2.11 he revealed his glory, and his disciples **believed** in him.
2.22 and they **believed** the scripture and what Jesus had
2.23 during the Passover Festival, many **believed** in him as they saw
3.12 You do not **believe** me when I tell you about the things
3.12 how will you ever **believe** me, then, when I tell you about
3.15 so that everyone who **believes** in him may have eternal life.
3.16 so that everyone who **believes** in him may not die but
3.18 Whoever **believes** in the Son is not judged;
3.18 but whoever does not **believe** has already been judged,
3.18 because he has not **believed** in God's only Son.
3.36 Whoever **believes** in the Son has eternal life;
4.21 Jesus said to her, **"Believe** me, woman, the time will come
4.39 Samaritans in that town **believed** in Jesus because the woman had
4.41 Many more **believed** because of his message,
4.42 said to the woman, "We **believe** now, not because of what you
4.48 "None of you will ever **believe** unless you see miracles and
4.50 The man **believed** Jesus' words and went.
4.53 So he and all his family **believed.**
5.24 whoever hears my words and **believes** in him who sent me
5.38 for you do not **believe** in the one whom he sent.
5.44 how, then, can you **believe** me?
5.46 If you had really **believed** Moses,
5.46 you would have **believed** me, because he wrote about me.
5.47 But since you do not **believe** what he wrote,
5.47 how can you **believe** what I say?"
6.29 wants you to do is to **believe** in the one he sent."
6.30 will you perform so that we may see it and **believe** you?
6.35 he who **believes** in me will never be thirsty.
6.36 I told you that you have seen me but will not **believe.**
6.40 who see the Son and **believe** in him should have eternal life.
6.47 he who **believes** has eternal life.
6.64 Yet some of you do not **believe."**
6.64 ones that would not **believe** and which one would betray him.)
6.69 And now we **believe** and know that you are the Holy One
7. 5 (Not even his brothers **believed** in him.)
7.31 But many in the crowd **believed** in him and said,
7.38 scripture says, 'Whoever **believes** in me, streams of life-giving
7.39 Spirit, which those who **believed** in him were going to receive.
7.48 one of the authorities or one Pharisee to **believe** in him?
8.24 sins if you do not **believe** that 'I Am Who I Am'."
8.30 Many who heard Jesus say these things **believed** in him.
8.31 Jesus said to those who **believed** in him, "If you obey
8.45 tell the truth, and that is why you do not **believe** me.
8.46 If I tell the truth, then why do you not **believe** me?
9.18 were not willing to **believe** that he had been blind
9.22 anyone who said he **believed** that Jesus was the Messiah
9.35 and asked him, "Do you **believe** in the Son of Man?"
9.36 me who he is, sir, so that I can **believe** in him!"
9.38 **"I believe,** Lord!"
10.25 "I have already told you, but you would not **believe** me.
10.26 but you will not **believe,** for you are not my sheep.
10.37 Do not **believe** me, then, if I am not doing the things

Jn 10.38 even though you do not **believe** me,
10.38 you should at least **believe** my deeds, in order that you
10.42 And many people there **believed** in him.
11.15 glad that I was not with him, so that you will **believe.**
11.25 Whoever **believes** in me will live, even though he dies;
11.26 and whoever lives and **believes** in me will never die.
11.26 Do you **believe** this?"
11.27 "I do **believe** that you are the Messiah, the Son of God,
11.40 I tell you that you would see God's glory if you **believed?"**
11.42 people here, so that they will **believe** that you sent me."
11.45 to visit Mary saw what Jesus did, and they **believed** in him.
11.48 in this way, everyone will **believe** in him, and the Roman
12.11 his account many Jews were rejecting them and **believing** in Jesus.
12.36 **Believe** in the light, then, while you have it,
12.37 their presence, they did not **believe** in him,
12.38 "Lord, who **believed** the message we told?
12.39 they were not able to **believe,** because Isaiah also said,
12.42 Even then, many of the Jewish authorities **believed** in Jesus;
12.44 "Whoever believes in me **believes** not only in me but also
12.46 so that everyone who **believes** in me should not remain in
13.19 it does happen, you will **believe** that 'I Am Who I Am.'
14. 1 **"Believe** in God and believe also in me.
14.10 Do you not **believe,** Philip, that I am in the Father and
14.11 **Believe** me when I say that I am in the Father and
14.11 If not, **believe** because of the things I do.
14.12 whoever **believes** in me will do what I do—
14.29 so that when it does happen, you will **believe.**
16. 9 They are wrong about sin, because they do not **believe** in me;
16.27 because you love me and have **believed** that I came from God.
16.30 This makes us **believe** that you came from God."
16.31 Jesus answered them, "Do you **believe** now?
17. 8 that I came from you, and they **believe** that you sent me.
17.20 also for those who **believe** in me because of their message.
17.21 so that the world will **believe** that you sent me.
19.35 this happen has spoken of it, so that you also may **believe.**
20. 8 he saw and **believed.**
20.25 those scars and my hand in his side, I will not **believe."**
20.27 Stop your doubting, and **believe!"**
20.29 Jesus said to him, "Do you **believe** because you see me?
20.29 How happy are those who **believe** without seeing me!"
20.31 in order that you may **believe** that Jesus is the Messiah,
Acts 2.41 Many of them **believed** his message and were baptized,
4. 4 But many who heard the message **believed;**
5.14 a crowd of men and women who **believed** in the Lord.
8.12 But when they **believed** Philip's message about the good news
8.13 Simon himself also **believed;**
9.26 But they would not **believe** that he was a disciple,
9.42 spread all over Joppa, and many people **believed** in the Lord.
10.43 saying that everyone who **believes** in him will have his sins
11.17 that he gave us when we **believed** in the Lord Jesus Christ;
11.21 a great number of people **believed** and turned to the Lord.
13.12 When the governor saw what had happened, he **believed;**
13.38 and that everyone who **believes** in him is set free from all
13.41 that you will not **believe,** even when someone explains it
14. 2 the Jews who would not **believe** stirred up the Gentiles
14. 9 Paul saw that he **believed** and could be healed, so he looked
14.27 how he had opened the way for the Gentiles to **believe.**
15. 7 Good News to the Gentiles, so that they could hear and **believe.**
15. 9 he forgave their sins because they **believed.**
15.11 We **believe** and are saved by the grace of the Lord Jesus,
16.31 answered, **"Believe** in the Lord Jesus, and you will be saved
16.34 family were filled with joy, because they now **believed** in God.
17.12 Many of them **believed;**
17.12 women of high social standing and many Greek men also **believed.**
17.34 Some men joined him and **believed,** among whom was Dionysius,
18. 8 the leader of the synagogue, **believed** in the Lord, together with
18. 8 people in Corinth heard the message, **believed,** and were baptized.
19. 4 the people of Israel to **believe** in the one who was coming
19. 9 were stubborn and would not **believe,** and before the whole group
20.21 turn from their sins to God and **believe** in our Lord Jesus.
22.19 synagogues and arrested and beat those who **believe** in you.
23. 8 but the Pharisees **believe** in all three.)
24.14 But I also **believe** in everything written in the Law of Moses
24.21 tried by you today for **believing** that the dead will rise
26. 8 here find it impossible to **believe** that God raises the dead?
26.27 King Agrippa, do you **believe** the prophets?
28.24 were convinced by his words, but others would not **believe.**
Rom 1. 5 in order to lead people of all nations to **believe** and obey.
1.16 power to save all who **believe,** first the Jews and also
3.22 does this to all who **believe** in Christ, because there is no
3.25 and that he puts right everyone who **believes** in Jesus.
3.27 No, but that we **believe.**
4. 3 scripture says, "Abraham **believed** God, and because of his faith
4. 5 on his deeds, and who **believes** in the God who declares
4. 9 quoted the scripture, "Abraham **believed** God, and because of his
4.11 spiritual father of all who **believe** in God and are accepted
4.13 but because he **believed** and was accepted as righteous
4.16 but also to those who **believe** as Abraham did.
4.17 of God, in whom Abraham **believed**—the God who brings the dead
4.18 Abraham **believed** and hoped, even when there was no reason for
4.24 be accepted as righteous, who **believe** in him who raised Jesus
6. 8 have died with Christ, we **believe** that we will also live
9.33 But whoever **believes** in him will not be disappointed."
10. 4 so that everyone who **believes** is put right with God.
10. 9 Jesus is Lord and **believe** that God raised him from death,
10.11 says, "Whoever **believes** in him will not be disappointed."
10.14 can they call to him for help if they have not **believed?**
10.14 And how can they **believe** if they have not heard the message?
10.16 Isaiah himself said, "Lord, who **believed** our message?"
11.20 because they did not **believe,**
Rom 11.20 while you remain in place because you do **believe.**
13.11 be saved is closer now than it was when we first **believed.**
14.14 but if a person **believes** that some food is unclean,
14.22 Keep what you **believe** about this matter, then, between
16. 5 the first man in the province of Asia to **believe** in Christ.
16.26 known to all nations, so that all may **believe** and obey.
1 Cor 1.21 message we preach, God decided to save those who **believe.**
3. 5 We are simply God's servants, by whom you were led to **believe.**
11.18 and this I **believe** is partly true.
15. 2 firmly to it—unless it was for nothing that you **believed.**
15.11 this is what we all preach, and this is what you **believe.**
15.14 we have nothing to preach and you have nothing to **believe.**
2 Cor 1.24 We are not trying to dictate to you what you must **believe;**
4. 4 They do not **believe,** because their minds have been kept in
4.13 The scripture says, "I spoke because I **believed."**
4.13 In the same spirit of faith, we also speak because we **believe.**
Gal 2.16 We, too, have **believed** in Christ Jesus in order to be put
3. 2 the Law requires or by hearing the gospel and **believing** it?
3. 5 Law requires or because you hear the gospel and **believe** it?
3. 6 the scripture says, "He **believed** God, and because of his faith
3. 9 Abraham **believed** and was blessed;
3. 9 so all who **believe** are blessed as he was.
3.22 of faith in Jesus Christ is given to those who **believe.**
Eph 1.13 You **believed** in Christ, and God put his stamp of ownership
1.19 how very great is his power at work in us who **believe.**
Phil 1.29 serving Christ, not only by **believing** in him, but also by
1 Thes 2.10 our conduct towards you who **believe** was pure, right, and without
2.13 For God is at work in you who **believe.**
4.14 We **believe** that Jesus died and rose again,
4.14 and so we **believe** that God will take
4.14 back with Jesus those who have died **believing** in him.
4.16 Those who have died **believing** in Christ will rise to life first;
2 Thes 1. 4 you continue to endure and **believe** through all the persecutions
1.10 glory from all his people and honour from all who **believe.**
1.10 because you have **believed** the message that we told you.
2.11 error to work in them so that they **believe** what is false.
2.12 all who have not **believed** the truth, but have taken pleasure
3. 2 for not everyone **believes** the message.
1 Tim 1.15 This is a true saying, to be completely accepted and **believed:**
1.16 those who would later **believe** in him and receive eternal life.
3.16 preached among the nations, was **believed** in throughout the world,
4. 9 This is a true saying, to be completely accepted and **believed.**
4.10 is the Saviour of all and especially of those who **believe.**
2 Tim 3.14 continue in the truths that you were taught and firmly **believe.**
Tit 3. 8 so that those who **believe** in God may be concerned
Heb 3.19 not able to enter the land, because they did not **believe.**
4. 3 We who **believe,** then, do receive that rest which God promised.
4. 6 Good News did not receive that rest, because they did not **believe.**
6. 1 of turning away from useless works and **believing** in God;
6.12 to be like those who **believe** and are patient, and so receive
10.38 My righteous people, however, will **believe** and live;
Jas 1. 6 But when you pray, you must **believe** and not doubt at all.
2.19 Do you **believe** that there is only one God?
2.19 The demons also **believe**—and tremble with fear.
2.23 came true that said, "Abraham **believed** God, and because of his
1 Pet 1. 8 not seen him, and you **believe** in him, although you do not
1.21 Through him you **believe** in God, who raised him from death
2. 6 and whoever **believes** in him will never be disappointed."
2. 7 This stone is of great value for you that **believe;**
2. 7 but for those who do not **believe:**
2. 8 They stumbled because they did not **believe** in the word;
3. 1 any of them do not **believe** God's word,
3. 1 your conduct will win them over to **believe.**
4.17 end with those who do not **believe** the Good News from God?
1 Jn 3.23 he commands is that we **believe** in his Son Jesus Christ
4. 1 My dear friends, do not **believe** all who claim to have
4.16 And we ourselves know and **believe** the love which God has
5. 1 Whoever **believes** that Jesus is the Messiah is a child of God;
5. 5 Only the person who **believes** that Jesus is the Son of God.
5. 9 We **believe** man's testimony;
5.10 So whoever **believes** in the Son of God has this testimony
5.10 but whoever does not **believe** God, has made him out to be
5.10 because he has not **believed** what God has said about his
5.13 you have eternal life—you that **believe** in the Son of God.
Jude 5 from Egypt, but afterwards destroyed those who did not **believe.**

BELIEVER

[FELLOW-BELIEVER]

Mk 16.17 **Believers** will be given the power to perform miracles:
Acts 1.15 a meeting of the **believers,** about a hundred and twenty
2. 1 Pentecost came, all the **believers** were gathered together in one
2. 6 of them heard the **believers** speaking in his own language.
2.13 made fun of the **believers,** saying, "These people are drunk!"
2.44 All the **believers** continued together in close fellowship
4.24 the **believers** heard it, they all joined together in prayer
4.32 The group of **believers** was one in mind and heart.
5.12 All the **believers** met together in Solomon's Porch.
6. 2 called the whole group of **believers** together and said,
8. 1 the **believers,** except the apostles, were scattered throughout
8. 3 he dragged out the **believers,** both men and women, and threw
8. 4 The **believers** who were scattered went everywhere, preaching the message.
8.15 they prayed for the **believers** that they might receive the Holy
8.18 been given to the **believers** when the apostles placed their hands
9.19 Saul stayed for a few days with the **believers** in Damascus.
9.30 the **believers** found out about this, they took Saul to Caesarea
9.36 In Joppa there was a woman named Tabitha, who was a **believer.**
9.38 and when the **believers** in Joppa heard that Peter was
9.41 Then he called all the **believers,** including the widows,

Acts 10.23 and some of the **believers** from Joppa went along with him.
10.45 Jewish **believers** who had come from Joppa with Peter were amazed
11. 1 The apostles and the other **believers** throughout Judaea heard
11.12 These six **fellow-believers** from Joppa accompanied me to Caesarea,
11.19 Some of the **believers** who were scattered by the persecution
11.20 other **believers,** men from Cyprus and Cyrene, went to Antioch
11.26 was at Antioch that the **believers** were first called Christians.
11.29 he could to help their **fellow-believers** who lived in Judaea.
12.17 "Tell this to James and the rest of the **believers,"** he
13.48 who had been chosen for eternal life became **believers.**
13.52 The **believers** in Antioch were full of joy and the Holy Spirit.
14. 1 that a great number of Jews and Gentiles became **believers.**
14. 2 stirred up the Gentiles and turned them against the **believers.**
14.20 But when the **believers** gathered round him, he got up and
14.22 strengthened the **believers** and encouraged them to remain true
14.28 And they stayed a long time there with the **believers.**
15. 1 started teaching the **believers,** "You cannot be saved unless you
15. 3 this news brought great joy to all the **believers.**
15. 5 But some of the **believers** who belonged to the party of
15.10 on the backs of the **believers** which neither our ancestors
15.22 were highly respected by the **believers,** Judas, called Barsabbas,
15.30 gathered the whole group of **believers** and gave them the letter.
15.33 off in peace by the **believers** and went back to those
15.40 and left, commended by the **believers** to the care of the
16. 2 All the **believers** in Lystra and Iconium spoke well of Timothy.
16. 4 they delivered to the **believers** the rules decided upon by the
16.15 you have decided that I am a true **believer** in the Lord."
16.40 they met the **believers,** spoke words of encouragement to them,
17. 6 Jason and some other **believers** before the city authorities
17.10 as night came, the **believers** sent Paul and Silas to Berea.
17.14 At once the **believers** sent Paul away to the coast;
18.18 Paul stayed on with the **believers** in Corinth for many days,
18.23 region of Galatia and Phrygia, strengthening all the **believers.**
18.27 go to Achaia, so the **believers** in Ephesus helped him
18.27 by writing to the **believers** in Achaia, urging them to welcome
18.27 help to those who through God's grace had become **believers.**
19. 2 "Did you receive the Holy Spirit when you became **believers?"**
19. 9 left them and took the **believers** with him, and every day
19.18 Many of the **believers** came, publicly admitting and revealing
19.30 to go before the crowd, but the **believers** would not let him.
20. 1 Paul called together the **believers** and with words of
20.30 group will tell lies to lead the **believers** away after them.
21. 4 There we found some **believers** and stayed with them a week.
21. 7 Ptolemais, where we greeted the **believers** and stayed with them
21.16 Mnason, from Cyprus, who had been a **believer** since the early
21.17 we arrived in Jerusalem, the **believers** welcomed us warmly.
21.20 thousands of Jews have become **believers,** and how devoted they
21.25 Gentiles who have become **believers,** we have sent them a letter
28.14 We found some **believers** there who asked us to stay with
28.15 The **believers** in Rome heard about us and came as far as
1 Cor 7.15 who is not a **believer** wishes to leave the Christian partner,
14.22 proof for unbelievers, not for **believers,** while the gift of
14.22 proclaiming God's message is proof for **believers,** not for
15.18 would also mean that the **believers** in Christ who have died
2 Cor 6.15 What does a **believer** have in common with an unbeliever?
Gal 2. 4 Pretending to be **fellow-believers,** these men slipped into our group as spies,
Eph 4.25 tell the truth to his **fellow-believer,** because we are all
Col 4. 5 towards those who are not **believers,** making good use of every
4.11 three are the only Jewish **believers** who work with me for
1 Thes 1. 7 you became an example to all **believers** in Macedonia and Achaia.
4. 9 need to write to you about love for your **fellow-believers.**
4.12 of those who are not **believers,** and you will not have to
5.26 Greet all the **believers** with a brotherly kiss.
5.27 of the Lord to read this letter to all the **believers.**
1 Tim 4. 3 by those who are **believers** and have come to know the
4.12 be an example for the **believers** in your speech, your conduct,
6. 2 those who benefit from their work are **believers** whom they love.
2 Tim 2.18 upsetting the faith of some **believers** by saying that our
Tit 1. 6 his children must be **believers** and not have the reputation of
Phlm 6 our fellowship with you as **believers** will bring about a deeper
Heb 3.12 My **fellow-believers,** be careful that no one among you
Jas 2. 1 My brothers, as **believers** in our Lord Jesus Christ, the Lord
1 Pet 1.22 a sincere love for your **fellow-believers,** love one another
2.17 Respect everyone, love your **fellow-believers,** honour God, and respect the Emperor.
5. 9 because you know that your **fellow-believers** in all the world

BELL

Ex 28.33 of blue, purple, and red wool, alternating with gold **bells.**
28.35 the sound of the **bells** will be heard, and he will
39.24 and red wool, alternating with **bells** of pure gold, just as
Zech 14.20 even the harness **bells** of the horses will be inscribed
1 Cor 13. 1 speech is no more than a noisy gong or a clanging **bell.**

BELLOW

Joel 1.18 cattle are **bellowing** in distress because there is no pasture

BELLY

Gen 3.14 you will crawl on your **belly,** and you will have to eat
Judg 3.21 from his right side and plunged it into the king's **belly.**
3.22 it out of the king's **belly,** and it stuck out behind, between
2 Sam 2.23 spear, struck him through the **belly** so that the spear came
3.27 privately with him, and there he stabbed him in the **belly.**
20.10 Joab stabbed him in the **belly,** and his entrails spilt out on
2 Kgs 15.16 He even ripped open the **bellies** of all the pregnant women.
Job 41.30 The scales on his **belly** are like jagged pieces of pottery;

BELONG

Gen 14.13 was living near the sacred trees **belonging** to Mamre the Amorite.
17. 8 whole land of Canaan will **belong** to your descendants for ever,
23.17 how the property which had **belonged** to Ephron at Machpelah,
23.20 the field which had **belonged** to the Hittites, and the cave
25. 9 east of Mamre that had **belonged** to Ephron son of Zohar the
26.20 with Isaac's shepherds and said, "This water **belongs** to us."
31. 1 "Jacob has taken everything that **belonged** to our father.
31.16 has taken from our father **belongs** to us and to our children.
31.19 Rachel stole the household gods that **belonged** to her father.
31.32 witnesses, look for anything that **belongs** to you and take
31.37 what household article have you found that **belongs** to you?
31.43 their children **belong** to me, and these flocks are mine.
31.43 In fact, everything you see here **belongs** to me.
32.18 you must answer, 'They **belong** to your servant Jacob.
37.32 Does it **belong** to your son?"
38. 9 that the children would not **belong** to him, so whenever he
46.32 your flocks and herds and everything else that **belongs** to you.
47.18 that our money is all gone and our livestock **belongs** to you.
47.22 he did not buy was the land that **belonged** to the priests.
47.26 Egypt that one-fifth of the harvest should **belong** to the king.
48. 5 born to you in Egypt before I came here, **belong** to me;
Ex 9. 4 and no animal that **belongs** to the Israelites will die.
9.29 so that you may know that the earth **belongs** to the Lord.
13. 2 male Israelite and every first-born male animal **belongs** to me."
13.12 first-born male of your animals **belongs** to the Lord,
21. 4 the woman and her children **belong** to the master, and the man
29.28 breast and the thigh of the animal **belong** to the priests.
34.19 and first-born male domestic animal **belongs** to me,
38. 8 base out of the mirrors **belonging** to the women who served at
Lev 2. 3 The rest of the grain-offering **belongs** to the priests;
2.10 The rest of the offering **belongs** to the priests;
3.16 All the fat **belongs** to the Lord.
5.13 The rest of the flour **belongs** to the priest, just as in
7. 7 the meat **belongs** to the priest who offers the sacrifice.
7. 8 animal offered as a burnt-offering **belongs** to the priest who
7. 9 pan or on a griddle **belongs** to the priest who has offered
7.10 mixed with oil or dry, **belong** to all the Aaronite priests
7.14 it **belongs** to the priest who takes the blood of the animal
7.31 on the altar, but the breast shall **belong** to the priests.
10.10 You must distinguish between what **belongs** to God and what
10.13 it is the part that **belongs** to you and your sons from
10.14 as the part that **belongs** to you from the fellowship-offerings
10.15 These parts **belong** to you and your children for ever, just
14.13 repayment-offering, like the sin-offering, **belongs** to the priest
20.26 You shall be holy and **belong** only to me, because I am
20.26 the other nations so that you would **belong** to me alone.
23. 3 The Sabbath **belongs** to the Lord, no matter where you live.
24. 9 The bread **belongs** to Aaron and his descendants,
24.18 who kills an animal **belonging** to someone else must replace it.
25.23 it **belongs** to God, and you are like foreigners who are
27.10 If he does, both animals **belong** to the Lord.
27.21 it shall **belong** to the priests.
27.23 the money **belongs** to the Lord.
27.26 first-born of an animal already **belongs** to the Lord, so no
27.26 a lamb, or a kid **belongs** to the Lord, [27] but the first-born
27.28 It **belongs** permanently to the Lord.
27.30 of the land, whether grain or fruit, **belongs** to the Lord.
27.32 One out of every ten domestic animals **belongs** to the Lord.
27.32 the animals are counted, every tenth one **belongs** to the Lord.
27.33 another, then both animals will **belong** to the Lord and may
Num 3.12 they will **belong** to me.
3.40 said to Moses, "All of Israel's first-born sons **belong** to me.
5. 9 Israelites offer to the Lord **belongs** to the priest to whom
6.20 the leg of the ram which by law **belong** to the priest.
8.14 the rest of the Israelites, so that they will **belong** to me.
8.16 first-born sons of the Israelites, and they **belong** to me alone.
15.40 keep all my commands, and you will **belong** completely to me.
16. 3 the members of the community **belong** to the Lord, and the
16. 5 "Tomorrow morning the Lord will show us who **belongs** to him;
16. 5 will let the one who **belongs** to him, that is, the one
16.26 these wicked men and don't touch anything that **belongs** to them.
18. 9 offerings not burnt on the altar, the following **belong** to you:
18. 9 to me as a sacred offering **belongs** to you and your sons.
18.13 It all **belongs** to you.
18.14 that has been unconditionally dedicated to me **belongs** to you.
18.15 or animal that the Israelites present to me **belongs** to you.
18.17 they **belong** completely to me and are to be sacrificed.
18.18 The meat from them **belongs** to you, like the breast and
18.28 present the special contribution that **belongs** to the Lord from
31.28 the part that **belongs** to the soldiers, withhold as a tax
35. 3 These cities will **belong** to the Levites, and they will live
36. 3 their property will then **belong** to that tribe, and the total
36. 8 an Israelite tribe must marry a man **belonging** to that tribe.
Deut 3. 6 we did in the towns that **belonged** to King Sihon of Heshbon.
4.38 give you their land, the land which still **belongs** to you.
4.45 the territory that had **belonged** to King Sihon of the Amorites,
7. 6 Do this because you **belong** to the Lord your God.
9. 1 occupy the land **belonging** to nations greater and more powerful
10. 6 out from the wells that **belonged** to the people of Jaakan,
10.14 To the Lord **belong** even the highest heavens;
11.23 occupy the land **belonging** to nations greater and more powerful
14. 2 You **belong** to the Lord your God;
14.21 But you **belong** to the Lord your God;
20.14 You may use everything that **belongs** to your enemies.
21.16 by giving him the share that **belongs** to the first-born son.
33. 3 Lord loves his people and protects those who **belong** to him.

Josh 7. 1 and grandson of Zabdi, and **belonged** to the clan of Zerah, a
13. 4 Canaanite country, and Mearah (which **belonged** to the
Sidonians),
14.14 Hebron still **belongs** to the descendants of Caleb
15.13 He received Hebron, the city **belonging** to Arba, father of Anak.
15.21 The cities farthest south that **belonged** to them, those that
17. 8 The land round Tappuah **belonged** to Manasseh, but the town of
17. 8 Tappuah, on the border, **belonged** to the descendants of Ephraim.
17. 9 cities south of the stream **belonged** to Ephraim, even though
18.11 territory **belonging** to the families of the tribe of Benjamin
18.14 (or Kiriath Jearim), which **belongs** to the tribe of Judah.
18.21 cities **belonging** to the families of the tribe of Benjamin were
Judg 6.11 sat under the oak-tree that **belonged** to Joash, a man of the
6.24 standing at Ophrah, which **belongs** to the clan of Abiezer.)
Ruth 1. 1 a man named Elimelech, who **belonged** to the clan of Ephrath
2. 1 and influential man who **belonged** to the family of her husband
2. 3 so happened that she was in a field that **belonged** to Boaz.
2.19 had been working in a field **belonging** to a man named Boaz.
4. 3 to sell the field that **belonged** to our relative Elimelech,
4. 4 the right to buy it **belongs** first to you and then to
4. 9 bought from Naomi everything that **belonged** to Elimelech
1 Sam 1. 1 and grandson of Elihu, and **belonged** to the family of Tohu,
1.28 As long as he lives, he will **belong** to the Lord."
2. 8 The foundations of the earth **belong** to the Lord;
2.14 and whatever the fork brought out **belonged** to the priest.
6. 2 it back where it **belongs,** what shall we send with it?"
6.14 wagon came to a field **belonging** to a man named Joshua, who
9. 1 and grandson of Zeror, and **belonged** to the family of Becorath,
9. 3 Some donkeys **belonging** to Kish had wandered off, so he said
9.21 Saul answered, "I **belong** to the tribe of Benjamin,
14.41 if it **belongs** to your people Israel, answer by the Thummim."
25. 7 Nothing that **belonged** to them was stolen all the time they
25.15 them in the fields, nothing that **belonged** to us was stolen.
25.21 Not a thing that **belonged** to him was stolen, and this is
27. 6 for this reason Ziklag has **belonged** to the kings of Judah
30.20 livestock in front of them and said, "This **belongs** to David!"
2 Sam 9. 7 back all the land that **belonged** to your grandfather Saul,
9. 9 your master's grandson, everything that **belonged** to Saul
16. 4 to Ziba, "Everything that **belonged** to Mephibosheth is yours."
20.19 Do you want to ruin what **belongs** to the Lord?"
1 Kgs 3.23 is hers and that the dead child **belongs** to the other one."
4.13 and the villages in Gilead **belonging** to the clan of Jair,
22. 3 It **belongs** to us!"
2 Kgs 9.21 They met him at the field which had **belonged** to Naboth.
9.25 his body and throw it in the field that **belonged** to Naboth.
9.26 it in the field that **belonged** to Naboth, so as to fulfil
11.10 spears and shields that had **belonged** to King David and had
12.16 it **belonged** to the priests.
14.25 all the territory that had **belonged** to Israel, from Hamath Pass
24. 7 all the territory that had **belonged** to Egypt, from the River
1 Chr 5. 1 concubines, he lost the rights **belonging** to the first-born son,
5.13 other members of the tribe **belonged** to the following seven clans:
6.56 fields and villages, however, that **belonged** to the city were
7.12 Shuppim and Huppim also **belonged** to this tribe.
7.21 tried to steal the livestock **belonging** to the native inhabitants
9.14 lived in the territory that **belonged** to the town of Netophah.
9.30 responsibility for mixing the spices **belonged** to the priests.
12. 2 members of the tribe of Benjamin, to which Saul **belonged.**
13.14 blessed Obed Edom's family and everything that **belonged** to him.
16.10 Be glad that we **belong** to him;
21.24 to the Lord something that **belongs** to you, something that costs
24. 1 These are the groups to which the descendants of Aaron **belong.**
26.31 and outstanding soldiers **belonging** to this family were found
28. 1 property and livestock that **belonged** to the king and his sons
29.16 name, but it all came from you and all **belongs** to you.
2 Chr 5.11 regardless of the group to which they **belonged,** had consecrated
23. 9 spears and shields that had **belonged** to King David and had
25. 5 according to the clans they **belonged** to, and placed officers in
31.19 or in the pasture lands **belonging** to these cities, there were
34.33 that were in the territory **belonging** to the people of Israel,
Ezra 2.59 There were 652 **belonging** to the clans of Delaiah,
Neh 7.61 There were 642 **belonging** to the clans of Delaiah,
11.22 Mattaniah and Mica, and he **belonged** to the clan of Asaph,
Job 15. 8 Does human wisdom **belong** to you alone?
24. 3 take donkeys that **belong** to orphans, and keep a widow's ox
32. 2 Barakel, a descendant of Buz, and **belonged** to the clan of Ram.)
Ps 24. 1 The world and all that is in it **belong** to the Lord;
61. 5 and you have given me what **belongs** to those who honour you.
62.11 heard God say that power **belongs** to him [12] and that his
83.12 "We will take for our own the land that **belongs** to God."
87. 5 be said that all nations **belong** there and that the Almighty
94. 5 they oppress those who **belong** to you.
94.14 he will not desert those who **belong** to him.
100. 3 He made us, and we **belong** to him;
105. 3 Be glad that we **belong** to him;
106. 5 your nation, in the glad pride of those who **belong** to you.
115.16 Heaven **belongs** to the Lord alone, but he gave the earth
Prov 5.10 and what you have worked for will **belong** to someone else.
Song 7.10 I **belong** to my lover, and he desires me.
Is 10. 2 how you take the property that **belongs** to widows and orphans.
34.17 land age after age, and it will **belong** to them for ever.
65. 9 will bless the Israelites who **belong** to the tribe of Judah,
Jer 2. 3 Israel, you **belonged** to me alone;
3.14 you **belong** to me.
15.16 I **belong** to you, Lord God Almighty, and so your words filled
Ezek 18. 4 The life of every person **belongs** to me, the life of the
33.25 What makes you think that the land **belongs** to you?
35.10 Israel, together with their lands, **belonged** to you and that you
43.19 priests **belonging** to the tribe of Levi who are descended from
44.15 Lord said, "Those priests **belonging** to the tribe of Levi who
45. 8 let the rest of the country **belong** to the tribes of Israel.
Ezek 46.16 as a present, it will **belong** to that son as a part
46.17 It **belongs** to him, and only he and his sons can own
48.12 area next to the area **belonging** to the Levites, and it will
48.14 It is holy and **belongs** to the Lord.
48.21 and the city, the remaining land **belongs** to the ruling prince.
48.21 the north by the section **belonging** to Judah
48.21 and on the south by the section **belonging** to Benjamin.
Hos 5. 1 Listen, you that **belong** to the royal family!
5. 7 their children do not **belong** to him.
Zech 9. 1 of Israel, but also the capital of Syria **belong** to the Lord.
9. 2 which borders on Hadrach, also **belongs** to him, and so do the
Mt 5. 3 the Kingdom of heaven **belongs** to them!
5.10 the Kingdom of heaven **belongs** to them!
10.32 anyone declares publicly that he **belongs** to me, I will do
12.29 house and take away his **belongings** unless he first ties up
13.38 the good seed is the people who **belong** to the Kingdom;
13.38 the weeds are the people who **belong** to the Evil One;
15. 5 or mother, but says, 'This **belongs** to God,' [6] he does not
19.14 because the Kingdom of heaven **belongs** to such as these."
20.23 These places **belong** to those for whom my Father has prepared
them."
22.21 pay the Emperor what **belongs** to the Emperor,
22.21 and pay God what **belongs** to God."
24.17 the time to go down and get his **belongings** from the house.
25.25 Here is what **belongs** to you.'
Mk 3.27 house and take away his **belongings** unless he first ties up
7.11 is Corban' (which means, it **belongs** to God),
9.38 told him to stop, because he doesn't **belong** to our group."
9.41 drink of water because you **belong** to me will certainly receive
10.14 because the Kingdom of God **belongs** to such as these.
12.17 pay the Emperor what **belongs** to the Emperor,
12.17 and pay God what **belongs** to God."
Lk 1. 5 named Zechariah, who **belonged** to the priestly order of Abijah.
1. 5 she also **belonged** to a priestly family.
5. 3 one of the boats—it **belonged** to Simon—and asked him
5.30 teachers of the Law who **belonged** to their group complained to
9.49 told him to stop, because he doesn't **belong** to our group."
11.21 weapons ready, guards his own house, all his **belongings** are safe.
12. 8 whoever declares publicly that he **belongs** to me, the Son of
12.33 Sell all your **belongings** and give the money to the poor.
16. 8 handling their affairs than the people who **belong** to the light."
16.12 not been faithful with what **belongs** to someone else,
16.12 who will give you what **belongs** to you?
17.31 house must not go down into the house to get his **belongings;**
18.16 because the Kingdom of God **belongs** to such as these.
19. 8 I will give half my **belongings** to the poor, and if I
20.25 pay the Emperor what **belongs** to the Emperor,
20.25 and pay God what **belongs** to God."
Jn 3. 1 named Nicodemus, who **belonged** to the party of the Pharisees.
3.29 The bridegroom is the one to whom the bride **belongs;**
3.31 who is from the earth **belongs** to the earth and speaks about
8.23 answered, "You **belong** to this world here below, but I come
8.35 A slave does not **belong** to a family permanently,
8.35 but a son **belongs** there for ever.
10.16 There are other sheep which **belong** to me that are not in
15.19 If you **belonged** to the world, then the world would love
15.19 chose you from this world, and you do not **belong** to it;
17. 6 They **belonged** to you, and you gave them to me.
17. 9 but for those you gave me, for they **belong** to you.
17.14 because they do not **belong** to the world,
17.14 just as I do not **belong** to the world.
17.16 Just as I do not **belong** to the world,
17.16 they do not **belong** to the world.
18.36 Jesus said, "My kingdom does not **belong** to this world;
18.36 if my kingdom **belonged** to this world, my followers would fight
18.36 No, my kingdom does not **belong** here!"
18.37 Whoever **belongs** to the truth listens to me."
Acts 1.25 of Judas, who left to go to the place where he **belongs."**
2.44 in close fellowship and shared their **belongings** with one another.
4. 6 and the others who **belonged** to the High Priest's family.
4.32 said that any of his **belongings** was his own, but they all
5. 1 with his wife Sapphira sold some property that **belonged** to them.
5. 4 Before you sold the property, it **belonged** to you;
7. 5 and that it would **belong** to him and to his descendants.
10.35 is acceptable to him, no matter what race he **belongs** to.
15. 5 some of the believers who **belonged** to the party of the
15.14 Gentiles by taking from among them a people to **belong** to him.
23. 9 teachers of the Law who **belonged** to the party of the
27.23 the God to whom I **belong** and whom I worship
28. 7 were some fields that **belonged** to Publius, the chief official
28.22 everywhere people speak against this party to which you **belong."**
Rom 1. 6 are in Rome, whom God has called to **belong** to Jesus Christ.
1.21 give him the honour that **belongs** to him, nor do they thank
4. 9 happiness that David spoke of **belong** only to those who are
4. 9 It **belongs** also to those who are not circumcised.
4.13 descendants that the world would **belong** to him, he did so,
7. 4 and now you **belong** to him who was raised from death
7. 7 "Do not desire what **belongs** to someone else,"
8. 9 does not have the Spirit of Christ does not **belong** to him.
9. 1 I **belong** to Christ and I do not lie.
9. 5 and Christ, as a human being, **belongs** to their race.
12.13 Share your **belongings** with your needy fellow-Christians,
13. 9 do not desire what **belongs** to someone else"—all these,
13.12 stop doing the things that **belong** to the dark, and let us
14. 8 So whether we live or die, we **belong** to the Lord.
16.10 Greetings to those who **belong** to the family of Aristobulus.
1 Cor 1. 2 God's holy people, who **belong** to him in union with Christ
2. 6 is not the wisdom that **belongs** to this world or to
3. 1 to you as though you **belonged** to this world, as children in
3. 3 doesn't this prove that you **belong** to this world, living by
3.21 Actually everything **belongs** to you:

1 Cor 3.23 and you belong to Christ, and Christ **belongs** to God.
6.19 You do not **belong** to yourselves but to God;
8. 7 they still think of it as food that **belongs** to an idol;
10.26 says, "The earth and everything in it **belong** to the Lord."
12.15 not a hand, I don't **belong** to the body," that would not
12.16 not an eye, I don't **belong** to the body," that would not
15.23 at the time of his coming, those who **belong** to him.
15.40 the beauty that **belongs** to heavenly bodies is different from
15.40 the beauty that **belongs** to earthly bodies.
15.48 Those who **belong** to the earth are like the one who was
2 Cor 3. 8 is the glory that **belongs** to the activity of the Spirit!
4. 7 to show that the supreme power **belongs** to God, not to us.
10. 7 Is there someone there who reckons himself to **belong** to Christ?
10. 7 because we **belong** to Christ just as much as
Gal 3.29 you **belong** to Christ, then you are the descendants of Abraham
5.24 And those who **belong** to Christ Jesus have put to death
6.10 especially to those who **belong** to our family in the faith.
Eph 2.12 You were foreigners and did not **belong** to God's chosen people.
5. 8 must live like people who **belong** to the light.
5.11 things that people do, things that **belong** to the darkness.
6. 9 you and your slaves **belong** to the same Master in heaven,
Phil 3.19 and they think only of things that **belong** to this world.
4.21 Greetings to each one of God's people who **belong** to Christ
4.22 send greetings, especially those who **belong** to the Emperor's
Col 2.20 Why, then, do you live as though you **belonged** to this world?
4. 9 that dear and faithful brother, who **belongs** to your group.
1 Thes 1. 1 the church in Thessalonica, who **belong** to God the Father
2.14 to the people there who **belong** to Christ Jesus.
3.13 when our Lord Jesus comes with all who **belong** to him.
5. 5 you are people who **belong** to the light,
5. 5 who **belong** to the day.
5. 5 We do not **belong** to the night or to the darkness.
5. 8 But we **belong** to the day, and we should be sober.
2 Thes 1. 1 the church in Thessalonica, who **belong** to God our Father
1 Tim 6. 2 Slaves **belonging** to Christian masters must not despise them,
2 Tim 2.19 "Whoever says that he **belongs** to the Lord must turn away
Tit 2.14 us a pure people who **belong** to him alone and are eager
Heb 6. 9 you have the better blessings that **belong** to your salvation.
7.13 whom these things are said, **belonged** to a different tribe,
10.34 and when all your **belongings** were seized, you endured your loss
Jas 3.15 it **belongs** to the world, it is unspiritual and demonic.
1 Pet 4.11 through Jesus Christ, to whom **belong** glory and power for ever
5.14 May peace be with all of you who **belong** to Christ.
1 Jn 2.15 Do not love the world or anything that **belongs** to the world.
2.16 Everything that **belongs** to the world—what the sinful self
2.19 These people really did not **belong** to our fellowship,
2.19 if they had **belonged** to our fellowship, they would have stayed
2.19 it might be clear that none of them really **belonged** to us.
3. 8 Whoever continues to sin **belongs** to the Devil,
3.12 **belonged** to the Evil One and murdered his own brother Abel.
3.19 is how we will know that we **belong** to the truth;
4. 4 But you **belong** to God, my children, and have defeated the
4. 4 powerful than the spirit in those who **belong** to the world.
4. 5 the world listens to them because they **belong** to the world.
4. 6 But we **belong** to God.
4. 6 whoever does not **belong** to God does not listen to us.
5.19 We know that we **belong** to God even though the whole
3 Jn 11 Whoever does good **belongs** to God;
Rev 1. 9 the suffering that comes to those who **belong** to his Kingdom.
2. 9 they are a group that **belongs** to Satan!
3. 5 of his angels I will declare openly that they **belong** to me.
3. 7 He has the key that **belonged** to David, and when he opens
3. 9 As for that group that **belongs** to Satan, those liars who
7.12 honour, power, and might **belong** to our God for ever
11.15 to rule over the world **belongs** now to our Lord and his
13. 8 of the living which **belongs** to the Lamb that was killed.
19. 1 Salvation, glory, and power **belong** to our God!

BELONGINGS

Gen 31.37 have searched through all my **belongings**, what household article
Judg 18.21 children, their livestock, and their **belongings** going ahead.
Neh 13. 8 I was furious and threw out all Tobiah's **belongings**.
Esth 3.13 slaughtered without mercy and their **belongings** were to be taken.
Ps 89.41 All who pass by steal his **belongings**;
Is 33. 4 Their **belongings** are pounced upon and taken as loot.
Jer 10.17 Gather up your **belongings**.

BELOVED see LOVE

BELOW

Gen 1. 9 God commanded, "Let the water **below** the sky come together
Deut 32.22 will reach to the world **below** and consume the roots of the
1 Kgs 8.23 is no god like you in heaven above or on earth **below!**
Ps 30. 3 on my way to the depths **below**, but you restored my life.
135. 6 heaven and on earth, in the seas and in the depths **below**.
Ezek 31.16 gone to the world **below** will be pleased at its downfall.
Jon 1. 5 Jonah had gone **below** and was lying in the ship's hold,
Jn 8.23 "You belong to this world here **below**, but I come from above.
Acts 2.19 miracles in the sky above and wonders on the earth **below**.
Rom 8.39 world above nor the world **below**—there is nothing in all
10. 7 are you to ask, Who will go down into the world **below?"**
Phil 2.10 and in the world **below** will fall on their knees,
Jude 6 eternal chains in the darkness **below**, where God is keeping them
Rev 5. 3 earth or in the world **below** who could open the scroll
5.13 on earth, in the world **below**, and in the sea—all living

BELSHAZZAR

Succeeded his father Nebuchadnezzar as king of Babylonia.

Dan 5. 1 King **Belshazzar** invited a thousand noblemen to a great banquet,
5. 2 While they were drinking, **Belshazzar** gave orders to bring in
5. 9 In his distress King **Belshazzar** grew even paler, and his
5.29 Immediately **Belshazzar** ordered his servants to dress
5.30 That same night **Belshazzar**, the king of Babylonia, was
7. 1 In the first year that **Belshazzar** was king of Babylonia, I
8. 1 In the third year that **Belshazzar** was king, I saw a second

BELT

Ex 28. 8 A finely woven **belt** made of the same materials is to be
28.27 of the ephod near the seam and above the finely woven **belt**.
28.28 the breast-piece rests above the **belt** and does not come loose.
29. 5 goes under the ephod, the ephod, the breast-piece, and the **belt**.
39. 5 finely woven **belt**, made of the same materials, was attached to
39.20 of the ephod, near the seam and above the finely woven **belt**.
39.21 the breast-piece rested above the **belt** and did not come loose.
Lev 8. 7 fastened it by putting its finely woven **belt** round his waist.
16. 4 the linen robe and shorts, the **belt**, and the turban.
1 Sam 18. 4 David, together with his armour and also his sword, bow, and **belt**.
2 Sam 18.11 would have given you ten pieces of silver and a **belt."**
20. 8 for battle, with a sword in its sheath fastened to his **belt**.
2 Kgs 1. 8 cloak made of animal skins, tied with a leather **belt**,"
Ps 109.19 cover him like clothes and always be round him like a **belt!**
Prov 31.24 She makes clothes and **belts**, and sells them to merchants.
Is 3.24 instead of fine **belts**, they will wear coarse ropes;
5.27 Not a **belt** is loose;
22.21 put your official robe and **belt** on him and give him all
Ezek 44.18 are to wear linen turbans and linen trousers, but no **belt**.
Dan 10. 5 who was wearing linen clothes and a **belt** of fine gold.
Mt 3. 4 he wore a leather **belt** round his waist, and his food
Mk 1. 6 camel's hair, with a leather **belt** round his waist, and his
Acts 12. 8 the angel said, "Fasten your **belt** and put on your sandals."
21.11 came to us, took Paul's **belt**, tied up his own feet
21.11 The owner of this **belt** will be tied up in this way
Eph 6.14 with truth as a **belt** tight round your waist, with righteousness
Rev 1.13 that reached to his feet, and a gold **belt** round his chest.
15. 6 clean shining linen and with gold **belts** tied around their chests.

BELTESHAZZAR

Another name for Daniel (1).

Dan 1. 7 **Belteshazzar**, Shadrach, Meshach, and Abednego.
2.26 Daniel (who was also called **Belteshazzar**), "Can you tell me
4. 8 (He is also called **Belteshazzar**, after the name of my god.)
4. 9 **Belteshazzar**, chief of the fortune-tellers, I know that the
4.18 "Now, **Belteshazzar**, tell me what it means.
4.19 Daniel, who is also called **Belteshazzar**, was so alarmed that
4.19 The king said to him, **"Belteshazzar**, don't let the dream and
4.19 **Belteshazzar** replied, "Your Majesty, I wish that the dream
5.12 Daniel, whom the king named **Belteshazzar**, and he will tell you
10. 1 a message was revealed to Daniel, who is also called **Belteshazzar**.

BENAIAH (1)

Jehoiada's son, in charge of David's bodyguard.

2 Sam 8.18 **Benaiah** son of Jehoiada was in charge of David's bodyguard
20.23 **Benaiah** son of Jehoiada was in charge of David's bodyguard;
23.20 **Benaiah** son of Jehoiada, from Kabzeel, was another famous
23.21 **Benaiah** attacked him with his club, snatched the spear from the
23.22 the brave deeds of **Benaiah**, who was one of "The Thirty."
1 Kgs 1. 8 But Zadok the priest, **Benaiah** son of Jehoiada, Nathan
1.10 or Nathan the prophet, or **Benaiah**, or the king's bodyguard.
1.26 not invite me, sir, or Zadok the priest, or **Benaiah**, or
1.32 Then King David sent for Zadok, Nathan, and **Benaiah**.
1.36 "It shall be done," answered **Benaiah**, "and may the Lord
1.38 Nathan, **Benaiah**, and the royal bodyguard put Solomon on King
1.44 sent Zadok, Nathan, **Benaiah**, and the royal bodyguard to escort
2.25 gave orders to **Benaiah**, who went out and killed Adonijah.
2.29 So King Solomon sent **Benaiah** to kill Joab.
2.30 **Benaiah** went back to the king and told him what Joab had
2.34 **Benaiah** went to the Tent of the Lord's presence and killed
2.35 The king made **Benaiah** commander of the army in Joab's place
2.46 king gave orders to **Benaiah**, who went out and killed Shimei.
4. 4 **Benaiah** son of Jehoiada
1 Chr 11.22 **Benaiah** son of Jehoiada from Kabzeel was a famous soldier;
11.23 **Benaiah** attacked him with a club, snatched the spear from the
11.24 the brave deeds of **Benaiah**, who was one of "The Thirty."
18.17 **Benaiah** son of Jehoiada was in charge of David's bodyguard;
27. 2 **Benaiah** son of Jehoiada the priest;

BEND

[BENT]

Gen 49.15 So he **bends** his back to carry the load And is forced
Ex 4. 4 the Lord said to Moses, **"Bend** down and pick it up by
4. 4 So Moses **bent** down and caught it, and it became a stick
Josh 16. 6 East of there the border **bent** towards Taanath Shiloh and went
Judg 15.15 He **bent** down and picked it up, and killed a thousand men
1 Sam 25.20 riding her donkey round a **bend** on a hillside when suddenly
2 Kgs 6. 7 out," he ordered, and the man **bent** down and picked it up.
Ps 7.12 He **bends** his bow and makes it ready;
35.14 I went about **bent** over in mourning, as one who mourns for
37.14 wicked draw their swords and **bend** their bows to kill the
113. 6 the heights above, [6] but he **bends** down to see the heavens
Is 42. 3 will not break off a **bent** reed or put out a flickering
Ezek 29.15 will not be able to **bend** any other nation to their will.
Hos 11. 4 I **bent** down to them and fed them.

Mt 11. 7 A blade of grass **bending** in the wind?
12.20 will not break off a **bent** reed, or put out a flickering
Mk 1. 7 am not good enough even to **bend** down and untie his sandals.
Lk 7.24 A blade of grass **bending** in the wind?
13.11 she was **bent** over and could not straighten up at all.
24.12 he **bent** down and saw the linen wrappings but nothing else.
Jn 8. 6 But he **bent** over and wrote on the ground with his finger.
8. 8 Then he **bent** over again and wrote on the ground.
20. 5 He **bent** over and saw the linen wrappings.
20.11 she was still crying, she **bent** over and looked in the tomb
Rom 11.10 and make them **bend** under their troubles at all times."

Am **BEND OVER** see **BOW (down)**

BENEFIT

Deut 10.13 I am giving them to you today for your **benefit.**
Job 13. 7 Do you think your lies will **benefit** God?
22. 3 Does your doing right **benefit** God, or does your being good
Prov 10.21 A good man's words will **benefit** many people, but you can
Ezek 13.18 death over my people and to use it for your own **benefit.**
1 Cor 9.11 Is it too much if we reap material **benefits** from you?
Eph 3.13 it is all for your **benefit.**
1 Tim 6. 2 because those who **benefit** from their work are believers
1 Pet 1.12 was not for their own **benefit,** but for yours, as they spoke

BENHADAD (1)

King of Syria, Tabrimmon's son.

1 Kgs 15.18 to Damascus, to King **Benhadad** of Syria, the son of Tabrimmon
15.20 **Benhadad** agreed to Asa's proposal and sent his commanding officers
2 Chr 16. 2 to Damascus, to King **Benhadad** of Syria, with this message:
16. 4 **Benhadad** agreed to Asa's proposal

BENHADAD (2)

King of Syria, son of Benhadad I.

1 Kgs 20. 1 King **Benhadad** of Syria gathered all his troops,
20. 2 of Israel to say, "King **Benhadad** demands that [3]you surrender
20. 4 "Tell my lord, King **Benhadad,** that I agree;
20. 5 the messengers came back to Ahab with another demand from **Benhadad:**
20. 9 Ahab replied to **Benhadad's** messengers, "Tell my lord the king
20.10 left and then returned with another message [10]from **Benhadad:**
20.11 Ahab answered, "Tell King **Benhadad** that a real soldier does
20.12 **Benhadad** received Ahab's answer as he and his allies,
20.16 attack began at noon, as **Benhadad** and his thirty-two allies
20.17 Scouts sent out by **Benhadad** reported to him that a group of
20.20 Israelites in hot pursuit, but **Benhadad** escaped on horseback,
20.23 **Benhadad's** officials said to him, "The gods of Israel are mountain
20.25 King **Benhadad** agreed and followed their advice.
20.30 **Benhadad** also escaped into the city and took refuge in the
20.32 said, "Your servant **Benhadad** pleads with you for his life."
20.33 **Benhadad's** officials were watching for a good sign,
20.33 once, and said, "As you say, **Benhadad** is your brother!"
20.33 When **Benhadad** arrived, Ahab invited him to get in the chariot
20.34 **Benhadad** said to him, "I will restore to you the towns
2 Kgs 6.24 time later King **Benhadad** of Syria led his entire army against
8. 7 to Damascus at a time when King **Benhadad** of Syria was ill.
8. 9 he said, "Your servant King **Benhadad** has sent me to ask you
8.14 went back to **Benhadad,** who asked him, "What did Elisha say?"
8.15 And Hazael succeeded **Benhadad** as king of Syria.

BENHADAD (3)

King of Syria, Hazael's son.

2 Kgs 13. 3 Syria and his son **Benhadad** to defeat Israel time after time.
13.24 death of King Hazael of Syria his son **Benhadad** became king.
13.25 Jehoash of Israel defeated **Benhadad** three times and recaptured
13.25 that had been taken by **Benhadad** during the reign of Jehoahaz,
Amos 1. 4 I will burn down the fortresses of King **Benhadad.**

BENHADAD (4)

A general name for kings of Syria.

Jer 49.27 of Damascus on fire and will burn down King **Benhadad's** palaces.

BENJAMIN (1)

Youngest son of Jacob and Rachel, his tribe and its territory.

Gen 35.18 named her son Benoni, but his father named him **Benjamin.**
35.24 The sons of Rachel were Joseph and **Benjamin.**
42. 4 did not send Joseph's full-brother **Benjamin** with them,
42.36 and now you want to take away **Benjamin.**
42.37 "If I do not bring **Benjamin** back to you, you can kill
43.14 so that he will give **Benjamin** and your other brother back to
43.15 twice as much money, and set out for Egypt with **Benjamin.**
43.16 When Joseph saw **Benjamin** with them, he said to the servant
43.29 When Joseph saw his brother **Benjamin,** he said, "So this is
43.34 from Joseph's table, and **Benjamin** was served five times as much
44.12 with the youngest, and the cup was found in **Benjamin's** sack.
45.12 of you, and you too, **Benjamin,** can see that I am really
45.14 He threw his arms round his brother **Benjamin** and began to cry;
45.14 **Benjamin** also cried as he hugged him.
45.22 of clothes, but he gave **Benjamin** three hundred pieces of silver
46.19 Joseph and **Benjamin.**
46.21 **Benjamin's** sons were Bela, Becher, Ashbel, Gera, Naaman,
49.27 **"Benjamin** is like a vicious wolf.
Ex 1. 3 Reuben, Simeon, Levi, Judah, [3]Issachar, Zebulun, **Benjamin,**
Num 1. 5 **Benjamin** Abidan son of Gideoni
1.20 **Benjamin** 35,400
2.18 **Benjamin** Abidan
7.12 9th **Benjamin** Abidan
10.24 Abidan son of Gideoni was in command of the tribe of **Benjamin.**
13. 3 **Benjamin** Palti son of Raphu
26.38 The tribe of **Benjamin:**
34.19 **Benjamin** Elidad son of Chislon
Deut 27.12 Simeon, Levi, Judah, Issachar, Joseph, and **Benjamin.**
33.12 About the tribe of **Benjamin** he said:
Josh 18.11 of the tribe of **Benjamin** was the first to be assigned.
18.20 families of the tribe of **Benjamin** received as their possession.
18.21 families of the tribe of **Benjamin** were Jericho, Beth Hoglah,
18.28 families of the tribe of **Benjamin** received as their possession.
21. 4 thirteen cities from the territories of Judah, Simeon, and **Benjamin.**
21.17 From the territory of **Benjamin** they were given four cities:
Judg 1.21 people of the tribe of **Benjamin** did not drive out the
1.21 continued to live there with the people of **Benjamin** ever since.
3.15 man, who was the son of Gera, from the tribe of **Benjamin.**
5.14 into the valley, behind the tribe of **Benjamin** and its people.
10. 9 crossed the Jordan to fight the tribes of Judah, **Benjamin,**
19.14 came to Gibeah in the territory of the tribe of **Benjamin.**
19.16 (The other people there were from the tribe of **Benjamin.)**
20. 3 the people of **Benjamin** heard that all the other Israelites had
20. 4 to Gibeah in the territory of **Benjamin** to spend the night.
20.12 territory of the tribe of **Benjamin** to say, "What is this
20.13 people of **Benjamin** paid no attention to the other Israelites.
20.14 From all the cities of **Benjamin** they came to Gibeah to
20.18 asked God, "Which tribe should attack the **Benjaminites** first?"
20.20 attack the army of **Benjamin,** and placed the soldiers in position
20.21 The army of **Benjamin** came out of the city, and before
20.22 we go again into battle against our brothers the **Benjaminites?"**
20.24 They marched against the army of **Benjamin** a second time.
20.25 for the second time the **Benjaminites** came out of Gibeah,
20.27 fight our brothers the **Benjaminites** again, or should we give up?"
20.30 marched against the army of **Benjamin** and placed their soldiers
20.31 The **Benjaminites** came out to fight and were led away from
20.32 **Benjaminites** said, "We've beaten them just as we did before."
20.34 **Benjaminites** had not realized that they were about to be destroyed.
20.35 The Lord gave Israel victory over the army of **Benjamin.**
20.36 and the **Benjaminites** realized they were defeated.
20.36 had retreated from the **Benjaminites** because they were relying
20.39 the **Benjaminites** had already killed the thirty Israelites.
20.40 **Benjaminites** looked behind them and were amazed to see the whole
20.41 turned round, and the **Benjaminites** were thrown into a panic
20.44 thousand of the best **Benjaminite** soldiers were killed.
20.46 In all, twenty-five thousand **Benjaminites** were killed
20.48 against the rest of the **Benjaminites** and killed them all—men,
21. 1 us will allow a **Benjaminite** to marry a daughter of ours."
21. 3 Why is the tribe of **Benjamin** about to disappear from Israel?"
21. 6 sorry for their brothers the **Benjaminites** and said, "Today
21. 7 do to provide wives for the men of **Benjamin** who are left?
21.13 assembly sent word to the **Benjaminites** who were at the Rock
21.14 The **Benjaminites** came back, and the other Israelites gave
21.15 people felt sorry for the **Benjaminites** because the Lord had
21.16 said, "There are no more women in the tribe of **Benjamin.**
21.17 for the tribe of **Benjamin** to survive, [18]but we cannot allow
21.18 who allows a **Benjaminite** to marry one of our daughters."
21.20 said to the **Benjaminites,** "Go and hide in the vineyards
21.21 and take her back to the territory of **Benjamin** with you.
21.23 The **Benjaminites** did this;
1 Sam 4.12 man from the tribe of **Benjamin** ran all the way from the
9. 1 wealthy and influential man named Kish, from the tribe of **Benjamin;**
9. 4 through the territory of **Benjamin,** but still did not find them.
9.16 time I will send you a man from the tribe of **Benjamin;**
9.21 belong to the tribe of **Benjamin,** the smallest tribe in Israel,
10. 2 near Rachel's tomb at Zelzah in the territory of **Benjamin.**
10.20 come forward, and the Lord picked the tribe of **Benjamin.**
10.21 families of the tribe of **Benjamin** come forward, and the family
13. 2 Jonathan to Gibeah, in the territory of the tribe of **Benjamin.**
13.15 They went from Gilgal to Gibeah in the territory of **Benjamin.**
13.16 and their men camped in Geba in the territory of **Benjamin;**
14.16 Gibeah in the territory of **Benjamin** saw the Philistines running
22. 7 found, [7]and he said to his officers, "Listen, men of **Benjamin!**
2 Sam 2. 9 Jezreel, Ephraim, and **Benjamin,** and indeed over all Israel.
2.15 and the tribe of **Benjamin,** fought twelve of David's men.
2.25 men from the tribe of **Benjamin** gathered round Abner again
2.31 had killed 360 of Abner's men from the tribe of **Benjamin.**
3.19 people of the tribe of **Benjamin** and then went to Hebron to
3.19 David what the people of **Benjamin** and of Israel had agreed
4. 2 Rechab, sons of Rimmon, from Beeroth in the tribe of **Benjamin.**
4. 2 (Beeroth is counted as part of **Benjamin.**
16.11 so why should you be surprised at this **Benjaminite?**
19.16 At the same time the **Benjaminite** Shimei son of Gera from
19.17 He had with him a thousand men from the tribe of **Benjamin.**
20. 1 character named Sheba son of Bikri, of the tribe of **Benjamin.**
21.14 Zela in the territory of **Benjamin,** doing all that the king
23.24 of Ribai from Gibeah in **Benjamin** Benaiah from Pirathon
1 Kgs 2. 8 Shimei son of Gera, from the town of Bahurim in **Benjamin.**
4.18 the territory of **Benjamin** [19]Geber son of Uri:
12.21 180,000 of the best soldiers from the tribes of Judah and **Benjamin.**
12.23 and to all the people of the tribes of Judah and **Benjamin:**
15.22 Asa fortified Mizpah and Geba, a city in the territory of **Benjamin.**
1 Chr 2. 2 Simeon, Levi, Judah, Issachar, Zebulun, [2]Dan, Joseph, **Benjamin,**
6.60 territory of **Benjamin** they were assigned the following towns
6.65 territories of Judah, Simeon, and **Benjamin,** mentioned above,
7. 6 **Benjamin** had three sons:

1 Chr 8. 1 **Benjamin** had five sons.
8.40 All those named above were members of the tribe of **Benjamin.**
9. 3 tribes of Judah, **Benjamin,** Ephraim, and Manasseh went to live
9. 7 following members of the tribe of **Benjamin** lived in Jerusalem:
11.26 of Ribai from Gibeah in **Benjamin** Benaiah from Pirathon
12. 2 members of the tribe of **Benjamin,** to which Saul belonged.
12.16 men from the tribes of **Benjamin** and Judah went out to the
12.23 **Benjamin** (Saul's own tribe):
12.23 (most of the people of **Benjamin** had remained loyal to Saul);
21. 6 did not take any census of the tribes of Levi and **Benjamin.**
27. 2 from Anathoth in the territory of the tribe of **Benjamin**
27.16 **Benjamin** Jaasiel son of Abner
2 Chr 11. 1 of the best soldiers from the tribes of **Benjamin** and Judah.
11. 3 and to all the people of the tribes of Judah and **Benjamin:**
11. 5 fortifications built for the following cities of Judah and **Benjamin:**
11.12 In this way he kept Judah and **Benjamin** under his control.
11.23 stationed them throughout Judah and **Benjamin** in the fortified
14. 8 and 280,000 men from **Benjamin,** armed with shields and bows.
15. 2 to me, King Asa, and all you people of Judah and **Benjamin!**
15. 8 the land of Judah and **Benjamin** and all the idols in the
15. 9 Asa summoned all of them and the people of Judah and **Benjamin.**
17.17 from the clans of **Benjamin** was Eliada, an outstanding soldier,
25. 5 the tribes of Judah and **Benjamin** into army units, according to
31. 1 the rest of Judah, and the territories of **Benjamin,** Ephraim,
34. 9 and from the people of Judah, **Benjamin,** and Jerusalem.)
34.32 He made the people of **Benjamin** and everyone else present
Ezra 1. 5 the tribes of Judah and **Benjamin,** the priests and Levites,
4. 1 people of Judah and **Benjamin** heard that those who had returned
10. 9 territory of Judah and **Benjamin** came to Jerusalem and assembled
Neh 11. 7 Members of the tribe of **Benjamin:**
11. 8 In all, 928 **Benjaminites** lived in Jerusalem.
11.31 people of the tribe of **Benjamin** lived in Geba, Michmash, Ai,
11.36 of Judah were assigned to live with the people of **Benjamin.**
Esth 2. 5 was from the tribe of **Benjamin** and was a descendant of Kish
Ps 68.27 First comes **Benjamin,** the smallest tribe, then the leaders
80. 2 reveal yourself to the tribes of Ephraim, **Benjamin,**
Jer 1. 1 of the town of Anathoth in the territory of **Benjamin.**
6. 1 People of **Benjamin,** run for safety!
17.26 come from the territory of **Benjamin,** from the foothills,
32. 7 in the territory of **Benjamin,** because I was his nearest relative
32.44 place in the territory of **Benjamin,** in the villages round
33.13 in the territory of **Benjamin,** in the villages round Jerusalem,
37.12 go to the territory of **Benjamin** to take possession of my
Ezek 48.21 Judah and on the south by the section belonging to **Benjamin.**
48.23 **Benjamin** Simeon Issachar Zebulun Gad
48.30 those in the east wall, after Joseph, **Benjamin,** and Dan;
Hos 5. 8 Into battle, men of **Benjamin!**
Obad 19 the people of **Benjamin** will take Gilead.
Acts 13.21 from the tribe of **Benjamin,** to be their king for forty
Rom 11. 1 a descendant of Abraham, a member of the tribe of **Benjamin.**
Phil 3. 5 an Israelite by birth, of the tribe of **Benjamin,** a pure-blooded
Rev 7. 5 Manasseh, Simeon, Levi, Issachar, Zebulun, Joseph, and **Benjamin.**

BENJAMIN GATE

Jer 20. 2 placed in chains near the upper **Benjamin Gate** in the Temple.
37.13 But when I reached the **Benjamin Gate,** the officer in charge
38. 7 At that time the king was holding court at the **Benjamin Gate.**
Zech 14.10 city will reach from the **Benjamin Gate** to the Corner Gate,

BENT see BEND

BERYL

A semi-precious stone, usually green or bluish green in colour.

Ex 28.20 and in the fourth row, a **beryl,** a carnelian, and a
39.13 and in the fourth row, a **beryl,** a carnelian, and a
Ezek 28.13 topaz, **beryl,** carnelian, and jasper;
Rev 21.20 seventh yellow quartz, the eighth **beryl,** the ninth topaz,

BESIEGE

Deut 28.53 "When your enemies are **besieging** your towns, you will
28.56 When the enemy **besieges** her town, she will become so desperate
1 Sam 11. 1 town of Jabesh in the territory of Gilead and **besieged** it.
23. 8 war, to march against Keilah and **besiege** David and his men.
2 Sam 11. 1 they defeated the Ammonites and **besieged** the city of Rabbah.
11.16 So while Joab was **besieging** the city, he sent Uriah to a
20.15 Sheba was there, and so they went and **besieged** the city.
1 Kgs 15.27 Nadab and his army were **besieging** the city of Gibbethon
16.15 The Israelite troops were **besieging** the city of Gibbethon
16.17 Omri and his troops left Gibbethon and went and **besieged** Tirzah.
2 Kgs 16. 5 attacked Jerusalem and **besieged** it, but could not defeat Ahaz.
17. 5 Shalmaneser invaded Israel and **besieged** Samaria.
18. 9 Shalmaneser of Assyria invaded Israel and **besieged** Samaria.
24.10 officers, marched against Jerusalem and **besieged** it.
1 Chr 20. 1 They **besieged** the city of Rabbah, attacked it, and destroyed it.
2 Chr 32. 1 He **besieged** the fortified cities and gave orders for his army
Is 29. 3 God will attack the city, surround it, and **besiege** it.
Jer 6. 6 cut down trees and build mounds in order to **besiege** Jerusalem.
21. 2 Nebuchadnezzar of Babylonia and his army are **besieging** the city.
37. 5 The Babylonian army had been **besieging** Jerusalem, but when
Ezek 4. 3 It is under siege, and you are the one **besieging** it.
Mic 5. 1 We are **besieged!**
Zech 12. 2 And when they **besiege** Jerusalem,
12. 2 the cities of the rest of Judah will also be **besieged.**

BEST

Gen 4. 4 killed it, and gave the **best** parts of it as an offering.
18. 6 "Quick, take a sack of your **best** flour, and bake some bread."
23. 6 bury your wife in the **best** grave that we have.
27.15 she took Esau's **best** clothes, which she kept in the house,
43.11 to be, then take the **best** products of the land in your
45.18 I will give them the **best** land in Egypt, and they will
45.20 the **best** in the whole land of Egypt will be theirs."
45.23 ten donkeys loaded with the **best** Egyptian goods and ten donkeys
47. 6 settle in the region of Goshen, the **best** part of the land.
47.11 giving them property in the **best** of the land near the city
49.11 young donkey to a grapevine, To the very **best** of the vines.
Ex 15. 4 the **best** of its officers were drowned in the Red Sea.
27.20 Israel to bring you the **best** olive-oil for the lamp, so that
29. 2 Use the **best** wheat flour, but no yeast, and make some
29.13 covers the internal organs, the **best** part of the liver, and
29.22 covering the internal organs, the **best** part of the liver,
Lev 3. 4 and the fat on them, and the **best** part of the liver.
3.10 and the fat on them, and the **best** part of the liver.
3.15 and the fat on them, and the **best** part of the liver.
4. 9 and the fat on them, and the **best** part of the liver.
7. 4 and the fat on them, and the **best** part of the liver.
8.16 on the internal organs, the **best** part of the liver, and the
8.25 covering the internal organs, the **best** part of the liver,
9.10 fat, the kidneys, and the **best** part of the liver, just as
23.40 day take some of the **best** fruit from your trees, take palm
Num 18.12 am giving you all the **best** of the first produce which the
18.29 Give it from the **best** that you receive.
18.30 When you have presented the **best** part, you may keep the rest,
18.32 long as you have presented the **best** of it to the Lord.
18.32 by eating any of the gifts before the **best** part is offered;
21.32 sent men to find the **best** way to attack the city of
28. 5 kilogramme of flour, mixed with one litre of the **best** olive-oil.
Deut 1.22 they can tell us the **best** route to take and what kind
32.14 they had the **best** sheep, goats, and cattle, the finest wheat,
33.14 sun-ripened fruit, Rich with the **best** fruits of each season.
33.21 They took the **best** of the land for themselves;
Josh 8. 3 out thirty thousand of his **best** troops and sent them out at
10. 7 whole army, including the **best** troops, started out from Gilgal.
Judg 3.29 they killed about ten thousand of the **best** Moabite soldiers;
14.20 to the man that had been his **best** man at the wedding.
20.44 thousand of the **best** Benjaminite soldiers were killed.
Ruth 2.21 Then Ruth said, **"Best** of all, he told me to keep
3. 3 put on some perfume, and get dressed in your **best** clothes.
1 Sam 1.23 Elkanah answered, "All right, do whatever you think **best;**
2.29 them fatten themselves on the **best** parts of all the sacrifices
3.18 he will do whatever seems **best** to him."
8.14 He will take your **best** fields, vineyards, and olive-groves,
8.16 take your servants and your **best** cattle and donkeys, and make
14.36 "Do whatever you think **best,"** they answered.
14.40 "Do whatever you think **best,"** they answered.
15. 9 and did not kill the **best** sheep and cattle,
15. 9 the **best** calves and lambs, or anything else
15.15 They kept the **best** sheep and cattle to offer as a sacrifice
15.21 did not kill the **best** sheep and cattle that they captured;
15.22 better to obey him than to sacrifice the **best** sheep to him.
24. 2 took three thousand of the **best** soldiers in Israel and went
25. 6 greetings, my friend, with his **best wishes** for you, your family,
26. 2 three thousand of the **best** soldiers in Israel to the wilderness
27. 1 The **best** thing for me to do is to escape to Philistia.
2 Sam 6. 1 David called together the **best** soldiers in Israel, a total of
10. 9 rear, so he chose the **best** of Israel's soldiers and put them
18. 4 "I will do whatever you think **best,"** the king answered.
19.37 with you, Your Majesty, and do for him as you think **best."**
1 Kgs 12.21 called together 180,000 of the **best** soldiers from the tribes of
2 Kgs 7. 1 Samaria three kilogrammes of the **best** wheat or six kilogrammes
7.16 three kilogrammes of the **best** wheat or six kilogrammes of barley
7.18 three kilogrammes of the **best** wheat or six kilogrammes of barley
10. 3 you are to choose the **best** qualified of the king's descendants,
10. 5 do whatever you think **best."**
1 Chr 12.23 knew what Israel should do and the **best** time to do it);
19.10 rear, so he chose the **best** of Israel's soldiers and put them
2 Chr 11. 1 thousand of the **best** soldiers from the tribes of Benjamin
11.21 he loved Maacah **best,** [22] and he favoured her son Abijah
13.17 defeat—half a million of Israel's **best** soldiers were killed.
Neh 5.18 one ox, six of the **best** sheep, and many chickens, and every
Esth 2. 4 take the girl you like **best** and make her queen in Vashti's
2. 9 He gave her the **best** place in the harem and assigned seven
3. 8 so it is not in your **best** interests to tolerate them.
Job 27.22 on them without pity while they try their **best** to escape.
Ps 41. 9 Even my **best** friend, the one I trusted most, the one who
78.31 and killed their strongest men, the **best** young men of Israel.
Prov 3. 9 an offering from the **best** of all that your land produces.
21.29 the wicked have to pretend as **best** they can.
31.29 women are good wives, but you are the **best** of them all."
Ecc 2. 3 that this might be the **best** way people can spend their short
2.24 The **best** thing a man can do is to eat and drink
3.12 be happy and do the **best** we can while we are still
3.22 I realized then that the **best** thing we can do is to
5.18 the **best** thing anyone can do is to eat and drink and
6.12 can anyone know what is **best** for a man in this short,
Song 4.16 lover come to his garden and eat the **best** of its fruits.
Is 30.24 that plough your fields will eat the finest and **best** fodder.
41.21 Bring the **best** arguments you have!
55. 2 what I say, and you will enjoy the **best** food of all.
64. 6 even our **best** actions are filthy through and through.
Jer 2.21 I planted you like a choice vine from the very **best** seed.
6.16 Ask for the ancient paths and where the **best** road is.
20. 9 I try my **best** to hold it in, but can no longer
31.20 "Israel, you are my dearest son, the child I love **best.**

Jer 38.22 'The king's **best** friends misled him, they overruled him.
Lam 3.26 in him, [26]So it is **best** for us to wait in patience
3.27 us— [27]And it is **best** to learn this patience in our
Ezek 16.10 gave you shoes of the **best** leather, a linen headband, and a
16.13 ate bread made from the **best** flour, and had honey and
16.19 I gave you food—the **best** flour, olive-oil, and honey—
17.21 His **best** soldiers will be killed in battle,
20.40 to bring me your sacrifices, your **best** offerings, and your
24. 4 Put in the **best** pieces of meat— the shoulders and the
34.18 Some of you are not satisfied with eating the **best** grass;
44.30 priests are to have the **best** of all the first harvest and
48.14 to the Lord is the **best** part of all the land, and
Dan 6.14 was upset and did his **best** to find some way to rescue
11.15 even the **best** of them will not have enough strength.
Hos 11. 6 destroy my people because they do what they themselves think **best.**
Jon 4. 2 That's why I did my **best** to run away to Spain!
Mic 6. 6 Shall I bring the **best** calves to burn as offerings to him?
7. 4 Even the **best** and most honest of them are as worthless as
Hab 1.16 because their nets provide them with the **best** of everything.
Mt 23. 6 They love the **best places** at feasts and the reserved seats
Mk 12.39 reserved seats in the synagogues and the **best places** at feasts.
Lk 1. 1 Many people have done their **best** to write a report of the
12.58 you to court, do your **best** to settle the dispute with him
13.24 answered them, [24]"Do your **best** to go in through the narrow
14. 7 guests were choosing the **best places,** so he told this parable
14. 8 to a wedding feast, do not sit down in the **best place.**
15.22 'Bring the **best** robe and put it on him.
20.46 reserved seats in the synagogues and the **best places** at feasts;
Jn 2.10 "Everyone else serves the **best** wine first, and after the guests
2.10 But you have kept the **best** wine until now!"
Acts 15.29 With our **best wishes."**
24.16 And so I do my **best** always to have a clear conscience
1 Cor 12.31 **Best** of all, however, is the following way.
Gal 1.13 the church of God and did my **best** to destroy it.
Eph 4. 3 Do your **best** to preserve the unity which the Spirit gives
Phil 1.10 so that you will be able to choose what is **best.**
3.13 is behind me and do my **best** to reach what is ahead.
Col 4.15 Give our **best wishes** to the brothers in Laodicea and to
1 Tim 6.12 Run your **best** in the race of faith, and win eternal life
2 Tim 2.15 Do your **best** to win full approval in God's sight,
4. 7 I have done my **best** in the race, I have run
4. 9 Do your **best** to come to me soon.
4.21 Do your **best** to come before winter.
Tit 3.12 Tychicus to you, do your **best** to come to me in Nicopolis,
3.13 Do your **best** to help Zenas the lawyer and Apollos to get
Heb 4.11 Let us, then, do our **best** to receive that rest,
Jas 2. 3 say to him, "Have this **best seat** here," but say to
2 Pet 1. 5 this very reason do your **best** to add goodness to your faith;
1.15 I will do my **best,** then, to provide a way for you
3.12 of God and do your **best** to make it come soon—
3.14 for that Day, do your **best** to be pure and faultless
Jude 3 friends, I was doing my **best** to write to you about

BET

Judg 14.12 I'll **bet** each one of you a piece of fine linen and

BETH HORON

Two cities near one another in Ephraim, distinguished as Lower and Upper Beth Horon.

Josh 10.10 down the mountain pass at **Beth Horon,** keeping up the attack
16. 3 of the Japhletites, as far as the area of Lower **Beth Horon.**
16. 5 Ataroth Addar eastwards to Upper **Beth Horon,** [6]and from there
18.13 to Ataroth Addar, on the mountain south of Lower **Beth Horon.**
21.22 Kibzaim, and **Beth Horon,** with their pasture lands.
1 Sam 13.18 another went towards **Beth Horon,** and the other one went
1 Kgs 9.17 Solomon also rebuilt Lower **Beth Horon,** [18]Baalath, Tamar in
1 Chr 6.68 the hills of Ephraim, Gezer, [68]Jokmeam, **Beth Horon,**
7.24 the towns of Upper and Lower **Beth Horon,** and Uzzen Sheerah.
2 Chr 8. 5 Upper **Beth Horon** and Lower Beth Horon (fortified cities with
25.13 between Samaria and **Beth Horon,** killed three thousand men,
Neh 2.10 Sanballat, from the town of **Beth Horon,** and Tobiah, an official
13.28 Sanballat, from the town of **Beth Horon,** so I made Joiada

BETH SHEMESH (1)

City in Judah.
see also HELIOPOLIS

Josh 15.10 (or Chesalon), down to **Beth Shemesh,** and on past Timnah.
21.16 Ain, Juttah, and **Beth Shemesh,** with their pasture lands:
Judg 1.33 the people living in the cities of **Beth Shemesh** and Bethanath.
1 Sam 6. 9 goes towards the town of **Beth Shemesh,** this means that it is
6.12 on the road to **Beth Shemesh** and headed straight towards it,
6.12 kings followed them as far as the border of **Beth Shemesh.**
6.13 people of **Beth Shemesh** were harvesting wheat in the valley,
6.14 named Joshua, who lived in **Beth Shemesh,** and it stopped there
6.15 Then the people of **Beth Shemesh** offered burnt-sacrifices
6.18 the field of Joshua of **Beth Shemesh,** on which they placed
6.19 seventy of the men of **Beth Shemesh** because they looked inside
6.20 So the men of **Beth Shemesh** said, "Who can stand before
1 Kgs 4. 9 cities of Makaz, Shaalbim, **Beth Shemesh,** Elon, and Beth Hanan
2 Kgs 14.11 his men and fought against him at **Beth Shemesh** in Judah.
1 Chr 6.57 Hilen, Debir, Ashan, and **Beth Shemesh,** with their pasture lands.
2 Chr 25.21 met at **Beth Shemesh** in Judah, [22]the Judaean army was defeated,
28.18 They captured the cities of **Beth Shemesh,** Aijalon, and Gederoth,

BETHANY (1)

Town near Jerusalem, home of Martha, Mary and Lazarus, where Jesus stayed in the period before his crucifixion.

Mt 21.17 went out of the city to **Bethany,** where he spent the night.
26. 6 Jesus was in **Bethany** at the house of Simon,
Mk 11. 1 the towns of Bethphage and **Bethany,** they came to the Mount
11.11 he went out to **Bethany** with the twelve disciples.
11.12 as they were coming back from **Bethany,** Jesus was hungry.
14. 3 Jesus was in **Bethany** at the house of Simon,
Lk 19.29 he came near Bethphage and **Bethany** at the Mount of Olives,
24.50 the city as far as **Bethany,** where he raised his hands
Jn 11. 1 A man named Lazarus, who lived in **Bethany,** was ill.
11. 1 **Bethany** was the town where Mary and her sister Martha lived.
11.18 **Bethany** was less than three kilometres from Jerusalem,
12. 1 the Passover, Jesus went to **Bethany,** the home of Lazarus,
12. 9 heard that Jesus was in **Bethany,** so they went there,

BETHANY (2)

Place to the east of the River Jordan.

Jn 1.28 All this happened in **Bethany** on the east side of the River

BETHEL (1)

Holy place at the s. edge of the n. kingdom (Israel).
see also LUZ (1)

Gen 12. 8 east of the city of **Bethel** and set up his camp
12. 8 between **Bethel** on the west and Ai
13. 3 there and moved from place to place, going towards **Bethel.**
13. 3 He reached the place between **Bethel** and Ai where he had
28.19 He named the place **Bethel.**
31.13 who appeared to you at **Bethel,** where you dedicated a stone
35. 1 God said to Jacob, "Go to **Bethel** at once, and live there.
35. 3 leave here and go to **Bethel,** where I will build an altar
35. 6 Luz, which is now known as **Bethel,** in the land of Canaan.
35. 7 place after the God of **Bethel,** because God had revealed himself
35. 8 Deborah died and was buried beneath the oak south of **Bethel.**
35.15 He named the place **Bethel.**
35.16 Jacob and his family left **Bethel,** and when they were still
Josh 7. 2 Ai, a city east of **Bethel,** near Bethaven, with orders to go
8. 9 place and waited there, west of Ai, between Ai and **Bethel.**
8.12 put them in hiding west of the city, between Ai and **Bethel.**
12. 9 Jericho, Ai (near **Bethel**), [10]Jerusalem, Hebron, [11]Jarmuth,
12.16 Hormah, Arad, [15]Libnah, Adullam, [16]Makkedah, **Bethel,**
16. 1 It went from Jericho up into the hill-country as far as **Bethel.**
16. 2 From **Bethel** it went to Luz, passing on to Ataroth Addar,
18.13 side of Luz (also called **Bethel**), then down to Ataroth Addar,
18.22 Emek Keziz, [22]Beth Arabah, Zemaraim, **Bethel,** [23]Avvim,
Judg 1.22 went to attack the city of **Bethel,** at that time called Luz.
4. 5 certain palm-tree between Ramah and **Bethel** in the hill-country
20.18 the place of worship at **Bethel,** and there they asked God,
20.26 Then all the people of Israel went up to **Bethel** and mourned.
20.27 Covenant Box was there at **Bethel** in those days, and Phinehas,
20.31 country on the road to **Bethel** and on the road to Gibeah.
21. 2 people of Israel went to **Bethel** and sat there in the
21.19 (Shiloh is north of **Bethel,** south of Lebonah,
21.19 and east of the road between **Bethel** and Shechem.)
1 Sam 7.16 he would go round to **Bethel,** Gilgal, and Mizpah, and in
10. 3 men on their way to offer a sacrifice to God at **Bethel.**
13. 2 and in the hill-country of **Bethel** and sending one thousand with
30.27 it to the people in **Bethel,** to the people in Ramah in
1 Kgs 12.29 one of the gold bull-calves in **Bethel** and the other in Dan.
12.30 the people sinned, going to worship in **Bethel** and in Dan.
12.32 altar in **Bethel** he offered sacrifices to the gold bull-calves
12.32 he placed there in **Bethel** the priests serving at the places
12.33 had set, he went to **Bethel** and offered a sacrifice on the
13. 1 prophet from Judah went to **Bethel** and arrived there as Jeroboam
13.11 At that time there was an old prophet living in **Bethel.**
13.11 from Judah had done in **Bethel** that day and what he had
13.18 Then the old prophet from **Bethel** said to him, "I, too,
13.25 They went on into **Bethel** and reported what they had seen.
13.29 and brought it back to **Bethel** to mourn over it and bury
13.32 command against the altar in **Bethel** and against all the places
16.34 During his reign Hiel from **Bethel** rebuilt Jericho.
2 Kgs 2. 2 the Lord has ordered me to go to **Bethel."**
2. 2 So they went on to **Bethel.**
2.23 left Jericho to go to **Bethel,** and on the way some boys
10.29 the gold bull-calves he set up in **Bethel** and in Dan.
17.28 Samaria went and lived in **Bethel,** where he taught the people
23. 4 of the Kidron, and then had the ashes taken to **Bethel.**
23.15 the place of worship in **Bethel** which had been built by King
23.17 The people of **Bethel** answered, "It is the tomb of the
23.19 He did to all those altars what he had done in **Bethel.**
1 Chr 7.28 took and settled in included **Bethel** and the towns round it,
2 Chr 13.19 **Bethel,** Jeshanah, and Ephron, and the villages near each of these cities.
Ezra 2.21 **Bethel** and Ai - 223
Neh 7.26 **Bethel** and Ai - 123
11.31 lived in Geba, Michmash, Ai, **Bethel** and the nearby villages,
Hos 10. 5 afraid and will mourn the loss of the gold bull at **Bethel.**
10.15 happen to you, people of **Bethel,** because of the terrible evil
12. 4 And at **Bethel** God came to our ancestor Jacob and spoke with
Amos 3.14 Israel for their sins, I will destroy the altars of **Bethel.**
4. 4 go to the holy place in **Bethel** and sin, if you must!
5. 5 not try to find me at **Bethel**—Bethel will come to nothing.
5. 6 burn up the people of **Bethel,** and no one will be able
7.10 Amaziah, the priest of **Bethel,** then sent a report
7.13 Don't prophesy here at **Bethel** any more.

BETHLEHEM (1)

City in Judah where David was born and brought up, and in which Jesus was born.

Gen 35.19 buried beside the road to Ephrath, now known as **Bethlehem.**
48. 7 (Ephrath is now known as **Bethlehem.)**
Judg 12. 8 After Jephthah, Ibzan from **Bethlehem** led Israel.
12.10 for seven years, [10] then he died and was buried at **Bethlehem.**
17. 7 Levite who had been living in the town of **Bethlehem** in Judah.
17. 8 He left **Bethlehem** to find somewhere else to live.
17. 9 He answered, "I am a Levite from **Bethlehem** in Judah.
19. 1 He took a girl from **Bethlehem** in Judah to be his concubine,
19. 2 father's house in **Bethlehem,** and stayed there four months.
19.18 answered, "We have been to **Bethlehem** in Judah, and now we
Ruth 1. 1 Ephrath and who lived in **Bethlehem** in Judah, went with his
1.19 They went on until they came to **Bethlehem.**
1.22 The barley harvest was just beginning when they arrived in **Bethlehem.**
2. 4 Some time later Boaz himself arrived from **Bethlehem**
4.11 become rich in the clan of Ephrath and famous in **Bethlehem.**
1 Sam 16. 1 some olive-oil and go to **Bethlehem,** to a man named Jesse,
16. 4 to do and went to **Bethlehem,** where the city leaders came
16.18 "Jesse, of the town of **Bethlehem,** has a son who is a
17.12 son of Jesse, who was an Ephrathite from **Bethlehem** in Judah.
17.15 David would go back to **Bethlehem** from time to time, to
17.58 "I am the son of your servant Jesse from **Bethlehem,"** David answered.
20. 6 permission to hurry home to **Bethlehem,** since it's the time
20.28 Jonathan answered, "He begged me to let him go to **Bethlehem.**
2 Sam 2.32 Asahel's body and buried it in the family tomb at **Bethlehem.**
21.19 Elhanan son of Jair from **Bethlehem** killed Goliath from Gath,
23.14 hill, and a group of Philistines had occupied **Bethlehem.**
23.15 a drink of water from the well by the gate at **Bethlehem!"**
23.24 Elhanan son of Dodo from **Bethlehem** Shammah and Elika from
1 Chr 2.51 his second son Salma founded **Bethlehem,** and his third
2.54 Salma, the founder of **Bethlehem,** was the ancestor of
4. 3 Caleb's wife Ephrath, and his descendants founded the city of **Bethlehem.**
4.22 Joash and Saraph, who married Moabite women and then settled in **Bethlehem.**
11.16 hill, and a group of Philistines had occupied **Bethlehem.**
11.17 a drink of water from the well by the gate in **Bethlehem!"**
11.26 Elhanan son of Dodo from **Bethlehem** Shammoth from Harod Helez
2 Chr 11. 6 **Bethlehem,** Etam, Tekoa, [7] Bethzur, Soco, Adullam, [8] Gath,
Ezra 2.21 **Bethlehem** - 123
Neh 7.26 **Bethlehem** and Netophah - 188
Ps 132. 6 In **Bethlehem** we heard about the Covenant Box, and we found
Jer 41.17 On the way, they stopped at Chimham, near **Bethlehem.**
Mic 5. 2 The Lord says, **"Bethlehem** Ephrathah, you are one of the
Mt 2. 1 born in the town of **Bethlehem** in Judaea, during the time
2. 5 "In the town of **Bethlehem** in Judaea," they answered.
2. 6 **'Bethlehem** in the land of Judah, you are by no means
2. 8 Then he sent them to **Bethlehem** with these instructions:
2.16 kill all the boys in **Bethlehem** and its neighbourhood
Lk 2. 4 to the town of **Bethlehem** in Judaea, the birthplace of King
2. 6 and while they were in **Bethlehem,** the time came for her to
2.15 "Let's go to **Bethlehem** and see this thing that has
Jn 7.42 and will be born in **Bethlehem,** the town where David lived."

BETRAY

2 Sam 3. 8 "Do you think that I would **betray** Saul?
19.26 so that I could ride along with you, but he **betrayed** me.
1 Chr 12.17 But if you intend to **betray** me to my enemies, even though
12.19 afraid that he would **betray** them to his former master Saul,
Job 17. 5 the old proverb a man **betrays** his friends for money, and his
Ps 7. 3 wronged anyone, if I have **betrayed** a friend or without cause
Prov 14.25 when he tells lies, he **betrays** people.
Is 21. 2 of cruel events, a vision of **betrayal** and destruction.
24.16 Traitors continue to **betray,** and their treachery grows worse
33. 1 They have robbed and **betrayed,** although no one has robbed them
33. 1 their time to rob and **betray** will end, and they themselves
Jer 5.11 The people of Israel and Judah have **betrayed** me completely.
12. 6 Even your brothers, members of your own family, have **betrayed** you;
Lam 1. 2 Her allies have **betrayed** her and all are now against her.
Ezek 37.23 them from all the ways in which they sin and **betray** me.
39.26 to forget how they were disgraced for having **betrayed** me.
Mt 10. 4 Simon the Patriot, and Judas Iscariot, who **betrayed** Jesus.
24.10 they will **betray** one another and hate one another.
26.15 "What will you give me if I **betray** Jesus to you?"
26.21 Jesus said, "I tell you, one of you will **betray** me."
26.23 who dips his bread in the dish with me will **betray** me.
26.24 but how terrible for that man who **betrays** the Son of Man!
26.46 Look, here is the man who is **betraying** me!"
27. 4 "I have sinned by **betraying** an innocent man to death!"
Mk 3.19 Simon the Patriot, [19] and Judas Iscariot, who **betrayed** Jesus.
14.10 off to the chief priests in order to **betray** Jesus to them.
14.18 that one of you will **betray** me—one who is eating
14.21 but how terrible for that man who **betrays** the Son of Man!
14.42 Look, here is the man who is **betraying** me!"
Lk 22. 4 the temple guard about how he could **betray** Jesus to them.
22.21 The one who **betrays** me is here at the table with me!
22.22 but how terrible for that man who **betrays** him!"
22.48 is it with a kiss that you **betray** the Son of Man?"
Jn 6.64 ones that would not believe and which one would **betray** him.)
6.71 was one of the twelve disciples, was going to **betray** him.
12. 4 one who was going to **betray** him—said, [5] "Why wasn't this
13. 2 Judas, the son of Simon Iscariot, the thought of **betraying** Jesus.
Jn 13.11 (Jesus already knew who was going to **betray** him;
13.21 one of you is going to **betray** me."
21.20 meal and had asked, "Lord, who is going to **betray** you?"
Acts 7.52 And now you have **betrayed** and murdered him.
1 Cor 11.23 on the night he was **betrayed,** took a piece of bread,

BETTER

Gen 41.38 "We will never find a **better** man than Joseph, a man who
49.14 "Issachar is no **better** than a donkey
Ex 14.12 It would be **better** to be slaves there than to die here
Num 11.18 you had some meat and that you were **better** off in Egypt.
14. 2 said, "It would have been **better** to die in Egypt or even
14. 3 Wouldn't it be **better** to go back to Egypt?"
20. 3 "It would have been **better** if we had died in front of
Deut 17.20 from thinking that he is **better** than his fellow-Israelites
Judg 11.25 you think you are any **better** than Balak son of Zippor, king
15.19 Samson drank it and began to feel much **better.**
18.25 from Dan said, "You had **better** not say anything else unless
Ruth 2.13 You have made me feel **better** by speaking gently to me, even
2.22 my daughter, it will be **better** for you to work with the
1 Sam 14.27 At once he felt much **better.**
14.29 See how much **better** I feel because I ate some honey!
14.30 How much **better** it would have been today if our people
15.22 It is **better** to obey him than to sacrifice the best sheep
15.28 and given it to someone who is a **better** man than you.
16.23 leave, and Saul would feel **better** and be all right again.
21. 9 "There is not a **better** sword anywhere!"
29. 4 What **better** way is there for him to win back his master's
2 Sam 1.26 was your love for me, **better** even than the love of women.
9. 8 again and said, "I am no **better** than a dead dog, sir!
14.32 It would have been **better** for me to have stayed there.' "
17.14 "Hushai's advice is **better** than Ahithophel's."
18. 3 It will be **better** if you stay here in the city and
1 Kgs 2.32 Joab killed two innocent men who were **better** men than he:
21. 2 I will give you a **better** vineyard for it, or, if you
2 Kgs 5.12 Abana and Pharpar, back in Damascus, **better** than any river in Israel?
2 Chr 21.13 You even murdered your brothers, who were **better** men than you are.
Esth 1.19 Then give her place as queen to some **better** woman.
Job 14.14 But I will wait for **better** times, wait till this time of
19. 5 You think you are **better** than I am, and regard my troubles
30.19 I am no **better** than dirt.
Ps 35.26 those who claim to be **better** than I am be covered with
63. 3 Your constant love is **better** than life itself, and so I
84.10 in your Temple is **better** than a thousand anywhere else;
118. 8 It is **better** to trust in the Lord than to depend on
118. 9 It is **better** to trust in the Lord than to depend on
Prov 8.11 "I am Wisdom, I am **better** than jewels;
8.19 better than the finest gold, **better** than the purest silver.
9.17 Stolen bread tastes **better."**
11.15 You are **better** off if you don't get involved.
12. 9 It is **better** to be an ordinary man working for a living
15.16 **Better** to be poor and fear the Lord than to be rich
15.17 **Better** to eat vegetables with people you love than to
15.30 Smiling faces make you happy, and good news makes you feel **better.**
16. 8 It is **better** to have a little, honestly earned, than to
16.16 It is **better**—much better—to have wisdom and knowledge
16.19 It is **better** to be humble and stay poor than to be
16.32 It is **better** to be patient than powerful.
16.32 It is **better** to win control over yourself than over whole cities.
17. 1 **Better** to eat a dry crust of bread with peace of mind
17.12 It is **better** to meet a mother bear robbed of her cubs
19. 1 It is **better** to be poor but honest than to be a
19.22 poor people are **better** off than liars.
19.25 so that people who don't know any **better** can learn a lesson.
21. 9 **Better** to live on the roof than share the house with a
21.19 **Better** to live out in the desert than with a nagging,
22.29 you a man who is **better** than most and worthy of the
24. 5 Being wise is **better** than being strong;
25. 7 It is **better** to be asked to take a higher position than
25.24 **Better** to live on the roof than share the house with a
26.12 The most stupid fool is **better** off than someone who
27. 5 **Better** to correct someone openly than to let him think you
28. 6 **Better** to be poor and honest than rich and dishonest.
28.11 a poor person who has insight into character knows **better.**
28.24 to steal from his parents is no **better** than a common thief.
28.25 You are much **better** off to trust the Lord.
Ecc 2.13 "Wisdom is better than foolishness, just as light is **better** than darkness.
3.18 testing us, to show us that we are no **better** than animals.
3.19 A human being is no **better** off than an animal, because life
4. 2 they are **better** off than those who are still alive.
4. 3 But **better** off than either are those who have never been born,
4. 6 Perhaps so, but it is **better** to have only a little, with
4. 9 Two are **better** off than one, because together they can
5. 1 It is **better** to go there to learn than to offer sacrifices
5. 5 **Better** not to promise at all than to make a promise and
6. 3 burial, then I say that a baby born dead is **better** off.
6. 8 How is a wise man **better** off than a fool?
6. 9 It is **better** to be satisfied with what you have than to
6.11 argue, the more useless it is, and you are no **better** off.
7. 1 A good reputation is **better** than expensive perfume;
7. 1 the day you die is **better** than the day you are born.
7. 2 It is **better** to go to a home where there is mourning
7. 3 Sorrow is **better** than laughter;
7. 5 It is **better** to have wise people reprimand you than to
7. 8 The end of anything is **better** than its beginning.
7. 8 Patience is **better** than pride.

Ecc 7.10 ask, "Oh, why were things so much **better** in the old days?"
9. 2 A good man is no **better** off than a sinner;
9. 2 takes an oath is no **better** off than one who does not.
9. 4 a live dog is **better** off than a dead lion.
9.16 always said that wisdom is **better** than strength, but no one
9.17 It is **better** to listen to the quiet words of a wise
11. 6 well or whether one sowing will do **better** than the other.
Song 1. 2 your love is **better** than wine.
4.10 Your love is **better** than wine;
Is 56.12 Tomorrow will be even **better** than today!' "
57. 3 You are no **better** than sorcerers, adulterers, and prostitutes.
Jer 3.11 from him, she had proved to be **better** than unfaithful Judah.
7.24 told them to do, and they became worse instead of **better.**
22.15 Does it make you a **better** king if you build houses of
Lam 4. 9 died in the war were **better** off than those who died later,
5. 8 by men who are no **better** than slaves, and no one can
Ezek 29. 6 Egyptians for support, but you were no **better** than a weak stick.
34. 8 as I am the living God, you had **better** listen to me.
Dan 6. 3 showed that he could do **better** work than the other
10.19 You have made me feel **better."**
Hos 2. 7 my first husband—I was **better** off then than I am now."
4. 5 day you blunder on, and the prophets do no **better** than you.
Amos 6. 2 Were they any **better** than the kingdoms of Judah and Israel?
Jon 4. 3 I am **better** off dead than alive."
4. 8 "I am **better** off dead than alive," he said.
Nah 3. 8 Nineveh, are you any **better** than Thebes, the capital of Egypt?
Hab 1. 4 Evil men get the **better** of the righteous, and so justice is
Mt 5.29 It is much **better** for you to lose a part of your
5.30 It is much **better** for you to lose one of your limbs
18. 6 it would be **better** for that person to have
18. 8 It is **better** for you to enter life without a hand
18. 9 It is **better** for you to enter life with only one eye
19.10 between a man and his wife, it is **better** not to marry."
26.24 It would have been **better** for that man if he had never
Mk 5.26 but instead of getting **better** she got worse all the time.
9.42 it would be **better** for that person to have
9.43 It is **better** for you to enter life without a hand than
9.45 It is **better** for you to enter life without a foot than
9.47 It is **better** for you to enter the Kingdom of God with
14.21 It would have been **better** for that man if he had never
Lk 5.39 'The old is **better,'** he says."
13. 9 Then if the tree bears figs next year, so much the **better;**
14.10 'Come on up, my friend, to a **better** place.'
17. 2 It would be **better** for him if a large millstone were tied
Jn 4.52 when his son got **better,** and they answered, "It was one
11.50 you realize that it is **better** for you to let one man
16. 7 it is **better** for you that I go away,
18.14 Jewish authorities that it was **better** that one man should die
Acts 7.31 and went near the bush to get a **better** look.
Rom 3. 9 are we Jews in any **better** condition than the Gentiles?
1 Cor 6. 7 Would it not be **better** for you to be wronged?
6. 7 Would it not be **better** for you to be robbed?
7. 8 say that it would be **better** for you to continue to live
7. 9 ahead and marry—it is **better** to marry than to burn with
7.26 I think it is **better** for a man to stay as
7.38 does well, but the one who doesn't marry does even **better.**
10.12 he is standing firm had **better** be careful that he does not
2 Cor 8.10 opinion is that it is **better** for you to finish now
11.23 like a madman—but I am a **better** servant than they are!
Phil 1.23 this life and be with Christ, which is a far **better** thing;
2. 3 one another, always considering others **better** than yourselves.
1 Tim 6. 2 to serve them even **better,** because those who benefit from their
Heb 6. 9 that you have the **better** blessings that belong to your salvation.
7.19 And now a **better** hope has been provided through which we
7.22 also makes Jesus the guarantee of a **better** covenant.
8. 6 and his people is a **better** one,
8. 6 because it is based on promises of **better** things.
9.23 the heavenly things themselves require much **better** sacrifices.
10.34 still possessed something much **better,** which would last for ever.
11. 4 that made Abel offer to God a **better** sacrifice than Cain's.
11.16 it was a **better** country they longed for, the heavenly country.
11.35 died under torture in order to be raised to a **better** life.
11.40 because God had decided on an even **better** plan for us.
12.24 blood that promises much **better** things than does the blood of
1 Pet 3.17 For it is **better** to suffer for doing good,
2 Pet 2.21 It would have been much **better** for them never to have

BEZALEL (1)

Craftsman who made the Tent and the Covenant Box.

Ex 31. 2 to Moses, [2]"I have chosen **Bezalel,** the son of Uri
35.30 Israelites, "The Lord has chosen **Bezalel,** the son of Uri
36. 1 **"Bezalel,** Oholiab, and all the other craftsmen
36. 2 Moses called **Bezalel,** Oholiab, and all the other skilled
37. 1 **Bezalel** made the Covenant Box out of acacia-wood, 110 centimetres long,
38.22 **Bezalel,** the son of Uri and grandson of Hur, from the
38.28 remaining 30 kilogrammes of silver **Bezalel** made the rods,
1 Chr 2.20 Hur's son was Uri, and his grandson was **Bezalel.**
2 Chr 1. 5 which had been made by **Bezalel,** the son of Uri and grandson

BIG

Ex 29.20 their right hands and on the **big** toes of their right feet.
Lev 8.23 his right hand, and on the **big** toe of his right foot.
8.24 their right hands, and on the **big** toes of their right feet.
14.14 right hand, and on the **big** toe of the right foot of
14.17 right hand, and on the **big** toe of the right foot of
14.25 his right hand, and on the **big** toe of his right foot.
14.28 his right hand, and on the **big** toe of his right foot.
Josh 10.18 He said, "Roll some **big** stones in front of the entrance
Josh 17.16 replied, "The hill-country is not **big** enough for us, but
Judg 1. 6 chased him, caught him, and cut off his thumbs and **big** toes.
1. 7 kings with their thumbs and **big** toes cut off have picked up
18.10 It is a **big** country;
20.38 When they saw a **big** cloud of smoke going up from the
1 Sam 14.33 "Roll a **big** stone over here to me."
17.25 has promised to give a **big** reward to the man who kills
2 Sam 6.20 "The king of Israel made a **big** name for himself today!"
1 Kgs 18.44 saw a little cloud no **bigger** than a man's hand, coming up
2 Kgs 4.38 his servant to put a **big** pot on the fire and make
Ezra 10.13 But they added, "The crowd is too **big,** and it's raining hard.
Job 38.18 Have you any idea how **big** the world is?
Prov 23. 2 If you have a **big** appetite, restrain yourself.
Is 5. 9 Lord Almighty say, "All these **big,** fine houses will be empty ruins.
30.14 that there is no piece **big** enough to pick up hot coals
Dan 4.11 It grew **bigger** and bigger until it reached the sky and
Zech 2. 4 in Jerusalem that it will be too **big** to have walls.
Mt 6. 2 do not make a **big** show of it, as the hypocrites
9.16 patch will shrink and make an even **bigger** hole in the coat.
12.40 days and nights in the **big** fish, so will the Son of
13.32 but when it grows up, it is the **biggest** of all plants.
17.20 if you have faith as **big** as a mustard seed, you can
Mk 2.21 tear off some of the old cloth, making an even **bigger** hole.
4.32 a while it grows up and becomes the **biggest** of all plants.
Lk 5.29 Then Levi had a **big** feast in his house for Jesus,
12.18 down my barns and build **bigger** ones, where I will store
17. 6 "If you had faith as **big** as a mustard seed, you could
Jn 21.11 the net ashore full of **big** fish, a hundred and fifty-three
1 Cor 2. 1 God's secret truth, I did not use **big** words and great learning.
Gal 6.11 See what **big** letters I make as I write to you now
Jas 3. 4 **big** as it is and driven by such strong winds,

BILHAH (1)

Rachel's slave-girl, wife of Jacob, and mother of Dan and Naphtali.

Gen 29.29 (Laban gave his slave-girl **Bilhah** to his daughter Rachel as her maid.)
30. 3 She said, "Here is my slave-girl **Bilhah;**
30. 4 So she gave **Bilhah** to her husband, and he had intercourse
30. 5 **Bilhah** became pregnant and bore Jacob a son.
30. 7 **Bilhah** became pregnant again and bore Jacob a second son.
35.22 Reuben had sexual intercourse with **Bilhah,** one of his father's concubines;
35.25 The sons of Rachel's slave **Bilhah** were Dan and Naphtali.
37. 2 the sons of **Bilhah** and Zilpah, his father's concubines.
46.25 the descendants of Jacob by **Bilhah,** the slave-girl whom
1 Chr 7.13 (They were descendants of **Bilhah.)**

BIND

[BOUND]

Gen 29.34 "Now my husband will be **bound** more tightly to me, because I
Ex 28.32 be reinforced with a woven **binding** to keep it from tearing.
39.23 was reinforced with a woven **binding** to keep it from tearing.
Num 6. 5 He is **bound** by the vow for the full time that he
15.15 come, the same rules are **binding** on you and on the
2 Sam 3.34 His hands were not tied, And his feet were not **bound;**
2 Chr 2.16 all the cedars you need, **bind** them together in rafts, and
Job 13.27 You **bind** chains on my feet;
33.11 He **binds** chains on my feet;
36. 8 But if people are **bound** in chains, suffering for what they
40.13 **bind** them in the world of the dead.
Ps 149. 8 to **bind** their kings in chains, their leaders in chains of iron;
Is 52. 2 Undo the chains that **bind** you, captive people of Zion!
Lam 3. 7 He has **bound** me in chains;
Nah 1.13 Assyria's power over you and break the chains that **bind** you."
Mt 23.16 'If someone swears by the Temple, he isn't **bound** by his vow;
23.16 if he swears by the gold in the Temple, he is **bound.'**
23.18 'If someone swears by the altar, he isn't **bound** by his vow;
23.18 if he swears by the gift on the altar, he is **bound.'**
Lk 13.16 descendant of Abraham whom Satan has kept **bound** up for eighteen
Jn 18.12 the Jewish guards arrested Jesus, **bound** him, [13]and took him
18.24 Annas sent him, still **bound,** to Caiaphas the High Priest.
21.18 hands and someone else will **bind** you and take you where you
Acts 21.33 Paul, arrested him, and ordered him to be **bound** with two chains.
28.20 matter of fact, I am **bound** in chains like this for the
Rom 7. 2 married woman, for example, is **bound** by the law to her
7. 2 then she is free from the law that **bound** her to him.
Eph 4. 3 Spirit gives by means of the peace that **binds** you together.
Col 2.14 of our debts with its **binding** rules and did away with it
3.14 add love, which **binds** all things together in perfect unity.
Jude 6 they are **bound** with eternal chains in the darkness below,
Rev 9.14 "Release the four angels who are **bound** at the great river

BIRD

Gen 1.20 of living beings, and let the air be filled with **birds."**
1.21 of creatures that live in the water, and all kinds of **birds.**
1.22 fill the sea, and he told the **birds** to increase in number.
1.26 the fish, the **birds,** and all animals, domestic and wild,
1.28 in charge of the fish, the **birds,** and all the wild animals.
1.30 animals and for all the **birds** I have provided grass and
2.19 the ground and formed all the animals and all the **birds.**
2.20 So the man named all the **birds** and all the animals;
6. 7 also the animals and the **birds,** because I am sorry that I
6.19 and of every kind of **bird,** in order to keep them alive.
7. 3 Take also seven pairs of each kind of **bird.**
7. 3 every kind of animal and **bird** will be kept alive to
7. 8 kind of animal and **bird,** whether ritually clean or unclean,

Gen	7.14	domestic and wild, large and small, and every kind of **bird.**
	7.21	the earth died—every **bird,** every animal, and every person.
	7.23	living beings on the earth—human beings, animals, and **birds.**
	8.17	Take all the **birds** and animals out with you, so that
	8.19	All the animals and **birds** went out of the boat in groups
	8.20	of ritually clean animal and **bird,** and burnt them whole as a
	9. 2	All the animals, **birds,** and fish will live in fear of you.
	9.10	with all living beings—all **birds** and all animals—everything
	15.10	but he did not cut up the **birds.**
	40.17	of pastries for the king, and the **birds** were eating them."
	40.19	your body on a pole, and the **birds** will eat your flesh."
Lev	1.14	the man is offering a **bird** as a burnt-offering, it must be
	5. 8	priest, who will first offer the **bird** for the sin-offering.
	5.10	he shall offer the second **bird** as a burnt-offering,
	7.26	they must never use the blood of **birds** or animals for food.
	11.13	You must not eat any of the following **birds:**
	11.46	the law about animals and **birds,** about everything that lives
	14. 4	shall order two ritually clean **birds** to be brought, together
	14. 5	shall order one of the **birds** to be killed over a clay
	14. 6	He shall take the other **bird** and dip it, together with the
	14. 6	and the hyssop, in the blood of the **bird** that was killed.
	14. 7	He shall let the live **bird** fly away over the open fields.
	14.49	house, he shall take two **birds,** some cedar-wood, a red cord,
	14.50	shall kill one of the **birds** over a clay bowl containing
	14.51	red cord, and the live **bird** and shall dip them
	14.51	in the blood of the **bird** that was killed
	14.52	purify the house with the **bird's** blood, the fresh water,
	14.52	the live **bird,** the cedar-wood, the hyssop,
	14.53	he shall let the live **bird** fly away outside the city over
	17.13	hunts an animal or a **bird** which is ritually clean, he must
	20.25	clear distinction between animals and **birds** that are
	20.25	Do not eat unclean animals or **birds.**
Deut	4.17	man or woman, [17]animal or **bird,** [18]reptile or fish.
	14.11	"You may eat any clean **bird.**
	14.12	But these are the kinds of **birds** you are not to eat:
	22. 6	you happen to find a **bird's** nest in a tree or on
	22. 6	the ground with the mother **bird** sitting either on the eggs
	22. 6	or with her young, you are not to take the mother **bird.**
	22. 7	You may take the young **birds,**
	22. 7	you must let the mother **bird** go, so that you will live
	28.26	When you die, **birds** and wild animals will come and eat
1 Sam	17.44	I will give your body to the **birds** and animals to eat."
	17.46	of the Philistine soldiers to the **birds** and animals to eat.
	26.20	Why should he hunt me down like a wild **bird?"**
2 Sam	21.10	day she would keep the **birds** away from the corpses, and at
1 Kgs	4.33	he talked about animals, **birds,** reptiles, and fish.
Job	12. 7	Even **birds** and animals have much they could teach you;
	28.21	No living creature can see it, Not even a **bird** in flight.
	35.11	to God, who makes us wise, wiser than any animal or **bird.**
	41. 5	a pet **bird,** like something to amuse your servant-girls?
Ps	8. 8	the **birds** and the fish and the creatures in the seas.
	11. 1	me, "Fly away like a **bird** to the mountains, [2]because the
	50.11	All the wild **birds** are mine and all living things in the
	78.27	his people he sent down **birds,** as many as the grains of
	102. 6	I am like a wild **bird** in the desert, like an owl
	102. 7	I am like a lonely **bird** on a house-top.
	104.12	In the trees near by, the **birds** make their nests and sing.
	104.17	There the **birds** build their nests;
	124. 7	We have escaped like a **bird** from a hunter's trap;
	148.10	all animals, tame and wild, reptiles and **birds.**
Prov	1.17	spread a net when the **bird** you want to catch is watching,
	6. 5	of the trap like a **bird** or a deer escaping from a
	7.23	He was like a **bird** going into a net—he did not
	26. 2	They are like **birds** that fly by and never settle.
	27. 8	man away from home is like a **bird** away from its nest.
Ecc	9.12	Like **birds** suddenly caught in a trap, like fish caught in a
	10.20	A **bird** might carry the message and tell them what you said.
	12. 4	but even the song of a **bird** will wake you from sleep.
Is	10.14	the world were like a **bird's** nest, and I gathered their
	16. 2	aimlessly to and fro, like **birds** driven from their nest.
	18. 6	will be left exposed to the **birds** and the wild animals.
	18. 6	In summer the **birds** will feed on them, and in winter, the
	31. 5	Just as a **bird** hovers over its nest to protect its young,
Jer	4.25	even the **birds** had flown away.
	5.26	who spread nets to catch **birds,** but they have set their
	5.27	hunter fills his cage with **birds,** they have filled their
	7.33	will be food for the **birds** and wild animals, and there will
	9.10	**birds** and wild animals have fled and gone."
	12. 4	Animals and **birds** are dying because of the wickedness of our people,
	12. 9	people are like a **bird** attacked from all sides by hawks.
	15. 3	**birds** will eat them, and wild animals will devour what is
	16. 4	bodies will be food for the **birds** and the wild animals.
	17.11	dishonestly is like a **bird** that hatches eggs it didn't lay.
	19. 7	their corpses to the **birds** and the wild animals as food.
	34.20	and their corpses will be eaten by **birds** and wild animals.
	50.39	be haunted by demons and evil spirits, and by unclean **birds.**
Lam	3.52	"I was trapped like a **bird** by enemies who had no cause
Ezek	17.23	**Birds** of every kind will live there and find shelter in its
	29. 5	I will give it to the **birds** and animals for food.
	31. 6	Every kind of **bird** built nests in its branches;
	31.13	The **birds** will come and perch on the fallen tree, and
	32. 4	ground and bring all the **birds** and animals of the world to
	38.20	Every fish and **bird,** every animal large and small, and
	39. 4	let their bodies be food for all the **birds** and wild animals.
	39.17	"Mortal man, call all the **birds** and animals to come from
	39.19	these people like sacrifices, the **birds** and animals are to
	44.31	priests must not eat any **bird** or animal that dies a natural
Dan	2.38	inhabited earth and ruler over all the animals and **birds.**
	4.12	rested in its shade, **birds** built nests in its branches,
	4.14	the animals from under it and the **birds** out of its branches.
Dan	4.21	under it, and **birds** made their nests in its branches.
	4.33	and his nails as long as **birds'** claws.
	7. 6	wings, like the wings of a **bird,** and it had four heads.
Hos	2.18	all the wild animals and **birds,** so that they will not harm
	4. 3	All the animals and **birds,** and even the fish, will die."
	7.12	out a net and catch them like **birds** as they go by.
	9. 8	Yet wherever I go, you try to trap me like a **bird.**
	9.11	will fly away like a **bird,** and there will be no more
	11.11	come from Egypt, as swiftly as **birds,** and from Assyria, like
Amos	3. 5	Does a **bird** get caught in a trap if the trap has
Zeph	1. 3	on earth, [3]all human beings and animals, **birds** and fish.
Mt	6.26	Look at the **birds:**
	6.26	Aren't you worth much more than **birds?**
	8.20	"Foxes have holes, and **birds** have nests, but the Son of
	13. 4	fell along the path, and the **birds** came and ate it up.
	13.32	becomes a tree, so that **birds** come and make their nests
Mk	4. 4	fell along the path, and the **birds** came and ate it up.
	4.32	such large branches that the **birds** come and make their nests
Lk	8. 5	where it was stepped on, and the **birds** ate it up.
	9.58	"Foxes have holes, and **birds** have nests, but the Son of
	12.24	You are worth so much more than **birds!**
	13.19	a tree, and the **birds** make their nests in its branches."
Acts	10.12	In it were all kinds of animals, reptiles, and wild **birds.**
	11. 6	and saw domesticated and wild animals, reptiles, and wild **birds.**
Rom	1.23	to look like mortal man or **birds** or animals or reptiles.
1 Cor	15.39	one kind of flesh, animals another, **birds** another, and fish
Jas	3. 7	tamed all other creatures—wild animals and **birds,** reptiles
Rev	18. 2	all kinds of filthy and hateful **birds** live in her.
	19.17	shouted in a loud voice to all the **birds** flying in midair:
	19.21	and all the **birds** ate all they could of their flesh.

BIRTH

Gen	3.16	your trouble in pregnancy and your pain in giving **birth.**
	4. 2	Later she gave **birth** to another son, Abel.
	4.20	Adah gave **birth** to Jabal, who was the ancestor of those
	4.22	Zillah gave **birth** to Tubal Cain, who made all kinds of
	25.13	Abraham, [13]had the following sons, listed in the order of their **birth:**
	25.23	You will give **birth** to two rival peoples.
	25.24	time came for her to give **birth,** and she had twin sons.
	29.32	Leah became pregnant and gave **birth** to a son.
	29.33	She became pregnant again and gave **birth** to another son.
	29.34	Once again she became pregnant and gave **birth** to another son.
	29.35	Then she became pregnant again and gave **birth** to another son.
	30.23	She became pregnant and gave **birth** to a son.
	30.25	After the **birth** of Joseph, Jacob said to Laban, "Let me
	38.27	came for her to give **birth,** it was discovered that she was
Ex	1.16	help the Hebrew women give **birth,"** he said to them, "kill
	1.19	they give **birth** easily, and their babies are born before
	28.10	in the order of their **birth,** with six on one stone and
Lev	12. 2	days after a woman gives **birth** to a son, she is ritually
	12. 5	days after a woman gives **birth** to a daughter, she is
	12. 7	This, then, is what a woman must do after giving **birth.**
Num	11.12	I didn't create them or bring them to **birth!**
Deut	28.54	most refined man of noble **birth** will become so desperate
	28.56	most refined woman of noble **birth,** so rich that she has
Judg	13. 5	from the day of his **birth** he will be dedicated to God
	13.24	The woman gave **birth** to a son and named him Samson.
1 Sam	1.20	it was that she became pregnant and gave **birth** to a son.
	4.19	were dead, she suddenly went into labour and gave **birth.**
2 Sam	3. 2	in the order of their **birth,** were born to David at Hebron:
1 Kgs	3.17	same house, and I gave **birth** to a baby boy at home
	3.18	my child was born she also gave **birth** to a baby boy.
2 Kgs	4.17	about that time the following year she gave **birth** to a son.
	19. 3	who is ready to give **birth,** but is too weak to do
1 Chr	4. 9	him the name Jabez, because his **birth** had been very painful.
	7.16	Maacah, Machir's wife, gave **birth** to two sons, whom
Job	21.10	Yes, all their cattle breed and give **birth** without trouble.
	39. 1	Have you watched wild deer give **birth?**
	39. 2	Do you know the time for their **birth?**
Ps	22. 9	who brought me safely through **birth,** and when I was a baby,
Ecc	3. 2	He sets the time for **birth** and the time for death, the
Is	26.18	We were in pain and agony, but we gave **birth** to nothing.
	37. 3	who is ready to give **birth,** but is too weak to do
	66. 7	a woman who suddenly gives **birth** to a child, without ever
	66. 9	people to the point of **birth** and not let them be born."
Jer	13.21	You will be in pain like a woman giving **birth.**
	20.14	Forget the day my mother gave me **birth!**
	30. 6	Can a man give **birth** to a child?
	31. 8	with them, pregnant women and those about to give **birth.**
Hos	1. 3	After the **birth** of their first child, a son, [4]the Lord said
Mic	4.10	Jerusalem, like a woman giving **birth,** for now you will have
	5. 3	enemies until the woman who is to give **birth** has her son.
Mt	1.12	exile in Babylon to the **birth** of Jesus, the following ancestors
	1.17	and fourteen from then to the **birth** of the Messiah.
	1.18	This was how the **birth** of Jesus Christ took place.
	1.25	sexual relations with her before she gave **birth** to her son.
Lk	1.15	From his very **birth** he will be filled with the Holy Spirit,
	1.31	will become pregnant and give **birth** to a son,
	1.57	Elizabeth to have her baby, and she gave **birth** to a son.
	2. 7	She gave **birth** to her first son, wrapped him in strips of
Jn	16.21	woman is about to give **birth,** she is sad because her hour
Acts	14. 8	who had been lame from **birth** and had never been able to
	15.23	all our brothers of Gentile **birth** who live in Antioch, Syria,
	22.28	"But I am one by **birth,"** Paul answered.
1 Cor	15. 8	even though I am like someone whose **birth** was abnormal.
Gal	2.15	Indeed, we are Jews by **birth** and not "Gentile sinners,"
Eph	2.11	Gentiles by **birth**—called "the uncircumcised" by the Jews,
Phil	3. 5	I am an Israelite by **birth,** of the tribe of Benjamin,
Tit	3. 5	Spirit, who gives us new **birth** and new life by washing us.

Heb 7. 3 no record of his **birth** or of his death.
Jas 1.15 Then his evil desire conceives and gives **birth** to sin;
1.15 and sin, when it is full-grown, gives **birth** to death.
Rev 12. 2 She was soon to give **birth,** and the pains and suffering
12. 5 Then she gave **birth** to a son, who will rule over all
12.13 began to pursue the woman who had given **birth** to the boy.

BIRTHDAY

Gen 40.20 On his **birthday** three days later the king gave a banquet
Mt 14. 6 On Herod's **birthday** the daughter of Herodias danced
Mk 6.21 It was on Herod's **birthday,** when he gave a feast for all

BIRTHPLACE

Lk 2. 4 Bethlehem in Judaea, the **birthplace** of King David.

BISCUIT

Ex 16.31 small white seed, and tasted like **biscuits** made with honey.
29. 2 it, and some in the form of **biscuits** brushed with oil.
29.23 made with olive-oil and one made without it and one **biscuit.**
Lev 2. 4 mixed with olive-oil or **biscuits** brushed with olive-oil.
7.12 flour mixed with olive-oil or **biscuits** brushed with
8.26 made with oil, and one **biscuit,** and he put them on top
Num 6.15 mixed with olive-oil and **biscuits** brushed with olive-oil,
6.19 loaf of bread and one **biscuit** from the basket, into the

AV BISHOP see CHURCH LEADER

BIT

2 Kgs 19.28 through your nose and a **bit** in your mouth, and take you
Ps 32. 9 be controlled with a **bit** and bridle to make it submit."
Is 37.29 through your nose and a **bit** in your mouth and will take
Jas 3. 3 We put a **bit** into the mouth of a horse to make

BITE

Gen 3.15 Her offspring will crush your head, and you will **bite** their heel."
Num 21. 6 snakes among the people, and many Israelites were **bitten**
21. 8 so that anyone who was **bitten** could look at it and be
21. 9 Anyone who had been **bitten** would look at the bronze snake
Deut 32.24 animals to attack them, and poisonous snakes to **bite** them.
Job 20.16 it kills him like the **bite** of a deadly snake.
37. 9 come from the south, and the **biting** cold from the north.
Prov 23.32 will feel as if you had been **bitten** by a poisonous snake.
Ecc 10. 8 if you break through a wall, a snake **bites** you.
10.11 snake is of no use if you let the snake **bite** first.
Jer 8.17 snakes that cannot be charmed, and they will **bite** you."
Amos 5.19 his hand on the wall—only to be **bitten** by a snake!
9. 3 of the sea, I will command the sea-monster to **bite** them.
Rev 16.10 and people **bit** their tongues because of their pain,

BITTER

Gen 27.34 he cried out loudly and **bitterly** and said, "Give me your
Ex 12. 8 be roasted, and eaten with **bitter** herbs and with bread made
15.23 the water there was so **bitter** that they could not drink it.
Num 5.17 Lord's presence and put it in the water to make it **bitter.**
5.18 the bowl containing the **bitter** water that brings a curse.
5.23 down and wash the writing off into the bowl of **bitter** water.
5.24 which may then cause her **bitter** pain, [25]the priest shall
5.27 If she has committed adultery, the water will cause **bitter** pain;
9.11 Celebrate it with unleavened bread and **bitter** herbs.
14.39 Moses told the Israelites what the Lord had said, they mourned **bitterly.**
Deut 29.18 like a root that grows to be a **bitter** and poisonous plant.
32.32 are like vines that bear **bitter** and poisonous grapes,
Judg 8. 1 They complained **bitterly** about it.
21. 2 Loudly and **bitterly** they mourned:
Ruth 1.20 "call me Marah, because Almighty God has made my life **bitter.**
1 Sam 1. 9 and she cried **bitterly** as she prayed to the Lord.
8.18 time comes, you will complain **bitterly** because of your king,
15.32 thinking to himself, "What a **bitter** thing it is to die!"
30. 6 his men were all very **bitter** about losing their children,
2 Sam 2.26 see that in the end there will be nothing but **bitterness?**
13.36 crying, and David and his officials also wept **bitterly.**
1 Kgs 2. 8 He cursed me **bitterly** the day I went to Mahanaim, but when
11.21 As king of Edom, Hadad was an evil, **bitter** enemy of Israel.
2 Kgs 20. 3 And he began to cry **bitterly.**
2 Chr 25.10 At this they went home, **bitterly** angry with the people of Judah.
Ezra 10. 1 Israelites—men, women, and children—gathered round him, weeping **bitterly.**
Esth 4. 1 the city, wailing loudly and **bitterly,** [2]until he came to
Job 7.11 I am angry and **bitter.**
9.18 he has filled my life with **bitterness.**
10. 1 Listen to my **bitter** complaint.
13.26 You bring **bitter** charges against me, even for what I did
17. 2 I watch how **bitterly** everyone mocks me.
20.14 the food turns bitter, as **bitter** as any poison could be.
21.25 they live and die with **bitter** hearts.
27. 1 justice and makes my life **bitter**— [3]as long as God gives
Ps 6.10 My enemies will know the **bitter** shame of defeat;
73.21 When my thoughts were **bitter** and my feelings were hurt,
106.33 They made him so **bitter** that he spoke without stopping to think.
Prov 5. 4 is all over, she leaves you nothing but **bitterness** and pain.
14.10 your **bitterness** is your own.
17.25 grief to his father and **bitter** regrets to his mother.
27. 7 but when you are hungry, even **bitter** food tastes sweet.
Ecc 7.26 I found something more **bitter** than death—woman.
Is 5.20 what is bitter sweet, and what is sweet you make **bitter.**
22. 4 leave me alone to weep **bitterly** over all those of my people
33. 7 The ambassadors who tried to bring about peace are crying **bitterly.**
38. 3 And he began to cry **bitterly.**
38.15 My heart is **bitter,** and I cannot sleep.
38.17 My **bitterness** will turn into peace.
Jer 2.19 You will learn how **bitter** and wrong it is to abandon me.
6.26 Mourn with **bitter** tears as you would for an only son,
9.15 I will give my people **bitter** plants to eat and poison to
13.17 I will cry **bitterly,** and my tears will flow because the
22.10 But weep **bitterly** for Joahaz, his son;
23.15 I will give them **bitter** plants to eat and poison to drink,
31.15 "A sound is heard in Ramah, the sound of **bitter** weeping.
47. 2 everyone on earth will cry **bitterly.**
Lam 3.15 **Bitter** suffering is all he has given me for food and drink.
3.19 The thought of my pain, my homelessness, is **bitter** poison;
Ezek 3.14 and as his spirit carried me off, I felt **bitter** and angry.
27.30 They all mourn **bitterly** for you, Throwing dust on their
27.31 Their hearts are **bitter** as they weep.
Hos 12.14 The people of Israel have made the Lord **bitterly** angry;
Amos 8.10 That day will be **bitter** to the end.
Obad 16 My people have drunk a **bitter** cup of punishment on my
16 nations will drink a still more **bitter** cup of punishment;
Zeph 1.14 That will be a **bitter** day, for even the bravest soldiers
Zech 12.10 They will mourn **bitterly,** like those who have lost their first-born son.
Mt 2.18 "A sound is heard in Ramah, the sound of **bitter** weeping.
26.75 He went out and wept **bitterly.**
27.34 There they offered Jesus wine mixed with a **bitter** substance;
Lk 11.53 Pharisees began to criticize him **bitterly** and ask him questions
22.62 Peter went out and wept **bitterly.**
Acts 8.23 that you are full of **bitter** envy and are a prisoner
Rom 3.14 their speech is filled with **bitter** curses.
Eph 4.31 Get rid of all **bitterness,** passion, and anger.
Heb 12.15 no one become like a **bitter** plant that grows up and causes
Jas 3.11 pours out sweet water and **bitter** water from the same opening.
3.14 heart you are jealous, **bitter,** and selfish, don't sin against
Rev 5. 4 I cried **bitterly** because no one could be found who was
8.11 (The name of the star is **"Bitterness.")**
8.11 third of the water turned **bitter,** and many people died
8.11 from drinking the water, because it had turned **bitter.**

BLACK

Gen 30.32 flocks today and take every **black** lamb and every spotted or
30.33 or any sheep that isn't **black,** you will know that it has
30.35 he also removed all the **black** sheep.
30.40 of the streaked and **black** animals of Laban's flock.
Ex 10.15 They covered the ground until it was **black** with them;
Song 5.11 his hair is wavy, **black** as a raven.
Jer 13.23 Can a **black** man change the colour of his skin, or a
Lam 4. 8 Now they lie unknown in the streets, their faces **blackened** in death;
Joel 2. 2 will be a dark and gloomy day, a **black** and cloudy day.
Zeph 1.15 of darkness and gloom, a **black** and cloudy day, [16]a day
Zech 6. 2 the second by **black** horses, [3]the third by white horses,
6. 6 The chariot pulled by the **black** horses was going north to Babylonia,
Mt 5.36 because you cannot make a single hair white or **black.**
Acts 13. 1 Barnabas, Simeon (called the **Black),** Lucius (from Cyrene),
Rev 6. 5 I looked, and there was a **black** horse.
6.12 and the sun became **black** like coarse black cloth,

BLACKSMITH

1 Sam 13.19 There were no **blacksmiths** in Israel because the
2 Kgs 24.14 the skilled workmen, including the **blacksmiths,** leaving only
24.16 thousand skilled workers, including the **blacksmiths,** all of
Is 54.16 "I create the **blacksmith,** who builds a fire and forges weapons.

BLADE

Job 5.25 as many children as there are **blades** of grass in a pasture.
Is 58. 5 your heads low like a **blade** of grass, and spread out
Mt 11. 7 A **blade** of grass bending in the wind?
Lk 7.24 A **blade** of grass bending in the wind?
Rev 8. 7 a third of the trees, and every **blade** of green grass.

BLAME

Gen 43. 9 back to you safe and sound, I will always bear the **blame.**
44.32 boy back to him, I would bear the **blame** all my life.
45. 5 not be upset or **blame** yourselves because you sold me here.
1 Sam 25.24 Let me take the **blame.**
2 Sam 14. 9 "whatever you do, my family and I will take the **blame;**
1 Kgs 2.37 Kidron, you will certainly die—and you yourself will be to **blame."**
Job 1.22 that had happened, Job did not sin by **blaming** God.
4. 6 You worshipped God, and your life was **blameless;**
12. 4 they laugh, although I am righteous and **blameless;**
32. 2 longer, because Job was justifying himself and **blaming** God.
Prov 19. 3 by their own stupid actions and then **blame** the Lord.
Ezek 18.13 He will be to **blame** for his own death.
33. 4 and kills him, then he is to **blame** for his own death.
Jon 1. 7 find out who is to **blame** for getting us into this danger."
1. 8 Who is to **blame** for this?
Mic 1. 5 Who is to **blame** for Israel's rebellion?
Acts 18. 6 "If you are lost, you yourselves must take the **blame** for it!
Phil 1.10 be free from all impurity and **blame** on the Day of Christ.
Tit 1. 6 an elder must be **blameless;**

Tit	1. 7	leader is in charge of God's work, he should be **blameless.**
Jude	16	These people are always grumbling and **blaming** others;

BLANK

Job	37.19	our minds are **blank;**

BLANKET

2 Sam	11.13	instead he slept on his **blanket** in the palace guardroom.
	20.12	from the road into the field and threw a **blanket** over it.
1 Kgs	1. 1	servants covered him with **blankets,** he could not keep warm.
2 Kgs	8.15	following day Hazael took a **blanket,** soaked it in water, and
Ps	147.16	He spreads snow like a **blanket** and scatters frost like dust.
Is	14.11	a bed of maggots and are covered with a **blanket** of worms.'
	28.20	out on, with a **blanket** too narrow to wrap himself in.

BLASPHEMY

Mt	9. 3	of the Law said to themselves, "This man is speaking **blasphemy!"**
	26.65	At this the High Priest tore his clothes and said, **"Blasphemy!**
	26.65	You have just heard his **blasphemy!**
Mk	2. 7	This is **blasphemy!**
	14.64	You heard his **blasphemy.**
Lk	5.21	to themselves, "Who is this man who speaks such **blasphemy!**
Jn	10.33	because of any good deeds, but because of your **blasphemy!**
	10.36	can you say that I **blaspheme** because I said that I am
1 Tim	1.20	this will teach them to stop their **blasphemy.**

BLAST

Ex	19.16	on the mountain, and a very loud trumpet **blast** was heard.
	20.18	the thunder and the trumpet **blast** and saw the lightning and
Num	10. 3	When long **blasts** are sounded on both trumpets, the whole
	10. 5	When short **blasts** are sounded, the tribes camped on the
	10. 6	When short **blasts** are sounded a second time, the tribes on
	10. 6	So short **blasts** are to be sounded to break camp, [7] but in
	10. 7	call the community together, long **blasts** are to be sounded.
2 Kgs	19.26	weeds growing on a roof when the hot east wind **blasts** them.
Job	39.25	At each **blast** of the trumpet they snort;
Ps	47. 5	shouts of joy and the **blast** of trumpets, as the Lord goes
Is	37.27	weeds growing on a roof when the hot east wind **blasts** them.
Jer	4.21	I see the battle raging and hear the **blasts** of trumpets?
Heb	12.19	the storm, [19] the **blast** of a trumpet, and the sound

BLAZE

Ex	15. 7	your anger **blazes** out and burns them up like straw.
Num	16.35	Lord sent a fire that **blazed** out and burnt up the 250
Deut	4.11	thick clouds of dark smoke and fire **blazing** up to the sky.
	4.20	But you are the people he rescued from Egypt, that **blazing** furnace.
Judg	9.15	If you don't, fire will **blaze** out of my thorny branches and
	9.20	But if not, may fire **blaze** out from Abimelech and burn
	9.20	May fire **blaze** out from the men of Shechem and Bethmillo and
1 Kgs	8.51	whom you brought out of Egypt, that **blazing** furnace.
Job	41.19	Flames **blaze** from his mouth, and streams of sparks fly out.
Ps	21. 9	He will destroy them like a **blazing** fire when he appears.
Jer	11. 4	of Egypt, the land that was like a **blazing** furnace to them.
Ezek	1.13	that looked like a **blazing** torch, constantly moving.
	1.13	The fire would **blaze** up and shoot out flashes of lightning.
	10. 4	the Temple, and the courtyard was **blazing** with the light.
	21.31	anger when I turn it loose on you like a **blazing** fire.
Dan	3. 6	worship will immediately be thrown into a **blazing** furnace."
	3.11	down and worship it is to be thrown into a **blazing** furnace.
	3.15	not, you will immediately be thrown into a **blazing** furnace.
	3.17	to save us from the **blazing** furnace and from your power,
	3.20	the three men up and throw them into the **blazing** furnace.
	3.21	caps, and all—and threw them into the **blazing** furnace.
	3.23	Abednego, still tied up, fell into the heart of the **blazing** fire.
	3.24	tie up three men and throw them into the **blazing** furnace?"
	3.26	up to the door of the **blazing** furnace and called out,
	7. 9	mounted on fiery wheels, was **blazing** with fire, [10] and a
	10. 6	as a flash of lightning, and his eyes **blazed** like fire.
Heb	12.18	Mount Sinai with its **blazing** fire, the darkness and the gloom,
Jas	1.11	The sun rises with its **blazing** heat and burns the plant;
Rev	1.14	white as wool, or as snow, and his eyes **blazed** like fire;
	2.18	Son of God, whose eyes **blaze** like fire, whose feet shine

BLEAT

1 Sam	15.14	Samuel asked, "Why, then, do I hear cattle mooing and sheep **bleating?"**

BLEED

Prov	30.33	If you hit someone's nose, it **bleeds.**
Mt	9.20	who had suffered from severe **bleeding** for twelve years
Mk	5.25	had suffered terribly from severe **bleeding** for twelve years,
	5.29	She touched his cloak, and her **bleeding** stopped at once;
Lk	8.43	a woman who had suffered from severe **bleeding** for twelve years;
	8.44	the edge of his cloak, and her **bleeding** stopped at once.

BLEMISH

Lev	13.39	white, it is only a **blemish** that has broken out on the

BLESS

Gen	1.22	He **blessed** them all and told the creatures that live in
	1.28	female, [28] **blessed** them, and said, "Have many children,
	2. 3	He **blessed** the seventh day and set it apart as a special
	5. 2	He created them male and female, **blessed** them, and named them "Mankind.")
	9. 1	God **blessed** Noah and his sons and said, "Have many children,
	12. 2	I will **bless** you and make your name famous,
	12. 2	so that you will be a **blessing.**
	12. 3	I will **bless** those who bless you, But I will curse those
	12. 3	And through you I will **bless** all the nations."
	14.19	bread and wine to Abram, [19] **blessed** him, and said,
	14.19	"May the Most High God, who made heaven and earth, **bless** Abram!
	17.16	I will **bless** her, and I will give you a son by
	17.16	I will **bless** her, and she will become the mother of nations,
	17.20	about Ishmael, so I will **bless** him and give him many
	18.18	nation, and through him I will **bless** all the nations.
	21. 1	The Lord **blessed** Sarah, as he had promised, [2] and she
	22.16	own name—the Lord is speaking—that I will richly **bless** you.
	22.18	bless them as I have **blessed** your descendants—all because
	24. 1	very old, and the Lord had **blessed** him in everything he did.
	24.31	You are a man whom the Lord has **blessed.**
	24.35	"The Lord has greatly **blessed** my master and made him a
	24.60	And they gave Rebecca their **blessing** in these words:
	25.11	the death of Abraham, God **blessed** his son Isaac, who lived
	26. 3	Live here, and I will be with you and **bless** you.
	26. 4	ask me to bless them as I have **blessed** your descendants.
	26. 5	I will **bless** you, because Abraham obeyed me and kept all
	26.12	times as much as he had sown, because the Lord **blessed** him.
	26.24	I will **bless** you and give you many descendants because of my
	26.29	Now it is clear that the Lord has **blessed** you."
	27. 4	eaten it, I will give you my final **blessing** before I die."
	27. 7	I will give you my **blessing** in the presence of the Lord
	27.10	to eat, and he will give you his **blessing** before he dies."
	27.12	way I will bring a curse on myself instead of a **blessing."**
	27.19	I have brought you, so that you can give me your **blessing."**
	27.23	about to give him his **blessing,** [24] but asked again, "Are
	27.25	After I have eaten it, I will give you my **blessing."**
	27.27	him, Isaac smelt his clothes—so he gave him his **blessing.**
	27.27	is like the smell of a field which the Lord has **blessed.**
	27.29	you be cursed, and may those who **bless** you be blessed."
	27.30	Isaac finished giving his **blessing,** and as soon as Jacob left,
	27.31	I have brought you, so that you can give me your **blessing."**
	27.33	I gave him my final **blessing,** and so it is his for
	27.34	loudly and bitterly and said, "Give me your **blessing** also,
	27.35	He has taken away your **blessing."**
	27.36	the first-born son, and now he has taken away my **blessing.**
	27.36	Haven't you saved a **blessing** for me?"
	27.38	"Have you only one **blessing,** father?
	27.38	**Bless** me too, father!"
	27.41	Esau hated Jacob, because his father had given Jacob the **blessing.**
	28. 3	May Almighty God **bless** your marriage and give you many children,
	28. 4	May he **bless** you and your descendants as he blessed Abraham,
	28. 6	Esau learnt that Isaac had **blessed** Jacob and sent him away
	28. 6	also learnt that when Isaac **blessed** him, he commanded him
	28.14	you and your descendants I will **bless** all the nations.
	30.27	by divination that the Lord has **blessed** me because of you.
	30.30	enormously, and the Lord has **blessed** you wherever I went.
	32.26	"I won't, unless you **bless** me," Jacob answered.
	32.29	Then he **blessed** Jacob.
	35. 9	Jacob returned from Mesopotamia, God appeared to him again and **blessed** him.
	39. 5	because of Joseph the Lord **blessed** the household of the
	39.21	Lord was with Joseph and **blessed** him, so that the jailer was
	43.29	God **bless** you, my son."
	47. 7	Jacob gave the king his **blessing,** [8] and the king asked him,
	47.10	Jacob gave the king a farewell **blessing** and left.
	48. 3	to me at Luz in the land of Canaan and **blessed** me.
	48. 9	Jacob said, "Bring them to me so that I may **bless** them."
	48.15	Then he **blessed** Joseph:
	48.15	God whom my fathers Abraham and Isaac served **bless** these boys!
	48.15	May God, who has led me to this very day, **bless** them!
	48.16	May the angel, who has rescued me from all harm, **bless**
	48.20	So he **blessed** them that day, saying,
	48.20	"The Israelites will use your names when they pronounce **blessings.**
	49.25	God who blesses you With **blessings** of rain from above
	49.25	**Blessings** of many cattle and children,
	49.26	Blessings of corn and flowers, **Blessings** of ancient mountains,
	49.26	May these **blessings** rest on the head of Joseph,
Ex	12.32	Also pray for a **blessing** on me."
	20.11	is why I, the Lord, **blessed** the Sabbath and made it holy.
	20.24	you to worship me, I will come to you and **bless** you.
	23.25	Lord your God, I will **bless** you with food and water and
	32.29	and brothers, so the Lord has given you his **blessing."**
	39.43	So Moses **blessed** them.
Lev	9.22	over the people and **blessed** them, and then stepped down.
	9.23	when they came out, they **blessed** the people, and the
	25.21	The Lord will **bless** the land in the sixth year so that
	26. 9	I will **bless** you and give you many children;
Num	6.23	use the following words in **blessing** the people of Israel:
	6.24	May the Lord **bless** you and take care of you;
	6.27	pronounce my name as a **blessing** upon the people of Israel,
	6.27	I will **bless** them."
	10.32	share with you all the **blessings** that the Lord gives us."
	22. 6	that when you pronounce a **blessing,** people are blessed, and
	22.12	on the people of Israel, because they have my **blessing."**
	23. 9	They know they are **blessed** more than other nations.
	23.11	to curse my enemies, but all you have done is **bless** them."
	23.20	I have been instructed to **bless,**

Num 23.20 And when God **blesses,** I cannot call it back.
23.25 the people of Israel, but at least don't **bless** them!"
24. 1 the Lord wanted him to **bless** the people of Israel, so he
24. 9 Whoever blesses Israel will be **blessed,** And whoever curses
24.10 enemies, but three times now you have **blessed** them instead.
Deut 2. 7 the Lord your God has **blessed** you in everything that you
7.13 He will love you and **bless** you, so that you will
7.13 he will **bless** your fields, so that you will have corn, wine,
7.13 and he will **bless** you by giving you a lot of livestock
7.13 will give you all these **blessings** in the land that he
7.14 No people in the world will be as richly **blessed** as you.
8.16 so that in the end he could **bless** you with good things.
10. 8 him as priests, and to pronounce **blessings** in his name.
11.26 the choice between a **blessing** and a curse—
11.27 a **blessing,** if you obey the commands of
11.29 you are to proclaim the **blessing** from Mount Gerizim and the
12. 7 Lord your God, who has **blessed** you, you and your families
14.24 the produce that the Lord has **blessed** you with, then do
14.29 and the Lord your God will **bless** you in everything you do.
15. 4 "The Lord your God will **bless** you in the land that he
15. 6 The Lord will **bless** you, as he has promised.
15.10 and the Lord will **bless** you in everything you do.
15.14 from what the Lord has **blessed** you with—sheep, corn, and
15.18 the Lord your God will **bless** you in all that you do.
16.10 offering in proportion to the **blessing** he has given you.
16.15 Be joyful, because the Lord has **blessed** your harvest and your work.
16.17 able, in proportion to the **blessings** that the Lord your God
21. 5 them to serve him and to pronounce **blessings** in his name.
23. 5 he turned the curse into a **blessing,** because he loved you.
23.20 the Lord your God will **bless** everything you do in the land
24.19 that the Lord your God will **bless** you in everything you do.
26.15 from your holy place in heaven and **bless** your people Israel;
26.15 **bless** also the rich and fertile land that you have given us,
27.12 Mount Gerizim when the **blessings** are pronounced on the people:
28. 2 Obey the Lord your God and all these **blessings** will be yours:
28. 3 "The Lord will **bless** your towns and your fields.
28. 4 "The Lord will **bless** you with many children, with abundant crops,
28. 5 "The Lord will **bless** your corn crops and the food you
28. 6 "The Lord will **bless** everything you do.
28. 8 "The Lord your God will **bless** your work and fill your
28. 8 He will **bless** you in the land that he is giving you.
28.12 storehouse in the sky and **bless** all your work, so that you
28.47 The Lord **blessed** you in every way, but you would not
30. 1 have now given you a choice between a **blessing** and a curse.
30.16 The Lord your God will **bless** you in the land that you
30.19 life and death, between God's **blessing** and God's curse, and
33. 1 These are the **blessings** that Moses, the man of God,
33.13 "May the Lord **bless** their land with rain And with water
33.14 May their land be **blessed** with sun-ripened fruit, Rich
33.16 with all that is good, **Blessed** by the goodness of the Lord,
33.16 May these **blessings** come to the tribe of Joseph, Because he
33.23 "Naphtali is richly **blessed** by the Lord's good favour;
33.24 "Asher is **blessed** more than the other tribes.
Josh 8.33 do this when the time came for them to receive the **blessing.**
8.34 the whole Law, including the **blessings** and the curses, just
14.13 Joshua **blessed** Caleb son of Jephunneh and gave him the
17.14 There are very many of us because the Lord has **blessed** us."
22. 6 Joshua sent them home with his **blessing** and with these words:
24.10 listen to Balaam, so he **blessed** you, and in this way I
Judg 13.24 The child grew and the Lord **blessed** him.
17. 2 His mother said, "May the Lord **bless** you, my son!"
Ruth 1. 6 heard that the Lord had **blessed** his people by giving them a
2. 4 "The Lord **bless** you!"
2.19 May God **bless** the man who took an interest in you!"
2.20 "May the Lord **bless** Boaz!"
3.10 "The Lord **bless** you," he said.
4.13 The Lord **blessed** her, and she became pregnant and had a son.
1 Sam 2.20 Then Eli would **bless** Elkanah and his wife, and say to Elkanah,
2.21 The Lord did **bless** Hannah, and she had three more sons
2.32 with envy on all the **blessings** I will give to the other
9.12 he gets there, because he has to **bless** the sacrifice first.
15.13 up to Saul, who greeted him, saying, "The Lord **bless** you,
23.21 Saul answered, "May the Lord **bless** you for being so
24.19 The Lord **bless** you for what you have done to me today!
25.31 And when the Lord has **blessed** you, sir, please do not forget
26.25 Saul said to David, "God **bless** you, my son!
2 Sam 2. 5 "May the Lord **bless** you for showing your loyalty to your
6.11 months, and the Lord **blessed** Obed Edom and his family.
6.12 Covenant Box the Lord had **blessed** Obed Edom's family and all
6.18 finished offering the sacrifices, he **blessed** the people in
7.29 I ask you to **bless** my descendants so that they will
7.29 and your **blessing** will rest on my descendants
14.22 David in respect, and said, "God **bless** you, Your Majesty!
16.12 misery and give me some **blessings** to take the place of his
19.39 gave him his **blessing,** and Barzillai went back home.
21. 3 done to you, so that you will **bless** the Lord's people."
22.21 he **blesses** me because I am innocent.
23. 5 that is how God will **bless** my descendants, because he has
1 Kgs 2.45 But he will **bless** me and he will make David's kingdom
8.14 Solomon turned to face them, and he asked God's **blessing** on them.
8.55 he asked God's **blessings** on all the people assembled there.
8.66 happy because of all the **blessings** that the Lord had given
1 Chr 4.10 to the God of Israel, **"Bless** me, God, and give me much
13.14 three months, and the Lord **blessed** Obed Edom's family and
16. 2 finished offering the sacrifices, he **blessed** the people in
17.27 I ask you to **bless** my descendants so that they will
17.27 blessed them, and your **blessing** will rest on them for ever."
23.13 Lord, to serve him, and to **bless** the people in his name.
1 Chr 26. 4 also Obed Edom, whom God **blessed** by giving him eight sons,
2 Chr 1. 1 the Lord his God **blessed** him and made him very powerful.
6. 3 The king turned to face them and asked God's **blessing** on them.
6.41 **Bless** your priests in all they do, and may all your people
7.10 were happy about all the **blessings** that the Lord had given
17. 3 The Lord **blessed** Jehoshaphat because he followed the
26. 5 living, he served the Lord faithfully, and God **blessed** him.
26.18 the Lord God, and you no longer have his **blessing."**
30.27 The priests and the Levites asked the Lord's **blessing** on the people.
31.10 We have all this because the Lord has **blessed** his people."
Ezra 6.10 of Heaven and pray for his **blessing** on me and my sons.
7. 6 Because Ezra had the **blessing** of the Lord his God, the
8.22 told him that our God **blesses** everyone who trusts him, but
Neh 9.35 With your **blessing,** kings ruled your people when they
13. 2 curse Israel, but our God turned the curse into a **blessing.**
Job 1.10 You **bless** everything he does, and you have given him enough
22.21 if you do, then he will **bless** you.
42.12 The Lord **blessed** the last part of Job's life
42.12 even more than he had **blessed** the first.
Ps 3. 8 Victory comes from the Lord— may he **bless** his people.
4. 6 "Give us more **blessings,** O Lord.
5.12 You **bless** those who obey you, Lord;
18.20 he **blesses** me because I am innocent.
21. 3 came to him with great **blessings** and set a crown of gold
21. 6 Your **blessings** are with him for ever and your presence
24. 5 The Lord will **bless** them and save them;
28. 9 Save your people, Lord, and **bless** those who are yours.
29.11 The Lord gives strength to his people and **blesses** them with peace.
37.22 Those who are **blessed** by the Lord will possess the land,
37.26 and lends to others, and his children are a **blessing.**
45. 2 God has always **blessed** you.
62. 4 You speak words of **blessing,** but in your heart you curse him.
65. 4 things of your house, the **blessings** of your sacred Temple.
67. 1 God, be merciful to us and **bless** us;
67. 6 God, our God, has **blessed** us.
67. 7 God has **blessed** us;
72.15 may God's **blessings** be on him always!
72.17 nations ask God to bless them as he has **blessed** the king.
84. 9 **Bless** our king, O God, the king you have chosen.
84.11 and glorious king, **blessing** us with kindness and honour.
87. 7 and sing, "In Zion is the source of all our **blessings."**
90.17 Lord our God, may your **blessings** be with us.
92.10 you have **blessed** me with happiness.
103. 4 keeps me from the grave and **blesses** me with love and mercy.
104.13 on the hills, and the earth is filled with your **blessings.**
107.38 He **blessed** his people, and they had many children;
109.17 He hated to give blessings—may no one **bless** him!
109.28 They may curse me, but you will **bless** me.
112. 2 his descendants will be **blessed.**
115.12 The Lord remembers us and will **bless** us;
115.12 he will **bless** the people of Israel and all the priests of
115.13 He will **bless** everyone who honours him, the great and
115.15 May you be **blessed** by the Lord, who made heaven and earth!
118.26 May God **bless** the one who comes in the name of the
118.26 From the Temple of the Lord we **bless** you.
119.135 **Bless** me with your presence and teach me your laws.
127. 3 they are a real **blessing.**
128. 4 A man who obeys the Lord will surely be **blessed** like this.
128. 5 May the Lord **bless** you from Zion!
129. 8 No one who passes by will say, "May the Lord **bless** you!
129. 8 We **bless** you in the name of the Lord."
132.16 I will **bless** her priests in all they do, and her people
133. 3 the Lord has promised his **blessing**— life that never ends.
134. 3 May the Lord, who made heaven and earth, **bless** you from Zion!
147.13 he **blesses** your people.
Prov 3.33 homes of wicked men, but **blesses** the homes of the righteous.
10. 6 A good man will receive **blessings.**
10. 7 will be remembered as a **blessing,** but the wicked will soon
10.22 It is the Lord's **blessing** that makes you wealthy.
11.11 A city becomes great when righteous men give it their **blessing;**
16. 3 Ask the Lord to **bless** your plans, and you will be
22. 9 You will be **blessed** for it.
Is 19.24 and these three nations will be a **blessing** to all the world.
19.25 The Lord Almighty will **bless** them and say,
19.25 "I will **bless** you, Egypt, my people;
44. 3 on your children and my **blessing** on your descendants.
45. 7 I bring both **blessing** and disaster.
48.18 Then **blessings** would have flowed for you like a stream that
51. 2 Abraham, he was childless, but I **blessed** him and gave him children;
55. 3 with you and give you the **blessings** I promised to David.
56. 2 I will **bless** those who always observe the Sabbath and do
56. 2 I will **bless** those who do nothing evil."
61. 9 will know That they are a people whom I have **blessed."**
63. 7 He has richly **blessed** the people of Israel because of his
65. 9 I will **bless** the Israelites who belong to the tribe of Judah,
65.16 for a blessing will ask to be **blessed** by the Faithful God.
65.23 I will **bless** them and their descendants for all time to come.
Jer 4. 2 will ask me to **bless** them, and they will praise me."
16. 5 I will no longer **bless** my people with peace or show them
17. 7 "But I will **bless** the person who puts his trust in me.
30.19 By my **blessing** they will increase in numbers;
30.19 my **blessing** will bring them honour.
31.23 'May the Lord **bless** the sacred hill of Jerusalem, the holy
Ezek 16.27 to punish you and to take away your share of my **blessing.**
34.26 "I will **bless** them and let them live round my sacred hill.
34.26 There I will **bless** them with showers of rain when they need
44.30 as an offering, and my **blessing** will rest on their homes.

Hos	10.12	plant righteousness, and reap the **blessings** that your devotion to me
	10.12	your Lord, and I will come and pour out **blessings** upon you.'
	12. 4	He wept and asked for a **blessing.**
	14. 8	I am the source of all their **blessings."**
Joel	2.14	God will change his mind and **bless** you with abundant crops.
Mic	2. 9	and you have robbed their children of my **blessings** for ever.
Hag	2.19	have not yet produced, yet from now on I will **bless** you."
Zech	7. 2	to pray for the Lord's **blessing** [3]and to ask the priests and
	8.12	I will give all these **blessings** to the people of my nation
	8.13	'May you receive the same **blessings** that came to Judah and Israel!'
	8.15	I am planning to **bless** the people of Jerusalem and Judah.
	8.21	to worship the Lord Almighty and pray for his **blessing.**
	8.22	Jerusalem to worship the Lord Almighty, and to pray for his **blessing.**
	9.12	you twice over with **blessing** for all you have suffered.
Mt	21. 9	God **bless** him who comes in the name of the Lord!
	23.39	until you say, 'God **bless** him who comes in the name
	25.34	on his right, 'Come, you that are **blessed** by my Father!
Mk	10.16	placed his hands on each of them, and **blessed** them.
	11. 9	God **bless** him who comes in the name of the Lord!
	11.10	God **bless** the coming kingdom of King David, our father!
	14.61	"Are you the Messiah, the Son of the **Blessed** God?"
Lk	1.28	The Lord is with you and has greatly **blessed** you!"
	1.42	"You are the most **blessed** of all women,
	1.42	and **blessed** is the child you will bear!
	2.34	Simeon **blessed** them and said to Mary, his mother,
	2.40	he was full of wisdom, and God's **blessings** were upon him.
	6.28	those who hate you, [28]**bless** those who curse you, and pray
	6.32	the people who love you, why should you receive a **blessing?**
	6.33	those who do good to you, why should you receive a **blessing?**
	6.34	you hope to get it back, why should you receive a **blessing?**
	13.35	comes when you say, 'God **bless** him who comes in the name
	14.14	and you will be **blessed,** because they are not able to
	19.38	"God **bless** the king who comes in the name of the Lord!
	24.30	to eat with them, took the bread, and said the **blessing;**
	24.50	far as Bethany, where he raised his hands and **blessed** them.
	24.51	As he was **blessing** them, he departed from them and was
Jn	1.16	he has blessed us all, giving us one **blessing** after another.
	12.13	God **bless** him who comes in the name of the Lord!
	12.13	God **bless** the King of Israel!"
Acts	3.25	'Through your descendants I will **bless** all the people on earth.'
	3.26	him first to you, to **bless** you by making every one of
	4.33	the Lord Jesus, and God poured rich **blessings** on them all.
	6. 8	Stephen, a man richly **blessed** by God and full of power,
	11.23	and saw how God had **blessed** the people, he was glad
	13.34	you the sacred and sure **blessings** that I promised to David.'
	20.32	and give you the **blessings** God has for all his people.
Rom	1.11	to share a spiritual **blessing** with you to make you strong.
	8.17	we will possess the **blessings** he keeps for his people,
	10.12	same Lord of all and richly **blesses** all who call to him.
	11.12	of the Jews brought rich **blessings** to the world, and
	11.12	their spiritual poverty brought rich **blessings** to the Gentiles.
	11.12	how much greater the **blessings** will be when the complete number
	11.29	God does not change his mind about whom he chooses and **blesses.**
	12.14	Ask God to **bless** those who persecute you—
	12.14	yes, ask him to **bless,** not to curse.
	15.27	the Jews shared their spiritual **blessings** with the Gentiles, the
	15.27	Gentiles ought to use their material **blessings** to help the Jews.
	15.29	I shall come with a full measure of the **blessing** of Christ.
1 Cor	1. 7	failed to receive a single **blessing,** as you wait for our
	4.12	When we are cursed, we **bless;**
	9.23	for the gospel's sake, in order to share in its **blessings.**
2 Cor	1.11	many prayers for us will be answered, and God will **bless** us;
	1.15	to visit you, in order that you might be **blessed** twice.
	11.31	and Father of the Lord Jesus—**blessed** be his name for ever!
Gal	3. 8	"Through you God will **bless** all mankind."
	3. 9	Abraham believed and was **blessed;**
	3. 9	so all who believe are **blessed** as he was.
	3.14	in order that the **blessing** which God promised to Abraham might
Eph	1. 3	union with Christ he has **blessed** us
	1. 3	by giving us every spiritual **blessing** in the heavenly world.
	1.18	how rich are the wonderful **blessings** he promises his people,
	3. 6	the Gentiles have a part with the Jews in God's **blessings;**
Col	1. 6	The gospel keeps bringing **blessings** and is spreading throughout
1 Tim	1.11	to announce, the Good News from the glorious and **blessed** God.
	6.15	right time by God, the **blessed** and only Ruler, the King
Tit	2.13	as we wait for the **blessed** Day we hope for,
Phlm	6	deeper understanding of every **blessing** which we have in our life
Heb	6. 7	God **blesses** the soil which drinks in the rain that often
	6. 9	you have the better **blessings** that belong to your salvation.
	6.14	you that I will **bless** you and give you many descendants."
	7. 1	Melchizedek met him and **blessed** him, [2]and Abraham gave him
	7. 6	a tenth from Abraham and **blessed** him, the man who received
	7. 7	the one who blesses is greater than the one who is **blessed.**
	9.15	by God may receive the eternal **blessings** that God has promised.
	11.20	faith that made Isaac promise **blessings** for the future to Jacob
	11.21	was faith that made Jacob **bless** each of the sons of Joseph
	12.17	you know, he wanted to receive his father's **blessing;**
Jas	1.25	that person will be **blessed** by God in what he does.
	2.16	What good is there in your saying to them, "God **bless** you!
1 Pet	1. 4	to possessing the rich **blessings** that God keeps for his people.
	1.13	your hope completely on the **blessing** which will be given you
	2.19	God will **bless** you for this, if you endure the pain
	2.20	even when you have done right, God will **bless** you for it.
	3. 9	instead, pay back with a **blessing,**
	3. 9	because a **blessing** is what God promised to give
Rev	20. 6	Happy and greatly **blessed** are those who are included in this

BLEW see BLOW (1)

BLIND

Gen	19.11	all the men outside with **blindness,** so that they couldn't
	27. 1	Isaac was now old and had become **blind.**
Ex	4.11	Who gives him sight or makes him **blind?**
	23. 8	for a bribe makes people **blind** to what is right and ruins
Lev	19.14	something in front of a **blind** man so as to make him
	21.18	no one who is **blind,** lame, disfigured, or deformed;
	22.22	Lord any animal that is **blind** or crippled or mutilated, or
	24.20	blinds him in one eye, one of his eyes shall be **blinded;**
	26.16	fevers that will make you **blind** and cause your life to waste
Deut	15.21	they are crippled or **blind** or have any other serious defect,
	16.19	to accept bribes, for gifts **blind** the eyes even of wise and
	27.18	on anyone who leads a **blind** man in the wrong direction.'
	28.28	he will strike you with **blindness** and confusion.
	28.29	in broad daylight like a **blind** man, and you will not be
1 Sam	2.33	But he will become **blind** and lose all hope, and all your
	3. 2	Eli, who was now almost **blind,** was sleeping in his own room;
	4.15	(Eli was now ninety-eight years old and almost completely **blind.)**
2 Sam	5. 6	even the **blind** and the crippled could keep you out."
	5. 8	the water tunnel and attack those poor **blind** cripples."
	5. 8	why it is said, "The **blind** and the crippled cannot enter
1 Kgs	14. 4	Old age had made Ahijah **blind.**
2 Kgs	6.18	Elisha prayed, "O Lord, strike these men **blind!"**
	6.18	The Lord answered his prayer and struck them **blind.**
Job	9.24	He made all the judges **blind.**
	17. 7	My grief has almost made me **blind;**
	23.16	me afraid— even though the darkness has made me **blind.**
	29.15	I was eyes for the **blind,** and feet for the lame.
	40.24	Who can **blind** his eyes and capture him?
Ps	69.23	Strike them with **blindness!**
	146. 8	The Lord sets prisoners free [8]and gives sight to the **blind.**
Is	6.10	ears deaf, and their eyes **blind,** so that they cannot see or
	29. 9	Go ahead and be **blind!**
	29.18	read aloud, and the **blind,** who have been living in darkness,
	35. 5	The **blind** will be able to see, and the deaf will hear.
	42. 7	open the eyes of the **blind** and set free those who sit
	42.16	"I will lead my **blind** people by roads they have never travelled.
	42.18	Look closely, you that are **blind!**
	42.19	Is anyone more **blind** than my servant, more deaf than the
	43. 8	They have eyes, but they are **blind;**
	44. 9	who worship these gods are **blind** and ignorant—and they will
	56.10	"All the leaders, who are supposed to warn my people, are **blind!**
	59.10	is only darkness, [10]and we grope about like **blind** people.
Jer	31. 8	The **blind** and the lame will come with them, pregnant women
Lam	4.14	wandered through the streets like **blind** men, so stained with
Zeph	1.17	on mankind that everyone will grope about like a **blind** man.
Zech	11.17	His arm will wither, and his right eye will go **blind."**
	12. 4	of Judah, but I will make the horses of their enemies **blind.**
Mal	1. 8	When you bring a **blind** or sick or lame animal to sacrifice
Mt	9.27	and as he walked along, two **blind** men started following him.
	9.28	had gone indoors, the two **blind** men came to him, and he
	11. 5	the **blind** can see, the lame can walk, those who suffer
	12.22	Jesus a man who was **blind** and could not talk because he
	15.14	They are **blind** leaders of the blind;
	15.14	when one **blind** man leads another, both fall into a ditch."
	15.30	with them the lame, the **blind,** the crippled, the dumb, and
	15.31	the crippled made whole, the lame walking, and the **blind** seeing;
	20.30	Two **blind** men who were sitting by the road heard that
	21.14	The **blind** and the crippled came to him in the Temple,
	23.16	"How terrible for you, **blind** guides!
	23.17	**Blind** fools!
	23.19	How **blind** you are!
	23.24	**Blind** guides!
	23.26	**Blind** Pharisee!
Mk	8.22	where some people brought a **blind** man to Jesus and begged
	8.23	Jesus took the **blind** man by the hand and led him out
	10.46	a large crowd, a **blind** beggar named Bartimaeus son of Timaeus
	10.49	So they called the **blind** man.
	10.51	"Teacher," the **blind** man answered, "I want to see again."
Lk	4.18	liberty to the captives and recovery of sight to the **blind;**
	6.39	"One **blind** man cannot lead another one;
	7.21	diseases, and evil spirits, and gave sight to many **blind** people.
	7.22	the **blind** can see, the lame can walk, those who suffer from
	14.13	invite the poor, the crippled, the lame, and the **blind;**
	14.21	bring back the poor, the crippled, the **blind,** and the lame.'
	18.35	there was a **blind** man sitting by the road, begging.
	18.40	Jesus stopped and ordered the **blind** man to be brought to him.
Jn	5. 3	lying in the porches—the **blind,** the lame, and the paralysed.
	9. 1	was walking along, he saw a man who had been born **blind.**
	9. 2	asked him, "Teacher, whose sin caused him to be born **blind?**
	9. 3	Jesus answered, "His **blindness** has nothing to do with his sins
	9. 3	He is **blind** so that God's power might be seen at work
	9.13	Then they took to the Pharisees the man who had been **blind.**
	9.14	made the mud and cured him of his **blindness** was a Sabbath.
	9.17	he cured you of your **blindness**—well, what do you say about
	9.18	believe that he had been **blind** and could now see, until they
	9.19	You say that he was born **blind;**
	9.20	he is our son, and we know that he was born **blind.**
	9.21	nor do we know who cured him of his **blindness.**
	9.24	man who had been born **blind,** and said to him, "Promise
	9.25	I was **blind,** and now I see."
	9.26	"How did he cure you of your **blindness?"**
	9.30	know where he comes from, but he cured me of my **blindness!**
	9.32	ever heard of anyone giving sight to a person born **blind.**
	9.39	blind should see and those who see should become **blind."**
	9.40	asked him, "Surely you don't mean that we are **blind,** too?"
	9.41	answered, "If you were **blind,** then you would not be guilty;

Jn 10.21 How could a demon give sight to **blind** people?"
11.37 of them said, "He gave sight to the **blind** man, didn't he?
12.40 "God has **blinded** their eyes and closed their minds,
Acts 13.11 you will be **blind** and will not see the light of day
22.11 I was **blind** because of the bright light, and so my
Rom 2.19 are a guide for the **blind,** a light for those who are
11.10 May their eyes be **blinded** so that they cannot see;
1 Jn 2.11 where he is going, because the darkness has made him **blind.**
Rev 3.17 You are poor, naked, and **blind.**

BLINDFOLDED

Is 29.10 be the eyes of the people, but God has **blindfolded** them.
Mk 14.65 to spit on Jesus, and they **blindfolded** him and hit him.
Lk 22.64 They **blindfolded** him and asked him, "Who hit you?

BLINKING

1 Cor 15.51 changed in an instant, as quickly as the **blinking** of an eye.

BLOCK (1)

1 Chr 22. 2 Some of them prepared stone **blocks** for building the Temple.
Ezra 5. 8 being rebuilt with large stone **blocks** and with wooden beams
Is 44.19 Here I am bowing down to a **block** of wood!"
Hab 2.19 or to a **block** of stone, "Get up!"
Acts 16.24 cell and fastened their feet between heavy **blocks** of wood.

BLOCK (2)

2 Chr 32.30 It was King Hezekiah who **blocked** the outlet for the
Job 19. 8 God has **blocked** the way, and I can't get through;
Is 30.11 Get out of our way and stop **blocking** our path.
Lam 3. 9 stone walls **block** me wherever I turn.
Hos 2. 6 her in with thorn-bushes and build a wall to **block** her way.

BLOCKADE

Lk 19.43 surround you with barricades, **blockade** you, and close in on you

BLOOD

[FIELD OF BLOOD, FLESH AND BLOOD, LIFE-BLOOD]
see also **BLEED**

Gen 4.10 Your brother's **blood** is crying out to me from the ground,
4.11 has soaked up your brother's **blood** as if it had opened its
9. 4 thing you must not eat is meat with **blood** still in it;
9. 4 I forbid this because the life is in the **blood.**
29.14 Laban said, "Yes, indeed, you are my own **flesh and blood."**
37.27 after all, he is our brother, our own **flesh and blood."**
37.31 Then they killed a goat and dipped Joseph's robe in its **blood.**
49.11 He washes his clothes in **blood-red** wine.
49.12 His eyes are **bloodshot** from drinking wine, His teeth
Ex 4. 9 The water will turn into **blood."**
4.25 she said to Moses, "You are a husband of **blood** to me."
7.17 with this stick, and the water will be turned into **blood.**
7.19 The water will become **blood,** and all over the land
7.19 there will be **blood,** even in the wooden tubs
7.20 the river, and all the water in it was turned into **blood.**
7.21 There was **blood** everywhere in Egypt.
12. 7 to take some of the **blood** and put it on the door-posts
12.13 The **blood** on the door-posts will be a sign
12.13 When I see the **blood,** I will pass over you
12.22 the animal's blood, and wipe the **blood** on the door-posts
12.23 Egyptians, he will see the **blood** on the beams and the
24. 6 Moses took half the **blood** of the animals and put it in
24. 8 Then Moses took the **blood** in the bowls and threw it on
24. 8 He said, "This is the **blood** that seals the covenant which
29.12 Take some of the bull's **blood** and with your finger put
29.12 out the rest of the **blood** at the base of the altar.
29.16 Kill it, and take its **blood** and throw it against all
29.20 and take some of its **blood** and put it on the lobes
29.20 Throw the rest of the **blood** against all four sides of the
29.21 Take some of the **blood** that is on the altar and some
30.10 four projections the **blood** of the animal sacrificed for sin.
Lev 1. 5 Aaronite priests shall present the **blood** to the Lord and
1.11 the priests shall throw its **blood** on all four sides of the
1.15 Its **blood** shall be drained out against the side of the altar.
3. 2 Aaronite priests shall throw the **blood** against all four
3. 8 The priests shall throw its **blood** against all four sides of
3.13 The priests shall throw its **blood** against all four sides of
3.17 No Israelite may eat any fat or any **blood;**
4. 5 take some of the bull's **blood** and carry it into the Tent.
4. 6 dip his finger in the **blood** and sprinkle it in front of
4. 7 shall put some of the **blood** on the projections at the
4. 7 out the rest of the **blood** at the base of the altar
4.16 take some of the bull's **blood** into the Tent, [17] dip his
4.18 shall put some of the **blood** on the projections at the
4.25 dip his finger in the **blood** of the animal, put it on
4.30 dip his finger in the **blood** of the animal, put it on
4.34 dip his finger in the **blood** of the animal, put it on
5. 9 and sprinkle some of its **blood** against the side of the altar.
5. 9 The rest of the **blood** will be drained out at the base
6.27 is spattered with the animal's **blood,** it must be washed in a
6.30 But if any of the **blood** is brought into the Tent and
7. 2 burnt-offerings are killed, and its **blood** is to be thrown
7.14 the priest who takes the **blood** of the animal and throws it
7.26 they must never use the **blood** of birds or animals for food.
7.33 who offers the **blood** and the fat of the fellowship-offering.
8.15 and took some of the **blood,** and with his finger put it
8.15 out the rest of the **blood** at the base of the altar.
Lev 8.19 killed it and threw the **blood** on all four sides of the
8.23 and took some of the **blood** and put it on the lobe
8.24 and put some of the **blood** on the lobes of their right
8.24 threw the rest of the **blood** on all four sides of the
8.30 oil and some of the **blood** that was on the altar and
9. 9 His sons brought him the **blood,** and he dipped his finger
9.12 His sons brought him the **blood,** and he threw it on all
9.18 His sons brought him the **blood,** and he threw it on all
10.18 Since its **blood** was not brought into the sacred tent,
12. 4 days before she is ritually clean from her loss of **blood;**
12. 5 days before she is ritually clean from her loss of **blood.**
14. 6 and the hyssop, in the **blood** of the bird that was killed.
14. 7 He shall sprinkle the **blood** seven times on the person who
14.14 shall take some of the **blood** of the lamb and put it
14.17 hand and some of the **blood** of the lamb and put them
14.25 and take some of the **blood** and put it on the lobe
14.28 of the oil on the same places as he put the **blood:**
14.51 shall dip them in the **blood** of the bird that was killed
14.52 the house with the bird's **blood,** the fresh water, the live
15.25 woman has a flow of **blood** for several days outside her
16.14 take some of the bull's **blood** and with his finger sprinkle
16.15 for the people, bring its **blood** into the Most Holy Place,
16.15 front of the Covenant Box, as he did with the bull's **blood.**
16.18 take some of the bull's **blood** and some of the goat's blood
16.19 he must sprinkle some of the **blood** on the altar seven times.
16.27 used for the sin-offering, whose **blood** was brought into the
17. 3 He has shed **blood** and shall no longer be considered one of
17. 6 The priest shall throw the **blood** against the sides of the
17.10 the community eats meat with **blood** still in it, the Lord
17.11 living thing is in the **blood,** and that is why the Lord
17.11 Lord has commanded that all **blood** be poured out on the altar
17.11 **Blood,** which is life, takes away sins.
17.12 among them shall eat any meat with **blood** still in it.
17.13 he must pour out its **blood** on the ground and cover it
17.14 living thing is in the **blood,** and that is why the Lord
17.14 not eat any meat with **blood** still in it and that anyone
19.26 "Do not eat any meat with **blood** still in it.
Num 18.17 Throw their **blood** against the altar and burn their fat as a
19. 4 to take some of its **blood** and with his finger sprinkle it
19. 5 whole animal, including skin, meat, **blood,** and intestines,
23.24 Until it has drunk the **blood** of those it has killed."
Deut 12.16 But you must not use their **blood** as food;
12.23 do not eat meat with **blood** still in it,
12.23 the life is in the **blood,**
12.24 Do not use the **blood** for food;
12.27 you eat the meat and pour the **blood** out on the altar.
15.23 But do not use their **blood** for food;
19.11 murders his enemy in cold **blood** and then escapes to one of
22.15 parents are to take the **blood-stained** wedding sheet that
22.17 look at the **bloodstains** on the wedding sheet!
32.42 arrows will drip with their **blood,** and my sword will kill
Judg 9. 2 Remember that Abimelech is your own **flesh and blood."**
1 Sam 14.32 the spot, and ate the meat with the **blood** still in it.
14.33 against the Lord by eating meat with the **blood** in it."
14.34 not sin against the Lord by eating meat with **blood** in it."
2 Sam 5. 1 Hebron and said to him, "We are your own **flesh and blood.**
19.12 You are my relatives, my own **flesh and blood;**
20.12 Amasa's body, covered with **blood,** was lying in the
23.17 would be like drinking the **blood** of these men who risked
1 Kgs 18.28 and daggers, according to their ritual, until **blood** flowed.
21.19 licked up Naboth's **blood** they will lick up your blood!' "
22.35 The **blood** from his wound ran down and covered the bottom of
22.38 dogs licked up his **blood** and prostitutes washed themselves,
2 Kgs 3.22 was shining on the water, making it look as red as **blood.**
3.23 "It's **blood!"**
9.33 her down, and her **blood** spattered the wall and the horses.
16.13 wine-offering and the **blood** of a fellowship-offering on it.
16.15 Pour on it the **blood** of all the animals that are sacrificed.
21.16 that the streets of Jerusalem were flowing with **blood;**
25.14 bowls used for catching the **blood** from the sacrifices, the
1 Chr 11. 1 Hebron and said to him, "We are your own **flesh and blood.**
11.19 would be like drinking the **blood** of these men who risked
22. 8 so, because of all the **bloodshed** I have caused, he would not
28. 3 it, because I am a soldier and have shed too much **blood.**
2 Chr 29.22 and sprinkled the **blood** of each sacrifice on the altar.
29.24 the goats and poured their **blood** on the altar as a sacrifice
30.16 The Levites gave the **blood** of the sacrifices to the priests,
35.11 Levites skinned them, and the priests sprinkled the **blood** on the altar.
Job 20.25 its shiny point drips with his **blood,** and terror grips his heart.
39.30 the eagles gather, and the young eagles drink the **blood.**
Ps 50.13 I eat the flesh of bulls or drink the **blood** of goats?
58.10 they will wade through the **blood** of the wicked.
68.23 you may wade in their **blood,** and your dogs may lap up
78.44 He turned the rivers into **blood,** and the Egyptians had
79. 3 They shed your people's **blood** like water;
79. 3 **blood** flowed like water all through Jerusalem, and no one
79.10 punish the nations for shedding the **blood** of your servants.
105.29 He turned their rivers into **blood** and killed all their fish.
Prov 23.29 His eyes are **bloodshot,** and he has bruises that could have
Is 1.11 I am tired of the **blood** of bulls and sheep and goats.
1.15 I will not listen, for your hands are covered with **blood.**
4. 4 guilt of Jerusalem and the **blood** that has been shed there.
9. 5 all their **bloodstained** clothing will be destroyed by fire.
15. 9 the river is red with **blood,** and God has something even
15. 9 Yes, there will be a **bloody** slaughter of everyone left in Moab.
29. 2 and the whole city will be like an altar covered with **blood.**
34. 3 and the mountains will be red with **blood.**
34. 6 will be covered with their **blood** and fat,
34. 6 like the **blood** and fat of lambs and goats
34. 7 and the earth will be red with **blood** and covered with fat.

Is	63. 3	in my anger, and their **blood** has stained all my clothing.
	63. 6	I poured out their **life-blood** on the ground."
	66. 3	whether they present a grain-offering or offer pigs' **blood;**
Jer	2.34	clothes are stained with the **blood** of the poor and innocent,
	2.34	not with the **blood** of burglars.
	19. 4	filled this place with the **blood** of innocent people, [5]and
	46.10	it is full, and drink their **blood** until it is satisfied.
	52.18	bowls used for catching the **blood** from the sacrifices, the
	52.19	holding the **blood** from the sacrifices, the ash containers,
Lam	4.14	men, so stained with **blood** that no one would touch them.
Ezek	16. 6	"Then I passed by and saw you squirming in your own **blood.**
	16. 6	You were covered with **blood,** but I wouldn't let you die.
	16. 9	"Then I took water and washed the **blood** off you.
	16.22	you were naked, squirming in your own **blood."**
	21.32	Your **blood** will be shed in your own country, and no one
	23.45	practise adultery and their hands are stained with **blood."**
	24. 7	in the city, but the **blood** was not spilt on the ground
	24. 8	I have left the **blood** there, where it cannot be hidden,
	28.23	send diseases on you and make **blood** flow in your streets.
	32. 6	I will pour out your **blood** until it spreads over the
	33.25	You eat meat with the **blood** still in it.
	38.22	I will punish him with disease and **bloodshed.**
	39.17	of Israel, where they can eat meat and drink **blood.**
	39.18	of soldiers and drink the **blood** of the rulers of the earth,
	39.19	fat they can hold and to drink **blood** until they are drunk.
	43.18	on it the **blood** of the animals that were sacrificed.
	43.20	to take some of its **blood** and put it on the projections
	43.22	Purify the altar with its **blood** in the same way as you
	44. 7	when the fat and the **blood** of the sacrifices are being
	44.15	to offer me the fat and the **blood** of the sacrifices.
	45.19	will take some of the **blood** of this sin-offering and put it
Joel	2.30	there will be **bloodshed,** fire, and clouds of smoke.
	2.31	moon will turn red as **blood** before the great and terrible
Zeph	1.17	me, and now their **blood** will be poured out like water,
Zech	9. 7	longer eat meat with **blood** in it, or other forbidden food.
	9.11	that was sealed by the **blood** of sacrifices, I will set your
	9.15	like drunken men and will shed the **blood** of their enemies;
	9.15	it will flow like the **blood** of a sacrifice poured on the
Mt	26.28	"this is my **blood,** which seals God's covenant,
	26.28	my **blood** poured out for many for the
	27. 6	coins and said, "This is **blood money,** and it is against our
	27. 8	that field is called **"Field of Blood"** to this very day.
Mk	14.24	Jesus said, "This is my **blood** which is poured out for many,
	14.24	my **blood** which seals God's covenant.
Lk	22.20	covenant sealed with my **blood,** which is poured out for you.
	22.44	his sweat was like drops of **blood** falling to the ground.
Jn	6.53	of Man and drink his **blood,** you will not have life in
	6.54	my flesh and drinks my **blood** has eternal life, and I will
	6.55	my **blood** is the real drink.
	6.56	my flesh and drinks my **blood** lives in me, and I live
	19.34	into Jesus' side, and at once **blood** and water poured out.
Acts	1.19	they call that field Akeldama, which means **"Field of Blood.")**
	2.19	There will be **blood,** fire, and thick smoke;
	2.20	moon will turn red as **blood,** before the great and glorious
	15.20	not to eat any animal that has been strangled, or any **blood.**
	15.29	eat no **blood;**
	21.25	offered to idols, or any **blood,** or any animal that has been
Rom	9. 3	pain in my heart [3] for my people, my own **flesh and blood!**
1 Cor	10.16	we drink from it, we are sharing in the **blood** of Christ.
	11.25	"This cup is God's new covenant, sealed with my **blood.**
	11.27	he is guilty of sin against the Lord's body and **blood.**
	15.50	is made of **flesh and blood** cannot share in God's Kingdom,
Phil	2.17	Perhaps my life's **blood** is to be poured out like an
Heb	2.14	them, are people of **flesh and blood,** Jesus himself became
	9. 7	He takes with him **blood** which he offers to God on behalf
	9.12	he did not take the **blood** of goats and bulls to offer
	9.12	he took his own **blood** and obtained eternal salvation for us.
	9.13	The **blood** of goats and bulls and the ashes of a burnt
	9.14	true, how much more is accomplished by the **blood** of Christ!
	9.14	His **blood** will purify our consciences from useless rituals,
	9.18	first covenant came into effect only with the use of **blood.**
	9.19	Then he took the **blood** of bulls and goats, mixed it with
	9.20	He said, "This is the **blood** which seals the covenant
	9.21	Moses also sprinkled the **blood** on the Covenant Tent and over
	9.22	almost everything is purified by **blood,**
	9.22	and sins are forgiven only if **blood** is poured out.
	9.25	the Most Holy Place every year with the **blood** of an animal.
	10. 4	For the **blood** of bulls and goats can never take away sins.
	10.29	as a cheap thing the **blood** of God's covenant which purified
	11.28	Passover and order the **blood** to be sprinkled on the doors,
	12.24	and to the sprinkled **blood** that promises much better things
	12.24	than does the **blood** of Abel.
	13.11	Jewish High Priest brings the **blood** of the animals into the
	13.12	in order to purify the people from sin with his own **blood.**
1 Pet	1. 2	to obey Jesus Christ and be purified by his **blood.**
1 Jn	1. 7	with one another, and the **blood** of Jesus, his Son, purifies
	5. 6	with the water of his baptism and the **blood** of his death.
	5. 6	only with the water, but with both the water and the **blood.**
	5. 8	the Spirit, the water, and the **blood;**
Rev	6.12	coarse black cloth, and the moon turned completely red like **blood.**
	7.14	their robes and made them white with the **blood** of the Lamb.
	8. 7	Hail and fire, mixed with **blood,** came pouring down on the earth.
	8. 8	the sea was turned into **blood,** [9]a third of the living
	11. 6	also over the springs of water, to turn them into **blood;**
	12.11	victory over him by the **blood** of the Lamb and by
	14.20	winepress outside the city, and **blood** came out of the winepress
	16. 3	The water became like the **blood** of a dead person, and every
	16. 4	rivers and the springs of water, and they turned into **blood.**
	16. 6	They poured out the **blood** of God's people and of the prophets,
	16. 6	and so you have given them **blood** to drink.
	17. 6	woman was drunk with the **blood** of God's people
Rev	17. 6	and the **blood** of those who were killed because
	18.24	Babylon was punished because the **blood** of prophets and of
	18.24	yes, the **blood** of all those who have been killed on earth.
	19.13	The robe he wore was covered with **blood.**

AV BLOOD

Gen	9. 5	If anyone takes human **life,** he will be punished.
	9. 6	made like God, so whoever **murders** a man will himself be
	37.22	him into this well in the wilderness, but don't **hurt** him."
	37.26	we gain by killing our brother and covering up the **murder?**
	42.22	And now we are being paid back for his **death."**
Ex	22. 2	is killed, the one who killed him is not guilty of **murder.**
	22. 2	But if it happens during the day, he is guilty of **murder.**
	23.18	bread made with yeast when you **sacrifice** an animal to me.
	34.25	bread made with yeast when you **sacrifice** an animal to me.
Lev	15.19	When a woman has her **monthly period,** she remains unclean
	17. 3	of the Tent of the Lord's presence has **broken** the Law.
	19.16	is on trial for his **life,** speak out if your testimony can
	20. 9	he is responsible for his own **death.**
	20.11	They are responsible for their own **death.**
	20.12	They have committed incest and are responsible for their own **death.**
	20.13	They are responsible for their own **death.**
	20.16	They are responsible for their own **death.**
	20.27	person who does this is responsible for his own **death."**
Num	35.19	The dead man's nearest **relative** has the responsibility
	35.21	The dead man's nearest **relative** has the responsibility for
	35.24	in favour of the dead man's **relative** who is seeking revenge.
	35.25	manslaughter from the dead man's **relative,** and they are to
	35.27	and if the dead man's **relative** finds him and kills him,
	35.27	this act of revenge is not **murder.**
	35.33	**Murder** defiles the land,
	35.33	and except by the **death** of the murderer there is no
	35.33	of purification for the land where a man has been **murdered.**
Deut	17. 8	that involve a distinction between **murder and manslaughter.**
	19. 6	be too great, and the **relative** who is responsible for taking
	19.10	that innocent people will not **die** and so that you will not
	19.10	be guilty of putting them **to death** in the land that the
	19.12	hand him over to the **relative** responsible for taking revenge
	19.13	Rid Israel of this **murderer,** so that all will go well with
	21. 7	and say, 'We did not **murder** the man, and we do not
	21. 8	not hold us responsible for the **murder** of an innocent man.'
	21. 9	Lord requires, you will not be held responsible for the **murder.**
	22. 8	will not be responsible if someone falls off and is **killed.**
	32.42	even the wounded and prisoners will **die.'**
	32.43	praise the Lord's people— he punishes all who **kill** them.
Josh	2.19	out of the house, his **death** will be his own fault, and
	20. 3	can go there and escape the man who is looking for **revenge.**
	20. 5	If the man looking for **revenge** follows him there, the
	20. 9	find protection there from the man looking for **revenge;**
Judg	9.24	Shechem, who encouraged him to **murder** Gideon's seventy sons,
1 Sam	19. 5	do wrong to an innocent **man** and kill David for no reason
	25.26	Lord who has kept you from taking revenge and **killing** your enemies.
	25.31	or remorse, sir, for having **killed** without cause
	25.33	me from the crime of **murder** and from taking my own revenge.
	26.20	Don't let me be **killed** on foreign soil, away from the Lord.
2 Sam	1.22	Saul was merciless, striking down the mighty, **killing** the enemy.
	3.27	Abner was murdered because he had **killed** Joab's brother Asahel.
	3.28	and I are completely innocent of the **murder** of Abner.
	4.11	take revenge on you for **murdering** him and will wipe you off
	14.11	your God, so that my **relative** who is responsible for
	16. 8	Lord is punishing you for **murdering** so many of Saul's family.
1 Kgs	2. 5	You remember how he **murdered** them in time of peace in
	2. 9	and you must see to it that he is put **to death."**
	2.31	responsible for what Joab did when he **killed** innocent men.
	2.32	will punish Joab for those **murders,** which he committed
	2.33	The punishment for their **murders** will fall on Joab and
2 Kgs	9. 7	may punish Jezebel for **murdering** my prophets and my other servants.
	21.16	Manasseh **killed** so many innocent people
	24. 4	especially because of all the innocent people he had **killed.**
1 Chr	22. 8	told me that I had **killed** too many people
2 Chr	19.10	before you a case of **homicide** or any other violation of a
	24.25	his bed to avenge the **murder** of the son of Jehoiada the
Job	16.18	O Earth, don't hide the **wrongs** done to me!
Ps	9.12	not forget their cry, and he punishes those who **wrong** them.
	16. 4	I will not take part in their **sacrifices;**
	30. 9	"What will you gain from my **death?**
	51.14	Spare my **life,** O God, and save me, and I will gladly
	72.14	their **lives** are precious to him.
	94.21	who plot against good men and sentence the innocent **to death.**
	106.38	They **killed** those innocent children,
	106.38	children, and the land was defiled by those **murders.**
Prov	1.11	let's find someone to **kill!**
	1.16	They're always ready to **kill.**
	1.18	a trap for themselves, a trap in which they will **die.**
	6.16	hands that **kill** innocent people,
	12. 6	words of wicked men are **murderous,** but the words of the
	28.17	A man guilty of **murder** is digging his own grave as fast
	30.33	If you hit someone's nose, it **bleeds.**
Is	26.21	The **murders** that were secretly committed on the earth will be
	33.15	those who plan to commit **murder** or to do other evil things.
	49.26	they will be drunk with **murder** and rage.
	59. 3	You are guilty of lying, violence, and **murder.**
	59. 7	You never hesitate to **murder** innocent people.
Jer	7. 6	Stop **killing** innocent people in this land.
	22. 3	and do not **kill** innocent people in this holy place.
	22.17	you **kill** the innocent and violently oppress your people.
	26.15	will be guilty of **killing** an innocent man,

Jer 48.10 Curse the man who does not slash and **kill!)**
51.35 "May Babylonia be held responsible for what we have **suffered!"**
Lam 4.13 priests were guilty of causing the **death** of innocent people.
Ezek 3.18 and I will hold you responsible for his **death.**
3.20 and I will hold you responsible for his **death.**
5.17 and will send sickness, **violence,** and war to kill you.
9. 9 They have committed **murder** all over the land and have filled
14.19 in my anger take many **lives,** killing people and animals,
16.36 and you **killed** your children as sacrifices to idols.
16.38 condemn you for adultery and **murder,** and in my anger and
16.38 and in my anger and fury I will punish you with **death.**
18.10 a son who robs and **kills,** who does any of these things
18.13 He will be to blame for his own **death.**
22. 3 Because you have **murdered** so many of your own people and
22. 4 You are guilty of those **murders** and are defiled by the
22. 6 All Israel's leaders trust in their own strength and commit **murder.**
22. 9 tell lies about others in order to have them put **to death.**
22.12 Some of your people **murder** for pay.
22.13 "I will bring my fist down on your robberies and **murders.**
22.27 They commit **murder** in order to get rich.
23.37 They have committed adultery and **murder—**
23.45 the charge of adultery and **murder,** because they practise
24. 7 There was **murder** in the city, but the blood was not spilt
33. 4 and kills him, then he is to blame for his own **death.**
33. 5 His **death** is his own fault, because he paid no attention
33. 6 but I will hold the watchman responsible for their **death.**
33. 8 and I will hold you responsible for his **death.**
33.25 You commit **murder.**
35. 6 Lord, am the living God—**death** is your fate, and you cannot
35. 6 You are guilty of **murder,** and murder will follow you.
36.18 my anger because of the **murders** they had committed in the
Hos 1. 4 king of Israel for the **murders** that his ancestor Jehu
4. 2 Crimes increase, and there is one **murder** after another.
6. 8 Gilead is a city full of evil men and **murderers.**
12.14 they deserve **death** for their crimes.
Joel 3.19 attacked the land of Judah and **killed** its innocent people.
3.20 I will avenge those who were **killed;**
Mic 3.10 God's city, Jerusalem, on a foundation of **murder** and injustice.
7. 2 Everyone is waiting for a chance to commit **murder.**
Hab 2. 8 plunder you because of the **murders** you have committed and
2.12 You founded a city on crime and built it up by **murder.**
2.17 will happen because of the **murders** you have committed and
Mt 9.20 who had suffered from severe **bleeding** for twelve years
23.30 would not have done what they did and **killed** the prophets.
23.35 result, the punishment for the **murder** of all innocent men will
23.35 fall on you, from the **murder** of innocent Abel
23.35 to the **murder** of Zachariah son of Berachiah,
27. 4 "I have sinned by betraying an innocent man to **death!"**
27.24 and said, "I am not responsible for the **death** of this man!
27.25 "Let the responsibility for his **death** fall on us and our children!"
Mk 5.25 had suffered terribly from severe **bleeding** for twelve years,
5.29 She touched his cloak, and her **bleeding** stopped at once;
Lk 8.43 a woman who had suffered from severe **bleeding** for twelve years;
8.44 the edge of his cloak, and her **bleeding** stopped at once.
11.50 will be punished for the **murder** of all the prophets killed
11.51 of the world, [51] from the **murder** of Abel
11.51 to the **murder** of Zechariah, who was killed between
13. 1 the Galileans whom Pilate had **killed** while they were offering
Acts 5.28 and you want to make us responsible for his **death!"**
17.26 From one **man** he created all races of mankind and made
18. 6 to them, "If you are **lost,** you yourselves must take the
20.26 if any of you should be **lost,** I am not responsible.
20.28 he made his own through the **sacrificial death** of his Son.
22.20 your witness Stephen was put **to death,** I myself was there,
Rom 3.15 They are quick to hurt and **kill;**
3.25 so that by his **sacrificial death** he should become the means
5. 9 By his **sacrificial death** we are now put right with God;
Eph 1. 7 For by the **sacrificial death** of Christ we are set free,
2.13 have been brought near by the **sacrificial death** of Christ.
Col 1.20 made peace through his Son's **sacrificial death** on the cross
Heb 10.19 into the Most Holy Place by means of the **death** of Jesus.
12. 4 have not yet had to resist to the point of being **killed.**
13.20 as the result of his **sacrificial death,** by which the eternal
1 Pet 1.19 it was the costly **sacrifice** of Christ, who was like a
Rev 1. 5 loves us, and by his **sacrificial death** he has freed us from
5. 9 and by your **sacrificial death** you bought for God people
6.10 judge the people on earth and punish them for **killing** us?"
19. 2 God has punished her because she **killed** his servants."

BLOODTHIRSTY

Prov 29.10 **Bloodthirsty** people hate anyone who's honest, but

BLOOM

Ps 90. 6 that grow and burst into **bloom,** then dry up and die in
Song 1.14 the wild flowers that **bloom** in the vineyards at Engedi.
2.12 in the countryside the flowers are in **bloom.**
2.15 the little foxes, before they ruin our vineyard in **bloom.**
7.12 blossoms are opening and the pomegranate-trees are in **bloom.**
Is 35. 1 The desert will rejoice, and flowers will **bloom** in the wilderness.

BLOSSOM

Gen 40.10 came out, the **blossoms** appeared, and the grapes ripened.
Ex 25.33 flowers shaped like almond **blossoms** with buds and petals.
25.34 flowers shaped like almond **blossoms** with buds and petals.
37.19 flowers shaped like almond **blossoms** with buds and petals.
37.20 flowers shaped like almond **blossoms** with buds and petals.
Num 17. 8 It had budded, **blossomed,** and produced ripe almonds!
Job 15.30 burnt by fire, whose **blossoms** are blown away by the wind.
Job 15.33 like an olive-tree that drops its **blossoms.**
Song 2.13 the air is fragrant with **blossoming** vines.
6.11 on the vines and the **blossoms** on the pomegranate-trees.
7.12 started to grow, whether the **blossoms** are opening and the
Is 5.24 roots will rot and your **blossoms** will dry up and blow away,
17.11 sprouted and **blossomed** the very morning you planted them,
18. 5 grapes are gathered, when the **blossoms** have all fallen and
27. 6 will take root like a tree, and they will **blossom** and bud.
45. 8 to receive it and will **blossom** with freedom and justice.
Hos 14. 5 They will **blossom** like flowers;

BLOT

Job 3. 5 cover it with clouds, and **blot** out the sun.
3. 6 **Blot** that night out of the year, and never let it be
Ezek 32. 7 destroy you, I will cover the sky and **blot** out the stars.

Am

BLOW

see also **SOUND**

BLOW (1)

[BLEW]

Gen 8. 1 he caused a wind to **blow,** and the water started going down.
Ex 10.13 wind from the east to **blow** on the land all that day
10.19 picked up the locusts and **blew** them into the Gulf of Suez.
14.21 It **blew** all night and turned the sea into dry land.
15. 8 You **blew** on the sea and the water piled up high;
19.13 But when the trumpet is **blown,** then the people are to go
Lev 25. 9 Atonement, send a man to **blow** a trumpet throughout the whole land.
26.36 the sound of a leaf **blowing** in the wind will make you
Num 10. 8 The trumpets are to be **blown** by Aaron's sons, the
10.10 religious festivals—you are to **blow** the trumpets when you
29. 1 On that day trumpets are to be **blown.**
Josh 6. 4 the city seven times while the priests **blow** the trumpets.
6. 8 started out ahead of the priests who were **blowing** trumpets;
6.12 next, the seven priests **blowing** the seven trumpets;
6.20 So the priests **blew** the trumpets.
Judg 3.27 the hill-country of Ephraim, he **blew** a trumpet to call the
6.34 control of Gideon, and he **blew** a trumpet to call the men
7.18 When my group and I **blow** our trumpets, then you blow
7.19 Then they **blew** the trumpets and broke the jars they were holding,
7.22 While Gideon's men were **blowing** their trumpets, the Lord
1 Sam 13. 3 Hebrews to war by **blowing** a trumpet throughout the whole country.
2 Sam 2.28 Then Joab **blew** the trumpet as a signal for his men to
18.16 ordered the trumpet to be **blown** to stop the fighting, and
20. 1 He **blew** the trumpet and called out, "Down with David!
20.22 He **blew** the trumpet as a signal for his men to leave
1 Kgs 1.34 Then **blow** the trumpet and shout, 'Long live King Solomon!'
1.39 They **blew** the trumpet, and all the people shouted, "Long
18.45 the wind began to **blow,** and heavy rain began to fall.
19.11 The wind stopped **blowing,** and then there was an earthquake—
2 Kgs 9.13 Jehu to stand on, **blew** trumpets, and shouted, "Jehu is king!"
11.14 the people were all shouting joyfully and **blowing** trumpets.
1 Chr 15.23 and Eliezer were chosen to **blow** trumpets in front of the
16. 6 Benaiah and Jahaziel, were to **blow** trumpets regularly in
2 Chr 7. 6 The priests **blew** trumpets while all the people stood.
13.12 here with trumpets, ready to **blow** them and call us to battle
13.14 to the Lord for help, and the priests **blew** the trumpets.
15.14 keep the covenant, and then they shouted and **blew** trumpets.
23.13 people were shouting joyfully and **blowing** trumpets, and the
Neh 12.33 The following priests, **blowing** trumpets, marched
12.41 my group included the following priests, **blowing** trumpets:
Job 1.19 It **blew** the house down and killed them all.
15.30 burnt by fire, whose blossoms are **blown** away by the wind.
20. 7 reaches the clouds, [7] but he will be **blown** away like dust.
21.18 the wicked in anger [18] and **blow** them away like straw in the
27.20 a wind in the night will **blow** them away;
27.22 it will **blow** down on them without pity while they try
30.22 You let the wind **blow** me away;
38.24 sun comes up, or the place from which the east wind **blows?**
39.24 when the trumpet **blows,** they can't stand still.
Ps 1. 4 they are like straw that the wind **blows** away.
18.42 so that they become like dust which the wind **blows** away.
35. 5 May they be like straw **blown** by the wind as the angel
58. 9 his fierce anger God will **blow** them away while they are
68. 2 As smoke is **blown** away, so he drives them off;
78.26 caused the east wind to **blow,** and by his power he stirred
78.39 only mortal beings, like a wind that **blows** by and is gone.
81. 3 **Blow** the trumpet for the festival, when the moon is new
83.13 them like dust, O God, like straw **blown** away by the wind.
98. 6 **Blow** trumpets and horns, and shout for joy to the Lord,
103.16 then the wind **blows** on it, and it is gone— no
107.25 and a mighty wind began to **blow** and stirred up the waves.
109.23 I am **blown** away like an insect.
Prov 10.25 come, and the wicked are **blown** away, but honest people are
Ecc 1. 6 The wind **blows** south, the wind blows north—round
Song 2.17 until the morning breezes **blow** and the darkness disappears.
4. 6 until the morning breezes **blow** and the darkness disappears.
4.16 South Wind, **blow** on my garden;
Is 5.24 blossoms will dry up and **blow** away, because you have
18. 3 Listen for the **blowing** of the bugle!
19. 7 the banks of the Nile will dry up and be **blown** away.
27.13 comes, a trumpet will be **blown** to call back from Assyria and
29. 5 who attack you will be **blown** away like dust, and their
40. 7 fade, when the Lord sends the wind **blowing** over them.
40.24 Lord sends a wind, they dry up and **blow** away like straw.
64. 6 are like leaves that wither and are **blown** away by the wind.

Jer 4. 5 **Blow** the trumpet throughout the land!
4.11 a scorching wind is **blowing** in from the desert towards them.
4.11 a gentle wind that only **blows** away the chaff—[12] the wind
13.24 you like straw that is **blown** away by the desert wind.
18.17 before their enemies, like dust **blown** by the east wind.
22.22 Your leaders will be **blown** away by the wind, your allies
49.36 I will make winds **blow** against Elam from all directions,
51. 2 to destroy Babylonia like a wind that **blows** straw away.
51.27 **Blow** the trumpet so that the nations can hear!
Ezek 13.11 will fall on it, and a strong wind will **blow** against it.
Dan 7. 2 Winds were **blowing** from all directions and lashing the
Hos 5. 8 **Blow** the war trumpets in Gibeah!
13. 3 like chaff which the wind **blows** from the threshing-place,
Joel 2. 1 **Blow** the trumpet;
2.15 **Blow** the trumpet on Mount Zion;
Zeph 2. 2 are driven away like chaff **blown** by the wind, before the
Hag 1. 9 And when you brought the harvest home, I **blew** it away.
Mt 7.25 rivers overflowed, and the wind **blew** hard against that house.
7.27 the rivers overflowed, the wind **blew** hard against that house,
14.24 tossed about by the waves, because the wind was **blowing** against
Mk 4.37 Suddenly a strong wind **blew** up, and the waves began to
Lk 8.23 Suddenly a strong wind **blew** down on the lake, and the boat
12.55 you feel the south wind **blowing**, you say that it is going
Jn 3. 8 The wind **blows** wherever it wishes;
6.18 By then a strong wind was **blowing** and stirring up the water.
Acts 2. 2 sounded like a strong wind **blowing**, and it filled the whole
27. 4 and because the winds were **blowing** against us, we sailed on
27.13 from the south began to **blow**, and the men thought that they
27.14 wind—the one called "North-easter"—**blew** down from the island.
27.20 sun or the stars, and the wind kept on **blowing** very hard.
27.40 so that the wind would **blow** the ship forward, and we headed
28.13 day a wind began to **blow** from the south, and in two
Eph 4.14 carried by the waves and **blown** about by every shifting wind
Jas 1. 6 in the sea that is driven and **blown** about by the wind.
2 Pet 2.17 are like dried-up springs, like clouds **blown** along by a storm;
Rev 7. 1 so that no wind should **blow** on the earth or the sea
8. 6 the seven angels with the seven trumpets prepared to **blow** them.
8. 7 The first angel **blew** his trumpet.
8. 8 Then the second angel **blew** his trumpet.
8.10 Then the third angel **blew** his trumpet.
8.12 Then the fourth angel **blew** his trumpet.
8.13 comes from the trumpets that the other three angels must **blow!"**
9. 1 Then the fifth angel **blew** his trumpet.
9.13 Then the sixth angel **blew** his trumpet.
10. 7 But when the seventh angel **blows** his trumpet, then God will
11.15 Then the seventh angel **blew** his trumpet, and there were loud

BLOW (2)

Judg 16.28 so that with this one **blow** I can get even with the
1 Sam 26. 8 ground with just one **blow**—I won't have to strike twice!"
1 Kgs 20.37 he hit him a hard **blow** and hurt him.
Ps 39.10 I am about to die from your **blows.**
Is 29.14 So I will startle them with one unexpected **blow** after another.
53. 5 he suffered, made whole by the **blows** he received.
Lam 3. 3 And beat me again and again with merciless **blows.**
Ezek 24.16 man," he said, "with one **blow** I am going to take away
1 Cor 9.27 harden my body with **blows** and bring it under complete control,

BLUE

Ex 24.10 what looked like a pavement of sapphire, as **blue** as the sky.
25. 4 **blue,** purple, and red wool;
26. 1 ten pieces of fine linen woven with **blue,** purple, and red
26. 4 Make loops of **blue** cloth on the edge of the outside piece
26.31 a curtain of fine linen woven with **blue,** purple, and red
26.36 of fine linen woven with **blue,** purple, and red wool and
27.16 of fine linen woven with **blue,** purple, and red wool, and
28. 5 The craftsmen are to use **blue,** purple, and red wool, gold
28. 6 to make the ephod of **blue,** purple, and red wool, gold
28.28 of the ephod with a **blue** cord, so that the breast-piece
28.31 goes under the ephod is to be made entirely of **blue** wool.
28.33 lower hem put pomegranates of **blue,** purple, and red wool,
28.37 Tie it to the front of the turban with a **blue** cord.
35. 6 **blue,** purple, and red wool;
35.23 **blue,** purple, or red wool;
35.25 linen thread and thread of **blue,** purple, and red wool, which
35.35 **blue,** purple, and red wool;
36. 8 of fine linen woven with **blue,** purple, and red wool and
36.11 They made loops of **blue** cloth on the edge of the outside
36.35 of fine linen, woven with **blue,** purple, and red wool and
36.37 of fine linen woven with **blue,** purple, and red wool and
38.18 of fine linen woven with **blue,** purple, and red wool and
38.23 a weaver of fine linen and of **blue,** purple, and red wool.
39. 1 With the **blue,** purple, and red wool they made the
39. 2 **blue,** purple, and red wool;
39. 3 into the fine linen and into the **blue,** purple, and red wool.
39.21 of the ephod with a **blue** cord, so that the breast-piece
39.22 that goes under the ephod was made entirely of **blue** wool.
39.24 of fine linen and of **blue,** purple, and red wool, alternating
39.29 of fine linen and of **blue,** purple, and red wool, decorated
39.31 of the turban with a **blue** cord, just as the Lord had
Num 4. 6 cover over it, spread a **blue** cloth on top, and then insert
4. 7 They shall spread a **blue** cloth over the table for the
4. 9 They shall take a **blue** cloth and cover the lampstand, with
4.11 Next they shall spread a **blue** cloth over the gold altar,
4.12 Place, wrap them in a **blue** cloth, put a fine leather cover
15.38 corners of your garments and put a **blue** cord on each tassel.
2 Chr 2. 7 bronze, and iron, and in making **blue,** purple and red cloth.
2.14 He can work with **blue,** purple, and red cloth, and with linen.
3.14 other material, which was dyed **blue,** purple, and red, with
Esth 1. 6 courtyard there was decorated with **blue** and white cotton curtains,
1. 6 red feldspar, shining mother-of-pearl, and **blue** turquoise.
8.15 palace, wearing royal robes of **blue** and white, a cloak of
Rev 9.17 breastplates red as fire, **blue** as sapphire, and yellow as sulphur.

BLUNDER

Hos 4. 5 Night and day you **blunder** on, and the prophets do no

BLUNT

Ecc 10.10 If your axe is **blunt** and you don't sharpen it, you have

BLUSH

Jer 6.15 they don't even know how to **blush.**
8.12 you don't even know how to **blush!**
Ezek 16.52 Now **blush** and bear your shame, because you make your sisters

BOARD (1)

Ezek 27.27 your merchants, Every soldier on **board** the ship— All, all
Acts 21. 6 and we went on **board** the ship while they went back
27.31 the sailors don't stay on **board,** you have no hope of being
27.37 There was a total of 276 of us on **board.**
28.10 we sailed, they put on **board** what we needed for the voyage.

BOARD (2)

[THRESHING-BOARD]

Ex 27. 8 Make the altar out of **boards** and leave it hollow,
38. 7 The altar was made of **boards** and was hollow.
2 Sam 24.22 are their yokes and the **threshing-boards** to use as fuel."
1 Kgs 6. 9 He put in a ceiling made of beams and **boards** of cedar.
6.16 was partitioned off by cedar **boards** reaching from the floor
1 Chr 21.23 altar, and here are the **threshing-boards** to use as fuel, and
Is 41.15 will make you like a **threshing-board,** with spikes that are

BOAST

Deut 32.27 let their enemies **boast** that they had defeated my people,
1 Sam 2. 3 Stop your loud **boasting;**
1 Kgs 20.11 soldier does his **boasting** after a battle, not before it."
2 Kgs 19.23 You sent your messengers to **boast** to me that with all
19.23 You **boasted** that there you cut down the tallest cedars and
19.24 You **boasted** that you dug wells and drank water in
2 Chr 25.19 Now Amaziah, you **boast** that you have defeated the Edomites,
Esth 5.11 He **boasted** to them how rich he was, how many sons he
Ps 12. 3 Close those **boastful** mouths that say, [4] "With our words
38.16 don't let them **boast** about my downfall!
49. 6 who trust in their riches and **boast** of their great wealth.
52. 1 Why do you **boast,** great man, of your evil?
55.12 if it were an opponent **boasting** over me, I could hide myself
75. 5 I tell them to stop their **boasting."**
94. 4 How much longer will criminals be proud and **boast** about their crimes?
Prov 27. 1 Never **boast** about tomorrow.
Is 10. 8 He **boasts,** "Every one of my commanders is a king!
10.12 of Assyria for all his **boasting** and all his pride."
10.13 The emperor of Assyria **boasts,** "I have done it all myself.
16. 6 are arrogant and conceited, but their **boasts** are empty."
20. 5 in Sudan and have **boasted** about Egypt will be disillusioned,
28.15 You **boast** that you have made a treaty with death and
37.24 You sent your servants to **boast** to me that with all your
37.24 You **boasted** that there you cut down the tallest cedars and
37.25 You **boasted** that you dug wells and drank water in foreign lands,
52. 5 Those who rule over you **boast** and brag and constantly show
Jer 9.23 "Wise men should not **boast** of their wisdom, nor strong men
9.24 If anyone wants to **boast,**
9.24 he should **boast** that he knows and understands me,
23.32 lead my people astray with their lies and their **boasting.**
48.30 Their **boasts** amount to nothing, and the things they do will
49. 4 Why do you unfaithful people **boast?**
Ezek 27. 3 Tyre, you **boasted** of your perfect beauty.
35.13 I have heard the wild, **boastful** way you have talked against me."
Dan 7. 8 This horn had human eyes and a mouth that was **boasting** proudly.
7.11 I could still hear the little horn bragging and **boasting.**
7.20 It had eyes and a mouth and was **boasting** proudly.
11.36 He will **boast** that he is greater than any god, superior even
Amos 4. 5 to God, and **boast** about the extra offerings you bring!
6.13 You **boast** about capturing the town of Lodebar.
6.13 You **boast,** "We were strong enough to take Karnaim."
Zeph 2. 8 my people, and **boasting** that they would seize their land.
Rom 1.30 they are hateful to God, insolent, proud, and **boastful;**
2.17 you depend on the Law and **boast** about God;
2.23 You **boast** about having God's law—but do you bring shame
3.27 What, then, can we **boast** about?
4. 2 would have something to **boast** about—but not in God's sight.
5. 2 And so we **boast** of the hope we have of sharing God's
5. 3 We also **boast** of our troubles, because we know that trouble
1 Cor 1.29 This means that no one can **boast** in God's presence.
1.31 "Whoever wants to boast must **boast** of what the Lord has done."
3.21 No one, then, should **boast** about what men can do.
4. 7 Well, then, how can you **boast,** as if what you have were
9.15 Nobody is going to turn my rightful **boast** into empty words!
9.16 I have no right to **boast** just because I preach the gospel.
2 Cor 3. 1 Does this sound as if we were again **boasting** about ourselves?
5.12 able to answer those who **boast** about a man's appearance
7.14 I did **boast** of you to him, and you have not disappointed
7.14 in the same way the **boast** we made to Titus has proved

2 Cor 8.24 and know that we are right in **boasting** about you.
9. 2 and I have **boasted** of you to the people in
9. 3 these brothers, so that our **boasting** about you in this matter
10. 8 even if I have **boasted** somewhat too much about the authority
10.13 for us, however, our **boasting** will not go beyond certain limits;
10.15 So we do not **boast** about the work that others have done
10.16 and shall not have to **boast** about work already done in
10.17 "Whoever wants to boast must **boast** about what the Lord has done."
11.10 I promise that this **boast** of mine will not be silenced
11.12 from having any reason for **boasting** and saying that they
11.16 a fool, so that I will have a little to **boast** of.
11.17 in this matter of **boasting** I am really talking like a fool.
11.18 there are so many who **boast** for merely human reasons,
11.21 But if anyone dares to **boast** about something—I am talking
11.30 If I must **boast,**
11.30 I will **boast** about things that show how weak
12. 1 I have to **boast,** even though it doesn't do any good.
12. 5 So I will **boast** about this man—
12. 5 but I will not **boast** about myself, except the things
12. 6 If I wanted to **boast,** I would not be a fool,
12. 6 But I will not **boast,** because I do not want anyone
Gal 6.12 ones who want to show off and **boast** about external matters.
6.13 circumcised so that they can **boast** that you submitted to this
6.14 for me, however, I will **boast** only about the cross of our
Eph 2. 8 but God's gift, so that no one can **boast** about it.
Phil 2. 3 a cheap desire to **boast,** but be humble towards one another,
1 Thes 2.19 and our reason for **boasting** of our victory in the presence
2 Thes 1. 4 That is why we ourselves **boast** about you in the churches
1. 4 We **boast** about the way you continue to endure and believe
2 Tim 3. 2 People will be selfish, greedy, **boastful,** and conceited;
Jas 3. 5 small as it is, it can **boast** about great things.
3.14 don't sin against the truth by **boasting** of your wisdom.
4.16 But now you are proud, and you **boast;**
4.16 all such **boasting** is wrong.
Jude 16 they **boast** about themselves and flatter others in order to get

BOAT

Gen 6.14 Build a **boat** for yourself out of good timber;
6.16 Make a roof for the **boat** and leave a space of 44
6.18 Go into the **boat** with your wife, your sons, and their wives.
6.19 Take into the **boat** with you a male and a female of
7. 1 Lord said to Noah, "Go into the **boat** with your whole family;
7. 7 and their wives, went into the **boat** to escape the flood.
7. 9 went into the **boat** with Noah, as God had commanded.
7.13 his wife went into the **boat** with their three sons, Shem,
7.15 went into the **boat** with Noah, [16]as God had commanded.
7.17 and the water became deep enough for the **boat** to float.
7.18 The water became deeper, and the **boat** drifted on the surface.
7.23 left were Noah and those who were with him in the **boat.**
8. 1 not forgotten Noah and all the animals with him in the **boat;**
8. 4 of the seventh month the **boat** came to rest on a mountain
8. 9 It flew back to the **boat,** and Noah reached out and took
8.13 removed the covering of the **boat,** looked round, and saw that
8.16 Noah, [16]"Go out of the **boat** with your wife, your sons,
8.18 Noah went out of the **boat** with his wife, his sons, and
8.19 birds went out of the **boat** in groups of their own kind.
9.10 all animals—everything that came out of the **boat** with you.
9.18 Noah who went out of the **boat** were Shem, Ham, and Japheth.
Job 9.26 life passes like the swiftest **boat,** as fast as an eagle
Is 18. 2 land ambassadors come down the Nile in **boats** made of reeds.
Mt 4.21 were in their **boat** with their father Zebedee, getting their nets
4.22 at once they left the **boat** and their father, and went with
8.23 Jesus got into a **boat,** and his disciples went with him.
8.24 storm hit the lake, and the **boat** was in danger of sinking.
9. 1 Jesus got into the **boat** and went back across the lake
13. 2 that he got into a **boat** and sat in it, while the
14.13 he left there in a **boat** and went to a lonely place
14.14 Jesus got out of the **boat,** and when he saw the large
14.22 the disciples get into the **boat** and go on ahead to the
14.24 and by this time the **boat** was far out in the lake,
14.29 Peter got out of the **boat** and started walking on the water
14.32 They both got into the **boat,** and the wind died down.
14.33 Then the disciples in the **boat** worshipped Jesus.
15.39 people away, got into a **boat,** and went to the territory of
24.38 women married, up to the very day Noah went into the **boat;**
Mk 1.19 They were in their **boat** getting their nets ready.
1.20 their father Zebedee in the **boat** with the hired men and went
3. 9 his disciples to get a **boat** ready for him, so that the
4. 1 so large that he got into a **boat** and sat in it.
4. 1 The **boat** was out in the water, and the crowd stood
4.36 disciples got into the **boat** in which Jesus was already sitting,
4.36 Other **boats** were there too.
4.37 to spill over into the **boat,** so that it was about to
4.38 in the back of the **boat,** sleeping with his head on
5. 2 Jesus got out of the **boat,** he was met by a man
5.18 Jesus was getting into the **boat,** the man who had had the
6.32 started out in a **boat** by themselves for a lonely place.
6.34 Jesus got out of the **boat,** he saw this large crowd,
6.45 his disciples get into the **boat** and go ahead of him
6.47 When evening came, the **boat** was in the middle of the lake,
6.51 Then he got into the **boat** with them, and the wind died
6.53 and came to land at Gennesaret, where they tied up the **boat.**
6.54 As they left the **boat,** people recognized Jesus at once.
8.10 at once got into a **boat** with his disciples and went to
8.13 got back into the **boat,** and started across to the other
8.14 enough bread and had only one loaf with them in the **boat.**
Lk 5. 2 He saw two **boats** pulled up on the beach;
5. 3 got into one of the **boats**—it belonged to Simon—and asked
5. 3 Jesus sat in the **boat** and taught the crowd.
Lk 5. 4 to Simon, "Push the **boat** out further to the deep water,
5. 7 to their partners in the other **boat** to come and help them.
5. 7 They came and filled both **boats** so full of fish
5. 7 that the **boats** were about to sink.
5.11 pulled the **boats** up on the beach, left everything, and followed
8.22 Jesus got into a **boat** with his disciples and said
8.23 on the lake, and the **boat** began to fill with water,
8.37 So Jesus got into the **boat** and left.
17.27 Noah went into the **boat** and the flood came and killed
Jn 6.17 got into a **boat,** and went back across the lake
6.19 on the water, coming near the **boat,** and they were terrified.
6.21 willingly took him into the **boat,**
6.21 and immediately the **boat** reached land at the place they
6.22 the lake realized that there had been only one **boat** there.
6.23 Other **boats,** which were from Tiberias, came to shore near
6.24 they got into those **boats** and went to Capernaum, looking for
21. 3 they went out in a **boat,** but all that night they did
21. 6 on the right side of the **boat,** and you will catch some."
21. 8 came to shore in the **boat,** pulling the net full of fish.
Acts 27.16 with some difficulty, we managed to make the ship's **boat** secure.
27.30 they lowered the **boat** into the water and pretended that they
27.32 soldiers cut the ropes that held the **boat** and let it go.
Heb 11. 7 obeyed God and built a **boat** in which he and his family
1 Pet 3.20 waited patiently during the days that Noah was building his **boat.**
3.20 The few people in the **boat**—eight in all—were saved

BOAZ (1)
Ruth's husband.

Ruth 2. 1 Naomi had a relative named **Boaz,** a rich and influential
2. 3 so happened that she was in a field that belonged to **Boaz.**
2. 4 Some time later **Boaz** himself arrived from Bethlehem
2. 5 **Boaz** asked the man in charge, "Who is that young woman?"
2. 8 Then **Boaz** said to Ruth, "Let me give you some advice.
2.10 the ground, and said to **Boaz,** "Why should you be so
2.11 **Boaz** answered, "I have heard about everything that you
2.14 At meal-time **Boaz** said to Ruth, "Come and have a piece
2.14 with the workers, and **Boaz** passed some roasted grain to her.
2.15 go on picking up corn, **Boaz** ordered the workers, "Let her
2.19 had been working in a field belonging to a man named **Boaz.**
2.20 "May the Lord bless **Boaz!"**
2.22 be better for you to work with the women in **Boaz'** field.
3. 2 Remember that this man **Boaz,** whose women you have been working with,
3. 7 When **Boaz** had finished eating and drinking, he was in a
3.14 her to be seen, because **Boaz** did not want anyone to know
3.15 **Boaz** said to her, "Take off your cloak and spread it
3.16 Ruth told her everything that **Boaz** had done for her.
3.18 **Boaz** will not rest today until he settles the matter."
4. 1 **Boaz** went to the meeting place at the town gate and sat
4. 1 nearest relative, the man whom **Boaz** had mentioned, came by,
4. 1 and **Boaz** called to him, "Come over here,
4. 2 Then **Boaz** got ten of the leaders of the town and asked
4. 5 **Boaz** said, "Very well, but if you buy the field from Naomi,
4. 8 when the man said to **Boaz,** "You buy it,"
4. 8 he took off his sandal and gave it to **Boaz.**
4. 9 Then **Boaz** said to the leaders and all the others there,
4.13 So **Boaz** took Ruth home as his wife.
4.18 Perez, Hezron, Ram, Amminadab, Nahshon, Salmon, **Boaz,** Obed,
1 Chr 2.11 prominent man of the tribe of Judah), [11]Salmon, **Boaz,**
Mt 1. 2 Amminadab, Nahshon, Salmon, **Boaz** (his mother was Rahab), Obed
Lk 3.32 of Obed, the son of **Boaz,** the son of Salmon, the son

BODILY see BODY

BODY
[BODILY, FULL-BODIED, HEAVENLY BODIES]

Gen 7.11 the outlets of the vast **body** of water beneath the earth
15.11 Vultures came down on the **bodies,** but Abram drove them off.
23. 3 place where his wife's **body** was lying, went to the Hittites,
37.20 kill him and throw his **body** into one of the dry wells.
40.19 Then he will hang your **body** on a pole, and the birds
47.18 is nothing left to give you except our **bodies** and our lands.
50. 2 Then Joseph gave orders to embalm his father's **body.**
50.13 they carried his **body** to Canaan and buried it in the
50.25 leads you to that land, you will take my **body** with you."
50.26 They embalmed his **body** and put it in a coffin.
Ex 2.12 he killed the Egyptian and hid his **body** in the sand.
4. 7 this time, it was healthy, just like the rest of his **body.**
13.19 Moses took the **body** of Joseph with him, as Joseph had
13.19 you, you must carry my **body** with you from this place."
Lev 1.17 wings and tear its **body** open, without tearing the wings off,
10. 4 here and carry your cousins' **bodies** away from the sacred
11. 8 Do not eat these animals or even touch their dead **bodies;**
11.11 You must not eat them or even touch their dead **bodies.**
11.24 Whoever touches the dead **bodies** of the following
11.24 Whoever carries their dead **bodies** must wash his clothes,
11.31 Whoever touches them or their dead **bodies** will be unclean
11.32 And if their dead **bodies** fall on anything, it will be unclean.
11.33 And if their **bodies** fall into a clay pot, everything
11.35 Anything on which the dead **bodies** fall is unclean;
11.36 anything else that touches their dead **bodies** is unclean.
11.40 anyone who carries the dead **body** must wash his clothes, but
13.13 actually has covered the whole **body,** he shall pronounce the
14. 9 his eyebrows, and all the rest of the hair on his **body;**
15.16 bathe his whole **body,** and he remains unclean until evening.
19.28 yourselves or cut gashes in your **body** to mourn for the dead.
21. 5 or cut gashes on his **body** to show that he is in

Lev	26.30	and throw your dead **bodies** on your fallen idols.
Num	5. 2	dreaded skin disease or a **bodily** discharge and everyone who
	8. 7	them to shave their whole **bodies** and to wash their clothes.
	19.18	had touched the human bone or the dead **body** or the grave.
Deut	14. 8	eat any of these animals or even touch their dead **bodies.**
	17. 8	of property rights or of **bodily** injury or those cases that
	21. 2	from the place where the **body** was found to each of the
	21. 3	town nearest to where the **body** was found are to select a
	21.22	for a crime and his **body** is hung on a post, [23] it
	21.23	same day, because a dead **body** hanging on a post brings God's
	21.23	Bury the **body,** so that you will not defile the land that
	28.26	will come and eat your **bodies,** and there will be no one
	28.27	He will make your **bodies** break out with sores.
Josh	8.29	of Ai from a tree and left his **body** there until evening.
	8.29	Joshua gave orders for the **body** to be removed, and it was
	10.26	them on five trees, where their **bodies** stayed until evening.
	10.27	Joshua gave orders, and their **bodies** were taken down and
	24.32	The **body** of Joseph, which the people of Israel had
Judg	14. 8	find a swarm of bees and some honey inside the dead **body.**
	14. 9	he had taken the honey from the dead **body** of a lion.
	16.31	and the rest of his family came down to get his **body.**
	19.28	So he put her **body** across the donkey and started on his
	19.29	He took his concubine's **body,** cut it into twelve pieces, and
	20. 1	They gathered in one **body** in the Lord's presence at Mizpah.
	20. 6	I took her **body,** cut it in pieces, and sent one piece
	20.36	The main **body** of the Israelite army had retreated from the
1 Sam	5. 4	only the **body** was left.
	17.44	"and I will give your **body** to the birds and animals to
	17.46	And I will give the **bodies** of the Philistine soldiers to the
	31. 8	corpses, and they found the **bodies** of Saul and his three
	31.10	Astarte, and they nailed his **body** to the wall of the city
	31.12	They took down the **bodies** of Saul and his sons from the
2 Sam	2.32	and his men took Asahel's **body** and buried it in the family
	18.17	They took Absalom's **body,** threw it into a deep pit in
	20.11	Joab's men stood by Amasa's **body** and called out, "Everyone
	20.12	Amasa's **body,** covered with blood, was lying in the
	20.12	stopping, so he dragged the **body** from the road into the
	20.13	After the **body** had been removed from the road, everyone
	21.12	the Philistines had hanged the **bodies** on the day they killed
1 Kgs	13.22	will be killed, and your **body** will not be buried in your
	13.24	His **body** lay on the road, and the donkey and the lion
	13.25	passed by and saw the **body** on the road, with the lion
	13.28	off and found the prophet's **body** lying on the road, with the
	13.28	The lion had not eaten the **body** or attacked the donkey.
	13.29	old prophet picked up the **body,** put it on the donkey, and
	13.31	bury me in this grave and lay my **body** next to his.
	21.23	says that dogs will eat her **body** in the city of Jezreel.
	22.37	His **body** was taken to Samaria and buried.
2 Kgs	4.34	out over the boy, the boy's **body** started to get warm.
	9.10	**body** will be eaten by dogs in the territory of Jezreel.' "
	9.25	his aide Bidkar, "Get his **body** and throw it in the field
	9.26	So take Joram's **body,"** Jehu ordered his aide, "and throw
	9.28	His officials took his **body** back to Jerusalem in a
	9.33	horses and chariot over her **body,** [34] entered the palace,
	9.36	'Dogs will eat Jezebel's **body** in the territory of Jezreel.
	10.25	swords, killed them all, and dragged the **bodies** outside.
	13.21	As soon as the **body** came into contact with Elisha's bones,
	14.20	His **body** was carried back to Jerusalem on a horse and
	23.30	His officials placed his **body** in a chariot and took it
1 Chr	10. 8	corpses, and they found the **bodies** of Saul and his sons
	10.12	men went and fetched the **bodies** of Saul and his sons and
2 Chr	16.14	perfumed oils to prepare his **body** for burial, and they built
	22. 9	But they did bury his **body** out of respect for his
	25.28	His **body** was carried to Jerusalem on a horse, and he was
Ezra	6.11	sharpened at one end, and then driven through his **body.**
Esth	9.13	And order the **bodies** of Haman's ten sons to be hung from
	9.14	The **bodies** of Haman's ten sons were publicly displayed.
Job	2. 5	now suppose you hurt his **body**—he will curse you to your
	2. 7	Lord's presence and made sores break out all over Job's **body.**
	4.14	my whole **body** shook with fear.
	6. 4	me with arrows, and their poison spreads through my **body.**
	6.12	Is my **body** bronze?
	7. 5	My **body** is full of worms;
	7.15	until I would rather be strangled than live in this miserable **body.**
	10.11	You formed my **body** with bones and sinews and covered the
	14.22	the pain of his own **body** and the grief of his own
	18.13	deadly disease spreads over his **body** and causes his arms and
	19.26	eaten by disease, while still in this **body** I will see God.
	20.11	His **body** used to be young and vigorous, but soon it will
	20.25	An arrow sticks through his **body;**
	21.23	they die happy and at ease, their **bodies** well-nourished.
	21.33	procession, and even the earth lies gently on his **body.**
	33.19	a man by sending sickness and filling his **body** with pain.
	33.21	His **body** wastes away to nothing;
	33.25	His **body** will grow young and strong again;
	39.30	Around dead **bodies** the eagles gather, and the young
	40.16	strength there is in his **body,** and what power there is in
Ps	38. 3	my whole **body** is diseased because of my sins.
	49.14	triumph over them, as their **bodies** quickly decay in the
	63.10	They will be killed in battle, and their **bodies** eaten by wolves.
	73.26	My mind and my **body** may grow weak, but God is my
	74.14	the monster Leviathan and fed his **body** to desert animals.
	79. 2	They left the **bodies** of your people for the vultures,
	79. 2	the **bodies** of your servants for wild animals
	83.10	You defeated them at Endor, and their **bodies** rotted on the ground.
	102. 3	my **body** is burning like fire.
	109.18	own curses soak into his **body** like water and into his bones
Prov	14.30	Peace of mind makes the **body** healthy, but jealousy is
Ecc	12. 7	Our **bodies** will return to the dust of the earth, and the
Song	5.14	His **body** is like smooth ivory, with sapphires set in it.
Is	1. 6	head to foot there is not a healthy spot on your **body.**
	5.25	mountains will shake, and the **bodies** of those who die will
	6. 2	with two wings, and its **body** with two, and used the other
	7.20	your beards, and the hair on your heads and your **bodies.**
	10.16	In their **bodies** there will be a fire that burns and burns.
	14.19	It is covered by the **bodies** of soldiers killed in battle,
	26.19	Their **bodies** will come back to life.
	66.24	they will see the dead **bodies** of those who have rebelled
Jer	9.22	Dead **bodies** are scattered everywhere, like piles of manure
	14.16	Their **bodies** will be thrown out into the streets of Jerusalem,
	14.18	into the fields, I see the **bodies** of men killed in war;
	15. 3	their **bodies** will be dragged off by dogs;
	16. 4	Their **bodies** will lie like piles of manure on the ground.
	16. 4	die of starvation, and their **bodies** will be food for the
	25.33	On that day the **bodies** of those whom the Lord has killed
	26.23	killed and his **body** thrown into the public burial-ground.)
	41. 7	and his men killed them and threw their **bodies** in a well.
	41. 9	into which Ishmael threw the **bodies** of the men he had killed
	41. 9	Ishmael filled the well with the **bodies.**
Lam	2.10	With dust on their heads and sackcloth on their **bodies.**
	2.20	Women are eating the **bodies** of the children they loved!
	3.13	He shot his arrows deep into my **body.**
Ezek	1. 9	When they moved, they moved as a group without turning their **bodies.**
	1.11	and their other two wings were folded against their **bodies.**
	1.23	next to it and covering its **body** with the other two wings.
	8. 2	From the waist down his **body** looked like fire, and from the
	10.12	Their **bodies,** backs, hands, wings, and wheels were covered with eyes.
	16. 8	I covered your naked **body** with my coat and promised to love
	29. 5	Your **body** will fall on the ground and be left unburied.
	32.27	under their heads and their shields over their **bodies.**
	35. 8	mountains with corpses, and the **bodies** of those who are
	37. 8	But there was no breath in the **bodies.**
	37. 9	to breathe into these dead **bodies,** and to bring them back to
	37.10	Breath entered the **bodies,** and they came to life and stood up.
	39. 4	and I will let their **bodies** be food for all the birds
	39.14	to find and bury those **bodies** remaining on the ground, so
	39.18	They are to eat the **bodies** of soldiers and drink the
Dan	4.33	The dew fell on his **body,** and his hair grew as long
	7.11	beast was killed, and its **body** was thrown into the flames
	10. 6	His **body** shone like a jewel.
Joel	2.20	Their dead **bodies** will stink.
Amos	4.10	your nostrils with the stink of dead **bodies** in your camps.
	6.10	charge of the funeral, will take the **body** out of the house.
	8. 3	There will be dead **bodies** everywhere.
Nah	3. 3	Corpses are piled high, dead **bodies** without number— men
Hab	3.16	My **body** goes limp, and my feet stumble beneath me.
Zeph	1.17	and their dead **bodies** will lie rotting on the ground."
Hag	2.13	"Suppose a man is defiled because he has touched a dead **body.**
Mal	2.15	Didn't God make you one **body** and spirit with her?
Mt	5.29	lose a part of your **body**
	5.29	than to have your whole **body** thrown into hell.
	5.30	of your limbs than for your whole **body** to go to hell.
	6.22	"The eyes are like a lamp for the **body.**
	6.22	your eyes are sound, your whole **body** will be full of light;
	6.23	if your eyes are no good, your **body** will be in darkness.
	6.25	need in order to stay alive, or about clothes for your **body.**
	6.25	And isn't the **body** worth more than clothes?
	10.28	afraid of those who kill the **body** but cannot kill the soul;
	10.28	afraid of God, who can destroy both **body** and soul in hell.
	14.12	John's disciples came, carried away his **body,** and buried
	15.17	goes into his stomach and then on out of his **body.**
	24.28	"Wherever there is a dead **body,** the vultures will gather.
	26.12	pour this perfume on my **body** to get me ready for burial.
	26.26	"this is my **body."**
	27.58	into the presence of Pilate and asked for the **body** of Jesus.
	27.58	Pilate gave orders for the **body** to be given to Joseph.
	27.64	to go and steal the **body,** and then tell the people that
	28.13	during the night and stole his **body** while you were asleep.
Mk	6.29	they came and took away his **body,** and buried it.
	7.19	but into his stomach and then goes on out of the **body."**
	12. 8	and killed him and threw his **body** out of the vineyard.
	14. 8	she poured perfume on my **body** to prepare it ahead of time
	14.22	"Take it," he said, "this is my **body."**
	15.42	the presence of Pilate and asked him for the **body** of Jesus.
	15.45	the officer's report, Pilate told Joseph he could have the **body.**
	15.46	a linen sheet, took the **body** down, wrapped it in the sheet,
	15.47	were watching and saw where the **body** of Jesus was placed.
	16. 1	and Salome bought spices to go and anoint the **body** of Jesus.
Lk	1.80	The child grew and developed in **body** and spirit.
	2.52	Jesus grew both in **body** and in wisdom, gaining favour
	3.22	Holy Spirit came down upon him in **bodily** form like a dove.
	11.34	Your eyes are like a lamp for the **body.**
	11.34	When your eyes are sound, your whole **body** is full of light;
	11.34	your eyes are no good, your whole **body** will be in darkness.
	11.36	If your whole **body** is full of light, with no part of
	12. 4	those who kill the **body** but cannot afterwards do anything worse.
	12.22	to stay alive or about the clothes you need for your **body.**
	12.23	than food, and the **body** much more important than clothes.
	17.37	"Wherever there is a dead **body,** the vultures will gather."
	22.19	saying, "This is my **body,** which is given for you.
	23.52	into the presence of Pilate and asked for the **body** of Jesus.
	23.53	Then he took the **body** down, wrapped it in a linen sheet,
	23.55	and saw the tomb and how Jesus' **body** was placed in it.
	23.56	home and prepared the spices and perfumes for the **body.**
	24. 3	but they did not find the **body** of the Lord Jesus.
	24.23	went at dawn to the tomb, [23] but could not find his **body.**
Jn	2.21	But the temple Jesus was speaking about was his **body.**
	11.52	together into one **body** all the scattered people of God.
	19.31	been crucified, and to take the **bodies** down from the crosses.

Jn 19.31 they did not want the **bodies** to stay on the crosses
19.38 of Arimathea, asked Pilate if he could take Jesus' **body.**
19.38 he could have the **body,** so Joseph went and took it
19.40 The two men took Jesus' **body** and wrapped it in linen
19.40 according to the Jewish custom of preparing a **body** for burial.
19.42 and because the tomb was close by, they placed Jesus' **body**
20.12 in white, sitting where the **body** of Jesus had been, one at
Acts 2.31 his **body** did not rot in the grave.'
5. 6 in, wrapped up his **body,** carried him out, and buried him.
7.16 Their **bodies** were taken to Shechem, where they were buried
9.37 Her **body** was washed and laid in a room upstairs.
9.40 then he turned to the **body** and said, "Tabitha, get up!"
13.36 buried with his ancestors, and his **body** rotted in the grave.
Rom 4.19 when he thought of his **body,** which was already practically dead,
6.12 longer rule in your mortal **bodies,** so that you obey the
7. 4 also have died because you are part of the **body** of Christ;
7. 5 were at work in our **bodies,** and all we did ended in
7.23 law at work in my **body**—a law that fights against
7.23 to the law of sin which is at work in my **body.**
7.24 will rescue me from this **body** that is taking me to death?
8.10 with God, even though your **bodies** are going to die because
8.11 give life to your mortal **bodies** by the presence of his
12. 4 many parts in the one **body,** and all these parts have
12. 5 are many, we are one **body** in union with Christ, and we
12. 5 are all joined to each other as different parts of one **body.**
1 Cor 5. 3 far away from you in **body,** still I am there with you
5. 5 over to Satan for his **body** to be destroyed, so that his
6.13 The **body** is not to be used for sexual immorality,
6.13 and the Lord provides for the **body.**
6.15 You know that your bodies are parts of the **body** of Christ.
6.15 take a part of Christ's **body**
6.15 and make it part of the **body** of a prostitute?
6.16 man who joins his **body** to a prostitute becomes physically one
6.16 The scripture says quite plainly, "The two will become one **body."**
6.18 Any other sin a man commits does not affect his **body;**
6.18 is guilty of sexual immorality sins against his own **body.**
6.19 Don't you know that your **body** is the temple of the Holy
6.20 So use your **bodies** for God's glory.
7. 4 is not the master of her own **body,** but her husband is;
7. 4 is not the master of his own **body,** but his wife is.
7.34 because she wants to be dedicated both in **body** and spirit;
9.27 harden my **body** with blows and bring it under complete control,
10. 5 and so their dead **bodies** were scattered over the desert.
10.16 when we eat it, we are sharing in the **body** of Christ.
10.17 though many, are one **body,** for we all share the same
11.24 broke it, and said, "This is my **body,** which is for you.
11.27 he is guilty of sin against the Lord's **body** and blood.
11.29 the meaning of the Lord's **body** when he eats the bread
12.12 Christ is like a single **body,** which has many parts;
12.12 it is still one **body,** even though it is made up of
12.13 been baptized into the one **body** by the same Spirit,
12.14 For the **body** itself is not made up of only one part,
12.15 I don't belong to the **body,"**
12.15 that would not keep it from being a part of the **body.**
12.16 I don't belong to the **body,"**
12.16 that would not keep it from being a part of the **body.**
12.17 If the whole **body** were just an eye, how could it hear?
12.18 every different part in the **body** just as he wanted it to
12.19 There would not be a **body** if it were all only one
12.20 As it is, there are many parts but one **body.**
12.22 do without the parts of the **body** that seem to be weaker;
12.23 while the parts of the **body** which don't look very nice
12.24 God himself has put the **body** together in such a way
12.25 is no division in the **body,** but all its different parts have
12.26 If one part of the **body** suffers, all the other parts
12.27 All of you are Christ's **body,** and each one is a part
13. 3 and even give up my **body** to be burnt
15.35 What kind of **body** will they have?"
15.37 not the **full-bodied** plant that will later grow up.
15.38 God provides that seed with the **body** he wishes;
15.38 he gives each seed its own proper **body.**
15.40 And there are **heavenly bodies** and earthly bodies;
15.40 the beauty that belongs to **heavenly bodies** is different from
15.40 from the beauty that belongs to earthly **bodies.**
15.42 When the **body** is buried, it is mortal;
15.44 When buried, it is a physical **body;**
15.44 when raised, it will be a spiritual **body.**
15.44 is, of course, a physical **body,**
15.44 so there has to be a spiritual **body.**
2 Cor 4.10 we carry in our mortal **bodies** the death of Jesus,
4.10 so that his life also may be seen in our **bodies.**
4.11 that his life may be seen in this mortal **body** of ours.
5. 1 tent we live in—our **body** here on earth—is torn down,
5. 3 by being clothed with it we shall not be without a **body.**
5. 4 get rid of our earthly **body,** but that we want to have
5. 6 are at home in the **body** we are away from the Lord's
5. 8 leave our home in the **body** and be at home with
5.10 everything he has done, good or bad, in his **bodily** life.
7. 1 ourselves from everything that makes **body** or soul unclean,
Gal 6.17 scars I have on my **body** show that I am the slave
Eph 1.23 The church is Christ's **body,** the completion of him who
2. 3 doing whatever suited the wishes of our own **bodies** and minds.
2.11 what men do to their **bodies**)—remember what you were in the
2.14 With his own **body** he broke down the wall that separated them
2.16 both races into one **body** and brought them back to God.
3. 6 are members of the same **body** and share in the promise
4. 4 There is one **body** and one Spirit, just as there is one
4.12 Christian service, in order to build up the **body** of Christ.
4.16 the different parts of the **body** fit together,
4.16 and the whole **body** is held together by every joint
4.16 as it should, the whole **body** grows and builds itself up
Eph 4.25 because we are all members together in the **body** of Christ.
5.23 and Christ is himself the Saviour of the church, his **body.**
5.28 to love their wives just as they love their own **bodies.**
5.29 (No one ever hates his own **body.**
5.30 for we are members of his **body.)**
Phil 3. 2 those dogs, those men who insist on cutting the **body.**
3.19 end up in hell, because their god is their **bodily** desires.
3.21 will change our weak mortal **bodies** and make them like his
3.21 like his own glorious **body,** using that power by which he
Col 1.18 He is the head of his **body,** the church;
1.18 he is the source of the **body's** life.
1.24 remains of Christ's sufferings on behalf of his **body,** the church.
2. 5 though I am absent in **body,** yet I am with you in
2.19 stopped holding on to Christ, who is the head of the **body.**
2.19 Christ's control the whole **body** is nourished and held together
2.23 and false humility, and severe treatment of the **body;**
3.15 this peace that God has called you together in the one **body.**
1 Thes 2.17 of course, but only in **body**—how we missed you
5.23 whole being—spirit, soul, and **body**—free from every fault
Heb 7.10 so to speak, in the **body** of his ancestor Abraham when
10. 5 sacrifices and offerings, but you have prepared a **body** for me.
10.10 offering that he made of his own **body** once and for all.
10.20 way, through the curtain—that is, through his own **body.**
10.22 purified from a guilty conscience and with **bodies** washed with
11.22 and leave instructions about what should be done with his **body.**
13.11 but the **bodies** of the animals are burnt outside the camp.
Jas 2.26 So then, as the **body** without the spirit is dead,
3. 6 occupying its place in our **bodies** and spreading evil through our
1 Pet 2.11 Do not give in to **bodily** passions, which are always at war
2.24 carried our sins in his **body** to the cross, so that we
3.21 not the washing away of **bodily** dirt, but the promise made
2 Pet 1.14 soon put off this mortal **body,** as our Lord Jesus Christ
2.10 those who follow their filthy **bodily** lusts and despise God's
2.13 in broad daylight that will satisfy their **bodily** appetites;
2.18 stupid statements, and use immoral **bodily** lusts to trap those
3.10 with a shrill noise, the **heavenly bodies** will burn up and be
3.12 and be destroyed, and the **heavenly bodies** will be melted by
Jude 8 people have visions which make them sin against their own **bodies;**
9 about who should have the **body** of Moses, Michael did not dare
Rev 11. 8 and kill them, [9]and their **bodies** will lie in the street
11. 9 races will look at their **bodies** for three and a half days

BODYGUARD

1 Sam 22.14 own son-in-law, captain of your **bodyguard,** and highly
28. 2 I will make you my permanent **bodyguard."**
2 Sam 8.18 Jehoiada was in charge of David's **bodyguard** and David's sons were priests.
15.18 to him as the royal **bodyguard** passed by in front of him.
16. 6 though David was surrounded by his men and his **bodyguard.**
20. 7 So Joab's men, the royal **bodyguard,** and all the other
20.23 Benaiah son of Jehoiada was in charge of David's **bodyguard;**
23.23 David put him in charge of his **bodyguard.**
1 Kgs 1. 8 Shimei, Rei, and David's **bodyguard** were not on Adonijah's side.
1.10 Solomon or Nathan the prophet, or Benaiah, or the king's **bodyguard.**
1.38 and the royal **bodyguard** put Solomon on King David's mule,
1.44 Zadok, Nathan, Benaiah, and the royal **bodyguard** to escort him.
2 Kgs 11. 4 in charge of the royal **bodyguard** and of the palace guards,
11.19 he, the officers, the royal **bodyguard,** and the palace guards
1 Chr 11.25 David put him in charge of his **bodyguard.**
18.17 Benaiah son of Jehoiada was in charge of David's **bodyguard;**
Neh 4.23 did any of my companions nor my servants nor my **bodyguard.**
Song 3. 7 sixty soldiers form the **bodyguard,** the finest soldiers in Israel.
Ezek 12.14 court and his advisers and **bodyguard,** and people will search
Dan 2.14 Arioch, commander of the king's **bodyguard,** who had been

BOIL (1)

Ex 12. 9 any of it raw or **boiled,** but eat it roasted whole, including
16.23 what you want to bake and **boil** what you want to boil.
29.31 of Aaron and his sons and **boil** it in a holy place.
Lev 6.28 in which the meat is **boiled** must be broken, and if a
8.31 Tent of the Lord's presence, **boil** it, and eat it there with
Num 6.19 shoulder of the ram is **boiled,** the priest shall take it and
11. 8 it into flour, and then **boil** it and make it into flat
Deut 16. 7 **Boil** the meat and eat it at the one place of worship;
1 Sam 2.15 he won't accept **boiled** meat from you, only raw meat."
2 Chr 35.13 to the regulations, and **boiled** the sacred offerings in pots,
Job 41.31 churns up the sea like **boiling** water and makes it bubble
Is 64. 2 They would tremble like water **boiling** over a hot fire.
Jer 1.13 answered, "I see a pot **boiling** in the north, and it is
1.14 said to me, "Destruction will **boil** over from the north on
Lam 4.10 loving mothers **boiled** their own children for food.
Ezek 24. 5 Let the water **boil;**
24. 5 **boil** the bones and the meat."
24.10 **Boil** away the broth!
46.20 where the priests are to **boil** the meat offered as sacrifices
46.24 servants are to **boil** the sacrifices the people offer."
Zech 14.21 will use them for **boiling** the meat of the sacrifices.

BOIL (2)

Ex 9. 9 and everywhere they will produce **boils** that become open
9.10 the air, and they produced **boils** that became open sores on
9.11 they were covered with **boils,** like all the other Egyptians.
Lev 13. 2 on his skin or a **boil** or an inflammation which could develop
13.18 If anyone has a **boil** that has healed [19]and if
13.19 reddish-white spot appears where the **boil** was, he shall go
13.20 It is a dreaded skin-disease that has started in the **boil.**

Lev 13.23 the scar left from the **boil,** and the priest shall pronounce
14.55 sores, **boils,** or inflammations;
Deut 28.27 The Lord will send **boils** on you, as he did on the
28.35 **boils** will cover you from head to foot.
2 Kgs 20. 7 attendants to put on his **boil** a paste made of figs, and
Is 38. 6 paste made of figs on his **boil,** and he would get well.

BOLD

Gen 18.27 "Please forgive my **boldness** in continuing to speak to you,
18.31 "Please forgive my **boldness** in continuing to speak to you,
Job 13.16 may even be that my **boldness** will save me, since no wicked
Prov 7.11 She was a **bold** and shameless woman who always walked the
Dan 11.25 "He will **boldly** raise a large army to attack the king
Mk 15.42 so Joseph went **boldly** into the presence of Pilate
Acts 4.13 were amazed to see how **bold** Peter and John were
4.29 allow us, your servants, to speak your message with all **boldness.**
4.31 the Holy Spirit and began to proclaim God's message with **boldness.**
9.27 He also told them how **boldly** Saul had preached in the name
9.28 all over Jerusalem, preaching **boldly** in the name of the Lord.
13.46 But Paul and Barnabas spoke out even more **boldly:**
14. 3 for a long time, speaking **boldly** about the Lord, who proved
18.26 He began to speak **boldly** in the synagogue.
19. 8 three months spoke **boldly** with the people, holding discussions
26.26 speak to you with all **boldness,** because you know about these
28.31 taught about the Lord Jesus Christ, speaking with all **boldness**
Rom 10.20 And Isaiah is even **bolder** when he says, "I was found
15.15 letter I have been quite **bold** about certain subjects
15.15 I have been **bold** because of the privilege God has given me
15.18 I will be **bold** and speak only about what Christ has done
2 Cor 3.12 Because we have this hope, we are very **bold.**
Eph 3.12 in him we have the **boldness** to go into God's presence with
6.19 that I may speak **boldly** and make known the gospel's secret.
6.20 Pray that I may be **bold** in speaking about the gospel
Phil 1.14 so that they grow **bolder** all the time to preach the
1 Tim 3.13 are able to speak **boldly** about their faith in Christ Jesus.
Phlm 8 reason I could be **bold** enough, as your brother in Christ,
Heb 13. 6 Let us be **bold,** then, and say, "The Lord is my helper,
2 Pet 2.10 These false teachers are **bold** and arrogant, and show no respect

BOLT

Neh 3. 3 place, and put in the **bolts** and bars for locking the gate.
3. 6 place, and put in the **bolts** and bars for locking the gate.
3.13 in place, put in the **bolts** and the bars for locking the
3.14 place, and put in the **bolts** and the bars for locking the
3.15 the gates in place, and put in the **bolts** and the bars.
Job 38.10 a boundary for the sea and kept it behind **bolted** gates.

BONDS

Job 38.31 the Pleiades together or loosen the **bonds** that hold Orion?

BONE
[BACKBONE, BONY, JAW-BONE]

Gen 2.23 kind— Bone taken from my **bone,** and flesh from my flesh.
41. 3 they were thin and **bony.**
41.19 Then seven other cows came up which were thin and **bony.**
Ex 12.46 And do not break any of the animal's **bones.**
Lev 3. 9 tail cut off near the **backbone,** all the fat covering the
24.20 If he breaks a **bone,** one of his bones shall be broken;
Num 9.12 morning and do not break any of the animal's **bones.**
19.16 if someone touches a human **bone** or a grave, he becomes
19.18 who had touched the human **bone** or the dead body or the
24. 8 They devour their enemies, Crush their **bones,** smash their arrows.
Judg 15.15 he found the **jaw-bone** of a donkey that had recently died.
15.16 "With the **jaw-bone** of a donkey I killed a thousand men;
15.16 With the **jaw-bone** of a donkey I piled them up in piles."
15.17 After that, he threw the **jaw-bone** away.
1 Sam 31.13 Then they took the **bones** and buried them under the
2 Sam 21.12 he went and got the **bones** of Saul and of his son
21.13 David took the **bones** of Saul and Jonathan
21.13 and also gathered up the **bones** of the seven men who had
21.14 Then they buried the **bones** of Saul and Jonathan in the
1 Kgs 13. 2 sacrifices on you, and he will burn human **bones** on you."
2 Kgs 9.35 except her skull, and the **bones** of her hands and feet.
13.21 came into contact with Elisha's **bones,** the man came back to
23.14 ground where they had stood he covered with human **bones.**
23.16 he had the **bones** taken out of them and burnt on the
23.18 "His **bones** are not to be moved."
23.18 So his **bones** were not moved, neither were those of the
23.20 where they served, and he burnt human **bones** on every altar.
2 Chr 34. 5 He burnt the **bones** of the pagan priests on the altars
Job 10.11 You formed my body with **bones** and sinews
10.11 and covered the **bones** with muscles and skin.
16. 8 I am skin and **bones,** and people take that as proof of
19.20 My skin hangs loose on my **bones;**
30.17 At night my **bones** all ache;
33.21 you can see all his **bones;**
40.18 His **bones** are as strong as bronze, and his legs are like
Ps 22.14 All my **bones** are out of joint;
22.17 All my **bones** can be seen.
31.10 even my **bones** are wasting away.
34.20 not one of his **bones** is broken.
53. 5 God will scatter the **bones** of the enemies of his people.
102. 5 I am nothing but skin and **bones.**
109.18 soak into his body like water and into his **bones** like oil!
109.24 I am nothing but skin and **bones.**
139.15 When my **bones** were being formed, carefully put together
Ps 141. 7 chopped into bits, so their **bones** are scattered at the edge
Prov 12. 4 brings shame on her husband is like a cancer in his **bones.**
Is 38.13 cried out with pain, As if a lion were breaking my **bones.**
Jer 8. 1 "At that time the **bones** of the kings and of the officials
8. 1 Judah, as well as the **bones** of the priests, of the prophets,
8. 2 being gathered and buried, their **bones** will be like manure
50.17 and then King Nebuchadnezzar of Babylonia gnawed their **bones.**
Lam 3. 4 has left my flesh open and raw, and has broken my **bones.**
4. 8 their skin, dry as wood, has shrivelled on their **bones.**
Ezek 6. 5 I will scatter their **bones** all round the altars.
24. 4 and the legs— fill it with choice **bony** pieces too.
24. 5 boil the **bones** and the meat."
24.10 Burn up the **bones!**
37. 1 me down in a valley where the ground was covered with **bones.**
37. 2 that there were very many **bones** and that they were very dry.
37. 3 to me, "Mortal man, can these **bones** come back to life?"
37. 4 He said, "Prophesy to the **bones.**
37. 4 Tell these dry **bones** to listen to the word of the Lord.
37. 7 I heard a rattling noise, and the **bones** began to join together.
37. 8 While I watched, the **bones** were covered with sinews and muscles,
37.11 me, "Mortal man, the people of Israel are like these **bones.**
39.15 time they find a human **bone,** they will put a marker beside
Dan 6.24 pit, the lions pounced on them and broke all their **bones.**
Amos 2. 1 They dishonoured the **bones** of the king of Edom by burning
Mic 3. 2 You skin my people alive and tear the flesh off their **bones.**
3. 3 off their skin, break their **bones,** and chop them up like
Zeph 3. 3 hungry wolves, too greedy to leave a **bone** until morning.
Mt 23.27 but are full of **bones** and decaying corpses on the inside.
Lk 24.39 ghost doesn't have flesh and **bones,** as you can see I have."
Jn 19.36 "Not one of his **bones** will be broken."

BONFIRE see FIRE

BONY see BONE

BOOK

Ex 24. 7 Then he took the **book** of the covenant, in which the Lord's
32.32 remove my name from the **book** in which you have written the
32.33 sinned against me whose names I will remove from my **book.**
Num 21.14 That is why The **Book of the Lord's Battles** speaks of
Deut 1. 1 In this **book** are the words that Moses spoke to the people
17.18 have a copy of the **book** of God's laws and teachings made
17.19 He is to keep this **book** near him and read from it
28.58 that are written in this **book** and if you do not honour
28.61 are not mentioned in this **book** of God's laws and teachings,
29.20 the disasters written in this **book** will fall on him until
29.21 that is written in this **book** of the Lord's teachings.
29.27 on their land all the disasters written in this **book.**
30.10 all his laws that are written in this **book** of his teachings.
31.24 wrote God's Law in a **book,** taking care not to leave out
31.26 Lord's Covenant Box, [26]"Take this **book** of God's Law and
Josh 1. 8 Be sure that the **book** of the Law is always read in
8.34 curses, just as they are written in the **book** of the Law.
10.13 This is written in The **Book of Jashar.**
23. 6 everything that is written in the **book** of the Law of Moses.
24.26 Joshua wrote these commands in the **book** of the Law of God.
1 Sam 10.25 then wrote them in a **book,** which he deposited in a holy
2 Sam 1.18 (It is recorded in The **Book of Jashar.)**
2 Kgs 22. 8 that he had found the **book** of the Law in the Temple.
22. 8 Hilkiah gave him the **book,** and Shaphan read it.
22.10 then he said, "I have here a **book** that Hilkiah gave me."
22.11 When the king heard the **book** being read, he tore his
22.13 all the people of Judah about the teachings of this **book.**
22.13 ancestors have not done what this **book** says must be done."
22.16 its people, as written in the **book** that the king has read.
22.18 what is written in the **book,** [19]and you repented and
23. 2 king read aloud the whole **book** of the covenant which had
23. 3 demands attached to the covenant, as written in the **book.**
23.21 the Lord their God, as written in the **book** of the covenant.
23.24 the laws written in the **book** that the High Priest Hilkiah
1 Chr 9. 1 was recorded in The **Book of the Kings of Israel.**
2 Chr 17. 9 They took the **book** of the Law of the Lord and went
24.27 The Commentary on the **Book of Kings** contains the stories
34.14 storeroom, Hilkiah found the **book** of the Law of the Lord,
34.15 Shaphan, "I have found the **book** of the Law here in the
34.15 He gave Shaphan the **book,** [16]and Shaphan took it to the king.
34.18 Then he added, "I have here a **book** that Hilkiah gave me."
34.19 When the king heard the **book** being read, he tore his
34.21 Find out about the teachings of this **book.**
34.21 Lord and have not done what this **book** says must be done."
34.24 the curses written in the **book** that was read to the king.
34.26 what is written in the **book,** [27]and you repented and
34.30 king read aloud the whole **book** of the covenant, which had
34.31 demands attached to the covenant, as written in the **book.**
Ezra 6.18 according to the instructions contained in the **book** of Moses.
Neh 8. 1 had given Israel through Moses, to get the **book** of the Law.
8. 5 As soon as he opened the **book,** they all stood up.
Job 19.23 someone would remember my words and record them in a **book!**
Ps 40. 7 your instructions for me are in the **book** of the Law.
56. 8 Aren't they listed in your **book?**
69.28 May their names be erased from the **book of the living;**
139.16 been recorded in your **book,** before any of them ever began.
Ecc 12.12 end to the writing of **books,** and too much study will wear
Is 1. 1 This **book** contains the messages about Judah and Jerusalem
29.18 be able to hear a **book** being read aloud, and the blind,
30. 8 to write down in a **book** what the people are like, so
34.16 Search in the Lord's **book** of living creatures and read

Jer 1. 1 This **book** is the account of what was said by Jeremiah son
25.13 I spoke through Jeremiah—all the disasters recorded in this **book.**
30. 2 "Write down in a **book** everything that I have told you,
51.60 I wrote in a **book** an account of all the destruction that
51.63 when you finish reading this **book** to the people, then tie it
Dan 7.10 The court began its session, and the **books** were opened.
9. 2 I was studying the sacred **books** and thinking about the
10.20 to reveal to you what is written in the **Book of Truth.**
12. 1 nation whose names are written in God's **book** will be saved.
12. 4 "And now, Daniel, close the **book** and put a seal on it
Mal 3.16 was written down in a **book** a record of those who feared
Mk 12.26 you ever read in the **Book of Moses** the passage about
Lk 3. 4 As it is written in the **book** of the prophet Isaiah:
4.17 and was handed the **book** of the prophet Isaiah.
20.42 David himself says in the **book** of Psalms, 'The Lord said
24.27 Scriptures, beginning with the **books** of Moses and the writings
Jn 1.45 Moses wrote about in the **book** of the Law and whom the
20.30 many other miracles which are not written down in this **book.**
21.25 whole world could not hold the **books** that would be written.
Acts 1. 1 In my first **book** I wrote about all the things that Jesus
1.20 it is written in the **book** of Psalms, 'May his house become
7.42 of heaven, as it is written in the **book** of the prophets:
8.27 along, he was reading from the **book** of the prophet Isaiah.
8.30 and heard him reading from the **book** of the prophet Isaiah.
19.19 had practised magic brought their **books** together and burnt them
19.19 up the price of the **books,** and the total came to fifty
24.14 written in the Law of Moses and the **books** of the prophets.
Rom 9.25 This is what he says in the **book** of Hosea:
2 Cor 3.14 the same veil as they read the **books** of the old covenant.
Gal 3.10 that is written in the **book** of the Law is under God's
Phil 4. 3 other fellow-workers, whose names are in God's **book of the living.**
2 Tim 4.13 the **books** too, and especially the ones made of parchment.
Heb 9.19 and sprinkled it on the **book** of the Law and all the
10. 7 as it is written of me in the **book** of the Law.' "
Rev 1. 1 This **book** is the record of the events that Jesus Christ
1. 3 the one who reads this **book,** and happy are those who listen
1. 3 prophetic message and obey what is written in this **book!**
1.11 you see, and send the **book** to the churches in these seven
3. 5 I will not remove their names from the **book of the living.**
13. 8 the world in the **book of the living** which belongs to the
17. 8 the world in the **book of the living,** will all be amazed
20.12 **Books** were opened,
20.12 and then another book was opened, the **book of the living.**
20.12 according to what they had done, as recorded in the **books.**
20.15 name written in the **book of the living** was thrown into
21.27 in the Lamb's **book of the living** will enter the city.
22. 7 Happy are those who obey the prophetic words in this **book!"**
22. 9 prophets and of all those who obey the words in this **book.**
22.10 the prophetic words of this **book** a secret, because the time
22.18 solemnly warn everyone who hears the prophetic words of this **book:**
22.18 God will add to his punishment the plagues described in this **book.**
22.19 the prophetic words of this **book,** God will take away from
22.19 and of the Holy City, which are described in this **book.**

AV BOOTHS see SHELTERS

BOOTS

Is 9. 5 The **boots** of the invading army and all their bloodstained

BORDER

Gen 10.19 spread out, [19]until the Canaanite **borders** reached from
12.11 was about to cross the **border** into Egypt, he said to his
12.14 When he crossed the **border** into Egypt, the Egyptians did
15.18 this land from the **border** of Egypt to the River Euphrates,
Ex 23.31 I will make the **borders** of your land extend from the
25.11 gold inside and out and put a gold **border** all round it.
25.24 Cover it with pure gold and put a gold **border** round it.
25.25 75 millimetres wide round it and a gold **border** round the rim.
30. 3 projections with pure gold, and put a gold **border** round it.
30. 4 and attach them below the **border** on two sides to hold the
37. 2 gold inside and out and put a gold **border** all round it.
37.11 covered it with pure gold and put a gold **border** round it.
37.12 wide round it and put a gold **border** round the rim.
37.26 projections with pure gold and put a gold **border** round it.
37.27 and attached them below the **border** on the two sides, to hold
Num 20.16 we are at Kadesh, a town at the **border** of your territory.
20.23 Kadesh and arrived at Mount Hor, [23]on the **border** of Edom.
21.13 (The Arnon was the **border** between the Moabites and the Amorites.)
21.15 extend to the town of Ar and towards the **border** of Moab."
21.24 Ammonites, because the Ammonite **border** was strongly defended.
22.36 Ar, a city on the River Arnon at the **border** of Moab.
34. 2 I am giving you, the **borders** of your territory will be as
34. 3 The southern **border** will extend from the wilderness of Zin
34. 3 along the **border** of Edom.
34. 5 towards the valley at the **border** of Egypt and end at the
34. 6 "The western **border** will be the Mediterranean Sea.
34. 7 "The northern **border** will follow a line from the
34.10 "The eastern **border** will follow a line from Hazar Enan to Shepham.
34.12 "These will be the four **borders** of your land."
Deut 3.14 that is, Bashan, as far as the **border** of Geshur and Maacah.
3.16 the River Jabbok, part of which formed the Ammonite **border.**
Josh 1. 4 Your **borders** will reach from the desert in the south to
12. 2 valley, as far as the River Jabbok, the **border** of Ammon;
13. 3 of Shihor, at the Egyptian **border,**
13. 3 as far north as the **border** of Ekron was considered Canaanite;
Josh 13. 4 to the Sidonians), as far as Aphek, at the Amorite **border;**
13.10 went as far as the **border** of Ammon and included all the
13.23 The Jordan was the western **border** of the tribe of Reuben.
13.26 Ramath Mizpeh and Betonim, from Mahanaim to the **border** of Lodebar.
13.27 Their western **border** was the River Jordan as far north as
15. 1 point of the wilderness of Zin, at the **border** of Edom.
15. 2 This southern **border** ran from the south end of the Dead Sea,
15. 4 followed the stream on the **border** of Egypt
15. 4 to the Mediterranean Sea, where the **border** ended.
15. 4 That was the southern **border** of Judah.
15. 5 The eastern **border** was the Dead Sea, all the way up to
15. 5 The northern **border** began there, [6]extended up to Beth Hoglah,
15. 8 The **border** then proceeded up to the top of the hill on
15.11 The **border** then went out to the hill north of Ekron,
15.12 It ended at the Mediterranean Sea, [12]which formed the western **border.**
15.12 Within these **borders** lived the people of the families of Judah.
15.21 those that were near the **border** of Edom, were Kabzeel, Eder,
15.47 to the stream on the **border** of Egypt and the coast of
16. 5 **border** ran from Ataroth Addar eastwards to Upper Beth Horon,
16. 6 East of there the **border** bent towards Taanath Shiloh and
16. 8 The **border** went west from Tappuah to the stream of Kanah
16. 9 villages that were within the **borders** of Manasseh, but given
17. 7 The **border** then went south to include the people of Entappuah.
17. 8 Tappuah, on the **border,** belonged to the descendants of Ephraim.
17. 9 The **border** then went down to the stream of Kanah.
17. 9 The **border** of Manasseh proceeded along the north side of the
17.10 north, with the Mediterranean Sea as their western **border.**
18.12 On the north their **border** began at the Jordan and then
18.13 The **border** then went to the slope on the south side of
18.14 The **border** then went in another direction, turning south
18.14 This was the western **border.**
18.15 The southern **border** started on the edge of Kiriath
18.17 The **border** then went down to the Stone of Bohan (Bohan was
18.19 This was the southern **border.**
18.20 The Jordan was the eastern **border.**
18.20 These were the **borders** of the land which the families of the
19.11 From there the **border** went west to Mareal, touching
19.12 it went east to the **border** of Chisloth Tabor, then to
19.14 On the north the **border** turned towards Hannathon, ending
19.22 The **border** also touched Tabor, Shahazumah, and Beth Shemesh,
19.27 As it turned east, the **border** went to Bethdagon,
19.29 The **border** then turned to Ramah, reaching the fortified city of Tyre;
19.33 Its **border** went from Heleph to the oak in Zaanannim, on
19.34 There the **border** turned west to Aznoth Tabor, from there to Hukkok,
Judg 1.36 North of Sela, the Edomite **border** ran through Akrabbim Pass.
12. 1 "Why did you cross the **border** to fight the Ammonites
12. 3 my life and crossed the **border** to fight them, and the Lord
1 Sam 6.12 Philistine kings followed them as far as the **border** of Beth Shemesh.
13.18 other one went to the **border** overlooking the Valley of
1 Kgs 4.21 the River Euphrates to Philistia and the Egyptian **border.**
5. 4 the Lord my God has given me peace on all my **borders.**
8.65 Hamath Pass in the north and the Egyptian **border** in the south.
2 Kgs 3.21 the youngest, were called out and stationed at the **border.**
24. 7 Egypt, from the River Euphrates to the northern **border** of Egypt.
1 Chr 13. 5 the country, from the Egyptian **border** in the south to Hamath
2 Chr 7. 8 Hamath Pass in the north and the Egyptian **border** in the south.
9.26 the River Euphrates to Philistia and the Egyptian **border.**
Neh 9.22 conquer nations and kingdoms, lands that **bordered** their own.
Ps 147.14 He keeps your **borders** safe and satisfies you with the finest wheat.
Is 15. 8 Everywhere at Moab's **borders** the sound of crying is heard.
19.19 Egypt and a stone pillar dedicated to him at the Egyptian **border.**
27.12 the Euphrates to the Egyptian **border,** the Lord will gather
Jer 37. 5 Egyptian army had crossed the Egyptian **border,** they retreated.
Ezek 25. 9 the cities that defend the **border** of Moab be attacked,
29.10 of Aswan in the south, all the way to the Sudanese **border.**
45. 7 will extend to the eastern **border** of the country, so that
47.16 of Ticon (located by the **border** of the district of Hauran).
47.17 city of Enon, with the **border** regions of Damascus and Hamath
47.19 north-west along the Egyptian **border** to the Mediterranean Sea.
48.28 north-west along the Egyptian **border** to the Mediterranean Sea.
Zech 9. 2 Hamath, which **borders** on Hadrach, also belongs to him, and
Lk 17.11 Jerusalem, he went along the **border** between Samaria and Galilee.
Acts 16. 7 When they reached the **border** of Mysia, they tried to go

BORE see BEAR (1), BEAR (2), BEAR (3)

BORN

[STILL-BORN]
see also **BEAR (3), FIRST-BORN, NEW-BORN**

Gen 4. 4 Abel brought the first lamb **born** to one of his sheep, killed
6. 1 world, and girls were being **born,** [2]some of the heavenly
17.11 eight days old, including slaves **born** in your homes and
17.21 son Isaac, who will be **born** to Sarah about this time next
17.23 his household, including the slaves **born** in his home and
21. 2 The boy was **born**
21. 2 at the time God had said he would be **born.**
21. 5 Abraham was a hundred years old when Isaac was **born.**
24. 4 the country where I was **born** and get a wife for my
25.22 twins, and before they were **born,** they struggled against
25.26 The second one was **born** holding on tightly to the heel
25.26 Isaac was sixty years old when they were **born.**
31.13 get ready to go back to the land where you were **born.'** "
35.26 These sons were **born** in Mesopotamia.

Gen 36. 5 All these sons were **born** to Esau in the land of Canaan.
37. 3 sons, because he had been **born** to him when he was old.
38. 5 Judah was at Achzib when the boy was **born.**
38.28 red thread round it, and said, "This one was **born** first."
38.29 But he pulled his arm back, and his brother was **born** first.
38.30 Then his brother was **born** with the red thread on his arm,
44.20 old and a younger brother, **born** to him in his old age.
46.27 Two sons were **born** to Joseph in Egypt, bringing to
48. 5 your two sons, who were **born** to you in Egypt before I
Ex 1.19 and their babies are **born** before either of us gets there."
Lev 22.11 with his own money or **born** in his home, may eat the
22.26 lamb or a kid is **born,** it must not be taken from
25.45 Such children **born** in your land may become your property,
Num 12.12 let her become like something **born** dead with half its flesh
26.59 who was married to Levi's daughter Jochebed, who was **born** in Egypt.
Deut 4.32 the time before you were **born,** all the way back to the
23. 2 "No one **born** out of wedlock or any descendant of such a
29.15 today and also with our descendants who are not yet **born.**
Judg 13. 5 and after your son is **born,** you must never cut his hair,
13. 8 us what we must do with the boy when he is **born."**
16.17 dedicated to God as a Nazirite from the time I was **born.**
Ruth 4.17 They told everyone, "A son has been **born** to Naomi!"
1 Sam 4.19 pregnant, and it was almost time for her baby to be **born.**
2 Sam 3. 2 in the order of their birth, were **born** to David at Hebron:
3. 5 All of these sons were **born** in Hebron.
5.14 The following children were **born** to him in Jerusalem:
1 Kgs 3.18 days after my child was **born** she also gave birth to a
13. 2 name will be Josiah, will be **born** to the family of David.
1 Chr 3. 1 age, are David's sons who were **born** while he was in Hebron:
3. 4 All six were **born** in Hebron during the seven and a half
3. 5 thirty-three years, [5]and many sons were **born** to him there.
14. 4 The following children were **born** to him in Jerusalem:
Neh 10.36 The first son **born** to each of us we will take to
10.36 also dedicate the first calf **born** to each of our cows,
10.36 the first lamb or kid **born** to each of our sheep
Job 1.21 He said, "I was **born** with nothing, and I will die with
3. 1 the silence and cursed the day on which he had been **born.**
3. 2 O God, put a curse on the day I was **born;**
3.10 night for letting me be **born,** for exposing me to trouble and
3.11 died in my mother's womb or died the moment I was **born.**
3.16 gold and silver, [16]or sleeping like a **still-born** child.
10.18 Why, God, did you let me be **born?**
11.12 Stupid men will start being wise when wild donkeys are **born** tame.
14. 1 We are all **born** weak and helpless.
15. 7 Do you think you were the first man **born?**
15.10 wisdom from grey-haired men— men **born** before your father.
39. 1 Do you know when mountain-goats are **born?**
Ps 22.10 since the day I was **born,** and you have always been my
22.31 People not yet **born** will be told:
51. 5 I have been evil from the day I was **born;**
58. 3 they tell lies from the day they are **born.**
58. 8 they be like a baby **born** dead that never sees the light.
71. 6 you have protected me since the day I was **born.**
102.18 Lord has done, so that people not yet **born** will praise him.
139.16 that I was there— [16]you saw me before I was **born.**
Prov 8.24 I was **born** before the oceans, when there were no springs
8.25 I was **born** before the mountains, before the hills were
Ecc 1.10 But no, it has all happened before, long before we were **born.**
2. 7 I bought many slaves, and there were slaves **born** in my household.
4. 3 those who have never been **born,** who have never seen the
6. 3 burial, then I say that a baby **born** dead is better off.
6. 4 It does that baby no good to be **born;**
7. 1 the day you die is better than the day you are **born.**
Song 3. 4 him to my mother's house, to the room where I was **born.**
8. 5 apple-tree I woke you, in the place where you were **born.**
Is 8. 3 When our son was **born,** the Lord said to me, "Name him
9. 6 A child is **born** to us!
44. 2 from the time you were **born,** I have helped you.
46. 3 I have cared for you from the time you were **born.**
49. 1 Before I was **born,** the Lord chose me and appointed me to
49. 5 Before I was **born,** the Lord appointed me;
49.20 Your people who were **born** in exile will one day say to
66. 8 Has a nation ever been **born** in a day?
66. 8 Zion will not have to suffer long, before the nation is **born.**
66. 9 people to the point of birth and not let them be **born."**
Jer 1. 5 life, and before you were **born** I selected you to be a
2.14 he was not **born** into slavery.
16. 3 to the children who are **born** here and to their parents.
20.14 Curse the day I was **born!**
20.17 at noon, [17]because he didn't kill me before I was **born.**
20.18 Why was I **born?**
22.10 to return, never again to see the land where he was **born.**
22.26 where neither of you was **born,** and both of you will die
Ezek 16. 3 "You were **born** in the land of Canaan.
16. 4 When you were **born,** no one cut your umbilical cord or
16. 5 When you were **born,** no one loved you.
21.30 where you were created, in the land where you were **born.**
47.22 and who have had children **born** here are also to receive
Hos 2. 3 her as naked as she was on the day she was **born.**
9.11 be no more children **born** to them, no more women pregnant,
13.13 a child about to be **born,** who refuses to come out of
Mt 2. 1 Jesus was **born** in the town of Bethlehem in Judaea,
2. 2 asked, "Where is the baby **born** to be the king of the
2. 4 the Law and asked them, "Where will the Messiah be **born?"**
19.12 some, because they were **born** that way;
26.24 have been better for that man if he had never been **born!"**
Mk 7.26 The woman was a Gentile, **born** in the region of Phoenicia
14.21 have been better for that man if he had never been **born!"**
Lk 1.14 and how happy many others will be when he is **born!**
2.11 day in David's town your Saviour was **born**—Christ the Lord!
Jn 1.13 that is, by being **born** as the children of a human
1.15 greater than I am, because he existed before I was **born.'"**
1.30 is greater than I am, because he existed before I was **born.'**
3. 3 one can see the Kingdom of God unless he is **born again."**
3. 4 "How can a grown man be **born again?"**
3. 4 cannot enter his mother's womb and be **born** a second time!"
3. 5 Kingdom of God unless he is **born** of water and the Spirit.
3. 6 A person is **born** physically of human parents,
3. 6 but he is **born** spiritually of the Spirit.
3. 7 because I tell you that you must all be **born again.**
3. 8 It is like that with everyone who is **born** of the Spirit."
7.42 and will be **born** in Bethlehem, the town where David
8.58 "Before Abraham was **born,** 'I Am'."
9. 1 was walking along, he saw a man who had been **born** blind.
9. 2 asked him, "Teacher, whose sin caused him to be **born** blind?
9.19 You say that he was **born** blind;
9.20 he is our son, and we know that he was **born** blind.
9.24 the man who had been **born** blind, and said to him, "Promise
9.32 ever heard of anyone giving sight to a person **born** blind.
9.34 They answered, "You were **born** and brought up in sin—
16.21 but when the baby is **born,** she forgets her suffering, because
16.21 she is happy that a baby has been **born** into the world.
18.37 I was **born** and came into the world for this one purpose,
Acts 4.36 that Joseph, a Levite **born** in Cyprus, whom the apostles called
7. 8 So Abraham circumcised Isaac a week after he was **born;**
7.20 at this time that Moses was **born,** a very beautiful child.
18. 2 met a Jew named Aquila, **born** in Pontus, who had recently
18.24 named Apollos, who had been **born** in Alexandria, came to Ephesus.
21.39 answered, "I am a Jew, **born** in Tarsus in Cilicia, a citizen
22. 3 "I am a Jew, **born** in Tarsus in Cilicia, but brought up
Rom 1. 3 as to his humanity, he was **born** a descendant of David;
9. 8 This means that the children **born** in the usual way are not
9. 8 the children **born** as a result of God's promise are regarded
9.11 said this before they were **born,** before they had done anything
1 Cor 11.12 made from man, in the same way man is **born** of woman;
Gal 1.15 me even before I was **born,** and called me to serve him.
4.23 son by the slave-woman was **born** in the usual way, but his
4.23 by the free woman was **born** as a result of God's promise.
4.24 The one whose children are **born** in slavery is Hagar,
4.29 time the son who was **born** in the usual way
4.29 persecuted the one who was **born** because of God's Spirit;
Heb 7.10 Levi had not yet been **born,** but was, so to speak, in
7.14 well known that he was **born** a member of the tribe of
11.23 of Moses hide him for three months after he was **born.**
1 Pet 1.23 of God you have been **born again** as the children of
2 Pet 2.12 by instinct, like wild animals **born** to be captured and killed;
Rev 12. 4 in order to eat her child as soon as it was **born.**

BORNE see BEAR (2), BEAR (3)

BORROW

Ex 22.14 "If a man **borrows** an animal from another man and it is
Deut 15. 6 to many nations, but you will not have to **borrow** from any;
28.12 to many nations, but you will not have to **borrow** from any.
2 Kgs 4. 3 "Go to your neighbours and **borrow** as many empty jars as
6. 5 "It was a **borrowed** axe!"
Neh 5. 4 others said, "We had to **borrow** money to pay the royal tax
5.10 I have let the people **borrow** money and corn from me, and
Ps 37.21 The wicked man **borrows** and never pays back, but the good
Prov 22. 7 **Borrow** money and you are the lender's slave.
Is 24. 2 and masters, buyers and sellers, lenders and **borrowers,**
Jer 15.10 I have not lent any money or **borrowed** any;
Ezek 18. 7 He returns what a **borrower** gives him as security;
18.12 he robs, he keeps what a **borrower** gives him as security.
18.16 He returns what a **borrower** gives him as security.
Mt 5.42 when someone wants to **borrow** something, lend it to him.
Lk 11. 5 say to him, 'Friend, let me **borrow** three loaves of bread.

BOTHER

1 Sam 25.15 they never **bothered** us, and all the time we were with them
Esth 7. 4 I would have kept quiet and not **bothered** you about it;
Job 9.29 Since I am held guilty, why should I **bother?**
Mt 26.10 so he said to them, "Why are you **bothering** this woman?
Mk 5.35 Why **bother** the Teacher any longer?"
14. 6 Why are you **bothering** her?
Lk 8.49 "don't **bother** the Teacher any longer."
11. 7 suppose your friend should answer from inside, 'Don't **bother** me!
Acts 18.17 But that did not **bother** Gallio a bit.
2 Cor 11. 9 with you I did not **bother** you for help when I needed
12.13 except that I did not **bother** you for financial help?

BOTTLE

Ecc 10. 1 flies can make a whole **bottle** of perfume stink, and a little
Is 5.22 Heroes of the wine **bottle!**

BOTTOM

Ex 15. 5 they sank to the **bottom** like a stone.
26.24 to be joined at the **bottom** and connected all the way to
36.29 frames were joined at the **bottom** and connected all the way
Num 8. 4 From top to **bottom** the lamp-stand was made of hammered gold,
Josh 7.21 buried inside my tent, with the silver at the **bottom."**
7.22 really were buried there, with the silver at the **bottom.**
1 Kgs 7.34 were four supports at the **bottom** corners of each cart, which
22.35 ran down and covered the **bottom** of the chariot, and at
Lam 3.55 "From the **bottom** of the pit, O Lord, I cried out to

Dan 6.24 Before they even reached the **bottom** of the pit, the lions
Amos 9. 3 hide from me at the **bottom** of the sea, I will command
Jon 2. 3 the depths, to the very **bottom** of the sea, where the waters
Mic 7.19 our sins underfoot and send them to the **bottom** of the sea!
Mt 27.51 hanging in the Temple was torn in two from top to **bottom.**
Mk 15.38 hanging in the Temple was torn in two, from top to **bottom.**

BOUGH

Ezek 31. 8 No fir-tree ever had such branches, And no plane-tree such **boughs.**
31.12 Its branches and broken **boughs** will fall on every mountain

BOUGHT see BUY

BOUND
see also **BIND**

BOUND (1)

Lk 17. 1 people fall into sin are **bound** to happen, but how terrible
Jn 15.25 This, however, was **bound** to happen so that what is
17.12 except the man who was **bound** to be lost—so that the

BOUND (2)

Song 4. 1 like a flock of goats **bounding** down the hills of Gilead.
6. 5 like a flock of goats **bounding** down the hills of Gilead.

BOUNDARY

Ex 19.12 Mark a **boundary** round the mountain that the people must not cross,
19.21 people not to cross the **boundary** to come and look at me;
19.23 the mountain sacred and to mark a **boundary** round it."
19.24 people must not cross the **boundary** to come up to me, or
Deut 3.16 the river was their southern **boundary,**
3.16 and their northern **boundary** was the River Jabbok,
19.14 "Do not move your neighbour's **boundary** mark,
27.17 "'God's curse on anyone who moves a neighbour's **boundary** mark.'
Josh 12. 5 Bashan as far as the **boundaries** of Geshur and Maacah, as
16. 1 The southern **boundary** of the land assigned to the
22.25 He made the Jordan a **boundary** between us and you people
Judg 11.18 did not cross the Arnon because it was the **boundary** of Moab.
Job 11. 7 you discover the limits and **bounds** of the greatness and
24. 2 Men move **boundary** stones to get more land;
38.10 I marked a **boundary** for the sea and kept it behind
Ps 104. 9 You set a **boundary** they can never pass, to keep them from
Prov 22.28 Never move an old **boundary-mark** that your ancestors established.
23.10 Never move an old **boundary-mark** or take over land owned by orphans.
30. 4 Or fixed the **boundaries** of the earth?
Is 10.13 I wiped out the **boundaries** between nations and took the
54. 3 You will extend your **boundaries** on all sides;
Jer 5.22 placed the sand as the **boundary** of the sea,
5.22 a permanent **boundary** that it cannot cross.
31.39 And the **boundary** line will continue from there on the
Lam 2.13 Your disaster is **boundless** as the ocean;
Ezek 45. 7 From the western **boundary** of the holy area it will extend
45. 7 and from the eastern **boundary** it will extend to the eastern
47.13 Lord said, "These are the **boundaries** of the land that is to
47.15 "The northern **boundary** runs eastwards from the
47.17 So the northern **boundary** runs from the Mediterranean
47.18 "The eastern **boundary** runs south from a point between
47.18 the River Jordan forming the **boundary** between the land of
47.19 "The southern **boundary** runs south-west from Tamar to
47.20 "The western **boundary** is formed by the Mediterranean
48. 1 The northern **boundary** of the land runs eastwards from
48. 1 city of Enon, to the **boundary** between the kingdoms of
48. 1 the eastern **boundary** westwards to the Mediterranean Sea,
48.21 the eastern **boundary** and westwards to the Mediterranean Sea,
48.21 and is **bounded** on the north by the section
48.23 the eastern **boundary** westwards to the Mediterranean Sea,
48.28 the tribe of Gad, the **boundary** runs south-west from Tamar to

BOW (1)

Gen 9.13 all living beings, [13] I am putting my **bow** in the clouds.
27. 3 Take your **bow** and arrows, go out into the country, and
48.22 which I took from the Amorites with my sword and my **bow."**
49.23 him fiercely And pursue him with their **bows** and arrows.
49.24 But his **bow** remains steady, And his arms are made strong
Josh 24.12 Your swords and **bows** had nothing to do with it.
Judg 16. 7 me up with seven new **bowstrings** that are not dried out, I'll
16. 8 Delilah seven new **bowstrings** that were not dried out,
16. 9 But he snapped the **bowstrings** just as thread breaks when
1 Sam 2. 4 The **bows** of strong soldiers are broken, but the weak grow strong.
18. 4 David, together with his armour and also his sword, **bow,** and
2 Sam 1.22 Jonathan's **bow** was deadly, the sword of Saul was merciless,
22.35 trains me for battle, so that I can use the strongest **bow.**
2 Kgs 9.24 Jehu drew his **bow,** and with all his strength shot an
13.15 "Get a **bow** and some arrows," Elisha ordered him.
1 Chr 5.18 44,760 soldiers, well-trained in the use of shields, swords, and **bows.**
2 Chr 14. 8 and 280,000 men from Benjamin, armed with shields and **bows.**
17.17 in command of 200,000 men armed with shields and **bows.**
26.14 coats of armour, **bows** and arrows, and stones for slinging.
Neh 4.13 people with swords, spears, and **bows,** and stationed them by
4.16 coats of armour and armed with spears, shields, and **bows.**
Job 20.24 from an iron sword, a bronze **bow** will shoot him down.
Ps 7.12 He bends his **bow** and makes it ready;
11. 2 the wicked have drawn their **bows** and aimed their arrows to
18.34 trains me for battle, so that I can use the strongest **bow.**
37.14 their swords and bend their **bows** to kill the poor and needy,
37.15 killed by their own swords, and their **bows** will be smashed.
44. 6 do not trust in my **bow** or in my sword to save
46. 9 he breaks **bows,** destroys spears, and sets shields on fire.
78. 9 The Ephraimites, armed with **bows** and arrows, ran away on
Is 5.28 Their arrows are sharp, and their **bows** are ready to shoot.
7.24 People will go hunting there with **bows** and arrows.
13.18 With their **bows** and arrows they will kill the young men.
21.15 ready to kill them, from **bows** that are ready to shoot, from
21.17 The **bowmen** are the bravest men of Kedar, but few of them
22. 6 Elam came riding on horseback, armed with **bows** and arrows.
66.19 Libya, and Lydia, with its skilled **bowmen,** and to Tubal and Greece.
Jer 4.29 At the noise of the horsemen and **bowmen** everyone will run away.
5.16 Their **bowmen** are mighty soldiers who kill without mercy.
6.23 They have taken up their **bows** and swords;
46. 9 and skilled **bowmen** from Lydia.' "
49.35 "I will kill all the **bowmen** who have made Elam so powerful.
50.14 **"Bowmen,** line up for battle against Babylon and surround it.
50.29 "Tell the **bowmen** to attack Babylon.
50.29 Send out everyone who knows how to use the **bow** and arrow.
50.42 They have taken their **bows** and swords;
51.56 its soldiers are captured, and their **bows** are broken.
Lam 3.12 He drew his **bow** and made me the target for his arrows.
Ezek 39. 3 Then I will knock his **bow** out of his left hand and
39. 9 build fires with the shields, **bows,** arrows, spears, and
Hos 1. 7 by war—with swords or **bows** and arrows or with horses and
2.18 the land, all swords and **bows,** and will let my people live
7.16 They are as unreliable as a crooked **bow.**
Amos 2.15 **Bowmen** will not stand their ground, fast runners will not get away,
Hab 3. 9 You got ready to use your **bow,** ready to shoot your arrows.
Zech 9.10 the **bows** used in battle will be destroyed.
9.13 use Judah like a soldier's **bow** and Israel like the arrows.
Rev 6. 2 Its rider held a **bow,** and he was given a crown.

BOW (2)

Gen 17. 3 Abram **bowed down** with his face touching the ground, and
17.17 Abraham **bowed down** with his face touching the ground,
18. 2 **Bowing down** with his face touching the ground, [3] he said,
19. 1 He **bowed down** before them [2] and said, "Sirs, I am here to
23. 7 Then Abraham **bowed** before them [8] and said, "If you are
23.12 But Abraham **bowed** before the Hittites [13] and said to Ephron,
24.52 Abraham heard this, he **bowed down** and worshipped the Lord.
27.29 May nations be your servants, and may peoples **bow down** before you.
27.29 and may your mother's descendants **bow down** before you.
33. 3 went ahead of them and **bowed down** to the ground seven times
33. 6 Then the concubines came up with their children and **bowed down;**
33. 7 and last of all Joseph and Rachel came and **bowed down.**
37. 7 Yours formed a circle round mine and **bowed down** to it."
37. 9 the sun, the moon, and eleven stars **bowing down** to me."
37.10 brothers, and I are going to come and **bow down** to you?"
42. 6 So Joseph's brothers came and **bowed down** before him with
43.26 the house to him and **bowed down** to the ground before him.
43.28 And they knelt and **bowed down** before him.
44.14 They **bowed down** before him, [15] and Joseph said, "What have you done?
48.12 them from Jacob's lap and **bowed down** before him with his
49. 8 Your brothers will **bow down** before you.
49.10 Nations will bring him tribute And **bow** in obedience before him.
50.18 Then his brothers themselves came and **bowed down** before him.
Ex 4.31 were being treated cruelly, they **bowed down** and worshipped.
11. 8 will come to me and **bow down** before me, and they will
18. 7 Moses went out to meet him, **bowed** before him, and kissed him.
20. 5 Do not **bow down** to any idol or worship it, because I
23.24 Do not **bow down** to their gods or worship them, and do
24. 1 while you are still some distance away, **bow down** in worship.
33.10 of cloud at the door of the Tent, they would **bow down.**
34. 8 Moses quickly **bowed down** to the ground and worshipped.
Lev 9.24 it, they all shouted and **bowed down** with their faces to the
Num 14. 5 Then Moses and Aaron **bowed** to the ground in front of all
16.22 But Moses and Aaron **bowed down** with their faces to the
16.45 The two of them **bowed down** with their faces to the ground,
20. 6 They **bowed down** with their faces to the ground, and the
Deut 5. 9 Do not **bow down** to any idol or worship it, for I
33. 3 So we **bow** at his feet and obey his commands.
Josh 23. 7 in taking vows or worship those gods or **bow down** to them.
Judg 2.12 They **bowed down** to them and made the Lord angry.
Ruth 2.10 Ruth **bowed down** with her face touching the ground, and
1 Sam 20.41 fell on his knees and **bowed** with his face to the ground
24. 8 Saul turned round, and David **bowed down** to the ground in
25.41 Abigail **bowed down** to the ground and said, "I am his servant,
28.14 that it was Samuel, and he **bowed** to the ground in respect.
2 Sam 1. 2 He went to David and **bowed** to the ground in respect.
9. 6 of Saul, arrived, he **bowed down** before David in respect.
9. 8 Mephibosheth **bowed** again and said, "I am no better than
14. 4 woman went to the king, **bowed down** to the ground in respect,
14.33 who went to him and **bowed down** to the ground in front
15. 5 the man approached Absalom to **bow down** before him, Absalom
18.21 The slave **bowed** and ran off.
22.45 Foreigners **bow** before me;
1 Kgs 1.16 Bathsheba **bowed** low before the king, and he asked,
1.23 was there, and Nathan went in and **bowed** low before the king.

1 Kgs 1.31 Bathsheba **bowed** low and said, "May my lord the king
1.47 Then King David **bowed** in worship on his bed [48]and prayed,
1.53 went to the king and **bowed** low before him, and the king
2.19 The king stood up to greet his mother and **bowed** to her.
18. 7 He recognized him, **bowed** low before him, and asked, "Is it
18.42 of Mount Carmel, where he **bowed down** to the ground, with his
19.18 to me and have not **bowed** to Baal or kissed his idol."
2 Kgs 2.15 They went to meet him, **bowed down** before him, [16]and said,
4.27 she came to Elisha she **bowed down** before him and took hold
17.35 do not **bow down** to them or serve them or offer sacrifices
17.36 you are to **bow down** to me and offer sacrifices to me.
1 Chr 16.29 **Bow down** before the Holy One when he appears;
21.16 of whom were wearing sackcloth—**bowed** low, with their faces
21.21 he left the threshing-place and **bowed** low, with his face
29.20 of their ancestors, and they **bowed** low and gave honour to
2 Chr 20.18 Then King Jehoshaphat **bowed** low,
20.18 and all the people **bowed** with him and worshipped the Lord.
Ezra 10. 1 While Ezra was **bowing** in prayer in front of the Temple,
Neh 9. 6 The heavenly powers **bow down** and worship you.
Esth 3. 2 show their respect for Haman by kneeling and **bowing** to him.
3. 4 "I am a Jew," he explained, "and I cannot **bow** to Haman."
3. 5 not going to kneel and **bow** to him, [6]and when he learnt
Ps 2.12 tremble [12]and **bow down** to him;
5. 7 in your holy Temple and **bow down** to you in reverence.
18.44 Foreigners **bow** before me;
22.29 All proud men will **bow down** to him;
22.29 all mortal men will **bow down** before him.
29. 2 **bow down** before the Holy One when he appears.
35.13 I prayed with my head **bowed** low, [14]as I would pray for
38. 6 I am **bowed down,** I am crushed;
66. 3 is so great that your enemies **bow down** in fear before you.
68.30 until they all **bow down** and offer you their silver.
72. 9 The peoples of the desert will **bow down** before him;
72.11 All kings will **bow down** before him;
81.15 Those who hate me would **bow** in fear before me;
86. 9 that you have created will come and **bow down** to you;
95. 6 Come, let us **bow down** and worship him;
96. 9 **Bow down** before the Holy One when he appears;
97. 7 all the gods **bow down** before the Lord.
138. 2 I face your holy Temple, **bow down,** and praise your name
Prov 14.19 Evil people will have to **bow down** to the righteous and
Is 44.17 makes into an idol, and then he **bows down** and worships it.
44.19 Here I am **bowing down** to a block of wood!"
45.14 They will **bow down** to you and confess, 'God is with you
46. 6 then they **bow down** and worship it!
49. 7 also will see it, and they will **bow** low to honour you."
49.23 They will **bow** low before you and honour you;
58. 5 you **bow** your heads low like a blade of grass, and spread
60.14 oppressed you will come And **bow** low to show their respect.
Jer 8.19 idols and by **bowing down** to your useless foreign gods?"
Lam 2.10 Young girls **bow** their heads to the ground.
3.29 We should **bow** in submission, for there may still be hope.
Ezek 8.16 to the sanctuary and were **bowing** low towards the east,
46. 3 the people are also to **bow down** and worship the Lord in
Dan 2.46 Then King Nebuchadnezzar **bowed** to the ground and gave
3. 5 music starts, you are to **bow down** and worship the gold
3. 6 Anyone who does not **bow down** and worship will immediately
3. 7 the nations, races, and languages **bowed down** and worshipped
3.10 starts, everyone is to **bow down** and worship the gold statue,
3.11 that anyone who does not **bow down** and worship it is to
3.12 not worship your god or **bow down** to the statue you set
3.14 worship my god and to **bow down** to the gold statue I
3.15 all the other instruments, **bow down** and worship the statue.
3.18 god, and we will not **bow down** to the gold statue that
3.28 risked their lives rather than **bow down** and worship any god
Mt 20.20 Jesus with her two sons, **bowed** before him, and asked him
Mk 15.19 spat on him, fell on their knees, and **bowed down** to him.
Lk 24. 5 Full of fear, the women **bowed down** to the ground,
Jn 19.30 Then he **bowed** his head and died.
Acts 10.25 Cornelius met him, fell at his feet, and **bowed down** before him.
1 Cor 14.25 and he will **bow down** and worship God, confessing,
Rev 3. 9 I will make them come and **bow down** at your feet.

BOWELS

Deut 23.13 that when you have a **bowel** movement you can dig a hole
Acts 1.18 he burst open and all his **bowels** spilt out.

BOWL

Ex 12.22 hyssop, dip it in the **bowl** containing the animal's blood,
24. 6 took half the blood of the animals and put it in **bowls;**
24. 8 took the blood in the **bowls** and threw it on the people.
25.29 Make plates, cups, jars, and **bowls** to be used for the wine-offerings.
27. 3 pans for the greasy ashes, and make shovels, **bowls,** hooks,
37.16 the jars, and the **bowls** to be used for the wine-offering.
38. 3 pans, the shovels, the **bowls,** the hooks, and the firepans.
Lev 14. 5 to be killed over a clay **bowl** containing fresh spring water.
14.50 of the birds over a clay **bowl** containing fresh spring water.
15.12 broken, and any wooden **bowl** that he touches must be washed.
Num 4. 7 bowls, the offering **bowls,** and the jars
5.17 holy water into a clay **bowl** and take some of the earth
5.18 the priest shall hold the **bowl** containing the bitter water
5.23 down and wash the writing off into the **bowl** of bitter water.
7.12 one silver **bowl** weighing 1.5 kilogrammes and one silver
7.84 twelve silver **bowls** and twelve silver basins weighing a
Judg 5.25 she brought him cream in a beautiful **bowl.**
6.38 wrung enough dew out of it to fill a **bowl** with water.
2 Sam 17.28 They brought **bowls,** clay pots, and bedding, and
1 Kgs 7.40 Huram also made pots, shovels, and **bowls.**
7.40 The two columns The two **bowl-shaped** capitals on top of the
7.40 The pots, shovels, and **bowls**
7.50 the cups, lamp snuffers, **bowls,** dishes for incense, and
17.12 handful of flour in a **bowl** and a drop of olive-oil in
17.14 'The **bowl** will not run out of flour or the jar run
17.16 had promised through Elijah, the **bowl** did not run out of
2 Kgs 2.20 some salt in a new **bowl,** and bring it to me," he
12.13 pay for making silver cups, **bowls,** trumpets, or tools for
25.14 the **bowls** used for catching the blood
25.14 the **bowls** used for burning incense,
25.15 or silver, including the small **bowls** and the pans used for
1 Chr 28.17 be used in making forks, **bowls,** and jars, how much silver
2 Chr 4. 7 They also made a hundred gold **bowls.**
4.11 Huram also made pots, shovels, and **bowls.**
4.11 The two columns The two **bowl-shaped** capitals on top of the
4.22 the lamp snuffers, the **bowls,** the dishes for incense,
24.14 who used it to have **bowls** and other utensils made for the
Ezra 1. 7 Cyrus gave them back the **bowls** and cups that King
1. 9 gold **bowls** for offerings 30
1. 9 silver **bowls** for offerings 1,000
1. 9 other **bowls** 29
1. 9 small gold **bowls** 30
1. 9 small silver **bowls** 410
1.11 were 5,400 gold and silver **bowls** and other articles which
8.26 20 gold **bowls** - 8.4 kilogrammes
8.26 2 fine bronze **bowls,** equal in value to gold bowls
Neh 7.70 50 ceremonial **bowls**
Song 7. 2 A **bowl** is there, that never runs out of spiced wine.
Is 22.24 will hang on him like pots and **bowls** hanging from a peg!
Jer 35. 5 Then I placed cups and **bowls** full of wine before the Rechabites,
52.18 the **bowls** used for catching the blood
52.18 the **bowls** used for burning incense,
52.19 the small **bowls,** the pans used for carrying live coals,
52.19 the **bowls** for holding the blood
52.19 the **bowls** used for incense,
52.19 and the **bowls** used for pouring out offerings
Dan 5. 2 gold and silver cups and **bowls** which his father
5. 3 once the gold cups and **bowls** were brought in, and they all
5.23 and brought in the cups and **bowls** taken from his Temple.
Amos 6. 6 You drink wine by the **bowlful** and use the finest perfumes,
Zech 4. 2 "At the top is a **bowl** for the oil.
9.15 the blood of a sacrifice poured on the altar from a **bowl.**
14.20 the Temple will be as sacred as the **bowls** before the altar.
Mt 5.15 No one lights a lamp and puts it under a **bowl;**
Mk 4.21 a lamp and put it under a **bowl** or under the bed?
7. 4 the proper way to wash cups, pots, copper **bowls,** and beds.
Lk 8.16 and covers it with a **bowl** or puts it under a bed.
11.33 a lamp and then hides it or puts it under a **bowl;**
Jn 4. 9 (Jews will not use the same cups and **bowls** that Samaritans use.)
19.29 A **bowl** was there, full of cheap wine;
2 Tim 2.20 In a large house there are dishes and **bowls** of all kinds:
Rev 5. 8 had a harp and gold **bowls** filled with incense, which are the
15. 7 the seven angels seven gold **bowls** full of the anger of God,
16. 1 and pour out the seven **bowls** of God's anger on the earth!"
16. 2 The first angel went and poured out his **bowl** on the earth.
16. 3 Then the second angel poured out his **bowl** on the sea.
16. 4 third angel poured out his **bowl** on the rivers and the
16. 8 fourth angel poured out his **bowl** on the sun,
16.10 fifth angel poured out his **bowl** on the throne of the beast.
16.12 angel poured out his **bowl** on the great river Euphrates.
16.17 Then the seventh angel poured out his **bowl** in the air.
17. 1 angels who had the seven **bowls** came to me and said, "Come,
21. 9 angels who had the seven **bowls** full of the seven last

BOX

see also **COVENANT BOX, OFFERING BOX**

1 Sam 6. 8 and place in a **box** beside it the gold models
6.11 together with the **box** containing the gold models
6.15 and the **box** with the gold models in it,
2 Kgs 12. 9 Then Jehoiada took a **box,** made a hole in the lid,
12. 9 and placed the **box** by the altar,
12. 9 put in the **box** all the money given by the
12.10 amount of money in the **box,** the royal secretary
12.16 and for the offerings for sin was not deposited in the **box;**
2 Chr 24. 8 the Levites to make a **box** for contributions
24.10 and they brought their tax money and filled the **box** with it.
24.11 the Levites would take the **box** to the royal official
24.11 would take the money out and return the **box** to its place.

BOXER

1 Cor 9.26 why I am like a **boxer** who does not waste his punches.

BOY

Gen 17.11 must circumcise every baby **boy** when he is eight days old,
21. 2 The **boy** was born at the time God had said he would
21.12 Abraham, "Don't be worried about the **boy** and your slave Hagar.
21.17 God heard the **boy** crying, and from heaven the angel of
21.17 God has heard the **boy** crying.
21.19 filled the leather bag with water and gave some to the **boy.**
21.20 God was with the **boy** as he grew up;
22. 5 The **boy** and I will go over there and worship, and then
22.12 "Don't hurt the **boy** or do anything to him," he said.
25.27 The **boys** grew up, and Esau became a skilled hunter, a
35.17 it's another **boy."**
37.30 He returned to his brothers and said, "The **boy** is not there!
38. 5 Judah was at Achzib when the **boy** was born.
42.22 "I told you not to harm the **boy,** but you wouldn't listen.
43. 8 to his father, "Send the **boy** with me, and we will leave

Gen 44.20 The **boy's** brother is dead, and he is the only one of
44.22 and we answered that the **boy** could not leave his father;
44.30 to my father without the **boy,**
44.30 as he sees that the **boy** is not with me,
44.30 with the life of the **boy,**
44.32 is more, I pledged my life to my father for the **boy.**
44.32 I did not bring the **boy** back to him, I would bear
44.33 I will stay here as your slave in place of the **boy;**
44.34 go back to my father if the **boy** is not with me?
48. 8 When Jacob saw Joseph's sons, he asked, "Who are these **boys?"**
48.10 Joseph brought the **boys** to him, and he hugged them and
48.15 God whom my fathers Abraham and Isaac served bless these **boys!**
48.16 of my fathers Abraham and Isaac live on through these **boys!**
48.18 This is the elder **boy;**
Ex 1.16 he said to them, "kill the baby if it is a **boy;**
1.17 instead, they let the **boys** live.
1.18 Why are you letting the **boys** live?"
1.22 "Take every new-born Hebrew **boy** and throw him into the Nile,
2. 6 The princess opened it and saw a baby **boy.**
21.31 If the bull kills a **boy** or a girl, the same rule
Num 31.17 So now kill every **boy** and kill every woman who has had
Josh 5. 4 the desert, none of the baby **boys** had been circumcised.
Judg 8.20 But the **boy** did not draw his sword.
8.20 He hesitated, because he was still only a **boy.**
13. 7 because the **boy** is to be dedicated to God
13. 8 us what we must do with the **boy** when he is born."
13.12 Manoah asked, "When your words come true, what must the **boy** do?
16.26 Samson said to the **boy** who was leading him by the hand,
Ruth 4.14 May the **boy** become famous in Israel!
4.17 The women of the neighbourhood named the **boy** Obed.
1 Sam 2.11 home to Ramah, but the **boy** Samuel stayed in Shiloh and
2.18 In the meantime the **boy** Samuel continued to serve the Lord,
2.21 The **boy** Samuel grew up in the service of the Lord.
2.26 The **boy** Samuel continued to grow and to gain favour
3. 1 In those days, when the **boy** Samuel was serving the Lord
3. 6 The **boy** did not know that it was the Lord, because the
3. 8 Lord who was calling the **boy,** [9] so he said to him, "Go
3.16 Eli called him, "Samuel, my **boy!"**
4.21 She named the **boy** Ichabod, explaining, "God's glory has left Israel"—
17.33 You're just a **boy,** and he has been a soldier all his
17.42 scorn for him because he was just a nice, good-looking **boy.**
20.35 He took a young **boy** with him [36] and said to him, "Run
20.36 The **boy** ran, and Jonathan shot an arrow beyond him.
20.37 When the **boy** reached the place where the arrow had fallen,
20.38 The **boy** picked up the arrow and returned to his master,
20.40 gave his weapons to the **boy** and told him to take them
20.41 After the **boy** had left, David got up from behind the
30.11 with David found an Egyptian **boy** out in the country and
2 Sam 12.24 The Lord loved the **boy** [25] and commanded the prophet Nathan
12.25 to name the **boy** Jedidiah, because the Lord loved him.
17.18 But one day a **boy** happened to see them, and he told
1 Kgs 3.17 gave birth to a baby **boy** at home while she was there.
3.18 my child was born she also gave birth to a baby **boy.**
17.19 "Give the **boy** to me," Elijah said.
17.19 He took the **boy** from her arms, carried him upstairs to the
17.21 stretched himself out on the **boy** three times and prayed, "O
17.23 Elijah took the **boy** back downstairs to his mother and
18.12 a devout worshipper of the Lord ever since I was a **boy.**
2 Kgs 2.23 and on the way some **boys** came out of a town and
2.24 out of the woods and tore forty-two of the **boys** to pieces.
4.18 later, at harvest time, the **boy** went out one morning to join
4.19 "Carry the **boy** to his mother," the father said to a servant.
4.20 The servant carried the **boy** back to his mother, who held
4.29 Go straight to the house and hold my stick over the **boy."**
4.31 back to meet Elisha and said, "The **boy** didn't wake up."
4.32 into the room and saw the **boy** lying dead on the bed.
4.34 he lay down on the **boy,** placing his mouth, eyes, and hands
4.34 on the **boy's** mouth, eyes, and hands.
4.34 lay stretched out over the **boy,**
4.34 the **boy's** body started to get warm.
4.35 and then went back and again stretched himself over the **boy.**
4.35 The **boy** sneezed seven times, and then opened his eyes.
4.36 Elisha called Gehazi and told him to call the **boy's** mother.
11. 3 Jehosheba took care of the **boy** and kept him hidden in the
Prov 4. 3 I was only a little **boy,** my parents' only son, [4] my father
17. 6 grandchildren, just as **boys** are proud of their fathers.
Is 3. 4 The Lord will let the people be governed by immature **boys.**
8. 4 Before the **boy** is old enough to say 'Mummy' and 'Daddy,'
Jer 20.15 my father glad when he brought him the news, "It's a **boy!**
51.22 old and young, to kill **boys** and girls, [23] to slaughter
Lam 5.13 **boys** go staggering under heavy loads of wood.
Joel 3. 3 They sold **boys** and girls into slavery to pay for prostitutes
Zech 8. 5 And the streets will again be full of **boys** and girls playing.
Mt 2.16 orders to kill all the **boys** in Bethlehem and its neighbourhood
17.17 Bring the **boy** here to me!"
17.18 it went out of the **boy,** and at that very moment he
Mk 9.19 Bring the **boy** to me!"
9.20 saw Jesus, it threw the **boy** into a fit, so that he
9.25 to come out of the **boy** and never go into him again!"
9.26 The spirit screamed, threw the **boy** into a bad fit, and
9.26 The **boy** looked like a corpse, and everyone said, "He is dead!"
9.27 But Jesus took the **boy** by the hand and helped him to
Lk 1.62 asking him what name he would like the **boy** to have.
2.43 they started back home, but the **boy** Jesus stayed in Jerusalem.
9.42 As the **boy** was coming, the demon knocked him to the
9.42 the evil spirit, healed the **boy,** and gave him back to his
Jn 4.51 met him with the news, "Your **boy** is going to live!"
6. 9 said, [9] "There is a **boy** here who has five loaves of
7.22 and so you circumcise a **boy** on the Sabbath.
Jn 7.23 If a **boy** is circumcised on the Sabbath so that Moses'
Rev 12.13 began to pursue the woman who had given birth to the **boy.**

BRACE

Is 50. 7 I **brace** myself to endure them.

BRACELET

Gen 24.22 in her nose and put two large gold **bracelets** on her arms.
24.30 seen the nose-ring and the **bracelets** on his sister's arms
24.47 put the ring in her nose and the **bracelets** on her arms.
Num 31.50 bringing the gold ornaments, armlets, **bracelets,** rings,
2 Sam 1.10 from his head and the **bracelet** from his arm, and I have
Is 3.16 They take dainty little steps, and the **bracelets** on their ankles jingle.
Ezek 16.11 I put jewels on you—**bracelets** and necklaces.
23.42 They put **bracelets** on the women's arms and beautiful crowns

Am **BRAG** see **BOAST**

BRAG

Prov 17.19 If you **brag** all the time, you are asking for trouble.
20.14 but then he goes off and **brags** about the bargain he got.
Is 52. 5 over you boast and **brag** and constantly show contempt for me.
Jer 46.17 Egypt a new name— 'Noisy **Braggart** Who Missed His Chance.'
Dan 7.11 I could still hear the little horn **bragging** and boasting.

BRAIDED

Song 7. 5 Your **braided** hair shines like the finest satin;

BRAMBLE BUSHES

Lk 6.44 pick figs from thorn bushes or gather grapes from **bramble bushes.**

BRANCH

Gen 30.37 Jacob got green **branches** of poplar, almond, and plane
30.37 of the bark so that the **branches** had white stripes on them.
30.38 He placed these **branches** in front of the flocks
30.39 of the **branches,** they produced young that were streaked,
30.41 were mating, Jacob put the **branches** in front of them
30.41 at the drinking-troughs, so that they would breed among the **branches.**
30.42 he did not put the **branches** in front of the weak animals.
40.10 a grapevine in front of me [10] with three **branches** on it.
40.12 the three **branches** are three days.
Ex 25.32 Six **branches** shall extend from its sides, three from each side.
25.33 Each of the six **branches** is to have three decorative
25.35 to be one bud below each of the three pairs of **branches.**
25.36 The buds, the **branches,** and the lamp-stand are to be a
37.18 Six **branches** extended from its sides, three from each side.
37.19 Each of the six **branches** had three decorative flowers
37.21 There was one bud below each of the three pairs of **branches.**
37.22 The buds, the **branches,** and the lamp-stand were a single
Lev 23.40 trees, take palm **branches** and the branches of leafy trees,
Num 13.23 there they cut off a **branch** which had one bunch of grapes
Judg 9.15 blaze out of my thorny **branches** and burn up the cedars of
9.48 took an axe, cut a **branch** off a tree, and put it
9.49 So every man cut off a **branch** of a tree;
2 Sam 18. 9 a large oak-tree, Absalom's head got caught in the **branches.**
Neh 8.15 to the hills and get **branches** from pines, olives, myrtles,
8.16 So the people got **branches** and built shelters on the
Job 15.30 be like a tree whose **branches** are burnt by fire, whose
15.32 will wither, wither like a **branch** and never be green again.
18.16 His roots and **branches** are withered and dry.
29.19 always have water and whose **branches** are wet with dew.
Ps 80.10 its **branches** overshadowed the giant cedars.
80.11 It extended its **branches** to the Mediterranean Sea and as
118.27 With **branches** in your hands, start the festival and march
Is 7.18 like flies from the farthest **branches** of the Nile, and for
10.33 Almighty will bring them crashing down like **branches** cut off a tree.
11. 1 but just as new **branches** sprout from a stump, so a new
17. 6 very top, or a few that are left on the lower **branches.**
18. 5 the Sudanese as easily as a knife cuts **branches** from a vine.
27.11 The **branches** of the trees are withered and broken, and
Jer 1.11 I answered, "A **branch** of an almond-tree."
5.10 strip away the **branches,** because those branches are not mine.
11.16 I will set its leaves on fire and break its **branches.**
48.32 are like a vine whose **branches** reach across the Dead Sea and
Ezek 15. 2 What good is a **branch** of a grapevine compared with the trees
17. 6 The **branches** grew upward towards the eagle, and the roots grew deep.
17. 6 The vine was covered with **branches** and leaves.
17. 9 the grapes, and break off the **branches** and let them wither?
17.23 It will grow **branches** and bear seed and become a magnificent cedar.
19.11 Its **branches** were strong, and grew to be royal sceptres.
19.12 Its **branches** were broken off;
19.14 fire burnt up its **branches** and fruit.
19.14 The **branches** will never again be strong, will never be royal sceptres.
31. 3 in Lebanon, With beautiful, shady **branches,** A tree so tall
31. 5 Its **branches** grew thick and long.
31. 6 Every kind of bird built nests in its **branches;**
31. 7 How beautiful the tree was— So tall, with such long **branches.**

Ezek 31. 8 No fir-tree ever had such **branches,** And no plane-tree such boughs.
31. 9 I made it beautiful, with spreading **branches.**
31.12 Its **branches** and broken boughs will fall on every mountain
31.13 tree, and the wild animals will walk over its **branches.**
Dan 4.12 birds built nests in its **branches,** and every kind of living
4.14 a loud voice, 'Cut the tree down and chop off its **branches;**
4.14 the animals from under it and the birds out of its **branches.**
4.21 under it, and birds made their nests in its **branches.**
Joel 1. 7 They have stripped off the bark, till the **branches** are white.
Zech 3. 8 I will reveal my servant, who is called The **Branch!**
4.12 meaning of the two olive **branches** beside the two gold pipes
6.12 man who is called The **Branch** will flourish where he is and
Mt 13.32 so that birds come and make their nests in its **branches."**
21. 8 while others cut **branches** from the trees and spread them
24.32 its **branches** become green and tender and it starts putting out
27.29 a crown out of thorny **branches** and placed it on his head,
Mk 4.32 It puts out such large **branches** that the birds come and make
11. 8 while others cut **branches** in the fields and spread them
13.28 its **branches** become green and tender and it starts putting out
15.17 a crown out of thorny **branches,** and put it on his head.
Lk 13.19 a tree, and the birds make their nests in its **branches."**
Jn 12.13 So they took **branches** of palm-trees and went out to meet him,
15. 2 He breaks off every **branch** in me that does not bear fruit,
15. 2 and he prunes every **branch** that does bear fruit, so that
15. 4 A **branch** cannot bear fruit by itself;
15. 5 "I am the vine, and you are the **branches.**
15. 6 remain in me is thrown out like a **branch** and dries up;
15. 6 such **branches** are gathered up and thrown into the fire,
19. 2 a crown out of thorny **branches** and put it on his head;
Rom 11.16 of a tree are offered to God, the **branches** are his also.
11.17 of the **branches** of the cultivated olive-tree have been broken
11.17 and a **branch** of a wild olive-tree has been
11.18 you must not despise those who were broken off like **branches.**
11.18 You are just a **branch;**
11.19 will say, "Yes, but the **branches** were broken off to make
11.21 God did not spare the Jews, who are like natural **branches;**
11.24 You Gentiles are like the **branch** of a wild olive-tree
11.24 God to join these broken-off **branches** to their own tree again.
Rev 7. 9 dressed in white robes and holding palm **branches** in their hands.

BRASS

1 Chr 15.17 they chose the following men to play the **brass** cymbals:
Rev 1.15 his feet shone like **brass** that has been refined and polished,
2.18 whose eyes blaze like fire, whose feet shine like polished **brass.**

BRAT

1 Sam 17.28 You cheeky **brat,** you!

BRAVE

Josh 6. 2 hands Jericho, with its king and all its **brave** soldiers.
Judg 6.12 and said, "The Lord is with you, **brave** and mighty man!"
11. 1 Jephthah, a **brave** soldier from Gilead, was the son of a prostitute.
20.46 Benjaminites were killed that day—all of them **brave** soldiers.
21.10 sent twelve thousand of their **bravest** men with the orders,
1 Sam 4. 9 Be **brave,** Philistines!
4.20 was dying, the women helping her said to her, "Be **brave!**
14.52 man who was strong or **brave,** he would enlist him in his
16.18 He is also a **brave** and handsome man, a good soldier, and
18.17 you serve me as a **brave** and loyal soldier, and fight the
31.12 had done to Saul, [12]the **bravest** men started out and
2 Sam 1.19 The **bravest** of our soldiers have fallen!
1.21 For the shields of the **brave** lie there in disgrace;
1.25 "The **brave** soldiers have fallen, they were killed in battle.
1.27 "The **brave** soldiers have fallen, their weapons abandoned and useless."
2. 7 Be strong and **brave!**
13.28 Be **brave** and don't hesitate!"
17.10 Then even the **bravest** men, as fearless as lions, will be
23.17 Those were the **brave** deeds of the three famous soldiers.
23.20 **brave** deeds, including killing two great Moabite warriors.
23.22 Those were the **brave** deeds of Benaiah, who was one of
1 Kgs 15.23 King Asa did, his **brave** deeds and the towns he fortified,
16. 5 Baasha did and all his **brave** deeds are recorded in The
22.45 that Jehoshaphat did, all his **bravery** and his battles, are
2 Kgs 10.34 that Jehu did, including his **brave** deeds, is recorded in The
13. 8 Jehoahaz did and all his **brave** deeds are recorded in The
13.12 that Jehoash did, including his **bravery** in the war against
14.15 that Jehoash did, including his **bravery** in the war against
14.28 that Jeroboam II did, his **brave** battles, and how he restored
20.20 that King Hezekiah did, his **brave** deeds, and an account of
1 Chr 10.12 had done to Saul, [12]the **bravest** men went and fetched the
11.19 These were the **brave** deeds of the three famous soldiers.
11.22 **brave** deeds, including killing two great Moabite warriors.
11.24 Those were the **brave** deeds of Benaiah, who was one of
2 Chr 14. 8 All of them were **brave,** well-trained men.
28. 5 Ahaz and kill 120,000 of the **bravest** Judaean soldiers in one day.
Ps 76. 5 Their **brave** soldiers have been stripped of all they had
147.10 is not in strong horses, nor his delight in **brave** soldiers;
Prov 28. 1 chasing them, but an honest person is as **brave** as a lion.
Ecc 9.11 win the race, and the **brave** do not always win the battle.
Is 5.22 **Brave** and fearless when it comes to mixing drinks!
21.17 The bowmen are the **bravest** men of Kedar, but few of them
33. 7 **Brave** men are calling for help.
Jer 48.14 do you claim to be heroes, **brave** soldiers tested in war?
Amos 2.16 On that day even the **bravest** soldiers will drop their
Zeph 1.14 day, for even the **bravest** soldiers will cry out in despair!
Jn 16.33 But be **brave!**
1 Cor 16.13 Be alert, stand firm in the faith, be **brave,** be strong.

BREAD

Gen 14.18 brought **bread** and wine to Abram, [19]blessed him,
18. 6 "Quick, take a sack of your best flour, and bake some **bread."**
19. 3 his servants to bake some **bread** and prepare a fine meal for
25.34 Then Jacob gave him some **bread** and some of the soup.
27.17 him the tasty food, together with the **bread** she had baked.
45.23 loaded with corn, **bread,** and other food for the journey.
Ex 12. 8 eaten with bitter herbs and with **bread** made without yeast.
12.15 not eat any bread made with yeast—eat only unleavened **bread.**
12.15 during those seven days eats **bread** made with yeast, he shall
12.18 day, you must not eat any **bread** made with yeast.
12.19 anyone, native-born or foreign, eats **bread** made with yeast,
12.39 They baked unleavened **bread** from the dough that they had
13. 3 No leavened **bread** is to be eaten.
13. 6 days you must eat unleavened **bread** and on the seventh day
13. 7 For seven days you must not eat any **bread** made with yeast;
13. 7 must be no yeast or leavened **bread** anywhere in your land.
16. 8 the evening and as much **bread** as you want in the morning,
16.12 and in the morning they will have all the **bread** they want.
23.15 celebrate the Festival of Unleavened **Bread** in the way that I
23.15 Do not eat any **bread** made with yeast during the seven days
23.18 "Do not offer **bread** made with yeast when you sacrifice
25.30 table there is always to be the sacred **bread** offered to me.
29. 2 yeast, and make some **bread** with olive-oil, some without it,
29.23 From the basket of **bread** which has been offered to me,
29.32 are to eat it along with the **bread** left in the basket.
29.34 meat or some of the **bread** is not eaten by morning, it
34.18 "Keep the Festival of Unleavened **Bread.**
34.18 have commanded you, eat unleavened **bread** for seven days in
34.25 "Do not offer **bread** made with yeast when you sacrifice
35.13 the **bread** offered to God;
39.36 the table and all its equipment, and the **bread** offered to God;
40.23 and placed on it the **bread** offered to the Lord, just as
Lev 2. 4 If the offering is **bread** baked in an oven, it must be
2. 5 If the offering is **bread** cooked on a griddle, it is to
2. 7 If the offering is **bread** cooked in a pan, it is to
6.16 It shall be made into **bread** baked without yeast and eaten in
7.12 to be sacrificed, an offering of **bread** made without yeast:
7.13 In addition, he shall offer loaves of **bread** baked without yeast.
7.14 part of each kind of **bread** as a special contribution to the
8. 2 the two rams, and the basket of unleavened **bread.**
8.26 took one loaf of **bread** from the basket of unleavened bread
8.31 eat it there with the **bread** that is in the basket of
8.32 Burn up any meat or **bread** that is left over.
10.12 to the Lord, make unleavened **bread** with it and eat it beside
23. 6 day the Festival of Unleavened **Bread** begins,
23. 6 for seven days you must not eat any **bread** made with yeast.
23.14 raw, roasted, or baked into **bread,** until you have brought
23.17 to bring two loaves of **bread** and present them to the Lord
23.18 And with the **bread** the community is to present seven one-year-old lambs,
23.20 The priest shall present the **bread** with the two lambs as
24. 5 Take twelve kilogrammes of flour and bake twelve loaves of **bread.**
24. 7 food-offering to the Lord to take the place of the **bread.**
24. 8 all time to come, the **bread** must be placed in the presence
24. 9 The **bread** belongs to Aaron and his descendants, and they
26.26 will need only one oven to bake all the **bread** they have.
Num 4. 7 over the table for the **bread** offered to the Lord and put
4. 7 There shall always be **bread** on the table.
6.15 He shall also offer a basket of **bread** made without yeast:
6.17 Lord as a fellowship-offering, and offer it with the basket of **bread;**
6.19 one thick loaf of **bread** and one biscuit from the basket,
9.11 Celebrate it with unleavened **bread** and bitter herbs.
11. 8 It tasted like **bread** baked with olive-oil.)
15.20 When you bake **bread,** the first loaf of the first bread
15.21 is to be given to the Lord from the **bread** you bake.
28.17 seven days, during which only **bread** prepared without yeast
Deut 8. 3 man must not depend on **bread** alone to sustain him, but on
16. 3 When you eat this meal, do not eat **bread** prepared with yeast.
16. 3 days you are to eat **bread** prepared without yeast, as you did
16. 3 Eat this **bread—**it will be called the bread of suffering—so
16. 8 days you are to eat **bread** prepared without yeast, and on the
29. 6 You did not have **bread** to eat or wine or beer to
Josh 5.11 roasted grain and **bread** made without yeast.
9. 5 The **bread** they took with them was dry and mouldy.
9.12 Look at our **bread.**
Judg 6.19 ten kilogrammes of flour to make **bread** without any yeast.
6.20 "Put the meat and the **bread** on this rock, and pour the
6.21 touched the meat and the **bread** with the end of the stick
6.21 out of the rock and burnt up the meat and the **bread.**
7.13 that a loaf of barley **bread** rolled into our camp and hit
8. 5 men of the town, "Please give my men some loaves of **bread.**
19.19 our donkeys, as well as **bread** and wine for my concubine and
Ruth 2.14 and have a piece of **bread,** and dip it in the sauce."
1 Sam 10. 3 be carrying three loaves of **bread,** and the third one will
16.20 goat, a donkey loaded with **bread,** and a leather bag full of
17.17 and these ten loaves of **bread,** and hurry with them to your
21. 3 Give me five loaves of **bread** or anything else you have."
21. 4 The priest said, "I haven't any ordinary **bread,** only sacred bread;
21. 6 priest gave David the sacred **bread,**
21. 6 because the only **bread** he had was the loaves offered
21. 6 removed from the sacred table and replaced by fresh **bread.**
25.11 not going to take my **bread** and water, and the animals I
25.18 two hundred loaves of **bread,** two leather bags full of wine,
28.24 some flour, prepared it, and baked some **bread** without yeast.
2 Sam 6.19 in Israel a loaf of **bread,** a piece of roasted meat, and

2 Sam 16. 1 two hundred loaves of **bread**, a hundred bunches of raisins,
16. 2 Majesty's family to ride, the **bread** and the fruit are for
1 Kgs 7.48 altar, the table for the **bread** offered to God, [49] the ten
14. 3 Take him ten loaves of **bread**, some cakes, and a jar of
17. 6 brook, and ravens brought him **bread** and meat every morning
17.11 get it, he called out, "And please bring me some **bread**,
17.12 living Lord your God I swear that I haven't got any **bread**.
19. 6 and saw a loaf of **bread** and a jar of water near
22.27 and to put him on **bread** and water until I return safely."
2 Kgs 4.42 bringing Elisha twenty loaves of **bread** made from the first
18.32 vineyards to give wine and there is corn for making **bread**;
23. 9 eat the unleavened **bread** provided for their fellow-priests.
1 Chr 9.32 preparing the sacred **bread** for the Temple every Sabbath.
16. 3 in Israel a loaf of **bread**, a piece of roasted meat, and
23.29 to be responsible for the **bread** offered to God, the
28.16 on which were placed the loaves of **bread** offered to God.
2 Chr 2. 4 will present offerings of sacred **bread** to him continuously,
4.19 the altar and the tables for the **bread** offered to God;
8.13 Festival of Unleavened **Bread**, the Harvest Festival,
13.11 They present the offerings of **bread** on a table that is
18.26 and to put him on **bread** and water until I return safely."
29.18 the table for the sacred **bread**, and all their equipment.
30.13 in the second month to celebrate the Festival of Unleavened **Bread**.
30.21 celebrated the Festival of Unleavened **Bread** with great joy,
35.17 the Passover and the Festival of Unleavened **Bread**.
Ezra 6.22 they joyfully celebrated the Festival of Unleavened **Bread**.
Neh 9.15 were hungry, you gave them **bread** from heaven, and water from
10.33 the sacred **bread**, the daily grain-offering, the animals to
Ps 78.20 he also provide us with **bread** and give his people meat?"
104.15 to make him cheerful, and **bread** to give him strength.
Prov 6.26 price of a loaf of **bread**, but adultery will cost him all
9.17 Stolen **bread** tastes better."
17. 1 eat a dry crust of **bread** with peace of mind than to
Is 36.17 vineyards to give wine and there is corn for making **bread**.
44.15 one part he builds a fire to warm himself and bake **bread**;
44.19 I baked some **bread** on the embers and I roasted meat and
62. 9 harvested the corn Will eat the **bread** and praise the Lord.
Jer 37.21 was given a loaf of **bread** from the bakeries
37.21 until all the **bread** in the city was gone.
Ezek 4. 9 Mix them all together and make **bread**.
4.10 be allowed 230 grammes of **bread** a day, and it will have
4.12 of dried human excrement, bake **bread** on the fire, and eat it
4.15 cow dung instead, and you can bake your **bread** on that."
4.16 I am going to cut off the supply of **bread** for Jerusalem.
4.17 They will run out of **bread** and water;
13.19 get a few handfuls of barley and a few pieces of **bread**.
16.13 You ate **bread** made from the best flour, and had honey and
44.30 Each time the people bake **bread**, they are to give the
45.21 For seven days everyone will eat **bread** made without yeast.
Hos 7. 8 "The people of Israel are like a half-baked loaf of **bread**.
8. 7 A field of corn that doesn't ripen can never produce any **bread**.
Amos 4. 5 Go ahead and offer your **bread** in thanksgiving to God, and
8.11 People will be hungry, but not for **bread**;
Hag 2.12 lets his robe touch any **bread**, cooked food, wine, olive-oil,
Mt 4. 3 "If you are God's Son, order these stones to turn into **bread**."
4. 4 'Man cannot live on **bread** alone, but needs every word that
7. 9 are fathers give your son a stone when he asks for **bread**?
12. 4 and his men ate the **bread** offered to God, even though it
12. 4 only the priests were allowed to eat that **bread**.
15.34 "How much **bread** have you?"
16. 5 the other side of the lake, they forgot to take any **bread**.
16. 7 "He says this because we didn't bring any **bread**."
16. 8 "Why are you discussing among yourselves about not having any **bread**?
16.11 don't understand that I was not talking to you about **bread**?
16.12 from the yeast used in **bread** but from the teaching of
26.23 answered, "One who dips his **bread** in the dish with me will
26.26 Jesus took a piece of **bread**, gave a prayer of thanks,
Mk 2.26 into the house of God and ate the **bread** offered to God.
2.26 the priests may eat this **bread**—but David ate it and even
6. 8 journey except a stick—no **bread**, no beggar's bag, no money
6.37 two hundred silver coins on **bread** in order to feed them?"
6.38 So Jesus asked them, "How much **bread** have you got?
6.43 baskets full of what was left of the **bread** and the fish.
8. 5 "How much **bread** have you got?"
8.14 had forgotten to bring enough **bread** and had only one loaf
8.16 "He says this because we haven't any **bread**."
8.17 them, "Why are you discussing about not having any **bread**?
14.20 you twelve, one who dips his **bread** in the dish with me.
14.22 Jesus took a piece of **bread**, gave a prayer of thanks,
Lk 4. 3 "If you are God's Son, order this stone to turn into **bread**."
4. 4 "The scripture says, 'Man cannot live on **bread** alone.'"
6. 4 house of God, took the **bread** offered to God, ate it,
6. 4 our Law for anyone except the priests to eat that **bread**."
11. 5 say to him, 'Friend, let me borrow three loaves of **bread**.
11. 8 and give you the **bread** because you are his friend,
22.19 he took a piece of **bread**, gave thanks to God, broke it,
24.30 to eat with them, took the **bread**, and said the blessing;
24.30 then he broke the **bread** and gave it to them.
24.35 how they had recognized the Lord when he broke the **bread**.
Jn 6. 7 more than two hundred silver coins to buy enough **bread**."
6. 9 boy here who has five loaves of barley **bread** and two fish.
6.11 Jesus took the **bread**, gave thanks to God, and distributed it
6.23 crowd had eaten the **bread** after the Lord had given thanks.
6.26 because you ate the **bread** and had all you wanted,
6.31 scripture says, 'He gave them **bread** from heaven to eat.'"
6.32 "What Moses gave you was not the **bread** from heaven;
6.32 it is my Father who gives you the real **bread** from heaven.
6.33 For the **bread** that God gives is he who comes down from
6.34 "Sir," they asked him, "give us this **bread** always."
Jn 6.35 "I am the **bread** of life," Jesus told them.
6.41 he said, "I am the **bread** that came down from heaven."
6.48 I am the **bread** of life.
6.50 But the **bread** that comes down from heaven is of such a
6.51 I am the living **bread** that came down from heaven.
6.51 If anyone eats this **bread**, he will live for ever.
6.51 The **bread** that I will give him is my flesh,
6.58 This, then, is the **bread** that came down from heaven;
6.58 it is not like the **bread** that your ancestors ate,
6.58 The one who eats this **bread** will live for ever."
13.26 answered, "I will dip some **bread** in the sauce and give it
13.26 he took a piece of **bread**, dipped it, and gave it to
13.27 As soon as Judas took the **bread**, Satan entered him.
13.30 Judas accepted the **bread** and went out at once.
21. 9 saw a charcoal fire there with fish on it and some **bread**.
21.13 So Jesus went over, took the **bread**, and gave it to them;
Acts 20.11 Then he went back upstairs, broke **bread**, and ate.
27.35 saying this, Paul took some **bread**, gave thanks to God before
Rom 11.16 If the first piece of **bread** is given to God,
1 Cor 5. 8 our Passover, then, not with **bread** having the old yeast of
5. 8 and wickedness, but with the **bread** that has no yeast,
5. 8 the **bread** of purity and truth.
10. 3 All ate the same spiritual **bread** [4] and drank the same spiritual
10.16 And the **bread** we break:
10.17 is the one loaf of **bread**, all of us, though many, are
11.23 took a piece of **bread**, [24] gave thanks to God, broke it,
11.26 every time you eat this **bread** and drink from this cup
11.27 if anyone eats the Lord's **bread** or drinks from his cup
11.28 first, and then eat the **bread** and drink from the cup.
11.29 body when he eats the **bread** and drinks from the cup,
2 Cor 9.10 supplies seed to sow and **bread** to eat, will also supply you
Heb 9. 2 the lampstand and the table with the **bread** offered to God.

BREAD-BASKETS see **BASKET**

BREAK

[BROKE, BROKEN, BROKEN-DOWN, BROKEN-HEARTED, BROKEN-OFF BRANCHES, UNBREAKABLE, UNBROKEN]

Gen 19. 9 They pushed Lot back and moved up to **break** down the door.
27.40 Yet when you rebel, You will **break** away from his control."
31.36 "What law have I **broken** that gives you the right to hunt
38.29 the midwife said, "So this is how you **break** your way out!"
43.30 He was about to **break down**, so he went to his room
Ex 6. 9 their spirit had been **broken** by their cruel slavery.
9.25 down all the plants in the fields and **broke** all the trees.
12.46 And do not **break** any of the animal's bones.
13.13 you do not want to buy back the donkey, **break** its neck.
15. 6 it **breaks** the enemy in pieces.
22. 2 "If a thief is caught **breaking** into a house at night and
23.24 Destroy their gods and **break** down their sacred stone pillars.
32.19 he threw down the tablets he was carrying and **broke** them.
34. 1 the words that were on the first tablets, which you **broke**.
34.20 If you do not buy it back, **break** its neck.
Lev 4. 2 that anyone who sinned and **broke** any of the Lord's commands
4.13 sins and becomes guilty of **breaking** one of the Lord's
4.22 sins and becomes guilty of **breaking** one of the Lord's
4.27 sins and becomes guilty of **breaking** one of the Lord's
5. 8 He will **break** its neck without pulling off its head [9] and
5.17 sins unintentionally by **breaking** any of the Lord's commands, he
6.28 meat is boiled must be **broken**, and if a metal pot is
7.27 Anyone who **breaks** this law will no longer be considered
11.33 is in it shall be unclean, and you must **break** the pot.
11.35 stove or oven shall be **broken**, [36] but a spring or a cistern
15.12 the man touches must be **broken**, and any wooden bowl that he
17. 3 of the Tent of the Lord's presence has **broken** the Law.
20.18 they have **broken** the regulations about ritual uncleanness.
24.20 If he **breaks** a bone, one of his bones shall be broken;
26.13 I **broke** the power that held you down and I let you
26.15 my laws and commands and **break** the covenant I have made with
26.19 I will **break** your stubborn pride;
26.25 you to punish you for **breaking** our covenant, and if you
Num 9.12 morning and do not **break** any of the animal's bones.
9.17 lifted, the people of Israel **broke** camp, and they set up
9.18 The people **broke** camp at the command of the Lord, and at
9.23 They set up camp and **broke** camp in obedience to the
10. 2 use for calling the people together and for **breaking** camp.
10.28 by company, whenever the Israelites **broke** camp and set out.
15.31 Lord said and has deliberately **broken** one of his commands.
18.19 This is an **unbreakable** covenant that I have made with you
30. 2 from something, he must not **break** his promise, but must do
Deut 7. 5 their altars, **break** their sacred stone pillars in pieces,
9.17 you I threw the stone tablets down and **broke** them to pieces.
9.21 Then I **broke** it in pieces, ground it to dust, and threw
10. 2 on the tablets that you **broke**, and then you are to put
17. 2 sinned against the Lord and **broken** his covenant [3] by
21. 4 ploughed or planted, and there they are to **break** its neck.
29.25 is because the Lord's people **broke** the covenant that they had
31.16 become unfaithful to me and **break** the covenant that I made
31.20 They will reject me and **break** my covenant, [21] and many
Josh 7.11 They have **broken** the agreement with me that I ordered them
7.15 brought terrible shame on Israel and has **broken** my covenant."
Judg 2. 1 I said, 'I will never **break** my covenant with you.
2.20 and say, "This nation has **broken** the covenant that I
7.19 they blew the trumpets and **broke** the jars they were holding,
11.35 You are **breaking** my heart!
15.14 made him strong, and he **broke** the ropes round his arms and
16. 9 the bowstrings just as thread **breaks** when fire touches it.
21.15 because the Lord had **broken** the unity of the tribes
21.22 to us, you are not guilty of **breaking** your promise.'"

1 Sam	2. 4	The bows of strong soldiers are **broken,** but the weak grow strong.
	4.18	old and fat that the fall **broke** his neck, and he died.
	5. 4	and both its arms were **broken** off and were lying in the
	17.49	him on the forehead and **broke** his skull, and Goliath fell
	20.16	may our promise to each other still be **unbroken.**
	20.16	If it is **broken,** the Lord will punish you."
2 Sam	5.20	He said, "The Lord has **broken** through my enemies like a flood."
	23. 5	agreement that will not be **broken,** a promise that will not
1 Kgs	2.43	Why, then, have you **broken** your promise and disobeyed my command?
	11.11	him, "Because you have deliberately **broken** your covenant
	15.19	Now **break** your alliance with King Baasha of Israel, so that
	19.10	the people of Israel have **broken** their covenant with you,
	19.14	the people of Israel have **broken** their covenant with you,
2 Kgs	8.21	his chariot commanders managed to **break** out and escape, and
	17.16	They **broke** all the laws of the Lord their God and made
	18. 4	the pagan places of worship, **broke** the stone pillars, and
	18. 4	He also **broke** in pieces the bronze snake that Moses had made,
	18.12	the Lord their God, but **broke** the covenant he had made with
	18.21	a reed as a walking-stick—it would **break** and jab your hand.
	23.14	King Josiah **broke** the stone pillars to pieces, cut down
	23.15	Josiah pulled down the altar, **broke** its stones into pieces,
	24.13	Nebuchadnezzar **broke** up all the gold utensils
	25. 4	nothing left to eat, [4]the city walls were **broken** through.
	25.13	The Babylonians **broke** in pieces the bronze columns and
1 Chr	14.11	"God has used me to **break** through the enemy army like a
2 Chr	13. 5	God of Israel, made an **unbreakable** covenant with David,
	14. 3	places of worship, **broke** down the sacred stone columns,
	16. 3	Now **break** your alliance with King Baasha of Israel so that
	21. 9	but during the night they managed to **break** out and escape.
	28.24	he took all the temple equipment and **broke** it in pieces.
	31. 1	every city in Judah and **broke** the stone pillars, cut down
	32. 1	orders for his army to **break** their way through the walls.
	34. 7	idols to dust, and **broke** in pieces all the incense-altars.
	36.19	its palaces and its wealth, and **broke** down the city wall.
Ezra	10. 2	said to Ezra, "We have **broken** faith with God by marrying
Neh	1. 3	walls of Jerusalem were still **broken** down and that the gates
	2.13	I went, I inspected the **broken** walls of the city and the
	10.29	of a curse if we **break** it, that we will live according
Job	2. 8	heap and took a piece of **broken** pottery to scrape his sores.
	3. 1	Finally Job **broke** the silence and cursed the day on which
	4.10	like lions, but God silences them and **breaks** their teeth.
	24.16	At night thieves **break** into houses, but by day they hide
	31.22	I could win in court, [22]then may my arms be **broken;**
	39.15	that a foot may crush them or a wild animal **break** them.
Ps	2. 9	You will **break** them with an iron rod;
	10.15	**Break** the power of wicked and evil men;
	18.12	the lightning before him and **broke** through the dark clouds.
	29. 5	The voice of the Lord **breaks** the cedars, even the cedars
	34.20	not one of his bones is **broken.**
	42. 4	My heart **breaks** when I remember the past, when I went with
	42. 6	in exile my heart is **breaking,** and so I turn my thoughts
	44.17	not forgotten you or **broken** the covenant you made with us.
	46. 9	he **breaks** bows, destroys spears, and sets shields on fire.
	51. 8	you have crushed me and **broken** me, I will be happy once
	55.20	he **broke** his promises.
	58. 6	**Break** the teeth of these fierce lions, O God.
	62. 3	attack a man who is no stronger than a **broken-down** fence?
	68.21	God will surely **break** the heads of his enemies, of those
	69.20	Insults have **broken** my heart, and I am in despair.
	75.10	He will **break** the power of the wicked, but the power of
	76. 3	There he **broke** the arrows of the enemy, their shields and swords,
	80.12	Why did you **break** down the fences round it?
	89.34	I will not **break** my covenant with him or take back even
	89.39	You have **broken** your covenant with your servant and
	105.33	he destroyed their grapevines and fig-trees and **broke** down all the trees.
	107.14	their gloom and darkness and **broke** their chains in pieces.
	107.16	He **breaks** down doors of bronze and smashes iron bars.
	119.53	When I see the wicked **breaking** your law, I am filled
	124. 7	the trap is **broken,** and we are free!
	147. 3	He heals the **broken-hearted** and bandages their wounds.
Prov	16.28	they stir up trouble and **break** up friendships.
	17. 9	Remembering wrongs can **break** up a friendship.
	17.14	start of an argument is like the first **break** in a dam;
	25.15	Patient persuasion can **break** down the strongest resistance
Ecc	4.12	A rope made of three cords is hard to **break.**
	9.14	He surrounded it and prepared to **break** through the walls.
	10. 8	if you **break** through a wall, a snake bites you.
	12. 6	chain will snap, and the golden lamp will fall and **break;**
	12. 6	rope at the well will **break,** and the water jar will be
Is	5. 5	the hedge round it, **break** down the wall that protects it,
	5.18	You are unable to **break** free from your sins.
	5.27	not a sandal strap is **broken.**
	9. 4	For you have **broken** the yoke that burdened them and the
	14.29	rod that beat you is **broken,** but you have no reason to
	19.10	weavers and skilled workmen will be **broken** and depressed.
	24. 5	have defiled the earth by **breaking** God's laws and by
	24.12	The city is in ruins, and its gates have been **broken** down.
	27.11	are withered and **broken,** and women gather them for firewood.
	30.14	a clay pot, so badly **broken** that there is no piece big
	33. 8	Treaties are **broken** and agreements are violated.
	33.20	whose pegs are never pulled up and whose ropes never **break.**
	36. 6	a reed as a walking-stick—it would **break** and jab your hand.
	38.13	cried out with pain, As if a lion were **breaking** my bones.
	42. 3	He will not **break** off a bent reed or put out a
	43.14	I will **break** down the city gates, and the shouts of her
	45. 2	I will **break** down bronze gates and smash their iron bars.
	61. 1	the poor, To heal the **broken-hearted,** To announce release to
	65.14	will sing for joy, but you will cry with a **broken** heart.
	66. 3	whether they sacrifice a lamb or **break** a dog's neck;
Jer	5.22	the waves may roar, but they cannot **break** through.
	10.20	the ropes that held them have **broken.**
	11.10	Both Israel and Judah have **broken** the covenant that I made
	11.16	I will set its leaves on fire and **break** its branches.
	14.21	Do not **break** the covenant you made with us.
	15.12	(No one can **break** iron, especially the iron from the
	17.18	Bring disaster on them and **break** them to pieces.
	18. 7	I am going to uproot, **break** down, or destroy any nation or
	19.10	the Lord told me to **break** the jar in front of the
	19.11	Almighty had said, "I will **break** this people and this city,
	19.11	it will be like this **broken** clay jar that cannot be put
	21.13	that no one can attack you or **break** through your defences.
	22.28	King Jehoiachin become like a **broken** jar that is thrown away
	23.29	like a fire, and like a hammer that **breaks** rocks in pieces.
	28. 2	"I have **broken** the power of the king of Babylonia.
	28. 4	Yes, I will **break** the power of the king of Babylonia.
	28.10	the yoke off my neck, **broke** it in pieces, [11]and said in
	28.11	this is how he will **break** the yoke that King Nebuchadnezzar
	28.13	you may be able to **break** a wooden yoke, but he will
	30. 8	that day comes, I will **break** the yoke that is round their
	33.20	and that covenant can never be **broken.**
	33.21	and those covenants can never be **broken.**
	34.18	But they **broke** the covenant and did not keep its terms.
	39. 2	the city walls were **broken** through.
	48.12	They will empty its wine-jars and **break** them in pieces.
	48.17	Say, 'Its powerful rule has been **broken;**
	48.38	but mourning, because I have **broken** Moab like a jar that no
	50. 5	They will make an eternal covenant with me and never **break** it.
	50.15	Its walls have been **broken** through and torn down.
	50.26	it from every side and **break** open the places where its grain
	51.30	The city gates are **broken** down, and the houses are on fire.
	51.31	Babylonia that his city has been **broken** into from every side.
	51.56	its soldiers are captured, and their bows are **broken.**
	52. 7	nothing left to eat, [7]the city walls were **broken** through.
	52.17	The Babylonians **broke** in pieces the bronze columns and
Lam	1.20	My heart is **broken** in sorrow for my sins.
	3. 4	has left my flesh open and raw, and has **broken** my bones.
	3.16	my face in the ground and **broke** my teeth on the gravel.
Ezek	6. 4	The altars will be torn down and the incense-altars **broken.**
	7.22	Temple is profaned, when robbers **break** into it and defile it.
	8. 8	He said, "Mortal man, **break** through the wall here."
	8. 8	I **broke** through it and found a door.
	11.12	you were **breaking** my laws and disobeying my commands."
	12. 5	While they are watching, **break** a hole through the wall of
	13.14	I intend to **break** down the wall they whitewashed, to
	16.59	because you ignored your promises and **broke** the covenant.
	17. 3	the Lebanon Mountains and **broke** off the top of a cedar-tree,
	17. 9	pull off the grapes, and **break** off the branches and let them
	17.15	He cannot **break** the treaty and go unpunished!
	17.16	die in Babylonia because he **broke** his oath and the treaty he
	17.18	He **broke** his oath and the treaty he had made.
	17.19	I will punish him for **breaking** the treaty which he swore in
	17.22	the top of a tall cedar and **break** off a tender sprout;
	19.12	Its branches were **broken** off;
	20.13	They **broke** my laws and rejected my commands, which bring
	20.16	they had rejected my commands, **broken** my laws, and profaned
	20.21	They **broke** my laws and did not keep my commands, which bring
	20.24	rejected my commands, **broken** my laws, profaned the Sabbath,
	21. 6	"Mortal man, groan as if your heart is **breaking** with despair.
	22.26	The priests **break** my law and have no respect for what is
	23.34	drain it dry, and with its **broken** pieces tear your breast.
	23.38	They profaned my Temple and **broke** the Sabbath, which I had established.
	29. 7	they leaned on you, you **broke,** pierced their armpits, and
	30.16	walls of Thebes will be **broken** down, and the city will be
	30.18	fall on Tahpanhes when I **break** the power of Egypt and put
	30.21	man," he said, "I have **broken** the arm of the king of
	30.22	I am going to **break** both his arms—the good one and
	30.22	one and the one already **broken**—and the sword will fall from
	30.24	But I will **break** the arms of the king of Egypt, and
	31.12	Its branches and **broken** boughs will fall on every mountain
	34.27	When I **break** my people's chains and set them free from those
	44. 7	So my people have **broken** my covenant by all the disgusting
Dan	2.34	at it, a great stone **broke** loose from a cliff without anyone
	2.40	as strong as iron, which shatters and **breaks** everything.
	2.45	You saw how a stone **broke** loose from a cliff without
	6.24	pit, the lions pounced on them and **broke** all their bones.
	8. 7	so angry that he smashed into him and **broke** the two horns.
	8. 8	but at the height of his power his horn was **broken.**
	8.22	when the first horn was **broken** represent the four kingdoms
	9.11	All Israel **broke** your laws and refused to listen to what
	11. 4	his power his empire will **break** up and be divided into four
Hos	4. 2	They make promises and **break** them;
	6. 7	the land at Adam, they **broke** the covenant I had made with
	7. 1	they **break** into houses and steal;
	8. 1	My people have **broken** the covenant I made with them and have
	8. 8	like any other nation and is as useless as a **broken** pot.
	10. 2	God will **break** down their altars and destroy their sacred pillars.
	11. 6	War will sweep through their cities and **break** down the city gates.
Joel	2.13	Let your **broken** heart show your sorrow;
Amos	3.14	of every altar will be **broken** off and will fall to the
	4. 3	dragged to the nearest **break** in the wall and thrown out."
	9. 1	**Break** them off and let them fall on the heads of the
Obad	11	You stood aside on that day when enemies **broke** down their gates.
Jon	1. 4	was so violent that the ship was in danger of **breaking** up.
Mic	2.13	They will **break** out of the city gates and go free.
	3. 3	You strip off their skin, **break** their bones, and chop them
	5. 5	Assyrians invade our country and **break** through our defences,
Nah	1.13	Assyria's power over you and **break** the chains that bind you."
	2. 8	Like water from a **broken** dam the people rush from Nineveh!
Zech	11.10	the stick called "Favour" and **broke** it, to cancel the

Zech 11.14 Then I **broke** the second stick, the one called "Unity,"
Mal 2. 4 the priests, the descendants of Levi, will not be **broken.**
2. 8 You have **broken** the covenant I made with you.
2.10 Then why do we **break** our promises to one another, and why
2.11 The people of Judah have **broken** their promise to God and
2.14 because he knows you have **broken** your promise to the wife
2.14 your partner, and you have **broken** your promise to her,
2.15 make sure that none of you **breaks** his promise to his wife.
2.16 sure that you do not **break** your promise to be faithful to
Mt 1.19 so he made plans to **break** the engagement privately.
5.33 in the past, 'Do not **break** your promise, but do what you
6.19 where moths and rust destroy, and robbers **break** in and steal.
6.20 and rust cannot destroy, and robbers cannot **break** in and steal.
12. 5 priests in the Temple actually **break** the Sabbath law, yet they
12.20 He will not **break** off a bent reed, or put out
12.29 "No one can **break** into a strong man's house and take
14.19 He **broke** the loaves and gave them to the disciples,
15.36 fish, gave thanks to God, **broke** them, and gave them to the
16. 9 Don't you remember when I **broke** the five loaves for the five
24.43 would stay awake and not let the thief **break** into his house.
26.26 gave a prayer of thanks, **broke** it, and gave it to his
27.52 split apart, [52] the graves **broke** open, and many of God's people
Mk 3.27 "No one can **break** into a strong man's house and take
5. 4 chained, but every time he **broke** the chains and smashed the
6.41 He **broke** the loaves and gave them to his disciples to
8. 6 loaves, gave thanks to God, **broke** them, and gave them to his
8.19 Don't you remember [19] when I **broke** the five loaves for the
8.20 "And when I **broke** the seven loaves for the four thousand
14. 3 She **broke** the jar and poured the perfume on Jesus' head.
14.22 gave a prayer of thanks, **broke** it, and gave it to his
14.72 And he **broke** down and cried.
Lk 2.35 And sorrow, like a sharp sword, will **break** your own heart."
5. 6 a large number of fish that the nets were about to **break.**
8.29 fastened with chains, he would **break** the chains and be driven
9.16 thanked God for them, **broke** them, and gave them to the
12.39 he would not let the thief **break** into his house.
22.19 bread, gave thanks to God, **broke** it, and gave it to them,
24.30 then he **broke** the bread and gave it to them.
24.35 how they had recognized the Lord when he **broke** the bread.
Jn 5.18 not only had he **broken** the Sabbath law, but he had said
7.23 that Moses' Law is not **broken,** why are you angry with me
15. 2 He **breaks** off every branch in me that does not bear fruit,
19.31 Pilate to allow them to **break** the legs of the men
19.32 So the soldiers went and **broke** the legs of the first man
19.33 that he was already dead, so they did not **break** his legs.
19.36 "Not one of his bones will be **broken."**
Acts 17. 7 They are all **breaking** the laws of the Emperor, saying that
20.11 Then he went back upstairs, **broke** bread, and ate.
21.13 "What are you doing, crying like this and **breaking** my heart?
23. 3 to the Law, yet you **break** the Law by ordering them to
25.11 If I have **broken** the law and done something for which I
27.35 thanks to God before them all, **broke** it, and began to eat.
27.41 the back part was being **broken** to pieces by the violence
27.44 on to the planks or to some **broken** pieces of the ship.
Rom 2.23 but do you bring shame on God by **breaking** his law?
2.27 by the Gentiles because you **break** the Law, even though you
11.17 the cultivated olive-tree have been **broken** off, and a branch of
11.18 you must not despise those who were **broken** off like branches.
11.19 "Yes, but the branches were **broken** off to make room for me."
11.20 They were **broken** off because they did not believe, while you
11.22 But if you do not, you too will be **broken** off.
11.24 wild olive-tree that is **broken** off and then, contrary to nature,
11.24 God to join these **broken-off branches** to their own tree again.
1 Cor 10.16 And the bread we **break:**
11.24 bread, [24] gave thanks to God, **broke** it, and said, "This is
Gal 2.18 then I show myself to be someone who **breaks** the Law.
3.15 an agreement, no one can **break** it or add anything to it.
3.17 years later, cannot **break** that covenant and cancel God's promise.
Eph 2.14 With his own body he **broke** down the wall that separated them
1 Tim 2.14 it was the woman who was deceived and **broke** God's law.
5.12 and so become guilty of **breaking** their earlier promise to him.
6.10 from the faith and have **broken** their hearts with many sorrows.
Jas 2.10 Whoever breaks one commandment is guilty of **breaking** them all.
1 Jn 3. 4 Whoever sins is guilty of **breaking** God's law,
3. 4 because sin is a **breaking** of the law.
Rev 2.26 an iron rod and to **break** them to pieces like clay pots.
5. 2 "Who is worthy to **break** the seals and open the scroll?"
5. 5 the victory, and he can **break** the seven seals and open the
5. 9 are worthy to take the scroll and to **break** open its seals.
6. 1 Then I saw the Lamb **break** open the first of the seven
6. 3 Then the Lamb **broke** open the second seal;
6. 5 Then the Lamb **broke** open the third seal;
6. 7 Then the Lamb **broke** open the fourth seal;
6. 9 Then the Lamb **broke** open the fifth seal.
6.12 And I saw the Lamb **break** open the sixth seal.
8. 1 When the Lamb **broke** open the seventh seal, there was silence

BREAK OUT

Gen 13. 7 So quarrels **broke out** between the men who took care of
Lev 13.39 it is only a blemish that has **broken out** on the skin;
14.43 If the mildew **breaks out** again in the house after the
Num 11.33 the people and caused an epidemic to **break out** among them.
16.46 The Lord's anger has already **broken out** and an epidemic has
18. 5 anger will not again **break out** against the people of Israel.
Deut 28.27 He will make your bodies **break out** with sores.
1 Sam 19. 8 War with the Philistines **broke out** again.
2 Sam 2.17 Then a furious battle **broke out,** and Abner and the
1 Chr 20. 4 Later on, war **broke out** again with the Philistines at Gezer.
2 Chr 13. 2 War **broke out** between Abijah and Jeroboam.
26.19 a dreaded skin-disease **broke out** on his forehead.
Job 2. 7 Lord's presence and made sores **break out** all over Job's body.
Ps 106.29 their actions, and a terrible disease **broke out** among them.
Is 7. 1 Jotham and grandson of Uzziah, ruled Judah, war **broke out.**
Mt 27.24 but that a riot might **break out,** he took some water, washed
Lk 9.46 An argument **broke out** among the disciples as to which one
22.24 An argument **broke out** among the disciples as to which one
Rev 12. 7 Then war **broke out** in heaven.

BREAST

Ex 29.26 "Take the **breast** of this ram and dedicate it to me as
29.27 a priest is ordained, the **breast** and the thigh of the ram
29.28 people make their fellowship-offerings, the **breast** and the
Lev 7.30 of the animal with its **breast** and present it as a special
7.31 on the altar, but the **breast** shall belong to the priests.
7.34 The **breast** of the animal is a special gift, and the
8.29 Then Moses took the **breast** and presented it as a special
9.20 ram [20] on top of the **breasts** of the animals and carried it
9.21 the altar [21] and presented the **breasts** and the right hind
10.14 your families may eat the **breast** and the hind leg that are
10.15 the hind leg and the **breast** at the time the fat is
Num 6.20 priest, in addition to the **breast** and the leg of the ram
18.18 belongs to you, like the **breast** and the right hind leg of
Job 3.12 Why did she feed me at her **breast?**
Song 1.13 lover has the scent of myrrh as he lies upon my **breasts.**
4. 5 Your **breasts** are like gazelles, twin deer feeding among lilies.
7. 3 Your **breasts** are like twin deer, like two gazelles.
7. 7 as a palm-tree, and your **breasts** are clusters of dates.
7. 8 To me your **breasts** are like bunches of grapes, your breath
8. 1 my brother, that my mother had nursed you at her **breast.**
8. 8 We have a young sister, and her **breasts** are still small.
8.10 I am a wall, and my **breasts** are its towers.
Is 32.12 Beat your **breasts** in grief because the fertile fields
66.11 You will enjoy her prosperity, like a child at its mother's **breast.**
Ezek 16. 7 Your **breasts** were well-formed, and your hair had grown, but
21.12 Beat your **breast** in despair!
23.21 Egypt, where men played with your **breasts** and you lost your virginity.)
23.34 drain it dry, and with its broken pieces tear your **breast.**
Nah 2. 7 her servants moan like doves and beat their **breasts** in sorrow.
Lk 18.13 but beat on his **breast** and said, 'God, have pity on
23.48 they all went back home, beating their **breasts** in sorrow.

BREAST-PIECE

Ex 25. 7 set in the ephod of the High Priest and in his **breast-piece.**
28. 4 Tell them to make a **breast-piece,** an ephod, a robe, an
28.15 "Make a **breast-piece** for the High Priest to use in
28.22 For the **breast-piece** make chains of pure gold,
28.23 the upper corners of the **breast-piece,** [24] and fasten the
28.26 the lower corners of the **breast-piece** on the inside edge
28.28 Tie the rings of the **breast-piece** to the rings of the
28.28 blue cord, so that the **breast-piece** rests above the belt and
28.29 Place, he will wear this **breast-piece** engraved with the
28.30 Urim and Thummim in the **breast-piece,** so that Aaron will carry
28.30 he must always wear this **breast-piece,** so that he can
29. 5 that goes under the ephod, the ephod, the **breast-piece,** and
35. 9 be set in the High Priest's ephod and in his **breast-piece.**
35.27 in the ephod and the **breast-piece** [28] and spices and oil for
39. 8 They made the **breast-piece** of the same materials as the
39.15 For the **breast-piece** they made chains of pure gold,
39.16 the two rings to the upper corners of the **breast-piece.**
39.19 the lower corners of the **breast-piece,** on the inside edge
39.21 tied the rings of the **breast-piece** to the rings of the ephod
39.21 blue cord, so that the **breast-piece** rested above the belt
Lev 8. 8 He put the **breast-piece** on him and put the Urim and

BREASTPLATE

Eph 6.14 with righteousness as your **breastplate,** [15] and as your shoes
1 Thes 5. 8 faith and love as a **breastplate,** and our hope of salvation
Rev 9. 9 with what looked like iron **breastplates,** and the sound made by
9.17 they had **breastplates** red as fire, blue as sapphire, and yellow

BREATH

Gen 2. 7 he breathed life-giving **breath** into his nostrils and the man
7.22 Everything on earth that **breathed** died.
35.18 was dying, and as she **breathed** her last, she named her son
Ex 15.10 But one **breath** from you, Lord, and the Egyptians were drowned;
1 Kgs 10. 5 It left her **breathless** and amazed.
17.22 the child started **breathing** again and revived.
2 Chr 9. 4 It left her **breathless** and amazed.
Job 7. 7 Remember, O God, my life is only a **breath;**
9.18 He won't let me get my **breath;**
17. 1 I can hardly **breathe;**
19.17 stand the smell of my **breath,** and my own brothers won't come
26.13 It is his **breath** that made the sky clear, and his hand
27. 3 long as God gives me **breath,** [4] my lips will never say
34.14 If God took back the **breath** of life, [15] then everyone
37.10 The **breath** of God freezes the waters, and turns them to
41.16 so tight to the next, not even a **breath** can come between.
41.21 His **breath** starts fires burning;
Ps 62. 9 Men are all like a puff of **breath;**
62. 9 they are lighter than a mere **breath.**
78.33 days like a **breath** and their lives with sudden disaster.
104.29 when you take away your **breath,** they die and go back to
104.30 But when you give them **breath,** they are created;
135.17 they are not even able to **breathe.**
Ecc 12. 7 of the earth, and the **breath** of life will go back to
Song 7. 8 bunches of grapes, your **breath** like the fragrance of apples,

Is 30.33 The Lord will **breathe** out a stream of flame to set it
42. 5 he gave life and **breath** to all its people.
Jer 4.31 Jerusalem gasping for **breath,** stretching out her hand and saying,
14. 6 stand on the hill-tops and pant for **breath** like jackals;
15. 9 The mother who lost her seven children has fainted, gasping for **breath.**
Ezek 37. 5 I am going to put **breath** into you and bring you back
37. 6 I will put **breath** into you and bring you back to life.
37. 8 But there was no **breath** in the bodies.
37. 9 from every direction, to **breathe** into these dead bodies,
37.10 **Breath** entered the bodies, and they came to life and stood up.
37.14 I will put my **breath** in them, bring them back to life,
Dan 10.17 I have no strength or **breath** left in me."
Mt 27.50 Jesus again gave a loud cry and **breathed** his last.
Jn 20.22 Then he **breathed** on them and said, "Receive the Holy Spirit.
Acts 17.25 who gives life and **breath** and everything else to everyone.
2 Thes 2. 8 will kill him with the **breath** from his mouth and destroy him
Rev 11.11 a life-giving **breath** came from God and entered them,
13.15 second beast was allowed to **breathe** life into the image of

BREATHTAKING

Song 6. 4 the city of Tirzah, as **breathtaking** as these great cities.

BRED see BREED

BREED
[BRED, CROSSBREED]

Gen 30.39 So when the goats **bred** in front of the branches, they
30.41 so that they would **breed** among the branches.
31.10 "During the **breeding** season I had a dream, and I saw
Lev 19.19 Do not **crossbreed** domestic animals.
2 Kgs 3. 4 King Mesha of Moab **bred** sheep, and every year he gave as
Job 21.10 Yes, all their cattle **breed** and give birth without trouble.

BREEZE

Job 4.15 A light **breeze** touched my face, and my hair bristled with fright.
Song 2.17 until the morning **breezes** blow and the darkness disappears.
4. 6 until the morning **breezes** blow and the darkness disappears.

BRIARS

Judg 8. 7 I will beat you with thorns and **briars** from the desert!"
8.16 He then took thorns and **briars** from the desert and used
Is 5. 6 instead I will let **briars** and thorns cover it.
7.23 of silver, will be overgrown with thorn-bushes and **briars.**
7.24 Yes, the whole country will be full of **briars** and thorn-bushes.
27. 4 only there were thorns and **briars** to fight against, then I
32.13 and thorn-bushes and **briars** are growing on my people's land.
55.13 Cypress-trees will grow where now there are **briars;**
Ezek 28.24 will ever again be like thorns and **briars** to hurt Israel.
Mt 7.16 Thorn bushes do not bear grapes, and **briars** do not bear figs.

BRIBE

Ex 18.21 God-fearing men who can be trusted and who cannot be **bribed.**
23. 8 Do not accept a **bribe,** for a bribe makes people blind to
Deut 10.17 He does not show partiality, and he does not accept **bribes.**
16.19 they are not to accept **bribes,** for gifts blind the eyes even
1 Sam 8. 3 so they accepted **bribes** and did not decide cases honestly.
12. 3 Have I accepted a **bribe** from anyone?
2 Chr 19. 7 God does not tolerate fraud or partiality or the taking of **bribes."**
Ezra 4. 5 They also **bribed** Persian government officials to work against them.
Neh 6.12 Tobiah and Sanballat had **bribed** him to give me this warning.
Job 6.22 me a gift or to **bribe** someone on my behalf [23] or to
15.34 men, and fire will destroy the homes built by **bribery.**
36.18 Be careful not to let **bribes** deceive you, or riches lead
Ps 15. 5 and cannot be **bribed** to testify against the innocent.
26.10 do evil all the time and are always ready to take **bribes.**
Prov 15.27 Don't take **bribes** and you will live longer.
17. 8 Some people think a **bribe** works like magic;
17.23 Corrupt judges accept secret **bribes,** and then justice is not done.
28.21 But some judges will do wrong to get even the smallest **bribe.**
Ecc 7. 7 If you take a **bribe,** you ruin your character.
Is 1.23 they are always accepting gifts and **bribes.**
5.23 But for just a **bribe** you let guilty men go free, and
33.15 Don't use your power to cheat the poor and don't accept **bribes.**
45.13 No one has hired him or **bribed** him to do this."
Ezek 16.33 to all your lovers and **bribed** them to come from everywhere
Amos 5.12 You persecute good men, take **bribes,** and prevent the poor
Mic 3.11 The city's rulers govern for **bribes,** the priests
7. 3 Officials and judges ask for **bribes.**
Lk 20.20 They **bribed** some men to pretend they were sincere, and
Acts 6.11 they **bribed** some men to say, "We heard him speaking against

BRICK

Gen 11. 3 Let's make **bricks** and bake them hard."
11. 3 So they had **bricks** to build with and tar to hold them
Ex 5. 7 "Stop giving the people straw for making **bricks.**
5. 8 the same number of **bricks** as before, not one brick less.
5.11 it, but you must still make the same number of **bricks."**
5.13 make the same number of **bricks** every day as they had made
5.14 making the same number of **bricks** as you made before?"
5.16 are given no straw, but we are still ordered to make **bricks!**
5.18 straw, but you must still make the same number of **bricks."**
5.19 make the same number of **bricks** every day as they had made
2 Sam 12.31 and iron axes, and forced them to work at making **bricks.**
Ps 81. 6 I let you put down your loads of **bricks.**
Is 9.10 They say, [10] "The **brick** buildings have fallen down, but we
Ezek 4. 1 said, "Mortal man, get a **brick,** put it in front of you,
Nah 3.14 Trample the clay to make bricks, and get the **brick** moulds ready!

BRIDE

Gen 34.12 and set the payment for the **bride** as high as you wish;
Ex 22.16 engaged, he must pay the **bride-price** for her and marry her.
22.17 a sum of money equal to the **bride-price** for a virgin.
Deut 22.29 the girl's father the **bride** price of fifty pieces of silver,
1 Sam 18.25 you as payment for the **bride** is the foreskins of a hundred
2 Sam 17. 3 all his men to you, like a **bride** returning to her husband.
Ps 45.10 **Bride** of the king, listen to what I say— forget your
Song 4. 8 Come with me from the Lebanon Mountains, my **bride;**
4. 9 your eyes, my sweetheart and **bride,** and the necklace you are
4.10 Your love delights me, my sweetheart and **bride.**
4.12 My sweetheart, my **bride,** is a secret garden, a walled garden,
5. 1 I have entered my garden, my sweetheart, my **bride.**
Is 49.18 of your people, as proud as a **bride** is of her jewels.
61.10 She is like a **bride** dressed for her wedding.
62. 5 taking a virgin as his **bride,** He who formed you will marry
62. 5 groom is delighted with his **bride,** So your God will delight
Jer 2.32 Does a young woman forget her jewellery, or a **bride** her wedding-dress?
Jn 3.29 The bridegroom is the one to whom the **bride** belongs;
Rev 18.23 more will the voices of **brides** and grooms be heard in you.
19. 7 of the Lamb, and his **bride** has prepared herself for it.
21. 2 prepared and ready, like a **bride** dressed to meet her husband.
21. 9 and I will show you the **Bride,** the wife of the Lamb."
22.17 The Spirit and the **Bride** say, "Come!"

BRIDEGROOM
[GROOM]

Ps 19. 5 the morning like a happy **bridegroom,** like an athlete eager
Is 62. 5 As a **groom** is delighted with his bride, So your God will
Mt 9.15 party to be sad as long as the **bridegroom** is with them?
9.15 will come when the **bridegroom** will be taken away from them,
25. 1 took their oil lamps and went out to meet the **bridegroom.**
25. 5 The **bridegroom** was late in coming, so the girls began to
25. 6 already midnight when the cry rang out, 'Here is the **bridegroom!**
25.10 and while they were gone, the **bridegroom** arrived.
25.12 I don't know you,' the **bridegroom** answered."
Mk 2.19 As long as the **bridegroom** is with them, they will not do
2.20 will come when the **bridegroom** will be taken away from them,
Lk 5.34 go without food as long as the **bridegroom** is with them?
5.35 will come when the **bridegroom** will be taken away from them,
Jn 2. 9 called the **bridegroom** [10] and said to him, "Everyone else serves
3.29 The **bridegroom** is the one to whom the bride belongs;
3.29 but the **bridegroom's** friend, who stands by and listens,
3.29 is glad when he hears the **bridegroom's** voice.
Rev 18.23 more will the voices of brides and **grooms** be heard in you.

BRIDESMAIDS

Ps 45.14 the king, followed by her **bridesmaids,** and they also are

BRIDLE

Ps 32. 9 be controlled with a bit and **bridle** to make it submit."
Prov 26. 3 a horse, you have to **bridle** a donkey, and you have to

BRIEF

Ps 119.54 During my **brief** earthly life I compose songs about your commands.
Is 54. 7 "For one **brief** moment I left you;
Mk 16. 9 friends and gave them a **brief** account of all they had been
Acts 24. 4 I beg you to be kind and listen to our **brief** account.
1 Cor 16. 7 I want to see you more than just **briefly** in passing;
Eph 3. 3 (I have written **briefly** about this, [4] and if you will read
1 Pet 5.12 I write you this **brief** letter with the help of Silas,

BRIGHT

Num 24.17 A king, like a **bright** star, will arise in that nation.
Job 11.17 Your life will be **brighter** than sunshine at noon, and
25. 5 his eyes even the moon is not **bright,** nor the stars pure.
31.26 worshipped the sun in its **brightness** or the moon in all its
37.21 the sky is dazzling, too **bright** for us to look at it;
38.15 light of day is too **bright** for the wicked and restrains them
Ps 38.10 strength is gone, and my eyes have lost their **brightness.**
139.12 dark for you, and the night is as **bright** as the day.
Prov 4.18 getting **brighter** and brighter until daylight has come.
13. 9 The righteous are like a light shining **brightly;**
23.18 If it is, you have a **bright** future.
24.14 Get wisdom and you have a **bright** future.
Song 6.10 She is beautiful and **bright,** as dazzling as the sun or the
Is 4. 5 cloud in the daytime and smoke and a **bright** flame at night.
14.12 "King of Babylonia, **bright** morning star, you have fallen from heaven!
30.26 The moon will be as **bright** as the sun,
30.26 sun will be seven times **brighter** than usual, like the light
58.10 the darkness around you will turn to the **brightness** of noon.
60. 2 The **brightness** of his presence will be with you.
Ezek 1.27 shone all over with a **bright** light [28] that had in it all
23.12 in **bright** uniforms—and for the cavalry officers,
23.14 into the wall and painted **bright** red, with sashes round
27.24 purple cloth, and embroidery, **brightly** coloured carpets,

Dan 2.31 before you a giant statue, **bright** and shining, and
5. 5 where the light from the lamps was shining most **brightly.**
10. 6 His face was as **bright** as a flash of lightning, and his
12. 3 The wise leaders will shine with all the **brightness** of the sky.
Amos 5.20 it will be a day of gloom, without any **brightness.**
Hab 3. 4 He comes with the **brightness** of lightning;
Lk 1.78 He will cause the **bright** dawn of salvation to rise on us
11.36 in darkness, it will be **bright** all over,
11.36 as when a lamp shines on you with its **brightness."**
24. 4 when suddenly two men in **bright** shining clothes stood by them.
Acts 22. 6 near Damascus, about midday a **bright** light from the sky flashed
22.11 was blind because of the **bright** light, and so my companions
26.13 I saw a light much **brighter** than the sun, coming from the
2 Cor 3. 7 Even though the **brightness** on Moses' face was fading,
3.10 that because of the far **brighter** glory
3.10 now the glory that was so **bright** in the past is gone.
3.13 people of Israel would not see the **brightness** fade and disappear.
Heb 1. 3 reflects the **brightness** of God's glory and is the exact likeness
1 Pet 5. 4 receive the glorious crown which will never lose its **brightness.**
Rev 1.16 His face was as **bright** as the midday sun.
8.12 stars, so that their light lost a third of its **brightness;**
18. 1 great authority, and his splendour **brightened** the whole earth.
22.16 I am the **bright** morning star."

BRILLIANCE

Prov 21.30 Human wisdom, **brilliance,** insight—they are of no help if

BRIM

Ps 23. 5 me as an honoured guest and fill my cup to the **brim.**
Prov 26.25 him, because his heart is filled to the **brim** with hate.
Jn 2. 7 They filled them to the **brim,** [8]and then he told them,

BRING

[BROUGHT, BROUGHT ABOUT]

Gen 1.28 live all over the earth and **bring** it under their control.
2.19 Then he **brought** them to the man to see what he would
2.22 formed a woman out of the rib and **brought** her to him.
4. 3 After some time, Cain **brought** some of his harvest and gave
4. 4 Then Abel **brought** the first lamb born to one of his sheep,
5.29 a curse, this child will **bring** us relief from all our hard
14.16 He also **brought** back his nephew Lot and his possessions,
14.18 of the Most High God, **brought** bread and wine to Abram,
15. 9 He answered, **"Bring** me a cow, a goat, and a ram, each
15.10 Abram **brought** the animals to God, cut them in half, and
18. 4 Let me **bring** some water for you to wash your feet;
18. 5 I will also **bring** a bit of food;
19. 5 **Bring** them out to us!"
19. 8 Let me **bring** them out to you, and you can do whatever
20. 2 So King Abimelech of Gerar had Sarah **brought** to him.
20. 9 to you to make you **bring** this disaster on me and my
21. 6 Sarah said, "God has **brought** me joy and laughter.
24. 7 Lord, the God of heaven, **brought** me from the home of my
24.14 'Drink, and I will also **bring** water for your camels,' may
24.19 she said, "I will also **bring** water for your camels and let
24.32 Then he **brought** water for Abraham's servant and his men to
24.33 When food was **brought,** the man said, "I will not eat
24.44 agrees and also offers to **bring** water for my camels, may she
24.53 Then he **brought** out clothing and silver and gold jewellery,
24.67 Then Isaac **brought** Rebecca into the tent that his mother
27. 4 of that tasty food that I like, and **bring** it to me.
27. 7 your father say to Esau, [7]**'Bring** me an animal and cook it
27.12 in this way I will **bring** a curse on myself instead of
27.14 went to get them and **brought** them to her, and she cooked
27.19 the meat that I have **brought** you, so that you can give
27.25 Isaac said, **"Bring** me some of the meat.
27.25 Jacob **brought** it to him,
27.25 and he also **brought** him some wine to drink.
27.31 the meat that I have **brought** you, so that you can give
27.33 was it, then, who killed an animal and **brought** it to me?
27.45 Then I will send someone to **bring** you back.
28.15 wherever you go, and I will **bring** you back to this land.
29. 7 and not yet time to **bring** the flocks in, why don't you
29.13 hugged him and kissed him, and **brought** him into the house.
30.14 and found mandrakes, which he **brought** to his mother Leah.
33.11 Please accept this gift which I have **brought** for you;
34.30 Jacob said to Simeon and Levi, "You have **brought** trouble on me;
37. 2 He **brought** bad reports to his father about what his brothers
39.14 This Hebrew that my husband **brought** to the house is insulting us.
39.17 "That Hebrew slave that you **brought** here came into my room
40.20 and his chief baker and **brought** them before his officials.
41.14 for Joseph, and he was immediately **brought** from the prison.
42.20 Then you must **bring** your youngest brother to me.
42.34 **Bring** your youngest brother to me.
42.37 father, "If I do not **bring** Benjamin back to you, you can
42.37 Put him in my care, and I will **bring** him back."
43. 2 the corn which had been **brought** from Egypt, Jacob said to
43. 7 know that he would tell us to **bring** our brother with us?"
43. 9 If I do not **bring** him back to you safe and sound,
43.18 As they were being **brought** to the house, they were afraid
43.18 and thought, "We are being **brought** here because of the money
43.21 We have **brought** it back to you.
43.22 We have also **brought** some more money with us to buy more
43.23 Then he **brought** Simeon to them.
44. 8 You know that we **brought** back to you from the land of
44.21 Sir, you told us to **bring** him here, so that you could
44.32 that if I did not **bring** the boy back to him, I
45.13 Then hurry and **bring** him here."
45.19 and small children and to **bring** their father with them.

Gen 46. 4 Egypt, and I will **bring** your descendants back to this land.
46.27 born to Joseph in Egypt, **bringing** to seventy the total
46.32 livestock and that you have **brought** your flocks and herds
47. 7 Then Joseph **brought** his father Jacob and presented him to the king.
47.16 Joseph answered, **"Bring** your livestock;
47.17 So they **brought** their livestock to Joseph, and he gave
48. 9 Jacob said, **"Bring** them to me so that I may bless them."
48.10 Joseph **brought** the boys to him, and he hugged them and
49.10 Nations will **bring** him tribute And bow in obedience before him.
Ex 2. 8 So the girl went and **brought** the baby's own mother.
3. 8 from the Egyptians and to **bring** them out of Egypt to a
3.11 I go to the king and **bring** the Israelites out of Egypt?"
3.12 with you, and when you **bring** the people out of Egypt, you
3.17 have decided that I will **bring** them out of Egypt, where they
6. 6 raise my mighty arm to **bring** terrible punishment upon them,
6. 8 I will **bring** you to the land that I solemnly promised to
7. 3 Then I will **bring** severe punishment on Egypt and lead the
7. 5 them and **bring** the Israelites out of their country."
8.12 to take away the frogs which he had **brought** on the king.
8.24 The whole land of Egypt was **brought** to ruin by the flies.
9.20 Lord had said, and they **brought** their slaves and animals
10. 4 then I will **bring** locusts into your country tomorrow.
10. 8 So Moses and Aaron were **brought** back to the king, and he
10.12 "Raise your hand over the land of Egypt to **bring** the locusts.
10.13 By morning it had **brought** the locusts.
12.17 was on this day that I **brought** your tribes out of Egypt.
12.39 the dough that they had **brought** out of Egypt, for they had
12.42 night when the Lord kept watch to **bring** them out of Egypt;
12.51 On that day the Lord **brought** the Israelite tribes out of Egypt.
13. 3 is the day the Lord **brought** you out by his great power.
13. 5 When he **brings** you into that rich and fertile land, you must
13. 9 the Lord, because the Lord **brought** you out of Egypt by his
13.11 "The Lord will **bring** you into the land of the Canaanites,
13.14 using great power the Lord **brought** us out of Egypt, the
13.16 remind us that the Lord **brought** us out of Egypt by his
14. 4 my victory over the king and his army will **bring** me honour.
14.11 Did you have to **bring** us out here in the desert to
14.11 Look what you have done by **bringing** us out of Egypt!
15.17 You **bring** them in and plant them on your mountain, the
15.19 into the sea, the Lord **brought** the water back, and it
15.26 with any of the diseases that I **brought** on the Egyptians.
16. 3 But you have **brought** us out into this desert to starve us
16. 5 sixth day they are to **bring** in twice as much as usual
16. 6 know that it was the Lord who **brought** you out of Egypt.
16.32 to eat in the desert when he **brought** us out of Egypt."
17. 3 They said, "Why did you **bring** us out of Egypt?
17.12 grew tired, Aaron and Hur **brought** a stone for him to sit
18. 2 So he came to Moses, **bringing** with him Moses' wife
18.12 Then Jethro **brought** an offering to be burnt whole and
18.19 the people before God and **bring** their disputes to him.
18.22 They can **bring** all the difficult cases to you, but they
18.26 people on a permanent basis, **bringing** the difficult cases to
19. 4 carries her young on her wings, and **brought** you here to me.
19.24 The Lord replied, "Go down and **bring** Aaron back with you.
20. 2 the Lord your God who **brought** you out of Egypt, where you
20. 5 I **bring** punishment on those who hate me and on their
22. 8 the valuables is to be **brought** to the place of worship and
22.13 wild animals, the man is to **bring** the remains as evidence;
23.15 Never come to worship me without **bringing** an offering.
23.19 "Each year **bring** to the house of the Lord your God the
23.20 as you travel and to **bring** you to the place which I
23.27 I will **bring** confusion among the people against whom you fight,
27.20 the people of Israel to **bring** you the best olive-oil for the
29. 4 **"Bring** Aaron and his sons to the entrance of the Tent of
29. 8 **"Bring** his sons and put shirts on them;
29.10 **"Bring** the bull to the front of the Tent of my presence
29.46 the Lord their God who **brought** them out of Egypt so that
32. 2 and your daughters are wearing, and **bring** them to me."
32. 3 took off their gold earrings and **brought** them to Aaron.
32. 6 Early the next morning they **brought** some animals to burn
32.12 your mind and do not **bring** this disaster on your people.
32.14 his mind and did not **bring** on his people the disaster he
32.23 has happened to this man Moses, who **brought** us out of Egypt;
32.24 I asked them to **bring** me their gold ornaments, and those
33. 1 you and the people you **brought** out of Egypt, and go to
34.26 "Each year **bring** to the house of the Lord the first
35. 5 to do so is to **bring** an offering of gold, silver, or
35.21 who wished to do so **brought** an offering to the Lord for
35.21 They **brought** everything needed for use in worship and for
35.22 to, both men and women, **brought** decorative pins, earrings,
35.23 or fine leather, **brought** it.
35.24 silver or bronze **brought** their offering for the Lord,
35.24 which could be used for any of the work **brought** it.
35.25 All the skilled women **brought** fine linen thread and thread of blue,
35.27 The leaders **brought** carnelians and other jewels to be
35.29 of Israel who wanted to **brought** their offering to the Lord
36. 3 the Israelites had **brought** for constructing the sacred Tent.
36. 3 Israel continued to **bring** Moses their offerings every morning.
36. 5 to Moses, "The people are **bringing** more than is needed for
36. 6 so the people did not **bring** any more.
36. 7 What had already been **brought** was more than enough to
39.33 They **brought** to Moses the Tent and all its equipment,
40. 4 **Bring** in the table and place the equipment on it.
40. 4 Also **bring** in the lamp-stand and set up the lamps on it.
40.12 **"Bring** Aaron and his sons to the entrance of the Tent,
40.14 **Bring** his sons and put the shirts on them.
Lev 1. 3 a burnt-offering, he must **bring** a bull without any defects.
2. 2 and incense on it [2]and **bring** it to the Aaronite priests.
2. 8 **Bring** it as an offering to the Lord and present it to
2.12 harvest each year shall be **brought** to the Lord, but it is

Lev 2.14 When you **bring** to the Lord an offering of the first corn
4. 3 Priest who sins and so **brings** guilt on the people, he shall
4. 4 He shall **bring** the bull to the entrance of the Tent, put
4.14 the community shall **bring** a young bull as a sin-offering.
4.14 They shall **bring** it to the Tent of the Lord's presence;
4.23 to the sin, he shall **bring** as his offering a male goat
4.28 to the sin, he shall **bring** as his offering a female goat
4.32 If a man **brings** a sheep as a sin-offering, it must be
5. 6 for his sin he must **bring** to the Lord a female sheep
5. 7 or a goat, he shall **bring** to the Lord as the payment
5. 8 He shall **bring** them to the priest, who will first offer
5.11 or two pigeons, he shall **bring** one kilogramme of flour as a
5.12 He shall **bring** it to the priest, who will take a handful
5.15 to the Lord, he shall **bring** as his repayment-offering to the
5.18 He must **bring** to the priest as a repayment-offering a
6. 6 He shall **bring** to the priest as his repayment-offering to
6.30 any of the blood is **brought** into the Tent and used in
7.16 If a man **brings** a fellowship-offering in fulfilment of a
7.29 Whoever offers a fellowship-offering must **bring** part of it
7.30 special gift to the Lord, [30]**bringing** it with his own hands
7.30 He shall **bring** the fat of the animal with its breast and
8. 2 Tent of my presence and **bring** the priestly garments, the anointing oil,
8. 6 Moses **brought** Aaron and his sons forward and told them to
8.13 Next, Moses **brought** the sons of Aaron forward and put
8.14 Then Moses **brought** the young bull for the sin-offering,
8.18 Next, Moses **brought** the ram for the burnt-offering, and
8.22 Then Moses **brought** the second ram, which was for the
8.24 Then he **brought** Aaron's sons forward and put some of the
9. 5 They **brought** to the front of the Tent everything that
9. 9 His sons **brought** him the blood, and he dipped his finger
9.12 His sons **brought** him the blood, and he threw it on all
9.16 He also **brought** the animal for the burnt-offering and
9.18 His sons **brought** him the blood, and he threw it on all
10.15 They shall **bring** the hind leg and the breast at the time
10.18 Since its blood was not **brought** into the sacred tent,
10.19 the Lord today, and they **brought** their burnt-offering, but
11.45 I am the Lord who **brought** you out of Egypt so that
12. 6 son or daughter, she shall **bring** to the priest at the
12. 8 afford a lamb, she shall **bring** two doves or two pigeons, one
13. 2 skin-disease, he shall be **brought** to the Aaronite priest.
13. 9 dreaded skin-disease, he shall be **brought** to the priest,
14. 2 pronounced clean, he shall be **brought** to the priest, [3]and
14. 4 birds to be **brought,** together with a piece of cedar-wood,
14.10 the eighth day he shall **bring** two male lambs and one female
14.21 afford any more, he shall **bring** for his purification only
14.21 He shall **bring** only one kilogramme of flour mixed with
14.22 He shall also **bring** two doves or two pigeons, one for
14.23 of his purification he shall **bring** them to the priest at the
16. 3 Place only after he has **brought** a young bull for a
16.12 of fine incense and **bring** them into the Most Holy Place.
16.15 the sin-offering for the people, **bring** its blood into the
16.27 the sin-offering, whose blood was **brought** into the Most Holy
17. 5 people of Israel shall now **bring** to the Lord the animals
17. 5 They shall now **bring** them to the priest at the entrance of
18.21 Molech, because that would **bring** disgrace on the name of God,
19.12 that **brings** disgrace on my name.
19.21 The man shall **bring** a ram to the entrance of the Tent
19.36 am the Lord your God, and I **brought** you out of Egypt.
20.22 by the land of Canaan, into which I am **bringing** you.
22. 2 his sons, "You must not **bring** disgrace on my holy name, so
22.16 this would **bring** guilt and punishment on such a person.
22.32 Do not **bring** disgrace on my holy name;
22.33 and I **brought** you out of Egypt to become your God.
23.14 into bread, until you have **brought** this offering to God.
23.15 the Sabbath on which you **bring** your sheaf of corn to present
23.17 Each family is to **bring** two loaves of bread and present
24. 2 **Bring** pure olive-oil of the finest quality for the lamps in
25.38 the Lord your God, who **brought** you out of Egypt in order
25.42 Israel are the Lord's slaves, and he **brought** them out of Egypt;
25.55 He **brought** them out of Egypt;
26.13 I, the Lord your God, **brought** you out of Egypt so that
26.16 I will **bring** disaster on you—incurable diseases and fevers
26.25 I will **bring** war on you to punish you for breaking our
26.33 I will **bring** war on you and scatter you in foreign lands.
26.45 the nations my power by **bringing** my people out of Egypt, in
27. 8 the standard price, he shall **bring** the person to the priest,
Num 3. 6 The Lord said to Moses, [6]"**Bring** forward the tribe of
5.15 a suspicious husband, made to **bring** the truth to light.
5.16 The priest shall **bring** the woman forward and make her
5.18 the bowl containing the bitter water that **brings** a curse.
5.19 you will not be harmed by the curse that this water **brings.**
6.10 the eighth day he shall **bring** two doves or two pigeons to
6.12 As a repayment offering he shall **bring** a one-year-old lamb.
7. 3 charge of the census, [3]**brought** their offerings to the Lord:
7.10 The leaders also **brought** offerings to celebrate the dedication of the altar.
7.12 The offerings each one **brought** were identical:
7.84 The totals of the offerings **brought** by the twelve
11.12 I didn't create them or **bring** them to birth!
11.16 as leaders of the people, **bring** them to me at the Tent
11.31 Lord sent a wind that **brought** quails from the sea, flying
12.14 for a week, and after that she can be **brought** back in."
12.15 the people did not move on until she was **brought** back in.
13.20 And be sure to **bring** back some of the fruit that grows
13.23 They also **brought** back some pomegranates and figs.
13.26 they had seen and showed them the fruit they had **brought.**
14.13 said to the Lord, "You **brought** these people out of Egypt by
14.16 you were not able to **bring** them into the land you promised
14.24 loyal to me, I will **bring** him into the land which he
14.31 be captured, but I will **bring** them into the land that you
Num 14.36 sent to explore the land **brought** back a false report which
15. 4 to the Lord is to **bring** with each animal a kilogramme of
15.25 mistake was unintentional and they **brought** their
15.41 I **brought** you out of Egypt to be your God.
16.13 it enough that you have **brought** us out of the fertile land
16.14 You certainly have not **brought** us into a fertile land or
16.15 to the Lord, "Do not accept any offerings these men **bring.**
18. 2 **Bring** in your relatives, the tribe of Levi, to work with
18.22 Tent and in this way **bring** on themselves the penalty of death.
19. 2 **Bring** to Moses and Aaron a red cow which has no defects
20. 4 Why have you **brought** us out into this wilderness?
20. 5 Why did you **bring** us out of Egypt into this miserable
20. 8 In this way you will **bring** water out of the rock for
21. 5 They complained, "Why did you **bring** us out of Egypt to die
21.16 the Lord said to Moses, "**Bring** the people together, and I
21.29 You worshippers of Chemosh are **brought** to ruin!
22. 5 They **brought** him this message from Balak:
22.23 Balaam beat the donkey and **brought** it back on to the road.
23. 1 here for me, and **bring** me seven bulls and seven rams."
23. 7 "Balak king of Moab has **brought** me From Syria, from the
23.11 I **brought** you here to curse my enemies, but all you have
23.21 I foresee that Israel's future Will **bring** her no misfortune or trouble.
23.22 God has **brought** them out of Egypt;
23.29 for me here and **bring** me seven bulls and seven rams."
24. 8 God **brought** them out of Egypt;
25.13 to me and **brought about** forgiveness for the people's sin."
31.12 prisoners and the animals, [12]and **brought** them to Moses and
31.16 That was what **brought** the epidemic on the Lord's people.
31.50 So we are **bringing** the gold ornaments, armlets,
32.14 of sinful men ready to **bring** down the fierce anger of the
Deut 1.17 is too difficult for you, **bring** it to me, and I will
1.25 They **brought** us back some fruit they found there, and
1.27 He **brought** us out of Egypt just to hand us over to
1.31 You saw how he **brought** you safely all the way to this
4.20 He **brought** you out to make you his own people, as you
4.34 he **brought** plagues and war, worked miracles and wonders, and
4.37 and by his great power he himself **brought** you out of Egypt.
4.38 you, so that he might **bring** you in and give you their
5. 9 I **bring** punishment on those who hate me and on their
6.11 When the Lord **brings** you into this land and you have all
6.23 freed us from Egypt to **bring** us here and give us this
7. 1 "The Lord your God will **bring** you into the land which you
7.15 sickness, and he will not **bring** on you any of the dreadful
7.15 in Egypt, but he will **bring** them on all your enemies.
7.26 Do not **bring** any of these idols into your homes, or the
8. 7 The Lord your God is **bringing** you into a fertile land—a
9. 4 say to yourselves that he **brought** you in to possess this
9.26 the people you rescued and **brought** out of Egypt by your
9.29 your own and whom you **brought** out of Egypt by your great
11.29 When the Lord **brings** you into the land that you are
12.11 worshipped, and there you must **bring** to him everything that
13.16 **Bring** together all the possessions of the people who
14.28 end of every third year **bring** the tithe of all your crops
16.10 the Lord your God, by **bringing** him a freewill offering in
16.16 Each man is to **bring** a gift [17]as he is able, in
21.23 dead body hanging on a post **brings** God's curse on the land.
22.19 because the man has **brought** disgrace on an Israelite girl.
23.18 in this way may be **brought** into the house of the Lord
24.11 wait outside and let him **bring** it to you himself.
24.19 your crops and fail to **bring** in some of the corn that
26. 9 He **brought** us here and gave us this rich and fertile land.
26.10 So now I **bring** to the Lord the first part of the
26.19 created, and you will **bring** praise and honour to his name.
28.20 reject the Lord, he will **bring** on you disaster, confusion,
28.49 The Lord will **bring** against you a nation from the ends
28.60 He will **bring** on you once again all the dreadful
28.63 take delight in destroying you and in **bringing** ruin on you.
29.21 tribes of Israel and will **bring** disaster on him in
29.22 and sufferings that the Lord has **brought** on your land.
29.25 God of their ancestors, when he **brought** them out of Egypt.
29.27 angry with his people and **brought** on their land all the
30. 3 He will **bring** you back from the nations where he has
30. 4 will gather you together and **bring** you back, [5]so that you
30.12 'Who will go up and **bring** it down for us, so that
30.13 go across the ocean and **bring** it to us, so that we
31.14 Call Joshua and **bring** him to the Tent, so that I may
32.23 "'I will **bring** on them endless disasters and use all my
32.25 War will **bring** death in the streets;
Josh 2. 3 **Bring** them out!"
6.18 if you do, you will **bring** trouble and destruction on the
6.22 the prostitute's house and **bring** her and her family out,
6.23 So they went and **brought** Rahab out, along with her
7. 7 Why did you **bring** us across the Jordan at all?
7.14 in the morning they will be **brought** forward, tribe by tribe.
7.15 he owns, for he has **brought** terrible shame on Israel and has
7.16 Early the next morning Joshua **brought** Israel forward, tribe by tribe,
7.17 He **brought** the tribe of Judah forward, clan by clan,
7.17 Then he **brought** the clan of Zerah forward, family by family,
7.18 He then **brought** Zabdi's family forward, man by man, and
7.23 They **brought** them out of the tent, took them to Joshua
7.25 And Joshua said, "Why have you **brought** such trouble on us?
7.25 The Lord will now **bring** trouble on you!"
9.22 people of Gibeon to be **brought** to him, and he asked them,
10.22 entrance to the cave and **bring** those five kings out to me."
10.23 Hebron, Jarmuth, Lachish, and Eglon were **brought** out [24]and taken to Joshua.
14. 7 I **brought** an honest report back to him.
18. 6 a description of these seven divisions and **bring** it to me.
24. 5 I sent Moses and Aaron, and I **brought** great trouble on Egypt.

Josh 24. 6 I **brought** your ancestors out of Egypt, and the Egyptians
24. 8 Then I **brought** you to the land of the Amorites, who lived
24.17 The Lord our God **brought** our fathers and us out of
24.32 of Israel had **brought** from Egypt, was buried at Shechem,
Judg 2. 1 you out of Egypt and **brought** you to the land that I
2.12 ancestors, the God who had **brought** them out of Egypt, and
4. 7 I will **bring** Sisera, the commander of Jabin's army, to
5.25 she **brought** him cream in a beautiful bowl.
6. 8 them a prophet who **brought** them this message from the Lord,
6. 8 "I **brought** you out of slavery in Egypt.
6.13 the Lord used to do—how he **brought** them out of Egypt?
6.18 Please do not leave until I **bring** you an offering of food."
6.19 the broth in a pot, **brought** them to the Lord's angel under
6.30 Then they said to Joash, **"Bring** your son out here, so
7.25 to pursue the Midianites and **brought** the heads of Oreb and
11. 5 leaders of Gilead went to **bring** Jephthah back from the land
11.20 He **brought** his whole army together, made camp at Jahaz, and
12. 4 Then Jephthah **brought** all the men of Gilead together,
12. 9 marriage outside the clan and **brought** thirty girls from
15.13 up with two new ropes and **brought** him back from the cliff.
16. 8 So the Philistine kings **brought** Delilah seven new
16.18 Then they came and **brought** the money with them.
16.24 When they **brought** Samson out of the prison, they made him
18. 3 Who **brought** you here?"
19.22 said to the old man, **"Bring** out that man that came home
19.24 I'll **bring** them out now, and you can have them.
21.12 young virgins, so they **brought** them to the camp at Shiloh,
Ruth 1.21 plenty, but the Lord has **brought** me back without a thing.
4.15 you a grandson, who will **bring** new life to you and give
1 Sam 2. 6 people to the world of the dead and **brings** them back again.
2.14 and whatever the fork **brought** out belonged to the priest.
4. 3 Let's go and **bring** the Lord's Covenant Box from Shiloh, so
5.10 people cried out, "They have **brought** the Covenant Box of
8. 8 Ever since I **brought** them out of Egypt, they have turned
9.23 Samuel said to the cook, **"Bring** the piece of meat I
9.24 So the cook **brought** the choice piece of the leg and
10.18 God of Israel, says, 'I **brought** you out of Egypt and rescued
10.23 So they ran and **brought** Saul out to the people, and
10.27 They despised Saul and did not **bring** him any gifts.
11. 2 everyone's right eye and so **bring** disgrace on all Israel."
12. 6 Moses and Aaron and who **brought** your ancestors out of Egypt.
12. 8 sent Moses and Aaron, who **brought** them out of Egypt and
13. 9 **"Bring** me the burnt-sacrifices and the fellowship-sacrifices."
14.18 **"Bring** the ephod here," Saul said to Ahijah the priest.
14.34 and tell them all to **bring** their cattle and sheep here.
14.34 So that night they all **brought** their cattle and slaughtered them there.
15.20 as he told me to, **brought** back King Agag, and killed all
15.21 instead, they **brought** them here to Gilgal to offer as a
15.32 **"Bring** King Agag here to me," Samuel ordered.
16. 8 Then Jesse called his son Abinadab and **brought** him to Samuel.
16. 9 Jesse then **brought** Shammah.
16.10 In this way Jesse **brought** seven of his sons to Samuel.
16.17 "Find me a man who plays well and **bring** him to me."
17.18 brothers are getting on and **bring** back something to show
20.31 Now go and **bring** him here—he must die!"
21.14 Why did you **bring** him to me?
21.15 Why **bring** another one to annoy me with his daft actions
23. 9 he said to the priest Abiathar, **"Bring** the ephod here."
23.23 hides, and be sure to **bring** back a report to me straight
25.27 accept this present I have **brought** you, and give it to your
25.35 David accepted what she had **brought** him and said to her,
29. 1 The Philistines **brought** all their troops together at Aphek,
30. 7 priest Abiathar son of Ahimelech, **"Bring** me the ephod,"
30. 7 and Abiathar **brought** it to him.
30.11 an Egyptian boy out in the country and **brought** him to David.
31.12 his sons from the wall, **brought** them back to Jabesh, and
2 Sam 1.10 bracelet from his arm, and I have **brought** them to you,
1.13 the young man who had **brought** him the news, "Where are you
1.16 and David said to the Amalekite, "You **brought** this on yourself.
3.13 you must **bring** Saul's daughter Michal to me when you come to
3.22 officials returned from a raid, **bringing** a large amount of
3.26 to get Abner, and they **brought** him back from the well of
4.10 told me of Saul's death thought he was **bringing** good news.
6. 2 in Judah, in order to **bring** from there God's Covenant Box,
6.16 As the Box was being **brought** into the city, Michal, Saul's daughter,
6.17 They **brought** the Box and put it in its place in the
9.10 your master Saul's family and **bring** in the harvest, to
11. 4 they **brought** her to him and he made love to her.
12.11 cause someone from your own family to **bring** trouble on you.
12.23 Could I **bring** the child back to life?
13.10 Then he said to her, **"Bring** the cakes here to my bed
14.10 replied, "If anyone threatens you, **bring** him to me, and he
14.14 Even God does not **bring** the dead back to life, but the
14.14 at least find a way to **bring** a man back from exile.
14.21 Go and get the young man Absalom and **bring** him back here."
14.23 up and went to Geshur and **brought** Absalom back to Jerusalem.
17. 3 only the king [3] and then **bring** back all his men to you,
17.11 My advice is that you **bring** all the Israelites together
17.13 city, our people will all **bring** ropes and just pull the city
17.28 They **brought** bowls, clay pots, and bedding, and
18. 1 King David **brought** all his men together, divided them into
18.25 the king said, "If he is alone, he is **bringing** good news."
18.26 The king answered, "This one also is **bringing** good news."
18.27 man," the king said, "and he is **bringing** good news."
19.10 So why doesn't somebody try to **bring** King David back?"
19.11 be the last to help **bring** the king back to his palace?
19.12 why should you be the last to **bring** me back?"
19.43 we were the first to talk about **bringing** the king back!"
23. 5 that will be my victory, and God will surely **bring it about.**
2 Sam 23.15 "How I wish someone would **bring** me a drink of water from
23.16 drew some water from the well, and **brought** it back to David.
24. 1 Israel once more, and he made David **bring** trouble on them.
1 Kgs 1. 3 such a girl named Abishag, and **brought** her to the king.
1.39 of olive-oil which he had **brought** from the Tent of the
1.42 "You're a good man—you must be **bringing** good news."
1.53 sent for Adonijah and had him **brought** down from the altar.
2.19 throne and had another one **brought** in on which she sat at
2.40 He found them and **brought** them back home.
3. 1 He **brought** her to live in David's City until he had finished
3.24 sword, and when it was **brought,** [25] he said, "Cut the
5. 9 My men will **bring** the logs down from Lebanon to the sea,
8.16 said, [16] 'From the time I **brought** my people out of Egypt, I
8.21 Lord made with our ancestors when he **brought** them out of Egypt."
8.31 of wronging another and is **brought** to your altar in this
8.34 sins of your people, and **bring** them back to the land which
8.51 whom you **brought** out of Egypt, that blazing furnace.
8.53 Moses when you **brought** our ancestors out of Egypt."
9. 9 Lord their God, who **brought** their ancestors out of Egypt.
9. 9 That is why the Lord has **brought** this disaster on them.'"
9.28 the land of Ophir, and **brought** back to Solomon more than
10. 2 She **brought** with her a large group of attendants, as well
10.10 She presented to King Solomon the gifts she had **brought:**
10.11 (Hiram's fleet, which had **brought** gold from Ophir, also brought
10.22 years his fleet would return, **bringing** gold, silver, ivory,
10.25 Everyone who came **brought** him a gift—articles of silver and gold,
12.15 will of the Lord to **bring about** what he had spoken to
12.28 Israel, here are your gods who **brought** you out of Egypt!"
13.29 it on the donkey, and **brought** it back to Bethel to mourn
13.34 This sin on his part **brought about** the ruin and total
14.10 Because of this I will **bring** disaster on your dynasty
17. 4 and I have commanded ravens to **bring** you food there."
17. 6 from the brook, and ravens **brought** him bread and meat every
17.10 "Please **bring** me a drink of water," he said to her.
17.11 get it, he called out, "And please **bring** me some bread,
17.13 from what you have and **bring** it to me, and then prepare
18.19 **Bring** along the 450 prophets of Baal and the 400 prophets of
18.23 **Bring** two bulls;
18.26 took the bull that was **brought** to them, prepared it, and
18.37 Lord, are God, and that you are **bringing** them back to yourself."
20.10 "I will **bring** enough men to destroy this city of yours and
20.33 **"Bring** him to me," Ahab ordered.
20.39 the battle when a soldier **brought** a captured enemy to me and
21.21 So the Lord says to you, 'I will **bring** disaster on you.
21.29 this, I will not **bring** disaster on him during his lifetime;
21.29 lifetime that I will **bring** disaster on Ahab's family."
2 Kgs 2.20 salt in a new bowl, and **bring** it to me," he ordered.
2.20 They **brought** it to him, [21] and he went to the spring, threw
4. 5 poured oil into the jars as her sons **brought** them to her.
4.39 He **brought** them back and sliced them up into the stew, not-
4.42 man came from Baal Shalishah, **bringing** Elisha twenty loaves
6.33 said, "It's the Lord who has **brought** this trouble on us!
8. 1 Shunem, whose son he had **brought** back to life, that the Lord
8. 5 the king how Elisha had **brought** a dead person back to life,
8. 5 and here is her son whom Elisha **brought** back to life!"
10. 6 ready to follow my orders, **bring** the heads of King Ahab's
10. 8 of Ahab's descendants had been **brought,** he ordered them to
10.22 of the sacred robes to **bring** the robes out and give them
10.26 inner sanctuary of the temple, [26] **brought** out the sacred
11. 9 officers obeyed Jehoiada's instructions and **brought** their
12. 5 be responsible for the money **brought** by those he served, and
14.10 that will only **bring** disaster on you and your people?"
17.27 "Send back one of the priests we **brought** as prisoners;
17.36 obey me, the Lord, who **brought** you out of Egypt with great
18.17 work, by the ditch that **brings** water from the upper pond.
20.20 and dug a tunnel to **bring** water into the city, are all
21.12 Lord God of Israel, will **bring** such a disaster on Jerusalem
22.20 which I am going to **bring** on Jerusalem will not come until
23. 4 entrance to the Temple to **bring** out of the Temple all the
23. 8 He **brought** to Jerusalem the priests who were in the cities
1 Chr 2. 7 Carmi, one of Zerah's descendants, **brought** disaster on the
11.17 "How I wish someone would **bring** me a drink of water from
11.18 drew some water from the well, and **brought** it back to David.
12.40 Zebulun, and Naphtali, people came **bringing** donkeys, camels,
12.40 They also **brought** cattle and sheep to kill and eat.
13. 5 the north, in order to **bring** the Covenant Box from Kiriath
13. 7 At Abinadab's house they **brought** out the Covenant Box and
15. 3 to Jerusalem in order to **bring** the Covenant Box to the place
15.12 fellow-Levites, so that you can **bring** the Covenant Box of
15.29 As the Box was being **brought** into the city, Michal, Saul's daughter,
16.29 **bring** an offering and come into his Temple.
18.10 Joram **brought** David presents made of gold, silver, and bronze.
19.16 by the Israelites, so they **brought** troops from the Syrian
21. 1 Satan wanted to **bring** trouble on the people of Israel, so
21.12 your land, using his angel to **bring** death throughout Israel?
22. 4 of Tyre and Sidon to **bring** him a large number of cedar
23. 2 King David **brought** together all the Israelite leaders and
26.28 Temple, including the gifts **brought** by the prophet Samuel,
29.16 Lord, our God, we have **brought** together all this wealth to
29.17 are gathered here have been happy to **bring** offerings to you.
29.21 They also **brought** the offerings of wine.
2 Chr 1. 4 David had set up when he **brought** the Box from Kiriath Jearim.)
6. 5 him, [5] 'From the time I **brought** my people out of Egypt until
6.22 of wronging another and is **brought** to your altar in this
6.25 sins of your people and **bring** them back to the land which
7.22 Lord their God, who **brought** their ancestors out of Egypt.
7.22 That is why the Lord has **brought** this disaster on them.'"
8.18 the land of Ophir and **brought** back to Solomon more than

2 Chr 9. 1 She **brought** with her a large group of attendants, as well as
9. 9 She presented to King Solomon the gifts she had **brought:**
9.10 and of King Solomon who **brought** gold from Ophir
9.10 also **brought** juniper wood and jewels.
9.12 he gave her in exchange for the gifts she **brought** to him.
9.14 of the Israelite districts also **brought** him silver and gold.
9.21 years his fleet would return, **bringing** gold, silver, ivory,
9.24 Each of them **brought** Solomon gifts—articles of silver and gold,
10.15 of the Lord God to **bring about** what he had spoken to
15. 6 city, because God was **bringing** trouble and distress on them.
15.11 sacrifices to the Lord from the loot they had **brought** back:
17. 5 Judah, and all the people **brought** him gifts, so that he
17.11 Some of the Philistines **brought** Jehoshaphat a large
17.11 and some Arabs **brought** him 7,700 sheep and 7,700 goats.
19. 2 What you have done has **brought** the Lord's anger on you.
19.10 from any of the cities **bring** before you a case of homicide
21.18 after all this, the Lord **brought** on the king a painful
22. 7 God used this visit to Joram to **bring about** Ahaziah's downfall.
23. 2 the cities of Judah and **brought** back with them to Jerusalem
23.20 Jehoiada in a procession that **brought** the king from the
24. 9 and Judah for everyone to **bring** to the Lord the tax which
24.10 and their leaders, and they **brought** their tax money and
24.18 Their guilt for these sins **brought** the Lord's anger on Judah
24.20 his commands and are **bringing** disaster on yourselves!
25.14 the Edomites, he **brought** their idols back with him,
25.19 that will only **bring** disaster on you and your people?"
28.13 They said, "Don't **bring** those prisoners here!
28.19 and had defied the Lord, the Lord **brought** troubles on Judah.
28.23 This **brought** disaster on him and on his nation.
28.25 In this way he **brought** on himself the anger of the Lord,
29.19 We have also **brought** back all the equipment which King
29.31 that you are ritually clean, **bring** sacrifices as offerings
29.31 **brought** animals to be sacrificed as burnt-offerings.
29.32 They **brought** seventy bulls, a hundred sheep, and two
29.33 they also **brought** six hundred bulls and three thousand
31. 4 the people of Jerusalem to **bring** the offerings to which the
31. 5 the people of Israel **brought** gifts of their finest corn,
31. 5 and they also **brought** the tithes of everything they had.
31. 6 cities of Judah **brought** tithes of their cattle and sheep,
31. 6 and they also **brought** large quantities of gifts,
31.10 "Since the people started **bringing** their gifts to the Temple,
32.23 Many people came to Jerusalem, **bringing** offerings to the
34.28 which I am going to **bring** on Jerusalem will not come until
36.17 So the Lord **brought** the king of Babylonia to attack them.
Ezra 3. 7 from Lebanon, which were to be **brought** by sea to Joppa.
4. 6 Judah and Jerusalem **brought** written charges against them.
6. 5 silver utensils which King Nebuchadnezzar **brought** to Babylon
8.28 and gold utensils **brought** to him as freewill offerings.
8.35 had returned from exile then **brought** offerings to be burnt
10.10 have been faithless and have **brought** guilt on Israel by
Neh 1. 9 have commanded you, I will **bring** you back to the place where
8. 2 So Ezra **brought** it to the place where the people had
10.31 If foreigners **bring** corn or anything else to sell to us
12.27 the Levites were **brought** in from wherever they were living,
13.11 And I **brought** the Levites and musicians back to the Temple
13.12 people of Israel again started **bringing** to the temple
13.16 living in Jerusalem, and they **brought** fish and all kinds of
13.18 God punished your ancestors when he **brought** destruction on this city.
13.18 And yet you insist on **bringing** more of God's anger down on
13.19 sure that nothing was **brought** into the city on the Sabbath.
13.31 burning the offerings to be **brought** at the proper times,
13.31 and for the people to **bring** their offerings of the first
Esth 1.11 He ordered them to **bring** in Queen Vashti, wearing her royal crown.
2. 3 empire and order them to **bring** all these beautiful young
2. 8 girls were being **brought** to Susa, Esther was among them.
2.16 month of Tebeth, Esther was **brought** to King Xerxes in the
6. 1 records of the empire to be **brought** and read to him.
6. 7 "Order royal robes to be **brought** for this man—robes that
Job 5. 7 Man **brings** trouble on himself, as surely as sparks fly up
7. 3 night after night **brings** me grief.
8.22 again, [22]but he will **bring** disgrace on those who hate you,
11.10 If God arrests you and **brings** you to trial, who is there
13.26 You **bring** bitter charges against me, even for what I did
19.29 sword— the sword that **brings** God's wrath on sin, so that
21. 9 God does not **bring** disaster on their homes;
21.29 Don't you know the reports they **bring** back?
22. 4 awe of God that he reprimands you and **brings** you to trial.
22.29 God **brings** down the proud and saves the humble.
28.11 to the sources of rivers And **bring** to light what is hidden.
31.35 If the charges my opponent **brings** against me were written
36.16 God **brought** you out of trouble, and let you enjoy security;
37. 7 He **brings** the work of men to a stop;
39. 3 they will crouch down and **bring** their young into the world?
39.12 Do you expect him to **bring** in your harvest and gather
40.12 Yes, look at them and **bring** them down;
42.11 him for all the troubles the Lord had **brought** on him.
Ps 7. 7 you demand, [7]so **bring** together all the peoples round you,
9.19 **Bring** the heathen before you and pronounce judgement on them.
16. 4 Those who rush to other gods **bring** many troubles on themselves.
16.11 your presence fills me with joy and **brings** me pleasure for ever.
22. 9 It was you who **brought** me safely through birth, and when I
43. 3 may they lead me and **bring** me back to Zion, your sacred
45.12 The people of Tyre will **bring** you gifts;
45.14 by her bridesmaids, and they also are **brought** to him.
46. 4 There is a river that **brings** joy to the city of God,
48. 2 the city of the great king **brings** joy to all the world.
50. 8 sacrifices and the burnt-offerings you always **bring** me.
55. 3 They **bring** trouble on me;
55.18 He will **bring** me safely back from the battles that I
Ps 55.23 But you, O God, will **bring** those murderers and liars to
62. 4 You only want to **bring** him down from his place of honour;
65. 4 whom you choose, whom you **bring** to live in your sanctuary.
65. 8 Your deeds **bring** shouts of joy from one end of the earth
66.12 flood, but now you have **brought** us to a place of safety.
66.13 I will **bring** burnt-offerings to your house;
68.22 The Lord has said, "I will **bring** your enemies back from Bashan;
68.22 I will **bring** them back from the depths of the ocean,
68.29 from your Temple in Jerusalem, where kings **bring** gifts to you.
69. 6 Don't let me **bring** shame on those who trust in you,
69. 6 Don't let me **bring** disgrace to those who worship you, O God
72.10 the kings of Sheba and Seba will **bring** him offerings.
74. 2 yourself long ago, whom you **brought** out of slavery to be
76.11 **bring** gifts to him, all you nearby nations.
78.41 God to the test and **brought** pain to the Holy God of
78.54 He **brought** them to his holy land, to the mountains which
80. 3 **Bring** us back, O God!
80. 7 **Bring** us back, Almighty God!
80. 8 You **brought** a grapevine out of Egypt;
80.19 **Bring** us back, Lord God Almighty.
81.10 I am the Lord your God, who **brought** you out of Egypt.
85. 4 **Bring** us back, O God our saviour, and stop being
90. 2 you created the hills or **brought** the world into being, you
90.10 yet all they **bring** us is trouble and sorrow;
90.11 Who knows what fear your fury can **bring?**
96. 8 **bring** an offering and come into his Temple.
99. 4 you have **brought** righteousness and fairness.
106.47 O Lord our God, and **bring** us back from among the nations,
107. 3 enemies [3]and has **brought** you back from foreign countries,
107.14 He **brought** them out of their gloom and darkness and broke
107.30 of the calm, and he **brought** them safe to the port they
116.13 I will **bring** a wine-offering to the Lord, to thank him
118.16 His power has **brought** us victory— his mighty power in battle!"
119.52 your judgements of long ago, and they **bring** me comfort, O
119.130 teachings gives light and **brings** wisdom to the ignorant.
119.143 trouble and anxiety, but your commandments **bring** me joy.
126. 1 When the Lord **brought** us back to Jerusalem, it was like a
126. 4 just as the rain **brings** water back to dry river-beds.
126. 6 come back singing for joy, as they **bring** in the harvest.
135. 7 He **brings** storm clouds from the ends of the earth;
135. 7 the storms, and he **brings** out the wind from his storeroom.
142. 2 I **bring** him all my complaints;
143. 5 all that you have done, I **bring** to mind all your deeds.
147. 2 he is **bringing** back the exiles.
Prov 1.27 on you like a storm, **bringing** fierce winds of trouble, and
4. 8 Embrace her, and she will **bring** you honour.
10. 1 a foolish one **brings** his mother grief.
11.11 but a city is **brought** to ruin by the words of the
11.29 The man who **brings** trouble on his family will have
12. 4 but a wife who **brings** shame on her husband is like a
13.17 but those who can be trusted **bring** peace.
14.32 Wicked people **bring about** their own downfall by their evil deeds,
15. 4 Kind words **bring** life, but cruel words crush your spirit.
15. 8 pray, but hates the sacrifices that wicked men **bring** him.
15.18 Hot tempers cause arguments, but patience **brings** peace.
16.15 is like the clouds that **bring** rain in the springtime—life is
17.25 A foolish son **brings** grief to his father and bitter
19.13 A stupid son can **bring** his father to ruin.
21. 3 that pleases the Lord more than **bringing** him sacrifices.
21.12 of the wicked, and he will **bring** the wicked down to ruin.
21.15 people are happy, but evil people are **brought** to despair.
21.18 The wicked **bring** on themselves the suffering they try to
22.21 sent to find it out, you will **bring** back the right answer.
25.14 never give are like clouds and wind that **bring** no rain.
25.23 Gossip **brings** anger just as surely as the north wind brings rain.
26.28 Insincere talk **brings** nothing but ruin.
29. 9 When an intelligent man **brings** a lawsuit against a fool,
29.23 Arrogance will **bring** your downfall, but if you are humble,
30. 9 I am poor, I might steal and **bring** disgrace on my God.
31.14 She **brings** home food from out-of-the-way places, as merchant ships do.
Ecc 2.17 because everything in it had **brought** me nothing but trouble.
2.23 everything you do **brings** nothing but worry and heartache.
10.12 What a wise man says **brings** him honour, but a fool is
Song 2. 4 He **brought** me to his banqueting hall and raised the banner
Is 1. 7 foreigners take over your land and **bring** everything to ruin.
1.12 Who asked you to **bring** me all this when you come to
1.13 It's useless to **bring** your offerings.
3. 9 They are doomed, and they have **brought** it on themselves.
3.14 The Lord is **bringing** the elders and leaders of his
7. 3 the end of the ditch that **brings** water from the upper pool.
7.17 "The Lord is going to **bring** on you, on your people, and
7.17 from Judah—he is going to **bring** the king of Assyria.
8. 7 Pekah, [7]I, the Lord, will **bring** the emperor of Assyria and
9. 1 disgraced, but the future will **bring** honour to this region,
10. 3 will you do when he **brings** disaster on you from a distant
10.23 Sovereign Lord Almighty will **bring** destruction,
10.33 The Lord Almighty will **bring** them crashing down like
11.11 again use his power and **bring** back home those of his people
11.12 of Israel and Judah and **bringing** them back from the four
11.15 of Suez, and he will **bring** a hot wind to dry up
12. 3 As fresh water **brings** joy to the thirsty, so God's people
13. 6 Lord is near, the day when the Almighty **brings** destruction.
13.11 The Lord says, "I will **bring** disaster on the earth and
14.15 But instead, you have been **brought** down to the deepest
14.22 Lord Almighty says, "I will attack Babylon and **bring** it to ruin.
19.21 and worship him, and **bring** him sacrifices and offerings.
20. 4 naked, with their buttocks exposed, **bringing** shame on Egypt.
21. 4 evening to come, but it has **brought** me nothing but terror.
22. 8 When that happened, you **brought** weapons out of the arsenal.
22.19 from office and **bring** you down from your high position."

Is 23. 8 was it that planned to **bring** all this on Tyre, that imperial
23.16 Play and sing your songs again to **bring** men back once more.
25.12 high walls and **bring** them tumbling down into the dust.
26.15 territory on every side, and this has **brought** you honour.
28. 7 are too drunk to decide the cases that are **brought** to them.
28.19 Each new message from God will **bring** new terror!
29. 2 festivals, [2]and then God will **bring** disaster on the city
33. 7 The ambassadors who tried to **bring about** peace are crying bitterly.
34.16 he himself will **bring** them together.
36. 2 work, by the ditch that **brings** water from the upper pond.
40.10 coming to rule with power, **bringing** with him the people he
40.23 He **brings** down powerful rulers and reduces them to nothing.
41. 2 "Who was it that **brought** the conqueror from the east, and
41. 9 I **brought** you from the ends of the earth;
41.21 **Bring** the best arguments you have!
41.23 Do something good or **bring** some disaster;
41.25 I will **bring** him to attack from the north.
42. 1 with my spirit, and he will **bring** justice to every nation.
42. 3 He will **bring** lasting justice to all.
42. 6 through you I will **bring** light to the nations.
43. 5 east and the farthest west, I will **bring** your people home.
43. 7 are my own people, and I created them to **bring** me glory."
43. 9 Let these gods **bring** in their witnesses to prove that they
43.23 You did not **bring** me your burnt-offerings of sheep;
43.26 **bring** your accusation!
43.28 So I **brought** destruction on Israel;
45. 7 I **bring** both blessing and disaster.
46.13 I am **bringing** the day of victory near— it is not
46.13 I will save Jerusalem and **bring** honour to Israel there."
49. 5 bring back his people, to **bring** back the scattered people of Israel.
49.22 to the nations, and they will **bring** your children home.
50. 8 Does anyone dare to **bring** charges against me?
50. 8 Let him **bring** his accusation!
51. 4 my laws will **bring** them light.
51. 6 But the deliverance I **bring** will last for ever;
51. 8 But the deliverance I **bring** will last for ever;
52. 7 the mountains, **bringing** good news, the news of peace!
53.10 his death was a sacrifice to **bring** forgiveness.
56. 7 "I will **bring** you to Zion, my sacred hill, give you joy
56. 8 The Sovereign Lord, who has **brought** his people Israel home from exile,
56. 8 that he will **bring** still other people to join them.
57. 6 You pour out wine as offerings to them and **bring** them grain-offerings.
57.20 whose waves never stop rolling in, **bringing** filth and muck.
60. 5 The wealth of the nations will be **brought** to you;
60. 6 They will come from Sheba, **bringing** gold and incense.
60. 7 Kedar and Nebaioth Will be **brought** to you as sacrifices And
60. 9 They are ships coming from distant lands, **Bringing** God's people home.
60. 9 They **bring** with them silver and gold To honour the name of
60.11 So that the kings of the nations May **bring** you their wealth.
60.13 forests of Lebanon, Will be **brought** to rebuild you,
60.17 "I will **bring** you gold instead of bronze, Silver and
61. 1 me and sent me To **bring** good news to the poor, To
62.11 is coming to save you, **Bringing** with him the people he has
63.14 He led his people and **brought** honour to his name.
66. 4 So I will **bring** disaster upon them—the very things they
66. 9 not think that I will **bring** my people to the point of
66.12 The Lord says, "I will **bring** you lasting prosperity;
66.20 They will **bring** back all your fellow-countrymen from the
66.20 They will **bring** them to my sacred hill in Jerusalem on horses,
66.20 and wagons, just as Israelites **bring** grain-offerings to the
Jer 2. 5 "What accusation did your ancestors **bring** against me?
2. 7 I **brought** them into a fertile land, to enjoy its harvests
2. 9 I will **bring** charges against their descendants.
2.11 me, the God who has **brought** them honour, for gods that can
2.17 Israel, you **brought** this on yourself!
3.14 from each clan, and I will **bring** you back to Mount Zion.
4. 6 The Lord is **bringing** disaster and great destruction from the north.
4.18 Judah, you have **brought** this on yourself by the way you
5.15 of Israel, the Lord is **bringing** a nation from afar to attack
6.19 all their schemes I am **bringing** ruin on these people,
6.20 care about the incense they **bring** me from Sheba, or the
7.19 No, they are hurting themselves and **bringing** shame on themselves.
7.22 other kinds of sacrifices, when I **brought** them out of Egypt.
10.13 he **brings** clouds from the ends of the earth.
11. 4 with their ancestors when I **brought** them out of Egypt, the
11. 7 When I **brought** their ancestors out of Egypt, I solemnly
11. 8 So I **brought** on them all the punishments described in it."
11.11 that I am going to **bring** destruction on them, and they will
11.17 They have **brought** this on themselves because they have done wrong;
11.23 set a time for **bringing** disaster on the people of Anathoth,
12.15 I will **bring** each nation back to its own land and to
13.11 be my people and would **bring** praise and honour to my name;
13.16 Lord, your God, before he **brings** darkness, and you stumble
14.21 do not **bring** disgrace on Jerusalem,
15.10 Why did my mother **bring** me into the world?
16.14 as the living God who **brought** the people of Israel out of
16.15 as the living God who **brought** the people of Israel out of
16.15 I will **bring** them back to their own country, to the land
17.16 But, Lord, I never urged you to **bring** disaster on them;
17.18 **Bring** disgrace on those who persecute me, but spare me,
17.18 **Bring** disaster on them and break them to pieces.
17.26 They will **bring** to my Temple burnt-offerings and sacrifices,
18.18 Let's **bring** charges against him, and stop listening to what he says."
Jer 19. 3 I am going to **bring** such a disaster on this place that
19. 8 I will **bring** such terrible destruction on this city that
19.15 said, "I am going to **bring** on this city and on every
20.15 my father glad when he **brought** him the news, "It's a boy!
22. 7 They will all **bring** their axes, cut down its beautiful cedar pillars,
22.23 You rest secure among the cedars **brought** from Lebanon;
23. 3 them, and I will **bring** them back to their homeland.
23. 7 as the living God who **brought** the people of Israel out of
23. 8 as the living God who **brought** the people of Israel out of
23.12 I am going to **bring** disaster on them;
23.40 I will **bring** on them everlasting shame and disgrace that
24. 6 I will watch over them and **bring** them back to this land.
24. 9 I will **bring** such a disaster on them that all the nations
24.10 I will **bring** war, starvation, and disease on them until
25. 7 your idols and have **brought** his punishment on yourselves.
25. 9 I am going to **bring** them to fight against Judah and its
25.13 disasters that I threatened to **bring** on the nations when I
25.31 He will **bring** all people to trial and put the wicked to
26. 3 the destruction I plan to **bring** on them for all their wicked
26.13 about the destruction that he said he would **bring** on you.
26.19 mind about the disaster that he said he would **bring** on them.
26.19 Now we are about to **bring** a terrible disaster on ourselves."
26.23 They **brought** him back to King Jehoiakim, who had him
27.16 temple treasures will soon be **brought** back from Babylonia.
27.22 Then I will **bring** them back and restore them to this place.
28. 3 Within two years I will **bring** back to this place all the
28. 4 I will also **bring** back the king of Judah, Jehoiachin son
28. 6 prophecy come true and will **bring** back from Babylonia all
29.10 concern for you and keep my promise to **bring** you back home.
29.11 have for you, plans to **bring** you prosperity and not disaster,
29.11 not disaster, plans to **bring about** the future you hope for.
29.14 scattered you, and I will **bring** you back to the land from
29.17 Lord Almighty says, 'I am **bringing** war, starvation, and disease on them,
29.22 Jerusalem to Babylonia want to **bring** a curse on someone,
30. 3 I will **bring** them back to the land that I gave their
30.19 my blessing will **bring** them honour.
31. 8 I will **bring** them from the north and gather them from the
31.18 **Bring** us back;
32.21 power and might to **bring** your people Israel out of Egypt.
32.23 And so you **brought** all this destruction on them.
32.37 and I am going to **bring** them back to this place and
32.42 "Just as I have **brought** this disaster on these people,
33. 9 Jerusalem and about the prosperity that I **bring** to the city."
33.11 You will hear people sing as they **bring** thank-offerings to my Temple;
35. 2 Then **bring** them into one of the rooms in the Temple and
35. 4 all his brothers and sons—[4]and **brought** them to the Temple.
35.17 the God of Israel, will **bring** on you people of Judah and
36. 3 destruction that I intend to **bring** on them, they will turn
36.14 Cushi) to tell Baruch to **bring** the scroll that he had read
36.14 Baruch **brought** them the scroll.
36.31 warnings, and so I will **bring** on all of you the disaster
38.14 occasion King Zedekiah had me **brought** to him at the third
39.14 king of Babylonia, [14]**brought** me from the palace courtyard.
39.16 would, I am going to **bring** upon this city destruction and
40.15 be scattered, and it would **bring** disaster on all the people
42.10 The destruction I **brought** on you has caused me great sorrow.
42.17 will escape the disaster that I am going to **bring** on them.'
43.10 of Israel, am going to **bring** my servant King Nebuchadnezzar
44. 2 have seen the destruction I **brought** on Jerusalem and all the
44. 7 Do you want to **bring** destruction on men and women, children
44.29 that my promise to **bring** destruction on you will come true.
45. 5 I am **bringing** disaster on all mankind, but you will at least
49. 5 I will **bring** terror on you from every side.
49. 5 there will be no one to **bring** your troops together again.
49.16 as high up as an eagle, the Lord will **bring** you down.
49.32 short, and I will **bring** disaster on them from every side.
50.34 up their cause and will **bring** peace to the earth, but
50.38 **Bring** a drought on its land and dry up its rivers.
51. 1 The Lord says, "I am **bringing** a destructive wind against
51.14 own life that he will **bring** many men to attack Babylonia
51.16 he **brings** clouds from the ends of the earth.
51.27 **Bring** up the horses like a swarm of locusts.
51.64 the destruction that the Lord is going to **bring** on it.' "
Lam 1.12 mine, Pain that the Lord **brought** on me in the time of
1.13 He set a trap for me and **brought** me to the ground.
1.21 My enemies are glad that you **brought** disaster on me.
1.21 **Bring** the day you promised;
2. 2 He **brought** disgrace on the kingdom and its rulers.
2. 5 He has **brought** on the people of Judah unending sorrow.
3.32 He may **bring** us sorrow, but his love for us is sure
4.10 The disaster that came to my people **brought** horror;
5.21 **Bring** us back to you, Lord!
5.21 **Bring** us back!
Ezek 7.24 I will **bring** the most evil nations here and let them
9. 1 **Bring** your weapons with you."
11. 8 I will **bring** men with swords to attack you.
11.24 God lifted me up and **brought** me back to the exiles in
14.17 "Or I might **bring** war on that country and send
14.22 that the punishment I am **bringing** on Jerusalem is justified;
16.37 Because of this I will **bring** all your former lovers together—
16.37 I will **bring** them round you in a circle, and then I
20. 9 not, since that would have **brought** dishonour to my name, for
20.11 them my laws, which **bring** life to anyone who obeys them.
20.13 my commands, which **bring** life to anyone who obeys them.
20.14 not, since that would have **brought** dishonour to my name
20.21 keep my commands, which **bring** life to anyone who obeys them.
20.22 not, since that would have **brought** dishonour to my name
20.22 the nations which had seen me **bring** Israel out of Egypt.
20.25 laws that are not good and commands that do not **bring** life.

Ezek	20.28	I **brought** them to the land I had promised to give them.
	20.28	they burnt and by the wine they **brought** as offerings.
	20.34	I gather you together and **bring** you back from all the
	20.35	I will **bring** you into the 'Desert of the Nations,' and
	20.40	expect you to **bring** me your sacrifices, your best offerings,
	20.41	After I **bring** you out of the countries where you have
	20.42	When I **bring** you back to Israel, the land that I
	21.26	**Bring** down those who are ruling!
	22.13	"I will **bring** my fist down on your robberies and murders.
	22.19	I will **bring** them all together in Jerusalem [20] in the same
	23.22	make them angry with you and **bring** them to surround you.
	23.23	I will **bring** all the Babylonians and Chaldeans, men from Pekod,
	23.24	attack you from the north, **bringing** a large army with
	23.30	Your lust and your prostitution [30] have **brought** this on you.
	23.42	could be heard, a group of men **brought** in from the desert.
	23.46	"**Bring** a mob to terrorize them and rob them.
	24.10	**Bring** more wood!
	25.12	Judah, and that revenge has **brought** lasting guilt on Edom.
	26. 3	I will **bring** many nations to attack you, and they will come
	26. 7	says, "I am going to **bring** the greatest king of all—King
	27.26	When your oarsmen **brought** you out to sea, An east wind
	28. 7	as a god, [7] I will **bring** ruthless enemies to attack you.
	28.25	Sovereign Lord said, "I will **bring** back the people of
	29.13	"After forty years I will **bring** the Egyptians back from the
	31.15	tree has died, I will **bring** darkness over the Lebanon
	32. 4	out on the ground and **bring** all the birds and animals of
	33. 2	"tell your people what happens when I **bring** war to a land.
	34. 4	those that are hurt, **brought** back those that wandered off,
	34.12	sheep that were scattered and are **brought** together again.
	34.12	I will **bring** them back from all the places where they were
	34.13	gather them together, and **bring** them back to their own land.
	34.16	for those that are lost, **bring** back those that wander off,
	36.12	I will **bring** you, my people Israel, back to live again
	36.20	Wherever they went, they **brought** disgrace on my holy name,
	36.21	the Israelites **brought** disgrace on it everywhere they went.
	36.24	nation and country and **bring** you back to your own land.
	37. 5	going to put breath into you and **bring** you back to life.
	37. 6	I will put breath into you and **bring** you back to life.
	37. 9	into these dead bodies, and to **bring** them back to life."
	37.12	to take them out and **bring** them back to the land of
	37.13	my people are buried and **bring** them out, they will know that
	37.14	put my breath in them, **bring** them back to life, and let
	37.21	gather them together, and **bring** them back to their own land.
	38. 8	country where the people were **brought** back together from
	38.17	in days to come I would **bring** someone to attack Israel."
	39.27	I am holy, I will **bring** my people back from all the
	39.28	and now gather them and **bring** them back into their own land,
	40. 4	I show you, because this is why you were **brought** here.
	40.44	Then he **brought** me into the inner courtyard.
	43.24	both of them without any defects, [24] and **bring** them to me.
	45.13	"You are to **bring** grain-offerings, animals to be burnt whole,
	46. 4	Sabbath the prince is to **bring** to the Lord, as sacrifices to
	46. 5	each ram he is to **bring** an offering of seventeen and a
	46. 5	with each lamb he is to **bring** whatever he wants to give.
	46. 5	For each such grain-offering he is to **bring** three litres of olive-oil.
	47. 9	Dead Sea fresh, and wherever it flows, it will **bring** life.
Dan	3.13	a rage and ordered the three men to be **brought** before him.
	4. 6	advisers in Babylon to be **brought** to me so that they could
	4. 7	magicians, wizards, and astrologers were **brought** in, and I
	5. 2	drinking, Belshazzar gave orders to **bring** in the gold and
	5. 3	gold cups and bowls were **brought** in, and they all drank wine
	5. 7	He shouted for someone to **bring** in the magicians,
	5.13	Daniel was **brought** at once into the king's presence,
	5.13	Jewish exile whom my father the king **brought** here from Judah?
	5.15	The advisers and magicians were **brought** in to read this
	5.23	the Lord of heaven and **brought** in the cups and bowls taken
	5.26	numbered the days of your kingdom and **brought** it to an end;
	8.24	He will **bring** destruction on powerful men and on God's own people.
	9. 7	is right, but we have always **brought** disgrace on ourselves.
	9.11	against you, and so you **brought** on us the curses that are
	9.15	you showed your power by **bringing** your people out of Egypt,
	9.26	will come like a flood, **bringing** the war and destruction
Hos	4. 1	Lord has an accusation to **bring** against the people who live
	5.12	I will **bring** destruction on Israel and ruin on the
	9. 4	of wine to the Lord, or **bring** their sacrifices to him.
	11.11	I will **bring** them to their homes again.
	12. 2	The Lord has an accusation to **bring** against the people of Judah;
	12.14	Lord will punish them for the disgrace they have **brought** on him.
	13.14	**Bring** on your plagues, death!
	13.14	**Bring** on your destruction, world of the dead!
	14. 4	"I will **bring** my people back to me.
Joel	1.15	the day when the Almighty **brings** destruction.
	1.15	What terror that day will **bring!**
	2.16	**bring** the old people;
	3. 2	all the nations and **bring** them to the Valley of Judgement.
	3. 7	Now I am going to **bring** them out of the places to
Amos	2.10	I **brought** you out of Egypt, led you through the desert
	3. 1	about you, the entire nation that he **brought** out of Egypt;
	4. 4	Go ahead and **bring** animals to be sacrificed morning after morning,
	4. 4	and **bring** your tithes every third day.
	4. 5	to God, and boast about the extra offerings you **bring!**
	4. 6	"I was the one who **brought** famine to all your cities,
	5. 9	He **brings** destruction on the mighty and their strongholds.
	5.20	The day of the Lord will **bring** darkness and not light;
	5.22	When you **bring** me burnt-offerings and grain-offerings,
	5.22	the animals you have fattened to **bring** me as offerings.
	6. 3	is coming, but what you do only **brings** that day closer.
	7. 9	I will **bring** the dynasty of King Jeroboam to an end."
	9. 2	Even if they climb up to heaven, I will **bring** them down.
Amos	9. 7	I **brought** the Philistines from Crete and the Syrians from Kir,
	9. 7	just as I **brought** you from Egypt.
	9.14	I will **bring** my people back to their land.
Jon	2. 6	you, O Lord my God, **brought** me back from the depths alive.
Mic	1.12	because the Lord has **brought** disaster close to Jerusalem.
	2. 3	says, "I am planning to **bring** disaster on you, and you will
	2.12	I will **bring** you together like sheep returning to the fold.
	4.12	in the same way that corn is **brought** in to be threshed.
	5. 2	out of you I will **bring** a ruler for Israel, whose family
	5. 5	will acknowledge his greatness, [5] and he will **bring** peace.
	6. 2	He is going to **bring** an accusation against Israel.
	6. 4	I **brought** you out of Egypt;
	6. 6	What shall I **bring** to the Lord, the God of heaven, when
	6. 6	Shall I **bring** the best calves to burn as offerings to him?
	6. 7	Lord be pleased if I **bring** him thousands of sheep or endless
	6.16	policies, and so I will **bring** you to ruin, and everyone will
	7. 9	He will **bring** us out to the light;
	7.15	you did in the days when you **brought** us out of Egypt.
Nah	3.18	the mountains, and there is no one to **bring** them home again.
Hab	1. 6	I am **bringing** the Babylonians to power, those fierce, restless people.
	2.10	But your schemes have **brought** shame on your family;
	2.10	many nations you have only **brought** ruin on yourself.
	3. 8	was your chariot, as you **brought** victory to your people.
Zeph	1. 3	I will **bring about** the downfall of the wicked.
	1.17	The Lord says, "I will **bring** such disasters on mankind
	3. 5	Every morning without fail, he **brings** justice to his people.
	3.10	my scattered people will **bring** offerings to me.
	3.19	I will rescue all the lame and **bring** the exiles home.
	3.20	I will **bring** your scattered people home;
Hag	1. 9	And when you **brought** the harvest home, I blew it away.
	1.11	I have **brought** drought on the land—on its hills,
	2. 7	and their treasures will be **brought** here, and the Temple
Zech	3. 1	Satan, ready to **bring** an accusation against him.
	8. 8	have been taken, [8] and will **bring** them back from east and
	8.16	In the courts, give real justice—the kind that **brings** peace.
	10. 6	I will have compassion on them and **bring** them all back home.
	10.10	Egypt and Assyria I will **bring** them home and settle them in
	14. 2	The Lord will **bring** all the nations together to make war
	14. 5	The Lord my God will come, **bringing** all the angels with him.
	14.12	The Lord will **bring** a terrible disease on all the
Mal	1. 8	When you **bring** a blind or sick or lame animal to sacrifice
	1.10	I will not accept the offerings you **bring** me.
	1.13	your offering to me you **bring** a stolen animal or one that
	2. 2	to what I say, then I will **bring** a curse on you.
	2.12	in the offerings our nation **brings** to the Lord Almighty.
	2.13	because he no longer accepts the offerings you **bring** him.
	3. 3	priests, so that they will **bring** to the Lord the right kind
	3. 4	people of Judah and Jerusalem **bring** to the Lord will be
	3.10	**Bring** the full amount of your tithes to the Temple, so
	4. 2	on you like the sun and **bring** healing like the sun's rays.
	4. 6	He will **bring** fathers and children together again;
Mt	2.11	They **brought** out their gifts of gold, frankincense, and myrrh,
	4.24	of Syria, so that people **brought** to him all those who were
	5.21	anyone who does will be **brought** to trial.'
	5.22	with his brother will be **brought** to trial, whoever calls his
	5.22	will be **brought** before the Council, and whoever calls his brother
	5.25	someone **brings** a lawsuit against you and takes you to court,
	6.13	Do not **bring** us to hard testing, but keep us safe from
	6.34	There is no need to add to the troubles each day **brings.**
	8.16	evening came, people **brought** to Jesus many who had demons in
	9. 2	where some people **brought** to him a paralysed man, lying
	9.32	men were leaving, some people **brought** to Jesus a man who
	10. 8	Heal the sick, **bring** the dead back to life, heal those who
	10.18	sake you will be **brought** to trial before rulers and kings,
	10.19	When they **bring** you to trial, do not worry about what
	10.34	not think that I have come to **bring** peace to the world.
	10.34	No, I did not come to **bring** peace, but a sword.
	11. 5	deaf hear, the dead are **brought** back to life, and the Good
	12.22	Then some people **brought** to Jesus a man who was blind
	12.35	A good person **brings** good things out of his treasure of
	12.35	a bad person **brings** bad things out of his treasure of bad
	12.45	it goes out and **brings** along seven other spirits even worse
	14.11	The head was **brought** in on a dish and given to the
	14.18	"Then **bring** them here to me," Jesus said.
	14.35	people in all the surrounding country and **brought** them to Jesus.
	15.30	crowds came to him, **bringing** with them the lame, the blind,
	16. 7	"He says this because we didn't **bring** any bread."
	17.16	I **brought** him to your disciples, but they could not heal him."
	17.17	**Bring** the boy here to me!"
	18.24	when one of them was **brought** in who owed him millions of
	19.13	people **brought** children to Jesus for him to place his hands
	21. 2	Untie them and **bring** them to me.
	21. 7	they **brought** the donkey and the colt, threw their cloaks over
	22.19	They **brought** him the coin, [20] and he asked them, "Whose face
Mk	1.32	and evening had come, people **brought** to Jesus all the sick
	4.21	Jesus continued, "Does anyone ever **bring** in a lamp and put
	4.22	is hidden away will be **brought** out into the open, and
	6.27	sent off a guard at once with orders to **bring** John's head.
	6.28	then he **brought** it on a dish and gave it to the
	6.55	they heard he was, they **brought** to him sick people lying on
	7.32	Some people **brought** him a man who was deaf and could
	8.14	disciples had forgotten to **bring** enough bread and had only one
	8.22	to Bethsaida, where some people **brought** a blind man to Jesus
	9.17	answered, "Teacher, I **brought** my son to you, because he
	9.19	**Bring** the boy to me!"
	9.20	They **brought** him to Jesus.
	10.13	people **brought** children to Jesus for him to place his hands
	11. 2	Untie it and **bring** it here.
	11. 7	**brought** the colt to Jesus, threw their cloaks over the animal,
	12.15	**Bring** a silver coin, and let me see it."

Mk 12.16 They **brought** him one, and he asked, "Whose face and
14.60 "Have you no answer to the accusation they **bring** against you?"
15.36 see if Elijah is coming to **bring** him down from the cross!"
Lk 1.16 and he will **bring** back many of the people
1.17 He will **bring** fathers and children together again;
1.52 He has **brought** down mighty kings from their thrones,
2.10 news for you, which will **bring** great joy to all the people.
2.27 When the parents **brought** the child Jesus into the Temple to
2.32 to the Gentiles and **bring** glory to your people Israel."
4.18 because he has chosen me to **bring** good news to the poor.
4.40 friends who were sick with various diseases **brought** them to Jesus;
6.45 A good person **brings** good out of the treasure of good
6.45 a bad person **brings** bad out of his treasure of bad things.
7.37 Pharisee's house, so she **brought** an alabaster jar full of perfume
8.17 is hidden away will be **brought** out into the open,
8.17 whatever is covered up will be found and **brought** to light.
9.41 Then he said to the man, "**Bring** your son here."
11. 4 And do not **bring** us to hard testing.'"
11.26 Then it goes out and **brings** seven other spirits even worse
12.11 "When they **bring** you to be tried in the synagogues or
12.51 Do you suppose that I came to **bring** peace to the world?
12.58 someone **brings** a lawsuit against you and takes you to court,
14.10 This will **bring** you honour in the presence of all the other
14.21 alleys of the town, and **bring** back the poor, the crippled,
15.22 '**Bring** the best robe and put it on him.
16.20 who used to be **brought** to the rich man's door,
18.15 Some people **brought** their babies to Jesus for him to place
18.40 Jesus stopped and ordered the blind man to be **brought** to him.
19.27 me to be their king, **bring** them here and kill them in
19.30 Untie it and **bring** it here.
21.12 you will be **brought** before kings and rulers for my sake.
22.66 the Law met together, and Jesus was **brought** before the Council.
23.14 and said to them, "You **brought** this man to me and said
Jn 1. 4 the source of life, and this life **brought** light to mankind.
4.33 asking among themselves, "Could somebody have **brought** him food?"
6.63 The words I have spoken to you **bring** God's life-giving Spirit.
7.45 priests and Pharisees asked them, "Why did you not **bring** him?"
8. 3 the Law and the Pharisees **brought** in a woman who had been
10. 4 When he has **brought** them out, he goes ahead of them,
10.16 I must **bring** them, too;
11. 4 has happened in order to **bring** glory to God, and it will
11.52 but also to **bring** together into one body all the
12.28 Father, **bring** glory to your name!"
12.28 spoke from heaven, "I have **brought** glory to it, and I will
12.50 And I know that his command **brings** eternal life.
18.16 spoke to the girl at the gate, and **brought** Peter inside.
18.30 "We would not have **brought** him to you if he had
19. 4 the crowd, "Look, I will **bring** him out here to you to
21.10 Then Jesus said to them, "**Bring** some of the fish you
21.19 the way in which Peter would die and **bring** glory to God.)
Acts 4.34 houses would sell them, **bring** the money received from the sale,
4.37 sold a field he owned, **brought** the money, and handed it
5.16 from the towns around Jerusalem, **bringing** those who were ill or
5.21 orders to the prison to have the apostles **brought** before them.
5.26 officer went off with his men and **brought** the apostles back.
5.27 They **brought** the apostles in, made them stand before the Council,
6.13 Then they **brought** in some men to tell lies about him.
7.10 God was with him [10] and **brought** him safely through all his
7.40 happened to that man Moses, who **brought** us out of Egypt.'
9. 2 both men and women, and **bring** them back to Jerusalem.
11.24 Holy Spirit and faith, and many people were **brought** to the Lord.
12. 6 before Herod was going to **bring** him out to the people, Peter
12.17 to them how the Lord had **brought** him out of prison.
13.17 God **brought** them out of Egypt by his great power,
13.32 And we are here to **bring** the Good News to you:
14.13 just outside the town, **brought** bulls and flowers to the gate,
15. 3 this news **brought** great joy to all the believers.
16.20 They **brought** them before the Roman officials and said,
17. 5 to find Paul and Silas and **bring** them out to the people.
17.19 took Paul, **brought** him before the city council, the Areopagus,
19.19 who had practised magic **brought** their books together and burnt
19.24 and his business **brought** a great deal of profit to
19.37 You have **brought** these men here even though they have not
21.28 And now he has even **brought** some Gentiles into the Temple
22. 5 to arrest these people and **bring** them back in chains to
23.15 to the Roman commander to **bring** Paul down to you, pretending
23.18 me and asked me to **bring** this young man to you,
24. 2 Your wise leadership has **brought** us a long period of peace,
24.13 give you proof of the accusations they now **bring** against me.
24.22 well informed about the Way, **brought** the hearing to a close.
25. 2 priests and the Jewish leaders **brought** their charges against Paul.
25. 3 do them the favour of **bringing** Paul to Jerusalem, for they
25. 6 in the court of judgement and ordered Paul to be **brought** in.
25.11 truth in the charges they **bring** against me, no one can hand
25.15 Jewish chief priests and elders **brought** charges against him
25.17 sat in the court and ordered the man to be **brought** in.
25.23 Festus gave the order, and Paul was **brought** in.
25.24 people, both here and in Jerusalem, have **brought** complaints to me.
25.26 So I have **brought** him here before you—and especially before you,
Rom 1.27 and as a result they **bring** upon themselves the punishment they
2.23 God's law—but do you **bring** shame on God by breaking his
3.19 stop all human excuses and **bring** the whole world under God's
4.15 The Law **brings** down God's anger;
4.17 Abraham believed—the God who **brings** the dead to life
4.17 and whose command **brings** into being what did not exist.
5. 2 He has **brought** us by faith into this experience of God's grace,
5. 4 endurance **brings** God's approval, and his approval creates
5.12 world through one man, and his sin **brought** death with it.
Rom 6.13 as those who have been **brought** from death to life, and
7.10 commandment which was meant to **bring** life,
7.10 in my case **brought** death.
7.13 using what is good, sin **brought** death to me, in order that
8. 2 law of the Spirit, which **brings** us life in union with Christ
10. 4 For Christ has **brought** the Law to an end, so that everyone
10. 6 (that is, to **bring** Christ down).
10. 7 (that is, to **bring** Christ up from death).
10.15 "How wonderful is the coming of messengers who **bring** good news!"
11.12 The sin of the Jews **brought** rich blessings to the world,
11.12 their spiritual poverty **brought** rich blessings to the Gentiles.
13. 2 and anyone who does so will **bring** judgement on himself.
14.19 aim at those things that **bring** peace and that help to
16.26 that truth has been **brought** out into the open through the
1 Cor 1.30 But God has **brought** you into union with Christ Jesus,
4. 5 he will **bring** to light the dark secrets and expose the
4.15 I have become your father by **bringing** the Good News to you.
9.27 my body with blows and **bring** it under complete control,
11.12 and it is God who **brings** everything into existence.
11.29 drinks from the cup, he **brings** judgement on himself as he
14. 6 Not a bit, unless I **bring** you some revelation from God
14.25 his secret thoughts will be **brought** into the open,
2 Cor 2.16 who are being saved, it is a fragrance that **brings** life.
3. 6 The written law **brings** death, but the Spirit gives life.
3. 7 If the Law, which **brings** death when it is in force, came
3. 9 The system which **brings** condemnation was glorious;
3. 9 much more glorious is the activity which **brings** salvation!
4. 6 shine in our hearts, to **bring** us the knowledge of God's
4.17 trouble we suffer will **bring** us a tremendous and eternal glory,
7.10 that is used by God **brings** a change of heart that leads
8.23 they represent the churches and **bring** glory to Christ.
9.13 which this service of yours **brings**, many will give glory to
10.14 when we came to you, **bringing** the Good News about Christ.
11. 9 brothers who came from Macedonia **brought** me everything I needed.
Gal 3.13 Christ has redeemed us from the curse that the Law **brings**;
3.21 received a law that could **bring** life, then everyone could be
Eph 1.10 time is right, is to **bring** all creation together, everything in
1.13 heard the true message, the Good News that **brought** you salvation.
2. 5 spiritually dead in our disobedience he **brought** us to life with
2.13 far away have been **brought** near by the sacrificial death of
2.14 Christ himself has **brought** us peace by making Jews and Gentiles
2.16 both races into one body and **brought** them back to God.
5. 9 it is the light that **brings** a rich harvest of every kind
5.11 Instead, **bring** them out to the light.
5.13 And when all things are **brought** out to the light,
6. 4 Instead, **bring** them up with Christian discipline and instruction.
Phil 1.20 my whole being I shall **bring** honour to Christ, whether I
1.21 Death, then, will **bring** more.
3.21 by which he is able to **bring** all things under his rule.
4.18 I need now that Epaphroditus has **brought** me all your gifts.
Col 1. 6 The gospel keeps **bringing** blessings and is spreading throughout
1.13 the power of darkness and **brought** us safe into the kingdom
1.20 God decided to **bring** the whole universe back to himself.
1.20 on the cross and so **brought** back to himself all things,
1.22 his friends, in order to **bring** you, holy, pure, and faultless,
1.28 teach them in order to **bring** each one into God's presence
2. 2 have the full wealth of assurance which true understanding **brings**.
2.13 But God has now **brought** you to life with Christ.
3.10 own image, in order to **bring** you to a full knowledge of
1 Thes 1. 5 For we **brought** the Good News to you, not with words only,
2.13 When we **brought** you God's message, you heard it and accepted it,
2.16 to the Gentiles the message that would **bring** them salvation.
2.16 In this way they have **brought** to completion all the sins
3. 6 come back, and he has **brought** us the welcome news about your
2 Thes 1. 6 he will **bring** suffering on those who make you suffer,
1 Tim 2. 5 and there is one who **brings** God and mankind together, the
5.19 an elder unless it is **brought** by two or more witnesses.
6. 4 quarrel about words, and this **brings** on jealousy, disputes,
6. 7 What did we **bring** into the world?
6.15 His appearing will be **brought** about at the right time by God,
2 Tim 2.10 that comes through Christ Jesus and **brings** eternal glory.
4.11 Get Mark and **bring** him with you, because he can help me
4.13 When you come, **bring** my coat that I left in Troas with
4.13 **bring** the books too, and especially the ones made of parchment.
Tit 2.10 and faithful, so as to **bring** credit to the teaching about
Phlm 6 with you as believers will **bring** about a deeper understanding
7 Your love, dear brother, has **brought** me great joy and much
Heb 2.10 suffering, in order to **bring** many sons to share his glory.
6. 4 those who abandon their faith be **brought** back to repent again?
6. 6 It is impossible to **bring** them back to repent again,
10.35 your courage, then, because it **brings** with it a great reward.
13.11 The Jewish High Priest **brings** the blood of the animals into
Jas 1.10 and the rich Christian must be glad when God **brings** him down.
1.18 By his own will he **brought** us into being through the
5.19 from the truth and another one **brings** him back again,
5.20 soul from death and **bring** about the forgiveness of many sins.
1 Pet 2.25 but now you have been **brought** back to follow the Shepherd
2 Pet 2. 1 They will **bring** in destructive, untrue doctrines, and will deny
2. 1 and so they will **bring** upon themselves sudden destruction.
2. 5 spare the ancient world, but **brought** the flood on the world
3.16 So they **bring** on their own destruction.
2 Jn 10 who does not **bring** this teaching, do not welcome him
Jude 12 like clouds carried along by the wind, but **bringing** no rain.
15 his holy angels [15] to **bring** judgement on all, to condemn them
24 you from falling, and to **bring** you faultless and joyful before
Rev 6. 4 was given the power to **bring** war on the earth,
11.10 because those two prophets **brought** much suffering upon mankind.

Rev 15. 8 until the seven plagues **brought** by the seven angels had come
16.14 kings of the world, to **bring** them together for the battle
16.16 Then the spirits **brought** the kings together in the place that
20. 8 Satan will **bring** them all together for battle, as many as
21.24 and the kings of the earth will **bring** their wealth into it.
21.26 and the wealth of the nations will be **brought** into the city.
22.12 I will **bring** my rewards with me, to give to each one

BRING UP
[BROUGHT UP]

Lev 18. 9 whether or not she was **brought up** in the same house with
1 Kgs 11.20 a son, Genubath, who was **brought up** by the queen in the
2 Kgs 10. 6 the leading citizens of Samaria, who were **bringing them up.**
Esth 2. 7 Mordecai had adopted her and **brought her up** as his own daughter.
Is 1. 2 The children I **brought up** have rebelled against me.
23. 4 I never **brought up** sons or daughters."
49.21 I was exiled and driven away— who **brought these children up?**
Hos 7.15 was the one who **brought them up** and made them strong, they
9.12 But even if they did **bring up** children, I would take
Lk 4.16 Nazareth, where he had been **brought up,** and on the Sabbath
Jn 9.34 answered, "You were born and **brought up** in sin—and you are
Acts 7.21 daughter adopted him and **brought him up** as her own son.
13. 1 Manaen (who had been **brought up** with Herod the governor),
22. 3 in Tarsus in Cilicia, but **brought up** here in Jerusalem as a
1 Tim 5.10 a woman who **brought up** her children well, received strangers

BRISTLED

Job 4.15 A light breeze touched my face, and my hair **bristled** with fright.

BROAD

Neh 9.35 when they lived in the **broad,** fertile land you gave them;
Job 11. 9 God's greatness is **broader** than the earth, wider than the sea.
Is 33.21 We will live beside **broad** rivers and streams, but hostile
Mt 10.27 dark you must repeat in **broad** daylight, and what you have
Lk 12. 3 will be heard in **broad** daylight, and whatever you have whispered
Jn 11. 9 So whoever walks in **broad** daylight does not stumble, for he
Eph 3.18 power to understand how **broad** and long, how high and deep,
2 Pet 2.13 to do anything in **broad** daylight that will satisfy their bodily

BROAD WALL

Neh 3. 8 of perfumes, built the next section, as far as **Broad Wall.**
12.38 of the Ovens to the **Broad Wall,** [39] and from there we went

BROKEN-DOWN see BREAK

BROKEN-HEARTED see BREAK, HEART

BRONZE

Gen 4.22 Cain, who made all kinds of tools out of **bronze** and iron.
Ex 25. 3 gold, silver, and **bronze;**
26.11 Make fifty **bronze** hooks and put them in the loops to
26.37 make five **bronze** bases for these posts.
27. 2 with the altar, and the whole is to be covered with **bronze.**
27. 3 All this equipment is to be made of **bronze.**
27. 4 Make a **bronze** grating and put four bronze carrying-rings on its corners.
27. 6 of acacia-wood, cover them with **bronze,** [7] and put them in
27.10 twenty bronze posts in twenty **bronze** bases, with hooks and
27.17 hooks are to be made of silver and their bases of **bronze.**
27.18 are to be made of fine linen and the bases of **bronze.**
27.19 the Tent and for the enclosure are to be made of **bronze.**
30.18 Lord said to Moses, [18] "Make a **bronze** basin with a bronze base.
31. 4 for planning skilful designs and working them in gold, silver, and **bronze;**
35. 5 do so is to bring an offering of gold, silver, or **bronze;**
35.16 to burn offerings, with its **bronze** grating attached, its
35.24 silver or **bronze** brought their offering for the Lord,
35.32 for planning skilful designs and working them in gold, silver and **bronze;**
36.18 They made fifty **bronze** hooks to join the two sets, so as
36.38 rods with gold, and made five **bronze** bases for the posts.
38. 2 He covered it all with **bronze.**
38. 3 All this equipment was made of **bronze.**
38. 4 He made a **bronze** grating and put it under the rim of
38. 6 of acacia-wood, covered them with **bronze,** [7] and put them in
38. 8 He made the **bronze** basin and its bronze base out of the
38.10 twenty bronze posts in twenty **bronze** bases, with hooks and
38.17 the posts were made of **bronze,** and the hooks, the rods, and
38.19 It was supported by four posts in four **bronze** bases.
38.20 Tent and for the surrounding enclosure were made of **bronze.**
38.29 The **bronze** which was dedicated to the Lord amounted to 2,425 kilogrammes.
38.30 the bronze altar with its **bronze** grating, all the equipment
39.39 the **bronze** altar with its bronze grating, its poles, and
Num 16.37 the priest to remove the **bronze** firepans from the remains of
21. 9 So Moses made a **bronze** snake and put it on a pole.
21. 9 been bitten would look at the **bronze** snake and be healed.
31.22 burn, such as gold, silver, **bronze,** iron, tin, or lead, is
Josh 6.19 Everything made of silver, gold, **bronze,** or iron is set
6.24 things made of gold, silver, **bronze,** and iron, which they
22. 6 of livestock, silver, gold, **bronze,** iron, and many clothes.
Judg 16.21 to Gaza, chained him with **bronze** chains, and put him to work
1 Sam 17. 5 wore **bronze** armour that weighed about fifty-seven kilogrammes
1 Sam 17. 5 and a **bronze** helmet.
17. 6 legs were also protected by **bronze** armour,
17. 6 and he carried a **bronze** javelin slung over his shoulder.
17.38 a **bronze** helmet, which he put on David's head, and a coat
2 Sam 8. 8 took a great quantity of **bronze** from Betah and Berothai,
8.10 Joram took David presents made of gold, silver, and **bronze.**
21.16 Ishbibenob, who was carrying a **bronze** spear that weighed
1 Kgs 4.13 fortified with walls and with **bronze** bars on the gates
7.13 living in the city of Tyre, who was skilled in **bronze** work.
7.14 was from Tyre, and had also been a skilled **bronze** craftsman;
7.14 King Solomon's invitation to be in charge of all the **bronze** work.
7.15 Huram cast two **bronze** columns, each one 8 metres tall
7.16 He also made two **bronze** capitals, each one 2.2 metres tall,
7.18 interwoven chains, [18] and two rows of **bronze** pomegranates.
7.21 Huram placed these two **bronze** columns in front of the
7.22 The lily-shaped **bronze** capitals were on top of the columns.
7.23 made a round tank of **bronze,** 2.2 metres deep, 4.4 metres in
7.24 tank were two rows of **bronze** gourds, which had been cast all
7.25 on the backs of twelve **bronze** bulls that faced outwards,
7.27 Huram also made ten **bronze** carts;
7.30 Each cart had four **bronze** wheels with bronze axles.
7.30 At the four corners were **bronze** supports for a basin;
7.33 their axles, rims, spokes, and hubs were all of **bronze.**
7.40 The four hundred **bronze** pomegranates, in two
7.40 Temple, which Huram made for King Solomon, was of polished **bronze.**
7.47 Solomon did not have these **bronze** objects weighed,
8.64 He did this because the **bronze** altar was too small for all
14.27 replace them, King Rehoboam made **bronze** shields and
2 Kgs 16.14 The **bronze** altar dedicated to the Lord was between the
16.15 But keep the **bronze** altar for me to use for divination."
16.17 King Ahaz took apart the **bronze** carts used in the
16.17 he also took the **bronze** tank from the backs
16.17 the backs of the twelve **bronze** bulls,
18. 4 also broke in pieces the **bronze** snake that Moses had made,
25.13 Babylonians broke in pieces the **bronze** columns and the carts
25.13 Temple, together with the large **bronze** tank,
25.13 and they took all the **bronze** to Babylon.
25.14 all the other **bronze** articles used in the temple service.
25.16 The **bronze** objects that King Solomon had made for the
25.17 metres high, with a **bronze** capital on top, 1.3 metres high.
25.17 bronze grating decorated with pomegranates made of **bronze.**
1 Chr 18. 8 took a great quantity of **bronze** from Tibhath and Kun, cities
18. 8 (Solomon later used this **bronze** to make the tank,
18. 8 the columns, and the **bronze** utensils for the Temple.)
18.10 Joram brought David presents made of gold, silver, and **bronze.**
22. 3 wooden gates, and so much **bronze** that no one could weigh it.
22.14 Besides that, there is an unlimited supply of **bronze** and iron.
22.16 of every sort who can work [16] with gold, silver, **bronze,**
29. 2 Temple—gold, silver, **bronze,** iron, timber, precious stones and gems,
29. 7 almost 620 metric tons of **bronze,** and more than 3,400 metric
2 Chr 1. 5 The **bronze** altar which had been made by Bezalel, the son
1. 6 the Lord by offering sacrifices on the **bronze** altar;
2. 7 working gold, silver, **bronze,** and iron, and in making blue,
2.14 to make things out of gold, silver, **bronze,** iron, stone, and
3.16 of interwoven chains and one hundred **bronze** pomegranates.
4. 1 King Solomon had a **bronze** altar made, which was nine
4. 2 made a round tank of **bronze,** 2.2 metres deep, 4.4 metres in
4. 4 on the backs of twelve **bronze** bulls that faced outwards,
4. 9 The doors in the gates between the courtyards were covered with **bronze.**
4.11 The four hundred **bronze** pomegranates arranged
4.11 out of polished **bronze,** as King Solomon had commanded,
4.18 that no one determined the total weight of the **bronze** used.
6.13 (Solomon had made a **bronze** platform and put it in the
7. 7 He did this because the **bronze** altar which he had made was
12.10 To replace them, Rehoboam made **bronze** shields and
Ezra 8.26 20 gold bowls - 8.4 kilogrammes 2 fine **bronze** bowls,
Job 6.12 Is my body **bronze?**
20.24 from an iron sword, a **bronze** bow will shoot him down.
40.18 bones are as strong as **bronze,** and his legs are like iron
41.27 is as flimsy as straw, and **bronze** as soft as rotten wood.
Ps 107.16 He breaks down doors of **bronze** and smashes iron bars.
Song 5.11 His face is **bronzed** and smooth;
Is 45. 2 I will break down **bronze** gates and smash their iron bars.
48. 4 to be stubborn, as rigid as iron and unyielding as **bronze.**
60.17 gold instead of **bronze,** Silver and bronze instead of iron
Jer 1.18 be like a fortified city, an iron pillar, and a **bronze** wall.
6.28 They are all stubborn rebels, hard as **bronze** and iron.
15.12 the iron from the north that is mixed with **bronze.)**
15.20 make you like a solid **bronze** wall as far as they are
27.19 he left the columns, the **bronze** tank, the carts, and some of
52.17 Babylonians broke in pieces the **bronze** columns and the carts
52.17 Temple, together with the large **bronze** tank,
52.17 and they took all the **bronze** to Babylon.
52.18 all the other **bronze** articles used in the temple service.
52.20 The **bronze** objects that King Solomon had made for the
52.21 of each column was a **bronze** capital 2.2 metres high, and all
52.21 with pomegranates, all of which was also made of **bronze.**
Ezek 1. 4 Where the lightning was flashing, something shone like **bronze.**
1. 7 They shone like polished **bronze.**
1.27 seemed to be shining like **bronze** in the middle of a fire.
8. 2 and from the waist up he was shining like polished **bronze.**
9. 2 They all came and stood by the **bronze** altar.
24.11 Now set the empty **bronze** pot on the coals and let it
27.13 Meshech and traded your goods for slaves and for articles of **bronze.**
40. 3 took me closer, and I saw a man who shone like **bronze.**
Dan 2.32 its waist and hips of **bronze;**
2.35 the iron, clay, **bronze,** silver, and gold crumbled

Dan 2.39 third, an empire of **bronze,** which will rule the whole earth.
2.45 it struck the statue made of iron, **bronze,** clay, silver, and
4.15 in the ground with a band of iron and **bronze** round it.
4.23 a band of iron and **bronze** round it, and leave it there
5. 4 and praised gods made of gold, silver, **bronze,** iron, wood,
5.23 gods made of gold, silver, **bronze,** iron, wood, and
7.19 crushed its victims with its **bronze** claws and iron teeth and
10. 6 and legs shone like polished **bronze,** and his voice sounded
Mic 4.13 you as strong as a bull with iron horns and **bronze** hoofs.
Zech 6. 1 I saw four chariots coming out from between two **bronze** mountains.
Jn 3.14 As Moses lifted up the **bronze** snake on a pole
Rev 9.20 idols of gold, silver, **bronze,** stone, and wood, which cannot see,
18.12 made of ivory and of expensive wood, of **bronze,** iron, and

BROOK

Josh 11. 5 and set up camp at Merom **Brook** to fight against Israel.
11. 7 Joshua and all his men attacked them by surprise at Merom **Brook.**
1 Sam 30. 9 when they arrived at the **brook** of Besor, some of them stayed
30.10 men were too tired to cross the **brook** and so stayed behind.
30.21 go with him and had stayed behind at the **brook** of Besor.
2 Sam 15.23 The king crossed the **brook** of Kidron, followed by his men,
1 Kgs 2.37 leave and go beyond the **brook** of Kidron, you will certainly
17. 3 hide yourself near the **brook** of Cherith, east of the Jordan.
17. 4 The **brook** will supply you with water to drink, and I have
17. 5 Lord's command, and went and stayed by the **brook** of Cherith.
17. 6 He drank water from the **brook,** and ravens brought him
17. 7 After a while the **brook** dried up because of the lack of
Song 4.15 water, **brooks** gushing down from the Lebanon Mountains.
5.12 as doves by a flowing **brook,** doves washed in milk and
Is 8. 6 the quiet waters from the **brook** of Shiloah, and tremble
15. 6 The **brook** of Nimrim is dry, the grass beside it has withered,
Jer 31.40 all the fields above the **brook** of Kidron as far as the
48.34 Even the **brook** of Nimrim has dried up.
Ezek 36. 4 mountains and hills, to you **brooks** and valleys, to you
36. 6 hills, **brooks,** and valleys what I, the Sovereign Lord,
Amos 6.14 in the north to the **brook** of the Arabah in the south."
Jn 18. 1 left with his disciples and went across the **brook** called Kidron.

BROOM

Is 14.23 I will sweep Babylon with a **broom** that will sweep everything away.

BROOM-TREE

Job 30. 4 and ate them, even the tasteless roots of the **broom-tree!**

BROTH

Judg 6.19 in a basket and the **broth** in a pot, brought them to
6.20 and the bread on this rock, and pour the **broth** over them."
Is 65. 4 They eat pork and drink **broth** made from meat offered in
Ezek 24.10 Boil away the **broth!**

BROTHER

[FULL-BROTHER]

Gen 4. 8 Then Cain said to his **brother** Abel, "Let's go out
4. 8 in the fields, Cain turned on his **brother** and killed him.
4. 9 The Lord asked Cain, "Where is your **brother** Abel?"
4. 9 Am I supposed to take care of my **brother?"**
4.10 Your **brother's** blood is crying out to me from the ground,
4.11 It has soaked up your **brother's** blood as if it had opened
4.21 His **brother** was Jubal, the ancestor of all musicians who
9.22 his father was naked, he went out and told his two **brothers.**
9.25 He will be a slave to his **brothers.**
10.21 Shem, the elder **brother** of Japheth, was the ancestor of
14.13 Mamre and his **brothers** Eshcol and Aner were Abram's allies.
20.13 are to me by telling everyone that I am your **brother.' "**
20.16 Sarah, "I am giving your **brother** a thousand pieces of
22.20 Abraham learnt that Milcah had borne eight children to his **brother** Nahor:
22.21 Uz the first-born, Buz his **brother,** Kemuel the father of Aram,
22.23 Milcah bore these eight sons to Nahor, Abraham's **brother.**
24.15 was the son of Abraham's **brother** Nahor and his wife Milcah.
24.29 Now Rebecca had a **brother** named Laban, and he ran
24.53 He also gave expensive gifts to her **brother** and to her mother.
24.55 But Rebecca's **brother** and her mother said, "Let the
27.30 soon as Jacob left, his **brother** Esau came in from hunting.
27.35 Isaac answered, "Your **brother** came and deceived me.
27.40 You will live by your sword, But be your **brother's** slave.
27.42 Jacob and said, "Listen, your **brother** Esau is planning to
27.43 Go at once to my **brother** Laban in Haran, [44]and stay with
27.44 for a while, until your **brother's** anger cools down [45]and
28. 5 Bethuel the Aramean and the **brother** of Rebecca, the mother
32. 3 ahead of him to his **brother** Esau in the country of Edom.
32. 6 said, "We went to your **brother** Esau, and he is already on
32.11 Save me, I pray, from my **brother** Esau.
32.13 Jacob chose from his livestock as a present for his **brother** Esau:
32.17 first servant, "When my **brother** Esau meets you and asks,
33. 3 down to the ground seven times as he approached his **brother.**
33. 9 But Esau said, "I have enough, my **brother;**
34.11 said to Dinah's father and **brothers,** "Do me this favour,
34.25 Simeon and Levi, the **brothers** of Dinah, took their swords,
35. 1 to you when you were running away from your **brother** Esau."
35. 7 to him there when he was running away from his **brother.**
36. 6 Canaan, and went away from his **brother** Jacob to another land.
37. 2 and goats with his **brothers,** the sons of Bilhah and Zilpah,

Gen 37. 2 brought bad reports to his father about what his **brothers** were doing.
37. 4 When his **brothers** saw that their father loved Joseph more
37. 4 loved them, they hated their **brother** so much that they would
37. 5 and when he told his **brothers** about it, they hated him even
37. 8 his **brothers** asked.
37. 9 dream and said to his **brothers,** "I had another dream, in
37.10 think that your mother, your **brothers,** and I are going to
37.11 Joseph's **brothers** were jealous of him, but his father
37.12 One day when Joseph's **brothers** had gone to Shechem to
37.13 Shechem, where your **brothers** are taking care of the flock."
37.14 "Go and see if your **brothers** are safe and if the flock
37.16 "I am looking for my **brothers,** who are taking care of
37.17 So Joseph went after his **brothers** and found them at Dothan.
37.23 Joseph came up to his **brothers,** they ripped off his long
37.26 Judah said to his **brothers,** "What will we gain
37.26 by killing our **brother** and covering up the murder?
37.27 after all, he is our **brother,** our own flesh and blood."
37.27 His **brothers** agreed, [28]and when some Midianite traders came
37.28 the **brothers** pulled Joseph out of the well
37.30 He returned to his **brothers** and said, "The boy is not there!
38. 1 that time Judah left his **brothers** and went to stay with a
38. 8 Then Judah said to Er's **brother** Onan,
38. 8 "Go and sleep with your **brother's** widow.
38. 8 brother, so that your **brother** may have descendants."
38. 9 he had intercourse with his **brother's** widow, he let the
38. 9 ground, so that there would be no children for his **brother.**
38.11 that Shelah would be killed, as his **brothers** had been.
38.29 But he pulled his arm back, and his **brother** was born first.
38.30 Then his **brother** was born with the red thread on his arm,
42. 4 Jacob did not send Joseph's **full-brother** Benjamin with them,
42. 6 So Joseph's **brothers** came and bowed down before him with
42. 7 When Joseph saw his **brothers,** he recognized them, but he
42. 8 Although Joseph recognized his **brothers,** they did not recognize him.
42.11 We are all **brothers.**
42.13 They said, "We were twelve **brothers** in all, sir, sons
42.13 One **brother** is dead, and the youngest is now with our father."
42.15 will never leave unless your youngest **brother** comes here.
42.20 Then you must bring your youngest **brother** to me.
42.21 suffering the consequences of what we did to our **brother;**
42.25 gave orders to fill his **brothers'** packs with corn, to put
42.26 The **brothers** loaded their donkeys with the corn they had bought,
42.28 "My money has been returned to me," he called to his **brothers.**
42.32 We were twelve **brothers** in all, sons of the same father.
42.32 One **brother** is dead, and the youngest is still in Canaan
42.34 Bring your youngest **brother** to me.
42.34 I will give your **brother** back to you, and you can stay
42.38 his **brother** is dead, and he is the only one left.
43. 3 admitted to his presence unless we had our **brother** with us.
43. 4 are willing to send our **brother** with us, we will go and
43. 5 admitted to his presence unless our **brother** was with us."
43. 6 trouble by telling the man that you had another **brother?"**
43. 7 Have you got another **brother?'**
43. 7 know that he would tell us to bring our **brother** with us?"
43.13 Take your **brother** and return at once.
43.14 he will give Benjamin and your other **brother** back to you.
43.15 So the **brothers** took the gifts and twice as much money,
43.17 he was commanded and took the **brothers** to Joseph's house.
43.24 The servant took the **brothers** into the house.
43.29 When Joseph saw his **brother** Benjamin, he said,
43.29 "So this is your youngest **brother,** the one you told me about.
43.30 his heart was full of tender feelings for his **brother.**
43.32 Joseph was served at one table and his **brothers** at another.
43.33 The **brothers** had been seated at table, facing Joseph, in
44. 2 the top of the youngest **brother's** sack, together with the
44. 3 Early in the morning the **brothers** were sent on their way
44.13 The **brothers** tore their clothes in sorrow, loaded their donkeys,
44.14 When Judah and his **brothers** came to Joseph's house, he
44.19 Sir, you asked us, 'Have you got a father or another **brother?'**
44.20 is old and a younger **brother,** born to him in his old
44.20 The boy's **brother** is dead, and he is the only one of
44.23 again unless your youngest **brother** comes with you.'
44.26 the man's presence unless our youngest **brother** is with us.
44.26 We can go only if our youngest **brother** goes also.'
44.33 let him go back with his **brothers.**
45. 1 else was with him when Joseph told his **brothers** who he was.
45. 3 Joseph said to his **brothers,** "I am Joseph.
45. 3 But when his **brothers** heard this, they were so terrified
45. 4 said, "I am your **brother** Joseph, whom you sold into Egypt.
45.14 He threw his arms round his **brother** Benjamin and began to cry;
45.15 Then, still weeping, he embraced each of his **brothers** and kissed them.
45.15 After that, his **brothers** began to talk with him.
45.16 reached the palace that Joseph's **brothers** had come, the king
45.17 said to Joseph, "Tell your **brothers** to load their animals
45.24 He sent his **brothers** off and as they left, he said to
46.31 Then Joseph said to his **brothers** and the rest of his
46.31 tell the king that my **brothers** and all my father's family,
47. 1 So Joseph took five of his **brothers** and went to the king.
47. 1 said, "My father and my **brothers** have come from Canaan
47. 2 He then presented his **brothers** to the king.
47. 5 that your father and your **brothers** have arrived, [6]the land
47.11 settled his father and his **brothers** in Egypt, giving them
47.12 food for his father, his **brothers,** and all the rest of his
48.19 But his younger **brother** will be greater than he, and his
48.22 you and not to your **brothers** that I am giving Shechem, that
49. 5 "Simeon and Levi are **brothers.**
49. 8 "Judah, your **brothers** will praise you.
49. 8 Your **brothers** will bow down before you.
49.26 Joseph, On the brow of the one set apart from his **brothers.**

Gen	50. 8	His family, his **brothers,** and the rest of his father's
	50.14	returned to Egypt with his **brothers** and all who had gone
	50.15	death of their father, Joseph's **brothers** said, "What if
	50.17	'Please forgive the crime your **brothers** committed
	50.18	Then his **brothers** themselves came and bowed down before him.
	50.24	He said to his **brothers,** "I am about to die, but God
Ex	1. 6	course of time Joseph, his **brothers,** and all the rest of
	4.14	angry with Moses and said, "What about your **brother** Aaron,
	7. 1	to the king, and your **brother** Aaron will speak to him as
	28. 1	"Summon your **brother** Aaron and his sons, Nadab, Abihu,
	28. 2	Make priestly garments for your **brother** Aaron, to provide
	28. 4	these priestly garments for your **brother** Aaron and his sons,
	28.41	Put these clothes on your **brother** Aaron and his sons.
	32.27	and kill his **brothers,** his friends, and his neighbours."
	32.29	by killing your sons and **brothers,** so the Lord has given you
Lev	16. 2	He said, "Tell your **brother** Aaron that only at the proper
	18.16	Do not have intercourse with your daughter-in-law [16] or with your **brother's** wife.
	20.21	If a man marries his **brother's** wife, they will die childless.
	20.21	He has done a ritually unclean thing and has disgraced his **brother.**
	21. 2	his mother, father, son, daughter, **brother,** [3] or unmarried
	25.48	One of his **brothers** [49] or his uncle or his cousin or
Num	6. 6	a corpse, not even that of his father, mother, **brother,** or
	27. 9	If he has no daughter, his **brothers** are to inherit it.
	27.10	If he has no **brothers,** his father's brothers are to inherit it.
	27.11	If he has no **brothers** or uncles, then his nearest
	27.13	you will die, as your **brother** Aaron did, [14] because both of
Deut	13. 6	"Even your **brother** or your son or your daughter or the
	25. 5	"If two **brothers** live on the same property and one of
	25. 5	it is the duty of the dead man's **brother** to marry her.
	25. 7	But if the dead man's **brother** does not want to marry her,
	25. 7	leaders and say, 'My husband's **brother** will not do his duty;
	25. 7	he refuses to give his **brother** a descendant among the people
	25. 9	refuses to marry her, [9] his **brother's** widow is to go up to
	25. 9	to the man who refuses to give his **brother** a descendant.'
	28.54	even give any to his **brother** or to the wife he loves
	32.50	on that mountain as your **brother** Aaron died on Mount Hor,
	33. 9	They showed greater loyalty to you Than to parents, **brothers,**
	33.16	of Joseph, Because he was the leader among his **brothers.**
	33.24	be the favourite of his **brothers,** And may his land be rich
Josh	2.13	and mother, my **brothers** and sisters, and all their families!
	2.18	your father and mother, your **brothers,** and all your father's
	6.23	father and mother, her **brothers,** and the rest of her family.
	15.17	Othniel, the son of Caleb's **brother** Kenaz, captured the city,
Judg	1.13	the son of Caleb's younger **brother** Kenaz, captured the city,
	3. 9	This was Othniel, the son of Caleb's younger **brother** Kenaz.
	8.19	Gideon said, "They were my **brothers,** my own mother's sons.
	9. 5	top of a single stone he killed his seventy **brothers,**
	9.21	he was afraid of his **brother** Abimelech, Jotham ran away and
	9.26	came to Shechem with his **brothers,** and the men of Shechem
	9.31	son of Ebed and his **brothers** have come to Shechem, and they
	9.41	Zebul drove Gaal and his **brothers** out of Shechem, so that
	9.56	against his father in killing his seventy **brothers.**
	11. 3	Jephthah fled from his **brothers** and lived in the land of Tob.
	16.31	His **brothers** and the rest of his family came down to
	20.22	"Should we go again into battle against our **brothers** the Benjaminites?"
	20.27	go out to fight our **brothers** the Benjaminites again, or
	21. 6	Israel felt sorry for their **brothers** the Benjaminites and said,
	21.22	If their fathers or **brothers** come to you and protest,
1 Sam	14. 3	Ahijah, the son of Ichabod's **brother** Ahitub, who was the son
	16.13	Samuel took the olive-oil and anointed David in front of his **brothers.**
	17.14	and while the three eldest **brothers** stayed with Saul,
	17.17	of bread, and hurry with them to your **brothers** in the camp.
	17.18	Find out how your **brothers** are getting on and bring back
	17.19	King Saul, your **brothers,** and all the other Israelites
	17.22	battle line, went to his **brothers,** and asked how they were
	17.28	Eliab, David's eldest **brother,** heard David talking to the men.
	20.29	feast in town, and my **brother** ordered me to be there.
	22. 1	When his **brothers** and the rest of the family heard that he
	26. 6	Hittite, and Abishai the **brother** of Joab (their mother was Zeruiah),
	30.23	But David answered, "My **brothers,** you can't do this
2 Sam	1.26	"I grieve for you, my **brother** Jonathan;
	2.22	How could I face your **brother** Joab?"
	3. 8	of your father Saul, his **brothers,** and his friends, and I
	3.27	And so Abner was murdered because he had killed Joab's **brother** Asahel.
	3.30	So Joab and his **brother** Abishai took revenge on Abner
	3.30	for killing their **brother** Asahel in the battle at Gibeon.
	10.10	under the command of his **brother** Abishai, who put them in
	13. 3	man named Jonadab, the son of David's **brother** Shammah.
	13.20	When her **brother** Absalom saw her, he asked, "Has Amnon molested you?
	13.26	"Well, then, will you at least let my **brother** Amnon come?"
	13.32	Jonadab, the son of David's **brother** Shammah, said, "Your Majesty,
	14. 7	them, so that they can kill him for murdering his **brother.**
	16.10	business," the king said to Abishai and his **brother** Joab.
	18. 2	with Joab and Joab's **brother** Abishai and Ittai from Gath,
	19.22	David said to Abishai and his **brother** Joab, "Who asked your opinion?
	19.41	"Your Majesty, why did our **brothers,** the men of Judah,
	20.10	Then Joab and his **brother** Abishai went on after Sheba.
	21.21	and Jonathan, the son of David's **brother** Shammah, killed him.
	23.18	Joab's **brother** Abishai (their mother was Zeruiah) was
	23.24	Asahel, Joab's **brother** Elhanan son of Dodo from Bethlehem
1 Kgs	1.10	not invite his half **brother** Solomon or Nathan the prophet,
	2. 7	kind to me when I was fleeing from your **brother** Absalom.
1 Kgs	2.15	it happened differently, and my **brother** became king, because
	2.21	She answered, "Let your **brother** Adonijah have Abishag as his wife."
	2.22	all, he is my elder **brother,** and Abiathar the priest and
	9.13	to Solomon, "So these, my **brother,** are the towns you have
	12.24	"Do not attack your own **brothers,** the people of Israel.
	13.30	sons mourned over it, saying, "Oh my **brother,** my brother!"
	20.32	He's like a **brother** to me!"
	20.33	and when Ahab said **"brother,"** they took it up at once,
	20.33	and said, "As you say, Benhadad is your **brother!"**
2 Kgs	1.17	had no sons, so his **brother** Joram succeeded him as king in
1 Chr	2. 6	His **brother** Zerah had five sons:
	2.30	Abishur's **brother** Nadab had two sons, Seled and Appaim,
	2.32	Jada, the **brother** of Shammai, had two sons,
	2.42	The eldest son of Caleb, Jerahmeel's **brother,** was named Mesha.
	2.44	Rekem, Shema's **brother,** was the father of Shammai, [45] who
	4.11	Caleb, the **brother** of Shuhah, had a son, Mehir.
	7.34	His **brother** Shomer had three sons:
	7.35	His **brother** Hotham had four sons:
	8.39	Azel's **brother** Eshek had three sons:
	11.20	Joab's **brother** Abishai was the leader of "The Famous Thirty."
	11.26	Asahel, Joab's **brother**
	11.26	Joel **brother** of Nathan
	18.15	Abishai's **brother** Joab was commander of the army;
	19.11	under the command of his **brother** Abishai, who put them in
	20. 5	of Jair killed Lahmi, the **brother** of Goliath from Gath,
	20. 7	and Jonathan, the son of David's **brother** Shammah, killed him.
	24. 2	so their **brothers** Eleazar and Ithamar became priests.
	24.25	Zechariah, a descendant of Uzziel through Isshiah, Micah's **brother;**
	24.31	one of his younger **brothers** drew lots for their assignments,
	26.25	Through Gershom's **brother** Eliezer he was related to Shelomith.
	27. 2	Asahel, **brother** of Joab (his son Zebadiah succeeded him)
	27.16	David's **brothers**
2 Chr	21. 2	Jehoram son of King Jehoshaphat of Judah had six **brothers:**
	21. 4	all his **brothers** killed, and also some Israelite officials.
	21.13	You even murdered your **brothers,** who were better men than you are.
	28.11	These prisoners are your **brothers** and sisters.
	31.12	Levite named Conaniah in charge and made his **brother** Shimei his assistant.
	35. 9	Levites—Conaniah, Shemaiah and his **brother** Nethanel,
	36. 4	Neco made Joahaz' **brother** Eliakim king of Judah and
Ezra	8.18	Mahli, and eighteen of his sons and **brothers** came with him.
	10.18	Clan of Joshua and his **brothers,** sons of Jehozadak:
Neh	1. 2	Hanani, one of my **brothers,** arrived from Judah with a
	5. 7	people and told them, "You are oppressing your **brothers!"**
	5. 8	been buying back our Jewish **brothers** who had to sell
	5. 8	you are forcing your own **brothers** to sell themselves to you,
	7. 2	**brother** Hanani and Hananiah, commanding officer of the fortress.
Job	1.13	their eldest **brother,** [14] a messenger came running to Job.
	19.13	God has made my **brothers** forsake me;
	19.17	smell of my breath, and my own **brothers** won't come near me.
	22. 6	To make your **brother** repay you the money he owed, you took
	42.11	All Job's **brothers** and sisters and former friends came
	42.15	them a share of the inheritance along with their **brothers.**
Ps	35.14	bowed low, [14] as I would pray for a friend or a **brother.**
	50.20	to accuse your own **brothers** and to find fault with them.
	69. 8	a stranger to my **brothers,** like a foreigner to my family.
Prov	17.17	What are **brothers** for if not to share trouble?
	18.19	Help your **brother** and he will protect you like a strong
	18.24	do not last, but some friends are more loyal than **brothers.**
	19. 7	Even the **brothers** of a poor man have no use for him;
	27.10	If you are in trouble, don't ask your **brother** for help;
	27.10	by can help you more than a **brother** who is far away.
Ecc	4. 8	He has no son, no **brother,** yet he is always working, never
Song	1. 6	My **brothers** were angry with me and made me work in the
	8. 1	wish that you were my **brother,** that my mother had nursed you
Is	19. 2	turn **brother** against brother and neighbour against neighbour.
Jer	9. 4	guard against his friend, and no one can trust his **brother;**
	9. 4	for every **brother** is as deceitful as Jacob, and everyone
	12. 6	your **brothers,** members of your own family, have betrayed you;
	35. 3	Habazziniah's son) and all his **brothers** and sons—[4] and brought
Ezek	44.25	one of his children or a **brother** or an unmarried sister.
Hos	12. 3	Jacob struggled with his twin **brother** Esau while the two of
Amos	1.11	They hunted down their **brothers,** the Israelites,
Obad	10	robbed and killed your **brothers,** the descendants of Jacob,
	12	have gloated over the misfortune of your **brothers** in Judah.
Mal	1. 2	answers, "Esau and Jacob were **brothers,** but I have loved
Mt	1. 2	Abraham, Isaac, Jacob, Judah and his **brothers;**
	1. 6	Manasseh, Amon, Josiah, and Jehoiachin and his **brothers.**
	4.18	Lake Galilee, he saw two **brothers** who were fishermen,
	4.18	Simon (called Peter) and his **brother** Andrew, catching fish in
	4.21	and saw two other **brothers,** James and John, the sons of
	5.22	whoever is angry with his **brother** will be brought to trial,
	5.22	whoever calls his **brother** 'You good-for-nothing!'
	5.22	and whoever calls his **brother** a worthless fool
	5.23	there you remember that your **brother** has something against you,
	5.24	and make peace with your **brother,** and then come back and
	7. 3	at the speck in your **brother's** eye, and pay no attention to
	7. 4	dare you say to your **brother,** 'Please, let me take that
	7. 5	to see clearly to take the speck out of your **brother's** eye.
	10. 2	first, Simon (called Peter) and his **brother** Andrew;
	10. 2	James and his **brother** John, the sons of Zebedee;
	10.21	will hand over their own **brothers** to be put to death,
	12.46	still talking to the people when his mother and **brothers** arrived.
	12.47	"Look, your mother and **brothers** are standing outside, and they
	12.48	Who are my **brothers?"**
	12.49	Here are my mother and my **brothers!**
	12.50	wants him to do is my **brother,** my sister, and my mother."
	13.55	and aren't James, Joseph, Simon, and Judas his **brothers?**

Mt 14. 3 He had done this because of Herodias, his **brother** Philip's wife.
17. 1 with him Peter and the **brothers** James and John and led them
18.15 "If your **brother** sins against you, go to him and show
18.15 If he listens to you, you have won your **brother** back.
18.21 and asked, "Lord, if my **brother** keeps on sinning against me,
18.35 of you unless you forgive your **brother** from your heart."
19.29 who has left houses or **brothers** or sisters or father or
20.24 heard about this, they became angry with the two **brothers.**
22.24 has no children dies, his **brother** must marry the widow so
22.25 Now, there were seven **brothers** who used to live here.
22.25 having children, so he left his widow to his **brother.**
22.26 thing happened to the second **brother,** to the third, and finally
23. 8 because you are all **brothers** of one another and have only
25.40 the least important of these **brothers** of mine, you did it
28.10 "Go and tell my **brothers** to go to Galilee, and there they
Mk 1.16 Simon and his **brother** Andrew, catching fish with a net.
1.19 and saw two other **brothers,** James and John, the sons of
3.17 James and his **brother** John, the sons of Zebedee
3.31 Then Jesus' mother and **brothers** arrived.
3.32 "Look, your mother and your **brothers** and sisters are outside,
3.33 Who are my **brothers?"**
3.34 Here are my mother and my **brothers!**
3.35 God wants him to do is my **brother,** my sister, my mother."
5.37 go on with him except Peter and James and his **brother** John.
6. 3 son of Mary, and the **brother** of James, Joseph, Judas, and
6.17 married, even though she was the wife of his **brother** Philip.
6.18 "It isn't right for you to be married to your **brother's** wife!"
10.29 anyone who leaves home or **brothers** or sisters or mother or
10.30 a hundred times more houses, **brothers,** sisters, mothers, children
12.19 but no children, that man's **brother** must marry the widow so
12.20 Once there were seven **brothers;**
12.21 thing happened to the third **brother,** [22] and then to the rest:
12.22 all seven **brothers** married the woman and died without having children.
13.12 will hand over their own **brothers** to be put to death,
Lk 3. 1 ruler of Galilee, and his **brother** Philip was ruler of the
3.19 he had married Herodias, his **brother's** wife, and had done many
6.14 Simon (whom he named Peter) and his **brother** Andrew;
6.41 at the speck in your **brother's** eye, but pay no attention to
6.42 to your brother, 'Please, **brother,** let me take that speck out
6.42 to see clearly to take the speck out of your **brother's** eye.
8.19 Jesus' mother and **brothers** came to him, but were unable to
8.20 "Your mother and **brothers** are standing outside and want to
8.21 "My mother and **brothers** are those who hear the word
12.13 "Teacher, tell my **brother** to divide with me the property
14.12 invite your friends or your **brothers** or your relatives or your
14.26 wife and his children, his **brothers** and his sisters, and himself
15.27 'Your **brother** has come back home,' the servant answered,
15.28 "The elder **brother** was so angry that he would not go
15.32 and be happy, because your **brother** was dead, but now he is
16.28 send Lazarus to my father's house, [28] where I have five **brothers.**
16.29 "Abraham said, 'Your **brothers** have Moses and the prophets
16.29 your **brothers** should listen to what they say.'
17. 3 "If your **brother** sins, rebuke him, and if he repents, forgive
18.29 leaves home or wife or **brothers** or parents or children for
20.28 but no children, that man's **brother** must marry the widow so
20.29 Once there were seven **brothers;**
21.16 handed over by your parents, your **brothers,** your relatives,
22.32 And when you turn back to me, you must strengthen your **brothers."**
Jn 1.40 One of them was Andrew, Simon Peter's **brother.**
1.41 At once he found his **brother** Simon and told him,
2.12 Jesus and his mother, **brothers,** and disciples went to Capernaum
6. 8 Andrew, who was Simon Peter's **brother,** said, [9] "There is a boy
7. 3 so Jesus' **brothers** said to him, "Leave this place
7. 5 (Not even his **brothers** believed in him.)
7.10 After his **brothers** had gone to the festival, Jesus also went;
11. 2 it was her **brother** Lazarus who was ill.)
11.19 see Martha and Mary to comfort them over their **brother's** death.
11.21 "If you had been here, Lord, my **brother** would not have died!
11.23 "Your **brother** will rise to life," Jesus told her.
11.32 "if you had been here, my **brother** would not have died!"
20.17 But go to my **brothers** and tell them that I am returning
Acts 1.14 and with Mary the mother of Jesus and with his **brothers.**
1.16 "My **brothers,"** he said, "the scripture had to come true
2.29 "My **brothers,** I must speak to you plainly about our famous
2.37 to Peter and the other apostles, "What shall we do, **brothers?"**
3.17 "And now, my **brothers,** I know that what you and your
6. 3 So then, **brothers,** choose seven men among you who are
7. 2 Stephen answered, **"Brothers** and fathers, listen to me!
7. 9 sons became jealous of their **brother** Joseph and sold him to
7.13 made himself known to his **brothers,** and the king of Egypt
9.17 **"Brother** Saul," he said, "the Lord has sent me—Jesus himself,
12. 2 He had James, the **brother** of John, put to death
13.15 **"Brothers,** we want you to speak to the people if you have
15. 7 stood up and said, "My **brothers,** you know that a long time
15.13 "Listen to me, my **brothers!**
15.23 apostles and the elders, your **brothers,**
15.23 send greetings to all our **brothers** of Gentile birth who live
15.36 go back and visit our **brothers** in every town where we
19.14 Seven **brothers,** who were the sons of a Jewish High Priest
21.20 Then they said, **"Brother** Paul, you can see how many thousands
22.13 came to me, stood by me, and said, **'Brother** Saul, see
Rom 1.13 must remember, my **brothers,** that many times I have planned
7. 1 am about to say, my **brothers,** because all of you know about
7. 4 That is how it is with you, my **brothers.**
8.12 So then, my **brothers,** we have an obligation, but it is
8.29 so that the Son would be the first among many **brothers.**
10. 1 My **brothers,** how I wish with all my heart that my own
11.25 is a secret truth, my **brothers,** which I want you to know,
12. 1 So then, my **brothers,** because of God's great mercy to us
Rom 12.10 one another warmly as Christian **brothers,** and be eager to show
14.10 only vegetables—why do you pass judgement on your **brother?**
14.10 And you who eat anything—why do you despise your **brother?**
14.13 anything that would make your **brother** stumble or fall into sin.
14.15 If you hurt your **brother** because of something you eat,
14.21 or doing anything else that will make your **brother** fall.
15. 2 we should all please our **brothers** for their own good, in
15.14 My **brothers:**
15.30 I urge you, **brothers,** by our Lord Jesus Christ and by
16.11 and to the Christian **brothers** in the family of Narcissus.
16.14 Patrobas, Hermas, and all the other Christian **brothers** with them.
16.16 Greet one another with a **brotherly** kiss.
16.17 I urge you, my **brothers:**
16.23 city treasurer, and our **brother** Quartus send you their greetings.
1 Cor 1. 1 Christ Jesus, and from our **brother** Sosthenes— [2] To the
1.10 to all of you, my **brothers,** to agree in what you say,
1.11 told me quite plainly, my **brothers,** that there are quarrels among
1.26 Now remember what you were, my **brothers,** when God called you.
2. 1 I came to you, my **brothers,** to preach God's secret truth,
3. 1 a matter of fact, my **brothers,** I could not talk to you
4. 6 For your sake, my **brothers,** I have applied all this to
5.11 person who calls himself a **brother** but is immoral or greedy
6. 8 wrong one another and rob one another, even your own **brothers!**
7.24 My **brothers,** each one should remain in fellowship with God
7.29 What I mean, my **brothers,** is this:
8.11 this weak person, your **brother** for whom Christ died, will perish
8.12 sinning against your Christian **brothers** and wounding their weak
8.13 then, if food makes my **brother** sin, I will never eat meat
8.13 again, so as not to make my **brother** fall into sin.
9. 5 apostles and the Lord's **brothers** and Peter, by taking a Christian
10. 1 want you to remember, my **brothers,** what happened to our ancestors
11.33 then, my **brothers,** when you gather together to eat the Lord's
12. 1 I want you to know the truth about them, my **brothers.**
14. 6 I come to you, my **brothers,** what use will I be to
14.20 Do not be like children in your thinking, my **brothers;**
14.26 This is what I mean, my **brothers.**
14.39 then, my **brothers,** set your heart on proclaiming God's message,
15. 1 want to remind you, my **brothers,** of the Good News which I
15.31 My **brothers,** I face death every day!
15.50 What I mean, **brothers,** is that what is made of flesh and
15.58 So then, my dear **brothers,** stand firm and steady.
16.11 for I am expecting him back with the **brothers.**
16.12 Now, about **brother** Apollos.
16.12 visit you with the other **brothers,** but he is not completely
16.15 I beg you, my **brothers,** [16] to follow the leadership of such
16.20 All the **brothers** here send greetings.
16.20 Greet one another with a **brotherly** kiss.
2 Cor 1. 1 God's will, and from our **brother** Timothy— To the church of
1. 8 We want to remind you, **brothers,** of the trouble we had in
2.13 I was deeply worried, because I could not find our **brother** Titus.
8. 1 **brothers,** we want you to know what God's grace has accomplished
8.18 we are sending the **brother** who is highly respected in all
8.22 So we are sending our **brother** with them;
8.23 as for the other **brothers** who are going with him, they
9. 2 "The **brothers** in Achaia," I said, "have been ready to help
9. 3 Now I am sending these **brothers,** so that our boasting
9. 5 was necessary to urge these **brothers** to go to you ahead of
11. 9 **brothers** who came from Macedonia brought me everything I needed.
12.18 Titus to go, and I sent the other Christian **brother** with him.
13.11 And now, my **brothers,** good-bye!
13.12 Greet one another with a **brotherly** kiss.
Gal 1. 2 All the **brothers** who are here join me in sending greetings
1.11 Let me tell you, my **brothers,** that the gospel I preach
1.19 did not see any other apostle except James, the Lord's **brother.**
2.12 arrived there, Peter had been eating with the Gentile **brothers.**
2.13 The other Jewish **brothers** also started acting like cowards
3.15 My **brothers,** I am going to use an everyday example:
4.12 I beg you, my **brothers,** be like me.
4.28 Now, you, my **brothers,** are God's children as a result of
4.31 my **brothers,** we are not the children of a slave-woman
5.11 But as for me, my **brothers,** if I continue to preach that
5.13 As for you, my **brothers,** you were called to be free.
6. 1 My **brothers,** if someone is caught in any kind of wrongdoing,
6.18 grace of our Lord Jesus Christ be with you all, my **brothers.**
Eph 6.21 Tychicus, our dear **brother** and faithful servant in the Lord's
6.23 Christ give to all Christian **brothers** peace and love with faith.
Phil 1.12 want you to know, my **brothers,** that the things that have
1.14 has given most of the **brothers** more confidence in the Lord,
2.25 to send you our **brother** Epaphroditus, who has worked and fought
2.29 Receive him, then, with joy, as a **brother** in the Lord.
3. 1 conclusion, my **brothers,** be joyful in your union with the Lord.
3.13 Of course, my **brothers,** I really do not think that I
3.17 Keep on imitating me, my **brothers.**
4. 1 So then, my **brothers,** how dear you are to me and how
4. 1 This then, dear **brothers,** is how you should stand firm in
4. 8 In conclusion, my **brothers,** fill your minds with those things
4.21 The **brothers** here with me send you their greetings.
Col 1. 1 Christ Jesus, and from our **brother** Timothy— [2] To God's
1. 2 in Colossae, who are our faithful **brothers** in union with Christ:
4. 7 Our dear **brother** Tychicus, who is a faithful worker and
4. 9 Onesimus, that dear and faithful **brother,** who belongs to your
4.15 our best wishes to the **brothers** in Laodicea and to Nympha
4.16 read the letter that the **brothers** in Laodicea will send you.
1 Thes 1. 4 Our **brothers,** we know that God loves you and has chosen
2. 1 Our **brothers,** you yourselves know that our visit to you
2. 9 Surely you remember, our **brothers,** how we worked and toiled!
2.14 Our **brothers,** the same things happened to you that happened

1 Thes	2.17	As for us, **brothers,** when we were separated from you for
	3. 2	while we sent Timothy, our **brother** who works with us for
	3. 7	trouble and suffering we have been encouraged about you, **brothers.**
	4. 1	Finally, our **brothers,** you learnt from us how you should live
	4.10	behaved like this towards all the **brothers** in all Macedonia.
	4.10	So we beg you, our **brothers,** to do even more.
	4.13	Our **brothers,** we want you to know the truth about those
	5. 1	need to write to you, **brothers,** about the times and occasions
	5. 4	But you, **brothers,** are not in the darkness, and the Day
	5.12	We beg you, our **brothers,** to pay proper respect to those
	5.14	urge you, our **brothers,** to warn the idle, encourage the timid,
	5.25	Pray also for us, **brothers.**
	5.26	Greet all the believers with a **brotherly** kiss.
2 Thes	1. 3	Our **brothers,** we must thank God at all times for you.
	2. 1	I beg you, my **brothers,** [2]not to be so easily confused
	2.13	God at all times for you, **brothers,** you whom the Lord loves.
	2.15	So then, our **brothers,** stand firm and hold on to those
	3. 1	Finally, our **brothers,** pray for us, that the Lord's message
	3. 6	Our **brothers,** we command you in the name of our Lord Jesus
	3. 6	to keep away from all **brothers** who are living a lazy life
	3.13	But you, **brothers,** must not get tired of doing good.
	3.15	instead, warn him as a **brother.**
1 Tim	4. 6	give these instructions to the **brothers,** you will be a good
	5. 1	the younger men as your **brothers,** [2]the older women as mothers,
	6. 2	masters must not despise them, for they are their **brothers.**
2 Tim	4.21	send their greetings, and so do all the other Christian **brothers.**
Phlm	1	Christ Jesus, and from our **brother** Timothy— To our
	4	**Brother** Philemon, every time I pray, I mention you and give
	7	Your love, dear **brother,** has brought me great joy and much
	8	be bold enough, as your **brother** in Christ, to order you
	16	he is a dear **brother** in Christ.
	16	both as a slave and as a **brother** in the Lord!
	20	So, my **brother,** please do me this favour for the Lord's sake;
	20	as a **brother** in Christ, cheer me up!
Heb	2.11	That is why Jesus is not ashamed to call them his **brothers.**
	2.12	says to God, "I will tell my **brothers** what you have done;
	2.17	had to become like his **brothers** in every way, in order to
	3. 1	My Christian **brothers,** who also have been called by God!
	10.19	have, then, my **brothers,** complete freedom to go into the Most
	13. 1	Keep on loving one another as Christian **brothers.**
	13.22	I beg you, my **brothers,** to listen patiently to this message
	13.23	you to know that our **brother** Timothy has been let out
	13.24	The **brothers** from Italy send you their greetings.
Jas	1. 2	**brothers,** consider yourselves fortunate when all kinds of trials
	1.16	Do not be deceived, my dear **brothers!**
	1.19	Remember this, my dear **brothers!**
	2. 1	My **brothers,** as believers in our Lord Jesus Christ,
	2. 5	Listen, my dear **brothers!**
	2.14	My **brothers,** what good is it for someone to say that he
	2.15	Suppose there are **brothers** or sisters who need clothes and
	3. 1	My **brothers,** not many of you should become teachers.
	3.10	My **brothers,** this should not happen!
	3.12	A fig-tree, my **brothers,** cannot bear olives;
	4.11	Do not criticize one another, my **brothers.**
	4.11	criticizes a Christian **brother** or judges him, criticizes the Law
	5. 7	Be patient, then, my **brothers,** until the Lord comes.
	5. 9	complain against one another, my **brothers,** so that God will not
	5.10	My **brothers,** remember the prophets who spoke in the name of
	5.12	Above all, my **brothers,** do not use an oath when you make
	5.19	My **brothers,** if one of you wanders away from the truth
1 Pet	3. 8	love one another as **brothers,** and be kind and humble with
	5.12	of Silas, whom I regard as a faithful Christian **brother.**
2 Pet	1. 7	to your godliness add **brotherly** affection;
	1. 7	and to your **brotherly** affection add love.
	1.10	So then, my **brothers,** try even harder to make God's call
	3.15	saved, just as our dear **brother** Paul wrote to you,
1 Jn	2. 9	the light, yet hates his **brother,** is in the darkness to this
	2.10	Whoever loves his **brother** lives in the light, and so
	2.11	But whoever hates his **brother** is in the darkness;
	3.10	or does not love his **brother** is not God's child.
	3.12	belonged to the Evil One and murdered his own **brother** Abel.
	3.12	did were wrong, but the things his **brother** did were right.
	3.13	do not be surprised, my **brothers,** if the people of the world
	3.14	we know it because we love our **brothers.**
	3.15	Whoever hates his **brother** is a murderer, and you know that
	3.16	We too, then, ought to give our lives for our **brothers!**
	3.17	a rich person sees his **brother** in need, yet
	3.17	closes his heart against his **brother,** how can he claim that
	4.20	says he loves God, but hates his **brother,** he is a liar.
	4.20	seen, if he does not love his **brother,** whom he has seen.
	4.21	whoever loves God must love his **brother** also.
	5.16	If you see your **brother** commit a sin that does not lead
3 Jn	3	so happy when some Christian **brothers** arrived and told me how
	10	will not receive the Christian **brothers** when they come, and even
Jude	1	servant of Jesus Christ, and **brother** of James— To those who
Rev	1. 9	I am John, your **brother,** and as a follower of Jesus I
	6.11	number of their fellow-servants and **brothers** had been killed,
	12.10	our God and accused our **brothers** day and night has been
	12.11	Our **brothers** won the victory over him by the blood of
	19.10	of yours and of your **brothers,** all those who hold to the
	22. 9	of yours and of your **brothers** the prophets and of all those

BROTHER-IN-LAW

Num	10.29	Moses said to his **brother-in-law** Hobab son of Jethro the Midianite,
Judg	4.11	Kenites, the descendants of Hobab, the **brother-in-law** of Moses.

BROUGHT ABOUT see BRING

BROW

Gen	49.26	head of Joseph, On the **brow** of the one set apart from

BROWN

Amos	1. 2	The pastures dry up, and the grass on Mount Carmel turns **brown."**
Nah	1. 4	Mount Carmel turns **brown,** and the flowers of Lebanon fade.

BRUISE

Ex	21.25	burn for burn, wound for wound, **bruise** for bruise.
Lev	22.24	any animal whose testicles have been crushed, cut, **bruised,**
Job	9.17	storms to batter and **bruise** me without any reason at all.
Prov	23.29	bloodshot, and he has **bruises** that could have been avoided.
Song	5. 7	they struck me and **bruised** me;
Is	1. 6	You are covered with **bruises** and sores and open wounds.
	28.28	it by driving a cart over it without **bruising** the grains.

BRUSH see THORN

BRUSH

Ex	29. 2	it, and some in the form of biscuits **brushed** with oil.
Lev	2. 4	mixed with olive-oil or biscuits **brushed** with olive-oil.
	7.12	mixed with olive-oil or biscuits **brushed** with olive-oil or
Num	6.15	mixed with olive-oil and biscuits **brushed** with olive-oil,

BRUTAL

Ezek	21.31	And I will hand you over to **brutal** men, experts at destruction.

BRUTE

Ps	10.10	**brute** strength has defeated them.

BUBBLE

Job	41.31	like boiling water and makes it **bubble** like a pot of oil.

BUCKET

Mt	13.48	good ones go into their **buckets,** the worthless ones are thrown
Jn	4.11	said, "you haven't got a **bucket,** and the well is deep.

BUCKLE

1 Sam	25.13	**"Buckle** on your swords!"
	25.13	David also **buckled** on his sword and left with about four
Ps	45. 3	**Buckle** on your sword, mighty king;

BUD

Ex	9.31	because the barley was ripe, and the flax was **budding.**
	25.31	its decorative flowers, including **buds** and petals, are to
	25.33	flowers shaped like almond blossoms with **buds** and petals.
	25.34	flowers shaped like almond blossoms with **buds** and petals.
	25.35	There is to be one **bud** below each of the three pairs
	25.36	The **buds,** the branches, and the lamp-stand are to be a
	37.17	including **buds** and petals, formed one piece with it.
	37.19	flowers shaped like almond blossoms with **buds** and petals.
	37.20	flowers shaped like almond blossoms with **buds** and petals.
	37.21	There was one **bud** below each of the three pairs of branches.
	37.22	The **buds,** the branches, and the lamp-stand were a single
Num	17. 8	It had **budded,** blossomed, and produced ripe almonds!
Is	27. 6	will take root like a tree, and they will blossom and **bud.**

BUGLE

Neh	4.18	who was to sound the alarm on the **bugle** stayed with me.
	4.20	If you hear the **bugle,** gather round me.
Is	18. 3	Listen for the blowing of the **bugle!**
1 Cor	14. 8	the man who plays the **bugle** does not sound a clear call,

BUILD
[WELL-BUILT]

Gen	4.17	Then Cain **built** a city and named it after his son.
	6.14	**Build** a boat for yourself out of good timber;
	6.16	**Build** it with three decks and put a door in the side.
	8.20	Noah **built** an altar to the Lord;
	10.11	he went to Assyria and **built** the cities of Nineveh, Rehoboth
	11. 3	So they had bricks to **build** with and tar to hold them
	11. 4	They said, "Now let's **build** a city with a tower that
	11. 5	tower which those men had **built,** [6]and he said, "Now then,
	11. 8	them all over the earth, and they stopped **building** the city.
	12. 7	Then Abram **built** an altar there to the Lord, who had
	12. 8	There also he **built** an altar and worshipped the Lord.
	13. 4	and Ai where he had camped before [4]and had **built** an altar.
	13.18	Mamre at Hebron, and there he **built** an altar to the Lord.
	22. 9	had told him about, Abraham **built** an altar and arranged the
	26.25	Isaac **built** an altar there and worshipped the Lord.
	30.40	In this way he **built** up his own flock and kept it
	33.17	went to Sukkoth, where he **built** a house for himself and
	35. 1	**Build** an altar there to me, the God who appeared to you
	35. 3	to Bethel, where I will **build** an altar to the God who
	35. 7	He **built** an altar there and named the place after the God
	39. 6	Joseph was **well-built** and good-looking, [7]and after a while
Ex	1.11	The Israelites **built** the cities of Pithom and Rameses to
	1.13	them work on their **building** projects and in their fields,

Ex 15.17 for your home, the Temple that you yourself have **built.**
17.15 Moses **built** an altar and named it "The Lord is my Banner."
20.25 stone for me, do not **build** it out of cut stones, because
20.26 Do not **build** an altar for me with steps leading up to
24. 4 Early the next morning he **built** an altar at the foot of
32. 5 Then Aaron **built** an altar in front of the gold bull and
36. 1 to make everything needed to **build** the sacred Tent, are to
Num 23. 1 He said to Balak, **"Build** seven altars here for me, and
23. 4 said to him, "I have **built** the seven altars and offered a
23.14 There also he **built** seven altars and offered a bull and a
23.29 Balaam said to him, **"Build** seven altars for me here and
32.16 said, "First, allow us to **build** stone enclosures here for
32.24 So **build** your towns and the enclosures for your sheep,
Deut 6.10 with large and prosperous cities which you did not **build.**
8.12 want to eat and have **built** good houses to live in [13] and
20. 5 man here who has just **built** a house, but has not yet
22. 8 "When you **build** a new house, be sure to put a railing
27. 5 **Build** an altar there made of stones that have had no iron
27. 6 them, [6] because any altar you **build** for the Lord your God
28.30 You will **build** a house—but never live in it.
Josh 2.15 Rahab lived in a house **built** into the city wall, so she
6.26 Whoever **builds** the gates will lose his youngest."
8.30 Then Joshua **built** on Mount Ebal an altar to the Lord,
11.13 burn any of the cities **built** on mounds, except Hazor, which
22.10 side of the Jordan, they **built** a large, impressive altar
22.11 Gad, and East Manasseh have **built** an altar at Geliloth, on
22.16 You have rebelled against the Lord by **building** this altar for yourselves!
22.19 rebels out of us by **building** an altar in addition to the
22.23 we disobeyed the Lord and **built** our own altar to burn
22.26 So we **built** an altar, not to burn sacrifices or make offerings,
22.29 stop following him now by **building** an altar to burn
22.29 We would not **build** any other altar than the altar of the
24.13 you had never cultivated and cities that you had not **built.**
Judg 1.26 the land of the Hittites, **built** a city there, and named it
6.24 Gideon **built** an altar to the Lord there and named it
6.26 **Build** a well-constructed altar to the Lord your God on
6.28 bull had been burnt on the altar that had been **built** there.
21. 4 the next morning the people **built** an altar there, offered
1 Sam 2. 8 on them he has **built** the world.
7.17 In Ramah he **built** an altar to the Lord.
14.35 Saul **built** an altar to the Lord,
14.35 the first one that he **built.**
15.12 of Carmel, where he had **built** a monument to himself, and
2 Sam 5. 9 He **built** the city round it, starting at the place where land
5.11 logs and with carpenters and stone-masons to **build** a palace.
7. 2 am living in a house **built** of cedar, but God's Covenant Box
7. 5 are not the one to **build** a temple for me to live
7. 7 why they had not **built** me a temple made of cedar.'
7.13 will be the one to **build** a temple for me, and I
18.18 During his lifetime Absalom had **built** a monument for
20.15 They **built** ramps of earth against the outer wall and also
24.18 "Go up to Araunah's threshing-place and **build** an altar to the Lord."
24.21 "To buy your threshing-place and **build** an altar for the Lord,
24.25 Then he **built** an altar to the Lord and offered
1 Kgs 2.36 Shimei and said to him, **"Build** a house for yourself here in
3. 1 City until he had finished **building** his palace, the Temple,
3. 2 temple had not yet been **built** for the Lord, and so the
5. 3 round him, he could not **build** a temple for the worship of
5. 5 I will make king after you, will **build** a temple for me.'
5. 5 I have now decided to **build** that temple for the worship of
5.18 Byblos prepared the stones and the timber to **build** the Temple.
6. 5 Temple, a three-storied annexe was **built,**
6. 6 rest on the wall without having their beams **built** into it.
6. 7 which the Temple was **built** had been prepared at the quarry,
6. 7 or any other iron tools as the Temple was being **built.**
6. 9 So King Solomon finished **building** the Temple.
6.10 storey 2.2 metres high, was **built** against the outside walls
6.13 Temple that you are **building,** and I will never abandon them."
6.14 So Solomon finished **building** the Temple.
6.16 the Most Holy Place, was **built** in the rear of the Temple.
6.19 Temple an inner room was **built,** where the Lord's Covenant
6.36 An inner court was **built** in front of the Temple,
6.38 It had taken Solomon seven years to **build** it.
7. 1 Solomon also **built** a palace for himself, and it took him
7. 8 He also **built** the same kind of house for his wife, the
8.13 Now I have **built** a majestic temple for you, a place for
8.16 which a temple should be **built** where I would be worshipped.
8.17 "My father David planned to **build** a temple for the worship
8.18 were right in wanting to **build** a temple for me,
8.19 but you will never **build** it.
8.19 It is your son, your own son, who will **build** my temple.'
8.20 of Israel, and I have **built** the Temple for the worship of
8.27 so how can this Temple that I have **built** be large enough?
8.43 that this Temple I have **built** is the place where you are
8.44 Temple which I have **built** for you, [45] listen to their prayers.
8.48 this Temple which I have **built** for you, [49] then listen to
9. 1 After King Solomon had finished **building** the Temple and
9. 1 else he wanted to **build,** [2] the Lord appeared to him again,
9. 3 this Temple which you have **built** as the place where I shall
9.10 It took Solomon twenty years to **build** the Temple and his palace.
9.15 Solomon used forced labour to **build** the Temple and the palace,
9.15 the east side of the city, and to **build** the city wall.
9.19 everything else he wanted to **build** in Jerusalem, in Lebanon,
9.23 labour working on Solomon's various **building** projects.
9.24 from David's City to the palace Solomon **built** for her.
9.25 fellowship-offerings on the altar he had **built** to the Lord.
9.25 And so he finished **building** the Temple.
9.26 King Solomon also **built** a fleet of ships at Eziongeber,
10. 4 Sheba heard Solomon's wisdom and saw the palace he had **built.**
1 Kgs 10.12 Solomon used the wood to **build** railings in the Temple
10.26 Solomon **built** up a force of fourteen hundred chariots
11. 7 east of Jerusalem he **built** a place to worship Chemosh,
11. 8 He also **built** places of worship where all his foreign
12.31 Jeroboam also **built** places of worship on hilltops, and
12.32 Bethel the priests serving at the places of worship he had **built.**
13.33 from ordinary families to serve at the altars he had **built.**
14.23 They **built** places of worship for false gods, and put up
16.24 Omri fortified the hill, **built** a town there, and named it Samaria,
16.32 He **built** a temple to Baal in Samaria, made an altar for
16.34 Jericho, and his youngest son Segub when he **built** the gates.
18.26 and kept dancing round the altar they had **built.**
20.22 and said, "Go back and **build** up your forces, and make
22.39 and all the cities he **built,** is recorded in The History of
22.48 King Jehoshaphat **built** ocean-going ships to sail to the
2 Kgs 4.10 Let's **build** a small room on the roof, put a bed, a
6. 2 down some trees, so that we can **build** a place to live."
12.20 killed him at the house **built** on the land that was filled
15.35 It was Jotham who **built** the North Gate of the Temple.
16.11 So Uriah **built** an altar just like it, and finished it
17. 9 They **built** pagan places of worship in all their towns, from
17.29 placed them in the shrines that the Israelites had **built.**
19.32 near the city, and no siege-mounds will be **built** round it.
20.20 an account of how he **built** a reservoir and dug a tunnel
21. 3 he **built** altars for the worship of Baal and made an image
21. 4 He **built** pagan altars in the Temple, the place that the
21. 5 courtyards of the Temple he **built** altars for the worship of
23. 8 near the gate **built** by Joshua, the city governor,
23.12 the kings of Judah had **built** on the palace roof above King
23.13 altars that King Solomon had **built** east of Jerusalem, south
23.15 Bethel which had been **built** by King Jeroboam son of Nebat,
23.19 of worship which had been **built** by the kings of Israel, who
25. 1 up camp outside the city, **built** siege walls round it, [2] and
1 Chr 6.10 the Temple which King Solomon **built** in Jerusalem),
6.32 Lord's presence during the time before King Solomon **built** the Temple.
7.24 She **built** the towns of Upper and Lower Beth Horon, and Uzzen
8.12 It was Shemed who **built** the cities of Ono and Lod and
14. 1 logs and with stone-masons and carpenters to **build** a palace.
15. 1 For his own use, David **built** houses in David's City.
17. 1 am living in a house **built** of cedar, but the Lord's Covenant
17. 4 are not the one to **build** a temple for me to live
17. 6 why they had not **built** me a temple made of cedar.'
17.12 will be the one to **build** a temple for me, and I
21.18 command David to go and **build** an altar to the Lord at
21.22 threshing-place, so that I can **build** an altar to the Lord,
21.26 He **built** an altar to the Lord there and offered
22. 2 Some of them prepared stone blocks for **building** the Temple.
22. 5 son Solomon is to **build** must be splendid and world-famous.
22. 6 Solomon and commanded him to **build** a temple for the Lord,
22. 7 "My son, I wanted to **build** a temple to honour the Lord
22. 8 have caused, he would not let me **build** a temple for him.
22.10 He will **build** a temple for me.
22.11 promise to make you successful in **building** a temple for him.
22.14 over 34,000 metric tons of silver to be used in **building** it.
22.19 Start **building** the Temple, so that you can place in it the
28. 2 I wanted to **build** a permanent home for the Covenant Box, the
28. 2 I have made preparations for **building** a temple to honour him,
28. 6 me, 'Your son Solomon is the one who will **build** my Temple.
28.10 that the Lord has chosen you to **build** his holy Temple.
29.16 together all this wealth to **build** a temple to honour your
29.19 that you command and to **build** the Temple for which I have
2 Chr 1.14 He **built** up a force of fourteen hundred chariots and
2. 1 King Solomon decided to **build** a temple where the Lord
2. 1 would be worshipped, and also to **build** a palace for himself.
2. 3 King David, when you sold him cedar logs for **building** his palace.
2. 4 I am **building** a temple to honour the Lord my God.
2. 5 I intend to **build** a great temple, because our God is
2. 6 Yet no one can really **build** a temple for God, because even
2. 6 How then can I **build** a temple that would be anything more
2. 9 this temple I intend to **build** will be large and magnificent.
2.12 skill, who now plans to **build** a temple for the Lord and
3. 3 The Temple which King Solomon **built** was twenty-seven
6. 2 Now I have **built** a majestic temple for you, a place for
6. 5 Israel as the place to **build** a temple where I would be
6. 7 "My father David planned to **build** a temple for the worship
6. 8 were right in wanting to **build** a temple for me,
6. 9 but you will never **build** it.
6. 9 It is your son, your own son, who will **build** my temple.'
6.10 of Israel, and I have **built** a temple for the worship of
6.18 so how can this Temple that I have **built** be large enough?
6.33 that this Temple I have **built** is where you are to be
6.34 Temple which I have **built** for you, [35] listen to their prayers.
6.38 this Temple which I have **built** for you, [39] then listen to
8. 1 It took Solomon twenty years to **build** the Temple and his palace.
8. 6 out all his plans for **building** in Jerusalem, in Lebanon, and
8.10 the forced labour working on the various **building** projects.
8.11 of Egypt, from David's City to a house he **built** for her.
8.12 on the altar which he had **built** in front of the Temple.
9. 3 Sheba heard Solomon's wisdom and saw the palace he had **built.**
11. 5 in Jerusalem and had fortifications **built** for the following
14. 6 He **built** fortifications for the cities of Judah during this time,
14. 7 us fortify the cities by **building** walls and towers, and
14. 7 And so they **built** and prospered.
16.14 body for burial, and they **built** a huge bonfire to mourn his
17.12 Throughout Judah he **built** fortifications and cities,
20. 8 have lived here and have **built** a temple to honour you,
20.36 At the port of Eziongeber they **built** ocean-going ships.
20.37 with Ahaziah, the Lord will destroy what you have **built."**
21.11 He even **built** pagan places of worship in the Judaean
26. 6 Gath, Jamnia, and Ashdod, and **built** fortified cities near

2 Chr 26. 9 of Jerusalem by **building** towers at the Corner Gate,
26.10 He also **built** fortified towers in the open country and
27. 3 It was Jotham who **built** the North Gate of the Temple and
27. 4 the mountains of Judah he **built** cities,
27. 4 and in the forests he **built** forts and towers.
28.25 and town in Judah, he **built** pagan places of worship, where
32. 5 the wall, building towers on it, and **building** an outer wall.
32. 5 addition, he repaired the defences **built** on the land that
32.27 He had storerooms **built** for his gold, silver, precious stones,
32.28 In addition, he had storehouses **built** for his corn,
32.29 cattle and so much other wealth that he **built** many cities.
33. 3 He **built** altars for the worship of Baal, made images of the
33. 4 He **built** pagan altars in the Temple, the place that the
33. 5 courtyards of the Temple he **built** altars for the worship of
35. 3 Box in the Temple that King Solomon, the son of David, **built.**
36.23 given me the responsibility of **building** a temple for him in
Ezra 1. 2 given me the responsibility of **building** a temple for him in
4. 2 clans and said, "Let us join you in **building** the Temple.
4. 3 don't need your help to **build** a temple for the Lord our
4. 3 We will **build** it ourselves, just as Cyrus, emperor of Persia,
4. 4 and frighten the Jews and keep them from **building.**
5. 3 "Who gave you orders to **build** this Temple and equip it?"
5. 4 names of all the men who were helping to **build** the Temple.
5.11 the Temple which was originally **built** and equipped many
6. 4 The walls are to be **built** with one layer of wood on
6.14 made good progress with the **building** of the Temple,
Neh 2.20 We are his servants, and we are going to start **building.**
3. 2 The men of Jericho **built** the next section.
3. 2 Zaccur son of Imri **built** the next section.
3. 3 The clan of Hassenaah **built** the Fish Gate.
3. 4 of Uriah and grandson of Hakkoz, **built** the next section.
3. 4 Berechiah and grandson of Meshezabel, **built** the next section.
3. 4 Zadok son of Baana **built** the next section.
3. 5 The men of Tekoa **built** the next section, but the leading
3. 7 men of Gibeon and Mizpah **built** the next section, as far as
3. 8 Uzziel son of Harhaiah, a goldsmith, **built** the next section.
3. 8 Hananiah, a maker of perfumes, **built** the next section,
3. 9 Hur, ruler of half the Jerusalem District, **built** the next section.
3.10 Jedaiah son of Harumaph **built** the next section, which
3.10 Hattush son of Hashabneiah **built** the next section.
3.11 Hasshub son of Pahath Moab **built** both the next section and
3.12 half of the Jerusalem District, **built** the next section.
3.15 the Pool of Shelah he **built** the wall next to the royal
3.16 of half the Bethzur District, **built** the next section, as far
3.17 Rehum son of Bani **built** the next section;
3.17 of half the Keilah District, **built** the next section on
3.18 other half of the Keilah District, **built** the next section;
3.19 of Jeshua, ruler of Mizpah, **built** the next section in front
3.20 Baruch son of Zabbai **built** the next section, as far as
3.21 Uriah and grandson of Hakkoz, **built** the next section, up to
3.22 Priests from the area around Jerusalem **built** the next section;
3.23 Benjamin and Hasshub **built** the next section, which was
3.23 Maaseiah and grandson of Ananiah, **built** the next section,
3.24 Binnui son of Henadad **built** the next section, from
3.25 Palal son of Uzai **built** the next section,
3.25 Pedaiah son of Parosh **built** the next section, to a point on
3.27 The men of Tekoa **built** the next section, their second one,
3.28 A group of priests **built** the next section, going north
3.28 Horse Gate, each one **building** in front of his own house.
3.29 Zadok son of Immer **built** the next section, which was in
3.29 Shecaniah, keeper of the East Gate, **built** the next section.
3.30 son of Zalaph, **built** the next section, their second one.
3.30 Meshullam son of Berechiah **built** the next section, which
3.31 Malchijah, a goldsmith, **built** the next section, as far as the building
3.32 The goldsmiths and the merchants **built** the last section,
4. 2 Can they make **building-stones** out of heaps of burnt rubble?"
4. 3 and he added, "What kind of wall could they ever **build?**
4. 5 their sins, for they have insulted us who are **building."**
4.10 How can we **build** the wall today?"
4.17 Even those who carried **building** materials worked with one
4.18 other, [18]and everyone who was **building** kept a sword
6. 1 heard that we had finished **building** the wall and that there
7. 4 were living in it, and not many houses had been **built** yet.
8. 4 on a wooden platform that had been **built** for the occasion.
8.16 the people got branches and **built** shelters on the flat roofs
8.17 come back from captivity **built** shelters and lived in them.
Esth 5.14 "Why don't you have a gallows **built,** twenty-two metres tall?
5.14 thought this was a good idea, so he had the gallows **built.**
7. 9 went so far as to **build** a gallows at his house so
7.10 Haman was hanged on the gallows that he had **built** for Mordecai.
Job 15.34 men, and fire will destroy the homes **built** by bribery.
20.19 the poor and seized houses someone else had **built.**
27.18 The wicked **build** houses like a spider's web or like the
39.27 for your command to **build** its nest high in the mountains?
Ps 24. 2 He **built** it on the deep waters beneath the earth and laid
78.69 There he **built** his Temple like his home in heaven;
84. 3 Even the sparrows have **built** a nest, and the swallows have
87. 1 The Lord **built** his city on the sacred hill;
104. 3 like a tent [3]and **built** your home on the waters above.
104.17 There the birds **build** their nests;
107.36 people settle there, and they **built** a city to live in.
127. 1 If the Lord does not **build** the house, the work of the
136. 6 he **built** the earth on the deep waters;
Prov 9. 1 Wisdom has **built** her house and made seven pillars for it.
24. 3 Homes are **built** on the foundation of wisdom and understanding.
24.27 Don't **build** your house and establish a home until your
Ecc 2. 4 I **built** myself houses and planted vineyards.
3. 3 the time for tearing down and the time for **building.**
Song 8. 9 If she is a wall, we will **build** her a silver tower.
Is 5. 2 He **built** a tower to guard them, dug a pit for treading
Is 13.21 where desert animals live and where owls **build** their nests.
22.11 order to store water, [11]you **built** a reservoir inside the
25. 2 The palaces which our enemies **built** are gone for ever.
34.15 Owls will **build** their nests, lay eggs, hatch their young,
37.33 near the city, and no siege-mounds will be **built** round it.
38. 8 On the stairway **built** by King Ahaz, the Lord will make the
44.15 With one part he **builds** a fire to warm himself and bake
54.12 I will **build** your towers with rubies, your gates with
54.16 "I create the blacksmith, who **builds** a fire and forges weapons.
57.14 **Build** the road, and make it ready!
58.12 long been in ruins, **building** again on the old foundations.
62.10 out of the city And **build** a road for your returning people!
65.21 People will **build** houses and live in them
66. 1 of house, then, could you **build** for me, what kind of place
Jer 1.10 down, to destroy and to overthrow, to **build** and to plant."
6. 1 trumpet in Tekoa and **build** a signal fire in Beth Haccherem.
6. 6 down trees and **build** mounds in order to besiege Jerusalem.
7.18 children gather firewood, the men **build** fires, and the women
7.31 Valley of Hinnom they have **built** an altar called Topheth, so
18. 9 am going to plant or **build** up any nation or kingdom, [10]but
19. 5 innocent people, [5]and they have **built** altars for Baal in
22.13 Doomed is the man who **builds** his house by injustice and
22.14 man who says, "I will **build** myself a mansion with spacious
22.15 a better king if you **build** houses of cedar, finer than those
24. 6 I will **build** them up and not tear them down;
29. 5 '**Build** houses and settle down.
29.28 a long time and should **build** houses, settle down, plant
31.28 I will take care to plant them and to **build** them up.
32.24 "The Babylonians have **built** siege mounds round the city to capture it,
32.31 have made me angry and furious from the day it was **built.**
32.34 disgusting idols in the Temple **built** for my worship, and
32.35 They have **built** altars to Baal in the Valley of Hinnom,
35. 7 also told us not to **build** houses or farm the land, and
35. 9 We do not **build** houses for homes—we live in
42.10 this land, then I will **build** you up and not tear you
45. 4 tearing down what I have **built** and pulling up what I have
51.26 stones from your ruins will ever be used again for **building.**
51.53 climb to the sky and **build** a strong fortress there, I would
52. 4 up camp outside the city, **built** siege walls round it, [5]and
Ezek 4.12 You are to **build** a fire out of dried human excrement,
11. 3 They say, 'We will soon be **building** houses again.
15. 4 It is only good for **building** a fire.
16.24 side of every road you **built** places to worship idols and
16.31 On every street you **built** places to worship idols and practise prostitution.
17.17 him fight when the Babylonians **build** earthworks and dig
22.21 will gather them in Jerusalem, **build** a fire under them, and
22.30 looked for someone who could **build** a wall, who could stand
26. 8 The enemy will dig trenches, **build** earthworks, and make a
28.26 They will **build** houses and plant vineyards.
31. 6 Every kind of bird **built** nests in its branches;
39. 9 They will **build** fires with the shields, bows, arrows,
40.17 There were thirty rooms **built** against the outer wall, and in
41. 7 rooms, two wide stairways were **built,** so that it was
42. 3 It was **built** on three levels, each one set further back than
43. 8 The kings **built** the thresholds and door-posts of their
43.18 When the altar is **built,** you are to dedicate it by burning
46.23 stone wall round it, with fireplaces **built** against the wall.
48.18 after the city has been **built** in the area immediately to the
Dan 4.12 rested in its shade, birds **built** nests in its branches, and
4.30 I **built** it as my capital city to display my power and
Hos 2. 6 her in with thorn-bushes and **build** a wall to block her way.
8.11 altars the people of Israel **build** for removing sin, the more
8.14 "The people of Israel have **built** palaces, but they
8.14 The people of Judah have **built** fortified cities.
10. 1 The more prosperous they were, the more altars they **built.**
Amos 1. 4 send fire upon the palace **built** by King Hazael and I will
5.11 the fine stone houses you **build** or drink wine from the
7. 7 a wall that had been **built** with the help of a plumb-line,
9. 6 The Lord **builds** his home in the heavens, and over the
Mic 3.10 You are **building** God's city, Jerusalem, on a foundation
Hab 2.12 You founded a city on crime and **built** it up by murder.
2.13 useless labour, and all they have **built** goes up in flames.
Zeph 1.13 in the houses they are **building** or drink wine from the
Hag 1. 4 should you be living in **well-built** houses while my Temple
Zech 4. 9 foundation of the Temple, and he will finish the **building.**
4.10 will see Zerubbabel continuing to **build** the Temple, and they
5.11 "To Babylonia, where they will **build** a temple for it.
6.13 is the one who will **build** it and receive the honour due
9. 3 Tyre has **built** fortifications for herself and has piled up
Mt 5.14 A city **built** on a hill cannot be hidden.
7.24 is like a wise man who **built** his house on rock.
7.25 But it did not fall, because it was **built** on rock.
7.26 is like a foolish man who **built** his house on sand.
16.18 this rock foundation I will **build** my church, and not even
21.33 dug a hole for the winepress, and **built** a watch-tower.
26.61 down God's Temple and three days later **build** it up again.'"
27.40 tear down the Temple and **build** it up again in three days!
Mk 12. 1 dug a hole for the winepress, and **built** a watch-tower.
14.58 after three days I will **build** one that is not made by
15.29 tear down the Temple and **build** it up again in three days!
Lk 4.29 to the top of the hill on which their town was **built.**
6.48 like a man who, in **building** his house, dug deep and laid
6.48 house but could not shake it, because it was well **built.**
6.49 like a man who **built** his house without laying a foundation;
7. 5 He loves our people and he himself **built** a synagogue for us."
11.48 they murdered the prophets, and you **build** their tombs.
12.18 tear down my barns and **build** bigger ones, where I will store
14.28 of you is planning to **build** a tower, he sits down first
14.30 'This man began to **build** but can't finish the job!'

Lk 17.28 eating and drinking, buying and selling, planting and **building.**
Jn 2.19 down this Temple, and in three days I will **build** it again."
2.20 "Are you going to **build** it again in three days?"
2.20 "It has taken forty-six years to **build** this Temple!"
18.18 servants and guards had **built** a charcoal fire and were standing
Acts 7.47 But it was Solomon who **built** him a house.
7.48 the Most High God does not live in houses **built** by men;
7.49 What kind of house would you **build** for me?
20.32 grace, which is able to **build** you up and give you the
Rom 15. 2 their own good, in order to **build** them up in the faith.
15.20 so as not to **build** on a foundation laid by someone
1 Cor 3.10 and laid the foundation, and another man is **building** on it.
3.10 But each one must be careful how he **builds.**
3.12 gold or silver or precious stones in **building** on the foundation;
3.14 If what was **built** on the foundation survives the fire,
8. 1 but love **builds** up.
14.12 greater use of those which help to **build** up the church.
2 Cor 10. 8 has given us—authority to **build** you up, not to tear you
13.10 has given me—authority to **build** you up, not to tear you
Eph 2.20 You, too, are **built** upon the foundation laid by the apostles
2.22 you too are being **built** together with all the others into
4.12 Christian service, in order to **build** up the body of Christ.
4.16 the whole body grows and **builds** itself up through love.
4.29 words, the kind that **build** up and provide what is needed,
6.10 Finally, **build** up your strength in union with the Lord
Col 2. 7 your roots deep in him, **build** your lives on him, and become
Heb 3. 3 A man who **builds** a house receives more honour than the
3. 4 Every house, of course, is **built** by someone—
3. 4 and God is the one who has **built** all things.
8. 5 When he was about to **build** the Covenant Tent, God said
11. 7 He obeyed God and **built** a boat in which he and his
11.10 God has designed and **built,** the city with permanent foundations.
1 Pet 2. 5 let yourselves be used in **building** the spiritual temple,
3.20 waited patiently during the days that Noah was **building** his boat.
Jude 20 my friends, keep on **building** yourselves up on your most sacred
Rev 13.14 The beast told them to **build** an image in honour of
17. 1 that great city that is **built** near many rivers.
21.14 The city's wall was **built** on twelve foundation-stones,

BUILDER

2 Kgs 12.11 the **builders,** [12] the masons, and the stone-cutters,
22. 6 to pay [6] the carpenters, the **builders,** and the masons, and
2 Chr 34.11 to [11] the carpenters and the **builders** to buy the stones and
Ps 118.22 The stone which the **builders** rejected as worthless
127. 1 not build the house, the work of the **builders** is useless;
Ezek 27. 4 Your **builders** made you like a beautiful ship;
Mt 21.42 'The stone which the **builders** rejected as worthless turned out
Mk 12.10 'The stone which the **builders** rejected as worthless turned out
Lk 20.17 'The stone which the **builders** rejected as worthless turned
Acts 4.11 'The stone that you the **builders** despised turned out to be
1 Cor 3.10 the work of an expert **builder** and laid the foundation,
3.14 foundation survives the fire, the **builder** will receive a reward.
1 Pet 2. 7 "The stone which the **builders** rejected as worthless turned out

BUILDING

Judg 16.26 hand, "Let me touch the pillars that hold up the **building.**
16.27 The **building** was crowded with men and women.
16.29 Samson took hold of the two middle pillars holding up the **building.**
16.30 all his might, and the **building** fell down on the five kings
1 Kgs 7. 8 the Hall of Judgement, were made like the other **buildings.**
7. 9 All these **buildings** and the great court were made of fine
1 Chr 9.33 of the temple **buildings** and were free from other duties,
28.11 plans for all the temple **buildings,** for the storerooms and
2 Chr 23. 6 is to enter the temple **buildings** except the priests and the
34.11 timber used to repair the **buildings** that the kings of Judah
Neh 3.31 section, as far as the **building** used by the temple workmen
Is 9.10 They say, [10] "The brick **buildings** have fallen down,
9.10 but we will replace them with stone **buildings.**
Jer 43. 9 the entrance to the government **building** here in the city,
Ezek 40. 2 front of me a group of **buildings** that looked like a city.
41. 5 inner wall of the temple **building,** and it was three metres.
41. 8 Between the terrace and the **buildings** used by the priests
41.12 the Temple there was a **building** forty-five metres long and
41.13 the far side of the **building** to the west, the distance was
41.15 measured the length of the **building** to the west, including
42. 1 and led me to a **building** on the north side of the
42. 1 Temple, not far from the **building** at the west end of the
42. 2 This **building** was fifty metres long and twenty-five metres wide.
42. 4 the north side of this **building** was a passage five metres
42. 5 the upper level of the **building** were narrower than those at
42. 6 by columns like the other **buildings** in the courtyard.
42. 7 outer wall of the **building** was solid for twenty-five metres,
42. 7 level there were rooms in the entire length of the **building.**
42. 9 the east end of the **building,** where the wall of the
42. 9 Temple there was an identical **building**
42. 9 not far from the **building** at the west end of the
42.12 the south side of the **building,** at the east end where the
42.13 The man said to me, "Both these **buildings** are holy.
Zeph 2.14 The cedar-wood of her **buildings** will be stripped away.
Mt 24. 1 came to him to call his attention to its **buildings.**
Mk 13. 1 What wonderful stones and **buildings!"**
13. 2 Jesus answered, "You see these great **buildings?**
1 Cor 3. 9 You are also God's **building.**
Eph 2.21 one who holds the whole **building** together and makes it grow

BUL

1 Kgs 6.38 eighth month, the month of **Bul,** in the eleventh year of

BULL

see also **BULL-CALF**

Gen 32.13 cows and ten **bulls,** twenty female donkeys and ten males.
49. 6 For they killed men in anger And they crippled **bulls** for sport.
Ex 21.28 "If a **bull** gores someone to death, it is to be stoned,
21.29 But if the **bull** had been in the habit of attacking
21.31 If the **bull** kills a boy or a girl, the same rule
21.32 If the **bull** kills a male or female slave, its owner
21.32 pieces of silver, and the **bull** shall be stoned to death.
21.33 not cover it, and a **bull** or a donkey falls into it,
21.35 If one man's **bull** kills another man's bull,
21.35 the two men shall sell the live **bull** and divide the money;
21.36 it was known that the **bull** had been in the habit of
21.36 the other man a live **bull,** but he may keep the dead
29. 1 Take one young **bull** and two rams without any defects.
29. 3 them to me when you sacrifice the **bull** and the two rams.
29.10 "Bring the **bull** to the front of the Tent of my presence
29.11 Kill the **bull** there in my holy presence at the entrance
29.12 Take some of the **bull's** blood and with your finger put
29.14 But burn the **bull's** flesh, its skin, and its intestines
29.36 day you must offer a **bull** as a sacrifice, so that sin
32. 5 in front of the gold **bull** and announced, "Tomorrow there
Lev 1. 3 a burnt-offering, he must bring a **bull** without any defects.
1. 5 He shall kill the **bull** there, and the Aaronite priests
3. 1 it is to be a **bull** or a cow without any defects.
4. 3 he shall present a young **bull** without any defects and
4. 4 He shall bring the **bull** to the entrance of the Tent, put
4. 5 shall take some of the **bull's** blood and carry it into the
4. 8 From this **bull** he shall take all the fat, the fat on
4.14 the community shall bring a young **bull** as a sin-offering.
4.16 shall take some of the **bull's** blood into the Tent, [17] dip
4.20 the same thing with this **bull**
4.20 as he does with the **bull** for the sin-offering,
4.21 Then he shall take the **bull** outside the camp and burn it,
4.21 just as he burns the **bull** offered for his own sin.
8. 2 the anointing oil, the young **bull** for the sin-offering, the
8.14 Then Moses brought the young **bull** for the sin-offering,
8.17 rest of the **bull,** including its skin, flesh, and intestines,
9. 2 to Aaron, "Take a young **bull** and a ram without any defects
9. 2 them to the Lord, the **bull** for a sin-offering and the ram
9. 4 and a **bull** and a ram for a fellowship-offering.
9. 8 killed the young **bull** which was for his own sin-offering.
9.18 He killed the **bull** and the ram as a fellowship-offering
9.19 the fat parts of the **bull** and the ram [20] on top of
16. 3 he has brought a young **bull** for a sin-offering and a ram
16. 6 He shall offer a **bull** as a sacrifice to take away his
16.11 When Aaron sacrifices the **bull** as the sin-offering for
16.14 shall take some of the **bull's** blood and with his finger
16.15 front of the Covenant Box, as he did with the **bull's** blood.
16.18 must take some of the **bull's** blood and some of the goat's
16.27 The **bull** and the goat used for the sin-offering, whose
23.18 present seven one-year-old lambs, one **bull,** and two rams,
Num 7.12 one young **bull,** one ram, and a one-year-old lamb,
7.12 and two **bulls,** five rams, five goats, and five one-year-old
7.84 twelve **bulls,** twelve rams, and twelve one-year-old lambs,
7.84 twenty-four **bulls,** sixty rams, sixty goats,
8. 8 are to take a young **bull** and the required grain-offering of
8. 8 and you are to take another **bull** for the sin-offering.
8.12 shall then put their hands on the heads of the two **bulls;**
15. 3 A **bull,** a ram, a sheep, or a goat may be presented
15. 8 When a **bull** is offered to the Lord as a burnt-offering or
15.11 is what shall be offered with each **bull,** ram, sheep, or
15.24 they are to offer a **bull** as a burnt-offering, a smell that
22. 4 round us, like a **bull** eating the grass in a pasture."
23. 1 here for me, and bring me seven **bulls** and seven rams."
23. 2 he and Balaam offered a **bull** and a ram on each altar.
23. 4 the seven altars and offered a **bull** and a ram on each."
23.14 seven altars and offered a **bull** and a ram on each of
23.29 for me here and bring me seven **bulls** and seven rams."
23.30 was told, and offered a **bull** and a ram on each altar.
28.11 two young **bulls,** one ram, seven one-year-old male lambs, all
28.12 with each **bull,** three kilogrammes of flour;
28.14 litres of wine with each **bull,** one and a half litres with
28.19 two young **bulls,** one ram, and seven one-year-old male lambs,
28.20 kilogrammes with each **bull,** two kilogrammes with the ram,
28.27 two young **bulls,** one ram, and seven one-year-old male lambs,
28.28 kilogrammes with each **bull,** two kilogrammes with the ram,
29. 2 one young **bull,** one ram, and seven one-year-old male lambs,
29. 3 of flour with the **bull,** two kilogrammes with the ram,
29. 8 one young **bull,** one ram, and seven one-year-old male lambs,
29. 9 of flour with the **bull,** two kilogrammes with the ram,
29.13 young **bulls,** two rams, and fourteen one-year-old male lambs,
29.14 of flour with each **bull,** two kilogrammes with each ram,
29.17 second day offer twelve young **bulls,** two rams, and fourteen
29.20 third day offer eleven young **bulls,** two rams, and fourteen
29.23 fourth day offer ten young **bulls,** two rams, and fourteen
29.26 fifth day offer nine young **bulls,** two rams, and fourteen
29.29 sixth day offer eight young **bulls,** two rams, and fourteen
29.32 seventh day offer seven young **bulls,** two rams, and fourteen
29.36 one young **bull,** one ram, and seven one-year-old male lambs,
Deut 33.17 has the strength of a **bull,** The horns of a wild ox.
Judg 6.25 Gideon, "Take your father's **bull** and another bull seven years old,
6.26 Then take the second **bull** and burn it whole as an offering,
6.28 down, and that the second **bull** had been burnt on the altar
1 Sam 1.24 Shiloh, taking along a three-year-old **bull,** ten kilogrammes of flour,
1.25 After they had killed the **bull,** they took the child to Eli.
2 Sam 6.13 offered the Lord a sacrifice of a **bull** and a fattened calf.
1 Kgs 1. 9 of sheep, **bulls,** and fattened calves at Snake Rock,
1.19 a sacrifice of many **bulls,** sheep, and fattened calves,

1 Kgs 1.25 a sacrifice of many **bulls,** sheep, and fattened calves.
7.25 the backs of twelve bronze **bulls** that faced outwards, three
7.29 figures of lions, **bulls,** and winged creatures on the panels;
7.29 the lions and **bulls,** there were spiral figures in relief.
7.40 The tank The twelve **bulls** supporting the tank The pots,
10.19 was the figure of a **bull's** head, and beside each of the
18.23 Bring two **bulls;**
18.23 I will do the same with the other **bull.**
18.25 so many of you, you take a **bull** and prepare it first.
18.26 They took the **bull** that was brought to them, prepared
18.33 on the altar, cut the **bull** in pieces, and laid it on
2 Kgs 16.17 backs of the twelve bronze **bulls,** and placed it on a stone
1 Chr 15.26 They sacrificed seven **bulls** and seven sheep, to make
29.21 addition, they sacrificed a thousand **bulls,** a thousand rams,
2 Chr 4. 3 were in the shape of **bulls,** which had been cast all in
4. 4 the backs of twelve bronze **bulls** that faced outwards, three
4.11 The tank The twelve **bulls** supporting the tank The pots,
13. 9 who comes along with a **bull** or seven sheep can get himself
29.21 the Temple, they took seven **bulls,** seven sheep, seven lambs,
29.22 The priests killed the **bulls** first, then the sheep, and
29.32 They brought seventy **bulls,** a hundred sheep, and two
29.33 they also brought six hundred **bulls** and three thousand
30.24 King Hezekiah contributed a thousand **bulls** and seven
30.24 gave them another thousand **bulls** and ten thousand sheep.
35. 7 sheep, lambs, and young goats, and three thousand **bulls.**
35. 8 and three hundred **bulls** for sacrifices during the festival.
35. 9 young goats and five hundred **bulls** for the Levites to offer
Ezra 6. 9 young **bulls,** sheep, or lambs to be burnt as offerings to the
6.17 dedication they offered a hundred **bulls,** two hundred sheep,
7.17 this money carefully and buy **bulls,** rams, lambs, corn, and
8.35 They offered 12 **bulls** for all Israel, 96 rams, and 77 lambs;
Job 42. 8 Now take seven **bulls** and seven rams to Job and offer them
Ps 22.12 Many enemies surround me like **bulls;**
22.12 all round me, like fierce **bulls** from the land of Bashan.
22.21 I am helpless before these wild **bulls.**
29. 6 like calves and makes Mount Hermon leap like a young **bull.**
50. 9 yet I do not need **bulls** from your farms or goats from
50.13 I eat the flesh of **bulls** or drink the blood of goats?
51.19 and **bulls** will be sacrificed on your altar.
66.15 I will sacrifice **bulls** and goats, and the smoke will go up
68.30 the nations, that herd of **bulls** with their calves, until
69.31 more than sacrificing a full-grown **bull.**
Is 1.11 I am tired of the blood of **bulls** and sheep and goats.
10.13 Like a **bull** I have trampled on the people who live there.
34. 7 like wild oxen and young **bulls,** and the earth will be red
66. 3 them whether they kill a **bull** as a sacrifice or sacrifice a
Jer 34.18 the two halves of a **bull** that they had cut in two.
34.18 I will do to these people what they did to the **bull.**
52.20 large tank, and the twelve **bulls** that supported it—were too
Ezek 1. 7 legs were straight, and they had hoofs like those of a **bull.**
1.10 face at the right, a **bull's** face at the left, and an
10.14 was the face of a **bull,** the second a human face, the
39.18 will be killed like rams or lambs or goats or fat **bulls.**
43.19 will give them a young **bull** to offer as a sacrifice for
43.21 You are to take the **bull** that is offered as a sacrifice
43.22 its blood in the same way as you did with the **bull.**
43.23 doing that, take a young **bull** and a young ram, both of
43.25 to offer a goat, a **bull,** and a ram as sacrifices for
45.18 you are to sacrifice a **bull** without any defects and purify
45.22 ruling prince must offer a **bull** as a sacrifice for his sins
45.23 sacrifice to the Lord seven **bulls** and seven rams without any
45.24 For each **bull** and each ram that is sacrificed, there is
46. 6 he will offer a young **bull,** six lambs, and a ram, all
46. 7 With each **bull** and each ram the offering is to be
46.11 a half litres with each **bull** or ram, and whatever the
Hos 8. 5 I hate the gold **bull** worshipped by the people of the city
8. 6 The gold **bull** worshipped in Samaria will be smashed to pieces!
10. 5 afraid and will mourn the loss of the gold **bull** at Bethel.
12.11 **Bulls** are sacrificed in Gilgal, and the altars there will
13. 2 How can men kiss those idols—idols in the shape of **bulls!**
Mic 4.13 you as strong as a **bull** with iron horns and bronze hoofs.
Acts 7.41 in the shape of a **bull,** offered sacrifice to it, and had
14.13 just outside the town, brought **bulls** and flowers to the gate,
Heb 9.12 take the blood of goats and **bulls** to offer as a sacrifice;
9.13 The blood of goats and **bulls** and the ashes of a burnt
9.19 he took the blood of **bulls** and goats, mixed it with water,
10. 4 For the blood of **bulls** and goats can never take away sins.
Rev 4. 7 the second looked like a **bull;**

BULL-CALF
see also **CALF**

Ex 32. 4 poured the gold into a mould, and made a gold **bull-calf.**
32. 8 they have made a **bull-calf** out of melted gold and have
32.19 the camp to see the **bull-calf** and to see the people dancing,
32.20 He took the **bull-calf** which they had made, melted it,
32.24 I threw the ornaments into the fire and out came this **bull-calf!"**
32.35 because they had caused Aaron to make the gold **bull-calf.**
Deut 9.16 making yourselves a metal idol in the form of a **bull-calf.**
9.21 had made—that metal **bull-calf**—and threw it into the fire.
1 Kgs 12.28 it over, he made two **bull-calves** of gold and said to his
12.29 placed one of the gold **bull-calves** in Bethel and the other
12.32 offered sacrifices to the gold **bull-calves** he had made, and
2 Kgs 10.29 sin of worshipping the gold **bull-calves** he set up in Bethel
17.16 Lord their God and made two metal **bull-calves** to worship;
2 Chr 11.15 demons and the idols he made in the form of **bull-calves.**
13. 8 have with you the gold **bull-calves** that Jeroboam made to be
Neh 9.18 in the shape of a **bull-calf** and said it was the god
Ps 106.19 They made a gold **bull-calf** at Sinai and worshipped that idol;

BULLOCKS

Mt 22. 4 my **bullocks** and prize calves have been butchered,

BUNCH

Num 13.23 a branch which had one **bunch** of grapes on it so heavy
13.24 of Eshcol because of the **bunch** of grapes the Israelites cut
Judg 9. 4 money he hired a **bunch** of worthless scoundrels to join him.
1 Sam 25.18 of roasted grain, a hundred **bunches** of raisins, and two
30.12 and water, [12]some dried figs, and two **bunches** of raisins.
2 Sam 16. 1 loaves of bread, a hundred **bunches** of raisins,
16. 1 a hundred **bunches** of fresh fruit, and a leather
Job 30. 2 They were a **bunch** of worn-out men, too weak to do any
30. 8 A worthless **bunch** of nameless nobodies!
Song 7. 8 me your breasts are like **bunches** of grapes, your breath like

BUNDLE

Ruth 2.15 it up even where the **bundles** are lying, and don't say
2.15 out some corn from the **bundles** and leave it for her to
Ps 129. 7 no one gathers it up or carries it away in **bundles.**
Ezek 12. 3 "Now, mortal man, pack a **bundle** just as a refugee would,
12. 4 is still daylight, pack your **bundle** for exile, so that they
12. 7 That day I packed a **bundle** as a refugee would, and that
Mt 13.30 weeds first, tie them in **bundles** and burn them, and then to
Acts 28. 3 Paul gathered up a **bundle** of sticks and was putting them

BURDEN

Ex 18.22 That will make it easier for you, as they share your **burden.**
2 Sam 19.35 I would only be a **burden** to Your Majesty.
1 Kgs 12. 4 "Your father Solomon treated us harshly and placed heavy **burdens** on us.
12. 4 If you make these **burdens** lighter and make life easier for us,
12. 9 people who are asking me to make their **burdens** lighter?"
12.11 Tell them, 'My father placed heavy **burdens** on you;
12.14 He said, "My father placed heavy **burdens** on you;
2 Chr 10. 4 "Your father placed heavy **burdens** on us.
10. 4 If you make these **burdens** lighter and make life easier for us,
10. 9 people who are asking me to make their **burdens** lighter?"
10.11 Tell them, 'My father placed heavy **burdens** on you;
10.14 He said, "My father placed heavy **burdens** on you;
Neh 4.10 "We grow weak carrying **burdens;**
5.15 before me had been a **burden** to the people and had demanded
5.18 But I knew what heavy **burdens** the people had to bear, so
Job 7.20 Am I so great a **burden** to you?
Ps 38. 4 they are a **burden** too heavy to bear.
66.11 us fall into a trap and placed heavy **burdens** on our backs.
68.19 Praise the Lord, who carries our **burdens** day after day;
81. 6 voice saying, [6]"I took the **burdens** off your backs;
88.15 I am worn out from the **burden** of your punishments.
Ecc 3.10 I know the heavy **burdens** that God has laid on us.
Is 1.14 they are a **burden** that I am tired of bearing.
9. 4 have broken the yoke that **burdened** them and the rod that
10.27 their yoke will no longer be a **burden** on your shoulders."
14.25 Assyrian yoke and from the **burdens** they have had to bear.
22.24 his relatives and dependants will become a **burden** to him.
43.23 I did not **burden** you by demanding offerings or wear you out
43.24 Instead you **burdened** me with your sins;
46. 1 loaded on donkeys, a **burden** for the backs of tired animals.
Jer 23.33 tell him, 'You are a **burden** to the Lord, and he is
23.34 uses the words 'the Lord's **burden,'** I will punish him and
23.36 use the words 'the Lord's **burden,'** because if anyone does,
23.36 I will make my message a real **burden** to him.
23.38 use the words 'the Lord's **burden,'** then tell them that [39]I
Ezek 33.10 'We are **burdened** with our sins and the wrongs we have done.
Mic 6. 3 How have I been a **burden** to you?
Acts 15.28 put any other **burden** on you besides these necessary rules:
Rom 15. 1 in the faith ought to help the weak to carry their **burdens.**
2 Cor 1. 8 The **burdens** laid upon us were so great and so heavy that
8.13 am not trying to relieve others by putting a **burden** on you;
11. 9 I will never be a **burden** to you!
12.16 You will agree, then, that I was not a **burden** to you.
Gal 6. 2 Help to carry one another's **burdens,** and in this way you
1 Tim 5.16 and not put the **burden** on the church, so that it
2 Tim 3. 6 over weak women who are **burdened** by the guilt of their sins
Rev 2.24 to you that I will not put any other **burden** on you.

BURGLARS

Jer 2.34 of the poor and innocent, not with the blood of **burglars.**

BURIAL see BURY

BURIAL CAVES see BURY

BURIAL-GROUND see BURY

BURN

Gen 8.20 clean animal and bird, and **burnt** them whole as a sacrifice
19.24 Suddenly the Lord rained **burning** sulphur on the cities
38.24 Judah ordered, "Take her out and **burn** her to death."
Ex 3. 2 the bush was on fire but that it was not **burning** up.
3. 3 "Why isn't the bush **burning** up?
12.10 if any is left over, it must be **burnt.**
15. 7 your anger blazes out and **burns** them up like straw.

Ex	18.12	brought an offering to be **burnt** whole and other sacrifices
	20.24	to be completely **burnt** and as fellowship-offerings.
	21.25	foot for foot, [25] **burn** for burn, wound for wound,
	22. 6	to another man's field and **burns** up corn that is growing or
	24. 5	sent young men, and they **burnt** sacrifices to the Lord and
	24.16	the light looked like a fire **burning** on top of the mountain.
	27.21	There in my presence it is to **burn** from evening until morning.
	29.13	the fat on them and **burn** them on the altar as an
	29.14	But **burn** the bull's flesh, its skin, and its intestines
	29.18	**Burn** the whole ram on the altar as a food offering.
	29.25	take it from them and **burn** it on the altar, on top
	29.34	the bread is not eaten by morning, it is to be **burnt;**
	30. 1	"Make an altar out of acacia-wood, for **burning** incense.
	30. 7	the lamps ready, he is to **burn** sweet-smelling incense on it.
	30.27	the altar for **burning** incense, [28] the altar for burning offerings,
	31. 8	altar for **burning** incense, [9] the altar for burnt-offerings
	32. 6	they brought some animals to **burn** as sacrifices and others
	35.15	the altar for **burning** incense and its poles;
	35.16	the altar on which to **burn** offerings, with its bronze grating attached,
	37.25	He made an altar out of acacia-wood, for **burning** incense.
	38. 1	For **burning** offerings, he made an altar out of acacia-wood.
	40. 5	Put the gold altar for **burning** incense in front of the
	40. 6	Put in front of the Tent the altar for **burning** offerings.
	40.27	of the curtain, [27] and **burnt** the sweet-smelling incense,
	40.29	of the curtain he placed the altar for **burning** offerings.
	40.38	the day and a fire **burning** above it during the night.
Lev	1. 9	priest will **burn** the whole sacrifice on the altar.
	1.13	sacrifice to the Lord and **burn** all of it on the altar.
	1.15	the altar, wring its neck, and **burn** its head on the altar.
	1.17	tearing the wings off, and then **burn** it whole on the altar.
	2. 2	all of the incense and **burn** it on the altar as a
	2. 9	offered to the Lord, and he will **burn** it on the altar.
	2.12	the Lord, but it is not to be **burnt** on the altar.
	2.16	The priest will **burn** that part of the meal and oil that
	3. 5	The priests shall **burn** all this on the altar along with
	3.11	The officiating priest shall **burn** all this on the altar
	3.16	The priest shall **burn** all this on the altar as a
	4. 7	of the altar used for **burning** sacrifices, which is at the
	4.10	shall take this fat and **burn** it on the altar used for
	4.12	poured out, and there he shall **burn** it on a wood fire.
	4.18	of the altar used for **burning** sacrifices, which is at the
	4.19	he shall take all its fat and **burn** it on the altar.
	4.21	bull outside the camp and **burn** it,
	4.21	just as he **burns** the bull offered for his own
	4.26	Then he shall **burn** all its fat on the altar,
	4.26	just as he **burns** the fat of the animals killed
	4.31	the fellowship-offerings, and he shall **burn** it on the altar
	4.35	the fellowship-offerings, and he shall **burn** it on the altar
	5.12	the Lord, and he will **burn** it on the altar as a
	6. 9	altar all night long, and the fire is to be kept **burning.**
	6.12	the altar must be kept **burning** and never allowed to go out.
	6.12	burnt-offering on it, and **burn** the fat of the fellowship-offering.
	6.13	fire must always be kept **burning** on the altar and never
	6.15	the incense on it, and **burn** it on the altar as a
	6.22	It shall be completely **burnt** as a sacrifice to the Lord.
	6.23	all of it must be **burnt.**
	6.25	altar, where the animals for the **burnt** offerings are killed.
	6.30	it must be **burnt.**
	7. 5	The priest shall **burn** all the fat on the altar as a
	7.17	Any meat that still remains on the third day must be **burnt.**
	7.19	ritually unclean, it must not be eaten, but must be **burned.**
	7.31	The priest shall **burn** the fat on the altar, but the
	8.16	with the fat on them, and **burnt** it all on the altar.
	8.17	skin, flesh, and intestines, and **burnt** it outside the camp,
	8.20	hind legs with water, and **burnt** the head, the fat, and all
	8.28	the food from them and **burnt** it on the altar, on top
	8.32	**Burn** up any meat or bread that is left over.
	9.10	Then he **burnt** on the altar the fat, the kidneys, and the
	9.11	But he **burnt** the meat and the skin outside the camp.
	9.13	other pieces of the animal, and he **burnt** them on the altar.
	9.14	and the hind legs and **burnt** them on the altar on top
	9.17	and took a handful of flour and **burnt** it on the altar.
	9.20	He **burnt** the fat on the altar [21] and presented the breasts
	10. 2	Lord sent fire, and it **burnt** them to death there in the
	10.16	the sin-offering and learnt that it had already been **burnt.**
	13.24	a person who has been **burnt,** if the raw flesh becomes white
	13.25	that has started in the **burn,** and the priest shall pronounce
	13.28	ritually clean, because it is only a scar from the **burn.**
	13.52	The priest shall **burn** it, because it is a spreading
	13.55	you must **burn** the object, whether the rot is on the front
	13.57	it is spreading again, and the owner shall **burn** the object.
	16.12	take a fire-pan full of **burning** coals from the altar and two
	16.25	He shall **burn** on the altar the fat of the animal for
	16.27	take away sin, shall be carried outside the camp and **burnt.**
	16.27	Skin, meat, and intestines shall all be **burnt.**
	16.28	The one who **burns** them must wash his clothes and have a
	17. 6	entrance of the Tent and **burn** the fat to produce a smell
	19. 6	third day must be **burnt,** [7] because it is ritually unclean,
	20.14	mother, all three shall be **burnt** to death because of the
	21. 9	she shall be **burnt** to death.
	24. 2	in the Tent, so that a light may be kept **burning** regularly.
	24. 3	light them and keep them **burning** until morning, there in the
	24. 4	must see that they **burn** regularly in the Lord's presence.
Num	5.26	of it as a token offering and **burn** it on the altar.
	6.18	the fire on which the fellowship-offering is being **burnt.**
	11. 1	It **burnt** among them and destroyed one end of the camp.
	11. 3	Taberah, because there the fire of the Lord **burnt** among them.
	16.35	fire that blazed out and **burnt** up the 250 men who had
	16.37	the men who have been **burnt,** and scatter the coals from the
	16.40	Aaron should come to the altar to **burn** incense for the Lord.
Num	18. 8	contributions made to me that are not **burnt** as sacrifices.
	18. 9	the most sacred offerings not **burnt** on the altar, the
	18.17	against the altar and **burn** their fat as a food-offering,
	19. 5	intestines, is to be **burnt** in the presence of the priest.
	19. 8	The man who **burnt** the cow must also wash his clothes and
	19.17	the red cow which was **burnt** to remove sin shall be taken
	28. 6	daily offering that is completely **burnt,** which was first
	31.10	all their wealth, [10] and **burnt** all their cities and camps.
	31.22	Everything that will not **burn,** such as gold,
Deut	7. 5	the symbols of their goddess Asherah, and **burn** their idols.
	7.25	**Burn** their idols.
	12. 3	**Burn** their symbols of the goddess Asherah and chop down their idols,
	12. 6	sacrifices that are to be **burnt** and your other sacrifices,
	12.11	sacrifices that are to be **burnt** and your other sacrifices,
	12.14	sacrifices that are to be **burnt** and do all the other things
	12.27	which are to be completely **burnt** on the Lord's altar.
	13.16	Then **burn** the town and everything in it as an offering to
	27. 6	sacrifices that are to be **burnt,** [7] and there you are to
	29.20	Instead, the Lord's **burning** anger will flame up against him,
	32.22	My anger will flame up like fire and **burn** everything on earth.
	33.16	the goodness of the Lord, Who spoke from the **burning** bush.
Josh	6.24	fire to the city and **burnt** it to the ground, along with
	7.15	the condemned goods will be **burnt,** along with his family and
	7.25	they also stoned and **burnt** his family and possessions.
	8.28	Joshua **burnt** Ai and left it in ruins.
	8.31	On it they offered **burnt** sacrifices to the Lord, and they
	11. 6	You are to cripple their horses and **burn** their chariots."
	11. 9	he crippled their horses and **burnt** their chariots.
	11.11	no one was left alive, and the city was **burnt.**
	11.13	However, the Israelites did not **burn** any of the cities
	11.13	built on mounds, except Hazor, which Joshua did **burn.**
	13.14	a share of the sacrifices **burnt** on the altar to the Lord
	22.23	built our own altar to **burn** sacrifices on or to use for
	22.26	not to **burn** sacrifices or make offerings, [27] but instead,
	22.27	Tent with our offerings to be **burnt** and with sacrifices
	22.28	It was not for **burning** offerings or for sacrifice, but as a
	22.29	by building an altar to **burn** offerings on or for
Judg	6.21	out of the rock and **burnt** up the meat and the bread.
	6.26	take the second bull and **burn** it whole as an offering, using
	6.28	the second bull had been **burnt** on the altar that had been
	9.15	of my thorny branches and **burn** up the cedars of Lebanon.'
	9.20	blaze out from Abimelech and **burn** up the men of Shechem and
	9.20	the men of Shechem and Bethmillo and **burn** Abimelech up."
	11.31	over the Ammonites, [31] I will **burn** as an offering the first
	12. 1	We'll **burn** the house down over your head!"
	13.15	you want to prepare it, **burn** it as an offering to the
	14.15	we'll set fire to your father's house and **burn** you with it.
	15. 5	In this way he **burnt** up not only the corn that had
	15. 6	So the Philistines went and **burnt** the woman to death
	15. 6	and **burnt** down her father's house.
	15.14	ropes round his arms and hands as if they were **burnt** thread.
	18.27	They killed the inhabitants and **burnt** the town.
	20.26	They offered fellowship sacrifices and **burnt** some sacrifices
	20.48	They **burnt** every town in the area.
	21. 4	fellowship sacrifices and **burnt** some sacrifices whole.
1 Sam	2.15	fat was taken off and **burnt,** the priest's servant would come
	2.16	answered, "Let us do what is right and **burn** the fat first;
	2.28	serve at the altar, to **burn** the incense, and to wear the
	2.28	right to keep a share of the sacrifices **burnt** on the altar.
	3. 3	while the lamp was still **burning,** [4] the Lord called Samuel.
	7. 9	killed a young lamb and **burnt** it whole as a sacrifice to
	30. 1	They had **burnt** down the town [2] and captured all the women;
	30. 3	that the town had been **burnt** down and that their wives,
	30.14	territory of the clan of Caleb, and we **burnt** down Ziklag."
	31.12	the wall, brought them back to Jabesh, and **burnt** them there.
2 Sam	22. 9	a consuming flame and **burning** coals from his mouth.
	22.13	**burning** coals flamed up from the lightning before him.
	23. 7	they will be **burnt** completely.
	24.22	Here are these oxen to **burn** as an offering on the altar;
1 Kgs	8.64	there the sacrifices **burnt** whole, the grain-offerings,
	9.25	He also **burnt** incense to the Lord.
	11. 8	all his foreign wives could **burn** incense and offer
	13. 2	sacrifices on you, and he will **burn** human bones on you."
	15.13	cut down the idol and **burnt** it in the valley of the
	18.38	sent fire down, and it **burnt** up the sacrifice, the wood, and
	22.43	people continued to offer sacrifices and **burn** incense there.
2 Kgs	10.26	brought out the sacred pillar that was there, and **burnt**
	12. 3	continued to offer sacrifices and **burn** incense there.
	14. 4	continued to offer sacrifices and **burn** incense there.
	15. 4	people continued to offer sacrifices and **burn** incense there.
	15.35	people continued to offer sacrifices and **burn** incense there.
	16. 4	shady tree, Ahaz offered sacrifices and **burnt** incense.
	16.13	so he **burnt** animal sacrifices and grain-offerings on it,
	17.11	Asherah, [11] and they **burnt** incense on all the pagan altars,
	18. 4	time the people of Israel had **burnt** incense in its honour.
	19.18	made their lands desolate, [18] and **burnt** up their gods—which
	23. 4	The king **burnt** all these objects outside the city near the
	23. 6	valley of the Kidron, **burnt** it, pounded its ashes to dust,
	23.11	of the sun, and he **burnt** the chariots used in this worship.
	23.15	he also **burnt** the image of Asherah.
	23.16	had the bones taken out of them and **burnt** on the altar.
	23.20	where they served, and he **burnt** human bones on every altar.
	25. 9	He **burnt** down the Temple, the palace, and the houses of
	25.14	sacrifices, the bowls used for **burning** incense, and all the
1 Chr	6.49	and offered the sacrifices that were **burnt** on the altar.
	14.12	idols behind, and David gave orders for them to be **burnt.**
	16.40	and evening they were to **burn** sacrifices whole on the altar
	21.23	Here are these oxen to **burn** as an offering on the altar,
	21.26	fire from heaven to **burn** the sacrifices on the altar.
	21.29	altar on which sacrifices were **burnt** were still at the place

1 Chr 23.13 sacred objects for ever, to **burn** incense in the worship of
23.31 offerings to the Lord are **burnt** on the Sabbath, the New Moon
28.18 altar on which incense was **burnt** and in making the chariot
29.21 and a thousand lambs, which they **burnt** whole on the altar.
2 Chr 1. 6 he had a thousand animals killed and **burnt** whole on it.
2. 4 I will worship him by **burning** incense of fragrant spices,
2. 6 would be anything more than a place to **burn** incense to God?
4. 6 the parts of the animals that were **burnt** as sacrifices.
4.20 fine gold that were to **burn** in front of the Most Holy
7. 1 came down from heaven and **burnt** up the sacrifices that had
7. 7 there the sacrifices **burnt** whole, the grain-offerings,
13.11 they offer him incense and animal sacrifices **burnt** whole.
15.16 idol, chopped it up, and **burnt** the pieces in the valley of
23.18 by King David and to **burn** the sacrifices offered to the Lord
25.14 set them up, worshipped them, and **burnt** incense to them.
26.16 into the Temple to **burn** incense on the altar of incense.
26.18 You have no right to **burn** incense to the Lord.
26.19 Temple beside the incense altar and was holding an incense **burner.**
27. 2 his father he did not sin by **burning** incense in the Temple.
28. 3 of Baal made, [3]**burnt** incense in the Valley of Hinnom,
28. 4 every shady tree Ahaz offered sacrifices and **burnt** incense.
28.25 of worship, where incense was to be **burnt** to foreign gods.
29. 7 go out, and failed to **burn** incense or offer burnt-offerings
29.11 the Lord has chosen to **burn** incense to him and to lead
29.28 the music continued until all the sacrifices had been **burnt.**
29.35 offering the sacrifices that were **burnt** whole,
29.35 the priests were responsible for **burning** the fat that was
30.14 Jerusalem for offering sacrifices and **burning** incense and
32.12 to worship and **burn** incense at one altar only.
34. 5 He **burnt** the bones of the pagan priests on the altars
35.14 burning the animals that were **burnt** whole and the fat of the
36.19 He **burnt** down the Temple and the city, with all its
Ezra 3. 2 Israel, so that they could **burn** sacrifices on it according
3. 3 they began once again to **burn** on it the regular morning and
3. 5 the regular sacrifices to be **burnt** whole and those to be
3. 6 day of the seventh month to **burn** sacrifices to the Lord.
6. 3 a place where sacrifices are made and offerings are **burnt.**
6. 9 sheep, or lambs to be **burnt** as offerings to the God of
8.35 then brought offerings to be **burnt** as sacrifices to the God
8.35 All these animals were **burnt** as sacrifices to the Lord.
Neh 1. 3 gates had not been restored since the time they were **burnt.**
4. 2 Can they make building-stones out of heaps of **burnt** rubble?"
10.33 the animals to be **burnt** each day as sacrifices,
10.34 are to provide wood to **burn** the sacrifices offered to the
13.31 for the wood used for **burning** the offerings to be brought at
Job 15.30 a tree whose branches are **burnt** by fire, whose blossoms are
18. 5 its flame will never **burn** again.
20.26 fire not lit by human hands **burns** him and all his family.
22.20 own is destroyed, and fire **burns** up anything that is left.
30.30 I am **burning** with fever.
41.20 out of his nose, like smoke from weeds **burning** under a pot.
41.21 His breath starts fires **burning;**
Ps 7.13 he takes up his deadly weapons and aims his **burning** arrows.
11. 6 He sends down flaming coals and **burning** sulphur on the wicked;
18. 8 a consuming flame and **burning** coals from his mouth.
38. 7 I am **burning** with fever and I am near to death.
40. 6 do not ask for animals **burnt** whole on the altar or for
66.15 I will offer sheep to be **burnt** on the altar;
69. 9 My devotion to your Temple **burns** in me like a fire;
74. 8 they **burnt** down every holy place in the land.
79. 5 Will your anger continue to **burn** like fire?
83.14 As fire **burns** the forest, as flames set the hills on fire,
89.46 How long will your anger **burn** like fire?
97. 3 goes in front of him and **burns** up his enemies round him.
102. 3 my body is **burning** like fire.
106.18 fire came down on their followers and **burnt** up those wicked people.
118.12 me like bees, but they **burnt** out as quickly as a fire
119.139 My anger **burns** in me like a fire, because my enemies
Prov 6.27 Can you carry fire against your chest without **burning** your clothes?
6.28 Can you walk on hot coals without **burning** your feet?
16.27 even their words **burn** with evil.
25.22 You will make him **burn** with shame, and the Lord will
26.21 the fire **burning,** and troublemakers keep arguments alive.
30.16 and a fire **burning** out of control.
Song 8. 6 It bursts into flame and **burns** like a raging fire.
Is 1. 7 devastated, and your cities have been **burnt** to the ground.
1.11 enough of the sheep you **burn** as sacrifices and of the fat
1.13 I am disgusted with the smell of the incense you **burn.**
5.24 and dry grass shrivel and **burn** in the fire, your roots will
6. 6 down to me, carrying a **burning** coal that he had taken from
6. 7 touched my lips with the **burning** coal and said, "This has
9.18 The wickedness of the people **burns** like a fire that
9.18 It **burns** like a forest fire that sends up columns of smoke.
9.19 Almighty is angry, his punishment **burns** like a fire
10.16 In their bodies there will be a fire that **burns** and burns.
10.17 in a single day will **burn** up everything, even the thorns and
13. 8 at each other in fear, and their faces will **burn** with shame.
17. 8 of the goddess Asherah and altars for **burning** incense.
25. 4 You give them shelter from storms and shade from the **burning** heat.
27. 4 to fight against, then I would **burn** them up completely.
30.27 He speaks, and his words **burn** like fire.
30.33 prepared where a huge fire will **burn** the emperor of Assyria.
31. 9 in Jerusalem and whose fire **burns** there for sacrifices.
33.12 You will crumble like rocks **burnt** to make lime,
33.12 like thorns **burnt** to ashes.
33.14 They say, "God's judgement is like a fire that **burns** for ever.
34. 9 The whole country will **burn** like tar.
Is 34.10 It will **burn** day and night, and smoke will rise from it
35. 7 the **burning** sand will become a lake, and dry land will
37.19 made their lands desolate, [19]and **burnt** up their gods—which
42.25 Like fire his anger **burned** throughout Israel, but we never
43. 2 When you pass through fire, you will not be **burnt;**
44.19 or the sense to say, "Some of the wood I **burnt** up.
47.14 be like bits of straw, and a fire will **burn** them up!
65. 3 in sacred gardens and **burn** incense on pagan altars.
65. 7 They have **burnt** incense at pagan hill shrines and spoken
66.24 die, and the fire that **burns** them will never be put out.
Jer 4. 4 you don't, my anger will **burn** like fire because of the evil
4. 4 It will **burn,** and there will be no one to put it
5.13 people will be like wood, and the fire will **burn** them up."
6.11 Your anger against them **burns** in me too, Lord, and I
6.29 The furnace **burns** fiercely, but the waste metals do not
7.21 "My people, some sacrifices you **burn** completely on the altar,
15.14 because my anger is like fire, and it will **burn** for ever."
17. 4 my anger is like a fire, and it will **burn** for ever."
17.27 Fire will **burn** down the palaces of Jerusalem, and no one
18.15 they **burn** incense to idols.
19. 5 for Baal in order to **burn** their children in the fire as
19.13 whose roofs incense has been **burnt** to the stars and where
20. 9 then your message is like a fire **burning** deep within me.
21.10 the king of Babylonia and he will **burn** it to the ground.
21.11 doing will make my anger **burn** like a fire that cannot be
21.14 on fire, and the fire will **burn** down everything round it.
32.29 They will **burn** it down, together with the houses where
32.29 have made me angry by **burning** incense to Baal on the
34. 2 over to the king of Babylonia, and he will **burn** it down.
34. 5 and as people **burnt** incense when they buried your ancestors,
34. 5 before you, in the same way they will **burn** incense for you.
34.22 They will attack it, capture it, and **burn** it down.
36.23 He kept doing this until the entire scroll was **burnt** up.
36.25 begged the king not to **burn** the scroll, he paid no attention
36.27 After King Jehoiakim had **burnt** the scroll that I had
36.29 to the king, "You have **burnt** the scroll, and you have asked
37. 8 come back, attack the city, capture it, and **burn** it down.
37.10 men would still get up and **burn** this city to the ground."
38.17 life will be spared, and this city will not be **burnt** down.
38.18 to the Babylonians, who will **burn** it down, and you will not
38.23 of Babylonia, and this city will be **burnt** to the ground."
39. 8 Meanwhile, the Babylonians **burnt** down the royal palace and
43.12 of Babylonia will either **burn** their gods or carry them off.
43.13 Heliopolis in Egypt and will **burn** down the temples of the
48.45 Fire has **burnt** up the frontiers and the mountain heights of
49. 2 will be left in ruins and its villages **burnt** to the ground.
49.27 Damascus on fire and will **burn** down King Benhadad's palaces.
51.58 be thrown to the ground, and its towering gates **burnt** down.
52.13 He **burnt** down the Temple, the palace, and the houses of
52.18 sacrifices, the bowls used for **burning** incense, and all the
Lam 1.13 "He sent fire from above, a fire that **burnt** inside me.
2. 4 Here in Jerusalem we felt his **burning** anger.
4.11 he lit a fire in Zion that **burnt** it to the ground.
5.10 Hunger has made us **burn** with fever, until our skin is as
Ezek 5. 2 **Burn** a third of it in the city when the siege is
5. 4 out again, throw them in the fire, and let them **burn** up.
6.13 in every place where they **burnt** sacrifices to their idols.
10. 2 under the creatures and fill your hands with **burning** coals.
15. 4 And when the ends are **burnt** up and the middle is charred,
15. 5 It was useless even before it was **burnt.**
15. 5 Now that the fire has **burnt** it and charred it, it is
15. 6 taken from the forest and **burnt,** so I will take the people
15. 7 They have escaped one fire, but now fire will **burn** them up.
16.41 They will **burn** your houses down and let crowds of women
19.12 they dried up and were **burnt.**
19.14 fire **burnt** up its branches and fruit.
20.28 angry by the sacrifices they **burnt** and by the wine they
20.41 accept the sacrifices that you **burn,** and the nations will
20.47 a fire, and it will **burn** up every tree in you, whether
23.25 take your sons and daughters from you and **burn** them alive.
23.47 swords, kill their children, and **burn** down their houses.
24.10 **Burn** up the bones!
24.11 again after the corrosion is **burnt** off, [12]although all
28.18 I set fire to the city and **burnt** it to the ground.
39.10 because they will have the abandoned weapons to **burn.**
40.38 carcasses of the animals to be **burnt** whole as sacrifices.
40.39 as sacrifices, either to be **burnt** whole or to be sacrifices
40.42 prepare the offerings to be **burnt** whole, were of cut stone.
43.15 which the sacrifices were **burnt,** was also two metres high.
43.18 are to dedicate it by **burning** sacrifices on it and by
43.21 a sacrifice for sin and **burn** it at the specified place
43.24 sprinkle salt on them and **burn** them as an offering to me.
45.13 to be **burnt** whole, and animals for fellowship-offerings,
45.17 provide the animals to be **burnt** whole, the grain-offerings,
45.17 offerings to be **burnt** whole, and the fellowship-offerings,
45.23 and seven rams without any defects and **burn** them whole.
45.25 the same offerings to be **burnt** whole, and the same offerings
46. 2 the gate while the priests **burn** his sacrifices whole and
46. 4 Lord, as sacrifices to be **burnt** whole, six lambs and one ram,
46.12 an offering to be **burnt** whole or a fellowship-offering,
46.13 any defects is to be **burnt** whole as an offering to the
Dan 3.22 made extremely hot, the flames **burnt** up the guards who took
3.27 singed, their clothes were not **burnt,** and there was no smell
11.33 killed in battle or be **burnt** to death, and some will be
Hos 2.13 she forgot me when she **burnt** incense to Baal and put on
4.13 on the hills they **burn** incense under tall, spreading trees,
6. 6 rather have my people know me than **burn** offerings to me.
7. 6 Yes, they **burned** like an oven with their plotting.
8.14 fire that will **burn** down their palaces and their cities."
11. 2 they **burnt** incense to idols.
Joel 1.19 and trees are dried up, as though a fire had **burnt** them.

Amos 1. 4 King Hazael and I will **burn** down the fortresses of King Benhadad.
1. 7 upon the city walls of Gaza and **burn** down its fortresses.
1.10 upon the city walls of Tyre and **burn** down its fortresses."
1.12 the city of Teman and **burn** down the fortresses of Bozrah."
1.14 upon the city walls of Rabbah and **burn** down its fortresses.
2. 1 the bones of the king of Edom by **burning** them to ashes.
2. 2 the land of Moab and **burn** down the fortresses of Kerioth.
2. 5 upon Judah and **burn** down the fortresses of Jerusalem."
4.11 who survived were like a **burning** stick saved from a fire.
5. 6 The fire will **burn** up the people of Bethel, and no one
7. 4 The fire **burnt** up the great ocean under the earth,
7. 4 and started to **burn** up the land.
Obad 18 they will destroy the people of Esau as fire **burns** stubble.
Mic 6. 6 Shall I bring the best calves to **burn** as offerings to him?
Nah 1.10 Like tangled thorns and dry straw, you drunkards will be **burnt** up!
2.13 "I will **burn** up your chariots.
3.15 do, you will still be **burnt** to death or killed in battle.
Zeph 2. 2 by the wind, before the **burning** anger of the Lord comes upon
Zech 9. 4 into the sea, and the city will be **burnt** to the ground.
11. 1 so that fire can **burn** down your cedar-trees!
Mal 1.11 Everywhere they **burn** incense to me and offer acceptable sacrifices.
4. 1 coming when all proud and evil people will **burn** like straw.
4. 1 On that day they will **burn** up, and there will be nothing
Mt 3.12 his barn, but he will **burn** the chaff in a fire that
6.30 that is here today and gone tomorrow, **burnt** up in the oven.
13. 6 But when the sun came up, it **burnt** the young plants;
13.30 tie them in bundles and **burn** them, and then to gather in
13.40 weeds are gathered up and **burnt** in the fire, so the same
22. 7 soldiers, who killed those murderers and **burnt** down their city.
Mk 4. 6 Then, when the sun came up, it **burnt** the young plants;
9.48 never die, and the fire that **burns** them is never put out.'
12.26 in the Book of Moses the passage about the **burning** bush?
Lk 1. 9 he was chosen by lot to **burn** incense on the altar.
1.10 people outside prayed during the hour when the incense was **burnt.**
1.11 on the right of the altar where the incense was **burnt.**
3.17 but he will **burn** the chaff in a fire that never goes
12.28 that is here today and gone tomorrow, **burnt** up in the oven.
20.37 In the passage about the **burning** bush he speaks of the Lord
24.32 "Wasn't it like a fire **burning** in us when he talked to
Jn 2.17 devotion to your house, O God, **burns** in me like a fire."
5.35 John was like a lamp, **burning** and shining, and you were
15. 6 gathered up and thrown into the fire, where they are **burnt.**
Acts 7.30 in the flames of a **burning** bush in the desert near Mount
7.35 help of the angel who appeared to him in the **burning** bush.
19.19 brought their books together and **burnt** them in public.
20. 8 Many lamps were **burning** in the upstairs room where we were
Rom 1.27 relations with women and **burn** with passion for each other.
12.20 for by doing this you will make him **burn** with shame."
1 Cor 3.15 But if anyone's work is **burnt** up, then he will lose it;
7. 9 and marry—it is better to marry than to **burn** with passion.
13. 3 up my body to be **burnt** —but if I have no
Eph 6.16 to put out all the **burning** arrows shot by the Evil One.
1 Tim 4. 2 whose consciences are dead, as if **burnt** with a hot iron.
Heb 9. 4 the gold altar for the **burning** of incense and the Covenant
9.13 and the ashes of a **burnt** calf are sprinkled on the people
10. 6 are not pleased with animals **burnt** whole on the altar or
10. 8 offerings or with animals **burnt** on the altar and the sacrifices
13.11 but the bodies of the animals are **burnt** outside the camp.
Jas 1.11 The sun rises with its blazing heat and **burns** the plant;
2 Pet 3.10 the heavenly bodies will **burn** up and be destroyed, and the
3.12 Day when the heavens will **burn** up and be destroyed, and the
Rev 4. 5 seven lighted torches were **burning,** which are the seven spirits
7.16 nor any scorching heat will **burn** them, [17] because the Lamb,
8. 4 The smoke of the **burning** incense went up with the prayers
8. 7 third of the earth was **burnt** up, a third of the trees,
8.10 A large star, **burning** like a torch, dropped from the sky
16. 8 and it was allowed to **burn** people with its fiery heat.
16. 9 They were **burnt** by the fierce heat, and they cursed the
18. 8 And she will be **burnt** with fire, because the Lord God, who
19.20 thrown alive into the lake of fire that **burns** with sulphur.
21. 8 for them is the lake **burning** with fire and sulphur, which is

BURNT-OFFERING

A kind of sacrifice in which all the parts of the animal were completely burnt on the altar; in other sacrifices only certain parts of the animal were burnt.

Gen 22.13 it and offered it as a **burnt-offering** instead of his son.
Ex 10.25 with animals for sacrifices and **burnt-offerings** to offer to
29.25 on top of the **burnt-offering,** as a food-offering to me.
29.42 all time to come, this **burnt-offering** is to be offered in my
31. 9 burning incense, [9] the altar for **burnt-offerings** and all its equipment,
40.29 On it he sacrificed the **burnt-offering** and the grain-offering,
Lev 1. 3 of his cattle as a **burnt-offering,** he must bring a bull
1.14 offering a bird as a **burnt-offering,** it must be a dove or
3. 5 burn all this on the altar along with the **burnt-offerings.**
4.10 the altar used for the **burnt-offerings,** just as he does with
4.24 altar, where the animals for the **burnt-offerings** are killed.
4.29 altar, where the animals for the **burnt-offerings** are killed.
4.33 altar, where the animals for the **burnt-offerings** are killed.
5. 7 one for a sin-offering and the other for a **burnt-offering.**
5.10 bird as a **burnt-offering,** according to the regulations.
6. 9 give Aaron and his sons the following regulations for **burnt-offerings.**
6. 9 A **burnt-offering** is to be left on the altar all night long,
6.12 firewood on it, arrange the **burnt-offering** on it, and burn
6.25 altar, where the animals for the **burnt offerings** are killed.
7. 2 where the animals for the **burnt-offerings** are killed, and
Lev 7. 8 an animal offered as a **burnt-offering** belongs to the priest
7.37 the regulations for the **burnt-offerings,**
8.18 brought the ram for the **burnt-offering,** and Aaron and his
8.20 This **burnt-offering** was a food-offering, and the smell was
8.28 on top of the **burnt-offering,** as an ordination offering.
9. 2 Lord, the bull for a sin-offering and the ram for a **burnt-offering.**
9. 3 without any defects for a **burnt-offering,** [4] and a bull and a
9. 7 offer the sin-offering and the **burnt-offering** to take away
9.12 He killed the animal which was for his own **burnt-offering.**
9.14 them on the altar on top of the rest of the **burnt-offering.**
9.16 brought the animal for the **burnt-offering** and offered it
9.17 (This was in addition to the daily **burnt-offering.)**
9.24 fire, and it consumed the **burnt-offering** and the fat parts
10.19 today, and they brought their **burnt-offering,** but still
12. 6 a one-year-old lamb for a **burnt-offering** and a pigeon or a
12. 8 one for a **burnt-offering** and the other for a sin-offering,
14.13 for the sin-offerings and the **burnt-offerings** are killed.
14.19 kill the animal for the **burnt-offering** [20] and offer it with
14.22 one for the sin-offering and one for the **burnt-offering.**
14.31 as the sin-offering and the other as the **burnt-offering**
15.15 of them as a sin-offering and the other as a **burnt-offering.**
15.30 and the other as a **burnt-offering,** and in this way he will
16. 3 bull for a sin-offering and a ram for a **burnt-offering."**
16. 5 goats for a sin-offering and a ram for a **burnt-offering.**
16.18 then go out to the altar for **burnt-offerings** and purify it.
16.24 go out and offer the **burnt-offering** to remove his own sins
17. 8 the community who offers a **burnt-offering** or any other
22.18 living in Israel presents a **burnt-offering,** whether in
23.12 corn, also sacrifice as a **burnt-offering** a one-year-old male
23.18 shall be offered as a **burnt-offering** to the Lord, together
23.37 presenting food-offerings, **burnt-offerings,**
Num 6.11 and the other as a **burnt-offering,** to perform the ritual of
6.14 one-year-old male lamb for a **burnt-offering,** a one-year-old
6.16 the Lord and offer the sin-offering and the **burnt-offering.**
7.12 one ram, and a one-year-old lamb, for the **burnt-offering;**
7.84 grain-offerings that go with them, for the **burnt-offerings**
8.12 and the other as a **burnt-offering,** in order to perform the
10.10 present your **burnt-offerings** and your fellowship-offerings.
15. 3 to the Lord as a **burnt-offering** or as a sacrifice in
15. 4 or a goat as a **burnt-offering** to the Lord is to bring
15. 8 to the Lord as a **burnt-offering** or as a sacrifice in
15.24 a bull as a **burnt-offering,** a smell that pleases the Lord,
23. 3 Balak, "Stand here by your **burnt-offering,** while I go to
23. 6 Balak still standing by his **burnt-offering,**
23.15 Balak, "Stand here by your **burnt-offering,** and I will meet
23.17 Balak still standing by his **burnt-offering,**
28. 3 **burnt-offering,** two one-year-old male lambs without any defects.
28.10 This **burnt-offering** is to be offered every Sabbath in
28.11 Present a **burnt-offering** to the Lord at the beginning of each month:
28.13 These **burnt-offerings** are food-offerings,
28.14 is the regulation for the **burnt-offering** for the first day
28.15 addition to the daily **burnt-offering** with its wine-offering,
28.19 Offer a **burnt-offering** as a food-offering to the Lord:
28.23 Offer these in addition to the regular morning **burnt-offering.**
28.24 Offer this in addition to the daily **burnt-offering**
28.27 Offer a **burnt-offering** as a smell pleasing to the Lord:
28.31 in addition to the daily **burnt-offering** and grain-offering.
29. 2 Present a **burnt-offering** to the Lord, a smell pleasing to him:
29. 6 in addition to the regular **burnt-offering** for the first day
29. 6 and the daily **burnt-offering** with its grain-offering
29. 8 Offer a **burnt-offering** to the Lord, a smell pleasing to him:
29.11 **burnt-offering** with its grain-offering and wine-offering.
29.16 **burnt-offering** with its grain-offering and wine-offering.
29.36 Offer a **burnt-offering** as a food-offering to the Lord, a
29.39 the **burnt-offerings,**
Josh 8.31 On it they offered **burnt sacrifices** to the Lord, and they
1 Sam 6.14 the cows and offered them as a **burnt-sacrifice** to the Lord.
6.15 Beth Shemesh offered **burnt-sacrifices** and other sacrifices
10. 8 Gilgal, where I will meet you and offer **burnt-sacrifices**
13. 9 so he said to them, "Bring me the **burnt-sacrifices**
13. 9 He offered a **burnt-sacrifice,** [10] and just as he was finishing,
2 Sam 24.25 Lord and offered **burnt-offerings** and fellowship-offerings.
1 Kgs 3. 4 He had offered hundreds of **burnt-offerings** there in the past.
3.15 Lord's Covenant Box and offered **burnt-offerings**
9.25 times a year Solomon offered **burnt-offerings** and
2 Kgs 5.17 sacrifices or **burnt-offerings** to any god except the Lord.
10.24 Jonadab went in to offer sacrifices and **burnt-offerings** to Baal.
16. 3 his own son as a **burnt-offering** to idols, imitating the
16.15 for the morning **burnt-offerings** and the evening grain-offerings,
16.15 for the **burnt-offerings** and grain-offerings of the king
17.17 their sons and daughters as **burnt-offerings** to pagan gods;
17.31 sacrificed their children as **burnt-offerings** to their gods
21. 6 He sacrificed his son as a **burnt-offering.**
23.10 his son or daughter as a **burnt-offering** to the god Molech.
1 Chr 21.26 and offered **burnt-offerings** and fellowship-offerings.
22. 1 where the people of Israel are to offer **burnt-offerings."**
2 Chr 2. 4 we will offer **burnt-offerings** every morning and evening,
8.13 He offered **burnt-offerings** according to the requirements
28. 3 sacrificed his own sons as **burnt-offerings** to idols,
29. 7 to burn incense or offer **burnt-offerings** in the Temple of
29.18 Temple, including the altar for **burnt-offerings,**
29.24 for the king had commanded **burnt-offerings** and sin-offerings
29.27 Hezekiah gave the order for the **burnt-offering** to be presented;
29.31 brought animals to be sacrificed as **burnt-offerings.**
29.32 and two hundred lambs as **burnt-offerings** for the Lord;
29.35 out the wine that was presented with the **burnt-offerings.**
30.15 and now they could sacrifice **burnt-offerings** in the Temple.
31. 2 These included offering the **burnt-offerings**
31. 3 animals for the **burnt-offerings** each morning and evening,
33. 6 He sacrificed his sons in the Valley of Hinnom as **burnt-offerings.**

2 Chr 35.12 family groups, the animals for **burnt-offerings,** so that they
35.16 and the offering of **burnt-offerings** on the altar.
Ps 50. 8 sacrifices and the **burnt-offerings** you always bring me.
51.16 you are not pleased with **burnt-offerings.**
51.19 pleased with proper sacrifices and with our **burnt-offerings;**
66.13 I will bring **burnt-offerings** to your house;
Is 43.23 You did not bring me your **burnt-offerings** of sheep;
Jer 7.22 about **burnt-offerings** or any other kinds of sacrifices,
14.12 even if they offer me **burnt-offerings** and grain-offerings, I
17.26 Temple **burnt-offerings** and sacrifices,
33.18 Levi to serve me and to offer **burnt-offerings,**
48.35 people of Moab from making **burnt-offerings** at their places
Ezek 43.27 **burnt-offerings** and the fellowship-offerings of the people.
44.11 the people offer for **burnt-offerings** and for sacrifices,
Amos 5.22 **burnt-offerings** and grain-offerings, I will not accept them;

BURST

Gen 7.11 of water beneath the earth **burst** open, all the floodgates of
Job 26. 8 with water and keeps them from **bursting** with the weight.
32.19 chance to speak, I will **burst** like a wineskin full of new
38. 8 back the sea when it **burst** from the womb of the earth?
Nah 2. 6 The gates by the river **burst** open;
Mt 9.17 wineskins, for the skins will **burst,** the wine will pour out,
Mk 2.22 because the wine will **burst** the skins, and both the wine
Lk 5.37 because the new wine will **burst** the skins, the wine will
Acts 1.18 he **burst** open and all his bowels spilt out.

BURY

[BURIAL, BURIAL CAVES, BURIAL-GROUND, UNBURIED]

Gen 15.15 live to a ripe old age, die in peace, and be **buried.**
23. 4 sell me some land, so that I can **bury** my wife."
23. 6 **bury** your wife in the best grave that we have.
23. 6 glad to give you a grave, so that you can **bury** her."
23. 8 are willing to let me **bury** my wife here, please ask Ephron
23. 9 your presence, so that I can own it as a **burial-ground."**
23.11 will give it to you, so that you can **bury** your wife."
23.13 Accept my payment, and I will **bury** my wife there."
23.15 **Bury** your wife in it."
23.19 Then Abraham **buried** his wife Sarah in that cave in the
23.20 in it, became the property of Abraham for a **burial-ground.**
25. 9 His sons Isaac and Ishmael **buried** him in Machpelah Cave,
25.10 both Abraham and his wife Sarah were **buried** there.
35. 4 He **buried** them beneath the oak-tree near Shechem.
35. 8 Deborah died and was **buried** beneath the oak south of Bethel.
35.19 When Rachel died, she was **buried** beside the road to Ephrath,
35.29 and his sons Esau and Jacob **buried** him.
47.29 make a solemn vow that you will not **bury** me in Egypt.
47.30 I want to be **buried** where my fathers are;
47.30 carry me out of Egypt and bury me where they are **buried."**
48. 7 I **buried** her there beside the road to Ephrath."
49.29 join my people in death, **bury** me with my fathers in the
49.30 Abraham bought this cave and field from Ephron for a **burial-ground.**
49.31 That is where they **buried** Abraham and his wife Sarah;
49.31 that is where they **buried** Isaac and his wife Rebecca;
49.31 and that is where I **buried** Leah.
49.32 **Bury** me there."
50. 5 promise him that I would **bury** him in the tomb which he
50. 5 please let me go and **bury** my father, and then I will
50. 6 The king answered, "Go and **bury** your father, as you
50. 7 So Joseph went to **bury** his father.
50.13 his body to Canaan and **buried** it in the cave at Machpelah,
50.13 Abraham had bought from Ephron the Hittite for a **burial-ground.**
50.14 After Joseph had **buried** his father, he returned to Egypt
Num 11.34 Craving"), because there they **buried** the people who had craved meat.
20. 1 There Miriam died and was **buried.**
33. 4 of the Egyptians, [4] who were **burying** the first-born sons
Deut 10. 6 There Aaron died and was **buried,** and his son Eleazar
21.23 It must be **buried** the same day, because a dead body hanging
21.23 **Bury** the body, so that you will not defile the land that
34. 6 The Lord **buried** him in a valley in Moab, opposite the town
34. 6 to this day no one knows the exact place of his **burial.**
Josh 7.21 You will find them **buried** inside my tent, with the silver at
7.22 the condemned things really were **buried** there, with the
24.30 They **buried** him on his own land at Timnath Serah in the
24.32 had brought from Egypt, was **buried** at Shechem, in the piece
24.33 of Aaron died and was **buried** at Gibeah, the town in the
Judg 2. 9 He was **buried** in his own part of the land at Timnath
8.32 ripe old age and was **buried** in the tomb of his father
10. 2 Then he died and was **buried** at Shamir.
10. 5 Jair died and was **buried** at Kamon.
12. 7 Then he died and was **buried** in his home town in Gilead.
12.10 then he died and was **buried** at Bethlehem.
12.12 Then he died and was **buried** at Aijalon in the territory
12.15 then he died and was **buried** at Pirathon in the territory
16.31 They took him back and **buried** him between Zorah and Eshtaol
Ruth 1.17 die, I will die, and that is where I will be **buried.**
1 Sam 25. 1 Then they **buried** him at his home in Ramah.
28. 3 mourned for him and had **buried** him in his own city of
31.13 they took the bones and **buried** them under the tamarisk-tree
2 Sam 2. 4 of Jabesh in Gilead had **buried** Saul, [5] he sent some men
2. 5 you for showing your loyalty to your king by **burying** him.
2.32 men took Asahel's body and **buried** it in the family tomb at
3.32 Abner was **buried** at Hebron, and the king wept aloud at
4.12 They took Ishbosheth's head and **buried** it in Abner's tomb
7.12 When you die and are **buried** with your ancestors, I will
13.19 and with her face **buried** in her hands went away crying.
·17.23 He was **buried** in the family grave.

2 Sam 21.14 Then they **buried** the bones of Saul and Jonathan in the
1 Kgs 2.10 David died and was **buried** in David's City.
2.31 "Kill him and **bury** him.
2.34 killed Joab, and he was **buried** at his home in the open
11.15 the commander of his army had gone there to **bury** the dead.
11.43 He died and was **buried** in David's City, and his son
13.22 and your body will not be **buried** in your family grave."
13.29 brought it back to Bethel to mourn over it and **bury** it.
13.30 He **buried** it in his own family grave, and he and his
13.31 After the **burial,** the prophet said to his sons,
13.31 "When I die, **bury** me in this grave and lay
14.13 All the people of Israel will mourn for him and **bury** him.
14.13 family who will be properly **buried,** because he is the only
14.18 Israel mourned for him and **buried** him, as the Lord had said
14.20 He died and was **buried,** and his son Nadab succeeded him as
14.31 Rehoboam died and was **buried** in the royal tombs in David's City,
15. 8 Abijah died and was **buried** in David's City, and his son
15.24 Asa died and was **buried** in the royal tombs in David's City,
16. 6 Baasha died and was **buried** in Tirzah, and his son Elah
16.28 Omri died and was **buried** in Samaria, and his son Ahab
22.37 His body was taken to Samaria and **buried.**
22.50 Jehoshaphat died and was **buried** in the royal tombs in David's City,
2 Kgs 8.24 Jehoram died and was **buried** in the royal tombs in David's City,
9.10 Jezebel will not be **buried;**
9.28 Jerusalem in a chariot and **buried** him in the royal tombs in
9.34 Only then did he say, "Take that damned woman and **bury** her;
9.35 men who went out to **bury** her found nothing except her skull,
10.35 He died and was **buried** in Samaria, and his son Jehoahaz
12.20 Joash was **buried** in the royal tombs in David's City, and his
13. 9 He died and was **buried** in Samaria, and his son Jehoash
13.13 Jehoash died and was **buried** in the royal tombs in Samaria,
13.20 Elisha died and was **buried.**
14.16 Jehoash died and was **buried** in the royal tombs in Samaria,
14.20 on a horse and was **buried** in the royal tombs in David's
14.29 Jeroboam died and was **buried** in the royal tombs, and his
15. 7 Uzziah died and was **buried** in the royal burial ground in
15.22 He died and was **buried,** and his son Pekahiah succeeded
15.38 Jotham died and was **buried** in the royal tombs in David's City,
16.20 Ahaz died and was **buried** in the royal tombs in David's City,
21.18 Manasseh died and was **buried** in the palace garden, the
21.26 Amon was **buried** in the tomb in the garden of Uzza, and
23. 6 to dust, and scattered it over the public **burial-ground.**
23.30 back to Jerusalem, where he was **buried** in the royal tombs.
1 Chr 10.12 They **buried** them there under an oak and fasted for seven days.
17.11 When you die and are **buried** with your ancestors, I will
2 Chr 9.31 He died and was **buried** in David's City, and his son
12.16 Rehoboam died and was **buried** in the royal tombs in
14. 1 King Abijah died and was **buried** in the royal tombs in
16.14 later he died [14] and was **buried** in the rock tomb which he
16.14 to prepare his body for **burial,** and they built a huge
21. 1 Jehoshaphat died and was **buried** in the royal tombs in
21.20 They **buried** him in David's City, but not in the royal tombs.
22. 9 But they did **bury** his body out of respect for his
24.16 They **buried** him in the royal tombs in David's City in
24.25 He was **buried** in David's City, but not in the royal tombs.
25.28 a horse, and he was **buried** in the royal tombs in David's
26.23 Uzziah died and was **buried** in the royal burial-ground,
26.23 because of his disease he was not **buried** in the royal tombs.
27. 9 He died and was **buried** in David's City and his son Ahaz
28.27 King Ahaz died and was **buried** in Jerusalem, but not in
32.33 Hezekiah died and was **buried** in the upper section of the
33.20 Manasseh died and was **buried** at the palace, and his son
35.24 There he died and was **buried** in the royal tombs.
Neh 2. 3 city where my ancestors are **buried** is in ruins and its gates
2. 5 city where my ancestors are **buried,** so that I can rebuild
Job 3.22 They are not happy till they are dead and **buried;**
21.26 But all alike die and are **buried;**
40.13 **Bury** them all in the ground;
Ps 79. 3 through Jerusalem, and no one was left to **bury** the dead.
106.17 up and swallowed Dathan and **buried** Abiram and his family;
Ecc 6. 3 does not receive a decent **burial,** then I say that a baby
8.10 I have seen wicked men **buried** and in their graves, but on
Is 14.20 your own people, you will not be **buried** like other kings.
34. 3 Their corpses will not be **buried,** but will lie there
53. 9 with evil men, he was **buried** with the rich, even though he
Jer 7.32 bury people there because there will be nowhere else to **bury** them.
8. 2 Instead of being gathered and **buried,** their bones will be
14.16 streets of Jerusalem, and there will be no one to **bury** them.
16. 4 diseases, and no one will mourn for them or **bury** them.
16. 6 this land, but no one will **bury** them or mourn for them.
19.11 People will **bury** their dead even in Topheth
19.11 because there will be nowhere else to **bury** them.
20. 6 you will die and be **buried,** along with all your friends to
25.33 mourn for them, and they will not be taken away and **buried.**
26.23 killed and his body thrown into the public **burial-ground.)**
31.40 valley, where the dead are **buried** and refuse is thrown, and
34. 5 people burnt incense when they **buried** your ancestors, who
43. 9 "Get some large stones and **bury** them in the mortar of the
43.10 over these stones that you **buried,** and will spread the royal
Lam 2. 9 The gates lie **buried** in rubble, their bars smashed to pieces.
Ezek 29. 5 Your body will fall on the ground and be left **unburied.**
32.27 They were not given honourable **burial** like the heroes of ancient times,
37.13 graves where my people are **buried** and bring them out, they
39.11 I will give Gog a **burial-ground** there in Israel, in
39.11 all his army will be **buried** there, and the valley will be
39.12 the Israelites seven months to **bury** all the corpses and make
39.13 the land will help to **bury** them, and they will be honoured
39.14 order to find and **bury** those bodies remaining on the ground,

Ezek 39.15 the grave-diggers can come and **bury** it in the Valley of
43. 7 worshipping other gods or by **burying** the corpses of their
Hos 9. 6 up—gather them for **burial** there at Memphis!
Mt 8.21 said, "Sir, first let me go back and **bury** my father."
8.22 Jesus answered, "and let the dead **bury** their own dead."
8.28 met by two men who came out of the **burial caves** there.
14.12 John's disciples came, carried away his body, and **buried**
26.12 pour this perfume on my body to get me ready for **burial.**
Mk 5. 2 met by a man who came out of the **burial caves** there.
6.29 they came and took away his body, and **buried** it.
14. 8 perfume on my body to prepare it ahead of time for **burial.**
Lk 8.27 not stay at home, but spent his time in the **burial caves.**
9.59 man said, "Sir, first let me go back and **bury** my father."
9.60 Jesus answered, "Let the dead **bury** their own dead.
16.22 rich man died and was **buried,** [23] and in Hades, where he was
Jn 11.17 he found that Lazarus had been **buried** four days before.
11.34 "Where have you **buried** him?"
11.39 He has been **buried** four days!"
12. 7 Let her keep what she has for the day of my **burial.**
19.40 according to the Jewish custom of preparing a body for **burial.**
19.41 there was a new tomb where no one had ever been **buried.**
Acts 2.29 He died and was **buried,** and his grave is here with us
5. 6 in, wrapped up his body, carried him out, and **buried** him.
5. 9 The men who **buried** your husband are now at the door,
5.10 so they carried her out and **buried** her beside her husband.
7.16 to Shechem, where they were **buried** in the grave which
8. 2 devout men **buried** Stephen, mourning for him with loud cries.
13.36 and then he died, was **buried** with his ancestors, and his
Rom 6. 4 then, we were **buried** with him and shared his death,
1 Cor 15. 4 that he was **buried** and that he was raised to life three
15.42 When the body is **buried,** it is mortal;
15.43 When **buried,** it is ugly and weak;
15.44 When **buried,** it is a physical body;
Col 2.12 you were baptized, you were **buried** with Christ, and in baptism
Rev 11. 9 and a half days and will not allow them to be **buried.**

BUSH
[THORN-BUSH]

Gen 21.15 left the child under a **bush** [16] and sat down about a hundred
22.13 round and saw a ram caught in a **bush** by its horns.
Ex 3. 2 to him as a flame coming from the middle of a **bush.**
3. 2 Moses saw that the **bush** was on fire but that it was
3. 3 "Why isn't the **bush** burning up?
3. 4 called to him from the middle of the **bush** and said, "Moses!
Deut 33.16 the goodness of the Lord, Who spoke from the burning **bush.**
Judg 9.14 trees said to the **thorn-bush,** 'You come and be our king.'
9.15 The **thorn-bush** answered, 'If you really want to make me your king,
2 Kgs 14. 9 "Once a **thorn bush** on the Lebanon Mountains sent a message
14. 9 A wild animal passed by and trampled the **bush** down.
2 Chr 25.18 "Once, a **thorn bush** in the Lebanon Mountains sent a message
25.18 A wild animal passed by and trampled the **bush** down.
Job 30. 7 howled like animals and huddled together under the **bushes.**
40.21 He lies down under the **thorn-bushes,** and hides among the
40.22 The **thorn-bushes** and the willows by the stream give him
Prov 24.31 They were full of **thorn bushes** and overgrown with weeds.
Is 7.19 and they will cover every **thorn-bush** and every pasture.
7.23 will be overgrown with **thorn-bushes** and briars.
7.24 the whole country will be full of briars and **thorn-bushes.**
9.18 burns like a fire that destroys **thorn-bushes** and thistles.
32.13 vineyards have been destroyed, [13] and **thorn-bushes** and
Jer 17. 6 He is like a **bush** in the desert, which grows in the
Hos 2. 6 to fence her in with **thorn-bushes** and build a wall to block
9. 6 once stood will be overgrown with weeds and **thorn-bushes.**
Mt 7.16 **Thorn bushes** do not bear grapes, and briars do not bear figs.
13. 7 the seed fell among **thorn bushes,** which grew up and choked
13.22 seeds that fell among **thorn bushes** stand for those who hear
Mk 4. 7 the seed fell among **thorn bushes,** which grew up and choked
4.18 Other people are like the seeds sown among the **thorn bushes.**
12.26 in the Book of Moses the passage about the burning **bush?**
Lk 6.44 not pick figs from **thorn bushes**
6.44 or gather grapes from bramble **bushes.**
8. 7 the seed fell among **thorn bushes,** which grew up with the
8.14 seeds that fell among **thorn bushes** stand for those who hear;
20.37 the passage about the burning **bush** he speaks of the Lord as
Acts 7.30 the flames of a burning **bush** in the desert near Mount Sinai.
7.31 he saw, and went near the **bush** to get a better look.
7.35 help of the angel who appeared to him in the burning **bush.**

BUSINESS

1 Sam 21. 2 "I am here on the king's **business,"** David answered.
2 Sam 16.10 "This is none of your **business,"** the king said to
2 Kgs 9.18 "That's none of your **business!"**
9.19 Again Jehu answered, "That's none of your **business!**
2 Chr 2. 3 "Do **business** with me as you did with my father, King David,
Ps 112. 5 is generous with his loans, who runs his **business** honestly.
Prov 9.15 to people passing by, who are minding their own **business:**
24.12 it is none of your **business,** but God knows and judges your
26.17 that is none of your **business** is like going down the street
Is 23. 3 that grew in Egypt and to do **business** with all the nations.
Ezek 16.29 Babylonians, that nation of **businessmen,**
27. 3 of the sea and does **business** with the people living on every
27. 9 Sailors from every sea-going ship Did **business** in your shops.
27.12 "You did **business** in Spain and took silver, iron, tin,
27.13 You did **business** in Greece, Tubal, and Meshech and
28. 5 You made clever **business** deals and kept on making profits.
Hos 12. 1 They make treaties with Assyria and do **business** with Egypt."
Mt 22. 5 invited guests paid no attention and went about their **business:**
27. 4 "That is your **business!"**
Acts 19.24 and his **business** brought a great deal of profit
19.27 the danger, then, that this **business** of ours will get a bad
1 Cor 5.12 After all, it is none of my **business** to judge outsiders.
1 Thes 4.11 to mind your own **business,** and to earn your own living,
2 Thes 3.11 and who do nothing except meddle in other people's **business.**
Jas 1.11 man will be destroyed while he goes about his **business.**
4.13 a year and go into **business** and make a lot of money."
Rev 18. 3 and the **businessmen** of the world grew rich from
18.11 The **businessmen** of the earth also cry and mourn for her,
18.14 The **businessmen** say to her, "All the good things you longed
18.15 **businessmen,** who became rich from doing business in that city,
18.23 Your **businessmen** were the most powerful in all the world,

BUSY

Ex 5. 9 work harder and keep them **busy,** so that they won't have time
18.13 the people, and he was kept **busy** from morning till night.
1 Kgs 20.40 But I got **busy** with other things, and the man escaped."
2 Chr 35.14 for the priests were kept **busy** until night, burning the
Ps 73. 7 out evil, and their minds are **busy** with wicked schemes.
Prov 17.12 her cubs than to meet some fool **busy** with a stupid project.
20.13 Keep **busy** and you will have plenty to eat.
31.13 She keeps herself **busy** making wool and linen cloth.
31.27 She is always **busy** and looks after her family's needs.
Ecc 4. 6 of mind, than to be **busy** all the time with both hands,
Ezek 28.16 You were **busy** buying and selling, and this led you to
Hag 1. 9 while every one of you is **busy** working on his own house.
1 Cor 15.58 Keep **busy** always in your work for the Lord, since you know

BUSYBODIES

1 Tim 5.13 to be gossips and **busybodies,** talking of things they should not.

BUTCHERED

Deut 28.31 Your cattle will be **butchered** before your very eyes, but
Jer 12. 3 Drag these evil men away like sheep to be **butchered;**
25.34 you to be slaughtered, and you will be **butchered** like rams.
Zech 11. 4 shepherd of a flock of sheep that are going to be **butchered.**
11. 7 the shepherd of the sheep that were going to be **butchered.**
Mt 22. 4 and prize calves have been **butchered,** and everything is ready.

BUTT

Ezek 34.21 the sick ones aside and **butted** them away from the flock.
Dan 8. 4 I watched the ram **butting** with his horns to the west, the

BUTTER

Prov 30.33 If you churn milk, you get **butter.**

BUTTOCKS

Is 20. 4 naked, with their **buttocks** exposed, bringing shame on Egypt.

BUY
[BOUGHT]

Gen 17.11 slaves born in your homes and slaves **bought** from foreigners.
17.23 the slaves born in his home and those he had **bought.**
23.13 I will **buy** the whole field.
25.10 It was the field that Abraham had **bought** from the Hittites;
33.19 He **bought** that part of the field from the descendants of
41.57 all over the world to **buy** corn from Joseph, because the
42. 2 go there and **buy** some to keep us from starving to death."
42. 3 Joseph's ten half-brothers went to **buy** corn in Egypt, [4] but
42. 5 Jacob came with others to **buy** corn, because there was famine
42. 7 "We have come from Canaan to **buy** food," they answered.
42.10 "We have come as your slaves, to **buy** food.
42.19 to your starving families the corn that you have **bought.**
42.26 donkeys with the corn they had **bought,** and then they left.
43. 2 to his sons, "Go back and **buy** a little food for us."
43. 4 our brother with us, we will go and **buy** food for you.
43.20 "If you please, sir, we came here once before to **buy** food.
43.22 have also brought some more money with us to **buy** more food.
44.25 Then he told us to return and **buy** a little food.
47.14 As they **bought** corn, Joseph collected all the money and
47.19 **Buy** us and our land in exchange for food.
47.20 Joseph **bought** all the land in Egypt for the king.
47.22 only land he did not **buy** was the land that belonged to
47.23 "You see, I have now **bought** you and your lands for the
49.30 Abraham **bought** this cave and field from Ephron for a burial-ground.
49.32 The field and the cave in it were **bought** from the Hittites.
50.13 the field which Abraham had **bought** from Ephron the Hittite
Ex 12.44 any slave that you have **bought** may eat it if you circumcise
13.13 the Lord, [13] but you must **buy** back from him every
13.13 you do not want to **buy** back the donkey, break its neck.
13.13 You must **buy** back every first-born male child of yours.
13.15 male animal to the Lord, but **buy** back our first-born sons.
21. 2 If you **buy** a Hebrew slave, he shall serve you for six
21. 9 If a man **buys** a female slave to give to his son,
34.20 me, [20] but you are to **buy** back every first-born donkey by
34.20 If you do not **buy** it back, break its neck.
34.20 **Buy** back every first-born son.
Lev 22.11 But a priest's slaves, **bought** with his own money or born
25.14 land to your fellow-Israelite or **buy** land from him, do not
25.24 of the original owner to **buy** it back must be recognized.
25.25 to sell his land, his closest relative is to **buy** it back.
25.26 who has no relative to **buy** it back may later become
25.26 and have enough to **buy** it back himself.

Lev 25.27 pay to the man who **bought** it a sum that will make
25.28 not have enough money to **buy** the land back, it remains under
25.28 control of the man who **bought** it until the next Year of
25.29 he has the right to **buy** it back during the first full
25.30 But if he does not **buy** it back within the year, he
25.31 owner has the right to **buy** them back, and they are to
25.32 Levites have the right to **buy** back at any time their
25.33 a Levite and is not **bought** back, it must be returned in
25.44 need slaves, you may **buy** them from the nations round you.
25.45 You may also **buy** the children of the foreigners who are
25.48 he is sold, he still has the right to be **bought** back.
25.49 cousin or another of his close relatives may **buy** him back;
25.49 or if he himself earns enough, he may **buy** his own freedom.
25.50 must consult the one who **bought** him, and they must count the
27.13 If the man wishes to **buy** it back, he must pay the
27.15 dedicated the house wishes to **buy** it back, he must pay the
27.19 dedicated the field wishes to **buy** it back, he must pay the
27.20 to someone else without first **buying** it back from the Lord,
27.20 he loses the right to **buy** it back.
27.22 a field that he has **bought,** [23]the priest shall estimate
27.27 an unclean animal may be **bought** back at the standard price
27.27 If it is not **bought** back, it may be sold to someone
27.28 No one may sell or **buy** back what he has unconditionally
27.29 who has been unconditionally dedicated may be **bought** back;
27.31 If a man wishes to **buy** any of it back, he must
27.33 animals will belong to the Lord and may not be **bought** back.
Num 3.46 the Levites by 273, you must **buy** back the extra sons.
18.15 you must accept payment to **buy** back every first-born child,
18.16 Children shall be **bought** back at the age of one month
18.17 of cows, sheep, and goats are not to be **bought** back;
Deut 2. 6 You may **buy** food and water from them.'
17.16 send people to Egypt to **buy** horses, because the Lord has
28.68 your enemies as slaves, but no one will want to **buy** you."
Josh 24.32 of land that Jacob had **bought** from the sons of Hamor, the
Ruth 4. 4 then, if you want it, **buy** it in the presence of these
4. 4 so, because the right to **buy** it belongs first to you and
4. 4 The man said, "I will **buy** it."
4. 5 "Very well, but if you **buy** the field from Naomi,
4. 5 then you are also **buying** Ruth, the Moabite widow, so
4. 6 give up my right to **buy** the field, because it would mean
4. 6 You **buy** it;
4. 7 seller to take off his sandal and give it to the **buyer.**
4. 8 man said to Boaz, "You **buy** it," he took off his sandal
4. 9 witnesses today that I have **bought** from Naomi everything
2 Sam 12. 3 while the poor man had only one lamb, which he had **bought.**
24.21 David answered, "To **buy** your threshing-place and build an
24.24 And he **bought** the threshing-place and the oxen for fifty
1 Kgs 16.24 in Tirzah, [24]and then he **bought** the hill of Samaria for
21. 6 I offered to **buy** his vineyard, or, if he preferred, to give
2 Kgs 7. 1 you will be able to **buy** in Samaria three kilogrammes of the
12.12 the masons, and the stone-cutters, **buy** the timber and
12.14 the workmen and to **buy** the materials used in the repairs.
22. 6 builders, and the masons, and **buy** the timber and the stones
2 Chr 34.11 carpenters and the builders to **buy** the stones and the timber
Ezra 7.17 spend this money carefully and **buy** bulls, rams, lambs, corn,
Neh 5. 8 been able, we have been **buying** back our Jewish brothers who
10.31 or on any other holy day, we will not **buy** from them.
Job 28.15 It cannot be **bought** with silver or gold.
31.19 in need, too poor to **buy** clothes, [20]I would give him
Prov 27.26 wool of your sheep and **buy** land with the money you get
31.16 She looks at land and **buys** it, and with money she has
Ecc 2. 7 I **bought** many slaves, and there were slaves born in my household.
Song 8. 7 But if anyone tried to **buy** love with his wealth, contempt is
Is 5. 8 You **buy** more houses and fields to add to those you already
23. 3 men [3]across the sea to **buy** and sell the corn that grew
23.18 will use her money to **buy** the food and the clothing they
24. 2 and masters, **buyers** and sellers, lenders and borrowers,
43.24 You didn't **buy** incense for me or satisfy me with the fat
55. 1 Come, you that have no money— **buy** corn and eat!
55. 1 **Buy** wine and milk— it will cost you nothing!
Jer 13. 1 told me to go and **buy** myself some linen shorts and to
13. 2 So I **bought** them and put them on.
19. 1 The Lord told me to go and **buy** a clay jar.
32. 7 me with the request to **buy** his field at Anathoth in the
32. 7 his nearest relative and had the right to **buy** it for myself.
32. 8 me there in the courtyard and asked me to **buy** the field.
32. 9 I **bought** the field from Hanamel and weighed out the money
32.15 fields, and vineyards will again be **bought** in this land."
32.25 one who ordered me to **buy** the field in the presence of
32.43 But fields will once again be **bought** in this land.
32.44 People will **buy** them, and the deeds will be signed,
35. 7 or farm the land, and not to plant vineyards or **buy** them.
Lam 5. 4 we must **buy** the wood we need for fuel.
Ezek 7.12 The day is near when **buying** and selling will have no more
27.16 The people of Syria **bought** your merchandise
27.18 The people of Damascus **bought** your merchandise
28.16 You were busy **buying** and selling, and this led you to
28.18 You did such evil in **buying** and selling that your places
Hos 3. 2 pieces of silver and 150 kilogrammes of barley to **buy** her.
Amos 8. 6 of a pair of sandals, and we'll **buy** him as a slave."
Zech 11. 7 Those who **bought** and sold the sheep hired me,
11.11 Those who **bought** and sold the sheep were watching me,
Mt 10.29 only a penny you can **buy** two sparrows, yet not one sparrow
13.44 everything he has, and then goes back and **buys** that field.
13.46 he goes and sells everything he has, and **buys** that pearl.
14.15 let them go to the villages to **buy** food for themselves."
21.12 Temple and drove out all those who were **buying** and selling there.
25. 9 Go to the shop and **buy** some for yourselves.'
25.10 So the foolish girls went off to **buy** some oil;
27. 7 they used the money to **buy** Potter's Field, as a cemetery for
Mt 27.10 and used the money to **buy** the potter's field, as the
Mk 6.36 farms and villages in order to **buy** themselves something to eat."
11.15 began to drive out all those who were **buying** and selling.
15.46 Joseph **bought** a linen sheet, took the body down, wrapped it
16. 1 mother of James, and Salome **bought** spices to go and anoint
Lk 9.13 you want us to go and **buy** food for this whole crowd?"
14.18 told the servant, 'I have **bought** a field and must go and
14.19 Another one said, 'I have **bought** five pairs of oxen and
17.28 Everybody kept on eating and drinking, **buying** and selling,
22.36 and whoever has no sword must sell his coat and **buy** one.
Jn 4. 8 (His disciples had gone into town to **buy** food.)
6. 5 asked Philip, "Where can we **buy** enough food to feed all
6. 7 take more than two hundred silver coins to **buy** enough bread."
13.29 told him to go and **buy** what they needed for the festival,
Acts 1.18 for his evil act he **bought** a field, where he fell to
7.16 the grave which Abraham had **bought** from the clan of Hamor
8.20 hell, for thinking that you can **buy** God's gift with money!
1 Cor 6.20 he **bought** you for a price.
7.23 God **bought** you for a price;
7.30 those who buy, as though they did not own what they **bought;**
Rev 3.18 I advise you, then, to **buy** gold from me, pure gold,
3.18 **Buy** also white clothing to dress yourself and cover up
3.18 **Buy** also some ointment to put on your eyes, so that you
5. 9 your sacrificial death you **bought** for God people from every tribe,
13.17 No one could **buy** or sell unless he had this mark,
18.11 mourn for her, because no one **buys** their goods any longer;
18.12 no one **buys** their gold, silver, precious stones, and

BUZZARD

Lev 11.13 **buzzards,** vultures, crows;
Deut 14.12 **buzzards,** vultures, crows;

BY MEANS OF see MEANS

BYSTANDER

Job 32. 2 But a **bystander** named Elihu could not control his anger any longer,
Mk 11. 5 some of the **bystanders** asked them, "What are you doing,
14.69 began to repeat to the **bystanders,** "He is one of them!"
14.70 A little while later the **bystanders** accused Peter again,

AV CAESAR see EMPEROR, AUGUSTUS, CLAUDIUS, TIBERIUS

CAESAREA

City on the Mediterranean coast n. of Mount Carmel, headquarters of Roman rule in Palestine.

Acts 8.40 he went on to **Caesarea,** and on the way he preached the
9.30 they took Saul to **Caesarea** and sent him away to Tarsus.
10. 1 There was a man in **Caesarea** named Cornelius, who was a
10.24 he arrived in **Caesarea,** where Cornelius was waiting for him,
11.11 been sent to me from **Caesarea** arrived at the house where I
11.12 from Joppa accompanied me to **Caesarea,** and we all went into
12.19 After this, Herod left Judaea and spent some time in **Caesarea.**
18.22 When he arrived at **Caesarea,** he went to Jerusalem and greeted
21. 8 On the following day we left and arrived in **Caesarea.**
21.16 Some of the disciples from **Caesarea** also went with us
23.23 soldiers ready to go to **Caesarea,** together with seventy horsemen
23.33 took him to **Caesarea,** delivered the letter to the governor,
24. 1 Priest Ananias went to **Caesarea** with some elders and a lawyer
25. 1 he went from **Caesarea** to Jerusalem, [2]where the chief priests
25. 4 being kept a prisoner in **Caesarea,** and I myself will be
25. 5 Let your leaders go to **Caesarea** with me and accuse the man
25. 6 eight or ten days with them and then went to **Caesarea.**
25.13 Agrippa and Bernice came to **Caesarea** to pay a visit of

CAESAREA PHILIPPI

City in n.e. Palestine, near Mount Hermon.

Mt 16.13 territory near the town of **Caesarea Philippi,** where he asked
Mk 8.27 and his disciples went away to the villages near **Caesarea Philippi.**

CAGE

Jer 5.27 as a hunter fills his **cage** with birds, they have filled
Ezek 19. 9 They put him in a **cage** and took him to the king

CAIAPHAS

High Priest and a Sadducee.

Mt 26. 3 together in the palace of **Caiaphas,** the High Priest, [4]and
26.57 him to the house of **Caiaphas,** the High Priest, where the
Lk 3. 2 Lysanias was ruler of Abilene, [2]and Annas and **Caiaphas** were high priests.
Jn 11.49 One of them, named **Caiaphas,** who was High Priest that year,
18.13 He was the father-in-law of **Caiaphas,** who was High Priest that year.
18.14 It was **Caiaphas** who had advised the Jewish authorities
18.24 Then Annas sent him, still bound, to **Caiaphas** the High Priest.
18.28 Jesus was taken from **Caiaphas'** house to the governor's palace.
Acts 4. 6 High Priest Annas and with **Caiaphas,** John, Alexander, and

CAIN

Adam's eldest son who murdered his brother Abel.
see also TUBAL CAIN, KAIN, **KENITE**

Gen 4. 1 So she named him **Cain.**
4. 2 Abel became a shepherd, but **Cain** was a farmer.
4. 3 After some time, **Cain** brought some of his harvest and gave
4. 5 Abel and his offering, [5] but he rejected **Cain** and his offering.
4. 5 **Cain** became furious, and he scowled in anger.
4. 6 Then the Lord said to **Cain,** "Why are you angry?
4. 8 Then **Cain** said to his brother Abel, "Let's go out in the
4. 8 were out in the fields, **Cain** turned on his brother and
4. 9 The Lord asked **Cain,** "Where is your brother Abel?"
4.13 And **Cain** said to the Lord, "This punishment is too hard
4.15 Lord put a mark on **Cain** to warn anyone who met him
4.16 And **Cain** went away from the Lord's presence and lived in
4.17 **Cain** and his wife had a son and named him Enoch.
4.17 Then **Cain** built a city and named it after his son.
4.24 taken to pay for killing **Cain,** Seventy-seven will be taken
4.25 "God has given me a son to replace Abel, whom **Cain** killed."
Heb 11. 4 that made Abel offer to God a better sacrifice than **Cain's.**
1 Jn 3.12 We must not be like **Cain;**
3.12 Why did **Cain** murder him?
Jude 11 They have followed the way that **Cain** took.

CAKE

Lev 7.12 with olive-oil or **cakes** made of flour mixed with olive-oil.
Num 11. 8 into flour, and then boil it and make it into flat **cakes.**
1 Sam 25.18 of raisins, and two hundred **cakes** of dried figs, and loaded
2 Sam 13. 6 come and make a few **cakes** here where I can see her,
13. 8 it, and made some **cakes** there where he could see her.
13. 8 Then she baked the **cakes** [9] and emptied them out of the pan
13.10 said to her, "Bring the **cakes** here to my bed and serve
13.10 She took the **cakes** and went over to him.
1 Kgs 14. 3 him ten loaves of bread, some **cakes,** and a jar of honey.
Jer 7.18 women mix dough to bake **cakes** for the goddess they call the
44.19 "When we baked **cakes** shaped like the Queen of Heaven,

CALAMITY

Is 57. 1 But when they die, no **calamity** can hurt them.
Ezek 38.21 I will terrify Gog with all sorts of **calamities.**

CALAMUS

Song 4.14 henna and nard, [14] of saffron, **calamus,** and cinnamon, or

CALEB (1)

Spy who represented Judah and gave a favourable report on his return to Kadesh.

Num 13. 3 Judah **Caleb** son of Jephunneh
13.30 **Caleb** silenced the people who were complaining against Moses,
13.31 men who had gone with **Caleb** said, "No, we are not strong
14. 6 Joshua son of Nun and **Caleb** son of Jephunneh, two of the
14.24 But because my servant **Caleb** has a different attitude
14.30 there, but not one of you will, except **Caleb** and Joshua.
14.38 Of the twelve spies only Joshua and **Caleb** survived.
26.65 the wilderness, and except for **Caleb** son of Jephunneh and
32.12 This included everyone, except **Caleb** son of Jephunneh
34.19 Judah **Caleb** son of Jephunneh
Deut 1.36 Only **Caleb** son of Jephunneh will enter it.
Josh 14. 6 One of them, **Caleb** son of Jephunneh the Kenizzite, said to
14.13 Joshua blessed **Caleb** son of Jephunneh and gave him the
14.14 to the descendants of **Caleb** son of Jephunneh the Kenizzite,
15.13 of Judah was given to **Caleb** son of Jephunneh, from the tribe
15.14 **Caleb** drove the descendants of Anak out of the city—the
15.16 **Caleb** said, "I will give my daughter Achsah in marriage
15.17 Othniel, the son of **Caleb's** brother Kenaz, captured the city,
15.17 so **Caleb** gave him his daughter Achsah
15.18 down from her donkey, and **Caleb** asked her what she wanted.
15.19 So **Caleb** gave her the upper and lower springs.
21.12 been given to **Caleb** son of Jephunneh as his possession.
Judg 1.12 One of them, called **Caleb,** said, "I will give my
1.13 Othniel, the son of **Caleb's** younger brother Kenaz,
1.13 so **Caleb** gave him his daughter Achsah
1.14 down from her donkey, and **Caleb** asked her what she wanted.
1.15 So **Caleb** gave her the upper and lower springs.
1.20 commanded, Hebron was given to **Caleb,** who drove out of the
3. 9 This was Othniel, the son of **Caleb's** younger brother Kenaz.
1 Sam 25. 2 man of the clan of **Caleb** named Nabal, who was from the
30.14 territory of the clan of **Caleb,** and we burnt down Ziklag."
1 Chr 2.46 **Caleb** had a concubine named Ephah, and by her he had
2.48 **Caleb** had another concubine, Maacah, who bore him two sons,
2.49 In addition, **Caleb** had a daughter named Achsah.
4.15 **Caleb** son of Jephunneh had three sons:
6.56 to the city were assigned to **Caleb** son of Jephunneh.

CALF

[CALVES]
see also **BULL-CALF**

Gen 18. 7 herd and picked out a **calf** that was tender and fat, and
Lev 9. 3 for a sin-offering, a one-year-old **calf,** and a one-year-old
22.26 When a **calf** or a lamb or a kid is born, it
22.28 sacrifice a cow and its **calf** or a sheep and its lamb
27.26 A **calf,** a lamb, or a kid belongs to the Lord, [27] but
1 Sam 6. 7 them to the wagon and drive their **calves** back to the barn.
6.10 hitched them to the wagon, and shut the **calves** in the barn.
15. 9 sheep and cattle, the best **calves** and lambs, or anything
1 Sam 16. 2 The Lord answered, "Take a **calf** with you and say that you
28.24 The woman quickly killed a **calf** which she had been fattening.
2 Sam 6.13 offered the Lord a sacrifice of a bull and a fattened **calf.**
1 Kgs 1. 9 of sheep, bulls, and fattened **calves** at Snake Rock, near the
1.19 bulls, sheep, and fattened **calves,** and he invited your sons,
1.25 a sacrifice of many bulls, sheep, and fattened **calves.**
Neh 10.36 will also dedicate the first **calf** born to each of our cows,
Ps 29. 6 mountains of Lebanon jump like **calves** and makes Mount Hermon
68.30 herd of bulls with their **calves,** until they all bow down and
Is 11. 6 **Calves** and lion cubs will feed together, and little children
11. 7 will eat together, and their **calves** and cubs will lie down
Jer 46.21 Even her hired soldiers are helpless as **calves.**
Mic 6. 6 Shall I bring the best **calves** to burn as offerings to him?
Mal 4. 2 be as free and happy as **calves** let out of a stall.
Mt 22. 4 my bullocks and prize **calves** have been butchered, and everything
Lk 15.23 go and get the prize **calf** and kill it, and let us
15.27 father has killed the prize **calf,** because he got him back
15.30 when he comes back home, you kill the prize **calf** for him!'
Heb 9.13 the ashes of a burnt **calf** are sprinkled on the people

CALL

see also **SO-CALLED**

Gen 3. 9 But the Lord God **called** out to the man, "Where are you?"
4.10 out to me from the ground, like a voice **calling** for revenge.
4.16 in a land **called** "Wandering," which is east of Eden.
11. 9 The city was **called** Babylon, because there the Lord mixed
14.14 nephew had been captured, he **called** together all the
14.17 him in the Valley of Shaveh (also **called** the King's Valley).
16.13 So she **called** the Lord who had spoken to her "A God
16.14 That is why people **call** the well between Kadesh and
17.15 God said to Abraham, "You must no longer **call** your wife Sarai;
19. 5 They **called** out to Lot and asked, "Where are the men who
19.22 Because Lot **called** it small, the town was named Zoar.
20. 8 Early the next morning Abimelech **called** all his officials
20. 9 Then Abimelech **called** Abraham and asked, "What have you done to us?
21.31 And so the place was **called** Beersheba, because it was
22. 1 he **called** to him, "Abraham!"
22.11 the angel of the Lord **called** to him from heaven, "Abraham,
22.15 The angel of the Lord **called** to Abraham from heaven a
24.57 They answered, "Let's **call** the girl and find out what
24.58 So they **called** Rebecca and asked, "Do you want to go
25.30 (That is why he was **called** Edom.)
28. 1 Isaac **called** Jacob, greeted him, and said to him, "Don't
30.13 Now women will **call** me happy";
32. 2 so he **called** the place Mahanaim.
36. 1 These are the descendants of Esau, also **called** Edom.
39.14 of the house, [14] she **called** to her house servants and said,
42.28 "My money has been returned to me," he **called** to his brothers.
46. 2 spoke to him in a vision at night and **called,** "Jacob,
46.33 When the king **calls** for you and asks what your occupation is,
47.29 for him to die, he **called** for his son Joseph and said
49. 1 Jacob **called** for his sons and said, "Gather round, and I
Ex 2. 7 her, "Shall I go and **call** a Hebrew woman to act as
3. 4 Moses was coming closer, he **called** to him from the middle of
3.14 'The one who is **called** I AM has sent me to you.'
3.15 this is what all future generations are to **call** me.
7.11 Then the king **called** for his wise men and magicians, and
8. 8 The king **called** for Moses and Aaron and said, "Pray to
8.25 Then the king **called** for Moses and Aaron and said, "Go
10.16 Then the king hurriedly **called** Moses and Aaron and said,
10.24 The king **called** Moses and said, "You may go and worship
12.21 Moses **called** for all the leaders of Israel and said to them,
15.23 they came to a place **called** Marah, but the water there was
16.31 The people of Israel **called** the food manna.
19. 3 The Lord **called** to him from the mountain and told him to
19. 7 So Moses went down and **called** the leaders of the people
19.20 top of Mount Sinai and **called** Moses to the top of the
24.16 on the seventh day the Lord **called** to Moses from the cloud.
28. 3 **Call** all the craftsmen to whom I have given ability, and
33. 7 It was **called** the Tent of the Lord's presence, and anyone
34. 6 in front of him and **called** out, "I, the Lord, am a
34.31 But Moses **called** them, and Aaron and all the leaders of
35. 1 Moses **called** together the whole community of the people of
36. 2 Moses **called** Bezalel, Oholiab, and all the other skilled
Lev 1. 1 The Lord **called** to Moses from the Tent of the Lord's
4.23 soon as his attention is **called** to the sin, he shall bring
4.28 soon as his attention is **called** to the sin, he shall bring
8. 3 Then **call** the whole community together there."
9. 1 ordination rites were completed, Moses **called** Aaron and his
10. 4 Moses **called** Mishael and Elzaphan, the sons of Uzziel,
13.45 cover the lower part of his face, and **call** out, "Unclean,
Num 1.18 twelve men Moses and Aaron [18] **called** together the whole
10. 2 hammered silver to use for **calling** the people together and
10. 7 camp, [7] but in order to **call** the community together, long
12. 5 cloud, stood at the entrance of the Tent, and **called** out,
13.22 Talmai, the descendants of a race of giants **called** the Anakim,
21.16 went on to a place **called** Wells, where the Lord said to
23.20 to bless, And when God blesses, I cannot **call** it back.
24.10 and said to Balaam, "I **called** you to curse my enemies, but
26. 3 Moses and Eleazar obeyed, and **called** together all the
Deut 2.10 (A mighty race of giants **called** the Emim used to live
2.11 but the Moabites **called** them Emim.
2.20 the Ammonites **called** them Zamzummim.
3. 9 (Mount Hermon is **called** Sirion by the Sidonians, and Senir
4. 7 He answers us whenever we **call** for help.
4.26 I **call** heaven and earth as witnesses against you today that,
5. 1 Moses **called** together all the people of Israel and said to them,

Deut	16. 3	this bread—it will be **called** the bread of suffering—so that
	28.65	You will find no peace anywhere, no place to **call** your own;
	29. 2	Moses **called** together all the people of Israel and said to them,
	30.19	and God's curse, and I **call** heaven and earth to witness the
	31. 7	Then Moses **called** Joshua and said to him in the presence
	31.12	**Call** together all the men, women, and children, and the
	31.14	**Call** Joshua and bring him to the Tent, so that I may
	31.28	I will **call** heaven and earth to be my witnesses against them.
Josh	4. 4	Then Joshua **called** the twelve men he had chosen, [5]and
	5. 3	the Israelites at a place **called** Circumcision Hill.
	6. 6	Joshua **called** the priests and said to them, "Take the Covenant Box,
	7.26	That is why that place is still **called** Trouble Valley.
	8.10	Early in the morning Joshua got up and **called** the soldiers together.
	8.16	in the city had been **called** together to go after them, and
	10.24	Joshua then **called** all the men of Israel to him and ordered
	11.21	destroyed the race of giants **called** the Anakim who lived in
	14.12	that the race of giants **called** the Anakim were there in
	14.15	Before this, Hebron was **called** the city of Arba.
	15.15	(This city used to be **called** Kiriath Sepher.)
	18.13	of Luz (also **called** Bethel), then down to Ataroth Addar,
	21.11	(Arba was Anak's father), now **called** Hebron, in the hill-country of Judah,
	22. 1	Then Joshua **called** together the people of the tribes of Reuben,
	23. 2	was very old, [2]so he **called** all Israel, the elders,
	24. 1	He **called** the elders, the leaders, the judges, and the
Judg	1.10	in the city of Hebron, which used to be **called** Kiriath Arba.
	1.11	the city of Debir, at that time **called** Kiriath Sepher.
	1.12	One of them, **called** Caleb, said, "I will give my
	1.22	went to attack the city of Bethel, at that time **called** Luz.
	2. 5	began to cry, [5]and that is why the place is **called** Bochim.
	3.27	he blew a trumpet to **call** the men of Israel to battle;
	4.10	Barak **called** the tribes of Zebulun and Naphtali to Kedesh,
	4.13	up to Mount Tabor, [13]he **called** out his nine hundred iron
	5.16	to listen to shepherds **calling** the flocks?
	6.34	he blew a trumpet to **call** the men of the clan of
	6.35	of both parts of Manasseh to **call** them to follow him.
	7.23	Manasseh were **called** out, and they pursued the Midianites.
	7.24	The men of Ephraim were **called** together, and they held the
	8. 1	to Gideon, "Why didn't you **call** us when you went to fight
	9.54	Then he quickly **called** the young man who was carrying
	10. 4	land of Gilead, which are still **called** the villages of Jair.
	12. 1	to fight the Ammonites without **calling** us to go with you?
	12. 2	I did **call** you, but you would not rescue me from them.
	15.18	became very thirsty, so he **called** to the Lord and said,
	16.19	in her lap and then **called** a man, who cut off Samson's
	16.24	enjoying themselves, so they said, "**Call** Samson, and let's
	18.12	That is why the place is still **called** Camp of Dan.
	18.22	the house when Micah **called** his neighbours out for battle.
	20. 1	as from the land of Gilead in the east, answered the **call.**
	20.15	They **called** out twenty-six thousand soldiers from their cities that day.
	21. 9	at the roll **call** of the army no one from Jabesh had
Ruth	1.20	"Don't **call** me Naomi," she answered;
	1.20	"**call** me Marah, because Almighty God has made my life bitter.
	1.21	Why **call** me Naomi when the Lord Almighty has condemned me
	4. 1	came by, and Boaz **called** to him, "Come over here,
1 Sam	3. 4	Before dawn, while the lamp was still burning, [4]the Lord **called** Samuel.
	3. 5	ran to Eli and said, "You **called** me, and here I am."
	3. 5	But Eli answered, "I didn't **call** you;
	3. 6	The Lord **called** Samuel again.
	3. 6	went to Eli, and said, "You **called** me, and here I am."
	3. 6	But Eli answered, "My son, I didn't **call** you;
	3. 8	The Lord **called** Samuel a third time;
	3. 8	went to Eli, and said, "You **called** me, and here I am."
	3. 8	was the Lord who was **calling** the boy, [9]so he said to
	3. 9	and if he **calls** you again, say, 'Speak, Lord, your servant
	3.10	Lord came and stood there, and **called** as he had before,
	3.16	Eli **called** him, "Samuel, my boy!"
	5. 8	So they sent messengers and **called** together all five of
	6. 2	for seven months, [2]the people **called** the priests and the
	9. 9	that time a prophet was **called** a seer, and so whenever
	9.26	At dawn Samuel **called** to Saul on the roof, "Get up, and
	10.17	Samuel **called** the people together for a religious
	13. 3	Then Saul sent messengers to **call** the Hebrews to war by
	13. 4	So the people answered the **call** to join Saul at Gilgal.
	14. 4	one was **called** Bozez and the other Seneh.
	14.12	Then they **called** out to Jonathan and the young man,
	15. 4	Saul **called** his forces together and inspected them at Telem:
	16. 8	Then Jesse **called** his son Abinadab and brought him to Samuel.
	17. 1	at a place **called** Ephes Dammim, between Socoh and Azekah.
	17.43	And he **called** down curses from his god on David.
	19. 7	So Jonathan **called** David and told him everything;
	23. 8	So Saul **called** his troops to war, to march against Keilah
	23.28	That is why that place is **called** Separation Hill.
	24. 8	Then David went out after him and **called** to him, "Your Majesty!"
	28. 8	"**Call** up the spirit of the man I name."
	28.11	"Whom shall I **call** up for you?"
	28.15	And so I have **called** you, for you to tell me what
	28.16	Samuel said, "Why do you **call** me when the Lord has
	29. 6	Achish **called** David and said to him, "I swear by the
2 Sam	1. 7	Then he turned round, saw me, and **called** to me.
	1.15	Then David **called** one of his men and said, "Kill him!"
	2.16	And so that place in Gibeon is **called** "Field of Swords."
	2.26	Abner **called** out to Joab, "Do we have to go on fighting
	5.20	And so that place is **called** Baal Perazim.
	6. 1	Once more David **called** together the best soldiers in Israel,
	6. 8	Box, [8]and so that place has been **called** Perez Uzzah ever since.
	9. 9	Then the king **called** Ziba, Saul's servant, and said, "I
2 Sam	10.15	by the Israelites, so they **called** all their troops together.
	13.17	he **called** in his personal servant and said, "Get this
	15. 2	king to settle, Absalom would **call** him over and ask him
	17. 5	Absalom said, "Now **call** Hushai, and let us hear what he
	18.25	He **called** down and told the king, and the king said,
	18.26	man running alone, and he **called** down to the gatekeeper,
	18.28	Ahimaaz **called** out a greeting to the king, threw
	20. 1	He blew the trumpet and **called** out, "Down with David!
	20. 4	The king said to Amasa, "**Call** the men of Judah together
	20. 5	Amasa went to **call** them, but he did not get back by
	20.11	stood by Amasa's body and **called** out, "Everyone who is for
	22. 4	I **call** to the Lord, and he saves me from my enemies.
	22. 7	In my trouble I **called** to the Lord;
	22. 7	I **called** to my God for help.
	22.42	they **call** to the Lord, but he does not answer.
1 Kgs	2. 1	was about to die, he **called** his son Solomon and gave him
	6.16	An inner room, **called** the Most Holy Place, was built in
	7. 7	The Throne Room, also **called** the Hall of Judgement, where
	8.52	and hear their prayer whenever they **call** to you for help.
	9.13	For this reason the area is still **called** Cabul.
	12.21	Rehoboam arrived in Jerusalem, he **called** together 180,000 of
	17.11	going to get it, he **called** out, "And please bring me some
	18. 3	at its worst, [3]so Ahab **called** in Obadiah, who was in charge
	20. 7	King Ahab **called** in all the leaders of the country and said,
	20.15	So the king **called** out the young soldiers who were
	20.15	Then he **called** out the Israelite army, a total of seven
	20.25	Then **call** up an army as large as the one that deserted
	20.26	The following spring he **called** up his men and marched
	20.27	The Israelites were **called** up and equipped;
	20.39	was passing by, the prophet **called** out to him and said,
	21. 9	"Proclaim a day of fasting, **call** the people together, and
	21.12	proclaimed a day of fasting, **called** the people together, and
	22. 6	So Ahab **called** in the prophets, about four hundred of them,
	22. 9	Then Ahab **called** in a court official and told him to go
2 Kgs	3.21	the youngest, were **called** out and stationed at the border.
	4.12	He told his servant Gehazi to go and **call** the woman.
	4.22	Then she **called** her husband and said to him, "Send a
	4.36	Elisha called Gehazi and told him to **call** the boy's mother.
	6.11	he **called** in his officers and asked them, "Which one of you
	7.10	went back to Samaria and **called** out to the guards at the
	8. 6	story, and so the king **called** an official and told him to
	9. 1	Meanwhile the prophet Elisha **called** one of the young
	9.17	he **called** out.
	9.31	As Jehu came through the gate, she **called** out, "You
	10.12	the way, at a place **called** "Shepherds' Camp," [13]he met
	10.18	Jehu **called** the people of Samaria together and said,
	10.19	**Call** together all the prophets of Baal, all his worshippers,
	12. 4	Joash **called** the priests and ordered them to save up the
	12. 7	So he **called** in Jehoiada and the other priests and asked them,
	14. 7	of Sela in battle and **called** it Joktheel, the name it still
	18. 4	snake that Moses had made, which was **called** Nehushtan.
1 Chr	9.33	from other duties, because they were on **call** day and night.
	11. 7	live in the fortress, it came to be **called** "David's City."
	12.18	became the commander of "The Thirty," and he **called** out,
	13.11	and so that place has been **called** Perez Uzzah ever since.
	14.11	So that place is **called** Baal Perazim.
	15.11	David **called** in the priests Zadok and Abiathar and the six Levites,
	19. 2	they arrived in Ammon and **called** on King Hanun, [3]the
2 Chr	3. 8	The inner room, **called** the Most Holy Place, was nine
	11. 1	Rehoboam arrived in Jerusalem, he **called** together a hundred
	13. 4	Mount Zemaraim and **called** out to Jeroboam and the Israelites:
	13.12	ready to blow them and **call** us to battle against you.
	15. 2	He **called** out, "Listen to me, King Asa, and all you people
	18. 5	So Ahab **called** in the prophets, about four hundred of them,
	18. 8	So King Ahab **called** in a court official and told him to
	19. 4	the north, in order to **call** the people back to the Lord,
	20.26	That is why the valley is **called** "Beracah."
	23.14	temple area, so he **called** out the army officers and said,
	24. 6	the Levites delayed, [6]so he **called** in Jehoiada, their
	24.20	people could see him and **called** out, "The Lord God asks why
	24.22	As Zechariah was dying, he **called** out, "May the Lord see
	27. 3	work on the city wall in the area of Jerusalem **called** Ophel.
	33.14	to the Fish Gate and the area of the city **called** Ophel.
Ezra	2. 3	Ater (also **called** Hezekiah) - 98
	10.23	Jozabad, Shimei, Kelaiah (also **called** Kelita), Pethahiah,
Neh	3.25	of the city **called** Ophel, where the temple workmen lived.)
	5. 7	I **called** a public assembly to deal with the problem [8]and said,
	5.12	I **called** in the priests and made the leaders swear in front
	7. 8	Ater (also **called** Hezekiah) -98
	9. 5	The following Levites gave a **call** to worship:
	9. 9	you heard their **call** for help at the Red Sea.
	9.27	In their trouble they **called** to you for help, and you
	11.21	in the part of Jerusalem **called** Ophel and worked under the
	13.25	I reprimanded the men, **called** down curses on them, beat
Esth	1.10	and feeling merry, so he **called** in the seven eunuchs who
	1.13	law and order, so he **called** for his advisers, who would know
	3. 7	be cast ("purim," they were **called**) to find out the right
	3.12	of the first month Haman **called** the king's secretaries and
	4. 5	Then she **called** Hathach, one of the palace eunuchs
	8. 9	Mordecai **called** the king's secretaries and dictated letters
	9.24	(or "purim," as they were **called**) to determine the day for
	9.26	That is why the holidays are **called** Purim.
Job	5. 1	**Call** out, Job.
	5. 3	who looked secure, but I **called** down a sudden curse on their
	14.15	Then you will **call**, and I will answer, and you will be
	16.18	Don't let my **call** for justice be silenced!
	17.14	I will **call** the grave my father,
	17.14	worms that eat me I will **call** my mother and my sisters.
	19.16	When I **call** a servant, he doesn't answer— even when I
	30.20	I **call** to you, O God, but you never answer;
	34.28	to cry out to God, and he heard their **calls** for help.

Job 42.14 He **called** the eldest daughter Jemimah, the second Keziah,
Ps 3. 4 I **call** to the Lord for help, and from his sacred hill
4. 3 for his own, and he hears me when I **call** to him.
18. 3 I **call** to the Lord, and he saves me from my enemies.
18. 6 In my trouble I **called** to the Lord;
18. 6 I **called** to my God for help.
18.41 they **call** to the Lord, but he does not answer.
20. 9 answer us when we **call.**
22. 2 During the day I **call** to you, my God, but you do
22. 2 I **call** at night, but get no rest.
22. 5 They **called** to you and escaped from danger;
22.24 turn away from them, but answers when they **call** for help."
27. 7 Hear me, Lord, when I **call** to you!
28. 1 O Lord, my defender, I **call** to you.
30. 8 I **called** to you, Lord;
31.17 I **call** to you, Lord;
31.22 But he heard my cry, when I **called** to him for help.
34. 6 The helpless **call** to him, and he answers;
34.17 The righteous **call** to the Lord, and he listens;
50. 1 he **calls** to the whole earth from east to west.
50. 4 He **calls** heaven and earth as witnesses to see him judge
50.15 **Call** to me when trouble comes;
55.16 But I **call** to the Lord God for help, and he will
56. 9 The day I **call** to you, my enemies will be turned back.
57. 2 I **call** to God, the Most High, to God, who supplies my
61. 2 In despair and far from home I **call** to you!
69. 3 I am worn out from **calling** for help, and my throat is
72.12 He rescues the poor who **call** to him, and those who are
81. 7 you were in trouble, you **called** to me, and I saved you.
86. 7 I **call** to you in times of trouble, because you answer my
88. 9 Lord, every day I **call** to you and lift my hands to
88.13 Lord, I **call** to you for help;
91.15 When they **call** to me, I will answer them;
99. 6 they **called** to the Lord, and he answered them.
102. 2 Listen to me, and answer me quickly when I **call!**
107. 6 Then in their trouble they **called** to the Lord, and he
107.13 Then in their trouble they **called** to the Lord, and he
107.19 Then in their trouble they **called** to the Lord, and he
107.28 Then in their trouble they **called** to the Lord, and he
116. 2 He listens to me every time I **call** to him.
116. 4 Then I **called** to the Lord, "I beg you, Lord, save me!"
118. 5 In my distress I **called** to the Lord;
119.145 With all my heart I **call** to you;
119.146 I **call** to you;
119.147 Before sunrise I **call** to you for help;
120. 1 I was in trouble, I **called** to the Lord, and he answered
130. 1 From the depths of my despair I **call** to you, Lord.
130. 2 listen to my **call** for help!
138. 3 You answered me when I **called** to you;
141. 1 I **call** to you, Lord;
141. 1 Listen to me when I **call** to you.
142. 1 I **call** to the Lord for help;
145.18 is near to those who **call** to him,
145.18 who **call** to him with sincerity.
147. 4 decided the number of the stars and **calls** each one by name.
147. 9 their food and feeds the young ravens when they **call.**
Prov 1.20 Wisdom is **calling** out in the streets and market-places,
1.21 **calling** loudly at the city gates
1.24 I have been **calling** you, inviting you to come, but you
1.28 Then you will **call** for wisdom, but I will not answer.
8. 1 Wisdom is **calling** out.
8. 3 At the entrance to the city, beside the gates, she **calls:**
8. 4 I **call** to everyone on earth.
9. 3 has sent her servant-girls to **call** out from the highest
9.15 part of the town, [15]and **calls** out to people passing by,
22.10 be no more arguments, quarrelling, or **calling** of names.
Song 5. 6 I **called** to him, but heard no answer.
8.11 Solomon has a vineyard in a place **called** Baal Hamon.
Is 1.26 Then Jerusalem will be **called** the righteous, faithful city."
4. 3 Jerusalem, whom God has chosen for survival, will be **called** holy.
5.20 You **call** evil good and call good evil.
5.26 The Lord gives a signal to **call** for a distant nation.
6. 3 They were **calling** out to each other:
9. 6 He will be **called,** "Wonderful Counsellor," "Mighty God," "Eternal Father,"
12. 4 **Call** for him to help you!
13. 3 The Lord has **called** out his proud and confident soldiers
14.10 They all **call** out to him, 'Now you are as weak as
19.18 One of the cities will be **called,** "City of the Sun."
19.20 there are oppressed and **call** out to the Lord for help,
21. 8 The sentry **calls** out, "Sir, I have been standing guard at
21.11 Someone **calls** to me from Edom, "Sentry, how soon will the
22.12 The Sovereign Lord Almighty was **calling** you then to weep and mourn,
27.13 trumpet will be blown to **call** back from Assyria and Egypt
29. 2 God will bring disaster on the city that is **called** "God's altar."
33. 7 Brave men are **calling** for help.
34.14 Wild animals will roam there, and demons will **call** to each other.
35. 8 There will be a highway there, **called** "The Road of Holiness."
40. 9 **Call** out with a loud voice, Zion;
40.26 he knows how many there are and **calls** each one by name!
41. 9 I **called** you from its farthest corners and said to you,
42. 6 servant, [6]"I, the Lord, have **called** you and given you
42.17 who trust in idols, who **call** images their gods, will be
43. 1 I have **called** you by name—you are mine.
44. 5 the Lord on his arm and **call** himself one of God's people."
45. 3 Lord, and that the God of Israel has **called** you by name.
46.11 I am **calling** a man to come from the east;
47. 5 no more will they **call** you the queen of nations!
48.12 "Listen to me, Israel, the people I have **called!**
48.15 I am the one who spoke and **called** him;
Is 50. 2 Why did they not answer when I **called?**
51. 2 When I **called** Abraham, he was childless, but I blessed him
54. 6 But the Lord **calls** you back to him and says:
56. 7 My Temple will be **called** a house of prayer for the people
58. 5 Is that what you **call** fasting?
58. 9 When you **call** to me, I will respond.
59. 1 to save you or too deaf to hear your **call** for help!
60.14 They will **call** you 'The City of the Lord,' 'Zion, the City
62. 2 You will be **called** by a new name, A name given by
62. 4 No longer will you be **called** "Forsaken,"
62. 4 Or your land be **called** "The Deserted Wife."
62. 4 Your land will be **called** "Happily Married," Because the
62.12 You will be **called** "God's Holy People," "The People
62.12 Jerusalem will be **called** "The City That God Loves," "The
65.12 did not answer when I **called** you or listen when I spoke.
65.19 There will be no weeping there, no **calling** for help.
66. 4 no one answered when I **called** or listened when I spoke.
Jer 1.15 this land, [15]because I am **calling** all the nations in the
3.17 comes, Jerusalem will be **called** 'The Throne of the Lord,'
3.19 I wanted you to **call** me father, and never again turn away
6.30 They will be **called** worthless dross, because I, the
7.13 You would not answer when I **called** you.
7.18 to bake cakes for the goddess they **call** the Queen of Heaven.
7.27 you will **call** them, but they will not answer.
7.31 they have built an altar **called** Topheth, so that they can
7.32 it will no longer be **called** Topheth or the Valley of Hinnom,
9.17 **Call** for the mourners to come, for the women who sing
11.14 they are in trouble and **call** to me for help, I will
11.16 I once **called** them a leafy olive-tree, full of beautiful fruit;
12. 9 **Call** the wild animals to come and join in the feast!
19. 6 will no longer be **called** Topheth or the Valley of Hinnom.
22.20 **call** out from the mountains of Moab, because all your allies
23. 6 He will be **called** 'The Lord Our Salvation.'
27. 9 either by dreams or by **calling** up the spirits of the dead
29.12 Then you will **call** to me.
31. 6 coming when watchmen will **call** out on the hills of Ephraim,
33. 3 name is the Lord said, [3]"**Call** to me, and I will answer
33.16 The city will be **called** 'The Lord Our Salvation.'
35.17 spoke to you, and you would not answer when I **called** you."
36. 4 So I **called** Baruch son of Neriah and dictated to him
42. 8 so I **called** together Johanan, all the army leaders who
42.13 war any more or hear the **call** to battle or go hungry.'
47. 2 People will **call** out for help;
Lam 1. 3 with no place to **call** their own— Surrounded by enemies,
1.17 The Lord has **called** enemies against me from every side;
1.19 "I **called** to my allies, but they refused to help me.
Ezek 9. 3 The Lord **called** to the man dressed in linen, [4]"Go through
20.29 So they have been **called** 'High Places' ever since.
36.13 It is true that people **call** the land a man-eater, and they
39.11 and the valley will be **called** 'The Valley of Gog's Army.'
39.17 said to me, "Mortal man, **call** all the birds and animals to
Dan 2.26 to Daniel (who was also **called** Belteshazzar), "Can you tell
3.26 up to the door of the blazing furnace and **called** out,
4. 8 (He is also **called** Belteshazzar, after the name of my god.)
4.19 this, Daniel, who is also **called** Belteshazzar, was so
6.20 When he got there, he **called** out anxiously, "Daniel,
8.16 I heard a voice **call** out over the River Ulai, "Gabriel,
10. 1 Persia, a message was revealed to Daniel, who is also **called** Belteshazzar.
Hos 2. 1 So **call** your fellow-Israelites "God's People" and "Loved-by-the-Lord."
2.16 Then once again she will **call** me her husband—
2.16 she will no longer **call** me her Baal.
2.23 love to those who were **called** "Unloved,"
2.23 and to those who were **called** "Not-My-People" I will say,
7.11 first her people **call** on Egypt for help, and then they run
8. 2 Even though they **call** me their God and claim that they are
10. 8 The people will **call** out to the mountains, "Hide us!"
11. 1 child, I loved him and **called** him out of Egypt as my
11. 2 But the more I **called** to him, the more he turned away
Joel 1.14 **call** an assembly!
2.15 give orders for a fast and **call** an assembly!
3. 9 **call** your warriors;
Amos 5. 8 He **calls** for the waters of the sea and pours them out
5.16 Even farmers will be **called** to mourn the dead along with
6.10 The relative will **call** to whoever is still left in the house,
9. 6 He **calls** for the waters of the sea and pours them out
Jon 2. 2 my distress, O Lord, I **called** to you, and you answered me.
Mic 6. 9 He **calls** to the city, "Listen, you people who assemble in
Hab 1. 2 Lord, how long must I **call** for help before you listen,
Zech 3. 8 I will reveal my servant, who is **called** The Branch!
6.12 says, 'The man who is **called** The Branch will flourish where
8. 3 hill of the Lord Almighty will be **called** the sacred hill.
10. 8 "I will **call** my people and gather them together.
11. 7 one I **called** "Favour," and the other "Unity."
11.10 Then I took the stick **called** "Favour" and broke it, to
11.14 the second stick, the one **called** "Unity," and the unity of
Mal 1. 4 People will **call** them 'The evil country' and 'The nation
3.12 people of all nations will **call** you happy, because your land
Mt 1.12 married Mary, the mother of Jesus, who was **called** the Messiah.
1.23 and he will be **called** Immanuel" (which means, "God is with
2. 4 He **called** together all the chief priests and the teachers of
2. 7 So Herod **called** the visitors from the east to a secret
2.15 the prophet come true, "I **called** my Son out of Egypt."
2.23 "He will be **called** a Nazarene."
4.18 who were fishermen, Simon **(called** Peter) and his brother Andrew,
4.21 Jesus **called** them, [22]and at once they left the boat and
5. 9 God will **call** them his children!
5.22 whoever **calls** his brother 'You good-for-nothing!'
5.22 and whoever **calls** his brother a worthless fool will

Mt 7.21 "Not everyone who **calls** me 'Lord, Lord' will enter the
9.13 I have not come to **call** respectable people, but outcasts."
10. 1 Jesus **called** his twelve disciples together and gave them
10. 2 first, Simon **(called** Peter) and his brother Andrew;
10.25 head of the family is **called** Beelzebul,
10.25 the members of the family will be **called** even worse names!
15.10 Then Jesus **called** the crowd to him and said to them,
15.32 Jesus **called** his disciples to him and said, "I feel sorry
18. 2 So Jesus **called** a child, made him stand in front of them,
18.32 So he **called** the servant in.
20. 8 the owner told his foreman, **'Call** the workers and pay them
20.25 So Jesus **called** them all together and said, "You know that
20.32 Jesus stopped and **called** them.
21.13 that God said, 'My Temple will be **called** a house of prayer.'
22. 8 Then he **called** his servants and said to them, 'My wedding
22.43 Jesus asked, "did the Spirit inspire David to **call** him 'Lord'?
22.45 If, then, David **called** him 'Lord,' how can the Messiah be
23. 7 with respect in the market-places and to be **called** 'Teacher.'
23. 8 You must not be **called** 'Teacher', because you are all brothers
23. 9 And you must not **call** anyone here on earth 'Father', because
23.10 Nor should you be **called** 'Leader', because your one and only
24. 1 came to him to **call** his attention to its buildings.
25.14 **called** his servants and put them in charge of his property.
26.36 disciples to a place **called** Gethsemane, and he said to them,
26.53 you know that I could **call** on my Father for help,
27. 8 is why that field is **called** "Field of Blood" to this very
27.17 Jesus Barabbas or Jesus **called** the Messiah?"
27.22 "What, then, shall I do with Jesus **called** the Messiah?"
27.33 came to a place **called** Golgotha, which means, "The Place of
27.47 standing there heard him and said, "He is **calling** for Elijah!"
Mk 1.20 As soon as Jesus saw them, he **called** them;
2.17 I have not come to **call** respectable people, but outcasts."
3.13 went up a hill and **called** to himself the men he wanted.
3.23 So Jesus **called** them to him and spoke to them in parables:
6. 7 **called** the twelve disciples together and sent them out two by
7.14 Then Jesus **called** the crowd to him once more and said
8. 1 left to eat, Jesus **called** the disciples to him and said,
8.34 Then Jesus **called** the crowd and his disciples to him.
9.35 Jesus sat down, **called** the twelve disciples, and said to them,
10.18 "Why do you **call** me good?"
10.42 So Jesus **called** them all together to him and said, "You
10.49 Jesus stopped and said, **"Call** him."
10.49 So they **called** the blind man.
10.49 "Get up, he is **calling** you."
11.17 said, 'My Temple will be **called** a house of prayer for the
12.37 David himself **called** him 'Lord';
12.43 He **called** his disciples together and said to them,
14.32 They came to a place **called** Gethsemane, and Jesus said
15.12 to do with the one you **call** the king of the Jews?"
15.16 governor's palace and **called** together the rest of the company.
15.22 took Jesus to a place **called** Golgotha, which means "The
15.23 wine mixed with a drug **called** myrrh, but Jesus would not
15.35 there heard him and said, "Listen, he is **calling** for Elijah!"
15.44 He **called** the army officer and asked him if Jesus had been
Lk 1.32 be great and will be **called** the Son of the Most High
1.35 this reason the holy child will be **called** the Son of God.
1.48 now on all people will **call** me happy, [49] because of the
1.76 "You, my child, will be **called** a prophet of the Most
5.32 I have not come to **call** respectable people to repent, but
6.13 day came, he **called** his disciples to him and chose twelve
6.15 and Simon (who was **called** the Patriot), [16] Judas son of James,
6.46 "Why do you **call** me, 'Lord, Lord,' and yet don't do
7.11 Jesus went to a town **called** Nain, accompanied by his disciples
7.18 about all these things, he **called** two of them [19] and sent
8. 2 Mary (who was **called** Magdalene), from whom seven demons had been
8.54 took her by the hand and **called** out, "Get up, my child!"
9. 1 Jesus **called** the twelve disciples together and gave them power
9.10 and they went off by themselves to a town **called** Bethsaida.
9.54 do you want us to **call** fire down from heaven to destroy
13.12 When Jesus saw her, he **called** out to her, "Woman, you
15. 6 he **calls** his friends and neighbours together and says to them,
15. 9 When she finds it, she **calls** her friends and neighbours
15.19 I am no longer fit to be **called** your son;
15.21 I am no longer fit to be **called** your son.'
15.22 But the father **called** his servants.
15.26 So he **called** one of the servants and asked him, 'What's
16. 2 his master's money, [2] so he **called** him in and said, 'What is
16. 5 "So he **called** in all the people who were in debt
16.24 So he **called** out, 'Father Abraham!
18.16 doing so, [16] but Jesus **called** the children to him and said,
18.19 "Why do you **call** me good?"
19.13 Before he left, he **called** his ten servants and gave them
19.46 that God said, 'My Temple will be **called** a house of prayer.'
20.44 David **called** him 'Lord';
22. 1 the Festival of Unleavened Bread, which is **called** the Passover.
22. 3 Satan entered Judas, **called** Iscariot, who was one of the twelve
23.13 Pilate **called** together the chief priests, the leaders, and
23.33 came to the place **called** "The Skull," they crucified Jesus
Jn 1.42 name is Simon son of John, but you will be **called** Cephas."
1.48 when you were under the fig-tree before Philip **called** you."
2. 9 so he **called** the bridegroom [10] and said to him, "Everyone else
4.16 "Go and **call** your husband," Jesus told her, "and come back."
5. 2 in Hebrew it is **called** Bethzatha.
6. 1 Lake Galilee (or, Lake Tiberias, as it is also **called).**
9.11 He answered, "The man **called** Jesus made some mud, rubbed it
9.18 could now see, until they **called** his parents [19] and asked them,
9.24 A second time they **called** back the man who had been born
10. 3 hear his voice as he **calls** his own sheep by name,
10.35 God **called** those people gods, the people to whom his message
11.16 Thomas **(called** the Twin) said to his fellow-disciples,
Jn 11.28 said this, she went back and **called** her sister Mary privately.
11.43 he had said this, he **called** out in a loud voice, "Lazarus,
12.17 been with Jesus when he **called** Lazarus out of the grave
13.13 "You **call** me Teacher and Lord, and it is right that you
15.15 I do not **call** you servants any longer, because a servant
15.15 Instead, I **call** you friends, because I have told you everything
18. 1 left with his disciples and went across the brook **called** Kidron.
18.33 Pilate went back into the palace and **called** Jesus.
19.13 on the judge's seat in the place **called** "The Stone Pavement."
19.17 and came to "The Place of the Skull," as it is **called.**
19.17 (In Hebrew it is **called** "Golgotha.")
20.24 of the twelve disciples, Thomas **(called** the Twin), was not with
21. 2 Thomas **(called** the Twin), Nathanael (the one from Cana
Acts 1.19 in their own language they **call** that field Akeldama, which means
1.23 Joseph, who was **called** Barsabbas (also known as Justus), and
2.21 And then, whoever **calls** out to the Lord for help will be
2.39 are far away—all whom the Lord our God **calls** to himself."
3. 2 Beautiful Gate, as it was **called,** was a man who had been
3.11 Solomon's Porch, as it was **called,** the people were amazed and
4.18 So they **called** them back in and told them that on no
4.36 the apostles **called** Barnabas (which means "One who Encourages"),
5.21 Priest and his companions **called** together all the Jewish elders
5.40 They **called** the apostles in, had them whipped, and ordered
6. 2 the twelve apostles **called** the whole group of believers together
6. 9 the Freedmen (as it was **called),** which included Jews from Cyrene
7.59 on stoning Stephen as he **called** out to the Lord, "Lord
9.41 Then he **called** all the believers, including the widows,
10. 1 a captain in the Roman regiment **called** "The Italian Regiment."
10. 7 angel went away, and Cornelius **called** two of his house servants
10.18 They **called** out and asked, "Is there a guest here by
11.26 was at Antioch that the believers were first **called** Christians.
13. 1 Barnabas, Simeon **(called** the Black), Lucius (from Cyrene),
13. 2 and Saul, to do the work to which I have **called** them."
13. 7 governor **called** Barnabas and Saul before him because he wanted
15.17 all the Gentiles whom I have **called** to be my own.
15.22 respected by the believers, Judas, **called** Barsabbas, and Silas,
16.10 we decided that God had **called** us to preach the Good News
16.29 The jailer **called** for a light, rushed in, and fell trembling
17. 5 the home of a man **called** Jason, in an attempt to find
19.25 So he **called** them all together with others whose work was
20. 1 the uproar died down, Paul **called** together the believers
23. 6 Pharisees, he **called** out in the Council, "Fellow-Israelites!
23.17 Then Paul **called** one of the officers and said to him,
23.18 and said, "The prisoner Paul **called** me and asked me to
23.23 Then the commander **called** two of his officers and said,
24. 2 Paul was **called** in, and Tertullus began to make his accusation,
24.21 for the one thing I **called** out when I stood before them:
24.25 I will **call** you again when I get the chance."
27. 1 officer in the Roman regiment **called** "The Emperor's Regiment."
27. 8 came to a place **called** Safe Harbours, not far from the
27.14 very strong wind—the one **called** "North-easter"—blew down from
28. 1 were safely ashore, we learnt that the island was **called** Malta.
28.11 on a ship from Alexandria, **called** "The Twin Gods," which had
28.17 three days Paul **called** the local Jewish leaders to a meeting.
Rom 1. 1 apostle chosen and **called by God** to preach his Good News.
1. 6 are in Rome, whom God has **called** to belong to Jesus Christ.
1. 7 Rome whom God loves and has **called** to be his own people:
2.17 You **call** yourself a Jew;
7. 3 her husband is alive, she will be **called** an adulteress;
8.28 love him, those whom he has **called** according to his purpose.
8.30 And so those whom God set apart, he **called;**
8.30 and those he **called,** he put right with himself, and he
9.11 choice was based on his **call,** and not on anything they had
9.24 we are the people he **called,** not only from among the Jews
9.25 "The people who were not mine I will **call** 'My People.'
9.25 The nation that I did not love I will **call** 'My Beloved.'
9.26 there they will be **called** the sons of the living God."
10.12 same Lord of all and richly blesses all who **call** to him.
10.13 scripture says, "Everyone who **calls** out to the Lord for help
10.14 But how can they **call** to him for help if they have
11. 7 the rest grew deaf to God's **call.**
1 Cor 1. 1 From Paul, who was **called** by the will of God to be
1. 2 Corinth, to all who are **called** to be God's holy people,
1. 9 be trusted, the God who **called** you to have fellowship with
1.24 for those whom God has **called,** both Jews and Gentiles, this
1.26 Now remember what you were, my brothers, when God **called** you.
5.11 with a person who **calls** himself a brother but is immoral
7.15 God has **called** you to live in peace.
7.17 Lord's gift to him, and as he was when God **called** him.
7.18 circumcised man has accepted God's **call,** he should not try to
7.18 an uncircumcised man has accepted God's **call,** he should not get
7.20 Everyone should remain as he was when he accepted God's **call.**
7.21 Were you a slave when God **called** you?
7.22 slave who has been **called by the Lord** is the Lord's free
7.22 a free man who has been **called by Christ** is his slave.
7.24 God in the same condition as he was when he was **called.**
9.27 being disqualified after having **called** others to the contest.
14. 8 does not sound a clear **call,** who will prepare for battle?
15. 9 not even deserve to be **called** an apostle, because I persecuted
2 Cor 1.23 I **call** God as my witness—he knows my heart!
Gal 1. 1 From Paul, whose **call** to be an apostle did not come from
1. 6 are deserting the one who **called** you by the grace of Christ,
1.15 me even before I was born, and **called** me to serve him.
2.15 Jews by birth and not "Gentile sinners," as they are **called.**
5. 8 It was not done by God, who **calls** you.
5.13 As for you, my brothers, you were **called** to be free.
Eph 1.18 hope to which he has **called** you, how rich are the wonderful

Eph 2.11 Gentiles by birth—**called** "the uncircumcised" by the Jews,
2.11 who **call** themselves "the circumcised"
4. 1 that measures up to the standard God set when he **called** you.
4. 4 just as there is one hope to which God has **called** you.
Phil 3.14 the prize, which is God's **call** through Christ Jesus to the
Col 3.15 this peace that God has **called** you together in the one body.
4.11 Joshua, also **called** Justus, sends greetings too.
1 Thes 2.12 life that pleases God, who **calls** you to share in his own
4. 7 God did not **call** us to live in immorality, but in holiness.
5.24 He who **calls** you will do it, because he is faithful.
2 Thes 1.11 make you worthy of the life he has **called** you to live.
2.14 God **called** you to this through the Good News we preached
2.14 he **called** you to possess your share of the glory of our
1 Tim 5.21 I solemnly **call** upon you to obey these instructions
6.12 to this life that God **called** you when you firmly professed
6.20 foolish arguments of what some people wrongly **call** "Knowledge."
2 Tim 1. 9 He saved us and **called** us to be his own people, not
2.22 who with a pure heart **call** out to the Lord for help.
Heb 2.11 That is why Jesus is not ashamed to **call** them his brothers.
2.14 Since the children, as he **calls** them, are people of
3. 1 My Christian brothers, who also have been **called by God!**
4. 7 fact that God sets another day, which is **called** "Today."
5. 4 It is only by God's **call** that a man is made
9. 2 was put up, the outer one, which was **called** the Holy Place.
9. 3 second curtain was the Tent **called** the Most Holy Place.
9.15 who have been **called by God** may receive the eternal blessings
11. 8 made Abraham obey when God **called** him to go out to a
11.16 not ashamed for them to **call** him their God, because he has
11.24 up, refuse to be **called** the son of the king's daughter.
Jas 2.23 And so Abraham was **called** God's friend.
5.11 We **call** them happy because they endured.
1 Pet 1.15 all that you do, just as God who **called** you is holy.
1.17 You **call** him Father, when you pray to God, who judges
2. 9 wonderful acts of God, who **called** you out of darkness into
2.21 was to this that God **called** you, for Christ himself suffered
3. 6 she obeyed Abraham and **called** him her master.
3. 9 is what God promised to give you when he **called** you.
5.10 God of all grace, who **calls** you to share his eternal glory
2 Pet 1. 3 knowledge of the one who **called** us to share in his own
1.10 even harder to make God's **call** and his choice of you a
1 Jn 3. 1 so great that we are **called** God's children—and so, in fact,
3 Jn 10 I come, then, I will **call** attention to everything he has done:
Jude 1 those who have been **called by God,** who live in the love
Rev 2.20 that woman Jezebel, who **calls** herself a messenger of God.
2.24 not learnt what the others **call** 'the deep secrets of Satan.'
6.16 They **called** out to the mountains and to the rocks,
7. 2 He **called** out in a loud voice to the four angels
7.10 They **called** out in a loud voice:
10. 3 foot on the land, [3]and **called** out in a loud voice that
10. 3 After he had **called** out, the seven thunders answered with a roar.
12. 9 that ancient serpent, **called** the Devil, or Satan, that deceived
13.10 This **calls** for endurance and faith on the part of God's people."
13.18 This **calls** for wisdom.
14.12 This **calls** for endurance on the part of God's people,
16.16 kings together in the place that in Hebrew is **called** Armageddon.
17. 9 "This **calls** for wisdom and understanding.
17.14 Lamb, together with his **called,** chosen, and faithful followers,
19.11 Its rider is **called** Faithful and True;

CALM

Neh 8.11 The Levites went about **calming** the people and telling
Job 15.11 We have spoken for him with **calm,** even words.
16. 6 I say helps, and being silent does not **calm** my pain.
40.23 he is **calm** when the Jordan dashes in his face.
Ps 65. 7 You **calm** the roar of the seas and the noise of the
65. 7 you **calm** the uproar of the peoples.
89. 9 you **calm** its angry waves.
107.29 He **calmed** the raging storm, and the waves became quiet.
107.30 were glad because of the **calm,** and he brought them safe to
Prov 14.17 wiser people remain **calm.**
14.29 If you stay **calm,** you are wise, but if you have a
17.27 People who stay **calm** have real insight.
21.14 angry with you, a gift given secretly will **calm** him down.
29. 8 Those who are wise keep things **calm.**
Ecc 10. 4 serious wrongs may be pardoned if you keep **calm.**
Is 7. 4 to keep alert, to stay **calm,** and not to be frightened or
Ezek 16.42 Then my anger will be over, and I will be **calm.**
32.14 waters settle and become clear and let your rivers run **calm.**
Jon 1.12 Jonah answered, "Throw me into the sea, and it will **calm** down.
1.15 and threw him into the sea, and it **calmed** down at once.
Zech 6. 8 north to Babylonia have **calmed** down the Lord's anger."
Mt 8.26 winds and the waves to stop, and there was a great **calm.**
Mk 4.39 The wind died down, and there was a great **calm.**
Lk 8.24 they died down, and there was a great **calm.**
Acts 19.35 At last the town clerk was able to **calm** the crowd.
19.36 So then, you must **calm** down and not do anything reckless.

CAMEL

Gen 12.16 of sheep and goats, cattle, donkeys, slaves, and **camels.**
24.10 took ten of his master's **camels** and went to the city where
24.11 he arrived, he made the **camels** kneel down at the well
24.14 also bring water for your **camels,'** may she be the one that
24.19 also bring water for your **camels** and let them have all they
24.20 to get more water, until she had watered all his **camels.**
24.30 who was standing by his **camels** at the well, [31]and said,
24.31 you in my house, and there is a place for your **camels."**
24.32 Laban unloaded the **camels** and gave them straw and fodder.
24.35 goats, cattle, silver, gold, male and female slaves, **camels,**
24.44 to bring water for my **camels,** may she be the one that
Gen 24.46 and said, 'Drink, and I will also water your **camels.'**
24.46 So I drank, and she watered the **camels.**
24.61 ready and mounted the **camels** to go with Abraham's servant,
24.63 evening to take a walk in the fields and saw **camels** coming.
24.64 she got down from her **camel** [65]and asked Abraham's servant,
30.43 He had many flocks, slaves, **camels,** and donkeys.
31.17 and his wives on the **camels,** and drove all his flocks ahead
31.34 and put them in a **camel's** saddlebag and was sitting on them.
32. 7 with him, and also his sheep, goats, cattle, and **camels.**
32.13 and twenty males, thirty milk **camels** with their young, forty
37.25 Their **camels** were loaded with spices and resins.
Ex 9. 3 on all your animals—your horses, donkeys, **camels,** cattle,
Lev 11. 4 chews the cud, [4-6]but you must not eat **camels,**
Deut 14. 7 You may not eat **camels,** rabbits, or rock-badgers.
Judg 6. 5 They and their **camels** were too many to count.
7.12 and they had as many **camels** as there were grains of sand
8.21 took the ornaments that were on the necks of their **camels.**
8.26 nor the collars that were round the necks of their **camels.**
1 Sam 15. 3 the cattle, sheep, **camels,** and donkeys."
27. 9 the sheep, cattle, donkeys, **camels,** and even the clothes.
30.17 hundred young men who mounted **camels** and got away, none of
1 Kgs 10. 2 of attendants, as well as **camels** loaded with spices, jewels,
2 Kgs 8. 9 So Hazael loaded forty **camels** with all kinds of the finest
1 Chr 5.21 the enemy 50,000 **camels,**
12.40 Naphtali, people came bringing donkeys, **camels,** mules, and
27.25 **Camels:**
2 Chr 9. 1 of attendants, as well as **camels** loaded with spices, jewels,
14.15 camps of some shepherds, capturing large numbers of sheep and **camels.**
Ezra 2.64 **Camels** - 435
Neh 7.66 **Camels** - 435
Job 1. 3 sheep, three thousand **camels,** one thousand head of cattle,
1.17 attacked us, took away the **camels,** and killed all your
42.12 sheep, six thousand **camels,** two thousand head of cattle,
Is 21. 7 on donkeys and **camels,** he is to observe them carefully."
30. 6 They load their donkeys and **camels** with expensive gifts for
60. 6 Great caravans of **camels** will come, from Midian and Ephah.
66.20 Jerusalem on horses, mules, and **camels,** and in chariots and wagons,
Jer 2.23 You are like a wild **camel** on heat, running about loose,
49.29 Take their **camels** and tell the people, 'Terror is all round you!'
49.32 "Take their **camels** and all their livestock!
Lam 5. 5 Driven hard like donkeys or **camels,** we are tired, but are
Ezek 25. 5 into a place to keep **camels,** and the whole country of Ammon
Zech 14.15 the horses, the mules, the **camels,** and the donkeys—on all
Mt 3. 4 John's clothes were made of **camel's** hair;
19.24 of God than for a **camel** to go through the eye of
23.24 You strain a fly out of your drink, but swallow a **camel!**
Mk 1. 6 John wore clothes made of **camel's** hair, with a leather belt
10.25 of God than for a **camel** to go through the eye of
Lk 18.25 of God than for a **camel** to go through the eye of

CAMP

Gen 12. 8 Bethel and set up his **camp** between Bethel on the west and
13. 3 and Ai where he had **camped** before [4]and had built an altar.
13.12 cities in the valley and **camped** near Sodom, [13]whose people
13.18 So Abram moved his **camp** and settled near the sacred
14.14 the fighting men in his **camp,** 318 in all, and pursued the
25.16 their names were given to their villages and **camping-places.**
26.17 left and set up his **camp** in the Valley of Gerar, where
26.25 Then he set up his **camp** there, and his servants dug another
28.11 At sunset he came to a holy place and **camped** there.
31.25 Jacob had set up his **camp** on a mountain,
31.25 and Laban set up his **camp** with his kinsmen in the
32. 2 When he saw them, he said, "This is God's **camp";**
32.21 the gifts on ahead of him and spent that night in **camp.**
33.18 Canaan and set up his **camp** in a field near the city.
35.21 on and set up his **camp** on the other side of the
43.21 When we set up **camp** on the way home, we opened our
Ex 4.24 At a **camping** place on the way to Egypt, the Lord met
13.20 The Israelites left Sukkoth and **camped** at Etham on the
14. 2 Israelites to turn back and **camp** in front of Pi Hahiroth,
14. 9 with them where they were **camped** by the Red Sea near Pi
15.27 there they **camped** by the water.
16.13 enough to cover the **camp,**
16.13 and in the morning there was dew all round the **camp.**
16.25 the Lord, and you will not find any food outside the **camp.**
17. 1 They made **camp** at Rephidim, but there was no water there to
18. 5 into the desert where Moses was **camped** at the holy mountain.
19. 1 There they set up **camp** at the foot of Mount Sinai, [3]and
19.16 All the people in the **camp** trembled with fear.
19.17 led them out of the **camp** to meet God, and they stood
24.14 leaders, "Wait here in the **camp** for us until we come back.
29.14 bull's flesh, its skin, and its intestines outside the **camp.**
32.17 said to Moses, "I hear the sound of battle in the **camp."**
32.19 came close enough to the **camp** to see the bull-calf and to
32.26 at the gate of the **camp** and shouted, "Everyone who is on
32.27 sword and go through the **camp** from this gate to the other
33. 7 people of Israel set up **camp,** Moses would take the sacred
33. 7 and put it up some distance away from the **camp.**
33.11 Then Moses would return to the **camp.**
36. 6 sent a command throughout the **camp** that no one was to make
40.36 The Israelites moved their **camp** to another place only
40.37 as the cloud stayed there, they did not move their **camp.**
Lev 4.12 carry it all outside the **camp** to the ritually clean
4.21 take the bull outside the **camp** and burn it, just as he
6.11 take the ashes outside the **camp** to a ritually clean place.
8.17 burnt it outside the **camp,** just as the Lord had commanded.
9.11 But he burnt the meat and the skin outside the **camp.**
10. 4 away from the sacred Tent and put them outside the **camp."**

Lev 10. 5 carried them outside the **camp**, just as Moses had commanded.
13.46 and he must live outside the **camp**, away from others.
14. 3 and the priest shall take him outside the **camp** and examine him.
14. 8 He may enter the **camp**, but he must live outside his tent
15.31 Tent of his presence, which was in the middle of the **camp**.
16.16 stands in the middle of the **camp**, which is ritually unclean.
16.26 his clothes and have a bath before he comes back into **camp**.
16.27 take away sin, shall be carried outside the **camp** and burnt.
16.28 wash his clothes and have a bath before he returns to **camp**.
24.10 There in the **camp** this man quarrelled with an Israelite.
24.14 The Lord said to Moses, [14]"Take that man out of the **camp**.
24.23 they took the man outside the **camp** and stoned him to death.
Num 1.50 its equipment, serve in it, and set up their **camp** round it.
1.51 Whenever you move your **camp**, the Levites shall take the
1.51 Tent down and set it up again at each new **camping** place.
1.52 the Israelites shall set up **camp**, company by company, each
1.53 But the Levites shall **camp** round the Tent to guard it,
2. 2 When the Israelites set up **camp**,
2. 2 each man will **camp** under the banner of his division
2. 2 The **camp** is to be set up all round the Tent.
2. 3 of Judah shall **camp** in their groups, under their leaders,
2.10 of Reuben shall **camp** in their groups, under their leaders,
2.17 same order as they **camp**, each in position under its banner.
2.18 of Ephraim shall **camp** in their groups, under their leaders,
2.25 of Dan shall **camp** in their groups, under their leaders,
2.34 They **camped**, each under his own banner, and they marched,
3.23 This clan was to **camp** on the west behind the Tent,
3.29 This clan was to **camp** on the south side of the Tent,
3.35 This clan was to **camp** on the north side of the Tent,
3.38 and his sons were to **camp** in front of the Tent on
4. 5 it is time to break **camp**, Aaron and his sons shall enter
4.15 it is time to break **camp**, the clan of Kohath shall come
5. 2 Israel to expel from the **camp** everyone with a dreaded skin
5. 3 will not defile the **camp**, where I live among my people."
5. 4 The Israelites obeyed and expelled them all from the **camp**.
9.17 the people of Israel broke **camp**, and they set up camp again
9.18 The people broke **camp** at the command of the Lord,
9.18 and at his command they set up **camp**.
9.18 cloud stayed over the Tent, they stayed in the same **camp**.
9.20 any case, they remained in **camp** or moved, according to the
9.23 They set up **camp** and broke camp in obedience to the
10. 2 use for calling the people together and for breaking **camp**.
10. 5 are sounded, the tribes **camped** on the east will move out.
10. 6 to be sounded to break **camp**, [7]but in order to call the
10.21 they arrived at the next **camp**, the Tent had been set up
10.28 by company, whenever the Israelites broke **camp** and set out.
10.31 "You know where we can **camp** in the wilderness, and you can
10.33 went ahead of them to find a place for them to **camp**.
10.34 they moved on from each **camp**, the cloud of the Lord was
11. 1 It burnt among them and destroyed one end of the **camp**.
11. 8 It fell on the **camp** at night along with the dew.
11.26 Medad, had stayed in the **camp** and had not gone out to
11.26 There in the **camp** the spirit came on them, and they too
11.30 Then Moses and the seventy leaders of Israel went back to **camp**.
11.31 They settled on the **camp** and all round it for many
11.32 They spread them out to dry all round the **camp**.
11.35 From there the people moved to Hazeroth, where they made **camp**.
12.14 be shut out of the **camp** for a week, and after that
12.15 was shut out of the **camp** for seven days, and the people
12.16 left Hazeroth and set up **camp** in the wilderness of Paran.
14.44 neither the Lord's Covenant Box nor Moses left the **camp**.
15.35 whole community is to stone him to death outside the **camp**."
15.36 community took him outside the **camp** and stoned him to death,
19. 3 is to be taken outside the **camp** and killed in his presence.
19. 7 and pour water over himself, and then he may enter the **camp**;
19. 9 ritually clean place outside the **camp**, where they are to be
20. 1 Israel came to the wilderness of Zin and **camped** at Kadesh.
20. 2 was no water where they **camped**, so the people gathered round
21.10 The Israelites moved on and **camped** at Oboth.
21.11 After leaving that place, they **camped** at the ruins of
21.12 Then they **camped** in the Valley of Zered.
21.13 there they moved again and **camped** on the north side of the
22. 1 moved on and set up **camp** in the plains of Moab east
24. 2 desert [2]and saw the people of Israel **camped** tribe by tribe.
25. 1 When the Israelites were **camped** in the Valley of Acacia,
31.10 all their wealth, [10]and burnt all their cities and **camps**.
31.12 Israel, who were at the **camp** on the plains of Moab across
31.13 of the community went out of the **camp** to meet the army.
31.19 touched a corpse must stay outside the **camp** for seven days.
31.24 ritually clean and will be permitted to enter the **camp**."
33. 1 where the Israelites set up **camp** after they left Egypt in
33. 2 down the name of the place each time they set up **camp**.
33. 5 The people of Israel left Rameses and set up **camp** at Sukkoth.
33. 6 Their next **camp** was at Etham on the edge of the desert.
33. 7 to Pi Hahiroth, east of Baal Zephon, and **camped** near Migdol.
33. 8 after a three days' march they **camped** at Marah.
33. 9 went to Elim, where they **camped**, because there were twelve
33.10 They left Elim and **camped** near the Gulf of Suez.
33.11 Their next **camp** was in the desert of Sin.
33.12 Then they **camped** at Dophkah, [13]and after that at Alush.
33.15 Rephidim to Mount Hor they set up **camp** at the following places:
33.41 of Moab the Israelites set up **camp** at the following places:
Deut 1. 7 Break **camp** and move on.
1.33 went ahead of you to find a place for you to **camp**.
23. 9 "When you are in **camp** in time of war, you are to
23.10 the night, he is to go outside the **camp** and stay there.
23.11 to wash himself, and at sunset he may come back into **camp**.
23.12 have a place outside the **camp** where you can go when you
23.14 Keep your **camp** ritually clean, because the Lord your God
23.14 is with you in your **camp** to protect you and to give

Josh 1.11 leaders to [11]go through the **camp** and say to the people,
2. 1 sent two spies from the **camp** at Acacia with orders to go
3. 1 got up early, left the **camp** at Acacia, and went to the
3. 1 to the Jordan, where they **camped** while waiting to cross it.
3. 2 the leaders went through the **camp** [3]and said to the people,
3. 3 Covenant Box of the Lord your God, break **camp** and follow them.
3.14 When the people left the **camp** to cross the Jordan, the
4. 3 with them and to put them down where you **camp** tonight."
4. 8 Israel, carried them to the **camping** place, and put them down there.
4.19 of the first month and made **camp** at Gilgal, east of Jericho.
5. 8 whole nation stayed in the **camp** until the wounds had healed.
5.10 Israelites were **camping** at Gilgal on the plain near Jericho,
6.11 Then they came back to **camp** and spent the night there.
6.14 again marched round the city once and then returned to **camp**.
6.18 will bring trouble and destruction on the Israelite **camp**.
6.23 all, family and slaves, to safety near the Israelite **camp**.
8. 9 Joshua spent the night in **camp**.
8.11 the city and set up **camp** on the north side, with a
8.13 for battle with the main **camp** north of the city and the
9. 6 Then they went to the **camp** at Gilgal and said to Joshua
10. 6 men of Gibeon sent word to Joshua at the **camp** in Gilgal:
10.15 this, Joshua and his army went back to the **camp** at Gilgal.
10.21 Joshua's men came back safe to him at the **camp** at Makkedah.
10.43 this, Joshua and his army went back to the **camp** at Gilgal.
11. 5 came together and set up **camp** at Merom Brook to fight
18. 9 Then they went back to Joshua in the **camp** at Shiloh.
Judg 6. 4 They would **camp** on the land and destroy the crops as far
6.33 the River Jordan, and **camped** in the Valley of Jezreel.
7. 1 his men got up early and **camped** beside the Spring of Harod.
7. 1 The Midianite **camp** was in the valley to the north of them
7. 8 The Midianite **camp** was below them in the valley.
7. 9 That night the Lord commanded Gideon, "Get up and attack the **camp**;
7.10 to attack, go down to the **camp** with your servant Purah.
7.11 his servant Purah went down to the edge of the enemy **camp**.
7.13 loaf of barley bread rolled into our **camp** and hit a tent.
7.15 Then he went back to the Israelite **camp** and said, "Get up!
7.17 to the edge of the **camp**, watch me, and do what I
7.18 blow yours all round the **camp** and shout, 'For the Lord and
7.19 to the edge of the **camp** a short while before midnight, just
7.21 in his place round the **camp**, and the whole enemy army ran
10.17 Then the Ammonite army prepared for battle and made **camp** in Gilead.
10.17 The men of Israel came together and **camped** at Mizpah in Gilead.
11.18 They made **camp** there, but they did not cross the Arnon
11.20 army together, made **camp** at Jahaz, and attacked Israel.
13.25 while he was between Zorah and Eshtaol in the **Camp** of Dan.
15. 9 The Philistines came and made **camp** in Judah, and attacked
18.12 They went up and made **camp** west of Kiriath Jearim in Judah.
18.12 That is why the place is still called **Camp** of Dan.
20.19 out the next morning and made **camp** near the city of Gibeah.
21.12 they brought them to the **camp** at Shiloh, which is in the
1 Sam 4. 1 The Israelites set up their **camp** at Ebenezer and the
4. 3 the survivors came back to **camp**, the leaders of Israel said,
4. 6 and said, "Listen to all that shouting in the Hebrew **camp!**
4. 6 had arrived in the Hebrew **camp**, [7]they were afraid,
4. 7 and said, "A god has come into their **camp!**
10. 5 the Hill of God in Gibeah, where there is a Philistine **camp**.
11.11 they rushed into the enemy **camp** and attacked the Ammonites.
13. 5 They went to Michmash, east of Bethaven, and **camped** there.
13.16 son Jonathan, and their men **camped** in Geba in the territory
13.16 the Philistine **camp** was at Michmash.
13.17 Philistine soldiers went out on raids from their **camp** in three groups:
14. 1 his weapons, "Let's go across to the Philistine **camp**."
14. 2 Saul, [2]who was **camping** under a pomegranate-tree in Migron,
14. 4 to the Philistine **camp**, there were two large jagged rocks,
14. 6 "Let's cross over to the **camp** of those heathen Philistines.
14.15 the raiders and the soldiers in the **camp** trembled with fear;
14.19 the confusion in the Philistine **camp** got worse and worse, so
14.21 gone with them to the **camp**, changed sides again and joined
17. 1 **camped** at a place called Ephes Dammim, between Socoh and Azekah.
17. 2 the Israelites assembled and **camped** in the Valley of Elah,
17. 4 came out from the Philistine **camp** to challenge the Israelites.
17.17 of bread, and hurry with them to your brothers in the **camp**.
17.20 He arrived at the **camp** just as the Israelites were going out
17.53 came back from pursuing the Philistines, they looted their **camp**.
17.57 So when David returned to **camp** after killing Goliath,
26. 3 look for David, [3]and **camped** by the road on Mount Hachilah.
26. 5 Saul slept inside the **camp**, and his men camped round him.
26. 6 Zeruiah), "Which of you two will go to Saul's **camp** with me?"
26. 7 David and Abishai entered Saul's **camp** and found Saul sleeping
26. 7 in the centre of the **camp** with his spear stuck in the
26.15 Just now someone entered the **camp** to kill your master.
28. 4 The Philistine troops assembled and **camped** near the town of Shunem;
28. 4 Saul gathered the Israelites and **camped** at Mount Gilboa.
29. 1 at Aphek, while the Israelites **camped** at the spring in the
2 Sam 1. 2 The next day a young man arrived from Saul's **camp**.
1. 3 "I have escaped from the Israelite **camp**," he answered.
8. 6 Then he set up military **camps** in their territory, and they
8.14 He set up military **camps** throughout Edom, and the people
11.11 commander Joab and his officers are **camping** out in the open.
17.26 Absalom and his men **camped** in the land of Gilead.
23.13 a band of Philistines was **camping** in the Valley of Rephaim.
23.16 through the Philistine **camp**, drew some water from the well,
24. 5 They crossed the Jordan and **camped** south of Aroer, the
1 Kgs 20.27 marched out and **camped** in two groups facing the Syrians.
20.29 Syrians and the Israelites stayed in their **camps**, facing each other.

2 Kgs 3.23 Let's go and loot their **camp!"**
3.24 But when they reached the **camp,** the Israelites attacked
6. 8 consulted his officers and chose a place to set up his **camp.**
7. 4 So let's go to the Syrian **camp;**
7. 5 they went to the Syrian **camp,** but when they reached it, no
7. 7 horses, and donkeys, and leaving the **camp** just as it was.
7. 8 reached the edge of the **camp,** they went into a tent, ate
7.10 So they left the Syrian **camp,** went back to Samaria and
7.10 "We went to the Syrian **camp** and didn't see or hear anybody;
7.12 so they have left their **camp** to go and hide in the
7.16 The people of Samaria rushed out and looted the Syrian **camp.**
10.12 at a place called "Shepherds' **Camp,"** [13]he met some
19.35 Lord went to the Assyrian **camp** and killed 185,000 soldiers.
25. 1 They set up **camp** outside the city, built siege walls round it,
1 Chr 9.18 had stood guard at the gates to the **camps** of the Levites.
9.19 had been when they were in charge of the Lord's **camp.**
11.15 a band of Philistines was **camping** in the Valley of Rephaim.
11.18 through the Philistine **camp,** drew some water from the well,
18. 6 Then he set up military **camps** in their territory, and they
18.13 He set up military **camps** throughout Edom, and the people
19. 7 the army of the king of Maacah came and **camped** near Medeba.
2 Chr 14.15 They also attacked the **camps** of some shepherds,
Ezra 8.15 runs to the town of Ahava, and we **camped** there three days.
Ps 69.25 May their **camps** be left deserted;
78.28 they fell in the middle of the **camp** all round the tents.
Is 21.13 Dedan, whose caravans **camp** in the barren country of Arabia,
29. 1 The city where David **camped** is doomed!
37.36 Lord went to the Assyrian **camp** and killed 185,000 soldiers.
Jer 6. 3 kings will **camp** there with their armies.
6. 3 round the city, and each one will **camp** wherever he wants.
52. 4 They set up **camp** outside the city, built siege walls round it,
Ezek 4. 2 earthworks, **camps,** and battering-rams all round it.
25. 4 They will set up their **camps** in your country and settle there.
Amos 4.10 your nostrils with the stink of dead bodies in your **camps.**
Mic 6. 5 that happened on the way from the **camp** at Acacia to Gilgal.
Zech 14.15 the donkeys—on all the animals in the **camps** of the enemy.
Heb 13.11 but the bodies of the animals are burnt outside the **camp.**
13.13 then, go to him outside the **camp** and share his shame.
Rev 20. 9 the earth and surrounded the **camp** of God's people and the

CAMP OF DAN

Judg 13.25 while he was between Zorah and Eshtaol in the **Camp of Dan.**
18.12 That is why the place is still called **Camp of Dan.**

CAMPAIGN

Josh 10.41 Joshua's **campaign** took him from Kadesh Barnea in the
10.42 and their territory in one **campaign** because the Lord
2 Sam 12.26 Meanwhile Joab continued his **campaign** against Rabbah,

CANAAN

Noah's grandson (or son) and ancestor of the Canaanites. Also the territory occupied by the Israelites.

Gen 9.18 (Ham was the father of **Canaan.)**
9.22 When Ham, the father of **Canaan,** saw that his father was naked,
9.25 "A curse on **Canaan!**
9.26 **Canaan** will be the slave of Shem.
9.27 **Canaan** will be the slave of Japheth."
10. 6 Ham—Cush, Egypt, Libya and **Canaan**—were the ancestors of the
10.15 **Canaan's** sons—Sidon, the eldest, and Heth—were the
10.16 **Canaan** was also the ancestor of the Jebusites, the Amorites, the Girgashites,
10.18 The different tribes of the **Canaanites** spread out,
10.19 until the **Canaanite** borders reached from Sidon southwards to
11.31 city of Ur in Babylonia to go to the land of **Canaan.**
12. 5 in Haran, and they started out for the land of **Canaan.**
12. 5 When they arrived in **Canaan,** [6]Abram travelled through the
12. 6 (At that time the **Canaanites** were still living in the land.)
12. 9 place to place, going towards the southern part of **Canaan.**
12.10 there was a famine in **Canaan,** and it was so bad that
13. 1 to the southern part of **Canaan** with his wife and everything
13. 7 (At that time the **Canaanites** and the Perizzites were still
13.12 stayed in the land of **Canaan,** and Lot settled among the
15.21 the **Canaanites,** the Girgashites, and the Jebusites."
16. 3 (This happened after Abram had lived in **Canaan** for ten years.)
17. 8 The whole land of **Canaan** will belong to your descendants for ever,
20. 1 southern part of **Canaan** and lived between Kadesh and Shur.
23. 2 Hebron in the land of **Canaan,** and Abraham mourned her death.
23.19 buried his wife Sarah in that cave in the land of **Canaan.**
24. 3 choose a wife for my son from the people here in **Canaan.**
24.37 wife for my son from the girls in the land of **Canaan.**
24.62 Who Sees Me" and was staying in the southern part of **Canaan.**
28. 1 Jacob, greeted him, and said to him, "Don't marry a **Canaanite** girl.
28. 6 Isaac blessed him, he commanded him not to marry a **Canaanite** woman.
28. 8 that his father Isaac did not approve of **Canaanite** women.
31.17 ready to go back to his father in the land of **Canaan.**
33.18 Shechem in the land of **Canaan** and set up his camp in
34. 1 Jacob and Leah, went to visit some of the **Canaanite** women.
34.30 now the **Canaanites,** the Perizzites, and everybody else in
35. 6 Luz, which is now known as Bethel, in the land of **Canaan.**
36. 2 Esau married **Canaanite** women:
36. 5 All these sons were born to Esau in the land of **Canaan.**
36. 6 acquired in the land of **Canaan,** and went away from his
37. 1 live in the land of **Canaan,** where his father had lived,
38. 2 There Judah met a **Canaanite** girl whose father was named Shua.
42. 5 to buy corn, because there was famine in the land of **Canaan.**
Gen 42. 7 "We have come from **Canaan** to buy food," they answered.
42.13 all, sir, sons of the same man in the land of **Canaan.**
42.29 to their father Jacob in **Canaan,** they told him all that had
42.32 dead, and the youngest is still in **Canaan** with our father.'
43. 1 The famine in **Canaan** got worse, [2]and when the family of
44. 8 you from the land of **Canaan** the money we found in the
45.17 to load their animals and to return to the land of **Canaan.**
45.25 Egypt and went back home to their father Jacob in **Canaan.**
46. 6 possessions they had acquired in **Canaan** and went to Egypt.
46.10 Jamin, Ohad, Jachin, Zohar, and Shaul, the son of a **Canaanite** woman.
46.12 (Judah's other sons, Er and Onan, had died in **Canaan.)**
46.31 father's family, who were living in **Canaan,** have come to me.
47. 1 my brothers have come from **Canaan** with their flocks, their
47. 4 because in the land of **Canaan** the famine is so severe that
47.13 and the people of Egypt and **Canaan** became weak with hunger.
47.15 the money in Egypt and **Canaan** was spent, the Egyptians came
48. 3 to me at Luz in the land of **Canaan** and blessed me.
48. 7 died in the land of **Canaan,** not far from Ephrath, as I
49.30 Hittite, [30]at Machpelah, east of Mamre, in the land of **Canaan.**
50. 5 in the tomb which he had prepared in the land of **Canaan.**
50.11 When the citizens of **Canaan** saw those people mourning at Atad,
50.13 they carried his body to **Canaan** and buried it in the
Ex 3. 8 the **Canaanites,** the Hittites, the Amorites, the Perizzites,
3.17 the **Canaanites,** the Hittites, the Amorites, the Perizzites,
6. 4 give them the land of **Canaan,** the land in which they had
6.15 Jamin, Ohad, Jachin, Zohar, and Shaul, the son of a **Canaanite** woman;
13. 5 you the land of the **Canaanites,** the Hittites, the Amorites,
13.11 into the land of the **Canaanites,** which he solemnly promised
15.15 the people of **Canaan** lose their courage.
16.35 until they reached the land of **Canaan,** where they settled.
23.23 the **Canaanites,** the Hivites, and the Jebusites,
23.28 Hivites, the **Canaanites,** and the Hittites as you advance.
33. 2 I will drive out the **Canaanites,** the Amorites, the Hittites, the Perizzites,
34.11 the Amorites, the **Canaanites,** the Hittites, the Perizzites,
Lev 14.34 Israel entered the land of **Canaan,** which the Lord was going
18. 3 people in the land of **Canaan,** where I am now taking you.
19.23 come into the land of **Canaan** and plant any kind of fruit
20.22 by the land of **Canaan,** into which I am bringing you.
25.38 to give you the land of **Canaan** and to be your God.
Num 13. 2 to explore the land of **Canaan,** which I am giving to the
13.17 of the land of **Canaan** and then on into the hill-country.
13.29 **Canaanites** live by the Mediterranean Sea and along the River Jordan."
14.25 in whose valleys the Amalekites and the **Canaanites** now live.
14.43 the Amalekites and the **Canaanites,** you will die in battle;
14.45 Then the Amalekites and the **Canaanites** who lived there
21. 1 When the **Canaanite** king of Arad in the southern part of Canaan
21. 3 The Lord heard them and helped them to conquer the **Canaanites.**
26.19 Judah's sons, Er and Onan, had died in the land of **Canaan.)**
32.30 share of the property in the land of **Canaan,** as you do."
32.32 cross into the land of **Canaan** and go into battle, so that
33.40 Arad in southern **Canaan** heard that the Israelites were coming.
33.51 Jordan into the land of **Canaan,** [52]you must drive out all
34. 2 "When you enter **Canaan,** the land which I am giving you, the
34.29 property for the people of Israel in the land of **Canaan.**
35.10 and enter the land of **Canaan,** [11]you are to choose cities
35.14 three east of the Jordan and three in the land of **Canaan.**
Deut 1. 7 Go to the land of **Canaan** and on beyond the Lebanon Mountains
7. 1 Girgashites, the Amorites, the **Canaanites,** the Perizzites,
11.30 territory of the **Canaanites** who live in the Jordan Valley.
20.17 the Hittites, the Amorites, the **Canaanites,** the Perizzites,
32.49 look at the land of **Canaan** that I am about to give
Josh 2. 1 explore the land of **Canaan,** especially the city of Jericho.
3.10 the **Canaanites,** the Hittites, the Hivites, the Perizzites,
5. 1 the Jordan and all the **Canaanite** kings along the
5.11 next day was the first time they ate food grown in **Canaan:**
5.12 From that time on they ate food grown in **Canaan.**
7. 9 The **Canaanites** and everyone else in the country will hear about it.
9. 1 the Hittites, the Amorites, the **Canaanites,** the Perizzites,
11. 3 sent word to the **Canaanites** on both sides of the Jordan,
12. 8 the Hittites, the Amorites, the **Canaanites,** the Perizzites,
13. 3 far north as the border of Ekron was considered **Canaanite;**
13. 4 There is still all the **Canaanite** country, and Mearah
14. 1 of how the land of **Canaan** west of the Jordan was divided
16.10 did not drive out the **Canaanites** who lived in Gezer,
16.10 so the **Canaanites** have lived among the Ephraimites
17.12 in those cities, so the **Canaanites** continued to live there.
17.13 not drive out all the **Canaanites,** but they did force them to
17.16 for us, but the **Canaanites** in the plains have iron chariots,
17.18 As for the **Canaanites,** you will drive them out, even though
21. 2 Shiloh in the land of **Canaan** they said to them, "The Lord
22. 9 Shiloh in the land of **Canaan** and started out for their own
22.32 Gilead and went back to **Canaan,** to the people of Israel, and
24. 3 the Euphrates and led him through the whole land of **Canaan.**
24.11 the **Canaanites,** the Hittites, the Girgashites,
Judg 1. 1 should be the first to go and attack the **Canaanites?"**
1. 3 assigned to us, and we will fight the **Canaanites** together.
1. 4 gave them victory over the **Canaanites** and the Perizzites,
1. 9 on to fight the **Canaanites** who lived in the hill-country,
1.10 They marched against the **Canaanites** living in the city of Hebron,
1.17 and together they defeated the **Canaanites** who lived in the
1.27 the **Canaanites** continued to live there.
1.28 stronger, they forced the **Canaanites** to work for them,
1.29 not drive out the **Canaanites** living in the city of Gezer,
1.29 and so the **Canaanites** continued to live there with them.
1.30 and Nahalal, and so the **Canaanites** continued to live there
1.32 Asher lived with the local **Canaanites,** since they did not

Judg 1.33 Naphtali lived with the local **Canaanites,** but forced them to
3. 1 the Israelites who had not been through the wars in **Canaan.**
3. 3 five Philistine cities, all the **Canaanites,** the Sidonians,
3. 5 Israel settled down among the **Canaanites,**
4. 2 be conquered by Jabin, a **Canaanite** king who ruled in the
4.23 God gave the Israelites victory over Jabin, the **Canaanite** king.
5.19 the kings of **Canaan** fought, but they took no silver away.
21.12 to the camp at Shiloh, which is in the land of **Canaan.**
1 Sam 7.14 And there was peace also between the Israelites and the **Canaanites.**
2 Sam 24. 7 of the Hivites and the **Canaanites,** and finally to Beersheba,
1 Kgs 9.20 descendants of the people of **Canaan** whom the Israelites had
2 Kgs 21.11 things, things far worse than what the **Canaanites** did;
1 Chr 1. 8 Ham—Cush, Egypt, Libya, and **Canaan**—were the ancestors of the
1.13 **Canaan's** sons—Sidon, the eldest, and Heth—were the
1.14 **Canaan** was also the ancestor of the Jebusites, the
2. 3 By his wife Bathshua, a **Canaanite,** he had three sons:
16.18 "I will give you the land of **Canaan,"** he said.
16.19 God's people were few in number, strangers in the land of **Canaan.**
2 Chr 8. 7 descendants of the people of **Canaan** whom the Israelites had
Ezra 9. 1 Moab, and Egypt or from the **Canaanites,** Hittites,
Neh 9. 8 him the land of the **Canaanites,** the land of the Hittites and
9.24 They conquered the land of **Canaan;**
9.24 to do as they pleased with the people and kings of **Canaan.**
Ps 105.11 "I will give you the land of **Canaan,"** he said.
105.12 God's people were few in number, strangers in the land of **Canaan.**
106.37 sons and daughters as sacrifices to the idols of **Canaan.**
135.11 Amorites, Og, king of Bashan, and all the kings in **Canaan.**
Ezek 16. 3 "You were born in the land of **Canaan.**
Hos 12. 7 Lord says, "The people of Israel are as dishonest as the **Canaanites;**
Mt 15.22 A **Canaanite** woman who lived in that region came to him.
Acts 7.11 a famine all over Egypt and **Canaan,** which caused much suffering.
13.19 nations in the land of **Canaan** and made his people the owners

CANAL

Ex 7.19 hold it out over all the rivers, **canals,** and pools in Egypt.
8. 5 stick over the rivers, the **canals,** and the pools, and make
Ezra 8.15 the entire group by the **canal** that runs to the town of
8.21 There by the Ahava **Canal** I gave orders for us all to
8.31 first month that we left the Ahava **Canal** to go to Jerusalem.

CANCEL

Deut 15. 1 seventh year you are to **cancel** the debts of those who owe
15. 2 has lent money to a fellow-Israelite is to **cancel** the debt;
15. 2 the Lord himself has declared the debt **cancelled.**
15. 9 just because the year when debts are **cancelled** is near.
31.10 the year that debts are **cancelled** comes round, read this
Neh 5.11 **Cancel** all the debts they owe you—money or corn or wine
10.31 we will not farm the land, and we will **cancel** all debts.
Ecc 10. 1 and a little stupidity can **cancel** out the greatest wisdom.
Is 28.18 your agreement with the world of the dead will be **cancelled.**
Zech 11.10 "Favour" and broke it, to **cancel** the covenant which the
11.11 So the covenant was **cancelled** on that day.
Mk 7.13 teaching you pass on to others **cancels** out the word of God.
Lk 7.42 them could pay him back, so he **cancelled** the debts of both.
Gal 3.17 years later, cannot break that covenant and **cancel** God's promise.
Col 2.14 he **cancelled** the unfavourable record of our debts with its

CANCER

Prov 12. 4 brings shame on her husband is like a **cancer** in his bones.
14.30 mind makes the body healthy, but jealousy is like a **cancer.**

CANE see STICK

CANE

Ex 30.23 cinnamon, three kilogrammes of sweet-smelling **cane,** [24]and

CAP

Ex 28.40 "Make shirts, sashes, and **caps** for Aaron's sons, to
29. 9 put sashes round their waists and tie **caps** on their heads.
39.28 sons, [28]and the turban, the **caps,** the linen shorts,
Lev 8.13 round their waists, and tied **caps** on their heads, just as
Dan 3.21 up, fully dressed—shirts, robes, **caps,** and all—and threw

CAPABLE

Gen 47. 6 And if there are any **capable** men among them, put them in
Ex 18.21 addition, you should choose some **capable** men and appoint
18.25 Jethro's advice [25]and chose **capable** men
Num 27.18 Joshua son of Nun, a **capable** man, and place your hands on
2 Sam 24. 9 king the total number of men **capable** of military service:
1 Chr 21. 5 King David the total number of men **capable** of military service:
Prov 31.10 How hard it is to find a **capable** wife!
Ecc 9.11 not always get rich, and **capable** men do not always rise to
1 Cor 6. 2 the world, aren't you **capable** of judging small matters?
2 Cor 2.16 Who, then, is **capable** of such a task?
3. 5 allows us to claim that we are **capable** of doing this work.
3. 5 The **capacity** we have comes from God;
3. 6 is he who made us **capable** of serving the new covenant,

CAPE

Song 5. 7 the guards at the city wall tore off my **cape.**

CAPE SALMONE see SALMONE

CAPERNAUM

Town on the shore of Lake Galilee.

Mt 4.13 but went to live in **Capernaum,** a town by Lake Galilee,
8. 5 Jesus entered **Capernaum,** a Roman officer met him and begged for
11.23 And as for you, **Capernaum!**
17.24 disciples came to **Capernaum,** the collectors of the temple-tax
Mk 1.21 came to the town of **Capernaum,** and on the next Sabbath Jesus
2. 1 later Jesus went back to **Capernaum,** and the news spread that
9.33 They came to **Capernaum,** and after going indoors Jesus asked
Lk 4.23 home town the same things you heard were done in **Capernaum.**
4.31 Jesus went to **Capernaum,** a town in Galilee, where he taught
7. 1 saying all these things to the people, he went to **Capernaum.**
10.15 And as for you, **Capernaum!**
Jn 2.12 and disciples went to **Capernaum** and stayed there a few days.
4.46 A government official was there whose son was ill in **Capernaum.**
4.47 asked him to go to **Capernaum** and heal his son, who was
6.17 into a boat, and went back across the lake towards **Capernaum.**
6.24 got into those boats and went to **Capernaum,** looking for him.
6.59 Jesus said this as he taught in the synagogue in **Capernaum.**

CAPITAL (1)

Num 21.26 Heshbon was the **capital city** of the Amorite king Sihon,
Josh 13.31 Ashtaroth and Edrei, the **capital cities** of Og's kingdom in Bashan.
1 Sam 27. 5 need, sir, for me to live with you in the **capital city."**
2 Sam 10. 8 entrance to Rabbah, their **capital city,** while the others,
12.26 his campaign against Rabbah, the **capital city** of Ammon, and
2 Kgs 3.25 At last only the **capital city** of Kir Heres was left, and
1 Chr 19. 9 the entrance to Rabbah, their **capital city,** and the kings
Neh 1. 1 of Persia, I, Nehemiah, was in Susa, the **capital city.**
Esth 1. 1 his royal throne in Persia's **capital city** of Susa, King
1. 5 all the men in the **capital city** of Susa, rich and poor
2. 3 young girls to your harem here in Susa, the **capital city.**
3.15 was made public in the **capital city** of Susa, and runners
8.14 The decree was also made public in Susa, the **capital city.**
9. 6 In Susa, the **capital city** itself, the Jews killed five hundred men.
Is 7. 8 no stronger than Damascus, its **capital city,** and Damascus is
7. 9 no stronger than Samaria, its **capital city,** and Samaria is
32.14 Even the palace will be abandoned and the **capital city** totally deserted.
Jer 49. 2 make the people of the **capital city** of Rabbah hear the noise
Ezek 30.14 I will punish the **capital city** of Thebes.
Dan 4.30 I built it as my **capital city** to display my power and
Amos 6. 8 I will give their **capital city** and everything in it to the
Obad 3 Your **capital** is a fortress of solid rock;
Mic 1. 5 Samaria, the **capital city** itself!
4. 8 once again be the **capital** of the kingdom that was yours.
Nah 3. 8 Nineveh, are you any better than Thebes, the **capital** of Egypt?
Zech 9. 1 of Israel, but also the **capital** of Syria belong to the Lord.

CAPITAL (2)

1 Kgs 7.16 He also made two bronze **capitals,** each one 2.2 metres tall,
7.19 The **capitals** were shaped like lilies, 1.8 metres tall,
7.20 There were two hundred pomegranates in two rows round each **capital.**
7.22 The lily-shaped bronze **capitals** were on top of the columns.
7.40 The two bowl-shaped **capitals** on top of the columns
7.40 chains on each **capital** The four hundred bronze pomegranates,
7.40 round the design on each **capital** The ten carts The ten
2 Kgs 25.17 metres high, with a bronze **capital** on top, 1.3 metres high.
25.17 All round each **capital** was a bronze grating decorated with
2 Chr 3.15 Each one had a **capital** 2.2 metres tall.
4.11 The two bowl-shaped **capitals** on top of the columns
4.11 of interwoven chains on each **capital** The four hundred bronze
4.11 round the design of each **capital** The ten carts The ten
Jer 52.21 each column was a bronze **capital** 2.2 metres high, and all

CAPTAIN

Gen 37.36 king's officers, who was the **captain** of the palace guard.
39. 1 king's officers, who was the **captain** of the palace guard.
40. 3 in the house of the **captain** of the guard, in the same
40. 4 prison, and the **captain** assigned Joseph as their servant.
41.10 us in prison in the house of the **captain** of the guard.
41.12 was there with us, a slave of the **captain** of the guard.
1 Sam 22.14 He is your own son-in-law, **captain** of your bodyguard, and
1 Kgs 9.22 as his soldiers, officers, commanders, chariot **captains,**
Jon 1. 6 The **captain** found him there and said to him, "What are
Acts 10. 1 named Cornelius, who was a **captain** in the Roman regiment called
10.22 **"Captain** Cornelius sent us," they answered.
27.11 was convinced by what the **captain** and the owner of the ship
Rev 18.17 All the ships' **captains** and passengers, the sailors and all

CAPTIVE

Num 21.29 And the women became **captives** of the Amorite king.
24.22 But you Kenites will be destroyed When Assyria takes you **captive."**
Judg 5.12 Forward, Barak son of Abinoam, lead your **captives** away!
1 Sam 30. 8 you will catch them and rescue the **captives."**
Neh 7. 5 who had first returned from **captivity,** and this is the
8.17 come back from **captivity** built shelters and lived in them.
Esth 2. 6 along with a group of **captives,** Mordecai was among them.
Ps 68.18 He goes up to the heights, taking many **captives** with him;

Song 6. 5 they are holding me **captive.**
7. 5 its beauty could hold a king **captive.**
Is 45.13 He will rebuild my city, Jerusalem, and set my **captive** people free.
50. 1 think I sold you into **captivity** like a man who sells his
50. 1 No, you went away **captive** because of your sins;
52. 2 Undo the chains that bind you, **captive** people of Zion!
52. 5 you are **captives,** and nothing was paid for you.
61. 1 To announce release to **captives** And freedom to those in prison.
Jer 13.17 because the Lord's people have been taken away as **captives.**
Lam 1.18 My young men and women have been taken away **captive.**
Ezek 12.11 what will happen to them—they will be refugees and **captives.**
39.28 because I sent them into **captivity** and now gather them and
Joel 3. 3 They threw dice to decide who would get the **captives.**
Amos 9. 4 they are taken away into **captivity** by their enemies, I will
Mic 2. 4 our land away And given it to those who took us **captive."**
Nah 2. 7 The queen is taken **captive;**
Hab 1. 9 Their **captives** are as numerous as grains of sand.
Lk 4.18 proclaim liberty to the **captives** and recovery of sight to the
2 Cor 10. 5 we take every thought **captive** and make it obey Christ.
Eph 4. 8 up to the very heights, he took many **captives** with him;
Col 2.15 them by leading them as **captives** in his victory procession.

CAPTURE

[RECAPTURED]

Gen 14.14 that his nephew had been **captured,** he called together all
31.26 me and carry off my daughters like women **captured** in war?
34.29 took everything of value, **captured** all the women and children,
Num 14. 3 in battle, and our wives and children will be **captured.**
14.31 that your children would be **captured,** but I will bring them
21. 1 way of Atharim, he attacked them and **captured** some of them.
21.25 So the people of Israel **captured** all the Amorite cities,
21.26 king of Moab and had **captured** all his land as far as
21.32 The Israelites **captured** it and its surrounding towns and
31. 9 The people of Israel **captured** the Midianite women and children,
31.11 they had **captured,** including the prisoners and the animals,
31.19 day purify yourselves and the women you have **captured.**
31.26 has been **captured,** including the prisoners and the animals.
31.32 a list of what was **captured** by the soldiers, in addition to
32.41 tribe of Manasseh, attacked and **captured** some villages and
32.42 Nobah attacked and **captured** Kenath and its villages, and
Deut 2.34 At the same time we **captured** and destroyed every town,
2.36 Lord our God let us **capture** all the towns from Aroer, on
3. 4 At the same time we **captured** all his towns—there was not
3. 4 In all we **captured** sixty towns—the whole region of Argob,
20.13 Lord your God lets you **capture** the city, kill every man in
20.16 "But when you **capture** cities in the land that the Lord
20.19 "When you are trying to **capture** a city, do not cut
20.20 use them in the siege mounds until the city is **captured.**
Josh 6.20 went straight up the hill into the city and **captured** it.
8. 7 Then you will come out of hiding and **capture** the city.
8.19 hiding got up quickly, ran into the city and **captured** it.
8.23 He was **captured** and taken to Joshua.
8.27 themselves the livestock and goods **captured** in the city, as
10. 1 Jerusalem, heard that Joshua had **captured** and totally
10.28 Joshua attacked and **captured** Makkedah and its king that day.
10.35 They **captured** it the same day and put everyone there to death,
10.37 Eglon up into the hills to Hebron, attacked it [37]and **captured** it.
10.39 He **captured** it, with its king and all the nearby towns.
11.10 Joshua then turned back, **captured** Hazor and killed its king.
11.12 Joshua **captured** all these cities and their kings, putting everyone to death,
11.16 Joshua **captured** all the land—the hill-country and foothills,
11.17 a long time, but he **captured** them all and put them to
11.23 Joshua **captured** the whole land, as the Lord had commanded Moses.
15.16 marriage to the man who succeeds in **capturing** Kiriath Sepher."
15.17 son of Caleb's brother Kenaz, **captured** the city, so Caleb
19.47 They **captured** it, killed its people, and claimed it for themselves.
Judg 1. 8 The men of Judah attacked Jerusalem and **captured** it.
1.12 marriage to the man who succeeds in **capturing** Kiriath Sepher."
1.13 of Caleb's younger brother Kenaz, **captured** the city, so
1.18 But they did not **capture** Gaza, Ashkelon, or Ekron, with
3.13 Israel and **captured** Jericho, the city of palm-trees.
3.28 they followed Ehud down and **captured** the place where the
5.30 are only finding things to **capture** and divide, a girl or two
7.25 They **captured** the two Midianite chiefs, Oreb and Zeeb;
8. 6 You haven't **captured** Zebah and Zalmunna yet."
8.12 but he pursued them and **captured** them, and caused their
8.14 way of Heres Pass, [14]he **captured** a young man from Sukkoth
8.15 army because I hadn't **captured** Zebah and Zalmunna yet.
9.45 Abimelech **captured** the city, killed its people, tore it
9.50 Abimelech went to Thebez, surrounded that city, and **captured** it.
12. 5 Ephraimites from escaping, the Gileadites **captured** the
15.18 of thirst and be **captured** by these heathen Philistines?"
16.21 The Philistines **captured** him and put his eyes out.
1 Sam 4.11 God's Covenant Box was **captured,** and Eli's sons,
4.17 Hophni and Phinehas were killed, and God's Covenant Box was **captured!"**
4.19 God's Covenant Box had been **captured** and that her
4.21 referring to the **capture** of the Covenant Box and the death
4.22 Israel," she said, "because God's Covenant Box has been **captured."**
5. 1 After the Philistines **captured** the Covenant Box, they
7.14 cities which the Philistines had **captured** between Ekron and
14.32 over to what they had **captured** from the enemy, took sheep
15. 8 he **captured** King Agag of Amalek alive and killed all the people.
15.21 did not kill the best sheep and cattle that they **captured;**
23.20 We know, Your Majesty, how much you want to **capture** him;
23.26 who were closing in on them and were about to **capture** them.
30. 2 They had burnt down the town [2]and **captured** all the women;
1 Sam 30.16 amount of loot they had **captured** from Philistia and Judah.
2 Sam 5. 7 (But David did **capture** their fortress of Zion, and it
5. 9 After **capturing** the fortress, David lived in it and named
5.17 made king of Israel, so their army set out to **capture** him.
8. 4 David **captured** seventeen hundred of his horsemen and
8. 7 David **captured** the gold shields carried by Hadadezer's
11.25 to launch a stronger attack on the city and **capture** it."
12.26 Rabbah, the capital city of Ammon, and was about to **capture** it.
12.27 "I have attacked Rabbah and have **captured** its water supply.
12.28 I don't want to get the credit for **capturing** it."
22.37 You have kept me from being **captured,** and I have never fallen.
1 Kgs 9.16 Egypt had attacked Gezer and **captured** it, killing its
15.20 They **captured** Ijon, Dan, Abel Beth Maacah, the area near Lake Galilee,
20.21 Ahab took to the field, **captured** the horses and chariots,
20.39 when a soldier brought a **captured** enemy to me and said,
2 Kgs 6.13 he is," the king ordered, "and I will **capture** him."
6.22 "Not even soldiers you had **captured** in combat would you put
7.12 and then they will take us alive and **capture** the city."
13.25 defeated Benhadad three times and **recaptured** the cities that
14. 7 **captured** the city of Sela in battle and called it Joktheel,
15.29 Pileser, the emperor of Assyria, **captured** the cities of Ijon,
16. 9 his army against Damascus, **captured** it, killed King Rezin,
17. 6 of Hoshea, the Assyrian emperor **captured** Samaria, took the
18.30 he will stop our Assyrian army from **capturing** your city.
25. 5 Babylonian army pursued King Zedekiah, **captured** him
1 Chr 5. 4 The Assyrian emperor, Tiglath Pileser, **captured** Beerah,
5.21 They **captured** from the enemy 50,000 camels,
11. 5 inside the city, but David **captured** their fortress of Zion,
14. 8 whole country of Israel, their army went out to **capture** him.
18. 4 David **captured** a thousand of his chariots,
18. 7 David **captured** the gold shields carried by Hadadezer's
26.27 some of the loot they **captured** in battle and dedicated it
2 Chr 8. 3 He **captured** the territory of Hamath and Zobah [4]and
12. 4 He **captured** the fortified cities of Judah and advanced as
14.14 plundered all those cities and **captured** large amounts of loot.
14.15 some shepherds, **capturing** large numbers of sheep and camels.
15. 8 the cities he had **captured** in the hill-country of Ephraim.
16. 4 They **captured** Ijon, Dan, Abel Beth Maacah, and all the
17. 2 cities which Asa had **captured** in the territory of Ephraim.
20. 2 They have already **captured** Hazazon Tamar."
25.12 Edomite soldiers [12]and **captured** another ten thousand.
25.13 killed three thousand men, and **captured** quantities of loot.
25.23 Jehoash **captured** Amaziah and took him to Jerusalem.
26. 2 Amaziah that Uzziah **recaptured** Elath and rebuilt the city.)
28. 8 their fellow-countrymen, the Israelite army **captured** 200,000
28.15 provide the prisoners with clothing from the **captured** loot.
28.16 to raid Judah again and **captured** many prisoners, so King
28.18 They **captured** the cities of Beth Shemesh, Aijalon, and
32.18 city wall, so that it would be easier to **capture** the city.
33.11 They **captured** Manasseh, stuck hooks in him, put him in chains,
36. 6 Nebuchadnezzar of Babylonia invaded Judah, **captured** Jehoiakim,
Neh 9.25 Your people **captured** fortified cities, fertile land,
Job 15.28 That is the man who **captured** cities and seized houses
40.24 Who can blind his eyes and **capture** him?
Ps 18.36 You have kept me from being **captured,** and I have never fallen.
21. 8 The king will **capture** all his enemies;
21. 8 he will **capture** everyone who hates him.
31. 8 You have not let my enemies **capture** me;
68.12 The women at home divided what was **captured:**
78.61 He allowed our enemies to **capture** the Covenant Box, the
137. 3 Those who **captured** us told us to sing;
137. 7 Remember, Lord, what the Edomites did the day Jerusalem was **captured.**
Is 7. 1 Remaliah, king of Israel, attacked Jerusalem, but were unable to **capture** it.
9. 3 harvest their corn or when they divide **captured** wealth.
10.28 The enemy army has **captured** the city of Ai!
14. 2 Those who once **captured** Israel will now be captured by Israel,
20. 3 When Ashdod was **captured,** the Lord said, "My servant
20. 4 naked the prisoners he **captures** from those two countries.
22. 3 ran away and were **captured** before they shot a single arrow.
30.25 of your enemies are **captured** and their people are killed,
36. 1 Assyria, attacked the fortified cities of Judah and **captured** them.
36.15 he will stop our Assyrian army from **capturing** your city.
46. 2 they are **captured** and carried away.
Jer 20. 6 family will also be **captured** and taken off to Babylonia.
21. 7 let all of you be **captured** by King Nebuchadnezzar and by
32. 3 let the king of Babylonia **capture** this city, [4]and King
32.24 mounds round the city to **capture** it, and they are attacking.
32.25 the city is about to be **captured** by the Babylonians."
32.28 they will **capture** it [29]and set it on fire.
34. 3 you will be **captured** and handed over to him.
34.22 They will attack it, **capture** it, and burn it down.
37. 8 come back, attack the city, **capture** it, and burn it down.
38. 3 city to the Babylonian army, and they will **capture** it."
38.28 the palace courtyard until the day Jerusalem was **captured.**
39. 3 (When Jerusalem was **captured,** all the high officials of
39. 5 Babylonian army pursued them and **captured** Zedekiah in the plains near Jericho.
48. 1 Kiriathaim is **captured,** its mighty fortress torn down, and
48. 2 The enemy have **captured** Heshbon and plot to destroy the
48.41 wings, [41]and the towns and fortresses will be **captured.**
50.33 All who **captured** them are guarding them closely and will not
51.32 The enemy have **captured** the river-crossing and have set
51.41 "The city that the whole world praised has been **captured!**
51.56 its soldiers are **captured,** and their bows are broken.
52. 8 Babylonian army pursued King Zedekiah, **captured** him in the plains near Jericho,
Lam 1. 5 Her children have been **captured** and taken away.

Lam 4.20 They **captured** the source of our life, the king the Lord
Ezek 21.23 of their sins and to warn them that they will be **captured.**
36. 3 nations **captured** and plundered the mountains of Israel,
36. 5 With glee and contempt, they **captured** my land and took
40. 1 exile and the fourteenth year after Jerusalem was **captured.**
Dan 1. 2 The Lord let him **capture** King Jehoiakim and seize some of
1. 2 and put the **captured** treasures in the temple storerooms.
11.11 to war against the king of Syria and **capture** his huge army.
11.15 of Syria will lay siege to a fortified city and **capture** it.
11.24 his followers the goods and property he has **captured** in war.
11.28 all the loot he has **captured,** determined to destroy the
Amos 6.13 You boast about **capturing** the town of Lodebar.
Obad 19 those from the western foothills will **capture** Philistia;
20 Jerusalem who are in Sardis will **capture** the towns of southern Judah.
Mic 1.15 you over to an enemy, who is going to **capture** your town.
Nah 3.10 were carried off in chains and divided among their **captors.**
Hab 1.10 can stop them—they pile up earth against it and **capture** it.
Mt 26.55 with swords and clubs to **capture** me, as though I were an
Mk 14.48 with swords and clubs to **capture** me, as though I were an
2 Pet 2.12 by instinct, like wild animals born to be **captured** and killed;
Rev 13.10 Whoever is meant to be **captured** will surely be captured;

CARAVAN

Judg 5. 6 the days of Jael, **caravans** no longer went through the land,
Job 6.18 **Caravans** get lost looking for water;
6.19 **Caravans** from Sheba and Tema search, [20] but their hope
Is 21.13 You people of Dedan, whose **caravans** camp in the barren
60. 6 Great **caravans** of camels will come, from Midian and Ephah.

CARCASS

Ezek 40.38 and there they washed the **carcasses** of the animals to be

CARE

Gen 4. 9 Am I supposed to take **care** of my brother?"
13. 7 between the men who took **care** of Abram's animals
13. 7 and those who took **care** of Lot's animals.
25.34 That was all Esau **cared** about his rights as the first-born son.
30.29 for you and how your flocks have prospered under my **care.**
30.31 I will continue to take **care** of your flocks if you agree
30.36 Jacob took **care** of the rest of Laban's flocks.
36.24 wilderness when he was taking **care** of his father's donkeys.)
37. 2 young man of seventeen, took **care** of the sheep and goats
37.12 gone to Shechem to take **care** of their father's flock,
37.13 Shechem, where your brothers are taking **care** of the flock."
37.16 for my brothers, who are taking **care** of their flock," he
39. 6 everything he had to the **care** of Joseph and did not concern
42.37 Put him in my **care,** and I will bring him back."
45.11 If you are in Goshen, I can take **care** of you.
46.32 you are shepherds and take **care** of livestock and that you
46.34 him that you have taken **care** of livestock all your lives,
50.21 I will take **care** of you and your children."
50.24 but God will certainly take **care** of you and lead you out
Ex 3. 1 day while Moses was taking **care** of the sheep and goats of
21.18 his lost time and take **care** of him until he gets well.
25.40 Take **care** to make them according to the plan that I
Lev 24. 4 Aaron shall take **care** of the lamps on the lampstand of
Num 6.24 May the Lord bless you and take **care** of you;
7. 9 the sacred objects they took **care** of had to be carried on
18.21 for their service in taking **care** of the Tent of my presence.
18.23 only the Levites will take **care** of the Tent and bear the
Deut 2. 7 He has taken **care** of you as you wandered through this vast
11.12 The Lord your God takes **care** of this land and watches
28.39 will plant vineyards and take **care** of them, but you will not
31.24 God's Law in a book, taking **care** not to leave out anything.
32.10 He protected them and **cared** for them, as he would protect himself.
Judg 13. 4 Take **care** not to drink any wine or beer, or eat any
18. 6 The Lord is taking **care** of you on this journey."
19.20 I'll take **care** of you;
Ruth 2.20 of ours, one of those responsible for taking **care** of us."
3. 9 a close relative, you are responsible for taking **care** of me.
4.14 He has given you a grandson today to take **care** of you.
4.16 Naomi took the child, held him close, and took **care** of him.
1 Sam 16.11 the youngest, but he is out taking **care** of the sheep."
16.19 me your son David, the one who takes **care** of the sheep."
17.15 Bethlehem from time to time, to take **care** of his father's sheep.
17.28 Who is taking **care** of those sheep of yours out there in
17.34 "Your Majesty," David said, "I take **care** of my father's sheep.
2 Sam 12. 3 He took **care** of it, and it grew up in his home
14. 8 the king answered, "and I will take **care** of the matter."
15.16 concubines, whom he left behind to take **care** of the palace.
16.21 concubines whom he left behind to take **care** of the palace.
18.22 Ahimaaz insisted, "I don't **care** what happens;
19.33 "Come with me to Jerusalem, and I will take **care** of you."
20. 3 he had left to take **care** of the palace, and put them
1 Kgs 1. 2 a young woman to stay with you and take **care** of you.
1. 4 on the king and took **care** of him, but he did not
1.15 and Abishag, the girl from Shunem, was taking **care** of him.
2. 7 Barzillai from Gilead and take **care** of them, because they
17.20 been kind enough to take **care** of me, and now you kill
2 Kgs 10. 6 King Ahab were under the **care** of the leading citizens of Samaria,
11. 3 For six years Jehosheba took **care** of the boy and kept him
1 Chr 23.28 worship, to take **care** of its courtyards and its rooms,
23.32 given the responsibility of taking **care** of the Tent of the
28.13 of the Temple, and to take **care** of all the temple utensils.
2 Chr 30. 1 He took special **care** to send letters to the tribes of
Ezra 5. 8 is being done with great **care** and is moving ahead steadily.
Esth 2. 3 Put them in the **care** of Hegai, the eunuch who is in
2. 8 the royal palace in the **care** of Hegai, who had charge of
2.14 harem and put in the **care** of Shaashgaz, the eunuch in charge
2.20 had obeyed him when she was a little girl under his **care.**
8. 5 Your Majesty, and if you **care** about me and if it seems
Job 9.21 I am innocent, but I no longer **care.**
10.12 me life and constant love, and your **care** has kept me alive.
18.21 of evil men, the fate of those who **care** nothing for God.
21.21 over, does he really **care** whether his children are happy?
31.18 All my life I have taken **care** of them.
Ps 8. 4 mere man, that you **care** for him?
10. 4 A wicked man does not **care** about the Lord;
10.11 The wicked man says to himself, "God doesn't **care!**
18.35 your **care** has made me great, and your power has kept me
27.10 mother may abandon me, but the Lord will take **care** of me.
28. 9 Be their shepherd, and take **care** of them for ever.
31. 5 I place myself in your **care.**
31.15 I am always in your **care;**
36. 6 Men and animals are in your **care.**
37.18 The Lord takes **care** of those who obey him, and the land
54. 3 trying to kill me— men who do not **care** about God.
65. 9 You show your **care** for the land by sending rain;
68. 5 his sacred Temple, **cares** for orphans and protects widows.
78.72 David took **care** of them with unselfish devotion and led
91. 4 you will be safe in his **care;**
95. 7 we are the people he **cares** for, the flock for which he
109.12 be kind to him or **care** for the orphans he leaves behind.
138. 6 are so high above, you **care** for the lowly, and the proud
142. 4 No one **cares** for me.
Prov 12.10 A good man takes **care** of his animals, but wicked men are
14. 9 Foolish people don't **care** if they sin, but good people
18. 2 A fool does not **care** whether he understands a thing or not;
27. 5 than to let him think you don't **care** for him at all.
27.18 Take **care** of a fig-tree and you will have figs to eat.
27.18 A servant who takes **care** of his master will be honoured.
Song 1. 6 I had no time to **care** for myself.
Is 11. 6 feed together, and little children will take **care** of them.
13.17 They **care** nothing for silver and are not tempted by gold.
34.15 nests, lay eggs, hatch their young, and **care** for them there.
40.11 He will take **care** of his flock like a shepherd;
40.27 Lord doesn't know your troubles or **care** if you suffer injustice?
42.23 From now on will you listen with **care?**
46. 3 I have **cared** for you from the time you were born.
46. 4 your God and will take **care** of you until you are old
46. 4 I made you and will **care** for you;
53. 8 and led off to die, and no one **cared** about his fate.
57. 1 Good people die, and no one understands or even **cares.**
60.16 Nations and kings will **care** for you As a mother nurses
61. 5 They will take **care** of your flocks And farm your land and
63. 9 He had always taken **care** of them in the past, [10] but they
Jer 2. 6 They did not **care** about me, even though I rescued them
6.20 What do I **care** about the incense they bring me from Sheba,
12. 2 speak well of you, yet they do not really **care** about you.
12.11 The whole land has become a desert, and no one **cares.**
13.20 the people entrusted to your **care,** your people you were so
23. 2 the rulers who were supposed to take **care** of his people:
23. 2 "You have not taken **care** of my people;
23. 4 I will appoint rulers to take **care** of them.
30.13 is no one to take **care** of you, no remedy for your
30.14 they no longer **care** about you.
30.17 no one **cares** about her.'
31.28 And just as I took **care** to uproot, to pull down, to
31.28 them, so I will take **care** to plant them and to build
39.12 "Go and find Jeremiah and take good **care** of him.
39.14 They put me under the **care** of Gedaliah, the son of Ahikam
40. 4 me, you may do so, and I will take **care** of you.
41.10 the commanding officer had placed under the **care** of Gedaliah.
43. 6 left under the **care** of Gedaliah, including Baruch and me.
49.11 Leave your orphans with me, and I will take **care** of them.
Ezek 16.49 they did not take **care** of the poor and the underprivileged.
23.42 The sound of a **carefree** crowd could be heard, a group of
34. 2 You take **care** of yourselves, but never tend the sheep.
34. 4 You have not taken **care** of the weak ones, healed those
34. 8 They were taking **care** of themselves and not the sheep.
34.10 never again will I let you take **care** only of yourselves.
34.11 for my sheep and take **care** of them [12] in the same way
34.12 as a shepherd takes **care** of his sheep that were scattered
34.23 to be their one shepherd, and he will take **care** of them.
Hos 11. 3 but they did not acknowledge that I took **care** of them.
12.12 wife, he worked for another man and took **care** of his sheep.
12.13 of Israel from slavery in Egypt and to take **care** of them.
13. 5 I took **care** of you in a dry, desert land.
14. 8 I will answer their prayers and take **care** of them;
Joel 1.11 cry, you that take **care** of the vineyards, because the wheat,
Amos 3. 2 earth, you are the only one I have known and **cared** for.
7.14 I am a herdsman, and I take **care** of fig-trees.
Nah 1. 7 he takes **care** of those who turn to him.
Zech 10. 3 are mine, and I, the Lord Almighty, will take **care** of them.
11. 7 And I took **care** of the flock.
Mt 6.26 yet your Father in heaven takes **care** of them!
8.33 men who had been taking **care** of the pigs ran away
16. 6 Jesus said to them, "Take **care;**
25.36 was sick and you took **care** of me, in prison and you
25.43 sick and in prison but you would not take **care** of me.'
27. 4 "What do we **care** about that?"
Mk 4.38 said, "Teacher, don't you **care** that we are about to die?"
5.14 men who had been taking **care** of the pigs ran away and
8.15 "Take **care,**" Jesus warned them, "and be on your guard
Lk 2. 8 spending the night in the fields, taking **care** of their flocks.
4.10 says, 'God will order his angels to take good **care** of you.'
8.34 men who had been taking **care** of the pigs saw what happened,

Lk 10.34 and took him to an inn, where he took **care** of him.
10.35 'Take **care** of him,' he told the innkeeper, 'and when I come
10.40 and said, "Lord, don't you **care** that my sister has left me
15.15 sent him out to his farm to take **care** of the pigs.
Jn 10.13 is only a hired man and does not **care** about the sheep.
10.29 and no one can snatch them away from the Father's **care.**
12. 6 said this, not because he **cared** about the poor, but because
21.15 Jesus said to him, "Take **care** of my lambs."
21.16 Jesus said to him, "Take **care** of my sheep."
21.17 Jesus said to him, "Take **care** of my sheep.
Acts 7.20 He was **cared** for at home for three months, [21] and when he
7.58 left their cloaks in the **care** of a young man named Saul.
13.40 Take **care,** then, so that what the prophets said may not
14.26 had been commended to the **care** of God's grace for the work
15.14 how God first showed his **care** for the Gentiles by taking
15.29 will do well if you take **care** not to do these things.
15.40 commended by the believers to the **care** of the Lord's grace.
20.28 all the flock which the Holy Spirit has placed in your **care.**
20.32 I commend you to the **care** of God and to the message
22.20 his murder and taking **care** of the cloaks of his murderers.'
1 Cor 12.23 very much are the ones which we treat with greater **care;**
2 Cor 8.20 We are taking **care** not to stir up any complaints about
Gal 4. 2 there are men who take **care** of him and manage his affairs
Eph 5.29 he feeds it and takes **care** of it, just as Christ does
Phil 2.20 one who shares my feelings and who really **cares** about you.
4.10 once more had the chance of showing that you **care** for me.
4.10 mean that you had stopped **caring** for me—you just had no
1 Thes 2. 7 we were with you, like a mother taking **care** of her children.
1 Tim 3. 5 own family, how can he take **care** of the church of God?
5. 5 with no one to take **care** of her, has placed her hope
5. 8 if anyone does not take **care** of his relatives, especially the
5.14 married, have children, and take **care** of their homes, so as
5.16 her family, she must take **care** of them and not put the
5.16 so that it may take **care** of the widows who are all
6.20 Timothy, keep safe what has been entrusted to your **care.**
Heb 2. 6 mere man, that you should **care** for him?
4. 1 Let us take **care,** then, that none of you will be found
Jas 1.27 to take **care** of orphans and widows in their suffering and to
1 Pet 5. 2 gave you and to take **care** of it willingly, as God wants
5. 3 have been put in your **care,** but be examples to the flock.
5. 7 Leave all your worries with him, because he **cares** for you.
Jude 12 They take **care** only of themselves.
Rev 12. 6 for her, where she will be taken **care** of for 1,260 days.
12.14 where she will be taken **care** of for three and a half

CAREER

1 Kgs 11.41 else that Solomon did, his **career** and his wisdom, are all

CAREFUL

Gen 13.14 Abram, "From where you are, look **carefully** in all directions.
31.24 and said to him, "Be **careful** not to threaten Jacob in any
44.12 Joseph's servant searched **carefully,** beginning with the
Lev 11.47 You must be **careful** to distinguish between what is
Deut 3.27 Look **carefully** at what you see, because you will never go
15. 5 if you obey him and **carefully** observe everything that I
Josh 22. 3 You have been **careful** to obey the commands of the Lord your
23. 6 So be **careful** to obey and do everything that is written in
23.11 Be **careful,** then, to love the Lord your God.
1 Sam 19. 2 Please be **careful** tomorrow morning;
1 Kgs 2. 4 as long as they were **careful** to obey his commands faithfully
8.25 of Israel, provided they obeyed you as **carefully** as he did.
20.22 up your forces, and make **careful** plans, because the king of
2 Kgs 18. 6 and never disobeyed him, but **carefully** kept all the commands
1 Chr 28. 7 if he continues to obey **carefully** all my laws and commands
28. 8 I charge you to obey **carefully** everything that the Lord our
2 Chr 6.16 of Israel, provided that they **carefully** obeyed your Law just
19. 6 "Be **careful** in pronouncing judgement;
19. 7 Honour the Lord and act **carefully,** because the Lord our
19.10 commandment, you must instruct them **carefully** how to conduct
Ezra 7.17 are to spend this money **carefully** and buy bulls, rams,
7.23 You must be **careful** to provide everything which the God
8.29 Guard them **carefully** until you reach the Temple.
Job 1. 1 He was a good man, **careful** not to do anything evil.
1. 8 He worships me and is **careful** not to do anything evil."
2. 3 He worships me and is **careful** not to do anything evil.
29.21 people were silent and listened **carefully** to what I said;
33. 1 And now, Job, listen **carefully** to all that I have to say.
36.18 Be **careful** not to let bribes deceive you, or riches lead
36.21 Be **careful** not to turn to evil;
Ps 39. 1 I said, "I will be **careful** what I do and will not
139.15 being formed, **carefully** put together in my mother's womb,
Prov 4.23 Be **careful** how you think;
4.26 Plan **carefully** what you do, and whatever you do will
7. 2 Be as **careful** to follow my teaching as you are to protect
13. 3 Be **careful** what you say and protect your life.
14.16 Wise people are **careful** to stay out of trouble, but
20.25 Think **carefully** before you promise an offering to God.
21. 5 Plan **carefully** and you will have plenty;
21.23 you want to stay out of trouble, be **careful** what you say.
24. 6 After all, you must make **careful** plans before you fight a battle,
27.23 your sheep and cattle as **carefully** as you can, [24] because
Ecc 5. 1 Be **careful** about going to the Temple.
Is 21. 7 on donkeys and camels, he is to observe them **carefully."**
Jer 8. 6 I listened **carefully,** but you did not speak the truth.
Ezek 18. 9 Such a man obeys my commands and **carefully** keeps my laws.
18.19 and followed them **carefully,** and so he will certainly live.
40. 4 Listen **carefully** and pay close attention to everything I show you,
44. 5 Note **carefully** which persons are allowed to go in and out of
47. 6 He said to me, "Mortal man, note all this **carefully."**
Dan 2.14 Choosing his words **carefully,** [15] he asked Arioch why the
10.11 Stand up and listen **carefully** to what I am going to say.
Amos 6.10 We must be **careful** not even to mention the Lord's name."
Mic 7. 5 Be **careful** what you say even to your wife.
Mt 2. 8 "Go and make a **careful** search for the child, and when you
27.64 for his tomb to be **carefully** guarded until the third day,
Lk 1. 3 because I have **carefully** studied all these matters from their
8.18 "Be **careful,** then, how you listen;
15. 8 sweeps her house, and looks **carefully** everywhere until she finds
Acts 5.35 "Fellow-Israelites, be **careful** what you do to these men.
1 Cor 3.10 But each one must be **careful** how he builds.
8. 9 Be **careful,** however, not to let your freedom of action make
10.12 standing firm had better be **careful** that he does not fall.
Eph 5.15 So be **careful** how you live.
Heb 3.12 My fellow-believers, be **careful** that no one among you has a
12.25 Be **careful,** then, and do not refuse to hear him who speaks.
1 Pet 1.10 that the prophets made **careful** search and investigation,

CARELESS

Lev 5. 4 If someone makes a **careless** vow, no matter what it is about,
Num 30. 6 or **carelessly,** or promises to abstain from something,
Prov 13. 3 A **careless** talker destroys himself.
14.16 but stupid people are **careless** and act too quickly.
22.15 Children just naturally do silly, **careless** things, but a

CARESS

Song 2. 6 left hand is under my head, and his right hand **caresses** me.
8. 3 hand is under my head, and your right hand **caresses** me.

CARGO

Ezek 27.25 Your merchandise was carried in fleets of the largest **cargo** ships.
27.25 You were like a ship at sea Loaded with heavy **cargo.**
Jon 1. 5 Then, in order to lessen the danger, they threw the **cargo** overboard.
Acts 21. 3 at Tyre, where the ship was going to unload its **cargo.**
27.10 be great damage to the **cargo** and to the ship, and loss
27.18 throw some of the ship's **cargo** overboard,

CARMEL (1)

Mountain on the Mediterranean coast.

Josh 12.22 Jokneam (in **Carmel**),
19.26 On the west it touched **Carmel** and Shihor Libnath.
1 Kgs 18.19 order all the people of Israel to meet me at Mount **Carmel.**
18.20 Israelites and the prophets of Baal to meet at Mount **Carmel.**
18.42 to the top of Mount **Carmel,** where he bowed down to the
2 Kgs 2.25 Elisha went on to Mount **Carmel,** and later returned to Samaria.
4.25 So she set out, and went to Mount **Carmel,** where Elisha was.
Song 7. 5 Your head is held high like Mount **Carmel.**
Is 33. 9 in Bashan and on Mount **Carmel** the leaves are falling from
35. 2 Lebanon Mountains and as fertile as the fields of **Carmel** and Sharon.
Jer 46.18 the mountains and Mount **Carmel** stands high above the sea,
50.19 food that grows on Mount **Carmel** and in the region of Bashan,
Amos 1. 2 The pastures dry up, and the grass on Mount **Carmel** turns brown."
9. 3 on the top of Mount **Carmel,** I will search for them and
Nah 1. 4 fields of Bashan wither, Mount **Carmel** turns brown, and the

CARNELIAN

A semi-precious stone, usually red in colour.

Ex 25. 7 **carnelians** and other jewels to be set in the ephod of the
28. 9 Take two **carnelian** stones and engrave on them the names of
28.20 and in the fourth row, a beryl, a **carnelian,** and a
35. 9 **carnelians** and other jewels to be set in the High Priest's
35.27 The leaders brought **carnelians** and other jewels to be
39. 6 They prepared the **carnelians** and mounted them in gold settings;
39.13 and in the fourth row, a beryl, a **carnelian,** and a
Ezek 28.13 topaz, beryl, **carnelian,** and jasper;
Rev 4. 3 precious stones as jasper and **carnelian,** and all round the throne
21.20 fifth onyx, the sixth **carnelian,** the seventh yellow quartz,

CARNIVAL

Lam 2.22 my enemies to hold a **carnival** of terror all round me, And

CAROUSING

Jude 12 With their shameless **carousing** they are like dirty spots

CARPENTER

2 Sam 5.11 logs and with **carpenters** and stone-masons to build a palace.
2 Kgs 12.11 would pay the **carpenters,** the builders, [12] the masons,
22. 6 They are to pay [6] the **carpenters,** the builders, and the masons,
1 Chr 14. 1 logs and with stone-masons and **carpenters** to build a palace.
22.15 and there are masons and **carpenters,** as well as a large
2 Chr 24.12 **carpenters,** and metalworkers to make the repairs.
34.11 they gave it to [11] the **carpenters** and the builders to buy
Ezra 3. 7 pay the stonemasons and the **carpenters** and gave food, drink,
Is 41. 7 The **carpenter** says to the goldsmith, 'Well done!'
44.13 The **carpenter** measures the wood.
Ezek 27. 9 The ship's **carpenters** Were well-trained men from Byblos.
27.27 in your crew, Your ship's **carpenters** and your merchants,
Mt 13.55 Isn't he the **carpenter's** son?
Mk 6. 3 Isn't he the **carpenter,** the son of Mary, and the brother

CARPET

Ezek	27.24	brightly coloured **carpets,** and well-made cords and ropes.

CARRIAGE

Acts	8.27	Jerusalem to worship God and was going back home in his **carriage.**
	8.29	Philip, "Go over to that **carriage** and stay close to it."
	8.31	invited Philip to climb up and sit in the **carriage** with him.
	8.38	official ordered the **carriage** to stop, and both Philip and the
Rev	18.13	and sheep, horses and **carriages,** slaves, and even human lives.

CARRY

Gen	22. 6	Abraham made Isaac **carry** the wood for the sacrifice,
	22. 6	and he himself **carried** a knife and live coals
	31.26	did you deceive me and **carry** off my daughters like women
	34.29	and children, and **carried** off everything in the houses.
	38.18	"Your seal with its cord and the stick you are **carrying.**"
	40.16	I was **carrying** three bread-baskets on my head.
	44. 1	much food as they can **carry,** and put each man's money in
	47.30	**carry** me out of Egypt and bury me where they are buried."
	49.15	he bends his back to **carry** the load And is forced to
	50.13	they **carried** his body to Canaan and buried it in the
Ex	3.22	and daughters and **carry** away the wealth of the Egyptians."
	4.20	out with them for Egypt, **carrying** the stick that God had
	12.34	them in clothing, and **carried** them on their shoulders.
	12.36	the Israelites **carried** away the wealth of the Egyptians.
	13.19	God rescues you, you must **carry** my body with you from this
	17. 9	of the hill holding the stick that God told me to **carry.**"
	19. 4	carried you as an eagle **carries** her young on her wings, and
	22.10	or is injured or is **carried** off in a raid, and if
	25.27	to hold the poles for **carrying** the table are to be placed
	27. 7	the rings on each side of the altar when it is **carried.**
	28.12	In this way Aaron will **carry** their names on his shoulders,
	28.30	breast-piece, so that Aaron will **carry** them when he comes
	30. 4	sides to hold the poles with which it is to be **carried.**
	32.15	went back down the mountain, **carrying** the two stone tablets
	32.19	he threw down the tablets he was **carrying** and broke them.
	34. 4	early the next morning he **carried** them up Mount Sinai, just
	34.29	went down from Mount Sinai **carrying** the Ten Commandments,
	37.14	to hold the poles for **carrying** the table were placed near
	37.27	sides, to hold the poles with which it was to be **carried.**
Lev	4. 5	take some of the bull's blood and **carry** it into the Tent.
	4.12	internal organs including the intestines, [12]**carry** it all
	9.20	the breasts of the animals and **carried** it all to the altar.
	10. 4	to them, "Come here and **carry** your cousins' bodies away
	10. 5	clothing on the corpses and **carried** them outside the camp,
	11.24	Whoever **carries** their dead bodies must wash his clothes, but
	11.40	anyone who **carries** the dead body must wash his clothes, but
	14.45	all its plaster must be **carried** out of the city to an
	15.10	Anyone who **carries** anything on which the man sat must wash
	16.22	The goat will **carry** all their sins away with him into
	16.27	take away sin, shall be **carried** outside the camp and burnt.
Num	1.50	They shall **carry** it and its equipment, serve in it, and set
	2.17	and the last two the Levites are to march **carrying** the Tent.
	4.10	in a fine leather cover and place it on a **carrying-frame.**
	4.12	leather cover over them, and place them on a **carrying-frame.**
	4.15	of Kohath shall come to **carry** the sacred objects only after
	4.19	and assign each man his task and tell him what to **carry.**
	4.24	They shall be responsible for **carrying** the following objects:
	4.27	perform all the duties and **carry** everything that Aaron and
	4.31	They shall be responsible for **carrying** the frames, bars,
	4.32	Each man will be responsible for **carrying** specific items.
	4.49	responsibility for his task of serving or **carrying.**
	7. 9	they took care of had to be **carried** on their shoulders.
	10.17	of Gershon and Merari, who **carried** it, would start out.
	10.21	clan of Kohath would start out, **carrying** the sacred objects.
	11.12	act like a nurse and **carry** them in my arms like babies
	13.23	it took two men to **carry** it on a pole between them.
Deut	1.31	way to this place, just as a father would **carry** his son.'
	9.15	and went down the mountain, **carrying** the two stone tablets
	14.24	your home for you to **carry** there the tithe of the produce
	23.13	**Carry** a stick as part of your equipment, so that when
	23.24	you want, but you must not **carry** any away in a container.
	29.11	who live among you and cut wood and **carry** water for you.
Josh	3. 3	"When you see the priests **carrying** the Covenant Box of the
	3. 8	Tell the priests **carrying** the Covenant Box that when they
	3.13	When the priests who **carry** the Covenant Box of the Lord
	3.14	the priests went ahead of them, **carrying** the Covenant Box.
	3.17	on dry ground, the priests **carrying** the Lord's Covenant Box
	4. 3	Tell them to **carry** these stones with them and to put them
	4. 8	of the tribes of Israel, **carried** them to the camping place,
	4. 9	Jordan, where the priests **carrying** the Covenant Box had stood.
	4.16	Joshua [16]to command the priests **carrying** the Covenant Box
	6. 4	Seven priests, each **carrying** a trumpet, are to go in front
	6. 6	Box, and seven of you go in front of it, **carrying** trumpets."
	6. 8	came the priests who were **carrying** the Covenant Box,
	6.12	then, the priests **carrying** the Lord's Covenant Box;
	8.33	Lord's Covenant Box, facing the levitical priests who **carried** it.
	9.21	but they will have to cut wood and **carry** water for us."
	9.23	be slaves, cutting wood and **carrying** water for the sanctuary
	9.27	slaves, to cut wood and **carry** water for the people of Israel
Judg	3.18	he told the men who had **carried** them to go back home.
	5. 8	thousand men in Israel, did anyone **carry** shield or spear?
	9.54	the young man who was **carrying** his weapons and ordered,
	16. 3	them on his shoulders and **carried** them all the way to the
	21.23	the girls who were dancing at Shiloh and **carried** her away.
1 Sam	5. 1	captured the Covenant Box, they **carried** it from Ebenezer to
	10. 3	goats, another one will be **carrying** three loaves of bread,
1 Sam	11. 7	pieces, and sent messengers to **carry** the pieces throughout
	14. 1	to the young man who **carried** his weapons, "Let's go across
	14. 3	(The priest **carrying** the ephod was Ahijah, the son of
	14.17	Jonathan and the young man who **carried** his weapons were missing.
	14.18	(On that day Ahijah was **carrying** it in front of the people
	14.27	with the stick he was **carrying,** dipped it in a honeycomb,
	16.21	very much and chose him as the man to **carry** his weapons.
	17. 6	by bronze armour, and he **carried** a bronze javelin slung over
	17. 7	A soldier walked in front of him **carrying** his shield.
	17.34	a lion or a bear **carries** off a lamb, [35]I go after
	17.57	David was still **carrying** Goliath's head.
	19.15	He ordered them, "**Carry** him here in his bed, and I will
	22.18	eighty-five priests who were qualified to **carry** the ephod.
	30. 3	that their wives, sons, and daughters had been **carried** away.
	31. 4	said to the young man **carrying** his weapons, "Draw your
2 Sam	5.21	idols behind, and David and his men **carried** them away.
	6.13	After the men **carrying** the Covenant Box had gone six steps,
	8. 7	David captured the gold shields **carried** by Hadadezer's
	15.24	with him were the Levites, **carrying** the sacred Covenant Box.
	21.16	giant named Ishbibenob, who was **carrying** a bronze spear that
1 Kgs	3.20	my side while I was asleep, and **carried** him to her bed;
	5.15	stone, with 70,000 men to **carry** it, [16]and he placed 3,300
	7.50	for incense, and the pans used for **carrying** live coals;
	8. 4	lifted the Covenant Box [4]and **carried** it to the Temple.
	8. 6	Then the priests **carried** the Covenant Box into the Temple
	8. 7	wings covered the box and the poles it was **carried** by.
	14.28	to the Temple, the guards **carried** the shields, and then
	15.22	everyone, without exception, to help **carry** away from Ramah
	17.19	the boy from her arms, **carried** him upstairs to the room
	18.12	the spirit of the Lord **carries** you off to some unknown place
	20.10	this city of yours and **carry** off the rubble in their hands.
2 Kgs	2.16	spirit of the Lord has **carried** him away and left him on
	4.19	"**Carry** the boy to his mother," the father said to a servant.
	4.20	The servant **carried** the boy back to his mother, who held
	4.21	She **carried** him up to Elisha's room, put him on the bed
	4.39	a wild vine, and picked as many gourds as he could **carry.**
	5. 2	Israel, the Syrians had **carried** off a little Israelite girl,
	5.24	Gehazi took the two bags and **carried** them into the house.
	14.14	all the palace treasures, and **carried** them back to Samaria.
	14.20	His body was **carried** back to Jerusalem on a horse and
	20.17	stored up to this day, will be **carried** off to Babylonia.
	24.13	he took Jehoiachin prisoner [13]and **carried** off to Babylon
	24.14	Nebuchadnezzar **carried** away as prisoners the people of Jerusalem,
	25.15	the small bowls and the pans used for **carrying** live coals.
	25.21	of Judah were **carried** away from their land into exile.
1 Chr	10. 4	said to the young man **carrying** his weapons, "Draw your
	15. 2	he said, "Only Levites should **carry** the Covenant Box,
	15. 2	ones the Lord chose to **carry** it and to serve him for
	15.13	you were not there to **carry** it the first time, the Lord
	15.15	The Levites **carried** it on poles on their shoulders, as
	15.26	God would help the Levites who were **carrying** the Covenant Box.
	15.27	Chenaniah their leader, and the Levites who **carried** the Box.
	18. 7	David captured the gold shields **carried** by Hadadezer's
	23.26	need for the Levites to **carry** the Tent of the Lord's
2 Chr	4.22	for incense, and the pans used for **carrying** live coals.
	5. 5	Levites lifted the Covenant Box [5]and **carried** it to the Temple.
	5. 7	Then the priests **carried** the Covenant Box of the Lord into
	12.11	to the Temple, the guards **carried** the shields and then
	16. 6	Judah and ordered them to **carry** off the stones and timber
	21.17	looted the royal palace, and **carried** off as prisoners all
	25.28	His body was **carried** to Jerusalem on a horse, and he was
	29.16	to purify it, and they **carried** out into the temple courtyard
	35. 3	You are no longer to **carry** it from place to place, but
	36. 7	Nebuchadnezzar **carried** off some of the treasures of the
	36.10	Babylonia as a prisoner, and **carried** off the treasures of the Temple.
Ezra	9. 7	been slaughtered, robbed, and **carried** away as prisoners.
Neh	4.10	"We grow weak **carrying** burdens;
	4.17	Even those who **carried** building materials worked with one
	12.36	and Hanani—all of whom **carried** musical instruments of the
Esth	3.15	city of Susa, and runners **carried** the news to the provinces.
Job	21.18	straw in the wind, or like dust **carried** away in a storm?
	21.32	When he is **carried** to the graveyard, to his well-guarded tomb,
	39. 2	Do you know how long they **carry** their young?
	39.23	The weapons which their riders **carry** rattle and flash in the sun.
Ps	7. 2	like a lion they will **carry** me off where no one can
	68.11	The Lord gave the command, and many women **carried** the news:
	68.19	Praise the Lord, who **carries** our burdens day after day;
	90. 5	You **carry** us away like a flood;
	105.37	they **carried** silver and gold, and all of them were healthy
	124. 4	then the flood would have **carried** us away, the water would
	126. 6	wept as they went out **carrying** the seed will come back
	129. 7	no one gathers it up or **carries** it away in bundles.
Prov	6.27	Can you **carry** fire against your chest without burning your clothes?
Ecc	10.20	A bird might **carry** the message and tell them what you said.
Song	3. 7	Solomon is coming, **carried** on his throne;
	3. 9	King Solomon is **carried** on a throne made of the finest wood.
Is	5.13	Lord is doing, [13]and so you will be **carried** away as prisoners.
	5.29	killed an animal and are **carrying** it off where no one can
	6. 6	creatures flew down to me, **carrying** a burning coal that he
	8. 4	of Samaria will be **carried** off by the king of Assyria."
	30.28	in front of him like a flood that **carries** everything away.
	39. 6	stored up to this day, will be **carried** off to Babylonia.
	40.11	he will gather the lambs together and **carry** them in his arms;
	41.16	the wind will **carry** them off, and they will be scattered
	46. 2	they are captured and **carried** away.
	46. 7	They lift it to their shoulders and **carry** it;
	52.11	leave Babylonia, all you that **carry** the temple equipment!

Is 57.13 A puff of wind will **carry** them off!
60. 4 Your daughters will be **carried** like children.
66.12 is nursed by its mother, **carried** in her arms, and treated
Jer 10. 5 they have to be **carried** because they cannot walk.
15.13 "I will send enemies to **carry** away the wealth and treasures
17.21 their lives, they must not **carry** any load on the Sabbath;
17.21 they must not **carry** anything in through the gates
17.22 of Jerusalem [22] or **carry** anything out of their houses
17.24 They must not **carry** any load in through the gates of this
17.27 They must not **carry** any load through the gates of Jerusalem
20. 5 the kings of Judah, and **carry** everything off to Babylonia.
43.12 of Babylonia will either burn their gods or **carry** them off.
46. 9 men from Sudan and Libya, **carrying** shields, and skilled bowmen from Lydia.' "
52.19 bowls, the pans used for **carrying** live coals, the bowls for
52.27 of Judah were **carried** away from their land into exile.
52.28 in his seventh year as king he **carried** away 3,023;
Ezek 3.14 force, and as his spirit **carried** me off, I felt bitter and
9. 2 outer north gate of the Temple, each one **carrying** a weapon.
9. 2 dressed in linen clothes, **carrying** something to write with.
17. 4 of a cedar-tree, [4] which he **carried** to a land of commerce,
27.25 Your merchandise was **carried** in fleets of the largest cargo ships.
29.18 He made his soldiers **carry** such heavy loads that their heads
29.19 loot and plunder it and **carry** off all the wealth of Egypt
38. 4 is enormous, and every soldier **carries** a shield and is armed
40. 1 the powerful presence of the Lord, and he **carried** me away.
46.20 so that nothing holy is **carried** to the outer courtyard,
Dan 2.35 The wind **carried** it all away, leaving not a trace.
5. 2 Nebuchadnezzar had **carried** off from the Temple in Jerusalem.
11. 8 He will **carry** back to Egypt the images of their gods and
Hos 4.19 They will be **carried** away as by the wind, and they will
10. 6 The idol will be **carried** off to Assyria as tribute to the
10. 7 Her king will be **carried** off, like a chip of wood on
Joel 3. 5 and gold and **carried** my rich treasures into your temples.
Amos 1. 6 They **carried** off a whole nation and sold them as slaves to
1. 9 They **carried** off a whole nation into exile in the land of
5.26 god, you will have to **carry** those images [27] when I take you
Obad 11 bad as those strangers who **carried** off Jerusalem's wealth
Mic 1. 7 will **carry** them off for temple prostitutes elsewhere."
6.14 You will **carry** things off, but you will not be able to
Nah 2. 3 The enemy soldiers **carry** red shields and wear uniforms of red.
3.10 Yet the people of Thebes were **carried** off into exile.
3.10 Their leading men were **carried** off in chains and divided
Hag 2.12 meat from a sacrifice and **carries** it in a fold of his
Mt 3.11 and I am not good enough even to **carry** his sandals.
5.41 occupation troops forces you to **carry** his pack one kilometre,
5.41 **carry** it two kilometres.
8.17 "He himself took our sickness and **carried** away our diseases."
10. 9 Do not **carry** any gold, silver, or copper money in your pockets;
10.10 do not **carry** a beggar's bag for the journey or an extra
11.28 you who are tired from **carrying** heavy loads, and I will give
14.12 John's disciples came, **carried** away his body, and buried
16.24 with me, he must forget self, **carry** his cross, and follow
23. 4 are heavy and hard to **carry**, yet they aren't willing
23. 4 even to lift a finger to help them **carry** those loads.
27.32 named Simon, and the soldiers forced him to **carry** Jesus' cross.
Mk 2. 3 when four men arrived, **carrying** a paralysed man to Jesus.
6. 9 Wear sandals, but don't **carry** an extra shirt."
8.34 told them, "he must forget self, **carry** his cross, and
11.16 would not let anyone **carry** anything through the temple courtyards.
14.13 the city, and a man **carrying** a jar of water will meet
15.21 the country, and the soldiers forced him to **carry** Jesus' cross.
Lk 5.18 Some men came **carrying** a paralysed man on a bed, and
5.19 So they **carried** him up on the roof, made an opening in
7.14 and touched the coffin, and the men **carrying** it stopped.
11.22 and defeats him, he **carries** away all the weapons the owner
11.46 backs which are hard to **carry**, but you yourselves will not
11.46 stretch out a finger to help them **carry** those loads.
14.22 said, 'Your order has been **carried** out, sir, but there is
14.27 Whoever does not **carry** his own cross and come after me
15. 6 that he puts it on his shoulders [6] and **carries** it back home.
16.22 poor man died and was **carried** by the angels to sit beside
22.10 into the city, a man **carrying** a jar of water will meet
23.26 put the cross on him, and made him **carry** it behind Jesus.
24. 1 women went to the tomb, **carrying** the spices they had prepared.
Jn 5.10 and it is against our Law for you to **carry** your mat."
12. 6 He **carried** the money bag and would help himself from it.
18. 3 they were armed and **carried** lanterns and torches.
19.17 He went out, **carrying** his cross, and came to "The Place
Acts 3. 2 Every day he was **carried** to the gate to beg for money
5. 6 in, wrapped up his body, **carried** him out, and buried him.
5. 9 are now at the door, and they will **carry** you out too!"
5.10 she was dead, so they **carried** her out and buried her beside
5.15 sick people were **carried** out into the streets and placed
7.43 the god Molech that you **carried**, and the image of Rephan,
7.45 the tent from their fathers **carried** it with them when they
15.10 which neither our ancestors nor we ourselves were able to **carry**?
21.35 then the soldiers had to **carry** him because the mob was so
23.31 The soldiers **carried** out their orders.
27.13 thought that they could **carry** out their plan, so they pulled
27.15 gave up trying and let it be **carried** along by the wind.
27.17 lowered the sail and let the ship be **carried** by the wind.
Rom 13. 4 He is God's servant and **carries** out God's punishment on those
15. 1 in the faith ought to help the weak to **carry** their burdens.
2 Cor 4.10 At all times we **carry** in our mortal bodies the death of
8.19 travel with us as we **carry** out this service of love for
Gal 6. 2 Help to **carry** one another's burdens, and in this way you
6. 5 For everyone has to **carry** his own load.
Eph 4.14 no longer be children, **carried** by the waves and blown about
6.16 At all times **carry** faith as a shield;
Phil 1. 6 good work in you, will **carry** it on until it is finished
1 Tim 5. 4 they should learn first to **carry** out their religious duties
Heb 2. 1 truths we have heard, so that we will not be **carried** away.
Jas 1. 4 Make sure that your endurance **carries** you all the way without
1 Pet 2.24 Christ himself **carried** our sins in his body to the cross,
Jude 12 They are like clouds **carried** along by the wind, but bringing
Rev 12.15 of water after the woman, so that it would **carry** her away.
17. 3 took control of me, and the angel **carried** me to a desert.
17. 7 and of the beast that **carries** her, the beast with seven
17.17 their hearts the will to **carry** out his purpose by acting
21.10 of me, and the angel **carried** me to the top of a

CARRYING-POLES

Ex 25.13 Make **carrying-poles** of acacia-wood and cover them with
27. 6 Make **carrying-poles** of acacia-wood, cover them with bronze,
37. 4 He made **carrying-poles** of acacia-wood, covered them with gold,
38. 6 He made **carrying-poles** of acacia-wood, covered them with bronze,
Num 4. 6 a blue cloth on top, and then insert the **carrying-poles.**
4. 8 leather cover over it, and then insert the **carrying-poles.**
4.11 leather cover over it, and then insert the **carrying-poles.**
4.14 a fine leather cover over it and insert the **carrying-poles.**
2 Chr 5. 8 Their outstretched wings covered the Box and the **carrying-poles.**

CARRYING-RINGS

Ex 25.12 Make four **carrying-rings** of gold for it and attach them
25.26 Make four **carrying-rings** of gold for it and put them at
27. 4 put four bronze **carrying-rings** on its corners.
30. 4 Make two gold **carrying-rings** for it and attach them below
37. 3 He made four **carrying-rings** of gold for it and attached
37.13 He made four **carrying-rings** of gold for it and put them
37.27 He made two gold **carrying-rings** for it and attached them
38. 5 He made four **carrying-rings** and put them on the four corners.

CART

2 Sam 6. 3 Abinadab's home on the hill and placed it on a new **cart.**
6. 3 Abinadab, were guiding the **cart,** [4] with Ahio walking in front.
1 Kgs 7.27 Huram also made ten bronze **carts;**
7.30 Each **cart** had four bronze wheels with bronze axles.
7.31 from the top of the **cart** and 18 centimetres down into it.
7.32 the panels, and the axles were of one piece with the **carts.**
7.34 corners of each cart, which were of one piece with the **cart.**
7.35 There was a 22 centimetre band round the top of each **cart;**
7.35 its supports and the panels were of one piece with the **cart.**
7.37 This, then, is how the **carts** were made;
7.38 Huram also made ten basins, one for each **cart.**
7.39 He placed five of the **carts** on the south side of the
7.40 on each capital The ten **carts** The ten basins The tank
2 Kgs 16.17 Ahaz took apart the bronze **carts** used in the Temple and
25.13 the bronze columns and the **carts** that were in the Temple,
25.16 Temple—the two columns, the **carts,** and the large tank—were
1 Chr 13. 7 brought out the Covenant Box and put it on a new **cart.**
13. 7 Uzzah and Ahio guided the **cart,** [8] while David and all the
2 Chr 4.11 of each capital The ten **carts** The ten basins The tank
Is 28.28 it by driving a **cart** over it without bruising the grains.
Jer 27.19 columns, the bronze tank, the **carts,** and some of the other
52.17 the bronze columns and the **carts** that were in the Temple,
52.20 Temple—the two columns, the **carts,** the large tank, and the
Amos 2.13 the ground, and you will groan like a **cart** loaded with corn.

CARVE

Ex 31. 5 for **carving** wood;
35.33 for **carving** wood;
Lev 26. 1 set up statues, stone pillars, or **carved** stones to worship.
Judg 3.19 himself turned back at the **carved** stones near Gilgal, went
3.26 He went past the **carved** stones and escaped to Seirah.
17. 4 metal-worker, who made an idol, **carving** it from wood and
1 Kgs 6.18 The cedar panels were decorated with **carvings** of gourds
6.29 were all decorated with **carved** figures of winged creatures,
6.32 The doors were decorated with **carved** figures
6.35 and decorated with **carved** figures of winged creatures,
7.31 It had **carvings** round it.
2 Chr 3. 7 On the walls the workmen **carved** designs of winged creatures.
16.14 tomb which he had **carved** out for himself in David's City.
Job 19.24 Or with a chisel **carve** my words in stone and write them
Is 22.16 What right have you to **carve** a tomb for yourself out of
44.13 outlines a figure with chalk, **carves** it out with his tools,
Jer 10. 3 it is **carved** by the tools of the woodcarver, [4] and
17. 1 a diamond point and **carved** on the corners of your altars.
Ezek 23.14 images of high Babylonian officials **carved** into the wall and
40.16 There were palm-trees **carved** on the inner walls
40.22 room, the windows, and the **carved** palm-trees were like those
40.26 There were palm-trees **carved** on the inner walls
40.31 and palm-trees were **carved** on the walls along the passage.
40.34 Palm-trees were **carved** on the walls along the passage.
40.37 Palm-trees were **carved** on the walls along the passage.
41.17 with **carvings** [18] of palm-trees and winged creatures.
41.25 were palm-trees and winged creatures **carved** on the doors of
2 Cor 3. 7 The Law was **carved** in letters on stone tablets, and God's

CASE (1)

Mt 26.54 in that **case,** how could the Scriptures come true which say
Acts 5.38 And so in this **case,** I tell you, do not take any
Rom 7.10 which was meant to bring life, in my **case** brought death.
1 Cor 7.15 In such **cases** the Christian partner, whether husband or wife,
7.36 In the **case** of an engaged couple who have decided not to

Heb 7. 8 In the **case** of the priests the tenth is collected by men
9.16 In the **case** of a will it is necessary to prove that
12. 9 In the **case** of our human fathers, they punished us and we

CASE (2)

Ex 18.22 can bring all the difficult **cases** to you, but they
18.26 permanent basis, bringing the difficult **cases** to Moses but
Lev 19.15 "Be honest and just when you make decisions in legal **cases;**
Num 5.29 This is the law in **cases** where a man is jealous
27. 5 Moses presented their **case** to the Lord, [6]and the Lord
35.24 In such **cases** the community shall judge in favour of the
Deut 1.17 If any **case** is too difficult for you, bring it to me,
17. 8 "It may be that some **cases** will be too difficult for the
17. 8 to decide, such as certain **cases** of property rights
17. 8 of bodily injury or those **cases** that involve a distinction
17. 9 your God, [9]and present your **case** to the levitical priests
17. 9 is in office at that time, and let them decide the **case.**
19.18 The judges will investigate the **case** thoroughly;
19.21 In such **cases** show no mercy;
21. 5 they are to decide every legal **case** involving violence.
22.26 This **case** is the same as when one man attacks another man
1 Sam 8. 3 so they accepted bribes and did not decide **cases** honestly.
2 Sam 15. 3 there is no representative of the king to hear your **case."**
1 Kgs 7. 7 of Judgement, where Solomon decided **cases,** had cedar panels
2 Chr 19. 8 leading citizens as judges in **cases** involving a violation of
19.10 cities bring before you a **case** of homicide or any other
19.11 final authority in all religious **cases,** and Zebadiah
19.11 governor of Judah, will have final authority in all civil **cases.**
Ezra 10.17 they investigated all the **cases** of men with foreign wives.
Job 5. 8 you, I would turn to God and present my **case** to him.
9. 1 But how can a man win his **case** against God?
13. 3 I want to argue my **case** with him.
13. 6 Listen while I state my **case.**
13. 8 Are you going to argue his **case** in court?
13.15 I am going to state my **case** to him.
13.18 am ready to state my **case,** because I know I am in
23. 4 I would state my **case** before him and present all the
34. 4 It is up to us to decide the **case.**
35.14 but wait patiently—your **case** is before him.
Prov 22.23 The Lord will argue their **case** for them and threaten the
23.11 defender, and he will argue their **case** against you.
Is 1.23 orphans in court or listen when widows present their **case.**
3.13 The Lord is ready to state his **case;**
28. 7 are too drunk to decide the **cases** that are brought to them.
41. 1 Get ready to present your **case** in court;
41.21 "You gods of the nations, present your **case.**
43.26 Present your **case** to prove you are in the right!
45.21 Come and present your **case** in court;
59. 4 You depend on lies to win your **case.**
Jer 2. 9 so I, the Lord, will state my **case** against my people again.
12. 1 Lord, if I argued my **case** with you, you would prove to
25.31 The Lord has a **case** against the nations.
Ezek 44.24 the priests are to decide the **case** according to my laws.
Mic 6. 1 Listen to the Lord's **case** against Israel.
6. 1 Arise, O Lord, and present your **case;**
6. 2 foundations of the earth, listen to the Lord's **case!**
6. 2 The Lord has a **case** against his people.
Acts 24.22 the commander arrives," he told them, "I will decide your **case."**
25.21 be kept under guard and to let the Emperor decide his **case.**
25.26 after investigating his **case,** I may have something to write.
Rom 3. 4 you must win your **case** when you are being tried."
1 Cor 6. 6 goes to court against another and lets unbelievers judge the **case!**

CASH

Lev 27.18 the priest shall estimate the **cash** value according to the

CASSIA

A spice made from the bark of a tree; it is very like cinnamon.

Ex 30.24 cane, [24]and six kilogrammes of **cassia** (all weighed

Am **CAST** see **THROW**

CAST (1)

1 Kgs 7.15 Huram **cast** two bronze columns, each one 8 metres tall
7.24 bronze gourds, which had been **cast** all in one piece with the
2 Chr 4. 3 of bulls, which had been **cast** all in one piece with the

CAST (2)

Esth 3. 7 ordered the lots to be **cast** ("purim," they were called) to
9.24 of the Jewish people—had **cast** lots (or "purim," as they
Prov 16.33 Men **cast** lots to learn God's will, but God himself
18.18 each other in court, **casting** lots can settle the issue.
Is 16. 3 like a tree that **casts** a cool shadow in the heat

CASTRATE

Deut 23. 1 "No man who has been **castrated** or whose penis has been
Is 56. 3 A man who has been **castrated** should never think that
Gal 5.12 let them go on and **castrate** themselves!

CATAPULT

1 Sam 17.40 With his **catapult** ready, he went out to meet Goliath.
17.50 David defeated and killed Goliath with a **catapult** and a stone!
1 Sam 25.29 throw them away, as a man hurls stones with his **catapult.**
Prov 26. 8 stupid makes as much sense as tying a stone in a **catapult.**

CATCH

[CAUGHT]

Gen 22.13 round and saw a ram **caught** in a bush by its horns.
31.23 for seven days until he **caught** up with him in the
33.14 and the children until I **catch** up with you in Edom."
38.28 the midwife **caught** it, tied a red thread round it, and said,
39.12 She **caught** him by his robe and said, "Come to bed with
44. 4 When you **catch** up with them, ask them, 'Why have you paid
44. 6 When the servant **caught** up with them, he repeated these words.
Ex 4. 4 So Moses bent down and **caught** it, and it became a stick
14. 9 and drivers, pursued them and **caught** up with them where they
15. 9 The enemy said, 'I will pursue them and **catch** them;
22. 2 "If a thief is **caught** breaking into a house at night and
Num 5.12 there was no witness, and she was not **caught** in the act.
11.32 and all the next day, the people worked **catching** quails;
Deut 19. 6 revenge for the killing might **catch** him and in his anger
22.22 "If a man is **caught** having intercourse with another man's wife,
22.23 "Suppose a man is **caught** in a town having intercourse
22.28 "Suppose a man is **caught** raping a girl who is not engaged.
32.11 young to fly, **catching** them safely on its spreading wings,
Josh 2. 4 but if you start after them quickly, you can **catch** them."
Judg 1. 6 away, but they chased him, **caught** him, and cut off his
14. 2 Philistine girl down at Timnah who has **caught** my attention.
15. 4 So he went and **caught** three hundred foxes.
18.22 They **caught** up with the men from Dan [23]and shouted at them.
20.42 They were **caught** between the main army and the men who were
1 Sam 9.12 If you hurry, you will **catch** up with him.
9.17 When Samuel **caught** sight of Saul, the Lord said to him,
15.27 turned to leave, but Saul **caught** hold of his cloak, and it
23.20 our territory, and we will make sure that you **catch** him."
24.19 How often does a man **catch** his enemy and then let him
30. 8 And will I **catch** them?"
30. 8 you will **catch** them and rescue the captives."
31. 2 But the Philistines **caught** up with them and killed three
2 Sam 2.16 Each man **caught** his opponent by the head and plunged his
17.16 so that he and his men won't all be **caught** and killed."
18. 9 a large oak-tree, Absalom's head got **caught** in the branches.
1 Kgs 21.20 saw Elijah, he said, "Have you **caught** up with me, my
2 Kgs 25.14 the bowls used for **catching** the blood from the sacrifices,
1 Chr 10. 2 But the Philistines **caught** up with them and killed three
Job 18. 8 He walks into a net, and his feet are **caught;**
18. 9 a trap **catches** his heels and holds him.
19. 6 He has set a trap to **catch** me.
40.24 Or who can **catch** his snout in a trap?
41. 1 Can you **catch** Leviathan with a fish-hook or tie his tongue
Ps 7. 5 my enemies pursue me and **catch** me, let them cut me down
7.15 But in the traps they set for others, they themselves get **caught.**
9.15 they have been **caught** in their own trap.
10. 2 **catch** them in the traps they have made.
10. 9 he **catches** them in his trap and drags them away.
18.37 I pursue my enemies and **catch** them;
35. 7 a trap for me and dug a deep hole to **catch** me.
35. 8 But destruction will **catch** them before they know it;
35. 8 they will be **caught** in their own trap and fall to their
40.12 My sins have **caught** up with me, and I can no longer
57. 6 My enemies have spread a net to **catch** me;
59.12 may they be **caught** in their pride!
71.11 let's go after him and **catch** him;
140. 5 snares and along the path they have set traps to **catch** me.
Prov 1.17 the bird you want to **catch** is watching, [18]but men like
5.22 He gets **caught** in the net of his own sin.
6. 2 Have you been **caught** by your own words, trapped by your
6.31 yet if he is **caught,** he must pay back seven times more
10. 9 Honest people are safe and secure, but the dishonest will be **caught.**
18. 7 he gets **caught** in the trap of his own words.
22. 5 away from the traps that **catch** the wicked along the way.
22.14 Adultery is a trap—it **catches** those with whom the Lord
26.27 People who set traps for others get **caught** themselves.
30. 4 Who has ever **caught** the wind in his hand?
Ecc 4. 6 all the time with both hands, trying to **catch** the wind.
5.16 We labour, trying to **catch** the wind, and what do we get?
7.26 love she offers you will **catch** you like a trap or like
7.26 who pleases God can get away, but she will **catch** the sinner.
9.12 Like birds suddenly **caught** in a trap,
9.12 like fish **caught** in a net, we are trapped
Song 2.15 **Catch** the foxes, the little foxes, before they ruin our
Is 8.14 like a trap that will **catch** the people of the kingdoms of
8.15 They will be **caught** in a trap."
13.15 Anyone who is **caught** will be stabbed to death.
24.18 anyone who escapes from the pit will be **caught** in a trap.
51.20 they are like deer **caught** in a hunter's net.
Jer 2.26 a thief is disgraced when **caught,** so all you people of
5.26 men who spread nets to **catch** birds,
5.26 but they have set their traps to **catch** men.
16.16 "I am sending for many fishermen to come and **catch** these people.
18.22 for me to fall in and have set traps to **catch** me.
20.10 "then we can **catch** him and get revenge."
23.11 I have **caught** them doing evil in the Temple itself.
48.27 them as though they had been **caught** with a gang of robbers.
48.44 of the pits will be **caught** in the traps, because the Lord
50.24 me, and you have been **caught** in the trap I set for
52.18 the bowls used for **catching** the blood from the sacrifices,
Ezek 17.20 I will spread out a hunter's net and **catch** him in it.
19. 8 They spread their hunting nets and **caught** him in their trap.
19.14 The stem of the vine **caught** fire;

Ezek 32. 3 many nations gather, I will **catch** you in my net and let

Hos 2. 7 She will run after her lovers but will not **catch** them.

7.12 spread out a net and **catch** them like birds as they go

10. 9 So at Gibeah war will **catch** up with them.

Amos 3. 4 young lion growl in his den unless he has **caught** something?

3. 5 Does a bird get **caught** in a trap if the trap has

9. 2 way down to the world of the dead, I will **catch** them.

9. 3 top of Mount Carmel, I will search for them and **catch** them.

Obad 14 stood at the cross-roads to **catch** those trying to escape.

Jon 1.12 it is my fault that you are **caught** in this violent storm."

Hab 1.15 The Babylonians **catch** people with hooks, as though they were fish.

1.15 drag them off in nets and shout for joy over their **catch!**

Mt 4.18 Peter) and his brother Andrew, **catching** fish in the lake with

4.19 "Come with me, and I will teach you to **catch** men."

13.47 their net out in the lake and **catch** all kinds of fish.

Mk 1.16 Simon and his brother Andrew, **catching** fish with a net.

1.17 "Come with me, and I will teach you to **catch** men."

Lk 5. 4 and you and your partners let down your nets for a **catch."**

5. 5 answered, "we worked hard all night long and **caught** nothing.

5. 6 They let them down and **caught** such a large number of fish

5. 9 were all amazed at the large number of fish they had **caught.**

5.10 from now on you will be **catching** men."

11.54 to lay traps for him and **catch** him saying something wrong.

20.26 the people they could not **catch** him out in anything, so they

21.34 life, or that Day may suddenly **catch** you [35]like a trap.

23. 2 **caught** this man misleading our people, telling them not to pay

Jn 8. 3 woman who had been **caught** committing adultery, and they made her

8. 4 to Jesus, "this woman was **caught** in the very act of

21. 3 a boat, but all that night they did not **catch** a thing.

21. 5 Then he asked them, "Young men, haven't you **caught** anything?"

21. 6 on the right side of the boat, and you will **catch** some."

21. 6 not pull it back in, because they had **caught** so many fish.

21.10 to them, "Bring some of the fish you have just **caught."**

Rom 11. 9 David says, "May they be **caught** and trapped at their feasts;

Gal 6. 1 My brothers, if someone is **caught** in any kind of wrongdoing,

1 Tim 6. 9 fall into temptation and are **caught** in the trap of many

2 Tim 2.26 of the Devil, who had **caught** them and made them obey his

2 Pet 2.20 and then are again **caught** and conquered by them, such people

CATTLE

Gen 12.16 gave him flocks of sheep and goats, **cattle,** donkeys, slaves,

13. 2 with sheep, goats, and **cattle,** as well as silver and gold.

13. 5 also had sheep, goats, and **cattle,** as well as his own family

20.14 and at the same time he gave him sheep, **cattle,** and slaves.

21.27 Abraham gave some sheep and **cattle** to Abimelech, and the two

32. 5 I own **cattle,** donkeys, sheep, goats, and slaves.

34.28 They took the flocks, the **cattle,** the donkeys, and

45.10 your goats, your **cattle,** and everything else that you have.

47.17 food in exchange for their horses, sheep, goats, **cattle,**

49.25 the ground, Blessings of many **cattle** and children,

50. 8 sheep, goats, and **cattle** stayed in the region of Goshen.

Ex 9. 3 on all your animals—your horses, donkeys, camels, **cattle,**

10. 9 sheep and goats, and our **cattle,** because we must hold a

10.24 But your sheep, goats, and **cattle** must stay here."

11. 5 The first-born of all the **cattle** will die also.

12.32 Take your sheep, goats, and **cattle,** and leave.

12.38 and many sheep, goats, and **cattle** also went with them.

20.17 his wife, his slaves, his **cattle,** his donkeys, or anything

20.24 sacrifice your sheep and your **cattle** as offerings to be

22. 9 about property, whether it involves **cattle,** donkeys, sheep,

22.30 Give me the first-born of your **cattle** and your sheep.

24. 5 the Lord and sacrificed some **cattle** as fellowship-offerings.

34. 3 and no sheep or **cattle** are to graze at the foot of

Lev 1. 2 may be one of his **cattle** or one of his sheep or

1. 3 is offering one of his **cattle** as a burnt-offering, he must

3. 1 anyone offers one of his **cattle** as a fellowship-offering, it

7.23 No fat of **cattle,** sheep, or goats shall be eaten.

Num 11.22 Could enough **cattle** and sheep be killed to satisfy them?

20.17 We and our **cattle** will not leave the road or go into

21.22 We and our **cattle** will not leave the road and go into

22.40 of Huzoth, [40]where Balak slaughtered **cattle** and sheep and

31. 9 women and children, took their **cattle** and their flocks,

32. 1 Jazer and Gilead was for **cattle,** [2]they went to Moses,

32.26 wives and children and our **cattle** and sheep will remain here

35. 3 land will be for their **cattle** and all their other animals.

Deut 5.21 his land, his slaves, his **cattle,** his donkeys, or anything

8.13 in [13]and when your **cattle** and sheep, your silver and gold,

12. 6 your freewill offerings, and the first-born of your **cattle**

12.17 nor the first-born of your **cattle** and sheep, the gifts that

12.21 may kill any of the **cattle** or sheep that the Lord has

14.23 and olive-oil, and the first-born of your **cattle** and sheep.

15.19 Lord your God all the first-born males of your **cattle** and sheep;

15.19 don't use any of these **cattle** for work and don't shear any

16. 2 one of your sheep or **cattle** for the Passover meal to honour

17. 1 to the Lord your God **cattle** or sheep that have any defects;

18. 3 "Whenever **cattle** or sheep are sacrificed, the priests

28. 4 with abundant crops, and with many **cattle** and sheep.

28.11 give you many children, many **cattle,** and abundant crops in

28.18 only a few children, poor crops, and few **cattle** and sheep.

28.31 Your **cattle** will be butchered before your very eyes, but

Josh 6.21 They also killed the **cattle,** sheep, and donkeys.

7.24 Achan's sons and daughters, his **cattle,** donkeys, and sheep,

14. 3 cities to live in, with fields for their **cattle** and flocks.

Judg 6. 4 would take all the sheep, **cattle,** and donkeys, and leave

1 Sam 14.32 enemy, took sheep and **cattle,** slaughtered them on the spot,

14.34 and tell them all to bring their **cattle** and sheep here.

14.34 they all brought their **cattle** and slaughtered them there.

15. 9 kill the best sheep and **cattle,** the best calves and lambs,

1 Sam 15.14 "Why, then, do I hear **cattle** mooing and sheep bleating?"

15.15 kept the best sheep and **cattle** to offer as a sacrifice to

15.21 did not kill the best sheep and **cattle** that they captured;

2 Sam 12. 2 The rich man had many **cattle** and sheep, [3]while the poor

1 Kgs 8. 5 a large number of sheep and **cattle**—too many to count.

1 Chr 12.40 They also brought **cattle** and sheep to kill and eat.

2 Chr 5. 6 a large number of sheep and **cattle**—too many to count.

18. 2 a large number of sheep and **cattle** slaughtered for a feast.

20.25 many **cattle,** supplies, clothing, and other valuable objects.

31. 6 Judah brought tithes of their **cattle** and sheep, and they

32.28 barns for his **cattle;**

32.29 God gave him sheep and **cattle** and so much other wealth that

Job 1.10 you have given him enough **cattle** to fill the whole country.

18. 3 What makes you think we are as stupid as **cattle?**

21.10 Yes, all their **cattle** breed and give birth without trouble.

36.33 Thunder announces the approaching storm, and the **cattle** know it is coming.

Ps 8. 7 sheep and **cattle,** and the wild animals too;

50.10 the forest are mine and the **cattle** on thousands of hills.

69.31 more than offering him **cattle,** more than sacrificing

78.48 He killed their **cattle** with hail and their flocks with lightning.

104.14 make grass grow for the **cattle** and plants for man to use,

107.38 he kept their herds of **cattle** from decreasing.

144.14 May our **cattle** reproduce plentifully without miscarriage or loss.

Prov 27.23 Look after your sheep and **cattle** as carefully as you can,

Is 1. 3 **Cattle** know who owns them, and donkeys know where their

7.25 It will be a place where **cattle** and sheep graze."

11. 7 Lions will eat straw as **cattle** do.

17. 2 a pasture for sheep and **cattle,** and no one will drive them

22.13 You killed sheep and **cattle** to eat, and you drank wine.

27.10 become a pasture for **cattle,** where they can rest and graze.

32.20 and safe pasture everywhere for the donkeys and **cattle.**

63.14 As **cattle** are led into a fertile valley, so the Lord

65.10 will lead their sheep and **cattle** to pasture in the Plain of

65.25 lions will eat straw, as **cattle** do, and snakes will no

Jer 31.12 of corn and wine and olive-oil, gifts of sheep and **cattle.**

Ezek 32.13 I will slaughter your **cattle** at every water-hole.

32.13 will be no people or **cattle** to muddy the water any more.

36.11 I will make people and **cattle** increase in number.

Hos 5. 6 They take their sheep and **cattle** to offer as sacrifices to

Joel 1.18 The **cattle** are bellowing in distress because there is no

3.18 with vineyards, and **cattle** will be found on every hill;

Jon 3. 7 persons, **cattle,** and sheep are forbidden to eat or drink.

Hab 3.17 sheep all die and the **cattle-stalls** are empty, [18]I will

Jn 2.14 Temple he found men selling **cattle,** sheep, and pigeons,

2.15 animals out of the Temple, both the sheep and the **cattle;**

Rev 18.13 flour and wheat, **cattle** and sheep, horses and carriages, slaves,

also Gen 24.35 Gen 26.14 Gen 32.7 Num 31.28 Num 31.30 Num 31.32 Num 31.36 Num 31.42 Deut 14.4 Deut 32.14 1 Sam 8.16 1 Sam 15.3 1 Sam 22.19 1 Sam 27.9 1 Kgs 4.23 1 Kgs 8.63 2 Kgs 5.26 1 Chr 27.25 2 Chr 7.5 2 Chr 15.11 Job 1.3 Job 42.12

CAULDRON

2 Chr 35.13 the sacred offerings in pots, **cauldrons,** and pans, and

CAUSE (1)

1 Sam 25.31 sir, for having killed without **cause** or for having taken

Ps 7. 3 a friend or without **cause** done violence to my enemy—

Lam 3.52 like a bird by enemies who had no **cause** to hate me.

Mt 5.29 So if your right eye **causes** you to sin, take it out

5.30 If your right hand **causes** you to sin, cut it off

5.32 divorces his wife, for any **cause** other than her unfaithfulness,

12.20 He will persist until he **causes** justice to triumph,

13.41 his Kingdom all those who **cause** people to sin and all others

18. 6 "If anyone should **cause** one of these little ones to lose

18. 7 always happen—but how terrible for the one who **causes** them!

19. 9 divorces his wife, for any **cause** other than her unfaithfulness

Mk 7.37 "He even **causes** the deaf to hear and the dumb to speak!"

9.42 "If anyone should **cause** one of these little ones to

Lk 1.78 He will **cause** the bright dawn of salvation to rise on us

17. 2 than for him to **cause** one of these little ones to

Jn 9. 2 asked him, "Teacher, whose sin **caused** him to be born blind?

Acts 7.11 a famine all over Egypt and Canaan, which **caused** much suffering.

10.40 three days later and **caused** him to appear, [41]not to everyone,

16.20 "These men are Jews, and they are **causing** trouble in our city.

17. 6 and shouted, "These men have **caused** trouble everywhere!

Rom 7.13 But does this mean that what is good **caused** my death?

8.15 does not make you slaves and **cause** you to be afraid;

14.20 eat anything that will **cause** someone else to fall into sin.

16.17 watch out for those who **cause** divisions and upset people's faith

1 Cor 10.32 such a way as to **cause** no trouble either to Jews or

2 Cor 7. 9 sadness was used by God, and so we **caused** you no harm.

7.10 But sadness that is merely human **causes** death.

Gal 5.11 my preaching about the cross of Christ would **cause** no trouble.

Tit 3.10 warnings to the person who **causes** divisions, and then have

Heb 12.15 plant that grows up and **causes** many troubles with its poison.

Jas 1.17 heavenly lights, who does not change or **cause** darkness by turning.

2 Pet 2.13 will be paid with suffering for the suffering they have **caused.**

1 Jn 2.10 there is nothing in him that will **cause** someone else to sin.

Jude 19 These are the people who **cause** divisions, who are controlled

Rev 9. 5 The pain **caused** by the torture is like

9. 5 the pain **caused** by a scorpion's sting.

CAUSE (2)

Ex 23. 8 is right and ruins the **cause** of those who are innocent.

2 Sam 3. 8 have been loyal to the **cause** of your father Saul, his

1 Kgs 1. 7 Abiathar the priest, and they agreed to support his **cause.**
Ps 35.23 rise up, my God, and plead my **cause.**
43. 1 O God, declare me innocent, and defend my **cause** against the ungodly;
74.22 Rouse yourself, God, and defend your **cause!**
119.154 Defend my **cause,** and set me free;
140.12 know that you defend the **cause** of the poor and the rights
Is 49. 4 Yet I can trust the Lord to defend my **cause;**
Jer 11.20 I have placed my **cause** in your hands;
20.12 on my enemies, for I have placed my **cause** in your hands.
50.34 himself will take up their **cause** and will bring peace to the
51.36 "I will take up your **cause** and will make your enemies pay
Acts 26. 9 do everything I could against the **cause** of Jesus of Nazareth.
2 Cor 9. 8 for yourselves and more than enough for every good **cause.**
Gal 2.17 does this mean that Christ is serving the **cause** of sin?
Phil 2.21 with his own affairs, not with the **cause** of Jesus Christ.

CAUTIOUS

Prov 11.24 Others are **cautious,** and yet grow poorer.
Mt 10.16 You must be as **cautious** as snakes and as gentle as doves.

CAVALRY

Josh 24. 6 Egypt, and the Egyptians pursued them with chariots and **cavalry.**
1 Sam 8.11 war chariots, others in his **cavalry,** and others will run
1 Kgs 4.26 for his chariot-horses and twelve thousand **cavalry** horses.
10.26 hundred chariots and twelve thousand **cavalry** horses.
20.20 Benhadad escaped on horseback, accompanied by some of the **cavalry.**
22. 4 Jehoshaphat answered, "and so are my soldiers and my **cavalry.**
2 Chr 1.14 hundred chariots and twelve thousand **cavalry** horses.
9.25 chariots and horses, and had twelve thousand **cavalry** horses.
Ezra 8.22 emperor for a troop of **cavalry** to guard us from any enemies
Is 36. 9 you expect the Egyptians to send you chariots and **cavalry.**
Ezek 23. 6 all of them were handsome young **cavalry** officers.
23.12 for the **cavalry** officers, all those handsome young men.
23.23 those important officials and high-ranking **cavalry** officers.
26. 7 with a huge army, with horses and chariots and with **cavalry.**

CAVE

Gen 19.30 two daughters moved up into the hills and lived in a **cave.**
23. 9 Zohar [9] to sell me Machpelah **Cave,** which is near the edge of
23.11 give you the whole field and the **cave** that is in it.
23.17 It included the field, the **cave** which was in it, and all
23.19 buried his wife Sarah in that **cave** in the land of Canaan.
23.20 to the Hittites, and the **cave** in it, became the property of
25. 9 Ishmael buried him in Machpelah **Cave,** in the field east of
49.29 with my fathers in the **cave** that is in the field of
49.30 Abraham bought this **cave** and field from Ephron for a burial-ground.
49.32 The field and the **cave** in it were bought from the Hittites.
50.13 and buried it in the **cave** at Machpelah, east of Mamre, in
Josh 10.16 had escaped and were hiding in the **cave** at Makkedah.
10.18 "Roll some big stones in front of the entrance to the **cave.**
10.22 "Open the entrance to the **cave** and bring those five kings
10.23 So the **cave** was opened, and the kings of Jerusalem,
10.27 and thrown into the same **cave** where they had hidden earlier.
10.27 at the entrance to the **cave,** and they are still there.
Judg 6. 2 Israel hid from them in **caves** and other safe places in the
15. 8 he went and stayed in the **cave** in the cliff at Etam.
15.11 of Judah went to the **cave** in the cliff at Etam and
1 Sam 13. 6 of the Israelites hid in **caves** and holes or among the rocks
22. 1 of Gath and went to a **cave** near the town of Adullam.
22. 4 they stayed there as long as David was hiding in the **cave.**
24. 3 He came to a **cave** close to some sheep pens by the
24. 3 happened to be the very **cave** in which David and his men
24. 3 were hiding far back in the **cave.**
24. 7 Saul got up, left the **cave,** and started on his way.
24.10 that just now in the **cave** the Lord put you in my
2 Sam 17. 9 now he is probably hiding in a **cave** or some other place.
23.13 Thirty" went down to the **cave** of Adullam, where David was,
1 Kgs 18. 4 of them, hid them in **caves** in two groups of fifty, and
18.13 a hundred of them in **caves,** in two groups of fifty, and
19. 9 There he went into a **cave** to spend the night.
19.13 cloak and went out and stood at the entrance of the **cave.**
1 Chr 11.15 David was staying near the **cave** of Adullam, while a band of
Job 30. 6 They had to live in **caves,** in holes dug in the sides
38.40 when they hide in their **caves,** or lie in wait in their
Ps 95. 4 whole earth, from the deepest **caves** to the highest hills.
Is 2.10 They will hide in **caves** in the rocky hills or dig holes
2.19 People will hide in **caves** in the rocky hills or dig
2.21 will hide in holes and **caves** in the rocky hills to try
7.19 rugged valleys and in the **caves** in the rocks, and they will
57. 5 as sacrifices in the rocky **caves** near the bed of a stream.
65. 4 At night they go to **caves** and tombs to consult the spirits
Jer 16.16 on every mountain and hill and in the **caves** among the rocks.
25.38 Lord has abandoned his people like a lion that leaves its **cave.**
Ezek 33.27 Those hiding in the mountains and in **caves** will die of disease.
Mic 1.15 leaders of Israel will go and hide in the **cave** at Adullam.
Mt 8.28 met by two men who came out of the burial **caves** there.
Mk 5. 2 met by a man who came out of the burial **caves** there.
Lk 8.27 not stay at home, but spent his time in the burial **caves.**
Jn 11.38 the tomb, which was a **cave** with a stone placed at the
Heb 11.38 deserts and hills, living in **caves** and holes in the ground.
Rev 6.15 hid themselves in **caves** and under rocks on the mountains.

CAW

Zeph 2.14 Crows will **caw** on the doorsteps.

CEASE

Ps 85. 5 Will your anger never **cease?**
Is 24. 8 and the joyful music of their harps and drums has **ceased.**
Lam 3.49 will pour out in a **ceaseless** stream [50] Until the Lord looks
1 Cor 13. 8 gifts of speaking in strange tongues, but they will **cease;**

CEDAR

Lev 14. 4 together with a piece of **cedar-wood,** a red cord, and a sprig
14. 6 together with the **cedar-wood,** the red cord, and the hyssop,
14.49 shall take two birds, some **cedar-wood,** a red cord, and a
14.51 Then he shall take the **cedar-wood,** the hyssop, the red
14.52 the live bird, the **cedar-wood,** the hyssop, and the red cord.
Num 19. 6 he is to take some **cedar-wood,** a sprig of hyssop, and a
24. 6 Like aloes planted by the Lord Or **cedars** beside the water.
Judg 9.15 of my thorny branches and burn up the **cedars** of Lebanon.'
2 Sam 5.11 he provided him with **cedar** logs and with carpenters and
7. 2 in a house built of **cedar,** but God's Covenant Box is kept
7. 7 why they had not built me a temple made of **cedar.'**
1 Kgs 4.33 and plants, from the Lebanon **cedars** to the hyssop that grows
5. 6 So send your men to Lebanon to cut down **cedars** for me.
5. 8 I will provide the **cedars** and the pine-trees.
5.10 Solomon with all the **cedar** and pine logs that he wanted,
6. 9 He put in a ceiling made of beams and boards of **cedar.**
6.10 walls of the Temple, and was joined to them by **cedar** beams.
6.15 inside walls were covered with **cedar** panels from the floor
6.16 and was partitioned off by **cedar** boards reaching from the
6.18 The **cedar** panels were decorated with carvings of gourds
6.18 whole interior was covered with **cedar,** so that the stones of
6.20 The altar was covered with **cedar** panels.
6.36 which had one layer of **cedar** beams for every three layers of
7. 2 It had three rows of **cedar** pillars, fifteen in each row,
7. 2 with **cedar** beams resting on them.
7. 2 The ceiling was of **cedar,** extending over store-rooms, which
7. 7 where Solomon decided cases, had **cedar** panels from the floor
7.11 of them were other stones, cut to measure, and **cedar** beams.
7.12 walls with one layer of **cedar** beams for every three layers
9.11 provided him with all the **cedar** and pine and with all the
10.27 and **cedar** was as plentiful as ordinary sycomore
2 Kgs 14. 9 bush on the Lebanon Mountains sent a message to a **cedar:**
19.23 you cut down the tallest **cedars** and the finest cypress-trees
1 Chr 14. 1 he provided him with **cedar** logs and with stone-masons and
17. 1 in a house built of **cedar,** but the Lord's Covenant Box is
17. 6 why they had not built me a temple made of **cedar.'**
22. 4 Tyre and Sidon to bring him a large number of **cedar** logs.
2 Chr 1.15 and **cedar** was as plentiful as ordinary sycomore.
2. 3 King David, when you sold him **cedar** logs for building his palace.
2. 8 so send me **cedar,** cypress, and juniper logs from Lebanon.
2.16 will cut down all the **cedars** you need, bind them together in
3. 5 room was panelled with **cedar** and overlaid with fine gold,
9.27 and **cedar** was as plentiful as ordinary sycomore
25.18 bush in the Lebanon Mountains sent a message to a **cedar:**
Ezra 3. 7 and Sidon in exchange for **cedar-trees** from Lebanon, which
Job 40.17 tail stands up like a **cedar,** and the muscles in his legs
Ps 29. 5 of the Lord breaks the **cedars,** even the cedars of Lebanon.
37.35 he towered over everyone like a **cedar** of Lebanon;
80.10 its branches overshadowed the giant **cedars.**
92.12 they will grow like the **cedars** of Lebanon.
104.16 The **cedars** of Lebanon get plenty of rain— the Lord's own
Song 1.17 the **cedars** will be the beams of our house, and the
5.15 He is majestic, like the Lebanon Mountains with their towering **cedars.**
8. 9 she is a gate, we will protect her with panels of **cedar.**
Is 2.13 He will destroy the tall **cedars** of Lebanon and all the
9.10 cut down, but we will replace them with the finest **cedar."**
14. 8 the **cedars** of Lebanon rejoice over the fallen king,
37.24 cut down the tallest **cedars** and the finest cypress-trees,
41.19 I will make **cedars** grow in the desert, and acacias and
44.14 He might cut down **cedars** to use, or choose oak or
Jer 22. 7 axes, cut down its beautiful **cedar** pillars, and throw them
22.14 in his house, panels it with **cedar,** and paints it red.
22.15 if you build houses of **cedar,** finer than those of others?
22.23 You rest secure among the **cedars** brought from Lebanon;
Ezek 17. 3 off the top of a **cedar-tree,** [4] which he carried to a land
17.22 the top of a tall **cedar** and break off a tender sprout;
17.23 It will grow branches and bear seed and become a magnificent **cedar.**
27. 5 Mount Hermon for timber And a **cedar** from Lebanon for your mast.
31. 3 You are like a **cedar** in Lebanon, With beautiful, shady branches,
31. 8 No **cedar** in God's garden could compare with it.
Hos 14. 6 They will be fragrant like the **cedars** of Lebanon.
Amos 2. 9 men who were as tall as **cedar-trees** and as strong as oaks.
Zeph 2.14 The **cedar-wood** of her buildings will be stripped away.
Zech 11. 1 Open your doors, Lebanon, so that fire can burn down your **cedar-trees!**
11. 2 Weep and wail, cypress-trees— the **cedars** have fallen;

CEILING

1 Kgs 6. 9 He put in a **ceiling** made of beams and boards of cedar.
6.15 from the floor to the **ceiling,** and the floor was made of
6.16 off by cedar boards reaching from the floor to the **ceiling.**
7. 2 The **ceiling** was of cedar, extending over store-rooms, which
Song 1.17 the beams of our house, and the cypress-trees the **ceiling.**

CELEBRATE

Gen 29.27 Wait until the week's marriage **celebrations** are over,
29.28 when the week of marriage **celebrations** was over, Laban gave

Ex 12.14 You must **celebrate** this day as a religious festival to
12.14 **Celebrate** it for all time to come."
12.17 all time to come you must **celebrate** this day as a festival.
12.21 and kill it, so that your families can **celebrate** Passover.
12.47 whole community of Israel must **celebrate** this festival,
12.48 you and wants to **celebrate** Passover to honour the Lord,
13. 5 and fertile land, you must **celebrate** this festival in the
13.10 **Celebrate** this festival at the appointed time each year.
23.14 "**Celebrate** three festivals a year to honour me.
23.15 **celebrate** the Festival of Unleavened Bread in
23.16 "**Celebrate** the Harvest Festival when you begin to harvest your crops.
23.16 "**Celebrate** the Festival of Shelters in the autumn, when
Lev 23. 5 The Passover, **celebrated** to honour the Lord, begins at
23.39 your fields, **celebrate** this festival for seven days,
23.41 **Celebrate** it for seven days.
Num 7.10 brought offerings to **celebrate** the dedication of the altar.
9.11 **Celebrate** it with unleavened bread and bitter herbs.
29.12 **Celebrate** this festival in honour of the Lord for seven days
Deut 16. 1 Lord your God by **celebrating** Passover in the month of Abib;
16.10 the corn, [10]and then **celebrate** the Harvest Festival,
16.13 pressed all your grapes, **celebrate** the Festival of Shelters
16.15 the Lord your God by **celebrating** this festival for seven
26.11 foreigners who live among you join in the **celebration.**
Judg 16.23 Philistine kings met together to **celebrate** and offer a great
1 Sam 11.15 and Saul and all the people of Israel **celebrated** the event.
18. 7 In their **celebration** the women sang, "Saul has killed thousands,
20.29 'because our family is **celebrating** the sacrificial feast in town,
30.16 the place, eating, drinking, and **celebrating** because of the
2 Sam 6.12 Obed's house to take it to Jerusalem with a great **celebration.**
1 Kgs 8.65 all the people of Israel **celebrated** the Festival of Shelters
12.33 sacrifice on the altar in **celebration** of the festival he had
2 Kgs 23.21 Josiah ordered the people to **celebrate** the Passover in
23.22 this one had ever been **celebrated** by any of the kings of
23.23 reign of Josiah, the Passover was **celebrated** in Jerusalem.
1 Chr 15.25 Edom to fetch the Covenant Box, and they had a great **celebration.**
2 Chr 7. 8 all the people of Israel **celebrated** the Festival of Shelters
7. 9 had a closing **celebration,** [10]and on the following day,
23.13 with their instruments were leading the **celebration.**
23.18 They were also in charge of the music and the **celebrations.**
30. 1 had not been able to **celebrate** the Passover Festival at the
30. 1 of Jerusalem agreed to **celebrate** it in the second month,
30. 1 the Temple in Jerusalem to **celebrate** the Passover in honour
30. 5 Jerusalem and **celebrate** the Passover according to the Law,
30.13 second month to **celebrate** the Festival of Unleavened Bread.
30.21 Jerusalem **celebrated** the Festival of Unleavened Bread
30.23 they all decided to **celebrate** for another seven days.
30.23 So they **celebrated** with joy.
35. 1 King Josiah **celebrated** the Passover at Jerusalem
35.17 of Israel who were present **celebrated** the Passover and the
35.18 Samuel, the Passover had never been **celebrated** like this.
35.18 the former kings had ever **celebrated** a Passover
35.18 like this one **celebrated** by King Josiah,
Ezra 3. 4 They **celebrated** the Festival of Shelters
6.19 who had returned from exile **celebrated** Passover on the
6.22 they joyfully **celebrated** the Festival of Unleavened Bread.
Neh 8.18 They **celebrated** for seven days, and on the eighth day there
12.27 that they could join in **celebrating** the dedication with
12.43 the children joined in the **celebration,** and the noise they
Esth 9.23 and the **celebration** became an annual custom.
Ps 20. 5 victory and **celebrate** your triumph by praising our God.
118.24 let us be happy, let us **celebrate!**
Prov 28.12 come to power, everybody **celebrates,** but when bad men rule,
Is 22. 1 people of the city **celebrating** on the roofs of the houses?
22.13 Instead, you laughed and **celebrated.**
33.20 Look at Zion, the city where we **celebrate** our religious festivals.
Ezek 7. 7 more **celebrations** at the mountain shrines, only confusion.
45.21 you will begin the **celebration** of the Passover Festival.
Hos 2.11 and her Sabbath **celebrations**—all her religious meetings.
7. 5 the day of the king's **celebration** they made the king and his
9. 1 People of Israel, stop **celebrating** your festivals like pagans.
Nah 1.15 People of Judah, **celebrate** your festivals and give God what
Zech 14.16 Lord Almighty as king, and to **celebrate** the Festival of Shelters.
14.18 If the Egyptians refuse to **celebrate** the Festival of Shelters,
14.19 nations if they do not **celebrate** the Festival of Shelters.
Mt 26.18 and I will **celebrate** the Passover at your house.'"
Lk 15. 6 Let us **celebrate!**'
15. 9 Let us **celebrate!**'
15.23 prize calf and kill it, and let us **celebrate** with a feast!
15.32 But we had to **celebrate** and be happy, because your brother
Jn 10.22 the Dedication of the Temple was being **celebrated** in Jerusalem.
1 Cor 5. 8 **celebrate** our Passover, then, not with bread having the old
Rev 11.10 will **celebrate** and send presents to each other, because those two

CELL

Jer 37.16 was put in an underground **cell** and kept there a long time.
Acts 12. 7 of the Lord stood there, and a light shone in the **cell.**
16.24 threw them into the inner **cell** and fastened their feet between

CELLAR

1 Chr 27.25 Wine **cellars:**

CEMETERY

Ecc 8.10 the way back from the **cemetery** people praise them in the
Mt 27. 7 the money to buy Potter's Field, as a **cemetery** for foreigners.

CENSUS

Ex 30.12 Moses, [12]"When you take a **census** of the people of Israel,
30.12 disaster will come on him while the **census** is being taken.
30.13 Everyone included in the **census** must pay the required amount
30.14 Everyone being counted in the **census,** that is, every man
38.25 The silver from the **census** of the community
38.26 enrolled in the **census,** each one paying the required amount,
38.26 603,550 men twenty years old or older enrolled in the **census.**
Num 1. 2 Aaron are to take a **census** of the people of Israel by
1.49 Moses, [49]"When you take a **census** of the men fit for
4. 2 told Moses [2]to take a **census** of the Levite clan of Kohath
4.22 told Moses [22]to take a **census** of the Levite clan of
4.29 told Moses to take a **census** of the Levite clan of Merari
4.34 of the community took a **census** of the three Levite clans,
7. 2 charge of the **census,** [3]brought their offerings to the Lord:
26. 2 son of Aaron, [2]"Take a **census** by families of the whole
26.63 Eleazar when they took a **census** of the Israelites in the
26.64 Aaron had listed in the first **census** in the Sinai Desert.
2 Sam 24.10 David had taken the **census,** his conscience began to trouble him,
1 Chr 21. 1 people of Israel, so he made David decide to take a **census.**
21. 6 he did not take any **census** of the tribes of Levi and
21.17 I am the one who ordered the **census.**
23. 3 He took a **census** of all the male Levites aged thirty or
27.23 David did not take a **census** of the people who were under
27.24 Zeruiah, began to take a **census,** but he did not complete it.
27.24 punished Israel because of this **census,** so the final figures
2 Chr 2.17 King Solomon took a **census** of all the foreigners living
2.17 of Israel, similar to the **census** his father David had taken.
Lk 2. 1 the Emperor Augustus ordered a **census** to be taken throughout the
2. 2 When this first **census** took place, Quirinius was the governor
Acts 5.37 Judas the Galilean appeared during the time of the **census;**

CENTIMETRE

Gen 6.16 Ex 25.10 Ex 25.10 Ex 25.10 Ex 25.17 Ex 25.17 Ex 25.23 Ex 25.23 Ex 25.23 Ex 26.13 Ex 26.16 Ex 28.16 Ex 28.16 Ex 30.2 Ex 30.2 Ex 30.2 Ex 36.21 Ex 37.1 Ex 37.1 Ex 37.1 Ex 37.6 Ex 37.6 Ex 37.10 Ex 37.10 Ex 37.10 Ex 37.25 Ex 37.25 Ex 37.25 Ex 39.9 Ex 39.9 Judg 3.16 1 Kgs 7.31 1 Kgs 7.31 1 Kgs 7.32 1 Kgs 7.35 Ezek 40.12 Ezek 40.12 Ezek 40.42 Ezek 40.42 Ezek 43.13 Ezek 43.13 Ezek 43.13 Ezek 43.14 Ezek 43.14 Ezek 43.17 Ezek 43.17

CENTRE

Ex 1.11 Pithom and Rameses to serve as supply **centres** for the king.
1 Sam 26. 7 found Saul sleeping in the **centre** of the camp with his spear
1 Kgs 8.64 day he also consecrated the **central** part of the courtyard,
20.34 may set up a commercial **centre** for yourself in Damascus,
2 Kgs 20. 4 he had passed through the **central** courtyard of the palace
2 Chr 3.11 touched each other in the **centre** of the room and reached the
7. 7 Solomon consecrated the **central** part of the courtyard,
8. 4 the cities in Hamath that were **centres** for storing supplies.
Is 23.11 He has ordered the Phoenician **centres** of commerce to be destroyed.
Jer 21. 4 pile up your soldiers' weapons in the **centre** of the city.
Ezek 1. 5 At the **centre** of the storm, I saw what looked like four
5. 5 I put her at the **centre** of the world, with other countries
41. 1 Next, the man took me into the **central** room, the Holy Place.
41. 4 This room was beyond the **central** room.
48. 9 In the **centre** of this section, a special area twelve and a
48.15 is to be in the **centre** of it, [16]and it will be
48.20 the total area in the **centre** of the section which was set
Lk 22.55 had been lit in the **centre** of the courtyard, and Peter
Rev 5. 6 a Lamb standing in the **centre** of the throne, surrounded by
7.17 Lamb, who is in the **centre** of the throne, will be their

CEREMONY

Gen 50.10 and Joseph performed mourning **ceremonies** for seven days.
50.11 "What a solemn **ceremony** of mourning the Egyptians are holding!"
Lev 21. 1 taking part in the funeral **ceremonies** when a relative dies,
Neh 7.70 50 **ceremonial** bowls
8.18 day there was a closing **ceremony,** as required in the Law.
12.45 Levites, [45]because they performed the **ceremonies** of
Lk 2.22 and Mary to perform the **ceremony** of purification, as the Law
Acts 7. 8 Then God gave Abraham the **ceremony** of circumcision as a sign
21.24 join them in the **ceremony** of purification and pay their expenses;
21.26 the next day performed the **ceremony** of purification with them.
24.18 in the Temple after I had completed the **ceremony** of purification.
25.23 came with great pomp and **ceremony** and entered the audience hall
Gal 6.13 they can boast that you submitted to this physical **ceremony.**
Phil 3. 3 We do not put any trust in external **ceremonies.**
3. 4 he can trust in external **ceremonies,** I have even more reason
Heb 9.10 to do only with food, drink, and various purification **ceremonies.**

CERTAIN (1)

[UNCERTAIN]

Num 5.12 the husband may not be **certain,** for his wife may have kept
Deut 4. 9 Make **certain** that you do not forget, as long as you live,
4.15 your own good, then, make **certain** [16]that you do not sin by
4.23 Be **certain** that you do not forget the covenant that the
6.12 you want to eat, [12]make **certain** that you do not forget the
8.11 "Make **certain** that you do not forget the Lord your God;
1 Sam 20. 9 "If I knew for **certain** that my father was determined to
23.22 find out for **certain** where he is and who has seen him

Neh 6. 7 His Majesty is **certain** to hear about this, so I suggest that
Ps 112. 8 he is **certain** to see his enemies defeated.
119.140 How **certain** your promise is!
Prov 11.18 if you do what is right, you are **certain** to be rewarded.
Is 28.15 You are **certain** that disaster will spare you when it comes,
Ezek 39. 8 Sovereign Lord said, "The day I spoke about is **certain** to come.
Mt 6. 1 "Make **certain** you do not perform your religious duties in
Lk 11.35 Make **certain,** then, that the light in you is not darkness.
Jn 8.52 said to him, "Now we are **certain** that you have a demon!
Acts 22.30 wanted to find out for **certain** what the Jews were accusing
Rom 2.20 You are **certain** that in the Law you have the full content
8.38 For I am **certain** that nothing can separate us from his love:
14.14 the Lord Jesus makes me **certain** that no food is of itself
1 Tim 6.17 hope, not in such an **uncertain** thing as riches, but in God,
Heb 11. 1 we hope for, to be **certain** of the things we cannot see.

CERTAIN (2)

Mt 26.18 "Go to a **certain** man in the city," he said to them,
Mk 14.51 **certain** young man, dressed only in a linen cloth, was following
Lk 11. 1 One day Jesus was praying in a **certain** place.
18. 2 "In a **certain** town there was a judge who neither feared
Acts 10. 5 men to Joppa for a **certain** man whose full name is Simon
13. 6 where they met a **certain** magician named Bar-Jesus, a Jew who
17.18 **Certain** Epicurean and Stoic teachers also debated with him.
19.24 A **certain** silversmith named Demetrius made silver models of
Rom 14. 5 One person thinks that a **certain** day is more important than
14. 6 Whoever thinks highly of a **certain** day does so in honour
14. 6 Whoever refuses to eat **certain** things does so in honour of
15.15 been quite bold about **certain** subjects of which I have reminded
2 Cor 10.13 however, our boasting will not go beyond **certain** limits;
12. 2 I know a **certain** Christian man who fourteen years ago was
Gal 4.10 You pay special attention to **certain** days, months, seasons, and
1 Tim 4. 3 teach that it is wrong to marry and to eat **certain** foods.
Jas 4.13 we will travel to a **certain** city, where we will stay a

CHAFF

Is 27.12 by one, like someone separating the wheat from the **chaff.**
Jer 4.11 that only blows away the **chaff—**[12] the wind that comes at
Hos 13. 3 They will be like **chaff** which the wind blows
Zeph 2. 2 you are driven away like **chaff** blown by the wind, before the
Mt 3.12 but he will burn the **chaff** in a fire that never goes
Lk 3.17 but he will burn the **chaff** in a fire that never goes
22.31 the bad, as a farmer separates the wheat from the **chaff.**

CHAIN

Gen 41.42 linen robe on him, and placed a gold **chain** round his neck.
Ex 28.14 settings [14] and two **chains** of pure gold twisted like cords,
28.22 For the breast-piece make **chains** of pure gold, twisted like cords.
39.15 For the breast-piece they made **chains** of pure gold,
Judg 16.21 They took him to Gaza, **chained** him with bronze chains, and
1 Kgs 6.21 covered with gold, and gold **chains** were placed across the
7.17 interwoven **chains,** [18] and two rows of bronze pomegranates.
7.20 on a rounded section which was above the **chain** design.
7.40 columns The design of interwoven **chains** on each capital
2 Kgs 25. 7 put out, placed him in **chains,** and took him to Babylon.
2 Chr 3. 5 which were worked designs of palm-trees and **chain** patterns.
3.16 of interwoven **chains** and one hundred bronze pomegranates.
4.11 columns The design of interwoven **chains** on each capital
16.10 so angry with the prophet that he had him put in **chains.**
33.11 hooks in him, put him in **chains,** and took him to Babylon.
36. 6 captured Jehoiakim, and took him to Babylonia in **chains.**
Job 13.27 You bind **chains** on my feet;
33.11 He binds **chains** on my feet;
36. 8 are bound in **chains,** suffering for what they have done,
Ps 105.18 His feet were kept in **chains,** and an iron collar was
107.10 and darkness, prisoners suffering in **chains,** [11] because
107.14 their gloom and darkness and broke their **chains** in pieces.
149. 8 to bind their kings in **chains,** their leaders in chains of iron;
Ecc 7.26 and her arms round you will hold you like a **chain.**
12. 6 The silver **chain** will snap, and the golden lamp will fall
Song 1.11 will make for you a **chain** of gold with ornaments of silver.
Is 45.14 they will follow you in **chains.**
52. 2 Undo the **chains** that bind you, captive people of Zion!
58. 6 Remove the **chains** of oppression and the yoke of injustice,
Jer 20. 2 be beaten and placed in **chains** near the upper Benjamin Gate
20. 3 had released me from the **chains,** I said to him, "The Lord
29.26 a prophet is placed in **chains** with an iron collar round his
30. 8 their necks and remove their **chains,** and they will no longer
39. 7 out and had him placed in **chains** to be taken to Babylonia.
40. 1 had been taken there in **chains,** along with all the other
40. 4 Now, I am taking the **chains** off your wrists and setting
52.11 put out and had him placed in **chains** and taken to Babylon.
Lam 3. 7 He has bound me in **chains;**
Ezek 34.27 When I break my people's **chains** and set them free from those
Dan 5. 7 royal purple, wear a gold **chain** of honour round his neck,
5.16 royal purple, wear a gold **chain** of honour round your neck,
5.29 purple and to hang a gold **chain** of honour round his neck.
Nah 1.13 Assyria's power over you and break the **chains** that bind you."
3.10 were carried off in **chains** and divided among their captors.
Mt 14. 3 John's arrest, and he had him **chained** and put in prison.
27. 2 They put him in **chains,** led him off, and handed him over
Mk 5. 3 Nobody could keep him **chained** up any more;
5. 4 feet and hands had been **chained,**
5. 4 every time he broke the **chains** and smashed the irons on his
6.17 John's arrest, and he had him **chained** and put in prison.
15. 1 They put Jesus in **chains,** led him away, and handed him over
Lk 8.29 hands and feet fastened with **chains,**
8.29 he would break the **chains** and be driven by the demon
Acts 12. 6 He was tied with two **chains,** and there were guards on duty
12. 7 At once the **chains** fell off Peter's hands.
16.26 the doors opened, and the **chains** fell off all the prisoners.
21.33 Paul, arrested him, and ordered him to be bound with two **chains.**
22. 5 and bring them back in **chains** to Jerusalem to be punished.
22.29 was a Roman citizen and that he had put him in **chains.**
22.30 next day he had Paul's **chains** taken off and ordered the
26.29 might become what I am—except, of course, for these **chains!"**
28.20 I am bound in **chains** like this for the sake of
Col 4.18 Do not forget my **chains!**
2 Tim 2. 9 I suffer and I am even **chained** like a criminal.
2. 9 of God is not in **chains,** [10] and so I endure everything for
Heb 11.36 and others were put in **chains** and taken off to prison.
2 Pet 2. 4 where they are kept **chained** in darkness, waiting for the Day
Jude 6 they are bound with eternal **chains** in the darkness below,
Rev 20. 1 in his hand the key of the abyss and a heavy **chain.**
20. 2 the Devil, or Satan—and **chained** him up for a thousand years.

CHAIR

2 Kgs 4.10 a bed, a table, a **chair,** and a lamp in it, and

CHALCEDONY

A semi-precious stone, usually milky or grey in colour.

Rev 21.20 the ninth topaz, the tenth **chalcedony,** the eleventh turquoise,

CHALK

Is 27. 9 altars are ground up like **chalk,** and no more incense-altars
44.13 He outlines a figure with **chalk,** carves it out with his tools,

CHALLENGE

Judg 11.25 He never **challenged** Israel, did he?
1 Sam 17. 4 Gath, came out from the Philistine camp to **challenge** the Israelites.
17.10 Here and now I **challenge** the Israelite army.
17.16 Goliath **challenged** the Israelites every morning and evening
17.23 them, Goliath came forward and **challenged** the Israelites as
17.25 "Listen to his **challenge!**
17.44 "Come on," he **challenged** David, "and I will give your
2 Sam 23. 9 One day he and David **challenged** the Philistines who had
2 Kgs 14. 8 messengers to King Jehoash of Israel, **challenging** him to fight.
2 Chr 25.17 of Jehoahaz and grandson of Jehu, **challenging** him to fight.
Job 40. 1 Job, you **challenged** Almighty God;
Ecc 8. 4 acts with authority, and no one can **challenge** what he does.
Jer 49.19 Who would dare **challenge** me?
50.44 Who would dare **challenge** me?
Dan 11. 2 power and wealth he will **challenge** the kingdom of Greece.
Amos 5.10 You people hate anyone who **challenges** injustice and

CHANCE

Deut 20. 6 but has not yet had the **chance** to harvest its grapes?
20.10 attack a city, first give its people a **chance** to surrender.
Judg 14. 4 the Lord was looking for a **chance** to fight the Philistines.
1 Sam 6. 9 it was only a matter of **chance."**
22. 8 this moment looking for a **chance** to kill me, and that my
22.13 turned against me and is waiting for a **chance** to kill me!"
24. 4 They said to him, "This is your **chance!**
2 Sam 3.18 Now here is your **chance.**
1 Kgs 22.34 By **chance,** however, a Syrian soldier shot an arrow which
2 Chr 18.33 By **chance,** however, a Syrian soldier shot an arrow which
Job 13.13 quiet and give me a **chance** to speak, and let the results
20.18 he will have no **chance** to enjoy his wealth, [19] because he
21. 3 Give me a **chance** to speak and then, when I am through,
32.19 If I don't get a **chance** to speak, I will burst like
37.20 why should I give him a **chance** to destroy me?
Ps 17.11 wherever I turn, watching for a **chance** to pull me down.
Is 41. 1 you will have your **chance** to speak.
Jer 46.17 Egypt a new name— 'Noisy Braggart Who Missed His **Chance.'**
Hos 13.13 Israel has a **chance** to live, but is too foolish to take
Mic 2. 1 soon as they have the **chance,** they do the evil they planned.
7. 2 Everyone is waiting for a **chance** to commit murder.
Mt 26.16 was looking for a good **chance** to hand Jesus over to them.
Mk 6.21 Finally Herodias got her **chance.**
14.11 looking for a good **chance** to hand Jesus over to them.
Lk 21.13 This will be your **chance** to tell the Good News.
22. 6 started looking for a good **chance** to hand Jesus over to them
Acts 16.19 her owners realized that their **chance** of making money was gone,
24.25 I will call you again when I get the **chance."**
25.16 has had the **chance** of defending himself against the accusation.
Rom 7. 8 that commandment sin found its **chance** to stir up all kinds
7.11 Sin found its **chance,** and by means of the commandment
1 Cor 7.21 but if you have a **chance** to become a free man, use
16.12 When he gets the **chance,** however, he will go.
Gal 6.10 often as we have the **chance,** we should do good to everyone,
Eph 4.27 Don't give the Devil a **chance.**
Phil 4.10 you once more had the **chance** of showing that you care for
4.10 stopped caring for me—you just had no **chance** to show it.
1 Tim 5.14 as to give our enemies no **chance** of speaking evil of us.
Heb 11.15 if they had, they would have had the **chance** to return.

CHANGE

[UNCHANGED, UNCHANGING]

Gen 31. 7 Yet he has cheated me and **changed** my wages ten times.
31.41 And even then, you **changed** my wages ten times.
38.14 So she **changed** from the widow's clothes she had been wearing,
41.14 After he had shaved and **changed** his clothes, he came into

Gen 45.22 gave each of them a **change** of clothes, but he gave Benjamin
45.22 Benjamin three hundred pieces of silver and five **changes** of clothes.
Ex 8.16 over the land of Egypt the dust will **change** into gnats."
10.19 And the Lord **changed** the east wind into a very strong
13.17 want the people to **change their minds** and return to Egypt
14. 5 he and his officials **changed their minds** and said, "What
29.28 It is my **unchanging** decision that when my people make their
32.12 **change your mind** and do not bring this disaster on your people.
32.14 So the Lord **changed his mind** and did not bring on his
Lev 6.11 Then he shall **change** his clothes and take the ashes
13.23 But if it remains **unchanged** and does not spread, it is
13.28 But if the spot remains **unchanged** and does not spread
13.55 if the mildew has not **changed** colour, even though it has not
Num 13.16 He **changed** the name of Hoshea son of Nun to Joshua.
14.19 to the greatness of your **unchanging** love, forgive, I pray,
23.19 He is not a human who **changes his mind.**
32.38 Baal Meon (this name was **changed**),
Deut 21.13 her head, cut her fingernails, [13]and **change** her clothes.
Josh 19.47 They settled there and **changed** the name of the city from
Judg 7.19 before midnight, just after the guard had been **changed.**
14.12 of fine linen and a **change** of fine clothes that you can't
18.29 They **changed** its name from Laish to Dan, after their ancestor Dan,
1 Sam 14.21 with them to the camp, **changed** sides again and joined Saul
15.29 Israel's majestic God does not lie or **change his mind.**
15.29 He is not a man—he does not **change his mind."**
26.19 me, an offering to him will make him **change his mind;**
2 Sam 12.20 floor, had a bath, combed his hair, and **changed** his clothes.
23. 5 will not be broken, a promise that will not be **changed.**
24.16 destroy Jerusalem, the Lord **changed his mind** about punishing
2 Kgs 5. 5 thousand pieces of gold, and ten **changes** of fine clothes.
5.22 pieces of silver and two **changes** of fine clothes."
5.23 bags, gave them and two **changes** of fine clothes to two of
23.34 Judah as successor to Josiah, and **changed** his name to Jehoiakim.
24.17 Jehoiachin's uncle Mattaniah king of Judah and **changed** his name to Zedekiah.
25.29 So Jehoiachin was permitted to **change** from his prison
1 Chr 21.15 Jerusalem, but he **changed his mind** and said to the angel,
2 Chr 36. 4 Joahaz' brother Eliakim king of Judah and **changed** his name to Jehoiakim.
Neh 9. 7 you **changed** his name to Abraham.
Esth 1.19 laws of Persia and Media, so that it can never be **changed.**
Job 14. 5 You have settled it, and it can't be **changed.**
23.13 He never **changes.**
Ps 7.12 If they do not **change** their ways, God will sharpen his sword.
30.11 You have **changed** my sadness into a joyful dance;
55.19 for they refuse to **change,** and they do not fear him.
66. 6 He **changed** the sea into dry land;
90. 3 you **change** him back to dust.
107.35 He **changed** deserts into pools of water and dry land into
114. 8 the God of Jacob, [8]who **changes** rocks into pools of water
119.159 Your love never **changes,** so save me!
Prov 20.30 Sometimes it takes a painful experience to make us **change** our ways.
22.25 You might learn their habits and not be able to **change.**
Is 43.13 no one can **change** what I do."
45.23 My promise is true, and it will not be **changed.**
55. 7 leave their way of life and **change** their way of thinking.
Jer 2.11 No other nation has ever **changed** its gods, even though
4.28 The Lord has spoken and will not **change his mind.**
7. 1 **"Change** the way you are living and the things you are doing,
7. 5 **"Change** the way you are living and stop doing the things
7. 7 If you **change,** I will let you go on living here in
8. 8 Look, the laws have been **changed** by dishonest scribes.
13.23 Can a black man **change** the colour of his skin, or a
18.11 stop living sinful lives—to **change** their ways and the things
26. 3 do, then I will **change my mind** about the destruction I plan
26.13 You must **change** the way you are living and the things
26.13 you do, he will **change his mind** about the destruction that
26.19 And the Lord **changed his mind** about the disaster that he
34.11 but later they **changed their minds,** took them back,
34.15 few days ago you **changed your minds** and did what pleased me.
34.16 But then you **changed your minds** again and dishonoured me.
52.33 So Jehoiachin was permitted to **change** from his prison
Ezek 3.18 do not warn him to **change** his ways so that he can
33. 8 do not warn him to **change** his ways so that he can
Dan 2. 9 me lies because you hope that in time things will **change.**
6. 8 a law of the Medes and Persians, which cannot be **changed."**
6.12 a law of the Medes and Persians, which cannot be **changed."**
6.15 Medes and Persians no order which the king issues can be **changed."**
7.25 He will try to **change** their religious laws and festivals,
10. 8 and my face was so **changed** that no one could have recognized
Joel 2. 7 straight ahead and do not **change** direction [8]or get in each
2.14 Lord your God will **change his mind** and bless you with
Amos 4.13 he **changes** day into night.
7. 3 The Lord **changed his mind** and said, "What you saw will
7. 6 The Lord **changed his mind** again and said, "This will not
7. 8 I will not **change my mind** again about punishing them.
8. 1 I will not **change my mind** again about punishing them.
8.10 festivals into funerals and **change** your glad songs into cries
Jon 3. 9 Perhaps God will **change his mind;**
3.10 So he **changed his mind** and did not punish them as he
4. 2 kind, and always ready to **change your mind** and not punish.
Zeph 3. 9 "Then I will **change** the people of the nations, and they
Zech 8.14 them and did not **change my mind,** but carried out my plans.
Mal 3. 6 "I am the Lord, and I do not **change.**
Mt 3.14 But John tried to make him **change** his mind.
17. 2 As they looked on, a **change** came over Jesus:
18. 3 assure you that unless you **change** and become like children,
Mt 21.29 to,' he answered, but later he **changed** his mind and went.
21.32 this, you did not later **change** your minds and believe him.
Mk 9. 2 As they looked on, a **change** came over Jesus, [3]and his
Lk 3.18 Good News to the people and urged them to **change** their ways.
9.29 he was praying, his face **changed** its appearance, and his clothes
Acts 6.14 tear down the Temple and **change** all the customs which have
28. 6 unusual happening to him, they **changed** their minds and said,
Rom 11.15 mankind was **changed** from God's enemies into his friends.
11.29 For God does not **change** his mind about whom he chooses
12. 2 God transform you inwardly by a complete **change** of your mind.
1 Cor 15.51 we shall all be **changed** in an instant, as quickly as
15.51 be raised, never to die again, and we shall all be **changed.**
15.53 For what is mortal must be **changed** into what is immortal;
15.53 what will die must be **changed** into what cannot die.
15.54 and the mortal has been **changed** into the immortal,
2 Cor 5. 5 has prepared us for this **change,** and he gave us his Spirit
5.18 God, who through Christ **changed** us from enemies into his friends
5.20 let God **change** you from enemies into his friends!
7. 9 you sad, but because your sadness made you **change** your ways.
7.10 used by God brings a **change** of heart that leads to salvation
Gal 1. 7 are upsetting you and trying to **change** the gospel of Christ.
Phil 3.21 He will **change** our weak mortal bodies and make them like
Heb 1.12 them up like a coat, and they will be **changed** like clothes.
6.17 make it very clear that he would never **change** his purpose;
6.18 things, then, that cannot **change** and about which God cannot lie.
7.12 For when the priesthood is **changed,**
7.12 there also has to be a **change** in the law.
12.17 not find any way to **change** what he had done, even though
Jas 1.17 heavenly lights, who does not **change** or cause darkness by turning.
4. 9 **change** your laughter into crying, your joy into gloom!

CHANNEL

2 Chr 32.30 the Spring of Gihon and **channelled** the water to flow through
Job 38.25 Who dug a **channel** for the pouring rain and cleared the
Is 19. 6 The **channels** of the river will stink as they slowly go dry.

CHANT

Ps 58. 5 of the snake-charmer, or the **chant** of the clever magician.
Ezek 27.32 They **chant** a funeral song for you:

CHAOS

Ps 42. 6 **chaos** roars at me like a flood, like waterfalls thundering
Is 24.10 the city everything is in **chaos,** and people lock themselves

CHARACTER

2 Sam 20. 1 be in Gilgal a worthless **character** named Sheba son of Bikri,
2 Chr 32.31 Hezekiah go his own way only in order to test his **character.**
Prov 1. 9 Their teaching will improve your **character** as a handsome
28.11 a poor person who has insight into **character** knows better.
Ecc 7. 7 If you take a bribe, you ruin your **character.**
1 Cor 15.33 "Bad companions ruin good **character."**
2 Cor 5.12 who boast about a man's appearance and not about his **character.**
1 Tim 3. 8 Church helpers must also have a good **character** and be sincere;
3.11 wives also must be of good **character** and must not gossip;

CHARCOAL

Ps 120. 4 With a soldier's sharp arrows, with red-hot **charcoal!**
Prov 26.21 **Charcoal** keeps the embers glowing, wood keeps the fire burning,
Jn 18.18 guards had built a **charcoal** fire and were standing round it,
21. 9 stepped ashore, they saw a **charcoal** fire there with fish on

CHARGE (1)

Gen 1.28 I am putting you in **charge** of the fish, the birds, and
24. 2 oldest servant, who was in **charge** of all that he had,
24.10 The servant, who was in **charge** of Abraham's property,
30.35 He put his sons in **charge** of them, [36]and then went away
32.16 herds and put one of his servants in **charge** of each herd.
32.19 and to all the others who were in **charge** of the herds:
39. 4 so he put him in **charge** of his house and everything he
39. 8 He has put me in **charge** of everything he has.
39.22 He put Joseph in **charge** of all the other prisoners and
41.33 wisdom and insight and put him in **charge** of the country.
41.40 I will put you in **charge** of my country, and all my
43.16 said to the servant in **charge** of his house, "Take these men
43.19 said to the servant in **charge,** [20]"If you please, sir, we
44. 1 Joseph commanded the servant in **charge** of his house,
44. 4 said to the servant in **charge** of his house, "Hurry after
45. 8 I am in **charge** of his whole country;
47. 6 men among them, put them in **charge** of my own livestock."
Ex 5.14 Israelite foremen, whom they had put in **charge** of the work.
Num 1.50 Instead, put the Levites in **charge** of the Tent of my
3. 8 They shall take **charge** of all the equipment of the Tent
3.32 He was in **charge** of those who carried out the duties in
7. 2 same men who were in **charge** of the census, [3]brought their
8.13 to me, and put Aaron and his sons in **charge** of them.
12. 7 I have put him in **charge** of all my people Israel.
31. 6 Eleazar the priest, who took **charge** of the sacred objects
31.30 them to the Levites who are in **charge** of the Lord's Tent."
31.47 them to the Levites who were in **charge** of the Lord's Tent.
Deut 1.13 from each tribe, and I will put them in **charge** of you.'
1.15 chose from your tribes, and I placed them in **charge** of you.
10. 8 of Levi to be in **charge** of the Covenant Box, to serve
26. 3 Go to the priest in **charge** at that time and say to
31. 9 priests, who were in **charge** of the Lord's Covenant Box,

Deut 31.25 priests, who were in **charge** of the Lord's Covenant Box,
Judg 20.27 son of Eleazar and grandson of Aaron, was in **charge** of it.
Ruth 2. 5 Boaz asked the man in **charge,** "Who is that young woman?"
1 Sam 7. 1 They consecrated his son Eleazar to be in **charge** of it.
8.12 some of them officers in **charge** of a thousand men,
8.12 and others in **charge** of fifty men.
17.20 morning, left someone else in **charge** of the sheep, took the
17.22 food with the officer in **charge** of the supplies, ran to the
2 Sam 8.16 Jehoshaphat son of Ahilud was in **charge** of the records;
8.18 son of Jehoiada was in **charge** of David's bodyguard and
19.13 I am putting you in **charge** of the army in place of
20.23 Benaiah son of Jehoiada was in **charge** of David's bodyguard;
20.24 Adoniram was in **charge** of the forced labour;
20.24 Jehoshaphat son of Ahilud was in **charge** of the records;
23.23 David put him in **charge** of his bodyguard.
1 Kgs 2.26 now, for you were in **charge** of the Lord's Covenant Box while
4. 3 In **charge** of the records:
4. 6 In **charge** of the palace servants:
4. 6 In **charge** of the forced labour:
4. 8 twelve officers and the districts they were in **charge** of:
5. 9 men will untie them, and your men will take **charge** of them.
5.14 all over Israel, [14]and put Adoniram in **charge** of them.
5.16 3,300 foremen in **charge** of them to supervise their work.
7.14 King Solomon's invitation to be in **charge** of all the bronze work.
9.23 There were 550 officials in **charge** of the forced labour
11.28 worked, he put him in **charge** of all the forced labour in
12.18 sent Adoniram, who was in **charge** of the forced labour, to go
16. 9 his officers who was in **charge** of half the king's chariots,
16. 9 in the home of Arza, who was in **charge** of the palace.
18. 3 so Ahab called in Obadiah, who was in **charge** of the palace.
2 Kgs 6. 1 prophets that Elisha was in **charge** of complained to him,
10. 2 "You are in **charge** of the king's descendants and you have
10. 5 So the officer in **charge** of the palace
10. 5 and the official in **charge** of the city, together with the
10.22 Jehu ordered the priest in **charge** of the sacred robes to
11. 4 sent for the officers in **charge** of the royal bodyguard and
12.11 over to the men in **charge** of the work in the Temple,
12.15 The men in **charge** of the work were thoroughly honest, so
18.18 Eliakim son of Hilkiah, who was in **charge** of the palace;
18.18 and Joah son of Asaph, who was in **charge** of the records.
19. 2 sent Eliakim, the official in **charge** of the palace, Shebna,
22. 5 the men who are in **charge** of the repairs in the Temple.
22. 7 The men in **charge** of the work are thoroughly honest, so
22. 9 have handed it over to the men in **charge** of the repairs."
22.14 Tikvah and grandson of Harhas, was in **charge** of the temple robes.)
25.19 assistant, who was in **charge** of military records,
25.22 Judah, and placed him in **charge** of all those who had not
1 Chr 6.31 whom King David put in **charge** of the music at the place
9.19 had been when they were in **charge** of the Lord's camp.
9.29 Others were in **charge** of the other sacred equipment, and
11.25 David put him in **charge** of his bodyguard.
15. 5 of Kohath came Uriel, in **charge** of 120 members of his clan;
15. 6 from the clan of Merari came Asaiah, in **charge** of 220;
15. 7 from the clan of Gershon, Joel, in **charge** of 130;
15. 8 from the clan of Elizaphan, Shemaiah, in **charge** of 200;
15. 9 from the clan of Hebron, Eliel, in **charge** of 80;
15.10 and from the clan of Uzziel, Amminadab, in **charge** of 112.
15.22 Chenaniah was chosen to be in **charge** of the levitical musicians.
16.37 and his fellow-Levites in permanent **charge** of the worship
16.38 Hosah and Obed Edom were in **charge** of guarding the gates.
16.39 his fellow-priests, however, were in **charge** of the worship
16.42 Heman and Jeduthun also had **charge** of the trumpets and
16.42 The members of Jeduthun's clan were in **charge** of guarding the gates.
17.14 I will put him in **charge** of my people and my kingdom
18.15 Jehoshaphat son of Ahilud was in **charge** of the records;
18.17 Benaiah son of Jehoiada was in **charge** of David's bodyguard;
23.13 set apart to be in **charge** of the sacred objects for ever,
25. 9 groups of twelve, with a leader in **charge** of each group.
26.20 of their fellow-Levites were in **charge** of the temple
26.22 Zetham and Joel, had **charge** of the temple treasury and storerooms.
26.26 of his family were in **charge** of all the gifts dedicated to
26.28 and his family were in **charge** of everything that had been
26.30 outstanding men, were put in **charge** of the administration of
26.32 relatives and put them in **charge** of administering all
27.32 son of Hachmoni were in **charge** of the education of the
2 Chr 1. 2 to all the officers in **charge** of units of a thousand men
8.10 There were 250 officials in **charge** of the forced labour
10.18 sent Adoniram, who was in **charge** of the forced labour, to go
21. 3 and placed each one in **charge** of one of the fortified cities
23.18 the priests and Levites in **charge** of the work of the Temple.
23.18 They were also in **charge** of the music and the celebrations.
24.11 the box to the royal official who was in **charge** of it.
24.12 to those who were in **charge** of repairing the Temple, and
31.12 a Levite named Conaniah in **charge** and made his brother
31.14 of the Temple, was in **charge** of receiving the gifts offered
34.10 to the three men in **charge** of the temple repairs, and they
34.13 Other Levites were in **charge** of transporting materials
34.22 Tikvah and grandson of Harhas, was in **charge** of the temple robes.)
35. 8 And the officials in **charge** of the Temple—Hilkiah, the High Priest,
Ezra 3. 8 or older were put in **charge** of the work of rebuilding the
3. 9 Hodaviah) joined together in taking **charge** of the rebuilding of the Temple.
8.30 priests and the Levites took **charge** of the silver, the gold,
10.14 Let our officials stay in Jerusalem and take **charge** of the matter.
Neh 4.22 I told the men in **charge** that they and all their helpers
7. 2 I put two men in **charge** of governing the city of Jerusalem:
Neh 11.16 prominent Levites in **charge** of the work outside the Temple.
12. 8 The following were in **charge** of the singing of hymns of thanksgiving:
12.25 following temple guards were in **charge** of guarding the
12.31 wall and put them in **charge** of two large groups to march
12.44 time men were put in **charge** of the storerooms where
13. 4 priest Eliashib, who was in **charge** of the temple storerooms,
13.13 I put the following men in **charge** of the storerooms:
Esth 2. 3 the eunuch who is in **charge** of your women, and let them
2. 8 palace in the care of Hegai, who had **charge** of the harem.
2.14 of Shaashgaz, the eunuch in **charge** of the king's concubines.
2.15 what Hegai, the eunuch in **charge** of the harem, advised her
8. 2 Esther put Mordecai in **charge** of Haman's property.
Job 29.25 I took **charge** and made the decisions;
34.13 Did someone put him in **charge** of the world?
Ps 77.20 people like a shepherd, with Moses and Aaron in **charge.**
91.11 will put his angels in **charge** of you to protect you wherever
105.21 He put him in **charge** of his government and made him
Is 36. 3 official in **charge** of the palace, Eliakim son of Hilkiah;
36. 3 the official in **charge** of the records, Joah son of Asaph.
37. 2 sent Eliakim, the official in **charge** of the palace, Shebna,
Jer 37.13 Benjamin Gate, the officer in **charge** of the soldiers on duty there,
40. 7 and had placed him in **charge** of all those who had not
41.16 the forces with him took **charge** of the people whom Ishmael
52.25 assistant, who was in **charge** of military records,
Ezek 44. 8 They have not taken **charge** of the sacred rituals in my Temple,
44. 8 but instead have put foreigners in **charge.**
44.11 in the Temple by taking **charge** of the gates and by
Dan 1.11 Ashpenaz had placed in **charge** of him and his three friends.
2.48 gifts, put him in **charge** of the province of Babylon,
2.49 Shadrach, Meshach, and Abednego in **charge** of the affairs of
3.12 Jews whom you put in **charge** of the province of Babylon
6. 3 king considered putting him in **charge** of the whole empire.
Amos 6.10 man's relative, the one in **charge** of the funeral, will take
Zech 3. 7 will continue to be in **charge** of my Temple and its courts,
11.16 have put a shepherd in **charge** of my flock, but he does
Mt 24.45 his master has placed in **charge** of the other servants to
24.47 master will put that servant in **charge** of all his property.
25.14 called his servants and put them in **charge** of his property.
25.21 small amounts, so I will put you in **charge** of large amounts.
25.23 small amounts, so I will put you in **charge** of large amounts.
Mk 3.21 set out to take **charge** of him, because people were saying,
13.34 and leaves his servants in **charge,** after giving to each one
Lk 12.42 his master will put in **charge,** to run the household and give
12.44 master will put that servant in **charge** of all his property.
19.17 in small matters, I will put you in **charge** of ten cities.'
19.19 this one he said, 'You will be in **charge** of five cities.'
Jn 2. 8 and take it to the man in **charge** of the feast."
13.29 Since Judas was in **charge** of the money bag, some of the
19.16 So they took **charge** of Jesus.
Acts 4. 1 some priests, the officer in **charge** of the temple guards, and
5.24 and the officer in **charge** of the temple guards heard this,
6. 3 and wisdom, and we will put them in **charge** of this matter.
8.27 an important official in **charge** of the treasury of the queen
12.20 convinced Blastus, the man in **charge** of the palace, that he
24.23 He ordered the officer in **charge** of Paul to keep him
1 Cor 4. 1 Christ's servants, who have been put in **charge** of God's secret
14.34 as the Jewish Law says, they must not be in **charge.**
Gal 3.24 so the Law was in **charge** of us until Christ came,
3.25 faith is here, the Law is no longer in **charge** of us.
Tit 1. 7 a church leader is in **charge** of God's work, he should be
Heb 3. 6 But Christ is faithful as the Son in **charge** of God's house.
10.21 We have a great priest in **charge** of the house of God.
Rev 9.11 ruling over them, who is the angel in **charge** of the abyss.
14.18 another angel, who is in **charge** of the fire, came from the
16. 5 I heard the angel in **charge** of the waters say,
21.12 twelve gates and with twelve angels in **charge** of the gates.

CHARGE (2)

[OVERCHARGE]

Gen 38.16 of the road and said, "All right, how much do you **charge?"**
Ex 22.15 a hired animal, the loss is covered by the hiring **charge.**
Lev 25.36 Do not **charge** him any interest, but obey God and let
Deut 23.19 else to a fellow-Israelite, do not **charge** him interest.
23.20 You may **charge** interest on what you lend to a foreigner,
1 Sam 13.21 the **charge** was one small coin for sharpening axes and
Ps 15. 5 He makes loans without **charging** interest and cannot be
Prov 28. 8 If you get rich by **charging** interest and taking advantage of people,
Ezek 22.12 Some **charge** interest on the loans they make to their
Amos 8. 5 Then we can **overcharge,** use false measures, and tamper with
1 Cor 9.18 preaching the Good News without **charging** for it,
2 Cor 11. 7 I did not **charge** you a thing when I preached the Good
Phlm 18 you any wrong or owes you anything, **charge** it to my account.

CHARGE (3)

Deut 22.14 So he makes up false **charges** against her, accusing her
22.17 He has made false **charges** against her, saying that she
22.20 "But if the **charge** is true and there is no proof that
Ezra 4. 6 Judah and Jerusalem brought written **charges** against them.
Job 10. 2 What is the **charge** against me?
13.23 What crimes am I **charged** with?
13.26 You bring bitter **charges** against me, even for what I did
31.35 If the **charges** my opponent brings against me were written
Is 50. 8 Does anyone dare to bring **charges** against me?
Jer 2. 9 I will bring **charges** against their descendants.
18.18 Let's bring **charges** against him, and stop listening to what he says."

Ezek 23.45 will condemn them on the **charge** of adultery and murder,
Acts 19.38 **charges** can be made there.
23.30 told his accusers to make their **charges** against him before you."
24. 1 They appeared before Felix and made their **charges** against Paul.
25. 2 and the Jewish leaders brought their **charges** against Paul.
25. 7 and started making many serious **charges** against him, which they
25. 9 Jerusalem and be tried on these **charges** before me there?"
25.11 is no truth in the **charges** they bring against me,
25.15 chief priests and elders brought **charges** against him and asked
25.20 to go to Jerusalem and be tried there on these **charges.**
25.27 a prisoner without clearly indicating the **charges** against him."

CHARGE (4)

Prov 20.18 don't go **charging** into battle without a plan.
Nah 3. 3 Horsemen **charge,** swords flash, spears gleam!

CHARGE (5)

1 Chr 28. 8 Israel, the Lord's people, I **charge** you to obey carefully
28. 9 he said, "My son, I **charge** you to acknowledge your father's

CHARIOT
[WAR CHARIOT]

Gen 41.43 gave him the second royal **chariot** to ride in, and his guard
46.29 arrived, [29] Joseph got in his **chariot** and went to Goshen to
50. 9 Men in **chariots** and men on horseback also went with him;
Ex 14. 6 The king got his **war chariot** and his army ready.
14. 7 out with all his **chariots,** including the six hundred finest,
14. 9 army, with all the horses, **chariots,** and drivers, pursued
14.17 over the king, his army, his **chariots,** and his drivers.
14.23 after them into the sea with all their horses, **chariots,** and
14.25 made the wheels of their **chariots** get stuck, so that they
14.26 back over the Egyptians and their **chariots** and drivers."
14.28 water returned and covered the **chariots,** the drivers, and
15. 4 "He threw Egypt's army and its **chariots** into the sea;
15.19 But when the Egyptian **chariots** with their horses and drivers
Deut 11. 4 along with their horses and **chariots,** by drowning them in
20. 1 your enemies and you see **chariots** and horses and an army
Josh 11. 4 They also had many horses and **chariots.**
11. 6 You are to cripple their horses and burn their **chariots."**
11. 9 he crippled their horses and burnt their **chariots.**
17.16 in the plains have iron **chariots,** both those who live in
17.18 they do have iron **chariots** and are a strong people."
24. 6 Egypt, and the Egyptians pursued them with **chariots** and cavalry.
Judg 1.18 along the coast had iron **chariots,** and so the people of
4. 3 Jabin had nine hundred iron **chariots,** and he ruled the
4. 7 He will have his **chariots** and soldiers, but I will give you
4.13 out his nine hundred iron **chariots** and all his men, and sent
4.15 Lord threw Sisera into confusion together with all his **chariots** and men.
4.15 Sisera got down from his **chariot** and fled on foot.
4.16 Barak pursued the **chariots** and the army to Harosheth-of-the-Gentiles,
5.28 "Why is his **chariot** so late in coming?"
1 Sam 8.11 them will serve in his **war chariots,** others in his cavalry,
8.11 and others will run before his **chariots.**
8.12 and make his weapons and the equipment for his **chariots.**
13. 5 had thirty thousand **war chariots,** six thousand horsemen,
2 Sam 1. 6 his spear and that the **chariots** and horsemen of the enemy
8. 4 horses for a hundred **chariots** and crippled all the rest.
10.18 hundred Syrian **chariot** drivers and forty thousand horsemen,
15. 1 After this, Absalom provided a **chariot** and horses for himself,
1 Kgs 1. 5 He provided for himself **chariots,** horses, and an escort of fifty men.
7.33 The wheels were like **chariot wheels;**
9.19 cities for his horses and **chariots,** and everything else he
9.22 as his soldiers, officers, commanders, **chariot** captains,
10.26 hundred **chariots** and twelve thousand cavalry horses.
10.29 Musri and Cilicia, [29] and the export of **chariots** from Egypt.
10.29 Syrian kings with horses and **chariots,**
10.29 selling **chariots** for 600 pieces of silver each
12.18 Rehoboam hurriedly got into his **chariot** and escaped to Jerusalem.
16. 9 in charge of half the king's **chariots,** plotted against him.
18.44 him to get into his **chariot** and go back home before the
18.45 Ahab got into his **chariot** and started back to Jezreel.
20. 1 rulers with their horses and **chariots,** he marched up, laid
20.21 field, captured the horses and **chariots,** and inflicted a
20.25 deserted you, with the same number of horses and **chariots.**
20.33 Benhadad arrived, Ahab invited him to get in the **chariot** with him.
22.31 Syria had ordered his thirty-two **chariot** commanders to
22.34 he cried out to his **chariot** driver.
22.35 King Ahab remained propped up in his **chariot,** facing the Syrians.
22.35 covered the bottom of the **chariot,** and at evening he died.
22.38 His **chariot** was cleaned up at the pool of Samaria, where
2 Kgs 2.11 then suddenly a **chariot** of fire pulled by horses of fire
5. 9 went with his horses and **chariot,** and stopped at the
5.21 he got down from his **chariot** to meet him, and asked, "Is
5.26 spirit when the man got out of his **chariot** to meet you?
6.14 Dothan, [14] he sent a large force there with horses and **chariots.**
6.15 Syrian troops with their horses and **chariots** surrounding the town.
6.17 covered with horses and **chariots** of fire all round Elisha.
7. 6 large army, with horses and **chariots,** and the Syrians
7.14 king sent them in two **chariots** with instructions to go and
8.21 set out with all his **chariots** for Zair, where the Edomite
8.21 the night he and his **chariot** commanders managed to break out
9.16 Then he got into his **chariot** and set off for Jezreel.
9.20 is driving his **chariot** like a madman, just like Jehu!"
2 Kgs 9.21 "Get my **chariot** ready," King Joram ordered.
9.21 King Ahaziah rode out, each in his own **chariot,** to meet
9.23 Joram cried out, as he turned his **chariot** round and fled.
9.24 Joram fell dead in his **chariot,** [25] and Jehu said to his
9.27 so he fled in his **chariot** towards the town of Beth Haggan,
9.27 him as he drove his **chariot** on the road up to Gur,
9.28 back to Jerusalem in a **chariot** and buried him in the royal
9.33 Jehu drove his horses and **chariot** over her body,
10. 2 disposal **chariots,** horses, weapons, and fortified cities.
10.15 helped him up into the **chariot,** [16] saying, "Come with me
13. 7 fifty horsemen, ten **chariots,** and ten thousand men on foot,
18.24 you expect the Egyptians to send you **chariots** and horsemen!
19.23 me that with all your **chariots** you had conquered the highest
23.11 of the sun, and he burnt the **chariots** used in this worship.
23.30 placed his body in a **chariot** and took it back to Jerusalem,
1 Chr 18. 4 a thousand of his **chariots,** seven thousand horsemen,
18. 4 horses for a hundred **chariots** and crippled all the rest.
19. 6 kilogrammes of silver to hire **chariots** and charioteers from
19. 7 The thirty-two thousand **chariots** they hired and the army
19.18 Syrian **chariot** drivers and forty thousand foot-soldiers.
28.18 burnt and in making the **chariot** for the winged creatures
2 Chr 1.14 hundred **chariots** and twelve thousand cavalry horses.
1.17 Musri and Cilicia, [17] and the export of **chariots** from Egypt.
1.17 Syrian kings with horses and **chariots,**
1.17 selling **chariots** for six hundred pieces of silver
8. 6 and the cities where his horses and **chariots** were stationed.
8. 9 but served as soldiers, officers, **chariot** commanders,
9.25 four thousand stalls for his **chariots** and horses, and had
10.18 Rehoboam hurriedly got into his **chariot** and escaped to Jerusalem.
12. 3 an army of twelve hundred **chariots,** sixty thousand horsemen,
14. 9 and three hundred **chariots** and advanced as far as Mareshah.
16. 8 the Libyans have large armies with many **chariots** and horsemen?
18.30 of Syria had ordered his **chariot** commanders to attack no one
18.32 The **chariot** commanders saw that he was not the king of Israel,
18.33 he cried out to his **chariot** driver.
18.34 King Ahab remained propped up in his **chariot,** facing the Syrians.
21. 9 So Jehoram and his officers set out with **chariots** and invaded Edom.
35.24 him out of his **chariot,** placed him in a second chariot
Ps 20. 7 Some trust in their **war-chariots** and others in their horses,
68.17 his many thousands of mighty **chariots** the Lord comes from
104. 3 use the clouds as your **chariot** and ride on the wings of
Song 1. 9 men as a mare excites the stallions of Pharaoh's **chariots.**
6.12 me as eager for love as a **chariot** driver is for battle.
Is 2. 7 is full of horses, and there is no end to their **chariots.**
5.28 as flint, and their **chariot-wheels** turn like a whirlwind.
22. 7 The fertile valleys of Judah were filled with **chariots;**
22.18 You will die there beside the **chariots** you were so proud of.
31. 1 They are relying on Egypt's vast military strength—horses, **chariots,**
36. 9 you expect the Egyptians to send you **chariots** and cavalry.
37.24 me that with all your **chariots** you had conquered the highest
43.17 mighty army to destruction, an army of **chariots** and horses.
66.20 mules, and camels, and in **chariots** and wagons, just as
Jer 4.13 His **war-chariots** are like a whirlwind, and his horses are
17.25 Jerusalem, they will ride in **chariots** and on horses, and the
22. 4 through the gates of this palace in **chariots** and on horses.
46. 9 Command the horses to go and the **chariots** to roll!
47. 3 of horses, the clatter of **chariots,** the rumble of wheels.
50.37 Destroy its horses and **chariots!**
51.21 horses and riders, to shatter **chariots** and their drivers,
Ezek 23.24 bringing a large army with **chariots** and supply wagons.
26. 7 with a huge army, with horses and **chariots** and with cavalry.
26.10 their horses pulling wagons and **chariots** will shake your
Dan 11.40 with all his power, using **chariots,** horses, and many ships.
Hos 10.13 "Because you trusted in your **chariots** and in the large
Joel 2. 5 on the tops of the mountains, they rattle like **chariots;**
Mic 1.13 You that live in Lachish, hitch the horses to the **chariots.**
5.10 time I will take away your horses and destroy your **chariots.**
Nah 2. 3 Their **chariots** flash like fire!
2. 4 **Chariots** dash wildly through the streets, rushing to and
2.13 "I will burn up your **chariots.**
3. 2 of wheels, the gallop of horses, the jolting of **chariots!**
Hab 3. 8 the storm cloud was your **chariot,** as you brought victory
Hag 2.22 I will overturn **chariots** and their drivers;
Zech 6. 1 This time I saw four **chariots** coming out from between two
6. 2 The first **chariot** was pulled by red horses, the second by
6. 4 Then I asked the angel, "Sir, what do these **chariots** mean?"
6. 6 The **chariot** pulled by the black horses was going north to Babylonia,
9.10 "I will remove the **war-chariots** from Israel and take the horses
Rev 9. 9 like the noise of many horse-drawn **chariots** rushing into battle.

CHARIOT-HORSES see HORSE

CHARITY

Acts 10. 4 prayers and works of **charity,** and is ready to answer you.
10.31 your prayer and has taken notice of your works of **charity.**

CHARM (1)

Num 23.23 There is no magic **charm,** no witchcraft, That can be used
Deut 18.11 omens or use spells [11] or **charms,** and don't let them
Ecc 10.11 Knowing how to **charm** a snake is of no use if you
Is 3.20 magic **charms** they wear on their arms and at their waists;
47.12 Keep all your magic spells and **charms;**
Jer 8.17 snakes that cannot be **charmed,** and they will bite you."

Mic 5.12 I will destroy the magic **charms** you use and leave you
Nah 3. 4 Attractive and full of deadly **charms,** she enchanted nations

CHARM (2)

Prov 5.19 Let her **charms** keep you happy;
5.20 Why should you prefer the **charms** of another man's wife?
7.21 she tempted him with her **charms,** and he gave in to her
31.30 **Charm** is deceptive and beauty disappears, but a woman

CHARRED

Ezek 15. 4 up and the middle is **charred,** can you make anything out of
15. 5 has burnt it and **charred** it, it is even more useless."

CHASE

Gen 14.15 He **chased** them as far as Hobah, north of Damascus, [16]and
Lev 26.17 so terrified that you will run when no one is **chasing** you.
26.37 another when no one is **chasing** you, and you will be unable
Deut 1.44 They **chased** you as far as Hormah and defeated you there in
2.12 descendants of Esau **chased** them out, destroyed their nation,
2.12 just as the Israelites later **chased** their enemies out of the
Josh 7. 5 The men of Ai **chased** them from the city gate as far
8.24 the enemy in the barren country where they had **chased** them.
Judg 1. 6 He ran away, but they **chased** him, caught him, and cut off
1 Sam 24.14 Look at what he is **chasing!**
2 Sam 2.19 deer, [19]started **chasing** Abner, running straight for him.
2.21 "Stop **chasing** me!"
2.21 But Asahel kept on **chasing** him.
2.22 Once more Abner said to him, "Stop **chasing** me!
2.26 will it be before you order your men to stop **chasing** us?"
2.27 men would have kept on **chasing** you until tomorrow morning."
2.30 When Joab gave up the **chase,** he gathered all his men
Ps 83.15 set the hills on fire, [15]**chase** them away with your storm
Prov 28. 1 run when no one is **chasing** them, but an honest person is
Ecc 1.14 It is like **chasing** the wind.
1.17 I found out that I might as well be **chasing** the wind.
2.11 It was like **chasing** the wind—of no use at all.
2.17 I had been **chasing** the wind.
2.26 It is like **chasing** the wind.
4. 4 It is like **chasing** the wind.
4.16 It is like **chasing** the wind.
6. 9 it is like **chasing** the wind.
Jer 2.25 let your throat become dry from **chasing** after other gods.
2.33 You certainly know how to **chase** after lovers.
50.17 "The people of Israel are like sheep, **chased** and scattered by lions.
Lam 3.11 He **chased** me off the road, tore me to pieces, and left
4.19 Swifter than eagles swooping from the sky, they **chased** us down.
Hos 2.13 Baal and put on her jewellery to go **chasing** after her lovers.
Mt 23.34 others in the synagogues and **chase** them from town to town.

AV CHASTEN

see also **PUNISH**

Deut 8. 5 that the Lord your God **corrects** and punishes you
8. 5 just as a father **disciplines** his children.
Job 5.17 Do not resent it when he **rebukes** you.
33.19 God **corrects** a man by sending sickness and filling his
Ps 94.12 happy is the person you **instruct,** the one to whom you teach
Prov 3.11 When the Lord **corrects** you, my son, pay close attention
13.24 If you do love him, you will **correct** him.
19.18 **Discipline** your children while they are young enough to learn.
Dan 10.12 you decided to **humble** yourself in order to gain understanding.
Heb 12. 5 pay attention when the Lord **corrects** you, and do not be
12. 6 the Lord **corrects** everyone he loves, and punishes everyone

AV CHASTISE

Lev 26.28 again make your **punishment** seven times worse than before.
Deut 11. 2 It was you, not your children, who had these **experiences.**
22.18 Then the town leaders are to take the husband and **beat** him.
1 Kgs 12.11 He **beat** you with a whip;
12.11 I'll **flog** you with a horsewhip!' "
12.14 He **beat** you with a whip;
12.14 I'll **flog** you with a horsewhip!"
2 Chr 10.11 He **beat** you with a whip;
10.11 I'll **flog** you with a horsewhip!' "
10.14 He **beat** you with a whip;
10.14 I'll **flog** you with a horsewhip!"
Ps 94.10 He **scolds** the nations—won't he punish them?
Is 53. 5 he suffered, made whole by the **blows** he received.
Jer 30.14 your **punishment** has been harsh because your sins are many
31.18 we were like an untamed animal, but you **taught us to obey.**
Hos 10.10 I will attack this sinful people and **punish** them.
Lk 23.16 So I will have him **whipped** and let him go."
23.22 I will have him **whipped** and set him free."
Heb 12. 8 If you are not **punished,** as all his sons are, it means

CHEAP

Prov 26.23 really thinking is like a fine glaze on a **cheap** clay pot.
Jer 2.36 You have **cheapened** yourself by turning to the gods of other nations.
Mt 27.48 a sponge, soaked it in **cheap** wine, put it on the end
Mk 15.36 a sponge, soaked it in **cheap** wine, and put it on the
Lk 23.36 and offered him **cheap** wine, [37]and said, "Save yourself if
Jn 19.29 A bowl was there, full of **cheap** wine;
2 Cor 2.17 who handle God's message as if it were **cheap** merchandise;
Phil 2. 3 selfish ambition or from a **cheap** desire to boast, but be
Heb 10.29 who treats as a **cheap** thing the blood of God's covenant

CHEAT

Gen 27.36 Esau said, "This is the second time that he has **cheated** me.
31. 7 Yet he has **cheated** me and changed my wages ten times.
Lev 6. 2 something from him or by **cheating** him [3]or by lying about
19.11 "Do not steal or **cheat** or lie.
19.35 "Do not **cheat** anyone by using false measures of length,
25.17 Do not **cheat** a fellow-Israelite, but obey the Lord your God.
Deut 24.14 "Do not **cheat** a poor and needy hired servant, whether
25.13 "Do not **cheat** when you use weights and measures.
25.16 The Lord hates people who **cheat.**
1 Sam 12. 3 Have I **cheated** or oppressed anyone?
12. 4 The people answered, "No, you have not **cheated** us or oppressed us;
Job 31.21 If I have ever **cheated** an orphan, knowing I could win in
Ecc 7. 7 When a wise man **cheats** someone, he is acting like a fool.
8. 8 we cannot **cheat** our way out.
Is 3.12 Money-lenders oppress my people, and their creditors **cheat** them.
33.15 Don't use your power to **cheat** the poor and don't accept bribes.
Jer 6.13 even prophets and priests **cheat** the people.
8.10 Even prophets and priests **cheat** the people.
21.11 the person who is being **cheated** from the one who is cheating
22. 3 the person who is being **cheated** from the one who is cheating
Ezek 18. 7 He doesn't **cheat** or rob anyone.
18.12 He **cheats** the poor, he robs, he keeps what a borrower
18.18 father, on the other hand, **cheated** and robbed, and always
22. 7 You **cheat** foreigners and take advantage of widows and orphans.
22.29 The wealthy **cheat** and rob.
Hos 7. 1 They **cheat** one another;
12. 7 they love to **cheat** their customers with false scales.
Amos 5. 7 that twist justice and **cheat** people out of their rights!
8. 5 measures, and tamper with the scales to **cheat** our customers.
Mal 1.14 A curse on the **cheat** who sacrifices a worthless animal to me,
3. 5 testimony, those who **cheat** employees out of their wages,
3. 8 I ask you, is it right for a person to **cheat** God?
3. 8 Of course not, yet you are **cheating** me.
3. 9 is on all of you because the whole nation is **cheating** me.
Mt 20.13 the owner answered one of them, 'I have not **cheated** you.
Mk 10.19 do not **cheat;**
Lk 19. 8 poor, and if I have **cheated** anyone, I will pay him back

CHEBAR

River in Babylonia near which the Jewish exiles were settled.

Ezek 1. 1 with the Jewish exiles by the River **Chebar** in Babylonia.
1. 3 in Babylonia beside the River **Chebar,** I heard the Lord speak
3.15 Tel Abib beside the River **Chebar,** where the exiles were living,
3.23 the Lord, just as I had seen it beside the River **Chebar.**
8. 4 as I had seen it when I was by the River **Chebar.**
10.15 the same creatures that I had seen by the River **Chebar.)**
10.20 I had seen beneath the God of Israel at the River **Chebar.**
10.22 exactly like the faces I had seen by the River **Chebar.**
43. 3 to destroy Jerusalem, and the one I saw by the River **Chebar.**

CHECK

Gen 30.33 When you come to **check** up on my wages, if I have
1 Chr 9.28 They **checked** them out and checked them back in every time
Neh 7. 5 leaders and officials and to **check** their family records.
Is 48. 9 people will praise my name, I am holding my anger in **check;**
Mt 18.23 there was a king who decided to **check** on his servants'

CHEEK

Song 1.10 hair is beautiful upon your **cheeks** and falls along your neck
4. 3 Your **cheeks** glow behind your veil.
5.13 His **cheeks** are as lovely as a garden that is full of
6. 7 Your **cheeks** glow behind your veil.
Lam 1. 2 tears run down her **cheeks.**
Hos 11. 4 I picked them up and held them to my **cheek;**
Mt 5.39 slaps you on the right **cheek,** let him slap your left cheek
Lk 6.29 anyone hits you on one **cheek,** let him hit the other one

CHEEKY

1 Sam 17.28 You **cheeky** brat, you!

CHEER (1)

1 Kgs 21. 7 "Get out of bed, **cheer** up and eat.
Job 29.24 my **cheerful** face encouraged them.
Ps 104.15 to make him **cheerful,** and bread to give him strength.
Prov 12.25 can rob you of happiness, but kind words will **cheer** you up.
17.22 Being **cheerful** keeps you healthy.
Ecc 2. 3 for wisdom, I decided to **cheer** myself up with wine and have
9. 7 drink your wine and be **cheerful.**
9. 8 Always look happy and **cheerful.**
10.19 makes you happy and wine **cheers** you up, but you can't have
Mk 10.49 **"Cheer** up!"
Rom 12. 8 whoever shows kindness to others should do it **cheerfully.**
1 Cor 16.18 for your absence [18]and have **cheered** me up,
16.18 just as they **cheered** you up.
2 Cor 2. 2 to make you sad, who would be left to **cheer** me up?
7. 7 not only his coming that **cheered** us, but also his report of
7.13 the way in which all of you helped to **cheer** him up!
Eph 6. 7 Do your work as slaves **cheerfully,** as though you served the
Col 4. 8 to you, in order to **cheer** you up by telling you how
2 Tim 1.16 the family of Onesiphorus, because he **cheered** me up many times.
Phlm 7 You have **cheered** the hearts of all God's people.
20 as a brother in Christ, **cheer** me up!

CHEER (2)

2 Chr 23.12 Athaliah heard the people **cheering** for the king, so she
Esth 8.15 Then the streets of Susa rang with **cheers** and joyful shouts.
Ezek 26. 2 is what the people in the city of Tyre are **cheering** about.

CHEESE

1 Sam 17.18 And take these ten **cheeses** to the commanding officer.
2 Sam 17.28 grain, beans, peas, honey, **cheese,** cream, and some sheep.

CHEMOSH

God worshipped by Moabites and Ammonites.

Num 21.29 You worshippers of **Chemosh** are brought to ruin!
Judg 11.24 You can keep whatever your god **Chemosh** has given you.
1 Kgs 11. 7 a place to worship **Chemosh,** the disgusting god of Moab,
11.33 **Chemosh,** the god of Moab;
2 Kgs 23.13 Astarte the goddess of Sidon, **Chemosh** the god of Moab, and
Jer 48. 7 your god **Chemosh** will go into exile, along with his princes
48.13 be disillusioned with their god **Chemosh,** just as the
48.46 The people who worshipped **Chemosh** have been destroyed, and

CHERISH

Deut 11.18 "Remember these commands and **cherish** them.

AV **CHERUBIM** see **(winged) CREATURES**

CHEST

2 Sam 18.14 plunged them into Absalom's **chest** while he was still alive,
Prov 6.27 Can you carry fire against your **chest** without burning your clothes?
Dan 2.32 its **chest** and arms were made of silver;
Zech 13. 6 Then if someone asks him, 'What are those wounds on your **chest?'**
Rev 1.13 that reached to his feet, and a gold belt round his **chest.**
9. 9 **chests** were covered with what looked like iron breastplates,
15. 6 clean shining linen and with gold belts tied around their **chests.**

CHEW

Lev 11. 3 divided hoofs and that also **chews** the cud, [4-6]but you
11. 4 they **chew** the cud, but do not have divided hoofs.
11. 7 they have divided hoofs, but do not **chew** the cud.
11.24 hoofs are divided and they **chew** the cud, and all four-footed
Deut 14. 6 any animals that have divided hoofs and that also **chew** the cud.
14. 7 eaten unless they have divided hoofs and also **chew** the cud.
14. 7 they **chew** the cud but do not have divided hoofs.
14. 8 they have divided hoofs but do not **chew** the cud.
Prov 25.19 crisis is like trying to **chew** with a loose tooth or walk
Ecc 12. 3 will be too few to **chew** your food, and your eyes too
Joel 1. 7 They have destroyed our grapevines and **chewed** up our fig-trees.

CHICK

Mt 23.37 as a hen gathers her **chicks** under her wings, but you would
Lk 13.34 as a hen gathers her **chicks** under her wings, but you would

CHICKEN

Neh 5.18 the best sheep, and many **chickens,** and every ten days I

CHIEF

Gen 34. 2 Hamor the Hivite, who was **chief** of that region, saw her, he
40. 1 Egypt's wine steward and his **chief** baker offended the king.
40. 5 the wine steward and the **chief** baker each had a dream, and
40.16 When the **chief** baker saw that the interpretation of the
40.20 his wine steward and his **chief** baker and brought them before
40.22 to his former position, [22]but he executed the **chief** baker.
41.10 You were angry with the **chief** baker and me, and you put
Num 1. 4 Ask one clan **chief** from each tribe to help you."
3.24 Tent, [24]with Eliasaph son of Lael as **chief** of the clan.
3.30 Tent, [30]with Elizaphan son of Uzziel as **chief** of the clan.
3.32 The **chief** of the Levites was Eleazar son of Aaron the priest.
3.35 the Tent, with Zuriel son of Abihail as **chief** of the clan.
7. 2 Then the clan **chiefs** who were leaders in the tribes of Israel,
25.15 Zur, her father, was **chief** of a group of Midianite clans.
Deut 5.23 darkness, your leaders and the **chiefs** of your tribes came to
Judg 7.25 They captured the two Midianite **chiefs,** Oreb and Zeeb;
8. 3 power of God you killed the two Midianite **chiefs,** Oreb and
1 Sam 21. 7 (Saul's **chief** herdsman, Doeg, who was from Edom, happened
1 Kgs 4. 5 **Chief** of the district governors: Azariah
2 Kgs 19. 4 Assyrian emperor has sent his **chief** official to insult the living God.
1 Chr 9.10 Azariah son of Hilkiah (the **chief** official in the Temple),
9.24 north, south, east, and west, and each had a **chief** guard.
9.26 The four **chief** guards were Levites and had the final responsibility.
26.24 Moses' son Gershom, was the **chief** official responsible for the temple treasury.
2 Chr 31.14 Imnah, a Levite who was **chief** guard at the East Gate of
Ezra 1. 8 handed them over to Mithredath, **chief** of the royal treasury,
9. 2 The leaders and officials were the **chief** offenders.
Prov 6. 7 They have no leader, **chief,** or ruler, [8]but they store up
Is 36. 2 Then he ordered his **chief** official to go from Lachish to
37. 4 Assyrian emperor has sent his **chief** official to insult the living God.
Jer 20. 1 of Immer, who was the **chief** officer of the Temple, heard me
Jer 29.26 Jehoiada, and you are now the **chief** officer in the Temple.
41. 1 and one of the king's **chief** officers, went to Mizpah with
Ezek 38. 2 man," he said, "denounce Gog, **chief** ruler of the nations
39. 1 "Mortal man, denounce Gog, the **chief** ruler of the nations
Dan 1. 3 The king ordered Ashpenaz, his **chief** official, to select
1. 7 The **chief** official gave them new names:
4. 9 Belteshazzar, **chief** of the fortune-tellers, I know that
5.11 Nebuchadnezzar, your father, made him **chief** of the fortune-tellers,
10.13 Then Michael, one of the **chief** angels, came to help me,
Mt 9.34 Pharisees said, "It is the **chief** of the demons who gives
Mk 3.22 It is the **chief** of the demons who gives him the power
6.21 a feast for all the **chief** government officials, the military
Lk 11.15 said, "It is Beelzebul, the **chief** of the demons, who gives
19. 2 was a **chief** tax collector there named Zacchaeus, who was rich.
Acts 14.12 and Paul the name Hermes, because he was the **chief** speaker.
25.23 audience hall with the military **chiefs** and the leading men of
28. 7 that belonged to Publius, the **chief** official of the island.
1 Pet 5. 4 when the **Chief** Shepherd appears, you will receive the glorious
Jude 9 Not even the **chief** angel Michael did this.
Rev 6.15 the rulers and the military **chiefs,** the rich and the powerful,

CHIEF PRIESTS

Mt 2. 4 He called together all the **chief priests** and the teachers of
16.21 much from the elders, the **chief priests,** and the teachers of
20.18 be handed over to the **chief priests** and the teachers of the
21.15 The **chief priests** and the teachers of the Law became angry
21.23 and as he taught, the **chief priests** and the elders came to
21.45 The **chief priests** and the Pharisees heard Jesus' parables
26. 3 the **chief priests** and the elders met together in the palace
26.14 Judas Iscariot—went to the **chief priests** [15]and asked,
26.47 and clubs and sent by the **chief priests** and the elders.
26.59 **chief priests** and the whole Council tried to find some false
27. 1 in the morning all the **chief priests** and the elders made
27. 3 the thirty silver coins to the **chief priests** and the elders.
27. 6 **chief priests** picked up the coins and said, "This is blood
27.12 nothing in response to the accusations of the **chief priests**
27.20 **chief priests** and the elders persuaded the crowd to ask Pilate
27.41 In the same way the **chief priests** and the teachers of
27.62 which was a Sabbath, the **chief priests** and the Pharisees met
28.11 to the city and told the **chief priests** everything that had
28.12 The **chief priests** met with the elders and made their plan;
Mk 8.31 rejected by the elders, the **chief priests,** and the teachers of
10.33 be handed over to the **chief priests** and the teachers of the
11.18 The **chief priests** and the teachers of the Law heard of this,
11.27 walking in the Temple, the **chief priests,** the teachers of the
14. 1 The **chief priests** and the teachers of the Law were looking
14.10 went off to the **chief priests** in order to betray Jesus
14.43 and sent by the **chief priests,** the teachers of the Law,
14.53 Priest's house, where all the **chief priests,** the elders, and
14.55 **chief priests** and the whole Council tried to find some evidence
15. 1 in the morning the **chief priests** met hurriedly with the elders,
15. 3 The **chief priests** were accusing Jesus of many things,
15.10 knew very well that the **chief priests** had handed Jesus over
15.11 But the **chief priests** stirred up the crowd to ask, instead,
15.31 In the same way the **chief priests** and the teachers of
Lk 9.22 rejected by the elders, the **chief priests,** and the teachers of
19.47 The **chief priests,** the teachers of the Law, and the leaders
20. 1 preaching the Good News, the **chief priests** and the teachers of
20.19 of the Law and the **chief priests** tried to arrest Jesus
22. 2 The **chief priests** and the teachers of the Law were afraid
22. 4 and spoke with the **chief priests** and the officers of the
22.52 Then Jesus said to the **chief priests** and the officers
22.66 day came, the elders, the **chief priests,** and the teachers of
23. 4 Then Pilate said to the **chief priests** and the crowds, "I
23.10 **chief priests** and the teachers of the Law stepped forward
23.13 Pilate called together the **chief priests,** the leaders, and
24.20 **chief priests** and rulers handed him over to be sentenced to
Jn 7.32 so they and the **chief priests** sent some guards to arrest
7.45 guards went back, the **chief priests** and Pharisees asked them,
11.47 So the Pharisees and the **chief priests** met with the Council
11.57 **chief priests** and the Pharisees had given orders that if anyone
12.10 So the **chief priests** made plans to kill Lazarus too,
18. 3 some temple guards sent by the **chief priests** and the Pharisees;
18.35 your own people and the **chief priests** who handed you over to
19. 6 the **chief priests** and the temple guards saw him, they shouted,
19.15 **chief priests** answered, "The only king we have is the Emperor!"
19.21 **chief priests** said to Pilate, "Do not write 'The King of
Acts 4.23 told them what the **chief priests** and the elders had said.
5.24 the **chief priests** and the officer in charge of the temple
9.14 with authority from the **chief priests** to arrest all who worship
9.21 arresting those people and taking them back to the **chief priests?"**
22.30 taken off and ordered the **chief priests** and the whole Council
23.14 Then they went to the **chief priests** and elders and said,
25. 2 to Jerusalem, [2]where the **chief priests** and the Jewish leaders
25.15 Jerusalem, the Jewish **chief priests** and elders brought charges
26.10 received authority from the **chief priests** and put many of God's
26.12 went to Damascus with authority and orders from the **chief priests.**

CHILD

see also **CHILD OF GOD, CHILDBIRTH, CHILDISH, CHILDLESS**

Gen 1.28 them, and said, "Have many **children,** so that your
5.29 Lord put a curse, this **child** will bring us relief from all
9. 1 sons and said, "Have many **children,** so that your
9. 7 "You must have many **children,** so that your descendants
11.30 Sarai was not able to have **children.**
15. 2 what good will your reward do me, since I have no **children?**
15. 3 You have given me no **children,** and one of my slaves will

Gen	16. 1	Abram's wife Sarai had not borne him any **children.**
	16. 2	said to Abram, "The Lord has kept me from having **children.**
	16. 2	Perhaps she can have a **child** for me."
	17.17	"Can a man have a **child** when he is a hundred years
	17.17	Can Sarah have a **child** at ninety?"
	17.20	I will bless him and give him many **children** and many descendants.
	18.13	say, 'Can I really have a **child** when I am so old?'
	19.31	the whole world to marry us so that we can have **children.**
	19.32	so that we can sleep with him and have **children** by him."
	19.34	Then each of us will have a **child** by our father."
	20.17	for any woman in Abimelech's palace to have **children.**
	20.17	wife and his slave-girls, so that they could have **children.**
	21. 7	"Who would have said to Abraham that Sarah would nurse **children?**
	21. 8	The **child** grew, and on the day that he was weaned, Abraham
	21.13	I will also give many **children** to the son of the slave-girl,
	21.14	He put the **child** on her back and sent her away.
	21.15	all gone, she left the **child** under a bush [16] and sat down
	21.16	She said to herself, "I can't bear to see my **child** die."
	21.23	God that you will not deceive me, my **children,** or my descendants.
	22.20	Abraham learnt that Milcah had borne eight **children**
	25.21	Because Rebecca had no **children,** Isaac prayed to the Lord for her.
	28. 3	marriage and give you many **children,** so that you will become
	29.31	for her to have **children,** but Rachel remained childless.
	29.35	Then she stopped having **children.**
	30. 1	had not borne Jacob any **children,** and so she became jealous
	30. 1	and said to Jacob, "Give me **children,** or I will die."
	30. 2	He is the one who keeps you from having **children."**
	30. 3	sleep with her, so that she can have a **child** for me.
	30. 9	that she had stopped having **children,** she gave her
	30.22	her prayer and made it possible for her to have **children.**
	30.26	Give me my wives and **children** that I have earned by
	31.16	has taken from our father belongs to us and to our **children.**
	31.17	He put his **children** and his wives on the camels, and drove
	31.43	their **children** belong to me, and these flocks are mine.
	31.43	keep my daughters and their **children,** [44] I am ready to make
	32.11	attack us and destroy us all, even the women and **children.**
	32.22	and his eleven **children,** and crossed the River Jabbok.
	33. 1	men, so he divided the **children** among Leah, Rachel, and the
	33. 2	and their **children** first, then Leah and her children,
	33. 5	saw the women and the **children,** he asked, "Who are these
	33. 5	"These, sir, are the **children** whom God has been good
	33. 6	Then the concubines came up with their **children** and bowed down;
	33. 7	then Leah and her **children** came, and last of all Joseph
	33.13	answered, "You know that the **children** are weak, and I must
	33.14	with the livestock and the **children** until I catch up with
	34.29	captured all the women and **children,** and carried off
	35.11	Have many **children.**
	38. 9	But Onan knew that the **children** would not belong to him,
	38. 9	ground, so that there would be no **children** for his brother.
	41.52	"God has given me **children** in the land of my trouble";
	42.36	to them, "Do you want to make me lose all my **children?**
	43.14	for me, if I must lose my **children,** I must lose them."
	44.20	and he is the only one of his mother's **children** still alive;
	45.10	be near me—you, your **children,** your grandchildren, your
	45.19	for their wives and small **children** and to bring their father
	46. 5	sons put him, their small **children,** and their wives in the
	47.27	of Goshen, where they became rich and had many **children.**
	48. 4	'I will give you many **children,** so that your descendants
	48.11	you again, and now God has even let me see your **children."**
	48.16	May they have many **children,** many descendants!"
	49. 3	my strength And the first **child** of my manhood, The proudest
	49.25	Blessings of many cattle and **children,**
	50. 8	Only their small **children** and their sheep, goats, and cattle
	50.21	I will take care of you and your **children."**
	50.23	He lived to see Ephraim's **children** and grandchildren.
	50.23	also lived to receive the **children** of Machir son of Manasseh
Ex	1. 7	descendants, the Israelites, had many **children** and became so
	2.10	Later, when the **child** was old enough, she took him to
	10. 2	be able to tell your **children** and grandchildren how I made
	10. 9	"We will all go, including our **children** and our old people.
	10.10	Lord that I will never let you take your women and **children!**
	10.24	even your women and **children** may go with you.
	12.24	You and your **children** must obey these rules for ever.
	12.26	When your **children** ask you, 'What does this ritual mean?'
	13.13	You must buy back every first-born male **child** of yours.
	17. 3	To kill us and our **children** and our livestock with thirst?"
	20.10	to work—neither you, your **children,** your slaves, your
	21. 4	daughters, the woman and her **children** belong to the master,
	21. 5	master, his wife, and his **children** and does not want to be
	21.22	so that she loses her **child,** but she is not injured in
	22.24	Your wives will become widows, and your **children** will be fatherless.
	23.26	no woman will have a miscarriage or be without **children.**
	34. 7	will not fail to punish **children** and grandchildren to the
Lev	10.14	given to you and your **children** as the part that belongs to
	10.15	belong to you and your **children** for ever, just as the Lord
	12. 3	On the eighth day, the **child** shall be circumcised.
	18.21	hand over any of your **children** to be used in the worship
	20. 2	who gives any of his **children** to be used in the worship
	20. 3	anyone gives one of his **children** to Molech and makes my
	20.20	neither of them will have **children.**
	21.15	his **children,** who ought to be holy, will be ritually unclean.
	22.13	divorced daughter who has no **children** and who has returned
	25.41	that time he and his **children** shall leave you and return to
	25.45	You may also buy the **children** of the foreigners who are
	25.45	Such **children** born in your land may become your property,
	25.54	these ways, he and his **children** must be set free in the
Lev	26. 9	I will bless you and give you many **children;**
	26.22	and they will kill your **children,** destroy your livestock,
	26.29	hunger will be so great that you will eat your own **children.**
Num	3. 4	They had no **children,** so Eleazar and Ithamar served as
	5.28	she will not be harmed and will be able to bear **children.**
	14. 3	in battle, and our wives and **children** will be captured.
	14.18	will not fail to punish **children** and grandchildren to the
	14.31	You said that your **children** would be captured, but I
	14.33	Your **children** will wander in the wilderness for forty years,
	16.27	the entrance of their tents, with their wives and **children.**
	18.15	"Every first-born **child** or animal that the Israelites
	18.15	to buy back every first-born **child,** and must also accept
	18.16	**Children** shall be bought back at the age of one month
	31. 9	Midianite women and **children,** took their cattle and their flocks,
	32.26	Our wives and **children** and our cattle and sheep will
Deut	1.39	to all of us, 'Your **children,** who are still too young to
	1.39	will enter the land—the **children** you said would be seized by
	2.34	town, and put everyone to death, men, women, and **children.**
	3. 6	all the men, women, and **children,** just as we did in the
	3.19	Only your wives, **children,** and livestock—I know you have
	4. 9	Tell your **children** and your grandchildren [10] about the day
	4.10	and so that they will teach their **children** to do the same.'
	4.11	"Tell your **children** how you went and stood at the foot
	4.25	a long time and have **children** and grandchildren, do not sin
	5.14	to work—neither you, your **children,** your slaves, your
	6. 7	Teach them to your **children.**
	6.20	"In time to come your **children** will ask you, 'Why did
	7. 3	and do not let your **children** marry any of them, [4] because
	7. 4	then they would lead your **children** away from the Lord to
	7.13	so that you will increase in number and have many **children;**
	8. 5	God corrects and punishes you just as a father disciplines his **children.**
	11. 2	It was you, not your **children,** who had these experiences.
	11.19	Teach them to your **children.**
	11.21	Then you and your **children** will live a long time in the
	12.12	his presence, together with your **children,** your servants,
	12.18	You and your **children,** together with your servants and
	12.31	They even sacrifice their **children** in the fires on their altars.
	16.11	Lord's presence, together with your **children,** your servants,
	16.14	Enjoy it with your **children,** your servants, and the Levites,
	18.10	Don't sacrifice your **children** in the fires on your altars;
	20.14	for yourselves the women, the **children,** the livestock, and
	21.15	but the first son is not the **child** of his favourite wife.
	21.16	divide his property among his **children,** he is not to show
	24.16	for crimes committed by their **children,** and children are not
	28. 4	will bless you with many **children,** with abundant crops, and
	28.11	Lord will give you many **children,** many cattle, and abundant
	28.18	giving you only a few **children,** poor crops, and few cattle
	28.32	your eyes, looking in vain for your **children** to return.
	28.53	you will even eat the **children** that the Lord your God has
	28.54	eat some of his own **children** because he has no other food.
	28.54	wife he loves or to any of his **children** who are left.
	28.56	secretly eat her newborn **child** and the afterbirth as well.
	28.56	with the husband she loves or with any of her **children.**
	29.11	officials, your men, [11] women, and **children,** and the
	30. 9	you will have many **children** and a lot of livestock, and your
	31.12	all the men, women, and **children,** and the foreigners who
	32.46	Repeat them to your **children,** so that they may faithfully
	33. 9	greater loyalty to you Than to parents, brothers, or **children.**
Josh	1.14	Your wives, your **children,** and your livestock will stay here,
	4. 6	In the future, when your **children** ask what these stones mean
	4.21	"In the future, when your **children** ask you what these stones mean,
	8.35	gathering, which included women and **children,** as well as the
	14. 9	Moses promised me that my **children** and I would certainly
	24. 4	but your ancestor Jacob and his **children** went down to Egypt.
Judg	11.34	She was his only **child.**
	13. 2	His wife had never been able to have **children.**
	13. 3	never been able to have **children,** but you will soon be
	13.24	The **child** grew and the Lord blessed him.
	18.21	and started off, with their **children,** their livestock, and
	21.10	"Go and kill everyone in Jabesh, including the women and **children.**
Ruth	4. 6	it would mean that my own **children** would not inherit it.
	4.11	like Rachel and Leah, who bore many **children** to Jacob.
	4.12	May the **children** that the Lord will give you by this
	4.16	Naomi took the **child,** held him close, and took care of him.
1 Sam	1. 2	Peninnah had **children,** but Hannah had none.
	1. 4	the meat to Peninnah and one share to each of her **children.**
	1. 5	share, because the Lord had kept her from having **children.**
	1.22	husband, "As soon as the **child** is weaned, I will take him
	1.23	So Hannah stayed at home and nursed her **child.**
	1.25	After they had killed the bull, they took the **child** to Eli.
	1.27	I asked him for this **child,** and he gave me what I
	2. 5	childless wife has borne seven **children,** but the mother of
	2.20	the Lord give you other **children** by this woman to take the
	15. 3	kill all the men, women, **children,** and babies;
	22.19	men and women, **children** and babies, cattle, donkeys, and
	30. 6	very bitter about losing their **children,** and they were
	30.22	They can take their wives and **children** and go away."
2 Sam	5.14	The following **children** were born to him in Jerusalem:
	6.23	Michal, Saul's daughter, never had any **children.**
	12. 3	of it, and it grew up in his home with his **children.**
	12.14	contempt for the Lord in doing this, your **child** will die."
	12.15	The Lord caused the **child** that Uriah's wife had borne to
	12.16	David prayed to God that the **child** would get well.
	12.18	A week later the **child** died, and David's officials were
	12.18	They said, "While the **child** was living, David wouldn't
	12.18	How can we tell him that his **child** is dead?
	12.19	to each other, he realized that the **child** had died.
	12.19	So he asked them, "Is the **child** dead?"

2 Sam	12.21	"While the **child** was alive, you wept for him and would not
	12.22	Lord might be merciful to me and not let the **child** die.
	12.23	Could I bring the **child** back to life?
1 Kgs	3.18	Two days after my **child** was born she also gave birth to
	3.20	then she put the dead **child** in my bed.
	3.21	at it more closely and saw that it was not my **child."**
	3.22	The living **child** is mine, and the dead one is yours!"
	3.22	The dead **child** is yours, and the living one is mine!"
	3.23	claims that the living **child** is hers
	3.23	and that the dead **child** belongs to the other one."
	3.25	he said, "Cut the living **child** in two and give each
	3.26	to the king, "Please, Your Majesty, don't kill the **child!**
	3.27	Then Solomon said, "Don't kill the **child!**
	11.17	(At that time Hadad was just a **child.)**
	13. 2	A **child,** whose name will be Josiah, will be born to the
	14.17	Just as she entered her home, the **child** died.
	17.21	and prayed, "O Lord my God, restore this **child** to life!"
	17.22	the **child** started breathing again and revived.
	20. 3	and gold, your women and the strongest of your **children."**
	20. 5	to me your silver and gold, your women and your **children.**
	20. 7	message demanding my wives and **children,** my silver and gold,
2 Kgs	4.31	held Elisha's stick over the **child,** but there was no sound
	5.14	His flesh became firm and healthy, like that of a **child.**
	6.28	suggested that we eat my **child,**
	6.28	and then eat her **child** the next day.
	8.12	finest young men, batter their **children** to death, and rip
	10.13	pay our respects to the **children** of Queen Jezebel and to the
	14. 6	he did not kill their **children** but followed what the Lord
	14. 6	for crimes committed by their **children,** and children are not
	17.31	people of Sepharvaim sacrificed their **children** as
1 Chr	4.27	but his relatives had fewer **children,** and the tribe of
	7. 4	had so many wives and **children** that their descendants were
	14. 4	The following **children** were born to him in Jerusalem:
2 Chr	11.22	Abijah over all his other **children,** choosing him as the one
	20.13	Judah, with their wives and **children,** were standing there at the Temple.
	21.14	severely punish your people, your **children,** and your wives,
	25. 4	did not, however, execute their **children,** but followed what
	25. 4	for crimes committed by their **children,** and children are not
	28. 8	army captured 200,000 women and **children** as prisoners and
	29. 9	our wives and **children** have been taken away as prisoners.
	31.18	together with their wives, **children,** and other dependants,
Ezra	8.21	and protect us and our **children** and all our possessions.
	10. 3	God that we will send these women and their **children** away.
	10.44	They divorced them and sent them and their **children** away.
Neh	4.14	your **children,** your wives, and your homes."
	5. 5	Aren't our **children** just as good as theirs?
	5. 5	But we have to make slaves of our **children.**
	8. 2	women, and the **children** who were old enough to understand.
	9.23	You gave them as many **children** as there are stars in the
	10.28	our wives and all our **children** old enough to understand,
	12.43	The women and the **children** joined in the celebration, and
	13.24	Half their **children** spoke the language of Ashdod or some
	13.25	would they or their **children** intermarry with foreigners.
Esth	3.13	Jews—young and old, women and **children**—were to be killed.
	8.11	attacked the Jewish men, their **children** or their women, the
Job	1. 5	sacrifices for each of his **children** in order to purify them.
	1.13	One day when Job's **children** were having a feast at the
	1.18	servant came and said, "Your **children** were having a feast
	3.16	gold and silver, [16]or sleeping like a still-born **child.**
	4.11	and eat, they die, and all their **children** are scattered.
	5.25	You will have as many **children** as there are blades of
	8. 4	Your **children** must have sinned against God, and so he
	17. 5	his friends for money, and his **children** suffer for it.
	19.18	**Children** despise me and laugh when they see me.
	21. 8	They have **children** and grandchildren, and live to watch
	21.11	Their **children** run and play like lambs [12]and dance to
	21.19	You claim God punishes a **child** for the sins of his father.
	21.21	over, does he really care whether his **children** are happy?
	24. 5	nowhere else can they find food for their **children.**
	24. 9	and take the poor man's **children** in payment for debts.
	27.14	their **children** never have enough to eat.
	29. 5	was with me then, and I was surrounded by all my **children.**
Ps	8. 2	it is sung by **children** and babies.
	17.14	children and some left over for their children's **children!**
	25.13	prosperous, and their **children** will possess the land.
	37.25	man abandoned by the Lord or his **children** begging for food.
	37.26	and lends to others, and his **children** are a blessing.
	48. 6	woman about to bear a **child,** [7]like ships tossing in a
	78. 4	We will not keep them from our **children;**
	78. 5	teach his laws to their **children,** [6]so that the next
	78. 6	might learn them and in turn should tell their **children.**
	102.28	Our **children** will live in safety, and under your
	103.13	father is kind to his **children,** so the Lord is kind to
	105.24	The Lord gave many **children** to his people and made them
	106.38	They killed those innocent **children,** and the land was
	107.38	He blessed his people, and they had many **children;**
	109. 9	May his **children** become orphans, and his wife a widow!
	109.10	May his **children** be homeless beggars;
	112. 2	The good man's **children** will be powerful in the land;
	113. 9	he makes her happy by giving her **children.**
	115.14	May the Lord give you **children**— you and your descendants!
	127. 3	**Children** are a gift from the Lord;
	131. 2	As a **child** lies quietly in its mother's arms, so my heart
	148.12	girls and young men, old people and **children** too.
Prov	5.16	**Children** that you have by other women will do you no good.
	5.17	Your **children** should grow up to help you, not strangers.
	19.18	Discipline your **children** while they are young enough to learn.
	20. 7	**Children** are fortunate if they have a father who is honest
	20.11	Even a **child** shows what he is by what he does;
	22. 6	Teach a **child** how he should live, and he will remember it
Prov	22.15	**Children** just naturally do silly, careless things, but a
	23.13	Don't hesitate to discipline a **child.**
	29.15	Correction and discipline are good for **children.**
	29.15	If a **child** has his own way, he will make his mother
	29.21	servant everything he wants from **childhood** on, some day he
	30.16	a woman without **children,**
	31.28	Her **children** show their appreciation, and her husband praises her.
Ecc	5.14	and end up with nothing left to pass on to their **children.**
	6. 3	man may have a hundred **children** and live a long time, but
Song	6. 9	She is her mother's only daughter, her mother's favourite **child.**
Is	1. 2	The **children** I brought up have rebelled against me.
	8.18	Here I am with the **children** the Lord has given me.
	9. 6	A **child** is born to us!
	9.20	They even eat their own **children!**
	10.19	trees left that even a **child** will be able to count them.
	11. 6	feed together, and little **children** will take care of them.
	13.18	will show no mercy to babies and take no pity on **children.**
	14.22	I will leave nothing—no **children,** no survivors at all.
	23. 4	ocean depths disown you and say, "I never had any **children.**
	29.23	When you see the **children** that I will give you, then you
	38.19	Fathers tell their **children** how faithful you are.
	44. 3	on your **children** and my blessing on your descendants.
	45.11	to question me about my **children** or to tell me what I
	47. 8	would never be a widow or suffer the loss of your **children.**
	47. 9	the magic you use, you will lose your husband and **children.**
	49.15	woman forget her own baby and not love the **child** she bore?
	49.15	a mother should forget her **child,** I will never forget you.
	49.21	will say to yourself, 'Who bore all these **children** for me?
	49.21	I lost my **children** and could have no more.
	49.21	I was exiled and driven away— who brought these **children** up?
	49.21	I was left all alone— where did these **children** come from?' "
	49.22	to the nations, and they will bring your **children** home.
	49.25	whoever fights you, and I will rescue your **children.**
	50. 1	into captivity like a man who sells his **children** as slaves?
	51. 2	Abraham, he was childless, but I blessed him and gave him **children;**
	54. 1	Now you will have more **children** than a woman whose husband
	56. 3	that because he cannot have **children,** he can never be part
	57. 5	You offer your **children** as sacrifices in the rocky caves
	59.21	obey me and teach your **children** and your descendants to obey
	60. 4	Your daughters will be carried like **children.**
	60.16	and kings will care for you As a mother nurses her **child.**
	65.23	successful, and their **children** will not meet with disaster.
	66. 7	gives birth to a **child,** without ever going into labour.
	66.11	You will enjoy her prosperity, like a **child** at its mother's breast.
	66.12	You will be like a **child** that is nursed by its mother,
	66.13	I will comfort you in Jerusalem, as a mother comforts her **child.**
Jer	3. 4	father, and you have loved me ever since I was a **child.**
	4.22	They are like foolish **children;**
	4.31	in labour, a scream like a woman bearing her first **child.**
	6.11	out my anger on the **children** in the streets and on the
	7.18	The **children** gather firewood, the men build fires, and
	9.21	it has cut down the **children** in the streets and the young
	10.20	Our **children** have all gone away;
	11.22	their **children** will die of starvation.
	15. 7	my people, I killed your **children** because you did not stop
	15. 9	The mother who lost her seven **children** has fainted, gasping for breath.
	16. 2	"Do not marry or have **children** in a place like this.
	16. 3	going to happen to the **children** who are born here and to
	18.21	But now, Lord, let their **children** starve to death;
	18.21	Let the women lose their husbands and **children;**
	19. 5	Baal in order to burn their **children** in the fire as sacrifices.
	19. 9	city will eat one another and even their own **children."**
	22.28	that why he and his **children** have been taken into exile to
	22.30	is condemned to lose his **children,** to be a man who will
	23. 3	They will have many **children** and increase in number.
	29. 6	Marry and have **children.**
	29. 6	children get married, so that they also may have **children.**
	30. 6	Can a man give birth to a **child?**
	31.15	Rachel is crying for her **children;**
	31.16	All that you have done for your **children** will not go unrewarded;
	31.17	your **children** will come back home.
	31.20	"Israel, you are my dearest son, the **child** I love best.
	31.29	ate the sour grapes, But the **children** got the sour taste.'
	38.23	added, "All your women and **children** will be taken out to
	41.16	Mizpah after murdering Gedaliah—soldiers, women, **children,**
	43. 6	the men, the women, the **children,** and the king's daughters.
	44. 7	destruction on men and women, **children** and babies, so that
	47. 3	Fathers will not turn back for their **children;**
	48. 4	listen to the **children** crying.
	49.20	Even their **children** will be dragged off,
	50.45	Even their **children** will be dragged off,
Lam	1. 5	Her **children** have been captured and taken away.
	2.11	**Children** and babies are fainting in the streets of the city.
	2.19	mercy on your children— **Children** starving to death on every
	2.20	Women are eating the bodies of the **children** they loved!
	2.22	They murdered my **children,** whom I had reared and loved.
	4. 4	**children** are begging for food that no one will give them.
	4.10	loving mothers boiled their own **children** for food.
Ezek	4.14	From **childhood** on I have never eaten meat from any animal
	5.10	will eat their **children,** and children will eat their parents.
	5.17	wild animals to kill your **children,** and will send sickness,
	9. 6	Kill the old men, young men, young women, mothers, and **children.**
	14.16	God—they would not be able to save even their own **children.**
	14.18	able to save even their **children,** but only their own lives.
	14.20	God—they would not be able to save even their own **children.**
	14.22	does survive and save his **children,** look at them when they
	16.21	without taking my **children** and sacrificing them to idols?

Ezek	16.22	never once remembered your **childhood**—when you were naked,
	16.36	idols, and you killed your **children** as sacrifices to idols.
	16.45	She detested her husband and her **children.**
	16.45	You are like your sisters, who hated their husbands and their **children.**
	18. 2	ate the sour grapes, But the **children** got the sour taste.'
	18. 4	the life of the parent as well as that of the **child.**
	20.31	same idols by sacrificing your **children** to them in the fire.
	23. 4	I married both of them, and they bore me **children.**
	23.25	will cut off your nose and your ears and kill your **children.**
	23.39	day that they killed my **children** as sacrifices to idols,
	23.47	swords, kill their **children,** and burn down their houses.
	36.11	of you than ever before, and you will have many **children.**
	36.12	own land, and it will never again let your **children** starve.
	36.13	and they say that it robs the nation of its **children.**
	36.14	will no longer be a man-eater who robs you of your **children.**
	36.15	The land will no longer rob the nation of its **children.**
	37.25	ever, and so will their **children** and all their descendants.
	44.25	his parents, one of his **children** or a brother or an
	47.22	you and who have had **children** born here are also to receive
Dan	6.24	wives and their **children,** into the pit filled with lions.
	11. 6	and she, her husband, her **child,** and the servants who went
Hos	1. 2	be unfaithful, and your **children** will be just like her.
	1. 3	the birth of their first **child,** a son, [4]the Lord said to
	1. 6	Gomer had a second **child**—this time it was a girl.
	1.10	say to them, "You are the **children** of the living God!"
	2. 2	My **children,** plead with your mother—though she is no
	2. 4	I will not show mercy to her **children;**
	2. 4	they are the **children** of a shameless prostitute.
	4.10	gods, but still have no **children,** because you have turned
	5. 7	their **children** do not belong to him.
	9.11	there will be no more **children** born to them,
	9.11	no more women pregnant, no more **children** conceived.
	9.12	if they did bring up **children,** I would take them away and
	9.13	Lord, I can see their **children** being hunted down and killed.
	9.16	They will have no **children,** but even if they did,
	9.16	I would kill the **children** so dear to them."
	10.14	Betharbel in battle, and mothers and their **children** were crushed to death.
	11. 1	"When Israel was a **child,** I loved him and called him out
	13.13	to take it—like a **child** about to be born, who refuses
Joel	1. 3	Tell your **children** about it;
	1. 3	they will tell their **children,** who in turn will tell the
	2.16	gather the **children** and the babies too.
Amos	7.17	on the streets, and your **children** will be killed in war.
Jon	4.11	has more than 120,000 innocent **children** in it, as well as
Mic	1.16	Judah, cut off your hair in mourning for the **children** you love.
	1.16	bald as vultures, because your **children** will be taken away
	2. 9	and you have robbed their **children** of my blessings for ever.
	6. 7	Shall I offer him my first-born **child** to pay for my sins?
Nah	3.10	At every street corner their **children** were beaten to death.
Zech	10. 9	They and their **children** will survive and return home together.
	12.10	will mourn for him like those who mourn for an only **child.**
Mal	2. 3	I will punish your **children** and rub your faces in the dung
	2.15	It was that you should have **children** who are truly God's people.
	4. 6	He will bring fathers and **children** together again;
Mt	2. 8	a careful search for the **child,** and when you find him,
	2. 9	until it stopped over the place where the **child** was.
	2.11	and when they saw the **child** with his mother Mary, they knelt
	2.13	"Herod will be looking for the **child** in order to kill him.
	2.13	So get up, take the **child** and his mother and escape to
	2.14	Joseph got up, took the **child** and his mother, and left
	2.18	Rachel is crying for her **children;**
	2.20	said, "Get up, take the **child** and his mother, and go back
	2.20	Israel, because those who tried to kill the **child** are dead."
	2.21	Joseph got up, took the **child** and his mother, and went back
	5. 9	God will call them his **children!**
	7.11	you know how to give good things to your **children.**
	10.21	to death, and fathers will do the same to their **children;**
	10.21	**children** will turn against their parents and have them put to
	11.16	They are like **children** sitting in the market-place.
	14.21	ate was about five thousand, not counting the women and **children.**
	15.26	isn't right to take the **children's** food and throw it to the
	15.38	ate was four thousand, not counting the women and **children.**
	18. 2	So Jesus called a **child,** made him stand in front of them,
	18. 3	and become like **children,** you will never enter the Kingdom
	18. 4	is the one who humbles himself and becomes like this **child.**
	18. 5	whoever welcomes in my name one such **child** as this,
	18.25	with his wife and his **children** and all that he had,
	19.13	people brought **children** to Jesus for him to place his hands
	19.14	Jesus said, "Let the **children** come to me and do not
	19.29	or father or mother or **children** or fields for my sake, will
	21.15	he was doing and the **children** shouting in the Temple, "Praise
	21.16	'You have trained **children** and babies to offer perfect praise.' "
	22.24	a man who has no **children** dies, his brother must marry the
	22.24	can have children who will be considered the dead man's **children.**
	22.25	married and died without having **children,** so he left his widow
	27.25	the responsibility for his death fall on us and our **children!"**
Mk	5.39	The **child** is not dead—she is only sleeping!"
	5.40	them all out, took the **child's** father and mother and his
	5.40	and went into the room where the **child** was lying.
	7.27	But Jesus answered, "Let us first feed the **children.**
	7.27	isn't right to take the **children's** food and throw it to the
	7.28	"even the dogs under the table eat the **children's** leftovers!"
	7.30	She went home and found her **child** lying on the bed;
	9.21	"Ever since he was a **child,"** he replied.
	9.36	Then he took a **child** and made him stand in front of
	9.37	welcomes in my name one of these **children,** welcomes me;
	10.13	people brought **children** to Jesus for him to place his hands
	10.14	to his disciples, "Let the **children** come to me, and do not
	10.15	the Kingdom of God like a **child** will never enter it."
Mk	10.16	Then he took the **children** in his arms, placed his hands
	10.24	went on to say, "My **children,** how hard it is to enter
	10.29	or mother or father or **children** or fields for me and for
	10.30	sisters, mothers, **children** and fields—and persecutions as well;
	12.19	leaves a wife but no **children,** that man's brother must marry
	12.19	can have children who will be considered the dead man's **children.'**
	12.20	the eldest got married and died without having **children.**
	12.21	one married the woman, and he also died without having **children.**
	12.22	seven brothers married the woman and died without having **children.**
	13.12	to death, and fathers will do the same to their **children.**
	13.12	**Children** will turn against their parents and have them put to
Lk	1. 7	They had no **children** because Elizabeth could not have any,
	1.17	He will bring fathers and **children** together again;
	1.35	For this reason the holy **child** will be called the Son of
	1.36	said that she cannot have **children,** but she herself is now
	1.42	of all women, and blessed is the **child** you will bear!
	1.66	about it and asked, "What is this **child** going to be?"
	1.76	"You, my **child,** will be called a prophet of the Most
	1.80	The **child** grew and developed in body and spirit.
	2.17	they told them what the angel had said about the **child.**
	2.22	So they took the **child** to Jerusalem to present him to the
	2.27	When the parents brought the **child** Jesus into the Temple to
	2.28	Simeon took the **child** in his arms and gave thanks
	2.33	**child's** father and mother were amazed at the things Simeon said
	2.34	to Mary, his mother, "This **child** is chosen by God for the
	2.38	and spoke about the **child** to all who were waiting for
	2.40	The **child** grew and became strong;
	7.32	They are like **children** sitting in the market-place.
	8.51	except Peter, John, and James, and the **child's** father and mother.
	8.52	Everyone there was crying and mourning for the **child.**
	8.52	the **child** is not dead—she is only sleeping!"
	8.54	took her by the hand and called out, "Get up, my **child!"**
	9.47	thinking, so he took a **child,** stood him by his side,
	9.48	"Whoever welcomes this **child** in my name, welcomes me;
	11. 7	door is already locked, and my **children** and I are in bed.
	11.13	you know how to give good things to your **children.**
	14.26	mother, his wife and his **children,** his brothers and his sisters,
	18.16	but Jesus called the **children** to him and said,
	18.16	"Let the **children** come to me and do not
	18.17	the Kingdom of God like a **child** will never enter it."
	18.29	or brothers or parents or **children** for the sake of the
	20.28	leaves a wife but no **children,** that man's brother must marry
	20.28	can have children who will be considered the dead man's **children.'**
	20.29	the eldest got married and died without having **children.**
	20.31	happened to all seven—they died without having **children.**
	23.28	Don't cry for me, but for yourselves and your **children.**
	23.29	women who never had **children,** who never bore babies, who never
Jn	1.13	that is, by being born as the **children** of a human father;
	4.49	replied the official, "come with me before my **child** dies."
	8.39	"If you really were Abraham's **children,"** Jesus replied,
	8.44	You are the **children** of your father, the Devil,
	13.33	My **children,** I shall not be with you very much longer.
Acts	2.39	made to you and your **children,** and to all who are far
	7. 5	At the time God made this promise, Abraham had no **children.**
	7.20	at this time that Moses was born, a very beautiful **child.**
	17.28	as some of your poets have said, 'We too are his **children.'**
	21. 5	together with their wives and **children,** went with us out of
	21.21	telling them not to circumcise their **children** or follow the
Rom	4.19	or of the fact that Sarah could not have **children.**
	8.17	Since we are his **children,** we will possess the blessings he
	9. 8	This means that the **children** born in the usual way are not
	9. 8	the **children** born as a result of God's promise are regarded
1 Cor	3. 1	you belonged to this world, as **children** in the Christian faith.
	4.14	feel ashamed, but to instruct you as my own dear **children.**
	7.14	If this were not so, their **children** would be like pagan children;
	13.11	When I was a **child,**
	13.11	my speech, feelings, and thinking were all those of a **child;**
	14.20	Do not be like **children** in your thinking, my brothers;
	14.20	be **children** so far as evil is concerned, but be grown-up in
2 Cor	6.13	I speak now as though you were my **children:**
	12.14	**children** should not have to provide for their parents,
	12.14	but parents should provide for their **children.**
Gal	4.19	My dear **children!**
	4.24	The one whose **children** are born in slavery is Hagar,
	4.27	deserted will have more **children** than the woman whose husband
	4.31	we are not the **children** of a slave-woman but of a
Eph	4.14	we shall no longer be **children,** carried by the waves and
	6. 1	**Children,** it is your Christian duty to obey your parents,
	6. 4	Parents, do not treat your **children** in such a way as to
Col	3.20	**Children,** it is your Christian duty to obey your parents
	3.21	do not irritate your **children,** or they will become discouraged.
1 Thes	2. 7	we were with you, like a mother taking care of her **children.**
	2.11	each one of you just as a father treats his own **children.**
1 Tim	1.18	Timothy, my **child,** I entrust to you this command, which is
	2.15	be saved through having **children,** if she perseveres in faith
	3. 4	family well and make his **children** obey him with all respect.
	3.12	wife, and be able to manage his **children** and family well.
	5. 4	if a widow has **children** or grandchildren, they should learn
	5.10	who brought up her **children** well, received strangers in her home,
	5.14	younger widows get married, have **children,** and take care of
2 Tim	3.15	since you were a **child,** you have known the Holy Scriptures,
Tit	1. 6	only one wife, and his **children** must be believers and not
	2. 4	to love their husbands and **children,** [5]to be self-controlled
Heb	2.13	says, "Here I am with the **children** that God has given me."
	2.14	Since the **children,** as he calls them, are people of
	5.13	drink milk is still a **child,** without any experience in the
	11.11	he was too old and Sarah herself could not have **children.**

Heb 11.23 that he was a beautiful **child,** and they were not afraid to
1 Pet 1.23 been born again as the **children** of a parent who is immortal,
1 Jn 2. 1 writing this to you, my **children,** so that you will not sin;
2.12 am writing to you, my **children,** because your sins are forgiven
2.14 I am writing to you, my **children,** because you know the Father.
2.18 My **children,** the end is near!
2.28 Yes, my **children,** remain in union with him, so that when
3. 7 Let no one deceive you, my **children!**
3.10 clear difference between God's children and the Devil's **children:**
3.18 My **children,** our love should not be just words and talk;
4. 4 belong to God, my **children,** and have defeated the false prophets,
5. 1 and whoever loves a father loves his **child** also.
5.21 My **children,** keep yourselves safe from false gods!
2 Jn 1 To the dear Lady and to her **children,** whom I truly love.
4 find that some of your **children** live in the truth, just as
13 The **children** of your dear Sister send you their greetings.
3 Jn 4 me happier than to hear that my **children** live in the truth.
Rev 12. 4 in order to eat her **child** as soon as it was born.
12. 5 But the **child** was snatched away and taken to God and his
also Gen 5.4 Gen 5.7 Gen 5.10 Gen 5.13 Gen 5.16 Gen 5.19 Gen 5.22
Gen 5.26 Gen 5.30 Gen 11.11 Gen 11.13 Gen 11.15 Gen 11.17
Gen 11.19 Gen 11.21 Gen 11.23 Gen 11.25 Ex 12.37 Judg 20.48
Ezra 10.1

CHILD OF GOD
[GOD'S CHILD, GOD'S CHILDREN, GOD'S SONS, SONS OF GOD]

Mt 5. 9 God will call them **his children!**
5.45 so that you may become the **sons** of your Father in heaven.
Lk 6.35 great reward, and you will be **sons** of the Most High God.
20.36 They are the **sons of God,** because they have risen from death.
Jn 1.12 so he gave them the right to become **God's children.**
1.13 They did not become **God's children** by natural means, that is,
Acts 17.28 as some of your poets have said, 'We too are **his children.'**
17.29 Since we are **God's children,** we should not suppose that
Rom 8.14 Those who are led by God's Spirit are **God's sons.**
8.15 the Spirit makes you **God's children,** and by the Spirit's power
8.16 to our spirits to declare that we are **God's children.**
8.17 Since we are **his children,** we will possess the blessings
8.19 waits with eager longing for God to reveal his **sons.**
8.21 and would share the glorious freedom of the **children of God.**
8.23 God to make us his **sons** and set our whole being free.
9. 4 he made them his **sons** and revealed his glory to them;
9. 7 Nor are all Abraham's descendants the **children of God.**
9. 8 children born in the usual way are not the **children of God;**
9.26 there they will be called the **sons** of the living God."
2 Cor 6.18 shall be my **sons** and daughters, says the Lord Almighty."
Gal 3.26 that all of you are **God's sons** in union with Christ Jesus.
4. 5 who were under the Law, so that we might become **God's sons.**
4. 6 show that you are his **sons,** God sent the Spirit of his
4. 7 So then, you are no longer a slave but a **son.**
4. 7 And since you are his **son,**
4. 7 God will give you all that he has for his **sons.**
4.28 Now, you, my brothers, are **God's children** as a result of
Eph 1. 5 he would make us his **sons**—this was his pleasure and purpose.
5. 1 Since you are **God's dear children,** you must try to be like
Phil 2.15 be innocent and pure as **God's perfect children,**
2.15 and pure as **God's perfect children,** who live in a world of
Heb 12. 5 the encouraging words which God speaks to you as his **sons?**
12. 6 he loves, and punishes everyone he accepts as a **son."**
12. 7 your suffering shows that God is treating you as his **sons.**
12. 8 not punished, as all his **sons** are,
12. 8 it means you are not real **sons,** but bastards.
12.23 of God's first-born **sons,** whose names are written in heaven.
1 Jn 2.29 then, that everyone who does what is right is **God's child.**
3. 1 great that we are called **God's children**—and so, in fact, we
3. 2 dear friends, we are now **God's children,** but it is not yet
3. 9 Whoever is a **child of God** does not continue to sin,
3.10 clear difference between **God's children** and the Devil's children:
3.10 is right or does not love his brother is not **God's child.**
4. 7 Whoever loves is a **child of God** and knows God.
5. 1 Whoever believes that Jesus is the Messiah is a **child of God;**
5. 2 This is how we know that we love **God's children:**
5. 4 because every **child of God** is able to defeat the
5.18 We know that no **child of God** keeps on sinning,
Rev 21. 7 I will be his God, and he will be my **son.**

CHILDBIRTH

Mt 24. 8 All these things are like the first pains of **childbirth.**
Mk 13. 8 These things are like the first pains of **childbirth.**
Rom 8.22 all of creation groans with pain, like the pain of **childbirth.**
Gal 4.19 just like a mother in **childbirth,** I feel the same kind of
4.27 cry with joy, you who never felt the pains of **childbirth!**
Rev 12. 2 and the pains and suffering of **childbirth** made her cry out.

CHILDISH

1 Cor 13.11 I am a man, I have no more use for **childish** ways.

CHILDLESS

Gen 29.31 for her to have children, but Rachel remained **childless.**
Lev 20.21 If a man marries his brother's wife, they will die **childless.**
Judg 11.38 because she was going to die unmarried and **childless.**
1 Sam 1. 6 and humiliate her, because the Lord had kept her **childless.**
2. 5 The **childless** wife has borne seven children, but the mother
15.33 sword has made many mothers **childless,**
15.33 so now will your mother become **childless."**
Job 24.21 widows and showed no kindness to **childless** women.
Ps 113. 9 He honours the **childless** wife in her home;
Is 51. 2 I called Abraham, he was **childless,** but I blessed him and
54. 1 you have been like a **childless** woman, but now you can sing
Gal 4.27 For the scripture says, "Be happy, you **childless** woman!

CHIMNEY

Hos 13. 3 blows from the threshing-place, like smoke from a **chimney.**

CHIN

Lev 13.29 on the head or the **chin,** [30] the priest shall examine it.

CHIP

Hos 10. 7 king will be carried off, like a **chip** of wood on water.

CHIRP

Is 8.19 from fortune-tellers and mediums, who **chirp** and mutter.

CHISEL

Ex 20.25 because when you use a **chisel** on stones, you make them unfit
Job 19.24 Or with a **chisel** carve my words in stone and write them

AV **CHISLEU** see **KISLEV**

CHOICE
see also **CHOOSE**

Deut 32.14 goats, and cattle, the finest wheat, and the **choicest** wine.
33.15 May their ancient hills be covered with **choice** fruit.
1 Sam 9.24 So the cook brought the **choice** piece of the leg and
Jer 2.21 I planted you like a **choice** vine from the very best seed.
Ezek 24. 4 and the legs— fill it with **choice** bony pieces too.
31.16 of Eden and all the **choice,** well-watered trees of Lebanon

CHOIR

1 Chr 6.33 Heman, the leader of the first **choir,** was the son of Joel.
6.39 Asaph was leader of the second **choir.**
6.44 of the clan of Merari was the leader of the third **choir.**
Neh 7. 1 the members of the sacred **choir,** and the other Levites had
10.39 and the members of the temple **choir** have their quarters.
11.17 He led the temple **choir** in singing the prayer of thanksgiving.
12. 9 The following formed the **choir** that sang the responses:

CHOKE

Job 6.16 The streams are **choked** with snow and ice, [17] but in the
Jon 2. 5 The water came over me and **choked** me;
Mt 13. 7 fell among thorn bushes, which grew up and **choked** the plants.
13.22 and the love for riches **choke** the message, and they don't
18.28 He grabbed him and started **choking** him.
Mk 4. 7 which grew up and **choked** the plants, and they didn't produce
4.19 of desires crowd in and **choke** the message, and they don't
Lk 8. 7 thorn bushes, which grew up with the plants and **choked** them.
8.14 life crowd in and **choke** them, and their fruit never ripens.

CHOOSE
[CHOICE, CHOSE, CHOSEN, CHOSEN PEOPLE]

Gen 13. 9 **Choose** any part of the land you want.
13.11 So Lot **chose** the whole Jordan Valley for himself and
18.19 I have **chosen** him in order that he may command his sons
24. 3 earth, that you will not **choose** a wife for my son from
24.14 she be the one that you have **chosen** for your servant Isaac.
24.37 He said, 'Do not **choose** a wife for my son from the
24.38 people, to my relatives, and **choose** a wife for him.'
24.44 the one that you have **chosen** as the wife for my master's
32.13 spending the night there, Jacob **chose** from his livestock as
41.33 "Now you should **choose** some man with wisdom and insight
Ex 12. 3 this month each man must **choose** either a lamb or a young
12. 5 You may **choose** either a sheep or a goat, but it must
12.21 "Each of you is to **choose** a lamb or a young goat
15.17 place that you, Lord, have **chosen** for your home, the Temple
18.21 But in addition, you should **choose** some capable men and
18.25 Moses took Jethro's advice [25] and **chose** capable men
19. 5 but you will be my **chosen people,** [6] a people dedicated to me
21.13 a place which I will **choose** for you, and there he will
31. 2 said to Moses, [2] "I have **chosen** Bezalel, the son of Uri and
33.13 Remember also that you have **chosen** this nation to be your own."
33.19 the Lord, and I show compassion and pity on those I **choose.**
35.30 the Israelites, "The Lord has **chosen** Bezalel, the son of
Lev 16. 9 Aaron shall sacrifice the goat **chosen** by lot for the Lord
16.10 The goat **chosen** for Azazel shall be presented alive to
16.20 shall present to the Lord the live goat **chosen** for Azazel.
27.33 that the poor animals are **chosen,** and he may not make any
Num 1. 5 tribes, who were **chosen** from the community for this work:
13. 2 The Lord said to Moses, [2] "**Choose** one of the leaders from
14. 4 said to one another, "Let's **choose** a leader and go back to
16. 1 Israelites, well-known leaders **chosen** by the community.
16. 5 that is, the one he has **chosen,** approach him at the altar.
16. 6 Then we will see which of us the Lord has **chosen.**
16.28 it is not by my own **choice** that I have done them.
17. 5 Then the stick of the man I have **chosen** will sprout.
18. 6 am the one who has **chosen** your relatives the Levites from
26. 9 (These are the Dathan and Abiram who were **chosen** by the
community.
31. 5 So a thousand men were **chosen** from each tribe, a total of

Num 34.19 These are the men the Lord **chose:**
35.11 of Canaan, [11] you are to **choose** cities of refuge to which a
35.13 **Choose** six cities, [14] three east of the Jordan and
Deut 1.13 **Choose** some wise, understanding, and experienced men from each tribe,
1.15 wise and experienced leaders you **chose** from your tribes, and
4.37 he loved your ancestors, he **chose** you, and by his great
7. 6 the peoples on earth he **chose** you to be his own special
7. 7 you and **choose** you because you outnumbered other peoples;
9.29 are the people whom you **chose** to be your own and whom
10.15 was so strong that he **chose** you instead of any other people,
10.15 and you are still his **chosen people.**
11.26 I am giving you the **choice** between a blessing and a curse
12. 5 your tribes the Lord will **choose** the one place where the
12.11 The Lord will **choose** a single place where he is to be
12.13 You are not to offer your sacrifices wherever you **choose;**
12.14 place that the Lord will **choose** in the territory of one of
12.18 in the one place of worship **chosen** by the Lord your God.
14. 2 he has **chosen** you to be his own people from among all
14.23 place where the Lord your God has **chosen** to be worshipped;
17. 8 the one place of worship **chosen** by the Lord your God, [9] and
17.15 sure that the man you **choose** to be king
17.15 is the one whom the Lord has **chosen.**
18. 5 The Lord **chose** from all your tribes the tribe of Levi to
20. 9 to the army, leaders are to be **chosen** for each unit.
20.12 city will not surrender, but **choose** to fight, surround it
21. 5 The Lord your God has **chosen** them to serve him and to
23.16 of your towns that he **chooses,** and you are not to treat
28.10 see that the Lord has **chosen** you to be his own people,
30. 1 have now given you a **choice** between a blessing and a curse.
30. 1 God has scattered you, you will remember the **choice** I gave you.
30.15 I am giving you a **choice** between good and evil, between life
30.19 am now giving you the **choice** between life and death, between
30.19 and I call heaven and earth to witness the **choice** you make.
30.19 **Choose** life.
32. 9 a god, [9] but Jacob's descendants he **chose** for himself.
Josh 3.12 Now **choose** twelve men, one from each of the tribes of Israel.
4. 2 Lord said to Joshua, [2] **"Choose** twelve men, one from each tribe,
4. 4 the twelve men he had **chosen,** [5] and said, "Go into the
9.27 in the place where the Lord has **chosen** to be worshipped.
20. 2 to the people of Israel, **"Choose** the cities of refuge that
20. 8 of Jericho, they **chose** Bezer in the territory of Reuben;
20. 9 were the cities of refuge **chosen** for all the people of
24.22 to the fact that you have **chosen** to serve the Lord."
Judg 5. 8 was war in the land when the Israelites **chose** new gods.
9. 8 time the trees got together to **choose** a king for themselves.
10.14 Go and cry out to the gods you have **chosen.**
18. 2 So the people of Dan **chose** five qualified men out of all
20. 9 we will draw lots and **choose** some men to attack Gibeah.
20.15 seven hundred specially **chosen** men who were left-handed.
20.34 Ten thousand men, specially **chosen** out of all Israel,
21.23 each of them **chose** a wife from the girls who were dancing
1 Sam 2.10 to his king, he will make his **chosen** king victorious."
2.28 the tribes of Israel I **chose** his family to be my priests,
2.35 I will **choose** a priest who will be faithful to me and
2.35 who will always serve in the presence of my **chosen** king.
8.18 your king, whom you yourselves **chose,** but the Lord will not
10. 1 you that the Lord has **chosen** you to be the ruler of
10.24 said to the people, "Here is the man the Lord has **chosen!**
12. 3 in the presence of the Lord and the king he has **chosen.**
12. 5 and the king he has **chosen** are witnesses today that you have
12. 6 Lord is the one who **chose** Moses and Aaron and who brought
12.13 "Now here is the king you **chose;**
16. 1 named Jesse, because I have **chosen** one of his sons to be
16. 6 in the Lord's presence is surely the one he has **chosen."**
16. 8 But Samuel said, "No, the Lord hasn't **chosen** him either."
16. 9 "No, the Lord hasn't **chosen** him either," Samuel said.
16.10 Samuel said to him, "No, the Lord hasn't **chosen** any of these."
16.21 liked him very much and **chose** him as the man to carry
17. 8 **Choose** one of your men to fight me.
24. 6 doing any harm to my master, whom the Lord **chose** as king!
24. 6 in the least, because he is the king **chosen** by the Lord!"
24.10 because you are the one whom the Lord **chose** to be king.
26. 9 The Lord will certainly punish whoever harms his **chosen** king.
2 Sam 1.14 "How is it that you dared to kill the Lord's **chosen** king?"
1.16 that you killed the one whom the Lord **chose** to be king."
3.39 though I am the king **chosen** by God, I feel weak today.
6.21 to honour the Lord, who **chose** me instead of your father and
7.10 I have **chosen** a place for my people Israel and
10. 9 from the rear, so he **chose** the best of Israel's soldiers and
16.18 the side of the one **chosen** by the Lord, by these people,
17. 1 said to Absalom, "Let me **choose** twelve thousand men, and
19.21 because he cursed the one whom the Lord **chose** as king."
21. 6 Lord at Gibeah, the town of Saul, the Lord's **chosen** king."
22.51 to the one he has **chosen,** to David and his descendants for
23. 1 whom the God of Jacob **chose** to be king, and who was
24.11 "Go and tell David that I am giving him three **choices.**
24.11 I will do whichever he **chooses."**
24.15 lasted from that morning until the time that he had **chosen.**
1 Kgs 1.35 is the one I have **chosen** to be the ruler of Israel
3. 8 among the people you have **chosen** to be your own, a people
5. 9 rafts to float them down the coast to the place you **choose.**
8.12 sky, yet you have **chosen** to live in clouds and darkness.
8.16 of Egypt, I have not **chosen** any city in all the land
8.16 But I **chose** you, David, to rule my people.' "
8.29 night, this place where you have **chosen** to be worshipped.
8.44 this city which you have **chosen** and this Temple which I have
8.48 this city which you have **chosen,** and this Temple which I
8.53 You **chose** them from all the peoples to be your own people,
11.32 Jerusalem, the city I have **chosen** to be my own from the
11.34 my servant David, whom I **chose** and who obeyed my laws and
1 Kgs 11.36 Jerusalem, the city I have **chosen** as the place where I am
12.31 worship on hilltops, and he **chose** priests from families who
13.33 evil ways, but continued to **choose** priests from ordinary
14. 7 'I **chose** you from among the people and made you the ruler
14.21 city which the Lord had **chosen** from all the territory of
2 Kgs 6. 8 He consulted his officers and **chose** a place to set up his
7.14 They **chose** some men, and the king sent them in two
10. 3 this letter, [3] you are to **choose** the best qualified of the
17.32 also worshipped the Lord and **chose** from among their own
21. 7 the place that I have **chosen** out of all the territory of
23.27 reject Jerusalem, the city I **chose,** and the Temple, the
23.30 The people of Judah **chose** Josiah's son Joahaz and anointed him king.
1 Chr 9.22 In all, 212 men were **chosen** as guards for the entrances
12.23 18,000 men **chosen** to go and make David king;
15. 2 are the ones the Lord **chose** to carry it and to serve
15.17 the clans of singers they **chose** the following men to play
15.17 To assist them they **chose** the following Levites to play the
15.17 To play the low-pitched harps they **chose** the following Levites:
15.22 skill in music Chenaniah was **chosen** to be in charge of the
15.23 Obed Edom and Jehiah, were **chosen** as guards for the Covenant Box.
15.23 Zechariah, Benaiah, and Eliezer were **chosen** to blow trumpets
16.12 descendants of Israel, whom God **chose,** remember the miracles
16.22 "Don't harm my **chosen** servants;
16.41 the others who were specifically **chosen** to sing praises to
17. 9 I have **chosen** a place for my people Israel and have
19.10 from the rear, so he **chose** the best of Israel's soldiers and
21.10 "Go and tell David that I am giving him three **choices.**
21.10 I will do whichever he **chooses."**
25. 1 the leaders of the Levites **chose** the following Levite clans
25. 1 is the list of persons **chosen** to lead the worship, with the
26.32 King David **chose** two thousand seven hundred outstanding
28. 4 Lord, the God of Israel, **chose** me and my descendants to rule
28. 4 He **chose** the tribe of Judah to provide leadership,
28. 4 and out of Judah he **chose** my father's family.
28. 5 out of them all he **chose** Solomon to rule over Israel, the
28. 6 I have **chosen** him to be my son, and I will be
28.10 that the Lord has **chosen** you to build his holy Temple.
29. 1 the one whom God has **chosen,** but he is still young and
2 Chr 1.11 God replied to Solomon, "You have made the right **choice.**
6. 1 "Lord, you have **chosen** to live in clouds and darkness.
6. 5 until now, I did not **choose** any city in the land of
6. 5 and I did not **choose** anyone to lead my people Israel.
6. 6 But now I have **chosen** Jerusalem as the place where I will
6.34 this city which you have **chosen** and this Temple which I have
6.38 this city which you have **chosen,** and this Temple which I
6.42 Lord God, do not reject the king you have **chosen.**
7.16 offered here, [16] because I have **chosen** it and consecrated
11.22 over all his other children, **choosing** him as the one to
12.13 city which the Lord had **chosen** from all the territory of
22. 7 Nimshi, whom the Lord had **chosen** to destroy the dynasty of Ahab.
24. 3 Jehoiada **chose** two wives for King Joash, and they bore him
26. 1 All the people of Judah **chose** Amaziah's sixteen-year-old
29.11 ones that the Lord has **chosen** to burn incense to him and
33. 7 the place that I have **chosen** out of all the territory of
36. 1 The people of Judah **chose** Josiah's son Joahaz and anointed
Ezra 6.12 May the God who **chose** Jerusalem as the place where he is
8.24 From among the leading priests I **chose** Sherebiah,
Neh 1. 9 the place where I have **chosen** to be worshipped, even though
9. 7 You, Lord God, **chose** Abram and led him out of Ur in
9.17 In their pride they **chose** a leader to take them back to
11. 1 the people drew lots to **choose** one family out of every ten
Esth 2. 9 and assigned seven girls specially **chosen** from the royal
Job 23.11 the road he **chooses,** and never wander to either side.
Ps 2. 2 together against the Lord and against the king he **chose.**
4. 3 Remember that the Lord has **chosen** the righteous for his own,
18.50 to the one he has **chosen,** to David and his descendants for
20. 6 Now I know that the Lord gives victory to his **chosen** king;
28. 8 he defends and saves his **chosen** king.
33.12 happy are the people he has **chosen** for his own!
45. 7 why God, your God, has **chosen** you and has poured out more
47. 4 He **chose** for us the land where we live, the proud
65. 4 Happy are those whom you **choose,** whom you bring to live in
68.16 look with scorn on the mountain on which God **chose** to live?
69.13 answer me, God, at a time you **choose.**
74. 2 Remember your people, whom you **chose** for yourself long ago,
78.68 Instead he **chose** the tribe of Judah and Mount Zion,
78.70 He **chose** his servant David;
80.17 the people you have **chosen,** the nation you made so strong.
84. 9 Bless our king, O God, the king you have **chosen.**
89. 3 You said, "I have made a covenant with the man I **chose;**
89.18 You, O Lord, **chose** our protector;
89.19 I have given the throne to one I **chose** from the people.
89.38 But you are angry with your **chosen** king;
89.51 Your enemies insult your **chosen** king, O Lord!
105. 5 you descendants of Jacob, the man he **chose:**
105.15 "Don't harm my **chosen** servants;
105.26 Then he sent his servant Moses, and Aaron, whom he had **chosen.**
105.43 So he led his **chosen people** out, and they sang and
106.23 would destroy his people, his **chosen** servant, Moses, stood
106.43 rescued his people, but they **chose** to rebel against him and
109. 6 **Choose** some corrupt judge to try my enemy, and let one of
119.30 I have **chosen** to be obedient;
132.10 do not reject your **chosen** king, Lord.
132.13 The Lord has **chosen** Zion;
132.17 here I will preserve the rule of my **chosen** king.
135. 4 He **chose** Jacob for himself, the people of Israel for his own.
Prov 8.10 **Choose** my instruction instead of silver;
8.10 **choose** knowledge rather than the finest gold.

Prov 22. 1 If you have to **choose** between a good reputation and great wealth,
22. 1 **choose** a good reputation.
Ecc 3. 1 Everything that happens in this world happens at the time God **chooses.**
Is 2. 3 we will walk in the paths he has **chosen.**
3. 6 members of a clan will **choose** one of their number and say
4. 3 Jerusalem, whom God has **chosen** for survival, will be called holy.
14. 1 be merciful to his people Israel and **choose** them as his own.
19.25 and you, Israel, my **chosen people.**"
40.20 afford silver or gold **chooses** wood that will not rot.
41. 8 the people that I have **chosen,** the descendants of Abraham,
41. 9 I did not reject you, but **chose** you.
41.25 "I have **chosen** a man who lives in the east;
42. 1 strengthen— the one I have **chosen,** with whom I am pleased.
43.10 I **chose** you to be my servant, so that you would know
43.20 flow in the desert to give water to my **chosen people.**
44. 1 "Listen now, Israel, my servant, my **chosen people,**
44. 2 you are my servant, my **chosen people** whom I love.
44.14 down cedars to use, or **choose** oak or cypress wood from the
45. 1 The Lord has **chosen** Cyrus to be king!
45. 4 to help my servant Israel, the people that I have **chosen.**
48.14 predict that the man I have **chosen** would attack Babylon;
49. 1 I was born, the Lord **chose** me and appointed me to be
49. 7 This will happen because the Lord has **chosen** his servant;
61. 1 He has **chosen** me and sent me To bring good news to
65. 9 My **chosen people,** who serve me, will live there.
65.12 You **chose** to disobey me and do evil.
65.15 My **chosen people** will use your name as a curse.
66. 4 They **chose** to disobey me and do evil."
Jer 1. 5 Lord said to me, [5] "I **chose** you before I gave you life,
7.12 the first place where I **chose** to be worshipped, and see what
10.16 made everything, and he has **chosen** Israel to be his very own
12. 7 I have rejected my **chosen** nation.
12. 8 My **chosen people** have turned against me;
12. 9 My **chosen people** are like a bird attacked from all sides
21. 8 Lord, am giving you a **choice** between the way that leads to
23. 5 is coming when I will **choose** as king a righteous descendant
27. 5 and I give it to anyone I **choose.**
33.15 At that time I will **choose** as king a righteous
33.24 I have rejected Israel and Judah, the two families that I **chose?**
33.26 I will **choose** one of David's descendants to rule over the
40. 4 have the whole country to **choose** from, and you may go
49.19 Then the leader I **choose** will rule the nation.
50.44 Then the leader I **choose** will rule the nation.
51.19 made everything, and he has **chosen** Israel to be his very own
Lam 4.20 the king the Lord had **chosen,** the one we had trusted to
Ezek 20. 5 When I **chose** Israel, I made them a promise.
20. 6 to a land I had **chosen** for them, a rich and fertile
21.27 the one whom I have **chosen** to punish the city has come.
33. 2 The people of that country **choose** one of their number to be
37.28 that I, the Lord, have **chosen** Israel to be my own people."
39.14 are over, men will be **chosen** to travel through the land in
Dan 1. 6 Among those **chosen** were Daniel, Hananiah, Mishael, and
2.14 **Choosing** his words carefully, [15] he asked Arioch why the
4.17 give them to anyone he **chooses**—even to the least important
4.25 kingdoms, and that he can give them to anyone he **chooses.**
4.32 kingdoms and that he can give them to anyone he **chooses.**"
5.21 all human kingdoms and can give them to anyone he **chooses.**
6. 2 In addition, he **chose** Daniel and two others to supervise
9.25 to rebuild Jerusalem, until God's **chosen** leader comes, seven
9.26 of that time God's **chosen** leader will be killed unjustly.
Hos 1.11 They will **choose** for themselves a single leader, and once
8. 4 "My people **chose** kings, but they did it on their own.
Joel 2.32 those whom I **choose** will survive.'
Amos 2.11 I **chose** some of your sons to be prophets, and some of
Mic 4. 2 we will walk in the paths he has **chosen.**
7.14 Be a shepherd to your people, Lord, the people you have **chosen.**
Hab 1.12 God and protector, you have **chosen** the Babylonians and made
3.13 You went out to save your people, to save your **chosen** king.
Hag 2.23 You are the one I have **chosen.**"
Zech 4.14 two men whom God has **chosen** and anointed to serve him, the
Mt 11.27 the Son and those to whom the Son **chooses** to reveal him.
12.18 my servant, whom I have **chosen,** the one I love,
20.23 not have the right to **choose** who will sit at my right
22.14 And Jesus concluded, "Many are invited, but few are **chosen.**"
24.22 For the sake of his **chosen people,** however, God will reduce
24.24 in order to deceive even God's **chosen people,** if possible.
24.31 and they will gather his **chosen people** from one end of the
Mk 3.14 came to him, [14] and he **chose** twelve, whom he named apostles.
3.14 "I have **chosen** you to be with me," he told them.
3.16 These are the twelve he **chose:**
10.40 not have the right to **choose** who will sit at my right
12.39 who **choose** the reserved seats in the synagogues
13.20 For the sake of his **chosen people,** however, he has reduced
13.22 in order to deceive even God's **chosen people,** if possible.
13.27 the earth to gather God's **chosen people** from one end of the
Lk 1. 9 by the priests, he was **chosen** by lot to burn incense on
2.34 his mother, "This child is **chosen** by God for the destruction
4. 6 over to me, and I can give it to anyone I **choose.**
4.18 upon me, because he has **chosen** me to bring good news to
6.13 his disciples to him and **chose** twelve of them, whom he named
9.35 "This is my Son, whom I have **chosen**—listen to him!"
10. 1 the Lord **chose** another seventy-two men and sent them out
10.22 the Son and those to whom the Son **chooses** to reveal him."
10.42 Mary has **chosen** the right thing, and it will not be taken
14. 7 some of the guests were **choosing** the best places, so he told
20.46 who **choose** the reserved seats in the synagogues and the best
23.35 him save himself if he is the Messiah whom God has **chosen!**"
Jn 6.70 Jesus replied, "I **chose** the twelve of you, didn't I?
10.36 As for me, the Father **chose** me and sent me into the
13.18 I know those I have **chosen.**
Jn 15.16 You did not **choose** me;
15.16 I **chose** you and appointed you to go and bear much fruit,
15.19 But I **chose** you from this world, and you do not belong
Acts 1. 2 the Holy Spirit to the men he had **chosen** as his apostles.
1.17 for he had been **chosen** to have a part in our
1.24 of these two you have **chosen** [25] to serve as an apostle in
1.26 Then they drew lots to **choose** between the two men,
1.26 two men, and the one **chosen** was Matthias, who was added to
3.20 Jesus, who is the Messiah he has already **chosen** for you.
3.26 And so God **chose** his Servant and sent him first to you,
6. 3 So then, brothers, **choose** seven men among you who are
6. 5 apostles' proposal, so they **chose** Stephen, a man full of faith
9.15 "Go, because I have **chosen** him to serve me, to make
10.41 witnesses that God had already **chosen,** that is, to us who
12.21 On a **chosen** day Herod put on his royal robes, sat on
13.17 of the people of Israel **chose** our ancestors and made the
13.48 those who had been **chosen** for eternal life became believers.
15. 7 a long time ago God **chose** me from among you to preach
15.22 the whole church, decided to **choose** some men from the group
15.22 They **chose** two men who were highly respected by the believers,
15.25 and have all agreed to **choose** some messengers and send them
15.40 while Paul **chose** Silas and left, commended by the
17.31 whole world with justice by means of a man he has **chosen.**
21. 8 the seven men who had been **chosen** as helpers in Jerusalem.
22.14 God of our ancestors has **chosen** you to know his will,
26.18 sins forgiven and receive their place among God's **chosen people.**'
Rom 1. 1 Christ Jesus and an apostle **chosen** and called by God to
2.18 and you have learnt from the Law to **choose** what is right;
5. 6 Christ died for the wicked at the time that God **chose.**
7.21 what is good, what is evil is the only **choice** I have.
8.29 Those whom God had already **chosen** he also set apart to
8.33 Who will accuse God's **chosen people?**
9.11 in order that the **choice** of one son might be completely
9.11 so God's **choice** was based on his call, and not on anything
11. 2 has not rejected his people, whom he **chose** from the beginning.
11. 5 left of those whom God has **chosen** because of his grace.
11. 6 His **choice** is based on his grace, not on what they have
11. 6 For if God's **choice** were based on what people do,
11. 7 It was only the small group that God **chose** who found it;
11.28 because of God's **choice,** they are his friends because of their
11.29 God does not change his mind about whom he **chooses** and blesses.
1 Cor 1.27 purposely **chose** what the world considers nonsense in order
1.27 shame the wise, and he **chose** what the world considers weak
1.28 He **chose** what the world looks down on and despises,
2. 7 but which he had already **chosen** for our glory even before
9.17 as a matter of free **choice,** then I could expect to be
2 Cor 8.19 besides that, he has been **chosen** and appointed by the churches
Gal 1.15 But God in his grace **chose** me even before I was born,
Eph 1. 4 was made, God had already **chosen** us to be his through our
1.11 and God **chose** us to be his own people in union with
2.12 You were foreigners and did not belong to God's **chosen people.**
Phil 1.10 so that you will be able to **choose** what is best.
1.22 worthwhile work, then I am not sure which I should **choose.**
Col 3.12 he loved you and **chose** you for his own.
1 Thes 1. 4 that God loves you and has **chosen** you to be his own.
5. 9 God did not **choose** us to suffer his anger, but to possess
2 Thes 2.13 For God **chose** you as the first to be saved by the
2 Tim 2.10 for the sake of God's **chosen people,** in order that they too
Tit 1. 1 I was **chosen** and sent to help
1. 1 help the faith of God's **chosen people** and to lead them to
Heb 1. 2 the one whom God has **chosen** to possess all things at the
1. 9 why God, your God, has **chosen** you and has given you the
3. 2 was faithful to God, who **chose** him to do this work,
5. 1 Every high priest is **chosen** from his fellow-men and appointed
5. 4 No one **chooses** for himself the honour of being a high priest.
Jas 2. 5 God **chose** the poor people of this world to be rich in
1 Pet 1. 1 To God's **chosen people** who live as refugees scattered
1. 2 You were **chosen** according to the purpose of God the Father
1.20 He had been **chosen** by God before the creation of the
2. 4 rejected by man as worthless but **chosen** by God as valuable.
2. 6 For the scripture says, "I **chose** a valuable stone, which I
2. 9 you are the **chosen** race, the King's priests, the holy nation,
2. 9 God's own people, **chosen** to proclaim the wonderful acts of
5.13 church in Babylon, also **chosen** by God, sends you greetings,
2 Pet 1.10 God's call and his **choice** of you a permanent experience;
Rev 17.14 Lamb, together with his called, **chosen,** and faithful followers,

CHOP

Deut 12. 3 of the goddess Asherah and **chop** down their idols, so that
19. 5 as one of them is **chopping** down a tree, the head of
1 Sam 6.14 The people **chopped** up the wooden wagon and killed the cows
2 Chr 15.16 Asa cut down the idol, **chopped** it up, and burnt the pieces
Ps 141. 7 wood that is split and **chopped** into bits, so their bones are
Jer 11.19 They were saying, "Let's **chop** down the tree while it is
Ezek 5. 2 Take another third and **chop** it up with your sword as you
Dan 4.14 a loud voice, 'Cut the tree down and **chop** off its branches;
Mic 3. 3 skin, break their bones, and **chop** them up like meat for the

CHOSEN see **CHOOSE**

CHOSEN PEOPLE see **CHOOSE, GOD'S PEOPLE**

CHRIST

Greek form of the title "Messiah", which developed into being a name for Jesus.
For CHRIST JESUS, JESUS CHRIST see **JESUS**

Mt 11. 2 prison about the things that **Christ** was doing, he sent some
Lk 2.11 day in David's town your Saviour was born—**Christ** the Lord!
Jn 1.41 (This word means **"Christ.")**
Rom 1. 5 apostle for the sake of **Christ,** in order to lead people of
3.22 to all who believe in **Christ,** because there is no difference
5. 6 when we were still helpless, **Christ** died for the wicked at
5. 8 it was while we were still sinners that **Christ** died for us!
5.10 God's friends, how much more will we be saved by **Christ's** life!
5.17 freely put right with him will rule in life through **Christ.**
6. 4 in order that, just as **Christ** was raised from death by the
6. 6 been put to death with **Christ** on his cross, in order that
6. 8 Since we have died with **Christ,** we believe that we will
6. 9 For we know that **Christ** has been raised from death and
7. 4 also have died because you are part of the body of **Christ;**
8. 9 does not have the Spirit of **Christ** does not belong to him.
8.10 But if **Christ** lives in you, the Spirit is life for you
8.11 then he who raised **Christ** from death will also give life
8.17 we will also possess with **Christ** what God has kept for him;
8.17 if we share **Christ's** suffering, we will also share his glory.
8.35 Who, then, can separate us from the love of **Christ?**
9. 1 I belong to **Christ** and I do not lie.
9. 3 that I myself were under God's curse and separated from **Christ.**
9. 5 and **Christ,** as a human being, belongs to their race.
10. 4 For **Christ** has brought the Law to an end, so that everyone
10. 6 (that is, to bring **Christ** down).
10. 7 (that is, to bring **Christ** up from death).
10.17 the message, and the message comes through preaching **Christ.**
12. 5 one body in union with **Christ,** and we are all joined to
14. 9 For **Christ** died and rose to life in order to be the
14.15 the food that you eat ruin the person for whom **Christ** died!
14.18 And when someone serves **Christ** in this way, he pleases God
15. 3 For **Christ** did not please himself.
15. 7 then, for the glory of God, as **Christ** has accepted you.
15. 8 For I tell you that **Christ's** life of service was on behalf
15.18 and speak only about what **Christ** has done through me to lead
15.19 to Illyricum, I have proclaimed fully the Good News about **Christ.**
15.20 Good News in places where **Christ** has not been heard of,
15.29 I shall come with a full measure of the blessing of **Christ.**
16. 5 the first man in the province of Asia to believe in **Christ.**
16. 9 Urbanus, our fellow-worker in **Christ's** service, and to Stachys,
16.10 Greetings to Apelles, whose loyalty to **Christ** has been proved.
16.16 All the churches of **Christ** send you their greetings.
16.18 are not serving **Christ** our Lord, but their own appetites.
1 Cor 1. 5 For in union with **Christ** you have become rich in all things,
1. 6 message about **Christ** has become so firmly established in you
1.12 and another, "I follow **Christ."**
1.13 **Christ** has been divided into groups!
1.17 **Christ** did not send me to baptize.
1.17 order to make sure that **Christ's** death on the cross is not
1.18 the message about **Christ's** death on the cross is nonsense to
1.23 proclaim the crucified **Christ,** a message that is offensive to
1.24 this message is **Christ,** who is the power of God
1.30 and God has made **Christ** to be our wisdom.
2.16 We, however, have the mind of **Christ.**
3.23 and you belong to **Christ,** and Christ belongs to God.
4. 1 should think of us as **Christ's** servants, who have been put
4.10 For **Christ's** sake we are fools;
4.10 but you are wise in union with **Christ!**
5. 7 now that **Christ,** our Passover lamb, has been sacrificed.
6.15 You know that your bodies are parts of the body of **Christ.**
6.15 I take a part of **Christ's** body and make it part of
7.22 a free man who has been called by **Christ** is his slave.
8.11 your brother for whom **Christ** died, will perish because of your
8.12 sinning against **Christ** by sinning against your Christian brothers
9.12 put any obstacle in the way of the Good News about **Christ.**
9.21 I am really under **Christ's** law.
10. 4 and that rock was **Christ** himself.
10.16 we drink from it, we are sharing in the blood of **Christ.**
10.16 when we eat it, we are sharing in the body of **Christ.**
11. 1 Imitate me, then, just as I imitate **Christ.**
11. 3 want you to understand that **Christ** is supreme over every man,
11. 3 is supreme over his wife, and God is supreme over **Christ.**
11. 4 message in public worship with his head covered disgraces **Christ.**
12.12 **Christ** is like a single body, which has many parts;
12.27 All of you are **Christ's** body, and each one is a part
15. 3 that **Christ** died for our sins, as written in the Scriptures;
15.12 since our message is that **Christ** has been raised from death,
15.13 If that is true, it means that **Christ** was not raised;
15.14 and if **Christ** has not been raised from death, then we
15.15 we said that he raised **Christ** from death—but if it is
15.15 dead are not raised to life, then he did not raise **Christ.**
15.16 if the dead are not raised, neither has **Christ** been raised.
15.17 And if **Christ** has not been raised, then your faith is a
15.18 mean that the believers in **Christ** who have died are lost.
15.19 If our hope in **Christ** is good for this life only
15.20 But the truth is that **Christ** has been raised from death,
15.22 will be raised to life because of their union with **Christ.**
15.23 **Christ,** first of all;
15.24 **Christ** will overcome all spiritual rulers, authorities, and powers,
15.25 For **Christ** must rule until God defeats all enemies and puts
15.27 do not include God himself, who puts all things under **Christ.**
15.28 have been placed under **Christ's** rule, then he himself, the Son,
2 Cor 1. 5 we have a share in **Christ's** many sufferings,
1. 5 so also through **Christ** we share in God's great help.
1.21 together with you, sure of our life in union with **Christ;**
2.10 I do it in **Christ's** presence because of you, [11]in order
2 Cor 2.12 preach the Good News about **Christ,** I found that the Lord had
2.14 For in union with **Christ** we are always led by God
2.14 as prisoners in **Christ's** victory procession.
2.14 knowledge about **Christ** spread everywhere like a sweet fragrance.
2.15 a sweet-smelling incense offered by **Christ** to God, which spreads
2.17 we speak with sincerity in his presence, as servants of **Christ.**
3. 3 It is clear that **Christ** himself wrote this letter and sent
3. 4 We say this because we have confidence in God through **Christ.**
3.14 The veil is removed only when a person is joined to **Christ.**
4. 4 News about the glory of **Christ,** who is the exact likeness of
4. 6 the knowledge of God's glory shining in the face of **Christ.**
5.10 all of us must appear before **Christ,** to be judged by him.
5.14 ruled by the love of **Christ,** now that we recognize that one
5.16 at one time we judged **Christ** according to human standards,
5.17 When anyone is joined to **Christ,** he is a new being;
5.18 done by God, who through **Christ** changed us from enemies into
5.19 God was making all mankind his friends through **Christ.**
5.20 we are, then, speaking for **Christ,** as though God himself were
5.20 We plead on **Christ's** behalf:
5.21 **Christ** was without sin, but for our sake God made him
6.15 How can **Christ** and the Devil agree?
8.23 they represent the churches and bring glory to **Christ.**
9.13 loyalty to the gospel of **Christ,** which you profess,
10. 1 the gentleness and kindness of **Christ** I beg you [2]not to
10. 5 we take every thought captive and make it obey **Christ.**
10. 7 Is there someone there who reckons himself to belong to **Christ?**
10. 7 because we belong to **Christ** just as much as he does.
10.14 when we came to you, bringing the Good News about **Christ.**
11. 2 I have promised in marriage to one man only, **Christ** himself.
11. 3 full and pure devotion to **Christ**—in the same way that Eve
11.10 By **Christ's** truth in me, I promise that this boast of
11.13 and disguise themselves to look like real apostles of **Christ.**
11.23 Are they **Christ's** servants?
12. 9 in order to feel the protection of **Christ's** power over me.
12.10 hardships, persecutions, and difficulties for **Christ's** sake.
12.19 We speak as **Christ** would wish us to speak in the presence
13. 3 have all the proof you want that **Christ** speaks through me.
Gal 1. 4 from this present evil age, **Christ** gave himself for our sins,
1. 6 called you by the grace of **Christ,** and are accepting another
1. 7 are upsetting you and trying to change the gospel of **Christ.**
1.10 trying to do so, I would not be a servant of **Christ.**
2.16 God through our faith in **Christ,** and not by doing what the
2.17 God by our union with **Christ,** we are found to be sinners
2.17 does this mean that **Christ** is serving the cause of sin?
2.19 been put to death with **Christ** on his cross,
2.20 longer I who live, but it is **Christ** who lives in me.
2.21 God through the Law, it means that **Christ** died for nothing!
3.13 becoming a curse for us **Christ** has redeemed us from the
3.14 **Christ** did this in order that the blessing which God promised
3.16 singular "descendant," meaning one person only, namely, **Christ.**
3.24 in charge of us until **Christ** came, in order that we might
3.27 were baptized into union with **Christ,** and now you are clothed,
3.27 so to speak, with the life of **Christ** himself.
4.19 kind of pain for you until **Christ's** nature is formed in you.
5. 1 Freedom is what we have—**Christ** has set us free!
5. 2 be circumcised, it means that **Christ** is of no use to you
5. 4 God by obeying the Law have cut yourselves off from **Christ.**
5.11 my preaching about the cross of **Christ** would cause no trouble.
6. 2 and in this way you will obey the law of **Christ.**
6.12 so that they may not be persecuted for the cross of **Christ.**
Eph 1. 3 For in our union with **Christ** he has blessed us by giving
1. 4 his through our union with **Christ,** so that we would be holy
1. 7 by the sacrificial death of **Christ** we are set free, that is,
1. 9 plan he had already decided to complete by means of **Christ.**
1.10 everything in heaven and on earth, with **Christ** as head.
1.11 own people in union with **Christ** because of his own purpose,
1.12 who were the first to hope in **Christ,** praise God's glory!
1.13 You believed in **Christ,** and God put his stamp of ownership
1.20 he used when he raised **Christ** from death and seated him at
1.21 **Christ** rules there above all heavenly rulers, authorities,
1.22 God put all things under **Christ's** feet and gave him to
1.23 The church is **Christ's** body, the completion of him who
2. 5 dead in our disobedience he brought us to life with **Christ.**
2.12 At that time you were apart from **Christ.**
2.13 have been brought near by the sacrificial death of **Christ.**
2.14 **Christ** himself has brought us peace by making Jews and Gentiles
2.16 By his death on the cross **Christ** destroyed their enmity;
2.17 So **Christ** came and preached the Good News of peace to
2.18 It is through **Christ** that all of us, Jews and Gentiles,
3. 4 you can learn about my understanding of the secret of **Christ.)**
3. 8 about the infinite riches of **Christ,** [9]and of making all people
3.12 In union with **Christ** and through our faith in him we
3.17 and I pray that **Christ** will make his home in your
3.18 how broad and long, how high and deep, is **Christ's** love.
4. 7 received a special gift in proportion to what **Christ** has given.
4.12 Christian service, in order to build up the body of **Christ.**
4.13 reaching to the very height of **Christ's** full stature.
4.15 must grow up in every way to **Christ,** who is the head.
4.20 That was not what you learnt about **Christ!**
4.25 we are all members together in the body of **Christ.**
4.32 and forgive one another, as God has forgiven you through **Christ.**
5. 2 controlled by love, just as **Christ** loved us and gave his
5. 5 ever receive a share in the Kingdom of **Christ** and of God.
5.14 and rise from death, and **Christ** will shine on you."
5.21 yourselves to one another because of your reverence for **Christ.**
5.23 over his wife just as **Christ** has authority over the church;
5.23 and **Christ** is himself the Saviour of the church, his body.
5.24 to their husbands just as the church submits itself to **Christ.**
5.25 love your wives just as **Christ** loved the church and gave his
5.29 and takes care of it, just as **Christ** does the church;

Eph	5.32	which I understand as applying to **Christ** and the church.
	6. 5	it with a sincere heart, as though you were serving **Christ.**
	6. 6	with all your heart do what God wants, as slaves of **Christ.**
Phil	1.13	that I am in prison because I am a servant of **Christ.**
	1.15	some of them preach **Christ** because they are jealous and
	1.17	others do not proclaim **Christ** sincerely, but from a spirit of
	1.18	so long as **Christ** is preached in every way possible,
	1.20	I shall bring honour to **Christ,** whether I live or die.
	1.21	To me, it is **Christ.**
	1.23	this life and be with **Christ,** which is a far better thing;
	1.27	be as the gospel of **Christ** requires, so that, whether or not
	1.29	the privilege of serving **Christ,** not only by believing in him,
	2. 1	Your life in **Christ** makes you strong, and his love comforts you.
	2.30	sake of the work of **Christ,** in order to give me the
	3. 7	count as profit I now reckon as loss for **Christ's** sake.
	3. 8	that I may gain **Christ** [9] and be completely united with him.
	3. 9	through faith in **Christ,** the righteousness that comes from God
	3.10	I want is to know **Christ** and to experience the power of
	3.18	whose lives make them enemies of **Christ's** death on the cross.
	4.13	strength to face all conditions by the power that **Christ** gives
Col	1. 2	in Colossae, who are our faithful brothers in union with **Christ:**
	1. 7	our dear fellow-servant, who is **Christ's** faithful worker
	1.15	**Christ** is the visible likeness of the invisible God.
	1.17	**Christ** existed before all things, and in union with him all
	1.24	what still remains of **Christ's** sufferings on behalf of his body,
	1.27	And the secret is that **Christ** is in you, which means that
	1.28	So we preach **Christ** to everyone.
	1.28	into God's presence as a mature individual in union with **Christ.**
	1.29	the mighty strength which **Christ** supplies and which is at work
	2. 2	In this way they will know God's secret, which is **Christ** himself.
	2. 5	firmness with which you stand together in your faith in **Christ.**
	2. 8	the ruling spirits of the universe, and not from **Christ.**
	2. 9	of divine nature lives in **Christ,** in his humanity,
	2.11	In union with **Christ** you were circumcised,
	2.11	the circumcision made by **Christ,** which consists of being freed
	2.12	you were buried with **Christ,** and in baptism you were also
	2.12	raised with **Christ** through your faith in the active
	2.13	But God has now brought you to life with **Christ.**
	2.15	And on that cross **Christ** freed himself from the power of
	2.17	the reality is **Christ.**
	2.19	has stopped holding on to **Christ,** who is the head of the
	2.19	Under **Christ's** control the whole body is nourished
	2.20	You have died with **Christ** and are set free from the
	3. 1	been raised to life with **Christ,** so set your hearts on the
	3. 1	that are in heaven, where **Christ** sits on his throne at the
	3. 3	you have died, and your life is hidden with **Christ** in God.
	3. 4	Your real life is **Christ** and when he appears, then you too
	3.11	slaves, and free men, but **Christ** is all, Christ is in all.
	3.15	The peace that **Christ** gives is to guide you in the
	3.16	**Christ's** message in all its richness must live in your hearts.
	3.24	For **Christ** is the real Master you serve.
	4. 3	good opportunity to preach his message about the secret of **Christ.**
1 Thes	2. 7	even though as apostles of **Christ** we could have made demands
	3. 2	with us for God in preaching the Good News about **Christ.**
	4.16	Those who have died believing in **Christ** will rise to life first;
2 Thes	3. 5	of God's love and the endurance that is given by **Christ.**
1 Tim	5.11	marry, they turn away from **Christ,** [12] and so become guilty of
2 Tim	1. 8	nor be ashamed of me, a prisoner for **Christ's** sake.
Phlm	6	blessing which we have in our life in union with **Christ.**
	8	enough, as your brother in **Christ,** to order you to do what
	10	you on behalf of Onesimus, who is my own son in **Christ;**
	16	he is a dear brother in **Christ.**
	20	as a brother in **Christ,** cheer me up!
Heb	3. 6	But **Christ** is faithful as the Son in charge of God's house.
	3.14	we are all partners with **Christ** if we hold firmly to the
	5. 5	In the same way, **Christ** did not take upon himself the
	9.11	But **Christ** has already come as the High Priest of the
	9.12	**Christ** went through the tent and entered once and for all
	9.14	true, how much more is accomplished by the blood of **Christ!**
	9.15	For this reason **Christ** is the one who arranges a new covenant,
	9.24	For **Christ** did not go into a man-made Holy Place,
	9.25	But **Christ** did not go in to offer himself many times,
	9.28	In the same manner **Christ** also was offered in sacrifice once
	10. 5	For this reason, when **Christ** was about to come into the world,
	10. 9	old sacrifices and puts the sacrifice of **Christ** in their place.
	10.12	**Christ,** however, offered one sacrifice for sins,
	13.20	And to **Christ** be the glory for ever and ever!
1 Pet	1.11	was the time to which **Christ's** Spirit in them was pointing,
	1.11	in predicting the sufferings that **Christ** would have to endure
	1.19	the costly sacrifice of **Christ,** who was like a lamb without
	2.21	that God called you, for **Christ** himself suffered for you and
	2.24	**Christ** himself carried our sins in his body to the cross,
	3.15	But have reverence for **Christ** in your hearts, and honour him
	3.16	good conduct as followers of **Christ** will be ashamed of what
	3.18	For **Christ** died for sins once and for all, a good man
	4. 1	**Christ** suffered physically, you too must strengthen yourselves
	4.13	glad that you are sharing **Christ's** sufferings, so that you may
	4.14	are you if you are insulted because you are **Christ's** followers;
	4.16	but thank God that you bear **Christ's** name.
	5. 1	I am a witness of **Christ's** sufferings, and I will share in
	5.10	eternal glory in union with **Christ,** will himself perfect you
1 Jn	2. 2	And **Christ** himself is the means by which our sins are forgiven,
	2. 8	because its truth is seen in **Christ** and also in you.
	2.12	because your sins are forgiven for the sake of **Christ.**
	2.18	You were told that the Enemy of **Christ** would come;
	2.18	and now many enemies of **Christ** have already appeared, and so
	2.20	poured out on you by **Christ,** and so all of you know
	2.22	person is the Enemy of **Christ**—he rejects both the Father and
	2.25	this is what **Christ** himself promised to give us—eternal life.
	2.27	But as for you, **Christ** has poured out his Spirit on you.
	2.27	Obey the Spirit's teaching, then, and remain in union with **Christ.**
1 Jn	2.29	You know that **Christ** is righteous;
	3. 2	But we know that when **Christ** appears, we shall be like him,
	3. 3	who has this hope in **Christ** keeps himself pure,
	3. 3	just as **Christ** is pure.
	3. 5	You know that **Christ** appeared in order to take away sins,
	3. 6	who lives in union with **Christ** does not continue to sin;
	3. 7	Whoever does what is right is righteous, just as **Christ** is
	3.16	**Christ** gave his life for us.
	3.23	and love one another, just as **Christ** commanded us.
	4. 3	The spirit that he has is from the Enemy of **Christ;**
	4.17	because our life in this world is the same as **Christ's.**
	4.21	The command that **Christ** has given us is this:
2 Jn	7	Such a person is a deceiver and the Enemy of **Christ.**
	9	stay with the teaching of **Christ,** but goes beyond it, does
3 Jn	7	journey in the service of **Christ** without accepting any help
Rev	1. 1	**Christ** made these things known to his servant John by
	20. 4	to life and ruled as kings with **Christ** for a thousand years.
	20. 6	priests of God and of **Christ,** and they will rule with him

CHRISTIAN

[FELLOW-CHRISTIAN]

Acts	9.10	There was a **Christian** in Damascus named Ananias.
	11.26	was at Antioch that the believers were first called **Christians.**
	16. 1	to Derbe and Lystra, where a **Christian** named Timothy lived.
	16. 1	mother, who was also a **Christian,** was Jewish, but his father
	26.28	this short time do you think you will make me a **Christian?"**
Rom	12.10	Love one another warmly as **Christian brothers,** and be eager
	12.13	needy **fellow-Christians,** and open your homes to strangers.
	16. 7	known among the apostles, and they became **Christians** before I
	16.11	and to the **Christian brothers** in the family of Narcissus.
	16.14	Patrobas, Hermas, and all the other **Christian brothers** with them.
	16.22	the writer of this letter, send you **Christian** greetings.
1 Cor	3. 1	you belonged to this world, as children in the **Christian** faith.
	4.15	ten thousand guardians in your **Christian** life, you have only one
	4.17	who is my own dear and faithful son in the **Christian** life.
	6. 1	has a dispute with a **fellow-Christian,** how dare he go before
	6. 5	who can settle a dispute between **fellow-Christians.**
	6. 6	Instead, one **Christian** goes to court against another
	7.12	if a **Christian** man has a wife who is an unbeliever
	7.13	And if a **Christian** woman is married to a man who is
	7.14	made acceptable to God by being united to her **Christian husband.**
	7.15	a believer wishes to leave the **Christian** partner, let it be
	7.15	In such cases the **Christian** partner, whether husband or wife,
	7.16	How can you be sure, **Christian wife,** that you will not
	7.16	how can you be sure, **Christian husband,** that you will not
	7.39	to any man she wishes, but only if he is a **Christian.**
	8.12	by sinning against your **Christian brothers** and wounding
	9. 5	and Peter, by taking a **Christian wife** with me on my travels?
	16.15	they are the first **Christian** converts in Achaia and have given
	16.19	church that meets in their house send warm **Christian** greetings.
2 Cor	12. 2	know a certain **Christian** man who fourteen years ago was snatched
	12.18	Titus to go, and I sent the other **Christian brother** with him.
Gal	6. 6	who is being taught the **Christian** message should share all the
Eph	4.12	people for the work of **Christian** service, in order to build
	6. 1	Children, it is your **Christian** duty to obey your parents,
	6. 4	Instead, bring them up with **Christian** discipline and instruction.
	6.23	Christ give to all **Christian brothers** peace and love with faith.
Col	3.18	husbands, for that is what you should do as **Christians.**
	3.20	Children, it is your **Christian** duty to obey your parents
	4.12	mature and fully convinced **Christians,** in complete obedience
1 Thes	4. 6	do wrong to his **fellow-Christian** or take advantage of him.
	5.12	among you, who guide and instruct you in the **Christian** life.
1 Tim	5.10	duties for **fellow-Christians,** helped people in trouble,
	5.16	But if any **Christian** woman has widows in her family, she
	6. 2	Slaves belonging to **Christian** masters must not despise them,
2 Tim	4.21	send their greetings, and so do all the other **Christian brothers.**
Heb	3. 1	My **Christian brothers,** who also have been called by God!
	6. 1	and leave behind us the first lessons of the **Christian** message.
	6.10	you gave and are still giving to your **fellow-Christians.**
	13. 1	Keep on loving one another as **Christian brothers.**
Jas	1. 9	The **Christian** who is poor must be glad when God lifts him
	1.10	and the rich **Christian** must be glad when God brings
	4.11	Whoever criticizes a **Christian brother** or judges him,
1 Pet	4.16	suffer because you are a **Christian,** don't be ashamed of it,
	5.12	of Silas, whom I regard as a faithful **Christian brother.**
	5.14	Greet one another with the kiss of **Christian** love.
3 Jn	3	so happy when some **Christian brothers** arrived and told me how
	5	do for your **fellow-Christians,** even when they are strangers.
	8	We **Christians,** then, must help these people, so that we may
	10	he will not receive the **Christian brothers** when they come,

CHRONIC

Lev	13.11	white and is full of pus, [11] it is a **chronic** skin-disease.

CHURCH

Mt	16.18	foundation I will build my **church,** and not even death will
	18.17	not listen to them, then tell the whole thing to the **church.**
	18.17	will not listen to the **church,** treat him as though he were
Acts	5.11	The whole **church** and all the others who heard of this
	8. 1	the **church** in Jerusalem began to suffer cruel persecution.
	8. 3	But Saul tried to destroy the **church;**
	9.31	so it was that the **church** throughout Judaea, Galilee, and
	11.22	news about this reached the **church** in Jerusalem, so they sent
	11.26	met with the people of the **church** and taught a large group.
	11.30	sent the money to the **church** elders by Barnabas and Saul.
	12. 1	King Herod began to persecute some members of the **church.**
	12. 5	but the people of the **church** were praying earnestly to God

Acts	13. 1	In the **church** at Antioch there were some prophets and teachers:
	14.23	In each **church** they appointed elders, and with prayers and
	14.27	gathered the people of the **church** together and told them
	15. 3	They were sent on their way by the **church;**
	15. 4	they were welcomed by the **church,** the apostles, and the elders,
	15.22	elders, together with the whole **church,** decided to choose some
	15.41	He went through Syria and Cilicia, strengthening the **churches.**
	16. 5	So the **churches** were made stronger in the faith and grew
	18.22	to Jerusalem and greeted the **church,** and then went to Antioch
	20.17	to Ephesus, asking the elders of the **church** to meet him.
	20.28	Be shepherds of the **church** of God, which he made his own
	21.18	and all the **church** elders were present.
Rom	15.26	For the **churches** in Macedonia and Achaia have freely decided
	16. 1	our sister Phoebe, who serves the **church** at Cenchreae.
	16. 4	to them—not only I, but all the Gentile **churches** as well.
	16. 5	Greetings also to the **church** that meets in their house.
	16.16	All the **churches** of Christ send you their greetings.
	16.23	Gaius, in whose house the **church** meets, sends you his greetings;
1 Cor	1. 2	Sosthenes— [2] To the **church** of God which is in Corinth,
	4.17	and which I teach in all the **churches** everywhere.
	6. 4	to be settled by people who have no standing in the **church?**
	7.17	This is the rule I teach in all the **churches.**
	10.32	trouble either to Jews or Gentiles or to the **church** of God.
	11.16	that neither we nor the **churches** of God have any other
	11.22	would you rather despise the **church** of God and put to shame
	12.28	In the **church** God has put all in place:
	14. 4	but the one who proclaims God's message helps the whole **church.**
	14. 5	what he says, so that the whole **church** may be helped.
	14.12	greater use of those which help to build up the **church.**
	14.19	But in **church** worship I would rather speak five words that
	14.23	If, then, the whole **church** meets together and everyone starts
	14.26	Everything must be of help to the **church.**
	14.33	As in all the **churches** of God's people, [34] the women should
	14.35	It is a disgraceful thing for a woman to speak in **church.**
	15. 9	deserve to be called an apostle, because I persecuted God's **church.**
	16. 1	You must do what I told the **churches** in Galatia to do.
	16.19	The **churches** in the province of Asia send you their greetings;
	16.19	Aquila and Priscilla and the **church** that meets in their house
2 Cor	1. 1	brother Timothy— To the **church** of God in Corinth, and to
	8. 1	what God's grace has accomplished in the **churches** in Macedonia.
	8.18	highly respected in all the **churches** for his work in preaching
	8.19	chosen and appointed by the **churches** to travel with us as we
	8.23	they represent the **churches** and bring glory to Christ.
	8.24	so that all the **churches** will be sure of it
	11. 8	While I was working among you, I was paid by other **churches.**
	11.28	I am under the pressure of my concern for all the **churches.**
	12.13	any worse than the other **churches,** except that I did not
Gal	1. 2	join me in sending greetings to the **churches** of Galatia:
	1.13	I persecuted without mercy the **church** of God and did my best
	1.22	the members of the **churches** in Judaea did not know me
Eph	1.22	and gave him to the **church** as supreme Lord over all things.
	1.23	The **church** is Christ's body, the completion of him who
	3.10	by means of the **church,** the angelic rulers and powers in
	3.21	be the glory in the **church** and in Christ Jesus for all
	5.23	over his wife just as Christ has authority over the **church;**
	5.23	and Christ is himself the Saviour of the **church,** his body.
	5.24	to their husbands just as the **church** submits itself to Christ.
	5.25	just as Christ loved the **church** and gave his life for it.
	5.26	did this to dedicate the **church** to God by his word,
	5.27	in order to present the **church** to himself in all its
	5.29	and takes care of it, just as Christ does the **church;**
	5.32	scripture, which I understand as applying to Christ and the **church.**
Phil	1. 1	union with Christ Jesus, including the **church** leaders and helpers:
	3. 6	Pharisee, [6] and I was so zealous that I persecuted the **church.**
	4.15	the Good News, you were the only **church** to help me;
Col	1.18	He is the head of his body, the **church;**
	1.24	of Christ's sufferings on behalf of his body, the **church.**
	1.25	made a servant of the **church** by God, who gave me this
	4.15	Laodicea and to Nympha and the **church** that meets in her house.
	4.16	make sure that it is read also in the **church** at Laodicea.
1 Thes	1. 1	To the people of the **church** in Thessalonica, who belong to
	2.14	you that happened to the **churches** of God in Judaea, to the
2 Thes	1. 1	To the people of the **church** in Thessalonica, who belong to
	1. 4	is why we ourselves boast about you in the **churches** of God.
1 Tim	2. 8	In every **church** service I want the men to pray, men who
	3. 1	eager to be a **church** leader, he desires an excellent work.
	3. 2	A **church** leader must be without fault;
	3. 5	own family, how can he take care of the **church** of God?
	3. 7	by the people outside the **church,** so that he will not be
	3. 8	**Church** helpers must also have a good character and be sincere;
	3.12	A **church** helper must have only one wife, and be able to
	3.15	God's household, which is the **church** of the living God,
	5.16	put the burden on the **church,** so that it may take care
Tit	1. 5	that still needed doing and appoint **church** elders in every town.
	1. 7	For since a **church** leader is in charge of God's work,
Phlm	2	fellow-worker Philemon, [2] and the **church** that meets in your house,
Jas	5.14	He should send for the **church** elders, who will pray for him
1 Pet	5. 1	am an elder myself, appeal to the **church** elders among you.
	5.13	sister **church** in Babylon, also chosen by God, sends you greetings,
3 Jn	6	They have spoken to the **church** here about your love.
	9	I wrote a short letter to the **church;**
	10	to receive them and tries to drive them out of the **church!**
Rev	1. 4	From John to the seven **churches** in the province of Asia:
	1.11	and send the book to the **churches** in these seven cities:
	1.20	the angels of the seven **churches,**
	1.20	and the seven lamp-stands are the seven **churches.**
	2. 1	"To the angel of the **church** in Ephesus write:
	2. 7	listen to what the Spirit says to the **churches!**
	2. 8	"To the angel of the **church** in Smyrna write:
Rev	2.11	listen to what the Spirit says to the **churches!**
	2.12	"To the angel of the **church** in Pergamum write:
	2.17	listen to what the Spirit says to the **churches!**
	2.18	"To the angel of the **church** in Thyatira write:
	2.23	and then all the **churches** will know that I am the
	2.29	listen to what the Spirit says to the **churches!**
	3. 1	"To the angel of the **church** in Sardis write:
	3. 6	listen to what the Spirit says to the **churches!**
	3. 7	"To the angel of the **church** in Philadelphia write:
	3.13	listen to what the Spirit says to the **churches!**
	3.14	"To the angel of the **church** in Laodicea write:
	3.22	listen to what the Spirit says to the **churches!"**
	22.16	my angel to announce these things to you in the **churches.**

CHURN

Job	41.31	He **churns** up the sea like boiling water and makes it
Prov	30.33	If you **churn** milk, you get butter.

CILICIA

Country in Asia Minor, centre of horse-breeding in Solomon's time.

1 Kgs	10.28	of horses from Musri and **Cilicia,** [29] and the export of
2 Chr	1.16	of horses from Musri and **Cilicia,** [17] and the export of
Acts	6. 9	Jews from the provinces of **Cilicia** and Asia started arguing with Stephen.
	15.23	of Gentile birth who live in Antioch, Syria, and **Cilicia.**
	15.41	He went through Syria and **Cilicia,** strengthening the churches.
	21.39	Jew, born in Tarsus in **Cilicia,** a citizen of an important city.
	22. 3	Jew, born in Tarsus in **Cilicia,** but brought up here in
	23.34	out that he was from **Cilicia,** [35] he said, "I will hear you
	27. 5	crossed over the sea off **Cilicia** and Pamphylia and came to
Gal	1.21	Afterwards I went to places in Syria and **Cilicia.**

CINNAMON

Ex	30.23	three kilogrammes of sweet-smelling **cinnamon,**
Prov	7.17	I've perfumed it with myrrh, aloes, and **cinnamon.**
Song	4.14	of saffron, calamus, and **cinnamon,** or incense of every kind.
Rev	18.13	and **cinnamon,** spice, incense, myrrh, and frankincense;

CIRCLE

Gen	37. 7	Yours formed a **circle** round mine and bowed down to it."
Josh	15.10	(or Kiriath Jearim), [10] where it **circled** west of Baalah
1 Kgs	7.31	There was a **circular** frame on top for the basin.
Job	16.16	my eyes are swollen and **circled** with shadows, [17] but I am
	26.10	light from darkness by a **circle** drawn on the face of the
Ezek	16.37	them round you in a **circle,** and then I will strip off
Rev	4. 4	In a **circle** round the throne were twenty-four other thrones,

CIRCUMCISE

[UNCIRCUMCISED]

To cut off the foreskin of the penis. As a sign of God's covenant with his people Israelite boys were circumcised eight days after they were born.

Gen	17.10	must all agree to **circumcise** every male among you.
	17.11	From now on you must **circumcise** every baby boy
	17.13	Each one must be **circumcised,** and this will be a
	17.14	male who has not been **circumcised** will no longer be
	17.23	day Abraham obeyed God and **circumcised** his son Ishmael and
	17.24	he was **circumcised,** [25] and his son Ishmael was thirteen.
	17.26	They were both **circumcised** on the same day, [27] together
	21. 4	Isaac was eight days old, Abraham **circumcised** him,
	34.14	"We cannot let our sister marry a man who is not **circumcised;**
	34.15	that you become like us by **circumcising** all your males.
	34.17	our terms and be **circumcised,** we will take her and leave."
	34.22	that we circumcise all our males, as they are **circumcised.**
	34.24	Hamor and Shechem proposed, and all the males were **circumcised.**
	34.25	still sore from their **circumcision,** two of Jacob's sons,
Ex	4.25	Because of the rite of **circumcision** she said to Moses, "You
	12.44	that you have bought may eat it if you **circumcise** him first.
	12.48	celebrate this festival, [48] but no **uncircumcised** man may eat it.
	12.48	Lord, you must first **circumcise** all the males of his household.
Lev	12. 3	On the eighth day, the child shall be **circumcised.**
Josh	5. 2	"Make some knives out of flint and **circumcise** the Israelites."
	5. 3	circumcised the Israelites at a place called **Circumcision Hill.**
	5. 4	Israel left Egypt, all the males were already **circumcised.**
	5. 4	the desert, none of the baby boys had been **circumcised.**
	5. 7	these men had never been **circumcised,**
	5. 7	and it was this new generation that Joshua **circumcised.**
	5. 8	After the **circumcision** was completed, the whole nation
Jer	9.25	All these people are **circumcised,** but have not kept the
Ezek	32.24	and they went down, **uncircumcised,** to the world of the dead.
	32.25	They are all **uncircumcised,** all killed in battle.
	32.26	They are all **uncircumcised,** all killed in battle.
	32.28	Egyptians will lie crushed among the **uncircumcised**
	32.29	the dead with the **uncircumcised** who were killed in battle.
	32.30	those killed in battle and are laid to rest, **uncircumcised.**
	32.32	laid to rest with all the **uncircumcised** who die in battle."
	44. 7	profaned my Temple by letting **uncircumcised** foreigners,
	44. 9	no **uncircumcised** foreigner, no one who disobeys me,
Lk	1.59	they came to **circumcise** him, and they were going to
	2.21	for the baby to be **circumcised,** he was named Jesus,
Jn	7.22	ordered you to **circumcise** your sons (although it was not Moses
	7.22	who started it), and so you **circumcise** a boy on the Sabbath.
	7.23	If a boy is **circumcised** on the Sabbath so that Moses'
Acts	7. 8	Abraham the ceremony of **circumcision** as a sign of the covenant.

Acts 7. 8 So Abraham **circumcised** Isaac a week after he was born;
7. 8 Isaac **circumcised** his son Jacob,
7. 8 and Jacob **circumcised** his twelve sons, the famous ancestors
11. 2 who were in favour of **circumcising** Gentiles criticized him,
11. 3 guest in the home of **uncircumcised** Gentiles, and you even ate
15. 1 unless you are **circumcised** as the Law of Moses requires."
15. 5 "The Gentiles must be **circumcised** and told to obey the Law
16. 3 wanted to take Timothy along with him, so he **circumcised** him.
21.21 telling them not to **circumcise** their children or follow the
Rom 2.25 If you obey the Law, your **circumcision** is of value;
2.25 disobey the Law, you might as well never have been **circumcised.**
2.26 Gentile, who is not **circumcised,** obeys the commands of the Law,
2.26 will God not regard him as though he were **circumcised?**
2.27 Law, even though you have it written down and are **circumcised;**
2.27 they obey the Law, even though they are not physically **circumcised.**
2.28 After all, who is a real Jew, truly **circumcised?**
2.28 a Jew on the outside, whose **circumcision** is a physical thing.
2.29 whose heart has been **circumcised,** and this is the work of
3. 1 Or is there any value in being **circumcised?**
4. 9 belong only to those who are **circumcised?**
4. 9 It belongs also to those who are not **circumcised.**
4.10 Was it before or after Abraham was **circumcised?**
4.11 He was **circumcised** later, and his circumcision was a sign
4.11 God had accepted him as righteous before he had been **circumcised.**
4.11 accepted as righteous by him, even though they are not **circumcised.**
4.12 father of those who are **circumcised,** that is, of those who,
4.12 in addition to being **circumcised,** also live the same life
4.12 of faith that our father Abraham lived before he was **circumcised.**
1 Cor 7.18 If a **circumcised** man has accepted God's call,
7.18 he should not try to remove the marks of **circumcision;**
7.18 if an **uncircumcised** man has accepted God's call,
7.18 he should not get **circumcised.**
7.19 For whether or not a man is **circumcised** means nothing;
Gal 2. 3 was not forced to be **circumcised,** [4] although some wanted it done.
2.12 was afraid of those who were in favour of **circumcising** them.
5. 2 allow yourselves to be **circumcised,** it means that Christ is of
5. 3 who allows himself to be **circumcised** that he is obliged to
5. 6 union with Christ Jesus, neither **circumcision** nor the lack of it
5.11 I continue to preach that **circumcision** is necessary,
6.12 to force you to be **circumcised** are the ones who want to
6.13 Even those who practise **circumcision** do not obey the Law;
6.13 they want you to be **circumcised** so that they can boast that
6.15 It does not matter at all whether or not one is **circumcised;**
Eph 2.11 Gentiles by birth—called "the **uncircumcised"** by the Jews,
2.11 Jews, who call themselves "the **circumcised"**
Phil 3. 3 have received the true **circumcision,** for we worship God by means
3. 5 I was **circumcised** when I was a week old.
Col 2.11 union with Christ you were **circumcised,**
2.11 not with the **circumcision** that is made by men,
2.11 but with the **circumcision** made by Christ, which consists of
3.11 between Gentiles and Jews, **circumcised** and uncircumcised,

CISTERN

Lev 11.36 but a spring or a **cistern** remains clean, although
2 Chr 26.10 open country and dug many **cisterns,** because he had large
Neh 9.25 **cisterns** already dug, olive-trees, fruit-trees, and vineyards.
Is 30.14 pick up hot coals with, or to scoop water from a **cistern."**
Jer 2.13 they have dug cisterns, cracked **cisterns** that can hold no water
14. 3 they go to the **cisterns,** but find no water;

CITIES OF REFUGE see CITY, REFUGE

CITIZEN

[FELLOW-CITIZEN]

Gen 34.24 All the **citizens** of the city agreed with what Hamor and
50.11 When the **citizens** of Canaan saw those people mourning at Atad,
Judg 20.15 Besides these, the **citizens** of Gibeah gathered seven hundred
1 Sam 23.11 Will the **citizens** of Keilah hand me over to Saul?
23.12 "And will the **citizens** of Keilah hand my men and me
1 Kgs 21. 8 sent them to the officials and leading **citizens** of Jezreel.
21.11 leading **citizens** of Jezreel did what Jezebel had commanded.
2 Kgs 10. 1 the city, to the leading **citizens,** and to the guardians of
10. 5 city, together with the leading **citizens** and the guardians,
10. 6 the care of the leading **citizens** of Samaria, who were
2 Chr 19. 8 and some of the leading **citizens** as judges in cases
19.10 Whenever your **fellow-citizens** from any of the cities bring
19.10 you and your **fellow-citizens** will feel the force of the
23.20 The army officers, the leading **citizens,** the officials,
Neh 11. 3 the list of the leading **citizens** of the province of Judah
Ps 87. 6 the peoples and include them all as **citizens** of Jerusalem.
Prov 31.23 Her husband is well known, one of the leading **citizens.**
Is 48. 2 to say that you are **citizens** of the holy city and that
Ezek 13. 9 will not be included in the list of the **citizens** of Israel;
47.22 be treated like full Israelite **citizens** and are to draw lots
Mt 17.25 The **citizens** of the country or the foreigners?"
17.26 replied Jesus, "that means that the **citizens** don't have to pay.
Mk 6.21 the military commanders, and the leading **citizens** of Galilee.
Lk 15.15 work for one of the **citizens** of that country, who sent him
Acts 16.21 we are Roman **citizens,** and we cannot accept these customs
16.37 yet they whipped us in public—and we are Roman **citizens!**
16.38 heard that Paul and Silas were Roman **citizens,** they were afraid.
17.21 (For all the **citizens** of Athens and the foreigners who lived
19.39 it will have to be settled in a legal meeting of **citizens.**
21.39 Jew, born in Tarsus in Cilicia, a **citizen** of an important city.
Acts 22.25 you to whip a Roman **citizen** who hasn't even been tried for
22.26 That man is a Roman **citizen!"**
22.27 to Paul and asked him, "Tell me, are you a Roman **citizen?"**
22.29 that Paul was a Roman **citizen** and that he had put him
23.27 that he was a Roman **citizen,** so I went with my soldiers
Eph 2.19 you are now **fellow-citizens** with God's people and members of
Phil 3.20 We, however, are **citizens** of heaven, and we eagerly wait for
Heb 8.11 to teach his **fellow-citizen** or say to his fellow-countryman,

CITY

[CITIES OF REFUGE, DAVID'S CITY, HOLY CITY]
see also **CITY OF THE SUN**

Gen 4.17 Then Cain built a **city** and named it after his son.
10.11 to Assyria and built the **cities** of Nineveh, Rehoboth Ir,
11. 4 said, "Now let's build a **city** with a tower that reaches the
11. 5 came down to see the **city** and the tower which those men
11. 8 them all over the earth, and they stopped building the **city.**
11. 9 The **city** was called Babylon, because there the Lord mixed
11.28 Haran died in his native **city,** Ur in Babylonia, while his
13.10 the Lord had destroyed the **cities** of Sodom and Gomorrah.)
13.12 and Lot settled among the **cities** in the valley and camped
18.24 people in the **city,** will you destroy the whole city?
18.26 in Sodom, I will spare the whole **city** for their sake."
18.28 Will you destroy the whole **city** because there are five too few?"
18.28 "I will not destroy the **city** if I find forty-five innocent people."
18.31 He said, "I will not destroy the **city** if I find twenty."
19. 1 to Sodom that evening, Lot was sitting at the **city gate.**
19. 2 "No, we will spend the night here in the **city** square."
19. 4 All the men of the **city,** both young and old, were there.
19.12 other relatives living in the **city**—get them out of here,
19.15 you will not lose your lives when the **city** is destroyed."
19.16 two daughters by the hand and led them out of the **city.**
19.24 rained burning sulphur on the **cities** of Sodom and Gomorrah
19.29 But when God destroyed the **cities** of the valley where
23.10 the other Hittites at the meeting-place at the **city gate;**
24.10 camels and went to the **city** where Nahor had lived in
24.11 he made the camels kneel down at the well outside the **city.**
24.13 the young women of the **city** will be coming to get water.
24.60 May your descendants conquer the **cities** of their enemies!"
33.18 Canaan and set up his camp in a field near the **city.**
34.20 at the **city gate** and spoke to their fellow-townsmen:
34.24 All the citizens of the **city** agreed with what Hamor and
34.25 their swords, went into the **city** without arousing suspicion,
34.28 donkeys, and everything else in the **city** and in the fields.
41.35 them authority to store up corn in the **cities** and guard it.
41.48 all of which Joseph collected and stored in the **cities.**
41.48 In each **city** he stored the food from the fields around it.
44. 4 a short distance from the **city,** Joseph said to the servant
44.13 in sorrow, loaded their donkeys, and returned to the **city.**
Ex 1.11 The Israelites built the **cities** of Pithom and Rameses to
9.29 I go out of the **city,** I will lift up my hands
9.33 king, went out of the **city,** and lifted up his hands in
Lev 14.40 removed and thrown into some unclean place outside the **city.**
14.41 and the plaster dumped in an unclean place outside the **city.**
14.45 plaster must be carried out of the **city** to an unclean place.
14.53 live bird fly away outside the **city** over the open fields.
25.29 a house in a walled **city,** he has the right to buy
25.32 at any time their property in the **cities** assigned to them.
25.33 house in one of these **cities** is sold by a Levite and
25.33 the Levites own in their **cities** are their permanent property
25.34 But the pasture land round the Levite **cities** shall never be sold;
26.25 if you gather in your **cities** for safety, I will send
26.31 disgust [31] I will turn your **cities** into ruins, destroy your
26.33 Your land will be deserted, and your **cities** left in ruins.
Num 13.19 the people live in open towns or in fortified **cities.**
13.28 and their **cities** are very large and well fortified.
21. 2 them and their **cities** to you and will destroy them."
21. 3 Israelites completely destroyed them and their **cities,**
21.25 Israel captured all the Amorite **cities,** including Heshbon
21.26 Heshbon was the capital **city** of the Amorite king Sihon,
21.27 "Come to Heshbon, to King Sihon's **city!**
22.36 meet him at Ar, a **city** on the River Arnon at the
31.10 all their wealth, [10] and burnt all their **cities** and camps.
35. 2 must give the Levites some **cities** to live in
35. 2 and pasture land round the **cities.**
35. 3 These **cities** will belong to the Levites, and they will live there.
35. 4 outwards from the **city walls** 450 metres in each direction,
35. 5 900 metres on each side, with the **city** in the middle.
35. 6 give the Levites six **cities of refuge** to which a man can
35. 6 give them forty-two other **cities** [7] with their pasture land,
35. 8 The number of Levite **cities** in each tribe is to be
35.11 you are to choose **cities of refuge** to which a man can
35.13 Choose six **cities,** [14] three east of the Jordan and
35.15 These will serve as **cities of refuge** for Israelites and
35.25 return him to the **city of refuge** to which he had escaped.
35.26 of manslaughter leaves the **city of refuge** to which he has
35.28 must remain in the **city of refuge** until the death of the
35.32 has fled to a **city of refuge,** do not allow him to
Deut 1.22 the best route to take and what kind of **cities** are there.'
1.28 and that they live in **cities** with walls that reach the sky.
2.36 of the Arnon, and the **city** in the middle of that valley,
3.10 **cities** on the plateau, the regions of Gilead and of Bashan,
4.41 Then Moses set aside three **cities** east of the River
4.42 escape to one of these **cities** and not be put to death.
6.10 with large and prosperous **cities** which you did not build.
9. 1 Their **cities** are large, with walls that reach the sky.
19. 1 you have taken their **cities** and houses and settled there,
19. 2 three parts, each with a **city** that can be easily reached.
19. 4 enemy, he may escape to any of these **cities** and be safe.
19. 5 he can run to one of those three **cities** and be safe.

Deut 19. 6 If there were only one **city**, the distance to it might be
19. 7 This is why I order you to set aside three **cities.**
19. 9 he has promised, [9]then you are to select three more **cities.**
19.11 and then escapes to one of those **cities** for protection.
20.10 you go to attack a **city**, first give its people a chance
20.12 if the people of that **city** will not surrender, but choose to
20.13 your God lets you capture the **city,** kill every man in it.
20.14 children, the livestock, and everything else in the **city.**
20.15 are to deal with those **cities** that are far away from the
20.16 "But when you capture **cities** in the land that the Lord
20.19 trying to capture a **city,** do not cut down its fruit-trees,
20.20 use them in the siege mounds until the **city** is captured.
21.21 Then the men of the **city** are to stone him to death,
22.21 where the men of her **city** are to stone her to death.
29.23 land will be like the **cities** of Sodom and Gomorrah, of Admah
34. 3 that reaches from Zoar to Jericho, the **city** of palm-trees.
Josh 2. 1 When they came to the **city,** they went to spend the night
2. 4 They left at sunset before the **city gate** was closed.
2. 7 The king's men left the **city,** and then the gate was shut.
2.15 a house built into the **city wall,** so she let the men
3.16 piled up, far upstream at Adam, the **city** beside Zarethan.
6. 1 No one could enter or leave the **city.**
6. 3 are to march round the **city** once a day for six days.
6. 4 are to march round the **city** seven times while the priests
6. 5 are to give a loud shout, and the **city walls** will collapse.
6. 5 Then the whole army will go straight into the **city."**
6. 7 to start marching round the **city,** with an advance guard
6.11 of men to take the Lord's Covenant Box round the **city** once.
6.12 and soldiers marched round the **city** in the same order as the
6.14 again marched round the **city** once and then returned to camp.
6.15 marched seven times round the **city** in the same way—this was
6.16 to shout, and he said, "The Lord has given you the **city!**
6.17 The **city** and everything in it must be totally destroyed
6.20 went straight up the hill into the **city** and captured it.
6.21 they killed everyone in the **city,** men and women, young and
6.24 they set fire to the **city** and burnt it to the ground,
7. 2 from Jericho to Ai, a **city** east of Bethel, near Bethaven,
7. 3 it is not a large **city."**
7. 5 Ai chased them from the **city gate** as far as some quarries
8. 1 his people, **city,** and land will be yours.
8. 2 Prepare to attack the **city** by surprise from the rear."
8. 4 the other side of the **city,** but not too far away from
8. 5 My men and I will approach the **city.**
8. 6 will pursue us until we have led them away from the **city.**
8. 7 Then you will come out of hiding and capture the **city.**
8. 8 After you have taken the **city,** set it on fire, just as
8.11 the main entrance to the **city** and set up camp on the
8.12 put them in hiding west of the **city,** between Ai and Bethel.
8.13 main camp north of the **city** and the rest of the men
8.16 All the men in the **city** had been called together
8.16 Joshua, they kept getting farther away from the **city.**
8.17 after the Israelites, and the **city** was left wide open, with
8.19 hiding got up quickly, ran into the **city** and captured it.
8.19 They immediately set the **city** on fire.
8.21 the others had taken the **city** and that it was on fire,
8.22 The Israelites in the **city** now came down to join the battle.
8.27 and goods captured in the **city,** as the Lord had told Joshua.
8.29 and it was thrown down at the entrance to the **city gate.**
9.17 days later arrived at the **cities** where these people lived:
10. 2 was as large as any of the **cities** that had a king;
10.19 don't let them get to their **cities!**
10.20 to find safety inside their **city walls** and were not killed.
10.28 He put everyone in the **city** to death;
10.30 Lord also gave the Israelites victory over this **city** and its king.
10.32 Libnah, they spared no one, but killed every person in the **city.**
10.37 and everyone else in the **city** as well as in the nearby
10.37 Joshua condemned the **city** to total destruction, just as he
11.11 no one was left alive, and the **city** was burnt.
11.12 Joshua captured all these **cities** and their kings,
11.13 not burn any of the **cities** built on mounds, except Hazor,
11.14 livestock from these **cities** and kept them for themselves.
11.19 The only **city** that made peace with the people of Israel
11.21 Joshua completely destroyed them and their **cities.**
12. 2 of the Arnon) and the **city** in the middle of that valley,
12. 9 The people of Israel defeated the kings of the following **cities:**
13. 9 the Arnon Valley) and the **city** in the middle of that valley
13.10 Ammon and included all the **cities** that had been ruled by the
13.16 the Arnon Valley) and the **city** in the middle of that valley
13.17 It included Heshbon and all the **cities** on the plateau:
13.21 It included all the **cities** of the plateau and the whole
13.23 These were the **cities** and towns given to the families of the
13.25 included Jazer and all the **cities** of Gilead, half the land
13.28 These were the **cities** and towns given to the families of
13.31 Ashtaroth and Edrei, the capital **cities** of Og's kingdom in Bashan.
14. 3 Instead, they received **cities** to live in, with fields for
14.12 giants called the Anakim were there in large walled **cities.**
15. 9 Springs of Nephtoah and out to the **cities** near Mount Ephron.
15.13 He received Hebron, the **city** belonging to Arba, father of Anak.
15.14 of Anak out of the **city**—the clans of Sheshai, Ahiman, and
15.15 (This **city** used to be called Kiriath Sepher.)
15.17 Caleb's brother Kenaz, captured the **city,** so Caleb gave him
15.21 The **cities** farthest south that belonged to them, those
15.32 twenty-nine **cities** in all, along with the towns round them.
15.33 The **cities** in the foothills were Eshtaol, Zorah, Ashnah,
15.36 fourteen **cities,** along with the towns round them.
15.41 sixteen **cities,** along with the towns round them.
15.44 nine **cities,** along with the towns round them.
15.46 and villages, [46]and all the **cities** and towns near Ashdod,
15.51 eleven **cities,** along with the towns round them.
15.54 nine **cities,** along with the towns round them.
15.57 ten **cities,** along with the towns round them.
Josh 15.59 six **cities,** along with the towns round them.
15.60 two **cities,** along with the towns round them.
15.62 Beth Arabah, Middin, Secacah, [62]Nibshan, the **city** of Salt,
15.62 six **cities,** along with the towns round them.
17. 9 The **cities** south of the stream belonged to Ephraim, even
17.12 the people living in those **cities,** so the Canaanites
18.21 The **cities** belonging to the families of the tribe of
18.24 twelve **cities,** along with the towns round them.
18.28 fourteen **cities,** along with the towns round them.
19. 6 thirteen **cities,** along with the towns round them.
19. 7 four **cities,** along with the towns round them.
19. 8 all the towns round these **cities** as far as Baalath Beer (or
19.15 twelve **cities,** along with the towns round them.
19.16 These **cities** and their towns were in the land which the
19.22 It included sixteen **cities** along with the towns round them.
19.23 These **cities** and their towns were in the land which the
19.30 twenty-two **cities,** along with the towns round them.
19.31 These **cities** and their towns were in the land which the
19.35 The fortified **cities** were Ziddim, Zer, Hammath, Rakkath,
19.38 nineteen **cities,** along with the towns round them.
19.39 These **cities** and their towns were in the land which the
19.47 changed the name of the **city** from Laish to Dan, naming it
19.48 These **cities** and their towns were in the land which the
19.50 the Lord had commanded, they gave him the **city** he asked for:
19.50 He rebuilt the **city** and settled there.
20. 2 of Israel, "Choose the **cities of refuge** that I commanded
20. 4 away to one of these **cities,** go to the place of judgement
20. 4 at the entrance to the **city,** and explain to the leaders what
20. 4 will let him into the **city** and give him a place to
20. 5 there, the people of the **city** must not hand him over to
20. 6 He may stay in the **city** until he has received a public
20. 9 These were the **cities of refuge** chosen for all the people
21. 2 we were to be given **cities** to live in, as well as
21. 3 Israel gave the Levites certain **cities** and pasture lands out
21. 4 Levite clan of Kohath were the first to be assigned **cities.**
21. 4 were assigned thirteen **cities** from the territories of Judah,
21. 5 Kohath was assigned ten **cities** from the territories of Ephraim,
21. 6 Gershon was assigned thirteen **cities** from the territories of Issachar,
21. 7 Merari were assigned twelve **cities** from the territories of Reuben,
21. 8 people of Israel assigned these **cities** and their pasture
21. 9 are the names of the **cities** from the territories of Judah
21.12 However, the fields of the **city,** as well as its towns,
21.13 the following **cities** were assigned to the descendants of
21.16 nine **cities** from the tribes of Judah and Simeon.
21.17 From the territory of Benjamin they were given four **cities:**
21.19 Thirteen **cities** in all, with their pasture lands, were
21.20 Kohath were assigned some **cities** from the territory of Ephraim.
21.21 They were given four **cities:**
21.23 From the territory of Dan they were given four **cities:**
21.25 From the territory of West Manasseh they were given two **cities:**
21.26 Kohath received ten **cities** in all, with their pasture lands.
21.27 Gershon, received from the territory of East Manasseh two **cities:**
21.28 From the territory of Issachar they received four **cities:**
21.30 From the territory of Asher they received four **cities:**
21.32 From the territory of Naphtali they received three **cities:**
21.33 Gershon received a total of thirteen **cities** with their pasture lands.
21.34 Merari, received from the territory of Zebulun four **cities:**
21.36 From the territory of Reuben they received four **cities:**
21.38 From the tribe of Gad they received four **cities:**
21.40 So the clan of Merari was assigned a total of twelve **cities.**
21.41 of forty-eight **cities,** with the pasture lands round them,
24.13 you had never cultivated and **cities** that you had not built.
Judg 1. 8 They killed its people and set fire to the **city.**
1.13 younger brother Kenaz, captured the **city,** so Caleb gave him
1.16 of Judah from Jericho, the **city** of palm-trees, into the
1.17 put a curse on the **city,** destroyed it, and named it Hormah.
1.20 drove out of the **city** the three clans descended from Anak.
1.22 They sent spies to the **city,** [24]who saw a man leaving and
1.24 us how to get into the **city,** and we won't hurt you."
1.25 Manasseh killed everyone in the **city,** except this man and his family.
1.26 of the Hittites, built a **city** there, and named it Luz, which
1.27 the people living in the **cities** of Beth Shan, Taanach, Dor,
1.30 the people living in the **cities** of Kitron and Nahalal, and
1.31 the people living in the **cities** of Acco, Sidon, Ahlab,
1.33 people living in the **cities** of Beth Shemesh and Bethanath.
3. 3 land were the five Philistine **cities,** all the Canaanites,
3.13 Israel and captured Jericho, the **city** of palm-trees.
5.11 Then the Lord's people marched down from their **cities.**
8.17 down the tower at Penuel and killed the men of that **city.**
9.30 Zebul, the ruler of the **city,** became angry when he
9.31 Shechem, and they are not going to let you into the **city.**
9.33 morning at sunrise and make a sudden attack on the **city.**
9.35 out and stand at the **city gate,** they got up from their
9.40 Many were wounded, even at the **city gate.**
9.43 people coming out of the **city,** he came out of hiding to
9.44 hurried forward to guard the **city gate,** the other two
9.45 Abimelech captured the **city,** killed its people, tore it
9.51 man and woman in the **city,** including the leaders, ran to it.
10. 4 They had thirty **cities** in the land of Gilead, which are
11.26 round them, and all the **cities** on the banks of the River
11.33 the area round Minnith, twenty **cities** in all, and as far as
14.18 went into the bedroom, the men of the **city** said to him,
16. 2 place and waited for him all night long at the **city gate.**
16. 3 and took hold of the **city gate** and pulled it up—doors,
19.10 we stop and spend the night here in this Jebusite **city?"**
19.12 going to stop in a **city** where the people are not Israelites.
19.15 They went into the **city** and sat down in the square, but
19.17 noticed the traveller in the **city** square and asked him,

Judg 20.14 From all the **cities** of Benjamin they came to Gibeah to
20.15 twenty-six thousand soldiers from their **cities** that day.
20.20 Benjamin, and placed the soldiers in position facing the **city.**
20.21 Benjamin came out of the **city,** and before the day was over
20.31 Benjaminites came out to fight and were led away from the **city.**
20.32 retreat and lead them away from the **city** on to the roads.
20.33 of their hiding places in the rocky country round the **city.**
20.37 they spread out in the **city** and killed everyone there.
20.40 and were amazed to see the whole **city** going up in flames.
20.42 were now coming out of the **city,** and they were destroyed.
1 Sam 5. 8 so they took it to Gath, another Philistine **city.**
5. 9 the Lord punished that **city** too and caused a great panic.
5. 9 in all the people of the **city,** young and old alike.
5.10 So they sent the Covenant Box to Ekron, another Philistine **city;**
5.11 There was panic throughout the **city** because God was
6.17 sins, one each for the **cities** of Ashdod, Gaza, Ashkelon,
6.18 for each of the **cities** ruled by the five Philistine kings,
7.14 All the **cities** which the Philistines had captured
16. 4 went to Bethlehem, where the **city** leaders came trembling to
21.13 would scribble on the **city gates** and dribble down his beard.
22.19 other inhabitants of Nob, the **city** of priests, to be put to
27. 5 need, sir, for me to live with you in the capital **city."**
2 Sam 5. 6 be able to conquer the **city,** and so they said to him,
5. 7 fortress of Zion, and it became known as **"David's City.")**
5. 9 fortress, David lived in it and named it **"David's City."**
5. 9 He built the **city** round it, starting at the place where land
6.16 was being brought into the **city,** Michal, Saul's daughter,
8. 8 bronze from Betah and Berothai, **cities** ruled by Hadadezer.
10. 3 as spies to explore the **city,** so that he can conquer us!"
10. 8 entrance to Rabbah, their capital **city,** while the others,
10.12 fight hard for our people and for the **cities** of our God.
10.14 Syrians running away, they fled from Abishai and retreated into the **city.**
11.16 while Joab was besieging the **city,** he sent Uriah to a place
11.17 The enemy troops came out of the **city** and fought Joab's forces;
11.20 you, 'Why did you go so near the **city** to fight them?
11.23 and came out of the **city** to fight us in the open,
11.23 but we drove them back to the **city gate.**
11.25 to launch a stronger attack on the **city** and capture it."
12.26 campaign against Rabbah, the capital **city** of Ammon, and was
12.28 rest of your forces, attack the **city** and take it yourself.
12.30 amount of loot from the **city** [31] and put its people to work
15. 2 early and go and stand by the road at the **city gate.**
15.14 soon be here and defeat us and kill everyone in the **city!"**
15.17 men were leaving the **city,** they stopped at the last house.
15.24 pick it up again until all the people had left the **city.**
15.25 said to Zadok, "Take the Covenant Box back to the **city.**
15.27 Abiathar's son Jonathan and go back to the **city** in peace.
15.34 me by returning to the **city** and telling Absalom that you
15.37 Hushai, David's friend, returned to the **city**
17.13 If he retreats into a **city,** our people will all bring
17.13 and just pull the **city** into the valley below.
17.17 Jerusalem, because they did not dare to be seen entering the **city.**
17.23 he saddled his donkey and went back to his own **city.**
18. 3 better if you stay here in the **city** and send us help."
18.24 in the space between the inner and outer gates of the **city.**
19. 3 They went back into the **city** quietly, like soldiers who
19. 8 the king got up, and went and sat near the **city gate.**
20.14 the clan of Bikri assembled and followed him into the **city.**
20.15 Sheba was there, and so they went and besieged the **city.**
20.16 a wise woman in the **city** who shouted from the wall,
20.19 Ours is a great **city,** one of the most peaceful and loyal
20.20 "I will never ruin or destroy your **city!**
20.21 Hand over this one man, and I will withdraw from the **city."**
20.22 to the people of the **city** with her plan, and they cut
20.22 for his men to leave the **city,** and they went back home.
24. 5 camped south of Aroer, the **city** in the middle of the valley,
24. 7 Tyre, on to all the **cities** of the Hivites and the Canaanites,
1 Kgs 1.41 asked, "What's the meaning of all that noise in the **city?"**
1.45 Then they went into the **city,** shouting for joy, and the
2.10 David died and was buried in **David's City.**
2.36 Live in it and don't leave the **city.**
3. 1 brought her to live in **David's City** until he had finished
4. 9 **cities** of Makaz, Shaalbim, Beth Shemesh, Elon, and Beth Hanan
4.10 the **cities** of Arubboth and Socoh and all the territory of
4.12 **cities** of Taanach, Megiddo, and all the region near Beth Shan,
8. 1 take the Lord's Covenant Box from Zion, **David's City,** to the
8.16 I have not chosen any **city** in all the land of Israel
8.44 wherever they are, facing this **city** which you have chosen
8.48 gave to our ancestors, this **city** which you have chosen, and
9.15 the east side of the city, and to build the **city wall.**
9.15 also used it to rebuild the **cities** of Hazor, Megiddo, and
9.16 it, killing its inhabitants and setting fire to the **city.**
9.19 the **cities** where his supplies were kept,
9.19 the **cities** for his horses and chariots,
9.24 the east side of the **city,** after his wife, the daughter of
9.24 of Egypt, had moved from **David's City** to the palace Solomon
10.26 Jerusalem and the rest he stationed in various other **cities.**
11.13 for the sake of Jerusalem, the **city** I have made my own."
11.27 on the east side of Jerusalem and repairing the **city walls.**
11.32 the sake of Jerusalem, the **city** I have chosen to be my
11.36 David ruling in Jerusalem, the **city** I have chosen as the
11.43 died and was buried in **David's City,** and his son Rehoboam
14.11 family who die in the **city** will be eaten by dogs, and
14.21 seventeen years in Jerusalem, the **city** which the Lord had
14.31 in the royal tombs in **David's City,** and his son Abijah
15. 8 died and was buried in **David's City,** and his son Asa
15.20 officers and their armies to attack the **cities** of Israel.
15.22 Asa fortified Mizpah and Geba, a **city** in the territory of Benjamin.
15.24 in the royal tombs in **David's City,** and his son Jehoshaphat
1 Kgs 16. 4 family who die in the **city** will be eaten by dogs, and
16.18 When Zimri saw that the **city** had fallen, he went into
19.15 near Damascus, then enter the **city** and anoint Hazael as king
20. 2 He sent messengers into the **city** to King Ahab of Israel to
20.10 enough men to destroy this **city** of yours and carry off the
20.12 get ready to attack the **city,** so they moved into position.
20.30 city of Aphek, where the **city walls** fell on twenty-seven
20.30 Benhadad also escaped into the **city** and took refuge in the
21.10 Then take him out of the **city** and stone him to death."
21.13 and so he was taken outside the **city** and stoned to death.
21.24 relatives who die in the **city** will be eaten by dogs, and
22.26 him to Amon, the governor of the **city,** and to Prince Joash.
22.36 "Every man go back to his own country and **city!"**
22.39 with ivory and all the **cities** he built, is recorded in The
22.50 in the royal tombs in **David's City,** and his son Jehoram
2 Kgs 2.19 sir, this is a fine **city,** but the water is bad and
3.19 You will conquer all their beautiful fortified **cities;**
3.25 slaughtering the Moabites [25] and destroying their **cities.**
3.27 and offered him on the **city wall** as a sacrifice to the
3.27 drew back from the **city** and returned to their own country.
6.20 they had entered the **city,** Elisha prayed, "Open their eyes,
6.25 the food shortage in the **city** was so severe that a donkey's
6.26 was walking by on the **city wall** when a woman cried out,
7. 4 no use going into the **city,** because we would starve to death
7.12 that we will leave the **city** to find food,
7.12 and then they will take us alive and capture the **city."**
7.13 "The people here in the **city** are doomed anyway, like those
7.17 of Israel had put the **city gate** under the command of the
7.20 he died, trampled to death by the people at the **city gate.**
8.24 in the royal tombs in **David's City,** and his son Ahaziah
9.28 chariot and buried him in the royal tombs in **David's City.**
10. 1 to the rulers of the **city,** to the leading citizens, and to
10. 2 disposal chariots, horses, weapons, and fortified **cities.**
10. 5 in charge of the **city,** together with the leading citizens
10. 8 in two heaps at the **city gate** and to be left there
11.20 filled with happiness, and the **city** was quiet, now that
12.20 in the royal tombs in **David's City,** and his son Amaziah
13.25 three times and recaptured the **cities** that had been taken by
14.13 Jerusalem, and tore down the **city wall** from Ephraim Gate to
14.20 a horse and was buried in the royal tombs in **David's City.**
15. 7 the royal burial ground in **David's City,** and his son Jotham
15.16 territory, because the **city** did not surrender to him.
15.29 of Assyria, captured the **cities** of Ijon, Abel Beth Maacah,
15.38 in the royal tombs in **David's City,** and his son Ahaz
16.20 in the royal tombs in **David's City,** and his son Hezekiah
17. 6 in the district of Gozan, and some in the **cities** of Media.
17. 9 their towns, from the smallest village to the largest **city.**
17.24 Assyria took people from the **cities** of Babylon, Cuth, Ivvah,
17.24 and settled them in the **cities** of Samaria, in place of the
17.24 They took possession of these **cities** and lived there.
17.26 he had settled in the **cities** of Samaria did not know the
17.29 Each different group made idols in the **cities** they were living in:
18. 8 largest **city,** including Gaza and its surrounding territory.
18.11 in the district of Gozan, and some in the **cities** of Media.
18.13 Assyria, attacked the fortified **cities** of Judah and conquered them.
18.30 he will stop our Assyrian army from capturing your **city.**
18.31 Assyria commands you to come out of the **city** and surrender.
19.12 My ancestors destroyed the **cities** of Gozan, Haran, and
19.13 are the kings of the **cities** of Hamath, Arpad, Sepharvaim,
19.25 you the power to turn fortified **cities** into piles of rubble.
19.32 'He will not enter this **city** or shoot a single arrow against
19.32 shields will come near the **city,** and no siege-mounds will be
19.33 back by the same road he came, without entering this **city.**
19.34 I will defend this **city** and protect it, for the sake of
20. 6 I will defend this **city,** for the sake of my own honour
20.20 to bring water into the **city,** are all recorded in The
23. 4 objects outside the **city** near the valley of the Kidron,
23. 5 the pagan altars in the **cities** of Judah and in places near
23. 6 took it out of the **city** to the valley of the Kidron,
23. 8 priests who were in the **cities** of Judah, and throughout the
23. 8 gate built by Joshua, the **city** governor, which was
23. 8 to the left of the main gate as one enters the **city.**
23.19 In every **city** of Israel King Josiah tore down all the
23.27 I will reject Jerusalem, the **city** I chose, and the Temple,
25. 1 set up camp outside the **city,** built siege walls round it,
25. 4 nothing left to eat, [4] the **city walls** were broken through.
25. 4 the Babylonians were surrounding the **city,**
25.10 in Jerusalem, [10] and his soldiers tore down the **city walls.**
25.11 who were left in the **city,** the remaining skilled workmen,
25.19 From the **city** he took the officer who had been in
25.19 who were still in the **city,** the commander's assistant, who
1 Chr 2.22 Jair ruled twenty-three **cities** in the territory of Gilead.
2.53 (The people of the **cities** of Zorah and Eshtaol were members
4.39 eastern side of the valley in which that **city** is located.
6.56 however, that belonged to the **city** were assigned to Caleb
6.57 Hebron, a **city of refuge,** Jattir, and the towns of Libnah,
6.67 Shechem, the **city of refuge** in the hills of Ephraim,
7.28 It also included the **cities** of Shechem and Ayyah, and the
7.29 descendants of Manasseh controlled the **cities** of Beth Shan,
8.12 was Shemed who built the **cities** of Ono and Lod and the
9. 2 to their property in the **cities** included Israelite laymen,
11. 5 would never get inside the **city,** but David captured their fortress
11. 5 fortress of Zion, and it became known as **"David's City."**
11. 7 live in the fortress, it came to be called **"David's City."**
11. 8 He rebuilt the **city,** starting at the place where land was
11. 8 side of the hill, and Joab restored the rest of the **city.**
15. 1 For his own use, David built houses in **David's City.**
15.29 was being brought into the **city,** Michal, Saul's daughter,
18. 8 of bronze from Tibhath and Kun, **cities** ruled by Hadadezer.
19. 7 too came out from all their **cities** and got ready to fight.

1 Chr 19. 9 entrance to Rabbah, their capital **city,** and the kings who
19.13 fight hard for our people and for the **cities** of our God.
19.15 Syrians running away, they fled from Abishai and retreated into the **city.**
20. 2 He also took a large amount of loot from the **city.**
20. 3 took the people of the **city** and put them to work with
2 Chr 1.14 Jerusalem, and the rest he stationed in various other **cities.**
5. 2 take the Lord's Covenant Box from Zion, **David's City,** to the
6. 5 I did not choose any **city** in the land of Israel as
6.34 wherever they are, facing this **city** which you have chosen
6.38 gave to our ancestors, this **city** which you have chosen, and
8. 2 He also rebuilt the **cities** that King Hiram had given him,
8. 4 He rebuilt all the **cities** in Hamath that were centres for
8. 5 Solomon also rebuilt the following **cities:**
8. 5 Lower Beth Horon (fortified **cities** with gates that could be barred),
8. 6 all the **cities** where he stored supplies,
8. 6 and the **cities** where his horses and chariots were
8.11 the king of Egypt, from **David's City** to a house he built
9.25 Jerusalem and the rest he stationed in various other **cities.**
9.31 died and was buried in **David's City,** and his son Rehoboam
11. 5 built for the following **cities** of Judah and Benjamin:
11.23 them throughout Judah and Benjamin in the fortified **cities.**
12. 4 He captured the fortified **cities** of Judah and advanced as
12.13 seventeen years in Jerusalem, the **city** which the Lord had
12.16 in the royal tombs in **David's City** and his son Abijah
13.19 Abijah pursued Jeroboam's army and occupied some of his **cities:**
13.19 Bethel, Jeshanah, and Ephron, and the villages near each of these **cities.**
14. 1 Abijah died and was buried in the royal tombs in **David's City.**
14. 5 the incense-altars from all the **cities** of Judah, the kingdom
14. 6 He built fortifications for the **cities** of Judah during this time,
14. 7 Judah, "Let us fortify the **cities** by building walls and towers,
14.14 were able to destroy the **cities** in the area around Gerar,
14.14 The army plundered all those **cities** and captured large amounts of loot.
15. 6 one city oppressed another **city,** because God was bringing trouble
15. 8 all the idols in the **cities** he had captured in the
16. 4 officers and their armies to attack the **cities** of Israel.
16. 4 Beth Maacah, and all the **cities** of Naphtali where supplies were stored.
16. 6 they used them to fortify the **cities** of Geba and Mizpah.
16.14 tomb which he had carved out for himself in **David's City.**
17. 2 the fortified **cities** of Judah, in the Judaean countryside,
17. 2 and in the **cities** which Asa had captured
17. 7 out the following officials to teach in the **cities** of Judah:
17.12 Judah he built fortifications and **cities,** [13]where supplies
17.19 other soldiers in the other fortified **cities** of Judah.
18.25 him to Amon, the governor of the **city,** and to Prince Joash.
19. 5 each of the fortified **cities** of Judah [6]and instructed them:
19. 8 Law of the Lord or legal disputes between inhabitants of the **city.**
19.10 fellow-citizens from any of the **cities** bring before you a
20. 4 From every **city** of Judah people hurried to Jerusalem to
20.28 When they reached the **city,** they marched to the Temple,
21. 1 in the royal tombs in **David's City** and his son Jehoram
21. 3 each one in charge of one of the fortified **cities** of Judah.
21.20 They buried him in **David's City,** but not in the royal tombs.
23. 2 They travelled to all the **cities** of Judah and brought back
23.21 filled with happiness, and the **city** was quiet, now that
24. 5 Levites to go to the **cities** of Judah and collect from all
24.16 in the royal tombs in **David's City** in recognition of the
24.25 He was buried in **David's City,** but not in the royal tombs.
25.13 attacked the Judaean **cities** between Samaria and Beth Horon,
25.23 There he tore down the **city wall** from Ephraim Gate to the
25.28 and he was buried in the royal tombs in **David's City.**
26. 2 Amaziah that Uzziah recaptured Elath and rebuilt the **city.)**
26. 6 down the walls of the **cities** of Gath, Jamnia, and Ashdod,
26. 6 and built fortified **cities** near Ashdod and in the rest
26.15 large stones from the towers and corners of the **city wall.**
27. 3 did extensive work on the **city wall** in the area of Jerusalem
27. 4 mountains of Judah he built **cities,** and in the forests he
27. 9 died and was buried in **David's City** and his son Ahaz
28. 9 was about to enter the **city,** and he said, "The Lord God
28.15 to Judaean territory at Jericho, the **city** of palm-trees.
28.18 They captured the **cities** of Beth Shemesh, Aijalon, and Gederoth,
28.18 and the **cities** of Soco, Timnah, and Gimzo
28.25 In every **city** and town in Judah, he built pagan places
29.16 took it all outside the **city** to the valley of the Kidron.
29.20 the leading men of the **city,** and together they went to the
30.10 The messengers went to every **city** in the territory of
31. 1 of Israel went to every **city** in Judah and broke the stone
31. 6 people who lived in the **cities** of Judah brought tithes of
31.15 In the other **cities** where priests lived, he was
31.19 who lived in the **cities** assigned to Aaron's descendants,
31.19 pasture lands belonging to these **cities,** there were responsible men
32. 1 He besieged the fortified **cities** and gave orders for his
32. 3 supply of water outside the **city** in order to prevent the
32. 5 The king strengthened the **city's** defences by repairing the wall,
32. 6 all the men in the **city** under the command of army officers
32. 6 them to assemble in the open square at the **city gate.**
32.18 Jerusalem who were on the **city wall,**
32.18 so that it would be easier to capture the **city.**
32.29 cattle and so much other wealth that he built many **cities.**
33.14 on the east side of **David's City,** from a point in the
33.14 to the Fish Gate and the area of the **city** called Ophel.
33.14 a unit of troops in each of the fortified **cities** of Judah.
33.15 took all these things outside the **city** and threw them away.
34. 6 thing in the **cities** and the devastated areas of Manasseh,
36.19 down the Temple and the **city,** with all its palaces
2 Chr 36.19 its palaces and its wealth, and broke down the **city wall.**
Ezra 2. 1 Babylon and returned to Jerusalem and Judah, each to his own **city.**
3. 7 to be sent to the **cities** of Tyre and Sidon in exchange
4.12 Jerusalem and are rebuilding that evil and rebellious **city.**
4.13 Your Majesty, if this **city** is rebuilt and its walls are completed,
4.15 you will discover that this **city** has always been rebellious
4.15 This is why the **city** was destroyed.
4.16 are convinced that if this **city** is rebuilt and its walls are
4.21 to stop rebuilding the **city** until I give further commands.
4.23 Jerusalem and forced the Jews to stop rebuilding the **city.**
10.14 time, together with the leaders and the judges of his **city.**
Neh 1. 1 of Persia, I, Nehemiah, was in Susa, the capital **city.**
2. 3 help looking sad when the **city** where my ancestors are buried
2. 5 land of Judah, to the **city** where my ancestors are buried,
2. 5 so that I can rebuild the **city."**
2. 8 guards the Temple, for the **city walls,** and for the house I
2.13 night as I left the **city** through the Valley Gate on the
2.13 the broken walls of the **city** and the gates that had been
2.14 the east side of the **city** I went north to the Fountain
2.15 come and went back into the **city** through the Valley Gate.
2.17 Let's rebuild the **city walls** and put an end to our disgrace."
3. 1 This is how the **city wall** was rebuilt.
3.15 garden, as far as the steps leading down from **David's City.**
3.25 near that part of the **city** called Ophel, where the temple
4. 2 Do they intend to rebuild the **city?**
4.22 that we could guard the **city** at night as well as work
7. 4 Jerusalem was a large **city,** but not many people were
7. 6 Babylon and returned to Jerusalem and Judah, each to his own **city.**
7.73 people of Israel—settled in the towns and **cities** of Judah.
8.15 them all through Jerusalem and the other **cities** and towns:
9.25 Your people captured fortified **cities,** fertile land,
11. 1 go and live in the **holy city** of Jerusalem,
11. 1 while the rest were to live in the other **cities** and towns.
11. 3 In the other towns and **cities** the people of Israel, the
11. 9 Judah son of Hassenuah was the second senior official in the **city.**
11.18 In all, 284 Levites lived in the **holy city** of Jerusalem.
11.20 their own property in the other **cities** and towns of Judah.
11.25 Kiriath Arba, Dibon, and Jekabzeel, and in the villages near these **cities.**
11.26 They also lived in the **cities** of Jeshua, Moladah, Bethpelet, [27]and Hazarshual,
12.27 When the **city wall** of Jerusalem was dedicated, the
12.30 for themselves, the people, the gates, and the **city wall.**
12.31 large groups to march round the **city,** giving thanks to God.
12.37 the steps that led to **David's City,** past David's palace, and
12.37 wall at the Water Gate, on the east side of the **city.**
12.44 the farms near the various **cities** the contributions for the
13.16 kinds of goods into the **city** to sell to our people on
13.18 God punished your ancestors when he brought destruction on this **city.**
13.19 I gave orders for the **city gates** to be shut at the
13.19 sure that nothing was brought into the **city** on the Sabbath.
13.20 kinds of goods spent Friday night outside the **city walls.**
Esth 2. 3 young girls to your harem here in Susa, the capital **city.**
4. 1 and walked through the **city,** wailing loudly and bitterly,
4. 6 went to Mordecai in the **city** square at the entrance of the
6. 9 and lead him, mounted on the horse, through the **city** square.
6.11 Haman led him through the **city** square, announcing to the
8.11 Jews in every **city** to organize themselves for self-defence.
8.14 The decree was also made public in Susa, the capital **city.**
8.17 In every **city** and province, wherever the king's proclamation was read,
9. 2 the Jewish quarter of every **city** in the empire the Jews
9. 6 In Susa, the capital **city** itself, the Jews killed five hundred men.
9.15 again and killed three hundred more men in the **city.**
9.28 in every province and every **city** should remember and observe
Job 15.28 is the man who captured **cities** and seized houses whose owners
15.28 had fled, but war will destroy those **cities** and houses.
24.12 In the **cities** the wounded and dying cry out, but God
29. 7 Whenever the **city** elders met and I took my place among them,
39. 7 far away from the noisy **cities,** and no one can tame them
Ps 9. 6 you have destroyed their **cities,** and they are completely forgotten.
46. 4 that brings joy to the **city** of God, to the sacred house
46. 5 God is in that **city,** and it will never be destroyed;
48. 1 be highly praised in the **city** of our God, on his sacred
48. 2 the **city** of the great king brings joy to all the world.
48. 3 there is safety with him inside the fortresses of the **city.**
48. 8 have seen it in the **city** of our God, the Lord Almighty;
48. 8 he will keep the **city** safe for ever.
48.11 let there be joy in the **cities** of Judah!
50. 2 God shines from Zion, the **city** perfect in its beauty.
55. 9 and riots in the **city,** [10]surrounding it day and night,
59. 6 the evening, snarling like dogs as they go about the **city.**
59.14 as they go about the **city,** [15]like dogs roaming about for
60. 9 Who, O God, will take me into the fortified **city?**
72.16 May the **cities** be filled with people, like fields full of grass.
87. 1 The Lord built his **city** on the sacred hill;
87. 3 Listen, **city** of God, to the wonderful things he says about you:
89.40 down the walls of his **city** and left his forts in ruins.
97. 8 Zion are glad, and the **cities** of Judah rejoice because of
101. 8 I will expel all evil men from the **city** of the Lord.
107. 4 and could not find their way to a **city** to live in.
107. 7 them by a straight road to a **city** where they could live.
107.36 people settle there, and they built a **city** to live in.
108.10 Who, O God, will take me into the fortified **city?**
122. 3 Jerusalem is a **city** restored in beautiful order and harmony.
127. 1 Lord does not protect the **city,** it is useless for the
Prov 1.21 calling loudly at the **city gates** and wherever people come together:

Prov 8. 3 At the entrance to the **city,** beside the gates, she calls:
11.10 A **city** is happy when honest people have good fortune,
11.11 A **city** becomes great when righteous men give it their blessing;
11.11 but a **city** is brought to ruin by the words of the
16.32 It is better to win control over yourself than over whole **cities.**
18.11 wealth protects them like high, strong walls round a **city.**
18.19 protect you like a strong **city wall,** but if you quarrel with
21.22 shrewd general can take a **city** defended by strong men, and
25.28 are as helpless as a **city** without walls, open to attack.
29. 8 People with no regard for others can throw whole **cities** into
turmoil.
Ecc 7.19 more for a person than ten rulers can do for a **city.**
8.10 praise them in the very **city** where they did their evil.
Song 3. 2 I went wandering through the **city,** through its streets and alleys.
3. 3 The watchmen patrolling the **city** saw me.
5. 7 The watchmen patrolling the **city** found me;
5. 7 the guards at the **city wall** tore off my cape.
6. 4 the city of Tirzah, as breathtaking as these great **cities.**
7. 4 in the city of Heshbon, near the gate of that great **city.**
Is 1. 7 devastated, and your **cities** have been burnt to the ground.
1. 8 Jerusalem alone is left, a **city** under siege—as defenceless
1.21 The **city** that once was faithful is behaving like a whore!
1.26 Then Jerusalem will be called the righteous, faithful **city."**
3.25 The men of the **city,** yes, even the strongest men, will
3.26 The **city gates** will mourn and cry,
3.26 and the **city** itself will be like a woman
4. 5 God's glory will cover and protect the whole **city.**
4. 6 His glory will shade the **city** from the heat of the day
5.17 In the ruins of the **cities** lambs will eat grass and
6.11 He answered, "Until the **cities** are ruined and empty—until
7. 8 stronger than Damascus, its capital **city,** and Damascus is no
7. 9 stronger than Samaria, its capital **city,** and Samaria is no
10. 9 I conquered the **cities** of Calno and Carchemish,
10. 9 the **cities** of Hamath and Arpad.
11.10 They will gather in his royal **city** and give him honour.
13. 2 the signal for them to attack the gates of the proud **city.**
14.17 this the man who destroyed **cities** and turned the world into
14.21 of them will ever rule the earth or cover it with **cities."**
14.31 Howl and cry for help, all you Philistine **cities!**
15. 1 The **cities** of Ar and Kir are destroyed in a single night,
15. 2 of Moab wail in grief over the **cities** of Nebo and Medeba;
15. 3 the **city** squares and on the house-tops people mourn and cry.
17. 1 The Lord said, "Damascus will not be a **city** any longer;
17. 2 The **cities** of Syria will be deserted for ever.
17. 9 When that day comes, well-defended **cities** will be deserted
17. 9 left in ruins like the **cities** that the Hivites and the
19. 2 Rival **cities** will fight each other, and rival kings will
19.18 the Hebrew language will be spoken in five Egyptian **cities.**
19.18 One of the cities will be called, **"City** of the Sun."
21. 2 Army of Media, lay siege to the **cities!**
22. 1 all the people of the **city** celebrating on the roofs of the
22. 2 The whole **city** is in an uproar, filled with noise and excitement.
22. 5 The walls of our **city** have been battered down, and cries for
22. 9 some of them down to get stones to repair the **city walls.**
22.11 built a reservoir inside the **city** to hold the water flowing
23. 7 Is this the **city** that sent settlers across the sea to
23. 8 this on Tyre, that imperial **city,** whose merchant princes
23.13 the fortifications of Tyre, and left the **city** in ruins.
23.14 The **city** you relied on has been destroyed.
24.10 In the **city** everything is in chaos, and people lock
24.12 The **city** is in ruins, and its gates have been broken down.
25. 2 You have turned **cities** into ruins and destroyed their fortifications.
25. 3 you will be feared in the **cities** of cruel nations.
26. 1 Our **city** is strong!
26. 2 Open the **city gates** and let the faithful nation enter, the
26. 5 he destroyed the strong **city** they lived in, and sent its
27.10 The fortified **city** lies in ruins.
28. 6 and courage to those who defend the **city gates** from attack.
29. 1 The **city** where David camped is doomed!
29. 2 God will bring disaster on the **city** that is called "God's altar."
29. 2 and wailing, and the whole **city** will be like an altar
29. 3 God will attack the **city,** surround it, and besiege it.
29. 7 of the nations attacking the **city** of God's altar, all their
30. 4 already arrived at the Egyptian **cities** of Zoan and Hanes,
32.13 people were happy and for the **city** that was full of life.
32.14 the palace will be abandoned and the capital **city** totally deserted.
32.19 will fall on the forests, and the **city** will be torn down.)
33.20 Look at Zion, the **city** where we celebrate our religious festivals.
36. 1 Assyria, attacked the fortified **cities** of Judah and captured them.
36.15 he will stop our Assyrian army from capturing your **city.**
36.16 Assyria commands you to come out of the **city** and surrender.
37.12 My ancestors destroyed the **cities** of Gozan, Haran, and
37.13 are the kings of the **cities** of Hamath, Arpad, Sepharvaim,
37.26 you the power to turn fortified **cities** into piles of rubble.
37.33 'He will not enter this **city** or shoot a single arrow against
37.33 shields will come near the **city,** and no siege-mounds will be
37.34 by the road on which he came, without entering this **city.**
37.35 I will defend this **city** and protect it, for the sake of
38. 6 of Assyria, and I will continue to protect the **city."**
43.14 I will break down the **city gates,** and the shouts of her
44.26 live there again, and the **cities** of Judah that they will be
44.26 Those **cities** will rise from the ruins.
45. 1 the Lord will open the gates of **cities** for him.
45.13 He will rebuild my **city,** Jerusalem, and set my captive people free.
47. 1 once like a virgin, a **city** unconquered, but you are soft and
48. 2 you are citizens of the **holy city** and that you depend on
52. 1 **Holy city** of God, clothe yourself with splendour!
52. 8 Those who guard the **city** are shouting, shouting together for joy!
52. 9 The Lord will rescue his **city** and comfort his people.
54. 3 **Cities** now deserted will be filled with people.
54.11 "O Jerusalem, you suffering, helpless **city,**
Is 55.12 you will be led out of the **city** in peace.
60.13 Jerusalem, To make my Temple beautiful, To make my **city**
glorious.
60.14 'The City of the Lord,' 'Zion, the **City** of Israel's Holy God.'
60.15 longer be forsaken and hated, A **city** deserted and desolate.
61. 4 They will rebuild **cities** that have long been in ruins.
62. 7 Jerusalem And makes it a **city** the whole world praises.
62.10 Jerusalem, go out of the **city** And build a road for your
62.12 "The City That God Loves," "The **City** That God Did Not Forsake."
64.10 Your sacred **cities** are like a desert;
66. 6 That loud noise in the **city,** that sound in the Temple, is
66. 7 "My **holy city** is like a woman who suddenly gives birth to
66.10 be glad for her, all you that love this **city!**
Jer 1.15 round its walls, and also round the other **cities** of Judah.
1.18 will be like a fortified **city,** an iron pillar, and a bronze
2.28 Judah, you have as many gods as you have **cities.**
4. 5 of Judah and Jerusalem to run to the fortified **cities.**
4. 7 The **cities** of Judah will be left in ruins, and no one
4.16 enemies will shout against the **cities** of Judah [17] and will
4.26 its **cities** were in ruins because of the Lord's fierce anger.
5.17 The fortified **cities** in which you trust will be destroyed by
6. 3 pitch their tents round the **city,** and each one will camp
6. 5 we'll destroy the **city's** fortresses."
6. 6 "I will punish this **city** because it is full of oppression.
6. 7 I hear violence and destruction in the **city;**
6. 8 I will turn your **city** into a desert, a place where no
7.17 they are doing in the **cities** of Judah and in the streets
7.34 In the **cities** of Judah and in the streets of Jerusalem I
8.14 "Come on, we will run to the fortified **cities,** and die
8.16 land and everything in it, our **city** and all its people."
9.11 the **cities** of Judah will become a desert, a place where no
10.22 its army will turn the **cities** of Judah into a desert, a
11. 6 to me, "Go to the **cities** of Judah and to the streets
11.13 many gods as they have **cities,** and the inhabitants of
11.13 that disgusting god Baal as there are streets in the **city.**
14. 2 its **cities** are dying, its people lie on the ground in sorrow,
17.19 Gate, through which the kings of Judah enter and leave the **city;**
17.24 any load in through the gates of this **city** on the Sabbath.
19. 8 such terrible destruction on this **city** that everyone who
19. 9 The enemy will surround the **city** and try to kill its people.
19. 9 that the people inside the **city** will eat one another and
19.11 break this people and this **city,** and it will be like this
19.12 that I will make this **city** and its inhabitants like Topheth.
19.15 going to bring on this **city** and on every nearby town all
20. 5 all the wealth of this **city** and seize all its possessions
20.16 May he be like those **cities** that the Lord destroyed without mercy.
21. 2 King Nebuchadnezzar of Babylonia and his army are besieging
the **city.**
21. 4 pile up your soldiers' weapons in the centre of the **city.**
21. 6 I will kill everyone living in this **city;**
21. 9 Anyone who stays in the **city** will be killed in war or
21. 9 Babylonians, who are now attacking the **city,** will not be killed;
21.10 up my mind not to spare this **city,** but to destroy it.
22. 8 I, the Lord, have done such a thing to this great **city.**
22.22 as prisoners of war, your **city** disgraced and put to shame
23.39 me, both them and the **city** that I gave to them and
25.19 the kings of the Philistine **cities** of Ashkelon, Gaza, Ekron,
25.19 the **cities** of Dedan, Tema, and Buz;
25.29 I will begin my work of destruction in my own **city.**
26. 6 the world will use the name of this **city** as a curse."
26. 9 like Shiloh and that this **city** will be destroyed and no one
26.11 sentenced to death because he has spoken against our **city.**
26.12 you heard me say against this Temple and against this **city.**
26.15 and the people of this **city** will be guilty of killing an
26.20 the Lord against this **city** and nation just as Jeremiah did.
27.17 Why should this **city** become a pile of ruins?
29. 7 for the good of the **cities** where I have made you go
29.16 about the people of this **city,** that is, your relatives who
31.38 will be rebuilt as my **city,** from Hananel Tower west to the
31.40 The **city** will never again be torn down or destroyed."
32. 3 Babylonia capture this **city,** [4] and King Zedekiah will not escape.
32.24 built siege mounds round the **city** to capture it, and they
32.24 War, starvation, and disease will make the **city** fall into their
hands.
32.25 of witnesses, even though the **city** is about to be captured
32.28 am going to give this **city** over to King Nebuchadnezzar of
32.31 The people of this **city** have made me angry and furious
32.36 and disease will make this **city** fall into the hands of the
33. 5 have turned away from this **city** because of the evil things
33. 6 But I will heal this **city** and its people and restore them
33. 9 Jerusalem and about the prosperity that I bring to the **city."**
33.16 The **city** will be called 'The Lord Our Salvation.'
34. 2 the Lord, will hand this **city** over to the king of Babylonia,
34. 7 while the army of the king of Babylonia was attacking the **city.**
34. 7 Lachish and Azekah, the only other fortified **cities** left in Judah.
34.22 I will give the order, and they will return to this **city.**
37. 8 come back, attack the **city,** capture it, and burn it down.
37.10 men would still get up and burn this **city** to the ground."
37.21 from the bakeries until all the bread in the **city** was gone.
38. 2 "Whoever stays on in the **city** will die in war or of
38. 3 am going to give the **city** to the Babylonian army, and they
38. 4 making the soldiers in the **city** lose their courage, and he
38. 4 is doing the same thing to everyone else left in the **city.**
38. 9 of starvation, since there is no more food in the **city."**
38.17 life will be spared, and this **city** will not be burnt down.
38.18 do not surrender, then this **city** will be handed over to the
38.23 of Babylonia, and this **city** will be burnt to the ground."
39. 2 Zedekiah's eleventh year as king, the **city walls** were broken
through.
39. 4 they tried to escape from the **city** during the night.
39. 5 Nebuchadnezzar, who was in the **city** of Riblah in the

Jer 39. 9 who were left in the **city,** together with those who had
39.16 I am going to bring upon this **city** destruction and not prosperity.
41. 7 as they were inside the **city,** Ishmael and his men killed
43. 9 government building here in the **city,** and let some of the
44. 1 living in Egypt, in the **cities** of Migdol, Tahpanhes, and
44. 2 I brought on Jerusalem and all the other **cities** of Judah.
46. 8 I will destroy **cities** and the people who live there.
47. 2 and everything on it, **cities** and the people who live there.
48.15 Moab and its **cities** are destroyed;
48.21 "Judgement has come on the **cities** of the plateau:
48.24 Judgement has come on all the **cities** of Moab, far and near.
48.32 **City** of Sibmah, you are like a vine whose branches reach
48.45 protection in Heshbon, the **city** that King Sihon once ruled,
49.23 "The people in the **cities** of Hamath and Arpad are worried
49.25 The famous **city** that used to be happy is completely deserted.
49.26 killed in the **city** streets, and all her soldiers destroyed.
49.31 Their **city** has no gates or locks and is completely unprotected.'
50.12 but your own great **city** will be humiliated and disgraced.
50.15 Raise the war cry all round the **city!**
50.29 Surround the **city** and don't let anyone escape.
50.30 will be killed in the **city** streets, and all its soldiers
50.32 I will set your **cities** on fire, and everything around will
50.44 and make the Babylonians run away suddenly from their **city.**
51. 4 They will be wounded and die in the streets of their **cities.**
51.30 The **city gates** are broken down, and the houses are on fire.
51.31 king of Babylonia that his **city** has been broken into from
51.34 He emptied the **city** like a jar;
51.41 "The **city** that the whole world praised has been captured!
52. 4 set up camp outside the **city,** built siege walls round it,
52. 7 nothing left to eat, [7] the **city walls** were broken through.
52. 7 the Babylonians were surrounding the **city,** all the soldiers
52.14 and his soldiers tore down the **city walls.**
52.15 who were left in the **city,** the remaining skilled workmen,
52.25 From the **city** he took the officer who had been in
52.25 who were still in the **city,** the commander's assistant, who
Lam 1. 1 The noblest of **cities** has fallen into slavery.
1. 4 The **city gates** stand empty, and Zion is in agony.
1.11 "Look at me, Lord," the **city** cries;
1.19 the leaders died in the **city** streets, Looking for food to
2.11 Children and babies are fainting in the streets of the **city.**
2.15 People passing by the **city** look at you in scorn.
2.15 "Is this that lovely **city?**
3.51 when I see what has happened to the women of the **city.**
5.14 no longer sit at the **city gate,** and the young people no
Ezek 4. 3 and set it up like a wall between you and the **city.**
4. 3 Face the **city.**
4. 7 Shake your fist at the **city** and prophesy against it.
5. 2 a third of it in the **city** when the siege is over.
5. 2 it up with your sword as you move about outside the **city.**
5.12 your people will die from sickness and hunger in the **city;**
5.12 a third will be cut down by swords outside the **city;**
6. 6 All the **cities** of Israel will be destroyed, so that all
7.15 fighting, and anyone in the **city** will be a victim of
7.23 land is full of murders and the **cities** are full of violence.
9. 1 "Come here, you men who are going to punish the **city.**
9. 4 of all the disgusting things being done in the **city."**
9. 5 say to the other men, "Follow him through the **city,** and
9. 7 So they began to kill the people in the **city.**
10. 2 Then scatter the coals over the **city."**
11. 2 these men make evil plans and give bad advice in this **city.**
11. 3 The **city** is like a cooking-pot, and we are like the meat
11. 6 many people here in the **city** that the streets are full of
11. 7 This **city** is indeed a cooking-pot, but what is the meat?
11. 7 will not be here—I will throw you out of the **city!**
11. 9 take you out of the **city** and hand you over to foreigners.
11.11 This **city** will not protect you as a pot protects the
11.23 the dazzling light left the **city** and moved to the mountain
12.20 **Cities** that are now full of people will be destroyed,
13. 4 are as useless as foxes living among the ruins of a **city.**
16.45 You and your sister **cities** had a Hittite mother and an
17. 4 to a land of commerce, and placed in a **city** of merchants.
21.15 I am threatening their **city** with a sword that flashes like
21.20 and the other the way to Judah, to the fortified **city,**
21.27 Yes, I will make the **city** a ruin.
21.27 the one whom I have chosen to punish the **city** has come.
22. 2 "are you ready to judge the **city** that is full of murderers?
22. 3 Tell the **city** what I, the Sovereign Lord, am saying:
22. 7 No one in the **city** honours his parents.
24. 6 "The **city** of murderers is doomed!
24. 7 There was murder in the **city,** but the blood was not spilt
24. 9 "The **city** of murderers is doomed!
25. 9 nations, [9] I will let the **cities** that defend the border of
25. 9 attacked, including even the finest **cities**—
26. 4 They will destroy your **city walls** and tear down your towers.
26.10 walls as they pass through the gates of the ruined **city.**
26.14 The **city** will never be rebuilt.
26.17 The famous **city** is destroyed!
26.17 The people of this **city** ruled the seas And terrified all who
26.19 make you as desolate as ruined **cities** where no one lives.
27. 3 funeral song for Tyre, [3] that **city** which stands at the edge
27. 8 Your oarsmen were from the **cities** of Sidon and Arvad.
27.23 The **cities** of Haran, Canneh, and Eden,
27.23 the merchants of Sheba, the **cities** of Asshur and Chilmad—
28.18 I set fire to the **city** and burnt it to the ground.
29.12 For forty years the **cities** of Egypt will lie in ruins,
29.12 ruins worse than those of any other **city.**
30. 7 in the world, and its **cities** will be left totally in ruins.
30.16 Thebes will be broken down, and the **city** will be flooded.
30.17 The young men of the **cities** of Heliopolis and Bubastis
30.18 Egypt, and the people of all her **cities** will be taken prisoner.
33.21 from Jerusalem came and told me that the **city** had fallen.
Ezek 33.24 are living in the ruined **cities** of the land of Israel are
33.27 God, the people who live in the ruined **cities** will be killed.
33.30 when they meet by the **city walls** or in the doorways of
35. 4 I will leave your **cities** in ruins And your land desolate;
35. 9 for ever, and no one will live in your **cities** again.
36. 4 ruins, and to you deserted **cities** which were plundered and
36.10 You will live in the **cities** and rebuild everything that was
36.33 let you live in your **cities** again and let you rebuild the
36.35 of Eden, and how the **cities** which were torn down, looted,
36.36 I, the Lord, rebuild ruined **cities** and replant waste fields.
36.38 The **cities** that are now in ruins will then be as full
38.12 loot the people who live in **cities** that were once in ruins.
39. 9 people who live in the **cities** of Israel will go out and
40. 2 front of me a group of buildings that looked like a **city.**
45. 6 be set aside for a **city** where any of the people of
47.16 city of Zedad, [16] to the **cities** of Berothah and Sibraim
48.15 The **city** is to be in the centre of it, [16] and it
48.17 All round the **city** on each side there will be an open
48.18 that is left after the **city** has been built in the area
48.18 used as farm land by the people who live in the **city.**
48.19 Anyone who lives in the **city,** no matter which tribe he
48.20 side, and it will include the area occupied by the **city.**
48.21 the Levites' land, and the **city,** the remaining land belongs
48.35 wall on all four sides of the **city** is nine thousand metres.
48.35 The name of the **city** from now on will be, "The-Lord-Is-Here!"
Dan 1. 1 Babylonia attacked Jerusalem and surrounded the **city.**
4.30 built it as my capital **city** to display my power and might,
9.12 more severely than any other **city** on earth, [13] giving us
9.16 It is your **city,** your sacred hill.
9.18 are in and the suffering of the **city** that bears your name.
9.19 This **city** and these people are yours."
9.24 freeing your people and your **holy city** from sin and evil.
9.26 The **city** and the Temple will be destroyed by the invading
11.15 of Syria will lay siege to a fortified **city** and capture it.
Hos 6. 8 Gilead is a **city** full of evil men and murderers.
8.14 The people of Judah have built fortified **cities.**
8.14 fire that will burn down their palaces and their **cities."**
11. 6 War will sweep through their **cities** and break down the city gates.
Joel 2. 9 They rush against the **city;**
3.17 Jerusalem will be a sacred **city;**
Amos 1. 5 I will smash the **city gates** of Damascus and remove the
1. 7 will send fire upon the **city walls** of Gaza and burn down
1. 8 I will remove the rulers of the **cities** of Ashdod and Ashkelon.
1.10 will send fire upon the **city walls** of Tyre and burn down
1.14 will send fire upon the **city walls** of Rabbah and burn down
3. 6 trumpet sound in a **city** without making the people afraid?
3. 6 Does disaster strike a **city** unless the Lord sends it?
4. 6 brought famine to all your **cities,** yet you did not come back
4. 7 I sent rain on one **city,** but not on another.
4. 8 cities went to a **city** where they hoped to find water,
5. 3 The Sovereign Lord says, "A **city** in Israel sends out a
5. 3 another **city** sends out a hundred, but only ten come back."
5.16 "There will be wailing and cries of sorrow in the **city** streets.
6. 8 I will give their capital **city** and everything in it to the
9.14 They will rebuild their ruined **cities** and live there;
Obad 13 should not have entered the **city** of my people to gloat over
Jon 1. 2 "Go to Nineveh, that great **city,** and speak out against it;
3. 2 "Go to Nineveh, that great **city,** and proclaim to the people
3. 3 and went to Nineveh, a **city** so large that it took three
3. 4 Jonah started through the **city,** and after walking a whole day,
4. 5 Jonah went out east of the **city** and sat down.
4.11 more, then, should I have pity on Nineveh, that great **city.**
Mic 1. 5 Samaria, the capital **city** itself!
1. 6 pour the rubble of the **city** down into the valley,
1. 6 and will lay bare the **city's** foundations.
1.11 Those who live in Zaanan dare not come out of their **city.**
2.13 They will break out of the **city gates** and go free.
3.10 You are building God's **city,** Jerusalem, on a foundation
3.11 The **city's** rulers govern for bribes, the priests
4.10 will have to leave the **city** and live in the open country.
4.11 We will see this **city** in ruins!"
5.11 I will destroy the **cities** in your land and tear down all
5.14 of the goddess Asherah in your land and destroy your **cities.**
6. 9 to the city, "Listen, you people who assemble in the **city!**
7.11 People of Jerusalem, the time to rebuild the **city walls** is coming.
Nah 2. 4 the streets, rushing to and fro through the **city** squares.
2. 9 The **city** is full of treasure!
2.11 Where now is the **city** that was like a den of lions,
3. 1 Doomed is the lying, murderous **city,** full of wealth to be
Hab 2. 8 violence against the people of the world and its **cities.**
2.12 You founded a **city** on crime and built it up by murder.
2.17 violence against the people of the world and its **cities.**
Zeph 1.10 the newer part of the **city** and a great crashing sound in
1.11 the lower part of the **city,** because all the merchants will
1.16 of soldiers attacking fortified **cities** and high towers.
2. 4 and the people of Ekron will be driven from their **city.**
2.15 what will happen to the **city** that is so proud of its
2.15 Its people think that their **city** is the greatest in the world.
3. 1 Jerusalem is doomed, that corrupt, rebellious **city**
3. 5 But the Lord is still in the **city;**
3. 6 I have destroyed their **cities** and left their walls and
3. 6 The **cities** are deserted;
Zech 1.12 Jerusalem and the **cities** of Judah for seventy years now.
1.14 concern for Jerusalem, my **holy city,** [15] and I am very angry
1.16 I have come back to Jerusalem to show mercy to the **city.**
1.16 My Temple will be restored, and the **city** will be rebuilt."
1.17 Lord Almighty says that his **cities** will be prosperous again
1.17 once again help Jerusalem and claim the **city** as his own."
2. 5 wall of fire round the **city** to protect it and that he
2.12 land, and Jerusalem will be the **city** he loves most of all.
7. 7 in the towns round the **city** but also in the southern region

Zech 8. 3 I will return to Jerusalem, my **holy city,** and live there.
8. 3 be known as the faithful **city,** and the hill of the Lord
8. 4 a stick when they walk, will be sitting in the **city** squares.
8.20 coming when people from many **cities** will come to Jerusalem.
8.21 Those from one **city** will say to those from another, 'We
9. 2 him, and so do the **cities** of Tyre and Sidon, with all
9. 4 into the sea, and the **city** will be burnt to the ground.
12. 2 when they besiege Jerusalem, the **cities** of the rest of Judah
12. 6 The people of Jerusalem will remain safe in the **city.**
14. 2 The **city** will be taken, the houses looted, and the women raped.
14. 2 the rest of them will not be taken away from the **city.**
14.10 **city** will reach from the Benjamin Gate to the Corner Gate,
Mt 2. 6 are by no means the least of the leading **cities** of Judah;
4. 5 took Jesus to Jerusalem, the **Holy City,** set him on the
5.14 A **city** built on a hill cannot be hidden.
5.35 nor by Jerusalem, for it is the **city** of the great King.
15.21 went off to the territory near the **cities** of Tyre and Sidon.
21. 5 "Tell the **city** of Zion, Look, your king is coming to you!
21.10 Jesus entered Jerusalem, the whole **city** was thrown into an uproar.
21.17 and went out of the **city** to Bethany, where he spent the
21.18 way back to the **city** early next morning, Jesus was hungry.
22. 7 soldiers, who killed those murderers and burnt down their **city.**
26.18 a certain man in the **city,"** he said to them, "and tell
27.53 they went into the **Holy City,** where many people saw them.
28.11 went back to the **city** and told the chief priests everything
Mk 1. 5 province of Judaea and the **city** of Jerusalem went out to
3. 8 Jordan, and from the region round the **cities** of Tyre and Sidon.
7.24 left and went away to the territory near the **city** of Tyre.
11.19 When evening came, Jesus and his disciples left the **city.**
14.13 "Go into the **city,** and a man carrying a jar of water
14.16 disciples left, went to the **city,** and found everything just as
15.21 who was coming into the **city** from the country, and the
Lk 6.17 from Jerusalem and from the coastal **cities** of Tyre and Sidon;
19.17 in small matters, I will put you in charge of ten **cities.'**
19.19 this one he said, 'You will be in charge of five **cities.'**
19.41 He came closer to the **city,** and when he saw it,
21.21 those who are in the **city** must leave, and those
21.21 who are out in the country must not go into the **city.**
22.10 "As you go into the **city,** a man carrying a jar of
22.39 Jesus left the **city** and went, as he usually did, to the
23.19 a riot that had taken place in the **city,** and for murder.)
23.26 named Simon who was coming into the **city** from the country.
24.49 you must wait in the **city** until the power from above comes
24.50 led them out of the **city** as far as Bethany, where he
Jn 7.35 go to the Greek **cities** where our people live, and teach
12.15 as the scripture says, [15]"Do not be afraid, **city** of Zion!
19.20 place where Jesus was crucified was not far from the **city.**
Acts 1.12 Mount of Olives, which is about a kilometre away from the **city.**
1.13 They entered the **city** and went up to the room where they
4.27 Pilate met together in this **city** with the Gentiles and the
7.58 threw him out of the **city,** and stoned him.
8. 5 Philip went to the principal **city** in Samaria and preached
8. 8 So there was great joy in that **city.**
8.10 and everyone in the **city,** from all classes of society, paid
9. 3 Saul was coming near the **city** of Damascus, suddenly a light
9. 6 up and go into the **city,** where you will be told what
9.24 and night they watched the **city gates** in order to kill him.
11. 5 I was praying in the **city** of Joppa, I had a vision.
12.10 and came at last to the iron gate leading into the **city.**
13.13 and came to Perga, a **city** in Pamphylia, where John Mark left
13.50 the leading men of the **city** and the Gentile women of high
14. 4 The people of the **city** were divided:
14. 6 they fled to the **cities** of Lystra and Derbe in Lycaonia
16.12 inland to Philippi, a **city** of the first district of Macedonia;
16.13 we went out of the **city** to the river-side, where we thought
16.20 "These men are Jews, and they are causing trouble in our **city.**
16.39 them out of the prison and asked them to leave the **city.**
17. 5 They set the whole **city** in an uproar and attacked the home
17. 6 some other believers before the **city** authorities and shouted,
17. 6 they have come to our **city,** [7]and Jason has kept them in
17. 8 they threw the crowd and the **city** authorities into an uproar.
17.16 upset when he noticed how full of idols the **city** was.
17.19 Paul, brought him before the **city** council, the Areopagus,
17.22 up in front of the **city** council and said, "I see that
17.23 as I walked through your **city** and looked at the places where
18.10 able to harm you, for many in this **city** are my people."
19.29 The uproar spread throughout the whole **city.**
19.35 "Everyone knows that the **city** of Ephesus is the keeper of
20.23 only know that in every **city** the Holy Spirit has warned me
21. 5 with us out of the **city** to the beach, where we all
21.29 Ephesus with Paul in the **city,** and they thought that Paul
21.30 Confusion spread through the whole **city,** and the people all
21.39 Jew, born in Tarsus in Cilicia, a citizen of an important **city.**
22.12 "In that **city** was a man named Ananias, a religious man
24.12 either in the synagogues or anywhere else in the **city.**
25.23 with the military chiefs and the leading men of the **city.**
26.11 I even went to foreign **cities** to persecute them.
28.12 We arrived in the **city** of Syracuse and stayed there for
28.13 From there we sailed on and arrived in the **city** of Rhegium.
Rom 16.23 Erastus, the **city** treasurer, and our brother Quartus send you
2 Cor 11.26 have been dangers in the **cities,** dangers in the wilds,
11.32 King Aretas placed guards at the **city gates** to arrest me.
Gal 4.25 a figure of the present **city** of Jerusalem, in slavery with
Heb 11.10 Abraham was waiting for the **city** which God has designed and built,
11.10 the **city** with permanent foundations.
11.16 him their God, because he has prepared a **city** for them.
12.22 Mount Zion and to the **city** of the living God, the heavenly
13.12 Jesus also died outside the **city,** in order to purify the
13.14 For there is no permanent **city** for us here on earth;
Heb 13.14 we are looking for the **city** which is to come.
Jas 4.13 will travel to a certain **city,** where we will stay a year
2 Pet 2. 6 God condemned the **cities** of Sodom and Gomorrah,
Rev 1.11 and send the book to the churches in these seven **cities:**
3.12 and the name of the **city** of my God, the new Jerusalem,
11. 2 who will trample on the **Holy City** for forty-two months.
11. 8 street of the great **city,** where their Lord was crucified.
11. 8 The symbolic name of that **city** is Sodom, or Egypt.
11.13 a tenth of the **city** was destroyed, and seven thousand people
14.20 in the winepress outside the **city,** and blood came out of the
16.19 The great **city** was split into three parts,
16.19 and the **cities** of all countries were destroyed.
17. 1 be punished, that great **city** that is built near many rivers.
17.18 you saw is the great **city** that rules over the kings of
18. 9 cry and weep over the **city** when they see the smoke from
18.10 This great and mighty **city** Babylon!
18.15 from doing business in that **city,** will stand a long way off,
18.16 How awful for the great **city!**
18.18 "There never has been another **city** like this great city!"
18.19 How awful for the great **city!**
18.19 She is the **city** where all who have ships sailing the seas
18.21 is how the great **city** Babylon will be violently thrown down
18.24 blood of prophets and of God's people was found in the **city;**
19. 3 that consume the great **city** goes up for ever and ever!"
20. 9 the camp of God's people and the **city** that he loves.
21. 2 And I saw the **Holy City,** the new Jerusalem, coming down
21.10 He showed me Jerusalem, the **Holy City,** coming down out of
21.11 The **city** shone like a precious stone, like a jasper, clear
21.14 The **city's** wall was built on twelve foundation-stones,
21.15 gold measuring-rod to measure the **city,** its gates, and its wall.
21.16 The **city** was perfectly square, as wide as it was long.
21.16 The angel measured the **city** with his measuring-rod:
21.18 made of jasper, and the **city** itself was made of pure gold,
21.19 The foundation-stones of the **city wall** were adorned with
21.21 The street of the **city** was of pure gold, transparent as glass.
21.22 see a temple in the **city,** because its temple is the Lord
21.23 The **city** has no need of the sun or the moon to
21.25 The gates of the **city** will stand open all day;
21.26 and the wealth of the nations will be brought into the **city.**
21.27 impure will enter the **city,** nor anyone who does shameful things
21.27 in the Lamb's book of the living will enter the **city.**
22. 2 and flowing down the middle of the **city's** street.
22. 3 Nothing that is under God's curse will be found in the **city.**
22. 3 Lamb will be in the **city,** and his servants will worship him.
22.14 tree of life and to go through the gates into the **city.**
22.15 outside the **city** are the perverts and those who practise magic,
22.19 of life and of the **Holy City,** which are described in this
also Josh 21.13 Josh 21.21 Josh 21.27 Josh 21.32 Josh 21.38

CITY OF THE SUN

Is 19.18 One of the cities will be called, **"City of the Sun."**

CIVIL

1 Chr 26.30 administration of all religious and **civil** matters in Israel
26.32 of administering all religious and **civil** matters in Israel
2 Chr 19.11 of Judah, will have final authority in all **civil** cases.
Is 19. 2 says, "I will stir up **civil** war in Egypt and turn brother

CIVILIAN

Is 3. 3 their statesmen, [3]their military and **civilian** leaders,
2 Tim 2. 4 so does not get mixed up in the affairs of **civilian life.**

CIVILIZED

Rom 1.14 to all peoples, to the **civilized** and to the savage, to the

CLAIM

Ex 22. 9 lost object, the two men **claiming** the property shall be
Num 3.40 But in place of them I **claim** all the Levites as mine!
3.40 I also **claim** the livestock of the Levites in place of all
8.16 I have **claimed** them in the place of all the first-born
Josh 19.47 They captured it, killed its people, and **claimed** it for themselves.
22. 4 to the land which you **claimed** for your own, the land on
22.19 **Claim** some land among us.
Judg 18. 1 was looking for territory to **claim** and occupy because they
1 Sam 18. 8 He said, "For David they **claim** tens of thousands, but only
2 Sam 15. 4 had a dispute or a **claim** could come to me, and I
19.43 have ten times as many **claims** on King David as you have,
19.43 more violent in making their **claims** than the men of Israel.
1 Kgs 3.23 Solomon said, "Each of you **claims** that the living child is
2 Kgs 19. 6 Assyrians frighten you with their **claims** that he cannot save you.
Neh 5.10 Now let's give up all our **claims** to repayment.
5.18 bear, so I did not **claim** the allowance that the governor is
Job 11. 4 You **claim** that what you say is true;
11. 4 you **claim** you are pure in the sight of God.
17. 8 Those who **claim** to be honest are shocked, and they all
17. 9 Those who **claim** to be respectable are more and more
21.16 They **claim** they succeed by their own strength, but their
21.19 You **claim** God punishes a child for the sins of his father.
27. 6 I will never give up my **claim** to be right;
32.13 How can you **claim** you have discovered wisdom?
34. 5 Job **claims** that he is innocent, that God refuses to give
37.24 of him, and that he ignores those who **claim** to be wise.
Ps 35.26 may those who **claim** to be better than I am be covered
Prov 1.19 Robbery always **claims** the life of the robber—this is
19. 6 **claims** the friendship of those who give out favours.
26.18 who misleads someone and then **claims** that he was only joking

Prov	30. 6	If you **claim** that he said something that he never said, he
Ecc	8.17	Wise men may **claim** to know, but they don't.
Is	10.15	Lord says, "Can an axe **claim** to be greater than the man
	29.13	The Lord said, "These people **claim** to worship me, but
	37. 6	Assyrians frighten you by their **claims** that he cannot save you.
	47. 8	You **claim** you are as great as God— that there is
	48. 1	name of the Lord and **claim** to worship the God of Israel
	48. 5	place, to prevent you from **claiming** that your idols and
	48. 7	If it had, you would **claim** that you knew all about it.
	58. 2	They worship me every day, **claiming** that they are eager to
Jer	5. 2	Even though you **claim** to worship the Lord, you do not mean
	23.25	lies in my name and **claim** that I have given them my
	23.31	who speak their own words and **claim** they came from me.
	27. 9	prophets or to anyone who **claims** he can predict the future,
	29. 8	you or by any others who **claim** they can predict the future.
	48.14	of Moab, why do you **claim** to be heroes, brave soldiers
Ezek	13. 6	They **claim** that they are speaking my message, but I have not
	22.28	They **claim** to speak the word of the Sovereign Lord, but I,
	28. 2	Puffed up with pride, you **claim** to be a god.
	28. 9	to kill you, will you still **claim** that you are a god?
Hos	8. 2	call me their God and **claim** that they are my people and
Amos	5.14	God Almighty really will be with you, as you **claim** he is.
Mic	3.11	for money—and they all **claim** that the Lord is with them.
Zech	1.17	once again help Jerusalem and **claim** the city as his own."
	13. 2	get rid of anyone who **claims** to be a prophet and will
	13. 3	put to death, because he **claimed** to speak the Lord's word,
Mt	22.23	Sadducees came to Jesus and **claimed** that people will not rise
	23.30	and you **claim** that if you had lived during the time of
	24. 5	Many men, **claiming** to speak for me, will come and say,
	27.43	He trusts in God and **claims** to be God's Son.
Mk	13. 6	Many men, **claiming** to speak for me, will come and say,
Lk	21. 8	Many men, **claiming** to speak for me, will come and say,
	22.25	and the rulers **claim** the title 'Friends of the People.'
	23. 2	to the Emperor and **claiming** that he himself is the Messiah,
Jn	4.12	You don't **claim** to be greater than Jacob, do you?"
	8.53	you do not **claim** to be greater than Abraham, do you?
	9.41	but since you **claim** that you can see, this means that you
	19. 7	ought to die, because he **claimed** to be the Son of God."
	19.12	Anyone who **claims** to be a king is a rebel against the
Acts	5.36	Theudas appeared some time ago, **claiming** to be somebody great,
	6. 1	Greek-speaking Jews **claimed** that their widows were being
	8. 9	He **claimed** that he was someone great, [10] and everyone in the
	13. 6	magician named Bar-Jesus, a Jew who **claimed** to be a prophet.
	25.19	but Paul **claims** that he is alive.
1 Cor	9.15	I writing this now in order to **claim** such rights for myself.
	9.18	without charging for it, without **claiming** my rights in my work
	15.29	it is true, as some **claim**, that the dead are not raised
2 Cor	3. 5	us that allows us to **claim** that we are capable of doing
Phil	3.12	I do not **claim** that I have already succeeded or have
Col	2.18	condemned by anyone who **claims** to be superior because of special
2 Thes	2. 2	thinking or upset by the **claim** that the Day of the Lord
	2. 4	and sit down in God's Temple and **claim** to be God.
1 Tim	2.10	deeds, as is proper for women who **claim** to be religious.
	6.21	For some have **claimed** to possess it, and as a result
Tit	1.16	They **claim** that they know God, but their actions deny it.
1 Jn	3.17	against his brother, how can he **claim** that he loves God?
	4. 1	do not believe all who **claim** to have the Spirit, but test
Rev	2. 9	against you by those who **claim** to be Jews but are not;
	3. 9	those liars who **claim** that they are Jews but are
	13. 5	was allowed to make proud **claims** which were insulting to God,

CLAMPS

1 Chr	22. 3	iron for making nails and **clamps** for the wooden gates, and

CLAN

[SUB-CLANS]

Gen	36.22	Lotan was the ancestor of the **clans** of Hori and Heman.
	36.23	was the ancestor of the **clans** of Alvan, Manahath, Ebal,
	36.25	was the ancestor of the **clans** of Hemdan, Eshban, Ithran, and
	36.27	Ezer was the ancestor of the **clans** of Bilhan, Zaavan,
	36.28	Dishan was the ancestor of the **clans** of Uz and Aran.
Ex	6.14	they were the ancestors of the **clans** that bear their names.
	6.15	they were the ancestors of the **clans** that bear their names.
	6.16	they were the ancestors of the **clans** that bear their names.
	6.19	These are the **clans** of Levi with their descendants.
	6.24	were the ancestors of the divisions of the **clan** of Korah.
	6.25	heads of the families and the **clans** of the tribe of Levi.
Lev	21.14	He shall marry only a virgin from his own **clan**.
Num	1. 2	take a census of the people of Israel by **clans** and families.
	1. 4	Ask one **clan** chief from each tribe to help you."
	1. 5	Tribe **Clan** chief
	1.18	month and registered all the people by **clans** and families.
	1.20	registered by name according to **clan** and family, beginning
	2. 2	the banner of his division and the flag of his own **clan**.
	2.34	his own banner, and they marched, each with his own **clan**.
	3.15	to register the Levites by **clans** and families, enrolling
	3.17	who were the ancestors of the **clans** that bear their names.
	3.21	The **clan** of Gershon was composed of the families of
	3.23	This **clan** was to camp on the west behind the Tent,
	3.24	with Eliasaph son of Lael as chief of the **clan**.
	3.27	The **clan** of Kohath was composed of the families of Amram,
	3.29	This **clan** was to camp on the south side of the Tent,
	3.30	with Elizaphan son of Uzziel as chief of the **clan**.
	3.33	The **clan** of Merari was composed of the families of Mahli
	3.35	This **clan** was to camp on the north side of the Tent,
	3.35	with Zuriel son of Abihail as chief of the **clan**.
	3.39	that Moses enrolled by **clans** at the command of the Lord,
Num	4. 2	Levite clan of Kohath by **sub-clans** and families, [3] and to
	4.15	time to break camp, the **clan** of Kohath shall come to carry
	4.15	The **clan** of Kohath must not touch the sacred objects,
	4.15	are the responsibilities of the **clan** of Kohath whenever the
	4.18	Aaron, [18] "Do not let the **clan** of Kohath [19] be killed by
	4.22	Levite clan of Gershon by **sub-clans** and families, [23] and to
	4.28	These are the responsibilities of the Gershon **clan** in the Tent;
	4.29	Levite clan of Merari by **sub-clans** and families, [30] and to
	4.33	of the Merari **clan** in their service in the Tent:
	4.34	took a census of the three Levite **clans**, Kohath, Gershon,
	4.34	They did this by **sub-clans** and families and registered all
	7. 2	Then the **clan** chiefs who were leaders in the tribes of Israel,
	10. 4	then only the leaders of the **clans** are to gather round you.
	10.17	be taken down, and the **clans** of Gershon and Merari, who
	10.21	Then the Levite **clan** of Kohath would start out, carrying
	13.22	came to Hebron, where the **clans** of Ahiman, Sheshai, and
	16. 1	of Izhar, from the Levite **clan** of Kohath, rebelled against
	25.15	Zur, her father, was chief of a group of Midianite **clans**.
	26. 5	the **clans** of Hanoch, Pallu, [6] Hezron, and Carmi.
	26. 7	These **clans** numbered 43,730 men.
	26.12	the **clans** of Nemuel, Jamin, Jachin, [13] Zerah, and Shaul.
	26.14	These **clans** numbered 22,200 men.
	26.15	the **clans** of Zephon, Haggi, Shuni, [16] Ozni, Eri, [17] Arod,
	26.18	These **clans** numbered 40,500 men.
	26.19	the **clans** of Shelah, Perez, Zerah, Hezron, and Hamul.
	26.22	These **clans** numbered 76,500 men.
	26.23	the **clans** of Tola, Puah, [24] Jashub, and Shimron.
	26.25	These **clans** numbered 64,300 men.
	26.26	the **clans** of Sered, Elon, and Jahleel.
	26.27	These **clans** numbered 60,500 men.
	26.29	and the following **clans** traced their ancestry to Gilead:
	26.30	the **clans** of Iezer, Helek, [31] Asriel, Shechem,
	26.34	These **clans** numbered 52,700 men.
	26.35	the **clans** of Shuthelah, Becher, and Tahan.
	26.36	The **clan** of Eran traced its descent from Shuthelah.
	26.37	These **clans** numbered 32,500 men.
	26.37	These are the **clans** descended from Joseph.
	26.38	the **clans** of Bela, Ashbel, Ahiram, [39] Shephupham, and
	26.40	The **clans** of Ard and Naaman traced their descent from Bela.
	26.41	These **clans** numbered 45,600 men.
	26.42	the **clan** of Shuham, [43] which numbered 64,400 men.
	26.44	the **clans** of Imnah, Ishvi, and Beriah.
	26.45	The **clans** of Heber and Malchiel traced their descent from Beriah.
	26.47	These **clans** numbered 53,400 men.
	26.48	the **clans** of Jahzeel, Guni, [49] Jezer, and Shillem.
	26.50	These **clans** numbered 45,400 men.
	26.57	tribe of Levi consisted of the **clans** of Gershon, Kohath, and
	26.58	Their descendants included the **subclans** of Libni,
	26.63	All these **clans** were listed by Moses and Eleazar when
	32.39	The **clan** of Machir son of Manasseh invaded the land of Gilead,
	32.40	Moses gave Gilead to the **clan** of Machir, and they lived there.
	33.54	among the various tribes and **clans** by drawing lots, giving a
	33.54	to a large clan and a small one to a small **clan**.
	36. 1	of the families in the **clan** of Gilead, the son of Machir
	36.12	They married within the **clans** of the tribe of Manasseh
Deut	3.15	"I assigned Gilead to the **clan** of Machir of the tribe
Josh	7. 1	Zabdi, and belonged to the **clan** of Zerah, a part of the
	7.14	tribe that I pick out will then come forward, **clan by clan**.
	7.14	The **clan** that I pick out will come forward, family by family.
	7.17	the tribe of Judah forward, **clan by clan**,
	7.17	and the **clan** of Zerah was picked out.
	7.17	Then he brought the **clan** of Zerah forward, family by family,
	15.14	Anak out of the city—the **clans** of Sheshai, Ahiman, and
	21. 4	The families of the Levite **clan** of Kohath were the first
	21. 5	The rest of the **clan** of Kohath was assigned ten cities
	21. 6	The **clan** of Gershon was assigned thirteen cities from the
	21. 7	The families of the **clan** of Merari were assigned twelve
	21.10	Aaron who were of the **clan** of Kohath, which was descended
	21.20	other families of the Levite **clan** of Kohath were assigned
	21.26	These families of the **clan** of Kohath received ten cities in all,
	21.27	Another group of Levites, the **clan** of Gershon, received
	21.33	The various families of the **clan** of Gershon received a
	21.34	rest of the Levites, the **clan** of Merari, received from the
	21.40	So the **clan** of Merari was assigned a total of twelve cities.
	22.14	tribes and each one the head of a family among the **clans**.
Judg	1.10	There they defeated the **clans** of Sheshai, Ahiman, and
	1.20	drove out of the city the three **clans** descended from Anak.
	6.11	that belonged to Joash, a man of the **clan** of Abiezer.
	6.15	My **clan** is the weakest in the tribe of Manasseh, and I
	6.24	standing at Ophrah, which belongs to the **clan** of Abiezer.)
	6.34	to call the men of the **clan** of Abiezer to follow him.
	8. 2	Ephraim did is worth more than what my whole **clan** has done.
	8.32	father Joash, at Ophrah, the town of the **clan** of Abiezer.
	9.28	Be loyal to your ancestor Hamor, who founded your **clan!**
	12. 9	daughters in marriage outside the **clan**
	12. 9	thirty girls from outside the **clan** for his sons to marry.
	14. 3	you find a girl in our own **clan**, among all our people?"
Ruth	1. 1	Elimelech, who belonged to the **clan** of Ephrath and who lived
	4.11	become rich in the **clan** of Ephrath and famous in Bethlehem.
1 Sam	1. 1	to the family of Tohu, a part of the **clan** of Zuph.
	2.30	that your family and your **clan** would serve me as priests for
	2.31	in your family and your **clan**, so that no man in your
	9. 1	to the family of Becorath, a part of the **clan** of Aphiah.
	10.19	yourselves before the Lord by tribes and by **clans**.' "
	25. 2	was a man of the **clan** of Caleb named Nabal, who was
	27.10	to the territory of the **clan** of Jerahmeel or to the
	30.14	and the territory of the **clan** of Caleb, and we burnt down
	30.29	to the **clan** of Jerahmeel, to the Kenites, [30] and to the
2 Sam	20.14	all the members of the **clan** of Bikri assembled and followed
	23. 9	famous three was Eleazar son of Dodo, of the **clan** of Ahoh.
1 Kgs	4.13	Gilead belonging to the **clan** of Jair, a descendant of Manasseh,

1 Kgs 8. 1 leaders of the tribes and **clans** of Israel to come to him
1 Chr 1.38 Lotan, who was the ancestor of the **clans** of Hori and Homam.
1.38 the ancestor of the **clans** of Alvan, Manahath, Ebal, Shephi,
1.38 the ancestor of the **clans** of Hamran, Eshban, Ithran, and Cheran.
1.38 who was the ancestor of the **clans** of Bilhan, Zaavan, and
1.38 Dishan, who was the ancestor of the **clans** of Uz and Aran.
2.53 and of the following **clans** that lived in Kiriath Jearim:
2.53 cities of Zorah and Eshtaol were members of these **clans.)**
2.54 of the Zorites, who were one of the two **clans** in Manahath.
2.55 (The following **clans** of experts in writing and copying
4. 8 ancestor of the **clans** descended from Aharhel son of Harum.
4.19 Their descendants founded the **clan** of Garm, which lived in the
4.19 town of Keilah, and the **clan** of Maacath, which lived in the
4.21 **clan** of linen-weavers, who lived in the town of Beth Ashbea;
4.34 The following men were the heads of their **clans:**
5. 7 list the following **clan** leaders in the tribe of Reuben:
5. 8 son of Azaz and grandson of Shema, of the **clan** of Joel.
5. 8 This **clan** lived in Aroer and in the territory from there
5.12 leading clan, and Shapham of the second most important **clan.**
5.12 Janai and Shaphat were founders of other **clans** in Bashan.
5.13 The other members of the tribe belonged to the following seven **clans:**
5.15 son of Abdiel and grandson of Guni, was head of these **clans.**
5.24 The following were the heads of their **clans:**
5.24 They were all outstanding soldiers, well-known leaders of their **clans.**
6.33 The **clan** of Kohath:
6.44 Ethan of the **clan** of Merari was the leader of the third
6.54 assigned to the descendants of Aaron of the **clan** of Kohath.
6.61 lot to the rest of the **clan** of Kohath, family by family.
6.62 To the **clan** of Gershon, family by family, were assigned
6.63 Zebulun were assigned to the **clan** of Merari, family by family.
6.66 of the families of the **clan** of Kohath were assigned towns
6.71 The families of the **clan** of Gershon were assigned the following towns,
6.77 The remaining families of the **clan** of Merari were
7. 2 of families of the **clan** of Tola and were famous soldiers.
7. 7 heads of families in the **clan** and were all famous soldiers.
7.11 heads of families in the **clan** and were all famous soldiers.
8.32 Their descendants lived in Jerusalem near other families of their **clan.**
9.14 Azrikam and Hashabiah, of the **clan** of Merari
9.18 that time members of their **clans** had been stationed at the
9.19 with his fellow-members of the **clan** of Korah, was
9.31 son of Shallum, of the **clan** of Korah, was responsible for
9.32 Members of the **clan** of Kohath were responsible for
9.38 Their descendants lived in Jerusalem near other families of their **clan.**
11.11 First was Jashobeam of the **clan** of Hachmon, the leader
11.12 "Three" was Eleazar son of Dodo, of the **clan** of Ahoh.
12. 3 and Jashobeam, of the **clan** of Korah
12.23 20,800 men famous in their own **clans;**
15. 5 From the Levite **clan** of Kohath came Uriel,
15. 5 in charge of 120 members of his **clan;**
15. 6 from the **clan** of Merari came Asaiah, in charge of 220;
15. 7 from the **clan** of Gershon, Joel, in charge of 130;
15. 8 from the **clan** of Elizaphan, Shemaiah, in charge of 200;
15. 9 from the **clan** of Hebron, Eliel, in charge of 80;
15.10 and from the **clan** of Uzziel, Amminadab, in charge of 112.
15.12 to the Levites, "You are the leaders of the Levite **clans.**
15.17 From the **clans** of singers they chose the following
15.17 Berechiah, and Ethan son of Kushaiah, of the **clan** of Merari.
16.38 Jeduthun and sixty-eight men of his **clan** were to assist them.
16.42 The members of Jeduthun's **clan** were in charge of guarding the gates.
23. 6 David divided the Levites into three groups, according to their **clans:**
23. 9 who were the heads of the **clans** descended from Ladan.
23.10 have many descendants, so they were counted as one **clan.**
23.18 son, Izhar, had a son, Shelomith, the head of the **clan.**
23.24 the descendants of Levi, by **clans** and families, every one of
25. 1 the following Levite **clans** to lead the services of worship:
26. 1 From the **clan** of Korah there was Meshelemiah son of Kore, of
26. 6 They were important men in their **clan** because of their great ability;
26.10 From the **clan** of Merari there was Hosah, who had four sons:
26.19 guard duty to the clan of Korah and the **clan** of Merari.
26.24 Shebuel, of the **clan** of Moses' son Gershom, was the
26.26 of families, leaders of **clan** groups, and army officers.
27. 1 Israelite heads of families and **clan** leaders and their
27. 2 was a member of the **clan** of Perez,
27. 2 was a member of the **clan** of Zerah,
27. 2 Netophah (he was a member of the **clan** of Zerah)
28. 1 kingdom, the leaders of the **clans,** the supervisors of the
29. 6 Then the heads of the **clans,** the officials of the tribes,
29. 8 was administered by Jehiel of the Levite **clan** of Gershon.
2 Chr 5. 2 of the tribes and **clans** of Israel to assemble in Jerusalem,
5.11 and the members of their **clans**—were wearing linen clothing.
17.14 he stationed outstanding officers, [14]according to their **clans.**
17.14 of the troops from the **clans** of Judah,
17.17 of the troops from the **clans** of Benjamin was Eliada, an
20.14 was a member of the **clan** of Asaph and was descended from
20.19 The members of the Levite **clans** of Kohath and Korah
23. 2 to Jerusalem the Levites and all the heads of the **clans.**
25. 5 army units, according to the **clans** they belonged to, and
29.12 From the **clan** of Kohath,
29.12 From the **clan** of Merari,
29.12 From the **clan** of Gershon,
29.12 From the **clan** of Elizaphan,
29.12 From the **clan** of Asaph,
29.12 From the **clan** of Heman,

2 Chr 29.12 From the **clan** of Jeduthun,
31.16 according to what their duties were, [16]and not by **clans.**
31.17 were assigned their duties by **clans,** and the Levites twenty
31.19 and to everyone who was on the rolls of the Levite **clans.**
34.12 Jahath and Obadiah of the **clan** of Merari,
34.12 and Zechariah and Meshullam of the **clan** of Kohath.
35. 4 places in the Temple by **clans,** according to the
35.15 following musicians of the Levite **clan** of Asaph were in the
Ezra 1. 5 Then the heads of the **clans** of the tribes of Judah and
2. 2 is the list of the **clans** of Israel,
2. 2 the number of those from each **clan** who returned from exile:
2.36 This is the list of the priestly **clans** that returned from exile:
2.40 **Clans** of Levites who returned from exile:
2.43 **Clans** of temple workmen who returned from exile:
2.55 **Clans** of Solomon's servants who returned from exile:
2.59 were 652 belonging to the **clans** of Delaiah, Tobiah, and
2.61 The following priestly **clans** could find no record to prove their ancestry:
2.61 (The ancestor of the priestly **clan** of Barzillai had married
2.61 a woman from the **clan** of Barzillai of Gilead
2.61 and had taken the name of his father-in-law's **clan.)**
2.68 of the leaders of the **clans** gave freewill offerings to help
3. 9 Kadmiel and his sons (the **clan** of Hodaviah) joined together
3. 9 (They were helped by the Levites of the **clan** of Henadad.)
3.10 the Levites of the **clan** of Asaph stood there with cymbals.
3.12 Levites, and heads of **clans** had seen the first Temple,
4. 2 and the heads of the **clans** and said, "Let us join you
4. 3 and the heads of the **clans** said to them, "We don't need
7.28 of the heads of the **clans** of Israel to return with me."
8. 1 of the heads of the **clans** who had been in exile in
8. 2 Gershom, of the **clan** of Phinehas
8. 2 Daniel, of the **clan** of Ithamar
8. 2 son of Shecaniah, of the **clan** of David
8. 2 Zechariah, of the **clan** of Parosh,
8. 2 150 men of his **clan** (there were records of their ancestry)
8. 2 son of Zerahiah, of the **clan** of Pahath Moab, with 200 men
8. 2 son of Jahaziel, of the **clan** of Zattu, with 300 men
8. 2 son of Jonathan, of the **clan** of Adin, with 50 men
8. 2 son of Athaliah, of the **clan** of Elam, with 70 men
8. 2 son of Michael, of the **clan** of Shephatiah, with 80 men
8. 2 son of Jehiel, of the **clan** of Joab, with 218 men
8. 2 son of Josiphiah, of the **clan** of Bani, with 160 men
8. 2 son of Bebai, of the **clan** of Bebai, with 28 men
8. 2 son of Hakkatan, of the **clan** of Azgad, with 110 men
8. 2 Jeuel, and Shemaiah, of the **clan** of Adonikam, with 60 men
8. 2 Uthai and Zaccur, of the **clan** of Bigvai, with 70 men
8.18 a Levite from the **clan** of Mahli,
8.19 Hashabiah and Jeshaiah of the **clan** of Merari, with twenty of
10. 2 son of Jehiel, of the **clan** of Elam, said to Ezra,
10.16 from among the heads of the **clans** and recorded their names.
10.18 Priests, listed by **clans:**
10.18 **Clan** of Joshua and his brothers, sons of Jehozadak:
10.20 **Clan** of Immer:
10.21 **Clan** of Harim:
10.22 **Clan** of Pashhur:
10.25 **Clan** of Parosh:
10.26 **Clan** of Elam:
10.27 **Clan** of Zattu:
10.28 **Clan** of Bebai:
10.29 **Clan** of Bani:
10.30 **Clan** of Pahath Moab:
10.31 **Clan** of Harim:
10.33 **Clan** of Hashum:
10.34 **Clan** of Bani:
10.38 **Clan** of Binnui:
10.43 **Clan** of Nebo:
Neh 3. 3 The **clan** of Hassenaah built the Fish Gate.
4.13 bows, and stationed them by **clans** behind the wall, wherever
7. 8 is the list of the **clans** of Israel,
7. 8 the number of those from each **clan** who returned from exile:
7.39 This is the list of the priestly **clans** that returned from exile:
7.43 **Clans** of Levites who returned from exile:
7.46 **Clans** of temple workmen who returned from exile:
7.57 **Clans** of Solomon's servants who returned from exile:
7.61 were 642 belonging to the **clans** of Delaiah, Tobiah, and
7.63 The following priestly **clans** could find no record to prove their ancestry:
7.63 (The ancestor of the priestly **clan** of Barzillai had married
7.63 a woman from the **clan** of Barzillai of Gilead
7.63 and taken the name of his father-in-law's **clan.)**
7.70 Heads of **clans** 168 kilogrammes of gold
8.13 day the heads of the **clans,** together with the priests and
10. 9 of Azaniah, Binnui of the **clan** of Henadad, Kadmiel,
10.34 each year to determine which **clans** are to provide wood to
11.12 In all, 822 members of this **clan** served in the Temple.
11.13 In all, 242 members of this **clan** were heads of families.
11.14 There were 128 members of this **clan** who were outstanding soldiers.
11.22 and he belonged to the **clan** of Asaph,
11.22 the **clan** that was responsible for the music
11.23 royal regulations stating how the **clans** should take turns in
11.24 son of Meshezabel, of the **clan** of Zerah and the tribe of
12.12 High Priest, the following priests were the heads of the priestly **clans:**
12.33 Mattaniah, Micaiah, and Zaccur, of the **clan** of Asaph.)
12.36 by other members of his **clan**—Shemaiah, Azarel, Milalai,
Job 32. 2 a descendant of Buz, and belonged to the **clan** of Ram.)
Is 3. 6 when the members of a **clan** will choose one of their number
Jer 3.14 town and two from each **clan,** and I will bring you back
35. 2 "Go to the members of the Rechabite **clan** and talk to them.

Jer 35. 3 I took the entire Rechabite **clan**—Jaazaniah (the son of another Jeremiah,
35.18 Then I told the Rechabite **clan** that the Lord Almighty,
Zech 9. 7 my people and be like a **clan** in the tribe of Judah.
12. 5 Then the **clans** of Judah will say to themselves, 'The Lord
12. 6 time I will make the **clans** of Judah like a fire in
Acts 7.16 Abraham had bought from the **clan** of Hamor for a sum of

CLANGING

1 Cor 13. 1 speech is no more than a noisy gong or a **clanging** bell.

CLAP

2 Kgs 11.12 The people **clapped** their hands and shouted, "Long live the king!"
Ps 47. 1 **Clap** your hands for joy, all peoples!
98. 8 **Clap** your hands, you rivers;
Ezek 21.14 **Clap** your hands, and the sword will strike again and again.
21.17 I also will **clap** my hands, and my anger will be over.
25. 6 You **clapped** your hands and jumped for joy.
Nah 3.19 hear the news of your destruction **clap** their hands for joy.

CLASH

2 Kgs 8.28 The armies **clashed** at Ramoth in Gilead, and Joram was
2 Chr 22. 5 The armies **clashed** at Ramoth in Gilead, and Joram was

CLASP

2 Kgs 10.15 They **clasped** hands, and Jehu helped him up into the chariot,

CLASS

Jer 42. 1 came with people of every **class** [2]and said to me, "Please
Acts 8.10 in the city, from all **classes** of society, paid close attention

CLASSIFY

2 Cor 10.12 we would not dare to **classify** ourselves or compare ourselves

CLATTER

Jer 47. 3 of horses, the **clatter** of chariots, the rumble of wheels.

CLAWS

Dan 4.33 as eagles' feathers and his nails as long as birds' **claws.**
7.19 its victims with its bronze **claws** and iron teeth and then

CLAY

Lev 6.28 Any **clay** pot in which the meat is boiled must be broken,
11.33 their bodies fall into a **clay** pot, everything that is in it
11.35 a **clay** stove or oven shall be broken, [36]but a spring or
14. 5 to be killed over a **clay** bowl containing fresh spring water.
14.50 of the birds over a **clay** bowl containing fresh spring water.
15.12 Any **clay** pot that the man touches must be broken, and
Num 5.17 some holy water into a **clay** bowl and take some of the
2 Sam 17.28 They brought bowls, **clay** pots, and bedding, and
Job 4.19 will trust a creature of **clay,** a thing of dust that can
10. 9 Remember that you made me from **clay;**
13.12 your arguments crumble like **clay.**
33. 6 the same in God's sight, both of us were formed from **clay.**
38.14 of a garment, clear as the imprint of a seal on **clay.**
Ps 2. 9 you will shatter them in pieces like a **clay** pot.' "
Prov 26.23 really thinking is like a fine glaze on a cheap **clay** pot.
Is 29.16 Which is more important, the potter or the **clay?**
30.14 will be shattered like a **clay** pot, so badly broken that
41.25 rulers as if they were mud, like a potter trampling **clay.**
45. 9 Does a **clay** pot dare to argue with its maker,
45. 9 Does the **clay** ask the potter what he is doing?
64. 8 We are like **clay,** and you are like the potter.
Jer 18. 4 he would take the **clay** and make it into something else.
18. 6 with you people of Israel what the potter did with the **clay?**
18. 6 You are in my hands just like **clay** in the potter's hands.
19. 1 The Lord told me to go and buy a **clay** jar.
19.11 will be like this broken **clay** jar that cannot be put
32.14 to place them in a **clay** jar, so that they may be
Lam 4. 2 us as gold, but now they are treated like common **clay** pots.
Dan 2.33 of iron, and its feet partly of iron and partly of **clay.**
2.34 it, struck the iron and **clay** feet of the statue, and
2.35 At once the iron, **clay,** bronze, silver, and gold crumbled
2.41 that the feet and the toes were partly **clay** and partly iron.
2.41 of iron, because there was iron mixed with the **clay.**
2.42 toes—partly iron and partly **clay**—mean that part of the
2.43 You also saw that the iron was mixed with the **clay.**
2.43 not be able to, any more than iron can mix with **clay.**
2.45 it struck the statue made of iron, bronze, **clay,** silver, and
Nah 3.14 Trample the **clay** to make bricks, and get the brick moulds ready!
Hab 2. 2 "Write down clearly on **clay** tablets what I reveal to you,
Rom 9.20 A **clay** pot does not ask the man who made it,
9.21 the right to use the **clay** as he wishes, and to make
9.21 from the same lump of **clay,** one for special occasions and
2 Cor 4. 7 spiritual treasure are like common **clay** pots, in order to show
2 Tim 2.20 some are made of silver and gold, others of wood and **clay;**
Rev 2.26 an iron rod and to break them to pieces like **clay** pots.

CLEAN

Gen 7. 2 of each kind of ritually **clean** animal, but only one pair of
7. 8 animal and bird, whether ritually **clean** or unclean, [9]went
8.20 of each kind of ritually **clean** animal and bird, and burnt
35. 2 purify yourselves and put on **clean** clothes.
Lev 4.12 the camp to the ritually **clean** place where the ashes are
6.11 take the ashes outside the camp to a ritually **clean** place.
7.19 Anyone who is ritually **clean** may eat the meat, [20]but if
7.20 if anyone who is not **clean** eats it, he shall no longer
10.10 use, between what is ritually **clean** and what is unclean.
10.14 You may eat them in any ritually **clean** place.
11.36 spring or a cistern remains **clean,** although anything else
11.37 on seed that is going to be sown, the seed remains **clean.**
11.47 distinguish between what is ritually **clean** and unclean,
12. 4 days before she is ritually **clean** from her loss of blood;
12. 5 days before she is ritually **clean** from her loss of blood.
12. 7 to take away her impurity, and she will be ritually **clean.**
12. 8 to take away her impurity, and she will be ritually **clean.**
13. 6 and has not spread, he shall pronounce him ritually **clean;**
13. 6 The person shall wash his clothes and be ritually **clean.**
13. 7 examined him and pronounced him **clean,** he must appear before
13.13 whole body, he shall pronounce the person ritually **clean.**
13.13 If his whole skin has turned white, he is ritually **clean.**
13.17 ritually clean, and the priest shall pronounce him **clean.**
13.23 boil, and the priest shall pronounce him ritually **clean.**
13.28 priest shall pronounce him ritually **clean,** because it is
13.34 the surrounding skin, he shall pronounce him ritually **clean.**
13.34 The person shall wash his clothes, and he will be **clean.**
13.35 pronounced **clean,** [36]the priest shall examine him again.
13.37 healed, and the priest shall pronounce him ritually **clean.**
13.39 the person is ritually **clean.**
13.58 he shall wash it again, and it will be ritually **clean.**
13.59 is made as to whether it is ritually **clean** or unclean.
14. 2 he is to be pronounced **clean,** he shall be brought to the
14. 4 priest shall order two ritually **clean** birds to be brought,
14. 7 his skin-disease, and then he shall pronounce him **clean.**
14. 8 he will then be ritually **clean.**
14. 9 and have a bath, and then he will be ritually **clean.**
14.14 right foot of the man who is to be declared ritually **clean.**
14.17 right foot of the man who is to be declared ritually **clean.**
14.20 ritual of purification, and the man will be ritually **clean.**
14.48 shall pronounce the house ritually **clean,** because the mildew
14.53 purification for the house, and it will be ritually **clean.**
14.57 These laws determine when something is unclean and when it is **clean.**
15. 8 on anyone who is ritually **clean,** that person must wash his
15.13 bathe in fresh spring water, and he will be ritually **clean.**
15.28 must wait seven days, and then she will be ritually **clean.**
16.30 from all their sins, so that they will be ritually **clean.**
17.13 a bird which is ritually **clean,** he must pour out its blood
17.15 a bath, and wait until evening before he is ritually **clean.**
20.25 and birds that are ritually **clean** and those that are not.
22. 4 eat any of the sacred offerings until he is ritually **clean.**
22. 7 the sun sets he is **clean,** and then he may eat the
Num 6. 9 and so he becomes ritually **clean.**
8. 7 Then they will be ritually **clean.**
9.13 But anyone who is ritually **clean** and not away on a
18.11 Every member of your family who is ritually **clean** may eat them.
18.13 Every member of your family who is ritually **clean** may eat it.
19. 9 a man who is ritually **clean** is to collect the ashes of
19. 9 put them in a ritually **clean** place outside the camp, where
19.12 day and on the seventh day, and then he will be **clean.**
19.12 both the third and the seventh day, he will not be **clean.**
19.18 someone who is ritually **clean** is to take a sprig of
19.18 someone who is ritually **clean** is to sprinkle the water on
19.19 the person who is ritually **clean** is to sprinkle the water on
19.19 water over himself, becomes ritually **clean** at sunset.
31.24 then you will be ritually **clean** and will be permitted to
Deut 12.15 All of you, whether ritually **clean** or unclean, may eat them,
12.22 Anyone, ritually **clean** or unclean, may eat that meat,
14.11 "You may eat any **clean** bird.
14.20 You may eat any **clean** insect.
15.22 All of you, whether ritually **clean** or unclean, may eat them,
23.14 Keep your camp ritually **clean,** because the Lord your God
1 Kgs 22.38 His chariot was **cleaned** up at the pool of Samaria, where
2 Kgs 21.13 I will wipe Jerusalem **clean** of its people,
21.13 as **clean** as a plate that has been
25.14 the ash containers used in **cleaning** the altar, the tools
2 Chr 13.11 a table that is ritually **clean,** and every evening they light
29.15 and they all made themselves ritually **clean.**
29.15 to make the Temple ritually **clean,** according to the Law of
29.31 "Now that you are ritually **clean,** bring sacrifices as
29.34 By then more priests had made themselves ritually **clean.**
29.34 Levites were more faithful in keeping ritually **clean** than the priests were.)
30. 1 not enough priests were ritually **clean** and not many people
30.15 Levites who were not ritually **clean** were so ashamed that
30.17 the people were not ritually **clean,** they could not kill the
30.19 all their heart, even though they are not ritually **clean."**
34. 5 By doing all this, he made Judah and Jerusalem ritually **clean** again.
35. 6 Now make yourselves ritually **clean** and prepare the
Ezra 6.20 the Levites had purified themselves and were ritually **clean.**
Job 14. 4 Nothing **clean** can ever come from anything as unclean as man.
37.21 and the sky has been swept **clean** by the wind.
Ps 51. 2 Wash away all my evil and make me **clean** from my sin!
51. 7 Remove my sin, and I will be **clean;**
Is 1. 6 Your wounds have not been **cleaned** or bandaged.
1.16 Wash yourselves **clean.**
1.18 red with sin, but I will wash you as **clean** as snow.
28. 8 are all covered with vomit, and not a **clean** spot is left.
66.20 grain-offerings to the Temple in ritually **clean** containers.
Jer 6. 9 me, "Israel will be stripped **clean** like a vineyard from
43.12 a shepherd picks his clothes **clean** of lice, so the king of

Jer 43.12 Babylonia will pick the land of Egypt **clean** and then leave victorious.
52.18 the ash containers used in **cleaning** the altar, the tools
Ezek 22.26 not teach the difference between **clean** and unclean things,
24. 6 It is like a corroded pot that is never **cleaned.**
36.25 I will sprinkle **clean** water on you
36.25 and make you **clean** from all your idols and everything
36.33 says, "When I make you **clean** from all your sins, I will
39.12 to bury all the corpses and make the land **clean** again.
39.14 on the ground, so that they can make the land **clean.**
39.16 And so the land will be made **clean** again."
44.23 is not, and between what is ritually **clean** and what is not.
44.26 After he has become **clean** again, he must wait seven days
Zech 3. 5 He commanded the attendants to put a **clean** turban on Joshua's head.
Mt 8. 2 and said, "Sir, if you want to, you can make me **clean."**
8. 3 "Be **clean!"**
11. 5 from dreaded skin-diseases are made **clean,** the deaf hear,
12.44 it goes back and finds the house empty, **clean,** and all tidy.
23.25 You **clean** the outside of your cup and plate, while the
23.26 **Clean** what is inside the cup first,
23.26 and then the outside will be **clean** too!
Mk 1.40 "If you want to," he said, "you can make me **clean."**
1.41 "Be **clean!"**
1.42 At once the disease left the man, and he was **clean.**
Lk 5.12 begged him, "Sir, if you want to, you can make me **clean!"**
5.13 "Be **clean!"**
7.22 from dreaded skin-diseases are made **clean,** the deaf can hear,
11.25 So it goes back and finds the house **clean** and tidy.
11.39 "Now then, you Pharisees **clean** the outside of your cup and
11.41 plates to the poor, and everything will be ritually **clean** for
17.14 On the way they were made **clean.**
Jn 13.10 had a bath is completely **clean** and does not have to wash
13.10 All of you are **clean**—all except one."
13.11 that is why he said, "All of you, except one, are **clean.")**
15. 2 bear fruit, so that it will be **clean** and bear more fruit.
15. 3 You have been made **clean** already by the teaching I have
18.28 wanted to keep themselves ritually **clean,** in order to be
Acts 10.15 "Do not consider anything unclean that God has declared **clean."**
11. 9 'Do not consider anything unclean that God has declared **clean.'**
Eph 5.26 his word, after making it **clean** by washing it in water,
2 Tim 2.21 If anyone makes himself **clean** from all those evil things,
Heb 10.22 and with bodies washed with **clean** water.
Rev 3. 4 a few of you there in Sardis have kept your clothes **clean.**
15. 6 the temple, dressed in **clean** shining linen and with gold belts
19. 8 She has been given **clean** shining linen to wear."
19.14 riding on white horses and dressed in **clean** white linen.
22.14 those who wash their robes **clean** and so have the right to

AV CLEANSE
see also **CLEAN, PURIFY**

Ps 19.12 **deliver** me, Lord, from hidden faults!
73.13 that I have kept myself **pure** and have not committed sin?
119. 9 How can a young man keep his life **pure?**
Prov 20.30 Sometimes it takes a painful experience to make us **change** our ways.
Dan 8.14 Then the Temple will be **restored."**
Mt 10. 8 **heal** those who suffer from dreaded skin-diseases,
Lk 4.27 not one of them was **healed,** but only Naaman the Syrian."
17.17 Jesus said, "There were ten men who were **healed;**
Jas 4. 8 **Wash** your hands, you sinners!

CLEAR

Gen 44.16 How can we **clear** ourselves?
Josh 17.15 go into the forests and **clear** ground for yourselves in the
17.18 is a forest, you will **clear** it and take possession of it
1 Sam 14.41 and the people were **cleared.**
Job 26.13 breath that made the sky **clear,** and his hand that killed the
38.14 the folds of a garment, **clear** as the imprint of a seal
38.25 the pouring rain and **cleared** the way for the thunderstorm?
Ps 49. 3 My thoughts will be **clear;**
80. 9 You **cleared** a place for it to grow;
Is 5. 2 He dug the soil and **cleared** it of stones;
40. 3 **Clear** the way in the desert for our God!
62.10 **clear** it of stones!
Ezek 32.14 waters settle and become **clear** and let your rivers run calm.
34.18 You drink the **clear** water and muddy what you don't drink!
Mt 7. 5 will be able to see **clearly** to take the speck out of
Mk 1. 2 send my messenger ahead of you to **clear** the way for you.'
8.25 his eyesight returned, and he saw everything **clearly.**
8.32 He made this very **clear** to them.
Lk 6.42 will be able to see **clearly** to take the speck out of
9.53 receive him, because it was **clear** that he was on his way
20.37 And Moses **clearly** proves that the dead are raised to life.
Jn 1.20 did not refuse to answer, but spoke out openly and **clearly,**
Acts 2.22 man whose divine authority was **clearly** proven to you
10. 3 a vision, in which he **clearly** saw an angel of God come
11.17 It is **clear** that God gave those Gentiles the same gift
23. 1 My conscience is perfectly **clear** about the way in which I
24.16 best always to have a **clear** conscience before God and man.
25.27 send a prisoner without **clearly** indicating the charges against
Rom 1.20 his eternal power and his divine nature, have been **clearly** seen;
3. 5 wrong serves to show up more **clearly** God's doing right?
3. 7 serves God's glory by making his truth stand out more **clearly?**
1 Cor 4. 4 My conscience is **clear,** but that does not prove that I am
11.19 that the ones who are in the right may be **clearly** seen.)
14. 8 does not sound a **clear** call, who will prepare for battle?
14. 9 if your message given in strange tongues is not **clear?**
15.27 It is **clear,** of course, that the words "all things" do not
2 Cor 3. 3 It is **clear** that Christ himself wrote this letter and sent
11. 6 we have made this **clear** to you at all times and in
Gal 2.11 I opposed him in public, because he was **clearly** wrong.
3. 1 very eyes you had a **clear** description of the death of Jesus
3.11 Now, it is **clear** that no one is put right with God
Eph 5.13 to the light, then their true nature is **clearly** revealed;
5.14 for anything that is **clearly** revealed becomes light.
Phil 3.15 have a different attitude, God will make this **clear** to you.
Col 4. 4 as I should, in such a way as to make it **clear.**
1 Tim 1. 5 from a pure heart, a **clear** conscience, and a genuine faith.
1.19 fight well, [19]and keep your faith and a **clear** conscience.
3. 9 to the revealed truth of the faith with a **clear** conscience.
4. 1 The Spirit says **clearly** that some people will abandon the faith
2 Tim 1. 3 God, whom I serve with a **clear** conscience, as my ancestors did.
Heb 2. 8 this **clearly** includes everything.
2.16 For it is **clear** that it is not the angels that he
6.17 wanted to make it very **clear** that he would never change his
9. 8 The Holy Spirit **clearly** teaches from all these arrangements
11.14 say such things make it **clear** that they are looking for
13.18 are sure we have a **clear** conscience, because we want to do
1 Pet 3.16 Keep your conscience **clear,** so that when you are insulted,
1 Jn 2.19 so that it might be **clear** that none of them really belonged
3. 2 God's children, but it is not yet **clear** what we shall become.
3.10 the **clear** difference between God's children and the Devil's
Rev 4. 6 was what looked like a sea of glass, **clear** as crystal.
21.11 like a precious stone, like a jasper, **clear** as crystal.
21.18 the city itself was made of pure gold, as **clear** as glass.

CLENCHED

Num 24.10 Balak **clenched** his fists in anger and said to Balaam,

CLEVER

2 Sam 14. 2 much, [2]so he sent for a **clever** woman who lived in Tekoa.
Job 15. 5 you are trying to hide behind **clever** words.
34. 1 You men are so wise, so **clever;**
Ps 58. 5 of the snake-charmer, or the chant of the **clever** magician.
Prov 1. 4 can make an inexperienced person **clever** and teach young men
14. 8 Why is a **clever** person wise?
14.18 deserves, but the **clever** are rewarded with knowledge.
18. 2 all he wants to do is to show how **clever** he is.
26. 5 asked it will realize that he's not as **clever** as he thinks.
30.24 animals in the world that are small, but very, very **clever:**
Ecc 9.15 who was poor, but so **clever** that he could have saved the
Is 5.21 You think you are wise, so very **clever.**
10.13 I am strong and wise and **clever.**
19.12 King of Egypt, where are those **clever** advisers of yours?
29.14 to be fools, and all their **cleverness** will be useless."
Ezek 28. 5 You made **clever** business deals and kept on making profits.
Amos 5.13 keeping quiet in such evil times is the **clever** thing to do!
Obad 7 they say of you, 'Where is all that **cleverness** he had?'
8 Edom, I will destroy their **clever** men and wipe out all their
Mk 7. 9 Jesus continued, "You have a **clever** way of rejecting God's law
1 Cor 3.19 As the scripture says, "God traps the wise in their **cleverness";**
2 Cor 11. 3 same way that Eve was deceived by the snake's **clever** lies.

CLIFF

Num 24.21 nest set high on a **cliff,** [22]But you Kenites will be
Judg 15. 8 he went and stayed in the cave in the **cliff** at Etam.
15.11 to the cave in the **cliff** at Etam and said to Samson,
15.13 up with two new ropes and brought him back from the **cliff.**
2 Chr 25.12 to the top of the **cliff** at the city of Sela and
Job 14.18 a time when mountains fall and solid **cliffs** are moved away.
30. 6 to live in caves, in holes dug in the sides of **cliffs.**
Ps 104.18 high mountains, and the rock-badgers hide in the **cliffs.**
114. 8 into pools of water and solid **cliffs** into flowing springs.
141. 6 are thrown down from rocky **cliffs,** the people will admit
Jer 48.28 Go and live on the **cliffs!**
49.16 You live on the rocky **cliffs,** high on top of the mountain;
Ezek 38.20 Mountains will fall, **cliffs** will crumble, and every wall will collapse.
Dan 2.34 stone broke loose from a **cliff** without anyone touching it,
2.45 stone broke loose from a **cliff** without anyone touching it
Mt 8.32 down the side of the **cliff** into the lake and was drowned.
Mk 5.13 down the side of the **cliff** into the lake and was drowned.
Lk 4.29 to throw him over the **cliff,** [30]but he walked through the
8.33 down the side of the **cliff** into the lake and was drowned.

CLIMB

Num 33.38 At the command of the Lord, Aaron the priest **climbed** Mount Hor.
Deut 32.49 **climb** Mount Nebo and look at the land of Canaan that I
1 Sam 14.13 Jonathan **climbed** up out of the pass on his hands and knees,
1 Kgs 18.42 Ahab went to eat, Elijah **climbed** to the top of Mount Carmel,
Song 7. 8 I will **climb** the palm-tree and pick its fruit.
Is 14.13 You were determined to **climb** up to heaven and to place
14.14 You said you would **climb** to the tops of the clouds and
15. 2 The people of Dibon **climb** the hill to weep at the shrine.
15. 5 Some **climb** the road to Luhith, weeping as they go;
57. 8 take off your clothes and **climb** into your large beds with
Jer 4.29 run to the forest, others will **climb** up among the rocks.
48.44 into the pits, and whoever **climbs** out of the pits will be
51.53 Even if Babylon could **climb** to the sky and build a
Joel 2. 7 they **climb** the walls like soldiers.
2. 9 they **climb** up the houses and go in through the windows
Amos 9. 2 Even if they **climb** up to heaven, I will bring them down.
Hab 2. 1 I will **climb** my watch-tower and wait to see what the Lord
Mt 15.29 He **climbed** a hill and sat down.
Lk 19. 4 ahead of the crowd and **climbed** a sycomore tree to see Jesus,

Jn 10. 1 sheepfold by the gate, but **climbs** in some other way, is a
Acts 8.31 And he invited Philip to **climb** up and sit in the carriage

CLING

Job 28. 4 There they work in loneliness, **Clinging** to ropes in the pits.
Ps 63. 8 I **cling** to you, and your hand keeps me safe.
Is 43.18 "Do not **cling** to events of the past or dwell on what
Jer 8. 5 You **cling** to your idols and refuse to return to me.

CLOAK

Ex 22.26 If you take someone's **cloak** as a pledge that he will pay
Josh 7.21 I saw a beautiful Babylonian **cloak,** about two kilogrammes of silver,
7.24 seized Achan, the silver, the **cloak,** and the bar of gold,
Ruth 3.15 said to her, "Take off your **cloak** and spread it out here."
1 Sam 15.27 to leave, but Saul caught hold of his **cloak,** and it tore.
28.14 "He is wearing a **cloak."**
1 Kgs 19.13 covered his face with his **cloak** and went out and stood at
19.19 Elijah took off his **cloak** and put it on Elisha.
2 Kgs 1. 8 "He was wearing a **cloak** made of animal skins, tied with
2. 8 Then Elijah took off his **cloak,** rolled it up, and struck
2.12 In grief, Elisha tore his **cloak** in two.
2.13 Then he picked up Elijah's **cloak** that had fallen from him,
2.14 water with Elijah's **cloak,** and said, "Where is the Lord,
9.13 once Jehu's fellow-officers spread their **cloaks** at the top
Esth 8.15 of blue and white, a **cloak** of fine purple linen, and a
Is 3.22 all their fine robes, gowns, **cloaks,** and purses;
Ezek 16.10 of the best leather, a linen headband, and a silk **cloak.**
Mt 9.20 came up behind Jesus and touched the edge of his **cloak.**
9.21 to herself, "If I only touch his **cloak,** I will get well."
14.36 those who were ill at least touch the edge of his **cloak;**
21. 7 the colt, threw their **cloaks** over them, and Jesus got on.
21. 8 crowd of people spread their **cloaks** on the road while others
23. 5 Notice also how long are the tassels on their **cloaks!**
24.18 is in the field must not go back to get his **cloak.**
Mk 5.29 She touched his **cloak,** and her bleeding stopped at once;
6.56 to let them at least touch the edge of his **cloak;**
10.50 He threw off his **cloak,** jumped up, and came to Jesus.
11. 7 colt to Jesus, threw their **cloaks** over the animal, and Jesus
11. 8 Many people spread their **cloaks** on the road,
13.16 the field must not go back to the house for his **cloak.**
Lk 8.44 the edge of his **cloak,** and her bleeding stopped at once.
19.35 Then they threw their **cloaks** over the animal and helped Jesus
19.36 As he rode on, people spread their **cloaks** on the road.
Acts 7.58 The witnesses left their **cloaks** in the care of a young man
12. 8 angel said, "Put your **cloak** round you and come with me."
22.20 his murder and taking care of the **cloaks** of his murderers.'

CLOSE (1)

Gen 2.21 took out one of the man's ribs and **closed** up the flesh.
8. 2 beneath the earth and the floodgates of the sky were **closed.**
19. 6 Lot went outside and **closed** the door behind him.
Ex 14. 3 about in the country and are **closed** in by the desert.
Num 16.33 The earth **closed** over them, and they vanished.
Josh 2. 4 They left at sunset before the city gate was **closed.**
Judg 3.23 Then Ehud went outside, **closed** the doors behind him,
1 Sam 23.26 and his men, who were **closing** in on them and were about
2 Sam 1. 6 chariots and horsemen of the enemy were **closing** in on him.
18.15 Then ten of Joab's soldiers **closed** in on Absalom and
2 Kgs 4. 4 sons go into the house, **close** the door, and start pouring
4. 5 her house with her sons, **closed** the door, took the small jar
4.21 put him on the bed and left, **closing** the door behind her.
4.33 He **closed** the door and prayed to the Lord.
16.18 and **closed** up the king's private entrance
2 Chr 7. 9 had a **closing** celebration, [10]and on the following day,
28.24 He **closed** the Temple and set up altars in every part of
29. 7 They **closed** the doors of the Temple, let the lamps go out,
Neh 4. 7 in the wall were being **closed,** and they were very angry.
7. 3 sunrise and to have them **closed** and barred before the guards
8.18 day there was a **closing** ceremony, as required in the Law.
Job 17. 4 You have **closed** their minds to reason;
38. 8 Who **closed** the gates to hold back the sea when it burst
Ps 10.11 He has **closed** his eyes and will never see me!"
12. 3 **Close** those boastful mouths that say, [4]"With our words
22.16 like a pack of dogs they **close** in on me;
51. 9 **Close** your eyes to my sins and wipe out all my evil.
88. 8 I am **closed** in and cannot escape;
88.17 they **close** in on me from every side.
116. 3 the horrors of the grave **closed** in on me;
Prov 18.19 if you quarrel with him, he will **close** his doors to you.
28.27 If you **close** your eyes to the poor, many people will curse
Song 8. 6 **Close** your heart to every love but mine;
Is 44.18 They **close** their eyes and their minds to the truth.
Lam 3.53 me alive into a pit and **closed** the opening with a stone.
3.54 Water began to **close** over me, and I thought death was near.
Ezek 44. 1 The gate was **closed,** [2]and the Lord said to me,
44. 2 "This gate will stay **closed** and will never be opened.
44. 2 It is to remain **closed.**
46. 1 courtyard must be kept **closed** during the six working days,
46.12 and the gate is to be **closed** after he goes out again."
Dan 12. 4 to me, "And now, Daniel, **close** the book and put a seal
Mic 7.16 In dismay they will **close** their mouths and cover their ears.
Zech 7.11 They **closed** their minds [12]and made their hearts as hard as rock.
Mal 1.10 wish one of you would **close** the temple doors so as to
Mt 6. 6 go to your room, **close** the door, and pray to your
13.15 they have stopped up their ears and have **closed** their eyes.
25.10 in with him to the wedding feast, and the door was **closed.**
Mk 9.25 noticed that the crowd was **closing** in on them, so he gave
Lk 12. 3 whispered in private in a **closed** room will be shouted from
13.25 The master of the house will get up and **close** the door;
19.43 blockade you, and **close** in on you from every side.
Jn 12.40 blinded their eyes and **closed** their minds, so that their eyes
Acts 21.30 At once the Temple doors were **closed.**
24.22 well informed about the Way, brought the hearing to a **close.**
28.27 and they have stopped up their ears and **closed** their eyes.
2 Cor 3.14 Their minds, indeed, were **closed;**
6.12 It is not we who have **closed** our hearts to you;
6.12 it is you who have **closed** your hearts to us.
1 Jn 3.17 his brother in need, yet **closes** his heart against his brother,
Rev 3. 7 a door, no one can **close** it,
3. 7 and when he **closes** it, no one can open it.
3. 8 opened a door in front of you, which no one can **close.**
21.25 will never be **closed,** because there will be no night there.

CLOSE (2)

Gen 27.21 said to Jacob, "Please come **closer** so that I can touch you.
27.22 Jacob moved **closer** to his father, who felt him and said,
27.26 his father said to him, "Come **closer** and kiss me, my son."
45. 4 Then Joseph said to them, "Please come **closer."**
Ex 3. 3 I will go **closer** and see."
3. 4 saw that Moses was coming **closer,** he called to him from the
3. 5 God said, "Do not come any **closer.**
32.19 When Moses came **close** enough to the camp to see the
Deut 32. 1 "Earth and sky, hear my words, listen **closely** to what I say.
Judg 4.11 had set up his tent **close** to Kedesh near the oak-tree at
Ruth 3.12 there is a man who is a **closer** relative than I am.
4.16 Naomi took the child, held him **close,** and took care of him.
1 Sam 17.41 He kept coming **closer,** [42]and when he got a good look at
24. 3 He came to a cave **close** to some sheep pens by the
1 Kgs 1. 2 She will lie **close** to you and keep you warm."
3.21 I looked at it more **closely** and saw that it was not
18.30 said to the people, "Come **closer** to me," and they all
21. 2 it is **close** to my palace, and I want to use the
2 Kgs 6.30 and the people who were **close** to the wall could see that
Esth 2. 2 the king's advisers who were **close** to him suggested, "Why
Job 13. 9 If God looks at you **closely,** will he find anything good?
Ps 73.23 Yet I always stay **close** to you, and you hold me by
88. 3 many troubles have fallen on me that I am **close** to death.
107.18 they couldn't stand the sight of food and were **close** to death.
119.150 My cruel persecutors are coming **closer,** people who never keep your law.
Is 42.18 Look **closely,** you that are blind!
48.16 "Now come **close** to me and hear what I say.
Jer 50.33 them are guarding them **closely** and will not let them go.
Ezek 40. 3 He took me **closer,** and I saw a man who shone like
Amos 6. 3 is coming, but what you do only brings that day **closer.**
Mic 1.12 because the Lord has brought disaster **close** to Jerusalem.
Mt 6. 3 a way that even your **closest** friend will not know about it.
24. 6 hear the noise of battles **close** by and the news of battles
Mk 3. 2 so they watched him **closely** to see whether he would heal the
13. 7 hear the noise of battles **close** by and news of battles far
Lk 6. 7 so they watched him **closely** to see if he would heal
14. 1 and people were watching Jesus **closely.**
15.25 way back, when he came **close** to the house, he heard the
19.41 He came **closer** to the city, and when he saw it, he
Jn 13.25 So that disciple moved **closer** to Jesus' side and asked,
19.25 Standing **close** to Jesus' cross were his mother,
19.42 because the tomb was **close** by, they placed Jesus' body there.
21.20 the one who had leaned **close** to Jesus at the meal and
Acts 2.44 The believers continued together in **close** fellowship and shared
8. 6 The crowds paid **close** attention to what Philip said,
8.10 from all classes of society, paid **close** attention to him.
8.13 after being baptized, he stayed **close** to Philip and was astounded
8.29 Philip, "Go over to that carriage and stay **close** to it."
10.24 together with relatives and **close** friends that he had invited.
11. 6 I looked **closely** inside and saw domesticated and wild animals,
23. 2 ordered those who were standing **close** to Paul to strike him
23. 4 The men **close** to Paul said to him, "You are insulting
27. 8 We kept **close** to the coast and with great difficulty came
27.13 the anchor and sailed as **close** as possible along the coast
27.27 the sailors suspected that we were getting **close** to land.
Rom 13.11 we will be saved is **closer** now than it was when we
Jas 1.25 whoever looks **closely** into the perfect law that sets people free,
Rev 6. 8 Its rider was named Death, and Hades followed **close** behind.

Am **CLOTH**
see also **WRAPPINGS**

CLOTH
[SADDLE-CLOTHS]

Ex 25. 4 **cloth** made of goats' hair;
26. 4 Make loops of blue **cloth** on the edge of the outside piece
26. 7 the Tent out of eleven pieces of **cloth** made of goats' hair.
35. 6 **cloth** made of goats' hair;
35.23 **cloth** of goats' hair;
35.35 and other **cloth.**
36.11 They made loops of blue **cloth** on the edge of the outside
36.14 the Tent out of eleven pieces of **cloth** made of goats' hair.
Lev 11.32 to any article of wood, **cloth,** leather, or sacking, no
13.48 any piece of linen or wool **cloth** or on leather or anything
13.59 or on linen or wool **cloth** or on anything made of leather;
15.17 Anything made of **cloth** or leather on which the semen
Num 4. 6 over it, spread a blue **cloth** on top, and then insert the
4. 7 They shall spread a blue **cloth** over the table for the
4. 8 They shall spread a red **cloth** over all this, put a fine
4. 9 They shall take a blue **cloth** and cover the lampstand, with

Num 4.11 they shall spread a blue **cloth** over the gold altar, put a
4.12 wrap them in a blue **cloth**, put a fine leather cover over
4.13 ashes from the altar and spread a purple **cloth** over it.
Deut 22.11 "Do not wear **cloth** made by weaving wool and linen together.
Judg 5.30 two for every soldier, rich **cloth** for Sisera, embroidered
8.25 They spread out a **cloth**, and everyone put on it the earrings
1 Sam 21. 9 it is behind the ephod, wrapped in a **cloth**.
2 Sam 6.14 David, wearing only a linen **cloth** round his waist,
1 Kgs 20.38 bandaged his face with a **cloth**, to disguise himself, and
20.41 The prophet tore the **cloth** from his face, and at once
2 Kgs 18.17 occupied the road where the **clothmakers** work, by the ditch
2 Chr 2. 7 bronze, and iron, and in making blue, purple and red **cloth**.
2.14 He can work with blue, purple, and red **cloth**, and with linen.
Prov 30. 4 Or wrapped up water in a piece of **cloth**?
31.13 She keeps herself busy making wool and linen **cloth**.
31.19 She spins her own thread and weaves her own **cloth**.
Song 3.10 over it is **cloth** embroidered with gold.
3.10 cushions are covered with purple **cloth**, lovingly woven by
Is 7. 3 on the road where the **cloth makers** work, at the end of
19. 9 Those who make linen **cloth** will be in despair;
36. 2 occupied the road where the **clothmakers** work, by the ditch
38.12 that is taken down, Like **cloth** that is cut from a loom.
50. 9 they will vanish like moth-eaten **cloth**.
Jer 10. 9 in violet and purple **cloth** woven by skilled weavers.
Ezek 16. 4 washed you or rubbed you with salt or wrapped you in **cloth**.
27. 7 awnings were made of finest **cloth**, Of purple from the island
27.16 They gave emeralds, purple **cloth**, embroidery, fine linen,
27.20 The people of Dedan exchanged **saddle-cloths** for your goods.
27.24 clothing, purple **cloth**, and embroidery, brightly coloured carpets,
Mt 9.16 with a piece of new **cloth**, for the new patch will shrink
Mk 2.21 uses a piece of new **cloth** to patch up an old coat,
2.21 tear off some of the old **cloth**, making an even bigger hole.
14.51 young man, dressed only in a linen **cloth**, was following Jesus.
14.52 but he ran away naked, leaving the **cloth** behind.
Lk 2. 7 wrapped him in strips of **cloth** and laid him in a manger
2.12 a baby wrapped in strips of **cloth** and lying in a manger."
5.36 and the piece of new **cloth** will not match the old.
Jn 11.44 wrapped in grave clothes, and with a **cloth** round his face.
19.23 made of one piece of woven **cloth** without any seams in it.
20. 7 and the **cloth** which had been round Jesus' head.
Acts 16.14 was Lydia from Thyatira, who was a dealer in purple **cloth**.
Rev 6.12 became black like coarse black **cloth**, and the moon turned
18.12 their goods of linen, purple **cloth**, silk, and scarlet cloth;

CLOTHE

Gen 3.21 And the Lord God made **clothes** out of animal skins for
3.21 for Adam and his wife, and he **clothed** them.
9.21 drunk, took off his **clothes**, and lay naked in his tent.
24.53 Then he brought out **clothing** and silver and gold jewellery,
27.15 Then she took Esau's best **clothes**, which she kept in the house,
27.27 him, Isaac smelt his **clothes**—so he gave him his blessing.
28.20 and give me food and **clothing**, [21] and if I return safely to
35. 2 purify yourselves and put on clean **clothes**.
37.29 that Joseph was not there, he tore his **clothes** in sorrow.
37.34 Jacob tore his **clothes** in sorrow and put on sackcloth.
38.14 she changed from the widow's **clothes** she had been wearing,
38.19 took off her veil, and put her widow's **clothes** back on.
41.14 and changed his **clothes**, he came into the king's presence.
44.13 The brothers tore their **clothes** in sorrow, loaded their donkeys,
45.22 of them a change of **clothes**, but he gave Benjamin
45.22 three hundred pieces of silver and five changes of **clothes**.
49.11 He washes his **clothes** in blood-red wine.
Ex 3.22 and will ask for **clothing** and for gold and silver jewellery.
12.34 them in **clothing**, and carried them on their shoulders.
12.35 Egyptians for gold and silver jewellery and for **clothing**.
19.10 They must wash their **clothes** [11] and be ready the day after tomorrow.
19.14 So they washed their **clothes**, [15] and Moses said to them,
21.10 same amount of food and **clothing** and the same rights that
22. 9 cattle, donkeys, sheep, **clothing**, or any other lost object,
28. 3 tell them to make Aaron's **clothes**, so that he may be
28.41 Put these **clothes** on your brother Aaron and his sons.
29.21 on Aaron and his clothes and on his sons and their **clothes**.
29.21 his sons, and their **clothes** will then be dedicated to me.
35.19 the Holy Place—the sacred **clothes** for Aaron the priest and
39.41 the Holy Place—the sacred **clothes** for Aaron the priest and
Lev 6.11 Then he shall change his **clothes** and take the ashes
6.27 If any article of **clothing** is spattered with the animal's blood,
8.30 sprinkled them on Aaron and his sons and on their **clothes**.
8.30 In this way he consecrated them and their **clothes** to the Lord.
10. 5 and took hold of the **clothing** on the corpses and carried
10. 6 hair uncombed or tear your **clothes** to show that you are in
11.24 dead bodies must wash his **clothes**, but he will still be
11.40 animal, he must wash his **clothes**, but he will still be
11.40 dead body must wash his **clothes**, but he will still be
13. 6 The person shall wash his **clothes** and be ritually clean.
13.34 The person shall wash his **clothes**, and he will be clean.
13.45 must wear torn **clothes**, leave his hair uncombed,
13.47 When there is mildew on **clothing**, whether wool or linen,
13.56 has faded, he shall tear it out of the **clothing** or leather.
13.59 law about mildew on **clothing**, whether it is wool or linen,
14. 8 The person shall wash his **clothes**, shave off all his hair,
14. 9 he shall wash his **clothes** and have a bath, and then he
14.47 who lies down or eats in the house must wash his **clothes**.
14.55 and about mildew in **clothes** or houses.
15. 6 sat on must wash his **clothes** and have a bath, and he
15. 7 the discharge must wash his **clothes** and have a bath, and he
15. 8 that person must wash his **clothes** and have a bath, and he
15.10 man sat must wash his **clothes** and have a bath, and he
15.11 that person must wash his **clothes** and have a bath, and he
Lev 15.13 and then wash his **clothes** and bathe in fresh spring water,
15.21 has sat must wash his **clothes** and have a bath, and he
15.27 them is unclean and must wash his **clothes** and have a bath;
16.24 must bathe in a holy place and put on his own **clothes**.
16.26 to Azazel must wash his **clothes** and have a bath before he
16.28 burns them must wash his **clothes** and have a bath before he
17.15 wild animals must wash his **clothes**, have a bath, and wait
19.19 Do not wear **clothes** made of two kinds of material.
21.10 hair uncombed or tear his **clothes** to show that he is in
Num 8. 7 them to shave their whole bodies and to wash their **clothes**.
8.21 purified themselves and washed their **clothes**, and Aaron
14. 6 of the spies, tore their **clothes** in sorrow [7] and said to the
19. 7 he is to wash his **clothes** and pour water over himself, and
19. 8 cow must also wash his **clothes** and pour water over himself,
19.10 must wash his **clothes**, but he remains unclean until evening.
19.19 after washing his **clothes** and pouring water over himself,
19.21 the water for purification must also wash his **clothes**;
31.20 every piece of **clothing** and everything made of leather,
31.24 On the seventh day you must wash your **clothes**;
Deut 8. 4 During these forty years your **clothes** have not worn out,
10.18 who live with our people, and gives them food and **clothes**.
21.13 her head, cut her fingernails, [13] and change her **clothes**.
22. 3 a donkey, a piece of **clothing**, or anything else that your
22. 5 men's clothing, and men are not to wear women's **clothing**;
22.12 "Sew tassels on the four corners of your **clothes**.
29. 5 the desert, and your **clothes** and sandals never wore out.
Josh 7. 6 leaders of Israel tore their **clothes** in grief, threw
9. 5 They put on ragged **clothes** and worn-out sandals that had been mended.
9.13 Our **clothes** and sandals are worn out from the long journey."
22. 6 of livestock, silver, gold, bronze, iron, and many **clothes**.
Judg 3.16 He had it fastened on his right side under his **clothes**.
8.26 necklaces, and purple **clothes** that the kings of Midian wore,
11.35 saw her, he tore his **clothes** in sorrow and said, "Oh, my
14.12 and a change of fine **clothes** that you can't tell me its
14.19 them, and gave their fine **clothes** to the men who had solved
17.10 ten pieces of silver a year, some **clothes**, and your food."
Ruth 3. 3 put on some perfume, and get dressed in your best **clothes**.
1 Sam 4.12 grief, he had torn his **clothes** and put earth on his head.
19.24 He took off his **clothes** and danced and shouted in Samuel's presence,
27. 9 the sheep, cattle, donkeys, camels, and even the **clothes**.
28. 8 he put on different **clothes**, and after dark he went with two
2 Sam 1. 2 grief, he had torn his **clothes** and put earth on his head.
1.11 David tore his **clothes** in sorrow, and all his men did
1.24 He **clothed** you in rich scarlet dresses and adorned you
3.31 to tear their **clothes**, wear sackcloth, and mourn for Abner.
10. 4 their beards, cut off their **clothes** at the hips, and sent
12.20 floor, had a bath, combed his hair, and changed his **clothes**.
13.18 with full sleeves, the usual **clothing** for an unmarried
13.31 king stood up, tore his **clothes** in sorrow, and threw himself
13.31 The servants who were there with him tore their **clothes** also.
14. 2 put on your mourning **clothes**, and don't comb your hair.
15.32 Archite met him with his **clothes** torn and with earth on his
19.24 his beard, or washed his **clothes** from the time the king left
1 Kgs 18.46 he fastened his **clothes** tight round his waist and ran ahead
21.27 finished speaking, Ahab tore his **clothes**, took them off, and
2 Kgs 5. 5 thousand pieces of gold, and ten changes of fine **clothes**.
5. 7 the letter, he tore his **clothes** in dismay and exclaimed,
5.22 pieces of silver and two changes of fine **clothes**."
5.23 and two changes of fine **clothes** to two of his servants, and
5.26 and **clothes**, olive-groves and vineyards,
6.30 this, the king tore his **clothes** in dismay, and the people
6.30 could see that he was wearing sackcloth under his **clothes**.
7. 8 grabbed the silver, gold, and **clothing** they found, and went
7.15 the road they saw the **clothes** and equipment that the Syrians
11.14 Athaliah tore her **clothes** in distress and shouted,
18.37 Shebna, and Joah tore their **clothes** in grief, and went and
19. 1 report, he tore his **clothes** in grief, put on sackcloth,
22.11 being read, he tore his **clothes** in dismay, [12] and gave the
22.19 yourself before me, tearing your **clothes** and weeping, when
25.29 to change from his prison **clothes** and to dine at the king's
1 Chr 19. 4 their beards, cut off their **clothes** at the hips, and sent
2 Chr 5.11 and the members of their clans—were wearing linen **clothing**.
9. 4 the uniforms they wore, the **clothing** of the servants who
20.25 many cattle, supplies, **clothing**, and other valuable objects.
23.13 She tore her **clothes** in distress and shouted, "Treason!
28.15 provide the prisoners with **clothing** from the captured loot.
28.15 They gave them **clothes** and sandals to wear, gave them enough
34.19 being read, he tore his **clothes** in dismay [20] and gave the
34.27 yourself before me, tearing your **clothes** and weeping, when
Ezra 9. 3 heard this, I tore my **clothes** in despair, tore my hair and
9. 5 and still wearing my torn **clothes**, I knelt in prayer and
Neh 4.23 I didn't take off my **clothes** even at night, neither did
9.21 their **clothing** never wore out, and their feet were not
Esth 4. 1 of all that had been done, he tore his **clothes** in anguish.
4. 4 She sent Mordecai some **clothes** to put on instead of the sackcloth,
Job 1.20 Then Job stood up and tore his **clothes** in grief.
2.12 weep and wail, tearing their **clothes** in grief and throwing
9.31 a pit of filth, and even my **clothes** are ashamed of me.
16.15 I mourn and wear **clothes** made of sackcloth, and I sit
22. 6 you took away his **clothes** and left him nothing to wear.
24.10 But the poor must go out with no **clothes** to protect them;
27.16 much silver to count and more **clothes** than anyone needs;
27.17 good man will wear the **clothes**, and some honest man will get
30.18 seizes me by my collar and twists my **clothes** out of shape.
31.19 need, too poor to buy **clothes**, [20] I would give him clothing
40.10 **clothe** yourself with majesty and glory.
Ps 22.18 They gamble for my **clothes** and divide them among themselves.
45. 8 The perfume of myrrh and aloes is on your **clothes**;
69.11 I dress myself in **clothes** of mourning, and they laugh at me.

Ps 93. 1 He is **clothed** with majesty and strength.
102.26 they will all wear out like **clothes.**
102.26 You will discard them like **clothes,** and they will vanish.
104. 1 You are **clothed** with majesty and glory;
109.19 May they cover him like **clothes** and always be round him
Prov 6.27 Can you carry fire against your chest without burning your **clothes?**
25.20 is like taking off his **clothes** on a cold day or like
27.26 You can make **clothes** from the wool of your sheep and buy
31.21 She doesn't worry when it snows, because her family has warm **clothing.**
31.22 She makes bedspreads and wears **clothes** of fine purple linen.
31.24 She makes **clothes** and belts, and sells them to merchants.
Song 4.11 Your **clothing** has all the fragrance of Lebanon.
Is 3. 7 I haven't any food or **clothes** either.
3.24 instead of fine **clothes,** they will be dressed in rags;
4. 1 say, "We can feed and **clothe** ourselves, but please let us
9. 5 all their bloodstained **clothing** will be destroyed by fire.
23.18 use her money to buy the food and the **clothing** they need.
32.11 Strip off your **clothes** and tie rags round your waist.
36.22 Shebna, and Joah tore their **clothes** in grief and went and
37. 1 report, he tore his **clothes** in grief, put on sackcloth,
47. 2 Strip off your fine **clothes!**
51. 6 will wear out like old **clothing,** and all its people will die
51. 8 they will vanish like moth-eaten **clothing!**
52. 1 Holy city of God, **clothe** yourself with splendour!
57. 8 you take off your **clothes** and climb into your large beds
58. 7 Give **clothes** to those who have nothing to wear, and do not
59. 5 you no good—they are as useless as **clothing** made of cobwebs!
59.17 He will **clothe** himself with the strong desire to set things
61.10 God has **clothed** her with salvation and victory.
63. 2 "Why is his **clothing** so red, like that of a man who
63. 3 in my anger, and their blood has stained all my **clothing.**
Jer 2.34 Your **clothes** are stained with the blood of the poor and innocent,
13.22 happened to you—why your **clothes** have been torn off and you
13.26 Lord himself will strip off your **clothes** and expose you to shame.
38.11 storeroom and got some worn-out **clothing** which he let down
41. 5 They had shaved off their beards, torn their **clothes,** and gashed themselves.
43.12 As a shepherd picks his **clothes** clean of lice, so the king
52.33 to change from his prison **clothes** and to dine at the king's
Ezek 5. 3 a few hairs and wrap them in the hem of your **clothes.**
9. 2 dressed in linen **clothes,** carrying something to write with.
9.11 Then the man wearing linen **clothes** returned and reported to the Lord,
10. 2 to the man wearing linen **clothes,** "Go between the wheels
10. 6 commanded the man wearing linen **clothes** to take some fire
16.13 and you always wore **clothes** of embroidered linen and silk.
16.16 You used some of your **clothes** to decorate your places of worship,
16.18 You took the embroidered **clothes** I gave you and put them
16.36 "You stripped off your **clothes** and, like a prostitute, you
16.37 I will strip off your **clothes** and let them see you naked.
16.39 They will take away your **clothes** and jewels and leave you
18. 7 he feeds the hungry and gives **clothing** to the naked.
18.16 He feeds the hungry and gives **clothing** to the naked.
23.26 They will tear off your **clothes** and take your jewels.
26.16 their embroidered **clothes** and sit trembling on the ground.
27.24 They sold you luxurious **clothing,**
34. 3 You drink the milk, wear **clothes** made from the wool, and
42.14 rooms the holy **clothing** they wore while serving the Lord.
42.14 They must put on other **clothes** before going out to the area
44.17 courtyard of the Temple, they are to put on linen **clothing.**
44.19 must first take off the **clothes** they wore on duty in the
44.19 are to put on other **clothing**
44.19 in order to keep their sacred **clothing** from harming the people.
Dan 3.27 hair was not singed, their **clothes** were not burnt, and there
7. 9 His **clothes** were white as snow, and his hair was like pure
10. 5 who was wearing linen **clothes** and a belt of fine gold.
12. 1 The angel wearing linen **clothes** said, "At that time the
Hos 2. 9 take away the wool and the linen I gave her for **clothing.**
Joel 2.13 tearing your **clothes** is not enough."
Amos 2. 8 of worship men sleep on **clothing** that they have taken from
Hag 1. 6 You have **clothing,** but not enough to keep you warm.
Zech 3. 3 Joshua was standing there, wearing filthy **clothes.**
3. 4 "Take away the filthy **clothes** this man is wearing."
3. 4 away your sin and will give you new **clothes** to wear."
3. 5 then they put the new **clothes** on him while the angel of
14.14 the nations—gold, silver, and **clothing** in great abundance.
Mt 3. 4 John's **clothes** were made of camel's hair;
6.25 need in order to stay alive, or about **clothes** for your body.
6.25 And isn't the body worth more than **clothes?**
6.28 "And why worry about **clothes?**
6.28 they do not work or make **clothes** for themselves.
6.29 with all his wealth had **clothes** as beautiful as one of these
6.30 It is God who **clothes** the wild grass—grass that is here
6.30 Won't he be all the more sure to **clothe** you?
6.31 or my **clothes?'**
11. 8 A man dressed up in fancy **clothes?**
17. 2 was shining like the sun, and his **clothes** were dazzling white.
22.11 guests and saw a man who was not wearing wedding **clothes.**
22.12 'Friend, how did you get in here without wedding **clothes?'**
25.36 you received me in your homes, [36]naked and you **clothed** me;
25.38 and welcome you in our homes, or naked and **clothe** you?
25.43 welcome me in your homes, naked but you would not **clothe** me;
26.65 the High Priest tore his **clothes** and said, "Blasphemy!
27.28 They stripped off his **clothes** and put a scarlet robe on him.
27.31 took the robe off and put his own **clothes** back on him.
27.35 and then divided his **clothes** among them by throwing dice.
28. 3 appearance was like lightning, and his **clothes** were white as snow.
Mk 1. 6 John wore **clothes** made of camel's hair, with a leather belt
5.15 He was sitting there, **clothed** and in his right mind;
Mk 5.28 herself, "If I just touch his **clothes,** I will get well."
5.30 round in the crowd and asked, "Who touched my **clothes?"**
9. 3 over Jesus, [3]and his **clothes** became shining white—whiter than
15.20 off the purple robe and put his own **clothes** back on him.
15.24 crucified him and divided his **clothes** among themselves,
15.24 throwing dice to see who would get which piece of **clothing.**
Lk 7.25 A man dressed up in fancy **clothes?**
8.27 man had gone without **clothes** and would not stay at home,
8.35 sitting at the feet of Jesus, **clothed** and in his right mind;
9.29 changed its appearance, and his **clothes** became dazzling white.
12.22 to stay alive or about the **clothes** you need for your body.
12.23 and the body much more important than **clothes.**
12.27 they don't work or make **clothes** for themselves.
12.27 with all his wealth had **clothes** as beautiful as one of these
12.28 It is God who **clothes** the wild grass—grass that is here
12.28 Won't he be all the more sure to **clothe** you?
16.19 dressed in the most expensive **clothes** and lived in great luxury
23.34 They divided his **clothes** among themselves by throwing dice.
24. 4 when suddenly two men in bright shining **clothes** stood by them.
Jn 11.44 and feet wrapped in grave **clothes,** and with a cloth round
19.23 they took his **clothes** and divided them into four parts,
19.24 divided my **clothes** among themselves and gambled for my robe."
21. 7 (for he had taken his **clothes** off) and jumped into the water.
Acts 10.30 a man dressed in shining **clothes** stood in front of me
14.14 they tore their **clothes** and ran into the middle of
16.22 Then the officials tore the **clothes** off Paul and Silas
18. 6 shaking the dust from his **clothes** and saying to them,
19.16 from his house, wounded and with their **clothes** torn off.
20.33 I have not wanted anyone's silver or gold or **clothing.**
22.23 They were screaming, waving their **clothes,** and throwing dust
1 Cor 4.11 we are **clothed** in rags;
2 Cor 5. 3 by being **clothed** with it we shall not be without a body.
11.27 I have often been without enough food, shelter, or **clothing.**
Gal 3.27 and now you are **clothed,** so to speak, with the life
Col 3.12 So then, you must **clothe** yourselves with compassion, kindness,
1 Tim 2. 9 be modest and sensible about their **clothes** and to dress properly;
6. 8 if we have food and **clothes,** that should be enough for us.
Heb 1.11 they will all wear out like **clothes.**
1.12 them up like a coat, and they will be changed like **clothes.**
11.37 They went round **clothed** in skins of sheep or goats—
Jas 2. 2 a gold ring and fine **clothes** comes to your meeting,
2. 2 and a poor man in ragged **clothes** also comes.
2.15 or sisters who need **clothes** and don't have enough to eat.
5. 2 have rotted away, and your **clothes** have been eaten by moths.
Jude 23 but hate their very **clothes,** stained by their sinful lusts.
Rev 3. 4 a few of you there in Sardis have kept your **clothes** clean.
3. 4 You will walk with me, **clothed** in white, because you are
3. 5 win the victory will be **clothed** like this in white,
3.18 Buy also white **clothing** to dress yourself and cover up
16.15 stays awake and guards his **clothes,** so that he will not walk

CLOUD

[THUNDERCLOUDS]

Gen 9.13 all living beings, [13]I am putting my bow in the **clouds.**
9.14 I cover the sky with **clouds** and the rainbow appears, [15]I
9.16 the rainbow appears in the **clouds,** I will see it and
Ex 13.21 them in a pillar of **cloud** to show them the way, and
13.22 The pillar of **cloud** was always in front of the people
14.19 The pillar of **cloud** also moved until it was [20]between the
14.20 The **cloud** made it dark for the Egyptians, but gave light to
14.24 the pillar of fire and **cloud** at the Egyptian army and threw
16.10 suddenly the dazzling light of the Lord appeared in a **cloud.**
19. 9 to you in a thick **cloud,** so that the people will hear
19.16 and lightning, a thick **cloud** appeared on the mountain,
20.21 off, and only Moses went near the dark **cloud** where God was.
24.15 Moses went up Mount Sinai, and a **cloud** covered it.
24.16 The **cloud** covered the mountain for six days,
24.16 on the seventh day the Lord called to Moses from the **cloud.**
24.18 Moses went on up the mountain into the **cloud.**
33. 9 gone in, the pillar of **cloud** would come down and stay at
33. 9 the Tent, and the Lord would speak to Moses from the **cloud.**
33.10 people saw the pillar of **cloud** at the door of the Tent,
34. 5 Lord came down in a **cloud,** stood with him there, and
40.34 Then the **cloud** covered the Tent and the dazzling light
40.36 to another place only when the **cloud** lifted from the Tent.
40.37 As long as the **cloud** stayed there, they did not move
40.38 wanderings they could see the **cloud** of the Lord's presence
Lev 16. 2 where I appear in a **cloud** above the lid on the Covenant
Num 9.15 the Lord's presence was set up, a **cloud** came and covered it.
9.15 At night the **cloud** looked like fire.
9.17 Whenever the **cloud** lifted, the people of Israel broke camp,
9.17 set up camp again in the place where the **cloud** came down.
9.18 As long as the **cloud** stayed over the Tent, they stayed in
9.19 When the **cloud** stayed over the Tent for a long time,
9.20 Sometimes the **cloud** remained over the Tent for only a few days;
9.21 Sometimes the **cloud** remained only from evening until morning,
9.21 and they moved on as soon as the **cloud** lifted.
9.21 Whenever the **cloud** lifted, they moved on.
9.22 longer, as long as the **cloud** remained over the Tent, they
10.11 the people left Egypt, the **cloud** over the Tent of the Lord's
10.12 The **cloud** came to rest in the wilderness of Paran.
10.34 on from each camp, the **cloud** of the Lord was over them
11.25 Then the Lord came down in the **cloud** and spoke to him.
12. 5 down in a pillar of **cloud,** stood at the entrance of the
12.10 as he departed [10]and the **cloud** left the Tent, Miriam's
14.14 are plainly seen when your **cloud** stops over us, and that you
14.14 us in a pillar of **cloud** by day and a pillar of
16.42 Tent and saw that the **cloud** was covering it and that the
Deut 1.33 of fire by night and in a pillar of **cloud** by day.
4.11 which was covered with thick **clouds** of dark smoke and fire

Deut 5.22 fire and from the thick **clouds,** he gave these commandments
31.15 there in a pillar of **cloud** that stood by the door of
33.26 the sky, riding through the **clouds** to come to your aid.
Judg 5. 4 Yes, water poured down from the **clouds.**
20.38 When they saw a big **cloud** of smoke going up from the
20.40 a **cloud** of smoke began to go up from the town.
2 Sam 22.10 sky apart and came down, with a dark **cloud** under his feet.
22.12 thick **clouds,** full of water, surrounded him;
23. 4 the sun shining on a **cloudless** dawn, the sun that makes the
1 Kgs 8.10 was suddenly filled with a **cloud** [11] shining with the
8.12 sky, yet you have chosen to live in **clouds** and darkness.
18.44 said, "I saw a little **cloud** no bigger than a man's hand,
18.45 sky was covered with dark **clouds,** the wind began to blow,
2 Chr 5.11 was suddenly filled with a **cloud** shining with the dazzling
6. 1 "Lord, you have chosen to live in **clouds** and darkness.
Neh 9.12 With a **cloud** you led them in day-time, and at night you
9.19 did not take away the **cloud** or the fire that showed them
Job 3. 5 cover it with **clouds,** and blot out the sun.
7. 9 Like a **cloud** that fades and is gone, a man dies and
20. 6 that his head reaches the **clouds,** [7] but he will be blown
22.13 He is hidden by **clouds**—how can he judge us?"
22.14 You think the thick **clouds** keep him from seeing, as he
26. 8 is God who fills the **clouds** with water and keeps them from
26. 9 He hides the full moon behind a **cloud.**
28.26 And the path that the **thunderclouds** travel;
30.15 gone like a puff of wind, and my prosperity like a **cloud.**
35. 5 See how high the **clouds** are!
36.28 the rain pour from the **clouds** in showers for all mankind.
36.29 No one knows how the **clouds** move or how the thunder
37.11 Lightning flashes from the **clouds,** [12] as they move at God's will.
37.15 God gives the command and makes lightning flash from the **clouds?**
37.16 Do you know how **clouds** float in the sky, the work of
38. 9 I who covered the sea with **clouds** and wrapped it in darkness.
38.34 you shout orders to the **clouds** and make them drench you with
38.37 wise enough to count the **clouds** and tilt them over to pour
Ps 18. 9 sky apart and came down with a dark **cloud** under his feet.
18.11 thick **clouds,** full of water, surrounded him.
18.12 the lightning before him and broke through the dark **clouds.**
68. 4 prepare a way for him who rides on the **clouds.**
77.17 The **clouds** poured down rain;
78.14 he led them with a **cloud** and all night long with the
97. 2 **Clouds** and darkness surround him;
99. 7 He spoke to them from the pillar of **cloud;**
104. 3 You use the **clouds** as your chariot and ride on the wings
105.39 God put a **cloud** over his people and a fire at night
135. 7 He brings storm **clouds** from the ends of the earth;
147. 8 He spreads **clouds** over the sky;
148. 8 snow and **clouds,** strong winds that obey his command.
Prov 3.20 rivers to flow and the **clouds** to give rain to the earth.
8.28 ocean, [28] when he placed the **clouds** in the sky, when he
16.15 king's favour is like the **clouds** that bring rain in the
25.14 never give are like **clouds** and wind that bring no rain.
Ecc 11. 3 When the **clouds** are full, it rains.
12. 2 grow dim for you, and the rain **clouds** will never pass away.
Is 4. 5 the Lord will send a **cloud** in the daytime and smoke and
5. 6 I will even forbid the **clouds** to let rain fall on it."
14.14 climb to the tops of the **clouds** and be like the Almighty.
14.31 A **cloud** of dust is coming from the north—it is an
19. 1 The Lord is coming to Egypt, riding swiftly on a **cloud.**
25. 5 the shouts of cruel men, as a **cloud** cools a hot day.
25. 7 he will suddenly remove the **cloud** of sorrow that has been
30.30 There will be flames, **cloudbursts,** hailstones, and torrents of rain.
44.22 I have swept your sins away like a **cloud.**
60. 8 that skim along like **clouds,** Like doves returning home?
Jer 4.13 Look, the enemy is coming like **clouds.**
10.13 he brings **clouds** from the ends of the earth.
51.16 he brings **clouds** from the ends of the earth.
Lam 3.44 by your anger, [44] By a **cloud** of fury too thick for our
Ezek 1. 4 was flashing from a huge **cloud,** and the sky round it was
10. 3 Temple when he went in, and a **cloud** filled the inner courtyard.
10. 4 Then the **cloud** filled the Temple, and the courtyard was
19.11 The vine grew tall enough to reach the **clouds;**
26.10 The **clouds** of dust raised by their horses will cover you.
30. 3 Lord will act, A day of **clouds** and trouble for the nations.
30.18 A **cloud** will cover Egypt, and the people of all her cities
31. 3 With beautiful, shady branches, A tree so tall it reaches the **clouds.**
31.10 happen to that tree that grew until it reached the **clouds.**
31.14 or push its top through the **clouds** and reach such a height.
32. 7 sun will hide behind the **clouds,** and the moon will give no
38. 9 will attack like a storm and cover the land like a **cloud."**
Dan 7.13 was approaching me, surrounded by **clouds,** and he went to the
Joel 2. 2 will be a dark and gloomy day, a black and **cloudy** day.
2.30 there will be bloodshed, fire, and **clouds** of smoke.
Nah 1. 3 the **clouds** are the dust raised by his feet!
Hab 3. 8 You rode upon the **clouds;**
3. 8 the storm **cloud** was your chariot, as you brought victory
Zeph 1.15 and gloom, a black and **cloudy** day, [16] a day filled with the
Zech 10. 1 the Lord who sends rain **clouds** and showers, making the
Mt 17. 5 he was talking, a shining **cloud** came over them,
17. 5 and a voice from the **cloud** said, "This is my own dear
24.30 of Man coming on the **clouds** of heaven with power and great
26.64 right of the Almighty and coming on the **clouds** of heaven!"
Mk 9. 7 Then a **cloud** appeared and covered them with its shadow, and
9. 7 a voice came from the **cloud,** "This is my own dear Son
13.26 Man will appear, coming in the **clouds** with great power and glory.
14.62 of the Almighty and coming with the **clouds** of heaven!"
Lk 9.34 he was still speaking, a **cloud** appeared and covered them
9.34 and the disciples were afraid as the **cloud** came over them.
9.35 A voice said from the **cloud,** "This is my Son, whom I
12.54 "When you see a **cloud** coming up in the west,
Lk 21.27 Man will appear, coming in a **cloud** with great power and glory.
Acts 1. 9 as they watched him, and a **cloud** hid him from their sight.
1 Cor 10. 1 under the protection of the **cloud,** and all passed safely through
10. 2 In the **cloud** and in the sea they were all baptized
1 Thes 4.17 along with them in the **clouds** to meet the Lord in the
2 Pet 2.17 like dried-up springs, like **clouds** blown along by a storm;
Jude 12 They are like **clouds** carried along by the wind, but bringing
Rev 1. 7 Look, he is coming on the **clouds!**
10. 1 He was wrapped in a **cloud** and had a rainbow round his
11.12 As their enemies watched, they went up into heaven in a **cloud.**
14.14 and there was a white **cloud,**
14.14 and sitting on the **cloud** was what looked like a human
14.15 who was sitting on the **cloud,** "Use your sickle and reap
14.16 one who sat on the **cloud** swung his sickle on the earth,

CLUB

2 Sam 23.21 Benaiah attacked him with his **club,** snatched the spear from
1 Chr 11.23 Benaiah attacked him with a **club,** snatched the spear from
Job 41.29 To him a **club** is a piece of straw, and he laughs
Prov 25.18 is as deadly as a sword, a **club,** or a sharp arrow.
Is 10. 5 I use Assyria like a **club** to punish those with whom I
10.15 A **club** doesn't lift up a man;
10.15 a man lifts up a **club."**
28.27 He never uses a heavy **club** to beat out dill seeds or
Ezek 39. 9 shields, bows, arrows, spears, and **clubs,** and will have
Mt 26.47 crowd armed with swords and **clubs** and sent by the chief
26.55 to come with swords and **clubs** to capture me, as though I
Mk 14.43 armed with swords and **clubs,** and sent by the chief priests,
14.48 to come with swords and **clubs** to capture me, as though I
Lk 22.52 to come with swords and **clubs,** as though I were an outlaw?

CLUSTER

Song 7. 7 as a palm-tree, and your breasts are **clusters** of dates.

COAL

Gen 22. 6 carried a knife and live **coals** for starting the fire.
22. 7 see that you have the **coals** and the wood, but where is
Lev 10. 1 took his fire-pan, put live **coals** in it, added incense, and
16.12 a fire-pan full of burning **coals** from the altar and two
Num 16. 6 followers take firepans, put live **coals** and incense on them,
16.18 took his firepan, put live **coals** and incense on it, and
16.37 and scatter the **coals** from the firepans somewhere else,
16.46 "Take your firepan, put live **coals** from the altar in it,
16.46 and put some incense on the **coals.**
16.47 put the incense on the **coals** and performed the ritual of
2 Sam 22. 9 a consuming flame and burning **coals** from his mouth.
22.13 burning **coals** flamed up from the lightning before him.
1 Kgs 7.50 for incense, and the pans used for carrying live **coals;**
2 Kgs 25.15 the small bowls and the pans used for carrying live **coals.**
2 Chr 4.22 for incense, and the pans used for carrying live **coals.**
Ps 11. 6 He sends down flaming **coals** and burning sulphur on the wicked;
18. 8 a consuming flame and burning **coals** from his mouth.
140.10 May red-hot **coals** fall on them;
Prov 6.28 Can you walk on hot **coals** without burning your feet?
Is 6. 6 to me, carrying a burning **coal** that he had taken from the
6. 7 my lips with the burning **coal** and said, "This has touched
30.14 enough to pick up hot **coals** with, or to scoop water from
Jer 52.19 pans used for carrying live **coals,** the bowls for holding the
Ezek 10. 2 under the creatures and fill your hands with burning **coals.**
10. 2 Then scatter the **coals** over the city."
10. 7 among them, picked up some **coals,** and put them in the hands
10. 7 The man took the **coals** and left.
24.11 the empty bronze pot on the **coals** and let it get red-hot.

Am **COALS**
see also **CHARCOAL, EMBERS, FIRE**

COARSE

Is 3.24 instead of fine belts, they will wear **coarse** ropes;
Zech 13. 4 wear a prophet's **coarse** garment in order to deceive people.
Rev 6.12 the sun became black like **coarse** black cloth, and the moon

COAST
[SEA-COAST]

Gen 10. 5 of the people who live along the **coast** and on the islands.
Ex 13.17 road that goes up the **coast** to Philistia, although it was
Deut 1. 7 to the southern region, and to the Mediterranean **coast.**
2.23 The land along the Mediterranean **coast** had been settled
Josh 9. 1 foothills, and all along the **coastal** plain of the
10.41 to Gaza near the **coast,** including all the area of Goshen,
11. 2 Lake Galilee, in the foothills, and on the **coast** near Dor.
12.23 (in Carmel), [23] Dor (on the **coast**), Goiim (in Galilee),
15.47 the border of Egypt and the **coast** of the Mediterranean Sea.
17.11 Dor (the one on the **coast**), Endor, Taanach, Megiddo, and
Judg 1.18 These people living along the **coast** had iron chariots, and
5.17 The tribe of Asher stayed by the **sea-coast;**
1 Kgs 5. 9 rafts to float them down the **coast** to the place you choose.
2 Chr 21.16 Arabs lived near where some Sudanese had settled along the **coast.**
Esth 10. 1 on the people of the **coastal** regions of his empire as well
Is 11.11 and Hamath, and in the **coastlands** and on the islands of the
20. 6 people who live along the **coast** of Philistia will say, 'Look
Jer 47. 7 to attack Ashkelon and the people who live on the **coast."**
Ezek 26.15 people who live along the **coast** will be terrified at the
26.17 ruled the seas And terrified all who lived on the **coast.**

Ezek 27. 3 sea and does business with the people living on every **seacoast.**
27.15 people of many **coastal** lands gave you ivory and ebony in
27.35 "Everyone who lives along the **coast** is shocked at your fate.
39. 6 Magog and along all the **coasts** where people live undisturbed,
Zeph 2. 5 You Philistines are doomed, you people who live along the **coast.**
Lk 6.17 from Jerusalem and from the **coastal** cities of Tyre and Sidon;
Acts 17.14 At once the believers sent Paul away to the **coast;**
27. 8 We kept close to the **coast** and with great difficulty came
27.13 and sailed as close as possible along the **coast** of Crete.
27.17 into the sandbanks off the **coast** of Libya, so they lowered
27.39 sailors did not recognize the **coast,** but they noticed a bay

COAT

1 Sam 17.38 helmet, which he put on David's head, and a **coat** of armour.
2 Chr 26.14 shields, spears, helmets, **coats** of armour, bows and arrows,
Neh 4.16 stood guard, wearing **coats** of armour and armed with spears,
Job 13.28 As a result, I crumble like rotten wood, like a moth-eaten **coat.**
41.13 can tear off his outer **coat** or pierce the armour he wears.
Is 59.17 will wear justice like a **coat** of armour and saving power
Ezek 16. 8 your naked body with my **coat** and promised to love you.
Mic 2. 8 there you are, waiting to steal the **coats** off their backs.
Mt 5.40 sue you for your shirt, let him have your **coat** as well.
9.16 one patches up an old **coat** with a piece of new cloth,
9.16 patch will shrink and make an even bigger hole in the **coat.**
Mk 2.21 to patch up an old **coat,** because the new patch will shrink
Lk 5.36 a piece off a new **coat** to patch up an old coat.
5.36 will have torn the new **coat,** and the piece of new cloth
6.29 if someone takes your **coat,** let him have your shirt as well.
12.37 he will take off his **coat,** ask them to sit down, and
22.36 and whoever has no sword must sell his **coat** and buy one.
Acts 9.39 all the shirts and **coats** that Dorcas had made while she
2 Tim 4.13 When you come, bring my **coat** that I left in Troas with
Heb 1.12 fold them up like a **coat,** and they will be changed

COBRA

Ps 58. 4 their ears like a deaf **cobra,** [5]which does not hear the
140. 3 their words are like a **cobra's** poison.

COBWEBS

Is 59. 5 you no good—they are as useless as clothing made of **cobwebs!**

COCK

Job 38.36 Nile will flood, or who tells the **cock** that rain will fall?
Prov 30.31 goats, strutting **cocks,** and kings in front of their people.
Mt 26.34 tell you that before the **cock** crows tonight, you will say
26.74 Just then a **cock** crowed, [75]and Peter remembered what Jesus had
26.75 "Before the **cock** crows, you will say three times that you
Mk 14.30 tell you that before the **cock** crows twice tonight, you will
14.68 Just then a **cock** crowed.
14.72 Just then a **cock** crowed a second time, and Peter remembered
14.72 said to him, "Before the **cock** crows twice, you will say
Lk 22.34 Peter," Jesus said, "the **cock** will not crow tonight until you
22.60 At once, while he was still speaking, a **cock** crowed.
22.61 said to him, "Before the **cock** crows tonight, you will say
Jn 13.38 before the **cock** crows you will say three times that you do
18.27 Again Peter said "No"—and at once a **cock** crowed.

COFFIN

Gen 50.26 They embalmed his body and put it in a **coffin.**
Deut 3.11 His **coffin,** made of stone, was four metres long and almost
2 Sam 3.31 And at the funeral King David himself walked behind the **coffin.**
Lk 7.14 and touched the **coffin,** and the men carrying it stopped.

COIN

[COPPER COINS, GOLD COIN, SILVER COIN]

1 Sam 9. 8 The servant answered, "I have a small **silver coin.**
13.21 the charge was one small **coin** for sharpening axes
13.21 and two **coins** for sharpening ploughs or hoes.)
1 Chr 21.25 And he paid Araunah six hundred **gold coins** for the threshing-place.
Neh 5.15 people and had demanded forty **silver coins** a day for food
Song 8.11 each one pays a thousand **silver coins.**
8.12 is welcome to his thousand **coins,** and the farmers to two
Mt 17.27 you will find a **coin** worth enough for my temple-tax and
20. 2 them the regular wage, a **silver coin** a day, and sent them
20. 9 begun to work at five o'clock were paid a **silver coin** each.
20.10 but they too were given a **silver coin** each.
20.13 all, you agreed to do a day's work for one **silver coin.**
22.19 Show me the **coin** for paying the tax!"
22.19 They brought him the **coin,** [20]and he asked them, "Whose face
25.15 one he gave five thousand **gold coins,** to another he gave two
25.16 who had received five thousand **coins** went at once and invested
25.17 servant who had received two thousand **coins** earned another two
25.18 who had received one thousand **coins** went off, dug a hole
25.20 who had received five thousand **coins** came in and handed over
25.20 'You gave me five thousand **coins,** sir,' he said.
25.22 had been given two thousand **coins** came in and said,
25.22 'You gave me two thousand **coins,** sir.
25.24 who had received one thousand **coins** came in and said,
25.28 and give it to the one who has ten thousand **coins.**
26.15 They counted out thirty **silver coins** and gave them to him.
27. 3 and took back the thirty **silver coins** to the chief priests
27. 5 Judas threw the **coins** down in the Temple and left;
27. 6 priests picked up the **coins** and said, "This is blood money,
27. 9 "They took the thirty **silver coins,** the amount the people
Mk 6.37 go and spend two hundred **silver coins** on bread in order to
12.15 Bring a **silver coin,** and let me see it."
12.42 and dropped in two little **copper coins,** worth about a penny.
14. 5 for more than three hundred **silver coins** and the money given
Lk 7.41 "One owed him five hundred **silver coins,** and the other owed
10.35 day he took out two **silver coins** and gave them to the
15. 8 a woman who has ten **silver coins** loses one of them—what
15. 9 'I am so happy I found the **coin** I lost.
19.13 and gave them each a **gold coin** and told them, 'See what
19.16 'Sir, I have earned ten **gold coins** with the one you gave
19.18 'Sir, I have earned five **gold coins** with the one you gave
19.20 "Another servant came and said, 'Sir, here is your **gold coin;**
19.24 were standing there, 'Take the **gold coin** away from him and
19.24 from him and give it to the servant who has ten **coins.'**
19.25 But they said to him, 'Sir, he already has ten **coins!'**
20.24 their trick and said to them, [24]"Show me a **silver coin.**
21. 2 saw a very poor widow dropping in two little **copper coins.**
Jn 2.15 the tables of the money-changers and scattered their **coins;**
6. 7 more than two hundred **silver coins** to buy enough bread."
12. 5 perfume sold for three hundred **silver coins** and the money
Acts 19.19 books, and the total came to fifty thousand **silver coins.**

COLD

Gen 8.22 There will always be **cold** and heat, summer and winter, day
31.40 from the heat during the day and from the **cold** at night.
Deut 19.11 deliberately murders his enemy in **cold** blood and then
Job 24. 7 nothing to cover them, nothing to keep them from the **cold.**
37. 9 come from the south, and the biting **cold** from the north.
Ps 147.17 no one can endure the **cold** he sends!
Prov 25.13 one who sends him, like **cold** water in the heat of harvest
25.20 off his clothes on a **cold** day or like rubbing salt in
25.25 is like a drink of **cold** water when you are dry and
Ecc 4.11 If it is **cold,** two can sleep together and stay warm, but
Nah 3.17 swarm of locusts that stay in the walls on a **cold** day.
Zech 14. 6 there will no longer be **cold** or frost, [7]nor any darkness.
Mt 10.42 gives even a drink of **cold** water to one of the least
24.12 the spread of evil that many people's love will grow **cold.**
Jn 18.18 It was **cold,** so the servants and guards had built a
Acts 28. 2 started to rain and was **cold,** so they lit a fire and
Rev 3.15 I know that you are neither **cold** nor hot.
3.16 are lukewarm, neither hot nor **cold,** I am going to spit you

COLLAPSE

Josh 6. 5 are to give a loud shout, and the city walls will **collapse.**
6.20 heard it, they gave a loud shout, and the walls **collapsed.**
Judg 7.13 The tent **collapsed** and lay flat on the ground."
Is 3. 8 Judah is **collapsing!**
24.20 it will **collapse** and never rise again.
30.13 suddenly you will **collapse.**
51.20 At the corner of every street your people **collapse** from weakness;
Ezek 13.12 The wall will **collapse,** and everyone will ask you what
13.14 It will **collapse** and kill you all.
38.20 Mountains will fall, cliffs will crumble, and every wall will **collapse.**
Amos 8.13 even healthy young men and women will **collapse** from thirst.

COLLAR

Judg 8.26 of Midian wore, nor the **collars** that were round the necks of
Job 30.18 God seizes me by my **collar** and twists my clothes out of
Ps 105.18 in chains, and an iron **collar** was round his neck, [19]until
133. 2 Aaron's head and beard, down to the **collar** of his robes.
Jer 29.26 is placed in chains with an iron **collar** round his neck.

COLLEAGUE

Ps 55.13 But it is you, my companion, my **colleague** and close friend.

COLLECT

Gen 41.35 Order them to **collect** all the food during the good years
41.48 all of which Joseph **collected** and stored in the cities.
47.14 As they bought corn, Joseph **collected** all the money and
Ex 30.16 **Collect** this money from the people of Israel and spend
Num 19. 9 is ritually clean is to **collect** the ashes of the cow and
19.10 The man who **collected** the ashes must wash his clothes,
Deut 15. 2 he must not try to **collect** the money;
15. 3 You may **collect** what a foreigner owes you,
15. 3 but you must not **collect** what any of your own people
1 Sam 25.18 Abigail quickly **collected** two hundred loaves of bread,
2 Kgs 22. 4 the entrance to the Temple have **collected** from the people.
23.35 King Jehoiakim **collected** a tax from the people in
2 Chr 24. 5 the cities of Judah and **collect** from all the people enough
24. 6 that the Levites **collect** from Judah and Jerusalem the tax
24. 9 Moses, God's servant, had first **collected** in the wilderness.
24.11 And so they **collected** a large sum of money.
34. 9 that the Levite guards had **collected** in the Temple was
34. 9 (It had been **collected** from the people of Ephraim and
35.25 The song is found in the **collection** of laments.
Ezra 4.20 province of West Euphrates, **collecting** taxes and revenue.
7.16 silver and gold which you **collect** throughout the province of
7.24 You are forbidden to **collect** any taxes from the priests,
Neh 5.12 We'll give the property back and not try to **collect** the debts."
10.37 to the Levites, who **collect** tithes in our farming villages,
10.38 the Levites when tithes are **collected,** and for use in the
10.38 temple storerooms one tenth of all the tithes they **collect.**
12.44 These men were responsible for **collecting** from the farms
Ecc 12.11 use to guide sheep, and **collected** proverbs are as lasting as
Ezek 39. 9 Israel will go out and **collect** the abandoned weapons for firewood.

Lk 3.13 "Don't **collect** more than is legal," he told them.
1 Cor 16. 2 there will be no need to **collect** money when I come.
2 Tim 4. 3 their own desires and will **collect** for themselves more and more
Heb 7. 5 commanded by the Law to **collect** a tenth from the people
7. 6 but he **collected** a tenth from Abraham and blessed
7. 8 case of the priests the tenth is **collected** by men who die;
7. 8 for Melchizedek the tenth was **collected** by one who lives,
7. 9 Levi (whose descendants **collect** the tenth) also paid it.

COLONY

Is 23. 7 that sent settlers across the sea to establish **colonies?**
23.10 Go and farm the land, you people in the **colonies** in Spain!
Acts 16.12 it is also a Roman **colony.**

COLOUR

Lev 13.21 skin, but is light in **colour,** the priest shall isolate him
13.26 skin, but is light in **colour,** the priest shall isolate him
13.28 and is light in **colour,** it is not a dreaded skin-disease.
13.55 has not changed **colour,** even though it has not spread,
Num 11. 7 (Manna was like small seeds, whitish yellow in **colour.**
Ps 45.14 In her **colourful** gown she is led to the king, followed
Prov 7.16 I've covered my bed with sheets of **coloured** linen from Egypt.
Song 1. 6 on me because of my **colour,** because the sun has tanned me.
Jer 13.23 a black man change the **colour** of his skin, or a leopard
Ezek 1.28 light [28] that had in it all the **colours** of the rainbow.
27.24 brightly **coloured** carpets, and well-made cords and ropes.
Rev 4. 3 the throne there was a rainbow the **colour** of an emerald.

COLT

Gen 49.22 a wild donkey by a spring, A wild **colt** on a hillside.
Zech 9. 9 on a donkey— on a **colt,** the foal of a donkey.
Mt 21. 2 you will find a donkey tied up with her **colt** beside her.
21. 5 on a donkey and on a **colt,** the foal of a donkey."
21. 7 brought the donkey and the **colt,** threw their cloaks over them,
Mk 11. 2 you will find a **colt** tied up that has never been
11. 4 they went and found a **colt** out in the street, tied to
11. 5 bystanders asked them, "What are you doing, untying that **colt?"**
11. 7 brought the **colt** to Jesus, threw their cloaks over the animal,
Lk 19.30 you will find a **colt** tied up that has never been
19.33 As they were untying the **colt,** its owners said to them,
19.35 and they took the **colt** to Jesus.

Am **COLUMN** see **PILLAR**

COLUMN

1 Kgs 7. 6 The Hall of **Columns** was 22 metres long and 13.5 metres wide.
7. 6 It had a covered porch, supported by **columns.**
7.15 Huram cast two bronze **columns,** each one 8 metres tall
7.16 one 2.2 metres tall, to be placed on top of the **columns.**
7.17 The top of each **column** was decorated with a design of
7.21 Huram placed these two bronze **columns** in front of the
7.22 The lily-shaped bronze capitals were on top of the **columns.**
7.22 And so the work on the **columns** was completed.
7.40 The two **columns** The two bowl-shaped capitals on top of the columns
2 Kgs 11.14 king standing by the **column** at the entrance of the Temple,
23. 3 He stood by the royal **column** and made a covenant with the
25.13 broke in pieces the bronze **columns** and the carts that were
25.16 for the Temple—the two **columns,** the carts, and the large
25.17 The two **columns** were identical:
1 Chr 18. 8 to make the tank, the **columns,** and the bronze utensils for
2 Chr 3.15 The king made two **columns,** each one fifteen and a half
3.16 The tops of the **columns** were decorated with a design of
3.17 The **columns** were set at the sides of the temple entrance:
4.11 The two **columns** The two bowl-shaped capitals on top of the columns
14. 3 broke down the sacred stone **columns,** and cut down the
23.13 temple entrance, standing by the **column** reserved for kings
34.31 He stood by the royal **column** and made a covenant with
Esth 1. 6 of fine purple linen to silver rings on marble **columns.**
Song 3. 6 from the desert like a **column** of smoke, fragrant with
5.15 His thighs are **columns** of alabaster set in sockets of gold.
Is 9.18 It burns like a forest fire that sends up **columns** of smoke.
Jer 27.19 and Jerusalem, he left the **columns,** the bronze tank, the
36.23 finished reading three or four **columns,** the king cut them
52.17 broke in pieces the bronze **columns** and the carts that were
52.20 for the Temple—the two **columns,** the carts, the large tank,
52.21 The two **columns** were identical:
52.21 On top of each **column** was a bronze capital 2.2 metres high,
52.23 On the grating of each **column** there were a hundred
Ezek 40.49 There were two **columns,** one on each side of the entrance.
42. 6 and were not supported by **columns** like the other buildings
Amos 9. 1 the tops of the temple **columns** so hard that the whole porch

COMB (1)
[UNCOMBED]

Lev 10. 6 "Do not leave your hair **uncombed** or tear your clothes to
13.45 torn clothes, leave his hair **uncombed,** cover the lower part
21.10 must not leave his hair **uncombed** or tear his clothes to show
2 Sam 12.20 floor, had a bath, **combed** his hair, and changed his clothes.
14. 2 put on your mourning clothes, and don't **comb** your hair.
Dan 10. 3 meat, drink any wine, or **comb** my hair until the three weeks
Mt 6.17 wash your face and **comb** your hair, [18] so that others cannot

COMB (2)

Prov 24.13 just as honey from the **comb** is sweet on your tongue, [14] you

COMBAT

2 Kgs 6.22 soldiers you had captured in **combat** would you put to death.

COME

Gen 16. 8 Sarai, where have you **come** from and where are you going?"
19. 2 Please **come** to my house.
24.31 his camels at the well, [31] and said, **"Come** home with me.
42. 7 He asked them harshly, "Where do you **come** from?"
45. 9 **come** to me without delay.
49. 2 **"Come** together and listen, sons of Jacob.
Ex 3. 5 God said, "Do not **come** any closer.
3. 8 sufferings, [8] and so I have **come** down to rescue them from
3.16 Tell them that I have **come** to them and have seen what
4.31 heard that the Lord had **come** to them and had seen how
19. 9 said to Moses, "I will **come** to you in a thick cloud,
19.11 On that day I will **come** down on Mount Sinai, where all
19.18 with smoke, because the Lord had **come** down on it in fire.
19.23 the Lord, "The people cannot **come** up, because you commanded
20.20 God has only **come** to test you and make you keep on
20.24 you to worship me, I will **come** to you and bless you.
24. 1 The Lord said to Moses, **"Come** up the mountain to me, you
24. 2 You alone, and none of the others, are to **come** near me.
24. 2 The people are not even to **come** up the mountain."
24.12 The Lord said to Moses, **"Come** up the mountain to me,
32.26 "Everyone who is on the Lord's side **come** over here!"
34. 3 No one is to **come** up with you;
Lev 19.23 "When you **come** into the land of Canaan and plant any
23. 9 When you **come** into the land that the Lord is giving
Num 10.29 to make Israel prosperous, so **come** with us, and we will
10.32 If you **come** with us, we will share with you all the
11.17 I will **come** down and speak with you there, and I will
16.12 for Dathan and Abiram, but they said, 'We will not **come!**
16.14 We will not **come!"**
21.27 **"Come** to Heshbon, to King Sihon's city!
22.37 to him, "Why didn't you **come** when I sent for you the
23.13 Then Balak said to Balaam, **"Come** with me to another
23.18 **"Come,** Balak son of Zippor, And listen to what I have to
23.27 Balak said, **"Come** with me, and I will take you to
24.16 And receive the knowledge that **comes** from the Most High.
24.17 Like a comet he will **come** from Israel.
Deut 10. 1 **Come** up to me on the mountain, [2] and I will write on
14.29 They are to **come** and get all they need.
18. 9 "When you **come** into the land that the Lord your God is
Josh 9. 8 Where do you **come** from?"
10. 6 **Come** at once and help us!
18. 4 Then they are to **come** back to me.
Judg 4.18 went out to meet Sisera and said to him, **"Come** in, sir;
4.18 **come** into my tent.
4.22 Jael went out to meet him and said to him, **"Come** here!
5.15 they could not decide whether to **come.**
5.16 they could not decide whether to **come.**
11. 7 Why **come** to me now that you're in trouble?"
17. 9 Micah asked him, "Where do you **come** from?"
19.17 in the city square and asked him, "Where do you **come** from?
Ruth 1.11 "Why do you want to **come** with me?
1 Sam 6.21 **Come** down and fetch it."
14. 9 to wait for them to **come** to us, then we will stay
14.12 called out to Jonathan and the young man, **"Come** on up here!
14.38 the leaders of the people, **"Come** here and find out what sin
16. 5 Purify yourselves and **come** with me."
16.11 "Tell him to **come** here," Samuel said.
21. 1 him and asked, "Why did you **come** here all by yourself?"
23.11 Will Saul really **come,** as I have heard?
23.11 The Lord answered, "Saul will **come."**
23.27 a messenger arrived and said to Saul, **"Come** back at once!
25.11 and give them to men who **come** from I don't know where!"
26.21 **Come** back, David, my son!
28.15 Why did you make me **come** back?"
2 Sam 1. 3 David asked him, "Where have you **come** from?"
12.23 to where he is, but he can never **come** back to me."
14.29 but Joab would not **come.**
14.29 Again Absalom sent for him, and again Joab refused to **come.**
20.16 Tell Joab to **come** here;
1 Kgs 12. 5 **"Come** back in three days and I will give you my answer,"
18.30 Elijah said to the people, **"Come** closer to me," and they
2 Kgs 1. 5 "Why have you **come** back?"
4.15 "Tell her to **come** here," Elisha ordered.
10.16 up into the chariot, [16] saying, **"Come** with me and see for
10.21 not one of them failed to **come.**
1 Chr 16.33 will shout for joy when the Lord **comes** to rule the earth.
2 Chr 10. 5 Then **come** back."
30. 8 **Come** to the Temple in Jerusalem, which the Lord your God has
Job 19.25 is someone in heaven who will **come** at last to my defence.
32. 8 of Almighty God that **comes** to men and gives them wisdom.
39. 4 they go away and don't **come** back.
Ps 3. 7 **Come,** Lord!
6. 4 **Come** and save me, Lord;
7. 1 O Lord, my God, I **come** to you for protection;
9.10 you do not abandon anyone who **comes** to you.
9.19 **Come,** Lord!
12. 5 "But now I will **come,"** says the Lord, "because the
16. 2 all the good things I have **come** from you."
17. 3 You have **come** to me at night;
17.13 **Come,** Lord!
22.19 **Come** quickly to my rescue!

Ps 22.26 those who **come** to the Lord will praise him.
24. 6 Such are the people who **come** to God,
24. 6 who **come** into the presence of the God
24. 7 open the ancient doors, and the great king will **come** in.
24. 9 open the ancient doors, and the great king will **come** in.
25.20 I **come** to you for safety.
27. 8 When you said, **"Come** and worship me," I answered, "I will come,
31. 1 I **come** to you, Lord, for protection;
39.12 **come** to my aid when I weep.
40.16 May all who **come** to you be glad and joyful.
44.26 **Come** to our aid!
46. 8 **Come** and see what the Lord has done.
50. 3 Our God is **coming,** but not in silence;
59.10 My God loves me and will **come** to me;
68. 8 down rain, because of the **coming** of the God of Sinai,
68. 8 the **coming** of the God of Israel.
68.17 chariots the Lord **comes** from Sinai into the holy place.
68.35 awesome is God as he **comes** from his sanctuary— the God
69.18 **Come** to me and save me;
70. 4 May all who **come** to you be glad and joyful.
70. 5 **come** to me quickly, O God.
71. 1 Lord, I have **come** to you for protection;
80. 2 **come** and save us!
80.14 **come** and save your people!
80.15 **Come** and save this grapevine that you planted, this
82. 8 **Come,** O God, and rule the world;
95. 2 Let us **come** before him with thanksgiving and sing joyful
96.13 shout for joy [13] when the Lord **comes** to rule the earth.
98. 9 joy before the Lord, [9] because he **comes** to rule the earth.
100. 2 **come** before him with happy songs!
101. 2 When will you **come** to me?
114. 7 Tremble, earth, at the Lord's **coming,** at the presence of
118.20 only the righteous can **come** in.
118.26 God bless the one who **comes** in the name of the Lord!
119.79 May those who honour you **come** to me— all those who
121. 1 where will my help **come** from?
121. 2 My help will **come** from the Lord, who made heaven and earth.
121. 8 will protect you as you **come** and go now and for ever.
132. 8 **Come** to the Temple, Lord, with the Covenant Box, the
134. 1 **Come,** praise the Lord, all his servants, all who serve in
144. 5 O Lord, tear the sky apart and **come** down;
Prov 9. 4 **"Come** in, ignorant people!"
9.16 **"Come** in, ignorant people!"
Song 2.10 **Come** then, my love;
2.10 my darling, **come** with me.
2.13 **Come** then, my love;
2.13 my darling, **come** with me.
4. 8 **Come** with me from the Lebanon Mountains, my bride;
4. 8 **come** with me from Lebanon.
4. 8 **Come** down from the top of Mount Amana, from Mount Senir and
5. 2 Let me **come** in, my darling, my sweetheart, my dove.
5. 5 I was ready to let him **come** in.
7.11 **Come,** darling, let's go out to the countryside and spend
8.14 **Come** to me, my lover, like a gazelle, like a young stag
Is 2.21 When the Lord **comes** to shake the earth, people will hide
5.26 And here they **come,** swiftly, quickly!
13. 5 In his anger the Lord is **coming** to devastate the whole country.
21. 9 Suddenly, here they **come!**
21.12 If you want to ask again, **come** back and ask."
26.21 The Lord is **coming** from his heavenly dwelling-place to
30.15 says to the people, **"Come** back and quietly trust in me.
31. 6 But now, **come** back to me!
34. 1 **Come,** people of all nations!
40. 9 Tell the towns of Judah that their God is **coming!**
40.10 The Sovereign Lord is **coming** to rule with power,
41. 5 So they all assemble and **come.**
44.22 **Come** back to me;
45.20 **"Come** together, people of the nations, all who survive the
48.16 "Now **come** close to me and hear what I say.
49. 9 and to those who are in darkness, **'Come** out to the light!'
51. 5 I will **come** quickly and save them;
51. 5 Distant lands wait for me to **come;**
55. 1 **"Come,** everyone who is thirsty— here is water!
55. 1 **Come,** you that have no money— buy corn and eat!
55. 1 **Come!**
55. 3 "Listen now, my people, and **come** to me;
55. 3 **come** to me, and you will have life!
57. 3 **Come** here to be judged, you sinners!
59.20 to his people, "I will **come** to Jerusalem to defend you and
62.11 Jerusalem That the Lord is **coming** to save you, Bringing with
63.17 **Come** back, for the sake of those who serve you, for the
64. 1 Why don't you tear the sky apart and **come** down?
64. 2 **Come** and reveal your power to your enemies, and make the
66.15 The Lord will **come** with fire.
Jer 2.31 do as you please, that you will never **come** back to me?
3.12 go and say to Israel, "Unfaithful Israel, **come** back to me.
3.14 "Unfaithful people, **come** back;
10.15 they will be destroyed when the Lord **comes** to deal with them.
29.12 You will **come** and pray to me, and I will answer you.
30.10 You will **come** back home and live in peace;
30.11 I will **come** to you and save you.
31. 8 They will **come** back a great nation.
31.17 your children will **come** back home.
31.21 **Come** back, people of Israel, come home to the towns you left.
46.27 You will **come** back home and live in peace.
46.28 I will **come** to you and save you.
50.44 land, I, the Lord, will **come** and make the Babylonians run
51.18 they will be destroyed when the Lord **comes** to deal with them.
Lam 4.18 the end had **come.**
Ezek 7. 3 "Israel, the end has **come.**
21. 7 The time has **come;**
Ezek 24.14 The time has **come** for me to act.
36. 8 You are going to **come** home soon.
Dan 3.26 **Come** out!"
9.25 God's chosen leader **comes,** seven times seven years will pass.
9.26 The end will **come** like a flood, bringing the war and
10.12 I have **come** in answer to your prayer.
11.35 continue until the end **comes,** the time that God has set.
12. 9 words are to be kept secret and hidden until the end **comes.**
Hos 6. 3 He will **come** to us as surely as the day dawns, as
11. 9 I will not **come** to you in anger.
Joel 2.13 **Come** back to the Lord your God.
2.16 Even newly married couples must leave their room and **come.**
2.31 blood before the great and terrible day of the Lord **comes.**
Amos 4. 6 to all your cities, yet you did not **come** back to me.
4. 8 Still you did not **come** back to me.
4. 9 Still you did not **come** back to me.
4.10 Still you did not **come** back to me.
4.11 Still you did not **come** back to me," says the Lord.
5. 4 to the people of Israel, **"Come** to me, and you will live.
Jon 1. 8 What country do you **come** from?
Mic 1. 3 he will **come** down and walk on the tops of the mountains.
5. 4 When he **comes,** he will rule his people with the strength
7. 4 The day has **come** when God will punish the people, as he
Hab 3. 4 He **comes** with the brightness of lightning;
Zeph 1. 6 me, those who do not **come** to me or ask me to
Zech 1.21 I asked, "What have these men **come** to do?"
6. 5 they have just **come** from the presence of the Lord of all
8.20 coming when people from many cities will **come** to Jerusalem.
8.21 **Come** with us!'
8.22 peoples and powerful nations will **come** to Jerusalem to
9. 9 He **comes** triumphant and victorious, but humble and riding on
14. 5 The Lord my God will **come,** bringing all the angels with him.
Mal 3. 1 Lord you are looking for will suddenly **come** to his Temple.
3. 1 The messenger you long to see will **come** and proclaim my covenant."
3. 2 But who will be able to endure the day when he **comes?**
3. 3 He will **come** to judge like one who refines and purifies silver.
4. 5 terrible day of the Lord **comes,** I will send you the prophet
Mt 4.19 Jesus said to them, **"Come with me,** and I will teach you
6.10 may your Kingdom **come;**
8. 9 and I order that one, **'Come!'**
11. 3 John said was going to **come,** or should we expect someone else?"
11.28 **"Come to me,** all of you who are tired from carrying
16.24 "If anyone wants to **come with me,** he must forget self,
19.14 said, "Let the children **come to me** and do not stop them,
21. 9 God bless him who **comes in the name of the Lord!**
22. 4 **Come** to the wedding feast!'
23.39 say, 'God bless him who **comes in the name of the Lord.'"**
24. 3 is the time for your **coming** and the end of the age."
24.37 The **coming** of the Son of Man will be like what happened
24.42 because you do not know what day your Lord will **come.**
25. 6 **Come** and meet him!'
25.21 **Come** on in and share my happiness!'
25.23 **Come** on in and share my happiness!'
25.34 the people on his right, **'Come,** you that are blessed by my
25.34 **Come** and possess the kingdom which has been prepared for you
27.40 **Come** on down from the cross!"
28. 2 an angel of the Lord **came down** from heaven, rolled the stone
28. 6 **Come** here and see the place where he was lying.
Mk 1.17 Jesus said to them, **"Come with me,** and I will teach you
3. 3 Jesus said to the man, **"Come** up here to the front."
8.34 "If anyone wants to **come with me,"** he told them, "he must
10.14 "Let the children **come to me,** and do not stop them,
10.21 then **come** and follow me."
11. 9 God bless him who **comes in the name of the Lord!**
15.30 Now **come** down from the cross and save yourself!"
15.42 Council, who was waiting for the **coming** of the Kingdom of God.
Lk 3.22 and the Holy Spirit **came down** upon him in bodily form
5.32 have not **come** to call respectable people to repent, but outcasts."
7. 8 I order that one, **'Come!'**
7.16 "God has **come** to save his people!"
7.19 John said was going to **come,** or should we expect someone else?"
9.23 "If anyone wants to **come with me,** he must forget self, take
10.40 Tell her to **come** and help me!"
11. 2 may your Kingdom **come.**
13.35 say, 'God bless him who **comes in the name of the Lord.'"**
14.10 come to you and say, **'Come** on up, my friend, to a
14.17 sent his servant to tell his guests, **'Come,** everything is ready!'
14.20 'I have just got married, and for that reason I cannot **come.'**
17.20 Some Pharisees asked Jesus when the Kingdom of God would **come.**
18.16 said, "Let the children **come to me** and do not stop them,
18.22 then **come** and follow me."
19.38 "God bless the king who **comes in the name of the Lord!**
21.31 you will know that the Kingdom of God is about to **come.**
23.42 to Jesus, "Remember me, Jesus, when you **come** as King!"
23.50 man, who was waiting for the **coming** of the Kingdom of God.
Jn 1.39 **"Come** and see," he answered.
1.43 He found Philip and said to him, **"Come with me!"**
1.46 **"Come** and see," answered Philip.
3.13 heaven except the Son of Man, who **came down** from heaven."
4.23 But the time is **coming** and is already here, when by the
4.29 said to the people there, [29] **"Come** and see the man who
4.49 "Sir," replied the official, **"come** with me before my child dies."
5.25 the time is **coming**—the time has already come—when the dead
5.40 are not willing to **come to me** in order to have life.
6.37 Everyone whom my Father gives me will **come to me.**
6.41 he said, "I am the bread that **came down** from heaven."
6.42 How, then, does he now say he **came down** from heaven?"
6.44 No one can **come to me** unless the Father who sent me
6.51 I am the living bread that **came down** from heaven.

Jn 6.58 This, then, is the bread that **came down** from heaven;
6.65 that no one can **come to me** unless the Father makes it
7.30 laid a hand on him, because his hour had not yet **come.**
7.37 voice, "Whoever is thirsty should **come to me** and drink.
8.20 And no one arrested him, because his hour had not **come.**
8.56 Abraham rejoiced that he was to see the time of my **coming;**
10.10 I have **come** in order that you might have life—life in
11.34 **"Come** and see, Lord," they answered.
11.43 he called out in a loud voice, "Lazarus, **come** out!"
12.13 God bless him who **comes in the name of the Lord!**
14.18 I will **come** back to you.
14.23 my Father and I will **come** to him and live with him.
14.28 to you, 'I am leaving, but I will **come** back to you.'
14.31 **"Come,** let us go from this place.
16.32 The time is **coming,** and is already here, when all of you
17. 1 looked up to heaven and said, "Father, the hour has **come.**
17.11 And now I am **coming** to you;
19. 9 into the palace and asked Jesus, "Where do you **come** from?"
21. 3 "We will **come** with you," they told him.
21.12 Jesus said to them, **"Come** and eat."
21.22 want him to live until I **come,** what is that to you?
Acts 7.52 God's messengers, who long ago announced the **coming** of his righteous Servant.
9.38 to him with the message, "Please hurry and **come** to us."
10.21 Why have you **come?"**
10.44 still speaking, the Holy Spirit **came down** on all those who
11.15 to speak, the Holy Spirit **came down** on them just as on
15.17 rest of mankind will **come to me,** all the Gentiles whom I
16. 9 standing and begging him, **"Come** over to Macedonia and help us!"
16.18 name of Jesus Christ I order you to **come** out of her!"
Rom 5.14 Adam was a figure of the one who was to **come.**
1 Cor 11.34 As for the other matters, I will settle them when I **come.**
15.23 then, at the time of his **coming,** those who belong to him.
16. 2 that there will be no need to collect money when I **come.**
16.22 Marana tha—Our Lord, **come!**
2 Cor 5.17 the old is gone, the new has **come.**
10. 2 beg you [2]not to force me to be harsh when I **come;**
Gal 3.19 meant to last until the **coming** of Abraham's descendant, to whom
3.23 as prisoners until this **coming** faith should be revealed.
Eph 4. 9 It means that first he **came down** to the lowest depths of
4.10 So the one who **came down** is the same one who went
Phil 4. 5 The Lord is **coming** soon.
1 Thes 5.23 from every fault at the **coming** of our Lord Jesus Christ.
2 Thes 2. 1 Concerning the **coming** of our Lord Jesus Christ and our being
2 Tim 1.10 revealed to us through the **coming** of our Saviour, Christ Jesus.
Heb 6. 5 is good, and they had felt the powers of the **coming** age.
7.25 to save those who **come to God** through him, because he lives
10. 1 of these sacrifices make perfect the people who **come to God?**
10.27 wait in fear for the **coming** Judgement and the fierce fire
10.37 "Just a little while longer, and he who is coming will **come;**
12.23 You have **come to God,** who is the judge of all mankind,
12.24 You have **come to Jesus,** who arranged the new covenant,
Jas 4. 8 **Come** near to God, and he will come near to you.
5. 8 your hopes high, for the day of the Lord's **coming** is near.
1 Pet 2. 4 **Come to the Lord,** the living stone rejected by man as
2. 5 **Come** as living stones, and let yourselves be used in
2.12 good deeds and so praise God on the Day of his **coming.**
2 Pet 1.16 known to you the mighty **coming** of our Lord Jesus Christ.
3. 4 will mock you [4]and will ask, "He promised to **come,** didn't
1 Jn 2.18 You were told that the Enemy of Christ would **come;**
Jude 14 "The Lord will **come** with many thousands of his holy angels
Rev 1. 4 was, and who is to **come,** and from the seven spirits in
1. 7 Look, he is **coming** on the clouds!
1. 8 Lord God Almighty, who is, who was, and who is to **come.**
2. 5 from your sins, I will **come** to you and take your lamp-stand
2.16 If you don't, I will **come** to you soon and fight against
2.25 But until I **come,** you must hold firmly to what you have.
3. 3 not wake up, I will **come** upon you like a thief,
3. 3 and you will not even know the time when I will **come.**
3.11 I am **coming** soon.
3.20 opens the door, I will **come** into his house and eat with
4. 1 speaking to me before, said, **"Come** up here, and I will show
4. 8 Lord God Almighty, who was, who is, and who is to **come."**
6. 1 living creatures say in a voice that sounded like thunder, **"Come!"**
6. 3 and I heard the second living creature say, **"Come!"**
6. 5 and I heard the third living creature say, **"Come!"**
6. 7 and I heard the fourth living creature say, **"Come!"**
11.12 a loud voice say to them from heaven, **"Come** up here!"
11.18 time for your anger has **come,** the time for the dead to
11.18 The time has **come** to reward your servants, the prophets, and
12.10 a loud voice in heaven saying, "Now God's salvation has **come!**
16.15 I am **coming** like a thief!
17. 1 came to me and said, **"Come,** and I will show you how
18. 4 heard another voice from heaven, saying, **"Come** out, my people!
18. 4 **Come** out from her!
19.17 **"Come** and gather together for God's great feast!
19.18 **Come** and eat the flesh of kings, generals, and soldiers,
20. 9 But fire **came down** from heaven and destroyed them.
21. 9 came to me and said, **"Come,** and I will show you the
22. 7 "I am **coming** soon!
22.12 "I am **coming** soon!
22.17 The Spirit and the Bride say, **"Come!"**
22.17 Everyone who hears this must also say, **"Come!"**
22.17 **Come,** whoever is thirsty;
22.20 I am **coming** soon!"
22.20 **Come,** Lord Jesus!

COMET

Num 24.17 Like a **comet** he will come from Israel.

COMFORT

Gen 21.18 Get up, go and pick him up, and **comfort** him.
24.67 and so he was **comforted** for the loss of his mother.
37.35 sons and daughters came to **comfort** him,
37.35 but he refused to be **comforted** and said, "I will go down
Deut 31.20 have all the food they want, and they will live **comfortably.**
2 Sam 12.24 Then David **comforted** his wife Bathsheba.
1 Chr 7.22 them for many days, and his relatives came to **comfort** him.
Job 2.11 Job had been suffering, they decided to go and **comfort** him.
15.11 God offers you **comfort;**
16. 1 the **comfort** you give is only torment.
16. 5 I could strengthen you with advice and keep talking to **comfort** you.
21. 1 that is all the **comfort** I ask from you.
21.34 You try to **comfort** me with nonsense!
29.18 to live a long life and to die at home in **comfort.**
29.25 leads his troops, and gave them **comfort** in their despair.
42.11 They expressed their sympathy and **comforted** him for all the
Ps 69.20 for **comfort,** but I found none.
71.21 you will **comfort** me again.
77. 2 long I lift my hands in prayer, but I cannot find **comfort.**
86.17 when they see that you have given me **comfort** and help.
94.19 I am anxious and worried, you **comfort** me and make me glad.
119.50 I was **comforted** because your promise gave me life.
119.52 your judgements of long ago, and they bring me **comfort,**
119.76 Let your constant love **comfort** me, as you have promised me,
Ecc 12.10 The Philosopher tried to find **comforting** words, but the
Is 12. 1 with me, but now you **comfort** me and are angry no longer.
22. 4 Don't try to **comfort** me.
28.12 He offered rest and **comfort** to all of you, but you
40. 1 **"Comfort** my people," says our God.
40. 1 **"Comfort** them!
49.13 The Lord will **comfort** his people;
52. 9 The Lord will rescue his city and **comfort** his people.
54.11 city, with no one to **comfort** you, I will rebuild your
57.18 lead them and help them, and I will **comfort** those who mourn.
61. 2 He has sent me to **comfort** all who mourn, [3]To give to
66.13 I will **comfort** you in Jerusalem, as a mother comforts her child.
Jer 16. 7 or drink with anyone to **comfort** him when a loved one dies.
31.13 I will **comfort** them and turn their mourning into joy, their
31.15 they are gone, and she refuses to be **comforted.**
Lam 1. 2 Of all her former friends, not one is left to **comfort** her.
1. 9 no one can **comfort** her.
1.16 No one can **comfort** me;
1.21 there is no one to **comfort** me.
2.13 How can I **comfort** you?
Ezek 32.31 in battle will be a **comfort** to the king of Egypt and
Dan 4. 4 "I was living **comfortably** in my palace, enjoying great prosperity.
Jon 4. 6 give him some shade, so that he would be more **comfortable.**
Nah 3. 7 Who will want to **comfort** her?' "
Zech 1.13 Lord answered the angel with **comforting** words, [14]and the
10. 2 the **comfort** they give is useless.
Mt 2.18 she refuses to be **comforted,** for they are dead."
5. 4 God will **comfort** them!
Jn 11.19 see Martha and Mary to **comfort** them over their brother's death.
11.31 with Mary, **comforting** her, followed her when they saw
Acts 20.12 They took the young man home alive and were greatly **comforted.**
1 Cor 14. 3 speaks to people and gives them help, encouragement, and **comfort.**
Phil 2. 1 Your life in Christ makes you strong, and his love **comforts** you.
1 Thes 2.12 We encouraged you, we **comforted** you, and we kept urging you

AV **COMFORTER** see **HELPER**

COMMAND

Gen 1. 3 Then God **commanded,** "Let there be light"—and light appeared.
1. 6 Then God **commanded,** "Let there be a dome to divide
1. 9 Then God **commanded,** "Let the water below the sky come
1.11 Then he **commanded,** "Let the earth produce all kinds of plants,
1.14 Then God **commanded,** "Let lights appear in the sky to
1.20 Then God **commanded,** "Let the water be filled with many
1.24 Then God **commanded,** "Let the earth produce all kinds of animal life:
6.22 Noah did everything that God **commanded.**
7. 5 And Noah did everything that the Lord **commanded.**
7. 9 went into the boat with Noah, as God had **commanded.**
7.16 went into the boat with Noah, [16]as God had **commanded.**
18.19 in order that he may **command** his sons and his descendants to
21. 4 Abraham circumcised him, as God had **commanded.**
22.18 I have blessed your descendants—all because you obeyed my **command."**
24.37 My master made me promise with a vow to obey his **command.**
26. 5 Abraham obeyed me and kept all my laws and **commands."**
28. 6 when Isaac blessed him, he **commanded** him not to marry a
43.17 servant did as he was **commanded** and took the brothers to
44. 1 Joseph **commanded** the servant in charge of his house,
47.11 land near the city of Rameses, as the king had **commanded.**
49.29 Then Jacob **commanded** his sons, "Now that I am going to
50.12 So Jacob's sons did as he had **commanded** them;
Ex 1.22 Finally the king issued a **command** to all his people:
5. 6 That same day the king **commanded** the Egyptian
6.13 The Lord **commanded** Moses and Aaron:
7. 2 Tell Aaron everything I **command** you, and he will tell the
7. 6 Moses and Aaron did what the Lord **commanded.**
7.10 Aaron went to the king and did as the Lord had **commanded.**
7.20 Then Moses and Aaron did as the Lord **commanded.**
8.27 sacrifices to the Lord our God, just as he **commanded** us."
12.28 went and did what the Lord had **commanded** Moses and Aaron.

Ex	12.50	did what the Lord had **commanded** Moses and Aaron.
	14. 7	the six hundred finest, **commanded** by their officers.
	15.26	right and by keeping my **commands,** I will not punish you with
	16.16	The Lord has **commanded** that each of you is to gather as
	16.23	to them, “The Lord has **commanded** that tomorrow is a holy
	16.24	As Moses had **commanded,** they kept what was left until
	16.28	“How much longer will you people refuse to obey my **commands?**
	16.32	Moses said, “The Lord has **commanded** us to save some manna,
	16.34	As the Lord had **commanded** Moses, Aaron put it in front
	17. 1	moving from one place to another at the **command** of the Lord.
	17.10	Joshua did as Moses **commanded** him and went out to fight
	18.16	them is right, and I tell them God’s **commands** and laws.”
	18.20	You should teach them God’s **commands** and explain to them
	18.23	do this, as God **commands,** you will not wear yourself out,
	19. 7	and told them everything that the Lord had **commanded** him.
	19.23	cannot come up, because you **commanded** us to consider the
	20.22	The Lord **commanded** Moses to say to the Israelites:
	23.15	Festival of Unleavened Bread in the way that I **commanded** you.
	23.22	him and do everything I **command,** I will fight against all
	24. 3	the people all the Lord’s **commands** and all the ordinances,
	24. 4	Moses wrote down all the Lord’s **commands.**
	24. 7	covenant, in which the Lord’s **commands** were written, and
	24. 7	“We will obey the Lord and do everything that he has **commanded.”**
	24. 8	the Lord made with you when he gave all these **commands.”**
	27.20	**“Command** the people of Israel to bring you the best
	27.21	This **command** is to be kept for ever by the Israelites and
	29.35	and his sons for seven days exactly as I have **commanded** you.
	31. 6	that they can make everything I have **commanded** to be made:
	31.11	things, they are to do exactly as I have **commanded** you.”
	31.12	The Lord **commanded** Moses [13] to say to the people of Israel,
	32. 8	They have already left the way that I **commanded** them to follow;
	32.27	“The Lord God of Israel **commands** every one of you to put
	33. 5	For the Lord had **commanded** Moses to say to them, “You are
	34. 4	them up Mount Sinai, just as the Lord had **commanded.**
	34.18	As I have **commanded** you, eat unleavened bread for seven days
	34.34	everything that he had been **commanded** to say, [35] and they
	35. 1	to them, “This is what the Lord has **commanded** you to do:
	35. 4	the people of Israel, “This is what the Lord has **commanded:**
	35.10	you are to come and make everything that the Lord **commanded:**
	35.29	the Lord for the work which he had **commanded** Moses to do.
	36. 1	are to make everything just as the Lord has **commanded.”**
	36. 5	needed for the work which the Lord **commanded** to be done.”
	36. 6	So Moses sent a **command** throughout the camp that no one
	38.22	tribe of Judah, made everything that the Lord had **commanded.**
	39. 1	garments for Aaron, as the Lord had **commanded** Moses.
	39. 5	to form one piece with it, as the Lord had **commanded** Moses.
	39. 7	tribes of Israel, just as the Lord had **commanded** Moses.
	39.21	Just as the Lord had **commanded** Moses, they tied the
	39.24	bells of pure gold, just as the Lord had **commanded** Moses.
	39.29	decorated with embroidery, as the Lord had **commanded** Moses.
	39.31	with a blue cord, just as the Lord had **commanded** Moses.
	39.32	The Israelites made everything just as the Lord had **commanded** Moses.
	39.42	had done all the work just as the Lord had **commanded** Moses.
	39.43	that they had made it all just as the Lord had **commanded.**
	40.16	Moses did everything just as the Lord had **commanded.**
	40.19	the outer covering over it, just as the Lord had **commanded.**
	40.21	off the Covenant Box, just as the Lord had **commanded.**
	40.23	bread offered to the Lord, just as the Lord had **commanded.**
	40.25	Lord’s presence he lit the lamps, just as the Lord had **commanded.**
	40.27	and burnt the sweet-smelling incense, just as the Lord had **commanded.**
	40.29	and the grain-offering, just as the Lord had **commanded.**
	40.32	the Tent or to the altar, just as the Lord had **commanded.**
Lev	4. 1	The Lord **commanded** Moses [2] to tell the people of Israel
	4. 2	broke any of the Lord’s **commands** without intending to, would
	4.13	breaking one of the Lord’s **commands** without intending to,
	4.22	breaking one of the Lord’s **commands** without intending to,
	4.27	breaking one of the Lord’s **commands** without intending to,
	5.17	breaking any of the Lord’s **commands,** he is guilty and must
	6. 8	The Lord **commanded** Moses [9] to give Aaron and his sons the
	6.24	The Lord **commanded** Moses [25] to give Aaron and his sons
	7.36	On that day the Lord **commanded** the people of Israel to
	7.38	desert, the Lord gave these **commands** to Moses on the day he
	8. 4	Lord had **commanded,** and when the community had assembled,
	8. 5	I am now about to do is what the Lord has **commanded.”**
	8. 9	sign of dedication, just as the Lord had **commanded** him.
	8.13	tied caps on their heads, just as the Lord had **commanded.**
	8.17	burnt it outside the camp, just as the Lord had **commanded.**
	8.20	of the ram on the altar, just as the Lord had **commanded.**
	8.29	Moses did everything just as the Lord had **commanded.**
	8.31	basket of ordination offerings, just as the Lord **commanded.**
	8.34	The Lord **commanded** us to do what we have done today, in
	8.35	and night for seven days, doing what the Lord has **commanded.**
	8.35	This is what the Lord has **commanded** me.”
	8.36	did everything that the Lord had **commanded** through Moses.
	9. 5	Tent everything that Moses had **commanded,** and the whole community
	9. 6	Moses said, “The Lord has **commanded** you to do all this,
	9. 7	away the sins of the people, just as the Lord **commanded.”**
	9.10	part of the liver, just as the Lord had **commanded** Moses.
	9.21	gift to the Lord for the priests, as Moses had **commanded.**
	10. 1	holy, because the Lord had not **commanded** them to present it.
	10. 5	carried them outside the camp, just as Moses had **commanded.**
	10.13	That is what the Lord **commanded** me.
	10.15	and your children for ever, just as the Lord **commanded.”**
	10.18	should have eaten the sacrifice there, as I **commanded.”**
	16.34	So Moses did as the Lord had **commanded.**
	17. 1	The Lord **commanded** Moses [2] to give Aaron and his sons and
	17. 5	The meaning of this **command** is that the people of Israel
Lev	17.11	is why the Lord has **commanded** that all blood be poured out
	18. 4	Obey my laws and do what I **command.**
	18.26	keep the Lord’s laws and **commands,** [28] and then the land
	18.30	the Lord said, “Obey the **commands** I give and do not follow
	19. 3	his father, and must keep the Sabbath, as I have **commanded.**
	19.19	“Obey my **commands.**
	19.37	Obey all my laws and **commands.**
	20.22	“Keep all my laws and **commands,** so that you will not be
	21. 1	The Lord **commanded** Moses to say to the Aaronite priests,
	21.16	The Lord **commanded** Moses [17] to say to Aaron, “None of
	22. 1	The Lord **commanded** Moses [2] to say to Aaron and his sons,
	22.17	The Lord **commanded** Moses [18] to give Aaron and his sons
	22.31	The Lord said, “Obey my **commands;**
	24.23	the people of Israel did what the Lord had **commanded** Moses.
	25. 1	Moses on Mount Sinai and **commanded** him [2] to give the
	25.18	all the Lord’s laws and **commands,** so that you may live in
	25.38	This is the **command** of the Lord your God, who brought
	26. 3	my laws and obey my **commands,** [4] I will send you rain at
	26.14	“If you will not obey my **commands,** you will be punished.
	26.15	to obey my laws and **commands** and break the covenant I have
	26.43	full penalty for having rejected my laws and my **commands.**
	26.46	these are the laws and **commands** that the Lord gave to Moses
	27.34	These are the **commands** that the Lord gave Moses on Mount
Num	1.19	were recorded and counted, [19] as the Lord had **commanded.**
	1.54	of Israel did everything that the Lord had **commanded** Moses.
	2.33	As the Lord had **commanded** Moses, the Levites were not
	2.34	Israel did everything the Lord had **commanded** Moses.
	3.14	the Sinai Desert the Lord **commanded** Moses [15] to register
	3.39	Moses enrolled by clans at the **command** of the Lord, was
	4.34	Following the Lord’s **command,** Moses, Aaron, and the leaders of the community
	4.49	Each man was registered as the Lord had **commanded** Moses;
	4.49	and at the **command** of the Lord given through Moses, each man
	5. 2	The Lord said to Moses, [2] **“Command** the people of Israel
	5.11	The Lord **commanded** Moses [12-14] to give the Israelites
	6. 1	The Lord **commanded** Moses [2] to give the following
	6.22	The Lord **commanded** Moses [23] to tell Aaron and his sons
	8.20	Israel dedicated the Levites, as the Lord **commanded** Moses.
	8.22	everything the Lord had **commanded** Moses concerning the Levites.
	9. 5	The people did everything just as the Lord had **commanded** Moses.
	9.18	people broke camp at the **command** of the Lord,
	9.18	and at his **command** they set up camp.
	9.20	in camp or moved, according to the **command** of the Lord.
	9.23	to the **commands** which the Lord gave through Moses.
	10.13	began to march at the **command** of the Lord through Moses,
	10.14	company by company, with Nahshon son of Amminadab in **command.**
	10.15	son of Zuar was in **command** of the tribe of Issachar, [16] and
	10.16	Eliab son of Helon was in **command** of the tribe of Zebulun.
	10.18	company by company, with Elizur son of Shedeur in **command.**
	10.19	son of Zurishaddai was in **command** of the tribe of Simeon,
	10.20	Eliasaph son of Deuel was in **command** of the tribe of Gad.
	10.22	company by company, with Elishama son of Ammihud in **command.**
	10.23	son of Pedahzur was in **command** of the tribe of Manasseh,
	10.24	Abidan son of Gideoni was in **command** of the tribe of Benjamin.
	10.25	company by company, with Ahiezer son of Ammishaddai in **command.**
	10.26	son of Ochran was in **command** of the tribe of Asher, [27] and
	10.27	Ahira son of Enan was in **command** of the tribe of Naphtali.
	15.23	community fails to do everything that the Lord **commanded**
	15.31	Lord said and has deliberately broken one of his **commands.**
	15.36	camp and stoned him to death, as the Lord had **commanded.**
	15.37	The Lord **commanded** Moses [38] to say to the people of Israel:
	15.39	see them you will remember all my **commands** and obey them;
	15.40	you to keep all my **commands,** and you will belong completely
	16.40	All this was done as the Lord had **commanded** Eleazar through Moses.
	17.11	Moses did as the Lord **commanded.**
	18.25	The Lord **commanded** Moses [26] to say to the Levites:
	19. 1	The Lord **commanded** Moses and Aaron [2] to give the
	20. 9	Moses went and got the stick, as the Lord had **commanded.**
	20.24	the two of you rebelled against my **command** at Meribah.
	20.27	Moses did what the Lord had **commanded.**
	22.18	I could not disobey the **command** of the Lord my God in
	24.13	I could not disobey the **command** of the Lord by doing
	25.16	The Lord **commanded** Moses, [17] “Attack the Midianites and destroy them,
	27.11	requirement, just as I, the Lord, have **commanded** you.”
	27.14	of you rebelled against my **command** in the wilderness of Zin.
	27.17	lead the people [17] and can **command** them in battle, so that
	27.22	Moses did as the Lord had **commanded** him.
	27.23	As the Lord had **commanded,** Moses put his hands on
	28. 1	The Lord **commanded** Moses [2] to instruct the Israelites to
	29.40	of Israel everything that the Lord had **commanded** him.
	31. 6	them to war under the **command** of Phinehas son of Eleazar the
	31. 7	as the Lord had **commanded** Moses, and killed all the men,
	31.31	Moses and Eleazar did what the Lord **commanded.**
	31.41	contribution to the Lord, as the Lord had **commanded.**
	31.47	and as the Lord had **commanded,** gave them to the Levites who
	31.48	Then the officers who had **commanded** the army went to
	31.49	counted the soldiers under our **command** and not one of them
	32.21	the Jordan and under the **command** of the Lord they are to
	32.25	of Gad and Reuben said, “Sir, we will do as you **command.**
	32.27	of us are ready to go into battle under the Lord’s **command.**
	32.28	So Moses gave these **commands** to Eleazar, Joshua, and the
	32.29	for battle at the Lord’s **command** and if with their help you
	32.31	Reuben answered, “Sir, we will do as the Lord has **commanded.**
	32.32	Under his **command** we will cross into the land of Canaan
	33. 2	At the **command** of the Lord, Moses wrote down the name of

Num	33.38	At the **command** of the Lord, Aaron the priest climbed Mount Hor.
	36. 2	They said, "The Lord **commanded** you to distribute the land
	36. 2	He also **commanded** you to give the property of our relative
	36. 5	Moses gave the people of Israel the following **command** from the Lord.
	36.10	Lord had **commanded** Moses, and they married their cousins.
Deut	1. 3	people everything the Lord had **commanded** him to tell them.
	1.19	"We did what the Lord our God **commanded** us.
	1.20	Go and occupy it as he **commanded.**
	1.26	"But you rebelled against the **command** of the Lord your God,
	1.41	now we will attack, just as the Lord our God **commanded** us.'
	2. 1	Aqaba, as the Lord had **commanded,** and we spent a long time
	2.37	place where the Lord our God had **commanded** us not to go.
	4. 2	add anything to what I **command** you, and do not take anything
	4. 2	Obey the **commands** of the Lord your God that I have given
	4.23	Obey his **command** not to make yourselves any kind of idol,
	5.12	keep it holy, as I, the Lord your God, have **commanded** you.
	5.15	That is why I **command** you to observe the Sabbath.
	5.16	I, the Lord your God, **command** you, so that all may go
	5.29	me and obey all my **commands,** so that everything would go
	5.31	with me, and I will give you all my laws and **commands.**
	5.32	you do everything that the Lord your God has **commanded** you.
	6. 1	the laws that the Lord your God **commanded** me to teach you.
	6. 6	Never forget these **commands** that I am giving you today.
	6.20	did the Lord our God **command** us to obey all these laws?'
	6.24	Then the Lord our God **commanded** us to obey all these
	6.25	obey everything that God has **commanded** us, he will be
	7. 9	love him and obey his **commands,** [10] but he will not hesitate
	7.12	"If you listen to these **commands** and obey them faithfully,
	8. 2	you intended to do and whether you would obey his **commands.**
	8. 6	So then, do as the Lord has **commanded** you:
	9.12	turned away from what I **commanded** them to do, and they have
	9.16	you had already disobeyed the **command** that the Lord your God
	10. 5	just as the Lord had **commanded,** I put them in the box
	10.12	Worship the Lord and do all that he **commands.**
	11.13	"So then, obey the **commands** that I have given you today;
	11.18	"Remember these **commands** and cherish them.
	11.22	Lord your God, do everything he **commands,** and be faithful to him.
	11.27	blessing, if you obey the **commands** of the Lord your God that
	11.28	curse, if you disobey these **commands** and turn away to
	12.11	you must bring to him everything that I have **commanded:**
	12.14	and do all the other things that I have **commanded** you.
	12.25	If you obey this **command,** the Lord will be pleased, and
	12.28	faithfully everything that I have **commanded** you, and all
	12.32	"Do everything that I have **commanded** you;
	13. 4	obey him and keep his **commands;**
	13. 5	away from the life that the Lord has **commanded** you to live.
	13.18	if you obey all his **commands** that I have given you today,
	15. 5	and carefully observe everything that I **command** you today.
	15.11	in need, and so I **command** you to be generous to them.
	15.15	that is why I am now giving you this **command.**
	16.12	Be sure that you obey these **commands;**
	17. 3	or the moon or the stars, contrary to the Lord's **command.**
	17.19	Lord and to obey faithfully everything that is **commanded** in it.
	17.20	and from disobeying the Lord's **commands** in any way.
	18.18	to say, and he will tell the people everything I **command.**
	18.20	name when I did not **command** him to do so, he must
	19. 9	you do everything that I **command** you today and if you love
	24.18	that is why I have given you this **command.**
	24.22	that is why I have given you this **command.**
	26.13	the orphans, and the widows, as you **commanded** me to do.
	26.13	or forgotten any of your **commands** concerning the tithe.
	26.14	I have done everything you **commanded** concerning the tithe.
	26.16	"Today the Lord your God **commands** you to obey all his laws;
	26.17	to keep all his laws, and to do all that he **commands.**
	26.18	and he **commands** you to obey all his laws.
	28. 1	faithfully keep all his **commands** that I am giving you today,
	28. 9	God and do everything he **commands,** he will make you his own
	28.13	obey faithfully all his **commands** that I am giving you today.
	28.15	not faithfully keep all his **commands** and laws that I am
	29. 1	the covenant that the Lord **commanded** Moses to make with the
	30. 2	all your heart obey his **commands** that I am giving you today,
	30. 8	him and keep all his **commands** that I am giving you today.
	30.11	"The **command** that I am giving you today is not too
	30.16	If you obey the **commands** of the Lord your God, which I
	31.10	He **commanded** them, "At the end of every seven years,
	32.46	you obey all these **commands** that I have given you today.
	33. 3	So we bow at his feet and obey his **commands.**
	33. 9	They obeyed your **commands** And were faithful to your covenant.
	33.21	They obeyed the Lord's **commands** and laws When the leaders of
	34. 9	obeyed Joshua and kept the **commands** that the Lord had given
Josh	1. 9	Remember that I have **commanded** you to be determined and confident!
	4. 3	one from each tribe, [3] and **command** them to take twelve
	4. 8	As the Lord had **commanded** Joshua, they took twelve stones
	4.10	This is what Moses had **commanded.**
	4.16	the Lord told Joshua [16] to **command** the priests carrying the
	5. 3	did as the Lord had **commanded,** and he circumcised the
	7. 1	The Lord's **command** to Israel not to take from Jericho
	8. 8	the city, set it on fire, just as the Lord has **commanded.**
	8.33	The Lord's servant Moses had **commanded** them to do this when
	9.24	the Lord your God had **commanded** his servant Moses to give
	10.40	This was what the Lord God of Israel had **commanded.**
	11. 9	Joshua did to them what the Lord had **commanded:**
	11.12	to death, just as Moses, the Lord's servant, had **commanded.**
	11.15	The Lord had given his **commands** to his servant Moses,
	11.15	He did everything that the Lord had **commanded** Moses.
	11.20	This was what the Lord had **commanded** Moses.
	11.23	Joshua captured the whole land, as the Lord had **commanded** Moses.
Josh	13. 6	among the Israelites, just as I have **commanded** you to do.
	14. 2	As the Lord had **commanded** Moses, the territories of the
	14. 5	of Israel divided the land as the Lord had **commanded** Moses.
	15.13	As the Lord **commanded** Joshua, part of the territory of
	17. 4	leaders, and said, "The Lord **commanded** Moses to give us, as
	17. 4	So, as the Lord had **commanded,** they were given land along
	19.50	As the Lord had **commanded,** they gave him the city he
	20. 2	cities of refuge that I **commanded** Moses to tell you about.
	21. 2	said to them, "The Lord **commanded** through Moses that we
	21. 3	in accordance with the Lord's **command** the people of Israel
	21. 8	to the Levites, as the Lord had **commanded** through Moses.
	22. 2	ordered you to do, and you have obeyed all my **commands.**
	22. 3	have been careful to obey the **commands** of the Lord your God.
	22. 5	Make sure you obey the law that Moses **commanded** you:
	22. 9	had taken as the Lord had **commanded** them through Moses.
	22.20	refused to obey the **command** about the things condemned
	23.16	which the Lord your God **commanded** you to keep and if you
	24.24	We will obey his **commands."**
	24.26	Joshua wrote these **commands** in the book of the Law of God.
Judg	1.20	As Moses had **commanded,** Hebron was given to Caleb, who
	2.17	fathers had obeyed the Lord's **commands,** but this new
	2.20	the covenant that I **commanded** their ancestors to keep.
	3. 4	the Israelites would obey the **commands** that the Lord had
	4. 6	"The Lord, the God of Israel, has given you this **command:**
	7. 9	That night the Lord **commanded** Gideon, "Get up and attack the camp;
1 Sam	12.14	to him, and obey his **commands,** and if you and your king
	12.15	the Lord but disobey his **commands,** he will be against you
	13.13	"You have not obeyed the **command** the Lord your God gave you.
	15.11	he has turned away from me and disobeyed my **commands."**
	15.13	I have obeyed the Lord's **command."**
	15.23	Because you rejected the Lord's **command,** he has rejected you as king."
	15.24	"I disobeyed the Lord's **command** and your instructions.
	15.26	"You rejected the Lord's **command,** and he has rejected you
	18.13	sent him away and put him in **command** of a thousand men.
	28.18	You disobeyed the Lord's **command** and did not completely
2 Sam	5.25	did what the Lord had **commanded,** and was able to drive the
	9.11	Ziba answered, "I will do everything Your Majesty **commands."**
	10.10	of his troops under the **command** of his brother Abishai, who
	10.16	came to Helam under the **command** of Shobach, commander of the
	11.22	to David and told him what Joab had **commanded** him to say.
	12. 9	Why, then, have you disobeyed my **commands?**
	12.25	Lord loved the boy [25] and **commanded** the prophet Nathan to
	17.25	(Absalom had put Amasa in **command** of the army in the
	18. 1	and of a hundred, and placed officers in **command** of them.
	18. 2	Abishai and Ittai from Gath, each in **command** of a group.
	18. 5	And all the troops heard David give this **command** to his officers.
	18.12	We all heard the king **command** you and Abishai and Ittai,
	20.23	Joab was in **command** of the army of Israel;
	21.14	of Benjamin, doing all that the king had **commanded.**
	22.23	I have not disobeyed his **commands.**
	24.19	David obeyed the Lord's **command** and went as Gad had told him.
1 Kgs	2. 3	Obey all his laws and **commands,** as written in the Law of
	2. 4	were careful to obey his **commands** faithfully with all their
	2.43	Why, then, have you broken your promise and disobeyed my **command?**
	3.14	and keep my laws and **commands,** as your father David did, I
	5.17	At King Solomon's **command** they quarried fine large
	6.12	obey all my laws and **commands,** I will do for you what
	8.44	"When you **command** your people to go into battle
	8.58	and keep all the laws and **commands** he gave our ancestors.
	8.61	God, obeying all his laws and **commands,** as you do today."
	9. 4	and do everything I have **commanded** you, [5] I will keep the
	9. 6	you disobey the laws and **commands** I have given you, and
	11. 2	even though the Lord had **commanded** the Israelites not to
	11. 9	Solomon twice and had **commanded** him not to worship foreign gods,
	11.11	with me and disobeyed my **commands,** I promise that I will
	11.33	has not kept my laws and **commands** as his father David did.
	11.34	David, whom I chose and who obeyed my laws and **commands.**
	11.38	approval by doing what I **command,** as my servant David did, I
	12.24	They all obeyed the Lord's **command** and went back home.
	13. 1	At the Lord's **command** a prophet from Judah went to Bethel
	13. 2	Following the Lord's **command,** the prophet denounced the altar:
	13. 9	The Lord has **commanded** me not to eat or drink a thing,
	13.17	here, [17] because the Lord has **commanded** me not to eat or
	13.18	you, and at the Lord's **command** an angel told me to take
	13.21	that you disobeyed him and did not do what he **commanded.**
	13.26	"That is the prophet who disobeyed the Lord's **command!**
	13.32	he spoke at the Lord's **command** against the altar in Bethel
	14. 8	loyal to me, obeyed my **commands,** and did only what I approve
	15. 5	never disobeyed any of his **commands,** except in the case of
	17. 4	and I have **commanded** ravens to bring you food there."
	17. 5	Elijah obeyed the Lord's **command,** and went and stayed by
	17. 9	I have **commanded** a widow who lives there to feed you."
	18.18	You are disobeying the Lord's **commands** and worshipping the idols of Baal.
	18.36	I am your servant and have done all this at your **command.**
	20.14	the young soldiers under the **command** of the district
	20.14	"Who will **command** the main force?"
	20.24	from their **commands** and replace them with field commanders.
	20.35	At the Lord's **command** a member of a group of prophets
	20.36	you have disobeyed the Lord's **command,** a lion will kill you
	21.11	leading citizens of Jezreel did what Jezebel had **commanded.**
2 Kgs	1. 3	angel of the Lord **commanded** Elijah, the prophet from Tishbe,
	1. 4	Elijah did as the Lord **commanded,** [5] and the messengers
	7.17	the city gate under the **command** of the officer who was his
	14. 6	followed what the Lord had **commanded** in the Law of Moses:
	16.16	Uriah did as the king **commanded.**

2 Kgs 17.12 and disobeyed the Lord's **command** not to worship idols.
17.13 evil ways and obey my **commands,** which are contained in the
17.15 nations, disobeying the Lord's **command** not to imitate them.
17.27 So the emperor **commanded:**
17.34 they obey the laws and **commands** which he gave to the
17.37 always obey the laws and **commands** that I wrote for you.
18. 6 kept all the **commands** that the Lord had given Moses.
18.17 it was **commanded** by his three highest officials.
18.31 The emperor of Assyria **commands** you to come out of the city
18.32 If you do what he **commands,** you will not die, but live.
21. 8 Israel will obey all my **commands** and keep the whole Law that
21.22 God of his ancestors, and disobeyed the Lord's **commands.**
23. 3 to keep his laws and **commands** with all his heart and soul,
24. 3 This happened at the Lord's **command,** in order to banish
24.10 Babylonian army, **commanded** by King Nebuchadnezzar's officers,
25.19 officer who had been in **command** of the troops, five of the
1 Chr 10.13 He disobeyed the Lord's **commands;**
12. 3 They were under the **command** of Ahiezer and Joash, sons of Shemaah,
12.14 Gad were senior officers in **command** of a thousand men,
12.14 and others were junior officers in **command** of a hundred.
12.20 In Manasseh they had all **commanded** units of a thousand men.
12.23 with the men under their **command** (these leaders knew what
13. 1 with all the officers in **command** of units of a thousand men
14.16 David did what God had **commanded,** and so he drove the
15.15 their shoulders, as the Lord had **commanded** through Moses.
15.16 David **commanded** the leaders of the Levites to assign
16.14 his **commands** are for all the world.
19.11 of his troops under the **command** of his brother Abishai, who
19.16 and placed them under the **command** of Shobach, commander of
21. 6 Joab disapproved of the king's **command,** he did not take any
21.18 the Lord told Gad to **command** David to go and build an
21.19 David obeyed the Lord's **command** and went, as Gad had
22. 6 for his son Solomon and **commanded** him to build a temple for
22.17 David **commanded** all the leaders of Israel to help Solomon.
24.19 Aaron in obedience to the **commands** of the Lord God of Israel.
25. 2 who proclaimed God's messages whenever the king **commanded.**
27. 2 a descendant of Ahohi (Mikloth was his second in **command)**
28. 1 King David **commanded** all the officials of Israel to assemble
28. 7 to obey carefully all my laws and **commands** as he does now.'
28. 8 the Lord our God has **commanded** us, so that you may continue
28.21 and all the people and their leaders are at your **command."**
29.19 to obey everything that you **command** and to build the Temple
29.20 Then David **commanded** the people, "Praise the Lord your God!"
2 Chr 1. 3 the rest of the people, [3] **commanding** them to go with him to
2. 4 He has **commanded** Israel to do this for ever.
4.11 bronze, as King Solomon had **commanded,** for use in the Temple
6.34 "When you **command** your people to go into battle
7.17 and doing everything I have **commanded** you, [18] I will keep
7.19 ever disobey the laws and **commands** I have given you, and
8.14 in accordance with the **commands** of David, the man of God.
8.18 sent him ships under the **command** of his own officers and
11. 4 They obeyed the Lord's **command** and did not go to fight Jeroboam.
13.11 We do what the Lord has **commanded,** but you have abandoned him.
14. 4 He **commanded** the people of Judah to do the will of the
14. 4 God of their ancestors, and to obey his teachings and **commands.**
17. 4 his father's God, obeyed God's **commands,** and did not act in
17.17 Eliada, an outstanding soldier, in **command** of 200,000 men
17.18 His second in **command** was Jehozabad with 180,000 men,
24.20 his **commands** and are bringing disaster on yourselves!
25. 4 followed what the Lord had **commanded** in the Law of Moses:
25. 5 to, and placed officers in **command** of units of a thousand
26.12 The army was **commanded** by 2,600 officers.
28. 7 Azrikam, and Elkanah, who was second in **command** to the king.
29.15 Then, as the king had **commanded** them to do, they began to
29.24 people, for the king had **commanded** burnt-offerings and
30. 6 Messengers went out at the **command** of the king and his
30.12 by following the **commands** of the king and his officials.
32. 6 in the city under the **command** of army officers and ordered
33. 8 Israel will obey all my **commands** and keep the whole Law that
33.14 stationed an army officer in **command** of a unit of troops in
33.16 He **commanded** all the people of Judah to worship the Lord,
34.16 He reported, "We have done everything that you **commanded.**
34.22 At the king's **command,** Hilkiah and the others went to
34.31 to keep his laws and **commands** with all his heart and soul,
35.10 and the Levites took their places, as **commanded** by the king.
35.16 So, as King Josiah had **commanded,** everything was done
36.22 Cyrus to issue the following **command** and send it out in
36.23 "This is the **command** of Cyrus, Emperor of Persia.
Ezra 1. 1 Cyrus to issue the following **command** and send it out in
1. 2 "This is the **command** of Cyrus, Emperor of Persia.
4. 3 just as Cyrus, emperor of Persia, **commanded** us."
4.21 to stop rebuilding the city until I give further **commands.**
6. 3 his reign Cyrus the emperor **commanded** that the Temple in
6. 8 I hereby **command** you to help them rebuild it.
6.11 I further **command** that if anyone disobeys this order, a
6.12 or nation that defies this **command** and tries to destroy the
6.13 their fellow-officials did exactly as the emperor had **commanded.**
6.14 Temple as they had been **commanded** by the God of Israel and
7.11 knowledge of the laws and **commands** which the Lord had given
7.13 "I **command** that throughout my empire all the Israelite people,
7.21 "I **command** all the treasury officials in the province
9.10 We have again disobeyed the **commands** [11] that you gave us
10. 3 and the others who honour God's **commands** advise us to do.
Neh 1. 5 covenant with those who love you and do what you **command.**
1. 7 wickedly against you and have not done what you **commanded.**
1. 9 and do what I have **commanded** you, I will bring you back
9.16 grew proud and stubborn and refused to obey your **commands.**
Neh 9.34 They did not listen to your **commands** and warnings.
10.29 that we will obey all that the Lord, our Lord, **commands** us;
12.45 purification and the other rituals that God had **commanded.**
Esth 1.12 Queen Vashti of the king's **command,** she refused to come.
1.15 to Queen Vashti with a **command,** and she refused to obey it!
1.17 They'll say, 'King Xerxes **commanded** Queen Vashti to come to him,
3. 3 service asked him why he was disobeying the king's **command;**
3.15 At the king's **command** the decree was made public in the
7. 9 the king **commanded.**
8.14 At the king's **command** the riders mounted royal horses
9.31 This was **commanded** by both Mordecai and Queen Esther.
9.32 Esther's **command,** confirming the rules for Purim, was
Job 3.18 Even prisoners enjoy peace, free from shouts and harsh **commands.**
6.10 I have never opposed what he **commands.**
23.12 I always do what God **commands;**
34.27 because they have stopped following him and ignored all his **commands.**
36.32 lightning with his hands and **commands** it to hit the mark.
37. 5 At God's **command** amazing things happen,
37. 6 He **commands** snow to fall on the earth, and sends torrents
37.12 They do all that God **commands,** everywhere throughout the world.
37.15 know how God gives the **command** and makes lightning flash
38.12 have you ever in all your life **commanded** a day to dawn?
38.35 And if you **command** the lightning to flash, will it come
39.25 get near, and they hear the officers shouting **commands.**
39.27 an eagle wait for your **command** to build its nest high in
Ps 17. 4 I have obeyed your **command** and have not followed paths of violence.
18.22 I have not disobeyed his **commands.**
19. 7 The **commands** of the Lord are trustworthy, giving wisdom to
19. 8 The **commands** of the Lord are just and give understanding to
25.10 he leads all who keep his covenant and obey his **commands.**
33. 6 created the heavens by his **command,** the sun, moon, and stars
33. 9 at his **command** everything appeared.
37.34 Put your hope in the Lord and obey his **commands;**
44.18 we have not disobeyed your **commands.**
50.17 you reject my **commands.**
51.13 I will teach sinners your **commands,** and they will turn back
68.11 The Lord gave the **command,** and many women carried the news:
78.23 he spoke to the sky above and **commanded** its doors to open;
89.30 not live according to my **commands,** [31] if they disregard my
95.10 They refuse to obey my **commands.'**
99. 7 they obeyed the laws and **commands** that he gave them.
103.18 true to his covenant and who faithfully obey his **commands.**
103.20 angels, who obey his **commands,** who listen to what he says.
104. 7 they rushed away when they heard your shout of **command.**
105. 7 his **commands** are for all the world.
105.28 on the country, but the Egyptians did not obey his **command.**
105.31 God **commanded,** and flies and gnats swarmed throughout the whole country.
105.34 He **commanded,** and the locusts came, countless millions of them;
105.45 his people would obey his laws and keep all his **commands.**
106. 3 those who obey his **commands,** who always do what is right.
106. 9 He gave a **command** to the Red Sea, and it dried up;
106.34 heathen, as the Lord had **commanded** them to do, [35] but they
107.11 they had rebelled against the **commands** of Almighty God and
107.20 He healed them with his **command** and saved them from the grave.
107.25 He **commanded,** and a mighty wind began to blow and
111. 7 all his **commands** are dependable.
111.10 he gives sound judgement to all who obey his **commands.**
112. 1 the Lord, who takes pleasure in obeying his **commands.**
119. 2 are those who follow his **commands,** who obey him with all
119. 6 pay attention to all your **commands,** then I will not be put
119. 9 By obeying your **commands.**
119.14 I delight in following your **commands** more than in having great wealth.
119.16 your **commands** I will not forget.
119.19 do not hide your **commands** from me.
119.21 cursed are those who disobey your **commands.**
119.32 I will eagerly obey your **commands,** because you will give
119.40 I want to obey your **commands;**
119.46 I will announce your **commands** to kings and I will not be
119.47 I find pleasure in obeying your **commands,** because I love them.
119.54 During my brief earthly life I compose songs about your **commands.**
119.56 I find my happiness in obeying your **commands.**
119.60 Without delay I hurry to obey your **commands.**
119.66 Give me wisdom and knowledge, because I trust in your **commands.**
119.68 Teach me your **commands.**
119.71 was good for me, because it made me learn your **commands.**
119.79 honour you come to me— all those who know your **commands.**
119.83 yet I have not forgotten your **commands.**
119.87 in killing me, but I have not neglected your **commands.**
119.91 of your **command,** because they are all your servants.
119.94 I have tried to obey your **commands.**
119.100 I have greater wisdom than old men, because I obey your **commands.**
119.108 Accept my prayer of thanks, O Lord, and teach me your **commands.**
119.110 lay a trap for me, but I have not disobeyed your **commands.**
119.115 I will obey the **commands** of my God.
119.117 be safe, and I will always pay attention to your **commands.**
119.124 Treat me according to your constant love, and teach me your **commands.**
119.127 I love your **commands** more than gold, more than the finest gold.
119.131 In my desire for your **commands** I pant with open mouth.

Ps 119.134 those who oppress me, so that I may obey your **commands.**
119.139 me like a fire, because my enemies disregard your **commands.**
119.145 answer me, Lord, and I will obey your **commands!**
119.151 are near to me, Lord, and all your **commands** are permanent.
119.158 I am filled with disgust, because they do not keep your **commands.**
119.166 for you to save me, Lord, and I do what you **command.**
119.168 I obey your **commands** and your instructions;
119.172 I will sing about your law, because your **commands** are just.
119.173 Always be ready to help me, because I follow your **commands.**
122. 4 to give thanks to the Lord according to his **command.**
125. 4 to those who are good, to those who obey your **commands.**
128. 1 Happy are those who obey the Lord, who live by his **commands.**
132.12 my covenant and to the **commands** I give them, their sons,
138. 2 have shown that your name and your **commands** are supreme.
147.15 He gives a **command** to the earth, and what he says is
147.18 Then he gives a **command,** and the ice melts;
148. 5 He **commanded,** and they were created;
148. 6 by his **command** they were fixed in their places for ever,
148. 8 snow and clouds, strong winds that obey his **command.**
149. 9 to punish the nations as God has **commanded.**
Ecc 8. 5 long as you obey his **commands,** you are safe, and a wise
12.13 for God, and obey his **commands,** because this is all that man
Is 11. 4 At his **command** the people will be punished, and evil persons
21. 5 Suddenly the **command** rings out:
34.16 The Lord has **commanded** it to be so;
36.16 The emperor of Assyria **commands** you to come out of the city
38. 4 Then the Lord **commanded** Isaiah [5] to go back to Hezekiah
44.27 With a word of **command** I dry up the ocean.
48.18 "If only you had listened to my **commands!**
50. 2 up the sea with a **command** and turn rivers into a desert,
Jer 1. 7 send you to, and tell them everything I **command** you to say.
1.17 go and tell them everything I **command** you to say.
2.12 And so I **command** the sky to shake with horror, to be
3.13 to foreign gods and that you have not obeyed my **commands.**
3.25 we have never obeyed his **commands."**
4.12 comes at the Lord's **command** will be much stronger than that!
5.31 as the prophets **command,** and my people offer no objections.
7.22 I gave your ancestors no **commands** about burnt-offerings
7.23 But I did **command** them to obey me, so that I would
7.23 to live as I had **commanded** them, so that things would go
7.31 I did not **command** them to do this—it did not even
10.13 At his **command** the waters above the sky roar;
11. 4 them to obey me and to do everything that I had **commanded.**
11. 8 I had **commanded** them to keep the covenant, but they refused.
14.17 The Lord **commanded** me to tell the people about my sorrow
17.22 observe it as a sacred day, as I **commanded** their ancestors.
17.24 "Tell these people that they must obey all my **commands.**
19. 5 I never **commanded** them to do this;
22. 3 "I, the Lord, **command** you to do what is just and right.
22. 4 really do as I have **commanded,** then David's descendants will
22. 5 you do not obey my **commands,** then I swear to you that
23.38 And if they disobey my **command** and use the words 'the
25.27 the God of Israel, am **commanding** them to drink until they
26. 2 and proclaim all I have **commanded** you to say to the people
26. 8 all that the Lord had **commanded** me to speak, they seized me
27. 4 of Israel, told me to **command** them to tell their kings that
32.23 not obey your **commands** or live according to your teaching;
32.35 I did not **command** them to do this, and it did not
35. 7 He **commanded** us always to live in tents, so that we might
35. 9 obeyed everything that our ancestor Jonadab **commanded** us.
35.14 Jonadab's descendants have obeyed his **command** not to drink wine,
35.16 Jonadab's descendants have obeyed the **command**
35.18 "You have obeyed the **command** that your ancestor Jonadab gave you;
35.18 instructions, and you have done everything he **commanded** you.
39.11 But King Nebuchadnezzar **commanded** Nebuzaradan,
42. 5 do not obey all the **commands** that the Lord our God gives
42.20 you promised that you would do everything that he **commands.**
43. 4 people would obey the Lord's **command** to remain in the land
43. 7 They disobeyed the Lord's **command** and went into Egypt as
44.23 sinned against the Lord by not obeying all his **commands."**
46. 9 **Command** the horses to go and the chariots to roll!
47. 7 I have **commanded** it to attack Ashkelon and the people who
50.21 Do everything I **command** you.
51.11 The attacking officers **command,** "Sharpen your arrows!
51.16 At his **command** the waters above the sky roar;
52.25 officer who had been in **command** of the troops, seven of the
Lam 3.38 Good and evil alike take place at his **command.**
Ezek 5. 6 But Jerusalem rebelled against my **commands**
5. 6 Jerusalem rejected my **commands** and refused to keep my laws.
5. 7 my laws or keeping my **commands,** you have caused more trouble
10. 6 When the Lord **commanded** the man wearing linen clothes to
11.12 you were breaking my laws and disobeying my **commands."**
11.20 Then they will keep my laws and faithfully obey all my **commands.**
18. 9 Such a man obeys my **commands** and carefully keeps my laws.
18.17 He keeps my laws and obeys my **commands.**
20.11 I gave them my **commands** and taught them my laws, which
20.13 my laws and rejected my **commands,** which bring life to anyone
20.16 because they had rejected my **commands,** broken my laws, and
20.19 Obey my laws and my **commands.**
20.21 and did not keep my **commands,** which bring life to anyone who
20.24 rejected my **commands,** broken my laws, profaned the Sabbath,
20.25 laws that are not good and **commands** that do not bring life.
28.10 I, the Sovereign Lord, have given the **command."**
36.27 follow my laws and keep all the **commands** I have given you.
36.29 I will **command** the corn to be plentiful, so that you will
37. 9 the Sovereign Lord **commands** it to come from every direction,
38. 7 to get ready and have all his troops ready at his **command.**
43.19 I, the Sovereign Lord, **command** this.
45.13 I, the Sovereign Lord, **command** it.
Ezek 46.16 The Sovereign Lord **commands:**
Dan 2.24 whom the king had **commanded** to execute the royal advisers.
3.20 And he **commanded** the strongest men in his army to tie
3.29 "And now I **command** that if anyone of any nation, race,
6.26 I **command** that throughout my empire everyone should fear
9. 4 love to those who love you and do what you **command.**
9. 5 We have rejected what you **commanded** us to do and have turned
9.25 From the time the **command** is given to rebuild Jerusalem,
Joel 2.11 The Lord thunders **commands** to his army.
Amos 2. 4 They have despised my teachings and have not kept my **commands.**
6.11 When the Lord gives the **command,** houses large and small
9. 1 He gave the **command:**
9. 3 of the sea, I will **command** the sea-monster to bite them.
9. 9 "I will give the **command** and shake the people of Israel
Jon 1.17 At the Lord's **command** a large fish swallowed Jonah, and
4. 7 the next day, at God's **command,** a worm attacked the plant,
Nah 1. 4 He **commands** the sea, and it dries up!
Hab 3. 5 He sends disease before him and **commands** death to follow him.
Zeph 2. 3 all you humble people of the land, who obey his **commands.**
Zech 1. 6 prophets I gave your ancestors **commands** and warnings, but
3. 5 He **commanded** the attendants to put a clean turban on Joshua's head.
6.15 happen if you fully obey the **commands** of the Lord your God.
7. 9 "Long ago I gave these **commands** to my people:
Mal 2. 1 The Lord Almighty says to the priests, "This **command** is for you:
2. 2 curse on them, because you do not take my **command** seriously.
2. 4 I have given you this **command,** so that my covenant with the
4. 4 servant Moses, the laws and **commands** which I gave him at
Mt 15. 3 why do you disobey God's **command** and follow your own teaching?
15. 6 you disregard God's **command,** in order to follow your own
17.18 Jesus gave a **command** to the demon, and it went out of
27.10 to buy the potter's field, as the Lord had **commanded** me."
28.20 and teach them to obey everything I have **commanded** you.
Mk 4.39 Jesus stood up and **commanded** the wind, "Be quiet!"
7. 8 "You put aside God's **command** and obey the teachings of men."
7.10 For Moses **commanded,** 'Respect your father and your mother,'
9.25 so he gave a **command** to the evil spirit.
Lk 1. 6 and obeyed fully all the Lord's laws and **commands.**
2.22 perform the ceremony of purification, as the Law of Moses **commanded.**
8.56 parents were astounded, but Jesus **commanded** them not to tell
9.42 Jesus gave a **command** to the evil spirit, healed the boy,
10.17 demons obeyed us when we gave them a **command** in your name!"
19.39 "Teacher," they said, **"command** your disciples to be quiet!"
23.56 On the Sabbath they rested, as the Law **commanded.**
Jn 8. 5 In our Law Moses **commanded** that such a woman must be
10.18 This is what my Father has **commanded** me to do."
12.49 Father who sent me has **commanded** me what I must say and
12.50 And I know that his **command** brings eternal life.
14.31 that is why I do everything as he **commands** me.
15.10 If you obey my **commands,** you will remain in my love,
15.10 I have obeyed my Father's **commands** and remain in his love.
15.14 And you are my friends if you do what I **command** you.
15.17 This, then, is what I **command** you:
Acts 10.42 And he **commanded** us to preach the gospel to the people
17.30 but now he **commands** all of them everywhere to turn
19.13 to the evil spirits, "I **command** you in the name of Jesus,
Rom 2.13 are put right with God, but by doing what the Law **commands.**
2.14 by instinct what the Law **commands,** they are their own law,
2.15 shows that what the Law **commands** is written in their hearts.
2.26 is not circumcised, obeys the **commands** of the Law, will God
3.28 only through faith, and not by doing what the Law **commands.**
4.17 dead to life and whose **command** brings into being what did
5.14 the same way that Adam did when he disobeyed God's **command.**
10. 5 "Whoever obeys the **commands** of the Law will live."
13. 9 summed up in the one **command,** "Love your neighbour as you
16.26 and by the **command** of the eternal God it is made known
1 Cor 7.10 married people I have a **command** which is not my own but
7.25 I do not have a **command** from the Lord, but I give
14.37 realize that what I am writing to you is the Lord's **command.**
Phil 3. 6 be righteous by obeying the **commands** of the Law, I was
1 Thes 4.16 will be the shout of **command,** the archangel's voice, the sound
2 Thes 3. 6 Our brothers, we **command** you in the name of our Lord Jesus
3.12 the Lord Jesus Christ we **command** these people and warn them
1 Tim 1.18 I entrust to you this **command,** which is in accordance with
6.13 before Pontius Pilate, I **command** you [14] to obey your orders
6.17 **Command** those who are rich in the things of this life
6.18 **Command** them to do good, to be rich in good works,
Heb 3.10 'They are always disloyal and refuse to obey my **commands.'**
7. 5 Levi who are priests are **commanded** by the Law to collect
9.20 which seals the covenant that God has **commanded** you to obey."
2 Pet 2.21 then turn away from the sacred **command** that was given them.
3. 2 the holy prophets, and the **command** from the Lord and Saviour
3. 5 long ago God gave a **command,** and the heavens and earth were
3. 7 being preserved by the same **command** of God, in order to be
1 Jn 2. 3 If we obey God's **commands,** then we are sure that we know
2. 4 but does not obey his **commands,** such a person is a liar
2. 7 My dear friends, this **command** I am writing to you is not
2. 7 it is the old **command,** the one you have had from the
2. 7 The old **command** is the message you have already heard.
2. 8 However, the **command** I am now writing to you is new,
3.22 because we obey his **commands** and do what pleases him.
3.23 What he **commands** is that we believe in his Son Jesus
3.23 and love one another, just as Christ **commanded** us.
3.24 Whoever obeys God's **commands** lives in union with God
4.21 The **command** that Christ has given us is this:
5. 2 it is by loving God and obeying his **commands.**
5. 3 For our love for God means that we obey his **commands.**
5. 3 And his **commands** are not too hard for us, [4] because every

2 Jn	4	children live in the truth, just as the Father **commanded** us.
	5	This is no new **command** I am writing to you;
	5	it is the **command** which we have had from the beginning.
	6	means that we must live in obedience to God's **commands.**
	6	The **command,** as you have all heard from the beginning, is
Rev	3.10	Because you have kept my **command** to endure, I will also

COMMANDER

Gen	21.22	Abimelech went with Phicol, the **commander** of his army, and
	26.26	adviser and Phicol the **commander** of his army to see Isaac.
Num	31.14	angry with the officers, the **commanders** of battalions and companies,
Josh	5.14	"I am here as the **commander** of the Lord's army."
	5.15	And the **commander** of the Lord's army told him, "Take
Judg	4. 2	The **commander** of his army was Sisera,
	4. 7	I will bring Sisera, the **commander** of Jabin's army, to
	5. 9	My heart is with the **commanders** of Israel, with the people
	5.14	The **commanders** came down from Machir, the officers down from Zebulun.
1 Sam	12. 9	king of Moab and Sisera, **commander** of the army of the city
	13. 3	Jonathan killed the Philistine **commander** in Geba, and all
	13. 4	Saul had killed the Philistine **commander**
	14.50	his army **commander** was his cousin Abner, the son of his
	17.18	And take these ten cheeses to the **commanding officer.**
	17.55	Goliath, he asked Abner, the **commander** of his army, "Abner,
	26. 5	where Saul and Abner son of Ner, **commander** of Saul's army,
	29. 3	The Philistine **commanders** saw them and asked, "What are
	29. 4	But the Philistine **commanders** were angry with Achish and said to him,
2 Sam	2. 8	The **commander** of Saul's army, Abner son of Ner, had fled
	8.16	Joab, whose mother was Zeruiah, was the **commander** of the army;
	10.16	under the command of Shobach, the **commander** of the army of King
	10.18	Shobach, the enemy **commander,** who died on the battlefield.
	11.11	**commander** Joab and his officers are camping out in the open.
	24. 2	So David gave orders to Joab, the **commander** of his army:
1 Kgs	1.19	priest, and Joab the **commander** of your army to the feast,
	1.25	all your sons, Joab the **commander** of your army, and Abiathar
	2. 5	me by killing the two **commanders** of Israel's armies, Abner
	2.32	Abner, **commander** of the army of Israel,
	2.32	and Amasa, **commander** of the army of Judah.
	2.35	The king made Benaiah **commander** of the army in Joab's
	4. 4	**Commander** of the army: Benaiah son of Jehoiada
	9.22	as his soldiers, officers, **commanders,** chariot captains,
	11.15	had conquered Edom, Joab the **commander** of his army had gone
	11.21	died and that Joab the **commander** of the army was dead, Hadad
	15.20	Asa's proposal and sent his **commanding officers** and their
	16.16	they all proclaimed their **commander** Omri king of Israel.
	20.15	the young soldiers who were under the district **commanders,**
	20.24	from their commands and replace them with field **commanders.**
	22.31	had ordered his thirty-two chariot **commanders** to attack no
2 Kgs	4.13	the king or the army **commander** and put in a good word
	5. 1	Naaman, the **commander** of the Syrian army, was highly
	8.21	and his chariot **commanders** managed to break out and escape,
	25. 8	to the king and **commander** of his army,
	25.18	In addition, Nebuzaradan, the **commanding officer,** took
	25.19	still in the city, the **commander's** assistant, who was in charge
1 Chr	11. 6	man to kill a Jebusite will be **commander** of the army!"
	11. 6	mother was Zeruiah, led the attack and became **commander.**
	12.18	Amasai, who later became the **commander** of "The Thirty,"
	15.25	of Israel, and the military **commanders** went to the house of
	18.15	Abishai's brother Joab was **commander** of the army;
	19.16	under the command of Shobach, **commander** of the army of King
	19.18	They also killed the Syrian **commander,** Shobach.
	27. 1	men was on duty under the **commander** for that month.
	27. 2	The following were the **commanders** for each month:
	27. 2	(his son Amizzabad succeeded him as **commander** of this group)
	27.34	Joab was **commander** of the royal army.
	29. 6	officials of the tribes, the **commanders** of the army, and the
2 Chr	8. 9	but served as soldiers, officers, chariot **commanders,**
	11.11	strongly fortified and appointed a **commander** for each of them,
	16. 4	Asa's proposal and sent his **commanding officers** and their
	17.14	Adnah was the **commander** of the troops from the clans of Judah,
	17.17	The **commander** of the troops from the clans of Benjamin was Eliada,
	18.30	Syria had ordered his chariot **commanders** to attack no one
	18.32	The chariot **commanders** saw that he was not the king of Israel,
	23. 8	Sabbath, so the **commanders** had available both those coming
	33.11	So the Lord let the **commanders** of the Assyrian army invade Judah.
Neh	7. 2	Hanani and Hananiah, **commanding officer** of the fortress.
Is	10. 8	He boasts, "Every one of my **commanders** is a king!
	20. 1	the **commander-in-chief** of the Assyrian army attacked
	55. 4	made him a leader and **commander** of nations,
Jer	39. 9	Finally Nebuzaradan, the **commanding officer,** took away as
	39.11	King Nebuchadnezzar commanded Nebuzaradan, the **commanding officer,** to give the following order:
	40. 1	to me after Nebuzaradan, the **commanding officer,** had set me
	40. 2	The **commanding officer** took me aside and said, "The Lord
	41.10	in Mizpah, whom Nebuzaradan the **commanding officer** had
	43. 6	took everyone whom Nebuzaradan the **commanding officer** had
	52.12	to the king and **commander** of his army,
	52.24	In addition, Nebuzaradan, the **commanding officer,** took
	52.25	still in the city, the **commander's** assistant, who was in charge
Dan	2.14	Then Daniel went to Arioch, **commander** of the king's bodyguard,
Hab	3.14	Your arrows pierced the **commander** of his army
Zech	10. 4	come rulers, leaders, and **commanders** to govern my people.
Mk	6.21	government officials, the military **commanders,** and the leading
Jn	18.12	Roman soldiers with their **commanding officer** and the Jewish
Acts	21.31	was sent up to the **commander** of the Roman troops that all
Acts	21.32	the **commander** took some officers and soldiers and rushed down
	21.33	**commander** went over to Paul, arrested him, and ordered him
	21.34	such confusion that the **commander** could not find out exactly what
	21.37	about to take Paul into the fort, he spoke to the **commander:**
	21.37	the **commander** asked.
	21.40	The **commander** gave him permission, so Paul stood on the steps
	22.24	Roman **commander** ordered his men to take Paul into the fort,
	22.26	he went to the **commander** and asked him, "What are you
	22.27	So the **commander** went to Paul and asked him, "Tell me,
	22.28	The **commander** said, "I became one by paying a large amount
	22.29	and the **commander** was frightened when he realized that Paul was
	22.30	**commander** wanted to find out for certain what the Jews were
	23.10	so violent that the **commander** was afraid that Paul would be
	23.15	send word to the Roman **commander** to bring Paul down to you,
	23.17	and said to him, "Take this young man to the **commander;**
	23.18	led him to the **commander,** and said, "The prisoner Paul called
	23.19	The **commander** took him by the hand, led him off by himself,
	23.22	**commander** said, "Don't tell anyone that you have reported this
	23.23	Then the **commander** called two of his officers and said,
	23.25	Then the **commander** wrote a letter that went like this:
	24.22	Lysias the **commander** arrives," he told them, "I will decide
2 Tim	2. 4	service wants to please his **commanding officer** and so does not

COMMANDMENT

Ex	25.16	I will give you, on which the **commandments** are written.
	31.18	tablets on which God himself had written the **commandments.**
	32.15	stone tablets with the **commandments** written on both sides.
	32.16	made the tablets and had engraved the **commandments** on them.
	34.28	the tablets the words of the covenant—the Ten **Commandments.**
	34.29	Mount Sinai carrying the Ten **Commandments,** his face was
	38.21	were kept on which the Ten **Commandments** were written.
	40. 3	Covenant Box containing the Ten **Commandments** and put the
Deut	4.13	you must obey the Ten **Commandments,** which he wrote on two
	5.22	"These are the **commandments** the Lord gave to all of you
	5.22	the thick clouds, he gave these **commandments** and no others.
	10. 4	the first time, the Ten **Commandments** that he gave you when
Josh	8.35	Every one of the **commandments** of Moses was read by
	22. 5	do his will, obey his **commandments,** be faithful to him, and
2 Chr	19.10	violation of a law or **commandment,** you must instruct them
Ezra	9.14	how can we ignore your **commandments** again and intermarry
Ps	50.16	But God says to the wicked, "Why should you recite my **commandments?**
	78. 5	of Israel and **commandments** to the descendants of Jacob.
	78. 7	forget what he has done, but always obey his **commandments.**
	78.56	They did not obey his **commandments,** [57] but were rebellious
	89.31	and do not keep my **commandments,** [32] then I will punish them
	119.10	keep me from disobeying your **commandments.**
	119.35	Keep me obedient to your **commandments,** because in them I find happiness.
	119.48	I respect and love your **commandments;**
	119.64	teach me your **commandments.**
	119.80	May I perfectly obey your **commandments** and be spared the
	119.86	Your **commandments** are all trustworthy;
	119.96	but your **commandment** is perfect.
	119.98	Your **commandment** is with me all the time and makes me
	119.111	Your **commandments** are my eternal possession;
	119.143	trouble and anxiety, but your **commandments** bring me joy.
Mt	5.19	the least important of the **commandments** and teaches others to
	19.17	Keep the **commandments** if you want to enter life."
	19.18	"What **commandments?"**
	19.20	have obeyed all these **commandments,"** the young man replied.
	22.36	he asked, "which is the greatest **commandment** in the Law?"
	22.38	This is the greatest and the most important **commandment.**
	22.39	The second most important **commandment** is like it:
	22.40	the teachings of the prophets depend on these two **commandments."**
Mk	10.19	You know the **commandments:**
	10.20	"ever since I was young, I have obeyed all these **commandments."**
	12.28	"Which **commandment** is the most important of all?"
	12.31	The second most important **commandment** is this:
	12.31	There is no other **commandment** more important than these two."
	12.33	important to obey these two **commandments** than to offer animals
Lk	18.20	You know the **commandments:**
	18.21	"Ever since I was young, I have obeyed all these **commandments."**
Jn	13.34	And now I give you a new **commandment:**
	14.15	"If you love me, you will obey my **commandments.**
	14.21	accepts my **commandments** and obeys them is the one
	15.12	My **commandment** is this:
Acts	13.47	For this is the **commandment** that the Lord has given us:
Rom	7. 8	But by means of that **commandment** sin found its chance to
	7. 9	when the **commandment** came, sin sprang to life, [10] and I died.
	7.10	And the **commandment** which was meant to bring life, in my
	7.11	by means of the **commandment** it deceived me and killed me.
	7.12	Law itself is holy, and the **commandment** is holy, right, and
	7.13	so, by means of the **commandment** sin is shown to be even
	13. 9	The **commandments,** "Do not commit adultery;
1 Cor	7.19	what matters is to obey God's **commandments.**
Gal	5.14	For the whole Law is summed up in one **commandment:**
Eph	2.15	the Jewish Law with its **commandments** and rules,
	6. 2	father and mother" is the first **commandment** that has a promise
Tit	1.14	Jewish legends and to human **commandments** which come from people
Heb	9. 4	and the two stone tablets with the **commandments** written on them.
	9.19	to the people all the **commandments** as set forth in the Law.
Jas	2.10	Whoever breaks one **commandment** is guilty of breaking them all.

Rev 12.17 those who obey God's **commandments** and are faithful to the truth
14.12 those who obey God's **commandments** and are faithful to Jesus.

COMMEND

Acts 14.23 with prayers and fasting they **commended** them to the Lord,
14.26 place where they had been **commended** to the care of God's
15.40 Paul chose Silas and left, **commended** by the believers to the
20.32 "And now I **commend** you to the care of God and to
2 Cor 4. 2 and try to **commend** ourselves to everyone's good conscience.

COMMENTARY

2 Chr 24.27 The **Commentary** on the Book of Kings contains the stories

COMMERCE

1 Kgs 20.34 you may set up a **commercial** centre for yourself in Damascus,
Is 23.11 He has ordered the Phoenician centres of **commerce** to be destroyed.
23.18 The money she earns by **commerce** will be dedicated to the Lord.
Ezek 17. 4 carried to a land of **commerce**, and placed in a city of
26. 2 Her **commercial** power is gone!

COMMISSION

2 Chr 7. 6 as they had been **commissioned** by David.
Dan 3. 2 princes, governors, lieutenant-governors, **commissioners,**

COMMIT

Ex 20.13 "Do not **commit murder.**
20.14 "Do not **commit adultery.**
Lev 20.10 If a man **commits adultery** with the wife of a fellow-Israelite,
24.17 "Anyone who **commits murder** shall be put to death,
Num 5.19 "If you have not **committed adultery,** you will not be harmed
5.20 But if you have **committed adultery,** [21] may the Lord
5.27 If she has **committed adultery,** the water will cause bitter pain;
5.29 and becomes suspicious that his wife has **committed adultery.**
Deut 5.17 "'Do not **commit murder.**
5.18 "'Do not **commit adultery.**
27.24 "'God's curse on anyone who secretly **commits murder.'**
Prov 6.32 But a man who **commits adultery** hasn't any sense.
30.20 she **commits adultery,** has a bath, and says, "But I haven't
Is 5. 7 to do what was good, but instead they **committed murder.**
33.15 with those who plan to **commit murder** or to do other evil
Jer 3. 9 and she **committed adultery** by worshipping stones and trees.
5. 7 they were full, but they **committed adultery** and spent their
7. 9 You steal, murder, **commit adultery,** tell lies under oath,
23.14 they **commit adultery** and tell lies;
29.23 of terrible sins—they have **committed adultery** and have told
Ezek 9. 9 They have **committed murder** all over the land and have filled
16.17 it to make male images, and **committed adultery** with them.
16.32 are like a woman who **commits adultery** with strangers instead
22. 6 All Israel's leaders trust in their own strength and **commit murder.**
22.11 Some **commit adultery,** and others seduce their daughters-in-law or their half-sisters.
22.27 They **commit murder** in order to get rich.
23.37 They have **committed adultery** and murder—adultery with
23.48 a warning to every woman not to **commit adultery** as they did.
33.25 You **commit murder.**
33.26 Everyone **commits adultery.**
Hos 3. 1 love for a woman who is **committing adultery** with a lover.
3. 3 for me without being a prostitute or **committing adultery;**
4. 2 they lie, murder, steal, and **commit adultery.**
4.13 as prostitutes, and your daughters-in-law **commit adultery.**
6. 9 on the road to the holy place at Shechem they **commit murder.**
Mic 7. 2 Everyone is waiting for a chance to **commit murder.**
Mt 5.21 that people were told in the past, 'Do not **commit murder;**
5.27 "You have heard that it was said, 'Do not **commit adultery.'**
5.28 is guilty of **committing adultery** with her in his heart.
5.32 guilty of making her **commit adultery** if she marries again;
5.32 and the man who marries her **commits adultery** also.
15.19 lead him to kill, **commit adultery,** and do other immoral things;
19. 9 other than her unfaithfulness **commits adultery** if he marries some
19.18 Jesus answered, "Do not **commit murder;**
19.18 do not **commit adultery;**
27.23 But Pilate asked, "What crime has he **committed?"**
Mk 3.29 will never be forgiven, because he has **committed** an eternal sin."
7.22 immoral things, to rob, kill, [22] **commit adultery,** be greedy,
10.11 divorces his wife and marries another woman **commits adultery**
10.12 who divorces her husband and marries another man **commits adultery."**
10.19 'Do not **commit murder;**
10.19 do not **commit adultery;**
15. 7 prison with the rebels who had **committed murder** in the riot.
15.14 "But what crime has he **committed?"**
Lk 16.18 who divorces his wife and marries another woman **commits adultery;**
16.18 and the man who marries a divorced woman **commits adultery.**
18.20 'Do not **commit adultery;**
18.20 do not **commit murder;**
23.22 to them the third time, "But what crime has he **committed?**
Jn 8. 3 who had been caught **committing adultery,** and they made her stand
8. 4 "this woman was caught in the very act of **committing adultery.**
8. 7 "Whichever one of you has **committed** no sin may throw the
18.30 have brought him to you if he had not **committed** a crime."
Acts 18.14 or wrong that has been **committed,** it would be reasonable for
Rom 2.22 say, "Do not **commit adultery"**—but do you commit adultery?
Rom 7. 3 free woman and does not **commit adultery** if she marries another
13. 9 The commandments, "Do not **commit adultery;**
13. 9 do not **commit murder;**
1 Cor 6.18 Any other sin a man **commits** does not affect his body;
7.28 But if you do marry, you haven't **committed** a sin;
7.28 if an unmarried woman marries, she hasn't **committed** a sin.
1 Thes 2.16 have brought to completion all the sins they have always **committed.**
1 Tim 5.20 Rebuke publicly all those who **commit** sins, so that the rest
Heb 9. 7 sins which the people have **committed** without knowing they were
13. 4 God will judge those who are immoral and those who **commit adultery.**
Jas 2.11 one who said, "Do not **commit adultery,"** also said, "Do
2.11 "Do not commit adultery," also said, "Do not **commit murder."**
2.11 Even if you do not **commit adultery,** you have become a
2.11 you have become a law-breaker if you **commit murder.**
5.15 to health, and the sins he has **committed** will be forgiven.
1 Pet 2.22 He **committed** no sin, and no one ever heard a lie come
1 Jn 5.16 If you see your brother **commit** a sin that does not lead
Jude 11 they have given themselves over to the error that Balaam **committed.**
Rev 2.22 where she and those who **committed adultery** with her will suffer

COMMON

Gen 34.31 "We cannot let our sister be treated like a **common** whore."
Lev 4.27 it is one of the **common** people who sins and becomes guilty
1 Kgs 10.27 his reign silver was as **common** in Jerusalem as stone, and
2 Chr 1.15 silver and gold became as **common** in Jerusalem as stone, and
9.27 his reign silver was as **common** in Jerusalem as stone, and
Prov 17.16 money on an education, because he has no **common** sense.
22. 2 The rich and the poor have this in **common:**
28.24 to steal from his parents is no better than a **common** thief.
29.13 his oppressor have this in **common**—the Lord gave eyes to both
Is 5.13 starve to death, and the **common** people will die of thirst.
5.14 of Jerusalem along with the noisy crowd of **common** people.
Lam 4. 2 us as gold, but now they are treated like **common** clay pots.
Ezek 16.31 But you are not out for money like a **common** prostitute.
Zech 9. 3 so much silver and gold that it is as **common** as dirt!
2 Cor 4. 7 spiritual treasure are like **common** clay pots, in order to show
6.15 What does a believer have in **common** with an unbeliever?
Phil 1.27 are standing firm with one **common** purpose and that with only
Tit 1. 4 Titus, my true son in the faith that we have in **common.**
Jude 3 the salvation we share in **common,** when I felt the need of

COMMOTION

2 Sam 18.29 me, I saw a great **commotion,** but I couldn't tell what it
Is 17.12 Powerful nations are in **commotion** with a sound like the
Jer 10.22 There is a great **commotion** in a nation to the north;

AV COMMUNION

1 Cor 10.16 we drink from it, we are **sharing** in the blood of Christ.
10.16 when we eat it, we are **sharing** in the body of Christ.
2 Cor 6.14 How can light and darkness live **together?**
13.13 love of God, and the **fellowship** of the Holy Spirit be with

COMMUNITY

Ex 12. 3 Give these instructions to the whole **community** of Israel:
12. 6 month, the whole **community** of Israel will kill the animals.
12.47 The whole **community** of Israel must celebrate this festival,
16. 1 The whole Israelite **community** set out from Elim, and on
16. 9 to Aaron, "Tell the whole **community** to come and stand
16.10 Aaron spoke to the whole **community,** they turned towards the desert,
16.22 All the leaders of the **community** came and told Moses about it,
17. 1 The whole Israelite **community** left the desert of Sin,
34.31 all the leaders of the **community** went to him, and Moses
35. 1 Moses called together the whole **community** of the people of
38.25 from the census of the **community** weighed 3,430 kilogrammes,
Lev 4.13 If it is the whole **community** of Israel that sins and
4.14 the sin becomes known, the **community** shall bring a young
4.15 the leaders of the **community** shall put their hands on its head,
4.21 This is an offering to take away the sin of the **community.**
8. 3 Then call the whole **community** together there."
8. 4 commanded, and when the **community** had assembled, [5] he said to them,
9. 5 and the whole **community** assembled there to worship the Lord.
10. 6 die, and the Lord will be angry with the whole **community.**
10.17 to you in order to take away the sin of the **community.**
16. 5 The **community** of Israel shall give Aaron two male goats
16.17 his family, and the whole **community,** [18] he must then go out
16.33 the altar, the priests, and all the people of the **community.**
17. 8 any foreigner living in the **community** who offers a
17.10 any foreigner living in the **community** eats meat with blood
17.13 any foreigner living in the **community** hunts an animal or a
19. 2 Moses [2] to say to the **community** of Israel, "Be holy,
20. 2 god Molech shall be stoned to death by the whole **community.**
20. 4 But if the **community** ignores what he has done and does not
20.17 shall be publicly disgraced and driven out of the **community.**
20.18 be driven out of the **community,** because they have broken the
23.18 with the bread the **community** is to present seven one-year-old lambs,
24.14 and then the whole **community** shall stone him to death.
24.16 the Lord shall be stoned to death by the whole **community.**
Num 1. 5 tribes, who were chosen from the **community** for this work:
1.18 Aaron [18] called together the whole **community** on the first
1.53 come near and cause my anger to strike the **community** of Israel."
3. 7 perform duties for the priests and for the whole **community.**

Num 4.34 and the leaders of the **community** took a census of the three
8. 9 Then assemble the whole **community** of Israel and make the
10. 3 on both trumpets, the whole **community** is to gather round you
10. 7 in order to call the **community** together, long blasts are to
13.26 Moses, Aaron, and the whole **community** of Israel at Kadesh in
14.10 The whole **community** was threatening to stone them to death,
15.23 that in the future the **community** fails to do everything that
15.24 of the ignorance of the **community,** they are to offer a bull
15.25 purification for the **community,** and they will be forgiven,
15.26 The whole **community** of Israel and the foreigners living
15.33 Aaron, and the whole **community,** [34] and was put under guard,
15.35 whole **community** is to stone him to death outside the camp."
15.36 So the whole **community** took him outside the camp and
16. 1 other Israelites, well-known leaders chosen by the **community.**
16. 3 All the members of the **community** belong to the Lord, and the
16. 3 Moses, do you set yourself above the Lord's **community?"**
16. 9 the rest of the **community,** so that you can approach him,
16. 9 Lord's Tent, and minister to the **community** and serve them?
16.19 Then Korah gathered the whole **community,** and they stood
16.19 presence appeared to the whole **community,** [20] and the Lord
16.22 When one man sins, do you get angry with the whole **community?"**
16.41 The next day the whole **community** complained against
19. 9 be kept for the Israelite **community** to use in preparing the
20. 1 the first month the whole **community** of Israel came to the
20. 8 Covenant Box, and then you and Aaron assemble the whole
community.
20.10 Aaron assembled the whole **community** in front of the rock,
20.22 The whole **community** of Israel left Kadesh and arrived at Mount
Hor,
20.27 the sight of the whole **community,** [28] and Moses removed
20.29 The whole **community** learnt that Aaron had died, and they
25. 6 of Moses and the whole **community,** while they were mourning
26. 2 by families of the whole **community** of Israel, of all men
26. 9 (These are the Dathan and Abiram who were chosen by the
community.
27. 2 the leaders, and the whole **community** at the entrance of the
27.14 When the whole **community** complained against me at Meribah,
27.17 in battle, so that your **community** will not be like sheep
27.19 the priest and the whole **community,** and there before them
27.20 so that the whole **community** of Israel will obey him.
27.21 Joshua and the whole **community** of Israel in all their affairs."
27.22 He made Joshua stand before Eleazar the priest and the whole
community.
31.12 and Eleazar and to the **community** of the people of Israel,
31.13 the other leaders of the **community** went out of the camp to
31.26 the other leaders of the **community,** are to count everything
31.27 soldiers and the other part for the rest of the **community.**
31.42 The share of the **community** was the same as that
32. 2 the other leaders of the **community** and said, [3-4] "This
35.24 In such cases the **community** shall judge in favour of the
35.25 The **community** is to rescue the man guilty of
Deut 26.12 widows, so that in every **community** they will have all they
Josh 9.15 The leaders of the **community** of Israel gave their solemn
18. 1 conquered the land, the entire **community** of Israel assembled
22.12 Israel heard this, the whole **community** came together at
22.16 and speaking for the whole **community** of the Lord, they
22.20 the whole **community** of Israel was punished for that.
22.30 ten leading men of the **community** who were with him, the
Ezra 8.17 to Iddo, head of the **community** at Casiphia, to ask him and
10. 8 he would lose his right to be a member of the **community.**
Neh 13. 3 they excluded all foreigners from the **community.**
Ezek 14. 7 who live in the Israelite **community** turns away from me and
14. 8 will remove him from the **community** of my people, so that you
20. 1 the leaders of the Israelite **community** came to consult me
Mal 2.12 Lord remove from the **community** of Israel those who did this,

COMPANION

Gen 2.18 I will make a suitable **companion** to help him."
2.20 but not one of them was a suitable **companion** to help him.
Judg 18.14 round Laish said to their **companions,** "Did you know that
1 Sam 2. 8 He makes them **companions** of princes and puts them in places
2 Kgs 9. 2 away from his **companions,** [3] pour this olive-oil on his head,
Neh 2.12 up and went out, taking a few of my **companions** with me.
4. 2 In front of his **companions** and the Samaritan troops he said,
4.23 did any of my **companions** nor my servants nor my bodyguard.
5.10 me, and so have my **companions** and the men who work for
Ps 55.13 But it is you, my **companion,** my colleague and close friend.
55.20 My former **companion** attacked his friends;
88.18 friends abandon me, and darkness is my only **companion.**
113. 8 their misery [8] and makes them **companions** of princes, the
Song 8.13 my **companions** are waiting to hear you speak.
Mk 1.36 But Simon and his **companions** went out searching for him,
16.10 She went and told his **companions.**
Lk 9.32 Peter and his **companions** were sound asleep, but they woke up
Acts 4.13 They realized then that they had been **companions** of Jesus.
5.17 High Priest and all his **companions,** members of the local
5.21 High Priest and his **companions** called together all the Jewish
13.13 Paul and his **companions** sailed from Paphos and came to Perga,
20.34 to provide everything that my **companions** and I have needed.
22.11 bright light, and so my **companions** took me by the hand and
1 Cor 15.33 "Bad **companions** ruin good character."
Gal 2. 3 My **companion** Titus, even though he is Greek, was not
Heb 1. 9 of an honour far greater than he gave to your **companions."**

COMPANY (1)

Num 1.52 Israelites shall set up camp, **company by company,**
10.14 Judah started out first, **company by company,** with Nahshon
10.18 Reuben would start out, **company by company,** with Elizur
10.22 Ephraim would start out, **company by company,** with Elishama
10.25 the divisions, would start out, **company by company,** with Ahiezer
10.28 order of march, **company by company,** whenever the Israelites
broke camp
31.14 commanders of battalions and **companies,** who had returned from
the war.
Judg 9.44 city gate, the other two **companies** attacked the people in
Mt 27.27 into the governor's palace, and the whole **company** gathered
round
Mk 15.16 the governor's palace and called together the rest of the **company.**

COMPANY (2)

Job 34. 8 He likes the **company** of evil men and goes about with sinners.
Ps 26. 4 I do not keep **company** with worthless people;
26. 5 I hate the **company** of evil men and avoid the wicked.
Prov 9. 6 Leave the **company** of ignorant people, and live.
13.20 Keep **company** with the wise and you will become wise.
22.29 who is better than most and worthy of the **company** of kings.
Ezek 26.20 world among eternal ruins, keeping **company** with the dead.
Heb 11.40 purpose was that only in **company** with us would they be made

COMPARE

Judg 8. 2 was able to do is nothing **compared** with what you have done.
8. 3 What have I done to **compare** with that?"
1 Kgs 20.27 two small flocks of goats **compared** with the Syrians, who
Job 8. 7 you lost will be nothing **compared** with what God will give
28.19 the purest gold Cannot **compare** with the value of wisdom.
41.33 There is nothing on earth to **compare** with him;
Prov 3.15 nothing you could want can **compare** with it.
8.11 nothing you want can **compare** with me.
27. 3 stone and sand is nothing **compared** to the trouble that
27. 4 Anger is cruel and destructive, but it is nothing **compared** to
jealousy.
Song 2. 3 of the forest, so is my dearest **compared** with other men.
Is 40.18 To whom can God be **compared?**
40.25 To whom can the holy God be **compared?**
46. 5 "With whom will you **compare** me?"
Jer 23.28 What good is straw **compared** with wheat?
30. 7 no other day can **compare** with it— a time of distress
49.19 Who can be **compared** to me?
50.44 Who can be **compared** to me?
Ezek 15. 2 "Mortal man," he said, "how does a vine **compare** with a tree?
15. 2 branch of a grapevine **compared** with the trees of the forest?
16.51 Your corruption makes your sisters look innocent by **comparison.**
27.32 'Who can be **compared** to Tyre, To Tyre now silent in the
31. 2 What can I **compare** you to?
31. 8 No cedar in God's garden could **compare** with it.
Dan 1.13 Then **compare** us with the young men who are eating the
Mt 11.16 "Now, to what can I **compare** the people of this day?
Lk 7.31 "Now to what can I **compare** the people of this day?
13.18 What shall I **compare** it with?
13.20 Jesus asked, "What shall I **compare** the Kingdom of God
Rom 8.18 this present time cannot be **compared** at all with the glory
2 Cor 10.12 classify ourselves or **compare** ourselves with those who rate
Gal 6. 4 without having to **compare** it with what someone else has

COMPASSION

Ex 33.19 the Lord, and I show **compassion** and pity on those I choose.
34. 6 God who is full of **compassion** and pity, who is not easily
Ps 69.16 in your great **compassion** turn to me!
77. 9 Has anger taken the place of his **compassion?"**
116. 5 our God is **compassionate.**
119.156 But your **compassion,** Lord, is great;
145. 9 He is good to everyone and has **compassion** on all he made.
Is 30.19 The Lord is **compassionate,** and when you cry to him for help,
51. 3 "I will show **compassion** to Jerusalem, to all who live in
63. 9 In his love and **compassion** he rescued them.
63.15 Where are your love and **compassion?**
Jer 13.14 No pity, **compassion,** or mercy will stop me from killing them."
Zech 10. 6 I will have **compassion** on them and bring them all back home.
Phil 2. 1 and you have kindness and **compassion** for one another.
Col 3.12 you must clothe yourselves with **compassion,** kindness, humility,
Jas 3.17 is full of **compassion** and produces a harvest of good deeds;
5.11 For the Lord is full of mercy and **compassion.**

COMPETENT

Prov 14.35 Kings are pleased with **competent** officials, but they

COMPLAIN

Gen 21.25 Abraham **complained** to Abimelech about a well which the
Ex 5.15 went to the king and **complained,** "Why do you do this to
15.24 The people **complained** to Moses and asked, "What are we
16. 2 in the desert they all **complained** to Moses and Aaron [3] and
16. 7 He has heard your **complaints** against him—yes, against him,
16. 8 he has heard how much you have **complained** against him.
16. 8 When you **complain** against us, you are really complaining
against the Lord."
16. 9 come and stand before the Lord, because he has heard their
complaints."
16.12 "I have heard the **complaints** of the Israelites.
17. 2 They **complained** to Moses and said, "Give us water to drink."
17. 2 Moses answered, "Why are you **complaining?**
17. 3 But the people were very thirsty and continued to **complain** to
Moses.
17. 7 and Meribah, because the Israelites **complained** and put the
Num 11. 1 The people began to **complain** to the Lord about their troubles.
11. 4 meat, and even the Israelites themselves began to **complain:**

Num 11.10 Moses heard all the people **complaining** as they stood
11.20 here among you and have **complained** to him that you should
13.30 silenced the people who were **complaining** against Moses, and
14. 2 They **complained** against Moses and Aaron, and said, "It
14.27 "How much longer are these wicked people going to **complain** against me?
14.27 I have heard enough of these **complaints!**
14.29 Because you have **complained** against me, none of you over
14.36 report which caused the people to **complain** against the Lord.
16.11 When you **complain** against Aaron, it is really against
16.41 whole community **complained** against Moses and Aaron and said,
17. 5 the constant **complaining** of these Israelites against you."
17.10 Israelites that they will die unless their **complaining** stops."
20. 3 the people gathered round Moses and Aaron [3]and **complained:**
20.13 where the people of Israel **complained** against the Lord and
21. 5 They **complained,** "Why did you bring us out of Egypt to die
27.14 When the whole community **complained** against me at Meribah,
Deut 1.34 "The Lord heard your **complaints** and became angry, and
Josh 9.18 All the people **complained** to the leaders about this, [19]but they answered,
Judg 8. 1 They **complained** bitterly about it.
1 Sam 8.18 time comes, you will **complain** bitterly because of your king,
8.18 chose, but the Lord will not listen to your **complaints."**
2 Kgs 6. 1 Elisha was in charge of **complained** to him, "The place where
Neh 5. 1 men and women, began to **complain** against their fellow-Jews.
5. 6 When I heard their **complaints,** I was angry [7]and decided to act.
Job 2.10 How can we **complain** when he sends us trouble?"
10. 1 Listen to my bitter **complaint.**
23. 1 I still rebel and **complain** against God;
31.13 When one of my servants **complained** against me, I would
33.13 Why do you accuse God of never answering a man's **complaints?**
Ps 55.17 Morning, noon, and night my **complaints** and groans go up to him,
142. 2 I bring him all my **complaints;**
Prov 20.14 The customer always **complains** that the price is too high,
21.19 out in the desert than with a nagging, **complaining** wife.
23.29 for himself, always causing trouble and always **complaining.**
Is 28. 9 They **complain** about me.
33.24 our land will ever again **complain** of being ill, and all sins
40.27 Israel, why then do you **complain** that the Lord doesn't
45. 9 Does the pot **complain** that its maker has no skill?
Jer 2.29 What is your **complaint?**
30.15 **Complain** no more about your injuries;
Lam 3.39 Why should we ever **complain** when we are punished for our sin?
Ezek 20.49 Everyone is already **complaining** that I always speak in riddles."
24.16 You are not to **complain** or cry or shed any tears.
Hos 4. 4 or reprimand them—my **complaint** is against you priests.
Hab 2. 1 me to say and what answer he will give to my **complaint.**
Lk 5.30 Law who belonged to their group **complained** to Jesus' disciples.
Acts 25.24 both here and in Jerusalem, have brought **complaints** to me.
1 Cor 10.10 We must not **complain,** as some of them did—and they were
2 Cor 8.20 not to stir up any **complaints** about the way we handle this
Phil 2.14 Do everything without **complaining** or arguing,
Col 3.13 whenever any of you has a **complaint** against someone else.
Jas 5. 4 Listen to their **complaints!**
5. 9 Do not **complain** against one another, my brothers, so that God
1 Pet 4. 9 Open your homes to each other without **complaining.**

COMPLETE

Gen 2. 1 And so the whole universe was **completed.**
2. 3 that day he had **completed** his creation and stopped working.
Ex 39.32 on the Tent of the Lord's presence was finally **completed.**
Lev 8.33 Tent for seven days, until your ordination rites are **completed.**
9. 1 after the ordination rites were **completed,** Moses called
12. 4 Tent until the time of her purification is **completed.**
12. 6 purification is **completed,** whether for a son or daughter,
Josh 5. 8 After the circumcision was **completed,** the whole nation
1 Kgs 7.22 And so the work on the columns was **completed.**
7.40 He **completed** all his work for King Solomon for the Lord's Temple.
1 Chr 27.24 Zeruiah, began to take a census, but he did not **complete** it.
2 Chr 4.11 He **completed** all the objects that he had promised King
8.16 By this time all Solomon's projects had been **completed.**
8.16 Lord's Temple to its **completion,** all the work had been successful.
29.18 "We have **completed** the ritual purification of the whole Temple,
Ezra 4.13 its walls are **completed,** the people will stop paying taxes,
4.16 rebuilt and its walls are **completed,** Your Majesty will no
6.14 They **completed** the Temple as they had been commanded by the
Ps 138. 8 **Complete** the work that you have begun.
Is 28.21 He will **complete** his work, his mysterious work.
Hag 2.18 day that the foundation of the Temple has been **completed.**
Mt 20.25 have power over them, and the leaders have **complete** authority.
Mk 10.42 have power over them, and the leaders have **complete** authority.
Lk 6.40 every pupil, when he has **completed** his training, will be like
16. 2 Hand in a **complete** account of your handling of my property,
Jn 3.29 This is how my own happiness is made **complete.**
13. 3 Jesus knew that the Father had given him **complete** power;
15.11 joy may be in you and that your joy may be **complete.**
16.24 you will receive, so that your happiness may be **complete.**
19.28 Jesus knew that by now everything had been **completed;**
Acts 11. 4 So Peter gave them a **complete** account of what had happened
14.26 care of God's grace for the work they had now **completed.**
20.24 I only want to **complete** my mission and finish the work that
21.19 greeted them and gave a **complete** report of everything that
24.18 in the Temple after I had **completed** the ceremony of purification.
Rom 1.16 I have **complete** confidence in the gospel;
1.21 Instead, their thoughts have become **complete** nonsense,
8.37 we have **complete** victory through him who loved us!
11.12 blessings will be when the **complete** number of Jews is included!
11.25 last only until the **complete** number of Gentiles comes to God.
12. 2 God transform you inwardly by a **complete** change of your mind.
1 Cor 7.37 he has his will under **complete** control and has already decided
9.27 and bring it under **complete** control, to keep myself from being
13.12 it will be **complete**—as complete as God's knowledge of me.
15.54 victory is **complete!"**
2 Cor 8. 6 continue it and help you **complete** this special service of love.
10. 6 after you have proved your **complete** loyalty, we will be
Eph 1. 9 plan he had already decided to **complete** by means of Christ.
1.10 This plan, which God will **complete** when the time is right,
1.14 that God will give **complete** freedom to those who are his.
1.23 church is Christ's body, the **completion** of him
1.23 who himself **completes** all things everywhere.
Phil 2.12 with fear and trembling to **complete** your salvation,
3. 8 I reckon everything as **complete** loss for the sake of what is
Col 1.24 helping to **complete** what still remains of Christ's sufferings
4.12 fully convinced Christians, in **complete** obedience to God's will.
1 Thes 1. 5 and the Holy Spirit, and with **complete** conviction of its truth.
2.16 they have brought to **completion** all the sins they have always
2 Thes 1.11 all your desire for goodness and **complete** your work of faith.
Heb 10.19 have, then, my brothers, **complete** freedom to go into the Most
Jas 1. 4 so that you may be perfect and **complete,** lacking nothing.
1 Pet 2.18 your masters and show them **complete** respect, not only to those
1 Jn 1. 4 We write this in order that our joy may be **complete.**
Rev 6.11 until the **complete** number of their fellow-servants and brothers

COMPLICATED

Ecc 7.29 and simple, but we have made ourselves very **complicated.**

COMPOSE

2 Sam 23. 1 and who was the **composer** of beautiful songs for Israel.
1 Kgs 4.32 He **composed** three thousand proverbs and more than a thousand songs.
2 Chr 35.25 The prophet Jeremiah **composed** a lament for King Josiah.
Ps 45. 1 words fill my mind, as I **compose** this song for the king.
119.54 During my brief earthly life I **compose** songs about your commands.
Amos 6. 5 You like to **compose** songs, as David did, and play them on

CONCEAL

Job 31.33 try to hide their sins, but I have never **concealed** mine.
Ps 32. 5 I did not **conceal** my wrongdoings.
Prov 25. 2 We honour God for what he **conceals;**
Is 45.15 who saves his people, is a God who **conceals** himself.

CONCEITED

Prov 3.34 He has no use for **conceited** people, but shows favour to
9. 7 If you correct a **conceited** man, you will only be insulted.
9. 8 Never correct a **conceited** man;
14. 6 **Conceited** people can never become wise, but intelligent people learn easily.
15.12 **Conceited** people do not like to be corrected;
19.29 A **conceited** fool is sure to get a beating.
21. 4 controlled by their **conceit** and arrogance, and this is sinful.
21.11 When someone who is **conceited** gets his punishment, even
21.24 Show me a **conceited** person and I will show you someone
22.10 Get rid of a **conceited** person, and then there will be no
Is 2.12 who is powerful, everyone who is proud and **conceited.**
16. 6 are arrogant and **conceited,** but their boasts are empty."
Jer 48.29 heard how proud, arrogant, and **conceited** the people are, how
1 Cor 13. 4 it is not jealous or **conceited** or proud;
2 Tim 3. 2 People will be selfish, greedy, boastful, and **conceited;**

CONCEIVE

Job 3. 2 put a curse on the night when I was **conceived!**
Ps 51. 5 from the time I was **conceived,** I have been sinful.
Hos 9.11 to them, no more women pregnant, no more children **conceived.**
Mt 1.20 For it is by the Holy Spirit that she has **conceived.**
Lk 2.21 which the angel had given him before he had been **conceived.**
Jas 1.15 Then his evil desire **conceives** and gives birth to sin;

CONCERN

[UNCONCERNED]

Gen 39. 6 of Joseph and did not **concern** himself with anything except
39. 8 does not have to **concern** himself with anything in the house,
Ex 2.25 He saw the slavery of the Israelites and was **concerned** for them.
Num 11.29 Moses answered, "Are you **concerned** about my interests?
Ruth 2.10 and said to Boaz, "Why should you be so **concerned** about me?
1 Sam 22. 8 No one is **concerned** about me or tells me that David, one
Job 39.16 not hers, and is **unconcerned** that her efforts were wasted.
Ps 41. 1 Happy are those who are **concerned** for the poor;
131. 1 I am not **concerned** with great matters or with subjects too
Prov 1.32 Stupid people are destroyed by their own lack of **concern.**
23.17 let reverence for the Lord be the **concern** of your life.
29. 4 When the king is **concerned** with justice, the nation will be strong,
29. 4 but when he is only **concerned** with money, he will ruin his
29.25 It is dangerous to be **concerned** with what others think of you,
Is 63.15 Where is your great **concern** for us?
Jer 29.10 over, I will show my **concern** for you and keep my promise
Lam 1. 9 was easily seen, but she showed no **concern** for her fate.
4.16 The Lord had no more **concern** for them;
Ezek 36.21 That made me **concerned** for my holy name, since the
Joel 2.18 Then the Lord showed **concern** for his land;
Mic 3. 1 You are supposed to be **concerned** about justice, [2]yet you
Zech 1.14 have a deep love and **concern** for Jerusalem, my holy city,
Mt 6.32 (These are the things the pagans are always **concerned** about.)
6.33 be **concerned** above everything else with the Kingdom of God

Lk 12.29 don't be all upset, always **concerned** about what you will eat
12.30 pagans of this world are always **concerned** about all these things.)
12.31 Instead, be **concerned** with his Kingdom, and he will provide
Rom 12.16 Have the same **concern** for everyone.
1 Cor 4. 3 I am not at all **concerned** about being judged by you
7.32 An unmarried man **concerns** himself with the Lord's work,
7.33 But a married man **concerns** himself with worldly matters,
7.34 unmarried woman or a virgin **concerns** herself with the Lord's work,
7.34 but a married woman **concerns** herself with worldly matters,
9. 9 Now, is God **concerned** about oxen?
12.25 all its different parts have the same **concern** for one another.
2 Cor 11.28 I am under the pressure of my **concern** for all the churches.
Phil 2.21 Everyone else is **concerned** only with his own affairs,
Tit 3. 8 believe in God may be **concerned** with giving their time to
Heb 10.24 Let us be **concerned** for one another, to help one another

CONCESSION

1 Cor 7. 6 tell you this not as an order, but simply as a **concession.**

CONCUBINE

A servant-woman who, although not a wife, had sexual relations with her master. She had important legal rights, and her master was referred to as her husband.

Gen 16. 3 So she gave Hagar to him to be his **concubine.**
22.24 Reumah, Nahor's **concubine,** bore Tebah, Gaham, Tahash,
32.22 his two wives, his two **concubines,** and his eleven children,
33. 1 the children among Leah, Rachel, and the two **concubines.**
33. 2 He put the **concubines** and their children first, then Leah
33. 6 Then the **concubines** came up with their children and bowed down;
35.22 Reuben had sexual intercourse with Bilhah, one of his father's **concubines;**
37. 2 the sons of Bilhah and Zilpah, his father's **concubines.**
49. 4 For you slept with my **concubine** And dishonoured your father's bed.
Lev 19.20 a slave-girl is the recognized **concubine** of a man and she
Judg 8.31 He also had a **concubine** in Shechem;
19. 1 Judah to be his **concubine,** [2]but she became angry with him,
19. 9 When the man, his **concubine,** and the servant once more
19.10 there, so he and his **concubine** started on their way, with
19.19 bread and wine for my **concubine** and me and for my servant.
19.24 Here is his **concubine** and my own daughter, who is a virgin.
19.25 So the Levite took his **concubine** and put her outside with them.
19.27 his way, he found his **concubine** lying in front of the house
19.29 He took his **concubine's** body, cut it into twelve pieces, and
20. 4 The Levite whose **concubine** had been murdered answered,
20. 4 "My **concubine** and I went to Gibeah
20. 5 instead they raped my **concubine,** and she died.
2 Sam 3. 7 Abner of sleeping with Saul's **concubine** Rizpah,
5.13 to Jerusalem, David took more **concubines** and wives, and had
15.16 and officials, except for ten **concubines,** whom he left
16.21 have intercourse with your father's **concubines** whom he left
16.22 Absalom went in and had intercourse with his father's **concubines.**
19. 5 of your sons and daughters and of your wives and **concubines.**
20. 3 Jerusalem, he took the ten **concubines** he had left to take
21.10 Then Saul's **concubine** Rizpah, the daughter of Aiah,
1 Kgs 11. 3 seven hundred princesses and also had three hundred **concubines.**
1 Chr 1.32 Abraham had a **concubine** named Keturah, who bore him six sons:
2.46 Caleb had a **concubine** named Ephah, and by her he had
2.48 Caleb had another **concubine,** Maacah, who bore him two sons,
3. 9 In addition to all these sons, David had sons by his **concubines.**
5. 1 with one of his father's **concubines,** he lost the rights
7.14 By his Aramean **concubine,** Manasseh had two sons, Asriel and Machir.
2 Chr 11.21 had eighteen wives and sixty **concubines,** and he fathered
11.21 Of all his wives and **concubines** he loved Maacah best,
Esth 2.14 of Shaashgaz, the eunuch in charge of the king's **concubines.**
Song 6. 8 Let the king have sixty queens, eighty **concubines,**
6. 9 queens and **concubines** sing her praises.
Dan 5. 2 his wives, and his **concubines** could drink out of them.
5.23 noblemen, your wives, and your **concubines** drank wine out of

CONDEMN

Ex 22.20 **"Condemn** to death anyone who offers sacrifices to any
23. 7 to death, for I will **condemn** anyone who does such an evil
Deut 13.17 for yourselves anything that was **condemned** to destruction,
Josh 7.11 They have taken some of the things **condemned** to destruction.
7.12 they themselves have now been **condemned** to destruction!
7.15 out and found with the **condemned** goods will be burnt, along
7.22 found that the **condemned** things really were buried there,
9.23 Because you did this, God has **condemned** you.
10.37 Joshua **condemned** the city to total destruction, just as he
11.20 so that they would be **condemned** to total destruction and all
22.20 to obey the command about the things **condemned** to destruction;
Ruth 1.21 Naomi when the Lord Almighty has **condemned** me and sent me trouble?"
2 Sam 1.16 You **condemned** yourself when you admitted that you killed the
14.13 exile, and so you have **condemned** yourself by what you have
2 Chr 21.12 God of your ancestor David, **condemns** you, because you did
Job 6.29 Don't **condemn** me.
9.20 sound guilty, and everything I say seems to **condemn** me.
10. 2 Don't **condemn** me, God.
15. 6 There is no need for me to **condemn** you;
15. 6 you are **condemned** by every word you speak.
17. 8 be honest are shocked, and they all **condemn** me as godless.
34.17 Are you **condemning** the righteous God?
Job 34.18 God **condemns** kings and rulers when they are worthless or wicked.
Ps 1. 5 Sinners will be **condemned** by God and kept apart from God's
5.10 **Condemn** and punish them, O God;
7.11 God is a righteous judge and always **condemns** the wicked.
9. 5 You have **condemned** the heathen and destroyed the wicked;
28. 3 Do not **condemn** me with the wicked, with those who do evil
36. 2 thinks that God will not discover his sin and **condemn** it.
37.33 enemy's power or let him be **condemned** when he is on trial.
51. 4 you are justified in **condemning** me.
75. 7 it is God who is the judge, **condemning** some and acquitting others.
79.11 by your great power free those who are **condemned** to die.
102.20 of prisoners and set free those who were **condemned** to die.
109.31 poor man and saves him from those who **condemn** him to death.
130. 3 a record of our sins, who could escape being **condemned?**
Prov 12. 2 Lord is pleased with good people, but **condemns** those who plan evil.
17.15 **Condemning** the innocent or letting the wicked go—both
Is 34. 2 He has **condemned** them to destruction.
34. 5 Edom, those people whom he has **condemned** to destruction.
Jer 2.19 will punish you, and your turning from me will **condemn** you.
8.14 The Lord our God has **condemned** us to die;
17. 5 "I will **condemn** the person who turns away from me and puts
22.30 "This man is **condemned** to lose his children, to be a
Lam 1.22 **"Condemn** them for all their wickedness;
Ezek 16.38 I will **condemn** you for adultery and murder, and in my
20.35 of the Nations,' and there I will **condemn** you to your face.
20.36 I will now **condemn** you
20.36 just as I **condemned** your fathers in the Sinai Desert,"
21.24 You stand **condemned,** and I will hand you over to your enemies.
23.45 Righteous men will **condemn** them on the charge of adultery and murder,
36.19 I **condemned** them for the way they lived and acted, and I
Zech 3. 2 of the Lord said to Satan, "May the Lord **condemn** you,
3. 2 May the Lord, who loves Jerusalem, **condemn** you.
Mt 12. 7 this means, you would not **condemn** people who are not guilty;
20.18 They will **condemn** him to death [19]and then hand him over to
23.33 How do you expect to escape from being **condemned** to hell?
27. 3 learnt that Jesus had been **condemned,** he repented and took back
Mk 10.33 They will **condemn** him to death and then hand him over to
16.16 whoever does not believe will be **condemned.**
Lk 6.37 do not condemn others, and God will not **condemn** you;
19.22 I will use your own words to **condemn** you!
23. 4 and the crowds, "I find no reason to **condemn** this man."
Jn 5.29 and those who have done evil will rise and be **condemned.**
7.51 to our Law we cannot **condemn** a man before hearing him and
8.10 Is there no one left to **condemn** you?"
8.11 "Well, then," Jesus said, "I do not **condemn** you either.
8.26 I have much to say about you, much to **condemn** you for.
18.38 and said to them, "I cannot find any reason to **condemn** him.
19. 4 let you see that I cannot find any reason to **condemn** him."
19. 6 I find no reason to **condemn** him."
Acts 13.27 Yet they made the prophets' words come true by **condemning** Jesus.
25.15 elders brought charges against him and asked me to **condemn** him.
Rom 2. 1 then do the same things which they do, you **condemn** yourself.
2.27 so you Jews will be **condemned** by the Gentiles because you
3. 7 Why should I still be **condemned** as a sinner?
3. 8 They will be **condemned,** as they should be.
5.18 as the one sin **condemned** all mankind, in the same way
8. 1 There is no **condemnation** now for those who live in union
8. 3 He **condemned** sin in human nature by sending his own Son,
8.20 creation was **condemned** to lose its purpose, not of its own
8.34 Who, then, will **condemn** them?
14.23 about what he eats, God **condemns** him when he eats it,
1 Cor 4. 9 to us apostles, like men **condemned** to die in public
11.32 so that we shall not be **condemned** together with the world.
2 Cor 3. 9 The system which brings **condemnation** was glorious;
7. 3 I do not say this to **condemn** you;
Gal 1. 8 the one we preached to you, may he be **condemned** to hell!
1. 9 from the one you accepted, may he be **condemned** to hell!
Col 2.18 not allow yourselves to be **condemned** by anyone who claims to
2 Thes 2.12 the truth, but have taken pleasure in sin, will be **condemned.**
1 Tim 3. 6 not swell up with pride and be **condemned,** as the Devil was.
Heb 11. 7 a result, the world was **condemned,** and Noah received from God
Jas 2. 9 guilty of sin, and the Law **condemns** you as a law-breaker.
5. 6 You have **condemned** and murdered innocent people,
2 Pet 2. 6 God **condemned** the cities of Sodom and Gomorrah,
1 Jn 3.20 If our conscience **condemns** us, we know that God is greater
3.21 if our conscience does not **condemn** us, we have courage in
Jude 4 the Scriptures predicted the **condemnation** they have received.
6 them for that great Day on which they will be **condemned.**
9 Michael did not dare to **condemn** the Devil with insulting words,
15 bring judgement on all, to **condemn** them all for the godless
Rev 18.20 For God has **condemned** her for what she did to you!
19. 2 He has **condemned** the prostitute who was corrupting the earth

AV CONDEMN

Ex 22. 9 whom God declares to be **guilty** shall pay double to the other
Deut 25. 1 dispute, and one is declared innocent and the other **guilty.**
1 Kgs 8.32 **Punish** the guilty one as he deserves, and acquit the one who
2 Chr 36. 3 him prisoner and made Judah **pay** 3,400 kilogrammes of silver
Job 9.20 faithful, but my words sound **guilty,** and everything I say
32. 3 Job, and this made it appear that God was in the **wrong.**
40. 8 to put me in the **wrong** and yourself in the right?
Ps 94.21 who plot against good men and **sentence** the innocent to death.
109. 7 May he be tried and found **guilty;**
Is 50. 9 Sovereign Lord himself defends me— who, then, can prove me **guilty?**

Is 54.17 you will have an **answer** for all who accuse you.
Mt 12.37 to judge you—to declare you either innocent or **guilty."**
12.41 Nineveh will stand up and **accuse** you, because they turned
12.42 Sheba will stand up and **accuse** you, because she travelled
Mk 14.64 They all **voted against** him:
Lk 11.31 Sheba will stand up and **accuse** the people of today,
11.32 Nineveh will stand up and **accuse** you, because they turned
23.40 You received the same **sentence** he did.
24.20 him over to be **sentenced** to death, and he was crucified.
Jn 3.17 into the world to be its **judge,** but to be its saviour.
3.18 Whoever believes in the Son is not **judged;**
3.18 not believe has already been **judged,** because he has not believed
3.19 This is how the **judgement** works:
5.24 He will not be **judged,** but has already passed from death to
Rom 5.16 After the one sin, came the judgement of **"Guilty";**
14.22 person who does not feel **guilty** when he does something he
1 Cor 11.34 you will not come under God's **judgement** as you meet together.
Tit 2. 8 sound words that cannot be **criticized,** so that your enemies may
3.11 a person is corrupt, and his sins prove that he is **wrong.**
Jas 3. 1 we teachers will be **judged** with greater strictness than others.
5. 9 one another, my brothers, so that God will not **judge** you.
5.12 mean no, and then you will not come under God's **judgement.**

CONDUCT

Rom 2.15 Their **conduct** shows that what the Law commands is
13.13 Let us **conduct** ourselves properly, as people who live in
Gal 6. 4 Each one should judge his own **conduct.**
1 Thes 2.10 that our **conduct** towards you who believe was pure,
1 Tim 2. 2 with all reverence towards God and with proper **conduct.**
3.15 you know how we should **conduct** ourselves in God's household,
4.12 in your speech, your **conduct,** your love, faith, and purity.
2 Tim 3.10 followed my teaching, my **conduct,** and my purpose in life;
Jas 1.21 So get rid of every filthy habit and all wicked **conduct.**
1 Pet 2.12 Your **conduct** among the heathen should be so good that when
3. 1 believe God's word, your **conduct** will win them over to believe.
3. 2 because they will see how pure and reverent your **conduct** is.
3.16 speak evil of your good **conduct** as followers of Christ
2 Pet 2. 7 who was distressed by the immoral **conduct** of lawless people.

CONFER

2 Kgs 9. 5 Ramoth, [5] where he found the army officers in a **conference.**
Acts 25.12 Then Festus, after **conferring** with his advisers, answered,

CONFESS

Gen 41. 9 to the king, "I must **confess** today that I have done wrong.
Lev 5. 5 person is guilty, he must **confess** the sin, [6] and as the
16.21 on the goat's head and **confess** over it all the evils, sins,
26.40 "But your descendants will **confess** their sins and the
Num 5. 7 someone, [7] he must **confess** his sin and make full repayment,
Josh 7.19 truth here before the Lord, the God of Israel, and **confess.**
1 Kgs 8.47 repent and pray to you, **confessing** how sinful and wicked
2 Chr 6.37 repent and pray to you, **confessing** how sinful and wicked
Ezra 9.15 We **confess** our guilt to you;
10. 1 of the Temple, weeping and **confessing** these sins, a large
10.11 Now then, **confess** your sins to the Lord, the God of your
Neh 1. 6 I **confess** that we, the people of Israel, have sinned.
9. 1 they stood and began to **confess** the sins that they and their
9. 3 the next three hours they **confessed** their sins and
Job 34.31 Job, have you **confessed** your sins to God and promised
Ps 32. 3 When I did not **confess** my sins, I was worn out from
32. 5 Then I **confessed** my sins to you;
32. 5 I decided to **confess** them to you, and you forgave all my
38.18 I **confess** my sins;
119.26 I **confessed** all I have done, and you answered me;
Prov 28.13 **Confess** them and give them up;
Is 45.14 bow down to you and **confess,** 'God is with you—he alone
Jer 3.13 **Confess** that under every green tree you have given your love
14.20 we **confess** our own sins and the sins of our ancestors.
Dan 9. 4 to the Lord my God and **confessed** the sins of my people.
9.20 I went on praying, **confessing** my sins and the sins of
Zech 13. 9 are my people, and they will **confess** that I am their God."
Mt 3. 6 They **confessed** their sins, and he baptized them in the Jordan.
Mk 1. 5 **confessed** their sins, and he baptized them in the River Jordan.
Rom 10. 9 If you **confess** that Jesus is Lord and believe that God
10.10 it is by our **confession** that we are saved.
14.11 kneel before me, and everyone will **confess** that I am God."
1 Cor 12. 3 and no one can **confess** "Jesus is Lord," unless he is
14.25 and worship God, **confessing,** "Truly God is here among you!"
Heb 13.15 is the offering presented by lips that **confess** him as Lord.
Jas 5.16 So then, **confess** your sins to one another and pray for
1 Jn 1. 9 But if we **confess** our sins to God, he will keep his

CONFIDENT

Deut 31. 6 Be determined and **confident.**
31. 7 of all the people of Israel, "Be determined and **confident;**
31.23 Joshua son of Nun and said to him, "Be **confident** and determined.
Josh 1. 6 Be determined and **confident,** for you will be the leader of
1. 7 Just be determined, be **confident;**
1. 9 Remember that I have commanded you to be determined and **confident!**
1.18 Be determined and **confident!"**
10.25 Be determined and **confident** because this is what the Lord is
Judg 9.26 and the men of Shechem put their **confidence** in him.
1 Kgs 2. 2 Be **confident** and determined, [3] and do what the Lord your God
2 Kgs 18.19 emperor wanted to know what made King Hezekiah so **confident.**
1 Chr 22.13 Be determined and **confident,** and don't let anything make you afraid.
28.20 King David said to his son Solomon, "Be **confident** and determined.
2 Chr 32. 7 "Be determined and **confident,** and don't be afraid
32.10 people the **confidence** to remain in Jerusalem under siege.
Job 4. 6 and so you should have **confidence** and hope.
29.24 I smiled on them when they had lost **confidence;**
Ps 57. 7 I have complete **confidence,** O God;
59. 9 I have **confidence** in your strength;
73. 2 But I had nearly lost **confidence;**
108. 1 I have complete **confidence,** O God!
116. 7 Be **confident,** my heart, because the Lord has been good to me.
Prov 3.32 who do evil, but he takes righteous men into his **confidence.**
4.25 Look straight ahead with honest **confidence;**
11. 7 **Confidence** placed in riches comes to nothing.
11.13 but you can put **confidence** in someone who is trustworthy.
14.26 Reverence for the Lord gives **confidence** and security to
31.11 Her husband puts his **confidence** in her, and he will
Is 2.22 Put no more **confidence** in mortal men.
13. 3 called out his proud and **confident** soldiers to fight a holy
36. 4 emperor wanted to know what made King Hezekiah so **confident.**
57.15 repentant, so that I can restore their **confidence** and hope.
Ezek 7.24 strongest men will lose their **confidence** when I let the
Mic 7. 7 I will wait **confidently** for God, who will save me.
Zeph 1.12 who are self-satisfied and **confident,** who say to themselves,
Rom 1.16 I have complete **confidence** in the gospel;
2 Cor 3. 4 We say this because we have **confidence** in God through Christ.
8.22 that he has so much **confidence** in you, he is all the
Gal 5.10 But I still feel **confident** about you.
5.10 with the Lord makes me **confident** that you will not take
Eph 3.12 the boldness to go into God's presence with all **confidence.**
Phil 1.14 most of the brothers more **confidence** in the Lord, so that
2 Thes 3. 4 And the Lord gives us **confidence** in you, and we are sure
1 Tim 1. 7 or the matters about which they speak with so much **confidence.**
2 Tim 1.12 I am still full of **confidence,** because I know whom I have
Heb 3. 6 keep up our courage and our **confidence** in what we hope for.
3.14 firmly to the end the **confidence** we had at the beginning.
4.16 Let us have **confidence,** then, and approach God's throne,
2 Pet 1.19 So we are even more **confident** of the message proclaimed by
1 Jn 3.19 this is how we will be **confident** in God's presence.

CONFINED

2 Sam 20. 3 They were kept **confined** for the rest of their lives, living

CONFIRM

Deut 29.13 that the Lord may now **confirm** you as his people and be
1 Kgs 1.14 with King David, I will come in and **confirm** your story."
1.36 answered Benaiah, "and may the Lord your God **confirm** it.
2 Kgs 8. 6 to the king's question, she **confirmed** Gehazi's story, and so
Esth 9.32 Esther's command, **confirming** the rules for Purim, was
Jn 3.33 whoever accepts his message **confirms** by this that God is truthful.

CONFISCATE

Ezra 7.26 or by **confiscation** of his property or by imprisonment."
10. 8 all his property would be **confiscated,** and he would lose his

CONFORM

Rom 12. 2 Do not **conform** yourselves to the standards of this world,

CONFUSE

Ex 23.27 I will bring **confusion** among the people against whom you fight,
Deut 28.20 you disaster, **confusion,** and trouble in everything you do,
28.28 he will strike you with blindness and **confusion.**
Judg 4.15 the Lord threw Sisera into **confusion** together with all his
1 Sam 7.10 They became completely **confused** and fled in panic.
14.16 Gibeah in the territory of Benjamin saw the Philistines running in **confusion.**
14.19 speaking to the priest, the **confusion** in the Philistine camp
14.20 who were fighting each other in complete **confusion.**
Neh 4. 8 and attack Jerusalem and create **confusion,** [9] but we prayed
Esth 3.15 while the city of Susa was being thrown into **confusion.**
Job 10.22 shadows, and **confusion,** where the light itself is darkness.
12.24 He makes their leaders foolish and lets them wander **confused** and lost;
Ps 6.10 in sudden **confusion** they will be driven away.
35. 4 May those who plot against me be turned back and **confused!**
35.26 May those who gloat over my suffering be completely defeated and **confused;**
40.14 May those who try to kill me be completely defeated and **confused.**
55. 9 **Confuse** the speech of my enemies, O Lord!
70. 2 May those who try to kill me be defeated and **confused.**
Is 9.16 Those who lead these people have misled them and totally **confused** them.
19.14 The Lord has made them give **confusing** advice.
22. 5 of panic, defeat, and **confusion** in the Valley of Vision,
28. 7 so much wine and liquor that they stumble in **confusion.**
Jer 8. 9 they are **confused** and trapped.
14. 3 Discouraged and **confused,** they hide their faces.
49. 3 Run about in **confusion.**
Ezek 7. 7 more celebrations at the mountain shrines, only **confusion.**
7.23 "Everything is in **confusion**—the land is full of murders
Mic 7. 4 Now they are in **confusion.**
Zech 14.13 Lord will make them so **confused** and afraid that everyone
Mk 5.38 where Jesus saw the **confusion** and heard all the loud crying
5.39 He went in and said to them, "Why all this **confusion?**
Lk 9. 7 he was very **confused,** because some people were saying that

Acts 2.12 Amazed and **confused,** they kept asking each other,
12.18 was a tremendous **confusion** among the guards—what had happened
21.30 **Confusion** spread through the whole city, and the people all ran
21.34 was such **confusion** that the commander could not find out exactly
2 Thes 2. 2 not to be so easily **confused** in your thinking or upset by

CONGRATULATE

2 Sam 8.10 King David and **congratulate** him on his victory over Hadadezer,
1 Chr 18.10 King David and **congratulate** him for his victory over Hadadezer,

AV CONGREGATION
see also **COMMUNITY**

Num 25. 7 Aaron the priest, saw this, he got up and left the **assembly.**
35.12 is not to be put to death without a **public** trial.
Deut 33. 4 Law that Moses gave us, our **nation's** most treasured possession.
Josh 8.35 Joshua to the whole **gathering,** which included women and children,
20. 6 until he has received a **public** trial and until the death of
20. 9 not be killed unless he had first received a **public** trial.
Judg 21. 5 not go to the **gathering** in the Lord's presence at Mizpah?"
21.10 So the **assembly** sent twelve thousand of their bravest
21.13 Then the whole **assembly** sent word to the Benjaminites
21.16 So the leaders of the **gathering** said, "There are no
1 Kgs 8.55 he asked God's blessings on all the people **assembled** there.
8.65 There was a huge **crowd** of people from as far away as
12. 3 and then they all went **together** to Rehoboam and said to him,
12.20 they invited him to a **meeting** of the people and made him
1 Chr 29. 1 King David announced to the whole **assembly:**
29.10 There in front of the whole **assembly** King David praised the Lord.
29.20 And the whole **assembly** praised the Lord, the God of their ancestors,
2 Chr 7. 8 There was a huge **crowd** of people from as far away as
20.14 the Lord came upon a Levite who was present in the **crowd.**
29.23 and to the other **worshippers,** who laid their hands on them.
Ezra 2.64 Total **number** of exiles who returned - 42,360
10. 1 confessing these sins, a large **group** of Israelites—men,
Neh 5.13 Everyone who was **present** said, "Amen!"
7.66 Total **number** of exiles who
Job 30.28 I stand up in **public** and plead for help.
Ps 22.22 I will praise you in their **assembly:**
22.25 In the full **assembly** I will praise you for what you have
26. 5 I hate the **company** of evil men and avoid the wicked.
26.12 in the **assembly** of his people I praise the Lord.
35.18 Then I will thank you in the **assembly** of your people;
40. 9 In the **assembly** of all your people, Lord, I told the good
40.10 In the **assembly** of all your people I have not been silent
58. 1 Do you **rulers** ever give a just decision?
68.26 "Praise God in the **meeting** of his people;
74. 4 Your enemies have shouted in triumph in your **Temple;**
75. 2 set a time for **judgement,"** says God, "and I will judge
82. 1 in the **assembly** of the gods he gives his decision:
107.32 proclaim his greatness in the **assembly** of the people and
149. 1 praise him in the **assembly** of his faithful people!
Prov 5.14 And suddenly I found myself **publicly** disgraced."
Is 14.13 king on that mountain in the north where the gods **assemble.**
Acts 13.43 the people had left the **meeting,** Paul and Barnabas were followed

CONQUER
[RECONQUERED, UNCONQUERED]

Gen 10. 8 named Nimrod, who became the world's first great **conqueror.**
14. 7 They **conquered** all the land of the Amalekites and defeated
22.17 Your descendants will **conquer** their enemies.
24.60 May your descendants **conquer** the cities of their enemies!"
Ex 34.24 try to **conquer** your country during the three festivals.
Lev 26.16 good, because your enemies will **conquer** you and eat what you
Num 13.30 we are strong enough to **conquer** it."
14. 9 We will **conquer** them easily.
21. 2 "If you will let us **conquer** these people, we will
21. 3 The Lord heard them and helped them to **conquer** the Canaanites.
24.18 He will **conquer** his enemies in Edom And make their land
24.24 They will **conquer** Assyria and Eber, But they, in turn, will
32.29 help you are able to **conquer** the land, then give them the
Josh 10.13 did not move until the nation had **conquered** its enemies.
10.40 Joshua **conquered** the whole land.
10.42 Joshua **conquered** all these kings and their territory in
11.19 All the others were **conquered** in battle.
12. 1 people of Israel had already **conquered** and occupied the land
18. 1 After they had **conquered** the land, the entire community of
23. 4 nations that I have already **conquered,** from the River Jordan
Judg 3. 8 King Cushan Rishathaim of Mesopotamia **conquer** them, and he
4. 2 the Lord let them be **conquered** by Jabin, a Canaanite king
10. 7 and let the Philistines and the Ammonites **conquer** them.
1 Sam 12. 9 of Hazor, fight against your ancestors and **conquer** them.
2 Sam 5. 6 would not be able to **conquer** the city, and so they said
8.11 from the nations he had **conquered**—[12]Edom, Moab, Ammon,
10. 3 as spies to explore the city, so that he can **conquer** us!"
12.29 went to Rabbah, attacked it, and **conquered** it.
1 Kgs 11.15 before this, when David had **conquered** Edom, Joab the
2 Kgs 3.19 You will **conquer** all their beautiful fortified cities;
10.32 King Hazael of Syria **conquered** all the Israelite territory
12.17 King Hazael of Syria attacked the city of Gath and **conquered** it;
14.22 Uzziah **reconquered** and rebuilt Elath after his father's death.
14.25 He **reconquered** all the territory that had belonged to Israel,
18.13 attacked the fortified cities of Judah and **conquered** them.
19.23 chariots you had **conquered** the highest mountains of Lebanon.
21.14 their enemies, who will **conquer** them and plunder their land.
1 Chr 1.10 named Nimrod, who became the world's first great **conqueror.)**
2.23 kingdoms of Geshur and Aram **conquered** sixty towns there,
18.11 took from the nations he **conquered**—Edom, Moab, Ammon,
19. 3 as spies to explore the land, so that he can **conquer** it!"
22.18 He let me **conquer** all the people who used to live in
2 Chr 12. 8 my anger, [8]but Shishak will **conquer** them, and they will
30. 6 You have survived the Assyrian **conquest** of the land.
Ezra 5.12 let them be **conquered** by King Nebuchadnezzar of Babylonia,
Neh 9.22 "You let them **conquer** nations and kingdoms,
9.22 They **conquered** the land of Heshbon, where Sihon ruled, and
9.23 the sky, and let them **conquer** and live in the land that
9.24 They **conquered** the land of Canaan;
9.27 time, [27]so you let their enemies **conquer** and rule them.
9.28 sinned again, and again you let their enemies **conquer** them.
9.30 were deaf, so you let them be **conquered** by other nations.
Job 26.12 It is his strength that **conquered** the sea;
Ps 44. 3 Your people did not **conquer** the land with their swords;
78.54 his holy land, to the mountains which he himself **conquered.**
81.14 I would quickly defeat their enemies and **conquer** all their foes.
Is 10. 9 I **conquered** the cities of Calno and Carchemish, the cities
10. 9 I **conquered** Samaria and Damascus.
11.14 They will **conquer** the people of Edom and Moab, and the
14. 6 never stopped persecuting the nations they had **conquered.**
14.12 In the past you **conquered** nations, but now you have been
37.24 chariots you had **conquered** the highest mountains of Lebanon.
41. 2 was it that brought the **conqueror** from the east, and makes
45. 1 He has appointed him to **conquer** nations;
47. 1 like a virgin, a city **unconquered,** but you are soft and
Jer 13.21 thought were your friends **conquer** you and rule over you?
46.24 they are **conquered** by the people of the north.
48. 7 and your wealth, but now even you will be **conquered;**
49.28 which were **conquered** by King Nebuchadnezzar of Babylonia:
50. 9 They will line up in battle against the country and **conquer** it.
Lam 1. 7 Her **conquerors** laughed at her downfall.
1.16 The enemy has **conquered** me;
Ezek 25. 4 I will let the tribes from the eastern desert **conquer** you.
25.10 of the eastern desert **conquer** Moab, together with Ammon,
26.15 "When you are being **conquered,** the people who live along
Dan 1.21 until Cyrus the emperor of Persia **conquered** Babylonia.
2.44 never be **conquered,** but will completely destroy all those empires,
7.21 that horn made war on God's people and **conquered** them.
11.18 will attack the nations by the sea and **conquer** many of them.
11.43 He will **conquer** Libya and Sudan.
Joel 3.17 foreigners will never **conquer** it again.
Amos 9.12 the people of Israel will **conquer** what is left of the land
Obad 7 People who were at peace with you have now **conquered** you.
20 Israel will return and **conquer** Phoenicia as far north as Zarephath.
Mic 5. 6 force of arms they will **conquer** Assyria, the land of Nimrod,
5. 9 Israel will **conquer** her enemies and destroy them all.
Hab 1. 6 They are marching out across the world to **conquer** other lands.
1. 9 "Their armies advance in violent **conquest,** and everyone
2. 5 That is why they **conquer** nation after nation for themselves.
2. 6 conquered people will taunt their **conquerors** and show their scorn for them.
2. 7 know it, you that have **conquered** others will be in debt
2.13 The nations you **conquered** wore themselves out in useless labour,
Rom 12.21 instead, **conquer** evil with good.
2 Pet 2.19 for a person is a slave of anything that has **conquered** him.
2.20 then are again caught and **conquered** by them, such people are
Rev 6. 2 He rode out as a conqueror to **conquer.**

CONSCIENCE

Gen 20. 5 this with a clear **conscience,** and I have done no wrong."
20. 6 "Yes, I know that you did it with a clear **conscience;**
1 Sam 24. 5 But then David's **conscience** began to trouble him, [6]and he
2 Sam 24.10 had taken the census, his **conscience** began to trouble him,
Job 27. 6 my **conscience** is clear.
Ps 16. 7 he guides me, and in the night my **conscience** warns me.
Prov 20. 9 anyone really say that his **conscience** is clear, that he has
20.27 The Lord gave us mind and **conscience;**
Acts 23. 1 My **conscience** is perfectly clear about the way in which I
24.16 best always to have a clear **conscience** before God and man.
Rom 1.31 they have no **conscience;**
2.15 Their **consciences** also show that this is true, since their
9. 1 My **conscience,** ruled by the Holy Spirit, also assures me
13. 5 because of God's punishment, but also as a matter of **conscience.**
1 Cor 4. 4 My **conscience** is clear, but that does not prove that I am
8. 7 their **conscience** is weak, and they feel they are defiled
8.10 Suppose a person whose **conscience** is weak in this matter sees
8.12 against your Christian brothers and wounding their weak **conscience.**
10.25 without asking any questions because of your **conscience.**
10.27 without asking any questions because of your **conscience.**
10.28 who told you and for **conscience'** sake—[29]that is,
10.29 not your own **conscience,** but the other person's conscience.
10.29 my freedom to act be limited by another person's **conscience?**
2 Cor 1.12 We are proud that our **conscience** assures us that our
4. 2 and try to commend ourselves to everyone's good **conscience.**
1 Tim 1. 5 from a pure heart, a clear **conscience,** and a genuine faith.
1.19 to fight well, [19]and keep your faith and a clear **conscience.**
1.19 have not listened to their **conscience** and have made a ruin
3. 9 to the revealed truth of the faith with a clear **conscience.**
4. 2 by deceitful liars, whose **consciences** are dead, as if burnt with
2 Tim 1. 3 God, whom I serve with a clear **conscience,** as my ancestors did.
Tit 1.15 unbelieving, for their minds and **consciences** have been defiled.
Heb 9.14 His blood will purify our **consciences** from useless rituals,
10.22 purified from a guilty **conscience** and with bodies washed with
13.18 sure we have a clear **conscience,** because we want to do the
1 Pet 3.16 Keep your **conscience** clear, so that when you are insulted,
3.21 but the promise made to God from a good **conscience.**

1 Jn 3.20 If our **conscience** condemns us, we know that God is
3.20 greater than our **conscience** and that he knows everything.
3.21 my dear friends, if our **conscience** does not condemn us, we

AV CONSCIENCE

1 Cor 8. 7 Some people have been so **used** to idols that to this day
2 Cor 5.11 and I hope that in your **hearts** you know me as well.
Heb 9. 9 God cannot make the worshipper's **heart** perfect, [10]since they
10. 2 sins, they would not feel **guilty** of sin any more, and all
1 Pet 2.19 undeserved suffering because you are **conscious** of his will.

CONSCIOUS

1 Pet 2.19 undeserved suffering because you are **conscious** of his will.

CONSECRATE
[RECONSECRATE]

Gen 35.14 up a memorial stone and **consecrated** it by pouring wine and
Ex 32.29 the Levites, "Today you have **consecrated** yourselves as
40.13 him, and in this way **consecrate** him, so that he can serve
Lev 8.30 In this way he **consecrated** them and their clothes to the Lord.
10. 7 die, because you have been **consecrated** by the anointing oil
16.32 properly ordained and **consecrated** to succeed his father, is to
21.10 head and has been **consecrated** to wear the priestly garments,
Num 3.12 first-born of the Egyptians, I **consecrated** as my own the
4.16 else in the Tent that has been **consecrated** to the Lord.
6. 8 long as he is a Nazirite, he is **consecrated** to the Lord.
6. 9 If the **consecrated** hair of a Nazirite is defiled because
6.11 same day the man shall **reconsecrate** his hair [12]and
6.12 doesn't count, because his **consecrated** hair was defiled.
8.17 the first-born in Egypt, I **consecrated** as my own the eldest
1 Sam 7. 1 They **consecrated** his son Eleazar to be in charge of it.
1 Kgs 8.64 That same day he also **consecrated** the central part of the courtyard,
9. 3 I **consecrate** this Temple which you have built as the place
9. 7 this Temple which I have **consecrated** as the place where I am
2 Chr 5.11 group to which they belonged, had **consecrated** themselves.
7. 7 Solomon **consecrated** the central part of the courtyard,
7.16 I have chosen it and **consecrated** it as the place where I
7.20 this Temple that I have **consecrated** as the place where I am
13. 9 seven sheep can get himself **consecrated** as a priest of those
23. 6 may enter, because they are **consecrated,** but the rest of the
26.18 are descended from Aaron have been **consecrated** to do this.
29. 5 said, "You Levites are to **consecrate** yourselves and purify
Ezek 43.20 In this way you will purify the altar and **consecrate** it.
43.26 days the priests are to **consecrate** the altar and make it
Hag 2.12 someone takes a piece of **consecrated** meat from a sacrifice
2.12 of food at all, will it make that food **consecrated** also?"

AV CONSECRATE

Ex 28. 3 so that he may be **dedicated** as a priest in my service.
28.41 Then **ordain** them and dedicate them by anointing them with olive-oil,
29. 9 That is how you are to **ordain** Aaron and his sons.
29.27 ram being used for the **ordination** are to be dedicated to me
29.29 after his death, for them to wear when they are **ordained.**
29.31 the ram used for the **ordination** of Aaron and his sons and
29.33 was used in the ritual of forgiveness at their **ordination.**
29.35 "Perform the rites of **ordination** for Aaron and his sons
30.30 Aaron and his sons, and **ordain** them as priests in my service.
Lev 7.37 the **ordination-offerings,** and the fellowship-offerings.
8.22 ram, which was for the **ordination** of priests, and Aaron and
8.28 on top of the burnt-offering, as an **ordination** offering.
8.29 It was Moses' part of the **ordination** ram.
8.31 basket of **ordination** offerings, just as the Lord commanded.
8.33 until your **ordination** rites are completed.
Num 3. 3 They were anointed and **ordained** as priests, [4]but Nadab
6. 6 is the sign of his **dedication** to God,
6.12 shall reconsecrate his hair [12]and **rededicate** to the Lord
Josh 6.19 of silver, gold, bronze, or iron is **set apart** for the Lord.
Judg 17. 5 idols and an ephod, and **appointed** one of his sons as his
17.12 Micah **appointed** him as his priest, and he lived in Micah's home.
1 Kgs 13.33 He **ordained** as priest anyone who wanted to be one.
1 Chr 29. 5 else is willing to **give** a generous offering to the Lord?"
2 Chr 29.31 "Now that you are ritually **clean,** bring sacrifices as
29.33 three thousand sheep as **sacrifices** for the people to eat.
31. 6 gifts, which they **dedicated** to the Lord their God.
Ezra 3. 5 at which the Lord is **worshipped,** as well as all the
Mic 4.13 got by violence you will **present** to me, the Lord of the
Heb 7.28 Law, appoints the Son, who has been made **perfect** for ever.
10.20 He **opened** for us a new way, a living way,

CONSENT

Is 54.15 If anyone attacks you, he does it without my **consent;**
Mt 10.29 not one sparrow falls to the ground without your Father's **consent.**
Acts 18.20 The people asked him to stay longer, but he would not **consent.**

CONSIDER

Mt 14. 5 the Jewish people, because they **considered** John to be a prophet.
21.46 afraid of the crowds, who **considered** Jesus to be a prophet.
22.24 have children who will be **considered** the dead man's children.
Mk 10.42 that the men who are **considered** rulers of the heathen have
12.19 have children who will be **considered** the dead man's children.'
Lk 7. 7 neither do I **consider** myself worthy to come to you
16.15 For the things that are **considered** of great value by man are
20.28 have children who will be **considered** the dead man's children.'
Lk 24.19 was a prophet and was **considered** by God and by all the
Acts 5.41 because God had **considered** them worthy to suffer disgrace for
10.15 "Do not **consider** anything unclean that God has declared
10.28 that I must not **consider** any person ritually unclean or defiled.
11. 9 'Do not **consider** anything unclean that God has declared
13.46 reject it and do not **consider** yourselves worthy of eternal life,
15. 6 apostles and the elders met together to **consider** this question.
26. 2 **consider** myself fortunate that today I am to defend myself before
Rom 8.18 I **consider** that what we suffer at this present time
12.17 Try to do what everyone **considers** to be good.
1 Cor 1.27 chose what the world **considers** nonsense in order to shame
1.27 he chose what the world **considers** weak in order to shame
3.19 For what this world **considers** to be wisdom is nonsense
7.26 **Considering** the present distress, I think it is better for
10.18 **Consider** the people of Israel;
Gal 3. 6 **Consider** the experience of Abraham;
Phil 2. 3 be humble towards one another, always **considering** others better
3. 8 I **consider** it all as mere refuse, so that I may gain
1 Tim 1.12 I thank him for **considering** me worthy and appointing me to
5.17 leaders should be **considered** worthy of receiving double pay,
6. 1 slaves must **consider** their masters worthy of all respect,
Jas 1. 2 **consider** yourselves fortunate when all kinds of trials come
1.27 What God the Father **considers** to be pure and genuine

CONSIDERATE

2 Chr 10. 7 please them by giving a **considerate** answer, they will always
1 Pet 2.18 those who are kind and **considerate,** but also to those who

CONSIST

2 Cor 3. 6 serving the new covenant, which **consists** not of a written
Col 2.11 circumcision made by Christ, which **consists** of being freed from
1 Pet 3. 4 Instead, your beauty should **consist** of your true inner self,

CONSPIRE

1 Sam 22.17 They **conspired** with David and did not tell me that he had
1 Kgs 16.20 including the account of his **conspiracy,** is recorded in The
2 Kgs 15.10 Shallum son of Jabesh **conspired** against King Zechariah,
15.15 including an account of his **conspiracy,** is recorded in The
2 Chr 24.21 King Joash joined in a **conspiracy** against Zechariah, and

CONSTANT
[LOVE IS CONSTANT]

Num 17. 5 the **constant** complaining of these Israelites against you."
Deut 7. 9 his covenant and show his **constant love** to a thousand
7.12 show you his **constant love,** as he promised your ancestors.
28.33 receive nothing but **constant** oppression and harsh treatment.
28.66 with terror, and you will live in **constant** fear of death.
2 Sam 22.51 he shows **constant love** to the one he has chosen, to David
1 Kgs 3. 6 show him your great and **constant love** by giving him a son
5. 3 know that because of the **constant** wars my father David had
Job 9.13 God's anger is **constant.**
10.12 have given me life and **constant love,** and your care has kept
Ps 13. 5 I rely on your **constant love;**
18.50 he shows **constant love** to the one he has chosen, to David
21. 7 and because of the Lord's **constant love** he will always be secure.
25. 6 O Lord, your kindness and **constant love** which you have shown
25. 7 In your **constant love** and goodness, remember me, Lord!
26. 3 Your **constant love** is my guide;
31. 7 I will be glad and rejoice because of your **constant love.**
31.16 save me in your **constant love.**
32.10 who trust in the Lord are protected by his **constant love.**
33. 5 his **constant love** fills the earth.
33.18 those who obey him, those who trust in his **constant love.**
33.22 May your **constant love** be with us, Lord, as we put our
36. 5 Lord, your **constant love** reaches the heavens;
36. 7 How precious, O God, is your **constant love!**
38.17 I am about to fall and am in **constant** pain.
40.10 I have not been silent about your loyalty and **constant love.**
42. 8 May the Lord show his **constant love** during the day, so
44.26 Because of your **constant love** save us!
48. 9 Inside your Temple, O God, we think of your **constant love.**
51. 1 Be merciful to me, O God, because of your **constant love.**
52. 8 I trust in his **constant love** for ever and ever.
57. 3 God will show me his **constant love** and faithfulness.
57.10 Your **constant love** reaches the heavens;
59.16 every morning I will sing aloud of your **constant love.**
61. 7 protect him with your **constant love** and faithfulness.
62.12 power belongs to him [12]and that his **love is constant.**
63. 3 Your **constant love** is better than life itself, and so I
66.20 reject my prayer or keep back his **constant love** from me.
69.16 Answer me, Lord, in the goodness of your **constant love;**
85. 7 Show us your **constant love,** O Lord, and give us your
86. 5 us and forgiving, full of **constant love** for all who pray to
86.13 How great is your **constant love** for me!
88.11 Is your **constant love** spoken of in the grave or your
89. 1 O Lord, I will always sing of your **constant love;**
90.14 us each morning with your **constant love,** so that we may sing
92. 2 High God, [2]to proclaim your **constant love** every morning and
94.18 but your **constant love,** O Lord, held me up.
98. 3 people of Israel with loyalty and **constant love** for them.
103. 8 and loving, slow to become angry and full of **constant love.**
107. 8 thank the Lord for his **constant love,** for the wonderful
107.15 thank the Lord for his **constant love,** for the wonderful
107.21 thank the Lord for his **constant love,** for the wonderful
107.31 thank the Lord for his **constant love,** for the wonderful
107.43 may they consider the Lord's **constant love.**
108. 4 Your **constant love** reaches above the heavens;

Ps	109.26	because of your **constant love,** save me!
	115. 1	be given because of your **constant love** and faithfulness.
	119.64	Lord, the earth is full of your **constant love;**
	119.76	Let your **constant love** comfort me, as you have promised me,
	119.88	Because of your **constant love** be good to me, so that I
	119.124	Treat me according to your **constant love,** and teach me your commands.
	119.149	Because your **love is constant,** hear me, O Lord;
	130. 7	the Lord, because his **love is constant** and he is always
	138. 2	your name because of your **constant love** and faithfulness,
	143. 8	me each morning of your **constant love,** for I put my trust
	145. 8	merciful, slow to become angry and full of **constant love.**
	147.11	who honour him, in those who trust in his **constant love.**
Prov	15.15	of the poor is a **constant** struggle, but happy people always
Is	51.13	Why should you live in **constant** fear of the fury of those
	63. 7	people of Israel because of his mercy and **constant love.**
Jer	9.24	understands me, because my **love is constant,** and I do what
	31. 3	loved you, so I continue to show you my **constant love.**
	32.18	You have shown **constant love** to thousands, but you also
Lam	1.13	Then he abandoned me and left me in **constant** pain.
Ezek	35. 5	"You were Israel's **constant** enemy and let her people be
Dan	9. 4	to your covenant and show **constant love** to those who love
Hos	2.19	I will show you **constant love** and mercy and make you mine
	6. 6	I want your **constant love,** not your animal sacrifices.
Mic	6. 8	what is just, to show **constant love,** and to live in humble
	7.18	but you take pleasure in showing us your **constant love.**
	7.20	show your faithfulness and **constant love** to your people,
Acts	10. 2	the Jewish poor people and was **constantly** praying to God.
Col	3.10	which God, its Creator, is **constantly** renewing in his own image,
1 Tim	6. 5	evil suspicions, [5]and **constant** arguments from people whose minds
Jas	4. 1	desires for pleasure, which are **constantly** fighting within you.

CONSTELLATION

Is	13.10	Every star and every **constellation** will stop shining,

CONSTRUCT

[WELL-CONSTRUCTED]

Ex	36. 3	the Israelites had brought for **constructing** the sacred Tent.
Judg	6.26	Build a **well-constructed** altar to the Lord your God on
2 Chr	3. 1	King Solomon began the **construction** [2]in the second month of
Ezra	5.16	**construction** has continued from then until the present, but
	6. 7	"Stay away from the Temple [7]and do not interfere with its **construction.**

CONSULT

Ex	18.14	standing here from morning till night to **consult** you?"
	33. 7	and anyone who wanted to **consult** the Lord would go out to
Lev	19.31	go for advice to people who **consult** the spirits of the dead.
	20. 6	for advice to people who **consult** the spirits of the dead, I
	20.27	"Any man or woman who **consults** the spirits of the dead
	25.50	He must **consult** the one who bought him, and they must
Deut	18.11	or charms, and don't let them **consult** the spirits of the dead.
Josh	9.14	some food from them, but did not **consult** the Lord about it.
	18. 6	I will draw lots to **consult** the Lord our God for you.
	18. 8	here in Shiloh I will **consult** the Lord for you by drawing
	18.10	Joshua drew lots to **consult** the Lord for them, and
	19.51	land by drawing lots to **consult** the Lord at Shiloh, at the
1 Sam	2.28	to burn the incense, and to wear the ephod to **consult** me.
	14.19	Saul said to him, "There's no time to **consult** the Lord!"
	14.36	But the priest said, "Let's **consult** God first."
	22.13	give him some food and a sword, and **consult** God for him?
	22.15	Yes, I **consulted** God for him, and it wasn't the first time.
	23. 4	So David **consulted** the Lord again, and the Lord said to him,
	28. 7	woman who is a medium, and I will go and **consult** her."
	28. 8	**"Consult** the spirits for me and tell me what is going to
2 Sam	5.23	Once more David **consulted** the Lord, who answered,
	21. 1	So David **consulted** the Lord about it, and the Lord said,
1 Kgs	12. 6	King Rehoboam **consulted** the older men who had served as
	22. 5	But first let's **consult** the Lord."
	22. 7	"Isn't there another prophet through whom we can **consult** the Lord?"
2 Kgs	1. 2	he sent some messengers to **consult** Baalzebub, the god of the
	1. 3	"Why are you going to **consult** Baalzebub, the god of Ekron?
	1. 6	'Why are you sending messengers to **consult** Baalzebub,
	1.16	'Because you sent messengers to **consult** Baalzebub, the god
	1.16	were no god in Israel to **consult**—you will not get well;
	3.11	"Is there a prophet here through whom we can **consult** the Lord?"
	3.13	"Go and **consult** those prophets
	3.13	that your father and mother **consulted."**
	6. 8	He **consulted** his officers and chose a place to set up his
	8. 8	prophet, and ask him to **consult** the Lord to find out whether
	17.17	they **consulted** mediums and fortune-tellers, and they devoted
	19. 8	so he went there to **consult** him.
	21. 6	He practised divination and magic and **consulted** fortune-tellers and mediums.
	22.13	"Go and **consult** the Lord for me and for all the people
	22.14	Shaphan, and Asaiah went to **consult** a woman named Huldah, a
1 Chr	10.13	tried to find guidance by **consulting** the spirits of the dead
	10.14	instead of **consulting** the Lord.
	13. 1	King David **consulted** with all the officers in command of
	14.14	Once more David **consulted** God, who answered, "Don't attack them from here,
2 Chr	9.23	They all **consulted** him, to hear the wisdom that God had
	10. 6	King Rehoboam **consulted** the older men who had served as
	18. 4	Then he added, "But first let's **consult** the Lord."
	18. 6	"Isn't there another prophet through whom we can **consult** the Lord?"
	20.21	After **consulting** with the people, the king ordered some
	33. 6	He practised divination and magic and **consulted** fortune-tellers
	34.21	"Go and **consult** the Lord for me and for the people who
	34.22	and the others went to **consult** a woman named Huldah, a
Is	8.19	messages from the spirits and **consult** the dead on behalf of
	19. 3	and they will go and **consult** mediums and ask the spirits of
	37. 8	so he went there to **consult** him.
	40.14	With whom does God **consult** in order to know and
	45.21	let the defendants **consult** one another.
	47.15	do you— those astrologers you've **consulted** all your life.
	65. 4	go to caves and tombs to **consult** the spirits of the dead.
Jer	8. 2	and served, and which they have **consulted** and worshipped.
Ezek	14. 1	of the Israelites came to **consult** me about the Lord's will.
	14. 4	and who then comes to **consult** a prophet, will get an answer
	14. 7	idols, and then goes to **consult** a prophet, I, the Lord, will
	14.10	and the one who **consults** him will get the same punishment.
	20. 1	Israelite community came to **consult** me about the Lord's will,
	21.21	he **consults** his idols;
Zech	10. 2	People **consult** idols and fortune-tellers, but the answers

CONSUME

Lev	9.24	sent a fire, and it **consumed** the burnt-offering and the fat
Deut	32.22	to the world below and **consume** the roots of the mountains.
2 Sam	22. 9	out of his nostrils, a **consuming** flame and burning coals
Job	31.12	like a destructive, hellish fire, **consuming** everything I have.
Ps	18. 8	out of his nostrils, a **consuming** flame and burning coals
	21. 9	Lord will devour them in his anger, and fire will **consume** them.
Rev	18. 9	when they see the smoke from the flames that **consume** her.
	18.18	as they saw the smoke from the flames that **consumed** her:
	19. 3	smoke from the flames that **consume** the great city goes up

CONTACT

Lev	7.19	If the meat comes into **contact** with anything ritually unclean,
	22. 4	anything which is unclean through **contact** with a corpse or
Num	5. 2	and everyone who is unclean by **contact** with a corpse.
	6.11	purification for him because of his **contact** with a corpse.
	18. 3	they must not have any **contact** with sacred objects in the
2 Kgs	13.21	as the body came into **contact** with Elisha's bones, the man

CONTAIN

Num	4. 9	its lamps, tongs, trays, and all the olive-oil **containers.**
Deut	23.24	you want, but you must not carry any away in a **container.**
1 Kgs	1.39	Zadok took the **container** of olive-oil which he had
2 Kgs	25.14	shovels and the ash **containers** used in cleaning the altar,
Is	66.20	bring grain-offerings to the Temple in ritually clean **containers.**
Jer	52.18	shovels and the ash **containers** used in cleaning the altar,
	52.19	from the sacrifices, the ash **containers,** the lampstands, the
Mt	25. 4	while the wise ones took **containers** full of oil for their lamps.
Heb	9. 4	all covered with gold and **containing** the gold jar with the

CONTAMINATED

Lev	15.24	during her period, he is **contaminated** by her impurity and
Ezra	9. 2	women, and so God's holy people had become **contaminated.**

CONTEMPT

Ex	18.11	the Egyptians treated the Israelites with such **contempt."**
Num	15.30	of treating the Lord with **contempt,** and he shall be put to
1 Sam	2.30	me, and I will treat with **contempt** those who despise me.
2 Sam	12.14	you have shown such **contempt** for the Lord in doing this,
1 Kgs	9. 7	People everywhere will ridicule Israel and treat her with **contempt.**
2 Chr	7.20	People everywhere will ridicule it and treat it with **contempt.**
Ps	31.11	All my enemies, and especially my neighbours, treat me with **contempt;**
	31.18	and arrogant who speak with **contempt** about righteous men.
	44.14	You have made us an object of **contempt** among the nations;
	107.40	he showed **contempt** for their oppressors
	123. 3	we have been treated with so much **contempt.**
Song	8. 7	to buy love with his wealth, **contempt** is all he would get.
Is	29.20	end of those who oppress others and show **contempt** for God.
	52. 5	over you boast and brag and constantly show **contempt** for me.
	58. 9	to every gesture of **contempt,** and to every evil word;
Jer	33.24	And so they look with **contempt** on my people and no longer
Lam	1. 8	she is naked and held in **contempt.**
Ezek	35.12	Lord, heard you say with **contempt** that the mountains of
	36. 5	With glee and **contempt,** they captured my land and took
Mic	6.16	People everywhere will treat you with **contempt."**
Nah	3. 6	I will treat you with **contempt** and cover you with filth.
Hab	1.10	They treat kings with **contempt** and laugh at high officials.
Mal	1. 7	I will tell you—by showing **contempt** for my altar.
Lk	23.11	Herod and his soldiers mocked Jesus and treated him with **contempt;**

CONTENT (1)

Rom	2.20	the Law you have the full **content** of knowledge and of truth.
Col	2. 9	For the full **content** of divine nature lives in Christ,

CONTENT (2)

Deut	15.16	he may love you and your family and be **content** to stay.
Job	6. 5	A donkey is **content** when eating grass, and a cow is quiet
Ps	131. 2	Instead, I am **content** and at peace.
Prov	19.23	and you will live a long life, **content** and safe from harm.
Song	8.10	My lover knows that with him I find **contentment** and peace.
Ezek	16.47	Were you **content** to follow in their footsteps and copy

Lk 3.14 Be **content** with your pay.”
2 Cor 12.10 I am **content** with weaknesses, insults, hardships,
Phil 4.12 at any time, I am **content,** whether I am full or hungry,

CONTEST

2 Sam 2.14 the young men from each side to fight an armed **contest.”**
1 Cor 9.27 being disqualified after having called others to the **contest.**

CONTINUE

Jn 12.35 **Continue** on your way while you have the light, so that
17.26 to them, and I will **continue** to do so, in order that
Acts 2.44 All the believers **continued** together in close fellowship
5.42 in people's homes they **continued** to teach and preach the Good
6. 7 And so the word of God **continued** to spread.
8.39 not see him again, but **continued** on his way, full of joy.
12.24 Meanwhile the word of God **continued** to spread and grow.
21. 7 We **continued** our voyage, sailing from Tyre to Ptolemais,
27. 9 until it became dangerous to **continue** the voyage, for by now
27.18 The violent storm **continued,** so on the next day they began
Rom 1.32 Yet, not only do they **continue** to do these very things, but
6. 1 Should we **continue** to live in sin so that God's grace will
11.22 but kind to you—if you **continue** in his kindness.
15.13 so that your hope will **continue** to grow by the power of
1 Cor 7. 8 be better for you to **continue** to live alone as I do.
16. 6 you can help me to **continue** my journey, wherever it is I
16.11 you must help him to **continue** his trip in peace,
2 Cor 8. 6 who began this work, to **continue** it and help you complete
Gal 5.11 if I **continue** to preach that circumcision is necessary,
Eph 4.17 do not **continue** to live like the heathen, whose thoughts are
Phil 1.18 And I will **continue** to be happy, [19] because I know that by
1.22 But if by **continuing** to live I can do more worthwhile work,
Col 1.23 must, of course, **continue** faithful on a firm and sure foundation,
2 Thes 1. 4 boast about the way you **continue** to endure and believe
3. 1 the Lord's message may **continue** to spread rapidly and be received
3. 4 you are doing and will **continue** to do what we tell you.
1 Tim 5. 5 her hope in God and **continues** to pray and ask him for
2 Tim 2.12 If we **continue** to endure, we shall also rule with him.
3.14 But as for you, **continue** in the truths that you were
Heb 7.23 other priests, because they died and could not **continue** their work.
2 Pet 3.18 But **continue** to grow in the grace and knowledge of our
1 Jn 3. 6 who lives in union with Christ does not **continue** to sin;
3. 6 whoever **continues** to sin has never seen him or known him.
3. 8 Whoever **continues** to sin belongs to the Devil,
3. 9 child of God does not **continue** to sin, for God's very nature
3. 9 and because God is his Father, he cannot **continue** to sin.
3 Jn 6 Please help them to **continue** their journey in a way that
Rev 2.26 who win the victory, who **continue** to the end to do what

CONTRACT

Jer 32.11 the sealed copy containing the **contract** and its conditions,

CONTRADICT

Lk 21.15 enemies will be able to refute or **contradict** what you say.

CONTRARY

Rom 11.24 is broken off and then, **contrary** to nature, is joined to a
1 Tim 1.10 false testimony or who do anything else **contrary** to sound doctrine.

CONTRIBUTE

Ex 35.24 All who were able to **contribute** silver or bronze brought
36. 6 was to make any further **contribution** for the sacred Tent;
Lev 7.14 of each kind of bread as a special **contribution** to the Lord;
7.32 be given as a special **contribution** [33] to the priest who
7.34 hind leg is a special **contribution** that the Lord has taken
10.14 and the special **contribution** to the Lord for the priests.
Num 5. 9 Also every special **contribution** which the Israelites offer
15.19 is to be set aside as a special **contribution** to the Lord.
15.20 is to be presented as a special **contribution** to the Lord.
15.20 same way as the special **contribution** you make from the corn
18. 8 giving you all the special **contributions** made to me that are
18.11 any other special **contributions** that the Israelites present
18.19 special **contributions** which the Israelites present to me.
18.24 the Israelites present to me as a special **contribution.**
18.26 present a tenth of it as a special **contribution** to the Lord.
18.27 This special **contribution** will be considered as the
18.28 also will present the special **contribution** that belongs to
18.28 are to give this special **contribution** for the Lord to Aaron
31.29 to Eleazar the priest as a special **contribution** to the Lord.
31.41 the tax as a special **contribution** to the Lord, as the Lord
31.52 The total **contribution** of the officers
2 Kgs 15.20 Israel by forcing each one to **contribute** fifty pieces of silver.
2 Chr 24. 8 to make a box for **contributions** and to place it at the
30.24 King Hezekiah **contributed** a thousand bulls and seven
35. 7 at the Passover, King Josiah **contributed** from his own herds
35. 8 His officials also made **contributions** for the people, the
35. 9 **contributed** five thousand lambs and young goats
Neh 7.70 Many of the people **contributed** to help pay the
10.32 Every year we will each **contribute** five grammes of
10.39 Levites are to take the **contributions** of corn, wine, and
12.44 the storerooms where **contributions** for the Temple were kept,
12.44 near the various cities the **contributions** for the priests

CONTROL

[UNCONTROLLABLE]

Gen 1.28 live all over the earth and bring it under their **control.**
14. 4 They had been under the **control** of Chedorlaomer for twelve years,
16. 6 Abram answered, “Very well, she is your slave and under your **control;**
27.40 Yet when you rebel, You will break away from his **control.”**
43.31 face, he came out, and **controlling** himself, he ordered the
45. 1 was no longer able to **control** his feelings in front of his
Ex 32.25 the people get out of **control** and make fools of themselves
Lev 25.28 back, it remains under the **control** of the man who bought it
Num 24. 2 The spirit of God took **control** of him, [3] and he uttered this
Deut 15. 6 you will have **control** over many nations,
15. 6 but no nation will have **control** over you.
Judg 1. 2 I am giving them **control** of the land.”
6.34 spirit of the Lord took **control** of Gideon, and he blew a
1 Sam 10. 6 of the Lord will take **control** of you, and you will join
10.10 the spirit of God took **control** of him, and he joined in
11. 6 spirit of God took **control** of him, and he became furious.
16.13 spirit of the Lord took **control** of David and was with him
18.10 spirit from God suddenly took **control** of Saul, and he raved
19. 9 One day an evil spirit from the Lord took **control** of Saul.
19.20 the spirit of God took **control** of Saul's men, and they also
19.23 the spirit of God took **control** of him also, and he danced
2 Sam 2. 1 “Shall I go and take **control** of one of the towns of
8. 1 defeated them, and ended their **control** over the land.
8. 3 his way to restore his **control** over the territory by the
1 Kgs 2.46 Solomon was now in complete **control.**
10.28 The king's agents **controlled** the export of horses
12.21 and restore his **control** over the northern tribes of Israel.
2 Kgs 16. 6 the king of Edom regained **control** of the city of Elath, and
24. 7 the king of Babylonia now **controlled** all the territory that
1 Chr 7.29 The descendants of Manasseh **controlled** the cities of Beth Shan,
10.14 Lord killed him and gave **control** of the kingdom to David son
12.18 God's spirit took **control** of one of them, Amasai, who
18. 1 He took out of their **control** the city of Gath and its
18. 3 Hadadezer was trying to gain **control** of the territory by the
2 Chr 1. 1 of King David, took firm **control** of the kingdom of Israel,
1.16 The king's agents **controlled** the export of horses
11. 1 and restore his **control** over the northern tribes of Israel.
11.12 In this way he kept Judah and Benjamin under his **control.**
14. 7 We have **control** of the land because we have done the will
17. 5 The Lord gave Jehoshaphat firm **control** over the kingdom of Judah,
21. 4 When Jehoram was in firm **control** of the kingdom, he had
24.20 the spirit of God took **control** of Zechariah son of Jehoiada
Ezra 4.16 longer be able to **control** the province of West Euphrates.”
Neh 9.15 You told them to take **control** of the land which you had
Esth 5.10 But he **controlled** himself and went home.
Job 3. 8 to curse that day, those who know how to **control** Leviathan.
32. 2 named Elihu could not **control** his anger any longer,
Ps 2. 3 “let us throw off their **control.”**
32. 9 a mule, which must be **controlled** with a bit and bridle to
Prov 16.32 It is better to win **control** over yourself than over whole cities.
19.11 If you are sensible, you will **control** your temper.
21. 1 The Lord **controls** the mind of a king as easily as he
21. 4 Wicked people are **controlled** by their conceit and arrogance,
25.28 If you cannot **control** your anger, you are as helpless as
30.16 and a fire burning out of **control.**
Ecc 7. 9 Keep your temper under **control;**
9. 1 this and saw that God **controls** the actions of wise and
10.17 proper time, who **control** themselves and don't get drunk.
Is 3. 3 politicians and everyone who uses magic to **control** events.
45.12 I **control** the sun, the moon, and the stars.
Jer 2.24 When she is on heat, who can **control** her?
10.23 no person has **control** over his own life.
14.10 to run away from me, and they will not **control** themselves.
15. 6 crushed you because I was tired of **controlling** my anger.
33.25 night, and I have made the laws that **control** earth and sky.
49.28 Kedar and the districts **controlled** by Hazor, which were conquered
51.28 officials, and the armies of all the countries they **control.**
Ezek 1.20 the creatures did, because the creatures **controlled** them.
10.17 went with them, because the creatures **controlled** them.
11. 5 spirit of the Lord took **control** of me, and the Lord told
13.20 that you use in your attempt to **control** life and death.
13.20 arms and set free the people that you were **controlling.**
20.37 “I will take firm **control** of you and make you obey my
Dan 2.21 He **controls** the times and the seasons;
4.25 admit that the Supreme God **controls** all human kingdoms, and
4.35 angels in heaven and people on earth are under his **control.**
5.21 admitted that the Supreme God **controls** all human kingdoms
5.23 whether you live or die and who **controls** everything you do.
Mk 5. 4 He was too strong for anyone to **control** him.
Acts 5. 3 did you let Satan take **control** of you and make you lie
Rom 8. 5 have their minds **controlled** by what human nature wants.
8. 5 have their minds **controlled** by what the Spirit wants.
8. 6 To be **controlled** by human nature results in death;
8. 6 to be **controlled** by the Spirit results in life and peace.
8. 7 an enemy of God when he is **controlled** by his human nature;
1 Cor 7.37 has his will under complete **control** and has already decided
9.27 and bring it under complete **control,** to keep myself from being
14.32 should be under the speaker's **control,** [33] because God does not
Gal 5.13 become an excuse for letting your physical desires **control** you.
5.25 he must also **control** our lives.
Eph 2. 2 the spirit who now **controls** the people who disobey God.
4.16 Under his **control** all the different parts of the body fit
5. 2 Your life must be **controlled** by love, just as Christ loved
Col 2.19 Christ's **control** the whole body is nourished and held together

Col 2.23 they have no real value in **controlling** physical passions.
2 Tim 3. 6 people's houses and gain **control** over weak women who are burdened
4. 5 But you must keep **control** of yourself in all circumstances;
Jas 1.26 If he does not **control** his tongue, his religion is worthless
3. 2 he is perfect and is also able to **control** his whole being.
3. 8 It is evil and **uncontrollable**, full of deadly poison.
1 Pet 4. 2 rest of your earthly lives **controlled** by God's will and not
2 Pet 1.21 but men were under the **control** of the Holy Spirit as they
3. 3 people will appear whose lives are **controlled** by their own lusts.
Jude 19 who cause divisions, who are **controlled** by their natural desires,
Rev 1.10 Lord's day the Spirit took **control** of me, and I heard a
4. 2 At once the Spirit took **control** of me.
17. 3 The Spirit took **control** of me, and the angel carried me to
21.10 The Spirit took **control** of me, and the angel carried me

CONVERSATION

1 Sam 18. 1 Saul and David finished their **conversation.**
Jer 38.24 let anyone know about this **conversation,** and your life will
38.27 could do, because no one had overheard the **conversation.**

CONVERT

Mt 23.15 You sail the seas and cross whole countries to win one **convert;**
Acts 2.11 both Jews and Gentiles **converted to Judaism,** and some of us
6. 5 a Gentile from Antioch who had earlier been **converted to Judaism.**
13.43 Jews and by many Gentiles who had been **converted to Judaism.**
Rom 1.13 I want to win **converts** among you also, as I have among
1 Cor 16.15 they are the first Christian **converts** in Achaia and have given
Tit 1.10 there are many, especially **converts** from Judaism, who rebel

AV CONVERT

Ps 19. 7 it gives new **strength.**
51.13 sinners your commands, and they will **turn back** to you.
Is 1.27 he will save Jerusalem and everyone there who **repents.**
6.10 If they did, they might **turn to me** and be healed."
Mt 13.15 understand, and they would **turn to me,** says God, and I would
18. 3 assure you that unless you **change** and become like children,
Mk 4.12 did, they would **turn to God,** and he would forgive them.'"
Lk 22.32 And when you **turn back to me,** you must strengthen your brothers."
Jn 12.40 and they would not **turn to me,** says God, for me to
Acts 3.19 Repent, then, and **turn to God,** so that he will forgive
28.27 understand, and they would **turn to me,** says God, and I would
Jas 5.19 from the truth and another one **brings** him back again,
5.20 whoever **turns** a sinner back from his wrong way will save

CONVICT

Deut 19.15 "One witness is not enough to **convict** a man of a crime;

CONVINCE

Ex 4. 8 not believe you or be **convinced** by the first miracle,
4. 8 then this one will **convince** them.
Deut 29.19 these solemn demands and yet **convinces** himself that all will
1 Sam 19. 6 Saul was **convinced** by what Jonathan said and made a vow
24. 7 So David **convinced** his men that they should not attack Saul.
24.11 This should **convince** you that I have no thought of rebelling
2 Sam 16. 3 Ziba answered, "because he is **convinced** that the Israelites
2 Chr 33.13 This **convinced** Manasseh that the Lord was God.
Ezra 4.16 We therefore are **convinced** that if this city is rebuilt
Job 6.25 Honest words are **convincing,** but you are talking nonsense.
17. 9 be respectable are more and more **convinced** they are right.
32. 1 Because Job was **convinced** of his own innocence, the three
Prov 25.15 down the strongest resistance and can even **convince** rulers.
Ecc 8.15 So I am **convinced** that a man should enjoy himself,
Ezek 5.13 this happens, you will be **convinced** that I, the Lord, have
14.22 evil they are, and be **convinced** that the punishment I am
Mt 21.26 because they are all **convinced** that John was a prophet."
28.14 hear of this, we will **convince** him that you are innocent,
Mk 11.32 because everyone was **convinced** that John had been a prophet.)
Lk 16.31 they will not be **convinced** even if someone were to rise
20. 6 us, because they are **convinced** that John was a prophet."
Acts 9.22 was the Messiah were so **convincing** that the Jews who lived
12.20 First they **convinced** Blastus, the man in charge of the palace,
17. 4 Some of them were **convinced** and joined Paul and Silas;
18. 4 synagogue every Sabbath, trying to **convince** both Jews and Greeks.
19. 8 and trying to **convince** them about the Kingdom of God.
19.26 he has succeeded in **convincing** many people, both here in Ephesus
21.14 We could not **convince** him, so we gave up and said,
27.11 But the army officer was **convinced** by what the captain and
28.23 and he tried to **convince** them about Jesus by quoting from
28.24 Some of them were **convinced** by his words, but others would
1 Cor 2. 4 of human wisdom, but with **convincing** proof of the power of
14.24 comes in, he will be **convinced** of his sin by what he
16.12 but he is not completely **convinced** that he should go at this
2 Cor 2. 3 For I am **convinced** that when I am happy, then all of
Col 4.12 as mature and fully **convinced** Christians, in complete obedience
1 Thes 1. 5 and the Holy Spirit, and with complete **conviction** of its truth.
2 Tim 4. 2 is right or not), to **convince,** reproach, and encourage, as

AV CONVINCE

Job 32.12 you have not **disproved** what Job has said.
Jn 8.46 Which one of you can **prove** that I am guilty of sin?
Acts 18.28 with his strong arguments he **defeated** the Jews in public debates
Tit 1. 9 and also to show the **error** of those who are opposed to
Jas 2. 9 guilty of sin, and the Law **condemns** you as a law-breaker.
Jude 15 bring judgement on all, to **condemn** them all for the godless

COOK

Gen 25.29 One day while Jacob was **cooking** some bean soup, Esau
27. 4 **Cook** me some of that tasty food that I like, and bring
27. 7 say to Esau, [7]'Bring me an animal and **cook** it for me.
27. 9 goats, so that I can **cook** them and make some of that
27.14 them to her, and she **cooked** the kind of food that his
27.31 He also **cooked** some tasty food and took it to his father.
Ex 23.19 "Do not **cook** a young sheep or goat in its mother's milk.
34.26 "Do not **cook** a young sheep or goat in its mother's milk."
Lev 2. 5 If the offering is bread **cooked** on a griddle, it is to
2. 7 If the offering is bread **cooked** in a pan, it is to
6.21 be mixed with oil and **cooked** on a griddle and then crumbled
Deut 14.21 "Do not **cook** a young sheep or goat in its mother's milk.
Judg 6.19 went into his house and **cooked** a young goat and used ten
13.15 Let us **cook** a young goat for you."
1 Sam 2.13 While the meat was still **cooking,** [14] he would stick the
2.14 stick the fork into the **cooking-pot,** and whatever the fork
8.13 make perfumes for him and work as his **cooks** and his bakers.
9.23 Samuel said to the **cook,** "Bring the piece of meat I
9.24 So the **cook** brought the choice piece of the leg and
2 Sam 12. 4 took the poor man's lamb and **cooked** a meal for his guest."
1 Kgs 19.21 of oxen, killed them, and **cooked** the meat, using the yoke as
2 Kgs 6.29 So we **cooked** my son and ate him.
Job 31.10 door, [10] then let my wife **cook** another man's food and sleep
Ezek 11. 3 The city is like a **cooking-pot,** and we are like the meat
11. 7 This city is indeed a **cooking-pot,** but what is the meat?
24.10 **Cook** the meat!
Hag 2.12 his robe touch any bread, **cooked** food, wine, olive-oil, or
Zech 14.20 The **cooking-pots** in the Temple will be as sacred as the
14.21 Every **cooking-pot** in Jerusalem and in all Judah will be
Lk 24.42 gave him a piece of **cooked** fish, [43] which he took and ate

COOL

Gen 27.44 while, until your brother's anger **cools** down [45] and he
Judg 3.20 sitting there alone in his **cool** room on the roof, Ehud went
Esth 2. 1 after the king's anger had **cooled** down, he kept thinking
7.10 Then the king's anger **cooled** down.
Job 7. 2 hard manual labour, [2] like a slave longing for **cool** shade;
Ps 42. 1 longs for a stream of **cool** water, so I long for you,
Is 16. 3 a tree that casts a **cool** shadow in the heat of noon,
25. 5 the shouts of cruel men, as a cloud **cools** a hot day.
Jer 18.14 Do its **cool** mountain streams ever run dry?
Lk 16.24 finger in some water and **cool** my tongue, because I am in

COPPER

Deut 8. 9 have iron in them, and from its hills you can mine **copper.**
Job 28. 2 iron out of the ground And melt **copper** out of the stones.
Ezek 22.18 are like the waste metal—**copper,** tin, iron, and lead—left
22.20 that the ore of silver, **copper,** iron, lead, and tin is put
Mt 10. 9 Do not carry any gold, silver, or **copper** money in your pockets;
Mk 7. 4 the proper way to wash cups, pots, **copper** bowls, and beds.
12.42 and dropped in two little **copper** coins, worth about a penny.
Lk 21. 2 saw a very poor widow dropping in two little **copper** coins.

COPY

Deut 17.18 he is to have a **copy** of the book of God's laws
17.18 made from the original **copy** kept by the levitical priests.
Josh 8.32 made on the stones a **copy** of the Law which Moses had
2 Kgs 10. 1 wrote a letter and sent **copies** to the rulers of the city,
11.12 head, and gave him a **copy** of the laws governing kingship.
1 Chr 2.55 of experts in writing and **copying** documents lived in the
2 Chr 23.11 head, and gave him a **copy** of the laws governing kingship.
Esth 4. 8 He gave Hathach a **copy** of the proclamation that had been
9.30 to all the Jews, and **copies** were sent to all the 127
Prov 25. 1 are more of Solomon's proverbs, **copied** by men at the court
Jer 32.11 Then I took both **copies** of the deed of purchase—the
32.11 sealed **copy** containing the contract and its conditions,
32.11 and the open **copy**—[12] and gave them to Baruch,
32.14 of purchase and the open **copy,** and to place them in a
Ezek 16.47 follow in their footsteps and **copy** their disgusting actions?
Heb 8. 5 priests is really only a **copy** and a shadow of what is
9.23 Those things, which are **copies** of the heavenly originals,
9.24 a man-made Holy Place, which was a **copy** of the real one.

CORAL

A brightly-coloured stony substance found in the sea; it was used as jewellery.

Job 28.18 The value of wisdom is more Than **coral** or crystal or rubies.
Ezek 27.16 purple cloth, embroidery, fine linen, **coral,** and rubies in

CORBAN

Mk 7.11 but says, 'This is **Corban**' (which means, it belongs to God),

CORD

Gen 38.18 "Your seal with its **cord** and the stick you are carrying."
38.25 whose they are—this seal with its **cord** and this stick."
Ex 28.14 gold twisted like **cords,** and attach them to the settings.
28.22 For the breast-piece make chains of pure gold, twisted like **cords.**
28.24 and fasten the two gold **cords** to the two rings.

Ex 28.25 other two ends of the **cords** to the two settings, and in
28.28 the ephod with a blue **cord,** so that the breast-piece rests
28.37 Tie it to the front of the turban with a blue **cord.**
39.15 For the breast-piece they made chains of pure gold, twisted like **cords.**
39.17 They fastened the two gold **cords** to the two rings
39.18 other two ends of the **cords** to the two settings and in
39.21 the ephod with a blue **cord,** so that the breast-piece rested
39.31 the turban with a blue **cord,** just as the Lord had commanded
Lev 14. 4 a piece of cedar-wood, a red **cord,** and a sprig of hyssop.
14. 6 with the cedar-wood, the red **cord,** and the hyssop, in the
14.49 birds, some cedar-wood, a red **cord,** and a sprig of hyssop.
14.51 cedar-wood, the hyssop, the red **cord,** and the live bird and
14.52 the live bird, the cedar-wood, the hyssop, and the red **cord.**
Num 15.38 corners of your garments and put a blue **cord** on each tassel.
19. 6 of hyssop, and a red **cord** and throw them into the fire.
Josh 2.18 your land, tie this red **cord** to the window you let us
2.21 When they had gone, she tied the red **cord** to the window.
Esth 1. 6 white cotton curtains, tied by **cords** of fine purple linen to
Ecc 4.12 A rope made of three **cords** is hard to break.
Ezek 16. 4 no one cut your umbilical **cord** or washed you or rubbed you
27.24 brightly coloured carpets, and well-made **cords** and ropes.
Jn 2.15 he made a whip from **cords** and drove all the animals out

CORINTH

Chief city and an important sea-port in the Roman province of Asia.

Acts 18. 1 After this, Paul left Athens and went on to **Corinth.**
18. 8 and many other people in **Corinth** heard the message,
18.18 on with the believers in **Corinth** for many days, then left
19. 1 While Apollos was in **Corinth,** Paul travelled through the
1 Cor 1. 2 of God which is in **Corinth,** to all who are called to
2 Cor 1. 1 the church of God in **Corinth,** and to all God's people
1.23 order to spare you that I decided not to go to **Corinth.**
6.11 Dear friends in **Corinth!**
2 Tim 4.20 Erastus stayed in **Corinth,** and I left Trophimus in Miletus,

CORMORANT

Lev 11.13 seagulls, storks, herons, pelicans, **cormorants;**
Deut 14.12 sea-gulls, storks, herons, pelicans, **cormorants;**

CORN

Gen 27.28 May he give you plenty of **corn** and wine!
27.37 I have given him **corn** and wine.
41. 5 Seven ears of **corn,** full and ripe, were growing on one stalk.
41. 6 Then seven other ears of **corn** sprouted, thin and scorched
41. 7 wind, [7]and the thin ears of **corn** swallowed the full ones.
41.22 I saw seven ears of **corn** which were full and ripe, growing
41.23 Then seven ears of **corn** sprouted, thin and scorched by
41.24 wind, [24]and the thin ears of **corn** swallowed the full ones.
41.26 years, and the seven full ears of **corn** are also seven years;
41.27 the seven thin ears of **corn** scorched by the desert wind are
41.35 them authority to store up **corn** in the cities and guard it.
41.49 There was so much **corn** that Joseph stopped measuring
41.56 Joseph opened all the storehouses and sold **corn** to the Egyptians.
41.57 over the world to buy **corn** from Joseph, because the famine
42. 1 Jacob learnt that there was **corn** in Egypt, he said to his
42. 2 I hear that there is **corn** in Egypt;
42. 3 ten half-brothers went to buy **corn** in Egypt, [4]but Jacob did
42. 5 came with others to buy **corn,** because there was famine in
42. 6 land of Egypt, was selling **corn** to people from all over the
42.19 to your starving families the **corn** that you have bought.
42.25 fill his brothers' packs with **corn,** to put each man's money
42.26 loaded their donkeys with the **corn** they had bought, and then
42.33 rest will take **corn** for your starving families and leave.
43. 2 Jacob had eaten all the **corn** which had been brought from Egypt,
44. 2 brother's sack, together with the money for his **corn."**
45.23 and ten donkeys loaded with **corn,** bread, and other food for
47.14 As they bought **corn,** Joseph collected all the money and
47.19 Give us **corn** to keep us alive and seed to sow in
49.26 Blessings of **corn** and flowers, Blessings of ancient mountains,
Ex 11. 5 the throne, to the son of the slave-woman who grinds **corn.**
22. 6 man's field and burns up **corn** that is growing or that has
22.29 me the offerings from your **corn,** your wine, and your
23.19 house of the Lord your God the first **corn** that you harvest.
34.26 to the house of the Lord the first **corn** that you harvest.
Lev 2.12 An offering of the first **corn** that you harvest each year
2.14 an offering of the first **corn** harvested, offer roasted grain
19. 9 fields, do not cut the **corn** at the edges of the fields,
19. 9 not go back to cut the ears of **corn** that were left.
23. 9 you and you harvest your **corn,** take the first sheaf to the
23.12 you present the offering of **corn,** also sacrifice as a
23.14 eat any of the new **corn,** whether raw, roasted, or baked into
23.15 which you bring your sheaf of **corn** to present to the Lord.
23.16 Sabbath, present to the Lord another new offering of **corn.**
23.17 the Lord as an offering of the first **corn** to be harvested.
23.22 fields, do not cut the **corn** at the edges of the fields,
23.22 not go back to cut the ears of **corn** that were left;
25. 5 Do not even harvest the **corn** that grows by itself without
25.11 your fields or harvest the **corn** that grows by itself or
26. 5 you will still be harvesting **corn** when it is time to pick
26. 5 will still be picking grapes when it is time to sow **corn.**
Num 6.15 and in addition the required offerings of **corn** and wine.
6.17 he shall also present the offerings of **corn** and wine.
15.20 bread made from the new **corn** is to be presented as a
15.20 the special contribution you make from the **corn** you thresh.
18.12 olive-oil, wine, and **corn.**
18.27 offering which the farmer makes of new **corn** and new wine.
Num 20. 5 There's no **corn,** no figs, no grapes, no pomegranates.
28.26 present the offering of new **corn** to the Lord, you are to
Deut 7.13 bless your fields, so that you will have **corn,** wine, and
11.14 so that there will be **corn,** wine, and olive-oil for you,
12.17 the tithes of your **corn,** your wine, or your olive-oil,
14.23 eat the tithes of your **corn,** wine, and olive-oil, and the
15.14 from what the Lord has blessed you with—sheep, **corn,** and
16. 9 the **corn,** [10]and then celebrate the Harvest Festival,
16.13 you have threshed all your **corn** and pressed all your grapes,
18. 4 to receive the first share of the **corn,** wine, olive-oil, and
23.25 you may eat all the **corn** you can pull off
23.25 but you must not cut any **corn** with a sickle.
24. 6 take as security his millstones used for grinding his **corn.**
24.19 bring in some of the **corn** that you have cut, do not
25. 4 not muzzle an ox when you are using it to thresh **corn.**
28. 5 "The Lord will bless your **corn** crops and the food you
28. 8 your God will bless your work and fill your barns with **corn.**
28.17 "The Lord will curse your **corn** crops and the food you
28.51 They will not leave you any **corn,** wine, olive-oil,
33.28 in a land full of **corn** and wine, where dew from the
Judg 15. 5 burnt up not only the **corn** that had been harvested
15. 5 but also the **corn** that was still in the fields,
Ruth 2. 2 fields to gather the **corn** that the harvest workers leave.
2. 3 behind the workers, picking up the **corn** which they left.
2. 7 me to let her follow the workers and pick up the **corn.**
2. 8 Don't pick up **corn** anywhere except in this field.
2.15 to go on picking up **corn,** Boaz ordered the workers, "Let
2.15 Besides that, pull out some **corn** from the bundles and leave
2.17 So Ruth went on gathering **corn** in the field until evening,
2.18 She took the **corn** back into town and showed her
2.21 me to keep picking up **corn** with his workers until they
2.23 worked with them and gathered **corn** until all the barley and
1 Sam 8.15 take a tenth of your **corn** and of your grapes for his
23. 1 town of Keilah and were stealing the newly-harvested **corn.**
2 Kgs 4.42 harvested that year, and some freshly-cut ears of **corn.**
18.32 vineyards to give wine and there is **corn** for making bread;
19.29 be able to sow your **corn** and harvest it, and plant vines
2 Chr 31. 5 brought gifts of their finest **corn,** wine, olive-oil, honey,
32.28 In addition, he had storehouses built for his **corn,**
Ezra 7.17 and buy bulls, rams, lambs, **corn,** and wine and offer them on
Neh 5. 2 "We have large families, we need **corn** to keep us alive."
5. 3 and houses to get enough **corn** to keep us from starving."
5.10 the people borrow money and **corn** from me, and so have my
5.11 the debts they owe you—money or **corn** or wine or olive-oil.
10.31 If foreigners bring **corn** or anything else to sell to us
10.35 an offering of the first **corn** we harvest and of the first
10.37 dough made from the first **corn** harvested each year and our
10.39 to take the contributions of **corn,** wine, and olive-oil to
12.44 tithes and the first **corn** and fruit that ripened each year.
13. 5 only for storing offerings of **corn** and incense, the
13. 5 priests, and the tithes of **corn,** wine, and olive-oil given
13.12 bringing to the temple storerooms their tithes of **corn,**
13.15 Others were loading **corn,** wine, grapes, figs, and other
13.31 of the first **corn** and the first fruits that ripened.
Job 24.24 a weed, like an ear of **corn** that has been cut off.
Ps 4. 7 more than they will ever have with all their **corn** and wine.
72.16 May there be plenty of **corn** in the land;
Prov 14. 4 will be empty, but with them it will be full of **corn.**
Is 5.10 litres of seed will produce only eighteen litres of **corn."**
9. 3 harvest their **corn** or when they divide captured wealth.
17. 5 like a field where the **corn** has been cut and harvested, as
23. 3 to buy and sell the **corn** that grew in Egypt and to
36.17 vineyards to give wine and there is **corn** for making bread.
37.30 be able to sow your **corn** and harvest it, and plant vines
55. 1 Come, you that have no money— buy **corn** and eat!
62. 8 "Your **corn** will no longer be food for your enemies, And
62. 9 that sowed and harvested the **corn** Will eat the bread and
Jer 9.22 manure on the fields, like **corn** cut and left behind
9.22 by the reapers, **corn** that no one gathers.
25.10 no oil for their lamps, and there will be no more **corn.**
31.12 my gifts— gifts of **corn** and wine and olive-oil, gifts of
35. 9 we live in tents—and we own no vineyards, fields, or **corn.**
41. 5 They were taking **corn** and incense to offer in the Temple.
50.11 about like a cow threshing **corn** or like a neighing horse,
51.33 them down and trample them like **corn** on a threshing-place.
Lam 5.13 Our young men are forced to grind **corn** like slaves;
Ezek 36.29 I will command the **corn** to be plentiful, so that you will
45.24 and a half litres of **corn** and three litres of olive-oil.
45.25 whole, and the same offerings of **corn** and olive-oil."
46. 5 and a half litres of **corn,** and with each lamb he is
46. 7 and a half litres of **corn,** and with each lamb the offering
46. 7 are to be offered with each such grain-offering of **corn.**
Hos 2. 8 one who gave her the **corn,** the wine, the olive-oil, and all
2. 9 take back my gifts of **corn** and wine, and will take away
2.21 and the earth will produce **corn** and grapes and olives.
7.14 When they pray for **corn** and wine, they gash themselves like pagans.
8. 7 A field of **corn** that doesn't ripen can never produce any bread.
9. 1 Baal and have loved the **corn** you thought he paid you with!
9. 2 you will not have enough **corn** and olive-oil, and there will
14. 7 They will grow **corn** and be fruitful like a vineyard.
Joel 1. 9 There is no **corn** or wine to offer in the Temple;
1.10 the ground mourns because the **corn** is destroyed, the grapes
1.13 There is no **corn** or wine to offer your God.
2.14 Then you can offer him **corn** and wine.
2.19 am going to give you **corn** and wine and olive-oil, and you
2.24 The threshing-places will be full of **corn;**
3.13 cut them down like **corn** at harvest time;
Amos 2.13 the ground, and you will groan like a cart loaded with **corn.**
8. 5 holy days to be over so that we can sell our **corn.**
9. 9 command and shake the people of Israel like **corn** in a sieve.

Amos 9.13 coming," says the Lord, "when **corn** will grow faster than
Mic 4.12 in the same way that **corn** is brought in to be threshed.
6.15 You will sow **corn,** but not harvest the crop.
Hab 3.17 and the fields produce no **corn,** even though the sheep all
Hag 1. 6 You have sown much **corn,** but have harvested very little.
2.16 to a heap of **corn** expecting to find two hundred kilogrammes,
2.19 Although there is no **corn** left, and the grapevines,
Zech 9.17 The young people will grow strong on its **corn** and wine.
12. 6 in a field of ripe **corn**—they will destroy all the
Mt 12. 1 so they began to pick ears of **corn** and eat the grain.
13. 3 "Once there was a man who went out to sow **corn.**
13. 8 But some seeds fell in good soil, and the plants produced **corn;**
13.26 grew and the ears of **corn** began to form, then the weeds
Mk 2.23 walked along with him, they began to pick the ears of **corn.**
4. 3 Once there was a man who went out to sow **corn.**
4. 7 up and choked the plants, and they didn't produce any **corn.**
4. 8 good soil, and the plants sprouted, grew, and produced **corn:**
4.28 appears, then the ear, and finally the ear full of **corn.**
4.29 When the **corn** is ripe, the man starts cutting it with
Lk 6. 1 to pick the ears of **corn,** rub them in their hands,
8. 5 "Once there was a man who went out to sow **corn.**
8. 8 the plants grew and produced **corn,** a hundred grains each."
12.18 where I will store my **corn** and all my other goods.
17.35 Two women will be grinding **corn** together:
Acts 7.12 Jacob heard that there was **corn** in Egypt, he sent his sons,
1 Cor 9. 9 not muzzle an ox when you are using it to thresh **corn."**
1 Tim 5.18 are using it to thresh **corn"** and "A worker should be given

CORNELIUS

Roman officer who became a Christian in the early days of the Church.

Acts 10. 1 a man in Caesarea named **Cornelius,** who was a captain in the
10. 3 saw an angel of God come in and say to him, **"Cornelius!"**
10. 7 angel went away, and **Cornelius** called two of his house servants
10.17 the men sent by **Cornelius** had learnt where Simon's house was,
10.22 "Captain **Cornelius** sent us," they answered.
10.24 he arrived in Caesarea, where **Cornelius** was waiting for him,
10.25 was about to go in, **Cornelius** met him, fell at his feet,
10.27 Peter kept on talking to **Cornelius** as he went into the house,
10.30 **Cornelius** said, "It was about this time three days ago
10.31 **"Cornelius!** God has heard your prayer
11.12 to Caesarea, and we all went into the house of **Cornelius.**

CORNER

Ex 25.26 it and put them at the four **corners,** where the legs are.
26.23 west, make six frames, [23]and two frames for the **corners.**
26.24 These **corner** frames are to be joined at the bottom and
26.24 frames that form the two **corners** are to be made in this
27. 2 Make projections at the top of the four **corners.**
27. 4 Make a bronze grating and put four bronze carrying-rings on its **corners.**
28.23 attach them to the upper **corners** of the breast-piece,
28.26 attach them to the lower **corners** of the breast-piece on the
30. 2 Its projections at the four **corners** are to form one piece
36.28 they made six frames [28]and two frames for the **corners.**
36.29 These **corner** frames were joined at the bottom and
36.29 frames that formed the two **corners** were made in this way.
37.13 it and put them at the four **corners,** where the legs were.
37.25 Its projections at the four **corners** formed one piece with it.
38. 2 the top of the four **corners,** so that they formed one piece
38. 5 He made four carrying-rings and put them on the four **corners.**
39.16 the two rings to the upper **corners** of the breast-piece.
39.19 attached them to the lower **corners** of the breast-piece, on
Lev 4. 7 projections at the **corners** of the incense-altar in the Tent.
4.18 on the projections at the **corners** of the incense-altar
4.25 on the projections at the **corners** of the altar, and pour out
4.30 on the projections at the **corners** of the altar, and pour out
4.34 on the projections at the **corners** of the altar, and pour out
8.15 on the projections at the **corners** of the altar, in order to
9. 9 on the projections at the **corners** of the altar, and poured
16.18 put it all over the projections at the **corners** of the altar.
Num 15.38 "Make tassels on the **corners** of your garments and put a
Deut 22.12 "Sew tassels on the four **corners** of your clothes.
30. 4 are scattered to the farthest **corners** of the earth, the Lord
1 Kgs 1.50 Lord's presence and took hold of the **corners** of the altar.
1.51 was holding on to the **corners** of the altar and had said,
2.28 Lord's presence and took hold of the **corners** of the altar.
7.30 At the four **corners** were bronze supports for a basin;
7.34 four supports at the bottom **corners** of each cart, which were
7.39 the tank he placed at the south-east **corner.**
2 Chr 4.10 The tank was placed near the south-east **corner** of the Temple.
26.15 large stones from the towers and **corners** of the city wall.
Neh 3.24 section, from Azariah's house to the **corner** of the wall;
3.25 next section, beginning at the **corner** of the wall and the
3.31 near the room on top of the north-east **corner** of the wall.
3.32 from the room at the **corner** as far as the Sheep Gate.
Ps 74.20 There is violence in every dark **corner** of the land.
144.12 like stately pillars which adorn the **corners** of a palace.
Prov 7. 8 the street near the **corner** where a certain woman lived.
7.12 or stood waiting at a **corner,** sometimes in the streets,
Is 11.12 Judah and bringing them back from the four **corners** of the earth.
41. 9 called you from its farthest **corners** and said to you, 'You
51.20 At the **corner** of every street your people collapse from weakness;
Jer 17. 1 a diamond point and carved on the **corners** of your altars.
Lam 2.19 Children starving to death on every street **corner!**
Ezek 41.22 Its **corner-posts,** its base, and its sides were all made of wood.
43.15 The projections on the four **corners** were higher than the
43.20 the projections on the top **corners** of the altar,
43.20 and on the **corners** of the middle section
45.19 the Temple, on the four **corners** of the altar, and on the
46.21 in each of its four **corners** there was a smaller courtyard,
Amos 3.14 The **corners** of every altar will be broken off and will fall
Nah 3.10 At every street **corner** their children were beaten to death.
Mt 6. 5 and on the street **corners,** so that everyone will see them.
24.31 his angels to the four **corners** of the earth, and they will
Mk 13.27 angels out to the four **corners** of the earth to gather God's
Acts 10.11 large sheet being lowered by its four **corners** to the earth.
11. 5 being lowered by its four **corners** from heaven, and it
26.26 for this thing has not happened hidden away in a **corner.**
Rev 7. 1 angels standing at the four **corners** of the earth, holding back
9.13 voice coming from the four **corners** of the gold altar standing

CORNER GATE

2 Kgs 14.13 from Ephraim Gate to the **Corner** Gate, a distance of nearly
2 Chr 25.23 from Ephraim Gate to the **Corner** Gate, a distance of nearly
26. 9 by building towers at the **Corner** Gate, at the Valley Gate,
Jer 31.38 as my city, from Hananel Tower west to the **Corner** Gate.
Zech 14.10 the Benjamin Gate to the **Corner** Gate, where there had been

CORNERSTONE

Job 38. 6 Who laid the **corner-stone** of the world?
Is 28.16 I am putting a solid **cornerstone** on which are written the words,
Eph 2.20 laid by the apostles and prophets, the **cornerstone** being Christ
1 Pet 2. 6 valuable stone, which I am placing as the **cornerstone** in Zion;

CORNFIELD

Deut 23.25 a path in someone else's **cornfield,** you may eat all the corn
Judg 15. 5 and turned the foxes loose in the Philistine **cornfields.**
Hag 1.11 the land—on its hills, **cornfields,** vineyards, and olive
Mt 12. 1 Jesus was walking through some **cornfields** on the Sabbath.
Mk 2.23 Jesus was walking through some **cornfields** on the Sabbath.
Lk 6. 1 Jesus was walking through some **cornfields** on the Sabbath.

CORPSE

Lev 10. 5 clothing on the **corpses** and carried them outside the camp,
22. 4 unclean through contact with a **corpse** or if he has an
Num 5. 2 and everyone who is unclean by contact with a **corpse.**
6. 6 himself by going near a **corpse,** not even that of his father,
6.11 purification for him because of his contact with a **corpse.**
9. 6 because they had touched a **corpse,** and they were not able to
9. 7* because we have touched a **corpse,** but why should we be
9.10 are unclean from touching a **corpse** or are far away on a
14.29 You will die and your **corpses** will be scattered across this wilderness.
19.11 Whoever touches a **corpse** is ritually unclean for seven days.
19.13 Whoever touches a **corpse** and does not purify himself remains unclean,
31.19 anyone or have touched a **corpse** must stay outside the camp
1 Sam 31. 8 Philistines went to plunder the **corpses,** and they found the
2 Sam 21.10 on the rock where the **corpses** were, and she stayed there
21.10 the birds away from the **corpses,** and at night she would
2 Kgs 13.21 the people threw the **corpse** into Elisha's tomb and ran off.
1 Chr 10. 8 Philistines went to plunder the **corpses,** and they found the
Job 15.23 kill him, [23]and vultures are waiting to eat his **corpse.**
Ps 110. 6 on the nations and fill the battlefield with **corpses;**
Is 14.19 you have no tomb, and your **corpse** is thrown out to rot.
18. 6 The **corpses** of their soldiers will be left exposed to the
34. 3 Their **corpses** will not be buried, but will lie there
Jer 7.33 The **corpses** will be food for the birds and wild animals,
16.18 that are as lifeless as **corpses,** and have filled it with
19. 7 I will give their **corpses** to the birds and the wild animals
33. 5 fill the houses with the **corpses** of those whom I am going
34.20 to kill them, and their **corpses** will be eaten by birds and
36.30 Your **corpse** will be thrown out where it will be exposed to
Ezek 6. 5 I will scatter the **corpses** of the people of Israel;
6.13 **Corpses** will be scattered among the idols and round the altars,
9. 7 Fill its courtyards with **corpses.**
11. 6 here in the city that the streets are full of **corpses.**
11. 7 The **corpses** of those you have killed!
30.11 Egypt with swords, and the land will be full of **corpses.**
32. 5 I will cover mountains and valleys with your rotting **corpse.**
35. 8 will cover the mountains with **corpses,** and the bodies of
39.12 to bury all the **corpses** and make the land clean again.
43. 7 gods or by burying the **corpses** of their kings in this place.
43. 9 other gods and remove the **corpses** of their kings.
44.25 ritually unclean by touching a **corpse,** unless it is one of
Nah 3. 3 **Corpses** are piled high, dead bodies without number— men
Mt 23.27 but are full of bones and decaying **corpses** on the inside.
Mk 9.26 The boy looked like a **corpse,** and everyone said, "He is dead!"

CORRECT

Deut 8. 5 that the Lord your God **corrects** and punishes you just as a
Job 5.17 Happy is the person whom God **corrects!**
33.19 God **corrects** a man by sending sickness and filling his
Ps 50.17 You refuse to let me **correct** you;
Prov 1.25 my advice and have not been willing to let me **correct** you.
1.30 wanted my advice or paid any attention when I **corrected** you.
3.11 When the Lord **corrects** you, my son, pay close attention
3.12 The Lord **corrects** those he loves, as a father corrects a
5.12 Why would I never let anyone **correct** me?
6.23 their **correction** can teach you how to live.
9. 7 If you **correct** a conceited man, you will only be insulted.
9. 8 Never **correct** a conceited man;
9. 8 But if you **correct** a wise man, he will respect you.
10.17 who listen when they are **corrected** will live, but those who

Prov 12. 1 It is stupid to hate being **corrected.**
13. 1 pays attention when his father **corrects** him, but an arrogant
13.18 Anyone who listens to **correction** is respected.
13.24 If you do love him, you will **correct** him.
15. 5 it is wise to accept his **correction.**
15.10 you will die if you do not let yourself be **corrected.**
15.12 Conceited people do not like to be **corrected;**
15.31 If you pay attention when you are **corrected,** you are
15.32 If you accept **correction,** you will become wiser.
19.25 If you are wise, you will learn when you are **corrected.**
27. 5 Better to **correct** someone openly than to let him think you
28.23 **Correct** someone, and afterwards he will appreciate it more than flattery.
29. 1 stubborn every time you are **corrected,** one day you will be
29.15 **Correction** and discipline are good for children.
29.19 You cannot **correct** a servant just by talking to him.
Jer 2.30 you would not let me **correct** you.
10.24 **Correct** your people, Lord;
Acts 18.25 he proclaimed and taught **correctly** the facts about Jesus.
18.26 them and explained to him more **correctly** the Way of God.
2 Tim 2.15 work, one who **correctly** teaches the message of God's truth.
2.25 who is gentle as he **corrects** his opponents, for it may
3.16 rebuking error, **correcting** faults, and giving instruction
Heb 12. 5 pay attention when the Lord **corrects** you, and do not be
12. 6 the Lord **corrects** everyone he loves, and punishes everyone

CORRESPONDENCE

Neh 6.17 the Jewish leaders had been in **correspondence** with Tobiah.

CORRIDOR

Ezek 41.15 to the west, including its **corridors** on both sides, and it

CORRODE

Ezek 24. 6 It is like a **corroded** pot that is never cleaned.
24.11 ritually pure again after the **corrosion** is burnt off,
24.12 although all that **corrosion** will not disappear in the flames.

CORRUPT

Deut 9.12 led out of Egypt, have become **corrupt** and have done evil.
32.32 Their enemies, **corrupt** as Sodom and Gomorrah, are like
2 Chr 24. 7 (The followers of Athaliah, that **corrupt** woman, had
Job 15.16 yes, man is **corrupt;**
Ps 14. 1 They are all **corrupt,** and they have done terrible things;
53. 1 They are all **corrupt,** and they have done terrible things;
82. 5 You are completely **corrupt,** and justice has disappeared
94.20 nothing to do with **corrupt** judges, who make injustice legal,
109. 6 Choose some **corrupt** judge to try my enemy, and let one of
Prov 17.23 **Corrupt** judges accept secret bribes, and then justice is not done.
Is 1. 4 You are doomed, you sinful nation, you **corrupt** and evil people!
1.13 they are all **corrupted** by your sins.
Jer 6.28 They are all **corrupt,** going round and spreading gossip.
Ezek 16.51 Your **corruption** makes your sisters look innocent by comparison.
28.18 and selling that your places of worship were **corrupted.**
37.23 disgusting idols any more or **corrupt** themselves with sin.
Zeph 3. 1 Jerusalem is doomed, that **corrupt,** rebellious city
Lk 18. 6 the Lord continued, "Listen to what that **corrupt** judge said.
Rom 1.28 has given them over to **corrupted** minds, so that they do the
2 Cor 11. 3 that your minds will be **corrupted** and that you will abandon
Phil 2.15 children, who live in a world of **corrupt** and sinful people.
Tit 3.11 that such a person is **corrupt,** and his sins prove that he
Jas 1.27 and to keep oneself from being **corrupted** by the world.
2 Pet 2.20 people have escaped from the **corrupting** forces of the world
Rev 19. 2 the prostitute who was **corrupting** the earth with her immorality.

COSMIC

Eph 6.12 the rulers, authorities, and **cosmic** powers of this dark age.

COST

Num 11. 5 to eat all the fish we wanted, and it **cost** us nothing.
Deut 15.18 you for six years at half the **cost** of a hired servant.
2 Sam 24.24 to the Lord my God sacrifices that have **cost** me nothing."
2 Kgs 6.25 severe that a donkey's head **cost** eighty pieces of silver,
6.25 two hundred grammes of dove's dung **cost** five pieces of silver.
1 Chr 21.24 Lord something that belongs to you, something that **costs** me nothing."
2 Chr 25. 6 from Israel at a **cost** of about 3,400 kilogrammes of silver.
Neh 7.70 contributed to help pay the **cost** of restoring the Temple:
Ps 15. 4 does what he promises, no matter how much it may **cost.**
Prov 6.26 a loaf of bread, but adultery will **cost** him all he has.
Is 55. 1 Buy wine and milk— it will **cost** you nothing!
Lk 14.28 works out what it will **cost,** to see if he has enough
1 Pet 1.19 it was the **costly** sacrifice of Christ, who was like a

COSY

Is 47.14 too hot for them, not a **cosy** fire to warm themselves by.

COTTON

Esth 1. 6 decorated with blue and white **cotton** curtains, tied by cords

COUCH

Esth 1. 6 **Couches** made of gold and silver had been placed in the courtyard,
7. 8 thrown himself down on Esther's **couch** to beg for mercy, when
Song 1.12 king was lying on his **couch,** and my perfume filled the air
Ezek 23.41 would sit on a beautiful **couch,** and in front of them they
Amos 3.12 of Samaria's people, who now recline on luxurious **couches.**
6. 4 out on your luxurious **couches,** feasting on veal and lamb!

COUNCIL

In the New Testament the word refers to the highest religious court of the Jews. It was made up of seventy leaders of the Jewish people. Its president was the High Priest.

Ps 82. 1 God presides in the heavenly **council;**
89. 7 You are feared in the **council** of the holy ones;
107.32 people and praise him before the **council** of the leaders.
Ecc 9.17 than to the shouts of a ruler at a **council** of fools.
Mt 5.22 will be brought before the **Council,** and whoever calls his brother
26.59 priests and the whole **Council** tried to find some false evidence
Mk 14.55 chief priests and the whole **Council** tried to find some evidence
15. 1 of the Law, and the whole **Council,** and made their plans.
15.42 respected member of the **Council,** who was waiting for the coming
Lk 22.66 Law met together, and Jesus was brought before the **Council.**
23.50 was a member of the **Council,** he had not agreed with their
Jn 11.47 priests met with the **Council** and said, "What shall we do?
Acts 4.13 The members of the **Council** were amazed to see how bold
4.15 them to leave the **Council** room, and then they started discussing
4.21 the **Council** warned them even more strongly and then set them
5.21 all the Jewish elders for a full meeting of the **Council;**
5.22 they returned to the **Council** and reported, [23] "When we arrived
5.27 made them stand before the **Council,** and the High Priest
5.33 the members of the **Council** heard this, they were so furious
5.34 highly respected by all the people, stood up in the **Council.**
5.35 said to the **Council,** "Fellow-Israelites, be careful what you do
5.39 The **Council** followed Gamaliel's advice.
5.41 As the apostles left the **Council,** they were happy,
6.12 They seized Stephen and took him before the **Council.**
6.15 All those sitting in the **Council** fixed their eyes on Stephen
7.54 the members of the **Council** listened to Stephen, they became
7.57 the members of the **Council** covered their ears with their hands.
17.19 brought him before the city **council,** the Areopagus, and said,
17.22 in front of the city **council** and said, "I see that in
17.34 and believed, among whom was Dionysius, a member of the **council;**
22. 5 High Priest and the whole **Council** can prove that I am
22.30 and ordered the chief priests and the whole **Council** to meet.
23. 1 Paul looked straight at the **Council** and said,
23. 6 he called out in the **Council,** "Fellow-Israelites!
23.15 Now then, you and the **Council** send word to the Roman
23.20 take Paul down to the **Council,** pretending that
23.20 the **Council** wants to get more accurate information
23.28 were accusing him of, so I took him down to their **Council.**
24.20 when I stood before the **Council**—[21] except for the one thing

COUNSEL

1 Chr 27.33 and Hushai the Archite was the king's friend and **counsellor.**
Ezra 7.14 I, together with my seven **counsellors,** send you to
7.15 offerings which I and my **counsellors** desire to give to the
7.28 of his **counsellors,** and of all his powerful officials;
Is 9. 6 He will be called, "Wonderful **Counsellor,**" "Mighty God,"
Jer 18.18 to give us **counsel,** and prophets to proclaim God's message.
Mic 4. 9 Is it because you have no king, and your **counsellors** are dead?

COUNT

Gen 13.16 many descendants that no one will be able to **count** them all;
13.16 would be as easy to **count** all the specks of dust on
15. 5 and said, "Look at the sky and try to **count** the stars;
16.10 so many descendants that no one will be able to **count** them.
32.12 more descendants than anyone could **count,** as many as the
Ex 30.14 Everyone being **counted** in the census, that is, every man
Lev 7.18 The offering will not be **counted** to his credit but will be
23.15 **Count** seven full weeks from the day after the Sabbath on
25. 8 **Count** seven times seven years, a total of forty-nine years.
25.50 bought him, and they must **count** the years from the time he
27.32 When the animals are **counted,** every tenth one belongs to the Lord.
Num 1.18 were recorded and **counted,** [19] as the Lord had commanded.
23.10 the dust— There are too many of them to be **counted.**
31.26 community, are to **count** everything that has been captured,
31.49 and reported, "Sir, we have **counted** the soldiers under
Deut 16. 9 **"Count** seven weeks from the time that you begin to
Judg 6. 5 They and their camels were too many to **count.**
1 Sam 14.17 Saul said to his men, **"Count** the soldiers and find out who
18.27 foreskins to the king and **counted** them all out to him, so
2 Sam 4. 2 (Beeroth is **counted** as part of Benjamin.
24. 1 to him, "Go and **count** the people of Israel and Judah."
24. 2 one end of the country to the other, and **count** the people.
24. 4 his presence and went out to **count** the people of Israel.
1 Kgs 3. 8 own, a people who are so many that they cannot be **counted.**
8. 5 a large number of sheep and cattle—too many to **count.**
1 Chr 21. 2 one end of the country to the other, and **count** the people.
23.10 have many descendants, so they were **counted** as one clan.
2 Chr 1. 9 many that they cannot be **counted,** [10] so give me the wisdom
5. 6 a large number of sheep and cattle—too many to **count.**
12. 3 could be **counted,** including Libyan, Sukkite, and Sudanese troops.
Ezra 8.34 Everything was **counted** and weighed, and a complete
Job 3. 6 night out of the year, and never let it be **counted** again;
25. 3 Can anyone **count** the angels who serve him?
27.16 much silver to **count** and more clothes than anyone needs;
36.26 fully know his greatness or **count** the number of his years.
38.37 Who is wise enough to **count** the clouds and tilt them
Ps 40.12 I am surrounded by many troubles— too many to **count!**

Ps 48.12 People of God, walk round Zion and **count** the towers;
104.25 where **countless** creatures live, large and small alike.
105.34 He commanded, and the locusts came, **countless** millions of them;
139.18 If I **counted** them, they would be more than the grains of
Prov 7.26 of many men and caused the death of too many to **count.**
Ecc 1.15 you can't **count** things that aren't there.
Is 10.19 trees left that even a child will be able to **count** them.
Jer 2.32 people have forgotten me for more days than can be **counted.**
33.13 towns of Judah, shepherds will once again **count** their sheep.
33.22 will be as impossible to **count** them
33.22 as it is to **count** the stars in the sky or
46.23 Their men are too many to **count;**
Hos 1.10 the sand of the sea, more than can be **counted** or measured.
8.12 I write down **countless** teachings for the people, but
Joel 1. 6 they are powerful and too many to **count;**
Mt 10.30 for you, even the hairs of your head have all been **counted.**
26.15 They **counted** out thirty silver coins and gave them to him.
Lk 12. 7 Even the hairs of your head have all been **counted.**
Phil 3. 7 those things that I might **count** as profit I now reckon as
2 Tim 4.16 May God not **count** it against them!
Rev 7. 9 was an enormous crowd—no one could **count** all the people!
11. 1 God and the altar, and **count** those who are worshipping in

COUNTRY

see also **COUNTRYMAN, COUNTRYSIDE**

Gen 2.11 it flows round the **country** of Havilah.
2.13 it flows round the **country** of Cush.
10. 5 tribes and **countries,** each group speaking its own language.
10.20 tribes and **countries,** each group speaking its own language.
10.31 tribes and **countries,** each group speaking its own language.
12. 1 "Leave your **country,** your relatives, and your father's home,
12. 7 to him, "This is the **country** that I am going to give
12.20 put him out of the **country,** together with his wife and
21.23 loyal to me and to this **country** in which you are living."
24. 4 must go back to the **country** where I was born and get
26.16 Then Abimelech said to Isaac, "Leave our **country.**
26.27 unfriendly to me before and made me leave your **country?"**
27. 3 arrows, go out into the **country,** and kill an animal for me.
32. 3 ahead of him to his brother Esau in the **country** of Edom.
34.10 Then you may stay here in our **country** with us;
36.31 in a battle in the **country** of Moab) Samlah from Masrekah
37.15 was wandering about in the **country** when a man saw him and
41.30 will be forgotten, because the famine will ruin the **country.**
41.33 wisdom and insight and put him in charge of the **country.**
41.36 a reserve supply for the **country** during the seven years of
41.40 you in charge of my **country,** and all my people will obey
41.54 in every other **country,** but there was food throughout Egypt.
41.56 and spread over the whole **country,** so Joseph opened all the
42. 9 you have come to find out where our **country** is weak."
42.12 You have come to find out where our **country** is weak."
42.30 harshly to us and accused us of spying against his **country.**
45. 8 I am in charge of his whole **country;**
47. 4 come to live in this **country,** because in the land of Canaan
Ex 1.10 to fight against us, and might escape from the **country.**
3.10 Egypt so that you can lead my people out of his **country."**
7. 2 will tell the king to let the Israelites leave his **country.**
7. 5 them and bring the Israelites out of their **country."**
8. 2 I will punish your **country** by covering it with frogs.
8.25 "Go and offer sacrifices to your God here in this **country."**
10. 4 then I will bring locusts into your **country** tomorrow.
10.14 They came in swarms and settled over the whole **country.**
11.10 and he would not let the Israelites leave his **country.**
12.31 Leave my **country;**
12.33 The Egyptians urged the people to hurry and leave the **country;**
14. 3 are wandering about in the **country** and are closed in by the
20.10 your animals, nor the foreigners who live in your **country.**
23.33 Do not let those people live in your **country;**
34.12 with the people of the **country** into which you are going,
34.15 with the people of the **country,** because when they worship
34.24 try to conquer your **country** during the three festivals.
Lev 17. 5 Lord the animals which they used to kill in the open **country.**
Num 13.18 Find out what kind of **country** it is, how many people
20.18 Edomites answered, "We refuse to let you pass through our **country!**
32.33 King Og of Bashan, including the towns and the **country** round them.
Deut 2.27 'Let us pass through your **country.**
2.28 is to pass through your **country,** [29] until we cross the
2.30 "But King Sihon would not let us pass through his **country.**
5.14 your animals, nor the foreigners who live in your **country.**
11. 3 he did to the king of Egypt and to his entire **country.**
28.37 In the **countries** to which the Lord will scatter you, the
29. 2 king of Egypt, to his officials, and to his entire **country.**
31. 4 Sihon and Og, kings of the Amorites, and destroyed their **country.**
34.11 the king of Egypt, his officials, and the entire **country.**
Josh 1. 4 the east, through the Hittite **country,** to the Mediterranean
2. 2 night to spy out the **country,** [3] so he sent word to Rahab:
2. 3 men in your house have come to spy out the whole **country!**
2. 9 Everyone in the **country** is terrified of you.
2.24 "We are sure that the Lord has given us the whole **country.**
6.27 Lord was with Joshua, and his fame spread through the whole **country.**
7. 9 The Canaanites and everyone else in the **country** will hear about it.
8.15 were retreating, and ran away towards the barren **country.**
8.20 towards the barren **country** now turned round to attack them.
8.24 the enemy in the barren **country** where they had chased them.
10.40 foothills, as well as those of the dry **country** in the south.
11.16 of Goshen and the dry **country** south of it, as well as
12. 8 the eastern slopes, and the dry **country** in the south.
Josh 13. 4 is still all the Canaanite **country,** and Mearah (which
15.19 The land you have given me is in the dry **country."**
18. 4 them out over the whole **country** to map out the territory
Judg 1. 9 in the foothills, and in the dry **country** to the south.
1.15 The land you have given me is in the dry **country."**
1.16 palm-trees, into the barren **country** south of Arad in Judah.
10. 8 Israelites who lived in Amorite **country** east of the River
11.12 Why have you invaded my **country?"**
11.19 for permission to go through his **country** to their own land.
11.21 all the territory of the Amorites who lived in that **country.**
18.10 It is a big **country;**
18.14 to explore the **country** round Laish said to their companions,
20.31 some Israelites in the open **country** on the road to Bethel
20.33 of their hiding places in the rocky **country** round the city.
20.42 ran towards the open **country,** but they could not escape.
20.45 and ran towards the open **country** to the Rock of Rimmon.
20.47 to escape to the open **country** to the Rock of Rimmon, and
Ruth 1. 1 and Chilion to live for a while in the **country** of Moab.
2.11 and mother and your own **country** and how you came to live
1 Sam 3.20 from one end of the **country** to the other, knew that Samuel
6. 5 mice that are ravaging your **country,** and you must give
8. 5 us, so that we will have a king, as other **countries** have."
13. 3 Hebrews to war by blowing a trumpet throughout the whole **country.**
20.31 as David is alive, you will never be king of this **country?**
21.11 said to Achish, "Isn't this David, the king of his **country?**
23.27 The Philistines are invading the **country!"**
25.10 The **country** is full of runaway slaves nowadays!
26.19 the Lord's land to a **country** where I can only worship
30.11 an Egyptian boy out in the **country** and brought him to David.
2 Sam 1.13 He answered, "I'm an Amalekite, but I live in your **country."**
3. 9 Israel and Judah, from one end of the **country** to the other.
15.19 You are a foreigner, a refugee away from your own **country.**
17.11 from one end of the **country** to the other, as many as
19. 9 All over the **country** they started quarrelling among themselves.
19. 9 but now he has fled from Absalom and left the **country.**
21.14 And after that, God answered their prayers for the **country.**
24. 2 from one end of the **country** to the other, and count the
24. 8 to Jerusalem, having travelled through the whole **country.**
24.15 From one end of the **country** to the other seventy thousand
1 Kgs 2.26 Abiathar the priest, "Go to your **country** home in Anathoth.
2.34 Joab, and he was buried at his home in the open **country.**
4.24 and he was at peace with all the neighbouring **countries.**
4.31 his fame spread throughout all the neighbouring **countries.**
5. 3 to fight against the enemy **countries** all round him, he could
10. 6 I heard in my own **country** about you and your wisdom is
11.21 said to the king, "Let me go back to my own **country."**
11.21 And he went back to his **country.**
11.29 from Shiloh, met him alone on the road in the open **country.**
14.11 any who die in the open **country** will be eaten by vultures.
14.24 of the land as the Israelites advanced into the **country.**
15.12 He expelled from the **country** all the male and female
16. 4 who die in the open **country** will be eaten by vultures."
18.10 has made a search for you in every **country** in the world.
18.10 Whenever the ruler of a **country** reported that
18.10 you were not in his **country,** Ahab would require that ruler
20. 7 all the leaders of the **country** and said, "You see that this
21.24 who die in the open **country** will be eaten by vultures."
22.36 "Every man go back to his own **country** and city!"
2 Kgs 1. 1 King Ahab of Israel, the **country** of Moab rebelled against Israel.
3.27 drew back from the city and returned to their own **country.**
15. 5 of all duties, while his son Jotham governed the **country.**
15.19 support in strengthening Menahem's power over the **country.**
15.20 So Tiglath Pileser went back to his own **country.**
17.33 to the customs of the **countries** from which they had come.
18.25 think I have attacked your **country** and destroyed it without
18.32 emperor resettles you in a **country** much like your own, where
18.33 nations save their **countries** from the emperor of Assyria?
18.35 the gods of all these **countries** ever save their country from
19. 7 go back to his own **country,** and the Lord will have him
19.11 Assyrian emperor does to any **country** he decides to destroy.
20.14 "They came from a very distant **country,** from Babylonia."
23. 8 Judah, and throughout the whole **country** he desecrated the
1 Chr 1.43 the Midianites in a battle in the **country** of Moab)
4.40 in a stretch of open **country** that was quiet and peaceful.
5.26 Emperor Pul of Assyria (also known as Tiglath Pileser) invade their **country.**
8. 8 when he lived in the **country** of Moab, he married Hodesh and
12.40 of the joy that was felt throughout the whole **country.**
13. 5 Israel from all over the **country,** from the Egyptian border
14. 8 made king over the whole **country** of Israel, their army went
16.20 They wandered from **country** to country, from one kingdom to another.
21. 2 from one end of the **country** to the other, and count the
21. 4 out, travelled through the whole **country** of Israel, and then
2 Chr 9. 5 I heard in my own **country** about you and your wisdom is
9.28 Solomon imported horses from Musri and from every other **country.**
20. 3 orders for a fast to be observed throughout the **country.**
20.16 of the valley that leads to the wild **country** near Jeruel.
20.20 morning the people went out to the wild **country** near Tekoa.
26.10 fortified towers in the open **country** and dug many cisterns,
26.21 of all duties, while his son Jotham governed the **country.**
32.14 gods of all those countries ever save their **country** from us?
32.22 He let the people live in peace with all the neighbouring **countries.**
Ezra 9. 1 the people in the neighbouring **countries** of Ammon, Moab, and
Job 1.10 you have given him enough cattle to fill the whole **country.**
Ps 44.11 you scattered us in foreign **countries.**
79. 7 they have ruined your **country.**
105.13 They wandered from **country** to country, from one kingdom to another.

Ps 105.16 Lord sent famine to their **country** and took away all their food.
105.23 Then Jacob went to Egypt and settled in that **country.**
105.28 God sent darkness on the **country,** but the Egyptians did
105.30 Their **country** was overrun with frogs, even the palace
105.31 God commanded, and flies and gnats swarmed throughout the whole **country.**
106.27 among the heathen, letting them die in foreign **countries.**
107. 3 brought you back from foreign **countries,** from east and west,
Prov 29. 4 he is only concerned with money, he will ruin his **country.**
Ecc 4.13 to become king of his **country,** or go from prison to the
10.16 A **country** is in trouble when its king is a youth and
10.17 But a **country** is fortunate to have a king who makes his
Is 1. 7 Your **country** has been devastated, and your cities have
5.30 Look at this **country!**
7.24 the whole **country** will be full of briars and thorn-bushes.
9.20 Everywhere in the **country** people snatch and eat any bit
10. 3 do when he brings disaster on you from a distant **country?**
10.23 whole **country** the Sovereign Lord Almighty will bring destruction,
13. 5 They are coming from far-off **countries** at the ends of the earth.
13. 5 In his anger the Lord is coming to devastate the whole **country.**
13.14 own **countries,** scattering like deer escaping from hunters,
14.20 Because you ruined your **country** and killed your own people,
16. 4 end, and those who are devastating the **country** will be gone.
19.23 The people of those two **countries** will travel to and fro
20. 4 naked the prisoners he captures from those two **countries.**
21.13 caravans camp in the barren **country** of Arabia, [14]give
22.18 up like a ball and throw you into a much larger **country.**
28.22 I have heard the Lord Almighty's decision to destroy the whole **country.**
30. 6 "The ambassadors travel through dangerous **country,** where
34. 9 The whole **country** will burn like tar.
34.12 no king to rule the **country,** and the leaders will all be
36.10 think I have attacked your **country** and destroyed it without
36.17 emperor resettles you in a **country** much like your own, where
36.18 nations save their **countries** from the emperor of Assyria?
36.20 the gods of all these **countries** ever save their country from
37. 7 go back to his own **country,** and the Lord will have him
37.11 Assyrian emperor does to any **country** he decides to destroy.
39. 3 "They came from a very distant **country,** from Babylonia."
40. 4 become a plain, and the rough **country** will be made smooth.
42.16 into light and make rough **country** smooth before them.
49.19 "Your **country** was ruined and desolate— but now it will
60.18 Destruction will not shatter your **country** again.
Jer 2. 7 they defiled the **country** I had given them.
3.18 come from exile in the **country** in the north and will return
4.16 Jerusalem that enemies are coming from a **country** far away.
4.20 the whole **country** is left in ruins.
6.22 The Lord says, "People are coming from a **country** in the north;
10.25 they have destroyed us completely and left our **country** in ruins.
12. 5 even stand up in open **country,** how will you manage in the
12.14 people away from their **countries** like an uprooted plant,
12.15 each nation back to its own land and to its own **country.**
16.15 out of all the other **countries** where I had scattered them.
16.15 them back to their own **country,** to the land that I gave
17. 3 on the hill-tops [3]and on the mountains in the open **country.**
20. 4 away as prisoners to his **country** and put others to death.
22.12 He will die in the **country** where they have taken him,
22.26 You will go to a **country** where neither of you was born,
22.27 to see this **country** again, but you will never return."
23. 3 of my people from the **countries** where I have scattered them,
23. 8 out of all the other **countries** where I had scattered them.
25.12 I will destroy that **country** and leave it in ruins for ever.
25.36 your nation and left your peaceful **country** in ruins.
25.38 Lord's fierce anger have turned the **country** into a desert.
27.10 and will cause you to be taken far away from your **country.**
29.14 will gather you from every **country** and from every place to
32.37 the people from all the **countries** where I have scattered
35.11 when King Nebuchadnezzar invaded the **country,** we decided to
37.19 the king of Babylonia would not attack you or the **country?**
40. 4 You have the whole **country** to choose from, and you may go
40.11 Moab, Ammon, Edom, and other **countries,** heard that the king
44. 1 and Memphis, and in the southern part of the **country.**
49.19 and make the Edomites run away suddenly from their **country.**
49.34 the Lord Almighty spoke to me about the **country** of Elam.
49.36 until there is no **country** where her refugees have not gone.
50. 8 Leave the **country!**
50. 9 They will line up in battle against the **country** and conquer it.
50.16 seeds be sown in that **country** or let a harvest be gathered.
50.18 punish King Nebuchadnezzar and his **country,** just as I
50.23 All the nations are shocked at what has happened to that **country.**
50.26 Destroy the **country!**
50.41 "People are coming from a **country** in the north, a
51.13 That **country** has many rivers and rich treasures, but its
51.28 officials, and the armies of all the **countries** they control.
51.37 That **country** will become a pile of ruins where wild animals live.
51.47 The whole **country** will be put to shame, and all its people
51.52 Babylon's idols, and the wounded will groan throughout the **country.**
Ezek 4.13 Law forbids, when I scatter them to foreign **countries."**
5. 5 the centre of the world, with other **countries** all round her.
5. 6 nations, more disobedient than the **countries** around her.
6.14 Yes, I will stretch out my hand and destroy their **country.**
7.15 who is out in the **country** will die in the fighting, and
8.12 He has abandoned the **country.'"**
8.17 here and with spreading violence throughout the **country.**
9. 9 have abandoned their **country** and that I don't see them.
11.10 and you will be killed in battle in your own **country.**
11.16 in far-off nations and scattered them in other **countries.**
11.17 gather them out of the **countries** where I scattered them, and
12.15 other nations and in foreign **countries,** they will know that
12.20 be destroyed, and the **country** will be made a wilderness.
Ezek 14.13 man," he said, "if a **country** sins and is unfaithful to me,
14.17 might bring war on that **country** and send destructive weapons
14.19 send an epidemic on that **country** and in my anger take many
15. 8 to me, and so I will make the **country** a wilderness."
20.32 who live in other **countries** and worship trees and rocks.
20.34 back from all the **countries** where you have been scattered.
20.41 bring you out of the **countries** where you have been scattered
21.19 Both of them are to start in the same **country.**
21.32 be shed in your own **country,** and no one will remember you
22. 4 let the nations mock you and all the **countries** sneer at you.
22. 5 **Countries** near by and countries far away sneer at you
22.15 scatter your people to every **country** and nation and will put
25. 2 "Mortal man," he said, "denounce the **country** of Ammon.
25. 4 They will set up their camps in your **country** and settle there.
25. 5 keep camels, and the whole **country** of Ammon into a place to
25. 7 be a nation any more or have a **country** of your own.
29.12 I will make Egypt the most desolate **country** in the world.
29.12 They will flee to every **country** and live among other peoples."
30. 4 The **country** will be plundered And left in ruins.
30.12 Foreigners will devastate the whole **country.**
31.12 will fall on every mountain and valley in the **country.**
32. 9 of your destruction through **countries** you never heard of.
33. 2 The people of that **country** choose one of their number to be
33.27 Those living in the **country** will be eaten by wild animals.
33.28 I will make the **country** a desolate waste, and the power
33.29 their sins and make the **country** a waste, then they will know
34.13 take them out of foreign **countries,** gather them together,
35. 2 "Mortal man," he said, "denounce the **country** of Edom.
36.19 and acted, and I scattered them through foreign **countries.**
36.22 you have disgraced in every **country** where you have gone.
36.24 you from every nation and **country** and bring you back to your
38. 8 order him to invade a **country** where the people were brought
38.11 decide to invade a helpless **country** where the people live in
39.15 go up and down the **country,** every time they find a human
39.27 people back from all the **countries** where their enemies live.
45. 4 a holy part of the **country,** set aside for the priests who
45. 7 the eastern border of the **country,** so that its length will
45. 8 let the rest of the **country** belong to the tribes of Israel.
Dan 9. 7 Israelites whom you scattered in **countries** near and far
9.16 the people in the neighbouring **countries** look down on
11.40 He will invade many **countries,** like the waters of a flood.
11.41 tens of thousands, but the **countries** of Edom, Moab, and what
11.42 When he invades all those **countries,** even Egypt will not be spared.
Joel 3. 2 the Israelites in foreign **countries** and divided up Israel,
3. 6 Jerusalem far from their own **country** and sold them to the Greeks.
Amos 6.14 I am going to send a foreign army to occupy your **country.**
7.10 His speeches will destroy the **country.**
7.17 to others, and you yourself will die in a heathen **country.**
8. 4 on the needy and try to destroy the poor of the **country.**
8. 8 The whole **country** will be shaken;
Obad 7 they have driven you from your **country.**
Jon 1. 8 What **country** do you come from?
Mic 1. 6 ruins in the open **country,** a place for planting grapevines.
4.10 will have to leave the city and live in the open **country.**
5. 5 When the Assyrians invade our **country** and break through our defences,
Nah 3.13 and your **country** stands defenceless before your enemies.
Zech 6. 6 the dappled horses were going to the **country** in the south.
7.14 Like a storm I swept them away to live in foreign **countries.**
10.10 I will bring them home and settle them in their own **country.**
Mal 1. 4 will call them 'The evil **country'** and 'The nation with whom
2.11 done a horrible thing in Jerusalem and all over the **country.**
4. 6 otherwise I would have to come and destroy your **country."**
Mt 2.12 Then they returned to their **country** by another road,
3. 5 of Judaea, and from all the **country** near the River Jordan.
4.24 spread through the whole **country** of Syria, so that people brought
9.26 The news about this spread all over that part of the **country.**
9.31 the news about Jesus all over that part of the **country.**
12.25 said to them, "Any **country** that divides itself into groups
12.42 all the way from her **country** to listen to King Solomon's
12.43 it travels over dry **country** looking for a place to rest.
14.35 in all the surrounding **country** and brought them to Jesus.
17.25 The citizens of the **country** or the foreigners?"
23.15 You sail the seas and cross whole **countries** to win one convert;
24. 7 **Countries** will fight each other, kingdoms will attack one another.
27.45 At noon the whole **country** was covered with darkness,
Mk 3.24 If a **country** divides itself into groups which fight each other,
3.24 that **country** will fall apart.
13. 8 **Countries** will fight each other;
15.21 into the city from the **country,** and the soldiers forced him
15.33 At noon the whole **country** was covered with darkness,
16.12 two of them while they were on their way to the **country.**
Lk 2. 8 in that part of the **country** who were spending the night in
4.44 So he preached in the synagogues throughout the **country.**
7.17 about Jesus went out through all the **country** and the surrounding
11.17 said to them, "Any **country** that divides itself into groups
11.24 it travels over dry **country** looking for a place to rest.
11.31 all the way from her **country** to listen to King Solomon's
14.23 'Go out to the **country** roads and lanes and make people
15.13 He went to a **country** far away, where he wasted his money
15.14 severe famine spread over that **country,** and he was left without
15.15 of the citizens of that **country,** who sent him out to his
19.12 who was going to a **country** far away to be made king,
21.10 He went on to say, **"Countries** will fight each other;
21.21 who are out in the **country** must not go into the city.
21.24 and others will be taken as prisoners to all **countries;**
21.25 On earth whole **countries** will be in despair, afraid of the
23.26 Cyrene named Simon who was coming into the city from the **country.**

Lk 23.44 and darkness covered the whole **country** until three o'clock;
Jn 1.11 He came to his own **country,** but his own people did not
4.44 had said, "A prophet is not respected in his own **country."**
11.55 people went up from the **country** to Jerusalem to perform the
Acts 2. 5 religious men who had come from every **country** in the world.
7. 3 'Leave your family and **country** and go to the land that
7. 4 And so he left his **country** and went to live in Haran.
7. 6 will live in a foreign **country,** where they will be slaves
7. 7 will come out of that **country** and will worship me in this
7.10 made Joseph governor over the **country** and the royal household.
12.20 because their country got its food supplies from the king's **country.**
21.21 Jews who live in Gentile **countries** to abandon the Law of Moses,
24. 2 reforms are being made for the good of our **country.**
26. 4 life, at first in my own **country** and then in Jerusalem.
2 Cor 10.16 the Good News in other **countries** beyond you and shall not
Heb 11. 8 to go out to a **country** which God had promised to give
11. 8 He left his own **country** without knowing where he was going.
11. 9 as a foreigner in the **country** that God had promised him.
11.14 it clear that they are looking for a **country** of their own.
11.15 They did not keep thinking about the **country** they had left;
11.16 it was a better **country** they longed for, the heavenly country.
11.33 Through faith they fought whole **countries** and won.
Rev 16.19 and the cities of all **countries** were destroyed.

COUNTRYMAN

[FELLOW-COUNTRYMAN]

Judg 18. 8 to Zorah and Eshtaol, their **countrymen** asked them what they
2 Sam 2.26 We are your **fellow-countrymen.**
15.20 Go back and take your **fellow-countrymen** with you—and may the
1 Chr 12.39 drink which their **fellow-countrymen** had prepared for them.
13. 2 to the rest of our **countrymen** and to the priests and Levites
28. 2 "My **countrymen,** listen to me.
2 Chr 28. 8 though the Judaeans were their **fellow-countrymen,** the
Ezra 3. 8 of their **fellow-countrymen,** the priests, and the Levites,
7.18 for whatever you and your **fellow-countrymen** desire, in
Neh 4.14 is, and fight for your **fellow-countrymen,** your children,
Is 66.20 will bring back all your **fellow-countrymen** from the nations
Jer 22.13 who makes his **countrymen** work for nothing and does not pay
31.34 will have to teach his **fellow-countryman** to know the Lord,
38.19 "I am afraid of our **countrymen** who have deserted to the Babylonians.
Ezek 3.11 Then go to your **countrymen** who are in exile and tell
Mic 5. 3 Then his **fellow-countrymen** who are in exile will be reunited
7. 2 Everyone hunts down his **fellow-countryman.**
Lk 19.14 Now, his **countrymen** hated him, and so they sent
1 Thes 2.14 same persecutions from your own **countrymen** that they suffered from
Heb 7. 5 that is, from their own **countrymen,**
7. 5 even though their **countrymen** are also descendants of Abraham.
8.11 or say to his **fellow-countryman,** 'Know the Lord.'

COUNTRYSIDE

Deut 22.25 a man out in the **countryside** rapes a girl who is engaged
22.27 girl in the **countryside,** and although she cried for help,
Josh 2.22 for them all over the **countryside** for three days, but they
1 Sam 14.15 All the Philistines in the **countryside** were terrified;
2 Sam 10. 8 Tob and Maacah, took up their position in the open **countryside.**
18. 6 army went out into the **countryside** and fought the Israelites
18. 8 The fighting spread over the **countryside,** and more men
1 Kgs 20.27 with the Syrians, who spread out over the **countryside.**
2 Kgs 7.12 they have left their camp to go and hide in the **countryside.**
1 Chr 19. 9 to help took up their position in the open **countryside.**
2 Chr 17. 2 of Judah, in the Judaean **countryside,** and in the cities
Song 2.12 in the **countryside** the flowers are in bloom.
7.11 let's go out to the **countryside** and spend the night in the
Jer 6.25 dare not go to the **countryside** or walk on the roads, because
Lam 5. 9 Murderers roam through the **countryside;**

COUPLE

Judg 19. 4 The **couple** had their meals and spent the nights there.
2 Sam 16. 1 who had with him a **couple** of donkeys loaded with two hundred
1 Kgs 21.10 Get a **couple** of scoundrels to accuse him to his face of
Joel 2.16 Even newly married **couples** must leave their room and come.
1 Cor 7.36 the case of an engaged **couple** who have decided not to marry:

COURAGE

Ex 15.15 the people of Canaan lose their **courage.**
Deut 20. 3 Do not be afraid of your enemies, or lose **courage,** or panic.
31. 8 you or abandon you, so do not lose **courage** or be afraid."
Josh 2.11 we have all lost our **courage** because of you.
5. 1 They became afraid and lost their **courage** because of the Israelites.
7. 5 Then the Israelites lost their **courage** and were afraid.
Judg 7.11 are saying, and then you will have the **courage** to attack."
1 Sam 30. 6 but the Lord his God gave him **courage.**
2 Sam 7.27 I have the **courage** to pray this prayer to you, because you
10.12 Be strong and **courageous!**
22.46 They lose their **courage** and come trembling from their fortresses.
1 Chr 17.25 I have the **courage** to pray this prayer to you, my God,
19.13 Be strong and **courageous!**
2 Chr 19.11 Be **courageous** and carry out these instructions, and may the
25.11 Amaziah summoned up his **courage** and led his army to the
26.17 accompanied by eighty strong and **courageous** priests,
Ezra 7.28 my God has given me **courage,** and I have been able to
Job 11.15 Then face the world again, firm and **courageous.**
19.27 My **courage** failed because you said, [28]"How can we torment him?"
Job 23.16 Almighty God has destroyed my **courage.**
41. 9 Anyone who sees Leviathan loses **courage** and falls to the ground.
Ps 3. 3 you give me victory and restore my **courage.**
10.17 you will give them **courage.**
18.45 They lose their **courage** and come trembling from their fortresses.
31.24 Be strong, be **courageous,** all you that hope in the Lord.
40.12 than the hairs of my head, and I have lost my **courage.**
107.26 In such danger the men lost their **courage;**
Is 13. 7 Everyone's hands will hang limp, and everyone's **courage** will fail.
15. 4 their **courage** is gone.
19. 1 before him, and the people of Egypt lose their **courage.**
28. 6 who serve as judges, and **courage** to those who defend the
42. 4 He will not lose hope or **courage;**
Jer 4. 9 Lord said, "On that day kings and officials will lose their **courage;**
38. 4 in the city lose their **courage,** and he is doing the same
51.30 They have lost their **courage** and have become like women.
51.46 Do not lose **courage** or be afraid because of the rumours
Lam 1.16 no one can give me **courage.**
Ezek 21. 7 hands will hang limp, their **courage** will fail, and their
21.15 It makes my people lose **courage** and stumble.
22.14 think you will have any **courage** left or have strength enough
Mic 3. 8 sense of justice and the **courage** to tell the people of
Zech 8. 9 "Have **courage!**
8.13 So have **courage** and don't be afraid."
Mt 9. 2 he said to the paralysed man, **"Courage,** my son!
9.22 turned round and saw her, and said, **"Courage,** my daughter!
14.27 **"Courage!"**
Mk 6.50 Jesus spoke to them at once, **"Courage!"**
Acts 15.32 spoke a long time with them, giving them **courage** and strength.
2 Cor 5. 6 So we are always full of **courage.**
5. 8 We are full of **courage** and would much prefer to leave our
7. 4 In all our troubles I am still full of **courage;**
Phil 1.20 I shall be full of **courage,** so that with my whole being
1.28 always be **courageous,** and this will prove to them that they
Col 2. 2 they may be filled with **courage** and may be drawn together in
1 Thes 2. 2 our God gave us **courage** to tell you the Good News
2 Thes 2.16 his grace gave us unfailing **courage** and a firm hope,
Heb 3. 6 if we keep up our **courage** and our confidence in what we
10.35 Do not lose your **courage,** then, because it brings with it
1 Jn 2.28 we may be full of **courage** and need not hide in shame
3.21 conscience does not condemn us, we have **courage** in God's presence.
4.17 in us in order that we may have **courage** on Judgement Day;
5.14 We have **courage** in God's presence, because we are sure

COURSE

Mt 24.29 and the powers in space will be driven from their **courses.**
Mk 13.25 and the powers in space will be driven from their **courses.**
Lk 21.26 for the powers in space will be driven from their **courses.**
Jas 3. 6 sets on fire the entire **course** of our existence with the

COURT (1)

Gen 12.15 Some of the **court** officials saw her and told the king
41.45 He left the king's **court** and travelled all over the land.
50. 7 the senior men of his **court,** and all the leading men of
Ex 23. 6 not deny justice to a poor man when he appears in **court.**
Lev 5. 1 summoned to give evidence in **court** and does not give
Deut 22.15 and they are to show it in **court** to the town leaders.
25. 1 "Suppose two Israelites go to **court** to settle a dispute,
1 Sam 8.15 of your grapes for his **court** officers and other officials.
22.14 and highly respected by everyone in the royal **court.**
2 Sam 8.17 Seraiah was the **court** secretary;
12.17 His **court** officials went to him and tried to make him
20.25 Sheva was the **court** secretary;
1 Kgs 1.33 in, [33]he said to them, "Take my **court** officials with you;
1.47 What is more, the **court** officials went in to pay their
4. 3 The **court** secretaries: Elihoreph and Ahijah
22. 9 Then Ahab called in a **court** official and told him to go
2 Kgs 18.18 Shebna, the **court** secretary;
19. 2 of the palace, Shebna, the **court** secretary, and the senior
22. 3 reign, King Josiah sent the **court** secretary Shaphan, the son
22.12 of Micaiah, to Shaphan, the **court** secretary, and to Asaiah,
1 Chr 18.16 Seraiah was **court** secretary;
2 Chr 18. 8 King Ahab called in a **court** official and told him to go
19.11 of seeing that the decisions of the **courts** are carried out.
34.20 of Micaiah, to Shaphan, the **court** secretary, and to Asaiah,
Neh 11.24 represented the people of Israel at the Persian **court.**
Esth 1. 4 of the imperial **court** with all its splendour and majesty.
Job 5. 4 no one stands up to defend them in **court.**
9.19 Should I take him to **court?**
9.32 we could go to **court** to decide our quarrel.
13. 8 Are you going to argue his case in **court?**
31.21 I could win in **court,** [22]then may my arms be broken;
Ps 45. 9 Among the ladies of your **court** are daughters of kings, and
94.15 again be found in the **courts,** and all righteous people will
Prov 18.17 first man to speak in **court** always seems right until his
18.18 each other in **court,** casting lots can settle the issue.
19. 5 If you tell lies in **court,** you will be punished—there will
19. 9 No one who tells lies in **court** can escape punishment;
22.22 don't take advantage of those who stand helpless in **court.**
25. 1 copied by men at the **court** of King Hezekiah of Judah.
25. 8 be too quick to go to **court** about something you have seen.
29.24 he tells the truth in **court,** and God will curse him if
Is 1.23 They never defend orphans in **court** or listen when widows
36. 3 the **court** secretary, Shebna;
37. 2 of the palace, Shebna, the **court** secretary, and the senior
41. 1 Get ready to present your case in **court;**
41.22 Explain to the **court** the events of the past, and tell us
43. 8 "Summon my people to **court.**

Is	43.26	"Let us go to **court;**
	45.21	Come and present your case in **court;**
	50. 8	Let us go to **court** together!
	59. 4	You go to **court,** but you haven't got justice on your side.
Jer	36.10	the room of Gemariah son of Shaphan, the **court** secretary.
	36.12	to the room of the **court** secretary, where all the officials
	36.12	Elishama, the **court** secretary,
	36.20	the room of Elishama, the **court** secretary,
	36.20	and went to the king's **court,** where they reported everything
	37.15	the house of Jonathan, the **court** secretary,
	38. 7	At that time the king was holding **court** at the Benjamin Gate.
Lam	3.36	When justice is perverted in **court,** he knows.
Ezek	12.14	all the members of his **court** and his advisers and bodyguard,
Dan	1. 4	so that they would be qualified to serve in the royal **court.**
	1. 5	the same food and wine as the members of the royal **court.**
	1. 8	the wine of the royal **court,** so he asked Ashpenaz to help
	1.13	the food of the royal **court,** and base your decision on how
	1.19	So they became members of the king's **court.**
	1.21	Daniel remained at the royal **court** until Cyrus the
	2.49	Daniel, however, remained at the royal **court.**
	7.10	The **court** began its session, and the books were opened.
	7.26	Then the heavenly **court** will sit in judgement, take away his power,
Amos	5.10	challenges injustice and speaks the whole truth in **court.**
	5.12	and prevent the poor from getting justice in the **courts.**
	5.15	what is right, and see that justice prevails in the **courts.**
Zech	8.16	In the **courts,** give real justice—the kind that brings peace.
Mt	5.25	and takes you to **court,** settle the dispute with him
	5.25	while there is time, before you get to **court.**
	5.40	if someone takes you to **court** to sue you for your shirt,
	10.17	and take you to **court,** and they will whip you in
Mk	13. 9	You will be arrested and taken to **court.**
	13.11	arrested and taken to **court,** do not worry beforehand about what
Lk	8. 3	Joanna, whose husband Chuza was an officer in Herod's **court;**
	12.58	and takes you to **court,** do your best to settle
	12.58	the dispute with him before you get to **court.**
Acts	18.12	the Jews got together, seized Paul, and took him into **court.**
	18.16	And he drove them out of the **court.**
	18.17	leader of the synagogue, and beat him in front of the **court.**
	19.38	we have the authorities and the regular days for **court;**
	25. 6	he sat down in the **court** of judgement and ordered Paul to
	25.10	standing before the Emperor's own **court** of judgement,
	25.17	day I sat in the **court** and ordered the man to be
1 Cor	6. 6	one Christian goes to **court** against another and lets unbelievers

COURT (2)

Num	3.26	entrance, [26] the curtains for the **court** which is round the
	3.26	the altar, and the curtain for the entrance of the **court.**
	3.37	for the posts, bases, pegs, and ropes for the outer **court.**
	4.26	curtains and ropes for the **court** that is round the Tent and
	4.26	for the entrance of the **court,** and all the fittings used in
	4.32	pegs, and ropes of the **court** round the Tent, with all the
1 Kgs	6.36	An inner **court** was built in front of the Temple,
	7. 8	quarters, in another **court** behind the Hall of Judgement,
	7. 9	these buildings and the great **court** were made of fine stones
	7.12	The palace **court,** the inner court of the Temple, and the
Neh	3.25	the tower of the upper palace near the **court** of the guard;
Ps	100. 4	Enter the temple gates with thanksgiving, go into its **courts** with praise.
Is	62. 9	grapes Will drink the wine in the **courts** of my Temple."
Jer	19.14	went and stood in the **court** of the Temple and told all
	26. 2	to me, "Stand in the **court** of the Temple and proclaim all
	36.10	room was in the upper **court** near the entrance of the New
Ezek	42. 3	on the other side it faced the pavement of the outer **court.**
Zech	3. 7	of my Temple and its **courts,** and I will hear your prayers,
Rev	11. 2	do not measure the outer **courts,** because they have been

COURT (3)

Song	8. 8	What will we do for her when a young man comes **courting?**

COURTYARD

Ex	8.13	frogs in the houses, the **courtyards,** and the fields died.
Lev	6.16	in a holy place, the **courtyard** of the Tent of the Lord's
	6.26	in a holy place, the **courtyard** of the Tent of the Lord's
1 Kgs	8.64	the central part of the **courtyard,** the area in front of the
2 Kgs	20. 4	had passed through the central **courtyard** of the palace the
	21. 5	In the two **courtyards** of the Temple he built altars for
	23.11	were kept in the temple **courtyard,** near the gate and not far
	23.12	put up by King Manasseh in the two **courtyards** of the Temple;
1 Chr	23.28	to take care of its **courtyards** and its rooms, and to keep
	28.12	had in mind for the **courtyards** and the rooms around them,
2 Chr	4. 9	courtyard for the priests, and also an outer **courtyard.**
	4. 9	doors in the gates between the **courtyards** were covered with bronze.
	6.13	a bronze platform and put it in the middle of the **courtyard.**
	7. 7	the central part of the **courtyard,** the area in front of the
	15. 8	the altar of the Lord that stood in the temple **courtyard.**
	20. 5	of Jerusalem gathered in the new **courtyard** of the Temple.
	23. 5	All the people will assemble in the temple **courtyard.**
	24.21	orders the people stoned Zechariah in the temple **courtyard.**
	29. 4	and Levites in the east **courtyard** of the Temple [5] and spoke
	29.16	the temple **courtyard** everything that was ritually unclean.
	33. 5	In the two **courtyards** of the Temple he built altars for
Neh	8.16	their yards, in the temple **courtyard,** and in the public
Esth	1. 6	The **courtyard** there was decorated with blue and white cotton curtains,
	1. 6	placed in the **courtyard,** which was paved with white marble,
	2.11	fro in front of the **courtyard** of the harem, in order to
Esth	4.11	woman, goes to the inner **courtyard** and sees the king without
	5. 1	and stood in the inner **courtyard** of the palace, facing the
	6. 4	Now Haman had just entered the **courtyard;**
Jer	32. 2	and I was locked up in the **courtyard** of the royal palace.
	32. 8	to me there in the **courtyard** and asked me to buy the
	32.12	purchase and of the men who were sitting in the **courtyard.**
	33. 1	still in prison in the **courtyard,** the Lord's message came to
	37.21	King Zedekiah ordered me to be locked up in the palace **courtyard.**
	38. 6	Prince Malchiah's well, which was in the palace **courtyard.**
	38.13	After that I was kept in the **courtyard.**
	38.28	the palace **courtyard** until the day Jerusalem was captured.
	39.14	king of Babylonia, [14] brought me from the palace **courtyard.**
	39.15	still imprisoned in the palace **courtyard,** the Lord told me
Ezek	8. 7	the entrance of the outer **courtyard** and showed me a hole in
	8.16	So he took me to the inner **courtyard** of the Temple.
	9. 7	Fill its **courtyards** with corpses.
	10. 3	Temple when he went in, and a cloud filled the inner **courtyard.**
	10. 4	the Temple, and the **courtyard** was blazing with the light.
	10. 5	the creatures' wings was heard even in the outer **courtyard.**
	40.14	The room at the far end led out to a **courtyard.**
	40.17	The man took me through the gateway into the **courtyard.**
	40.18	paved with stones, [18] which extended round the **courtyard.**
	40.18	This outer **courtyard** was at a lower level than the inner courtyard.
	40.19	a gateway at a higher level that led to the inner **courtyard.**
	40.20	gateway on the north side that led into the outer **courtyard.**
	40.22	and the entrance room was at the end facing the **courtyard.**
	40.23	Across the **courtyard** from this north gateway was another gateway
	40.23	leading to the inner **courtyard,**
	40.26	its entrance room was also at the end facing the **courtyard.**
	40.27	Here, too, there was a gateway leading to the inner **courtyard.**
	40.28	The man took me through the south gateway into the inner **courtyard.**
	40.31	entrance room faced the other **courtyard,** and palm-trees were
	40.32	The man took me through the east gateway into the inner **courtyard.**
	40.34	The entrance room faced the outer **courtyard.**
	40.37	The entrance room faced the outer **courtyard.**
	40.38	In the outer **courtyard** there was an annexe attached to
	40.38	entrance room that faced the **courtyard,** and there they
	40.41	four inside the room and four out in the **courtyard.**
	40.44	Then he brought me into the inner **courtyard.**
	40.44	rooms opening on the inner **courtyard,** one facing south
	40.47	The man measured the inner **courtyard,** and it was fifty metres
	42. 1	took me into the outer **courtyard** and led me to a building
	42. 6	by columns like the other buildings in the **courtyard.**
	42. 9	where the wall of the **courtyard** began,
	42. 9	there was an entrance into the outer **courtyard.**
	42.14	to go to the outer **courtyard,** they must leave in these rooms
	43. 5	took me into the inner **courtyard,** where I saw that the
	44.17	the gateway to the inner **courtyard** of the Temple,
	44.17	they are on duty in the inner **courtyard** or in the Temple.
	44.19	they go to the outer **courtyard** where the people are, they
	44.21	Priests must not drink any wine before going into the inner **courtyard.**
	44.27	then go into the inner **courtyard** of the Temple and offer a
	45.19	and on the posts of the gateways to the inner **courtyard.**
	46. 1	east gateway to the inner **courtyard** must be kept closed
	46. 2	will go from the outer **courtyard** into the entrance room by
	46.12	the east gate to the inner **courtyard** will be opened for him.
	46.19	near the gate on the south side of the inner **courtyard.**
	46.20	to the outer **courtyard,** where it might harm the people."
	46.21	led me to the outer **courtyard** and showed me that in each
	46.21	corners there was a smaller **courtyard,** twenty metres long
Mt	26.58	as far as the **courtyard** of the High Priest's house.
	26.58	He went into the **courtyard** and sat down with the guards
	26.69	sitting outside in the **courtyard** when one of the High Priest's
	26.71	and went on out to the entrance of the **courtyard.**
Mk	11.16	would not let anyone carry anything through the temple **courtyards.**
	14.54	and went into the **courtyard** of the High Priest's house.
	14.66	was still down in the **courtyard** when one of the High
	15.16	Jesus inside to the **courtyard** of the governor's palace
Lk	22.55	in the centre of the **courtyard,** and Peter joined those who
Jn	18.15	went with Jesus into the **courtyard** of the High Priest's house,

COUSIN

Lev	10. 4	"Come here and carry your **cousins'** bodies away from the
	25.49	or his uncle or his **cousin** or another of his close
Num	36.10	Lord had commanded Moses, and they married their **cousins.**
1 Sam	14.50	his army commander was his **cousin** Abner, the son of his
1 Chr	23.22	His daughters married their **cousins,** the sons of Kish.
Esth	2. 7	He had a **cousin,** Esther, whose Hebrew name was Hadassah;
	2.15	daughter of Abihail and the **cousin** of Mordecai, who had
Col	4.10	sends you greetings, and so does Mark, the **cousin** of Barnabas.

Are you looking for

a word? Continue in this section.
a theme? Turn to the **Thematic Index.**
a name? Turn to the **Concordance of Biblical Names.**
For more detailed instructions, turn to 'How to use the Concordance' on page ix.

COVENANT

[NEW COVENANT]

An agreement, either between people, or between God and a person or a group of people. God made a covenant with Noah (Genesis 9.8-17) and with Abraham (Genesis 17.1-8), but in the Old Testament the term usually refers to the covenant made between God and the people of Israel at the time of Moses (Exodus 24.4-8).

see also **COVENANT BOX**

Gen 6.18 the earth will die, [18] but I will make a **covenant** with you.
9. 9 "I am now making my **covenant** with you and with your descendants,
9.11 With these words I make my **covenant** with you:
9.12 a sign of this everlasting **covenant** which I am making with
9.13 It will be the sign of my **covenant** with the world.
9.16 it and remember the everlasting **covenant** between me and all
15.18 Then and there the Lord made a **covenant** with Abram.
17. 2 I will make my **covenant** with you and give you many descendants."
17. 4 the ground, and God said, [4] "I make this **covenant** with you:
17. 7 in future generations as an everlasting **covenant.**
17. 9 must agree to keep the **covenant** with me, both you and your
17.11 This will show that there is a **covenant** between you and me.
17.13 sign to show that my **covenant** with you is everlasting.
17.14 my people, because he has not kept the **covenant** with me."
17.19 I will keep my **covenant** with him and with his descendants
17.19 It is an everlasting **covenant.**
17.21 But I will keep my **covenant** with your son Isaac, who
Ex 2.24 their groaning and remembered his **covenant** with Abraham,
6. 4 I also made my **covenant** with them, promising to give them
6. 5 Egyptians have enslaved, and I have remembered my **covenant.**
19. 5 obey me and keep my **covenant,** you will be my own people.
24. 7 took the book of the **covenant,** in which the Lord's commands
24. 8 the blood that seals the **covenant** which the Lord made with
31.16 Israel are to keep this day as a sign of the **covenant.**
34.10 to Moses, "I now make a **covenant** with the people of Israel.
34.27 that I am making a **covenant** with you and with Israel."
34.28 the tablets the words of the **covenant**—the Ten Commandments.
Lev 2.13 because salt represents the **covenant** between you and God.
26. 9 will keep my part of the **covenant** that I made with you.
26.15 and commands and break the **covenant** I have made with you,
26.25 punish you for breaking our **covenant,** and if you gather in
26.42 rebellion, [42] I will remember my **covenant** with Jacob and
26.44 put an end to my **covenant** with them, and I am the
26.45 I will renew the **covenant** that I made with their
Num 18.19 This is an unbreakable **covenant** that I have made with you
25.12 that I am making a **covenant** with him that is valid for
Deut 4.13 must do to keep the **covenant** he made with you—you must
4.23 you do not forget the **covenant** that the Lord your God made
4.31 he will not forget the **covenant** that he himself made with
5. 2 Lord our God made a **covenant,** [3] not only with our fathers,
7. 9 He will keep his **covenant** and show his constant love to a
7.12 will continue to keep his **covenant** with you and will show
8.18 today to the **covenant** that he made with your ancestors.
9. 9 on which was written the **covenant** that the Lord had made
9.11 the two stone tablets on which he had written the **covenant.**
9.15 the two stone tablets on which the **covenant** was written.
17. 2 the Lord and broken his **covenant** [3] by worshipping and
29. 1 are the terms of the **covenant** that the Lord commanded Moses
29. 1 was in addition to the **covenant** which the Lord had made with
29. 9 all the terms of this **covenant,** so that you will be
29.12 today to enter into this **covenant** that the Lord your God is
29.14 whom the Lord is making this **covenant** with its obligations.
29.21 the curses listed in the **covenant** that is written in this
29.25 the Lord's people broke the **covenant** they had made with him,
31.16 to me and break the **covenant** that I made with them.
31.20 reject me and break my **covenant,** [21] and many terrible
33. 9 They obeyed your commands And were faithful to your **covenant.**
Josh 7.15 terrible shame on Israel and has broken my **covenant."**
23.16 you do not keep the **covenant** which the Lord your God
24.25 So Joshua made a **covenant** for the people that day, and
Judg 2. 1 I said, 'I will never break my **covenant** with you.
2. 2 You must not make any **covenant** with the people who live in
2.20 "This nation has broken the **covenant** that I commanded their
2 Sam 23. 5 he has made an eternal **covenant** with me, an agreement that
1 Kgs 8. 9 when the Lord made a **covenant** with the people of Israel as
8.21 the stone tablets of the **covenant** which the Lord made with
8.23 You keep your **covenant** with your people and show them your
11.11 broken your **covenant** with me and disobeyed my commands,
19.10 Israel have broken their **covenant** with you, torn down your altars,
19.14 Israel have broken their **covenant** with you, torn down your altars,
2 Kgs 11.17 the people enter into a **covenant** with the Lord that they
11.17 he also made a **covenant** between the king and the people.
13.23 but helped them, because of his **covenant** with Abraham,
17.15 did not keep the **covenant** he had made with their ancestors,
17.35 The Lord had made a **covenant** with them and had ordered them:
17.38 and you shall not forget the **covenant** I made with you.
18.12 their God, but broke the **covenant** he had made with them and
23. 2 the whole book of the **covenant** which had been found in the
23. 3 royal column and made a **covenant** with the Lord to obey him,
23. 3 demands attached to the **covenant,** as written in the book.
23. 3 And all the people promised to keep the **covenant.**
23.21 the Lord their God, as written in the book of the **covenant.**
1 Chr 16.15 Never forget God's **covenant,** which he made to last for ever,
16.16 to last for ever, [16] the **covenant** he made with Abraham, the
16.17 The Lord made a **covenant** with Jacob, one that will last
2 Chr 5.10 when the Lord made a **covenant** with the people of Israel as
6.11 the stone tablets of the **covenant** which the Lord made with
6.14 You keep your **covenant** with your people and show them your
13. 5 of Israel, made an unbreakable **covenant** with David, giving
2 Chr 15.12 They made a **covenant** in which they agreed to worship the Lord,
15.14 that they would keep the **covenant,** and then they shouted and
15.15 because they had made this **covenant** with all their heart.
21. 7 because he had made a **covenant** with David and promised that
23. 3 and there they made a **covenant** with Joash, the king's son.
23.16 join him in making a **covenant** that they would be the Lord's
29.10 now decided to make a **covenant** with the Lord, the God of
34.30 the whole book of the **covenant,** which had been found in the
34.31 royal column and made a **covenant** with the Lord to obey him,
34.31 demands attached to the **covenant,** as written in the book.
34.32 everyone else present in Jerusalem promise to keep the **covenant.**
34.32 obeyed the requirements of the **covenant** they had made with
Neh 1. 5 You faithfully keep your **covenant** with those who love you
9. 8 he was faithful to you, and you made a **covenant** with him.
9.32 You faithfully keep your **covenant** promises.
13.29 office of priest and the **covenant** you made with the priests
Ps 25.10 he leads all who keep his **covenant** and obey his commands.
25.14 those who obey him and he affirms his **covenant** with them.
44.17 not forgotten you or broken the **covenant** you made with us.
50. 5 who made a **covenant** with me by offering a sacrifice."
50.16 Why should you talk about my **covenant?**
74.20 Remember the **covenant** you made with us.
78.10 They did not keep their **covenant** with God;
78.37 they were not faithful to their **covenant** with him.
89. 3 You said, "I have made a **covenant** with the man I chose;
89.28 to him, and my **covenant** with him will last for ever.
89.34 I will not break my **covenant** with him or take back even
89.39 You have broken your **covenant** with your servant and
103.18 true to his **covenant** and who faithfully obey his commands.
105. 8 He will keep his **covenant** for ever, his promises for a
105.10 The Lord made a **covenant** with Jacob, one that will last
106.45 their sake he remembered his **covenant,** and because of his
111. 5 he never forgets his **covenant.**
111. 9 He set his people free and made an eternal **covenant** with them.
132.12 sons are true to my **covenant** and to the commands I give
Is 24. 5 laws and by violating the **covenant** he made to last for ever.
42. 6 Through you I will make a **covenant** with all peoples;
49. 8 you and through you make a **covenant** with all peoples.
55. 3 I will make a lasting **covenant** with you and give you the
56. 4 me and faithfully keep my **covenant,** [5] then your name will be
56. 6 who observe the Sabbath and faithfully keep his **covenant:**
59.21 And I make a **covenant** with you:
61. 8 reward my people And make an eternal **covenant** with them.
Jer 4. 4 Keep your **covenant** with me, your Lord,
9.25 circumcised, but have not kept the **covenant** it symbolizes.
9.25 and none of the people of Israel have kept my **covenant."**
11. 2 The Lord said to me, [2] "Listen to the terms of the **covenant.**
11. 3 on everyone who does not obey the terms of this **covenant.**
11. 4 It is the **covenant** I made with their ancestors when I
11. 6 to listen to the terms of the **covenant** and to obey them.
11. 8 I had commanded them to keep the **covenant,** but they refused.
11.10 Judah have broken the **covenant** that I made with their ancestors.
14.21 Do not break the **covenant** you made with us.
22. 9 because you have abandoned your **covenant** with me, your God,
31.31 when I will make a **new covenant** with the people of Israel
31.32 not be like the old **covenant** that I made with their
31.32 was like a husband to them, they did not keep that **covenant.**
31.33 The **new covenant** that I will make with the people of
32.40 I will make an eternal **covenant** with them.
33.20 me, [20] "I have made a **covenant** with the day and with the
33.20 and that **covenant** can never be broken.
33.21 way I have made a **covenant** with my servant David that he
33.21 and I have made a **covenant** with the priests from the tribe
33.21 and those **covenants** can never be broken.
33.25 I, the Lord, have a **covenant** with day and night, and I
33.26 so I will maintain my **covenant** with Jacob's descendants and
34.13 "I made a **covenant** with your ancestors when I rescued them
34.15 free, and you made a **covenant** in my presence, in the Temple
34.18 all the leaders, made a **covenant** with me by walking between
34.18 But they broke the **covenant** and did not keep its terms.
50. 5 They will make an eternal **covenant** with me and never break it.
Ezek 16. 8 I made a marriage **covenant** with you, and you became mine."
16.59 because you ignored your promises and broke the **covenant.**
16.60 But I will honour the **covenant** I made with you when you
16.60 and I will make a **covenant** with you that will last for
16.61 you, even though this was not part of my **covenant** with you.
16.62 I will renew my **covenant** with you, and you will know
20.20 be a sign of the **covenant** we made, and will remind you
20.37 will take firm control of you and make you obey my **covenant.**
34.25 I will make a **covenant** with them that guarantees their security.
37.26 I will make a **covenant** with them that guarantees their
44. 7 my people have broken my **covenant** by all the disgusting
Dan 9. 4 You are faithful to your **covenant** and show constant love to
Hos 2.18 time I will make a **covenant** with all the wild animals and
6. 7 land at Adam, they broke the **covenant** I had made with them.
8. 1 My people have broken the **covenant** I made with them and have
Zech 9.11 "Because of my **covenant** with you that was sealed by the
11.10 broke it, to cancel the **covenant** which the Lord had made
11.11 So the **covenant** was cancelled on that day.
Mal 2. 4 this command, so that my **covenant** with the priests, the
2. 5 "In my **covenant** I promised them life and well-being, and
2. 8 You have broken the **covenant** I made with you.
2.10 do we despise the **covenant** that God made with our ancestors?
3. 1 The messenger you long to see will come and proclaim my **covenant."**
Mt 26.28 my blood, which seals God's **covenant,** my blood poured out
Mk 14.24 is poured out for many, my blood which seals God's **covenant.**
Lk 1.72 show mercy to our ancestors and remember his sacred **covenant.**
22.20 saying, "This cup is God's **new covenant** sealed with my blood,
Acts 3.25 you share in the **covenant** which God made with your ancestors.
7. 8 Abraham the ceremony of circumcision as a sign of the **covenant.**

Rom 9. 4 he made his **covenants** with them and gave them the Law;
11.27 I will make this **covenant** with them when I take away
1 Cor 11.25 "This cup is God's **new covenant,** sealed with my blood.
2 Cor 3. 6 us capable of serving the **new covenant,** which consists not
3.14 the same veil as they read the books of the old **covenant.**
Gal 3.17 is that God made a **covenant** with Abraham and promised to
3.17 later, cannot break that **covenant** and cancel God's promise.
4.24 the two women represent two **covenants.**
4.24 is Hagar, and she represents the **covenant** made at Mount Sinai.
Eph 2.12 had no part in the **covenants,** which were based on God's
Heb 7.22 also makes Jesus the guarantee of a better **covenant.**
8. 5 was about to build the **Covenant Tent,** God said to him, "Be
8. 6 just as the **covenant** which he arranged between God and
8. 7 nothing wrong with the first **covenant,** there would have been
8. 8 I will draw up a **new covenant** with the people of Israel
8. 9 will not be like the **covenant** that I made with their
8. 9 were not faithful to the **covenant** I made with them,
8.10 Now, this is the **covenant** that I will make with the
8.13 By speaking of a **new covenant,** God has made the first
9. 1 The first **covenant** had rules for worship and a man-made
9.15 the one who arranges a **new covenant,** so that those who have
9.15 the wrongs they did while the first **covenant** was in force.
9.18 is why even the first **covenant** came into effect only with
9.20 the blood which seals the **covenant** that God has commanded
9.21 sprinkled the blood on the **Covenant Tent** and over all the
10.16 he says, [16]"This is the **covenant** that I will make with
10.29 the blood of God's **covenant** which purified him from sin?
12.24 Jesus, who arranged the **new covenant,** and to the sprinkled blood
13.20 his sacrificial death, by which the eternal **covenant** is sealed.

COVENANT BOX

[BOX]

A wooden chest covered with gold. The two stone tablets with the Ten Commandments written on them were kept in it. It is often called "the Ark of the Covenant".

Ex 16.34 it in front of the **Covenant Box,** so that it could be
25.10 "Make a **box** out of acacia-wood,
25.14 and put them through the rings on each side of the **box.**
25.16 Then put in the **box** the two stone tablets that I will
25.21 two stone tablets inside the **box** and put the lid on top
25.30 placed in front of the **Covenant Box,** and on the table there
26.33 put the **Covenant Box** containing the two stone tablets.
26.34 Put the lid on the **Covenant Box.**
27.21 outside the curtain which is in front of the **Covenant Box.**
30. 6 the curtain which hangs in front of the **Covenant Box.**
30.26 Tent of my presence, the **Covenant Box,** [27]the table and all
30.36 my presence, and sprinkle it in front of the **Covenant Box.**
31. 7 Tent of my presence, the **Covenant Box** and its lid, all the
35.12 the **Covenant Box,** its poles, its lid, and the curtain to
37. 1 Bezalel made the **Covenant Box** out of acacia-wood,
37. 5 and put them through the rings on each side of the **box.**
39.35 the **Covenant Box** containing the stone tablets, its
40. 3 Place in it the **Covenant Box** containing the Ten
40. 5 incense in front of the **Covenant Box** and hang the curtain at
40.20 took the two stone tablets and put them in the **Covenant Box.**
40.20 in the rings of the **box** and put the lid on it.
40.21 Then he put the **box** in the Tent and hung up the
40.21 way he screened off the **Covenant Box,** just as the Lord had
Lev 16. 2 I appear in a cloud above the lid on the **Covenant Box.**
16.13 hide the lid of the **Covenant Box** so that he will not
16.14 some of it seven times in front of the **Covenant Box.**
16.15 then in front of the **Covenant Box,** as he did with the
24. 3 curtain in front of the **Covenant Box,** which is in the Most
Num 3.31 They were responsible for the **Covenant Box,**
4. 5 curtain in front of the **Covenant Box,** and cover the Box with
7.89 lid on the **Covenant Box,** between the two winged creatures.
10.33 The Lord's **Covenant Box** always went ahead of them to find a
10.35 Whenever the **Covenant Box** started out, Moses would say,
14.44 neither the Lord's **Covenant Box** nor Moses left the camp.
17. 4 put them in front of the **Covenant Box,** where I meet you.
17. 7 the sticks in the Tent in front of the Lord's **Covenant Box.**
17.10 "Put Aaron's stick back in front of the **Covenant Box.**
20. 8 is in front of the **Covenant Box,** and then you and Aaron
Deut 10. 1 the first ones and make a wooden **box** to put them in.
10. 2 you broke, and then you are to put them in the **box.'**
10. 3 "So I made a **box** of acacia-wood and cut two stone
10. 5 I put them in the **box** that I had made—and they
10. 8 be in charge of the **Covenant Box,** to serve him as priests,
31. 9 in charge of the Lord's **Covenant Box,** and to the leaders of
31.25 in charge of the Lord's **Covenant Box,** [26]"Take this book
31.26 and place it beside the **Covenant Box** of the Lord your God,
Josh 3. 3 the priests carrying the **Covenant Box** of the Lord your God,
3. 4 But do not get near the **Covenant Box;**
3. 6 the priests to take the **Covenant Box** and go with it ahead
3. 8 Tell the priests carrying the **Covenant Box** that when they
3.11 is among you [11] when the **Covenant Box** of the Lord of all
3.13 the priests who carry the **Covenant Box** of the Lord of all
3.14 the priests went ahead of them, carrying the **Covenant Box.**
3.17 the priests carrying the Lord's **Covenant Box** stood on dry
4. 5 the Jordan ahead of the **Covenant Box** of the Lord your God.
4. 7 Jordan stopped flowing when the Lord's **Covenant Box** crossed the river.
4. 9 where the priests carrying the **Covenant Box** had stood.
4.11 the priests with the Lord's **Covenant Box** went on ahead of
4.16 command the priests carrying the **Covenant Box** to come up out
6. 4 carrying a trumpet, are to go in front of the **Covenant Box.**
6. 6 said to them, "Take the **Covenant Box,** and seven of you go
6. 7 an advance guard going on ahead of the Lord's **Covenant Box.**
6. 8 who were carrying the **Covenant Box,** followed by a rearguard.
6.11 of men to take the Lord's **Covenant Box** round the city once.
Josh 6.12 then, the priests carrying the Lord's **Covenant Box;**
7. 6 before the Lord's **Covenant Box,** and lay there till evening,
8.33 two sides of the Lord's **Covenant Box,** facing the levitical
Judg 20.27 God's **Covenant Box** was there at Bethel in those days,
1 Sam 3. 3 sleeping in the sanctuary, where the sacred **Covenant Box** was.
4. 3 go and bring the Lord's **Covenant Box** from Shiloh, so that he
4. 4 to Shiloh and fetched the **Covenant Box** of the Lord Almighty;
4. 4 Hophni and Phinehas, came along with the **Covenant Box.**
4. 5 When the **Covenant Box** arrived, the Israelites gave such a
4. 6 found out that the Lord's **Covenant Box** had arrived in the
4.11 God's **Covenant Box** was captured, and Eli's sons, Hophni and Phinehas,
4.13 was very anxious about the **Covenant Box,** was sitting on a
4.17 Hophni and Phinehas were killed, and God's **Covenant Box** was captured!"
4.18 When the man mentioned the **Covenant Box,** Eli fell
4.19 When she heard that God's **Covenant Box** had been captured and
4.21 to the capture of the **Covenant Box** and the death of her
4.22 she said, "because God's **Covenant Box** has been captured."
5. 1 After the Philistines captured the **Covenant Box,** they
5. 3 downwards on the ground in front of the Lord's **Covenant Box.**
5. 4 statue had again fallen down in front of the **Covenant Box.**
5. 7 We can't let the **Covenant Box** stay here any longer."
5. 8 shall we do with the **Covenant Box** of the God of Israel?"
5.10 So they sent the **Covenant Box** to Ekron, another Philistine city;
5.10 "They have brought the **Covenant Box** of the God of Israel
5.11 kings and said, "Send the **Covenant Box** of Israel back to
6. 1 After the Lord's **Covenant Box** had been in Philistia for seven months,
6. 2 asked, "What shall we do with the **Covenant Box** of the Lord?
6. 3 "If you return the **Covenant Box** of the God of Israel,
6. 3 The **Covenant Box** must not go back without a gift.
6. 8 Take the Lord's **Covenant Box,** put it on the wagon,
6.11 They put the **Covenant Box** in the wagon,
6.13 when suddenly they looked up and saw the **Covenant Box.**
6.15 The Levites lifted off the **Covenant Box** of the Lord
6.18 which they placed the Lord's **Covenant Box,** is still there as
6.19 of Beth Shemesh because they looked inside the **Covenant Box.**
6.21 "The Philistines have returned the Lord's **Covenant Box.**
7. 1 Kiriath Jearim fetched the Lord's **Covenant Box** and took it
7. 2 The **Covenant Box** of the Lord stayed in Kiriath Jearim a
2 Sam 6. 2 to bring from there God's **Covenant Box,** bearing the name of
6. 6 and Uzzah reached out and took hold of the **Covenant Box.**
6. 7 Uzzah died there beside the **Covenant Box,** [8]and so that
6. 9 and said, "How can I take the **Covenant Box** with me now?"
6.12 heard that because of the **Covenant Box** the Lord had blessed
6.12 so he fetched the **Covenant Box** from Obed's house to take it
6.13 After the men carrying the **Covenant Box** had gone six steps,
6.15 all the Israelites took the **Covenant Box** up to Jerusalem
6.16 As the **Box** was being brought into the city, Michal,
6.17 They brought the **Box** and put it in its place in the
7. 2 built of cedar, but God's **Covenant Box** is kept in a tent!"
11.11 are away at the war, and the **Covenant Box** is with them;
15.24 with him were the Levites, carrying the sacred **Covenant Box.**
15.25 said to Zadok, "Take the **Covenant Box** back to the city.
15.29 Zadok and Abiathar took the **Covenant Box** back into Jerusalem
1 Kgs 2.26 in charge of the Lord's **Covenant Box** while you were with my
3.15 in front of the Lord's **Covenant Box** and offered
6.19 was built, where the Lord's **Covenant Box** was to be placed.
8. 1 order to take the Lord's **Covenant Box** from Zion, David's
8. 3 gathered, the priests lifted the **Covenant Box** [4]and carried
8. 5 assembled in front of the **Covenant Box** and sacrificed a
8. 6 Then the priests carried the **Covenant Box** into the Temple
8. 7 Their outstretched wings covered the **box**
8. 9 There was nothing inside the **Covenant Box** except the two
8.21 in the Temple for the **Covenant Box** containing the stone
1 Chr 6.31 worship in Jerusalem after the **Covenant Box** was moved there.
13. 3 will go and fetch God's **Covenant Box,** which was ignored
13. 5 to bring the **Covenant Box** from Kiriath Jearim to Jerusalem.
13. 6 of Judah, to fetch the **Covenant Box** of God, which bears the
13. 7 house they brought out the **Covenant Box** and put it on a
13. 9 Uzzah stretched out his hand and took hold of the **Covenant Box.**
13.10 Lord became angry with Uzzah and killed him for touching the **box.**
13.12 and said, "How can I take the **Covenant Box** with me now?"
15. 1 prepared a place for God's **Covenant Box** and put up a tent
15. 2 "Only Levites should carry the **Covenant Box,** because they
15. 3 in order to bring the **Covenant Box** to the place he had
15.12 that you can bring the **Covenant Box** of the Lord God of
15.14 in order to move the **Covenant Box** of the Lord God of
15.23 Obed Edom and Jehiah, were chosen as guards for the **Covenant Box.**
15.23 Eliezer were chosen to blow trumpets in front of the **Covenant Box.**
15.25 Obed Edom to fetch the **Covenant Box,** and they had a great
15.26 God would help the Levites who were carrying the **Covenant Box.**
15.27 Chenaniah their leader, and the Levites who carried the **Box.**
15.28 all the Israelites accompanied the **Covenant Box** up to
15.29 As the **Box** was being brought into the city, Michal,
16. 1 They took the **Covenant Box** to the tent which David had
16. 4 in front of the **Covenant Box,** by singing and praising him.
16. 6 to blow trumpets regularly in front of the **Covenant Box.**
16.37 that was held at the place where the **Covenant Box** was kept.
17. 1 of cedar, but the Lord's **Covenant Box** is kept in a tent!"
22.19 can place in it the **Covenant Box** of the Lord and all
28. 2 a permanent home for the **Covenant Box,** the footstool of the
28.18 that spread their wings over the Lord's **Covenant Box.**
2 Chr 1. 4 (The **Covenant Box,** however, was in Jerusalem, kept in a
1. 4 David had set up when he brought the **Box** from Kiriath Jearim.)
5. 2 order to take the Lord's **Covenant Box** from Zion, David's
5. 4 then the Levites lifted the **Covenant Box** [5]and carried it to

2 Chr 5. 6 assembled in front of the **Covenant Box** and sacrificed a
5. 7 Then the priests carried the **Covenant Box** of the Lord into
5. 8 Their outstretched wings covered the **Box** and the carrying-poles.
5.10 There was nothing inside the **Covenant Box** except the two
6.11 placed in the Temple the **Covenant Box**, which contains the
6.41 Lord God, and with the **Covenant Box**, the symbol of your power,
8.11 any place where the **Covenant Box** has been is holy."
35. 3 "Put the sacred **Covenant Box** in the Temple that King Solomon,
Ps 78.61 our enemies to capture the **Covenant Box**, the symbol of his
132. 6 Bethlehem we heard about the **Covenant Box**, and we found it
132. 8 Lord, with the **Covenant Box**, the symbol of your power,
Jer 3.16 that land, people will no longer talk about my **Covenant Box**.
Heb 9. 4 burning of incense and the **Covenant Box** all covered with
9. 5 Above the **Box** were the winged creatures representing God's
Rev 11.19 in heaven was opened, and the **Covenant Box** was seen there.

COVENANT TENT see TENT (2)

COVER

Gen 1. 2 The raging ocean that **covered** everything
3. 7 so they sewed fig leaves together and **covered** themselves.
6.14 make rooms in it and **cover** it with tar inside and out.
7.19 It became so deep that it **covered** the highest mountains;
8. 9 but since the water still **covered** all the land, the dove
8.13 Noah removed the **covering** of the boat, looked round, and saw
9.14 Whenever I **cover** the sky with clouds and the rainbow appears,
9.23 backwards into the tent and **covered** their father, keeping
24.65 So she took her scarf and **covered** her face.
37.26 we gain by killing our brother and **covering** up the murder?
38.14 clothes she had been wearing, **covered** her face with a veil,
38.15 that she was a prostitute, because she had her face **covered**.
Ex 2. 3 basket made of reeds and **covered** it with tar to make it
3. 6 So Moses **covered** his face, because he was afraid to look at
4. 6 his hand out, it was diseased, **covered** with white spots,
8. 2 I will punish your country by **covering** it with frogs.
8. 5 pools, and make frogs come up and **cover** the land of Egypt."
8. 6 all the water, and the frogs came out and **covered** the land.
8.17 turned into gnats, which **covered** the people and the animals.
8.21 be full of flies, and the ground will be **covered** with them.
9.11 before Moses, because they were **covered** with boils, like all
10. 5 There will be so many that they will completely **cover** the ground.
10.15 They **covered** the ground until it was black with them;
10.21 thick enough to be felt will **cover** the land of Egypt."
14.28 The water returned and **covered** the chariots, the
15. 5 The deep sea **covered** them;
15.19 sea, the Lord brought the water back, and it **covered** them.
16.13 quails flew in, enough to **cover** the camp, and in the morning
19.18 whole of Mount Sinai was **covered** with smoke, because the
21.33 "If a man takes the **cover** off a pit or if he
21.33 digs one and does not **cover** it, and a bull or a
22.15 a hired animal, the loss is **covered** by the hiring charge.
22.27 because it is the only **covering** he has to keep him warm.
24.15 Moses went up Mount Sinai, and a cloud **covered** it.
24.16 The cloud **covered** the mountain for six days, and on the
25.11 **Cover** it with pure gold inside and out and put a gold
25.13 Make carrying-poles of acacia-wood and **cover** them with
25.20 across the lid, and their outspread wings are to **cover** it.
25.24 **Cover** it with pure gold and put a gold border round it.
25.28 Make the poles of acacia-wood and **cover** them with gold.
26. 7 "Make a **cover** for the Tent out of eleven pieces of cloth
26.11 loops to join the two sets so as to form one **cover**.
26.13 is to hang over the sides of the Tent to **cover** it.
26.14 "Make two more **coverings**, one of rams' skin dyed red
26.14 and the other of fine leather, to serve as the outer **cover**.
26.29 **Cover** the frames with gold and fit them with gold rings
26.29 hold the cross-bars, which are also to be **covered** with gold.
26.32 posts of acacia-wood **covered** with gold, fitted with hooks,
26.37 make five posts of acacia-wood **covered** with gold and fitted
27. 2 with the altar, and the whole is to be **covered** with bronze.
27. 6 Make carrying-poles of acacia-wood, **cover** them with bronze,
29.13 take all the fat which **covers** the internal organs, the best
29.22 the fat tail, the fat **covering** the internal organs, the best
30. 3 **Cover** its top, all four sides, and its projections with pure gold,
30. 5 Make these poles of acacia-wood and **cover** them with gold.
33.22 opening in the rock and **cover** you with my hand until I
34.33 finished speaking to them, he **covered** his face with a veil.
35.11 the Tent, its **covering** and its outer covering,
36.14 Then they made a **cover** for the Tent out of eleven pieces
36.18 hooks to join the two sets, so as to form one **cover**.
36.19 They made two more **coverings**, one of rams' skin dyed red
36.19 and the other of fine leather, to serve as an outer **cover**.
36.34 They **covered** the frames with gold and fitted them with
36.34 to hold the cross-bars, which were also **covered** with gold.
36.36 acacia-wood to hold the curtain, **covered** them with gold, and
36.38 five posts fitted with hooks, **covered** their tops and their
37. 2 He **covered** it with pure gold inside and out and put a
37. 4 He made carrying-poles of acacia-wood, **covered** them with gold,
37. 9 other across the lid, and their outspread wings **covered** it.
37.11 He **covered** it with pure gold and put a gold border round
37.15 He made the poles of acacia-wood and **covered** them with gold.
37.26 He **covered** its top, all four sides, and its projections
37.28 He made the poles of acacia-wood and **covered** them with gold.
38. 2 He **covered** it all with bronze.
38. 6 He made carrying-poles of acacia-wood, **covered** them with bronze,
38.17 hooks, the rods, and the **covering** of the tops of the posts
38.19 Their hooks, the **covering** of their tops, and their rods were
38.28 the hooks for the posts, and the **covering** for their tops.
39.34 the **covering** of rams' skin dyed red;
Ex 39.34 the **covering** of fine leather;
40.19 He spread out the **covering** over the Tent
40.19 and put the outer **covering** over it, just as the Lord
40.34 Then the cloud **covered** the Tent and the dazzling light
Lev 3. 9 the backbone, all the fat **covering** the internal organs,
7. 3 the fat tail, the fat **covering** the internal organs, [4] the
8.25 fat tail, all the fat **covering** the internal organs, the best
13.12 If the skin-disease spreads and **covers** the person from head to foot,
13.13 finds that it actually has **covered** the whole body, he shall
13.45 leave his hair uncombed, **cover** the lower part of his face,
14.42 removed, and new plaster will be used to **cover** the walls.
17.13 pour out its blood on the ground and **cover** it with earth.
24. 6 each row, on the table **covered** with pure gold, which is in
Num 3.25 for the Tent, its inner **cover**, its outer cover, the curtain
4. 5 in front of the Covenant Box, and **cover** the Box with it.
4. 6 shall put a fine leather **cover** over it, spread a blue cloth
4. 8 this, put a fine leather **cover** over it, and then insert the
4. 9 take a blue cloth and **cover** the lampstand, with its lamps,
4.10 in a fine leather **cover** and place it on a carrying-frame.
4.11 altar, put a fine leather **cover** over it, and then insert the
4.12 cloth, put a fine leather **cover** over them, and place them on
4.14 a fine leather **cover** over it and insert the carrying-poles.
4.15 Aaron and his sons have finished **covering** them
4.25 the Tent, its inner **cover**, its outer cover,
4.25 the fine leather **cover** on top of it,
9.15 the Lord's presence was set up, a cloud came and **covered** it.
12.10 Tent, Miriam's skin was suddenly **covered** with a dreaded
12.10 and saw that she was **covered** with the disease, [11] he said
16.38 them into thin plates, and make a **covering** for the altar.
16.39 beaten into thin plates to make a **covering** for the altar.
16.42 saw that the cloud was **covering** it and that the dazzling
Deut 4.11 of the mountain which was **covered** with thick clouds of dark
23.13 a bowel movement you can dig a hole and **cover** it up.
27. 2 set up some large stones, **cover** them with plaster, [3] and
27. 4 as I am instructing you today, and **cover** them with plaster.
27. 8 On the stones **covered** with plaster write clearly every
28.27 You will be **covered** with scabs, and you will itch, but there
28.35 The Lord will **cover** your legs with incurable, painful
28.35 boils will **cover** you from head to foot.
29.23 The fields will be a barren waste, **covered** with sulphur and salt;
33.15 May their ancient hills be **covered** with choice fruit.
Josh 8.29 They **covered** it with a huge pile of stones, which is still
Judg 3.22 sword went in, handle and all, and the fat **covered** it up.
9.45 its people, tore it down, and **covered** the ground with salt.
17. 3 It will be used to make a wooden idol **covered** with silver.
17. 4 idol, carving it from wood and **covering** it with the silver.
18.14 of these houses there is a wooden idol **covered** with silver?
18.17 took the wooden idol **covered** with silver, the other idols,
Ruth 3. 4 asleep, go and lift the **covers** and lie down at his feet.
3. 7 over quietly, lifted the **covers** and lay down at his feet.
1 Sam 19.13 made of goats'-hair at its head, and put a **cover** over it.
2 Sam 15.30 was barefoot and had his head **covered** as a sign of grief.
15.30 All who followed him **covered** their heads and wept also.
17.19 The man's wife took a **covering**, spread it over the
18.17 pit in the forest, and **covered** it with a huge pile of
19. 4 The king **covered** his face and cried loudly, "O my son!
20.12 Amasa's body, **covered** with blood, was lying in the
22.12 He **covered** himself with darkness;
1 Kgs 1. 1 man, and although his servants **covered** him with blankets, he
6.15 The inside walls were **covered** with cedar panels from
6.18 the whole interior was **covered** with cedar, so that the
6.20 wide, and nine metres high, all **covered** with pure gold.
6.20 The altar was **covered** with cedar panels.
6.21 inside of the Temple was **covered** with gold, and gold chains
6.21 of the inner room, which was also **covered** with gold.
6.22 interior of the Temple was **covered** with gold, as well as the
6.28 The two winged creatures were **covered** with gold.
6.30 Even the floor was **covered** with gold.
6.32 the winged creatures, and the palm-trees were **covered** with gold.
6.35 and flowers, which were evenly **covered** with gold.
7. 6 It had a **covered** porch, supported by columns.
8. 7 Their outstretched wings **covered** the box and the poles it
10.18 Part of it was **covered** with ivory
10.18 and the rest of it was **covered** with the finest gold.
18.45 little while the sky was **covered** with dark clouds, the wind
19.13 When Elijah heard it, he **covered** his face with his
22.35 his wound ran down and **covered** the bottom of the chariot,
2 Kgs 3.19 all their fertile fields by **covering** them with stones."
3.20 flowing from the direction of Edom, and **covered** the ground.
3.25 a stone on it until finally all the fields were **covered**;
6.17 up and saw the hillside **covered** with horses and chariots of
18.16 with which he himself had **covered** the doorposts, and he sent
23.14 ground where they had stood he **covered** with human bones.
2 Chr 3. 8 of gold were used to **cover** the walls of the Most Holy
3. 9 the walls of the upper rooms were also **covered** with gold.
3.10 winged creatures out of metal, **cover** them with gold, and
4. 9 doors in the gates between the courtyards were **covered** with bronze.
5. 8 Their outstretched wings **covered** the Box and the carrying-poles.
9.15 shields, each of which was **covered** with about seven
9.16 three hundred smaller shields, each **covered** with about three
9.17 Part of it was **covered** with ivory
9.17 and the rest of it was **covered** with pure gold.
9.18 and there was a footstool attached to it, **covered** with gold.
Neh 3.15 He **covered** the gateway, put the gates in place, and put in
Esth 4. 1 Then he dressed in sackcloth, **covered** his head with ashes,
6.12 Haman hurried home, **covering** his face in embarrassment.
7. 8 no sooner said this than the eunuchs **covered** Haman's head.
Job 3. 5 **cover** it with clouds, and blot out the sun.
7. 5 it is **covered** with scabs;

Job 10.11 and sinews and **covered** the bones with muscles and skin:
10.15 I am miserable and **covered** with shame.
13. 4 You **cover** up your ignorance with lies;
21.26 they all are **covered** with worms.
24. 7 they sleep with nothing to **cover** them, nothing to keep them
24.15 he **covers** his face so that no one can see him.
26. 6 no **covering** shields it from his sight.
38. 9 It was I who **covered** the sea with clouds and wrapped it
Ps 18.11 He **covered** himself with darkness;
35.26 to be better than I am be **covered** with shame and disgrace.
44.15 I am **covered** with shame [16]from hearing the sneers and
65.13 The fields are **covered** with sheep;
68.13 figures of doves **covered** with silver,
69. 7 that I have been insulted and that I am **covered** with shame.
72.16 may the hills be **covered** with crops, as fruitful as those
80.10 It **covered** the hills with its shade;
83.16 **Cover** their faces with shame, O Lord, and make them
89.45 made him old before his time and **covered** him with disgrace.
91. 4 He will **cover** you with his wings;
104. 2 you **cover** yourself with light.
104. 6 over it like a robe, and the water **covered** the mountains.
104. 9 can never pass, to keep them from **covering** the earth again.
109.19 May they **cover** him like clothes and always be round him
109.29 May my enemies be **covered** with disgrace;
124. 4 away, the water would have **covered** us, [5]the raging torrent
132.18 I will **cover** his enemies with shame, but his kingdom
Prov 7.16 I've **covered** my bed with sheets of coloured linen from Egypt.
Song 1. 2 Your lips **cover** me with kisses;
3.10 Its posts are **covered** with silver;
3.10 Its cushions are **covered** with purple cloth, lovingly woven
5. 5 My hands were **covered** with myrrh, my fingers with liquid myrrh,
Is 1. 5 Israel, your head is already **covered** with wounds, and your
1. 6 You are **covered** with bruises and sores and open wounds.
1.15 I will not listen, for your hands are **covered** with blood.
4. 5 God's glory will **cover** and protect the whole city.
5. 6 instead I will let briars and thorns **cover** it.
6. 2 Each creature **covered** its face with two wings, and its body
7.19 and they will **cover** every thorn-bush and every pasture.
8. 8 Judah in a flood, rising shoulder high and **covering** everything."
14.11 a bed of maggots and are **covered** with a blanket of worms.'
14.19 It is **covered** by the bodies of soldiers killed in battle,
14.21 of them will ever rule the earth or **cover** it with cities."
15. 1 in a single night, and silence **covers** the land of Moab.
27. 6 The earth will be **covered** with the fruit they produce.
28. 8 where they sit are all **covered** with vomit, and not a clean
29. 2 and the whole city will be like an altar **covered** with blood.
30.22 with silver and your idols **covered** with gold, and will throw
34. 6 His sword will be **covered** with their blood and fat, like
34. 7 and the earth will be red with blood and **covered** with fat.
40.19 that workmen make, that metalworkers **cover** with gold and set
60. 2 Other nations will be **covered** by darkness, But on you the
Jer 3.25 We should lie down in shame and let our disgrace **cover** us.
10. 9 Their idols are **covered** with silver from Spain and with
46. 8 Egypt said, 'I will rise and **cover** the world;
47. 2 They will **cover** the land and everything on it, cities and
51.42 The sea has rolled over Babylon and **covered** it with roaring waves.
Lam 2. 1 The Lord in his anger has **covered** Zion with darkness.
Ezek 1.18 The rims of the wheels were **covered** with eyes.
1.23 ones next to it and **covering** its body with the other two
8.10 The walls were **covered** with drawings of snakes
10.12 backs, hands, wings, and wheels were **covered** with eyes.
12. 6 the dark with your eyes **covered**, so that you can't see where
12.12 He will **cover** his eyes and not see where he is going.
13.10 then the prophets have come and **covered** it with whitewash.
13.15 "The wall and those who **covered** it with whitewash will
16. 6 You were **covered** with blood, but I wouldn't let you die.
16. 8 I **covered** your naked body with my coat and promised to love
17. 6 The vine was **covered** with branches and leaves.
19.10 of water, the vine was **covered** with leaves and fruit.
22.28 hidden these sins like men **covering** a wall with whitewash.
23.41 they would have a table **covered** with good things, including
24.17 Don't **cover** your face or eat the food that mourners eat."
24.22 You will not **cover** your faces or eat the food that mourners
26.10 The clouds of dust raised by their horses will **cover** you.
26.19 I will **cover** you with the water of the ocean depths.
30.18 A cloud will **cover** Egypt, and the people of all her cities
31.15 make the underground waters **cover** it as a sign of mourning.
32. 5 I will **cover** mountains and valleys with your rotting corpse.
32. 7 I destroy you, I will **cover** the sky and blot out the
35. 8 I will **cover** the mountains with corpses, and the bodies of
35. 8 who are killed in battle will **cover** the hills and valleys.
37. 1 me down in a valley where the ground was **covered** with bones.
37. 6 I will give you sinews and muscles, and **cover** you with skin.
37. 8 I watched, the bones were **covered** with sinews and muscles,
38. 9 will attack like a storm and **cover** the land like a cloud."
41.16 These windows could be **covered.**
41.17 above the doors, were completely **covered** with carvings
41.25 And there was a wooden **covering** over the outside of the
Dan 2.35 stone grew to be a mountain that **covered** the whole earth.
Hos 10. 8 and to the hills, **"Cover** us!"
Joel 3.18 time the mountains will be **covered** with vineyards, and
Jon 2. 5 the sea **covered** me completely, and seaweed was wrapped round my head.
Mic 7.16 In dismay they will close their mouths and **cover** their ears.
Nah 3. 6 I will treat you with contempt and **cover** you with filth.
Hab 2.16 You in turn will be **covered** with shame instead of honour.
2.19 It may be **covered** with silver and gold, but there is no
3. 3 His splendour **covers** the heavens;
Mt 10.26 Whatever is now **covered** up will be uncovered, and every secret
Mt 13.44 He **covers** it up again, and is so happy that he goes
27.45 noon the whole country was **covered** with darkness, which lasted
Mk 4.22 into the open, and whatever is **covered** up will be uncovered.
9. 7 Then a cloud appeared and **covered** them with its shadow,
11.13 in the distance a fig-tree **covered** with leaves, so he went
15.33 noon the whole country was **covered** with darkness, which lasted
Lk 7.46 for my head, but she has **covered** my feet with perfume.
8.16 one lights a lamp and **covers** it with a bowl or puts
8.17 and whatever is **covered** up will be found and brought
9.34 still speaking, a cloud appeared and **covered** them with its shadow;
12. 2 Whatever is **covered** up will be uncovered, and every secret
16.20 a poor man named Lazarus, **covered** with sores, who used to be
23.44 sun stopped shining and darkness **covered** the whole country
Acts 7.57 the members of the Council **covered** their ears with their hands.
13.11 Elymas felt a dark mist **cover** his eyes, and he walked about
1 Cor 11. 4 in public worship with his head **covered** disgraces Christ.
11. 6 If the woman does not **cover** her head, she might as well
11. 6 shave her head or cut her hair, she should **cover** her head.
11. 7 man has no need to **cover** his head, because he reflects the
11.10 a woman should have a **covering** over her head to show that
11.15 Her long hair has been given her to serve as a **covering.**
2 Cor 3.14 their minds are **covered** with the same veil as they
3.15 read the Law of Moses, the veil still **covers** their minds.
1 Thes 2. 5 did we use words to **cover** up greed—God is our witness!
Heb 9. 4 Covenant Box all **covered** with gold and containing the gold
Jas 5. 3 Your gold and silver are **covered** with rust, and this rust
1 Pet 2.16 however, use your freedom to **cover** up any evil, but live as
4. 8 love one another earnestly, because love **covers** over many sins.
Rev 3.18 to dress yourself and **cover** up your shameful nakedness.
4. 6 four living creatures **covered** with eyes in front and behind.
4. 8 six wings, and they were **covered** with eyes, inside and out.
5. 1 it was **covered** with writing on both sides and was sealed
9. 9 Their chests were **covered** with what looked like iron breastplates,
17. 4 and scarlet, and **covered** with gold ornaments, precious stones,
18.16 linen, purple, and scarlet, and **cover** herself with gold ornaments,
19.13 The robe he wore was **covered** with blood.

COW

Gen 15. 9 He answered, "Bring me a **cow,** a goat, and a ram, each
32.13 camels with their young, forty **cows** and ten bulls, twenty
41. 2 the River Nile, [2]when seven **cows,** fat and sleek, came up
41. 3 Then seven other **cows** came up;
41. 3 and stood by the other **cows** on the river-bank, [4]and the
41. 4 on the river-bank, [4]and the thin **cows** ate up the fat cows.
41.18 of the Nile, [18]when seven **cows,** fat and sleek, came up out
41.19 Then seven other **cows** came up which were thin and bony.
41.19 They were the poorest **cows** I have ever seen anywhere in Egypt.
41.20 The thin **cows** ate up the fat ones, [21]but no one would
41.26 The seven fat **cows** are seven years, and the seven full
41.27 The seven thin **cows** which came up later and the seven
Ex 22. 1 "If a man steals a **cow** or a sheep and kills it
22. 1 pay five cows for one **cow** and four sheep for one sheep.
22. 2 the stolen animal, whether a **cow,** a donkey, or a sheep, is
22.10 another man's donkey, **cow,** sheep, or other animal for him,
23. 4 happen to see your enemy's **cow** or donkey running loose, take
Lev 3. 1 it is to be a bull or a **cow** without any defects.
17. 3 An Israelite who kills a **cow** or a sheep or a goat
22.28 Do not sacrifice a **cow** and its calf or a sheep and
Num 18.17 But the first-born of **cows,** sheep, and goats are not to
19. 2 Moses and Aaron a red **cow** which has no defects and which
19. 8 The man who burnt the **cow** must also wash his clothes and
19. 9 collect the ashes of the **cow** and put them in a ritually
19.17 some ashes from the red **cow** which was burnt to remove sin
Deut 21. 3 are to select a young **cow** that has never been used for
21. 6 wash their hands over the **cow** [7]and say, 'We did not murder
22. 1 "If you see a fellow-Israelite's **cow** or sheep running loose,
22. 4 "If a fellow-Israelite's donkey or **cow** has fallen down,
32.14 Their **cows** and goats gave plenty of milk;
Judg 14.18 ploughing with my **cow,** You wouldn't know the answer now."
1 Sam 6. 7 prepare a new wagon and two **cows** that have never been yoked;
6.10 they took two **cows** and hitched them to the wagon, and shut
6.12 The **cows** started off on the road to Beth Shemesh and
6.14 wooden wagon and killed the **cows** and offered them as a
12. 3 Have I taken anybody's **cow** or anybody's donkey?
Neh 10.36 born to each of our **cows,** and the first lamb or kid
Job 6. 5 when eating grass, and a **cow** is quiet when eating hay.
29. 6 My **cows** and goats gave plenty of milk, and my olive-trees
40.15 He eats grass like a **cow,** [16]but what strength there is in
Is 7.21 to save only one young **cow** and two goats, [22]they will give
11. 7 **Cows** and bears will eat together, and their calves and
Jer 46.20 Egypt is like a splendid **cow,** attacked by a stinging fly
50.11 glad, going about like a **cow** threshing corn or like a
Ezek 4.15 I will let you use **cow** dung instead, and you can bake
Hos 10.11 a well-trained young **cow,** ready and willing to thresh grain.
Amos 4. 1 like the well-fed **cows** of Bashan, who ill-treat the weak,

COWARD

Ps 64. 4 they destroy good men with **cowardly** slander.
Is 14.31 the north—it is an army with no **cowards** in its ranks.
Gal 2.13 Jewish brothers also started acting like **cowards** along with Peter;
2.13 and even Barnabas was swept along by their **cowardly** action.
Rev 21. 8 But **cowards,** traitors, perverts, murderers, the immoral,

CRACK

Is 24.19 The earth will **crack** and shatter and split open.
30.13 You are like a high wall with a **crack** running down it;
Jer 2.13 and they have dug cisterns, **cracked** cisterns that can hold

Jer 2.16 Yes, the men of Memphis and Tahpanhes have **cracked** his skull.
Nah 3. 2 The **crack** of the whip, the rattle of wheels, the gallop of

CRACKLE

Ecc 7. 6 When a fool laughs, it is like thorns **crackling** in a fire.
Joel 2. 5 they **crackle** like dry grass on fire.

CRAFTSMAN
[VALLEY OF CRAFTSMEN]

Ex 28. 3 Call all the **craftsmen** to whom I have given ability, and
28. 5 The **craftsmen** are to use blue, purple, and red wool, gold
31. 6 to all the other skilful **craftsmen,** so that they can make
35.34 tribe of Dan, the ability to teach their **crafts** to others.
36. 1 Oholiab, and all the other **craftsmen** to whom the Lord has
1 Kgs 7.13 a man named Huram, a **craftsman** living in the city of Tyre,
7.14 was from Tyre, and had also been a skilled bronze **craftsman;**
7.14 Huram was an intelligent and experienced **craftsman.**
1 Chr 4.14 founder of the **Valley of Craftsmen,** where all the people
22.15 as a large number of **craftsmen** of every sort who can work
29. 5 Temple [5] and for all the objects which the **craftsmen** are to make.
2 Chr 2. 7 He will work with the **craftsmen** of Judah and Jerusalem whom
2.13 I am sending you a wise and skilful master **craftsman** named Huram.
2.14 Let him work with your **craftsmen** and with those who worked
4.11 Huram the master **craftsman** made all these objects
Neh 11.35 Lod, and Ono, and in the **Valley of Craftsmen.**
Is 40.20 He finds a skilful **craftsman** to make an image that won't
41. 6 The **craftsmen** help and encourage one another.
Jer 24. 1 leaders of Judah, the **craftsmen,** and the skilled workers.)
29. 2 Judah and of Jerusalem, the **craftsmen,** and the skilled
Hos 8. 6 An Israelite **craftsman** made the idol, and it is not a god

CRAFTY

2 Cor 12.16 will say that I was **crafty,** and trapped you with lies.

CRASH

Job 30.14 holes in my defences and come **crashing** down on top of me;
Ps 77.17 thunder **crashed** from the sky, and lightning flashed
77.18 The **crash** of your thunder rolled out, and flashes of
Is 10.33 Lord Almighty will bring them **crashing** down like branches
17.12 like the roar of the sea, like the **crashing** of huge waves.
26. 5 they lived in, and sent its walls **crashing** into the dust.
Zeph 1.10 part of the city and a great **crashing** sound in the hills.
Lk 6.49 house it fell at once—and what a terrible **crash** that was!"

CRAVE
[GRAVES OF CRAVING]

Num 11. 4 They had a strong **craving** for meat, and even the Israelites
11.34 Hattaavah (which means **"Graves of Craving"),**
11.34 because there they buried the people who had **craved** meat.
33.15 Kibroth Hattaavah (or **"Graves of Craving"),** Hazeroth,
Ps 78.30 had not yet satisfied their **craving** and were still eating,
106.14 They were filled with **craving** in the desert and put God
Prov 31. 4 Kings should not drink wine or have a **craving** for alcohol.

Am **CRAWL (skin)** see **(hair) BRISTLE**

CRAWL

Gen 3.14 From now on you will **crawl** on your belly, and you will
Lev 11.23 that have wings and also **crawl** must be considered unclean.
11.42 on the ground, [42] whether they **crawl,** or walk on four legs,
Mic 7.17 They will **crawl** in the dust like snakes;

Am **CRAZY** see **MAD**

CRAZY

2 Kgs 9.11 What did that **crazy** fellow want with you?"
1 Cor 14.23 unbelievers come in, won't they say that you are all **crazy?**

CREAM

Gen 18. 8 He took some **cream,** some milk, and the meat, and set the
Judg 5.25 she brought him **cream** in a beautiful bowl.
2 Sam 17.28 grain, beans, peas, honey, cheese, **cream,** and some sheep.
Ps 55.21 His words were smoother than **cream,** but there was hatred

CREATE

Gen 1. 1 In the beginning, when God **created** the universe,
1.21 So God **created** the great sea-monsters, all kinds of creatures
1.27 So God **created** human beings, making them to be like himself.
1.27 He **created** them male and female, [28] blessed them, and said,
2. 3 that day he had completed his **creation** and stopped working.
2. 4 And that is how the universe was **created.**
5. 1 (When God **created** human beings, he made them like himself.
5. 2 He **created** them male and female, blessed them,
6. 7 out these people I have **created,** and also the animals and
Num 11.12 I didn't **create** them or bring them to birth!
Deut 4.32 way back to the time when God **created** man on the earth.
26.19 other nation that he has **created,** and you will bring praise
2 Kgs 19.15 You **created** the earth and the sky.
1 Chr 16.26 nations are only idols, but the Lord **created** the heavens.
Neh 4. 8 come and attack Jerusalem and **create** confusion, [9] but we
Job 31.15 The same God who **created** me created my servants also.
34.19 favour the rich against the poor, for he **created** everyone.
40.15 I **created** him and I created you.
Ps 8. 6 you placed him over all **creation:**
33. 6 The Lord **created** the heavens by his command, the sun,
33. 9 When he spoke, the world was **created;**
51.10 **Create** a pure heart in me, O God, and put a new
74.16 You **created** the day and the night;
86. 9 the nations that you have **created** will come and bow down to
89.12 You **created** the north and the south;
89.47 remember that you **created** all of us mortal!
90. 2 Before you **created** the hills or brought the world into being,
96. 5 nations are only idols, but the Lord **created** the heavens.
102.25 long ago you **created** the earth, and with your own
104.19 You **created** the moon to mark the months;
104.30 But when you give them breath, they are **created;**
119.73 You **created** me, and you keep me safe;
139.13 You **created** every part of me;
148. 5 He commanded, and they were **created;**
Prov 3.19 The Lord **created** the earth by his wisdom;
8.22 "The Lord **created** me first of all, the first of his works,
Ecc 12.13 his commands, because this is all that man was **created** for.
Is 19.25 you, Assyria, whom I **created;**
34.11 make it a barren waste again, as it was before the **creation.**
37.16 You **created** the earth and the sky.
40.26 Who **created** the stars you see?
40.28 he **created** all the world.
42. 5 God **created** the heavens and stretched them out;
43. 1 Israel, the Lord who **created** you says,
43. 7 are my own people, and I **created** them to bring me glory."
43.15 I **created** you, Israel, and I am your king."
44. 2 I am the Lord who **created** you;
44.21 I **created** you to be my servant, and I will never forget
44.24 I am the one who **created** you.
45. 7 I **create** both light and darkness;
45.12 one who made the earth and **created** mankind to live there.
45.18 The Lord **created** the heavens— he is the one who is
54.16 "I **create** the blacksmith, who builds a fire and forges weapons.
54.16 I also **create** the soldier, who uses the weapons to kill.
64. 8 You **created** us, [9] so do not be too angry with us or
65.18 Be glad and rejoice for ever in what I **create.**
66. 2 I myself **created** the whole universe!
Jer 10.12 by his wisdom he **created** the world and stretched out the heavens.
27. 5 great power and strength I **created** the world, mankind, and
31.22 I have **created** something new and different, as different as
51.15 by his wisdom he **created** the world and stretched out the heavens.
Ezek 21.30 the place where you were **created,** in the land where you were
28.13 They were made for you on the day you were **created.**
28.15 from the day you were **created** until you began to do evil.
Amos 4.13 God is the one who made the mountains and **created** the winds.
7. 1 In it I saw him **create** a swarm of locusts just after
Zech 12. 1 who spread out the skies, **created** the earth, and gave life
Mal 2.10 Didn't the same God **create** us all?
Mt 13.35 I will tell them things unknown since the **creation** of the world."
19. 8 But it was not like that at the time of **creation.**
25.34 been prepared for you ever since the **creation** of the world.
Mk 10. 6 at the time of **creation,** 'God made them male and female,'
13.19 very beginning when God **created** the world until the present time.
Lk 11.50 the prophets killed since the **creation** of the world,
Jn 1. 1 Before the world was **created,** the Word already existed;
1. 3 not one thing in all **creation** was made without him.
Acts 17.26 From one man he **created** all races of mankind and made
Rom 1.20 Ever since God **created** the world, his invisible qualities,
1.25 and serve what God has **created** instead of the Creator himself,
5. 4 endurance brings God's approval, and his approval **creates** hope.
8.19 All of **creation** waits with eager longing for God to
8.20 For **creation** was condemned to lose its purpose, not of
8.21 there was the hope [21] that **creation** itself would one day be
8.22 the present time all of **creation** groans with pain, like the
8.23 But it is not just **creation** alone which groans;
8.39 there is nothing in all **creation** that will ever be able to
11.36 For all things were **created** by him, and all things exist
1 Cor 8. 6 Christ, through whom all things were **created** and through whom we live.
11. 8 for man was not **created** from woman, but woman from man.
11. 9 Nor was man **created** for woman's sake,
11. 9 but woman was **created** for man's sake.
15.45 scripture says, "The first man, Adam, was **created** a living being";
Eph 1.10 is to bring all **creation** together, everything in heaven and on
2.10 with Christ Jesus he has **created** us for a life of good
2.15 and rules, in order to **create** out of the two races one
4.24 new self, which is **created** in God's likeness and reveals itself
Col 1.15 He is the first-born Son, superior to all **created** things.
1.16 For through him God **created** everything in heaven and on earth,
1.16 God **created** the whole universe through him and for him.
1 Tim 2.13 For Adam was **created** first, and then Eve.
4. 3 But God **created** those foods to be eaten, after a prayer of
4. 4 Everything that God has **created** is good;
Heb 1. 2 the one through whom God **created** the universe, the one whom
1.10 "You, Lord, in the beginning **created** the earth, and with
2.10 only right that God, who **creates** and preserves all things,
4. 3 work had been finished from the time he **created** the world.
4.13 everything in all **creation** is exposed and lies open before his
9.11 that is, it is not a part of this **created** world.
9.26 to suffer many times ever since the **creation** of the world.
11. 3 understand that the universe was **created** by God's word,
12.27 plainly show that the **created** things will be shaken and removed,
Jas 2. 4 then you are guilty of **creating** distinctions among yourselves
3. 9 curse our fellow-man, who is **created** in the likeness of God.
1 Pet 1.20 chosen by God before the **creation** of the world and was

2 Pet 3. 4 still the same as it was since the **creation** of the world!"
3. 5 God gave a command, and the heavens and earth were **created.**
Rev 3.14 true witness, who is the origin of all that God has **created.**
4.11 For you **created** all things, and by your will they were given
10. 6 for ever and ever, who **created** heaven, earth, and the sea,
13. 8 names were written before the **creation** of the world in the
16.18 There has never been such an earthquake since the **creation** of man;
17. 8 not been written before the **creation** of the world in the

CREATOR

Deut 32. 6 He is your father, your **Creator,** he made you into a nation.
32.15 They abandoned God their **Creator** and rejected their mighty saviour.
2 Chr 2.12 Praise the Lord God of Israel, **Creator** of heaven and earth!
Job 4.17 in the sight of God or be pure before his **Creator?**
35.10 don't turn to God, their **Creator,** who gives them hope in
36. 3 use what I know to show that God, my **Creator,** is just.
40.19 Only his **Creator** can defeat him.
Ps 146. 6 the Lord his God, [6]the **Creator** of heaven, earth, and sea,
149. 2 Be glad, Israel, because of your **Creator;**
Ecc 12. 1 So remember your **Creator** while you are still young, before
Is 17. 7 will turn for help to their **Creator,** the holy God of Israel.
27.11 have understood nothing, God their **Creator** will not pity
44.24 I am the Lord, the **Creator** of all things.
54. 5 Your **Creator** will be like a husband to you— the Lord
Mt 19. 4 that in the beginning the **Creator** made people male and female?
Acts 4.24 "Master and **Creator** of heaven, earth, and sea, and all that
Rom 1.25 has created instead of the **Creator** himself, who is to be
1 Cor 8. 6 the Father, who is the **Creator** of all things and for whom
Eph 3. 9 God, who is the **Creator** of all things, kept his secret
Col 3.10 new being which God, its **Creator,** is constantly renewing
Jas 1.17 comes down from God, the **Creator** of the heavenly lights,
1 Pet 4.19 trust themselves completely to their **Creator,** who always keeps

CREATURE

Gen 1.21 sea-monsters, all kinds of **creatures** that live in the water,
1.22 them all and told the **creatures** that live in the water to
3.24 the garden he put living **creatures** and a flaming sword which
Ex 25.18 Make two winged **creatures** of hammered gold, [19]one for
25.20 The winged **creatures** are to face each other across the lid,
25.22 lid between the two winged **creatures** I will give you all my
26. 1 Embroider them with figures of winged **creatures.**
26.31 Embroider it with figures of winged **creatures.**
36. 8 red wool and embroidered with figures of winged **creatures.**
36.35 wool and embroidered it with figures of winged **creatures.**
37. 7 He made two winged **creatures** of hammered gold, [8]one for
37. 9 The winged **creatures** faced each other across the lid, and
Lev 11.11 Such **creatures** must be considered unclean.
Num 7.89 lid on the Covenant Box, between the two winged **creatures.**
1 Sam 4. 4 who is enthroned above the winged **creatures.**
2 Sam 6. 2 Lord Almighty, who is enthroned above the winged **creatures.**
22.11 He flew swiftly on his winged **creature;**
1 Kgs 6.23 Two winged **creatures** were made of olive wood and placed
6.28 The two winged **creatures** were covered with gold.
6.29 were all decorated with carved figures of winged **creatures,**
6.32 were decorated with carved figures of winged **creatures,**
6.32 the winged **creatures,** and the palm-trees were covered with gold.
6.35 with carved figures of winged **creatures,** palm-trees, and
7.29 with the figures of lions, bulls, and winged **creatures** on the panels;
7.36 with figures of winged **creatures,** lions, and palm-trees,
8. 6 put it in the Most Holy Place, beneath the winged **creatures.**
2 Kgs 19.15 enthroned above the winged **creatures,** you alone are God,
1 Chr 13. 6 the name of the Lord enthroned above the winged **creatures.**
16.32 Roar, sea, and every **creature** in you;
28.18 the chariot for the winged **creatures** that spread their wings
2 Chr 3. 7 On the walls the workmen carved designs of winged **creatures.**
3.10 workmen to make two winged **creatures** out of metal, cover
3.14 red, with designs of the winged **creatures** worked into it.
5. 7 put it in the Most Holy Place, beneath the winged **creatures.**
Job 4.19 think he will trust a **creature** of clay, a thing of dust
12. 8 ask the **creatures** of earth and sea for their wisdom.
12.10 It is God who directs the lives of his **creatures;**
14.15 I will answer, and you will be pleased with me, your **creature.**
28.21 No living **creature** can see it, Not even a bird in flight.
40.19 The most amazing of all my **creatures!**
41.33 he is a **creature** that has no fear.
Ps 8. 8 the birds and the fish and the **creatures** in the seas.
18.10 He flew swiftly on a winged **creature;**
69.34 Praise God, O heaven and earth, seas and all **creatures** in them.
75. 3 Though every living **creature** tremble and the earth itself be shaken,
80. 1 your throne above the winged **creatures,** [2]reveal yourself to
96.11 Roar, sea, and every **creature** in you;
98. 7 Roar, sea, and every **creature** in you;
99. 1 He is enthroned above the winged **creatures** and the earth shakes.
103.22 Praise the Lord, all his **creatures** in all the places he rules.
104.24 The earth is filled with your **creatures.**
104.25 where countless **creatures** live, large and small alike.
136.25 He gives food to every living **creature;**
145.10 All your **creatures,** Lord, will praise you, and all your
145.21 let all his **creatures** praise his holy name for ever.
150. 6 Praise the Lord, all living **creatures!**
Ecc 3.19 They are both the same kind of **creature.**
Is 6. 2 Round him flaming **creatures** were standing,
6. 2 Each **creature** covered its face with two wings, and its body
6. 6 Then one of the **creatures** flew down to me, carrying a
34.16 the Lord's book of living **creatures** and read what it says.
34.16 Not one of these **creatures** will be missing, and not one will
Is 37.16 enthroned above the winged **creatures,** you alone are God,
42.10 praise him, all **creatures** of the sea!
Jer 51.62 would be no living **creature** in it, neither man nor animal,
Ezek 1. 5 what looked like four living **creatures** in human form, [6]but
1. 9 Two wings of each **creature** were spread out
1. 9 so that the **creatures** formed a square with their wing
1.10 Each living **creature** had four different faces:
1.11 Two wings of each **creature** were raised so that they
1.11 of the wings of the **creatures** next to it, and their other
1.12 Each **creature** faced all four directions, and so the
1.13 Among the **creatures** there was something that looked like
1.14 The **creatures** themselves darted to and fro
1.15 was looking at the four **creatures,** I saw four wheels
1.19 Whenever the **creatures** moved, the wheels moved with them,
1.19 and if the **creatures** rose up from the earth, so
1.20 The **creatures** went wherever they wished, and the wheels
1.20 did exactly what the **creatures** did, because the creatures controlled them.
1.21 So every time the **creatures** moved or stopped or rose in
1.22 Above the heads of the **creatures** there was something
1.23 under the dome stood the **creatures,** each stretching out two
3.13 the wings of the **creatures** beating together in the air,
9. 3 rose up from the winged **creatures,** where it had been, and
10. 1 the heads of the living **creatures** and above them was
10. 2 between the wheels under the **creatures** and fill your hands
10. 3 The **creatures** were standing to the south of the Temple
10. 4 presence rose up from the **creatures** and moved to the
10. 5 The noise made by the **creatures'** wings was heard even in
10. 6 wheels that were under the **creatures,** the man went in and
10. 7 One of the **creatures** put his hand into the fire that was
10. 8 I saw that each **creature** had what looked like a human hand
10. 9 there were four wheels, all alike, one beside each **creature.**
10.11 When the **creatures** moved, they could go in any direction
10.14 Each **creature** had four faces.
10.15 (They were the same **creatures** that I had seen by the
10.15 When the **creatures** rose in the air [16]and moved, the wheels
10.17 When the **creatures** stopped, the wheels stopped;
10.17 and when the **creatures** flew,
10.17 the wheels went with them, because the **creatures** controlled them.
10.18 of the Temple and moved to a place above the **creatures.**
10.20 recognized them as the same **creatures** which I had seen
10.22 Each **creature** moved straight ahead.
11.22 The living **creatures** began to fly, and the wheels went with them.
41.18 with carvings [18]of palm-trees and winged **creatures.**
41.18 Palm-trees alternated with **creatures,** one following the other,
41.18 Each **creature** had two faces:
41.25 There were palm-trees and winged **creatures** carved on the
Gal 6.15 what does matter is being a new **creature.**
Heb 9. 5 the Box were the winged **creatures** representing God's presence,
Jas 1.18 so that we should have first place among all his **creatures.**
3. 7 has tamed all other **creatures**—wild animals and birds, reptiles
Rev 4. 6 were four living **creatures** covered with eyes in front and
4. 8 one of the four living **creatures** had six wings, and they
4. 9 The four living **creatures** sing songs of glory and honour
5. 6 throne, surrounded by the four living **creatures** and the elders.
5. 8 the four living **creatures** and the twenty-four elders fell down
5.11 throne, the four living **creatures,** and the elders, [12]and sang
5.13 And I heard every **creature** in heaven, on earth, in the
5.14 The four living **creatures** answered, "Amen!"
6. 1 one of the four living **creatures** say in a voice that sounded
6. 3 and I heard the second living **creature** say, "Come!"
6. 5 and I heard the third living **creature** say, "Come!"
6. 6 among the four living **creatures,** which said, "A litre of wheat
6. 7 and I heard the fourth living **creature** say, "Come!"
7.11 stood round the throne, the elders, and the four living **creatures.**
8. 9 a third of the living **creatures** in the sea died, and a
14. 3 stood before the throne, the four living **creatures,** and the elders;
15. 7 one of the four living **creatures** gave the seven angels seven
16. 3 a dead person, and every living **creature** in the sea died.
19. 4 elders and the four living **creatures** fell down and worshipped God,

CREDIT

Lev 7.18 not be counted to his **credit** but will be considered unclean,
Judg 4. 9 but you won't get any **credit** for the victory, because the
7. 2 that they had won by themselves, and so give me no **credit.**
2 Sam 12.28 I don't want to get the **credit** for capturing it."
Neh 5.19 O God, remember to my **credit** everything that I have done for
13.31 Remember all this, O God, and give me **credit** for it.
Job 10.15 trouble with you, but when I do right, I get no **credit.**
Prov 31.31 Give her **credit** for all she does.
Tit 2.10 faithful, so as to bring **credit** to the teaching about God
1 Pet 2.20 For what **credit** is there if you endure the beatings you

CREDITORS

Ps 109.11 May his **creditors** take away all his property, and may
Is 3.12 Money-lenders oppress my people, and their **creditors** cheat them.

CREEP

1 Sam 24. 4 David **crept** over and cut off a piece of Saul's robe without

CREST

Judg 9.37 are men coming down the **crest** of the mountain and one group

CRETE
Island in the Mediterranean south of Greece.

Gen 10.14 and of **Crete** from whom the Philistines are descended.
Deut 2.23 Mediterranean coast had been settled by people from the island of **Crete.**
1 Chr 1.12 and of **Crete** (from whom the Philistines were descended).
Jer 47. 4 the Philistines, all who came from the shores of **Crete.**
Amos 9. 7 I brought the Philistines from **Crete** and the Syrians from Kir,
Acts 2.11 some of us are from **Crete** and Arabia—yet all of us
27. 7 sheltered side of the island of **Crete,** passing by Cape Salmone.
27.12 Phoenix is a harbour in **Crete** that faces south-west and north-west.
27.13 and sailed as close as possible along the coast of **Crete.**
27.21 should have listened to me and not have sailed from **Crete;**
Tit 1. 5 I left you in **Crete,** so that you could put in order
1.12 It was a **Cretan** himself, one of their own prophets,
1.12 the truth when he said, **"Cretans** are always liars, wicked beasts,

CREVICE

Song 2.14 are like a dove that hides in the **crevice** of a rock.

CREW

Ezek 27.27 All the sailors in your **crew,**
Jon 1. 3 and went aboard with the **crew** to sail to Spain, where he

CRICKET

Lev 11.22 You may eat locusts, **crickets,** or grasshoppers.

CRIME

Gen 31.36 "What **crime** have I committed?"
44. 5 You have committed a serious **crime!"**
50.17 ask you, 'Please forgive the **crime** your brothers committed
Deut 19.15 "One witness is not enough to convict a man of a **crime;**
19.16 falsely accusing him of a **crime,** [17]both are to go to the
21.22 put to death for a **crime** and his body is hung on
24.16 be put to death for **crimes** committed by their children, and
24.16 to be put to death for **crimes** committed by their parents;
24.16 be put to death only for a **crime** he himself has committed.
25. 2 The number of lashes will depend on the **crime** he has committed.
Judg 9.24 to murder Gideon's seventy sons, would pay for their **crime.**
9.56 paid Abimelech back for the **crime** that he committed against
20. 3 The Israelites asked, "Tell us, how was this **crime** committed?"
20.12 Benjamin to say, "What is this **crime** that you have committed?
1 Sam 20. 1 "What **crime** have I committed?
25.33 in keeping me from the **crime** of murder and from taking my
26.18 What **crime** have I committed?
2 Sam 3.34 He died like someone killed by **criminals!"**
3.39 May the Lord punish these **criminals** as they deserve!"
13.16 away like this is a greater **crime** than what you just did!"
14.11 will not commit a greater **crime** by killing my other son."
16. 7 **Criminal!**
2 Kgs 14. 6 be put to death for **crimes** committed by their children, and
14. 6 to be put to death for **crimes** committed by their parents;
14. 6 put to death only for a **crime** he himself has committed."
2 Chr 25. 4 be put to death for **crimes** committed by their children, and
25. 4 to be put to death for **crimes** committed by their parents;
25. 4 put to death only for a **crime** he himself has committed."
Job 13.23 What **crimes** am I charged with?
Ps 35.11 against me and accuse me of **crimes** I know nothing about.
55.10 surrounding it day and night, filling it with **crime** and trouble.
58. 2 evil you can do, and commit **crimes** of violence in the land.
64. 6 They make evil plans and say, "We have planned a perfect **crime."**
94. 4 How much longer will **criminals** be proud
94. 4 and boast about their **crimes?**
109. 7 may even his prayer be considered a **crime!**
Prov 29.16 When evil men are in power, **crime** increases.
Ecc 8.11 Why do people commit **crimes** so readily?
8.11 Because **crime** is not punished quickly enough.
8.12 A sinner may commit a hundred **crimes** and still live.
Is 29.21 who prevent the punishment of **criminals,** and those who tell
50. 1 you were sent away because of your **crimes.**
53. 9 though he had never committed a **crime** or ever told a lie."
59.12 "Lord, our **crimes** against you are many.
59.15 who stops doing evil finds himself the victim of **crime."**
61. 8 "I love justice and I hate oppression and **crime.**
Jer 16.10 They will ask what **crime** they are guilty of and what sin
37.18 Then I asked, "What **crime** have I committed against you
41.11 with him heard of the **crime** that Ishmael had committed.
Ezek 9. 9 all over the land and have filled Jerusalem with **crime.**
Hos 4. 2 **Crimes** increase, and there is one murder after another.
12.14 they deserve death for their **crimes.**
Amos 3. 9 see the great disorder and the **crimes** being committed there."
3.10 fill their mansions with things taken by **crime** and violence.
5.12 your sins are and how many **crimes** you have committed.
Hab 2.12 You founded a city on **crime** and built it up by murder.
Mt 27.23 But Pilate asked, "What **crime** has he committed?"
Mk 15.14 "But what **crime** has he committed?"
Lk 22.37 'He shared the fate of **criminals,'** must come true about me,
23.14 found him guilty of any of the **crimes** you accuse him of.
23.22 to them the third time, "But what **crime** has he committed?
23.32 other men, both of them **criminals,** were also led out to be
23.33 Jesus there, and the two **criminals,** one on his right and the
23.39 One of the **criminals** hanging there hurled insults at him:
Jn 18.30 have brought him to you if he had not committed a **crime."**
Acts 16.37 not found guilty of any **crime,** yet they whipped us in public
18.14 matter of some evil **crime** or wrong that has been committed,
22.25 a Roman citizen who hasn't even been tried for any **crime?"**
24.20 these men here tell what **crime** they found me guilty of
25.16 any man accused of a **crime** before he has met his accusers
25.18 him of any of the evil **crimes** that I thought they would.
1 Tim 1. 9 but for lawbreakers and **criminals,** for the godless and sinful,
2 Tim 2. 9 Good News, I suffer and I am even chained like a **criminal.**
1 Pet 4.15 or a thief or a **criminal** or a meddler in other people's

CRIPPLE

Gen 49. 6 For they killed men in anger And they **crippled** bulls for sport.
Lev 21.19 no one with a **crippled** hand or foot;
22.22 animal that is blind or **crippled** or mutilated, or that has a
Deut 15.21 the animals, if they are **crippled** or blind or have any other
Josh 11. 6 You are to **cripple** their horses and burn their chariots."
11. 9 he **crippled** their horses and burnt their chariots.
2 Sam 4. 4 such a hurry that she dropped him, and he became **crippled.**
5. 6 even the blind and the **crippled** could keep you out."
5. 8 the water tunnel and attack those poor blind **cripples."**
5. 8 "The blind and the **crippled** cannot enter the Lord's house.")
8. 4 horses for a hundred chariots and **crippled** all the rest.
9. 3 He is **crippled."**
9.13 So Mephibosheth, who was **crippled** in both feet, lived in Jerusalem,
19.26 He answered, "As you know, Your Majesty, I am **crippled.**
1 Kgs 15.23 But in his old age he was **crippled** by a foot disease.
1 Chr 18. 4 horses for a hundred chariots and **crippled** all the rest.
2 Chr 16.12 that Asa was king, he was **crippled** by a severe foot disease;
Ps 35.16 men who would mock a **cripple,** they glared at me with hate.
Prov 25.19 to chew with a loose tooth or walk with a **crippled** foot.
26. 7 proverb about as well as a **crippled** man can use his legs.
Mic 4. 7 They are **crippled** and far from home, but I will make a
Mt 15.30 the lame, the blind, the **crippled,** the dumb, and many other
15.31 saw the dumb speaking, the **crippled** made whole, the lame walking,
21.14 The blind and the **crippled** came to him in the Temple,
Lk 14.13 a feast, invite the poor, the **crippled,** the lame, and the
14.21 and bring back the poor, the **crippled,** the blind, and the

CRISIS

Prov 24.10 If you are weak in a **crisis,** you are weak indeed.
25.19 an unreliable person in a **crisis** is like trying to chew with

CRITICIZE

Num 12. 1 a Cushite woman, and Miriam and Aaron **criticized** him for it.
Job 34.29 God decided to do nothing at all, no one could **criticize** him.
Prov 10.10 trouble, but one who openly **criticizes** works for peace.
27.11 I will have an answer for anyone who **criticizes** me.
30.10 Never **criticize** a servant to his master.
Ecc 10.20 Don't **criticize** the king, even silently,
10.20 and don't **criticize** the rich, even in the privacy
Mk 14. 5 And they **criticized** her harshly.
Lk 11.53 Pharisees began to **criticize** him bitterly and ask him questions
Acts 11. 2 in favour of circumcising Gentiles **criticized** him, saying,
11.18 heard this, they stopped their **criticism** and praised God, saying,
1 Cor 9. 3 When people **criticize** me, this is how I defend myself:
10.30 why should anyone **criticize** me about food for which I
Tit 2. 8 sound words that cannot be **criticized,** so that your enemies may
Jas 4.11 Do not **criticize** one another, my brothers.
4.11 Whoever **criticizes** a Christian brother or judges him,
4.11 **criticizes** the Law and judges it.

CROCODILE

Ezek 29. 3 I am your enemy, you monster **crocodile,** lying in the river.
32. 2 but you are more like a **crocodile** splashing through a river.

CROOKED

Ps 78.57 disloyal like their fathers, unreliable as a **crooked** arrow.
Prov 21. 8 Guilty people walk a **crooked** path;
Ecc 1.15 You can't straighten out what is **crooked;**
7.13 How can anyone straighten out what God has made **crooked?**
Is 59. 8 You follow a **crooked** path, and no one who walks that path
Hos 7.16 They are as unreliable as a **crooked** bow.

CROP (1)
[OLIVE-CROP]

Gen 4.12 If you try to grow **crops,** the soil will not produce anything;
41.34 take a fifth of the **crops** during the seven years of plenty.
41.47 the land produced abundant **crops,** [48]all of which Joseph collected
Ex 22. 5 and eat up the **crops** growing in another man's field,
22. 5 the loss with the **crops** from his own fields or vineyards.
23.16 "Celebrate the Harvest Festival when you begin to harvest your **crops.**
34.22 begin to harvest the first **crop** of your wheat, and keep the
Lev 25. 3 prune your vineyards, and gather your **crops** for six years.
25.15 land can produce **crops** before the next Year of Restoration.
25.16 is being sold is the number of **crops** the land can produce.
25.19 The land will produce its **crops,** and you will have all
25.20 seventh year, when no fields are sown and no **crops** gathered.
25.22 to eat until the **crops** you plant that year are harvested.
26. 4 the land will produce **crops** and the trees will bear fruit.
26. 5 Your **crops** will be so plentiful that you will still be
26.20 your land will not produce **crops** and the trees will not bear
Deut 11.17 rain, and your ground will become too dry for **crops** to grow.
14.28 the tithe of all your **crops** and store it in your towns.
22. 9 "Do not plant any **crop** in the same field as your grapevines;
22. 9 to use either the grapes or the produce of the other **crop.**

Deut 24.19 “When you gather your **crops** and fail to bring in some
26. 2 the first part of each **crop** that you harvest and you must
26.12 tithe—a tenth of your **crops**—to the Levites, the foreigners,
28. 4 with abundant **crops**, and with many cattle and sheep.
28. 5 Lord will bless your corn **crops** and the food you prepare
28.11 children, many cattle, and abundant **crops** in the land that
28.17 Lord will curse your corn **crops** and the food you prepare
28.18 only a few children, poor **crops**, and few cattle and sheep.
28.22 will send drought and scorching winds to destroy your **crops**.
28.33 nation will take all the **crops** that you have worked so hard
28.38 a small harvest, because the locusts will eat your **crops**.
28.42 All your trees and **crops** will be devoured by insects.
28.51 your livestock and your **crops**, and you will starve to death.
30. 9 of livestock, and your fields will produce abundant **crops**.
Judg 6. 4 the land and destroy the **crops** as far south as the area
1 Sam 8.12 plough his fields, harvest his **crops**, and make his weapons
1 Kgs 8.37 or an epidemic, or the **crops** are destroyed by scorching
2 Kgs 8. 6 the value of all the **crops** that her fields had produced
2 Chr 6.28 or an epidemic or the **crops** are destroyed by scorching winds
7.13 locusts to eat up the **crops** or send an epidemic on my
Neh 10.37 villages, the tithes from the **crops** that grow on our land.
Job 5. 5 people will eat the fool's **crops**— even the grain growing
31. 8 with sin, [8]then let my **crops** be destroyed, or let others
Ps 65. 9 you provide the earth with **crops**.
72.16 be covered with **crops**, as fruitful as those of Lebanon.
78.46 He sent locusts to eat their **crops** and to destroy their fields.
104.14 that he can grow his **crops** [15]and produce wine to make him
105.35 they ate all the **crops**.
144.13 May our barns be filled with **crops** of every kind.
Prov 10. 5 A sensible man gathers the **crops** when they are ready;
27.25 on the hillsides while the next **crop** of hay is growing.
28. 3 poor people is like a driving rain that destroys the **crops**.
Is 4. 2 take delight and pride in the **crops** that the land produces.
7.25 All the hills where **crops** used to grow will be so
19. 7 will wither, [7]and all the **crops** sown along the banks of the
32.15 The waste land will become fertile, and fields will produce rich **crops**.
32.20 plenty of water for the **crops** and safe pasture everywhere
55.10 They make the **crops** grow and provide seed for sowing and
Jer 5.17 They will devour your **crops** and your food;
7.20 and animals alike, and even on the trees and the **crops**.
12.13 Because of my fierce anger their **crops** have failed.”
50.19 all they want of the **crops** that grow in the territories of
Ezek 34.27 fruit, the fields will produce **crops**, and everyone will live
Joel 1. 4 Swarm after swarm of locusts settled on the **crops**;
1.11 the wheat, the barley, yes all the **crops** are destroyed.
1.16 We look on helpless as our **crops** are destroyed.
2.14 God will change his mind and bless you with abundant **crops**.
2.25 lost in the years when swarms of locusts ate your **crops**.
Amos 4. 7 I held back the rain when your **crops** needed it most.
4. 9 “I sent a scorching wind to dry up your **crops**.
Mic 6.15 You will sow corn, but not harvest the **crop**.
Nah 3.15 You will be wiped out like **crops** eaten up by locusts.
Hab 3.17 the vines, even though the **olive-crop** fails and the fields
Hag 1.11 and olive orchards—on every **crop** the ground produces, on men
Zech 8.12 They will sow their **crops** in peace.
8.12 the earth will produce **crops**, and there will be plenty
Mal 3.11 not let insects destroy your **crops**, and your grapevines will
Mt 25.24 sow, and you gather **crops** where you did not scatter seed.
25.26 did not sow, and gather **crops** where I did not scatter seed?
Lk 12.16 was once a rich man who had land which bore good **crops**.
12.17 think to himself, ‘I haven't anywhere to keep all my **crops**.
Jn 4.35 the **crops** are now ripe and ready to be harvested!
4.36 is being paid and gathers the **crops** for eternal life;
Acts 14.17 he gives you rain from heaven and **crops** at the right times;
1 Cor 9.10 their work in the hope of getting a share of the **crop**.
2 Cor 9. 6 that the person who sows few seeds will have a small **crop**;
9. 6 the one who sows many seeds will have a large **crop**.
Jas 5. 4 those who gather in your **crops** have reached the ears of God,
5. 7 is as he waits for his land to produce precious **crops**.
5.18 sky poured out its rain and the earth produced its **crops**.

CROP (2)

Lev 1.16 He shall remove the **crop** and its contents and throw them

Am

CROPS

see also **SEED**

CROSS (1)

Mt 10.38 does not take up his **cross** and follow in my steps is
16.24 he must forget self, carry his **cross**, and follow me.
27.32 named Simon, and the soldiers forced him to carry Jesus' **cross**.
27.40 Come on down from the **cross**!”
27.42 he comes down off the **cross** now, we will believe in him!
Mk 8.34 “he must forget self, carry his **cross**, and follow me.
15.21 country, and the soldiers forced him to carry Jesus' **cross**.
15.30 Now come down from the **cross** and save yourself!”
15.32 come down from the **cross** now, and we will believe in
15.36 see if Elijah is coming to bring him down from the **cross**!”
15.39 standing there in front of the **cross** saw how Jesus had died.
Lk 9.23 forget self, take up his **cross** every day, and follow me.
14.27 does not carry his own **cross** and come after me cannot be
23.26 They seized him, put the **cross** on him, and made him carry
Jn 19.17 He went out, carrying his **cross**, and came to “The Place
19.19 Pilate wrote a notice and had it put on the **cross**.
19.25 Standing close to Jesus' **cross** were his mother, his mother's
19.31 crucified, and to take the bodies down from the **crosses**.
19.31 bodies to stay on the **crosses** on the Sabbath, since the
Acts 5.30 after you had killed him by nailing him to a **cross**.
10.39 Then they put him to death by nailing him to a **cross**.
13.29 took him down from the **cross** and placed him in a tomb.
Rom 6. 6 death with Christ on his **cross**, in order that the power of
1 Cor 1.13 Was it Paul who died on the **cross** for you?
1.17 Christ's death on the **cross** is not robbed of its power.
1.18 about Christ's death on the **cross** is nonsense to those who
2. 2 except Jesus Christ and especially his death on the **cross**.
2 Cor 13. 4 put to death on the **cross**, it is by God's power that
Gal 2.19 death with Christ on his **cross**, [20]so that it is no longer
3. 1 clear description of the death of Jesus Christ on the **cross**!
5.11 my preaching about the **cross** of Christ would cause no trouble.
6.12 so that they may not be persecuted for the **cross** of Christ.
6.14 I will boast only about the **cross** of our Lord Jesus Christ;
6.14 for by means of his **cross** the world is dead to me,
Eph 2.16 By his death on the **cross** Christ destroyed their enmity;
2.16 by means of the **cross** he united both races into one body
Phil 2. 8 obedience all the way to death— his death on the **cross**.
3.18 lives make them enemies of Christ's death on the **cross**.
Col 1.20 sacrificial death on the **cross** and so brought back to himself
2.14 and did away with it completely by nailing it to the **cross**.
2.15 And on that **cross** Christ freed himself from the power of
Heb 12. 2 He did not give up because of the **cross**!
12. 2 disgrace of dying on the **cross**, and he is now seated at
1 Pet 2.24 in his body to the **cross**, so that we might die to

CROSS (2)

[RIVER CROSSING]

Gen 12.11 When he was about to **cross** the border into Egypt, he
12.14 When he **crossed** the border into Egypt, the Egyptians did
31.21 He **crossed** the River Euphrates
32.10 I **crossed** the Jordan with nothing but a walking-stick, and
32.22 and his eleven children, and **crossed** the River Jabbok.
48.14 But Jacob **crossed** his hands, and put his right hand on
Ex 19.12 that the people must not **cross**, and tell them not to go
19.21 warn the people not to **cross** the boundary to come and look
19.24 and the people must not **cross** the boundary to come up to
Num 32. 5 do not make us **cross** the River Jordan and settle there.”
32. 7 the people of Israel from **crossing** the Jordan into the land
32.21 your fighting men are to **cross** the Jordan and under the
32.27 We will **cross** the Jordan and fight, just as you have said.”
32.29 men of Gad and Reuben **cross** the Jordan ready for battle at
32.30 But if they do not **cross** the Jordan and go into battle
32.32 Under his command we will **cross** into the land of Canaan
33.51 “When you **cross** the Jordan into the land of Canaan, [52]you
35.10 “When you **cross** the River Jordan and enter the land of Canaan,
Deut 2.13 “Then we **crossed** the River Zered as the Lord told us
2.24 Lord said to us, ‘Now, start out and **cross** the River Arnon.
2.29 through your country, [29]until we **cross** the River Jordan
3.25 Let me **cross** the River Jordan, Lord, and see the fertile
4.21 declared that I would not **cross** the River Jordan to enter
4.22 in this land and never **cross** the river, but you are about
9. 1 Today you are about to **cross** the River Jordan and occupy the
11. 8 you will be able to **cross** the river and occupy the land
11.31 You are about to **cross** the River Jordan and occupy the
12.10 When you **cross** the River Jordan, the Lord will let you
27. 2 On the day you **cross** the River Jordan and enter the land
27.12 of Israel, [12]“After you have **crossed** the Jordan, the
31. 2 the Lord has told me that I will not **cross** the Jordan.
Josh 1. 2 the people of Israel, and **cross** the River Jordan into the
1.11 days you are going to **cross** the River Jordan to occupy the
1.14 soldiers, armed for battle, will **cross** over ahead of their
2. 7 as far as the place where the road **crosses** the Jordan.
2.23 came down from the hills, **crossed** the river, and went back
3. 1 to the Jordan, where they camped while waiting to **cross** it.
3.11 the Lord of all the earth **crosses** the Jordan ahead of you.
3.14 people left the camp to **cross** the Jordan, the priests went
3.16 off, and the people were able to **cross** over near Jericho.
3.17 middle of the Jordan until all the people had **crossed** over.
4. 1 When the whole nation had **crossed** the Jordan, the Lord
4. 7 when the Lord's Covenant Box **crossed** the river.
4.12 of Manasseh, ready for battle, **crossed** ahead of the rest of
4.13 men ready for war **crossed** over to the plain near Jericho.
4.19 The people **crossed** the Jordan on the tenth day of the
4.22 about the time when Israel **crossed** the Jordan on dry ground.
4.23 for you until you had **crossed**, just as he dried up the
5. 1 up the Jordan until the people of Israel had **crossed** it.
5. 4 forty years the people spent **crossing** the desert, none of
24.11 You **crossed** the Jordan and came to Jericho.
Judg 3.28 the place where the Moabites were to **cross** the Jordan;
3.28 they did not allow a single man to **cross**.
6.33 and the desert tribes assembled, **crossed** the River Jordan,
7.24 as Bethbarah, to keep the Midianites from **crossing** them.”
8. 4 hundred men had come to the River Jordan and had **crossed** it.
10. 9 The Ammonites even **crossed** the Jordan to fight the tribes of Judah,
11.18 there, but they did not **cross** the Arnon because it was the
11.32 So Jephthah **crossed** the river to fight the Ammonites,
12. 1 **crossed** the River Jordan to Zaphon and said to Jephthah,
12. 1 “Why did you **cross** the border to fight the Ammonites
12. 3 I risked my life and **crossed** the border to fight them, and
12. 5 Gileadites captured the places where the Jordan could be **crossed**.
12. 5 asked permission to **cross**, the men of Gilead would ask,
12. 6 and kill him there at one of the **crossings** of the Jordan.
1 Sam 13. 7 others **crossed** the River Jordan into the territories of Gad and Gilead.
14. 6 to the young man, “Let's **cross** over to the camp of those
26.13 Then David **crossed** over to the other side of the valley
30.10 men were too tired to **cross** the brook and so stayed behind.

2 Sam 2.29 **crossed** the River Jordan, and after marching all the next morning,
10.17 he gathered the Israelite troops, **crossed** the River Jordan,
15.23 The king **crossed** the brook of Kidron, followed by his men,
15.28 I will wait at the **river crossings** in the wilderness until I
17.16 spend the night at the **river crossings** in the wilderness,
17.16 but to **cross** the Jordan at once,
17.20 "They **crossed** the river," she answered.
17.21 against him and said, "Hurry up and **cross** the river."
17.22 David and his men started **crossing** the Jordan, and by
17.24 Absalom and the Israelites had **crossed** the Jordan.
19.18 They **crossed** the river to escort the royal party across
19.18 king was getting ready to **cross**, Shimei threw himself down
19.39 Then David and all his men **crossed** the Jordan.
19.40 When the king had **crossed**, escorted by all the men of
24. 5 They **crossed** the Jordan and camped south of Aroer, the
2 Kgs 2. 8 divided, and he and Elisha **crossed** to the other side on dry
1 Chr 12.15 Jordan overflowed its banks, they **crossed** the river,
19.17 he gathered the Israelite troops, **crossed** the Jordan, and
Job 36.12 will die in ignorance and **cross** the stream into the world of
Ps 66. 6 our ancestors **crossed** the river on foot.
77.19 you **crossed** the deep sea, but your footprints could not be seen.
Is 10.29 They have **crossed** the pass and are spending the night at Geba!
47. 2 Lift up your skirts to **cross** the streams!
51.10 the water, so that those you were saving could **cross**.
Jer 5.22 of the sea, a permanent boundary that it cannot **cross**.
37. 5 Egyptian army had **crossed** the Egyptian border, they retreated.
51.32 The enemy have captured the **river-crossing** and have set
Ezek 47. 5 It was too deep to **cross** except by swimming.
Mt 14.34 They **crossed** the lake and came to land at Gennesaret,
16. 5 When the disciples **crossed** over to the other side of the lake,
23.15 You sail the seas and **cross** whole countries to win one convert;
Mk 6.53 They **crossed** the lake and came to land at Gennesaret,
10. 1 went to the province of Judaea, and **crossed** the River Jordan.
Lk 16.26 that those who want to **cross** over from here to you cannot
16.26 do so, nor can anyone **cross** over to us from where you
Acts 27. 5 We **crossed** over the sea off Cilicia and Pamphylia and came
Heb 11.29 made the Israelites able to **cross** the Red Sea as if on

CROSS (3)

Jer 3. 5 you won't be **cross** with me for ever.'

CROSS-BAR

Ex 26.26 "Make fifteen **cross-bars** of acacia-wood, five for the
26.28 The middle **cross-bar**, set half-way up the frames, is to
26.29 gold rings to hold the **cross-bars**, which are also to be
35.11 its hooks and its frames, its **cross-bars**, its posts, and its
36.31 They made fifteen **cross-bars** of acacia-wood, five for
36.33 The middle **cross-bar**, set half-way up the frames,
36.34 to hold the **cross-bars**, which were also covered with gold.
39.33 equipment, its hooks, its frames, its **cross-bars**, its posts,
40.18 its frames, attached its **cross-bars**, and put up its posts.
Jer 27. 2 of leather straps and wooden **crossbars** and to put it on my

CROSSBREED see BREED

CROSSROADS

Prov 8. 2 On the hilltops near the road and at the **cross-roads** she stands.
Jer 6.16 The Lord said to his people, "Stand at the **crossroads** and look.
Ezek 38.12 and property and live at the **crossroads** of the world.
Obad 14 stood at the **cross-roads** to catch those trying to escape.

CROUCH

Gen 4. 7 because you have done evil, sin is **crouching** at your door.
Job 39. 3 you know when they will **crouch** down and bring their young

CROW (1)

Lev 11.13 buzzards, vultures, **crows**;
Deut 14.12 buzzards, vultures, **crows**;
Zeph 2.14 **Crows** will caw on the doorsteps.
Lk 12.24 Look at the **crows**:

CROW (2)

Mt 26.34 you that before the cock **crows** tonight, you will say three
26.74 Just then a cock **crowed**, [75] and Peter remembered what Jesus
26.75 "Before the cock **crows**, you will say three times that you
Mk 14.30 you that before the cock **crows** twice tonight, you will say
14.68 Just then a cock **crowed**.
14.72 Just then a cock **crowed** a second time, and Peter
14.72 to him, "Before the cock **crows** twice, you will say three
Lk 22.34 "the cock will not **crow** tonight until you have said three
22.60 At once, while he was still speaking, a cock **crowed**.
22.61 "Before the cock **crows** tonight, you will say three times
Jn 13.38 before the cock **crows** you will say three times that you do
18.27 Again Peter said "No"—and at once a cock **crowed**.

CROWD

Judg 5.11 **crowds** round the wells are telling of the Lord's victories,
16.27 The building was **crowded** with men and women.
2 Sam 13.34 sentry duty saw a large **crowd** coming down the hill on the
1 Kgs 8.65 There was a huge **crowd** of people from as far away as
2 Kgs 11.13 so she hurried to the Temple, where the **crowd** had gathered.
2 Chr 7. 8 There was a huge **crowd** of people from as far away as
20.14 the Lord came upon a Levite who was present in the **crowd**.
23.12 so she hurried to the Temple, where the **crowd** had gathered.
Ezra 10.13 But they added, "The **crowd** is too big, and it's raining hard.
Job 16.10 they **crowd** round me and slap my face.
Ps 42. 4 when I went with the **crowds** to the house of God and
42. 4 along, a happy **crowd**, singing and shouting praise to God.
Is 5.14 of Jerusalem along with the noisy **crowd** of common people.
13. 4 the sound of a great **crowd** of people, the sound of nations
24.22 God will **crowd** kings together like prisoners in a pit.
Jer 26. 9 Then the people **crowded** round me.
44.15 in southern Egypt—a large **crowd** in all—said to me, [16] "We
Ezek 16.40 "They will stir up a **crowd** to stone you, and they will
16.41 houses down and let **crowds** of women see your punishment.
23.42 The sound of a carefree **crowd** could be heard, a group of
33.31 So my people **crowd** in to hear what you have to say,
Dan 10. 6 and his voice sounded like the roar of a great **crowd**.
Mt 4.25 Large **crowds** followed him from Galilee and the Ten Towns,
5. 1 Jesus saw the **crowds** and went up a hill, where he sat
7.28 finished saying these things, the **crowd** was amazed at the way
8. 1 When Jesus came down from the hill, large **crowds** followed him.
8.18 When Jesus noticed the **crowd** round him, he ordered his disciples
9.36 As he saw the **crowds**, his heart was filled with pity
11. 7 John's disciples were leaving, Jesus spoke about him to the **crowds**:
12.15 and large **crowds** followed him.
12.23 The **crowds** were all amazed at what Jesus had done.
13. 2 The **crowd** that gathered round him was so large that he got
13. 2 boat and sat in it, while the **crowd** stood on the shore.
13.34 Jesus used parables to tell all these things to the **crowds**;
13.36 When Jesus had left the **crowd** and gone indoors, his disciples
14.14 when he saw the large **crowd**, his heart was filled with pity
15.10 Then Jesus called the **crowd** to him and said to them,
15.30 Large **crowds** came to him, bringing with them the lame,
15.33 we find enough food in this desert to feed this **crowd?"**
15.35 So Jesus ordered the **crowd** to sit down on the ground.
17.14 When they returned to the **crowd**, a man came to Jesus,
19. 2 Large **crowds** followed him, and he healed them there.
20.29 his disciples were leaving Jericho, a large **crowd** was following.
20.31 The **crowd** scolded them and told them to be quiet.
21. 8 A large **crowd** of people spread their cloaks on the road
21. 9 The **crowds** walking in front of Jesus and those walking behind
21.11 prophet Jesus, from Nazareth in Galilee," the **crowds** answered.
21.46 they were afraid of the **crowds**, who considered Jesus to be
22.33 When the **crowds** heard this, they were amazed at his teaching.
23. 1 Then Jesus spoke to the **crowds** and to his disciples.
26.47 With him was a large **crowd** armed with swords and clubs
26.48 The traitor had given the **crowd** a signal:
26.55 Then Jesus spoke to the **crowd**, "Did you have to come
27.15 habit of setting free any one prisoner the **crowd** asked for.
27.17 So when the **crowd** gathered, Pilate asked them, "Which
27.20 the elders persuaded the **crowd** to ask Pilate to set Barabbas
27.21 But Pilate asked the **crowd**, "Which one of these two do
27.24 hands in front of the **crowd**, and said, "I am not
27.25 The whole **crowd** answered, "Let the responsibility for his death
Mk 2. 4 Because of the **crowd**, however, they could not get the man
2.13 A **crowd** came to him, and he started teaching them.
3. 7 went away to Lake Galilee, and a large **crowd** followed him.
3. 9 The **crowd** was so large that Jesus told his disciples to
3.20 Again such a large **crowd** gathered that Jesus and his disciples
3.32 A **crowd** was sitting round Jesus, and they said to him,
4. 1 The **crowd** that gathered round him was so large that he got
4. 1 in the water, and the **crowd** stood on the shore at the
4.19 all other kinds of desires **crowd** in and choke the message,
4.36 So they left the **crowd**;
5.21 There at the lakeside a large **crowd** gathered round him.
5.24 along with Jesus that they were **crowding** him from every side.
5.27 so she came in the **crowd** behind him, [28] saying to herself,
5.30 turned round in the **crowd** and asked, "Who touched my clothes?"
5.31 disciples answered, "You see how the people are **crowding** you;
6.34 he saw this large **crowd**, and his heart was filled with
6.45 the other side of the lake, while he sent the **crowd** away.
7.14 Then Jesus called the **crowd** to him once more and said to
7.17 When he left the **crowd** and went into the house, his
7.33 off alone, away from the **crowd**, put his fingers in the man's
8. 1 Not long afterwards another large **crowd** came together.
8. 6 He ordered the **crowd** to sit down on the ground.
8. 6 and gave them to his disciples to distribute to the **crowd**;
8.34 Then Jesus called the **crowd** and his disciples to him.
9.14 disciples, they saw a large **crowd** round them and some
9.17 A man in the **crowd** answered, "Teacher, I brought my son
9.25 Jesus noticed that the **crowd** was closing in on them,
10. 1 **Crowds** came flocking to him again, and he taught them,
10.46 his disciples and a large **crowd**, a blind beggar named Bartimaeus
11.18 of him, because the whole **crowd** was amazed at his teaching.
12.12 they were afraid of the **crowd**, so they left him and went
12.37 A large **crowd** was listening to Jesus gladly.
14.43 With him was a **crowd** armed with swords and clubs,
14.44 The traitor had given the **crowd** a signal:
15. 8 When the **crowd** gathered and began to ask Pilate for the
15.11 chief priests stirred up the **crowd** to ask, instead, for
15.12 Pilate spoke again to the **crowd**, "What, then, do you
15.15 Pilate wanted to please the **crowd**, so he set Barabbas
Lk 1.10 while the **crowd** of people outside prayed during the
3. 7 **Crowds** of people came out to John to be baptized by him.
4.30 he walked through the middle of the **crowd** and went his way.
5. 3 Jesus sat in the boat and taught the **crowd**.
5.15 all the more widely, and **crowds** of people came to hear him
5.19 Because of the **crowd**, however, they could find no way to
6.17 A large **crowd** of people was there from all over Judaea and
7. 9 and said to the **crowd** following him, "I tell you, I
7.11 town called Nain, accompanied by his disciples and a large **crowd**.

Lk	7.12	a widow, and a large **crowd** from the town was with her.
	7.24	had left, Jesus began to speak about him to the **crowds:**
	8. 4	and when a great **crowd** gathered, Jesus told this parable:
	8.14	and pleasures of this life **crowd** in and choke them, and
	8.19	to him, but were unable to join him because of the **crowd.**
	8.42	Jesus went along, the people were **crowding** him from every side.
	8.44	She came up in the **crowd** behind Jesus and touched the
	8.45	"Master, the people are all round you and **crowding** in on you."
	9.11	When the **crowds** heard about it, they followed him.
	9.13	you want us to go and buy food for this whole **crowd?"**
	9.18	"Who do the **crowds** say I am?"
	9.37	went down from the hill, and a large **crowd** met Jesus.
	9.38	A man shouted from the **crowd,** "Teacher!
	11.14	The **crowds** were amazed, [15] but some of the people said,
	11.27	woman spoke up from the **crowd** and said to him, "How happy
	11.29	As the people **crowded** round Jesus, he went on to say,
	12. 1	As thousands of people **crowded** together, so that they were
	12.13	A man in the **crowd** said to Jesus, "Teacher, tell my
	14.25	Once when large **crowds** of people were going along with Jesus,
	18.36	When he heard the **crowd** passing by, he asked, "What is this?"
	18.43	When the **crowd** saw it, they all praised God.
	19. 3	a little man and could not see Jesus because of the **crowd.**
	19. 4	he ran ahead of the **crowd** and climbed a sycomore tree to
	19.37	Mount of Olives, the large **crowd** of his disciples began to
	19.39	Then some of the Pharisees in the **crowd** spoke to Jesus.
	20. 6	say 'From man,' this whole **crowd** here will stone us,
	22.47	was still speaking when a **crowd** arrived, led by Judas, one
	23. 4	the chief priests and the **crowds,** "I find no reason to
	23.18	The whole **crowd** cried out, "Kill him!
	23.20	wanted to set Jesus free, so he appealed to the **crowd** again.
	23.27	A large **crowd** of people followed him;
Jn	5. 3	A large **crowd** of sick people were lying in the porches—
	5.13	for there was a **crowd** in that place, and Jesus had
	6. 2	A large **crowd** followed him, because they had seen his miracles
	6. 5	and saw that a large **crowd** was coming to him, so he
	6.22	Next day the **crowd** which had stayed on the other side of
	6.23	near the place where the **crowd** had eaten the bread after the
	6.24	When the **crowd** saw that Jesus was not there, nor his disciples,
	7.12	There was much whispering about him in the **crowd.**
	7.20	the **crowd** answered.
	7.31	But many in the **crowd** believed in him and said,
	7.32	Pharisees heard the **crowd** whispering these things about Jesus,
	7.40	of the people in the **crowd** heard him say this and said,
	7.43	So there was a division in the **crowd** because of Jesus.
	7.49	This **crowd** does not know the Law of Moses, so they are
	12.12	The next day the large **crowd** that had come to the
	12.18	That was why the **crowd** met him—because they heard that
	12.29	The **crowd** standing there heard the voice, and some of
	12.34	**crowd** answered, "Our Law tells us that the Messiah will live
	19. 4	and said to the **crowd,** "Look, I will bring him out
	19. 7	The **crowd** answered back, "We have a law that says he
	19.12	But the **crowd** shouted back, "If you set him free, that
Acts	2. 6	When they heard this noise, a large **crowd** gathered.
	2.14	and in a loud voice began to speak to the **crowd:**
	5.14	added to the group—a **crowd** of men and women who believed
	5.16	And **crowds** of people came in from the towns around Jerusalem,
	5.37	he drew a **crowd** after him, but he also was killed,
	8. 6	The **crowds** paid close attention to what Philip said,
	9.39	where all the widows **crowded** round him, crying and showing him
	13.45	When the Jews saw the **crowds,** they were filled with jealousy;
	14.11	When the **crowds** saw what Paul had done, they started shouting
	14.13	for he and the **crowds** wanted to offer sacrifice to the
	14.14	middle of the **crowd,** shouting, [15] "Why are you doing this?
	14.18	could hardly keep the **crowd** from offering a sacrifice to them.
	14.19	they won the **crowd** over to their side, stoned Paul and
	16.22	And the **crowd** joined in the attack against Paul and Silas.
	17. 8	these words they threw the **crowd** and the city authorities into
	19.28	As the **crowd** heard these words, they became furious and started
	19.30	wanted to go before the **crowd,** but the believers would not
	19.35	At last the town clerk was able to calm the **crowd.**
	21.27	They stirred up the whole **crowd** and seized Paul.
	21.32	took some officers and soldiers and rushed down to the **crowd.**
	21.34	Some in the **crowd** shouted one thing, others something else.
	24.18	There was no **crowd** with me and no disorder.
Heb	12. 1	As for us, we have this large **crowd** of witnesses round us.
Rev	7. 9	and there was an enormous **crowd**—no one could count all the
	19. 1	the roar of a large **crowd** of people in heaven, saying,
	19. 6	what sounded like a large **crowd,** like the sound of a roaring

CROWN

2 Sam	1.10	Then I took the **crown** from his head and the bracelet from
	12.30	David took a gold **crown** which weighed about thirty-five kilogrammes
	12.30	David took the jewel and put it in his own **crown.**
2 Kgs	11.12	led Joash out, placed the **crown** on his head, and gave him
	14.21	The people of Judah then **crowned** his sixteen-year-old son
1 Chr	20. 2	a gold **crown** which weighed about thirty-four kilogrammes.
	20. 2	was a jewel, which David took and put in his own **crown.**
2 Chr	23.11	led Joash out, placed the **crown** on his head, and gave him
Esth	1.11	He ordered them to bring in Queen Vashti, wearing her royal **crown.**
	2.17	He placed the royal **crown** on her head and made her queen
	8.15	a cloak of fine purple linen, and a magnificent gold **crown.**
Job	31.36	on my shoulder and place them on my head like a **crown.**
Ps	8. 5	you **crowned** him with glory and honour.
	21. 3	with great blessings and set a **crown** of gold on his head.
	89.39	covenant with your servant and thrown his **crown** in the mud.
Prov	4. 9	She will be your **crowning** glory."
	16.31	grey hair is a glorious **crown.**
Song	3.11	He is wearing the **crown** that his mother placed on his head
Is	28. 1	glory is fading like the **crowns** of flowers on the heads of
	28. 5	will be like a glorious **crown** of flowers for his people who
	62. 3	You will be like a beautiful **crown** for the Lord.
Jer	13.18	their beautiful **crowns** have fallen from their heads.
Ezek	16.12	you a nose-ring and earrings and a beautiful **crown** to wear.
	21.26	Take off your **crown** and your turban.
	23.42	on the women's arms and beautiful **crowns** on their heads.
Zech	6.11	Make a **crown** out of the silver and gold they have given,
	6.14	The **crown** will be a memorial in the Lord's Temple in
	9.16	They will shine in his land like the jewels of a **crown.**
Mt	27.29	Then they made a **crown** out of thorny branches and placed
Mk	15.17	robe on Jesus, made a **crown** out of thorny branches, and put
Jn	19. 2	The soldiers made a **crown** out of thorny branches and put
	19. 5	Jesus came out, wearing the **crown** of thorns and the purple robe.
1 Cor	9.25	discipline, in order to be **crowned** with a wreath that will
Heb	2. 7	you **crowned** him with glory and honour, [8] and made him
	2. 9	We see him now **crowned** with glory and honour because of the
1 Pet	5. 4	receive the glorious **crown** which will never lose its brightness.
Rev	4. 4	twenty-four elders dressed in white and wearing **crowns** of gold.
	4.10	They throw their **crowns** down in front of the throne and say,
	6. 2	Its rider held a bow, and he was given a **crown.**
	9. 7	had what seemed to be **crowns** of gold, and their faces were
	12. 1	under her feet and a **crown** of twelve stars on her head.
	12. 3	and ten horns and a **crown** on each of his heads.
	13. 1	its horns there was a **crown,** and on each of its heads
	14.14	a human being, with a **crown** of gold on his head and
	19.12	a flame of fire, and he wore many **crowns** on his head.

CRUCIFY

Mt	20.19	the Gentiles, who will mock him, whip him, and **crucify** him;
	23.34	will kill some of them, **crucify** others, and whip others
	26. 2	and the Son of Man will be handed over to be **crucified."**
	27.22	**"Crucify** him!"
	27.23	**"Crucify** him!"
	27.26	he had Jesus whipped, he handed him over to be **crucified.**
	27.31	Then they led him out to **crucify** him.
	27.35	They **crucified** him and then divided his clothes among them
	27.38	Then they **crucified** two bandits with Jesus, one on his
	27.44	the bandits who had been **crucified** with him insulted him in
	28. 5	"I know you are looking for Jesus, who was **crucified.**
Mk	15.13	They shouted back, **"Crucify** him!"
	15.14	They shouted all the louder, **"Crucify** him!"
	15.15	Then he had Jesus whipped and handed him over to be **crucified.**
	15.20	Then they led him out to **crucify** him.
	15.24	Then they **crucified** him and divided his clothes among themselves,
	15.25	It was nine o'clock in the morning when they **crucified** him.
	15.27	They also **crucified** two bandits with Jesus, one on his
	15.32	And the two who were **crucified** with Jesus insulted him also.
	16. 6	"I know you are looking for Jesus of Nazareth, who was **crucified.**
Lk	23.21	But they shouted back, **"Crucify** him!
	23.21	**Crucify** him!"
	23.23	Jesus should be **crucified,** and finally their shouting succeeded.
	23.33	place called "The Skull," they **crucified** Jesus there,
	24. 7	over to sinful men, be **crucified,** and three days later rise
	24.20	him over to be sentenced to death, and he was **crucified.**
Jn	19. 6	and the temple guards saw him, they shouted, **"Crucify** him!
	19. 6	**Crucify** him!"
	19. 6	Pilate said to them, "You take him, then, and **crucify** him.
	19.10	authority to set you free and also to have you **crucified."**
	19.15	**Crucify** him!"
	19.15	Pilate asked them, "Do you want me to **crucify** your king?"
	19.16	Then Pilate handed Jesus over to them to be **crucified.**
	19.18	There they **crucified** him;
	19.18	and they also **crucified** two other men, one on each side,
	19.20	place where Jesus was **crucified** was not far from the city.
	19.23	After the soldiers had **crucified** Jesus, they took his clothes
	19.31	the men who had been **crucified,** and to take the bodies down
	19.32	and then of the other man who had been **crucified** with Jesus.
Acts	2.23	and you killed him by letting sinful men **crucify** him.
	2.36	that this Jesus, whom you **crucified,** is the one that God has
	4.10	Christ of Nazareth—whom you **crucified** and whom God raised from death.
1 Cor	1.23	for us, we proclaim the **crucified** Christ, a message that is
	2. 8	known it, they would not have **crucified** the Lord of glory.
Heb	6. 6	because they are again **crucifying** the Son of God and exposing
Rev	11. 8	street of the great city, where their Lord was **crucified.**

CRUEL

Gen	15.13	there and will be treated **cruelly** for four hundred years.
	16. 6	Then Sarai treated Hagar so **cruelly** that she ran away.
	49. 7	is so fierce, And on their fury, because it is so **cruel.**
Ex	1.13	made their lives miserable by forcing them into **cruel** slavery.
	3. 7	said, "I have seen how **cruelly** my people are being treated
	3.17	where they are being treated **cruelly,** and will take them to
	4.31	were being treated **cruelly,** they bowed down and worshipped.
	5.23	to the king to speak for you, he has treated them **cruelly.**
	6. 9	their spirit had been broken by their **cruel** slavery.
Num	11.15	so that I won't have to endure your **cruelty** any longer."
Judg	4. 3	people of Israel with **cruelty** and violence for twenty years.
2 Sam	12. 6	For having done such a **cruel** thing, he must pay back four
2 Kgs	17.20	and handing them over to **cruel** enemies until at last he had
2 Chr	16.10	time that Asa began treating some of the people **cruelly.**
Job	10. 3	Is it right for you to be so **cruel?**
	29.17	I destroyed the power of **cruel** men and rescued their victims.
	30.21	You are treating me **cruelly;**
Ps	41. 5	My enemies say **cruel** things about me.
	42. 9	Why must I go on suffering from the **cruelty** of my enemies?"
	43. 2	Why must I go on suffering from the **cruelty** of my enemies?

Ps 54. 3 **cruel** men are trying to kill me— men who do not
59. 3 **cruel** men are gathering against me.
64. 3 They sharpen their tongues like swords and aim **cruel** words like arrows.
71. 4 me from wicked men, from the power of **cruel** and evil men.
74.19 Don't abandon your helpless people to their **cruel** enemies;
86.14 a gang of **cruel** men is trying to kill me— people
107.39 defeated and humiliated by **cruel** oppression and suffering,
119.150 My **cruel** persecutors are coming closer,
129. 2 have persecuted me **cruelly,** but they have not overcome me.
144.11 Save me from my **cruel** enemies;
Prov 11.17 If you are **cruel,** you only hurt yourself.
12.10 care of his animals, but wicked men are **cruel** to theirs.
15. 4 Kind words bring life, but **cruel** words crush your spirit.
17.11 Death will come like a **cruel** messenger to wicked people
27. 4 Anger is **cruel** and destructive,
28.16 A ruler without good sense will be a **cruel** tyrant.
30.14 There are people who take **cruel** advantage of the poor and needy;
Is 13. 9 the Lord is coming—that **cruel** day of his fierce anger and
13.11 who is proud and punish everyone who is arrogant and **cruel.**
14. 4 "The **cruel** king has fallen!
19. 4 over to a tyrant, to a **cruel** king who will rule them.
21. 2 have seen a vision of **cruel** events, a vision of betrayal and
25. 3 you will be feared in the cities of **cruel** nations.
25. 4 **Cruel** men attack like a winter storm, [5]like drought in a
25. 5 you silence the shouts of **cruel** men, as a cloud cools a
27. 8 He took them away with a **cruel** wind from the east.
Jer 6.23 they are **cruel** and merciless.
50.42 they are **cruel** and merciless.
Lam 4. 3 but my people are like ostriches, **cruel** to their young.
Ezek 25.12 "The people of Edom took **cruel** revenge on Judah, and that
25.15 said, "The Philistines have taken **cruel** revenge on their
32.12 I will let soldiers from **cruel** nations draw their swords
34. 4 Instead, you treated them **cruelly.**
Dan 5.20 he became proud, stubborn, and **cruel,** he was removed from
Amos 1. 3 They treated the people of Gilead with savage **cruelty.**
Nah 3.19 Did anyone escape your endless **cruelty?**
Mal 2.16 when one of you does such a **cruel** thing to his wife.
Acts 7.19 tricked our ancestors and was **cruel** to them, forcing them to
7.34 I have seen the **cruel** suffering of my people in Egypt.
8. 1 the church in Jerusalem began to suffer **cruel** persecution.

CRUMBLE

Lev 2. 6 **Crumble** it up and pour the oil on it when you present
6.21 griddle and then **crumbled** and presented as a grain-offering,
Job 13.12 your arguments **crumble** like clay.
13.28 As a result, I **crumble** like rotten wood, like a moth-eaten coat.
Is 22. 8 All Judah's defences **crumbled.**
31. 3 acts, the strong nation will **crumble,** and the weak nation it
33.12 You will **crumble** like rocks burnt to make lime, like
34. 4 The sun, moon, and stars will **crumble** to dust.
41.15 hills will **crumble** into dust.
54.10 The mountains and hills may **crumble,** but my love for you
Ezek 13. 5 the walls have **crumbled,** nor do they rebuild the walls,
22.30 places where the walls have **crumbled** and defend the land
38.20 Mountains will fall, cliffs will **crumble,**
Dan 2.35 clay, bronze, silver, and gold **crumbled** and became like the
Nah 1. 6 rocks **crumble** to dust before him.

CRUSH

Gen 3.15 Her offspring will **crush** your head, and you will bite their heel."
Ex 1.11 Egyptians put slave-drivers over them to **crush** their spirits
Lev 22.24 any animal whose testicles have been **crushed,** cut, bruised,
Num 22.25 over against the wall and **crushed** Balaam's foot against it.
24. 8 They devour their enemies, **Crush** their bones, smash their arrows.
Deut 32.27 my people, when it was I myself who had **crushed** them.'
33.11 **Crush** all their enemies;
Judg 5.26 she struck Sisera and **crushed** his skull;
6.16 You will **crush** the Midianites as easily as if they were only
2 Sam 22.43 I **crush** them, and they become like dust;
2 Chr 13.17 army dealt the Israelites a **crushing** defeat—half a million
Ezra 9. 3 tore my hair and my beard, and sat down **crushed** with grief.
Job 4.19 clay, a thing of dust that can be **crushed** like a moth?
9.13 He **crushed** his enemies who helped Rahab, the sea-monster,
10. 9 are you going to **crush** me back to dust?
13.21 stop punishing me, and don't **crush** me with terror.
16.12 God took me by the throat and battered me and **crushed** me.
20.22 of his success all the weight of misery will **crush** him.
28. 5 But underneath the same earth All is torn up and **crushed.**
34.25 what they do he overthrows them and **crushes** them by night.
39.15 unaware that a foot may **crush** them or a wild animal break
40.12 **crush** the wicked where they stand.
Ps 9.18 the hope of the poor will not be **crushed** for ever.
10.10 The helpless victims lie **crushed;**
18.42 I **crush** them, so that they become like dust which the
38. 6 I am bowed down, I am **crushed;**
38. 8 I am worn out and utterly **crushed;**
42.10 I am **crushed** by their insults, as they keep on asking me,
44.25 We fall **crushed** to the ground;
51. 8 and though you have **crushed** me and broken me, I will be
55. 3 of my enemies, **crushed** by the oppression of the wicked.
55. 4 I am terrified, and the terrors of death **crush** me.
58. 7 may they be **crushed** like weeds on a path.
74. 8 They wanted to **crush** us completely;
74.14 you **crushed** the heads of the monster Leviathan and fed
88. 7 anger lies heavy on me, and I am **crushed** beneath its waves.
88.16 Your furious anger **crushes** me;
89.10 You **crushed** the monster Rahab and killed it;
89.23 I will **crush** his foes and kill everyone who hates him.
Ps 94. 5 They **crush** your people, Lord;
116.10 I said, "I am completely **crushed,**" [11]even when I was
147. 6 He raises the humble, but **crushes** the wicked to the ground.
Prov 13.12 When hope is **crushed,** the heart is crushed,
15. 4 Kind words bring life, but cruel words **crush** your spirit.
26.27 People who start landslides get **crushed.**
29. 1 corrected, one day you will be **crushed** and never recover.
Is 1.28 But he will **crush** everyone who sins and rebels against him;
3.15 You have no right to **crush** my people and take advantage
8.15 they will fall and be **crushed.**
59. 5 **Crush** an egg, out comes a snake!
Jer 5. 3 he **crushed** you, but you refused to learn.
8.21 My heart has been **crushed** because my people are crushed;
10.18 he is going to **crush** you until not one of you is
15. 6 stretched out my hand and **crushed** you because I was tired of
23. 9 My heart is **crushed,** and I am trembling.
48.25 Moab's might has been **crushed;**
50. 2 Babylon's idols are put to shame, her disgusting images are **crushed!**
51.20 I used you to **crush** nations and kingdoms, [21]to shatter
51.23 and their horses, to **crush** rulers and high officials."
Lam 1.15 He **crushed** my people like grapes in a winepress.
3.34 The Lord knows when our spirits are **crushed** in prison;
Ezek 32.28 how the Egyptians will lie **crushed** among the uncircumcised
Dan 2.40 it will shatter and **crush** all the earlier empires.
7. 7 its huge iron teeth it **crushed** its victims, and then it
7.19 others—the terrifying beast which **crushed** its victims with
7.23 It will **crush** the whole earth and trample it down.
Hos 10.14 and mothers and their children were **crushed** to death.
Joel 3.13 **crush** them as grapes are crushed in a full winepress
Amos 2.13 And now I will **crush** you to the ground, and you will
Mic 4.13 You will **crush** many nations, and the wealth they got by
Zech 1.21 overthrow the nations that completely **crushed** the land of
Mt 26.38 sorrow in my heart is so great that it almost **crushes** me.
Mk 3. 9 boat ready for him, so that the people would not **crush** him.
14.34 sorrow in my heart is so great that it almost **crushes** me.
Lk 20.18 if that stone falls on someone, it will **crush** him to dust."
Rom 16.20 God, our source of peace, will soon **crush** Satan under your feet.
2 Cor 4. 8 We are often troubled, but not **crushed;**

CRUST

Prov 17. 1 Better to eat a dry **crust** of bread with peace of mind

CRY

[WAR-CRY]

Gen 4.10 Your brother's blood is **crying** out to me from the ground,
16.11 Ishmael, because the Lord has heard your **cry** of distress.
21.16 While she was sitting there, she began to **cry.**
21.17 God heard the boy **crying,** and from heaven the angel of
21.17 God has heard the boy **crying.**
27.34 When Esau heard this, he **cried** out loudly and bitterly and said,
27.38 He began to **cry.**
29.11 Then he kissed her and began to **cry** for joy.
33. 4 They were both **crying.**
41.43 guard of honour went ahead of him and **cried** out, "Make way!
41.55 began to be hungry, they **cried** out to the king for food.
42.24 Joseph left them and began to **cry.**
43.30 about to break down, so he went to his room and **cried.**
45. 2 He **cried** with such loud sobs that the Egyptians heard it,
45.14 He threw his arms round his brother Benjamin and began to **cry;**
45.14 Benjamin also **cried** as he hugged him.
46.29 his arms round his father's neck and **cried** for a long time.
50. 1 Joseph threw himself on his father, **crying** and kissing his face.
50.17 Joseph **cried** when he received this message.
Ex 2. 6 He was **crying,** and she felt sorry for him.
2.23 still groaning under their slavery and **cried** out for help.
2.23 Their **cry** went up to God, [24]who heard their groaning and
3. 7 I have heard them **cry** out to be rescued from their slave-drivers.
3. 9 I have indeed heard the **cry** of my people, and I see
11. 6 There will be loud **crying** all over Egypt, such as there
12.30 There was loud **crying** throughout Egypt, because there was
14.10 they were terrified and **cried** out to the Lord for help.
14.15 The Lord said to Moses, "Why are you **crying** out for help?
22.23 will answer them when they **cry** out to me for help, [24]and
22.27 When he **cries** out to me for help, I will answer him
32.18 doesn't sound like a shout of victory or a **cry** of defeat;
Num 11. 2 The people **cried** out to Moses for help;
12.13 So Moses **cried** out to the Lord, "O God, heal her!"
14. 1 All night long the people **cried** out in distress.
16.34 of Israel who were there fled when they heard their **cry.**
20.16 our ancestors and us, [16]and we **cried** to the Lord for help.
20.16 He heard our **cry** and sent an angel, who led us out
Deut 1.45 So you **cried** out to the Lord for help, but he would
15. 9 make the loan, he will **cry** out to the Lord against you,
22.24 die because she did not **cry** out for help, although she was
22.27 the countryside, and although she **cried** for help, there was
24.15 not pay him, he will **cry** out against you to the Lord,
26. 7 Then we **cried** out for help to the Lord, the God of
33. 7 "Lord, listen to their **cry** for help;
Josh 24. 7 to the Red Sea [7]they **cried** out to me for help, and
Judg 2. 4 people of Israel began to **cry,** [5]and that is why the place
3. 9 Then the Israelites **cried** out to the Lord, and he sent a
3.15 Then the Israelites **cried** out to the Lord, and he sent
4. 3 Then the people of Israel **cried** out to the Lord for help.
6. 7 Then the people of Israel **cried** out to the Lord for help
10.10 Then the Israelites **cried** out to the Lord and said,
10.12 Maonites oppressed you in the past, and you **cried** out to me.
10.14 Go and **cry** out to the gods you have chosen.
14.17 She **cried** about it for the whole seven days of the feast.

Ruth	1. 9	But they started **crying** [10]and said to her, "No!
	1.14	Again they started **crying.**
1 Sam	1. 7	Hannah so much that she would **cry** and refuse to eat anything.
	1. 8	Her husband Elkanah would ask her, "Hannah, why are you **crying?**
	1. 9	was deeply distressed, and she **cried** bitterly as she prayed
	4.13	news throughout the town, and everyone **cried** out in fear.
	5.10	it arrived there, the people **cried** out, "They have brought
	5.12	tumours and the people **cried** out to their gods for help.
	7. 2	During this time all the Israelites **cried** to the Lord for help.
	9.16	of my people and have heard their **cries** for help."
	11. 4	they told the news, the people started **crying** in despair.
	11. 5	Why is everyone **crying?"**
	12. 8	Egyptians oppressed them, your ancestors **cried** to the Lord for help,
	12.10	Then they **cried** to the Lord for help and said, 'We have
	14.33	Saul **cried** out.
	17.20	Israelites were going out to their battle line, shouting the **war-cry.**
	20.41	Both he and Jonathan were **crying** as they kissed each other;
	24.16	And he started **crying.**
	30. 4	David and his men started **crying** and did not stop until
2 Sam	3.16	all the way to the town of Bahurim, **crying** as he went.
	13.19	and with her face buried in her hands went away **crying.**
	13.36	**crying,** and David and his officials also wept bitterly.
	15.23	The people **cried** loudly as David's followers left.
	18.33	As he went, he **cried,** "O my son!
	19. 4	The king covered his face and **cried** loudly, "O my son!
	22. 7	he listened to my **cry** for help.
1 Kgs	13.21	old prophet, [21]and he **cried** out to the prophet from Judah,
	22.32	But when he **cried** out, [33]they realized that he was not the
	22.34	he **cried** out to his chariot driver.
2 Kgs	2.12	Elisha saw it and **cried** out to Elijah, "My father, my
	4.19	Suddenly he **cried** out to his father, "My head hurts!
	6.26	wall when a woman **cried** out, "Help me, Your Majesty!"
	8.12	"Why are you **crying,** sir?"
	9.23	Joram **cried** out, as he turned his chariot round and fled.
	20. 3	And he began to **cry** bitterly.
2 Chr	13.14	They **cried** to the Lord for help, and the priests blew the
	18.33	he **cried** out to his chariot driver.
	32.20	of Amoz prayed to God and **cried** out to him for help.
Ezra	3.12	foundation of this Temple being laid, they **cried** and wailed.
	3.13	the joyful shouts and the **crying,** because the noise they
Neh	8. 9	the Law required, they were so moved that they began to **cry.**
	8. 9	the Lord your God, so you are not to mourn or **cry.**
Esth	7. 8	Seeing this, the king **cried** out, "Is this man going to rape
	8. 3	to the king again, throwing herself at his feet and **crying.**
Job	16.16	I have **cried** until my face is red, and my eyes are
	19. 7	no one hears my **cry** for justice.
	24.12	wounded and dying **cry** out, but God ignores their prayers.
	27. 9	When trouble comes, will God hear their **cries?**
	29.12	When the poor **cried** out, I helped them;
	30.29	sad and lonely as the **cries** of a jackal or an ostrich.
	34.28	They forced the poor to **cry** out to God, and he heard
	35. 9	they **cry** for someone to save them.
	35.12	They **cry** for help, but God doesn't answer, for they are
	35.13	It is useless for them to **cry** out;
	36.19	It will do you no good to **cry** out for help;
	38.41	wander about hungry, when their young **cry** to me for food?
Ps	5. 2	Listen to my **cry** for help, my God and king!
	6. 9	he listens to my **cry** for help and will answer my prayer.
	9.12	he does not forget their **cry,** and he punishes those who
	10.18	You will hear the **cries** of the oppressed and the orphans;
	17. 1	pay attention to my **cry** for help!
	18. 6	he listened to my **cry** for help.
	18.41	They **cry** for help, but no one saves them;
	22. 1	I have **cried** desperately for help, but still it does not come.
	28. 1	Listen to my **cry!**
	28. 2	Hear me when I **cry** to you for help, when I lift
	28. 6	he has heard my **cry** for help.
	30. 2	I **cried** to you for help, O Lord my God, and you
	31. 9	my eyes are tired from so much **crying;**
	31.22	But he heard my **cry,** when I called to him for help.
	32. 3	confess my sins, I was worn out from **crying** all day long.
	34.15	The Lord watches over the righteous and listens to their **cries;**
	39.12	Hear my prayer, Lord, and listen to my **cry;**
	40. 1	then he listened to me and heard my **cry.**
	42. 3	Day and night I **cry,** and tears are my only food;
	61. 1	Hear my **cry,** O God;
	66.17	I **cried** to him for help;
	77. 1	I **cry** aloud to God;
	77. 1	I **cry** aloud, and he hears me.
	86. 6	hear my **cries** for help.
	88. 1	Lord God, my saviour, I **cry** out all day, and at night
	88. 2	listen to my **cry** for help!
	92.11	the defeat of my enemies and heard the **cries** of the wicked.
	102. 1	Listen to my prayer, O Lord, and hear my **cry** for help!
	106.44	Lord heard them when they **cried** out, and he took notice of
	119.169	Let my **cry** for help reach you, Lord!
	130. 2	Hear my **cry,** O Lord;
	140. 6	Hear my **cry** for help, Lord!
	142. 5	Lord, I **cry** to you for help;
	142. 6	Listen to my **cry** for help, for I am sunk in despair.
	144.14	May there be no **cries** of distress in our streets.
	145.19	he hears their **cries** and saves them.
Prov	21.13	refuse to listen to the **cry** of the poor,
	21.13	your own **cry** for help will not be heard.
Is	3.26	city gates will mourn and **cry,** and the city itself will be
	5. 7	do what was right, but their victims **cried** out for justice.
	13.22	and palaces will echo with the **cries** of hyenas and jackals.
	14.31	Howl and **cry** for help, all you Philistine cities!
	15. 3	the city squares and on the house-tops people mourn and **cry.**
Is	15. 4	people of Heshbon and Elealeh **cry** out,
	15. 4	and their **cry** can be heard
	15. 5	My heart **cries** out for Moab!
	15. 8	Everywhere at Moab's borders the sound of **crying** is heard.
	19. 8	earns his living by fishing in the Nile will groan and **cry;**
	22. 5	have been battered down, and **cries** for help have echoed
	26.17	You, Lord, have made us **cry** out,
	26.17	as a woman in labour **cries** out in pain.
	30.19	is compassionate, and when you **cry** to him for help, he will
	33. 7	The ambassadors who tried to bring about peace are **crying** bitterly.
	38. 3	And he began to **cry** bitterly.
	38.13	All night I **cried** out with pain, As if a lion were
	40. 3	A voice **cries** out, "Prepare in the wilderness a road for
	40. 6	A voice **cries** out, "Proclaim a message!"
	42.13	He gives a **war-cry,** a battle-shout;
	42.14	I **cry** out like a woman in labour.
	43.14	gates, and the shouts of her people will turn into **crying.**
	49. 8	you, I will show you favour and answer your **cries** for help.
	57.13	When you **cry** for help, let those idols of yours save you!
	65.14	will sing for joy, but you will **cry** with a broken heart.
Jer	3.21	is the people of Israel **crying** and pleading, because they
	4.31	I heard a **cry,** like a woman in labour,
	4.31	It was the **cry** of Jerusalem gasping for breath,
	7.16	Do not **cry** or pray on their behalf;
	8.19	land I hear my people **crying** out, "Is the Lord no longer
	8.20	The people **cry** out, "The summer is gone, the harvest is over,
	9. 1	tears, so that I could **cry** day and night for my people
	9.18	fill with tears, and our eyelids are wet from **crying."**
	9.19	Listen to the sound of **crying** in Zion,
	10.19	The people of Jerusalem **cried** out,
	11.11	And when they **cry** out to me for help, I will not
	11.12	they offer sacrifices and will **cry** out to them for help.
	13.17	I will **cry** in secret because of your pride;
	13.17	I will **cry** bitterly, and my tears will flow
	14. 2	on the ground in sorrow, and Jerusalem **cries** out for help.
	14. 7	My people **cry** out to me, 'Even though our sins accuse us,
	14.12	if they fast, I will not listen to their **cry** for help;
	18.22	make them **cry** out in terror.
	20. 8	Whenever I speak, I have to **cry** out and shout, "Violence!
	20.16	May he hear **cries** of pain in the morning and the battle
	22.18	No one will weep for him or **cry,** 'My lord!
	22.20	to Lebanon and shout, go to the land of Bashan and **cry;**
	25.34	**Cry,** you leaders, you shepherds of my people, cry out
	25.36	You moan and **cry** out in distress because the Lord
	30. 5	a cry of terror, a **cry** of fear and not of peace.
	31.15	Rachel is **crying** for her children;
	31.16	Stop your **crying** and wipe away your tears.
	46.12	everyone has heard you **cry.**
	47. 2	everyone on earth will **cry** bitterly.
	47. 6	You **cry** out, 'Sword of the Lord!
	48. 3	The people of Horonaim **cry** out, 'Violence!
	48. 4	listen to the children **crying.**
	48. 5	road up to Luhith, the **cries** of distress on the way down
	48.32	I will **cry** for the people of Sibmah, even more than for
	48.34	people of Heshbon and Elealeh **cry** out,
	48.34	and their **cry** can be heard
	48.39	**Cry** out!
	49. 3	People of Heshbon, **cry** out!
	49.21	earth will shake, and the **cries** of alarm will be heard as
	50.15	Raise the **war cry** all round the city!
	50.46	earth will shake, and the **cries** of alarm will be heard by
	51.54	"Listen to the sound of **crying** in Babylon, of mourning for
Lam	1. 2	All night long she **cries;**
	1. 9	Her enemies have won, and she **cries** to the Lord for mercy.
	1.11	"Look at me, Lord," the city **cries;**
	1.12	she **cries** to everyone who passes by.
	2.12	Hungry and thirsty, they **cry** to their mothers;
	2.18	O Jerusalem, let your very walls **cry** out to the Lord!
	2.19	night get up again and again to **cry** out to the Lord;
	3. 8	I **cry** aloud for help, but God refuses to listen;
	3.55	the pit, O Lord, I **cried** out to you, [56]And when I
	3.56	And when I begged you to listen to my **cry,** you heard.
Ezek	2.10	was writing on both sides—**cries** of grief were written there,
	6.11	**Cry** in sorrow because of all the evil, disgusting things the
	24.16	You are not to complain or **cry** or shed any tears.
	24.23	You will not go bareheaded or barefoot or mourn or **cry.**
Hos	5. 5	The arrogance of the people of Israel **cries** out against them.
	5. 8	Raise the **war-cry** at Bethaven!
	7.10	The arrogance of the people of Israel **cries** out against them.
	11. 7	They will **cry** out because of the yoke that is on them,
Joel	1. 5	**cry,** you wine-drinkers;
	1. 8	**Cry,** you people, like a girl who mourns the death of the
	1.11	**cry,** you that take care of the vineyards, because the wheat,
	1.14	the Temple of the Lord your God and **cry** out to him.
	1.19	I **cry** out to you, Lord, because the pastures and trees
	1.20	Even the wild animals **cry** out to you because the streams
Amos	5.16	"There will be wailing and **cries** of sorrow in the city streets.
	8. 3	day the songs in the palace will become **cries** of mourning.
	8.10	funerals and change your glad songs into **cries** of grief.
Jon	1. 5	The sailors were terrified and **cried** out for help, each
	1.14	So they **cried** out to the Lord, "O Lord, we pray, don't
	2. 2	world of the dead I **cried** for help, and you heard me.
Mic	3. 4	is coming when you will **cry** out to the Lord, but he
	4. 9	Why do you **cry** out so loudly?
Nah	2. 8	the **cry** rings out— but no one turns back.
Hab	2.11	the stones of the walls **cry** out against you,
	2.11	and the rafters echo the **cry.**
Zeph	1.10	will hear the sound of **crying** at the Fish Gate in Jerusalem.
	1.11	Wail and **cry** when you hear this, you that live in the
	1.14	day, for even the bravest soldiers will **cry** out in despair!

Zech 6. 8 Then the angel **cried** out to me, "The horses that went
11. 3 The rulers **cry** out in grief;
Mt 2.18 Rachel is **crying** for her children;
8.12 into the darkness, where they will **cry** and grind their teeth."
11.17 We sang funeral songs, but you wouldn't **cry!**'
13.42 fiery furnace, where they will **cry** and grind their teeth.
13.50 fiery furnace, where they will **cry** and grind their teeth.
22.13 There he will **cry** and grind his teeth.'"
24.51 There he will **cry** and grind his teeth.
25. 6 already midnight when the **cry** rang out, 'Here is the bridegroom!
25.30 there he will **cry** and grind his teeth.'
27.46 At about three o'clock Jesus **cried** out with a loud shout,
27.50 Jesus again gave a loud **cry** and breathed his last.
Mk 5.38 Jesus saw the confusion and heard all the loud **crying** and wailing.
5.39 Why are you **crying?**
9.24 The father at once **cried** out, "I do have faith, but not
14.72 And he broke down and **cried.**
15.34 At three o'clock Jesus **cried** out with a loud shout,
15.37 With a loud **cry** Jesus died.
16.10 They were mourning and **crying;**
Lk 7.13 filled with pity for her, and he said to her, "Don't **cry.**"
7.32 We sang funeral songs, but you wouldn't **cry!**'
7.38 behind Jesus, by his feet, **crying** and wetting his feet with
8.28 Jesus, he gave a loud **cry,** threw himself down at his feet,
8.52 Everyone there was **crying** and mourning for the child.
8.52 Jesus said, "Don't **cry;**
13.28 How you will **cry** and grind your teeth when you see Abraham,
18. 7 of his own people who **cry** to him day and night for
18.38 He **cried** out, "Jesus!
23.18 The whole crowd **cried** out, "Kill him!
23.28 Don't **cry** for me, but for yourselves and your children.
23.46 Jesus **cried** out in a loud voice, "Father!
Jn 1.15 He **cried** out, "This is the one I was talking about
16.20 you will **cry** and weep, but the world will be glad;
20.11 Mary stood **crying** outside the tomb.
20.11 While she was still **crying,** she bent over and looked in the
20.13 "Woman, why are you **crying?**"
20.15 "Woman, why are you **crying?**"
Acts 7.57 With a loud **cry** the members of the Council covered their
7.60 He knelt down and **cried** out in a loud voice, "Lord!
8. 2 Some devout men buried Stephen, mourning for him with loud **cries.**
8. 7 many people with a loud **cry,** and many paralysed and lame
9.39 widows crowded round him, **crying** and showing him all the shirts
20.37 They were all **crying** as they hugged him and kissed him good-bye.
21.13 "What are you doing, **crying** like this and breaking my heart?
Rom 8.15 and by the Spirit's power we **cry** out to God, "Father!
Gal 4. 6 into our hearts, the Spirit who **cries** out, "Father, my Father."
4.27 Shout and **cry** with joy, you who never felt the pains of
Heb 5. 7 prayers and requests with loud **cries** and tears to God,
Jas 4. 9 Be sorrowful, **cry,** and weep;
4. 9 change your laughter into **crying,** your joy into gloom!
5. 4 The **cries** of those who gather in your crops have reached the
Rev 5. 4 I **cried** bitterly because no one could be found who was
5. 5 Then one of the elders said to me, "Don't **cry.**
12. 2 and the pains and suffering of childbirth made her **cry** out.
14.15 out from the temple and **cried** out in a loud voice to
18. 2 He **cried** out in a loud voice:
18. 9 her immorality and lust will **cry** and weep over the city when
18.11 businessmen of the earth also **cry** and mourn for her, because
18.15 They will **cry** and mourn, [16]and say, "How terrible!
18.18 a long way off, [18]and **cried** out as they saw the smoke
18.19 threw dust on their heads, they **cried** and mourned, saying,
21. 4 will be no more death, no more grief or **crying** or pain.
also Mt 14.30 Mt 15.22 Mt 25.11

CRYSTAL

Job 28.18 The value of wisdom is more Than coral or **crystal** or rubies.
Ezek 1.22 something that looked like a dome made of dazzling **crystal.**
Rev 4. 6 was what looked like a sea of glass, clear as **crystal.**
21.11 like a precious stone, like a jasper, clear as **crystal.**
22. 1 water of life, sparkling like **crystal,** and coming from the throne

CUB

2 Sam 17. 8 they are as fierce as a mother bear robbed of her **cubs.**
Prov 17.12 mother bear robbed of her **cubs** than to meet some fool busy
Is 11. 6 Calves and lion **cubs** will feed together, and little children
11. 7 together, and their calves and **cubs** will lie down in peace.
Jer 51.38 The Babylonians all roar like lions and growl like lion **cubs.**
Lam 4. 3 wolf will nurse her **cubs,** but my people are like ostriches,
Ezek 19. 2 She reared her **cubs** among the fierce male lions.
19. 3 She reared a **cub** and taught him to hunt;
19. 5 she reared another of her **cubs,** and he grew into a fierce
Hos 13. 8 bear that has lost her **cubs,** and I will tear you open.
Nah 2.11 lion and the lioness would go and their **cubs** would be safe?
2.12 prey and tore it to pieces for his mate and her **cubs;**

CUCUMBER

Num 11. 5 Remember the **cucumbers,** the water-melons, the leeks, the
Is 1. 8 watchman's hut in a vineyard or a shed in a **cucumber** field.

CUD

Lev 11. 3 that also chews the **cud,** [4-6]but you must not eat camels,
11. 4 they chew the **cud,** but do not have divided hoofs.
11. 7 they have divided hoofs, but do not chew the **cud.**
11.24 they chew the **cud,** and all four-footed animals with paws.
Deut 14. 6 any animals that have divided hoofs and that also chew the **cud.**
Deut 14. 7 eaten unless they have divided hoofs and also chew the **cud.**
14. 7 they chew the **cud** but do not have divided hoofs.
14. 8 they have divided hoofs but do not chew the **cud.**

CULTIVATE

Gen 2. 5 sent any rain, and there was no one to **cultivate** the land;
2.15 man in the Garden of Eden to **cultivate** it and guard it.
3.23 of Eden and made him **cultivate** the soil from which he had
Lev 25. 2 the Lord by not **cultivating** the land every seventh year.
25. 6 the land has not been **cultivated** during that year, it will
Josh 24.13 land that you had never **cultivated** and cities that you had
Rom 11.17 the branches of the **cultivated** olive-tree have been broken off,
11.24 then, contrary to nature, is joined to a **cultivated** olive-tree.
11.24 The Jews are like this **cultivated** tree;
Heb 6. 7 plants that are useful to those for whom it is **cultivated.**

CUMIN

A small plant whose seeds are crushed and used for seasoning foods.

Is 28.25 soil, he sows the seeds of herbs such as dill and **cumin.**
28.27 uses a heavy club to beat out dill seeds or **cumin** seeds;
Mt 23.23 such as mint, dill, and **cumin,** but you neglect to obey

CUNNING

Gen 3. 1 the snake was the most **cunning** animal that the Lord God had
1 Sam 23.22 I hear that he is very **cunning.**
Job 5.12 He upsets the plans of **cunning** men, and traps wise
Dan 8.25 Because he is **cunning,** he will succeed in his deceitful ways.

CUP

Gen 40.11 I was holding the king's **cup;**
40.11 grapes and squeezed them into the **cup** and gave it to him."
40.13 You will give him his **cup** as you did before when you
44. 2 Put my silver **cup** in the top of the youngest brother's sack,
44. 5 Why did you steal my master's silver **cup?**
44.10 one who has taken the **cup** will become my slave, and the
44.12 with the youngest, and the **cup** was found in Benjamin's sack.
44.16 slaves and not just the one with whom the **cup** was found."
44.17 Only the one who had the **cup** will be my slave.
Ex 25.29 Make plates, **cups,** jars, and bowls to be used for the wine-offerings.
37.16 the plates, the **cups,** the jars, and the bowls to be used
2 Sam 12. 3 let it drink from his **cup,** and hold it in his lap.
1 Kgs 7.26 like the rim of a **cup,** curving outwards like the petals of
7.50 the **cups,** lamp snuffers, bowls, dishes for incense, and
10.21 All of Solomon's drinking **cups** were made of gold, and
2 Kgs 12.13 to pay for making silver **cups,** bowls, trumpets, or tools for
2 Chr 4. 5 like the rim of a **cup,** curving outwards like the petals of
9.20 All King Solomon's **cups** were made of gold, and all the
Ezra 1. 7 them back the bowls and **cups** that King Nebuchadnezzar had
Esth 1. 7 Drinks were served in gold **cups,** no two of them alike, and
Ps 23. 5 me as an honoured guest and fill my **cup** to the brim.
75. 8 The Lord holds a **cup** in his hand, filled with the strong
80. 5 given us sorrow to eat, a large **cup** of tears to drink.
Prov 23.31 though it sparkles in the **cup,** and it goes down smoothly.
Is 40.12 of the earth in a **cup** or weigh the mountains and hills
51.17 You have drunk the **cup** of punishment that the Lord in his
51.22 "I am taking away the **cup** that I gave you in my
Jer 25.15 said to me, "Here is a wine **cup** filled with my anger.
25.17 So I took the **cup** from the Lord's hand, gave it to
25.19 list of all the others who had to drink from the **cup:**
25.28 they refuse to take the **cup** from your hand and drink from
35. 5 Then I placed **cups** and bowls full of wine before the Rechabites,
49.12 had to drink from the **cup** of punishment, do you think that
49.12 No, you must drink from the **cup!**
51. 7 Babylonia was like a gold **cup** in my hand, making the whole
Ezek 4.11 have a limited amount of water to drink, two **cups** a day.
23.31 so I will give you the same **cup** of punishment to drink."
23.32 "You will drink from your sister's **cup;**
23.32 the **cup** is full.
23.33 that cup of fear and ruin, your sister Samaria's **cup.**
Dan 5. 2 in the gold and silver **cups** and bowls which his father
5. 3 At once the gold **cups** and bowls were brought in, and they
5.23 and brought in the **cups** and bowls taken from his Temple.
Obad 16 have drunk a bitter **cup** of punishment on my sacred hill.
16 nations will drink a still more bitter **cup** of punishment;
Hab 2.16 make you drink your own **cup** of punishment, and your honour
Zech 12. 2 He says, [2]"I will make Jerusalem like a **cup** of wine;
Mt 20.22 "Can you drink the **cup of suffering** that I am about to
20.23 will indeed drink from my **cup,**" Jesus told them, "but I do
23.25 clean the outside of your **cup** and plate, while the inside is
23.26 Clean what is inside the **cup** first, and then the outside
26.27 Then he took a **cup,** gave thanks to God, and gave it
26.39 Father, if it is possible, take this **cup of suffering** from me!
26.42 "My Father, if this **cup of suffering** cannot be taken away
Mk 7. 4 as the proper way to wash **cups,** pots, copper bowls, and
10.38 Can you drink the **cup of suffering** that I must drink?
10.39 "You will indeed drink the **cup** I must drink and be baptized
14.23 Then he took a **cup,** gave thanks to God, and handed it
14.36 Take this **cup of suffering** away from me.
Lk 11.39 clean the outside of your **cup** and plate, but inside you are
11.41 give what is in your **cups** and plates to the poor,
22.17 Then Jesus took a **cup,** gave thanks to God, and said,
22.20 he gave them the **cup** after the supper, saying,
22.20 "This **cup** is God's new covenant
22.42 "if you will, take this **cup of suffering** away from me.
Jn 4. 9 (Jews will not use the same **cups** and bowls that Samaritans use.)

Jn	18.11	will not drink the **cup of suffering** which my Father has
1 Cor	10.16	The **cup** we use in the Lord's Supper and for which we
	10.21	cannot drink from the Lord's **cup** and
	10.21	also from the **cup** of demons;
	11.25	the cup and said, "This **cup** is God's new covenant, sealed
	11.26	bread and drink from this **cup** you proclaim the Lord's death
	11.27	bread or drinks from his **cup** in a way that dishonours him,
	11.28	first, and then eat the bread and drink from the **cup.**
	11.29	bread and drinks from the **cup,** he brings judgement on himself
Rev	14.10	he has poured at full strength into the **cup** of his anger!
	16.19	drink the wine from his **cup**—the wine of his furious anger.
	17. 4	hand she held a gold **cup** full of obscene and filthy things,
	18. 6	Fill her **cup** with a drink twice as strong as the drink

CURE

Lev	14. 2	purification of a person **cured** of a dreaded skin-disease.
	15.13	After the man is **cured** of his discharge, he must wait
Deut	28.27	with scabs, and you will itch, but there will be no **cure.**
2 Kgs	5. 3	He would **cure** him of his disease."
	5. 6	I want you to **cure** him of his disease."
	5. 7	"How can the king of Syria expect me to **cure** this man?
	5.10	River Jordan, and he would be completely **cured** of his disease.
	5.11	his God, wave his hand over the diseased spot, and **cure** me!
	5.12	I could have washed in them and been **cured!"**
	5.13	can't you just wash yourself, as he said, and be **cured?"**
	5.14	as Elisha had instructed, and he was completely **cured.**
Jer	30.15	there is no **cure** for you.
Hos	5.13	for help, but he could not **cure** them or heal their wounds.
Mt	8. 4	that you are **cured,** offer the sacrifice that Moses ordered."
Mk	1.44	that you are **cured,** offer the sacrifice that Moses ordered."
Lk	5.14	that you are **cured,** offer the sacrifice as Moses ordered."
	7.21	At that very time Jesus **cured** many people of their sicknesses,
	8.36	had seen it told the people how the man had been **cured.**
	8.43	had on doctors, but no one had been able to **cure** her.
	9. 1	and authority to drive out all demons and to **cure** diseases.
	13.32	driving out demons and performing **cures** today and tomorrow,
Jn	9.14	Jesus made the mud and **cured** him of his blindness
	9.17	once more, "You say he **cured** you of your blindness—well,
	9.21	nor do we know who **cured** him of his blindness.
	9.24	We know that this man who **cured** you is a sinner."
	9.26	"How did he **cure** you of your blindness?"
	9.30	know where he comes from, but he **cured** me of my blindness!

CURL

Lam	2.16	They **curl** their lips and sneer, "We have destroyed it!

CURSE

Gen	3.14	you alone of all the animals must bear this **curse:**
	3.17	of what you have done, the ground will be under a **curse.**
	4.11	You are placed under a **curse** and can no longer farm the
	5.29	which the Lord put a **curse,** this child will bring us relief
	8.21	I put the earth under a **curse** because of what man does;
	9.25	"A **curse** on Canaan!
	12. 3	those who bless you, But I will **curse** those who curse you.
	27.12	way I will bring a **curse** on myself instead of a blessing."
	27.13	His mother answered, "Let any **curse** against you fall on me,
	27.29	those who curse you be **cursed,** and may those who bless you
	49. 7	A **curse** be on their anger, because it is so fierce, And
Ex	21.17	"Whoever **curses** his father or his mother is to be put
	22.28	evil of God, and do not **curse** a leader of your people.
Lev	19.14	Do not **curse** a deaf man or put something in front of
	20. 9	Anyone who **curses** his father or his mother shall be put to
	24.10	During the quarrel he **cursed** God, so they took him to Moses,
	24.14	Everyone who heard him **curse** shall put his hands on the
	24.15	of Israel that anyone who **curses** God must suffer the
	24.16	foreigner living in Israel who **curses** the Lord shall be
Num	5.18	the bowl containing the bitter water that brings a **curse.**
	5.19	you will not be harmed by the **curse** that this water brings.
	5.21	may the Lord make your name a **curse** among your people.
	5.23	the priest shall write this **curse** down and wash the writing
	5.27	Her name will become a **curse** among her people.
	22. 6	us, so please come and put a **curse** on them for me.
	22. 6	you pronounce a **curse,** they are placed under a curse."
	22. 7	them the payment for the **curse,** went to Balaam, and gave him
	22.11	He wants me to **curse** them for him, so that he can
	22.12	and do not put a **curse** on the people of Israel, because
	22.17	Please come and **curse** these people for me."
	23. 7	'Put a **curse** on the people of Israel.'
	23. 8	How can I **curse** what God has not cursed,
	23.11	I brought you here to **curse** my enemies, but all you have
	23.13	**Curse** them for me from there."
	23.25	to Balaam, "You refuse to **curse** the people of Israel, but
	23.27	will be willing to let you **curse** them for me from there."
	24. 9	Israel will be blessed, And whoever curses Israel will be **cursed."**
	24.10	Balaam, "I called you to **curse** my enemies, but three times
Deut	7.26	your homes, or the same **curse** will be on you that is
	7.26	these idols, because they are under the Lord's **curse.**
	11.26	between a blessing and a **curse**—[27] a blessing, if you obey
	11.28	but a **curse,** if you disobey these commands
	11.29	blessing from Mount Gerizim and the **curse** from Mount Ebal.
	21.23	dead body hanging on a post brings God's **curse** on the land.
	23. 4	of Beor, from the city of Pethor in Mesopotamia, to **curse**
	23. 5	he turned the **curse** into a blessing, because he loved you.
	27.13	will stand on Mount Ebal when the **curses** are pronounced:
	27.15	" 'God's **curse** on anyone who makes an idol of stone,
	27.16	" 'God's **curse** on anyone who dishonours his father or mother.'
	27.17	" 'God's **curse** on anyone who moves a neighbour's boundary mark.'
Deut	27.18	" 'God's **curse** on anyone who leads a blind man in the
	27.19	" 'God's **curse** on anyone who deprives foreigners, orphans, and widows
	27.20	" 'God's **curse** on anyone who disgraces his father by having intercourse
	27.21	" 'God's **curse** on anyone who has sexual relations with an animal.'
	27.22	" 'God's **curse** on anyone who has intercourse with his sister
	27.23	" 'God's **curse** on anyone who has intercourse with his mother-in-law.'
	27.24	" 'God's **curse** on anyone who secretly commits murder.'
	27.25	" 'God's **curse** on anyone who accepts money to murder an innocent person.'
	27.26	" 'God's **curse** on anyone who does not obey all of God's
	28.16	"The Lord will **curse** your towns and your fields.
	28.17	"The Lord will **curse** your corn crops and the food you
	28.18	"The Lord will **curse** you by giving you only a few children,
	28.19	"The Lord will **curse** everything you do.
	29.21	in accordance with all the **curses** listed in the covenant
	30. 1	have now given you a choice between a blessing and a **curse.**
	30. 7	He will turn all these **curses** against your enemies, who
	30.19	between God's blessing and God's **curse,** and I call heaven
Josh	6.26	rebuild the city of Jericho will be under the Lord's **curse.**
	8.34	including the blessings and the **curses,** just as they are
	24. 9	son of Beor and asked him to put a **curse** on you.
Judg	1.17	They put a **curse** on the city, destroyed it, and named it
	5.23	"Put a **curse** on Meroz," says the angel of the Lord,
	5.23	"a curse, a **curse** on those who live there.
	9.57	Jotham, Gideon's son, said they would when he **cursed** them.
	17. 2	pieces of silver from you, you put a **curse** on the thief.
	17. 3	she said, "To stop the **curse** from falling on my son, I
	21.18	because we have put a **curse** on anyone of us who allows
1 Sam	14.24	"A **curse** be on anyone who eats any food today before I
	14.26	ate any of it because they were all afraid of Saul's **curse.**
	14.27	Jonathan had not heard his father threaten the people with a **curse;**
	14.28	threatened us and said, 'A **curse** be on anyone who eats any
	17.43	And he called down **curses** from his god on David.
	26.19	if men have done it, may the Lord's **curse** fall on them.
2 Sam	16. 5	of Gera, came out to meet him, **cursing** him as he came.
	16. 7	Shimei **cursed** him and said, "Get out!
	16. 9	the king, "Your Majesty, why do you let this dog **curse** you?
	16.10	"If he **curses** me because the Lord told him to, who has
	16.11	The Lord told him to **curse;**
	16.12	and give me some blessings to take the place of his **curse."**
	16.13	he was **cursing** and throwing stones and earth at them as he
	19.21	put to death because he **cursed** the one whom the Lord chose
1 Kgs	2. 8	He **cursed** me bitterly the day I went to Mahanaim, but when
	21.10	to accuse him to his face of **cursing** God and the king.
	21.13	scoundrels publicly accused him of **cursing** God and the king,
2 Kgs	2.24	round, glared at them, and **cursed** them in the name of the
	22.19	sight, a place whose name people will use as a **curse.**
2 Chr	34.24	all its people with the **curses** written in the book that was
Neh	10.29	oath, under penalty of a **curse** if we break it, that we
	13. 2	paid money to Balaam to **curse** Israel,
	13. 2	but our God turned the **curse** into a blessing.
	13.25	reprimanded the men, called down **curses** on them, beat them,
Job	1.11	away everything he has—he will **curse** you to your face!"
	2. 5	suppose you hurt his body—he will **curse** you to your face!"
	2. 9	Why don't you **curse** God and die?"
	3. 1	Job broke the silence and **cursed** the day on which he had
	3. 2	O God, put a **curse** on the day I was born;
	3. 2	put a **curse** on the night when I was conceived!
	3. 8	Tell the sorcerers to **curse** that day, those who know how
	3.10	**Curse** that night for letting me be born, for exposing me
	5. 3	secure, but I called down a sudden **curse** on their homes.
	24.18	away by floods, and the land he owns is under God's **curse;**
Ps	10. 3	the greedy man **curses** and rejects the Lord.
	10. 7	His speech is filled with **curses,** lies, and threats;
	37.22	land, but those who are **cursed** by him will be driven out.
	59.12	Because they **curse** and lie, [13] destroy them in your anger;
	62. 4	You speak words of blessing, but in your heart you **curse** him.
	89.50	am insulted, how I endure all the **curses** of the heathen.
	102. 8	those who mock me use my name in **cursing.**
	109.17	He loved to **curse**—may he be cursed!
	109.18	He **cursed** as naturally as he dressed himself;
	109.18	may his own **curses** soak into his body like water and into
	109.28	They may **curse** me, but you will bless me.
	119.21	**cursed** are those who disobey your commands.
Prov	3.33	The Lord puts a **curse** on the homes of wicked men, but
	11.26	People **curse** a man who hoards grain, waiting for a higher price,
	20.20	If you **curse** your parents, your life will end like a
	24.24	person innocent, he will be **cursed** and hated by everyone.
	26. 2	**Curses** cannot hurt you unless you deserve them.
	27.14	You might as well **curse** your friend as wake him up early
	28.27	close your eyes to the poor, many people will **curse** you.
	29.24	the truth in court, and God will **curse** him if he doesn't.
	30.10	You will be **cursed** and suffer for it.
	30.11	There are people who **curse** their fathers and do not show
Is	8.21	and their anger they will **curse** their king and their God.
	24. 6	So God has pronounced a **curse** on the earth.
	65.15	My chosen people will use your name as a **curse.**
Jer	11. 3	of Israel, have placed a **curse** on everyone who does not obey
	15.10	yet everyone **curses** me.
	15.11	Lord, may all their **curses** come true if I have not
	20.14	**Curse** the day I was born!
	20.15	**Curse** the man who made my father glad when he brought
	23.10	Because of the Lord's **curse** the land mourns and the pastures
	24. 9	and use their name as a **curse** everywhere I scatter them.
	25.18	people would use their name as a **curse**—as they still do.
	26. 6	the world will use the name of this city as a **curse."**
	29.18	People will mock them and use their name as a **curse.**

Jer 29.22 Babylonia want to bring a **curse** on someone, they will say,
42.18 will treat you with scorn and use your name as a **curse.**
44. 8 will treat you with scorn and use your name as a **curse?**
44.12 will treat them with scorn and use their name as a **curse.**
44.22 use its name as a **curse** because the Lord could no longer
48.10 (**Curse** the man who does not do the Lord's work with all
48.10 **Curse** the man who does not slash and kill!)
49.13 people will jeer at it and use its name as a **curse.**
Lam 3.65 **Curse** them and fill them with despair!
Dan 9.11 you brought on us the **curses** that are written in the Law
Mic 2. 7 Do you think the people of Israel are under a **curse?**
Zech 5. 3 "On it is written the **curse** that is to go out over
5. 4 that he will send this **curse** out, and it will enter the
8.13 In the past foreigners have **cursed** one another by saying,
Mal 1.14 A **curse** on the cheat who sacrifices a worthless animal to me,
2. 2 to what I say, then I will bring a **curse** on you.
2. 2 I will put a **curse** on the things you receive for your
2. 2 I have already put a **curse** on them, because you do not
3. 9 A **curse** is on all of you because the whole nation is
Mt 15. 4 and your mother,' and 'Whoever **curses** his father or his mother
25.41 on his left, 'Away from me, you that are under God's **curse!**
Mk 7.10 and your mother,' and, 'Whoever **curses** his father or his mother
11.21 "Look, Teacher, the fig-tree you **cursed** has died!"
Lk 6.28 bless those who **curse** you, and pray for those who
Jn 7.49 not know the Law of Moses, so they are under God's **curse!"**
9.28 They **cursed** him and said, "You are that fellow's disciple;
Rom 3.14 their speech is filled with bitter **curses.**
9. 3 that I myself were under God's **curse** and separated from Christ.
12.14 those who persecute you—yes, ask him to bless, not to **curse.**
1 Cor 4.12 When we are **cursed,** we bless;
12. 3 who is led by God's Spirit can say "A **curse** on Jesus!"
16.22 Whoever does not love the Lord—a **curse** on him!
Gal 3.10 Those who depend on obeying the Law live under a **curse.**
3.10 is written in the book of the Law is under God's **curse!"**
3.13 But by becoming a **curse** for us Christ has redeemed us
3.13 from the **curse** that the Law brings;
3.13 "Anyone who is hanged on a tree is under God's **curse."**
Heb 6. 8 is in danger of being **cursed** by God and will be destroyed
Jas 3. 9 and Father and also to **curse** our fellow-man, who is created
3.10 Words of thanksgiving and **cursing** pour out from the same mouth.
1 Pet 3. 9 Do not pay back evil with evil or **cursing** with cursing;
2 Pet 2.14 They are under God's **curse!**
Rev 13. 6 It began to **curse** God, his name, the place where he lives,
16. 9 the fierce heat, and they **cursed** the name of God, who has
16.11 of their pain, [11] and they **cursed** the God of heaven for
16.21 the sky on people, who **cursed** God on account of the plague
22. 3 Nothing that is under God's **curse** will be found in the city.

CURTAIN

Ex 26.31 "Make a **curtain** of fine linen woven with blue, purple,
26.33 Place the **curtain** under the row of hooks in the roof of
26.33 the Tent, and behind the **curtain** put the Covenant Box
26.33 The **curtain** will separate the Holy Place from the Most Holy Place.
26.36 of the Tent make a **curtain** of fine linen woven with blue,
26.37 For this **curtain** make five posts of acacia-wood covered
27. 9 Tent of my presence make an enclosure out of fine linen **curtains.**
27. 9 On the south side the **curtains** are to be 44 metres long,
27.12 side there are to be **curtains** 22 metres long, with ten posts
27.14 be 6.6 metres of **curtains,** with three posts and three bases.
27.16 there is to be a **curtain** 9 metres long made of fine
27.18 The **curtains** are to be made of fine linen and the bases
27.21 of my presence outside the **curtain** which is in front of the
30. 6 Put this altar outside the **curtain** which hangs in front of
35.12 Box, its poles, its lid, and the **curtain** to screen it off;
35.15 the **curtain** for the entrance of the Tent;
35.17 the **curtains** for the enclosure, its posts and bases;
35.17 the **curtain** for the entrance of the enclosure;
36.35 They made a **curtain** of fine linen, woven with blue,
36.36 of acacia-wood to hold the **curtain,** covered them with gold,
36.37 the Tent they made a **curtain** of fine linen woven with blue,
36.38 For this **curtain** they made five posts fitted with hooks,
38. 9 Lord's presence he made the enclosure out of fine linen **curtains.**
38. 9 On the south side the **curtains** were 44 metres long,
38.12 the west side there were **curtains** 22 metres long, with ten
38.14 6.6 metres of **curtains,** with three posts and three bases.
38.16 All the **curtains** round the enclosure were made of fine linen.
38.18 The **curtain** for the entrance of the enclosure was made
38.18 long and 2 metres high, like the **curtains** of the enclosure.
38.27 Tent and for the **curtain,** 34 kilogrammes for each base.
39.34 the **curtain;**
39.38 the **curtain** for the entrance of the Tent;
39.40 the **curtains** for the enclosure and its posts and bases;
39.40 the **curtain** for the entrance of the enclosure and its ropes;
40. 3 the Ten Commandments and put the **curtain** in front of it.
40. 5 Covenant Box and hang the **curtain** at the entrance of the Tent.
40. 8 enclosure and hang the **curtain** at its entrance.
40.21 he put the box in the Tent and hung up the **curtain.**
40.22 the north side outside the **curtain,** [23] and placed on it the
40.26 of the **curtain,** [27] and burnt the sweet-smelling incense,
40.28 He hung the **curtain** at the entrance of the Tent, [29] and
40.29 there in front of the **curtain** he placed the altar for
40.33 altar and hung the **curtain** at the entrance of the enclosure.
Lev 4. 6 and sprinkle it in front of the sacred **curtain** seven times.
4.17 in it, and sprinkle it in front of the **curtain** seven times.
16. 2 he to go behind the **curtain** into the Most Holy Place,
21.23 not come near the sacred **curtain** or approach the altar.
24. 3 outside the **curtain** in front of the Covenant Box,
Num 3.26 curtain for the entrance, [26] the **curtains** for the court
3.26 the altar, and the **curtain** for the entrance of the court.
Num 3.31 the Holy Place, and the **curtain** at the entrance to the Most
4. 5 Tent, take down the **curtain** in front of the Covenant Box,
4.26 curtain for the entrance, [26] the **curtains** and ropes for the court
4.26 Tent and the altar, the **curtains** for the entrance of the court,
Judg 4.18 So he went in, and she hid him behind a **curtain.**
2 Chr 3.14 A **curtain** for the Most Holy Place was made of linen and
Esth 1. 6 with blue and white cotton **curtains,** tied by cords of fine
Song 1. 5 but beautiful as the **curtains** in Solomon's palace.
Is 40.22 out the sky like a **curtain,** like a tent in which to
Jer 4.20 their **curtains** are torn to pieces.
10.20 there is no one to hang their **curtains."**
49.29 their tent **curtains** and everything in their tents.
Mt 27.51 Then the **curtain** hanging in the Temple was torn in two
Mk 15.38 The **curtain** hanging in the Temple was torn in two, from
Lk 23.45 and the **curtain** hanging in the Temple was torn in two.
Heb 6.19 and goes through the **curtain** of the heavenly temple into the
9. 3 Behind the second **curtain** was the Tent called the Most Holy Place.
10.20 way, through the **curtain**—that is, through his own body.

CURVE

1 Kgs 7.26 the rim of a cup, **curving** outwards like the petals
2 Chr 4. 5 the rim of a cup, **curving** outwards like the petals
Song 7. 1 The **curve** of your thighs is like the work of an artist.

CUSHION

Song 3.10 Its **cushions** are covered with purple cloth, lovingly woven

CUSTOM

Gen 29.26 answered, "It is not the **custom** here to give the younger
Lev 20.23 Do not adopt the **customs** of people who live there;
Judg 11.39 was the origin of the **custom** in Israel [40] that the young
14.10 This was a **custom** among the young men.
Ruth 4. 7 of property, it was the **custom** for the seller to take off
1 Kgs 10.13 for, besides all the other **customary** gifts that he had
2 Kgs 11.14 the column at the entrance of the Temple, as was the **custom.**
17. 8 worshipped other gods, [8] followed the **customs** of the people
17. 8 and adopted **customs** introduced by the kings of Israel.
17.15 and they followed the **customs** of the surrounding nations,
17.19 they imitated the **customs** adopted by the people of Israel.
17.33 own gods according to the **customs** of the countries from
17.34 They still carry on their old **customs** to this day.
17.40 not listen, and they continued to follow their old **customs.**
2 Chr 35.25 It has become a **custom** in Israel for the singers, both men
Esth 1.13 Now it was the king's **custom** to ask for expert opinion
3. 8 They observe **customs** that are not like those of any other people.
9.23 and the celebration became an annual **custom.**
Is 2. 6 The people follow foreign **customs.**
Ezek 5. 7 You have followed the **customs** of other nations.
20.18 follow their **customs** or defile yourselves with their idols.
Zeph 1. 8 the king's sons, and all who practise foreign **customs.**
Lk 1. 9 According to the **custom** followed by the priests, he was chosen
Jn 18.39 But according to the **custom** you have, I always set free
19.40 according to the Jewish **custom** of preparing a body for burial.
Acts 6.14 Temple and change all the **customs** which have come down to us
16.21 They are teaching **customs** that are against our law;
16.21 and we cannot accept these **customs** or practise them."
21.21 not to circumcise their children or follow the Jewish **customs.**
26. 3 since you know so well all the Jewish **customs** and disputes.
28.17 our people or the **customs** that we received from our ancestors,
1 Cor 11.16 nor the churches of God have any other **custom** in worship.

CUSTOMER

Prov 20.14 The **customer** always complains that the price is too high,
Hos 12. 7 they love to cheat their **customers** with false scales.
Amos 8. 5 and tamper with the scales to cheat our **customers.**

CUT

[FRESHLY-CUT]

Gen 15.10 brought the animals to God, **cut** them in half, and placed the
15.10 but he did not **cut** up the birds.
22. 3 Early the next morning Abraham **cut** some wood for the sacrifice,
40.19 the king will release you—and have your head **cut** off!
Ex 4.25 wife, took a sharp stone, **cut** off the foreskin of her son,
20.25 not build it out of **cut** stones,
22. 6 growing or that has been **cut** and stacked,
29.17 **Cut** the ram in pieces;
29.22 "**Cut** away the ram's fat, the fat tail, the fat covering
31. 5 for **cutting** jewels to be set;
34. 1 The Lord said to Moses, "**Cut** two stone tablets like the
34. 4 So Moses **cut** two more stone tablets,
34.13 destroy their sacred pillars, and **cut** down the symbols of
35.33 for **cutting** jewels to be set;
39. 3 out sheets of gold and **cut** them into thin strips
Lev 1. 6 shall skin the animal and **cut** it up,
1.12 After the man **cuts** it up, the officiating priest shall
3. 9 fat, the entire fat tail **cut** off near the backbone,
8.20 He **cut** the ram in pieces, washed the internal
19. 9 harvest your fields, do not **cut** the corn at the edges
19. 9 do not go back to **cut** the ears of corn
19.27 Do not **cut** the hair on the sides of your head or
19.28 beard [28] or tattoo yourselves or **cut** gashes in your body to
21. 5 or trim his beard or **cut** gashes on his body to show
22.24 any animal whose testicles have been crushed, **cut,** bruised,
23.22 harvest your fields, do not **cut** the corn at the edges of
23.22 do not go back to **cut** the ears of corn that were

Lev 26.26 I will **cut** off your food supply, so that ten women will
Num 6. 5 under the Nazirite vow, he must not **cut** his hair or shave.
13.23 of Eshcol, and there they **cut** off a branch which had one
13.24 because of the bunch of grapes the Israelites **cut** off there.)
Deut 7. 5 sacred stone pillars in pieces, **cut** down the symbols of
10. 1 the Lord said to me, '**Cut** two stone tablets like the first
10. 3 a box of acacia-wood and **cut** two stone tablets like the
19. 5 into the forest together to **cut** wood and if, as one of
20.19 capture a city, do not **cut** down its fruit-trees, even though
20.20 You may **cut** down the other trees and use them in the
21.12 her head, **cut** her fingernails, [13]and change her clothes.
23. 1 or whose penis has been **cut** off may be included among the
23.25 your hands, but you must not **cut** any corn with a sickle.
24.19 the corn that you have **cut**, do not go back for it;
25.12 **cut** off her hand.
29.11 who live among you and **cut** wood and carry water for you.
Josh 3.16 the Dead Sea was completely **cut** off, and the people were
8.31 made of stones which have not been **cut** with iron tools."
9.21 but they will have to **cut** wood and carry water for us."
9.23 people will always be slaves, **cutting** wood and carrying
9.27 he made them slaves, to **cut** wood and carry water for the
Judg 1. 6 chased him, caught him, and **cut** off his thumbs and big toes.
1. 7 their thumbs and big toes **cut** off have picked up scraps
6.25 father's altar to Baal, and **cut** down the symbol of the
6.26 for firewood the symbol of Asherah you have **cut** down."
6.28 symbol of Asherah had been **cut** down, and that the second
6.30 the altar to Baal and **cut** down the symbol of Asherah beside
9.48 There he took an axe, **cut** a branch off a tree, and
9.49 So every man **cut** off a branch of a tree;
13. 5 is born, you must never **cut** his hair, because from the day
16.17 "My hair has never been **cut**," he said.
16.17 If my hair were **cut**, I would lose my strength and be
16.19 then called a man, who **cut** off Samson's seven locks of hair.
19.29 He took his concubine's body, **cut** it into twelve pieces, and
20. 6 I took her body, **cut** it in pieces, and sent one piece
1 Sam 1.11 his whole life and that he will never have his hair **cut**."
11. 7 He took two oxen, **cut** them in pieces, and sent messengers
15.33 And he **cut** Agag to pieces in front of the altar in
17.46 I will defeat you and **cut** off your head.
17.51 out of its sheath, and **cut** off his head and killed him.
24. 4 David crept over and **cut** off a piece of Saul's robe without
24.11 I could have killed you, but instead I only **cut** this off.
31. 9 They **cut** off Saul's head, stripped off his armour, and
2 Sam 4. 7 Then they **cut** off his head, took it with them, and walked
4.12 killed Rechab and Baanah and **cut** off their hands and feet,
10. 4 one side of their beards, **cut** off their clothes at the hips,
14.26 thick, and he had to **cut** it once a year, when it
16. 9 Let me go over there and **cut** off his head!"
20.22 with her plan, and they **cut** off Sheba's head and threw it
1 Kgs 3.25 it was brought, [25]he said, "**Cut** the living child in two
3.26 go ahead and **cut** it in two."
5. 6 So send your men to Lebanon to **cut** down cedars for me.
5. 6 men don't know how to **cut** down trees as well as yours
7. 9 prepared at the quarry and **cut** to measure, with their inner
7.11 of them were other stones, **cut** to measure, and cedar beams.
7.12 layer of cedar beams for every three layers of **cut** stones.
15.13 Asa **cut** down the idol and burnt it in the valley of
15.17 fortify Ramah in order to **cut** off all traffic in and out
18.23 Baal take one, kill it, **cut** it in pieces, and put it
18.28 prayed louder and **cut** themselves with knives and daggers,
18.33 the wood on the altar, **cut** the bull in pieces, and laid
2 Kgs 3.19 will **cut** down all their fruit-trees, stop all their springs,
3.25 also stopped up the springs and **cut** down the fruit-trees.
4.42 barley harvested that year, and some **freshly-cut** ears of corn.
6. 2 go to the Jordan and **cut** down some trees, so that we
6. 5 As one of them was **cutting** down a tree, suddenly his iron
6. 6 him the place, and Elisha **cut** off a stick, threw it in
18. 4 broke the stone pillars, and **cut** down the images of the
19.23 You boasted that there you **cut** down the tallest cedars and
23.14 the stone pillars to pieces, **cut** down the symbols of the
1 Chr 10. 9 They **cut** off Saul's head, stripped off his armour, and
19. 4 shaved off their beards, **cut** off their clothes at the hips,
2 Chr 2.16 of Lebanon we will **cut** down all the cedars you need,
2.18 materials and 80,000 to **cut** stones in the mountains,
14. 3 the sacred stone columns, and **cut** down the symbols of the
15.16 Asa **cut** down the idol, chopped it up, and burnt the pieces
16. 1 fortify Ramah in order to **cut** off all traffic in and out
31. 1 and broke the stone pillars, **cut** down the symbols of the
32. 3 and his officials decided to **cut** off the supply of water
Job 8.12 first to wither, while still too small to be **cut** and used.
14. 7 There is hope for a tree that has been **cut** down;
24.24 a weed, like an ear of corn that has been **cut** off.
30.13 They **cut** off my escape and try to destroy me;
41. 6 Will merchants **cut** him up to sell?
Ps 7. 5 and catch me, let them **cut** me down and kill me and
55.21 were as soothing as oil, but they **cut** like sharp swords.
58. 9 Before they know it, they are **cut** down like weeds;
60. 2 You have made the land tremble, and you have **cut** it open;
74. 5 They looked like woodmen **cutting** down trees with their axes.
80.16 Our enemies have set it on fire and **cut** it down;
90. 9 Our life is **cut** short by your anger;
129. 3 They **cut** deep wounds in my back and made it like a
Prov 7.27 It is a short **cut** to death.
26. 6 deliver a message, you might as well **cut** off your own feet;
27.25 You **cut** the hay and then cut the grass on the hillsides
Is 6.13 be like the stump of an oak-tree that has been **cut** down."
9.10 of sycomore wood have been **cut** down, but we will replace
9.14 he will **cut** them off, head and tail.
10.33 Almighty will bring them crashing down like branches **cut** off a tree.
10.33 The proudest and highest of them will be **cut** down and humiliated.
Is 10.34 The Lord will **cut** them down as trees in the
10.34 heart of the forest are **cut** down with an axe,
11. 1 line of David is like a tree that has been **cut** down;
14. 8 there is no one to **cut** them down, now that he is
17. 5 where the corn has been **cut** and harvested, as desolate as a
18. 5 the Sudanese as easily as a knife **cuts** branches from a vine.
37.24 You boasted that there you **cut** down the tallest cedars and
38.12 My life was **cut** off and ended, Like a tent
38.12 that is taken down, Like cloth that is **cut** from a loom.
44.14 He might **cut** down cedars to use, or choose oak or
51. 9 It was you that **cut** the sea-monster Rahab to pieces.
Jer 5.10 I will send enemies to **cut** down my people's vineyards,
6. 6 has ordered these kings to **cut** down trees and build mounds
7.29 **cut** off your hair and throw it away.
9.21 it has **cut** down the children in the streets and the young
9.22 on the fields, like corn **cut** and left behind by the reapers,
9.25 Moab, and the desert people, who have their hair **cut** short.
10. 3 A tree is **cut** down in the forest;
22. 7 all bring their axes, **cut** down its beautiful cedar pillars,
25.19 all the people who **cut** their hair short;
34.18 the two halves of a bull that they had **cut** in two.
36.23 or four columns, the king **cut** them off with a small knife
46.22 her with axes, like men **cutting** down trees [23]and
47. 4 come to destroy Philistia, to **cut** off from Tyre and Sidon
48.37 All of them have shaved their heads and **cut** off their beards.
49.32 every direction those people who **cut** their hair short, and I
51.13 but its time is up, and its thread of life is **cut**.
51.33 Soon the enemy will **cut** them down and trample them like
51.34 The king of Babylonia **cut** Jerusalem up and ate it.
Ezek 4.16 man, I am going to **cut** off the supply of bread for
5.11 things you did, I will **cut** you down without mercy.
5.12 a third will be **cut** down by swords outside the city;
5.16 I will **cut** off your supply of food and let you starve.
16. 4 you were born, no one **cut** your umbilical cord or washed you
16.40 you, and they will **cut** you to pieces with their swords.
17.24 I **cut** down the tall trees and make the small trees grow
21.16 **Cut** to the right and the left, you sharp sword!
21.16 **Cut** wherever you turn.
23.25 They will **cut** off your nose and your ears and kill your
31.12 Ruthless foreigners will **cut** it down and leave it.
39.10 firewood in the fields or **cut** down trees in the forest,
40.42 prepare the offerings to be burnt whole, were of **cut** stone.
Dan 4.14 proclaimed in a loud voice, '**Cut** the tree down and chop off
4.23 from heaven and said, '**Cut** the tree down and destroy it,
Joel 3.13 **cut** them down like corn at harvest time;
Amos 7. 1 of the hay had been **cut** and the grass was starting to
Mic 1.16 People of Judah, **cut** off your hair in mourning for the
Hab 2.17 You have **cut** down the forests of Lebanon;
2.17 now you will be **cut** down.
Zech 11. 2 wail, oaks of Bashan— the dense forest has been **cut** down!
Mt 3.10 The axe is ready to **cut** down the trees at the roots;
3.10 bear good fruit will be **cut** down and thrown in the fire.
5.30 hand causes you to sin, **cut** it off and throw it away!
7.19 not bear good fruit is **cut** down and thrown in the fire.
18. 8 makes you lose your faith, **cut** it off and throw it away!
21. 8 on the road while others **cut** branches from the trees and
24.51 The master will **cut** him in pieces and make him share
26.51 and struck at the High Priest's slave, **cutting** off his ear.
Mk 4.29 the man starts **cutting** it with his sickle, because harvest
5. 5 through the hills, screaming and **cutting** himself with stones.
6.16 I had his head **cut** off, but he has come back to
6.27 The guard left, went to the prison, and **cut** John's head off;
9.43 So if your hand makes you lose your faith, **cut** it off!
9.45 And if your foot makes you lose your faith, **cut** it off!
11. 8 on the road, while others **cut** branches in the fields and
14.47 and struck at the High Priest's slave, **cutting** off his ear.
Lk 3. 9 The axe is ready to **cut** down the trees at the roots;
3. 9 bear good fruit will be **cut** down and thrown in the fire."
9. 9 Herod said, "I had John's head **cut** off;
12.46 The master will **cut** him in pieces and make him share
13. 7 **Cut** it down!
13. 9 if not, then you can have it **cut** down.'"
20.18 Everyone who falls on that stone will be **cut** to pieces;
22.50 struck the High Priest's slave and **cut** off his right ear.
Jn 18.10 struck the High Priest's slave, **cutting** off his right ear.
18.26 relative of the man whose ear Peter had **cut** off, spoke up.
Acts 8.32 sound when its wool is **cut** off, he did not say a
27.32 So the soldiers **cut** the ropes that held the boat and let
27.40 So they **cut** off the anchors and let them sink in the
1 Cor 11. 6 does not cover her head, she might as well **cut** her hair.
11. 6 to shave her head or **cut** her hair, she should cover her
Gal 5. 4 by obeying the Law have **cut** yourselves off from Christ.
Phil 3. 2 those dogs, those men who insist on **cutting** the body.
Heb 4.12 It **cuts** all the way through, to where soul and spirit meet,
Rev 14.18 "Use your sickle, and **cut** the grapes from the vineyard of
14.19 his sickle on the earth, **cut** the grapes from the vine,

CYMBALS

2 Sam 6. 5 They were playing harps, lyres, drums, rattles, and **cymbals.**
1 Chr 13. 8 They sang and played musical instruments—harps, drums, **cymbals,**
15.16 Levites to sing and to play joyful music on harps and **cymbals.**
15.17 they chose the following men to play the brass **cymbals:**
15.28 of trumpets, horns, and **cymbals,** and the music of harps.
16. 5 Asaph was to sound the **cymbals,**
16.42 charge of the trumpets and **cymbals** and the other instruments
25. 1 God's messages, accompanied by the music of harps and **cymbals.**
25. 6 All his sons played **cymbals** and harps under their father's direction,
2 Chr 5.11 side of the altar with **cymbals** and harps, and with them were

2 Chr 5.11 perfect harmony by trumpets, **cymbals,** and other instruments,
29.25 the Temple, with harps and **cymbals,** [26]instruments like
Ezra 3.10 the Levites of the clan of Asaph stood there with **cymbals.**
Neh 12.27 of thanksgiving and with the music of **cymbals** and harps.
Ps 150. 5 Praise him with **cymbals.**
150. 5 Praise him with loud **cymbals.**

CYPRESS

2 Kgs 19.23 tallest cedars and the finest **cypress-trees** and that you
2 Chr 2. 8 so send me cedar, **cypress,** and juniper logs from Lebanon.
Song 1.17 the beams of our house, and the **cypress-trees** the ceiling.
Is 14. 8 The **cypress-trees** and the cedars of Lebanon rejoice
37.24 tallest cedars and the finest **cypress-trees,** and that you
41.19 in barren land, forests of pine and juniper and **cypress.**
44.14 to use, or choose oak or **cypress** wood from the forest.
55.13 **Cypress-trees** will grow where now there are briars;
60.13 pine, the juniper, and the **cypress,** The finest wood from the
Zech 11. 2 Weep and wail, **cypress-trees**— the cedars have fallen;

CYPRUS
Island in the Mediterranean which became a Roman province.

Gen 10. 4 descendants of Javan were the people of Elishah, Spain, **Cyprus,**
Num 24.24 Invaders will sail from **Cyprus;**
1 Chr 1. 7 descendants of Javan were the people of Elishah, Spain, **Cyprus,**
Is 23. 1 As your ships return from **Cyprus,** you learn the news.
23.12 Even if they escape to **Cyprus,** they will still not be safe.
Jer 2.10 west to the island of **Cyprus,** and send someone eastwards to
Ezek 27. 6 your deck out of pine from **Cyprus** And inlaid it with ivory.
27. 7 made of finest cloth, Of purple from the island of **Cyprus.**
Acts 4.36 a Levite born in **Cyprus,** whom the apostles called Barnabas
11.19 as far as Phoenicia, **Cyprus,** and Antioch, telling the message
11.20 But other believers, men from **Cyprus** and Cyrene, went to Antioch
13. 4 to Seleucia and sailed from there to the island of **Cyprus.**
15.39 and sailed off for **Cyprus,** [40]while Paul chose Silas and left,
21. 3 to where we could see **Cyprus,** and then sailed south of it
21.16 to stay with —Mnason, from **Cyprus,** who had been a believer
27. 4 we sailed on the sheltered side of the island of **Cyprus.**

CYRUS
King of Persia who conquered Babylonia in 538 BC and enabled the Jews to return to Jerusalem.

2 Chr 36.22 In the first year that **Cyrus** of Persia was emperor,
36.22 He prompted **Cyrus** to issue the following command and send it
36.23 "This is the command of **Cyrus,** Emperor of Persia.
Ezra 1. 1 In the first year that **Cyrus** of Persia was emperor,
1. 1 He prompted **Cyrus** to issue the following command and send it
1. 2 "This is the command of **Cyrus,** Emperor of Persia.
1. 7 **Cyrus** gave them back the bowls and cups that King
3. 7 All this was done with the permission of **Cyrus,** emperor of Persia.
4. 3 just as **Cyrus,** emperor of Persia, commanded us."
4. 5 throughout the reign of **Cyrus** and into the reign of Darius.
5.13 Cyrus as emperor of Babylonia, **Cyrus** issued orders for the
5.14 **Cyrus** handed these utensils over to a man named Sheshbazzar,
5.17 to find whether or not **Cyrus** gave orders for this Temple
6. 3 first year of his reign **Cyrus** the emperor commanded that the
6.14 by **Cyrus,** Darius, and Artaxerxes, emperors of Persia.
Is 44.28 I say to **Cyrus,** 'You are the one who will rule
45. 1 The Lord has chosen **Cyrus** to be king!
45. 1 To **Cyrus** the Lord says, [2]"I myself will prepare your way,
45.13 I myself have stirred **Cyrus** to action
Dan 1.21 until **Cyrus** the emperor of Persia conquered Babylonia.
6.28 the reign of Darius and the reign of **Cyrus** the Persian.
10. 1 (In the third year that **Cyrus** was emperor of Persia,

DADDY

Is 8. 4 to say 'Mummy' and **'Daddy,'** all the wealth of Damascus

DAFT

1 Sam 21.15 to annoy me with his **daft** actions right here

DAGGER

1 Kgs 18.28 with knives and **daggers,** according to their ritual,

DAILY

Lev 6.20 (the same amount as the **daily** grain-offering),
9.17 (This was in addition to the **daily** burnt-offering.)
23. 7 you shall gather for worship and do none of your **daily** work.
23. 8 for worship, but you shall do none of your **daily** work.
23.21 that day do none of your **daily** work, but gather for worship.
23.25 a food-offering to the Lord and do none of your **daily** work.
23.35 come together for worship and do none of your **daily** work.
Num 28. 3 **daily** burnt-offering, two one-year-old male lambs without any defects.
28. 6 This is the **daily** offering that is completely burnt,
28.10 Sabbath in addition to the **daily** offering with its wine-offering.
28.15 And in addition to the **daily** burnt-offering with its wine-offering,
28.24 Offer this in addition to the **daily** burnt-offering and wine-offering.
28.31 in addition to the **daily** burnt-offering and grain-offering.
29. 6 **daily** burnt-offering with its grain-offering and wine-offering.
29.11 **daily** burnt-offering with its grain-offering and wine-offering.
29.16 **daily** burnt-offering with its grain-offering and wine-offering.
1 Kgs 8.59 of Israel and to their king, according to their **daily** needs.
1 Chr 26.17 Four guards were stationed at the storerooms **daily,**
2 Chr 8.14 he organized the **daily** work of the priests
8.14 in sections for performing their **daily** duties at each gate,
31.16 age or older who had **daily** responsibilities in the Temple
Neh 10.33 the sacred bread, the **daily** grain-offering, the animals
12.47 the people of Israel gave **daily** gifts for the support of the
Ps 61. 8 praises to you, as I offer you **daily** what I have promised.
Prov 8.30 I was his **daily** source of joy, always happy
Dan 8.11 stopped the **daily** sacrifices offered to him,
8.12 instead of offering the proper **daily** sacrifices,
8.13 How long will an awful sin replace the **daily** sacrifices?
11.31 They will stop the **daily** sacrifices and set up The Awful Horror.
12.11 "From the time the **daily** sacrifices are stopped,
Lk 1. 8 priest in the Temple, taking his turn in the **daily** service.
Acts 6. 1 widows were being neglected in the **daily** distribution of funds.

DAINTY

Is 3.16 They take **dainty** little steps, and the bracelets on their ankles jingle.

DAM

Prov 17.14 start of an argument is like the first break in a **dam;**
Nah 2. 8 Like water from a broken **dam** the people rush from Nineveh!

DAMAGE

Ex 22. 6 the one who started the fire is to pay for the **damage.**
2 Chr 24. 7 Athaliah, that corrupt woman, had **damaged** the Temple
Acts 27.10 there will be great **damage** to the cargo and to the ship,
27.21 then we would have avoided all this **damage** and loss.
Rev 6. 6 But do not **damage** the olive-trees and the vineyards!"
7. 2 God had given the power to **damage** the earth and the sea.

DAMASCUS
Capital of the kingdom of Syria (later the Roman province of Syria).

Gen 14.15 far as Hobah, north of **Damascus,** [16]and recovered the loot
15. 2 My only heir is Eliezer of **Damascus.**
2 Sam 8. 5 When the Syrians of **Damascus** sent an army to help King Hadadezer,
1 Kgs 11.24 men went and lived in **Damascus,** where his men made him king
15.18 of his officials to **Damascus,** to King Benhadad of Syria,
19.15 "Return to the wilderness near **Damascus,** then enter the
20.34 commercial centre for yourself in **Damascus,** just as my
2 Kgs 5.12 Abana and Pharpar, back in **Damascus,** better than any river in Israel?
8. 7 Elisha went to **Damascus** at a time when King Benhadad of
8. 9 kinds of the finest products of **Damascus** and went to Elisha.
14.28 battles, and how he restored **Damascus** and Hamath to Israel,
16. 9 his army against **Damascus,** captured it, killed King Rezin,
16.10 When King Ahaz went to **Damascus** to meet Emperor Tiglath Pileser,
16.12 On his return from **Damascus,** Ahaz saw that the altar was finished,
1 Chr 18. 5 When the Syrians of **Damascus** sent an army to help King Hadadezer,
2 Chr 16. 2 palace and sent it to **Damascus,** to King Benhadad of Syria,
24.23 leaders, and took large amounts of loot back to **Damascus.**
28. 5 a large number of Judaeans back to **Damascus** as prisoners.
Song 7. 4 as the tower of Lebanon that stands guard at **Damascus.**
Is 7. 8 Syria is no stronger than **Damascus,** its capital city,
7. 8 and **Damascus** is no stronger than King Rezin.
8. 4 all the wealth of **Damascus** and all the loot of Samaria
10. 9 I conquered Samaria and **Damascus.**
17. 1 The Lord said, **"Damascus** will not be a city any longer;
17. 3 Israel will be defenceless, and **Damascus** will lose its independence.
Jer 49.23 This is what the Lord said about **Damascus:**
49.24 The people of **Damascus** are weak and have fled in terror.
49.27 will set the walls of **Damascus** on fire and will burn down
Ezek 27.18 The people of **Damascus** bought your merchandise and your products,
47.16 territory of the kingdom of **Damascus** and that of the kingdom
47.17 with the border regions of **Damascus** and Hamath to the north
47.18 point between the territory of **Damascus** and that of Hauran,
48. 1 to the boundary between the kingdoms of **Damascus** and Hamath.
Amos 1. 3 Lord says, "The people of **Damascus** have sinned again and again,
1. 5 smash the city gates of **Damascus** and remove the inhabitants
5.27 exile in a land beyond **Damascus,"** says the Lord, whose name
Zech 9. 1 for the land of Hadrach and for the city of **Damascus.**
Acts 9. 2 to the synagogues in **Damascus,** so that if he should find
9. 3 near the city of **Damascus,** suddenly a light from the sky
9. 8 So they took him by the hand and led him into **Damascus.**
9.10 There was a Christian in **Damascus** named Ananias.
9.14 he has come to **Damascus** with authority from the chief priests
9.19 Saul stayed for a few days with the believers in **Damascus.**
9.22 that the Jews who lived in **Damascus** could not answer him.
9.27 boldly Saul had preached in the name of Jesus in **Damascus.**
22. 5 written to fellow-Jews in **Damascus,** so I went there to arrest
22. 6 and coming near **Damascus,** about midday a bright light from
22.10 'Get up and go into **Damascus,** and there you will be told
22.11 my companions took me by the hand and led me into **Damascus.**
26.12 that I went to **Damascus** with authority and orders from the
26.20 First in **Damascus** and in Jerusalem and then in all Judaea
2 Cor 11.32 When I was in **Damascus,** the governor under King Aretas placed
Gal 1.17 I went at once to Arabia, and then I returned to **Damascus.**

AV DAMNATION

Mt 23.33 How do you expect to escape from being **condemned** to hell?
Mk 12.40 Their **punishment** will be all the worse!"
16.16 whoever does not believe will be **condemned.**
Lk 20.47 Their **punishment** will be all the worse!"
Jn 5.29 and those who have done evil will rise and be **condemned.**
Rom 3. 8 They will be **condemned,** as they should be.
13. 2 and anyone who does so will bring **judgement** on himself.
14.23 about what he eats, God **condemns** him when he eats it,
1 Cor 11.29 from the cup, he brings **judgement** on himself as he eats and
2 Thes 2.12 the truth, but have taken pleasure in sin, will be **condemned.**
1 Tim 5.12 and so become **guilty** of breaking their earlier promise to
2 Pet 2. 1 They will bring in **destructive,** untrue doctrines, and will deny
2. 3 Judge has been ready, and their **Destroyer** has been wide awake!

DAMP

Ps 6. 6 every night my bed is **damp** from my weeping;
Song 5. 2 is wet with dew, and my hair is **damp** from the mist.

DAN (1)

Jacob and Bilhah's son, and the tribe descended from him, associated with Samson and a migration to n. Israel.

Gen 30. 6 so she named him **Dan.**
35.25 The sons of Rachel's slave Bilhah were **Dan** and Naphtali.
46.23 **Dan** and his son Hushim.
49.16 **"Dan** will be a ruler for his people.
49.17 **Dan** will be a snake at the side of the road,
Ex 1. 4 Reuben, Simeon, Levi, Judah, [3] Issachar, Zebulun, Benjamin, [4] **Dan,**
31. 6 son of Ahisamach, from the tribe of **Dan,** to work with him.
35.34 Ahisamach, from the tribe of **Dan,** the ability to teach
38.23 Ahisamach, from the tribe of **Dan,** was an engraver,
Lev 24.10 Israelite named Shelomith, the daughter of Dibri from the tribe of **Dan.**
Num 2.25 banner of the division of **Dan** shall camp in their groups,
2.25 The division of **Dan** shall march last.
10.25 led by the tribe of **Dan,** serving as the rearguard
Deut 33.22 About the tribe of **Dan** he said:
33.22 **"Dan** is a young lion;
Josh 19.40 assignment made was for the families of the tribe of **Dan.**
19.47 city from Laish to **Dan,** naming it after their ancestor Dan.
19.48 families of the tribe of **Dan** received as their possession.
21. 5 from the territories of Ephraim, **Dan,** and West Manasseh.
21.23 From the territory of **Dan** they were given four cities:
Judg 1.34 people of the tribe of **Dan** into the hill-country
5.17 and the tribe of **Dan** remained by the ships.
13. 2 He was a member of the tribe of **Dan.**
13.25 while he was between Zorah and Eshtaol in the Camp of **Dan.**
18. 1 those days the tribe of **Dan** was looking for territory
18. 2 So the people of **Dan** chose five qualified men
18.11 men from the tribe of **Dan** left Zorah and Eshtaol,
18.12 That is why the place is still called Camp of **Dan.**
18.16 the six hundred soldiers from **Dan,** ready for battle,
18.22 They caught up with the men from **Dan** [23] and shouted at them.
18.23 The men from **Dan** turned round and asked Micah, "What's the matter?
18.25 The men from **Dan** said, "You had better not say
18.27 After the men from **Dan** had taken the priest
18.27 The men from **Dan** rebuilt the town and settled down there.
18.29 Laish to Dan, after their ancestor **Dan,** the son of Jacob.
18.30 The men from **Dan** set up the idol to be worshipped,
18.30 priest for the tribe of **Dan,** and his descendants served
1 Chr 2. 2 Simeon, Levi, Judah, Issachar, Zebulun, [2] **Dan,** Joseph,
7.12 **Dan** had one son, Hushim.
2 Chr 2.14 member of the tribe of **Dan** and his father was a native
Ezek 48. 1 **Dan** Asher Naphtali Manasseh Ephraim Reuben Judah
48.30 those in the east wall, after Joseph, Benjamin, and **Dan;**
also Num 1.5 Num 1.20 Num 2.25 Num 7.12 Num 13.3 Num 26.42 Num 34.19 Deut 27.13 1 Chr 12.23 1 Chr 27.16

DAN (2)

City at the northernmost point of Israel's territory, previously known as Laish.

Gen 14.14 in all, and pursued the four kings all the way to **Dan.**
Deut 34. 1 the territory of Gilead as far north as the town of **Dan;**
Josh 19.47 When the people of **Dan** lost their land,
Judg 20. 1 the people of Israel from **Dan** in the north to Beersheba
2 Sam 24. 6 they went to Dan, and from **Dan** they went west to Sidon.
1 Kgs 12.29 one of the gold bull-calves in Bethel and the other in **Dan.**
12.30 the people sinned, going to worship in Bethel and in **Dan.**
15.20 They captured Ijon, **Dan,** Abel Beth Maacah, the area near Lake Galilee,
2 Kgs 10.29 the gold bull-calves he set up in Bethel and in **Dan.**
2 Chr 16. 4 They captured Ijon, **Dan,** Abel Beth Maacah,
30. 5 invited all the Israelites, from **Dan** in the north
Jer 4.15 Messengers from the city of **Dan** and from the hills
8.16 Our enemies are already in the city of **Dan;**
Amos 8.14 say, 'By the god of **Dan,'** or, 'By the god of Beersheba'

DANCE

Ex 15.20 all the women followed her, playing tambourines and **dancing.**
32.19 the bull-calf and to see the people **dancing,** he was furious.
Judg 11.34 coming out to meet him, **dancing** and playing the tambourine.
21.21 of Shiloh come out to **dance** during the festival,
21.23 the girls who were **dancing** at Shiloh and carried her away.
1 Sam 10. 5 They will be **dancing** and shouting.
10. 6 will join in their religious **dancing** and shouting and will
1 Sam 10.10 him, and he joined in their ecstatic **dancing** and shouting.
10.13 When Saul finished his ecstatic **dancing** and shouting,
18. 6 They were singing joyful songs, **dancing,** and playing tambourines and lyres.
19.20 saw the group of prophets **dancing** and shouting, with Samuel
19.20 of Saul's men, and they also began to **dance** and shout.
19.21 more messengers, and they also began to **dance** and shout.
19.23 of him also, and he **danced** and shouted all the way to
19.24 off his clothes and **danced** and shouted in Samuel's presence,
21.11 the women sang, as they **danced,** 'Saul has killed thousands,
29. 5 the women sang, as they **danced,** 'Saul has killed thousands,
2 Sam 6. 5 and all the Israelites were **dancing** and singing with all
6.14 linen cloth round his waist, **danced** with all his might
6.16 window and saw King David **dancing** and jumping around
6.16 around in the sacred **dance,** and she was disgusted with him.
6.21 David answered, "I was **dancing** to honour the Lord,
6.21 And I will go on **dancing** to honour the Lord,
1 Kgs 18.26 and kept **dancing** round the altar they had built.
1 Chr 13. 8 David and all the people **danced** with all their might
15.29 window and saw King David **dancing** and leaping for joy,
Job 21.12 and play like lambs [12] and **dance** to the music of harps
Ps 30.11 You have changed my sadness into a joyful **dance;**
87. 7 They **dance** and sing, "In Zion is the source of all our
149. 3 Praise his name with **dancing;**
150. 4 Praise him with drums and **dancing.**
Ecc 3. 4 mourning and the time for **dancing,** [5] the time for making love
Song 4. 1 Your hair **dances,** like a flock of goats bounding down
6. 5 Your hair **dances,** like a flock of goats bounding down
6.13 **Dance,** dance, girl of Shulam.
6.13 Let us watch you as you **dance.**
6.13 want to watch me as I **dance** between the rows of onlookers?
Is 35. 6 The lame will leap and **dance,** and those who cannot speak
Jer 31. 4 Once again you will take up your tambourines and **dance** joyfully.
31.13 Then the girls will **dance** and be happy, and men, young
Lam 5.15 grief has taken the place of our **dances.**
Mt 11.17 'We played wedding music for you, but you wouldn't **dance!**
14. 6 the daughter of Herodias **danced** in front of the whole group.
Mk 6.22 came in and **danced,** and pleased Herod and his guests.
Lk 6.23 glad when that happens, and **dance** for joy,
7.32 'We played wedding music for you, but you wouldn't **dance!**
15.25 he came close to the house, he heard the music and **dancing.**

DANGER

Gen 15. 1 I will shield you from **danger** and give you a great reward."
Lev 26. 6 will get rid of the **dangerous** animals in the land, and there
26.22 I will send **dangerous** animals among you, and they will
Deut 28.66 Your life will always be in **danger.**
Josh 23.13 Rather, they will be as **dangerous** for you as a trap or
1 Sam 20.21 swear by the living Lord that you will be in no **danger.**
2 Sam 4. 9 vow by the living Lord, who has saved me from all **dangers!**
22. 6 The **danger** of death was round me, and the grave set its
22.20 He helped me out of **danger;**
1 Kgs 5. 4 I have no enemies, and there is no **danger** of attack.
18. 9 want to put me in **danger** of being killed by King Ahab?
Ps 3. 3 But you, O Lord, are always my shield from **danger;**
18. 4 The **danger** of death was all round me;
18. 5 The **danger** of death was round me, and the grave set its
18.19 He helped me out of **danger;**
22. 5 They called to you and escaped from **danger;**
25.15 Lord for help at all times, and he rescues me from **danger.**
26.12 I am safe from all **dangers;**
27. 1 The Lord protects me from all **danger;**
31. 4 shelter me from **danger.**
34. 7 those who honour the Lord and rescues them from **danger.**
40. 2 me out of a **dangerous** pit, out of the deadly quicksand.
49. 5 afraid in times of **danger** when I am surrounded by enemies,
91. 3 safe from all hidden **dangers** and from all deadly diseases.
91. 5 You need not fear any **dangers** at night or sudden attacks
107.26 In such **danger** the men lost their courage;
116. 3 The **danger** of death was all round me;
116. 6 when I was in **danger,** he saved me.
121. 7 The Lord will protect you from all **danger;**
Prov 6.29 It is just as **dangerous** to sleep with another man's wife.
7.23 a net—he did not know that his life was in **danger.**
10.17 those who will not admit that they are wrong are in **danger.**
13.14 they will help you escape when your life is in **danger.**
28.15 he is as **dangerous** as a growling lion or a prowling bear.
29.25 It is **dangerous** to be concerned with what others think of you,
Ecc 8. 3 don't stay in such a **dangerous** place.
12. 5 You will be afraid of high places, and walking will be **dangerous.**
Is 7. 4 King Pekah is no more **dangerous** than the smoke from two
21.15 bows that are ready to shoot, from all the **dangers** of war.
30. 6 "The ambassadors travel through **dangerous** country, where
33. 8 The highways are so **dangerous** that no one travels on them.
38.17 You save my life from all **danger;**
65.25 straw, as cattle do, and snakes will no longer be **dangerous.**
Jer 2. 6 and sand-dunes, a dry and **dangerous** land where no one lives
2.31 been like a desert to you, like a dark and **dangerous** land?
38.24 this conversation, and your life will not be in **danger.**
Lam 3.47 we live in **danger** and fear.
Ezek 3.20 I put him in a **dangerous** situation, he will die if you
14.15 people, making the land so **dangerous** that no one could
34.25 get rid of all the **dangerous** animals in the land, so that
Jon 1. 4 was so violent that the ship was in **danger** of breaking up.
1. 5 order to lessen the **danger,** they threw the cargo overboard.
1. 7 find out who is to blame for getting us into this **danger."**
Hab 2. 9 have tried to make your own home safe from harm and **danger!**
Zech 9.16 save his people, as a shepherd saves his flock from **danger.**
Mt 5.22 worthless fool will be in **danger** of going to the fire of
8.24 storm hit the lake, and the boat was in **danger** of sinking.

Lk 8.23 to fill with water, so that they were all in great **danger.**
Acts 19.27 There is the **danger,** then, that this business of ours
19.27 but there is also the **danger** that the temple of the great
19.40 happened today, there is the **danger** that we will be accused
24. 5 We found this man to be a **dangerous** nuisance;
27. 9 time there, until it became **dangerous** to continue the voyage,
27.10 "Men, I see that our voyage from here on will be **dangerous;**
Rom 3.13 off their tongues, and **dangerous** threats, like snake's poison,
8.35 or persecution or hunger or poverty or **danger** or death?
8.36 "For your sake we are in **danger** of death at all times;
1 Cor 15.30 for us—why would we run the risk of **danger** every hour?
2 Cor 1.10 From such terrible **dangers** of death he saved us, and
4.11 we are always in **danger** of death for Jesus' sake,
11.26 travels I have been in **danger** from floods and from robbers,
11.26 in **danger** from fellow-Jews and from Gentiles;
11.26 there have been **dangers** in the cities, dangers in the wilds,
11.26 dangers on the high seas, and **dangers** from false friends.
Heb 6. 8 it is in **danger** of being cursed by God and will be

DANIEL (1)

Young man of noble family taken into exile in Babylon.

Dan 1.1-21 **The young men at Nebuchadnezzar's court**
2.1-13 **Nebuchadnezzar's dream**
14-23 **God shows Daniel what the dream means**
24-45 **Daniel tells the king the dream and explains it**
46-49 **The king rewards Daniel**
4.1-18 **Nebuchadnezzar's second dream**
19-33 **Daniel explains the dream**
5.1-12 **Belshazzar's banquet**
13-31 **Daniel explains the writing**
6.1-28 **Daniel in the pit of lions**
9.20-27 **Gabriel explains the prophecy**
10.1–11.2a **Daniel's vision by the river Tigris**
11.2b-20 **The kingdoms of Egypt and Syria**
12.1-13 **The time of the End**
Mt 24.15 will see 'The Awful Horror' of which the prophet **Daniel** spoke.

DAPPLED

Zech 1. 8 a valley, and behind him were other horses—red, **dappled,**
6. 3 the third by white horses, and the fourth by **dappled** horses.
6. 6 and the **dappled** horses were going to the country
6. 7 As the **dappled** horses came out, they were impatient to go

DARE

Gen 49. 9 No one **dares** disturb him.
Num 12. 8 How **dare** you speak against my servant Moses?"
14.44 Yet they still **dared** to go up into the hill-country,
24. 9 When it is sleeping, no one **dares** wake it.
32. 7 How **dare** you try to discourage the people of Israel
Deut 4.34 Has any god ever **dared** to go and take a people
17.12 Anyone who **dares** to disobey either the judge
17.13 and no one else will **dare** to act in such a way.
18.20 But if any prophet **dares** to speak a message in my name
Josh 10.21 No one in the land **dared** even to speak against the Israelites.
1 Sam 17.10 I **dare** you to pick someone to fight me!"
2 Sam 1.14 "How is it that you **dared** to kill the Lord's chosen king?"
17.17 because they did not **dare** to be seen entering the city.
Esth 7. 5 King Xerxes asked Queen Esther, "Who **dares** to do such a thing?
Job 9.12 no one **dares** ask him, "What are you doing?"
13.16 will save me, since no wicked man would **dare** to face God.
41.10 no one would **dare** to stand before him.
42. 3 You ask how I **dare** question your wisdom when I am so
Is 19.11 How **dare** they tell the king that they are successors to the
45. 9 Does a clay pot **dare** to argue with its maker, a pot
45.10 Does anyone **dare** to say to his parents, "Why did you
50. 8 Does anyone **dare** to bring charges against me?
Jer 6.25 We **dare** not go to the countryside or walk on the roads,
30.21 me when I invite him, for who would **dare** come uninvited?
49. 4 in your power and say that no one would **dare** attack you?
49.19 Who would **dare** challenge me?
50.44 Who would **dare** challenge me?
Mic 1.11 Those who live in Zaanan **dare** not come out of their city.
Mt 7. 4 How **dare** you say to your brother, 'Please, let me take
8.28 and were so fierce that no one **dared** travel on that road.
22.46 that day on no one **dared** to ask him any more questions.
Mk 2. 7 thought to themselves, [7]"How does he **dare** to talk like this?
12.34 After this nobody **dared** to ask Jesus any more questions.
Lk 20.40 For they did not **dare** ask him any more questions.
Jn 18.22 slapped him and said, "How **dare** you talk like that to
21.12 None of the disciples **dared** ask him, "Who are you?"
Acts 5.13 Nobody outside the group **dared** to join them, even though
7.32 Moses trembled with fear and **dared** not look.
Rom 5. 7 even be that someone might **dare** to die for a good person.
1 Cor 6. 1 with a fellow-Christian, how **dare** he go before heathen judges
2 Cor 10.12 we would not **dare** to classify ourselves or compare ourselves
11.21 But if anyone **dares** to boast about something—
11.21 I am talking like a fool—I will be just as **daring.**
Jude 9 Michael did not **dare** to condemn the Devil with insulting

DARING see DARE

DARIUS (1)

Emperor of Persia in Haggai and Zechariah's time, end of 6th century BC.

Ezra 4. 5 throughout the reign of Cyrus and into the reign of **Darius.**
4.24 the second year of the reign of **Darius,** emperor of Persia.
5. 5 action until they could write to **Darius** and receive a reply.
5. 7 "To Emperor **Darius,** may you rule in peace.
6. 1 So **Darius** the emperor issued orders for a search to be
6. 6 Then **Darius** sent the following reply:
6.12 I, **Darius,** have given this order.
6.14 and by Cyrus, **Darius,** and Artaxerxes, emperors of Persia.
6.15 Adar in the sixth year of the reign of **Darius** the emperor.
Hag 1. 1 During the second year that **Darius** was emperor of Persia,
1.15 the sixth month of the second year that **Darius** was emperor.
2.10 of the second year that **Darius** was emperor, the Lord
Zech 1. 1 of the second year that **Darius** was emperor of Persia, the
1. 7 In the second year that **Darius** was emperor, on the
7. 1 In the fourth year that **Darius** was emperor, on the fourth

DARIUS (2)

"Darius the Mede", conqueror of Babylon.

Dan 5.31 and **Darius** the Mede, who was then sixty-two years old,
6. 1 **Darius** decided to appoint a hundred and twenty governors
6. 6 and said, "King **Darius,** may Your Majesty live for ever!
6. 9 And so King **Darius** signed the order.
6.25 Then King **Darius** wrote to the people of all nations,
6.28 prospered during the reign of **Darius** and the reign of Cyrus
9. 1 **Darius** the Mede, who was the son of Xerxes, ruled

DARIUS (3)

Darius III, reigned 4th century BC.

Neh 12.22 This record was finished when **Darius** was emperor of Persia.

DARK

Gen 1. 2 everything was engulfed in total **darkness,**
1. 4 separated the light from the **darkness,**
1. 5 and he named the light "Day" and the **darkness** "Night".
1.18 the day and the night, and to separate light from **darkness.**
15.17 had set and it was **dark,** a smoking fire-pot and a flaming
Ex 10.21 towards the sky, and a **darkness** thick enough to be felt
10.22 there was total **darkness** throughout Egypt for three days.
14.20 The cloud made it **dark** for the Egyptians, but gave light
20.21 off, and only Moses went near the **dark** cloud where God was.
Deut 4.11 covered with thick clouds of **dark** smoke and fire blazing up
5.23 heard the voice from the **darkness,** your leaders
Josh 24. 7 for help, and I put **darkness** between them and the Egyptians.
Judg 19. 9 It will be **dark** soon;
1 Sam 2. 9 his faithful people, but the wicked disappear in **darkness;**
28. 8 on different clothes, and after **dark** he went with two of his
2 Sam 22.10 sky apart and came down, with a **dark** cloud under his feet.
22.12 He covered himself with **darkness;**
22.29 you dispel my **darkness.**
1 Kgs 8.12 sky, yet you have chosen to live in clouds and **darkness.**
18.45 sky was covered with **dark** clouds, the wind began to blow,
2 Kgs 7. 5 as it began to get **dark,** they went to the Syrian camp,
2 Chr 6. 1 "Lord, you have chosen to live in clouds and **darkness.**
Job 3. 4 Turn that day into **darkness,** God.
3. 5 Make it a day of gloom and thick **darkness;**
5.14 even at noon they grope in **darkness.**
10.21 to a land that is **dark** and gloomy, [22]a land of darkness,
10.22 darkness, shadows, and confusion, where the light itself is **darkness.**
11.17 at noon, and life's **darkest** hours will shine like the dawn.
12.22 He sends light to places **dark** as death.
12.25 they grope in the **dark** and stagger like drunkards.
15.22 no hope of escaping from **darkness,** for somewhere a sword is
15.23 He knows his future is **dark;**
15.30 Even his shadow will vanish, [30]and he will not escape from **darkness.**
17.12 say that light is near, but I know I remain in **darkness.**
17.13 the dead, where I will lie down to sleep in the **dark.**
18. 6 The lamp in his tent will be **darkened.**
18.18 of the land of the living, driven from light into **darkness.**
19. 8 he has hidden my path in **darkness.**
22.11 It has grown so **dark** that you cannot see, and a flood
23.16 It is God, not the **dark,** that makes me afraid— even
23.16 me afraid— even though the **darkness** has made me blind.
24.17 the light of day, but **darkness** holds no terror for them.
26.10 He divided light from **darkness** by a circle drawn on the
28. 3 Men explore the deepest **darkness.**
28. 3 the depths of the earth And dig for rocks in the **darkness.**
29. 3 me then and gave me light as I walked through the **darkness.**
30.26 I hoped for happiness and light, but trouble and **darkness** came instead.
30.30 My skin has turned **dark;**
34.22 There is no **darkness** dark enough to hide a sinner from God.
34.22 There is no darkness **dark** enough to hide a sinner from God.
35.10 their Creator, who gives them hope in their **darkest** hours.
36.30 through all the sky, but the depths of the sea remain **dark.**
38. 9 I who covered the sea with clouds and wrapped it in **darkness.**
38.17 shown you the gates that guard the **dark** world of the dead?
38.19 the light comes from or what the source of **darkness** is?
Ps 18. 9 sky apart and came down with a **dark** cloud under his feet.
18.11 He covered himself with **darkness;**
18.12 the lightning before him and broke through the **dark** clouds.
18.28 you dispel my **darkness.**
23. 4 I go through the deepest **darkness,** I will not be afraid,
35. 6 May their path be **dark** and slippery while the angel of the
44.19 you abandoned us in deepest **darkness.**
49.19 his ancestors in death, where the **darkness** lasts for ever.
74.20 There is violence in every **dark** corner of the land.
88. 6 the depths of the tomb, into the **darkest** and deepest pit.
88.12 seen in that place of **darkness** or your goodness in the land

Ps	88.18	friends abandon me, and **darkness** is my only companion.
	91. 6	plagues that strike in the **dark** or the evils that kill in
	97. 2	Clouds and **darkness** surround him;
	104.20	night, and in the **darkness** all the wild animals come out.
	105.28	God sent **darkness** on the country, but the Egyptians did
	107.10	living in gloom and **darkness,** prisoners suffering in chains,
	107.14	their gloom and **darkness** and broke their chains in pieces.
	112. 4	Light shines in the **darkness** for good men,
	139.11	I could ask the **darkness** to hide me
	139.12	but even **darkness** is not dark for you,
	139.12	**Darkness** and light are the same to you.
	143. 3	has put me in a **dark** prison, and I am like those
Prov	2.13	to live in the **darkness** of sin, [14] men who find pleasure
	4.19	The road of the wicked, however, is **dark** as night.
	7. 9	passing near her house [9] in the evening after it was **dark.**
	20.20	life will end like a lamp that goes out in the **dark.**
Ecc	2.13	"Wisdom is better than foolishness, just as light is better than **darkness.**
	5.17	to live our lives in **darkness** and grief, worried, angry, and
	6. 4	it disappears into **darkness,** where it is forgotten.
Song	1. 5	Women of Jerusalem, I am **dark** but beautiful,
	1. 5	**dark** as the desert tents of Kedar,
	2.17	until the morning breezes blow and the **darkness** disappears.
	4. 6	until the morning breezes blow and the **darkness** disappears.
Is	5.20	You turn **darkness** into light and light into darkness.
	5.30	**Darkness** and distress!
	5.30	The light is swallowed by **darkness.**
	8.22	see nothing but trouble and **darkness,**
	8.22	terrifying **darkness** into which they are being driven.
	9. 2	The people who walked in **darkness** have seen a great light.
	13.10	shining, the sun will be **dark** when it rises, and the moon
	24.23	The moon will grow **dark,** and the sun will no longer shine,
	29.18	have been living in **darkness,** will open their eyes and see.
	42. 7	of the blind and set free those who sit in **dark** prisons.
	42.16	I will turn their **darkness** into light and make rough country
	45. 3	I will give you treasures from **dark,** secret places;
	45. 7	I create both light and **darkness;**
	47. 5	"Sit in silence and **darkness;**
	49. 9	and to those who are in **darkness,** 'Come out to the light!'
	50. 3	can make the sky turn **dark,** as if it were in mourning
	50.10	path you walk may be **dark** indeed, but trust in the Lord,
	58.10	are in need, then the **darkness** around you will turn to the
	59. 9	but there is only **darkness,** [10] and we grope about like blind
	59.10	night, as if we were in the **dark** world of the dead.
	60. 2	nations will be covered by **darkness,** But on you the light of
Jer	2.31	been like a desert to you, like a **dark** and dangerous land?
	4.28	the sky will grow **dark.**
	13.16	he brings **darkness,** and you stumble on the mountains;
	13.16	before he turns into deep **darkness** the light you hoped for.
	15. 9	Her daylight has turned to **darkness;**
	23.12	The paths they follow will be slippery and **dark;**
Lam	2. 1	The Lord in his anger has covered Zion with **darkness.**
	3. 2	me deeper and deeper into **darkness** [3] And beat me again and
	3. 6	He has forced me to live in the stagnant **darkness** of death.
Ezek	12. 6	and going out into the **dark** with your eyes covered, so that
	12. 7	evening as it was getting **dark** I dug a hole in the
	12.12	shoulder his pack in the **dark** and escape through a hole that
	30.18	**Darkness** will fall on Tahpanhes when I break the power
	31.15	I will bring **darkness** over the Lebanon Mountains
	32. 8	the lights of heaven and plunge your world into **darkness.**
	34.12	where they were scattered on that **dark,** disastrous day.
Dan	2.22	knows what is hidden in **darkness,** and he himself is surrounded
Joel	2. 2	It will be a **dark** and gloomy day, a black and cloudy
	2. 2	army of locusts advances like **darkness** spreading over the mountains.
	2.10	sun and the moon grow **dark,** and the stars no longer shine.
	2.31	The sun will be **darkened,** and the moon will turn red as
	3.15	sun and the moon grow **dark,** and the stars no longer shine.
Amos	5. 8	He turns **darkness** into daylight, and day into night.
	5.18	it will be a day of **darkness** and not of light.
	5.20	The day of the Lord will bring **darkness** and not light;
	8. 9	sun go down at noon and the earth grow **dark** in daytime.
Mic	7. 8	We are in **darkness** now, but the Lord will give us light.
Zeph	1.15	a day of **darkness** and gloom,
Zech	14. 7	there will no longer be cold or frost, [7] nor any **darkness.**
Mt	4.16	The people who live in **darkness** will see a great light.
	4.16	those who live in the **dark** land of death the light will
	6.23	if your eyes are no good, your body will be in **darkness.**
	6.23	the light in you is darkness, how terribly **dark** it will be!
	8.12	thrown out into the **darkness,** where they will cry and grind
	10.27	telling you in the **dark** you must repeat in broad daylight,
	16. 3	'It is going to rain, because the sky is red and **dark.'**
	22.13	him up hand and foot, and throw him outside in the **dark.**
	24.29	the sun will grow **dark,** the moon will no longer shine,
	25.30	As for this useless servant—throw him outside in the **darkness;**
	27.45	country was covered with **darkness,** which lasted for three hours.
Mk	13.24	the sun will grow **dark,** the moon will no longer shine,
	15.33	country was covered with **darkness,** which lasted for three hours.
Lk	1.79	those who live in the **dark** shadow of death, to guide our
	11.34	your eyes are no good, your whole body will be in **darkness.**
	11.35	Make certain, then, that the light in you is not **darkness.**
	11.36	no part of it in **darkness,** it will be bright all over,
	12. 3	you have said in the **dark** will be heard in broad daylight,
	22.53	is your hour to act, when the power of **darkness** rules."
	23.44	the sun stopped shining and **darkness** covered the whole country
	24.29	the day is almost over and it is getting **dark."**
Jn	1. 5	The light shines in the **darkness,**
	1. 5	and the **darkness** has never put it out.
	3.19	but people love the **darkness** rather than the light,
	8.12	have the light of life and will never walk in **darkness."**
	12.35	have the light, so that the **darkness** will not come upon you;
Jn	12.35	one who walks in the **dark** does not know where he is
	12.46	everyone who believes in me should not remain in the **darkness.**
	20. 1	while it was still **dark,** Mary Magdalene went to the tomb
Acts	2.20	the sun will be **darkened,** and the moon will turn red
	13.11	At once Elymas felt a **dark** mist cover his eyes,
	26.18	and turn them from the **darkness** to the light and from the
Rom	1.21	and their empty minds are filled with **darkness.**
	2.19	for those who are in **darkness,** [20] an instructor for the foolish,
	13.12	things that belong to the **dark,** and let us take up weapons
1 Cor	4. 5	bring to light the **dark secrets** and expose the hidden purposes
2 Cor	4. 4	have been kept in the **dark** by the evil god of this
	4. 6	The God who said, "Out of **darkness** the light shall shine!"
	6.14	How can light and **darkness** live together?
Eph	4.18	whose thoughts are worthless [18] and whose minds are in the **dark.**
	5. 8	used to be in the **darkness,** but since you have become
	5.11	things that people do, things that belong to the **darkness.**
	6.12	the rulers, authorities, and cosmic powers of this **dark** age.
Col	1.13	us from the power of **darkness** and brought us safe into the
1 Thes	5. 4	brothers, are not in the **darkness,** and the Day should not
	5. 5	We do not belong to the night or to the **darkness.**
Heb	12.18	with its blazing fire, the **darkness** and the gloom, the storm,
Jas	1.17	who does not change or cause **darkness** by turning.
1 Pet	2. 9	God, who called you out of **darkness** into his own marvellous light.
2 Pet	1.19	a lamp shining in a **dark** place until the Day dawns
	2. 4	kept chained in **darkness,** waiting for the Day of Judgement.
	2.17	God has reserved a place for them in the deepest **darkness.**
1 Jn	1. 5	God is light, and there is no **darkness** at all in him.
	1. 6	same time live in the **darkness,** we are lying both in our
	2. 8	For the **darkness** is passing away, and the real light is
	2. 9	yet hates his brother, is in the **darkness** to this very hour.
	2.11	But whoever hates his brother is in the **darkness;**
	2.11	where he is going, because the **darkness** has made him blind.
Jude	6	eternal chains in the **darkness** below, where God is keeping them
	13	God has reserved a place for ever in the deepest **darkness.**
Rev	9. 2	and the air were **darkened** by the smoke from the abyss.
	16.10	**Darkness** fell over the beast's kingdom, and people bit

DARLING

Song	2. 2	Like a lily among thorns is my **darling** among women.
	2.10	my **darling,** come with me.
	2.13	my **darling,** come with me.
	2.17	Return, my **darling,** like a gazelle, like a stag on the
	4.11	The taste of honey is on your lips, my **darling;**
	5. 2	Let me come in, my **darling,** my sweetheart, my dove.
	7.11	Come, **darling,** let's go out to the countryside and spend
	7.13	**Darling,** I have kept for you the old delights and the new.

DART

Ezek	1.14	The creatures themselves **darted** to and fro
Nah	2. 4	They flash like torches and **dart** about like lightning.

DASH (1)

Nah	2. 4	Chariots **dash** wildly through the streets, rushing to and

DASH (2)

Job	40.23	he is calm when the Jordan **dashes** in his face.
Hos	13.16	babies will be **dashed** to the ground, and pregnant women will

DATE (1)

Song	7. 7	and your breasts are clusters of **dates.**

DATE (2)

Acts	28.23	So they fixed a **date** with Paul, and a large number of

DATHAN

Abiram's fellow-conspirator in rebelling against Moses.

Num	16. 1	of the tribe of Reuben—**Dathan** and Abiram, the sons of Eliab,
	16.12	Then Moses sent for **Dathan** and Abiram, but they said,
	16.24	people to move away from the tents of Korah, **Dathan,** and
	16.25	by the leaders of Israel, went to **Dathan** and Abiram.
	16.27	So they moved away from the tents of Korah, **Dathan,**
	16.27	**Dathan** and Abiram had come out and were standing at the
	16.31	finished speaking, the ground under **Dathan** and Abiram split
	26. 9	of Pallu were Eliab [9] and his sons Nemuel, **Dathan,**
	26. 9	(These are the **Dathan** and Abiram who were chosen by the community.
Deut	11. 6	recall what he did to **Dathan** and Abiram, the sons of Eliab
Ps	106.17	swallowed **Dathan** and buried Abiram and his family;

DAUGHTER

Gen	19. 8	Look, I have two **daughters** who are still virgins.
	19.12	have anyone else here—sons, **daughters,** sons-in-law,
	19.14	to the men that his **daughters** were going to marry, and said,
	19.15	your wife and your two **daughters** and get out,
	19.16	his wife, and his two **daughters** by the hand and led them
	19.30	Zoar, he and his two **daughters** moved up into the hills
	19.31	The elder **daughter** said to her sister, "Our father is getting old,
	19.33	to drink, and the elder **daughter** had intercourse with him.
	19.34	The next day the elder **daughter** said to her sister,
	19.35	drunk, and the younger **daughter** had intercourse with him.
	19.36	both of Lot's **daughters** became pregnant by their own father.
	19.37	The elder **daughter** had a son, whom she named Moab.
	19.38	The younger **daughter** also had a son, whom she named Benammi.

Gen 20.12 She is the **daughter** of my father, but not of my mother,
24.48 relative, where I found his **daughter** for my master's son.
28. 2 one of the girls there, one of your uncle Laban's **daughters.**
28. 9 of Abraham and married his **daughter** Mahalath,
29. 6 "Look, here comes his **daughter** Rachel with his flock."
29.16 Laban had two **daughters;**
29.21 let me marry your **daughter."**
29.24 (Laban gave his slave-girl Zilpah to his **daughter** Leah as her maid.)
29.26 to give the younger **daughter** in marriage before the elder.
29.28 was over, Laban gave him his **daughter** Rachel as his wife.
29.29 (Laban gave his slave-girl Bilhah to his **daughter** Rachel as her maid.)
30.21 Later she bore a **daughter,** whom she named Dinah.
31.26 me and carry off my **daughters** like women captured in war?
31.28 even let me kiss my grandchildren and my **daughters** good-bye.
31.31 I thought that you might take your **daughters** away from me.
31.41 to win your two **daughters**—and six years for your flocks.
31.43 Laban answered Jacob, "These girls are my **daughters;**
31.43 do nothing to keep my **daughters** and their children,
31.50 "If you ill-treat my **daughters** or if you marry other women,
31.55 kissed his grandchildren and his **daughters** good-bye, and
34. 1 One day Dinah, the **daughter** of Jacob and Leah, went to
34. 5 Jacob learnt that his **daughter** had been disgraced, but
34. 7 insulted the people of Israel by raping Jacob's **daughter.**
34. 8 him, "My son Shechem has fallen in love with your **daughter;**
34.19 was suggested, because he was in love with Jacob's **daughter.**
34.21 Let us marry their **daughters** and give them ours in marriage.
36. 6 his wives, his sons, his **daughters,** and all the people of
36.25 Anah also had a **daughter** named Oholibamah.
37.35 All his sons and **daughters** came to comfort him, but he
46. 7 his sons, his grandsons, his **daughters,** and his granddaughters.
46.15 Leah had borne to Jacob in Mesopotamia, besides his **daughter** Dinah.
46.18 Jacob by Zilpah, the slave-girl whom Laban gave to his **daughter** Leah.
46.25 Jacob by Bilhah, the slave-girl whom Laban gave to his **daughter** Rachel.

Ex 2. 5 The king's **daughter** came down to the river to bathe, while
2.10 took him to the king's **daughter,** who adopted him as her own
2.15 by a well, seven **daughters** of Jethro, the priest of Midian,
2.17 But some shepherds drove Jethro's **daughters** away.
2.20 he asked his **daughters.**
2.21 and Jethro gave him his **daughter** Zipporah in marriage,
3.22 things on their sons and **daughters** and carry away the wealth
6.23 Aaron married Elisheba, the **daughter** of Amminadab and sister of Nahshon;
6.25 Eleazar, Aaron's son, married one of Putiel's **daughters,**
10. 9 will take our sons and **daughters,** our sheep and goats, and
21. 4 she bore him sons or **daughters,** the woman and her children
21. 7 "If a man sells his **daughter** as a slave, she is not
21. 9 give to his son, he is to treat her like a **daughter.**
32. 2 wives, your sons, and your **daughters** are wearing, and bring

Lev 12. 5 woman gives birth to a **daughter,** she is ritually unclean, as
12. 6 whether for a son or **daughter,** she shall bring to the priest
18.17 not have intercourse with the **daughter** or granddaughter of a
19.29 "Do not disgrace your **daughters** by making them temple prostitutes;
21. 2 is his mother, father, son, **daughter,** brother,
21. 9 If a priest's **daughter** becomes a prostitute, she disgraces her father;
22.12 A priest's **daughter** who marries someone who is not a
22.13 But a widowed or divorced **daughter** who has no children

Num 18.11 to you, your sons, and your **daughters** for all time to come.
18.19 your sons, and to your **daughters,** for all time to come,
26.33 Zelophehad son of Hepher had no sons, but only **daughters;**
26.46 Asher had a **daughter** named Serah.
26.59 who was married to Levi's **daughter** Jochebed, who was born in Egypt.
26.59 She bore Amram two sons, Aaron and Moses, and a **daughter,**
27. 1 and Tirzah were the **daughters** of Zelophehad son of Hepher,
27. 7 "What the **daughters** of Zelophehad request is right;
27. 8 leaving a son, his **daughter** is to inherit his property.
27. 9 If he has no **daughter,** his brothers are to inherit it.
36. 2 the property of our relative Zelophehad to his **daughters.**
36. 4 owners, the property of Zelophehad's **daughters** will be
36. 6 the Lord says that the **daughters** of Zelophehad are free
36.10 Hoglah, Milcah, and Noah, the **daughters** of Zelophehad,

Deut 13. 6 or your son or your **daughter** or the wife you love
22.16 to them, 'I gave my **daughter** to this man in marriage,
22.17 But here is the proof that my **daughter** was a virgin;
28.32 Your sons and **daughters** will be given as slaves
28.41 You will have sons and **daughters,** but you will lose them,
32.19 Lord saw this, he was angry and rejected his sons and **daughters.**

Josh 7.24 together with Achan's sons and **daughters,** his cattle,
15.16 said, "I will give my **daughter** Achsah in marriage to the
15.17 the city, so Caleb gave him his **daughter** Achsah in marriage.
17. 3 son of Manasseh, did not have any sons, but only **daughters.**

Judg 1.12 said, "I will give my **daughter** Achsah in marriage to the
1.13 the city, so Caleb gave him his **daughter** Achsah in marriage.
11.34 to Mizpah, there was his **daughter** coming out to meet him,
11.35 he tore his clothes in sorrow and said, "Oh, my **daughter!**
11.40 year to grieve for the **daughter** of Jephthah of Gilead.
12. 9 He had thirty sons and thirty **daughters.**
12. 9 He gave his **daughters** in marriage outside the clan
19.24 Here is his concubine and my own **daughter,** who is a virgin.
21. 1 us will allow a Benjaminite to marry a **daughter** of ours."
21. 7 the Lord that we will not give them any of our **daughters."**
21.18 allow them to marry our **daughters,** because we have put a
21.18 who allows a Benjaminite to marry one of our **daughters."**

Ruth 1.11 "You must go back, my **daughters,"** Naomi answered.
1.13 No, my **daughters,** you know that's impossible.
2. 2 Naomi answered, "Go ahead, my **daughter."**
2.22 said to Ruth, "Yes, my **daughter,** it will be better for you
3.16 asked her, "How did you get on, my **daughter?"**

1 Sam 2.21 bless Hannah, and she had three more sons and two **daughters.**
8.13 Your **daughters** will have to make perfumes for him
14.49 His elder **daughter** was named Merab, and the younger one Michal.
14.50 His wife was Ahinoam, the **daughter** of Ahimaaz;
17.25 will also give him his **daughter** to marry
18.17 Then Saul said to David, "Here is my elder **daughter** Merab.
18.20 Saul's **daughter** Michal, however, fell in love with David,
18.22 now is a good time for you to marry his **daughter."**
18.27 So Saul had to give his **daughter** Michal in marriage to David.
18.28 Lord was with David and also that his **daughter** Michal loved him.
25.44 Saul had given his **daughter** Michal, who had been David's wife,
30. 3 that their wives, sons, and **daughters** had been carried away.
30.19 all his men's sons and **daughters,** and all the loot

2 Sam 1.20 do not let the **daughters** of pagans rejoice.
3. 3 mother was Maacah, the **daughter** of King Talmai of Geshur;
3.13 you must bring Saul's **daughter** Michal to me when you come to
5.13 David took more concubines and wives, and had more sons and **daughters.**
6.16 Michal, Saul's **daughter,** looked out
6.23 Michal, Saul's **daughter,** never had any children.
11. 3 that she was Bathsheba, the **daughter** of Eliam and the wife
12. 3 The lamb was like a **daughter** to him.
14.27 sons and one **daughter** named Tamar, a very beautiful woman.
17.25 his mother was Abigail, the **daughter** of Nahash
19. 5 of your sons and **daughters** and of your wives and concubines.
21. 8 two sons that Rizpah the **daughter** of Aiah had borne to Saul;
21. 8 the five sons of Saul's **daughter** Merab, whom she had borne
21.10 Then Saul's concubine Rizpah, the **daughter** of Aiah,

1 Kgs 3. 1 an alliance with the king of Egypt by marrying his **daughter.**
4.11 Benabinadab, who was married to Solomon's **daughter** Taphath:
4.15 Ahimaaz, who was married to Basemath, another of Solomon's **daughters:**
7. 8 of house for his wife, the **daughter** of the king of Egypt.
9.16 a wedding present to his **daughter** when she married Solomon,
9.24 city, after his wife, the **daughter** of the king of Egypt,
11. 1 Besides the **daughter** of the king of Egypt he married Hittite
15. 2 His mother was Maacah, the **daughter** of Absalom.
15.10 His grandmother was Maacah, the **daughter** of Absalom.
16.31 and married Jezebel, the **daughter** of King Ethbaal of Sidon,
22.42 His mother was Azubah, the **daughter** of Shilhi.

2 Kgs 8.18 His wife was Ahab's **daughter,**
8.26 His mother was Athaliah, the **daughter** of King Ahab
9.34 after all, she is a king's **daughter."**
11. 2 who was King Jehoram's **daughter** and Ahaziah's half-sister.
14. 9 'Give your **daughter** in marriage to my son.'
17.17 They sacrificed their sons and **daughters** as burnt-offerings
23.10 his son or **daughter** as a burnt-offering to the god

1 Chr 2.16 He also had two **daughters,** Zeruiah and Abigail.
2.16 Jesse's **daughter** Zeruiah had three sons:
2.17 His other **daughter** Abigail married Jether, a descendant of Ishmael,
2.18 Hezron's son Caleb married Azubah and had a **daughter** named Jerioth.
2.21 old, he married Machir's **daughter,** the sister of Gilead.
2.34 Sheshan had no sons, only **daughters.**
2.35 Jarha, [35] to whom he gave one of his **daughters** in marriage.
2.49 In addition, Caleb had a **daughter** named Achsah.
3. 1 was Maacah, **daughter** of King Talmai of Geshur
3. 5 His wife Bathsheba, **daughter** of Ammiel, bore him four sons:
3. 9 He also had a **daughter,** Tamar.
3.19 of two sons, Meshullam and Hananiah, and one **daughter,**
4. 3 Jezreel, Ishma, and Idbash, and one **daughter,** Hazzelelponi.
4.17 Mered married Bithiah, a **daughter** of the king of Egypt,
4.17 and they had a **daughter,** Miriam, and two sons,
4.27 and six **daughters,** but his relatives had fewer children,
6. 3 Amram had two sons, Aaron and Moses, and one **daughter,**
7.15 Machir's second son was Zelophehad, and he had only **daughters.**
7.24 Ephraim had a **daughter** named Sheerah.
7.30 and one **daughter,** Serah.
7.32 and one **daughter,** Shua.
14. 3 David married more wives and had more sons and **daughters.**
15.29 into the city, Michal, Saul's **daughter,** looked out of the
23.22 but Eleazar died without having any sons, only **daughters.**
23.22 His **daughters** married their cousins, the sons of Kish.
25. 5 fourteen sons and also three **daughters,** as he had promised,

2 Chr 8.11 Solomon moved his wife, the **daughter** of the king of Egypt,
11.18 Abihail, the **daughter** of Eliab and granddaughter of Jesse.
11.20 Later he married Maacah, the **daughter** of Absalom, and
11.21 and he fathered twenty-eight sons and sixty **daughters.**
13.21 fathered twenty-two sons and sixteen **daughters.**
20.31 His mother was Azubah, the **daughter** of Shilhi.
21. 6 of Israel, because he had married one of Ahab's **daughters.**
22. 2 since his mother Athaliah—the **daughter** of King Ahab and
24. 3 wives for King Joash, and they bore him sons and **daughters.**
25.18 'Give your **daughter** in marriage to my son.'
27. 1 His mother was Jerushah, the **daughter** of Zadok.
29. 1 His mother was Abijah, the **daughter** of Zechariah.

Neh 3.12 (His **daughters** helped with the work.)
5. 5 Some of our **daughters** have already been sold as slaves.
6.18 Jehohanan had married the **daughter** of Meshullam son of Berechiah.
13.28 of Joiada's sons married the **daughter** of Sanballat, from the

Esth 2. 7 Mordecai had adopted her and brought her up as his own **daughter.**
2.15 Esther—the **daughter** of Abihail and the cousin of Mordecai,

Esth	2.15	who had adopted her as his **daughter;**
	9.29	Then Queen Esther, the **daughter** of Abihail, along with Mordecai,
Job	1. 2	had seven sons and three **daughters,** ³and owned seven thousand sheep,
	42.13	He was the father of seven sons and three **daughters.**
	42.14	He called the eldest **daughter** Jemimah, the second Keziah,
	42.15	women in the whole world as beautiful as Job's **daughters.**
Ps	45. 9	ladies of your court are **daughters** of kings, and on the
	106.37	offered their own sons and **daughters** as sacrifices to the
	144.12	May our **daughters** be like stately pillars which adorn the
Prov	30.15	A leech has two **daughters,** and both are named "Give me!"
Song	6. 9	She is her mother's only **daughter,** her mother's favourite child.
Is	23. 4	I never brought up sons or **daughters."**
	56. 5	among my people longer than if you had sons and **daughters.**
	60. 4	Your **daughters** will be carried like children.
Jer	3.24	flocks and herds, sons and **daughters**—everything that our
	5.17	they will kill your sons and your **daughters.**
	7.31	they can sacrifice their sons and **daughters** in the fire.
	9.20	Teach your **daughters** how to mourn, and your friends how to
	14.16	them—including their wives, their sons, and their **daughters.**
	32.35	to sacrifice their sons and **daughters** to the god Molech.
	35. 8	wine, and neither do our wives, our sons, or our **daughters.**
	41.10	made prisoners of the king's **daughters** and all the rest of
	43. 6	the men, the women, the children, and the king's **daughters.**
	48.46	their sons and **daughters** have been taken away as prisoners.
	52. 1	mother's name was Hamutal, the **daughter** of the Jeremiah who
Lam	5.11	in every Judaean village our **daughters** have been forced to submit.
Ezek	16.20	took the sons and the **daughters** you had borne me and offered
	16.44	'Like mother, like **daughter.'**
	16.45	You really are your mother's **daughter.**
	16.49	She and her **daughters** were proud because they had plenty
	16.61	will let them be like **daughters** to you, even though this was
	23.10	naked, seized her sons and **daughters,** and then killed her
	23.25	take your sons and **daughters** from you and burn them alive.
	24.25	And I will take away their sons and **daughters.**
Dan	11. 6	the king of Syria and give him his **daughter** in marriage.
	11.17	an alliance with him and offer him his **daughter** in marriage;
Hos	1. 3	So Hosea married a woman named Gomer, the **daughter** of Diblaim.
	1. 8	After Gomer had weaned her **daughter,** she became pregnant
	4.13	"As a result, your **daughters** serve as prostitutes,
Joel	2.28	your sons and **daughters** will proclaim my message;
	3. 8	will let your sons and **daughters** be sold to the people of
Mic	7. 6	their fathers like fools, **daughters** oppose their mothers,
Mt	9.18	knelt down before him, and said, "My **daughter** has just died;
	9.22	Jesus turned round and saw her, and said, "Courage, my **daughter!**
	10.35	sons against their fathers, **daughters** against their mothers,
	10.37	whoever loves his son or **daughter** more than me is not fit
	14. 6	On Herod's birthday the **daughter** of Herodias danced in front of
	15.22	My **daughter** has a demon and is in a terrible condition."
	15.28	And at that very moment her **daughter** was healed.
Mk	5.23	and begged him earnestly, "My little **daughter** is very ill.
	5.34	Jesus said to her, "My **daughter,** your faith has made you well.
	5.35	came from Jairus' house and told him, "Your **daughter** has died.
	6.22	The **daughter** of Herodias came in and danced, and pleased Herod
	7.25	A woman, whose **daughter** had an evil spirit in her, heard
	7.26	She begged Jesus to drive the demon out of her **daughter.**
	7.29	will find that the demon has gone out of your **daughter!"**
Lk	2.36	prophetess, a widow named Anna, **daughter** of Phanuel
	8.42	because his only **daughter,** who was twelve years old, was
	8.48	Jesus said to her, "My **daughter,** your faith has made you well.
	8.49	"Your **daughter** has died," he told Jairus;
	12.53	mothers will be against their **daughters,**
	12.53	and **daughters** against their mothers;
Acts	2.17	Your sons and **daughters** will proclaim my message;
	7.21	the king's **daughter** adopted him and brought him up
	21. 9	He had four unmarried **daughters** who proclaimed God's message.
2 Cor	6.18	shall be my sons and **daughters,** says the Lord Almighty."
Heb	11.24	up, refuse to be called the son of the king's **daughter.**
1 Pet	3. 6	You are now her **daughters** if you do good and are not
	also	Gen 11.29 Gen 24.15 Gen 25.20 Gen 26.34 Gen 36.2 Gen 36.3 Gen 36.14 Gen 36.18 Gen 36.31 Gen 41.45 Gen 46.20 Lev 24.10 2 Sam 3.7 2 Kgs 15.33 2 Kgs 18.2 2 Kgs 21.19 2 Kgs 22.1 2 Kgs 23.31 2 Kgs 23.36 2 Kgs 24.8 2 Kgs 24.18 1 Chr 1.43 2 Chr 13.2

DAUGHTER-IN-LAW

Gen	11.31	son of Haran, and his **daughter-in-law** Sarai, Abram's wife,
	38.11	Then Judah said to his **daughter-in-law** Tamar, "Return
	38.16	(He did not know that she was his **daughter-in-law.)**
	38.24	someone said to Judah, "Your **daughter-in-law** Tamar has been
Lev	18.15	Do not have intercourse with your **daughter-in-law**
	20.12	man has intercourse with his **daughter-in-law,** they shall
Ruth	1. 6	so she got ready to leave Moab with her **daughters-in-law.**
	1.22	Naomi came back from Moab with Ruth, her Moabite **daughter-in-law.**
	4.15	Your **daughter-in-law** loves you, and has done more for
1 Sam	4.19	Eli's **daughter-in-law,** the wife of Phinehas, was
1 Chr	2. 4	By his **daughter-in-law** Tamar, Judah had two more sons,
Ezek	22.11	Some commit adultery, and others seduce their **daughters-in-law**
Hos	4.13	and your **daughters-in-law** commit adultery.
Mt	10.35	**daughters-in-law** against their mothers-in-law;
Lk	12.53	mothers-in-law will be against their **daughters-in-law,**
	12.53	and **daughters-in-law** against their mothers-in-law."

DAVID

[DESCENDANT OF DAVID]

Son of Jesse chosen to succeed Saul as king of Israel.

see also **SON OF DAVID**

Ruth	4.13-22	**Boaz and his descendants**
1 Sam	16.1-13	**David is anointed king**
	14-23	**David in Saul's court**
	17.12-40	**David in Saul's camp**
	41-54	**David defeats Goliath**
	17.55–18.5	**David is presented to Saul**
	18.6-16	**Saul becomes jealous of David**
	17-30	**David marries Saul's daughter**
	19.1-24	**David is persecuted by Saul**
	20.1-42	**Jonathan helps David**
	21.1-15	**David flees from Saul**
	22.1-23	**The slaughter of the priests**
	23.1-13	**David saves the town of Keilah**
	14-29	**David in the hill-country**
	24.1-22	**David spares Saul's life**
	25.1b-44	**David and Abigail**
	26.1-25	**David spares Saul's life again**
	27.1–28.2	**David among the Philistines**
	28.3-25	**Saul consults a medium**
	29.1-11	**David is rejected by the Philistines**
	30.1-31	**The war against the Amalekites**
2 Sam	1.1-16	**David learns of Saul's death**
	17-27	**David's lament for Saul and Jonathan**
	2.1-7	**David is made king of Judah**
	8-11	**Ishbosheth is made king of Israel**
	2.12–3.1	**War between Israel and Judah**
	3.2-5	**David's sons**
	6-21	**Abner joins David**
	22-30	**Abner is murdered**
	31-39	**Abner is buried**
	4.1-12	**Ishbosheth is murdered**
	5.1-16	**David becomes king of Israel and Judah**
	17-25	**Victory over the Philistines**
	6.1-23	**The Covenant Box is brought to Jerusalem**
	7.1-17	**Nathan's message to David**
	18-29	**David's prayer of thanksgiving**
	8.1-18	**David's military victories**
	9.1-13	**David and Mephibosheth**
	10.1-19	**David defeats the Ammonites and the Syrians**
	11.1-27	**David and Bathsheba**
	12.1-15a	**Nathan's message and David's repentance**
	15b-23	**David's son dies**
	24-25	**Solomon is born**
	26-31	**David captures Rabbah**
	13.1-22	**Amnon and Tamar**
	23-39	**Absalom's revenge**
	14.1-24	**Joab arranges for Absalom's return**
	25-33	**Absalom is reconciled to David**
	15.1-12	**Absalom plans rebellion**
	13-37	**David flees from Jerusalem**
	16.1-4	**David and Ziba**
	5-14	**David and Shimei**
	15-23	**Absalom in Jerusalem**
	17.1-14	**Hushai misleads Absalom**
	15-29	**David is warned and escapes**
	18.1-18	**Absalom is defeated and killed**
	19-33	**David is told of Absalom's death**
	19.1-8a	**Joab reprimands David**
	8b-18a	**David starts back to Jerusalem**
	18b-23	**David shows kindness to Shimei**
	24-30	**David shows kindness to Mephibosheth**
	31-39	**David shows kindness to Barzillai**
	40-43	**Judah and Israel argue over the king**
	20.1-22	**Sheba's rebellion**
	23-26	**David's officials**
	21.1-14	**Saul's descendants are put to death**
	15-22	**Battles against Philistine giants**
	22.1-51	**David's song of victory**
	23.1-7	**David's last words**
	8-39	**David's famous soldiers**
	24.1-25	**David takes a census**
1 Kgs	1.1-4	**King David in his old age**
	5-10	**Adonijah claims the throne**
	11-53	**Solomon is made king**
	2.1-9	**David's last instructions to Solomon**
	10-12	**The death of David**
1 Chr	2.9-17	**The family tree of King David**
	3.1-9	**King David's children**
	4.24-43	**The descendants of Simeon**
	6.31-48	**The Temple musicians**
	9.17-27	**The Temple guards who lived in Jerusalem**
	10.1-14	**The death of King Saul**
	11.1-9	**David becomes king of Israel and Judah**
	10-47	**David's famous soldiers**
	12.1-7	**David's early followers from the tribe of Benjamin**
	8-15	**David's followers from the tribe of Gad**
	16-18	**Followers from Benjamin and Judah**
	19-22	**Followers from Manasseh**
	23-40	**List of David's forces**
	13.1-14	**The Covenant Box is moved from Kiriath Jearim**
	14.1-7	**David's activities in Jerusalem**
	8-17	**Victory over the Philistines**
	15.1-24	**Getting ready to move the Covenant Box**
	15.25–16.7	**Moving the Covenant Box to Jerusalem**
	16.37-43	**Worship at Jerusalem and Gibeon**
	17.1-15	**Nathan's message to David**

1 Chr 16-27 **David's prayer of thanksgiving**
18.1-17 **David's military victories**
19.1-19 **David defeats the Ammonites and the Syrians**
20.1-3 **David captures Rabbah**
4-8 **Battles against Philistine giants**
21.1–22.1 **David takes a census**
22.2–23.1 **Preparations for building the Temple**
23.2-32 **The work of the Levites**
24.1-19 **The work assigned to the priests**
20-31 **The list of the Levites**
25.1-31 **The Temple musicians**
26.20-28 **Other Temple duties**
29-32 **Duties of other Levites**
27.16-24 **Administration of the tribes of Israel**
32-34 **David's personal advisers**
28.1-21 **David's instructions for the Temple**
29.1-9 **Gifts for building the Temple**
10-25 **David praises God**
26-30 **Summary of David's reign**

2 Sam 5. 7 fortress of Zion, and it became known as **"David's City."**)
5. 9 fortress, David lived in it and named it **"David's City."**

1 Kgs 2.10 David died and was buried in **David's City.**
2.24 Lord has firmly established me on the throne of my father **David;**
2.26 you were with my father **David,** and you shared in all his
2.31 I nor any other of **David's** descendants will any longer be
2.32 which he committed without my father **David's** knowledge.
2.33 success to **David's** descendants who sit on his throne."
2.44 very well all the wrong that you did to my father **David.**
2.45 me and he will make **David's** kingdom secure for ever."
3. 1 brought her to live in **David's City** until he had finished
3. 3 the instructions of his father **David,** but he also
3. 6 love for my father **David,** your servant, and he was good,
3.14 and commands, as your father **David** did, I will give you a
5. 1 always been a friend of **David's,** and when he heard that
5. 1 Solomon had succeeded his father **David** as king he sent
5. 3 the constant wars my father **David** had to fight against the
5. 5 The Lord promised my father **David,** 'Your son, whom I will
5. 7 the Lord today for giving **David** such a wise son to succeed
6.12 I will do for you what I promised your father **David.**
7.51 the things that his father **David** had dedicated to the
8. 1 take the Lord's Covenant Box from Zion, **David's City,** to the
8.15 he made to my father **David,** when he said, [16] 'From the time
8.16 But I chose you, **David,** to rule my people.' "
8.17 And Solomon continued, "My father **David** planned to
8.24 You have kept the promise you made to my father **David;**
8.26 everything come true that you promised to my father **David,**
8.66 the Lord had given his servant **David** and his people Israel.
9. 4 and integrity, as your father **David** did, and if you obey my
9. 5 I made to your father **David** when I told him that Israel
9.24 of Egypt, had moved from **David's City** to the palace Solomon
11. 4 faithful to the Lord his God, as his father **David** had been.
11. 6 and was not true to him as his father **David** had been.
11.12 the sake of your father **David** I will not do this in
11.13 the sake of my servant **David** and for the sake of Jerusalem,
11.15 Long before this, when **David** had conquered Edom,
11.21 reached Hadad in Egypt that **David** had died and that Joab the
11.24 (This happened after **David** had defeated Hadadezer and had
11.32 the sake of my servant **David** and for the sake of Jerusalem,
11.33 has not kept my laws and commands as his father **David** did.
11.34 the sake of my servant **David,** whom I chose and who obeyed
11.36 a descendant of my servant **David** ruling in Jerusalem, the
11.38 I command, as my servant **David** did, I will always be with
11.38 descendants rule after you, just as I have done for **David.**
11.39 I will punish the descendants of **David,** but not for all time.' "
11.43 died and was buried in **David's City,** and his son Rehoboam
12.16 to them, they shouted, "Down with **David** and his family!
12.19 Israel have been in rebellion against the dynasty of **David.**
12.20 Only the tribe of Judah remained loyal to **David's** descendants.
13. 2 name will be Josiah, will be born to the family of **David.**
14. 8 kingdom away from **David's** descendants and gave it to you.
14. 8 been like my servant **David,** who was completely loyal to me,
14.31 in the royal tombs in **David's City,** and his son Abijah
15. 3 the Lord his God, as his great-grandfather **David** had been.
15. 4 But for **David's** sake, the Lord his God gave Abijah a son
15. 5 The Lord did this because **David** had done what pleased him
15. 8 died and was buried in **David's City,** and his son Asa
15.11 Asa did what pleased the Lord, as his ancestor **David** had done.
15.24 in the royal tombs in **David's City,** and his son Jehoshaphat
22.50 in the royal tombs in **David's City,** and his son Jehoram

2 Kgs 8.19 he had promised his servant **David** that his descendants would
8.24 in the royal tombs in **David's City,** and his son Ahaziah
9.28 chariot and buried him in the royal tombs in **David's City.**
11.10 that had belonged to King **David** and had been kept in the
12.20 in the royal tombs in **David's City,** and his son Amaziah
14. 3 to the Lord, but he was not like his ancestor King **David;**
14.20 a horse and was buried in the royal tombs in **David's City.**
15. 7 the royal burial ground in **David's City,** and his son Jotham
15.38 in the royal tombs in **David's City,** and his son Ahaz
16. 2 He did not follow the good example of his ancestor King **David;**
16.20 in the royal tombs in **David's City,** and his son Hezekiah
18. 3 example of his ancestor King **David,** he did what was pleasing
19.34 and because of the promise I made to my servant **David.' "**
20. 5 the God of your ancestor **David,** have heard your prayer and
20. 6 and because of the promise I made to my servant **David."**
21. 7 about which the Lord had said to **David** and his son Solomon:
22. 2 example of his ancestor King **David,** strictly obeying all the

1 Chr 7. 2 At the time of King **David** their descendants numbered 22,600.
11. 5 fortress of Zion, and it became known as **"David's City."**
11. 7 live in the fortress, it came to be called **"David's City."**
15. 1 For his own use, David built houses in **David's City.**

2 Chr 1. 1 Solomon, the son of King **David,** took firm control
1. 4 in a tent which King **David** had set up when he brought
1. 8 great love for my father **David,** and now you have let me
2. 3 did with my father, King **David,** when you sold him cedar logs
2. 7 craftsmen of Judah and Jerusalem whom my father **David** selected.
2.12 He has given King **David** a wise son, full of understanding
2.14 craftsmen and with those who worked for your father, King **David.**
2.17 of Israel, similar to the census his father **David** had taken.
3. 1 King **David,** Solomon's father, had already prepared a place
3. 1 where the Lord appeared to **David,** the place which Araunah
5. 1 the things that his father **David** had dedicated to the Lord—
5. 2 take the Lord's Covenant Box from Zion, **David's City,** to the
6. 4 he made to my father **David** when he said to him,
6. 6 I will be worshipped, and you, **David,** to rule my people.' "
6. 7 Solomon continued, "My father **David** planned to build a temple
6.15 You have kept the promise you made to my father **David;**
6.17 let everything come true that you promised to your servant **David.**
6.42 Remember the love you had for your servant **David."**
7. 6 the musical instruments that King **David** had provided
7. 6 as they had been commissioned by **David.**
7.10 Lord had given to his people Israel, to **David,** and to Solomon.
7.17 me faithfully as your father **David** did, obeying my laws
7.18 I made to your father **David** when I told him that Israel
8.11 the king of Egypt, from **David's City** to a house he built
8.11 in the palace of King **David** of Israel, because any place
8.14 laid down by his father **David,** he organized the daily work
8.14 in accordance with the commands of **David,** the man of God.
8.15 The instructions which **David** had given the priests
9.31 died and was buried in **David's City,** and his son Rehoboam
10.16 they shouted, "Down with **David** and his family!
10.19 Israel have been in rebellion against the dynasty of **David.**
11.17 as they had under the rule of King **David** and King Solomon.
11.18 father was Jerimoth son of **David,** and whose mother was Abihail,
12.16 in the royal tombs in **David's City** and his son Abijah
13. 5 made an unbreakable covenant with **David,**
13. 8 royal authority that the Lord gave to **David's** descendants.
14. 1 Abijah died and was buried in the royal tombs in **David's City.**
16.14 tomb which he had carved out for himself in **David's City.**
21. 1 in the royal tombs in **David's City** and his son Jehoram
21. 7 to destroy the dynasty of **David,** because he had made a
21. 7 covenant with **David** and promised that his descendants
21.12 the God of your ancestor **David,** condemns you,
21.20 They buried him in **David's City,** but not in the royal tombs.
23. 3 as the Lord promised that King **David's** descendants would be.
23. 9 that had belonged to King **David** and had been kept in the
23.18 assigned to them by King **David** and to burn the sacrifices
24.16 in the royal tombs in **David's City** in recognition of the
24.25 He was buried in **David's City,** but not in the royal tombs.
25.28 and he was buried in the royal tombs in **David's City.**
27. 9 died and was buried in **David's City** and his son Ahaz
28. 1 He did not follow the good example of his ancestor King **David;**
29. 2 example of his ancestor King **David,** he did what was pleasing
29.25 Lord had given to King **David** through Gad, the king's prophet,
29.26 instruments like those that King **David** had used.
29.30 praise that were written by **David** and by Asaph the prophet.
30.26 happened since the days of King Solomon, the son of **David.**
33. 7 place about which God had said to **David** and his son Solomon:
33.14 on the east side of **David's City,** from a point in the
34. 2 example of his ancestor King **David,** strictly obeying all
34. 3 he began to worship the God of his ancestor King **David.**
35. 3 Box in the Temple that King Solomon, the son of **David,**
35. 4 assigned to you by King **David** and his son King Solomon,
35.15 in the places assigned to them by King **David's** instructions:

Ezra 3.10 the instructions handed down from the time of King **David.**
8. 2 Shecaniah, of the clan of **David**
8.20 had been designated by King **David** and his officials

Neh 3.15 garden, as far as the steps leading down from **David's City.**
3.16 as far as **David's** tomb, the pool, and the barracks.
12.24 accordance with the instructions given by King **David,**
12.36 of the kind played by King **David,** the man of God.
12.37 the steps that led to **David's City,**
12.37 past **David's** palace, and back to the wall
12.45 accordance with the regulations made by King **David**
12.46 From the time of King **David** and the musician Asaph

Ps 18.50 one he has chosen, to **David** and his descendants for ever.
72.20 This is the end of the prayers of **David** son of Jesse.
78.70 He chose his servant **David;**
78.72 **David** took care of them with unselfish devotion
89. 3 I have promised my servant **David,**
89.20 I have made my servant **David** king by anointing him
89.33 I will not stop loving **David** or fail to keep my promise
89.35 I will never lie to **David.**
89.49 Where are the promises you made to **David?**
132. 1 Lord, do not forget **David** and all the hardships he endured.
132.10 You made a promise to your servant **David;**
132.11 made a solemn promise to **David—**
132.17 Here I will make one of **David's** descendants a great king;
144.10 You give victory to kings and rescue your servant **David.**

Prov 1. 1 The proverbs of Solomon, son of **David** and king of Israel.

Ecc 1. 1 of the Philosopher, **David's** son, who was king in Jerusalem.

Song 4. 4 is like the tower of **David,** round and smooth, with a

Is 7.13 Isaiah replied, "Listen, now, descendants of King **David.**
9. 7 He will rule as King **David's** successor, basing his power on
11. 1 The royal line of **David** is like a tree that has been
11. 1 so a new king will arise from among **David's** descendants.
11.10 from the royal line of **David** will be a symbol to the
16. 5 Then one of **David's** descendants will be king, and he will
22.22 complete authority under the king, the **descendant of David.**
29. 1 The city where **David** camped is doomed!
37.35 and because of the promise I made to my servant **David.' "**

Is 38. 5 the God of your ancestor **David,** have heard your prayer
55. 3 with you and give you the blessings I promised to **David.**
Jer 13.13 the kings, who are **David's** descendants, the priests, the
17.25 of Jerusalem and have the same royal power that **David** had.
21.11 to the royal house of Judah, the descendants of **David:**
22. 1 of Judah, the **descendant of David,** and there tell the king,
22. 4 then **David's** descendants will continue to be kings.
22.30 descendants who will rule in Judah as **David's** successors.
23. 5 when I will choose as king a righteous **descendant of David.**
29.16 who rules the kingdom that **David** ruled
30. 9 their God, and a **descendant of David,** whom I will enthrone
33.15 time I will choose as king a righteous **descendant of David.**
33.17 will always be a **descendant of David** to be king of Israel
33.21 a covenant with my servant **David** that he would always have a
33.22 descendants of my servant **David** and the number of priests
33.26 covenant with Jacob's descendants and with my servant **David.**
33.26 I will choose one of **David's** descendants to rule over the
36.30 no descendant of yours will ever rule over **David's** kingdom.
Ezek 34.23 a king like my servant **David** to be their one shepherd,
34.24 and a king like my servant **David** will be their ruler.
37.24 A king like my servant **David** will be their king.
37.25 A king like my servant **David** will rule over them for ever.
Hos 3. 5 the Lord their God, and to a **descendant of David** their king.
Amos 6. 5 like to compose songs, as **David** did, and play them on harps.
9.11 will restore the kingdom of **David,** which is like a house
Zech 12. 7 honour which the descendants of **David** and the people of Jerusalem
12. 8 the weakest among them will become as strong as **David** was.
12. 8 The descendants of **David** will lead them like the angel
12.10 will fill the descendants of **David** and the other people
12.12 the family descended from **David,**
13. 1 to purify the descendants of **David** and the people of Jerusalem
Mt 1. 1 ancestors of Jesus Christ, a **descendant of David,**
1. 2 From Abraham to King **David,** the following ancestors are listed:
1. 2 Obed (his mother was Ruth), Jesse, and King **David.**
1. 6 From **David** to the time when the people of Israel
1. 6 **David,** Solomon (his mother was the woman who had been Uriah's wife),
1.17 fourteen generations from Abraham to **David,**
1.17 and fourteen from **David** to the exile in Babylon,
1.20 dream and said, "Joseph, **descendant of David,** do not be afraid
12. 3 "Have you never read what **David** did that time when he and
22.42 "He is **David's descendant,"** they answered.
22.43 Jesus asked, "did the Spirit inspire **David** to call him 'Lord'?
22.43 **David** said, [44]'The Lord said to my Lord:
22.45 If, then, **David** called him 'Lord,'
22.45 how can the Messiah be **David's descendant?"**
Mk 2.25 "Have you never read what **David** did that time when he
2.26 may eat this bread—but **David** ate it and even gave it
11.10 God bless the coming kingdom of King **David,** our father!
12.35 Law say that the Messiah will be the **descendant of David?**
12.36 The Holy Spirit inspired **David** to say:
12.37 **David** himself called him 'Lord';
12.37 so how can the Messiah be **David's descendant?"**
Lk 1.27 to a man named Joseph, who was a **descendant of King David.**
1.32 a king, as his ancestor **David** was, [33]and he will be the
1.69 a mighty Saviour, a **descendant of his servant David.**
2. 4 town of Bethlehem in Judaea, the birthplace of King **David.**
2. 4 Joseph went there because he was a **descendant of David.**
2.11 This very day in **David's** town your Saviour
3.31 the son of **David,** [32]the son of Jesse,
6. 3 "Haven't you read what **David** did when he and his men
20.41 it be said that the Messiah will be the **descendant of David?**
20.42 For **David** himself says in the book of Psalms, 'The Lord
20.44 **David** called him 'Lord';
20.44 how, then, can the Messiah be **David's descendant?"**
Jn 7.42 the Messiah will be a **descendant of King David** and will be
7.42 and will be born in Bethlehem, the town where **David** lived."
Acts 1.16 Spirit, speaking through **David,** made a prediction about Judas,
2.25 For **David** said about him, 'I saw the Lord before me at
2.29 I must speak to you plainly about our famous ancestor King **David.**
2.30 make one of David's descendants a king, just as **David** was.
2.31 **David** saw what God was going to do in the future,
2.34 For it was not **David** who went up into heaven;
4.25 you spoke through our ancestor **David,** your servant, when he said,
7.45 And it stayed there until the time of **David.**
13.22 After removing him, God made **David** their king.
13.22 'I have found that **David** son of Jesse is the kind of
13.23 It was Jesus, a **descendant of David,** whom God made the
13.34 you the sacred and sure blessings that I promised to **David.'**
13.36 For **David** served God's purposes in his own time, and
15.16 I will return, says the Lord, and restore the kingdom of **David.**
Rom 1. 3 as to his humanity, he was born a **descendant of David;**
4. 6 This is what **David** meant when he spoke of the happiness of
4. 9 Does this happiness that **David** spoke of belong only to those
11. 9 **David** says, "May they be caught and trapped at their feasts;
2 Tim 2. 8 from death, who was a **descendant of David,** as is taught in
Heb 4. 7 he spoke of it through **David** in the scripture already quoted:
11.32 Gideon, Barak, Samson, Jephthah, **David,** Samuel, and the prophets.
Rev 3. 7 the key that belonged to **David,** and when he opens a door,
5. 5 the great **descendant of David,** has won the victory,
22.16 I am descended from the family of **David;**

DAVID'S SON see **SON OF DAVID**

DAWN

Gen 19.15 At **dawn** the angels tried to make Lot hurry.
Ex 14.24 Just before **dawn** the Lord looked down from the pillar of
Judg 19.26 At **dawn** the woman came and fell down at the door of
1 Sam 3. 3 Before **dawn,** while the lamp was still burning,
9.26 At **dawn** Samuel called to Saul on the roof, "Get up, and
11.11 into three groups, and at **dawn** they rushed into the enemy
14.36 plunder them until **dawn,** and kill them all."
30.17 At **dawn** the next day David attacked them and fought until evening.
2 Sam 2.32 Then they marched all night and at **dawn** arrived back at Hebron.
23. 4 sun shining on a cloudless **dawn,** the sun that makes the
2 Kgs 19.35 At **dawn** the next day, there they lay, all dead!
Neh 4.21 So every day, from **dawn** until the stars came out at night,
8. 3 the Law to them from **dawn** until noon, and they all listened
Job 3. 9 give that night no hope of **dawn.**
7. 4 I toss all night and long for **dawn.**
11.17 at noon, and life's darkest hours will shine like the **dawn.**
24.14 At **dawn** the murderer gets up and goes out to kill the
38. 7 In the **dawn** of that day the stars sang together, and the
38.12 have you ever in all your life commanded a day to **dawn?**
38.13 Have you ordered the **dawn** to seize the earth and shake
Ps 46. 5 at early **dawn** he will come to its aid.
130. 6 wait for the dawn— than watchmen wait for the **dawn.**
Song 6.10 Who is this whose glance is like the **dawn?**
Is 37.36 At **dawn** the next day there they lay, all dead!
60. 3 to your light, And kings to the **dawning** of your new day.
Dan 6.19 At **dawn** the king got up and hurried to the pit.
Hos 6. 3 as surely as the day **dawns,** as surely as the spring rains
Jon 4. 7 But at **dawn** the next day, at God's command, a worm
Mt 28. 1 as Sunday morning was **dawning,** Mary Magdalene and the other Mary
Mk 13.35 in the evening or at midnight or before **dawn** or at sunrise.
Lk 1.78 He will cause the bright **dawn** of salvation to rise on us
24.22 they went at **dawn** to the tomb, [23]but could not find his
Acts 5.21 The apostles obeyed, and at **dawn** they entered the Temple
27.33 Just before **dawn,** Paul begged them all to eat some food:
2 Pet 1.19 dark place until the Day **dawns** and the light of the morning

DAY

[EVERY DAY, NIGHT AND DAY, SEVENTH DAY, THIS DAY]
see also **DAY OF JUDGEMENT, DAY OF THE LORD, DAYBREAK, DAYLIGHT**

Gen 1. 5 and he named the light **"Day"** and the darkness "Night".
1. 5 Evening passed and morning came—that was the first **day.**
1. 8 Evening passed and morning came—that was the second **day.**
1.13 Evening passed and morning came—that was the third **day.**
1.14 in the sky to separate **day** from night and to show the
1.14 the time when **days,** years, and religious festivals begin;
1.16 sun to rule over the **day** and the moon to rule over
1.18 earth, [18]to rule over the **day** and the night, and to
1.19 Evening passed and morning came—that was the fourth **day.**
1.23 Evening passed and morning came—that was the fifth **day.**
1.31 Evening passed and morning came—that was the sixth **day.**
2. 2 By the **seventh day** God finished what he had been doing and
2. 3 He blessed the **seventh day** and set it apart as a special
2. 3 as a special **day,**
2. 3 because by that **day** he had completed his creation
2.17 if you do, you will die the same **day."**
6. 4 In those **days,** and even later, there were giants on the
7. 4 Seven **days** from now I am going to send rain
7. 4 that will fall for forty **days** and nights,
7.10 Seven **days** later the flood came.
7.11 years old, on the seventeenth **day** of the second month all
7.12 and rain fell on the earth for forty **days** and nights.
7.13 On that same **day** Noah and his wife went into the boat
7.17 The flood continued for forty **days,**
7.24 did not start going down for a hundred and fifty **days.**
8. 3 and the water gradually went down for a hundred and fifty **days.**
8. 4 On the seventeenth **day** of the seventh month the boat came
8. 5 down, and on the first **day** of the tenth month the tops
8. 6 After forty **days** Noah opened a window [7]and sent out a raven.
8.10 He waited another seven **days** and sent out the dove again.
8.12 Then he waited another seven **days** and sent out the dove
8.13 years old, on the first **day** of the first month, the water
8.14 By the twenty-seventh **day** of the second month the earth
8.22 be cold and heat, summer and winter, **day** and night."
17.11 boy when he is eight **days** old, including slaves born in your
18. 1 the hottest part of the **day,** [2]he looked up and saw three
21. 4 and when Isaac was eight **days** old, Abraham circumcised him,
22. 4 On the third **day** Abraham saw the place in the distance.
24.55 with us a week or ten **days,** and then she may go."
29.20 seemed like only a few **days** to him, because he loved her.
30.36 with this flock as far as he could travel in three **days.**
31.22 Three **days** later Laban was told that Jacob had fled.
31.23 and pursued Jacob for seven **days** until he caught up with him
31.39 anything that was stolen during the **day** or during the night.
31.40 from the heat during the **day** and from the cold at night.
33.13 are driven hard for even one **day,** the whole herd will die.
34.25 Three **days** later, when the men were still sore
40.12 the three branches are three **days.**
40.13 In three **days** the king will release you, pardon you, and
40.18 the three baskets are three **days.**
40.19 In three **days** the king will release you—and have your
40.20 On his birthday three **days** later the king gave a banquet
42.17 Then he put them in prison for three **days.**
42.18 On the third **day** Joseph said to them, "I am a
48.15 May God, who has led me to this very **day,** bless them!
50. 3 It took forty **days,** the normal time for embalming.

Gen 50. 3 The Egyptians mourned for him seventy **days.**
50.10 and Joseph performed mourning ceremonies for seven **days.**
Ex 3.18 us to travel for three **days** into the desert to offer
5. 3 us to travel for three **days** into the desert to offer
5.13 the same number of bricks **every day** as they had made when
5.19 same number of bricks **every day** as they had made before.
7.25 Seven **days** passed after the Lord struck the river.
8.27 We must travel three **days** into the desert to offer
10.13 to blow on the land all that **day** and all that night.
10.22 there was total darkness throughout Egypt for three **days.**
12. 3 On the tenth **day** of this month each man must choose either
12. 6 the evening of the fourteenth **day** of the month, the whole
12.14 You must celebrate this **day** as a religious festival to
12.15 The Lord said, "For seven **days** you must not eat any
12.15 On the first **day** you are to get rid of all the
12.15 if anyone during those seven **days** eats bread made with yeast,
12.16 On the first **day**
12.16 and again on the **seventh day** you are to meet
12.16 is to be done on those **days,** but you may prepare food.
12.17 because it was on this **day** that I brought your tribes out
12.17 all time to come you must celebrate this **day** as a festival.
12.18 the evening of the fourteenth **day** of the first month to the
12.18 the evening of the twenty-first **day,** you must not eat any
12.19 For seven **days** no yeast must be found in your houses,
13. 3 "Remember this day—the **day** on which you left Egypt,
13. 3 This is the **day** the Lord brought you out by his great
13. 4 are leaving Egypt on this **day** in the first month, the month
13. 6 For seven **days** you must eat unleavened bread and on the
13. 6 unleavened bread and on the **seventh day** there is to be a
13. 7 For seven **days** you must not eat any bread made with yeast;
13.21 During the **day** the Lord went in front of them in a
13.21 to give them light, so that they could travel night and **day.**
13.22 of the people during the **day,** and the pillar of fire at
15.22 For three **days** they walked through the desert,
16. 1 Elim, and on the fifteenth **day** of the second month after
16. 4 The people must go out **every day**
16. 4 and gather enough for that **day.**
16. 5 On the sixth **day** they are to bring in twice as much
16.22 On the sixth **day** they gathered twice as much food, four
16.23 that tomorrow is a holy **day of rest,** dedicated to him.
16.25 is the Sabbath, a **day of rest** dedicated to the Lord, and
16.26 must gather food for six **days,** but on the seventh day, the
16.26 six days, but on the **seventh day,**
16.26 the **day of rest,** there will be none."
16.27 On the **seventh day** some of the people went out to gather
16.29 have given you a **day of rest,** and that is why on
16.29 sixth day I will always give you enough food for two **days.**
16.29 where he is on the **seventh day** and not leave his home."
16.30 So the people did no work on the **seventh day.**
19. 1 Rephidim, and on the first **day** of the third month after they
19.11 They must wash their clothes [11]and be ready the **day** after tomorrow.
19.15 them, "Be ready by the **day** after tomorrow and don't have
19.16 morning of the third **day** there was thunder and lightning,
20. 9 You have six **days** in which to do your work, [10]but the
20.10 do your work, [10]but the **seventh day** is a day of rest
20.10 but the seventh day is a **day of rest** dedicated to me.
20.11 In six **days** I, the Lord, made the earth, the sky, the
20.11 and everything in them, but on the **seventh day** I rested.
22. 2 But if it happens during the **day,** he is guilty of murder.
22.30 for seven days, and on the eighth **day** offer it to me.
23.12 "Work six **days** a week, but do no work on the seventh
23.12 do no work on the **seventh day,** so that your slaves and
23.15 made with yeast during the seven **days** of this festival.
24.16 covered the mountain for six **days,** and on the seventh day
24.16 six days, and on the **seventh day** the Lord called to Moses
24.18 There he stayed for forty **days** and nights.
29.30 in the Holy Place is to wear these garments for seven **days.**
29.35 and his sons for seven **days** exactly as I have commanded you.
29.36 Each **day** you must offer a bull as a sacrifice, so that
29.37 Do this **every day** for seven days.
29.38 **"Every day** for all time to come, sacrifice on the altar
31.13 "Keep the Sabbath, my **day of rest,** because it is a sign
31.14 You must keep the **day of rest,** because it is sacred.
31.14 it, but works on that **day,** is to be put to death.
31.15 You have six **days** in which to do your work, but the
31.15 do your work, but the **seventh day**
31.15 is a solemn **day of rest** dedicated to me.
31.15 does any work on that **day** is to be put to death.
31.16 Israel are to keep this **day** as a sign of the covenant.
31.17 heaven and earth in six **days,**
31.17 and on the **seventh day** I stopped working and rested."
34.18 eat unleavened bread for seven **days** in the month of Abib,
34.21 "You have six **days** in which to do your work, but do
34.21 do not work on the **seventh day,** not even during ploughing
34.28 the Lord forty **days** and nights, eating and drinking nothing.
35. 2 You have six **days** in which to do your work, but the
35. 2 do your work, but the **seventh day** is to be sacred, a
35. 2 be sacred, a solemn **day of rest** dedicated to me, the Lord.
35. 2 does any work on that **day** is to be put to death.
40. 2 to Moses, [2]"On the first **day** of the first month set up
40.17 So on the first **day** of the first month of the second
40.38 over the Tent during the **day** and a fire burning above it
Lev 7.17 Any meat that still remains on the third **day** must be burnt.
7.18 is eaten on the third **day,** God will not accept the man's
8.33 Tent for seven **days,** until your ordination rites are completed.
8.35 day and night for seven **days,** doing what the Lord has commanded.
12. 2 For seven **days** after a woman gives birth to a son, she
12. 3 On the eighth **day,** the child shall be circumcised.
12. 4 it will be thirty-three more **days** before she is ritually
Lev 12. 5 For fourteen **days** after a woman gives birth to a daughter,
12. 5 it will be sixty-six more **days** before she is ritually clean
13. 4 white, the priest shall isolate the person for seven **days.**
13. 5 examine him again on the **seventh day,** and if in his opinion
13. 5 has not spread, he shall isolate him for another seven **days.**
13. 6 examine him again on the **seventh day,** and if the sore has
13.21 in colour, the priest shall isolate him for seven **days.**
13.26 in colour, the priest shall isolate him for seven **days.**
13.27 him again on the **seventh day,** and if it is spreading,
13.31 no healthy hairs in it, he shall isolate him for seven **days.**
13.32 the sore again on the **seventh day,** and if it has not
13.33 The priest shall then isolate him for another seven **days.**
13.34 On the **seventh day** the priest shall again examine the sore,
13.50 shall examine it and put the object away for seven **days.**
13.51 examine it again on the **seventh day,** and if the mildew has
13.54 order it to be washed and put away for another seven **days.**
14. 8 the camp, but he must live outside his tent for seven **days.**
14. 9 On the **seventh day** he shall again shave his head, his
14.10 On the eighth **day** he shall bring two male lambs and one
14.23 On the eighth **day** of his purification he shall bring
14.38 he shall leave the house and lock it up for seven **days.**
14.39 On the **seventh day** he shall return and examine it again.
15.13 discharge, he must wait seven **days** and then wash his clothes
15.14 On the eighth **day** he shall take two doves or two pigeons
15.19 has her monthly period, she remains unclean for seven **days.**
15.24 and remains unclean for seven **days,** and any bed on which he
15.25 flow of blood for several **days** outside her monthly period or
15.28 stops, she must wait seven **days,** and then she will be
15.29 On the eighth **day** she shall take two doves or two
16.29 On the tenth **day** of the seventh month the Israelites and the
16.31 That **day** is to be a very holy day, one on which
19. 6 meat left on the third **day** must be burnt, [7]because it is
22.26 from its mother for seven **days,** but after that it is
23. 3 You have six **days** in which to do your work,
23. 3 but remember that the **seventh day,** the Sabbath,
23. 3 the Sabbath, is a **day of rest.**
23. 3 On that **day** do not work, but gather for worship.
23. 5 begins at sunset on the fourteenth **day** of the first month.
23. 6 On the fifteenth **day** the Festival of Unleavened Bread begins,
23. 6 Bread begins, and for seven **days** you must not eat any bread
23. 7 On the first of these **days** you shall gather for worship
23. 8 Offer your food-offerings to the Lord for seven **days.**
23. 8 On the **seventh day** you shall again gather for worship, but
23.16 On the fiftieth **day,**
23.16 the **day** after the seventh Sabbath,
23.23 On the first **day** of the seventh month
23.23 month observe a special **day of rest,** and come together for
23.26 The tenth **day** of the seventh month
23.26 is the **day** when the annual ritual is to
23.32 From sunset on the ninth **day** of the month to sunset on
23.32 day as a special **day of rest,** during which nothing may be
23.33 Shelters begins on the fifteenth **day** of the seventh month
23.33 day of the seventh month and continues for seven **days.**
23.35 On the first of these **days** come together for worship and
23.36 Each day for seven **days** you shall present a food-offering.
23.36 On the eighth **day** come together again for worship and
23.36 It is a **day** for worship, and you shall do no work.
23.39 this festival for seven **days,** beginning on the fifteenth day
23.39 days, beginning on the fifteenth **day** of the seventh month.
23.39 The first day shall be a special **day of rest.**
23.41 Celebrate it for seven **days.**
23.42 live in shelters for seven **days,** [43]so that your
25. 9 Then, on the tenth **day** of the seventh month,
25. 9 the **Day of Atonement,** send a man to blow
Num 1. 1 On the first **day** of the second month in the second year
1.18 whole community on the first **day** of the second month and
6. 9 dies, he must wait seven **days** and then shave off his hair
6.10 On the eighth **day** he shall bring two doves or two
7.11 for a period of twelve **days** one of the leaders is to
9. 2 "On the fourteenth **day** of this month, beginning at sunset,
9. 5 the evening of the fourteenth **day** of the first month they
9.11 on the evening of the fourteenth **day** of the second month.
9.20 Sometimes the cloud remained over the Tent for only a few **days;**
9.22 Whether it was two **days,** a month, a year, or longer, as
10.11 On the twentieth **day** of the second month in the second
10.33 Sinai, the holy mountain, they travelled for three **days.**
10.34 each camp, the cloud of the Lord was over them by **day.**
11.19 just for one or two **days,** or five, or ten,
11.19 or even twenty **days,** [20]but for a whole month,
12.14 face, she would have to bear her disgrace for seven **days.**
12.15 of the camp for seven **days,** and the people did not move
13.25 the land for forty **days,** the spies returned [26]to Moses,
14.14 a pillar of cloud by **day** and a pillar of fire by
14.34 for each of the forty **days** you spent exploring the land.
19.11 Whoever touches a corpse is ritually unclean for seven **days.**
19.12 third day and on the **seventh day,** and then he will be
19.12 both the third and the **seventh day,** he will not be clean.
19.14 or who enters it becomes ritually unclean for seven **days.**
19.16 a human bone or a grave, he becomes unclean for seven **days.**
19.19 On the third **day** and on the seventh the person who is
19.19 On the **seventh day** he is to purify the man, who, after
20.29 Aaron had died, and they all mourned for him for thirty **days.**
23.10 Let me end my **days** like one of God's people;
28. 9 On the Sabbath **day** offer two one-year-old male lambs
28.14 for the first **day** of each month throughout the year.
28.16 is to be held on the fourteenth **day** of the first month.
28.17 On the fifteenth **day** a religious festival begins
28.17 festival begins which lasts seven **days,** during which only
28.18 On the first **day** of the festival you are to gather for
28.24 same way, for seven **days** offer to the Lord a food-offering,
28.25 Meet for worship on the **seventh day** and do no work.

Num 28.26 On the first **day** of the Harvest Festival, when you
29. 1 On the first **day** of the seventh month you are to gather
29. 6 for the first **day** of the month with its grain-offering,
29. 7 Gather for worship on the tenth **day** of the seventh month;
29.12 Gather for worship on the fifteenth **day** of the seventh month.
29.12 in honour of the Lord for seven **days** and do no work.
29.13 On this first **day** offer a food-offering to the Lord,
29.17 On the second **day** offer twelve young bulls, two rams,
29.18 Offer with them all the other offerings required for the first **day.**
29.20 On the third **day** offer eleven young bulls, two rams,
29.21 Offer with them all the other offerings required for the first **day.**
29.23 On the fourth **day** offer ten young bulls, two rams,
29.24 Offer with them all the other offerings required for the first **day.**
29.26 On the fifth **day** offer nine young bulls, two rams,
29.27 Offer with them all the other offerings required for the first **day.**
29.29 On the sixth **day** offer eight young bulls, two rams,
29.30 Offer with them all the other offerings required for the first **day.**
29.32 On the **seventh day** offer seven young bulls, two rams,
29.33 Offer with them all the other offerings required for the first **day.**
29.35 On the eighth **day** gather for worship and do no work.
29.37 Offer with them all the other offerings required for the first **day.**
31.19 touched a corpse must stay outside the camp for seven **days.**
31.19 third day and on the **seventh day** purify yourselves
31.24 On the **seventh day** you must wash your clothes;
33. 3 left Egypt on the fifteenth **day** of the first month of the
33. 8 after a three **days'** march they camped at Marah.
33.38 died there on the first **day** of the fifth month of the
Deut 1. 2 (It takes eleven **days** to travel from Mount Sinai to Kadesh
1. 3 On the first **day** of the eleventh month of the fortieth
1.33 of fire by night and in a pillar of cloud by **day.**
4.10 and your grandchildren [10]about the **day** you stood
5.13 You have six **days** in which to do your work,
5.14 do your work, [14]but the **seventh day**
5.14 is a **day of rest** dedicated to me.
9. 9 I stayed there forty **days** and nights and did not eat
9.11 Yes, after those forty **days** and nights the Lord gave me
9.18 the Lord's presence for forty **days** and nights
9.25 the Lord's presence those forty **days** and nights,
10.10 stayed on the mountain forty **days** and nights,
16. 3 For seven **days** you are to eat bread prepared without yeast,
16. 4 For seven **days** no one in your land is to have any
16. 4 the evening of the first **day** must be eaten that same night.
16. 8 For the next six **days** you are to eat bread prepared
16. 8 without yeast, and on the **seventh day** assemble to worship
16. 8 and do no work on that **day.**
16.13 grapes, celebrate the Festival of Shelters for seven **days.**
16.15 this festival for seven **days** at the one place of worship.
24.15 Each day before sunset pay him for that **day's** work;
28.32 **Every day** you will strain your eyes, looking in vain
28.66 **Day** and night you will be filled with terror,
32.35 the **day** of their doom is near.
33.12 He guards them all the **day** long, And he dwells in their
34. 8 Israel mourned for him for thirty **days** in the plains of Moab.
Josh 1. 8 Study it **day** and night, and make sure that you obey
1.11 food ready, because in three **days** you are going to cross
2.16 Hide there for three **days** until they come back.
2.22 the countryside for three **days,** but they did not find them,
3. 2 Three **days** later the leaders went through the camp
4.19 the Jordan on the tenth **day** of the first month and made
5.10 Passover on the evening of the fourteenth **day** of the month.
6. 3 are to march round the city once a day for six **days.**
6. 4 On the **seventh day** you and your soldiers are to march round
6.14 On this second **day** they again marched round the city
6.14 They did this for six **days.**
6.15 On the **seventh day** they got up at daybreak and marched seven
9.16 Three **days** after the treaty had been made,
9.17 Israel started out and three **days** later arrived
10.13 of the sky and did not go down for a whole **day.**
10.32 Israelites victory over Lachish on the second **day** of the battle.
Judg 5. 6 In the **days** of Shamgar son of Anath,
5. 6 in the **days** of Jael, caravans no longer went
6.27 town to do it by **day,** so he did it at night.
11.40 would go away for four **days** every year to grieve
14. 8 A few **days** later Samson went back to marry her.
14.12 before the seven **days** of the wedding feast are over."
14.14 Three **days** later they had still not solved the riddle.
14.15 On the fourth **day** they said to Samson's wife, "Trick
14.17 She cried about it for the whole seven **days** of the feast.
14.17 But on the **seventh day** he told her what the riddle meant,
14.18 So on the **seventh day,** before Samson went into the bedroom,
18. 1 In those **days** the tribe of Dan was looking for territory
19. 1 In those **days,** before Israel had a king,
19. 4 insisted that he stay, and so he stayed for three **days.**
19. 5 the morning of the fourth **day** they woke up early
19. 8 the morning of the fifth **day** he started to leave,
19.16 came by at the end of a **day's** work in the fields.
20.21 the city, and before the **day** was over they had killed
20.27 there at Bethel in those **days,** and Phinehas,
20.30 Then for the third successive **day** they marched against
Ruth 1. 1 Long ago, in the **days** before Israel had a king,
4. 7 Now in those **days,** to settle a sale or an exchange of
1 Sam 3. 1 In those **days,** when the boy Samuel was serving the Lord
9.20 that were lost three **days** ago, don't worry about them;
10. 8 Wait there seven **days** until I come and tell you what to
11. 3 Jabesh said, "Give us seven **days** to send messengers
11.13 death today, for this is the **day** the Lord rescued Israel."
13. 8 He waited seven **days** for Samuel, as Samuel had instructed
14.23 The Lord saved Israel that **day.**
14.24 So nobody had eaten anything all **day.**
14.37 But God did not answer that **day.**
1 Sam 17.16 challenged the Israelites every morning and evening for forty **days.**
17.46 This very **day** the Lord will put you in my power;
18.10 the harp, as he did **every day,** and Saul was holding a
19.24 Samuel's presence, and lay naked all that **day** and all that night.
20.34 nothing that day—the second **day** of the New Moon Festival.
25. 8 have come on a feast **day,** and David asks you to receive
25.16 They protected us **day** and night the whole time we were
25.38 Some ten **days** later the Lord struck Nabal and he died.
27. 1 David said to himself, "One of these **days** Saul will kill me.
28.20 because he had not eaten anything all **day** and all night.
30. 1 Two **days** later David and his men arrived back at Ziklag.
30.12 had not had anything to eat or drink for three full **days.**
30.13 "My master left me behind three **days** ago because I was ill.
31.13 the tamarisk-tree in the town, and fasted for seven **days.**
2 Sam 1. 1 over the Amalekites and stayed in Ziklag for two **days.**
3.35 All **day** long the people tried to get David to eat something,
3.35 strike me dead if I eat anything before the **day** is over!"
13.18 the usual clothing for an unmarried princess in those **days.**
16.23 that Ahithophel gave in those **days** was accepted
21.10 During the **day** she would keep the birds away from the corpses,
23.10 The Lord won a great victory that **day.**
23.12 The Lord won a great victory that **day.**
24. 8 nine months and twenty **days** they returned to Jerusalem,
24.13 from your enemies or three **days** of an epidemic in your land?
1 Kgs 3.18 Two **days** after my child was born she also gave birth
8.29 Watch over this Temple **day** and night,
8.65 Israel celebrated the Festival of Shelters for seven **days.**
8.66 On the eighth **day** Solomon sent the people home.
12. 5 "Come back in three **days** and I will give you my answer,"
12.12 Three **days** later Jeroboam and all the people returned
12.32 religious festival on the fifteenth **day** of the eighth month,
12.33 And on the fifteenth **day** of the eighth month,
12.33 the **day** that he himself had set,
16.15 Asa of Judah, Zimri ruled in Tirzah over Israel for seven **days.**
17.15 told her, and all of them had enough food for many **days.**
19. 4 Elijah walked a whole **day** into the wilderness.
19. 8 strength to walk forty **days** to Sinai, the holy mountain.
20.29 For seven **days** the Syrians and the Israelites stayed in their camps,
20.29 On the **seventh day** they started fighting, and the Israelites
21. 9 "Proclaim a **day** of fasting, call the people together,
21.12 They proclaimed a **day** of fasting, called the people together,
22.46 altars who were still left from the **days** of his father Asa.
2 Kgs 2.17 high and low for Elijah for three **days,** but didn't find him.
3. 9 After marching for seven **days,** they ran out of water,
6.31 me dead if Elisha is not beheaded before the **day** is over!"
10.20 "Proclaim a **day** of worship in honour of Baal!"
19. 3 "Today is a **day** of suffering;
20. 5 heal you, and in three **days** you will go to the Temple.
20. 8 heal me and that three **days** later I will be able to
25. 1 attacked Jerusalem on the tenth **day** of the tenth month
25. 3 On the ninth **day** of the fourth month of that same year,
25. 8 On the seventh **day** of the fifth month of the nineteenth
25.27 This happened on the twenty-seventh **day** of the twelfth month
1 Chr 5.17 records were compiled in the **days** of King Jotham of Judah
7.22 mourned for them for many **days,** and his relatives came to
9.25 to take turns at guard duty for seven **days** at a time.
9.33 from other duties, because they were on call **day** and night.
10.12 They buried them there under an oak and fasted for seven **days.**
12.22 Almost **every day** new men joined David's forces,
12.39 They spent three **days** there with David, feasting on
16.23 Proclaim **every day** the good news that he has saved us.
21.12 Or three **days** during which the Lord attacks you
29.15 Our **days** are like a passing shadow, and we cannot escape death.
2 Chr 2. 4 New Moon Festivals, and other holy **days** honouring the Lord our God.
6.20 Watch over this Temple **day** and night.
7. 8 Israel celebrated the Festival of Shelters for seven **days.**
7. 9 They had spent seven **days** for the dedication of the altar
7. 9 and then seven more **days** for the festival.
7.10 following day, the twenty-third **day** of the seventh month,
8.13 to the requirements of the Law of Moses for each holy **day:**
10. 5 Rehoboam replied, "Give me three **days** to consider the matter.
10.12 Three **days** later Jeroboam and all the people returned to King Rehoboam,
15. 5 In those **days** no one could come and go in safety,
20.25 They spent three **days** gathering the loot,
20.26 On the fourth **day** they assembled in the Valley
24.11 **Every day** the Levites would take the box to the royal
28. 5 Ahaz and kill 120,000 of the bravest Judaean soldiers in one **day.**
29.17 was begun on the first **day** of the first month,
29.17 and by the eighth **day** they had finished it all,
29.17 for the next eight **days,** until the sixteenth of the month,
30.15 And on the fourteenth **day** of the month they killed the
30.21 For seven **days** the people who had gathered in Jerusalem
30.22 After the seven **days** during which they offered sacrifices
30.23 they all decided to celebrate for another seven **days.**
30.26 this had happened since the **days** of King Solomon, the son of
35. 1 on the fourteenth **day** of the first month they killed the
35.17 For seven **days** all the people of Israel who were present
35.18 Since the **days** of the prophet Samuel, the Passover had
36. 9 and he ruled in Jerusalem for three months and ten **days.**
Ezra 3. 4 each day they offered the sacrifices required for that **day;**
3. 6 they began on the first **day** of the seventh month to burn
6.15 the Temple on the third **day** of the month Adar in the
6.19 celebrated Passover on the fourteenth **day** of the first month
6.22 For seven **days** they joyfully celebrated the Festival
7. 8 left Babylonia on the first **day** of the first month, and with
7. 8 arrived in Jerusalem on the first **day** of the fifth month.
8.15 runs to the town of Ahava, and we camped there three **days.**

Ezra	8.31	It was on the twelfth **day** of the first month that we
	8.32	When we reached Jerusalem, we rested for three **days.**
	8.33	Then on the fourth **day** we went to the Temple, weighed
	9. 7	From the **days** of our ancestors until now, we, your people,
	10. 8	within three **days,** all his property would be confiscated,
	10. 9	Within the three **days,** on the twentieth day of the ninth month,
	10.13	done in one or two **days,** because so many of us are
	10.16	On the first **day** of the tenth month they began their investigation,
Neh	1. 4	For several **days** I mourned and did not eat.
	1. 6	my prayer, as I pray **day** and night for your servants, the
	1.11	In those **days** I was the emperor's wine steward.
	2.11	to Jerusalem, and for three **days** [12]I did not tell anyone
	4. 2	by offering sacrifices they can finish the work in one **day?**
	4. 9	our God and kept men on guard against them **day** and night.
	4.21	So **every day,** from dawn until the stars came out at night,
	4.22	guard the city at night as well as work in the **daytime.**
	5.15	and had demanded forty silver coins a **day** for food and wine.
	5.18	**Every day** I served one ox, six of the best sheep, and
	5.18	many chickens, and every ten **days** I provided a fresh supply
	6.15	After fifty-two **days** of work the entire wall was
	6.15	was finished on the twenty-fifth **day** of the month of Elul.
	8. 1	On the first **day** of that month they all assembled in Jerusalem,
	8. 9	told all the people, "This **day** is holy to the Lord your
	8.11	and telling them not to be sad on such a holy **day.**
	8.17	had been done since the **days** of Joshua son of Nun, and
	8.18	From the first **day** of the festival to the last they read
	8.18	to the last they read a part of God's Law **every day.**
	8.18	They celebrated for seven **days,**
	8.18	and on the eighth **day** there was a closing ceremony, as
	9. 1	On the twenty-fourth **day** of the same month the people
	9.12	cloud you led them in **day-time,** and at night you lighted
	9.19	or the fire that showed them the path by **day** and night.
	10.31	or on any other holy **day,** we will not buy from them.
	12. 2	among all their fellow-priests in the **days** of Joshua.
Esth	1.10	On the seventh **day** of his banquet the king was drinking
	2.11	**Every day** Mordecai would walk to and fro in front of the
	3. 7	to find out the right **day** and month to carry out his
	3. 7	The thirteenth **day** of the twelfth month, the month of Adar,
	3.12	So on the thirteenth **day** of the first month Haman called
	3.13	that on a single **day,** the thirteenth day of Adar,
	3.14	so that everyone would be prepared when that **day** came.
	4.16	Don't eat or drink anything for three **days** and nights.
	5. 1	On the third **day** of her fast Esther put on her royal
	8. 9	This happened on the twenty-third **day** of the third month,
	8.13	ready to take revenge on their enemies when that **day** came.
	9. 1	The thirteenth **day** of Adar came,
	9. 1	the **day** on which the royal proclamation was
	9. 1	was to take effect, the **day** when the enemies of the Jews
	9.15	On the fourteenth **day** of Adar the Jews of Susa got
	9.17	This was on the thirteenth **day** of Adar.
	9.17	no more killing, and they made it a joyful **day** of feasting.
	9.19	small towns observe the fourteenth **day** of the month of Adar
	9.21	and fifteenth **days** of Adar as holidays every year.
	9.22	These were the **days** on which the Jews had rid themselves
	9.22	were told to observe these **days** with feasts and parties,
	9.24	were called) to determine the **day** for destroying the Jews;
	9.27	time each year these two **days** would be regularly observed
	9.28	should remember and observe the **days** of Purim for all time
	9.31	descendants to observe the **days** of Purim at the proper time,
Job	1. 6	When the **day** came for the heavenly beings to appear before
	2. 1	When the **day** came for the heavenly beings to appear before
	2.13	with him for seven **days** and nights without saying a word,
	3. 4	Turn that **day** into darkness, God.
	3. 4	Never again remember that **day;**
	3. 5	Make it a **day** of gloom and thick darkness;
	3. 8	the sorcerers to curse that **day,** those who know how to
	7. 6	My **days** pass by without hope, pass faster than a weaver's shuttle.
	9.25	My **days** race by, not one of them good.
	17.11	My **days** have passed;
	24.16	into houses, but by **day** they hide and avoid the light.
	24.17	They fear the light of **day,** but darkness holds no terror
	29. 4	Those were the **days** when I was prosperous, and the
	38. 7	In the dawn of that **day** the stars sang together, and the
	38.12	have you ever in all your life commanded a **day** to dawn?
	38.15	The light of **day** is too bright for the wicked and
	38.23	ready for times of trouble, for **days** of battle and war.
Ps	1. 2	the Law of the Lord, and they study it **day** and night.
	13. 2	How long will sorrow fill my heart **day** and night?
	19. 2	Each **day** announces it to the following day;
	22. 2	During the **day** I call to you, my God, but you do
	32. 3	confess my sins, I was worn out from crying all **day** long.
	32. 4	**Day** and night you punished me, Lord;
	35.28	your righteousness, and I will praise you all **day** long.
	38. 6	I mourn all **day** long.
	42. 3	**Day** and night I cry, and tears are my only food;
	42. 8	his constant love during the **day,** so that I may have a
	44. 1	things you did in their time, in the **days** of long ago:
	55.10	in the city, [10]surrounding it **day** and night, filling it
	56. 2	All **day** long my opponents attack me.
	56. 5	My enemies make trouble for me all **day** long;
	71. 8	All **day** long I praise you and proclaim your glory.
	71.15	all **day** long I will speak of your salvation, though it is
	71.24	speak of your righteousness all **day** long, because those who
	73.14	O God, you have made me suffer all **day** long;
	74.16	You created the **day** and the night;
	74.22	Remember that godless people laugh at you all **day** long.
	77. 5	I think of **days** gone by and remember years of long ago.
	78.14	By **day** he led them with a cloud and all night long
	78.33	So he ended their **days** like a breath and their lives
	78.42	his great power and the **day** when he saved them from their
	84.10	One **day** spent in your Temple is better than a thousand
Ps	86. 3	I pray to you all **day** long.
	88. 1	saviour, I cry out all **day,** and at night I come before
	88. 9	Lord, **every day** I call to you and lift my hands to
	88.17	All **day** long they surround me like a flood;
	89.16	of you they rejoice all **day** long, and they praise you for
	90. 4	A thousand years to you are like one **day;**
	91. 5	or sudden attacks during the **day** [6]or the plagues that
	94.13	You give him rest from **days** of trouble until a pit is
	96. 2	Proclaim **every day** the good news that he has saved us.
	102. 8	All **day** long my enemies insult me;
	118.24	This is the **day** of the Lord's victory;
	119.97	I think about it all **day** long.
	119.164	Seven times each **day** I thank you for your righteous judgements.
	121. 6	not hurt you during the **day,** nor the moon during the night.
	128. 5	May you see Jerusalem prosper all the **days** of your life!
	136. 8	the sun to rule over the **day;**
	139.12	dark for you, and the night is as bright as the **day.**
	139.16	The **days** allotted to me had all been recorded in your book,
	143. 5	I remember the **days** gone by;
	144. 4	his **days** are like a passing shadow.
	145. 2	**Every day** I will thank you;
Prov	6.22	travel, protect you at night, and advise you during the **day.**
	8.34	who stays at my door **every day,** waiting at the entrance to
Ecc	1.11	past, and no one in **days** to come will remember what happens
	2.16	In **days** to come, we will all be forgotten.
	6. 5	never sees the light of **day** or knows what life is like,
	7. 1	the day you die is better than the **day** you are born.
	7.10	ask, "Oh, why were things so much better in the old **days?"**
	8.16	could stay awake night and **day** [17]and never be able to
	9. 9	Enjoy every useless **day** of it, because that is all you will
	11. 1	foreign trade, and one of these **days** you will make a profit.
	11. 7	is good to be able to enjoy the pleasant light of **day.**
	12. 1	still young, before those dismal **days** and years come when
Song	3.11	on his wedding day, on the **day** of his gladness and joy.
Is	1.14	I hate your New Moon Festivals and holy **days;**
	2. 2	In **days** to come the mountain where the Temple stands will
	2.11	A **day** is coming when human pride will be ended and human
	2.12	On that **day** the Lord Almighty will humble everyone who is powerful,
	2.17	disappear, and the Lord alone will be exalted on that **day.**
	2.20	When that **day** comes, they will throw away the gold and
	3.18	A **day** is coming when the Lord will take away from the
	4. 5	send a cloud in the **daytime** and smoke and a bright flame
	4. 6	from the heat of the **day** and make it a place of
	5.30	When that **day** comes, they will roar over Israel as
	7.17	on the whole royal family, **days** of trouble worse than any
	9.14	In a single **day** the Lord will punish Israel's leaders
	10.17	flame, which in a single **day** will burn up everything, even
	11.10	A **day** is coming when the new king from the royal line
	11.11	When that **day** comes, the Lord will once again use his
	12. 1	A **day** is coming when people will sing,
	12. 4	A **day** is coming when people will sing,
	13. 6	The **day** of the Lord is near,
	13. 6	the **day** when the Almighty brings destruction.
	13. 9	The **day** of the Lord is coming—
	13. 9	that cruel **day** of his fierce anger and fury.
	13.13	on that **day** when I, the Lord Almighty, show
	13.22	Her **days** are almost over."
	17. 4	The Lord said, "A **day** is coming when Israel's greatness
	17. 7	When that **day** comes, people will turn for help to their Creator,
	17. 9	When that **day** comes, well-defended cities will be deserted
	18. 4	as serenely as the sun shines in the heat of the **day.**
	21. 8	"Sir, I have been standing guard at my post **day** and night."
	25. 5	the shouts of cruel men, as a cloud cools a hot **day.**
	26. 1	A **day** is coming when the people will sing this song
	27. 1	On that **day** the Lord will use his powerful and deadly
	27. 2	On that **day** the Lord will say of his pleasant vineyard,
	27. 3	I guard it night and **day** so that no one will harm
	27. 6	In **days** to come the people of Israel, the descendants of Jacob,
	27.12	On that **day,** from the Euphrates to the Egyptian border,
	27.13	When that **day** comes, a trumpet will be blown
	28. 5	A **day** is coming when the Lord Almighty will be like a
	28.19	You will have to bear it **day** and night.
	29.18	When that **day** comes, the deaf will be able to hear
	30.25	On the **day** when the forts of your enemies are captured
	30.26	brighter than usual, like the light of seven **days** in one.
	34.10	It will burn **day** and night, and smoke will rise from it
	37. 3	"Today is a **day** of suffering;
	46.13	I am bringing the **day** of victory near— it is not
	47. 9	moment, in a single **day,** both of these things will happen.
	58. 2	They worship me **every day,** claiming that they are eager to
	58.13	if you value my holy **day** and honour it by not travelling,
	58.13	or talking idly on that **day,** [14]then you will find the joy
	60. 3	to your light, And kings to the dawning of your new **day.**
	60.11	**Day** and night your gates will be open, So that the kings
	60.19	sun be your light by **day** Or the moon be your light
	60.20	Your **days** of grief will come to an end.
	62. 6	They must never be silent **day** or night.
	63.11	they remembered the past, the **days** of Moses, the servant of
	66. 8	Has a nation ever been born in a **day?**
Jer	2.32	people have forgotten me for more **days** than can be counted.
	5.18	says, "Yet even in those **days** I will not completely destroy
	6. 4	say, "It's too late, the **day** is almost over, and the
	9. 1	so that I could cry **day** and night for my people who
	14.17	my eyes flow with tears **day** and night, may I never stop
	16.13	you will serve other gods **day** and night, and I will show
	17.22	observe it as a sacred **day,** as I commanded their ancestors.
	17.24	the Sabbath as a sacred **day** and must not do any work
	17.27	they must obey me and observe the Sabbath as a sacred **day.**
	20. 7	they mock me all **day** long.
	21.11	See that justice is done **every day.**

Jer 23.20 In **days** to come his people will understand this clearly."
30. 7 A terrible **day** is coming;
30. 7 no other **day** can compare with it— a time of distress
30. 8 "When that **day** comes, I will break the yoke that is round
30.23 In **days** to come his people will understand this clearly.
31.35 the sun for light by **day**, the moon and the stars to
33.20 made a covenant with the **day** and with the night, so that
33.25 Lord, have a covenant with **day** and night, and I have made
34.15 Just a few **days** ago you changed your minds and did what
36.30 to the sun during the **day** and to the frost at night.
39. 2 On the ninth **day** of the fourth month of Zedekiah's
42. 7 Ten **days** later the Lord spoke to me;
46.10 This is the **day** of the Sovereign Lord Almighty:
46.21 The **day** of their doom had arrived, the time of their destruction.
48.47 But in **days** to come the Lord will make Moab prosperous again.
51. 2 When that **day** of destruction comes, they will attack from
52. 4 attacked Jerusalem on the tenth **day** of the tenth month of
52. 6 On the ninth **day** of the fourth month of that same year,
52.12 On the tenth **day** of the fifth month of the nineteenth
52.31 This happened on the twenty-fifth **day** of the twelfth month
Lam 1. 4 one comes to the Temple now to worship on the holy **days.**
1.21 Bring the **day** you promised;
2. 1 On the **day** of his anger he abandoned even his Temple.
2. 6 He has put an end to holy **days** and Sabbaths.
2.16 This is the **day** we have waited for!"
2.18 Let your tears flow like rivers night and **day;**
2.21 You slaughtered them without mercy on the **day** of your anger.
2.22 me, And no one could escape on that **day** of your anger.
3.14 People laugh at me all **day** long;
3.62 All **day** long they talk about me and make their plans.
4.18 Our **days** were over;
Ezek 1. 1 On the fifth **day** of the fourth month of the thirtieth year,
3.15 were living, and for seven **days** I stayed there, overcome by
3.16 After the seven **days** had passed, the Lord spoke to me.
4. 4 For 390 **days** you will stay there and suffer because of their
4. 4 have sentenced you to one **day** for each year their punishment
4. 6 guilt of Judah for forty **days—**
4. 6 one **day** for each year of their punishment.
4. 9 to eat during the 390 **days** you are lying on your left
4.10 230 grammes of bread a **day,**
4.10 and it will have to last until the next **day.**
4.11 have a limited amount of water to drink, two cups a **day.**
7.10 The **day** of disaster is coming for Israel.
7.12 The **day** is near when buying and selling will have no more
8. 1 On the fifth **day** of the sixth month of the sixth year
13. 5 cannot be defended when war comes on the **day** of the Lord.
16.25 who came by, and you were more of a prostitute **every day.**
16.56 joke about Sodom in those **days** when you were proud [57] and
20. 1 It was the tenth **day** of the fifth month of the seventh
20.20 Make the Sabbath a holy **day,** so that it will be a
21.25 ruler of Israel, your **day,** the day of your final punishment,
21.29 and your day is coming, the **day** of your final punishment.
22. 4 you made, and so your **day** is coming, your time is up!
24. 1 On the tenth **day** of the tenth month of the ninth year
24.26 On the **day** that I do this, someone who escapes the
29. 1 On the twelfth **day** of the tenth month of the tenth year
29.17 On the first **day** of the first month of the
30. 2 A **day** of terror is coming!
30. 3 The **day** is near, the day when the Lord will act,
30. 3 A **day** of clouds and trouble
30. 9 "When that **day** comes and Egypt is destroyed, I will send
30. 9 That **day** is coming!"
30.20 On the seventh **day** of the first month of the eleventh
31. 1 On the first **day** of the third month of the eleventh year
32. 1 On the first **day** of the twelfth month of the twelfth year
32.17 On the fifteenth **day** of the first month of the twelfth
33.21 On the fifth **day** of the tenth month of the twelfth year
34.12 where they were scattered on that dark, disastrous **day.**
38.17 prophets of Israel, that in **days** to come I would bring
38.19 my anger that on that **day** there will be a severe earthquake
39. 8 The Sovereign Lord said, "The **day** I spoke about is
39.13 they will be honoured for this on the **day** of my victory.
40. 1 It was the tenth **day** of the new year, which was the
43.25 Each day for seven **days** you are to offer a goat, a
43.26 For seven **days** the priests are to consecrate the altar
44.26 again, he must wait seven **days** [27] and then go into the
45.18 Lord said, "On the first **day** of the first month you are
45.20 On the seventh **day** of the month you are to do the
45.21 "On the fourteenth **day** of the first month you will
45.21 For seven **days** everyone will eat bread made without yeast.
45.22 On the first **day** of the festival the ruling prince must
45.23 On each of the seven **days** of the festival he is to
45.25 which begins on the fifteenth **day** of the seventh month, the
45.25 on each of the seven **days** the same sacrifice for sin, the
46. 1 closed during the six working **days,** but it is to be opened
46.11 On the feast **days** and at the festivals the
46.13 This offering must be made **every day.**
Dan 1. 5 king also gave orders that **every day** they were to be given
1.12 "Test us for ten **days,"** he said.
1.14 He agreed to let them try it for ten **days.**
5.26 number, God has numbered the **days** of your kingdom and
6. 7 Give orders that for thirty **days** no one be permitted to
6.12 that for the next thirty **days** anyone who requested anything
8.14 "It will continue for 1,150 **days,** during which evening and
8.27 I was depressed and ill for several **days.**
10. 4 On the twenty-fourth **day** of the first month of the year,
10.13 of the kingdom of Persia opposed me for twenty-one **days.**
12.11 is, from the time of The Awful Horror, 1,290 **days** will pass.
12.12 Happy are those who remain faithful until 1,335 **days** are over!
Hos 1.10 not my people," but the **day** is coming when he will say
1.11 Yes, the day of Jezreel will be a great **day!**
4. 5 Night and **day** you blunder on, and the prophets do no
5. 9 The **day** of punishment is coming, and Israel will be ruined.
6. 2 In two or three **days** he will revive us, and we will
6. 3 us as surely as the **day** dawns, as surely as the spring
6. 4 it is like dew, that vanishes early in the **day.**
7. 9 Their **days** are numbered, but they don't even know it.
13. 3 morning mist, like the dew that vanishes early in the **day.**
Joel 1.15 The **day** of the Lord is near;
1.15 the **day** when the Almighty brings destruction.
1.15 What terror that **day** will bring!
2. 1 The **day** of the Lord is coming soon.
2. 2 will be a dark and gloomy **day,** a black and cloudy day.
2.11 How terrible is the **day** of the Lord!
2.30 will give warnings of that **day** in the sky and on the
2.31 blood before the great and terrible **day** of the Lord comes.
3.14 It is there that the **day** of the Lord will soon come.
Amos 2.16 On that **day** even the bravest soldiers will drop their
3.14 "On the **day** when I punish the people of Israel for
4. 2 holy, he has promised, "The **days** will come when they will
4. 4 after morning, and bring your tithes every third **day.**
4.13 he changes **day** into night.
5. 8 He turns darkness into daylight, and **day** into night.
5.18 will be for you who long for the **day** of the Lord!
5.18 What good will that **day** do you?
5.18 you it will be a **day** of darkness and not of light.
5.20 The **day** of the Lord will bring darkness and not light;
5.20 it will be a **day** of gloom, without any brightness.
6. 3 refuse to admit that a **day** of disaster is coming,
6. 3 but what you do only brings that **day** closer.
8. 3 On that **day** the songs in the palace will become cries of
8. 5 hardly wait for the holy **days** to be over so that we
8. 9 sun go down at noon and the earth grow dark in **daytime.**
8.10 That **day** will be bitter to the end.
8.13 On that **day** even healthy young men and women will
9.11 The Lord says, "A **day** is coming when I will restore
9.13 "The **days** are coming," says the Lord, "when corn will
Obad 8 "On the **day** I punish Edom, I will destroy their clever
15 "The **day** is near when I, the Lord, will judge all nations.
Jon 1.17 and he was inside the fish for three **days** and nights.
3. 3 city so large that it took three **days** to walk through it.
3. 4 and after walking a whole **day,** he proclaimed,
3. 4 "In forty **days** Nineveh will be destroyed!"
Mic 3. 6 "Prophets, your **day** is almost over;
4. 1 In **days** to come the mountain where the Temple stands will
7.15 as you did in the **days** when you brought us out of
Zeph 1. 7 The **day** is near when the Lord will sit in judgement;
1. 8 "On that **day** of slaughter," says the Lord, "I will
1.10 "On that **day,"** says the Lord, "you will hear the
1.14 The great **day** of the Lord is near—very near and coming
1.14 That will be a bitter **day,** for even the bravest soldiers
1.15 It will be a **day** of fury,
1.15 a **day** of trouble and distress,
1.15 a **day** of ruin and destruction,
1.15 a **day** of darkness and gloom,
1.15 a black and cloudy **day,**
1.16 a **day** filled with the sound of war-trumpets
1.18 On the **day** when the Lord shows his fury, not even all
2. 2 Lord comes upon you, before the **day** when he shows his fury.
2. 3 escape punishment on the **day** when the Lord shows his anger.
2. 4 driven out in half a **day,** and the people of Ekron will
3. 8 "Wait for the **day** when I rise to accuse the nations.
Hag 1. 1 on the first **day** of the sixth month,
1.15 on the twenty-fourth **day** of the sixth month
2. 1 On the twenty-first **day** of the seventh month of that same year,
2.10 On the twenty-fourth **day** of the ninth month of the
2.18 Today is the twenty-fourth **day** of the ninth month,
2.18 the **day** that the foundation of the Temple
2.20 On that same **day,** the twenty-fourth of the month, the
2.23 On that **day** I will take you, Zerubbabel my servant, and
Zech 1. 7 was emperor, on the twenty-fourth **day** of the eleventh month
3. 9 it, and in a single **day** I will take away the sin
3.10 When that **day** comes, each of you will invite his
7. 1 was emperor, on the fourth **day** of the ninth month (the month
8.23 In those **days** ten foreigners will come to one Jew and say,
9.16 When that **day** comes, the Lord will save his people, as a
14. 1 The **day** when the Lord will sit in judgement is near.
14. 8 When that **day** comes, fresh water will flow from Jerusalem,
Mal 2. 5 In those **days** they did respect and fear me.
3. 2 But who will be able to endure the **day** when he comes?
3.17 "On the **day** when I act, they will be my very own.
4. 1 The Lord Almighty says, "The **day** is coming when all proud
4. 1 On that **day** they will burn up, and there will be nothing
4. 3 On the **day** when I act, you will overcome the wicked, and
4. 5 before the great and terrible **day** of the Lord comes, I will
Mt 4. 2 After spending forty **days and nights** without food, Jesus was hungry.
6.34 There is no need to add to the troubles each **day** brings.
9.15 But the **day** will come when the bridegroom will be taken away
11.12 until this very **day** the Kingdom of heaven has suffered
11.16 "Now, to what can I compare the people of **this day?**
12.39 "How evil and godless are the people of **this day!"**
12.40 that Jonah spent three **days and nights** in the big fish, so
12.40 of Man spend three **days and nights** in the depths of the
12.45 This is what will happen to the evil people of **this day."**
13. 1 That same **day** Jesus left the house and went to the lake-side,
15.32 been with me for three **days** and now have nothing to eat.
16. 4 How evil and godless are the people of **this day!**
16.21 put to death, but three **days** later I will be raised to
17. 1 Six **days** later Jesus took with him Peter and the brothers
17.23 but three **days** later he will be raised to life."
20. 2 wage, a silver coin a **day,** and sent them to work in

Mt	20. 6	'Why are you wasting the whole **day** here doing nothing?'
	20.12	put up with a whole **day's** work in the hot sun—
	20.13	you agreed to do a **day's** work for one silver coin.
	20.19	but three **days** later he will be raised to life."
	22.23	That same **day** some Sadducees came to Jesus and claimed
	22.28	Now, on the **day** when the dead rise to life, whose wife
	22.46	any answer, and from that **day** on no one dared to ask
	23.36	for all these murders will fall on the people of **this day!**
	24.19	it will be in those **days** for women who are pregnant and
	24.21	ever been, from the beginning of the world to this very **day.**
	24.22	But God has already reduced the number of **days;**
	24.22	of his chosen people, however, God will reduce the **days.**
	24.29	after the trouble of those **days,** the sun will grow dark,
	24.36	one knows, however, when that **day** and hour will come—neither
	24.38	In the **days** before the flood people ate and drank,
	24.38	women married, up to the very **day** Noah went into the boat;
	24.42	because you do not know what **day** your Lord will come.
	25.13	guard, then, because you do not know the **day** or the hour.
	26. 2	to his disciples, [2]"In two **days,** as you know, it will be
	26.17	On the first **day** of the Festival of Unleavened Bread the
	26.29	drink this wine until the **day** I drink the new wine with
	26.55	**Every day** I sat down and taught in the Temple, and you
	26.61	down God's Temple and three **days** later build it up again.'"
	27. 8	that field is called "Field of Blood" to this very **day.**
	27.40	tear down the Temple and build it up again in three **days!**
	27.62	The next **day,** which was a Sabbath, the chief priests and
	27.63	he said, 'I will be raised to life three **days** later.'
	27.64	guarded until the third **day,** so that his disciples will not
	28.15	is the report spread round by the Jews to this very **day.**
Mk	1.13	into the desert, [13]where he stayed forty **days,** being tempted
	2. 1	A few **days** later Jesus went back to Capernaum, and the
	2.20	But the **day** will come when the bridegroom will be taken
	4.27	up and about during the **day,** and all the while the seeds
	4.35	the evening of that same **day** Jesus said to his disciples,
	5. 5	**Day and night** he wandered among the tombs and through the hills,
	8. 2	been with me for three **days** and now have nothing to eat.
	8.12	said, "Why do the people of **this day** ask for a miracle?
	8.31	put to death, but three **days** later he will rise to life."
	8.38	in this godless and wicked **day,** then the Son of Man will
	9. 2	Six **days** later Jesus took with him Peter, James, and John,
	9.31	Three **days** later, however, he will rise to life."
	10.34	but three **days** later he will rise to life."
	11.11	was already late in the **day,** he went out to Bethany with
	11.12	The next **day,** as they were coming back from Bethany,
	12.23	rise to life on the **day** of resurrection, whose wife will she
	13.17	it will be in those **days** for women who are pregnant and
	13.19	For the trouble of those **days** will be far worse than any
	13.20	But the Lord has reduced the number of those **days;**
	13.20	of his chosen people, however, he has reduced those **days.**
	13.24	"In the **days** after that time of trouble the sun will
	13.32	one knows, however, when that **day** or hour will come—neither
	14. 1	It was now two **days** before the Festival of Passover
	14.12	On the first **day** of the Festival of Unleavened Bread,
	14.12	the **day** the lambs for the Passover meal
	14.25	drink this wine until the **day** I drink the new wine in
	14.49	**Day after day** I was with you teaching in the Temple, and
	14.58	have made, and after three **days** I will build one that is
	15.29	tear down the Temple and build it up again in three **days!**
	15.42	It was Preparation **day** (that is, the day before the Sabbath),
Lk	1.20	remain silent until the **day** my promise to you comes true."
	1.75	be holy and righteous before him all the **days** of our life.
	1.80	in the desert until the **day** when he appeared publicly to the
	2.11	This very **day** in David's town your Saviour was
	2.36	**day and night** she worshipped God, fasting and praying.
	2.44	so they travelled a whole **day** and then started looking for
	2.46	On the third **day** they found him in the Temple, sitting
	4. 2	desert, [2]where he was tempted by the Devil for forty **days.**
	5.35	But the **day** will come when the bridegroom will be taken
	6.13	When **day** came, he called his disciples to him and chose
	7.31	"Now to what can I compare the people of **this day?**
	9.22	put to death, but three **days** later he will be raised to
	9.23	must forget self, take up his cross **every day,** and follow
	9.37	The next **day** Jesus and the three disciples went down from
	10.35	The next **day** he took out two silver coins and gave them
	11. 3	Give us **day by day** the food we need.
	11.29	went on to say, "How evil are the people of **this day!**
	11.30	of Man will be a sign for the people of **this day.**
	13.14	to the people, "There are six **days** in which we should work;
	13.14	so come during those **days** and be healed, but not on the
	13.32	and tomorrow, and on the third **day** I shall finish my work.'
	13.33	I must be on my way today, tomorrow, and the next **day;**
	14.14	will repay you on the **day** the good people rise from death."
	15.13	After a few **days** the younger son sold his part of the
	16.19	most expensive clothes and lived in great luxury **every day.**
	17. 4	you seven times in one **day,** and each time he comes to
	17.22	could see one of the **days** of the Son of Man,
	17.24	the other, so will the Son of Man be in his **day.**
	17.25	must suffer much and be rejected by the people of **this day.**
	17.26	so shall it be in the **days** of the Son of Man.
	17.27	up to the very **day** Noah went into the boat and
	17.29	On the **day** Lot left Sodom, fire and sulphur rained down
	17.30	it will be on the **day** the Son of Man is revealed.
	17.31	"On that **day** the man who is on the roof of his
	18. 7	his own people who cry to him **day and night** for help?
	18.12	I fast two **days** a week, and I give you a tenth
	18.33	and kill him, but three **days** later he will rise to life."
	19.47	**Every day** Jesus taught in the Temple.
	20.33	Now, on the **day** when the dead rise to life, whose wife
	21.22	For those will be 'The **Days** of Punishment,' to make all
	21.23	it will be in those **days** for women who are pregnant and
Lk	21.37	Jesus spent those **days** teaching in the Temple,
	22. 7	The **day** came during the Festival of Unleavened Bread when the
	22.53	with you in the Temple **every day,** and you did not try
	22.66	When **day** came, the elders, the chief priests, and the teachers
	23.12	On that very **day** Herod and Pilate became friends;
	23.29	For the **days** are coming when people will say, 'How lucky
	24. 7	men, be crucified, and three **days** later rise to life.'"
	24.13	On that same **day** two of Jesus' followers were going to
	24.18	the things that have been happening there these last few **days?"**
	24.21	Besides all that, this is now the third **day** since it happened.
	24.29	the **day** is almost over and it is getting dark."
	24.46	must rise from death three **days** later,
Jn	1.29	The next **day** John saw Jesus coming to him, and said,
	1.35	The next **day** John was standing there again with two of
	1.39	where he lived, and spent the rest of that **day** with him.
	1.43	The next **day** Jesus decided to go to Galilee.
	2. 1	Two **days** later there was a wedding in the town of Cana
	2.12	and disciples went to Capernaum and stayed there a few **days.**
	2.19	down this Temple, and in three **days** I will build it again."
	2.20	"Are you going to build it again in three **days?"**
	4.40	him to stay with them, and Jesus stayed there two **days.**
	4.43	After spending two **days** there, Jesus left and went to Galilee.
	5. 9	**day** this happened was a Sabbath, [10]so the Jewish authorities
	6.22	Next **day** the crowd which had stayed on the other side of
	6.39	that I should raise them all to life on the last **day.**
	6.40	And I will raise them to life on the last **day."**
	6.44	and I will raise him to life on the last **day.**
	6.54	and I will raise him to life on the last **day.**
	7.37	the last and most important **day** of the festival Jesus stood
	9. 4	As long as it is **day,** we must keep on doing the
	9.14	The **day** that Jesus made the mud and cured him of his
	11. 6	Lazarus was ill, he stayed where he was for two more **days.**
	11. 9	Jesus said, "A **day** has twelve hours, hasn't it?
	11.17	he found that Lazarus had been buried four **days** before.
	11.24	she replied, "that he will rise to life on the last **day."**
	11.39	He has been buried four **days!"**
	11.53	From that **day** on the Jewish authorities made plans to kill Jesus.
	12. 1	Six **days** before the Passover, Jesus went to Bethany,
	12. 7	Let her keep what she has for the **day** of my burial.
	12.12	The next **day** the large crowd that had come to the
	12.48	words I have spoken will be his judge on the last **day!**
	13. 1	It was now the **day** before the Passover Festival.
	14.20	When that **day** comes, you will know that I am in my
	16.23	"When that **day** comes, you will not ask me for anything.
	16.26	When that **day** comes, you will ask him in my name;
	19.14	It was then almost noon of the **day** before the Passover.
	19.42	Since it was the **day** before the Sabbath and because the
Acts	1. 2	began his work [2]until the **day** he was taken up to heaven.
	1. 3	For forty **days** after his death he appeared to them many
	1. 5	water, but in a few **days** you will be baptized with the
	1.15	A few **days** later there was a meeting of the believers,
	1.21	message of baptism until the **day** Jesus was taken up from us
	2. 1	When the **day** of Pentecost came, all the believers were gathered
	2.17	'This is what I will do in the last **days,** God says:
	2.18	my Spirit in those **days,** and they will proclaim my message.
	2.29	buried, and his grave is here with us to this very **day.**
	2.41	three thousand people were added to the group that **day.**
	2.46	**Day after day** they met as a group in the Temple, and
	2.47	And **every day** the Lord added to their group those who were
	3. 2	**Every day** he was carried to the gate to beg for money
	3.24	after him, also announced what has been happening these **days.**
	4. 3	them in jail until the next **day,** since it was already late.
	4. 5	The next **day** the Jewish leaders, the elders, and the teachers
	5.42	**every day** in the Temple and in people's homes they continued
	7.26	The next **day** he saw two Israelites fighting, and he
	8. 1	That very **day** the church in Jerusalem began to suffer cruel
	9. 9	For three **days** he was not able to see, and during that
	9.19	Saul stayed for a few **days** with the believers in Damascus.
	9.23	After many **days** had gone by, the Jews met together and
	9.24	**Day and night** they watched the city gates in order to kill
	9.43	in Joppa for many **days** with a tanner of leather named
	10. 9	The next **day,** as they were on their way and coming near
	10.23	The next **day** he got ready and went with them;
	10.24	The following **day** he arrived in Caesarea, where Cornelius was waiting
	10.30	was about this time three **days** ago that I was praying in
	10.40	him from death three **days** later and caused him to appear,
	10.48	Then they asked him to stay with them for a few **days.**
	12.21	On a chosen **day** Herod put on his royal robes, sat on
	13.11	blind and will not see the light of **day** for a time."
	13.31	from death, [31]and for many **days** he appeared to those who
	14.20	The next **day** he and Barnabas went to Derbe.
	16. 5	made stronger in the faith and grew in numbers **every day.**
	16.11	straight across to Samothrace, and the next **day** to Neapolis.
	16.12	We spent several **days** there.
	16.18	She did this for many **days,** until Paul became so upset
	17.11	and **every day** they studied the Scriptures
	17.17	also in the public square **every day** with the people
	17.31	For he has fixed a **day** in which he will judge the
	18.18	believers in Corinth for many **days,** then left them and
	19. 9	the believers with him, and **every day** he held discussions
	19.38	we have the authorities and the regular **days** for court;
	20. 6	Unleavened Bread, and five **days** later we joined them in Troas,
	20. 7	until midnight, since he was going to leave the next **day.**
	20.15	We sailed from there and arrived off Chios the next **day.**
	20.15	A **day** later we came to Samos,
	20.15	and the following **day** we reached Miletus.
	20.16	in Jerusalem by the **day** of Pentecost, if at all possible.
	20.18	with you, from the first **day** I arrived in the province of
	20.26	So I solemnly declare to you this very **day:**
	20.31	that with many tears, **day and night,** I taught every one of

Acts 21. 1 the next **day** we reached Rhodes, and from there we went on
21. 7 we greeted the believers and stayed with them for a **day.**
21. 8 On the following **day** we left and arrived in Caesarea.
21.10 been there for several **days** when a prophet named Agabus arrived
21.16 Mnason, from Cyprus, who had been a believer since the early **days.**
21.18 The next **day** Paul went with us to see James;
21.26 and the next **day** performed the ceremony of purification with
21.26 gave notice of how many **days** it would be until the end
21.27 But just when the seven **days** were about to come to an
22.30 so the next **day** he had Paul's chains taken off and ordered
23. 1 way in which I have lived before God to this very **day."**
23.32 The next **day** the foot-soldiers returned to the fort
24. 1 Five **days** later the High Priest Ananias went to Caesarea
24.11 was no more than twelve **days** ago that I went to Jerusalem
24.24 After some **days** Felix came with his wife Drusilla,
25. 1 Three **days** after Festus arrived in the province, he went
25. 6 spent another eight or ten **days** with them and then went to
25. 6 On the next **day** he sat down in the court of judgement
25.14 had been there several **days,** Festus explained Paul's situation
25.17 but on the very next **day** I sat in the court and
25.23 next **day** Agrippa and Bernice came with great pomp and ceremony
26. 7 people hope to receive, as they worship God **day and night.**
26.22 But to this very **day** I have been helped by God,
27. 3 The next **day** we arrived at Sidon.
27. 7 We sailed slowly for several **days** and with great difficulty
27. 9 voyage, for by now the **Day** of Atonement was already past.
27.18 so on the next **day** they began to throw some of
27.19 and on the following **day** they threw part of the ship's
27.20 For many **days** we could not see the sun or the stars,
27.33 have been waiting for fourteen **days** now, and all this time
27.39 When **day** came, the sailors did not recognize the coast,
28. 7 He welcomed us kindly and for three **days** we were his guests.
28.12 in the city of Syracuse and stayed there for three **days.**
28.13 The next **day** a wind began to blow from the south,
28.13 the south, and in two **days** we came to the town of
28.17 After three **days** Paul called the local Jewish leaders to
28.23 number of them came that **day** to the place where Paul was
Rom 10.21 concerning Israel he says, "All **day** long I held out my
11. 8 to this very **day** they cannot see or hear."
13.12 The night is nearly over, **day** is almost here.
13.13 live in the light of **day**—no orgies or drunkenness, no
14. 5 thinks that a certain **day** is more important than other days,
14. 5 while someone else thinks that all **days** are the same.
14. 6 thinks highly of a certain **day** does so in honour of the
1 Cor 8. 7 to idols that to this **day** when they eat such food they
10. 8 and in one **day** twenty-three thousand of them fell dead.
15. 4 raised to life three **days** later, as written in the Scriptures;
15.31 My brothers, I face death **every day!**
16. 8 I will stay here in Ephesus until the **day** of Pentecost.
2 Cor 3.14 and to this very **day** their minds are covered with the same
4.16 decaying, yet our spiritual being is renewed **day after day.**
6. 2 when the **day** arrived for me to save you I helped you."
6. 2 today is the **day** to be saved!
11.28 not to mention other things, **every day** I am under the
Gal 4.10 You pay special attention to certain **days,** months, seasons,
Eph 4.26 anger lead you into sin, and do not stay angry all **day.**
5.16 of every opportunity you have, because these are evil **days.**
6.13 Then when the evil **day** comes, you will be able to resist
Phil 1. 5 the work of the gospel from the very first **day** until now.
4.15 left Macedonia in the early **days** of preaching the Good News,
Col 1. 6 among you ever since the **day** you first heard about the grace
2.16 or drink or about holy **days** or the New Moon Festival or
1 Thes 2. 9 We worked **day and night** so that we would not be any
3.10 **Day and night** we ask him with all our heart to let
4.15 who are alive on the **day** the Lord comes will not go
5. 5 are people who belong to the light, who belong to the **day.**
5. 8 But we belong to the **day,** and we should be sober.
2 Thes 3. 8 we kept working **day and night** so as not to be an
1 Tim 5. 5 continues to pray and ask him for his help **night and day.**
2 Tim 1. 3 him as I remember you always in my prayers **night and day.**
3. 1 Remember that there will be difficult times in the last **days.**
Heb 1. 2 but in these last **days** he has spoken to us through
3. 8 as they were that **day** in the desert when they put
3.13 you must help one another **every day,** as long as the word
4. 4 For somewhere in the Scriptures this is said about the seventh **day:**
4. 4 "God rested on the seventh **day** from all his work."
4. 7 fact that God sets another **day,** which is called "Today."
4. 8 God would not have spoken later about another **day.**
4. 9 God's people a rest like God's resting on the seventh **day.**
7.27 not need to offer sacrifices **every day** for his own sins
8. 8 when he says, "The **days** are coming, says the Lord, when
8. 9 with their ancestors on the **day** I took them by the hand
8.10 the people of Israel in the **days** to come, says the Lord:
9. 6 go into the outer Tent **every day** to perform their duties,
10.11 Jewish priest performs his services **every day** and offers the same
10.16 will make with them in the **days** to come, says the Lord:
10.32 In those **days,** after God's light had shone on you, you
11.30 after the Israelites had marched round them for seven **days.**
Jas 5. 3 You have piled up riches in these last **days.**
5. 5 You have made yourselves fat for the **day** of slaughter.
5. 8 your hopes high, for the **day** of the Lord's coming is near.
1 Pet 1.20 and was revealed in these last **days** for your sake.
3.20 waited patiently during the **days** that Noah was building his boat.
2 Pet 2. 8 lived among them, and **day after day** he suffered agony as he
3. 3 understand that in these last **days** some people will appear whose
3. 7 are being kept for the **day** when godless people will be
3. 8 in the Lord's sight between one **day** and a thousand years;
Jude 18 "When the last **days** come, people will appear who will
Rev 1.10 On the Lord's **day** the Spirit took control of me, and I
2.10 thrown into prison, and your troubles will last ten **days.**
4. 8 **Day and night** they never stop singing:
6. 6 litre of wheat for a **day's** wages,
6. 6 and three litres of barley for a **day's** wages.
6.17 The terrible **day** of their anger is here, and who can
7.15 God's throne and serve him **day and night** in his temple.
8.12 during a third of the **day** and a third of the night.
9.15 very hour of this very **day** of this very month and year
11. 3 and they will proclaim God's message during those 1,260 **days."**
11. 9 for three and a half **days** and will not allow them to
11.11 After three and a half **days** a life-giving breath came
12. 6 for her, where she will be taken care of for 1,260 **days.**
12.10 and accused our brothers **day and night** has been thrown out
14.11 There is no relief **day** or night for those who worship the
18. 8 Because of this, in one **day** she will be struck with
20.10 and they will be tormented **day and night** for ever and ever.
21.25 The gates of the city will stand open all **day;**

DAY OF JUDGEMENT

[JUDGEMENT DAY]

Mt 7.22 When **Judgement Day** comes, many will say to me, 'Lord,
10.15 assure you that on the **Judgement Day** God will show more
11.22 assure you that on the **Judgement Day** God will show more
11.24 be sure that on the **Judgement Day** God will show more mercy
12.36 can be sure that on **Judgement Day** everyone will have to give
12.41 On **Judgement Day** the people of Nineveh will stand up and
12.42 On **Judgement Day** the Queen of Sheba will stand up and
Lk 10.12 I assure you that on **Judgement Day** God will show more
10.14 will show more mercy on **Judgement Day** to Tyre and Sidon than
11.31 On **Judgement Day** the Queen of Sheba will stand up and
11.32 On **Judgement Day** the people of Nineveh will stand up and
Acts 24.25 and the coming **Day of Judgement,** Felix was afraid and said,
2 Pet 2. 4 kept chained in darkness, waiting for the **Day of Judgement.**
2. 9 under punishment for the **Day of Judgement,** [10] especially those
1 Jn 4.17 in us in order that we may have courage on **Judgement Day;**

DAY OF PREPARATION see PREPARATION DAY

DAY OF THE LORD

Is 13. 6 The **day of the Lord** is near, the day when the Almighty
13. 9 The **day of the Lord** is coming—that cruel day of his
Ezek 13. 5 cannot be defended when war comes on the **day of the Lord.**
Joel 1.15 The **day of the Lord** is near;
2. 1 The **day of the Lord** is coming soon.
2.11 How terrible is the **day of the Lord!**
2.31 blood before the great and terrible **day of the Lord** comes.
3.14 It is there that the **day of the Lord** will soon come.
Amos 5.18 will be for you who long for the **day of the Lord!**
5.20 The **day of the Lord** will bring darkness and not light;
Zeph 1.14 The great **day of the Lord** is near—very near and coming
Mal 4. 5 the great and terrible **day of the Lord** comes, I will send
Lk 21.34 of this life, or that **Day** may suddenly catch you [35] like a
Acts 2.20 blood, before the great and glorious **Day of the Lord** comes.
Rom 2. 5 punishment even greater on the **Day** when God's anger and righteous
2.16 it will be on that **Day** when God through Jesus Christ will
1 Cor 1. 8 you will be faultless on the **Day of our Lord** Jesus Christ.
3.13 work will be seen when the **Day of Christ** exposes it.
3.13 For on that **Day** fire will reveal everyone's work;
5. 5 that his spirit may be saved in the **Day of the Lord.**
2 Cor 1.13 so that in the **Day of our Lord** Jesus you can be
Eph 4.30 a guarantee that the **Day** will come when God will set
Phil 1. 6 it on until it is finished on the **Day of Christ** Jesus.
1.10 be free from all impurity and blame on the **Day of Christ.**
2.16 of you on the **Day of Christ,** because it will show that
1 Thes 5. 2 very well that the **Day of the Lord** will come as a
5. 4 in the darkness, and the **Day** should not take you by surprise
2 Thes 1.10 when he comes on that **Day** to receive glory from all his
2. 2 upset by the claim that the **Day of the Lord** has come.
2. 3 For the **Day** will not come until the final Rebellion takes
1 Tim 6.14 keep them faithfully until the **Day** when our Lord Jesus Christ
2 Tim 1.12 to keep safe until that **Day** what he has entrusted to me.
1.18 May the Lord grant him his mercy on that **Day!**
4. 8 will give me on that **Day**—and not only to me, but
Tit 2.13 we wait for the blessed **Day** we hope for, when the glory
Heb 10.25 since you see that the **Day of the Lord** is coming nearer.
1 Pet 1. 7 glory and honour on the **Day** when Jesus Christ is revealed.
2.12 good deeds and so praise God on the **Day** of his coming.
2 Pet 1.19 a dark place until the **Day** dawns and the light of the
3.10 But the **Day of the Lord** will come like a thief.
3.10 On that **Day** the heavens will disappear with a shrill noise,
3.12 you wait for the **Day of God** and do your best to
3.12 make it come soon—the **Day** when the heavens will burn up
3.14 as you wait for that **Day,** do your best to be pure
1 Jn 2.28 need not hide in shame from him on the **Day** he comes.
Jude 6 them for that great **Day** on which they will be condemned.
Rev 16.14 together for the battle on the great **Day of Almighty God.**

DAY-DREAMING see DREAM

DAY-TIME see DAY

DAYBREAK

Gen 32.24 Then a man came and wrestled with him until just before **daybreak.**
Ex 14.27 over the sea, and at **daybreak** the water returned to its
Josh 6.15 day they got up at **daybreak** and marched seven times round
Judg 16. 2 "We'll wait until **daybreak,** and then we'll kill him."
2 Sam 17.22 the Jordan, and by **daybreak** they had all gone across.
Lk 4.42 At **daybreak** Jesus left the town and went off to a lonely

DAYLIGHT

Gen 29. 7 "Since it is still broad **daylight** and not yet time to bring
32.26 **daylight** is coming."
Num 25. 4 me, execute them in broad **daylight,** and then I will no
Deut 28.29 will grope about in broad **daylight** like a blind man, and you
Judg 19.26 She was still there when **daylight** came.
2 Sam 12.11 and he will have intercourse with them in broad **daylight.**
12.12 this happen in broad **daylight** for all Israel to see.' "
Job 17.12 But my friends say night is **daylight;**
38.14 **Daylight** makes the hills and valleys stand out like the
Ps 91. 6 that strike in the dark or the evils that kill in **daylight.**
Prov 4.18 getting brighter and brighter until **daylight** has come.
31.15 She gets up before **daylight** to prepare food for her
Jer 15. 9 Her **daylight** has turned to darkness;
Ezek 12. 4 While it is still **daylight,** pack your bundle for exile, so
Amos 5. 8 He turns darkness into **daylight,** and day into night.
Zech 14. 7 There will always be **daylight,** even at night-time.
Mt 10.27 you must repeat in broad **daylight,** and what you have heard
Mk 1.35 the next morning, long before **daylight,** Jesus got up and left
Lk 12. 3 will be heard in broad **daylight,** and whatever you have whispered
Jn 11. 9 So whoever walks in broad **daylight** does not stumble, for he
Acts 27.29 anchors from the back of the ship and prayed for **daylight.**
2 Pet 2.13 to do anything in broad **daylight** that will satisfy their bodily

DAZZLING

Ex 16. 7 you will see the **dazzling** light of the Lord's presence.
16.10 the desert, and suddenly the **dazzling** light of the Lord
24.16 The **dazzling** light of the Lord's presence came down on the mountain.
29.43 people of Israel, and the **dazzling** light of my presence will
33.18 "Please, let me see the **dazzling** light of your presence."
33.22 When the **dazzling** light of my presence passes by, I will
40.34 covered the Tent and the **dazzling** light of the Lord's
Lev 9. 6 all this, so that the **dazzling** light of his presence can
9.23 blessed the people, and the **dazzling** light of the Lord's
Num 14.10 suddenly the people saw the **dazzling** light of the Lord's
14.22 They have seen the **dazzling** light of my presence and the
16.19 Suddenly the **dazzling** light of the Lord's presence appeared
16.42 covering it and that the **dazzling** light of the Lord's
20. 6 to the ground, and the **dazzling** light of the Lord's presence
1 Kgs 8.11 shining with the **dazzling** light of the Lord's presence,
2 Chr 5.11 shining with the **dazzling** light of the Lord's presence,
7. 1 had been offered, and the **dazzling** light of the Lord's
7. 2 Temple was full of the **dazzling** light, the priests could not
Job 37.21 light in the sky is **dazzling,** too bright for us to look
Song 6.10 beautiful and bright, as **dazzling** as the sun or the moon.
Ezek 1.22 something that looked like a dome made of **dazzling** crystal.
1.28 This was the **dazzling** light that shows the presence of the Lord.
8. 4 There I saw the **dazzling** light that shows the presence of
9. 3 Then the **dazzling** light of the presence of the God of
10. 4 The **dazzling** light of the Lord's presence rose up from the
10.18 Then the **dazzling** light of the Lord's presence left the
10.19 gate of the Temple, and the **dazzling** light was over them.
11.22 The **dazzling** light of the presence of the God of Israel was
11.23 Then the **dazzling** light left the city and moved to the
16.13 Your beauty was **dazzling,** and you became a queen.
43. 2 coming from the east the **dazzling** light of the presence of
43. 2 of the sea, and the earth shone with the **dazzling** light.
43. 4 The **dazzling** light passed through the east gate and went
44. 4 the Lord was filled with the **dazzling** light of his presence.
Mt 17. 2 shining like the sun, and his clothes were **dazzling** white.
Lk 9.29 changed its appearance, and his clothes became **dazzling** white.
2 Thes 2. 8 breath from his mouth and destroy him with his **dazzling** presence.

AV DEACON see HELPER (1)

DEAD

Gen 42.13 One brother is **dead,** and the youngest is now with our father."
42.32 One brother is **dead,** and the youngest is still in Canaan
42.38 his brother is **dead,** and he is the only one left.
44.20 The boy's brother is **dead,** and he is the only one of
Ex 4.19 to Egypt, for all those who wanted to kill you are **dead."**
8.15 saw that the frogs were **dead,** he became stubborn again and,
12.30 was not one home in which there was not a **dead** son.
12.33 they said, "We will all be **dead** if you don't leave."
14.30 and the Israelites saw them lying **dead** on the seashore.
21.34 pay the money to the owner and may keep the **dead** animal.
21.35 they shall also divide up the meat from the **dead** animal.
21.36 other man a live bull, but he may keep the **dead** animal.
Lev 5. 2 ritually unclean, such as a **dead** animal, he is unclean and
11. 8 Do not eat these animals or even touch their **dead** bodies;
11.11 You must not eat them or even touch their **dead** bodies.
11.24 Whoever touches the **dead** bodies of the following
11.24 Whoever carries their **dead** bodies must wash his clothes,
11.31 Whoever touches them or their **dead** bodies will be unclean
11.32 And if their **dead** bodies fall on anything, it will be unclean.
11.35 Anything on which the **dead** bodies fall is unclean;
Lev 11.36 anything else that touches their **dead** bodies is unclean.
11.40 anyone who carries the **dead** body must wash his clothes, but
19.28 yourselves or cut gashes in your body to mourn for the **dead.**
19.31 go for advice to people who consult the spirits of the **dead.**
20. 6 consult the spirits of the **dead,** I will turn against him and
20.27 consults the spirits of the **dead** shall be stoned to death;
21.11 house where there is a **dead** person, even if it is his
26.30 and throw your **dead** bodies on your fallen idols.
Num 12.12 like something born **dead** with half its flesh eaten away."
16.48 and he was left standing between the living and the **dead.**
17.13 the Tent must die, then we are all as good as **dead!"**
19.18 had touched the human bone or the **dead** body or the grave.
32.13 that whole generation that had displeased him was **dead.**
35.12 will be safe from the **dead** man's relative who seeks revenge.
35.19 The **dead** man's nearest relative has the responsibility
35.21 The **dead** man's nearest relative has the responsibility for
35.24 in favour of the **dead** man's relative who is seeking revenge.
35.25 guilty of manslaughter from the **dead** man's relative, and
35.27 has escaped [27] and if the **dead** man's relative finds him and
Deut 14. 1 when you mourn for the **dead,** don't gash yourselves or shave
14. 8 eat any of these animals or even touch their **dead** bodies.
18.11 or charms, and don't let them consult the spirits of the **dead.**
21.23 the same day, because a **dead** body hanging on a post brings
25. 5 it is the duty of the **dead** man's brother to marry her.
25. 6 considered the son of the **dead** man, so that his family line
25. 7 But if the **dead** man's brother does not want to marry her,
26.14 have not given any of it as an offering for the **dead.**
31.27 my lifetime, and they will rebel even more after I am **dead.**
Josh 1. 2 He said, "My servant Moses is **dead.**
Judg 3.25 And there was their master, lying **dead** on the floor.
4.22 Sisera on the ground, **dead,** with the tent-peg through his head.
5.27 he fell to the ground, **dead.**
9.55 When the Israelites saw that Abimelech was **dead,**
14. 8 find a swarm of bees and some honey inside the **dead** body.
14. 9 he had taken the honey from the **dead** body of a lion.
Ruth 2.20 "The Lord always keeps his promises to the living and the **dead."**
4. 5 so that the field will stay in the **dead** man's family."
4.10 keep the property in the **dead** man's family, and his family
1 Sam 4.19 father-in-law and her husband were **dead,** she suddenly went
14.44 him, "May God strike me **dead** if you are not put to
17.51 When the Philistines saw that their hero was **dead,** they ran
18.25 of a hundred **dead** Philistines, as revenge on his enemies."
19.11 "If you don't get away tonight, tomorrow you will be **dead."**
20.13 may the Lord strike me **dead** if I don't let you know
24.14 A **dead** dog, a flea!
25.22 May God strike me **dead** if I don't kill every last one
25.34 me, all of Nabal's men would have been **dead** by morning!"
31. 5 man saw that Saul was **dead,** so he too threw himself on
2 Sam 1. 5 "How do you know that Saul and Jonathan are **dead?"**
1.19 "On the hills of Israel our leaders are **dead!**
1.25 Jonathan lies **dead** in the hills.
2. 7 Saul your king is **dead,** and the people of Judah have
2.16 so that all twenty-four of them fell down **dead** together.
2.23 Asahel dropped to the ground **dead,** and everyone who came to
3. 9 Now may God strike me **dead** if I don't make this come
3.35 promise, "May God strike me **dead** if I eat anything before
9. 8 again and said, "I am no better than a **dead** dog, sir!
12.18 How can we tell him that his child is **dead?**
12.19 So he asked them, "Is the child **dead?"**
12.23 But now that he is **dead,** why should I fast?
13.32 Only Amnon is **dead.**
13.33 So don't believe the news that all your sons are **dead;**
14. 5 "My husband is **dead.**
14.14 God does not bring the **dead** back to life, but the king
18.20 may do so, but not today, for the king's son is **dead."**
19. 6 happy if Absalom were alive today and all of us were **dead.**
19.13 May God strike me **dead** if I don't!"
23.10 to where Eleazar was and stripped the armour from the **dead.**
1 Kgs 1. 5 Now that Absalom was **dead,** Adonijah, the son of David
1.21 as soon as you are **dead** my son Solomon and I will
2.23 name, "May God strike me **dead** if I don't make Adonijah pay
3.20 then she put the **dead** child in my bed.
3.21 was going to feed my baby, I saw that it was **dead.**
3.22 The living child is mine, and the **dead** one is yours!"
3.22 The **dead** child is yours, and the living one is mine!"
3.23 is hers and that the **dead** child belongs to the other one."
11.15 the commander of his army had gone there to bury the **dead.**
11.21 commander of the army was **dead,** Hadad said to the king,
19. 2 "May the gods strike me **dead** if by this time tomorrow
19. 4 I might as well be **dead!"**
20.10 May the gods strike me **dead** if I don't!"
21.15 Jezebel received the message, she said to Ahab, "Naboth is **dead.**
2 Kgs 4.32 into the room and saw the boy lying **dead** on the bed.
6.31 exclaimed, "May God strike me **dead** if Elisha is not beheaded
8. 5 how Elisha had brought a **dead** person back to life,
9.24 Joram fell **dead** in his chariot,
19.35 At dawn the next day, there they lay, all **dead!**
1 Chr 10. 5 man saw that Saul was **dead,** so he too threw himself on
10.13 the spirits of the **dead** [14] instead of consulting the Lord.
2 Chr 20.24 enemy and saw that they were all lying on the ground, **dead.**
24.17 But once Jehoiada was **dead,** the leaders of Judah
Job 3.22 They are not happy till they are **dead** and buried;
26. 5 The spirits of the **dead** tremble in the waters under the earth.
39.30 Around **dead** bodies the eagles gather, and the young
Ps 22.15 You have left me for **dead** in the dust.
30. 9 Are **dead** people able to praise you?
31.12 Everyone has forgotten me, as though I were **dead;**
58. 8 they be like a baby born **dead** that never sees the light.
76. 6 O God of Jacob, the horses and their riders fell **dead.**
79. 3 through Jerusalem, and no one was left to bury the **dead.**
88. 5 I am abandoned among the **dead;**

Ps 88.10 Do you perform miracles for the **dead?**
91. 7 A thousand may fall **dead** beside you, ten thousand all round you,
115.17 is not praised by the **dead,** by any who go down to
Prov 1.12 find them, but they'll be **dead** when we're through with them!
27.22 a fool until he's half **dead,** you still can't beat his
Ecc 4. 2 I envy those who are **dead** and gone;
6. 3 burial, then I say that a baby born **dead** is better off.
9. 4 a live dog is better off than a **dead** lion.
9. 5 know they are going to die, but the **dead** know nothing.
10. 1 **Dead** flies can make a whole bottle of perfume stink, and a
11. 8 long you live, remember that you will be **dead** much longer.
Is 8.19 the spirits and consult the **dead** on behalf of the living."
14.16 "The **dead** will stare and gape at you.
19. 3 consult mediums and ask the spirits of the **dead** for advice.
22.13 Tomorrow we'll be **dead."**
26.14 Now they are **dead** and will not live again;
26.19 so the Lord will revive those who have long been **dead.**
37.36 At dawn the next day there they lay, all **dead!**
38.18 The **dead** cannot trust in your faithfulness.
50. 3 sky turn dark, as if it were in mourning for the **dead."**
65. 4 go to caves and tombs to consult the spirits of the **dead.**
66.24 leave, they will see the **dead** bodies of those who have
Jer 7.28 Faithfulness is **dead.**
9.22 **Dead** bodies are scattered everywhere, like piles of manure
19.11 People will bury their **dead** even in Topheth because there
27. 9 or by calling up the spirits of the **dead** or by magic.
31.40 The entire valley, where the **dead** are buried and refuse is thrown,
34. 5 They will mourn over you and say, 'Our king is **dead!'**
Lam 2.21 Young and old alike lie **dead** in the streets, Young men
Ezek 11.13 While I was prophesying, Pelatiah dropped **dead.**
26.20 world among eternal ruins, keeping company with the **dead.**
32.24 In life they spread terror, but now they lie **dead** and disgraced.
32.25 terror, but now they lie **dead** and disgraced, sharing the
37. 9 direction, to breathe into these **dead** bodies, and to bring
39. 4 and his allies will fall **dead** on the mountains of Israel,
39. 5 They will fall **dead** in the open field.
Joel 2.20 Their **dead** bodies will stink.
Amos 4.10 your nostrils with the stink of **dead** bodies in your camps.
5.16 be called to mourn the **dead** along with those who are paid
6.10 The **dead** man's relative, the one in charge of the funeral,
8. 3 There will be **dead** bodies everywhere.
Jon 4. 3 I am better off **dead** than alive."
4. 8 So he wished he were **dead.**
4. 8 "I am better off **dead** than alive," he said.
Mic 4. 9 Is it because you have no king, and your counsellors are **dead?**
Nah 3. 3 Corpses are piled high, **dead** bodies without number— men
3.18 of Assyria, your governors are **dead,** and your noblemen are
Zeph 1.11 part of the city, because all the merchants will be **dead!**
1.17 out like water, and their **dead** bodies will lie rotting on
Hag 2.13 "Suppose a man is defiled because he has touched a **dead** body.
Mt 2.18 she refuses to be comforted, for they are **dead."**
2.20 because those who tried to kill the child are **dead."**
8.22 "Follow me," Jesus answered, "and let the **dead** bury their own dead."
9.24 The little girl is not **dead**—she is only sleeping!"
10. 8 Heal the sick, bring the **dead** back to life, heal those who
11. 5 the deaf hear, the **dead** are brought back to life,
22.24 have children who will be considered the **dead** man's children.
22.28 on the day when the **dead** rise to life, whose wife will
22.30 For when the **dead** rise to life, they will be like the
22.31 Now, as for the **dead** rising to life:
22.32 He is the God of the living, not of the **dead."**
24.28 "Wherever there is a **dead** body, the vultures will gather.
28. 4 were so afraid that they trembled and became like **dead** men.
Mk 5.39 The child is not **dead**—she is only sleeping!"
9.26 The boy looked like a corpse, and everyone said, "He is **dead!"**
11.20 It was **dead** all the way down to its roots.
12.19 have children who will be considered the **dead** man's children.'
12.23 Now, when all the **dead** rise to life on the day of
12.25 For when the **dead** rise to life, they will be like the
12.26 Now, as for the **dead** being raised:
12.27 He is the God of the living, not of the **dead.**
15.44 Pilate was surprised to hear that Jesus was already **dead.**
15.44 officer and asked him if Jesus had been **dead** a long time.
Lk 7.12 The **dead** man was the only son of a woman who was
7.15 The **dead** man sat up and began to talk, and Jesus gave
7.22 the deaf can hear, the **dead** are raised to life, and the
8.52 the child is not **dead**—she is only sleeping!"
8.53 They all laughed at him, because they knew that she was **dead.**
9.60 Jesus answered, "Let the **dead** bury their own dead.
10.30 him, stripped him, and beat him up, leaving him half **dead.**
15.24 For this son of mine was **dead,** but now he is alive;
15.32 happy, because your brother was **dead,** but now he is alive;
17.37 "Wherever there is a **dead** body, the vultures will gather."
20.28 have children who will be considered the **dead** man's children.'
20.33 on the day when the **dead** rise to life, whose wife will
20.37 And Moses clearly proves that the **dead** are raised to life.
20.38 the living, not of the **dead,** for to him all are alive."
24. 5 "Why are you looking among the **dead** for one who is alive?
Jn 5.21 as the Father raises the **dead** and gives them life, in the
5.25 has already come—when the **dead** will hear the voice of the
5.28 is coming when all the **dead** will hear his voice [29] and come
11.14 told them plainly, "Lazarus is **dead,** [15] but for your sake
11.39 the **dead** man's sister, answered, "There will be a bad smell,
19.33 saw that he was already **dead,** so they did not break his
Acts 2.27 because you will not abandon me in the world of the **dead;**
2.31 he said, 'He was not abandoned in the world of the **dead;**
4. 2 from death, which proved that the **dead** will rise to life.
5. 5 As soon as Ananias heard this, he fell down **dead;**
5.10 and saw that she was **dead,** so they carried her out
10.42 one whom God has appointed judge of the living and the **dead.**
Acts 14.19 and dragged him out of the town, thinking that he was **dead.**
20. 9 When they picked him up, he was **dead.**
23. 6 the hope I have that the **dead** will rise to life!"
24.21 you today for believing that the **dead** will rise to life.'"
26. 8 find it impossible to believe that God raises the **dead?**
28. 6 were waiting for him to swell up or suddenly fall down **dead.**
Rom 4.17 the God who brings the **dead** to life and whose command brings
4.19 body, which was already practically **dead,** or of the fact that
6.11 to think of yourselves as **dead,** so far as sin is concerned,
7. 8 Apart from law, sin is a **dead** thing.
11.15 It will be life for the **dead!**
14. 9 order to be the Lord of the living and of the **dead.**
1 Cor 10. 5 and so their **dead** bodies were scattered over the desert.
10. 8 and in one day twenty-three thousand of them fell **dead.**
15.12 of you say that the **dead** will not be raised to life?
15.15 it is true that the **dead** are not raised to life, then
15.16 For if the **dead** are not raised, neither has Christ been raised.
15.29 Now, what about those people who are baptized for the **dead?**
15.29 as some claim, that the **dead** are not raised to life,
15.29 why are those people being baptized for the **dead?**
15.32 But if the **dead** are not raised to life, then,
15.35 Someone will ask, "How can the **dead** be raised to life?
15.42 is how it will be when the **dead** are raised to life.
15.51 when the trumpet sounds, the **dead** will be raised, never to
2 Cor 1. 9 not on ourselves, but only on God, who raises the **dead.**
6. 9 as though we were **dead,** but, as you see, we live on.
Gal 2.19 is concerned, however, I am **dead**—killed by the Law itself—
6.14 world is dead to me, and I am **dead** to the world.
Eph 2. 1 you were spiritually **dead** because of your disobedience and sins.
2. 5 while we were spiritually **dead** in our disobedience he brought us
Col 2.13 were at one time spiritually **dead** because of your sins
1 Thes 5.10 with him, whether we are alive or **dead** when he comes.
1 Tim 4. 2 deceitful liars, whose consciences are **dead,** as if burnt with
2 Tim 4. 1 judge the living and the **dead,** and because he is coming to
Heb 3.17 With the people who sinned, who fell down **dead** in the desert.
6. 2 of the resurrection of the **dead** and the eternal judgement.
11. 4 of his faith Abel still speaks, even though he is **dead.**
11.12 Though Abraham was practically **dead,** from this one man came
11.35 Through faith women received their **dead** relatives raised back to
Jas 2.17 if it is alone and includes no actions, then it is **dead.**
2.26 body without the spirit is **dead,**
2.26 so also faith without actions is **dead.**
1 Pet 4. 5 to God, who is ready to judge the living and the **dead.**
4. 6 was preached also to the **dead,** to those who had been judged
Jude 12 have been pulled up by the roots and are completely **dead.**
Rev 1.17 saw him, I fell down at his feet like a **dead** man.
1.18 I was **dead,** but now I am alive for ever and ever.
1.18 I have authority over death and the world of the **dead.**
3. 1 the reputation of being alive, even though you are **dead!**
11.18 your anger has come, the time for the **dead** to be judged.
16. 3 like the blood of a **dead** person, and every living creature
20. 5 (The rest of the **dead** did not come to life until the
20. 5 This is the first raising of the **dead.**
20. 6 those who are included in this first raising of the **dead.**
20.12 And I saw the **dead,** great and small alike, standing before
20.12 The **dead** were judged according to what they had done,
20.13 Then the sea gave up its **dead.**
20.13 the world of the dead also gave up the **dead** they held.
20.14 and the world of the **dead** were thrown into the lake of

DEAD SEA

Inland sea in s. Palestine.

Gen 14. 3 forces in the Valley of Siddim, which is now the **Dead Sea.**
Num 34. 3 begin on the east at the southern end of the **Dead Sea.**
34.12 then south along the River Jordan to the **Dead Sea.**
Deut 2. 8 Elath and Eziongeber to the **Dead Sea,** and we turned
3.17 the north down to the **Dead Sea** in the south and to
4.49 as far south as the **Dead Sea** and east to the foot
Josh 3.16 The flow downstream to the **Dead Sea** was completely cut off,
12. 3 Beth Jeshimoth (east of the **Dead Sea)** and on towards the
15. 2 the south end of the **Dead Sea,** [3] went southwards from the
15. 5 The eastern border was the **Dead Sea,** all the way up to
18.19 the northern inlet on the **Dead Sea,** where the River Jordan
2 Kgs 14.25 Hamath Pass in the north to the **Dead Sea** in the south.
2 Chr 20. 2 come from the other side of the **Dead Sea** to attack you.
Is 16. 8 the desert, and westwards to the other side of the **Dead Sea.**
Jer 48.32 whose branches reach across the **Dead Sea** and go as far as
Ezek 39.11 in Israel, in Travellers' Valley, east of the **Dead Sea.**
47. 8 east and down into the Jordan Valley and to the **Dead Sea.**
47. 8 When it flows into the **Dead Sea,** it replaces the salt water
47. 9 make the water of the **Dead Sea** fresh, and wherever it flows,
47.18 Gilead on the east, as far as Tamar on the **Dead Sea.**
Joel 2.20 will be driven into the **Dead Sea,** their rear ranks into the
Amos 8.12 People will wander from the **Dead Sea** to the
Zech 14. 8 half of it to the **Dead Sea** and the other half to

DEADLY

2 Sam 1.22 Jonathan's bow was **deadly,** the sword of Saul was merciless,
Job 18.13 A **deadly** disease spreads over his body and causes his
20.16 it kills him like the bite of a **deadly** snake.
Ps 5. 9 Their words are flattering and smooth, but full of **deadly** deceit.
7.13 he takes up his **deadly** weapons and aims his burning arrows.
17. 9 **Deadly** enemies surround me;
40. 2 me out of a dangerous pit, out of the **deadly** quicksand.
91. 3 safe from all hidden dangers and from all **deadly** diseases.
140. 3 Their tongues are like **deadly** snakes;
Prov 23.27 Prostitutes and immoral women are a **deadly** trap.
25.18 A false accusation is as **deadly** as a sword, a club, or
26.18 only joking is like a madman playing with a **deadly** weapon.

Is 27. 1 and **deadly** sword to punish Leviathan, that wriggling,
59. 5 plots you make are as **deadly** as the eggs of a poisonous
Jer 9. 8 Their tongues are like **deadly** arrows;
Nah 3. 4 Attractive and full of **deadly** charms, she enchanted nations
Rom 3.13 Their words are full of **deadly** deceit;
2 Cor 2.16 those who are being lost, it is a **deadly** stench that kills;
Jas 3. 8 It is evil and uncontrollable, full of **deadly** poison.

DEAF

Ex 4.11 Who makes him **deaf** or dumb?
Lev 19.14 Do not curse a **deaf** man or put something in front of
Neh 9.30 speak, but your people were **deaf**, so you let them be
Ps 38.13 I am like a **deaf** man and cannot hear, like a dumb
58. 4 up their ears like a **deaf** cobra, [5]which does not hear the
Ecc 12. 4 Your ears will be **deaf** to the noise of the street.
Is 6.10 these people dull, their ears **deaf**, and their eyes blind, so
29.18 When that day comes, the **deaf** will be able to hear a
35. 5 The blind will be able to see, and the **deaf** will hear.
42.18 "Listen, you **deaf** people!
42.19 blind than my servant, more **deaf** than the messenger I send?
43. 8 they have ears, but they are **deaf!**
59. 1 to save you or too **deaf** to hear your call for help!
Mt 11. 5 skin-diseases are made clean, the **deaf** hear, the dead are brought
Mk 7.32 him a man who was **deaf** and could hardly speak, and they
7.37 "He even causes the **deaf** to hear and the dumb to speak!"
9.25 "**Deaf** and dumb spirit," he said, "I order you to come out
Lk 7.22 made clean, the **deaf** can hear, the dead are raised
Acts 7.51 "How heathen your hearts, how **deaf** you are to God's message!
Rom 11. 7 the rest grew **deaf** to God's call.

DEAL (1)

Lev 25.14 fellow-Israelite or buy land from him, do not **deal** unfairly.
Ecc 5.14 it all in some unlucky **deal** and end up with nothing left
Ezek 28. 5 You made clever business **deals** and kept on making profits.
Acts 16.14 Lydia from Thyatira, who was a **dealer** in purple cloth.
1 Cor 7.31 those who **deal** in material goods, as though they were not

DEAL (2)

Deut 20.15 is how you are to **deal** with those cities that are far
Judg 18. 7 the Sidonians and had no **dealings** with any other people.
18.27 from Sidon, and they had no **dealings** with any other people.
1 Kgs 8.39 **Deal** with each person as he deserves, [40]so that your
2 Chr 6.30 **Deal** with each person as he deserves, [31]so that your
9.29 Iddo the Prophet, which also **deal** with the reign of King
13.17 Abijah and his army **dealt** the Israelites a crushing
Neh 5. 7 a public assembly to **deal** with the problem [8]and said,
Job 37.23 he is righteous and just in his **dealings** with men.
Ps 101. 4 I will not be dishonest, and will have no **dealings** with evil.
Jer 10.15 they will be destroyed when the Lord comes to **deal** with them.
18.20 their behalf, so that you would not **deal** with them in anger.
18.23 down in defeat and **deal** with them while you are angry."
32. 5 Babylonia, and he will remain there until I **deal** with him.
51.18 they will be destroyed when the Lord comes to **deal** with them.
51.47 the time is coming when I will **deal** with Babylonia's idols.
51.52 is coming when I will **deal** with Babylon's idols, and the
Ezek 20.44 Lord, because I do not **deal** with you as your wicked, evil
23.25 with you, I will let them **deal** with you in their anger.
Rom 3.25 in the present time he **deals** with their sins, in order to
1 Cor 7. 1 Now, to **deal** with the matters you wrote about.
2 Cor 10. 2 I am sure I can **deal** harshly with those who say that
13. 3 When he **deals** with you, he is not weak;
13.10 I will not have to **deal** harshly with you in using the
1 Tim 1.16 his full patience in **dealing** with me, the worst of sinners,
Heb 9.28 a second time, not to **deal** with sin, but to save those

DEAR

1 Sam 25. 8 can to us your servants and to your **dear** friend David."
2 Sam 1.23 "Saul and Jonathan, so wonderful and **dear;**
1.26 how **dear** you were to me!
Ps 78.68 the tribe of Judah and Mount Zion, which he **dearly** loves.
148.14 people praise him— the people of Israel, so **dear** to him.
Prov 31. 2 "You are my own **dear** son, the answer to my prayers.
Song 1.16 How handsome you are, my **dearest;**
2. 3 of the forest, so is my **dearest** compared with other men.
Jer 31.20 "Israel, you are my **dearest** son, the child I love best.
Hos 9.16 if they did, I would kill the children so **dear** to them."
Mt 3.17 "This is my own **dear** Son, with whom I am pleased."
17. 5 said, "This is my own **dear** Son, with whom I am pleased
Mk 1.11 And a voice came from heaven, "You are my own **dear** Son.
9. 7 from the cloud, "This is my own **dear** Son—listen to him!"
12. 6 The only one left to send was the man's own **dear** son.
Lk 1. 1 **Dear** Theophilus:
3.22 And a voice came from heaven, "You are my own **dear** Son.
7. 2 Roman officer there had a servant who was very **dear** to him;
20.13 I will send my own **dear** son;
Jn 11. 3 "Lord, your **dear** friend is ill."
Acts 1. 1 **Dear** Theophilus:
15.25 They will go with our **dear** friends Barnabas and Paul,
Rom 16. 5 Greetings to my **dear** friend Epaenetus, who was the first
16. 8 My greetings to Ampliatus, my **dear** friend in the fellowship
16. 9 fellow-worker in Christ's service, and to Stachys, my **dear** friend.
16.12 Lord's service, and to my **dear** friend Persis, who has done
1 Cor 4.14 feel ashamed, but to instruct you as my own **dear** children.
4.17 Timothy, who is my own **dear** and faithful son in the
10.14 So then, my **dear friends,** keep away from the worship of idols.
15.58 So then, my **dear** brothers, stand firm and steady.
2 Cor 6.11 **Dear friends** in Corinth!
7. 1 All these promises are made to us, my **dear friends.**
7. 3 said before, you are so **dear** to us that we are always
12.19 and everything we do, **dear friends,** is done to help you.
Gal 4.19 My **dear** children!
Eph 1. 6 grace, for the free gift he gave us in his **dear** Son!
5. 1 Since you are God's **dear** children, you must try to be like
6.21 Tychicus, our **dear** brother and faithful servant in the Lord's
Phil 2.12 So then, **dear friends,** as you always obeyed me when I
4. 1 So then, my brothers, how **dear** you are to me and how
4. 1 This then, **dear** brothers, is how you should stand firm in
Col 1. 7 from Epaphras, our **dear** fellow-servant, who is Christ's faithful
1.13 into the kingdom of his **dear** Son, [14]by whom we are set
4. 7 Our **dear** brother Tychicus, who is a faithful worker and
4. 9 With him goes Onesimus, that **dear** and faithful brother,
4.14 Luke, our **dear** doctor, and Demas send you their greetings.
1 Thes 2. 8 You were so **dear** to us!
2 Tim 1. 2 have in union with Christ Jesus— [2]To Timothy, my **dear** son:
Phlm 7 Your love, **dear** brother, has brought me great joy and much
16 he is a **dear** brother in Christ.
Heb 6. 9 if we speak like this, **dear friends,** we feel sure about you.
Jas 1.16 Do not be deceived, my **dear** brothers!
1.19 Remember this, my **dear** brothers!
2. 5 Listen, my **dear** brothers!
1 Pet 4.12 My **dear friends,** do not be surprised at the painful test
2 Pet 1.17 saying, "This is my own **dear** Son, with whom I am pleased!"
3. 1 My **dear friends,** this is now the second letter I have
3. 8 But do not forget one thing, my **dear friends!**
3.15 be saved, just as our **dear** brother Paul wrote to you, using
1 Jn 2. 7 My **dear friends,** this command I am writing to you is not
3. 2 My **dear friends,** we are now God's children, but it is not
3.21 And so, my **dear friends,** if our conscience does not condemn us,
4. 1 My **dear friends,** do not believe all who claim to have the
4. 7 **Dear friends,** let us love one another, because love comes from God.
4.11 **Dear friends,** if this is how God loved us, then we
2 Jn 1 the Elder— To the **dear** Lady and to her children, whom
5 And so I ask you, **dear** Lady:
13 The children of your **dear** Sister send you their greetings.
3 Jn 1 From the Elder— To my **dear** Gaius, whom I truly love.
2 My **dear friend,** I pray that everything may go well with
5 My **dear friend,** you are so faithful in the work you do
11 My **dear friend,** do not imitate what is bad, but imitate
Jude 3 My **dear friends,** I was doing my best to write to you

DEATH (1)

[SACRIFICIAL DEATH]
see also **DEATH (2) (from DEATH), DEATH (3) (to DEATH)**

Gen 9. 5 I will punish with **death** any animal that takes a human life.
23. 2 Hebron in the land of Canaan, and Abraham mourned her **death.**
25.11 After the **death** of Abraham, God blessed his son Isaac,
26.11 who ill-treats this man or his wife will be put to **death."**
26.18 which the Philistines had stopped up after Abraham's **death.**
27.41 He thought, "The time to mourn my father's **death** is near;
42. 2 go there and buy some to keep us from starving to **death."**
42.22 And now we are being paid back for his **death."**
43. 8 Then none of us will starve to **death.**
49.29 to join my people in **death,** bury me with my fathers in
50.15 After the **death** of their father, Joseph's brothers said,
Ex 8.26 them where they can see us, they will stone us **to death.**
12.23 not let the Angel of **Death** enter your houses and kill you.
16. 3 us out into this desert to starve us all **to death."**
29.29 to his sons after his **death,** for them to wear when they
Lev 7.24 that has died a natural **death** or has been killed by a
10. 6 are allowed to mourn this **death** caused by the fire which the
16. 1 spoke to Moses after the **death** of the two sons of Aaron
17.15 that has died a natural **death** or has been killed by wild
20. 9 he is responsible for his own **death.**
20.11 They are responsible for their own **death.**
20.12 They have committed incest and are responsible for their own **death.**
20.13 They are responsible for their own **death.**
20.16 They are responsible for their own **death.**
20.27 person who does this is responsible for his own **death."**
21. 4 make himself unclean at the **death** of those related to him by
22. 8 that has died a natural **death** or has been killed by wild
Num 15.31 He is responsible for his own **death.**
16.29 men die a natural **death** without some punishment from God,
18.22 Tent and in this way bring on themselves the penalty of **death.**
19.14 tent at the time of **death** or who enters it becomes ritually
19.16 or has died a natural **death** out of doors or if someone
35.24 the man who caused the **death** and not in favour of the
35.25 must live there until the **death** of the man who is then
35.28 city of refuge until the **death** of the High Priest,
35.32 in order to return home before the **death** of the High Priest.
35.33 land, and except by the **death** of the murderer there is no
Deut 5.25 But why should we risk **death** again?
14.21 "Do not eat any animal that dies a natural **death.**
22.26 girl, because she has not committed a sin worthy of **death.**
28.51 your livestock and your crops, and you will starve to **death.**
28.66 with terror, and you will live in constant fear of **death.**
30.15 you a choice between good and evil, between life and **death.**
30.19 the choice between life and **death,** between God's blessing
31.16 and after your **death** the people will become unfaithful
31.29 I know that after my **death** the people will become wicked
32.25 War will bring **death** in the streets;
Josh 1. 1 After the **death** of the Lord's servant Moses, the Lord spoke
2.19 out of the house, his **death** will be his own fault, and
20. 6 public trial and until the **death** of the man who is then
24.31 the Lord, and after his **death** they continued to do so as
Judg 1. 1 After Joshua's **death** the people of Israel asked the Lord,

Judg	2. 7	the Lord, and after his **death** they continued to do so as
	2.23	them, nor did he drive them out soon after Joshua's **death.**
	8.33	After Gideon's **death** the people of Israel were again
	10. 1	After Abimelech's **death** Tola, the son of Puah
	16.30	killed more people at his **death** than he had killed during
Ruth	1.17	upon me if I let anything but **death** separate me from you!"
1 Sam	2.33	and all your other descendants will die a violent **death.**
	4.21	Covenant Box and the **death** of her father-in-law and her husband.
	20. 3	the living Lord that I am only a step away from **death!"**
	22.22	So I am responsible for the **death** of all your relatives.
	26.10	comes to die a natural **death** or when he dies in battle.
	29. 4	win back his master's favour than by the **death** of our men?
2 Sam	1. 1	After Saul's **death** David came back from his victory
	1.23	together in life, together in **death;**
	4. 4	When the news about their **death** came from the city of Jezreel,
	4.10	told me of Saul's **death** thought he was bringing good news.
	12.10	descendants will die a violent **death** because you have disobeyed
	13.39	when he got over Amnon's **death,** he was filled with longing
	14.11	is responsible for avenging the **death** of my son
	15.21	go with you wherever you go, even if it means **death."**
	22. 5	The waves of **death** were all round me;
	22. 6	The danger of **death** was round me,
1 Kgs	2. 5	of peace in revenge for **deaths** they had caused in time of
	2. 6	you must not let him die a natural **death.**
	3.11	yourself or riches or the **death** of your enemies,
	11.40	to King Shishak of Egypt and stayed there until Solomon's **death.**
	17.12	will be our last meal, and then we will starve to **death."**
	17.18	to remind God of my sins and so cause my son's **death?"**
	22.40	At his **death** his son Ahaziah succeeded him as king.
2 Kgs	1. 1	After the **death** of King Ahab of Israel, the country of
	2.21	and it will not cause any more **deaths** or miscarriages.' "
	5. 7	think that I am God, with the power of life and **death?**
	7. 4	into the city, because we would starve to **death** in there;
	13.24	At the **death** of King Hazael of Syria his son Benhadad
	14.17	Judah lived fifteen years after the **death** of King Jehoash
	14.22	Uzziah reconquered and rebuilt Elath after his father's **death.**
	15.18	until the day of his **death** he followed the wicked example
	15.18	Nebat, who led Israel into sin till the day of his **death.**
	22.20	to bring on Jerusalem will not come until after your **death.**
1 Chr	2.19	After the **death** of Azubah, Caleb married Ephrath,
	21.12	using his angel to bring **death** throughout Israel?
	29.15	Our days are like a passing shadow, and we cannot escape **death.**
2 Chr	1.11	treasure or fame or the **death** of your enemies or even for
	16.14	burial, and they built a huge bonfire to mourn his **death.**
	22. 4	after his father's **death** other members of King Ahab's family
	26. 2	after the **death** of Amaziah that Uzziah recaptured Elath
	32.26	the Lord did not punish the people until after Hezekiah's **death.**
	32.33	of Judah and Jerusalem paid him great honour at his **death.**
	34.28	to bring on Jerusalem will not come until after your **death.**
	35.24	All the people of Judah and Jerusalem mourned his **death.**
Ezra	7.26	by **death** or by exile or by confiscation of his property or
Esth	2. 7	At the **death** of her parents, Mordecai had adopted her
Job	3.21	They wait for **death,** but it never comes;
	5. 2	To worry yourself to **death** with resentment
	11.20	Their one hope is that **death** will come.
	12.22	He sends light to places dark as **death.**
	14.20	his face is twisted in **death.**
	18.14	he lived secure, and is dragged off to face King **Death.**
	27.15	and even their widows will not mourn their **death.**
	28.22	**death** and destruction Admit they have heard only rumours.
	30.23	taking me off to my **death,** to the fate in store
	31.11	Such wickedness should be punished by **death.**
	31.28	Such a sin should be punished by **death;**
	31.30	I never sinned by praying for their **death.**
Ps	9.17	**Death** is the destiny of all the wicked,
	16.10	completely secure, [10] because you protect me from the power of **death.**
	18. 4	The danger of **death** was all round me;
	18. 5	The danger of **death** was round me, and the grave set its
	30. 9	"What will you gain from my **death?**
	38. 7	I am burning with fever and I am near to **death.**
	49.14	doomed to die like sheep, and **Death** will be their shepherd.
	49.15	he will save me from the power of **death.**
	49.19	join all his ancestors in **death,** where the darkness lasts
	55. 4	I am terrified, and the terrors of **death** crush me.
	76. 5	of all they had and now are sleeping the sleep of **death;**
	78.49	anger and fierce rage, which came as messengers of **death.**
	88. 3	many troubles have fallen on me that I am close to **death.**
	88.15	Ever since I was young, I have suffered and been near **death;**
	107.18	they couldn't stand the sight of food and were close to **death.**
	116. 3	The danger of **death** was all round me;
Prov	2.18	you go to her house, you are travelling the road to **death.**
	5. 5	the road she walks is the road to **death.**
	5.11	will lie groaning on your **deathbed,**
	7.26	of many men and caused the **death** of too many to count.
	7.27	It is a short cut to **death.**
	8.36	anyone who hates me loves **death."**
	11. 4	on the day you face **death,** but honesty can save your life.
	12.28	wickedness is the road to **death.**
	14.12	What you think is the right road may lead to **death.**
	14.27	Do you want to avoid **death?**
	15.24	upwards to life, not the road that leads downwards to **death.**
	16.25	What you think is the right road may lead to **death.**
	17.11	**Death** will come like a cruel messenger to wicked people
	17.22	It is slow **death** to be gloomy all the time.
	21. 6	but not before they lead you into the jaws of **death.**
	21.16	**Death** is waiting for anyone who wanders away from good sense.
Ecc	3. 2	birth and the time for **death,** the time for planting and the
	4. 5	a fool to fold his hands and let himself starve to **death.**
	7. 2	always remind themselves that **death** is waiting for us all.
	7. 4	A wise person thinks about **death.**
Ecc	7.26	I found something more bitter than **death**—woman.
	8. 8	keep himself from dying or put off the day of his **death.**
Song	8. 6	Love is as powerful as **death;**
	8. 6	passion is as strong as **death** itself.
Is	5.13	Your leaders will starve to **death,**
	25. 8	The Sovereign Lord will destroy **death** for ever!
	28.15	have made a treaty with **death** and reached an agreement
	28.18	treaty you have made with **death** will be abolished,
	53.10	his **death** was a sacrifice to bring forgiveness.
	57. 2	Those who live good lives find peace and rest in **death.**
	65.12	to die a violent **death,** because you did not answer
Jer	9.21	**Death** has come in through our windows
	14.18	when I go into the towns, I see people starving to **death.**
	18.21	But now, Lord, let their children starve to **death;**
	21. 8	way that leads to life and the way that leads to **death.**
	22.10	do not mourn his **death.**
	22.18	"No one will mourn his **death** or say, 'How terrible,
	31. 2	desert I showed mercy to those people who had escaped **death.**
	44.28	few of you will escape **death** and return from Egypt to Judah.
	50.35	**"Death** to Babylonia!
	50.35	**Death** to its people, to its rulers, to its men of wisdom.
	50.36	**Death** to its lying prophets— what fools they are!
	50.36	**Death** to its soldiers— how terrified they are!
	50.37	**Death** to its hired soldiers— how weak they are!
	51.49	Babylonia caused the **death** of people all over the world,
	51.49	Babylonia will fall because it caused the **death** of so many
	51.50	"You have escaped **death!**
Lam	1.20	even indoors there is **death.**
	2.19	Children starving to **death** on every street corner!
	3. 6	He has forced me to live in the stagnant darkness of **death.**
	3.54	Water began to close over me, and I thought **death** was near.
	4. 8	lie unknown in the streets, their faces blackened in **death;**
	4. 9	who starved slowly to **death,**
	4.13	priests were guilty of causing the **death** of innocent people.
Ezek	3.18	and I will hold you responsible for his **death.**
	3.20	and I will hold you responsible for his **death.**
	4.14	that died a natural **death** or was killed by wild animals.
	6.12	those who survive will starve to **death.**
	8.14	showed me women weeping over the **death** of the god Tammuz.
	13.18	the power of life and **death** over my people
	13.20	wristbands that you use in your attempt to control life and **death.**
	16.38	and in my anger and fury I will punish you with **death.**
	18.13	He will be to blame for his own **death.**
	33. 4	and kills him, then he is to blame for his own **death.**
	33. 5	His **death** is his own fault, because he paid no attention
	33. 6	but I will hold the watchman responsible for their **death.**
	33. 8	and I will hold you responsible for his **death.**
	35. 6	Lord, am the living God—**death** is your fate, and you cannot
	44.31	that dies a natural **death** or is killed by another animal."
Hos	7.16	they will die a violent **death,** and the Egyptians will laugh."
	12.14	they deserve **death** for their crimes.
	13.14	world of the dead or rescue them from the power of **death.**
	13.14	Bring on your plagues, **death!**
Joel	1. 8	a girl who mourns the **death** of the man she was going
Jon	1.14	don't punish us with **death** for taking this man's life!
Nah	1. 8	he sends to their **death** those who oppose him.
Hab	2. 5	proud and restless—like **death** itself they are never satisfied.
	3. 5	He sends disease before him and commands **death** to follow
Mt	4.16	who live in the dark land of **death** the light will shine."
	16.18	my church, and not even **death** will ever be able to overcome
	27. 4	"I have sinned by betraying an innocent man to **death!"**
	27.24	and said, "I am not responsible for the **death** of this man!
	27.25	"Let the responsibility for his **death** fall on us and our children!"
Lk	1.79	in the dark shadow of **death,** to guide our steps
	23.15	There is nothing this man has done to deserve **death.**
	23.22	I cannot find anything he has done to deserve **death!**
Jn	11. 4	result of this illness will not be the **death** of Lazarus;
	11.19	Martha and Mary to comfort them over their brother's **death.**
	12.33	this he indicated the kind of **death** he was going to suffer.)
	18.32	he used when he indicated the kind of **death** he would die.)
Acts	1. 3	For forty days after his **death** he appeared to them
	1.18	evil act he bought a field, where he fell to his **death;**
	2.24	because it was impossible that **death** should hold him prisoner.
	5.28	and you want to make us responsible for his **death!"**
	13.28	no reason to pass the **death sentence** on him,
	20.28	he made his own through the **sacrificial death** of his Son.
	22. 4	I persecuted to the **death** the people who followed this Way.
	25.11	for which I deserve the **death** penalty, I do not ask to
	25.25	he had done anything for which he deserved the **death** sentence.
Rom	1.32	God's law says that people who live in this way deserve **death.**
	3.25	so that by his **sacrificial death** he should become the means
	5. 9	By his **sacrificial death** we are now put right with God;
	5.10	but he made us his friends through the **death** of his Son.
	5.12	world through one man, and his sin brought **death** with it.
	5.12	As a result, **death** has spread to the whole human race
	5.14	to the time of Moses **death** ruled over all mankind,
	5.17	the sin of one man **death** began to rule
	5.21	sin ruled by means of **death,** so also God's grace rules
	6. 3	with Christ Jesus, we were baptized into union with his **death.**
	6. 4	with him and shared his **death,** in order that, just as Christ
	6. 9	and will never die again—**death** will no longer rule over him.
	6.16	of sin, which results in **death,** or of obedience, which results
	6.21	The result of those things is **death!**
	6.23	For sin pays its wage—**death;**
	7. 5	at work in our bodies, and all we did ended in **death.**
	7.10	which was meant to bring life, in my case brought **death.**
	7.13	But does this mean that what is good caused my **death?**
	7.13	sin brought **death** to me,
	7.24	will rescue me from this body that is taking me to **death?**
	8. 2	Jesus, has set me free from the law of sin and **death.**
	8. 6	To be controlled by human nature results in **death;**

Rom 8.35 hardship or persecution or hunger or poverty or danger or **death?**
8.36 "For your sake we are in danger of **death** at all times;
8.38 neither **death** nor life, neither angels nor other heavenly rulers
1 Cor 1.17 to make sure that Christ's **death** on the cross is not robbed
1.18 For the message about Christ's **death** on the cross is
2. 2 except Jesus Christ and especially his **death** on the cross.
3.22 this world, life and **death**, the present and the future—
10.10 and they were destroyed by the Angel of **Death.**
11.26 from this cup you proclaim the Lord's **death** until he comes.
15.20 guarantee that those who sleep in **death** will also be raised.
15.21 For just as **death** came by means of a man,
15.26 The last enemy to be defeated will be **death.**
15.31 My brothers, I face **death** every day!
15.54 **"Death** is destroyed;
15.55 "Where, **Death,** is your victory?
15.55 Where, **Death,** is your power to hurt?"
15.56 **Death** gets its power to hurt from sin,
2 Cor 1. 9 We felt that the **death** sentence had been passed on us.
1.10 From such terrible dangers of **death** he saved us,
3. 6 The written law brings **death,** but the Spirit gives life.
3. 7 If the Law, which brings **death** when it is in force, came
4.10 in our mortal bodies the **death** of Jesus, so that his life
4.11 are always in danger of **death** for Jesus' sake,
4.12 This means that **death** is at work in us,
5.14 died for everyone, which means that all share in his **death.**
7.10 But sadness that is merely human causes **death.**
11.23 whipped much more, and I have been near **death** more often.
Gal 3. 1 clear description of the **death** of Jesus Christ on the cross!
6. 8 desires, from it he will gather the harvest of **death;**
Eph 1. 7 For by the **sacrificial death** of Christ we are set free,
2.13 have been brought near by the **sacrificial death** of Christ.
2.16 By his **death** on the cross Christ destroyed their enmity;
Phil 1.21 **Death,** then, will bring more.
2. 8 obedience all the way to **death**— his death on the cross.
3.10 become like him in his **death,** [11] in the hope that I myself
3.18 lives make them enemies of Christ's **death** on the cross.
Col 1.20 made peace through his Son's **sacrificial death** on the cross
1.22 by means of the physical **death** of his Son, God has made
2 Tim 1.10 ended the power of **death** and through the gospel has revealed
Heb 2. 9 crowned with glory and honour because of the **death** he suffered.
2.14 so that through his **death** he might destroy the Devil,
2.14 who has the power over **death,** [15] and in this way set free
2.15 were slaves all their lives because of their fear of **death.**
5. 7 loud cries and tears to God, who could save him from **death.**
7. 3 no record of his birth or of his **death.**
9.15 because there has been a **death** which sets people free
9.17 it comes into effect only after his **death.**
10.19 into the Most Holy Place by means of the **death** of Jesus.
11.28 so that the Angel of **Death** would not kill the first-born
13.20 as the result of his **sacrificial death,** by which the eternal
Jas 1.15 and sin, when it is full-grown, gives birth to **death.**
2 Pet 1.15 you to remember these matters at all times after my **death.**
1 Jn 3.14 We know that we have left **death** and come over into life;
3.14 Whoever does not love is still under the power of **death.**
5. 6 with the water of his baptism and the blood of his **death.**
5.16 that does not lead to **death,** you should pray to God,
5.16 This applies to those whose sins do not lead to **death.**
5.16 is sin which leads to **death,** and I do not say that
5.17 is sin, but there is sin which does not lead to **death.**
Rev 1. 5 loves us, and by his **sacrificial death** he has freed us from
1.18 I have authority over **death** and the world of the dead.
2.10 even if it means **death,** and I will give you life
2.11 who win the victory will not be hurt by the second **death.**
5. 9 and by your **sacrificial death** you bought for God people
6. 8 Its rider was named **Death,** and Hades followed close behind.
9. 6 five months they will seek **death,** but will not find it;
9. 6 they will want to die, but **death** will flee from them.
11.10 the earth will be happy because of the **death** of these two.
20. 6 The second **death** has no power over them;
20.13 **Death** and the world of the dead also gave up the dead
20.14 Then **death** and the world of the dead were thrown into
20.14 (This lake of fire is the second **death.**)
21. 4 There will be no more **death,** no more grief or crying
21. 8 burning with fire and sulphur, which is the second **death."**

DEATH (2) (FROM DEATH)

2 Chr 22.11 she saved him **from death** at the hands of Athaliah.
Job 5.15 But God saves the poor **from death;**
5.20 he will keep you alive, and in war protect you **from death.**
33.18 he saves them **from death** itself.
Ps 6. 4 in your mercy rescue me **from death.**
9.13 Rescue me **from death,** O Lord,
33.19 He saves them **from death;**
49.12 A man's greatness cannot save him **from death;**
49.20 A man's greatness cannot save him **from death;**
56.13 you have rescued me **from death** and kept me from defeat.
68.20 he is the Lord, our Lord, who rescues us **from death.**
86. 2 Save me **from death,** because I am loyal to you;
116. 8 The Lord saved me **from death;**
116.16 You have saved me **from death.**
Mt 17. 9 until the Son of Man has been raised **from death."**
22.23 and claimed that people will not rise **from death.**
27.53 and after Jesus rose **from death,** they went into the Holy
27.64 and then tell the people that he was raised **from death.**
28. 7 'He has been raised **from death,** and now he is going
Mk 9. 9 until the Son of Man has risen **from death."**
9.10 "What does this 'rising **from death'** mean?"
12.18 that people will not rise **from death,**
16. 9 After Jesus rose **from death** early on Sunday,
Lk 14.14 will repay you on the day the good people rise **from death."**
Lk 16.30 if someone were to rise **from death** and go to them,
16.31 not be convinced even if someone were to rise **from death.' "**
20.27 people will not rise **from death,** came to Jesus and said,
20.35 who are worthy to rise **from death** and live in the age
20.36 They are the sons of God, because they have risen **from death.**
24.46 must suffer and must rise **from death** three days later,
Jn 2.22 So when he was raised **from death,** his disciples remembered
5.24 not be judged, but has already passed **from death** to life.
12. 1 Bethany, the home of Lazarus, the man he had raised **from death.**
12. 9 Jesus but also to see Lazarus, whom Jesus had raised **from death.**
12.17 and raised him **from death** had reported what had happened.
20. 9 the scripture which said that he must rise **from death.)**
21.14 Jesus appeared to the disciples after he was raised **from death.**
Acts 2.24 But God raised him **from death,** setting him free from its power,
2.32 has raised this very Jesus **from death,**
3.15 but God raised him **from death**—and we are witnesses
4. 2 people that Jesus had risen **from death,** which proved that
4.10 of Nazareth—whom you crucified and whom God raised **from death.**
5.30 raised Jesus **from death,** after you had killed him
10.40 But God raised him **from death** three days later
10.41 us who ate and drank with him after he rose **from death.**
13.30 But God raised him **from death,**
13.34 God said about raising him **from death,** never to rot away
13.37 this did not happen to the one whom God raised **from death.**
17. 3 that the Messiah had to suffer and rise **from death.**
17.31 proof of this to everyone by raising that man **from death!"**
17.32 Paul speak about a raising **from death,** some of them made fun
23. 8 that people will not rise **from death** and that there are no
24.15 both the good and the bad, will rise **from death.**
26.23 the first one to rise **from death,** to announce the light
Rom 1. 4 power to be the Son of God by being raised **from death.**
4.24 who believe in him who raised Jesus our Lord **from death.**
6. 4 just as Christ was raised **from death** by the glorious power
6. 9 that Christ has been raised **from death** and will never die
6.13 those who have been brought **from death** to life,
7. 4 to him who was raised **from death** in order that we might
8.11 God, who raised Jesus **from death,** lives in you,
8.11 then he who raised Christ **from death** will also give life
10. 7 (that is, to bring Christ up **from death).**
10. 9 believe that God raised him **from death,** you will be saved.
1 Cor 6.14 God raised the Lord **from death,** and he will also raise
15.12 that Christ has been raised **from death,** how can some of you
15.14 Christ has not been raised **from death,** then we have nothing
15.15 said that he raised Christ **from death**—but if it is true
15.20 that Christ has been raised **from death,** as the guarantee
15.21 the same way the rising **from death** comes by means of a
Gal 1. 1 Jesus Christ and God the Father, who raised him **from death.**
Eph 1.20 used when he raised Christ **from death** and seated him at his
5.14 "Wake up, sleeper, and rise **from death,** and Christ will shine
Phil 3.11 the hope that I myself will be raised **from death** to life.
Col 1.18 first-born Son, who was raised **from death,** in order that he
2.12 the active power of God, who raised him **from death.**
1 Thes 1.10 Son Jesus, whom he raised **from death** and who rescues us
2 Tim 2. 8 Jesus Christ, who was raised **from death,**
Heb 5. 7 cries and tears to God, who could save him **from death.**
11.19 was able to raise Isaac **from death**—
11.19 so to speak, Abraham did receive Isaac back **from death.**
13.20 God has raised **from death** our Lord Jesus,
Jas 5.20 sinner's soul **from death** and bring about the forgiveness
1 Pet 1. 3 he gave us new life by raising Jesus Christ **from death.**
1.21 in God, who raised him **from death** and gave him glory;
Rev 1. 5 the first to be raised **from death** and who is also the

DEATH (3) (TO DEATH)

Gen 26.11 who ill-treats this man or his wife will be put **to death."**
31.32 that anyone here has your gods, he will be put **to death.**
38.24 Judah ordered, "Take her out and burn her **to death."**
42. 2 go there and buy some to keep us from starving **to death."**
42.20 been telling the truth, and I will not put you **to death."**
43. 8 Then none of us will starve **to death.**
44. 9 he will be put **to death,** and the rest of us
Ex 8.26 them where they can see us, they will stone us **to death.**
16. 3 us out into this desert to starve us all **to death."**
19.12 anyone sets foot on it, he is to be put **to death;**
19.13 they must be put **to death.**
21.12 hits a man and kills him is to be put **to death.**
21.14 he is to be put **to death,** even if he has run
21.15 hits his father or his mother is to be put **to death.**
21.16 to keep him as a slave, is to be put **to death.**
21.17 curses his father or his mother is to be put **to death.**
21.28 "If a bull gores someone **to death,** it is to be stoned,
21.29 then if it gores someone **to death,** it is to be stoned,
21.29 and its owner is to be put **to death** also.
21.32 pieces of silver, and the bull shall be stoned **to death.**
22.18 "Put **to death** any woman who practises magic.
22.19 "Put **to death** any man who has sexual relations with an animal.
22.20 "Condemn **to death** anyone who offers sacrifices to any god
23. 7 not put an innocent person **to death,** for I will condemn
31.14 it, but works on that day, is to be put **to death.**
31.15 does any work on that day is to be put **to death.**
35. 2 does any work on that day is to be put **to death.**
Lev 10. 2 fire, and it burnt them **to death** there in the presence of
19.20 be punished but not put **to death,** since she is a slave.
20. 2 god Molech shall be stoned **to death** by the whole community.
20. 4 and does not put him **to death,** [5] I myself will turn against
20. 9 who curses his father or his mother shall be put **to death;**
20.10 both he and the woman shall be put **to death.**
20.11 father, and both he and the woman shall be put **to death.**
20.12 with his daughter-in-law, they shall both be put **to death.**

Lev 20.13 done a disgusting thing, and both shall be put **to death.**
20.14 all three shall be burnt **to death** because of the disgraceful
20.15 with an animal, he and the animal shall be put **to death.**
20.16 with an animal, she and the animal shall be put **to death.**
20.27 consults the spirits of the dead shall be stoned **to death;**
21. 9 she shall be burnt **to death.**
23.30 work on that day, the Lord himself will put him **to death.**
24.14 and then the whole community shall stone him **to death.**
24.16 must suffer the consequences [16]and be put **to death.**
24.16 the Lord shall be stoned **to death**
24.17 commits murder shall be put **to death,** [18]and anyone who
24.21 replace it, but whoever kills a man shall be put **to death.**
24.23 they took the man outside the camp and stoned him **to death.**
27.29 he must be put **to death.**
Num 1.51 Anyone else who comes near the Tent shall be put **to death.**
3.10 anyone else who tries to do so shall be put **to death."**
3.38 else who tried to do so was to be put **to death.**
14.10 was threatening to stone them **to death,** but suddenly the
15.30 and he shall be put **to death,** [31]because he has rejected
15.35 the Lord said to Moses, "The man must be put **to death;**
15.35 whole community is to stone him **to death** outside the camp."
15.36 camp and stoned him **to death,** as the Lord had commanded.
16.38 these men who were put **to death** for their sin,
18. 3 If they do, both they and you will be put **to death.**
18. 7 who comes near the sacred objects shall be put **to death."**
18.32 if you do, you will be put **to death."**
35.12 is not to be put **to death** without a public trial.
35.16 he is guilty of murder and is to be put **to death.**
35.19 has the responsibility for putting the murderer **to death.**
35.21 he is guilty of murder and is to be put **to death.**
35.21 has the responsibility for putting the murderer **to death.**
35.30 be found guilty and put **to death** only on the evidence of
35.31 A murderer must be put **to death.**
Deut 2.34 destroyed every town, and put everyone **to death,** men, women,
3. 6 all the towns and put **to death** all the men, women,
4.42 escape to one of these cities and not be put **to death.**
7. 2 power and you defeat them, you must put them all **to death.**
13. 5 But put **to death** any interpreter of dreams or prophet
13. 5 He must be put **to death,** in order to rid yourselves
13.10 Stone him **to death!**
17. 5 then take that person outside the town and stone him **to death.**
17. 6 However, he may be put **to death** only if two or more
17. 6 is not to be put **to death** if there is only one
17.12 judge or the priest on duty is to be put **to death;**
19.10 be guilty of putting them **to death** in the land that the
19.12 revenge for the murder, so that he may be put **to death.**
21.21 city are to stone him **to death,** and so you will get
21.22 a man has been put **to death** for a crime
22.21 where the men of her city are to stone her **to death.**
22.22 another man's wife, both of them are to be put **to death.**
22.24 are to take them outside the town and stone them **to death.**
22.25 Then only the man is to be put **to death;**
24. 7 slave or sells him into slavery is to be put **to death.**
24.16 are not to be put **to death** for crimes committed by their children,
24.16 are not to be put **to death** for crimes committed by their parents;
24.16 person is to be put **to death** only for a crime
28.51 your livestock and your crops, and you will starve **to death.**
Josh 1.18 or disobeys any of your orders will be put **to death.**
7.25 All the people then stoned Achan **to death;**
10.28 He put everyone in the city **to death;**
10.35 day and put everyone there **to death,** just as they had done
10.39 They put everyone there **to death.**
10.40 everyone was put **to death.**
11.11 They put everyone there **to death;**
11.12 and their kings, putting everyone **to death,** just as Moses,
11.14 But they put every person **to death;**
11.17 long time, but he captured them all and put them **to death.**
Judg 15. 6 went and burnt the woman **to death** and burnt down
21. 5 anyone who had not gone to Mizpah would be put **to death.)**
1 Sam 11.13 "No one will be put **to death** today,
14.39 guilty one will be put **to death,**
14.44 "May God strike me dead if you are not put **to death!"**
14.45 who won this great victory for Israel, be put **to death?**
14.45 So the people saved Jonathan from being put **to death.**
17.35 me, I grab it by the throat and beat it **to death.**
22.19 inhabitants of Nob, the city of priests, to be put **to death:**
2 Sam 4.10 I seized him and had him put **to death.**
8. 2 ground and put two out of every three of them **to death.**
14.32 king, and if I'm guilty, then let him put me **to death."**
19.21 "Shimei should be put **to death** because he cursed the one
19.22 Israel now, and no Israelite will be put **to death** today."
19.23 give you my word that you will not be put **to death."**
19.28 family deserved to be put **to death** by Your Majesty,
21. 1 he put the people of Gibeon **to death."**
21. 9 of the barley harvest, when they were put **to death.**
1 Kgs 1.51 swear to me that he will not have me put **to death."**
2. 9 and you must see to it that he is put **to death."**
2.26 will not have you put **to death** now,
12.18 to go to the Israelites, but they stoned him **to death.**
16.11 Every male relative and friend was put **to death.**
17.12 will be our last meal, and then we will starve **to death."**
18.12 here, and he can't find you, he will put me **to death.**
19. 1 and how he had put all the prophets of Baal **to death.**
19.17 Anyone who escapes being put **to death** by Hazael
21.10 Then take him out of the city and stone him **to death."**
21.13 and so he was taken outside the city and stoned **to death.**
21.14 "Naboth has been put **to death."**
2 Kgs 6.22 soldiers you had captured in combat would you put **to death.**
7. 4 into the city, because we would starve **to death** in there;
7.17 The officer was trampled **to death** there by the people and died,
7.20 he died, trampled **to death** by the people

2 Kgs 8.12 young men, batter their children **to death,** and rip open
10.11 Then Jehu put **to death** all the other relatives of Ahab
10.14 seized them, and he put them **to death** near a pit there.
10.19 to Baal, and whoever is not present will be put **to death."**
14. 6 are not to be put **to death** for crimes committed by their
14. 6 are not to be put **to death** for crimes committed by their
14. 6 person is to be put **to death** only for a crime
25. 7 While Zedekiah was looking on, his sons were put **to death;**
25.21 There the king had them beaten and put **to death.**
2 Chr 10.18 to go to the Israelites, but they stoned him **to death.**
15.13 female, who did not worship him was to be put **to death.**
22. 9 They took him to Jehu and put him **to death.**
25. 4 are not to be put **to death** for crimes committed by their children,
25. 4 are not to be put **to death** for crimes committed by their parents;
25. 4 person is to be put **to death** only for a crime
Esth 3. 9 Majesty, issue a decree that they are to be put **to death.**
Job 5. 2 To worry yourself **to death** with resentment would be a foolish,
Ps 94.21 who plot against good men and sentence the innocent **to death.**
109.31 poor man and saves him from those who condemn him **to death.**
Ecc 4. 5 a fool to fold his hands and let himself starve **to death.**
Is 5.13 Your leaders will starve **to death,** and the common people
13.15 Anyone who is caught will be stabbed **to death.**
13.16 their babies will be battered **to death,**
53. 8 He was put **to death** for the sins of our people.
65.15 I, the Sovereign Lord, will put you **to death.**
66.16 world whom he finds guilty—and many will be put **to death.**
Jer 14.18 when I go into the towns, I see people starving **to death.**
18.21 But now, Lord, let their children starve **to death;**
20. 4 away as prisoners to his country and put others **to death.**
21. 7 Nebuchadnezzar will put you **to death.**
25.31 will bring all people to trial and put the wicked **to death.**
26.11 man deserves to be sentenced **to death** because he has spoken
26.16 he should not be put **to death."**
26.19 Hezekiah and the people of Judah did not put Micah **to death.**
29.21 of Babylonia, who will put them **to death** before your eyes.
38. 4 to the king and said, "This man must be put **to death.**
38.15 you will put me **to death,**
38.16 I will not put you **to death** or hand you over
38.25 promise not to put you **to death** if you tell them everything.
39. 6 he put Zedekiah's sons **to death** while Zedekiah was looking on,
39.18 will keep you safe, and you will not be put **to death.**
52.10 he put Zedekiah's sons **to death**
52.27 There the king had them beaten and put **to death.**
Lam 2.19 Children starving **to death** on every street corner!
4. 9 died later, who starved slowly **to death,** with no food
Ezek 6.12 those who survive will starve **to death.**
11. 9 I have sentenced you **to death,** [10]and you will be killed
22. 9 tell lies about others in order to have them put **to death.**
Dan 2.24 He said to him, "Don't put them **to death.**
11.33 in battle or be burnt **to death,** and some will be robbed
Hos 10.14 and mothers and their children were crushed **to death.**
Amos 9. 4 by their enemies, I will order them to be put **to death.**
Nah 3.10 At every street corner their children were beaten **to death.**
3.15 do, you will still be burnt **to death** or killed in battle.
Zeph 2.12 The Lord will also put the people of Sudan **to death.**
Zech 12.10 the one whom they stabbed **to death,** and they will mourn
13. 3 that he must be put **to death,** because he claimed to speak
13. 3 his own father and mother will stab him **to death.**
Mt 10.21 own brothers to be put **to death,** and fathers will do the
10.21 will turn against their parents and have them put **to death.**
15. 4 curses his father or his mother is to be put **to death.'**
16.21 I will be put **to death,** but three days later I will
24. 9 arrested and handed over to be punished and be put **to death.**
26. 4 and made plans to arrest Jesus secretly and put him **to death.**
26.59 to find some false evidence against Jesus to put him **to death;**
27. 1 elders made their plans against Jesus to put him **to death.**
27.20 ask Pilate to set Barabbas free and have Jesus put **to death.**
Mk 7.10 curses his father or his mother is to be put **to death.'**
8.31 He will be put **to death,** but three days later he will
13.12 own brothers to be put **to death,** and fathers will do the
13.12 Children will turn against their parents and have them put **to death.**
14. 1 for a way to arrest Jesus secretly and put him **to death.**
14.55 in order to put him **to death,** but they could not find
14.64 he was guilty and should be put **to death.**
Lk 9.22 He will be put **to death,** but three days later he will
21.16 and some of you will be put **to death.**
22. 2 trying to find a way of putting Jesus **to death** secretly.
23.32 criminals, were also led out to be put **to death** with Jesus.
Jn 8. 5 Law Moses commanded that such a woman must be stoned **to death.**
18.31 They replied, "We are not allowed to put anyone **to death."**
19.41 where Jesus had been put **to death,** and in it there was
Acts 5.33 furious that they wanted to have the apostles put **to death.**
10.39 Then they put him **to death** by nailing him to a cross.
12. 2 had James, the brother of John, put **to death** by the sword.
12.19 the guards questioned and ordered them to be put **to death.**
13.28 sentence on him, they asked Pilate to have him put **to death.**
22.20 your witness Stephen was put **to death,** I myself was there,
Rom 6. 6 old being has been put **to death** with Christ on his cross,
8.13 by the Spirit you put **to death** your sinful actions,
2 Cor 13. 4 weakness that he was put **to death** on the cross,
Gal 2.19 I have been put **to death** with Christ on his cross,
5.24 to Christ Jesus have put **to death** their human nature with
Col 3. 5 You must put **to death,** then, the earthly desires at work
Heb 10.28 Law of Moses is put **to death** without any mercy when judged
12.20 animal touches the mountain, it must be stoned **to death."**
1 Pet 3.18 He was put **to death** physically, but made alive spiritually,
Rev 13.15 image could talk and put **to death** all those who would not

DEBATE

Job 32.21 I will not take sides in this **debate**;
Acts 15. 7 After a long **debate** Peter stood up and said, "My brothers,
17.18 Certain Epicurean and Stoic teachers also **debated** with him.
18.28 defeated the Jews in public **debates** by proving from the Scriptures
1 Cor 1.20 or the skilful **debaters** of this world?

DEBORAH (1)

Prophet and judge in Israel.

Judg 4. 4 Now **Deborah,** the wife of Lappidoth, was a prophet,
4. 9 So **Deborah** set off for Kedesh with Barak.
4.10 **Deborah** went with him.
4.14 Then **Deborah** said to Barak, "Go!
5. 1 On that day **Deborah** and Barak son of Abinoam sang this song:
5. 7 The towns of Israel stood abandoned, **Deborah;**
5.12 Lead on, **Deborah,** lead on!
5.15 The leaders of Issachar came with **Deborah;**

DEBT

Deut 15. 1 you are to cancel the **debts** of those who owe you money.
15. 2 has lent money to a fellow-Israelite is to cancel the **debt;**
15. 2 the Lord himself has declared the **debt** cancelled.
15. 9 just because the year when **debts** are cancelled is near.
31.10 when the year that **debts** are cancelled comes round,
1 Sam 22. 2 who were oppressed or in **debt** or dissatisfied went to him,
2 Kgs 4. 1 my two sons as slaves in payment for my husband's **debt."**
4. 7 pay all your **debts,** and there will be enough money
Neh 5.11 Cancel all the **debts** they owe you—money or corn or wine
5.12 We'll give the property back and not try to collect the **debts."**
10.31 we will not farm the land, and we will cancel all **debts.**
Job 24. 3 to orphans, and keep a widow's ox till she pays her **debts.**
24. 9 and take the poor man's children in payment for **debts.**
Prov 6. 1 Have you promised to be responsible for someone else's **debts,**
11.15 If you promise to pay a stranger's **debt,** you will regret it.
17.18 would promise to be responsible for someone else's **debts.**
20.16 responsible for a stranger's **debts** ought to have his own
22.26 Don't promise to be responsible for someone else's **debts.**
27.13 responsible for a stranger's **debts** deserves to have his own
Amos 2. 6 men who cannot pay their **debts,** poor men who cannot repay
2. 8 that they have taken from the poor as security for **debts.**
8. 6 man who can't pay his **debts,** not even the price
Hab 2. 6 you go on getting rich by forcing your **debtors** to pay up?"
2. 7 will be in **debt** yourselves and be forced to pay
Mt 18.25 have enough to pay his **debt,** so the king ordered him to
18.25 children and all that he had, in order to pay the **debt.**
18.27 so he forgave him the **debt** and let him go.
18.30 he had him thrown into jail until he should pay the **debt.**
Lk 7.42 them could pay him back, so he cancelled the **debts** of both.
16. 5 called in all the people who were in **debt** to his master.
Col 2.14 the unfavourable record of our **debts** with its binding rules

DECAY

2 Chr 34.11 the buildings that the kings of Judah had allowed to **decay.**
Ps 49.14 them, as their bodies quickly **decay** in the world of the dead
Is 24. 4 both earth and sky **decay.**
Mt 23.27 but are full of bones and **decaying** corpses on the inside.
Rom 8.21 free from its slavery to **decay** and would share the glorious
2 Cor 4.16 our physical being is gradually **decaying,** yet our spiritual being
1 Pet 1. 4 in heaven, where they cannot **decay** or spoil or fade away.

DECEIVE

Gen 21.23 that you will not **deceive** me, my children, or my descendants.
27.12 father will touch me and find out that I am **deceiving** him;
27.35 Isaac answered, "Your brother came and **deceived** me.
31.20 Jacob **deceived** Laban by not letting him know that he was leaving.
31.26 to Jacob, "Why did you **deceive** me and carry off my
31.27 Why did you **deceive** me and slip away without telling me?
34.13 answered Shechem and his father Hamor in a **deceitful** way.
Ex 8.29 But you must not **deceive** us again and prevent the people
Num 16.14 and now you are trying to **deceive** us.
25.18 when they **deceived** you at Peor,
Deut 32. 5 unworthy to be his people, a sinful and **deceitful** nation.
Josh 9. 4 done to Jericho and Ai, and they decided to **deceive** him.
9.22 asked them, "Why did you **deceive** us and tell us that you
2 Sam 3.25 He came here to **deceive** you and to find out everything
1 Kgs 22.20 The Lord asked, 'Who will **deceive** Ahab so that he will
22.21 approached the Lord, and said, 'I will **deceive** him.'
22.22 The Lord said, 'Go and **deceive** him.
2 Kgs 18.29 He warns you not to let Hezekiah **deceive** you.
19.10 will not fall into my hands, but don't let that **deceive** you.
2 Chr 18.19 The Lord asked, 'Who will **deceive** Ahab so that he will
18.20 approached the Lord, and said, 'I will **deceive** him.'
18.21 The Lord said, 'Go and **deceive** him.
32.11 but Hezekiah is **deceiving** you and will let you die
32.15 Now don't let Hezekiah **deceive** you or mislead you
Job 6.15 you, my friends, you **deceive** me like streams that go dry
12.16 both **deceived** and deceiver are in his power.
15.35 their hearts are always full of **deceit.**
31. 5 I have never acted wickedly and never tried to **deceive** others.
36.18 not to let bribes **deceive** you, or riches lead you astray.
Ps 5. 6 You destroy all liars and despise violent, **deceitful** men.
5. 9 Their words are flattering and smooth, but full of deadly **deceit.**
7.14 they plan trouble and practise **deception.**
12. 2 they **deceive** each other with flattery.
Ps 32. 2 not accuse of doing wrong and who is free from all **deceit.**
105.25 the Egyptians hate his people and treat his servants with **deceit.**
119.118 their **deceitful** schemes are useless.
120. 2 Save me, Lord, from liars and **deceivers.**
Prov 6.13 wink and make gestures to **deceive** you,
12. 5 the wicked only want to **deceive** you.
13. 2 but those who are **deceitful** are hungry for violence.
16.29 Violent people **deceive** their friends
31.30 Charm is **deceptive** and beauty disappears,
Is 28.15 because you depend on lies and **deceit** to keep you safe.
30.12 "You ignore what I tell you and rely on violence and **deceit.**
36.14 He warns you not to let Hezekiah **deceive** you.
37.10 will not fall into my hands, but don't let that **deceive** you.
63. 8 they will not **deceive** me."
Jer 4.10 you have completely **deceived** the people of Jerusalem!
7. 4 Stop believing those **deceitful** words, 'We are safe!
7. 8 "Look, you put your trust in **deceitful** words.
9. 4 for every brother is as **deceitful** as Jacob,
9. 5 and one **deceitful** act follows another.
17. 9 There is nothing else so **deceitful;**
20. 7 Lord, you have **deceived** me, and I was deceived.
27.10 They are **deceiving** you and will cause you to be taken
27.14 They are **deceiving** you.
29. 8 not to let yourselves be **deceived** by the prophets
37. 9 not to **deceive** yourselves into thinking that the Babylonians
49.16 Your pride has **deceived** you.
Lam 2.14 Their preaching **deceived** you by never exposing your sin.
Ezek 14. 9 "If a prophet is **deceived** into giving a false answer,
14. 9 it is because I, the Lord, have **deceived** him.
Dan 8.23 there will be a stubborn, vicious, and **deceitful** king.
8.25 he is cunning, he will succeed in his **deceitful** ways.
11.23 By making treaties, he will **deceive** other nations,
11.25 king of Egypt will be **deceived** and will not be successful.
11.32 By **deceit** the king will win the support of those who
Hos 7. 3 The Lord says, "People **deceive** the king and his officers
10. 2 The people whose hearts are **deceitful** must now suffer
11.12 surrounded me with lies and **deceit,**
Obad 3 Your pride has **deceived** you.
7 Your allies have **deceived** you;
Mic 2.11 about full of lies and **deceit** and says, 'I prophesy that
3. 5 My people are **deceived** by prophets who promise peace
Hab 2. 5 Wealth is **deceitful.**
Zeph 3.13 do no wrong to anyone, tell no lies, nor try to **deceive.**
Zech 13. 4 or wear a prophet's coarse garment in order to **deceive** people.
Mt 24. 4 "Be on your guard, and do not let anyone **deceive** you.
24. 5 and they will **deceive** many people.
24.11 Then many false prophets will appear and **deceive** many people.
24.24 in order to **deceive** even God's chosen people, if possible.
Mk 7.22 **deceit,** indecency, jealousy, slander, pride, and folly—
13. 5 to them, "Be on guard, and don't let anyone **deceive** you.
13. 6 and they will **deceive** many people.
13.22 in order to **deceive** even God's chosen people, if possible.
Lk 21. 8 don't be **deceived.**
Rom 1.29 they are full of jealousy, murder, fighting, **deceit,** and
3.13 Their words are full of deadly **deceit;**
7.11 by means of the commandment it **deceived** me and killed me.
16.18 fine words and flattering speech they **deceive** innocent people.
2 Cor 4. 2 we do not act with **deceit,** nor do we falsify the word
11. 3 same way that Eve was **deceived** by the snake's clever lies.
Gal 6. 3 somebody when really he is nobody, he is only **deceiving** himself.
6. 7 Do not **deceive** yourselves;
Eph 4.14 of the teaching of **deceitful** men, who lead others into error
4.22 the old self that was being destroyed by its **deceitful** desires.
5. 6 Do not let anyone **deceive** you with foolish words;
Col 2. 4 do not let anyone **deceive** you with false arguments, no matter
2. 8 by means of the worthless **deceit** of human wisdom, which comes
2 Thes 2. 3 Do not let anyone **deceive** you in any way.
2.10 and use every kind of wicked **deceit** on those who will perish.
1 Tim 2.14 And it was not Adam who was **deceived;**
2.14 it was the woman who was **deceived** and broke God's law.
4. 2 Such teachings are spread by **deceitful** liars, whose consciences
2 Tim 3.13 bad to worse, deceiving others and being **deceived** themselves.
Tit 1.10 especially converts from Judaism, who rebel and **deceive** others
Heb 3.13 that none of you be **deceived** by sin and become stubborn,
Jas 1.16 Do not be **deceived,** my dear brothers!
1.22 Do not **deceive** yourselves by just listening to his word;
1.26 his religion is worthless and he **deceives** himself.
2 Pet 2.13 in your meals, all the while enjoying their **deceitful** ways!
1 Jn 1. 8 we have no sin, we **deceive** ourselves, and there is no truth
2.26 this to you about those who are trying to **deceive** you.
3. 7 Let no one **deceive** you, my children!
2 Jn 7 Many **deceivers** have gone out all over the world, people
7 Such a person is a **deceiver** and the Enemy of Christ.
Rev 12. 9 called the Devil, or Satan, that **deceived** the whole world.
13.14 And it **deceived** all the people living on earth
18.23 false magic you **deceived** all the peoples of the world!"
19.20 those miracles that he had **deceived** those who had the mark
20. 3 so that he could not **deceive** the nations any more
20. 8 he will go out to **deceive** the nations scattered over the
20.10 Then the Devil, who **deceived** them, was thrown into the

DECIDE

[UNDECIDED]

Gen 6.13 said to Noah, "I have **decided** to put an end
24.49 if not, say so, and I will **decide** what to do."
24.50 from the Lord, it is not for us to make a **decision.**
31.37 see it, and let them **decide** which one of us is right.
37.18 they plotted against him and **decided** to kill him.
Ex 3.17 I have **decided** that I will bring them out of Egypt,
18.16 come to me, and I **decide** which one of them is right,

Ex 18.22 but they themselves can **decide** all the smaller disputes.
18.26 cases to Moses but **deciding** the smaller disputes themselves.
29.28 It is my unchanging **decision** that when my people make
33. 5 off your jewellery, and I will **decide** what to do with you."
Lev 13.59 this is how the **decision** is made as to whether it is
19.15 honest and just when you make **decisions** in legal cases;
Deut 1.17 Show no partiality in your **decisions;**
1.17 afraid of anyone, for the **decisions** you make come from God.
1.17 difficult for you, bring it to me, and I will **decide** it.'
16.19 wise and honest men, and cause them to give wrong **decisions.**
17. 8 the local judges to **decide,** such as certain cases of property
17. 9 is in office at that time, and let them **decide** the case.
17.10 They will give their **decision,** and you are to do exactly
17.14 settled there, then you will **decide** you need a king like all
21. 5 because they are to **decide** every legal case involving violence.
21.16 the man **decides** how he is going to divide his property
22.13 man marries a girl and later he **decides** he doesn't want her.
24. 1 marries a woman and later **decides** that he doesn't want her,
24. 3 and he also **decides** that he doesn't want her,
Josh 9. 4 done to Jericho and Ai, [4]and they **decided** to deceive him.
24.15 not willing to serve him, **decide** today whom you will serve,
Judg 4. 5 and the people of Israel would go there for her **decisions.**
5.15 they could not **decide** whether to come.
5.16 they could not **decide** whether to come.
6.36 "You say that you have **decided** to use me to rescue Israel.
9. 3 and the men of Shechem **decided** to follow Abimelech
11.27 He will **decide** today between the Israelites and the Ammonites."
19. 3 Then the man **decided** to go after her and try to persuade
1 Sam 2.25 to their father, for the Lord had **decided** to kill them.
8. 3 so they accepted bribes and did not **decide** cases honestly.
12.22 abandon you, for he has **decided** to make you his own people.
14.42 Then Saul said, **"Decide** between my son Jonathan and me."
20. 3 like me, and he has **decided** not to let you know what
24.15 will judge, and he will **decide** which one of us is wrong.
25.17 Please think this over and **decide** what to do.
2 Sam 6.10 So he **decided** not to take it with him to Jerusalem;
14.21 king said to Joab, "I have **decided** to do what you want.
17.14 The Lord had **decided** that Ahithophel's good advice would not
19.29 I have **decided** that you and Ziba will share Saul's property."
1 Kgs 3.28 Israel heard of Solomon's **decision,** they were all filled with
5. 5 And I have now **decided** to build that temple for the worship
5. 6 work with them, and I will pay your men whatever you **decide.**
7. 7 Hall of Judgement, where Solomon **decided** cases,
2 Kgs 12.17 then he **decided** to attack Jerusalem.
19.11 Assyrian emperor does to any country he **decides** to destroy.
1 Chr 21. 1 people of Israel, so he made David **decide** to take a census.
23. 4 thousand to keep records and **decide** disputes,
2 Chr 2. 1 King Solomon **decided** to build a temple
19.11 seeing that the **decisions** of the courts are carried out.
23. 1 Jehoiada the priest **decided** that it was time to take
24. 4 Joash **decided** to have the Temple repaired.
25.16 I know that God has **decided** to destroy you
29.10 "I have now **decided** to make a covenant with the Lord,
30.23 they all **decided** to celebrate for another seven days.
32. 3 he and his officials **decided** to cut off the supply
Ezra 5. 5 leaders, and the Persian officials **decided** to take no action
Neh 5. 7 When I heard their complaints, I was angry [7]and **decided** to act.
Esth 3. 6 he **decided** to do more than punish Mordecai
3. 7 of the twelfth month, the month of Adar, was **decided** on.
Job 2.11 Job had been suffering, they **decided** to go and comfort him.
9.32 we could go to court to **decide** our quarrel.
14. 5 length of his life is **decided** beforehand— the number of
28.26 When God **decided** where the rain would fall,
29.25 I took charge and made the **decisions;**
34. 4 It is up to us to **decide** the case.
34.29 If God **decided** to do nothing at all, no one could
34.33 The **decision** is yours, not mine;
38. 5 Who **decided** how large it would be?
Ps 32. 5 I **decided** to confess them to you, and you forgave all
58. 1 Do you rulers ever give a just **decision?**
82. 1 in the assembly of the gods he gives his **decision:**
119.112 I have **decided** to obey your laws until the day I die.
147. 4 He has **decided** the number of the stars
Prov 3.31 jealous of violent people or **decide** to act as they do,
16.10 his **decisions** are always right.
Ecc 2. 1 I **decided** to enjoy myself and find out what happiness is.
2. 3 my desire for wisdom, I **decided** to cheer myself up with wine
10.17 king who makes his own **decisions** and leaders who eat at the
Is 7.15 to make his own **decisions,** people will be drinking milk
28. 7 priests are too drunk to **decide** the cases that are brought
28.22 the Lord Almighty's **decision** to destroy the whole country.
37.11 Assyrian emperor does to any country he **decides** to destroy.
41. 1 Let us come together to **decide** who is right.
63. 4 I **decided** that the time to save my people had come;
65. 6 "I have already **decided** on their punishment,
Jer 4.28 He has made his **decision** and will not turn back.
13.25 This is what he has **decided** to do with you,
15. 3 I, the Lord, have **decided** that four terrible things
16.10 will ask you why I have **decided** to punish them so harshly.
32.31 I have **decided** to destroy it [32]because of all the evil
35.11 Nebuchadnezzar invaded the country, we **decided** to come to Jerusalem
Ezek 13. 9 You will not be there when my people gather to make **decisions;**
18. 8 to do evil and gives an honest **decision** in any dispute.
20.17 I **decided** not to kill them there in the desert.
38.11 You will **decide** to invade a helpless country
39.21 them how I use my power to carry out my just **decisions.**
44.24 the priests are to **decide** the case according to my laws.
Dan 1.10 to Daniel, "The king has **decided** what you are to eat
1.13 the royal court, and base your **decision** on how we look."
4.17 This is the **decision** of the alert and watchful angels.
Dan 6. 1 Darius **decided** to appoint a hundred and twenty governors
10.12 since the first day you **decided** to humble yourself
Hos 10.11 But I **decided** to put a yoke on her beautiful neck
Joel 3. 3 They threw dice to **decide** who would get the captives.
Jon 3. 5 So they **decided** that everyone should fast,
Mt 18.23 there was a king who **decided** to check on his servants'
Mk 14.64 What is your **decision?"**
Lk 14.31 will sit down first and **decide** if he is strong enough to
22.22 will die as God has **decided,** but how terrible for that man
23.50 the Council, he had not agreed with their **decision** and action.
Jn 1.43 The next day Jesus **decided** to go to Galilee.
Acts 2.23 own plan God had already **decided** that Jesus would be handed
3.13 even after Pilate had **decided** to set him free.
4.28 you by your power and will had already **decided** would happen.
5. 4 Why, then, did you **decide** to do such a thing?
5. 9 did you and your husband **decide** to put the Lord's Spirit to
5.17 so they **decided** to take action.
7.23 he **decided** to find out how his fellow-Israelites
11.29 The disciples **decided** that each of them would send as
14. 5 together with their leaders, **decided** to ill-treat the apostles
15. 2 so it was **decided** that Paul and Barnabas and some
15.22 together with the whole church, **decided** to choose some men from
16. 4 the believers the rules **decided** upon by the apostles and elders
16.10 leave for Macedonia, because we **decided** that God had called
16.15 my house if you have **decided** that I am a true believer
18.27 Apollos then **decided** to go to Achaia, so the believers
20. 3 so he **decided** to go back through Macedonia.
20.16 Paul had **decided** to sail on past Ephesus, so as not to
21.25 a letter telling them we **decided** that they must not eat any
23.21 are now ready to do it and are waiting for your **decision."**
23.30 plot against him, at once I **decided** to send him to you.
24.22 Lysias the commander arrives," he told them, "I will **decide** your case."
25.20 was **undecided** about how I could get information on these matters,
25.21 be kept under guard and to let the Emperor **decide** his case.
25.25 made an appeal to the Emperor, I have **decided** to send him.
27. 1 When it was **decided** that we should sail to Italy, they
27.39 bay with a beach and **decided** that, if possible, they would
Rom 11.33 Who can explain his **decisions?**
14. 4 his own Master who will **decide** whether he succeeds or fails.
14.13 Instead, you should **decide** never to do anything that would make
15.26 and Achaia have freely **decided** to give an offering to help
15.27 That **decision** was their own;
1 Cor 1.21 message we preach, God **decided** to save those who believe.
7.36 the case of an engaged couple who have **decided** not to marry:
7.37 complete control and has already **decided** in his own mind what
10.27 to a meal and you **decide** to go, eat what is set
2 Cor 1.23 order to spare you that I **decided** not to go to Corinth.
8.17 that of his own free will he **decided** to go to you.
9. 7 give, then, as he has **decided,** not with regret or out of
Gal 1.15 And when he **decided** [16]to reveal his Son to me, so that
Eph 1. 5 God had already **decided** that through Jesus Christ he would
1. 9 plan he had already **decided** to complete by means of Christ.
1.11 All things are done according to God's plan and **decision;**
1.11 purpose, based on what he had **decided** from the very beginning.
Col 1.19 it was by God's own **decision** that the Son has in himself
1.20 the Son, then, God **decided** to bring the whole universe back
3.15 that Christ gives is to guide you in the **decisions** you make;
1 Thes 3. 1 So we **decided** to stay on alone in Athens [2]while we sent
Tit 3.12 in Nicopolis, because I have **decided** to spend the winter there.
Heb 11.40 because God had **decided** on an even better plan for
Jas 1. 7 make up his mind and **undecided** in all he does, must not

DECK

Gen 6.16 Build it with three **decks** and put a door in the side.
Ezek 27. 6 They made your **deck** out of pine from Cyprus

DECLARE

Mt 10.32 "If anyone **declares** publicly that he belongs to me, I
12.37 to judge you—to **declare** you either innocent or guilty."
Mk 7.19 (In saying this, Jesus **declared** that all foods are fit to be
Lk 12. 8 that whoever **declares** publicly that he belongs to me,
Jn 13. 8 Peter **declared,** "Never at any time will you wash my feet!"
13.21 he was deeply troubled and **declared** openly, "I am telling you
Acts 10.15 "Do not consider anything unclean that God has **declared** clean."
11. 9 'Do not consider anything unclean that God has **declared** clean.'
20.24 to do, which is to **declare** the Good News about the grace
20.26 So I solemnly **declare** to you this very day:
Rom 4. 5 believes in the God who **declares** the guilty to be innocent,
8.16 himself to our spirits to **declare** that we are God's children.
8.33 God himself **declares** them not guilty!
1 Cor 15.31 in union with Christ Jesus our Lord, makes me **declare** this.
15.34 I **declare** to your shame that some of you do not know
Heb 5.10 who obey him, [10]and God **declared** him to be high priest,
1 Jn 4.15 If anyone **declares** that Jesus is the Son of God, he
Rev 3. 5 of his angels I will **declare** openly that they belong to me.
15. 4 Who will refuse to **declare** your greatness?

DECORATE

Ex 25.31 its **decorative** flowers, including buds and petals,
25.33 three **decorative** flowers shaped like almond blossoms
25.34 four **decorative** flowers shaped like almond blossoms
26.36 with blue, purple, and red wool and **decorated** with embroidery.
27.16 with blue, purple, and red wool, and **decorated** with embroidery.
28. 6 gold thread, and fine linen, **decorated** with embroidery.
28.39 and also a sash **decorated** with embroidery.

Ex 35.22 both men and women, brought **decorative** pins, earrings, rings,
36.37 with blue, purple, and red wool and **decorated** with embroidery.
37.17 its **decorative** flowers, including buds and petals,
37.19 three **decorative** flowers shaped like almond blossoms
37.20 four **decorative** flowers shaped like almond blossoms
38.18 with blue, purple, and red wool and **decorated** with embroidery.
39.29 blue, purple, and red wool, **decorated** with embroidery,
1 Kgs 6.18 The cedar panels were **decorated** with carvings of gourds
6.29 were all **decorated** with carved figures of winged creatures,
6.32 doors were **decorated** with carved figures of winged creatures,
6.35 doors made of pine [35] and **decorated** with carved figures
7.17 each column was **decorated** with a design of interwoven chains,
7.30 the supports were **decorated** with spiral figures in relief.
7.36 The supports and panels were **decorated** with figures
22.39 an account of his palace **decorated** with ivory
2 Kgs 25.17 a bronze grating **decorated** with pomegranates made of bronze.
1 Chr 29. 4 pure silver for **decorating** the walls of the Temple
2 Chr 3. 6 The king **decorated** the Temple with beautiful precious stones
3.16 tops of the columns were **decorated** with a design
4. 3 the tank were two rows of **decorations,** one above the other.
4. 3 The **decorations** were in the shape of bulls,
4.21 the flower **decorations,** the lamps, and the tongs;
Esth 1. 6 courtyard there was **decorated** with blue and white cotton curtains,
Ps 45. 8 musicians entertain you in palaces **decorated** with ivory.
Jer 10. 4 and **decorated** with silver and gold.
52.21 round it was a grating **decorated** with pomegranates,
Ezek 16.16 some of your clothes to **decorate** your places of worship,
40.36 it also had guardrooms, **decorated** inner walls,
41.26 windows, and the walls were **decorated** with palm-trees.
Amos 3.15 The houses **decorated** with ivory will fall in ruins;
Mt 23.29 tombs for the prophets and **decorate** the monuments of those

DECREASE

Ezra 4.13 will stop paying taxes, and your royal revenues will **decrease.**
Ps 107.38 he kept their herds of cattle from **decreasing.**
Jer 29. 6 You must increase in numbers and not **decrease.**
Lk 12.33 heaven, where they will never **decrease,** because no thief can get

DECREE

1 Kgs 22.23 But he himself has **decreed** that you will meet with disaster!"
2 Chr 18.22 But he himself has **decreed** that you will meet with disaster!"
Esth 3. 9 please Your Majesty, issue a **decree** that they are to be put
3.15 At the king's command the **decree** was made public
8.12 This **decree** was to take effect throughout the Persian
8.14 The **decree** was also made public in Susa, the capital city.
Nah 1.14 This is what the Lord has **decreed** about the Assyrians:
Zech 9. 1 He has **decreed** punishment for the land of Hadrach and for

DEDICATE
[REDEDICATE]

Gen 28.18 Then he poured olive-oil on it to **dedicate** it to God.
31.13 Bethel, where you **dedicated** a stone as a memorial
Ex 12.42 this same night is **dedicated** to the Lord for all time
13. 2 **"Dedicate** all the first-born males to me,
16.23 tomorrow is a holy day of rest, **dedicated** to him.
16.25 Sabbath, a day of rest **dedicated** to the Lord,
19. 6 my chosen people, [6] a people **dedicated** to me alone,
20.10 but the seventh day is a day of rest **dedicated** to me.
28. 3 so that he may be **dedicated** as a priest in my service.
28.36 pure gold and engrave on it **'Dedicated to the Lord.'**
28.38 the offerings that the Israelites **dedicate** to me,
28.41 ordain them and **dedicate** them by anointing them with olive-oil,
29. 1 Aaron and his sons to **dedicate** them as priests in my service.
29. 6 the sacred sign of dedication engraved **'Dedicated to the Lord.'**
29.19 the ram used for **dedication**—and tell Aaron and his sons
29.21 his sons, and their clothes will then be **dedicated** to me.
29.24 sons and tell them to **dedicate** it to me as a special
29.26 breast of this ram and **dedicate** it to me as a special
29.27 the ordination are to be **dedicated** to me as a special gift
30.10 This altar is to be completely holy, **dedicated** to me,
30.29 **Dedicate** these things in this way,
30.37 Treat it as a holy thing **dedicated** to me.
31.15 the seventh day is a solemn day of rest **dedicated** to me.
35. 2 be sacred, a solemn day of rest **dedicated** to me, the Lord.
35.22 all kinds of gold jewellery and **dedicated** them to the Lord.
38.24 the gold that had been **dedicated** to the Lord for the sacred
38.29 The bronze which was **dedicated** to the Lord amounted to
39.30 ornament, the sacred sign of **dedication,** out of pure gold,
39.30 gold, and they engraved on it **"Dedicated to the Lord."**
40. 9 "Then **dedicate** the Tent and all its equipment
40.10 **dedicate** the altar and all its equipment by anointing it,
40.11 Also **dedicate** the wash-basin and its base in the same way.
Lev 8. 9 the sacred sign of **dedication,** just as the Lord had commanded
8.10 it, and in this way he **dedicated** it all to the Lord.
8.11 basin and its base, in order to **dedicate** them to the Lord.
8.15 at the corners of the altar, in order to **dedicate** it.
8.15 In this way he **dedicated** it and purified it.
8.26 the basket of unleavened bread **dedicated** to the Lord,
19. 8 treating as ordinary what is **dedicated** to me,
19.24 all the fruit shall be **dedicated** as an offering to show your
21.11 He has been **dedicated** to me
22. 2 the sacred offerings that the people of Israel **dedicate** to me.
22. 3 the people of Israel have **dedicated** to me,
25. 4 of complete rest for the land, a year **dedicated** to the Lord.
27.14 When someone **dedicates** his house to the Lord,
27.15 If the one who **dedicated** the house wishes to buy it back,
27.16 If a man **dedicates** part of his land to the Lord,
Lev 27.17 If he **dedicates** the land immediately after a Year of
27.18 If he **dedicates** it later, the priest shall estimate
27.19 If the man who **dedicated** the field wishes to buy it back,
27.22 If a man **dedicates** to the Lord a field that he has
27.26 so no one may **dedicate** it to him as a freewill
27.28 what he has unconditionally **dedicated** to the Lord,
27.29 a human being who has been unconditionally **dedicated**
Num 3.45 Lord said to Moses, [45] "Now **dedicate** the Levites as mine
3.45 and **dedicate** the livestock of the Levites
5.25 hold it out in **dedication** to the Lord, and present it
6. 2 to become a Nazirite and **dedicates** himself to the Lord
6. 5 full time that he is **dedicated** to the Lord,
6. 6 is the sign of his **dedication** to God,
6.12 shall reconsecrate his hair [12] and **rededicate** to the Lord
7. 1 he anointed and **dedicated** the Tent and all its equipment,
7.10 brought offerings to celebrate the **dedication** of the altar.
7.11 is to present his gifts for the **dedication** of the altar."
7.84 the twelve leaders for the **dedication** of the altar
8.11 and then Aaron shall **dedicate** the Levites to me
8.13 **"Dedicate** the Levites as a special gift to me,
8.15 After you have purified and **dedicated** the Levites,
8.20 all the people of Israel **dedicated** the Levites,
8.21 their clothes, and Aaron **dedicated** them as a special gift
18. 6 They are **dedicated** to me, so that they can carry out their
18.14 that has been unconditionally **dedicated** to me belongs to you.
21. 2 we will unconditionally **dedicate** them and their cities to you
Deut 5.14 but the seventh day is a day of rest **dedicated** to me.
20. 5 who has just built a house, but has not yet **dedicated** it?
20. 5 killed in battle, someone else will **dedicate** his house.
Judg 13. 5 of his birth he will be **dedicated** to God as a Nazirite.
13. 7 the boy is to be **dedicated** to God as a Nazirite
16.17 "I have been **dedicated** to God as a Nazirite from the time
17. 3 I myself am solemnly **dedicating** the silver to the Lord.
1 Sam 1.11 I promise that I will **dedicate** him to you
1.28 So I am **dedicating** him to the Lord.
2.20 woman to take the place of the one you **dedicated** to him."
7. 3 **Dedicate** yourselves completely to the Lord
2 Sam 8.11 King David **dedicated** them for use in worship,
1 Kgs 7.51 that his father David had **dedicated** to the Lord—
8.63 And so the king and all the people **dedicated** the Temple.
15.15 the objects his father had **dedicated** to God,
15.15 as the gold and silver objects that he himself **dedicated.**
2 Kgs 12.18 Jehoshaphat, Jehoram, and Ahaziah had **dedicated** to the Lord,
16.14 The bronze altar **dedicated** to the Lord was between the
23. 8 also tore down the altars **dedicated** to the goat-demons
23.11 the kings of Judah had **dedicated** to the worship of the sun,
1 Chr 18.11 King David **dedicated** them for use in worship,
26.20 and the storerooms for gifts **dedicated** to God.
26.26 charge of all the gifts **dedicated** to God by King David,
26.27 captured in battle and **dedicated** it for use in the Temple.
26.28 everything that had been **dedicated** for use in the Temple,
28.12 the temple equipment and the gifts **dedicated** to the Lord.
29.21 they killed animals as sacrifices, **dedicating** them to the Lord,
2 Chr 5. 1 that his father David had **dedicated** to the Lord—the silver,
7. 5 And so he and all the people **dedicated** the Temple.
7. 9 spent seven days for the **dedication** of the altar
15.18 objects his father Abijah had **dedicated** to God,
15.18 as the gold and silver objects that he himself **dedicated.**
29.19 years he was unfaithful to God, and we have **rededicated** it.
30.15 were so ashamed that they **dedicated** themselves to the Lord,
30.17 Levites did it for them, and **dedicated** the lambs to the Lord.
31. 6 gifts, which they **dedicated** to the Lord their God.
35. 3 the teachers of Israel, who were **dedicated** to the Lord:
Ezra 6.16 others who had returned from exile—joyfully **dedicated** the Temple.
6.17 For the **dedication** they offered a hundred bulls,
Neh 3. 1 fellow-priests rebuilt the Sheep Gate, **dedicated** it,
3. 1 They **dedicated** the wall as far as the Tower of the Hundred
10.36 there, as required by the Law, **dedicate** him to God.
10.36 We will also **dedicate** the first calf born to each of our
12.27 city wall of Jerusalem was **dedicated,** the Levites were
12.27 join in celebrating the **dedication** with songs of thanksgiving
Is 19.19 a stone pillar **dedicated** to him at the Egyptian border.
23.18 money she earns by commerce will be **dedicated** to the Lord.
Jer 4. 4 and **dedicate** yourselves to me, you people
Ezek 43.18 you are to **dedicate** it by burning sacrifices on it
45. 1 one part is to be **dedicated** to the Lord.
48. 9 by ten kilometres is to be **dedicated** to the Lord.
48.14 The area **dedicated** to the Lord is the best part of all
Dan 3. 2 the **dedication** of the statue which King Nebuchadnezzar
3. 3 these officials gathered for the **dedication**
9.24 will come true, and the holy Temple will be **rededicated.**
11. 8 the articles of gold and silver **dedicated** to those gods.
Zech 14.20 horses will be inscribed with the words **"Dedicated to the Lord."**
Lk 2.23 "Every first-born male is to be **dedicated** to the Lord."
Jn 17.17 **Dedicate** them to yourself by means of the truth;
17.19 And for their sake I **dedicate** myself to you, in order
17.19 in order that they, too, may be truly **dedicated** to you.
Acts 22. 3 ancestors and was just as **dedicated** to God as are all of
Rom 6.22 gain is a life fully **dedicated** to him, and the result is
12. 1 living sacrifice to God, **dedicated** to his service and pleasing
15.16 offering acceptable to God, **dedicated** to him by the Holy Spirit.
1 Cor 6.11 you have been **dedicated** to God;
7.34 because she wants to be **dedicated** both in body and spirit;
Eph 2.21 makes it grow into a sacred temple **dedicated** to the Lord.
5.26 He did this to **dedicate** the church to God by his word,
1 Tim 2. 8 to pray, men who are **dedicated** to God and can lift up
5.22 lay hands on someone to **dedicate** him to the Lord's service.
2 Tim 2.21 because he is **dedicated** and useful to his Master, ready
2 Pet 3.11 lives should be holy and **dedicated** to God, [12] as you wait

DEDICATION

A Jewish festival in which people remembered how Judas Maccabeus rededicated the altar in the Temple in 165 BC. The festival began on the 25th day of the month Kislev (about December 10th) and lasted eight days. The Jewish name for this festival is Hanukkah.

Jn 10.22 **Festival of the Dedication** of the Temple was being celebrated

DEED (1)

Jer 32.10 I signed and sealed the **deed,** had it witnessed,
32.11 took both copies of the **deed** of purchase—the sealed copy
32.12 witnesses who had signed the **deed** of purchase
32.14 deeds, both the sealed **deed** of purchase and the open copy,
32.16 After I had given the **deed** of purchase to Baruch,
32.44 will buy them, and the **deeds** will be signed, sealed, and

DEED (2)

Mt 16.27 and then he will reward each one according to his **deeds.**
Jn 3.19 darkness rather than the light, because their **deeds** are evil.
3.20 because he does not want his evil **deeds** to be shown up.
5.36 that is, the **deeds** my Father gave me to do,
10.32 "I have done many good **deeds** in your presence which the
10.33 stone you because of any good **deeds,** but because of
10.38 should at least believe my **deeds,** in order that you may know
Acts 4. 9 questioned today about the good **deed** done to the lame man
7.22 of the Egyptians and became a great man in words and **deeds.**
Rom 4. 5 his faith, not on his **deeds,** and who believes in the God
15.18 by means of words and **deeds,** [19]by the power of miracles
2 Cor 4. 2 We put aside all secret and shameful **deeds;**
Eph 2.10 for a life of good **deeds,** which he has already prepared for
Col 1.10 produce all kinds of good **deeds,** and you will grow in your
1 Tim 2.10 dresses, [10]but with good **deeds,** as is proper for women who
5.10 been married only once [10]and have a reputation for good **deeds:**
5.25 In the same way good **deeds** are plainly seen, and even
2 Tim 2.21 useful to his Master, ready to be used for every good **deed.**
3.17 fully qualified and equipped to do every kind of good **deed.**
Tit 3. 5 not because of any good **deeds** that we ourselves had done,
3. 8 their time to doing good **deeds,** which are good and useful
Heb 10.17 "I will not remember their sins and evil **deeds** any longer."
Jas 3.13 good life, by his good **deeds** performed with humility and wisdom.
3.17 is full of compassion and produces a harvest of good **deeds;**
1 Pet 2.12 have to recognize your good **deeds** and so praise God on the
Jude 13 of the sea, with their shameful **deeds** showing up like foam.
15 them all for the godless **deeds** they have performed and for
Rev 15. 3 "Lord God Almighty, how great and wonderful are your **deeds!**
19. 8 (The linen is the good **deeds** of God's people.)
22.15 idols and those who are liars both in words and **deeds.**

DEEP

[DEPTHS]

Gen 7.17 and the water became **deep** enough for the boat to float.
7.18 water became **deeper,** and the boat drifted on the surface.
7.19 It became so **deep** that it covered the highest mountains;
49.25 rain from above And of **deep** waters from beneath the ground,
Ex 15. 5 The **deep** sea covered them;
15. 8 the **deepest** part of the sea became solid.
2 Sam 18.17 body, threw it into a **deep** pit in the forest, and covered
22.17 he pulled me out of the **deep** waters.
1 Kgs 6. 3 entrance room was 4.5 metres **deep** and 9 metres wide, as wide
7.23 tank of bronze, 2.2 metres **deep,** 4.4 metres in diameter,
2 Kgs 19.23 and that you reached the **deepest** parts of the forests.
19.30 like plants that send roots **deep** into the ground
2 Chr 4. 2 tank of bronze, 2.2 metres **deep,** 4.4 metres in diameter,
Neh 9.11 who pursued them drowned in **deep** water, as a stone sinks
Job 11. 6 there are things too **deep** for human knowledge.
28. 3 They search the **depths** of the earth
28.14 The **depths** of the oceans and seas Say that wisdom is not
36.30 through all the sky, but the **depths** of the sea remain dark.
38.16 Have you been to the springs in the **depths** of the sea?
Ps 18.16 he pulled me out of the **deep** waters.
24. 2 He built it on the **deep** waters beneath the earth and laid
24. 2 the earth and laid its foundations in the ocean **depths.**
29.10 The Lord rules over the **deep** waters;
30. 3 on my way to the **depths** below, but you restored my life.
33. 7 he shut up the ocean **depths** in storerooms.
35. 7 a trap for me and dug a **deep** hole to catch me.
36. 6 your justice is like the **depths** of the sea.
46. 2 earth is shaken and mountains fall into the ocean **depths;**
68.22 bring them back from the **depths** of the ocean, [23]so that
69. 2 I am sinking in **deep** mud, and there is no solid ground;
69. 2 I am out in **deep** water, and the waves are about to
69.14 keep me safe from my enemies, safe from the **deep** water.
69.15 don't let me drown in the **depths** or sink into the grave.
77.16 O God, they were afraid, and the **depths** of the sea trembled.
77.19 you crossed the **deep** sea, but your footprints could not be
78.15 open in the desert and gave them water from the **depths.**
80. 9 its roots went **deep,** and it spread out over the whole land.
88. 6 have thrown me into the **depths** of the tomb,
88. 6 into the darkest and **deepest** pit.
92. 5 How **deep** are your thoughts!
93. 3 The ocean **depths** raise their voice, O Lord;
95. 4 whole earth, from the **deepest** caves to the highest hills.
106.43 they chose to rebel against him and sank **deeper** into sin.
107.26 lifted high in the air and plunged down into the **depths.**
109.22 I am hurt to the **depths** of my heart.
129. 3 They cut **deep** wounds in my back
130. 1 From the **depths** of my despair I call to you, Lord.
Ps 135. 6 heaven and on earth, in the seas and in the **depths** below.
136. 6 he built the earth on the **deep** waters;
139. 6 Your knowledge of me is too **deep;**
144. 7 from above, pull me out of the **deep** water, and rescue me;
148. 7 Praise the Lord from the earth, sea-monsters and all ocean **depths;**
Prov 9.18 have already entered are now **deep** in the world of the dead.
18. 4 be a source of wisdom, **deep** as the ocean,
20. 5 are like water in a **deep** well, but someone with insight can
24. 7 Wise sayings are too **deep** for a stupid person to understand.
25. 3 like the heights of the sky or the **depths** of the ocean.
Ecc 7.24 It is too **deep** for us, too hard to understand.
Song 1. 4 We will be happy together, drink **deep,** and lose ourselves in love.
Is 7.11 It can be from **deep** in the world of the dead
14.15 been brought down to the **deepest** part of the world of the
23. 4 sea and the great ocean **depths** disown you and say, "I never
30.33 It is **deep** and wide, and piled high with wood.
37.24 and that you reached the **deepest** parts of the forests.
37.31 like plants that send roots **deep** into the ground
43. 2 When you pass through **deep** waters, I will be with you;
44.23 Shout, **deep** places of the earth!
63.12 leading his people through the **deep** water, to win everlasting
Jer 20. 9 then your message is like a fire burning **deep** within me.
Lam 3. 2 He drove me **deeper** and deeper into darkness
3.13 He shot his arrows **deep** into my body.
Ezek 17. 6 branches grew upward towards the eagle, and the roots grew **deep.**
23.14 "She sank **deeper** and deeper in her immorality.
23.32 it is large and **deep.**
26.19 I will cover you with the water of the ocean **depths.**
27.34 You have sunk to the ocean **depths.**
31. 7 Its roots reached down to the **deep-flowing** streams.
32.23 their graves are in the **deepest** parts of the world of the
40. 6 it was three metres **deep.**
40. 8 He measured this room, and found it was four metres **deep.**
40.48 two and a half metres **deep** and seven metres wide,
40.49 room, which was ten metres wide and six metres **deep.**
41. 1 it was three metres **deep** [2]and five metres wide,
41. 3 it was one metre **deep** and three metres wide,
43.13 a gutter fifty centimetres **deep** and fifty centimetres wide,
47. 5 there the stream was so **deep** I could not wade through it.
47. 5 It was too **deep** to cross except by swimming.
Dan 2.22 He reveals things that are **deep** and secret;
Hos 5. 2 spread on Mount Tabor, [2]a **deep** pit at Acacia City, and I
Jon 2. 1 From **deep** inside the fish Jonah prayed to the Lord his God:
2. 2 From **deep** in the world of the dead I cried for help,
2. 3 threw me down into the **depths,** to the very bottom
2. 6 you, O Lord my God, brought me back from the **depths** alive.
Zech 10.11 strike the waves, and the **depths** of the Nile will go dry.
Mt 12.11 a sheep and it falls into a **deep** hole on the Sabbath?
12.40 spend three days and nights in the **depths** of the earth.
13. 5 The seeds soon sprouted, because the soil wasn't **deep.**
13. 6 roots had not grown **deep** enough, the plants soon dried up.
13.21 But it does not sink **deep** into them, and they don't last
18. 6 tied round his neck and be drowned in the **deep** sea.
Mk 4. 5 The seeds soon sprouted, because the soil wasn't **deep.**
4. 6 roots had not grown **deep** enough, the plants soon dried up.
4.17 But it does not sink **deep** into them, and they don't last
7.34 up to heaven, gave a **deep** groan, and said to the man,
8.12 But Jesus gave a **deep** groan and said, "Why do the
Lk 1.29 Mary was **deeply** troubled by the angel's message,
2.19 Mary remembered all these things and thought **deeply** about them.
5. 4 boat out further to the **deep** water, and you and your
6.48 his house, dug **deep** and laid the foundation on rock.
8.13 But it does not sink **deep** into them;
16.26 all that, there is a **deep** pit lying between us, so that
Jn 4.11 said, "you haven't got a bucket, and the well is **deep.**
11.33 his heart was touched, and he was **deeply** moved.
11.38 **Deeply** moved once more, Jesus went to the tomb, which
13.21 had said this, he was **deeply** troubled and declared openly,
Acts 2.37 people heard this, they were **deeply** troubled and said to Peter
24. 3 and at all times, and we are **deeply** grateful to you.
27.28 tied to it and found that the water was forty metres **deep;**
27.28 they did the same and found that it was thirty metres **deep.**
Rom 10. 2 I can assure you that they are **deeply** devoted to God;
11.33 How **deep** are his wisdom and knowledge!
1 Cor 2.10 The Spirit searches everything, even the hidden **depths** of God's purposes.
2 Cor 2.13 But I was **deeply** worried, because I could not find our
7.12 in God's sight, how **deep** your devotion to us really is.
9.14 And so with **deep** affection they will pray for you
Gal 4.17 other people show a **deep** interest in you, but their intentions
4.18 good to have such a **deep** interest if the purpose is good
Eph 3.18 how broad and long, how high and **deep,** is Christ's love.
4. 9 that first he came down to the lowest **depths** of the earth.
5.32 There is a **deep** secret truth revealed in this scripture,
Phil 1. 8 when I say that my **deep** feeling for you all comes from
1.20 My **deep** desire and hope is that I shall never fail in
Col 2. 7 Keep your roots **deep** in him, build your lives on him,
Phlm 6 bring about a **deeper** understanding of every blessing which we
2 Pet 2.17 God has reserved a place for them in the **deepest** darkness.
Jude 13 God has reserved a place for ever in the **deepest** darkness.
Rev 2.24 not learnt what the others call 'the **deep** secrets of Satan.'
14.20 a flood three hundred kilometres long and nearly two metres **deep.**

DEER

Gen 49.21 "Naphtali is a **deer** that runs free, Who bears lovely fawns.
Deut 12.15 them, just as you would eat the meat of **deer** or antelope.
12.22 meat, just as he would eat the meat of **deer** or antelope.
14. 5 cattle, sheep, goats, [5]**deer,** wild sheep, wild goats,
15.22 or unclean, may eat them, just as you eat **deer** or antelope.

2 Sam 2.18 as fast as a wild **deer,** [19] started chasing Abner, running
22.34 He makes me sure-footed as a **deer;**
1 Kgs 4.23 pasture-fed cattle, and a hundred sheep, besides **deer,**
1 Chr 12. 8 as fierce-looking as lions and as quick as mountain **deer.**
Job 39. 1 Have you watched wild **deer** give birth?
Ps 18.33 He makes me sure-footed as a **deer;**
42. 1 As a **deer** longs for a stream of cool water, so I
Prov 5.19 with the girl you married—[19] pretty and graceful as a **deer.**
6. 5 the trap like a bird or a **deer** escaping from a hunter.
7.22 to be slaughtered, like a **deer** prancing into a trap
Song 2. 7 swear by the swift **deer** and the gazelles that you will not
3. 5 swear by the swift **deer** and the gazelles that you will not
4. 5 Your breasts are like gazelles, twin **deer** feeding
7. 3 Your breasts are like twin **deer,** like two gazelles.
Is 13.14 scattering like **deer** escaping from hunters,
51.20 they are like **deer** caught in a hunter's net.
Jer 14. 5 In the field the mother **deer** abandons her new-born fawn
Lam 1. 6 Her leaders are like **deer** that are weak from hunger,
Hab 3.19 makes me sure-footed as a **deer,** and keeps me safe
Acts 9.36 (Her name in Greek is Dorcas, meaning "a **deer.")**

DEFEAT

Gen 14. 5 came with their armies and **defeated** the Rephaim
14. 7 and **defeated** the Amorites who lived in Hazazon
14.15 attacked the enemy by night, and **defeated** them.
36.31 of Bedad from Avith (he **defeated** the Midianites in a battle
Ex 14.18 When I **defeat** them, the Egyptians will know that I am
14.31 with which the Lord had **defeated** the Egyptians,
17.13 In this way Joshua totally **defeated** the Amalekites.
32.18 doesn't sound like a shout of victory or a cry of **defeat;**
Lev 26. 8 you will be able to **defeat** a hundred,
26. 8 and a hundred will be able to **defeat** ten thousand.
26.17 so that you will be **defeated,** and those who hate you will
Num 14. 9 Lord is with us and has **defeated** the gods who protected them;
14.42 The Lord is not with you, and your enemies will **defeat** you.
14.45 who lived there attacked and **defeated** them, and pursued them
22. 6 we will be able to **defeat** them and drive them out of
32.21 our enemies until the Lord **defeats** them [22] and takes possession
Deut 1. 4 was after the Lord had **defeated** King Sihon of the Amorites,
1.42 I will not be with them, and their enemies will **defeat** them.'
1.44 as far as Hormah and **defeated** you there in the hill-country
2.30 so that we could **defeat** him and take his territory,
4.45 and the people of Israel **defeated** him when they came out of
7. 2 in your power and you **defeat** them, you must put them all
9. 3 He will **defeat** them as you advance, so that you will drive
28. 7 "The Lord will **defeat** your enemies when they attack you.
29. 7 But we **defeated** them, [8] took their land, and divided it
31. 4 those people, just as he **defeated** Sihon and Og, kings of the
32.27 enemies boast that they had **defeated** my people, when it was
32.29 They fail to see why they were **defeated;**
32.30 Why were a thousand **defeated** by one, and ten thousand by
Josh 1. 5 one will be able to **defeat** you as long as you live.
10.33 aid of Lachish, but Joshua **defeated** him and his army and
10.40 He **defeated** the kings of the hill-country, the eastern slopes,
12. 1 They **defeated** two kings.
12. 4 They also **defeated** King Og of Bashan, who was one of the
12. 6 These two kings were **defeated** by Moses and the people of Israel.
12. 7 and the people of Israel **defeated** all the kings in the
12. 9 The people of Israel **defeated** the kings of the following cities:
13.12 Moses had **defeated** these people and driven them out.
13.21 Moses **defeated** him, as well as the rulers of Midian:
Judg 1. 4 the Perizzites, and they **defeated** ten thousand men at Bezek.
1.10 There they **defeated** the clans of Sheshai, Ahiman, and
1.17 of Simeon, and together they **defeated** the Canaanites
3.13 **defeated** Israel and captured Jericho, the city of palm-trees.
3.30 That day the Israelites **defeated** Moab,
8.28 So Midian was **defeated** by the Israelites
11.33 There was a great slaughter, and the Ammonites were **defeated**
12. 4 Gilead together, fought the men of Ephraim and **defeated** them.
20.36 and the Benjaminites realized they were **defeated.**
1 Sam 4. 2 and after fierce fighting they **defeated** the Israelites
4. 3 "Why did the Lord let the Philistines **defeat** us today?
4.10 The Philistines fought hard and **defeated** the Israelites,
4.17 it was a terrible **defeat** for us!
7.13 So the Philistines were **defeated,**
14.30 eaten the food they took when they **defeated** the enemy.
14.31 That day the Israelites **defeated** the Philistines,
14.48 He fought heroically and **defeated** even the people of Amalek.
15. 7 Saul **defeated** the Amalekites,
17.46 I will **defeat** you and cut off your head.
17.50 so, without a sword, David **defeated** and killed Goliath
19. 8 David attacked them and **defeated** them so thoroughly that they fled.
2 Sam 2.17 Abner and the Israelites were **defeated** by David's men.
3. 8 and I have saved you from being **defeated** by David;
5.20 So David went to Baal Perazim and there he **defeated** the Philistines.
5.24 I will be marching ahead of you to **defeat** the Philistine army."
7. 9 I have **defeated** all your enemies as you advanced.
8. 1 David attacked the Philistines again, **defeated** them,
8. 2 Then he **defeated** the Moabites.
8. 3 Then he **defeated** the king of the Syrian state of Zobah,
8. 9 Toi of Hamath heard that David had **defeated** all of Hadadezer's army.
10.11 see that the Syrians are **defeating** me, come and help me,
10.11 and if the Ammonites are **defeating** you, I will go and help
10.15 realized that they had been **defeated** by the Israelites,
10.19 realized that they had been **defeated** by the Israelites,
11. 1 they **defeated** the Ammonites and besieged the city of Rabbah.
15.14 will soon be here and **defeat** us and kill everyone in the
2 Sam 17. 9 hears about it will say that your men have been **defeated.**
18. 7 The Israelites were **defeated** by David's men;
18. 7 it was a terrible **defeat,** with twenty thousand men killed
22.38 I pursue my enemies and **defeat** them;
22.39 they lie **defeated** before me.
1 Kgs 8.33 "When your people Israel are **defeated** by their enemies
8.46 you let their enemies **defeat** them and take them as prisoners
11.24 (This happened after David had **defeated** Hadadezer
20.21 and inflicted a severe **defeat** on the Syrians.
20.23 mountain gods, and that is why the Israelites **defeated** us.
20.23 But we will certainly **defeat** them if we fight them
20.25 Israelites in the plains, and this time we will **defeat** them."
22.11 you will fight the Syrians and totally **defeat** them.' "
2 Kgs 13. 3 of Syria and his son Benhadad to **defeat** Israel
13.17 You will fight the Syrians in Aphek until you **defeat** them."
13.19 but now you will **defeat** them only three times."
13.25 Then King Jehoash of Israel **defeated** Benhadad three times
14.10 Now Amaziah, you have **defeated** the Edomites,
14.12 Amaziah's army was **defeated,** and all his soldiers fled
16. 5 attacked Jerusalem and besieged it, but could not **defeat** Ahaz.
18. 8 He **defeated** the Philistines, and raided their settlements,
1 Chr 1.43 (he **defeated** the Midianites in a battle
14.11 So David attacked them at Baal Perazim and **defeated** them.
14.15 I will be marching ahead of you to **defeat** the Philistine army."
17. 8 and I have **defeated** all your enemies as you advanced.
17. 9 I promise to **defeat** all your enemies and to give you
18. 1 King David attacked the Philistines again and **defeated** them.
18. 2 He also **defeated** the Moabites, who became his subjects
18. 9 Toi of Hamath heard that David had **defeated** Hadadezer's entire army.
18.12 Abishai, whose mother was Zeruiah, **defeated** the Edomites
19.12 see that the Syrians are **defeating** me, come and help me,
19.12 and if the Ammonites are **defeating** you, I will go and help
19.16 realized that they had been **defeated** by the Israelites,
19.19 realized that they had been **defeated** by Israel,
20. 4 killed a giant named Sippai, and the Philistines were **defeated.**
2 Chr 6.24 "When your people Israel are **defeated** by their enemies
6.36 you let their enemies **defeat** them and take them as prisoners
13.15 God **defeated** Jeroboam and the Israelite army.
13.17 dealt the Israelites a crushing **defeat**—
14.11 no one can hope to **defeat** you."
14.12 The Lord **defeated** the Sudanese army
18.10 'With these you will fight the Syrians and totally **defeat** them.' "
20.27 in triumph, because the Lord had **defeated** their enemies.
20.29 heard how the Lord had **defeated** Israel's enemies
24.24 but the Lord let them **defeat** a much larger Judaean army
25. 8 power to give victory or **defeat,**
25. 8 and he will let your enemies **defeat** you."
25.14 When Amaziah returned from **defeating** the Edomites,
25.19 you boast that you have **defeated** the Edomites,
25.20 for Amaziah to be **defeated,** because he had worshipped the
25.22 the Judaean army was **defeated,** and the soldiers fled
26. 7 God helped him to **defeat** the Philistines,
27. 5 against the king of Ammon and his army and **defeated** them.
28. 5 let the king of Syria **defeat** him and take a large number
28. 5 Pekah son of Remaliah, **defeat** Ahaz and kill 120,000
28. 9 with Judah and let you **defeat** them, but now he has heard
28.23 sacrifices to the gods of the Syrians, who had **defeated** him.
Neh 4.15 and they realized that God had **defeated** their plans.
Esth 6.13 He will certainly **defeat** you."
Job 12.23 makes nations strong and great, but then he **defeats** and destroys
16.15 made of sackcloth, and I sit here in the dust **defeated.**
40.19 Only his Creator can **defeat** him.
Ps 6.10 My enemies will know the bitter shame of **defeat;**
10.10 brute strength has **defeated** them.
13. 4 Don't let my enemies say, "We have **defeated** him."
17.13 Oppose my enemies and **defeat** them!
18.38 they lie **defeated** before me.
25. 2 Save me from the shame of **defeat;**
25. 3 **Defeat** does not come to those who trust in you,
25.20 keep me from **defeat.**
30. 6 I felt secure and said to myself, "I will never be **defeated."**
31. 1 never let me be **defeated.**
35. 4 May those who try to kill me be **defeated** and disgraced!
35.19 Don't let my enemies, those liars, gloat over my **defeat.**
35.26 May those who gloat over my suffering be completely **defeated**
40.14 May those who try to kill me be completely **defeated** and confused.
40.15 May those who jeer at me be dismayed by their **defeat.**
44. 5 and by your power we **defeat** our enemies.
44. 7 saved us from our enemies and **defeated** those who hate us.
44. 9 But now you have rejected us and let us be **defeated;**
44.25 we lie **defeated** in the dust.
53. 5 God has rejected them, and so Israel will totally **defeat** them.
54. 7 from all my troubles, and I have seen my enemies **defeated.**
55.19 God, who has ruled from eternity, will hear me and **defeat**
55.22 he never lets honest men be **defeated.**
56. 7 **defeat** those people in your anger!
56.13 you have rescued me from death and kept me from **defeat.**
57. 3 he will **defeat** my oppressors.
59.10 he will let me see my enemies **defeated.**
59.11 Scatter them by your strength and **defeat** them, O Lord,
60. 1 You have rejected us, God, and **defeated** us;
60.12 he will **defeat** our enemies.
62. 2 he is my defender, and I shall never be **defeated.**
62. 6 he is my defender, and I shall never be **defeated.**
65. 3 Our faults **defeat** us, but you forgive them.
68. 1 Those who hate him run away in **defeat.**
70. 2 May those who try to kill me be **defeated** and confused.
70. 3 May those who jeer at me be dismayed by their **defeat.**
71. 1 never let me be **defeated!**
71.13 May those who attack me be **defeated** and destroyed.

Ps 71.24 those who tried to harm me have been **defeated** and disgraced.
72. 4 may he help the needy and **defeat** their oppressors.
76. 4 as you return from the mountains where you **defeated** your foes.
78.66 He drove his enemies back in lasting and shameful **defeat.**
81.14 I would quickly **defeat** their enemies
83.10 You **defeated** them at Endor, and their bodies rotted
83.11 **defeat** all their rulers as you did Zebah and Zalmunna,
83.17 May they be **defeated** and terrified for ever;
89.10 with your mighty strength you **defeated** your enemies.
89.22 the wicked will not **defeat** him.
89.43 made his weapons useless and let him be **defeated** in battle.
92. 9 your enemies will die, and all the wicked will be **defeated.**
92.11 I have seen the **defeat** of my enemies and heard the cries
107.39 When God's people were **defeated** and humiliated
108.13 he will **defeat** our enemies.
109.28 May my persecutors be **defeated,** and may I, your servant,
110. 5 when he becomes angry, he will **defeat** kings.
110. 6 he will **defeat** kings all over the earth.
112. 8 he is certain to see his enemies **defeated.**
116. 8 he stopped my tears and kept me from **defeat.**
118. 7 the Lord who helps me, and I will see my enemies **defeated.**
118.13 fiercely attacked and was being **defeated,** but the Lord helped me.
119.25 I lie **defeated** in the dust;
119.80 obey your commandments and be spared the shame of **defeat.**
127. 5 He will never be **defeated** when he meets his enemies
129. 5 May everyone who hates Zion be **defeated** and driven back.
136.23 He did not forget us when we were **defeated;**
143. 3 My enemy has hunted me down and completely **defeated** me.
149. 7 swords in their hands [7]to **defeat** the nations
Ecc 4.12 Two men can resist an attack that would **defeat** one man
Is 9. 4 You have **defeated** the nation that oppressed and exploited
9. 4 people, just as you **defeated** the army of Midian long ago.
22. 5 a time of panic, **defeat,** and confusion
41.11 "Those who are angry with you will know the shame of **defeat.**
61. 2 When the Lord will save his people And **defeat** their enemies.
Jer 1.18 They will not **defeat** you, for I will be with you
15.20 They will fight against you, but they will not **defeat** you.
18.23 Throw them down in **defeat** and deal with them
21. 4 "Zedekiah, I am going to **defeat** your army that is fighting
22.20 of Moab, because all your allies have been **defeated.**
37.10 Even if you **defeat** the whole Babylonian army,
43.11 Nebuchadnezzar will come and **defeat** Egypt.
46. 2 which King Nebuchadnezzar of Babylonia **defeated** at Carchemish
Ezek 39.23 and let their enemies **defeat** them and kill them in battle.
Dan 11. 7 of the king of Syria, enter their fortress, and **defeat** them.
11.14 of a vision they have seen, but they will be **defeated.**
11.18 But a foreign leader will **defeat** him and put an end
11.19 land, but he will be **defeated,** and that will be the end
Mic 1.10 Don't tell our enemies in Gath about our **defeat;**
7.10 We will see them **defeated,** trampled down like mud in the streets.
Zech 10. 5 Lord is with them, and they will **defeat** even the enemy horsemen.
Lk 9.25 if he wins the whole world but is himself lost or **defeated?**
11.22 stronger man attacks him and **defeats** him, he carries away
Jn 16.33 I have **defeated** the world!"
Acts 5.39 but if it comes from God, you cannot possibly **defeat** them.
18.28 with his strong arguments he **defeated** the Jews in public debates
Rom 12.21 Do not let evil **defeat** you;
1 Cor 15.25 Christ must rule until God **defeats** all enemies and puts them
15.26 The last enemy to be **defeated** will be death.
Heb 7. 1 battle in which he **defeated** the four kings, Melchizedek met him
10.32 you suffered many things, yet were not **defeated** by the struggle.
11.34 were mighty in battle and **defeated** the armies of foreigners.
1 Jn 2.13 to you, young men, because you have **defeated** the Evil One.
2.14 of God lives in you, and you have **defeated** the Evil One.
4. 4 and have **defeated** the false prophets, because the Spirit
5. 4 because every child of God is able to **defeat** the world.
5. 5 Who can **defeat** the world?
Rev 11. 7 He will **defeat** them and kill them, [8]and their bodies will
12. 8 but the dragon was **defeated,** and he and his angels were
13. 7 against God's people and to **defeat** them, and it was given
17.14 and faithful followers, will **defeat** them, because he is Lord
19.15 came a sharp sword, with which he will **defeat** the nations.

DEFECT

Ex 12. 5 but it must be a one-year-old male without any **defects.**
29. 1 Take one young bull and two rams without any **defects.**
Lev 1. 3 a burnt-offering, he must bring a bull without any **defects.**
1.10 his sheep or goats, it must be a male without any **defects.**
3. 1 it is to be a bull or a cow without any **defects.**
3. 6 may be male or female, but it must be without any **defects.**
4. 3 a young bull without any **defects** and sacrifice it to the
4.23 shall bring as his offering a male goat without any **defects.**
4.28 bring as his offering a female goat without any **defects.**
4.32 as a sin-offering, it must be a female without any **defects.**
5.15 to the Lord a male sheep or goat without any **defects.**
5.18 repayment-offering a male sheep or goat without any **defects.**
6. 6 to the Lord a male sheep or goat without any **defects.**
9. 2 and a ram without any **defects** and offer them to the Lord,
9. 3 a one-year-old lamb without any **defects** for a burnt-offering,
14.10 that are without any **defects,**
21.17 descendants who has any physical **defect** may present the food-offering
21.18 No man with any physical **defect** may make the offering:
21.21 priest who has any physical **defect** may present the food-offering
21.23 because he has a physical **defect,** he shall not come near
22.18 as a freewill offering, the animal must not have any **defects.**
22.19 To be accepted, it must be a male without any **defects.**
22.20 any animal that has any **defect,** the Lord will not accept it.
22.21 animal must be without any **defect** if it is to be accepted.
Lev 22.25 Such animals are considered **defective** and are not acceptable.
23.12 a one-year-old male lamb that has no **defects.**
23.18 one bull, and two rams, none of which may have any **defects.**
Num 6.14 and present to the Lord three animals without any **defects:**
19. 2 red cow which has no **defects**
28. 3 two one-year-old male lambs without any **defects.**
28. 9 one-year-old male lambs without any **defects,**
28.11 one ram, seven one-year-old male lambs, all without any **defects.**
28.19 and seven one-year-old male lambs, all without any **defects.**
28.27 and seven one-year-old male lambs, all without any **defects.**
29. 2 and seven one-year-old male lambs, all without any **defects.**
29. 8 and seven one-year-old male lambs, all without any **defects.**
29.13 and fourteen one-year-old male lambs, all without any **defects.**
29.17 and fourteen one-year-old male lambs, all without any **defects.**
29.20 and fourteen one-year-old male lambs, all without any **defects.**
29.23 and fourteen one-year-old male lambs, all without any **defects.**
29.26 and fourteen one-year-old male lambs, all without any **defects.**
29.29 and fourteen one-year-old male lambs, all without any **defects.**
29.32 and fourteen one-year-old male lambs, all without any **defects.**
29.36 and seven one-year-old male lambs, all without any **defects.**
Deut 15.21 or have any other serious **defect,** you must not sacrifice them
17. 1 to the Lord your God cattle or sheep that have any **defects;**
2 Sam 14.25 he had no **defect** from head to foot.
Ezek 43.22 a male goat without any **defects** and offer it as a sacrifice
43.23 both of them without any **defects,** [24]and bring them to me.
43.25 All of them must be without any **defects.**
45.18 sacrifice a bull without any **defects** and purify the Temple.
45.23 seven rams without any **defects** and burn them whole.
46. 4 burnt whole, six lambs and one ram, all without any **defects.**
46. 6 a young bull, six lambs, and a ram, all without any **defects.**
46.13 a one-year-old lamb without any **defects** is to be burnt whole
Dan 1. 4 and free from physical **defects,** so that they would be qualified
1 Pet 1.19 of Christ, who was like a lamb without **defect** or flaw.

DEFENCELESS see DEFEND

DEFEND

[SELF-DEFENCE, WELL-DEFENDED]

Ex 15. 2 The Lord is my strong **defender;**
Num 10. 9 at war in your land, **defending** yourselves against an enemy
21.24 to the Ammonites, because the Ammonite border was strongly **defended.**
Deut 32. 4 "The Lord is your mighty **defender,** perfect and just
33.27 God has always been your **defence;**
33.29 shield and your sword, to **defend** you and give you victory.
Josh 8.17 the city was left wide open, with no one to **defend** it.
Judg 6.31 Are you **defending** him?
6.31 If Baal is a god, let him **defend** himself.
6.32 because Joash said, "Let Baal **defend** himself;
1 Sam 2.25 If a man sins against another man, God can **defend** him;
2.25 but who can **defend** a man who sins against the Lord?"
13.23 sent a group of soldiers to **defend** the pass of Michmash.
24.15 look into the matter, **defend** me, and save me from you."
2 Sam 18.13 about everything—and you would not have **defended** me."
22. 3 he **defends** me and keeps me safe.
22.30 to attack my enemies and power to overcome their **defences.**
22.32 God alone is our **defence.**
22.47 Praise my **defender!**
23.12 in the field, **defended** it, and killed the Philistines.
2 Kgs 2.12 Mighty **defender** of Israel!
10. 3 make him king, and fight to **defend** him."
13.14 "You have been the mighty **defender** of Israel!"
19.34 I will **defend** this city and protect it,
20. 6 I will **defend** this city, for the sake of my own honour
2 Chr 32. 5 The king strengthened the city's **defences** by repairing the wall,
32. 5 In addition, he repaired the **defences** built on the land
Esth 8.11 Jews in every city to organize themselves for **self-defence.**
9.16 Jews in the provinces also organized and **defended** themselves.
Job 5. 4 no one stands up to **defend** them in court.
13. 8 Are you trying to **defend** him?
15. 3 talk as you do or **defend** himself with such meaningless words.
19.25 is someone in heaven who will come at last to my **defence.**
30.14 through the holes in my **defences** and come crashing down
Ps 4. 1 Answer me when I pray, O God, my **defender!**
18. 1 You are my **defender.**
18. 2 he **defends** me and keeps me safe.
18.29 strength to attack my enemies and power to overcome their **defences.**
18.31 God alone is our **defence.**
18.46 Praise my **defender!**
28. 1 O Lord, my **defender,** I call to you.
28. 7 The Lord protects and **defends** me;
28. 8 he **defends** and saves his chosen king.
31. 2 my **defence** to save me.
31. 3 You are my refuge and **defence;**
35.23 Rouse yourself, O Lord, and **defend** me;
42. 9 To God, my **defender,** I say, "Why have you forgotten me?
43. 1 O God, declare me innocent, and **defend** my cause against the ungodly;
45. 4 in majesty to victory for the **defence** of truth and justice!
54. 4 The Lord is my **defender.**
55.22 Leave your troubles with the Lord, and he will **defend** you;
59.17 I will praise you, my **defender.**
61. 3 for you are my protector, my strong **defence** against my enemies.
62. 2 he is my **defender,** and I shall never be defeated.
62. 6 he is my **defender,** and I shall never be defeated.
71. 3 you are my refuge and **defence.**
71. 7 example to many, because you have been my strong **defender.**
74.22 Rouse yourself, God, and **defend** your cause!

Ps 81. 1 Shout for joy to God our **defender;**
82. 3 **Defend** the rights of the poor and the orphans;
91. 2 can say to him, "You are my **defender** and protector.
91. 4 his faithfulness will protect and **defend** you.
91. 9 have made the Lord your **defender,** the Most High your protector,
94.22 But the Lord **defends** me;
109.31 because he **defends** the poor man and saves him
119.114 You are my **defender** and protector;
119.154 **Defend** my cause, and set me free;
135.14 The Lord will **defend** his people;
140. 7 My Sovereign Lord, my strong **defender,** you have protected me
140.12 Lord, I know that you **defend** the cause of the poor and
144. 2 He is my protector and **defender,** my shelter and saviour,
Prov 21.22 general can take a city **defended** by strong men,
23.11 The Lord is their powerful **defender,**
29.14 If a king **defends** the rights of the poor, he will rule
Is 1. 8 a city under siege—as **defenceless** as a watchman's hut
1.17 give orphans their rights, and **defend** widows."
1.23 They never **defend** orphans in court
11. 4 the poor fairly and **defend** the rights of the helpless.
17. 3 Israel will be **defenceless,**
17. 9 When that day comes, **well-defended** cities will be deserted
22. 8 All Judah's **defences** crumbled.
26. 1 God himself **defends** its walls!
28. 6 and courage to those who **defend** the city gates from attack.
30.29 way to the Temple of the Lord, the **defender** of Israel.
31. 5 I, the Lord Almighty, will protect Jerusalem and **defend** it."
37.35 I will **defend** this city and protect it,
49. 4 Yet I can trust the Lord to **defend** my cause;
50. 9 The Sovereign Lord himself **defends** me— who, then, can
51.22 the Lord your God **defends** you and says, "I am taking
54.17 I will **defend** my servants and give them victory."
59.20 will come to Jerusalem to **defend** you and to save all of
60.18 I will protect and **defend** you like a wall;
Jer 21.13 that no one can attack you or break through your **defences.**
46.14 'Get ready to **defend** yourselves;
49. 1 Is there no one to **defend** their land?
Lam 2. 2 And tore down the forts that **defended** the land.
Ezek 13. 5 and so Israel cannot be **defended** when war comes on the day
22.30 the walls have crumbled and **defend** the land when my anger is
25. 9 let the cities that **defend** the border of Moab be attacked,
30. 6 all Egypt's **defenders** will be killed in battle.
30. 8 to Egypt and all her **defenders** are killed,
38.11 peace and security in unwalled towns that have no **defences.**
Dan 3.16 "Your Majesty, we will not try to **defend** ourselves.
9.16 You have **defended** us in the past, so do not be angry
9.25 rebuilt with streets and strong **defences,**
11. 1 He is responsible for helping and **defending** me.
11.39 To **defend** his fortresses, he will use people who worship
Joel 2. 8 They swarm through **defences,** and nothing can stop them.
3.16 But he will **defend** his people.
Amos 3.11 enemy will surround their land, destroy their **defences,**
Mic 5. 5 and break through our **defences,** we will send our strongest
5.11 the cities in your land and tear down all your **defences.**
7. 9 in the end he will **defend** us and right the wrongs
Nah 2. 1 Man the **defences!**
3. 8 river to protect her like a wall—the Nile was her **defence.**
3.13 your country stands **defenceless** before your enemies.
Zech 14.14 The men of Judah will fight to **defend** Jerusalem.
Lk 12.11 about how you will **defend** yourself or what you will say.
21.14 worry about how you will **defend** yourselves, [15]because I will
Acts 19.33 to be silent, and he tried to make a speech of **defence.**
22. 1 fellow-Israelites, listen to me as I make my **defence** before you!"
24.10 many years, and so I am happy to **defend** myself before you.
25. 8 But Paul **defended** himself:
25.16 has had the chance of **defending** himself against the accusation.
26. 1 Paul stretched out his hand and **defended** himself as follows:
26. 2 that today I am to **defend** myself before you from all the
26.24 As Paul **defended** himself in this way, Festus shouted at him,
Rom 2.15 their thoughts sometimes accuse them and sometimes **defend** them.
1 Cor 9. 3 When people criticize me, this is how I **defend** myself:
2 Cor 6. 7 as our weapon, both to attack and to **defend** ourselves.
7. 7 how sorry you are, how ready you are to **defend** me;
12.19 all along we have been trying to **defend** ourselves before you.
Phil 1. 7 I was free to **defend** the gospel and establish it firmly.
1.16 know that God has given me the work of **defending** the gospel.
2 Tim 4.16 No one stood by me the first time I **defended** myself;

DEFENDANT

Is 45.21 let the **defendants** consult one another.

DEFIANT see DEFY

DEFILE
[UNDEFILED]

To make a person unfit to worship God. Some foods and actions were forbidden by the Law of Moses. If people broke these laws they were not allowed into the place where they worshipped God. Such people could not take part in worship until they had gone through certain rituals.

Lev 15.31 so that they would not **defile** the Tent of his presence,
21.11 unclean nor is he to **defile** my sacred Tent by leaving it
Num 5. 3 so that they will not **defile** the camp, where I live among
5.12 and has **defiled** herself by having intercourse with another
6. 6 and so he must not **defile** himself by going near a corpse,
6. 9 hair of a Nazirite is **defiled** because he is right beside
Num 6.12 period of time doesn't count, because his consecrated hair was **defiled.**
19.13 He **defiles** the Lord's Tent, and he will no longer be
19.20 He **defiles** the Lord's Tent and will no longer be considered
35.33 did this, you would **defile** the land where you are living.
35.33 Murder **defiles** the land, and except by the death of the
35.34 Do not **defile** the land where you are living, because I
Deut 21.23 so that you will not **defile** the land that the Lord your
24. 4 he is to consider her **defiled.**
1 Chr 23.28 its rooms, and to keep **undefiled** everything that is sacred;
2 Chr 29. 5 Remove from the Temple everything that **defiles** it.
36.14 worshipping idols, and so they **defiled** the Temple,
Neh 13.29 O God, how those people **defiled** both the office of priest
Ps 106.38 killed those innocent children, and the land was **defiled**
Is 24. 5 The people have **defiled** the earth by breaking God's laws
Jer 2. 7 they **defiled** the country I had given them.
2.23 you say you have not **defiled** yourself,
3. 1 This would completely **defile** the land.
3. 2 You have **defiled** the land with your prostitution.
3. 9 She **defiled** the land, and she committed adultery
7.30 their idols, which I hate, in my Temple and have **defiled** it.
16.18 and wickedness, because they have **defiled** my land with idols
19. 4 abandoned me and **defiled** this place by offering sacrifices
32.34 the Temple built for my worship, and they have **defiled** it.
Lam 4. 7 Our princes were **undefiled** and pure as snow, vigorous and strong,
4.15 "You're **defiled!**
Ezek 4.14 I have never **defiled** myself.
5.11 because you **defiled** my Temple with all the evil,
7.21 "and law-breakers will take all their wealth and **defile** it.
7.22 Temple is profaned, when robbers break into it and **defile** it.
9. 7 God said to them, **"Defile** the Temple.
14.11 keep the Israelites from deserting me and **defiling** themselves
20.18 follow their customs or **defile** yourselves with their idols.
20.26 I let them **defile** themselves with their own offerings,
20.31 offer the same gifts and **defile** yourselves with the same idols
20.43 the disgraceful things you did and how you **defiled** yourselves.
22. 3 and have **defiled** yourself by worshipping idols,
22. 4 of those murders and are **defiled** by the idols you made,
23. 7 her lust led her to **defile** herself by worshipping Assyrian idols.
23.17 They used her and **defiled** her so much that finally she
23.30 and **defiled** yourself with their idols.
24.13 Jerusalem, your immoral actions have **defiled** you.
24.13 Although I tried to purify you, you remained **defiled.**
36.17 living in their land, they **defiled** it by the way they lived
36.18 land and because of the idols by which they had **defiled** it.
36.25 from all your idols and everything else that has **defiled** you.
36.29 I will save you from everything that **defiles** you.
37.23 They will not **defile** themselves with disgusting idols
Hos 6.10 my people have **defiled** themselves by worshipping idols.
9. 4 Their food will **defile** everyone who eats it,
Zeph 3. 4 the priests **defile** what is sacred, and twist the law of God
Hag 2.13 asked, "Suppose a man is **defiled** because he has touched a
2.13 touches any of these foods, will that make them **defiled** too?"
2.14 and so everything they offer on the altar is **defiled."**
Mal 2.11 They have **defiled** the Temple which the Lord loves.
Acts 10.14 I have never eaten anything ritually unclean or **defiled."**
10.28 that I must not consider any person ritually unclean or **defiled.**
11. 8 No ritually unclean or **defiled** food has ever entered my mouth.'
21.28 some Gentiles into the Temple and **defiled** this holy place!"
24. 6 He also tried to **defile** the Temple, and we arrested him.
1 Cor 8. 7 is weak, and they feel they are **defiled** by the food.
Tit 1.15 pure to those who are **defiled** and unbelieving,
1.15 for their minds and consciences have been **defiled.**

DEFINITE

Acts 25.26 But I have nothing **definite** about him to write to the Emperor.

DEFORMED

Lev 21.18 no one who is blind, lame, disfigured, or **deformed;**

DEFY
[DEFIANT]

Lev 26.23 to me, but continue to **defy** me, [24]then I will turn on
26.27 this you still continue to **defy** me and refuse to obey me,
Num 26. 9 They **defied** Moses and Aaron and joined the followers of Korah
1 Sam 17.26 heathen Philistine to **defy** the army of the living God?"
17.36 Philistine, who has **defied** the army of the living God.
17.45 the God of the Israelite armies, which you have **defied.**
2 Sam 21.21 He **defied** the Israelites,
1 Chr 20. 7 He **defied** the Israelites,
2 Chr 26.16 He **defied** the Lord his God by going into the Temple
28.19 of his people and had **defied** the Lord, the Lord brought
32.17 that the emperor wrote **defied** the Lord, the God of Israel.
Ezra 6.12 any king or nation that **defies** this command and tries to
Job 15.25 the man who shakes his fist at God and **defies** the Almighty.
Ps 9.19 Do not let men **defy** you!
Is 1.20 But if you **defy** me, you are doomed to die.
Ezek 2. 6 They will **defy** and despise you;
3. 7 All of them are stubborn and **defiant.**
20. 8 But they **defied** me and refused to listen.
20.13 But even in the desert they **defied** me.
20.21 "But that generation also **defied** me.
Dan 8.11 It even **defied** the Prince of the heavenly army,
8.25 He will even **defy** the greatest King of all,

DEGRADING

2 Sam 13.12 “Don't force me to do such a **degrading** thing!
Ezek 6. 9 because of the evil and **degrading** things they have done.

DEGREE

2 Cor 3.18 into his likeness in an ever greater **degree** of glory.

DELAY

Gen 32. 4 with Laban and that I have **delayed** my return until now.
45. 9 come to me without **delay**.
2 Chr 24. 5 but the Levites **delayed**, [6]so he called in Jehoiada,
29.20 Without **delay** King Hezekiah assembled the leading men
Ps 119.60 Without **delay** I hurry to obey your commands.
Is 46.13 My triumph will not be **delayed.**
Jer 4. 6 Don't **delay!**
Ezek 12.25 There will be no more **delay.**
12.28 There will be no more **delay.**
Dan 9.19 that everyone will know that you are God, do not **delay!**
Hab 2. 3 it will certainly take place, and it will not be **delayed.**
1 Tim 3.15 But if I am **delayed,** this letter will let you know how
Heb 10.37 he will not **delay.**
Rev 10. 6 The angel said, “There will be no more **delay!**

DELIBERATE

Ex 21.14 a man gets angry and **deliberately** kills another man, he is
Num 15.30 But any person who sins **deliberately,** whether he is a native
15.31 Lord said and has **deliberately** broken one of his commands.
30. 6 woman makes a vow, whether **deliberately** or carelessly,
Deut 19.11 “But suppose a man **deliberately** murders his enemy
1 Kgs 11.11 “Because you have **deliberately** broken your covenant with me
Ps 78.18 They **deliberately** put God to the test by demanding the food
Hos 6. 9 And they do all this evil **deliberately!**

DELICATE

Ex 16.14 It was as **delicate** as frost.
Is 47. 1 a city unconquered, but you are soft and **delicate** no longer!

DELIGHT

Gen 49.15 the resting-place is good And that the land is **delightful.**
49.26 Blessings of ancient mountains, **Delightful** things from everlasting hills.
Deut 28.63 Just as the Lord took **delight** in making you prosper
28.63 so he will take **delight** in destroying you
1 Sam 18.26 had said, and David was **delighted** with the thought of becoming
2 Chr 15.15 They took **delight** in worshipping the Lord, and he accepted them
Ps 35.19 hate me for no reason smirk with **delight** over my sorrow.
111. 2 All who are **delighted** with them want to understand them.
119.14 I **delight** in following your commands more than in having great wealth.
147.10 nor his **delight** in brave soldiers;
Song 1.16 how you **delight** me!
4.10 Your love **delights** me, my sweetheart and bride.
7. 6 how complete the **delights** of your love.
7.13 Darling, I have kept for you the old **delights** and the new.
Is 4. 2 Israel who survive will take **delight** and pride in the crops
62. 5 As a groom is **delighted** with his bride,
62. 5 So your God will **delight** in you.
Jer 3.19 and give you a **delightful** land, the most beautiful land
31.12 on Mount Zion and be **delighted** with my gifts— gifts of
Lam 2. 4 He killed all those who were our joy and **delight.**
Ezek 25. 3 You were **delighted** to see my Temple profaned,
Hos 4.18 After drinking much wine, they **delight** in their prostitution,
Zeph 3.17 The Lord will take **delight** in you, and in his love he
Rom 7.22 My inner being **delights** in the law of God.

DELILAH

Philistine woman who lured Samson to his destruction.

Judg 16. 4 love with a woman named **Delilah,** who lived in the Valley of
16. 6 So **Delilah** said to Samson, “Please tell me what makes
16. 8 So the Philistine kings brought **Delilah** seven new bowstrings
16.10 **Delilah** said to Samson, “Look, you've been making a fool
16.12 So **Delilah** got some new ropes and tied him up.
16.13 **Delilah** said to Samson, “You're still making a fool of me
16.14 **Delilah** then lulled him to sleep, took his seven locks of hair,
16.18 When **Delilah** realized that he had told her the truth,
16.19 **Delilah** lulled Samson to sleep in her lap

DELIVER (1)

Gen 49.18 “I wait for your **deliverance,** Lord.
Ps 19.12 **deliver** me, Lord, from hidden faults!
43. 1 **deliver** me from lying and evil men!
119.123 watching for your saving help, for the **deliverance** you promised.
Is 51. 6 But the **deliverance** I bring will last for ever;
51. 8 But the **deliverance** I bring will last for ever;

DELIVER (2)

1 Sam 25. 9 David's men **delivered** this message to Nabal in David's name.
2 Kgs 22. 8 Shaphan **delivered** the king's order to Hilkiah,
Esth 8.10 They were **delivered** by riders mounted on fast horses
Prov 26. 6 If you let a fool **deliver** a message, you might as well
Acts 16. 4 the towns, they **delivered** to the believers the rules decided
Acts 23.33 took him to Caesarea, **delivered** the letter to the governor,
1 Cor 2. 4 teaching and message were not **delivered** with skilful words of

AV DELIVER

see also **RESCUE, SAVE, VICTORY**

Ex 5.23 And you have done nothing to **help** them!”
12.27 He killed the Egyptians, but **spared** us.’ ”
Deut 23.14 you in your camp to **protect** you and to give you victory
25.11 wife of one tries to **help** her husband by grabbing hold of
Josh 9.26 he **protected** them and did not allow the people of Israel to
Judg 3. 9 out to the Lord, and he sent a man who **freed** them.
6.13 abandoned us and left us to the **mercy** of the Midianites.”
1 Sam 26.24 Lord do the same to me and **free** me from all troubles!”
2 Sam 22.49 me victory over my enemies and **protect** me from violent men.
2 Kgs 3.10 the three of us at the **mercy** of the king of Moab!”
3.13 put us three kings at the **mercy** of the king of Moab.”
Ezra 8.31 God was with us and **protected** us from enemy attacks and from
Job 5. 4 no one stands up to **defend** them in court.
29.12 When the poor cried out, I **helped** them;
33.24 In mercy the angel will say, **“Release** him!
33.28 **He kept me from** going to the world of the dead, and
Ps 18.48 me victory over my enemies and **protect** me from violent men.
22. 5 They called to you and **escaped** from danger;
34. 4 he **freed** me from all my fears.
35.10 You **protect** the weak from the strong, the poor from the oppressor.”
41. 1 the Lord will **help** them when they are in trouble.
51.14 **Spare** my life, O God, and save me, and I will gladly
69.14 **keep me safe** from my enemies, safe from the deep water.
71. 2 Because you are righteous, **help** me and rescue me.
89.48 How can man **keep himself from** the grave?
91. 3 He will **keep you safe** from all hidden dangers
119.154 Defend my cause, and **set me free;**
Prov 2.12 protect you [12]and **prevent** you from doing the wrong thing.
2.16 You will be able to **resist** any immoral woman who tries
11. 8 The righteous are **protected** from trouble;
11.21 evil men will be punished, but righteous men will **escape.**
Is 20. 6 we relied on to **protect** us from the emperor of Assyria!
37.11 Do you think that you can **escape?**
43.13 No one can **escape** from my power;
44.20 His foolish ideas have so misled him that he is beyond **help.**
Jer 1. 8 afraid of them, for I will be with you to **protect** you.
1.18 not defeat you, for I will be with you to **protect** you.
15.20 I will be with you to protect you and **keep you safe.**
21.11 **Protect** the person who is being cheated from the one who is
22. 3 **Protect** the person who is being cheated from the one who is
39.17 But I, the Lord, will **protect** you, and you will not be
39.18 I **will keep you safe,** and you will not be put to
Ezek 3.19 he will die, still a sinner, but your life will be **spared.**
3.21 he will stay alive, and your life will also be **spared.”**
13.21 scarves and let my people **escape** from your power once and
17.15 He cannot break the treaty and go **unpunished!**
33. 5 If he had paid attention, he could have **escaped.**
33. 9 will die, still a sinner, but your life will be **spared.”**
34.27 chains and **set them free** from those who made them slaves,
Dan 8. 4 No animal could stop him or **escape** his power.
Amos 2.15 away, and men on horses will not **escape** with their lives.
Zech 2. 6 But now, you exiles, **escape** from Babylonia and return to Jerusalem.
Acts 7.25 to use him to **set them free,** but they did not understand.)
7.34 heard their groans, and I have come down to **set them free.**
Rom 7. 6 Now, however, we are **free** from the Law, because we died to
8.21 itself would one day be **set free** from its slavery to decay
Gal 1. 4 In order to **set us free** from this present evil age, Christ
Heb 2.15 death, [15]and in this way **set free** those who were slaves
2 Pet 2. 4 into hell, where they are **kept** chained in darkness, waiting for

DELUSION

1 Cor 15.17 then your faith is a **delusion** and you are still lost in

DEMAND

Gen 31.39 You **demanded** that I make good anything that was stolen
Ex 7. 9 “If the king **demands** that you prove yourselves
21.22 whatever amount the woman's husband **demands,**
Deut 10.12 Israel, listen to what the Lord your God **demands** of you:
29.19 who hears these solemn **demands** and yet convinces himself
1 Sam 2.13 regulations concerning what the priests could **demand** from the people.
2 Sam 14. 7 turned against me and are **demanding** that I hand my son over
1 Kgs 20. 2 “King Benhadad **demands** that [3]you surrender to him
20. 5 messengers came back to Ahab with another **demand** from Benhadad:
20. 7 He sent me a message **demanding** my wives and children, my
20. 9 I agreed to his first **demand,** but I cannot agree to the
2 Kgs 18.14 stop your attack, and I will pay whatever you **demand.”**
23. 3 to put into practice the **demands** attached to the covenant,
23.35 needed to pay the tribute **demanded** by the king of Egypt.
2 Chr 34.31 to put into practice the **demands** attached to the covenant,
Ezra 10. 3 We will do what God's Law **demands.**
Neh 5.15 to the people and had **demanded** forty silver coins a day for
Job 27. 8 for godless men in the hour when God **demands** their life?
Ps 7. 6 Justice is what you **demand,** [7]so bring together all the peoples
78.18 put God to the test by **demanding** the food they wanted.
Is 36. 2 force to **demand** that King Hezekiah should surrender.
43.23 did not burden you by **demanding** offerings or wear you out by
Ezek 24. 8 it cannot be hidden, where it **demands** angry revenge.”
Dan 2.10 has ever made such a **demand** of his fortune-tellers, magicians,

Amos	4. 1	oppress the poor, and **demand** that your husbands keep you supplied
	5.25	I did not **demand** sacrifices and offerings
Nah	2.13	The **demands** of your envoys will no longer be heard."
Mk	6.25	once to the king and **demanded,** "I want you to give me
Lk	7.29	obeyed God's righteous **demands** and had been baptized by John.
Rom	8. 4	so that the righteous **demands** of the Law might be fully
2 Cor	12.14	to visit you—and I will not make any **demands** on you.
1 Thes	2. 7	as apostles of Christ we could have made **demands** on you.
2 Thes	3. 9	this, not because we have no right to **demand** our support;

DEMOLISH

Jer	31.28	to destroy, and to **demolish** them,

DEMON

[GOAT-DEMONS]

An evil spirit with the power to harm people; it was regarded as a messenger and servant of the Devil.

Lev	17. 7	animals in the fields as sacrifices to the **goat-demons.**
2 Kgs	23. 8	dedicated to the **goat-demons** near the gate built by Joshua,
2 Chr	11.15	of worship and to worship **demons** and the idols he made
Is	34.14	Wild animals will roam there, and **demons** will call to each other.
Jer	50.39	Babylon will be haunted by **demons** and evil spirits,
Mt	4.24	people with **demons,** and epileptics, and paralytics—
	7.22	your name we drove out many **demons** and performed many miracles!'
	8.16	people brought to Jesus many who had **demons** in them.
	8.28	These men had **demons** in them and were so fierce that no
	8.31	So the **demons** begged Jesus, "If you are going to drive
	8.33	story and what had happened to the men with the **demons.**
	9.32	a man who could not talk because he had a **demon.**
	9.33	But as soon as the **demon** was driven out, the man started
	9.34	is the chief of the **demons** who gives him
	9.34	the power to drive out **demons."**
	10. 8	those who suffer from dreaded skin-diseases, and drive out **demons.**
	11.18	drank no wine, and everyone said, 'He has a **demon** in him!'
	12.22	who was blind and could not talk because he had a **demon.**
	12.24	"He drives out **demons** only because their ruler Beelzebul gives
	12.27	that I drive out **demons** because Beelzebul gives me the power
	12.28	the power to drive out **demons,** which proves that the Kingdom
	15.22	My daughter has a **demon** and is in a terrible condition."
	17.18	gave a command to the **demon,** and it went out of the
	17.19	and asked him, "Why couldn't we drive the **demon** out?"
Mk	1.32	brought to Jesus all the sick and those who had **demons.**
	1.34	sick with all kinds of diseases and drove out many **demons.**
	1.34	He would not let the **demons** say anything, because they knew
	1.39	over Galilee, preaching in the synagogues and driving out **demons.**
	3.15	to preach, [15]and you will have authority to drive out **demons."**
	3.22	is the chief of the **demons** who gives him the power to
	5.15	the man who used to have the mob of **demons** in him.
	5.16	happened to the man with the **demons,** and about the pigs.
	5.18	man who had had the **demons** begged him, "Let me go with
	6.13	drove out many **demons,** and rubbed olive-oil on many sick people
	7.26	She begged Jesus to drive the **demon** out of her daughter.
	7.29	will find that the **demon** has gone out of your daughter!"
	7.30	the **demon** had indeed gone out of her.
	9.38	man who was driving out **demons** in your name, and we told
	16. 9	to Mary Magdalene, from whom he had driven out seven **demons.**
	16.17	they will drive out **demons** in my name;
Lk	4.33	a man who had the spirit of an evil **demon** in him;
	4.35	The **demon** threw the man down in front of them and went
	4.41	**Demons** also went out from many people, screaming, "You
	4.41	Jesus gave the **demons** an order and would not let them speak,
	7.33	drank no wine, and you said, 'He has a **demon** in him!'
	8. 2	called Magdalene), from whom seven **demons** had been driven out;
	8.27	met by a man from the town who had **demons** in him.
	8.29	the chains and be driven by the **demon** out into the desert.
	8.30	is 'Mob,' " he answered—because many **demons** had gone into him.
	8.31	The **demons** begged Jesus not to send them into the abyss.
	8.32	So the **demons** begged Jesus to let them go into the pigs,
	8.35	the man from whom the **demons** had gone out sitting at the
	8.38	The man from whom the **demons** had gone out begged Jesus,
	9. 1	and authority to drive out all **demons** and to cure diseases.
	9.42	the boy was coming, the **demon** knocked him to the ground and
	9.49	saw a man driving out **demons** in your name, and we told
	10.17	"Lord," they said, "even the **demons** obeyed us when we gave
	11.14	Jesus was driving out a **demon** that could not talk;
	11.14	and when the **demon** went out, the man began to talk.
	11.15	Beelzebul, the chief of the **demons,** who gives him the power
	11.18	say that I drive out **demons** because Beelzebul gives me the
	11.20	power that I drive out **demons,** and this proves that the
	13.32	'I am driving out **demons** and performing cures today and tomorrow,
Jn	7.20	"You have a **demon** in you!"
	8.48	saying that you are a Samaritan and have a **demon** in you?"
	8.49	"I have no **demon,"** Jesus answered.
	8.52	said to him, "Now we are certain that you have a **demon!**
	10.20	Many of them were saying, "He has a **demon!**
	10.21	"A man with a **demon** could not talk like this!
	10.21	How could a **demon** give sight to blind people?"
1 Cor	10.20	is sacrificed on pagan altars is offered to **demons,** not to
	10.20	And I do not want you to be partners with **demons.**
	10.21	drink from the Lord's cup and also from the cup of **demons;**
	10.21	eat at the Lord's table and also at the table of **demons.**
1 Tim	4. 1	will obey lying spirits and follow the teachings of **demons.**
Jas	2.19	The **demons** also believe—and tremble with fear.
	3.15	it belongs to the world, it is unspiritual and **demonic.**
Rev	9.20	They did not stop worshipping **demons,** nor the idols of gold,
	16.14	They are the spirits of **demons** that perform miracles.
	18. 2	She is now haunted by **demons** and unclean spirits;

DEMONSTRATE

Ezek	36.23	When I **demonstrate** to the nations the holiness of my
Rom	3.25	God did this in order to **demonstrate** that he is righteous.
	3.25	deals with their sins, in order to **demonstrate** his righteousness.
Eph	2. 7	did this to **demonstrate** for all time to come the extraordinary

DEN

Gen	49. 9	and returning to his **den,** Stretching out and lying down.
Job	37. 8	The wild animals go to their **dens.**
	38.40	they hide in their caves, or lie in wait in their **dens?**
Ps	104.22	the sun rises, they go back and lie down in their **dens.**
Amos	3. 4	young lion growl in his **den** unless he has caught something?
Nah	2.11	city that was like a **den** of lions,
	2.12	he filled his **den** with torn flesh.

AV DEN (lions')

see also **PIT**

DENOUNCE

1 Kgs	13. 2	Following the Lord's command, the prophet **denounced** the altar:
Neh	5. 7	I **denounced** the leaders and officials of the people
Job	15.13	You are angry with God and **denounce** him.
Ezek	11. 4	Now then, **denounce** them, mortal man."
	13. 2	"Mortal man," he said, **"denounce** the prophets of Israel
	13.17	**Denounce** them [18]and tell them what the Sovereign Lord is saying
	21. 2	"Mortal man," he said, **"denounce** Jerusalem.
	21. 2	**Denounce** the places where people worship.
	25. 2	"Mortal man," he said, **"denounce** the country of Ammon.
	28.21	The Lord said to me, [21]"Mortal man, **denounce** the city of Sidon.
	29. 2	"Mortal man," he said, **"denounce** the king of Egypt.
	34. 2	"Mortal man," he said, **"denounce** the rulers of Israel.
	35. 2	"Mortal man," he said, **"denounce** the country of Edom.
	38. 2	"Mortal man," he said, **"denounce** Gog,
	38. 2	**Denounce** him, [3]and tell him that I, the Sovereign Lord,
	39. 1	Sovereign Lord said, "Mortal man, **denounce** Gog,
Dan	3. 8	some Babylonians took the opportunity to **denounce** the Jews.

DENSE

Is	29.17	before long the **dense** forest will become farmland,
Zech	11. 2	wail, oaks of Bashan— the **dense** forest has been cut down!

DENY

Gen	18.15	Because Sarah was afraid, she **denied** it.
Ex	23. 6	"Do not **deny** justice to a poor man when he appears in
Job	24.25	Can anyone **deny** that this is so?
	31.28	it **denies** Almighty God.
Ecc	2.10	I did not **deny** myself any pleasure.
	4. 8	For whom is he working so hard and **denying** himself any pleasure?
	5. 8	the government oppresses the poor and **denies** them justice
Jer	2.35	Lord, will punish you because you **deny** that you have sinned.
	5.12	The Lord's people have **denied** him and have said, "He won't
Lam	3.35	He knows when we are **denied** the rights he gave us;
Mt	26.70	But he **denied** it in front of them all.
	26.72	Again Peter **denied** it and answered, "I swear that I
Mk	14.68	But he **denied** it.
	14.70	But Peter **denied** it again.
	14.70	Peter again, "You can't **deny** that you are one of them,
Lk	8.45	Everyone **denied** it, and Peter said, "Master, the people are
	22.57	But Peter **denied** it, "Woman, I don't even know him!"
Jn	18.25	But Peter **denied** it.
Acts	4.16	miracle has been performed by them, and we cannot **deny** it.
	8.33	He was humiliated, and justice was **denied** him.
	19.36	Nobody can **deny** these things.
	26.11	in the synagogues and tried to make them **deny** their faith.
1 Cor	7. 5	Do not **deny** yourselves to each other, unless you first agree
1 Tim	3.16	No one can **deny** how great is the secret of our religion:
	5. 8	his own family, he has **denied** the faith and is worse than
2 Tim	2.12	If we **deny** him, he also will deny us.
Tit	1.16	They claim that they know God, but their actions **deny** it.
2 Pet	2. 1	untrue doctrines, and will **deny** the Master who redeemed them,
1 Jn	4. 3	But anyone who **denies** this about Jesus does not have the

DEPART

Num	12. 9	and so as he **departed** [10]and the cloud left the Tent,
Ps	37.31	law of his God in his heart and never **departs** from it.
	119.51	scornful of me, but I have not **departed** from your law.
Ecc	8. 3	The king can do anything he likes, so **depart** from his presence;
Lk	24.51	he was blessing them, he **departed** from them and was taken up
Heb	11.22	speak of the **departure** of the Israelites from Egypt,

DEPEND

Lev	22.13	her father's house as a **dependant** may eat the food her
Num	27.21	He will **depend** on Eleazar the priest, who will learn my
	32.16	enclosures here for our sheep and fortified towns for our **dependants.**
	32.17	In the meantime, our **dependants** can live here
Deut	8. 3	you that man must not **depend** on bread alone to sustain him,
	25. 2	The number of lashes will **depend** on the crime he has committed.

2 Sam 15.22 So Ittai went on with all his men and their **dependants.**
22.31 This God—how perfect are his deeds, how **dependable** his words!
2 Chr 20.15 The battle **depends** on God, not on you.
31.18 their wives, children, and other **dependants,**
Ps 18.30 How **dependable** his words!
33. 4 of the Lord are true and all his works are **dependable.**
52. 7 a man who did not **depend** on God for safety, but trusted
62. 1 I **depend** on him alone.
62. 5 I **depend** on God alone;
62. 7 My salvation and honour **depend** on God;
62.10 even if your riches increase, don't **depend** on them.
104.27 All of them **depend** on you to give them food when they
111. 7 all his commands are **dependable.**
118. 8 is better to trust in the Lord than to **depend** on man.
118. 9 to trust in the Lord than to **depend** on human leaders.
123. 2 As a servant **depends** on his master,
123. 2 as a maid **depends** on her mistress,
146. 5 to help him and who **depends** on the Lord his God,
Prov 11.28 Those who **depend** on their wealth will fall like the
12.14 Your reward **depends** on what you say and what you do;
14.28 A king's greatness **depends** on how many people he rules;
25.19 **Depending** on an unreliable person in a crisis
Ecc 5. 9 Even a king **depends** on the harvest.
Is 3. 1 everything and everyone that the people **depend** on.
22.24 "But all his relatives and **dependants** will become a burden
28.15 when it comes, because you **depend** on lies and deceit to keep
28.17 away all the lies you **depend** on, and floods will destroy
48. 2 holy city and that you **depend** on Israel's God, whose name is
59. 4 You **depend** on lies to win your case.
Jer 49.11 Your widows can **depend** on me.
Ezek 29.16 Israel will never again **depend** on them for help.
Mic 5. 7 They will **depend** on God, not man.
Mt 22.40 the teachings of the prophets **depend** on these two commandments."
Lk 11.22 the weapons the owner was **depending** on and divides up what
Rom 2.17 you **depend** on the Law and boast about God;
4. 5 But the person who **depends** on his faith, not on his deeds,
9.16 So then, everything **depends,** not on what man wants or does,
9.32 Because they did not **depend** on faith but on what they did.
2 Cor 7.16 How happy I am that I can **depend** on you completely!
Gal 3.10 Those who **depend** on obeying the Law live under a curse.
3.18 For if God's gift **depends** on the Law,
3.18 then it no longer **depends** on his promise.
1 Thes 4.12 you will not have to **depend** on anyone for what you need.
Heb 12. 2 on Jesus, on whom our faith **depends** from beginning to end.
2 Pet 1.16 We have not **depended** on made-up stories in making known

DEPORT

2 Kgs 17.28 Israelite priest who had been **deported** from Samaria
24.14 He also **deported** all the skilled workmen,
24.16 Nebuchadnezzar **deported** all the important men to Babylonia,
1 Chr 5. 4 captured Beerah, a leader of the tribe, and **deported** him.
5.26 He **deported** the tribes of Reuben, Gad, and East Manasseh
6.15 King Nebuchadnezzar **deported** Jehozadak
9. 1 people of Judah had been **deported** to Babylon as punishment

DEPOSIT

Lev 6. 2 fellow-Israelite has left as a **deposit** or by stealing
1 Sam 10.25 wrote them in a book, which he **deposited** in a holy place.
2 Kgs 12.16 and for the offerings for sin was not **deposited** in the box;
Mt 25.27 Well, then, you should have **deposited** my money in the bank,

DEPRESSED

1 Kgs 20.43 The king went back home to Samaria, worried and **depressed.**
21. 4 Ahab went home, **depressed** and angry over what Naboth had said
21. 5 Jezebel went to him and asked, "Why are you so **depressed?**
21.27 slept in the sackcloth, and went about gloomy and **depressed.**
Prov 15.13 they smile, but when they are sad, they look **depressed.**
25.20 to a person who is **depressed** is like taking off his clothes
Is 19.10 weavers and skilled workmen will be broken and **depressed.**
Lam 3.20 I think of it constantly and my spirit is **depressed.**
Dan 8.27 I was **depressed** and ill for several days.

DEPRIVE

Deut 24.17 "Do not **deprive** foreigners and orphans of their rights;
27.19 " 'God's curse on anyone who **deprives** foreigners, orphans,
Ps 35.13 I **deprived** myself of food;

DEPTH(S) see DEEP

DEPUTY

1 Kgs 22.47 it was ruled by a **deputy** appointed by the king of Judah.

DESCENDANT

[DAVID'S DESCENDANT]

Gen 1.28 many children, so that your **descendants** will live all over
5. 1 This is the list of the **descendants** of Adam.
6. 4 on the earth who were **descendants** of human women and the
9. 1 so that your **descendants** will live all over the earth.
9. 7 so that your **descendants** will live all over the earth."
9. 9 with you and with your **descendants,** [10]and with all living
9.27 May his **descendants** live with the people of Shem!
10. 1 These are the **descendants** of Noah's sons, Shem, Ham, and
Gen 10. 3 The **descendants** of Gomer were the people of Ashkenaz,
10. 4 The **descendants** of Javan were the people of Elishah, Spain, Cyprus,
10. 5 These are the **descendants** of Japheth,
10. 7 The **descendants** of Cush were the people of Seba, Havilah,
10. 7 The **descendants** of Raamah were the people of Sheba and Dedan.
10.13 The **descendants** of Egypt were the people of Lydia, Anam,
10.14 of Crete from whom the Philistines are **descended.**
10.20 These are the **descendants** of Ham,
10.23 The **descendants** of Aram were the people of Uz, Hul, Gether,
10.26 The **descendants** of Joktan were the people of Almodad, Sheleph,
10.29 All of them were **descended** from Joktan.
10.31 These are the **descendants** of Shem,
10.32 All these peoples are the **descendants** of Noah,
10.32 nation by nation, according to their different lines of **descent.**
10.32 nations of the earth were **descended** from the sons of Noah.
11.10 These are the **descendants** of Shem.
11.27 These are the **descendants** of Terah,
12. 2 I will give you many **descendants,**
12. 7 the country that I am going to give to your **descendants."**
13.15 to give you and your **descendants** all the land that you see,
13.16 to give you so many **descendants** that no one will be able
15. 5 you will have as many **descendants** as that."
15.13 Lord said to him, "Your **descendants** will be strangers in a
15.16 be four generations before your **descendants** come back here,
15.18 "I promise to give your **descendants** all this land from the
16.10 will give you so many **descendants** that no one will be able
17. 2 I will make my covenant with you and give you many **descendants."**
17. 6 I will give you many **descendants,** and some of them will be
17. 6 You will have so many **descendants** that they will become nations.
17. 7 to you and to your **descendants** in future generations
17. 7 I will be your God and the God of your **descendants.**
17. 8 to you and to your **descendants** this land in which you are
17. 8 Canaan will belong to your **descendants** for ever, and I will
17. 9 both you and your **descendants** in future generations.
17.10 You and your **descendants** must all agree to circumcise every male
17.16 nations, and there will be kings among her **descendants."**
17.19 keep my covenant with him and with his **descendants** for ever.
17.20 I will bless him and give him many children and many **descendants.**
17.20 princes, and I will make a great nation of his **descendants.**
18.18 His **descendants** will become a great and mighty nation,
18.19 command his sons and his **descendants** to obey me and to do
21.12 Isaac that you will have the **descendants** I have promised.
21.18 I will make a great nation out of his **descendants."**
21.23 God that you will not deceive me, my children, or my **descendants.**
22.17 will give you as many **descendants** as there are stars in the
22.17 Your **descendants** will conquer their enemies.
22.18 I have blessed your **descendants**—all because you obeyed my command."
24. 7 promised me that he would give this land to my **descendants.**
24.60 May your **descendants** conquer the cities of their enemies!"
25. 3 Sheba and Dedan, and the **descendants** of Dedan were the Asshurim,
25. 4 All these were Keturah's **descendants.**
25.18 The **descendants** of Ishmael lived in the territory between
25.18 They lived apart from the other **descendants** of Abraham.
26. 3 to give all this territory to you and to your **descendants.**
26. 4 will give you as many **descendants** as there are stars in the
26. 4 ask me to bless them as I have blessed your **descendants.**
26.24 you and give you many **descendants** because of my promise
27.29 and may your mother's **descendants** bow down before you.
28. 4 he bless you and your **descendants** as he blessed Abraham, and
28.13 to you and to your **descendants** this land on which you are
28.14 you and your **descendants** I will bless all the nations.
32.12 and to give me more **descendants** than anyone could count, as
32.32 Even today the **descendants** of Israel do not eat the muscle
33.19 of the field from the **descendants** of Hamor father of Shechem
35.11 Nations will be **descended** from you, and you will be the
35.12 and I will also give it to your **descendants** after you."
36. 1 These are the **descendants** of Esau, also called Edom.
36. 9 These are the **descendants** of Esau, the ancestor of the Edomites.
36.15 These are the tribes **descended** from Esau.
36.16 These were all **descendants** of Esau's wife Adah.
36.17 These were all **descendants** of Esau's wife Basemath.
36.18 The following tribes were **descended** from Esau
36.19 All these tribes were **descended** from Esau.
36.20 which traced their ancestry to the following **descendants** of Seir,
38. 8 brother, so that your brother may have **descendants."**
45. 7 way and to make sure that you and your **descendants** survive.
46. 3 I will make your **descendants** a great nation there.
46. 4 Egypt, and I will bring your **descendants** back to this land.
46. 6 Jacob took all his **descendants** with him:
46.15 In all, his **descendants** by Leah numbered thirty-three.
46.18 These sixteen are the **descendants** of Jacob by Zilpah,
46.22 These fourteen are the **descendants** of Jacob by Rachel.
46.25 These seven are the **descendants** of Jacob by Bilhah,
46.26 total number of the direct **descendants** of Jacob who went to
48. 4 many children, so that your **descendants** will become many nations;
48. 4 land to your **descendants** as their possession for ever.' "
48.16 May they have many children, many **descendants!"**
48.19 Manasseh's **descendants** will also become a great people.
48.19 and his **descendants** will become great nations."
49.10 hold the royal sceptre, And his **descendants** will always rule.
Ex 1. 5 The total number of these people directly **descended** from Jacob
1. 7 but their **descendants,** the Israelites, had many children
6.17 Libni and Shimei, and they had many **descendants.**
6.19 These are the clans of Levi with their **descendants.**

Ex 16.32 to be kept for our **descendants,** so that they can see the
16.33 it in the Lord's presence to be kept for our **descendants."**
19. 3 told him to say to the Israelites, Jacob's **descendants:**
20. 5 hate me and on their **descendants** down to the third and
27.21 be kept for ever by the Israelites and their **descendants.**
28.43 This is a permanent rule for Aaron and his **descendants.**
29. 9 They and their **descendants** are to serve me as priests for ever.
30.21 which they and their **descendants** are to observe for ever."
32.10 Then I will make you and your **descendants** into a great nation."
32.13 to give them as many **descendants** as there are stars in the
32.13 sky and to give their **descendants** all that land you promised
33. 1 give to Abraham, Isaac, and Jacob and to their **descendants.**
Lev 6.18 come any of the male **descendants** of Aaron may eat it as
6.22 to be made by every **descendant** of Aaron who is serving as
10. 9 This is a law to be kept by all your **descendants.**
21.17 to Aaron, "None of your **descendants** who has any physical
21.21 No **descendant** of Aaron the priest who has any physical defect
22. 3 If any of your **descendants,** while he is ritually unclean,
22. 4 "None of the **descendants** of Aaron who has a dreaded skin-disease
23.14 be observed by all your **descendants** for all time to come.
23.21 Your **descendants** are to observe this regulation for all time
23.31 This regulation applies to all your **descendants,**
23.41 is to be kept by your **descendants** for all time to come.
23.43 so that your **descendants** may know that the Lord
24. 9 belongs to Aaron and his **descendants,** and they shall eat it
25.10 the original owner or his **descendants,** and anyone who has been
25.30 the permanent property of the purchaser and his **descendants;**
26.40 "But your **descendants** will confess their sins
26.41 At last, when your **descendants** are humbled and they have paid
27.24 be returned to the original owner or to his **descendants.**
Num 9.10 you or your **descendants** are unclean from touching a corpse
13.22 Ahiman, Sheshai, and Talmai, the **descendants** of a race of giants
13.28 Even worse, we saw the **descendants** of the giants there.
13.33 and we even saw giants there, the **descendants** of Anak.
14.24 and his **descendants** will possess the land
16.40 one who was not a **descendant** of Aaron should come to the
18. 8 to you and to your **descendants** as the part assigned to you
18.19 covenant that I have made with you and your **descendants."**
18.23 This is a permanent rule that applies also to your **descendants.**
21.30 But now their **descendants** are destroyed,
23.10 The **descendants** of Israel are like the dust—
25.13 He and his **descendants** are permanently established as priests,
26. 8 The **descendants** of Pallu were Eliab [9] and his sons
26.36 The clan of Eran traced its **descent** from Shuthelah.
26.37 These are the clans **descended** from Joseph.
26.40 The clans of Ard and Naaman traced their **descent** from Bela.
26.45 clans of Heber and Malchiel traced their **descent** from Beriah.
26.58 Their **descendants** included the subclans of Libni, Hebron,
35.29 These rules apply to you and your **descendants**
Deut 1. 8 ancestors, Abraham, Isaac, and Jacob, and to their **descendants.**
1.36 give him and his **descendants** the land that he has explored.'
2. 4 the territory of your distant relatives, the **descendants** of Esau.
2. 5 I have given Edom to Esau's **descendants.**
2. 9 the people of Moab, the **descendants** of Lot, or start a war
2.12 live in Edom, but the **descendants** of Esau chased them out,
2.19 be near the land of the Ammonites, the **descendants** of Lot.
2.22 thing for the Edomites, the **descendants** of Esau, who live in
2.29 The **descendants** of Esau, who live in Edom, and the Moabites,
4.40 today, and all will go well with you and your **descendants.**
5. 9 hate me and on their **descendants** down to the third and
5.29 everything would go well with them and their **descendants** for ever.
6. 2 you and your **descendants** are to honour the Lord
11. 9 the Lord promised to give your ancestors and their **descendants.**
12.25 pleased, and all will go well for you and your **descendants.**
12.28 well for you and your **descendants** for ever, because you will
17.20 and his **descendants** will rule Israel for many generations.
23. 2 out of wedlock or any **descendant** of such a person, even in
23. 3 Moabite—or any of their **descendants,** even in the tenth generation—
23. 8 their **descendants** may be included among the Lord's
25. 7 to give his brother a **descendant** among the people of Israel.'
25. 9 to the man who refuses to give his brother a **descendant.'**
28.46 evidence of God's judgement on you and your **descendants**
28.59 on you and on your **descendants** incurable diseases
29.15 today and also with our **descendants** who are not yet born.
29.22 "In future generations your **descendants** and foreigners
29.29 Law, and we and our **descendants** are to obey it for ever.
30. 2 If you and your **descendants** will turn back to the Lord and
30. 6 will give you and your **descendants** obedient hearts,
30.20 and then you and your **descendants** will live long in the land
31.13 In this way your **descendants** who have never heard the Law
32. 9 but Jacob's **descendants** he chose for himself.
33.28 So Jacob's **descendants** live in peace,
34. 4 I promised Abraham, Isaac, and Jacob I would give to their **descendants.**
Josh 6.25 (Her **descendants** have lived in Israel to this day.)
13.31 half the families **descended** from Machir son of Manasseh.
14. 3 (The **descendants** of Joseph were divided into two tribes:
14.14 Hebron still belongs to the **descendants** of Caleb
15.14 Caleb drove the **descendants** of Anak out of the city—
16. 1 the land assigned to the **descendants** of Joseph
16. 4 The **descendants** of Joseph, the tribes of Ephraim and West Manasseh,
17. 1 some of the families **descended** from Joseph s elder son Manasseh.
17. 2 These were male **descendants** of Manasseh
17. 6 descendants as well as his male **descendants** were assigned land.
17. 6 Gilead was assigned to the rest of the **descendants** of Manasseh.
17. 8 Tappuah, on the border, belonged to the **descendants** of Ephraim.
17.14 The **descendants** of Joseph said to Joshua,
Josh 21. 4 The families who were **descended** from Aaron the priest
21.10 which were given [10] to the **descendants** of Aaron
21.10 were of the clan of Kohath, which was **descended** from Levi.
21.13 the following cities were assigned to the **descendants** of Aaron
21.19 lands, were given to the priests, the **descendants** of Aaron.
22.24 that in the future your **descendants** would say to ours,
22.25 Then your **descendants** might make our descendants stop worshipping the Lord.
22.27 This was to keep your **descendants** from saying that ours have
22.28 if this should ever happen, our **descendants** could say, 'Look!
24. 3 I gave him many **descendants.**
24.32 This land was inherited by Joseph's **descendants.**
Judg 1.16 The **descendants** of Moses' father-in-law, the Kenite,
1.20 drove out of the city the three clans **descended** from Anak.
4.11 Kenites, the **descendants** of Hobab, the brother-in-law of Moses.
8.22 Gideon, "Be our ruler—you and your **descendants** after you.
18.30 tribe of Dan, and his **descendants** served as their priests
1 Sam 2.33 will keep one of your **descendants** alive, and he will serve
2.33 and all your other **descendants** will die a violent death.
2.35 I will give him **descendants,** who will always serve
2.36 Any of your **descendants** who survive will have to go to
13.13 have let you and your **descendants** rule over Israel for ever.
20.42 you and I, and your **descendants** and mine, will for ever keep
24.21 that you will spare my **descendants,** so that my name and my
25.28 make you king, and your **descendants** also,
2 Sam 3. 9 away from Saul and his **descendants** and would make David king
4. 4 Another **descendant** of Saul was Jonathan's son Mephibosheth,
4. 8 Your Majesty to take revenge on Saul and his **descendants."**
7.10 you safe from all your enemies and to give you **descendants.**
7.16 You will always have **descendants,**
7.19 made promises about my **descendants** in the years to come.
7.25 made about me and my **descendants,** and do what you said you
7.27 and have told me that you will make my **descendants** kings.
7.29 ask you to bless my **descendants** so that they will continue
7.29 and your blessing will rest on my **descendants** for ever."
12.10 every generation some of your **descendants** will die a violent death
21. 6 over seven of his male **descendants,** and we will hang them
21.22 These four were **descendants** of the giants of Gath,
22.51 one he has chosen, to David and his **descendants** for ever.
23. 5 how God will bless my **descendants,** because he has made an
1 Kgs 1.48 today made one of my **descendants** succeed me as king,
2. 4 he told me that my **descendants** would rule Israel
2.24 his promise and given the kingdom to me and my **descendants.**
2.27 Shiloh about the priest Eli and his **descendants** come true.
2.31 David's **descendants** will any longer be held responsible
2.33 murders will fall on Joab and on his **descendants** for ever.
2.33 give success to David's **descendants** who sit on his throne."
4.13 the clan of Jair, a **descendant** of Manasseh, and the region
8.25 always be one of his **descendants** ruling as king of Israel,
9. 5 I told him that Israel would always be ruled by his **descendants.**
9. 6 But if you or your **descendants** stop following me,
9.20 Solomon used the **descendants** of the people of Canaan
9.20 Hivites, and Jebusites, whose **descendants** continue to be slaves
11.36 I will always have a **descendant** of my servant David ruling
11.38 will make sure that your **descendants** rule after you,
11.39 sin I will punish the **descendants** of David,
12.20 Only the tribe of Judah remained loyal to David's **descendants.**
14. 8 kingdom away from David's **descendants** and gave it to you.
14.10 and will kill all your male **descendants,** young and old alike.
2 Kgs 5.27 and you and your **descendants** will have it for ever!"
8.19 David that his **descendants** would always continue to rule.
9. 8 All Ahab's family and **descendants** are to die;
10. 1 There were seventy **descendants** of King Ahab living in the city
10. 1 to the leading citizens, and to the guardians of Ahab's **descendants.**
10. 2 in charge of the king's **descendants** and you have at your
10. 3 best qualified of the king's **descendants,** make him king,
10. 6 the heads of King Ahab's **descendants** to me at Jezreel by
10. 6 The seventy **descendants** of King Ahab were under the care of
10. 7 killed all seventy of Ahab's **descendants,**
10. 8 that the heads of Ahab's **descendants** had been brought,
10.10 the Lord said about the **descendants** of Ahab will come true.
10.30 "You have done to Ahab's **descendants** everything I wanted
10.30 I promise you that your **descendants,** down to the fourth generation,
15.12 "Your **descendants,** down to the fourth generation, will be kings of Israel."
17.34 which he gave to the **descendants** of Jacob,
17.41 and to this day their **descendants** continue to do the same.
20.18 Some of your own direct **descendants** will be taken away
21.13 as I did King Ahab of Israel and his **descendants.**
1 Chr 1. 6 The **descendants** of Gomer were the people of Ashkenaz, Riphath,
1. 7 The **descendants** of Javan were the people of Elishah, Spain,
1. 9 The **descendants** of Cush were the people of Seba, Havilah,
1. 9 The **descendants** of Raamah were the people of Sheba and Dedan.
1.11 The **descendants** of Egypt were the people of Lydia, Anam,
1.12 Crete (from whom the Philistines were **descended).**
1.20 The **descendants** of Joktan were the people of Almodad,
1.38 inhabitants of Edom were **descended** from the following sons of Seir:
2. 7 one of Zerah's **descendants,** brought disaster on the people
2.17 daughter Abigail married Jether, a **descendant** of Ishmael,
2.23 people who lived there were **descendants** of Machir,
2.33 All these were **descendants** of Jerahmeel.
2.50 The following are also **descendants** of Caleb.
3.10 This is the line of King Solomon's **descendants**
3.17 These are the **descendants** of King Jehoiachin,
4. 1 These are some of the **descendants** of Judah:
4. 3 and his **descendants** founded the city of Bethlehem.
4. 8 ancestor of the clans **descended** from Aharhel son of Harum.
4.12 The **descendants** of these men lived in Recah.

1 Chr 4.19 Their **descendants** founded the clan of Garm,
4.21 His **descendants** included Er, who founded the town of Lecah;
4.26 Then from Mishma the line **descended** through Hammuel,
4.28 King David the **descendants** of Simeon lived in the following
4.34 Shiphi, the son of Allon, a **descendant** of Jedaiah,
5. 1 These are the **descendants** of Reuben,
5. 4 These are the **descendants** of Joel
5.14 They were **descendants** of Abihail son of Huri,
6. 4 The **descendants** of Eleazar from generation to generation
6.20 These are the **descendants** of Gershon
6.22 These are the **descendants** of Kohath
6.26 These are Ahimoth's **descendants**
6.29 These are the **descendants** of Merari
6.49 Aaron and his **descendants** presented the offerings
6.50 This is the line of Aaron's **descendants:**
6.54 the territory assigned to the **descendants** of Aaron
6.57 The following towns were assigned to Aaron's **descendants:**
7. 2 At the time of King David their **descendants** numbered 22,600.
7. 4 their **descendants** were able to provide 36,000 men
7. 7 Their **descendants** included 22,034 men eligible for military
7. 9 The official record of their **descendants** by families
7.11 Their **descendants** included 17,200 men
7.13 (They were **descendants** of Bilhah.)
7.17 These are all **descendants** of Gilead,
7.20 These are the **descendants** of Ephraim
7.25 Ephraim also had a son named Rephah, whose **descendants** were
7.29 The **descendants** of Manasseh controlled the cities
7.29 the places where the **descendants** of Joseph son of Jacob lived.
7.30 These are the **descendants** of Asher.
7.36 The **descendants** of Zophah were Suah, Harnepher,
7.38 The **descendants** of Jether were Jephunneh,
7.39 and the **descendants** of Ulla were Arah, Hanniel,
7.40 All these were **descendants** of Asher.
7.40 Asher's **descendants** included 26,000 men
8. 3 The **descendants** of Bela were Addar, Gera,
8. 6 The **descendants** of Ehud were Naaman, Ahijah, and
8.14 Beriah's **descendants** included Ahio, Shashak, Jeremoth,
8.17 Elpaal's **descendants** included Zebadiah, Meshullam,
8.19 Shimei's **descendants** included Jakim, Zichri, Zabdi,
8.22 Shashak's **descendants** included Ishpan, Eber, Eliel,
8.26 Jeroham's **descendants** included Shamsherai, Sheheriah,
8.28 heads of families and their principal **descendants**
8.32 Their **descendants** lived in Jerusalem
9. 4 The **descendants** of Judah's son Perez had as their leader Uthai,
9. 4 The **descendants** of Judah's son Shelah had as their leader Asaiah,
9. 4 The **descendants** of Judah's son Zerah had Jeuel as their leader.
9.23 They and their **descendants** continued to guard the gates
9.38 Their **descendants** lived in Jerusalem
10. 6 sons all died together and none of his **descendants** ever ruled.
12.23 Followers of Jehoiada, **descendant** of Aaron:
15. 4 Next he sent for the **descendants** of Aaron and for the Levites.
16.12 You **descendants** of Jacob, God's servant,
16.12 **descendants** of Israel, whom God chose, remember
17. 9 I promise to defeat all your enemies and to give you **descendants.**
17.17 have made promises about my **descendants** in the years to come,
17.23 made about me and my **descendants,** and do what you said you
17.25 and have told me that you will make my **descendants** kings.
17.27 ask you to bless my **descendants** so that they will continue
20. 6 He was a **descendant** of the ancient giants.
20. 8 David and his men, were **descendants** of the giants at Gath.
23. 9 who were the heads of the clans **descended** from Ladan.
23.10 Beriah did not have many **descendants,** so they were counted
23.13 (Aaron and his **descendants** were set apart to be in charge of
23.17 but Rehabiah had many **descendants.**
23.24 These were the **descendants** of Levi,
23.24 Each of his **descendants,** twenty years of age or older,
23.28 to help the priests **descended** from Aaron with the temple worship,
23.32 assisting their relatives, the priests **descended** from Aaron,
24. 1 These are the groups to which the **descendants** of Aaron belong.
24. 2 and left no **descendants,** so their brothers Eleazar and Ithamar
24. 3 King David organized the **descendants** of Aaron into groups
24. 3 in this by Zadok, a **descendant** of Eleazar,
24. 3 and by Ahimelech, a **descendant** of Ithamar.
24. 4 The **descendants** of Eleazar were organized into sixteen groups,
24. 4 while the **descendants** of Ithamar were organized into eight;
24. 4 more male heads of families among the **descendants** of Eleazar.
24. 5 and spiritual leaders among the **descendants** of both Eleazar
24. 6 The **descendants** of Eleazar and of Ithamar took turns
24.20 These are other heads of families **descended** from Levi:
24.20 Jehdeiah, a **descendant** of Amram through Shebuel;
24.21 Isshiah, a **descendant** of Rehabiah;
24.22 Jahath, a **descendant** of Izhar through Shelomith;
24.24 Shamir, a **descendant** of Uzziel through Micah;
24.25 Zechariah, a **descendant** of Uzziel through Isshiah,
24.26 Mahli, Mushi, and Jaaziah, **descendants** of Merari.
24.31 just as their relatives, the priests **descended** from Aaron,
26.23 were also assigned to the **descendants** of Amram, Izhar,
26.29 Among the **descendants** of Izhar, Chenaniah and his sons
26.30 Among the **descendants** of Hebron, Hashabiah
26.31 Jeriah was the leader of the **descendants** of Hebron.
26.31 the family line of Hebron's **descendants,**
27. 2 Dodai, a **descendant** of Ahohi (Mikloth was his second in command)
27. 2 Shamhuth, a **descendant** of Izhar
27. 2 Heldai from Netophah (he was a **descendant** of Othniel)
28. 4 Israel, chose me and my **descendants** to rule Israel for ever.
2 Chr 6.16 always be one of his **descendants** ruling as king of Israel,
7.18 I told him that Israel would always be ruled by his **descendants.**
8. 7 in forced labour all the **descendants** of the people of Canaan
8. 7 Hivites, and Jebusites, whose **descendants** continue to be slaves

2 Chr 13. 5 giving him and his **descendants** kingship over Israel for ever?
13. 8 the royal authority that the Lord gave to David's **descendants.**
13. 9 the Lord's priests, the **descendants** of Aaron,
13.10 Priests **descended** from Aaron perform their duties,
20. 7 gave the land to the **descendants** of Abraham,
20.14 and was **descended** from Asaph through Mattaniah,
21. 7 promised that his **descendants** would always continue to rule.
23. 3 as the Lord promised that King David's **descendants** would be.
25.24 temple equipment guarded by the **descendants** of Obed Edom,
26.18 the priests who are **descended** from Aaron have been consecrated
29.21 priests, who were **descendants** of Aaron, to offer the animals
31.10 Azariah the High Priest, a **descendant** of Zadok, said to him,
31.19 the cities assigned to Aaron's **descendants,**
35.14 and for the priests **descended** from Aaron,
36.20 they served him and his **descendants** as slaves
Ezra 2. 3 Pahath Moab (**descendants** of Jeshua and Joab) - 2,812
2.36 Jedaiah (**descendants** of Jeshua) - 973
2.40 Jeshua and Kadmiel (**descendants** of Hodaviah) - 74
2.40 Temple musicians (**descendants** of Asaph) - 128
2.40 Temple guards (**descendants** of Shallum, Ater, Talmon, Akkub,
2.58 The total number of **descendants** of the temple workmen
2.59 they could not prove that they were **descendants** of Israelites.
9.12 enjoy the land and pass it on to our **descendants** for ever.
Neh 7. 8 Pahath Moab (**descendants** of Jeshua
7.39 Jedaiah (**descendants** of Jeshua) - 973
7.43 Jeshua and Kadmiel (**descendants** of
7.43 Temple musicians (**descendants** of
7.43 Temple guards (**descendants** of
7.60 The total number of **descendants** of the temple workmen
7.61 they could not prove that they were **descendants** of Israelites.
9. 8 to be a land where his **descendants** would live.
10.38 Priests who are **descended** from Aaron
11. 3 the temple workmen, and the **descendants** of Solomon's servants
11. 4 **descendants** of Judah's son Perez.
11. 5 **descendants** of Judah's son Shelah.
11. 6 Of the **descendants** of Perez, 468 outstanding men
11.17 son of Mica and grandson of Zabdi, a **descendant** of Asaph.
11.17 of Shammua and grandson of Galal, a **descendant** of Jeduthun.
Esth 2. 5 tribe of Benjamin and was a **descendant** of Kish and Shimei.
3. 1 Haman was the son of Hammedatha, a **descendant** of Agag.
3.10 Haman son of Hammedatha, the **descendant** of Agag.
8. 3 evil plot that Haman, the **descendant** of Agag, had made
8. 5 the son of Hammedatha the **descendant** of Agag gave
9.24 Haman son of Hammedatha—the **descendant** of Agag
9.27 a rule for themselves, their **descendants,** and anyone who might
9.31 directed them and their **descendants** to observe the days of Purim
10. 3 his people and for the security of all their **descendants.**
Job 15.34 There will be no **descendants** for godless men,
18.19 He has no **descendants,** no survivors.
32. 2 the son of Barakel, a **descendant** of Buz,
Ps 18.50 one he has chosen, to David and his **descendants** for ever.
21.10 None of their **descendants** will survive;
22.23 Honour him, you **descendants** of Jacob!
37.27 do good, and your **descendants** will always live in the land;
37.28 them for ever, but the **descendants** of the wicked will be
37.37 a peaceful man has **descendants,** [38] but sinners are completely destroyed,
37.38 and their **descendants** are wiped out.
49.10 They all leave their riches to their **descendants.**
68.26 praise the Lord, all you **descendants** of Jacob!"
69.36 the **descendants** of his servants will inherit it,
77.15 saved your people, the **descendants** of Jacob and of Joseph.
78. 5 people of Israel and commandments to the **descendants** of Jacob.
78.67 But he rejected the **descendants** of Joseph;
83. 8 ally of the Ammonites and Moabites, the **descendants** of Lot.
89. 4 my servant David, 'A **descendant** of yours will always be king;
89.29 a **descendant** of his will always be king.
89.30 "But if his **descendants** disobey my law
89.36 He will always have **descendants,**
90.16 let our **descendants** see your glorious might.
102.28 and under your protection their **descendants** will be secure.
105. 5 You **descendants** of Abraham, his servant;
105. 5 you **descendants** of Jacob, the man he chose:
106.27 and scatter their **descendants** among the heathen,
109.13 May all his **descendants** die,
112. 2 his **descendants** will be blessed.
114. 1 when Jacob's **descendants** left that foreign land,
115.14 May the Lord give you children— you and your **descendants!**
132.17 Here I will make one of David's **descendants** a great king;
Prov 12. 7 their downfall and leave no **descendants,** but the families of
Is 2. 5 Now, **descendants** of Jacob, let us walk in the light
2. 6 O God, you have forsaken your people, the **descendants** of Jacob!
7.13 Isaiah replied, "Listen, now, **descendants** of King David.
9. 8 judgement on the kingdom of Israel, on the **descendants** of Jacob.
11. 1 so a new king will arise from among David's **descendants.**
16. 5 Then one of David's **descendants** will be king, and he will
22.22 complete authority under the king, the **descendant of David.**
27. 6 the people of Israel, the **descendants** of Jacob, will take root
39. 7 Some of your own direct **descendants** will be taken away and
41. 8 the people that I have chosen, the **descendants** of Abraham,
44. 1 Israel, my servant, my chosen people, the **descendants** of Jacob.
44. 3 on your children and my blessing on your **descendants.**
45.25 Lord, will rescue all the **descendants** of Israel,
46. 3 "Listen to me, **descendants** of Jacob, all who are left
48. 1 you that are **descended** from Judah:
48.19 Your **descendants** would be as numerous as grains of sand,
51. 2 Abraham, and of Sarah, from whom you are **descended.**
51. 2 I made his **descendants** numerous.
53.10 And so he will see his **descendants;**
59.21 teach your children and your **descendants** to obey me for all
65. 9 and their **descendants** will possess my land of mountains.

Is	65.23	I will bless them and their **descendants** for all time to come.
	66.22	by my power, so your **descendants** and your name will endure.
Jer	2. 4	Lord's message, you **descendants** of Jacob, you tribes of Israel.
	2. 9	I will bring charges against their **descendants.**
	5.20	The Lord says, "Tell the **descendants** of Jacob,
	13.13	the kings, who are David's **descendants,** the priests, the prophets,
	21.11	message to the royal house of Judah, the **descendants** of David:
	22. 1	of Judah, the **descendant of David,** and there tell the king,
	22. 4	then David's **descendants** will continue to be kings.
	22.30	He will have no **descendants** who will rule in Judah
	23. 5	when I will choose as king a righteous **descendant of David.**
	29.31	"I, the Lord, will punish Shemaiah and all his **descendants.**
	29.31	He will have no **descendants** among you.
	30. 9	their God, and a **descendant of David,** whom I will enthrone
	32.39	time, for their own good and the good of their **descendants.**
	33.15	time I will choose as king a righteous **descendant of David.**
	33.17	will always be a **descendant of David** to be king of Israel
	33.21	he would always have a **descendant** to be king, and I have
	33.22	will increase the number of **descendants** of my servant David
	33.26	will maintain my covenant with Jacob's **descendants**
	33.26	will choose one of David's **descendants**
	33.26	to rule over the **descendants** of Abraham, Isaac, and Jacob.
	35. 6	neither we nor our **descendants** were ever to drink any wine.
	35.14	Jonadab's **descendants** have obeyed his command not to drink wine,
	35.16	Jonadab's **descendants** have obeyed the command
	35.19	of Rechab will always have a male **descendant** to serve me."
	36.30	King Jehoiakim, that no **descendant** of yours will ever rule
	36.31	I will punish you, your **descendants,** and your officials
	49. 8	am going to destroy Esau's **descendants,**
	49.10	But I have stripped Esau's **descendants** completely
Ezek	37.25	and so will their children and all their **descendants.**
	39.25	will be merciful to Jacob's **descendants,** the people of Israel,
	40.46	All the priests are **descended** from Zadok;
	43.19	tribe of Levi who are **descended** from Zadok are the only ones
	44.15	tribe of Levi who are **descended** from Zadok,
	48.11	area is to be for the priests who are **descendants** of Zadok.
Dan	11. 4	Kings not **descended** from him will rule in his place,
Hos	3. 5	the Lord their God, and to a **descendant of David** their king.
	12. 6	So now, **descendants** of Jacob, trust in your God
Amos	3.13	Listen now, and warn the **descendants** of Jacob,"
	7. 9	The places where Isaac's **descendants** worship will be destroyed.
	9. 8	But I will not destroy all the **descendants** of Jacob.
Obad	6	**Descendants** of Esau, your treasures have been looted.
	10	killed your brothers, the **descendants** of Jacob,
	18	No **descendant** of Esau will survive.
Mic	7.20	love to your people, the **descendants** of Abraham and of Jacob,
Nah	1.14	"They will have no **descendants** to carry on their name.
Zeph	1. 1	(Zephaniah was **descended** from King Hezekiah through Amariah,
Zech	10. 7	Their **descendants** will remember this victory
	12. 7	the honour which the **descendants** of David and the people
	12. 8	The **descendants** of David will lead them like the angel
	12.10	"I will fill the **descendants** of David
	12.12	the family **descended** from David,
	12.12	the family **descended** from Nathan,
	12.12	the family **descended** from Levi,
	12.12	the family **descended** from Shimei, and all the other
	13. 1	to purify the **descendants** of David and the people
Mal	1. 2	have loved Jacob and his **descendants,**
	1. 3	and have hated Esau and his **descendants.**
	1. 4	If Esau's **descendants,** the Edomites, say, "Our towns
	2. 4	covenant with the priests, the **descendants** of Levi,
	3. 6	you, the **descendants** of Jacob, are not yet completely lost.
Mt	1. 1	ancestors of Jesus Christ, a **descendant of David,**
	1. 1	who was a **descendant** of Abraham.
	1.20	dream and said, "Joseph, **descendant of David,** do not be afraid
	3. 9	God can take these stones and make **descendants** for Abraham!
	22.42	Whose **descendant** is he?"
	22.42	"He is **David's descendant,"** they answered.
	22.45	David called him 'Lord,' how can the Messiah be **David's descendant?"**
	23.31	you are the **descendants** of those who murdered the prophets!
Mk	12.35	Law say that the Messiah will be the **descendant of David?**
	12.37	so how can the Messiah be **David's descendant?"**
Lk	1.27	to a man named Joseph, who was a **descendant of King David.**
	1.33	he will be the king of the **descendants** of Jacob for ever;
	1.55	show mercy to Abraham and to all his **descendants** for ever!"
	1.69	a mighty Saviour, a **descendant of his servant David.**
	2. 4	Joseph went there because he was a **descendant of David.**
	3. 8	God can take these stones and make **descendants** for Abraham!
	13.16	Now here is this **descendant** of Abraham whom Satan has kept
	19. 9	for this man, also, is a **descendant** of Abraham.
	20.41	it be said that the Messiah will be the **descendant of David?**
	20.44	how, then, can the Messiah be **David's descendant?"**
Jn	7.42	the Messiah will be a **descendant of King David** and will be
	8.33	"We are the **descendants** of Abraham," they answered,
	8.37	I know you are Abraham's **descendants.**
Acts	2.30	make one of **David's descendants** a king, just as David was.
	3.25	said to Abraham, 'Through your **descendants** I will bless all the
	7. 5	and that it would belong to him and to his **descendants.**
	7. 6	'Your **descendants** will live in a foreign country, where they
	8.33	able to tell about his **descendants,** because his life on earth
	13.23	It was Jesus, a **descendant of David,** whom God made the
	13.26	"My fellow-Israelites, **descendants** of Abraham, and all Gentiles here
	13.32	for us, who are their **descendants,** by raising Jesus to life.
Rom	1. 3	as to his humanity, he was born a **descendant of David;**
	4.13	promised Abraham and his **descendants** that the world would belong
	4.16	gift to all of Abraham's **descendants**—not just to those who
	4.18	the scripture says, "Your **descendants** will be as many as the
	9. 5	they are **descended** from the famous Hebrew ancestors;
	9. 7	Nor are all Abraham's **descendants** the children of God.
	9. 7	through Isaac that you will have the **descendants** I promised you."
	9. 8	of God's promise are regarded as the true **descendants.**
	9.29	left us some **descendants,** we would have become like Sodom,
	11. 1	myself am an Israelite, a **descendant** of Abraham, a member of
	11.26	and remove all wickedness from the **descendants** of Jacob.
	15.12	And again, Isaiah says, "A **descendant** of Jesse will appear;
2 Cor	11.22	Are they Abraham's **descendants?**
Gal	3. 7	that the real **descendants** of Abraham are the people who
	3.16	Now, God made his promises to Abraham and to his **descendant.**
	3.16	not use the plural **"descendants,"** meaning many people, but the
	3.16	singular **"descendant,"** meaning one person only, namely, Christ.
	3.19	the coming of Abraham's **descendant,** to whom the promise was made.
	3.29	then you are the **descendants** of Abraham and will receive what
2 Tim	2. 8	from death, who was a **descendant of David,** as is taught in
Heb	2.16	as the scripture says, "He helps the **descendants** of Abraham."
	6.14	you that I will bless you and give you many **descendants."**
	7. 5	And those **descendants** of Levi who are priests are commanded
	7. 5	even though their countrymen are also **descendants** of Abraham.
	7. 6	Melchizedek was not **descended** from Levi, but he collected
	7. 9	Levi (whose **descendants** collect the tenth) also paid it.
	11.12	one man came as many **descendants** as there are stars in the
	11.18	is through Isaac that you will have the **descendants** I promised."
Jude	14	was Enoch, the sixth direct **descendant** from Adam, who long ago
Rev	5. 5	the great **descendant of David,** has won the victory,
	12.17	against the rest of her **descendants,** all those who obey God's
	22.16	I am **descended** from the family of David;

DESCRIBE

Josh	15. 1	of Judah received a part of the land **described** as follows:
	18. 6	Write down a **description** of these seven divisions
2 Kgs	22.14	They **described** to her what had happened,
2 Chr	34.22	They **described** to her what had happened,
Job	41.12	Leviathan's legs and **describe** how great and strong he is.
Is	40.18	How can you **describe** what he is like?
Jer	11. 8	So I brought on them all the punishments **described** in it."
Dan	9.13	giving us all the punishment **described** in the Law of Moses.
Gal	3. 1	you had a clear **description** of the death of Jesus Christ
Rev	22.18	God will add to his punishment the plagues **described** in this book.
	22.19	and of the Holy City, which are **described** in this book.

DESECRATE

2 Kgs	23. 8	throughout the whole country he **desecrated** the altars
	23.10	King Josiah also **desecrated** Topheth, the pagan place
	23.13	Josiah **desecrated** the altars that King Solomon had built
	23.16	In this way he **desecrated** the altar,
Ps	74. 7	they **desecrated** the place where you are worshipped.
	79. 1	They have **desecrated** your holy Temple
Dan	8.11	stopped the daily sacrifices offered to him, and **desecrated** the Temple.
	11.31	Some of his soldiers will **desecrate** the Temple.

DESERT (1)

Gen	14. 6	pursuing them as far as Elparan on the edge of the **desert.**
	16. 7	at a spring in the **desert** on the road to Shur
	41. 6	thin and scorched by the **desert** wind,
	41.23	thin and scorched by the **desert** wind,
	41.27	corn scorched by the **desert** wind are seven years of famine.
Ex	3. 1	led the flock across the **desert** and came to Sinai, the holy
	3.18	three days into the **desert** to offer sacrifices to the Lord,
	4.27	Lord had said to Aaron, "Go into the **desert** to meet Moses."
	5. 1	they can hold a festival in the **desert** to honour me.' "
	5. 3	for three days into the **desert** to offer sacrifices to the
	7.16	his people go, so that they can worship him in the **desert.**
	8.27	travel three days into the **desert** to offer sacrifices to the
	8.28	Lord, your God, in the **desert,** if you do not go very
	13.18	in a roundabout way through the **desert** towards the Red Sea.
	13.20	left Sukkoth and camped at Etham on the edge of the **desert.**
	14. 3	about in the country and are closed in by the **desert.**
	14.11	you have to bring us out here in the **desert** to die?
	14.12	better to be slaves there than to die here in the **desert."**
	15.22	of Israel away from the Red Sea into the **desert** of Shur.
	15.22	For three days they walked through the **desert,** but found no water.
	16. 1	Egypt, they came to the **desert** of Sin, which is between Elim
	16. 2	There in the **desert** they all complained to Moses and Aaron
	16. 3	us out into this **desert** to starve us all to death."
	16.10	they turned towards the **desert,**
	16.14	was something thin and flaky on the surface of the **desert.**
	16.32	us to eat in the **desert** when he brought us out of
	17. 1	whole Israelite community left the **desert** of Sin,
	18. 5	her two sons into the **desert** where Moses was camped at the
	19. 1	after they had left Egypt they came to the **desert** of Sinai.
	23.31	and from the **desert** to the Euphrates River.
Lev	7.38	on Mount Sinai in the **desert,** the Lord gave these commands
	16.10	and sent off into the **desert** to Azazel, in order to take
	16.21	be driven off into the **desert** by a man appointed to do
	16.26	drove the goat into the **desert** to Azazel must wash his
Num	1. 1	Moses there in the Tent of his presence in the Sinai **Desert.**
	1.19	In the Sinai **Desert,** Moses registered the people.
	3. 4	they offered unholy fire to the Lord in the Sinai **Desert.**
	3.14	In the Sinai **Desert** the Lord commanded Moses [15] to register
	9. 1	to Moses in the Sinai **Desert** in the first month of the
	9. 5	day of the first month they did so in the Sinai **Desert.**
	10.12	the Israelites started on their journey out of the Sinai **Desert.**

Num 21. 5 Egypt to die in this **desert,** where there is no food
21.20 below the top of Mount Pisgah, looking out over the **desert.**
23.28 took Balaam to the top of Mount Peor overlooking the **desert.**
24. 1 He turned towards the **desert** [2]and saw the people of Israel
26.64 Aaron had listed in the first census in the Sinai **Desert.**
33. 6 Their next camp was at Etham on the edge of the **desert.**
33. 8 Hahiroth and passed through the Red Sea into the **desert** of Shur;
33.11 Their next camp was in the **desert** of Sin.
33.15 the Sinai **Desert,** Kibroth Hattaavah (or "Graves of Craving"),
Deut 1.19 through that vast and fearful **desert** on the way to the
1.31 just as you saw him do in Egypt [31] and in the **desert.**
1.40 and go back into the **desert** along the road to the Gulf
2. 1 turned and went into the **desert,** along the road to the Gulf
2. 7 taken care of you as you wandered through this vast **desert.**
2.26 I sent messengers from the **desert** of Kedemoth to King Sihon
4.43 Reuben there was the city of Bezer, on the **desert** plateau;
8. 2 this long journey through the **desert** these past forty years,
8.15 that vast and terrifying **desert** where there were poisonous snakes
8.16 In the **desert** he gave you manna to eat,
9. 7 forget how you made the Lord your God angry in the **desert.**
9.28 your people out into the **desert** to kill them, because you
11. 5 the Lord did for you in the **desert** before you arrived here.
11.24 territory will extend from the **desert** in the south to the
29. 5 Lord led you through the **desert,**
32.10 "He found them wandering through the **desert,**
Josh 1. 4 borders will reach from the **desert** in the south to the
5. 4 the people spent crossing the **desert,** none of the baby boys
14.10 Israel was going through the **desert,** and the Lord, as he promised,
15.61 In the **desert** there were Beth Arabah, Middin, Secacah,
16. 1 east of the springs of Jericho, and went into the **desert.**
18.12 through the hill-country as far as the **desert** of Bethaven.
20. 8 of the Jordan, on the **desert** plateau east of Jericho, they
24. 7 'You lived in the **desert** a long time.
Judg 6. 3 come with the Amalekites and the **desert** tribes and attack them.
6.33 Midianites, the Amalekites, and the **desert** tribes assembled,
7.12 Midianites, the Amalekites, and the **desert** tribesmen were
8. 7 I will beat you with thorns and briars from the **desert!"**
8.10 Of the whole army of **desert** tribesmen, only about 15,000 were left;
8.11 by the edge of the **desert,** east of Nobah and Jogbehah,
8.16 thorns and briars from the **desert** and used them to punish
8.24 (The Midianites, like other **desert** people, wore gold earrings.)
11.16 Egypt, they went through the **desert** to the Gulf of Aqaba and
11.18 they went on through the **desert,** going round the land of
11.22 the north and from the **desert** on the east to the Jordan
1 Sam 4. 8 They are the gods who slaughtered the Egyptians in the **desert!**
1 Chr 5. 9 as far east as the **desert** that stretches all the way to
12. 8 Gad who joined David's troops when he was at the **desert** fort.
2 Chr 8. 4 Hamath and Zobah [4]and fortified the city of Palmyra in the **desert.**
20.24 tower that was in the **desert,** they looked towards the enemy
Neh 9.19 abandon them there in the **desert,** for your mercy is great.
9.21 forty years in the **desert** you provided all that they needed;
Job 1.19 your eldest son, [19] when a storm swept in from the **desert.**
6.18 they wander and die in the **desert.**
30. 4 up the plants of the **desert** and ate them, even the tasteless
39. 6 I gave them the **desert** to be their home, and let them
Ps 29. 8 His voice makes the **desert** shake;
29. 8 he shakes the **desert** of Kadesh.
68. 7 when you marched across the **desert,** [8]the earth shook,
72. 9 The peoples of the **desert** will bow down before him;
74.14 the monster Leviathan and fed his body to **desert** animals.
78.15 split rocks open in the **desert** and gave them water
78.17 and in the **desert** they rebelled against the Most High.
78.19 against God and said, "Can God supply food in the **desert?**
78.40 How often they rebelled against him in the **desert;**
78.52 out like a shepherd and guided them through the **desert.**
95. 8 at Meribah, as they were that day in the **desert** at Massah.
102. 6 a wild bird in the **desert,** like an owl in abandoned ruins.
105.41 rock, and water gushed out, flowing through the **desert**
106.14 filled with craving in the **desert** and put God to the test;
106.16 There in the **desert** they were jealous of Moses and of Aaron,
106.26 make them die in the **desert** [27]and scatter their descendants
107. 4 Some wandered in the trackless **desert** and could not find
107.35 He changed **deserts** into pools of water
107.40 and made them wander in trackless **deserts.**
136.16 He led his people through the **desert;**
Prov 21.19 out in the **desert** than with a nagging, complaining wife.
Song 1. 5 but beautiful, dark as the **desert** tents of Kedar,
3. 6 is this coming from the **desert** like a column of smoke,
8. 5 is this coming from the **desert,** arm in arm with her lover?
Is 13.21 will be a place where **desert** animals live and where owls
14.17 man who destroyed cities and turned the world into a **desert?**
16. 1 city of Sela in the **desert** the people of Moab send a
16. 8 eastwards into the **desert,** and westwards to the other side
21. 1 a whirlwind sweeping across the **desert,**
30. 6 This is God's message about the animals of the southern **desert:**
32. 2 like streams flowing in a **desert,**
33. 9 of Sharon is like a **desert,** and in Bashan and on Mount
35. 1 The **desert** will rejoice, and flowers will bloom in the wilderness.
35. 2 The **desert** will sing and shout for joy;
35. 6 Streams of water will flow through the **desert;**
40. 3 Clear the way in the **desert** for our God!
41.18 I will turn the **desert** into pools of water and the dry
41.19 cedars grow in the **desert,** and acacias and myrtles and olive-trees.
42.11 Let the **desert** and its towns praise God;
42.15 turn the river valleys into **deserts** and dry up the pools
43.20 make rivers flow in the **desert** to give water to my chosen
48.21 through a hot, dry **desert,** they did not suffer from thirst.
49.10 Sun and **desert** heat will not hurt them, for they will be
50. 2 and turn rivers into a **desert,** so that the fish in them
51. 3 Though her land is a **desert,** I will make it a garden,
64.10 Your sacred cities are like a **desert;**
Jer 2. 2 you followed me through the **desert,** through a land that had
2. 6 a land of **deserts** and sand-dunes, a dry and dangerous land
2.15 have made his land a **desert,** and his towns lie in ruins,
2.24 running about loose, [24] rushing into the **desert.**
2.31 Have I been like a **desert** to you, like a dark and
3. 2 the roadside, as an Arab waits for victims in the **desert.**
4.11 a scorching wind is blowing in from the **desert** towards them.
4.26 The fertile land had become a **desert;**
5. 6 wolves from the **desert** will tear them to pieces,
6. 8 turn your city into a **desert,** a place where no one lives."
7.34 The land will become a **desert.**
9. 2 place to stay in the **desert** where I could get away from
9.11 Judah will become a **desert,** a place where no one lives."
9.12 devastated and dry as a **desert,** so that no one travels
9.25 Edom, Ammon, Moab, and the **desert** people, who have their
10.22 of Judah into a **desert,** a place where jackals live."
12.10 they have turned my lovely land into a **desert.**
12.11 The whole land has become a **desert,** and no one cares.
12.12 Across all the **desert** highlands men have come to plunder.
13.24 you like straw that is blown away by the **desert** wind.
17. 6 a bush in the **desert,** which grows in the dry wilderness,
25.18 that they would become a **desert,** a terrible and shocking sight,
25.19 all the kings of the **desert** tribes;
25.38 Lord's fierce anger have turned the country into a **desert.**
31. 2 In the **desert** I showed mercy to those people who had
32.43 will be like a **desert** where neither people nor animals live,
33.10 this place is like a **desert,** that it has no people or
33.12 land that is like a **desert** and where no people or animals
34.22 make the towns of Judah like a **desert** where no one lives.
46.19 Memphis will be made a **desert,** a ruin where no one lives.
48. 6 'Run like a wild **desert** donkey!'
49.13 city of Bozrah will become a horrifying sight and a **desert;**
49.33 Hazor will be made a **desert** for ever, a place where only
50. 3 has come to attack Babylonia and will make it a **desert.**
50.12 it will become a dry and waterless **desert.**
51.26 You will be like a **desert** for ever.
51.29 out his plan to make Babylonia a **desert,** where no one lives.
51.43 and are like a waterless **desert,** where no one lives or even
51.62 man nor animal, and it would be like a **desert** for ever.'
Lam 4.19 they took us by surprise in the **desert.**
Ezek 6.14 a waste from the southern **desert** to the city of Riblah in
19.13 it is planted in the **desert,** in a dry and waterless land.
20.10 "And so I led them out of Egypt into the **desert.**
20.13 But even in the **desert** they defied me.
20.13 the force of my anger there in the **desert** and destroy them.
20.15 made a promise in the **desert** that I would not take them
20.17 I decided not to kill them there in the **desert.**
20.21 force of my anger there in the **desert** and kill them all.
20.23 So I made another promise in the **desert.**
20.35 will bring you into the **'Desert** of the Nations,'
20.36 I condemned your fathers in the Sinai **Desert,"**
23.42 could be heard, a group of men brought in from the **desert.**
25. 4 I will let the tribes from the eastern **desert** conquer you.
25.10 the tribes of the eastern **desert** conquer Moab,
29. 5 I will throw you and all those fish into the **desert.**
Hos 2.14 So I am going to take her into the **desert** again;
9.10 Israel, it was like finding grapes growing in the **desert.**
12. 9 again, as you did when I came to you in the **desert.**
13. 5 I took care of you in a dry, **desert** land.
13.15 hot east wind from the **desert,** and it will dry up their
Joel 2. 3 the Garden of Eden, but behind them it is a barren **desert.**
2.20 from the north and will drive some of them into the **desert.**
3.19 "Egypt will become a **desert,** and Edom a ruined waste,
Amos 2.10 Egypt, led you through the **desert** for forty years, and gave
5.25 during those forty years that I led you through the **desert.**
Mic 7.13 the earth will become a **desert** because of the wickedness
Zeph 2.13 the city of Nineveh a deserted ruin, a waterless **desert.**
Mt 3. 1 John the Baptist came to the **desert** of Judaea and started
3. 3 "Someone is shouting in the **desert,** 'Prepare a road for the Lord;
4. 1 Spirit led Jesus into the **desert** to be tempted by the Devil.
11. 7 out to John in the **desert,** what did you expect to see?
15.33 we find enough food in this **desert** to feed this crowd?"
24.26 if people should tell you, 'Look, he is out in the **desert!"**
Mk 1. 3 Someone is shouting in the **desert,** 'Get the road ready for
1. 4 So John appeared in the **desert,** baptizing and preaching.
1.12 made him go into the **desert,** [13] where he stayed forty days,
8. 4 "Where in this **desert** can anyone find enough food to
Lk 1.80 He lived in the **desert** until the day when he appeared
3. 2 word of God came to John son of Zechariah in the **desert.**
3. 4 "Someone is shouting in the **desert:**
4. 1 by the Spirit into the **desert,** [2] where he was tempted by the
7.24 out to John in the **desert,** what did you expect to see?
8.29 the chains and be driven by the demon out into the **desert.**
Jn 1.23 "I am 'the voice of someone shouting in the **desert:**
3.14 on a pole in the **desert,** in the same way the Son
6.31 ancestors ate manna in the **desert,** just as the scripture says,
6.49 Your ancestors ate manna in the **desert,** but they died.
11.54 to a place near the **desert,** to a town named Ephraim, where
Acts 7.30 the flames of a burning bush in the **desert** near Mount Sinai.
7.36 and at the Red Sea and for forty years in the **desert.**
7.38 who was with the people of Israel assembled in the **desert;**
7.42 slaughtered and sacrificed animals for forty years in the **desert.**
7.44 had the Tent of God's presence with them in the **desert.**
13.18 and for forty years he endured them in the **desert.**
21.38 and led four thousand armed terrorists out into the **desert?"**
1 Cor 10. 5 and so their dead bodies were scattered over the **desert.**
Heb 3. 8 were that day in the **desert** when they put him to the
3.17 With the people who sinned, who fell down dead in the **desert.**
11.38 wandered like refugees in the **deserts** and hills, living in caves
Rev 12. 6 The woman fled to the **desert,** to a place God had prepared

Rev 12.14 to her place in the **desert,** where she will be taken care
17. 3 took control of me, and the angel carried me to a **desert.**

DESERT (2)

Gen 47.19 Don't let our fields be **deserted.**
Ex 23.29 the land would become **deserted,**
Lev 26.22 and leave so few of you that your roads will be **deserted.**
26.33 Your land will be **deserted,** and your cities left in ruins.
Josh 22. 3 you have never once **deserted** your fellow-Israelites.
Judg 12. 4 "You Gileadites in Ephraim and Manasseh, you are **deserters**
1 Sam 13. 8 The people began to **desert** Saul, [9] so he said to them,
13.11 Saul answered, "The people were **deserting** me,
2 Sam 20. 2 So the Israelites **deserted** David and went with Sheba,
1 Kgs 20.25 large as the one that **deserted** you, with the same number of
2 Kgs 25. 5 in the plains near Jericho, and all his soldiers **deserted** him.
25.11 skilled workmen, and those who had **deserted** to the Babylonians.
1 Chr 5.25 God of their ancestors and **deserted** him to worship the gods
Job 18. 4 Will the earth be **deserted** because you are angry?
Ps 69.25 May their camps be left **deserted;**
89.38 you have **deserted** and rejected him.
94.14 he will not **desert** those who belong to him.
Is 7.16 lands of those two kings who terrify you will be **deserted.**
17. 2 The cities of Syria will be **deserted** for ever.
17. 9 well-defended cities will be **deserted** and left in ruins
27.10 It is **deserted** like an empty wilderness.
32.14 the palace will be abandoned and the capital city totally **deserted.**
33. 9 The land lies idle and **deserted.**
54. 3 Cities now **deserted** will be filled with people.
54. 6 like a young wife, **deserted** by her husband
60.15 no longer be forsaken and hated, A city **deserted** and desolate.
62. 4 Or your land be called "The **Deserted** Wife."
64.10 Jerusalem is a **deserted** ruin, [11] and our Temple,
Jer 2.17 You **deserted** me, the Lord your God,
37.13 stopped me and said, "You are **deserting** to the Babylonians!"
37.14 I'm not **deserting."**
38.19 "I am afraid of our countrymen who have **deserted** to the Babylonians.
39. 9 together with those who had **deserted** to him.
49.25 The famous city that used to be happy is completely **deserted.**
52. 8 in the plains near Jericho, and all his soldiers **deserted** him.
52.15 skilled workmen, and those who had **deserted** to the Babylonians.
Lam 2. 7 The Lord rejected his altar and **deserted** his holy Temple;
5.18 because Mount Zion lies lonely and **deserted,**
Ezek 6. 9 because their faithless hearts **deserted** me
14.11 to keep the Israelites from **deserting** me and defiling themselves
27.29 "Every ship is now **deserted,** And every sailor has gone ashore.
36. 4 and to you **deserted** cities which were plundered
38. 8 Israel, which were desolate and **deserted** so long,
44.10 the people of Israel, **deserted** me and worshipped idols.
Nah 2.10 Nineveh is destroyed, **deserted,** desolate!
Zeph 2. 4 Ashkelon will be **deserted.**
2.13 the city of Nineveh a **deserted** ruin, a waterless desert.
3. 6 The cities are **deserted;**
Zech 9. 5 Gaza will lose her king, and Ashkelon will be left **deserted.**
Gal 1. 6 time at all you are **deserting** the one who called you by
4.27 For the woman who was **deserted** will have more children than
2 Tim 1.15 of Asia, including Phygelus and Hermogenes, has **deserted** me.
4.10 present world and has **deserted** me, going off to Thessalonica.
4.16 all **deserted** me.

DESERTED WIFE

Is 62. 4 "Forsaken," Or your land be called **"The Deserted Wife."**

DESERVE

[UNDESERVED]

Gen 40.15 Egypt I didn't do anything to **deserve** being put in prison."
Deut 9. 4 brought you in to possess this land because you **deserved** it.
9. 6 Lord is not giving you this fertile land because you **deserve** it.
Judg 9.16 and treat his family properly, as his actions **deserved?**
1 Sam 26.16 Lord that all of you **deserve** to die, because you have not
2 Sam 3.39 May the Lord punish these criminals as they **deserve!"**
19.28 All my father's family **deserved** to be put to death
19.36 I don't **deserve** such a great reward.
1 Kgs 2.26 You **deserve** to die, but I will not have you put to
8.32 the guilty one as he **deserves,** and acquit the one who is
8.39 with each person as he **deserves,** [40] so that your people may
2 Chr 6.23 the guilty one as he **deserves** and acquit the one who is
6.30 with each person as he **deserves,** [31] so that your people may
Ezra 9.13 us less than we **deserve** and have allowed us to survive.
Job 8. 4 against God, and so he punished them as they **deserved.**
11. 6 God is punishing you less than you **deserve.**
34.11 people for what they do and treats them as they **deserve.**
36.17 But now you are being punished as you **deserve.**
42. 8 I will answer his prayer and not disgrace you as you **deserve.**
Ps 28. 4 give them what they **deserve!**
31.23 The Lord protects the faithful, but punishes the proud as they **deserve.**
94. 2 rise and give the proud what they **deserve!**
103.10 not punish us as we **deserve** or repay us according to our
Prov 1.31 you will get what you **deserve,** and your own actions will
12.14 you will get what you **deserve.**
14.14 Bad people will get what they **deserve.**
14.18 people get what their foolishness **deserves,**
26. 2 Curses cannot hurt you unless you **deserve** them.
27.13 responsible for a stranger's debts **deserves** to have his own property
31.31 She **deserves** the respect of everyone.
Is 10.22 Destruction is in store for the people, and it is fully **deserved.**
53. 6 punishment fall on him, the punishment all of us **deserved.**
65. 7 So I will punish them as their past deeds **deserve."**
Jer 10. 7 You **deserve** to be honoured.
26.11 "This man **deserves** to be sentenced to death
49.12 even those who did not **deserve** to be punished had to drink
51. 6 I am now taking my revenge and punishing it as it **deserves.**
51.56 God who punishes evil, and I will treat Babylon as it **deserves.**
Ezek 13.19 You kill people who don't **deserve** to die,
13.19 and you keep people alive who don't **deserve** to live.
14. 4 an answer from me—the answer that his many idols **deserve!**
16.59 will treat you as you **deserve,** because you ignored your promises
20.44 I do not deal with you as your wicked, evil actions **deserve."**
31.11 He will give that tree what it **deserves** for its wickedness.
39.24 I gave them what they **deserved** for their uncleanness
Hos 9. 7 has come, the time when people will get what they **deserve.**
12.14 they **deserve** death for their crimes.
Nah 1.14 a grave for the Assyrians—they don't **deserve** to live!"
Zech 1. 6 had punished them as they **deserved** and as I had determined
Mt 8. 8 "I do not **deserve** to have you come into my house.
22. 8 feast is ready, but the people I invited did not **deserve** it.
23.15 you make him twice as **deserving** of going to hell as you
Lk 7. 4 and begged him earnestly, "This man really **deserves** your help.
7. 6 I do not **deserve** to have you come into my house, [7] neither
12.48 something for which he **deserves** a whipping, will be punished
17. 9 servant does not **deserve** thanks for obeying orders, does he?
23.15 There is nothing this man has done to **deserve** death.
23.22 I cannot find anything he has done to **deserve** death!
23.41 because we are getting what we **deserve** for what we did;
Acts 23.29 done anything for which he **deserved** to die or be put in
25.11 done something for which I **deserve** the death penalty, I do
25.25 he had done anything for which he **deserved** the death sentence.
28.18 found that I had done nothing for which I **deserved** to die.
Rom 1.27 result they bring upon themselves the punishment they **deserve** for their
1.32 God's law says that people who live in this way **deserve** death.
5.16 after so many sins, comes the **undeserved** gift of "Not guilty!"
1 Cor 4. 5 And then everyone will receive from God the praise he **deserves.**
15. 9 I do not even **deserve** to be called an apostle, because
15.19 and no more, then we **deserve** more pity than anyone else in
16.18 Such men as these **deserve** notice.
2 Cor 5.10 will receive what he **deserves,** according to everything he
11.15 In the end they will get exactly what their actions **deserve.**
Phil 4. 8 minds with those things that are good and that **deserve** praise:
Heb 2. 2 follow it or obey it received the punishment he **deserved.**
10.29 Just think how much worse is the punishment he will **deserve!**
1 Pet 2.19 you endure the pain of **undeserved** suffering because you are
2.20 if you endure the beatings you **deserve** for having done wrong?
Rev 16. 6 They are getting what they **deserve!"**

DESIGN

Ex 31. 4 for planning skilful **designs** and working them in gold,
35.32 for planning skilful **designs** and working them in gold,
35.35 work done by engravers, **designers,** and weavers of fine linen;
35.35 are able to do all kinds of work and are skilful **designers.**
38.23 Dan, was an engraver, a **designer,** and a weaver of fine linen
1 Kgs 7.17 column was decorated with a **design** of interwoven chains,
7.20 on a rounded section which was above the chain **design.**
7.40 The **design** of interwoven chains on each capital
7.40 a hundred each round the **design** on each capital
2 Chr 2.14 of engraving and can follow any **design** suggested to him.
3. 5 fine gold, in which were worked **designs** of palm-trees
3. 7 On the walls the workmen carved **designs** of winged creatures.
3.14 blue, purple, and red, with **designs** of the winged creatures
3.16 columns were decorated with a **design** of interwoven chains
4.11 The **design** of interwoven chains on each capital
4.11 in two rows round the **design** of each capital
Prov 25.11 An idea well-expressed is like a **design** of gold, set in silver.
Ezek 42.11 the same measurements, the same **design,**
43.11 its **design,** its entrances and exits, its shape,
Hos 13. 2 to worship—idols of silver, **designed** by human minds,
Heb 11.10 city which God has **designed** and built, the city with permanent

DESIRE

Gen 3.16 you will still have **desire** for your husband,
39. 7 his master's wife began to **desire** Joseph
Ex 20.17 "Do not **desire** another man's house;
20.17 do not **desire** his wife, his slaves, his cattle, his donkeys,
Num 15.39 turn away from me and follow your own wishes and **desires.**
Deut 5.21 "'Do not **desire** another man's wife;
5.21 do not **desire** his house, his land, his slaves, his cattle,
7.25 Do not **desire** the silver or gold that is on them,
2 Sam 23. 5 That is all I **desire;**
1 Chr 28. 9 He knows all our thoughts and **desires.**
29.19 my son Solomon a wholehearted **desire** to obey everything
Ezra 7.13 priests, and Levites that so **desire** be permitted to go with
7.15 which I and my counsellors **desire** to give to the God of
7.18 whatever you and your fellow-countrymen **desire,**
Job 23.12 I follow his will, not my own **desires.**
27.10 They should have **desired** the joy he gives;
Ps 7. 9 You are a righteous God and judge our thoughts and **desires.**
10. 3 The wicked man is proud of his evil **desires;**
17. 3 you have examined me completely and found no evil **desire** in me.
19.10 They are more **desirable** than the finest gold;
20. 4 give you what you **desire** and make all your plans succeed.
21. 2 You have given him his heart's **desire;**
26. 2 judge my **desires** and thoughts.
37. 4 in the Lord, and he will give you your heart's **desire.**
45.11 Your beauty will make the king **desire** you;
63. 1 My whole being **desires** you;

Ps 102. 4 I have lost my **desire** for food.
119.36 Give me the **desire** to obey your laws rather than to get
119.131 In my **desire** for your commands I pant with open mouth.
Prov 27.20 Human **desires** are like the world of the dead—
Ecc 2. 3 Driven on by my **desire** for wisdom, I decided to cheer
3.11 He has given us a **desire** to know the future, but never
11. 9 Do what you want to do, and follow your heart's **desire.**
12. 5 able to drag yourself along, and all **desire** will have gone.
Song 7.10 I belong to my lover, and he **desires** me.
Is 26. 8 you are all that we **desire.**
59.17 clothe himself with the strong **desire** to set things right
Jer 5. 8 stallions wild with **desire,** each lusting for his neighbour's wife.
24. 7 I will give them the **desire** to know
34.16 had set free as they **desired,** and you forced them into
Ezek 7.19 They cannot use it to satisfy their **desires** or fill their stomachs.
Zech 13. 2 be a prophet and will take away the **desire** to worship idols.
Mt 5. 6 "Happy are those whose greatest **desire** is to do what God
Mk 4.19 all other kinds of **desires** crowd in and choke the message,
Jn 8.44 father, the Devil, and you want to follow your father's **desires.**
Rom 1.24 filthy things their hearts **desire,** and they do shameful things
6.12 bodies, so that you obey the **desires** of your natural self.
7. 5 our human nature, the sinful **desires** stirred up by the Law
7. 7 had not said, "Do not **desire** what belongs to someone else,"
7. 7 I would not have known such a **desire.**
7. 8 its chance to stir up all kinds of selfish **desires** in me.
7.18 For even though the **desire** to do good is in me,
13. 9 do not **desire** what belongs to someone else"—all these, and
13.14 paying attention to your sinful nature and satisfying its **desires.**
1 Cor 7. 9 if you cannot restrain your **desires,** go ahead and marry—
10. 6 to warn us not to **desire** evil things, as they did,
2 Cor 5. 2 so great is our **desire** that our home which comes from
Gal 5.13 become an excuse for letting your physical **desires** control you.
5.16 and you will not satisfy the **desires** of the human nature.
5.24 death their human nature with all its passions and **desires.**
6. 8 the field of his natural **desires,** from it he will gather the
Eph 2. 3 lived according to our natural **desires,** doing whatever suited
4.22 the old self that was being destroyed by its deceitful **desires.**
Phil 1.20 My deep **desire** and hope is that I shall never fail in
1.27 and that with only one **desire** you are fighting together for
2. 3 ambition or from a cheap **desire** to boast, but be humble
3.19 end up in hell, because their god is their bodily **desires.**
Col 3. 5 to death, then, the earthly **desires** at work in you, such as
3. 7 live according to such **desires,** when your life was dominated by
1 Thes 4. 5 not with a lustful **desire,** like the heathen who do not
2 Thes 1.11 by his power all your **desire** for goodness and complete your
1 Tim 3. 1 eager to be a church leader, he **desires** an excellent work.
5.11 when their **desires** make them want to marry, they turn away
6. 4 He has an unhealthy **desire** to argue and quarrel about words,
6. 9 many foolish and harmful **desires,** which pull them down to ruin
2 Tim 3. 6 driven by all kinds of **desires,** [7] women who are always
4. 3 will follow their own **desires** and will collect for themselves
Heb 4.12 It judges the **desires** and thoughts of man's heart.
6.11 Our great **desire** is that each one of you keep up his
Jas 1.14 when he is drawn away and trapped by his own evil **desire.**
1.15 Then his evil **desire** conceives and gives birth to sin;
4. 1 your **desires** for pleasure, which are constantly fighting within
4. 2 strongly **desire** things, but you cannot get them, so you quarrel
4. 5 "The spirit that God placed in us is filled with fierce **desires.**"
1 Pet 1.14 to be shaped by those **desires** you had when you were still
4. 2 earthly lives controlled by God's will and not by human **desires.**
5. 2 work, not for mere pay, but from a real **desire** to serve.
1 Jn 2.16 what the sinful self **desires,** what people see and want,
2.17 world and everything in it that people **desire** is passing away;
Jude 16 they follow their own evil **desires;**
18 who will mock you, people who follow their own godless **desires.**"
19 controlled by their natural **desires,** who do not have the Spirit.

DESOLATE

Gen 1. 2 the earth was formless and **desolate.**
Deut 32.10 wandering through the desert, a **desolate,** wind-swept wilderness.
1 Sam 23.24 wilderness of Maon, in a **desolate** valley
2 Kgs 19.17 made their lands **desolate,** [18] and burnt up their gods—
2 Chr 36.21 "The land will lie **desolate** for seventy years,
Job 30. 3 would gnaw dry roots— at night, in wild, **desolate** places.
Ps 68. 6 freedom, but rebels will have to live in a **desolate** land.
Is 6.11 until the land itself is a **desolate** waste.
6.12 send the people far away and make the whole land **desolate.**
17. 5 been cut and harvested, as **desolate** as a field in the valley
24. 1 The Lord is going to devastate the earth and leave it **desolate.**
37.18 made their lands **desolate,** [19] and burnt up their gods—
45.18 did not make it a **desolate** waste, but a place for people
45.19 the people of Israel to look for me in a **desolate** waste.
49.19 "Your country was ruined and **desolate**— but now it will
60.15 longer be forsaken and hated, A city deserted and **desolate.**
Jer 12.11 it lies **desolate** before me.
22. 6 but I will make it a **desolate** place where no one lives.
Ezek 26.19 "I will make you as **desolate** as ruined cities where no one
29.12 I will make Egypt the most **desolate** country in the world.
30. 7 land will be the most **desolate** in the world, and its cities
30.14 I will make southern Egypt **desolate** and set fire to the
32.15 When I make Egypt a **desolate** waste and destroy all who
33.28 will make the country a **desolate** waste, and the power they
35. 3 I will make you a **desolate** waste.
35. 4 I will leave your cities in ruins And your land **desolate;**
35. 9 I will make you **desolate** for ever, and no one will live
35.12 the mountains of Israel were **desolate** and that they were
35.14 "I will make you so **desolate** that the whole world will
35.15 of Seir, yes, all the land of Edom, will be **desolate.**
38. 8 mountains of Israel, which were **desolate** and deserted so long,
Mic 1. 7 destroyed by fire, and all its images will become a **desolate** heap.
Nah 2.10 Nineveh is destroyed, deserted, **desolate!**
Zeph 2.15 What a **desolate** place it will become, a place where wild
Zech 7.14 good land was left a **desolate** place, with no one living in

AV **DESOLATE** see **DESERTED WIFE**

DESPAIR

Deut 28.53 towns, you will become so **desperate** for food that you will
28.54 noble birth will become so **desperate** during the siege that
28.56 town, she will become so **desperate** for food that she will
28.65 Lord will overwhelm you with anxiety, hopelessness, and **despair.**
1 Sam 1.15 I am **desperate,** and I have been praying, pouring out my
11. 4 they told the news, the people started crying in **despair.**
13. 6 against the Israelites, putting them in a **desperate** situation.
2 Sam 24.14 David answered, "I am in a **desperate** situation!
1 Chr 21.13 David replied to Gad, "I am in a **desperate** situation!
Ezra 9. 3 I tore my clothes in **despair,** tore my hair and my beard,
Esth 9.22 a time of grief and **despair** into a time of joy and
Job 6.26 then why do you answer my words of **despair?**
11.20 wicked will look round in **despair** and find that there is no
29.25 leads his troops, and gave them comfort in their **despair.**
31.16 I let widows live in **despair** [17] or let orphans go hungry
Ps 22. 1 I have cried **desperately** for help, but still it does not come.
27.14 Have faith, do not **despair.**
35.12 They pay me back evil for good, and I sink in **despair.**
61. 2 In **despair** and far from home I call to you!
69.20 Insults have broken my heart, and I am in **despair.**
69.29 But I am in pain and **despair;**
130. 1 From the depths of my **despair** I call to you, Lord.
142. 6 Listen to my cry for help, for I am sunk in **despair.**
143. 4 I am in deep **despair.**
Prov 21.15 people are happy, but evil people are brought to **despair.**
Is 16. 7 They will be driven to **despair.**
19. 9 Those who make linen cloth will be in **despair;**
32.10 year you will be in **despair** because there will be no grapes
54. 4 and your **desperate** loneliness as a widow.
Lam 3.65 Curse them and fill them with **despair!**
Ezek 4.17 they will be in **despair,** and they will waste away because of
7.25 **Despair** is coming.
21. 6 "Mortal man, groan as if your heart is breaking with **despair.**
21.12 Beat your breast in **despair!**
Mic 1.10 People of Beth Leaphrah, show your **despair** by rolling in the dust!
2. 4 and they will sing this song of **despair** about your experience:
Zeph 1.14 day, for even the bravest soldiers will cry out in **despair!**
Lk 21.25 whole countries will be in **despair,** afraid of the roar of
2 Cor 4. 8 sometimes in doubt, but never in **despair;**

DESPISE

Gen 16. 4 she became proud and **despised** Sarai.
16. 5 Sarai said to Abram, "It's your fault that Hagar **despises** me.
16. 5 she found out that she was pregnant, she has **despised** me.
Deut 7.26 You must hate and **despise** these idols,
23. 7 "Do not **despise** the Edomites;
23. 7 And do not **despise** the Egyptians;
1 Sam 2.30 me, and I will treat with contempt those who **despise** me.
10.27 They **despised** Saul and did not bring him any gifts.
2 Kgs 19.21 Jerusalem laughs at you, Sennacherib, and **despises** you.
Job 10. 3 To **despise** what you yourself have made?
19.18 Children **despise** me and laugh when they see me.
36. 5 He **despises** no one;
Ps 5. 6 You destroy all liars and **despise** violent, deceitful men.
10.13 How can a wicked man **despise** God and say to himself,
15. 4 He **despises** those whom God rejects,
22. 6 I am a worm, **despised** and scorned by everyone!
74.18 laugh at you, that they are godless and **despise** you.
119.141 I am unimportant and **despised,** but I do not neglect your teachings.
139.21 How I **despise** those who rebel against you!
Prov 6.30 People don't **despise** a thief if he steals food when he
14.21 it is a sin to **despise** anyone.
15.20 Only a fool **despises** his mother.
30.17 fun of his father or **despises** his mother in her old age
Is 37.22 Jerusalem laughs at you, Sennacherib, and **despises** you.
49. 7 the one who is deeply **despised,** who is hated by the nations
53. 3 We **despised** him and rejected him;
60.14 All who once **despised** you will worship at your feet.
Jer 10.15 They are worthless and should be **despised;**
14.21 Remember your promises and do not **despise** us;
18.16 made this land a thing of horror, to be **despised** for ever.
51.18 They are worthless and should be **despised;**
Ezek 2. 6 They will defy and **despise** you;
25. 6 You **despised** the land of Israel.
Joel 2.17 Do not let other nations **despise** us and mock us by saying,
2.19 Other nations will no longer **despise** you.
2.26 My people will never be **despised** again.
2.27 My people will never be **despised** again.
Amos 2. 4 They have **despised** my teachings and have not kept my commands.
6. 8 I **despise** their luxurious mansions.
Obad 2 everyone will **despise** you.
Mic 6.16 so I will bring you to ruin, and everyone will **despise** you.
Mal 1. 6 You **despise** me, and yet you ask, 'How have we despised you?'
1.12 is worthless and when you offer on it food that you **despise.**
2. 9 make the people of Israel **despise** you because you do not
2.10 another, and why do we **despise** the covenant that God made
Mt 6.24 he will be loyal to one and **despise** the other.
18.10 "See that you don't **despise** any of these little ones.
Lk 16.13 he will be loyal to one and **despise** the other.

Lk 18. 9 who were sure of their own goodness and **despised** everybody else.
Acts 4.11 stone that you the builders **despised** turned out to be the
Rom 2. 4 perhaps you **despise** his great kindness, tolerance, and patience.
11.18 So then, you must not **despise** those who were broken off
14. 3 who will eat anything is not to **despise** the one who doesn't;
14.10 And you who eat anything—why do you **despise** your brother?
1 Cor 1.28 world looks down on and **despises,** and thinks is nothing,
4. 6 None of you should be proud of one person and **despise** another.
4.10 We are **despised,** but you are honoured!
11.22 Or would you rather **despise** the church of God and put to
Gal 4.14 a great trial to you, you did not **despise** or reject me.
1 Thes 5.20 do not **despise** inspired messages.
1 Tim 6. 2 to Christian masters must not **despise** them, for they are
Heb 10.29 What, then, of the person who **despises** the Son of God?
2 Pet 2.10 follow their filthy bodily lusts and **despise** God's authority.
Jude 8 **despise** God's authority and insult the glorious beings above.

DESTINY

Ps 9.17 Death is the **destiny** of all the wicked,
Prov 16. 4 Everything the Lord has made has its **destiny;**
16. 4 and the **destiny** of the wicked is destruction.
Jer 10.23 I know that no one is the master of his own **destiny;**
Zech 8.23 want to share in your **destiny,** because we have heard that
Eph 2. 3 we, like everyone else, were **destined** to suffer God's anger.
2 Thes 2. 3 and the Wicked One appears, who is **destined** for hell.

DESTROY

Gen 6.13 I will **destroy** them completely,
6.17 to send a flood on the earth to **destroy** every living being.
7. 4 and nights, in order to **destroy** all the living beings that I
7.23 The Lord **destroyed** all living beings on the earth—
8.21 Never again will I **destroy** all living beings, as I have done
9.11 never again will all living beings be **destroyed** by a flood;
9.11 never again will a flood **destroy** the earth.
9.15 a flood will never again **destroy** all living beings.
13.10 before the Lord had **destroyed** the cities of Sodom and Gomorrah.)
18.23 "Are you really going to **destroy** the innocent with the guilty?
18.24 innocent people in the city, will you **destroy** the whole city?
18.28 Will you **destroy** the whole city because there are five too few?"
18.28 Lord answered, "I will not **destroy** the city if I find
18.29 He replied, "I will not **destroy** it if there are forty."
18.31 He said, "I will not **destroy** the city if I find twenty."
18.32 He said, "I will not **destroy** it if there are ten."
19.13 out of here, [13] because we are going to **destroy** this place.
19.13 and has sent us to **destroy** Sodom."
19.14 the Lord is going to **destroy** this place."
19.15 you will not lose your lives when the city is **destroyed."**
19.21 I won't **destroy** that town.
19.25 Sodom and Gomorrah [25] and **destroyed** them and the whole valley,
19.29 But when God **destroyed** the cities of the valley
20. 4 Would you **destroy** me and my people?
32.11 coming to attack us and **destroy** us all,
34.30 me and attack me, our whole family will be **destroyed."**
Ex 9.15 you would have been completely **destroyed.**
10. 5 that the hail did not **destroy,** even the trees that are left.
17.14 Tell Joshua that I will completely **destroy** the Amalekites."
23.23 the Hivites, and the Jebusites, and I will **destroy** them.
23.24 **Destroy** their gods and break down their sacred stone pillars.
32.10 I am angry with them, and I am going to **destroy** them.
32.12 planning to kill them in the mountains and **destroy** them completely?
33. 3 a stubborn people, and I might **destroy** you on the way."
33. 5 with you even for a moment, I would completely **destroy** you.
34.13 Instead, tear down their altars, **destroy** their sacred pillars,
Lev 13.52 it is a spreading mildew which must be **destroyed** by fire.
26.22 they will kill your children, **destroy** your livestock,
26.30 I will **destroy** your places of worship on the hills,
26.31 turn your cities into ruins, **destroy** your places of worship,
26.32 I will **destroy** your land so completely that the enemies
26.32 enemies who occupy it will be shocked at the **destruction.**
26.44 I will not completely abandon or **destroy** them.
Num 11. 1 It burnt among them and **destroyed** one end of the camp.
14.12 will send an epidemic and **destroy** them,
16.21 "Stand back from these people, and I will **destroy** them
16.40 Otherwise he would be **destroyed** like Korah and his men.
16.45 from these people, and I will **destroy** them on the spot!"
21. 2 dedicate them and their cities to you and will **destroy** them."
21. 3 So the Israelites completely **destroyed** them and their cities,
21.28 It **destroyed** the city of Ar in Moab And devoured the hills
21.30 But now their descendants are **destroyed,**
22. 4 Midianites, "This horde will soon **destroy** everything round us,
24.22 you Kenites will be **destroyed** When Assyria takes you captive."
25. 8 the epidemic that was **destroying** Israel was stopped,
25.11 and that is why I did not **destroy** them in my anger.
25.17 "Attack the Midianites and **destroy** them,
26.10 died with Korah and his followers when fire **destroyed** 250 men;
32.15 and you will be responsible for their **destruction."**
33.52 **Destroy** all their stone and metal idols
33.56 I will destroy you, as I planned to **destroy** them."
Deut 2.12 chased them out, **destroyed** their nation, and settled there
2.15 The Lord kept on opposing them until he had **destroyed** them all.
2.21 But the Lord **destroyed** them, so that the Ammonites took over
2.22 He **destroyed** the Horites, so that the Edomites took over their
2.23 They had **destroyed** the Avvim, the original inhabitants,
2.34 same time we captured and **destroyed** every town,
3. 6 We **destroyed** all the towns and put to death all the men,
4. 3 He **destroyed** everyone who worshipped Baal there,
4.26 You will be completely **destroyed.**
4.31 will not abandon you or **destroy** you, and he will not forget
Deut 5.25 That terrible fire will **destroy** us.
6.15 like fire and will **destroy** you completely,
7. 4 the Lord will be angry with you and **destroy** you at once.
7.16 **Destroy** every nation that the Lord your God places in your power,
7.19 destroyed the Egyptians, he will **destroy** all these people
7.20 panic among them and will **destroy** those who escape
7.22 will not be able to **destroy** them all at once,
7.23 in your power and make them panic until they are **destroyed.**
7.24 you will **destroy** everyone.
8.19 then I warn you today that you will certainly be **destroyed.**
8.20 then you will be **destroyed** just like those nations
8.20 those nations that he is going to **destroy** as you advance.
9. 3 drive them out and **destroy** them quickly, as he promised.
9. 8 Mount Sinai you made the Lord angry—angry enough to **destroy** you.
9.14 I intend to **destroy** them so that no one will remember them
9.19 Lord's fierce anger, because he was furious enough to **destroy** you;
9.25 because I knew that he was determined to **destroy** you.
9.26 I prayed, 'Sovereign Lord, don't **destroy** your own people,
10.10 Lord listened to me once more and agreed not to **destroy** you.
12. 2 land that you are taking, **destroy** all the places where the
12.29 "The Lord your God will **destroy** the nations as you invade
12.30 After the Lord **destroys** those nations,
13.15 **Destroy** that town completely.
13.17 anything that was condemned to **destruction,** and then the Lord
19. 1 the Lord your God has **destroyed** the people whose land he is
20. 8 Otherwise, he will **destroy** the morale of the others.'
20.17 Completely **destroy** all the people:
20.19 Eat the fruit, but do not **destroy** the trees;
28.20 until you are quickly and completely **destroyed.**
28.22 will send drought and scorching winds to **destroy** your crops.
28.24 duststorms and sandstorms until you are **destroyed.**
28.45 with you until you are **destroyed,** because you did not obey
28.48 The Lord will oppress you harshly until you are **destroyed.**
28.61 book of God's laws and teachings, and you will be **destroyed.**
28.63 he will take delight in **destroying** you
29.19 That would **destroy** all of you, good and evil alike.
29.20 fall on him until the Lord has **destroyed** him completely.
29.23 Admah and Zeboiim, which the Lord **destroyed**
30.18 gods, [18] you will be **destroyed**—I warn you here and now.
31. 3 will go before you and **destroy** the nations living there, so
31. 4 The Lord will **destroy** those people, just as he defeated Sihon
31. 4 Sihon and Og, kings of the Amorites, and **destroyed** their country.
31.17 I will abandon them, and they will be **destroyed.**
32.26 I would have **destroyed** them completely,
33.27 enemies as you advanced, and told you to **destroy** them all.
Josh 6.17 in it must be totally **destroyed** as an offering to the Lord.
6.18 But you are not to take anything that is to be **destroyed;**
6.18 you will bring trouble and **destruction** on the Israelite camp.
7. 1 Jericho anything that was to be **destroyed** was not obeyed.
7. 7 To **destroy** us?
7.11 They have taken some of the things condemned to **destruction.**
7.12 because they themselves have now been condemned to **destruction!**
7.12 you any longer unless you **destroy** the things you were
7.13 your possession some things that I ordered you to **destroy!**
10. 1 Joshua had captured and totally **destroyed** Ai
10.37 condemned the city to total **destruction,**
11.20 would be condemned to total **destruction** and all be killed
11.21 this time Joshua went and **destroyed** the race of giants
11.21 Joshua completely **destroyed** them and their cities.
22.20 to obey the command about the things condemned to **destruction;**
24. 8 You took their land, and I **destroyed** them as you advanced.
24.20 He will **destroy** you, even though he was good to you before."
Judg 1.17 put a curse on the city, **destroyed** it, and named it Hormah.
4.24 pressed harder and harder against him until they **destroyed** him.
6. 4 camp on the land and **destroy** the crops as far south as
20.34 The Benjaminites had not realized that they were about to be **destroyed.**
20.41 because they realized that they were about to be **destroyed.**
20.42 were now coming out of the city, and they were **destroyed.**
1 Sam 2.10 The Lord's enemies will be **destroyed;**
12.25 you continue to sin, you and your king will be **destroyed."**
15. 3 Go and attack the Amalekites and completely **destroy** everything
15. 9 they **destroyed** only what was useless or worthless.
15.15 Lord your God, and the rest we have **destroyed** completely."
15.18 out with orders to **destroy** those wicked people of Amalek.
20.15 when the Lord has completely **destroyed** all your enemies,
23.10 to come to Keilah and **destroy** it on account of me,
28.18 did not completely **destroy** the Amalekites and all they had.
2 Sam 14. 7 They will **destroy** my last hope and leave my husband without
20.19 Why are you trying to **destroy** it?
20.20 "I will never ruin or **destroy** your city!
21. 2 but Saul had tried to **destroy** them because of his zeal
21. 5 They answered, "Saul wanted to **destroy** us
22. 5 the waves of **destruction** rolled over me.
22.38 I do not stop until I **destroy** them.
22.41 I **destroy** those who hate me.
24.16 Lord's angel was about to **destroy** Jerusalem,
1 Kgs 8.37 epidemic, or the crops are **destroyed** by scorching winds
13.34 brought about the ruin and total **destruction** of his dynasty.
15.14 Even though Asa did not **destroy** all the pagan places
20.10 will bring enough men to **destroy** this city of yours and
20.42 and your army will be **destroyed** for letting his army escape.' "
22.43 places of worship were not **destroyed,** and the people continued to
2 Kgs 3.25 slaughtering the Moabites [25] and **destroying** their cities.
8.19 Lord was not willing to **destroy** Judah, because he had
10.27 So they **destroyed** the sacred pillar and the temple,
12. 3 places of worship were not **destroyed,** and the people continued
13. 7 the king of Syria had **destroyed** the rest,
13.23 would not let them be **destroyed,** but helped them,

2 Kgs 14.27 not the Lord's purpose to **destroy** Israel completely and for ever,
15. 4 places of worship were not **destroyed,** and the people continued
15.16 he completely **destroyed** the city of Tappuah,
15.35 places of worship were not **destroyed,** and the people continued
18. 4 He **destroyed** the pagan places of worship,
18.22 shrines and altars that Hezekiah **destroyed,** when he told
18.25 attacked your country and **destroyed** it without the Lord's help?
18.25 The Lord himself told me to attack it and **destroy** it."
19.11 Assyrian emperor does to any country he decides to **destroy.**
19.12 My ancestors **destroyed** the cities of Gozan, Haran,
19.17 the emperors of Assyria have **destroyed** many nations,
21. 3 pagan places of worship that his father Hezekiah had **destroyed;**
23. 7 He **destroyed** the living-quarters in the Temple occupied by
24. 2 Ammonites against Jehoiakim to **destroy** Judah,
1 Chr 4.41 went to Gerar and **destroyed** the tents and huts
20. 1 They besieged the city of Rabbah, attacked it, and **destroyed** it.
21.15 he sent an angel to **destroy** Jerusalem, but he changed his
21.16 holding his sword in his hand, ready to **destroy** Jerusalem.
2 Chr 6.28 epidemic or the crops are **destroyed** by scorching winds
12. 7 "Because they admit their sin, I will not **destroy** them.
12.12 Lord's anger did not completely **destroy** him,
14.14 Then they were able to **destroy** the cities in the area
15.17 Even though Asa did not **destroy** all the pagan places
17. 6 in serving the Lord and **destroyed** all the pagan places of
20.10 so our ancestors went round them and did not **destroy** them.
20.23 the Edomite army and completely **destroyed** it,
20.33 but the pagan places of worship were not **destroyed.**
20.37 with Ahaziah, the Lord will **destroy** what you have built."
21. 7 Lord was not willing to **destroy** the dynasty of David,
21.14 your children, and your wives, and will **destroy** your possessions.
22. 7 whom the Lord had chosen to **destroy** the dynasty of Ahab.
25.16 that God has decided to **destroy** you because you have done
31. 1 **destroyed** the altars and the pagan places
32.12 He is the one who **destroyed** the Lord's shrines and altars
33. 3 pagan places of worship that his father Hezekiah had **destroyed.**
34. 3 years later he began to **destroy** the pagan places of worship,
34.33 King Josiah **destroyed** all the disgusting idols
35.21 on my side, so don't oppose me, or he will **destroy** you."
Ezra 4.15 This is why the city was **destroyed.**
5.12 The Temple was **destroyed,** and the people were taken into exile
6.12 nation that defies this command and tries to **destroy** the Temple
9.14 so angry that you will **destroy** us completely
Neh 2. 3 is in ruins and its gates have been **destroyed** by fire?"
2.13 of the city and the gates that had been **destroyed** by fire.
2.17 because Jerusalem is in ruins and its gates are **destroyed!**
9.31 your mercy is great, you did not forsake or **destroy** them.
13.18 punished your ancestors when he brought **destruction** on this city.
Esth 4. 8 issued in Susa, ordering the **destruction** of the Jews.
7. 4 but we are about to be **destroyed**—exterminated!"
8. 5 of Agag gave for the **destruction** of all the Jews
8.11 the Jews could fight back and **destroy** the attackers;
9.24 to determine the day for **destroying** the Jews;
Job 4. 9 Like a storm, God **destroys** them in his anger.
5.21 he will save you when **destruction** comes.
9. 5 he moves mountains and in anger he **destroys** them.
9.21 innocent or guilty, God will **destroy** us.
10. 8 formed and shaped me, and now those same hands **destroy** me.
12.23 strong and great, but then he defeats and **destroys** them.
14.19 so you **destroy** man's hope for life.
15.28 but war will **destroy** those cities and houses.
15.34 and fire will **destroy** the homes built by bribery.
19. 9 He has taken away all my wealth and **destroyed** my reputation.
20.26 Everything he has saved is **destroyed;**
20.28 All his wealth will be **destroyed** in the flood of God's anger.
22.20 that the wicked own is **destroyed,** and fire burns up anything
23.16 Almighty God has **destroyed** my courage.
24.20 he is eaten by worms and **destroyed** like a fallen tree.
24.22 God, in his strength, **destroys** the mighty;
26.12 by his skill he **destroyed** the monster Rahab.
27.23 frightening them with **destructive** power.
28.22 death and **destruction** Admit they have heard only rumours.
29.17 I **destroyed** the power of cruel men and rescued their victims.
30.13 They cut off my escape and try to **destroy** me;
31. 8 then let my crops be **destroyed,** or let others eat the food
31.12 It would be like a **destructive,** hellish fire,
33.18 He will not let them be **destroyed;**
37.20 why should I give him a chance to **destroy** me?
Ps 5. 6 You **destroy** all liars and despise violent, deceitful men.
5. 9 they only want to **destroy.**
9. 5 You have condemned the heathen and **destroyed** the wicked;
9. 6 you have **destroyed** their cities,
18. 4 the waves of **destruction** rolled over me.
18.37 I do not stop until I **destroy** them.
18.40 I **destroy** those who hate me.
21. 9 He will **destroy** them like a blazing fire when he appears.
26. 9 Do not **destroy** me with the sinners;
28. 5 so he will punish them and **destroy** them for ever.
35. 8 But **destruction** will catch them before they know it;
35. 8 be caught in their own trap and fall to their **destruction!**
37.13 wicked men, because he knows they will soon be **destroyed.**
37.38 but sinners are completely **destroyed,**
39.11 by your rebukes, and like a moth you **destroy** what he loves.
46. 5 God is in that city, and it will never be **destroyed;**
46. 9 he breaks bows, **destroys** spears, and sets shields on fire.
50.22 ignore me, or I will **destroy** you, and there will be no
54. 5 He will **destroy** them because he is faithful.
55.11 There is **destruction** everywhere;
59.13 Because they curse and lie, [13]**destroy** them in your anger;
59.13 **destroy** them completely.
60. 4 those who show you reverence, so that they might escape **destruction.**
Ps 64. 4 they **destroy** good men with cowardly slander.
64. 8 He will **destroy** them because of those words;
71.13 May those who attack me be defeated and **destroyed.**
73.18 them in slippery places and make them fall to **destruction!**
73.19 They are instantly **destroyed;**
73.27 you will **destroy** those who are unfaithful to you.
74. 3 our enemies have **destroyed** everything in the Temple.
78.38 He forgave their sin and did not **destroy** them.
78.46 He sent locusts to eat their crops and to **destroy** their fields.
80.16 look at them in anger and **destroy** them!
83. 4 "Come," they say, "let us **destroy** their nation,
88.11 or your faithfulness in the place of **destruction?**
88.16 your terrible attacks **destroy** me.
90. 7 We are **destroyed** by your anger;
92. 7 yet they will be totally **destroyed,**
94.23 punish them for their wickedness and **destroy** them for their sins;
94.23 the Lord our God will **destroy** them.
101. 8 Day after day I will **destroy** the wicked in our land;
102.14 Your servants love her, even though she is **destroyed;**
104.35 May sinners be **destroyed** from the earth;
105.33 he **destroyed** their grapevines and fig-trees
106.23 God said that he would **destroy** his people,
106.23 stood up against God and prevented his anger from **destroying** them.
106.36 God's people worshipped idols, and this caused their **destruction.**
118.10 but I **destroyed** them by the power of the Lord!
118.11 but I **destroyed** them by the power of the Lord!
118.12 by the power of the Lord I **destroyed** them.
124. 6 us thank the Lord, who has not let our enemies **destroy** us.
135.10 He **destroyed** many nations and killed powerful kings:
137. 8 Babylon, you will be **destroyed.**
140.11 may evil overtake violent men and **destroy** them.
143.12 kill my enemies and **destroy** all my oppressors,
145.20 He protects everyone who loves him, but he will **destroy** the wicked.
Prov 1.32 Stupid people are **destroyed** by their own lack of concern.
6.32 He is just **destroying** himself.
10.15 poverty **destroys** the poor.
10.29 The Lord protects honest people, but **destroys** those who do wrong.
11. 3 People who can't be trusted are **destroyed** by their own dishonesty.
13. 3 A careless talker **destroys** himself.
14. 1 by the wisdom of women, but are **destroyed** by foolishness.
14.11 be standing after an evil man's house has been **destroyed.**
15.25 The Lord will **destroy** the homes of arrogant men,
16. 4 and the destiny of the wicked is **destruction.**
16.18 Pride leads to **destruction,** and arrogance to downfall.
18. 9 A lazy person is as bad as someone who is **destructive.**
18.21 What you say can preserve life or **destroy** it;
19.18 If you don't, you are helping them to **destroy** themselves.
21.22 and **destroy** the walls they relied on.
24.16 but disaster **destroys** the wicked.
27. 4 Anger is cruel and **destructive,**
28. 3 like a driving rain that **destroys** the crops.
31. 3 they have **destroyed** kings.
Ecc 5. 6 Why let him **destroy** what you have worked for?
10.12 brings him honour, but a fool is **destroyed** by his own words.
Is 1. 9 Jerusalem would have been totally **destroyed,**
1.31 so powerful men will be **destroyed** by their own evil deeds,
1.31 and no one will be able to stop the **destruction.**
2.11 human pride will be ended and human arrogance **destroyed.**
2.13 He will **destroy** the tall cedars of Lebanon
2.17 Human pride will be ended, and human arrogance will be **destroyed.**
6.13 out of ten remains in the land, he too will be **destroyed;**
9. 5 all their bloodstained clothing will be **destroyed** by fire.
9.18 burns like a fire that **destroys** thorn-bushes and thistles.
9.19 fire throughout the land and **destroys** the people,
10. 7 He is determined to **destroy** many nations.
10.11 I have **destroyed** Samaria and all its idols,
10.18 farmlands will be totally **destroyed,**
10.18 in the same way that a fatal sickness **destroys** a man.
10.20 no longer rely on the nation that almost **destroyed** them.
10.22 **Destruction** is in store for the people, and it is fully deserved.
10.23 the Sovereign Lord Almighty will bring **destruction,**
10.25 I will finish punishing you, and then I will **destroy** them.
13. 6 Lord is near, the day when the Almighty brings **destruction.**
13. 9 be made a wilderness, and every sinner will be **destroyed.**
14.17 Is this the man who **destroyed** cities
14.25 I will **destroy** the Assyrians in my land of Israel
15. 1 Ar and Kir are **destroyed** in a single night,
16. 4 Protect us from those who want to **destroy** us."
16. 4 (Oppression and **destruction** will end,
16. 8 the vineyards of Sibmah are **destroyed**—
18. 5 the enemy will **destroy** the Sudanese
19. 3 frustrate the plans of the Egyptians and **destroy** their morale.
21. 2 of cruel events, a vision of betrayal and **destruction.**
23. 1 Your home port of Tyre has been **destroyed;**
23. 5 shocked and dismayed when they learn that Tyre has been **destroyed.**
23.11 He has ordered the Phoenician centres of commerce to be **destroyed.**
23.14 The city you relied on has been **destroyed.**
25. 2 turned cities into ruins and **destroyed** their fortifications.
25. 8 The Sovereign Lord will **destroy** death for ever!
25.12 He will **destroy** the fortresses of Moab with their high walls
26. 5 he **destroyed** the strong city they lived in,
26.14 for you have punished them and **destroyed** them.
28.17 and floods will **destroy** your security.
28.22 the Lord Almighty's decision to **destroy** the whole country.

Is 29.20 Every sinner will be **destroyed.**
29.21 God will **destroy** those who slander others,
30.28 It sweeps nations to **destruction** and puts an end to their
31. 3 Both of them will be **destroyed.**
31. 8 Assyria will be **destroyed** in war, but not by human power.
32.12 the vineyards have been **destroyed,**
33.11 My spirit is like a fire that will **destroy** you.
34. 2 He has condemned them to **destruction.**
34. 5 Edom, those people whom he has condemned to **destruction.**
36. 7 altars that Hezekiah **destroyed** when he told the people
36.10 attacked your country and **destroyed** it without the Lord's help?
36.10 The Lord himself told me to attack it and **destroy** it."
37.11 Assyrian emperor does to any country he decides to **destroy.**
37.12 My ancestors **destroyed** the cities of Gozan, Haran,
37.18 the emperors of Assyria have **destroyed** many nations,
41.15 You will thresh mountains and **destroy** them;
42.15 I will **destroy** the hills and mountains and dry up the
43.17 mighty army to **destruction,** an army of chariots and horses.
43.28 So I brought **destruction** on Israel;
48. 9 I am keeping it back and will not **destroy** you.
48.19 and I would have made sure they were never **destroyed."**
49.17 and those who **destroyed** you will leave.
50.11 plot to destroy others will be **destroyed** by your own plots.
51.13 who oppress you, of those who are ready to **destroy** you?
59. 7 You leave ruin and **destruction** wherever you go,
60.12 But nations that do not serve you Will be completely **destroyed.**
60.18 **Destruction** will not shatter your country again.
64.11 place where our ancestors praised you, has been **destroyed** by fire.
65. 8 The Lord says, "No one **destroys** good grapes;
65. 8 Neither will I **destroy** all my people—I will save those who
Jer 1.10 and to pull down, to **destroy** and to overthrow, to build and
1.14 He said to me, **"Destruction** will boil over from the north
4. 6 The Lord is bringing disaster and great **destruction**
4. 7 from its hiding place, a **destroyer** of nations has set out.
4. 7 He is coming to **destroy** Judah.
4.20 Suddenly our tents are **destroyed;**
4.27 a wilderness, but that he will not completely **destroy** it.)
5.10 my people's vineyards, but not to **destroy** them completely.
5.17 slaughter your flocks and your herds and **destroy** your vines
5.17 cities in which you trust will be **destroyed** by their army.
5.18 "Yet even in those days I will not completely **destroy** my people.
6. 1 Disaster and **destruction** are about to come from the north.
6. 2 The city of Zion is beautiful, but it will be **destroyed;**
6. 5 we'll **destroy** the city's fortresses."
6. 7 I hear violence and **destruction** in the city;
6.26 because the one who comes to **destroy** you will suddenly attack.
7. 6 Stop worshipping other gods, for that will **destroy** you.
8.16 Our enemies have come to **destroy** our land and everything in it,
9.16 armies against them until I have completely **destroyed** them."
10.11 who did not make the earth and the sky will be **destroyed.**
10.15 they will be **destroyed** when the Lord comes to deal with them.
10.25 they have **destroyed** us completely and left our country in ruins.
11.11 I am going to bring **destruction** on them,
11.12 will not be able to save them when this **destruction** comes.
12.10 Many foreign rulers have **destroyed** my vineyard;
12.12 I have sent war to **destroy** the entire land;
12.17 not obey, then I will completely uproot it and **destroy** it.
13. 9 "This is how I will **destroy** the pride of Judah and the
15. 7 I **destroyed** you, my people, I killed your children
18. 7 to uproot, break down, or **destroy** any nation or kingdom,
19. 8 I will bring such terrible **destruction** on this city
20. 8 **Destruction!"**
20.16 May he be like those cities that the Lord **destroyed**
21.10 up my mind not to spare this city, but to **destroy** it.
22. 7 I am sending men to **destroy** it.
23. 1 judgement on those rulers who **destroy** and scatter his people!
25. 9 I am going to **destroy** this nation and its neighbours and
25.12 I will **destroy** that country and leave it in ruins for ever.
25.29 I will begin my work of **destruction** in my own city.
25.36 Lord in his anger has **destroyed** your nation
26. 3 change my mind about the **destruction** I plan to bring on them
26. 9 that this city will be **destroyed** and no one will live
26.13 change his mind about the **destruction** that he said he would
27. 8 until I have let Nebuchadnezzar **destroy** it completely.
27.10 I will drive you out, and you will be **destroyed.**
30.11 I will **destroy** all the nations where I have scattered you,
30.11 but I will not **destroy** you.
31.28 pull down, to overthrow, to **destroy,** and to demolish them,
31.40 The city will never again be torn down or **destroyed."**
32.23 And so you brought all this **destruction** on them.
32.31 I have decided to **destroy** it [32] because of all the evil
35.17 Judah and of Jerusalem all the **destruction** that I promised.
36. 3 Judah hear about all the **destruction** that I intend to bring
36.29 of Babylonia would come and **destroy** this land and kill its
39.16 I am going to bring upon this city **destruction** and not prosperity.
40. 2 God threatened this land with **destruction,**
42.10 The **destruction** I brought on you has caused me great sorrow.
43.13 He will **destroy** the sacred stone monuments at Heliopolis
44. 2 "You yourselves have seen the **destruction** I brought
44. 7 Do you want to bring **destruction** on men and women,
44. 8 doing this just to **destroy** yourselves,
44.11 God of Israel, will turn against you and **destroy** all Judah.
44.12 Egypt, I will see to it that all of them are **destroyed.**
44.27 see to it that you will not prosper, but will be **destroyed.**
44.29 that my promise to bring **destruction** on you will come true.
46. 8 I will **destroy** cities and the people who live there.
46.14 all you have will be **destroyed** in war!
46.21 The day of their doom had arrived, the time of their **destruction.**
46.23 like men cutting down trees [23] and **destroying** a thick forest.
46.28 I will **destroy** all the nations where I have scattered you,
46.28 but I will not **destroy** you.
Jer 47. 4 The time has come to **destroy** Philistia, to cut off from
47. 4 I, the Lord, will **destroy** the Philistines, all who came from
48. 1 "Pity the people of Nebo— their town is **destroyed!**
48. 2 captured Heshbon and plot to **destroy** the nation of Moab.
48. 3 **Destruction!"**
48. 4 "Moab has been **destroyed;**
48. 8 Not a town will escape the **destruction;**
48. 9 it will soon be **destroyed.**
48.15 Moab and its cities are **destroyed;**
48.18 Moab's **destroyer** is here and has left its forts in ruins.
48.20 Announce along the River Arnon that Moab is **destroyed!"**
48.25 its power has been **destroyed.**
48.32 But now your summer fruits and your grapes have been **destroyed.**
48.42 Moab will be **destroyed** and will no longer be a nation,
48.44 because the Lord has set the time for Moab's **destruction.**
48.46 who worshipped Chemosh have been **destroyed,**
49. 3 Ai is **destroyed!**
49. 8 I am going to **destroy** Esau's descendants,
49.10 All the people of Edom are **destroyed.**
49.17 The Lord said, "The **destruction** that will come on Edom
49.18 Sodom and Gomorrah, when they and the near-by towns were **destroyed.**
49.26 killed in the city streets, and all her soldiers **destroyed.**
49.28 "Attack the people of Kedar and **destroy** that tribe
49.37 my great anger I will **destroy** the people of Elam and send
49.38 I will **destroy** their kings and leaders, and set up my
50.21 Kill and **destroy** them.
50.22 battle is heard in the land, and there is great **destruction.**
50.26 **Destroy** the country!
50.30 and all its soldiers will be **destroyed** on that day.
50.32 your cities on fire, and everything around will be **destroyed."**
50.37 **Destroy** its horses and chariots!
50.37 **Destroy** its treasures;
50.40 Sodom and Gomorrah, when I **destroyed** them and the near-by towns.
51. 1 "I am bringing a **destructive** wind against Babylonia
51. 2 I will send foreigners to **destroy** Babylonia
51. 2 When that day of **destruction** comes, they will attack
51. 3 **Destroy** the whole army!
51. 8 Babylonia has suddenly fallen and is **destroyed!**
51. 9 Babylonia with all his might and has **destroyed** it completely.' "
51.11 because he intends to **destroy** Babylonia.
51.11 how he will take revenge for the **destruction** of his Temple.
51.18 they will be **destroyed** when the Lord comes to deal with them.
51.25 are like a mountain that **destroys** the whole world,
51.48 falls to the people who come from the north to **destroy** it.
51.53 fortress there, I would still send people to **destroy** it.
51.54 crying in Babylon, of mourning for the **destruction** in the land.
51.55 I am **destroying** Babylon and putting it to silence.
51.56 They have come to **destroy** Babylon;
51.60 an account of all the **destruction** that would come on Babylonia,
51.62 have said that you would **destroy** this place, so that there
51.64 rise again, because of the **destruction** that the Lord is
Lam 1.15 He sent an army to **destroy** my young men.
2. 2 The Lord **destroyed** without mercy every village in Judah
2. 3 He raged against us like fire, **destroying** everything.
2. 5 Like an enemy, the Lord has **destroyed** Israel;
2. 8 He measured them off to make sure of total **destruction.**
2.11 I am exhausted with grief at the **destruction** of my people.
2.16 They curl their lips and sneer, "We have **destroyed** it!
2.17 He has **destroyed** us without mercy, as he warned us long ago.
3.48 flow with rivers of tears at the **destruction** of my people.
Ezek 5.16 the pains of hunger like sharp arrows sent to **destroy** you.
6. 3 a sword to **destroy** the places where people worship idols.
6. 6 cities of Israel will be **destroyed,** so that all their altars
6.14 Yes, I will stretch out my hand and **destroy** their country.
12.20 full of people will be **destroyed,** and the country will be
13.13 pouring rain, and hailstones to **destroy** the wall.
14.13 I will stretch out my hand and **destroy** its supply of food.
14.17 send **destructive** weapons to wipe out people
14.21 and disease—to **destroy** people and animals alike.
16.50 things that I hate, so I **destroyed** them, as you well know.
18.30 the evil you are doing, and don't let your sin **destroy** you.
20.13 the force of my anger there in the desert and **destroy** them.
21.28 'A sword is ready to **destroy;**
21.31 And I will hand you over to brutal men, experts at **destruction.**
21.32 You will be **destroyed** by fire.
22.30 my anger is about to **destroy** it, but I could find no
22.31 like a fire I will **destroy** them for what they have done."
24.26 someone who escapes the **destruction** will come and tell you
25. 7 I will **destroy** you so completely that you will not be a
25.15 their age-long enemies and **destroyed** them in their hate.
25.16 I will **destroy** everyone left living there on the Philistine Plain.
26. 4 They will **destroy** your city walls and tear down your towers.
26.17 The famous city is **destroyed!**
26.18 And their people are shocked at such **destruction."**
28. 7 They will **destroy** all the beautiful things
30. 6 Egypt's proud army will be **destroyed.**
30. 9 day comes and Egypt is **destroyed,** I will send messengers
30.13 "I will **destroy** the idols and the false gods
30.15 I will **destroy** the wealth of Thebes.
32. 7 When I **destroy** you, I will cover the sky and blot out
32. 9 spread the news of your **destruction**
32.12 and everything else that you are proud of will be **destroyed.**
32.15 Egypt a desolate waste and **destroy** all who live there,
34.16 fat and strong I will **destroy,** because I am a shepherd
43. 3 seen when God came to **destroy** Jerusalem, and the one I saw
43. 8 things they did, and so in my anger I **destroyed** them.
Dan 2.44 be conquered, but will completely **destroy** all those empires,
4.23 'Cut the tree down and **destroy** it, but leave the stump in
6.26 His kingdom will never be **destroyed,**

Dan 7.11 and its body was thrown into the flames and **destroyed.**
7.26 take away his power, and **destroy** him completely.
8.24 He will cause terrible **destruction**
8.24 He will bring **destruction** on powerful men
8.25 He will be proud of himself and **destroy** many people
8.25 all, but he will be **destroyed** without the use of any human
9.17 Restore your Temple, which has been **destroyed;**
9.26 and the Temple will be **destroyed** by the invading army of a
9.26 bringing the war and **destruction** which God has prepared.
11.17 Then, in order to **destroy** his enemy's kingdom,
11.28 determined to **destroy** the religion of God's people.
11.30 in a rage and try to **destroy** the religion of God's people.
Hos 1. 5 I will at that time **destroy** Israel's military power."
2.12 I will **destroy** her grapevines and her fig-trees,
2.12 wild animals will **destroy** them.
4. 5 I am going to **destroy** Israel, your mother.
5. 7 So now they and their lands will soon be **destroyed.**
5.12 I will bring **destruction** on Israel
6. 5 to you with my message of judgement and **destruction.**
7.13 They will be **destroyed.**
8. 4 silver and gold and made idols—for their own **destruction.**
10. 2 God will break down their altars and **destroy** their sacred pillars.
10. 8 Aven, where the people of Israel worship idols, will be **destroyed.**
10.14 to your people, and all your fortresses will be **destroyed.**
10.14 the day when King Shalman **destroyed** the city of Betharbel
11. 6 It will **destroy** my people because they do what they themselves
11. 8 Could I ever **destroy** you as I did Admah, or treat you
11. 9 I will not **destroy** Israel again.
12. 1 Israel do from morning to night is useless and **destructive.**
13. 9 "I will **destroy** you, people of Israel!
13.14 Bring on your **destruction,** world of the dead!
Joel 1. 5 the grapes for making new wine have been **destroyed.**
1. 7 They have **destroyed** our grapevines and chewed up our fig-trees.
1.10 mourns because the corn is **destroyed,** the grapes are dried up,
1.11 the wheat, the barley, yes all the crops are **destroyed.**
1.15 the day when the Almighty brings **destruction.**
1.16 We look on helpless as our crops are **destroyed.**
2.20 I will **destroy** them because of all they have done to you.
Amos 2. 9 your sake that I totally **destroyed** the Amorites,
3.11 enemy will surround their land, **destroy** their defences,
3.14 Israel for their sins, I will **destroy** the altars of Bethel.
3.15 I will **destroy** winter houses and summer houses.
3.15 every large house will be **destroyed."**
4.11 "I **destroyed** some of you as I destroyed Sodom and Gomorrah.
5. 9 He brings **destruction** on the mighty and their strongholds.
7. 9 The places where Isaac's descendants worship will be **destroyed.**
7.10 His speeches will **destroy** the country.
8. 4 on the needy and try to **destroy** the poor of the country.
9. 4 I am determined to **destroy** them, not to help them."
9. 8 of Israel, and I will **destroy** it from the face of the
9. 8 But I will not **destroy** all the descendants of Jacob.
Obad 8 I punish Edom, I will **destroy** their clever men and wipe out
10 the descendants of Jacob, you will be **destroyed** and dishonoured
18 they will **destroy** the people of Esau as fire burns stubble.
Jon 3. 4 he proclaimed, "In forty days Nineveh will be **destroyed!"**
Mic 1. 7 its temple prostitutes will be **destroyed** by fire,
1. 9 **destruction** has reached the gates of Jerusalem itself,
2.10 Your sins have doomed this place to **destruction.**
4.11 They say, "Jerusalem must be **destroyed!**
5. 9 Israel will conquer her enemies and **destroy** them all.
5.10 time I will take away your horses and **destroy** your chariots.
5.11 I will **destroy** the cities in your land and tear down all
5.12 I will **destroy** the magic charms you use and leave you
5.13 I will **destroy** your idols and sacred stone pillars;
5.14 of the goddess Asherah in your land and **destroy** your cities.
6.13 I have already begun your ruin and **destruction**
6.14 anything you do save I will **destroy** in war.
Nah 1. 8 Like a great rushing flood he completely **destroys** his enemies;
1. 9 He will **destroy** you.
1.12 the Assyrians are strong and numerous, they will be **destroyed**
1.14 I will **destroy** the idols that are in the temples
1.15 They have been totally **destroyed!**
2.10 Nineveh is **destroyed,** deserted, desolate!
3.13 Fire will **destroy** the bars across your gates.
3.19 hear the news of your **destruction** clap their hands for joy.
Hab 1. 3 **Destruction** and violence are all round me,
1.13 are you silent while they **destroy** people who are more righteous
1.17 use their swords for ever and keep on **destroying** nations
2.10 **destroying** many nations you have only brought ruin on yourself.
3.13 the leader of the wicked and completely **destroyed** his followers.
Zeph 1. 2 "I am going to **destroy** everything on earth,
1. 3 I will **destroy** all mankind, and no survivors will be left.
1. 4 I will **destroy** the last trace of the worship of Baal there,
1. 5 I will **destroy** anyone who goes up on the roof and worships
1. 5 I will also **destroy** those who worship me
1. 6 I will **destroy** those who have turned back
1.13 Their wealth will be looted and their houses **destroyed.**
1.15 a day of ruin and **destruction,** a day of darkness and gloom,
1.18 The whole earth will be **destroyed** by the fire of his anger.
2. 5 He will **destroy** you, and not one of you will be left.
2. 9 Moab and Ammon are going to be **destroyed** like Sodom and Gomorrah.
2.13 The Lord will use his power to **destroy** Assyria.
3. 6 I have **destroyed** their cities
3. 8 The whole earth will be **destroyed** by the fire of my fury.
Zech 7. 3 to mourn because of the **destruction** of the Temple,
9.10 the bows used in battle will be **destroyed.**
9.15 will protect his people, and they will **destroy** their enemies.
11. 2 those glorious trees have been **destroyed!**
11. 3 their forest home along the Jordan is **destroyed!**
11. 9 Let those who are to be **destroyed,** be destroyed.
Zech 11. 9 Those who are left will **destroy** one another."
11.16 does not help the sheep that are threatened by **destruction;**
11.17 War will totally **destroy** his power.
12. 6 they will **destroy** all the surrounding nations.
12. 9 At that time I will **destroy** every nation that tries to
14.11 live there in safety, no longer threatened by **destruction.**
Mal 1. 4 "Our towns have been **destroyed,** but we will rebuild them,"
3.11 I will not let insects **destroy** your crops,
4. 6 otherwise I would have to come and **destroy** your country."
Mt 6.19 where moths and rust **destroy,** and robbers break in and steal.
6.20 where moths and rust cannot **destroy,** and robbers cannot break in
10.28 afraid of God, who can **destroy** both body and soul in hell.
Mk 1.24 Are you here to **destroy** us?
3. 4 To save a man's life or to **destroy** it?"
Lk 2.34 chosen by God for the **destruction** and the salvation of many
4.34 Are you here to **destroy** us?
6. 9 To save a man's life or **destroy** it?"
9.54 you want us to call fire down from heaven to **destroy** them?"
12.33 no thief can get to them, and no moth can **destroy** them.
19.44 will completely **destroy** you and the people within your walls;
21.20 armies, then you will know that she will soon be **destroyed.**
Jn 10.10 The thief comes only in order to steal, kill, and **destroy.**
11.48 Roman authorities will take action and **destroy** our Temple and
11.50 die for the people, instead of having the whole nation **destroyed?"**
Acts 3.23 shall be separated from God's people and **destroyed.'**
8. 3 But Saul tried to **destroy** the church;
13.19 He **destroyed** seven nations in the land of Canaan and made
19.27 her greatness will be **destroyed**—the goddess worshipped by everyone
Rom 3.16 they leave ruin and **destruction** wherever they go.
6. 6 the sinful self might be **destroyed,** so that we should no
9.22 the objects of his anger, who were doomed to **destruction.**
14.20 Do not, because of food, **destroy** what God has done.
1 Cor 1.19 The scripture says, "I will **destroy** the wisdom of the wise
1.28 in order to **destroy** what the world thinks is important.
3.17 So if anyone destroys God's temple, God will **destroy** him.
5. 5 for his body to be **destroyed,** so that his spirit may be
10.10 of them did—and they were **destroyed** by the Angel of Death.
15.54 "Death is **destroyed;**
2 Cor 4. 9 and though badly hurt at times, we are not **destroyed.**
10. 4 God's powerful weapons, which we use to **destroy** strongholds.
10. 4 We **destroy** false arguments;
Gal 1.13 mercy the church of God and did my best to **destroy** it.
1.23 is now preaching the faith that he once tried to **destroy!"**
5.15 then watch out, or you will completely **destroy** one another.
Eph 2.16 By his death on the cross Christ **destroyed** their enmity;
4.22 the old self that was being **destroyed** by its deceitful desires.
1 Thes 5. 3 is quiet and safe," then suddenly **destruction** will hit them!
2 Thes 1. 9 suffer the punishment of eternal **destruction,** separated from the
2. 8 breath from his mouth and **destroy** him with his dazzling presence.
1 Tim 6. 9 and harmful desires, which pull them down to ruin and **destruction.**
Heb 2.14 through his death he might **destroy** the Devil, who has the
6. 8 of being cursed by God and will be **destroyed** by fire.
10.27 and the fierce fire which will **destroy** those who oppose God!
12.29 because our God is indeed a **destroying** fire.
Jas 1.11 its flower falls off and its beauty is **destroyed.**
1.11 man will be **destroyed** while he goes about his business.
4.12 He alone can save and **destroy.**
1 Pet 1. 7 Even gold, which can be **destroyed,** is tested by fire;
1.18 not something that can be **destroyed,** such as silver or gold;
2 Pet 1. 4 may escape from the **destructive** lust that is in the world,
2. 1 They will bring in **destructive,** untrue doctrines, and will deny
2. 1 and so they will bring upon themselves sudden **destruction.**
2. 6 cities of Sodom and Gomorrah, **destroying** them with fire,
2.12 They will be **destroyed** like wild animals, [13] and they will be
2.19 they themselves are slaves of **destructive** habits—
3. 6 the water of the flood, that the old world was **destroyed.**
3. 7 the same command of God, in order to be **destroyed** by fire.
3. 7 the day when godless people will be judged and **destroyed.**
3. 9 not want anyone to be **destroyed,** but wants all to turn away
3.10 will burn up and be **destroyed,** and the earth with everything
3.11 all these things will be **destroyed** in this way, what kind of
3.12 will burn up and be **destroyed,** and the heavenly bodies will
3.16 So they bring on their own **destruction.**
1 Jn 3. 8 for this very reason, to **destroy** what the Devil had done.
Jude 5 from Egypt, but afterwards **destroyed** those who did not believe.
10 like wild animals, are the very things that **destroy** them.
11 have rebelled as Korah rebelled, and like him they are **destroyed.**
Rev 8. 9 in the sea died, and a third of the ships were **destroyed.**
11. 5 fire comes out of their mouths and **destroys** their enemies;
11.13 tenth of the city was **destroyed,** and seven thousand people were
11.18 The time has come to **destroy** those who destroy the earth!"
16.19 into three parts, and the cities of all countries were **destroyed.**
17. 8 come up from the abyss and will go off to be **destroyed.**
17.11 is one of the seven and is going off to be **destroyed.**
17.16 they will eat her flesh and **destroy** her with fire.
18.20 Be glad, heaven, because of her **destruction!**
20. 9 But fire came down from heaven and **destroyed** them.

DESTROYER

2 Pet 2. 3 Judge has been ready, and their **Destroyer** has been wide awake!
Rev 9.11 in Greek the name is Apollyon (meaning "The **Destroyer**").

AV DESTROYER

Ex 12.23 and will not let the **Angel of Death** enter your houses and
Job 15.21 scream in his ears, and **robbers** attack when he thinks he is

Ps 17. 4 I have obeyed your command and have not followed paths of **violence.**
1 Cor 10.10 and they were destroyed by the **Angel of Death.**

DETAIL

Mt 5.18 least point nor the smallest **detail** of the Law will be done
Lk 16.17 disappear than for the smallest **detail** of the Law to be done
Heb 9. 5 But now is not the time to explain everything in **detail.**

DETERMINE

Ex 28.15 for the High Priest to use in **determining** God's will.
28.30 so that he can **determine** my will for the people
32.22 you know how **determined** these people are to do evil.
Lev 5.15 Its value is to be **determined** according to the official standard.
5.18 Its value is to be **determined** according to the official standard.
6. 6 Its value is to be **determined** according to the official standard.
14.57 These laws **determine** when something is unclean
Num 35. 8 each tribe is to be **determined** according to the size of its
Deut 1.38 But strengthen the **determination** of your helper, Joshua son
3.28 Strengthen his **determination,** because he will lead the people
9.25 because I knew that he was **determined** to destroy you.
31. 6 Be **determined** and confident.
31. 7 of all the people of Israel, "Be **determined** and confident;
31.23 Joshua son of Nun and said to him, "Be confident and **determined.**
32. 8 he **determined** where peoples should live.
Josh 1. 6 Be **determined** and confident, for you will be the leader
1. 7 Just be **determined,** be confident;
1. 9 Remember that I have commanded you to be **determined** and confident!
1.18 Be **determined** and confident!"
10.25 Be **determined** and confident because this is what the Lord
11.20 The Lord had made them **determined** to fight the Israelites,
14. 2 tribes west of the Jordan were **determined** by drawing lots.
Judg 5. 2 The Israelites were **determined** to fight;
Ruth 1.18 Naomi saw that Ruth was **determined** to go with her,
1 Sam 13.19 because the Philistines were **determined** to keep the Hebrews from
20. 7 angry, you will know that he is **determined** to harm me.
20. 9 certain that my father was **determined** to harm you,
20.33 Jonathan realized that his father was really **determined** to kill David.
1 Kgs 2. 2 Be confident and **determined,**
7.47 too many of them, and so their weight was never **determined.**
2 Kgs 19.31 because the Lord is **determined** to make this happen.
1 Chr 12.38 went to Hebron, **determined** to make David king
22.13 Be **determined** and confident,
25. 8 To **determine** the assignment of duties they all drew lots,
28.10 Now do it—and do it with **determination."**
28.20 King David said to his son Solomon, "Be confident and **determined.**
2 Chr 4.18 no one **determined** the total weight of the bronze
30.12 united the people in their **determination** to obey his will
32. 7 "Be **determined** and confident, and don't be afraid
35.22 But Josiah was **determined** to fight.
Neh 10.34 draw lots each year to **determine** which clans are to provide
Esth 7. 7 see that the king was **determined** to punish him for this,
9.24 to **determine** the day for destroying the Jews;
Job 22.15 Are you **determined** to walk in the paths that evil men
28.25 gave the wind its power And **determined** the size of the sea;
Prov 11.19 Anyone who is **determined** to do right will live,
16.33 lots to learn God's will, but God himself **determines** the answer.
19.28 no justice where a witness is **determined** to hurt someone.
20.24 The Lord has **determined** our path;
Ecc 1.13 I **determined** that I would examine and study all the things
1.17 **determined** to learn the difference between knowledge and foolishness,
6.10 Everything that happens was already **determined** long ago,
7.23 I was **determined** to be wise, but it was beyond me.
7.25 I was **determined** to find wisdom and the answers to my questions,
Is 9. 7 The Lord Almighty is **determined** to do all this.
10. 7 He is **determined** to destroy many nations.
14.13 You were **determined** to climb up to heaven
14.24 What I have **determined** to do will be done.
14.27 The Lord Almighty is **determined** to do this;
37.32 because the Lord Almighty is **determined** to make this happen.
41. 4 Who has **determined** the course of history?
Jer 42.13 says, 'If you are **determined** to go and live in Egypt,
42.17 All the people who are **determined** to go and live in
44.12 who are left and are **determined** to go and live in Egypt,
Lam 2. 8 The Lord was **determined** that the walls of Zion should fall;
Dan 5.23 not honour the God who **determines** whether you live or die
11.28 the loot he has captured, **determined** to destroy the religion
Amos 9. 4 I am **determined** to destroy them, not to help them."
Zech 1. 6 them as they deserved and as I had **determined** to do."
Jn 5.18 made the Jewish authorities all the more **determined** to kill him;
Acts 22.10 be told everything that God has **determined** for you to do.'
Heb 12. 1 let us run with **determination** the race that lies before us.

DETEST

Ps 119.163 I hate and **detest** all lies, but I love your law.
Ezek 16.45 She **detested** her husband and her children.
Rom 2.22 You **detest** idols—but do you rob temples?

DETHRONES see THRONE

DEVASTATE

Josh 22.33 about going to war to **devastate** the land
Judg 6. 5 They came and **devastated** the land, [6]and Israel was helpless
16.24 victory over our enemy, who **devastated** our land
2 Chr 34. 6 in the cities and the **devastated** areas of Manasseh, Ephraim,
Is 1. 7 Your country has been **devastated,**
13. 5 In his anger the Lord is coming to **devastate** the whole country.
16. 4 and those who are **devastating** the country will be gone.
24. 1 The Lord is going to **devastate** the earth and leave it desolate.
51.19 your land has been **devastated** by war,
Jer 9.12 "Lord, why is the land **devastated** and dry as a desert,
Ezek 25. 3 see the land of Israel **devastated,** to see the people of
30.11 He and his ruthless army will come to **devastate** the land.
30.12 Foreigners will **devastate** the whole country.
35.15 just as you rejoiced at the **devastation** of Israel,
Zech 11. 6 Those rulers will **devastate** the earth, and I will not save
Mal 1. 3 I have **devastated** Esau's hill-country

DEVELOP

Lk 1.80 The child grew and **developed** in body and spirit.

DEVIL

Mt 4. 1 Spirit led Jesus into the desert to be tempted by the **Devil.**
4. 3 Then the **Devil** came to him and said, "If you are God's
4. 5 Then the **Devil** took Jesus to Jerusalem, the Holy City, set
4. 8 Then the **Devil** took Jesus to a very high mountain and
4. 9 I will give you," the **Devil** said, "if you kneel down and
4.11 Then the **Devil** left Jesus;
13.39 and the enemy who sowed the weeds is the **Devil.**
25.41 fire which has been prepared for the **Devil** and his angels!
Lk 4. 2 desert, [2]where he was tempted by the **Devil** for forty days.
4. 3 The **Devil** said to him, "If you are God's Son, order this
4. 5 Then the **Devil** took him up and showed him in a second
4. 6 all this power and all this wealth," the **Devil** told him.
4. 9 Then the **Devil** took him to Jerusalem and set him on the
4.13 the **Devil** finished tempting Jesus in every way, he left him
8.12 the **Devil** comes and takes the message away from their hearts
Jn 6.70 Yet one of you is a **devil!"**
8.44 children of your father, the **Devil,** and you want to follow
13. 2 The **Devil** had already put into the heart of Judas, the son
Acts 10.38 were under the power of the **Devil,** for God was with him.
13.10 straight at the magician [10]and said, "You son of the **Devil!**
2 Cor 6.15 How can Christ and the **Devil** agree?
Eph 4.27 Don't give the **Devil** a chance.
6.11 will be able to stand up against the **Devil's** evil tricks.
1 Thes 3. 5 could not be that the **Devil** had tempted you and all our
1 Tim 3. 6 not swell up with pride and be condemned, as the **Devil** was.
3. 7 he will not be disgraced and fall into the **Devil's** trap.
2 Tim 2.26 from the trap of the **Devil,** who had caught them and made
Heb 2.14 he might destroy the **Devil,** who has the power over death,
Jas 4. 7 Resist the **Devil,** and he will run away from you.
1 Pet 5. 8 Your enemy, the **Devil,** roams round like a roaring lion,
1 Jn 3. 8 to sin belongs to the **Devil,**
3. 8 because the **Devil** has sinned from the very beginning.
3. 8 for this very reason, to destroy what the **Devil** had done.
3.10 clear difference between God's children and the **Devil's** children:
Jude 9 In his quarrel with the **Devil,** when they argued about who
9 not dare to condemn the **Devil** with insulting words, but said,
Rev 2.10 The **Devil** will put you to the test by having some of
12. 9 serpent, called the **Devil,** or Satan, that deceived the whole
12.12 For the **Devil** has come down to you, and he is filled
20. 2 ancient serpent—that is, the **Devil,** or Satan—and chained him
20.10 Then the **Devil,** who deceived them, was thrown into the

DEVOTE

1 Kgs 21.20 "You have **devoted** yourself completely to doing what is wrong
21.25 no one else who had **devoted** himself so completely to doing
2 Kgs 10.16 see for yourself how **devoted** I am to the Lord."
16. 7 "I am your **devoted** servant.
17.17 and they **devoted** themselves completely to doing what is
1 Chr 2. 7 of Israel by keeping loot that had been **devoted** to God.
29.18 keep such **devotion** for ever strong
2 Chr 31.21 in a spirit of complete loyalty and **devotion** to his God.
32.32 King Hezekiah did and his **devotion** to the Lord are recorded
35.26 Everything that Josiah did—his **devotion** to the Lord,
Ezra 7.10 Ezra had **devoted** his life to studying the Law of the Lord,
Ps 69. 9 My **devotion** to your Temple burns in me like a fire;
78.72 took care of them with unselfish **devotion**
86.11 teach me to serve you with complete **devotion.**
Prov 2. 8 others fairly, and guards those who are **devoted** to him.
Ecc 7.25 But I **devoted** myself to knowledge and study;
Is 53.11 My **devoted** servant, with whom I am pleased,
Hos 10.12 reap the blessings that your **devotion** to me will produce.
Jn 2.17 the scripture says, "My **devotion** to your house, O God, burns
Acts 13.35 'You will not allow your **devoted** servant to rot in the grave.'
21.20 become believers, and how **devoted** they all are to the Law.
Rom 10. 2 I can assure you that they are deeply **devoted** to God;
10. 2 but their **devotion** is not based on true knowledge.
12.11 Serve the Lord with a heart full of **devotion.**
2 Cor 7.11 such feelings, such **devotion,** such readiness to punish
7.12 in God's sight, how deep your **devotion** to us really is.
11. 3 abandon your full and pure **devotion** to Christ—in the same
Gal 1.13 to live when I was **devoted** to the Jewish religion, how I
1.14 and was much more **devoted** to the traditions of our ancestors.
1 Tim 4.15 Practise these things and **devote** yourself to them, in order
5.10 helped people in trouble, and **devoted** herself to doing good.
Heb 5. 7 Because he was humble and **devoted,** God heard him.

DEVOUR

Gen 49.27 Morning and evening he kills and **devours.”**
Num 21.28 of Ar in Moab And **devoured** the hills of the upper Arnon.
23.24 until it has torn and **devoured,** Until it has drunk the blood
24. 8 They **devour** their enemies, Crush their bones, smash their arrows.
Deut 28.42 All your trees and crops will be **devoured** by insects.
Ps 21. 9 The Lord will **devour** them in his anger, and fire will
Is 9.12 Philistia on the west have opened their mouths to **devour** Israel.
56. 9 nations to come like wild animals and **devour** his people.
Jer 5.17 They will **devour** your crops and your food;
15. 3 eat them, and wild animals will **devour** what is left over.
30.16 But now, all who **devour** you will be devoured, and all
Ezek 35.12 of Israel were desolate and that they were yours to **devour.**
Hos 13. 8 Like a lion I will **devour** you on the spot, and will
Joel 1. 4 what one swarm left, the next swarm **devoured.**
1 Pet 5. 8 roams round like a roaring lion, looking for someone to **devour.**

DEVOUT

1 Kgs 18. 3 (Obadiah was a **devout** worshipper of the Lord,
18.12 that I have been a **devout** worshipper of the Lord ever since
Acts 8. 2 Some **devout** men buried Stephen, mourning for him with loud cries.
1 Pet 3. 5 For the **devout** women of the past who placed their hope in

DEW

Gen 27.28 May God give you **dew** from heaven and make your fields fertile!
27.39 “No **dew** from heaven for you, No fertile fields for you.
Ex 16.13 camp, and in the morning there was **dew** all round the camp.
16.14 When the **dew** evaporated, there was something thin and flaky
Num 11. 8 It fell on the camp at night along with the **dew.**
Deut 32. 2 fall like drops of rain and form on the earth like **dew.**
33.28 of corn and wine, where **dew** from the sky waters the ground.
Judg 6.37 in the morning there is **dew** only on the wool but not
6.38 the wool and wrung enough **dew** out of it to fill a
6.40 morning the wool was dry, but the ground was wet with **dew.**
2 Sam 1.21 “May no rain or **dew** fall on Gilboa's hills;
1 Kgs 17. 1 that there will be no **dew** or rain for the next two
Job 29.19 always have water and whose branches are wet with **dew.**
38.28 Does either the rain or the **dew** have a father?
Ps 110. 3 Like the **dew** of early morning your young men will come to
133. 3 It is like the **dew** on Mount Hermon, falling on the hills
Song 5. 2 My head is wet with **dew,** and my hair is damp from
Is 18. 4 heaven as quietly as the **dew** forms in the warm nights of
26.19 As the sparkling **dew** refreshes the earth, so the Lord will
Dan 4.15 “‘Now let the **dew** fall on this man, and let him live
4.23 Let the **dew** fall on this man, and let him live there
4.25 sleep in the open air, where the **dew** will fall on you.
4.33 The **dew** fell on his body, and his hair grew as long
5.21 in the open air with nothing to protect him from the **dew.**
Hos 6. 4 it is like **dew,** that vanishes early in the day.
13. 3 morning mist, like the **dew** that vanishes early in the day.
Mic 5. 7 survive will be like refreshing **dew** sent by the Lord for

DIAMOND

Ex 28.18 in the second row, an emerald, a sapphire, and a **diamond;**
39.11 in the second row, an emerald, a sapphire, and a **diamond;**
Jer 17. 1 on your hearts with a **diamond** point and carved on the
Ezek 3. 9 make you as firm as a rock, as hard as a **diamond;**
28.13 rubies and **diamonds;**

DICE

Job 6.27 You would even throw **dice** for orphan slaves
Joel 3. 3 They threw **dice** to decide who would get the captives.
Mt 27.35 and then divided his clothes among them by throwing **dice.**
Mk 15.24 clothes among themselves, throwing **dice** to see who would get
Lk 23.34 They divided his clothes among themselves by throwing **dice.**
Jn 19.24 let's throw **dice** to see who will get it.”

DICTATE

Esth 3.12 called the king's secretaries and **dictated** a proclamation
8. 9 called the king's secretaries and **dictated** letters to the Jews
Jer 36. 4 Baruch son of Neriah and **dictated** to him everything that the
36. 6 Lord has said to me and that I have **dictated** to you.
36.17 Did Jeremiah **dictate** it to you?”
36.18 Baruch answered, “Jeremiah **dictated** every word of it to me,
36.27 the scroll that I had **dictated** to Baruch,
36.32 my secretary Baruch, and he wrote down everything that I **dictated.**
36.32 and similar messages that I **dictated** to him.
45. 1 Baruch wrote down what I had **dictated** to him.
2 Cor 1.24 We are not trying to **dictate** to you what you must believe;

DIE

Gen 2.17 if you do, you will **die** the same day.”
3. 3 if we do, we will **die.”**
3. 4 you will not **die.**
5. 5 He had other children [5] and **died** at the age of 930.
5. 8 He had other children [8] and **died** at the age of 912.
5.11 He had other children [11] and **died** at the age of 905.
5.14 He had other children [14] and **died** at the age of 910.
5.17 He had other children [17] and **died** at the age of 895.
5.20 He had other children [20] and **died** at the age of 962.
5.27 He had other children [27] and **died** at the age of 969.
5.31 He had other children [31] and **died** at the age of 777.
Gen 6.17 Everything on the earth will **die,** [18] but I will make a
7.21 living being on the earth **died**—every bird, every animal,
7.22 Everything on earth that breathed **died.**
9.29 Noah lived for 350 years [29] and **died** at the age of 950.
11.28 father of Lot, [28] and Haran **died** in his native city, Ur in
11.32 Terah **died** there at the age of two hundred and five.
15.15 live to a ripe old age, **die** in peace, and be buried.
19.19 will overtake me, and I will **die** before I get there.
20. 3 “You are going to **die,** because you have taken this woman;
20. 7 and he will pray for you, so that you will not **die.**
20. 7 you that you are going to **die,** you and all your people.”
21.16 She said to herself, “I can't bear to see my child **die.”**
23. 2 She **died** in Hebron in the land of Canaan, and Abraham
25. 7 Abraham **died** at the ripe old age of a hundred and seventy-five.
25.17 Ishmael was a hundred and thirty-seven years old when he **died.**
25.32 I am about to **die;**
27. 2 Isaac said, “You see that I am old and may **die** soon.
27. 4 eaten it, I will give you my final blessing before I **die.”**
27. 7 you my blessing in the presence of the Lord before I **die.’**
27.10 to eat, and he will give you his blessing before he **dies.”**
27.46 marries one of these Hittite girls, I might as well **die.”**
30. 1 and said to Jacob, “Give me children, or I will **die.”**
33.13 are driven hard for even one day, the whole herd will **die.**
35. 8 Rebecca's nurse Deborah **died**
35.18 But she was **dying,** and as she breathed her last,
35.19 When Rachel **died,** she was buried beside the road to Ephrath,
35.29 hundred and eighty years old [29] and **died** at a ripe old age;
38.12 After some time Judah's wife **died.**
44.22 if he did, his father would **die.**
44.30 he sees that the boy is not with me, he will **die.**
45.28 I must go and see him before I **die.”**
46. 4 Joseph will be with you when you **die.”**
46.12 (Judah's other sons, Er and Onan, had **died** in Canaan.)
46.30 Joseph, “I am ready to **die,** now that I have seen you
47.15 Don't let us **die.**
47.19 Don't let us **die.**
47.29 drew near for him to **die,** he called for his son Joseph
48. 7 To my great sorrow she **died** in the land of Canaan, not
48.21 see, I am about to **die,** but God will be with you
49.33 giving instructions to his sons, he lay down again and **died.**
50. 5 my father was about to **die,** he made me promise him that
50.16 “Before our father **died,** [17] he told us to ask you,
50.22 he was a hundred and ten years old when he **died.**
50.24 brothers, “I am about to **die,** but God will certainly take
50.26 So Joseph **died** in Egypt at the age of a hundred and
Ex 1. 6 the rest of that generation **died,**
2.23 later the king of Egypt **died,** but the Israelites were still
7.18 The fish will **die,** and the river will stink so much that
7.21 The fish in the river **died,**
8.13 frogs in the houses, the courtyards, and the fields **died.**
9. 4 and no animal that belongs to the Israelites will **die.**
9. 6 the animals of the Egyptians **died,**
9. 6 but not one of the animals of the Israelites **died.**
9. 7 told that none of the animals of the Israelites had **died.**
9.19 people and animals left outside unprotected, and they will all **die.’ ”**
10.28 On the day I do, you will **die!”**
11. 5 first-born son in Egypt will **die,** from the king's son, who
11. 5 The first-born of all the cattle will **die** also.
14.11 you have to bring us out here in the desert to **die?**
14.12 better to be slaves there than to **die** here in the desert.”
19.21 if they do, many of them will **die.**
20.19 we are afraid that if God speaks to us, we will **die.”**
21.20 or female, and the slave **dies** on the spot, the man is
21.21 if the slave does not **die** for a day or two, the
22.10 for him, and the animal **dies** or is injured or is carried
22.14 and it is injured or **dies** when its owner is not present,
30.21 must wash their hands and feet, so that they will not **die.**
Lev 7.24 of an animal that has **died** a natural death or has been
8.35 If you don't, you will **die.**
10. 6 If you do, you will **die,** and the Lord will be angry
10. 7 the Tent or you will **die,** because you have been consecrated
10. 9 if you do, you will **die.**
11.39 animal that may be eaten **dies,** anyone who touches it will be
16.13 the Covenant Box so that he will not see it and **die.**
17.15 from an animal that has **died** a natural death or has been
20.21 If a man marries his brother's wife, they will **die** childless.
21. 1 funeral ceremonies when a relative **dies,**
22. 8 of any animal that has **died** a natural death or has been
22. 9 they will be guilty and **die,** because they have disobeyed
26.38 You will **die** in exile, swallowed up by the land of your
Num 4.15 Kohath must not touch the sacred objects, or they will **die.**
4.20 preparing the sacred objects for moving, they will **die.”**
5. 8 But if that person has **died** and has no near relative to
6. 9 right beside someone who suddenly **dies,** he must wait seven days
11. 2 he prayed to the Lord, and the fire **died** down.
14. 2 would have been better to **die** in Egypt or even here in
14.29 You will **die** and your corpses will be scattered
14.32 You will **die** here in this wilderness.
14.33 suffering for your unfaithfulness, until the last one of you **dies.**
14.35 Here in the wilderness every one of you will **die.**
14.36 And so the Lord struck them with a disease, and they **died.**
14.43 face the Amalekites and the Canaanites, you will **die** in battle;
16.29 If these men **die** a natural death without some punishment
16.49 The number of people who **died** was 14,700,
16.49 not counting those who **died** in Korah's rebellion.
17.10 Israelites that they will **die** unless their complaining stops.”
17.13 comes near the Tent must **die,** then we are all as good
19.14 If someone **dies** in a tent, anyone who is in the tent
19.16 has been killed or has **died** a natural death out of doors
20. 1 There Miriam **died** and was buried.

Num 20. 3 been better if we had **died** in front of the Lord's Tent
20. 4 Just so that we can **die** here with our animals?
20.24 he is going to **die,** because the two of you rebelled against
20.26 Aaron is going to **die** there."
20.28 top of the mountain Aaron **died,** and Moses and Eleazar came
20.29 community learnt that Aaron had **died,**
21. 5 us out of Egypt to **die** in this desert, where there is
21. 6 and many Israelites were bitten and **died.**
23.10 Let me **die** in peace like the righteous."
26.10 swallowed them, and they **died** with Korah and his followers
26.19 Judah's sons, Er and Onan, had **died** in the land of Canaan.)
26.61 Nadab and Abihu **died** when they offered unholy fire
26.65 that all of them would **die** in the wilderness, and except for
27. 3 said, [3]"Our father **died** in the wilderness
27. 3 he **died** because of his own sin.
27. 8 that whenever a man **dies** without leaving a son, his daughter
27.13 have seen it, you will **die,** as your brother Aaron did,
31. 2 After you have done that, you will **die."**
33.38 the age of 123 he **died** there on the first day of
Deut 2.14 men of that generation had **died,** as the Lord had said they
2.16 "After they had all **died,** [17]the Lord said to us,
4.22 I will **die** in this land and never cross the river, but
5.25 We are sure to **die** if we hear the Lord our God
10. 6 There Aaron **died** and was buried, and his son Eleazar
11.17 Then you will soon **die** there, even though it is a good
14.21 "Do not eat any animal that **dies** a natural death.
18.16 presence any more, because you were afraid you would **die.**
18.20 to do so, he must **die** for it, and so must any
19.10 that innocent people will not **die** and so that you will not
22.24 The girl is to **die** because she did not cry out for
22.24 And the man is to **die** because he had intercourse with a
24. 3 Or suppose her second husband **dies.**
25. 5 property and one of them **dies,** leaving no son, then his
28.22 These disasters will be with you until you **die.**
28.26 When you **die,** birds and wild animals will come and eat
28.51 and you will **die.**
31.16 to Moses, "You will soon **die,** and after your death the
32.24 They will **die** from hunger and fever;
32.24 they will **die** from terrible diseases.
32.25 Young men and young women will **die;**
32.42 even the wounded and prisoners will **die.'**
32.50 You will **die** on that mountain as your brother Aaron died
32.50 as your brother Aaron **died** on Mount Hor,
33. 1 of God, pronounced on the people of Israel before he **died.**
33. 6 "May Reuben never **die** out, Although their people are few."
34. 5 So Moses, the Lord's servant, **died** there in the land of Moab,
34. 7 Moses was a hundred and twenty years old when he **died;**
Josh 5. 4 left Egypt had **died** because they had disobeyed the Lord.
22.20 Achan was not the only one who **died** because of his sin."
23.14 "Now my time has come to **die.**
24.29 servant Joshua son of Nun **died** at the age of a hundred
24.33 Eleazar son of Aaron **died** and was buried at Gibeah, the
Judg 1. 7 He was taken to Jerusalem, where he **died.**
2. 8 servant Joshua son of Nun **died** at the age of a hundred
2.10 That whole generation also **died,**
2.19 But when the leader **died,** the people used to return
2.21 of the nations that were still in the land when Joshua **died.**
3.11 peace in the land for forty years, and then Othniel **died.**
4. 1 After Ehud **died,** the people of Israel sinned against the Lord
5.31 May all your enemies **die** like that, O Lord, but may your
6.23 You will not **die."**
8.28 The land was at peace for forty years, until Gideon **died.**
8.32 Gideon son of Joash **died** at a ripe old age
9.49 the people of the fort **died**—about a thousand men and women.
9.54 So the young man ran him through, and he **died.**
10. 2 Then he **died** and was buried at Shamir.
10. 5 Jair **died** and was buried at Kamon.
11.37 in the mountains and grieve that I must **die** a virgin."
11.38 grieved because she was going to **die** unmarried and childless.
11.39 what he had promised the Lord, and she **died** still a virgin.
12. 7 Then he **died** and was buried in his home town in Gilead.
12.10 then he **died** and was buried at Bethlehem.
12.12 Then he **died** and was buried at Aijalon in the territory
12.15 for eight years, [15]then he **died** and was buried at Pirathon
13.22 his wife, "We are sure to **die,** because we have seen God!"
15.15 Then he found the jaw-bone of a donkey that had recently **died.**
15.18 am I now going to **die** of thirst and be captured
16.30 and shouted, "Let me **die** with the Philistines!"
18.25 Then you and your whole family would **die."**
20. 5 instead they raped my concubine, and she **died.**
Ruth 1. 3 Elimelech **died,** and Naomi was left alone
1. 5 Mahlon and Chilion also **died,** and Naomi was left all alone,
1. 8 as you have been to me and to those who have **died.**
1.17 Wherever you **die,** I will die, and that is where I will
2.11 that you have done for your mother-in-law since your husband **died.**
1 Sam 2.33 and all your other descendants will **die** a violent death.
2.34 sons Hophni and Phinehas both **die** on the same day, this will
4.18 old and fat that the fall broke his neck, and he **died.**
4.20 As she was **dying,** the women helping her said to her,
5.12 Even those who did not **die** developed tumours
12.19 to the Lord your God for us, so that we won't **die.**
14.43 Here I am—I am ready to **die."**
15.32 thinking to himself, "What a bitter thing it is to **die!"**
20. 2 Jonathan answered, "God forbid that you should **die!**
20.14 but if I **die,** [15]show the same kind of loyalty to my
20.31 Now go and bring him here—he must **die!"**
20.32 "Why should he **die?"**
22.16 "Ahimelech, you and all your relatives must **die."**
25. 1 Samuel **died,** and all the Israelites came together
25.38 Some ten days later the Lord struck Nabal and he **died.**
1 Sam 25.39 When David heard that Nabal had **died,** he said,
26.10 when his time comes to **die** a natural death
26.10 or when he **dies** in battle.
26.16 all of you deserve to **die,** because you have not protected
28. 3 Now Samuel had **died,** and all the Israelites had mourned
31. 5 he too threw himself on his own sword and **died** with Saul.
31. 6 that is how Saul, his three sons, and the young man **died;**
31. 6 all of Saul's men **died** that day.
2 Sam 1. 9 I have been badly wounded, and I'm about to **die.'**
1.10 I knew that he would **die** anyway as soon as he fell.
3.33 "Why did Abner have to **die** like a fool?
3.34 He **died** like someone killed by criminals!"
3.38 you realize that this day a great leader in Israel has **died?**
6. 7 Uzzah **died** there beside the Covenant Box,
7.12 When you **die** and are buried with your ancestors,
10. 1 King Nahash of Ammon **died,** and his son Hanun became king.
10.18 Shobach, the enemy commander, who **died** on the battlefield.
11.25 be upset, since you never can tell who will **die** in battle.
12. 5 the living Lord that the man who did this ought to **die!**
12.10 some of your descendants will **die** a violent death
12.13 you will not **die.**
12.14 contempt for the Lord in doing this, your child will **die."**
12.18 A week later the child **died,**
12.19 to each other, he realized that the child had **died.**
12.21 but as soon as he **died,** you got up and ate!"
12.22 Lord might be merciful to me and not let the child **die.**
14.14 We will all **die;**
18. 8 and more men **died** in the forest than were killed
18.33 If only I had **died** in your place, my son!
19.37 Then let me go back home and **die** near my parents' grave.
20.10 He **died** immediately, and Joab did not have to strike again.
21. 9 before the Lord—and all seven of them **died** together.
24.15 the country to the other seventy thousand Israelites **died.**
1 Kgs 1.52 but if he is not, he will **die."**
2. 1 When David was about to **die,** he called his son Solomon and
2. 2 "My time to **die** has come.
2. 6 you must not let him **die** a natural death.
2.10 David **died** and was buried in David's City.
2.24 by the living Lord that Adonijah will **die** this very day!"
2.26 You deserve to **die,** but I will not have you put to
2.30 "I will **die** here."
2.37 of Kidron, you will certainly **die**—and you yourself will be
2.42 I warned you that if you ever did, you would certainly **die.**
11.21 in Egypt that David had **died** and that Joab the commander of
11.43 He **died** and was buried in David's City, and his son
13.31 to his sons, "When I **die,** bury me in this grave and
14.11 members of your family who **die** in the city will be eaten
14.11 by dogs, and any who **die** in the open country will be
14.12 As soon as you enter the town your son will **die.**
14.17 Just as she entered her home, the child **died.**
14.20 He **died** and was buried, and his son Nadab succeeded him as
14.31 Rehoboam **died** and was buried in the royal tombs
15. 8 Abijah **died** and was buried in David's City, and his son
15.24 Asa **died** and was buried in the royal tombs in David's City,
16. 4 members of your family who **die** in the city will be eaten
16. 4 by dogs, and any who **die** in the open country will be
16. 6 Baasha **died** and was buried in Tirzah,
16.18 set the palace on fire, and **died** in the flames.
16.22 Tibni **died** and Omri became king.
16.28 Omri **died** and was buried in Samaria,
17.17 he got worse and worse, and finally he **died.**
19. 4 down in the shade of a tree and wished he would **die.**
21.24 Any of your relatives who **die** in the city will be eaten
21.24 by dogs, and any who **die** in the open country will be
22.35 covered the bottom of the chariot, and at evening he **died.**
22.37 So **died** King Ahab.
22.50 Jehoshaphat **died** and was buried in the royal tombs
2 Kgs 1. 4 you will **die!'**
1. 6 you will **die!' "**
1.16 you will **die!' "**
1.17 Ahaziah **died,** as the Lord had said through Elijah.
3. 5 But when King Ahab of Israel **died,** Mesha rebelled against
4. 1 went to Elisha and said, "Sir, my husband has **died!**
4.20 held him in her lap until noon, at which time he **died.**
7. 3 said to one another, "Why should we wait here until we **die?**
7. 4 but if we stay here, we'll **die** also.
7.13 city are doomed anyway, like those that have already **died.**
7.17 there by the people and **died,** as Elisha had predicted
7.20 he **died,** trampled to death by the people
8.10 "The Lord has revealed to me that he will **die;**
8.24 Jehoram **died** and was buried in the royal tombs
9. 8 All Ahab's family and descendants are to **die;**
9.27 going until he reached the city of Megiddo, where he **died.**
10.35 He **died** and was buried in Samaria,
13. 9 He **died** and was buried in Samaria,
13.13 Jehoash **died** and was buried in the royal tombs in Samaria,
13.14 disease, and as he lay **dying** King Jehoash of Israel went to
13.20 Elisha **died** and was buried.
14.16 Jehoash **died** and was buried in the royal tombs in Samaria,
14.29 Jeroboam **died** and was buried in the royal tombs,
15. 7 Uzziah **died** and was buried in the royal burial ground
15.22 He **died** and was buried,
15.38 Jotham **died** and was buried in the royal tombs
16.20 Ahaz **died** and was buried in the royal tombs in David's City,
18.32 If you do what he commands, you will not **die,** but live.
20. 1 About this time King Hezekiah fell ill and almost **died.**
20. 1 Get ready to **die."**
20.21 Hezekiah **died,** and his son Manasseh succeeded him as king.
21.18 Manasseh **died** and was buried in the palace garden,
22.17 My anger is aroused against Jerusalem, and it will not **die** down.
22.20 I will let you **die** in peace."

2 Kgs 23.26 King Manasseh had done, and even now it did not **die** down.
23.34 Joahaz was taken to Egypt by King Neco, and there he **died.**
24. 6 Jehoiakim **died,** and his son Jehoiachin succeeded him as king.
1 Chr 2.24 After Hezron **died,** his son Caleb married Ephrath,
2.30 but Seled **died** without having any sons.
2.32 but Jether **died** without having any sons.
10. 5 so he too threw himself on his sword and **died.**
10. 6 and his three sons all **died** together
10. 7 Saul and his sons had **died,** they abandoned their towns
10.13 Saul **died** because he was unfaithful to the Lord.
13.10 He **died** there in God's presence,
17.11 When you **die** and are buried with your ancestors,
19. 1 King Nahash of Ammon **died,** and his son Hanun became king.
21.14 on the people of Israel, and seventy thousand of them **died.**
22. 5 So David got large amounts of the materials ready before he **died.**
23.22 but Eleazar **died** without having any sons, only daughters.
24. 2 Nadab and Abihu **died** before their father did,
27.34 After Ahithophel **died,** Abiathar and Jehoiada son of Benaiah
29.28 He **died** at a ripe old age, wealthy and respected,
2 Chr 9.31 He **died** and was buried in David's City,
12.16 Rehoboam **died** and was buried in the royal tombs
13.20 Finally the Lord struck him down, and he **died.**
14. 1 King Abijah **died** and was buried in the royal tombs
16.13 Two years later he **died** [14]and was buried in the rock
18.34 At sunset he **died.**
21. 1 Jehoshaphat **died** and was buried in the royal tombs
21.19 it grew steadily worse until finally the king **died** in agony.
21.20 Nobody was sorry when he **died.**
24.15 reaching the very old age of a hundred and thirty, he **died.**
24.22 As Zechariah was **dying,** he called out, "May the Lord see
26.23 Uzziah **died** and was buried in the royal burial-ground,
27. 9 He **died** and was buried in David's City
28.27 King Ahaz **died** and was buried in Jerusalem,
32.11 is deceiving you and will let you **die** of hunger and thirst.
32.24 About this time King Hezekiah fell ill and almost **died.**
32.33 Hezekiah **died** and was buried in the upper section
33.20 Manasseh **died** and was buried at the palace,
34.25 My anger is aroused against Jerusalem, and it will not **die** down.
34.28 I will let you **die** in peace."
35.24 There he **died** and was buried in the royal tombs.
Esth 4.11 sees the king without being summoned, that person must **die.**
4.14 be saved, but you will **die** and your father's family will
4.16 If I must **die** for doing it, I will die."
Job 1.21 "I was born with nothing, and I will **die** with nothing.
2. 9 Why don't you curse God and **die?"**
3.11 died in my mother's womb or **died** the moment I was born.
3.13 If I had **died** then, I would be at rest now, [14]sleeping
4.11 and eat, they **die,** and all their children are scattered.
4.20 alive in the morning, but **die** unnoticed before evening comes.
4.21 he **dies,** still lacking wisdom."
6.18 they wander and **die** in the desert.
6.20 but their hope **dies** beside dry streams.
7. 9 cloud that fades and is gone, a man **dies** and never returns;
9.23 When an innocent man suddenly **dies,** God laughs.
10.18 I should have **died** before anyone saw me.
12. 1 When you **die,** wisdom will die with you.
13.19 If you do, I am ready to be silent and **die.**
14. 8 grow old, and its stump **dies** in the ground,
14.10 But a man **dies,** and that is the end of him;
14.10 he **dies,** and where is he then?
14.12 people **die,** never to rise.
14.14 If a man **dies,** can he come back to life?
19.10 He uproots my hope and leaves me to wither and **die.**
21.13 and quietly **die** without suffering.
21.23 Some men stay healthy till the day they **die;**
21.23 they **die** happy and at ease, their bodies well-nourished.
21.25 they live and **die** with bitter hearts.
21.26 But all alike **die** and are buried;
24.12 the cities the wounded and **dying** cry out, but God ignores
24.22 God acts—and the wicked man **dies.**
27. 5 I will insist on my innocence to my **dying** day.
27.15 Those who survive will **die** from disease,
29.18 to live a long life and to **die** at home in comfort.
30.16 Now I am about to **die;**
34.15 then everyone living would **die** and turn into dust again.
34.20 A man may suddenly **die** at night.
36.12 But if not, they will **die** in ignorance and cross the
36.14 They **die** while they are still young, worn out by a life
42.17 And then he **died** at a very great age.
Ps 2.12 anger will be quickly aroused, and you will suddenly **die.**
9. 3 they fall down and **die.**
13. 3 don't let me **die.**
34.16 do evil, so that when they **die,** they are soon forgotten.
37. 2 they will **die** like plants that wither.
37.20 But the wicked will **die;**
39. 4 When will I **die?**
39.10 I am about to **die** from your blows.
41. 5 They want me to **die** and be forgotten.
49.10 see that even wise men **die,** as well as foolish and stupid
49.12 he will still **die** like the animals.
49.14 they are doomed to **die** like sheep, and Death will be
49.17 he cannot take it with him when he **dies;**
49.20 he will still **die** like the animals.
55.15 May my enemies **die** before their time;
78.64 Priests **died** by violence,
79.11 by your great power free those who are condemned to **die.**
82. 7 But you will **die** like men;
83.17 may they **die** in complete disgrace.
88. 4 I am like all others who are about to **die;**
89.48 Who can live and never **die?**
90. 6 and burst into bloom, then dry up and **die** in the evening.
Ps 92. 9 know that your enemies will **die,** and all the wicked will be
102.20 of prisoners and set free those who were condemned to **die.**
104.29 take away your breath, they **die** and go back to the dust
106.26 that he would make them **die** in the desert [27]and scatter
106.27 letting them **die** in foreign countries.
109.13 May all his descendants **die,** and may his name be
116.15 painful it is to the Lord when one of his people **dies!**
118.17 I will not **die;**
118.18 He has punished me severely, but he has not let me **die.**
119.92 the source of my joy, I would have **died** from my sufferings.
119.112 I have decided to obey your laws until the day I **die.**
141. 8 don't let me **die!**
143. 3 a dark prison, and I am like those who **died** long ago.
146. 4 When they **die,** they return to the dust;
Prov 1.18 a trap for themselves, a trap in which they will **die.**
1.32 Inexperienced people **die** because they reject wisdom.
5. 9 once had, and you will **die** young at the hands of merciless
5.23 He **dies** because he has no self-control.
9.18 not know that the people **die** who go to her house, that
10.27 The wicked **die** before their time.
11. 7 When a wicked man **dies,** his hope dies with him.
11.10 fortune, and there are joyful shouts when wicked men **die.**
11.19 will live, but anyone who insists on doing wrong will **die.**
15.10 you will **die** if you do not let yourself be corrected.
16.14 if the king becomes angry, someone may **die.**
19.16 if you ignore them, you will **die.**
30. 7 ask you, God, to let me have two things before I **die:**
31. 6 is for people who are **dying,** for those who are in misery.
Ecc 2.16 We must all **die**—wise and foolish alike.
3.19 One **dies** just like the other.
3.22 no way for us to know what will happen after we **die.**
6.12 anyone know what will happen in the world after he **dies?**
7. 1 and the day you **die** is better than the day you are
7.15 A good man may **die** while another man lives on, even though
7.17 wicked or too foolish, either—why **die** before you have to?
8. 8 one can keep himself from **dying** or put off the day of
8.13 a shadow and they will **die** young, because they do not obey
9. 3 minds are full of evil and madness, and suddenly they **die.**
9. 5 know they are going to **die,** but the dead know nothing.
9. 6 Their loves, their hates, their passions, all **died** with them.
10.14 and no one can tell us what will happen after we **die.**
Is 1.20 But if you defy me, you are doomed to **die.**
1.30 You will wither like a **dying** oak,
5.13 starve to death, and the common people will **die** of thirst.
5.25 the bodies of those who **die** will be left in the streets
6. 1 In the year that King Uzziah **died,** I saw the Lord.
11. 4 the people will be punished, and evil persons will **die.**
14.21 The sons of this king will **die** because of their ancestors'
14.28 that was proclaimed in the year that King Ahaz **died.**
14.29 When one snake **dies,** a worse one comes in its place.
22. 2 Your men who **died** in this war did not die fighting.
22. 4 to weep bitterly over all those of my people who have **died.**
22.18 You will **die** there beside the chariots you are so proud of.
26.19 Those of our people who have **died** will live again!
29. 8 hungry, or like a man **dying** of thirst who dreams he is
38. 1 About this time King Hezekiah fell ill and almost **died.**
38. 1 Get ready to **die."**
41.11 who fight against you will **die** [12]and will disappear
50. 2 desert, so that the fish in them **die** for lack of water.
51. 6 like old clothing, and all its people will **die** like flies.
53. 8 sentenced and led off to **die,** and no one cared about his
57. 1 Good people **die,** and no one understands or even cares.
57. 1 But when they **die,** no calamity can hurt them.
65.12 will be your fate to **die** a violent death, because you did
65.20 Babies will no longer **die** in infancy,
65.20 To **die** before that would be a sign that I had punished
66.24 that eat them will never **die,** and the fire that burns them
Jer 6.21 Fathers and sons will **die,** and so will friends and neighbours."
8. 3 them, will prefer to **die** rather than to go on living.
8.14 "Come on, we will run to the fortified cities, and **die**
8.14 The Lord our God has condemned us to **die;**
11.22 their children will **die** of starvation.
12. 4 Animals and birds are **dying** because of the wickedness
14. 2 its cities are **dying,** its people lie on the ground in sorrow,
15. 2 Some are doomed to **die** by disease— that's where they will
15. 2 Others are doomed to **die** in war— that's where they will
15. 2 Some are doomed to **die** of starvation— that's where they will
16. 4 They will **die** of terrible diseases, and no one will mourn
16. 4 be killed in war or **die** of starvation, and their bodies will
16. 6 rich and the poor will **die** in this land, but no one
16. 7 or drink with anyone to comfort him when a loved one **dies.**
18.21 let the men **die** of disease and the young men be killed
20. 6 There you will **die** and be buried, along with all your
21. 6 people and animals alike will **die** of a terrible disease.
22.12 He will **die** in the country where they have taken him,
22.26 neither of you was born, and both of you will **die** there.
27.13 should you and your people **die** in war or of starvation or
28.16 year is over you will **die** because you have told the people
28.17 And Hananiah **died** in the seventh month of that same year.
31.30 and everyone will **die** because of his own sin."
34. 5 You will **die** in peace, and as people burnt incense when
34.17 the freedom to **die** by war, disease, and starvation.
37.20 If you do, I will surely **die** there."
38. 2 on in the city will **die** in war or of starvation or
38. 9 where he is sure to **die** of starvation, since there is no
38.10 men and to pull me out of the well before I **died.**
38.26 begging me not to send you back to prison to **die** there."
42.16 you dread will follow you, and you will **die** there in Egypt.
42.17 and live in Egypt will **die** either in war or of starvation
42.22 you will **die** in war or of starvation or disease in the
43.11 people who are doomed to **die** of disease will die of disease,

Jer	44.12	them, great and small, will **die** in Egypt, either in war or
	44.18	and our people have **died** in war and of starvation."
	44.27	All of you will **die,** either in war or of disease, until
	51. 4	They will be wounded and **die** in the streets of their cities.
	52.11	Zedekiah remained in prison in Babylon until the day he **died.**
Lam	1.19	The priests and the leaders **died** in the city streets,
	2.12	And slowly **die** in their mothers' arms.
	4. 4	They let their babies **die** of hunger and thirst;
	4. 5	People who once ate the finest foods **die** starving
	4. 9	Those who **died** in the war were better off than
	4. 9	those who **died** later, who starved slowly to death,
Ezek	3.18	evil man is going to **die** but you do not warn him
	3.18	save his life, he will **die,** still a sinner, and I will
	3.19	doesn't stop sinning, he will **die,** still a sinner,
	3.20	a dangerous situation, he will **die** if you do not warn him.
	3.20	He will **die** because of his sins—I will not remember the
	4.14	meat from any animal that **died** a natural death or was killed
	5.12	third of your people will **die** from sickness and hunger
	6.11	They are going to **die** in war, by famine, and by disease.
	6.12	Those far away will fall ill and **die;**
	7.15	out in the country will **die** in the fighting, and anyone in
	12.13	city of Babylon, where he will **die** without having seen it.
	13.19	people who don't deserve to **die,** and you keep people alive
	16. 6	You were covered with blood, but I wouldn't let you **die.**
	17.16	Sovereign Lord, "this king will **die** in Babylonia
	18. 4	The person who sins is the one who will **die.**
	18.13	He has done all these disgusting things, and so he will **die.**
	18.17	He will not **die** because of his father's sins, but he will
	18.18	And so he **died** because of the sins he himself had committed.
	18.20	It is the one who sins who will **die.**
	18.21	if he does what is right and good, he will not **die;**
	18.23	Do you think I enjoy seeing an evil man **die?"**
	18.24	He will **die** because of his unfaithfulness and his sins.
	18.26	starts doing evil and then **dies,** he dies because of the evil
	18.28	sinning, so he will certainly not **die,** but go on living.
	18.31	Why do you Israelites want to **die?**
	18.32	I do not want anyone to **die,"** says the Sovereign Lord.
	24.18	That evening my wife **died,** and the next day I did as
	28.10	You will **die** like a dog at the hand of godless foreigners.
	30.17	of Heliopolis and Bubastis will **die** in the war, and the
	30.24	Egypt, and he will groan and **die** in front of his enemy.
	31.14	of them are doomed to **die** like mortal men, doomed to join
	31.15	Because the tree has **died,** I will bring darkness over the
	32.32	laid to rest with all the uncircumcised who **die** in battle."
	33. 8	evil man is going to **die** but you do not warn him
	33. 8	his life, then he will **die,** still a sinner, and I will
	33. 9	doesn't stop sinning, he will **die,** still a sinner, but your
	33.11	am the living God, I do not enjoy seeing a sinner **die.**
	33.11	Why do you want to **die?**
	33.13	He will **die** because of his sins.
	33.14	that he is going to **die,** but if he stops sinning and
	33.15	follows the laws that give life, he will not **die,** but live.
	33.18	stops doing good and starts doing evil, he will **die** for it.
	33.27	Those hiding in the mountains and in caves will **die** of disease.
	44.31	any bird or animal that **dies** a natural death or is killed
Dan	5.23	determines whether you live or **die** and who controls everything
	11.45	But he will **die,** with no one there to help him."
	12. 2	Many of those who have already **died** will live again:
	12.13	Then you will **die,** but you will rise to receive your reward
Hos	2. 3	like a dry and barren land, and she will **die** of thirst.
	4. 3	land will dry up, and everything that lives on it will **die.**
	4. 3	All the animals and birds, and even the fish, will **die."**
	7.16	leaders talk arrogantly, they will **die** a violent death,
	10.15	As soon as the battle begins, the king of Israel will **die."**
	12.11	worshipped in Gilead, and those who worship them will **die.**
	13. 1	sinned by worshipping Baal, and for this they will **die.**
	13.16	Her people will **die** in war;
Joel	1.12	all the fruit-trees have wilted and **died.**
	1.17	The seeds **die** in the dry earth.
Amos	1. 8	of Ekron, and all the Philistines who are left will **die."**
	1.11	Their anger had no limits, and they never let it **die.**
	2. 2	The people of Moab will **die** in the noise of battle while
	6. 9	If there are ten men left in a family, they will **die.**
	7.11	'Jeroboam will **die** in battle, and the people of Israel will
	7.17	to others, and you yourself will **die** in a heathen country.
Jon	3. 9	perhaps he will stop being angry, and we will not **die!"**
	4. 3	Now, Lord, let me **die.**
	4. 7	at God's command, a worm attacked the plant, and it **died.**
	4. 9	"I have every right to be angry—angry enough to **die!"**
Hab	3.17	even though the sheep all **die** and the cattle-stalls are empty,
Hag	2.22	the horses will **die,** and their riders will kill one another.
Zech	11. 9	Let those who are to **die,** die.
	13. 8	and throughout the land two-thirds of the people will **die.**
Mt	2.15	during the night for Egypt, [15] where he stayed until Herod **died.**
	2.19	After Herod **died,** an angel of the Lord appeared in a
	8.25	"We are about to **die!"**
	9.18	knelt down before him, and said, "My daughter has just **died;**
	14.32	They both got into the boat, and the wind **died** down.
	16.28	some here who will not **die** until they have seen the Son
	22.24	man who has no children **dies,** his brother must marry the
	22.25	The eldest got married and **died** without having children,
	22.27	Last of all, the woman **died.**
	24.34	things will happen before the people now living have all **died.**
	26.24	The Son of Man will **die** as the Scriptures say he will,
	26.35	will never say that, even if I have to **die** with you!"
	26.52	"All who take the sword will **die** by the sword.
	26.66	They answered, "He is guilty and must **die."**
	27.52	and many of God's people who had **died** were raised to life.
Mk	4.38	said, "Teacher, don't you care that we are about to **die?"**
	4.39	The wind **died** down, and there was a great calm.
	5.35	came from Jairus' house and told him, "Your daughter has **died.**
Mk	6.51	he got into the boat with them, and the wind **died** down.
	9. 1	some here who will not **die** until they have seen the Kingdom
	9.48	worms that eat them never **die,** and the fire that burns them
	11.21	said to Jesus, "Look, Teacher, the fig-tree you cursed has **died!"**
	12.19	'If a man **dies** and leaves a wife but no children,
	12.20	the eldest got married and **died** without having children.
	12.21	married the woman, and he also **died** without having children.
	12.22	brothers married the woman and **died** without having children.
	12.22	Last of all, the woman **died.**
	13.30	things will happen before the people now living have all **died.**
	14.21	The Son of Man will **die** as the Scriptures say he will;
	14.31	will never say that, even if I have to **die** with you!"
	15.37	With a loud cry Jesus **died.**
	15.39	standing there in front of the cross saw how Jesus had **died.**
Lk	2.26	him that he would not **die** before he had seen the Lord's
	7. 2	the man was sick and about to **die.**
	8.24	We are about to **die!"**
	8.24	they **died** down, and there was a great calm.
	8.42	because his only daughter, who was twelve years old, was **dying.**
	8.49	"Your daughter has **died,"** he told Jairus;
	9.27	some here who will not **die** until they have seen the Kingdom
	9.31	he would soon fulfil God's purpose by **dying** in Jerusalem.
	13. 3	not turn from your sins, you will all **die** as they did.
	13. 5	not turn from your sins, you will all **die** as they did."
	16.22	"The poor man **died** and was carried by the angels to sit
	16.22	The rich man **died** and was buried, [23] and in Hades, where he
	20.28	'If a man **dies** and leaves a wife but no children,
	20.29	the eldest got married and **died** without having children.
	20.31	happened to all seven—they **died** without having children.
	20.32	Last of all, the woman **died.**
	20.36	They will be like angels and cannot **die.**
	21.32	will take place before the people now living have all **died.**
	22.22	The Son of Man will **die** as God has decided, but how
	22.33	ready to go to prison with you and to **die** with you!"
	23.46	He said this and **died.**
Jn	3.16	who believes in him may not **die** but have eternal life.
	4.47	go to Capernaum and heal his son, who was about to **die.**
	4.49	replied the official, "come with me before my child **dies."**
	6.49	Your ancestors ate manna in the desert, but they **died.**
	6.50	is of such a kind that whoever eats it will not **die.**
	6.58	like the bread that your ancestors ate, but then later **died.**
	8.21	you will look for me, but you will **die** in your sins.
	8.24	is why I told you that you will **die** in your sins.
	8.24	And you will **die** in your sins if you do not believe
	8.51	whoever obeys my teaching will never **die."**
	8.52	Abraham died, and the prophets **died,**
	8.52	yet you say that whoever obeys your teaching will never **die.**
	8.53	Our father Abraham **died;**
	8.53	And the prophets also **died.**
	10.11	am the good shepherd, who is willing to **die** for the sheep.
	10.14	And I am willing to **die** for them.
	10.28	I give them eternal life, and they shall never **die.**
	11.13	Jesus meant that Lazarus had **died,** but they thought he meant
	11.16	all go with the Teacher, so that we may **die** with him!"
	11.21	"If you had been here, Lord, my brother would not have **died!**
	11.25	Whoever believes in me will live, even though he **dies;**
	11.26	and whoever lives and believes in me will never **die.**
	11.32	"if you had been here, my brother would not have **died!"**
	11.37	Could he not have kept Lazarus from **dying?"**
	11.50	you to let one man **die** for the people, instead of having
	11.51	that Jesus was going to **die** for the Jewish people, [52] and
	12.24	single grain unless it is dropped into the ground and **dies.**
	12.24	If it does **die,** then it produces many grains.
	13.37	"I am ready to **die** for you!"
	13.38	Jesus answered, "Are you really ready to **die** for me?
	18.14	it was better that one man should **die** for all the people.
	18.32	he used when he indicated the kind of death he would **die.)**
	19. 7	that says he ought to **die,** because he claimed to be the
	19.30	Then he bowed his head and **died.**
	21.19	the way in which Peter would **die** and bring glory to God.)
	21.23	among the followers of Jesus that this disciple would not **die.**
	21.23	But Jesus did not say that he would not **die;**
Acts	2.29	He **died** and was buried, and his grave is here with us
	5.10	At once she fell down at his feet and **died.**
	5.36	all his followers were scattered, and his movement **died** out.
	7. 4	After Abraham's father **died,** God made him move to this land
	7.15	Then Jacob went to Egypt, where he and his sons **died.**
	7.19	put their babies out of their homes, so that they would **die.**
	7.60	He said this and **died.**
	9.37	At that time she became ill and **died.**
	12.23	He was eaten by worms and **died.**
	13.36	own time, and then he **died,** was buried with his ancestors,
	13.41	Be astonished and **die!**
	20. 1	After the uproar **died** down, Paul called together the believers
	21.13	in Jerusalem but even to **die** there for the sake of the
	23.29	anything for which he deserved to **die** or be put in prison;
	25.19	own religion and about a man named Jesus, who has **died;**
	26.31	done anything for which he should **die** or be put in prison."
	28.18	found that I had done nothing for which I deserved to **die.**
Rom	4.25	he was handed over to **die,** and he was raised to life
	5. 6	we were still helpless, Christ **died** for the wicked at the
	5. 7	a difficult thing for someone to **die** for a righteous person.
	5. 7	even be that someone might dare to **die** for a good person.
	5. 8	it was while we were still sinners that Christ **died** for us!
	5.15	is true that many people **died** because of the sin of that
	6. 2	We have **died** to sin—how then can we go on living
	6. 5	become one with him in **dying** as he did, in the same
	6. 7	For when a person **dies,** he is set free from the power
	6. 8	Since we have **died** with Christ, we believe that we will
	6. 9	from death and will never **die** again—death will no longer
	6.10	And so, because he **died,** sin has no power over him;

Rom 7. 2 but if he **dies,** then she is free from the law that
7. 3 but if her husband **dies,** she is legally a free woman
7. 4 is concerned, you also have **died** because you are part of the
7. 6 from the Law, because we **died** to that which once held us
7.10 the commandment came, sin sprang to life, [10]and I **died.**
8.10 even though your bodies are going to **die** because of sin.
8.13 live according to your human nature, you are going to **die;**
8.34 Not Christ Jesus, who **died,** or rather, who was raised to
14. 7 lives for himself only, none of us **dies** for himself only.
14. 8 and if we die, it is for the Lord that we **die.**
14. 8 So whether we live or **die,** we belong to the Lord.
14. 9 For Christ **died** and rose to life in order to be the
14.15 the food that you eat ruin the person for whom Christ **died!**
1 Cor 1.13 Was it Paul who **died** on the cross for you?
4. 9 apostles, like men condemned to **die** in public as a spectacle
7.39 but if her husband **dies,** then she is free to be married
8.11 your brother for whom Christ **died,** will perish because of your
9.15 I would rather **die** first!
11.30 why many of you are weak and ill, and several have **died.**
15. 3 that Christ **died** for our sins, as written in the Scriptures;
15. 6 once, most of whom are still alive, although some have **died.**
15.18 mean that the believers in Christ who have **died** are lost.
15.22 For just as all people **die** because of their union with Adam,
15.32 goes, "Let us eat and drink, for tomorrow we will **die."**
15.36 in the ground, it does not sprout to life unless it **dies.**
15.51 we shall not all **die,** but when the last trumpet sounds, we
15.51 will be raised, never to **die** again, and we shall all be
15.53 what will **die** must be changed into what cannot die.
2 Cor 5.14 we recognize that one man **died** for everyone, which means that
5.15 He **died** for all, so that those who live should no longer
5.15 but only for him who **died** and was raised to life for
7. 3 to us that we are always together, whether we live or **die.**
Gal 2.21 through the Law, it means that Christ **died** for nothing!
Phil 1.20 being I shall bring honour to Christ, whether I live or **die.**
2.27 Indeed he was ill and almost **died.**
2.30 risked his life and nearly **died** for the sake of the work
Col 2.20 You have **died** with Christ and are set free from the
3. 3 For you have **died,** and your life is hidden with Christ in
1 Thes 4.13 truth about those who have **died,** so that you will not be
4.14 We believe that Jesus **died** and rose again, and so we
4.14 take back with Jesus those who have **died** believing in him.
4.15 the Lord comes will not go ahead of those who have **died.**
4.16 Those who have **died** believing in Christ will rise to life first;
5.10 our Lord Jesus Christ, [10]who **died** for us in order that we
1 Tim 5. 6 who gives herself to pleasure has already **died,** even though
2 Tim 2.11 "If we have **died** with him, we shall also live with him.
Heb 2. 9 so that through God's grace he should **die** for everyone.
7. 8 case of the priests the tenth is collected by men who **die;**
7.23 priests, because they **died** and could not continue their work.
9.16 person who made it has **died,** [17]for a will means nothing
9.27 Everyone must **die** once, and after that be judged by God.
11. 5 It was faith that kept Enoch from **dying.**
11.13 It was in faith that all these persons **died.**
11.21 Jacob bless each of the sons of Joseph just before he **died.**
11.22 when he was about to **die,** speak of the departure of the
11.35 Others, refusing to accept freedom, **died** under torture in order
12. 2 nothing of the disgrace of **dying** on the cross, and he is
13. 7 Think back on how they lived and **died,** and imitate their faith.
13.12 For this reason Jesus also **died** outside the city, in
1 Pet 2.24 so that we might **die** to sin and live for righteousness.
3.18 For Christ **died** for sins once and for all, a good man
2 Pet 3. 4 Our fathers have already **died,** but everything is still the same
Rev 2. 8 who is the first and the last, who **died** and lived again.
3. 2 and strengthen what you still have before it **dies** completely.
8. 9 living creatures in the sea **died,** and a third of the ships
8.11 turned bitter, and many people **died** from drinking the water,
9. 6 they will want to **die,** but death will flee from them.
12.11 and they were willing to give up their lives and **die.**
14.13 those who from now on **die** in the service of the Lord!"
16. 3 a dead person, and every living creature in the sea **died.**

DIET

Esth 2. 9 beginning her beauty treatment of massage and special **diet.**

DIFFERENT

Gen 10. 5 of Japheth, living in their **different** tribes and countries,
10.18 The **different** tribes of the Canaanites spread out,
10.20 of Ham, living in their **different** tribes and countries,
10.31 of Shem, living in their **different** tribes and countries,
10.32 nation by nation, according to their **different** lines of descent.
40. 5 each had a dream, and the dreams had **different** meanings.
41.11 of us had a dream, and the dreams had **different** meanings.
Lev 19.17 against anyone, but settle your **differences** with him,
Num 12. 7 It is **different** when I speak with my servant Moses;
14.24 my servant Caleb has a **different** attitude and has remained loyal
1 Sam 10. 6 dancing and shouting and will become a **different** person.
28. 8 he put on **different** clothes,
2 Sam 18. 3 "It won't make any **difference** to the enemy
1 Kgs 2.15 But it happened **differently,** and my brother became king,
3. 2 people were still offering sacrifices at many **different** altars.
3. 9 and to know the **difference** between good and evil.
18. 6 each one would explore, and set off in **different** directions.
2 Kgs 17.29 Each **different** group made idols in the cities
1 Chr 27. 1 month of the year a **different** group of twenty-four thousand men
2 Chr 12. 8 they will learn the **difference** between serving me and serving
Neh 5.15 But I acted **differently,** because I honoured God.
Prov 25. 9 and your neighbour have a **difference** of opinion, settle it
Ecc 1.17 to learn the **difference** between knowledge and foolishness,
9. 2 It makes no **difference.**
Song 5. 9 is your lover **different** from everyone else?
Is 55. 8 "are not like yours, and my ways are **different** from yours.
65.11 "But it will be **different** for you that forsake me,
Jer 31.22 have created something new and **different,**
31.22 as **different** as a woman protecting a man."
51.46 Every year a **different** rumour spreads—
Ezek 1.10 Each living creature had four **different** faces:
16.34 Yes, you are **different."**
22.26 They do not teach the **difference** between clean and unclean things,
44.23 to teach my people the **difference** between what is holy and
47.10 There will be as many **different** kinds of fish there
Dan 7. 3 up out of the ocean, each one **different** from the others.
7.23 on the earth and will be **different** from all other empires.
7.24 he will be very **different** from the earlier ones
8. 8 prominent horns came up, each pointing in a **different** direction.
11.29 but this time things will turn out **differently.**
Zech 8.11 But now I am treating the survivors of this nation **differently.**
Mal 3.18 will see the **difference** between what happens to the righteous
Mt 19.12 For there are **different** reasons why men cannot marry:
Mk 16.12 Jesus appeared in a **different** manner to two of them while
Lk 3.18 In many **different** ways John preached the Good News to the
Acts 15. 9 He made no **difference** between us and them;
Rom 3.22 who believe in Christ, because there is no **difference** at all:
5.16 And there is a **difference** between God's gift and the sin
7.23 But I see a **different** law at work in my body—
10.12 because there is no **difference** between Jews and Gentiles;
12. 4 in the one body, and all these parts have **different** functions.
12. 5 are all joined to each other as **different** parts of one body.
12. 6 we are to use our **different** gifts in accordance with the
1 Cor 1.12 each one of you says something **different.**
3. 8 There is no **difference** between the man who sows and the
11. 5 there is no **difference** between her and a woman whose head
12. 4 There are **different** kinds of spiritual gifts, but the same Spirit
12. 5 There are **different** ways of serving, but the same Lord is served.
12. 6 are **different** abilities to perform service, but the same God
12.10 the ability to tell the **difference** between gifts that come from
12.11 as he wishes, he gives a **different** gift to each person.
12.12 one body, even though it is made up of **different** parts.
12.18 however, God put every **different** part in the body just as
12.25 the body, but all its **different** parts have the same concern
14.10 There are many **different** languages in the world, yet none of
15.40 to heavenly bodies is **different** from the beauty that belongs to
15.41 the moon another beauty, and the stars a **different** beauty;
15.41 and even among stars there are **different** kinds of beauty.
2 Cor 10.11 understand that there is no **difference** between what we write in
11. 4 you and preaches a **different** Jesus, not the one we preached;
11. 4 and a gospel completely **different** from the Spirit and the gospel
12.20 there I will find you **different** from what I would like you
12.20 and you will find me **different** from what you would like me
Gal 1. 8 you a gospel that is **different** from the one we preached to
1. 9 you a gospel that is **different** from the one you accepted,
2. 6 this because it makes no **difference** to me what they were;
3.28 So there is no **difference** between Jews and Gentiles,
4.20 now, so that I could take a **different** attitude towards you.
5. 6 circumcision nor the lack of it makes any **difference** at all;
5.10 you will not take a **different** view and that the man who
Eph 3.10 world might learn of his wisdom in all its **different** forms.
4.16 his control all the **different** parts of the body fit together,
Phil 3.15 some of you have a **different** attitude, God will make this
1 Tim 6. 3 Whoever teaches a **different** doctrine and does not agree with
Heb 7.11 been no need for a **different** kind of priest to appear,
7.13 are said, belonged to a **different** tribe, and no member of
7.15 a **different** priest has appeared, who is like Melchizedek.
7.22 This **difference,** then, also makes Jesus the guarantee of
7.23 There is another **difference:**
Jas 2. 1 never treat people in **different** ways according to their outward
2.25 Israelite spies and helping them to escape by a **different** road.
1 Pet 4.10 a good manager of God's **different** gifts, must use for the
2 Pet 3. 8 There is no **difference** in the Lord's sight between one day
1 Jn 3.10 This is the clear **difference** between God's children and the Devil's
4. 6 then, is how we can tell the **difference** between the Spirit

DIFFICULT

Gen 35.16 Rachel to have her baby, and she was having **difficult** labour.
47. 9 years have been few and **difficult,**
Ex 14.25 get stuck, so that they moved with great **difficulty.**
18.22 They can bring all the **difficult** cases to you,
18.26 a permanent basis, bringing the **difficult** cases to Moses
Deut 1.17 If any case is too **difficult** for you, bring it to me,
17. 8 cases will be too **difficult** for the local judges to decide,
30.11 giving you today is not too **difficult** or beyond your reach.
1 Sam 10.19 your troubles and **difficulties,** but today you have rejected me
1 Kgs 10. 1 she travelled to Jerusalem to test him with **difficult** questions.
10. 3 there was nothing too **difficult** for him to explain.
2 Kgs 2.10 "That is a **difficult** request to grant," Elijah replied.
5.13 told you to do something **difficult,** you would have done it.
2 Chr 9. 1 she travelled to Jerusalem to test him with **difficult** questions.
9. 2 there was nothing too **difficult** for him to explain.
Neh 1. 3 the homeland were in great **difficulty** and that the foreigners
Ps 73.16 through, but it was too **difficult** for me [17]until I went
131. 1 with great matters or with subjects too **difficult** for me.
139.17 O God, how **difficult** I find your thoughts;
Prov 15.19 lazy, you will meet **difficulty** everywhere,
Jer 32.17 nothing is too **difficult** for you.
32.27 Nothing is too **difficult** for me.
Ezek 3. 5 a nation that speaks a **difficult** foreign language,
3. 6 nations that spoke **difficult** languages you didn't understand,
Dan 2.11 is asking for is so **difficult** that no one can do it

Acts 27. 7 days and with great **difficulty** finally arrived off the town of
27. 8 the coast and with great **difficulty** came to a place called
27.16 with some **difficulty,** we managed to make the ship's boat secure.
Rom 5. 7 It is a **difficult** thing for someone to die for a righteous
2 Cor 6. 4 by patiently enduring troubles, hardships, and **difficulties.**
12.10 hardships, persecutions, and **difficulties** for Christ's sake.
2 Tim 3. 1 Remember that there will be **difficult** times in the last days.
1 Pet 4.18 scripture says, "It is **difficult** for good people to be saved;
2 Pet 3.16 There are some **difficult** things in his letters which ignorant

DIG
[DUG]

Gen 21.30 you admit that I am the one who **dug** this well."
26.15 the servants of his father Abraham had **dug**
26.18 He **dug** once again the wells
26.18 which had been **dug** during the time of Abraham
26.19 Isaac's servants **dug** a well in the valley and found water.
26.21 Isaac's servants **dug** another well, and there was a quarrel
26.22 He moved away from there and **dug** another well.
26.25 set up his camp there, and his servants **dug** another well.
26.32 came and told him about the well which they had **dug.**
Ex 7.24 All the Egyptians **dug** along the bank of the river
21.33 a pit or if he **digs** one and does not cover it,
Num 21.18 a song— [18] The well **dug** by princes And by
21.18 leaders of the people, **Dug** with a royal sceptre
Deut 6.11 wells that you did not **dig,** and vineyards and olive orchards
23.13 a bowel movement you can **dig** a hole and cover it up.
2 Sam 20.15 wall and also began to **dig** under the wall
1 Kgs 18.32 He **dug** a trench round it,
2 Kgs 3.16 '**Dig** ditches all over this dry stream bed.
19.24 You boasted that you **dug** wells and drank water
20.20 he built a reservoir and **dug** a tunnel to bring water
2 Chr 26.10 in the open country and **dug** many cisterns, because he had
Neh 9.25 houses full of wealth, cisterns already **dug,**
Job 19.12 they **dig** trenches and lay siege to my tent.
28. 1 There are mines where silver is **dug;**
28. 2 Men **dig** iron out of the ground And melt copper
28. 3 And **dig** for rocks in the darkness.
28. 4 Or human feet ever travel, Men **dig** the shafts of mines.
28. 9 Men **dig** the hardest rocks, Dig mountains away at their base.
28.11 They **dig** to the sources of rivers
30. 6 to live in caves, in holes **dug** in the sides of cliffs.
38.25 Who **dug** a channel for the pouring rain
Ps 9.15 The heathen have **dug** a pit and fallen in;
35. 7 a trap for me and **dug** a deep hole to catch me.
57. 6 They **dug** a pit in my path, but fell into it themselves.
94.13 days of trouble until a pit is **dug** to trap the wicked.
119.85 who do not obey your law, have **dug** pits to trap me.
Prov 28.17 man guilty of murder is **digging** his own grave
Ecc 2. 6 I **dug** ponds to irrigate them.
10. 8 If you **dig** a pit, you fall in it;
Is 2.10 in the rocky hills or **dig** holes in the ground
2.19 in the rocky hills or **dig** holes in the ground
5. 2 He **dug** the soil and cleared it of stones;
5. 2 a tower to guard them, **dug** a pit for treading the grapes.
37.25 You boasted that you **dug** wells and drank water
51. 1 from which you came, the quarry from which you were **dug.**
Jer 2.13 and they have **dug** cisterns, cracked cisterns
18.20 Yet they have **dug** a pit for me to fall in.
18.22 They have **dug** a pit for me to fall in and have
41. 9 one that King Asa had **dug** when he was being attacked by
Ezek 12. 7 it was getting dark I **dug** a hole in the wall with
12.12 escape through a hole that they **dig** for him in the wall.
17.17 the Babylonians build earthworks and **dig** trenches
21.22 to throw up earthworks, and to **dig** trenches.
26. 8 The enemy will **dig** trenches, build earthworks,
Amos 9. 2 Even if they **dig** their way down to the world of the
Mt 21.33 put a fence around it, **dug** a hole for the winepress,
25.18 one thousand coins went off, **dug** a hole in the ground,
27.60 own tomb, which he had just recently **dug** out of solid rock.
Mk 12. 1 put a fence round it, **dug** a hole for the winepress,
15.46 it in a tomb which had been **dug** out of solid rock.
Lk 6.48 who, in building his house, **dug** deep and laid the foundation
13. 8 I will **dig** round it and put in some manure.
16. 3 am not strong enough to **dig** ditches, and I am ashamed to
23.53 a tomb which had been **dug** out of solid rock and which

DIGESTION

1 Tim 5.23 wine to help your **digestion,** since you are ill so often.

DIGNITY

Gen 43.32 they considered it beneath their **dignity** to eat with Hebrews.
Ex 28. 2 garments for your brother Aaron, to provide him with **dignity**
28.40 caps for Aaron's sons, to provide them with **dignity** and beauty.
Job 30.15 my **dignity** is gone like a puff of wind,
Is 53. 2 He had no **dignity** or beauty to make us take notice
Dan 5.18 Nebuchadnezzar a great king and gave him **dignity** and majesty.

DILL
A small plant whose stems, leaves, and seeds are used for seasoning food.

Is 28.25 soil, he sows the seeds of herbs such as **dill** and cumin.
28.27 uses a heavy club to beat out **dill** seeds or cumin seeds;
Mt 23.23 seasoning herbs, such as mint, **dill,** and cumin, but you neglect

DIM

Ecc 12. 2 and the stars will grow **dim** for you, and the rain clouds
12. 3 to chew your food, and your eyes too **dim** to see clearly.
1 Cor 13.12 What we see now is like a **dim** image in a mirror;

DINE

2 Kgs 25.29 his prison clothes and to **dine** at the king's table
Neh 2. 1 when Emperor Artaxerxes was **dining,** I took the wine to him.
Jer 52.33 his prison clothes and to **dine** at the king's table

DINNER

Lk 7.36 Pharisee invited Jesus to have **dinner** with him, and Jesus went
14.12 give a lunch or a **dinner,** do not invite your friends or
14.24 none of those men who were invited will taste my **dinner!'** "
Jn 12. 2 prepared a **dinner** for him there, which Martha helped to serve;

Am DIP
see also **SCOOP**

DIP

Gen 37.31 Then they killed a goat and **dipped** Joseph's robe in its blood.
Ex 12.22 Take a sprig of hyssop, **dip** it in the bowl containing
Lev 4. 6 He shall **dip** his finger in the blood and sprinkle it in
4.17 bull's blood into the Tent, [17] **dip** his finger in it,
4.25 The priest shall **dip** his finger in the blood of the animal,
4.30 The priest shall **dip** his finger in the blood of the animal,
4.34 The priest shall **dip** his finger in the blood of the animal,
9. 9 the blood, and he **dipped** his finger in it,
11.32 It shall be **dipped** in water, but it will remain unclean
14. 6 take the other bird and **dip** it, together with the cedar-wood,
14.16 of his own left hand, [16] **dip** a finger of his right hand
14.51 the live bird and shall **dip** them in the blood of the
Num 19.18 take a sprig of hyssop, **dip** it in the water, and sprinkle
Ruth 2.14 and have a piece of bread, and **dip** it in the sauce."
1 Sam 14.27 the stick he was carrying, **dipped** it in a honeycomb, and ate
2 Kgs 5.14 went down to the Jordan, **dipped** himself in it seven times,
Mt 26.23 Jesus answered, "One who **dips** his bread in the dish
Mk 14.20 of you twelve, one who **dips** his bread in the dish with
Lk 16.24 and send Lazarus to **dip** his finger in some water and
Jn 13.26 Jesus answered, "I will **dip** some bread in the sauce and
13.26 took a piece of bread, **dipped** it, and gave it to Judas,

Am DIPPER see (Great) BEAR, (Little) BEAR

DIRECT

Ex 38.21 Levites who worked under the **direction** of Ithamar son of Aaron
Num 4.28 carry them out under the **direction** of Ithamar son of Aaron
4.33 carry them out under the **direction** of Ithamar son of Aaron
7. 8 was to be done under the **direction** of Ithamar son of Aaron.
27.21 In this way Eleazar will **direct** Joshua and the whole community
1 Sam 3. 1 serving the Lord under the **direction** of Eli,
1 Chr 25. 2 They were under the **direction** of Asaph,
25. 3 Under the **direction** of their father they proclaimed God's message,
25. 6 cymbals and harps under their father's **direction,**
2 Chr 34. 4 Under his **direction** his men smashed the altars
Neh 12.24 Under the **direction** of Hashabiah, Sherebiah, Jeshua,
Esth 9.31 peace and security [31] and **directed** them and their descendants
Job 12.10 It is God who **directs** the lives of his creatures;
38.32 season by season and **direct** the Great and the Little Bear?
Prov 16. 9 You may make your plans, but God **directs** your actions.
21. 1 a king as easily as he **directs** the course of a stream.
Is 48.17 for your own good and **direct** you in the way you should
Hab 1.14 like a swarm of insects that have no ruler to **direct** them?
1 Cor 12.28 to help others or to **direct** them or to speak in strange
Gal 5.16 let the Spirit **direct** your lives, and you will not satisfy

DIRECTION

Gen 3.24 and a flaming sword which turned in all **directions.**
13.14 "From where you are, look carefully in all **directions.**
28.14 extend their territory in all **directions,**
30.40 made them face in the **direction** of the streaked and black
Num 11.31 and all round it for many kilometres in every **direction.**
14.25 the wilderness in the **direction** of the Gulf of Aqaba."
19. 4 finger sprinkle it seven times in the **direction** of the Tent.
35. 4 walls 450 metres in each **direction,** [5] so that there is a
Deut 27.18 on anyone who leads a blind man in the wrong **direction.'**
28. 7 They will attack from one **direction,** but they will run from
28. 7 but they will run from you in all **directions.**
28.25 will attack them from one **direction,** but you will run from
28.25 run from them in all **directions,** and all the people on earth
Josh 18.14 border then went in another **direction,** turning south
19.13 and Ethkazin, turning in the **direction** of Neah on the way to
1 Kgs 7.25 bronze bulls that faced outwards, three facing in each **direction.**
18. 6 each one would explore, and set off in different **directions.**
2 Kgs 3.20 water came flowing from the **direction** of Edom,
25. 4 two walls, and fled in the **direction** of the Jordan Valley.
1 Chr 9.24 a gate facing in each **direction,** north, south, east, and west,
2 Chr 4. 4 bronze bulls that faced outwards, three facing in each **direction.**
Ps 77.17 and lightning flashed in all **directions.**
Prov 17.24 but a fool starts off in many **directions.**
20.24 can anyone understand the **direction** his own life is taking?
Ecc 11. 3 No matter in which **direction** a tree falls, it will lie

Is 33.17 ruling in splendour over a land that stretches in all **directions.**
Jer 39. 4 and escaped in the **direction** of the Jordan Valley.
41.10 and started off in the **direction** of the territory of Ammon.
49.32 I will scatter in every **direction** those people who cut their
49.36 blow against Elam from all **directions,** and I will scatter her
50. 5 will ask the way to Zion and then go in that **direction.**
52. 7 two walls, and fled in the **direction** of the Jordan Valley.
Ezek 1.12 Each creature faced all four **directions,**
1.17 so that the wheels could move in any of the four **directions.**
5.10 you and scatter in every **direction** any who are left alive.
10.11 When the creatures moved, they could go in any **direction**
10.11 all moved together in the **direction** they wanted to go,
12.14 I will scatter in every **direction** all the members
17.21 and the survivors will be scattered in every **direction.**
37. 9 from every **direction,** to breathe into these dead bodies,
39. 2 turn him in a new **direction** and lead him out
47. 1 flowing east, the **direction** the Temple faced.
Dan 7. 2 Winds were blowing from all **directions**
8. 8 prominent horns came up, each pointing in a different **direction.**
Joel 2. 7 and do not change **direction** [8] or get in each other's way.
Jon 1. 3 set out in the opposite **direction** in order to get away
Zech 2. 6 "I scattered you in all **directions.**
Acts 27. 7 any further in that **direction,** so we sailed down the sheltered
1 Cor 7.34 and so he is pulled in two **directions.**
Phil 1.23 I am pulled in two **directions.**

DIRECTLY

Mt 16.17 but it was given to you **directly** by my Father in heaven.

Am **DIRT**
see also **MUD**

DIRT

Job 30.19 I am no better than **dirt.**
Song 5. 3 why should I get them **dirty** again?
Is 10. 6 steal and trample on the people like **dirt** in the streets."
51.23 in the streets and trampled on you as if you were **dirt."**
Zech 9. 3 so much silver and gold that it is as common as **dirt!**
1 Pet 3.21 the washing away of bodily **dirt,** but the promise made to God
Jude 12 carousing they are like **dirty** spots in your fellowship meals.

DISABLED

Heb 12.13 the lame foot may not be **disabled,** but instead be healed.

DISAGREE

Prov 18. 1 they will **disagree** with what everyone else knows is right.
Acts 28.25 they left, **disagreeing** among themselves, after Paul had said

DISAPPEAR

Gen 5.24 and then he **disappeared,** because God took him away.
Lev 13.58 the object and the spot **disappears,** he shall wash it again,
Num 27. 4 why should our father's name **disappear** from Israel?
Deut 4.26 if you disobey me, you will soon **disappear** from the land.
Judg 6.21 Then the angel **disappeared.**
21. 3 Why is the tribe of Benjamin about to **disappear** from Israel?"
1 Sam 2. 9 but the wicked **disappear** in darkness;
Job 6.17 but in the heat they **disappear,** and the stream beds lie
14. 2 we **disappear** like shadows.
20. 9 He will **disappear** from the place where he used to live;
Ps 37. 2 They will soon **disappear** like grass that dries up;
37.10 Soon the wicked will **disappear;**
37.20 they will **disappear** like smoke.
58. 7 May they **disappear** like water draining away;
73.20 when you rouse yourself, O Lord, they **disappear.**
82. 5 You are completely corrupt, and justice has **disappeared**
102. 3 My life is **disappearing** like smoke;
102.26 They will **disappear,** but you will remain;
112.10 they glare in hate and **disappear;**
Prov 21. 6 you get by dishonesty soon **disappear,** but not before they lead
31.30 Charm is deceptive and beauty **disappears,**
Ecc 6. 4 it **disappears** into darkness, where it is forgotten.
8. 1 Wisdom makes him smile and makes his frowns **disappear.**
Song 2.17 until the morning breezes blow and the darkness **disappears.**
4. 6 until the morning breezes blow and the darkness **disappears.**
Is 2.17 Idols will completely **disappear,** and the Lord alone will be exalted
16.14 "In exactly three years Moab's great wealth will **disappear.**
28. 4 of those proud leaders will **disappear** like the first figs
34. 4 The sky will **disappear** like a scroll being rolled up,
41.12 and will **disappear** from the earth.
50. 9 All my accusers will **disappear;**
51. 6 The heavens will **disappear** like smoke;
Jer 17.13 They will **disappear** like names written in the dust,
49. 7 Has all their wisdom **disappeared?**
Ezek 6. 6 and everything they made will **disappear.**
24.12 although all that corrosion will not **disappear** in the flames.
Hos 6. 4 Your love for me **disappears** as quickly as morning mist,
13. 3 And so these people will **disappear** like morning mist,
Jon 4.10 "This plant grew up in one night and **disappeared** the next;
Nah 1.12 strong and numerous, they will be destroyed and **disappear.**
Zech 4. 7 Obstacles as great as mountains will **disappear** before you.
Lk 16.17 for heaven and earth to **disappear** than for the smallest detail
24.31 and they recognized him, but he **disappeared** from their sight.
Acts 5.38 human origin, it will **disappear,** [39] but if it comes from God,
1 Cor 13.10 when what is perfect comes, then what is partial will **disappear.**
2 Cor 3.13 people of Israel would not see the brightness fade and **disappear.**
Phil 2.28 again when you see him, and my own sorrow will **disappear.**
Heb 1.11 They will **disappear,** but you will remain;
8.13 anything that becomes old and worn out will soon **disappear.**
Jas 4.14 of smoke, which appears for a moment and then **disappears.**
2 Pet 3.10 that Day the heavens will **disappear** with a shrill noise,
Rev 6.14 The sky **disappeared** like a scroll being rolled up,
16.20 All the islands **disappeared,** all the mountains vanished.
18.14 you longed to own have **disappeared,** and all your wealth
21. 1 The first heaven and the first earth **disappeared,** and the sea
21. 4 The old things have **disappeared."**

DISAPPOINT

Ps 22. 5 they trusted you and were not **disappointed.**
34. 5 they will never be **disappointed.**
119.116 don't let me be **disappointed** in my hope!
Is 49.23 no one who waits for my help will be **disappointed."**
Jer 2.36 You will be **disappointed** by Egypt, just as you were by Assyria.
15.18 Do you intend to **disappoint** me like a stream that goes dry
Zech 4.10 **disappointed** because so little progress is being made.
Rom 5. 5 This hope does not **disappoint** us, for God has poured out
9.33 But whoever believes in him will not be **disappointed."**
10.11 "Whoever believes in him will not be **disappointed."**
2 Cor 7.14 did boast of you to him, and you have not **disappointed** me.
1 Pet 2. 6 and whoever believes in him will never be **disappointed."**

DISAPPROVE

2 Kgs 17. 9 Israelites did things that the Lord their God **disapproved** of.
1 Chr 21. 6 Because Joab **disapproved** of the king's command,

DISASTER

Gen 19.19 the **disaster** will overtake me, and I will die before I get
20. 9 you to make you bring this **disaster** on me and my kingdom?
44.34 I cannot bear to see this **disaster** come upon my father."
Ex 30.12 his life, so that no **disaster** will come on him while the
32.12 your mind and do not bring this **disaster** on your people.
32.14 did not bring on his people the **disaster** he had threatened.
Lev 26.16 I will bring **disaster** on you—
Num 8.19 protect the Israelites from the **disaster** that would strike them
Deut 28.20 he will bring on you **disaster,** confusion, and trouble
28.22 These **disasters** will be with you until you die.
28.45 "All these **disasters** will come on you,
29.20 against him, and all the **disasters** written in this book will
29.21 of Israel and will bring **disaster** on him in accordance with
29.22 distant lands will see the **disasters** and sufferings
29.27 on their land all the **disasters** written in this book.
31.17 Many terrible **disasters** will come upon them,
31.21 and many terrible **disasters** will come on them.
31.29 they will meet with **disaster,** because they will have made
32.23 will bring on them endless **disasters** and use all my arrows
1 Sam 6. 9 God of the Israelites who has sent this terrible **disaster** on us.
25.17 This could be **disastrous** for our master and all his family.
2 Sam 17.14 so that **disaster** would come on Absalom.
19. 7 That would be the worst **disaster** you have suffered
1 Kgs 9. 9 That is why the Lord has brought this **disaster** on them.' "
14.10 I will bring **disaster** on your dynasty
21.21 So the Lord says to you, 'I will bring **disaster** on you.
21.29 this, I will not bring **disaster** on him during his lifetime;
21.29 his son's lifetime that I will bring **disaster** on Ahab's family."
22.23 But he himself has decreed that you will meet with **disaster!"**
2 Kgs 14.10 that will only bring **disaster** on you and your people?"
21.12 will bring such a **disaster** on Jerusalem and Judah
1 Chr 2. 7 one of Zerah's descendants, brought **disaster** on the people
2 Chr 7.22 That is why the Lord has brought this **disaster** on them.' "
18.22 But he himself has decreed that you will meet with **disaster!"**
20. 9 knowing [9] that if any **disaster** struck them to punish them—
24.20 disobeyed his commands and are bringing **disaster** on yourselves!
25.19 trouble that will only bring **disaster** on you and your people?"
28.23 This brought **disaster** on him and on his nation.
Esth 8. 6 I endure it if this **disaster** comes on my people,
Job 4. 7 Name a single case where a righteous man met with **disaster.**
15.24 **disaster,** like a powerful king, is waiting to attack him.
18.12 **disaster** stands and waits at his side.
21. 9 God does not bring **disaster** on their homes;
21.17 Did one of them ever meet with **disaster?**
31. 3 He sends **disaster** and ruin to those who do wrong.
31.29 enemies suffered, or pleased when they met with **disaster;**
Ps 78.33 days like a breath and their lives with sudden **disaster.**
91.10 and so no **disaster** will strike you, no violence
Prov 3.25 have to worry about sudden **disasters,** such as come on the
6.15 Because of this, **disaster** will strike them without warning,
16.29 Violent people deceive their friends and lead them to **disaster.**
17.20 speaks evil can expect to find nothing good—only **disaster.**
22. 8 sow the seeds of injustice, **disaster** will spring up,
24.16 but **disaster** destroys the wicked.
24.17 when your enemy meets **disaster,** and don't rejoice
24.22 Do you realize the **disaster** that God or the king can cause?
Is 10. 3 do when he brings **disaster** on you from a distant country?
13.11 Lord says, "I will bring **disaster** on the earth
21. 1 **disaster** will come from a terrifying land.
28.15 You are certain that **disaster** will spare you when it comes,
28.18 When **disaster** sweeps down, you will be overcome.
29. 2 and then God will bring **disaster** on the city
30. 3 powerless to help them, and Egypt's protection will end in **disaster.**
31. 2 He sends **disaster.**
41.23 Do something good or bring some **disaster;**
45. 7 I bring both blessing and **disaster.**

Is 46. 7 prays to it, it cannot answer or save him from **disaster.**
47.11 **Disaster** will come upon you, and none of your magic can
51.19 A double **disaster** has fallen on you:
65.23 and their children will not meet with **disaster.**
66. 4 So I will bring **disaster** upon them—
Jer 2. 3 I sent suffering and **disaster** on everyone who hurt you.
4. 6 The Lord is bringing **disaster** and great destruction
4.20 One **disaster** follows another;
6. 1 **Disaster** and destruction are about to come from the north.
11.15 they think they can prevent **disaster** by making promises
11.17 but now I threaten them with **disaster.**
11.23 set a time for bringing **disaster** on the people of Anathoth,
14. 8 you are the one who saves us from **disaster.**
17.16 But, Lord, I never urged you to bring **disaster** on them;
17.18 Bring **disaster** on them and break them to pieces.
18.17 I will not help them when the **disaster** comes."
19. 3 going to bring such a **disaster** on this place that everyone
23.12 I am going to bring **disaster** on them;
23.17 who is stubborn that **disaster** will never touch him."
24. 9 I will bring such a **disaster** on them that all the nations
25.13 punish Babylonia with all the **disasters** that I threatened
25.13 spoke through Jeremiah—all the **disasters** recorded in this book.
25.32 The Lord Almighty says that **disaster** is coming on
26.19 changed his mind about the **disaster** that he said he would
26.19 Now we are about to bring a terrible **disaster** on ourselves."
29.11 bring you prosperity and not **disaster,**
32.42 as I have brought this **disaster** on these people, so I am
36.31 bring on all of you the **disaster** that I have threatened."
40.15 and it would bring **disaster** on all the people
42.17 not one will escape the **disaster** that I am going to bring
44.23 **disaster** has come on you because you offered sacrifices
45. 5 I am bringing **disaster** on all mankind, but you will at least
49.32 short, and I will bring **disaster** on them from every side.
Lam 1.21 My enemies are glad that you brought **disaster** on me.
2.13 Your **disaster** is boundless as the ocean;
3.47 We have been through **disaster** and ruin;
4.10 The **disaster** that came to my people brought horror;
4.21 Your **disaster** is coming too;
Ezek 7. 5 "One **disaster** after another is coming on you.
7.10 The day of **disaster** is coming for Israel.
7.26 One **disaster** will follow another,
34.12 places where they were scattered on that dark, **disastrous** day.
35. 5 in the time of her **disaster,** the time of final punishment
Hos 9. 6 When the **disaster** comes and the people are scattered,
Amos 3. 6 Does **disaster** strike a city unless the Lord sends it?
6. 3 admit that a day of **disaster** is coming, but what you do
Obad 13 and to seize their riches on the day of their **disaster.**
Mic 1.12 because the Lord has brought **disaster** close to Jerusalem.
2. 3 "I am planning to bring **disaster** on you,
2. 4 story as an example of **disaster,** and they will sing this
Zeph 1.17 "I will bring such **disasters** on mankind that everyone will grope
Zech 8.13 by saying, 'May the same **disasters** fall on you that fell
8.14 made me angry, I planned **disaster** for them and did not

DISCARD

Ps 102.26 You will **discard** them like clothes, and they will vanish.
119.83 I am as useless as a **discarded** wineskin;

DISCHARGE

Lev 15. 2 discharge from his penis, the **discharge** is unclean,
15. 7 touches the man with the **discharge** must wash his clothes
15. 8 If the man with the **discharge** spits on anyone
15. 9 or seat on which the man with the **discharge** sits is unclean.
15.11 a man who has a **discharge** touches someone
15.13 man is cured of his **discharge,** he must wait seven days
15.32 a man who has a **discharge** or an emission of semen,
22. 4 a dreaded skin-disease or a **discharge** may eat any of the
Num 5. 2 skin disease or a bodily **discharge** and everyone who is unclean

DISCIPLE

[FELLOW-DISCIPLES]
A person who follows and learns from someone else. In the New Testament the word is used of the followers of John the Baptist and especially of the followers of Jesus, particularly the twelve apostles.
see also **APOSTLE**

Is 8.16 You, my **disciples** are to guard and preserve the messages
Jer 35. 4 into the room of the **disciples** of the prophet Hanan
Mt 5. 1 His **disciples** gathered round him, [2]and he began to teach them:
8.18 round him, he ordered his **disciples** to go to the other side
8.21 Another man, who was a **disciple,** said, "Sir, first let
8.23 Jesus got into a boat, and his **disciples** went with him.
8.25 The **disciples** went to him and woke him up.
9.10 outcasts came and joined Jesus and his **disciples** at the table.
9.11 and asked his **disciples,** "Why does your teacher eat with
9.14 the Pharisees fast often, but your **disciples** don't fast at all?"
9.19 up and followed him, and his **disciples** went along with him.
9.37 So he said to his **disciples,** "The harvest is large, but
10. 1 Jesus called his twelve **disciples** together and gave them
10.37 or mother more than me is not fit to be my **disciple;**
10.37 or daughter more than me is not fit to be my **disciple.**
10.38 and follow in my steps is not fit to be my **disciple.**
11. 1 these instructions to his twelve **disciples,** he left that place
11. 2 that Christ was doing, he sent some of his **disciples** to him.
11. 7 While John's **disciples** were leaving, Jesus spoke about him
12. 1 His **disciples** were hungry, so they began to pick ears of
12. 2 our Law for your **disciples** to do this on the Sabbath!"
12.49 Then he pointed to his **disciples** and said, "Look!
Mt 13.10 Then the **disciples** came to Jesus and asked him, "Why do
13.36 crowd and gone indoors, his **disciples** came to him and said,
13.52 the Law who becomes a **disciple** in the Kingdom of heaven is
14.12 John's **disciples** came, carried away his body, and buried
14.15 evening his **disciples** came to him and said, "It is already
14.19 and gave them to the **disciples,**
14.19 and the **disciples** gave them to the people.
14.20 Then the **disciples** took up twelve baskets full of what was
14.22 Then Jesus made the **disciples** get into the boat and go
14.25 the morning Jesus came to the **disciples,** walking on the water.
14.33 Then the **disciples** in the boat worshipped Jesus.
15. 2 "Why is it that your **disciples** disobey the teaching handed down
15.12 Then the **disciples** came to him and said, "Do you know
15.23 His **disciples** came to him and begged him, "Send her away!
15.32 Jesus called his **disciples** to him and said, "I feel
15.33 The **disciples** asked him, "Where will we find enough food
15.36 thanks to God, broke them, and gave them to the **disciples;**
15.36 and the **disciples** gave them to the people.
15.37 the **disciples** took up seven baskets full of pieces left over.
16. 5 When the **disciples** crossed over to the other side of the lake,
16.12 the **disciples** understood that he was not warning them to guard
16.13 where he asked his **disciples,** "Who do people say the Son
16.20 Jesus ordered his **disciples** not to tell anyone that he was
16.21 to say plainly to his **disciples,** "I must go to Jerusalem
16.24 Then Jesus said to his **disciples,** "If anyone wants to come
17. 3 the three **disciples** saw Moses and Elijah talking with Jesus.
17. 6 When the **disciples** heard the voice, they were so terrified
17.10 the **disciples** asked Jesus, "Why do the teachers of the Law
17.13 the **disciples** understood that he was talking to them about John
17.16 I brought him to your **disciples,** but they could not heal him."
17.19 Then the **disciples** came to Jesus in private and asked him,
17.22 the **disciples** all came together in Galilee, Jesus said to them,
17.23 The **disciples** became very sad.
17.24 When Jesus and his **disciples** came to Capernaum, the collectors
18. 1 At that time the **disciples** came to Jesus, asking, "Who is
19.10 His **disciples** said to him, "If this is how it is
19.13 and to pray for them, but the **disciples** scolded the people.
19.23 Jesus then said to his **disciples,** "I assure you:
19.25 When the **disciples** heard this, they were completely amazed.
20.17 he took the twelve **disciples** aside and spoke to them privately,
20.24 the other ten **disciples** heard about this, they became angry
20.29 Jesus and his **disciples** were leaving Jericho, a large crowd
21. 1 As Jesus and his **disciples** approached Jerusalem, they came to
21. 1 sent two of the **disciples** on ahead [2]with these instructions:
21. 6 So the **disciples** went and did what Jesus had told them to
21.20 The **disciples** saw this and were astounded.
22.16 some of their **disciples** and some members of Herod's party.
23. 1 Then Jesus spoke to the crowds and to his **disciples.**
24. 1 from the Temple when his **disciples** came to him to call his
24. 3 the Mount of Olives, the **disciples** came to him in private.
26. 1 he said to his **disciples,** [2]"In two days, as you know,
26. 8 The **disciples** saw this and became angry.
26.14 one of the twelve **disciples**—the one named Judas Iscariot—went
26.17 of Unleavened Bread the **disciples** came to Jesus and asked him,
26.18 **disciples** and I will celebrate the Passover at your house.'"
26.19 **disciples** did as Jesus had told them and prepared the Passover
26.20 was evening, Jesus and the twelve **disciples** sat down to eat.
26.22 The **disciples** were very upset and began to ask him, one
26.26 a prayer of thanks, broke it, and gave it to his **disciples.**
26.35 And all the other **disciples** said the same thing.
26.36 Jesus went with his **disciples** to a place called Gethsemane,
26.40 he returned to the three **disciples** and found them asleep;
26.43 He returned once more and found the **disciples** asleep;
26.45 he returned to the **disciples** and said, "Are you still sleeping
26.47 still speaking when Judas, one of the twelve **disciples,** arrived.
26.56 Then all the **disciples** left him and ran away.
27.57 his name was Joseph, and he also was a **disciple** of Jesus.
27.64 third day, so that his **disciples** will not be able to go
28. 7 quickly now, and tell his **disciples,** 'He has been raised
28. 8 and yet filled with joy, and ran to tell his **disciples.**
28.13 are to say that his **disciples** came during the night and
28.16 The eleven **disciples** went to the hill in Galilee where Jesus
28.19 Go, then, to all peoples everywhere and make them my **disciples:**
Mk 1.21 Jesus and his **disciples** came to the town of Capernaum,
1.29 Jesus and his **disciples,** including James and John, left the
2.15 and many of them joined him and his **disciples** at the table.
2.16 so they asked his **disciples,** "Why does he eat with such
2.18 "Why is it that the **disciples** of John the Baptist and
2.18 the **disciples** of the Pharisees fast, but yours
2.23 As his **disciples** walked along with him, they began to pick
2.24 our Law for your **disciples** to do that on the Sabbath!"
3. 7 Jesus and his **disciples** went away to Lake Galilee, and a
3. 9 that Jesus told his **disciples** to get a boat ready for
3.20 gathered that Jesus and his **disciples** had no time to eat.
4.10 to him with the twelve **disciples** and asked him to explain
4.34 alone with his **disciples,** he would explain everything to them.
4.35 day Jesus said to his **disciples,** "Let us go across to the
4.36 **disciples** got into the boat in which Jesus was already sitting,
4.38 The **disciples** woke him up and said, "Teacher, don't you care
4.40 Then Jesus said to his **disciples,** "Why are you frightened?
5. 1 Jesus and his **disciples** arrived on the other side of Lake
5.31 His **disciples** answered, "You see how the people are crowding
5.40 and mother and his three **disciples,** and went into the room
6. 1 and went back to his home town, followed by his **disciples.**
6. 7 called the twelve **disciples** together and sent them out two by
6.29 John's **disciples** heard about this, they came and took away his
6.31 that Jesus and his **disciples** didn't even have time to eat.
6.33 and arrived at the place ahead of Jesus and his **disciples.**
6.35 it was getting late, his **disciples** came to him and said,
6.39 then told his **disciples** to make all the people divide into
6.41 and gave them to his **disciples** to distribute to the people.

Mk 6.43 the **disciples** took up twelve baskets full of what was left
6.45 At once Jesus made his **disciples** get into the boat and
6.48 He saw that his **disciples** were straining at the oars,
6.51 The **disciples** were completely amazed, [52] because they had not
7. 2 noticed that some of his **disciples** were eating their food with
7. 5 "Why is it that your **disciples** do not follow the teaching
7.17 into the house, his **disciples** asked him to explain this saying.
8. 1 to eat, Jesus called the **disciples** to him and said, [2] "I
8. 4 His **disciples** asked him, "Where in this desert can anyone find
8. 6 and gave them to his **disciples** to distribute to the crowd;
8. 6 and the **disciples** did so.
8. 7 gave thanks for these and told the **disciples** to distribute them
8. 8 Then the **disciples** took up seven baskets full of pieces left
8.10 into a boat with his **disciples** and went to the district of
8.14 The **disciples** had forgotten to bring enough bread and had only
8.27 Jesus and his **disciples** went away to the villages near Caesarea
8.31 Then Jesus began to teach his **disciples:**
8.33 Jesus turned round, looked at his **disciples,** and rebuked Peter.
8.34 Then Jesus called the crowd and his **disciples** to him.
9. 4 the three **disciples** saw Elijah and Moses talking with Jesus.
9.14 joined the rest of the **disciples,** they saw a large crowd
9.16 asked his **disciples,** "What are you arguing with them about?"
9.18 I asked your **disciples** to drive the spirit out, but they
9.28 indoors, his **disciples** asked him privately, "Why couldn't we
9.30 Jesus and his **disciples** left that place and went on through
9.31 to know where he was, [31] because he was teaching his **disciples:**
9.33 Jesus asked his **disciples,** "What were you arguing about on
9.35 called the twelve **disciples,** and said to them, "Whoever wants
10.10 into the house, the **disciples** asked Jesus about this matter.
10.13 his hands on them, but the **disciples** scolded the people.
10.14 and said to his **disciples,** "Let the children come to me,
10.23 looked round at his **disciples** and said to them, "How hard
10.24 The **disciples** were shocked at these words, but Jesus went on
10.26 this the **disciples** were completely amazed and asked one another,
10.32 Jesus and his **disciples** were now on the road going up to
10.32 Jesus was going ahead of the **disciples,** who were filled with alarm;
10.32 Jesus took the twelve **disciples** aside and spoke of the things
10.41 When the other ten **disciples** heard about it, they became angry
10.46 Jesus was leaving with his **disciples** and a large crowd,
11. 1 sent two of his **disciples** on ahead [2] with these instructions:
11.11 the day, he went out to Bethany with the twelve **disciples.**
11.14 And his **disciples** heard him.
11.19 When evening came, Jesus and his **disciples** left the city.
12.43 called his **disciples** together and said to them, "I tell you
13. 1 leaving the Temple, one of his **disciples** said, "Look, Teacher!
14.10 Iscariot, one of the twelve **disciples,** went off to the chief
14.12 Jesus' **disciples** asked him, "Where do you want
14.14 is the room where my **disciples** and I will eat the Passover
14.16 **disciples** left, went to the city, and found everything just as
14.17 When it was evening, Jesus came with the twelve **disciples.**
14.19 The **disciples** were upset and began to ask him, one after
14.22 a prayer of thanks, broke it, and gave it to his **disciples.**
14.31 And all the other **disciples** said the same thing.
14.32 and Jesus said to his **disciples,** "Sit here while I pray."
14.37 Then he returned and found the three **disciples** asleep.
14.40 Then he came back to the **disciples** and found them asleep;
14.43 still speaking when Judas, one of the twelve **disciples,** arrived.
14.50 Then all the **disciples** left him and ran away.
16. 7 Now go and give this message to his **disciples,** including Peter:
16.10 sent out through his **disciples** from the east to the west
16.14 Jesus appeared to the eleven **disciples** as they were eating.
16.20 **disciples** went and preached everywhere, and the Lord worked with

Lk 5.30 Law who belonged to their group complained to Jesus' **disciples.**
5.33 said to Jesus, "The **disciples** of John fast frequently and
5.33 offer prayers, and the **disciples** of the Pharisees do the same;
5.33 but your **disciples** eat and drink."
6. 1 His **disciples** began to pick the ears of corn, rub them in
6.13 day came, he called his **disciples** to him and chose twelve of
6.17 stood on a level place with a large number of his **disciples.**
6.20 Jesus looked at his **disciples** and said, "Happy are you poor;
7.11 called Nain, accompanied by his **disciples** and a large crowd.
7.18 When John's **disciples** told him about all these things,
8. 1 The twelve **disciples** went with him, [2] and so did some women
8. 3 who used their own resources to help Jesus and his **disciples.**
8. 9 His **disciples** asked Jesus what this parable meant,
8.22 into a boat with his **disciples** and said to them, "Let us
8.24 **disciples** went to Jesus and woke him up, saying, "Master, Master!
8.25 Then he said to the **disciples,** "Where is your faith?"
8.26 Jesus and his **disciples** sailed on over to the territory of
9. 1 Jesus called the twelve **disciples** together and gave them power
9. 6 **disciples** left and travelled through all the villages, preaching
9.12 beginning to set, the twelve **disciples** came to him and said,
9.14 said to his **disciples,** "Make the people sit down in groups
9.15 the **disciples** had done so, [16] Jesus took the five loaves
9.16 and gave them to the **disciples** to distribute to the people.
9.17 and had enough, and the **disciples** took up twelve baskets of
9.18 when Jesus was praying alone, the **disciples** came to him.
9.34 and the **disciples** were afraid as the cloud came over them.
9.36 The **disciples** kept quiet about all this, and told no one at
9.37 Jesus and the three **disciples** went down from the hill,
9.40 I begged your **disciples** to drive it out, but they couldn't."
9.43 he said to his **disciples,** [44] "Don't forget what I am about
9.45 But the **disciples** did not know what this meant.
9.46 argument broke out among the **disciples** as to which one of
9.50 to the other **disciples,** "because whoever is not against you
9.54 When the **disciples** James and John saw this, they said, "Lord,
9.56 Then Jesus and his **disciples** went on to another village.
10.16 said to his **disciples,** "Whoever listens to you listens to me;
10.23 Then Jesus turned to the **disciples** and said to them privately,
10.38 As Jesus and his **disciples** went on their way, he came to
11. 1 one of his **disciples** said to him,
11. 1 "Lord, teach us to pray, just as John taught his **disciples."**
11. 5 Jesus said to his **disciples,** "Suppose one of you should go
12. 1 Jesus said first to his **disciples,** "Be on guard against the
12.22 Then Jesus said to the **disciples,** "And so I tell you
14.26 to me cannot be my **disciple** unless he loves me more than
14.27 his own cross and come after me cannot be my **disciple.**
14.33 of you can be my **disciple** unless he gives up everything he
16. 1 Jesus said to his **disciples,** "There was once a rich man
17. 1 said to his **disciples,** "Things that make people fall into sin
17.22 Then he said to the **disciples,** "The time will come when
17.37 The **disciples** asked him, "Where, Lord?"
18. 1 Then Jesus told his **disciples** a parable to teach them that
18.15 The **disciples** saw them and scolded them for doing so,
18.31 took the twelve **disciples** aside and said to them, "Listen!
18.34 But the **disciples** did not understand any of these things;
19.29 the Mount of Olives, he sent two **disciples** ahead [30] with these
19.37 the large crowd of his **disciples** began to thank God and
19.39 "Teacher," they said, "command your **disciples** to be quiet!"
20.45 Jesus said to his **disciples,** [46] "Be on your guard against the
21. 5 Some of the **disciples** were talking about the Temple,
22. 3 Judas, called Iscariot, who was one of the twelve **disciples.**
22.11 is the room where my **disciples** and I will eat the Passover
22.24 argument broke out among the **disciples** as to which one of
22.35 Jesus asked his **disciples,** "When I sent you out that time
22.38 The **disciples** said, "Look!
22.39 and the **disciples** went with him.
22.45 he went back to the **disciples** and found them asleep, worn
22.47 a crowd arrived, led by Judas, one of the twelve **disciples.**
22.49 When the **disciples** who were with Jesus saw what was
24. 9 all these things to the eleven **disciples** and all the rest.
24.33 found the eleven **disciples** gathered together with the others

Jn 1.35 with two of his **disciples,** [36] when he saw Jesus walking by.
1.37 The two **disciples** heard him say this and went with Jesus.
2. 2 and Jesus and his **disciples** had also been invited to the
2.11 he revealed his glory, and his **disciples** believed in him.
2.12 and his mother, brothers, and **disciples** went to Capernaum
2.17 His **disciples** remembered that the scripture says, "My devotion
2.22 raised from death, his **disciples** remembered that he had said
3.22 Jesus and his **disciples** went to the province of Judaea,
3.25 Some of John's **disciples** began arguing with a Jew about the
4. 1 that Jesus was winning and baptizing more **disciples** than John.
4. 2 only his **disciples** did.)
4. 8 (His **disciples** had gone into town to buy food.)
4.27 Jesus' **disciples** returned, and they were greatly surprised to
4.31 the **disciples** were begging Jesus, "Teacher, have something to
4.33 the **disciples** started asking among themselves, "Could somebody
6. 3 Jesus went up a hill and sat down with his **disciples.**
6. 8 Another of his **disciples,** Andrew, who was Simon Peter's brother,
6.12 full, he said to his **disciples,** "Gather the pieces left over;
6.16 When evening came, Jesus' **disciples** went down to the lake,
6.19 **disciples** had rowed about five or six kilometres when they saw
6.22 gone in it with his **disciples,** but that they had left
6.24 was not there, nor his **disciples,** they got into those boats
6.67 he asked the twelve **disciples,** "And you—would you also like
6.71 was one of the twelve **disciples,** was going to betray him.
8.31 "If you obey my teaching, you are really my **disciples;**
9. 2 His **disciples** asked him, "Teacher, whose sin caused him to be
9.27 Maybe you, too, would like to be his **disciples?"**
9.28 They cursed him and said, "You are that fellow's **disciple;**
9.28 but we are Moses' **disciples.**
11. 7 Then he said to the **disciples,** "Let us go back to Judaea."
11. 8 **disciples** answered, "just a short time ago the people there
11.12 **disciples** answered, "If he is asleep, Lord, he will get well."
11.16 the Twin) said to his **fellow-disciples,** "Let us all go with
11.54 to a town named Ephraim, where he stayed with the **disciples.**
12. 4 One of Jesus' **disciples,** Judas Iscariot—the one who was going
12.16 His **disciples** did not understand this at the time;
13. 2 Jesus and his **disciples** were at supper.
13. 5 and began to wash the **disciples'** feet and dry them with the
13. 8 your feet," Jesus answered, "you will no longer be my **disciple."**
13.22 The **disciples** looked at one another, completely puzzled
13.23 One of the **disciples,** the one whom Jesus loved, was sitting
13.25 So that **disciple** moved closer to Jesus' side and asked,
13.29 some of the **disciples** thought that Jesus had told him
13.35 then everyone will know that you are my **disciples."**
14.10 you," Jesus said to his **disciples,** "do not come from me.
15. 8 and in this way you become my **disciples.**
16.17 Some of his **disciples** asked among themselves, "What does this
16.29 **disciples** said to him, "Now you are speaking plainly, without
18. 1 he left with his **disciples** and went across the brook called
18. 1 a garden in that place, and Jesus and his **disciples** went in.
18. 2 because many times Jesus had met there with his **disciples.**
18.15 Simon Peter and another **disciple** followed Jesus.
18.15 That other **disciple** was well known to the High Priest, so he
18.16 Then the other **disciple** went back out, spoke to the girl
18.17 Peter, "Aren't you also one of the **disciples** of that man?"
18.19 The High Priest questioned Jesus about his **disciples** and about
18.25 "Aren't you also one of the **disciples** of that man?"
19.26 Jesus saw his mother and the **disciple** he loved standing there;
19.27 Then he said to the **disciple,** "She is your mother."
19.27 From that time the **disciple** took her to live in his home.
20. 2 Peter and the other **disciple,** whom Jesus loved, and told them,
20. 3 Then Peter and the other **disciple** went to the tomb.
20. 4 but the other **disciple** ran faster than Peter and reached
20. 8 the other **disciple,** who had reached the tomb first, also went
20.10 Then the **disciples** went back home.
20.18 Magdalene went and told the **disciples** that she had seen the
20.19 and the **disciples** were gathered together behind locked doors,

Jn 20.20 The **disciples** were filled with joy at seeing the Lord.
20.24 One of the twelve **disciples,** Thomas (called the Twin), was not
20.25 So the other **disciples** told him, "We have seen the Lord!"
20.26 A week later the **disciples** were together again indoors,
20.30 In his **disciples'** presence Jesus performed many other miracles
21. 1 Jesus appeared once more to his **disciples** at Lake Tiberias.
21. 2 sons of Zebedee, and two other **disciples** of Jesus were all
21. 4 the water's edge, but the **disciples** did not know that it was
21. 7 The **disciple** whom Jesus loved said to Peter, "It is the Lord!"
21. 8 The other **disciples** came to shore in the boat, pulling the
21.12 None of the **disciples** dared ask him, "Who are you?"
21.14 Jesus appeared to the **disciples** after he was raised from death.
21.20 saw behind him that other **disciple,** whom Jesus loved—the one
21.23 among the followers of Jesus that this **disciple** would not die.
21.24 He is the **disciple** who spoke of these things, the one
Acts 6. 1 as the number of **disciples** kept growing, there was a quarrel
6. 7 The number of **disciples** in Jerusalem grew larger and larger,
9.26 Saul went to Jerusalem and tried to join the **disciples.**
9.26 believe that he was a **disciple,** and they were all afraid of
11.29 The **disciples** decided that each of them would send as
14.21 Barnabas preached the Good News in Derbe and won many **disciples.**
19. 1 he found some **disciples** [2]and asked them, "Did you receive
21.16 Some of the **disciples** from Caesarea also went with us
1 Cor 1.13 Were you baptized as Paul's **disciples?**
1.15 No one can say, then, that you were baptized as my **disciples.**

DISCIPLINE

Deut 8. 5 God corrects and punishes you just as a father **disciplines** his children.
Prov 19.18 **Discipline** your children while they are young enough to learn.
23.13 Don't hesitate to **discipline** a child.
29.15 Correction and **discipline** are good for children.
29.17 **Discipline** your son and you can always be proud of him.
Zeph 3. 2 It has not listened to the Lord or accepted his **discipline.**
3. 7 for me and accept my **discipline,** that they would never forget
1 Cor 9.25 in training submits to strict **discipline,** in order to be crowned
Eph 6. 4 bring them up with Christian **discipline** and instruction.
Tit 1. 8 He must be self-controlled, upright, holy, and **disciplined.**
Heb 12.11 those who have been **disciplined** by such punishment reap the

DISCOURAGE

Num 32. 7 How dare you try to **discourage** the people of Israel
32. 9 they **discouraged** the people from entering the land
Josh 1. 9 Don't be afraid or **discouraged,** for I, the Lord your God,
8. 1 Don't be afraid or **discouraged.**
10.25 Joshua said to his officers, "Don't be afraid or **discouraged.**
2 Sam 17. 2 I will attack him while he is tired and **discouraged.**
2 Chr 15. 7 But you must be strong and not be **discouraged.**
20.15 that you must not be **discouraged** or be afraid
32.18 in order to frighten and **discourage** the people of Jerusalem
Ezra 4. 4 tried to **discourage** and frighten the Jews
Ps 34.18 The Lord is near to those who are **discouraged;**
77. 3 when I meditate, I feel **discouraged.**
Is 8.21 The people will wander through the land, **discouraged**
35. 4 Tell everyone who is **discouraged,** "Be strong
Jer 14. 3 **Discouraged** and confused, they hide their faces.
Ezek 13.22 "By your lies you **discourage** good people,
Hag 2. 4 But now don't be **discouraged,** any of you.
Lk 18. 1 that they should always pray and never become **discouraged.**
2 Cor 4. 1 given us this work to do, and so we are not **discouraged.**
4.16 For this reason we never become **discouraged.**
Eph 3.13 then, not to be **discouraged** because I am suffering for you;
Col 3.21 do not irritate your children, or they will become **discouraged.**
Heb 12. 3 So do not let yourselves become **discouraged** and give up.
12. 5 Lord corrects you, and do not be **discouraged** when he rebukes you.

DISCOVER

Gen 29.25 Not until the next morning did Jacob **discover** that it was Leah.
38.27 to give birth, it was **discovered** that she was going to have
2 Sam 11. 5 Afterwards she **discovered** that she was pregnant
Ezra 4.15 If you do, you will **discover** that this city has always been
Neh 8.14 They **discovered** that the Law, which the Lord gave
13.23 At that time I also **discovered** that many of the Jewish
Esth 2.23 an investigation, and it was **discovered** that the report was true,
Job 11. 7 Can you **discover** the limits and bounds of the greatness
28.10 They **discover** precious stones.
32.13 How can you claim you have **discovered** wisdom?
Ps 36. 2 thinks that God will not **discover** his sin and condemn it.
44.21 you would surely have **discovered** it, because you know
139.23 test me, and **discover** my thoughts.
Ecc 2. 2 I **discovered** that laughter is foolish,
7.24 How can anyone **discover** what life means?
Ezek 21.21 To **discover** which way to go, he shakes the arrows;
Dan 5.15 me what it means, but they could not **discover** the meaning.
Acts 20. 3 to Syria when he **discovered** that the Jews were plotting against

DISCUSS

Prov 24. 7 He has nothing to say when important matters are being **discussed.**
Mt 16. 7 started **discussing** among themselves, "He says this because we
16. 8 "Why are you **discussing** among yourselves about not having any
Mk 8.16 They started **discussing** among themselves:
8.17 asked them, "Why are you **discussing** about not having any bread?
9.10 they started **discussing** the matter, "What does this 'rising
12.28 A teacher of the Law was there who heard the **discussion.**
Lk 6.11 with rage and began to **discuss** among themselves what they could
24.15 they talked and **discussed,** Jesus himself drew near and walked
Acts 4.15 Council room, and then they started **discussing** among themselves.
17. 2 during three Sabbaths he held **discussions** with the people,
17.17 So he held **discussions** in the synagogue with the Jews
18. 4 **discussions** in the synagogue every Sabbath, trying to convince both
18.19 He went into the synagogue and held **discussions** with the Jews.
19. 8 boldly with the people, holding **discussions** with them and trying
19. 9 day he held **discussions** in the lecture hall of Tyrannus.
24.25 But as Paul went on **discussing** about goodness, self-control,
1 Tim 1. 6 away from these and have lost their way in foolish **discussions.**
2 Tim 2.16 profane and foolish **discussions,** which only drive people further

DISEASE

[SKIN-DISEASE]

Gen 12.17 Sarai, the Lord sent terrible **diseases** on him and on the
Ex 4. 6 his hand out, it was **diseased,** covered with white spots,
5. 3 he will kill us with **disease** or by war."
9. 3 by sending a terrible **disease** on all your animals—
9.15 people with **disease,** you would have been completely destroyed.
15.26 with any of the **diseases** that I brought on the Egyptians.
32.35 So the Lord sent a **disease** on the people,
Lev 13. 2 could develop into a dreaded **skin-disease,** he shall be
13. 3 skin, it is a dreaded **skin-disease,** and the priest shall
13. 8 it is a dreaded **skin-disease.**
13. 9 If anyone has a dreaded **skin-disease,** he shall be brought
13.11 white and is full of pus, [11]it is a chronic **skin-disease.**
13.12 If the **skin-disease** spreads and covers the person
13.15 An open sore means a dreaded **skin-disease,**
13.20 It is a dreaded **skin-disease** that has started in the boil.
13.22 he is **diseased.**
13.25 it is a dreaded **skin-disease** that has started in the burn,
13.27 spreading, it is a dreaded **skin-disease,** and the priest
13.28 and is light in colour, it is not a dreaded **skin-disease.**
13.30 thin, it is a dreaded **skin-disease,** and he shall pronounce
13.42 sore appears on the bald spot, it is a dreaded **skin-disease.**
13.44 unclean, because of the dreaded **skin-disease** on his head.
13.45 who has a dreaded **skin-disease** must wear torn clothes,
13.46 long as he has the **disease,** and he must live outside
14. 2 purification of a person cured of a dreaded **skin-disease.**
14. 3 If the **disease** is healed, [4]the priest shall order two ritually
14. 7 to be purified from his **skin-disease,** and then he shall
14.32 man who has a dreaded **skin-disease** but who cannot afford the
14.54 These are the laws about dreaded **skin-diseases;**
21.20 no one with any eye or **skin disease;**
22. 4 Aaron who has a dreaded **skin-disease** or a discharge may eat
26.16 bring disaster on you—incurable **diseases** and fevers
26.25 I will send incurable **diseases** among you,
Num 5. 2 camp everyone with a dreaded **skin disease** or a bodily
12.10 covered with a dreaded **disease** and turned as white as snow.
12.10 she was covered with the **disease,** [11]he said to Moses,
14.36 And so the Lord struck them with a **disease,** and they died.
Deut 7.15 any of the dreadful **diseases** that you experienced in Egypt,
24. 8 are suffering from a dreaded **skin-disease,** be sure to do
28.21 He will send **disease** after disease on you
28.22 The Lord will strike you with infectious **diseases,**
28.59 and on your descendants incurable **diseases** and horrible epidemics
28.60 once again all the dreadful **diseases** you experienced in Egypt,
28.61 also send all kinds of **diseases** and epidemics
32.24 they will die from terrible **diseases.**
2 Sam 3.29 has gonorrhoea or a dreaded **skin disease** or is fit only to
1 Kgs 8.37 enemies, or when there is **disease** or sickness among them,
15.23 But in his old age he was crippled by a foot **disease.**
2 Kgs 5. 1 a great soldier, but he suffered from a dreaded **skin-disease.**
5. 3 He would cure him of his **disease."**
5. 6 I want you to cure him of his **disease."**
5.10 River Jordan, and he would be completely cured of his **disease.**
5.11 his God, wave his hand over the **diseased** spot, and cure me!
5.27 And now Naaman's **disease** will come upon you, and you and
5.27 Gehazi left, he had the **disease**—his skin was as white as
7. 3 a dreaded **skin-disease** were outside the gates of Samaria,
13.14 fell ill with a fatal **disease,** and as he lay dying King
15. 5 struck Uzziah with a dreaded **skin-disease** that stayed with
2 Chr 6.28 or when there is **disease** or sickness among them,
16.12 that Asa was king, he was crippled by a severe foot **disease;**
21.15 yourself will suffer a painful **disease** of the intestines
21.18 Lord brought on the king a painful **disease** of the intestines.
26.19 a dreaded **skin-disease** broke out on his forehead.
26.21 King Uzziah was ritually unclean because of his **disease.**
26.23 burial-ground, but because of his **disease** he was not buried in
Job 18.13 A deadly **disease** spreads over his body
19.26 my skin is eaten by **disease,**
27.15 who survive will die from **disease,**
Ps 38. 3 my whole body is **diseased** because of my sins.
91. 3 safe from all hidden dangers and from all deadly **diseases.**
103. 3 He forgives all my sins and heals all my **diseases.**
106.15 but also sent a terrible **disease** among them.
106.29 and a terrible **disease** broke out among them.
Is 10.16 Almighty is going to send **disease** to punish those
Jer 14.12 I will kill them in war and by starvation and **disease."**
15. 2 are doomed to die by **disease**— that's where they will go!
16. 4 They will die of terrible **diseases,** and no one will mourn
18.21 let the men die of **disease** and the young men be killed
21. 6 people and animals alike will die of a terrible **disease.**
21. 7 war, the famine, and the **disease**—I will let all of you
21. 9 the city will be killed in war or by starvation or **disease.**

Jer 24.10 will bring war, starvation, and **disease** on them
27. 8 by war, starvation, and **disease** until I have let Nebuchadnezzar
27.13 you and your people die in war or of starvation or **disease?**
28. 8 predicted that war, starvation, and **disease** would come
29.17 am bringing war, starvation, and **disease** on them,
29.18 with war, starvation, and **disease,** and all the nations
32.24 War, starvation, and **disease** will make the city fall
32.36 saying that war, starvation, and **disease** will make this city fall
34.17 the freedom to die by war, **disease,** and starvation.
38. 2 in the city will die in war or of starvation or **disease.**
42.17 in Egypt will die either in war or of starvation or **disease.**
42.22 war or of starvation or **disease** in the land where you want
43.11 are doomed to die of **disease** will die of disease, those
44.13 just as I punished Jerusalem—with war, starvation, and **disease.**
44.27 either in war or of **disease,** until not one of you is
Ezek 6.11 They are going to die in war, by famine, and by **disease.**
12.16 the famine, and the **diseases,** so that there among the nations
14.21 famine, wild animals, and **disease**—to destroy people and animals
28.23 I will send **diseases** on you and make blood flow in your
33.27 Those hiding in the mountains and in caves will die of **disease.**
38.22 I will punish him with **disease** and bloodshed.
Hab 3. 5 He sends **disease** before him and commands death to follow him.
Zech 14.12 Lord will bring a terrible **disease** on all the nations that
14.15 A terrible **disease** will also fall on the horses, the mules,
14.18 be struck by the same **disease** that the Lord will send on
Mt 4.23 and healing people who had all kinds of **disease** and sickness.
4.24 sick, suffering from all kinds of **diseases** and disorders:
8. 2 man suffering from a dreaded **skin-disease** came to him, knelt down
8. 3 At once the man was healed of his **disease.**
8.17 "He himself took our sickness and carried away our **diseases."**
9.35 and healed people with every kind of **disease** and sickness.
10. 1 drive out evil spirits and to heal every **disease** and every
10. 8 heal those who suffer from dreaded **skin-diseases,** and drive out demons.
11. 5 those who suffer from dreaded **skin-diseases** are made clean,
26. 6 Simon, a man who had suffered from a dreaded **skin-disease.**
Mk 1.34 sick with all kinds of **diseases** and drove out many demons.
1.40 man suffering from a dreaded **skin-disease** came to Jesus, knelt down,
1.42 At once the **disease** left the man, and he was clean.
14. 3 Simon, a man who had suffered from a dreaded **skin-disease.**
Lk 4.27 people suffering from a dreaded **skin-disease** who lived in Israel
4.40 who were sick with various **diseases** brought them to Jesus;
5.12 there was a man who was suffering from a dreaded **skin-disease.**
5.13 At once the **disease** left the man.
5.15 people came to hear him and be healed from their **diseases.**
6.18 had come to hear him and to be healed of their **diseases.**
7.21 many people of their sicknesses, **diseases,** and evil spirits,
7.22 those who suffer from dreaded **skin-diseases** are made clean,
8. 2 some women who had been healed of evil spirits and **diseases:**
9. 1 and authority to drive out all demons and to cure **diseases.**
17.12 he was met by ten men suffering from a dreaded **skin-disease.**
Acts 19.12 who were ill, and their **diseases** were driven away, and the
1 Cor 12.30 or to heal **diseases** or to speak in strange tongues
Rev 6. 8 to kill by means of war, famine, **disease,** and wild animals.
18. 8 she will be struck with plagues— **disease,** grief, and famine.

DISFIGURED

Lev 21.18 no one who is blind, lame, **disfigured,** or deformed;
Is 52.14 he was so **disfigured** that he hardly looked human.

DISGRACE

Gen 30.23 said, "God has taken away my **disgrace** by giving me a son.
34. 5 that his daughter had been **disgraced,** but because his sons
34.13 Because Shechem had **disgraced** their sister Dinah,
34.14 that would be a **disgrace** for us.
34.27 looted the town to take revenge for their sister's **disgrace.**
Lev 18. 7 Do not **disgrace** your father by having intercourse with your mother.
18. 7 You must not **disgrace** your own mother.
18. 8 Do not **disgrace** your father by having intercourse with any of
18.10 that would be a **disgrace** to you.
18.21 Molech, because that would bring **disgrace** on the name of God,
19.12 that brings **disgrace** on my name.
19.29 "Do not **disgrace** your daughters by making them temple prostitutes;
20. 3 my sacred Tent unclean and **disgraces** my holy name, I will
20.11 one of his father's wives **disgraces** his father, and both he
20.14 to death because of the **disgraceful** thing they have done;
20.17 they shall be publicly **disgraced** and driven out
20.20 with his uncle's wife, he **disgraces** his uncle, and he and
20.21 He has done a ritually unclean thing and has **disgraced** his brother.
21. 6 He must be holy and must not **disgrace** my name.
21. 9 priest's daughter becomes a prostitute, she **disgraces** her father;
22. 2 "You must not bring **disgrace** on my holy name,
22.32 Do not bring **disgrace** on my holy name;
Num 12.14 she would have to bear her **disgrace** for seven days.
Deut 22.19 because the man has brought **disgrace** on an Israelite girl.
22.30 "No man is to **disgrace** his father by having intercourse with
27.20 " 'God's curse on anyone who **disgraces** his father
Josh 5. 9 I have removed from you the **disgrace** of being slaves in Egypt."
1 Sam 11. 2 everyone's right eye and so bring **disgrace** on all Israel."
17.26 who kills this Philistine and frees Israel from this **disgrace?**
20.30 are **disgracing** yourself and that mother of yours!
2 Sam 1.21 For the shields of the brave lie there in **disgrace;**
6.22 dancing to honour the Lord, [22] and will **disgrace** myself even more.
13.13 And you—you would be completely **disgraced** in Israel.
2 Kgs 19. 3 we are being punished and are in **disgrace.**
2 Chr 32.21 So the emperor went back to Assyria **disgraced.**
Ezra 9. 7 We have been totally **disgraced,** as we still are today.
Neh 2.17 Let's rebuild the city walls and put an end to our **disgrace."**
Job 8.22 but he will bring **disgrace** on those who hate you,
12.21 He **disgraces** those in power
14.21 he never knows it, nor is he told when they are **disgraced.**
36.14 while they are still young, worn out by a life of **disgrace.**
42. 8 I will answer his prayer and not **disgrace** you as you deserve.
Ps 31.17 don't let me be **disgraced.**
31.17 May the wicked be **disgraced;**
35. 4 May those who try to kill me be defeated and **disgraced!**
35.26 to be better than I am be covered with shame and **disgrace.**
40.14 happy because of my troubles be turned back and **disgraced.**
44.15 I am always in **disgrace;**
69. 6 Don't let me bring **disgrace** to those who worship you, O God
69.19 You know how I am insulted, how I am **disgraced**
70. 2 happy because of my troubles be turned back and **disgraced.**
71.13 May those who try to hurt me be shamed and **disgraced.**
71.24 who tried to harm me have been defeated and **disgraced.**
83.17 may they die in complete **disgrace.**
89.45 made him old before his time and covered him with **disgrace.**
109.29 May my enemies be covered with **disgrace;**
Prov 3.35 but stupid men will only add to their own **disgrace.**
5.14 And suddenly I found myself publicly **disgraced."**
6.33 he will be permanently **disgraced.**
10. 5 it is a **disgrace** to sleep through the time of harvest.
11. 2 People who are proud will soon be **disgraced.**
11.16 is respected, but a woman without virtue is a **disgrace.**
13. 5 the words of wicked people are shameful and **disgraceful.**
13.18 Someone who will not learn will be poor and **disgraced.**
14.34 sin is a **disgrace** to any nation.
19.22 It is a **disgrace** to be greedy;
19.26 Only a shameful, **disgraceful** person would ill-treat his father
28. 7 One who makes friends with good-for-nothings is a **disgrace**
30. 9 I am poor, I might steal and bring **disgrace** on my God.
Is 2. 9 Everyone will be humiliated and **disgraced.**
5.15 Everyone will be **disgraced,** and all who are proud
9. 1 Zebulun and Naphtali was once **disgraced,**
17. 3 Syrians who survive will be in **disgrace** like the people of Israel.
22.18 You are a **disgrace** to your master's household.
23. 4 City of Sidon, you are **disgraced!**
25. 8 eyes and take away the **disgrace** his people have suffered
29.22 you will not be **disgraced** any longer,
37. 3 we are being punished and are in **disgrace.**
42.17 who call images their gods, will be humiliated and **disgraced."**
44. 9 gods are blind and ignorant—and they will be **disgraced.**
44.11 trial—they will be terrified and will suffer **disgrace.**
45.16 all of them will be **disgraced.**
45.17 her people will never be **disgraced.'"**
45.24 but all who hate me will suffer **disgrace.**
50. 7 that I will not be **disgraced,** [8] for God is near, and he
54. 4 Do not be afraid—you will not be **disgraced** again;
61. 7 Your shame and **disgrace** are ended.
65.13 They will be happy, but you will be **disgraced.**
66. 5 But they themselves will be **disgraced!**
Jer 2.26 "Just as a thief is **disgraced** when caught, so all you
2.26 people of Israel will be **disgraced**—your kings and officials,
2.27 You will all be **disgraced**—you that say that a tree is
3.25 We should lie down in shame and let our **disgrace** cover us.
9.19 We are completely **disgraced!**
14.21 do not bring **disgrace** on Jerusalem,
15. 9 she is **disgraced** and sick at heart.
17.18 Bring **disgrace** on those who persecute me, but spare me,
20.11 They will be **disgraced** for ever, because they cannot succeed.
20.11 Their **disgrace** will never be forgotten.
20.18 to have trouble and sorrow, to end my life in **disgrace?**
22.22 prisoners of war, your city **disgraced** and put to shame
23.40 bring on them everlasting shame and **disgrace**
31.19 We were ashamed and **disgraced,** because we sinned
48.20 it is **disgraced.**
48.39 Moab has been **disgraced.**
50.12 but your own great city will be humiliated and **disgraced.**
51.51 You say, 'We've been **disgraced** and made ashamed;
Lam 2. 2 He brought **disgrace** on the kingdom and its rulers.
5. 1 Look at us, and see our **disgrace.**
Ezek 6. 9 I have punished them and **disgraced** them,
7.18 Their heads will be shaved, and they will all be **disgraced.**
8. 6 You will see even more **disgraceful** things than this."
16.52 And now you will have to endure your **disgrace.**
16.54 ashamed of yourself, and your **disgrace** will show your sisters
20.43 you will remember all the **disgraceful** things you did
32.24 In life they spread terror, but now they lie dead and **disgraced.**
32.25 now they lie dead and **disgraced,** sharing the fate of those
32.30 now they go down in **disgrace** with those killed in battle
32.30 They share the **disgrace** of those who go down to the world
36.20 Wherever they went, they brought **disgrace** on my holy name,
36.21 holy name, since the Israelites brought **disgrace** on it
36.22 holy name, which you have **disgraced** in every country
36.23 great name—the name you **disgraced** among them—then they will
36.30 will be no more famines to **disgrace** you among the nations.
36.32 you to feel the shame and **disgrace** of what you are doing.
39. 7 name, and I will not let my name be **disgraced** any more.
39.26 to forget how they were **disgraced** for having betrayed me.
43. 7 their kings will ever again **disgrace** my holy name
43. 8 They **disgraced** my holy name by all the disgusting things they did,
Dan 5.19 He honoured or **disgraced** anyone he wanted to.
9. 7 but we have always brought **disgrace** on ourselves.
12. 2 enjoy eternal life, and some will suffer eternal **disgrace.**
Hos 4. 7 against me, and so I will turn your honour into **disgrace.**

Hos 4.18 they delight in their prostitution, preferring **disgrace** to honour.
10. 6 Israel will be **disgraced** and put to shame because of the
12.14 Lord will punish them for the **disgrace** they have brought on him.
Mic 2. 6 God is not going to **disgrace** us.
3. 7 Those who predict the future will be **disgraced** by their failure.
7.10 will see this and be **disgraced**—the same enemies who taunted
Hab 2.15 In your fury you humiliated and **disgraced** your neighbours;
2.16 of punishment, and your honour will be turned to **disgrace.**
Zeph 3.18 "I have ended the threat of doom and taken away your **disgrace.**
Mt 1.19 was right, but he did not want to **disgrace** Mary publicly;
Lk 1.25 "He has taken away my public **disgrace!"**
Acts 5.41 considered them worthy to suffer **disgrace** for the sake of Jesus.
1 Cor 11. 4 message in public worship with his head covered **disgraces** Christ.
11. 5 public worship with nothing on her head **disgraces** her husband;
11.14 on a man is a **disgrace,** [15] but on a woman it is
14.35 It is a **disgraceful** thing for a woman to speak in church.
2 Cor 6. 8 We are honoured and **disgraced;**
1 Tim 3. 7 he will not be **disgraced** and fall into the Devil's trap.
Heb 12. 2 he thought nothing of the **disgrace** of dying on the cross,
2 Pet 2.13 are a shame and a **disgrace** as they join you in your

DISGUISE

1 Sam 28. 8 So Saul **disguised** himself;
1 Kgs 14. 2 Jeroboam said to his wife, **"Disguise** yourself
20.38 face with a cloth, to **disguise** himself, and went and stood
22.30 go into battle, I will **disguise** myself, but you wear your
22.30 So the king of Israel went into battle in **disguise.**
2 Chr 18.29 go into battle, I will **disguise** myself, but you wear your
18.29 So the king of Israel went into battle in **disguise.**
35.22 through King Neco, so he **disguised** himself and went into battle
Prov 26.26 He may **disguise** his hatred,
2 Cor 11.13 about their work and **disguise** themselves to look like real apostles
11.14 Even Satan can **disguise** himself to look like an angel of light!
11.15 if his servants **disguise** themselves to look like servants of

DISGUST

Lev 18.26 They did all these **disgusting** things
18.29 whoever does any of these **disgusting** things will no longer
20.13 they have done a **disgusting** thing,
20.23 They have **disgusted** me with all their evil practices.
26.30 In utter **disgust** [31] I will turn your cities into ruins,
Deut 12.31 they do all the **disgusting** things that the Lord hates.
18. 9 don't follow the **disgusting** practices of the nations
18.12 hates people who do these **disgusting** things,
20.18 you to do all the **disgusting** things that they do
29.17 You saw their **disgusting** idols made of wood, stone, silver,
2 Sam 6.16 in the sacred dance, and she was **disgusted** with him.
1 Kgs 11. 5 and Molech the **disgusting** god of Ammon.
11. 7 place to worship Chemosh, the **disgusting** god of Moab,
11. 7 and a place to worship Molech, the **disgusting** god of Ammon.
2 Kgs 16. 3 burnt-offering to idols, imitating the **disgusting** practice
21. 2 Following the **disgusting** practices of the nations
21.11 "King Manasseh has done these **disgusting** things,
23.13 for the worship of **disgusting** idols—
1 Chr 15.29 dancing and leaping for joy, and she was **disgusted** with him.
2 Chr 28. 3 burnt-offerings to idols, imitating the **disgusting** practice
33. 2 Following the **disgusting** practices of the nations
34.33 King Josiah destroyed all the **disgusting** idols
36. 8 Jehoiakim did, including his **disgusting** practices and the evil
Ezra 9. 1 They were doing the same **disgusting** things that those people did.
9.11 from one end to the other with **disgusting,** filthy actions.
Job 19.19 My closest friends look at me with **disgust;**
30.10 They treat me with **disgust;**
Ps 95.10 For forty years I was **disgusted** with those people.
106.40 he was **disgusted** with them.
119.158 I am filled with **disgust,** because they do not keep
Is 1.13 I am **disgusted** with the smell of the incense you burn.
41.24 those who worship you are **disgusting!**
66. 3 They take pleasure in **disgusting** ways of worship.
66.17 and who eat pork and mice and other **disgusting** foods.
66.24 The sight of them will be **disgusting** to all mankind."
Jer 6.15 Were they ashamed because they did these **disgusting** things?
8.12 were you ashamed because you did these **disgusting** things?
11.13 altars for sacrifices to that **disgusting** god Baal
32.34 They even placed their **disgusting** idols in the Temple
50. 2 idols are put to shame, her **disgusting** images are crushed!
Ezek 5.11 Temple with all the evil, **disgusting** things you did,
5.15 They will look at you with **disgust** and will mock you.
6. 9 And they will be **disgusted** with themselves because of the evil
6.11 all the evil, **disgusting** things the Israelites have done.
7. 3 I will pay you back for all your **disgusting** conduct.
7. 4 to punish you for the **disgusting** things you have done,
7. 8 and I will pay you back for all your **disgusting** conduct.
7. 9 to punish you for the **disgusting** things you have done,
7.20 beautiful jewels, but they used them to make **disgusting** idols.
8. 6 Look at the **disgusting** things the people of Israel are doing
8. 9 look at the evil, **disgusting** things they are doing there."
8.13 to see them do even more **disgusting** things than that."
8.15 You will see even more **disgusting** things."
8.17 with merely doing all the **disgusting** things you have seen
9. 4 because of all the **disgusting** things being done in the city."
11.18 to get rid of all the filthy, **disgusting** idols they find.
11.21 the people who love to worship filthy, **disgusting** idols.
12.16 they will realize how **disgusting** their actions have been
14. 6 Turn back and leave your **disgusting** idols.
16. 2 "point out to Jerusalem what **disgusting** things she has done.
16.22 During your **disgusting** life as a prostitute you never once
16.27 the Philistines, who hate you and are **disgusted**
16.36 to all your **disgusting** idols, and you killed your children
Ezek 16.43 you add sexual immorality to all the other **disgusting** things
16.47 to follow in their footsteps and copy their **disgusting** actions?
16.51 You have acted more **disgustingly** than she ever did.
16.58 You must suffer for the obscene, **disgusting** things
18.12 goes to pagan shrines, worships **disgusting** idols,
18.13 He has done all these **disgusting** things, and so he will die.
18.24 starts doing all the evil, **disgusting** things that evil men do,
20. 4 Remind them of the **disgusting** things their fathers did.
20. 7 them to throw away the **disgusting** idols they loved
20. 8 did not throw away their **disgusting** idols
20.43 You will be **disgusted** with yourselves because of all the evil
22. 2 Make clear to her all the **disgusting** things she has done.
23.17 so much that finally she became **disgusted** with them.
23.18 I was as **disgusted** with her as I had been with her
23.28 hand you over to people you hate and are **disgusted** with.
23.36 Accuse them of the **disgusting** things they have done.
33.26 Your actions are **disgusting.**
36.31 and you will be **disgusted** with yourselves because of your sins
37.23 will not defile themselves with **disgusting** idols any more
43. 8 holy name by all the **disgusting** things they did,
44. 6 will no longer tolerate the **disgusting** things
44. 7 broken my covenant by all the **disgusting** things they have done.
44.13 This is the punishment for the **disgusting** things they have done.
Hos 9.10 and soon became as **disgusting** as the gods they loved.
1 Pet 4. 3 orgies, drinking parties, and the **disgusting** worship of idols.

DISH

Ex 37.16 He made the **dishes** of pure gold for the table:
Num 4. 7 put on it the **dishes,** the incense bowls, the offering bowls,
7.12 one gold **dish** weighing 110 grammes, full of incense;
7.84 twelve gold **dishes** weighing a total of 1.32 kilogrammes,
1 Kgs 7.50 the cups, lamp snuffers, bowls, **dishes** for incense,
1 Chr 28.17 silver and gold in making **dishes,**
2 Chr 4.22 lamp snuffers, the bowls, the **dishes** for incense,
Mt 14. 8 here and now the head of John the Baptist on a **dish!"**
14.11 was brought in on a **dish** and given to the girl,
26.23 who dips his bread in the **dish** with me will betray me.
Mk 6.25 here and now the head of John the Baptist on a **dish!"**
6.28 he brought it on a **dish** and gave it to the girl,
14.20 you twelve, one who dips his bread in the **dish** with me.
2 Tim 2.20 In a large house there are **dishes** and bowls of all kinds:

DISHONEST

Lev 6. 4 ways, he must repay whatever he got by **dishonest** means.
Ps 101. 4 I will not be **dishonest,** and will have no dealings with evil.
Prov 10. 2 Wealth that you get by **dishonesty** will do you no good,
10. 9 safe and secure, but the **dishonest** will be caught.
11. 1 The Lord hates people who use **dishonest** scales.
11. 3 People who can't be trusted are destroyed by their own **dishonesty.**
14. 2 be **dishonest** and you show that you do not.
15.27 try to make a profit **dishonestly,** you will get your family
16. 8 honestly earned, than to have a large income gained **dishonestly.**
20.10 The Lord hates people who use **dishonest** weights and measures.
20.17 What you get by **dishonesty** you may enjoy like the finest food,
20.23 The Lord hates people who use **dishonest** scales and weights.
21. 6 The riches you get by **dishonesty** soon disappear,
28. 6 Better to be poor and honest than rich and **dishonest.**
28.16 One who hates **dishonesty** will rule a long time.
28.18 If you are **dishonest,** you will suddenly fall.
Jer 6.13 Everyone, great and small, tries to make money **dishonestly;**
8. 8 Look, the laws have been changed by **dishonest** scribes.
8.10 Everyone, great and small, tries to make money **dishonestly.**
9. 3 **dishonesty** instead of truth rules the land.
12. 1 Why do **dishonest** men succeed?
17.11 The person who gets money **dishonestly** is like a bird
22.13 his house by injustice and enlarges it by **dishonesty;**
Dan 6. 4 Daniel was reliable and did not do anything wrong or **dishonest.**
Hos 12. 7 "The people of Israel are as **dishonest** as the Canaanites;
12. 8 And no one can accuse us of getting rich **dishonestly.'**
Mic 6.10 houses of evil men are treasures which they got **dishonestly.**
Lk 16. 8 the master of this **dishonest** manager praised him for doing such
16.10 whoever is **dishonest** in small matters
16.10 will be **dishonest** in large ones.
18.11 am not greedy, **dishonest,** or an adulterer, like everybody else.

DISHONOUR

Gen 49. 4 you slept with my concubine And **dishonoured** your father's bed.
Deut 27.16 " 'God's curse on anyone who **dishonours** his father or mother.'
32.51 the wilderness of Zin, you **dishonoured** me in the presence
Ps 69.19 You know how I am insulted, how I am disgraced and **dishonoured;**
Prov 6.33 He will be **dishonoured** and beaten up;
Is 48.11 not let my name be **dishonoured** or let anyone else share
Jer 34.16 But then you changed your minds again and **dishonoured** me.
Ezek 13.19 You **dishonour** me in front of my people
20. 9 since that would have brought **dishonour** to my name,
20.14 that would have brought **dishonour** to my name among the nations
20.22 that would have brought **dishonour** to my name among the nations
20.39 to obey me and stop **dishonouring** my holy name by offering
22.16 so the other nations will **dishonour** you,
Amos 2. 1 They **dishonoured** the bones of the king of Edom by burning
Obad 10 you will be destroyed and **dishonoured** for ever.
Mal 1.12 But you **dishonour** me when you say that my altar is
Jn 8.49 "I honour my Father, but you **dishonour** me.
1 Cor 11.27 cup in a way that **dishonours** him, he is guilty of sin
Jas 2. 6 But you **dishonour** the poor!

DISILLUSIONED

Is 20. 5 boasted about Egypt will be **disillusioned,** their hopes shattered.
Jer 10.14 those who make idols are **disillusioned,**
48.13 Then the Moabites will be **disillusioned** with their god Chemosh,
48.13 just as the Israelites were **disillusioned** with Bethel,
51.17 those who make idols are **disillusioned**

DISINFECT

Job 18.15 in his tent— after sulphur is sprinkled to **disinfect** it!

DISLOYAL

Josh 23.12 If you are **disloyal** and join with the nations
2 Chr 12. 2 their **disloyalty** to the Lord was punished.
Ps 44.18 We have not been **disloyal** to you;
78.57 but were rebellious and **disloyal** like their fathers,
95.10 I said, 'How **disloyal** they are!
Hos 7. 4 They are all treacherous and **disloyal.**
2 Cor 10. 6 we will be ready to punish any act of **disloyalty.**
Heb 3.10 'They are always **disloyal** and refuse to obey my commands.'

DISMAL

Ecc 12. 1 are still young, before those **dismal** days and years come

DISMAY

2 Kgs 5. 7 he tore his clothes in **dismay** and exclaimed, "How can the
6.30 king tore his clothes in **dismay,** and the people who were
22.11 he tore his clothes in **dismay,** [12]and gave the following order
2 Chr 34.19 he tore his clothes in **dismay** [20]and gave the following order
Ps 40.15 May those who jeer at me be **dismayed** by their defeat.
70. 3 May those who jeer at me be **dismayed** by their defeat.
Is 23. 5 Egyptians will be shocked and **dismayed** when they learn that Tyre
Jer 8.21 I am completely **dismayed.**
Mic 7.16 In **dismay** they will close their mouths and cover their ears.

DISMISS

1 Kgs 2.27 Then Solomon **dismissed** Abiathar from serving as a priest
2 Chr 23. 8 The men were not **dismissed** when they went off duty
Lk 16. 3 to himself, 'My master is going to **dismiss** me from my job.
Acts 19.41 After saying this, he **dismissed** the meeting.

DISMOUNT

1 Sam 25.23 Abigail saw David, she quickly **dismounted**

DISOBEY

Lev 16. 2 If he **disobeys,** he will be killed.
22. 9 die, because they have **disobeyed** the sacred regulations.
Num 14.41 But Moses said, "Then why are you **disobeying** the Lord now?
22.18 his palace, I could not **disobey** the command of the Lord
24.13 your palace, I could not **disobey** the command of the Lord
Deut 4.26 you today that, if you **disobey** me, you will soon disappear
5.32 Do not **disobey** any of his laws.
9.16 saw that you had already **disobeyed** the command that the Lord
11.28 but a curse, if you **disobey** these commands and turn away
17.12 Anyone who dares to **disobey** either the judge or the priest
17.20 and from **disobeying** the Lord's commands in any way.
26.13 I have not **disobeyed** or forgotten any of your commands
28.14 But you must never **disobey** them in any way, or worship
28.15 "But if you **disobey** the Lord your God
30.17 But if you **disobey** and refuse to listen, and are led
Josh 1.18 questions your authority or **disobeys** any of your orders
5. 4 they left Egypt had died because they had **disobeyed** the Lord.
7. 1 A man named Achan **disobeyed** that order,
22.23 If we **disobeyed** the Lord and built our own altar to burn
1 Sam 12.15 listen to the Lord but **disobey** his commands, he will be
13.14 Because you have **disobeyed** him, the Lord will find the kind
15.11 he has turned away from me and **disobeyed** my commands."
15.24 "I **disobeyed** the Lord's command and your instructions.
28.18 You **disobeyed** the Lord's command and did not completely
2 Sam 12. 9 Why, then, have you **disobeyed** my commands?
12.10 death because you have **disobeyed** me and have taken Uriah's wife.
18.13 But if I had **disobeyed** the king and killed Absalom,
22.23 I have not **disobeyed** his commands.
1 Kgs 2.43 broken your promise and **disobeyed** my command?
9. 6 stop following me, if you **disobey** the laws and commands I
11.11 your covenant with me and **disobeyed** my commands,
11.33 Solomon has **disobeyed** me;
13.21 "The Lord says that you **disobeyed** him
13.26 "That is the prophet who **disobeyed** the Lord's command!
15. 5 pleased him and had never **disobeyed** any of his commands,
18.18 You are **disobeying** the Lord's commands and worshipping the idols
20.36 "Because you have **disobeyed** the Lord's command, a lion will
2 Kgs 17.12 and **disobeyed** the Lord's command not to worship
17.15 of the surrounding nations, **disobeying** the Lord's command
18. 6 to the Lord and never **disobeyed** him, but carefully kept all
18.12 made with them and **disobeyed** all the laws given by Moses,
21.22 the God of his ancestors, and **disobeyed** the Lord's commands.
1 Chr 10.13 He **disobeyed** the Lord's commands;
2 Chr 7.19 you and your people ever **disobey** the laws and commands I
24.20 God asks why you have **disobeyed** his commands
Ezra 6.11 further command that if anyone **disobeys** this order,
Ezra 7.26 If anyone **disobeys** the laws of your God
9.10 We have again **disobeyed** the commands [11]that you gave us
Neh 9.26 "But your people rebelled and **disobeyed** you;
13.27 your example and **disobey** our God by marrying foreign women?"
Esth 3. 3 asked him why he was **disobeying** the king's command;
Ps 18.22 I have not **disobeyed** his commands.
44.18 we have not **disobeyed** your commands.
78. 8 their ancestors, a rebellious and **disobedient** people,
89.30 "But if his descendants **disobey** my law
119.10 keep me from **disobeying** your commandments.
119.21 cursed are those who **disobey** your commands.
119.110 lay a trap for me, but I have not **disobeyed** your commands.
119.118 You reject everyone who **disobeys** your laws;
119.126 for you to act, because people are **disobeying** your law.
148. 6 fixed in their places for ever, and they cannot **disobey.**
Is 65.12 You chose to **disobey** me and do evil.
66. 4 They chose to **disobey** me and do evil."
Jer 18.10 but then that nation **disobeys** me and does evil,
23.38 And if they **disobey** my command and use the words 'the
26. 6 If you continue to **disobey,** then I will do to this Temple
34.17 So now, I, the Lord, say that you have **disobeyed** me:
40. 3 because your people sinned against the Lord and **disobeyed** him.
42.13 left in Judah must not **disobey** the Lord your God and refuse
42.21 told you, but you are **disobeying** everything that the Lord
43. 7 They **disobeyed** the Lord's command and went into Egypt
Lam 1.18 "But the Lord is just, for I have **disobeyed** him.
Ezek 5. 6 more **disobedient** than the countries around her.
11.12 you were breaking my laws and **disobeying** my commands."
44. 9 no one who **disobeys** me, will enter my Temple,
Dan 3.12 Shadrach, Meshach, and Abednego—who are **disobeying** Your Majesty's
3.28 They **disobeyed** my orders and risked their lives rather than bow
Mt 5.19 whoever **disobeys** even the least important of the commandments
15. 2 that your disciples **disobey** the teaching handed down by our
15. 3 "And why do you **disobey** God's command and follow your own
Lk 1.17 he will turn **disobedient** people back to the way of thinking
12.46 in pieces and make him share the fate of the **disobedient.**
15.29 you like a slave, and I have never **disobeyed** your orders.
Jn 3.36 whoever **disobeys** the Son will not have life, but will remain
Acts 26.19 King Agrippa, I did not **disobey** the vision I had from heaven.
Rom 1.30 they **disobey** their parents;
2.25 but if you **disobey** the Law, you might as well never have
4.15 where there is no law, there is no **disobeying** of the law.
5.14 the same way that Adam did when he **disobeyed** God's command.
5.19 as the result of the **disobedience** of one man, in the same
10.21 held out my hands to welcome a **disobedient** and rebellious people."
11.30 As for you Gentiles, you **disobeyed** God in the past;
11.30 you have received God's mercy because the Jews were **disobedient.**
11.31 the Jews now **disobey** God, in order that they also
11.32 made all people prisoners of **disobedience,** so that he might show
Eph 2. 1 you were spiritually dead because of your **disobedience** and sins.
2. 2 the spirit who now controls the people who **disobey** God.
2. 5 were spiritually dead in our **disobedience** he brought us to life
2 Tim 3. 2 they will be insulting, **disobedient** to their parents, ungrateful,
Tit 1. 6 and not have the reputation of being wild or **disobedient.**
1.16 They are hateful and **disobedient,** not fit to do anything good.
3. 3 For we ourselves were once foolish, **disobedient,** and
Heb 10.28 Anyone who **disobeys** the Law of Moses is put to death
11.23 and they were not afraid to **disobey** the king's order.
11.31 killed with those who **disobeyed** God, for she gave the Israelite

DISORDER

2 Chr 15. 5 because there was trouble and **disorder** in every land.
Amos 3. 9 see the great **disorder** and the crimes being committed there."
Mt 4.24 who were sick, suffering from all kinds of diseases and **disorders:**
Acts 24.18 There was no crowd with me and no **disorder.**
1 Cor 14.33 not want us to be in **disorder** but in harmony and peace.
2 Cor 12.20 and selfishness, insults and gossip, pride and **disorder.**
Jas 3.16 and selfishness, there is also **disorder** and every kind of evil.

DISOWN

Is 23. 4 and the great ocean depths **disown** you and say, "I never had

DISPEL

2 Sam 22.29 you **dispel** my darkness.
Ps 18.28 you **dispel** my darkness.

AV DISPENSATION

1 Cor 9.17 matter of duty, because God has entrusted me with this **task.**
Eph 1.10 This **plan,** which God will complete when the time is right,
3. 2 heard that God in his **grace** has given me this work to
Col 1.25 by God, who gave me this **task** to perform for your good.

DISPERSE

Gen 49. 7 I will **disperse** them among its people.

DISPLAY

Esth 9.14 The bodies of Haman's ten sons were publicly **displayed.**
Dan 4.30 as my capital city to **display** my power and might, my glory

DISPLEASE

Gen 38. 7 conduct was evil, and it **displeased** the Lord, so the Lord
38.10 What he did **displeased** the Lord, and the Lord killed him also.
Num 11.11 Why are you **displeased** with me?
32.13 until that whole generation that had **displeased** him was dead.
1 Sam 8. 6 Samuel was **displeased** with their request for a king;
15.19 to seize the loot, and so do what **displeases** the Lord?"
29. 7 and don't do anything that would **displease** them."
1 Kgs 16.19 Like his predecessor Jeroboam he **displeased** the Lord
1 Chr 21. 7 God was **displeased** with what had been done,
2 Chr 29. 6 to the Lord our God and did what was **displeasing** to him.
Ezra 8.22 but that he is **displeased** with and punishes anyone who turns
Ps 85. 4 O God our saviour, and stop being **displeased** with us!
Is 59.15 and he is **displeased** that there is no justice.
Jer 32.30 the people of Judah have **displeased** me and made me angry
1 Thes 2.15 How **displeasing** they are to God!

DISPROVE

Job 32.12 you have not **disproved** what Job has said.
Prov 22.12 that truth is kept safe by **disproving** the words of liars.

DISPUTE

Gen 26.22 There was no **dispute** about this one, so he named it "Freedom."
Ex 18.13 next day Moses was settling **disputes** among the people,
18.16 When two people have a **dispute,** they come to me, and I
18.19 represent the people before God and bring their **disputes** to him.
18.22 but they themselves can decide all the smaller **disputes.**
18.23 and all these people can go home with their **disputes** settled."
18.26 but deciding the smaller **disputes** themselves.
22. 9 "In every case of a **dispute** about property,
24.14 and so whoever has a **dispute** to settle can go to them."
Deut 1.12 I alone bear the heavy responsibility for settling your **disputes?**
1.16 'Listen to the **disputes** that come up among your people.
1.16 Judge every **dispute** fairly, whether it concerns only your own
25. 1 to court to settle a **dispute,** and one is declared innocent
Judg 18. 7 They were a peaceful, quiet people, with no **disputes** with anyone;
1 Sam 7. 6 at Mizpah that Samuel settled **disputes** among the Israelites.)
7.16 and in these places he would settle **disputes.**
2 Sam 15. 2 someone came there with a **dispute** that he wanted the king to
15. 4 Then anyone who had a **dispute** or a claim could come to
1 Kgs 3.28 God had given him the wisdom to settle **disputes** fairly.
1 Chr 23. 4 to keep records and decide **disputes,**
26.29 records and settling **disputes** for the people of Israel.
2 Chr 19. 8 or legal **disputes** between inhabitants of the city.
Job 13. 3 But my **dispute** is with God, not you;
Is 2. 4 He will settle **disputes** among great nations.
Ezek 18. 8 to do evil and gives an honest decision in any **dispute.**
44.24 When a legal **dispute** arises, the priests are to decide
Mic 4. 3 He will settle **disputes** among the nations,
Mt 5.25 to court, settle the **dispute** with him while there is time,
Lk 12.58 your best to settle the **dispute** with him before you get to
Acts 9.29 He also talked and **disputed** with the Greek-speaking Jews,
13.45 they **disputed** what Paul was saying and insulted him.
26. 3 since you know so well all the Jewish customs and **disputes.**
1 Cor 6. 1 one of you has a **dispute** with a fellow-Christian, how dare
6. 5 wise person in your fellowship who can settle a **dispute** between
6. 7 fact that you have legal **disputes** among yourselves shows that
1 Tim 6. 4 and this brings on jealousy, **disputes,** insults, evil suspicions,

DISQUALIFY

1 Cor 9.27 keep myself from being **disqualified** after having called others

DISREGARD

2 Kgs 17.15 made with their ancestors, and they **disregarded** his warnings.
Ps 89.31 if they **disregard** my instructions
119.139 because my enemies **disregard** your commands.
Ezek 21.10 be no rejoicing, for my people have **disregarded** every warning
Zech 1. 6 warnings, but they **disregarded** them and suffered the consequences.
Mt 15. 6 In this way you **disregard** God's command, in order to follow

DISRESPECT

1 Sam 2.17 because they treated the offerings to the Lord with such **disrespect.**
2 Kgs 19.22 You have been **disrespectful** to me, the holy God of Israel.
Is 37.23 You have been **disrespectful** to me, the holy God of Israel.
Dan 3.29 speaks **disrespectfully** of the God of Shadrach, Meshach,

DISSATISFY

1 Sam 22. 2 oppressed or in debt or **dissatisfied** went to him,

DISSOLVE

Ps 46. 6 God thunders, and the earth **dissolves.**
58. 8 May they be like snails that **dissolve** into slime;

DISTANCE

Gen 22. 4 On the third day Abraham saw the place in the **distance.**
35.16 when they were still some **distance** from Ephrath,
37.18 They saw him in the **distance,** and before he reached them,
44. 4 had gone only a short **distance** from the city, Joseph said to
Ex 2. 4 The baby's sister stood some **distance** away to see
24. 1 while you are still some **distance** away, bow down in worship.
Ex 33. 7 sacred Tent and put it up some **distance** away from the camp.
Deut 19. 6 were only one city, the **distance** to it might be too great,
21. 2 go out and measure the **distance** from the place where the
29.22 and foreigners from **distant** lands will see the disasters
32.52 at the land from a **distance,** but you will not enter
Josh 9. 6 and the men of Israel, "We have come from a **distant** land.
9. 9 have come from a very **distant** land, sir, because we have
Judg 18.22 They had travelled a good **distance** from the house
1 Sam 26.13 a safe **distance** away, [14]and shouted to Saul's troops
1 Kgs 6.24 so that the **distance** from one wing-tip to the other
8.41 foreigner who lives in a **distant** land hears of your fame and
2 Kgs 2. 7 and the fifty prophets stood a short **distance** away.
4.25 while she was still some **distance** away, and said to his
5.19 had gone only a short **distance,** [20]when Elisha's servant Gehazi
14.13 to the Corner Gate, a **distance** of nearly two hundred metres.
20.14 Hezekiah answered, "They came from a very **distant** country,
2 Chr 6.32 foreigner who lives in a **distant** land hears how great
25.23 to the Corner Gate, a **distance** of nearly two hundred metres.
Neh 4.19 spread out over such a **distance** that we are widely separated
Job 36.25 but we can only watch from a **distance.**
Ps 65. 5 over the world and across the **distant** seas trust in you.
Prov 25.25 hearing good news from a **distant** land is like a drink of
Is 5.26 The Lord gives a signal to call for a **distant** nation.
8. 9 Listen, you **distant** parts of the earth.
10. 3 do when he brings disaster on you from a **distant** country?
24.16 From the most **distant** parts of the world we will hear
30.27 The Lord's power and glory can be seen in the **distance.**
39. 3 Hezekiah answered, "They came from a very **distant** country,
40.15 the **distant** islands are as light as dust.
41. 1 "Be silent and listen to me, you **distant** lands!
41. 5 "The people of **distant** lands have seen what I have done;
42. 4 **Distant** lands eagerly wait for his teaching."
42.10 Sing, **distant** lands and all who live there!
42.12 Let those who live in **distant** lands give praise and glory
43. 5 "From the **distant** east and the farthest west,
43. 6 Let my people return from **distant** lands,
49. 1 Listen to me, **distant** nations, you people who live far away!
51. 5 **Distant** lands wait for me to come;
59.18 what they have done, even those who live in **distant** lands.
60. 9 They are ships coming from **distant** lands,
66.19 to the nations and the **distant** lands that have not heard of
Jer 6.20 they bring me from Sheba, or the spices from a **distant** land?
30.10 will rescue you from that **distant** land,
46.27 will rescue you from that **distant** land,
Ezek 5.14 you who passes by will sneer at you and keep his **distance.**
12.27 visions and prophecies are about the **distant** future.
23.40 invite men to come from a great **distance,** and the men came.
40.13 Then he measured the **distance** from the back wall of one
40.19 The man measured the **distance** between the two gateways,
40.23 The man measured the **distance** between these two gateways,
40.27 The man measured the **distance** to this second gateway,
41.13 the **distance** was also fifty metres.
41.14 The **distance** across the front of the Temple,
Mic 7.12 from the region of the Euphrates, from **distant** seas
Hab 1. 8 Their horsemen come riding from **distant** lands;
Zeph 3.10 from **distant** Sudan my scattered people will bring offerings
Mt 26.58 Peter followed from a **distance,** as far as the courtyard
27.55 looking on from a **distance,** who had followed Jesus from Galilee
Mk 5. 6 He was some **distance** away when he saw Jesus;
11.13 He saw in the **distance** a fig-tree covered with leaves,
14.54 Peter followed from a **distance** and went into the courtyard
15.40 Some women were there, looking on from a **distance.**
Lk 17.12 They stood at a **distance** [13]and shouted, "Jesus!
18.13 tax collector stood at a **distance** and would not even raise
22.41 off from them about the **distance** of a stone's throw and
22.54 and Peter followed at a **distance.**
23.49 followed him from Galilee, stood at a **distance** to watch.
2 Tim 4. 7 I have run the full **distance,** and I have kept the faith.

DISTINCT

1 Cor 14. 7 tune that is being played unless the notes are sounded **distinctly?**

DISTINGUISH

Ex 8.23 I will make a **distinction** between my people and your people.
9. 4 I will make a **distinction** between the animals of the Israelites
11. 7 make a **distinction** between the Egyptians and the Israelites.' "
33.16 Your presence with us will **distinguish** us from any other people
Lev 10.10 You must **distinguish** between what belongs to God and what
11.47 You must be careful to **distinguish** between what is ritually
20.25 you must make a clear **distinction** between animals and birds that
Deut 17. 8 cases that involve a **distinction** between murder and manslaughter.
2 Sam 14.17 is like God's angel and can **distinguish** good from evil.
Ezra 3.13 No one could **distinguish** between the joyful shouts and the crying,
Ezek 22.26 They make no **distinction** between what is holy and what is not.
Col 3.11 there is no longer any **distinction** between Gentiles and Jews,
Heb 5.14 through practice are able to **distinguish** between good and evil.
Jas 2. 4 you are guilty of creating **distinctions** among yourselves and of

DISTORT

Jude 4 unnoticed among us, persons who **distort** the message about

DISTRESS

Gen 16.11 Ishmael, because the Lord has heard your cry of **distress.**
Num 11.10 He was **distressed** because the Lord was angry with them,
14. 1 All night long the people cried out in **distress.**

Judg 2.15 They were in great **distress.**
10. 9 Israel was in great **distress.**
10.16 and he became troubled over Israel's **distress.**
1 Sam 1. 9 She was deeply **distressed,** and she cried bitterly as she prayed
20.34 He was deeply **distressed** about David, because Saul had insulted
2 Kgs 4.27 Can't you see she's deeply **distressed?**
11.14 Athaliah tore her clothes in **distress** and shouted,
2 Chr 15. 6 another city, because God was bringing trouble and **distress** on them.
23.13 She tore her clothes in **distress** and shouted, "Treason!
Neh 9.37 with us and our livestock, and we are in deep **distress!"**
Job 36.15 God teaches men through suffering and uses **distress** to open their eyes.
Ps 25.18 Consider my **distress** and suffering and forgive all my sins.
38.16 Don't let my enemies gloat over my **distress;**
57. 6 I am overcome with **distress.**
78.49 He caused them great **distress** by pouring out his anger
106.44 when they cried out, and he took notice of their **distress.**
107. 6 called to the Lord, and he saved them from their **distress.**
107.13 called to the Lord, and he saved them from their **distress.**
107.19 called to the Lord, and he saved them from their **distress.**
107.28 called to the Lord, and he saved them from their **distress.**
118. 5 In my **distress** I called to the Lord;
142. 7 Set me free from my **distress;**
144.14 May there be no cries of **distress** in our streets.
Is 5.30 Darkness and **distress!**
54. 6 young wife, deserted by her husband and deeply **distressed.**
59.11 We are frightened and **distressed.**
Jer 15.11 behalf of my enemies when they were in trouble and **distress.**
25.36 moan and cry out in **distress** because the Lord in his anger
30. 7 it— a time of **distress** for my people, but they will
48. 5 Luhith, the cries of **distress** on the way down to Horonaim.
Ezek 4.16 The people there will be **distressed** and anxious as they measure
9. 4 forehead of everyone who is **distressed** and troubled
30. 4 There will be war in Egypt And great **distress** in Sudan.
Dan 5. 9 In his **distress** King Belshazzar grew even paler,
Joel 1.18 cattle are bellowing in **distress** because there is no pasture
Amos 8. 8 will quake, and everyone in the land will be in **distress.**
Obad 12 You should not have laughed at them in their **distress.**
14 handed them over to the enemy on the day of their **distress.**
Jon 2. 2 "In my **distress,** O Lord, I called to you, and you
Zeph 1.15 day of trouble and **distress,** a day of ruin and destruction,
Mk 14.33 **Distress** and anguish came over him, [34]and he said to them,
16. 8 they went out and ran from the tomb, **distressed** and terrified.
Lk 12.50 to receive, and how **distressed** I am until it is over!
21.23 Terrible **distress** will come upon this land, and God's punishment
1 Cor 7.26 the present **distress,** I think it is better for a man
2 Cor 2. 4 a greatly troubled and **distressed** heart and with many tears;
11.29 when someone is led into sin, I am filled with **distress.**
2 Pet 2. 7 good man, who was **distressed** by the immoral conduct of lawless

DISTRIBUTE

Num 36. 2 "The Lord commanded you to **distribute** the land to the people
2 Sam 6.19 of the Lord Almighty [19]and **distributed** food to them all.
1 Chr 16. 3 in the name of the Lord [3]and **distributed** food to them all.
2 Chr 31.14 the gifts offered to the Lord and of **distributing** them.
31.15 They **distributed** the food equally to their fellow-Levites
31.19 there were responsible men who **distributed** the food
35.13 and quickly **distributed** the meat to the people.
Neh 13.13 honest in **distributing** the supplies to their fellow-workers.
Esth 2.18 and **distributed** gifts worthy of a king.
Ps 60. 6 I will divide Shechem and **distribute** the Valley of Sukkoth
108. 7 I will divide Shechem and **distribute** the Valley of Sukkoth
Mk 6.41 and gave them to his disciples to **distribute** to the people.
8. 6 and gave them to his disciples to **distribute** to the crowd;
8. 7 gave thanks for these and told the disciples to **distribute** them
Lk 9.16 and gave them to the disciples to **distribute** to the people.
Jn 6.11 gave thanks to God, and **distributed** it to the people who
Acts 2.45 property and possessions, and **distribute** the money among all,
4.35 money was **distributed** to each one according to his need.
6. 1 widows were being neglected in the daily **distribution** of funds.
Heb 2. 4 and wonders and by **distributing** the gifts of the Holy Spirit

DISTRICT

1 Kgs 4. 5 Chief of the **district** governors: Azariah
4. 7 Solomon appointed twelve men as **district** governors in Israel.
4. 7 food from their **districts** for the king and his household,
4. 8 twelve officers and the **districts** they were in charge of:
4.14 the **district** of Mahanaim
10.15 the Arabian kings and the governors of the Israelite **districts.**
20.14 under the command of the **district** governors are to do it."
20.15 the young soldiers who were under the **district** commanders,
2 Kgs 17. 6 the River Habor in the **district** of Gozan,
18.11 the River Habor in the **district** of Gozan,
2 Chr 9.14 the governors of the Israelite **districts** also brought him silver
Neh 3. 9 ruler of half the Jerusalem **District,** built the next
3.12 of the other half of the Jerusalem **District,** built the next
3.14 ruler of the Beth Haccherem **District,** rebuilt the Rubbish Gate.
3.15 ruler of the Mizpah **District,** rebuilt the Fountain Gate.
3.16 ruler of half the Bethzur **District,** built the next section,
3.17 ruler of half the Keilah **District,**
3.17 built the next section on behalf of his **district;**
3.18 other half of the Keilah **District,** built the next section;
Jer 49.28 tribe of Kedar and the **districts** controlled by Hazor,
Ezek 47.16 of Ticon (located by the border of the **district** of Hauran).
Mk 8.10 boat with his disciples and went to the **district** of Dalmanutha.
Acts 16.12 inland to Philippi, a city of the first **district** of Macedonia;

DISTURB

[UNDISTURBED]

Gen 49. 9 No one dares **disturb** him.
1 Sam 28.15 Samuel said to Saul, "Why have you **disturbed** me?
Esth 4. 4 told her what Mordecai was doing, she was deeply **disturbed.**
Job 4.13 Like a nightmare it **disturbed** my sleep.
Is 7. 4 alert, to stay calm, and not to be frightened or **disturbed.**
Jer 10. 2 do not be **disturbed** by unusual sights in the sky,
48.11 like wine left to settle **undisturbed** and never poured from
Ezek 39. 6 the coasts where people live **undisturbed,** and everyone will
Dan 5.10 Please do not be so **disturbed** and look so pale.
7.15 The visions I saw alarmed me, and I was deeply **disturbed.**
Mk 6.20 even though he became greatly **disturbed** every time he heard him.

DITCH

2 Kgs 3.16 'Dig **ditches** all over this dry stream bed.
18.17 by the **ditch** that brings water
Is 7. 3 at the end of the **ditch** that brings water
36. 2 by the **ditch** that brings water
Mt 15.14 when one blind man leads another, both fall into a **ditch."**
Lk 6.39 if he does, both will fall into a **ditch.**
16. 3 not strong enough to dig **ditches,** and I am ashamed to beg.

DIVIDE

Gen 1. 6 a dome to **divide** the water and to keep it
2.10 beyond Eden it **divided** into four rivers.
10.25 during his time the people of the world were **divided;**
14.15 There he **divided** his men into groups,
32. 7 He **divided** into two groups the people who were with him, and
32.16 He **divided** them into herds and put one of his servants
33. 1 four hundred men, so he **divided** the children among Leah, Rachel,
36.20 the land of Edom were **divided** into tribes which traced their
Ex 6.24 were the ancestors of the **divisions** of the clan of Korah.
14.16 The water will **divide,** and the Israelites will be able to
14.21 water was **divided,** [22]and the Israelites went through the sea
15. 9 I will **divide** their wealth and take all I want;
21.35 the two men shall sell the live bull and **divide** the money;
21.35 they shall also **divide** up the meat from the dead animal.
Lev 11. 3 any land animal [3]that has **divided** hoofs and that also chews
11. 4 they chew the cud, but do not have **divided** hoofs.
11. 7 they have **divided** hoofs, but do not chew the cud.
11.24 unless their hoofs are **divided** and they chew the cud,
Num 2. 2 under the banner of his **division** and the flag of his own
2. 3 under the banner of the **division** of Judah shall camp in
2. 3 The **division** of Judah shall march first.
2.10 under the banner of the **division** of Reuben shall camp in
2.10 The **division** of Reuben shall march second.
2.17 Then, between the first two **divisions** and the last two
2.17 Each **division** shall march in the same order as they camp,
2.18 under the banner of the **division** of Ephraim shall camp in
2.18 The **division** of Ephraim shall march third.
2.25 under the banner of the **division** of Dan shall camp in their
2.25 The **division** of Dan shall march last.
2.32 people of Israel enrolled in the **divisions,** group by group,
10.14 under the banner of the **division** led by the tribe of Judah
10.18 under the banner of the **division** led by the tribe of Reuben
10.22 under the banner of the **division** led by the tribe of Ephraim
10.25 under the banner of the **division** led by the tribe of Dan,
10.25 the rearguard of all the **divisions,** would start out,
26.53 The Lord said to Moses, [53]**"Divide** the land among the tribes,
26.54 **Divide** the land by drawing lots,
31.27 **Divide** what was taken into two equal parts,
33.54 **Divide** the land among the various tribes and clans
34.14 received their property, **divided** according to their families,
34.17 and Joshua son of Nun will **divide** the land for the people.
34.18 Take also one leader from each tribe to help them **divide** it."
34.29 that the Lord assigned to **divide** the property for the people
Deut 14. 6 any animals that have **divided** hoofs and that also chew the
14. 7 eaten unless they have **divided** hoofs and also chew the cud.
14. 7 they chew the cud but do not have **divided** hoofs.
14. 8 they have **divided** hoofs but do not chew the cud.
19. 2 **divide** the territory into three parts,
21.16 how he is going to **divide** his property among his children,
29. 8 took their land, and **divided** it among the tribes of Reuben
Josh 11.23 Israelites as their own and **divided** it into portions,
12. 7 Joshua **divided** this land among the tribes and gave it to
13. 6 You must **divide** the land among the Israelites,
13. 7 Now then, **divide** this land among the other nine tribes
13.32 That is how Moses **divided** the land east of Jericho
14. 1 Canaan west of the Jordan was **divided** among the people of Israel.
14. 1 families of the Israelite tribes **divided** it among the population.
14. 3 (The descendants of Joseph were **divided** into two tribes:
14. 5 The people of Israel **divided** the land as the Lord had
18. 5 The land will be **divided** among them in seven parts;
18. 6 a description of these seven **divisions** and bring it to me.
18. 9 down in writing how they **divided** it into seven parts,
19.49 the people of Israel finished **dividing** up the land,
19.51 In this way they finished **dividing** the land.
Judg 5.15 But the tribe of Reuben was **divided;**
5.16 Yes, the tribe of Reuben was **divided;**
5.30 finding things to capture and **divide,** a girl or two for
7.16 He **divided** his three hundred men into three groups
9.43 so he took his men, **divided** them into three groups,
1 Sam 11.11 That night Saul **divided** his men into three groups,
2 Sam 18. 1 all his men together, **divided** them into units of a thousand
1 Kgs 5.14 He **divided** them into three groups of 10,000 men,

1 Kgs 16.21 The people of Israel were **divided:**
2 Kgs 2. 8 the water **divided,** and he and Elisha crossed to the other
2.14 the water again, and it **divided,** and he walked over
1 Chr 1.19 of the world were **divided,** and the other was named Joktan.
1.51 The people of Edom were **divided** into the following tribes:
23. 6 David **divided** the Levites into three groups,
25. 9 These 288 men were **divided** according to families
26.12 The temple guards were **divided** into groups,
26.16 Guard duty was **divided** into assigned periods, one after
2 Chr 35.12 Then they **divided** among the people, by family groups,
Job 26.10 He **divided** light from darkness by a circle drawn on the
Ps 22.18 They gamble for my clothes and **divide** them among themselves.
60. 6 "In triumph I will **divide** Shechem
68.12 The women at home **divided** what was captured:
74.13 With your mighty strength you **divided** the sea
78.13 He **divided** the sea and took them through it;
78.55 he **divided** their land among the tribes of Israel
108. 7 "In triumph I will **divide** Shechem
136.13 He **divided** the Red Sea;
Is 9. 3 when they harvest their corn or when they **divide** captured wealth.
18. 2 message back to your land **divided** by rivers,
18. 7 receive offerings from this land **divided** by rivers,
34.17 the Lord who will **divide** the land among them
63.12 did great things through Moses, **dividing** the waters of the sea
Ezek 5. 1 Then weigh the hair on scales and **divide** it into three parts.
37.22 they will no longer be **divided** into two nations
45. 1 When the land is **divided** to give each tribe a share,
47.13 land that is to be **divided** among the twelve tribes,
47.14 now **divide** it equally among you.
47.21 **"Divide** this land among your tribes;
47.22 also to receive their share of the land when you **divide** it.
48.29 the land is to be **divided** into sections for the tribes
Dan 2.41 This means that it will be a **divided** empire.
5.25 'Number, number, weight, **divisions.'**
5.28 divisions, your kingdom is **divided** up and given to the Medes
8.22 which that nation will be **divided** and which will not be as
11. 4 his empire will break up and be **divided** into four parts.
11.24 Then he will **divide** among his followers the goods and property
Joel 3. 2 Israelites in foreign countries and **divided** up Israel, my land.
Amos 7.17 Your land will be **divided** up and given to others,
Obad 11 carried off Jerusalem's wealth and **divided** it among themselves.
Nah 3.10 carried off in chains and **divided** among their captors.
Zech 14. 1 and the loot will be **divided** up before your eyes.
14. 5 through this valley that **divides** the mountain in two.
Mt 12.25 "Any country that **divides** itself into groups which fight each
12.25 town or family that **divides** itself into groups which fight each
12.26 means that it is already **divided** into groups and will soon
13.48 they pull it to shore and sit down to **divide** the fish:
25.32 Then he will **divide** them into two groups, just as a shepherd
27.35 They crucified him and then **divided** his clothes among them
Mk 3.24 If a country **divides** itself into groups which fight each other,
3.25 If a family **divides** itself into groups which fight each other,
3.26 So if Satan's kingdom **divides** into groups, it cannot last,
6.39 to make all the people **divide** into groups and sit down on
6.41 He also **divided** the two fish among them all.
15.24 they crucified him and **divided** his clothes among themselves,
Lk 11.17 "Any country that **divides** itself into groups which fight each
11.17 a family **divided** against itself falls apart.
11.22 the owner was depending on and **divides** up what he stole.
12.13 tell my brother to **divide** with me the property our father
12.14 right to judge or to **divide** the property between you two?"
12.51 No, not peace, but **division.**
12.52 family of five will be **divided,** three against two
15.12 So the man **divided** his property between his two sons.
23.34 They **divided** his clothes among themselves by throwing dice.
Jn 7.43 So there was a **division** in the crowd because of Jesus.
9.16 And there was a **division** among them.
10.19 there was a **division** among the people because of these words.
19.23 they took his clothes and **divided** them into four parts,
19.24 **divided** my clothes among themselves and gambled for my robe."
Acts 14. 4 The people of the city were **divided:**
23. 7 and Sadducees started to quarrel, and the group was **divided.**
Rom 16.17 out for those who cause **divisions** and upset people's faith
1 Cor 1.10 what you say, so that there will be no **divisions** among you.
1.13 Christ has been **divided** into groups!
11.19 (No doubt there must be **divisions** among you so that the
12.25 And so there is no **division** in the body, but all its
Tit 3.10 the person who causes **divisions,** and then have nothing more to
Jude 19 people who cause **divisions,** who are controlled by their natural

DIVINATION

The attempt to discover a message from God or the gods by examining such things as marked stones or the liver of a sacrificed animal.

Gen 30.27 I have learnt by **divination** that the Lord has blessed me
44. 5 is the one he drinks from, the one he uses for **divination.**
44.15 my position could find you out by practising **divination?"**
Deut 18.10 don't let your people practise **divination** or look for omens
18.14 advice of those who practise **divination** and look for omens,
2 Kgs 16.15 But keep the bronze altar for me to use for **divination."**
21. 6 He practised **divination** and magic and consulted fortune-tellers
2 Chr 33. 6 He practised **divination** and magic and consulted fortune-tellers
Hos 3. 4 sacred stone pillars, without idols or images to use for **divination.**

AV DIVINATION

Num 22. 7 them the payment for the **curse,** went to Balaam, and gave him
23.23 is no magic charm, no **witchcraft,** That can be used against
2 Kgs 17.17 they consulted mediums and **fortune-tellers,** and they devoted
Jer 14.14 **predictions** are worthless things that they have imagined.
Ezek 12.24 Israel there will be no more false visions or misleading **prophecies.**
13. 6 Their visions are false, and their **predictions** are lies.
13. 7 you see are false, and the **predictions** you make are lies.
13.23 So now your false visions and misleading **predictions** are over.
21.21 To **discover** which way to go, he shakes the arrows;
21.23 people of Jerusalem won't **believe** this, because of the treaties
Acts 16.16 had an evil spirit that enabled her to **predict** the future.

DIVINE

Prov 16.10 The king speaks with **divine** authority;
Ezek 28. 2 pretend to be a god, but, no, you are mortal, not **divine.**
28. 9 your murderers, you will be mortal and not at all **divine.**
Acts 2.22 was a man whose **divine** authority was clearly proven to you
3.13 God of our ancestors, has given **divine** glory to his Servant Jesus.
Rom 1. 4 as to his **divine** holiness, he was shown with great power
1.20 his eternal power and his **divine** nature, have been clearly seen;
Col 2. 9 For the full content of **divine** nature lives in Christ,
Heb 8. 1 at the right of the throne of the **Divine** Majesty in heaven.
12.25 the one who gave the **divine** message on earth did not escape.
2 Pet 1. 3 God's **divine** power has given us everything we need to live
1. 4 is in the world, and may come to share the **divine** nature.

DIVORCE

[NOTICE OF DIVORCE]

Lev 21. 7 or a woman who is not a virgin or who is **divorced;**
21.14 not a widow or a **divorced** woman or a woman who has
22.13 But a widowed or **divorced** daughter who has no children
Num 30. 9 A widow or a **divorced** woman must keep every vow she makes
Deut 22.19 wife, and he can never **divorce** her as long as he lives.
22.29 He can never **divorce** her as long as he lives.
24. 1 So he writes out **divorce** papers, gives them to her,
24. 3 so he also writes out **divorce** papers, gives them to her,
1 Chr 8. 8 Shaharaim **divorced** two wives, Hushim and Baara.
Ezra 10.19 They promised to **divorce** their wives,
10.44 They **divorced** them and sent them and their children away.
Is 50. 1 I sent my people away like a man who **divorces** his wife?
50. 1 Where, then, are the papers of **divorce?**
Jer 3. 1 Lord says, "If a man **divorces** his wife, and she leaves him
3. 8 Judah also saw that I **divorced** Israel and sent her away
Ezek 44.22 No priest may marry a **divorced** woman;
Mal 2.16 "I hate **divorce,"** says the Lord God of Israel.
Mt 5.31 who divorces his wife must give her a written **notice of divorce.'**
5.32 if a man **divorces** his wife, for any cause other than her
19. 3 Law allow a man to **divorce** his wife for whatever reason he
19. 7 man to hand his wife a **divorce notice** and send her away?"
19. 8 "Moses gave you permission to **divorce** your wives because you
19. 9 that any man who **divorces** his wife, for any cause other
Mk 10. 2 asked, "does our Law allow a man to **divorce** his wife?"
10. 4 a man to write a **divorce notice** and send his wife away."
10.11 "A man who **divorces** his wife and marries another woman
10.12 a woman who **divorces** her husband and marries another man
Lk 16.18 **divorces** his wife and marries another woman commits adultery;
16.18 and the man who marries a **divorced** woman commits adultery.
1 Cor 7.11 and a husband must not **divorce** his wife.
7.12 agrees to go on living with him, he must not **divorce** her.
7.13 agrees to go on living with her, she must not **divorce** him.

DO

Gen 1. 6 and to keep it in two separate places"—and it was **done.**
1. 9 one place, so that the land will appear"—and it was **done.**
1.11 that bear grain and those that bear fruit"—and it was **done.**
1.15 the sky to give light to the earth"—and it was **done.**
1.24 domestic and wild, large and small"—and it was **done.**
1.30 provided grass and leafy plants for food"—and it was **done.**
20. 9 No one should ever do what you have **done** to me.
41.25 God has told you what he is going to **do.**
41.28 told you—God has shown you what he is going to **do.**
Ex 12.14 festival to remind you of what I, the Lord, have **done.**
13. 8 because of what the Lord **did** for you when you left Egypt.
14.13 you will see what the Lord will **do** to save you today;
18. 1 about everything that God had **done** for Moses and the people
18. 8 everything that the Lord had **done** to the king and the people
18.18 This is too much for you to **do** alone.
19. 4 saw what I, the Lord, **did** to the Egyptians and how I
34.10 In their presence I will **do** great things such as have never
34.10 such as have never been **done** anywhere on earth among any of
34.10 things I, the Lord, can **do,**
34.10 because I am going to **do** an awesome thing for you.
Num 16.30 But if the Lord **does** something unheard of, and the earth
23.19 Whatever he promises, he **does;**
23.19 He speaks, and it is **done.**
23.23 Now people will say about Israel, 'Look what God has **done!'**
Deut 3.21 that the Lord your God **did** to those two kings, Sihon and
3.24 on earth who can do the mighty things that you have **done!**
4. 3 You yourselves saw what the Lord **did** at Mount Peor.
7.18 what the Lord your God **did** to the king of Egypt and
10.21 the great and astounding things that he has **done** for you.
11. 3 You saw what he **did** to the king of Egypt and to
11. 5 You know what the Lord **did** for you in the desert before
11. 7 have seen all these great things that the Lord has **done.**
12.18 are to be happy there over everything that you have **done.**
15. 2 This is how it is to be **done.**
24. 9 what the Lord your God **did** to Miriam as you were coming
29. 2 for yourselves what the Lord **did** to the king of Egypt, to
32. 4 he **does** what is right and fair.
32.39 wound and I heal, and no one can oppose what I **do.**
Josh 2.18 This is what you must **do.**

Josh 4. 6 These stones will remind the people of what the Lord has **done.**
4.14 What the Lord **did** that day made the people of Israel
5.14 What do you want me to **do?"**
7.19 Tell me now what you have **done.**
10.25 is what the Lord is going to **do** to all your enemies."
23. 3 the Lord your God has **done** to all these nations because of
24.31 themselves everything that the Lord had **done** for Israel.
Judg 1. 7 God has now **done** to me what I did to them."
2. 7 all the great things that the Lord had **done** for Israel.
2.10 generation forgot the Lord and what he had **done** for Israel.
6.13 us the Lord used to **do**—how he brought them out of
7.17 the edge of the camp, watch me, and **do** what I do.
15.11 He answered, "I **did** to them just what they did to me."
18.14 What do you think we should **do?"**
19.30 We have to **do** something about this!
20. 7 What are we going to **do** about this?"
20. 9 This is what we will **do:**
Ruth 3. 4 He will tell you what to **do."**
3.11 I will **do** everything you ask;
1 Sam 2. 1 how happy I am because of what he has **done!**
3.18 he will **do** whatever seems best to him."
12. 7 mighty actions the Lord **did** to save you and your ancestors.
12.16 will see the great thing which the Lord is going to **do.**
12.24 Remember the great things he has **done** for you.
14.36 **"Do** whatever you think best," they answered.
14.40 **"Do** whatever you think best," they answered.
14.45 What he **did** today was done with God's help."
22. 3 until I find out what God is going to **do** for me."
25.30 And when the Lord has **done** all the good things he has
25.35 I will **do** what you want."
2 Sam 7.18 of what you have already **done** for me, Sovereign Lord, nor is
7.21 you have **done** all these great things in order to teach me.
10.12 And may the Lord's will be **done!"**
1 Kgs 8.41 the great things you have **done** for your people, and comes to
17.20 my God, why have you **done** such a terrible thing to this
2 Kgs 3.18 continued, "But this is an easy thing for the Lord to **do;**
4. 2 "What shall I **do** for you?"
6. 5 "What shall I **do,** sir?"
6.15 What shall we **do?"**
10. 5 **do** whatever you think best."
23.27 said, "I will do to Judah what I have **done** to Israel:
1 Chr 16. 8 tell the nations what he has **done.**
16. 9 tell the wonderful things he has **done.**
17.16 of what you have already **done** for me, Lord God, nor is
19.13 And may the Lord's will be **done."**
2 Chr 23. 4 This is what we will **do.**
32.25 for what the Lord had **done** for him, and Judah and Jerusalem
Neh 9.17 they forgot all you **did;**
Esth 6. 6 What should I **do** for this man?"
10. 2 great and wonderful things he **did,** as well as the whole
Job 5. 9 understand the great things he **does,** and to his miracles
7.17 Why pay attention to what he **does?**
9.10 understand the great things he **does,** and to his miracles
31. 2 What does Almighty God **do** to us?
34.10 Will Almighty God **do** what is wrong?
34.12 Almighty God does not **do** evil;
34.29 If God decided to **do** nothing at all, no one could
34.33 you object to what God **does,** can you expect him to do
34.33 what God does, can you expect him to **do** what you want?
36.24 He has always been praised for what he **does;**
36.25 Everyone has seen what he has **done;**
37. 7 he shows them what he can **do.**
37.14 consider the wonderful things God **does.**
42. 2 that you can **do** everything you want.
Ps 9. 1 I will tell of all the wonderful things you have **done.**
9.11 Tell every nation what he has **done!**
19. 1 How plainly it shows what he has **done!**
22.22 I will tell my people what you have **done;**
22.25 the full assembly I will praise you for what you have **done;**
28. 5 of what the Lord has **done** or of what he has made;
30. 4 Remember what the Holy One has **done,** and give him thanks!
32.11 be glad and rejoice because of what the Lord has **done.**
33. 1 are righteous, shout for joy for what the Lord has **done;**
34. 2 I will praise him for what he has **done;**
40. 5 You have **done** many things for us, O Lord our God;
44. 1 about the great things you **did** in their time, in the days
44.13 Our neighbours see what you **did** to us, and they mock us
46. 8 Come and see what the Lord has **done.**
46. 8 See what amazing things he has **done** on earth.
48. 8 have heard what God has **done,** and now we have seen it
52. 9 I will always thank you, God, for what you have **done;**
64. 9 think about what God has **done** and tell about his deeds.
64.10 All righteous people will rejoice because of what the Lord has **done.**
65. 5 giving us victory and you **do** wonderful things to save us.
65. 8 world stands in awe of the great things that you have **done.**
66. 3 Say to God, "How wonderful are the things you **do!**
66. 5 Come and see what God has **done,** his wonderful acts among men.
66. 6 There we rejoiced because of what he **did.**
66.16 God, and I will tell you what he has **done** for me.
71.19 You have **done** great things;
72.18 He alone **does** these wonderful things.
73.28 the Sovereign Lord and to proclaim all that he has **done!**
75. 1 you are and tell of the wonderful things you have **done.**
77.11 I will recall the wonders you **did** in the past.
77.12 I will think about all that you have **done;**
77.13 Everything you **do,** O God, is holy.
78. 4 and his great deeds and the wonderful things he has **done.**
78. 7 forget what he has **done,** but always obey his commandments.
78.11 They forgot what he had **done,** the miracles they had seen
83. 9 Do to them what you **did** to the Midianites, and to Sisera
Ps 83.11 Do to their leaders what you **did** to Oreb and Zeeb;
86. 8 like you, O Lord, not one has **done** what you have done.
86.10 You are mighty and **do** wonderful things;
89. 5 The heavens sing of the wonderful things you **do;**
89.14 love and faithfulness are shown in all you **do.**
92. 4 because of what you have **done,** I sing for joy.
95. 9 and tried me, although they had seen what I **did** for them.
97.12 are righteous be glad because of what the Lord has **done!**
97.12 Remember what the holy God has **done,** and give thanks to him.
98. 1 he has **done** wonderful things!
102.18 generation what the Lord has **done,** so that people not yet
105. 1 tell the nations what he has **done.**
105. 2 tell of the wonderful things he has **done.**
106. 2 Who can tell all the great things he has **done?**
106.22 What wonderful things he **did** there!
107. 8 constant love, for the wonderful things he **did** for them.
107.15 constant love, for the wonderful things he **did** for them.
107.21 constant love, for the wonderful things he **did** for them.
107.22 and with songs of joy must tell all that he has **done.**
107.24 saw what the Lord can **do,** his wonderful acts on the seas.
107.31 constant love, for the wonderful things he **did** for them.
111. 2 How wonderful are the things the Lord **does!**
111. 3 All he **does** is full of honour and majesty;
111. 7 In all he **does** he is faithful and just;
115. 3 he **does** whatever he wishes.
118.17 instead, I will live and proclaim what the Lord has **done.**
120. 3 You liars, what will God **do** to you?
125. 4 Lord, **do** good to those who are good, to those who obey
126. 2 said about us, "The Lord **did** great things for them."
126. 3 Indeed he **did** great things for us;
135. 6 He **does** whatever he wishes in heaven and on earth, in the
138. 5 sing about what you have **done** and about your great glory.
138. 8 You will **do** everything you have promised;
139.14 all you **do** is strange and wonderful.
143. 5 about all that you have **done,** I bring to mind all your
145. 4 What you have **done** will be praised from one generation to
145.17 Lord is righteous in all he **does,** merciful in all his acts.
150. 2 Praise him for the mighty things he has **done.**
Prov 2. 9 You will know what you should **do.**
19.21 kinds of things, but the Lord's will is going to be **done.**
24.29 Don't say, "I'll **do** to him just what he did to me!
24.29 Don't say, "I'll do to him just what he **did** to me!
Ecc 1. 9 What has been **done** before will be done again.
3.14 I know that everything God **does** will last for ever.
3.14 And one thing God **does** is to make us stand in awe
7.13 Think about what God has **done.**
Is 3.11 what they have **done** to others will now be done to them.
5.19 the Lord hurry up and **do** what he says he will, so
12. 4 Tell all the nations what he has **done!**
12. 5 Sing to the Lord because of the great things he has **done.**
14.24 What I have determined to **do** will be done.
24. 3 The Lord has spoken and it will be **done.**
25. 1 You have **done** amazing things;
33.13 and far hear what I have **done** and acknowledge my power."
40.13 Can anyone tell the Lord what to **do?**
41. 5 "The people of distant lands have seen what I have **done;**
41.24 You and all you **do** are nothing;
43.13 no one can change what I **do."**
43.19 Watch for the new thing I am going to **do.**
44. 7 Could anyone else have **done** what I did?
44.28 you will **do** what I want you to do:
45. 7 I, the Lord, **do** all these things.
46. 8 consider what I have **done.**
46.10 never fail, that I would **do** everything I intended to do.
46.11 I have spoken, and it will be **done.**
48.11 What I **do** is done for my own sake— I will
48.14 he will **do** what I want him to do.
55.11 it will not fail to **do** what I plan for it;
55.11 it will **do** everything I send it to do.
55.13 last for ever, a reminder of what I, the Lord, have **done."**
60. 6 People will tell the good news of what the Lord has **done!**
61. 3 is right, And God will be praised for what he has **done.**
61.10 Jerusalem rejoices because of what the Lord has **done.**
63. 7 I praise him for all he has **done** for us.
63.12 Lord, who by his power **did** great things through Moses,
64. 3 you came and did terrifying things that we **did** not expect;
66.18 see what my power can **do** [19]and will know that I am
Jer 5.19 When they ask why I **did** all these things, tell them,
7.12 worshipped, and see what I **did** to it because of the sins
7.14 And so, what I **did** to Shiloh I will do to this
7.14 you, I will do the same thing that I **did** to Shiloh.
9.15 to what I, the Lord Almighty, the God of Israel, will **do:**
9.24 my love is constant, and I **do** what is just and right.
12. 3 you see what I **do,** and how I love you.
13.25 what he has decided to **do** with you, because you have
14.15 what I am going to **do** to those prophets whom I did
14.22 Lord our God, because you are the one who **does** these things.
16.17 I see everything they **do.**
18. 6 "Haven't I the right to **do** with you people of Israel what
18. 8 from its evil, I will not **do** what I said I would.
18.10 and does evil, I will not **do** what I said I would.
22. 8 why I, the Lord, have **done** such a thing to this great
23.20 will not end until he has **done** everything he intends to do.
26. 6 to this Temple what I **did** to Shiloh, and all the nations
29.31 that I am going to **do** for my people, because he told
30.23 not end until he has **done** all that he intends to do.
33. 9 the good things that I **do** for the people of Jerusalem and
34.17 every nation in the world horrified at what I **do** to you.
40. 3 destruction, [3]and now he has **done** what he said he would.
49.20 to what I intend to **do** to the people of the city
50.45 of Babylon and to what I intend to **do** to its people.

Jer	51.10	the people in Jerusalem what the Lord our God has **done.'** "
	51.12	The Lord has **done** what he said he would do to the
Lam	2.17	The Lord has finally **done** what he threatened to do:
Ezek	9.10	I will **do** to them what they have done to others."
	12.25	Lord, will speak to them, and what I say will be **done.**
	12.25	rebels, I will do what I have warned you I would **do.**
	12.28	What I have said will be **done.**
	14.23	will know that there was good reason for everything I **did."**
	17.24	I will **do** what I have said I would do."
	18.25	"But you say, 'What the Lord **does** isn't right.'
	18.29	And you Israelites say, 'What the Lord **does** isn't right.'
	23.38	And that is not all they **did.**
	24.22	Then you will **do** what I have done.
	24.24	you will **do** everything I have done.
	28.22	people will praise me because of what I **do** to you.
	32.10	What I **do** to you will shock many nations.
	33.17	"And your people say that what I **do** isn't right!
	33.20	But Israel, you say that what I **do** isn't right.
	34.16	destroy, because I am a shepherd who **does** what is right.
	36.22	What I am going to **do** is not for the sake of
	38.16	I am, to show my holiness by what I **do** through you.
Dan	4.35	No one can oppose his will or question what he **does.**
	4.37	Everything he **does** is right and just, and he can humble
	9. 7	You, Lord, always **do** what is right, but we have always
	9.12	did what you said you would **do** to us and our rulers.
	9.14	you did, because you always **do** what is right, and we did
	11.36	God will **do** exactly what he has planned.
Hos	6. 4	says, "Israel and Judah, what am I going to **do** with you?
Joel	2.21	joyful and glad because of all the Lord has **done** for you.
	2.23	Zion, rejoice at what the Lord your God has **done** for you.
	2.26	the Lord your God, who has **done** wonderful things for you.
	3. 7	I will **do** to you what you have done to them.
Amos	3. 7	The Sovereign Lord never **does** anything without revealing
Mic	2. 7	Would he really **do** such things?
	6. 5	and you will realize what I **did** in order to save you."
Hab	1. 5	I am going to **do** something that you will not believe when
	3. 2	heard of what you have **done,** and I am filled with awe.
	3. 2	do again in our times the great deeds you used to **do.**
Zeph	1.12	'The Lord never **does** anything, one way or the other.'
	3. 5	he **does** what is right and never what is wrong.
Zech	10. 7	this victory and be glad because of what the Lord has **done.**
Mal	2.13	This is another thing you **do.**
Mt	3. 8	**Do** those things that will show that you have turned from
	5.33	promise, but do what you have vowed to the Lord to **do.'**
	6.10	may your will be **done** on earth as it is in heaven.
	7.12	"Do for others what you want them to **do** for you:
	7.16	You will know them by what they **do.**
	7.20	So then, you will know the false prophets by what they **do.**
	7.21	those who do what my Father in heaven wants them to **do.**
	8. 9	and I order my slave, **'Do** this!'
	8. 9	and he **does** it."
	12.27	What your own followers **do** proves that you are wrong!
	17.20	You could **do** anything!"
	19.16	"what good thing must I **do** to receive eternal life?"
	19.20	"What else do I need to **do?"**
	23.30	would not have done what they **did** and killed the prophets.
	25.40	'I tell you, whenever you **did** this for one of the least
	25.40	important of these brothers of mine, you **did** it for me!'
	27.24	This is your **doing!"**
	28.15	guards took the money and **did** what they were told to do.
Mk	3. 8	to Jesus because they had heard of the things he was **doing.**
	7.13	And there are many other things like this that you **do."**
	7.37	"How well he **does** everything!"
	8. 6	and the disciples **did** so.
	10.17	"Good Teacher, what must I **do** to receive eternal life?"
	14. 8	She **did** what she could;
Lk	1.37	For there is nothing that God cannot **do."**
	2.27	Jesus into the Temple to **do** for him what the Law required,
	2.48	said to him, "My son, why have you **done** this to us?
	3. 8	**Do** those things that will show that you have turned from
	3.10	The people asked him, "What are we to **do,** then?"
	3.12	and they asked him, "Teacher, what are we to **do?"**
	3.14	What are we to **do?"**
	6.31	**Do** for others just what you want them to do for you.
	7. 8	and I order my slave, **'Do** this!'
	7. 8	and he **does** it."
	10.25	"Teacher," he asked, "what must I **do** to receive eternal life?"
	12.17	What can I **do?**
	12.18	This is what I will **do,'** he told himself;
	16. 3	What shall I **do?**
	16. 4	Now I know what I will **do!**
	17. 3	So watch what you **do!**
	17.10	when you have **done** all you have been told to do, say,
	17.10	we have only **done** our duty.'
	18.18	"Good Teacher, what must I **do** to receive eternal life?"
	20.13	Then the owner of the vineyard said, 'What shall I **do?**
	22.19	**Do** this in memory of me."
	22.42	Not my will, however, but your will be **done."**
	23.34	They don't know what they are **doing."**
Jn	2. 4	"You must not tell me what to **do,"** Jesus replied.
	2. 5	mother then told the servants, **"Do** whatever he tells you."
	2.18	perform to show us that you have the right to **do** this?"
	4.29	and see the man who told me everything I have ever **done.**
	4.34	sent me and to finish the work he gave me to **do.**
	4.39	woman had said, "He told me everything I have ever **done."**
	5.12	asked him, "Who is the man who told you to **do** this?"
	5.19	the Son can **do** nothing on his own;
	5.19	he **does** only what he sees his Father doing.
	5.19	What the Father **does,** the Son also does.
	5.20	him even greater things to **do** than this, and you will all
	5.30	"I can **do** nothing on my own authority;
Jn	5.30	I am not trying to **do** what I want, but only what
	5.36	what I **do,** that is, the deeds my Father
	6.28	we do in order to do what God wants us to **do?"**
	6.30	What will you **do?**
	8.39	Jesus replied, "you would do the same things that he **did.**
	8.41	You are doing what your father **did."**
	9.26	"What did he **do** to you?"
	9.33	came from God, he would not be able to **do** a thing."
	11.47	priests met with the Council and said, "What shall we **do?**
	14.12	whoever believes in me will **do** what I do—yes, he will
	14.14	you ask me for anything in my name, I will **do** it.
	15. 5	for you can **do** nothing without me.
	15.21	But they will **do** all this to you because you are mine;
	15.24	not done among them the things that no one else ever **did;**
	16. 3	People will **do** these things to you because they have not
	16. 4	time comes for them to **do** these things, you will remember
	18.35	What have you **done?"**
Acts	2.37	to Peter and the other apostles, "What shall we **do,** brothers?"
	4.16	"What shall we **do** with these men?"
	5.28	"but see what you have **done!**
	13.22	like, a man who will **do** all I want him to do.'
	16.30	them out and asked, "Sirs, what must I **do** to be saved?"
	21.22	What should be **done,** then?
	21.23	This is what we want you to **do.**
	21.33	Then he asked, "Who is this man, and what has he **done?"**
	22.10	I asked, 'What shall I **do,** Lord?'
Rom	1.28	so that they do the things that they should not **do.**
	2. 1	you judge others and then **do** the same things which they do,
	4. 6	God accepts as righteous, apart from anything that person **does:**
	7.15	I do not understand what I **do;**
	7.15	for I don't **do** what I would like to do,
	7.15	but instead I **do** what I hate.
	7.16	Since what I **do** is what I don't want to do,
	7.17	So I am not really the one who **does** this thing;
	7.18	I am not able to **do** it.
	7.19	I don't **do** the good I want to do;
	7.19	instead, I **do** the evil that I do not want to do.
	7.20	If I **do** what I don't want to do, this means that
	7.20	this means that I am no longer the one who **does** it;
	8. 3	Law could not do, because human nature was weak, God **did.**
	9.11	was based on his call, and not on anything they had **done.**
	9.16	not on what man wants or **does,** but only on God's mercy.
	9.31	Because they did not depend on faith but on what they **did.**
	11. 6	choice is based on his grace, not on what they have **done.**
	11. 6	were based on what people **do,** then his grace would not be
1 Cor	11.24	**Do** this in memory of me."
	14.15	What should I **do,** then?
	15.10	not really my own **doing,** but God's grace working with me.
2 Cor	10.11	and what we will **do** when we are there with you.
	11.12	I will go on **doing** what I am doing now, in order
Gal	5.17	and this means that you cannot **do** what you want to do.
	6. 4	of what he himself has **done,** without having to
	6. 4	compare it with what someone else has **done.**
Eph	3.20	in us is able to **do** so much more than we can
Col	2.21	you obey such rules as [21] **"Don't** handle this,"
	2.21	**"Don't** taste that," "Don't touch the other"?
	3.17	Everything you **do** or say, then,
2 Thes	3. 7	know very well that you should do just what we **did.**
2 Tim	1. 9	because of what we have **done,** but because of his own purpose
	4.14	the Lord will reward him according to what he has **done.**
Tit	3. 5	deeds that we ourselves had **done,** but because of his own
Heb	10.10	Because Jesus Christ **did** what God wanted him to do, we
	13. 6	What can anyone **do** to me?"
1 Pet	1.17	by the same standard, according to what each one has **done;**
Rev	2. 2	I know what you have **done;**
	2. 5	Turn from your sins and do what you **did** at first.
	2.19	know that you are doing more now than you **did** at first.
	2.23	will repay each one of you according to what he has **done.**
	3.15	I know what you have **done;**
	16.17	came from the throne in the temple, saying, "It is **done!"**
	20.12	according to what they had **done,** as recorded in the books.
	20.13	And all were judged according to what they had **done.**
	21. 6	And he said, "It is **done!**
	22.12	to give to each one according to what he has **done.**

DO AWAY WITH

Mt	5.17	I have come to **do away with** the Law of Moses and
	5.17	have not come to **do away with** them, but to make their
	5.18	the Law will be **done away with**—not until the end of
Lk	16.17	for the smallest detail of the Law to be **done away with.**
Rom	3.31	this mean that by this faith we **do away with** the Law?
	8. 3	with a nature like man's sinful nature, to **do away with** sin.
Col	2.14	its binding rules and **did away with** it completely by nailing
Heb	10. 9	So God **does away with** all the old sacrifices and puts the

DOCTOR

2 Chr	16.12	he did not turn to the Lord for help, but to **doctors.**
Job	13. 4	you are like **doctors** who can't heal anyone.
Jer	8.22	Are there no **doctors** there?
Mt	9.12	well do not need a **doctor,** but only those who are sick.
Mk	2.17	well do not need a **doctor,** but only those who are sick.
	5.26	even though she had been treated by many **doctors.**
Lk	4.23	that you will quote this proverb to me, **'Doctor,** heal yourself.'
	5.31	well do not need a **doctor,** but only those who are sick.
	8.43	spent all she had on **doctors,** but no one had been able
Col	4.14	Luke, our dear **doctor,** and Demas send you their greetings.

DOCTRINE

1 Tim 1. 3 people there are teaching false **doctrines,** and you must order
1.10 or who do anything else contrary to sound **doctrine.**
6. 3 Whoever teaches a different **doctrine** and does not agree with
2 Tim 4. 3 not listen to sound **doctrine,** but will follow their own desires
Tit 1. 9 message which can be trusted and which agrees with the **doctrine.**
2. 1 But you must teach what agrees with sound **doctrine.**
2 Pet 2. 1 bring in destructive, untrue **doctrines,** and will deny the Master

AV DOCTRINE

see also **MESSAGE, TEACH**

Is 28. 9 Who needs his **message?**
Mt 15. 9 because they teach man-made rules as though they were my **laws!'"**
Mk 7. 7 because they teach man-made rules as though they were God's **laws!'**
Acts 2.42 spent their time in **learning** from the apostles, taking part in

DOCUMENT

1 Chr 2.55 experts in writing and copying **documents**
Ezra 7.11 Artaxerxes gave the following **document** to Ezra,
8.36 They also took the **document** the emperor had given them

DODGE

1 Sam 18.11 but David **dodged** each time.
19.10 with his spear, but David **dodged,** and the spear stuck in the

DOG

[WATCHDOGS]

Ex 11. 7 But not even a **dog** will bark at the Israelites or their
22.31 instead, give it to the **dogs.**
Judg 7. 5 with his tongue like a **dog,** from everyone who gets down on
1 Sam 17.43 Do you think I'm a **dog?"**
24.14 A dead **dog,** a flea!
2 Sam 9. 8 again and said, "I am no better than a dead **dog,** sir!
16. 9 the king, "Your Majesty, why do you let this **dog** curse you?
1 Kgs 14.11 city will be eaten by **dogs,** and any who die in the
16. 4 city will be eaten by **dogs,** and any who die in the
21.19 the very place that the **dogs** licked up Naboth's blood
21.23 Jezebel, the Lord says that **dogs** will eat her body
21.24 city will be eaten by **dogs,** and any who die in the
22.38 the pool of Samaria, where **dogs** licked up his blood
2 Kgs 9.10 body will be eaten by **dogs** in the territory of Jezreel.'"
9.36 **'Dogs** will eat Jezebel's body in the territory of Jezreel.
Job 30. 1 that I wouldn't let them help my **dogs** guard sheep.
Ps 22.16 like a pack of **dogs** they close in on me;
22.20 save my life from these **dogs.**
59. 6 the evening, snarling like **dogs** as they go about the city.
59.14 the evening, snarling like **dogs** as they go about the city,
59.15 go about the city, [15] like **dogs** roaming about for food
68.23 in their blood, and your **dogs** may lap up as much as
Prov 26.11 a second time is like a **dog** going back to its vomit.
26.17 like going down the street and grabbing a **dog** by the ears.
Ecc 9. 4 a live **dog** is better off than a dead lion.
Is 56.10 They are like **watchdogs** that don't bark—they only lie about
56.11 They are like greedy **dogs** that never get enough.
66. 3 whether they sacrifice a lamb or break a **dog's** neck;
Jer 15. 3 their bodies will be dragged off by **dogs;**
Ezek 28.10 You will die like a **dog** at the hand of godless foreigners.
Mt 7. 6 give what is holy to **dogs**—they will only turn and attack
15.26 to take the children's food and throw it to the **dogs."**
15.27 even the **dogs** eat the leftovers that fall from their masters'
Mk 7.27 to take the children's food and throw it to the **dogs."**
7.28 she answered, "even the **dogs** under the table eat the children's
Lk 16.21 Even the **dogs** would come and lick his sores.
Phil 3. 2 who do evil things, those **dogs,** those men who insist on
2 Pet 2.22 "A **dog** goes back to what it has vomited"

DOME

Gen 1. 6 commanded, "Let there be a **dome** to divide the water
1. 6 So God made a **dome,** and it separated the water under it
1. 8 He named the **dome** "Sky."
Job 22.14 him from seeing, as he walks on the **dome** of the sky.
Ezek 1.22 something that looked like a **dome** made of dazzling crystal.
1.23 There under the **dome** stood the creatures,
1.25 still a sound coming from above the **dome** over their heads.
1.26 Above the **dome** there was something that looked like a throne
10. 1 I looked at the **dome** over the heads of the living
Amos 9. 6 heavens, and over the earth he puts the **dome** of the sky.

DOMESTIC

Gen 1.24 **domestic** and wild, large and small"—and it was done.
1.26 and all animals, **domestic** and wild, large and small."
7.14 went every kind of animal, **domestic** and wild, large and small,
Ex 34.19 first-born son and first-born male **domestic** animal belongs to me,
Lev 19.19 Do not crossbreed **domestic** animals.
25. 7 your **domestic** animals, and the wild animals
27.32 One out of every ten **domestic** animals belongs to the Lord.
Acts 11. 6 looked closely inside and saw **domesticated** and wild animals,

DOMINATE

Col 3. 7 to such desires, when your life was **dominated** by them.

DOMINION

1 Tim 6.16 To him be honour and eternal **dominion!**

DONKEY

Gen 12.16 gave him flocks of sheep and goats, cattle, **donkeys,** slaves,
16.12 But your son will live like a wild **donkey;**
22. 3 for the sacrifice, loaded his **donkey,** and took Isaac
22. 5 Then he said to the servants, "Stay here with the **donkey.**
24.35 silver, gold, male and female slaves, camels, and **donkeys.**
30.43 He had many flocks, slaves, camels, and **donkeys.**
32. 5 I own cattle, **donkeys,** sheep, goats, and slaves.
32.13 twenty female **donkeys** and ten males.
34.28 the flocks, the cattle, the **donkeys,** and everything else
36.24 wilderness when he was taking care of his father's **donkeys.)**
42.26 The brothers loaded their **donkeys** with the corn
42.27 his sack to feed his **donkey** and found his money at the
43.18 attack us, take our **donkeys,** and make us his slaves."
43.24 that they could wash their feet, and he fed their **donkeys.**
44. 3 the brothers were sent on their way with their **donkeys.**
44.13 loaded their **donkeys,** and returned to the city.
45.23 ten **donkeys** loaded with the best Egyptian goods
45.23 and ten **donkeys** loaded with corn,
47.17 in exchange for their horses, sheep, goats, cattle, and **donkeys.**
49.11 He ties his young **donkey** to a grapevine, To the very
49.14 is no better than a **donkey** That lies stretched out between
49.22 "Joseph is like a wild **donkey** by a spring, A wild colt
Ex 4.20 sons, put them on a **donkey,** and set out with them for
9. 3 on all your animals—your horses, **donkeys,** camels, cattle,
13.13 from him every first-born male **donkey** by offering a lamb in
13.13 you do not want to buy back the **donkey,** break its neck.
20.17 his cattle, his **donkeys,** or anything else that he owns."
21.33 and a bull or a **donkey** falls into it, [34] he must pay
22. 2 animal, whether a cow, a **donkey,** or a sheep, is found alive
22. 9 property, whether it involves cattle, **donkeys,** sheep, clothing,
22.10 agrees to keep another man's **donkey,** cow, sheep, or other animal
23. 4 see your enemy's cow or **donkey** running loose, take it back
23. 5 If his **donkey** has fallen under its load,
23. 5 help him get the **donkey** to its feet again;
34.20 to buy back every first-born **donkey** by offering a lamb in
Num 16.15 I have not even taken one of their **donkeys."**
22.21 next morning Balaam saddled his **donkey** and went with the Moabite
22.22 was riding along on his **donkey,** accompanied by his two servants,
22.23 When the **donkey** saw the angel standing there holding a sword,
22.23 Balaam beat the **donkey** and brought it back on to the road.
22.25 When the **donkey** saw the angel, it moved over against the
22.25 Again Balaam beat the **donkey.**
22.27 This time, when the **donkey** saw the angel, it lay down.
22.27 lost his temper and began to beat the **donkey** with his stick.
22.28 Then the Lord gave the **donkey** the power of speech, and
22.30 The **donkey** replied, "Am I not the same donkey on which
22.32 angel demanded, "Why have you beaten your **donkey** three times
22.33 But your **donkey** saw me and turned aside three times.
22.33 If it hadn't, I would have killed you and spared the **donkey."**
31.28 the same proportion of the cattle, **donkeys,** sheep, and goats.
31.30 the same proportion of the cattle, **donkeys,** sheep, and goats.
31.32 72,000 cattle, 61,000 **donkeys,** and 32,000 virgins.
31.36 30,500 **donkeys** for the soldiers,
31.42 36,000 cattle, 30,500 **donkeys,** and 16,000 virgins.
Deut 5.21 his cattle, his **donkeys,** or anything else that he owns.'
22. 3 thing if you find a **donkey,** a piece of clothing, or anything
22. 4 "If a fellow-Israelite's **donkey** or cow has fallen down,
22.10 "Do not hitch an ox and a **donkey** together for ploughing.
28.31 Your **donkeys** will be dragged away while you look on,
Josh 6.21 They also killed the cattle, sheep, and **donkeys.**
7.24 sons and daughters, his cattle, **donkeys,** and sheep,
9. 4 loaded their **donkeys** with worn-out sacks and patched-up wineskins.
15.18 She got down from her **donkey,** and Caleb asked her what she
Judg 1.14 She got down from her **donkey,** and Caleb asked her what she
5.10 you that ride on white **donkeys,** sitting on saddles,
6. 4 cattle, and **donkeys,** and leave nothing for the Israelites
10. 4 He had thirty sons who rode thirty **donkeys.**
12.14 He had forty sons and thirty grandsons, who rode on seventy **donkeys.**
15.15 Then he found the jaw-bone of a **donkey** that had recently died.
15.16 "With the jaw-bone of a **donkey** I killed a thousand men;
15.16 With the jaw-bone of a **donkey** I piled them up in piles."
19. 3 He took his servant and two **donkeys** with him.
19.10 with their servant and two **donkeys** with pack saddles.
19.19 fodder and straw for our **donkeys,** as well as bread and wine
19.21 So he took them home with him and fed their **donkeys.**
19.28 put her body across the **donkey** and started on his way home.
1 Sam 8.16 your best cattle and **donkeys,** and make them work for him.
9. 3 Some **donkeys** belonging to Kish had wandered off,
9. 3 of the servants with you and go and look for the **donkeys."**
9. 4 the region of Shaalim, but the **donkeys** were not there.
9. 5 stop thinking about the **donkeys** and start worrying about us."
9. 6 and maybe he can tell us where we can find the **donkeys."**
9.20 As for the **donkeys** that were lost three days ago,
10. 2 will tell you that the **donkeys** you were looking for have
10.14 "Looking for the **donkeys,"** Saul answered.
12. 3 Have I taken anybody's cow or anybody's **donkey?**
15. 3 the cattle, sheep, camels, and **donkeys."**
16.20 with a young goat, a **donkey** loaded with bread, and a leather
22.19 cattle, **donkeys,** and sheep—they were all killed.
25.18 two hundred cakes of dried figs, and loaded them on **donkeys.**
25.20 She was riding her **donkey** round a bend on a hillside
25.42 She rose quickly and mounted her **donkey.**

1 Sam 27. 9 taking the sheep, cattle, **donkeys,** camels, and even the clothes.
2 Sam 16. 1 with him a couple of **donkeys** loaded with two hundred loaves
16. 2 Ziba answered, "The **donkeys** are for Your Majesty's family
17.23 been followed, he saddled his **donkey** and went back to his
19.26 my servant to saddle my **donkey** so that I could ride along
1 Kgs 2.40 in Gath, [40] he saddled his **donkey** and went to King Achish
13.13 the road [13] and he told them to saddle his **donkey** for him.
13.23 the old prophet saddled the **donkey** for the prophet from Judah,
13.24 on the road, and the **donkey** and the lion stood beside it.
13.27 Then he said to his sons, "Saddle my **donkey** for me."
13.28 on the road, with the **donkey** and the lion still standing by
13.28 The lion had not eaten the body or attacked the **donkey.**
13.29 body, put it on the **donkey,** and brought it back to Bethel
2 Kgs 4.22 and said to him, "Send a servant here with a **donkey.**
4.24 Then she had the **donkey** saddled, and ordered the servant,
4.24 "Make the **donkey** go as fast as it can,
6.25 so severe that a **donkey's** head cost eighty pieces of silver,
7. 7 abandoning their tents, horses, and **donkeys,** and leaving the camp
7.10 the horses and **donkeys** have not been untied,
1 Chr 5.21 and 2,000 **donkeys,** and took 100,000 prisoners of war.
12.40 people came bringing **donkeys,** camels, mules,
27.25 **Donkeys:**
2 Chr 28.15 to walk were put on **donkeys,** and all the prisoners were
Ezra 2.64 **Donkeys** - 6,720
Neh 2.12 The only animal we took was the **donkey** that I rode on.
2.14 The **donkey** I was riding could not find any path through the
7.66 **Donkeys** - 6,720
13.15 other things on their **donkeys** and taking them into Jerusalem;
Job 1. 3 one thousand head of cattle, and five hundred **donkeys.**
1.14 oxen," he said, "and the **donkeys** were in a nearby pasture.
6. 5 A **donkey** is content when eating grass, and a cow is quiet
11.12 Stupid men will start being wise when wild **donkeys** are born tame.
24. 3 They take **donkeys** that belong to orphans,
24. 5 So the poor, like wild **donkeys,** search for food
39. 5 Who gave the wild **donkeys** their freedom?
42.12 two thousand head of cattle, and one thousand **donkeys.**
Ps 104.11 there the wild **donkeys** quench their thirst.
Prov 26. 3 you have to bridle a **donkey,** and you have to beat a
Is 1. 3 and **donkeys** know where their master feeds them.
21. 7 and men riding on **donkeys** and camels,
30. 6 They load their **donkeys** and camels with expensive gifts
30.24 The oxen and **donkeys** that plough your fields will eat
32.14 Wild **donkeys** will roam there, and sheep will find pasture there.
32.20 safe pasture everywhere for the **donkeys** and cattle.
46. 1 now they are loaded on **donkeys,** a burden for the backs
Jer 14. 6 The wild **donkeys** stand on the hill-tops and pant for breath
22.19 the funeral honours of a **donkey,** he will be dragged away and
48. 6 'Run like a wild desert **donkey!'**
Lam 5. 5 Driven hard like **donkeys** or camels, we are tired,
Ezek 23.20 oversexed men who had all the lustfulness of **donkeys**
Dan 5.21 He lived with wild **donkeys,** ate grass like an ox,
Hos 8. 9 Stubborn as wild **donkeys,** the people of Israel go their own way.
Zech 9. 9 humble and riding on a **donkey**—
9. 9 on a colt, the foal of a **donkey.**
14.15 mules, the camels, and the **donkeys**—on all the animals in the
Mt 21. 2 you will find a **donkey** tied up with her colt beside
21. 5 on a donkey and on a colt, the foal of a **donkey."**
21. 7 they brought the **donkey** and the colt, threw their cloaks over
Lk 13.15 untie his ox or his **donkey** from the stall and take it
Jn 12.14 Jesus found a **donkey** and rode on it, just as the
12.15 Here comes your king, riding on a young **donkey."**
2 Pet 2.16 **donkey** spoke with a human voice and stopped the prophet's insane

DOOM

Num 23. 8 has not cursed, Or speak of **doom** when the Lord has not?
Deut 32.35 the day of their **doom** is near.
2 Kgs 6.15 He went back to Elisha and exclaimed, "We are **doomed,** sir!
7.13 here in the city are **doomed** anyway, like those that have
Ps 1. 6 the Lord, but the evil are on the way to their **doom.**
49.14 they are **doomed** to die like
Prov 19. 9 he is **doomed.**
21. 7 The wicked are **doomed** by their own violence;
Is 1. 4 You are **doomed,** you sinful nation, you corrupt and evil people!
1.20 But if you defy me, you are **doomed** to die.
3. 8 Yes, Jerusalem is **doomed!**
3. 9 They are **doomed,** and they have brought it on themselves.
3.11 But evil men are **doomed;**
5. 8 You are **doomed!**
5.11 You are **doomed!**
5.18 You are **doomed!**
5.20 You are **doomed!**
5.21 You are **doomed!**
5.22 You are **doomed!**
6. 5 I am **doomed** because every word that passes my lips is sinful,
10. 1 You are **doomed!**
28. 1 The kingdom of Israel is **doomed!**
29. 1 God's altar, Jerusalem itself, is **doomed!**
29. 1 The city where David camped is **doomed!**
29.15 Those who try to hide their plans from the Lord are **doomed!**
30. 1 "Those who rule Judah are **doomed** because they rebel against me.
31. 1 Those who go to Egypt for help are **doomed!**
33. 1 Our enemies are **doomed!**
Jer 4.13 We are **doomed!**
4.30 Jerusalem, you are **doomed!**
4.31 stretching out her hand and saying, "I am **doomed!**
13.27 People of Jerusalem, you are **doomed!**
15. 2 Some are **doomed** to die by disease— that's where they will
15. 2 Others are **doomed** to die in war— that's where they will
Jer 15. 2 Some are **doomed** to die of starvation— that's where they will
15. 2 Others are **doomed** to be taken away as prisoners— that's
22.13 **Doomed** is the man who builds his house by injustice
22.14 **Doomed** is the man who says, "I will build myself a
43.11 Those people who are **doomed** to die of disease will die
43.11 of disease, those **doomed** to be taken away as prisoners
43.11 and those **doomed** to be killed in war will
46.21 The day of their **doom** had arrived, the time of their destruction.
48.16 Moab's **doom** approaches;
50.27 The people of Babylonia are **doomed!**
Lam 5.16 We sinned, and now we are **doomed.**
Ezek 13. 3 "These foolish prophets are **doomed!**
13.18 "You women are **doomed!**
16.23 The Sovereign Lord said, "You are **doomed!**
16.23 **Doomed!**
24. 6 "The city of murderers is **doomed!**
24. 9 "The city of murderers is **doomed!**
31.14 All of them are **doomed** to die like mortal men,
31.14 **doomed** to join those who go down
34. 2 You are **doomed,** you shepherds of Israel!
Hos 4. 6 My people are **doomed** because they do not acknowledge me.
7.13 "They are **doomed!**
Amos 5. 5 Do not go to Gilgal—her people are **doomed** to exile."
5. 7 You are **doomed,** you that twist justice and cheat people
Mic 2.10 Your sins have **doomed** this place to destruction.
Nah 3. 1 **Doomed** is the lying, murderous city, full of wealth to be
Hab 2. 6 They will say, "You take what isn't yours, but you are **doomed!**
2. 9 You are **doomed!**
2.12 You are **doomed!**
2.15 You are **doomed!**
2.19 You are **doomed!**
Zeph 2. 5 You Philistines are **doomed,** you people who live along the coast.
3. 1 Jerusalem is **doomed,** that corrupt, rebellious city
3.18 "I have ended the threat of **doom** and taken away your disgrace.
Zech 11.17 That worthless shepherd is **doomed!**
Rom 9.22 were the objects of his anger, who were **doomed** to destruction.

DOOR

Gen 4. 7 because you have done evil, sin is crouching at your **door.**
6.16 Build it with three decks and put a **door** in the side.
7.16 Then the Lord shut the **door** behind Noah.
18.10 Sarah was behind him, at the **door** of the tent, listening.
19. 6 Lot went outside and closed the **door** behind him.
19. 9 They pushed Lot back and moved up to break down the **door.**
19.10 out, pulled Lot back into the house, and shut the **door.**
19.11 with blindness, so that they couldn't find the **door.**
43.19 So at the **door** of the house, they said to the servant
Ex 12. 7 and put it on the **door-posts** and above the doors of the
12. 7 the door-posts and above the **doors** of the houses in which
12.13 The blood on the **door-posts** will be a sign to mark the
12.22 and wipe the blood on the **door-posts**
12.22 and the beam above the **door** of your house.
12.23 on the beams and the **door-posts** and will not let the Angel
21. 6 make him stand against the **door** or the door-post and pierce
21. 6 stand against the door or the **door-post** and pierce his ear.
33. 8 people would stand at the **door** of their tents and watch
33. 9 down and stay at the **door** of the Tent, and the Lord
33.10 pillar of cloud at the **door** of the Tent, they would bow
Num 19.16 a natural death out of **doors** or if someone touches a human
Deut 6. 9 Write them on the **door-posts** of your houses and on your gates.
11.20 Write them on the **door-posts** of your houses and on your gates.
15.17 Then take him to the **door** of your house and there pierce
31.15 a pillar of cloud that stood by the **door** of the Tent.
Judg 3.23 Ehud went outside, closed the **doors** behind him, locked them,
3.24 came and saw that the **doors** were locked, but they only
3.25 still did not open the **door,** they took the key and opened
4.20 told her, "Stand at the **door** of the tent, and if anyone
9.52 he went up to the **door** to set the tower on fire.
16. 3 the city gate and pulled it up—**doors,** posts, lock, and all.
19.22 town surrounded the house and started beating on the **door.**
19.26 and fell down at the **door** of the old man's house, where
19.27 and when he opened the **door** to go on his way, he
19.27 in front of the house with her hands reaching for the **door.**
1 Sam 1. 9 Eli the priest was sitting in his place by the **door.**
3.15 got up and opened the **doors** of the house of the Lord.
5. 4 both its arms were broken off and were lying in the **doorway;**
2 Sam 4. 6 The woman at the **door** had become drowsy while she was
13.17 Throw her out and lock the **door!"**
13.18 The servant put her out and locked the **door.**
1 Kgs 6.31 A double **door** made of olive wood was set in place at
6.31 the top of the **doorway** was a pointed arch.
6.32 The **doors** were decorated with carved figures
6.32 The **doors,** the winged creatures, and the palm-trees
6.33 main room a rectangular **door-frame** of olive wood was made.
6.34 There were two folding **doors** made of pine
7. 5 The **doorways** and the windows had rectangular frames, and
7.50 and the hinges for the **doors** of the Most Holy Place
7.50 and of the outer **doors** of the Temple.
14. 6 when Ahijah heard her coming in the **door,** he said, "Come
2 Kgs 4. 4 into the house, close the **door,** and start pouring oil into
4. 5 her sons, closed the **door,** took the small jar of olive-oil,
4.15 came and stood in the **doorway,** [16] and Elisha said to her,
4.21 put him on the bed and left, closing the **door** behind her.
4.33 He closed the **door** and prayed to the Lord.
6.32 he gets here, shut the **door** and don't let him come in.
18.16 the gold from the temple **doors** and the gold with which he
18.16 he himself had covered the **doorposts,** and he sent it all to
2 Chr 3. 7 the temple walls, the rafters, the thresholds, and the **doors.**
4. 9 The **doors** in the gates between the courtyards were covered
4.22 The outer **doors** of the Temple

2 Chr 4.22 and the **doors** to the Most Holy Place were
29. 7 They closed the **doors** of the Temple, let the lamps go out,
Neh 6.10 the Temple and lock the **doors,** because they are coming to
Job 31. 9 and waited, hidden, outside her **door,**
Ps 24. 7 the gates, open the ancient **doors,** and the great king will
24. 9 the gates, open the ancient **doors,** and the great king will
78.23 he spoke to the sky above and commanded its **doors** to open;
107.16 He breaks down **doors** of bronze and smashes iron bars.
141. 3 guard at my mouth, a sentry at the **door** of my lips.
Prov 5. 8 Don't even go near her **door!**
8.34 man who stays at my **door** every day, waiting at the entrance
9.14 She sits at the **door** of her house or on a seat
18.19 if you quarrel with him, he will close his **doors** to you.
26.14 He gets no farther than a **door** swinging on its hinges.
Song 5. 2 I dreamt my lover knocked at the **door.**
5. 4 put his hand to the **door,** and I was thrilled that he
5. 5 with liquid myrrh, as I grasped the handle of the **door.**
5. 6 I opened the **door** for my lover, but he had already gone.
7.13 mandrakes, and all the pleasant fruits are near our **door.**
Is 26.20 Go into your houses, my people, and shut the **door** behind you.
57. 8 You set up your obscene idols just inside your front **doors.**
Ezek 8. 8 I broke through it and found a **door.**
33.30 meet by the city walls or in the **doorways** of their houses.
41. 8 there was one **door** into the rooms on the north side of
41.17 as high as above the **doors,** were completely covered with carvings
41.20 all round the wall, [20] from the floor to above the **doors.**
41.21 The **door-posts** of the Holy Place were square.
41.23 There was a **door** at the end of the passage leading to
41.24 They were double **doors** that swung open in the middle.
41.25 winged creatures carved on the **doors** of the Holy Place, just
41.25 wooden covering over the outside of the **doorway** of the entrance
42.12 There was a **door** under the rooms on the south side of
43. 8 kings built the thresholds and **door-posts** of their palace
43. 8 right against the thresholds and **door-posts** of my Temple,
45.19 and put it on the **door-posts** of the Temple, on the four
Dan 3.26 Nebuchadnezzar went up to the **door** of the blazing furnace
Hos 2.15 vineyards she had and make Trouble Valley a **door** of hope.
Zeph 2.14 Crows will caw on the **doorsteps.**
Zech 11. 1 Open your **doors,** Lebanon, so that fire can burn down your
Mal 1.10 you would close the temple **doors** so as to prevent you from
Mt 6. 6 to your room, close the **door,** and pray to your Father,
7. 7 knock, and the **door** will be opened to you.
7. 8 seeks will find, and the **door** will be opened to him who
23.13 You lock the **door** to the Kingdom of heaven in people's faces,
25.10 in with him to the wedding feast, and the **door** was closed.
Mk 2. 2 was no room left, not even out in front of the **door.**
11. 4 colt out in the street, tied to the **door** of a house.
Lk 11. 7 The **door** is already locked, and my children and I are in
11. 9 knock, and the **door** will be opened to you.
11.10 seeks will find, and the **door** will be opened to anyone who
11.52 kept the key that opens the **door** to the house of knowledge;
12.36 comes and knocks, they will open the **door** for him at once.
13.24 "Do your best to go in through the narrow **door;**
13.25 The master of the house will get up and close the **door;**
13.25 knock on the door and say, 'Open the **door** for us, sir!'
16.20 brought to the rich man's **door,** [21] hoping to eat the bits
Jn 20.19 gathered together behind locked **doors,** because they were afraid
20.26 The **doors** were locked, but Jesus came and stood among them
Acts 5. 9 husband are now at the **door,** and they will carry you out
12.13 Peter knocked at the outside **door,** and a servant-girl
12.14 back in without opening the **door,** and announced that Peter was
12.16 At last they opened the **door,** and when they saw him,
16.26 At once all the **doors** opened, and the chains fell off all
16.27 when he saw the prison **doors** open, he thought that the
21.30 At once the Temple **doors** were closed.
Heb 11.28 to be sprinkled on the **doors,** so that the Angel of Death
Rev 3. 7 and when he opens a **door,** no one can close it,
3. 8 I have opened a **door** in front of you, which no one
3.20 I stand at the **door** and knock;
3.20 my voice and opens the **door,** I will come into his house
4. 1 I had another vision and saw an open **door** in heaven.

DOORKEEPER

Mk 13.34 work to do and after telling the **doorkeeper** to keep watch.

Am **DOORSILL** see **THRESHOLD**

DOUBLE

Ex 22. 7 his house, the thief, if he is found, shall repay **double.**
22. 9 God declares to be guilty shall pay **double** to the other man.
26. 9 Fold the sixth piece **double** over the front of the Tent.
28.16 to be square and folded **double,** 22 centimetres long and 22
39. 9 It was square and folded **double,** 22 centimetres long and 22
Deut 21.17 He is to give a **double** share of his possessions to his
1 Kgs 6.31 A **double** door made of olive wood was set in place
Is 51.19 A **double** disaster has fallen on you:
61. 7 live in your own land, And your wealth will be **doubled;**
Jer 16.18 I will make them pay **double** for their sin and wickedness,
Ezek 41.24 They were **double** doors that swung open in the middle.
1 Tim 5.17 worthy of receiving **double** pay, especially those who work hard
Rev 18. 6 pay her back **double** for all she has done.

DOUBLE-EDGED
see also **TWO-EDGED**

Judg 3.16 Ehud had made himself a **double-edged** sword
Heb 4.12 of God is alive and active, sharper than any **double-edged** sword.

DOUBT

Mt 11. 6 How happy are those who have no **doubts** about me!"
14.31 Why did you **doubt?"**
21.21 you believe and do not **doubt,** you will be able to do
28.17 saw him, they worshipped him, even though some of them **doubted.**
Mk 11.23 the sea and does not **doubt** in his heart, but believes that
Lk 7.23 How happy are those who have no **doubts** about me!"
22.59 "There isn't any **doubt** that this man was with Jesus,
24.38 Why are these **doubts** coming up in your minds?
Jn 20.27 Stop your **doubting,** and believe!"
Acts 1. 3 times in ways that proved beyond **doubt** that he was alive.
Rom 4.20 faith did not leave him, and he did not **doubt** God's promise;
14.23 But if he has **doubts** about what he eats, God condemns
1 Cor 11.19 (No **doubt** there must be divisions among you so that the
2 Cor 4. 8 sometimes in **doubt,** but never in despair;
Heb 7. 7 There is no **doubt** that the one who blesses is greater than
Jas 1. 6 But when you pray, you must believe and not **doubt** at all.
1. 6 Whoever **doubts** is like a wave in the sea that is driven
Jude 22 Show mercy towards those who have **doubts;**

DOUGH

Ex 12.34 filled their baking-pans with unleavened **dough,**
12.39 baked unleavened bread from the **dough** that they had brought
12.39 time to get their food ready or to prepare leavened **dough.**
2 Sam 13. 8 She took some **dough,** prepared it, and made some cakes there
Neh 10.37 the **dough** made from the first corn harvested
Jer 7.18 and the women mix **dough** to bake cakes for the goddess
Hos 7. 4 not stirred by the baker until the **dough** is ready to bake.
Mt 13.33 litres of flour until the whole batch of **dough** rises."
Lk 13.21 litres of flour until the whole batch of **dough** rises."
1 Cor 5. 6 "A little bit of yeast makes the whole batch of **dough** rise."
5. 7 like a new batch of **dough** without any yeast, as indeed I
Gal 5. 9 yeast to make the whole batch of **dough** rise," as they say.

DOVE

Gen 8. 8 Meanwhile, Noah sent out a **dove** to see if the water
8. 9 covered all the land, the **dove** did not find a place to
8.10 He waited another seven days and sent out the **dove** again.
8.12 waited another seven days and sent out the **dove** once more;
15. 9 each of them three years old, and a **dove** and a pigeon."
Lev 1.14 bird as a burnt-offering, it must be a **dove** or a pigeon.
5. 7 payment for his sin two **doves** or two pigeons, one for a
5.11 a man cannot afford two **doves** or two pigeons, he shall bring
12. 6 a burnt-offering and a pigeon or a **dove** for a sin-offering.
12. 8 lamb, she shall bring two **doves** or two pigeons, one for a
14.22 He shall also bring two **doves** or two pigeons, one for
14.30 shall offer one of the **doves** or pigeons [31] as the sin-offering
15.14 day he shall take two **doves** or two pigeons to the entrance
15.29 day she shall take two **doves** or two pigeons to the priest
Num 6.10 day he shall bring two **doves** or two pigeons to the priest
2 Kgs 6.25 hundred grammes of **dove's** dung cost five pieces of silver.
Ps 55. 6 I wish I had wings, like a **dove.**
68.13 figures of **doves** covered with silver,
Song 2.12 the song of **doves** is heard in the fields.
2.14 You are like a **dove** that hides in the crevice of a
5. 2 Let me come in, my darling, my sweetheart, my **dove.**
5.12 eyes are as beautiful as **doves** by a flowing brook,
5.12 **doves** washed in milk and standing by
6. 9 I love only one, and she is as lovely as a **dove.**
Is 38.14 My voice was thin and weak, And I moaned like a **dove.**
60. 8 ships that skim along like clouds, Like **doves** returning
Jer 8. 7 **doves,** swallows, and thrushes know when it is time to migrate.
48.28 Be like the **dove** that makes its nest in the sides of
Ezek 7.16 Some will escape to the mountains like **doves** frightened from
Hos 11.11 Egypt, as swiftly as birds, and from Assyria, like **doves.**
Nah 2. 7 her servants moan like **doves** and beat their breasts in sorrow.
Mt 3.16 Spirit of God coming down like a **dove** and alighting on him.
10.16 You must be as cautious as snakes and as gentle as **doves.**
Mk 1.10 opening and the Spirit coming down on him like a **dove.**
Lk 2.24 sacrifice of a pair of **doves** or two young pigeons, as
3.22 Holy Spirit came down upon him in bodily form like a **dove.**
Jn 1.32 Spirit come down like a **dove** from heaven and stay on him.

DOWNFALL

2 Chr 22. 4 King Ahab's family became his advisers, and they led to his **downfall.**
22. 7 God used this visit to Joram to bring about Ahaziah's **downfall.**
26.16 Uzziah became strong, he grew arrogant, and that led to his **downfall.**
Ps 13. 4 Don't let them gloat over my **downfall.**
38.16 don't let them boast about my **downfall!**
69.22 may their sacred feasts cause their **downfall.**
140. 4 keep me safe from violent men who plot my **downfall.**
Prov 11. 5 life easier, but a wicked man will cause his own **downfall.**
12. 7 Wicked men meet their **downfall** and leave no descendants,
13. 6 wickedness is the **downfall** of sinners.
14.32 people bring about their own **downfall** by their evil deeds,
16.18 Pride leads to destruction, and arrogance to **downfall.**
29.16 But the righteous will live to see the **downfall** of such men.
29.23 Arrogance will bring your **downfall,**
Jer 20.10 Even my close friends wait for my **downfall.**
Lam 1. 7 Her conquerors laughed at her **downfall.**
1. 9 Her **downfall** was terrible;
2.17 He gave our enemies victory, gave them joy at our **downfall.**
4. 6 which met with a sudden **downfall** at the hands of God.
Ezek 31.16 the dead, the noise of its **downfall** will shake the nations.

Ezek 31.16 gone to the world below will be pleased at its **downfall.**
35.14 world will rejoice at your **downfall,** [15]just as you rejoiced
Zeph 1. 3 I will bring about the **downfall** of the wicked.

DOWNHEARTED

2 Cor 7. 6 But God, who encourages the **downhearted,** encouraged us with

DOWNSTAIRS

1 Kgs 17.23 Elijah took the boy back **downstairs** to his mother

DOWNSTREAM

Josh 3.13 and the water coming **downstream** will pile up in one place."
3.16 The flow **downstream** to the Dead Sea was completely cut off,
Ezek 47. 3 man measured five hundred metres **downstream** to the east

DOZE

Ps 121. 4 The protector of Israel never **dozes** or sleeps.
Is 5.27 They never **doze** or sleep.

DRAFTED

Deut 24. 5 he is not to be **drafted** into military service
1 Kgs 5.13 King Solomon **drafted** 30,000 men as forced labour

DRAG

Deut 28.31 Your donkeys will be **dragged** away while you look on, and
2 Sam 20.12 everybody was stopping, so he **dragged** the body from the road
2 Kgs 10.25 killed them all, and **dragged** the bodies outside.
Job 7. 4 When I lie down to sleep, the hours **drag;**
18.14 he lived secure, and is **dragged** off to face King Death.
Ps 10. 9 he catches them in his trap and **drags** them away.
Ecc 12. 5 will hardly be able to **drag** yourself along,
Is 1. 4 Your sins **drag** you down!
10. 4 You will be killed in battle or **dragged** off as prisoners.
Jer 12. 3 **Drag** these evil men away like sheep to be butchered;
15. 3 their bodies will be **dragged** off by dogs;
22.19 he will be **dragged** away and thrown outside Jerusalem's gates."
49.20 Even their children will be **dragged** off,
50.45 Even their children will be **dragged** off,
Ezek 16.25 You **dragged** your beauty through the mud.
19. 4 With hooks they **dragged** him off to Egypt.
32. 3 catch you in my net and let them **drag** the net ashore.
38. 4 hooks in his jaws, and **drag** him and all his troops away.
Hos 5.14 When I **drag** them off, no one will be able to save
Amos 4. 2 "The days will come when they will **drag** you away with hooks;
4. 3 You will be **dragged** to the nearest break in the wall
Hab 1.15 They **drag** them off in nets and shout for joy over their
Lk 4.29 They rose up, **dragged** Jesus out of the town, and took
12.58 If you don't, he will **drag** you before the judge, who will
Jn 21.11 Simon Peter went aboard and **dragged** the net ashore full of
Acts 8. 3 from house to house, he **dragged** out the believers, both men
14.19 stoned Paul and **dragged** him out of the town, thinking
16.19 seized Paul and Silas and **dragged** them to the authorities
17. 6 did not find them, they **dragged** Jason and some other believers
21.30 ran together, seized Paul, and **dragged** him out of the Temple.
Jas 2. 6 the ones who oppress you and **drag** you before the judges?
Rev 12. 4 With his tail he **dragged** a third of the stars out of

DRAGON

A beast in old legends, thought to be like a huge lizard. It is also called a serpent and appears as a picture of the Devil (Revelation 12.3-13.4; 20.2-3).

Is 14.29 A snake's egg hatches a flying **dragon.**
27. 1 punish Leviathan, that wriggling, twisting **dragon,**
30. 6 where there are poisonous snakes and flying **dragons.**
30. 7 So I have nicknamed Egypt, 'The Harmless **Dragon.'** "
Rev 12. 3 There was a huge red **dragon** with seven heads and ten horns
12. 7 fought against the **dragon,** who fought back with his angels;
12. 8 but the **dragon** was defeated, and he and his angels were
12. 9 **dragon** was thrown out—that ancient serpent, called the Devil,
12.13 When the **dragon** realized that he had been thrown down to
12.14 for three and a half years, safe from the **dragon's** attack.
12.15 then from his mouth the **dragon** poured out a flood of water
12.16 and swallowed the water that had come from the **dragon's** mouth.
12.17 The **dragon** was furious with the woman and went off to
12.18 And the **dragon** stood on the sea-shore.
13. 2 The **dragon** gave the beast his own power, his throne, and his
13. 4 worshipped the **dragon** because he had given his authority to
13.11 two horns like a lamb's horns, and it spoke like a **dragon.**
16.13 of the mouth of the **dragon,** the mouth of the beast, and
20. 2 He seized the **dragon,** that ancient serpent—that is, the Devil,

DRAGON'S FOUNTAIN

Neh 2.13 and went south past **Dragon's Fountain** to the Rubbish Gate.

DRAIN

Lev 1.15 Its blood shall be **drained** out against the side of the altar.
5. 9 of the blood will be **drained** out at the base of the
Ps 32. 4 my strength was completely **drained,** as moisture is dried up
58. 7 May they disappear like water **draining** away;
Ezek 23.34 You will drink and **drain** it dry, and with its broken

Am **DRAPERIES** see **CURTAIN**

DRAUGHT

1 Kgs 4.28 for the chariot-horses and the **draught** animals.
Ezek 27.14 You sold your goods for **draught-horses,** war-horses,

DRAW

[DREW, DRAW BACK, DRAW LOTS, DRAW NEAR, DRAW UP, DRAW WATER]

Gen 14. 8 Gomorrah, Admah, Zeboiim, and Bela **drew up** their armies
47.29 When the time **drew near** for him to die,
Ex 2.15 priest of Midian, came to **draw water** and fill the troughs
2.19 they answered, "and he even **drew water** for us
15. 9 I will **draw my sword** and take all they have.'
Lev 16. 8 There he shall **draw lots,** using two stones,
Num 26.54 Divide the land by **drawing lots,**
33.54 various tribes and clans by **drawing lots,**
34.13 that you will receive by **drawing lots,** the land that the
36. 2 distribute the land to the people of Israel by **drawing lots.**
Josh 14. 2 tribes west of the Jordan were determined by **drawing lots.**
18. 6 Then I will **draw lots** to consult the Lord our God for
18. 8 in Shiloh I will consult the Lord for you by **drawing lots."**
18.10 Joshua **drew lots** to consult the Lord for them,
19.51 parts of the land by **drawing lots** to consult the Lord
21. 8 By **drawing lots,** the people of Israel assigned these cities
Judg 8.20 But the boy did not **draw his sword.**
9.54 and ordered, **"Draw your sword** and kill me.
20. 9 we will **draw lots** and choose some men to attack Gibeah.
1 Sam 7. 6 They **drew some water** and poured it out as an offering
9. 9 town, they met some girls who were coming out to **draw water.**
31. 4 man carrying his weapons, **"Draw your sword** and kill me,
2 Sam 23.16 through the Philistine camp, **drew some water** from the well,
2 Kgs 3.27 were terrified and so they **drew back** from the city and
9.24 Jehu **drew his bow,** and with all his strength shot an
10.25 They went in with **drawn swords,** killed them all,
11. 8 to guard King Joash with **drawn swords** and stay with him
11.11 he stationed the men with **drawn swords** all round
1 Chr 6.65 Benjamin, mentioned above, were also assigned by **drawing lots.)**
10. 4 man carrying his weapons, **"Draw your sword** and kill me,
11.18 through the Philistine camp, **drew some water** from the well,
24. 5 Eleazar and Ithamar, assignments were made by **drawing lots.**
24. 6 descendants of Eleazar and of Ithamar took turns in **drawing lots.**
24.31 one of his younger brothers **drew lots** for their assignments,
25. 8 they all **drew lots,** whether they were young
26.13 Each family, regardless of size, **drew lots** to see which gate
26.14 Shelemiah **drew** the east gate,
26.14 a man who always gave good advice, **drew** the north gate.
2 Chr 23. 7 the king, with their **swords drawn,** and are to stay with the
23.10 He stationed the men with **drawn swords** all round
Neh 10.34 people, priests, and Levites, will **draw lots** each year
11. 1 the rest of the people **drew lots** to choose one family
Job 6.21 streams to me, you see my fate and **draw back** in fear.
26.10 from darkness by a circle **drawn** on the face of the sea.
Ps 11. 2 because the wicked have **drawn their bows**
37.14 The wicked **draw their swords** and bend their bows to kill
Prov 20. 5 in a deep well, but someone with insight can **draw** them out.
Is 53. 2 nothing attractive about him, nothing that would **draw** us to him.
60. 3 Nations will be **drawn** to your light, And kings to the
Lam 3.12 He **drew his bow** and made me the target for his arrows.
Ezek 8.10 The walls were covered with **drawings** of snakes
21. 3 I will **draw my sword** and kill all of you, good and
21. 5 I, the Lord, have **drawn my sword** and that I will not
32.12 cruel nations **draw their swords** and kill all your people.
47.22 Israelite citizens and are to **draw lots** for shares of the
Hos 11. 4 I **drew** them to me with affection and love.
Jon 1. 7 said to one another, "Let's **draw lots** and find out who is
1. 7 They did so, and Jonah's name was **drawn.**
Nah 3.14 **Draw water** to prepare for a siege,
Hag 2.16 You would go to **draw** a hundred litres of wine
Mt 26.51 those who were with Jesus **drew his sword** and struck at the
28.18 Jesus **drew near** and said to them, "I have been given
Mk 14.47 one of those standing there **drew his sword** and struck at the
Lk 9.51 As the time **drew near** when Jesus would be taken up to
24.15 Jesus himself **drew near** and walked along with them;
Jn 2. 8 then he told them, "Now **draw some water** out and take it
2. 9 (but, of course, the servants who had **drawn out** the water knew);
4. 7 A Samaritan woman came to **draw some water,** and Jesus said
4.15 thirsty again, nor will I have to come here to **draw water."**
6.44 to me unless the Father who sent me **draws** him to me;
12.32 am lifted up from the earth, I will **draw** everyone to me."
18.10 Peter, who had a sword, **drew** it and struck the High Priest's
Acts 1.26 Then they **drew lots** to choose between the two men,
5.37 he **drew** a crowd after him, but he also was killed,
7.17 "When the time **drew near** for God to keep the promise he
11.10 and finally the whole thing was **drawn back** up into heaven.
22.29 the men who were going to question Paul **drew back** from him;
Gal 2.12 after these men arrived, he **drew back** and would not eat with
Col 2. 2 with courage and may be **drawn together** in love, and so have
Heb 8. 8 the Lord, when I will **draw up** a new covenant with the
Jas 1.14 is tempted when he is **drawn away** and trapped by his own

DREAD

see also **DISEASE**

Ex 15.16 Terror and **dread** fall upon them.
Deut 7.15 any of the **dreadful** diseases that you experienced in Egypt,
28.60 once again all the **dreadful** diseases you experienced in Egypt,

Job 3.25 Everything I fear and **dread** comes true.
Jer 42.16 you, and the hunger you **dread** will follow you, and you will

DREAM
[DAY-DREAMING, WET DREAM]

Gen 20. 3 One night God appeared to him in a **dream** and said:
20. 6 God replied in the **dream,** "Yes, I know that you did it
28.12 He **dreamt** that he saw a stairway reaching from earth to heaven,
31.10 breeding season I had a **dream,** and I saw that the male
31.11 angel of God spoke to me in the **dream** and said, 'Jacob!'
31.24 In a **dream** that night God came to Laban and said to
37. 5 One night Joseph had a **dream,** and when he told his
37. 6 He said, "Listen to the **dream** I had.
37. 8 even more because of his **dreams** and because of what he said
37. 9 Then Joseph had another **dream** and said to his brothers,
37. 9 "I had another **dream,** in which I saw the sun,
37.10 He also told the **dream** to his father, and his father
37.10 "What kind of a **dream** is that?
37.19 They said to one another, "Here comes that **dreamer.**
37.20 Then we will see what becomes of his **dreams."**
40. 5 each had a **dream,** and the dreams had different meanings.
40. 8 "Each of us had a **dream,** and there is no one here
40. 8 and there is no one here to explain what the **dreams** mean."
40. 8 "It is God who gives the ability to interpret **dreams,"**
40. 8 "Tell me your **dreams."**
40. 9 wine steward said, "In my **dream** there was a grapevine in
40.16 interpretation of the wine steward's **dream** was favourable,
40.16 he said to Joseph, "I had a **dream** too;
41. 1 the king of Egypt **dreamt** that he was standing by the
41. 5 He fell asleep again and had another **dream.**
41. 7 The king woke up and realized that he had been **dreaming.**
41. 8 He told them his **dreams,** but no one could explain them to
41.11 of us had a **dream,** and the dreams had different meanings.
41.12 We told him our **dreams,** and he interpreted them for us.
41.15 him, "I have had a **dream,** and no one can explain it.
41.15 I have been told that you can interpret **dreams."**
41.17 The king said, "I **dreamt** that I was standing on the
41.22 I also **dreamt** that I saw seven ears of corn which were
41.24 I told the **dreams** to the magicians, but none of them could
41.25 Joseph said to the king, "The two **dreams** mean the same thing;
41.32 The repetition of your **dream** means that the matter is fixed
42. 9 He remembered the **dreams** he had dreamt about them and said,
Num 12. 6 myself to them in visions and speak to them in **dreams.**
Deut 13. 1 prophet or an interpreter of **dreams** may promise a miracle or
13. 5 to death any interpreter of **dreams** or prophet that tells you
23.10 he has had a **wet dream** during the night, he is to
Judg 7.13 Gideon arrived, he heard a man telling a friend about a **dream.**
7.13 He was saying, "I **dreamt** that a loaf of barley bread rolled
7.15 Gideon heard about the man's **dream** and what it meant, he
1 Sam 28. 6 him at all, either by **dreams** or by the use of Urim
28.15 He doesn't answer me any more, either by prophets or by **dreams.**
1 Kgs 3. 5 appeared to him in a **dream** and asked him, "What would you
3.15 up and realized that God had spoken to him in the **dream.**
18.27 Maybe he is **day-dreaming** or relieving himself,
Job 7.14 But you—you terrify me with **dreams;**
20. 8 He will vanish like a **dream,** like a vision at night,
33.15 At night when men are asleep, God speaks in **dreams**
Ps 73.20 They are like a **dream** that goes away in the morning;
90. 5 we last no longer than a **dream.**
126. 1 the Lord brought us back to Jerusalem, it was like a **dream!**
Ecc 5. 3 you are to have bad **dreams,** and the more you talk,
5. 7 No matter how much you **dream,** how much useless work you do,
Song 3. 1 my bed, night after night I **dreamt** of the one I love;
5. 2 I **dreamt** my lover knocked at the door.
Is 29. 7 everything—will vanish like a **dream,** like something imagined
29. 8 like a starving man who **dreams** he is eating and wakes up
29. 8 man dying of thirst who **dreams** he is drinking and wakes
47.11 Ruin will come on you suddenly— ruin you never **dreamt** of!
56.10 watchdogs that don't bark—they only lie about and **dream.**
Jer 23.25 claim that I have given them my messages in their **dreams.**
23.27 think that the **dreams** they tell will make my people forget
23.28 prophet who has had a **dream** should say
23.28 say it is only a **dream,** but the prophet who has heard
23.32 the prophets who tell their **dreams** that are full of lies.
23.32 They tell these **dreams** and lead my people astray with their
27. 9 predict the future, either by **dreams** or by calling up the
29. 8 Do not pay any attention to their **dreams.**
Dan 1.17 In addition, he gave Daniel skill in interpreting visions and **dreams.**
2. 1 In the second year that Nebuchadnezzar was king, he had a **dream.**
2. 2 sorcerers, and wizards to come and explain the **dream** to him.
2. 3 he said to them, "I'm worried about a **dream** I have had.
2. 4 Tell us your **dream,** and we will explain it to you."
2. 5 you must tell me the **dream** and then tell me what it
2. 6 can tell me both the **dream** and its meaning, I will reward
2. 6 Now then, tell me what the **dream** was and what it means."
2. 7 will only tell us what the **dream** was, we will explain it."
2. 9 of you the same punishment if you don't tell me the **dream.**
2. 9 Tell me what the **dream** was, and then I will know that
2.16 time, so that he could tell the king what the **dream** meant.
2.24 to the king, and I will tell him what his **dream** means."
2.25 Jewish exiles, who can tell Your Majesty the meaning of your **dream."**
2.26 "Can you tell me what I **dreamt** and what it means?"
2.28 I will tell you the **dream,** the vision you had while you
2.29 "While Your Majesty was sleeping, you **dreamt** about the future;
2.30 learn the meaning of your **dream** and understand the thoughts
2.36 "This was the **dream.**
2.45 told you exactly what you **dreamt,** and have given you its
Dan 4. 5 But I had a frightening **dream** and saw terrifying visions
4. 6 to me so that they could tell me what the **dream** meant.
4. 7 and I told them my **dream,** but they could not explain it
4. 8 so I told him what I had **dreamt.**
4. 9 This is my **dream.**
4.18 "This is the **dream** I had," said King Nebuchadnezzar.
4.19 "Belteshazzar, don't let the **dream** and its message alarm you."
4.19 Majesty, I wish that the **dream** and its explanation applied
5.12 is wise and skilful in interpreting **dreams,** solving riddles,
7. 1 of Babylonia, I had a **dream** and saw a vision in the
7. 1 I wrote the **dream** down, and this is the record
Joel 2.28 your old men will have **dreams,**
Zech 10. 2 Some interpret **dreams,** but only mislead you;
Mt 1.20 appeared to him in a **dream** and said, "Joseph, descendant of
2.12 had warned them in a **dream** not to go back to Herod.
2.13 the Lord appeared in a **dream** to Joseph and said, "Herod
2.19 Lord appeared in a **dream** to Joseph in Egypt [20] and said,
2.22 given more instructions in a **dream,** so he went to the
27.19 innocent man, because in a **dream** last night I suffered much
Acts 2.17 men will see visions, and your old men will have **dreams.**

DRENCH

Job 24. 8 They are **drenched** by the rain that falls on the mountains,
37. 6 to fall on the earth, and sends torrents of **drenching** rain.
38.34 orders to the clouds and make them **drench** you with rain?

DRESS
[UNDRESSED, WEDDING-DRESS, WELL-DRESSED]

Ex 12.11 for you are to be **dressed** for travel, with your sandals on
29. 5 Then **dress** Aaron in the priestly garments—
40.13 **Dress** Aaron in the priestly garments, anoint him,
Ruth 3. 3 put on some perfume, and get **dressed** in your best clothes.
2 Sam 1.24 clothed you in rich scarlet **dresses** and adorned you with jewels
20. 8 Joab was **dressed** for battle, with a sword in its sheath
1 Kgs 22.10 The two kings, **dressed** in their royal robes,
2 Chr 18. 9 The two kings, **dressed** in their royal robes,
Esth 4. 1 Then he **dressed** in sackcloth, covered his head with ashes,
6. 9 of your highest noblemen to **dress** the man in these robes
Ps 35.13 But when they were sick, I **dressed** in mourning;
69.11 I **dress** myself in clothes of mourning, and they laugh at me.
109.18 He cursed as naturally as he **dressed** himself;
Prov 7.10 she was **dressed** like a prostitute and was making plans.
Song 5. 3 I have already **undressed;**
5. 3 why should I get **dressed** again?
Is 3.24 instead of fine clothes, they will be **dressed** in rags;
15. 3 The people in the streets are **dressed** in sackcloth;
61.10 She is like a bride **dressed** for her wedding.
63. 1 Who is this so splendidly **dressed** in red,
Jer 2.32 Does a young woman forget her jewellery, or a bride her **wedding-dress?**
4.30 Why do you **dress** in scarlet?
10. 9 they are **dressed** in violet and purple cloth
Ezek 9. 2 With them was a man **dressed** in linen clothes,
9. 3 Lord called to the man **dressed** in linen, [4] "Go through
16.10 I **dressed** you in embroidered gowns
27.31 They shave their heads for you And **dress** themselves in sackcloth.
Dan 3.21 they tied them up, fully **dressed**—shirts, robes, caps, and all—
5. 7 what it means will be **dressed** in robes of royal purple,
5.16 you will be **dressed** in robes of royal purple,
5.29 Belshazzar ordered his servants to **dress** Daniel in a robe
Mt 11. 8 A man **dressed** up in fancy clothes?
11. 8 People who **dress** like that live in palaces!
Mk 14.51 certain young man, **dressed** only in a linen cloth, was following
Lk 7.25 A man **dressed** up in fancy clothes?
7.25 People who **dress** like that and live in luxury are found in
12.35 "Be ready for whatever comes, **dressed** for action and with
16.19 once a rich man who **dressed** in the most expensive clothes
Jn 20.12 saw two angels there **dressed** in white, sitting where the body
Acts 1.10 when two men **dressed** in white suddenly stood beside them
10.30 Suddenly a man **dressed** in shining clothes stood in front of
1 Tim 2. 9 modest and sensible about their clothes and to **dress** properly;
2. 9 ornaments or pearls or expensive **dresses,** [10] but with good deeds,
Jas 2. 3 show more respect to the **well-dressed** man and say to him,
1 Pet 3. 3 or the jewellery you put on, or the **dresses** you wear.
Rev 3.18 Buy also white clothing to **dress** yourself and cover up your
4. 4 seated twenty-four elders **dressed** in white and wearing crowns
7. 9 throne and of the Lamb, **dressed** in white robes and holding
7.13 "Who are these people **dressed** in white robes, and where do
11. 3 will send my two witnesses **dressed** in sackcloth, and they will
12. 1 There was a woman, whose **dress** was the sun and who had
15. 6 came out of the temple, **dressed** in clean shining linen and
17. 4 woman was **dressed** in purple and scarlet, and covered with gold
18.16 She used to **dress** herself in linen, purple, and scarlet,
19.14 riding on white horses and **dressed** in clean white linen.
21. 2 prepared and ready, like a bride **dressed** to meet her husband.

DRIBBLE

1 Sam 21.13 would scribble on the city gates and **dribble** down his beard.

DRIED-UP see DRY

DRIFT

Gen 7.18 The water became deeper, and the boat **drifted** on the surface.

DRINK
[DRANK, DRUNK, WINE-DRINKERS]

Gen	9.21	After he **drank** some of the wine, he became drunk, took
	19.33	gave him wine to **drink,** and the elder daughter had intercourse
	24.14	'Please, lower your jar and let me have a **drink.'**
	24.14	If she says, **'Drink,** and I will also bring water for your
	24.17	said, "Please give me a **drink** of water from your jar."
	24.18	She said, **"Drink,** sir," and quickly lowered her jar
	24.18	her jar from her shoulder and held it while he **drank.**
	24.43	ask her to give me a **drink** of water from her jar.
	24.45	I said to her, 'Please give me a **drink.'**
	24.46	from her shoulder and said, **'Drink,** and I will also water
	24.46	So I **drank,** and she watered the camels.
	24.54	the men with him ate and **drank,** and spent the night there.
	25.34	He ate and **drank** and then got up and left.
	26.30	Isaac prepared a feast for them, and they ate and **drank.**
	27.25	it to him, and he also brought him some wine to **drink.**
	30.38	there, because the animals mated when they came to **drink.**
	43.34	So they ate and **drank** with Joseph until they were drunk.
	44. 5	It is the one he **drinks** from, the one he uses for
	49.12	His eyes are bloodshot from **drinking** wine,
	49.12	His teeth white from **drinking** milk.
Ex	7.18	that the Egyptians will not be able to **drink** from it.' "
	7.21	it smelt so bad that the Egyptians could not **drink** from it.
	7.24	bank of the river for **drinking** water, because they were not
	7.24	because they were not able to **drink** water from the river.
	15.23	the water there was so bitter that they could not **drink** it.
	15.24	to Moses and asked, "What are we going to **drink?"**
	15.25	and the water became fit to **drink.**
	17. 1	camp at Rephidim, but there was no water there to **drink.**
	17. 2	They complained to Moses and said, "Give us water to **drink."**
	17. 6	and water will come out of it for the people to **drink."**
	24.11	they saw God, and then they ate and **drank** together.
	32. 6	to a feast, which turned into an orgy of **drinking** and sex.
	32.20	Then he made the people of Israel **drink** it.
	34.28	forty days and nights, eating and **drinking** nothing.
Lev	10. 9	enter the Tent of my presence after **drinking** wine or beer;
	11.34	be unclean, and anything **drinkable** in such a pot is unclean.
Num	5.24	Before he makes the woman **drink** the water,
	5.26	Finally, he shall make the woman **drink** the water.
	6. 3	He shall not **drink** any kind of drink made from grapes
	6.20	After that, the Nazirite may **drink** wine.
	20. 5	There is not even any water to **drink!"**
	20. 8	rock for the people, for them and their animals to **drink."**
	20.11	of water gushed out, and all the people and animals **drank.**
	20.17	fields or vineyards, and we will not **drink** from your wells.
	20.19	if we or our animals **drink** any of your water, we will
	21.22	or vineyards, and we will not **drink** water from your wells;
	23.24	and devoured, Until it has **drunk** the blood of those it has
	33.14	Next was Rephidim, where there was no water for them to **drink.**
Deut	2.28	will pay for the food we eat and the water we **drink.**
	9. 9	forty days and nights and did not eat or **drink** anything.
	9.18	for forty days and nights and did not eat or **drink** anything.
	28.39	not gather their grapes or **drink** wine from them,
	29. 6	or wine or beer to **drink,** but the Lord provided for your
	32.38	the fat of your sacrifices and offered them wine to **drink.**
Judg	4.19	He said to her, "Please give me a **drink** of water;
	4.19	leather bag of milk, gave him a **drink,** and hid him again.
	7. 5	a dog, from everyone who gets down on his knees to **drink."**
	7. 6	all the others got down on their knees to **drink.**
	9.27	where they ate and **drank** and spoke scornfully of Abimelech.
	13. 4	Take care not to **drink** any wine or beer, or eat any
	13. 7	He told me not to **drink** any wine or beer, or eat
	13.14	she must not **drink** any wine or beer, or eat any forbidden
	15.19	Samson **drank** it and began to feel much better.
	19. 6	So the two men sat down and ate and **drank** together.
Ruth	2. 9	you are thirsty, go and **drink** from the water jars that they
	3. 3	you are there until he has finished eating and **drinking.**
	3. 7	Boaz had finished eating and **drinking,** he was in a good mood.
1 Sam	1.14	Stop your **drinking** and sober up!"
	1.15	"I haven't been **drinking!**
	30.12	had not had anything to eat or **drink** for three full days.
	30.16	all over the place, eating, **drinking,** and celebrating
2 Sam	11.11	could I go home, eat and **drink,** and sleep with my wife?
	12. 3	his own food, let it **drink** from his cup, and hold it
	13.28	has had too much to **drink,** and then when I give the
	16. 2	wine is for them to **drink** when they get tired in the
	19.35	taste what I eat and **drink,** and I can't hear the voices
	23.15	someone would bring me a **drink** of water from the well by
	23.16	But he would not **drink** it;
	23.17	and said, "Lord, I could never **drink** this!
	23.17	It would be like **drinking** the blood of these men who risked
	23.17	So he refused to **drink** it.
1 Kgs	4.20	they ate and **drank,** and were happy.
	10.21	All of Solomon's **drinking** cups were made of gold,
	13. 8	would not go with you or eat or **drink** anything with you.
	13. 9	me not to eat or **drink** a thing, and not to return
	13.16	And I won't eat or **drink** anything with you here,
	13.17	me not to eat or **drink** a thing, and not to return
	17. 4	supply you with water to **drink,** and I have commanded ravens
	17. 6	He **drank** water from the brook, and ravens brought him bread
	17.10	"Please bring me a **drink** of water," he said to her.
	19. 6	He ate and **drank,** and lay down again.
	19. 8	Elijah got up, ate and **drank,** and the food gave him enough
	20.12	the other rulers, were **drinking** in their tents.
2 Kgs	3.17	and your pack-animals will have plenty to **drink.'**
	6.22	them something to eat and **drink,** and let them return to
	6.23	after they had eaten and **drunk,** he sent them back
	7. 8	a tent, ate and **drank** what was there, grabbed the silver,
	18.27	their excrement and **drink** their urine, just as you will."
2 Kgs	18.31	your own trees, and to **drink** water from your own wells—
	19.24	that you dug wells and **drank** water in foreign lands and that
1 Chr	11.17	someone would bring me a **drink** of water from the well by
	11.18	But he would not **drink** it;
	11.19	and said, "I could never **drink** this!
	11.19	It would be like **drinking** the blood of these men who risked
	11.19	So he refused to **drink** it.
	12.39	feasting on the food and **drink** which their fellow-countrymen
	29.22	happy as they ate and **drank** in the presence of the Lord.
2 Chr	28.15	enough to eat and **drink,** and put olive-oil on their wounds.
Ezra	3. 7	and gave food, **drink,** and olive-oil to be sent
	10. 6	He did not eat or **drink** anything.
Neh	8.12	went home and ate and **drank** joyfully and shared what they
	9.20	you fed them with manna and gave them water to **drink.**
Esth	1. 7	**Drinks** were served in gold cups, no two of them alike,
	1. 8	There were no limits on the **drinks;**
	1.10	his banquet the king was **drinking** and feeling merry,
	3.15	sat down and had a **drink** while the city of Susa was
	4.16	Don't eat or **drink** anything for three days and nights.
Job	15.16	And man **drinks** evil as if it were water;
	39.30	the eagles gather, and the young eagles **drink** the blood.
Ps	36. 8	you let us **drink** from the river of your goodness.
	50.13	I eat the flesh of bulls or **drink** the blood of goats?
	75. 8	He pours it out, and all the wicked **drink** it;
	75. 8	they **drink** it down to the last drop.
	78.44	rivers into blood, and the Egyptians had no water to **drink.**
	80. 5	given us sorrow to eat, a large cup of tears to **drink.**
	102. 9	ashes are my food, and my tears are mixed with my **drink.**
	110. 7	The king will **drink** from the stream by the road,
Prov	4.17	Wickedness and violence are like food and **drink** to them.
	9. 5	"Come, eat my food and **drink** the wine that I have mixed.
	20. 1	**Drinking** too much makes you loud and foolish.
	23.20	Don't associate with people who **drink** too much wine
	23.29	Show me someone who **drinks** too much,
	23.29	to try out some new **drink,** and I will show you someone
	23.35	I need another **drink."**
	25.21	if he is thirsty, give him a **drink.**
	25.25	distant land is like a **drink** of cold water when you are
	31. 4	Kings should not **drink** wine or have a craving for alcohol.
	31. 5	When they **drink,** they forget the laws
	31. 7	Let them **drink** and forget their poverty and unhappiness.
Ecc	2.24	do is to eat and **drink** and enjoy what he has earned.
	3.13	of us should eat and **drink** and enjoy what we have worked
	5.18	do is to eat and **drink** and enjoy what he has worked
	8.15	in this life is eating and **drinking** and enjoying himself.
	9. 7	**drink** your wine and be cheerful.
Song	1. 4	We will be happy together, **drink** deep,
	5. 1	I am **drinking** my wine and milk.
	5. 1	Eat, lovers, and **drink** until you are drunk with love!
	8. 2	I would give you spiced wine, my pomegranate wine to **drink.**
Is	5.11	in the morning to start **drinking,** and you spend long evenings
	5.22	Brave and fearless when it comes to mixing **drinks!**
	7.15	people will be **drinking** milk and eating honey.
	21. 5	They are eating and **drinking.**
	22.13	You killed sheep and cattle to eat, and you **drank** wine.
	22.13	You said, "We might as well eat and **drink!**
	28. 7	They have **drunk** so much wine and liquor that they stumble
	29. 8	who dreams he is **drinking** and wakes with a dry throat.
	29. 9	Stagger without **drinking** a drop!
	32. 6	feeds the hungry or gives thirsty people anything to **drink.**
	33.16	You will have food to eat and water to **drink.**
	36.12	to eat their excrement and **drink** their urine,
	36.16	and to **drink** water from your own wells—
	37.25	that you dug wells and **drank** water in foreign lands, and
	51.17	You have **drunk** the cup of punishment that the Lord in his
	51.17	of punishment that the Lord in his anger gave you to **drink;**
	51.17	you **drank** it down, and it made you stagger.
	51.22	no longer have to **drink** the wine that makes you stagger.
	56.12	some wine,' these drunkards say, 'and **drink** all we can hold!
	62. 8	And foreigners will no longer **drink** your wine.
	62. 9	and gathered the grapes Will **drink** the wine in the courts of
	65. 4	They eat pork and **drink** broth made from meat offered in
	65.13	have plenty to eat and **drink,** but you will be hungry and
	65.21	enjoy the wine—it will not be **drunk** by others.
Jer	2.18	will gain by going to Egypt to **drink** water from the Nile?
	2.18	gain by going to Assyria to **drink** water from the Euphrates?
	8.14	us poison to **drink,** because we have sinned against him.
	9.15	give my people bitter plants to eat and poison to **drink.**
	16. 7	No one will eat or **drink** with anyone to comfort him when
	16. 8	Do not sit down with them to eat and **drink.**
	23.15	and poison to **drink,** because they have spread ungodliness
	25.15	nations to whom I send you, and make them **drink** from it.
	25.16	When they **drink** from it, they will stagger and go out of
	25.17	whom the Lord had sent me, and made them **drink** from it.
	25.18	and leaders, were made to **drink** from it, so that they would
	25.19	list of all the others who had to **drink** from the cup:
	25.19	nation on the face of the earth had to **drink** from it.
	25.19	Last of all, the king of Babylonia will **drink** from it.
	25.27	am commanding them to **drink** until they are drunk and vomit,
	25.28	cup from your hand and **drink** from it, then tell them that
	25.28	Almighty has said that they will still have to **drink** from it.
	35. 6	But they answered, "We do not **drink** wine.
	35. 6	neither we nor our descendants were ever to **drink** any wine.
	35. 8	We ourselves never **drink** wine, and neither do our wives,
	35.14	obeyed his command not to **drink** wine,
	35.14	and to this very day none of them **drink** any.
	46.10	it is full, and **drink** their blood until it is satisfied.
	49.12	to be punished had to **drink** from the cup of punishment,
	49.12	No, you must **drink** from the cup!
	51. 7	The nations **drank** its wine and went out of their minds.
Lam	3.15	Bitter suffering is all he has given me for food and **drink.**

Lam 5. 4 We must pay for the water we **drink;**
Ezek 4.11 have a limited amount of water to **drink,** two cups a day.
4.16 they measure out the food they eat and the water they **drink.**
12.18 "tremble when you eat, and shake with fear when you **drink.**
12.19 tremble when they eat and shake with fear when they **drink.**
23.31 so I will give you the same cup of punishment to **drink."**
23.32 "You will **drink** from your sister's cup;
23.34 You will **drink** and drain it dry, and with its broken
25. 4 will eat the fruit and **drink** the milk that should have been
34. 3 You **drink** the milk, wear clothes made from the wool, and
34.18 You **drink** the clear water and muddy what you don't drink!
34.19 the grass you trample down and **drink** the water you muddy.
39.17 of Israel, where they can eat meat and **drink** blood.
39.18 the bodies of soldiers and **drink** the blood of the rulers of
39.19 fat they can hold and to **drink** blood until they are drunk.
44.21 Priests must not **drink** any wine before going into the inner
Dan 1. 8 by eating the food and **drinking** the wine of the royal court,
1.10 you are to eat and **drink,** and if you don't look as
1.12 "Give us vegetables to eat and water to **drink.**
5. 1 noblemen to a great banquet, and they **drank** wine together.
5. 2 While they were **drinking,** Belshazzar gave orders to bring
5. 2 his wives, and his concubines could **drink** out of them.
5. 3 brought in, and they all **drank** wine out of them [4]and
5.23 your wives, and your concubines **drank** wine out of them
10. 3 rich food or any meat, **drink** any wine, or comb my hair
Hos 4.18 After **drinking** much wine, they delight in their prostitution,
Joel 1. 5 cry, you **wine-drinkers;**
Amos 2. 8 temple of their God they **drink** wine which they have taken
2.12 But you made the Nazirites **drink** wine,
4. 8 they hoped to find water, but there was not enough to **drink.**
5.11 houses you build or **drink** wine from the beautiful vineyards
6. 6 You **drink** wine by the bowlful and use the finest perfumes,
9.14 they will plant vineyards and **drink** the wine;
Obad 16 My people have **drunk** a bitter cup of punishment
16 all the surrounding nations will **drink** a still more bitter cup
16 they will **drink** it all and vanish away.
Jon 3. 7 persons, cattle, and sheep are forbidden to eat or **drink.**
Mic 6.15 You will make wine, but never **drink** it.
Hab 2.16 You yourself will **drink** and stagger.
2.16 The Lord will make you **drink** your own cup of punishment,
Zeph 1.13 houses they are building or **drink** wine from the vineyards
Hag 1. 6 You have wine to **drink,** but not enough to get drunk on!
Zech 7. 6 And when they ate and **drank,** it was for their own satisfaction."
10. 7 happy like men who have been **drinking** wine.
12. 2 nations round her will **drink** and stagger like drunken men.
Mt 6.25 worried about the food and **drink** you need in order to stay
6.31 or my **drink?**
10.42 that whoever gives even a **drink** of cold water to one of
11.18 John came, he fasted and **drank** no wine, and everyone said,
11.19 Man came, he ate and **drank,** and everyone said, 'Look at this
20.22 you drink the cup of suffering that I am about to **drink?"**
20.23 "You will indeed **drink** from my cup," Jesus told them,
23.24 You strain a fly out of your **drink,** but swallow a camel!
24.38 the flood people ate and **drank,** men and women married, up to
24.49 to beat his fellow-servants and to eat and **drink** with drunkards.
25.35 hungry and you fed me, thirsty and you gave me a **drink;**
25.37 you hungry and feed you, or thirsty and give you a **drink?**
25.42 not feed me, thirsty but you would not give me a **drink;**
26.27 **"Drink** it, all of you," he said;
26.29 you, I will never again **drink** this wine
26.29 until the day I **drink** the new wine with you in
26.42 cannot be taken away unless I **drink** it, your will be done."
27.34 but after tasting it, he would not **drink** it.
27.48 the end of a stick, and tried to make him **drink** it.
Mk 9.41 anyone who gives you a **drink** of water because you belong to
10.38 Can you **drink** the cup of suffering that I must drink?
10.39 to them, "You will indeed **drink** the cup I must drink and
14.23 and they all **drank** from it.
14.25 you, I will never again **drink** this wine
14.25 until the day I **drink** the new wine in the Kingdom
15.23 with a drug called myrrh, but Jesus would not **drink** it.
16.18 they pick up snakes or **drink** any poison, they will not be
Lk 1.15 He must not drink any wine or strong **drink.**
5.30 "Why do you eat and **drink** with tax collectors and other outcasts?"
5.33 but your disciples eat and **drink."**
5.39 And no one wants new wine after **drinking** old wine.
7.33 came, and he fasted and **drank** no wine, and you said,
7.34 came, and he ate and **drank,** and you said, 'Look at this
10. 7 that same house, eating and **drinking** whatever they offer you,
12.19 Take life easy, eat, **drink,** and enjoy yourself!'
12.29 all upset, always concerned about what you will eat and **drink.**
12.45 and eats and **drinks** and gets drunk, [46]then the master
13.26 Then you will answer, 'We ate and **drank** with you;
17. 8 on your apron and wait on me while I eat and **drink;**
17.27 Everybody kept on eating and **drinking,** and men and women
17.28 Everybody kept on eating and **drinking,** buying and selling,
21.34 too much feasting and **drinking** and with the worries of this
22.18 now on I will not **drink** this wine until the Kingdom of
22.30 You will eat and **drink** at my table in my Kingdom,
Jn 2.10 guests have had plenty to **drink,** he serves the ordinary wine.
4. 7 and Jesus said to her, "Give me a **drink** of water."
4. 9 am a Samaritan—so how can you ask me for a **drink?"**
4.10 is asking you for a **drink,** you would ask him, and he
4.12 he and his sons and his flocks all **drank** from it.
4.13 answered, "Whoever **drinks** this water will be thirsty again,
4.14 but whoever **drinks** the water that I will give
6.53 the Son of Man and **drink** his blood, you will not have
6.54 Whoever eats my flesh and **drinks** my blood has eternal life,
6.55 my blood is the real **drink.**
6.56 Whoever eats my flesh and **drinks** my blood lives in me,
7.37 voice, "Whoever is thirsty should come to me and **drink.**
Jn 18.11 think that I will not **drink** the cup of suffering which my
19.30 Jesus **drank** the wine and said, "It is finished!"
Acts 9. 9 and during that time he did not eat or **drink** anything.
10.41 to us who ate and **drank** with him after he rose from
23.12 would not eat or **drink** anything until they had killed Paul.
23.21 a vow not to eat or **drink** until they have killed him.
Rom 12.20 if he is thirsty, give him a **drink;**
14.17 matter of eating and **drinking,** but of the righteousness, peace,
14.21 to keep from eating meat, **drinking** wine, or doing anything else
1 Cor 9. 4 I the right to be given food and **drink** for my work?
10. 4 ate the same spiritual bread [4]and **drank** the same spiritual drink.
10. 4 They **drank** from the spiritual rock that went with them;
10. 7 to a feast which turned into an orgy of **drinking** and sex."
10.16 when we **drink** from it, we are sharing in the blood of
10.21 You cannot **drink** from the Lord's cup and also from the
10.31 do, whether you eat or **drink,** do it all for God's glory.
11.22 Haven't you got your own homes in which to eat and **drink?**
11.25 Whenever you **drink** it, do so in memory of me."
11.26 you eat this bread and **drink** from this cup you proclaim the
11.27 eats the Lord's bread or **drinks** from his cup in a way
11.28 first, and then eat the bread and **drink** from the cup.
11.29 he eats the bread and **drinks** from the cup,
11.29 he brings judgement on himself as he eats and **drinks.**
12.13 and we have all been given the one Spirit to **drink.**
15.32 goes, "Let us eat and **drink,** for tomorrow we will die."
Col 2.16 about what you eat or **drink** or about holy days or the
1 Tim 3. 8 they must not **drink** too much wine or be greedy for money;
5.23 Do not **drink** water only, but take a little wine to help
Heb 5.12 Instead of eating solid food, you still have to **drink** milk.
5.13 Anyone who has to **drink** milk is still a child, without
6. 7 God blesses the soil which **drinks** in the rain that often
9.10 they have to do only with food, **drink,** and various purification
1 Pet 2. 2 spiritual milk, so that by **drinking** it you may grow up and
4. 3 lust, drunkenness, orgies, **drinking** parties, and the disgusting
Rev 8.11 many people died from **drinking** the water, because it had turned
14. 8 She made all peoples **drink** her wine—the strong wine of her
14.10 on his hand [10]will himself **drink** God's wine, the wine of
16. 6 of the prophets, and so you have given them blood to **drink.**
16.19 great Babylon and made her **drink** the wine from his cup—
17. 2 the world became drunk from **drinking** the wine of her immorality."
18. 3 For all the nations have **drunk** her wine—the strong wine of
18. 6 a drink twice as strong as the **drink** she prepared for you.
21. 6 will give the right to **drink** from the spring of the water

DRINKER

Mt 11.19 is a glutton and a **drinker,** a friend of tax collectors and
Lk 7.34 is a glutton and a **drinker,** a friend of tax collectors and

DRINKING-TROUGH see TROUGH

DRIP

Deut 32.42 My arrows will **drip** with their blood,
Job 20.25 its shiny point **drips** with his blood,
Prov 19.13 A nagging wife is like water going **drip-drip-drip.**
27.15 A nagging wife is like water going **drip-drip-drip**
Amos 9.13 The mountains will **drip** with sweet wine,

DRIVE

[DROVE]

Gen 4.14 You are **driving** me off the land and away from your presence.
15.11 Vultures came down on the bodies, but Abram **drove** them off.
15.16 because I will not **drive** out the Amorites
31.17 wives on the camels, and **drove** all his flocks ahead of him,
33.13 If they are **driven** hard for even one day, the whole herd
Ex 2.17 But some shepherds **drove** Jethro's daughters away.
6. 1 fact, I will force him to **drive** them out of his land."
10.11 Moses and Aaron were **driven** out of the king's presence.
11. 1 In fact, he will **drive** all of you out of here.
12.39 for they had been **driven** out of Egypt so suddenly
14. 9 all the horses, chariots, and **drivers,** pursued them
14.17 over the king, his army, his chariots, and his **drivers.**
14.21 the sea, and the Lord **drove** the sea back with a strong
14.23 into the sea with all their horses, chariots, and **drivers.**
14.26 over the Egyptians and their chariots and **drivers."**
14.28 and covered the chariots, the **drivers,** and all the Egyptian army
15.19 chariots with their horses and **drivers** went into the sea,
23.28 I will **drive** out the Hivites, the Canaanites,
23.29 I will not **drive** them out within one year;
23.30 Instead, I will **drive** them out little by little,
23.31 of the land, and you will **drive** them out as you advance.
33. 2 and I will **drive** out the Canaanites, the Amorites,
34.11 I will **drive** out the Amorites, the Canaanites,
34.24 After I have **driven** out the nations before you
Lev 16.21 the goat is to be **driven** off into the desert
16.26 The man who **drove** the goat into the desert to Azazel
18.24 and whom the Lord is **driving** out so that you can go
20.17 they shall be publicly disgraced and **driven** out of the community.
20.18 are to be **driven** out of the community,
20.23 I am **driving** out those pagans so that you can enter
Num 21.32 surrounding towns and **drove** out the Amorites living there.
22. 6 be able to defeat them and **drive** them out of the land.
22.11 for him, so that he can fight them and **drive** them out."
25. 8 into the tent, and **drove** the spear through both of them.
32.39 of Gilead, occupied it, and **drove** out the Amorites
33.52 you must **drive** out all the inhabitants
33.55 But if you do not **drive** out the inhabitants of the land,

Num	33.56	If you do not **drive** them out, I will destroy you,
Deut	4.38	As you advanced, he **drove** out nations
	6.19	and you will **drive** out your enemies, as he promised.
	7. 1	going to occupy, and he will **drive** many nations out of it.
	7. 1	As you advance, he will **drive** out seven nations larger and
	7.17	these peoples outnumber you and that you cannot **drive** them out.
	7.22	Little by little he will **drive** out these nations
	9. 3	so that you will **drive** them out and destroy them quickly,
	9. 4	the Lord your God has **driven** them out for you,
	9. 4	the Lord is going to **drive** these people out for you
	9. 5	He will **drive** them out because they are wicked
	11.23	Then he will **drive** out all those nations as you advance,
	18.12	that is why he is **driving** those nations out of the land
	33.27	He **drove** out your enemies as you advanced,
Josh	3.10	he will surely **drive** out the Canaanites, the Hittites,
	13. 6	I will **drive** all these peoples out as the people of Israel
	13.12	Moses had defeated these people and **driven** them out.
	13.13	the Israelites did not **drive** out the people of Geshur
	14.12	and I will **drive** them out, just as the Lord
	15.14	Caleb **drove** the descendants of Anak out of the city—
	15.63	Judah were not able to **drive** out the Jebusites,
	16.10	But they did not **drive** out the Canaanites who lived in Gezer,
	17.12	were not able to **drive** out the people living in those
	17.13	they did not **drive** out all the Canaanites,
	17.18	the Canaanites, you will **drive** them out, even though
	23. 5	and he will **drive** them away as you advance.
	23. 9	The Lord has **driven** great and powerful nations out
	23.13	God will no longer **drive** these nations out as you advance.
	24.12	into panic in order to **drive** out the two Amorite kings.
	24.18	into this land, the Lord **drove** out all the Amorites who
Judg	1.18	so the people of Judah were not able to **drive** them out.
	1.20	was given to Caleb, who **drove** out of the city the three
	1.21	Benjamin did not **drive** out the Jebusites living in Jerusalem,
	1.27	tribe of Manasseh did not **drive** out the people
	1.28	but still they did not **drive** them all out.
	1.29	tribe of Ephraim did not **drive** out the Canaanites
	1.30	tribe of Zebulun did not **drive** out the people
	1.31	tribe of Asher did not **drive** out the people
	1.32	the local Canaanites, since they did not **drive** them out.
	1.33	tribe of Naphtali did not **drive** out the people
	2. 3	now that I will not **drive** these people out as you advance.
	2.21	I will no longer **drive** out any of the nations
	2.23	nor did he **drive** them out soon after Joshua's death.
	4.21	and killed him by **driving** the peg right through the side
	6. 9	I **drove** them out as you advanced, and I gave you their
	9.41	lived in Arumah, and Zebul **drove** Gaal and his brothers out
	11.23	God of Israel, who **drove** out the Amorites for his people,
1 Sam	6. 7	to the wagon and **drive** their calves back to the barn.
	26.19	For they have **driven** me out from the Lord's land
	30.20	his men **drove** all the livestock in front of them and said,
2 Sam	5.25	and was able to **drive** the Philistines back from Geba
	7.23	You **drove** out other nations and their gods
	10.18	and the Israelites **drove** the Syrian army back.
	10.18	killed seven hundred Syrian chariot **drivers**
	11.23	but we **drove** them back to the city gate.
1 Kgs	14.24	people whom the Lord had **driven** out of the land as the
	21.26	whom the Lord had **driven** out of the land
	22.34	he cried out to his chariot **driver.**
2 Kgs	3.24	the Israelites attacked them and **drove** them back.
	9.20	leader of the group is **driving** his chariot like a madman,
	9.27	they wounded him as he **drove** his chariot on the road up
	9.33	Jehu **drove** his horses and chariot over her body,
	16. 3	people whom the Lord had **driven** out of the land
	16. 6	city of Elath, and **drove** out the Judaeans who lived there.
	17. 8	people whom the Lord had **driven** out as his people advanced,
	17.11	of the people whom the Lord had **driven** out of the land.
	21. 2	nations whom the Lord had **driven** out of the land
	21. 8	not allow them to be **driven** out of the land
	21. 9	nations whom the Lord had **driven** out of the land
1 Chr	4.41	They **drove** the people out and settled there permanently
	5.25	gods of the nations whom God had **driven** out of the land.
	8.13	the city of Aijalon and **drove** out the people who lived in
	14.16	and so he **drove** the Philistines back from Gibeon
	17.21	from Egypt and **drove** out other nations
	19.18	and the Israelites **drove** the Syrian army back.
	19.18	his men killed seven thousand Syrian chariot **drivers**
2 Chr	13. 9	You **drove** out the Lord's priests, the descendants of Aaron,
	13. 9	and you **drove** out the Levites.
	18.33	he cried out to his chariot **driver.**
	20. 7	moved into this land, you **drove** out the people
	20.11	repay us—they come to **drive** us out of the land that
	28. 3	people whom the Lord had **driven** out of the land
	33. 2	nations whom the Lord had **driven** out of the land
	33. 8	not allow them to be **driven** out of the land
	33. 9	nations whom the Lord had **driven** out of the land
Ezra	6.11	sharpened at one end, and then **driven** through his body.
Job	18.18	He will be **driven** out of the land of the living,
	18.18	**driven** from light into darkness.
	30. 5	Everyone **drove** them away with shouts,
	30. 8	They were **driven** out of the land.
Ps	5.10	**Drive** them out of your presence because of their many sins
	6.10	in sudden confusion they will be **driven** away.
	31.22	and thought that he had **driven** me out of his presence.
	37. 9	Lord will possess the land, but the wicked will be **driven** out.
	37.22	land, but those who are cursed by him will be **driven** out.
	37.28	ever, but the descendants of the wicked will be **driven** out.
	37.34	you the land, and you will see the wicked **driven** out.
	44. 2	how you yourself **drove** out the heathen
	68. 2	As smoke is blown away, so he **drives** them off;
	78.55	He **drove** out the inhabitants as his people advanced;
	78.66	He **drove** his enemies back in lasting and shameful defeat.
Ps	80. 8	you **drove** out other nations and planted it in their land.
	109.10	may they be **driven** from the ruins they live in!
	129. 5	May everyone who hates Zion be defeated and **driven** back.
Prov	28. 3	oppresses poor people is like a **driving** rain
Ecc	2. 3	**Driven** on by my desire for wisdom, I decided to cheer
	12.11	collected proverbs are as lasting as firmly **driven** nails.
Song	6.12	me as eager for love as a chariot **driver** is for battle.
Is	8.22	terrifying darkness into which they are being **driven.**
	16. 2	move aimlessly to and fro, like birds **driven** from their nest.
	16. 7	They will be **driven** to despair.
	17. 2	for sheep and cattle, and no one will **drive** them away.
	17.13	they retreat, **driven** away like dust on a hillside,
	28.28	how to thresh it by **driving** a cart over it
	49.21	I was exiled and **driven** away— who brought these children up?
	59.14	Justice is **driven** away, and right cannot come near.
	63.18	We, your holy people, were **driven** out by our enemies
Jer	7.15	I will **drive** you out of my sight
	7.15	as I **drove** out your relatives, the people of
	23. 2	you have scattered them and **driven** them away.
	27.10	I will **drive** you out, and you will be destroyed.
	27.15	And so he will **drive** you out, and you will be killed,
	51.21	to shatter chariots and their **drivers,**
Lam	3. 2	He **drove** me deeper and deeper into darkness
	5. 5	**Driven** hard like donkeys or camels, we are tired,
Ezek	8. 6	Israel are doing here, **driving** me farther and farther away
	28.16	who guarded you **drove** you away from the sparkling gems.
	45. 9	You must never again **drive** my people off their land.
Dan	4.14	**Drive** the animals from under it and the birds out of its
	4.25	You will be **driven** away from human society
	4.32	You will be **driven** away from human society,
	4.33	Nebuchadnezzar was **driven** out of human society
	5.21	He was **driven** away from human society,
Hos	9.15	evil they have done, I will **drive** them out of my land.
Joel	2.20	from the north and will **drive** some of them into the desert.
	2.20	Their front ranks will be **driven** into the Dead Sea,
Obad	7	they have **driven** you from your country.
Mic	2. 9	You **drive** the women of my people out of the homes they
Zeph	2. 2	your senses [2] before you are **driven** away like chaff
	2. 4	people of Ashdod will be **driven** out in half a day,
	2. 4	and the people of Ekron will be **driven** from their city.
Hag	2.22	I will overturn chariots and their **drivers;**
Mt	7.22	by your name we **drove** out many demons and performed many
	8.16	Jesus **drove** out the evil spirits with a word and healed all
	8.31	"If you are going to **drive** us out, send us into that
	9.33	soon as the demon was **driven** out, the man started talking,
	9.34	of the demons who gives him the power to **drive** out demons."
	10. 1	and gave them authority to **drive** out evil spirits and to
	10. 8	who suffer from dreaded skin-diseases, and **drive** out demons.
	12.24	they replied, "He **drives** out demons only because their ruler
	12.27	You say that I **drive** out demons because Beelzebul gives me
	12.27	Well, then, who gives your followers the power to **drive** them out?
	12.28	gives me the power to **drive** out demons, which proves that
	17.19	and asked him, "Why couldn't we **drive** the demon out?"
	21.12	went into the Temple and **drove** out all those who were buying
	24.29	and the powers in space will be **driven** from their courses.
Mk	1.34	sick with all kinds of diseases and **drove** out many demons.
	1.39	over Galilee, preaching in the synagogues and **driving** out demons.
	3.15	to preach, [15] and you will have authority to **drive** out demons."
	3.22	of the demons who gives him the power to **drive** them out."
	3.23	"How can Satan **drive** out Satan?
	6.13	**drove** out many demons, and rubbed olive-oil on many sick people
	7.26	She begged Jesus to **drive** the demon out of her daughter.
	9.18	I asked your disciples to **drive** the spirit out, but they
	9.28	asked him privately, "Why couldn't we **drive** the spirit out?"
	9.29	"Only prayer can **drive** this kind out," answered Jesus;
	9.38	saw a man who was **driving** out demons in your name,
	11.15	the Temple and began to **drive** out all those who were buying
	13.25	and the powers in space will be **driven** from their courses.
	16. 9	to Mary Magdalene, from whom he had **driven** out seven demons.
	16.17	they will **drive** out demons in my name;
Lk	8. 2	called Magdalene), from whom seven demons had been **driven** out;
	8.29	break the chains and be **driven** by the demon out into the
	9. 1	them power and authority to **drive** out all demons and to cure
	9.40	I begged your disciples to **drive** it out, but they couldn't."
	9.49	"Master, we saw a man **driving** out demons in your name,
	11.14	Jesus was **driving** out a demon that could not talk;
	11.15	of the demons, who gives him the power to **drive** them out."
	11.18	You say that I **drive** out demons because Beelzebul gives me
	11.19	If this is how I **drive** them out,
	11.19	how do your followers **drive** them out?
	11.20	of God's power that I **drive** out demons, and this proves that
	13.32	'I am **driving** out demons and performing cures today and tomorrow,
	19.45	the Temple and began to **drive** out the merchants,
	21.26	for the powers in space will be **driven** from their courses.
Jn	2.15	a whip from cords and **drove** all the animals out of the
Acts	7.45	land from the nations that God **drove** out as they advanced.
	18.16	And he **drove** them out of the court.
	19.12	ill, and their diseases were **driven** away, and the evil spirits
	19.13	Jews who travelled round and **drove** out evil spirits also tried
	26.24	Your great learning is **driving** you mad!"
	27.26	But we will be **driven** ashore on some island."
	27.27	and we were being **driven** about in the Mediterranean by the
2 Tim	2.16	discussions, which only **drive** people further away from God.
	3. 6	guilt of their sins and **driven** by all kinds of desires,
Jas	1. 6	in the sea that is **driven** and blown about by the wind.
	3. 4	big as it is and **driven** by such strong winds, it can
1 Jn	4.18	perfect love **drives** out all fear.
3 Jn	10	to receive them and tries to **drive** them out of the church!

DROP

Deut 28.40 will not have any olive-oil, because the olives will **drop** off.
32. 2 My teaching will fall like **drops** of rain
2 Sam 2.23 Asahel **dropped** to the ground dead,
4. 4 she **dropped** him, and he became crippled.
1 Kgs 17.12 flour in a bowl and a **drop** of olive-oil in a jar.
Job 15.33 like an olive-tree that **drops** its blossoms.
29.22 My words sank in like **drops** of rain;
36.27 takes water from the earth and turns it into **drops** of rain.
Ps 75. 8 they drink it down to the last **drop.**
Is 29. 9 Stagger without drinking a **drop!**
34. 4 will fall like leaves **dropping** from a vine or a fig-tree.
40.15 Lord the nations are nothing, no more than a **drop** of water;
Ezek 11.13 While I was prophesying, Pelatiah **dropped** dead.
Amos 2.16 even the bravest soldiers will **drop** their weapons and run."
Mt 17.27 So go to the lake and **drop** in a line.
Mk 12.41 treasury, he watched the people as they **dropped** in their money.
12.41 Many rich men **dropped** in a lot of money;
12.42 poor widow came along and **dropped** in two little copper coins,
Lk 21. 1 and saw rich men **dropping** their gifts in the temple treasury,
21. 2 saw a very poor widow **dropping** in two little copper coins.
22.44 his sweat was like **drops** of blood falling to the ground.
Jn 12.24 single grain unless it is **dropped** into the ground and dies.
Acts 27.28 So they **dropped** a line with a weight tied to it and
Rev 8.10 star, burning like a torch, **dropped** from the sky and fell on

DROSS

Jer 6.30 They will be called worthless **dross,**

DROUGHT

Deut 28.22 will send **drought** and scorching winds to destroy your crops.
1 Kgs 18. 1 the third year of the **drought,** the Lord said to Elijah,
Job 12.15 **Drought** comes when God withholds rain;
24.19 snow vanishes in heat and **drought,** so a sinner vanishes
Is 25. 5 attack like a winter storm, [5] like **drought** in a dry land.
Jer 14. 1 The Lord said to me concerning the **drought,**
50.38 Bring a **drought** on its land and dry up its rivers.
Hag 1.11 I have brought **drought** on the land—on its hills,

DROWN

Ex 15. 4 the best of its officers were **drowned** in the Red Sea.
15.10 But one breath from you, Lord, and the Egyptians were **drowned;**
Deut 11. 4 their horses and chariots, by **drowning** them in the Red Sea
Josh 24. 7 I made the sea come rolling over the Egyptians and **drown** them.
Neh 9.11 Those who pursued them **drowned** in deep water, as a stone
Job 16. 4 shake my head wisely and **drown** you with a flood of words.
Ps 38. 4 I am **drowning** in the flood of my sins;
69. 2 out in deep water, and the waves are about to **drown** me.
69.15 don't let me **drown** in the depths or sink into the grave.
106.11 But the water **drowned** their enemies;
124. 5 the raging torrent would have **drowned** us."
136.15 but he **drowned** the king of Egypt and his army;
Song 8. 7 no flood can **drown** it.
Ezek 27.28 The shouts of the **drowning** sailors Echoed on the shore.
Mal 2.13 You **drown** the Lord's altar with tears,
Mt 8.32 down the side of the cliff into the lake and was **drowned.**
18. 6 tied round his neck and be **drowned** in the deep sea.
Mk 5.13 down the side of the cliff into the lake and was **drowned.**
Lk 8.33 down the side of the cliff into the lake and was **drowned.**

DROWSY

2 Sam 4. 6 at the door had become **drowsy** while she was sifting wheat
Is 29.10 The Lord has made you **drowsy,** ready to fall into a deep

DRUG

Mk 15.23 him wine mixed with a **drug** called myrrh, but Jesus would not

DRUM

1 Sam 10. 5 playing harps, **drums,** flutes, and lyres.
2 Sam 6. 5 They were playing harps, lyres, **drums,** rattles, and
1 Chr 13. 8 They sang and played musical instruments—harps, **drums,** cymbals,
Ps 149. 3 play **drums** and harps in praise of him.
150. 4 Praise him with **drums** and dancing.
Is 24. 8 and the joyful music of their harps and **drums** has ceased.
30.32 his people will keep time with the music of **drums** and harps.

DRUNK
see also **DRINK**

Gen 9.21 he became **drunk,** took off his clothes,
19.32 let's make our father **drunk,** so that we can sleep with
19.33 But he was so **drunk** that he didn't know it.
19.34 let's make him **drunk** again tonight, and you sleep with him.
19.35 they made him **drunk,** and the younger daughter had intercourse
19.35 Again he was so **drunk** that he didn't know it.
43.34 So they ate and drank with Joseph until they were **drunk.**
Deut 21.20 he wastes money and is a **drunkard.'**
1 Sam 1.13 Eli thought that she was **drunk,** [14] and said to her, "Stop
1.14 and said to her, "Stop making a **drunken** show of yourself!
1.15 "No, I'm not **drunk,** sir," she answered.
25.36 He was **drunk** and in a good mood,
2 Sam 11.13 David invited him to supper and made him **drunk.**
1 Kgs 16. 9 Elah was getting **drunk** in the home of Arza,
1 Kgs 20.16 Benhadad and his thirty-two allies were getting **drunk**
Job 12.25 they grope in the dark and stagger like **drunkards.**
Ps 60. 3 we stagger around as though we were **drunk.**
69.12 me in the streets, and **drunkards** make up songs about me.
107.27 they stumbled and staggered like **drunken** men—
Prov 20. 1 It's stupid to get **drunk.**
23.21 **Drunkards** and gluttons will be reduced to poverty.
26. 9 saying reminds you of a **drunk** man trying to pick a thorn
Ecc 10.17 who control themselves and don't get **drunk.**
Song 5. 1 Eat, lovers, and drink until you are **drunk** with love!
Is 5.11 and you spend long evenings getting **drunk.**
16. 8 whose wine used to make the rulers of the nations **drunk.**
19.14 staggers like a **drunken** man slipping on his own vomit.
24.20 itself will stagger like a **drunken** man and sway like a hut
28. 1 the crowns of flowers on the heads of its **drunken** leaders.
28. 1 Their proud heads are well perfumed, but there they lie, dead **drunk.**
28. 3 The pride of those **drunken** leaders will be trampled underfoot.
28. 7 Even the prophets and the priests are so **drunk**
28. 7 The prophets are too **drunk** to understand the visions
28. 7 and the priests are too **drunk** to decide the cases
29. 9 Get **drunk** without any wine!
49.26 they will be **drunk** with murder and rage.
51.21 stagger as though you were **drunk,**
56.12 'Let's get some wine,' these **drunkards** say,
Jer 13.13 fill the people in this land with wine until they are **drunk:**
23. 9 like a man who is **drunk,** a man who has had too
25.27 to drink until they are **drunk** and vomit, until they fall
48.26 The Lord said, "Make Moab **drunk,** because it has rebelled
51. 7 like a gold cup in my hand, making the whole world **drunk.**
51.39 I will prepare them a feast and make them **drunk** and happy.
51.57 I will make its rulers **drunk—** men of wisdom, leaders,
Ezek 23.33 make you miserable and **drunk,** that cup of fear and ruin,
39.19 fat they can hold and to drink blood until they are **drunk.**
Hos 7. 5 made the king and his officials **drunk** and foolish with wine.
Joel 1. 5 Wake up and weep, you **drunkards;**
Nah 1.10 you **drunkards** will be burnt up!
3.11 Nineveh, you too will fall into a **drunken** stupor!
Hab 2.15 you made them stagger as though they were **drunk.**
Hag 1. 6 You have wine to drink, but not enough to get **drunk** on!
Zech 9.15 will shout in battle like **drunken** men and will shed the
12. 2 nations round her will drink and stagger like **drunken** men.
Mt 24.49 beat his fellow-servants and to eat and drink with **drunkards.**
Lk 12.45 eats and drinks and gets **drunk,** [46] then the master will come
Acts 2.13 made fun of the believers, saying, "These people are **drunk!"**
2.15 These people are not **drunk,** as you suppose;
Rom 13.13 no orgies or **drunkenness,** no immorality or indecency,
1 Cor 5.11 worships idols or is a slanderer or a **drunkard** or a thief.
6.10 or are greedy or are **drunkards** or who slander others or are
11.21 own meal, so that some are hungry while others get **drunk.**
Gal 5.21 they are envious, get **drunk,** have orgies, and do other things
Eph 5.18 Do not get **drunk** with wine, which will only ruin you;
1 Thes 5. 7 it is at night that they get **drunk.**
1 Tim 3. 3 he must not be a **drunkard** or a violent man, but gentle
Tit 1. 7 quick-tempered, or a **drunkard** or violent or greedy for money.
1 Pet 4. 3 spent in indecency, lust, **drunkenness,** orgies, drinking parties,
Rev 17. 2 people of the world became **drunk** from drinking the wine of
17. 6 saw that the woman was **drunk** with the blood of God's people

DRY
[DRIED-UP]

Gen 8.13 looked round, and saw that the ground was getting **dry.**
8.14 twenty-seventh day of the second month the earth was completely **dry.**
37.20 kill him and throw his body into one of the **dry** wells.
37.24 they took him and threw him into the well, which was **dry.**
Ex 14.16 Israelites will be able to walk through the sea on **dry** ground.
14.21 It blew all night and turned the sea into **dry** land.
14.22 went through the sea on **dry** ground, with walls of water on
14.29 walked through the sea on **dry** ground, with walls of water on
15.19 The Israelites walked through the sea on **dry** ground.
16.36 (The standard **dry** measure then in use equalled twenty litres.)
Lev 7.10 whether mixed with oil or **dry,**
26.19 rain, and your land will be **dry** and as hard as iron.
Num 11.32 They spread them out to **dry** all round the camp.
Deut 8.15 In that **dry** and waterless land he made water flow out of
11.17 rain, and your ground will become too **dry** for crops to grow.
21. 4 a stream that never runs **dry** and where the ground has never
Josh 2.10 have heard how the Lord **dried** up the Red Sea
3.17 the people walked across on **dry** ground, the priests carrying
3.17 Lord's Covenant Box stood on **dry** ground in the middle of the
4.22 about the time when Israel crossed the Jordan on **dry** ground.
4.23 that the Lord your God **dried** up the water of the Jordan
4.23 had crossed, just as he **dried** up the Red Sea for us.
5. 1 heard that the Lord had **dried** up the Jordan until the people
9. 5 The bread they took with them was **dry** and mouldy.
9.12 Now it is **dry** and mouldy.
10.40 foothills, as well as those of the **dry** country in the south.
11.16 area of Goshen and the **dry** country south of it, as well
12. 8 the eastern slopes, and the **dry** country in the south.
15.19 The land you have given me is in the **dry** country."
Judg 1. 9 in the foothills, and in the **dry** country to the south.
1.15 The land you have given me is in the **dry** country."
6.39 This time let the wool be **dry,** and the ground be wet."
6.40 next morning the wool was **dry,** but the ground was wet
16. 7 new bowstrings that are not **dried** out, I'll be as weak as
16. 8 bowstrings that were not **dried** out, and she tied Samson up.
1 Sam 12.17 It's the **dry** season, isn't it?
15. 5 the city of Amalek and waited in ambush in a **dry** river-bed.
25.18 two hundred cakes of **dried** figs, and loaded them on donkeys.

1 Sam	30.12	some food and water, [12]some **dried** figs,
1 Kgs	17. 7	After a while the brook **dried** up because of the lack of
	18.38	scorched the earth and **dried** up the water in the trench.
2 Kgs	2. 8	and he and Elisha crossed to the other side on **dry** ground.
	3.16	'Dig ditches all over this **dry** stream bed.
	19.24	that the feet of your soldiers tramped the River Nile **dry.**
Neh	9.11	a path for your people and led them through on **dry** ground.
Job	6.15	you deceive me like streams that go **dry** when no rain comes.
	6.17	heat they disappear, and the stream beds lie bare and **dry.**
	6.20	but their hope dies beside **dry** streams.
	8.12	If the water **dries** up, they are the first to wither,
	13.25	you are attacking a piece of **dry** straw.
	14.11	and lakes that go **dry,** [12]people die, never to rise.
	18.16	His roots and branches are withered and **dry.**
	22.24	dump your finest gold in the **dry** stream bed.
	24. 5	like wild donkeys, search for food in the **dry** wilderness;
	30. 3	hungry that they would gnaw **dry** roots—
	38.27	Who waters the **dry** and thirsty land,
Ps	1. 3	fruit at the right time, and whose leaves do not **dry** up.
	22.15	My throat is as **dry** as dust,
	32. 4	drained, as moisture is **dried** up by the summer heat.
	37. 2	They will soon disappear like grass that **dries** up;
	63. 1	like a **dry,** worn-out, and waterless land, my soul is thirsty
	66. 6	He changed the sea into **dry** land;
	74.15	you **dried** up large rivers.
	84. 6	As they pass through the **dry** valley of Baca,
	90. 6	and burst into bloom, then **dry** up and die in the evening.
	102. 4	I am beaten down like **dry** grass;
	102.11	I am like **dry** grass.
	106. 9	He gave a command to the Red Sea, and it **dried** up;
	106. 9	he led his people across on **dry** land.
	107.33	The Lord made rivers **dry** up completely
	107.35	deserts into pools of water and **dry** land into flowing springs.
	126. 4	just as the rain brings water back to **dry** river-beds.
	129. 6	on the house-tops, which **dries** up before it can grow;
	143. 6	like **dry** ground my soul is thirsty for you.
Prov	17. 1	Better to eat a **dry** crust of bread with peace of mind
	25.25	like a drink of cold water when you are **dry** and thirsty.
	30.16	**dry** ground that needs rain,
Is	5.24	now, just as straw and **dry** grass shrivel and burn in the
	5.24	rot and your blossoms will **dry** up and blow away, because you
	11.15	The Lord will **dry** up the Gulf of Suez, and he will
	11.15	bring a hot wind to **dry** up the Euphrates, leaving only seven
	15. 6	The brook of Nimrim is **dry,** the grass beside it has withered,
	19. 5	be low in the Nile, and the river will gradually **dry** up.
	19. 6	The channels of the river will stink as they slowly go **dry.**
	19. 7	the banks of the Nile will **dry** up and be blown away.
	24. 4	The earth **dries** up and withers;
	25. 5	attack like a winter storm, [5]like drought in a **dry** land.
	29. 8	who dreams he is drinking and wakes with a **dry** throat.
	35. 7	become a lake, and **dry** land will be filled with springs.
	37.25	that the feet of your soldiers tramped the River Nile **dry.**
	40.24	Lord sends a wind, they **dry** up and blow away like straw.
	41.17	water, when their throats are **dry** with thirst, then I, the
	41.18	into pools of water and the **dry** land into flowing springs.
	42.15	the hills and mountains and **dry** up the grass and trees.
	42.15	river valleys into deserts and **dry** up the pools of water.
	44. 3	the thirsty land and make streams flow on the **dry** ground.
	44.27	With a word of command I **dry** up the ocean.
	48.18	have flowed for you like a stream that never goes **dry!**
	48.21	his people through a hot, **dry** desert, they did not suffer
	50. 2	I can **dry** up the sea with a command and turn rivers
	51.10	It was you also who **dried** up the sea and made a
	53. 2	servant should grow like a plant taking root in **dry** ground.
	58.11	plenty of water, like a spring of water that never runs **dry.**
	66.12	nations will flow to you like a river that never goes **dry.**
Jer	2. 6	of deserts and sand-dunes, a **dry** and dangerous land where no
	2.25	let your throat become **dry** from chasing after other gods.
	9.10	pastures, because they have **dried** up, and no one travels through
	9.12	is the land devastated and **dry** as a desert, so that no
	12. 4	long will our land be **dry,** and the grass in every field
	14. 4	rain and the ground is **dried** up, the farmers are sick at
	15.18	disappoint me like a stream that goes **dry** in the summer?"
	17. 6	desert, which grows in the **dry** wilderness, on salty ground
	18.14	Do its cool mountain streams ever run **dry?**
	23.10	the Lord's curse the land mourns and the pastures are **dry.**
	48.34	Even the brook of Nimrim has **dried** up.
	50.12	it will become a **dry** and waterless desert.
	50.38	Bring a drought on its land and **dry** up its rivers.
	51.36	I will **dry** up the source of Babylonia's water
	51.36	and make its rivers go **dry.**
Lam	4. 8	their skin, **dry** as wood, has shrivelled on their bones.
Ezek	4.12	build a fire out of **dried** human excrement, bake bread on the
	17.24	up the green trees and make the **dry** trees become green.
	19.12	The east wind **dried** up its fruit.
	19.12	they **dried** up and were burnt.
	19.13	it is planted in the desert, in a **dry** and waterless land.
	20.47	it will burn up every tree in you, whether green or **dry.**
	23.34	will drink and drain it **dry,** and with its broken pieces tear
	26. 5	Fishermen will **dry** their nets on it, there where it stands
	26.14	leave only a bare rock where fishermen can **dry** their nets.
	30.12	I will **dry** up the Nile and put Egypt under the power
	37. 2	that there were very many bones and that they were very **dry.**
	37. 4	Tell these **dry** bones to listen to the word of the Lord.
	37.11	They say that they are **dried** up, without any hope and with
	45.11	"The ephah for **dry** measure is to be equal to the bath
	47.10	the sea, and they will spread out their nets there to **dry.**
Hos	2. 3	will make her like a **dry** and barren land, and she will
	4. 3	And so the land will **dry** up, and everything that lives on
	9.16	a plant whose roots have **dried** up and which bears no fruit.
	13. 5	I took care of you in a **dry,** desert land.
Hos	13.15	from the desert, and it will **dry** up their springs and wells.
	14. 5	be to the people of Israel like rain in a **dry** land.
Joel	1.10	the grapes are **dried** up, and the olive-trees are withered.
	1.17	The seeds die in the **dry** earth.
	1.19	the pastures and trees are **dried** up, as though a fire had
	1.20	animals cry out to you because the streams have become **dry.**
	2. 5	they crackle like **dry** grass on fire.
Amos	1. 2	The pastures **dry** up, and the grass on Mount Carmel turns brown."
	4. 7	Rain fell on one field, but another field **dried** up.
	4. 9	"I sent a scorching wind to **dry** up your crops.
	5.24	stream, and righteousness like a river that never goes **dry.**
Nah	1. 4	He commands the sea, and it **dries** up!
	1. 4	He makes the rivers go **dry.**
	1.10	Like tangled thorns and **dry** straw, you drunkards will be burnt up!
Zech	10.11	strike the waves, and the depths of the Nile will go **dry.**
	14. 8	the year round, in the **dry** season as well as the wet.
Mt	12.43	a person, it travels over **dry** country looking for a place to
	13. 6	roots had not grown deep enough, the plants soon **dried** up.
	21.19	At once the fig-tree **dried** up.
	21.20	"How did the fig-tree **dry** up so quickly?"
Mk	4. 6	roots had not grown deep enough, the plants soon **dried** up.
Lk	7.38	Then she **dried** his feet with her hair, kissed them, and
	7.44	washed my feet with her tears and **dried** them with her hair.
	8. 6	when the plants sprouted, they **dried** up because the soil had
	11.24	a person, it travels over **dry** country looking for a place to
	23.31	when the wood is green, what will happen when it is **dry?"**
Jn	13. 5	wash the disciples' feet and **dry** them with the towel round
	15. 6	remain in me is thrown out like a branch and **dries** up;
Heb	11.29	Israelites able to cross the Red Sea as if on **dry** land;
2 Pet	2.17	These men are like **dried-up** springs, like clouds blown along
Rev	16.12	The river **dried** up, to provide a way for the kings who

DUE (1)

Ex	22.29	corn, your wine, and your olive-oil when they are **due.**

DUE (2)

Zech	6.13	and receive the honour **due** to a king,

DUE (3)

2 Kgs	12. 4	the **dues** paid for the regular sacrifices

DUG see DIG

Am DULL

see also **BLUNT**

DULL

Lev	13.39	If the spots are **dull** white, it is only a blemish
Is	6.10	the minds of these people **dull,** their ears deaf,
Lam	4. 1	Our glittering gold has grown **dull;**
Mt	13.15	because their minds are **dull,** and they have stopped up their
Mk	8.17	Are your minds so **dull?**
Acts	28.27	because this people's minds are **dull,** and they have stopped up
Rom	11. 8	As the scripture says, "God made their minds and hearts **dull;**

DUMB

Ex	4.11	Who makes him deaf or **dumb?**
Ps	38.13	like a **dumb** man and cannot speak.
Mt	15.30	the blind, the crippled, the **dumb,** and many other sick people,
	15.31	amazed as they saw the **dumb** speaking, the crippled made whole,
Mk	7.37	"He even causes the deaf to hear and the **dumb** to speak!"
	9.25	"Deaf and **dumb** spirit," he said, "I order you to come out

Am DUMP see HEAP, THROW

DUMP

Lev	14.41	walls scraped and the plaster **dumped** in an unclean place
Job	22.24	**dump** your finest gold in the dry stream bed.
Ezek	26.12	and wood and all the rubble, and **dump** them into the sea.

DUNG

1 Kgs	14.10	they will be swept away like **dung.**
2 Kgs	6.25	two hundred grammes of dove's **dung** cost five pieces of silver.
	9.37	will be scattered there like **dung,** so that no one will be
Ezek	4.15	will let you use cow **dung** instead, and you can bake your
Mal	2. 3	rub your faces in the **dung** of the animals you sacrifice—
	2. 3	you sacrifice—and you will be taken out to the **dunghill.**

DUNGEON

Ex	12.29	to the throne, to the son of the prisoner in the **dungeon;**
Is	42.22	they are locked up in **dungeons** and hidden away in prisons.

DUST

Gen	3.14	and you will have to eat **dust** as long as you live.
	13.16	be as easy to count all the specks of **dust** on earth!
	28.14	be as numerous as the specks of **dust** on the earth.
Ex	8.16	over the land of Egypt the **dust** will change into gnats."
	8.17	his stick, and all the **dust** in Egypt was turned into gnats,
	9. 9	will spread out like fine **dust** over all the land of Egypt,

Num 23.10 of Israel are like the **dust**— There are too many of
Deut 9.21 in pieces, ground it to **dust,**
9.21 and threw the **dust** into the stream that flowed down
28.24 the Lord will send down **duststorms** and sandstorms
Josh 7. 6 lay there till evening, with **dust** on their heads to
1 Sam 2. 8 lifts the poor from the **dust** and raises the needy
2 Sam 22.43 I crush them, and they become like **dust;**
2 Kgs 13. 7 had destroyed the rest, trampling them down like **dust.**
23. 6 pounded its ashes to **dust,** and scattered it
23.15 broke its stones into pieces, and pounded them to **dust;**
2 Chr 34. 4 They ground to **dust** the images of Asherah
34. 4 and then scattered the **dust** on the graves of the people
34. 7 ground the idols to **dust,** and broke in pieces all the
Neh 9. 1 They wore sackcloth and put **dust** on their heads
Job 2.12 clothes in grief and throwing **dust** into the air
4.19 of clay, a thing of **dust** that can be crushed
10. 9 are you going to crush me back to **dust?**
16.15 and I sit here in the **dust** defeated.
20. 7 reaches the clouds, [7]but he will be blown away like **dust.**
20.11 young and vigorous, but soon it will turn to **dust.**
21.18 straw in the wind, or like **dust** carried away in a storm?
28. 6 the earth contain sapphires, And its **dust** contains gold.
34.15 everyone living would die and turn into **dust** again.
38.38 the rain, [38]rain that hardens the **dust** into lumps?
42. 6 ashamed of all I have said and repent in **dust** and ashes.
Ps 18.42 so that they become like **dust** which the wind blows away.
22.15 throat is as dry as **dust,** and my tongue sticks to the
22.15 You have left me for dead in the **dust.**
44.25 we lie defeated in the **dust.**
83.13 Scatter them like **dust,** O God, like straw blown away
90. 3 you change him back to **dust.**
103.14 he remembers that we are **dust.**
104.29 they die and go back to the **dust** from which they came.
113. 7 He raises the poor from the **dust;**
119.25 I lie defeated in the **dust;**
146. 4 When they die, they return to the **dust;**
147.16 He spreads snow like a blanket and scatters frost like **dust.**
Ecc 3.20 They are both going to the same place—the **dust.**
12. 7 bodies will return to the **dust** of the earth,
Is 14.31 A cloud of **dust** is coming from the north—
17.13 they retreat, driven away like **dust** on a hillside,
25.12 high walls and bring them tumbling down into the **dust.**
26. 5 they lived in, and sent its walls crashing into the **dust.**
29. 4 under the ground, a muffled voice coming from the **dust.**
29. 5 will be blown away like **dust,** and their terrifying armies
34. 4 The sun, moon, and stars will crumble to **dust.**
40.15 the distant islands are as light as **dust.**
41. 2 His sword strikes them down as if they were **dust.**
41.15 hills will crumble into **dust.**
47. 1 down from your throne, and sit in the **dust** on the ground.
52. 2 Rise from the **dust** and sit on your throne!
Jer 17.13 like names written in the **dust,** because they have abandoned you,
18.17 before their enemies, like **dust** blown by the east wind.
25.34 Mourn and roll in the **dust.**
48.18 your place of honour and sit on the ground in the **dust;**
Lam 2.10 in silence, With **dust** on their heads and sackcloth
Ezek 24. 7 was not spilt on the ground where the **dust** could hide it;
26. 4 will sweep away all the **dust** and leave only a bare rock.
26.10 The clouds of **dust** raised by their horses will cover you.
27.30 mourn bitterly for you, Throwing **dust** on their heads
Dan 2.35 gold crumbled and became like the **dust** on a threshing-place
Mic 1.10 People of Beth Leaphrah, show your despair by rolling in the **dust!**
7.17 They will crawl in the **dust** like snakes;
Nah 1. 3 the clouds are the **dust** raised by his feet!
1. 6 rocks crumble to **dust** before him.
Mal 4. 3 the wicked, and they will be like **dust** under your feet.
Mt 10.14 then leave that place and shake the **dust** off your feet.
Mk 6.11 listen to you, leave it and shake the **dust** off your feet.
Lk 9. 5 that town and shake the **dust** off your feet as a warning
10.11 streets and say, [11]'Even the **dust** from your town that sticks
20.18 if that stone falls on someone, it will crush him to **dust."**
Acts 13.51 apostles shook the **dust** off their feet in protest against them
18. 6 he protested by shaking the **dust** from his clothes and saying
22.23 waving their clothes, and throwing **dust** up in the air.
Rev 18.19 They threw **dust** on their heads, they cried and mourned,

DUTY (1)

Ex 21.11 he does not fulfil these **duties** to her, he must set her
Lev 24. 8 This is Israel's **duty** for ever.
Num 3. 7 of my presence and perform **duties** for the priests and for
3. 8 Tent and perform the **duties** for the rest of the Israelites.
3.10 Aaron and his sons to carry out the **duties** of the priesthood;
3.32 of those who carried out the **duties** in the Holy Place.
4.27 the Gershonites perform all the **duties** and carry everything
8.24 Levite shall perform his **duties** in the Tent of my presence,
8.26 his fellow-Levites in performing their **duties** in the Tent,
8.26 This is how you are to regulate the **duties** of the Levites."
18. 3 They are to fulfil their **duties** to you
18. 6 me, so that they can carry out their **duties** in the Tent.
Deut 10. 8 And these are still their **duties.**
17.12 judge or the priest on **duty** is to be put to death;
24. 5 be drafted into military service or any other public **duty;**
24. 5 is to be excused from **duty** for one year, so that he
25. 5 it is the **duty** of the dead man's brother to marry her.
25. 7 leaders and say, 'My husband's brother will not do his **duty;**
1 Sam 10.25 the people the rights and **duties** of a king, and then wrote
26.16 You failed in your **duty,** Abner!
2 Sam 13.34 then the soldier on sentry **duty** saw a large crowd coming
1 Kgs 8.11 and they could not go back in to perform their **duties.**
2 Kgs 9.17 A guard on **duty** in the watch-tower at Jezreel saw Jehu
11. 5 "When you come on **duty** on the Sabbath, one third of you
11. 7 two groups that go off **duty** on the Sabbath are to stand
11. 9 those going off duty on the Sabbath and those going on **duty.**
11.18 Jehoiada put guards on **duty** at the Temple,
12. 9 The priests on **duty** at the entrance put in the box all
15. 5 relieved of all **duties,** while his son Jotham governed
22. 4 money that the priests on **duty** at the entrance to the Temple
23. 4 priests, and the guards on **duty** at the entrance to the
24.16 all of them able-bodied men fit for military **duty.**
1 Chr 6.32 They took regular turns of **duty** at the Tent of the
6.48 fellow-Levites were assigned all the other **duties**
9.25 to take turns at guard **duty** for seven days at a time.
9.27 Temple, because it was their **duty** to guard it and to open
9.33 and were free from other **duties,** because they were on call
16.37 They were to perform their **duties** there day by day.
23. 5 four thousand to do guard **duty,** and four thousand to praise
23.28 age of twenty, [28]and were assigned the following **duties:**
23.31 The Levites were assigned the **duty** of worshipping the Lord
24. 3 descendants of Aaron into groups according to their **duties.**
24.19 performing the **duties** established by their ancestor Aaron
25. 8 To determine the assignment of **duties** they all drew lots,
25. 9 This is the order in which they were on **duty:**
26.12 and they were assigned **duties** in the Temple,
26.16 Guard **duty** was divided into assigned periods, one after another.
26.17 east, six guards were on **duty** each day, on the north, four,
26.19 is the assignment of guard **duty** to the clan of Korah and
26.23 **Duties** were also assigned to the descendants of Amram,
26.29 Chenaniah and his sons were assigned administrative **duties:**
27. 1 was on **duty** under the commander for that month.
28.13 and Levites to perform their **duties,** to do the work of the
28.21 Levites have been assigned **duties** to perform in the Temple.
2 Chr 8.14 sections for performing their daily **duties** at each gate,
13.10 Priests descended from Aaron perform their **duties,**
19. 9 "You must perform your **duties** in reverence for the Lord,
19.10 But if you do your **duty,** you will not be guilty.
23. 4 priests and Levites come on **duty** on the Sabbath,
23. 6 except the priests and the Levites who are on **duty.**
23. 8 when they went off **duty** on the Sabbath, so the commanders
23. 8 had available both those coming on **duty** and those going off.
23.18 were to carry out the **duties** assigned to them by King David
23.19 Jehoiada also put guards on **duty** at the temple gates to
26.21 relieved of all **duties,** while his son Jotham governed
31. 2 priests and Levites, under which they each had specific **duties.**
31.15 according to what their **duties** were, [16]and not by clans.
31.17 The priests were assigned their **duties** by clans,
31.18 to be ready to perform their sacred **duties** at any time.
35. 2 assigned to the priests the **duties** they were to perform
Neh 7. 3 closed and barred before the guards went off **duty** at sunset.
10.39 the priests who are on **duty,** the temple guards, and the
12.45 temple guards also performed their **duties**
13.30 and the Levites so that each one would know his **duty;**
Job 33.23 of God's thousands of angels, who remind men of their **duty.**
Jer 29.26 It is your **duty** to see that every madman who pretends to
37.13 charge of the soldiers on **duty** there, a man by the name
Ezek 44.11 sacrifices, and they are to be on **duty** to serve the people.
44.17 wool when they are on **duty** in the inner courtyard or in
44.19 the clothes they wore on **duty** in the Temple and leave them
45.17 It will be his **duty** to provide the animals to be burnt
Zech 3. 7 my laws and perform the **duties** I have assigned to you,
Mal 2. 7 It is the **duty** of priests to teach the true knowledge of
Mt 6. 1 do not perform your religious **duties** in public so that people
Lk 17.10 we have only done our **duty.'"**
Acts 12. 6 chains, and there were guards on **duty** at the prison gate.
Rom 12.16 Do not be proud, but accept humble **duties.**
13. 6 the authorities are working for God when they fulfil their **duties.**
1 Cor 7. 3 A man should fulfil his **duty** as a husband, and
7. 3 a woman should fulfil her **duty** as a wife, and each should
9.17 as a matter of **duty,** because God has entrusted me with
2 Cor 9. 7 has decided, not with regret or out of a sense of **duty;**
Eph 6. 1 Children, it is your Christian **duty** to obey your parents,
Phil 1.20 shall never fail in my **duty,** but that at all times, and
Col 3.20 Children, it is your Christian **duty** to obey your parents
1 Tim 5. 4 carry out their religious **duties** towards their own family and
5.10 in her home, performed humble **duties** for fellow-Christians,
2 Tim 4. 5 Good News, and perform your whole **duty** as a servant of God.
Heb 9. 6 every day to perform their **duties,** [7]but only the High Priest

DUTY (2)

Mt 17.25 Who pays **duties** or taxes to the kings of this world?

DWARF

Lev 21.20 no one who is a hunchback or a **dwarf;**

DWELL

Deut 33.12 them all the day long, And he **dwells** in their midst."
2 Chr 29. 6 him and turned their backs on the place where he **dwells.**
Job 36.29 or how the thunder roars through the sky, where God **dwells.**
Ps 26. 8 where you live, O Lord, the place where your glory **dwells.**
Is 26.21 coming from his heavenly **dwelling-place** to punish the people
43.18 to events of the past or **dwell** on what happened long ago.
Zech 2.13 for he is coming from his holy **dwelling-place.**
Acts 7.46 allow him to provide a **dwelling place** for the God of Jacob.
Jude 6 of their proper authority, but abandoned their own **dwelling place:**

DYE

Ex 25. 5 rams' skin **dyed** red;
26.14 coverings, one of rams' skin **dyed** red

Ex 35. 7 rams' skin **dyed** red;
35.23 rams' skin **dyed** red;
36.19 coverings, one of rams' skin **dyed** red
39.34 the covering of rams' skin **dyed** red;
2 Chr 3.14 other material, which was **dyed** blue, purple, and red,

DYNASTY

2 Sam 7.13 and I will make sure that his **dynasty** continues for ever.
7.16 Your **dynasty** will never end.' "
7.26 And you will preserve my **dynasty** for all time.
1 Kgs 12.19 Israel have been in rebellion against the **dynasty** of David.
13.34 brought about the ruin and total destruction of his **dynasty.**
14.10 will bring disaster on your **dynasty**
14.14 king over Israel who will put an end to Jeroboam's **dynasty.**
1 Chr 17.12 and I will make sure that his **dynasty** continues for ever.
17.14 His **dynasty** will never end.' "
17.24 And you will preserve my **dynasty** for all time.
22.10 His **dynasty** will rule Israel for ever.' "
2 Chr 10.19 Israel have been in rebellion against the **dynasty** of David.
21. 7 not willing to destroy the **dynasty** of David,
22. 7 whom the Lord had chosen to destroy the **dynasty** of Ahab.
22. 8 out God's sentence on the **dynasty,** he came across a group
Ezra 5.12 King Nebuchadnezzar of Babylonia, a king of the Chaldean **dynasty.**
Ps 89. 4 I will preserve your **dynasty** for ever.' "
89.29 His **dynasty** will be as permanent as the sky;
Hos 1. 4 I am going to put an end to Jehu's **dynasty.**
Amos 7. 9 I will bring the **dynasty** of King Jeroboam to an end."

DYSENTERY

Acts 28. 8 Publius' father was in bed, sick with fever and **dysentery.**

EACH OTHER

see also **ONE ANOTHER**

Gen 3.15 I will make you and the woman hate **each other;**
15.10 and placed the halves opposite **each other** in two rows;
25.22 before they were born, they struggled against **each other**
31.49 keep an eye on us while we are separated from **each other."**
Ex 10.23 The Egyptians could not see **each other,**
14.20 the armies could not come near **each other** all night.
16.15 know what it was and asked **each other,** "What is it?"
18. 7 They asked about **each other's** health
25.20 winged creatures are to face **each other** across the lid,
37. 9 The winged creatures faced **each other** across the lid,
Judg 6.29 They asked **each other,** "Who did this?"
7.22 the Lord made the enemy troops attack **each other**
9.23 hostile to **each other,** and they rebelled against him.
1 Sam 14.20 the Philistines, who were fighting **each other** in complete confusion.
17.21 Israelite armies took up positions for battle, facing **each other.**
17.25 they said to **each other.**
20.16 may our promise to **each other** still be unbroken.
20.23 promise we have made to **each other,** the Lord will make sure
20.41 Both he and Jonathan were crying as they kissed **each other;**
20.42 ever keep the sacred promise we have made to **each other."**
23.18 of them made a sacred promise of friendship to **each other.**
2 Sam 12.19 David noticed them whispering to **each other,**
21. 7 and Jonathan had made to **each other,** David spared Jonathan's son
1 Kgs 5.12 Hiram and Solomon, and they made a treaty with **each other.**
6.27 their outstretched wings touched **each other** in the middle
14.30 Rehoboam and Jeroboam were constantly at war with **each other.**
15.16 were constantly at war with **each other** as long as they were
15.32 were constantly at war with **each other** as long as they were
20.29 Syrians and the Israelites stayed in their camps, facing **each other.**
2 Kgs 3.23 "The three enemy armies must have fought and killed **each other!**
7. 9 But then they said to **each other,** "We shouldn't be doing this!
2 Chr 3.11 out so that they touched **each other** in the centre of the
12.15 Rehoboam and Jeroboam were constantly at war with **each other.**
20.23 and then they turned on **each other** in savage fighting.
Ps 12. 2 they deceive **each other** with flattery.
41. 7 who hate me whisper to **each other** about me,
55.14 We had intimate talks with **each other** and worshipped together
64. 5 They encourage **each other** in their evil plots;
Prov 7.18 We'll be happy in **each other's** arms.
18.18 two powerful men are opposing **each other** in court,
Is 6. 3 They were calling out to **each other:**
9.21 the people of Ephraim attack **each other,**
13. 8 They will look at **each other** in fear,
19. 2 Rival cities will fight **each other,**
34.14 Wild animals will roam there, and demons will call to **each other.**
49.26 I will make your oppressors kill **each other;**
Jer 23.30 those prophets who take **each other's** words and proclaim them
Dan 11.27 their motives will be evil, and they will lie to **each other.**
Joel 2. 8 and do not change direction [8] or get in **each other's** way.
Mt 12.25 into groups which fight **each other** will not last very long.
12.25 itself into groups which fight **each other** will fall apart.
24. 7 Countries will fight **each other,** kingdoms will attack one another.
Mk 3.24 into groups which fight **each other,** that country will fall apart.
3.25 into groups which fight **each other,** that family will fall apart.
13. 8 Countries will fight **each other;**
15.31 jeered at Jesus, saying to **each other,** "He saved others,
Lk 11.17 into groups which fight **each other** will not last very long;
11.18 Satan's kingdom has groups fighting **each other,** how can it last?
12. 1 that they were stepping on **each other,** Jesus said first to
21.10 He went on to say, "Countries will fight **each other;**
24.14 and they were talking to **each other** about all the things
24.17 "What are you talking about to **each other,** as you walk along?"
Lk 24.32 They said to **each other,** "Wasn't it like a fire burning
Acts 2.12 confused, they kept asking **each other,** "What does this mean?"
26.31 after leaving they said to **each other,** "This man has not
Rom 1.24 their hearts desire, and they do shameful things with **each other.**
1.27 sexual relations with women and burn with passion for **each other.**
1.27 Men do shameful things with **each other,** and as a result they
12. 5 we are all joined to **each other** as different parts of one
1 Cor 7. 3 duty as a wife, and **each** should satisfy the other's needs.
7. 5 Do not deny yourselves to **each other,** unless you first agree
Gal 5.15 wild animals, hurting and harming **each other,** then watch out,
Col 3.16 Teach and instruct **each other** with all wisdom.
Heb 13. 4 and husbands and wives must be faithful to **each other.**
1 Pet 4. 9 Open your homes to **each other** without complaining.
Rev 6. 4 bring war on the earth, so that men should kill **each other.**
11.10 celebrate and send presents to **each other,** because those two

EAGER

1 Chr 28.21 every kind of skill are **eager** to help you,
Neh 4. 6 its full height, because the people were **eager** to work.
Job 39.21 They **eagerly** paw the ground in the valley;
Ps 19. 5 a happy bridegroom, like an athlete **eager** to run a race.
73.10 God's people turn to them and **eagerly** believe whatever they say.
84. 5 comes from you, who are **eager** to make the pilgrimage
119.32 I will **eagerly** obey your commands,
130. 5 I wait **eagerly** for the Lord's help,
130. 6 more **eagerly** than watchmen wait for the dawn
Prov 18.15 Intelligent people are always **eager** and ready to learn.
Song 6.12 you have made me as **eager** for love as a chariot driver
Is 42. 4 Distant lands **eagerly** wait for his teaching."
42.13 he is ready and **eager** for battle.
42.21 is a God who is **eager** to save,
50. 4 Every morning he makes me **eager** to hear what he is going
58. 2 day, claiming that they are **eager** to know my ways and obey
Acts 17.11 the message with great **eagerness,** and every day they studied
Rom 1.15 So then, I am **eager** to preach the Good News to you
8.19 All of creation waits with **eager** longing for God to reveal
12.10 brothers, and be **eager** to show respect for one another.
1 Cor 14.12 Since you are **eager** to have the gifts of the Spirit,
2 Cor 7.11 earnest it has made you, how **eager** to prove your innocence!
8. 7 and knowledge, in your **eagerness** to help and in your love
8. 8 But by showing how **eager** others are to help, I am trying
8.11 Be as **eager** to finish it as you were to plan it,
8.12 If you are **eager** to give, God will accept your gift
8.16 God for making Titus as **eager** as we are to help you!
8.17 he was so **eager** to help that of his own free will
8.22 him many times and found him always very **eager** to help.
8.22 much confidence in you, he is all the more **eager** to help.
9. 2 Your **eagerness** has stirred up most of them.
Gal 2.10 group, which is the very thing I have been **eager** to do.
Phil 2.28 I am all the more **eager,** then, to send him to you,
3.20 citizens of heaven, and we **eagerly** wait for our Saviour,
1 Tim 3. 1 If a man is **eager** to be a church leader, he desires
6.10 Some have been so **eager** to have it that they have wandered
Tit 2.14 people who belong to him alone and are **eager** to do good.
Heb 6.11 of you keep up his **eagerness** to the end, so that the
1 Pet 3.13 will harm you if you are **eager** to do what is good?

EAGLE

Ex 19. 4 I carried you as an **eagle** carries her young on her wings,
Lev 11.13 **eagles,** owls, hawks, falcons;
Deut 14.12 **eagles,** owls, hawks, falcons;
28.49 They will swoop down on you like an **eagle.**
32.11 Like an **eagle** teaching its young to fly, catching them
2 Sam 1.23 swifter than **eagles,** stronger than lions.
Job 9.26 boat, as fast as an **eagle** swooping down on a rabbit.
39.27 Does an **eagle** wait for your command to build its nest
39.30 Around dead bodies the **eagles** gather,
39.30 and the young **eagles** drink the blood.
Ps 103. 5 good things, so that I stay young and strong like an **eagle.**
Prov 23. 5 as if it had grown wings and flown away like an **eagle.**
30.19 an **eagle** flying in the sky,
Is 40.31 They will rise on wings like **eagles;**
Jer 4.13 are like a whirlwind, and his horses are faster than **eagles.**
48.40 down on Moab like an **eagle** with its outspread wings, [41] and
49.16 as high up as an **eagle,** the Lord will bring you down.
49.22 Bozrah like an **eagle** swooping down with outspread wings.
Lam 4.19 Swifter than **eagles** swooping from the sky, they chased us down.
Ezek 1.10 bull's face at the left, and an **eagle's** face at the back.
10.14 face of a lion, and the fourth the face of an **eagle.**
17. 3 There was a giant **eagle** with beautiful feathers and huge wings,
17. 6 The branches grew upward towards the **eagle,** and the roots grew deep.
17. 7 "There was another giant **eagle** with huge wings and thick plumage.
17. 9 Won't the first **eagle** pull it up by its roots, pull off
Dan 4.33 hair grew as long as **eagles'** feathers and his nails as long
7. 4 first one looked like a lion, but had wings like an **eagle.**
Hos 8. 1 Enemies are swooping down on my land like **eagles!**
Obad 4 home as high as an **eagle's** nest, so that it seems to
Hab 1. 8 They come swooping down like **eagles** attacking their prey.
Rev 4. 7 and the fourth looked like an **eagle** in flight.
8.13 looked, and I heard an **eagle** that was flying high in the
12.14 two wings of a large **eagle** in order to fly to her

EAR

Ex 21. 6 stand against the door or the door-post and pierce his **ear.**
29.20 the lobes of the right **ears** of Aaron and his sons, on
Lev 8.23 the lobe of Aaron's right **ear,** on the thumb of his right

Lev 8.24 the lobes of their right **ears,** on the thumbs of their right
14.14 the lobe of the right **ear,** on the thumb of the right
14.17 the lobe of the right **ear,** on the thumb of the right
14.25 lobe of the man's right **ear,** on the thumb of his right
14.28 lobe of the man's right **ear,** on the thumb of his right
Num 11.20 it comes out of your **ears,** until you are sick of it.
Deut 15.17 him to the door of your house and there pierce his **ear;**
Job 12.11 tongue enjoys tasting food, your **ears** enjoy hearing words.
15.21 terror will scream in his **ears,** and robbers attack when he
Ps 40. 6 Instead, you have given me **ears** to hear you, [7]and so I
44. 1 With our own **ears** we have heard it, O God— our
58. 4 they stop up their **ears** like a deaf cobra, [5]which does
94. 9 God made our **ears**—can't he hear?
115. 6 They have **ears,** but cannot hear, and noses, but cannot smell.
135.17 They have **ears,** but cannot hear;
Prov 20.12 has given us eyes to see with and **ears** to listen with.
26.17 like going down the street and grabbing a dog by the **ears.**
Ecc 1. 8 our **ears** can never hear enough.
12. 4 Your **ears** will be deaf to the noise of the street.
Is 6.10 of these people dull, their **ears** deaf, and their eyes blind,
32. 3 Their eyes and **ears** will be open to the needs of the
42.20 You have **ears** to hear with, but what have you really heard?"
43. 8 they have **ears,** but they are deaf!
48. 8 at all, why no word of it ever came to your **ears.**
Jer 5.21 have eyes, but cannot see, and have **ears,** but cannot hear.
26.11 You heard him with your own **ears.**"
Ezek 12. 2 **ears,** but they hear nothing, because they are rebellious.
23.25 will cut off your nose and your **ears** and kill your children.
Amos 3.12 only two legs or an **ear** of a sheep that a lion
Mic 7.16 In dismay they will close their mouths and cover their **ears.**
Mt 11.15 Listen, then, if you have **ears!**
13. 9 And Jesus concluded, "Listen, then, if you have **ears!**"
13.15 they have stopped up their **ears** and have closed their eyes.
13.15 their eyes would see, their **ears** would hear, their minds would
13.16 Your eyes see and your **ears** hear.
13.43 Listen, then, if you have **ears!**
26.51 and struck at the High Priest's slave, cutting off his **ear.**
Mk 4. 9 And Jesus concluded, "Listen, then, if you have **ears!**"
4.23 Listen, then, if you have **ears!**"
7.33 fingers in the man's **ears,** spat, and touched the man's tongue.
8.18 You have **ears**—can't you hear?
14.47 and struck at the High Priest's slave, cutting off his **ear.**
Lk 8. 8 And Jesus concluded, "Listen, then, if you have **ears!**"
14.35 Listen, then, if you have **ears!**"
22.50 struck the High Priest's slave and cut off his right **ear.**
22.51 He touched the man's **ear** and healed him.
Jn 18.10 and struck the High Priest's slave, cutting off his right **ear.**
18.26 relative of the man whose **ear** Peter had cut off, spoke up.
Acts 7.57 the members of the Council covered their **ears** with their hands.
28.27 and they have stopped up their **ears** and closed their eyes.
28.27 their eyes would see, their **ears** would hear, their minds would
1 Cor 12.16 And if the **ear** were to say, "Because I am not an
12.17 And if it were only an **ear,** how could it smell?
Jas 5. 4 your crops have reached the **ears** of God, the Lord Almighty.
Rev 2. 7 "If you have **ears,** then, listen to what the Spirit says
2.11 "If you have **ears,** then, listen to what the Spirit says
2.17 "If you have **ears,** then, listen to what the Spirit says
2.29 "If you have **ears,** then, listen to what the Spirit says
3. 6 "If you have **ears,** then, listen to what the Spirit says
3.13 "If you have **ears,** then, listen to what the Spirit says
3.22 "If you have **ears,** then, listen to what the Spirit says
13. 9 "Listen, then, if you have **ears!**

EAR OF CORN

Gen 41. 5 Seven **ears of corn,** full and ripe, were growing on one stalk.
41. 6 Then seven other **ears of corn** sprouted, thin and scorched
41. 7 wind, [7]and the thin **ears of corn** swallowed the full ones.
41.22 that I saw seven **ears of corn** which were full and ripe,
41.23 Then seven **ears of corn** sprouted, thin and scorched by
41.24 wind, [24]and the thin **ears of corn** swallowed the full ones.
41.26 years, and the seven full **ears of corn** are also seven years;
41.27 and the seven thin **ears of corn** scorched by the desert wind
Lev 19. 9 not go back to cut the **ears of corn** that were left.
23.22 not go back to cut the **ears of corn** that were left;
2 Kgs 4.42 harvested that year, and some freshly-cut **ears of corn.**
Job 24.24 a weed, like an **ear of corn** that has been cut off.
Mt 12. 1 so they began to pick **ears of corn** and eat the grain.
13.26 plants grew and the **ears of corn** began to form, then the
Mk 2.23 walked along with him, they began to pick the **ears of corn.**
4.28 appears, then the ear, and finally the **ear full of corn.**
Lk 6. 1 began to pick the **ears of corn,** rub them in their hands,

EARN

Gen 30.26 and children that I have **earned** by working for you, and I
Lev 25.49 or if he himself **earns** enough, he may buy his own freedom.
Deut 23.18 Also, no money **earned** in this way may be brought into
Ps 107.23 over the ocean in ships, **earning** their living on the seas.
Prov 13.11 The harder it is to **earn,** the more you will have.
14.22 You will **earn** the trust and respect of others if you
14.23 Work and you will **earn** a living;
16. 8 to have a little, honestly **earned,** than to have a large
24. 8 planning evil, you will **earn** a reputation as a troublemaker.
24.27 are ready, and you are sure that you can **earn** a living.
31.16 it, and with money she has **earned** she plants a vineyard.
Ecc 2.18 I had worked for and **earned** meant a thing to me, because
2.19 for, everything my wisdom has **earned** for me in this world.
2.24 do is to eat and drink and enjoy what he has **earned.**
2.26 but he makes sinners work, **earning** and saving, so that what
9.11 Wise men do not always **earn** a living, intelligent men do not
Is 19. 8 Everyone who **earns** his living by fishing in the Nile will
23.18 The money she **earns** by commerce will be dedicated to the Lord.
Hag 1. 6 And the working man cannot **earn** enough to live on.
Mt 25.16 at once and invested his money and **earned** another five thousand.
25.17 who had received two thousand coins **earned** another two thousand.
25.20 Here are another five thousand that I have **earned.'**
25.22 Here are another two thousand that I have **earned.'**
Lk 19.13 'See what you can **earn** with this while I am gone.'
19.15 before him, in order to find out how much they had **earned.**
19.16 and said, 'Sir, I have **earned** ten gold coins with the one
19.18 and said, 'Sir, I have **earned** five gold coins with the one
Acts 16.16 She **earned** a lot of money for her owners by telling fortunes.
18. 3 worked with them, because he **earned** his living by making tents,
Rom 4. 4 they are something that he has **earned.**
1 Cor 16. 2 proportion to what he has **earned,** and save it up, so that
Eph 4.28 start working, in order to **earn** an honest living for himself
1 Thes 4.11 your own business, and to **earn** your own living, just as we
2 Thes 3.12 to lead orderly lives and work to **earn** their own living.
Rev 18.17 sailors and all others who **earn** their living on the sea,

EARNEST

Ex 15.25 Moses prayed **earnestly** to the Lord, and the Lord showed
17. 4 Moses prayed **earnestly** to the Lord and said, "What can I
Deut 3.23 "At that time I **earnestly** prayed, [24]'Sovereign Lord,
Ps 78.34 they would repent and pray **earnestly** to him.
Dan 9. 3 And I prayed **earnestly** to the Lord God, pleading with him,
Jon 3. 8 Everyone must pray **earnestly** to God and must give up his
Mk 5.23 and begged him **earnestly,** "My little daughter is very ill.
Lk 7. 4 and begged him **earnestly,** "This man really deserves your help.
Acts 12. 5 people of the church were praying **earnestly** to God for him.
2 Cor 7.11 **earnest** it has made you, how eager to prove your innocence!
Heb 13.19 I beg you even more **earnestly** to pray that God will send
Jas 5.17 He prayed **earnestly** that there would be no rain, and no rain
1 Pet 1.22 fellow-believers, love one another **earnestly** with all your heart.
4. 8 love one another **earnestly,** because love covers over many sins.
Rev 3.19 Be in **earnest,** then, and turn from your sins.

EARRINGS

Gen 35. 4 that they had and also the **ear-rings** that they were wearing.
Ex 32. 2 them, "Take off the gold **earrings** which your wives, your
32. 3 took off their gold **earrings** and brought them to Aaron.
32. 4 He took the **earrings,** melted them, poured the gold into a mould,
35.22 and women, brought decorative pins, **earrings,** rings,
Num 31.50 gold ornaments, armlets, bracelets, rings, **earrings,** and
Judg 8.24 Every one of you give me the **earrings** you took."
8.24 (The Midianites, like other desert people, wore gold **earrings.**)
8.25 and everyone put on it the **earrings** that he had taken.
8.26 The gold **earrings** that Gideon received
Ezek 16.12 you a nose-ring and **earrings** and a beautiful crown to wear.

EARTH

[END OF THE EARTH, HEAVEN AND EARTH, NEW EARTH]

Gen 1. 2 God created the universe, [2]the **earth** was formless and desolate.
1.10 He named the land **"Earth,"** and the water which had
1.11 Then he commanded, "Let the **earth** produce all kinds of plants,
1.12 So the **earth** produced all kinds of plants, and God was
1.15 the sky to give light to the **earth"**—and it was done.
1.17 sky to shine on the **earth,** [18]to rule over the day and
1.24 "Let the **earth** produce all kinds of animal life:
1.28 live all over the **earth** and bring it under their control.
2. 5 were no plants on the **earth** and no seeds had sprouted,
4.12 you will be a homeless wanderer on the **earth.**"
4.14 a homeless wanderer on the **earth,** and anyone who finds me
6. 4 there were giants on the **earth** who were descendants of human
6. 5 saw how wicked everyone on **earth** was and how evil their
6. 6 that he had ever made them and put them on the **earth.**
6.17 to send a flood on the **earth** to destroy every living being.
6.17 Everything on the **earth** will die, [18]but I will make a
7. 3 and bird will be kept alive to reproduce again on the **earth.**
7. 6 was six hundred years old when the flood came on the **earth.**
7.11 body of water beneath the **earth** burst open, all the
7.12 and rain fell on the **earth** for forty days and nights.
7.21 Every living being on the **earth** died—every bird, every
7.22 Everything on **earth** that breathed died.
7.23 destroyed all living beings on the **earth**—human beings,
8. 2 of the water beneath the **earth** and the floodgates of the sky
8.14 day of the second month the **earth** was completely dry.
8.17 so that they may reproduce and spread over all the **earth.**"
8.21 again will I put the **earth** under a curse because of what
9. 1 so that your descendants will live all over the **earth.**
9. 7 so that your descendants will live all over the **earth.**"
9.11 never again will a flood destroy the **earth.**
9.16 covenant between me and all living beings on **earth.**
9.19 sons of Noah were the ancestors of all the people on **earth.**
10.32 all the nations of the **earth** were descended from the sons of
11. 4 for ourselves and not be scattered all over the **earth.**"
11. 8 them all over the **earth,** and they stopped building the city.
11. 9 and from there he scattered them all over the **earth.**
13.16 be as easy to count all the specks of dust on **earth!**
14.19 the Most High God, who made **heaven and earth,** bless Abram!
14.22 High God, Maker of **heaven and earth,** [23]that I will not
18.25 The judge of all the **earth** has to act justly."
24. 3 Lord, the God of **heaven and earth,** that you will not choose
28.12 a stairway reaching from **earth to heaven,** with angels going
28.14 will be as numerous as the specks of dust on the **earth.**
Ex 9.29 so that you may know that the **earth** belongs to the Lord.
15.12 your right hand, and the **earth** swallowed our enemies.

Ex 19. 5 The whole **earth** is mine, but you will be my chosen people,
20. 4 in heaven or on earth or in the water under the **earth.**
20.11 the Lord, made the **earth, the sky,** the sea, and everything
20.24 Make an altar of **earth** for me, and on it sacrifice your
31.17 I, the Lord, made **heaven and earth** in six days,
33.16 us will distinguish us from any other people on **earth."**
34.10 never been done anywhere on **earth** among any of the nations.
Lev 17.13 pour out its blood on the ground and cover it with **earth.**
Num 5.17 and take some of the **earth** that is on the floor of
12. 3 (Moses was a humble man, more humble than anyone else on **earth.)**
14.21 as my presence fills the **earth,** [22]none of these people
16.30 something unheard of, and the **earth** opens up and swallows
16.33 The **earth** closed over them, and they vanished.
16.34 The **earth** might swallow us too!"
Deut 3.24 god in heaven or on **earth** who can do the mighty things
4.26 I call **heaven and earth** as witnesses against you today
4.32 way back to the time when God created man on the **earth.**
4.32 Search the entire **earth.**
4.36 and here on **earth** he let you see his holy fire, and
4.39 the Lord is God in **heaven and on earth.**
5. 8 in heaven or on earth or in the water under the **earth.**
7. 6 From all the peoples on **earth** he chose you to be his
7. 7 you were the smallest nation on **earth.**
10.14 the **earth** is his also, and everything on it.
11. 6 sight of everyone the **earth** opened up and swallowed them,
11.21 live there as long as there is a sky above the **earth.**
14. 2 own people from among all the peoples who live on **earth.**
28. 1 he will make you greater than any other nation on **earth.**
28.10 Then all the peoples on **earth** will see that the Lord has
28.25 and all the people on **earth** will be terrified when they see
28.49 a nation from the **ends of the earth,** a nation whose language
28.64 the nations, from one **end of the earth** to the other, and
30. 4 the farthest corners of the **earth,** the Lord your God will
30.19 curse, and I call **heaven and earth** to witness the choice you
31.28 I will call **heaven and earth** to be my witnesses against them.
32. 1 **"Earth and sky,** hear my words, listen closely to what I say.
32. 2 fall like drops of rain and form on the **earth** like dew.
32.22 My anger will flame up like fire and burn everything on **earth.**
33.13 their land with rain And with water from under the **earth.**
33.17 the nations And pushes them to the **ends of the earth."**
Josh 2.11 Lord your God is God in heaven above and here on **earth.**
3.11 the Lord of all the **earth** crosses the Jordan ahead of you.
3.13 the Lord of all the **earth** put their feet in the water,
4.24 Because of this everyone on **earth** will know how great
Judg 5. 4 the region of Edom, the **earth** shook, and rain fell from the
1 Sam 2. 8 The foundations of the **earth** belong to the Lord;
4. 5 Israelites gave such a loud shout of joy that the **earth** shook.
4.12 grief, he had torn his clothes and put **earth** on his head.
14.15 the **earth** shook, and there was great panic.
28.13 "I see a spirit coming up from the **earth,"** she answered.
2 Sam 1. 2 grief, he had torn his clothes and put **earth** on his head.
4.11 murdering him and will wipe you off the face of the **earth!"**
7.23 is no other nation on **earth** like Israel, whom you rescued
15.32 met him with his clothes torn and with **earth** on his head.
16.13 cursing and throwing stones and **earth** at them as he went.
20.15 They built ramps of **earth** against the outer wall and also
22. 8 Then the **earth** trembled and shook;
22.16 and the foundations of the **earth** were uncovered when the
1 Kgs 8.23 is no god like you in heaven above or on **earth** below!
8.27 "But can you, O God, really live on **earth?**
18.38 and the stones, scorched the **earth** and dried up the water in
2 Kgs 5.17 me have two mule-loads of **earth** to take home with me,
19.15 You created the **earth and the sky.**
1 Chr 16.28 Praise the Lord, all people on **earth,** praise his glory and might.
16.30 tremble before him, all the **earth!**
16.30 The **earth** is set firmly in place and cannot be moved.
16.31 Be glad, **earth and sky!**
16.33 will shout for joy when the Lord comes to rule the **earth.**
17.21 is no other nation on **earth** like Israel, whom you rescued
29.11 Everything in **heaven and earth** is yours, and you are king,
2 Chr 2.12 Praise the Lord God of Israel, Creator of **heaven and earth!**
6.14 of Israel, in all **heaven and earth** there is no god like
6.18 can you, O God, really live on **earth** among men and women?
12. 8 difference between serving me and serving **earthly** rulers."
Ezra 5.11 of the God of **heaven and earth,** and we are rebuilding the
Neh 1. 9 even though you are scattered to the **ends of the earth.'**
Job 1. 7 "I have been walking here and there, roaming round the **earth."**
1. 8 "There is no one on **earth** as faithful and good as he
2. 2 "I have been walking here and there, roaming round the **earth."**
2. 3 "There is no one on **earth** as faithful and good as he
8. 9 we pass like shadows across the **earth.**
9. 6 he rocks the pillars that support the **earth.**
11. 9 God's greatness is broader than the **earth,** wider than the sea.
12. 8 ask the creatures of **earth** and sea for their wisdom.
16.18 O **Earth,** don't hide the wrongs done to me!
18. 4 Will the **earth** be deserted because you are angry?
20. 4 man was first placed on **earth,** [5]no wicked man has been
20.27 and the **earth** gives testimony against him.
21.33 procession, and even the **earth** lies gently on his body.
26. 5 The spirits of the dead tremble in the waters under the **earth.**
26. 7 out the northern sky and hung the **earth** in empty space.
28. 3 search the depths of the **earth** And dig for rocks in the
28. 5 Food grows out of the **earth,**
28. 5 But underneath the same **earth** All is torn up and crushed.
28. 6 The stones of the **earth** contain sapphires,
28.24 Because he sees the **ends of the earth,** Sees everything
36.27 who takes water from the **earth** and turns it into drops of
37. 3 across the sky, from one **end of the earth** to the other.
37. 6 to fall on the **earth,** and sends torrents of drenching rain.
37.13 God sends rain to water the **earth;**
Job 38. 6 What holds up the pillars that support the **earth?**
38. 8 back the sea when it burst from the womb of the **earth?**
38.13 the dawn to seize the **earth** and shake the wicked from their
38.33 govern the skies, and can you make them apply to the **earth?**
41.33 There is nothing on **earth** to compare with him;
Ps 2. 8 the whole **earth** will be yours.
18. 7 Then the **earth** trembled and shook;
18.15 and the foundations of the **earth** were uncovered, when you
19. 4 all the world and is heard to the **ends of the earth.**
24. 1 the **earth** and all who live on it are his.
24. 2 the deep waters beneath the **earth** and laid its foundations
33. 5 his constant love fills the **earth.**
33. 8 Worship the Lord, all the **earth!**
33.14 where he rules, he looks down on all who live on **earth.**
45.16 kings, and you will make them rulers over the whole **earth.**
46. 2 be afraid, even if the **earth** is shaken and mountains fall
46. 6 God thunders, and the **earth** dissolves.
46. 8 See what amazing things he has done on **earth.**
48.10 everywhere, and your fame extends over all the **earth.**
50. 1 he calls to the whole **earth** from east to west.
50. 4 He calls **heaven and earth** as witnesses to see him judge
57. 5 in the sky, O God, and your glory over all the **earth.**
57.11 in the sky, O God, and your glory over all the **earth.**
59.13 God rules in Israel, that his rule extends over all the **earth.**
65. 8 shouts of joy from one **end of the earth** to the other.
65. 9 you provide the **earth** with crops.
66. 4 Everyone on **earth** worships you;
67. 4 the peoples with justice and guide every nation on **earth.**
68. 8 marched across the desert, [8]the **earth** shook, and the sky
69.34 Praise God, O **heaven and earth,** seas and all creatures
72. 8 sea to sea, from the Euphrates to the **ends of the earth.**
73. 9 arrogant orders to men on **earth,** [10]so that even God's
73.25 Since I have you, what else could I want on **earth?**
74.17 you set the limits of the **earth;**
75. 3 living creature tremble and the **earth** itself be shaken, I
76. 9 to pronounce judgement, to save all the oppressed on **earth.**
77.18 the **earth** trembled and shook.
78.69 he made it firm like the **earth** itself, secure for all time.
83.18 you alone are the Lord, supreme ruler over all the **earth.**
85.11 will reach up from the **earth,** and God's righteousness will
89.11 Heaven is yours, the **earth** also;
93. 1 The **earth** is set firmly in place and cannot be moved.
95. 4 He rules over the whole **earth,** from the deepest caves to
96. 7 Praise the Lord, all people on **earth;**
96. 9 tremble before him, all the **earth!**
96.10 The **earth** is set firmly in place and cannot be moved;
96.11 Be glad, **earth and sky!**
96.13 shout for joy [13]when the Lord comes to rule the **earth.**
97. 1 **Earth,** be glad!
97. 4 the **earth** sees it and trembles.
97. 5 like wax before the Lord, before the Lord of all the **earth.**
97. 9 Lord Almighty, you are ruler of all the **earth;**
98. 4 Sing for joy to the Lord, all the **earth;**
98. 7 sing, **earth,** and all who live on you!
98. 9 joy before the Lord, [9]because he comes to rule the **earth.**
99. 1 He is enthroned above the winged creatures and the **earth** shakes.
102.15 all the kings of the **earth** will fear his power.
102.19 holy place on high, he looked down from heaven to **earth.**
102.25 long ago you created the **earth,** and with your own
103.11 the sky is above the **earth,** so great is his love for
104. 5 You have set the **earth** firmly on its foundations, and it
104. 9 can never pass, to keep them from covering the **earth** again.
104.13 on the hills, and the **earth** is filled with your blessings.
104.24 The **earth** is filled with your creatures.
104.30 you give new life to the **earth.**
104.32 He looks at the **earth,** and it trembles;
104.35 May sinners be destroyed from the **earth;**
106.17 Then the **earth** opened up and swallowed Dathan and buried
108. 5 in the sky, O God, and your glory over all the **earth.**
110. 6 he will defeat kings all over the **earth.**
113. 6 but he bends down to see the **heavens and the earth.**
114. 7 Tremble, **earth,** at the Lord's coming, at the presence of
115.15 May you be blessed by the Lord, who made **heaven and earth!**
115.16 belongs to the Lord alone, but he gave the **earth** to man.
119.19 I am here on **earth** for just a little while;
119.54 During my brief **earthly** life I compose songs about your commands.
119.64 Lord, the **earth** is full of your constant love;
119.90 you have set the **earth** in place, and it remains.
121. 2 My help will come from the Lord, who made **heaven and earth.**
124. 8 Our help comes from the Lord, who made **heaven and earth.**
134. 3 the Lord, who made **heaven and earth,** bless you from Zion!
135. 6 whatever he wishes in **heaven and on earth,** in the seas and
135. 7 He brings storm clouds from the **ends of the earth;**
136. 6 he built the **earth** on the deep waters;
146. 6 God, [6]the Creator of heaven, **earth,** and sea, and all that
147. 8 he provides rain for the **earth** and makes grass grow on the
147.15 gives a command to the **earth,** and what he says is quickly
148. 7 Praise the Lord from the **earth,** sea-monsters and all ocean depths;
148.13 his glory is above **earth and heaven.**
Prov 3.19 The Lord created the **earth** by his wisdom;
3.20 rivers to flow and the clouds to give rain to the **earth.**
8. 4 I call to everyone on **earth.**
8.16 Every ruler on **earth** governs with my help,
8.26 place, [26]before God made the **earth** and its fields or even
8.29 I was there when he laid the **earth's** foundations.
11.31 good are rewarded here on **earth,** so you can be sure that
30. 4 Or fixed the boundaries of the **earth?**
30.21 There are four things that the **earth** itself cannot tolerate:
Ecc 2. 3 the best way people can spend their short lives on **earth.**
5. 2 heaven and you are on **earth,** so don't say any more than

Ecc 7.20 There is no one on **earth** who does what is right all
12. 7 to the dust of the **earth,** and the breath of life will
Is 1. 2 The Lord said, **"Earth and sky,** listen to what I am saying!
2.19 from his power and glory, when he comes to shake the **earth.**
2.21 Lord comes to shake the **earth,** people will hide in holes and
5.26 He whistles for them to come from the **ends of the earth.**
8. 9 Listen, you distant parts of the **earth.**
11.12 Judah and bringing them back from the four corners of the **earth.**
13. 5 They are coming from far-off countries at the **ends of the earth.**
13. 9 The **earth** will be made a wilderness, and every sinner will
13.11 will bring disaster on the **earth** and punish all wicked
13.13 the heavens tremble, and the **earth** will be shaken out of its
14. 9 The ghosts of those who were powerful on **earth** are stirring about.
14.16 'Is this the man who shook the **earth** and made kingdoms tremble?
14.18 All the kings of the **earth** lie in their magnificent tombs,
14.21 of them will ever rule the **earth** or cover it with cities."
18. 3 Listen, everyone who lives on **earth!**
23. 8 whose merchant princes were the most honoured men on **earth?**
24. 1 The Lord is going to devastate the **earth** and leave it desolate.
24. 1 He will twist the **earth's** surface and scatter its people.
24. 3 The **earth** will lie shattered and ruined.
24. 4 The **earth** dries up and withers;
24. 4 both **earth and sky** decay.
24. 5 The people have defiled the **earth** by breaking God's laws
24. 6 So God has pronounced a curse on the **earth.**
24.18 will pour from the sky, and **earth's** foundations will shake.
24.19 The **earth** will crack and shatter and split open.
24.20 The **earth** itself will stagger like a drunken man and
24.21 Lord will punish the powers above and the rulers of the **earth.**
26. 9 when you judge the **earth** and its people, they will all
26.19 the sparkling dew refreshes the **earth,** so the Lord will
26.21 to punish the people of the **earth** for their sins.
26.21 were secretly committed on the **earth** will be revealed, and
27. 6 The **earth** will be covered with the fruit they produce.
34. 1 Let the whole **earth** and everyone living on it come here and
34. 7 and young bulls, and the **earth** will be red with blood and
37.16 You created the **earth and the sky.**
40.12 hold the soil of the **earth** in a cup or weigh the
40.22 who sits on his throne above the **earth** and beyond the sky;
41. 9 I brought you from the **ends of the earth;**
41.12 against you will die [12]and will disappear from the **earth.**
42. 4 he will establish justice on the **earth.**
42. 5 he fashioned the **earth** and all that lives there;
42. 6 and given you power to see that justice is done on **earth.**
44.23 Shout, deep places of the **earth!**
44.24 when I made the **earth,** no one helped me.
45. 8 the **earth** will open to receive it and will blossom with
45.12 one who made the **earth** and created mankind to live there.
45.18 He formed and made the **earth**— he made it firm and
48.13 My hands made the **earth's** foundations and spread the heavens out.
48.13 When I summon **earth and sky,** they come at once and present
49.13 Shout for joy, **earth!**
51. 6 look at the **earth!**
51. 6 the **earth** will wear out like old clothing, and all its
51.13 stretched out the heavens and laid the **earth's** foundations?
51.16 I stretched out the heavens and laid the **earth's** foundations;
54. 9 the time of Noah I promised never again to flood the **earth.**
55. 9 the heavens are above the **earth,** so high are my ways and
55.10 the rain that come down from the sky to water the **earth.**
62.11 can know [11]That the Lord is announcing to all the **earth:**
65.17 The Lord says, "I am making a **new earth** and new heavens.
66. 1 Lord says, "Heaven is my throne, and the **earth** is my footstool.
66.22 "Just as the **new earth** and the new heavens will endure
Jer 4.23 I looked at the **earth**—it was a barren waste;
4.27 has said that the whole **earth** will become a wilderness, but
4.28 The **earth** will mourn;
6.19 Listen, **earth!**
10.11 who did not make the **earth and the sky** will be destroyed.
10.11 They will no longer exist anywhere on **earth.)**
10.12 The Lord made the **earth** by his power;
10.13 he brings clouds from the **ends of the earth.**
16.19 to you from the **ends of the earth** and say, "Our ancestors
23.24 you not know that I am everywhere in **heaven and on earth?**
25.19 nation on the face of the **earth** had to drink from it.
25.29 I am going to send war on all the people on **earth.**
25.30 Everyone on **earth** will hear him, [31]and the sound will echo
25.31 him, [31]and the sound will echo to the **ends of the earth.**
25.32 a great storm is gathering at the far **ends of the earth.**
25.33 will lie scattered from one **end of the earth** to the other.
27. 5 world, mankind, and all the animals that live on the **earth;**
31. 8 from the north and gather them from the **ends of the earth.**
31.37 and the foundations of the **earth** explored, only then would
32.17 Lord, you made the **earth and the sky** by your great power
33. 2 The Lord, who made the **earth,** who formed it and set it
33.25 night, and I have made the laws that control **earth and sky.**
44. 8 so that every nation on **earth** will treat you with scorn and
45. 4 I will do this to the entire **earth.**
47. 2 everyone on **earth** will cry bitterly.
49.21 a noise that the entire **earth** will shake, and the cries of
50.34 will bring peace to the **earth,** but trouble to the people of
50.46 a noise that the entire **earth** will shake, and the cries of
51.15 The Lord made the **earth** by his power;
51.16 he brings clouds from the **ends of the earth.**
51.29 The **earth** trembles and shakes because the Lord is
51.48 Everything on **earth** and in the sky will shout for joy
Lam 3.66 Hunt them down and wipe them off the **earth!"**
Ezek 1.19 if the creatures rose up from the **earth,** so did the wheels.
10.19 and flew up from the **earth** while I was watching, and the
34. 6 over the face of the **earth,** and no one looked for them
38.20 on the face of the **earth** will tremble for fear of me.
Ezek 39.18 of the rulers of the **earth,** all of whom will be killed
43. 2 of the sea, and the **earth** shone with the dazzling light.
Dan 2.10 on the face of the **earth** who can tell Your Majesty what
2.35 stone grew to be a mountain that covered the whole **earth.**
2.38 ruler of all the inhabited **earth** and ruler over all the
2.39 third, an empire of bronze, which will rule the whole **earth.**
4.10 a vision of a huge tree in the middle of the **earth.**
4.35 He looks on the people of the **earth** as nothing;
4.35 angels in heaven and people on **earth** are under his control.
6.25 the people of all nations, races, and languages on **earth:**
6.27 he performs wonders and miracles in **heaven and on earth.**
7.17 "These four huge beasts are four empires which will arise on **earth.**
7.23 that will be on the **earth** and will be different from all
7.23 It will crush the whole **earth** and trample it down.
7.27 of all the kingdoms on **earth** will be given to the people
7.27 end and all rulers on **earth** will serve and obey them."
9.12 than any other city on **earth,** [13]giving us all the
Hos 2.21 make rain fall on the **earth,** and the earth will produce corn
6. 3 as surely as the spring rains that water the **earth."**
Joel 1.17 The seeds die in the dry **earth.**
2.10 The **earth** shakes as they advance;
2.30 give warnings of that day in the sky and on the **earth;**
3.16 **earth and sky** tremble.
Amos 3. 2 "Of all the nations on **earth,** you are the only one I
4.13 He walks on the heights of the **earth.**
5. 8 the waters of the sea and pours them out on the **earth.**
7. 4 the great ocean under the **earth,** and started to burn up the
8. 8 And so the **earth** will quake, and everyone in the land will
8. 9 sun go down at noon and the **earth** grow dark in daytime.
9. 5 The Sovereign Lord Almighty touches the **earth,** and it quakes;
9. 6 the heavens, and over the **earth** he puts the dome of the
9. 6 the waters of the sea and pours them out on the **earth.**
9. 8 Israel, and I will destroy it from the face of the **earth.**
Mic 1. 2 listen to this, all who live on **earth!**
5. 4 people all over the **earth** will acknowledge his greatness,
6. 2 foundations of the **earth,** listen to the Lord's case!
7.13 But the **earth** will become a desert because of the
Nah 1. 5 The **earth** shakes when the Lord appears;
Hab 1.10 can stop them—they pile up **earth** against it and capture it.
2.14 But the **earth** will be as full of the knowledge of the
2.20 let everyone on **earth** be silent in his presence.
3. 3 and the **earth** is full of his praise.
3. 6 When he stops, the **earth** shakes;
3. 9 Your lightning split open the **earth.**
3.10 The waters under the **earth** roared, and their waves rose high.
3.12 You marched across the **earth** in anger;
Zeph 1. 2 destroy everything on **earth,** [3]all human beings and animals,
1.18 The whole **earth** will be destroyed by the fire of his anger.
1.18 put an end—a sudden end—to everyone who lives on **earth.**
2.11 reduce the gods of the **earth** to nothing, and then every
3. 8 The whole **earth** will be destroyed by the fire of my fury.
Hag 2. 6 "Before long I will shake **heaven and earth,** land and sea.
2.21 am about to shake **heaven and earth** [22]and overthrow kingdoms
Zech 1.10 The Lord sent them to go and inspect the **earth."**
4.10b the seven eyes of the Lord, which see all over the **earth."**
4.14 and anointed to serve him, the Lord of the whole **earth."**
6. 5 just come from the presence of the Lord of all the **earth."**
6. 7 came out, they were impatient to go and inspect the **earth.**
6. 7 The angel said, "Go and inspect the **earth!"**—
8.12 vines will bear grapes, the **earth** will produce crops, and
9.10 sea, from the River Euphrates to the **ends of the earth."**
11. 6 (The Lord said, "I will no longer pity anyone on **earth.**
11. 6 Those rulers will devastate the **earth,** and I will not save
12. 1 out the skies, created the **earth,** and gave life to man.
14. 9 Then the Lord will be king over all the **earth;**
Mt 5.18 that as long as **heaven and earth** last, not the least point
5.35 nor by **earth,** for it is the resting place for his feet;
6.10 may your will be done on **earth** as it is in heaven.
6.19 riches for yourselves here on **earth,** where moths and rust destroy,
9. 6 the Son of Man has authority on **earth** to forgive sins."
11.25 At that time Jesus said, "Father, Lord of **heaven and earth!**
12.40 Man spend three days and nights in the depths of the **earth.**
16.19 what you prohibit on **earth** will be prohibited in heaven,
16.19 and what you permit on **earth** will be permitted in heaven."
18.18 what you prohibit on **earth** will be prohibited in heaven,
18.18 and what you permit on **earth** will be permitted in heaven.
18.19 two of you on **earth** agree about anything you pray for,
23. 9 not call anyone here on **earth** 'Father', because you have only
24.30 and all the peoples of **earth** will weep as they see the
24.31 the four corners of the **earth,** and they will gather his
24.35 **Heaven and earth** will pass away, but my words will never
27.51 The **earth** shook, the rocks split apart, [52]the graves broke
28.18 "I have been given all authority in **heaven and on earth.**
Mk 2.10 the Son of Man has authority on **earth** to forgive sins."
13.27 the four corners of the **earth** to gather God's chosen people
13.31 **Heaven and earth** will pass away, but my words will never
Lk 2.14 highest heaven, and peace on **earth** to those with whom he is
5.24 the Son of Man has authority on **earth** to forgive sins."
10.21 Holy Spirit and said, "Father, Lord of **heaven and earth!**
12.49 "I came to set the **earth** on fire, and how I wish
12.56 You can look at the **earth** and the sky and predict the
16.17 it is easier for **heaven and earth** to disappear than for the
18. 8 will the Son of Man find faith on **earth** when he comes?"
21.25 On **earth** whole countries will be in despair, afraid of the
21.26 is coming over the whole **earth,** for the powers in space will
21.33 **Heaven and earth** will pass away, but my words will never
21.35 For it will come upon all people everywhere on **earth.**
Jn 3.31 He who is from the **earth** belongs to the earth
3.31 and speaks about **earthly** matters, but he who comes from

Jn 12.32 am lifted up from the **earth,** I will draw everyone to me."
17. 4 I have shown your glory on **earth;**
Acts 1. 8 in all Judaea and Samaria, and to the **ends of the earth."**
2.19 miracles in the sky above and wonders on the **earth** below.
3.25 'Through your descendants I will bless all the people on **earth.'**
4.24 "Master and Creator of heaven, **earth,** and sea, and all that
4.26 The kings of the **earth** prepared themselves, and the rulers
7.49 is my throne, says the Lord, and the **earth** is my footstool.
8.33 descendants, because his life on **earth** has come to an end."
10.11 large sheet being lowered by its four corners to the **earth.**
11.28 that a severe famine was about to come over all the **earth.**
14.15 living God, who made heaven, **earth,** sea, and all that is in
17.24 it, is Lord of **heaven and earth** and does not live in
17.26 races of mankind and made them live throughout the whole **earth.**
Rom 10.18 their words reached the **ends of the earth."**
1 Cor 4.13 we are the scum of the **earth** to this very moment!
8. 5 whether in heaven or on **earth,** and even though there are
10.26 the scripture says, "The **earth** and everything in it belong to
15.40 And there are heavenly bodies and **earthly** bodies;
15.40 is different from the beauty that belongs to **earthly** bodies.
15.47 The first Adam, made of **earth,** came from the earth;
15.48 Those who belong to the **earth** are like
15.48 the one who was made of **earth;**
15.49 of the man made of **earth,** so we will wear the likeness
2 Cor 5. 1 our body here on **earth**—is torn down, God will have
5. 4 While we live in this **earthly** tent, we groan with a
5. 4 to get rid of our **earthly** body, but that we want to
Eph 1.10 together, everything in **heaven and on earth,** with Christ as head.
3.15 every family in **heaven and on earth** receives its true name.
4. 9 that first he came down to the lowest depths of the **earth.**
Phil 2.10 all beings in heaven, on **earth,** and in the world below will
Col 1.16 God created everything in **heaven and on earth,** the seen and
1.20 back to himself all things, both on **earth** and in heaven.
3. 2 minds fixed on things there, not on things here on **earth.**
3. 5 put to death, then, the **earthly** desires at work in you,
Heb 1.10 in the beginning created the **earth,** and with your own hands
5. 7 In his life on **earth** Jesus made his prayers and requests
8. 4 If he were on **earth,** he would not be a priest at
11.13 admitted openly that they were foreigners and refugees on **earth.**
12.25 the one who gave the divine message on **earth** did not escape.
12.26 His voice shook the **earth** at that time, but now he has
12.26 once more shake not only the **earth** but heaven as well."
13.14 For there is no permanent city for us here on **earth;**
Jas 5. 5 Your life here on **earth** has been full of luxury and pleasure.
5.12 Do not swear by heaven or by **earth** or by anything else.
5.18 sky poured out its rain and the **earth** produced its crops.
1 Pet 1.17 the rest of your lives here on **earth** in reverence for him.
4. 2 live the rest of your **earthly** lives controlled by God's will
2 Pet 3. 5 God gave a command, and the heavens and **earth** were created.
3. 5 The **earth** was formed out of water and by water,
3. 7 the heavens and the **earth** that now exist are being preserved
3.10 be destroyed, and the **earth** with everything in it will vanish.
3.13 and a new **earth,** where righteousness will be at home.
Rev 1. 7 All peoples on **earth** will mourn over him.
3.10 is coming upon the world to test all the people on **earth.**
5. 3 one in heaven or on **earth** or in the world below who
5. 6 spirits of God that have been sent throughout the whole **earth.**
5.10 priests to serve our God, and they shall rule on **earth."**
5.13 every creature in heaven, on **earth,** in the world below,
6. 4 to bring war on the **earth,** so that men should kill each
6. 8 over a quarter of the **earth,** to kill by means of war,
6.10 judge the people on **earth** and punish them for killing us?"
6.13 stars fell down to the **earth,** like unripe figs falling from
6.15 the kings of the **earth,** the rulers and the military chiefs,
7. 1 the four corners of the **earth,** holding back the four winds
7. 1 wind should blow on the **earth** or the sea or against any
7. 2 God had given the power to damage the **earth** and the sea.
7. 3 "Do not harm the **earth,** the sea, or the trees, until
8. 5 with fire from the altar, and threw it on the **earth.**
8. 7 Hail and fire, mixed with blood, came pouring down on the **earth.**
8. 7 A third of the **earth** was burnt up, a third of the
8.13 for all who live on **earth** when the sound comes from the
9. 1 had fallen down to the **earth,** and it was given the key
9. 3 of the smoke upon the **earth,** and they were given the same
10. 6 who created heaven, **earth,** and the sea, and everything in
11. 4 and the two lamps that stand before the Lord of the **earth.**
11. 6 authority also to strike the **earth** with every kind of plague
11.10 The people of the **earth** will be happy because of the
11.18 The time has come to destroy those who destroy the **earth!"**
12. 4 stars out of the sky and threw them down to the **earth.**
12. 9 He was thrown down to **earth,** and all his angels with him.
12.12 But how terrible for the **earth** and the sea!
12.13 been thrown down to the **earth,** he began to pursue the woman
12.16 But the **earth** helped the woman;
13. 3 The whole **earth** was amazed and followed the beast.
13. 8 All people living on **earth** will worship it, except those whose
13.11 Then I saw another beast, which came up out of the **earth.**
13.12 It forced the **earth** and all who live on it to worship
13.13 come down out of heaven to **earth** in the sight of everyone.
13.14 all the people living on **earth** by means of the miracles
14. 6 to the peoples of the **earth,** to every race, tribe, language,
14. 7 Worship him who made heaven, **earth,** sea, and the springs
14.15 the **earth** is ripe for the harvest!"
14.16 swung his sickle on the **earth,**
14.16 and the **earth's** harvest was reaped.
14.18 from the vineyard of the **earth,** because the grapes are ripe!"
14.19 swung his sickle on the **earth,** cut the grapes from the vine,
16. 1 and pour out the seven bowls of God's anger on the **earth!"**
16. 2 The first angel went and poured out his bowl on the **earth.**
17. 2 The kings of the **earth** practised sexual immorality with her,
17. 8 The people living on **earth** whose names have not been written
Rev 17.18 is the great city that rules over the kings of the **earth."**
18. 1 had great authority, and his splendour brightened the whole **earth.**
18. 3 The kings of the **earth** practised sexual immorality with her,
18. 9 The kings of the **earth** who took part in her immorality
18.11 The businessmen of the **earth** also cry and mourn for her,
18.24 yes, the blood of all those who have been killed on **earth.**
19. 2 the prostitute who was corrupting the **earth** with her immorality.
19.19 and the kings of the **earth** and their armies gathered to
20. 9 They spread out over the **earth** and surrounded the camp of
20.11 **Earth** and heaven fled from his presence and were seen no more.
21. 1 Then I saw a new heaven and a new **earth.**
21. 1 The first heaven and the first **earth** disappeared, and the sea
21.24 and the kings of the **earth** will bring their wealth into it.

EARTHQUAKE
see also **QUAKE**

1 Kgs 19.11 and then there was an **earthquake**—
19.11 but the Lord was not in the **earthquake.**
19.12 After the **earthquake,** there was a fire—but the Lord was
Job 9. 6 God sends **earthquakes** and shakes the ground;
Is 29. 6 Almighty will rescue you with violent thunderstorms and **earthquakes.**
Ezek 3.13 air, and the noise of the wheels, as loud as an **earthquake.**
38.19 day there will be a severe **earthquake** in the land of Israel.
Amos 1. 1 Two years before the **earthquake,** when Uzziah was king of
Zech 14. 5 your ancestors did when the **earthquake** struck in the time of
Mt 24. 7 There will be famines and **earthquakes** everywhere.
27.54 saw the **earthquake** and everything else that happened,
28. 2 Suddenly there was a violent **earthquake;**
Mk 13. 8 There will be **earthquakes** everywhere, and there will be famines.
Lk 21.11 There will be terrible **earthquakes,** famines, and plagues
Acts 16.26 there was a violent **earthquake,** which shook the prison
Rev 6.12 There was a violent **earthquake,** and the sun became black like
8. 5 peals of thunder, flashes of lightning, and an **earthquake.**
11.13 At that very moment there was a violent **earthquake;**
11.19 rumblings and peals of thunder, an **earthquake,** and heavy hail.
16.18 rumblings and peals of thunder, and a terrible **earthquake.**
16.18 has never been such an **earthquake** since the creation of man;
16.18 this was the worst **earthquake** of all!

EARTHWORKS

Ezek 4. 2 **earthworks,** camps, and battering-rams all round it.
17.17 fight when the Babylonians build **earthworks** and dig trenches
21.22 the gates, to throw up **earthworks,** and to dig trenches.
26. 8 enemy will dig trenches, build **earthworks,** and make a solid

EASE
[ILL AT EASE]

2 Kgs 8.11 horrified look on his face until Hazael became **ill at ease.**
Job 21.23 they die happy and at **ease,** their bodies well-nourished.
Prov 3. 8 good medicine, healing your wounds and **easing** your pains.

EAST

Gen 2. 8 garden in Eden, in the **East,** and there he put the man
2.14 is the Tigris, which flows **east** of Assyria, and the fourth
3.24 Then at the **east** side of the garden he put living
4.16 in a land called "Wandering," which is **east** of Eden.
10.19 to Gerar near Gaza, and **eastwards** to Sodom, Gomorrah, Admah,
10.30 extended from Mesha to Sephar in the **eastern** hill-country.
11. 2 they wandered about in the **East,** they came to a plain in
12. 8 on south to the hill-country **east** of the city of Bethel and
12. 8 his camp between Bethel on the west and Ai on the **east.**
13.11 Jordan Valley for himself and moved away towards the **east.**
23.17 to Ephron at Machpelah, **east** of Mamre, became Abraham's.
25. 6 sons to the land of the **East,** away from his son Isaac.
25. 9 Machpelah Cave, in the field **east** of Mamre that had belonged
25.18 Havilah and Shur, to the **east** of Egypt on the way to
29. 1 continued on his way and went towards the land of the **East.**
49.30 Ephron the Hittite, [30] at Machpelah, **east** of Mamre, in the
50.10 the threshing-place at Atad **east of the Jordan,** they mourned
50.13 in the cave at Machpelah, **east** of Mamre, in the field which
Ex 10.13 caused a wind from the **east** to blow on the land all
10.19 And the Lord changed the **east** wind into a very strong
14.21 and the Lord drove the sea back with a strong **east** wind.
27.13 On the **east** side, where the entrance is, the enclosure
38.13 On the **east** side, where the entrance was, the enclosure
Lev 1.16 throw them away on the **east** side of the altar where the
Num 2. 3 On the **east** side, those under the banner of the
3.38 sons were to camp in front of the Tent on the **east.**
10. 5 are sounded, the tribes camped on the **east** will move out.
21.11 ruins of Abarim in the wilderness **east** of Moabite territory.
22. 1 the plains of Moab **east of the Jordan** and opposite Jericho.
23. 7 Moab has brought me From Syria, from the **eastern** mountains.
32.19 we have received our share here **east of the Jordan."**
32.22 Lord will acknowledge that this land **east of the Jordan** is yours.
32.32 that we can retain our property here **east of the Jordan."**
33. 7 turned back to Pi Hahiroth, **east** of Baal Zephon, and camped
34. 3 It will begin on the **east** at the southern end of the
34.10 "The **eastern** border will follow a line from Hazar Enan to Shepham.
34.11 then go south to Harbel, **east** of Ain, and on to the
34.11 to the hills on the **eastern** shore of Lake Galilee, [12] then
34.15 on the **eastern side of the Jordan,** opposite Jericho."
35.14 Choose six cities, [14] three **east of the Jordan** and
Deut 1. 1 Israel when they were in the wilderness **east of the River Jordan.**
1. 5 while the people were **east of the Jordan** in the territory of
3. 8 Amorite kings the land **east of the River Jordan,** from the

Deut	3.10	and of Bashan, as far **east** as the towns of Salecah and
	3.17	the south and to the foot of Mount Pisgah on the **east.**
	3.18	God has given you this land **east of the Jordan** to occupy.
	3.27	north and to the south, to the **east** and to the west.
	4.41	set aside three cities **east of the River Jordan** [42] to which
	4.45	were in the valley **east of the River Jordan,** opposite the
	4.47	Bashan, the other Amorite king who lived **east of the Jordan.**
	4.49	included all the region **east of the River Jordan** as far
	4.49	as the Dead Sea and **east** to the foot of Mount Pisgah.
	11.24	the River Euphrates in the **east** to the Mediterranean Sea in
	34. 1	the top of Mount Pisgah **east** of Jericho, and there the Lord
Josh	1. 4	River Euphrates in the **east,** through the Hittite country,
	1.13	this land on the **east side of the Jordan** as your home.
	1.15	in your own land **east of the Jordan,** which Moses, the Lord's
	2.10	Sihon and Og, the two Amorite kings **east of the Jordan.**
	4.19	of the first month and made camp at Gilgal, **east** of Jericho.
	7. 2	Jericho to Ai, a city **east** of Bethel, near Bethaven, with
	9.10	what he did to the two Amorite kings **east of the Jordan:**
	10.40	hill-country, the **eastern** slopes, and the western foothills,
	11. 8	Maim and Sidon, and as far **east** as the valley of Mizpah.
	12. 1	and occupied the land **east of the Jordan,** from the Arnon
	12. 3	Galilee south to Beth Jeshimoth (**east** of the Dead Sea) and
	12. 8	Valley and its foothills, the **eastern** slopes, and the dry
	13. 5	all of Lebanon to the **east,** from Baalgad, which is south of
	13. 8	it was on the **east side of the River Jordan.**
	13.25	land of Ammon as far as Aroer, which is **east** of Rabbah;
	13.32	how Moses divided the land **east** of Jericho and the Jordan
	14. 3	already assigned the land **east of the Jordan** to the other
	15. 5	The **eastern** border was the Dead Sea, all the way up to
	16. 1	near Jericho, at a point **east** of the springs of Jericho, and
	16. 5	border ran from Ataroth Addar **eastwards** to Upper Beth Horon,
	16. 6	**East** of there the border bent towards Taanath Shiloh
	16. 6	and went past it on the **east** to Janoah.
	17. 1	Gilead and Bashan, **east of the Jordan,** were assigned to him.
	17. 5	Bashan on the **east side of the Jordan,** [6] since his female
	17. 7	Manasseh reached from Asher to Michmethath, **east** of Shechem.
	18. 7	already received their land **east of the Jordan,** which Moses,
	18.20	The Jordan was the **eastern** border.
	19.11	Mareal, touching Dabbesheth and the stream **east** of Jokneam.
	19.12	side of Sarid it went **east** to the border of Chisloth Tabor,
	19.13	It continued **east** from there to Gath Hepher and Ethkazin,
	19.27	As it turned **east,** the border went to Bethdagon,
	19.34	the south, Asher on the west, and the Jordan on the **east.**
	20. 8	**East of the Jordan,** on the desert plateau east of Jericho,
	22. 4	land on the **east side of the Jordan,** that Moses, the Lord's
	22. 6	Moses had given land **east of the Jordan** to one half of
	22.12	together at Shiloh to go to war against the **eastern** tribes.
	23. 4	the River Jordan in the **east** to the Mediterranean Sea in the
	24. 8	of the Amorites, who lived on the **east side of the Jordan.**
Judg	5.17	tribe of Gad stayed **east of the Jordan,** and the tribe of
	7.25	Oreb and Zeeb to Gideon, who was now **east of the Jordan.**
	8.11	the edge of the desert, **east** of Nobah and Jogbehah, and
	10. 8	lived in Amorite country **east of the River Jordan** in Gilead.
	11.18	until they came to the **east** side of Moab, on the other
	11.22	from the desert on the **east** to the Jordan on the west.
	20. 1	as from the land of Gilead in the **east,** answered the call.
	20.43	as far as a point **east** of Gibeah, killing them as they
	21.19	Bethel, south of Lebonah, and **east** of the road between
1 Sam	13. 5	They went to Michmash, **east** of Bethaven, and camped there.
	15. 7	Amalekites, fighting all the way from Havilah to Shur, **east**
	24. 2	went looking for David and his men **east** of Wild Goat Rocks.
	31. 7	Valley of Jezreel and **east of the River Jordan** heard that
2 Sam	2.24	Ammah, which is to the **east** of Giah on the road to
	5. 9	where land was filled in on the **east** side of the hill.
	10.16	Syrians who were on the **east** side of the River Euphrates,
1 Kgs	4.30	the wise men of the **East** or the wise men of Egypt.
	9.15	fill in land on the **east** side of the city, and to
	9.24	in the land on the **east** side of the city, after his
	11. 7	On the mountain **east** of Jerusalem he built a place to
	11.27	in the land on the **east** side of Jerusalem and repairing the
	17. 3	"Leave this place and go **east**
	17. 3	hide yourself near the brook of Cherith, **east of the Jordan.**
2 Kgs	10.33	all the Israelite territory [33] **east of the Jordan,** as far
	12.20	was filled in on the **east** side of Jerusalem, on the road
	19.26	weeds growing on a roof when the hot **east** wind blasts them.
	23.13	that King Solomon had built **east** of Jerusalem, south of the
1 Chr	4.39	pastured their sheep on the **eastern** side of the valley in
	4.42	other members of the tribe of Simeon went **east** to Edom.
	5. 9	occupied the land as far **east** as the desert that stretches
	5.10	and occupied their land in the **eastern** part of Gilead.
	5.11	of Reuben in the land of Bashan as far **east** as Salecah.
	6.78	In the territory of Reuben, **east of the River Jordan** beyond Jericho:
	7.28	towns round it, as far **east** as Naaran and as far west
	9.18	been stationed at the **eastern** entrance to the King's Gate.
	9.24	in each direction, north, south, **east,** and west, and each
	11. 8	was filled in on the **east** side of the hill, and Joab
	12.15	who lived in the valleys both **east** and west of the river.
	12.23	Tribes **east of the Jordan**—Reuben, Gad, and East Manasseh:
	19.16	the Syrian states on the **east** side of the River Euphrates
	26.14	Shelemiah drew the **east** gate, and his son Zechariah, a
	26.17	On the **east,** six guards were on duty each day, on the
	26.32	civil matters in Israel **east of the River Jordan**—the
2 Chr	5.11	The Levites stood near the **east** side of the altar with
	29. 4	priests and Levites in the **east** courtyard of the Temple
	32. 5	was filled in on the **east** side of the old part of
	33.14	the outer wall on the **east** side of David's City, from a
Neh	2.14	Then on the **east** side of the city I went north to
	3.25	to a point on the **east** near the Water Gate and the
	12.37	wall at the Water Gate, on the **east** side of the city.
Job	1. 3	number of servants and was the richest man in the **East.**
Job	18.20	From **east** to west, all who hear of his fate shudder and
	23. 8	I have searched in the **east,** but God is not there;
	27.21	the **east** wind will sweep them from their homes;
	38.24	sun comes up, or the place from which the **east** wind blows?
Ps	50. 1	he calls to the whole earth from **east** to west.
	75. 6	does not come from the **east** or from the west, from the
	78.26	He also caused the **east** wind to blow, and by his power
	103.12	As far as the **east** is from the west, so far does
	107. 3	countries, from **east** and west, from north and south.
	113. 3	From the **east** to the west praise the name of the Lord!
	139. 9	I flew away beyond the **east** or lived in the farthest place
Is	2. 6	full of magic practices from the **east** and from Philistia.
	9. 1	this region, from the Mediterranean **eastwards** to the land on
	9.12	Syria on the **east** and Philistia on the west have opened
	11.14	on the west and plunder the people who live to the **east.**
	16. 8	the city of Jazer, and **eastwards** into the desert, and
	24.15	the Lord is, [15] and those in the **east** will praise him.
	27. 8	He took them away with a cruel wind from the **east.**
	37.27	weeds growing on a roof when the hot **east** wind blasts them.
	41. 2	brought the conqueror from the **east,** and makes him
	41.25	"I have chosen a man who lives in the **east;**
	43. 5	"From the distant **east** and the farthest west, I will bring
	46.11	I am calling a man to come from the **east;**
	59.19	From **east** to west everyone will fear him and his great power.
	65.10	in the west and in the Valley of Trouble in the **east.**
Jer	2.10	of Cyprus, and send someone **eastwards** to the land of Kedar.
	18.17	before their enemies, like dust blown by the **east** wind.
	31.40	as the Horse Gate to the **east,** will be sacred to me.
	49.28	"Attack the people of Kedar and destroy that tribe of **eastern** people!
Ezek	8.16	bowing low towards the **east,** worshipping the rising sun.
	10.19	They paused at the **east** gate of the Temple, and the dazzling
	11. 1	me up and took me to the **east** gate of the Temple.
	11.23	light left the city and moved to the mountain **east** of it.
	17.10	Won't it wither when the **east** wind strikes it?
	19.12	The **east** wind dried up its fruit.
	25. 4	I will let the tribes from the **eastern** desert conquer you.
	25.10	of the **eastern** desert conquer Moab, together with Ammon,
	27.26	you out to sea, An **east** wind wrecked you far from land.
	39.11	in Israel, in Travellers' Valley, **east** of the Dead Sea.
	40. 6	Then he went to the gateway that faced **east.**
	40.21	all had the same measurements as those in the **east** gateway.
	40.22	and the carved palm-trees were like those in the **east** gate.
	40.23	to the inner courtyard, just as there was on the **east** side.
	40.32	The man took me through the **east** gateway into the inner courtyard.
	42. 9	these two rooms at the **east** end of the building, where the
	42.12	side of the building, at the **east** end where the wall began.
	42.15	took me out through the **east** gate and then measured the
	42.16	and measured the **east** side, and it was 250 metres.
	43. 1	to the gate that faces **east,** [2] and there I saw
	43. 2	I saw coming from the **east** the dazzling light of the
	43. 4	passed through the **east** gate and went into the Temple.
	43.17	The steps going up the altar were on the **east** side.
	44. 1	to the outer gate at the **east** side of the temple area.
	45. 7	and from the **eastern** boundary it will extend
	45. 7	extend to the **eastern** border of the country, so that
	46. 1	The Sovereign Lord says, "The **east** gateway to the inner
	46.12	whole or a fellowship-offering, the **east** gate to the inner
	47. 1	entrance and flowing **east,** the direction the Temple faced.
	47. 2	north gate and led me round to the gate that faces **east.**
	47. 3	hundred metres downstream to the **east** and told me to wade
	47. 8	through the land to the **east** and down into the Jordan Valley
	47.15	"The northern boundary runs **eastwards** from the
	47.17	runs from the Mediterranean **eastwards** to the city of Enon,
	47.18	"The **eastern** boundary runs south from a point between
	47.18	west and Gilead on the **east,** as far as Tamar on the
	48. 1	boundary of the land runs **eastwards** from the Mediterranean
	48. 1	the **eastern** boundary westwards to the Mediterranean Sea,
	48. 8	and the same length from **east** to west as the sections given
	48.10	From **east** to west their portion is to measure twelve and a
	48.13	and a half kilometres from **east** to west, by five kilometres
	48.18	a half kilometres on the **east** and five kilometres by two and
	48.21	To the **east** and to the west of this area which
	48.21	It extends **eastwards** to the eastern boundary and westwards
	48.23	the **eastern** boundary westwards to the Mediterranean Sea,
	48.30	those in the **east** wall, after Joseph, Benjamin, and Dan;
Dan	8. 9	the south and the **east** and towards the Promised Land.
	11.44	that comes from the **east** and the north will frighten him,
Hos	13.15	I will send a hot **east** wind from the desert, and it
Amos	8.12	to the Mediterranean and then on from the north to the **east.**
Jon	4. 5	Jonah went out **east** of the city and sat down.
	4. 8	risen, God sent a hot **east** wind, and Jonah was about to
Mic	7.12	Assyria in the **east,** from Egypt in the south,
Zech	8. 8	bring them back from **east** and west to live in Jerusalem.
	14. 4	will stand on the Mount of Olives, to the **east** of Jerusalem.
	14. 4	be split in two from **east** to west by a large valley.
Mt	2. 1	the stars came from the **east** to Jerusalem [2] and asked,
	2. 2	it came up in the **east,** and we have come to worship
	2. 7	called the visitors from the **east** to a secret meeting and
	2. 9	way they saw the same star they had seen in the **east.**
	2.16	the visitors from the **east** had tricked him, he was furious.
	8.11	many will come from the **east** and the west and sit down
	24.27	flashes across the whole sky from the **east** to the west.
Mk	3. 8	from the territory on the **east side of the Jordan,** and from
	16.10	through his disciples from the **east** to the west the sacred
Lk	13.29	People will come from the **east** and the west, from the
Jn	1.28	happened in Bethany on the **east side of the River Jordan,**
	3.26	was with you on the **east side of the Jordan,** the one
Rev	7. 2	angel coming up from the **east** with the seal of the living

Rev 16.12 to provide a way for the kings who come from the **east.**
21.13 three on the **east,** three on the south, three on the north,

EAST GATE

2 Chr 31.14 was chief guard at the **East Gate** of the Temple, was in
Neh 3.29 Shecaniah, keeper of the **East Gate,** built the next section.

EAST MANASSEH see MANASSEH (1)

EASY

Gen 13.16 it would be as **easy** to count all the specks of dust
26.10 "One of my men might **easily** have slept with your wife, and
30.33 In the future you can **easily** find out if I have been
Ex 1.19 they give birth **easily,** and their babies are born before
18.22 That will make it **easier** for you, as they share your burden.
34. 6 and pity, who is not **easily** angered and who shows great love
Num 14. 9 We will conquer them **easily.**
14.18 'I, the Lord, am not **easily** angered, and I show great
Deut 1.41 thinking it would be **easy** to invade the hill-country.
19. 2 three parts, each with a city that can be **easily** reached.
Judg 6.16 will crush the Midianites as **easily** as if they were only one
1 Kgs 12. 4 burdens lighter and make life **easier** for us, we will be your
2 Kgs 3.18 continued, "But this is an **easy** thing for the Lord to do;
20.10 "It's **easy** to make the shadow go forward ten steps!
2 Chr 10. 4 burdens lighter and make life **easier** for us, we will be your
14.11 you can help a weak army as **easily** as a powerful one.
32.18 city wall, so that it would be **easier** to capture the city.
Prov 11. 5 makes a good man's life **easier,** but a wicked man will cause
13.11 The more **easily** you get your wealth, the sooner you will
14. 6 can never become wise, but intelligent people learn **easily.**
18.16 Take him a gift and it will be **easy.**
20.21 The more **easily** you get your wealth, the less good it
21. 1 mind of a king as **easily** as he directs the course of
Is 10.14 and I gathered their wealth as **easily** as gathering eggs.
18. 5 will destroy the Sudanese as **easily** as a knife cuts branches
32. 9 You women who live an **easy** life, free from worries, listen
32.11 You have been living an **easy** life, free from worries;
Lam 1. 9 Her uncleanness was **easily** seen, but she showed no concern
Ezek 27. 7 Embroidered linen from Egypt, **Easily** recognized from afar.
Amos 6. 1 you that have such an **easy** life in Zion and for you
Nah 1. 3 The Lord does not **easily** become angry, but he is powerful
Mt 7.13 that leads to it is **easy,** and there are many who travel
9. 5 Is it **easier** to say, 'Your sins are forgiven,' or to say,
11.30 I will give you is **easy,** and the load I will put
Mk 2. 9 Is it **easier** to say to this paralysed man, 'Your sins are
Lk 5.23 Is it **easier** to say, 'Your sins are forgiven you,' or to
6.24 you have had your **easy** life!
12.19 Take life **easy,** eat, drink, and enjoy yourself!'
16.17 But it is **easier** for heaven and earth to disappear than
Rom 11.24 and it will be much **easier** for God to join these broken-off
2 Thes 2. 2 not to be so **easily** confused in your thinking or upset

EAT
[ATE]

Gen 1.29 kinds of grain and all kinds of fruit for you to **eat;**
2.16 said to him, "You may **eat** the fruit of any tree in
2.17 You must not **eat** the fruit of that tree;
3. 1 really tell you not to **eat** fruit from any tree in the
3. 2 "We may **eat** the fruit of any tree in the garden," the
3. 3 God told us not to **eat** the fruit of that tree or
3. 5 he knows that when you **eat** it you will be like God
3. 6 its fruit would be to **eat,** and she thought how wonderful it
3. 6 So she took some of the fruit and **ate** it.
3. 6 Then she gave some to her husband, and he also **ate** it.
3. 7 As soon as they had **eaten** it, they were given
3.11 "Did you **eat** the fruit that I told you not to eat?"
3.12 put here with me gave me the fruit, and I **ate** it."
3.13 She replied, "The snake tricked me into **eating** it."
3.14 and you will have to **eat** dust as long as you live.
3.17 listened to your wife and **ate** the fruit which I told you
3.17 wife and ate the fruit which I told you not to **eat.**
3.18 weeds and thorns, and you will have to **eat** wild plants.
3.22 from the tree that gives life, **eat** it, and live for ever."
9. 3 Now you can **eat** them, as well as green plants;
9. 4 one thing you must not **eat** is meat with blood still in
18. 8 There under the tree he served them himself, and they **ate.**
19. 3 When it was ready, they **ate** it.
24.33 man said, "I will not **eat** until I have said what I
24.54 and the men with him **ate** and drank, and spent the night
25.28 Esau, because he enjoyed **eating** the animals Esau killed,
25.34 He **ate** and drank and then got up and left.
26.30 Isaac prepared a feast for them, and they **ate** and drank.
27. 4 After I have **eaten** it, I will give you my final blessing
27. 7 After I have **eaten** it, I will give you my blessing in
27.10 take it to him to **eat,** and he will give you his
27.19 Please sit up and **eat** some of the meat that I have
27.25 After I have **eaten** it, I will give you my blessing."
27.31 "Please, father, sit up and **eat** some of the meat that I
27.33 I **ate** it just before you came.
31.38 reproduce, and I have not **eaten** any rams from your flocks.
31.46 Then they **ate** a meal beside the pile of rocks.
31.54 After they had **eaten,** they spent the night on the mountain.
32.32 descendants of Israel do not **eat** the muscle which is on the
37.25 While they were **eating,** they suddenly saw a group of
39. 6 not concern himself with anything except the food he **ate.**
40.17 of pastries for the king, and the birds were **eating** them."
40.19 your body on a pole, and the birds will **eat** your flesh."
Gen 41. 4 on the river-bank, [4]and the thin cows **ate** up the fat cows.
41.20 The thin cows **ate** up the fat ones, [21]but no one would
43. 2 the family of Jacob had **eaten** all the corn which had been
43.16 They are going to **eat** with me at noon, so kill an
43.25 because they had been told that they were to **eat** with him.
43.32 The Egyptians who were **eating** there were served separately,
43.32 considered it beneath their dignity to **eat** with Hebrews.
43.34 So they **ate** and drank with Joseph until they were drunk.
Ex 2.20 Go and invite him to **eat** with us."
10. 5 They will **eat** everything that the hail did not destroy, even
10.12 They will come and **eat** everything that grows, everything
10.15 they **ate** everything that the hail had left, including all
12. 4 family is too small to **eat** a whole animal, he and his
12. 4 number of people and the amount that each person can **eat.**
12. 7 doors of the houses in which the animals are to be **eaten.**
12. 8 is to be roasted, and **eaten** with bitter herbs and with bread
12. 9 Do not **eat** any of it raw or boiled,
12. 9 but **eat** it roasted whole, including the head,
12.11 You are to **eat** it quickly, for you are to be dressed
12.15 seven days you must not **eat** any bread made with yeast—
12.15 **eat** only unleavened bread.
12.15 anyone during those seven days **eats** bread made with yeast,
12.18 day, you must not **eat** any bread made with yeast.
12.19 anyone, native-born or foreign, **eats** bread made with yeast,
12.43 No foreigner shall **eat** the Passover meal, [44]but any slave
12.44 that you have bought may **eat** it if you circumcise him first.
12.45 No temporary resident or hired worker may **eat** it.
12.46 The whole meal must be **eaten** in the house in which it
12.48 but no uncircumcised man may **eat** it.
13. 3 No leavened bread is to be **eaten.**
13. 6 For seven days you must **eat** unleavened bread and on the
13. 7 For seven days you must not **eat** any bread made with yeast;
16. 3 at least sit down and **eat** meat and as much other food
16. 8 will give you meat to **eat** in the evening and as much
16.12 they will have meat to **eat,** and in the morning they will
16.15 "This is the food that the Lord has given you to **eat.**
16.25 Moses said, "**Eat** this today, because today is the Sabbath,
16.32 which he gave us to **eat** in the desert when he brought
16.35 The Israelites **ate** manna for the next forty years, until
18.12 Israel went with him to **eat** the sacred meal as an act
21.28 it is to be stoned, and its flesh shall not be **eaten;**
22. 5 and they stray away and **eat** up the crops growing in another
22.31 people, so you must not **eat** the meat of any animal that
23.11 The poor may **eat** what grows there, and the wild animals can
23.15 Do not **eat** any bread made with yeast during the seven days
24.11 they saw God, and then they **ate** and drank together.
29.32 my presence they are to **eat** it along with the bread left
29.33 They shall **eat** what was used in the ritual of
29.33 Only priests may **eat** this food, because it is sacred.
29.34 of the bread is not **eaten** by morning, it is to be
29.34 it is not to be **eaten,** for it is sacred.
32. 6 as sacrifices and others to **eat** as fellowship-offerings.
34.15 you will be tempted to **eat** the food they offer to their
34.18 As I have commanded you, **eat** unleavened bread for seven days
34.28 the Lord forty days and nights, **eating** and drinking nothing.
Lev 3.17 No Israelite may **eat** any fat or any blood;
6.16 The priests shall **eat** the rest of it.
6.16 bread baked without yeast and **eaten** in a holy place, the
6.18 male descendants of Aaron may **eat** it as their continuing
6.23 No part of a grain-offering that a priest makes may be **eaten;**
6.26 who sacrifices the animal shall **eat** it in a holy place, the
6.29 Any male of the priestly families may **eat** this offering;
6.30 the ritual to take away sin, the animal must not be **eaten;**
7. 6 the priestly families may **eat** it,
7. 6 but it must be **eaten** in a holy place,
7.15 of the animal must be **eaten** on the day it is sacrificed;
7.16 of it has to be **eaten** on the day it is offered,
7.16 any that is left over may be **eaten** on the following day.
7.18 If any of it is **eaten** on the third day, God will
7.18 unclean, and whoever **eats** it will suffer the consequences.
7.19 ritually unclean, it must not be **eaten,** but must be burned.
7.19 who is ritually clean may **eat** the meat, [20]but if anyone
7.20 anyone who is not clean **eats** it, he shall no longer be
7.21 Also, if anyone **eats** the meat of this offering after he
7.23 No fat of cattle, sheep, or goats shall be **eaten.**
7.24 wild animal must not be **eaten,** but it may be used for
7.25 Anyone who **eats** the fat of an animal that may be offered
8.31 Lord's presence, boil it, and **eat** it there with the bread
10.12 unleavened bread with it and **eat** it beside the altar,
10.13 **Eat** it in a holy place;
10.14 you and your families may **eat** the breast and the hind leg
10.14 You may **eat** them in any ritually clean place.
10.17 "Why didn't you **eat** the sin-offering in a sacred place?
10.18 should have **eaten** the sacrifice there, as I commanded."
10.19 Aaron answered, "If I had **eaten** the sin-offering today,
11. 2 You may **eat** any land animal [3]that has divided hoofs and
11. 4 chews the cud, [4-6]but you must not **eat** camels,
11. 7 Do not **eat** pigs.
11. 8 Do not **eat** these animals or even touch their dead bodies;
11. 9 You may **eat** any kind of fish that has fins and scales,
11.10 water that does not have fins and scales must not be **eaten.**
11.11 You must not **eat** them or even touch their dead bodies.
11.12 You must not **eat** anything that lives in the water and
11.13 You must not **eat** any of the following birds:
11.22 You may **eat** locusts, crickets, or grasshoppers.
11.34 food which could normally be **eaten,** but on which water from
11.39 any animal that may be **eaten** dies, anyone who touches it
11.40 And if anyone **eats** any part of the animal, he must wash
11.41 You must not **eat** any of the small animals that move on
11.43 Do not make yourselves unclean by **eating** any of these.
11.47 between animals that may be **eaten** and those that may not.

Lev 14.37 spots that appear to be **eating** into the wall, [38]he shall
14.47 Anyone who lies down or **eats** in the house must wash his
17.10 living in the community **eats** meat with blood still in it,
17.12 foreigner living among them shall **eat** any meat with blood
17.14 Israel that they shall not **eat** any meat with blood still in
17.15 person, Israelite or foreigner, who **eats** meat from an animal
19. 6 The meat must be **eaten** on the day the animal is killed
19. 7 ritually unclean, and if anyone **eats** it, I will not accept
19. 8 Anyone who **eats** it will be guilty of treating as ordinary
19.23 During that time you must not **eat** it.
19.25 But in the fifth year you may **eat** the fruit.
19.26 "Do not **eat** any meat with blood still in it.
20.25 Do not **eat** unclean animals or birds.
20.25 declared them unclean, and **eating** them would make you unclean.
21.22 Such a man may **eat** the food offered to me, both the
22. 4 skin-disease or a discharge may **eat** any of the sacred
22. 6 even then he may not **eat** any of the sacred offerings until
22. 7 clean, and then he may **eat** the sacred offerings, which are
22. 8 He shall not **eat** the meat of any animal that has died
22.10 of a priestly family may **eat** any of the sacred offerings;
22.10 no one else may **eat** them—not even someone staying with a
22.11 or born in his home, may **eat** the food the priest receives.
22.12 is not a priest may not **eat** any of the sacred offerings.
22.13 house as a dependant may **eat** the food her father receives as
22.13 Only a member of a priestly family may **eat** any of it.
22.14 member of a priestly family **eats** any of the sacred offerings
22.16 offerings [16]by letting any unauthorized person **eat** them;
22.30 **eat** it the same day and leave none of it until the
23. 6 for seven days you must not **eat** any bread made with yeast.
23.14 Do not **eat** any of the new corn, whether raw, roasted, or
23.26 On that day do not **eat** anything at all;
23.29 Anyone who **eats** anything on that day will no longer be
23.32 a special day of rest, during which nothing may be **eaten.**
24. 9 his descendants, and they shall **eat** it in a holy place,
25. 7 Everything that it produces may be **eaten.**
25.12 you shall **eat** only what the fields produce of themselves.
25.19 will have all you want to **eat** and will live in safety.
25.20 what there will be to **eat** during the seventh year, when no
25.22 year, you will still be **eating** what you harvested during the
25.22 you will have enough to **eat** until the crops you plant that
26. 5 all that you want to **eat,** and you will live in safety
26.16 your enemies will conquer you and **eat** what you have grown.
26.26 out, and when you have **eaten** it all, you will still be
26.29 hunger will be so great that you will **eat** your own children.
Num 6. 3 kind of drink made from grapes or **eat** any grapes or raisins.
6. 4 he shall not **eat** anything that comes from a grapevine,
11. 5 In Egypt we used to **eat** all the fish we wanted, and
11. 6 is nothing at all to **eat**—nothing but this manna day after
11.18 you will have meat to **eat.**
11.18 Lord will give you meat, and you will have to **eat** it.
11.19 You will have to **eat** it not just for one or two
11.33 of meat for them to **eat,** the Lord became angry with the
12.12 like something born dead with half its flesh **eaten** away."
15.19 any food produced there is **eaten,** some of it is to be
18.10 You must **eat** these things in a holy place,
18.10 and only males may **eat** them;
18.11 Every member of your family who is ritually clean may **eat** them.
18.13 Every member of your family who is ritually clean may **eat** it.
18.31 You and your families may **eat** the rest anywhere, because
18.32 not become guilty when you **eat** it, as long as you have
18.32 gifts of the Israelites by **eating** any of the gifts before
22. 4 round us, like a bull **eating** the grass in a pasture."
25. 2 The Israelites **ate** the food and worshipped the god [3]Baal of Peor.
28.17 which only bread prepared without yeast is to be **eaten.**
29. 7 **eat** no food and do no work.
Deut 2.28 will pay for the food we **eat** and the water we drink.
4.28 wood and stone, gods that cannot see or hear, **eat** or smell.
6.11 have all you want to **eat,** [12]make certain that you do not
8. 3 he gave you manna to **eat,**
8. 3 food that you and your ancestors had never **eaten** before.
8.10 have all you want to **eat,** and you will give thanks
8.12 have all you want to **eat** and have built good houses
8.16 he gave you manna to **eat,**
8.16 food that your ancestors had never **eaten.**
9. 9 forty days and nights and did not **eat** or drink anything.
9.18 for forty days and nights and did not **eat** or drink anything.
12. 7 you and your families will **eat** and enjoy the good things
12.15 you are free to kill and **eat** your animals wherever you live.
12.15 You may **eat** as many as the Lord gives you.
12.15 ritually clean or unclean, may **eat** them,
12.15 just as you would **eat** the meat of deer or antelope.
12.17 is to be **eaten** in the places where you live:
12.18 in your towns, are to **eat** these offerings only in the
12.20 as he has promised, you may **eat** meat whenever you wish.
12.21 given you, and you may **eat** the meat at home, as I
12.22 ritually clean or unclean, may **eat** that meat,
12.22 just as he would **eat** the meat of deer or antelope.
12.23 Only do not **eat** meat with blood still in it, for the
12.23 the blood, and you must not **eat** the life with the meat.
12.27 those sacrifices in which you **eat** the meat and pour the
14. 3 "Do not **eat** anything that the Lord has declared unclean.
14. 4 You may **eat** these animals:
14. 7 But no animals may be **eaten** unless they have divided hoofs
14. 7 You may not **eat** camels, rabbits, or rock-badgers.
14. 8 Do not **eat** pigs.
14. 8 Do not **eat** any of these animals or even touch their dead
14. 9 "You may **eat** any kind of fish that has fins and scales,
14.10 water that does not have fins and scales may not be **eaten;**
14.11 "You may **eat** any clean bird.
14.12 But these are the kinds of birds you are not to **eat:**
14.19 do not **eat** them.
Deut 14.20 You may **eat** any clean insect.
14.21 "Do not **eat** any animal that dies a natural death.
14.21 foreigners who live among you **eat** it, or you may sell it
14.23 and there in his presence **eat** the tithes of your corn, wine,
14.26 God, you and your families are to **eat** and enjoy yourselves.
15.20 and your family are to **eat** them in the Lord's presence at
15.22 You may **eat** such animals at home.
15.22 or unclean, may eat them, just as you **eat** deer or antelope.
16. 3 When you **eat** this meal, do not eat bread prepared with yeast.
16. 3 seven days you are to **eat** bread prepared without yeast, as
16. 3 **Eat** this bread—it will be called the bread of suffering—so
16. 4 the evening of the first day must be **eaten** that same night.
16. 7 Boil the meat and **eat** it at the one place of worship;
16. 8 six days you are to **eat** bread prepared without yeast, and on
20.19 **Eat** the fruit, but do not destroy the trees;
23.24 else's vineyard, you may **eat** all the grapes you want,
23.25 someone else's cornfield, you may **eat** all the corn you can
26.12 that in every community they will have all they need to **eat.**
26.14 I have not **eaten** any of it when I was mourning;
27. 7 you are to sacrifice and **eat** your fellowship-offerings and
28.26 wild animals will come and **eat** your bodies, and there will
28.30 You will plant a vineyard—but never **eat** its grapes.
28.31 your very eyes, but you will not **eat** any of the meat.
28.38 a small harvest, because the locusts will **eat** your crops.
28.39 or drink wine from them, because worms will **eat** the vines.
28.51 They will **eat** your livestock and your crops, and you
28.53 food that you will even **eat** the children that the Lord your
28.54 the siege that he will **eat** some of his own children because
28.56 food that she will secretly **eat** her newborn child and the
29. 6 did not have bread to **eat** or wine or beer to drink,
32.13 rule the highlands, and they **ate** what grew in the fields.
Josh 5.11 next day was the first time they **ate** food grown in Canaan:
5.12 From that time on they **ate** food grown in Canaan.
24.13 you are living there and **eating** grapes from vines that you
Judg 9.27 of their god, where they **ate** and drank and spoke scornfully
13. 4 not to drink any wine or beer, or **eat** any forbidden food;
13. 7 any wine or beer, or **eat** any forbidden food, because the boy
13.14 She must not **eat** anything that comes from the grapevine;
13.14 must not drink any wine or beer, or **eat** any forbidden food.
13.15 angel said, "If I do stay, I will not **eat** your food.
14. 9 honey out into his hands and **ate** it as he walked along.
14. 9 They **ate** it, but Samson did not tell them that he had
14.14 "Out of the **eater** came something to eat;
19. 5 father said to the Levite, "Have something to **eat** first.
19. 6 So the two men sat down and **ate** and drank together.
19. 8 to leave, but the girl's father said, **"Eat** something,
19. 8 So the two men **ate** together.
20.26 there in the Lord's presence and did not **eat** until evening.
Ruth 2.14 She **ate** until she was satisfied, and she still had some food
3. 3 you are there until he has finished **eating** and drinking.
3. 7 When Boaz had finished **eating** and drinking, he was in a
1 Sam 1. 7 Hannah so much that she would cry and refuse to **eat** anything.
1. 8 Why won't you **eat?**
1.18 Then she went away, **ate** some food, and was no longer sad.
2.36 to help the priests, in order to have something to **eat."**
9.12 who are invited won't start **eating** until he gets there,
9.12 you will find him before he goes up the hill to **eat."**
9.19 Both of you are to **eat** with me today.
9.24 **Eat** it.
9.24 saved it for you to **eat** at this time with the people
9.24 So Saul **ate** with Samuel that day.
14.24 curse be on anyone who **eats** any food today before I take
14.24 So nobody had **eaten** anything all day.
14.26 of honey, but no one **ate** any of it because they were
14.27 was carrying, dipped it in a honeycomb, and **ate** some honey.
14.28 said, 'A curse be on anyone who **eats** any food today.' "
14.29 See how much better I feel because I **ate** some honey!
14.30 today if our people had **eaten** the food they took when they
14.32 them on the spot, and **ate** the meat with the blood still
14.33 against the Lord by **eating** meat with the blood in it."
14.34 They are to slaughter them and **eat** them here;
14.34 not sin against the Lord by **eating** meat with blood in it."
14.43 Jonathan answered, "I **ate** a little honey with the stick I
17.44 I will give your body to the birds and animals to **eat."**
17.46 of the Philistine soldiers to the birds and animals to **eat.**
20. 5 David replied, "and I am supposed to **eat** with the king.
20.34 table in a rage and **ate** nothing that day—the second day
28.20 because he had not **eaten** anything all day and all night.
28.22 You must **eat** so that you will be strong enough to travel."
28.23 Saul refused and said he would not **eat** anything.
28.23 But his officers also urged him to **eat.**
28.25 set the food before Saul and his officers, and they **ate** it.
30.12 After he had **eaten,** his strength returned;
30.12 had not had anything to **eat** or drink for three full days.
30.16 scattered all over the place, **eating,** drinking, and
2 Sam 3.29 work or is killed in battle or hasn't enough to **eat!"**
3.35 tried to get David to **eat** something, but he made a solemn
3.35 strike me dead if I **eat** anything before the day is over!"
9.11 So Mephibosheth **ate** at the king's table, just like one of
9.13 both feet, lived in Jerusalem, **eating** all his meals at the
11.11 How could I go home, **eat** and drink, and sleep with my
12.16 He refused to **eat** anything, and every night he went into his
12.17 get up, but he refused and would not **eat** anything with them.
12.20 he asked for food and **ate** it as soon as it was
12.21 the child was alive, you wept for him and would not **eat;**
12.21 but as soon as he died, you got up and **ate!"**
13. 9 them out of the pan for him to **eat,** but he wouldn't.
16. 2 are for the men to **eat,** and the wine is for them
19.28 Majesty, but you gave me the right to **eat** at your table.
19.35 I can't taste what I **eat** and drink, and I can't hear
1 Kgs 4.20 they **ate** and drank, and were happy.

1 Kgs 4.27 Solomon needed for himself and for all who **ate** in the palace;
13. 7 the prophet, "Come home with me and have something to **eat.**
13. 8 would not go with you or **eat** or drink anything with you.
13. 9 has commanded me not to **eat** or drink a thing, and not
13.16 And I won't **eat** or drink anything with you here, [17] because
13.17 has commanded me not to **eat** or drink a thing, and not
13.22 Instead, you returned and **ate** a meal in a place he had
13.22 meal in a place he had ordered you not to **eat** in.
13.23 After they had finished **eating,** the old prophet saddled
13.28 The lion had not **eaten** the body or attacked the donkey.
14.11 in the city will be **eaten** by dogs, and
14.11 any who die in the open country will be **eaten** by vultures.
16. 4 in the city will be **eaten** by dogs, and
16. 4 who die in the open country will be **eaten** by vultures."
18.41 Then Elijah said to King Ahab, "Now, go and **eat.**
18.42 While Ahab went to **eat,** Elijah climbed to the top of
19. 5 Suddenly an angel touched him and said, "Wake up and **eat."**
19. 6 He **ate** and drank, and lay down again.
19. 7 time, saying, "Get up and **eat,** or the journey will be too
19. 8 Elijah got up, **ate** and drank, and the food gave him enough
19.21 He gave the meat to the people, and they **ate** it.
21. 4 lay down on his bed, facing the wall, and would not **eat.**
21. 5 Why won't you **eat?"**
21. 7 "Get out of bed, cheer up and **eat.**
21.23 Lord says that dogs will **eat** her body in the city of
21.24 in the city will be **eaten** by dogs, and
21.24 who die in the open country will be **eaten** by vultures."
2 Kgs 4.40 out for the men to **eat,** but as soon as they tasted
4.40 and wouldn't **eat** it.
4.43 "Give it to them to **eat,** because the Lord says
4.43 that they will **eat** and still have some left over."
4.44 Lord had said, they all **ate** and there was still some left
6.22 Give them something to **eat** and drink, and let them return to
6.23 and after they had **eaten** and drunk, he sent them back to
6.28 woman here suggested that we **eat** my child,
6.28 and then **eat** her child the next day.
6.29 So we cooked my son and **ate** him.
6.29 told her that we would **eat** her son, but she had hidden
7. 2 but you will never **eat** any of the food," Elisha replied.
7. 8 they went into a tent, **ate** and drank what was there, grabbed
7.19 see it happen, but you will never **eat** any of the food."
9.10 body will be **eaten** by dogs in the territory of Jezreel.' "
9.36 'Dogs will **eat** Jezebel's body in the territory of Jezreel.
18.27 who will have to **eat** their excrement and drink their urine,
18.31 will all be allowed to **eat** grapes from your own vines, and
19.29 have only wild grain to **eat,** but the following year you will
19.29 your corn and harvest it, and plant vines and **eat** grapes.
23. 9 the Temple, but they could **eat** the unleavened bread provided
25. 3 nothing left to **eat,** [4] the city walls were broken through.
1 Chr 12.40 They also brought cattle and sheep to kill and **eat.**
29.21 to the Lord, and then gave them to the people to **eat.**
29.22 were very happy as they **ate** and drank in the presence of
2 Chr 7.13 rain or send locusts to **eat** up the crops or send an
28.15 wear, gave them enough to **eat** and drink, and put olive-oil
29.33 three thousand sheep as sacrifices for the people to **eat.**
29.35 the sacrifices which the people **ate,** and for pouring out the
30.24 the people to kill and **eat,** and the officials gave them
31.10 there has been enough to **eat** and a large surplus besides.
Ezra 2.63 them that they could not **eat** the food offered to God until
6.21 The sacrifices were **eaten** by all the Israelites who had
10. 6 He did not **eat** or drink anything.
Neh 1. 4 For several days I mourned and did not **eat.**
5.14 neither my relatives nor I **ate** the food I was entitled to
7.65 them that they could not **eat** the food offered to God until
8.12 the people went home and **ate** and drank joyfully and shared
9.25 They **ate** all they wanted and grew fat;
Esth 4.16 Don't **eat** or drink anything for three days and nights.
7. 1 king and Haman went to **eat** with Esther [2] for a second time.
Job 3.24 Instead of **eating,** I mourn, and I can never stop groaning.
4.11 with nothing to kill and **eat,** they die, and all their
5. 5 Hungry people will **eat** the fool's crops— even the grain
6. 5 A donkey is content when **eating** grass,
6. 5 and a cow is quiet when **eating** hay.
6. 6 But who can **eat** tasteless, unsalted food?
6. 7 for food like that, and everything I **eat** makes me sick.
15.23 kill him, [23] and vultures are waiting to **eat** his corpse.
17.14 father, and the worms that **eat** me I will call my mother
19.26 Even after my skin is **eaten** by disease, while still in
20.21 When he **eats,** there is nothing left over, but now his
20.23 Let him **eat** all he wants!
24.20 he is **eaten** by worms and destroyed like a fallen tree.
27.14 their children never have enough to **eat.**
30. 4 plants of the desert and **ate** them, even the tasteless roots
31. 8 my crops be destroyed, or let others **eat** the food I grow.
31.17 live in despair [17] or let orphans go hungry while I **ate.**
31.39 owners— [39] if I have **eaten** the food that grew there but
38.39 find food for lions to **eat,** and satisfy hungry young lions
39. 8 they feed, where they search for anything green to **eat.**
39.29 it watches near and far for something to kill and **eat.**
40.15 He **eats** grass like a cow, [16] but what strength there is in
Ps 22.26 The poor will **eat** as much as they want;
50.13 Do I **eat** the flesh of bulls or drink the blood of
63.10 They will be killed in battle, and their bodies **eaten** by wolves.
78.24 grain from heaven, by sending down manna for them to **eat.**
78.25 So they **ate** the food of angels, and God gave them all
78.29 So the people **ate** and were satisfied;
78.30 their craving and were still **eating,** [31] when God became
78.46 He sent locusts to **eat** their crops and to destroy their fields.
79. 2 the bodies of your servants for wild animals to **eat.**
80. 5 have given us sorrow to **eat,** a large cup of tears to
104.28 You give it to them, and they **eat** it;
Ps 105.35 they **ate** all the plants in the land;
105.35 they **ate** all the crops.
106.20 glory of God for the image of an animal that **eats** grass.
106.28 of Baal, and **ate** sacrifices offered to lifeless gods.
Prov 5.11 flesh and muscles being **eaten** away, [12] and you will say,
9. 5 foolish man she says, [5] "Come, **eat** my food and drink the
12.11 hard-working farmer has plenty to **eat,** but it is stupid to
13.25 The righteous have enough to **eat,** but the wicked are always hungry.
15.17 Better to **eat** vegetables with people you love
15.17 than to **eat** the finest meat where there is
17. 1 Better to **eat** a dry crust of bread with peace of mind
20.13 Keep busy and you will have plenty to **eat.**
23. 1 When you sit down to **eat** with an important man, keep in
23. 6 Don't **eat** at the table of a stingy man or be greedy
23. 8 vomit up what you have **eaten,** and all your flattery will be
23.21 If all you do is **eat** and sleep, you will soon be
24.13 Son, **eat** honey;
25.16 Never **eat** more honey than you need;
27.18 Take care of a fig-tree and you will have figs to **eat.**
28.19 A hard-working farmer has plenty to **eat.**
30.17 old age ought to be **eaten** by vultures or have his eyes
30.22 a fool who has all he wants to **eat,**
Ecc 2.24 man can do is to **eat** and drink and enjoy what he
2.25 could you have anything to **eat** or enjoy yourself at all?
3.13 All of us should **eat** and drink and enjoy what we have
5.12 may not have enough to **eat,** but at least he can get
5.18 anyone can do is to **eat** and drink and enjoy what he
6. 7 work just to get something to **eat,** but he never has enough.
8.15 in this life is **eating** and drinking and enjoying himself.
9. 7 Go ahead—**eat** your food and be happy;
10.17 own decisions and leaders who **eat** at the proper time, who
Song 4.16 lover come to his garden and **eat** the best of its fruits.
5. 1 I am **eating** my honey and honeycomb;
5. 1 **Eat,** lovers, and drink until you are drunk with love!
Is 1.19 obey me, you will **eat** the good things the land produces.
5. 5 it, and let wild animals **eat** it and trample it down.
5.17 of the cities lambs will **eat** grass and young goats will find
7.15 decisions, people will be drinking milk and **eating** honey.
7.22 survivors left in the land will have milk and honey to **eat.**
9.20 the country people snatch and **eat** any bit of food they can
9.20 They even **eat** their own children!
11. 7 Cows and bears will **eat** together, and their calves and
11. 7 Lions will **eat** straw as cattle do.
16. 7 fine food they used to **eat** in the city of Kir Heres.
21. 5 They are **eating** and drinking.
22.13 You killed sheep and cattle to **eat,** and you drank wine.
22.13 You said, "We might as well **eat** and drink!
28. 4 of the season, picked and **eaten** as soon as they are ripe.
29. 8 man who dreams he is **eating** and wakes up hungry, or like
30.24 that plough your fields will **eat** the finest and best fodder.
33.16 You will have food to **eat** and water to drink.
36.12 who will have to **eat** their excrement and drink their urine,
36.16 will all be allowed to **eat** grapes from your own vines and
37.30 have only wild grain to **eat,** but the following year you will
37.30 your corn and harvest it, and plant vines and **eat** grapes.
44.16 he roasts meat, **eats** it, and is satisfied.
44.19 some bread on the embers and I roasted meat and **ate** it.
44.20 It makes as much sense as **eating** ashes.
55. 1 Come, you that have no money— buy corn and **eat!**
55.10 the crops grow and provide seed for sowing and food to **eat.**
62. 9 harvested the corn Will **eat** the bread and praise the Lord.
65. 4 They **eat** pork and drink broth made from meat offered in
65.13 me will have plenty to **eat** and drink, but you will be
65.25 Wolves and lambs will **eat** together;
65.25 lions will **eat** straw, as cattle do, and snakes will no
66.17 to sacred gardens, and who **eat** pork and mice and other
66.24 The worms that **eat** them will never die, and the fire that
Jer 7.21 completely on the altar, and some you are permitted to **eat.**
7.21 the Lord, say is that you might as well **eat** them all.
9.15 give my people bitter plants to **eat** and poison to drink.
15. 3 birds will **eat** them, and wild animals will devour what is
16. 7 No one will **eat** or drink with anyone to comfort him when
16. 8 Do not sit down with them to **eat** and drink.
19. 9 people inside the city will **eat** one another and even their
23.15 give them bitter plants to **eat** and poison to drink, because
24. 2 the other one contained bad figs, too bad to **eat.**
24. 3 good, and the bad ones are very bad, too bad to **eat."**
24. 8 them all like these figs that are too bad to be **eaten.**
29. 5 Plant gardens and **eat** what you grow in them.
29.17 will make them like figs that are too rotten to be **eaten.**
29.28 settle down, plant gardens, and **eat** what they grow."
31. 5 those who plant them will **eat** what the vineyards produce.
31.29 'The parents **ate** the sour grapes, But the children got the
31.30 Instead, whoever **eats** sour grapes will have his own
34.20 and their corpses will be **eaten** by birds and wild animals.
41. 1 While they were all **eating** a meal together, [2] Ishmael and
46.10 His sword will **eat** them until it is full, and drink their
50.19 They will **eat** the food that grows on Mount Carmel and in
50.19 of Bashan, and they will **eat** all they want of the crops
51.34 The king of Babylonia cut Jerusalem up and **ate** it.
52. 6 nothing left to **eat,** [7] the city walls were broken through.
Lam 1.11 Her people groan as they look for something to **eat;**
2.20 Women are **eating** the bodies of the children they loved!
4. 5 People who once **ate** the finest foods die starving in the streets;
Ezek 2. 8 Open your mouth and **eat** what I am going to give you."
3. 1 God said, "Mortal man, **eat** this scroll;
3. 2 I opened my mouth, and he gave me the scroll to **eat.**
3. 3 He said, "Mortal man, **eat** this scroll that I give you;
3. 3 I **ate** it, and it tasted as sweet as honey.
4. 9 is what you are to **eat** during the 390 days you are

Ezek 4.12 bread on the fire, and **eat** it where everyone can see you."
4.13 the Israelites will have to **eat** food which the Law forbids,
4.14 childhood on I have never **eaten** meat from any animal that
4.14 I have never **eaten** any food considered unclean."
4.16 they measure out the food they **eat** and the water they drink.
5.10 result, parents in Jerusalem will **eat** their children,
5.10 and children will **eat** their parents.
12.18 he said, "tremble when you **eat**, and shake with fear when
12.19 They will tremble when they **eat** and shake with fear when
16.13 You **ate** bread made from the best flour,
16.13 and had honey and olive-oil to **eat**.
16.49 because they had plenty to **eat** and lived in peace and quiet,
18. 2 'The parents **ate** the sour grapes, But the children got the
18. 6 Israelites or **eat** the sacrifices offered at forbidden shrines.
18.11 He **eats** sacrifices offered at forbidden shrines
18.15 Israelites or **eat** the sacrifices offered at forbidden shrines.
22. 9 Some of them **eat** sacrifices offered to idols.
24.17 Don't cover your face or **eat** the food that mourners eat."
24.22 will not cover your faces or **eat** the food that mourners eat.
25. 4 They will **eat** the fruit and drink the milk that should have
33.25 You **eat** meat with the blood still in it.
33.27 Those living in the country will be **eaten** by wild animals.
34. 3 made from the wool, and kill and **eat** the finest sheep.
34. 5 they were scattered, and wild animals killed and **ate** them.
34. 8 that killed and **ate** them because there was no shepherd.
34.10 will rescue my sheep from you and not let you **eat** them.
34.18 Some of you are not satisfied with **eating** the best grass;
34.18 you even trample down what you don't **eat!**
34.19 My other sheep have to **eat** the grass you trample down
34.28 any more, and the wild animals will not kill and **eat** them.
39.17 come from all round to **eat** the sacrifice I am preparing for
39.17 of Israel, where they can **eat** meat and drink blood.
39.18 They are to **eat** the bodies of soldiers and drink the
39.19 birds and animals are to **eat** all the fat they can hold
39.20 At my table they will **eat** all they can hold of horses
42.13 who enter the Lord's presence **eat** the holiest offerings.
44. 3 however, may go there to **eat** a holy meal in my presence.
44.31 The priests must not **eat** any bird or animal that dies a
45.21 For seven days everyone will **eat** bread made without yeast.
Dan 1. 8 himself become ritually unclean by **eating** the food and
1.10 decided what you are to **eat** and drink, and if you don't
1.12 "Give us vegetables to **eat** and water to drink.
1.13 the young men who are **eating** the food of the royal court,
1.15 stronger than all those who had been **eating** the royal food.
1.16 guard let them continue to **eat** vegetables instead of what
4.12 loaded down with fruit—enough for the whole world to **eat**.
4.12 its branches, and every kind of living being **ate** its fruit.
4.25 For seven years you will **eat** grass like an ox, and sleep
4.32 live with wild animals, and **eat** grass like an ox for seven
4.33 was driven out of human society and **ate** grass like an ox.
5.21 He lived with wild donkeys, **ate** grass like an ox, and slept
7. 5 said to it, "Go on, **eat** as much meat as you can!"
10. 3 I did not **eat** any rich food or any meat, drink any
11.27 kings will sit down to **eat** at the same table, but their
Hos 4.10 You will **eat** your share of the sacrifices, but still be hungry.
8. 7 But even if it did, foreigners would **eat** it up.
8.13 They offer sacrifices to me and **eat** the meat of the sacrifices.
9. 3 to Egypt and will have to **eat** forbidden food in Assyria.
9. 4 defile everyone who **eats** it, like food eaten at funerals.
10.13 You have **eaten** the fruit produced by your lies.
Joel 2. 3 Like fire they **eat** up the plants.
2.25 lost in the years when swarms of locusts **ate** your crops.
2.26 Now you will have plenty to **eat**, and be satisfied.
Amos 3.12 sheep that a lion has **eaten**, so only a few will survive
4. 9 The locusts **ate** up all your gardens and vineyards, your
7. 2 vision I saw the locusts **eat** up every green thing in the
9.14 they will plant gardens and **eat** what they grow.
Obad 7 Those friends who **ate** with you have laid a trap for you;
Jon 3. 7 No one is to **eat** anything;
3. 7 persons, cattle, and sheep are forbidden to **eat** or drink.
Mic 3. 3 You **eat** my people up.
6.14 You will **eat**, but not be satisfied—in fact you will
Nah 3.15 You will be wiped out like crops **eaten** up by locusts.
Hag 1. 6 You have food to **eat**, but not enough to make you full.
Zech 7. 6 And when they **ate** and drank, it was for their own satisfaction."
9. 7 They will no longer **eat** meat with blood in it, or other
11.16 Instead, he **eats** the meat of the fattest sheep and tears off
Mt 9.11 "Why does your teacher **eat** with such people?"
11.19 Son of Man came, he **ate** and drank, and everyone said,
12. 1 so they began to pick ears of corn and **eat** the grain.
12. 4 and he and his men **ate** the bread offered to God,
12. 4 the Law for them to **eat** it—
12. 4 only the priests were allowed to **eat** that bread.
13. 4 fell along the path, and the birds came and **ate** it up.
14.16 "You yourselves give them something to **eat!"**
14.20 Everyone **ate** and had enough.
14.21 The number of men who **ate** was about five thousand,
15. 2 They don't wash their hands in the proper way before they **eat!"**
15.20 But to **eat** without washing your hands as they say you should
15.27 even the dogs **eat** the leftovers that fall from their masters'
15.32 been with me for three days and now have nothing to **eat**.
15.37 They all **ate** and had enough.
15.38 The number of men who **ate** was four thousand,
24.38 before the flood people **ate** and drank, men and women married,
24.49 to beat his fellow-servants and to **eat** and drink with drunkards.
26. 7 While Jesus was **eating**, a woman came to him with an
26.20 was evening, Jesus and the twelve disciples sat down to **eat**.
26.26 While they were **eating**, Jesus took a piece of bread,
26.26 "Take and **eat** it," he said;
Mk 2.16 saw that Jesus was **eating** with these outcasts and tax collectors,
2.16 they asked his disciples, "Why does he **eat** with such people?"

Mk 2.25 what David did that time when he needed something to **eat?**
2.26 into the house of God and **ate** the bread offered to God.
2.26 Law only the priests may **eat** this bread—but David ate it
3.20 gathered that Jesus and his disciples had no time to **eat**.
4. 4 fell along the path, and the birds came and **ate** it up.
5.43 to tell anyone, and he said, "Give her something to **eat."**
6.31 that Jesus and his disciples didn't even have time to **eat**.
6.36 farms and villages in order to buy themselves something to **eat."**
6.37 "You yourselves give them something to **eat,"** Jesus answered.
6.42 Everyone **ate** and had enough.
7. 2 some of his disciples were **eating** their food with hands that
7. 3 they do not **eat** unless they wash their hands in the proper
7. 4 nor do they **eat** anything that comes from the market unless
7. 5 by our ancestors, but instead **eat** with ritually unclean hands?"
7.19 this, Jesus declared that all foods are fit to be **eaten.)**
7.28 "even the dogs under the table **eat** the children's leftovers!"
8. 1 people had nothing left to **eat**, Jesus called the disciples
8. 2 been with me for three days and now have nothing to **eat**.
8. 8 Everybody **ate** and had enough—there were about four thousand
9.48 There 'the worms that **eat** them never die, and the fire
11.14 the fig-tree, "No one shall ever **eat** figs from you again!"
14. 3 While Jesus was **eating**, a woman came in with an alabaster
14.14 room where my disciples and I will **eat** the Passover meal?'
14.18 they were at the table **eating**, Jesus said, "I tell you that
14.18 one of you will betray me—one who is **eating** with me."
14.22 While they were **eating**, Jesus took a piece of bread,
16.14 Jesus appeared to the eleven disciples as they were **eating**.
Lk 4. 2 In all that time he **ate** nothing, so that he was hungry
5.30 "Why do you **eat** and drink with tax collectors and other outcasts?"
5.33 but your disciples **eat** and drink."
6. 1 ears of corn, rub them in their hands, and **eat** the grain.
6. 4 the bread offered to God, **ate** it, and gave it also to
6. 4 our Law for anyone except the priests to **eat** that bread."
7.34 of Man came, and he **ate** and drank, and you said,
7.36 and Jesus went to his house and sat down to **eat**.
7.37 She heard that Jesus was **eating** in the Pharisee's house,
8. 5 path, where it was stepped on, and the birds **ate** it up.
8.55 once, and Jesus ordered them to give her something to **eat**.
9.13 Jesus said to them, "You yourselves give them something to **eat."**
9.17 They all **ate** and had enough, and the disciples took up
10. 7 in that same house, **eating** and drinking whatever they offer you,
10. 8 town and are made welcome, **eat** what is set before you,
11.37 Jesus finished speaking, a Pharisee invited him to **eat** with him;
11.37 so he went in and sat down to **eat**.
11.38 surprised when he noticed that Jesus had not washed before **eating**.
12.19 Take life easy, **eat**, drink, and enjoy yourself!'
12.29 all upset, always concerned about what you will **eat** and drink.
12.45 men and the women, and **eats** and drinks and gets drunk,
13.26 Then you will answer, 'We **ate** and drank with you;
14. 1 One Sabbath Jesus went to **eat** a meal at the home of
15. 2 "This man welcomes outcasts and even **eats** with them!"
15.16 pods the pigs ate, but no one gave him anything to **eat**.
15.17 have more than they can **eat**, and here I am about to
16.21 rich man's door, [21] hoping to **eat** the bits of food that
17. 7 the field, do you tell him to hurry and **eat** his meal?
17. 8 on your apron and wait on me while I **eat** and drink;
17.27 Everybody kept on **eating** and drinking, and men and women
17.28 Everybody kept on **eating** and drinking, buying and selling,
22. 8 "Go and get the Passover meal ready for us to **eat."**
22.11 room where my disciples and I will **eat** the Passover meal?'
22.15 have wanted so much to **eat** this Passover meal with you
22.16 tell you, I will never **eat** it until it is given its
22.27 one who sits down to **eat** or the one who serves him?
22.30 You will **eat** and drink at my table in my Kingdom,
24.30 He sat down to **eat** with them, took the bread, and said
24.41 so he asked them, "Have you anything here to **eat?"**
24.43 of cooked fish, [43] which he took and **ate** in their presence.
Jn 4.31 disciples were begging Jesus, "Teacher, have something to **eat!"**
4.32 "I have food to **eat** that you know nothing about."
6.13 from the five barley loaves which the people had **eaten**.
6.23 place where the crowd had **eaten** the bread after the Lord had
6.26 looking for me because you **ate** the bread and had all you
6.31 Our ancestors **ate** manna in the desert, just as the scripture
6.31 scripture says, 'He gave them bread from heaven to **eat.'**
6.49 Your ancestors **ate** manna in the desert, but they died.
6.50 is of such a kind that whoever **eats** it will not die.
6.51 If anyone **eats** this bread, he will live for ever.
6.52 "How can this man give us his flesh to **eat?"**
6.53 if you do not **eat** the flesh of the Son of Man
6.54 Whoever **eats** my flesh and drinks my blood has eternal life,
6.56 Whoever **eats** my flesh and drinks my blood lives in me,
6.57 In the same way whoever **eats** me will live because of me.
6.58 like the bread that your ancestors **ate**, but then later died.
6.58 The one who **eats** this bread will live for ever."
18.28 clean, in order to be able to **eat** the Passover meal.
21.12 Jesus said to them, "Come and **eat."**
21.15 After they had **eaten**, Jesus said to Simon Peter, "Simon son
Acts 2.46 together in their homes, **eating** with glad and humble hearts,
9. 9 and during that time he did not **eat** or drink anything.
9.19 and after he had **eaten**, his strength came back.
10.10 He became hungry and wanted something to **eat;**
10.13 kill and **eat!"**
10.14 I have never **eaten** anything ritually unclean or defiled."
10.41 that is, to us who **ate** and drank with him after he
11. 3 the home of uncircumcised Gentiles, and you even **ate** with them!"
11. 7 kill and **eat!'**
12.23 He was **eaten** by worms and died.
15.20 telling them not to **eat** any food that is ritually unclean
15.20 and not to **eat** any animal that has been strangled, or any
15.29 **eat** no food that has been offered to idols;

Acts 15.29 **eat** no blood;
15.29 **eat** no animal that has been strangled;
16.34 Silas up into his house and gave them some food to **eat.**
20.11 Then he went back upstairs, broke bread, and **ate.**
21.25 decided that they must not **eat** any food that has been
23.12 vow that they would not **eat** or drink anything until they had
23.14 solemn vow together not to **eat** a thing until we have killed
23.21 taken a vow not to **eat** or drink until they have killed
27.33 Just before dawn, Paul begged them all to **eat** some food:
27.33 days now, and all this time you have not **eaten** anything.
27.34 I beg you, then, **eat** some food;
27.35 thanks to God before them all, broke it, and began to **eat.**
27.36 They took heart, and every one of them also **ate** some food.
27.38 After everyone had **eaten** enough, they lightened the ship
Rom 14. 2 person's faith allows him to **eat** anything, but the person who
14. 2 the person who is weak in the faith **eats** only vegetables.
14. 3 The person who will **eat** anything is not to despise the one
14. 3 while the one who **eats** only vegetables is not to pass
14. 3 is not to pass judgement on the one who will **eat** anything;
14. 6 whoever will **eat** anything does so in honour of the Lord,
14. 6 Whoever refuses to **eat** certain things does so in honour of
14.10 You then, who **eat** only vegetables—why do you pass judgement
14.10 And you who **eat** anything—why do you despise your brother?
14.15 because of something you **eat,** then you are no longer acting
14.15 let the food that you **eat** ruin the person for whom Christ
14.17 not a matter of **eating** and drinking, but of the righteousness,
14.20 All foods may be **eaten,**
14.20 but it is wrong to **eat** anything that will cause someone else
14.21 keep from **eating** meat, drinking wine, or doing anything
14.23 has doubts about what he **eats,**
14.23 God condemns him when he **eats** it, because his action is not
1 Cor 5.11 Don't even sit down to **eat** with such a person.
8. 4 So then, about **eating** the food offered to idols:
8. 7 to this day when they **eat** such food they still think of
8. 8 anything if we do not **eat,**
8. 8 nor shall we gain anything if we do **eat.**
8.10 have so-called "knowledge," **eating** in the temple of an idol;
8.10 will not this encourage him to **eat** food offered to idols?
8.13 brother sin, I will never **eat** meat again, so as not to
9. 7 What farmer does not **eat** the grapes from his own vineyard?
10. 3 All **ate** the same spiritual bread [4] and drank the same spiritual
10.16 when we **eat** it, we are sharing in the body of Christ.
10.18 those who **eat** what is offered in sacrifice share in the
10.21 you cannot **eat** at the Lord's table and also at the table
10.25 You are free to **eat** anything sold in the meat-market,
10.27 and you decide to go, **eat** what is set before you, without
10.28 to idols," then do not **eat** that food, for the sake of
10.31 whatever you do, whether you **eat** or drink, do it all for
11.20 as a group, it is not the Lord's Supper that you **eat.**
11.21 For as you **eat,** each one goes ahead with his own meal,
11.22 Haven't you got your own homes in which to **eat** and drink?
11.26 means that every time you **eat** this bread and drink from this
11.27 It follows that if anyone **eats** the Lord's bread or drinks
11.28 examine himself first, and then **eat** the bread and drink from
11.29 the Lord's body when he **eats** the bread and drinks from
11.29 cup, he brings judgement on himself as he **eats** and drinks.
11.33 when you gather together to **eat** the Lord's Supper, wait for
11.34 anyone is hungry, he should **eat** at home, so that you will
15.32 the saying goes, "Let us **eat** and drink, for tomorrow we
2 Cor 9.10 to sow and bread to **eat,** will also supply you with all
Gal 2.12 arrived there, Peter had been **eating** with the Gentile brothers.
2.12 drew back and would not **eat** with the Gentiles, because he
Col 2.16 make rules about what you **eat** or drink or about holy days
2 Thes 3.10 to you, "Whoever refuses to work is not allowed to **eat."**
1 Tim 4. 3 teach that it is wrong to marry and to **eat** certain foods.
4. 3 created those foods to be **eaten,** after a prayer of thanks,
2 Tim 2.17 Such teaching is like an open sore that **eats** away the flesh.
Heb 5.12 Instead of **eating** solid food, you still have to drink milk.
13.10 worship have no right to **eat** any of the sacrifice on our
Jas 2.15 or sisters who need clothes and don't have enough to **eat.**
2.16 Keep warm and **eat** well!"
5. 2 have rotted away, and your clothes have been **eaten** by moths.
5. 3 a witness against you and will **eat** up your flesh like fire.
Rev 2. 7 will give the right to **eat** the fruit of the tree of
2.14 sin by persuading them to **eat** food that had been offered to
2.20 sexual immorality and **eating** food that has been offered to
3.20 his house and eat with him, and he will **eat** with me.
10. 9 He said to me, "Take it and **eat** it;
10.10 scroll from his hand and **ate** it, and it tasted sweet
12. 4 the woman, in order to **eat** her child as soon as it
17.16 they will **eat** her flesh and destroy her with fire.
19.18 Come and **eat** the flesh of kings, generals, and soldiers,
19.21 and all the birds **ate** all they could of their flesh.
22.14 so have the right to **eat** the fruit from the tree of

EAVES

1 Kgs 7. 9 were made of fine stones from the foundations to the **eaves.**

EBONY

Ezek 27.15 lands gave you ivory and **ebony** in exchange for your goods.

ECHO

Ps 29. 3 the glorious God thunders, and his voice **echoes** over the ocean.
Is 13.22 The towers and palaces will **echo** with the cries of
22. 5 down, and cries for help have **echoed** among the hills.
Jer 25.31 him, [31] and the sound will **echo** to the ends of the earth.
Ezek 27.28 The shouts of the drowning sailors **Echoed** on the shore.
Hab 2.11 walls cry out against you, and the rafters **echo** the cry.

ECSTATIC

1 Sam 10.10 him, and he joined in their **ecstatic** dancing and shouting.
10.13 When Saul finished his **ecstatic** dancing and shouting, he

EDEN (1)

Garden of Eden.

Gen 2. 8 God planted a garden in **Eden,** in the East, and there he
2.10 A stream flowed in **Eden** and watered the garden;
2.10 beyond **Eden** it divided into four rivers.
2.15 man in the Garden of **Eden** to cultivate it and guard it.
3.23 out of the Garden of **Eden** and made him cultivate the soil
4.16 in a land called "Wandering," which is east of **Eden.**
Is 51. 3 will make it a garden, like the garden I planted in **Eden.**
Ezek 28.13 You lived in **Eden,** the garden of God, and wore gems of
31. 9 was the envy of every tree in **Eden,** the garden of God.
31.16 All the trees of **Eden** and all the choice, well-watered trees
31.18 Not even the trees in **Eden** were so tall and impressive.
31.18 now, like the trees of **Eden,** it will go down to the
36.35 become like the Garden of **Eden,** and how the cities which
Joel 2. 3 is like the Garden of **Eden,** but behind them it is a

EDGE

Gen 14. 6 pursuing them as far as Elparan on the **edge** of the desert.
23. 9 sell me Machpelah Cave, which is near the **edge** of his field.
23.17 the trees in the field up to the **edge** of the property.
Ex 2. 3 placed it in the tall grass at the **edge** of the river.
13.20 left Sukkoth and camped at Etham on the **edge** of the desert.
26. 4 of blue cloth on the **edge** of the outside piece in each
26.10 Put fifty loops on the **edge** of the last piece of one
26.10 and fifty loops on the **edge** of the other set.
28.26 of the breast-piece on the inside **edge** next to the ephod.
36.11 of blue cloth on the **edge** of the outside piece in each
36.17 put fifty loops on the **edge** of the last piece of one
36.17 and fifty loops on the **edge** of the other set.
39.19 of the breast-piece, on the inside **edge** next to the ephod.
Lev 19. 9 cut the corn at the **edges** of the fields, and do not
23.22 cut the corn at the **edges** of the fields, and do not
Num 33. 6 Their next camp was at Etham on the **edge** of the desert.
33.15 Kadesh), and Mount Hor, at the **edge** of the land of Edom.
Deut 2.36 towns from Aroer, on the **edge** of the valley of the Arnon,
4.48 town of Aroer, on the **edge** of the River Arnon, all the
22. 8 be sure to put a railing round the **edge** of the roof.
Josh 12. 2 from Aroer (on the **edge** of the valley of the Arnon) and
13. 9 extended to Aroer (on the **edge** of the Arnon Valley) and the
13.16 extended to Aroer (on the **edge** of the Arnon Valley) and the
18.15 southern border started on the **edge** of Kiriath Jearim and
Judg 7.11 his servant Purah went down to the **edge** of the enemy camp.
7.17 "When I get to the **edge** of the camp, watch me, and
7.19 hundred men came to the **edge** of the camp a short while
8.11 along the road by the **edge** of the desert, east of Nobah
1 Sam 9.27 When they arrived at the **edge** of the town, Samuel said
26. 1 on Mount Hachilah at the **edge** of the Judaean wilderness.
1 Kgs 7.24 All round the outer **edge** of the rim of the tank were
2 Kgs 7. 8 the four men reached the **edge** of the camp, they went into
2 Chr 4. 3 All round the outer **edge** of the rim of the tank were
19. 4 in the south to the **edge** of the hill-country of Ephraim in
Ps 141. 7 so their bones are scattered at the **edge** of the grave.
Is 28.25 and barley, and at the **edges** of his fields he sows other
Jer 31.30 eats sour grapes will have his own teeth set on **edge;**
Ezek 27. 3 city which stands at the **edge** of the sea and does business
40.43 Ledges seventy-five millimetres wide ran round the **edge**
43.13 with a rim at the outside **edge** twenty-five centimetres high.
43.14 was set back from the **edge** fifty centimetres all round, and
43.14 was also set back from the **edge** fifty centimetres all round.
43.17 with a rim at the outside **edge** twenty-five centimetres high.
43.20 of the middle section of the altar, and all round its **edges.**
Mt 9.20 came up behind Jesus and touched the **edge** of his cloak.
14.36 those who were ill at least touch the **edge** of his cloak;
Mk 4. 1 and the crowd stood on the shore at the water's **edge.**
6.56 him to let them at least touch the **edge** of his cloak;
Lk 8.44 behind Jesus and touched the **edge** of his cloak, and her
Jn 21. 4 Jesus stood at the water's **edge,** but the disciples did not

EDOM

Country s.e. of Canaan, near the Dead Sea, whose people were descended from Esau.
see also **OBED EDOM**

Gen 14. 6 Horites in the mountains of **Edom,** pursuing them as far as
25.30 (That is why he was called **Edom.)**
32. 3 ahead of him to his brother Esau in the country of **Edom.**
33.14 and the children until I catch up with you in **Edom."**
33.16 So that day Esau started on his way back to **Edom.**
36. 1 These are the descendants of Esau, also called **Edom.**
36. 8 So Esau lived in the hill-country of **Edom.**
36. 9 These are the descendants of Esau, the ancestor of the **Edomites.**
36.20 inhabitants of the land of **Edom** were divided into tribes
36.29 These are the Horite tribes in the land of **Edom:**
36.31 following kings ruled over the land of **Edom** in succession:
36.40 Esau was the ancestor of the following **Edomite** tribes:
Ex 15.15 The leaders of **Edom** are terrified;
Num 20.14 Moses sent messengers from Kadesh to the king of **Edom.**
20.18 But the **Edomites** answered, "We refuse to let you pass
20.20 The **Edomites** repeated, "We refuse!"
20.21 Because the **Edomites** would not let the Israelites pass
20.23 Kadesh and arrived at Mount Hor, [23] on the border of **Edom.**
21. 4 Gulf of Aqaba, in order to go round the territory of **Edom.**
24.18 his enemies in **Edom** And make their land his property,

Num	33.15	Kadesh), and Mount Hor, at the edge of the land of **Edom.**
	34. 3	extend from the wilderness of Zin along the border of **Edom.**
Deut	1. 2	Mount Sinai to Kadesh Barnea by way of the hill-country of **Edom.)**
	1.44	Hormah and defeated you there in the hill-country of **Edom.**
	2. 1	a long time wandering about in the hill-country of **Edom.**
	2. 4	of **Edom,** the territory of your distant relatives,
	2. 5	I have given **Edom** to Esau's descendants.
	2.12	Horites used to live in **Edom,** but the descendants of Esau
	2.22	Edomites, the descendants of Esau, who live in the hill-country of **Edom.**
	2.22	the Horites, so that the **Edomites** took over their land and
	2.29	of Esau, who live in **Edom,** and the Moabites, who live in
	23. 7	"Do not despise the **Edomites;**
	33. 2	rose like the sun over **Edom** and shone on his people from
Josh	11.17	Halak in the south near **Edom,** as far as Baalgad in the
	12. 7	the valley of Lebanon to Mount Halak in the south near **Edom.**
	15. 1	point of the wilderness of Zin, at the border of **Edom.**
	15.10	Baalah towards the hill-country of **Edom,** went on the north
	15.21	were near the border of **Edom,** were Kabzeel, Eder, Jagur,
	24. 4	gave Esau the hill-country of **Edom** as his possession, but
Judg	1.36	North of Sela, the **Edomite** border ran through Akrabbim Pass.
	5. 4	out of the region of **Edom,** the earth shook, and rain fell
	11.17	messengers to the king of **Edom** to ask permission to go
	11.17	But the king of **Edom** would not let them.
	11.18	going round the land of **Edom** and the land of Moab until
1 Sam	14.47	Moab, of Ammon, and of **Edom,** the kings of Zobah, and the
	21. 7	Doeg, who was from **Edom,** happened to be there that day,
2 Sam	8.12	the nations he had conquered—[12] **Edom,** Moab, Ammon,
	8.13	killing eighteen thousand **Edomites** in the Valley of Salt.
	8.14	set up military camps throughout **Edom,** and the people there
1 Kgs	9.26	the shore of the Gulf of Aqaba, in the land of **Edom.**
	11. 1	he married Hittite women and women from Moab, Ammon, **Edom,**
	11.14	Hadad, of the royal family of **Edom,** to turn against Solomon.
	11.15	when David had conquered **Edom,** Joab the commander of his army
	11.15	and his men remained in **Edom** six months, and during that
	11.15	they killed every male in **Edom** [17] except Hadad and some of
	11.17	Hadad and some of his father's **Edomite** servants,
	11.21	As king of **Edom,** Hadad was an evil, bitter enemy of Israel.
	22.47	The land of **Edom** had no king;
2 Kgs	3. 8	long way, through the wilderness of **Edom,"** Joram answered.
	3. 9	So King Joram and the kings of Judah and **Edom** set out.
	3.20	flowing from the direction of **Edom,** and covered the ground.
	8.20	During Jehoram's reign **Edom** revolted against Judah
	8.21	chariots for Zair, where the **Edomite** army surrounded them.
	8.22	**Edom** has been independent of Judah ever since.
	14. 7	Amaziah killed ten thousand **Edomite** soldiers in Salt Valley;
	14.10	have defeated the **Edomites,** and you are filled with pride.
	16. 6	same time, the king of **Edom** regained control of the city of
	16. 6	The **Edomites** settled in Elath, and still live there.)
1 Chr	1.38	The original inhabitants of **Edom** were descended
	1.43	kings ruled the land of **Edom** one after the other, in the
	1.51	The people of **Edom** were divided into the following tribes:
	4.42	other members of the tribe of Simeon went east to **Edom.**
	18.11	took from the nations he conquered—**Edom,** Moab, Ammon,
	18.12	mother was Zeruiah, defeated the **Edomites** in the Valley of
	18.13	set up military camps throughout **Edom,** and the people there
2 Chr	8.17	the shore of the Gulf of Aqaba, in the land of **Edom.**
	20. 2	"A large army from **Edom** has come from the other side of
	20.10	"Now the people of Ammon, Moab, and **Edom** have attacked us.
	20.23	Moabites attacked the **Edomite** army and completely destroyed it,
	21. 8	During Jehoram's reign **Edom** revolted against Judah
	21. 9	So Jehoram and his officers set out with chariots and invaded **Edom.**
	21. 9	There the **Edomite** army surrounded them, but during the night
	21.10	**Edom** has been independent of Judah ever since.
	25.11	**Edomite** soldiers [12] and captured another ten thousand.
	25.14	Amaziah returned from defeating the **Edomites,** he brought
	25.19	that you have defeated the **Edomites,** but I advise you to
	25.20	because he had worshipped the **Edomite** idols.
	28.16	The **Edomites** began to raid Judah again and captured many prisoners,
Ps	60. 8	will throw my sandals on **Edom,** as a sign that I own
	60. 9	Who will lead me to **Edom?**
	83. 6	the people of **Edom** and the Ishmaelites;
	108. 9	will throw my sandals on **Edom,** as a sign that I own
	108.10	Who will lead me to **Edom?**
	137. 7	what the **Edomites** did the day Jerusalem was captured.
Is	11.14	will conquer the people of **Edom** and Moab, and the people of
	21.11	This is a message about **Edom.**
	21.11	Someone calls to me from **Edom,** "Sentry, how soon will the
	34. 5	and now it will strike **Edom,** those people whom he has
	34. 6	he will make this a great slaughter in the land of **Edom.**
	34. 9	The rivers of **Edom** will turn into tar, and the soil will
	63. 1	"Who is this coming from the city of Bozrah in **Edom?**
Jer	9.25	of Egypt, Judah, **Edom,** Ammon, Moab, and the desert people,
	25.19	all the people of **Edom,** Moab, and Ammon;
	27. 3	message to the kings of **Edom,** Moab, Ammon, Tyre, and Sidon
	40.11	who were in Moab, Ammon, **Edom,** and other countries, heard
	49. 7	This is what the Lord Almighty said about **Edom:**
	49. 7	"Have the people of **Edom** lost their good judgement?
	49.10	All the people of **Edom** are destroyed.
	49.14	I said, **"Edom,** I have received a message from the Lord.
	49.17	destruction that will come on **Edom** will be so terrible that
	49.18	thing will happen to **Edom** as happened to Sodom and Gomorrah,
	49.19	and make the **Edomites** run away suddenly from their country.
	49.20	made against the people of **Edom,** and to what I intend to
	49.21	When **Edom** falls, there will be such a noise that the
	49.22	On that day **Edom's** soldiers will be as frightened as a woman
Lam	4.21	Laugh on, people of **Edom** and Uz;
Lam	4.22	But **Edom,** the Lord will punish you;
Ezek	16.57	her—a joke to the **Edomites,** the Philistines, and your other
	25.12	Lord said, "The people of **Edom** took cruel revenge on Judah,
	25.12	and that revenge has brought lasting guilt on **Edom.**
	25.13	announce that I will punish **Edom** and kill every man and
	25.14	Israel will take revenge on **Edom** for me,
	25.14	and they will make **Edom** feel my furious anger.
	25.14	**Edom** will know what it means to be the object of my
	32.29	**"Edom** is there with her kings and rulers.
	35. 2	"Mortal man," he said, "denounce the country of **Edom.**
	35. 3	I am your enemy, mountains of **Edom!**
	35. 7	will make the hill-country of **Edom** a waste and kill everyone
	35.15	of Seir, yes, all the land of **Edom,** will be desolate.
	36. 5	the surrounding nations, and especially against **Edom.**
Dan	11.41	thousands, but the countries of **Edom,** Moab, and what is left
Joel	3.19	will become a desert, and **Edom** a ruined waste, because they
Amos	1. 6	whole nation and sold them as slaves to the people of **Edom.**
	1. 9	exile in the land of **Edom,** and did not keep the treaty
	1.11	Lord says, "The people of **Edom** have sinned again and again,
	2. 1	the bones of the king of **Edom** by burning them to ashes.
	9.12	left of the land of **Edom** and all the nations that were
Obad	1	Obadiah—what the Sovereign Lord said about the nation of **Edom.**
	1	Let us go to war against **Edom!"**
	2	The Lord says to **Edom,** "I will make you weak;
	8	"On the day I punish **Edom,** I will destroy their clever
	9	Teman will be terrified, and every soldier in **Edom** will be killed.
	15	**Edom,** what you have done will be done to you.
	19	"People from southern Judah will occupy **Edom;**
	21	The victorious men of Jerusalem will attack **Edom** and rule over it.
Hab	3. 3	God is coming again from **Edom;**
Mal	1. 4	the **Edomites,** say, "Our towns have been destroyed,

EDUCATE

1 Chr	27.32	Hachmoni were in charge of the **education** of the king's sons.
Prov	1. 5	and give guidance to the **educated,** [6] so that they can
	4.13	Your **education** is your life—guard it well.
	15.33	Reverence for the Lord is an **education** in itself.
	16.22	the wise, but trying to **educate** stupid people is a waste of
	17.16	money on an **education,** because he has no common sense.
Acts	4.13	and to learn that they were ordinary men of no **education.**
Rom	1.14	and to the savage, to the **educated** and to the ignorant.

EFFECT

2 Chr	26.13	able to fight **effectively** for the king against his enemies.
Esth	8.12	This decree was to take **effect** throughout the Persian
	9. 1	royal proclamation was to take **effect,** the day when the
Ecc	4. 9	than one, because together they can work more **effectively.**
Lk	16.16	of the prophets were in **effect** up to the time of John
1 Cor	15.10	and the grace that he gave me was not without **effect.**
Eph	3. 9	people see how God's secret plan is to be put into **effect.**
Heb	9.17	it comes into **effect** only after his death.
	9.18	first covenant came into **effect** only with the use of blood.
	10.12	an offering that is **effective** for ever, and then he sat
Jas	5.16	The prayer of a good person has a powerful **effect.**
2 Pet	1. 8	make you active and **effective** in your knowledge of our Lord

EFFORT

1 Chr	22.14	for the Temple, by my **efforts** I have accumulated more than
	29. 2	I have made every **effort** to prepare materials for the Temple—gold,
Job	34.20	he kills the mighty with no **effort** at all.
	39.16	not hers, and is unconcerned that her **efforts** were wasted.
Jer	51.58	their **efforts** go up in flames.
Dan	12. 4	their **efforts** trying to understand what is happening."
Eph	2. 8	the result of your own **efforts,** but God's gift, so that no
Phil	2.16	will show that all my **effort** and work have not been wasted.
1 Tim	4.13	give your time and **effort** to the public reading of the

EGG

Deut	22. 6	bird sitting either on the **eggs** or with her young, you are
Job	6. 6	What flavour is there in the white of an **egg?**
	39.14	The ostrich leaves her **eggs** on the ground for the heat
	39.16	She acts as if the **eggs** were not hers,
Is	10.14	and I gathered their wealth as easily as gathering **eggs.**
	14.29	A snake's **egg** hatches a flying dragon.
	34.15	will build their nests, lay **eggs,** hatch their young,
	59. 5	you make are as deadly as the **eggs** of a poisonous snake.
	59. 5	Crush an **egg,** out comes a snake!
Jer	17.11	dishonestly is like a bird that hatches **eggs** it didn't lay.
Lk	11.12	would you give him a scorpion when he asks for an **egg?**

EGYPT

[KING OF EGYPT]

Country s.w. of Palestine in which the Israelites lived as slaves, and to which Jesus was taken for safety as a child.

Gen	10. 6	The sons of Ham—Cush, **Egypt,** Libya and Canaan—were the
	10.13	The descendants of **Egypt** were the people of Lydia, Anam,
	12.10	Abram went farther south to **Egypt,** to live there for a while.
	12.11	to cross the border into **Egypt,** he said to his wife Sarai,
	12.12	When the **Egyptians** see you, they will assume that you
	12.14	he crossed the border into **Egypt,**
	12.14	the **Egyptians** did see that his wife was
	13. 1	Abram went north out of **Egypt** to the southern part of
	13.10	like the Garden of the Lord or like the land of **Egypt.**
	15.18	land from the border of **Egypt** to the River Euphrates,

Gen 16. 1 But she had an **Egyptian** slave-girl named Hagar, [2]and so she
21. 9 day Ishmael, whom Hagar the **Egyptian** had borne to Abraham,
21.21 His mother found an **Egyptian** wife for him.
25.12 Ishmael, whom Hagar, the **Egyptian** slave of Sarah, bore to Abraham,
25.18 and Shur, to the east of **Egypt** on the way to Assyria.
26. 2 had appeared to Isaac and had said, "Do not go to **Egypt;**
37.25 saw a group of Ishmaelites travelling from Gilead to **Egypt.**
37.28 pieces of silver to the Ishmaelites, who took him to **Egypt.**
37.36 Meanwhile, in **Egypt,** the Midianites had sold Joseph to Potiphar,
39. 1 Ishmaelites had taken Joseph to **Egypt** and sold him to Potiphar,
39. 2 in the house of his **Egyptian** master, [3]who saw that the Lord
39. 5 blessed the household of the **Egyptian** and everything that he
40. 1 Some time later the **king of Egypt's** wine steward
40.15 Hebrews, and even here in **Egypt** I didn't do anything to
41. 1 the **king of Egypt** dreamt that he was standing
41. 8 so he sent for all the magicians and wise men of **Egypt.**
41.19 They were the poorest cows I have ever seen anywhere in **Egypt.**
41.29 be seven years of great plenty in all the land of **Egypt.**
41.36 the seven years of famine which are going to come on **Egypt.**
41.41 I now appoint you governor over all **Egypt."**
41.43 And so Joseph was appointed governor over all **Egypt.**
41.44 and no one in all **Egypt** shall so much as lift a
41.45 He gave Joseph the **Egyptian** name Zaphenath Paneah,
41.45 thirty years old when he began to serve the **king of Egypt.**
41.53 plenty that the land of **Egypt** had enjoyed came to an end,
41.54 in every other country, but there was food throughout **Egypt.**
41.55 When the **Egyptians** began to be hungry, they cried out to
41.56 Joseph opened all the storehouses and sold corn to the **Egyptians.**
41.57 People came to **Egypt** from all over the world to buy corn
42. 1 that there was corn in **Egypt,** he said to his sons, "Why
42. 2 I hear that there is corn in **Egypt;**
42. 3 went to buy corn in **Egypt,** [4]but Jacob did not send Joseph's
42. 6 governor of the land of **Egypt,** was selling corn to people
42.30 "The governor of **Egypt** spoke harshly to us and accused
43. 2 which had been brought from **Egypt,** Jacob said to his sons,
43.15 twice as much money, and set out for **Egypt** with Benjamin.
43.32 The **Egyptians** who were eating there were served separately,
45. 2 such loud sobs that the **Egyptians** heard it, and the news was
45. 4 said, "I am your brother Joseph, whom you sold into **Egypt.**
45. 8 I am the ruler of all **Egypt.**
45. 9 'God has made me ruler of all **Egypt;**
45.13 powerful I am here in **Egypt** and tell him about everything
45.18 them the best land in **Egypt,** and they will have more than
45.19 take wagons with them from **Egypt** for their wives and small
45.20 the best in the whole land of **Egypt** will be theirs."
45.23 donkeys loaded with the best **Egyptian** goods and ten donkeys
45.25 They left **Egypt** and went back home to their father Jacob
45.26 "He is the ruler of all **Egypt!"**
45.27 had sent to take him to **Egypt,** he recovered from the shock.
46. 3 "Do not be afraid to go to **Egypt;**
46. 4 will go with you to **Egypt,** and I will bring your descendants
46. 5 their wives in the wagons which the **king of Egypt** had sent.
46. 6 possessions they had acquired in Canaan and went to **Egypt.**
46. 8 Jacob's family who went to **Egypt** with him were his eldest
46.20 In **Egypt** Joseph had two sons, Manasseh and Ephraim, by
46.26 Jacob who went to **Egypt** was sixty-six, not including his sons'
46.27 were born to Joseph in **Egypt,** bringing to seventy the total
46.34 because **Egyptians** will have nothing to do with shepherds.
47. 6 your brothers have arrived, [6]the land of **Egypt** is theirs.
47.11 father and his brothers in **Egypt,** giving them property in
47.13 and the people of **Egypt** and Canaan became weak with hunger.
47.15 When all the money in **Egypt** and Canaan was spent,
47.15 the **Egyptians** came to Joseph and said,
47.20 Joseph bought all the land in **Egypt** for the king.
47.20 Every **Egyptian** was forced to sell his land, because the
47.21 slaves of the people from one end of **Egypt** to the other.
47.26 law for the land of **Egypt** that one-fifth of the harvest
47.27 The Israelites lived in **Egypt** in the region of Goshen,
47.28 Jacob lived in **Egypt** for seventeen years, until he was a
47.29 make a solemn vow that you will not bury me in **Egypt.**
47.30 carry me out of **Egypt** and bury me where they are buried."
48. 5 were born to you in **Egypt** before I came here, belong to
48. 9 "These are my sons, whom God has given me here in **Egypt."**
50. 3 The **Egyptians** mourned for him seventy days.
50. 7 court, and all the leading men of **Egypt** went with Joseph.
50.11 "What a solemn ceremony of mourning the **Egyptians** are holding!"
50.14 his father, he returned to **Egypt** with his brothers and all
50.22 Joseph continued to live in **Egypt** with his father's family;
50.26 So Joseph died in **Egypt** at the age of a hundred and

Ex 1. 1 of Jacob who went to **Egypt** with him, each with his family,
1. 5 His son Joseph was already in **Egypt.**
1. 7 so numerous and strong that **Egypt** was filled with them.
1. 8 king, who knew nothing about Joseph, came to power in **Egypt.**
1.11 So the **Egyptians** put slave-drivers over them to crush
1.12 But the more the **Egyptians** oppressed the Israelites, the
1.12 The **Egyptians** came to fear the Israelites [13-14]and made
1.15 Then the **king of Egypt** spoke to Shiphrah and Puah,
1.19 They answered, "The Hebrew women are not like **Egyptian** women;
2.11 He even saw an **Egyptian** kill a Hebrew, one of Moses' own
2.12 was watching, he killed the **Egyptian** and hid his body in the
2.14 Are you going to kill me just as you killed that **Egyptian?"**
2.19 "An **Egyptian** rescued us from the shepherds," they
2.23 Years later the **king of Egypt** died,
3. 7 "I have seen how cruelly my people are being treated in **Egypt;**
3. 8 to rescue them from the **Egyptians** and to bring them out of
3. 8 to bring them out of **Egypt** to a spacious land, one which
3. 9 my people, and I see how the **Egyptians** are oppressing them.
3.10 sending you to the **king of Egypt** so that you can lead

Ex 3.11 I go to the king and bring the Israelites out of **Egypt?"**
3.12 bring the people out of **Egypt,** you will worship me on this
3.16 to them and have seen what the **Egyptians** are doing to them.
3.17 them out of **Egypt,** where they are being treated cruelly,
3.18 Israel to the **king of Egypt** and say to him,
3.19 I know that the **king of Egypt** will not let you go
3.20 and will punish **Egypt** by doing terrifying things there.
3.21 "I will make the **Egyptians** respect you so that when my
3.22 woman will go to her **Egyptian** neighbours
3.22 and to any **Egyptian** woman living in her house
3.22 and daughters and carry away the wealth of the **Egyptians."**
4.18 back to my relatives in **Egypt** to see if they are still
4.19 to him, "Go back to **Egypt,** for all those who wanted to
4.20 set out with them for **Egypt,** carrying the stick that God had
4.21 you are going back to **Egypt,** be sure to perform before the
4.24 place on the way to **Egypt,** the Lord met Moses and tried
4.28 the Lord had said when he told him to return to **Egypt;**
4.29 Moses and Aaron went to **Egypt** and gathered all the Israelite
5. 1 Aaron went to the **king of Egypt** and said, "The Lord,
5. 5 You people have become more numerous than the **Egyptians.**
5. 6 the **Egyptian** slave-drivers and the Israelite foremen:
5.12 So the people went all over **Egypt** looking for straw.
5.14 The **Egyptian** slave-drivers beat the Israelite foremen,
6. 5 of the Israelites, whom the **Egyptians** have enslaved, and I
6. 6 you and set you free from your slavery to the **Egyptians.**
6. 7 Lord your God when I set you free from slavery in **Egypt.**
6.11 "Go and tell the **king of Egypt** that he must let
6.13 the Israelites and the **king of Egypt** that I have ordered you
6.13 I have ordered you to lead the Israelites out of **Egypt."**
6.26 the Lord said, "Lead the tribes of Israel out of **Egypt."**
6.27 the men who told the **king of Egypt** to free the Israelites.
6.28 Moses in the land of **Egypt,** [29]he said, "I am the Lord.
6.29 Tell the **king of Egypt** everything I tell you."
7. 3 to you, no matter how many terrifying things I do in **Egypt.**
7. 3 will bring severe punishment on **Egypt** and lead the tribes of
7. 5 The **Egyptians** will then know that I am the Lord, when I
7.18 stink so much that the **Egyptians** will not be able to drink
7.19 hold it out over all the rivers, canals, and pools in **Egypt.**
7.21 it smelt so bad that the **Egyptians** could not drink from it.
7.21 There was blood everywhere in **Egypt.**
7.24 All the **Egyptians** dug along the bank of the river for
8. 5 pools, and make frogs come up and cover the land of **Egypt."**
8.14 The **Egyptians** piled them up in great heaps, until the
8.16 over the land of **Egypt** the dust will change into gnats."
8.17 and all the dust in **Egypt** was turned into gnats, which
8.21 The houses of the **Egyptians** will be full of flies, and the
8.24 The whole land of **Egypt** was brought to ruin by the flies.
8.26 that," Moses answered, "because the **Egyptians** would be
8.26 these animals and offend the **Egyptians** by sacrificing them
9. 4 Israelites and those of the **Egyptians,** and no animal that
9. 6 all the animals of the **Egyptians** died, but not one of the
9. 9 over all the land of **Egypt,** and everywhere they will produce
9.11 they were covered with boils, like all the other **Egyptians.**
9.18 a heavy hailstorm, such as **Egypt** has never known in all its
9.22 over the whole land of **Egypt**—on the people, the animals, and
9.24 was the worst storm that **Egypt** had ever known in all its
9.25 All over **Egypt** the hail struck down everything in the open,
10. 2 I made fools of the **Egyptians** when I performed the miracles.
10. 7 Don't you realize that **Egypt** is ruined?"
10.12 "Raise your hand over the land of **Egypt** to bring the locusts.
10.15 left on any tree or plant in all the land of **Egypt.**
10.19 Not one locust was left in all **Egypt.**
10.21 thick enough to be felt will cover the land of **Egypt."**
10.22 there was total darkness throughout **Egypt** for three days.
10.23 The **Egyptians** could not see each other, and no one left
11. 1 one more punishment on the **king of Egypt** and his people.
11. 3 The Lord made the **Egyptians** respect the Israelites.
11. 4 midnight I will go through **Egypt,**
11. 5 and every first-born son in **Egypt** will die, from the king's son,
11. 6 be loud crying all over **Egypt,** such as there has never been
11. 7 a distinction between the **Egyptians** and the Israelites.' "
11. 9 in order that I may do more of my miracles in **Egypt."**
12. 1 The Lord spoke to Moses and Aaron in **Egypt:**
12.12 go through the land of **Egypt,** killing every first-born male,
12.12 both human and animal, and punishing all the gods of **Egypt.**
12.13 over you and will not harm you when I punish the **Egyptians.**
12.17 was on this day that I brought your tribes out of **Egypt.**
12.23 When the Lord goes through **Egypt** to kill the Egyptians,
12.27 he passed over the houses of the Israelites in **Egypt.**
12.27 He killed the **Egyptians,** but spared us.' "
12.29 all the first-born sons in **Egypt,** from the king's son, who
12.30 his officials, and all the other **Egyptians** were awakened.
12.30 There was loud crying throughout **Egypt,** because there was
12.33 The **Egyptians** urged the people to hurry and leave the country;
12.35 said, and had asked the **Egyptians** for gold and silver
12.36 The Lord made the **Egyptians** respect the people and give
12.36 In this way the Israelites carried away the wealth of the **Egyptians.**
12.39 they had brought out of **Egypt,** for they had been
12.39 had been driven out of **Egypt** so suddenly that they did not
12.40 The Israelites had lived in **Egypt** for 430 years.
12.41 430 years ended, all the tribes of the Lord's people left **Egypt.**
12.42 night when the Lord kept watch to bring them out of **Egypt;**
12.51 On that day the Lord brought the Israelite tribes out of **Egypt.**
13. 3 on which you left **Egypt,** the place where you were slaves.
13. 4 You are leaving **Egypt** on this day in the first month, the
13. 8 because of what the Lord did for you when you left **Egypt.**
13. 9 the Lord brought you out of **Egypt** by his great power.
13.14 Lord brought us out of **Egypt,** the place where we were slaves.
13.15 When the **king of Egypt** was stubborn and refused to let
13.15 first-born male in the land of **Egypt,** both human and animal.

Ex 13.16 the Lord brought us out of **Egypt** by his great power.' "
13.17 When the **king of Egypt** let the people go,
13.17 their minds and return to **Egypt** when they see that they are
14. 4 Then the **Egyptians** will know that I am the Lord."
14. 5 When the **king of Egypt** was told that the people had escaped,
14. 9 The **Egyptian** army, with all the horses, chariots, and
14.11 They said to Moses, "Weren't there any graves in **Egypt?**
14.11 Look what you have done by bringing us out of **Egypt!**
14.12 us alone and let us go on being slaves of the **Egyptians.**
14.13 you will never see these **Egyptians** again.
14.17 I will make the **Egyptians** so stubborn that they will go
14.18 When I defeat them, the **Egyptians** will know that I am
14.20 until it was [20] between the **Egyptians** and the Israelites.
14.20 made it dark for the **Egyptians,** but gave light to the people
14.23 The **Egyptians** pursued them and went after them into the
14.24 fire and cloud at the **Egyptian** army and threw them into a
14.25 The **Egyptians** said, "The Lord is fighting for the Israelites
14.26 back over the **Egyptians** and their chariots and drivers."
14.27 The **Egyptians** tried to escape from the water, but the Lord
14.28 the drivers, and all the **Egyptian** army that had followed the
14.30 people of Israel from the **Egyptians,** and the Israelites saw
14.31 the Lord had defeated the **Egyptians,** they stood in awe of
15. 4 "He threw **Egypt's** army and its chariots into the sea;
15.10 But one breath from you, Lord, and the **Egyptians** were drowned;
15.19 But when the **Egyptian** chariots with their horses and drivers
15.26 with any of the diseases that I brought on the **Egyptians.**
16. 1 month after they had left **Egypt,** they came to the desert of
16. 3 to them, "We wish that the Lord had killed us in **Egypt.**
16. 6 know that it was the Lord who brought you out of **Egypt.**
16.32 to eat in the desert when he brought us out of **Egypt."**
17. 3 They said, "Why did you bring us out of **Egypt?**
18. 1 and the people of Israel when he led them out of **Egypt.**
18. 4 saved me from being killed by the **king of Egypt";**
18. 8 and the people of **Egypt** in order to rescue the Israelites.
18.10 Lord, who saved you from the king and the people of **Egypt!**
18.11 the **Egyptians** treated the Israelites with such contempt."
19. 1 month after they had left **Egypt** they came to the desert of
19. 4 the Lord, did to the **Egyptians** and how I carried you as
20. 2 God who brought you out of **Egypt,** where you were slaves.
22.21 remember that you were foreigners in **Egypt.**
23. 9 to be a foreigner, because you were foreigners in **Egypt.**
23.15 month in which you left **Egypt,** celebrate the Festival of
29.46 who brought them out of **Egypt** so that I could live among
32. 1 has happened to this man Moses, who led us out of **Egypt;**
32. 4 said, "Israel, this is our god, who led us out of **Egypt!"**
32. 7 whom you led out of **Egypt,** have sinned and rejected me.
32. 8 saying that this is their god, who led them out of **Egypt.**
32.11 whom you rescued from **Egypt** with great might and power?
32.12 Why should the **Egyptians** be able to say that you led
32.12 led your people out of **Egypt,** planning to kill them in the
32.23 has happened to this man Moses, who brought us out of **Egypt;**
33. 1 people you brought out of **Egypt,** and go to the land that
34.18 of Abib, because it was in that month that you left **Egypt.**
40.17 second year after they left **Egypt,** the Tent of the Lord's
Lev 11.45 who brought you out of **Egypt** so that I could be your
18. 3 practices of the people of **Egypt,** where you once lived, or
19.34 Remember that you were once foreigners in the land of **Egypt.**
19.36 am the Lord your God, and I brought you out of **Egypt.**
22.33 and I brought you out of **Egypt** to become your God.
23.43 Israel live in simple shelters when he led them out of **Egypt.**
24.10 man whose father was an **Egyptian** and whose mother was an
25.38 who brought you out of **Egypt** in order to give you the
25.42 Israel are the Lord's slaves, and he brought them out of **Egypt;**
25.55 He brought them out of **Egypt;**
26.13 God, brought you out of **Egypt** so that you would no longer
26.45 bringing my people out of **Egypt,** in order that I, the Lord,
Num 1. 1 the people of Israel left **Egypt,** the Lord spoke to Moses
3.12 all the first-born of the **Egyptians,** I consecrated as my own
8.17 killed all the first-born in **Egypt,** I consecrated as my own
9. 1 the second year after the people of Israel had left **Egypt.**
10.11 year after the people left **Egypt,** the cloud over the Tent of
11. 5 In **Egypt** we used to eat all the fish we wanted, and
11.18 you had some meat and that you were better off in **Egypt.**
11.20 to him that you should never have left **Egypt.'** "
13.22 (Hebron was founded seven years before Zoan in **Egypt.)**
14. 2 been better to die in **Egypt** or even here in the wilderness!
14. 3 Wouldn't it be better to go back to **Egypt?"**
14. 4 another, "Let's choose a leader and go back to **Egypt!"**
14.13 Lord, "You brought these people out of **Egypt** by your power.
14.13 When the **Egyptians** hear what you have done to your people,
14.19 as you have forgiven them ever since they left **Egypt."**
14.22 miracles that I performed in **Egypt** and in the wilderness,
15.41 I brought you out of **Egypt** to be your God.
16.13 of the fertile land of **Egypt** to kill us here in the
20. 5 you bring us out of **Egypt** into this miserable place where
20.15 how our ancestors went to **Egypt,** where we lived many years.
20.15 The **Egyptians** ill-treated our ancestors and us, [16] and we
20.16 our cry and sent an angel, who led us out of **Egypt.**
21. 5 you bring us out of **Egypt** to die in this desert, where
22. 5 want you to know that a whole nation has come from **Egypt;**
22.11 a people who came from **Egypt** has spread out over the whole
23.22 God has brought them out of **Egypt;**
24. 8 God brought them out of **Egypt;**
26. 3 These were the Israelites who came out of **Egypt:**
26.59 who was married to Levi's daughter Jochebed, who was born in **Egypt.**
32.11 older who came out of **Egypt** will enter the land that I
33. 1 up camp after they left **Egypt** in their tribes under the
33. 3 The people of Israel left **Egypt** on the fifteenth day of
33. 3 in full view of the **Egyptians,** [4] who were burying the
33. 4 Lord showed that he was more powerful than the gods of **Egypt.**
Num 33.38 of the fortieth year after the Israelites had left **Egypt.**
34. 5 valley at the border of **Egypt** and end at the Mediterranean.
Deut 1. 3 year after they had left **Egypt,** Moses told the people
1.27 He brought us out of **Egypt** just to hand us over to
1.30 just as you saw him do in **Egypt** [31] and in the desert.
4.20 But you are the people he rescued from **Egypt,** that blazing furnace.
4.34 his own, as the Lord your God did for you in **Egypt?**
4.37 and by his great power he himself brought you out of **Egypt.**
4.45 they had come out of **Egypt** and were in the valley east
4.45 people of Israel defeated him when they came out of **Egypt.**
5. 6 Lord your God, who rescued you from **Egypt,** where you were slaves.
5.15 that you were slaves in **Egypt,** and that I, the Lord your
6.12 the Lord who rescued you from **Egypt,** where you were slaves.
6.21 were slaves of the **king of Egypt,** and the Lord rescued us
6.22 do terrifying things to the **Egyptians** and to their king and
6.23 He freed us from **Egypt** to bring us here and give us
7. 8 and set you free from slavery to the **king of Egypt.**
7.15 diseases that you experienced in **Egypt,** but he will bring
7.18 God did to the **king of Egypt** and to all his people.
7.19 way that he destroyed the **Egyptians,** he will destroy all
8.14 Lord your God who rescued you from **Egypt,** where you were slaves.
9. 7 the day that you left **Egypt** until the day you arrived here,
9.12 whom you led out of **Egypt,** have become corrupt and have done
9.26 and brought out of **Egypt** by your great strength and power.
9.28 Otherwise, the **Egyptians** will say that you were unable
9.29 you brought out of **Egypt** by your great power and might.'
10.19 those foreigners, because you were once foreigners in **Egypt.**
10.22 When your ancestors went to **Egypt,** there were only seventy of them.
11. 3 he did to the **king of Egypt** and to his entire country.
11. 4 Lord completely wiped out the **Egyptian** army, along with
11.10 is not like the land of **Egypt,** where you lived before.
13. 5 the Lord, who rescued you from **Egypt,** where you were slaves.
13.10 Lord your God, who rescued you from **Egypt,** where you were slaves.
15.15 that you were slaves in **Egypt** and the Lord your God set
16. 1 on a night in that month that he rescued you from **Egypt.**
16. 3 you did when you had to leave **Egypt** in such a hurry.
16. 3 the day you came out of **Egypt,** that place of suffering.
16. 5 Do it at sunset, the time of day when you left **Egypt.**
16.12 do not forget that you were slaves in **Egypt.**
17.16 not to send people to **Egypt** to buy horses, because the Lord
20. 1 Lord your God, who rescued you from **Egypt,** will be with you.
21. 8 Lord, forgive your people Israel, whom you rescued from **Egypt.**
23. 4 on your way out of **Egypt,** and they hired Balaam son of
23. 7 And do not despise the **Egyptians;**
24. 9 Lord your God did to Miriam as you were coming from **Egypt.**
24.18 that you were slaves in **Egypt** and that the Lord your God
24.22 Never forget that you were slaves in **Egypt;**
25.17 the Amalekites did to you as you were coming from **Egypt.**
26. 5 a wandering Aramean, who took his family to **Egypt** to live.
26. 6 The **Egyptians** treated us harshly and forced us to work as slaves.
26. 8 By his great power and strength he rescued us from **Egypt.**
28.27 Lord will send boils on you, as he did on the **Egyptians.**
28.60 you experienced in **Egypt,** and you will never recover.
28.68 will send you back to **Egypt** in ships, even though he said
29. 2 Lord did to the **king of Egypt,** to his officials,
29.16 what life was like in **Egypt** and what it was like to
29.25 God of their ancestors, when he brought them out of **Egypt.**
34.11 to perform against the **king of Egypt,** his officials,
Josh 2.10 the Red Sea in front of you when you were leaving **Egypt.**
5. 4 Israel left **Egypt,** all the males were already circumcised.
5. 4 fighting age when they left **Egypt** had died because they had
5. 9 I have removed from you the disgrace of being slaves in **Egypt."**
9. 9 everything that he did in **Egypt** [10] and what he did to the
13. 3 stream of Shihor, at the **Egyptian** border, as far north as
15. 4 stream on the border of **Egypt** to the Mediterranean Sea,
15.47 stream on the border of **Egypt** and the coast of the
24. 4 but your ancestor Jacob and his children went down to **Egypt.**
24. 5 I sent Moses and Aaron, and I brought great trouble on **Egypt.**
24. 6 brought your ancestors out of **Egypt,**
24. 6 and the **Egyptians** pursued them with chariots and cavalry.
24. 7 for help, and I put darkness between them and the **Egyptians.**
24. 7 I made the sea come rolling over the **Egyptians** and drown them.
24. 7 You know what I did to **Egypt.**
24.14 in Mesopotamia and in **Egypt,** and serve only the Lord.
24.17 us out of slavery in **Egypt,** and we saw the miracles that
24.32 of Israel had brought from **Egypt,** was buried at Shechem, in
Judg 2. 1 "I took you out of **Egypt** and brought you to the land
2.12 had brought them out of **Egypt,** and they began to worship
6. 8 "I brought you out of slavery in **Egypt.**
6. 9 I rescued you from the **Egyptians** and from the people who
6.13 the Lord used to do—how he brought them out of **Egypt?**
10.11 "The **Egyptians,** the Amorites, the Ammonites,
11.13 the Israelites came out of **Egypt,** they took away my land
11.16 when the Israelites left **Egypt,** they went through the desert
19.30 Nothing like this has ever happened since the Israelites left **Egypt!**
1 Sam 2.27 slaves of the **king of Egypt,** I revealed myself to Aaron.
4. 8 They are the gods who slaughtered the **Egyptians** in the desert!
6. 6 stubborn, as the **king of Egypt** and the Egyptians were?
6. 6 be stubborn, as the king of Egypt and the **Egyptians** were?
6. 6 God made fools of them until they let the Israelites leave **Egypt.**
8. 8 I brought them out of **Egypt,** they have turned away from me
10.18 'I brought you out of **Egypt**
10.18 and rescued you from the **Egyptians** and all the other peoples
12. 6 Moses and Aaron and who brought your ancestors out of **Egypt.**
12. 8 his family went to **Egypt** and the Egyptians oppressed them,
12. 8 who brought them out of **Egypt** and settled them in this land.

1 Sam 15. 2 opposed the Israelites when they were coming from **Egypt.**
15. 6 had been kind to the Israelites when they came from **Egypt:**
15. 7 fighting all the way from Havilah to Shur, east of **Egypt;**
27. 8 all the way down to **Egypt,** [9] killing all the men and women
30.11 men with David found an **Egyptian** boy out in the country and
30.13 "I am an **Egyptian,** the slave of an Amalekite," he
2 Sam 7. 6 the people of Israel from **Egypt** until now, I have never
7.23 the people whom you set free from **Egypt** to be your own.
23.21 He also killed an **Egyptian,** a huge man who was armed
23.21 the spear from the **Egyptian's** hand, and killed him with it.
1 Kgs 3. 1 alliance with the **king of Egypt** by marrying his daughter.
4.21 the River Euphrates to Philistia and the **Egyptian** border.
4.30 the wise men of the East or the wise men of **Egypt.**
6. 1 the people of Israel left **Egypt,** during the fourth year of
7. 8 for his wife, the daughter of the **king of Egypt.**
8. 9 with the people of Israel as they were coming from **Egypt.**
8.16 brought my people out of **Egypt,** I have not chosen any city
8.21 Lord made with our ancestors when he brought them out of **Egypt."**
8.51 whom you brought out of **Egypt,** that blazing furnace.
8.53 Moses when you brought our ancestors out of **Egypt."**
8.65 Hamath Pass in the north and the **Egyptian** border in the south.
9. 9 Lord their God, who brought their ancestors out of **Egypt.**
9.16 (The **king of Egypt** had attacked Gezer and captured it,
9.24 daughter of the **king of Egypt,** had moved from David's City
10.29 Musri and Cilicia, [29] and the export of chariots from **Egypt.**
11. 1 the daughter of the **king of Egypt** he married Hittite women
11.17 Hadad and some of his father's Edomite servants, who escaped to **Egypt.**
11.18 Then they travelled to **Egypt** and went to the king, who gave
11.21 the news reached Hadad in **Egypt** that David had died and that
11.40 King Shishak of **Egypt** and stayed there until Solomon's death.
12. 2 who had gone to **Egypt** to escape from King Solomon,
12. 2 heard this news, he returned from **Egypt.**
12.20 that Jeroboam had returned from **Egypt,** they invited him to a
12.28 Israel, here are your gods who brought you out of **Egypt!"**
14.25 Rehoboam's reign King Shishak of **Egypt** attacked Jerusalem.
2 Kgs 7. 6 Israel had hired Hittite and **Egyptian kings** and their armies
17. 4 sent messengers to So, **king of Egypt,** asking for his help,
17. 7 rescued them from the **king of Egypt**
17. 7 and had led them out of **Egypt.**
17.36 who brought you out of **Egypt** with great power and strength;
18.21 You are expecting **Egypt** to help you, but that would be
18.21 That is what the **king of Egypt** is like when anyone relies
18.24 you expect the **Egyptians** to send you chariots and horsemen!
19. 9 reached the Assyrians that the **Egyptian** army, led by King
21.15 the time their ancestors came out of **Egypt** to this day."
23.29 was king, King Neco of **Egypt** led an army to the River
23.29 Josiah tried to stop the **Egyptian** army at Megiddo and was
23.33 ended when King Neco of **Egypt** took him prisoner in Riblah,
23.34 Joahaz was taken to **Egypt** by King Neco, and there he died.
23.35 needed to pay the tribute demanded by the **king of Egypt.**
24. 7 The **king of Egypt** and his army never marched out of Egypt
24. 7 territory that had belonged to **Egypt,**
24. 7 from the River Euphrates to the northern border of **Egypt.**
25.26 officers, left and went to **Egypt,** because they were afraid
1 Chr 1. 8 The sons of Ham—Cush, **Egypt,** Libya, and Canaan—were the
1.11 The descendants of **Egypt** were the people of Lydia, Anam,
2.34 He had an **Egyptian** servant named Jarha, [35] to whom he gave
4.17 a daughter of the **king of Egypt,** and they had a daughter,
11.23 He also killed an **Egyptian,** a huge man over two metres tall,
11.23 the spear from the **Egyptian's** hand, and killed him with it.
13. 5 over the country, from the **Egyptian** border in the south to
17. 5 the people of Israel from **Egypt** until now, I have never
17.21 You rescued your people from **Egypt** and drove out other
2 Chr 1.17 Musri and Cilicia, [17] and the export of chariots from **Egypt.**
5.10 with the people of Israel as they were coming from **Egypt.**
6. 5 brought my people out of **Egypt** until now, I did not choose
7. 8 Hamath Pass in the north and the **Egyptian** border in the south.
7.22 Lord their God, who brought their ancestors out of **Egypt.**
8.11 the daughter of the **king of Egypt,** from David's City
9.26 the River Euphrates to Philistia and the **Egyptian** border.
10. 2 who had gone to **Egypt** to escape from King Solomon, heard
12. 2 King Shishak of **Egypt** attacked Jerusalem [3] with an army of
20.10 our ancestors came out of **Egypt,** you did not allow them to
26. 8 he became so powerful that his fame spread even to **Egypt.**
35.20 the Temple, King Neco of **Egypt** led an army to fight at
35.23 During the battle King Josiah was struck by **Egyptian** arrows.
36. 3 King Neco of **Egypt** took him prisoner and made Judah pay
36. 4 Joahaz was taken to **Egypt** by Neco.
Ezra 9. 1 countries of Ammon, Moab, and **Egypt** or from the Canaanites,
Neh 9. 9 "You saw how our ancestors suffered in **Egypt;**
9.17 they chose a leader to take them back to slavery in **Egypt.**
9.18 bull-calf and said it was the god who led them from **Egypt!**
13. 2 food and water to the Israelites on their way out of **Egypt.**
Ps 68.30 Rebuke **Egypt,** that wild animal in the reeds;
68.31 Ambassadors will come from **Egypt;**
78.12 miracles in the plain of Zoan in the land of **Egypt.**
78.43 and miracles in the plain of Zoan in the land of **Egypt.**
78.44 rivers into blood, and the **Egyptians** had no water to drink.
78.51 He killed the first-born sons of all the families of **Egypt.**
80. 8 You brought a grapevine out of **Egypt;**
81. 5 to the people of Israel when he attacked the land of **Egypt.**
81.10 I am the Lord your God, who brought you out of **Egypt.**
87. 4 "I will include **Egypt** and Babylonia when I list the
105.20 Then the **king of Egypt** had him released;
105.23 Then Jacob went to **Egypt** and settled in that country.
105.25 He made the **Egyptians** hate his people and treat his
105.27 They did God's mighty acts and performed miracles in **Egypt.**
105.28 on the country, but the **Egyptians** did not obey his command.
105.36 He killed the first-born sons of all the families of **Egypt.**
Ps 105.38 The **Egyptians** were afraid of them and were glad when they left.
106. 7 Our ancestors in **Egypt** did not understand God's wonderful acts;
106.21 the God who had saved them by his mighty acts in **Egypt.**
114. 1 the people of Israel left **Egypt,** when Jacob's descendants
135. 8 In **Egypt** he killed all the first-born of men and animals alike.
136.10 He killed the first-born sons of the **Egyptians;**
136.11 He led the people of Israel out of **Egypt;**
136.15 but he drowned the **king of Egypt** and his army;
Prov 7.16 I've covered my bed with sheets of coloured linen from **Egypt.**
Is 7.18 as a signal for the **Egyptians** to come like flies from the
10.24 even though they oppress you as the **Egyptians** used to do.
10.26 I will punish Assyria as I punished **Egypt.**
11.11 are left in Assyria and **Egypt,** in the lands of Pathros,
11.16 just as there was for their ancestors when they left **Egypt.**
19. 1 This is a message about **Egypt.**
19. 1 The Lord is coming to **Egypt,** riding swiftly on a cloud.
19. 1 The **Egyptian** idols tremble before him,
19. 1 and the people of **Egypt** lose their courage.
19. 2 stir up civil war in **Egypt** and turn brother against brother
19. 3 the plans of the **Egyptians** and destroy their morale.
19. 4 I will hand the **Egyptians** over to a tyrant, to a cruel
19.11 **Egypt's** wisest men give stupid advice!
19.12 **King of Egypt,** where are those clever advisers of yours?
19.12 can tell you what plans the Lord Almighty has for **Egypt.**
19.14 As a result, **Egypt** does everything wrong and staggers like a
19.15 No one in **Egypt,** rich or poor, important or unknown, can
19.16 coming when the people of **Egypt** will be as timid as women.
19.17 The people of **Egypt** will be terrified of Judah every
19.18 the Hebrew language will be spoken in five **Egyptian** cities.
19.19 Lord in the land of **Egypt** and a stone pillar
19.19 stone pillar dedicated to him at the **Egyptian** border.
19.20 They will be symbols of the Lord Almighty's presence in **Egypt.**
19.21 will reveal himself to the **Egyptian** people, and then they
19.22 The Lord will punish the **Egyptians,** but then he will heal them.
19.23 comes, there will be a highway between **Egypt** and Assyria.
19.24 comes, Israel will rank with **Egypt** and Assyria, and these
19.25 will bless them and say, "I will bless you, **Egypt,** my
20. 3 This is a sign of what will happen to **Egypt** and Sudan.
20. 4 naked, with their buttocks exposed, bringing shame on **Egypt.**
20. 5 have boasted about **Egypt** will be disillusioned,
23. 3 the corn that grew in **Egypt** and to do business with all
23. 5 Even the **Egyptians** will be shocked and dismayed when they
27.12 from the Euphrates to the **Egyptian** border, the Lord will
27.13 call back from Assyria and **Egypt** all the Israelites who are
30. 2 They go to **Egypt** for help without asking for my advice.
30. 2 They want **Egypt** to protect them,
30. 2 so they put their trust in **Egypt's king.**
30. 3 to help them, and **Egypt's** protection will end in disaster.
30. 4 already arrived at the **Egyptian** cities of Zoan and Hanes,
30. 7 The help that **Egypt** gives is useless.
30. 7 So I have nicknamed **Egypt,** 'The Harmless Dragon.'"
31. 1 Those who go to **Egypt** for help are doomed!
31. 1 They are relying on **Egypt's** vast military strength—horses,
31. 3 The **Egyptians** are not gods—they are only human.
36. 6 You are expecting **Egypt** to help you, but that would be
36. 6 That is what the **king of Egypt** is like when anyone relies
36. 9 you expect the **Egyptians** to send you chariots and cavalry.
37. 9 reached the Assyrians that the **Egyptian** army, led by King
43. 3 I will give up **Egypt** to set you free;
45.14 "The wealth of **Egypt** and Sudan will be yours, and the tall
52. 4 you went to live in **Egypt** as foreigners, you did so of
Jer 2. 6 I rescued them from **Egypt** and led them through the wilderness:
2.18 will gain by going to **Egypt** to drink water from the Nile?
2.36 You will be disappointed by **Egypt,** just as you were by Assyria.
2.37 You will turn away from **Egypt,** hanging your head in shame.
7.22 other kinds of sacrifices, when I brought them out of **Egypt.**
7.25 your ancestors came out of **Egypt** until this very day, I have
9.25 will punish the people of **Egypt,** Judah, Edom, Ammon, Moab,
11. 4 I brought them out of **Egypt,** the land that was like a
11. 7 brought their ancestors out of **Egypt,** I solemnly warned them
16.14 who brought the people of Israel out of the land of **Egypt.**
23. 7 who brought the people of Israel out of the land of **Egypt.**
24. 8 this land or moved to **Egypt**—I, the Lord, will treat them
25.19 the **king of Egypt,** his officials and leaders;
25.19 all the Egyptians and all the foreigners in **Egypt;**
26.21 so he fled in terror and escaped to **Egypt.**
26.22 son of Achbor and some other men to **Egypt** to get Uriah.
31.32 I took them by the hand and led them out of **Egypt.**
32.20 performed miracles and wonders in **Egypt,** and you have
32.21 power and might to bring your people Israel out of **Egypt.**
34.13 I rescued them from **Egypt** and set them free from slavery.
37. 5 when they heard that the **Egyptian** army
37. 5 had crossed the **Egyptian** border, they retreated.
37. 7 to say to Zedekiah, "The **Egyptian** army is on its way to
37.11 from Jerusalem because the **Egyptian** army was approaching.
41.17 So they set out for **Egypt,** in order to get away from
42.13 will go and live in **Egypt,** where we won't face war any
42.13 to go and live in **Egypt,** [16] then the war that you fear
42.16 you dread will follow you, and you will die there in **Egypt.**
42.17 to go and live in **Egypt** will die either in war or
42.18 fury will be poured out on you if you go to **Egypt.**
42.19 you people who are left in Judah not to go to **Egypt.**
43. 2 send you to tell us not to go and live in **Egypt.**
43. 5 left in Judah away to **Egypt,** together with all the people
43. 7 Lord's command and went into **Egypt** as far as the city of
43.11 Nebuchadnezzar will come and defeat **Egypt.**
43.12 fire to the temples of **Egypt's** gods, and the king of
43.12 Babylonia will pick the land of **Egypt** clean
43.13 stone monuments at Heliopolis in **Egypt**
43.13 and will burn down the temples of the **Egyptian** gods."
44. 1 all the Israelites living in **Egypt,** in the cities of Migdol,

Jer	44. 8	to other gods here in **Egypt,** where you have come to live?
	44.12	to go and live in **Egypt,** I will see to it that
	44.12	small, will die in **Egypt,** either in war or of starvation.
	44.13	punish those who live in **Egypt,** just as I punished
	44.14	left and have come to **Egypt** to live will escape or survive.
	44.15	Israelites who lived in southern **Egypt**—a large crowd in
	44.24	Israel, was saying to the people of Judah living in **Egypt:**
	44.26	have made in my mighty name to all you Israelites in **Egypt:**
	44.28	few of you will escape death and return from **Egypt** to Judah.
	44.30	hand over King Hophra of **Egypt** to his enemies who want to
	46. 2	The Lord spoke to me about the nations, [2] beginning with **Egypt.**
	46. 2	army of King Neco of **Egypt,** which King Nebuchadnezzar of
	46. 3	"The **Egyptian** officers shout, 'Get your shields ready
	46. 8	It is **Egypt,** rising like the Nile, like a river flooding
	46. 8	**Egypt** said, 'I will rise and cover the world;
	46.11	People of **Egypt,** go to Gilead and look for medicine!
	46.13	Nebuchadnezzar of Babylonia came to attack **Egypt,**
	46.14	"Proclaim it in the towns of **Egypt,**
	46.17	"Give the **king of Egypt** a new name— 'Noisy
	46.19	Get ready to be taken prisoner, you people of **Egypt!**
	46.20	**Egypt** is like a splendid cow, attacked by a stinging fly
	46.22	**Egypt** runs away, hissing like a snake,
	46.24	The people of **Egypt** are put to shame;
	46.25	god of Thebes, together with **Egypt** and its gods and kings.
	46.25	going to take the **king of Egypt** and all who put their
	46.26	on, people will live in **Egypt** again, as they did in times
	47. 1	Before the **king of Egypt** attacked Gaza, the Lord spoke to
Lam	5. 6	enough to stay alive, we went begging to **Egypt** and Assyria.
Ezek	16.26	your lustful neighbours, the **Egyptians,** go to bed with you,
	17.15	rebelled and sent agents to **Egypt** to get horses and a large
	17.17	powerful army of the **king of Egypt** will not be able
	19. 4	With hooks they dragged him off to **Egypt.**
	20. 5	I revealed myself to them in **Egypt** and told them:
	20. 6	to take them out of **Egypt** and lead them to a land
	20. 7	with the false gods of **Egypt,** because I am the Lord their
	20. 8	away their disgusting idols or give up the **Egyptian** gods.
	20. 8	let them feel the full force of my anger there in **Egypt.**
	20. 9	to Israel that I was going to lead them out of **Egypt.**
	20.10	"And so I led them out of **Egypt** into the desert.
	20.14	the nations which had seen me lead Israel out of **Egypt.**
	20.22	the nations which had seen me bring Israel out of **Egypt.**
	23. 3	they were young, living in **Egypt,** they lost their virginity
	23. 8	as a prostitute in **Egypt,** where she lost her virginity.
	23.19	she did as a girl, when she was a prostitute in **Egypt.**
	23.21	of as a girl in **Egypt,** where men played with your breasts
	23.27	obscenities you have committed ever since you were in **Egypt.**
	23.27	look at any more idols or think about **Egypt** any more."
	27. 7	Embroidered linen from **Egypt,** Easily recognized from afar.
	29. 2	"Mortal man," he said, "denounce the **king of Egypt.**
	29. 2	him how he and all the land of **Egypt** will be punished.
	29. 3	is what the Sovereign Lord is telling the **king of Egypt:**
	29. 6	Then all the people of **Egypt** will know that I am the
	29. 6	"The Israelites relied on you **Egyptians** for support, but
	29. 9	**Egypt** will become an empty waste.
	29.10	I will make all of **Egypt** an empty waste, from the city
	29.12	I will make **Egypt** the most desolate country in the world.
	29.12	forty years the cities of **Egypt** will lie in ruins, ruins
	29.12	I will make the **Egyptians** refugees.
	29.13	years I will bring the **Egyptians** back from the nations where
	29.14	and I will let them live in southern **Egypt,** their original home.
	29.16	**Egypt's** fate will remind Israel how wrong it was to rely on
	29.19	I am giving the land of **Egypt** to King Nebuchadnezzar.
	29.19	and carry off all the wealth of **Egypt** as his army's pay.
	29.20	I am giving him **Egypt** in payment for his services,
	30. 4	There will be war in **Egypt** And great distress in Sudan.
	30. 4	Many in **Egypt** will be killed;
	30. 6	Aswan in the south, all **Egypt's** defenders will be killed in battle.
	30. 6	**Egypt's** proud army will be destroyed.
	30. 8	When I set fire to **Egypt** and all her defenders are killed,
	30. 9	"When that day comes and **Egypt** is destroyed, I will send
	30.10	King Nebuchadnezzar of Babylonia to put an end to **Egypt's** wealth.
	30.11	They will attack **Egypt** with swords, and the land will be
	30.12	up the Nile and put **Egypt** under the power of evil men.
	30.13	no one to rule over **Egypt,** and I will terrify all the
	30.14	I will make southern **Egypt** desolate and set fire to the
	30.15	will let the city of Pelusium, **Egypt's** great fortress, feel
	30.16	I will set fire to **Egypt,** and Pelusium will be in agony.
	30.18	I break the power of **Egypt** and put an end to the
	30.18	A cloud will cover **Egypt,** and the people of all her cities
	30.19	When I punish **Egypt** in this way, they will know that I
	30.21	he said, "I have broken the arm of the **king of Egypt.**
	30.22	I am the enemy of the **king of Egypt.**
	30.23	I am going to scatter the **Egyptians** throughout the world.
	30.24	the arms of the **king of Egypt,** and he will groan
	30.25	and he points it towards **Egypt,** everyone will know that I am
	30.26	I will scatter the **Egyptians** throughout the world.
	31. 2	he said, "say to the **king of Egypt** and all his people:
	31.18	"The tree is the **king of Egypt** and all his people.
	32. 2	he said, "give a solemn warning to the **king of Egypt.**
	32.11	Lord says to the **king of Egypt,** "You will face the sword
	32.15	When I make **Egypt** a desolate waste and destroy all who
	32.16	nations will sing it to mourn for **Egypt** and all its people.
	32.18	"Mortal man," he said, "mourn for all the many people of **Egypt.**
	32.20	"The people of **Egypt** will fall with those who are
	32.21	Egyptian side welcome the **Egyptians** to the world of the dead.
	32.28	"That is how the **Egyptians** will lie crushed among the
	32.31	a comfort to the **king of Egypt** and his army,"
	32.32	"I made the **king of Egypt** terrorize the living,
	47.19	along the **Egyptian** border to the Mediterranean Sea.
	48.28	along the **Egyptian** border to the Mediterranean Sea.

Dan	9.15	people out of **Egypt,** and your power is still remembered.
	11. 5	"The **king of Egypt** will be strong.
	11. 6	number of years the **king of Egypt** will make an alliance
	11. 8	He will carry back to **Egypt** the images of their gods and
	11. 9	king of Syria will invade **Egypt,** but he will be forced to
	11.11	In his anger the **king of Egypt** will go to war
	11.14	Then many people will rebel against the **king of Egypt.**
	11.15	The soldiers of **Egypt** will not continue to fight;
	11.25	army to attack the **king of Egypt,** who will prepare to fight
	11.25	But the **king of Egypt** will be deceived
	11.29	"Later on he will invade **Egypt** again, but this time
	11.40	has almost come, the **king of Egypt** will attack him,
	11.42	When he invades all those countries, even **Egypt** will not be spared.
	11.43	He will take away **Egypt's** hidden treasures of gold and
Hos	2.15	as she did when she was young, when she came from **Egypt.**
	7.11	first her people call on **Egypt** for help, and then they run
	7.16	will die a violent death, and the **Egyptians** will laugh."
	8.13	I will send them back to **Egypt!**
	9. 3	have to go back to **Egypt** and will have to eat forbidden
	9. 6	the people are scattered, the **Egyptians** will gather them
	11. 1	I loved him and called him out of **Egypt** as my son.
	11. 5	so they must return to **Egypt,** and Assyria will rule them.
	11.11	They will come from **Egypt,** as swiftly as birds, and from Assyria,
	12. 1	They make treaties with Assyria and do business with **Egypt."**
	12. 9	who led you out of **Egypt,** I will make you live in
	12.13	of Israel from slavery in **Egypt** and to take care of them.
	13. 4	"I am the Lord your God, who led you out of **Egypt.**
Joel	3.19	**"Egypt** will become a desert, and Edom a ruined waste,
Amos	2.10	I brought you out of **Egypt,** led you through the desert
	3. 1	about you, the entire nation that he brought out of **Egypt;**
	3. 9	Announce to those who live in the palaces of **Egypt** and Ashdod:
	4.10	sent a plague on you like the one I sent on **Egypt.**
	9. 7	and the Syrians from Kir, just as I brought you from **Egypt.**
Mic	6. 4	I brought you out of **Egypt;**
	7.12	Assyria in the east, from **Egypt** in the south, from the
	7.15	you did in the days when you brought us out of **Egypt.**
Nah	3. 8	Nineveh, are you any better than Thebes, the capital of **Egypt?**
	3. 9	She ruled Sudan and **Egypt,** there was no limit to her power;
Hag	2. 5	When you came out of **Egypt,** I promised that I would always
Zech	10.10	From **Egypt** and Assyria I will bring them home and settle
	10.11	and mighty **Egypt** will lose her power.
	14.18	If the **Egyptians** refuse to celebrate the Festival of Shelters,
	14.19	punishment that will fall on **Egypt** and on all the other
Mt	2.13	his mother and escape to **Egypt,** and stay there until I tell
	2.14	left during the night for **Egypt,** [15] where he stayed until
	2.15	the prophet come true, "I called my Son out of **Egypt."**
	2.19	a dream to Joseph in **Egypt** [20] and said, "Get up, take the
Acts	2.10	Phrygia and Pamphylia, from **Egypt** and the regions of Libya near
	7. 9	their brother Joseph and sold him to be a slave in **Egypt.**
	7.10	Joseph appeared before the **king of Egypt,** God gave him a
	7.11	a famine all over **Egypt** and Canaan, which caused much suffering.
	7.12	that there was corn in **Egypt,** he sent his sons, our
	7.13	his brothers, and the **king of Egypt** came to know about
	7.14	the whole family, seventy-five people in all, to come to **Egypt.**
	7.15	Then Jacob went to **Egypt,** where he and his sons died.
	7.17	the number of our people in **Egypt** had grown much larger.
	7.18	king who did not know about Joseph began to rule in **Egypt.**
	7.22	all the wisdom of the **Egyptians** and became a great man in
	7.24	being ill-treated by an **Egyptian,** so he went to his help
	7.24	and took revenge on the **Egyptian** by killing him.
	7.28	to kill me, just as you killed that **Egyptian** yesterday?'
	7.29	heard this, he fled from **Egypt** and went to live in the
	7.34	I have seen the cruel suffering of my people in **Egypt.**
	7.34	I will send you to **Egypt.'**
	7.36	led the people out of **Egypt,** performing miracles
	7.36	and wonders in **Egypt** and at the Red Sea and
	7.39	him aside and wished that they could go back to **Egypt.**
	7.40	happened to that man Moses, who brought us out of **Egypt.'**
	13.17	nation during the time they lived as foreigners in **Egypt.**
	13.17	God brought them out of **Egypt** by his great power,
	21.38	"Then you are not that **Egyptian** fellow who some time ago
Rom	9.17	scripture says to the **king of Egypt,** "I made you king in
Heb	3.16	All those who were led out of **Egypt** by Moses.
	8. 9	I took them by the hand and led them out of **Egypt.**
	11.22	departure of the Israelites from **Egypt,** and leave instructions
	11.26	than all the treasures of **Egypt,** for he kept his eyes on
	11.27	faith that made Moses leave **Egypt** without being afraid
	11.29	the **Egyptians** tried to do it, the water swallowed them up.
Jude	5	the people of Israel from **Egypt,** but afterwards destroyed those
Rev	11. 8	The symbolic name of that city is Sodom, or **Egypt.**

EHUD (1)

Israelite leader in the period before the monarchy.

Judg	3.15	This was **Ehud,** a left-handed man, who was the son of Gera,
	3.15	The people of Israel sent **Ehud** to King Eglon of Moab
	3.16	**Ehud** had made himself a double-edged sword
	3.18	When **Ehud** had given him the gifts, he told the men
	3.19	But **Ehud** himself turned back at the carved stones near Gilgal,
	3.20	cool room on the roof, **Ehud** went over to him and said,
	3.21	With his left hand **Ehud** took the sword from his right
	3.22	**Ehud** did not pull it out of the king's belly, and it
	3.23	Then **Ehud** went outside, closed the doors behind him,
	3.26	**Ehud** got away while they were waiting.
	3.28	So they followed **Ehud** down and captured the place
	4. 1	After **Ehud** died, the people of Israel sinned

EIGHT

Gen	17.11	baby boy when he is **eight** days old, including slaves born in
	21. 4	and when Isaac was **eight** days old, Abraham circumcised him,
	22.20	Abraham learnt that Milcah had borne **eight** children
	22.23	Milcah bore these **eight** sons to Nahor, Abraham's brother.
Ex	22.30	for seven days, and on the **eighth** day offer it to me.
	26.25	So there will be **eight** frames with their sixteen silver bases,
	36.30	So there were **eight** frames and sixteen silver bases, two
Lev	12. 3	On the **eighth** day, the child shall be circumcised.
	14.10	On the **eighth** day he shall bring two male lambs and one
	14.23	On the **eighth** day of his purification he shall bring
	15.14	On the **eighth** day he shall take two doves or two pigeons
	15.29	On the **eighth** day she shall take two doves or two
	23.36	On the **eighth** day come together again for worship and
	25.22	sow your fields in the **eighth** year, you will still be eating
Num	6.10	On the **eighth** day he shall bring two doves or two
	7. 8	and four wagons and **eight** oxen to the Merarites.
	29.29	On the sixth day offer **eight** young bulls, two rams, and
	29.35	On the **eighth** day gather for worship and do no work.
Judg	3. 8	Mesopotamia conquer them, and he ruled over them for **eight** years.
	12.14	Abdon led Israel for **eight** years, [15]then he died and was
1 Sam	17.12	Jesse had **eight** sons, and at the time Saul was king, he
1 Kgs	6.38	In the **eighth** month, the month of Bul, in the eleventh
	8.66	On the **eighth** day Solomon sent the people home.
	12.32	day of the **eighth** month, like the festival in Judah.
	12.33	the fifteenth day of the **eighth** month, the day that he
2 Kgs	8.17	of thirty-two, and he ruled in Jerusalem for **eight** years.
	22. 1	Josiah was **eight** years old when he became king of Judah,
	24.12	In the **eighth** year of Nebuchadnezzar's reign he took
	25.17	one was **eight** metres high, with a bronze capital on top,
1 Chr	24. 4	while the descendants of Ithamar were organized into **eight;**
	26. 4	God blessed by giving him **eight** sons, listed in order of age:
	27. 2	**Eighth** month:
2 Chr	21. 5	of thirty-two, and he ruled in Jerusalem for **eight** years.
	21.20	of thirty-two and had ruled in Jerusalem for **eight** years.
	29.17	first month, and by the **eighth** day they had finished it all,
	29.17	they worked for the next **eight** days, until the sixteenth of
	34. 1	Josiah was **eight** years old when he became king of Judah,
	34. 3	In the **eighth** year that Josiah was king, while he was
Neh	8.18	days, and on the **eighth** day there was a closing ceremony,
Is	5.10	ten hectares of land will yield only **eight** litres of wine.
Jer	41.15	But Ishmael and **eight** of his men got away from Johanan
Ezek	40.31	**Eight** steps led up to this gate.
	40.34	**Eight** steps led up to this gate.
	40.37	**Eight** steps led up to this gate.
	40.41	Altogether there were **eight** tables on which the animals
Zech	1. 1	In the **eighth** month of the second year that Darius was
Acts	9.33	had not been able to get out of bed for **eight** years.
	25. 6	Festus spent another **eight** or ten days with them and then
1 Pet	3.20	few people in the boat—**eight** in all—were saved by the
Rev	17.11	no longer, is itself an **eighth** king who is one of the
	21.20	the seventh yellow quartz, the **eighth** beryl, the ninth topaz,
	also	Num 7.12 1 Kgs 7.15 1 Chr 24.7 1 Chr 25.9 Neh 7.70 Jer 52.21

EKRON

One of the five chief cities of the Philistines.

Josh	13. 3	far north as the border of **Ekron** was considered Canaanite;
	13. 3	Philistines lived at Gaza, Ashdod, Ashkelon, Gath, and **Ekron.)**
	15.11	north of **Ekron,** turned towards Shikkeron, past Mount Baalah,
	15.45	There was **Ekron** with its towns and villages,
	15.46	and towns near Ashdod, from **Ekron** to the Mediterranean Sea.
	19.43	Shaalbim, Aijalon, Ithlah, [43]Elon, Timnah, **Ekron,**
Judg	1.18	Ashkelon, or **Ekron,** with their surrounding territories.
1 Sam	5.10	So they sent the Covenant Box to **Ekron,** another Philistine city;
	6.16	them do this and then went back to **Ekron** that same day.
	6.17	for the cities of Ashdod, Gaza, Ashkelon, Gath, and **Ekron.**
	7.14	captured between **Ekron** and Gath were returned to Israel,
	17.52	them all the way to Gath and to the gates of **Ekron.**
	17.52	the road that leads to Shaaraim, as far as Gath and **Ekron.**
2 Kgs	1. 2	of the Philistine city of **Ekron,** in order to find out
	1. 3	"Why are you going to consult Baalzebub, the god of **Ekron?**
	1. 6	'Why are you sending messengers to consult Baalzebub, the god of **Ekron?**
	1.16	consult Baalzebub, the god of **Ekron**—as if there were no god
Jer	25.19	cities of Ashkelon, Gaza, **Ekron,** and what remains of Ashdod;
Amos	1. 8	will punish the city of **Ekron,** and all the Philistines
Zeph	2. 4	day, and the people of **Ekron** will be driven from their city.
Zech	9. 5	So will **Ekron,** and her hopes will be shattered.
	9. 7	**Ekron** will become part of my people, as the Jebusites did.

ELAM (1)

A country s.e. of Mesopotamia, inhabited by descendants of Shem's son.

Gen	10.22	Shem's sons—**Elam,** Asshur, Arpachshad, Lud, and Aram—
	14. 1	Arioch of Ellasar, Chedorlaomer of **Elam,** and Tidal of Goiim,
	14. 9	fought [9]against the kings of **Elam,** Goiim, Babylonia, and
1 Chr	1.17	Shem's sons—**Elam,** Asshur, Arpachshad, Lud, Aram, Uz,
Ezra	4. 9	Susa in the land of **Elam,** [10]together with the other
Is	11.11	the lands of Pathros, Sudan, **Elam,** Babylonia, and Hamath,
	21. 2	Army of **Elam,** attack!
	22. 6	soldiers from the land of **Elam** came riding on horseback,
Jer	25.19	all the kings of Zimri, **Elam,** and Media;
	49.34	the Lord Almighty spoke to me about the country of **Elam.**
	49.35	"I will kill all the bowmen who have made **Elam** so powerful.
	49.36	will make winds blow against **Elam** from all directions,
	49.37	will make the people of **Elam** afraid of their enemies,
	49.37	will destroy the people of **Elam** and send armies against them
Jer	49.39	But later on I will make the people of **Elam** prosperous again.
Ezek	32.24	**"Elam** is there, with the graves of her soldiers all around.
	32.25	**Elam** lies down among those killed in battle, and the
Dan	8. 2	myself in the walled city of Susa in the province of **Elam.**
Acts	2. 9	We are from Parthia, Media, and **Elam;**

ELDER (1)

Gen	10.15	Canaan's sons—Sidon, the **eldest,** and Heth—
	10.21	Shem, the **elder** brother of Japheth, was the ancestor of
	19.31	The **elder** daughter said to her sister, "Our father is getting old,
	19.33	to drink, and the **elder** daughter had intercourse with him.
	19.34	The next day the **elder** daughter said to her sister,
	19.37	The **elder** daughter had a son, whom she named Moab.
	27. 1	He sent for his **elder** son Esau and said to him,
	27.19	Jacob answered, "I am your **elder** son Esau;
	27.32	"Your **elder** son Esau," he answered.
	29.16	the **elder** was named Leah, and the younger Rachel.
	29.26	to give the younger daughter in marriage before the **elder.**
	35.23	of Leah were Reuben (Jacob's **eldest** son), Simeon, Levi,
	43.33	in the order of their age from the **eldest** to the youngest.
	44.12	beginning with the **eldest** and ending with the youngest,
	46. 8	Egypt with him were his **eldest** son Reuben [9]and Reuben's sons:
	48.14	his left hand on the head of Manasseh, who was the **elder.**
	48.18	This is the **elder** boy;
Num	1.20	beginning with the tribe of Reuben, Jacob's **eldest** son.
	3. 2	Nadab, the **eldest,** Abihu, Eleazar, and Ithamar.
	3.12	consecrated as my own the **eldest** son of each Israelite
	8.17	consecrated as my own the **eldest** son of each Israelite
	26. 5	The tribe of Reuben (Reuben was the **eldest** son of Jacob):
Josh	6.26	Whoever lays the foundation will lose his **eldest** son;
	17. 1	of the families descended from Joseph's **elder** son Manasseh.
	17. 1	of Gilead, was Manasseh's **eldest** son and a military hero,
Judg	8.20	Then he said to Jether, his **eldest** son, "Go ahead, kill
1 Sam	8. 2	The **elder** son was named Joel and the younger one Abijah;
	14.49	His **elder** daughter was named Merab, and the younger one Michal.
	17.13	His three **eldest** sons had gone with Saul to war.
	17.13	The **eldest** was Eliab, the next was Abinadab, and the third
	17.14	son, and while the three **eldest** brothers stayed with Saul,
	17.28	Eliab, David's **eldest** brother, heard David talking to the men.
	18.17	Then Saul said to David, "Here is my **elder** daughter Merab.
1 Kgs	1. 5	the son of David and Haggith, was the **eldest** surviving son.
	2.22	After all, he is my **elder** brother, and Abiathar the priest
	16.34	of Nun, Hiel lost his **eldest** son Abiram when he laid the
2 Kgs	3.27	So he took his **eldest** son, who was to succeed him as
1 Chr	1.13	Canaan's sons—Sidon, the **eldest,** and Heth—were the
	1.29	(from the name of Ishmael's **eldest** son), Kedar, Adbeel,
	2. 3	His **eldest** son, Er, was so evil that the Lord killed him.
	2.25	Jerahmeel, the **eldest** son of Hezron, had five sons:
	2.25	Ram, the **eldest,** Bunah, Oren, Ozem, and Ahijah.
	2.42	The **eldest** son of Caleb, Jerahmeel's brother, was named Mesha.
	2.50	Hur was the **eldest** son of Caleb and his wife Ephrath.
	4. 3	Hur was the **eldest** son of his father Caleb's wife Ephrath,
	5. 1	These are the descendants of Reuben, the **eldest** of Jacob's sons.
	5. 3	Reuben, the **eldest** of Jacob's sons, had four sons:
	6.28	Joel, the **elder,** and Abijah, the younger.
	8.30	His wife was named Maacah, [30]and his **eldest** son, Abdon.
	9.31	A Levite named Mattithiah, **eldest** son of Shallum, of
	9.36	His **eldest** son was Abdon, and his other sons were Zur,
	23.13	His **eldest** son, Amram, was the father of Aaron and Moses.
	26. 6	Obed Edom's **eldest** son, Shemaiah, had six sons:
	26.10	even though he was not the **eldest** son), [11]Hilkiah,
2 Chr	21. 3	because Jehoram was the **eldest,** Jehoshaphat made him his successor.
Job	1.13	at the home of their **eldest** brother, [14]a messenger came
	1.18	at the home of your **eldest** son, [19]when a storm swept in
	42.14	He called the **eldest** daughter Jemimah, the second Keziah,
Is	3. 5	people will not respect their **elders,** and worthless people
Jer	31. 9	am like a father to Israel, and Ephraim is my **eldest** son."
Ezek	16.46	"Your **elder** sister is Samaria, in the north, with her villages.
	16.61	when you get your **elder** sister and your younger sister back.
Mt	21.28	He went to the **elder** one and said, 'Son, go and work
	21.31	"The **elder** one," they answered.
	22.25	The **eldest** got married and died without having children,
Mk	12.20	the **eldest** got married and died without having children.
Lk	15.25	"In the meantime the **elder** son was out in the field.
	15.28	"The **elder** brother was so angry that he would not go
	20.29	the **eldest** got married and died without having children.
Rom	9.11	God said to her, "The **elder** will serve the younger."
Heb	12.16	who for a single meal sold his rights as the **elder** son.

ELDER (2)

In the Old Testament this is a name given to certain respected leaders of a tribe, nation, or city. In the New Testament three different groups are called elders: (1) in the Gospels the elders are important Jewish religious leaders, some of whom were members of their highest Council; (2) in Acts 11-21 and the Letters, the elders are Christian church officers who were responsible for the work of the church; (3) in Revelation the twenty-four elders are part of God's court in heaven, perhaps as representatives of God's people.

Josh	23. 2	he called all Israel, the **elders,** leaders, judges, and
	24. 1	He called the **elders,** the leaders, the judges, and the
2 Kgs	6.32	Elisha was at home with some **elders** who were visiting him.
	6.32	arrived, Elisha said to the **elders,** "That murderer is
Job	29. 7	Whenever the city **elders** met and I took my place among them,
Is	3.14	The Lord is bringing the **elders** and leaders of his
Jer	19. 1	to take some of the **elders** of the people and some of
	26.17	After that, some of the **elders** stood up and said to the

Ezek 7.26 the people, and the **elders** will have no advice to give.
Mt 16.21 suffer much from the **elders,** the chief priests, and the teachers
21.23 the chief priests and the **elders** came to him and asked,
26. 3 the chief priests and the **elders** met together in the palace
26.47 and clubs and sent by the chief priests and the **elders.**
26.57 the teachers of the Law and the **elders** had gathered together.
27. 1 the chief priests and the **elders** made their plans against Jesus
27. 3 the thirty silver coins to the chief priests and the **elders.**
27.12 in response to the accusations of the chief priests and **elders.**
27.20 chief priests and the **elders** persuaded the crowd to ask Pilate
27.41 and the teachers of the Law and the **elders** jeered at him:
28.12 The chief priests met with the **elders** and made their plan;
Mk 8.31 be rejected by the **elders,** the chief priests, and the teachers
11.27 of the Law, and the **elders** came to him [28]and asked him,
14.43 the chief priests, the teachers of the Law, and the **elders.**
14.53 all the chief priests, the **elders,** and the teachers of the
15. 1 priests met hurriedly with the **elders,** the teachers of the Law,
Lk 7. 3 Jesus, he sent some Jewish **elders** to ask him to come and
9.22 be rejected by the **elders,** the chief priests, and the teachers
20. 1 together with the **elders,** came [2]and said to him, "Tell
22.52 the temple guard and the **elders** who had come there to get
22.66 When day came, the **elders,** the chief priests, and the
Acts 4. 5 day the Jewish leaders, the **elders,** and the teachers of the
4. 8 Holy Spirit, answered them, "Leaders of the people and **elders:**
4.23 told them what the chief priests and the **elders** had said.
5.21 called together all the Jewish **elders** for a full meeting of
6.12 up the people, the **elders,** and the teachers of the Law.
11.30 sent the money to the church **elders** by Barnabas and Saul.
14.23 In each church they appointed **elders,** and with prayers and
15. 2 to Jerusalem and see the apostles and **elders** about this matter.
15. 4 church, the apostles, and the **elders,** to whom they told all
15. 6 apostles and the **elders** met together to consider this question.
15.22 apostles and the **elders,** together with the whole church, decided
15.23 "We, the apostles and the **elders,** your brothers, send greetings
16. 4 upon by the apostles and **elders** in Jerusalem, and told them
20.17 to Ephesus, asking the **elders** of the church to meet him.
21.18 and all the church **elders** were present.
23.14 to the chief priests and **elders** and said, "We have taken a
24. 1 Ananias went to Caesarea with some **elders** and a lawyer named
25.15 the Jewish chief priests and **elders** brought charges against him
1 Tim 4.14 the prophets spoke and the **elders** laid their hands on you.
5.17 **elders** who do good work as leaders should be considered worthy
5.19 to an accusation against an **elder** unless it is brought by
Tit 1. 5 that still needed doing and appoint church **elders** in every town.
1. 6 an **elder** must be blameless;
Jas 5.14 should send for the church **elders,** who will pray for him
1 Pet 5. 1 am an elder myself, appeal to the church **elders** among you.
Rev 4. 4 on which were seated twenty-four **elders** dressed in white and
4.10 the twenty-four **elders** fall down before the one who
5. 5 Then one of the **elders** said to me, "Don't cry.
5. 6 throne, surrounded by the four living creatures and the **elders.**
5. 8 creatures and the twenty-four **elders** fell down before the Lamb.
5.11 living creatures, and the **elders,** [12]and sang in a loud voice:
5.14 And the **elders** fell down and worshipped.
7.11 angels stood round the throne, the **elders,** and the four living
7.13 One of the **elders** asked me, "Who are these people
11.16 Then the twenty-four **elders** who sit on their thrones in front
14. 3 before the throne, the four living creatures, and the **elders;**
19. 4 The twenty-four **elders** and the four living creatures fell down

ELDER (3)

2 Jn 1 From the **Elder**— To the dear Lady and to her children,
3 Jn 1 From the **Elder**— To my dear Gaius, whom I truly love.

ELEAZAR (1)

Aaron's son and his successor as priest.

Ex 6.23 she bore him Nadab, Abihu, **Eleazar,** and Ithamar.
6.25 **Eleazar,** Aaron's son, married one of Putiel's daughters,
28. 1 "Summon your brother Aaron and his sons, Nadab, Abihu, **Eleazar,**
Lev 10. 6 Aaron and to his sons **Eleazar** and Ithamar, "Do not leave
10.12 and his two remaining sons, **Eleazar** and Ithamar, "Take the
10.16 This made him angry with **Eleazar** and Ithamar, and he demanded,
Num 3. 2 Nadab, the eldest, Abihu, **Eleazar,** and Ithamar.
3. 4 They had no children, so **Eleazar** and Ithamar served as
3.32 The chief of the Levites was **Eleazar** son of Aaron the priest.
4.16 **Eleazar** son of Aaron the priest shall be responsible for
16.37 Lord said to Moses, [37]"Tell **Eleazar** son of Aaron the
16.39 So **Eleazar** the priest took the firepans and had them
16.40 All this was done as the Lord had commanded **Eleazar** through Moses.
19. 3 put to work, [3]and they will give it to **Eleazar** the priest.
19. 4 Then **Eleazar** is to take some of its blood and with his
20.25 Take Aaron and his son **Eleazar** up Mount Hor,
20.26 and there remove Aaron's priestly robes and put them on **Eleazar.**
20.28 and Moses removed Aaron's priestly robes and put them on **Eleazar.**
20.28 mountain Aaron died, and Moses and **Eleazar** came back down.
25. 7 When Phinehas, the son of **Eleazar** and grandson of Aaron the priest,
26. 1 Lord said to Moses and **Eleazar** son of Aaron, [2]"Take a
26. 3 Moses and **Eleazar** obeyed, and called together all the
26.60 Aaron had four sons, Nadab, Abihu, **Eleazar,** and Ithamar.
26.63 were listed by Moses and **Eleazar** when they took a census of
27. 2 went and stood before Moses, **Eleazar** the priest, the
27.19 in front of **Eleazar** the priest and the whole community,
27.21 He will depend on **Eleazar** the priest, who will learn my
27.21 In this way **Eleazar** will direct Joshua and the whole
Num 27.22 He made Joshua stand before **Eleazar** the priest
31. 6 command of Phinehas son of **Eleazar** the priest, who took
31.12 brought them to Moses and **Eleazar** and to the community of
31.13 Moses, **Eleazar,** and all the other leaders of the
31.21 **Eleazar** the priest said to the men who had returned from battle,
31.26 said to Moses, [26]"You and **Eleazar,** together with the
31.29 Give them to **Eleazar** the priest as a special
31.31 Moses and **Eleazar** did what the Lord commanded.
31.41 So Moses gave **Eleazar** the tax as a special contribution
31.51 Moses and **Eleazar** received the gold, all of which was in
31.54 So Moses and **Eleazar** took the gold to the Tent, so that
32. 2 cattle, [2]they went to Moses, **Eleazar,** and the other leaders
32.28 Moses gave these commands to **Eleazar,** Joshua, and the other
34.17 The Lord said to Moses, [17]**"Eleazar** the priest and
Deut 10. 6 and was buried, and his son **Eleazar** succeeded him as priest.
Josh 14. 1 **Eleazar** the priest, Joshua son of Nun, and the leaders of
17. 4 They went to **Eleazar** the priest and to Joshua son of Nun
19.51 **Eleazar** the priest, Joshua son of Nun, and the leaders
21. 1 Levite families went to **Eleazar** the priest, Joshua son of Nun,
22.13 sent Phinehas, the son of **Eleazar** the priest, to the people
22.31 Phinehas, the son of **Eleazar** the priest, said to them,
24.33 **Eleazar** son of Aaron died and was buried at Gibeah, the
Judg 20.27 and Phinehas, the son of **Eleazar** and grandson of Aaron, was
1 Chr 6. 3 Nadab, Abihu, **Eleazar,** and Ithamar.
6. 4 The descendants of **Eleazar** from generation to generation
6.50 **Eleazar,** Phinehas, Abishua, [51]Bukki, Uzzi, Zerahiah,
9.20 Phineas son of **Eleazar**—may the Lord be with him!—
24. 1 Nadab, Abihu, **Eleazar,** and Ithamar.
24. 2 so their brothers **Eleazar** and Ithamar became priests.
24. 3 by Zadok, a descendant of **Eleazar,** and by Ahimelech, a
24. 4 The descendants of **Eleazar** were organized into sixteen groups,
24. 4 male heads of families among the descendants of **Eleazar.**
24. 5 among the descendants of both **Eleazar** and Ithamar,
24. 6 The descendants of **Eleazar** and of Ithamar took turns
Ezra 7. 5 son of Abishua, son of Phinehas, son of **Eleazar,** son of

AV ELECT see GOD'S PEOPLE

AV ELECTION see CHOICE, CHOOSE

ELEVEN

Gen 32.22 and his **eleven** children, and crossed the River Jabbok.
37. 9 the sun, the moon, and **eleven** stars bowing down to me."
Ex 26. 7 for the Tent out of **eleven** pieces of cloth made of goats'
36.14 for the Tent out of **eleven** pieces of cloth made of goats'
Num 29.20 On the third day offer **eleven** young bulls, two rams, and
Deut 1. 2 (It takes **eleven** days to travel from Mount Sinai to Kadesh
1. 3 the first day of the **eleventh** month of the fortieth year
Josh 15.51 **eleven** cities, along with the towns round them.
1 Kgs 6.38 month of Bul, in the **eleventh** year of Solomon's reign, the
19.19 there were **eleven** teams ahead of him, and he was ploughing
2 Kgs 9.29 king of Judah in the **eleventh** year that Joram son of Ahab
23.36 king of Judah, and he ruled in Jerusalem for **eleven** years.
24.18 king of Judah, and he ruled in Jerusalem for **eleven** years.
25. 2 and kept it under siege until Zedekiah's **eleventh** year.
1 Chr 27. 2 **Eleventh** month:
2 Chr 36. 5 king of Judah, and he ruled in Jerusalem for **eleven** years.
36.11 king of Judah, and he ruled in Jerusalem for **eleven** years.
Jer 1. 3 until the **eleventh** year of the reign of Zedekiah
39. 2 the fourth month of Zedekiah's **eleventh** year as king, the
52. 1 king of Judah, and he ruled in Jerusalem for **eleven** years.
52. 5 and kept it under siege until Zedekiah's **eleventh** year.
Ezek 26. 1 month of the **eleventh** year of our exile, the Lord spoke to
30.20 the first month of the **eleventh** year of our exile, the Lord
31. 1 the third month of the **eleventh** year of our exile, the Lord
Zech 1. 7 day of the **eleventh** month (the month of Shebat),
Mt 28.16 The **eleven** disciples went to the hill in Galilee where Jesus
Mk 16.14 Jesus appeared to the **eleven** disciples as they were eating.
Lk 24. 9 all these things to the **eleven** disciples and all the rest.
24.13 a village named Emmaus, about **eleven** kilometres from Jerusalem,
24.33 found the **eleven** disciples gathered together with the others
Acts 1.26 was Matthias, who was added to the group of **eleven** apostles.
2.14 stood up with the other **eleven** apostles and in a loud voice
Rev 21.20 tenth chalcedony, the **eleventh** turquoise, the twelfth amethyst.
also Num 7.12 1 Chr 24.7 1 Chr 25.9

ELI (1)

Priest and civil leader in the period preceding the monarchy.

1 Sam 1. 3 and Phinehas, the two sons of **Eli,** were priests of the Lord.
1. 9 **Eli** the priest was sitting in his place by the door.
1.12 to the Lord for a long time, and **Eli** watched her lips.
1.13 So **Eli** thought that she was drunk, [14]and said to her,
1.17 "Go in peace," **Eli** said, "and may the God of Israel
1.25 After they had killed the bull, they took the child to **Eli.**
2.11 Samuel stayed in Shiloh and served the Lord under the priest **Eli.**
2.12 The sons of **Eli** were scoundrels.
2.17 sin of the sons of **Eli** was extremely serious in the Lord's
2.20 Then **Eli** would bless Elkanah and his wife, and say to Elkanah,
2.22 **Eli** was now very old.
2.27 A prophet came to **Eli** with this message from the Lord:
2.29 Why, **Eli,** do you honour your sons more than me by letting
3. 1 Lord under the direction of **Eli,** there were very few
3. 2 One night **Eli,** who was now almost blind, was sleeping in
3. 5 and ran to **Eli** and said, "You called me, and here I
3. 5 But **Eli** answered, "I didn't call you;
3. 6 he got up, went to **Eli,** and said, "You called me, and

1 Sam 3. 6 But **Eli** answered, "My son, I didn't call you;
3. 8 he got up, went to **Eli**, and said, "You called me, and
3. 8 Then **Eli** realized that it was the Lord who was calling the
3.12 all my threats against **Eli's** family, from beginning to end.
3.13 **Eli** knew they were doing this, but he did not stop them.
3.14 declare to the family of **Eli** that no sacrifice or offering
3.15 He was afraid to tell **Eli** about the vision.
3.16 **Eli** called him, "Samuel, my boy!"
3.17 **Eli** asked.
3.18 **Eli** said, "He is the Lord;
4. 4 And **Eli's** two sons, Hophni and Phinehas, came along with the
4.11 Covenant Box was captured, and **Eli's** sons, Hophni and Phinehas,
4.13 **Eli**, who was very anxious about the Covenant Box, was
4.14 **Eli** heard the noise and asked, "What is all this noise about?"
4.14 The man hurried to **Eli** to tell him the news.
4.15 (**Eli** was now ninety-eight years old and almost completely blind.)
4.16 **Eli** asked him, "What happened, my son?"
4.18 man mentioned the Covenant Box, **Eli** fell backwards from his
4.19 **Eli's** daughter-in-law, the wife of Phinehas, was
14. 3 of Phinehas and grandson of **Eli**, the priest of the Lord in
1 Kgs 2.27 Shiloh about the priest **Eli** and his descendants come true.

ELI (2)
see also **ELOI**

Mt 27.46 Jesus cried out with a loud shout, **"Eli, Eli, lema sabachthani?"**

ELIASHIB (1)
A High Priest.

Ezra 10. 6 living-quarters of Jehohanan son of **Eliashib**, and spent the
Neh 3. 1 The High Priest **Eliashib** and his fellow-priests rebuilt the Sheep Gate,
3.20 as the entrance to the house of the High Priest **Eliashib;**
3.21 the next section, up to the far end of **Eliashib's** house.
12.10 Joiakim was the father of **Eliashib;**
12.10 **Eliashib** was the father of Joiada;
12.23 only until the time of Jonathan, the grandson of **Eliashib.**
13. 4 The priest **Eliashib**, who was in charge of the temple storerooms,
13. 7 was shocked to find that **Eliashib** had allowed Tobiah to use
13.28 Joiada was the son of **Eliashib** the High Priest, but one

ELIJAH (1)
One of the earliest prophets, who strongly supported the traditional faith of Israel against Canaanite religion.

1 Kgs 17.1-7 **Elijah and the drought**
8-24 **Elijah and the widow in Zarephath**
18.1-40 **Elijah and the prophets of Baal**
41-46 **The end of the drought**
19.1-18 **Elijah on Mount Sinai**
19-21 **The call of Elisha**
21.1-29 **Naboth's vineyard**
2 Kgs 1.1-18 **Elijah and King Ahaziah**
2.1-18 **Elijah is taken up to heaven**

2 Kgs 3.11 He was **Elijah's** assistant."
9.36 Lord said would happen, when he spoke through his servant **Elijah:**
10.10 The Lord has done what he promised through his prophet **Elijah."**
10.17 This is what the Lord had told **Elijah** would happen.
2 Chr 21.12 The prophet **Elijah** sent Jehoram a letter, which read as follows:
Mal 4. 5 day of the Lord comes, I will send you the prophet **Elijah.**
Mt 11.14 their message, John is **Elijah,** whose coming was predicted.
16.14 say **Elijah,** while others say Jeremiah or some other prophet."
17. 3 the three disciples saw Moses and **Elijah** talking with Jesus.
17. 4 here, one for you, one for Moses, and one for **Elijah."**
17.10 the teachers of the Law say that **Elijah** has to come first?"
17.11 **"Elijah** is indeed coming first," answered Jesus,
17.12 But I tell you that **Elijah** has already come and people
27.47 standing there heard him and said, "He is calling for **Elijah!"**
27.49 said, "Wait, let us see if **Elijah** is coming to save him!"
Mk 6.15 Others, however, said, "He is **Elijah."**
8.28 "others say that you are **Elijah,** while others say that you
9. 4 the three disciples saw **Elijah** and Moses talking with Jesus.
9. 5 tents, one for you, one for Moses, and one for **Elijah."**
9.11 the teachers of the Law say that **Elijah** has to come first?"
9.12 His answer was, **"Elijah** is indeed coming first in order to
9.13 I tell you, however, that **Elijah** has already come and that
15.35 heard him and said, "Listen, he is calling for **Elijah!"**
15.36 Let us see if **Elijah** is coming to bring him down from
Lk 1.17 of the Lord, strong and mighty like the prophet **Elijah.**
4.25 Israel during the time of **Elijah,** when there was no rain for
4.26 Yet **Elijah** was not sent to anyone in Israel, but only to
9. 8 Others were saying that **Elijah** had appeared,
9.19 "Others say that you are **Elijah,** while others say that one
9.30 They were Moses and **Elijah,** [31] who appeared in heavenly glory
9.33 tents, one for you, one for Moses, and one for **Elijah."**
Jn 1.21 "Are you **Elijah?"**
1.25 are not the Messiah nor **Elijah** nor the Prophet, why do you
Rom 11. 2 says in the passage where **Elijah** pleads with God against Israel:
Jas 5.17 **Elijah** was the same kind of person as we are.

ELISHA
Elijah's successor, who took an active part as a prophet in the politics of the n. kingdom (Israel).

1 Kgs 19.1-18 **Elijah on Mount Sinai**
19-21 **The call of Elisha**
2 Kgs 2.1-18 **Elijah is taken up to heaven**
19-25 **Miracles of Elisha**
3.1-27 **War between Israel and Moab**

2 Kgs 4.1-7 **Elisha helps a poor widow**
8-37 **Elisha and the rich woman from Shunem**
38-44 **Two more miracles**
5.1-27 **Naaman is cured**
6.1-7 **The recovery of the axe-head**
8-23 **The Syrian army is defeated**
6.24–7.2 **The siege of Samaria**
7.3-20 **The Syrian army leaves**
8.1-6 **The woman from Shunem returns**
7-15 **Elisha and King Benhadad of Syria**
9.1-13 **Jehu is anointed king of Israel**
13.14-21 **The death of Elisha**
Lk 4.27 who lived in Israel during the time of the prophet **Elisha;**

ELIZABETH
Wife of Zechariah (1) and mother of John the Baptist.

Lk 1. 5 His wife's name was **Elizabeth;**
1. 7 They had no children because **Elizabeth** could not have any,
1.13 your prayer, and your wife **Elizabeth** will bear you a son.
1.24 Some time later his wife **Elizabeth** became pregnant
1.26 In the sixth month of **Elizabeth's** pregnancy God sent the angel
1.36 Remember your relative **Elizabeth.**
1.40 She went into Zechariah's house and greeted **Elizabeth.**
1.41 **Elizabeth** heard Mary's greeting, the baby moved within her.
1.41 **Elizabeth** was filled with the Holy Spirit
1.56 Mary stayed about three months with **Elizabeth**
1.57 The time came for **Elizabeth** to have her baby,

ELKANAH (1)
Samuel's father.

1 Sam 1. 1 There was a man named **Elkanah,** from the tribe of Ephraim,
1. 2 **Elkanah** had two wives, Hannah and Peninnah.
1. 3 Every year **Elkanah** went from Ramah to worship
1. 4 Each time **Elkanah** offered his sacrifice, he would give one
1. 8 Her husband **Elkanah** would ask her, "Hannah, why are you crying?
1.19 The next morning **Elkanah** and his family got up early,
1.19 **Elkanah** had intercourse with his wife Hannah,
1.21 The time came again for **Elkanah** and his family to go
1.23 **Elkanah** answered, "All right, do whatever you think best;
2.11 Then **Elkanah** went back home to Ramah,
2.20 Then Eli would bless **Elkanah** and his wife,
2.20 and say to **Elkanah,** "May the Lord give you other
1 Chr 6.27 Eliab, Jeroham, **Elkanah.**
6.34 Heman, Joel, Samuel, [34] **Elkanah,** Jeroham, Eliel, Toah,

ELOI
see also **ELI (2)**

Mk 15.34 Jesus cried out with a loud shout, **"Eloi, Eloi, lema sabachthani?"**

ELOQUENT

Ps 45. 2 you are an **eloquent** speaker.
Lk 4.22 impressed with him and marvelled at the **eloquent** words
Acts 18.24 He was an **eloquent** speaker and had a thorough knowledge

ELUL
The sixth month of the Hebrew calendar.

Neh 6.15 was finished on the twenty-fifth day of the month of **Elul.**

EMBALM

Gen 50. 2 Then Joseph gave orders to **embalm** his father's body.
50. 3 It took forty days, the normal time for **embalming.**
50.26 They **embalmed** his body and put it in a coffin.

EMBARRASS

Gen 2.25 the woman were both naked, but they were not **embarrassed.**
Esth 6.12 Haman hurried home, covering his face in **embarrassment.**
Lk 14. 9 Then you would be **embarrassed** and have to sit in the lowest

EMBERS

Prov 26.21 Charcoal keeps the **embers** glowing, wood keeps the fire burning,
Is 44.19 baked some bread on the **embers** and I roasted meat and ate

EMBRACE

Gen 45.15 Then, still weeping, he **embraced** each of his brothers
Ps 85.10 righteousness and peace will **embrace.**
Prov 4. 8 **Embrace** her, and she will bring you honour.

EMBROIDER

Ex 26. 1 **Embroider** them with figures of winged creatures.
26.31 **Embroider** it with figures of winged creatures.
26.36 blue, purple, and red wool and decorated with **embroidery.**
27.16 blue, purple, and red wool, and decorated with **embroidery.**
28. 4 an ephod, a robe, an **embroidered** shirt, a turban, and a
28. 6 gold thread, and fine linen, decorated with **embroidery.**
28.15 the same materials as the ephod and with similar **embroidery.**
28.39 of fine linen and also a sash decorated with **embroidery.**
36. 8 red wool and **embroidered** with figures of winged creatures.
36.35 wool and **embroidered** it with figures of winged creatures.
36.37 blue, purple, and red wool and decorated with **embroidery.**

Ex 38.18 blue, purple, and red wool and decorated with **embroidery.**
39. 8 the same materials as the ephod and with similar **embroidery.**
39.29 decorated with **embroidery,** as the Lord had commanded Moses.
Judg 5.30 soldier, rich cloth for Sisera, **embroidered** pieces for the
Song 3.10 over it is cloth **embroidered** with gold.
Ezek 16.10 I dressed you in **embroidered** gowns and gave you shoes of
16.13 and you always wore clothes of **embroidered** linen and silk.
16.18 You took the **embroidered** clothes I gave you and put them
26.16 off their robes and their **embroidered** clothes and sit
27. 7 sails were made of linen, **Embroidered** linen from Egypt,
27.16 They gave emeralds, purple cloth, **embroidery,** fine linen,
27.24 purple cloth, and **embroidery,** brightly coloured carpets,

EMERALD

Ex 28.18 in the second row, an **emerald,** a sapphire, and a
39.11 in the second row, an **emerald,** a sapphire, and a
Ezek 27.16 They gave **emeralds,** purple cloth, embroidery, fine linen,
28.13 sapphires, **emeralds,** and garnets.
Rev 4. 3 the throne there was a rainbow the colour of an **emerald.**
21.19 the third agate, the fourth **emerald,** [20] the fifth onyx,

EMISSION

Lev 15.16 When a man has an **emission** of semen, he must bathe his
15.32 has a discharge or an **emission** of semen,
22. 4 or if he has an **emission** of semen [5] or if he has

EMPEROR

[ASSYRIAN EMPEROR, ROMAN EMPEROR]

2 Kgs 15.19 Tiglath Pileser, the **emperor of Assyria,** invaded Israel,
15.29 Tiglath Pileser, the **emperor of Assyria,** captured the cities
16. 7 Tiglath Pileser, the **emperor of Assyria,** with this message:
16. 8 the palace treasury and sent it as a present to the **emperor.**
16.10 went to Damascus to meet **Emperor** Tiglath Pileser, he saw the
16.18 in order to please the **Assyrian emperor,** Ahaz also removed
17. 3 **Emperor Shalmaneser of Assyria** made war against him;
17. 6 the reign of Hoshea, the **Assyrian emperor** captured Samaria,
17.24 The **emperor of Assyria** took people from the cities of Babylon,
17.26 The **emperor of Assyria** was told that the people he had
17.27 So the **emperor** commanded:
18. 7 He rebelled against the **emperor of Assyria** and refused to
18. 9 Hoshea's reign over Israel—**Emperor Shalmaneser of Assyria**
18.11 The **Assyrian emperor** took the Israelites to Assyria as
18.13 King Hezekiah, Sennacherib, the **emperor of Assyria,** attacked
18.14 The **emperor's** answer was that Hezekiah should send him ten
18.17 The **Assyrian emperor** sent a large army from Lachish to
18.19 officials told them that the **emperor** wanted to know what
18.23 will make a bargain with you in the name of the **emperor.**
18.27 are the only ones the **emperor** sent me to say all these
18.28 "Listen to what the **emperor of Assyria** is telling you!
18.31 The **emperor of Assyria** commands you to come out of the city
18.32 your own wells—[32] until the **emperor** resettles you in a
18.33 nations save their countries from the **emperor of Assyria?**
18.35 these countries ever save their country from our **emperor?**
19. 4 The **Assyrian emperor** has sent his chief official to insult
19. 7 The Lord will cause the **emperor** to hear a rumour that will
19. 8 Assyrian official learnt that the **emperor** had left Lachish
19. 9 When the **emperor** heard this, he sent a letter to King
19.11 You have heard what an **Assyrian emperor** does to any
19.17 that the **emperors** of Assyria have destroyed many nations,
19.32 "This is what the Lord has said about the **Assyrian emperor:**
19.36 Then the **Assyrian emperor** Sennacherib withdrew and returned to Nineveh.
19.37 Another of his sons, Esarhaddon, succeeded him as **emperor.**
20. 6 you and this city of Jerusalem from the **emperor of Assyria.**
23.29 army to the River Euphrates to help the **emperor of Assyria.**
1 Chr 5. 4 The **Assyrian emperor,** Tiglath Pileser, captured Beerah,
5.26 So God made **Emperor Pul of Assyria** (also known as Tiglath Pileser)
2 Chr 28.16 King Ahaz asked Tiglath Pileser, the **emperor of Assyria,** to
28.20 The **Assyrian emperor,** instead of helping Ahaz, opposed
28.21 and gave it to the **emperor,** but even this did not help.
32. 1 Sennacherib, the **emperor of Assyria,** invaded Judah.
32. 7 don't be afraid of the **Assyrian emperor** or of the army he
32.10 "I, Sennacherib, **Emperor of Assyria,** ask what gives you
32.13 other nation save their people from the **emperor of Assyria?**
32.15 ever been able to save his people from any **Assyrian emperor.**
32.17 The letter that the **emperor** wrote defied the Lord, the
32.21 So the **emperor** went back to Assyria disgraced.
32.22 power of Sennacherib, the **emperor of Assyria,** and also from
36.22 that Cyrus of Persia was **emperor,** the Lord made what he had
36.23 "This is the command of Cyrus, **Emperor of Persia.**
Ezra 1. 1 that Cyrus of Persia was **emperor,** the Lord made what he had
1. 2 "This is the command of Cyrus, **Emperor of Persia.**
3. 7 All this was done with the permission of Cyrus, **emperor of Persia.**
4. 2 Esarhaddon, **emperor of Assyria,** sent us here to live."
4. 3 just as Cyrus, **emperor of Persia,** commanded us."
4. 6 the reign of Xerxes the **emperor,** the enemies of the people
4. 7 the reign of Artaxerxes, **emperor of Persia,** Bishlam,
4. 7 Tabeel, and their associates wrote a letter to the **emperor.**
4.11 "To **Emperor** Artaxerxes from his servants, the men of West Euphrates.
4.17 The **emperor** sent this answer:
4.24 the second year of the reign of Darius, **emperor of Persia.**
5. 6 This is the report that they sent to the **emperor:**
5. 7 "To **Emperor** Darius, may you rule in peace.
5.13 of King Cyrus as **emperor of Babylonia,** Cyrus issued orders
5.15 The **emperor** told him to take them and return them to the
6. 1 So Darius the **emperor** issued orders for a search to be
Ezra 6. 3 of his reign Cyrus the **emperor** commanded that the Temple in
6.13 their fellow-officials did exactly as the **emperor** had commanded.
6.14 Cyrus, Darius, and Artaxerxes, **emperors** of Persia.
6.15 Adar in the sixth year of the reign of Darius the **emperor.**
6.22 Lord had made the **emperor of Assyria** favourable to them, so
7. 1 later, when Artaxerxes was **emperor of Persia,** there was a
7. 6 Lord his God, the **emperor** gave him everything he asked for.
7.12 "From Artaxerxes the **emperor** to Ezra the priest,
7.27 He has made the **emperor** willing to honour in this way the
7.28 won the favour of the **emperor,** of his counsellors, and of
8. 1 who returned with Ezra to Jerusalem when Artaxerxes was **emperor:**
8.22 been ashamed to ask the **emperor** for a troop of cavalry to
8.25 the utensils which the **emperor,** his advisers and officials,
8.36 also took the document the **emperor** had given them and gave
9. 9 You made the **emperors** of Persia favour us and permit us to
Neh 1. 1 year that Artaxerxes was **emperor of Persia,** I, Nehemiah, was
1.11 Give me success today and make the **emperor** merciful to me."
1.11 In those days I was the **emperor's** wine steward.
2. 1 day four months later, when **Emperor** Artaxerxes was dining, I
2. 4 The **emperor** asked, "What is it that you want?"
2. 5 then I said to the **emperor,** "If Your Majesty is pleased
2. 6 The **emperor,** with the empress sitting at his side,
2. 8 The **emperor** gave me all I asked for, because God was with
2. 9 The **emperor** sent some army officers and a troop of
2. 9 There I gave the **emperor's** letters to the governors.
2.18 me and helped me, and what the **emperor** had said to me.
2.19 Are you going to rebel against the **emperor?"**
5.14 that Artaxerxes was **emperor** until his thirty-second year,
12.22 This record was finished when Darius was **emperor of Persia.**
Is 7.20 a barber from across the Euphrates—the **emperor of Assyria!—**
8. 7 Lord, will bring the **emperor of Assyria** and all his forces
10. 7 But the **Assyrian emperor** has his own violent plans in mind.
10.12 I will punish the **emperor of Assyria** for all his boasting
10.13 The **emperor of Assyria** boasts, "I have done it all myself.
20. 1 the orders of Sargon, **emperor of Assyria,** the
20. 4 The **emperor of Assyria** will lead away naked the prisoners
20. 6 we relied on to protect us from the **emperor of Assyria!**
30.33 prepared where a huge fire will burn the **emperor of Assyria.**
31. 9 Their **emperor** will run away in terror, and the officers
36. 1 of Judah, Sennacherib, the **emperor of Assyria,** attacked the
36. 4 official told them that the **emperor** wanted to know what made
36. 8 will make a bargain with you in the name of the **emperor.**
36.12 are the only ones the **emperor** sent me to say all these
36.13 "Listen to what the **emperor of Assyria** is telling you.
36.16 The **emperor of Assyria** commands you to come out of the city
36.17 your own wells—[17] until the **emperor** resettles you in a
36.18 nations save their countries from the **emperor of Assyria?**
36.20 these countries ever save their country from our **emperor?**
37. 4 The **Assyrian emperor** has sent his chief official to insult
37. 7 The Lord will cause the **emperor** to hear a rumour that will
37. 8 Assyrian official learnt that the **emperor** had left Lachish
37. 9 When the **emperor** heard this, he sent a letter to King
37.11 You have heard what an **Assyrian emperor** does to any
37.18 that the **emperors** of Assyria have destroyed many nations,
37.33 "This is what the Lord has said about the **Assyrian emperor:**
37.37 Then the **Assyrian emperor** Sennacherib withdrew and returned to Nineveh.
37.38 Another of his sons, Esarhaddon, succeeded him as **emperor.**
38. 6 of Jerusalem from the **emperor of Assyria,** and I will
Jer 50.17 were attacked by the **emperor of Assyria,** and then King
50.18 just as I punished the **emperor of Assyria.**
Dan 1.21 until Cyrus the **emperor of Persia** conquered Babylonia.
2.37 of heaven has made you **emperor** and given you power, might,
10. 1 year that Cyrus was **emperor of Persia,** a message was
Hos 5.13 Assyria to ask the great **emperor** for help, but he could not
8.10 writhe in pain, when the **emperor of Assyria** oppresses them.
10. 6 be carried off to Assyria as tribute to the great **emperor.**
Nah 3.18 **Emperor of Assyria,** your governors are dead, and your
Hag 1. 1 year that Darius was **emperor of Persia,** on the first day of
1.15 the sixth month of the second year that Darius was **emperor.**
2.10 second year that Darius was **emperor,** the Lord Almighty spoke
Zech 1. 1 year that Darius was **emperor of Persia,** the Lord gave this
1. 7 second year that Darius was **emperor,** on the twenty-fourth
7. 1 fourth year that Darius was **emperor,** on the fourth day of
Mt 22.17 against our Law to pay taxes to the **Roman Emperor,** or not?"
22.21 "The **Emperor's,"** they answered.
22.21 "Well, then, pay the **Emperor** what belongs to the Emperor,
Mk 12.14 is it against our Law to pay taxes to the **Roman Emperor?**
12.16 "The **Emperor's,"** they answered.
12.17 "Well, then, pay the **Emperor** what belongs to the Emperor,
Lk 2. 1 At that time the **Emperor Augustus** ordered a census to be
3. 1 It was the fifteenth year of the rule of the **Emperor Tiberius;**
20.22 Law for us to pay taxes to the **Roman Emperor,** or not?"
20.24 "The **Emperor's,"** they answered.
20.25 "Well, then, pay the **Emperor** what belongs to the Emperor,
23. 2 to pay taxes to the **Emperor** and claiming that he himself is
Jn 19.12 him free, that means that you are not the **Emperor's** friend!
19.12 who claims to be a king is a rebel against the **Emperor!"**
19.15 chief priests answered, "The only king we have is the **Emperor!"**
Acts 11.28 (It came when Claudius was **emperor.)**
17. 7 breaking the laws of the **Emperor,** saying that there is another
18. 2 Priscilla, for the **Emperor Claudius** had ordered all the Jews
25. 8 Jews or against the Temple or against the **Roman Emperor."**
25.10 "I am standing before the **Emperor's** own court of judgement,
25.11 I appeal to the **Emperor."**
25.12 appealed to the Emperor, so to the **Emperor** you will go."
25.21 be kept under guard and to let the **Emperor** decide his case.
25.21 be kept under guard until I could send him to the **Emperor."**
25.25 made an appeal to the **Emperor,** I have decided to send him.
25.26 But I have nothing definite about him to write to the **Emperor.**

Acts 26.32 have been released if he had not appealed to the **Emperor."**
27. 1 officer in the Roman regiment called "The **Emperor's Regiment."**
27.24 You must stand before the **Emperor.**
28.19 forced to appeal to the **Emperor,** even though I had no
Phil 4.22 greetings, especially those who belong to the **Emperor's** palace.
1 Pet 2.13 to the **Emperor,** who is the supreme authority,
2.17 love your fellow-believers, honour God, and respect the **Emperor.**

EMPHASIS

Tit 3. 8 want you to give special **emphasis** to these matters, so that

EMPIRE

2 Chr 36.20 descendants as slaves until the rise of the Persian **Empire.**
36.22 out in writing to be read aloud everywhere in his **empire:**
Ezra 1. 1 out in writing to be read aloud everywhere in his **empire:**
7.13 "I command that throughout my **empire** all the Israelite people,
7.26 or the laws of the **empire,** he is to be punished promptly:
Esth 1.16 but also his officials—in fact, every man in the **empire!**
1.17 Every woman in the **empire** will begin to look down on her
1.20 known all over this huge **empire,** every woman will treat her
2. 3 in every province of the **empire** and order them to bring all
2.18 a holiday for the whole **empire** and distributed gifts worthy
2.23 to be written down in the official records of the **empire.**
3. 6 He made plans to kill every Jew in the whole Persian **Empire.**
3. 8 scattered all over your **empire** and found in every province.
3. 8 obey the laws of the **empire,** so it is not in your
3. 9 the royal treasury for the administration of the **empire."**
3.12 of writing used in the **empire** and to be sent to all
3.13 Runners took this proclamation to every province of the **empire.**
5. 3 and you shall have it—even if it is half my **empire."**
5. 6 grant your request, even if you ask for half my **empire."**
6. 1 the official records of the **empire** to be brought and read to
7. 2 I'll even give you half the **empire."**
8. 5 Agag gave for the destruction of all the Jews in the **empire.**
8.12 take effect throughout the Persian **Empire** on the day set for
9. 2 of every city in the **empire** the Jews organized themselves to
9. 4 was well known throughout the **empire** that Mordecai was now a
9.20 and far, throughout the Persian **Empire,** [21] telling them to
9.30 were sent to all the 127 provinces of the Persian **Empire.**
10. 1 the coastal regions of his **empire** as well as on those of
Is 45.20 of the nations, all who survive the fall of the **empire;**
Dan 2.39 you there will be another **empire,** not as great as yours, and
2.39 after that a third, an **empire** of bronze, which will rule the
2.40 there will be a fourth **empire,** as strong as iron, which
2.40 it will shatter and crush all the earlier **empires.**
2.41 This means that it will be a divided **empire.**
2.42 mean that part of the **empire** will be strong and part of
2.43 that the rulers of that **empire** will try to unite their
2.44 destroy all those **empires,** and then last for ever.
6. 1 and twenty governors to hold office throughout his **empire.**
6. 3 king considered putting him in charge of the whole **empire.**
6. 4 the way Daniel administered the **empire,** but they couldn't,
6. 7 who administer your **empire**—the supervisors,
6.26 I command that throughout my **empire** everyone should fear
7.17 "These four huge beasts are four **empires** which will arise on earth.
7.23 fourth beast is a fourth **empire** that will be on the earth
7.23 on the earth and will be different from all other **empires.**
7.24 The ten horns are ten kings who will rule that **empire.**
11. 3 He will rule over a huge **empire** and do whatever he wants.
11. 4 height of his power his **empire** will break up and be divided
Lk 2. 1 Augustus ordered a census to be taken throughout the Roman **Empire.**

EMPLOY

2 Chr 8. 7 Solomon **employed** in forced labour all the descendants
Prov 26.10 An **employer** who hires any fool that comes along is only
Mal 3. 5 testimony, those who cheat **employees** out of their wages,
Mt 20.11 They took their money and started grumbling against the **employer.**

EMPRESS

Neh 2. 6 The emperor, with the **empress** sitting at his side,

EMPTY

Gen 24.20 She quickly **emptied** her jar into the animals'
31.42 with me, you would have already sent me away **empty-handed.**
42.35 Then when they **emptied** out their sacks, every one of
Ex 3.21 so that when my people leave, they will not go **empty-handed.**
Deut 15.13 When you set him free, do not send him away **empty-handed.**
32.47 These teachings are not **empty** words;
Josh 15. 5 the way up to the inlet where the Jordan **empties** into it.
18.19 on the Dead Sea, where the River Jordan **empties** into it.
Judg 5. 7 they stood **empty** until you came, came like a mother for Israel.
Ruth 3.17 not come back to you **empty-handed,** so he gave me all this
1 Sam 20.25 David's place was **empty,** [26] but Saul said nothing that day,
20.27 David's place was still **empty,** and Saul asked Jonathan,
2 Sam 13. 9 she baked the cakes [9] and **emptied** them out of the pan for
2 Kgs 4. 3 neighbours and borrow as many **empty** jars as you can,"
Job 15. 1 **Empty** words, Job!
15. 1 **Empty** words!
26. 7 out the northern sky and hung the earth in **empty** space.
38. 2 to question my wisdom with your ignorant, **empty** words?
Prov 14. 4 plough your barn will be **empty,** but with them it will be
Is 5. 9 "All these big, fine houses will be **empty** ruins.
6.11 the cities are ruined and **empty**—until the houses are
Is 16. 6 are arrogant and conceited, but their boasts are **empty."**
27.10 It is deserted like an **empty** wilderness.
Jer 4.29 Every town will be left **empty,** and no one will live in
14. 3 they come back with their jars **empty.**
33.10 the towns of Judah and the streets of Jerusalem are **empty;**
48.12 They will **empty** its wine-jars and break them in pieces.
51.34 He **emptied** the city like a jar;
Lam 1. 4 The city gates stand **empty,** and Zion is in agony.
Ezek 6.10 I am the Lord and that my warnings were not **empty** threats."
24.11 Now set the **empty** bronze pot on the coals and let it
29. 9 Egypt will become an **empty** waste.
29.10 make all of Egypt an **empty** waste, from the city of Migdol
Hos 10. 4 They utter **empty** words and make false promises
Joel 1.17 to be stored, and so the **empty** granaries are in ruins.
Hab 3.17 die and the cattle-stalls are **empty,** [18] I will still be
Zeph 3. 6 the streets are **empty**—no one is left.
Mt 12.44 it goes back and finds the house **empty,** clean, and all tidy.
23.38 And so your Temple will be abandoned and **empty.**
Lk 1.53 with good things, and sent the rich away with **empty** hands.
Acts 1.20 written in the book of Psalms, 'May his house become **empty;**
Rom 1.21 nonsense, and their **empty** minds are filled with darkness.
1 Cor 9.15 Nobody is going to turn my rightful boast into **empty** words!
2 Cor 9. 3 you in this matter may not turn out to be **empty** words.

ENABLE see ABLE

ENCHANT

Song 2.14 Let me see your lovely face and hear your **enchanting** voice.
5.16 everything about him **enchants** me.
Nah 3. 4 she **enchanted** nations and enslaved them.

ENCLOSURE

Ex 27. 9 Tent of my presence make an **enclosure** out of fine linen curtains.
27.11 same is to be done on the north side of the **enclosure.**
27.13 where the entrance is, the **enclosure** is also to be 22 metres
27.17 All the posts round the **enclosure** are to be connected
27.18 The **enclosure** is to be 44 metres long, 22 metres wide,
27.19 the Tent and for the **enclosure** are to be made of bronze.
35.17 the curtains for the **enclosure,** its posts and bases;
35.17 the curtain for the entrance of the **enclosure;**
35.18 the pegs and ropes for the Tent and the **enclosure;**
38. 9 Lord's presence he made the **enclosure** out of fine linen curtains.
38.11 The **enclosure** was the same on the north side.
38.13 the entrance was, the **enclosure** was also 22 metres wide.
38.16 All the curtains round the **enclosure** were made of fine linen.
38.17 All the posts round the **enclosure** were connected with silver rods.
38.18 for the entrance of the **enclosure** was made of fine linen
38.18 long and 2 metres high, like the curtains of the **enclosure.**
38.20 Tent and for the surrounding **enclosure** were made of bronze.
38.31 the bases for the surrounding **enclosure** and
38.31 for the entrance of the **enclosure,**
38.31 and all the pegs for the Tent and the surrounding **enclosure.**
39.40 the curtains for the **enclosure** and its posts and bases;
39.40 the curtain for the entrance of the **enclosure** and its ropes;
40. 8 Put up the surrounding **enclosure** and hang the curtain
40.33 Moses set up the **enclosure** round the Tent and the altar
40.33 and hung the curtain at the entrance of the **enclosure.**
Num 32.16 allow us to build stone **enclosures** here for our sheep and
32.24 build your towns and the **enclosures** for your sheep, but do
1 Kgs 6.36 in front of the Temple, **enclosed** with walls which had one
2 Chr 32.28 and **enclosures** for his sheep.
Ezek 42.20 metres, [20] so that the wall **enclosed** a square 250 metres on

ENCOURAGE

Deut 13. 6 friend may secretly **encourage** you to worship other gods,
13. 7 One of them may **encourage** you to worship the gods of the
Judg 9.24 Shechem, who **encouraged** him to murder Gideon's seventy sons,
20.22 So the Israelite army was **encouraged,** and they placed their
1 Sam 22. 8 a chance to kill me, and that my son has **encouraged** him!"
23.16 and **encouraged** him with assurances of God's protection,
2 Sam 11.25 David said to the messenger, **"Encourage** Joab and tell
16.21 his enemy, and your followers will be greatly **encouraged."**
2 Chr 15. 8 that Azariah son of Oded had spoken, he was **encouraged.**
26.10 Because he loved farming, he **encouraged** the people to plant
32. 8 The people were **encouraged** by these words of their king.
35. 2 perform in the Temple and **encouraged** them to do them well.
Ezra 6.14 the Temple, **encouraged** by the prophets Haggai and Zechariah.
Job 4. 4 your words **encouraged** him to stand.
29.24 my cheerful face **encouraged** them.
Ps 64. 5 They **encourage** each other in their evil plots;
69.32 those who worship God will be **encouraged.**
Is 40. 2 **Encourage** the people of Jerusalem.
41. 6 The craftsmen help and **encourage** one another.
41. 7 the idol smooth **encourages** the one who nails it together.
62. 1 I will speak out to **encourage** Jerusalem;
Acts 4.36 Barnabas (which means "One who **Encourages"),** [37] sold a field
13.15 people if you have a message of **encouragement** for them."
13.43 apostles spoke to them and **encouraged** them to keep on living
14.22 strengthened the believers and **encouraged** them to remain true
15.31 they were filled with joy by the message of **encouragement.**
16.40 they met the believers, spoke words of **encouragement** to them,
20. 1 believers and with words of **encouragement** said goodbye to them.
20. 2 those regions and **encouraged** the people with many messages.
28.15 When Paul saw them, he thanked God and was greatly **encouraged.**
Rom 12. 8 if it is to **encourage** others, we should do so.
15. 4 the patience and **encouragement** which the Scriptures give us.

Rom	15. 5	the source of patience and **encouragement,** enable you to have
1 Cor	8.10	will not this **encourage** him to eat food offered to idols?
	14. 3	God's message speaks to people and gives them help, **encouragement,**
	14.31	one by one, so that everyone will learn and be **encouraged.**
	16.12	I have often **encouraged** him to visit you with the other
2 Cor	2. 7	you should forgive him and **encourage** him, in order to keep
	7. 6	But God, who **encourages** the downhearted,
	7. 6	**encouraged** us with the coming of Titus.
	7. 7	cheered us, but also his report of how you **encouraged** him.
	7.13	That is why we were **encouraged.**
	7.13	Not only were we **encouraged;**
Eph	6.22	you how all of us are getting on, and to **encourage** you.
Phil	2.19	you soon, so that I may be **encouraged** by news about you.
1 Thes	2.12	We **encouraged** you, we comforted you, and we kept urging you
	3. 7	our trouble and suffering we have been **encouraged** about you,
	3. 7	It was your faith that **encouraged** us, [8] because now we really
	4.18	So then, **encourage** one another with these words.
	5.11	And so **encourage** one another and help one another, just as
	5.14	brothers, to warn the idle, **encourage** the timid, help the weak,
2 Thes	2.17	courage and a firm hope, [17] **encourage** you and strengthen you
2 Tim	4. 2	reproach, and **encourage,** as you teach with all patience.
Tit	1. 9	he will be able to **encourage** others with the true teaching
	2.15	your full authority as you **encourage** and rebuke your hearers.
Phlm	7	dear brother, has brought me great joy and much **encouragement!**
Heb	6.18	with him are greatly **encouraged** to hold firmly to the hope
	10.25	Instead, let us **encourage** one another all the more,
	12. 5	Have you forgotten the **encouraging** words which God speaks
	13.22	my brothers, to listen patiently to this message of **encouragement;**
1 Pet	5.12	I want to **encourage** you and give my testimony that this is
Jude	3	of writing at once to **encourage** you to fight on for the

END

Gen	6.13	to Noah, "I have decided to put an **end** to all mankind.
	41.53	had enjoyed came to an **end,** [54] and the seven years of
	44.12	beginning with the eldest and **ending** with the youngest, and
	47.21	slaves of the people from one **end** of Egypt to the other.
Ex	12.41	the day the 430 years **ended,** all the tribes of the Lord's
	25.19	creatures of hammered gold, [19] one for each **end** of the lid.
	26.27	and five for the frames on the west **end,** at the back.
	26.28	is to extend from one **end** of the Tent to the other.
	28.25	Fasten the other two **ends** of the cords to the two settings,
	36.32	and five for the frames on the west **end,** at the back.
	36.33	the frames, extended from one **end** of the Tent to the other.
	37. 8	creatures of hammered gold, [8] one for each **end** of the lid.
	39.18	and fastened the other two **ends** of the cords to the two
Lev	26.44	That would put an **end** to my covenant with them, and I
Num	11. 1	It burnt among them and destroyed one **end** of the camp.
	17.12	people of Israel said to Moses, "Then that's the **end** of us!
	23.10	Let me **end** my days like one of God's people;
	24.20	nation of all, But at the **end** it will perish for ever."
	34. 3	begin on the east at the southern **end** of the Dead Sea.
	34. 5	valley at the border of Egypt and **end** at the Mediterranean.
	34. 9	to Zedad [9] and to Ziphron, and will **end** at Hazar Enan.
Deut	8.16	you, so that in the **end** he could bless you with good
	14.28	At the **end** of every third year bring the tithe of all
	15. 1	"At the **end** of every seventh year you are to cancel the
	28.44	In the **end** they will be your rulers.
	28.49	a nation from the **ends of the earth,** a nation whose language
	28.64	the nations, from one **end of the earth** to the other, and
	31.10	He commanded them, "At the **end** of every seven years,
	32.23	"'I will bring on them **endless** disasters and use all my
	33.17	the nations And pushes them to the **ends of the earth."**
Josh	5. 4	Also, by the **end** of that time all the men who were
	15. 2	border ran from the south **end** of the Dead Sea, [3] went
	15. 4	of Egypt to the Mediterranean Sea, where the border **ended.**
	15. 8	Valley of Hinnom, at the northern **end** of the Valley of Rephaim.
	15.11	It **ended** at the Mediterranean Sea,
	16. 3	on from there to Gezer and **ended** at the Mediterranean Sea.
	16. 7	reaching Jericho and **ending** at the Jordan.
	16. 8	and **ended** at the Mediterranean Sea.
	17. 9	north side of the stream and **ended** at the Mediterranean Sea.
	17.18	it and take possession of it from one **end** to the other.
	18.16	Valley of Hinnom, at the north **end** of the Valley of Rephaim.
	18.19	ridge of Beth Hoglah, and **ended** at the northern inlet on the
	19.14	turned towards Hannathon, **ending** at the Valley of Iphtahel.
	19.22	Tabor, Shahazumah, and Beth Shemesh, **ending** at the Jordan.
	19.29	then it turned to Hosah and **ended** at the Mediterranean Sea.
	19.33	and to Jamnia, as far as Lakkum, and **ended** at the Jordan.
Judg	6.21	and the bread with the **end** of the stick he was holding.
	19.16	man came by at the **end** of a day's work in the
	21.13	were at the Rock of Rimmon and offered to **end** the war.
1 Sam	3.12	all my threats against Eli's family, from beginning to **end.**
	3.20	people of Israel, from one **end** of the country to the other,
2 Sam	2.26	see that in the **end** there will be nothing but bitterness?
	3. 9	Israel and Judah, from one **end** of the country to the other.
	7.16	Your dynasty will never **end.' "**
	8. 1	defeated them, and **ended** their control over the land.
	17.11	Israelites together from one **end** of the country to the other,
	24. 2	tribes of Israel from one **end** of the country to the other,
	24.15	From one **end** of the country to the other seventy thousand
1 Kgs	8. 8	The **ends** of the poles could be seen by anyone standing
	10.19	of a lion at each **end** of every step, a total of
	14.14	king over Israel who will put an **end** to Jeroboam's dynasty.
	16.22	In the **end,** those in favour of Omri won;
2 Kgs	8. 3	At the **end** of the seven years, she returned to Israel and
	10.21	the temple of Baal, filling it from one **end** to the other.
	23.33	His reign **ended** when King Neco of Egypt took him
1 Chr	17.14	His dynasty will never **end.' "**
	21. 2	"Go through Israel, from one **end** of the country to the other,
1 Chr	29.29	King David from beginning to **end** is recorded in the records
2 Chr	5. 9	The **ends** of the poles could be seen by anyone standing
	9.19	lions were on the steps, one at either **end** of each step.
	9.29	of Solomon from beginning to **end** is recorded in The History
	12.15	Rehoboam's acts from beginning to **end** and his family
	16.11	Asa's reign from beginning to **end** are recorded in The
	20.16	will meet them at the **end** of the valley that leads to
	20.34	of his reign to its **end,** is recorded in The History of
	25.26	from the beginning to the **end** of his reign are recorded in
	28.26	his reign, from beginning to **end,** are recorded in The
	31. 1	After the festival **ended,** all the people of Israel went to
	34. 8	land and the Temple by **ending** pagan worship, King Josiah
	35.27	his history from beginning to **end**—is all recorded in The
Ezra	6.11	sharpened at one **end,** and then driven through his body.
	9.11	it filled it from one **end** to the other with disgusting,
Neh	1. 9	even though you are scattered to the **ends of the earth.'**
	2.17	Let's rebuild the city walls and put an **end** to our disgrace."
	3.21	the next section, up to the far **end** of Eliashib's house.
	4.11	already upon us, killing us and putting an **end** to our work.
	12.39	We **ended** our march near the gate to the Temple.
Esth	4.14	you will die and your father's family will come to an **end.**
Job	3.26	I have no peace, no rest, and my troubles never **end.**
	5. 9	great things he does, and to his miracles there is no **end.**
	7. 7	my happiness has already **ended.**
	9.10	great things he does, and to his miracles there is no **end.**
	12.21	those in power and puts an **end** to the strength of rulers.
	14.10	But a man dies, and that is the **end** of him;
	14.14	for better times, wait till this time of trouble is **ended.**
	17. 1	The **end** of my life is near.
	18.17	His fame is **ended** at home and abroad;
	20.21	nothing left over, but now his prosperity comes to an **end.**
	22.23	to God and put an **end** to all the evil that is
	28.24	Because he sees the **ends of the earth,** Sees everything
	31.40	The words of Job are **ended.**
	37. 3	across the sky, from one **end of the earth** to the other.
Ps	19. 4	all the world and is heard to the **ends of the earth.**
	19. 6	It starts at one **end** of the sky and goes across to
	39. 4	Tell me how soon my life will **end."**
	65. 8	shouts of joy from one **end of the earth** to the other.
	72. 8	sea to sea, from the Euphrates to the **ends of the earth.**
	72.20	This is the **end** of the prayers of David son of Jesse.
	73.19	they go down to a horrible **end.**
	73.24	instruction and at the **end** you will receive me with honour.
	78.33	So he **ended** their days like a breath and their lives
	82. 7	your life will **end** like that of any prince."
	102.27	But you are always the same, and your life never **ends.**
	109. 8	May his life soon be **ended;**
	133. 3	the Lord has promised his blessing— life that never **ends.**
	135. 7	He brings storm clouds from the **ends of the earth;**
	146. 4	on that day all their plans come to an **end.**
Prov	11.29	brings trouble on his family will have nothing at the **end.**
	20.20	your parents, your life will **end** like a lamp that goes out
	22. 8	will spring up, and your oppression of others will **end.**
Ecc	5.14	in some unlucky deal and **end** up with nothing left to pass
	7. 8	The **end** of anything is better than its beginning.
	10.13	He starts out with silly talk and **ends** up with pure madness.
	12.12	There is no **end** to the writing of books, and too much
Is	2. 7	of silver and gold, and there is no **end** to their treasures.
	2. 7	is full of horses, and there is no **end** to their chariots.
	2.11	human pride will be **ended** and human arrogance destroyed.
	2.17	Human pride will be **ended,** and human arrogance will be destroyed.
	5.25	Lord's anger will not be **ended,** but his hand will still be
	5.26	He whistles for them to come from the **ends of the earth.**
	7. 3	cloth makers work, at the **end** of the ditch that brings water
	9. 7	power on right and justice, from now until the **end** of time.
	9.12	Yet even so the Lord's anger is not **ended;**
	9.17	Lord's anger will not be **ended,** but his hand will still be
	9.21	Yet even so the Lord's anger is not **ended;**
	10. 4	Yet even so the Lord's anger will not be **ended;**
	13. 5	They are coming from far-off countries at the **ends of the earth.**
	14. 5	The Lord has **ended** the power of the evil rulers [6] who
	16. 4	(Oppression and destruction will **end,** and those who are
	16.10	the shouts of joy are **ended.**
	17. 4	greatness will come to an **end,** and its wealth will be
	21. 2	God will put an **end** to the suffering which Babylon has caused.
	21.11	Tell me how soon it will **end."**
	21.16	the greatness of the tribes of Kedar will be at an **end.**
	22.25	And that will be the **end** of everything that was hanging on
	23. 9	in order to put an **end** to their pride in what they
	23.12	City of Sidon, your happiness has **ended,**
	24.13	It will be like the **end** of harvest, when the olives have
	28.28	the wheat by threshing it **endlessly,** and he knows how to
	29.20	It will be the **end** of those who oppress others and show
	30. 3	to help them, and Egypt's protection will **end** in disaster.
	30.28	nations to destruction and puts an **end** to their evil plans.
	33. 1	to rob and betray will **end,** and they themselves will become
	38.12	life was cut off and **ended,** Like a tent that is taken
	38.12	I thought that God was **ending** my life.
	38.13	I thought that God was **ending** my life.
	41. 4	the beginning, and I, the Lord, will be there at the **end.**
	41. 9	I brought you from the **ends of the earth;**
	44. 7	would happen from the very beginning to the **end** of time?
	45. 6	so that everyone from one **end** of the world to the other
	46. 1	"This is the **end** for Babylon's gods!
	46. 2	This is the **end** for Babylon's gods!
	47. 7	take these things to heart or think how it all would **end,**
	54.10	and hills may crumble, but my love for you will never **end;**
	58. 9	"If you put an **end** to oppression, to every gesture of contempt,
	60.20	Your days of grief will come to an **end.**
	61. 7	Your shame and disgrace are **ended.**

Is 66.17 The Lord says, "The **end** is near for those who purify
Jer 5.31 But what will they do when it all comes to an **end?"**
6.15 when I punish them, that will be the **end** of them.
7.34 Jerusalem I will put an **end** to the sounds of joy and
8.12 when I punish you, that will be the **end** of you.
10.13 he brings clouds from the **ends of the earth.**
10.24 that would be the **end** of us.
16.19 to you from the **ends of the earth** and say, "Our ancestors
17.11 his riches, and in the **end** he is nothing but a fool.
20.18 to have trouble and sorrow, to **end** my life in disgrace?
23.20 wicked, [20] and it will not **end** until he has done everything
25.31 him, [31] and the sound will echo to the **ends of the earth.**
25.32 a great storm is gathering at the far **ends of the earth.**
25.33 will lie scattered from one **end of the earth** to the other.
30.23 It will not **end** until he has done all that he intends
31. 8 from the north and gather them from the **ends of the earth.**
51.16 he brings clouds from the **ends of the earth.**
51.64 The words of Jeremiah **end** here.
Lam 2. 6 He has put an **end** to holy days and Sabbaths.
4.18 the **end** had come.
5.19 are king for ever, and will rule to the **end** of time.
Ezek 7. 2 This is the **end** for the whole land!
7. 3 "Israel, the **end** has come.
7. 6 This is the **end.**
7. 7 The **end** is coming for you people who live in the land.
12.23 I will put an **end** to that proverb.
15. 4 And when the **ends** are burnt up and the middle is charred,
22.15 country and nation and will put an **end** to your evil actions.
26.13 I will put an **end** to all your songs, and I will
26.21 you a terrifying example, and that will be the **end** of you.
30.10 King Nebuchadnezzar of Babylonia to put an **end** to Egypt's wealth.
30.18 of Egypt and put an **end** to the strength they were so
33.28 the power they were so proud of will come to an **end.**
34.29 them fertile fields and put an **end** to hunger in the land.
37.17 Then hold the two sticks **end** to end in your hand so
40. 8 It formed that **end** of the gateway which was nearest the Temple,
40. 8 and at its far **end** the walls were one metre thick.
40.14 The room at the far **end** led out to a courtyard.
40.22 and the entrance room was at the **end** facing the courtyard.
40.26 its entrance room was also at the **end** facing the courtyard.
41.12 At the far **end** of the open space on the west side
41.23 was a door at the **end** of the passage leading to the
41.23 and one also at the **end** of the passage leading to the
42. 1 not far from the building at the west **end** of the Temple.
42. 9 two rooms at the east **end** of the building, where the wall
42. 9 not far from the building at the west **end** of the Temple.
42.12 side of the building, at the east **end** where the wall began.
44. 3 the gateway through the entrance room at the inner **end."**
Dan 1.18 At the **end** of three years set by the king, Ashpenaz took
2.44 God of heaven will establish a kingdom that will never **end.**
5.26 numbered the days of your kingdom and brought it to an **end;**
6.26 be destroyed, and his power will never come to an **end.**
7.14 His authority would last for ever, and his kingdom would never **end.**
7.27 Their royal power will never **end** and all rulers on earth
7.28 This is the **end** of the account.
8.17 The vision has to do with the **end** of the world."
8.19 The vision refers to the time of the **end.**
8.23 "When the **end** of those kingdoms is near and they have
9.26 And at the **end** of that time God's chosen leader will be
9.26 The **end** will come like a flood, bringing the war and
9.27 is past, he will put an **end** to sacrifices and offerings.
9.27 it there meets the **end** which God has prepared for him."
11.18 leader will defeat him and put an **end** to his arrogance;
11.19 he will be defeated, and that will be the **end** of him.
11.35 This will continue until the **end** comes, the time that God
12. 4 and put a seal on it until the **end** of the world.
12. 6 will it be until these amazing events come to an **end?"**
12. 7 God's people **ends,** all these things will have happened."
12. 8 So I asked, "But, sir, how will it all **end?"**
12. 9 words are to be kept secret and hidden until the **end** comes.
12.13 "And you, Daniel, be faithful to the **end.**
12.13 you will rise to receive your reward at the **end** of time."
Hos 1. 4 I am going to put an **end** to Jehu's dynasty.
2.11 I will put an **end** to all her festivities—her annual and
Amos 6. 7 Your feasts and banquets will come to an **end.**
7. 9 I will bring the dynasty of King Jeroboam to an **end."**
8. 1 Lord said to me, "The **end** has come for my people Israel.
8. 5 When will the Sabbath **end,** so that we can start selling again?
8.10 That day will be bitter to the **end.**
Mic 6. 7 I bring him thousands of sheep or **endless** streams of olive-oil?
7. 9 But in the **end** he will defend us and right the wrongs
Nah 1.13 I will now **end** Assyria's power over you and break the
3.19 Did anyone escape your **endless** cruelty?
Zeph 1.18 put an end—a sudden **end**—to everyone who lives on earth.
3.15 The Lord has **ended** your punishment;
3.18 "I have **ended** the threat of doom and taken away your disgrace.
Hag 2.22 and earth [22] and overthrow kingdoms and **end** their power.
Zech 9.10 sea, from the River Euphrates to the **ends of the earth."**
Mal 1.11 People from one **end** of the world to the other honour me.
Mt 5.18 will be done away with—not until the **end** of all things.
10.22 But whoever holds out to the **end** will be saved.
13.39 The harvest is the **end** of the age, and the harvest workers
13.40 so the same thing will happen at the **end** of the age:
13.49 It will be like this at the **end** of the age:
20. 8 were hired last and **ending** with those who were hired first.'
24. 3 is the time for your coming and the **end** of the age."
24. 6 must happen, but they do not mean that the **end** has come.
24.13 But whoever holds out to the **end** will be saved.
24.14 and then the **end** will come.
Mt 24.31 his chosen people from one **end** of the world to the other.
27.48 wine, put it on the **end** of a stick, and tried to
28.20 I will be with you always, to the **end** of the age."
Mk 3.26 it cannot last, but will fall apart and come to an **end.**
13. 7 must happen, but they do not mean that the **end** has come.
13.10 But before the **end** comes, the gospel must be preached to
13.13 But whoever holds out to the **end** will be saved.
13.27 God's chosen people from one **end** of the world to the other.
15.36 in cheap wine, and put it on the **end** of a stick.
Lk 1.33 his kingdom will never **end!"**
21. 9 happen first, but they do not mean that the **end** is near."
Jn 13. 1 who were his own, and he loved them to the very **end.**
Acts 1. 8 in all Judaea and Samaria, and to the **ends of the earth."**
8.33 descendants, because his life on earth has come to an **end."**
15.38 stayed with them to the **end** of their mission, but had turned
21.26 it would be until the **end** of the period of purification,
21.27 about to come to an **end,** some Jews from the province of
Rom 1.17 it is through faith from beginning to **end.**
7. 5 at work in our bodies, and all we did **ended** in death.
9. 2 great is my sorrow, how **endless** the pain in my heart
10. 4 brought the Law to an **end,** so that everyone who believes is
10.18 their words reached the **ends of the earth."**
1 Cor 1. 8 keep you firm to the **end,** so that you will be faultless
6.13 but God will put an **end** to both.
10.11 we live at a time when the **end** is about to come.
15.24 Then the **end** will come;
2 Cor 11.15 In the **end** they will get exactly what their actions deserve.
Eph 6.13 after fighting to the **end,** you will still hold your ground.
Phil 3.19 They are going to **end** up in hell, because their god is
2 Tim 1.10 He has **ended** the power of death and through the gospel has
2.23 you know that they **end** up in quarrels.
Heb 1. 2 one whom God has chosen to possess all things at the **end.**
1.12 But you are always the same, and your life never **ends."**
3.14 we hold firmly to the **end** the confidence we had at the
6.11 up his eagerness to the **end,** so that the things you hope
7.16 but through the power of a life which has no **end.**
9.26 of time are nearing the **end,** he has appeared once and for
12. 2 on Jesus, on whom our faith depends from beginning to **end.**
Jas 5.11 and you know how the Lord provided for him in the **end.**
1 Pet 1. 5 salvation which is ready to be revealed at the **end** of time.
4. 7 The **end** of all things is near.
4.17 with us, how will it **end** with those who do not believe
2 Pet 2.20 a worse state at the **end** than they were at the beginning.
1 Jn 2.18 My children, the **end** is near!
2.18 have already appeared, and so we know that the **end** is near.
Rev 2.26 victory, who continue to the **end** to do what I want, I
15. 8 plagues brought by the seven angels had come to an **end.**
21. 6 I am the first and the last, the beginning and the **end.**
22.13 I am the first and the last, the beginning and the **end."**

ENDURE

Num 11.15 so that I won't have to **endure** your cruelty any longer."
Esth 8. 6 How can I **endure** it if this disaster comes on my people,
Job 14.12 They will never wake up while the sky **endures;**
Ps 13. 2 How long must I **endure** trouble?
33.11 But his plans **endure** for ever;
55.12 If it were an enemy that mocked me, I could **endure** it;
89.50 am insulted, how I **endure** all the curses of the heathen.
103.17 for ever, and his goodness **endures** for all generations
119.90 Your faithfulness **endures** through all the ages;
132. 1 Lord, do not forget David and all the hardships he **endured.**
147.17 no one can **endure** the cold he sends!
Prov 28. 2 and **endure** when it has intelligent, sensible leaders.
Is 4. 1 we won't have to **endure** the shame of being unmarried."
7. 9 "If your faith is not **enduring,** you will not endure."
40. 7 People are no more **enduring** than grass.
40. 8 flowers fade, but the word of our God **endures** for ever."
50. 7 I brace myself to **endure** them.
51. 8 my victory will **endure** for all time."
51.12 you fear mortal man, who is no more **enduring** than grass?
53. 3 he **endured** suffering and pain.
53. 4 "But he **endured** the suffering that should have been ours,
53. 7 "He was treated harshly, but **endured** it humbly;
64.12 to do nothing and make us suffer more than we can **endure?**
66.22 and the new heavens will **endure** by my power, so your
66.22 so your descendants and your name will **endure.**
Jer 10.10 the nations cannot **endure** your anger.
10.19 And we thought this was something we could **endure!**
44.22 Lord could no longer **endure** your wicked and evil practices.
Ezek 16.52 And now you will have to **endure** your disgrace.
Mic 7. 9 the Lord, so now we must **endure** his anger for a while.
Hab 1. 3 How can you **endure** to look on such wrongdoing?
Mal 3. 2 But who will be able to **endure** the day when he comes?
Jn 15.16 to go and bear much fruit, the kind of fruit that **endures.**
Acts 13.18 and for forty years he **endured** them in the desert.
Rom 5. 4 trouble produces endurance, [4] **endurance** brings God's approval,
9.22 he was very patient in **enduring** those who were the objects
1 Cor 4.12 when we are persecuted, we **endure;**
9.12 we have **endured** everything in order not to put any obstacle
10.13 give you the strength to **endure** it, and so provide you with
2 Cor 1. 6 to endure with patience the same sufferings that we also **endure.**
6. 4 we are God's servants by patiently **enduring** troubles, hardships,
Col 1.11 so that you may be able to **endure** everything with patience.
2 Thes 1. 4 you continue to **endure** and believe through all the persecutions
3. 5 of God's love and the **endurance** that is given by Christ.
1 Tim 6.11 Strive for righteousness, godliness, faith, love, **endurance,**
2 Tim 2.10 in chains, [10] and so I **endure** everything for the sake of
2.12 If we continue to **endure,** we shall also rule with him.
3.10 faith, my patience, my love, my **endurance,** [11] my persecutions,
3.11 Antioch, Iconium, and Lystra, the terrible persecutions I **endured!**

2 Tim 4. 5 **endure** suffering, do the work of a preacher of the Good News,
Tit 2. 2 to be sound in their faith, love, and **endurance.**
Heb 10.34 your belongings were seized, you **endured** your loss gladly,
12. 7 **Endure** what you suffer as being a father's punishment;
Jas 1. 3 in facing such trials, the result is the ability to **endure.**
1. 4 Make sure that your **endurance** carries you all the way without
5.10 Take them as examples of patient **endurance** under suffering.
5.11 We call them happy because they **endured.**
1 Pet 1. 7 than gold, must also be tested, so that it may **endure.**
1.11 Christ would have to **endure** and the glory that would follow.
2.19 for this, if you **endure** the pain of undeserved suffering
2.20 credit is there if you **endure** the beatings you deserve for
2.20 But if you **endure** suffering even when you have done right,
2 Pet 1. 6 to your self-control add **endurance;**
1. 6 to your **endurance** add godliness;
Rev 1. 9 am your partner in patiently **enduring** the suffering that comes
3.10 have kept my command to **endure,** I will also keep you safe
13.10 This calls for **endurance** and faith on the part of God's people."
14.12 This calls for **endurance** on the part of God's people,

ENEMY

Gen 3.15 her offspring and yours will always be **enemies.**
14.15 into groups, attacked the **enemy** by night, and defeated them.
14.20 Most High God, who gave you victory over your **enemies,** be
22.17 Your descendants will conquer their **enemies.**
24.60 May your descendants conquer the cities of their **enemies!"**
49. 8 You hold your **enemies** by the neck.
49.23 His **enemies** attack him fiercely And pursue him with
Ex 1.10 they might join our **enemies** in order to fight against us,
15. 6 it breaks the **enemy** in pieces.
15. 9 The **enemy** said, 'I will pursue them and catch them;
15.12 stretched out your right hand, and the earth swallowed our **enemies.**
23. 4 you happen to see your **enemy's** cow or donkey running loose,
23.22 everything I command, I will fight against all your **enemies.**
23.27 and I will make all your **enemies** turn and run from you.
23.28 I will throw your **enemies** into a panic;
32.25 and make fools of themselves in front of their **enemies.**
Lev 26. 7 You will be victorious over your **enemies;**
26.16 you no good, because your **enemies** will conquer you and eat
26.25 you, and you will be forced to surrender to your **enemies.**
26.32 land so completely that the **enemies** who occupy it will be
26.34 rest while you are in exile in the land of your **enemies.**
26.36 battle, and you will fall when there is no **enemy** near you.
26.37 you, and you will be unable to fight against any **enemy.**
26.38 will die in exile, swallowed up by the land of your **enemies.**
26.39 in the land of your **enemies** will waste away because of your
26.41 them and send them into exile in the land of their **enemies.**
26.44 in the land of their **enemies,** I will not completely abandon
Num 10. 9 defending yourselves against an **enemy** who has attacked you,
10. 9 Lord your God, will help you and save you from your **enemies.**
10.35 scatter your **enemies** and put to flight those who hate you!"
14.42 The Lord is not with you, and your **enemies** will defeat you.
21.24 Israelites killed many of the **enemy** in battle and occupied
23.11 you here to curse my **enemies,** but all you have done is
24. 8 They devour their **enemies,** Crush their bones, smash their arrows.
24.10 called you to curse my **enemies,** but three times now you have
24.18 He will conquer his **enemies** in Edom And make their land
32.21 they are to attack our **enemies** until the Lord defeats them
35.23 he did not intend to hurt and who was not his **enemy.**
Deut 1.39 land—the children you said would be seized by your **enemies.**
1.42 I will not be with them, and their **enemies** will defeat them.'
2.12 the Israelites later chased their **enemies** out of the land
4.42 had accidentally killed someone who had not been his **enemy.**
6.19 and you will drive out your **enemies,** as he promised.
7.15 in Egypt, but he will bring them on all your **enemies.**
7.23 The Lord will put your **enemies** in your power and make
12.10 you safe from all your **enemies,** and you will live in peace.
19. 4 someone who is not his **enemy,** he may escape to any of
19. 6 by accident that he killed a man who was not his **enemy.**
19.11 a man deliberately murders his **enemy** in cold blood and then
20. 1 out to fight against your **enemies** and you see chariots and
20. 3 Do not be afraid of your **enemies,** or lose courage, or panic.
20.14 You may use everything that belongs to your **enemies.**
20.19 the trees are not your **enemies.**
23.14 to protect you and to give you victory over your **enemies.**
25.19 you safe from all your **enemies** who live around you, be sure
28. 7 "The Lord will defeat your **enemies** when they attack you.
28.25 "The Lord will give your **enemies** victory over you.
28.31 will be given to your **enemies,** and there will be no one
28.48 then, you will serve the **enemies** that the Lord is going to
28.53 "When your **enemies** are besieging your towns, you will
28.56 When the **enemy** besieges her town, she will become so
28.68 to sell yourselves to your **enemies** as slaves, but no one
30. 7 against your **enemies,** who hated you and oppressed you,
32.27 I could not let their **enemies** boast that they had defeated
32.31 Their **enemies** know that their own gods are weak, not
32.32 Their **enemies,** corrupt as Sodom and Gomorrah, are like
32.34 "The Lord remembers what their **enemies** have done;
32.41 take revenge on my **enemies** and punish those who hate me.
32.43 He takes revenge on his **enemies** and forgives the sins of his
33. 7 Fight for them, Lord, And help them against their **enemies."**
33.11 Crush all their **enemies;**
33.27 He drove out your **enemies** as you advanced, and told you to
33.29 Your **enemies** will come begging for mercy, and you will
Josh 5.13 and asked, "Are you one of our soldiers, or an **enemy?"**
7. 8 I say, O Lord, now that Israel has retreated from the **enemy?**
7.12 This is why the Israelites cannot stand against their **enemies.**
7.13 You cannot stand against your **enemies** until you get rid of
8.24 killed every one of the **enemy** in the barren country where
Josh 10.13 did not move until the nation had conquered its **enemies.**
10.19 Keep on after the **enemy** and attack them from the rear;
10.25 is what the Lord is going to do to all your **enemies."**
11. 8 The fight continued until none of the **enemy** was left alive.
21.44 Not one of all their **enemies** had been able to stand against
21.44 Lord gave the Israelites the victory over all their **enemies.**
22. 6 Share with your fellow-tribesmen what you took from your **enemies."**
23. 1 the Lord gave Israel security from their **enemies** around them.
Judg 2. 3 They will be your **enemies,** and you will be trapped by the
2.14 He let **enemies** all around overpower them, and the Israelites
2.18 the people from their **enemies** as long as that leader lived.
3.28 The Lord has given you victory over your **enemies,** the Moabites."
5.31 May all your **enemies** die like that, O Lord, but may your
7.11 his servant Purah went down to the edge of the **enemy** camp.
7.21 round the camp, and the whole **enemy** army ran away yelling.
7.22 trumpets, the Lord made the **enemy** troops attack each other
8. 4 They were exhausted, but were still pursuing the **enemy.**
8.34 God, who had saved them from all their **enemies** round them.
11.36 Lord has given you revenge on your **enemies,** the Ammonites."
16.23 They sang, "Our god has given us victory over our **enemy** Samson!"
16.24 given us victory over our **enemy,** who devastated our land and
20.35 Israelites killed 25,100 of the **enemy** that day, [36]and the
20.43 The Israelites had the **enemy** trapped, and without
1 Sam 2. 1 I laugh at my **enemies;**
2.10 The Lord's **enemies** will be destroyed;
4. 3 that he will go with us and save us from our **enemies."**
10. 1 You will rule his people and protect them from all their **enemies.**
11.11 they rushed into the **enemy** camp and attacked the Ammonites.
12.10 Rescue us from our **enemies,** and we will worship you!'
12.11 us rescued you from your **enemies,** and you lived in safety.
14.24 eats any food today before I take revenge on my **enemies."**
14.30 had eaten the food they took when they defeated the **enemy.**
14.32 they had captured from the **enemy,** took sheep and cattle,
14.47 he fought against all his **enemies** everywhere:
18.25 of a hundred dead Philistines, as revenge on his **enemies."**
18.29 afraid of David and was his **enemy** as long as he lived.
19.17 "Why have you tricked me like this and let my **enemy** escape?"
20.15 has completely destroyed all your **enemies,** [16]may our
24. 4 that he would put your **enemy** in your power and you could
24.19 does a man catch his **enemy** and then let him get away
25.26 Lord who has kept you from taking revenge and killing your **enemies.**
25.26 the living Lord that your **enemies** and all who want to harm
25.29 As for your **enemies,** however, he will throw them away, as a
26. 8 to David, "God has put your **enemy** in your power tonight.
28.16 me when the Lord has abandoned you and become your **enemy?**
29. 8 I go with you, my master and king, and fight your **enemies?"**
30.26 for you from the loot we took from the Lord's **enemies."**
31. 3 and he himself was hit by **enemy** arrows and badly wounded.
2 Sam 1. 6 chariots and horsemen of the **enemy** were closing in on him.
1.22 Saul was merciless, striking down the mighty, killing the **enemy.**
3.18 Israel from the Philistines and from all their other **enemies.'"**
4. 8 the son of your **enemy** Saul, who tried to kill you.
5.20 He said, "The Lord has broken through my **enemies** like a flood."
7. 1 his palace, and the Lord kept him safe from all his **enemies.**
7. 9 gone, and I have defeated all your **enemies** as you advanced.
7.10 you safe from all your **enemies** and to give you descendants.
10. 6 they had made David their **enemy,** so they hired twenty
10. 9 Joab saw that the **enemy** troops would attack him in front
10.18 Shobach, the **enemy** commander, who died on the battlefield.
11.16 sent Uriah to a place where he knew the **enemy** was strong.
11.17 The **enemy** troops came out of the city and fought Joab's forces;
11.23 He said, "Our **enemies** were stronger than we were and
16.21 father regards you as his **enemy,** and your followers will be
18. 3 make any difference to the **enemy** if the rest of us turn
18.19 good news that the Lord has saved him from his **enemies."**
18.32 would happen to all your **enemies,** sir, and to all who rebel
19. 9 "King David saved us from our **enemies,"** they said to one another.
22. 1 from Saul and his other **enemies,** David sang this song to the
22. 4 I call to the Lord, and he saves me from my **enemies.**
22.15 He shot his arrows and scattered his **enemies;**
22.16 the Lord rebuked his **enemies** and roared at them in anger.
22.18 rescued me from my powerful **enemies** and from all those who
22.30 to attack my **enemies** and power to overcome their defences.
22.38 I pursue my **enemies** and defeat them;
22.40 You give me strength for the battle and victory over my **enemies.**
22.41 You make my **enemies** run from me;
22.48 He gives me victory over my **enemies;**
22.49 me victory over my **enemies** and protect me from violent men.
24.13 of running away from your **enemies** or three days of an
1 Kgs 3.11 or the death of your **enemies,** [12]I will do what you have
5. 3 had to fight against the **enemy** countries all round him, he
5. 3 God until the Lord had given him victory over all his **enemies.**
5. 4 I have no **enemies,** and there is no danger of attack.
8.33 Israel are defeated by their **enemies** because they have sinned against you,
8.37 people are attacked by their **enemies,** or when there is
8.44 go into battle against their **enemies** and they pray to you,
8.46 your anger you let their **enemies** defeat them and take them
8.50 you, and make their **enemies** treat them with kindness.
11.21 As king of Edom, Hadad was an evil, bitter **enemy** of Israel.
11.25 He was an **enemy** of Israel during the lifetime of Solomon.
20.39 a soldier brought a captured **enemy** to me and said, 'Guard
21.20 Elijah, he said, "Have you caught up with me, my **enemy?"**
2 Kgs 3.23 "The three **enemy** armies must have fought and killed each other!
3.26 force his way through the **enemy** lines and escape to the king
9.17 "Send a horseman to find out if they are friends or **enemies."**
14.19 Lachish, but his **enemies** followed him there and killed him.
17.20 handing them over to cruel **enemies** until at last he had

2 Kgs	17.39	Lord your God, and I will rescue you from your **enemies."**
	21.14	hand them over to their **enemies,** who will conquer them and
1 Chr	5.21	They captured from the **enemy** 50,000 camels,
	5.22	They killed many of the **enemy,** because the war was God's will.
	10. 3	Saul, and he was hit by **enemy** arrows and badly wounded.
	12.17	to betray me to my **enemies,** even though I have not tried
	14.11	has used me to break through the **enemy** army like a flood."
	17. 8	gone, and I have defeated all your **enemies** as you advanced.
	17. 9	I promise to defeat all your **enemies** and to give you descendants.
	19. 6	they had made David their **enemy,** so they paid thirty-four
	19.10	Joab saw that the **enemy** troops would attack him in
	21.12	Or three months of running away from the armies of your **enemies?**
	22. 9	peace, because I will give him peace from all his **enemies.**
2 Chr	1.11	or the death of your **enemies** or even for long life for
	6.24	Israel are defeated by their **enemies** because they have
	6.28	people are attacked by their **enemies,** or when there is
	6.34	go into battle against their **enemies** and they pray to you,
	6.36	your anger you let their **enemies** defeat them and take them
	20.24	desert, they looked towards the **enemy** and saw that they were
	20.27	Jerusalem in triumph, because the Lord had defeated their **enemies.**
	20.29	the Lord had defeated Israel's **enemies** was terrified, [30]so
	24.25	severely wounded, and when the **enemy** withdrew, two of his
	25. 8	or defeat, and he will let your **enemies** defeat you."
	25.27	Lachish, but his **enemies** followed him there and killed him.
	26.13	able to fight effectively for the king against his **enemies.**
	32.22	the emperor of Assyria, and also from their other **enemies.**
	35.21	you, but to fight my **enemies,** and God has told me to
Ezra	4. 1	The **enemies** of the people of Judah and Benjamin heard that
	4. 6	of Xerxes the emperor, the **enemies** of the people living in
	8.22	to guard us from any **enemies** during our journey, because I
	8.31	us and protected us from **enemy** attacks and from ambush as we
Neh	4.11	Our **enemies** thought we would not see them or know what
	4.12	who were living among our **enemies** came to warn us
	4.12	of the plans our **enemies** were making against us.
	4.14	leaders and officials, "Don't be afraid of our **enemies.**
	4.15	Our **enemies** heard that we had found out what they were plotting,
	5. 9	you would not give our **enemies,** the Gentiles, any reason to
	6. 1	and the rest of our **enemies** heard that we had finished
	6.16	When our **enemies** in the surrounding nations heard this,
	9.27	time, [27]so you let their **enemies** conquer and rule them.
	9.28	sinned again, and again you let their **enemies** conquer them.
Esth	3.10	and gave it to the **enemy** of the Jewish people, Haman son
	7. 6	"Our **enemy,** our persecutor, is this evil man Haman!"
	8. 1	Queen Esther all the property of Haman, the **enemy** of the Jews.
	8.13	ready to take revenge on their **enemies** when that day came.
	9. 1	effect, the day when the **enemies** of the Jews were hoping to
	9. 5	So the Jews could do what they wanted with their **enemies.**
	9. 7	ten sons of Haman son of Hammedatha, the **enemy** of the Jews:
	9.16	They rid themselves of their **enemies** by killing seventy-five
	9.18	since they had slaughtered their **enemies** on the thirteenth
	9.22	days on which the Jews had rid themselves of their **enemies;**
	9.24	descendant of Agag and the **enemy** of the Jewish people—had
Job	6.23	on my behalf [23]or to save me from some **enemy** or tyrant?
	9.13	He crushed his **enemies** who helped Rahab, the sea-monster,
	11.19	You won't be afraid of your **enemies;**
	13.24	Why do you treat me like an **enemy?**
	16. 8	you are my **enemy.**
	19.11	he treats me like his worst **enemy.**
	22.21	make peace with God and stop treating him like an **enemy;**
	31.29	never been glad when my **enemies** suffered, or pleased when
	33.10	God finds excuses for attacking me and treats me like an **enemy.**
Ps	3. 1	I have so many **enemies,** Lord, so many who turn against me!
	3. 6	of the thousands of **enemies** who surround me on every side.
	3. 7	You punish all my **enemies** and leave them powerless to harm me.
	5. 8	Lord, I have so many **enemies!**
	5. 9	What my **enemies** say can never be trusted;
	6. 7	my eyes are so swollen from the weeping caused by my **enemies.**
	6.10	My **enemies** will know the bitter shame of defeat;
	7. 3	cause done violence to my **enemy**— if I have done any
	7. 5	things— [5]then let my **enemies** pursue me and catch me, let
	7. 6	Stand up against the fury of my **enemies;**
	8. 2	You are safe and secure from all your **enemies;**
	9. 3	My **enemies** turn back when you appear;
	9. 6	Our **enemies** are finished for ever;
	9.13	See the sufferings my **enemies** cause me!
	10. 5	he sneers at his **enemies.**
	13. 2	How long will my **enemies** triumph over me?
	13. 4	Don't let my **enemies** say, "We have defeated him."
	17. 7	at your side I am safe from my **enemies.**
	17. 9	Deadly **enemies** surround me;
	17.13	Oppose my **enemies** and defeat them!
	18. 3	I call to the Lord, and he saves me from my **enemies.**
	18.14	He shot his arrows and scattered his **enemies;**
	18.15	uncovered, when you rebuked your **enemies,** Lord, and roared
	18.17	rescued me from my powerful **enemies** and from all those who
	18.29	to attack my **enemies** and power to overcome their defences.
	18.37	I pursue my **enemies** and catch them;
	18.39	You give me strength for the battle and victory over my **enemies.**
	18.40	You make my **enemies** run from me;
	18.47	He gives me victory over my **enemies;**
	18.48	me victory over my **enemies** and protect me from violent men.
	21. 8	The king will capture all his **enemies;**
	22.12	Many **enemies** surround me like bulls;
	22.17	My **enemies** look at me and stare.
	23. 5	prepare a banquet for me, where all my **enemies** can see me;
	25. 2	don't let my **enemies** gloat over me!
	25.19	See how many **enemies** I have;
	27. 3	even if **enemies** attack me, I will still trust God.
	27. 6	So I will triumph over my **enemies** around me.
Ps	27.11	and lead me along a safe path, because I have many **enemies.**
	27.12	Don't abandon me to my **enemies,** who attack me with lies
	30. 1	have saved me and kept my **enemies** from gloating over me.
	31. 8	You have not let my **enemies** capture me;
	31.11	All my **enemies,** and especially my neighbours,
	31.13	I hear many **enemies** whispering;
	31.15	save me from my **enemies,** from those who persecute me.
	31.20	shelter you hide them from the insults of their **enemies.**
	35.19	Don't let my **enemies,** those liars, gloat over my defeat.
	35.24	don't let my **enemies** gloat over me.
	37.20	the **enemies** of the Lord will vanish like wild flowers;
	37.33	not abandon him to his **enemy's** power or let him be condemned
	38.16	Don't let my **enemies** gloat over my distress;
	38.19	My **enemies** are healthy and strong;
	41. 2	he will not abandon them to the power of their **enemies.**
	41. 5	My **enemies** say cruel things about me.
	41.10	and restore my health, and I will pay my **enemies** back.
	42. 3	all the time my **enemies** ask me, "Where is your God?"
	42. 9	Why must I go on suffering from the cruelty of my **enemies?"**
	43. 2	Why must I go on suffering from the cruelty of my **enemies?**
	44. 5	to your people, [5]and by your power we defeat our **enemies.**
	44. 7	saved us from our **enemies** and defeated those who hate us.
	44.10	made us run from our **enemies,** and they took for themselves
	44.16	the sneers and insults of my **enemies** and those who hate me.
	45. 5	Your arrows are sharp, they pierce the hearts of your **enemies;**
	49. 5	when I am surrounded by **enemies,** [6]by evil men who trust in
	53. 5	God will scatter the bones of the **enemies** of his people.
	54. 5	May God use their own evil to punish my **enemies.**
	54. 7	from all my troubles, and I have seen my **enemies** defeated.
	55. 3	by the threats of my **enemies,** crushed by the oppression of
	55. 9	Confuse the speech of my **enemies,** O Lord!
	55.12	If it were an **enemy** that mocked me, I could endure it;
	55.15	May my **enemies** die before their time;
	55.18	back from the battles that I fight against so many **enemies.**
	56. 1	my **enemies** persecute me all the time.
	56. 5	My **enemies** make trouble for me all day long;
	56. 9	The day I call to you, my **enemies** will be turned back.
	57. 4	I am surrounded by **enemies,** who are like man-eating lions.
	57. 6	My **enemies** have spread a net to catch me;
	59. 1	Save me from my **enemies,** my God;
	59.10	he will let me see my **enemies** defeated.
	59.14	My **enemies** come back in the evening, snarling like dogs
	60.11	Help us against the **enemy;**
	60.12	he will defeat our **enemies.**
	61. 3	for you are my protector, my strong defence against my **enemies.**
	64. 1	I am afraid of my **enemies**—save my life!
	66. 3	is so great that your **enemies** bow down in fear before you.
	66.12	You let our **enemies** trample over us;
	68. 1	God rises up and scatters his **enemies.**
	68.21	break the heads of his **enemies,** of those who persist in
	68.22	The Lord has said, "I will bring your **enemies** back from Bashan;
	69. 4	My **enemies** tell lies against me;
	69.14	keep me safe from my **enemies,** safe from the deep water.
	69.18	rescue me from my **enemies.**
	69.19	you see all my **enemies.**
	71.10	My **enemies** want to kill me;
	72. 9	his **enemies** will throw themselves to the ground.
	74. 3	our **enemies** have destroyed everything in the Temple.
	74. 4	Your **enemies** have shouted in triumph in your Temple;
	74.10	How long, O God, will our **enemies** laugh at you?
	74.18	remember, O Lord, that your **enemies** laugh at you, that they
	74.19	Don't abandon your helpless people to their cruel **enemies;**
	74.23	the angry shouts of your **enemies,** the continuous noise made
	76. 3	broke the arrows of the **enemy,** their shields and swords,
	78.42	he saved them from their **enemies** [43]and performed his
	78.53	but the sea came rolling over their **enemies.**
	78.61	He allowed our **enemies** to capture the Covenant Box, the
	78.62	his own people and let them be killed by their **enemies.**
	78.66	He drove his **enemies** back in lasting and shameful defeat.
	80. 6	our **enemies** insult us.
	80.16	Our **enemies** have set it on fire and cut it down;
	81.14	I would quickly defeat their **enemies** and conquer all their foes.
	83. 2	Your **enemies** are in revolt, and those who hate you are rebelling.
	89.10	with your mighty strength you defeated your **enemies.**
	89.22	His **enemies** will never succeed against him;
	89.42	You have given the victory to his **enemies;**
	89.51	Your **enemies** insult your chosen king, O Lord!
	92. 9	We know that your **enemies** will die, and all the wicked
	92.11	seen the defeat of my **enemies** and heard the cries of the
	97. 3	goes in front of him and burns up his **enemies** round him.
	102. 8	All day long my **enemies** insult me;
	105.24	to his people and made them stronger than their **enemies.**
	106.10	he rescued them from their **enemies.**
	106.11	But the water drowned their **enemies;**
	106.41	power of the heathen, and their **enemies** ruled over them.
	106.42	They were oppressed by their **enemies** and were in
	107. 2	has rescued you from your **enemies** [3]and has brought you back
	108.12	Help us against the **enemy;**
	108.13	he will defeat our **enemies.**
	109. 6	corrupt judge to try my **enemy,** and let one of his own
	109. 6	try my enemy, and let one of his own **enemies** accuse him.
	109.20	Lord, punish my **enemies** in that way— those who say such
	109.27	Make my **enemies** know that you are the one who saves me.
	109.29	May my **enemies** be covered with disgrace;
	110. 1	at my right until I put your **enemies** under your feet."
	110. 2	"Rule over your **enemies,"** he says.
	110. 3	On the day you fight your **enemies,** your people will volunteer.
	112. 8	he is certain to see his **enemies** defeated.
	118. 7	the Lord who helps me, and I will see my **enemies** defeated.
	118.10	Many **enemies** were round me;
	119.98	with me all the time and makes me wiser than my **enemies.**

Ps 119.121 don't abandon me to my **enemies!**
119.139 me like a fire, because my **enemies** disregard your commands.
119.157 I have many **enemies** and oppressors, but I do not fail
124. 2 on our side when our **enemies** attacked us, [3]then they would
124. 6 us thank the Lord, who has not let our **enemies** destroy us.
127. 5 when he meets his **enemies** in the place of judgement.
129. 1 Israel, tell us how your **enemies** have persecuted you ever
129. 2 since I was young, my **enemies** have persecuted me cruelly,
132.18 I will cover his **enemies** with shame, but his kingdom
136.24 he freed us from our **enemies;**
138. 7 You oppose my angry **enemies** and save me by your power.
139.22 I regard them as my **enemies.**
140. 9 Don't let my **enemies** be victorious;
142. 3 path where I walk, my **enemies** have hidden a trap for me.
142. 6 Save me from my **enemies;**
143. 3 My **enemy** has hunted me down and completely defeated me.
143. 9 rescue me from my **enemies.**
143.12 love for me, kill my **enemies** and destroy all my oppressors,
144. 6 Send flashes of lightning and scatter your **enemies;**
144.11 Save me from my cruel **enemies;**
Prov 16. 7 When you please the Lord, you can make your **enemies** into friends.
24.17 Don't be glad when your **enemy** meets disaster, and don't
25.21 If your **enemy** is hungry, feed him;
27. 6 But when an **enemy** puts his arm round your shoulder—watch out!
29.24 A thief's partner is his own worst **enemy.**
Is 1.24 take revenge on you, my **enemies,** and you will cause me no
9.11 The Lord has stirred up their **enemies** to attack them.
10.28 The **enemy** army has captured the city of Ai!
10.32 Today the **enemy** are in the town of Nob, and there they
11.13 Judah any more, and Judah will not be the **enemy** of Israel.
18. 5 the grapes are ripening, the **enemy** will destroy the Sudanese
25. 2 The palaces which our **enemies** built are gone for ever.
25. 5 But you, Lord, have silenced our **enemies;**
26.11 Your **enemies** do not know that you will punish them.
27. 5 But if the **enemies** of my people want my protection, let
27. 7 Lord as severely as its **enemies,** nor has she lost as many
30.16 you plan to escape from your **enemies** by riding fast horses.
30.17 away when you see one **enemy** soldier, and five soldiers will
30.25 when the forts of your **enemies** are captured and their people
33. 1 Our **enemies** are doomed!
33.22 seize all the wealth of **enemy** armies, and there will be so
34. 8 Lord will rescue Zion and take vengeance on her **enemies.**
35. 4 God is coming to your rescue, coming to punish your **enemies."**
42.13 he shows his power against his **enemies.**
47.12 perhaps you can frighten your **enemies.**
59.18 He will punish his **enemies** according to what they have done,
61. 2 When the Lord will save his people And defeat their **enemies.**
62. 8 longer be food for your **enemies,** And foreigners will no
63. 4 it was time to punish their **enemies.**
63.10 So the Lord became their **enemy** and fought against them.
63.18 people, were driven out by our **enemies** for a little while;
64. 2 reveal your power to your **enemies,** and make the nations
66. 6 the Temple, is the sound of the Lord punishing his **enemies!**
66.14 who obey me, and I show my anger against my **enemies."**
Jer 2.14 Why then do his **enemies** hunt him down?
4.13 Look, the **enemy** is coming like clouds.
4.16 and to tell Jerusalem that **enemies** are coming from a country
4.16 These **enemies** will shout against the cities of Judah [17]and
5.10 I will send **enemies** to cut down my people's vineyards,
6.25 on the roads, because our **enemies** are armed and terror is
8.16 Our **enemies** are already in the city of Dan;
8.16 Our **enemies** have come to destroy our land and everything in it,
11.18 me of the plots that my **enemies** were making against me.
12. 7 given the people I love into the power of their **enemies.**
13.20 Your **enemies** are coming down from the north!
15. 9 I will let your **enemies** kill those of you who are still
15.11 you on behalf of my **enemies** when they were in trouble and
15.13 to me, "I will send **enemies** to carry away the wealth and
15.14 will make them serve their **enemies** in a land they know
17. 3 I will make your **enemies** take away your wealth and your
17. 4 will make you serve your **enemies** in a land you know nothing
18.17 scatter my people before their **enemies,** like dust blown by
18.19 am saying and listen to what my **enemies** are saying about me.
19. 7 I will let their **enemies** triumph over them and kill them in
19. 9 The **enemy** will surround the city and try to kill its people.
20. 4 you will see them all killed by the swords of their **enemies.**
20. 5 I will also let their **enemies** plunder all the wealth of
20.12 you take revenge on my **enemies,** for I have placed my cause
21. 7 King Nebuchadnezzar and by your **enemies,** who want to kill you.
30.14 I have attacked you like an **enemy;**
30.16 and all your **enemies** will be taken away as prisoners.
30.17 your wounds, though your **enemies** say, 'Zion is an outcast;
31.16 they will return from the **enemy's** land.
32.21 and wonders that terrified our **enemies,** you used your power
34.20 hand them over to their **enemies,** who want to kill them, and
44.30 Hophra of Egypt to his **enemies** who want to kill him, just
44.30 Nebuchadnezzar of Babylonia, who was his **enemy**
46.10 today he will punish his **enemies.**
46.16 Let's go home to our people and escape the **enemy's** sword!'
46.22 runs away, hissing like a snake, as the **enemy's** army approaches.
48. 2 The **enemy** have captured Heshbon and plot to destroy the
49.22 The **enemy** will attack Bozrah like an eagle swooping down
49.37 of Elam afraid of their **enemies,** who want to kill them.
50. 7 Their **enemies** say, 'They sinned against the Lord, and so
51.25 destroys the whole world, but I, the Lord, am your **enemy.**
51.32 The **enemy** have captured the river-crossing and have set
51.33 Soon the **enemy** will cut them down and trample them like
51.36 cause and will make your **enemies** pay for what they did to
Lam 1. 3 their own— Surrounded by **enemies,** with no way to escape.
1. 5 Her **enemies** succeeded;
Lam 1. 7 When she fell to the **enemy,** there was no one to help
1. 9 Her **enemies** have won, and she cries to the Lord for mercy.
1.10 Her **enemies** robbed her of all her treasures.
1.16 The **enemy** has conquered me;
1.17 The Lord has called **enemies** against me from every side;
1.21 My **enemies** are glad that you brought disaster on me.
1.21 make my **enemies** suffer as I do.
2. 3 He refused to help us when the **enemy** came.
2. 4 He aimed his arrows at us like an **enemy;**
2. 5 Like an **enemy,** the Lord has destroyed Israel;
2. 7 He allowed the **enemy** to tear down its walls.
2.16 All your **enemies** mock you and glare at you with hate.
2.17 He gave our **enemies** victory, gave them joy at our downfall.
2.21 the streets, Young men and women, killed by **enemy** swords.
2.22 You invited my **enemies** to hold a carnival of terror all
3.46 "We are insulted and mocked by all our **enemies.**
3.52 trapped like a bird by **enemies** who had no cause to hate
3.60 You know how my **enemies** hate me and how they plot
4.18 The **enemy** was watching for us;
5. 3 been killed by the **enemy,** and now our mothers are widows.
Ezek 5. 8 I, the Sovereign Lord, am telling you that I am your **enemy.**
21. 3 I am your **enemy.**
21.24 You stand condemned, and I will hand you over to your **enemies.**
25.15 on their age-long **enemies** and destroyed them in their hate.
26. 3 I am your **enemy,** city of Tyre.
26. 8 The **enemy** will dig trenches, build earthworks, and make a
26.12 Your **enemies** will help themselves to your wealth and merchandise.
28. 7 as a god, [7]I will bring ruthless **enemies** to attack you.
28.22 I am your **enemy,** Sidon;
29. 3 I am your **enemy,** you monster crocodile, lying in the river.
29.10 made it, [10]I am your **enemy** and the enemy of your Nile.
30.22 I am the **enemy** of the king of Egypt.
30.24 Egypt, and he will groan and die in front of his **enemy.**
33. 3 When he sees the **enemy** approaching, he sounds the alarm to
33. 4 pays no attention and the **enemy** comes and kills him, then he
33. 6 however, the watchman sees the **enemy** coming and does not sound
33. 6 sound the alarm, the **enemy** will come and kill those sinners,
34.10 I, the Sovereign Lord, declare that I am your **enemy.**
35. 3 I am your **enemy,** mountains of Edom!
35. 5 "You were Israel's constant **enemy** and let her people be
36. 2 **enemies** gloated and said, 'Now those ancient hills are ours!'
38. 3 and tell him that I, the Sovereign Lord, am his **enemy.**
39. 1 of Meshech and Tubal, and tell him that I am his **enemy.**
39.23 from them and let their **enemies** defeat them and kill them in
39.27 people back from all the countries where their **enemies** live.
Dan 4.19 and its explanation applied to your **enemies** and not to you.
6.11 When Daniel's **enemies** observed him praying to God,
11.10 will sweep on like a flood and attack an **enemy** fortress.
11.17 in order to destroy his **enemy's** kingdom, he will make an
Hos 8. 1 **Enemies** are swooping down on my land like eagles!
8. 3 Because of this their **enemies** will pursue them.
9. 8 Even in God's Temple the people are the prophet's **enemies.**
11.10 will follow me when I roar like a lion at their **enemies.**
Amos 3.11 And so an **enemy** will surround their land, destroy their defences,
6. 8 their capital city and everything in it to the **enemy."**
9. 4 away into captivity by their **enemies,** I will order them to
Obad 5 But your **enemies** have wiped you out completely.
11 You stood aside on that day when **enemies** broke down their gates.
14 handed them over to the **enemy** on the day of their distress.
Mic 1. 7 fertility rites, and now her **enemies** will carry them off for
1.10 Don't tell our **enemies** in Gath about our defeat;
1.15 hand you over to an **enemy,** who is going to capture your
2. 8 The Lord replies, "You attack my people like **enemies.**
4.10 Babylon, but there the Lord will save you from your **enemies.**
4.13 The Lord says, "People of Jerusalem, go and punish your **enemies!**
5. 3 abandon his people to their **enemies** until the woman who is
5. 9 Israel will conquer her **enemies** and destroy them all.
7. 6 a man's **enemies** are the members of his own family.
7. 8 Our **enemies** have no reason to gloat over us.
7.10 Then our **enemies** will see this and be disgraced—
7.10 the same **enemies** who taunted us by asking, "Where
Nah 1. 8 Like a great rushing flood he completely destroys his **enemies;**
2. 2 of Israel, as it was before her **enemies** plundered her.)
2. 3 The **enemy** soldiers carry red shields and wear uniforms of red.
2.13 "I am your **enemy!"**
3.11 You too will try to escape from your **enemies.**
3.13 and your country stands defenceless before your **enemies.**
Hab 2. 7 **Enemies** will come and make you tremble.
Zeph 1. 7 his people and has invited **enemies** to plunder Judah.
3.15 he has removed all your **enemies.**
Zech 8. 2 her people, a love which has made me angry with her **enemies.**
8.10 either men or animals, and no one was safe from his **enemies.**
9.15 will protect his people, and they will destroy their **enemies.**
9.15 like drunken men and will shed the blood of their **enemies;**
10. 5 who trample their **enemies** into the mud of the streets.
10. 5 Lord is with them, and they will defeat even the **enemy** horsemen.
12. 4 of Judah, but I will make the horses of their **enemies** blind.
14.15 the donkeys—on all the animals in the camps of the **enemy.**
Mt 5.43 heard that it was said, 'Love your friends, hate your **enemies.'**
5.44 love your **enemies** and pray for those who persecute you,
10.36 a man's worst **enemies** will be the members of his own family.
13.25 when everyone was asleep, an **enemy** came and sowed weeds among
13.28 'It was some **enemy** who did this,' he answered.
13.39 and the **enemy** who sowed the weeds is the Devil.
22.44 here on my right until I put your **enemies** under your feet.'
Mk 12.36 here on my right until I put your **enemies** under your feet.'
Lk 1.71 would save us from our **enemies,** from the power of all those
1.73 to rescue us from our **enemies** and allow us to serve him

Lk 6.27 Love your **enemies,** do good to those who hate you,
6.35 Love your **enemies** and do good to them;
10.19 all the power of the **Enemy,** and nothing will hurt you.
13.17 answer made his **enemies** ashamed of themselves, while the people
19.27 Now, as for those **enemies** of mine who did not want me
19.43 will come when your **enemies** will surround you with barricades, blockade
20.43 until I put your **enemies** as a footstool under your feet.'
21.15 wisdom that none of your **enemies** will be able to refute or
23.12 before this they had been **enemies.**
Acts 2.35 until I put your **enemies** as a footstool under your feet.'
13.10 You are the **enemy** of everything that is good.
Rom 5.10 We were God's **enemies,** but he made us his friends
8. 7 so a person becomes an **enemy** of God when he is controlled
11.15 mankind was changed from God's **enemies** into his friends.
11.28 the Jews are God's **enemies** for the sake of you Gentiles.
12.20 "If your **enemy** is hungry, feed him;
1 Cor 15.25 until God defeats all **enemies** and puts them under his feet.
15.26 The last **enemy** to be defeated will be death.
2 Cor 4. 9 there are many **enemies,** but we are never without a friend;
5.18 through Christ changed us from **enemies** into his friends and gave
5.20 let God change you from **enemies** into his friends!
Gal 4.16 Have I now become your **enemy** by telling you the truth?
5.17 These two are **enemies,** and this means that you cannot do
5.20 People become **enemies** and they fight;
Eph 2.14 down the wall that separated them and kept them **enemies.**
6.13 day comes, you will be able to resist the **enemy's** attacks;
Phil 1.28 Don't be afraid of your **enemies;**
3.18 whose lives make them **enemies** of Christ's death on the cross.
Col 1.21 from God and were his **enemies** because of the evil things you
2 Thes 3.15 But do not treat him as an **enemy;**
1 Tim 5.14 so as to give our **enemies** no chance of speaking evil of
Tit 2. 8 be criticized, so that your **enemies** may be put to shame by
Heb 1.13 until I put your **enemies** as a footstool under your feet."
10.13 until God puts his **enemies** as a footstool under his feet.
Jas 4. 4 know that to be the world's friend means to be God's **enemy?**
4. 4 Whoever wants to be the world's friend makes himself God's **enemy.**
1 Pet 5. 8 Your **enemy,** the Devil, roams round like a roaring lion,
1 Jn 2.18 You were told that the **Enemy of Christ** would come;
2.18 and now many **enemies** of Christ have already appeared,
2.22 a person is the **Enemy of Christ**—he rejects both the Father
4. 3 The spirit that he has is from the **Enemy of Christ;**
2 Jn 7 Such a person is a deceiver and the **Enemy of Christ.**
Rev 11. 5 fire comes out of their mouths and destroys their **enemies;**
11.12 As their **enemies** watched, they went up into heaven in a cloud.

ENERGY

Neh 5.16 I put all my **energy** into rebuilding the wall and did not
Prov 31. 3 Don't spend all your **energy** on sex and all your money on

ENFORCE

2 Kgs 23.24 In order to **enforce** the laws written in the book that
Dan 6. 7 Your Majesty should issue an order and **enforce** it strictly.

ENGAGE

Ezek 16.39 places where you **engage** in prostitution and worship idols.

ENGAGED

Ex 22.16 a virgin who is not **engaged,** he must pay the bride-price for
Deut 20. 7 Is there anyone here who is **engaged** to be married?
20. 7 someone else will marry the woman he is **engaged** to.'
22.23 intercourse with a girl who is **engaged** to someone else.
22.24 die because he had intercourse with a girl who was **engaged.**
22.25 the countryside rapes a girl who is **engaged** to someone else.
22.27 The man raped the **engaged** girl in the countryside, and
22.28 "Suppose a man is caught raping a girl who is not **engaged.**
28.30 "You will be **engaged** to a girl—but someone else will
Mt 1.18 mother Mary was **engaged** to Joseph, but before they were married,
1.19 so he made plans to break the **engagement** privately.
1 Cor 7.36 In the case of an **engaged** couple who have decided not to

ENGRAVE

Gen 41.42 from his finger the ring **engraved** with the royal seal and
Ex 28. 9 Take two carnelian stones and **engrave** on them the names of
28.11 Get a skilful jeweller to **engrave** on the two stones the
28.21 twelve stones is to have **engraved** on it the name of one
28.29 he will wear this breast-piece **engraved** with the names of
28.36 of pure gold and **engrave** on it 'Dedicated to the Lord.'
29. 6 sacred sign of dedication **engraved** 'Dedicated to the Lord.'
32.16 made the tablets and had **engraved** the commandments on them.
35.35 done by **engravers,** designers, and weavers of fine linen;
38.23 tribe of Dan, was an **engraver,** a designer, and a weaver of
39. 6 they were skilfully **engraved** with the names of the twelve
39.14 of the twelve stones had **engraved** on it the name of one
39.30 gold, and they **engraved** on it "Dedicated to the Lord."
2 Chr 2. 7 a man with skill in **engraving,** in working gold, silver,
2.14 can do all sorts of **engraving** and can follow any design
Jer 17. 1 it is **engraved** on your hearts with a diamond point and
Zech 3. 9 I will **engrave** an inscription on it, and in a single day

ENGULF

Gen 1. 2 that covered everything was **engulfed** in total darkness,

ENJOY

Gen 18.12 that I am old and worn out, can I still **enjoy** sex?
25.28 because he **enjoyed** eating the animals Esau killed,
41.53 the land of Egypt had **enjoyed** came to an end, [54] and the
Lev 26.34 Then the land will **enjoy** the years of complete
26.43 people, so that it can **enjoy** its complete rest, and they
Deut 12. 7 your families will eat and **enjoy** the good things that you
14.26 God, you and your families are to eat and **enjoy** yourselves.
16.14 **Enjoy** it with your children, your servants, and the Levites,
20. 6 if he is killed in battle, someone else will **enjoy** the wine.
Judg 16.24 They were **enjoying** themselves, so they said,
19. 6 to him, "Please spend the night here and **enjoy** yourself."
19.22 They were **enjoying** themselves when all of a sudden some
2 Sam 7.29 descendants so that they will continue to **enjoy** your favour.
1 Chr 17.27 descendants so that they will continue to **enjoy** your favour.
2 Chr 14. 1 as king, and under Asa the land **enjoyed** peace for ten years.
Ezra 9.12 succeed if we wanted to **enjoy** the land and pass it on
Neh 9.25 they **enjoyed** all the good things you gave them.
Job 3.18 Even prisoners **enjoy** peace, free from shouts and harsh commands.
10.20 Let me **enjoy** the time I have left.
12.11 tongue enjoys tasting food, your ears **enjoy** hearing words.
14. 6 let him **enjoy** his hard life—if he can.
20.12 him that he keeps some in his mouth to **enjoy** its flavour.
20.18 will have no chance to **enjoy** his wealth, [19] because he
36.16 God brought you out of trouble, and let you **enjoy** security;
Ps 34.12 Would you like to **enjoy** life?
37.11 the humble will possess the land and **enjoy** prosperity and peace.
72. 3 May the land **enjoy** prosperity;
Prov 1.22 How long will you **enjoy** pouring scorn on knowledge?
2.14 in doing wrong and who **enjoy** senseless evil, [15] unreliable
10.23 It is foolish to **enjoy** doing wrong.
15.15 is a constant struggle, but happy people always **enjoy** life.
20.17 get by dishonesty you may **enjoy** like the finest food, but
24.25 however, will be prosperous and **enjoy** a good reputation.
Ecc 2. 1 I decided to **enjoy** myself and find out what happiness is.
2.24 do is to eat and drink and **enjoy** what he has earned.
2.25 could you have anything to eat or **enjoy** yourself at all?
3.13 us should eat and drink and **enjoy** what we have worked for.
3.22 thing we can do is to **enjoy** what we have worked for.
5.18 to eat and drink and **enjoy** what he has worked for during
5.19 and property and lets him **enjoy** them,
5.19 he should be grateful and **enjoy** what he has worked for.
6. 2 everything he wants, but then will not let him **enjoy** it.
6. 2 Some stranger will **enjoy** it instead.
6. 6 than the man who never **enjoys** life, though he may live two
8.15 convinced that a man should **enjoy** himself, because the only
8.15 in this life is eating and drinking and **enjoying** himself.
9. 9 **Enjoy** life with the woman you love, as long as you live
9. 9 **Enjoy** every useless day of it, because that is all you will
11. 7 is good to be able to **enjoy** the pleasant light of day.
11. 9 Young people, **enjoy** your youth.
12. 1 and years come when you will say, "I don't **enjoy** life."
Is 3.10 They will be able to **enjoy** what they have worked for.
14. 7 at last the whole world **enjoys** rest and peace, and everyone
24. 9 no one **enjoys** its taste any more.
55. 2 what I say, and you will **enjoy** the best food of all.
58.14 the world, and you will **enjoy** the land I gave to your
61. 6 You will **enjoy** the wealth of the nations And be proud that
65.21 They will plant vineyards and **enjoy** the wine—it will not be
65.21 They will fully **enjoy** the things that they have worked for.
66.11 You will **enjoy** her prosperity,
Jer 2. 7 into a fertile land, to **enjoy** its harvests and its other
22.15 Your father **enjoyed** a full life.
Ezek 18.23 Do you think I **enjoy** seeing an evil man die?"
33.11 am the living God, I do not **enjoy** seeing a sinner die.
Dan 4. 4 "I was living comfortably in my palace, **enjoying** great prosperity.
12. 2 **enjoy** eternal life, and some will suffer eternal disgrace.
Zech 1.15 I am very angry with the nations that **enjoy** quiet and peace.
3.10 his neighbour to come and **enjoy** peace and security,
Lk 12.19 Take life easy, eat, drink, and **enjoy** yourself!'
16.25 But now he is **enjoying** himself here, while you are in pain.
Jn 5.35 and you were willing for a while to **enjoy** his light.
Acts 2.47 praising God, and **enjoying** the good will of all the
Rom 15.24 to go there, after I have **enjoyed** visiting you for a while.
15.32 if it is God's will, and **enjoy** a refreshing visit to you.
1 Tim 6.17 but in God, who generously gives us everything for our **enjoyment.**
Heb 11.25 God's people rather than to **enjoy** sin for a little while.
1 Pet 3.10 scripture says, "Whoever wants to **enjoy** life and wishes to see
2 Pet 2.13 join you in your meals, all the while **enjoying** their deceitful
Rev 14.13 "They will **enjoy** rest from their hard work, because the results

ENLARGE

Deut 12.20 "When the Lord your God **enlarges** your territory, as he has promised,
19. 8 "When the Lord your God **enlarges** your territory, as he
Is 26.15 made our nation grow, **enlarging** its territory on every side,
Jer 22.13 his house by injustice and **enlarges** it by dishonesty;
Mic 7.11 At that time your territory will be **enlarged.**

ENLIST

1 Sam 14.52 who was strong or brave, he would **enlist** him in his army.

ENMITY

Gen 26.21 a quarrel about that one also, so he named it **"Enmity."**
Eph 2.16 By his death on the cross Christ destroyed their **enmity;**

ENOCH (1)
Methuselah's father.

Gen 5.18 162, he had a son, **Enoch,** [19] and then lived another 800 years.
5.21 When **Enoch** was 65, he had a son, Methuselah.
5.22 After that, **Enoch** lived in fellowship with God for 300
1 Chr 1. 3 Jared was the father of **Enoch,** who was the father of Methuselah;
Lk 3.37 of Methuselah, the son of **Enoch,** the son of Jared, the son
Heb 11. 5 It was faith that kept **Enoch** from dying.
11. 5 scripture says that before **Enoch** was taken up, he had pleased
Jude 14 was **Enoch,** the sixth direct descendant from Adam, who long ago

ENORMOUS

Gen 30.30 before I came has grown **enormously,** and the Lord has blessed
1 Sam 30.16 and celebrating because of the **enormous** amount of loot they
1 Chr 12.22 joined David's forces, so that his army was soon **enormous.**
Ezek 38. 4 horses and uniformed riders, is **enormous,** and every soldier
Rev 7. 9 looked, and there was an **enormous** crowd—no one could count

ENOUGH

Gen 3.17 hard all your life to make it produce **enough** food for you.
7.17 and the water became deep **enough** for the boat to float.
13. 6 And so there was not **enough** pasture land for the two of
19.20 It is near **enough.**
30.15 "Isn't it **enough** that you have taken away my husband?
33. 5 whom God has been good **enough** to give me," Jacob answered.
33. 9 But Esau said, "I have **enough,** my brother;
34.21 The land is large **enough** for them also.
40.14 you, and please be kind **enough** to mention me to the king
45.18 in Egypt, and they will have more than **enough** to live on.
Ex 2.10 when the child was old **enough,** she took him to the king's
5. 8 They haven't **enough** work to do, and that is why they keep
9.28 We have had **enough** of this thunder and hail!
10.21 sky, and a darkness thick **enough** to be felt will cover the
16. 4 people must go out every day and gather **enough** for that day.
16.13 flock of quails flew in, **enough** to cover the camp, and in
16.29 sixth day I will always give you **enough** food for two days.
21.21 The loss of his property is punishment **enough.**
23.30 by little, until there are **enough** of you to take possession
32.19 When Moses came close **enough** to the camp to see the
36. 7 been brought was more than **enough** to finish all the work.
Lev 25.21 year so that it will produce **enough** food for two years.
25.22 year, and you will have **enough** to eat until the crops you
25.26 become prosperous and have **enough** to buy it back himself.
25.28 if he does not have **enough** money to buy the land back,
25.49 or if he himself earns **enough,** he may buy his own freedom.
Num 11.13 Where could I get **enough** meat for all these people?
11.21 you say that you will give them **enough** meat for a month?
11.22 Could **enough** cattle and sheep be killed to satisfy them?
11.22 Are all the fish in the sea **enough** for them?"
13.30 we are strong **enough** to conquer it."
13.31 Caleb said, "No, we are not strong **enough** to attack them;
13.32 "That land doesn't even produce **enough** to feed the people
14.27 I have heard **enough** of these complaints!
16.13 Isn't it **enough** that you have brought us out of the
20.12 "Because you did not have **enough** faith to acknowledge my
22.37 Did you think I wasn't able to reward you **enough?"**
Deut 1. 6 God said to us, 'You have stayed long **enough** at this mountain.
2. 3 me [3] that we had spent **enough** time wandering about in those
3.26 Instead, he said, 'That's **enough!**
9. 8 Mount Sinai you made the Lord angry—angry **enough** to destroy you.
9.19 Lord's fierce anger, because he was furious **enough** to destroy you;
9.20 The Lord was also angry **enough** with Aaron to kill him,
19.15 "One witness is not **enough** to convict a man of a crime;
Josh 14.11 I am still strong **enough** for war or for anything else.
17.16 "The hill-country is not big **enough** for us, but the
22.17 Wasn't that sin **enough?**
Judg 6.38 squeezed the wool and wrung **enough** dew out of it to fill
21.14 But there were not **enough** of them.
Ruth 3.14 up before it was light **enough** for her to be seen, because
1 Sam 21.15 Haven't I got **enough** madmen already?
23. 3 said to him, "We have **enough** to be afraid of here in
28.22 You must eat so that you will be strong **enough** to travel."
2 Sam 3.29 work or is killed in battle or hasn't **enough** to eat!"
5. 8 **Enough** to kill them?
8. 4 He kept **enough** horses for a hundred chariots and crippled
12. 8 If this had not been **enough,** I would have given you twice
19.30 "It's **enough** for me that Your Majesty has come home safely."
24.16 That's **enough!"**
1 Kgs 1.40 playing flutes, making **enough** noise to shake the ground.
8.27 even all heaven is large **enough** to hold you,
8.27 so how can this Temple that I have built be large **enough?**
12.28 "You have been going long **enough** to Jerusalem to worship.
16.31 It was not **enough** for him to sin like King Jeroboam;
17.15 told her, and all of them had **enough** food for many days.
17.20 She has been kind **enough** to take care of me, and now
18. 5 see if we can find **enough** grass to keep the horses and
18.32 a trench round it, large **enough** to hold almost fourteen
19. 8 and the food gave him **enough** strength to walk forty days to
20.10 "I will bring **enough** men to destroy this city of yours and
2 Kgs 4. 7 debts, and there will be **enough** money left over for you and
4.43 "Do you think this is **enough** for a hundred men?"
1 Chr 18. 4 He kept **enough** horses for a hundred chariots and crippled
21.15 That's **enough!"**
2 Chr 6.18 even all heaven is large **enough** to hold you,
6.18 so how can this Temple that I have built be large **enough?**
24. 5 collect from all the people **enough** money to make the annual
28.13 against the Lord and made him angry **enough** to punish us.
2 Chr 28.15 sandals to wear, gave them **enough** to eat and drink, and put
29.34 Since there were not **enough** priests to kill all these animals,
30. 1 the first month, because not **enough** priests were ritually
31.10 the Temple, there has been **enough** to eat and a large surplus
Neh 5. 3 and houses to get **enough** corn to keep us from starving."
8. 2 women, and the children who were old **enough** to understand.
8.10 Share your food and wine with those who haven't **enough.**
9. 5 glorious name, although no human praise is great **enough."**
10.28 and all our children old **enough** to understand, [29] do hereby
13.10 the people had not been giving them **enough** to live on.
Esth 2.14 again unless he liked her **enough** to ask for her by name.
5. 8 "If Your Majesty is kind **enough** to grant my request, I
Job 1.10 you have given him **enough** cattle to fill the whole country.
6.29 You have gone far **enough.**
7.19 Won't you look away long **enough** for me to swallow my spittle?
15.31 If he is foolish **enough** to trust in evil, then evil will
19.22 Haven't you tormented me **enough?**
21. 5 Isn't that **enough** to make you stare in shocked silence?
27.14 their children never have **enough** to eat.
34.22 There is no darkness dark **enough** to hide a sinner from God.
38.37 Who is wise **enough** to count the clouds and tilt them
42.16 **enough** to see his grandchildren and great-grandchildren.
Ps 17.14 may there be **enough** for their children and some left over
37.19 they will have **enough** in time of famine.
49. 8 pay would never be **enough** [9] to keep him from the grave,
59.15 about for food and growling if they do not find **enough.**
106. 2 Who can praise him **enough?**
145.16 You give them **enough** and satisfy the needs of all.
Prov 13.25 The righteous have **enough** to eat, but the wicked are always hungry.
19.18 Discipline your children while they are young **enough** to learn.
20.16 Anyone stupid **enough** to promise to be responsible for a
21. 5 if you act too quickly, you will never have **enough.**
23. 4 Be wise **enough** not to wear yourself out trying to get rich.
27.13 Anyone stupid **enough** to promise to be responsible for a
30.32 If you have been foolish **enough** to be arrogant and plan evil,
Ecc 1. 8 Our eyes can never see **enough** to be satisfied;
1. 8 our ears can never hear **enough.**
5.12 may or may not have **enough** to eat, but at least he
6. 7 work just to get something to eat, but he never has **enough.**
8.11 Because crime is not punished quickly **enough.**
Is 1.11 I have had more than **enough** of the sheep you burn as
7.13 It's bad **enough** for you to wear out the patience of men
7.15 the time he is old **enough** to make his own decisions, people
8. 4 Before the boy is old **enough** to say 'Mummy' and 'Daddy,'
30.14 there is no piece big **enough** to pick up hot coals with,
30.16 think your horses are fast **enough,** but those who pursue you
30.17 and five soldiers will be **enough** to make you all run away.
40. 2 have suffered long **enough** and their sins are now forgiven.
40.16 of Lebanon are not **enough** for a sacrifice to our God,
56.11 They are like greedy dogs that never get **enough.**
Jer 9.12 Who is wise **enough** to understand this?
15. 5 Who will stop long **enough** to ask how you are?
Lam 5. 6 To get food **enough** to stay alive, we went begging to Egypt
Ezek 7.13 No merchant will live long **enough** to get back what he
16. 5 No one took **enough** pity on you to do any of these
16.20 Wasn't it bad **enough** to be unfaithful to me, [21] without
19.11 The vine grew tall **enough** to reach the clouds;
22.14 courage left or have strength **enough** to lift your hand when
30.21 it could heal and be strong **enough** to hold a sword again.
32.27 These heroes were once powerful **enough** to terrify the living.
33.13 that his past goodness is **enough** and begins to sin, I will
37.10 There were **enough** of them to form an army.
39. 9 and clubs, and will have **enough** to last for seven years.
Dan 4.12 loaded down with fruit—**enough** for the whole world to eat.
4.21 were beautiful, and it had **enough** fruit on it to feed the
8.10 It grew strong **enough** to attack the army of heaven, the
11.15 even the best of them will not have **enough** strength.
Hos 5.15 people until they have suffered **enough** for their sins and
9. 2 soon you will not have **enough** corn and olive-oil, and there
Joel 2.13 tearing your clothes is not **enough."**
Amos 4. 8 they hoped to find water, but there was not **enough** to drink.
6.13 You boast, "We were strong **enough** to take Karnaim."
7.12 Amaziah then said to Amos, "That's **enough,** prophet!
Jon 4. 9 "I have every right to be angry—angry **enough** to die!"
Hag 1. 6 You have food to eat, but not **enough** to make you full.
1. 6 You have wine to drink, but not **enough** to get drunk on!
1. 6 You have clothing, but not **enough** to keep you warm.
1. 6 And the working man cannot earn **enough** to live on.
Mt 3.11 and I am not good **enough** even to carry his sandals.
6.34 it will have **enough** worries of its own.
13. 6 roots had not grown deep **enough,** the plants soon dried up.
13.12 will be given more, so that he will have more than **enough;**
14.20 Everyone ate and had **enough.**
15.33 "Where will we find **enough** food in this desert to feed
15.37 They all ate and had **enough.**
17.20 "It was because you haven't **enough** faith," answered Jesus.
17.27 will find a coin worth **enough** for my temple-tax and yours.
18.25 The servant did not have **enough** to pay his debt,
25. 9 wise ones answered, 'there is not **enough** for you and for us.
25.29 even more will be given, and he will have more than **enough;**
Mk 1. 7 I am not good **enough** even to bend down and untie his
4. 6 roots had not grown deep **enough,** the plants soon dried up.
6.42 Everyone ate and had **enough.**
8. 4 this desert can anyone find **enough** food to feed all these
8. 8 Everybody ate and had **enough**—there were about four thousand
8.14 disciples had forgotten to bring **enough** bread and had only
9.24 father at once cried out, "I do have faith, but not **enough.**
14.41 **Enough!** The hour has come!
Lk 3.16 I am not good **enough** even to untie his sandals.
9.17 They all ate and had **enough,** and the disciples took up

Lk	14.28	cost, to see if he has **enough** money to finish the job.
	14.31	and decide if he is strong **enough** to face that other king.
	16. 3	I am not strong **enough** to dig ditches, and I am ashamed
	16.30	The rich man answered, 'That is not **enough,** father Abraham!
	22.38	"That is **enough!"**
	22.51	But Jesus said, **"Enough** of this!"
Jn	1.27	but I am not good **enough** even to untie his sandals."
	2. 6	each one large **enough** to hold about a hundred litres.
	6. 5	"Where can we buy **enough** food to feed all these people?"
	6. 7	take more than two hundred silver coins to buy **enough** bread."
	6. 9	But they will certainly not be **enough** for all these people."
	9.21	he is old **enough,** and he can answer for himself!"
	9.23	That is why his parents said, "He is old **enough;**
Acts	10.33	for you at once, and you have been good **enough** to come.
	13.25	and I am not good **enough** to take his sandals off his
	27.38	After everyone had eaten **enough,** they lightened the ship
2 Cor	2. 6	It is **enough** that this person has been punished in this
	9. 8	need for yourselves and more than **enough** for every good cause.
	9.11	always make you rich **enough** to be generous at all times,
	11.27	I have often been without **enough** food, shelter, or clothing.
Phil	4.12	be in need and what it is to have more than **enough.**
	4.18	you have given me—and it has been more than **enough!**
1 Tim	6. 8	if we have food and clothes, that should be **enough** for us.
Phlm	8	reason I could be bold **enough,** as your brother in Christ,
Heb	5.12	There has been **enough** time for you to be teachers—yet
	11.32	There isn't **enough** time for me to speak of Gideon, Barak,
	11.38	The world was not good **enough** for them!
	13.23	If he comes soon **enough,** I will have him with me when
Jas	2.15	or sisters who need clothes and don't have **enough** to eat.
1 Pet	4. 3	You have spent **enough** time in the past doing what the
3 Jn	10	But that is not **enough** for him;

ENROL

Ex	38.26	total paid by all persons **enrolled** in the census, each one
	38.26	603,550 men twenty years old or older **enrolled** in the census.
Num	2.32	people of Israel **enrolled** in the divisions, group by group,
	3.15	Levites by clans and families, **enrolling** every male a month
	3.22	males one month old or older that were **enrolled** was 7,500.
	3.28	males one month old or older that were **enrolled** was 8,600.
	3.34	males one month old or older that were **enrolled** was 6,200.
	3.39	old or older that Moses **enrolled** by clans at the command of

ENSLAVE see SLAVE

ENTER

Ex	12.23	not let the Angel of Death **enter** your houses and kill you.
	12.25	When you **enter** the land that the Lord has promised to
	28.29	"When Aaron **enters** the Holy Place, he will wear this
	33. 8	the door of their tents and watch Moses until he **entered** it.
Lev	10. 9	your sons are not to **enter** the Tent of my presence after
	12. 4	anything that is holy or **enter** the sacred Tent until the
	14. 8	He may **enter** the camp, but he must live outside his tent
	14.34	after the people of Israel **entered** the land of Canaan, which
	14.46	Anyone who **enters** the house while it is locked up will
	16. 3	He may **enter** the Most Holy Place only after he has brought
	16.17	From the time Aaron **enters** the Most Holy Place to
	16.23	he had put on before **entering** the Most Holy Place, and leave
	20.23	am driving out those pagans so that you can **enter** the land.
	21.11	Tent by leaving it and **entering** a house where there is a
	25. 2	When you **enter** the land that the Lord is giving you, you
Num	4. 5	Aaron and his sons shall **enter** the Tent, take down the
	4.20	But if the Kohathites **enter** the Tent and see the priests
	5.22	May this water **enter** your stomach and cause it to swell
	14.22	none of these people will live to **enter** that land.
	14.23	never **enter** the land which I promised to their ancestors.
	14.23	None of those who have rejected me will ever **enter** it.
	14.29	none of you over twenty years of age will **enter** that land.
	19. 7	and pour water over himself, and then he may **enter** the camp;
	19.14	time of death or who **enters** it becomes ritually unclean for
	20.24	"Aaron is not going to **enter** the land which I promised
	31.24	ritually clean and will be permitted to **enter** the camp."
	32. 9	they discouraged the people from **entering** the land which the
	32.11	came out of Egypt will **enter** the land that I promised to
	34. 2	"When you **enter** Canaan, the land which I am giving you, the
	35.10	cross the River Jordan and **enter** the land of Canaan, [11] you
Deut	1.26	of the Lord your God, and you would not **enter** the land.
	1.35	from this evil generation will **enter** the fertile land that I
	1.36	Only Caleb son of Jephunneh will **enter** it.
	1.37	with me and said, 'Not even you, Moses, will **enter** the land.
	1.39	know right from wrong, will **enter** the land—the children you
	4.21	cross the River Jordan to **enter** the fertile land which he is
	6. 1	them in the land that you are about to **enter** and occupy.
	11. 8	the river and occupy the land that you are about to **enter.**
	11.11	that you are about to **enter** is a land of mountains and
	12. 9	because you have not yet **entered** the land that the Lord
	15. 9	Do not let such an evil thought **enter** your mind.
	26. 3	my God that I have **entered** the land that he promised our
	27. 2	cross the River Jordan and **enter** the land that the Lord your
	27. 3	When you have **entered** the rich and fertile land that the Lord,
	29.12	You are here today to **enter** into this covenant that the
	31.16	worship the pagan gods of the land they are about to **enter.**
	32.52	distance, but you will not **enter** the land that I am giving
Josh	6. 1	No one could **enter** or leave the city.
1 Sam	16.21	David came to Saul and **entered** his service.
	26. 7	that night David and Abishai **entered** Saul's camp and found
	26.15	Just now someone **entered** the camp to kill your master.
2 Sam	5. 8	"The blind and the crippled cannot **enter** the Lord's house.")
	7.10	Ever since they **entered** this land, they have been attacked
2 Sam	16.15	Israelites with him **entered** Jerusalem,
	17.17	because they did not dare to be seen **entering** the city.
1 Kgs	14.12	As soon as you **enter** the town your son will die.
	14.17	Just as she **entered** her home, the child died.
	16.10	Zimri **entered** the house, assassinated Elah,
	19.15	the wilderness near Damascus, then **enter** the city and anoint
2 Kgs	6.20	As soon as they had **entered** the city, Elisha prayed,
	7. 8	they returned, **entered** another tent, and did the same thing.
	9.34	over her body, [34] **entered** the palace, and had a meal.
	11.17	King Joash and the people **enter** into a covenant with the
	11.19	Joash **entered** by the Guard Gate and took his place on the
	12. 9	by the altar, on the right side as one **enters** the Temple.
	19.32	'He will not **enter** this city or shoot a single arrow against
	19.33	back by the same road he came, without **entering** this city.
	23. 8	to the left of the main gate as one **enters** the city.
	25. 8	to the king and commander of his army, **entered** Jerusalem.
1 Chr	17. 9	Ever since they **entered** this land they have been attacked by
2 Chr	6.41	the symbol of your power, **enter** the Temple and stay here for
	7. 2	full of the dazzling light, the priests could not **enter** it.
	20.10	did not allow them to **enter** those lands, so our ancestors
	23. 6	No one is to **enter** the temple buildings except the priests
	23. 6	They may **enter,** because they are consecrated, but the rest
	23. 7	Anyone who tries to **enter** the Temple is to be killed."
	23.20	They **entered** by the main gate, and the king took his place
	26.21	Unable to **enter** the Temple again, he lived in his own house,
	28. 9	as it was about to **enter** the city, and he said, "The
Esth	6. 4	Now Haman had just **entered** the courtyard;
	8. 1	then on Mordecai was allowed to **enter** the king's presence.
Ps	15. 1	Lord, who may **enter** your Temple?
	24. 3	Who may **enter** his holy Temple?
	45.15	With joy and gladness they come and **enter** the king's palace.
	95.11	'You will never **enter** the land where I would have given
	100. 4	**Enter** the temple gates with thanksgiving,
Prov	9.18	that those who have already **entered** are now deep in the
Ecc	5.15	We leave this world just as we **entered** it—with nothing.
Song	5. 1	I have **entered** my garden, my sweetheart, my bride.
Is	26. 2	and let the faithful nation **enter,** the nation whose people
	37.33	'He will not **enter** this city or shoot a single arrow against
	37.34	by the road on which he came, without **entering** this city.
	52. 1	The heathen will never **enter** your gates again.
Jer	7.31	command them to do this—it did not even **enter** my mind.
	9.21	Death has come in through our windows and **entered** our palaces;
	16. 5	"You must not **enter** a house where there is mourning.
	16. 8	"Do not **enter** a house where people are feasting.
	17.19	through which the kings of Judah **enter** and leave the city;
	17.20	who lives in Jerusalem and **enters** these gates, to listen to
	17.25	their kings and princes will **enter** the gates of Jerusalem
	19. 5	it never even **entered** my mind.
	32.35	and it did not even **enter** my mind that they would do
	52.12	to the king and commander of his army, **entered** Jerusalem.
Lam	1.10	She saw them **enter** the Temple itself, Where the Lord had
	4.12	believed that any invader could **enter** Jerusalem's gates.
Ezek	2. 2	voice was speaking, God's spirit **entered** me and raised me to
	3.24	the ground, [24] but God's spirit **entered** me and raised me to
	37.10	Breath **entered** the bodies, and they came to life and stood up.
	42.13	In them the priests who **enter** the Lord's presence eat the
	44. 2	because I, the Lord God of Israel, have **entered** through it.
	44. 3	He is to **enter** and leave the gateway through the entrance
	44. 7	who do not obey me, **enter** the Temple when the fat and
	44. 9	one who disobeys me, will **enter** my Temple, not even a
	44.13	that is holy to me or to **enter** the Most Holy Place.
	44.16	They alone will **enter** my Temple, serve at my altar, and
	44.17	When they **enter** the gateway to the inner courtyard of the Temple,
	46. 9	at any festival, those who **enter** by the north gate are to
	46. 9	have worshipped, and those who **enter** by the south gate are
	46. 9	the same way as he **entered,** but must leave by the opposite
Dan	5.10	the king and his noblemen and **entered** the banqueting-hall.
	11. 7	of the king of Syria, **enter** their fortress, and defeat them.
Hos	6. 7	"But as soon as they **entered** the land at Adam, they broke
	7. 2	It never **enters** their heads that I will remember all this evil;
	13. 6	But when you **entered** the good land, you became full and satisfied,
Obad	13	You should not have **entered** the city of my people to
Zech	5. 4	curse out, and it will **enter** the house of every thief and
Mt	5.20	you will be able to **enter** the Kingdom of heaven only if
	7.21	calls me 'Lord, Lord' will **enter** the Kingdom of heaven, but
	8. 5	Jesus **entered** Capernaum, a Roman officer met him and begged
	18. 3	like children, you will never **enter** the Kingdom of heaven.
	18. 8	is better for you to **enter** life without a hand or
	18. 9	is better for you to **enter** life with only one eye than
	19.17	Keep the commandments if you want to **enter** life."
	19.23	be very hard for rich people to **enter** the Kingdom of heaven.
	19.24	for a rich person to **enter** the Kingdom of God than for
	21.10	When Jesus **entered** Jerusalem, the whole city was thrown into
	23.13	nor do you allow in those who are trying to **enter!**
Mk	5.13	the evil spirits went out of the man and **entered** the pigs.
	9.43	is better for you to **enter** life without a hand than to
	9.45	is better for you to **enter** life without a foot than to
	9.47	is better for you to **enter** the Kingdom of God with only
	10.15	the Kingdom of God like a child will never **enter** it."
	10.23	it will be for rich people to **enter** the Kingdom of God!"
	10.24	"My children, how hard it is to **enter** the Kingdom of God!
	10.25	for a rich person to **enter** the Kingdom of God than for
	11.11	Jesus **entered** Jerusalem, went into the Temple, and looked
	14.14	to the house he **enters,** and say to the owner of
	16. 5	So they **entered** the tomb, where they saw a young man
Lk	18.17	the Kingdom of God like a child will never **enter** it."
	18.24	hard it is for rich people to **enter** the Kingdom of God!
	18.25	for a rich person to **enter** the Kingdom of God than for
	22. 3	Satan **entered** Judas, called Iscariot, who was one of the twelve
	22.10	into the house that he **enters,** [11] and say to the owner of

Lk 24.26 Messiah to suffer these things and then to **enter** his glory?"
Jn 3. 4 certainly cannot **enter** his mother's womb and be born a second
3. 5 "No one can **enter** the Kingdom of God unless he is born
10. 1 the man who does not **enter** the sheepfold by the gate, but
13.27 As soon as Judas took the bread, Satan **entered** him.
Acts 1.13 They **entered** the city and went up to the room where they
5.21 and at dawn they **entered** the Temple and started teaching.
9.17 Ananias went, **entered** the house where Saul was, and placed his
11. 8 No ritually unclean or defiled food has ever **entered** my mouth.'
14.22 pass through many troubles to **enter** the Kingdom of God,"
25.23 great pomp and ceremony and **entered** the audience hall with the
Heb 3.11 'They will never **enter** the land where I would have given
3.18 "They will never **enter** the land where I would have
3.19 they were not able to **enter** the land, because they did not
4. 3 'They will never **enter** the land where I would have given
4. 5 "They will never **enter** that land where I would have given
9.12 went through the tent and **entered** once and for all into the
2 Pet 1.11 given the full right to **enter** the eternal Kingdom of our
Rev 11.11 life-giving breath came from God and **entered** them, and they
21.27 nothing that is impure will **enter** the city, nor anyone who
21.27 in the Lamb's book of the living will **enter** the city.

ENTERTAIN

Judg 16.24 said, "Call Samson, and let's make him **entertain** us!"
16.24 the prison, they made him **entertain** them and made him stand
16.27 men and women on the roof, watching Samson **entertain** them.
Ps 45. 8 musicians **entertain** you in palaces decorated with ivory.
137. 3 they told us to **entertain** them:
Ecc 2. 8 Men and women sang to **entertain** me, and I had all the
Ezek 33.32 are nothing more than an **entertainer** singing love songs or
Dan 6.18 sleepless night, without food or any form of **entertainment.**

ENTHRONE see THRONE

ENTHUSIASM

Prov 19. 2 **Enthusiasm** without knowledge is not good;
Acts 18.25 and with great **enthusiasm** he proclaimed and taught correctly

ENTIRE

Rom 6.19 you surrendered yourselves **entirely** as slaves to impurity and
6.19 now surrender yourselves **entirely** as slaves of righteousness
1 Cor 5. 7 the old yeast of sin so that you will be **entirely** pure.
Jas 3. 6 It sets on fire the **entire** course of our existence with the

ENTITLED

Deut 21.17 first son and give him the share he is legally **entitled** to.
2 Chr 31. 4 priests and the Levites were **entitled,** so that they could
Neh 5.14 nor I ate the food I was **entitled** to have as governor.
5.18 I did not claim the allowance that the governor is **entitled** to.

ENTRAILS

2 Sam 20.10 him in the belly, and his **entrails** spilt out on the ground.

ENTRANCE

Gen 18. 1 Abraham was sitting at the **entrance** of his tent during the
38.14 and sat down at the **entrance** to Enaim, a town on the
Ex 26.36 "For the **entrance** of the Tent make a curtain of fine
27.13 the east side, where the **entrance** is, the enclosure is also
27.14 On each side of the **entrance** there are to be 6.6
27.16 For the **entrance** itself there is to be a curtain 9
29. 4 and his sons to the **entrance** of the Tent of my presence,
29.11 bull there in my holy presence at the **entrance** of the Tent.
29.32 At the **entrance** of the Tent of my presence they are to
29.42 in my presence at the **entrance** of the Tent of my presence.
35.15 the curtain for the **entrance** of the Tent;
35.17 the curtain for the **entrance** of the enclosure;
36.37 For the **entrance** of the Tent they made a curtain of fine
38. 8 women who served at the **entrance** of the Tent of the Lord's
38.13 the east side, where the **entrance** was, the enclosure was
38.14 On each side of the **entrance** there were 6.6 metres of curtains,
38.18 The curtain for the **entrance** of the enclosure was made
38.30 made the bases for the **entrance** of the Tent of the Lord's
38.31 surrounding enclosure and for the **entrance** of the enclosure,
39.38 the curtain for the **entrance** of the Tent;
39.40 the curtain for the **entrance** of the enclosure and its ropes;
40. 5 Covenant Box and hang the curtain at the **entrance** of the Tent.
40. 8 Put up the surrounding enclosure and hang the curtain at its **entrance.**
40.12 and his sons to the **entrance** of the Tent, and tell them
40.28 hung the curtain at the **entrance** of the Tent, [29] and there
40.33 altar and hung the curtain at the **entrance** of the enclosure.
Lev 1. 3 must present it at the **entrance** of the Tent of the Lord's
1. 5 sides of the altar which is at the **entrance** of the Tent.
3. 2 and kill it at the **entrance** of the Tent of the Lord's
4. 4 bring the bull to the **entrance** of the Tent, put his hand
4. 7 burning sacrifices, which is at the **entrance** of the Tent.
4.18 burning sacrifices, which is at the **entrance** of the Tent.
8. 2 and his sons to the **entrance** of the Tent of my presence
8.31 "Take the meat to the **entrance** of the Tent of the Lord's
8.33 You shall not leave the **entrance** of the Tent for seven days,
8.35 You must stay at the **entrance** of the Tent day and night
10. 7 Do not leave the **entrance** of the Tent or you will die,
12. 6 to the priest at the **entrance** of the Tent of the Lord's
14.11 and these offerings to the **entrance** of the Tent of the
Lev 14.23 shall bring them to the priest at the **entrance** of the Tent.
15.14 or two pigeons to the **entrance** of the Tent of the Lord's
15.29 to the priest at the **entrance** of the Tent of the Lord's
16. 7 the two goats to the **entrance** of the Tent of the Lord's
17. 3 Lord anywhere except at the **entrance** of the Tent of the
17. 5 to the priest at the **entrance** of the Tent and kill them
17. 6 of the altar at the **entrance** of the Tent and burn the
17. 9 Lord anywhere except at the **entrance** of the Tent shall no
19.21 bring a ram to the **entrance** of the Tent of my presence
Num 3.25 cover, the curtain for the **entrance,** [26] the curtains for
3.26 the altar, and the curtain for the **entrance** of the court.
3.31 and the curtain at the **entrance** to the Most Holy Place.
4.25 it, the curtain for the **entrance,** [26] the curtains and ropes
4.26 altar, the curtains for the **entrance** of the court, and all
6.10 to the priest at the **entrance** of the Tent of the Lord's
6.13 He shall go to the **entrance** of the Tent [14] and present to
6.18 At the **entrance** of the Tent the Nazirite shall shave off
10. 3 gather round you at the **entrance** to the Tent of my presence.
11.10 they stood about in groups at the **entrances** of their tents.
12. 5 of cloud, stood at the **entrance** of the Tent, and called out,
16.18 it, and stood at the **entrance** of the Tent with Moses and
16.19 stood facing Moses and Aaron at the **entrance** of the Tent.
16.27 and were standing at the **entrance** of their tents, with their
16.50 Aaron returned to Moses at the **entrance** of the Tent.
20. 6 away from the people and stood at the **entrance** of the Tent.
25. 6 they were mourning at the **entrance** of the Tent of the Lord's
27. 2 the whole community at the **entrance** of the Tent of the
Deut 22.21 take her out to the **entrance** of her father's house, where
Josh 8.11 him went towards the main **entrance** to the city and set up
8.29 and it was thrown down at the **entrance** to the city gate.
10.18 "Roll some big stones in front of the **entrance** to the cave.
10.22 Then Joshua said, "Open the **entrance** to the cave and
10.27 stones were placed at the **entrance** to the cave, and they are
19.51 Lord at Shiloh, at the **entrance** of the Tent of the Lord's
20. 4 place of judgement at the **entrance** to the city, and explain
1 Sam 2.22 women who worked at the **entrance** to the Tent of the Lord's
10. 5 At the **entrance** to the town you will meet a group of
2 Sam 10. 8 position at the **entrance** to Rabbah, their capital city,
1 Kgs 6. 3 The **entrance** room was 4.5 metres deep and 9 metres wide,
6. 8 The **entrance** to the lowest storey of the annexe was on
6.21 chains were placed across the **entrance** of the inner room,
6.31 was set in place at the **entrance** of the Most Holy Place;
6.33 For the **entrance** to the main room a rectangular
7.12 of the Temple, and the **entrance** room of the Temple had walls
7.15 and placed them at the **entrance** of the Temple.
7.21 two bronze columns in front of the **entrance** of the Temple:
19.13 cloak and went out and stood at the **entrance** of the cave.
2 Kgs 5. 9 and chariot, and stopped at the **entrance** to Elisha's house.
11.14 by the column at the **entrance** of the Temple, as was the
12. 9 priests on duty at the **entrance** put in the box all the
16.18 and closed up the king's private **entrance** to the Temple.
22. 4 priests on duty at the **entrance** to the Temple have collected
23. 4 guards on duty at the **entrance** to the Temple to bring out
1 Chr 9.18 been stationed at the eastern **entrance** to the King's Gate.
9.19 was responsible for guarding the **entrance** to the Tent of the
9.21 also a guard at the **entrance** to the Tent of the Lord's
9.22 212 men were chosen as guards for the **entrances** and gates.
19. 9 position at the **entrance** to Rabbah, their capital city,
2 Chr 3. 4 The **entrance** room was the full width of the Temple, nine
3.11 where they stood side by side facing the **entrance.**
3.17 The columns were set at the sides of the temple **entrance:**
23.13 new king at the temple **entrance,** standing by the column
29.17 finished it all, including the **entrance** room to the Temple.
Neh 3.20 section, as far as the **entrance** to the house of the High
Esth 2.21 palace eunuchs who guarded the **entrance** to the king's rooms,
4. 2 and bitterly, [2] until he came to the **entrance** of the palace.
4. 6 Mordecai in the city square at the **entrance** of the palace.
5. 1 The king was inside, seated on the royal throne, facing the **entrance.**
5. 9 he saw Mordecai at the **entrance** of the palace, and when
5.13 I see that Jew Mordecai sitting at the **entrance** of the palace."
6.10 You will find him sitting at the **entrance** of the palace."
6.12 went back to the palace **entrance** while Haman hurried home,
Prov 8. 3 At the **entrance** to the city, beside the gates, she calls:
8.34 at my door every day, waiting at the **entrance** to my home.
Jer 36.10 the upper court near the **entrance** of the New Gate of the
38.14 to him at the third **entrance** to the Temple, and he said,
43. 9 pavement in front of the **entrance** to the government building
Ezek 8. 3 took me to the inner **entrance** of the north gate of the
8. 5 near the altar by the **entrance** of the gateway I saw the
8. 7 He took me to the **entrance** of the outer courtyard and
8.16 There near the **entrance** of the sanctuary, between the altar
9. 3 where it had been, and moved to the **entrance** of the Temple.
10. 4 from the creatures and moved to the **entrance** of the Temple.
10.18 the Lord's presence left the **entrance** of the Temple and
40. 6 went up the steps, and at the top he measured the **entrance;**
40. 7 long that led to an **entrance** room which faced the Temple.
40.21 walls between them, and the **entrance** room all had the same
40.22 The **entrance** room, the windows, and the carved
40.22 to the gate, and the **entrance** room was at the end facing
40.24 its inner walls and its **entrance** room, and they were the
40.26 up to it, and its **entrance** room was also at the end
40.29 Its guardrooms, its **entrance** room, and its inner
40.31 Its **entrance** room faced the other courtyard, and
40.33 Its guardrooms, its **entrance** room, and its inner walls
40.33 There were windows all round, and in the **entrance** room also.
40.34 The **entrance** room faced the outer courtyard.
40.36 inner walls, an **entrance** room, and windows all round.
40.37 The **entrance** room faced the outer courtyard.
40.38 It opened into the **entrance** room that faced the courtyard,
40.39 In this **entrance** room there were four tables, two on

Ezek 40.40 two on either side of the **entrance** of the north gate.
40.48 Then he took me into the **entrance** room of the Temple.
40.48 He measured the **entrance:**
40.49 Steps led up to the **entrance** room, which was ten metres
40.49 There were two columns, one on each side of the **entrance.**
41.15 The **entrance** room of the Temple, the Holy Place, and the
41.21 In front of the **entrance** of the Most Holy Place there was
41.25 over the outside of the doorway of the **entrance** room.
42. 4 wide and fifty metres long, with **entrances** on that side.
42. 9 began, there was an **entrance** into the outer courtyard.
42.11 the same design, and the same kind of **entrances.**
43.11 **entrances** and exits, its shape, the arrangement of everything,
44. 3 the gateway through the **entrance** room at the inner end."
46. 2 the outer courtyard into the **entrance** room by the gateway
46. 8 The prince must leave the **entrance** room of the gateway and
46.19 man took me to the **entrance** of the rooms facing north near
47. 1 The man led me back to the **entrance** of the Temple.
47. 1 coming out from under the **entrance** and flowing east, the
48.30 There are twelve **entrances** to the city of Jerusalem.
Joel 2.17 between the altar and the **entrance** of the Temple, must weep
Mt 26.71 and went on out to the **entrance** of the courtyard.
27.60 a large stone across the **entrance** to the tomb and went away.
Mk 15.46 Then he rolled a large stone across the **entrance** to the tomb.
16. 3 roll away the stone for us from the **entrance** to the tomb?"
Lk 24. 2 stone rolled away from the **entrance** to the tomb, [3]so they
Jn 11.38 tomb, which was a cave with a stone placed at the **entrance.**
20. 1 saw that the stone had been taken away from the **entrance.**

ENTRUST

1 Kgs 14.27 Rehoboam made bronze shields and **entrusted** them to the
2 Chr 12.10 Rehoboam made bronze shields and **entrusted** them to the
Ezra 7.14 your God, which has been **entrusted** to you, is being obeyed.
Jer 13.20 Where are the people **entrusted** to your care, your people you
1 Cor 9.17 matter of duty, because God has **entrusted** me with this task.
1 Thes 2. 4 he has judged us worthy to be **entrusted** with the Good News.
1 Tim 1.11 in the gospel that was **entrusted** to me to announce, the Good
1.18 Timothy, my child, **I entrust** to you this command, which
6.20 Timothy, keep safe what has been **entrusted** to your care.
2 Tim 1.12 to keep safe until that Day what he has **entrusted** to me.
1.14 us, keep the good things that have been **entrusted** to you.
2. 2 presence of many witnesses, and **entrust** them to reliable people,
Tit 1. 3 This was **entrusted** to me, and I proclaim it by order of

ENVIOUS see ENVY

ENVOY

Nah 2.13 The demands of your **envoys** will no longer be heard."

ENVY
[ENVIOUS]

1 Sam 2.32 be troubled and look with **envy** on all the blessings I will
Job 5. 5 among thorns— and thirsty people will **envy** his wealth.
Prov 23.17 Don't be **envious** of sinful people;
24. 1 Don't be **envious** of evil people, and don't try to make
24.19 don't be **envious** of them.
Ecc 4. 2 I **envy** those who are dead and gone;
4. 4 it is because they **envy** their neighbours.
Ezek 31. 9 It was the **envy** of every tree in Eden, the garden of
Acts 8.23 you are full of bitter **envy** and are a prisoner of sin."
Gal 5.21 they are **envious,** get drunk, have orgies, and do other things
Tit 3. 3 We spent our lives in malice and **envy;**

EPHAH (1)
Measure of capacity, about 17.5 litres.

Ezek 45.11 "The **ephah** for dry measure is to be equal to the bath
45.11 1 homer = 10 **ephahs** = 10 baths

EPHESUS
[FELLOW-EPHESIANS]
Chief city in the Roman province of Asia.

Acts 18.19 They arrived in **Ephesus,** where Paul left Priscilla and Aquila.
18.21 And so he sailed from **Ephesus.**
18.24 Jew named Apollos, who had been born in Alexandria, came to **Ephesus.**
18.27 so the believers in **Ephesus** helped him by writing to the
19. 1 through the interior of the province and arrived in **Ephesus.**
19.17 the Jews and Gentiles who lived in **Ephesus** heard about this;
19.23 there was serious trouble in **Ephesus** because of the Way of
19.26 many people, both here in **Ephesus** and in nearly the whole
19.28 and started shouting, "Great is Artemis of **Ephesus!"**
19.34 "Great is Artemis of **Ephesus!"**
19.35 **"Fellow-Ephesians!"**
19.35 knows that the city of **Ephesus** is the keeper of the temple
20.16 decided to sail on past **Ephesus,** so as not to lose any
20.17 Paul sent a message to **Ephesus,** asking the elders of the
21.29 they had seen Trophimus from **Ephesus** with Paul in the city,
1 Cor 15.32 "wild beasts" here in **Ephesus** simply from human motives,
16. 8 I will stay here in **Ephesus** until the day of Pentecost.
Eph 1. 1 To God's people in **Ephesus,** who are faithful in their life
1 Tim 1. 3 want you to stay in **Ephesus,** just as I urged you when
2 Tim 1.18 you know very well how much he did for me in **Ephesus.**
4.12 I sent Tychicus to **Ephesus.**
Rev 1.11 **Ephesus,** Smyrna, Pergamum, Thyatira, Sardis, Philadelphia,
2. 1 "To the angel of the church in **Ephesus** write:

EPHOD (1)
Piece of cloth worn by the High Priest which had the Urim and Thummim attached to it.
Also something the people worshipped and an object used to foretell future events.

Ex 25. 7 to be set in the **ephod** of the High Priest
28. 4 make a breast-piece, an **ephod,** a robe, an embroidered shirt,
28. 6 "They are to make the **ephod** of blue, purple, and red
28. 8 to be attached to the **ephod** so as to form one piece
28.12 on the shoulder-straps of the **ephod** to represent the twelve
28.15 the same materials as the **ephod** and with similar embroidery.
28.25 attach them in front to the shoulder-straps of the **ephod.**
28.26 of the breast-piece on the inside edge next to the **ephod.**
28.27 the two shoulder-straps of the **ephod** near the seam and above
28.28 to the rings of the **ephod** with a blue cord, so that
28.31 robe that goes under the **ephod** is to be made entirely of
29. 5 robe that goes under the **ephod,** the ephod, the breast-piece,
35. 9 be set in the High Priest's **ephod** and in his breast-piece.
35.27 to be set in the **ephod** and the breast-piece [28]and spices
39. 2 They made the **ephod** of fine linen;
39. 4 for the **ephod** and attached them to its sides,
39. 5 materials, was attached to the **ephod** so as to form one piece
39. 7 on the shoulder-straps of the **ephod** to represent the twelve
39. 8 the same materials as the **ephod** and with similar embroidery.
39.18 attached them in front to the shoulder-straps of the **ephod.**
39.19 of the breast-piece, on the inside edge next to the **ephod.**
39.20 two shoulder straps of the **ephod,** near the seam and above
39.21 to the rings of the **ephod** with a blue cord,
39.22 that goes under the **ephod** was made entirely of blue wool.
Lev 8. 7 He put the **ephod** on him and fastened it by putting its
Judg 17. 5 made some idols and an **ephod,** and appointed one of his sons
18.14 There are also other idols and an **ephod.**
18.17 the other idols, and the **ephod,** while the priest stayed at
1 Sam 2.28 to burn the incense, and to wear the **ephod** to consult me.
14. 3 (The priest carrying the **ephod** was Ahijah,
14.18 "Bring the **ephod** here," Saul said to Ahijah the priest.
21. 9 it is behind the **ephod,** wrapped in a cloth.
22.18 eighty-five priests who were qualified to carry the **ephod.**
23. 6 and joined David in Keilah, he took the **ephod** with him.
23. 9 he said to the priest Abiathar, "Bring the **ephod** here."
30. 7 "Bring me the **ephod,"** and Abiathar brought it to him.
1 Chr 15.27 David also wore a linen **ephod.**

EPHPHATHA

Mk 7.34 and said to the man, **"Ephphatha,"** which means, "Open up!"

EPHRAIM (1)
Joseph's son and Jacob's grandson, the tribe descended from him and its territory.

Gen 41.52 so he named his second son **Ephraim.**
46.20 Manasseh and **Ephraim,** by Asenath, the daughter of Potiphera,
48. 1 his two sons, Manasseh and **Ephraim,** and went to see Jacob.
48. 5 **Ephraim** and Manasseh are just as much my sons as Reuben and
48. 6 inheritance they get will come through **Ephraim** and Manasseh.
48.13 Joseph put **Ephraim** at Jacob's left and Manasseh at his right.
48.14 hand on the head of **Ephraim,** even though he was the younger,
48.17 that his father had put his right hand on **Ephraim's** head;
48.17 hand to move it from **Ephraim's** head to the head of Manasseh.
48.20 They will say, 'May God make you like **Ephraim** and Manasseh.' "
48.20 In this way Jacob put **Ephraim** before Manasseh.
50.23 He lived to see **Ephraim's** children and grandchildren.
Num 2.18 of the division of **Ephraim** shall camp in their groups,
2.18 The division of **Ephraim** shall march third.
10.22 by the tribe of **Ephraim** would start out, company by company,
13. 3 **Ephraim** Hoshea son of Nun
26.28 who was the father of two sons, Manasseh and **Ephraim.**
26.35 The tribe of **Ephraim:**
34.19 **Ephraim** Kemuel son of Shiphtan
Deut 33.17 His horns are Manasseh's thousands And **Ephraim's** ten thousands.
34. 2 the territories of **Ephraim** and Manasseh;
Josh 16. 4 of Joseph, the tribes of **Ephraim** and West Manasseh, received
16. 5 This was the territory of the **Ephraimite** families:
16. 8 families of the tribe of **Ephraim** as their possession,
16. 9 the borders of Manasseh, but given to the **Ephraimites.**
16.10 Canaanites have lived among the **Ephraimites** to this day, but
17. 8 on the border, belonged to the descendants of **Ephraim.**
17. 9 of the stream belonged to **Ephraim,** even though they were in
17.10 **Ephraim** was to the south, and Manasseh was to the north,
17.15 you and the hill-country of **Ephraim** is too small for you,
17.17 said to the tribes of **Ephraim** and West Manasseh, "There are
19.50 Timnath Serah, in the hill-country of **Ephraim.**
20. 7 Shechem, in the hill-country of **Ephraim;**
21. 5 from the territories of **Ephraim,** Dan, and West Manasseh.
21.20 Kohath were assigned some cities from the territory of **Ephraim.**
21.21 the hill-country of **Ephraim** (one of the cities of refuge),
24.30 Timnath Serah in the hill-country of **Ephraim** north of Mount Gaash.
24.33 town in the hill-country of **Ephraim** which had been given to
Judg 1.22 The tribes of **Ephraim** and Manasseh went to attack
1.25 them, and the people of **Ephraim** and Manasseh killed everyone
1.29 The tribe of **Ephraim** did not drive out the Canaanites
1.35 Heres, but the tribes of **Ephraim** and Manasseh kept them
2. 9 Timnath Serah in the hill-country of **Ephraim** north of Mount Gaash.
3.27 there in the hill-country of **Ephraim,** he blew a trumpet to
4. 5 Bethel in the hill-country of **Ephraim,** and the people of
5.14 They came from **Ephraim** into the valley, behind the tribe
7.24 through all the hill-country of **Ephraim** to say, "Come down

Judg 7.24 The men of **Ephraim** were called together, and they held the
8. 1 Then the men of **Ephraim** said to Gideon, "Why didn't you
8. 2 little that you men of **Ephraim** did is worth more than what
10. 1 Issachar and lived at Shamir in the hill-country of **Ephraim.**
10. 9 Jordan to fight the tribes of Judah, Benjamin, and **Ephraim.**
12. 1 The men of **Ephraim** prepared for battle;
12. 4 Gilead together, fought the men of **Ephraim** and defeated them.
12. 4 (The **Ephraimites** had said, "You Gileadites in Ephraim
12. 4 you are deserters from **Ephraim!")**
12. 5 In order to keep the **Ephraimites** from escaping, the
12. 5 When any **Ephraimite** who was trying to escape asked permission
12. 5 the men of Gilead would ask, "Are you an **Ephraimite?"**
12. 6 At that time forty-two thousand of the **Ephraimites** were killed.
12.15 Pirathon in the territory of **Ephraim** in the hill-country of the Amalekites.
17. 1 a man named Micah, who lived in the hill-country of **Ephraim.**
17. 8 he came to Micah's house in the hill-country of **Ephraim.**
18. 2 the hill-country of **Ephraim,** they stayed at Micah's house.
18.13 and came to Micah's house in the hill-country of **Ephraim.**
19. 1 was a Levite living far back in the hill-country of **Ephraim.**
19.16 originally from the hill-country of **Ephraim,** but he was now
19.18 we are on our way home deep in the hill-country of **Ephraim.**
1 Sam 1. 1 Elkanah, from the tribe of **Ephraim,**
1. 1 lived in the town of Ramah in the hill-country of **Ephraim.**
9. 4 the hill-country of **Ephraim** and the region of Shalishah,
14.22 hiding in the hills of **Ephraim,** heard that the Philistines
2 Sam 2. 9 territories of Gilead, Asher, Jezreel, **Ephraim,** and
20.21 of **Ephraim,** started a rebellion against King David.
1 Kgs 4. 8 the hill-country of **Ephraim**
11.26 officials, Jeroboam son of Nebat, from Zeredah in **Ephraim.**
11.28 in the territory of the tribes of Manasseh and **Ephraim.**
12.25 in the hill-country of **Ephraim** and lived there for a while.
2 Kgs 5.22 prophets in the hill-country of **Ephraim** arrived, and he
1 Chr 6.66 assigned towns and pasture lands in the territory of **Ephraim:**
6.67 refuge in the hills of **Ephraim,** Gezer, [68] Jokmeam, Beth
7.20 These are the descendants of **Ephraim**
7.21 **Ephraim** had two other sons besides Shuthelah:
7.22 Their father **Ephraim** mourned for them for many days, and
7.24 **Ephraim** had a daughter named Sheerah.
7.25 **Ephraim** also had a son named Rephah,
9. 3 the tribes of Judah, Benjamin, **Ephraim,** and Manasseh went to
27. 2 Helez, an **Ephraimite** from Pelon
27. 2 Pirathon in the territory of the tribe of **Ephraim**
27.16 **Ephraim** Hoshea son of
2 Chr 13. 4 The armies met in the hill-country of **Ephraim.**
15. 8 the cities he had captured in the hill-country of **Ephraim.**
15. 9 over to Asa's side from **Ephraim,** Manasseh, and Simeon, and
17. 2 cities which Asa had captured in the territory of **Ephraim.**
19. 4 edge of the hill-country of **Ephraim** in the north, in order
30. 1 letters to the tribes of **Ephraim** and Manasseh, inviting them
30.10 territory of the tribes of **Ephraim** and Manasseh, and as far
30.18 come from the tribes of **Ephraim,** Manasseh, Issachar, and
31. 1 the rest of Judah, and the territories of Benjamin, **Ephraim,**
34. 6 the devastated areas of Manasseh, **Ephraim,** and Simeon, and
34. 9 collected from the people of **Ephraim** and Manasseh and the
Ps 60. 7 **Ephraim** is my helmet and Judah my royal sceptre.
78. 9 The **Ephraimites,** armed with bows and arrows, ran away on
78.67 he did not select the tribe of **Ephraim.**
80. 2 creatures, [2] reveal yourself to the tribes of **Ephraim,**
108. 8 **Ephraim** is my helmet and Judah my royal sceptre.
Is 9.21 Manasseh and the people of **Ephraim** attack each other, and
Jer 4.15 of Dan and from the hills of **Ephraim** announce the bad news.
31. 6 out on the hills of **Ephraim,** 'Let's go up to Zion, to
31. 9 am like a father to Israel, and **Ephraim** is my eldest son."
50.19 crops that grow in the territories of **Ephraim** and Gilead.
Ezek 48. 1 Dan Asher Naphtali Manasseh **Ephraim** Reuben Judah
Hos 13. 1 past, when the tribe of **Ephraim** spoke, the other tribes of
13. 1 they looked up to **Ephraim.**
Obad 19 Israelites will possess the territory of **Ephraim** and Samaria;
also Num 1.5 Num 1.20 Num 2.18 Num 7.12 Josh 14.3 1 Chr 12.23

EPHRAIM GATE

2 Kgs 14.13 down the city wall from **Ephraim Gate** to the Corner Gate, a
2 Chr 25.23 down the city wall from **Ephraim Gate** to the Corner Gate, a
Neh 8.16 public squares by the Water Gate and by the **Ephraim Gate.**
12.39 from there we went past **Ephraim Gate,** Jeshanah Gate, the

EPHRON (1)

Hittite who sold a cave at Hebron to Abraham.

Gen 23. 8 my wife here, please ask **Ephron** son of Zohar [9] to sell me
23.10 **Ephron** himself was sitting with the other Hittites at
23.13 Hittites [13] and said to **Ephron,** so that everyone could hear,
23.14 **Ephron** answered, [15] "Sir, land worth only four hundred
23.16 weighed out the amount that **Ephron** had mentioned in the
23.17 property which had belonged to **Ephron** at Machpelah, east of
25. 9 Mamre that had belonged to **Ephron** son of Zohar the Hittite.
49.29 is in the field of **Ephron** the Hittite, [30] at Machpelah,
49.30 Abraham bought this cave and field from **Ephron** for a burial-ground.
50.13 Abraham had bought from **Ephron** the Hittite for a burial-ground.

EPICUREAN

Those who followed the teaching of Epicurus (died 270 B.C.), a Greek philosopher who taught that happiness is the highest good in life.

Acts 17.18 Certain **Epicurean** and Stoic teachers also debated with him.

EPIDEMIC

Num 11.33 the people and caused an **epidemic** to break out among them.
14.12 I will send an **epidemic** and destroy them,
16.46 an **epidemic** has already begun."
25. 8 In this way the **epidemic** that was destroying Israel was stopped,
25.18 who was killed at the time of the **epidemic** at Peor."
26. 1 After the **epidemic** the Lord said to Moses and Eleazar
31.16 That was what brought the **epidemic** on the Lord's people.
Deut 28.59 diseases and horrible **epidemics** that can never be stopped.
28.61 all kinds of diseases and **epidemics** that are not mentioned
Josh 22.17 when the Lord punished his own people with an **epidemic?**
2 Sam 24.13 from your enemies or three days of an **epidemic** in your land?
24.15 So the Lord sent an **epidemic** on Israel,
24.21 an altar for the Lord, in order to stop the **epidemic."**
24.25 and the **epidemic** in Israel was stopped.
1 Kgs 8.37 in the land or an **epidemic,** or the crops are destroyed
1 Chr 21.12 his sword and sends an **epidemic** on your land, using his
21.14 So the Lord sent an **epidemic** on the people of Israel,
21.22 I can build an altar to the Lord, to stop the **epidemic.**
2 Chr 6.28 in the land or an **epidemic** or the crops are destroyed by
7.13 the crops or send an **epidemic** on my people, [14] if they pray
20. 9 punish them—a war, an **epidemic,** or a famine—then they could
Ezek 14.19 "If I send an **epidemic** on that country and in my anger

EPILEPTIC

A person who suffers from a nervous disease which causes fits and fainting.

Mt 4.24 and **epileptics,** and paralytics—and Jesus healed them all.
17.15 He is an **epileptic** and has such terrible fits that he often

EQUAL

Ex 16.36 (The standard dry measure then in use **equalled** twenty litres.)
22.17 a sum of money **equal** to the bride-price for a virgin.
30.34 said to Moses, "Take an **equal** part of each of the following
38.26 This amount **equalled** the total paid by all persons
Lev 7.10 the Aaronite priests and must be shared **equally** among them.
Num 31.27 what was taken into two **equal** parts, one part for the
Ruth 2.13 even though I am not the **equal** of one of your servants."
2 Chr 31.15 They distributed the food **equally** to their fellow-Levites
Ezra 8.26 2 fine bronze bowls, **equal** in value
Neh 7. 2 Hananiah was a reliable and God-fearing man without an **equal.**
Job 28.16 The finest gold and jewels Cannot **equal** its value.
Ps 14. 3 they are all **equally** bad.
53. 3 they are all **equally** bad.
89. 6 none of the heavenly beings is your **equal.**
Ezek 45.11 dry measure is to be **equal** to the bath for liquid measure.
47.14 now divide it **equally** among you.
Jn 5.18 own Father and in this way had made himself **equal** with God.
2 Cor 6.14 to work together as **equals** with unbelievers, for it cannot be
8.13 In this way both are treated **equally.**
Phil 2. 6 think that by force he should try to become **equal** with God.

EQUIP

[WELL-EQUIPPED]

1 Kgs 20.27 The Israelites were called up and **equipped;**
1 Chr 12.23 6,800 **well-equipped** men, armed with shields and spears;
2 Chr 17.18 Jehozabad with 180,000 men, **well-equipped** for battle.
Ezra 5. 3 "Who gave you orders to build this Temple and **equip** it?"
5. 9 given them authority to rebuild the Temple and to **equip** it.
5.11 which was originally built and **equipped** many years ago by a
Dan 11.13 time comes, he will return with a large, **well-equipped** army.
2 Tim 3.17 may be fully qualified and **equipped** to do every kind of good

EQUIPMENT

Ex 25.39 of pure gold to make the lamp-stand and all this **equipment.**
27. 3 All this **equipment** is to be made of bronze.
27.19 All the **equipment** that is used in the Tent and all the
30.27 the table and all its **equipment,**
30.27 the lamp-stand and its **equipment,** the altar for burning incense,
30.28 with all its **equipment,** and the wash-basin with its base.
31. 8 Tent, [8] the table and its **equipment,** the lamp-stand of pure
31. 8 gold and all its **equipment,** the altar for burning incense,
31. 9 and all its **equipment,** the wash-basin and its base,
35.13 the table, its poles, and all its **equipment;**
35.14 the lamp-stand for the light and its **equipment;**
35.16 bronze grating attached, its poles, and all its **equipment;**
37.24 of pure gold to make the lamp-stand and all its **equipment.**
38. 3 He also made all the **equipment** for the altar:
38. 3 All this **equipment** was made of bronze.
38.30 its bronze grating, all the **equipment** for the altar, [31] the
39.33 Tent and all its **equipment,** its hooks, its frames, its cross-bars,
39.36 the table and all its **equipment,** and the bread offered to God;
39.37 its lamps, all its **equipment,** and the oil for the lamps;
39.39 with its bronze grating, its poles, and all its **equipment;**
39.40 all the **equipment** to be used in the Tent;
40. 4 Bring in the table and place the **equipment** on it.
40. 9 the Tent and all its **equipment** by anointing it with the
40.10 the altar and all its **equipment** by anointing it, and it will
Lev 8.11 on the altar and its **equipment** and on the basin and its
Num 1.50 in charge of the Tent of my presence and all its **equipment.**
1.50 shall carry it and its **equipment,** serve in it, and set up
3. 8 take charge of all the **equipment** of the Tent and perform the
4.10 wrap it and all its **equipment** in a fine leather cover and
4.14 put on it all the **equipment** used in the service at the
4.15 Aaron and his sons have finished covering them and all their **equipment.**

Num 7. 1 Tent and all its equipment, and the altar and all its **equipment.**
Deut 23.13 stick as part of your **equipment,** so that when you have a
1 Sam 8.12 and make his weapons and the **equipment** for his chariots.
1 Kgs 7.40 shovels, and bowls All this **equipment** for the Temple, which
8. 4 Tent of the Lord's presence and all its **equipment** to the Temple.
2 Kgs 7.15 they saw the clothes and **equipment** that the Syrians had
14.14 find, all the temple **equipment** and all the palace treasures,
20.13 his spices and perfumes, and all his military **equipment.**
1 Chr 9.29 charge of the other sacred **equipment,** and of the flour,
23.26 Tent of the Lord's presence and all the **equipment** used in worship."
28.12 the storerooms for the temple **equipment** and the gifts
2 Chr 5. 5 Tent of the Lord's presence and all its **equipment** to the Temple.
25.24 in the Temple, the temple **equipment** guarded by the
26.15 In Jerusalem his inventors made **equipment** for shooting
28.24 he took all the temple **equipment** and broke it in pieces.
29.18 the table for the sacred bread, and all their **equipment.**
29.19 also brought back all the **equipment** which King Ahaz took
Neh 13. 5 of corn and incense, the **equipment** used in the Temple, the
13. 9 purified and for the temple **equipment,** grain-offerings, and
Is 29. 7 weapons and **equipment**—everything—will vanish like a dream,
39. 2 his spices and perfumes, and all his military **equipment.**
52.11 leave Babylonia, all you that carry the temple **equipment!**
Ezek 40.42 All the **equipment** used in killing the sacrificial animals
Acts 27.19 following day they threw part of the ship's **equipment** overboard.

EQUIVALENT

Num 18.27 will be considered as the **equivalent** of the offering which

ERASE

Ps 69.28 May their names be **erased** from the book of the living;

ERROR

Ex 28.38 me, even if the people commit some **error** in offering them.
Ps 19.12 No one can see his own **errors;**
25. 7 Forgive the sins and **errors** of my youth.
Eph 4.14 deceitful men, who lead others into **error** by the tricks they
1 Thes 2. 3 is not based on **error** or impure motives, nor do we
2 Thes 2.11 God sends the power of **error** to work in them so that
2 Tim 3.16 for teaching the truth, rebuking **error,** correcting faults,
Tit 1. 9 and also to show the **error** of those who are opposed to
2 Pet 2.18 beginning to escape from among people who live in **error.**
3.17 be led away by the **errors** of lawless people and fall from
1 Jn 4. 6 difference between the Spirit of truth and the spirit of **error.**
Jude 11 have given themselves over to the **error** that Balaam committed.

ERUPTION

Lev 22.22 or that has a running sore or a skin **eruption** or scabs.

ESAU

Isaac and Rebecca's elder son and ancestor of the Edomites.

Gen 25.19-26 **The birth of Esau and Jacob**
27-34 **Esau sells his rights as the first-born son**
26.34-35 **Esau's foreign wives**
27.1-29 **Isaac blesses Jacob**
30-45 **Esau begs for Isaac's blessing**
27.46–28.5 **Isaac sends Jacob to Laban**
28.6-9 **Esau takes another wife**
32.1-21 **Jacob prepares to meet Esau**
33.1-20 **Jacob meets Esau**
35.1-15 **God blesses Jacob at Bethel**
27-29 **The death of Isaac**
36.1-19 **The descendants of Esau**
1 Chr 1.34-37 **The descendants of Esau**

Gen 36.40 **Esau** was the ancestor of the following Edomite tribes:
Deut 2. 4 of your distant relatives, the descendants of **Esau.**
2. 5 I have given Edom to **Esau's** descendants.
2.12 descendants of **Esau** chased them out, destroyed their nation,
2.22 the Edomites, the descendants of **Esau,** who live in the
2.29 The descendants of **Esau,** who live in Edom, and the Moabites,
Josh 24. 4 I gave him Isaac, [4]and to Isaac I gave Jacob and **Esau.**
24. 4 I gave **Esau** the hill-country of Edom as his possession, but
Jer 49. 8 I am going to destroy **Esau's** descendants, because the time
49.10 But I have stripped **Esau's** descendants completely
Hos 12. 3 struggled with his twin brother **Esau** while the two of them
Obad 6 Descendants of **Esau,** your treasures have been looted.
18 they will destroy the people of **Esau** as fire burns stubble.
18 No descendant of **Esau** will survive.
Mal 1. 2 The Lord answers, **"Esau** and Jacob were brothers, but I
1. 3 Jacob and his descendants, [3]and have hated **Esau** and his descendants.
1. 3 I have devastated **Esau's** hill-country
1. 4 If **Esau's** descendants, the Edomites, say,
Rom 9.13 As the scripture says, "I loved Jacob, but I hated **Esau."**
Heb 11.20 made Isaac promise blessings for the future to Jacob and **Esau.**
12.16 immoral or unspiritual like **Esau,** who for a single meal sold

ESCAPE

Gen 7. 7 and their wives, went into the boat to **escape** the flood.
14.10 but the other three kings **escaped** to the mountains.
14.13 But a man **escaped** and reported all this to Abram, the
19.29 kept Abraham in mind and allowed Lot to **escape** to safety.
32. 8 attacks the first group, the other may be able to **escape."**
39.12 But he **escaped** and ran outside, leaving his robe in her hand.
Ex 1.10 to fight against us, and might **escape** from the country.
Ex 14. 5 told that the people had **escaped,** he and his officials
14. 5 We have let the Israelites **escape,** and we have lost them as
14.27 The Egyptians tried to **escape** from the water, but the Lord
21.13 kill the man, he can **escape** to a place which I will
Num 35. 6 to which a man can **escape** if he kills someone accidentally.
35.11 to which a man can **escape** if he kills someone accidentally.
35.15 Anyone who kills someone accidentally can **escape** to one of them.
35.25 return him to the city of refuge to which he had **escaped.**
35.26 refuge to which he has **escaped** [27]and if the dead man's
35.31 He cannot **escape** this penalty by the payment of money.
Deut 4.42 to which a man could **escape** and be safe if he had
4.42 He could **escape** to one of these cities and not be put
7.20 them and will destroy those who **escape** and go into hiding.
19. 2 will be able to **escape** to one of them for protection.
19. 4 not his enemy, he may **escape** to any of these cities and
19.11 in cold blood and then **escapes** to one of those cities for
Josh 8.20 no way for them to **escape,** because the Israelites who had
10.16 five Amorite kings, however, had **escaped** and were hiding in
20. 3 accidentally can go there and **escape** the man who is looking
Judg 3.26 He went past the carved stones and **escaped** to Seirah.
3.29 none of them **escaped.**
12. 5 to keep the Ephraimites from **escaping,** the Gileadites
12. 5 Ephraimite who was trying to **escape** asked permission to cross,
20.42 ran towards the open country, but they could not **escape.**
20.47 hundred men were able to **escape** to the open country to the
1 Sam 4.16 The man said, "I have **escaped** from the battle and have
19.10 David ran away and **escaped.**
19.12 let him down from a window, and he ran away and **escaped.**
19.17 "Why have you tricked me like this and let my enemy **escape?"**
19.17 said he would kill me if I didn't help him to **escape."**
19.18 David **escaped** and went to Samuel in Ramah and told him
22.20 But Abiathar, one of Ahimelech's sons, **escaped,**
23. 6 When Abiathar son of Ahimelech **escaped** and joined David in Keilah,
23.13 Saul heard that David had **escaped** from Keilah, he gave up
27. 1 The best thing for me to do is to **escape** to Philistia.
30.17 men who mounted camels and got away, none of them **escaped.**
2 Sam 1. 3 "I have **escaped** from the Israelite camp," he answered.
15.14 must get away at once if we want to **escape** from Absalom!
20. 6 he may occupy some fortified towns and **escape** from us."
1 Kgs 11.17 some of his father's Edomite servants, who **escaped** to Egypt.
11.40 to kill Jeroboam, but he **escaped** to King Shishak of Egypt
12. 2 gone to Egypt to **escape** from King Solomon, heard this news,
12.18 Rehoboam hurriedly got into his chariot and **escaped** to Jerusalem.
19.17 Anyone who **escapes** being put to death by Hazael will be
19.17 Jehu, and anyone who **escapes** Jehu will be killed by Elisha.
20.20 in hot pursuit, but Benhadad **escaped** on horseback,
20.30 Benhadad also **escaped** into the city and took refuge in the
20.39 if he **escapes,** you will pay for it with your life or
20.40 But I got busy with other things, and the man **escaped."**
20.42 you allowed the man to **escape** whom I had ordered to be
20.42 army will be destroyed for letting his army **escape.'"**
2 Kgs 3.26 through the enemy lines and **escape** to the king of Syria, but
8.21 managed to break out and **escape,** and his soldiers scattered
10.24 who lets one of them **escape** will pay for it with his
10.25 don't let anyone **escape!"**
11. 2 Only Ahaziah's son Joash **escaped.**
19.11 Do you think that you can **escape?**
19.37 with their swords, and then **escaped** to the land of Ararat.
25. 4 all the soldiers **escaped** during the night.
1 Chr 12. 1 in Ziklag, where he had gone to **escape** from King Saul.
29.15 Our days are like a passing shadow, and we cannot **escape** death.
2 Chr 10. 2 gone to Egypt to **escape** from King Solomon, heard this news,
10.18 Rehoboam hurriedly got into his chariot and **escaped** to Jerusalem.
12. 5 Judaean leaders who had gathered in Jerusalem to **escape** Shishak.
16. 7 the army of the king of Israel has **escaped** from you.
20.24 Not one had **escaped.**
21. 9 but during the night they managed to break out and **escape.**
36.16 against his people was so great that there was no **escape.**
Ezra 9. 8 have let some of us **escape** from slavery and live in safety
Job 1.15 I am the only one who **escaped** to tell you."
1.16 I am the only one who **escaped** to tell you."
1.17 I am the only one who **escaped** to tell you."
1.19 I am the only one who **escaped** to tell you."
11.20 round in despair and find that there is no way to **escape.**
15.22 He has no hope of **escaping** from darkness, for somewhere
15.30 and he will not **escape** from darkness.
19.20 I have barely **escaped** with my life.
20.24 When he tries to **escape** from an iron sword, a bronze bow
26.13 sky clear, and his hand that killed the **escaping** monster.
27.22 on them without pity while they try their best to **escape.**
30.13 They cut off my **escape** and try to destroy me;
Ps 22. 5 They called to you and **escaped** from danger;
60. 4 show you reverence, so that they might **escape** destruction.
88. 8 I am closed in and cannot **escape;**
124. 7 We have **escaped** like a bird from a hunter's trap;
130. 3 a record of our sins, who could **escape** being condemned?
139. 7 Where could I go to **escape** from you?
Prov 6. 5 the trap like a bird or a deer **escaping** from a hunter.
11.21 evil men will be punished, but righteous men will **escape.**
13.14 they will help you **escape** when your life is in danger.
16. 5 he will never let them **escape** punishment.
19. 5 in court, you will be punished—there will be no **escape.**
19. 9 No one who tells lies in court can **escape** punishment;
Ecc 8. 8 That is a battle we cannot **escape;**
Is 2.10 the ground to try to **escape** from the Lord's anger and to
2.19 the ground to try to **escape** from the Lord's anger and to
2.21 rocky hills to try to **escape** from his anger and to hide

Is 9. 1 be no way for them to **escape** from this time of trouble.
9.17 any of the young men **escape,** and he will not show pity
13.14 own countries, scattering like deer **escaping** from hunters,
15. 5 some **escape** to Horonaim, grieving loudly.
15. 7 Valley of Willows, trying to **escape** with all their possessions.
21.15 People are fleeing to **escape** from swords that are ready
23. 6 Try to **escape** to Spain!
23.12 Even if they **escape** to Cyprus, they will still not be safe.
24.18 Anyone who tries to **escape** from the terror will fall
24.18 a pit, and anyone who **escapes** from the pit will be caught
28.22 If you do, it will be even harder for you to **escape.**
30.16 you plan to **escape** from your enemies by riding fast horses.
30.16 And you are right—**escape** is what you will have to do!
37.11 Do you think that you can **escape?**
37.38 with their swords and then **escaped** to the land of Ararat.
43.13 No one can **escape** from my power;
52.12 you will not be trying to **escape.**
Jer 6. 1 **Escape** from Jerusalem!
11.11 to bring destruction on them, and they will not **escape.**
16.17 their sins do not **escape** my sight.
21. 9 he will at least **escape** with his life.
25.35 There will be no way for you to **escape.**
26.21 so he fled in terror and **escaped** to Egypt.
31. 2 desert I showed mercy to those people who had **escaped** death.
32. 4 Babylonia capture this city, [4]and King Zedekiah will not **escape.**
34. 3 You will not **escape;**
38. 2 he will at least **escape** with his life."
38.18 who will burn it down, and you will not **escape** from them."
38.23 the Babylonians, and you yourself will not **escape** from them.
39. 4 they tried to **escape** from the city during the night.
39. 4 connecting the two walls, and **escaped** in the direction of
39.18 You will **escape** with your life because you have put your
41.15 men got away from Johanan and **escaped** to the land of Ammon.
42.17 will survive, not one will **escape** the disaster that I am
44.14 left and have come to Egypt to live will **escape** or survive.
44.28 a few of you will **escape** death and return from Egypt to
45. 5 you will at least **escape** with your life, wherever you go.
46. 6 the soldiers cannot **escape.**
46.16 Let's go home to our people and **escape** the enemy's sword!'
48. 8 Not a town will **escape** the destruction;
48.44 Whoever tries to **escape** the terror will fall into the pits,
50.28 (Refugees **escape** from Babylonia and come to Jerusalem,
50.29 Surround the city and don't let anyone **escape.**
51.50 "You have **escaped** death!
52. 7 all the soldiers **escaped** during the night.
Lam 1. 3 their own— Surrounded by enemies, with no way to **escape.**
2.22 me, And no one could **escape** on that day of your anger.
3. 7 I am a prisoner with no hope of **escape.**
Ezek 6. 8 "I will let some **escape** the slaughter and be scattered
7.16 Some will **escape** to the mountains
12.12 pack in the dark and **escape** through a hole that they dig
13.21 scarves and let my people **escape** from your power once and
15. 7 They have **escaped** one fire, but now fire will burn them up.
17.18 He did all these things, and now he will not **escape."**
24.26 I do this, someone who **escapes** the destruction will come and
33. 5 If he had paid attention, he could have **escaped.**
33.21 exile, a man who had **escaped** from Jerusalem came and told me
35. 6 the living God—death is your fate, and you cannot **escape** it.
Dan 8. 4 No animal could stop him or **escape** his power.
11.41 of Edom, Moab, and what is left of Ammon will **escape.**
Joel 2. 3 Nothing **escapes** them.
2.32 As the Lord has said, 'Some in Jerusalem will **escape;**
Amos 2.14 Not even fast runners will **escape;**
2.15 away, and men on horses will not **escape** with their lives.
9. 1 not one will **escape.**
Obad 14 stood at the cross-roads to catch those trying to **escape.**
17 on Mount Zion some will **escape,** and it will be a sacred
Mic 2. 3 disaster on you, and you will not be able to **escape** it.
Nah 3.11 You too will try to **escape** from your enemies.
3.19 Did anyone **escape** your endless cruelty?
Zeph 2. 3 Perhaps you will **escape** punishment on the day when the Lord
Zech 2. 6 But now, you exiles, **escape** from Babylonia and return to Jerusalem.
14. 5 You will **escape** through this valley
Mt 2.13 child and his mother and **escape** to Egypt, and stay there
3. 7 told you that you could **escape** from the punishment God is
3. 9 don't think you can **escape** punishment by saying that Abraham is
23.33 How do you expect to **escape** from being condemned to hell?
Lk 3. 7 told you that you could **escape** from the punishment God is
Acts 16.27 the prison doors open, he thought that the prisoners had **escaped;**
25.11 I deserve the death penalty, I do not ask to **escape** it.
27.30 Then the sailors tried to **escape** from the ship;
27.42 in order to keep them from swimming ashore and **escaping.**
28. 4 not let him live, even though he **escaped** from the sea."
Rom 2. 3 Do you think you will **escape** God's judgement?
1 Cor 3.15 will be saved, as if he had **escaped** through the fire.
2 Cor 11.33 basket through an opening in the wall and **escaped** from him.
13. 2 the next time I come nobody will **escape** punishment.
1 Thes 5. 3 come upon a woman in labour, and people will not **escape.**
2 Tim 2.26 come to their senses and **escape** from the trap of the Devil,
Heb 2. 3 How, then, shall we **escape** if we pay no attention to such
11.34 put out fierce fires, **escaped** being killed by the sword.
12.25 the one who gave the divine message on earth did not **escape.**
12.25 How much less shall we **escape,** then, if we turn away from
Jas 2.25 Israelite spies and helping them to **escape** by a different road.
2 Pet 1. 4 of these gifts you may **escape** from the destructive lust that
2.18 who are just beginning to **escape** from among people who live
2.20 If people have **escaped** from the corrupting forces of the world

ESCORT

2 Sam 15. 1 chariot and horses for himself, and an **escort** of fifty men.
19.15 who had come to Gilgal to **escort** him across the river.
19.18 They crossed the river to **escort** the royal party across
19.31 come down from Rogelim to **escort** the king across the Jordan.
19.40 When the king had crossed, **escorted** by all the men of
19.41 to take you away and **escort** you, your family, and your men
1 Kgs 1. 5 chariots, horses, and an **escort** of fifty men.
1.33 ride my own mule, and **escort** him down to the spring of
1.38 King David's mule, and **escorted** him to the spring of Gihon.
1.44 and the royal bodyguard to **escort** him.
2 Kgs 11.19 bodyguard, and the palace guards **escorted** the king from the

ESTABLISH

[RE-ESTABLISHED]

Num 25.13 and his descendants are permanently **established** as priests,
Deut 19.14 move your neighbour's boundary mark, **established** long ago in
2 Sam 5.12 realized that the Lord had **established** him as king of Israel
1 Kgs 2.12 David as king, and his royal power was firmly **established.**
2.24 The Lord has firmly **established** me on the throne of my
1 Chr 14. 2 realized that the Lord had **established** him as king of Israel
24.19 Temple and performing the duties **established** by their
29.23 father David on the throne which the Lord had **established.**
2 Chr 12. 1 As soon as Rehoboam had **established** his authority as king,
31. 2 King Hezekiah **re-established** the organization of the priests
Ps 44. 2 out the heathen and **established** your people in their land;
99. 4 you have **established** justice in Israel;
Prov 22.28 Never move an old boundary-mark that your ancestors **established.**
24.27 Don't build your house and **establish** a home until your
Is 14.32 them that the Lord has **established** Zion and that his
23. 7 that sent settlers across the sea to **establish** colonies?
42. 4 he will **establish** justice on the earth.
Jer 30.20 the nation's ancient power and **establish** it firmly again;
32.41 them, and I will **establish** them permanently in this land.
Ezek 23.38 They profaned my Temple and broke the Sabbath, which I had **established.**
37.26 I will **establish** them and increase their population, and put
Dan 2.44 God of heaven will **establish** a kingdom that will never end.
9.24 be forgiven and eternal justice **established,** so that the
Hos 2.23 I will **establish** my people in the land and make them prosper.
1 Cor 1. 6 Christ has become so firmly **established** in you [7]that you have
Phil 1. 7 I was free to defend the gospel and **establish** it firmly.
Heb 9.10 only until the time when God will **establish** the new order.
11.28 faith that made him **establish** the Passover and order the blood

ESTEEM

2 Kgs 5. 1 was highly respected and **esteemed** by the king of Syria,

ESTHER

Jewish wife of King Xerxes who saved her people from being killed.
see also HADASSAH

Esth 2.1-18 **Esther becomes queen**
19-23 **Mordecai saves the king's life**
4.1-17 **Mordecai asks for Esther's help**
5.1-8 **Esther invites the king and Haman to a banquet**
9-14 **Haman plots to kill Mordecai**
6.14–7.10 **Haman is put to death**
8.1-17 **The Jews are told to fight back**
9.1-19 **The Jews destroy their enemies**
20-32 **The Festival of Purim**

ESTIMATE

Lev 27.18 it later, the priest shall **estimate** the cash value according
27.23 has bought, [23]the priest shall **estimate** its value

ETERNAL

[LIFE ETERNAL]

Deut 33.27 his **eternal** arms are your support.
1 Sam 18. 3 Jonathan swore **eternal** friendship with David because of
2 Sam 23. 5 because he has made an **eternal** covenant with me, an
1 Kgs 10. 9 his love for Israel is **eternal,** he has made you their king
1 Chr 16.34 his love is **eternal.**
16.41 chosen to sing praises to the Lord for his **eternal** love.
2 Chr 5.11 "Praise the Lord, because he is good, And his love is **eternal."**
7. 3 God and praising him for his goodness and his **eternal** love.
7. 6 King David had provided and singing the hymn, "His Love Is **Eternal!"**
20.21 His love is **eternal!"**
Ezra 3.11 "The Lord is good, and his love for Israel is **eternal."**
Ps 33.11 his purposes last **eternally.**
52. 1 God's faithfulness is **eternal.**
55.19 God, who has ruled from **eternity,** will hear me and defeat them;
90. 2 world into being, you were **eternally** God, and will be God
93. 5 Your laws are **eternal,** Lord, and your Temple is holy indeed,
100. 5 his love is **eternal** and his faithfulness lasts for ever.
106. 1 his love is **eternal.**
107. 1 his love is **eternal!"**
111. 3 his righteousness is **eternal.**
111. 9 He set his people free and made an **eternal** covenant with them.
117. 2 His love for us is strong and his faithfulness is **eternal.**
118. 1 to the Lord, because he is good, and his love is **eternal.**
118. 2 Let the people of Israel say, "His love is **eternal."**
118. 3 Let the priests of God say, "His love is **eternal."**

Ps 118. 4 Let all who worship him say, "His love is **eternal.**"
118.29 to the Lord, because he is good, and his love is **eternal.**
119.89 it is **eternal** in heaven.
119.111 Your commandments are my **eternal** possession;
119.160 is truth, and all your righteous judgements are **eternal.**
136 his love is **eternal.**
138. 8 Lord, your love is **eternal.**
145.13 Your rule is **eternal,** and you are king for ever.
Is 9. 6 "Wonderful Counsellor," "Mighty God," "**Eternal** Father,"
60.19 I, the Lord, will be your **eternal** light;
60.20 the Lord, will be your **eternal** light, More lasting than the
61. 8 reward my people And make an **eternal** covenant with them.
Jer 10.10 the true God, you are the living God and the **eternal** king.
32.40 I will make an **eternal** covenant with them.
33.11 Lord Almighty, because he is good and his love is **eternal.'**
50. 5 They will make an **eternal** covenant with me and never break it.
Ezek 26.20 world among **eternal** ruins, keeping company with the dead.
Dan 9.24 Sin will be forgiven and **eternal** justice established, so
12. 2 some will enjoy **eternal life,**
12. 2 and some will suffer **eternal** disgrace.
12. 7 and made a solemn promise in the name of the **Eternal** God.
Hab 1.12 You are my God, holy and **eternal.**
3. 6 The **eternal** mountains are shattered;
Mt 18. 8 hands and both feet and be thrown into the **eternal** fire.
19.16 "what good thing must I do to receive **eternal life?"**
19.29 receive a hundred times more and will be given **eternal life.**
25.41 Away to the **eternal** fire which has been prepared for the
25.46 will be sent off to **eternal** punishment,
25.46 but the righteous will go to **eternal life."**
Mk 3.29 never be forgiven, because he has committed an **eternal** sin."
10.17 "Good Teacher, what must I do to receive **eternal life?"**
10.30 and in the age to come he will receive **eternal life.**
16.10 the sacred and ever-living message of **eternal** salvation.
Lk 10.25 "Teacher," he asked, "what must I do to receive **eternal life?"**
16. 9 when it gives out, you will be welcomed in the **eternal** home.
18.18 "Good Teacher, what must I do to receive **eternal life?"**
18.30 in this present age and **eternal life** in the age to come."
Jn 3.15 so that everyone who believes in him may have **eternal life.**
3.16 who believes in him may not die but have **eternal life.**
3.36 Whoever believes in the Son has **eternal life;**
4.14 provide him with life-giving water and give him **eternal life."**
4.36 is being paid and gathers the crops for **eternal life;**
5.24 my words and believes in him who sent me has **eternal life.**
5.39 because you think that in them you will find **eternal life.**
6.27 instead, work for the food that lasts for **eternal life.**
6.40 who see the Son and believe in him should have **eternal life.**
6.47 he who believes has **eternal life.**
6.54 and drinks my blood has **eternal life,** and I will raise him
6.68 You have the words that give **eternal life.**
10.28 I give them **eternal life,** and they shall never die.
12.25 his own life in this world will keep it for **life eternal.**
12.50 And I know that his command brings **eternal life.**
17. 2 so that he might give **eternal life** to all those you gave
17. 3 And **eternal life** means knowing you, the only true God,
Acts 13.46 not consider yourselves worthy of **eternal life,** we will leave
13.48 those who had been chosen for **eternal life** became believers.
Rom 1.20 his invisible qualities, both his **eternal** power and his divine
2. 7 to them God will give **eternal life.**
5.21 righteousness, leading us to **eternal life** through Jesus Christ
6.22 life fully dedicated to him, and the result is **eternal life.**
6.23 but God's free gift is **eternal life** in union with Christ
16.26 by the command of the **eternal** God it is made known to
1 Cor 13. 8 Love is **eternal.**
2 Cor 4.17 a tremendous and **eternal** glory, much greater than the trouble.
Gal 6. 8 from the Spirit he will gather the harvest of **eternal life.**
Eph 3.11 according to his **eternal** purpose, which he achieved through
2 Thes 1. 9 suffer the punishment of **eternal** destruction, separated from
1 Tim 1.16 those who would later believe in him and receive **eternal life.**
1.17 To the **eternal** King, immortal and invisible, the only God—
6.12 in the race of faith, and win **eternal life** for yourself;
6.16 To him be honour and **eternal** dominion!
2 Tim 2.10 that comes through Christ Jesus and brings **eternal** glory.
Tit 1. 2 our religion, [2]which is based on the hope for **eternal life.**
3. 7 God and come into possession of the **eternal life** we hope for.
Heb 5. 9 became the source of **eternal** salvation for all those who obey
6. 2 of the resurrection of the dead and the **eternal** judgement.
9.12 he took his own blood and obtained **eternal** salvation for us.
9.14 Through the **eternal** Spirit he offered himself as a perfect
9.15 may receive the **eternal** blessings that God has promised.
13.20 his sacrificial death, by which the **eternal** covenant is sealed.
1 Pet 1.23 For through the living and **eternal** word of God you have
5.10 calls you to share his **eternal** glory in union with Christ,
2 Pet 1.11 full right to enter the **eternal** Kingdom of our Lord and
1 Jn 1. 2 and tell you about the **eternal life** which was with the
2.25 this is what Christ himself promised to give us—**eternal life.**
3.15 you know that a murderer has not got **eternal life** in him.
5.11 God has given us **eternal life,** and this life has its source
5.13 may know that you have **eternal life**—you that believe in the
5.20 This is the true God, and this is **eternal life.**
Jude 6 they are bound with **eternal** chains in the darkness below,
7 they suffer the punishment of **eternal** fire as a plain warning
21 Lord Jesus Christ in his mercy to give you **eternal life.**
Rev 14. 6 in the air, with an **eternal** message of Good News to announce

ETHANIM

Seventh month of the Hebrew calendar.

1 Kgs 8. 2 Festival of Shelters in the seventh month, in the month of **Ethanim.**

EUNUCH

A man who has had an operation which prevents him from having normal sexual relations. Eunuchs were often important officials in the courts of ancient kings, and the word may have come to be used of such officials, even if they had not had the operation.

Lev 21.20 and no **eunuch.**
2 Kgs 20.18 be taken away and made **eunuchs** to serve in the palace of
Esth 1.10 called in the seven **eunuchs** who were his personal servants,
2. 3 the care of Hegai, the **eunuch** who is in charge of your
2.14 of Shaashgaz, the **eunuch** in charge of the king's concubines.
2.15 wore just what Hegai, the **eunuch** in charge of the harem,
2.21 Teresh, two of the palace **eunuchs** who guarded the entrance
4. 4 When Esther's servant-girls and **eunuchs** told her
4. 5 Hathach, one of the palace **eunuchs** appointed as her servant
6. 2 the two palace **eunuchs** who had guarded the king's rooms.
6.14 were still talking, the palace **eunuchs** arrived in a hurry to
7. 8 no sooner said this than the **eunuchs** covered Haman's head.
Is 39. 7 be taken away and made **eunuchs** to serve in the palace of
Jer 38. 7 Ebedmelech the Sudanese, a **eunuch** who worked in the royal palace,
41.16 after murdering Gedaliah—soldiers, women, children, and **eunuchs.**
Acts 8.27 Now an Ethiopian **eunuch,** who was an important official in

EUPHRATES (1)

One of two main rivers in Mesopotamia.

Gen 2.14 east of Assyria, and the fourth river is the **Euphrates.**
15.18 to the River **Euphrates,** [19]including the lands of the Kenites,
31.21 He crossed the River **Euphrates**
Ex 23.31 Mediterranean Sea and from the desert to the **Euphrates** River.
Num 22. 5 was at Pethor near the River **Euphrates** in the land of Amaw.
Deut 1. 7 the Lebanon Mountains as far as the great River **Euphrates.**
11.24 north, and from the River **Euphrates** in the east to the
Josh 1. 4 River **Euphrates** in the east, through the Hittite country,
24. 2 other side of the River **Euphrates** and worshipped other gods.
24. 3 from the land beyond the **Euphrates** and led him through the
2 Sam 8. 3 his control over the territory by the upper **Euphrates.**
10.16 east side of the River **Euphrates,** and they came to Helam
1 Kgs 4.21 the River **Euphrates** to Philistia and the Egyptian border.
4.24 land west of the River **Euphrates,**
4.24 from Tiphsah on the **Euphrates** as far west as the city
4.24 the kings west of the **Euphrates** were subject to him, and he
14.15 scatter them beyond the River **Euphrates,** because they have
2 Kgs 23.29 army to the River **Euphrates** to help the emperor of Assyria.
24. 7 from the River **Euphrates** to the northern border of Egypt.
1 Chr 5. 9 desert that stretches all the way to the River **Euphrates.**
18. 3 to gain control of the territory by the upper **Euphrates.**
19.16 east side of the River **Euphrates** and placed them under the
2 Chr 9.26 the River **Euphrates** to Philistia and the Egyptian border.
35.20 Egypt led an army to fight at Carchemish on the River **Euphrates.**
Ps 72. 8 sea to sea, from the **Euphrates** to the ends of the earth.
80.11 to the Mediterranean Sea and as far as the River **Euphrates.**
89.25 extend his kingdom from the Mediterranean to the River **Euphrates.**
Is 7.20 a barber from across the **Euphrates**—the emperor of Assyria!—
8. 7 waters of the River **Euphrates,** overflowing all its banks.
11.15 to dry up the **Euphrates,** leaving only seven tiny streams,
27.12 On that day, from the **Euphrates** to the Egyptian border,
Jer 2.18 gain by going to Assyria to drink water from the **Euphrates?**
13. 4 said, [4]"Go to the River **Euphrates** and hide the shorts in a
13. 5 So I went and hid them near the **Euphrates.**
13. 6 told me to go back to the **Euphrates** and get the shorts.
46. 2 at Carchemish near the River **Euphrates** in the fourth year
46. 6 In the north, by the **Euphrates,** they stumble and fall.
46.10 sacrifices his victims in the north, by the **Euphrates.**
51.63 throw it into the River **Euphrates,** [64]and say, 'This is
Mic 7.12 of the **Euphrates,** from distant seas and far-off mountains.
Zech 9.10 sea, from the River **Euphrates** to the ends of the earth."
Rev 9.14 "Release the four angels who are bound at the great river **Euphrates!"**
16.12 angel poured out his bowl on the great river **Euphrates.**

EUPHRATES (2)

[WEST EUPHRATES]

West Euphrates, a Persian province.

Ezra 4.10 Samaria and elsewhere in the province of **West Euphrates."**
4.11 "To Emperor Artaxerxes from his servants, the men of **West Euphrates.**
4.16 longer be able to control the province of **West Euphrates."**
4.17 who live in Samaria and in the rest of **West Euphrates,**
4.20 province of **West Euphrates,** collecting taxes and revenue.
5. 3 once Tattenai, governor of **West Euphrates,** Shethar Bozenai,
6. 6 "To Tattenai, governor of **West Euphrates,** Shethar Bozenai,
6. 6 and your fellow-officials in **West Euphrates.**
6. 8 received from taxes in **West Euphrates,** so that the work is
7.21 the province of **West Euphrates** to provide promptly for Ezra,
7.25 all the people in **West Euphrates** who live by the Law of
8.36 of the province of **West Euphrates,** who then gave their
Neh 2. 7 to the governors of **West Euphrates** Province, instructing
2. 9 horsemen with me, and I made the journey to **West Euphrates.**
3. 7 as far as the residence of the governor of **West Euphrates.**

AV **EUROCLYDON** see **NORTH-EASTER**

EVANGELIST

Acts	21. 8	the house of Philip the **evangelist,** one of the seven men who
Eph	4.11	be prophets, others to be **evangelists,** others to be pastors

EVAPORATE

Ex	16.14	When the dew **evaporated,** there was something thin and

EVE
Adam's wife.

Gen	3.20	Adam named his wife **Eve,** because she was the mother of
2 Cor	11. 3	in the same way that **Eve** was deceived by the snake's clever
1 Tim	2.13	For Adam was created first, and then **Eve.**

EVEN

Gen	27.42	brother Esau is planning to get **even** with you and kill you.
Judg	16.28	one blow I can get **even** with the Philistines for putting out
1 Kgs	6.35	and flowers, which were **evenly** covered with gold.
Job	15.11	We have spoken for him with calm, **even** words.
Prov	24.29	I'll get **even** with him!"

EVENING

Gen	1. 5	**Evening** passed and morning came—that was the first day.
	1. 8	**Evening** passed and morning came—that was the second day.
	1.13	**Evening** passed and morning came—that was the third day.
	1.19	**Evening** passed and morning came—that was the fourth day.
	1.23	**Evening** passed and morning came—that was the fifth day.
	1.31	**Evening** passed and morning came—that was the sixth day.
	3. 8	That **evening** they heard the Lord God walking in the garden,
	8.11	returned to him in the **evening** with a fresh olive leaf in
	19. 1	angels came to Sodom that **evening,** Lot was sitting at the
	24.63	went out in the early **evening** to take a walk in the
	30.16	from the fields in the **evening,** Leah went out to meet him
	49.27	Morning and **evening** he kills and devours."
Ex	12. 6	Then, on the **evening** of the fourteenth day of the month,
	12.18	From the **evening** of the fourteenth day of the first month
	12.18	to the **evening** of the twenty-first day, you must
	16. 6	to all the Israelites, "This **evening** you will know that it
	16. 8	meat to eat in the **evening** and as much bread as you
	16.13	In the **evening** a large flock of quails flew in, enough
	27.20	olive-oil for the lamp, so that it can be lit each **evening.**
	27.21	There in my presence it is to burn from **evening** until morning.
	29.39	of the lambs in the morning and the other in the **evening.**
	29.41	the second lamb in the **evening,** and offer with it the same
	30. 8	must do the same when he lights the lamps in the **evening.**
Lev	6.20	half in the morning and half in the **evening.**
	11.24	of the following animals will be unclean until **evening:**
	11.24	his clothes, but he will still be unclean until **evening.**
	11.31	touches them or their dead bodies will be unclean until **evening.**
	11.32	dipped in water, but it will remain unclean until **evening.**
	11.39	dies, anyone who touches it will be unclean until **evening.**
	11.40	his clothes, but he will still be unclean until **evening;**
	11.40	his clothes, but he will still be unclean until **evening.**
	14.46	house while it is locked up will be unclean until **evening.**
	15. 6	and have a bath, and he remains unclean until **evening.**
	15. 7	and have a bath, and he remains unclean until **evening.**
	15. 8	and have a bath, and he remains unclean until **evening.**
	15.10	anything on which the man sat is unclean until **evening.**
	15.10	and have a bath, and he remains unclean until **evening.**
	15.11	and have a bath, and he remains unclean until **evening.**
	15.16	bathe his whole body, and he remains unclean until **evening.**
	15.17	falls must be washed, and it remains unclean until **evening.**
	15.18	must have a bath, and they remain unclean until **evening.**
	15.19	Anyone who touches her is unclean until **evening.**
	15.21	and have a bath, and he remains unclean until **evening.**
	15.27	he remains unclean until **evening.**
	17.15	a bath, and wait until **evening** before he is ritually clean.
	22. 6	becomes unclean remains unclean until **evening,** and even then
	24. 3	Each **evening** Aaron shall light them
Num	9. 5	the Passover, [5] and on the **evening** of the fourteenth day of
	9.11	month later instead, on the **evening** of the fourteenth day of
	9.21	the cloud remained only from **evening** until morning, and they
	19. 7	but he remains ritually unclean until **evening.**
	19. 8	over himself, but he also remains unclean until **evening.**
	19.10	must wash his clothes, but he remains unclean until **evening.**
	19.21	touches the water remains ritually unclean until **evening.**
	19.22	anyone else who touches it remains unclean until **evening.**
	28. 4	and the second in the **evening,** [5] each with a grain-offering
	28. 8	In the **evening** offer the second lamb in the same way as
Deut	16. 4	the animal killed on the **evening** of the first day must be
	23.11	Towards **evening** he is to wash himself, and at sunset he
	24.13	return it to him each **evening,** so that he can have it
	28.67	Every morning you will wish for **evening;**
	28.67	every **evening** you will wish for morning.
Josh	5.10	they observed Passover on the **evening** of the fourteenth day
	7. 6	Box, and lay there till **evening,** with dust on their heads to
	8.29	of Ai from a tree and left his body there until **evening.**
	10.26	them on five trees, where their bodies stayed until **evening.**
Judg	19. 9	to leave, the father said, "Look, it's almost **evening** now;
	20.22	and mourned in the presence of the Lord until **evening.**
	20.26	there in the Lord's presence and did not eat until **evening.**
	21. 2	Bethel and sat there in the presence of God until **evening.**
Ruth	2.17	corn in the field until **evening,** and when she had beaten it
	3. 2	This **evening** he will be threshing the barley.
1 Sam	17.16	Goliath challenged the Israelites every morning and **evening**
	20. 5	in the fields until the **evening** of the day after tomorrow.
1 Sam	30.17	At dawn the next day David attacked them and fought until **evening.**
2 Sam	1.12	and mourned and fasted until **evening** for Saul and Jonathan
1 Kgs	17. 6	brought him bread and meat every morning and every **evening.**
	22.35	covered the bottom of the chariot, and at **evening** he died.
2 Kgs	7. 7	So that **evening** the Syrians had fled for their lives,
	16.15	the morning burnt-offerings and the **evening** grain-offerings,
1 Chr	16.40	Every morning and **evening** they were to burn sacrifices
	23.30	Lord every morning and every **evening** [31] and whenever
2 Chr	2. 4	every morning and **evening,** as well as on Sabbaths,
	13.11	Every morning and every **evening** they offer him incense
	13.11	is ritually clean, and every **evening** they light the lamps on
	31. 3	the burnt-offerings each morning and **evening,** and for those
Ezra	3. 3	to burn on it the regular morning and **evening** sacrifices.
	9. 4	until the time for the **evening** sacrifice to be offered, and
	9. 5	the time came for the **evening** sacrifice, I got up from where
Neh	13.19	every Sabbath, as soon as **evening** began to fall, and not to
Esth	2.14	would go there in the **evening,** and the next morning she
Job	4.20	in the morning, but die unnoticed before **evening** comes.
Ps	59. 6	They come back in the **evening,** snarling like dogs as they
	59.14	enemies come back in the **evening,** snarling like dogs as they
	90. 6	and burst into bloom, then dry up and die in the **evening.**
	102.11	My life is like the **evening** shadows;
	104.23	go out to do their work and keep working until **evening.**
	109.23	Like an **evening** shadow I am about to vanish;
	141. 2	my uplifted hands as an **evening** sacrifice.
Prov	7. 9	passing near her house [9] in the **evening** after it was dark.
Ecc	11. 6	Do your sowing in the morning and in the **evening,** too.
Is	5.11	start drinking, and you spend long **evenings** getting drunk.
	17.14	In the **evening** they cause terror, but by morning they are gone.
	21. 4	I had been longing for **evening** to come, but it has brought
Jer	6. 4	is almost over, and the **evening** shadows are growing long.
Ezek	12. 4	watch you leave in the **evening** as if you were going into
	12. 7	a refugee would, and that **evening** as it was getting dark I
	24.18	That **evening** my wife died, and the next day I did as
	33.22	The **evening** before he came, I had felt the powerful
	46. 2	The gate must not be shut until **evening.**
Dan	8.14	for 1,150 days, during which **evening** and morning sacrifices
	8.26	This vision about the **evening** and morning sacrifices
	9.21	It was the time for the **evening** sacrifice to be offered.
Mt	8.16	**evening** came, people brought to Jesus many who had demons in
	14.15	That **evening** his disciples came to him and said, "It is
	14.23	When **evening** came, Jesus was there alone;
	20. 8	"When **evening** came, the owner told his foreman, 'Call the
	26.20	When it was **evening,** Jesus and the twelve disciples sat down
	27.57	When it was **evening,** a rich man from Arimathea arrived;
Mk	1.32	the sun had set and **evening** had come, people brought to
	4.35	On the **evening** of that same day Jesus said to his disciples,
	6.47	When **evening** came, the boat was in the middle of the lake,
	11.19	When **evening** came, Jesus and his disciples left the city.
	13.35	it might be in the **evening** or at midnight or before dawn
	14.17	When it was **evening,** Jesus came with the twelve disciples.
	15.42	It was towards **evening** when Joseph of Arimathea arrived.
Lk	21.37	in the Temple, and when **evening** came, he would go out and
Jn	6.16	When **evening** came, Jesus' disciples went down to the lake,
	20.19	It was late that Sunday **evening,** and the disciples were
Acts	20. 7	On Saturday **evening** we gathered together for the fellowship meal.

EVENT

1 Sam	11.15	and Saul and all the people of Israel celebrated the **event.**
2 Chr	16.11	All the **events** of Asa's reign from beginning to end are
	27. 7	The other **events** of Jotham's reign, his wars, and his policies,
	28.26	All the other **events** of his reign, from beginning to end,
	32. 1	After these **events,** in which King Hezekiah served the Lord
	32.31	about the unusual **event** that had happened in the land,
Esth	9.20	Mordecai had these **events** written down and sent letters
Is	3. 3	politicians and everyone who uses magic to control **events.**
	21. 2	of cruel **events,** a vision of betrayal and destruction.
	41.22	Explain to the court the **events** of the past, and tell us
	43.18	"Do not cling to **events** of the past or dwell on what
	48. 5	future long ago, announcing **events** before they took place,
	48. 6	of new things to come, **events** that I did not reveal before.
	65.17	The **events** of the past will be completely forgotten.
Dan	12. 6	will it be until these amazing **events** come to an end?"
Acts	10.37	know of the great **event** that took place throughout the land
Rev	1. 1	This book is the record of the **events** that Jesus Christ revealed.

EVER
[FOR EVER]

Gen	3.22	from the tree that gives life, eat it, and live **for ever."**
	6. 3	the Lord said, "I will not allow people to live **for ever;**
	13.15	the land that you see, and it will be yours **for ever.**
	17. 8	will belong to your descendants **for ever,** and I will be
	17.19	keep my covenant with him and with his descendants **for ever.**
	27.33	gave him my final blessing, and so it is his **for ever."**
	48. 4	give this land to your descendants as their possession **for ever.'"**
Ex	3.15	This is my name **for ever;**
	12.24	You and your children must obey these rules **for ever.**
	15.18	You, Lord, will be king **for ever** and ever."
	17.16	The Lord will continue to fight against the Amalekites **for ever!"**
	27.21	command is to be kept **for ever** by the Israelites and their
	29. 9	They and their descendants are to serve me as priests **for ever.**
	30.21	which they and their descendants are to observe **for ever."**
	32.13	all that land you promised would be their possession **for ever."**
Lev	3.17	a rule to be kept **for ever** by all Israelites wherever they
	10.15	and your children **for ever,** just as the Lord commanded."
	24. 8	This is Israel's duty **for ever.**
	25.34	it is their property **for ever.**

Num	18. 8	to your descendants as the part assigned to you **for ever.**
	24.20	nation of all, But at the end it will perish **for ever.**"
	24.24	Assyria and Eber, But they, in turn, will perish **for ever.**"
Deut	4.40	the Lord your God is giving you to be yours **for ever.**"
	5.29	everything would go well with them and their descendants **for ever.**
	12.28	for you and your descendants **for ever,** because you will be
	13.16	must be left in ruins **for ever** and never again be rebuilt.
	18. 5	tribes the tribe of Levi to serve him as priests **for ever.**
	28.46	evidence of God's judgement on you and your descendants **for ever.**
	29.29	Law, and we and our descendants are to obey it **for ever.**
Josh	4.24	power is, and you will honour the Lord your God **for ever.**"
1 Sam	3.13	to punish his family **for ever** because his sons have spoken
	13.13	have let you and your descendants rule over Israel **for ever.**
	20.15	show the same kind of loyalty to my family **for ever.**
	20.23	the Lord will make sure that we will keep it **for ever.**"
	20.42	your descendants and mine, will **for ever** keep the sacred promise
2 Sam	2.26	out to Joab, "Do we have to go on fighting **for ever?**
	7.13	and I will make sure that his dynasty continues **for ever.**
	7.16	descendants, and I will make your kingdom last **for ever.**
	7.24	made Israel your own people **for ever,** and you, Lord, have
	7.26	be great, and people will **for ever** say, 'The Lord Almighty
	7.29	and your blessing will rest on my descendants **for ever.**"
	22.51	one he has chosen, to David and his descendants **for ever.**
1 Kgs	1.31	bowed low and said, "May my lord the king live **for ever!**"
	2.33	murders will fall on Joab and on his descendants **for ever.**
	2.45	me and he will make David's kingdom secure **for ever.**"
	8.13	temple for you, a place for you to live in **for ever.**"
	9. 3	built as the place where I shall be worshipped **for ever.**
2 Kgs	5.27	you, and you and your descendants will have it **for ever!**"
	14.27	to destroy Israel completely and **for ever,** so he rescued them
1 Chr	15. 2	the Lord chose to carry it and to serve him **for ever.**"
	16.15	which he made to last **for ever,** [16] the covenant he made
	16.17	Lord made a covenant with Jacob, one that will last **for ever.**
	16.36	Praise him now and **for ever!**
	17.12	and I will make sure that his dynasty continues **for ever.**
	17.14	put him in charge of my people and my kingdom **for ever.**
	17.22	made Israel your own people **for ever,** and you, Lord, have
	17.24	be great, and people will **for ever** say, 'The Lord Almighty
	17.27	them, and your blessing will rest on them **for ever.**"
	22.10	His dynasty will rule Israel **for ever.'** "
	23.13	charge of the sacred objects **for ever,** to burn incense in
	23.25	his people, and he himself will live in Jerusalem **for ever.**
	28. 4	Israel, chose me and my descendants to rule Israel **for ever.**
	28. 7	will make his kingdom last **for ever** if he continues to obey
	28. 8	you may hand it on to succeeding generations **for ever.**"
	28. 9	if you turn away from him, he will abandon you **for ever.**
	29.10	of our ancestor Jacob, may you be praised **for ever** and ever!
	29.18	keep such devotion **for ever** strong in your people's hearts
2 Chr	2. 4	He has commanded Israel to do this **for ever.**
	6. 2	temple for you, a place for you to live in **for ever.**"
	6.41	of your power, enter the Temple and stay here **for ever.**
	7.16	it as the place where I will be worshipped **for ever.**
	9. 8	and wants to preserve them **for ever,** he has made you their
	13. 5	giving him and his descendants kingship over Israel **for ever?**
	20. 7	descendants of Abraham, your friend, to be theirs **for ever.**
	30. 8	your God has made holy **for ever,** and worship him so that
	33. 4	Lord had said was where he should be worshipped **for ever.**
Ezra	9.12	enjoy the land and pass it on to our descendants **for ever.**
Neh	2. 3	I was startled [3] and answered, "May Your Majesty live **for ever!**
	9. 5	praise him **for ever** and ever!
Job	14.20	You overpower a man and send him away **for ever;**
	16. 3	Are you going to keep on talking **for ever?**
	19.24	in stone and write them so that they would last **for ever.**
	36. 7	them to rule like kings and lets them be honoured **for ever.**
	41. 4	an agreement with you and promise to serve you **for ever?**
Ps	9. 6	Our enemies are finished **for ever;**
	9. 7	But the Lord is king **for ever;**
	9.18	the hope of the poor will not be crushed **for ever.**
	10.16	The Lord is king **for ever** and ever.
	13. 1	**For ever?**
	16.11	your presence fills me with joy and brings me pleasure **for ever.**
	18.50	one he has chosen, to David and his descendants **for ever.**
	19. 9	it will continue **for ever.**
	21. 6	Your blessings are with him **for ever** and your presence fills
	22.26	May they prosper **for ever!**
	28. 5	so he will punish them and destroy them **for ever.**
	28. 9	Be their shepherd, and take care of them **for ever.**
	29.10	he rules as king **for ever.**
	30.12	Lord, you are my God, I will give you thanks **for ever.**
	33.11	But his plans endure **for ever;**
	37.18	those who obey him, and the land will be theirs **for ever.**
	37.28	He protects them **for ever,** but the descendants of the wicked
	37.29	The righteous will possess the land and live in it **for ever.**
	41.12	you will keep me in your presence **for ever.**
	41.13	Praise him now and **for ever!**
	44. 8	We will always praise you and give thanks to you **for ever.**
	44.23	Don't reject us **for ever!**
	45. 6	kingdom that God has given you will last **for ever** and ever.
	45.17	will keep your fame alive **for ever,** and everyone will praise
	48. 8	he will keep the city safe **for ever.**
	48.14	"This God is our God **for ever** and ever;
	49. 9	to keep him from the grave, to let him live **for ever.**
	49.11	Their graves are their homes **for ever;**
	49.19	his ancestors in death, where the darkness lasts **for ever.**
	52. 5	So God will ruin you **for ever;**
	52. 8	I trust in his constant love **for ever** and ever.
	61. 7	May he rule **for ever** in your presence, O God;
	66. 7	He rules **for ever** by his might and keeps his eyes on
	68.16	The Lord will live there **for ever!**
Ps	72.19	Praise his glorious name **for ever!**
	74. 1	Will you be angry with your own people **for ever?**
	74.10	Will they insult your name **for ever?**
	79. 5	Lord, will you be angry with us **for ever?**
	79.13	your flock, will thank you **for ever** and praise you for all
	81.15	their punishment would last **for ever.**
	83. 4	destroy their nation, so that Israel will be forgotten **for ever.**"
	83.17	May they be defeated and terrified **for ever;**
	85. 5	Will you be angry with us **for ever?**
	86.12	I will proclaim your greatness **for ever.**
	89. 1	I will proclaim your faithfulness **for ever.**
	89. 4	I will preserve your dynasty **for ever.'** "
	89.28	to him, and my covenant with him will last **for ever.**
	89.46	Lord, will you hide yourself **for ever?**
	89.52	Praise the Lord **for ever!**
	90. 2	being, you were eternally God, and will be God **for ever.**
	92. 8	be totally destroyed, [8] because you, Lord, are supreme **for ever.**
	93. 5	Lord, and your Temple is holy indeed, **for ever** and ever.
	100. 5	his love is eternal and his faithfulness lasts **for ever.**
	102.12	But you, O Lord, are king **for ever;**
	102.24	O Lord, you live **for ever;**
	103. 9	he is not angry **for ever.**
	103.17	Lord, his love lasts **for ever,** and his goodness endures for
	104.31	May the glory of the Lord last **for ever!**
	105. 8	will keep his covenant **for ever,** his promises for a thousand
	105.10	Lord made a covenant with Jacob, one that will last **for ever.**
	106.48	praise him now and **for ever!**
	110. 4	"You will be a priest **for ever** in the priestly order of
	111.10	He is to be praised **for ever.**
	112. 3	be wealthy and rich, and he will be prosperous **for ever.**
	112.10	their hopes are gone **for ever.**
	113. 2	May his name be praised, now and **for ever.**
	115.18	we, the living, will give thanks to him now and **for ever.**
	119.44	I will always obey your law, **for ever** and ever.
	119.89	Your word, O Lord, will last **for ever;**
	119.142	Your righteousness will last **for ever,** and your law is
	119.152	you made them to last **for ever.**
	121. 8	will protect you as you come and go now and **for ever.**
	125. 2	so the Lord surrounds his people now and **for ever.**
	131. 3	Israel, trust in the Lord now and **for ever!**
	132. 8	Covenant Box, the symbol of your power, and stay here **for ever.**
	132.14	"This is where I will live **for ever;**
	145. 1	I will thank you **for ever** and ever.
	145. 2	I will praise you **for ever** and ever.
	145.13	Your rule is eternal, and you are king **for ever.**
	145.21	let all his creatures praise his holy name **for ever.**
	146.10	The Lord is king **for ever.**
	148. 6	were fixed in their places **for ever,** and they cannot disobey.
Prov	12.19	A lie has a short life, but truth lives on **for ever.**
	27.24	Not even nations last **for ever.**
Ecc	3.14	I know that everything God does will last **for ever.**
Is	17. 2	The cities of Syria will be deserted **for ever.**
	24. 5	laws and by violating the covenant he made to last **for ever.**
	24.11	Happiness is gone **for ever;**
	25. 2	The palaces which our enemies built are gone **for ever.**
	25. 8	The Sovereign Lord will destroy death **for ever!**
	26. 4	Trust in the Lord **for ever;**
	32.14	and the forts that guarded them will be in ruins **for ever.**
	32.17	do what is right, there will be peace and security **for ever.**
	33.14	They say, "God's judgement is like a fire that burns **for ever.**
	34.10	burn day and night, and smoke will rise from it **for ever.**
	34.17	land age after age, and it will belong to them **for ever.**
	35.10	be happy for ever, **for ever** free from sorrow and grief.
	40. 8	flowers fade, but the word of our God endures **for ever.**"
	45.17	Israel is saved by the Lord, and her victory lasts **for ever;**
	51. 6	But the deliverance I bring will last **for ever;**
	51. 8	But the deliverance I bring will last **for ever;**
	51.11	be happy for ever, **for ever** free from sorrow and grief.
	54. 8	only a moment, but I will show you my love **for ever.**"
	54.10	I will keep **for ever** my promise of peace."
	55.13	a sign that will last **for ever,** a reminder of what I,
	57.15	"I am the high and holy God, who lives **for ever.**
	57.16	not continue to accuse them or be angry with them **for ever.**
	59.21	my teachings to be yours **for ever,** and from now on you
	60.15	you great and beautiful, A place of joy **for ever** and ever.
	60.21	all do what is right, And will possess the land **for ever.**
	61. 7	Your joy will last **for ever.**
	64. 9	too angry with us or hold our sins against us **for ever.**
	65.18	Be glad and rejoice **for ever** in what I create.
Jer	3. 5	you won't be cross with me **for ever.'**
	3.12	I will not be angry with you **for ever.**
	15.14	because my anger is like fire, and it will burn **for ever.**"
	17. 4	my anger is like a fire, and it will burn **for ever.**"
	18.16	made this land a thing of horror, to be despised **for ever.**
	20.11	They will be disgraced **for ever,** because they cannot succeed.
	25. 9	leave them in ruins **for ever,** a terrible and shocking sight.
	25.12	I will destroy that country and leave it in ruins **for ever.**
	49.13	All the near-by villages will be in ruins **for ever.**
	49.33	will be made a desert **for ever,** a place where only jackals
	51.26	You will be like a desert **for ever.**
	51.62	man nor animal, and it would be like a desert **for ever.'**
Lam	3.31	The Lord is merciful and will not reject us **for ever.**
	5.19	you, O Lord, are king **for ever,** and will rule to the
	5.22	Or have you rejected us **for ever?**
Ezek	16.60	I will make a covenant with you that will last **for ever.**
	27.36	You are gone, gone **for ever,** and merchants all over the
	28.19	You are gone, gone **for ever,** and all the nations that
	35. 9	I will make you desolate **for ever,** and no one will live
	37.25	They will live there **for ever,** and so will their children
	37.25	A king like my servant David will rule over them **for ever.**

Ezek 37.26 make a covenant with them that guarantees their security **for ever.**
37.26 put my Temple in their land, where it will stay **for ever.**
37.28 there to be among them **for ever,** then the nations will know
43. 7 here among the people of Israel and rule over them **for ever.**
43. 9 If they do, I will live among them **for ever."**
46.14 this offering to the Lord are to be in force **for ever.**
46.15 are to be offered to the Lord every morning **for ever."**
Dan 2. 4 answered the king in Aramaic, "May Your Majesty live **for ever!**
2.20 praise him **for ever** and ever.
2.44 will completely destroy all those empires, and then last **for ever.**
3. 9 said to King Nebuchadnezzar, "May Your Majesty live **for ever!**
4. 3 God is king **for ever;**
4.34 and gave honour and glory to the one who lives **for ever.**
4.34 "He will rule **for ever,** and his kingdom will last for all
5.10 She said, "May Your Majesty live **for ever!**
6. 6 and said, "King Darius, may Your Majesty live **for ever!**
6.21 Daniel answered, "May Your Majesty live **for ever!**
6.26 "He is a living God, and he will rule **for ever.**
7. 9 One who had been living **for ever** sat down on one of
7.13 one who had been living **for ever** and was presented to him.
7.14 His authority would last **for ever,** and his kingdom would never
7.18 God will receive royal power and keep it **for ever** and ever."
7.22 one who had been living **for ever** came and pronounced judgement
12. 3 to do what is right will shine like the stars **for ever."**
Hos 2.19 you constant love and mercy and make you mine **for ever.**
Joel 3.20 and Jerusalem will be inhabited **for ever,** and I the Lord,
Obad 10 you will be destroyed and dishonoured **for ever.**
Jon 2. 6 mountains, into the land whose gates lock shut **for ever.**
Mic 2. 9 and you have robbed their children of my blessings **for ever.**
4. 5 will worship and obey the Lord our God **for ever** and ever.
4. 7 over them on Mount Zion from that time on and **for ever."**
7.18 You do not stay angry **for ever,** but you take pleasure in
Nah 3.18 your governors are dead, and your noblemen are asleep **for ever!**
Hab 1.17 to use their swords **for ever** and keep on destroying nations
Mal 1. 4 and 'The nation with whom the Lord is angry **for ever.'"**
Lk 1.33 he will be the king of the descendants of Jacob **for ever;**
1.55 show mercy to Abraham and to all his descendants **for ever!"**
Jn 6.51 If anyone eats this bread, he will live **for ever.**
6.58 The one who eats this bread will live **for ever."**
8.35 to a family permanently, but a son belongs there **for ever.**
10.35 We know that what the scripture says is true **for ever;**
12.34 "Our Law tells us that the Messiah will live **for ever.**
14.16 give you another Helper, who will stay with you **for ever.**
Rom 1.25 of the Creator himself, who is to be praised **for ever!**
9. 5 May God, who rules over all, be praised **for ever!**
11.36 To God be the glory **for ever!**
16.27 God, who alone is all-wise, be glory through Jesus Christ **for ever!**
1 Cor 9.25 but we do it for one that will last **for ever.**
2 Cor 3.11 how much more glory is there in that which lasts **for ever!**
4.18 only for a time, but what cannot be seen lasts **for ever.**
5. 1 in, a home he himself has made, which will last **for ever.**
9. 9 his kindness lasts **for ever."**
11.31 and Father of the Lord Jesus—blessed be his name **for ever!**
Gal 1. 5 To God be the glory **for ever** and ever!
Eph 3.21 church and in Christ Jesus for all time, **for ever** and ever!
Phil 4.20 To our God and Father be the glory **for ever** and ever!
1 Tim 1.17 only God—to him be honour and glory **for ever** and ever!
2 Tim 4.18 To him be the glory **for ever** and ever!
Heb 1. 8 "Your kingdom, O God, will last **for ever** and ever!
5. 6 "You will be a priest **for ever,** in the priestly order of
6.20 has become a high priest **for ever,** in the priestly order of
7. 3 he remains a priest **for ever.**
7.17 "You will be a priest **for ever,** in the priestly order of
7.21 'You will be a priest **for ever.'"**
7.24 But Jesus lives on **for ever,** and his work as priest does
7.25 through him, because he lives **for ever** to plead with God for
7.28 Law, appoints the Son, who has been made perfect **for ever.**
10. 1 The same sacrifices are offered **for ever,** year after year.
10.12 an offering that is effective **for ever,** and then he sat down
10.14 then, he has made perfect **for ever** those who are purified
10.34 possessed something much better, which would last **for ever.**
13. 8 Jesus Christ is the same yesterday, today, and **for ever.**
13.20 And to Christ be the glory **for ever** and ever!
1 Pet 1.25 fall, [25] but the word of the Lord remains **for ever."**
4.11 Jesus Christ, to whom belong glory and power **for ever** and ever.
5.11 To him be the power **for ever!**
2 Pet 3.18 To him be the glory, now and **for ever!**
1 Jn 2.17 but he who does the will of God lives **for ever.**
2 Jn 2 the truth remains in us and will be with us **for ever.**
Jude 13 God has reserved a place **for ever** in the deepest darkness.
25 from all ages past, and now, and **for ever** and ever!
Rev 1. 6 To Jesus Christ be the glory and power **for ever** and ever!
1.18 I was dead, but now I am alive **for ever** and ever.
4. 9 one who sits on the throne, who lives **for ever** and ever.
4.10 on the throne, and worship him who lives **for ever** and ever.
5.13 Lamb, be praise and honour, glory and might, **for ever** and ever!"
7.12 power, and might belong to our God **for ever** and ever!
10. 6 of God, who lives **for ever** and ever, who created heaven,
11.15 Lord and his Messiah, and he will rule **for ever** and ever!"
14.11 of the fire that torments them goes up **for ever** and ever.
15. 7 full of the anger of God, who lives **for ever** and ever.
19. 3 that consume the great city goes up **for ever** and ever!"
20.10 and they will be tormented day and night **for ever** and ever.
22. 5 their light, and they will rule as kings **for ever** and ever.

EVER-LIVING see **LIVE (1)**

EVERGREEN

Hos 14. 8 Like an **evergreen** tree I will shelter them;

EVERLASTING

Gen 9.12 As a sign of this **everlasting** covenant which I am making
9.16 see it and remember the **everlasting** covenant between me and
17. 7 in future generations as an **everlasting** covenant.
17.13 sign to show that my covenant with you is **everlasting.**
17.19 It is an **everlasting** covenant.
21.33 in Beersheba and worshipped the Lord, the **Everlasting** God.
49.26 Delightful things from **everlasting** hills.
Ps 139.24 is any evil in me and guide me in the **everlasting** way.
Is 40.28 The Lord is the **everlasting** God;
63.12 the deep water, to win **everlasting** fame for himself?"
Jer 23.40 I will bring on them **everlasting** shame and disgrace that
Mic 6. 2 You mountains, you **everlasting** foundations of the earth,
Hab 3. 6 the **everlasting** hills sink down, the hills where he walked
Zeph 2. 9 of salt pits and **everlasting** ruin, overgrown with weeds.

EVERY DAY see **DAY**

EVERYDAY

Rom 6.19 (I use **everyday** language because of the weakness of your
1 Cor 7.28 rather spare you the **everyday** troubles that married people
9. 8 limit myself to these **everyday** examples, because the Law says
Gal 3.15 My brothers, I am going to use an **everyday** example:

EVIDENCE

Ex 22.13 wild animals, the man is to bring the remains as **evidence;**
23. 1 and do not help a guilty man by giving false **evidence.**
23. 2 do wrong or when they give **evidence** that perverts justice.
Lev 5. 1 is officially summoned to give **evidence** in court and does
Num 35.30 put to death only on the **evidence** of two or more witnesses;
35.30 the **evidence** of one witness is not sufficient to support an
Deut 28.46 They will be the **evidence** of God's judgement on you and
31.19 of Israel, so that it will stand as **evidence** against them.
31.21 still be sung, and it will stand as **evidence** against them.
Job 15. 5 Your wickedness is **evident** by what you say;
Prov 24.28 Don't give **evidence** against someone else without good reason,
Ecc 10. 3 His stupidity will be **evident** even to strangers he meets
Mt 26.59 tried to find some false **evidence** against Jesus to put him
Mk 14.55 Council tried to find some **evidence** against Jesus in order to
Acts 14.17 But he has always given **evidence** of his existence by the
2 Cor 13. 1 must be upheld by the **evidence** of two or more witnesses"—
Heb 10.28 when judged guilty on the **evidence** of two or more witnesses.

EVIL

see also **EVIL ONE**

Gen 4. 7 because you have done **evil,** sin is crouching at your door.
6. 5 on earth was and how **evil** their thoughts were all the time,
6.11 God, [11] but everyone else was **evil** in God's sight, and
6.12 and saw that it was **evil,**
6.12 for the people were all living **evil** lives.
8.21 know that from the time he is young his thoughts are **evil.**
38. 7 Er's conduct was **evil,** and it displeased the Lord, so the
44. 4 with them, ask them, 'Why have you paid back **evil** for good?
50.20 You plotted **evil** against me, but God turned it into good,
Ex 20. 7 not use my name for **evil** purposes, for I, the Lord your
22.28 "Do not speak **evil** of God, and do not curse a leader
23. 7 for I will condemn anyone who does such an **evil** thing.
32.22 you know how determined these people are to do **evil.**
34. 7 for thousands of generations and forgive **evil** and sin;
34. 9 are stubborn, but forgive our **evil** and our sin, and accept
Lev 16.21 confess over it all the **evils,** sins, and rebellions of the
20.23 They have disgusted me with all their **evil** practices.
Num 25.18 destroy them, [18] because of the **evil** they did to you when
Deut 1.35 one of you from this **evil** generation will enter the fertile
4.25 This is **evil** in the Lord's sight, and it will make him
5.11 not use my name for **evil** purposes, for I, the Lord your
9.12 led out of Egypt, have become corrupt and have done **evil.**
13. 5 Such a man is **evil** and is trying to lead you away
13. 5 be put to death, in order to rid yourselves of this **evil.**
13.11 afraid, and no one will ever again do such an **evil** thing.
13.14 it is true that this **evil** thing did happen, [15] then kill
15. 9 Do not let such an **evil** thought enter your mind.
17. 4 it is true that this **evil** thing has happened in Israel,
17. 7 in this way you will get rid of this **evil.**
17.12 in this way you will remove this **evil** from Israel.
19.19 In this way you will get rid of this **evil.**
19.20 afraid, and no one will ever again do such an **evil** thing.
21.21 him to death, and so you will get rid of this **evil.**
22.21 In this way you will get rid of this **evil.**
22.22 In this way you will get rid of this **evil.**
22.24 In this way you will get rid of this **evil.**
24. 7 In this way you will get rid of this **evil.**
28.15 giving you today, all these **evil** things will happen to you:
28.20 "If you do **evil** and reject the Lord, he will bring on
29.19 That would destroy all of you, good and **evil** alike.
30.15 you a choice between good and **evil,** between life and death.
31.18 because they have done **evil** and worshipped other gods.
32.16 the **evil** they did made him angry.
Josh 22.16 "Why have you done this **evil** thing against the God of Israel?
Judg 2.19 other gods, and refused to give up their own **evil** ways.
19.23 Don't do such an **evil,** immoral thing!
20. 6 These people have committed an **evil** and immoral act among us.

Judg 20.13 so that we can kill them and remove this **evil** from Israel."
1 Sam 2.23 Everybody tells me about the **evil** you are doing.
3.13 ever because his sons have spoken **evil** things against me.
12.20 you have done such an **evil** thing, do not turn away from
16.14 spirit left Saul, and an **evil** spirit sent by the Lord
16.15 him, "We know that an **evil** spirit sent by God is tormenting
16.16 Then when the **evil** spirit comes on you, the man can play
16.23 From then on, whenever the **evil** spirit sent by God came
16.23 The **evil** spirit would leave, and Saul would feel better and
18.10 The next day an **evil** spirit from God suddenly took
19. 9 One day an **evil** spirit from the Lord took control of Saul.
24.13 You know the old saying, '**Evil** is done only by evil men.'
25.28 and you will not do anything **evil** as long as you live.
25.39 The Lord has punished Nabal for his **evil."**
2 Sam 4.11 worse it will be for **evil** men who murder an innocent man
12. 9 Why did you do this **evil** thing?
14.17 is like God's angel and can distinguish good from **evil.**
1 Kgs 3. 9 justice and to know the difference between good and **evil.**
11.21 As king of Edom, Hadad was an **evil,** bitter enemy of Israel.
13.33 did not turn from his **evil** ways, but continued to choose
16. 7 not only because of the **evil** he did, just as King Jeroboam
2 Kgs 8.18 of Ahab he followed the **evil** ways of the kings of Israel.
13. 2 he never gave up his **evil** ways.
13.11 the Lord and followed the **evil** example of King Jeroboam, who
17.13 "Abandon your **evil** ways and obey my commands, which are
1 Chr 2. 3 His eldest son, Er, was so **evil** that the Lord killed him.
4.10 and keep me from anything **evil** that might cause me pain."
2 Chr 7.14 and turn away from the **evil** they have been doing, then I
12.14 He did what was **evil,** because he did not try to find
22. 2 King Omri of Israel—gave him advice that led him into **evil.**
33.19 committed before he repented—the **evil** he did, the pagan
36. 8 his disgusting practices and the **evil** he committed, is
Ezra 4.12 Jerusalem and are rebuilding that **evil** and rebellious city.
Neh 4. 5 Don't forgive the **evil** they do and don't forget their sins,
13.17 Jewish leaders and said, "Look at the **evil** you're doing!
Esth 7. 6 "Our enemy, our persecutor, is this **evil** man Haman!"
8. 3 do something to stop the **evil** plot that Haman, the
Job 1. 1 He was a good man, careful not to do anything **evil.**
1. 8 He worships me and is careful not to do anything **evil."**
2. 3 He worships me and is careful not to do anything **evil.**
3.17 grave wicked men stop their **evil,** and tired workmen find
4. 8 people plough fields of **evil** and sow wickedness like seed;
4. 8 now they harvest wickedness and **evil.**
5. 6 **Evil** does not grow in the soil, nor does trouble grow out
8.16 **Evil** men sprout like weeds in the sun, like weeds that
8.19 Yes, that's all the joy **evil** men have;
8.20 never abandon the faithful or ever give help to **evil** men.
11.11 he sees all their **evil** deeds.
11.14 Put away **evil** and wrong from your home.
15.16 And man drinks **evil** as if it were water;
15.31 enough to trust in **evil,** then evil will be his reward.
15.35 These are the men who plan trouble and do **evil;**
16.11 God has handed me over to **evil** men.
18.21 That is the fate of **evil** men, the fate of those who
20.12 **Evil** tastes so good to him that he keeps some in
20.16 What the **evil** man swallows is like poison;
21. 7 Why does God let **evil** men live, let them grow old and
21.28 house of the great man now, the man who practised **evil?"**
22. 5 it's because of all the **evil** you do.
22.15 to walk in the paths that **evil** men have always followed?
22.23 an end to all the **evil** that is done in your house.
24. 9 **Evil** men make slaves of fatherless infants and take the
27. 4 lips will never say anything **evil,** my tongue will never tell
28.28 To understand, you must turn from **evil."**
31. 7 let myself be attracted to **evil,** if my hands are stained
34. 8 He likes the company of **evil** men and goes about with sinners.
34.12 Almighty God does not do **evil;**
34.32 you your faults, and have you agreed to stop doing **evil?**
34.36 you will see that he talks like an **evil** man.
35.12 but God doesn't answer, for they are proud and **evil** men.
36.10 He makes them listen to his warning to turn away from **evil.**
36.21 Be careful not to turn to **evil;**
36.23 can tell God what to do or accuse him of doing **evil.**
Ps 1. 1 who reject the advice of **evil** men, who do not follow the
1. 4 But **evil** men are not like this at all;
1. 6 by the Lord, but the **evil** are on the way to their
5. 4 you allow no **evil** in your presence.
6. 8 Keep away from me, you **evil** men!
7. 9 Stop the wickedness of **evil** men and reward those who are good.
7.14 See how wicked people think up **evil;**
7.16 are punished by their own **evil** and are hurt by their own
10. 3 The wicked man is proud of his **evil** desires;
10. 7 he is quick to speak hateful, **evil** words.
10.15 Break the power of wicked and **evil** men;
12. 7 Wicked men are everywhere, and everyone praises what is **evil.**
14. 4 "Are all these **evildoers** ignorant?
14. 6 **Evildoers** frustrate the plans of the humble man, but the
17. 3 you have examined me completely and found no **evil** desire in me.
17. 4 I speak no **evil** as others do;
19.13 Then I shall be perfect and free from the **evil** of sin.
22.16 A gang of **evil** men is round me;
26. 5 I hate the company of **evil** men and avoid the wicked.
26.10 murderers— [10]men who do **evil** all the time and are always
27. 2 When **evil** men attack me and try to kill me, they stumble
28. 3 with those who do **evil**— men whose words are friendly,
28. 4 for what they have done, for the **evil** they have committed.
34.13 Then hold back from speaking **evil** and from telling lies.
34.14 Turn away from **evil** and do good;
34.16 he opposes those who do **evil,** so that when they die, they
34.21 **Evil** will kill the wicked;
35.11 **Evil** men testify against me and accuse me of crimes I

Ps 35.12 They pay me back **evil** for good, and I sink in despair.
36. 4 He makes **evil** plans as he lies in bed;
36. 4 nothing he does is good, and he never rejects anything **evil.**
36.12 See where **evil** men have fallen.
37. 7 those who prosper or those who succeed in their **evil** plans.
37.27 Turn away from **evil** and do good, and your descendants
38.20 Those who pay back **evil** for good are against me because
39. 1 I will not say anything while **evil** men are near."
43. 1 deliver me from lying and **evil** men!
45. 7 you love what is right and hate what is **evil.**
49. 6 am surrounded by enemies, [6]by **evil** men who trust in their
50.19 "You are always ready to speak **evil;**
51. 2 Wash away all my **evil** and make me clean from my sin!
51. 4 you—only against you— and done what you consider **evil.**
51. 5 I have been **evil** from the day I was born;
51. 9 Close your eyes to my sins and wipe out all my **evil.**
52. 1 Why do you boast, great man, of your **evil?**
52. 3 You love **evil** more than good and falsehood more than truth.
53. 4 "Are these **evildoers** ignorant?
54. 5 May God use their own **evil** to punish my enemies.
55.15 **Evil** is in their homes and in their hearts.
56. 7 Punish them, O God, for their **evil;**
58. 2 You think only of the **evil** you can do, and commit crimes
58. 3 **Evil** men go wrong all their lives;
59. 2 Save me from those **evil** men;
59. 5 show no mercy to **evil** traitors!
64. 2 me from the plots of the wicked, from mobs of **evil** men.
64. 5 They encourage each other in their **evil** plots;
64. 6 They make **evil** plans and say, "We have planned a perfect crime."
71. 4 me from wicked men, from the power of cruel and **evil** men.
73. 7 their hearts pour out **evil,** and their minds are busy with
73. 8 They laugh at other people and speak of **evil** things;
73. 9 They speak **evil** of God in heaven and give arrogant orders
82. 4 Rescue them from the power of **evil** men.
91. 6 that strike in the dark or the **evils** that kill in daylight.
94.16 Who took my side against the **evildoers?**
97.10 The Lord loves those who hate **evil;**
101. 3 a pure life in my house, [3]and will never tolerate **evil.**
101. 4 I will not be dishonest, and will have no dealings with **evil.**
101. 5 rid of anyone who whispers **evil** things about someone else;
101. 8 I will expel all **evil** men from the city of the Lord.
106. 6 we have been wicked and **evil.**
107.17 suffering because of their sins and because of their **evil;**
109. 3 about me [3]and they say **evil** things about me, attacking me
109. 5 They pay me back **evil** for good and hatred for love.
109.14 May the Lord remember the **evil** of his ancestors and
109.20 in that way— those who say such **evil** things against me!
119.101 I have avoided all **evil** conduct, because I want to
119.133 don't let me be overcome by **evil.**
125. 3 if they did, the righteous themselves might do **evil.**
139.20 they speak **evil** things against your name.
139.24 out if there is any **evil** in me and guide me in
140. 1 Save me, Lord, from **evil** men;
140. 2 They are always plotting **evil,** always stirring up quarrels.
140.11 may **evil** overtake violent men and destroy them.
141. 4 to do wrong and from joining **evil** men in their wickedness.
141. 5 will never accept honour from **evil** men,
141. 5 because I am always praying against their **evil** deeds.
141. 9 they have set for me, from the snares of those **evildoers.**
Prov 2.14 senseless **evil,** [15]unreliable men who cannot be trusted.
3.32 Lord hates people who do **evil,** but he takes righteous men
4.14 Do not go where **evil** men go.
4.15 Keep away from **evil!**
4.27 Avoid **evil** and walk straight ahead.
6.14 all the while planning **evil** in their perverted minds,
6.16 feet that hurry off to do **evil,**
8.13 To honour the Lord is to hate **evil;**
8.13 I hate pride and arrogance, **evil** ways and false words.
9. 7 If you reprimand an **evil** man, you will only get hurt.
10.31 wisdom, but the tongue that speaks **evil** will be stopped.
11.20 The Lord hates **evil-minded** people, but loves those who do right.
11.21 You can be sure that **evil** men will be punished, but
12. 2 Lord is pleased with good people, but condemns those who plan **evil.**
12.12 people want is to find **evil** things to do, but the righteous
12.20 Those who plan **evil** are in for a rude surprise, but
13.19 Stupid people refuse to turn away from **evil.**
14.11 be standing after an **evil** man's house has been destroyed.
14.19 **Evil** people will have to bow down to the righteous and
14.22 if you work for **evil,** you are making a mistake.
14.32 their own downfall by their **evil** deeds, but good people are
15. 3 he is watching us, whether we do good or **evil.**
15. 9 Lord hates the ways of **evil** people, but loves those who do
15.26 The Lord hates **evil** thoughts,
15.28 **Evil** people have a quick reply, but it causes trouble.
15.29 pray, the Lord listens, but he ignores those who are **evil.**
16. 6 Obey the Lord and nothing **evil** will happen to you.
16.12 Kings cannot tolerate **evil,**
16.17 Those who are good travel a road that avoids **evil;**
16.27 **Evil** people look for ways to harm others;
16.27 even their words burn with **evil.**
16.30 they have thought of something **evil.**
17. 4 **Evil** people listen to evil ideas, and liars listen to lies.
17.13 If you repay good with **evil,**
17.13 you will never get **evil** out of your house.
17.20 Anyone who thinks and speaks **evil** can expect to find
19.28 Wicked people love the taste of **evil.**
20. 8 The king sits in judgement and knows **evil** when he sees it.
21.10 Wicked people are always hungry for **evil;**
21.15 people are happy, but **evil** people are brought to despair.
21.27 him sacrifices, especially if they do it from **evil** motives.

Prov	24. 1	Don't be envious of **evil** people, and don't try to make
	24. 8	If you are always planning **evil,** you will earn a
	24.19	Don't let **evil** people worry you;
	25. 5	Keep **evil** advisers away from the king and his government
	25.26	in to someone who is **evil** reminds you of a polluted spring
	26.26	his hatred, but everyone will see the **evil** things he does.
	28. 5	**Evil** people do not know what justice is, but those who
	28.10	an honest person into doing **evil,** you will fall into your
	29. 6	**Evil** people are trapped in their own sins, while honest
	29.16	When **evil** men are in power, crime increases.
	30.32	foolish enough to be arrogant and plan **evil,** stop and think!
Ecc	3.17	judge the righteous and the **evil** alike, because every thing,
	7.15	may die while another man lives on, even though he is **evil.**
	8.10	praise them in the very city where they did their **evil.**
	9. 3	minds are full of **evil** and madness, and suddenly they die.
	9.12	we are trapped at some **evil** moment when we least expect it.
Is	1. 4	You are doomed, you sinful nation, you corrupt and **evil** people!
	1.16	Stop all this **evil** that I see you doing.
	1.16	Yes, stop doing **evil** [17] and learn to do right.
	1.31	be destroyed by their own **evil** deeds, and no one will be
	3.11	But **evil** men are doomed;
	5.20	You call **evil** good and call good evil.
	9.17	are godless and wicked and everything they say is **evil.**
	11. 4	the people will be punished, and **evil** persons will die.
	11. 9	On Zion, God's sacred hill, there will be nothing harmful or **evil.**
	14. 5	ended the power of the **evil** rulers [6] who angrily oppressed
	14.20	None of your **evil** family will survive.
	22.14	to me and said, "This **evil** will never be forgiven them as
	30. 8	that there would be a permanent record of how **evil** they are.
	30.28	nations to destruction and puts an end to their **evil** plans.
	31. 2	his threats to punish **evil** men and those who protect them.
	32. 6	A fool speaks foolishly and thinks up **evil** things to do.
	32. 7	A stupid person is **evil** and does evil things;
	33.15	those who plan to commit murder or to do other **evil** things.
	47.10	"You felt sure of yourself in your **evil;**
	53. 5	our sins he was wounded, beaten because of the **evil** we did.
	53. 9	placed in a grave with **evil** men, he was buried with the
	53.12	He willingly gave his life and shared the fate of **evil** men.
	56. 2	I will bless those who do nothing **evil."**
	57.20	But **evil** men are like the restless sea, whose waves
	58. 9	to every gesture of contempt, and to every **evil** word;
	59. 5	The **evil** plots you make are as deadly as the eggs of
	59. 7	You are always planning something **evil,** and you can hardly
	59.15	who stops doing **evil** finds himself the victim of crime."
	65. 7	burnt incense at pagan hill shrines and spoken **evil** of me.
	65.12	You chose to disobey me and do **evil.**
	65.25	On Zion, my sacred hill, there will be nothing harmful or **evil."**
	66. 4	They chose to disobey me and do **evil."**
Jer	2.19	Your own **evil** will punish you, and your turning from me
	3. 5	is what you said, but you did all the **evil** you could."
	3.17	no longer do what their stubborn and **evil** hearts tell them.
	4. 4	burn like fire because of the **evil** things you have done.
	4.14	Jerusalem, wash the **evil** from your heart, so that you
	4.22	experts at doing what is **evil,** but failures at doing what is
	5.26	**"Evil** men live among my people;
	5.28	There is no limit to their **evil** deeds.
	6. 7	keeps its water fresh, so Jerusalem keeps its **evil** fresh.
	6.29	my people, because those who are **evil** are not taken away.
	7.24	did whatever their stubborn and **evil** hearts told them to do,
	7.30	"The people of Judah have done an **evil** thing.
	8. 3	And the people of this **evil** nation who survive, who live
	9. 3	"My people do one **evil** thing after another, and do not
	9. 7	My people have done **evil**— what else can I do with
	11. 8	everyone continued to be as stubborn and **evil** as ever.
	11.15	The Lord says, "The people I love are doing **evil** things.
	11.19	that it was against me that they were planning **evil** things.
	12. 3	Drag these **evil** men away like sheep to be butchered;
	13.10	These **evil** people have refused to obey me.
	13.23	you that do nothing but **evil** could learn to do what is
	15. 7	I killed your children because you did not stop your **evil** ways.
	16.12	of you are stubborn and **evil,** and you do not obey me.
	18. 8	that nation turns from its **evil,** I will not do what I
	18.10	nation disobeys me and does **evil,** I will not do what I
	18.12	all be just as stubborn and **evil** as we want to be.' "
	18.20	Is **evil** the payment for good?
	18.23	Do not forgive their **evil** or pardon their sin.
	20.13	He rescues the oppressed from the power of **evil** men.
	21.11	If you don't, the **evil** you are doing will make my anger
	22.22	and put to shame because of all the **evil** you have done.
	23. 2	I am going to punish you for the **evil** you have done.
	23.11	I have caught them doing **evil** in the Temple itself.
	23.14	to do wrong, so that no one stops doing what is **evil.**
	23.22	made them give up the **evil** lives they live and the wicked
	25. 5	of life and from the **evil** things you are doing, so that
	26. 3	Perhaps the people will listen and give up their **evil** ways.
	32.32	it [32] because of all the **evil** that has been done by the
	33. 5	city because of the **evil** things that its people have done.
	35.15	you to give up your **evil** ways and to do what is
	36. 3	to bring on them, they will turn from their **evil** ways.
	36. 7	Lord and turn from their **evil** ways, because the Lord has
	44. 3	because their people had done **evil** and had made me angry.
	44. 5	not give up your **evil** practice of sacrificing to other gods.
	44. 7	now ask why you are doing such an **evil** thing to yourselves.
	44.22	Lord could no longer endure your wicked and **evil** practices.
	50.39	be haunted by demons and **evil** spirits, and by unclean birds.
	51.24	Babylonia and its people for all the **evil** they did to Jerusalem.
	51.56	am a God who punishes **evil,** and I will treat Babylon as
Lam	3.38	Good and **evil** alike take place at his command.
Ezek	3.18	If I announce that an **evil** man is going to die but
	3.19	If you do warn an **evil** man and he doesn't stop sinning,
	3.20	truly good man starts doing **evil** and I put him in a
Ezek	5.11	my Temple with all the **evil,** disgusting things you did, I
	6. 9	because of the **evil** and degrading things they have done.
	6.11	of all the **evil,** disgusting things the Israelites have done.
	7.13	Those who are **evil** cannot survive.
	7.24	I will bring the most **evil** nations here and let them
	8. 9	look at the **evil,** disgusting things they are doing there."
	11. 2	"Mortal man, these men make **evil** plans and give bad advice
	13.22	You prevent **evil** people from giving up evil and saving their lives.
	14.22	See how **evil** they are, and be convinced that the punishment
	16.23	You did all that **evil,** and then [24] by the side of every
	16.48	her villages never did the **evil** that you and your villages
	16.57	were proud [57] and before the **evil** you did had been exposed?
	18. 8	He refuses to do **evil** and gives an honest decision in any
	18.17	He refuses to do **evil** and doesn't lend money for profit.
	18.18	hand, cheated and robbed, and always did **evil** to everyone.
	18.20	and an evil man will suffer for the **evil** he does.
	18.21	"If an **evil** man stops sinning and keeps my laws, if he
	18.23	Do you think I enjoy seeing an **evil** man die?"
	18.24	starts doing all the **evil,** disgusting things that evil men do,
	18.26	doing good and starts doing **evil** and then dies,
	18.26	he dies because of the **evil** he has done.
	18.27	When an **evil** man stops sinning and does what is right
	18.30	Turn away from all the **evil** you are doing, and don't let
	18.31	Give up all the **evil** you have been doing, and get
	20.43	with yourselves because of all the **evil** things you did.
	20.44	I do not deal with you as your wicked, **evil** actions deserve."
	21. 3	draw my sword and kill all of you, good and **evil** alike.
	21.29	You are wicked and **evil,** and your day is coming, the day
	22.15	country and nation and will put an end to your **evil** actions.
	28.15	from the day you were created until you began to do **evil.**
	28.18	You did such **evil** in buying and selling that your places
	30.12	up the Nile and put Egypt under the power of **evil** men.
	33. 8	If I announce that an **evil** man is going to die but
	33. 9	If you do warn an **evil** man and he doesn't stop sinning,
	33.11	Israel, stop the **evil** you are doing.
	33.12	If an **evil** man stops doing evil, he won't be punished,
	33.14	I may warn an **evil** man that he is going to die,
	33.18	stops doing good and starts doing **evil,** he will die for it.
	33.19	When an **evil** man gives up sinning and does what is right
	36.31	You will remember your **evil** conduct
	38.10	"When that time comes, you will start thinking up an **evil** plan.
Dan	9. 5	"We have sinned, we have been **evil,** we have done wrong.
	9.16	people because of our sins and the **evil** our ancestors did.
	9.24	freeing your people and your holy city from sin and **evil.**
	11.21	of Syria will be an **evil** man who has no right to
	11.27	but their motives will be **evil,** and they will lie to each
Hos	4. 9	will punish you and make you pay for the **evil** you do.
	5. 4	The **evil** that the people have done prevents them from
	6. 8	Gilead is a city full of **evil** men and murderers.
	6. 9	And they do all this **evil** deliberately!
	7. 1	all I can see is their wickedness and the **evil** they do.
	7. 2	It never enters their heads that I will remember all this **evil;**
	7. 3	"People deceive the king and his officers by their **evil** plots.
	7.12	I will punish them for the **evil** they have done.
	9. 9	They are hopelessly **evil** in what they do, just as they
	9.15	The Lord says, "All their **evil-doing** began in Gilgal.
	9.15	And because of the **evil** they have done, I will drive them
	10.13	But instead you planted **evil** and reaped its harvest.
	10.15	of Bethel, because of the terrible **evil** that you have done.
Amos	5.13	so, keeping quiet in such **evil** times is the clever thing to
	5.14	what is right, not what is **evil,** so that you may live.
	5.15	Hate what is **evil,** love what is right, and see that
	8. 7	God of Israel, has sworn, "I will never forget their **evil** deeds.
Jon	3. 8	God and must give up his wicked behaviour and his **evil** actions.
Mic	2. 1	terrible it will be for those who lie awake and plan **evil!**
	2. 1	soon as they have the chance, they do the **evil** they planned.
	3. 2	yet you hate what is good and you love what is **evil.**
	3. 4	He will not listen to your prayers, for you have done **evil.**
	6.10	In the houses of **evil** men are treasures which they got dishonestly.
	6.16	because you have followed the **evil** practices of King Omri
	7. 3	They are all experts at doing **evil.**
Hab	1. 4	**Evil** men get the better of the righteous, and so justice is
	1.13	But how can you stand these treacherous, **evil** men?
	1.13	too holy to look at **evil,** and you cannot stand the sight
	2. 4	'Those who are **evil** will not survive, but those who are
Zech	1. 4	telling them not to live **evil,** sinful lives any longer.
Mal	1. 4	People will call them 'The **evil** country' and 'The nation
	2. 6	but they also helped many others to stop doing **evil.**
	2.17	By saying, "The Lord Almighty thinks all **evildoers** are good;
	3.15	**Evil** men not only prosper, but they test God's patience
	3.15	with their **evil** deeds and get away with it.' "
	4. 1	coming when all proud and **evil** people will burn like straw.
Mt	5.11	and tell all kinds of **evil** lies against you because you are
	5.45	rain to those who do good and to those who do **evil.**
	9. 4	thinking, so he said, "Why are you thinking such **evil** things?
	12.31	people can be forgiven any sin and any **evil** thing they say;
	12.31	but whoever says **evil** things against the Holy Spirit will not
	12.34	You snakes—how can you say good things when you are **evil?**
	12.39	"How **evil** and godless are the people of this day!"
	12.45	This is what will happen to the **evil** people of this day."
	13.41	and all others who do **evil** things, [42] and they will throw
	13.49	out and gather up the **evil** people from among the good
	15.19	from his heart come the **evil** ideas which lead him to kill,
	16. 4	How **evil** and godless are the people of this day!
	21.41	"He will certainly kill those **evil** men," they answered,
	22.18	however, was aware of their **evil** plan, and so he said,
	24.12	will be the spread of **evil** that many people's love will grow
Mk	3.28	all their sins and all the **evil** things they may say.
	3.29	whoever says **evil** things against the Holy Spirit will never be
	7.21	a person's heart, come the **evil** ideas which lead him to do
	7.22	commit adultery, be greedy, and do all sorts of **evil** things;

Mk 7.23 and folly—[23] all these **evil** things come from inside a person
9.39 will be able soon afterwards to say **evil** things about me.
Lk 3.19 his brother's wife, and had done many other **evil** things.
4.33 a man who had the spirit of an **evil** demon in him;
6.22 and say that you are **evil,** all because of the Son of
11.29 went on to say, "How **evil** are the people of this day!
11.39 cup and plate, but inside you are full of violence and **evil.**
12.10 whoever says **evil** things against the Holy Spirit will not be
Jn 3.19 the darkness rather than the light, because their deeds are **evil.**
3.20 Anyone who does **evil** things hates the light and will not
3.20 because he does not want his **evil** deeds to be shown up.
5.29 and those who have done **evil** will rise and be condemned.
Acts 1.18 that Judas got for his **evil** act he bought a field, where
8.22 Repent, then, of this **evil** plan of yours, and pray to
13.10 full of all kinds of **evil** tricks, and you always keep trying
17.30 all of them everywhere to turn away from their **evil** ways.
18. 6 they opposed him and said **evil** things about him, he
18.14 were a matter of some **evil** crime or wrong that has been
19. 9 the whole group they said **evil** things about the Way of the
19.37 have not robbed temples or said **evil** things about our goddess.
23. 5 'You must not speak **evil** of the ruler of your people.'"
25.18 him of any of the **evil** crimes that I thought they would.
Rom 1.18 against all the sin and **evil** of the people
1.18 whose **evil** ways prevent the truth from being
1.29 filled with all kinds of wickedness, **evil,** greed, and vice;
1.30 They gossip [30] and speak **evil** of one another;
1.30 they think of more ways to do **evil;**
2. 9 those who do what is **evil,** for the Jews first and also
2.24 "Because of you Jews, the Gentiles speak **evil** of God."
3. 8 not say, then, "Let us do **evil** so that good may come"?
7.19 instead, I do the **evil** that I do not want to do.
7.21 what is good, what is **evil** is the only choice I have.
12. 9 Hate what is **evil,** hold on to what is good.
12.21 Do not let **evil** defeat you;
12.21 instead, conquer **evil** with good.
13. 3 feared by those who do good, but by those who do **evil.**
13. 4 But if you do **evil,** then be afraid of him, because his
13. 4 and carries out God's punishment on those who do **evil.**
16.19 be wise about what is good, but innocent in what is **evil.**
1 Cor 5.12 As the scripture says, "Remove the **evil** man from your group."
10. 6 warn us not to desire **evil** things, as they did, [7] nor to
13. 6 love is not happy with **evil,** but is happy with the truth.
14.20 be children so far as **evil** is concerned, but be grown-up in
2 Cor 4. 4 been kept in the dark by the **evil** god of this world.
Gal 1. 4 free from this present **evil** age, Christ gave himself for our
Eph 2. 2 At that time you followed the world's **evil** way;
5.16 use of every opportunity you have, because these are **evil** days.
6.11 will be able to stand up against the Devil's **evil** tricks.
6.13 Then when the **evil** day comes, you will be able to resist
Phil 3. 2 out for those who do **evil** things, those dogs, those men who
Col 1.21 his enemies because of the **evil** things you did and thought.
3. 5 as sexual immorality, indecency, lust, **evil** passions, and greed
1 Thes 5.22 keep what is good [22] and avoid every kind of **evil.**
2 Thes 3. 2 Pray also that God will rescue us from wicked and **evil** people;
1 Tim 1.13 in the past I spoke **evil** of him and persecuted and insulted
5.14 as to give our enemies no chance of speaking **evil** of us.
6. 1 that no one will speak **evil** of the name of God and
6. 4 brings on jealousy, disputes, insults, **evil** suspicions,
6.10 the love of money is a source of all kinds of **evil.**
2 Tim 2.21 himself clean from all those **evil** things, he will be used
3.13 and **evil** persons and impostors will keep on going from
4.18 will rescue me from all **evil** and take me safely into his
Tit 2. 5 that no one will speak **evil** of the message that comes from
3. 2 Tell them not to speak **evil** of anyone, but to be peaceful
Heb 3.12 has a heart so **evil** and unbelieving that he will turn
5.14 through practice are able to distinguish between good and **evil.**
10.17 "I will not remember their sins and **evil** deeds any longer."
Jas 1.13 God cannot be tempted by **evil,** and he himself tempts no one.
1.14 when he is drawn away and trapped by his own **evil** desire.
1.15 Then his **evil** desire conceives and gives birth to sin;
2. 4 among yourselves and of making judgements based on **evil** motives.
2. 7 are the ones who speak **evil** of that good name which has
3. 6 place in our bodies and spreading **evil** through our whole being.
3. 8 It is **evil** and uncontrollable, full of deadly poison.
3.16 and selfishness, there is also disorder and every kind of **evil.**
1 Pet 2. 1 Rid yourselves, then, of all **evil;**
2.12 they accuse you of being **evildoers,** they will have to
2.14 by him to punish the **evildoers** and to praise those who do
2.16 your freedom to cover up any **evil,** but live as God's slaves.
3. 9 Do not pay back **evil** with evil or cursing with cursing;
3.10 good times, must keep from speaking **evil** and stop telling lies.
3.11 He must turn away from **evil** and do good;
3.12 but he opposes those who do **evil."**
3.16 those who speak **evil** of your good conduct as followers
3.17 good, if this should be God's will, than for doing **evil.**
2 Pet 2. 2 what they do, others will speak **evil** of the Way of truth.
2. 8 he suffered agony as he saw and heard their **evil** actions.
2 Jn 11 him peace becomes his partner in the **evil** things he does.
Jude 16 they follow their own **evil** desires;
Rev 2. 2 know that you cannot tolerate **evil** men and that you have
2. 9 I know the **evil** things said against you by those who claim
2.24 rest of you in Thyatira have not followed this **evil** teaching;
16.11 But they did not turn from their **evil** ways.
22.11 Whoever is **evil** must go on doing evil, and whoever is

EVIL ONE

Mt 5.37 'Yes' or 'No'—anything else you say comes from the **Evil One.**
6.13 us to hard testing, but keep us safe from the **Evil One.'**
13.19 The **Evil One** comes and snatches away what was sown in them.
13.38 the weeds are the people who belong to the **Evil One;**
Jn 17.15 I do ask you to keep them safe from the **Evil One.**
Eph 6.16 to put out all the burning arrows shot by the **Evil One.**
2 Thes 3. 3 he will strengthen you and keep you safe from the **Evil One.**
1 Jn 2.13 to you, young men, because you have defeated the **Evil One.**
2.14 of God lives in you, and you have defeated the **Evil One.**
3.12 belonged to the **Evil One** and murdered his own brother Abel.
5.18 of God keeps him safe, and the **Evil One** cannot harm him.
5.19 though the whole world is under the rule of the **Evil One.**

EVIL SPIRIT see SPIRIT (2)

EWE

Num 6.14 burnt-offering, a one-year-old **ewe** lamb for a sin-offering,

EXALTED

Is 2.11 Then the Lord alone will be **exalted.**
2.17 disappear, and the Lord alone will be **exalted** on that day.
6. 1 on his throne, high and **exalted,** and his robe filled the
42.21 eager to save, so he **exalted** his laws and teachings, and he

EXAMINE

Ex 39.43 Moses **examined** everything and saw that they had made it
Lev 13. 3 The priest shall **examine** the sore, and if the hairs in it
13. 5 The priest shall **examine** him again on the seventh day, and
13. 6 The priest shall **examine** him again on the seventh day, and
13. 7 after the priest has **examined** him and pronounced him clean,
13. 8 The priest will **examine** him again, and if it has spread,
13.10 he shall be brought to the priest, [10] who will **examine** him.
13.13 from head to foot, [13] the priest shall **examine** him again.
13.15 The priest shall **examine** him again, and if he sees an
13.17 shall go to the priest, [17] who will **examine** him again.
13.20 The priest shall **examine** him, and if the spot seems to
13.21 But if the priest **examines** it and finds that the hairs
13.25 white or reddish-white, [25] the priest shall **examine** him.
13.27 The priest shall **examine** him again on the seventh day,
13.30 on the head or the chin, [30] the priest shall **examine** it.
13.31 If, when the priest **examines** him, the sore does not
13.32 The priest shall **examine** the sore again on the seventh day,
13.34 day the priest shall again **examine** the sore, and if it has
13.36 pronounced clean, [36] the priest shall **examine** him again.
13.39 spots on the skin, [39] the priest shall **examine** that person.
13.43 The priest shall **examine** him, and if there is a reddish-white sore,
13.50 The priest shall **examine** it and put the object away for
13.51 He shall **examine** it again on the seventh day, and if the
13.53 But if, when he **examines** it, the priest finds that the
13.55 Then he shall **examine** it, and if the mildew has not
13.56 But if, when the priest **examines** it again, the mildew has faded,
14. 3 and the priest shall take him outside the camp and **examine** him.
14.36 moved out of the house before he goes to **examine** the mildew;
14.37 Then he shall go to the house [37] and **examine** the mildew.
14.39 On the seventh day he shall return and **examine** it again.
Job 13.27 you watch every step I take, and even **examine** my footprints.
Ps 11. 5 He **examines** the good and the wicked alike;
17. 3 you have **examined** me completely and found no evil desire in me.
26. 2 **Examine** me and test me, Lord;
48.13 notice of the walls and **examine** the fortresses, so that you
119.15 I **examine** your teachings.
139. 1 Lord, you have **examined** me and you know me.
139.23 **Examine** me, O God, and know my mind;
Ecc 1.13 I determined that I would **examine** and study all the
Lam 3.40 Let us **examine** our ways and turn back to the Lord.
Ezek 21.21 he **examines** the liver of a sacrificed animal.
Mt 8. 4 but go straight to the priest and let him **examine** you;
Mk 1.44 But go straight to the priest and let him **examine** you;
Lk 5.14 but go straight to the priest and let him **examine** you;
17.14 and said to them, "Go and let the priests **examine** you."
23.14 Now, I have **examined** him here in your presence, and I have
1 Cor 11.28 So then, everyone should **examine** himself first, and then
11.31 If we would **examine** ourselves first, we would not come

EXAMPLE

Deut 29.21 The Lord will make an **example** of him before all the
1 Sam 8. 3 But they did not follow their father's **example;**
8. 5 "Look, you are getting old and your sons don't follow your **example.**
1 Kgs 22.52 the Lord, following the wicked **example** of his father Ahab,
2 Kgs 10.31 followed the **example** of Jeroboam, who led Israel into sin.
13.11 Lord and followed the evil **example** of King Jeroboam, who had
14.24 the Lord, following the wicked **example** of his predecessor
15. 3 Following the **example** of his father, he did what was
15. 9 He followed the wicked **example** of King Jeroboam son of Nebat,
15.18 followed the wicked **example** of King Jeroboam son of Nebat,
15.24 following the wicked **example** of King Jeroboam son of Nebat,
15.28 following the wicked **example** of King Jeroboam son of Nebat,
15.34 Following the **example** of his father Uzziah, Jotham did
16. 2 He did not follow the good **example** of his ancestor King David;
16. 3 Lord his God [3] and followed the **example** of the kings of Israel.
18. 3 Following the **example** of his ancestor King David, he did
22. 2 he followed the **example** of his ancestor King David, strictly
23.32 Following the **example** of his ancestors, he sinned against the Lord.
23.37 Following the **example** of his ancestors, Jehoiakim sinned
24. 9 Following the **example** of his father, Jehoiachin sinned against the Lord.
2 Chr 17. 3 Jehoshaphat because he followed the **example** of his father's

2 Chr 21. 6 He followed the wicked **example** of King Ahab and the other
21.12 did not follow the **example** of your father, King Jehoshaphat,
21.13 Instead, you have followed the **example** of the kings of
22. 2 Ahaziah also followed the **example** of King Ahab's family,
26. 4 Following the **example** of his father, he did what was
28. 1 He did not follow the good **example** of his ancestor King David;
28. 2 the Lord [2]and followed the **example** of the kings of Israel.
29. 2 Following the **example** of his ancestor King David, he did
34. 2 he followed the **example** of his ancestor King David, strictly
36.14 the people followed the sinful **example** of the nations round
Neh 13.27 we then to follow your **example** and disobey our God by
Ps 1. 1 who do not follow the **example** of sinners or join those who
71. 7 My life has been an **example** to many, because you have been
Prov 2.20 So you must follow the **example** of good men and live a
4.14 Do not follow the **example** of the wicked.
23.26 Pay close attention, son, and let my life be your **example.**
Ecc 9.13 else I saw, a good **example** of how wisdom is regarded in
Ezek 14. 8 I will make an **example** of him.
18.14 sins his father practised, but does not follow his **example.**
26.21 will make you a terrifying **example,** and that will be the end
28.12 You were once an **example** of perfection.
Mic 2. 4 use your story as an **example** of disaster, and they will sing
Jn 13.15 I have set an **example** for you, so that you will do
Rom 7. 2 A married woman, for **example,** is bound by the law to her
15. 5 among yourselves by following the **example** of Christ Jesus,
1 Cor 4. 6 two of us as an **example,** so that you may learn what
4.16 I beg you, then, to follow my **example.**
9. 5 the right to follow the **example** of the other apostles and
9. 8 limit myself to these everyday **examples,** because the Law
10. 6 Now, all this is an **example** for us, to warn us not
10.11 things happened to them as **examples** for others, and they
Gal 3.15 My brothers, I am going to use an everyday **example:**
Phil 3.17 those who follow the right **example** that we have set for you.
1 Thes 1. 7 So you became an **example** to all believers in Macedonia and Achaia.
2 Thes 3. 9 we did it to be an **example** for you to follow.
1 Tim 1.16 worst of sinners, as an **example** for all those who would
4.12 young, but be an **example** for the believers in your speech,
2 Tim 1.13 I taught you, as the **example** for you to follow, and remain
Tit 2. 7 In all things you yourself must be an **example** of good behaviour.
Jas 5.10 Take them as **examples** of patient endurance under suffering.
1 Pet 2.21 you and left you an **example,** so that you would follow in
5. 3 have been put in your care, but be **examples** to the flock.
2 Pet 2. 6 fire, and made them an **example** of what will happen to the

EXCELLENCY

Lk 1. 3 And so, your **Excellency,** because I have carefully studied
Acts 23.26 "Claudius Lysias to His **Excellency,** the governor Felix:
24. 2 "Your **Excellency!**
26.25 Paul answered, "I am not mad, Your **Excellency!**

EXCELLENT

Num 14. 7 to the people, "The land we explored is an **excellent** land.
Ps 16. 3 How **excellent** are the Lord's faithful people!
Prov 8. 6 Listen to my **excellent** words;
1 Tim 3. 1 eager to be a church leader, he desires an **excellent** work.

EXCHANGE

Gen 47.16 will give you food in **exchange** for it if your money is
47.17 he gave them food in **exchange** for their horses, sheep,
47.17 them with food in **exchange** for all their livestock.
47.19 Buy us and our land in **exchange** for food.
Ruth 4. 7 settle a sale or an **exchange** of property, it was the custom
2 Chr 9.12 what he gave her in **exchange** for the gifts she brought to
Ezra 3. 7 of Tyre and Sidon in **exchange** for cedar-trees from Lebanon,
Ps 106.20 they **exchanged** the glory of God for the image of an
Jer 2.11 But my people have **exchanged** me, the God who has brought
Lam 1.11 They **exchange** their treasures for food to keep themselves alive.
Ezek 27.15 lands gave you ivory and ebony in **exchange** for your goods.
27.18 They **exchanged** wrought iron and spices for your goods.
27.20 The people of Dedan **exchanged** saddle-cloths for your goods.
27.22 Sheba and Raamah **exchanged** jewels, gold, and the finest spices.
48.14 it may be sold or **exchanged** or transferred to anyone else.
Rom 1.25 They **exchange** the truth about God for a lie;

EXCITE

Ruth 1.19 the whole town got **excited,** and the women there exclaimed,
Neh 8.17 of Joshua son of Nun, and everybody was **excited** and happy.
Job 15.12 But you are **excited** and glare at us in anger.
39.24 Trembling with **excitement,** the horses race ahead;
Ps 78.65 he was like a strong man **excited** by wine.
Song 1. 9 You, my love, **excite** men as a mare excites the stallions
Is 22. 2 The whole city is in an uproar, filled with noise and **excitement.**
60. 5 You will tremble with **excitement.**
Acts 2. 6 They were all **excited,** because each one of them heard the
17.13 came there and started **exciting** and stirring up the mob.

EXCLUDE

Num 9. 7 but why should we be **excluded** from presenting the Lord's
Neh 13. 3 they **excluded** all foreigners from the community.

EXCREMENT

2 Kgs 18.27 will have to eat their **excrement** and drink their urine, just
Is 36.12 will have to eat their **excrement** and drink their urine, just
Ezek 4.12 fire out of dried human **excrement,** bake bread on the fire,

EXCUSE

Ex 5.21 You have given them an **excuse** to kill us."
Deut 24. 5 he is to be **excused** from duty for one year, so that
1 Sam 1.26 Hannah said to him, **"Excuse** me, sir.
2 Kgs 10.19 No one is **excused;**
Job 19.28 You looked for some **excuse** to attack me.
33.10 But God finds **excuses** for attacking me and treats me
Ezek 8.12 Their **excuse** is:
Mk 7.12 God), [12]he is **excused** from helping his father or mother.
Lk 14.18 But they all began, one after another, to make **excuses.**
Jn 15.22 as it is, they no longer have any **excuse** for their sin.
Acts 19.40 There is no **excuse** for all this uproar, and we would not
Rom 1.20 So those people have no **excuse** at all!
2. 1 You have no **excuse** at all, whoever you are.
3.19 order to stop all human **excuses** and bring the whole world
Gal 5.13 let this freedom become an **excuse** for letting your physical
Jude 4 our God in order to **excuse** their immoral ways, and who

EXECUTE

Gen 40.22 to his former position, [22]but he **executed** the chief baker.
41.13 restored me to my position, but you **executed** the baker."
Num 25. 4 and, in obedience to me, **execute** them in broad daylight, and
2 Kgs 14. 5 was firmly in power, he **executed** the officials who had
2 Chr 25. 3 was firmly in power, he **executed** the officials who had
25. 4 He did not, however, **execute** their children, but followed
Prov 24.11 rescue someone who is about to be **executed** unjustly.
Jer 39. 6 and he also **executed** the officials of Judah.
52.10 looking on and he also had the officials of Judah **executed.**
Dan 2.12 a rage and ordered the **execution** of all the royal advisers
2.14 bodyguard, who had been ordered to carry out the **execution.**
2.24 whom the king had commanded to **execute** the royal advisers.
Rev 20. 4 of those who had been **executed** because they had proclaimed

EXERCISE

1 Tim 4. 8 Physical **exercise** has some value,
4. 8 but spiritual **exercise** is valuable in every way, because

EXHAUSTED

Deut 25.18 when you were tired and **exhausted,** and killed all who were
Judg 8. 4 They were **exhausted,** but were still pursuing the enemy.
8. 5 They are **exhausted,** and I am pursuing Zebah and Zalmunna,
8.15 give any food to my **exhausted** army because I hadn't captured
1 Sam 30. 4 and did not stop until they were completely **exhausted.**
Ps 6. 2 I am completely **exhausted** [3]and my whole being is deeply troubled.
31.10 I am **exhausted** by sorrow, and weeping has shortened my life.
Is 40.30 young men can fall **exhausted.**
Lam 2.11 I am **exhausted** with grief at the destruction of my people.

EXILE

[FELLOW-EXILES]

Lev 26.34 rest while you are in **exile** in the land of your enemies.
26.36 of you who are in **exile** so terrified that the sound of
26.38 You will die in **exile,** swallowed up by the land of your
26.41 them and send them into **exile** in the land of their enemies.
Judg 18.30 their priests until the people were taken away into **exile.**
2 Sam 14.13 own son to return from **exile,** and so you have condemned
14.14 at least find a way to bring a man back from **exile.**
2 Kgs 17.23 Israel were taken into **exile** to Assyria, where they still live.
17.24 in the cities of Samaria, in place of the **exiled** Israelites.
25.21 of Judah were carried away from their land into **exile.**
25.28 gave the other kings who were **exiles** with him in Babylonia.
1 Chr 5.22 And they went on living in that territory until the **exile.**
6.15 of Judah and Jerusalem whom the Lord sent into **exile.**
29.15 life like **exiles** and strangers, as our ancestors did.
Ezra 1. 4 any of his people in **exile** need help to return, their
1.11 he and the other **exiles** went from Babylon to Jerusalem.
2. 1 Many of the **exiles** left the province of Babylon and
2. 1 families had been living in **exile** in Babylonia ever since
2. 2 the number of those from each clan who returned from **exile:**
2.36 This is the list of the priestly clans that returned from **exile:**
2.40 Clans of Levites who returned from **exile:**
2.43 Clans of temple workmen who returned from **exile:**
2.55 Clans of Solomon's servants who returned from **exile:**
2.58 and of Solomon's servants who returned from **exile** was 392.
2.64 Total number of **exiles** who returned – 42,360
2.68 When the **exiles** arrived at the Lord's Temple in Jerusalem,
3. 3 Even though the returning **exiles** were afraid of the people
3. 8 in fact all the **exiles** who had come back to Jerusalem,
4. 1 those who had returned from **exile** were rebuilding the Temple
5.12 and the people were taken into **exile** in Babylonia.
6.16 who had returned from **exile**—joyfully dedicated the Temple.
6.19 people who had returned from **exile** celebrated Passover on
6.21 Israelites who had returned from **exile** and by all those who
7.26 by death or by **exile** or by confiscation of his property or
8. 1 clans who had been in **exile** in Babylonia and who returned
8.35 those who had returned from **exile** then brought offerings to
9. 4 said about the sins of those who had returned from **exile.**
10. 6 night there grieving over the unfaithfulness of the **exiles.**
10. 7 those who had returned from **exile** were to meet in Jerusalem
10.16 The returned **exiles** accepted the plan, so Ezra the
Neh 1. 2 our fellow-Jews who had returned from **exile** in Babylonia.
7. 6 Many of the **exiles** left the province of Babylon and
7. 6 families had been living in **exile** in Babylonia ever since
7. 8 the number of those from each clan who returned from **exile:**
7.39 This is the list of the priestly clans that returned from **exile:**

Neh	7.43	Clans of Levites who returned from **exile:**
	7.46	Clans of temple workmen who returned from **exile:**
	7.57	Clans of Solomon's servants who returned from **exile:**
	7.60	and of Solomon's servants who returned from **exile** was 392.
	7.66	Total number of **exiles** who
	12. 1	and Levites who returned from **exile** with Zerubbabel son of
Esth	2. 6	King Jehoiachin of Judah into **exile** from Jerusalem, along
Ps	42. 6	Here in **exile** my heart is breaking, and so I turn my
	147. 2	he is bringing back the **exiles.**
Is	27. 8	The Lord punished his people by sending them into **exile.**
	27.13	Assyria and Egypt all the Israelites who are in **exile** there.
	49.20	people who were born in **exile** will one day say to you,
	49.21	I was **exiled** and driven away— who brought these children up?
	56. 8	his people Israel home from **exile,** has promised that he will
Jer	1. 3	of that year the people of Jerusalem were taken into **exile.**
	3.18	together they will come from **exile** in the country in the
	13.19	All the people of Judah have been taken away into **exile."**
	22.26	I am going to force you and your mother into **exile.**
	22.28	children have been taken into **exile** to a land they know
	28. 4	all the people of Judah who went into **exile** in Babylonia.
	29. 2	and the skilled workmen had been taken into **exile.**
	29.14	to the land from which I had sent you away into **exile.**
	29.20	you whom I sent into **exile** in Babylonia, listen to what I,
	48. 7	Chemosh will go into **exile,** along with his princes and priests.
	48.11	"Moab has always lived secure and has never been taken into **exile.**
	49. 3	Molech will be taken into **exile,** together with his priests
	52.27	of Judah were carried away from their land into **exile.**
	52.32	gave the other kings who were **exiles** with him in Babylonia.
Lam	2. 9	The king and the noblemen now are in **exile.**
	4.22	the Lord will not keep us in **exile** any longer.
Ezek	1. 1	with the Jewish **exiles** by the River Chebar in Babylonia.
	1. 2	fifth year since King Jehoiachin had been taken into **exile.)**
	3.11	your countrymen who are in **exile** and tell them what I, the
	3.15	the River Chebar, where the **exiles** were living, and for
	6. 9	among the nations, [9] where they will live in **exile.**
	8. 1	the sixth year of our **exile,** the leaders of the exiles from
	8. 1	exile, the leaders of the **exiles** from Judah were sitting in
	11.15	talking about you and your fellow-Israelites who are in **exile.**
	11.15	They say, 'The **exiles** are too far away to worship the Lord.
	11.16	"Now tell your **fellow-exiles** what I am saying.
	11.24	lifted me up and brought me back to the **exiles** in Babylonia.
	11.25	faded, [25] and I told the **exiles** everything that the Lord
	12. 4	pack your bundle for **exile,** so that they can see you,
	12. 4	you leave in the evening as if you were going into **exile.**
	20. 1	day of the fifth month of the seventh year of our **exile.**
	24. 1	of the ninth year of our **exile,** the Lord spoke to me.
	25. 3	Israel devastated, to see the people of Judah go into **exile.**
	26. 1	of the eleventh year of our **exile,** the Lord spoke to me.
	29. 1	of the tenth year of our **exile,** the Lord spoke to me.
	29.17	the twenty-seventh year of our **exile,** the Lord spoke to me.
	30.20	of the eleventh year of our **exile,** the Lord spoke to me.
	31. 1	of the eleventh year of our **exile,** the Lord spoke to me.
	32. 1	of the twelfth year of our **exile,** the Lord spoke to me.
	32.17	of the twelfth year of our **exile,** the Lord spoke to me.
	33.21	the twelfth year of our **exile,** a man who had escaped from
	39.23	that the Israelites went into **exile** because of the sins
	40. 1	we had been taken into **exile** and the fourteenth year after
Dan	1. 3	select from among the Israelite **exiles** some young men of the
	2.25	found one of the Jewish **exiles,** who can tell Your Majesty
	5.13	"Are you Daniel, that Jewish **exile** whom my father the king
	6.13	king, "Daniel, one of the **exiles** from Judah, does not
Amos	1. 9	off a whole nation into **exile** in the land of Edom, and
	1.15	Their king and his officers will go into **exile."**
	5. 5	Do not go to Gilgal—her people are doomed to **exile."**
	5.27	when I take you into **exile** in a land beyond Damascus,"
	6. 7	So you will be the first to go into **exile.**
	7.11	Israel will be taken away from their land into **exile.' "**
	7.17	Israel will certainly be taken away from their own land into **exile.' "**
Obad	20	The army of **exiles** from northern Israel will return and
	20	The **exiles** from Jerusalem who are in Sardis will capture the
Mic	1.11	You people of Shaphir, go into **exile,** naked and ashamed.
	1.16	your children will be taken away from you into **exile.**
	2.13	will open the way for them and lead them out of **exile.**
	4. 6	the people I punished, those who have suffered in **exile.**
	5. 3	his fellow-countrymen who are in **exile** will be reunited with
Nah	3.10	Yet the people of Thebes were carried off into **exile.**
Zeph	3.19	I will rescue all the lame and bring the **exiles** home.
Hag	1.12	who had returned from the **exile** in Babylonia, did what the
	1.14	High Priest, and all the people who had returned from the **exile.**
Zech	2. 6	you **exiles,** escape from Babylonia and return to Jerusalem.
	6.10	the gifts given by the **exiles** Heldai, Tobijah, and Jedaiah,
	6.10	All these men have returned from **exile** in Babylonia.
	9.11	set your people free— free from the waterless pit of **exile.**
	9.12	Return, you **exiles** who now have hope;
	14. 2	the people will go into **exile,** but the rest of them will
Mt	1. 6	of Israel were taken into **exile** in Babylon, the following
	1.12	From the time after the **exile** in Babylon to the
	1.17	fourteen from David to the **exile** in Babylon, and fourteen
Acts	7.43	And so I will send you into **exile** beyond Babylon.'

EXIST

Gen	8.22	As long as the world **exists,** there will be a time for
1 Kgs	10.19	No throne like this had ever **existed** in any other kingdom.
2 Chr	9.19	No throne like this had ever **existed** in any other kingdom.
Job	10.19	to the grave would have been as good as never **existing.**
Ps	93. 2	firm from the beginning, and you **existed** before time began.
Prov	23.22	without him you would not **exist.**
Jer	10.11	They will no longer **exist** anywhere on earth.)
Dan	12. 1	troubles, the worst since nations first came into **existence.**
Mt	11.23	performed in Sodom, it would still be in **existence** today!
Jn	1. 1	Before the world was created, the Word already **existed;**
	1.15	greater than I am, because he **existed** before I was born.' "
	1.30	is greater than I am, because he **existed** before I was born.'
Acts	14.17	given evidence of his **existence** by the good things he does:
	17.28	as someone has said, 'In him we live and move and **exist.'**
Rom	4.17	life and whose command brings into being what did not **exist.**
	11.36	by him, and all things **exist** through him and for him.
	13. 1	because no authority **exists** without God's permission,
	13. 1	and the **existing** authorities have been put there by
	13. 2	Whoever opposes the **existing** authority opposes what God has ordered;
1 Cor	8. 4	an idol stands for something that does not really **exist;**
	11.12	and it is God who brings everything into **existence.**
Col	1.17	Christ **existed** before all things, and in union with him
Heb	11. 6	have faith that God **exists** and rewards those who seek him.
Jas	3. 6	the entire course of our **existence** with the fire that comes
1 Pet	3.19	spiritually, [19] and in his spiritual **existence** he went and
	4. 6	judged in their physical **existence** as everyone is judged;
	4. 6	in their spiritual **existence** they may live as God lives.
2 Pet	3. 7	and the earth that now **exist** are being preserved by the same
1 Jn	1. 1	the Word of life, which has **existed** from the very beginning.
	2.13	because you know him who has **existed** from the beginning.
	2.14	because you know him who has **existed** from the beginning.
Rev	4.11	and by your will they were given **existence** and life."

EXIT

Ezek	43.11	and **exits,** its shape, the arrangement of everything,

EXPECT
[UNEXPECTED]

Gen	48.11	said to Joseph, "I never **expected** to see you again, and now
1 Kgs	2.15	I should have become king and that everyone in Israel **expected** it.
2 Kgs	5. 7	"How can the king of Syria **expect** me to cure this man?
	18.21	You are **expecting** Egypt to help you, but that would be
	18.24	Assyrian official, and yet you **expect** the Egyptians to send
Job	29.18	I always **expected** to live a long life and to die at
	34.33	what God does, can you **expect** him to do what you want?
	39.11	on his great strength and **expect** him to do your heavy work?
	39.12	Do you **expect** him to bring in your harvest and gather
Prov	17.20	speaks evil can **expect** to find nothing good—only disaster.
Ecc	9.12	we are trapped at some evil moment when we least **expect** it.
Is	5. 4	it produce sour grapes and not the good grapes I **expected?**
	5. 7	He **expected** them to do what was good, but instead they
	5. 7	He **expected** them to do what was right, but their victims
	29. 5	Suddenly and **unexpectedly** [6] the Lord Almighty will rescue
	29.14	So I will startle them with one **unexpected** blow after another.
	30. 5	nation, a nation that fails them when they **expect** help."
	36. 6	You are **expecting** Egypt to help you, but that would be
	36. 9	Assyrian official, and yet you **expect** the Egyptians to send
	64. 3	you came and did terrifying things that we did not **expect;**
Ezek	13. 6	Yet they **expect** their words to come true!
	20.40	with you and will **expect** you to bring me your sacrifices,
Dan	11.21	but he will come **unexpectedly** and seize power by trickery.
Hag	2.16	to a heap of corn **expecting** to find two hundred kilogrammes,
Mt	9.15	Jesus answered, "Do you **expect** the guests at a wedding
	11. 3	John said was going to come, or should we **expect** someone else?"
	11. 7	out to John in the desert, what did you **expect** to see?
	23.33	How do you **expect** to escape from being condemned to hell?
	24.44	Man will come at an hour when you are not **expecting** him.
	24.50	when the servant does not **expect** him and at a time he
Mk	2.19	Jesus answered, "Do you **expect** the guests at a wedding
Lk	6.35	lend and **expect** nothing back.
	7.19	John said was going to come, or should we **expect** someone else?"
	7.20	was going to come, or if we should **expect** someone else."
	7.24	out to John in the desert, what did you **expect** to see?
	12.40	Man will come at an hour when you are not **expecting** him."
	12.46	when the servant does not **expect** him and at a time he
Acts	3. 5	So he looked at them, **expecting** to get something from them.
	12.11	Herod's power and from everything the Jewish people **expected** to happen."
1 Cor	9.12	others have the right to **expect** this from you, haven't we an
	9.17	a matter of free choice, then I could **expect** to be paid;
	11.22	What do you **expect** me to say to you about this?
	16.11	for I am **expecting** him back with the brothers.

EXPEDITION

Dan	11.17	"The king of Syria will plan an **expedition,** using his whole army.

EXPEL

Num	5. 2	the people of Israel to **expel** from the camp everyone with a
	5. 4	The Israelites obeyed and **expelled** them all from the camp.
1 Kgs	15.12	**expelled** from the country all the male and female prostitutes
Ps	101. 8	I will **expel** all evil men from the city of the Lord.
Jn	9.22	Jesus was the Messiah would be **expelled** from the synagogue.
	9.34	And they **expelled** him from the synagogue.
	12.42	it openly, so as not to be **expelled** from the synagogue.
	16. 2	You will be **expelled** from the synagogues, and the time
1 Cor	5. 2	done such a thing should be **expelled** from your fellowship.

EXPENSE

Gen	24.22	finished, the man took an **expensive** gold ring and put it in
	24.53	He also gave **expensive** gifts to her brother and to her mother.
2 Kgs	12.12	used in the repairs, and pay all other necessary **expenses.**
Ezra	6. 4	All **expenses** are to be paid by the royal treasury.

Ezra 6. 8 Their **expenses** are to be paid promptly out of the royal
Neh 10.32 grammes of silver to help pay the **expenses** of the Temple.
Ecc 7. 1 A good reputation is better than **expensive** perfume;
Is 30. 6 their donkeys and camels with **expensive** gifts for a nation
Mt 26. 7 alabaster jar filled with an **expensive** perfume, which she
Mk 14. 3 jar full of a very **expensive** perfume made of pure nard.
Lk 16.19 who dressed in the most **expensive** clothes and lived in great
Jn 12. 3 a litre of a very **expensive** perfume made of pure nard,
Acts 21.24 them in the ceremony of purification and pay their **expenses;**
1 Cor 9. 7 What soldier ever has to pay his own **expenses** in the army?
2 Thes 3. 8 night so as not to be an **expense** to any of you.
1 Tim 2. 9 or pearls or **expensive** dresses, [10] but with good deeds,
Rev 18.12 made of ivory and of **expensive** wood, of bronze, iron, and

EXPERIENCE

Deut 1.13 Choose some wise, understanding, and **experienced** men
1.15 I took the wise and **experienced** leaders you chose from your tribes,
7.15 the dreadful diseases that you **experienced** in Egypt, but he
11. 2 learned about the Lord through your **experiences** with him.
11. 2 It was you, not your children, who had these **experiences.**
28.60 all the dreadful diseases you **experienced** in Egypt, and you
29. 4 day he has not let you understand what you have **experienced.**
2 Sam 17. 8 Your father is an **experienced** soldier and does not stay with
1 Kgs 7.14 Huram was an intelligent and **experienced** craftsman.
9.27 King Hiram sent some **experienced** seamen from his fleet
1 Chr 12. 1 he was joined by many **experienced,** reliable soldiers,
12. 8 the names of the famous, **experienced** soldiers from the tribe
29. 1 God has chosen, but he is still young and lacks **experience.**
2 Chr 8.18 of his own officers and manned by **experienced** sailors.
Ps 72. 3 may it **experience** righteousness.
Prov 20.30 Sometimes it takes a painful **experience** to make us change our ways.
25.12 A warning given by an **experienced** person to someone
Mic 2. 4 they will sing this song of despair about your **experience:**
Rom 4. 1 What was his **experience?**
5. 2 us by faith into this **experience** of God's grace, in which we
1 Cor 10.13 Every test that you have **experienced** is the kind that
Gal 3. 4 Did all your **experience** mean nothing at all?
3. 6 Consider the **experience** of Abraham;
Phil 3.10 know Christ and to **experience** the power of his resurrection,
2 Thes 1. 4 all the persecutions and sufferings you are **experiencing.**
Heb 5.13 still a child, without any **experience** in the matter of right
6. 5 they knew from **experience** that God's word is good, and
2 Pet 1.10 God's call and his choice of you a permanent **experience;**

EXPERT

1 Chr 2.55 (The following clans of **experts** in writing and copying
9.13 They were **experts** in all the work carried on in the Temple.
12. 8 They were **experts** with shields and spears, as fierce-looking
25. 7 All these twenty-four men were **experts;**
25. 8 lots, whether they were young or old, **experts** or beginners.
Esth 1.13 king's custom to ask for **expert** opinion on questions of law
Jer 4.22 They are **experts** at doing what is evil, but failures at
Ezek 21.31 And I will hand you over to brutal men, **experts** at destruction.
Mic 7. 3 They are all **experts** at doing evil.
1 Cor 3.10 did the work of an **expert** builder and laid the foundation,

EXPLAIN

Gen 40. 8 and there is no one here to **explain** what the dreams mean."
41. 8 told them his dreams, but no one could **explain** them to him.
41.15 him, "I have had a dream, and no one can **explain** it.
41.24 the magicians, but none of them could **explain** them to me."
Ex 13. 8 When the festival begins, **explain** to your sons that you do
18.20 teach them God's commands and **explain** to them how they
Deut 1. 5 Moab that Moses began to **explain** God's laws and teachings.
Josh 20. 4 to the city, and **explain** to the leaders what happened.
1 Sam 1.20 She named him Samuel, and **explained,** "I asked the Lord for him."
4.21 named the boy Ichabod, **explaining,** "God's glory has left Israel"—
8. 9 warnings and **explain** how their kings will treat them."
8.11 "This is how your king will treat you," Samuel **explained.**
10.25 Samuel **explained** to the people the rights and duties of a king,
1 Kgs 10. 3 there was nothing too difficult for him to **explain.**
2 Chr 9. 2 there was nothing too difficult for him to **explain.**
Neh 8. 7 places, and the following Levites **explained** the Law to them:
8. 8 translation of God's Law and **explained** it so that the people
8. 9 the Levites who were **explaining** the Law told all the people,
Esth 3. 4 "I am a Jew," he **explained,** "and I cannot bow to Haman."
4. 8 to take it to Esther, **explain** the situation to her, and ask
8.11 These letters **explained** that the king would allow the
Job 13.17 Now listen to my words of **explanation.**
27.11 is God's power, and **explain** what Almighty God has planned.
Ps 49. 4 my attention to proverbs and **explain** their meaning as I play
78. 2 to use wise sayings and **explain** mysteries from the past,
119.34 **Explain** your law to me, and I will obey it;
119.130 The **explanation** of your teachings gives light and
Prov 25. 2 we honour kings for what they **explain.**
Is 41.22 **Explain** to the court the events of the past, and tell us
Jer 9.12 To whom have you **explained** it so that he can tell others?"
Ezek 43.11 of what they have done, **explain** the plan of the Temple to
Dan 2. 2 sorcerers, and wizards to come and **explain** the dream to him.
2. 4 Tell us your dream, and we will **explain** it to you."
2. 7 will only tell us what the dream was, we will **explain** it."
2.18 and to ask him to **explain** the mystery to them so that
2.47 I know this because you have been able to **explain** this mystery."
4. 7 told them my dream, but they could not **explain** it to me.
4.19 that the dream and its **explanation** applied to your enemies
5.12 dreams, solving riddles, and **explaining** mysteries;
Dan 5.16 you can find hidden meanings and **explain** mysteries.
7.16 one of those standing there and asked him to **explain** it all.
7.23 This is the **explanation** I was given:
8.16 over the River Ulai, "Gabriel, **explain** to him the meaning
8.26 sacrifices which has been **explained** to you will come true.
9.22 He **explained,** "Daniel, I have come here to help you
9.23 Now pay attention while I **explain** the vision.
10. 1 It was **explained** to him in a vision.)
11.21 The angel went on to **explain:**
Mt 15.15 Peter spoke up, **"Explain** this saying to us."
Mk 4.10 the twelve disciples and asked him to **explain** the parables.
4.30 "What parable shall we use to **explain** it?
4.34 with his disciples, he would **explain** everything to them.
7.17 the house, his disciples asked him to **explain** this saying.
Lk 24.27 And Jesus **explained** to them what was said about himself
24.32 to us on the road and **explained** the Scriptures to us?"
24.35 The two then **explained** to them what had happened on the road,
Acts 8.31 "How can I understand unless someone **explains** it to me?"
9.27 He **explained** to them how Saul had seen the Lord on the
12.17 to be quiet, and he **explained** to them how the Lord had
13.41 will not believe, even when someone **explains** it to you!'"
15.14 Simon has just **explained** how God first showed his care
17. 3 with the people, quoting [3] and **explaining** the Scriptures and
18.26 him home with them and **explained** to him more correctly the
25.14 several days, Festus **explained** Paul's situation to the king:
28.23 From morning till night he **explained** to them his message
Rom 11.33 Who can **explain** his decisions?
1 Cor 2.13 by the Spirit, as we **explain** spiritual truths to those who
12.10 and to another he gives the ability to **explain** what is said.
12.30 or to speak in strange tongues or to **explain** what is said.
14. 5 is someone present who can **explain** what he says, so that the
14.13 then, must pray for the gift to **explain** what he says.
14.26 tongues, and still another the **explanation** of what is said.
14.27 the other, and someone else must **explain** what is being said.
14.28 one is there who can **explain,** then the one who speaks in
Gal 2. 2 meeting with the leaders I **explained** the gospel message that
Heb 5.11 but it is hard to **explain** to you, because you are so
9. 5 But now is not the time to **explain** everything in detail.
1 Pet 3.15 anyone who asks you to **explain** the hope you have in you,
2 Pet 1.20 remember that no one can **explain** by himself a prophecy in
3.16 which ignorant and unstable people **explain** falsely, as they

EXPLOIT

Is 9. 4 the nation that oppressed and **exploited** your people, just as
Mic 6.12 Your rich men **exploit** the poor, and all of you are liars.

EXPLORE

Num 13. 2 send them as spies to **explore** the land of Canaan, which I
13.16 These are the spies Moses sent to **explore** the land.
13.21 the men went north and **explored** the land from the wilderness
13.25 After **exploring** the land for forty days, the spies returned
13.27 They said to Moses, "We **explored** the land and found it
13.32 among the Israelites about the land they had **explored.**
14. 7 to the people, "The land we **explored** is an excellent land.
14.24 into the land which he **explored,** and his descendants will
14.34 for each of the forty days you spent **exploring** the land.
14.36 men Moses had sent to **explore** the land brought back a false
32. 8 did when I sent them from Kadesh Barnea to **explore** the land.
Deut 1.24 hill-country as far as the Valley of Eshcol and **explored** it.
1.36 give him and his descendants the land that he has **explored.'**
Josh 2. 1 orders to go and secretly **explore** the land of Canaan,
7. 2 near Bethaven, with orders to go and **explore** the land.
Judg 18. 2 of Zorah and Eshtaol with instructions to **explore** the land.
18.14 men who had gone to **explore** the country round Laish said to
2 Sam 10. 3 them here as spies to **explore** the city, so that he can
1 Kgs 18. 6 one would **explore,** and set off in different directions.
1 Chr 19. 3 them here as spies to **explore** the land, so that he can
Job 28. 3 Men **explore** the deepest darkness.
Jer 31.37 the foundations of the earth **explored,** only then would he

EXPORT

1 Kgs 10.28 The king's agents controlled the **export** of horses
10.29 and the **export** of chariots from Egypt.
2 Chr 1.16 The king's agents controlled the **export** of horses
1.17 and the **export** of chariots from Egypt.

EXPOSE

Ex 20.26 if you do, you will **expose** yourselves as you go up the
28.42 to the thighs, so that they will not **expose** themselves.
28.43 so that they will not be killed for **exposing** themselves.
2 Sam 6.20 "He **exposed** himself like a fool in the sight of the
Job 3.10 letting me be born, for **exposing** me to trouble and grief.
Is 18. 6 their soldiers will be left **exposed** to the birds and the
20. 4 naked, with their buttocks **exposed,** bringing shame on Egypt.
57.12 is right, but I will **expose** your conduct, and your idols
Jer 13.26 Lord himself will strip off your clothes and **expose** you to shame.
36.30 out where it will be **exposed** to the sun during the day
Lam 2.14 Their preaching deceived you by never **exposing** your sin.
4.22 he will **expose** your guilty deeds.
Ezek 16.57 were proud [57] and before the evil you did had been **exposed?**
21.24 Your sins are **exposed.**
23.18 **exposed** herself publicly and let everyone know she was a whore.
23.29 for and leave you stripped naked, **exposed** like a prostitute.
1 Cor 3.13 work will be seen when the Day of Christ **exposes** it.
4. 5 secrets and **expose** the hidden purposes of people's minds.
Heb 4.13 in all creation is **exposed** and lies open before his eyes.
6. 6 crucifying the Son of God and **exposing** him to public shame.

EXPRESS

[WELL-EXPRESSED]

2 Sam 10. 2 So David sent messengers to **express** his sympathy.
10. 3 that David has sent these men to **express** sympathy to you?
1 Chr 12.40 All this was an **expression** of the joy that was felt
19. 2 So David sent messengers to **express** his sympathy.
19. 3 that David has sent these men to **express** sympathy to you?
Job 42.11 They **expressed** their sympathy and comforted him for all the
Prov 25.11 An idea **well-expressed** is like a design of gold, set in silver.
29.11 Stupid people **express** their anger openly, but sensible
Rom 8.26 pleads with God for us in groans that words cannot **express.**
1 Pet 1. 8 glorious joy which words cannot **express,** [9]because you are
Rev 15. 1 ones, because they are the final **expression** of God's anger.

EXTEND

Gen 10.30 land in which they lived **extended** from Mesha to Sephar in
28.14 They will **extend** their territory in all directions, and
Ex 23.31 the borders of your land **extend** from the Gulf of Aqaba to
25.32 Six branches shall **extend** from its sides, three from each side.
26.28 up the frames, is to **extend** from one end of the Tent
34.24 the nations before you and **extended** your territory, no one
36.33 set half-way up the frames, **extended** from one end of the
37.18 Six branches **extended** from its sides, three from each side.
Num 21.13 in the wilderness which **extends** into Amorite territory.
21.15 slope of the valleys that **extend** to the town of Ar and
24. 7 than Agag, And his rule shall be **extended** far and wide.
34. 3 The southern border will **extend** from the wilderness of Zin
35. 4 The pasture land is to **extend** outwards from the city walls
Deut 3.17 On the west their territory **extended** to the River Jordan,
4.48 This land **extended** from the town of Aroer, on the edge
11.24 Your territory will **extend** from the desert in the south to
Josh 11.17 The territory **extended** from Mount Halak in the south near Edom,
13. 9 Their territory **extended** to Aroer
13.16 Their territory **extended** to Aroer
13.26 their land **extended** from Heshbon to Ramath Mizpeh and Betonim,
13.30 Their territory **extended** to Mahanaim and included all of
15. 6 The northern border began there, [6]**extended** up to Beth Hoglah,
19. 1 Its territory **extended** into the land assigned to the tribe
1 Kgs 7. 2 The ceiling was of cedar, **extending** over store-rooms, which
2 Chr 27. 3 of the Temple and did **extensive** work on the city wall in
Ps 36. 5 your faithfulness **extends** to the skies.
48.10 everywhere, and your fame **extends** over all the earth.
59.13 God rules in Israel, that his rule **extends** over all the earth.
80.11 It **extended** its branches to the Mediterranean Sea and as
89.25 I will **extend** his kingdom from the Mediterranean to the River
110. 2 From Zion the Lord will **extend** your royal power.
Is 54. 3 You will **extend** your boundaries on all sides;
Ezek 40.18 paved with stones, [18]which **extended** round the courtyard.
45. 7 the holy area it will **extend** west to the Mediterranean Sea;
45. 7 the eastern boundary it will **extend** to the eastern border of
48. 1 receive one section of land **extending** from the eastern
48.21 It **extends** eastwards to the eastern boundary and westwards
Dan 4.22 reach the sky, and your power **extends** over the whole world.
8. 9 a little horn, whose power **extended** towards the south and

EXTERMINATE

Esth 7. 4 but we are about to be destroyed—**exterminated!"**

EXTERNAL

Jn 7.24 Stop judging by **external** standards, and judge by true standards."
Gal 6.12 ones who want to show off and boast about **external** matters.
Phil 3. 3 We do not put any trust in **external** ceremonies.
3. 4 thinks he can trust in **external** ceremonies, I have even more

EXTRAORDINARY

Acts 4.16 Jerusalem knows that this **extraordinary** miracle has been performed by them,
2 Cor 9.14 you because of the **extraordinary** grace God has shown you.
Eph 2. 7 all time to come the **extraordinary** greatness of his grace in

EYE

Gen 21.19 Then God opened her **eyes,** and she saw a well.
29.17 Leah had lovely **eyes,** but Rachel was shapely and beautiful.
31.49 "May the Lord keep an **eye** on us while we are separated
49.12 His **eyes** are bloodshot from drinking wine, His teeth
Ex 21.24 shall be life for life, [24]**eye for eye,** tooth for tooth,
21.26 or female slave in the **eye** so that he loses the use
21.26 he is to free the slave as payment for the **eye.**
Lev 21.20 no one with any **eye** or skin disease;
24.20 blinds him in one eye, one of his **eyes** shall be blinded;
Num 24. 4 With staring **eyes** I see in a trance A vision from Almighty
24.16 With staring **eyes** I see in a trance A vision from Almighty
33.55 as splinters in your **eyes** and thorns in your sides,
Deut 4. 9 long as you live, what you have seen with your own **eyes.**
4.34 Before your very **eyes** he used his great power and strength;
6.22 With our own **eyes** we saw him work miracles and do
7.19 you saw with your own **eyes,** the miracles and wonders, and
10.21 have seen with your own **eyes** the great and astounding things
16.19 for gifts blind the **eyes** even of wise and honest men,
19.21 an **eye for an eye,** a tooth for a tooth,
28.31 be butchered before your very **eyes,** but you will not eat any
28.32 day you will strain your **eyes,** looking in vain for your
Josh 23.13 painful as a whip on your back or thorns in your **eyes.**
Judg 16.21 The Philistines captured him and put his **eyes** out.
16.28 get even with the Philistines for putting out my two **eyes."**
1 Sam 11. 2 will put out everyone's right **eye** and so bring disgrace on
16.12 He was a handsome, healthy young man, and his **eyes** sparkled.
2 Kgs 4.34 his mouth, eyes, and hands on the boy's mouth, **eyes,** and
4.35 The boy sneezed seven times, and then opened his **eyes.**
6.17 Then he prayed, "O Lord, open his **eyes** and let him see!"
6.20 Elisha prayed, "Open their **eyes,** Lord, and let them see."
25. 7 Nebuchadnezzar had Zedekiah's **eyes** put out, placed him in chains,
Neh 8. 5 above the people, they all kept their **eyes** fixed on him.
Job 16.16 is red, and my **eyes** are swollen and circled with shadows,
16.20 my **eyes** pour out tears to God.
19.27 see him with my own **eyes,** and he will not be a
24.23 him live secure, but keeps an **eye** on him all the time.
25. 5 In his **eyes** even the moon is not bright, nor the stars
25. 6 What is man worth in God's **eyes?**
29.15 I was **eyes** for the blind, and feet for the lame.
36.15 teaches men through suffering and uses distress to open their **eyes.**
40.24 Who can blind his **eyes** and capture him?
41.18 when he sneezes, and his **eyes** glow like the rising sun.
42. 5 told me, but now I have seen you with my own **eyes.**
Ps 6. 7 my **eyes** are so swollen from the weeping caused by my enemies.
10.11 He has closed his **eyes** and will never see me!"
17. 8 Protect me as you would your very **eyes;**
31. 9 my **eyes** are tired from so much crying;
38.10 strength is gone, and my **eyes** have lost their brightness.
51. 9 Close your **eyes** to my sins and wipe out all my evil.
66. 7 for ever by his might and keeps his **eyes** on the nations.
69. 3 I have strained my **eyes,** looking for your help.
88. 9 my **eyes** are weak from suffering.
94. 9 He made our **eyes**—can't he see?
115. 5 They have mouths, but cannot speak, and **eyes,** but cannot see.
119.18 Open my **eyes,** so that I may see the wonderful truths in
119.82 My **eyes** are tired from watching for what you promised,
119.123 My **eyes** are tired from watching for your saving help,
135.16 They have mouths, but cannot speak, and **eyes,** but cannot see.
Prov 6.25 don't be trapped by their flirting **eyes.**
7. 2 to follow my teaching as you are to protect your **eyes.**
7.13 looked him straight in the **eye,** and said, [14]"I made my
10.26 irritating as vinegar on your teeth or smoke in your **eyes.**
20.12 The Lord has given us **eyes** to see with and ears to
23.29 His **eyes** are bloodshot, and he has bruises that could have
23.33 sights will appear before your **eyes,** and you will not be
28.27 If you close your **eyes** to the poor, many people will curse
29.13 have this in common—the Lord gave **eyes** to both of them.
30.17 by vultures or have his **eyes** picked out by wild ravens.
Ecc 1. 8 Our **eyes** can never see enough to be satisfied;
12. 3 to chew your food, and your **eyes** too dim to see clearly.
Song 1.15 how your **eyes** shine with love!
4. 1 How your **eyes** shine with love behind your veil.
4. 9 The look in your **eyes,** my sweetheart and bride, and the
5.12 His **eyes** are as beautiful as doves by a flowing brook,
6. 5 Turn your **eyes** away from me;
7. 4 Your **eyes** are like the pools in the city of Heshbon, near
Is 6. 5 And yet, with my own **eyes,** I have seen the King, the
6.10 their ears deaf, and their **eyes** blind, so that they cannot
25. 8 away the tears from everyone's **eyes** and take away the
29.10 The prophets should be the **eyes** of the people, but God has
29.18 have been living in darkness, will open their **eyes** and see.
32. 3 Their **eyes** and ears will be open to the needs of the
38.14 My **eyes** grew tired from looking to heaven.
42. 7 You will open the **eyes** of the blind and set free those
43. 8 They have **eyes,** but they are blind;
44.18 They close their **eyes** and their minds to the truth.
52. 8 can see with their own **eyes** the return of the Lord to
Jer 4.30 Why do you put on jewellery and paint your **eyes?**
5.21 and stupid people, who have **eyes,** but cannot see, and have
9. 1 well of water, and my **eyes** a fountain of tears, so that
9.18 song for us, until our **eyes** fill with tears, and our eyelids
14.17 "May my **eyes** flow with tears day and night, may I never
29.21 Babylonia, who will put them to death before your **eyes.**
39. 7 After that, he had Zedekiah's **eyes** put out and had him
52.11 After that, he had Zedekiah's **eyes** put out and had him
Lam 1.16 "That is why my **eyes** are overflowing with tears.
2.11 My **eyes** are worn out with weeping;
3.48 My **eyes** flow with rivers of tears at the destruction
Ezek 1.18 The rims of the wheels were covered with **eyes.**
4. 7 "Fix your **eyes** on the siege of Jerusalem.
10.12 Their bodies, backs, hands, wings, and wheels were covered with **eyes.**
12. 2 They have **eyes,** but they see nothing;
12. 6 into the dark with your **eyes** covered, so that you can't see
12.12 He will cover his **eyes** and not see where he is going.
Dan 7. 8 This horn had human **eyes** and a mouth that was boasting proudly.
7.20 It had **eyes** and a mouth and was boasting proudly.
8. 5 He had one prominent horn between his **eyes.**
8.21 and the prominent horn between his **eyes** is the first king.
10. 6 as a flash of lightning, and his **eyes** blazed like fire.
Hab 1.13 Your **eyes** are too holy to look at evil, and you cannot
Zech 4.10b seven lamps are the seven **eyes** of the Lord, which see all
11.17 His arm will wither, and his right **eye** will go blind."
14. 1 be looted, and the loot will be divided up before your **eyes.**
14.12 their **eyes** and their tongues will rot away.
Mal 1. 5 see this with their own **eyes,** and they will say, "The Lord
Mt 5.29 So if your right **eye** causes you to sin, take it out
5.38 said, 'An **eye for an eye,** and a tooth for a tooth.'
6.22 "The **eyes** are like a lamp for the body.
6.22 If your **eyes** are sound, your whole body will be full of
6.23 but if your **eyes** are no good, your body will be in
7. 3 the speck in your brother's **eye,**

Mt 7. 3 and pay no attention to the log in your own **eye?**
7. 4 that speck out of your **eye,'**
7. 4 when you have a log in your own **eye?**
7. 5 log out of your own **eye,** and then you will be able
7. 5 to see clearly to take the speck out of your brother's **eye.**
9.29 Then Jesus touched their **eyes** and said, "Let it happen,
13.15 they have stopped up their ears and have closed their **eyes.**
13.15 Otherwise, their **eyes** would see, their ears would hear,
13.16 Your **eyes** see and your ears hear.
18. 9 And if your **eye** makes you lose your faith, take it out
18. 9 enter life with only one **eye**
18. 9 than to keep both **eyes** and be thrown into the fire
20.34 Jesus had pity on them and touched their **eyes;**
26.43 they could not keep their **eyes** open.
Mk 8.18 You have **eyes**—can't you see?
8.23 After spitting on the man's **eyes,** Jesus placed his hands on
8.25 Jesus again placed his hands on the man's **eyes.**
9.47 And if your **eye** makes you lose your faith, take it out!
9.47 of God with only one **eye**
9.47 than to keep both **eyes** and be thrown into hell.
14.40 they could not keep their **eyes** open.
Lk 2.30 With my own **eyes** I have seen your salvation, [31] which
4.20 in the synagogue had their **eyes** fixed on him, [21] as he said
6.41 the speck in your brother's **eye,**
6.41 but pay no attention to the log in your own **eye?**
6.42 that speck out of your **eye,'**
6.42 yet cannot even see the log in your own **eye?**
6.42 log out of your own **eye,** and then you will be able
6.42 to see clearly to take the speck out of your brother's **eye.**
11.34 Your **eyes** are like a lamp for the body.
11.34 When your **eyes** are sound, your whole body is full of light;
11.34 but when your **eyes** are no good, your whole body will be
24.31 Then their **eyes** were opened and they recognized him, but
Jn 9. 6 the mud on the man's **eyes** [7] and said, "Go and wash your
9.11 mud, rubbed it on my **eyes,** and told me to go to
9.15 He told them, "He put some mud on my **eyes;**
12.40 "God has blinded their **eyes** and closed their minds,
12.40 so that their **eyes** would not see, and their minds
Acts 1.10 They still had their **eyes** fixed on the sky as he went
6.15 in the Council fixed their **eyes** on Stephen and saw that his
9. 8 the ground and opened his **eyes,** but could not see a thing.
9.18 fish scales fell from Saul's **eyes,** and he was able to see
9.40 She opened her **eyes,** and when she saw Peter, she sat up.
13.11 a dark mist cover his **eyes,** and he walked about trying to
26.18 You are to open their **eyes** and turn them from the
28.27 and they have stopped up their ears and closed their **eyes.**
28.27 Otherwise, their **eyes** would see, their ears would hear,
Rom 11.10 May their **eyes** be blinded so that they cannot see;
1 Cor 12.16 "Because I am not an **eye,** I don't belong to the body,"
12.17 If the whole body were just an **eye,** how could it hear?
12.21 So then, the **eye** cannot say to the hand, "I don't need
15.51 changed in an instant, as quickly as the blinking of an **eye.**
2 Cor 3. 7 the people of Israel could not keep their **eyes** fixed on him.
Gal 3. 1 Before your very **eyes** you had a clear description of the
4.15 have taken out your own **eyes,** if you could, and given them
6. 1 And keep an **eye** on yourselves, so that you will not be
Heb 4.13 in all creation is exposed and lies open before his **eyes.**
11.26 of Egypt, for he kept his **eyes** on the future reward.
12. 2 Let us keep our **eyes** fixed on Jesus, on whom our faith
2 Pet 1.16 With our own **eyes** we saw his greatness.
1 Jn 1. 1 We have heard it, and we have seen it with our **eyes;**
Rev 1.14 white as wool, or as snow, and his **eyes** blazed like fire;
2.18 the Son of God, whose **eyes** blaze like fire, whose feet shine
3.18 some ointment to put on your **eyes,** so that you may see.
4. 6 four living creatures covered with **eyes** in front and behind.
4. 8 six wings, and they were covered with **eyes,** inside and out.
5. 6 had seven horns and seven **eyes,** which are the seven spirits
6.16 and hide us from the **eyes** of the one who sits on
7.17 And God will wipe away every tear from their **eyes."**
19.12 His **eyes** were like a flame of fire, and he wore many
21. 4 He will wipe away all tears from their **eyes.**

EYE OF A NEEDLE

Mt 19.24 than for a camel to go through the **eye of a needle."**
Mk 10.25 than for a camel to go through the **eye of a needle."**
Lk 18.25 than for a camel to go through the **eye of a needle."**

EYEBROW

Lev 14. 9 his head, his beard, his **eyebrows,** and all the rest of the

EYELID

Jer 9.18 eyes fill with tears, and our **eyelids** are wet from crying."

EYESHADOW

2 Kgs 9.30 what had happened, put on **eyeshadow,** arranged her hair, and
Ezek 23.40 The two sisters would bathe and put on **eye-shadow** and jewellery.

EYESIGHT see SIGHT

EZRA (1)

A priest and scholar.

Ezra 7. 1 Artaxerxes was emperor of Persia, there was a man named **Ezra.**
7. 1 **Ezra** was the son of Seraiah, son of Azariah, son of Hilkiah,
7. 6 **Ezra** was a scholar with a thorough knowledge of the
7. 6 Because **Ezra** had the blessing of the Lord his God, the
7. 6 of the reign of Artaxerxes, **Ezra** set out from Babylonia for
7.10 **Ezra** had devoted his life to studying the Law of the Lord,
7.11 gave the following document to **Ezra,** the priest and scholar,
7.12 "From Artaxerxes the emperor to **Ezra** the priest,
7.21 Euphrates to provide promptly for **Ezra,** the priest and
7.25 "You, **Ezra,** using the wisdom which your God has given you,
7.27 **Ezra** said, "Praise the Lord, the God of our ancestors!
8. 1 who returned with **Ezra** to Jerusalem when Artaxerxes was emperor:
10. 1 While **Ezra** was bowing in prayer in front of the Temple,
10. 2 clan of Elam, said to **Ezra,** "We have broken faith with God
10. 5 So **Ezra** began by making the leaders of the priests, of the
10.10 **Ezra** the priest stood up and spoke to them.
10.16 exiles accepted the plan, so **Ezra** the priest appointed men
Neh 8. 1 They asked **Ezra,** the priest and scholar of the Law which the
8. 2 So **Ezra** brought it to the place where the people had
8. 4 **Ezra** was standing on a wooden platform that had been built
8. 5 As **Ezra** stood there on the platform high above the people,
8. 6 **Ezra** said, "Praise the Lord, the great God!"
8. 9 Nehemiah, who was the governor, **Ezra,** the priest and scholar
8.13 and the Levites, went to **Ezra** to study the teachings of the
12.26 governor, and the time of **Ezra,** the priest who was a scholar
12.33 Azariah, **Ezra,** Meshullam, Judah, Benjamin, Shemaiah, and
12.36 **Ezra** the scholar led this group in the procession.

Am **FACE**
see also **STARE**

FACE (1)

Gen 4. 6 Why that scowl on your **face?**
9.23 covered their father, keeping their **faces** turned away so as
17. 3 Abram bowed down with his **face** touching the ground, and
17.17 Abraham bowed down with his **face** touching the ground,
18. 2 Bowing down with his **face** touching the ground, [3] he said,
24.65 So she took her scarf and covered her **face.**
32.30 "I have seen God **face to face,** and I am still alive";
33.10 To see your **face** is for me like
33.10 like seeing the **face** of God, now that you have
38.14 had been wearing, covered her **face** with a veil, and sat down
38.15 that she was a prostitute, because she had her **face** covered.
42. 6 and bowed down before him with their **faces** to the ground.
43.31 After he had washed his **face,** he came out, and controlling himself,
48.12 lap and bowed down before him with his **face** to the ground.
50. 1 Joseph threw himself on his father, crying and kissing his **face.**
Ex 3. 6 So Moses covered his **face,** because he was afraid to look at
33.11 would speak with Moses **face to face,** just as a man speaks
33.20 not let you see my **face,** because no one can see me
33.23 hand away, and you will see my back but not my **face."**
34.29 carrying the Ten Commandments, his **face** was shining because
34.30 Moses and saw that his **face** was shining, and they were
34.33 finished speaking to them, he covered his **face** with a veil.
34.35 to say, [35] and they would see that his **face** was shining.
Lev 9.24 all shouted and bowed down with their **faces** to the ground.
13.45 cover the lower part of his **face,** and call out, "Unclean,
Num 12. 8 I speak to him **face to face,** clearly and not in riddles;
12.14 father had spat in her **face,** she would have to bear her
16.22 Aaron bowed down with their **faces** to the ground and said,
16.45 them bowed down with their **faces** to the ground, [46] and
20. 6 They bowed down with their **faces** to the ground, and the
22.31 and Balaam threw himself **face downwards** on the ground.
Deut 5. 4 mountain the Lord spoke to you **face-to-face** from the fire.
9.18 Then once again I lay **face downwards** in the Lord's
9.25 "So I lay **face downwards** in the Lord's presence those
25. 2 is to make him lie **face downwards** and have him whipped.
25. 9 his sandals, spit in his **face,** and say, 'This is what
34.10 the Lord spoke with him **face to face.**
Judg 6.22 I have seen your angel **face to face!"**
13.20 and his wife threw themselves **face downwards** on the ground.
Ruth 2.10 Ruth bowed down with her **face** touching the ground, and
1 Sam 5. 3 statue of Dagon had fallen **face downwards** on the ground in
17.49 his skull, and Goliath fell **face downwards** on the ground.
20.41 his knees and bowed with his **face** to the ground three times.
2 Sam 4.11 murdering him and will wipe you off the **face of the earth!"**
13.19 her robe, and with her **face** buried in her hands went away
19. 4 The king covered his **face** and cried loudly, "O my son!
1 Kgs 19.13 heard it, he covered his **face** with his cloak and went out
20.38 The prophet bandaged his **face** with a cloth, to disguise himself,
20.41 tore the cloth from his **face,** and at once the king
21.10 to accuse him to his **face** of cursing God and the king.
22.24 up to Micaiah, slapped his **face,** and asked, "Since when did
2 Kgs 4.37 She fell at Elisha's feet, with her **face** touching the ground;
8.11 horrified look on his **face** until Hazael became ill at ease.
20. 2 Hezekiah turned his **face** to the wall and prayed:
1 Chr 21.16 sackcloth—bowed low, with their **faces** touching the ground.
21.21 and bowed low, with his **face** touching the ground.
2 Chr 7. 3 fill the Temple, they fell **face downwards** on the pavement,
18.23 up to Micaiah, slapped his **face,** and asked, "Since when did
20.12 we are helpless in the **face** of this large army that is
20.18 Jehoshaphat bowed low, with his **face** touching the ground,
Neh 6.16 realized that they had lost **face,** since everyone knew that
8. 6 They knelt in worship, with their **faces** to the ground.
Esth 6.12 Haman hurried home, covering his **face** in embarrassment.
Job 1.11 away everything he has—he will curse you to your **face!"**
1.20 He shaved his head and threw himself **face downwards** on the ground.
2. 5 suppose you hurt his body—he will curse you to your **face!"**
4.15 A light breeze touched my **face,** and my hair bristled with fright.
6.28 Look me in the **face.**

Job	14.20	his **face** is twisted in death.
	16.10	they crowd round me and slap my **face.**
	16.16	I have cried until my **face** is red, and my eyes are
	17. 6	they come and spit in my **face.**
	24.15	he covers his **face** so that no one can see him.
	26.10	from darkness by a circle drawn on the **face** of the sea.
	29.24	my cheerful **face** encouraged them.
	30.10	too good for me, and even come and spit in my **face.**
	34.29	If he hid his **face,** men would be helpless.
	38.30	turn the waters to stone and freeze the **face** of the sea?
	40.23	he is calm when the Jordan dashes in his **face.**
Ps	83.16	Cover their **faces** with shame, O Lord, and make them
Prov	15.30	Smiling **faces** make you happy, and good news makes you feel better.
	27.19	It is your own **face** that you see reflected in the water
Ecc	7. 3	may sadden your **face,** but it sharpens your understanding.
Song	2.14	Let me see your lovely **face** and hear your enchanting voice.
	5.11	His **face** is bronzed and smooth;
Is	6. 2	Each creature covered its **face** with two wings, and its body
	13. 8	at each other in fear, and their **faces** will burn with shame.
	29.22	disgraced any longer, and your **faces** will no longer be pale
	38. 2	Hezekiah turned his **face** to the wall and prayed:
	50. 6	pulled out the hairs of my beard and spat in my **face.**
Jer	14. 3	Discouraged and confused, they hide their **faces.**
	14. 4	they hide their **faces.**
	25.19	Every nation on the **face of the earth** had to drink from
	32. 4	he will see him **face to face** and will speak to him
	34. 3	You will see him **face to face** and talk to him in
Lam	1. 8	She groans and hides her **face** in shame.
	3.16	He rubbed my **face** in the ground and broke my teeth on
	4. 8	they lie unknown in the streets, their **faces** blackened in death;
Ezek	1. 6	form, [6]but each of them had four **faces** and four wings.
	1. 8	In addition to their four **faces** and four wings, they each
	1.10	Each living creature had four different **faces:**
	1.10	a human **face** in front, a lion's face at the right,
	1.10	bull's face at the left, and an eagle's **face** at the back.
	1.28	When I saw this, I fell **face downwards** on the ground.
	3.23	I fell **face downwards** on the ground, [24]but God's spirit
	9. 8	I threw myself **face downwards** on the ground and shouted,
	10.14	Each creature had four **faces.**
	10.14	The first was the **face** of a bull,
	10.14	the second a human **face,**
	10.14	the third the **face** of a lion,
	10.14	and the fourth the **face** of an eagle.
	10.21	Each of them had four **faces,** four wings, and what looked
	10.22	faces looked exactly like the **faces** I had seen by the River
	11.13	I threw myself **face downwards** on the ground and shouted,
	20.35	of the Nations,' and there I will condemn you to your **face.**
	24.17	Don't cover your **face** or eat the food that mourners eat."
	24.22	You will not cover your **faces** or eat the food that mourners
	27.35	Even their kings are terrified, and fear is written on their **faces.**
	34. 6	were scattered over the **face of the earth,** and no one looked
	38.20	human being on the **face of the earth** will tremble for fear
	41.18	Each creature had two **faces:**
	41.19	human **face** that was turned towards the palm-tree on one side,
	41.19	and a lion's **face** that was turned towards the tree
	43. 3	Then I threw myself **face downwards** on the ground.
	44. 4	I threw myself **face downwards** on the ground, [5]and the Lord
Dan	2.10	no one on the **face of the earth** who can tell Your
	3.19	his temper, and his **face** turned red with anger at Shadrach,
	10. 6	His **face** was as bright as a flash of lightning, and his
	10. 8	no strength left, and my **face** was so changed that no one
	10. 9	I fell to the ground unconscious and lay there **face downwards.**
Joel	2. 6	every **face** turns pale.
Amos	9. 8	Israel, and I will destroy it from the **face of the earth.**
Nah	2.10	**faces** grow pale.
Mal	2. 3	your children and rub your **faces** in the dung of the animals
Mt	6.16	fast, do not put on a sad **face** as the hypocrites do.
	6.17	go without food, wash your **face** and comb your hair, [18]so
	17. 2	his **face** was shining like the sun, and his clothes were
	17. 6	that they threw themselves **face downwards** on the ground.
	22.20	and he asked them, "Whose **face** and name are these?"
	23.13	Kingdom of heaven in people's **faces,** and you yourselves don't go in,
	26.39	farther on, threw himself **face downwards** on the ground,
	26.67	Then they spat in his **face** and beat him;
Mk	10.22	this, gloom spread over his **face,** and he went away sad,
	12.16	him one, and he asked, "Whose **face** and name are these?"
Lk	9.29	While he was praying, his **face** changed its appearance,
	18.13	would not even raise his **face** to heaven, but beat on his
	20.24	Whose **face** and name are these on it?"
	24.17	They stood still, with sad **faces.**
Jn	5.37	his voice or seen his **face,** [38]and you do not keep his
	9. 7	and said, "Go and wash your **face** in the Pool of Siloam."
	9. 7	So the man went, washed his **face,** and came back seeing.
	9.11	eyes, and told me to go to Siloam and wash my **face.**
	9.15	I washed my **face,** and now I can see."
	11.44	wrapped in grave clothes, and with a cloth round his **face.**
Acts	6.15	and saw that his face looked like the **face** of an angel.
	25.16	met his accusers **face to face** and has had the chance of
1 Cor	13.12	then we shall see **face to face.**
2 Cor	3. 7	though the brightness on Moses' **face** was fading, it was so
	3.13	put a veil over his **face** so that the people of Israel
	3.18	then, reflect the glory of the Lord with uncovered **faces;**
	4. 6	the knowledge of God's glory shining in the **face** of Christ.
	11.20	you or looks down on you or slaps you in the **face.**
Rev	1.16	His **face** was as bright as the midday sun.
	4. 3	His **face** gleamed like such precious stones as jasper and carnelian,
	4. 7	the third had a **face** like a man's face;
	7.11	Then they threw themselves **face downwards** in front of the
Rev	9. 7	to be crowns of gold, and their **faces** were like men's faces.
	10. 1	his **face** was like the sun, and his legs were like pillars
	11.16	of God threw themselves **face downwards** and worshipped God,
	22. 4	They will see his **face,** and his name will be written on

FACE (2)

[FACING]

Gen	30.40	the goats and made them **face** in the direction of the
	43.33	had been seated at table, **facing** Joseph, in the order of
Ex	18. 8	the hardships the people had **faced** on the way and how the
	25.20	The winged creatures are to **face** each other across the lid,
	37. 9	The winged creatures **faced** each other across the lid, and
Num	8. 3	placed the lamps **facing** the front of the lamp-stand.
	14.43	When you **face** the Amalekites and the Canaanites, you
	16.19	whole community, and they stood **facing** Moses and Aaron at
Josh	8.33	Lord's Covenant Box, **facing** the levitical priests who carried it.
	15. 7	turned north towards Gilgal, which **faces** Adummim Pass on the
Judg	20.20	and placed the soldiers in position **facing** the city.
	20.30	in battle position **facing** Gibeah, as they had done before.
1 Sam	14. 5	north side of the pass, **facing** Michmash,
	14. 5	and the other was on the south side, **facing** Geba.
	17.21	Israelite armies took up positions for battle, **facing** each other.
2 Sam	2.22	How could I **face** your brother Joab?"
	10. 9	Israel's soldiers and put them in position **facing** the Syrians.
	10.10	Abishai, who put them in position **facing** the Ammonites.
	10.17	Helam, where the Syrians took up their position **facing** him.
1 Kgs	7. 5	three rows of windows in each wall **faced** the opposite rows.
	7.25	bulls that **faced** outwards, three facing in each direction.
	7.25	bulls that faced outwards, three **facing** in each direction.
	8.14	there, King Solomon turned to **face** them, and he asked God's
	8.29	Hear me when I **face** this Temple and pray.
	8.30	prayers of your people when they **face** this place and pray.
	8.35	they repent and **face** this Temple, humbly praying to you,
	8.44	to you, wherever they are, **facing** this city which you have
	8.48	pray to you as they **face** towards this land which you gave
	20.27	marched out and camped in two groups **facing** the Syrians.
	20.29	Israelites stayed in their camps, **facing** each other.
	21. 4	lay down on his bed, **facing** the wall, and would not eat.
	22.35	King Ahab remained propped up in his chariot, **facing** the Syrians.
2 Kgs	13.17	the king opened the window that **faced** towards Syria.
1 Chr	9.24	There was a gate **facing** in each direction, north, south,
	19.10	Israel's soldiers and put them in position **facing** the Syrians.
	19.11	Abishai, who put them in position **facing** the Ammonites.
	19.17	the Jordan, and put them in position **facing** the Syrians.
2 Chr	3.11	where they stood side by side **facing** the entrance.
	4. 4	bulls that **faced** outwards, three facing in each direction.
	6. 3	The king turned to **face** them and asked God's blessing on them.
	6.20	be worshipped, so hear me when I **face** this Temple and pray.
	6.21	of your people Israel when they **face** this place and pray.
	6.26	they repent and **face** this Temple, humbly praying to you,
	6.34	to you, wherever they are, **facing** this city which you have
	6.38	pray to you as they **face** towards this land which you gave
	7. 6	were assigned to them, and **facing** them stood the Levites,
	13.13	from the rear, while the rest **faced** them from the front.
	18.34	King Ahab remained propped up in his chariot, **facing** the Syrians.
	20.15	not be discouraged or be afraid to **face** this large army.
Esth	5. 1	the inner courtyard of the palace, **facing** the throne room.
	5. 1	seated on the royal throne, **facing** the entrance.
Job	4. 5	to be in trouble, and you are too stunned to **face** it.
	11.15	Then **face** the world again, firm and courageous.
	13.16	will save me, since no wicked man would dare to **face** God.
	18.14	he lived secure, and is dragged off to **face** King Death.
	31.14	If I did not, how could I then **face** God?
Ps	138. 2	I **face** your holy Temple, bow down, and praise your name
Prov	11. 4	good on the day you **face** death, but honesty can save your
Ecc	6. 8	does it do a poor man to know how to **face** life?
Jer	42.13	in Egypt, where we won't **face** war any more or hear the
Ezek	1.12	Each creature **faced** all four directions, and so the
	4. 3	**Face** the city.
	28. 9	When you **face** your murderers, you will be mortal and not at
	32.11	king of Egypt, "You will **face** the sword of the king of
	40. 6	Then he went to the gateway that **faced** east.
	40. 7	long that led to an entrance room which **faced** the Temple.
	40.16	palm-trees carved on the inner walls that **faced** the passage.
	40.22	and the entrance room was at the end **facing** the courtyard.
	40.26	its entrance room was also at the end **facing** the courtyard.
	40.26	palm-trees carved on the inner walls that **faced** the passage.
	40.31	Its entrance room **faced** the other courtyard, and
	40.34	The entrance room **faced** the outer courtyard.
	40.37	The entrance room **faced** the outer courtyard.
	40.38	into the entrance room that **faced** the courtyard, and there
	40.44	the inner courtyard, one **facing** south beside the north gateway
	40.44	and the other **facing** north beside the south gateway.
	40.45	me that the room which **faced** south was for the priests who
	40.46	Temple, [46]and the room which **faced** north was for the
	42. 3	On one side it **faced** the space ten metres wide which was
	42. 3	on the other side it **faced** the pavement of the outer court.
	43. 1	me to the gate that **faces** east, [2]and there I saw coming
	46.19	the entrance of the rooms **facing** north near the gate on the
	47. 1	entrance and flowing east, the direction the Temple **faced.**
	47. 2	north gate and led me round to the gate that **faces** east.
Dan	6.10	his house there were windows that **faced** towards Jerusalem.
Amos	4.12	I am going to do this, get ready to **face** my judgement!"
Mt	27.61	Mary Magdalene and the other Mary were sitting there, **facing** the tomb.
Lk	14.31	and decide if he is strong enough to **face** that other king.
Acts	27.12	Phoenix is a harbour in Crete that **faces** south-west and north-west.
1 Cor	15.31	My brothers, I **face** death every day!
Phil	4.13	I have the strength to **face** all conditions by the power
Jas	1. 3	when your faith succeeds in **facing** such trials, the result

FACET
Zech 3. 9 placing in front of Joshua a single stone with seven **facets.**

FACING see FACE (2)

FACT
Acts 2.32 Jesus from death, and we are all witnesses to this **fact.**
18.25 he proclaimed and taught correctly the **facts** about Jesus.
Rom 4.19 dead, or of the **fact** that Sarah could not have children.
1 Cor 6. 7 The very **fact** that you have legal disputes among
9. 2 you yourselves are proof of the **fact** that I am an apostle.
Heb 4. 7 This is shown by the **fact** that God sets another day, which
2 Pet 3. 5 They purposely ignore the **fact** that long ago God gave a command,

FADE
Lev 13. 6 and if the sore has **faded** and has not spread, he shall
13.56 it again, the mildew has **faded,** he shall tear it out of
Job 7. 9 Like a cloud that **fades** and is gone, a man dies and
11.16 Then all your troubles will **fade** from your memory, like
Ps 90. 9 it **fades** away like a whisper.
Is 28. 1 Its glory is **fading** like the crowns of flowers on the heads
28. 4 The **fading** glory of those proud leaders will disappear
40. 7 Grass withers and flowers **fade,** when the Lord sends the
40. 8 Yes, grass withers and flowers **fade,** but the word of our
Ezek 11.24 Then the vision **faded,** [25] and I told the exiles everything
Nah 1. 4 Mount Carmel turns brown, and the flowers of Lebanon **fade.**
2 Cor 3. 7 brightness on Moses' face was **fading,** it was so strong that
3.13 of Israel would not see the brightness **fade** and disappear.
1 Pet 1. 4 in heaven, where they cannot decay or spoil or **fade** away.

FAIL
Gen 31.38 and your goats have not **failed** to reproduce, and I have not
38.26 I have **failed** in my obligation to her—I should have given
48.10 Jacob's eyesight was **failing** because of his age, and he
Ex 8.18 to use their magic to make gnats appear, but they **failed.**
34. 7 but I will not **fail** to punish children and grandchildren to
Lev 5.15 If anyone sins unintentionally by **failing** to hand over
5.16 make the payments he has **failed** to hand over and must pay
Num 14.18 Yet I will not **fail** to punish children and grandchildren to
15.22 But suppose someone unintentionally **fails** to keep some
15.23 in the future the community **fails** to do everything that the
30.15 suffer the consequences for the **failure** to fulfil the vow.
Deut 8.11 do not **fail** to obey any of his laws that I am
24.19 you gather your crops and **fail** to bring in some of the
28.13 will always prosper and never **fail** if you obey faithfully
31. 6 He will not **fail** you or abandon you."
31. 8 He will not **fail** you or abandon you, so do not lose
32.29 They **fail** to see why they were defeated;
Josh 23.14 not one has **failed.**
1 Sam 26.16 You **failed** in your duty, Abner!
1 Kgs 11.22 "Have I **failed** to give you something?
2 Kgs 3.26 enemy lines and escape to the king of Syria, but he **failed.**
10.21 not one of them **failed** to come.
2 Chr 29. 7 the lamps go out, and **failed** to burn incense or offer
Ezra 6. 9 Day by day, without **fail,** you are to give the priests in
10. 8 If anyone **failed** to come within three days, all his property
Neh 9.35 but they **failed** to turn from sin and serve you.
Job 8. 3 he never **fails** to do what is right.
17.11 my plans have **failed;**
19.27 My courage **failed** because you said, [28] "How can we torment him?"
29.20 Everyone was always praising me, and my strength never **failed** me.
32.12 I paid close attention and heard you **fail;**
32.13 God must answer Job, for you have **failed.**
32.15 Words have **failed** them, Job;
Ps 10. 6 He says to himself, "I will never **fail;**
89.33 not stop loving David or **fail** to keep my promise to him.
112. 6 A good person will never **fail;**
112. 9 He gives generously to the needy, and his kindness never **fails;**
119.157 and oppressors, but I do not **fail** to obey your laws.
Prov 14.35 competent officials, but they punish those who **fail** them.
15.22 without it you will **fail.**
Ecc 2. 9 had ever lived in Jerusalem, and my wisdom never **failed** me.
Is 5. 4 Is there anything I **failed** to do for it?
13. 7 Everyone's hands will hang limp, and everyone's courage will **fail.**
30. 5 nation, a nation that **fails** them when they expect help."
42.16 These are my promises, and I will keep them without **fail.**
46.10 that my plans would never **fail,** that I would do everything I
50. 2 "Why did my people **fail** to respond when I went to them
55.11 speak— it will not **fail** to do what I plan for
Jer 4.22 doing what is evil, but **failures** at doing what is good."
10.21 This is why they have **failed,** and our people have been scattered.
12.13 Because of my fierce anger their crops have **failed."**
14. 6 their eyesight **fails** them because they have no food.
20.11 strong and mighty, and those who persecute me will **fail.**
25. 3 me, and I have never **failed** to tell you what he said.
49. 4 Your strength is **failing.**
Ezek 21. 7 limp, their courage will **fail,** and their knees will tremble.
Mic 3. 7 Those who predict the future will be disgraced by their **failure.**
Hab 3.17 though the olive-crop **fails** and the fields produce no corn,
Zeph 3. 5 Every morning without **fail,** he brings justice to his people.
Mal 1. 7 Then you ask, 'How have we **failed** to respect you?'
Lk 22.32 I have prayed for you, Simon, that your faith will not **fail.**
Rom 9. 6 I am not saying that the promise of God has **failed;**
14. 4 his own Master who will decide whether he succeeds or **fails.**
1 Cor 1. 7 you [7] that you have not **failed** to receive a single blessing,
6. 7 among yourselves shows that you have **failed** completely.
13. 7 and its faith, hope, and patience never **fail.**
2 Cor 13. 5 unless you have completely **failed.**
13. 6 I trust you will know that we are not **failures.**
13. 7 do what is right, even though we may seem to be **failures.**
Gal 2. 2 work in the past or in the present to be a **failure.**
Phil 1.20 is that I shall never **fail** in my duty, but that at
1 Thes 2. 1 you yourselves know that our visit to you was not a **failure.**
2 Tim 3. 8 minds do not function and who are **failures** in the faith.
Heb 4. 1 will be found to have **failed** to receive that promised rest.
4.11 no one of us will **fail** as they did because of their
Jas 1. 4 you all the way without **failing,** so that you may be perfect

FAINT (1)
Jer 15. 9 The mother who lost her seven children has **fainted,**
Lam 2.11 Children and babies are **fainting** in the streets of the city.
Jon 4. 8 and Jonah was about to **faint** from the heat of the sun
Mt 15.32 feeding them, for they might **faint** on their way home."
Mk 8. 3 without feeding them, they will **faint** as they go, because
Lk 21.26 People will **faint** from fear as they wait for what is

FAINT (2)
Heb 10. 1 it is only a **faint** outline of the good things to come.

FAIR
[UNFAIR]
Gen 24.49 towards my master and treat him **fairly,** please tell me;
34.18 These terms seemed **fair** to Hamor and his son Shechem,
Ex 21. 8 sell her to foreigners, because he has treated her **unfairly.**
Lev 25.14 fellow-Israelite or buy land from him, do not deal **unfairly.**
Deut 1.16 Judge every dispute **fairly,** whether it concerns only your
10.18 He makes sure that orphans and widows are treated **fairly;**
16.20 Always be **fair** and just, so that you will occupy the
32. 4 he does what is right and **fair.**
2 Sam 8.15 sure that his people were always treated **fairly** and justly.
1 Kgs 3.28 God had given him the wisdom to settle disputes **fairly.**
21. 2 it, or, if you prefer, I will pay you a **fair** price."
1 Chr 18.14 sure that his people were always treated **fairly** and justly.
Job 29.14 I have always acted justly and **fairly.**
31.13 complained against me, I would listen and treat him **fairly.**
Ps 9. 4 You are **fair** and honest in your judgements, and you have
19. 9 they are always **fair.**
37.30 A good man's words are wise, and he is always **fair.**
58. 1 Do you judge all men **fairly?**
72. 4 May the king judge the poor **fairly;**
75. 2 judgement," says God, "and I will judge with **fairness.**
82. 3 be **fair** to the needy and the helpless.
96.13 He will rule the peoples of the world with justice and **fairness.**
98. 9 He will rule the peoples of the world with justice and **fairness.**
99. 4 you have brought righteousness and **fairness.**
119.138 The rules that you have given are completely **fair** and right.
Prov 1. 3 to live intelligently and how to be honest, just, and **fair.**
2. 8 protects those who treat others **fairly,** and guards those who
2. 9 listen to me, you will know what is right, just, and **fair.**
12. 5 Honest people will treat you **fairly;**
16.11 and measures to be honest and every sale to be **fair.**
20.28 in power as long as his rule is honest, just, and **fair.**
21. 3 Do what is right and **fair;**
21.21 others will respect you and treat you **fairly.**
Is 11. 4 he will judge the poor **fairly** and defend the rights of
Jer 7. 5 Be **fair** in your treatment of one another.
22.15 He was always just and **fair,** and he prospered in
22.16 He gave the poor a **fair** trial, and all went well with
26.14 Do with me whatever you think is **fair** and right.
30.11 but when I punish you, I will be **fair.**
46.28 but when I punish you, I will be **fair.**
Mt 20. 4 work in the vineyard, and I will pay you a **fair** wage.'
2 Cor 8.13 this time, it is only **fair** that you should help those who
12.13 Please forgive me for being so **unfair!**
Col 4. 1 Masters, be **fair** and just in the way you treat your slaves.
Heb 6.10 God is not **unfair.**

FAITH
Ex 14.31 and they had **faith** in the Lord and in his servant Moses.
Num 20.12 you did not have enough **faith** to acknowledge my holy power
Josh 22.22 rebelled and did not keep **faith** with the Lord, do not let
2 Sam 15.11 they knew nothing of the plot and went in all good **faith.**
Ezra 10. 2 "We have broken **faith** with God by marrying foreign women,
Ps 27.14 Have **faith,** do not despair.
73. 2 my **faith** was almost gone [3] because I was jealous of the
78.22 grew, [22] because they had no **faith** in him and did not
112. 7 his **faith** is strong, and he trusts in the Lord.
Is 7. 9 "If your **faith** is not enduring, you will not endure."
28.16 are written the words, '**Faith** that is firm is also patient.'
Mt 6.30 How little **faith** you have!
8.10 I have never found anyone in Israel with **faith** like this.
8.26 "How little **faith** you have!"
9. 2 When Jesus saw how much **faith** they had, he said to the
9.22 Your **faith** has made you well."
13.58 Because they did not have **faith,** he did not perform many
14.31 grabbed hold of him and said, "How little **faith** you have!
15.28 So Jesus answered her, "You are a woman of great **faith!**
16. 8 How little **faith** you have!
17.20 "It was because you haven't enough **faith,**" answered Jesus.
17.20 you that if you have **faith** as big as a mustard seed,
18. 6 little ones to lose his **faith** in me, it would be better

Mt 18. 7 that there are things that make people lose their **faith!**
18. 8 foot makes you lose your **faith,** cut it off and throw it
18. 9 eye makes you lose your **faith,** take it out and throw it
24.10 Many will give up their **faith** at that time;
Mk 2. 5 Seeing how much **faith** they had, Jesus said to the paralysed man,
4.40 Have you still no **faith?"**
5.34 Jesus said to her, "My daughter, your **faith** has made you well.
6. 6 He was greatly surprised, because the people did not have **faith.**
9.23 Everything is possible for the person who has **faith."**
9.24 father at once cried out, "I do have **faith,** but not enough.
9.42 little ones to lose his **faith** in me, it would be better
9.43 So if your hand makes you lose your **faith,** cut it off!
9.45 And if your foot makes you lose your **faith,** cut it off!
9.47 And if your eye makes you lose your **faith,** take it out!
10.52 "Go," Jesus told him, "your **faith** has made you well."
11.22 Jesus answered them, "Have **faith** in God.
16.14 because they did not have **faith** and because they were too
Lk 5.20 When Jesus saw how much **faith** they had, he said to the
7. 9 I have never found **faith** like this, not even in Israel!"
7.50 But Jesus said to the woman, "Your **faith** has saved you;
8.25 Then he said to the disciples, "Where is your **faith?"**
8.48 Jesus said to her, "My daughter, your **faith** has made you well.
12.28 How little **faith** you have!
17. 5 The apostles said to the Lord, "Make our **faith** greater."
17. 6 Lord answered, "If you had **faith** as big as a mustard seed,
17.19 your **faith** has made you well."
18. 8 will the Son of Man find **faith** on earth when he comes?"
18.42 Your **faith** has made you well."
22.32 I have prayed for you, Simon, that your **faith** will not fail.
Jn 16. 1 told you this, so that you will not give up your **faith.**
20.31 God, and that through your **faith** in him you may have life.
Acts 3.16 What you see and know was done by **faith** in his name;
3.16 it was **faith** in Jesus that has made him well, as you
6. 5 Stephen, a man full of **faith** and the Holy Spirit, and
6. 7 larger, and a great number of priests accepted the **faith.**
11.24 of the Holy Spirit and **faith,** and many people were brought
13. 8 Greek), who tried to turn the governor away from the **faith.**
14.22 believers and encouraged them to remain true to the **faith.**
16. 5 made stronger in the **faith** and grew in numbers every day.
24.24 listened to him as he talked about **faith** in Christ Jesus.
26.11 in the synagogues and tried to make them deny their **faith.**
26.18 God, so that through their **faith** in me they will have their
Rom 1. 8 of you, because the whole world is hearing about your **faith.**
1.12 at the same time, you by my **faith** and I by yours.
1.17 it is through **faith** from beginning to end.
1.17 "The person who is put right with God through **faith** shall live."
3.22 God puts people right through their **faith** in Jesus Christ.
3.25 which people's sins are forgiven through their **faith** in him.
3.28 right with God only through **faith,** and not by doing what the
3.30 on the basis of their **faith,**
3.30 and will put the Gentiles right through their **faith.**
3.31 this mean that by this **faith** we do away with the Law?
4. 3 God, and because of his **faith** God accepted him as righteous."
4. 5 person who depends on his **faith,** not on his deeds, and who
4. 5 be innocent, it is his **faith** that God takes into account in
4. 9 God, and because of his **faith** God accepted him as righteous."
4.11 show that because of his **faith** God had accepted him as
4.12 live the same life of **faith** that our father Abraham lived
4.14 obey the Law, then man's **faith** means nothing and God's
4.16 the promise was based on **faith,** in order that the promise
4.19 but his **faith** did not weaken when he thought of his body,
4.20 His **faith** did not leave him, and he did not doubt God's
4.20 his **faith** filled him with power, and he gave praise to God.
4.22 That is why Abraham, through **faith,** "was accepted as righteous by God."
5. 1 put right with God through **faith,** we have peace with God
5. 2 He has brought us by **faith** into this experience of God's grace,
9.30 right with God, were put right with him through **faith;**
9.32 Because they did not depend on **faith** but on what they did.
10. 6 says about being put right with God through **faith** is this:
10. 8 your heart"—that is, the message of **faith** that we preach.
10.10 For it is by our **faith** that we are put right with
10.17 So then, **faith** comes from hearing the message, and the
12. 3 according to the amount of **faith** that God has given you.
12. 6 we should do it according to the **faith** that we have;
14. 1 person who is weak in **faith,** but do not argue with him
14. 2 One person's **faith** allows him to eat anything,
14. 2 the person who is weak in the **faith** eats only vegetables.
14.23 when he eats it, because his action is not based on **faith.**
14.23 And anything that is not based on **faith** is sin.
15. 1 who are strong in the **faith** ought to help the weak to
15. 2 their own good, in order to build them up in the **faith.**
15.13 peace by means of your **faith** in him, so that your hope
16.17 cause divisions and upset people's **faith** and go against the
16.25 you stand firm in your **faith,** according to the Good News I
1 Cor 2. 5 Your **faith,** then, does not rest on human wisdom but on
3. 1 belonged to this world, as children in the Christian **faith.**
8. 9 action make those who are weak in the **faith** fall into sin.
9.22 Among the weak in **faith** I become weak like one of them,
12. 9 and the same Spirit gives **faith** to one person, while to
13. 2 I may have all the **faith** needed to move mountains—but if
13. 7 and its **faith,** hope, and patience never fail.
13.13 **faith,** hope, and love;
15. 1 which you received, and on which your **faith** stands firm.
15.17 not been raised, then your **faith** is a delusion and you are
16.13 Be alert, stand firm in the **faith,** be brave, be strong.
2 Cor 1.24 we know that you stand firm in the **faith.**
4.13 In the same spirit of **faith,** we also speak because we believe.
5. 7 For our life is a matter of **faith,** not of sight.
8. 7 in **faith,** speech, and knowledge, in your eagerness to help
10.15 Instead, we hope that your **faith** may grow and that we may
2 Cor 13. 5 yourselves, to find out whether you are living in **faith.**
Gal 1.23 is now preaching the **faith** that he once tried to destroy!"
2.16 right with God only through **faith** in Jesus Christ, never by
2.16 right with God through our **faith** in Christ, and not by doing
2.20 live now, I live by **faith** in the Son of God, who
3. 6 God, and because of his **faith** God accepted him as righteous."
3. 7 real descendants of Abraham are the people who have **faith.**
3. 8 God would put the Gentiles right with himself through **faith.**
3.11 person who is put right with God through **faith** shall live."
3.12 But the Law has nothing to do with **faith.**
3.14 Christ Jesus, so that through **faith** we might receive the
3.22 promised on the basis of **faith** in Jesus Christ is given to
3.23 But before the time for **faith** came, the Law kept us all
3.23 locked up as prisoners until this coming **faith** should be revealed.
3.24 that we might then be put right with God through **faith.**
3.25 Now that the time for **faith** is here, the Law is no
3.26 It is through **faith** that all of you are God's sons in
5. 5 for by the power of God's Spirit working through our **faith.**
5. 6 what matters is **faith** that works through love.
6.10 especially to those who belong to our family in the **faith.**
Eph 1.15 since I heard of your **faith** in the Lord Jesus and your
2. 8 it is by God's grace that you have been saved through **faith.**
3.12 with Christ and through our **faith** in him we have the
3.17 that Christ will make his home in your hearts through **faith.**
4. 5 There is one Lord, one **faith,** one baptism;
4.13 to that oneness in our **faith** and in our knowledge of the
6.16 At all times carry **faith** as a shield;
6.23 Jesus Christ give to all Christian brothers peace and love with **faith.**
Phil 1.25 progress and joy in the **faith,** [26] so that when I am with
1.27 you are fighting together for the **faith** of the gospel.
2.17 an offering on the sacrifice that your **faith** offers to God.
3. 9 righteousness that is given through **faith** in Christ,
3. 9 the righteousness that comes from God and is based on **faith.**
Col 1. 4 we have heard of your **faith** in Christ Jesus and of your
1. 5 So your **faith** and love are based on what you hope for,
2. 5 with which you stand together in your **faith** in Christ.
2. 7 him, and become stronger in your **faith,** as you were taught.
2.12 with Christ through your **faith** in the active power of God,
1 Thes 1. 3 Father how you put your **faith** into practice, how your love
1. 8 Achaia, but the news about your **faith** in God has gone everywhere.
3. 2 strengthen you and help your **faith,** [3] so that none of you
3. 5 any longer, so I sent him to find out about your **faith.**
3. 6 has brought us the welcome news about your **faith** and love.
3. 7 It was your **faith** that encouraged us, [8] because now we
3.10 see you personally and supply what is needed in your **faith.**
5. 8 We must wear **faith** and love as a breastplate, and our hope
2 Thes 1. 3 to do so, because your **faith** is growing so much and the
1.11 your desire for goodness and complete your work of **faith.**
2.13 make you his holy people and by your **faith** in the truth.
1 Tim 1. 2 Jesus our hope— [2] To Timothy, my true son in the **faith:**
1. 4 they do not serve God's plan, which is known by **faith.**
1. 5 from a pure heart, a clear conscience, and a genuine **faith.**
1.13 I did not yet have **faith** and so did not know what
1.14 me and gave me the **faith** and love which are ours in
1.19 fight well, [19] and keep your **faith** and a clear conscience.
1.19 to their conscience and have made a ruin of their **faith.**
2. 7 of the Gentiles, to proclaim the message of **faith** and truth.
2.15 children, if she perseveres in **faith** and love and holiness,
3. 6 must be mature in the **faith,** so that he will not swell
3. 9 to the revealed truth of the **faith** with a clear conscience.
3.13 are able to speak boldly about their **faith** in Christ Jesus.
4. 1 that some people will abandon the **faith** in later times;
4. 6 spiritually on the words of **faith** and of the true teaching
4.12 believers in your speech, your conduct, your love, **faith,**
5. 8 he has denied the **faith** and is worse than an unbeliever.
6.10 have wandered away from the **faith** and have broken their
6.11 Strive for righteousness, godliness, **faith,** love, endurance, and gentleness.
6.12 in the race of **faith,** and win eternal life for yourself;
6.12 God called you when you firmly professed your **faith** before many witnesses.
6.13 Jesus, who firmly professed his **faith** before Pontius Pilate,
6.21 it, and as a result they have lost the way of **faith.**
2 Tim 1. 5 I remember the sincere **faith** you have,
1. 5 the kind of **faith** that your grandmother Lois and your
1.13 follow, and remain in the **faith** and love that are ours in
2.18 truth and are upsetting the **faith** of some believers by
2.22 youth, and strive for righteousness, **faith,** love, and peace,
3. 8 minds do not function and who are failures in the **faith.**
3.10 you have observed my **faith,** my patience, my love, my
3.15 that leads to salvation through **faith** in Christ Jesus.
4. 7 I have run the full distance, and I have kept the **faith.**
Tit 1. 1 and sent to help the **faith** of God's chosen people and to
1. 4 Titus, my true son in the **faith** that we have in common.
1.12 they may have a healthy **faith** [14] and no longer hold on to
2. 2 to be sound in their **faith,** love, and endurance.
3.15 Give our greetings to our friends in the **faith.**
Phlm 5 all God's people and the **faith** you have in the Lord Jesus.
Heb 3. 1 God sent to be the High Priest of the **faith** we profess.
4. 2 when they heard it, they did not accept it with **faith.**
4.11 us will fail as they did because of their lack of **faith.**
4.14 Let us, then, hold firmly to the **faith** we profess.
6. 4 who abandon their **faith** be brought back to repent again?
6. 6 And then they abandoned their **faith!**
10.22 sincere heart and a sure **faith,** with hearts that have been
10.39 Instead, we have **faith** and are saved.
11. 1 To have **faith** is to be sure of the things we hope
11. 2 It was by their **faith** that people of ancient times won
11. 3 It is by **faith** that we understand that the universe was

Heb 11. 4 It was **faith** that made Abel offer to God a better
11. 4 Through his **faith** he won God's approval as a righteous man,
11. 4 By means of his **faith** Abel still speaks, even though he is
11. 5 It was **faith** that kept Enoch from dying.
11. 6 can please God without **faith,** for whoever comes to God
11. 6 must have **faith** that God exists and rewards those
11. 7 It was **faith** that made Noah hear God's warnings about
11. 7 and Noah received from God the righteousness that comes by **faith.**
11. 8 It was **faith** that made Abraham obey when God called him to
11. 9 By **faith** he lived as a foreigner in the country that God
11.11 It was **faith** that made Abraham able to become a father,
11.13 It was in **faith** that all these persons died.
11.17 It was **faith** that made Abraham offer his son Isaac as a
11.20 It was **faith** that made Isaac promise blessings for the
11.21 It was **faith** that made Jacob bless each of the sons of
11.22 It was **faith** that made Joseph, when he was about to die,
11.23 It was **faith** that made the parents of Moses hide him for
11.24 It was **faith** that made Moses, when he had grown up,
11.27 It was **faith** that made Moses leave Egypt without being
11.28 It was **faith** that made him establish the Passover and
11.29 It was **faith** that made the Israelites able to cross the
11.30 It was **faith** that made the walls of Jericho fall down
11.31 It was **faith** that kept the prostitute Rahab from being
11.33 Through **faith** they fought whole countries and won.
11.35 Through **faith** women received their dead relatives raised back to life.
11.39 What a record all of these have won by their **faith!**
12. 2 on Jesus, on whom our **faith** depends from beginning to end.
13. 7 Think back on how they lived and died, and imitate their **faith.**
Jas 1. 3 know that when your **faith** succeeds in facing such trials,
2. 5 world to be rich in **faith** and to possess the kingdom which
2.14 to say that he has **faith** if his actions do not prove
2.14 Can that **faith** save him?
2.17 So it is with **faith:**
2.18 But someone will say, "One person has **faith,** another has actions."
2.18 My answer is, "Show me how anyone can have **faith** without actions.
2.18 I will show you my **faith** by my actions."
2.20 Do you want to be shown that **faith** without actions is useless?
2.22 His **faith** and his actions worked together;
2.22 his **faith** was made perfect through his actions.
2.23 God, and because of his **faith** God accepted him as righteous."
2.24 person is put right with God, and not by his **faith** alone.
2.26 the spirit is dead, so also **faith** without actions is dead.
5.15 This prayer made in **faith** will heal the sick person;
1 Pet 1. 5 are for you, who through **faith** are kept safe by God's power
1. 7 Their purpose is to prove that your **faith** is genuine.
1. 7 and so your **faith,** which is much more precious than gold,
1. 9 of your souls, which is the purpose of your **faith** in him.
1.21 and so your **faith** and hope are fixed on God.
5. 9 Be firm in your **faith** and resist him, because you know
2 Pet 1. 1 Saviour Jesus Christ have been given a **faith** as precious as ours:
1. 5 this very reason do your best to add goodness to your **faith;**
1.10 if you do so, you will never abandon your **faith.**
1 Jn 5. 4 we win the victory over the world by means of our **faith.**
Jude 3 to fight on for the **faith** which once and for all God
20 keep on building yourselves up on your most sacred **faith.**
Rev 2.13 you did not abandon your **faith** in me even during the time
13.10 This calls for endurance and **faith** on the part of God's people."

FAITHFUL

Gen 24.27 Abraham, who has **faithfully** kept his promise to my master.
32.10 all the kindness and **faithfulness** that you have shown me,
Ex 15.13 **Faithful** to your promise, you led the people you had rescued;
34. 6 easily angered and who shows great love and **faithfulness.**
Num 14.18 I show great love and **faithfulness** and forgive sin and rebellion.
Deut 1.36 He has remained **faithful** to me, and I will give him and
4. 4 those of you who were **faithful** to the Lord your God are
4. 6 Obey them **faithfully,** and this will show the people of
6.25 If we **faithfully** obey everything that God has commanded us,
7. 9 Lord your God is the only God and that he is **faithful.**
7.12 these commands and obey them **faithfully,** then the Lord your
8. 1 "Obey **faithfully** all the laws that I have given you today,
8.18 this because he is still **faithful** today to the covenant that
10.20 Be **faithful** to him and make your promises in his name alone.
11.22 "Obey **faithfully** all the laws that I have given you:
11.22 Lord your God, do everything he commands, and be **faithful** to him.
12.28 Obey **faithfully** everything that I have commanded you,
13. 4 worship him and be **faithful** to him.
17.19 Lord and to obey **faithfully** everything that is commanded in it.
18.13 Be completely **faithful** to the Lord."
26.16 so obey them **faithfully** with all your heart.
28. 1 the Lord your God and **faithfully** keep all his commands that
28.13 never fail if you obey **faithfully** all his commands that I am
28.15 your God and do not **faithfully** keep all his commands and
28.58 "If you do not obey **faithfully** all God's teachings
29. 9 Obey **faithfully** all the terms of this covenant, so that
30.20 God, obey him and be **faithful** to him, and then you and
31.12 the Lord your God and to obey his teachings **faithfully.**
32. 4 Your God is **faithful** and true;
32.46 so that they may **faithfully** obey all God's teachings.
33. 8 will by the Urim and Thummim Through your **faithful** servants,
33. 9 They obeyed your commands And were **faithful** to your covenant.
Josh 14. 8 But I **faithfully** obeyed the Lord my God.
14.14 Jephunneh the Kenizzite, because he **faithfully** obeyed the Lord,
22. 5 will, obey his commandments, be **faithful** to him, and serve
23. 8 Instead, be **faithful** to the Lord, as you have been till now.
24.14 "honour the Lord and serve him sincerely and **faithfully.**
Judg 5.13 Then the **faithful** ones came down to their leaders;
1 Sam 2. 9 protects the lives of his **faithful** people, but the wicked
2.35 a priest who will be **faithful** to me and do everything I
12.24 Obey the Lord and serve him **faithfully** with all your heart.
22.14 Ahimelech answered, "David is the most **faithful** officer you have!
26.23 The Lord rewards those who are **faithful** and righteous.
2 Sam 2. 6 And now may the Lord be kind and **faithful** to you.
15.20 with you—and may the Lord be kind and **faithful** to you."
15.34 will now serve him as **faithfully** as you served his father.
22.26 O Lord, you are **faithful** to those who are faithful to you,
1 Kgs 2. 4 obey his commands **faithfully** with all their heart and soul.
8.61 you, his people, always be **faithful** to the Lord our God,
11. 4 He was not **faithful** to the Lord his God, as his father
15.14 of worship, he remained **faithful** to the Lord all his life.
2 Kgs 18. 6 He was **faithful** to the Lord and never disobeyed him, but
20. 3 that I have served you **faithfully** and loyally, and that I
1 Chr 29.18 your people's hearts and keep them always **faithful** to you.
2 Chr 7.17 If you serve me **faithfully** as your father David did,
15.17 in the land, he remained **faithful** to the Lord all his life.
19. 9 for the Lord, **faithfully** obeying him in everything you do.
26. 5 living, he served the Lord **faithfully,** and God blessed him.
27. 6 Jotham grew powerful because he **faithfully** obeyed the Lord his God.
29.34 (The Levites were more **faithful** in keeping ritually clean
31.15 lived, he was **faithfully** assisted in this by other Levites:
32. 1 King Hezekiah served the Lord **faithfully,**
Neh 1. 5 You **faithfully** keep your covenant with those who love you
9. 8 You found that he was **faithful** to you, and you made a
9. 8 You kept your promise, because you are **faithful.**
9.32 You **faithfully** keep your covenant promises.
9.33 you have been **faithful,** even though we have sinned.
Job 1. 1 the land of Uz, who worshipped God and was **faithful** to him.
1. 8 is no one on earth as **faithful** and good as he is.
2. 3 is no one on earth as **faithful** and good as he is.
2. 3 no reason at all, but Job is still as **faithful** as ever."
2. 9 said to him, "You are still as **faithful** as ever, aren't
8.20 God will never abandon the **faithful** or ever give help to
9.20 I am innocent and **faithful,** but my words sound guilty,
23.11 I follow **faithfully** the road he chooses, and never
Ps 16. 3 How excellent are the Lord's **faithful** people!
16.10 I have served you **faithfully,** and you will not abandon me
18.25 O Lord, you are **faithful** to those who are faithful to you;
25.10 With **faithfulness** and love he leads all who keep his
26. 3 your **faithfulness** always leads me.
30. 4 Sing praise to the Lord, all his **faithful** people!
31. 5 you are a **faithful** God.
31.23 Love the Lord, all his **faithful** people.
31.23 The Lord protects the **faithful,** but punishes the proud
36. 5 your **faithfulness** extends to the skies.
37.28 Lord loves what is right and does not abandon his **faithful** people.
40.10 I have always spoken of your **faithfulness** and help.
50. 5 He says, "Gather my **faithful** people to me, those who made
52. 1 God's **faithfulness** is eternal.
54. 5 He will destroy them because he is **faithful.**
57. 3 God will show me his constant love and **faithfulness.**
57.10 your **faithfulness** touches the skies.
61. 7 protect him with your constant love and **faithfulness.**
71.22 I will praise your **faithfulness,** my God.
78. 8 God was never firm and who did not remain **faithful** to him.
78.37 they were not **faithful** to their covenant with him.
85.10 Love and **faithfulness** will meet;
86.11 what you want me to do, and I will obey you **faithfully;**
86.15 and loving God, always patient, always kind and **faithful.**
88.11 the grave or your **faithfulness** in the place of destruction?
89. 1 I will proclaim your **faithfulness** for ever.
89. 2 time, that your **faithfulness** is as permanent as the sky.
89. 5 the holy ones sing of your **faithfulness,** Lord.
89. 8 in all things you are **faithful,** O Lord.
89.14 love and **faithfulness** are shown in all you do.
89.19 ago you said to your **faithful** servants, "I have given help
89.37 permanent as the moon, that **faithful** witness in the sky."
91. 4 his **faithfulness** will protect and defend you.
92. 2 love every morning and your **faithfulness** every night, [3] with
100. 5 his love is eternal and his **faithfulness** lasts for ever.
101. 6 approve of those who are **faithful** to God and will let them
103.18 true to his covenant and who **faithfully** obey his commands.
108. 4 your **faithfulness** touches the skies.
111. 7 In all he does he is **faithful** and just;
115. 1 be given because of your constant love and **faithfulness.**
117. 2 His love for us is strong and his **faithfulness** is eternal.
119. 4 given us your laws and told us to obey them **faithfully.**
119. 5 How I hope that I shall be **faithful** in keeping your instructions!
119.75 Lord, and that you punished me because you are **faithful.**
119.90 Your **faithfulness** endures through all the ages;
138. 2 of your constant love and **faithfulness,** because you have
143. 1 answer me in your **faithfulness!**
145.13 The Lord is **faithful** to his promises, and he is merciful in
149. 1 praise him in the assembly of his **faithful** people!
Prov 3. 3 Never let go of loyalty and **faithfulness.**
5.15 Be **faithful** to your own wife and give your love to her
16. 6 Be loyal and **faithful,** and God will forgive your sin.
20. 6 talks about how loyal and **faithful** he is, but just try to
Is 1.21 The city that once was **faithful** is behaving like a whore!
1.26 Then Jerusalem will be called the righteous, **faithful** city."
16. 5 and he will rule the people with **faithfulness** and love.
25. 1 you have **faithfully** carried out the plans you made long ago.
26. 2 city gates and let the **faithful** nation enter, the nation
38. 3 that I have served you **faithfully** and loyally, and that I
38.18 The dead cannot trust in your **faithfulness.**
38.19 Fathers tell their children how **faithful** you are.
56. 4 do what pleases me and **faithfully** keep my covenant, [5] then

Is 56. 6 who observe the Sabbath and **faithfully** keep his covenant:
61. 8 I will **faithfully** reward my people And make an eternal
65.16 for a blessing will ask to be blessed by the **Faithful** God.
65.16 takes an oath will swear by the name of the **Faithful** God.
66. 5 "Because you are **faithful** to me, some of your own people
Jer 2. 2 "I remember how **faithful** you were when you were young, how
3.20 But like an unfaithful wife, you have not been **faithful** to me.
3.22 he will heal you and make you **faithful.**
4. 1 If you are **faithful** to me and remove the idols I hate,
5. 1 who does what is right and tries to be **faithful** to God?
5. 3 Surely the Lord looks for **faithfulness.**
7.28 **Faithfulness** is dead.
23.28 heard my message should proclaim that message **faithfully.**
42. 5 Lord be a true and **faithful** witness against us if we do
50. 7 and they themselves should have remained **faithful** to him.'
Ezek 11.20 Then they will keep my laws and **faithfully** obey all my commands.
37.24 be united under one ruler and will obey my laws **faithfully.**
44.15 however, continued to serve me **faithfully** in the Temple when
48.11 They served me **faithfully** and did not join the rest of the
Dan 9. 4 You are **faithful** to your covenant and show constant love to
12.12 Happy are those who remain **faithful** until 1,335 days are over!
12.13 "And you, Daniel, be **faithful** to the end.
Hos 2.19 I will be true and **faithful;**
4. 1 "There is no **faithfulness** or love in the land, and the
11.12 Judah are still rebelling against me, the **faithful** and holy God.
Mic 7.20 You will show your **faithfulness** and constant love to your people,
Hab 2. 4 righteous will live because they are **faithful** to God.' "
Zech 8. 3 will be known as the **faithful** city, and the hill of the
8. 8 I will be their God, ruling over them **faithfully** and justly.
Mal 2.14 you promised before God that you would be **faithful** to her.
2.16 do not break your promise to be **faithful** to your wife."
Mt 5.20 only if you are more **faithful** than the teachers of the Law
24.45 "Who, then, is a **faithful** and wise servant?
25.21 'Well done, you good and **faithful** servant!'
25.21 'You have been **faithful** in managing small amounts, so I will
25.23 'Well done, you good and **faithful** servant!'
25.23 'You have been **faithful** in managing small amounts, so I will
Lk 12.42 The Lord answered, "Who, then, is the **faithful** and wise servant?
16.10 Whoever is **faithful** in small matters will be faithful in large ones;
16.11 then, you have not been **faithful** in handling worldly wealth,
16.12 have not been **faithful** with what belongs to someone else,
19.17 Since you were **faithful** in small matters, I will put you in
Acts 2.27 you will not allow your **faithful** servant to rot in the grave.
11.23 urged them all to be **faithful** and true to the Lord with
Rom 3. 3 But what if some of them were not **faithful?**
3. 3 Does this mean that God will not be **faithful?**
15. 8 to show that God is **faithful,** to make his promises to their
1 Cor 4. 2 of such a servant is that he be **faithful** to his master.
4.17 who is my own dear and **faithful** son in the Christian life.
Gal 5.22 Spirit produces love, joy, peace, patience, kindness, goodness, **faithfulness,** [23] humility, and self-control.
Eph 1. 1 people in Ephesus, who are **faithful** in their life in union
6.21 Tychicus, our dear brother and **faithful** servant in the Lord's work,
Phil 4. 3 And you too, my **faithful** partner, I want you to help these
Col 1. 2 Colossae, who are our **faithful** brothers in union with Christ:
1. 7 Epaphras, our dear fellow-servant, who is Christ's **faithful** worker on our behalf.
1.23 You must, of course, continue **faithful** on a firm and sure foundation,
4. 7 brother Tychicus, who is a **faithful** worker and
4. 9 Onesimus, that dear and **faithful** brother, who belongs to your group.
1 Thes 5.24 He who calls you will do it, because he is **faithful.**
2 Thes 3. 3 But the Lord is **faithful,** and he will strengthen you and
1 Tim 6.14 your orders and keep them **faithfully** until the Day when our
2 Tim 2.13 If we are not **faithful,** he remains faithful,
Tit 2.10 they are always good and **faithful,** so as to bring credit to
Heb 2.17 in order to be their **faithful** and merciful High Priest in
3. 2 He was **faithful** to God, who chose him to do this work,
3. 2 just as Moses was **faithful** in his work in God's house.
3. 5 Moses was **faithful** in God's house as a servant, and he
3. 6 But Christ is **faithful** as the Son in charge of God's house.
8. 9 They were not **faithful** to the covenant I made with them, and
10. 1 Law is not a full and **faithful** model of the real things;
13. 4 all, and husbands and wives must be **faithful** to each other.
Jas 1.12 is the person who remains **faithful** under trials, because
1 Pet 5.12 of Silas, whom I regard as a **faithful** Christian brother.
3 Jn 3 arrived and told me how **faithful** you are to the truth—just
5 dear friend, you are so **faithful** in the work you do for
Rev 1. 5 and from Jesus Christ, the **faithful** witness, the first to
2.10 Be **faithful** to me, even if it means death, and I will
2.13 the time when Antipas, my **faithful** witness, was killed there
2.19 I know your love, your **faithfulness,** your service, and your patience.
3. 8 you have followed my teaching and have been **faithful** to me.
3.14 message from the Amen, the **faithful** and true witness, who is
6. 9 God's word and had been **faithful** in their witnessing.
12.17 God's commandments and are **faithful** to the truth revealed by Jesus.
14.12 God's people, those who obey God's commandments and are **faithful** to Jesus.
17.14 called, chosen, and **faithful** followers, will defeat them,
19.11 Its rider is called **Faithful** and True;

FAITHLESS

1 Sam 20.30 "How rebellious and **faithless** your mother was!
Ezra 10.10 He said, "You have been **faithless** and have brought guilt on
Prov 2.17 her smooth talk, [17] who is **faithless** to her own husband and
Jer 31.22 How long will you hesitate, **faithless** people?
Ezek 6. 9 and disgraced them, because their **faithless** hearts deserted

FALCON

Lev 11.13 eagles, owls, hawks, **falcons;**
Deut 14.12 eagles, owls, hawks, **falcons;**

FALL

[FELL]
for FALL ASLEEP see **ASLEEP**
for FALL IN LOVE see **LOVE**

Gen 7. 4 to send rain that will **fall** for forty days and nights, in
7.12 sky were opened, [12] and rain **fell** on the earth for forty
14.10 tried to run away from the battle, they **fell** into the pits;
27.13 mother answered, "Let any curse against you **fall** on me, my
35. 5 started to leave, great fear **fell** on the people of the
Ex 9.19 Hail will **fall** on the people and animals left outside unprotected,
9.22 the sky, and hail will **fall** over the whole land of Egypt
15.16 Terror and dread **fall** upon them.
21.33 a bull or a donkey **falls** into it, [34] he must pay for
23. 5 If his donkey has **fallen** under its load, help him get the
Lev 11.32 And if their dead bodies **fall** on anything, it will be unclean.
11.33 And if their bodies **fall** into a clay pot, everything
11.35 Anything on which the dead bodies **fall** is unclean;
11.37 If one of them **falls** on seed that is going to be
11.38 water and one of them **falls** on it, the seed is unclean.
15.17 leather on which the semen **falls** must be washed, and it
19.10 that were missed or to pick up the grapes that have **fallen;**
26.30 and throw your dead bodies on your **fallen** idols.
26.36 in battle, and you will **fall** when there is no enemy near
Num 11. 8 It **fell** on the camp at night along with the dew.
Deut 22. 4 "If a fellow-Israelite's donkey or cow has **fallen** down,
22. 8 will not be responsible if someone **falls** off and is killed.
28.23 No rain will **fall,** and your ground will become as hard
28.52 and the high, fortified walls in which you trust will **fall.**
29.20 written in this book will **fall** on him until the Lord has
32. 2 My teaching will **fall** like drops of rain and form on the
32. 2 My words will **fall** like showers on young plants, like gentle
32.11 on its spreading wings, the Lord kept Israel from **falling.**
32.35 the time will come when they will **fall;**
Josh 5.12 The manna stopped **falling** then,
10.11 the Lord made large hailstones **fall** down on them all the way
Judg 5. 4 of Edom, the earth shook, and rain **fell** from the sky.
5.27 He sank to his knees, **fell** down and lay still
5.27 At her feet he sank to his knees and **fell;**
5.27 he **fell** to the ground, dead.
7.15 and what it meant, he **fell** to his knees and worshipped the
16.30 his might, and the building **fell** down on the five kings and
17. 3 "To stop the curse from **falling** on my son, I myself am
19.26 dawn the woman came and **fell** down at the door of the
1 Sam 4.18 mentioned the Covenant Box, Eli **fell** backwards from his seat
4.18 old and fat that the **fall** broke his neck, and he died.
5. 3 the statue of Dagon had **fallen** face downwards on the ground
5. 4 that the statue had again **fallen** down in front of the
17.49 his skull, and Goliath **fell** face downwards on the ground.
17.52 The Philistines **fell** wounded all along the road
20.37 place where the arrow had **fallen,** Jonathan shouted to him,
20.41 behind the pile of stones, **fell** on his knees and bowed with
26.19 if men have done it, may the Lord's curse **fall** on them.
28.20 At once Saul **fell** down and lay stretched out on the ground,
2 Sam 1.10 I knew that he would die anyway as soon as he **fell.**
1.19 The bravest of our soldiers have **fallen!**
1.21 "May no rain or dew **fall** on Gilboa's hills;
1.25 "The brave soldiers have **fallen,** they were killed in battle.
1.27 "The brave soldiers have **fallen,** their weapons abandoned
2.16 so that all twenty-four of them **fell** down dead together.
3.29 May the punishment for it **fall** on Joab and all his family!
20. 8 As he came forward, the sword **fell** out.
20.15 also began to dig under the wall to make it **fall** down.
22.37 You have kept me from being captured, and I have never **fallen.**
23. 9 The Israelites **fell** back, [10] but he stood his ground and
1 Kgs 2.33 punishment for their murders will **fall** on Joab and on his
13. 3 to say, "This altar will **fall** apart, and the ashes on it
13. 5 The altar suddenly **fell** apart and the ashes spilt to the ground,
16.18 saw that the city had **fallen,** he went into the palace's
18.45 the wind began to blow, and heavy rain began to **fall.**
20.30 where the city walls **fell** on twenty-seven thousand of them.
2 Kgs 1. 2 King Ahaziah of Israel **fell** off the balcony on the roof
1.13 He went up the hill, **fell** on his knees in front of
2.13 up Elijah's cloak that had **fallen** from him, and went back
4.37 She **fell** at Elisha's feet, with her face touching the ground;
6. 5 down a tree, suddenly his iron axe-head **fell** in the water.
6. 6 "Where did it **fall?"**
9.24 Joram **fell** dead in his chariot, [25] and Jehu said to his
17. 7 Samaria **fell** because the Israelites sinned against the Lord
18.10 In the third year of the siege, Samaria **fell;**
18.12 Samaria **fell** because the Israelites did not obey the Lord
19.10 you that you will not **fall** into my hands, but don't let
2 Chr 7. 3 of Israel saw the fire **fall** from heaven and the light fill
7. 3 fill the Temple, they **fell** face downwards on the pavement,
Ezra 9. 7 and our priests have **fallen** into the hands of foreign kings,
Neh 4. 4 Let their ridicule **fall** on their own heads.
Job 12. 5 you hit a man who is about to **fall.**
14.18 a time when mountains **fall** and solid cliffs are moved away.
18. 7 he **falls**—a victim of his own advice.
24. 8 drenched by the rain that **falls** on the mountains, and they
24.20 he is eaten by worms and destroyed like a **fallen** tree.
28.26 decided where the rain would **fall,** And the path that the
37. 6 He commands snow to **fall** on the earth, and sends torrents

Job 38.26 Who makes rain **fall** where no one lives?
38.36 Nile will flood, or who tells the cock that rain will **fall?**
41. 9 Anyone who sees Leviathan loses courage and **falls** to the ground.
Ps 9. 3 they **fall** down and die.
9.15 The heathen have dug a pit and **fallen** in;
11. 3 There is nothing a good man can do when everything **falls** apart."
18.36 You have kept me from being captured, and I have never **fallen.**
20. 8 Such people will stumble and **fall,** but we will rise and
27. 2 men attack me and try to kill me, they stumble and **fall.**
35. 8 be caught in their own trap and **fall** to their destruction!
36.12 See where evil men have **fallen.**
37.24 If they **fall,** they will not stay down, because the Lord
38.17 I am about to **fall** and am in constant pain.
44.25 We **fall** crushed to the ground;
45. 5 nations **fall** down at your feet.
46. 2 earth is shaken and mountains **fall** into the ocean depths;
57. 6 They dug a pit in my path, but **fell** into it themselves.
60. 2 now heal its wounds, because it is **falling** apart.
66. 9 He has kept us alive and has not allowed us to **fall.**
66.11 You let us **fall** into a trap and placed heavy burdens on
68. 9 You caused abundant rain to **fall** and restored your worn-out land;
68.14 the kings on Mount Zalmon, he caused snow to **fall** there.
69. 9 the insults which are hurled at you **fall** on me.
72. 6 like rain on the fields, like showers **falling** on the land.
73.18 them in slippery places and make them **fall** to destruction!
76. 6 O God of Jacob, the horses and their riders **fell** dead.
78.28 they **fell** in the middle of the camp all round the tents.
88. 3 So many troubles have **fallen** on me that I am close to
91. 7 A thousand may **fall** dead beside you, ten thousand all round you,
94.18 I said, "I am **falling";**
107.12 they would **fall** down, and no one would help.
119.133 As you have promised, keep me from **falling;**
119.165 security, and there is nothing that can make them **fall.**
121. 3 He will not let you **fall;**
133. 3 like the dew on Mount Hermon, **falling** on the hills of Zion.
140. 9 make their threats against me **fall** back on them.
140.10 May red-hot coals **fall** on them;
141.10 May the wicked **fall** into their own traps while I go by
145.14 he lifts those who have **fallen.**
146. 8 He lifts those who have **fallen;**
Prov 3.26 He will not let you **fall** into a trap.
4.19 They **fall,** but cannot see what they have stumbled over.
11.14 A nation will **fall** if it has no guidance.
11.28 depend on their wealth will **fall** like the leaves of autumn,
24.16 how often an honest man **falls,** he always gets up again;
24.31 The stone wall round them had **fallen** down.
28.10 person into doing evil, you will **fall** into your own trap.
28.18 If you are dishonest, you will suddenly **fall.**
28.28 But when they **fall** from power, righteous men will rule again.
Ecc 4.10 If one of them **falls** down, the other can help him up.
4.10 if someone is alone and **falls,** it's just too bad, because
10. 8 If you dig a pit, you **fall** in it;
10.18 repair his roof, it will leak, and the house will **fall** in.
11. 3 in which direction a tree **falls,** it will lie where it fell.
12. 6 chain will snap, and the golden lamp will **fall** and break;
Is 5. 6 I will even forbid the clouds to let rain **fall** on it."
8.15 they will **fall** and be crushed.
9.10 say, [10] "The brick buildings have **fallen** down, but we will
10.34 down with an axe, as even the finest trees of Lebanon **fall!**
14. 4 "The cruel king has **fallen!**
14. 8 of Lebanon rejoice over the **fallen** king, because there is no
14.12 bright morning star, you have **fallen** from heaven!
16. 9 My tears **fall** for Heshbon and Elealeh, because there is no
18. 5 the blossoms have all **fallen** and the grapes are ripening,
21. 9 The sentry gives the news, "Babylon has **fallen!**
22.25 the peg that was firmly fastened will work loose and **fall.**
24.18 escape from the terror will **fall** into a pit, and anyone who
31. 3 will crumble, and the weak nation it helped will **fall.**
32.19 ([19] But hail will **fall** on the forests, and the city will be
33. 9 on Mount Carmel the leaves are **falling** from the trees.
34. 4 up, and the stars will **fall** like leaves dropping from a vine
34. 7 The people will **fall** like wild oxen and young bulls, and
37.10 you that you will not **fall** into my hands, but don't let
40.20 a skilful craftsman to make an image that won't **fall** down.
40.30 young men can **fall** exhausted.
43.17 Down they **fell,** never to rise, snuffed out like the flame of
45.20 of the nations, all who survive the **fall** of the empire;
51.19 A double disaster has **fallen** on you:
53. 6 the Lord made the punishment **fall** on him, the punishment all
54.15 whoever fights against you will **fall.**
Jer 6.15 And so they will **fall** as others have fallen;
6.15 And so they will fall as others have **fallen;**
6.21 And so I will make these people stumble and **fall.**
8. 4 people, "When someone **falls** down, doesn't he get back up?
8.12 And so you will **fall** as others have fallen;
10. 4 It is fastened down with nails to keep it from **falling** over.
13.18 their beautiful crowns have **fallen** from their heads.
14.22 the sky by itself cannot make showers **fall.**
18.20 Yet they have dug a pit for me to **fall** in.
18.22 a pit for me to **fall** in and have set traps to
22. 5 then I swear to you that this palace will **fall** into ruins.
23.12 I will make them stumble and **fall.**
25.27 drunk and vomit, until they **fall** down and cannot get up,
27. 7 grandson until the time comes for his own nation to **fall.**
32.24 and disease will make the city **fall** into their hands.
32.36 disease will make this city **fall** into the hands of the king
46. 6 In the north, by the Euphrates, they stumble and **fall.**
46.12 trips over another, and both of them **fall** to the ground.
46.15 Why has your mighty god Apis **fallen?**
46.16 Your soldiers have stumbled and **fallen;**
48.20 'Moab has **fallen,'** they will answer, 'weep for it;
Jer 48.44 to escape the terror will **fall** into the pits, and whoever
49.21 When Edom **falls,** there will be such a noise that the
50. 2 Babylon has **fallen!**
50.32 proud nation will stumble and **fall,** and no one will help you
50.46 When Babylon **falls,** there will be such a noise that the
51. 8 Babylonia has suddenly **fallen** and is destroyed!
51.44 "Babylon's walls have **fallen.**
51.48 shout for joy when Babylonia **falls** to the people who come
51.49 world, and now Babylonia will **fall** because it caused the
Lam 1. 1 The noblest of cities has **fallen** into slavery.
1. 7 When she **fell** to the enemy, there was no one to help
2. 8 The Lord was determined that the walls of Zion should **fall;**
2.12 They **fall** in the streets as though they were wounded, And
Ezek 1.28 When I saw this, I **fell** face downwards on the ground.
3.23 I **fell** face downwards on the ground, [24] but God's spirit
7.12 because God's punishment will **fall** on everyone alike.
7.14 off to war, for God's anger will **fall** on everyone alike.
13.11 Tell the prophets that their wall is going to **fall** down.
13.11 Hailstones will **fall** on it, and a strong wind will blow
21.29 The sword is going to **fall** on your necks.
26.18 on the day it has **fallen,** The islands are trembling, And
29. 5 Your body will **fall** on the ground and be left unburied.
30.18 Darkness will **fall** on Tahpanhes when I break the power
30.22 one already broken—and the sword will **fall** from his hand.
31.12 branches and broken boughs will **fall** on every mountain and
31.13 come and perch on the **fallen** tree, and the wild animals will
31.17 world of the dead to join those that have already **fallen.**
32.10 On the day you **fall,** all of them will tremble in fear
32.20 "The people of Egypt will **fall** with those who are
32.23 All her soldiers **fell** in battle,
33.21 from Jerusalem came and told me that the city had **fallen.**
38.20 Mountains will **fall,** cliffs will crumble,
39. 4 and his allies will **fall** dead on the mountains of Israel,
39. 5 They will **fall** dead in the open field.
Dan 3.23 and Abednego, still tied up, **fell** into the heart of the
4.15 " 'Now let the dew **fall** on this man, and let him live
4.23 Let the dew **fall** on this man, and let him live there
4.25 sleep in the open air, where the dew will **fall** on you.
4.33 The dew **fell** on his body, and his hair grew as long
7.20 had come up afterwards and had made three of the horns **fall.**
8.17 me, and I was so terrified that I **fell** to the ground.
8.18 While he was talking, I **fell** to the ground unconscious.
10. 9 I heard his voice, I **fell** to the ground unconscious and lay
Hos 2.21 I will make rain **fall** on the earth, and the earth will
5. 1 to judge with justice—so judgement will **fall** on you!
5. 5 sins make them stumble and **fall,**
5. 5 and the people of Judah **fall** with them.
14. 1 Your sin has made you stumble and **fall.**
14. 9 but sinners stumble and **fall** because they ignore them.
Amos 3.14 every altar will be broken off and will **fall** to the ground.
3.15 The houses decorated with ivory will **fall** in ruins;
4. 7 Rain **fell** on one field, but another field dried up.
5. 2 Virgin Israel has **fallen,** Never to rise again!
8. 8 it will rise and **fall** like the River Nile.
8.14 of Beersheba'—those people will **fall** and not rise again."
9. 1 them off and let them **fall** on the heads of the people.
9. 5 The whole world rises and **falls** like the River Nile.
9.11 kingdom of David, which is like a house **fallen** into ruins.
Mic 7. 8 We have **fallen,** but we will rise again.
Nah 3.12 shake the trees, and the fruit **falls** right into your mouth!
Zech 8.13 saying, 'May the same disasters **fall** on you that fell on
8.13 same disasters fall on you that **fell** on Judah and Israel!'
11. 2 Weep and wail, cypress-trees— the cedars have **fallen;**
14.15 A terrible disease will also **fall** on the horses, the
14.17 Lord Almighty as king, then rain will not **fall** on their land.
14.19 be the punishment that will **fall** on Egypt and on all the
Mt 7.25 But it did not **fall,** because it was built on rock.
7.27 the wind blew hard against that house, and it **fell.**
7.27 And what a terrible **fall** that was!"
10.29 sparrows, yet not one sparrow **falls** to the ground without
12.11 has a sheep and it **falls** into a deep hole on the
12.25 itself into groups which fight each other will **fall** apart.
12.26 it is already divided into groups and will soon **fall** apart!
13. 4 the field, some of it **fell** along the path, and the birds
13. 5 Some of it **fell** on rocky ground, where there was little soil.
13. 7 Some of the seed **fell** among thorn bushes, which grew up
13. 8 But some seeds **fell** in good soil, and the plants produced corn;
13.19 understand it are like the seeds that **fell** along the path.
13.20 The seeds that **fell** on rocky ground stand for those who
13.22 The seeds that **fell** among thorn bushes stand for those
15.14 when one blind man leads another, both **fall** into a ditch."
15.25 At this the woman came and **fell** at his feet.
15.27 the dogs eat the leftovers that **fall** from their masters'
17.15 terrible fits that he often **falls** in the fire or into water.
18.26 The servant **fell** on his knees before the king.
18.29 His fellow-servant **fell** down and begged him, 'Be patient with me,
23.35 of all innocent men will **fall** on you, from the murder of
23.36 for all these murders will **fall** on the people of this day!
24.29 longer shine, the stars will **fall** from heaven, and the
26.41 Keep watch and pray that you will not **fall** into temptation.
27.25 "Let the responsibility for his death **fall** on us and our children!"
Mk 3.11 them saw him, they would **fall** down before him and scream,
3.24 groups which fight each other, that country will **fall** apart.
3.25 groups which fight each other, that family will **fall** apart.
3.26 it cannot last, but will **fall** apart and come to an end.
4. 4 the field, some of it **fell** along the path, and the birds
4. 5 Some of it **fell** on rocky ground, where there was little soil.
4. 7 Some of the seed **fell** among thorn bushes, which grew up
4. 8 But some seeds **fell** in good soil, and the plants sprouted.
4.15 Some people are like the seeds that **fall** along the path;
4.16 Other people are like the seeds that **fall** on rocky ground.

Mk	5. 6	so he ran, **fell** on his knees before him, [7]and screamed in
	7.25	Jesus and came to him at once and **fell** at his feet.
	9.20	a fit, so that he **fell** on the ground and rolled round,
	13.25	longer shine, [25]the stars will **fall** from heaven, and the
	14.38	"Keep watch, and pray that you will not **fall** into temptation.
	15.19	a stick, spat on him, **fell** on their knees, and bowed down
Lk	5. 8	saw what had happened, he **fell** on his knees before Jesus and
	6.39	if he does, both will **fall** into a ditch.
	6.49	flood hit that house it **fell** at once—and what a terrible
	8. 5	the field, some of it **fell** along the path, where it was
	8. 6	Some of it **fell** on rocky ground, and when the plants sprouted,
	8. 7	Some of the seed **fell** among thorn bushes, which grew up
	8. 8	And some seeds **fell** in good soil;
	8.12	The seeds that **fell** along the path stand for those who hear;
	8.13	The seeds that **fell** on rocky ground stand for those who
	8.13	a while but when the time of testing comes, they **fall** away.
	8.14	The seeds that **fell** among thorn bushes stand for those who hear;
	8.15	The seeds that **fell** in good soil stand for those who
	10.18	Jesus answered them, "I saw Satan **fall** like lightning from heaven.
	11.17	a family divided against itself **falls** apart.
	13. 4	in Siloam who were killed when the tower **fell** on them?
	14. 5	an ox that happened to **fall** in a well on a Sabbath,
	16.21	eat the bits of food that **fell** from the rich man's table.
	17. 1	"Things that make people **fall** into sin are bound to happen,
	20.18	Everyone who **falls** on that stone will be cut to pieces;
	20.18	and if that stone **falls** on someone, it will crush him to
	21.23	this land, and God's punishment will **fall** on this people.
	22.40	to them, "Pray that you will not **fall** into temptation."
	22.44	his sweat was like drops of blood **falling** to the ground.
	22.46	Get up and pray that you will not **fall** into temptation."
	23.30	time when people will say to the mountains, **'Fall** on us!'
Jn	11.32	and as soon as she saw him, she **fell** at his feet.
	18. 6	them, "I am he," they moved back and **fell** to the ground.
Acts	1.18	evil act he bought a field, where he **fell** to his death;
	5. 5	As soon as Ananias heard this, he **fell** down dead;
	5.10	At once she **fell** down at his feet and died.
	5.15	at least Peter's shadow might **fall** on some of them as he
	9. 4	He **fell** to the ground and heard a voice saying to him,
	9.18	once something like fish scales **fell** from Saul's eyes, and
	10.25	go in, Cornelius met him, **fell** at his feet, and bowed down
	12. 7	At once the chains **fell** off Peter's hands.
	16.26	the doors opened, and the chains **fell** off all the prisoners.
	16.29	a light, rushed in, and **fell** trembling at the feet of Paul
	19.35	Artemis and of the sacred stone that **fell** down from heaven.
	20. 9	finally went sound asleep and **fell** from the third storey to
	22. 7	I **fell** to the ground and heard a voice saying to me,
	26.14	All of us **fell** to the ground, and I heard a voice
	28. 6	were waiting for him to swell up or suddenly **fall** down dead.
Rom	9.33	will make people stumble, a rock that will make them **fall.**
	11. 9	may they **fall,** may they be punished!
	11.11	When the Jews stumbled, did they **fall** to their ruin?
	11.22	severe towards those who have **fallen,** but kind to you—if you
	14.13	that would make your brother stumble or **fall** into sin.
	14.20	eat anything that will cause someone else to **fall** into sin.
	14.21	or doing anything else that will make your brother **fall.**
	15. 3	"The insults which are hurled at you have **fallen** on me."
1 Cor	8. 9	action make those who are weak in the faith **fall** into sin.
	8.13	meat again, so as not to make my brother **fall** into sin.
	10. 8	were—and in one day twenty-three thousand of them **fell** dead.
	10.12	standing firm had better be careful that he does not **fall.**
Eph	3.14	For this reason I **fall** on my knees before the Father,
Phil	2.10	in the world below will **fall** on their knees, [11]and all
1 Tim	3. 7	he will not be disgraced and **fall** into the Devil's trap.
	6. 9	who want to get rich **fall** into temptation and are caught in
Heb	3.17	With the people who sinned, who **fell** down dead in the desert.
	6. 7	in the rain that often **falls** on it and which grows plants
	10.31	is a terrifying thing to **fall** into the hands of the living
	11.30	made the walls of Jericho **fall** down after the Israelites had
Jas	1.11	its flower **falls** off, and its beauty is destroyed.
	5.17	no rain, and no rain **fell** on the land for three and
1 Pet	1.24	grass withers, and the flowers **fall,** [25]but the word of the
	2. 8	make people stumble, the rock that will make them **fall."**
2 Pet	3.17	errors of lawless people and **fall** from your safe position.
Jude	24	able to keep you from **falling,** and to bring you faultless
Rev	1.17	When I saw him, I **fell** down at his feet like a
	2. 5	Think how far you have **fallen!**
	4.10	do so, [10]the twenty-four elders **fall** down before the one
	5. 8	and the twenty-four elders **fell** down before the Lamb.
	5.14	And the elders **fell** down and worshipped.
	6.13	The stars **fell** down to the earth,
	6.13	like unripe figs **falling** from the tree
	6.16	mountains and to the rocks, **"Fall** on us and hide us from
	8.10	dropped from the sky and **fell** on a third of the rivers
	9. 1	saw a star which had **fallen** down to the earth, and it
	14. 8	A second angel followed the first one, saying, "She has **fallen!**
	14. 8	Great Babylon has **fallen!**
	16.10	Darkness **fell** over the beast's kingdom, and people bit their
	16.21	as much as fifty kilogrammes, **fell** from the sky on people,
	17.10	five of them have **fallen,** one still rules, and the other
	18. 2	"She has **fallen!**
	18. 2	Great Babylon has **fallen!**
	19. 4	and the four living creatures **fell** down and worshipped God,
	19.10	I **fell** down at his feet to worship him, but he said
	22. 8	hearing and seeing them, I **fell** down at the feet of the

FALSE

Ex	20.16	"Do not accuse anyone **falsely.**
	23. 1	"Do not spread **false** rumours,
	23. 1	and do not help a guilty man by giving **false** evidence.
	23. 7	Do not make **false** accusations, and do not put an innocent
Lev	19.35	not cheat anyone by using **false** measures of length, weight,
Num	13.32	So they spread a **false** report among the Israelites about
	14.36	the land brought back a **false** report which caused the people
Deut	5.20	" 'Do not accuse anyone **falsely.**
	19.16	tries to harm another by **falsely** accusing him of a crime,
	19.18	has made a **false** accusation against his fellow-Israelite,
	22.14	So he makes up **false** charges against her, accusing her
	22.17	He has made **false** charges against her, saying that she
1 Sam	12.21	Don't go after **false gods;**
1 Kgs	14.23	built places of worship for **false gods,** and put up stone
Job	36. 4	Nothing I say to you is **false;**
Ps	4. 2	will you love what is worthless and go after what is **false?**
	24. 4	thought, who do not worship idols or make **false** promises.
	31. 6	You hate those who worship **false gods,** but I trust in you.
	40. 4	do not turn to idols or join those who worship **false gods.**
	52. 3	You love evil more than good and **falsehood** more than truth.
	119.78	May the proud be ashamed for **falsely** accusing me;
	140.11	May those who accuse others **falsely** not succeed;
Prov	8. 8	nothing is **false** or misleading.
	8.13	I hate pride and arrogance, evil ways and **false** words.
	25.18	A **false** accusation is as deadly as a sword, a club, or
	29.12	a ruler pays attention to **false** information, all his
Is	59.13	Our thoughts are **false;**
Jer	10.14	because the gods they make are **false** and lifeless.
	13.25	you have forgotten him and have trusted in **false gods.**
	16.18	as corpses, and have filled it with their **false gods."**
	16.19	"Our ancestors had nothing but **false gods,**
	23.16	they are filling you with **false** hopes.
	51.17	because the gods they make are **false** and lifeless.
Ezek	12.24	there will be no more **false** visions or misleading prophecies.
	13. 6	Their visions are **false,** and their predictions are lies.
	13. 7	Those visions you see are **false,** and the predictions you
	13. 8	to them, "Your words are **false,** and your visions are lies.
	13. 9	who have **false** visions and make misleading predictions.
	13.23	So now your **false** visions and misleading predictions are over.
	14. 9	is deceived into giving a **false** answer, it is because I, the
	20. 7	make themselves unclean with the **false gods** of Egypt,
	21.29	visions that you see are **false,** and the predictions you make
	22.28	They see **false** visions and make false predictions.
	30.13	"I will destroy the idols and the **false gods** in Memphis.
Hos	7.13	I wanted to save them, but their worship of me was **false.**
	10. 4	utter empty words and make **false** promises and useless treaties.
	12. 7	they love to cheat their customers with **false** scales.
Amos	2. 4	astray by the same **false gods** that their ancestors served.
	8. 5	Then we can overcharge, use **false** measures, and tamper with
Mic	6.10	They use **false** measures, a thing that I hate.
	6.11	How can I forgive men who use **false** scales and weights?
Zech	8.17	Do not give **false** testimony under oath.
Mal	3. 5	adulterers, against those who give **false** testimony, those
Mt	7.15	"Be on your guard against **false prophets;**
	7.20	So then, you will know the **false prophets** by what they do.
	19.18	do not accuse anyone **falsely;**
	24.11	Then many **false prophets** will appear and deceive many people.
	24.24	For false Messiahs and **false prophets** will appear;
	26.59	Council tried to find some **false** evidence against Jesus to
Mk	10.19	do not accuse anyone **falsely;**
	13.22	For false Messiahs and **false prophets** will appear.
Lk	3.14	"Don't take money from anyone by force or accuse anyone **falsely.**
	6.26	said the very same things about the **false prophets.**
	18.20	do not accuse anyone **falsely;**
Jn	1.47	there is nothing **false** in him!"
	7.18	who sent him is honest, and there is nothing **false** in him.
Acts	24.14	our ancestors by following that Way which they say is **false.**
Rom	11. 4	thousand men who have not worshipped the **false god** Baal."
2 Cor	4. 2	not act with deceit, nor do we **falsify** the word of God.
	10. 4	We destroy **false** arguments;
	11.13	not true apostles—they are **false** apostles, who lie about
	11.26	dangers on the high seas, and dangers from **false** friends.
Col	2. 4	let anyone deceive you with **false** arguments, no matter how
	2.18	and who insists on **false** humility and the worship of angels.
	2.23	forced worship of angels, and **false** humility, and severe
2 Thes	2. 9	and perform all kinds of **false** miracles and wonders, [10]and
	2.11	error to work in them so that they believe what is **false.**
1 Tim	1. 3	Some people there are teaching **false** doctrines, and you must
	1.10	those who lie and give **false** testimony or who do anything
2 Tim	2.13	remains faithful, because he cannot be **false** to himself."
2 Pet	2. 1	**False prophets** appeared in the past among the people, and
	2. 1	and in the same way **false** teachers will appear among you.
	2. 3	In their greed these **false** teachers will make a profit out
	2.10	These **false** teachers are bold and arrogant, and show no
	2.11	stronger and mightier than these **false** teachers, do not
	3.16	ignorant and unstable people explain **falsely,** as they do
1 Jn	2.27	about everything, and what he teaches is true, not **false.**
	4. 1	For many **false prophets** have gone out everywhere.
	4. 4	children, and have defeated the **false prophets,** because the
	4. 5	Those **false prophets** speak about matters of the world, and
	5.21	My children, keep yourselves safe from **false gods!**
Rev	16.13	the mouth of the beast, and the mouth of the **false prophet.**
	18.23	the world, and with your **false** magic you deceived all the
	19.20	taken prisoner, together with the **false prophet** who had
	19.20	The beast and the **false prophet** were both thrown alive into
	20.10	the beast and the **false prophet** had already been thrown;

FALSE GOD(S) see **GOD (2)**

FAME see **FAMOUS**

FAMILY

Gen 7. 1 Lord said to Noah, "Go into the boat with your whole **family;**
13. 5 goats, and cattle, as well as his own **family** and servants.
24.40 my son a wife from my own people, from my father's **family.**
24.59 let Rebecca and her old **family** servant go with Abraham's
34.19 He was the most important member of his **family.**
34.30 me and attack me, our whole **family** will be destroyed."
35. 2 So Jacob said to his **family** and to all who were with
35.16 Jacob and his **family** left Bethel, and when they were
37. 2 had lived, [2]and this is the story of Jacob's **family.**
41.51 me forget all my sufferings and all my father's **family";**
42.19 to your starving **families** the corn that you have bought.
42.33 rest will take corn for your starving **families** and leave.
43. 2 got worse, [2]and when the **family** of Jacob had eaten all the
43. 7 about us and our **family,** 'Is your father still living?
45.11 I do not want you, your **family,** and your livestock to starve.' "
45.18 Let them get their father and their **families** and come back here.
46. 8 The members of Jacob's **family** who went to Egypt with him
46.27 seventy the total number of Jacob's **family** who went there.
46.31 the rest of his father's **family,** "I must go and tell the
46.31 and all my father's **family,** who were living in Canaan,
47.12 rest of his father's **family,** including the very youngest.
47.24 for seed and for food for yourselves and your **families."**
50. 8 His **family,** his brothers, and the rest
50. 8 the rest of his father's **family** all went with him.
50.22 Joseph continued to live in Egypt with his father's **family;**
50.23 the children of Machir son of Manasseh into the **family.**
Ex 1. 1 with him, each with his **family,** were [2]Reuben, Simeon, Levi,
1.20 he was good to them and gave them **families** of their own.
6.25 were the heads of the **families** and the clans of the tribe
12. 4 If his **family** is too small to eat a whole animal, he
12.21 and kill it, so that your **families** can celebrate Passover.
Lev 6.29 Any male of the priestly **families** may eat this offering;
7. 6 Any male of the priestly **families** may eat it, but it must
10.14 But you and your **families** may eat the breast and the
16. 6 sacrifice to take away his own sins and those of his **family.**
16.11 sin-offering for himself and his **family,** [12]he shall take a
16.17 the ritual for himself, his **family,** and the whole community,
20. 5 the man and his whole **family** and against all who join him
22.10 a member of a priestly **family** may eat any of the sacred
22.13 Only a member of a priestly **family** may eat any of it.
22.14 a member of a priestly **family** eats any of the sacred
23.17 Each **family** is to bring two loaves of bread and present
25.10 who has been sold as a slave shall return to his **family.**
25.41 you and return to his **family** and to the property of his
25.47 a slave to that foreigner or to a member of his **family.**
Num 1. 2 take a census of the people of Israel by clans and **families.**
1.18 month and registered all the people by clans and **families.**
1.20 to clan and **family,** beginning with the tribe of Reuben,
3. 1 This is the **family** of Aaron and Moses at the time the
3.12 of each Israelite **family** and the first-born of every animal.
3.15 the Levites by clans and **families,** enrolling every male a
3.17 They were the ancestors of the **families** that bear their names.
3.21 of Gershon was composed of the **families** of Libni and Shimei.
3.27 Kohath was composed of the **families** of Amram, Izhar, Hebron,
3.33 of Merari was composed of the **families** of Mahli and Mushi.
4. 2 of Kohath by sub-clans and **families,** [3]and to register all
4.22 of Gershon by sub-clans and **families,** [23]and to register
4.29 of Merari by sub-clans and **families,** [30]and to register all
4.34 did this by sub-clans and **families** and registered all the
8.17 of each Israelite **family** and the first-born of every animal.
10.36 "Return, Lord, to the thousands of **families** of Israel."
16.32 and swallowed them and their **families,** together with all
18.11 Every member of your **family** who is ritually clean may eat them.
18.13 Every member of your **family** who is ritually clean may eat it.
18.31 You and your **families** may eat the rest anywhere, because
25.14 of Salu, the head of a **family** in the tribe of Simeon.
26. 2 "Take a census by **families** of the whole community of Israel,
34.14 property, divided according to their **families,** [15]on the
36. 1 The heads of the **families** in the clan of Gilead, the son
Deut 11. 6 swallowed them, along with their **families,** their tents, and
12. 7 blessed you, you and your **families** will eat and enjoy the
14.26 God, you and your **families** are to eat and enjoy yourselves.
15.16 he may love you and your **family** and be content to stay.
15.20 Each year you and your **family** are to eat them in the
18. 8 priests, and he may keep whatever his **family** sends him.
24. 6 This would take away the **family's** means of preparing food to
25. 5 widow is not to be married to someone outside the **family;**
25. 6 dead man, so that his **family** line will continue in Israel.
25.10 His **family** will be known in Israel as 'the family of the
26. 5 a wandering Aramean, who took his **family** to Egypt to live.
26.11 things that the Lord your God has given you and your **family;**
29.18 sure that no man, woman, **family,** or tribe standing here
Josh 2.12 that you will treat my **family** as kindly as I have treated
2.13 and mother, my brothers and sisters, and all their **families!**
2.18 and all your father's **family** together in your house.
6.22 and bring her and her **family** out, as you promised her."
6.23 father and mother, her brothers, and the rest of her **family.**
6.23 They took them all, **family** and slaves, to safety near the
7.14 The clan that I pick out will come forward, **family by family.**
7.14 The **family** that I pick out will come forward, man by man.
7.15 be burnt, along with his **family** and everything he owns, for
7.17 the clan of Zerah forward, **family by family,**
7.17 and the **family** of Zabdi was picked out.,
7.18 He then brought Zabdi's **family** forward, man by man, and
7.25 they also stoned and burnt his **family** and possessions.
13.15 of the land to the **families** of the tribe of Reuben as
13.23 and towns given to the **families** of the tribe of Reuben as
13.24 of the land to the **families** of the tribe of Gad as
13.28 and towns given to the **families** of the tribe of Gad as
Josh 13.29 of the land to the **families** of half the tribe of Manasseh
13.31 to half the **families** descended from Machir son of Manasseh.
14. 1 and the leaders of the **families** of the Israelite tribes
15. 1 The **families** of the tribe of Judah received a part of the
15.12 Within these borders lived the people of the **families** of Judah.
15.20 is the land that the **families** of the tribe of Judah received
16. 5 This was the territory of the Ephraimite **families:**
16. 8 the land given to the **families** of the tribe of Ephraim as
17. 1 of the **families** descended from Joseph's elder son Manasseh.
17. 2 Jordan was assigned to the rest of the **families** of Manasseh:
17. 2 of Manasseh son of Joseph, and they were heads of **families.**
18.11 The territory belonging to the **families** of the tribe of
18.20 of the land which the **families** of the tribe of Benjamin
18.21 The cities belonging to the **families** of the tribe of
18.28 is the land which the **families** of the tribe of Benjamin
19. 1 assignment made was for the **families** of the tribe of Simeon.
19. 8 was the land which the **families** of the tribe of Simeon
19.10 made was for the **families** of the tribe of Zebulun.
19.16 in the land which the **families** of the tribe of Zebulun
19.17 made was for the **families** of the tribe of Issachar.
19.23 in the land which the **families** of the tribe of Issachar
19.24 assignment made was for the **families** of the tribe of Asher.
19.31 in the land which the **families** of the tribe of Asher
19.32 made was for the **families** of the tribe of Naphtali.
19.39 in the land which the **families** of the tribe of Naphtali
19.40 assignment made was for the **families** of the tribe of Dan.
19.48 in the land which the **families** of the tribe of Dan received
19.51 and the leaders of the **families** of the tribes of Israel
21. 1 The leaders of the Levite **families** went to Eleazar the priest,
21. 1 to the heads of the **families** of all the tribes of Israel.
21. 4 The **families** of the Levite clan of Kohath were the first
21. 4 The **families** who were descended from Aaron the priest were
21. 7 The **families** of the clan of Merari were assigned twelve
21.20 The other **families** of the Levite clan of Kohath were
21.26 These **families** of the clan of Kohath received ten cities in all,
21.33 The various **families** of the clan of Gershon received a
22.14 tribes and each one the head of a **family** among the clans.
22.21 answered the heads of the **families** of the western tribes:
22.30 with him, the heads of **families** of the western tribes, heard
24.15 As for my **family** and me, we will serve the Lord."
Judg 1.25 Manasseh killed everyone in the city, except this man and his **family.**
4.17 King Jabin of Hazor was at peace with Heber's **family.**
6.15 and I am the least important member of my **family."**
6.27 was too afraid of his **family** and the people of the town
8.27 It was a trap for Gideon and his **family.**
8.35 were not grateful to the **family** of Gideon for all the good
9.16 treat his **family** properly, as his actions deserved?
9.18 But today you turned against my father's **family.**
9.19 today to Gideon and his **family** was sincere and honest, then
16.31 and the rest of his **family** came down to get his body.
18. 2 men out of all the **families** in the tribe and sent them
18.19 a whole Israelite tribe than for the **family** of one man?"
18.25 Then you and your whole **family** would die."
21.24 back to his own tribe and **family** and to his own property.
Ruth 2. 1 man who belonged to the **family** of her husband Elimelech.
3.10 "You are showing even greater **family** loyalty in what you
4. 5 so that the field will stay in the dead man's **family."**
4.10 property in the dead man's **family,**
4.10 and his **family** line will continue among his people
4.12 this young woman make your **family** like the family of Perez,
4.18 This is the **family** line from Perez to David:
1 Sam 1. 1 Elihu, and belonged to the **family** of Tohu, a part of the
1.19 next morning Elkanah and his **family** got up early, and after
1.21 again for Elkanah and his **family** to go to Shiloh and offer
2.27 your ancestor Aaron and his **family** were slaves of the king
2.28 of Israel I chose his **family** to be my priests, to serve
2.30 in the past that your **family** and your clan would serve me
2.31 the young men in your **family** and your clan,
2.31 so that no man in your **family** will live to be old.
2.32 but no one in your **family** will ever again live to old
3.12 all my threats against Eli's **family,** from beginning to end.
3.13 am going to punish his **family** for ever because his sons have
3.14 I solemnly declare to the **family** of Eli that no sacrifice or
5.11 its own place, so that it won't kill us and our **families."**
9. 1 Zeror, and belonged to the **family** of Becorath, a part of the
9.20 It is you—you and your father's **family."**
9.21 tribe in Israel, and my **family** is the least important one in
10.21 Samuel made the **families** of the tribe of Benjamin come forward,
10.21 Benjamin come forward, and the **family** of Matri was picked out.
10.21 Then the men of the **family** of Matri came forward, and Saul
12. 8 When Jacob and his **family** went to Egypt and the Egyptians
17.25 and will not require his father's **family** to pay taxes."
18.18 I and what is my **family** that I should become the king's
20. 6 the time for the annual sacrifice there for my whole **family.**
20.15 show the same kind of loyalty to my **family** for ever.
20.29 go,' he said, 'because our **family** is celebrating the
22. 1 and the rest of the **family** heard that he was there, they
22.15 Your Majesty must not accuse me or anyone else in my **family.**
24.21 and my **family's** name will not be completely forgotten."
25. 6 his best wishes for you, your **family,** and all that is yours.
25.17 This could be disastrous for our master and all his **family.**
27. 3 David and his men settled there in Gath with their **families.**
2 Sam 2. 3 took his men and their **families,** and they settled in the
2.32 Asahel's body and buried it in the **family** tomb at Bethlehem.
3. 1 between the forces supporting Saul's **family** and those
3. 6 the forces loyal to Saul's **family,** Abner became more and
3.29 May the punishment for it fall on Joab and all his **family!**
3.29 be some man in his **family** who has gonorrhoea or a dreaded
6.11 months, and the Lord blessed Obed Edom and his **family.**
6.12 the Lord had blessed Obed Edom's **family** and all that he had;

2 Sam 6.20 went home to greet his **family,** Michal came out to meet him.
6.21 of your father and his **family** to make me the leader of
7.18 have already done for me, Sovereign Lord, nor is my **family.**
9. 1 One day David asked, "Is there anyone left of Saul's **family?**
9. 2 was a servant of Saul's **family** named Ziba, and he was told
9. 3 there anyone left of Saul's **family** to whom I can show
9. 9 grandson, everything that belonged to Saul and his **family.**
9.10 land for your master Saul's **family** and bring in the harvest,
9.12 All the members of Ziba's **family** became servants of Mephibosheth.
12.11 cause someone from your own **family** to bring trouble on you.
14. 9 "whatever you do, my **family** and I will take the blame;
14. 9 you and the royal **family** are innocent."
15.16 by all his **family** and officials, except for ten concubines,
16. 2 donkeys are for Your Majesty's **family** to ride, the bread and
16. 8 Lord is punishing you for murdering so many of Saul's **family.**
17.23 He was buried in the **family** grave.
19.17 Ziba, the servant of Saul's **family,** also came with his
19.28 All my father's **family** deserved to be put to death by
19.41 escort you, your **family,** and your men across the Jordan?"
21. 1 the Lord said, "Saul and his **family** are guilty of murder;
21. 4 quarrel with Saul and his **family** can't be settled with
24.17 You should punish me and my **family."**
1 Kgs 4.25 each **family** with its own grapevines and fig-trees.
11.14 Hadad, of the royal **family** of Edom, to turn against Solomon.
12.16 to them, they shouted, "Down with David and his **family!**
12.31 and he chose priests from **families** who were not of the tribe
13. 2 name will be Josiah, will be born to the **family** of David.
13.22 and your body will not be buried in your **family** grave."
13.30 buried it in his own **family** grave, and he and his sons
13.33 to choose priests from ordinary **families** to serve at the
14.10 I will get rid of your **family;**
14.11 Any members of your **family** who die in the city will be
14.13 member of Jeroboam's **family** who will be properly buried,
15.29 At once he began killing all the members of Jeroboam's **family.**
15.29 Ahijah from Shiloh, all Jeroboam's **family** were killed;
16. 3 away with you and your **family,** just as I did with Jeroboam.
16. 4 Any members of your **family** who die in the city will be
16. 7 Lord against Baasha and his **family** was given by the prophet
16. 7 him, but also because he killed all Jeroboam's **family.**
16.11 Zimri became king he killed off all the members of Baasha's **family.**
16.12 Zimri killed all the **family** of Baasha.
21.21 get rid of every male in your **family,** young and old alike.
21.22 Your **family** will become like the family of King Jeroboam
21.22 and like the **family** of King Baasha son of Ahijah,
21.29 lifetime that I will bring disaster on Ahab's **family."**
2 Kgs 8. 1 should leave with her **family** and go and live somewhere else.
8. 2 and had gone with her **family** to live in Philistia for the
8.18 Ahab's daughter, and like the **family** of Ahab he followed the
8.27 he sinned against the Lord, just as Ahab's **family** did.
9. 8 All Ahab's **family** and descendants are to die;
9. 8 get rid of every male in his **family,** young and old alike.
9. 9 I will treat his **family**
9. 9 as I did the **families** of King Jeroboam of Israel
10.13 of Queen Jezebel and to the rest of the royal **family."**
11. 1 orders for all the members of the royal **family** to be killed.
25.25 a member of the royal **family,** went to Mizpah with ten men,
1 Chr 1.24 The **family** line from Shem to Abram is as follows:
2.10 The **family** line from Ram to Jesse is as follows:
2.36 The **family** line from Attai to Elishama is as follows:
4. 9 Jabez, who was the most respected member of his **family.**
4.33 which they kept of their **families** and of the places where
4.34 Because their **families** continued to grow, [39] they spread
5. 7 The **family** records list the following clan leaders in the
6.33 The **family** lines of those who held this office are as follows:
6.33 His **family** line went back to Jacob as follows:
6.39 His **family** line went back to Levi as follows:
6.44 His **family** line went back to Levi as follows:
6.60 a total of thirteen towns for all their **families** to live in.
6.61 lot to the rest of the clan of Kohath, **family by family.**
6.62 To the clan of Gershon, **family by family,** were assigned
6.63 Zebulun were assigned to the clan of Merari, **family by family.**
6.66 Some of the **families** of the clan of Kohath were
6.71 The **families** of the clan of Gershon
6.77 The remaining **families** of the clan of Merari were
7. 2 They were heads of **families** of the clan of Tola and were
7. 3 Obadiah, Joel, and Isshiah, were all heads of **families.**
7. 5 official records of all the **families** of the tribe of
7. 7 They were heads of **families** in the clan and were all famous
7. 9 record of their descendants by **families** listed 20,200 men
7.11 They were heads of **families** in the clan and were all famous
7.23 because of the trouble that had come to their **family.**
7.40 They were heads of **families,** famous fighting men,
8. 6 They were heads of **families** that lived in Geba, but which
8.10 His sons all became heads of **families.**
8.13 and Shema were heads of **families** that settled in the city of
8.28 were the ancestral heads of **families** and their principal
8.32 Their descendants lived in Jerusalem near other **families**
9. 1 were listed according to their **families,** and this
9. 4 There were 690 **families** of the tribe of Judah who
9. 4 had as their leader Asaiah, who was the head of his **family.**
9. 9 There were 956 **families** of this tribe living there.
9. 9 All the men named above were heads of **families.**
9.13 The priests who were heads of **families** totalled 1,760.
9.33 Some Levite **families** were responsible for the temple music.
9.33 The heads of these **families** lived in some of the temple
9.34 of Levite **families,** according to their ancestral lines.
9.38 Their descendants lived in Jerusalem near other **families**
13.14 blessed Obed Edom's **family** and everything that belonged to him.
16.43 and David went home to spend some time with his **family.**
1 Chr 17.16 you have already done for me, Lord God, nor is my **family.**
21.17 my God, punish me and my **family,** and spare your people."
23.24 of Levi, by clans and **families,** every one of them registered
24. 4 male heads of **families** among the descendants of Eleazar.
24. 6 the heads of the priestly **families**
24. 6 and of the Levite **families,** were all witnesses.
24. 7 the twenty-four **family** groups were given their assignments:
24.20 These are other heads of **families** descended from Levi:
24.30 These are the **families** of the Levites.
24.31 The head of each **family** and one of his younger brothers
24.31 Ahimelech, and the heads of **families** of the priests and of
25. 9 according to **families** into twenty-four groups of twelve,
25. 9 Joseph of the **family** of Asaph
26. 1 Korah there was Meshelemiah son of Kore, of the **family** of Asaph.
26. 8 Obed Edom's **family** furnished a total of sixty-two highly
26. 9 Meshelemiah's **family** furnished eighteen qualified men.
26.11 thirteen members of Hosah's **family** who were temple guards.
26.12 divided into groups, according to **families,** and they were
26.13 Each **family,** regardless of size, drew lots to see which
26.21 was the ancestor of several **family** groups,
26.21 including the **family** of his son Jehiel.
26.26 and the members of his **family** were in charge of all the
26.26 King David, the heads of **families,** leaders of clan groups,
26.28 Shelomith and his **family** were in charge of everything
26.31 investigation was made of the **family** line of Hebron's descendants,
26.31 outstanding soldiers belonging to this **family** were found
26.32 seven hundred outstanding heads of **families** from Jeriah's
27. 1 of the Israelite heads of **families** and clan leaders and
28. 4 leadership, and out of Judah he chose my father's **family.**
28. 4 From all that **family** it was his pleasure to take me and
2 Chr 1. 2 officials, all the heads of **families,** and all the rest of
10.16 to them, they shouted, "Down with David and his **family!**
12.15 beginning to end and his **family** records are found in The
18. 1 between a member of his **family** and the family of King Ahab
22. 2 the example of King Ahab's **family,** since his mother
22. 4 other members of King Ahab's **family** became his advisers, and
22. 9 No member of Ahaziah's **family** was left who could rule the kingdom.
22.10 all the members of the royal **family** of Judah to be killed.
29.21 the sins of the royal **family** and of the people of Judah
31.19 the males in the priestly **families** and to everyone who was
35. 5 be available to help each **family** of the people of Israel.
35.12 people, by **family** groups, the animals for burnt-offerings,
Ezra 2. 1 Their **families** had been living in exile in Babylonia ever
Neh 5. 2 Some said, "We have large **families,** we need corn to keep
7. 5 leaders and officials and to check their **family** records.
7. 6 Their **families** had been living in exile in Babylonia ever
11. 1 drew lots to choose one **family** out of every ten to go
11.13 In all, 242 members of this clan were heads of **families.**
11.14 Their leader was Zabdiel, a member of a leading **family.**
12.22 the heads of the Levite **families** and
12.22 of the priestly **families** during the lifetimes of the following
12.23 The heads of the Levite **families,** however, were recorded
12.28 The Levite **families** of singers gathered from the area
Esth 4.14 you will die and your father's **family** will come to an end.
9.28 was resolved that every Jewish **family** of every future
Job 1.10 You have always protected him and his **family**
16. 7 you have let my **family** be killed.
20.26 fire not lit by human hands burns him and all his **family.**
Ps 38.11 even my **family** keeps away from me.
69. 8 a stranger to my brothers, like a foreigner to my **family.**
78.51 He killed the first-born sons of all the **families** of Egypt.
105.36 He killed the first-born sons of all the **families** of Egypt.
106.17 up and swallowed Dathan and buried Abiram and his **family;**
107.41 their misery and made their **families** increase like flocks.
112. 3 His **family** will be wealthy and rich, and he will be
Prov 11.29 brings trouble on his **family** will have nothing at the end.
12. 7 no descendants, but the **families** of righteous men live on.
14.26 Lord gives confidence and security to a man and his **family.**
15.27 a profit dishonestly, you will get your **family** into trouble.
27.27 you and your **family,** and for your servant-girls as well.
31.15 to prepare food for her **family** and to tell her servant-girls
31.21 doesn't worry when it snows, because her **family** has warm clothing.
31.27 She is always busy and looks after her **family's** needs.
Is 7.17 and on the whole royal **family,** days of trouble worse than
14.20 None of your evil **family** will survive.
22.23 and he will be a source of honour to his whole **family.**
60.22 Even your smallest and humblest **family** Will become as
Jer 12. 6 Even your brothers, members of your own **family,** have betrayed you;
20. 6 Pashhur, you and all your **family** will also be captured and
23.34 words 'the Lord's burden,' I will punish him and his **family.**
30.18 my people to their land and have mercy on every **family;**
33.24 I have rejected Israel and Judah, the two **families** that I chose?
37.12 Benjamin to take possession of my share of the **family** property.
38.17 Both you and your **family** will be spared.
41. 1 a member of the royal **family** and one of the king's chief
Ezek 17.13 took one of the king's **family,** made a treaty with him, and
24.21 the younger members of your **families** who are left in
46.16 will belong to that son as a part of his **family** property.
Dan 1. 3 young men of the royal **family**
1. 3 and of the noble **families.**
2.43 will try to unite their **families** by intermarriage, but they
Hos 5. 1 Listen, you that belong to the royal **family!**
Amos 6. 9 If there are ten men left in a **family,** they will die.
Mic 2. 2 No man's **family** or property is safe.
5. 2 for Israel, whose **family** line goes back to ancient times."
7. 6 a man's enemies are the members of his own **family.**
Hab 2. 9 You have made your **family** rich with what you took by violence,

Hab 2.10 But your schemes have brought shame on your **family;**
Zech 12.12 Each **family** in the land will mourn by itself:
12.12 family descended from David, the **family** descended from Nathan,
12.12 family descended from Levi, the **family** descended from Shimei,
12.12 family descended from Shimei, and all the other **families.**
12.12 Each **family** will mourn by itself,
12.12 men of each **family** will mourn separately from the women.
Mt 10.25 If the head of the **family** is called Beelzebul,
10.25 the members of the **family** will be called even worse names!
10.36 a man's worst enemies will be the members of his own **family.**
12.25 And any town or **family** that divides itself into groups which
13.57 everywhere except in his home town and by his own **family."**
Mk 3.21 When his **family** heard about it, they set out to take
3.25 If a **family** divides itself into groups which fight each other,
3.25 that **family** will fall apart.
5.19 "Go back home to your **family** and tell them how much the
6. 4 in his own home town and by his relatives and his **family."**
Lk 1. 5 she also belonged to a priestly **family.**
9.61 but first let me go and say good-bye to my **family."**
11.17 a **family** divided against itself falls apart.
12.52 From now on a **family** of five will be divided, three
Jn 4.53 So he and all his **family** believed.
8.35 does not belong to a **family** permanently, but a son belongs
Acts 4. 6 John, Alexander, and the others who belonged to the High Priest's **family.**
7. 3 said to him, 'Leave your **family** and country and go to the
7.13 and the king of Egypt came to know about Joseph's **family.**
7.14 him and the whole **family,** seventy-five people in all,
10. 2 he and his whole **family** worshipped God.
11.14 to you by which you and all your **family** will be saved.'
16.31 the Lord Jesus, and you will be saved—you and your **family."**
16.33 and he and all his **family** were baptized at once.
16.34 He and his **family** were filled with joy, because they now
18. 8 believed in the Lord, together with all his **family;**
Rom 16.10 Greetings to those who belong to the **family** of Aristobulus.
16.11 and to the Christian brothers in the **family** of Narcissus.
1 Cor 1.11 For some people from Chloe's **family** have told me quite plainly,
1.16 (Oh yes, I also baptized Stephanas and his **family;**
16.15 You know about Stephanas and his **family;**
Gal 6.10 especially to those who belong to our **family** in the faith.
Eph 2.19 with God's people and members of the **family** of God.
3.15 the Father, [15] from whom every **family** in heaven and on
1 Tim 3. 4 able to manage his own **family** well and make his children
3. 5 how to manage his own **family,** how can he take care of
3.12 wife, and be able to manage his children and **family** well.
5. 4 religious duties towards their own **family** and in this way
5. 8 the members of his own **family,** he has denied the faith and
5.16 woman has widows in her **family,** she must take care of them
2 Tim 1.16 Lord show mercy to the **family** of Onesiphorus, because he
4.19 to Priscilla and Aquila and to the **family** of Onesiphorus.
Tit 1.11 upsetting whole **families** by teaching what they should not,
Heb 11. 7 and built a boat in which he and his **family** were saved.
Rev 22.16 I am descended from the **family** of David;

FAMINE

Gen 12.10 But there was a **famine** in Canaan, and it was so bad
26. 1 There was another **famine** in the land besides the earlier
41.27 corn scorched by the desert wind are seven years of **famine.**
41.30 will be seven years of **famine,** and all the good years
41.30 will be forgotten, because the **famine** will ruin the country.
41.31 because the **famine** which follows will be so terrible.
41.36 during the seven years of **famine** which are going to come on
41.50 Before the years of **famine** came, Joseph had two sons by Asenath.
41.54 and the seven years of **famine** began, just as Joseph had said.
41.54 There was **famine** in every other country, but there was food
41.56 The **famine** grew worse and spread over the whole country,
41.57 corn from Joseph, because the **famine** was severe everywhere.
42. 5 to buy corn, because there was **famine** in the land of Canaan.
43. 1 The **famine** in Canaan got worse, [2] and when the family of
45. 6 This is only the second year of **famine** in the land;
45.11 There will still be five years of **famine;**
47. 4 the land of Canaan the **famine** is so severe that there is
47.13 The **famine** was so severe that there was no food anywhere,
47.20 forced to sell his land, because the **famine** was so severe;
Ruth 1. 1 before Israel had a king, there was a **famine** in the land.
2 Sam 21. 1 there was a severe **famine** which lasted for three full years.
24.13 Three years of **famine** in your land or three months of
1 Kgs 8.37 "When there is **famine** in the land or an epidemic, or
18. 2 The **famine** in Samaria was at its worst, [3] so Ahab called in
2 Kgs 4.38 Once, when there was a **famine** throughout the land,
7.12 They know about the **famine** here, so they have left their
8. 1 the Lord was sending a **famine** on the land, which would last
25. 3 that same year, when the **famine** was so bad that the people
1 Chr 21.12 Three years of **famine?**
2 Chr 6.28 "When there is **famine** in the land or an epidemic or
20. 9 war, an epidemic, or a **famine**—then they could come and stand
Job 5.20 when **famine** comes, he will keep you alive, and in war
Ps 33.19 he keeps them alive in times of **famine.**
37.19 they will have enough in time of **famine.**
105.16 The Lord sent **famine** to their country and took away all
Is 14.30 he will send a terrible **famine** on you Philistines, and it
Jer 5.12 we won't have war or **famine."**
21. 7 who survive the war, the **famine,** and the disease—I will let
52. 6 that same year, when the **famine** was so bad that the people
Ezek 6.11 They are going to die in war, by **famine,** and by disease.
12.16 them survive the war, the **famine,** and the diseases, so that
14.13 I will send a **famine** and kill people and animals alike.
14.21 worst punishments on Jerusalem—war, **famine,** wild animals,
36.29 to be plentiful, so that you will not have any more **famines.**
36.30 will be no more **famines** to disgrace you among the nations.
Amos 4. 6 was the one who brought **famine** to all your cities, yet you
8.11 "The time is coming when I will send **famine** on the land.
Mt 24. 7 There will be **famines** and earthquakes everywhere.
Mk 13. 8 There will be earthquakes everywhere, and there will be **famines.**
Lk 4.25 years and a severe **famine** spread throughout the whole land.
15.14 Then a severe **famine** spread over that country, and he was
21.11 There will be terrible earthquakes, **famines,** and plagues everywhere;
Acts 7.11 Then there was a **famine** all over Egypt and Canaan, which
11.28 Spirit predicted that a severe **famine** was about to come over
Rev 6. 8 to kill by means of war, **famine,** disease, and wild animals.
18. 8 will be struck with plagues— disease, grief, and **famine.**

FAMOUS
[FAME, WORLD-FAMOUS]

Gen 6. 4 They were the great heroes and **famous** men of long ago.
12. 2 you and make your name **famous,** so that you will be a
Ex 9.16 you live so that my **fame** might spread over the whole world.
Num 14.15 who have heard of your **fame** will say [16] that you killed
Josh 6.27 Lord was with Joshua, and his **fame** spread
Ruth 4.11 become rich in the clan of Ephrath and **famous** in Bethlehem.
4.14 May the boy become **famous** in Israel!
1 Sam 18.30 As a result David became very **famous.**
2 Sam 7. 9 I will make you as **famous** as the greatest leaders in the
7.23 you did for them have spread your **fame** throughout the world.
7.26 Your **fame** will be great, and people will for ever say,
8.13 David became even more **famous** when he returned from
14.25 no one in Israel as **famous** for his good looks as Absalom;
23. 8 These are the names of David's **famous** soldiers:
23. 9 The second of the **famous** three was Eleazar son of Dodo, of
23.11 The third of the **famous** three was Shammah son of Agee,
23.16 The three **famous** soldiers forced their way through
23.17 Those were the brave deeds of the three **famous** soldiers.
23.18 the leader of "The **Famous** Thirty."
23.18 and killed them, and became **famous** among "The Thirty."
23.19 He was the most **famous** of "The Thirty" and became
23.19 their leader, but he was not as **famous** as "The Three."
23.20 Benaiah son of Jehoiada, from Kabzeel, was another **famous** soldier;
23.23 among them, but was not as **famous** as "The Three."
23.24 There were thirty-seven **famous** soldiers in all.
1 Kgs 1.47 God make Solomon even more **famous** than you, and may
3. 4 sacrifices because that was where the most **famous** altar was.
4.31 his **fame** spread throughout all the neighbouring countries.
8.41 distant land hears of your **fame** and of the great things you
10. 1 of Sheba heard of Solomon's **fame,** and she travelled to
2 Kgs 14.10 Be satisfied with your **fame** and stay at home.
1 Chr 7. 2 of families of the clan of Tola and were **famous** soldiers.
7. 7 heads of families in the clan and were all **famous** soldiers.
7.11 heads of families in the clan and were all **famous** soldiers.
7.40 They were heads of families, **famous** fighting men,
11.10 This is the list of David's **famous** soldiers.
11.12 Next among the **famous** "Three" was Eleazar son of Dodo,
11.18 The three **famous** soldiers forced their way through
11.19 These were the brave deeds of the three **famous** soldiers.
11.20 Joab's brother Abishai was the leader of "The **Famous** Thirty."
11.20 and killed them, and became **famous** among "The Thirty."
11.21 He was the most **famous** of "The Thirty" and became
11.21 their leader, but he was not as **famous** as "The Three."
11.22 Benaiah son of Jehoiada from Kabzeel was a **famous** soldier;
11.25 among "The Thirty," but not as **famous** as "The Three."
12. 3 Ishmaiah from Gibeon, a **famous** soldier and one of the leaders
12. 8 are the names of the **famous,** experienced soldiers from the
12.23 20,800 men **famous** in their own clans;
14.17 David's **fame** spread everywhere, and the Lord made every
17. 8 I will make you as **famous** as the greatest leaders in the
17.21 you did for them spread your **fame** throughout the world.
17.24 Your **fame** will be great, and people will for ever say,
22. 5 son Solomon is to build must be splendid and **world-famous.**
2 Chr 1.11 for wealth or treasure or **fame** or the death of your enemies
1.12 you more wealth, treasure, and **fame** than any king has ever
9. 1 Sheba heard of King Solomon's **fame,** and she travelled to
18. 1 of Judah became rich and **famous,** he arranged a marriage
26. 8 he became so powerful that his **fame** spread even to Egypt.
26.15 His **fame** spread everywhere, and he became very powerful
Neh 9.10 You won then the **fame** you still have today.
Job 3.19 Everyone is there, the **famous** and the unknown, and
18.17 His **fame** is ended at home and abroad;
Ps 21. 5 you have given him **fame** and majesty.
45.17 My song will keep your **fame** alive for ever, and everyone
48.10 everywhere, and your **fame** extends over all the earth.
72.17 may his **fame** last as long as the sun.
89.19 faithful servants, "I have given help to a **famous** soldier;
136.18 he killed **famous** kings;
Is 61. 9 They will be **famous** among the nations;
63.12 the deep water, to win everlasting **fame** for himself?"
66.19 have not heard of my **fame** or seen my greatness and power:
Jer 48.17 you that live near by, all of you that know its **fame.**
49.25 The **famous** city that used to be happy is completely deserted.
Ezek 16.14 You became **famous** in every nation for your perfect beauty,
16.15 advantage of your beauty and **fame** to sleep with everyone who
26.17 The **famous** city is destroyed!
28.17 of being handsome, and your **fame** made you act like a fool.
Hos 14. 7 They will be as **famous** as the wine of Lebanon.
Zeph 3.20 I will make you **famous** throughout the world and make you
Acts 2.29 I must speak to you plainly about our **famous** ancestor King David.
7. 8 Jacob circumcised his twelve sons, the **famous** ancestors of our race.
Rom 9. 5 they are descended from the **famous** Hebrew ancestors;
9.17 show my power and to spread my **fame** over the whole world."

Heb 7. 4 Abraham, our **famous** ancestor, gave him a tenth of all he got
Rev 17. 1 will show you how the **famous** prostitute is to be punished,

FAN

Ezek 24.10 **Fan** the flames!

Am FANCY
see also **NEW**

FANCY

Ezek 23.14 sashes round their waists and **fancy** turbans on their heads.
Mt 11. 8 A man dressed up in **fancy** clothes?
Lk 7.25 A man dressed up in **fancy** clothes?
1 Tim 2. 9 not with **fancy** hair styles or with gold ornaments or pearls

FAR
[FURTHER]

Gen 12.10 so bad that Abram went **farther** south to Egypt, to live there
19.19 But the hills are too **far away;**
Ex 8.28 your God, in the desert, if you do not go very **far.**
Num 9.10 touching a corpse or are **far away** on a journey, but still
16. 3 Moses and Aaron and said to them, "You have gone too **far!**
16. 6 You Levites are the ones who have gone too **far!"**
24. 7 than Agag, And his rule shall be extended **far** and wide.
Deut 12.21 place of worship is too **far away,** then, whenever you wish,
13. 7 live near you or the gods of those who live **far away.**
14.24 place of worship is too **far** from your home for you to
20.15 with those cities that are **far away** from the land you will
30. 4 you are scattered to the **farthest** corners of the earth, the
Josh 3.16 stopped flowing and piled up, **far** upstream at Adam, the city
8. 4 other side of the city, but not too **far away** from it;
8.16 Joshua, they kept getting **farther away** from the city.
9.22 us that you were from **far away,** when you live right here?
15.21 The cities **farthest** south that belonged to them, those
Judg 18. 7 They lived **far away** from the Sidonians and had no dealings
19.12 on and go a little **farther** and spend the night at Gibeah
1 Kgs 8.46 that land is **far away,** [47] listen to your people's prayers.
2 Chr 6.36 that land is **far away,** [37] listen to your people's prayers.
Ezra 3.13 made was so loud that it could be heard **far** and wide.
Neh 12.43 and the noise they all made could be heard **far** and wide.
Esth 7. 9 said, "Haman even went so **far** as to build a gallows at
9.20 all the Jews, near and **far,** throughout the Persian Empire,
Job 6.29 You have gone **far** enough.
28. 4 **Far** from where anyone lives Or human feet ever travel, Men
38.11 I told it, "So **far** and no farther!
38.20 Can you show them how **far** to go, or send them back
39. 7 They keep **far away** from the noisy cities, and no one can
39.29 it watches near and **far** for something to kill and eat.
Ps 10. 1 Why are you so **far away,** O Lord?
35.22 don't keep yourself **far away!**
49.14 decay in the world of the dead **far** from their homes.
55. 7 I would fly **far away** and live in the wilderness.
61. 2 In despair and **far** from home I call to you!
71.12 Don't stay so **far away,** O God;
103.12 As **far** as the east is from the west,
103.12 so **far** does he remove our sins from
139. 2 from **far away** you understand all my thoughts.
139. 9 east or lived in the **farthest** place in the west, [10] you
Prov 10.14 they can, but when fools speak, trouble is not **far** off.
26.14 He gets no **farther** than a door swinging on its hinges.
27.10 by can help you more than a brother who is **far away.**
Is 6.12 I will send the people **far away** and make the whole land
7.18 come like flies from the **farthest** branches of the Nile, and
13. 5 They are coming from **far-off** countries at the ends of the earth.
33.13 Let everyone near and **far** hear what I have done and
41. 9 I called you from its **farthest** corners and said to you,
43. 5 the distant east and the **farthest** west, I will bring your
46.12 me, you stubborn people who think that victory is **far away.**
46.13 day of victory near— it is not **far away** at all.
49. 1 Listen to me, distant nations, you people who live **far away!**
49.12 My people will come from **far away,** from the north and
49.19 those who left you in ruins will be **far** removed from you.
57. 9 to worship, you send messengers **far** and wide, even to the
57.19 I offer peace to all, both near and **far!**
60. 4 Your sons will come from **far away;**
Jer 4.16 Jerusalem that enemies are coming from a country **far away.**
6.22 a mighty nation **far away** is preparing for war.
23.39 them up and throw them **far away** from me, both them and
25.19 the kings of the north, **far** and near, one after another.
25.32 a great storm is gathering at the **far** ends of the earth.
27.10 and will cause you to be taken **far away** from your country.
31. 3 Israel longed for rest, [3] I appeared to them from **far away.**
31.10 listen to me, and proclaim my words on the **far-off** shores.
48.24 Judgement has come on all the cities of Moab, **far** and near.
49.30 Hazor, I, the Lord, warn you to run **far away** and hide.
50.41 from a country in the north, a mighty nation **far away;**
51.50 Though you are **far** from home, think about me, your Lord, and
Ezek 6.12 Those **far away** will fall ill and die;
8. 6 driving me farther and **farther away** from my holy place.
11.15 They say, 'The exiles are too **far away** to worship the Lord.
11.16 sent them to live in **far-off** nations and scattered them in
22. 5 Countries near by and countries **far away** sneer at you
27.26 you out to sea, An east wind wrecked you **far** from land.
38.15 from your place in the **far** north, leading a large,
39. 2 lead him out of the **far** north until he comes to the
Dan 9. 7 countries near and **far** because they were unfaithful to you.
Joel 3. 6 people of Judah and Jerusalem **far** from their own country and
Joel 3. 8 they will sell them to the **far-off** Sabeans.
Mic 4. 3 among the nations, among the great powers near and **far.**
4. 7 They are crippled and **far** from home, but I will make a
7.12 of the Euphrates, from distant seas and **far-off** mountains.
Zech 6.15 Men who live **far away** will come and help to rebuild the
10. 9 the nations, yet in **far-off** places they will remember me.
Mt 8.30 Not **far away** there was a large herd of pigs feeding.
14.24 this time the boat was **far** out in the lake, tossed about
15. 8 their words, but their heart is really **far away** from me.
18.13 I tell you, he feels **far** happier over this one sheep than
24. 6 noise of battles close by and the news of battles **far away;**
24.21 at that time will be **far** more terrible than any there has
26.39 He went a little **farther** on, threw himself face
Mk 1.19 He went a little **farther** on and saw two other brothers,
7. 6 their words, but their heart is really **far away** from me.
12.34 he told him, "You are not **far** from the Kingdom of God."
13. 7 the noise of battles close by and news of battles **far away.**
13.19 of those days will be **far** worse than any the world has
14.35 He went a little **farther** on, threw himself on the ground,
Lk 5. 4 Simon, "Push the boat out **further** to the deep water, and
7. 6 He was not **far** from the house when the officer sent friends
15.13 He went to a country **far away,** where he wasted his money
16.23 up and saw Abraham, **far away,** with Lazarus at his side.
19.12 was going to a country **far away** to be made king, after
24.28 they were going, Jesus acted as if he were going **farther;**
Jn 3.23 was baptizing in Aenon, not **far** from Salim, because there
4. 5 named Sychar, which was not **far** from the field that Jacob
19.20 place where Jesus was crucified was not **far** from the city.
21. 8 They were not very **far** from land, about a hundred metres away.
Acts 2.39 and to all who are **far away**—all whom the Lord our
4.17 this matter from spreading any **further** among the people,
9.38 Joppa was not very **far** from Lydda, and when the
17.27 Yet God is actually not **far** from any one of us;
22.21 to me, 'for I will send you **far away** to the Gentiles.'"
27. 7 not let us go any **further** in that direction, so we sailed
27. 8 place called Safe Harbours, not **far** from the town of Lasea.
28. 7 Not **far** from that place were some fields that belonged to Publius,
Rom 3.23 everyone has sinned and is **far away** from God's saving presence.
1 Cor 5. 3 And even though I am **far away** from you in body, still
2 Cor 3.10 say that because of the **far** brighter glory now the glory
Eph 2.13 you who used to be **far away** have been brought near by
2.17 to you Gentiles, who were **far away** from God, and to the
Phil 1.23 this life and be with Christ, which is a **far** better thing;
4. 7 And God's peace, which is **far** beyond human understanding,
Col 1.21 At one time you were **far away** from God and were his
2 Tim 2.16 discussions, which only drive people **further away** from God.
3. 9 they will not get very **far,** because everyone will see how
Heb 1. 9 the joy of an honour **far** greater than he gave to your
11.26 for the Messiah was worth **far** more than all the treasures of
Rev 2. 5 Think how **far** you have fallen!

Am FARAWAY see DISTANT

FARE

Jon 1. 3 He paid his **fare** and went aboard with the crew to sail

FAREWELL

Gen 47.10 Jacob gave the king a **farewell** blessing and left.
49.28 said as he spoke a suitable word of **farewell** to each son.

FARM

Gen 4. 2 Abel became a shepherd, but Cain was a **farmer.**
4.11 are placed under a curse and can no longer **farm** the soil.
9.20 Noah, who was a **farmer,** was the first man to plant a
Num 18.27 of the offering which the **farmer** makes of new corn and new
18.30 the rest, just as the **farmer** keeps what is left after he
2 Sam 9.10 sons, and your servants will **farm** the land for your master
1 Chr 27.25 **Farm** labour:
2 Chr 26.10 Because he loved **farming,** he encouraged the people to plant
26.10 vineyards in the hill-country and to **farm** the fertile land.
31. 5 wine, olive-oil, honey, and other **farm** produce, and they
Neh 10.31 seventh year we will not **farm** the land, and we will cancel
10.37 who collect tithes in our **farming** villages, the tithes from
11.25 Many of the people lived in towns near their **farms.**
11.30 in Lachish and on the **farms** near by, and in Azekah and
12.44 responsible for collecting from the **farms** near the various
13.10 and gone back to their **farms,** because the people had not
Job 29.23 everyone welcomed them just as **farmers** welcome rain in spring.
31.38 have stolen the land I **farm** and taken it from its rightful
31.39 grew there but let the **farmers** that grew it starve— [40] then
Ps 50. 9 not need bulls from your **farms** or goats from your flocks;
Prov 12.11 A hard-working **farmer** has plenty to eat, but it is
13.23 for the poor, but unjust men keep them from being **farmed.**
20. 4 A **farmer** who is too lazy to plough his fields at the
28.19 A hard-working **farmer** has plenty to eat.
Song 8.11 There are **farmers** who rent it from him;
8.12 coins, and the **farmers** to two hundred as their share;
Is 7.21 time comes, even if a **farmer** has been able to save only
10.18 The rich forests and **farmlands** will be totally destroyed,
16. 8 The **farms** near Heshbon and the vineyards of Sibmah are
23.10 Go and **farm** the land, you people in the colonies in Spain!
28.24 No **farmer** goes on constantly ploughing his fields and
29.17 the dense forest will become **farmland,**
29.17 and the **farmland** will go back to forest.
61. 5 of your flocks And **farm** your land and tend your vineyards.
Jer 14. 4 and the ground is dried up, the **farmers** are sick at heart;
27.11 stay on in its own land, to **farm** it and live there.

Jer 31.24 and there will be **farmers,** and shepherds with their flocks.
35. 7 not to build houses or **farm** the land, and not to plant
Ezek 36.34 and wild they were, but I will let you **farm** them again.
48.18 is to be used as **farm** land by the people who live
48.19 no matter which tribe he comes from, may **farm** that land.
Joel 1.11 Grieve, you **farmers;**
Amos 5.16 Even **farmers** will be called to mourn the dead along with
Zech 13. 5 I am a farmer—I have **farmed** the land all my life.'
Mt 22. 5 one went to his **farm,** another to his shop, [6]while others
Mk 5.14 away and spread the news in the town and among the **farms.**
6.36 them go to the nearby **farms** and villages in order to buy
6.56 went, to villages, towns, or **farms,** people would take those
Lk 8.34 off and spread the news in the town and among the **farms.**
9.12 go to the villages and **farms** round here and find food and
15.15 sent him out to his **farm** to take care of the pigs.
22.31 the bad, as a **farmer** separates the wheat from the chaff.
1 Cor 9. 7 What **farmer** does not eat the grapes from his own vineyard?
2 Tim 2. 6 The **farmer** who has done the hard work should have the
Jas 5. 7 See how patient a **farmer** is as he waits for his land

FASHIONED

Is 42. 5 he **fashioned** the earth and all that lives there;

FAST (1)

Gen 33.14 will follow slowly, going as **fast** as I can with the
2 Sam 2.18 Asahel, who could run as **fast** as a wild deer, [19]started
2 Kgs 4.24 "Make the donkey go as **fast** as it can, and don't slow
9. 3 Then leave there as **fast** as you can."
Esth 8.10 by riders mounted on **fast** horses from the royal stables.
Job 7. 6 My days pass by without hope, pass **faster** than a weaver's shuttle.
9.26 like the swiftest boat, as **fast** as an eagle swooping down on
39.13 How **fast** the wings of an ostrich beat!
Prov 21.20 but stupid people spend their money as **fast** as they get it.
28.17 of murder is digging his own grave as **fast** as he can.
Ecc 9.11 thing, that in this world **fast** runners do not always win the
Is 8. 1 'Quick Loot, **Fast** Plunder.'
30.16 you plan to escape from your enemies by riding **fast** horses.
30.16 You think your horses are **fast** enough,
30.16 but those who pursue you will be **faster!**
41. 3 safely on, so **fast** that he hardly touches the ground!
Jer 4.13 are like a whirlwind, and his horses are **faster** than eagles.
46. 5 with fear, they run as **fast** as they can and do not
46. 6 Those who run **fast** cannot get away;
Dan 8. 5 of the west, moving so **fast** that his feet didn't touch the
Amos 2.14 Not even **fast** runners will escape;
2.15 will not stand their ground, **fast** runners will not get away,
9.13 "when corn will grow **faster** than it can be harvested,
9.13 and grapes will grow **faster** than the wine can be made.
Hab 1. 8 "Their horses are **faster** than leopards, fiercer than hungry wolves.
Zeph 1.14 great day of the Lord is near—very near and coming **fast!**
Jn 20. 4 but the other disciple ran **faster** than Peter and reached the

FAST (2)

To go without food for a while as a religious duty.

Lev 16.29 living among them must **fast** and must not do any work.
16.31 day, one on which they **fast** and do no work at all.
1 Sam 7. 6 out as an offering to the Lord and **fasted** that whole day.
31.13 the tamarisk-tree in the town, and **fasted** for seven days.
2 Sam 1.12 They grieved and mourned and **fasted** until evening for
12.22 "Yes," David answered, "I did **fast** and weep while he
12.23 But now that he is dead, why should I **fast?**
1 Kgs 21. 9 "Proclaim a day of **fasting,** call the people together, and
21.12 They proclaimed a day of **fasting,** called the people together,
1 Chr 10.12 They buried them there under an oak and **fasted** for seven days.
2 Chr 20. 3 orders for a **fast** to be observed throughout the country.
Ezra 8.21 orders for us all to **fast** and humble ourselves before our
8.23 So we **fasted** and prayed for God to protect us, and he
Neh 9. 1 people of Israel assembled to **fast** in order to show sorrow
Esth 4. 3 They **fasted,** wept and wailed, and most of them put on
4.16 hold a **fast** and pray for me.
5. 1 the third day of her **fast** Esther put on her royal robes
9.31 rules for the observance of **fasts** and times of mourning.
Ps 69.10 I humble myself by **fasting,** and people insult me;
Is 58. 3 The people ask, "Why should we **fast** if the Lord never notices?
58. 3 the same time as you **fast,** you pursue your own interests and
58. 4 Your **fasting** makes you violent, and you quarrel and fight.
58. 4 you think this kind of **fasting** will make me listen to your
58. 5 When you **fast,** you make yourselves suffer;
58. 5 Is that what you call **fasting?**
58. 6 "The kind of **fasting** I want is this:
Jer 14.12 Even if they **fast,** I will not listen to their cry for
36. 6 want you to go there the next time the people are **fasting.**
36. 9 king of Judah, the people **fasted** to gain the Lord's favour.
36. 9 The **fast** was kept by all who lived in Jerusalem and by
Dan 9. 3 **fasting,** wearing sackcloth, and sitting in ashes.
Joel 1.14 Give orders for a **fast;**
2.12 "repent sincerely and return to me with **fasting**
2.15 give orders for a **fast** and call an assembly!
Jon 3. 5 they decided that everyone should **fast,** and all the people,
Zech 7. 3 destruction of the Temple, by **fasting** in the fifth month as
7. 5 the priests that when they **fasted** and mourned in the fifth
8.19 "The **fasts** held in the fourth, fifth, seventh, and
Mt 6.16 "And when you **fast,** do not put on a sad face as
6.16 appearance so that everyone will see that they are **fasting.**
6.18 cannot know that you are **fasting**—only your Father, who is
9.14 Pharisees fast often, but your disciples don't **fast** at all?"
9.15 will be taken away from them, and then they will **fast.**
Mt 11.18 When John came, he **fasted** and drank no wine, and everyone said,
Mk 2.18 of John the Baptist and the Pharisees were **fasting.**
2.18 Baptist and the disciples of the Pharisees **fast,** but yours do not?"
2.20 will be taken away from them, and then they will **fast.**
Lk 2.36 day and night she worshipped God, **fasting** and praying.
5.33 Jesus, "The disciples of John **fast** frequently and offer prayers,
5.35 will be taken away from them, and then they will **fast."**
7.33 the Baptist came, and he **fasted** and drank no wine, and you
18.12 I **fast** two days a week, and I give you a tenth
Acts 13. 2 serving the Lord and **fasting,** the Holy Spirit said to them,
13. 3 They **fasted** and prayed, placed their hands on them, and
14.23 with prayers and **fasting** they commended them to the Lord,

FASTEN

Ex 28. 7 by which it can be **fastened,** are to be attached to the
28.24 corners of the breast-piece, [24]and **fasten** the two gold
28.25 **Fasten** the other two ends of the cords to the two settings,
39. 4 attached them to its sides, so that it could be **fastened.**
39.17 They **fastened** the two gold cords to the two rings
39.18 and **fastened** the other two ends of the
Lev 8. 7 the ephod on him and **fastened** it by putting its finely woven
Judg 3.16 He had it **fastened** on his right side under his clothes.
2 Sam 20. 8 for battle, with a sword in its sheath **fastened** to his belt.
1 Kgs 18.46 he **fastened** his clothes tight round his waist and ran ahead
Job 41.15 of rows of shields, **fastened** together and hard as stone.
41.17 They all are **fastened** so firmly together that nothing
Is 22.23 I will **fasten** him firmly in place like a peg, and he
22.25 the peg that was firmly **fastened** will work loose and fall.
41. 7 is good'— and they **fasten** the idol in place with nails.
Jer 10. 4 It is **fastened** down with nails to keep it from falling over.
Lk 8.29 prisoner, his hands and feet **fastened** with chains, he would
Acts 12. 8 Then the angel said, **"Fasten** your belt and put on your sandals."
16.24 into the inner cell and **fastened** their feet between heavy
27.17 it aboard and then **fastened** some ropes tight round the ship.
28. 3 out on account of the heat and **fastened** itself to his hand.

FAT (1)

Ex 23.18 The **fat** of animals sacrificed to me during these festivals
29.13 Next, take all the **fat** which covers the internal organs,
29.13 the two kidneys with the **fat** on them and burn them on
29.22 "Cut away the ram's **fat,** the fat tail,
29.22 the **fat** covering the internal organs,
29.22 the two kidneys with the **fat** on them, and the right thigh.
Lev 1. 8 the pieces of the animal, including the head and the **fat.**
1.12 on the fire all the parts, including the head and the **fat.**
3. 3 all the **fat** on the internal organs,
3. 4 the kidneys and the **fat** on them, and the best part
3. 9 the **fat,** the entire fat tail cut off near the backbone,
3. 9 all the **fat** covering the internal organs,
3.10 the kidneys and the **fat** on them, and the best part
3.14 all the **fat** on the internal organs,
3.15 the kidneys and the **fat** on them, and the best part
3.16 All the **fat** belongs to the Lord.
3.17 No Israelite may eat any **fat** or any blood;
4. 8 he shall take all the **fat,** the fat on the internal organs,
4. 9 the kidneys and the **fat** on them, and the best part
4.10 The priest shall take this **fat** and burn it on the altar
4.10 as he does with the **fat** from the animal killed for the
4.19 he shall take all its **fat** and burn it on the altar.
4.26 he shall burn all its **fat** on the altar,
4.26 just as he burns the **fat** of the animals killed for the
4.31 he shall remove all its **fat,**
4.31 just as the **fat** is removed from the animals killed
4.35 he shall remove all its **fat,**
4.35 just as the **fat** is removed from the sheep killed
6.12 on it, and burn the **fat** of the fellowship-offering.
7. 3 All its **fat** shall be removed and offered on the altar:
7. 3 the **fat** tail, the fat covering the internal organs,
7. 4 the kidneys and the **fat** on them, and the best part
7. 5 priest shall burn all the **fat** on the altar as a
7.23 No **fat** of cattle, sheep, or goats shall be eaten.
7.24 The **fat** of an animal that has died a natural death or
7.25 Anyone who eats the **fat** of an animal that may be offered
7.30 He shall bring the **fat** of the animal with its breast and
7.31 The priest shall burn the **fat** on the altar, but the
7.33 who offers the blood and the **fat** of the fellowship-offering.
8.16 Moses took all the **fat** on the internal organs, the best
8.16 and the kidneys with the **fat** on them, and burnt it all
8.20 and burnt the head, the **fat,** and all the rest of the
8.25 He took the **fat,** the fat tail,
8.25 all the **fat** covering the internal organs,
8.25 liver, the kidneys with the **fat** on them, and the right hind
8.26 put them on top of the **fat** and the right hind leg.
9.10 burnt on the altar the **fat,** the kidneys, and the best part
9.19 Aaron put the **fat** parts of the bull and the ram [20]on
9.20 He burnt the **fat** on the altar [21]and presented the breasts
9.24 consumed the burnt-offering and the **fat** parts on the altar.
10.15 breast at the time the **fat** is presented as a food-offering
16.25 on the altar the **fat** of the animal for the sin-offering.
17. 6 the Tent and burn the **fat** to produce a smell that is
Num 18.17 the altar and burn their **fat** as a food-offering, a smell
Deut 32.38 You fed them with the **fat** of your sacrifices and offered
Judg 3.22 sword went in, handle and all, and the **fat** covered it up.
1 Sam 2.15 In addition, even before the **fat** was taken off and burnt,
2.16 answered, "Let us do what is right and burn the **fat** first;
1 Kgs 8.64 and the **fat** of the animals for the fellowship-offerings.
2 Chr 7. 7 grain-offerings, and the **fat** from the fellowship-offerings.
29.35 were responsible for burning the **fat** that was offered from
35.14 animals that were burnt whole and the **fat** of the sacrifices.

Is 1.11 you burn as sacrifices and of the **fat** of your fine animals.
34. 6 covered with their blood and **fat,**
34. 6 like the blood and **fat** of lambs and goats that are
34. 7 and the earth will be red with blood and covered with **fat.**
43.24 incense for me or satisfy me with the **fat** of your animals.
Ezek 39.19 are to eat all the **fat** they can hold and to drink
44. 7 enter the Temple when the **fat** and the blood of the
44.15 to offer me the **fat** and the blood of the sacrifices.

FAT (2)

Gen 18. 7 calf that was tender and **fat,** and gave it to a servant,
27. 9 flock and pick out two **fat** young goats, so that I can
41. 2 River Nile, [2]when seven cows, **fat** and sleek, came up out of
41. 4 on the river-bank, [4]and the thin cows ate up the **fat** cows.
41.18 the Nile, [18]when seven cows, **fat** and sleek, came up out of
41.20 thin cows ate up the **fat** ones, [21]but no one would have
41.26 The seven **fat** cows are seven years, and the seven full
Deut 32.15 they were **fat** and stuffed with food.
Judg 3.17 he took the gifts to Eglon, who was a very **fat** man.
1 Sam 2.29 than me by letting them **fatten** themselves on the best parts
4.18 He was so old and **fat** that the fall broke his neck,
28.24 The woman quickly killed a calf which she had been **fattening.**
2 Sam 6.13 offered the Lord a sacrifice of a bull and a **fattened** calf.
1 Kgs 1. 9 of sheep, bulls, and **fattened** calves at Snake Rock,
1.19 bulls, sheep, and **fattened** calves, and he invited your sons,
1.25 a sacrifice of many bulls, sheep, and **fattened** calves.
Neh 9.25 They ate all they wanted and grew **fat;**
Jer 5.28 are powerful and rich, [28]why they are **fat** and well fed.
Ezek 34.16 but those that are **fat** and strong I will destroy, because I
39.18 will be killed like rams or lambs or goats or **fat** bulls.
Amos 4. 1 of Samaria, who grow **fat** like the well-fed cows of Bashan,
5.22 the animals you have **fattened** to bring me as offerings.
Zech 11.16 the meat of the **fattest** sheep and tears off their hoofs.
Jas 5. 5 You have made yourselves **fat** for the day of slaughter.

FATAL

Ex 10.17 Lord your God to take away this **fatal** punishment from me."
23.33 you worship their gods, it will be a **fatal** trap for you."
34.12 you are going, because this could be a **fatal** trap for you.
Deut 7.16 Do not worship their gods, for that would be **fatal.**
7.25 If you do, that will be **fatal,** because the Lord hates idolatry.
12.30 their religious practices, because that would be **fatal.**
2 Kgs 13.14 Elisha fell ill with a **fatal** disease, and as he lay dying
Job 34. 6 I am **fatally** wounded, but I am sinless."
Ps 41. 8 They say, "He is **fatally** ill;
Prov 6.15 them without warning, and they will be **fatally** wounded.
Is 10.18 in the same way that a **fatal** sickness destroys a man.
Jer 42.20 so I warn you now [20]that you are making a **fatal** mistake.
Rev 13. 3 to have been **fatally** wounded, but the wound had healed.

FATE

Esth 9.25 result that Haman suffered the **fate** he had planned for the
Job 6.21 streams to me, you see my **fate** and draw back in fear.
15.25 That is the **fate** of the man who shakes his fist at
18.20 all who hear of his **fate** shudder and tremble with fear.
18.21 That is the **fate** of evil men,
18.21 the **fate** of those who care nothing
20.29 This is the **fate** of wicked men,
20.29 the **fate** that God assigns to them.
30.23 me off to my death, to the **fate** in store for everyone.
Ps 26. 9 spare me from the **fate** of murderers— [10]men who do evil
49.13 who trust in themselves, the **fate** of those who are satisfied
Ecc 1.13 God has laid a miserable **fate** upon us.
2.14 I also know that the same **fate** is waiting for us all.
2.15 I thought to myself, "I will suffer the same **fate** as fools.
3.19 After all, the same **fate** awaits man and animal alike.
5.18 this is man's **fate.**
9. 2 The same **fate** comes to the righteous and the wicked, to the
9. 3 One **fate** comes to all alike, and this is as wrong as
Is 17.14 That is the **fate** of everyone who plunders our land.
19.17 they are reminded of the **fate** that the Lord Almighty has
24. 2 Everyone will meet the same **fate**—the priests and the people,
50.11 you will suffer a miserable **fate.**
53. 8 and led off to die, and no one cared about his **fate.**
53.12 He willingly gave his life and shared the **fate** of evil men.
65.11 hill, and worship Gad and Meni, the gods of luck and **fate.**
65.12 It will be your **fate** to die a violent death, because you
Jer 13.25 He has said that this will be your **fate.**
29.23 This will be their **fate** because they are guilty of
Lam 1. 9 was easily seen, but she showed no concern for her **fate.**
Ezek 23.10 Women everywhere gossiped about her **fate.**
26.16 be so terrified at your **fate** that they will not be able
27.35 "Everyone who lives along the coast is shocked at your **fate.**
27.36 are terrified, afraid that they will share your **fate."**
28.12 he said, "grieve for the **fate** that is waiting for the king
28.19 you are terrified, afraid that they will share your **fate."**
29.16 Egypt's **fate** will remind Israel how wrong it was to rely on
32.25 and disgraced, sharing the **fate** of those killed in battle.
35. 6 the living God—death is your **fate,** and you cannot escape it.
Mt 24.51 him in pieces and make him share the **fate** of the hypocrites.
Lk 12.46 in pieces and make him share the **fate** of the disobedient.
22.37 which says, 'He shared the **fate** of criminals,' must come
Acts 28. 4 must be a murderer, but **Fate** will not let him live, even

FATHER (1)

Gen 2.24 a man leaves his **father and mother** and is united with his
4.18 named Irad, who was the **father** of Mehujael, and Mehujael had
4.18 had a son named Methushael, who was the **father** of Lamech.
9.18 (Ham was the **father** of Canaan.)
9.22 Ham, the **father** of Canaan, saw that his father was naked,
9.23 the tent and covered their **father,** keeping their faces
10.24 Arpachshad was the **father** of Shelah,
10.24 who was the **father** of Eber.
11.26 70 years old, he became the **father** of Abram, Nahor, and
11.27 descendants of Terah, who was the **father** of Abram, Nahor,
11.27 Haran was the **father** of Lot, [28]and Haran died in his
11.28 native city, Ur in Babylonia, while his **father** was still living.
11.29 the daughter of Haran, who was also the **father** of Iscah.
12. 1 country, your relatives, and your **father's** home, and go to a
17.20 He will be the **father** of twelve princes, and I will make
19.31 said to her sister, "Our **father** is getting old, and there
19.32 Come on, let's make our **father** drunk, so that we can
19.34 Then each of us will have a child by our **father."**
19.36 both of Lot's daughters became pregnant by their own **father.**
20.12 is the daughter of my **father,** but not of my mother, and
20.13 God sent me from my **father's** house into foreign lands,
22. 7 As they walked along together, [7]Isaac said, **"Father!"**
22.21 Buz his brother, Kemuel the **father** of Aram, [22]Chesed,
22.23 and Bethuel, [23]Rebecca's **father.**
24. 7 from the home of my **father** and from the land of my
24.23 He said, "Please tell me who your **father** is.
24.24 "My **father** is Bethuel son of Nahor and Milcah," she
24.38 Instead, go to my **father's** people, to my relatives, and
24.40 my son a wife from my own people, from my **father's** family.
24.47 I asked her, 'Who is your **father?'**
24.47 And she answered, 'My **father** is Bethuel son of Nahor and Milcah.'
25. 3 Jokshan was the **father** of Sheba and Dedan, and the
26. 3 I will keep the promise I made to your **father** Abraham.
26.15 which the servants of his **father** Abraham had dug while
26.18 the wells the same names that his **father** had given them.
26.24 to him and said, "I am the God of your **father** Abraham.
27. 6 "I have just heard your **father** say to Esau, [7]'Bring me an
27. 9 them and make some of that food your **father** likes so much.
27.12 Perhaps my **father** will touch me and find out that I am
27.14 her, and she cooked the kind of food that his **father** liked.
27.18 Then Jacob went to his **father** and said, "Father!"
27.22 Jacob moved closer to his **father,** who felt him and said,
27.26 Then his **father** said to him, "Come closer and kiss me,
27.31 He also cooked some tasty food and took it to his **father.**
27.31 He said, "Please, **father,** sit up and eat some of the meat
27.34 bitterly and said, "Give me your blessing also, **father!"**
27.38 Esau continued to plead with his **father:**
27.38 "Have you only one blessing, **father?**
27.38 Bless me too, **father!"**
27.41 Esau hated Jacob, because his **father** had given Jacob the blessing.
27.41 He thought, "The time to mourn my **father's** death is near;
28. 3 so that you will become the **father** of many nations!
28. 7 Jacob had obeyed his **father and mother** and had gone to Mesopotamia.
28. 8 Esau then understood that his **father** Isaac did not approve
28.21 I return safely to my **father's** home, then you will be my
29.12 He told her, "I am your **father's** relative, the son of Rebecca."
29.12 She ran to tell her **father;**
31. 1 "Jacob has taken everything that belonged to our **father.**
31. 1 All his wealth has come from what our **father** owned."
31. 3 "Go back to the land of your **fathers** and to your relatives.
31. 5 "I have noticed that your **father** is not as friendly towards
31. 5 but my **father's** God has been with me.
31. 6 that I have worked for your **father** with all my strength.
31. 9 taken flocks away from your **father** and given them to me.
31.14 "There is nothing left for us to inherit from our **father.**
31.16 God has taken from our **father** belongs to us and to our
31.17 ready to go back to his **father** in the land of Canaan.
31.19 Rachel stole the household gods that belonged to her **father.**
31.29 night the God of your **father** warned me not to threaten you
31.35 Rachel said to her **father,** "Do not be angry with me,
31.42 If the God of my **fathers,** the God of Abraham and Isaac,
31.53 of the God whom his **father** Isaac worshipped, Jacob solemnly
32. 9 of my grandfather Abraham and God of my **father** Isaac, hear
33.19 from the descendants of Hamor **father** of Shechem for a
34. 4 He said to his **father,** "I want you to get this girl
34. 6 Shechem's **father** Hamor went out to talk with Jacob, [7]just
34.11 Shechem said to Dinah's **father** and brothers, "Do me this favour,
34.13 Jacob's sons answered Shechem and his **father** Hamor in
35.18 named her son Benoni, but his **father** named him Benjamin.
35.22 sexual intercourse with Bilhah, one of his **father's** concubines;
35.27 Jacob went to his **father** Isaac at Mamre, near Hebron,
36.24 wilderness when he was taking care of his **father's** donkeys.)
36.25 Anah was the **father** of Dishon, who was the
37. 1 land of Canaan, where his **father** had lived, [2]and this is
37. 2 the sons of Bilhah and Zilpah, his **father's** concubines.
37. 2 reports to his **father** about what his brothers were doing.
37. 4 his brothers saw that their **father** loved Joseph more than he
37.10 told the dream to his **father,** and his father scolded him:
37.11 him, but his **father** kept thinking about the whole matter.
37.12 take care of their **father's** flock, [13]Jacob said to Joseph,
37.14 His **father** said, "Go and see if your brothers are safe
37.14 So his **father** sent him on his way from the Valley of
37.22 to save him from them and send him back to his **father.**
37.32 They took the robe to their **father** and said, "We found this.
38. 2 There Judah met a Canaanite girl whose **father** was named Shua.
38.11 daughter-in-law Tamar, "Return to your **father's** house and
41.51 me forget all my sufferings and all my **father's** family";
42.13 One brother is dead, and the youngest is now with our **father."**
42.29 When they came to their **father** Jacob in Canaan, they
42.32 We were twelve brothers in all, sons of the same **father.**
42.32 dead, and the youngest is still in Canaan with our **father.'**
42.35 they saw the money, they and their **father** Jacob were afraid.

Gen 42.36 Their **father** said to them, "Do you want to make me lose
42.37 Reuben said to his **father,** "If I do not bring Benjamin
43. 7 about us and our family, 'Is your **father** still living?
43. 8 Judah said to his **father,** "Send the boy with me, and we
43.11 Their **father** said to them, "If that is how it has to
43.23 God, the God of your **father,** must have put the money in
43.27 then said, "You told me about your old **father**—how is he?
43.28 "Your humble servant, our **father,** is still alive and well."
44.17 rest of you may go back safe and sound to your **father."**
44.19 Sir, you asked us, 'Have you got a **father** or another brother?'
44.20 We answered, 'We have a **father** who is old and a younger
44.20 his **father** loves him very much.'
44.22 and we answered that the boy could not leave his **father;**
44.22 if he did, his **father** would die.
44.24 we went back to our **father,** we told him what you had
44.27 Our **father** said to us, 'You know that my wife Rachel
44.30 I go back to my **father** without the boy, as soon as
44.32 is more, I pledged my life to my **father** for the boy.
44.34 I go back to my **father** if the boy is not with
44.34 I cannot bear to see this disaster come upon my **father."**
45. 3 Is my **father** still alive?"
45. 9 "Now hurry back to my **father** and tell him that this is
45.13 Tell my **father** how powerful I am here in Egypt and tell
45.18 Let them get their **father** and their families and come back here.
45.19 and small children and to bring their **father** with them.
45.23 He sent his **father** ten donkeys loaded with the best
45.25 Egypt and went back home to their **father** Jacob in Canaan.
46. 1 where he offered sacrifices to the God of his **father** Isaac.
46. 3 "I am God, the God of your **father,"** he said.
46.29 got in his chariot and went to Goshen to meet his **father.**
46.29 threw his arms round his **father's** neck and cried for a long
46.31 and the rest of his **father's** family, "I must go and tell
46.31 and all my **father's** family, who were living in Canaan,
47. 1 He said, "My **father** and my brothers have come from Canaan
47. 5 "Now that your **father** and your brothers have arrived,
47. 7 Then Joseph brought his **father** Jacob and presented him to the king.
47.11 Then Joseph settled his **father** and his brothers in Egypt,
47.12 Joseph provided food for his **father,** his brothers, and
47.12 rest of his **father's** family, including the very youngest.
47.30 I want to be buried where my **fathers** are;
48. 1 Some time later Joseph was told that his **father** was ill.
48.15 "May the God whom my **fathers** Abraham and Isaac served bless
48.16 and the name of my **fathers** Abraham and Isaac live on through
48.17 when he saw that his **father** had put his right hand on
48.17 so he took his **father's** hand to move it from Ephraim's head
48.18 He said to his **father,** "Not that way, father.
48.19 His **father** refused, saying, "I know, my son, I know.
49. 2 Listen to your **father** Israel.
49. 4 For you slept with my concubine And dishonoured your **father's** bed.
49.25 It is your **father's** God who helps you, The Almighty God
49.28 and this is what their **father** said as he spoke a suitable
49.29 death, bury me with my **fathers** in the cave that is in
50. 1 Joseph threw himself on his **father,** crying and kissing his face.
50. 2 Then Joseph gave orders to embalm his **father's** body.
50. 5 'When my **father** was about to die, he made me promise him
50. 5 me go and bury my **father,** and then I will come back.' "
50. 6 "Go and bury your **father,** as you promised you would."
50. 7 So Joseph went to bury his **father.**
50. 8 and the rest of his **father's** family all went with him.
50.14 After Joseph had buried his **father,** he returned to Egypt
50.15 After the death of their **father,** Joseph's brothers said,
50.16 "Before our **father** died, [17] he told us to ask you, 'Please
50.17 the wrong that we, the servants of your **father's** God, have
50.22 Joseph continued to live in Egypt with his **father's** family;

Ex 2.15 and fill the troughs for their **father's** sheep and goats.
2.18 When they returned to their **father,** he asked, "Why have
6.20 Amram married his **father's** sister Jochebed,
15. 2 I will praise him, my **father's** God, and I will sing about
18. 4 said, "The God of my **father** helped me and saved me from
20.12 "Respect your **father and your mother,** so that you may
21. 8 like her, then she is to be sold back to her **father;**
21.15 "Whoever hits his **father or his mother** is to be put to
21.17 "Whoever curses his **father or his mother** is to be put
22.17 But if her **father** refuses to let him marry her,
22.17 he must pay the **father** a sum of money equal to
22.24 Your wives will become widows, and your children will be **fatherless.**
40.15 just as you anointed their **father,** so that they can serve me

Lev 16.32 and consecrated to succeed his **father,** is to perform the
18. 7 Do not disgrace your **father** by having intercourse with your mother.
18. 8 Do not disgrace your **father** by having intercourse with any
18.12 whether she is your **father's** sister or your mother's sister.
19. 3 his mother and his **father,** and must keep the Sabbath,
20. 9 Anyone who curses his **father or his mother** shall be put to
20.11 with one of his **father's** wives disgraces his father,
21. 2 unless it is his mother, **father,** son, daughter, brother,
21. 9 If a priest's daughter becomes a prostitute, she disgraces her **father;**
21.11 a dead person, even if it is his own **father or mother.**
22.13 returned to live in her **father's** house as a dependant may
22.13 dependant may eat the food her **father** receives as a priest.
24.10 There was a man whose **father** was an Egyptian and

Num 6. 6 a corpse, not even that of his **father,** mother, brother, or
12.14 The Lord answered, "If her **father** had spat in her face,
14.12 I will make you the **father** of a nation that is larger
25.15 Zur, her **father,** was chief of a group of Midianite clans.
26.28 who was the **father** of two sons, Manasseh and Ephraim.
26.29 son of Manasseh was the **father** of Gilead, and the following
26.58 Kohath was the **father** of Amram, [59] who was married to
27. 3 Lord's presence and said, [3] "Our **father** died in the
27. 4 no sons, why should our **father's** name disappear from Israel?
27. 4 Give us property among our **father's** relatives."
27. 7 give them property among their **father's** relatives.
27.10 If he has no brothers, his **father's** brothers are to inherit it.
30. 3 woman still living in her **father's** house makes a vow to give
30. 4 vowed or promised unless her **father** raises an objection when
30. 5 But if her **father** forbids her to fulfil the vow when he
30. 5 forgive her, because her **father** refused to let her keep it.
30.16 woman living in her **father's** house or by a married woman.
32. 8 That is what your **fathers** did when I sent them from Kadesh
32.14 now you have taken your **fathers'** place, a new generation of
36.12 and their property remained in their **father's** tribe.

Deut 1.31 way to this place, just as a **father** would carry his son.'
5. 3 covenant, [3] not only with our **fathers,** but with all of us
5.16 " 'Respect your **father and your mother,** as I, the Lord your God,
8. 5 punishes you just as a **father** disciplines his children.
9.14 I will make you the **father** of a nation larger and more
22.16 The girl's **father** will say to them, 'I gave my daughter
22.19 the money to the girl's **father,** because the man has brought
22.21 to the entrance of her **father's** house, where the men of her
22.21 married, while she was still living in her **father's** house.
22.29 is to pay the girl's **father** the bride price of fifty pieces
22.30 man is to disgrace his **father**
22.30 by having intercourse with any of his **father's** wives.
27.16 " 'God's curse on anyone who dishonours his **father or mother.'**
27.20 on anyone who disgraces his **father**
27.20 by having intercourse with any of his **father's** wives.'
32. 7 ask your **fathers** to tell you what happened, ask the old

Josh 2.13 you will save my **father and mother,** my brothers and sisters,
2.18 Get your **father and mother,** your brothers,
2.18 and all your **father's** family together in your house.
6.23 out, along with her **father and mother,** her brothers, and the
15.13 He received Hebron, the city belonging to Arba, **father** of Anak.
15.18 wedding day Othniel urged her to ask her **father** for a field.
17. 1 Machir, the **father** of Gilead, was Manasseh's eldest son and
21.11 of Arba (Arba was Anak's **father),** now called Hebron, in the
24. 2 One of those ancestors was Terah, the **father** of Abraham and Nahor.
24.17 Lord our God brought our **fathers** and us out of slavery in
24.32 the sons of Hamor, the **father** of Shechem, for a hundred

Judg 1.14 wedding day Othniel urged her to ask her **father** for a field.
2.17 Their **fathers** had obeyed the Lord's commands, but this new
6.13 the wonderful things that our **fathers** told us the Lord used
6.25 Lord told Gideon, "Take your **father's** bull and another bull
6.25 tear down your **father's** altar to Baal, and cut down
8.32 in the tomb of his **father** Joash, at Ophrah, the town of
9. 5 He went to his **father's** house at Ophrah, and there on the
9.17 Remember that my **father** fought for you.
9.18 But today you turned against my **father's** family.
9.56 against his **father** in killing his seventy brothers.
11. 1 His **father** Gilead [2] had other sons by his wife, and when
11. 2 They said to him, "You will not inherit anything from our **father;**
11. 7 me so much that you forced me to leave my **father's** house.
11.37 But she asked her **father,** "Do this one thing for me.
11.39 After two months she came back to her **father.**
14. 2 and said to his **father and mother,** "There is a Philistine
14. 3 But his **father and mother** asked him, "Why do you have to
14. 3 But Samson said to his **father,** "She is the one I want
14. 5 So Samson went down to Timnah with his **father and mother.**
14. 9 Then he went to his **father and mother** and gave them some.
14.10 His **father** went to the girl's house, and Samson gave a
14.15 we'll set fire to your **father's** house and burn you with it.
14.16 He said, "Look, I haven't even told my **father and mother.**
15. 1 He said to her **father,** "I want to go to my wife's
15. 6 burnt the woman to death and burnt down her **father's** house.
16.31 between Zorah and Eshtaol in the tomb of his **father** Manoah.
19. 2 him, went back to her **father's** house in Bethlehem, and
19. 3 the house, and when her **father** saw him, he gave him a
19. 4 The **father** insisted that he stay, and so he stayed for
19. 5 But the girl's **father** said to the Levite, "Have something
19. 6 Then the girl's **father** said to him, "Please spend the night
19. 7 up to go, but the **father** urged him to stay, so he
19. 8 to leave, but the girl's **father** said, "Eat something,
19. 9 to leave, the **father** said, "Look, it's almost evening now;
21.22 If their **fathers** or brothers come to you and protest,

Ruth 2.11 how you left your **father and mother** and your own country and
4.17 Obed became the **father** of Jesse, who was the father of David.

1 Sam 2.25 would not listen to their **father,** for the Lord had decided
8. 3 But they did not follow their **father's** example;
9. 5 go back home, or my **father** might stop thinking about the
9.20 It is you—you and your **father's** family."
10. 2 been found, so that your **father** isn't worried any more about
10.12 "How about these other prophets—who do you think their **fathers** are?"
14. 1 Jonathan did not tell his **father** Saul, [2] who was camping
14.27 Jonathan had not heard his **father** threaten the people with a curse;
14.28 weak with hunger, but your **father** threatened us and said, 'A
14.29 "What a terrible thing my **father** has done to our people!
14.51 Saul's **father** Kish and Abner's father Ner were sons of Abiel.
17.15 Bethlehem from time to time, to take care of his **father's** sheep.
17.25 and will not require his **father's** family to pay taxes."
17.34 "Your Majesty," David said, "I take care of my **father's** sheep.
19. 2 so he said to him, "My **father** is trying to kill you.
19. 3 go and stand by my **father** in the field where you are
20. 1 have I done to your **father** to make him want to kill
20. 2 My **father** tells me everything he does, important or not, and
20. 3 But David answered, "Your **father** knows very well how
20. 6 If your **father** notices that I am not at table, tell him

1 Sam 20. 8 Why take me to your **father** to be killed?"
20. 9 knew for certain that my **father** was determined to harm you,
20.10 "Who will let me know if your **father** answers you angrily?"
20.12 tomorrow and on the following day I will question my **father.**
20.13 May the Lord be with you as he was with my **father!**
20.33 realized that his **father** was really determined to kill David.
22. 3 Moab, "Please let my **father and mother** come and stay with
23.17 My **father** Saul won't be able to harm you.
24.11 Look, my **father,** look at the piece of your robe I am
2 Sam 3. 8 cause of your **father** Saul, his brothers, and his friends,
6.21 chose me instead of your **father** and his family to make me
7.14 does wrong, I will punish him as a **father** punishes his son.
9. 7 will be kind to you for the sake of your **father** Jonathan.
10. 2 loyal friendship to Hanun, as his **father** Nahash did to me."
10. 3 that it is in your **father's** honour that David has sent these
13. 5 When your **father** comes to see you, say to him, 'Please ask
15.34 will now serve him as faithfully as you served his **father.**
16.19 As I served your **father,** so now I will serve you."
16.21 and have intercourse with your **father's** concubines whom he
16.21 Israel will know that your **father** regards you as his enemy,
16.22 Absalom went in and had intercourse with his **father's** concubines.
17. 8 You know that your **father** David and his men are hard
17. 8 Your **father** is an experienced soldier and does not stay with
17.10 in Israel knows that your **father** is a great soldier and that
19.28 All my **father's** family deserved to be put to death by
21.14 in the grave of Saul's **father** Kish, in Zela in the territory
1 Kgs 2.12 Solomon succeeded his **father** David as king, and his
2.24 Lord has firmly established me on the throne of my **father** David;
2.26 while you were with my **father** David, and you shared in all
2.32 which he committed without my **father** David's knowledge.
2.44 very well all the wrong that you did to my **father** David.
3. 3 followed the instructions of his **father** David, but he also
3. 6 showed great love for my **father** David, your servant, and he
3. 7 have let me succeed my **father** as king, even though I am
3.14 laws and commands, as your **father** David did, I will give you
5. 1 that Solomon had succeeded his **father** David as king he sent
5. 3 of the constant wars my **father** David had to fight against
5. 5 The Lord promised my **father** David, 'Your son, whom I will
6.12 I will do for you what I promised your **father** David.
7.14 His **father,** who was no longer living, was from Tyre, and
7.51 all the things that his **father** David had dedicated to the
8.15 promise he made to my **father** David, when he said, [16]'From
8.17 And Solomon continued, "My **father** David planned to
8.20 I have succeeded my **father** as king of Israel, and I have
8.24 You have kept the promise you made to my **father** David;
8.25 promise you made to my **father** when you told him that there
8.26 everything come true that you promised to my **father** David,
9. 4 honesty and integrity, as your **father** David did, and if you
9. 5 promise I made to your **father** David when I told him that
11. 4 faithful to the Lord his God, as his **father** David had been.
11. 6 and was not true to him as his **father** David had been.
11.12 for the sake of your **father** David I will not do this
11.17 Hadad and some of his **father's** Edomite servants,
11.33 has not kept my laws and commands as his **father** David did.
12. 4 and said to him, [4]"Your **father** Solomon treated us harshly
12. 6 older men who had served as his **father** Solomon's advisers.
12.10 'My little finger is thicker than my **father's** waist!'
12.11 Tell them, 'My **father** placed heavy burdens on you;
12.14 He said, "My **father** placed heavy burdens on you;
15. 3 the same sins as his **father** and was not completely loyal to
15.15 Temple all the objects his **father** had dedicated to God, as
15.19 "Let us be allies, as our **fathers** were.
15.26 Like his **father** before him, he sinned against the Lord
18.18 "You are—you and your **father.**
19.20 "Let me kiss my **father and mother** good-bye, and then I will
20.34 to you the towns my **father** took from your father,
20.34 in Damascus, just as my **father** did in Samaria."
22.43 Like his **father** Asa before him, he did what was right in
22.46 altars who were still left from the days of his **father** Asa.
22.52 the wicked example of his **father** Ahab, his mother Jezebel,
22.53 served Baal, and like his **father** before him, he aroused the
2 Kgs 2.12 Elisha saw it and cried out to Elijah, "My father, my **father!**
3. 2 he was not as bad as his **father** or his mother Jezebel;
3. 2 pulled down the image his **father** had made for the worship of
3.13 "Go and consult those prophets that your **father and mother** consulted."
4.18 one morning to join his **father,** who was in the field with
4.19 Suddenly he cried out to his **father,** "My head hurts!
4.19 "Carry the boy to his mother," the **father** said to a servant.
9.25 riding together behind King Joram's **father** Ahab, the Lord
13.14 "My **father,** my father!"
13.25 Benhadad during the reign of Jehoahaz, the **father** of Jehoash.
14. 3 instead, he did what his **father** Joash had done.
14. 5 power, he executed the officials who had killed his **father,**
14.22 reconquered and rebuilt Elath after his **father's** death.
15. 3 Following the example of his **father,** he did what was
15.34 Following the example of his **father** Uzziah, Jotham did
21. 3 places of worship that his **father** Hezekiah had destroyed;
21.20 Like his **father** Manasseh, he sinned against the Lord;
21.21 he imitated his **father's** actions,
21.21 and he worshipped the idols that his **father** had worshipped.
24. 9 Following the example of his **father,** Jehoiachin sinned
1 Chr 2.24 his son Caleb married Ephrath, his **father's** widow.
3.10 This is the line of King Solomon's descendants from **father** to son:
5. 1 intercourse with one of his **father's** concubines, he lost the
17.13 I will be his **father** and he will be my son.
19. 2 loyal friendship to Hanun, as his **father** Nahash did to me."
19. 3 that it is in your **father's** honour that David has sent these
22.10 He will be my son, and I will be his **father.**
23.13 His eldest son, Amram, was the **father** of Aaron and Moses.
24. 2 Abihu died before their **father** did, and left no descendants,
1 Chr 25. 3 Under the direction of their **father** they proclaimed God's message,
25. 6 their **father's** direction, to accompany the temple worship.
26.10 Shimri (his **father** made him the leader, even though he was
28. 4 leadership, and out of Judah he chose my **father's** family.
28. 6 chosen him to be my son, and I will be his **father.**
28. 9 charge you to acknowledge your **father's** God and to serve him
29.23 So Solomon succeeded his **father** David on the throne
2 Chr 1. 8 showed great love for my **father** David, and now you have let
1. 9 O Lord God, fulfil the promise you made to my **father.**
2. 3 as you did with my **father,** King David, when you sold him
2. 7 of Judah and Jerusalem whom my **father** David selected.
2.14 the tribe of Dan and his **father** was a native of Tyre.
2.14 your craftsmen and with those who worked for your **father,**
2.17 of Israel, similar to the census his **father** David had taken.
3. 1 King David, Solomon's **father,** had already prepared a place
5. 1 all the things that his **father** David had dedicated to the
6. 4 promise he made to my **father** David when he said to him,
6. 7 And Solomon continued, "My **father** David planned to build
6.10 I have succeeded my **father** as king of Israel, and I have
6.15 You have kept the promise you made to my **father** David;
6.16 promise you made to my **father** when you told him that there
7.17 serve me faithfully as your **father** David did, obeying my
7.18 promise I made to your **father** David when I told him that
8.14 rules laid down by his **father** David, he organized the daily
10. 4 "Your **father** placed heavy burdens on us.
10. 6 older men who had served as his **father** Solomon's advisers.
10.10 'My little finger is thicker than my **father's** waist.'
10.11 Tell them, 'My **father** placed heavy burdens on you;
10.14 He said, "My **father** placed heavy burdens on you;
11.18 Rehoboam married Mahalath, whose **father** was Jerimoth
11.21 and he **fathered** twenty-eight sons and sixty daughters.
13.21 He had fourteen wives and **fathered** twenty-two sons
15.18 Temple all the objects his **father** Abijah had dedicated to God,
16. 3 "Let us be allies, as our **fathers** were.
17. 1 Jehoshaphat succeeded his **father** Asa as king and
17. 3 followed the example of his **father's** early life and did not
17. 4 He served his **father's** God, obeyed God's commands, and did
20.32 Like his **father** Asa before him, he did what was right in
21. 3 Their **father** gave them large amounts of gold, silver, and
21.12 follow the example of your **father,** King Jehoshaphat, or that
22. 1 of Jerusalem made Ahaziah king as his **father's** successor.
22. 4 the Lord, because after his **father's** death other members of
24.22 service that Zechariah's **father** Jehoiada had given him,
25. 3 he executed the officials who had murdered his **father.**
26. 1 Uzziah to succeed his **father** as king.
26. 4 Following the example of his **father,** he did what was
27. 2 what was pleasing to the Lord, just as his **father** had done;
27. 2 but unlike his **father** he did not sin by burning incense in
29. 9 Our **fathers** were killed in battle, and our wives and
33. 3 places of worship that his **father** Hezekiah had destroyed.
33.22 Like his **father** Manasseh, he sinned against the Lord,
33.22 and he worshipped the idols that his **father** had worshipped.
33.23 But unlike his **father,** he did not become humble and turn
33.23 he was even more sinful than his **father** had been.
Esth 4.14 you will die and your **father's** family will come to an end.
Job 8. 8 consider the truths our **fathers** learnt.
10.10 You gave my **father** strength to beget me;
15.10 wisdom from grey-haired men— men born before your **father.**
15.18 learnt from their **fathers,** and they kept no secrets hidden.
17.14 will call the grave my **father,** and the worms that eat me
21.19 You claim God punishes a child for the sins of his **father.**
24. 9 Evil men make slaves of **fatherless** infants and take the
29.16 I was like a **father** to the poor and took the side
30. 1 Their **fathers** have always been so worthless that I wouldn't
38.28 Does either the rain or the dew have a **father?**
42.13 He was the **father** of seven sons and three daughters.
42.15 Their **father** gave them a share of the inheritance along with
Ps 27.10 My **father and mother** may abandon me, but the Lord will
78. 3 things we have heard and known, things that our **fathers** told us.
78.57 disloyal like their **fathers,** unreliable as a crooked arrow.
103.13 As a **father** is kind to his children, so the Lord is
Prov 1. 8 Pay attention to what your **father and mother** tell you, my
3.12 those he loves, as a **father** corrects a son of whom he
4. 1 Listen to what your **father** teaches you, my sons.
4. 4 boy, my parents' only son, [4]my **father** would teach me.
6.20 Do what your **father** tells you, my son, and never forget
10. 1 A wise son makes his **father** proud of him;
13. 1 son pays attention when his **father** corrects him, but an
15. 5 It is foolish to ignore what your **father** taught you;
15.20 A wise son makes his **father** happy.
17. 6 grandchildren, just as boys are proud of their **fathers.**
17.21 and sorrow for a **father** whose son does foolish things.
17.25 grief to his **father** and bitter regrets to his mother.
19.13 A stupid son can bring his **father** to ruin.
19.26 disgraceful person would ill-treat his **father** or turn his
20. 7 fortunate if they have a **father** who is honest and does what
23.22 Listen to your **father;**
23.24 A righteous man's **father** has good reason to be happy.
23.25 Make your **father and mother** proud of you;
27.10 Do not forget your friends or your **father's** friends.
28. 7 makes friends with good-for-nothings is a disgrace to his **father.**
29. 3 If you appreciate wisdom, your **father** will be proud of you.
30.11 are people who curse their **fathers** and do not show their
30.17 who makes fun of his **father** or despises his mother in her
Is 9. 6 "Wonderful Counsellor," "Mighty God," "Eternal **Father,"**
22.21 He will be like a **father** to the people of Jerusalem and
38.19 **Fathers** tell their children how faithful you are.
49.23 Kings will be like **fathers** to you;
Jer 2.27 that a tree is your **father** and that a rock is your
6.21 **Fathers** and sons will die, and so will friends and neighbours."

Jer	9.14	the idols of Baal as their **fathers** taught them to do.
	16. 7	not even for someone who has lost his **father or mother.**
	20.15	the man who made my **father** glad when he brought him the
	22.11	son Joahaz, who succeeded his **father** as king of Judah, "He
	22.15	Your **father** enjoyed a full life.
	23.27	me, just as their **fathers** forgot me and turned to Baal.
	47. 3	**Fathers** will not turn back for their children;
Lam	5. 3	Our **fathers** have been killed by the enemy, and now our
Ezek	16. 3	Your **father** was an Amorite, and your mother was a Hittite.
	16.45	sister cities had a Hittite mother and an Amorite **father.**
	18.11	who does any of these things [11] that the **father** never did.
	18.14	sees all the sins his **father** practised, but does not follow
	18.17	because of his **father's** sins, but he will certainly live.
	18.18	His **father,** on the other hand, cheated and robbed, and
	18.19	'Why shouldn't the son suffer because of his **father's** sins?'
	18.20	his father's sins, nor a **father** because of the sins of his
	20. 4	Remind them of the disgusting things their **fathers** did.
	20.27	This is another way their **fathers** insulted me
	20.30	commit the same sins your **fathers** did and go running after
	20.36	just as I condemned your **fathers** in the Sinai Desert," says
	22.10	Some of them sleep with their **father's** wife.
Dan	5. 2	cups and bowls which his **father** Nebuchadnezzar had carried
	5.11	When your **father** was king, this man showed good sense,
	5.11	And King Nebuchadnezzar, your **father,** made him chief
	5.13	Jewish exile whom my **father** the king brought here from Judah?
	5.18	"The Supreme God made your **father** Nebuchadnezzar a
Joel	1. 2	ever happened in your time or the time of your **fathers?**
Amos	2. 7	A man and his **father** have intercourse with the same slave-girl,
Mic	7. 6	their **fathers** like fools, daughters oppose their mothers,
Zech	13. 3	on prophesying, his own **father and mother** will tell him that
	13. 3	his own **father and mother** will stab him to death.
Mal	1. 6	"A son honours his **father,** and a servant honours his master.
	3.17	merciful to them, as a **father** is merciful to the son who
	4. 6	He will bring **fathers** and children together again;
Mt	2.22	that Archelaus had succeeded his **father** Herod as king of Judaea,
	4.21	boat with their **father** Zebedee, getting their nets ready.
	4.22	they left the boat and their **father,** and went with him.
	7. 9	any of you who are **fathers** give your son a stone when
	8.21	said, "Sir, first let me go back and bury my **father."**
	10.21	be put to death, and **fathers** will do the same to their
	10.35	set sons against their **fathers,** daughters against their mothers,
	10.37	"Whoever loves his **father or mother** more than me is not
	15. 4	God said, 'Respect your **father and your mother,'**
	15. 4	and 'Whoever curses his **father** or his mother is to be
	15. 5	use to help his **father or mother,** but says, 'This belongs to
	15. 6	'This belongs to God,' [6]he does not need to honour his **father.**
	19. 5	will leave his **father and mother** and unite with his wife,
	19.19	respect your **father and your mother;**
	19.29	brothers or sisters or **father or mother** or children or fields
	21.30	Then the **father** went to the other son and said the same
	21.31	Which one of the two did what his **father** wanted?"
	23. 9	call anyone here on earth **'Father',**
Mk	1.20	they left their **father** Zebedee in the boat with the hired
	5.40	out, took the child's **father and mother** and his three disciples,
	7.10	Moses commanded, 'Respect your **father and your mother,'**
	7.10	and, 'Whoever curses his **father** or his mother is to be
	7.11	use to help his **father or mother,** but says, 'This is Corban'
	7.12	he is excused from helping his **father or mother.**
	9.21	Jesus asked the **father.**
	9.24	The **father** at once cried out, "I do have faith, but not
	10. 7	will leave his **father and mother** and unite with his wife,
	10.19	respect your **father and your mother.' "**
	10.29	or sisters or mother or **father** or children or fields for me
	11.10	God bless the coming kingdom of King David, our **father!**
	13.12	be put to death, and **fathers** will do the same to their
	15.21	(Simon was from Cyrene and was the **father** of Alexander and Rufus.)
Lk	1.17	He will bring **fathers** and children together again;
	1.59	and they were going to name him Zechariah, after his **father.**
	1.62	they made signs to his **father,** asking him what name he would
	1.67	John's **father** Zechariah was filled with the Holy Spirit,
	2.33	child's **father and mother** were amazed at the things Simeon said
	2.48	Your **father** and I have been terribly worried trying to find you."
	8.51	except Peter, John, and James, and the child's **father and mother.**
	9.42	spirit, healed the boy, and gave him back to his **father.**
	9.59	man said, "Sir, first let me go back and bury my **father."**
	11.11	any of you who are **fathers** give your son a snake
	12.13	brother to divide with me the property our **father** left us."
	12.53	**Fathers** will be against their sons,
	12.53	and sons against their **fathers;**
	14.26	more than he loves his **father** and his mother, his wife and
	15.12	younger one said to him, **'Father,** give me my share of the
	15.17	and said, 'All my **father's** hired workers have more than they
	15.18	to my father and say, **Father,** I have sinned against God and
	15.20	So he got up and started back to his **father.**
	15.20	was still a long way from home when his **father** saw him;
	15.21	**'Father,'** the son said, 'I have sinned against God and against you.
	15.22	But the **father** called his servants.
	15.27	the servant answered, 'and your **father** has killed the prize calf,
	15.28	so his **father** came out and begged him to come in.
	15.29	But he answered his **father,** 'Look, all these years I
	15.31	'My son,' the **father** answered, 'you are always here with me,
	16.24	So he called out, **'Father** Abraham!
	16.27	said, 'Then I beg you, **father** Abraham,
	16.27	send Lazarus to my **father's** house, [28] where I have five brothers.
	16.30	The rich man answered, 'That is not enough, **father** Abraham!
	18.20	respect your **father and your mother.' "**
Jn	1.13	that is, by being born as the children of a human **father;**
	4.53	Then the **father** remembered that it was at that very hour
	6.42	We know his **father and mother.**
	8.19	"Where is your **father?"**
	8.38	has shown me, but you do what your **father** has told you."
	8.39	They answered him, "Our **father** is Abraham."
	8.41	You are doing what your **father** did."
	8.44	are the children of your **father,** the Devil,
	8.44	and you want to follow your **father's** desires.
	8.44	because he is a liar and the **father** of all lies.
	8.53	Our **father** Abraham died;
	8.56	Your **father** Abraham rejoiced that he was to see the time
Acts	7. 2	Stephen answered, "Brothers and **fathers,** listen to me!
	7. 4	After Abraham's **father** died, God made him move to this land
	7.14	sent a message to his **father** Jacob, telling him and the
	7.45	received the tent from their **fathers** carried it with them
	16. 1	also a Christian, was Jewish, but his **father** was a Greek.
	16. 3	Jews who lived in those places knew that Timothy's **father** was Greek.
	28. 8	Publius' **father** was in bed, sick with fever and dysentery.
Rom	4. 1	What shall we say, then, of Abraham, the **father** of our race?
	4.11	so Abraham is the spiritual **father** of all who believe in God
	4.12	He is also the **father** of those who are circumcised, that
	4.12	that our **father** Abraham lived before he was circumcised.
	4.16	For Abraham is the spiritual **father** of us all;
	4.17	as the scripture says, "I have made you **father** of many nations."
	4.18	for hoping, and so became "the **father** of many nations."
	9.10	For Rebecca's two sons had the same **father,** our ancestor Isaac.
1 Cor	4.15	guardians in your Christian life, you have only one **father.**
	4.15	I have become your **father** by bringing the Good News
Gal	4. 1	son who will receive his **father's** property is treated just like
	4. 2	him and manage his affairs until the time set by his **father.**
	4.30	have a part of the **father's** property along with the son
Eph	5.31	will leave his **father and mother** and unite with his wife,
	6. 2	"Respect your **father and mother"** is the first commandment that
Phil	2.22	like a son and his **father,** have worked together for the sake
1 Thes	2.11	each one of you just as a **father** treats his own children.
1 Tim	1. 9	for those who kill their **fathers** or mothers, for murderers,
	5. 1	older man, but appeal to him as if he were your **father.**
Phlm	10	for while in prison I have become his spiritual **father.**
Heb	7. 3	no record of Melchizedek's **father or mother** or of any of his
	11.11	Abraham able to become a **father,** even though he was too old
	12. 7	Endure what you suffer as being a **father's** punishment;
	12. 7	Was there ever a son who was not punished by his **father?**
	12. 9	the case of our human **fathers,** they punished us and we
	12.10	Our human **fathers** punished us for a short time,
	12.17	Afterwards, you know, he wanted to receive his **father's** blessing;
2 Pet	3. 4	Our **fathers** have already died, but everything is still the same
1 Jn	2.13	I am writing to you, **fathers,** because you know him
	2.14	I am writing to you, **fathers,** because you know him
	5. 1	and whoever loves a **father** loves his child also.

FATHER (2) (GOD)

[MY FATHER, OUR FATHER]

Deut	32. 6	He is your **father,** your Creator, he made you into a nation.
2 Sam	7.14	I will be his **father,** and he will be my son.
Ps	2. 7	today I have become your **father.**
	89.26	He will say to me, 'You are my **father** and my God;
Is	63.16	You are our **father.**
	63.16	but you, Lord, are our **father,** the one who has always
	64. 8	But you are our **father,** Lord.
Jer	3. 4	to me, 'You are my **father,** and you have loved me ever
	3.19	wanted you to call me **father,** and never again turn away from
	31. 9	I am like a **father** to Israel, and Ephraim is my eldest
Mal	1. 6	I am your **father**—why don't you honour me?
	2.10	Don't we all have the same **father?**
Mt	5.16	the good things you do and praise your **Father** in heaven.
	5.45	so that you may become the sons of your **Father** in heaven.
	5.48	You must be perfect—just as your **Father** in heaven is perfect!
	6. 1	you will not have any reward from your **Father** in heaven.
	6. 4	And your **Father,** who sees what you do in private, will
	6. 6	room, close the door, and pray to your **Father,** who is
	6. 6	And your **Father,** who sees what you do in private, will
	6. 8	Your **Father** already knows what you need before you ask him.
	6. 9	**'Our Father** in heaven:
	6.14	done to you, your **Father** in heaven will also forgive you.
	6.15	not forgive others, then your **Father** will not forgive the
	6.18	that you are fasting—only your **Father,** who is unseen, will
	6.18	And your **Father,** who sees what you do in private, will
	6.26	yet your **Father** in heaven takes care of them!
	6.32	Your **Father** in heaven knows that you need all these things.
	7.11	much more, then, will your **Father** in heaven give good things
	7.21	only those who do what **my Father** in heaven wants them to
	10.20	come from the Spirit of your **Father** speaking through you.
	10.29	not one sparrow falls to the ground without your **Father's** consent.
	10.32	I will do the same for him before **my Father** in heaven.
	10.33	me publicly, I will reject him before **my Father** in heaven.
	11.25	At that time Jesus said, **"Father,** Lord of heaven and earth!
	11.26	Yes, **Father,** this was how you wanted it to happen.
	11.27	**"My Father** has given me all things.
	11.27	knows the Son except the **Father,**
	11.27	and no one knows the **Father** except the Son and those to
	12.50	Whoever does what **my Father** in heaven wants him to do is
	13.43	God's people will shine like the sun in their **Father's** Kingdom.
	15.13	"Every plant which **my Father** in heaven did not plant
	16.17	but it was given to you directly by **my Father** in heaven.
	16.27	in the glory of his **Father** with his angels,
	18.10	tell you, are always in the presence of **my Father** in heaven.
	18.14	just the same way your **Father** in heaven does not want any
	18.19	for, it will be done for you by **my Father** in heaven.
	18.35	Jesus concluded, "That is how **my Father** in heaven will treat
	20.23	These places belong to those for whom **my Father** has prepared them."
	23. 9	because you have only the one **Father** in heaven.

Mt 24.36 the **Father** alone knows.
25.34 on his right, 'Come, you that are blessed by **my Father!**
26.29 day I drink the new wine with you in **my Father's** Kingdom."
26.39 on the ground, and prayed, **"My Father,** if it is possible,
26.42 Jesus went away and prayed, **"My Father,** if this cup of
26.53 that I could call on **my Father** for help, and at once
28.19 in the name of the **Father,** the Son, and the Holy Spirit,
Mk 8.38 he comes in the glory of his **Father** with the holy angels."
11.25 against anyone, so that your **Father** in heaven will forgive
13.32 only the **Father** knows.
14.36 "Father," he prayed, **"my Father!**
Lk 2.49 Didn't you know that I had to be in **my Father's** house?"
6.36 Be merciful just as your **Father** is merciful.
9.26 and in the glory of the **Father** and of the holy angels.
10.21 Holy Spirit and said, **"Father,** Lord of heaven and earth!
10.21 Yes, **Father,** this was how you wanted it to happen.
10.22 **"My Father** has given me all things.
10.22 No one knows who the Son is except the **Father,** and
10.22 no one knows who the **Father** is except the Son and those
11. 2 **'Father:** May your holy name be honoured;
11.13 much more, then, will the **Father** in heaven give the Holy
12.30 Your **Father** knows that you need these things.
12.32 afraid, little flock, for your **Father** is pleased to give you
22.29 and just as **my Father** has given me the right to rule,
22.42 **"Father,"** he said, "if you will, take this cup of
23.34 Jesus said, "Forgive them, **Father!**
23.46 Jesus cried out in a loud voice, **"Father!**
24.49 And I myself will send upon you what **my Father** has promised.
Jn 1.13 God himself was their **Father.**
1.14 the glory which he received as the **Father's** only Son.
1.18 and is at the **Father's** side, he has made him known.
2.16 Stop making **my Father's** house a market-place!"
3.35 The **Father** loves his Son and has put everything in his power.
4.21 people will not worship the **Father** either on this mountain
4.23 people will worship the **Father** as he really is, offering him
5.17 Jesus answered them, **"My Father** is always working, and I too
5.18 that God was his own **Father** and in this way had made
5.19 he does only what he sees his **Father** doing.
5.19 What the **Father** does, the Son also does.
5.20 For the **Father** loves the Son and shows him all that he
5.21 Just as the **Father** raises the dead and gives them life,
5.22 Nor does the **Father** himself judge anyone.
5.23 honour the Son in the same way as they honour the **Father.**
5.23 not honour the Son does not honour the **Father** who sent him.
5.26 Just as the **Father** is himself the source of life,
5.36 that is, the deeds **my Father** gave me to do, these
5.36 speak on my behalf and show that the **Father** has sent me.
5.37 And the **Father,** who sent me, also testifies on my behalf.
5.43 I have come with **my Father's** authority, but you have not
5.45 that I am the one who will accuse you to **my Father.**
6.27 give you, because God, the **Father,** has put his mark of
6.32 it is **my Father** who gives you the real bread from heaven.
6.37 Everyone whom **my Father** gives me will come to me.
6.40 For what **my Father** wants is that all who see the Son
6.44 come to me unless the **Father** who sent me draws him to
6.45 Anyone who hears the **Father** and learns from him comes to me.
6.46 This does not mean that anyone has seen the **Father;**
6.46 is from God is the only one who has seen the **Father.**
6.57 The living **Father** sent me, and because of him I live also.
6.65 come to me unless the **Father** makes it possible for him to
8.16 the **Father** who sent me is with me.
8.18 my own behalf, and the **Father** who sent me also testifies on
8.19 "You know neither me nor **my Father,"** Jesus answered.
8.19 "If you knew me, you would know **my Father** also."
8.27 understand that Jesus was talking to them about the **Father.**
8.28 but I say only what the **Father** has instructed me to say.
8.38 I talk about what **my Father** has shown me, but you do
8.41 "God himself is the only **Father** we have," they answered,
8.42 "If God really were your **Father,** you would love me,
8.49 "I honour **my Father,** but you dishonour me.
8.54 one who honours me is **my Father**—the very one you say
10.14 As the **Father** knows me and I know the Father,
10.17 "The **Father** loves me because I am willing to give up my
10.18 This is what **my Father** has commanded me to do."
10.25 The things I do by **my Father's** authority speak on my behalf;
10.29 What **my Father** has given me is greater than everything,
10.29 and no one can snatch them away from the **Father's** care.
10.30 The **Father** and I are one."
10.32 good deeds in your presence which the **Father** gave me to do;
10.36 As for me, the **Father** chose me and sent me
10.37 I am not doing the things **my Father** wants me to do.
10.38 the Father is in me and that I am in the **Father."**
11.41 and said, "I thank you, **Father,** that you listen to me.
12.26 And **my Father** will honour anyone who serves me.
12.27 Shall I say, **'Father,** do not let this hour come upon me'?
12.28 **Father,** bring glory to your name!"
12.49 my own authority, but the **Father** who sent me has commanded
12.50 I say, then, is what the **Father** has told me to say."
13. 1 come for him to leave this world and go to the **Father.**
13. 3 Jesus knew that the **Father** had given him complete power;
14. 2 There are many rooms in **my Father's** house, and I am going
14. 6 no one goes to the **Father** except by me.
14. 7 to them, "you will know **my Father** also, and from now on
14. 8 Philip said to him, "Lord, show us the **Father;**
14. 9 Whoever has seen me has seen the **Father.**
14. 9 Why, then, do you say, 'Show us the **Father'?**
14.10 that I am in the **Father** and the Father is in me?
14.10 The **Father,** who remains in me, does his own work.
14.11 that I am in the **Father** and the Father is in me.
14.12 do even greater things, because I am going to the **Father.**
14.13 my name, so that the **Father's** glory will be shown through
Jn 14.16 I will ask the **Father,** and he will give you another Helper,
14.20 know that I am in **my Father** and that you are in
14.21 **My Father** will love whoever loves me;
14.23 **My Father** will love him, and my Father and I will come
14.24 heard is not mine, but comes from the **Father,** who sent me.
14.26 the Holy Spirit, whom the **Father** will send in my name,
14.28 you would be glad that I am going to the **Father;**
14.31 but the world must know that I love the **Father;**
15. 1 "I am the real vine, and **my Father** is the gardener.
15. 8 **My Father's** glory is shown by your bearing much fruit;
15. 9 I love you just as the **Father** loves me;
15.10 just as I have obeyed **my Father's** commands and remain in his
15.15 I have told you everything I have heard from **my Father.**
15.16 And so the **Father** will give you whatever you ask of him
15.23 Whoever hates me hates **my Father** also.
15.24 seen what I did, and they hate both me and **my Father.**
15.26 reveals the truth about God and who comes from the **Father.**
15.26 him to you from the **Father,** and he will speak about me.
16. 3 to you because they have not known either the **Father** or me.
16.10 I am going to the **Father** and you will not see me
16.15 All that **my Father** has is mine;
16.17 he also says, 'It is because I am going to the **Father.'**
16.23 the **Father** will give you whatever you ask him for in my
16.25 of speech, but will speak to you plainly about the **Father.**
16.27 him on your behalf, [27] for the **Father** himself loves you.
16.28 I did come from the **Father,** and I came into the world;
16.28 and now I am leaving the world and going to the **Father."**
16.32 But I am not really alone, because the **Father** is with me.
17. 1 looked up to heaven and said, **"Father,** the hour has come.
17. 5 **Father!** Give me glory
17.11 Holy **Father!** Keep them safe
17.21 **Father!** May they be in us,
17.24 **"Father!** You have given them to me,
17.25 Righteous **Father!** The world does not know you,
18. 9 **"Father,** I have not lost even one of those you gave me.")
18.11 drink the cup of suffering which **my Father** has given me?"
20.17 her, "because I have not yet gone back up to the **Father.**
20.17 who is my Father and their **Father,** my God and their God."
20.21 As the **Father** sent me, so I send you."
Acts 1. 4 for the gift I told you about, the gift **my Father** promised.
1. 7 and occasions are set by **my Father's** own authority, and it
2.33 right-hand side of God, his **Father,** and has received from
13.32 today I have become your **Father.'**
Rom 1. 7 May God **our Father** and the Lord Jesus Christ give you grace
6. 4 the glorious power of the **Father,** so also we might live a
8.15 and by the Spirit's power we cry out to God, **"Father!**
8.15 **my Father!"**
15. 6 with one voice the God and **Father** of our Lord Jesus Christ.
1 Cor 1. 3 May God **our Father** and the Lord Jesus Christ give you
8. 6 us only one God, the **Father,** who is the Creator of all
15.24 powers, and will hand over the Kingdom to God the **Father.**
2 Cor 1. 2 May God **our Father** and the Lord Jesus Christ give you
1. 3 thanks to the God and **Father** of our Lord Jesus Christ, the
1. 3 Lord Jesus Christ, the merciful **Father,** the God from whom
6.18 I will be your **father,** and you shall be my sons and
11.31 The God and **Father** of the Lord Jesus—blessed be his name
Gal 1. 1 Jesus Christ and God the **Father,** who raised him from death.
1. 3 May God **our Father** and the Lord Jesus Christ give you
1. 4 our sins, in obedience to the will of our God and **Father.**
4. 6 into our hearts, the Spirit who cries out, "Father, **my Father."**
Eph 1. 2 May God **our Father** and the Lord Jesus Christ give you
1. 3 give thanks to the God and **Father** of our Lord Jesus Christ!
1.17 the glorious **Father,** to give you the Spirit, who
2.18 to come in the one Spirit into the presence of the **Father.**
3.14 my knees before the **Father,** [15] from whom every family in heaven
4. 6 there is one God and **Father** of all mankind, who is Lord
5.20 always give thanks for everything to God the **Father.**
6.23 May God the **Father** and the Lord Jesus Christ give to all
Phil 1. 2 May God **our Father** and the Lord Jesus Christ give you
2.11 that Jesus Christ is Lord, to the glory of God the **Father.**
4.20 To our God and **Father** be the glory for ever and ever!
Col 1. 2 May God **our Father** give you grace and peace.
1. 3 give thanks to God, the **Father** of our Lord Jesus Christ,
1.11 joy give thanks to the **Father,** who has made you fit to
3.17 Lord Jesus, as you give thanks through him to God the **Father.**
1 Thes 1. 1 Thessalonica, who belong to God the **Father** and the Lord Jesus Christ:
1. 3 remember before our God and **Father** how you put your faith
3.11 May our God and **Father** himself and our Lord Jesus
3.13 presence of our God and **Father** when our Lord Jesus comes
2 Thes 1. 1 who belong to God **our Father** and the Lord Jesus Christ:
1. 2 May God **our Father** and the Lord Jesus Christ give you
2.16 Jesus Christ himself and God **our Father,** who loved us and in
1 Tim 1. 2 May God the **Father** and Christ Jesus our Lord give you grace,
2 Tim 1. 2 May God the **Father** and Christ Jesus our Lord give you grace,
Tit 1. 4 May God the **Father** and Christ Jesus our Saviour give you
Phlm 3 May God **our Father** and the Lord Jesus Christ give you
Heb 1. 5 today I have become your **Father."**
1. 5 angel, "I will be his **Father,** and he will be my Son."
2.11 he and those who are made pure all have the same **Father.**
5. 5 today I have become your **Father."**
12. 9 then, should we submit to our spiritual **Father** and live!
Jas 1.27 What God the **Father** considers to be pure and genuine
3. 9 to our Lord and **Father** and also to curse our fellow-man,
1 Pet 1. 2 the purpose of God the **Father** and were made a holy people
1. 3 give thanks to the God and **Father** of our Lord Jesus Christ!
1.17 You call him **Father,** when you pray to God, who judges
2 Pet 1.17 and glory by God the **Father,** when the voice came to him
1 Jn 1. 2 life which was with the **Father** and was made known to us.
1. 3 that we have with the **Father** and with his Son Jesus Christ.
2. 1 someone who pleads with the **Father** on our behalf—Jesus Christ,

1 Jn	2.14	I am writing to you, my children, because you know the **Father.**
	2.15	If you love the world, you do not love the **Father.**
	2.16	people are so proud of—none of this comes from the **Father;**
	2.22	the Enemy of Christ—he rejects both the **Father** and the Son.
	2.23	For whoever rejects the Son also rejects the **Father;**
	2.23	whoever accepts the Son has the **Father** also.
	2.24	you will always live in union with the Son and the **Father.**
	3. 1	See how much the **Father** has loved us!
	3. 9	and because God is his **Father,** he cannot continue to sin.
	4.14	and tell others that the **Father** sent his Son
2 Jn	3	May God the **Father** and Jesus Christ, the Father's Son,
	4	children live in the truth, just as the **Father** commanded us.
	9	does stay with the teaching has both the **Father** and the Son.
Jude	1	love of God the **Father** and the protection of Jesus Christ:
Rev	1. 6	made us a kingdom of priests to serve his God and **Father.**
	2.26	I will give the same authority that I received from **my Father:**
	3. 5	In the presence of **my Father** and of his angels I will
	3.21	been victorious and now sit by **my Father** on his throne.
	14. 1	have his name and his **Father's** name written on their foreheads.

FATHER-IN-LAW

Gen	38.13	Someone told Tamar that her **father-in-law** was going to
	38.25	As she was being taken out, she sent word to her **father-in-law:**
Ex	3. 1	and goats of his **father-in-law** Jethro, the priest of Midian,
	4.18	went back to Jethro, his **father-in-law,** and said to him,
	18. 1	Moses' **father-in-law** Jethro, the priest of Midian, heard
Judg	1.16	The descendants of Moses' **father-in-law,** the Kenite,
	15. 6	had done it because his **father-in-law,** a man from Timnah,
1 Sam	4.19	and that her **father-in-law** and her husband were dead,
	4.21	Covenant Box and the death of her **father-in-law** and her husband.
Ezra	2.61	and had taken the name of his **father-in-law's** clan.)
Neh	6.18	because of his Jewish **father-in-law,** Shecaniah son of Arah.
	7.63	and taken the name of his **father-in-law's** clan.)
Jn	18.13	was the **father-in-law** of Caiaphas, who was High Priest that year.

FATHERLESS see FATHER (1), ORPHAN

FATTEN see FAT (2)

FAULT

Gen	6. 9	Noah had no **faults** and was the only good man of his
	16. 5	Sarai said to Abram, "It's your **fault** that Hagar despises me.
	31.39	take it to you to show that it was not my **fault.**
Ex	5.16	It is your people that are at **fault."**
Josh	2.19	death will be his own **fault,** and we will not be responsible;
1 Sam	29. 3	done nothing I can find **fault** with since the day he came
	29. 6	I have not found any **fault** in you from the day you
	29. 8	say, you haven't found any **fault** in me since the day I
2 Sam	3. 8	yet today you find **fault** with me about a woman!
	22.24	He knows that I am **faultless,** that I have kept myself
Job	4.18	he finds **fault** even with his angels.
	6.24	tell me my **faults.**
	10. 6	track down all my sins and hunt down every **fault** I have?
	34.32	God to show you your **faults,** and have you agreed to stop
Ps	18.23	He knows that I am **faultless,** that I have kept myself
	19.12	deliver me, Lord, from hidden **faults!**
	50.20	to accuse your own brothers and to find **fault** with them.
	51. 3	I recognize my **faults;**
	59. 4	done, [4] nor because of any **fault** of mine, O Lord, that they
	65. 3	Our **faults** defeat us, but you forgive them.
	101. 2	My conduct will be **faultless.**
	119. 1	are those whose lives are **faultless,** who live according to
Ezek	33. 5	His death is his own **fault,** because he paid no attention
Jon	1.12	I know it is my **fault** that you are caught in this
Mal	1. 9	He will not answer your prayer, and it will be your **fault.**
Mt	18.15	brother sins against you, go to him and show him his **fault.**
Rom	9.19	me, "If this is so, how can God find **fault** with anyone?
1 Cor	1. 8	so that you will be **faultless** on the Day of our Lord
2 Cor	6. 3	not want anyone to find **fault** with our work, so we try
	7.11	You have shown yourselves to be without **fault** in the whole matter.
Eph	1. 4	Christ, so that we would be holy and without **fault** before him.
	5.27	all its beauty—pure and **faultless,** without spot or wrinkle
Phil	3. 6	by obeying the commands of the Law, I was without **fault.**
Col	1.22	to bring you, holy, pure, and **faultless,** into his presence.
1 Thes	2.10	towards you who believe was pure, right, and without **fault.**
	5.23	and body—free from every **fault** at the coming of our Lord
1 Tim	3. 2	A church leader must be without **fault;**
	5. 7	instructions, so that no one will find **fault** with them.
2 Tim	3.16	correcting **faults,** and giving instruction for right living,
Heb	7.26	he has no **fault** or sin in him;
	8. 8	But God finds **fault** with his people when he says, "The
2 Pet	3.14	best to be pure and **faultless** in God's sight and to be
Jude	24	falling, and to bring you **faultless** and joyful before his
Rev	14. 5	they are **faultless.**

FAVOUR

Gen	19.19	You have done me a great **favour** and saved my life.
	30. 6	Rachel said, "God has judged in my **favour.**
	32. 5	you word, sir, in the hope of gaining your **favour."**
	33. 8	Jacob answered, "It was to gain your **favour."**
	33.10	"No, please, if I have gained your **favour,** accept my gift.
	33.15	no need for that for I only want to gain your **favour."**
	34.11	and brothers, "Do me this **favour,** and I will give you
Num	6.26	May the Lord look on you with **favour** and give you peace.
	35.24	the community shall judge in **favour** of the man who caused
Num	35.24	the death and not in **favour** of the dead man's relative who
Deut	33.23	"Naphtali is richly blessed by the Lord's good **favour;**
1 Sam	2.26	to grow and to gain **favour** both with the Lord and with
	13.12	in Gilgal, and I have not tried to win the Lord's **favour.'**
	20. 8	Please do me this **favour,** and keep the sacred promise you
	29. 4	to win back his master's **favour** than by the death of our
2 Sam	7.29	descendants so that they will continue to enjoy your **favour.**
	19.28	no right to ask for any more **favours** from Your Majesty."
1 Kgs	2.20	She said, "I have a small **favour** to ask of you;
	8.52	may you always look with **favour** on your people Israel and
	16.21	son of Ginath king, and the others were in **favour** of Omri.
	16.22	In the end, those in **favour** of Omri won;
1 Chr	17.27	descendants so that they will continue to enjoy your **favour.**
2 Chr	11.22	loved Maacah best, [22] and he **favoured** her son Abijah over
Ezra	7.28	I have won the **favour** of the emperor, of his counsellors,
	9. 9	made the emperors of Persia **favour** us and permit us to go
Neh	2. 7	him to grant me the **favour** of giving me letters to the
Esth	2. 9	Hegai liked Esther, and she won his **favour.**
	2.17	than any of the others she won his **favour** and affection.
	5. 2	standing outside, she won his **favour,** and he held out to her
Job	23. 4	case before him and present all the arguments in my **favour.**
	34.19	the side of rulers nor **favour** the rich against the poor, for
	37.13	may send it to punish men, or to show them his **favour.**
Ps	7. 8	Judge in my **favour,** O Lord;
	9. 4	in your judgements, and you have judged in my **favour.**
	10.18	you will judge in their **favour,** so that mortal men may
	17. 2	You will judge in my **favour,** because you know what is right.
	45.12	rich people will try to win your **favour.**
	103. 6	The Lord judges in **favour** of the oppressed and gives them
	106.31	has been remembered in his **favour** ever since and will be for
	146. 7	he judges in **favour** of the oppressed and gives food to
Prov	3.34	conceited people, but shows **favour** to those who are humble.
	11.17	You do yourself a **favour** when you are kind.
	14.19	to bow down to the righteous and humbly beg their **favour.**
	16.13	wants to hear the truth and will **favour** those who speak it.
	16.15	The king's **favour** is like the clouds that bring rain in
	18. 5	It is not right to **favour** the guilty and prevent the
	19. 6	Everyone tries to gain the **favour** of important people;
	19. 6	claims the friendship of those who give out **favours.**
	19. 8	Do yourself a **favour** and learn all you can;
	19.12	the roar of a lion, but his **favour** is like welcome rain.
Is	49. 8	you, I will show you **favour** and answer your cries for help.
	58. 8	"Then my **favour** will shine on you like the morning sun,
	60.10	punished you, But now I will show you my **favour** and mercy.
Jer	26.19	Hezekiah honoured the Lord and tried to win his **favour.**
	36. 9	king of Judah, the people fasted to gain the Lord's **favour.**
Lam	3.59	Judge in my **favour;**
Ezek	16.19	you offered it as a sacrifice to win the **favour** of idols."
Dan	7.22	came and pronounced judgement in **favour** of the people of the
Zech	11. 7	one I called **"Favour,"** and the other "Unity."
	11.10	I took the stick called **"Favour"** and broke it, to cancel
Mal	1. 8	Would he be pleased with you or grant you any **favours?"**
Mt	20.20	her two sons, bowed before him, and asked him a **favour.**
Mk	15. 8	ask Pilate for the usual **favour,** [9] he asked them, "Do you
Lk	2.52	in body and in wisdom, gaining **favour** with God and men.
	18. 7	will God not judge in **favour** of his own people who cry
	18. 8	tell you, he will judge in their **favour** and do it quickly.
Jn	8.50	is one who is seeking it and who judges in my **favour.**
Acts	3.14	Pilate to do you the **favour** of turning loose a murderer.
	7.46	He won God's **favour** and asked God to allow him to
	11. 2	those who were in **favour** of circumcising Gentiles criticized him,
	24.27	Felix wanted to gain **favour** with the Jews so he left Paul
	25. 3	Festus [3] to do them the **favour** of bringing Paul to Jerusalem,
	25. 9	But Festus wanted to gain **favour** with the Jews, so he
	27.12	of the men were in **favour** of putting out to sea
2 Cor	6. 2	the time came for me to show you **favour** I heard you;
	6. 2	This is the hour to receive God's **favour;**
Gal	2.12	was afraid of those who were in **favour** of circumcising them.
1 Tim	5.21	without showing any prejudice or **favour** to anyone
Phlm	20	So, my brother, please do me this **favour** for the Lord's sake;
1 Pet	5. 5	"God resists the proud, but shows **favour** to the humble."
Rev	2. 6	But this is what you have in your **favour:**

FAVOURABLE
[UNFAVOURABLE]

Gen	40.16	the wine steward's dream was **favourable,** he said to Joseph,
	41.16	but God will give a **favourable** interpretation."
1 Kgs	12. 7	this people well, give a **favourable** answer to their request,
Ezra	6.22	made the emperor of Assyria **favourable** to them, so that he
Col	2.14	he cancelled the **unfavourable** record of our debts with its

FAVOURITE

Lev	19.15	do not show **favouritism** to the poor or fear the rich.
Deut	21.15	but the first son is not the child of his **favourite** wife.
	21.16	to the son of his **favourite** wife by giving him the share
	21.17	son, even though he is not the son of his **favourite** wife.
	33.24	May he be the **favourite** of his brothers, And may his land
Song	6. 9	She is her mother's only daughter, her mother's **favourite** child.

FAWN

Gen	49.21	"Naphtali is a deer that runs free, Who bears lovely **fawns.**
Jer	14. 5	deer abandons her new-born **fawn** because there is no grass.

FEAR
see also **GOD-FEARING**

Gen	9. 2	All the animals, birds, and fish will live in **fear** of you.
	15.12	fell into a deep sleep, and **fear** and terror came over him.

Gen 35. 5 sons started to leave, great **fear** fell on the people of the
42.28 Their hearts sank, and in **fear** they asked one another,
50.21 You have nothing to **fear**.
Ex 1.12 The Egyptians came to **fear** the Israelites [13-14] and made
1.17 But the midwives **feared** God and so did not obey the king;
1.20 Because the midwives **feared** God, he was good to
9.30 that you and your officials do not yet **fear** the Lord God."
15.14 The nations have heard, and they tremble with **fear;**
15.16 Lord, and stand helpless with **fear** until your people have
19.16 All the people in the camp trembled with **fear.**
20.18 mountain, they trembled with **fear** and stood a long way off.
Lev 19.15 do not show favouritism to the poor or **fear** the rich.
Deut 1.19 went through that vast and **fearful** desert on the way to the
2.25 Everyone will tremble with **fear** at the mention of your name.'
7.19 he will destroy all these people that you now **fear.**
7.21 he is a great God and one to be **feared.**
10.17 He is great and mighty, and he is to be **feared.**
11.25 God will make the people **fear** you, as he has promised, and
18.22 spoken on his own authority, and you are not to **fear** him.
25.18 They had no **fear** of God, and so they attacked you from
28.66 with terror, and you will live in constant **fear** of death.
28.67 Your hearts will pound with **fear** at everything you see.
Josh 9.24 we were in **fear** of our lives.
1 Sam 4.13 news throughout the town, and everyone cried out in **fear.**
13. 7 at Gilgal, and the people with him were trembling with **fear.**
14.15 the raiders and the soldiers in the camp trembled with **fear;**
15.32 came to him, trembling with **fear,** thinking to himself,
2 Sam 17.10 even the bravest men, as **fearless** as lions, will be afraid
1 Kgs 1.50 Adonijah, in great **fear** of Solomon, went to the Tent of
Neh 1. 5 You are great, and we stand in **fear** of you.
Job 3.25 Everything I **fear** and dread comes true.
4.14 my whole body shook with **fear.**
6.21 streams to me, you see my fate and draw back in **fear.**
15. 4 If you had your way, no one would **fear** God;
18.20 all who hear of his fate shudder and tremble with **fear.**
22.10 pitfalls all round you, and suddenly you are full of **fear.**
23.15 I tremble with **fear** before him.
24.17 They **fear** the light of day, but darkness holds no terror
26.11 that hold up the sky, they shake and tremble with **fear.**
31.23 Because I **fear** God's punishment, I could never do such a thing.
31.34 I have never **feared** what people would say;
31.34 kept quiet or stayed indoors because I **feared** their scorn.
33. 7 So you have no reason to **fear** me;
39.22 not know the meaning of **fear,** and no sword can turn them
41.24 His stony heart is without **fear,** as unyielding and hard
41.25 they are helpless with **fear.**
41.33 he is a creature that has no **fear.**
Ps 2.11 Serve the Lord with **fear;**
4. 4 Tremble with **fear** and stop sinning;
27. 1 I will **fear** no one.
34. 4 he freed me from all my **fears.**
47. 2 The Lord, the Most High, is to be **feared;**
48. 6 There they were seized with **fear** and anguish, like a woman
55. 5 I am gripped by **fear** and trembling;
55.19 for they refuse to change, and they do not **fear** him.
66. 3 is so great that your enemies bow down in **fear** before you.
76. 7 But you, Lord, are **feared** by all.
76.11 God makes men **fear** him;
81.15 Those who hate me would bow in **fear** before me;
89. 7 You are **feared** in the council of the holy ones;
90.11 Who knows what **fear** your fury can bring?
91. 5 You need not **fear** any dangers at night or sudden attacks
102.15 The nations will **fear** the Lord;
102.15 all the kings of the earth will **fear** his power.
116. 3 I was filled with **fear** and anxiety.
119.39 Save me from the insults I **fear;**
119.120 I am filled with **fear** because of your judgements.
139.14 I praise you because you are to be **feared;**
Prov 2. 5 know what it means to **fear** the Lord and you will succeed
10.24 they want, but the wicked will get what they **fear** most.
15.16 Better to be poor and **fear** the Lord than to be rich
20. 2 **Fear** an angry king as you would a growling lion;
Is 5.22 Brave and **fearless** when it comes to mixing drinks!
8. 9 Gather together in **fear,** you nations!
8.12 people and do not be afraid of the things that they **fear.**
8.13 I am the one you must **fear.**
13. 8 look at each other in **fear,** and their faces will burn with
18. 2 smooth-skinned people, who are **feared** all over the world.
18. 7 smooth-skinned people, who are **feared** all over the world.
21. 4 My head is spinning, and I am trembling with **fear.**
25. 3 you will be **feared** in the cities of cruel nations.
32.11 but now, tremble with **fear!**
33.18 Your old **fears** of foreign tax-collectors and spies will
41. 5 they are frightened and tremble with **fear.**
41.23 fill us with **fear** and awe!
51.12 Why should you **fear** mortal man, who is no more enduring
51.13 should you live in constant **fear** of the fury of those who
59.19 From east to west everyone will **fear** him and his great power.
64. 1 The mountains would see you and shake with **fear.**
64. 3 the mountains saw you and shook with **fear.**
66. 2 who are humble and repentant, who **fear** me and obey me.
66. 5 to what the Lord says, you that **fear** him and obey him:
Jer 5.22 why don't you **fear** me?
30. 5 a cry of terror, a cry of **fear** and not of peace.
32.40 and I will make them **fear** me with all their heart, so
33. 9 nation in the world will **fear** and tremble when they hear
42.16 then the war that you **fear** will overtake you, and the
46. 5 overcome with **fear,** they run as fast as they can and do
49.16 No one **fears** you as much as you think they do.
Lam 3.47 we live in danger and **fear.**
Ezek 7.27 will give up hope, and the people will shake with **fear.**
Ezek 12.18 "tremble when you eat, and shake with **fear** when you drink.
12.19 tremble when they eat and shake with **fear** when they drink.
21. 7 hearts will be filled with **fear,** their hands will hang limp,
23.33 that cup of **fear** and ruin, your sister Samaria's cup.
27.35 their kings are terrified, and **fear** is written on their faces.
32.10 all of them will tremble in **fear** for their own lives."
38. 8 from many nations and have lived without **fear** of war.
38.20 on the face of the earth will tremble for **fear** of me.
Dan 6.26 my empire everyone should **fear** and respect Daniel's God.
Hos 3. 5 Then they will **fear** the Lord and will receive his good gifts.
10. 3 saying, "We have no king because we did not **fear** the Lord.
Mic 6. 9 It is wise to **fear** the Lord.
7.17 They will turn in **fear** to the Lord our God.
Nah 2.10 Hearts melt with **fear;**
Hab 1. 7 They spread **fear** and terror, and in their pride they are a
3.16 my lips quiver with **fear.**
Mal 1.14 I am a great king, and people of all nations **fear** me."
2. 5 In those days they did respect and **fear** me.
3.16 Then the people who **feared** the Lord spoke to one another,
3.16 a record of those who **feared** the Lord and respected him.
Mt 14.26 they said, and screamed with **fear.**
Mk 5.33 so she came, trembling with **fear,** knelt at his feet, and
Lk 1.65 neighbours were all filled with **fear,** and the news about
1.73 to serve him without **fear,** [75] so that we might be holy
5.26 Full of **fear,** they praised God, saying, "What marvellous
7.16 They all were filled with **fear** and praised God.
12. 5 I will show you whom to **fear:**
12. 5 **fear** God, who, after killing, has the authority to throw into hell.
12. 5 Believe me, he is the one you must **fear!**
18. 2 there was a judge who neither **feared** God nor respected man.
18. 4 'Even though I don't **fear** God or respect man,
21.26 People will faint from **fear** as they wait for what is
23.40 The other one, however, rebuked him, saying, "Don't you **fear** God?
24. 5 Full of **fear,** the women bowed down to the ground,
Acts 7.32 Moses trembled with **fear** and dared not look.
10. 4 stared at the angel in **fear** and said, "What is it, sir?"
19.17 they were all filled with **fear,** and the name of the Lord
Rom 13. 3 rulers are not to be **feared** by those who do good,
1 Cor 2. 3 and trembled all over with **fear,** [4] and my teaching and message
2 Cor 5.11 know what it means to **fear** the Lord, and so we try
7. 5 troubles everywhere, quarrels with others, **fears** in our hearts.
7.15 how you welcomed him with **fear** and trembling.
Eph 6. 5 Slaves, obey your human masters with **fear** and trembling;
Phil 1.14 they grow bolder all the time to preach the message **fearlessly.**
2.12 Keep on working with **fear** and trembling to complete your salvation,
Heb 2.15 were slaves all their lives because of their **fear** of death.
10.27 to wait in **fear** for the coming Judgement
Jas 2.19 The demons also believe—and tremble with **fear.**
1 Jn 4.18 There is no **fear** in love;
4.18 perfect love drives out all **fear.**
4.18 who is afraid, because **fear** has to do with punishment.
Jude 23 others show mercy mixed with **fear,** but hate their very clothes,

AV **FEAR**
see also **OBEY**

FEAST
[WEDDING-FEAST]

Gen 21. 8 on the day that he was weaned, Abraham gave a great **feast.**
26.30 Isaac prepared a **feast** for them, and they ate and drank.
29.22 So Laban gave a **wedding-feast** and invited everyone.
Ex 32. 6 people sat down to a **feast,** which turned into an orgy of
Num 25. 2 women invited them to sacrificial **feasts,** where the god of
Judg 14.12 before the seven days of the **wedding feast** are over."
14.17 She cried about it for the whole seven days of the **feast.**
1 Sam 20.29 family is celebrating the sacrificial **feast** in town, and my
25. 8 We have come on a **feast** day, and David asks you to
25.36 Nabal, who was at home having a **feast** fit for a king.
2 Sam 3.20 David at Hebron with twenty men, David gave a **feast** for them.
1 Kgs 1. 9 to come to this sacrificial **feast,** [10] but he did not invite
1.19 of your army to the **feast,** but he did not invite your
1.25 and just now they are **feasting** with him and shouting, 'Long
1.41 his guests were finishing the **feast,** they heard the noise.
3.15 After that he gave a **feast** for all his officials.
10. 5 who waited on him at **feasts,** and the sacrifices he offered
2 Kgs 6.23 So the king of Israel provided a great **feast** for them;
1 Chr 12.39 three days there with David, **feasting** on the food and drink
2 Chr 9. 4 who waited on him at **feasts,** and the sacrifices he offered
18. 2 a large number of sheep and cattle slaughtered for a **feast.**
Neh 8.10 Now go home and have a **feast.**
Esth 8.17 the Jews held a joyful holiday with **feasting** and happiness.
9.17 no more killing, and they made it a joyful day of **feasting.**
9.19 joyous holiday, a time for **feasting** and giving gifts of food
9.22 to observe these days with **feasts** and parties, giving gifts
Job 1. 4 in turns to give a **feast,** to which all the others would
1. 5 The morning after each **feast,** Job would get up early and
1.13 Job's children were having a **feast** at the home of their
1.18 "Your children were having a **feast** at the home of your
42.11 friends came to visit him and **feasted** with him in his house.
Ps 36. 8 We **feast** on the abundant food you provide;
63. 5 My soul will **feast** and be satisfied, and I will sing glad
69.22 may their sacred **feasts** cause their downfall.
141. 4 May I never take part in their **feasts.**
Prov 9. 2 an animal killed for a **feast,** mixed spices in the wine, and
Ecc 10.16 its king is a youth and its leaders **feast** all night long.
10.19 **Feasting** makes you happy and wine cheers you up, but you

Is	5.12	At your **feasts** you have harps and tambourines and flutes—and wine.
	29. 1	come and go, with its **feasts** and festivals, [2]and then God
Jer	7.34	joy and gladness and to the happy sounds of **wedding feasts.**
	12. 9	Call the wild animals to come and join in the **feast!**
	16. 8	"Do not enter a house where people are **feasting.**
	16. 9	of joy and gladness and the happy sounds of **wedding feasts.**
	25.10	of joy and gladness and the happy sounds of **wedding feasts.**
	33.11	of gladness and joy and the happy sounds of **wedding feasts.**
	51.39	I will prepare them a **feast** and make them drunk and happy.
Ezek	39.17	It will be a huge **feast** on the mountains of Israel, where
	46.11	On the **feast** days and at the festivals the
Amos	6. 4	out on your luxurious couches, **feasting** on veal and lamb!
	6. 7	Your **feasts** and banquets will come to an end.
Mt	8.11	Abraham, Isaac, and Jacob at the **feast** in the Kingdom of heaven.
	22. 2	there was a king who prepared a **wedding feast** for his son.
	22. 3	guests to come to the **feast,** but they did not want to
	22. 4	'My **feast** is ready now;
	22. 4	Come to the **wedding feast!'**
	22. 8	and said to them, 'My **wedding feast** is ready, but the people
	22. 9	streets and invite to the **feast** as many people as you find.'
	23. 6	love the best places at **feasts** and the reserved seats
	25.10	in with him to the **wedding feast,** and the door was closed.
Mk	6.21	when he gave a **feast** for all the chief government officials,
	12.39	seats in the synagogues and the best places at **feasts.**
Lk	5.29	Then Levi had a big **feast** in his house for Jesus,
	12.36	waiting for their master to come back from a **wedding feast.**
	13.29	and sit down at the **feast** in the Kingdom of God.
	14. 8	someone invites you to a **wedding feast,** do not sit down in
	14.13	When you give a **feast,** invite the poor, the crippled,
	14.15	who will sit down at the **feast** in the Kingdom of God!"
	14.16	was giving a great **feast** to which he invited many people.
	14.17	it was time for the **feast,** he sent his servant to tell
	15.23	prize calf and kill it, and let us celebrate with a **feast!**
	15.24	And so the **feasting** began.
	15.29	even a goat for me to have a **feast** with my friends!
	16.22	to sit beside Abraham at the **feast** in heaven.
	20.46	seats in the synagogues and the best places at **feasts;**
	21.34	become occupied with too much **feasting** and drinking
Jn	2. 8	take it to the man in charge of the **feast."**
Acts	7.41	and had a **feast** in honour of what they themselves
Rom	11. 9	And David says, "May they be caught and trapped at their **feasts;**
1 Cor	10. 7	people sat down to a **feast** which turned into an orgy
Rev	19. 9	those who have been invited to the **wedding-feast** of the Lamb."
	19.17	"Come and gather together for God's great **feast!**

AV **FEAST**
see also **FESTIVAL**

FEATHERS

Ezek	17. 3	was a giant eagle with beautiful **feathers** and huge wings,
Dan	4.33	grew as long as eagles' **feathers** and his nails as long as

FEEBLE

Job	4. 3	You have taught many people and given strength to **feeble** hands.
Ps	2. 4	in heaven the Lord laughs and mocks their **feeble** plans.
	71. 9	do not abandon me now that I am **feeble.**

FEED
[FED, WELL-FED]

Gen	41. 2	up out of the river and began to **feed** on the grass.
	41.18	came up out of the river and began **feeding** on the grass.
	42.27	them opened his sack to **feed** his donkey and found his money
	43.24	that they could wash their feet, and he **fed** their donkeys.
Num	13.32	even produce enough to **feed** the people who live there.
Deut	32.38	You **fed** them with the fat of your sacrifices and offered
Judg	19.21	So he took them home with him and **fed** their donkeys.
1 Sam	2. 5	people who once were well **fed** now hire themselves out to get
2 Sam	12. 3	He would **feed** it with some of his own food, let it
	13. 5	to him, 'Please ask my sister Tamar to come and **feed** me.
1 Kgs	3.21	up and was going to **feed** my baby, I saw that it
	5.11	litres of pure olive-oil every year to **feed** his men.
	17. 9	I have commanded a widow who lives there to **feed** you."
2 Kgs	4.42	Elisha told his servant to **feed** the group of prophets with this,
Neh	5.17	I regularly **fed** at my table a hundred and fifty of the
	9.20	you **fed** them with manna and gave them water to drink.
Job	3.12	Why did she **feed** me at her breast?
	22. 7	who were tired, and refused to **feed** those who were hungry.
	36.31	This is how he **feeds** the people and provides an
	38.41	Who is it that **feeds** the ravens when they wander about hungry,
	39. 8	are the pastures where they **feed,** where they search for
	40.20	Grass to **feed** him grows on the hills where wild beasts play.
Ps	74.14	the monster Leviathan and **fed** his body to desert animals.
	80.13	wild pigs trample it down, and wild animals **feed** on it.
	81.10	Open your mouth, and I will **feed** you.
	81.16	But I would **feed** you with the finest wheat and satisfy
	147. 9	their food and **feeds** the young ravens when they call.
Prov	25.21	If your enemy is hungry, **feed** him;
Ecc	5.11	The richer you are, the more mouths you must **feed.**
Song	2.16	He **feeds** his flock among the lilies [17]until the morning
	4. 5	Your breasts are like gazelles, twin deer **feeding** among lilies.
	6. 2	He is **feeding** his flock in the garden and gathering lilies.
	6. 3	he **feeds** his flock among the lilies.
Is	1. 3	owns them, and donkeys know where their master **feeds** them.
	4. 1	man and say, "We can **feed** and clothe ourselves, but please
	10.16	going to send disease to punish those who are now **well-fed.**
	11. 6	Calves and lion cubs will **feed** together, and little children
Is	18. 6	In summer the birds will **feed** on them, and in winter, the
	32. 6	the Lord, and he never **feeds** the hungry or gives thirsty
Jer	5. 7	I **fed** my people until they were full, but they committed
	5. 8	They were like **well-fed** stallions wild with desire, each
	5.28	are powerful and rich, [28]why they are fat and well **fed.**
Ezek	18. 7	he **feeds** the hungry and gives clothing to the naked.
	18.16	He **feeds** the hungry and gives clothing to the naked.
	31. 4	water to make it grow, And underground rivers to **feed** it.
	32. 4	all the birds and animals of the world to **feed** on you.
	34.13	streams of Israel and will **feed** them in pleasant pastures.
	34.31	sheep, the flock that I **feed,** are my people, and I am
Dan	4.21	and it had enough fruit on it to **feed** the whole world.
Hos	4.16	How can I **feed** them like lambs in a meadow?
	11. 4	I bent down to them and **fed** them.
Amos	4. 1	who grow fat like the **well-fed** cows of Bashan, who ill-treat
Mic	7.14	Let them go and **feed** in the rich pastures of Bashan and
Nah	2.11	place where young lions were **fed,** where the lion and the
Zech	11.16	the lost, or heal those that are hurt, or **feed** the healthy.
Mt	8.30	Not far away there was a large herd of pigs **feeding.**
	15.32	to send them away without **feeding** them, for they might faint
	15.33	we find enough food in this desert to **feed** this crowd?"
	25.35	I was hungry and you **fed** me, thirsty and you gave me
	25.37	ever see you hungry and **feed** you, or thirsty and give you
	25.42	hungry but you would not **feed** me, thirsty but you would not
Mk	5.11	was a large herd of pigs near by, **feeding** on a hillside.
	6.37	two hundred silver coins on bread in order to **feed** them?"
	6.44	The number of men who were **fed** was five thousand.
	6.52	the real meaning of the **feeding** of the five thousand;
	7.27	But Jesus answered, "Let us first **feed** the children.
	8. 3	I send them home without **feeding** them, they will faint as
	8. 4	can anyone find enough food to **feed** all these people?"
Lk	8.32	was a large herd of pigs near by, **feeding** on a hillside.
	12.24	God **feeds** them!
Jn	6. 5	Philip, "Where can we buy enough food to **feed** all these people?"
Rom	12.20	"If your enemy is hungry, **feed** him;
1 Cor	3. 2	I had to **feed** you with milk, not solid food, because you
Eph	5.29	Instead, he **feeds** it and takes care of it, just as Christ
1 Tim	4. 6	of Christ Jesus, as you **feed** yourself spiritually on the

FEEL
[FELT]

Gen	27.22	closer to his father, who **felt** him and said, "Your voice
	27.22	like Jacob's voice, but your arms **feel** like Esau's arms."
	43.30	his heart was full of tender **feelings** for his brother.
	45. 1	able to control his **feelings** in front of his servants,
Ex	10.21	thick enough to be **felt** will cover the land of Egypt."
	23. 9	you know how it **feels** to be a foreigner, because you were
Num	13.33	We **felt** as small as grasshoppers, and that is how we must
Deut	5.29	If only they would always **feel** like this!
Judg	15.19	Samson drank it and began to **feel** much better.
Ruth	2.13	You have made me **feel** better by speaking gently to me, even
1 Sam	13.12	So I **felt** I had to offer a sacrifice."
	14.27	At once he **felt** much better.
	14.29	See how much better I **feel** because I ate some honey!
	16.23	leave, and Saul would **feel** better and be all right again.
	25.31	you will not have to **feel** regret or remorse, sir, for having
2 Sam	3.39	though I am the king chosen by God, I **feel** weak today.
	23.15	David **felt** homesick and said, "How I wish someone would
1 Chr	12.40	of the joy that was **felt** throughout the whole country.
2 Chr	12. 7	Jerusalem will not **feel** the full force of my anger, [8]but
	19.10	fellow-citizens will **feel** the force of the Lord's anger.
Esth	1.10	the king was drinking and **feeling** merry, so he called in the
Job	14.22	He **feels** only the pain of his own body and the grief
	21.20	let them **feel** the wrath of Almighty God.
Ps	16. 9	thankful and glad, and I **feel** completely secure, [10]because
	30. 6	I **felt** secure and said to myself, "I will never be defeated."
	73.21	thoughts were bitter and my **feelings** were hurt, [22]I was as
	77. 3	when I meditate, I **feel** discouraged.
	90.11	Who has **felt** the full power of your anger?
	115. 7	They have hands, but cannot **feel,** and feet, but cannot walk;
Prov	15.30	good news makes you **feel** better.
	23.32	The next morning you will **feel** as if you had been bitten
	23.34	You will **feel** as if you were out on the ocean, sea-sick,
	27. 9	and fragrant oils make you **feel** happier, but trouble
Is	30.30	hear his majestic voice and **feel** the force of his anger.
	30.31	hear the Lord's voice and **feel** the force of his punishment.
	42.25	So he made us **feel** the force of his anger and suffer
	47.10	"You **felt** sure of yourself in your evil;
	51.20	They have **felt** the force of God's anger.
Jer	10.14	At the sight of this, men **feel** stupid and senseless;
	11.20	you test people's thoughts and **feelings.**
	49.31	We'll attack those people that **feel** safe and secure!
	51.17	At the sight of this, men **feel** stupid and senseless;
	51.51	we **feel** completely helpless because foreigners have taken
Lam	2. 4	Here in Jerusalem we **felt** his burning anger.
	2. 6	King and priest alike have **felt** the force of his anger.
Ezek	1. 3	I heard the Lord speak to me and I **felt** his power.
	3.14	and as his spirit carried me off, I **felt** bitter and angry.
	3.22	I **felt** the powerful presence of the Lord and heard him
	5.13	"You will **feel** all the force of my anger and rage until
	5.16	You will **feel** the pains of hunger like sharp arrows sent to
	6.12	They will **feel** all the force of my anger.
	7. 3	You will **feel** my anger, because I am judging you for what
	7. 8	"Very soon now you will **feel** all the force of my anger.
	8.18	They will **feel** all the force of my anger.
	13.15	covered it with whitewash will **feel** the force of my anger.
	20. 8	was ready to let them **feel** the full force of my anger
	20.13	was ready to let them **feel** the force of my anger there
	20.21	was ready to let them **feel** the force of my anger there
	20.47	to north, and everyone will **feel** the heat of the flames.

Ezek	21.31	You will **feel** my anger when I turn it loose on you
	22.22	will know that they are **feeling** the anger of the Lord."
	24.13	pure again until you have **felt** the full force of my anger.
	25.14	Edom for me, and they will make Edom **feel** my furious anger.
	25.17	They will **feel** my anger.
	30.15	will let the city of Pelusium, Egypt's great fortress, **feel**
	33.22	he came, I had **felt** the powerful presence of the Lord.
	36.18	I let them **feel** the force of my anger because of the
	36.32	I want you to **feel** the shame and disgrace of what you
	37. 1	I **felt** the powerful presence of the Lord, and his spirit
	40. 1	On that day I **felt** the powerful presence of the Lord, and
Dan	10.18	Once more he took hold of me, and I **felt** stronger.
	10.19	he had said this, I **felt** even stronger and said, "Sir, tell
	10.19	You have made me **feel** better."
Amos	6. 1	Zion and for you that **feel** safe in Samaria—you great men
Jon	2. 7	When I **felt** my life slipping away, then, O Lord, I prayed
Zeph	3. 8	kingdoms, in order to let them **feel** the force of my anger.
Mt	15.12	the Pharisees had their **feelings** hurt by what you said?"
	15.32	to him and said, "I **feel** sorry for these people, because
	18.13	I tell you, he **feels** far happier over this one sheep
	18.27	The king **felt** sorry for him, so he forgave him the debt
Mk	3. 5	at the same time he **felt** sorry for them, because they were
	5.29	and she had the **feeling** inside herself that she was healed
	8. 2	to him and said, [2]"I **feel** sorry for these people, because
Lk	1.12	When Zechariah saw him, he was alarmed and **felt** afraid.
	12.55	And when you **feel** the south wind blowing, you say that
	24.39	**Feel** me, and you will know, for a ghost doesn't have flesh
Acts	13.11	At once Elymas **felt** a dark mist cover his eyes, and he
	17.27	for him, and perhaps find him as they **felt** about for him.
Rom	14.22	the person who does not **feel** guilty when he does something
	15.14	I myself **feel** sure that you are full of goodness, that you
1 Cor	4.14	I want to make you **feel** ashamed, but to instruct you as
	7.36	if the man **feels** that he is not acting properly towards the girl
	7.36	are too strong and he **feels** that they ought to marry,
	8. 7	is weak, and they **feel** they are defiled by the food.
	13.11	was a child, my speech, **feelings,** and thinking were all
	16.10	be sure to make him **feel** welcome among you, because he is
2 Cor	1. 9	We **felt** that the death sentence had been passed on us.
	5. 4	in this earthly tent, we groan with a **feeling** of oppression;
	6.13	show us the same **feelings** that we have for you.
	7.11	Such indignation, such alarm, such **feelings,** such devotion,
	9. 4	not to speak of your shame—for **feeling** so sure of you!
	11.29	When someone is weak, then I **feel** weak too;
	12. 9	my weaknesses, in order to **feel** the protection of Christ's
Gal	4.19	a mother in childbirth, I **feel** the same kind of pain for
	4.27	cry with joy, you who never **felt** the pains of childbirth!
	5.10	But I still **feel** confident about you.
Eph	4.19	They have lost all **feeling** of shame;
	4.31	No more shouting or insults, no more hateful **feelings** of any sort.
Phil	1. 7	is only right for me to **feel** as I do about you.
	1. 8	I say that my deep **feeling** for you all comes from the
	2.20	one who shares my **feelings** and who really cares about you.
	3. 4	ceremonies, I have even more reason to **feel** that way.
	4.11	not saying this because I **feel** neglected, for I have learnt
Col	3. 8	anger, passion, and hateful **feelings.**
Heb	4.15	High Priest is not one who cannot **feel** sympathy for our weaknesses.
	6. 5	is good, and they had **felt** the powers of the coming age.
	6. 9	if we speak like this, dear friends, we **feel** sure about you.
	10. 2	their sins, they would not **feel** guilty of sin any more, and
	12.18	came, to what you can **feel,** to Mount Sinai with its blazing
1 Pet	3. 8	you must all have the same attitude and the same **feelings;**
Jude	3	share in common, when I **felt** the need of writing at once

FELDSPAR

A colourful, rather hard rock, often glassy in appearance.

Esth	1. 6	red **feldspar,** shining mother-of-pearl, and blue turquoise.

FELIX

Roman governor of Judaea when Paul was imprisoned in Caesarea.

Acts	23.24	Paul to ride and get him safely through to the governor **Felix."**
	23.26	"Claudius Lysias to His Excellency, the governor **Felix:**
	24. 1	They appeared before **Felix** and made their charges against Paul.
	24.22	Then **Felix,** who was well informed about the Way, brought
	24.24	After some days **Felix** came with his wife Drusilla, who was Jewish.
	24.25	the coming Day of Judgement, **Felix** was afraid and said,
	24.27	After two years had passed, Porcius Festus succeeded **Felix** as governor.
	24.27	**Felix** wanted to gain favour with the Jews so he left Paul
	25.14	"There is a man here who was left a prisoner by **Felix;**

FELLOW- *Where not listed below, see under main part of word. e.g. for "fellow-Jew" see JEW*

FELLOW-TOWNSMEN

Gen	34.20	at the city gate and spoke to their **fellow-townsmen:**

FELLOWSHIP

Gen	5.22	After that, Enoch lived in **fellowship** with God for 300
	5.24	He spent his life in **fellowship** with God, and then he disappeared,
	6. 9	He lived in **fellowship** with God, [11]but everyone else was
Mic	6. 8	love, and to live in humble **fellowship** with our God.
Acts	2.42	taking part in the **fellowship,** and sharing in the fellowship
	2.44	believers continued together in close **fellowship** and shared
Rom	6.10	and now he lives his life in **fellowship** with God.
	6.11	but living in **fellowship** with God through Christ Jesus.
	16. 8	to Ampliatus, my dear friend in the **fellowship** of the Lord.
1 Cor	1. 9	who called you to have **fellowship** with his Son Jesus Christ,
	5. 2	done such a thing should be expelled from your **fellowship.**
	5.12	But should you not judge the members of your own **fellowship?**
	6. 5	one wise person in your **fellowship** who can settle a dispute
	7.24	each one should remain in **fellowship** with God in the same
2 Cor	13.13	love of God, and the **fellowship** of the Holy Spirit be with
Phil	2. 1	You have **fellowship** with the Spirit, and you have kindness
Phlm	6	My prayer is that our **fellowship** with you as believers
1 Jn	1. 3	join with us in the **fellowship** that we have with the Father
	1. 6	we say that we have **fellowship** with him, yet at the same
	1. 7	the light—then we have **fellowship** with one another, and the
	2.19	did not belong to our **fellowship,** and that is why they left
	2.19	belonged to our **fellowship,** they would have stayed with us.

FELLOWSHIP MEAL

Acts	2.42	fellowship, and sharing in the **fellowship meals** and the prayers.
	20. 7	On Saturday evening we gathered together for the **fellowship meal.**
Jude	12	they are like dirty spots in your **fellowship meals.**

FELLOWSHIP-OFFERING

A sacrifice offered to restore or keep a right relationship with God. Only a part of the animal was burnt on the altar; the rest was eaten by the worshippers or the priests.

Ex	20.24	to be completely burnt and as **fellowship-offerings.**
	24. 5	the Lord and sacrificed some cattle as **fellowship-offerings.**
	29.28	when my people make their **fellowship-offerings,** the breast
	32. 6	as sacrifices and others to eat as **fellowship-offerings.**
Lev	3. 1	of his cattle as a **fellowship-offering,** it is to be a bull
	3. 6	is used as a **fellowship-offering,** it may be male or female,
	4.10	the fat from the animal killed for the **fellowship-offering.**
	4.26	the fat of the animals killed for the **fellowship-offerings.**
	4.31	the animals killed for the **fellowship-offerings,** and he
	4.35	the sheep killed for the **fellowship-offerings,** and he shall
	6.12	on it, and burn the fat of the **fellowship-offering.**
	7.11	The following are the regulations for the **fellowship-offerings**
	7.16	If a man brings a **fellowship-offering** in fulfilment of a
	7.29	Whoever offers a **fellowship-offering** must bring part of it
	7.33	who offers the blood and the fat of the **fellowship-offering.**
	7.37	the ordination-offerings, and the **fellowship-offerings.**
	9. 4	and a bull and a ram for a **fellowship-offering.**
	9.18	bull and the ram as a **fellowship-offering** for the people.
	10.14	you from the **fellowship-offerings** of the people of Israel.
	17. 5	entrance of the Tent and kill them as **fellowship-offerings.**
	19. 5	kill an animal for a **fellowship-offering,** keep the
	22.21	When anyone presents a **fellowship-offering** to the Lord,
	23.19	and two one-year-old male lambs as a **fellowship-offering.**
Num	6.14	for a sin-offering, and a ram for a **fellowship-offering.**
	6.17	to the Lord as a **fellowship-offering,** and offer it with the
	6.18	the fire on which the **fellowship-offering** is being burnt.
	7.12	and five one-year-old lambs for the **fellowship-offering.**
	7.84	sixty one-year-old lambs, for the **fellowship-offerings**
	10.10	present your burnt-offerings and your **fellowship-offerings.**
	15. 8	a vow or as a **fellowship-offering,** [9]a grain-offering of
	29.39	grain-offerings, wine-offerings, and **fellowship-offerings**
Deut	27. 7	to sacrifice and eat your **fellowship-offerings** and be
Josh	8.31	Lord, and they also presented their **fellowship-offerings.**
	22.23	or **fellowship-offerings,** let the Lord himself punish us.
	22.27	to be burnt and with sacrifices and **fellowship-offerings.**
2 Sam	6.17	Then he offered sacrifices and **fellowship-offerings** to the Lord.
	24.25	Lord and offered burnt-offerings and **fellowship-offerings.**
1 Kgs	3.15	offered burnt-offerings and **fellowship-offerings** to the Lord.
	8.63	and 120,000 sheep as **fellowship-offerings.**
	8.64	and the fat of the animals for the **fellowship-offerings.**
	9.25	Solomon offered burnt-offerings and **fellowship-offerings**
2 Kgs	16.13	wine-offering and the blood of a **fellowship-offering** on it.
1 Chr	16. 1	Then they offered sacrifices and **fellowship-offerings** to God.
	21.26	Lord there and offered burnt-offerings and **fellowship-offerings.**
2 Chr	7. 5	and 120,000 sheep as **fellowship-offerings.**
	7. 7	grain-offerings, and the fat from the **fellowship-offerings.**
	31. 2	the **fellowship-offerings,** taking part in the temple worship,
	33.16	and he sacrificed **fellowship-offerings** and thanksgiving-offerings
Ezek	43.27	burnt-offerings and the **fellowship-offerings** of the people.
	45.13	burnt whole, and animals for **fellowship-offerings,** so that
	45.17	be burnt whole, and the **fellowship-offerings,** to take away
	46. 2	his sacrifices whole and offer his **fellowship-offerings.**
	46.12	be burnt whole or a **fellowship-offering,** the east gate to

FELLOWSHIP-SACRIFICE

Judg	20.26	They offered **fellowship sacrifices** and burnt some sacrifices
	21. 4	**fellowship sacrifices** and burnt some sacrifices whole.
1 Sam	10. 8	I will meet you and offer burnt-sacrifices and **fellowship-sacrifices.**
	11.15	They offered **fellowship-sacrifices,** and Saul and all the people of Israel celebrated
	13. 9	"Bring me the burnt-sacrifices and the **fellowship-sacrifices."**

FEMALE

Gen	1.27	He created them male and **female,** [28]blessed them, and said,
	5. 2	He created them male and **female,** blessed them,
	6.19	you a male and a **female** of every kind of animal and
	7. 8	A male and a **female** of every kind of animal and bird,
	7.15	A male and a **female** of each kind of living being went
	24.35	and goats, cattle, silver, gold, male and **female** slaves,

Gen 30.35 or spots and all the **females** that were speckled and spotted
32.13 two hundred **female** goats and twenty males,
32.13 two hundred **female** sheep and twenty males,
32.13 forty cows and ten bulls, twenty **female** donkeys and ten males.
Ex 21. 9 If a man buys a **female** slave to give to his son,
21.20 his slave, whether male or **female,** and the slave dies on the
21.26 man hits his male or **female** slave in the eye so that
21.32 bull kills a male or **female** slave, its owner shall pay the
Lev 3. 6 it may be male or **female,** but it must be without any
4.28 bring as his offering a **female** goat without any defects.
4.32 as a sin-offering, it must be a **female** without any defects.
5. 6 bring to the Lord a **female** sheep or goat as an offering.
14.10 two male lambs and one **female** lamb a year old that are
27. 3 —adult **female:**
27. 3 —young **female:**
27. 3 —infant **female:**
27. 3 —**female** above sixty:
Num 15.27 he is to offer a one-year-old **female** goat as a sin-offering.
Deut 15.17 Treat your **female** slave in the same way.
Josh 17. 6 of the Jordan, [6]since his **female** descendants as well as his
1 Kgs 15.12 country all the male and **female** prostitutes serving at the
22.46 of all the male and **female** prostitutes serving at the pagan
2 Chr 15.13 young or old, male or **female,** who did not worship him was
Ezra 2.64 Their male and **female** servants - 7,337
2.64 Male and **female** musicians - 200
Neh 7.66 Their male and **female** servants - 7,337
7.66 Male and **female** musicians - 245
Jer 34. 9 Hebrew slaves, both male and **female,** so that no one would
Mt 19. 4 in the beginning the Creator made people male and **female?**
Mk 10. 6 'God made them male and **female,**' as the scripture says.

FENCE

Ps 62. 3 attack a man who is no stronger than a broken-down **fence?**
80.12 Why did you break down the **fences** round it?
Hos 2. 6 So I am going to **fence** her in with thorn-bushes and build
Mt 21.33 planted a vineyard, put a **fence** around it, dug a hole for
Mk 12. 1 planted a vineyard, put a **fence** round it, dug a hole for

FERTILE

Gen 27.28 May God give you dew from heaven and make your fields **fertile!**
27.39 "No dew from heaven for you, No **fertile** fields for you.
48.22 I am giving Shechem, that **fertile** region which I took from
Ex 3. 8 one which is rich and **fertile** and in which the Canaanites,
3.17 them to a rich and **fertile** land—the land of the Canaanites,
13. 5 you into that rich and **fertile** land, you must celebrate this
33. 3 You are going to a rich and **fertile** land.
Lev 20.24 promised you this rich and **fertile** land as your possession,
Num 13.20 whether the soil is **fertile** and whether the land is wooded.
13.27 "We explored the land and found it to be rich and **fertile;**
14. 8 will take us there and give us that rich and **fertile** land.
16.13 brought us out of the **fertile** land of Egypt to kill us
16.14 not brought us into a **fertile** land or given us fields and
Deut 1.25 land which the Lord our God was giving us was very **fertile.**
1.35 evil generation will enter the **fertile** land that I promised
3.25 Jordan, Lord, and see the **fertile** land on the other side,
4.21 River Jordan to enter the **fertile** land which he is giving you.
4.22 but you are about to go across and occupy that **fertile** land.
6. 3 live in that rich and **fertile** land, just as the Lord, the
6.18 to take possession of the **fertile** land that the Lord
8. 7 is bringing you into a **fertile** land—a land that has rivers
8.10 Lord your God for the **fertile** land that he has given you.
9. 6 Lord is not giving you this **fertile** land because you deserve it.
11. 9 time in the rich and **fertile** land that the Lord promised to
26. 9 He brought us here and gave us this rich and **fertile** land.
26.15 bless also the rich and **fertile** land that you have given us,
27. 3 have entered the rich and **fertile** land that the Lord, the
31.20 this rich and **fertile** land, as I promised their ancestors.
Josh 5. 4 to see the rich and **fertile** land that he had promised their
2 Kgs 3.19 all their **fertile** fields by covering them with stones."
3.25 As they passed a **fertile** field, every Israelite would throw
1 Chr 4.40 They found plenty of **fertile** pasture lands there in a
2 Chr 26.10 vineyards in the hill-country and to farm the **fertile** land.
Neh 9.25 Your people captured fortified cities, **fertile** land,
9.35 when they lived in the broad, **fertile** land you gave them;
9.36 that you gave us, this **fertile** land which gives us food.
Ps 65. 9 you make it rich and **fertile.**
Is 5. 1 My friend had a vineyard on a very **fertile** hill.
16.10 No one is happy now in the **fertile** fields.
22. 7 The **fertile** valleys of Judah were filled with chariots;
32.12 breasts in grief because the **fertile** fields and the
32.15 The waste land will become **fertile,**
33. 9 of Lebanon have withered, the **fertile** valley of Sharon is
35. 2 the Lebanon Mountains and as **fertile** as the fields of Carmel
63.14 cattle are led into a **fertile** valley, so the Lord gave his
Jer 2. 7 I brought them into a **fertile** land, to enjoy its harvests
4.26 The **fertile** land had become a desert;
11. 5 give them the rich and **fertile** land which they now have."
32.22 gave them this rich and **fertile** land, as you had promised
48.33 and joy have been taken away from the **fertile** land of Moab.
Ezek 17. 5 and planted it in a **fertile** field, where there was always
17. 8 already been planted in a **fertile,** well-watered field so
20. 6 for them, a rich and **fertile** land, the finest land of all.
20.15 given them, a rich and **fertile** land, the finest land of all.
34.29 I will give them **fertile** fields and put an end to hunger
Mic 7.14 apart in the wilderness, there is **fertile** land around them.

FERTILITY

1 Kgs 15.13 had made an obscene idol of the **fertility** goddess Asherah.
2 Chr 15.16 had made an obscene idol of the **fertility** goddess Asherah.
Is 57. 5 You worship the **fertility** gods by having sex under those
Jer 2.20 and under every green tree you worshipped **fertility** gods.
Hos 4.10 You will worship the **fertility** gods, but still have no children,
Mic 1. 7 acquired these things for its **fertility** rites, and now her

FERVENT

Lk 22.44 In great anguish he prayed even more **fervently;**
Rom 15.30 join me in praying **fervently** to God for me.
Col 4.12 He always prays **fervently** for you, asking God to make you

FESTIVAL

Gen 1.14 the time when days, years, and religious **festivals** begin;
Ex 5. 1 they can hold a **festival** in the desert to honour me.' "
10. 9 because we must hold a **festival** to honour the Lord."
12.11 It is the Passover **Festival** to honour me, the Lord.
12.14 this day as a religious **festival** to remind you of what I,
12.17 Keep this **festival,** because it was on this day that I
12.17 all time to come you must celebrate this day as a **festival.**
12.47 of Israel must celebrate this **festival,** [48]but no
12.48 like a native-born Israelite and may join in the **festival.**
13. 5 land, you must celebrate this **festival** in the first month of
13. 6 seventh day there is to be a **festival** to honour the Lord.
13. 8 When the **festival** begins, explain to your sons that you do
13.10 Celebrate this **festival** at the appointed time each year.
23.14 "Celebrate three **festivals** a year to honour me.
23.15 Egypt, celebrate the **Festival** of Unleavened Bread in the way
23.15 made with yeast during the seven days of this **festival.**
23.16 "Celebrate the Harvest **Festival** when you begin to harvest
23.16 "Celebrate the **Festival** of Shelters in the autumn,
23.17 Every year at these three **festivals** all your men must
23.18 sacrificed to me during these **festivals** is not to be left
32. 5 "Tomorrow there will be a **festival** to honour the Lord."
34.18 "Keep the **Festival** of Unleavened Bread.
34.22 "Keep the Harvest **Festival** when you begin to harvest
34.22 and keep the **Festival** of Shelters in the autumn when you
34.24 try to conquer your country during the three **festivals.**
34.25 any part of the animal killed at the Passover **Festival.**
Lev 23. 2 following regulations for the religious **festivals,** when the
23. 4 Proclaim the following **festivals** at the appointed times.
23. 6 fifteenth day the **Festival** of Unleavened Bread begins, and
23.33 The **Festival** of Shelters begins on the fifteenth day
23.37 (These are the religious **festivals** on which you honour
23.38 These **festivals** are in addition to the regular Sabbaths,
23.39 your fields, celebrate this **festival** for seven days,
23.40 and begin a religious **festival** to honour the Lord your God.
23.44 observing the religious **festivals** to honour the Lord.
26. 2 Keep the religious **festivals**
Num 10.10 joyful occasions—at your New Moon **Festivals** and your other
10.10 and your other religious **festivals**—you are to blow the trumpets
15. 3 or as an offering at your regular religious **festivals;**
28.16 The Passover **Festival** in honour of the Lord is to be
28.17 day a religious **festival** begins which lasts seven days,
28.18 the first day of the **festival** you are to gather for worship,
28.26 first day of the Harvest **Festival,** when you present the
29.12 Celebrate this **festival** in honour of the Lord for seven days
29.39 you are to make to the Lord at your appointed **festivals.**
Deut 16.10 and then celebrate the Harvest **Festival,** to honour the Lord
16.13 celebrate the **Festival** of Shelters for seven days.
16.15 your God by celebrating this **festival** for seven days at the
16.16 at Passover, Harvest **Festival,** and the Festival of Shelters.
31.10 read this aloud at the **Festival** of Shelters.
Judg 9.27 picked the grapes, made wine from them, and held a **festival.**
21.19 Then they thought, "The yearly **festival** of the Lord at
21.21 to dance during the **festival,** you come out of the vineyards.
1 Sam 20. 5 "Tomorrow is the New Moon **Festival,**" David replied,
20.18 "Since tomorrow is the New Moon **Festival,** your absence will
20.24 At the New Moon **Festival,** King Saul came to the meal [25]and
20.27 after the New Moon **Festival,** David's place was still empty,
20.34 nothing that day—the second day of the New Moon **Festival.**
1 Kgs 8. 2 assembled during the **Festival** of Shelters in the seventh month,
8.65 Israel celebrated the **Festival** of Shelters for seven days.
12.32 Jeroboam also instituted a religious **festival** on the
12.32 day of the eighth month, like the **festival** in Judah.
12.33 altar in celebration of the **festival** he had instituted for
2 Kgs 4.23 "It's neither a Sabbath nor a New Moon **Festival.**"
23.16 predicted long before during the **festival** as King Jeroboam
1 Chr 23.31 on the Sabbath, the New Moon Festival, and other **festivals.**
2 Chr 2. 4 well as on Sabbaths, New Moon **Festivals,** and other holy days
5. 3 They all assembled at the time of the **Festival** of Shelters.
7. 8 Israel celebrated the **Festival** of Shelters for seven days.
7. 9 of the altar and then seven more days for the **festival.**
8.13 Sabbaths, New Moon **Festivals,**
8.13 and the three annual **festivals**—the Festival of Unleavened Bread,
8.13 the Harvest **Festival,** and the Festival of Shelters.
30. 1 able to celebrate the Passover **Festival** at the proper time,
30.13 to celebrate the **Festival** of Unleavened Bread.
30.21 celebrated the **Festival** of Unleavened Bread with great joy, and
31. 1 After the **festival** ended, all the people of Israel went to
31. 3 the Sabbath, at the New Moon **Festival,**
31. 3 and at the other **festivals** which are required by the Law
35. 1 of the first month they killed the animals for the **festival.**
35. 8 and three hundred bulls for sacrifices during the **festival.**
35.16 Lord, the keeping of the Passover **Festival,** and the offering
35.17 the Passover and the **Festival** of Unleavened Bread.

Ezra	3. 4	They celebrated the **Festival** of Shelters according to the
	3. 5	be offered at the New Moon **Festival** and at all the other
	6.22	they joyfully celebrated the **Festival** of Unleavened Bread.
Neh	8.18	the first day of the **festival** to the last they read a
	10.33	for Sabbaths, New Moon **Festivals,** and other festivals,
Ps	76.10	those who survive the wars will keep your **festivals.**
	81. 3	Blow the trumpet for the **festival,** when the moon is new
	118.27	your hands, start the **festival** and march round the altar.
Is	1.13	I cannot stand your New Moon **Festivals,** your Sabbaths, and
	1.14	I hate your New Moon **Festivals** and holy days;
	29. 1	go, with its feasts and **festivals,** [2]and then God will bring
	30.29	and sing as you do on the night of a sacred **festival.**
	33.20	Look at Zion, the city where we celebrate our religious **festivals.**
	66.23	On every New Moon **Festival** and every Sabbath, people of
Ezek	36.38	of the sheep which were offered as sacrifices at a **festival.**
	44.24	religious **festivals** according to my rules and regulations,
	45.17	at the New Moon Festivals, the Sabbaths, and the other **festivals.**
	45.21	you will begin the celebration of the Passover **Festival.**
	45.22	the first day of the **festival** the ruling prince must offer a
	45.23	the seven days of the **festival** he is to sacrifice to the
	45.25	"For the **Festival** of Shelters, which begins on the fifteenth
	46. 1	to be opened on the Sabbath and at the New Moon **Festival.**
	46. 3	Each Sabbath and each New Moon **Festival** all the people are
	46. 6	At the New Moon **Festival** he will offer a young bull, six
	46. 9	worship the Lord at any **festival,** those who enter by the
	46.11	feast days and at the **festivals** the grain-offering will be
Dan	7.25	change their religious laws and **festivals,** and God's people
Hos	2.11	festivities—her annual and monthly **festivals** and her Sabbath
	9. 1	People of Israel, stop celebrating your **festivals** like pagans.
	9. 5	comes for the appointed **festivals** in honour of the Lord,
Amos	5.21	The Lord says, "I hate your religious **festivals;**
	8.10	I will turn your **festivals** into funerals and change your
Nah	1.15	People of Judah, celebrate your **festivals** and give God what
Zeph	3.18	joyful over you, [18]as joyful as people at a **festival."**
Zech	8.19	and tenth months will become **festivals** of joy and gladness
	14.16	Lord Almighty as king, and to celebrate the **Festival** of Shelters.
	14.18	to celebrate the **Festival** of Shelters, then they will be
	14.19	nations if they do not celebrate the **Festival** of Shelters.
Mt	26. 2	it will be the Passover **Festival,** and the Son of Man
	26. 5	not do it during the **festival,"** they said, "or the people
	26.17	the first day of the **Festival** of Unleavened Bread the
	27.15	At every Passover **Festival** the Roman governor was in the habit
Mk	14. 1	days before the **Festival** of Passover and Unleavened Bread.
	14. 2	not do it during the **festival,"** they said, "or the people
	14.12	the first day of the **Festival** of Unleavened Bread, the day
	15. 6	every Passover **Festival** Pilate was in the habit of setting free
Lk	2.41	the parents of Jesus went to Jerusalem for the Passover **Festival.**
	2.42	Jesus was twelve years old, they went to the **festival** as usual.
	2.43	When the **festival** was over, they started back home, but
	22. 1	time was near for the **Festival** of Unleavened Bread, which is
	22. 7	The day came during the **Festival** of Unleavened Bread when
Jn	2.13	almost time for the Passover **Festival,** so Jesus went to Jerusalem.
	2.23	in Jerusalem during the Passover **Festival,** many believed in him
	4.45	they had gone to the Passover **Festival** in Jerusalem
	4.45	and had seen everything that he had done during the **festival.**
	5. 1	After this, Jesus went to Jerusalem for a religious **festival.**
	6. 4	The time for the Passover **Festival** was near.
	7. 2	The time for the **Festival** of Shelters was near, [3]so
	7. 8	You go on to the **festival.**
	7. 8	am not going to this **festival,** because the right time has
	7.10	After his brothers had gone to the **festival,** Jesus also went;
	7.11	The Jewish authorities were looking for him at the **festival.**
	7.14	The **festival** was nearly half over when Jesus went to the
	7.37	most important day of the **festival** Jesus stood up and said
	10.22	It was winter, and the **Festival** of the Dedication of the
	11.55	The time for the Passover **Festival** was near, and many people
	11.55	Jerusalem to perform the ritual of purification before the **festival.**
	11.56	Surely he will not come to the **festival,** will he?"
	12.12	that had come to the Passover **Festival** heard that Jesus was
	12.20	who had gone to Jerusalem to worship during the **festival.**
	13. 1	It was now the day before the Passover **Festival.**
	13.29	what they needed for the **festival,** or to give something to
Acts	12. 3	(This happened during the time of the **Festival** of Unleavened Bread.)
	20. 6	sailed from Philippi after the **Festival** of Unleavened Bread,
1 Cor	5. 7	For our Passover **Festival** is ready,
Col	2.16	or about holy days or the New Moon **Festival** or the Sabbath.

FESTIVITIES

2 Sam	13.24	Will you and your officials come and take part in the **festivities?"**
Hos	2.11	end to all her **festivities—**her annual and monthly festivals

FESTUS

[PORCIUS FESTUS]

Porcius Festus, successor of Felix as governor of Judaea.

Acts	24.27	two years had passed, **Porcius Festus** succeeded Felix as governor.
	25. 1	Three days after **Festus** arrived in the province, he went
	25. 2	They begged **Festus** [3]to do them the favour of bringing Paul
	25. 4	**Festus** answered, "Paul is being kept a prisoner in Caesarea,
	25. 6	**Festus** spent another eight or ten days with them and then
	25. 9	But **Festus** wanted to gain favour with the Jews, so he
	25.12	Then **Festus,** after conferring with his advisers,
	25.13	Bernice came to Caesarea to pay a visit of welcome to **Festus.**
	25.14	several days, **Festus** explained Paul's situation to the king:
	25.22	Agrippa said to **Festus,** "I would like to hear this man myself."
	25.22	"You will hear him tomorrow," **Festus** answered.
	25.23	**Festus** gave the order, and Paul was brought in.
	25.24	**Festus** said, "King Agrippa and all who are here with us:
Acts	26.24	defended himself in this way, **Festus** shouted at him, "You
	26.32	And Agrippa said to **Festus,** "This man could have been

FEVER

Lev	26.16	on you—incurable diseases and **fevers** that will make you
Deut	28.22	will strike you with infectious diseases, with swelling and **fever;**
	32.24	They will die from hunger and **fever;**
Job	30.30	I am burning with **fever.**
Ps	38. 7	I am burning with **fever** and I am near to death.
Lam	5.10	has made us burn with **fever,** until our skin is as hot
Mt	8.14	there he saw Peter's mother-in-law sick in bed with a **fever.**
	8.15	the **fever** left her, and she got up and began to wait
Mk	1.30	sick in bed with a **fever,** and as soon as Jesus arrived,
	1.31	The **fever** left her, and she began to wait on them.
Lk	4.38	was sick with a high **fever,** and they spoke to Jesus about
	4.39	and stood at her bedside and ordered the **fever** to leave her.
	4.39	The **fever** left her, and she got up at once and began
Jn	4.52	"It was one o'clock yesterday afternoon when the **fever** left him."
Acts	28. 8	Publius' father was in bed, sick with **fever** and dysentery.

FEW

Gen	18.28	Will you destroy the whole city because there are five too **few?"**
	29.20	time seemed like only a **few** days to him, because he loved
	47. 9	Those years have been **few** and difficult, unlike the long
Ex	9. 8	Moses and Aaron, "Take a **few** handfuls of ashes from a furnace;
Lev	25.16	if there are only a **few** years, the price shall be lower,
	26.22	your livestock, and leave so **few** of you that your roads will
	26.39	The **few** of you who survive in the land of your enemies
Num	9.20	Sometimes the cloud remained over the Tent for only a **few** days;
Deut	4.27	among other nations, where only a **few** of you will survive.
	26. 5	They were **few** in number when they went there, but they
	28.18	by giving you only a **few** children,
	28.18	poor crops, and **few** cattle and sheep.
	28.62	in the sky, only a **few** of you will survive, because you
	33. 6	"May Reuben never die out, Although their people are **few."**
Josh	11.22	a **few,** however, were left in Gaza, Gath, and Ashdod.
Judg	14. 8	A **few** days later Samson went back to marry her.
1 Sam	3. 1	of Eli, there were very **few** messages from the Lord, and
	14. 6	giving us the victory, no matter how **few** of us there are."
2 Sam	13. 6	Tamar come and make a **few** cakes here where I can see
1 Chr	4.27	daughters, but his relatives had **fewer** children, and the
	16.19	God's people were **few** in number, strangers in the land of Canaan.
Neh	2.12	up and went out, taking a **few** of my companions with me.
Ps	105.12	God's people were **few** in number, strangers in the land of Canaan.
Prov	19. 4	new friends, but the poor cannot keep the **few** they have.
Ecc	12. 3	Your teeth will be too **few** to chew your food, and your
Is	7.22	Yes, the **few** survivors left in the land will have milk and
	10.19	There will be so **few** trees left that even a child will
	10.21	A **few** of the people of Israel will come back to their
	10.22	grains of sand by the sea, only a **few** will come back.
	16.14	its many people, only a **few** will survive, and they will be
	17. 6	Only a **few** people will survive, and Israel will be like an
	17. 6	the very top, or a **few** that are left on the lower
	21.17	the bravest men of Kedar, but **few** of them will be left.
	24. 6	**Fewer and fewer** remain alive.
	40.16	our God, and its trees are too **few** to kindle the fire.
Jer	34.15	Just a **few** days ago you changed your minds and did what
	42. 2	but now only a **few** of us are left, as you can
	44.14	No one will return except a **few** refugees."
	44.28	But a **few** of you will escape death and return from Egypt
	49. 9	pick grapes, they leave a **few** on the vines, and when robbers
Ezek	5. 3	Keep back a **few** hairs and wrap them in the hem of
	5. 4	Then take a **few** of them out again, throw them in the
	12.16	I will let a **few** of them survive the war, the famine,
	13.19	get a few handfuls of barley and a **few** pieces of bread.
Amos	3.12	has eaten, so only a **few** will survive of Samaria's people,
Obad	5	When people gather grapes, they always leave a **few.**
Mt	7.14	to it is hard, and there are **few** people who find it.
	9.37	harvest is large, but there are **few** workers to gather it in.
	15.34	"Seven loaves," they answered, "and a **few** small fish."
	18.28	met one of his fellow-servants who owed him a **few** pounds.
	22.14	And Jesus concluded, "Many are invited, but **few** are chosen."
Mk	2. 1	A **few** days later Jesus went back to Capernaum, and the
	6. 5	he placed his hands on a **few** sick people and healed them.
	8. 7	They also had a **few** small fish.
Lk	10. 2	"There is a large harvest, but **few** workers to gather it in.
	13.23	Someone asked him, "Sir, will just a **few** people be saved?"
	15.13	After a **few** days the younger son sold his part of the
	24.18	things that have been happening there these last **few** days?"
Jn	2.12	disciples went to Capernaum and stayed there a **few** days.
Acts	1. 5	with water, but in a **few** days you will be baptized with
	1.15	A **few** days later there was a meeting of the believers,
	9.19	Saul stayed for a **few** days with the believers in Damascus.
	10.48	Then they asked him to stay with them for a **few** days.
Rom	9.27	by the sea, yet only a **few** of them will be saved;
1 Cor	1.26	the human point of view **few** of you were wise or powerful
2 Cor	9. 6	that the person who sows **few** seeds will have a small crop;
1 Pet	3.20	The **few** people in the boat—eight in all—were saved by
Rev	2.14	But there are a **few** things I have against you:
	3. 4	But a **few** of you there in Sardis have kept your clothes

FICKLE

2 Cor	1.17	In planning this, did I appear **fickle?**

FIELD
[BARLEY-FIELD]
see also **CORNFIELD**

Gen 4. 8 Cain said to his brother Abel, "Let's go out in the **fields.**"
4. 8 they were out in the **fields,** Cain turned on his brother and
23. 9 sell me Machpelah Cave, which is near the edge of his **field.**
23.11 will give you the whole **field** and the cave that is in
23.13 I will buy the whole **field.**
23.17 It included the **field,** the cave which was in it, and all
23.17 the trees in the **field** up to the edge of the
23.20 So the **field** which had belonged to the Hittites, and the
24.63 evening to take a walk in the **fields** and saw camels coming.
24.65 "Who is that man walking towards us in the **field?"**
25. 9 in Machpelah Cave, in the **field** east of Mamre that had
25.10 It was the **field** that Abraham had bought from the Hittites;
27.27 is like the smell of a **field** which the Lord has blessed.
27.28 May God give you dew from heaven and make your **fields** fertile!
27.39 "No dew from heaven for you, No fertile **fields** for you.
29. 2 a well out in the **fields** with three flocks of sheep lying
30.14 Reuben went into the **fields** and found mandrakes,
30.16 Jacob came in from the **fields** in the evening, Leah went out
31. 4 and Leah to meet him in the **field** where his flocks were.
33.18 Canaan and set up his camp in a **field** near the city.
33.19 bought that part of the **field** from the descendants of Hamor
34. 5 sons were out in the **fields** with his livestock, he did
34. 7 just as Jacob's sons were coming in from the **fields.**
34.28 donkeys, and everything else in the city and in the **fields.**
37. 7 We were all in the **field** tying up sheaves of wheat, when
39. 5 and everything that he had in his house and in his **fields.**
41.48 In each city he stored the food from the **fields** around it.
47.19 Don't let our **fields** be deserted.
47.19 corn to keep us alive and seed to sow in our **fields."**
47.23 Here is seed for you to sow in your **fields.**
49.29 is in the **field** of Ephron the Hittite, [30]at Machpelah,
49.30 Abraham bought this cave and **field** from Ephron for a burial-ground.
49.32 The **field** and the cave in it were bought from the Hittites.
50.13 east of Mamre, in the **field** which Abraham had bought from

Ex 1.13 building projects and in their **fields,** and they had no mercy
8.13 frogs in the houses, the courtyards, and the **fields** died.
9.22 the people, the animals, and all the plants in the **fields."**
9.25 down all the plants in the **fields** and broke all the trees.
22. 5 his animals graze in a **field** or a vineyard and they stray
22. 5 crops growing in another man's **field,** he must make good the
22. 5 the loss with the crops from his own **fields** or vineyards.
22. 6 starts a fire in his **field** and it spreads through the weeds
22. 6 to another man's **field** and burns up corn that is
23.10 "For six years sow your **field** and gather in what it produces.

Lev 14. 7 He shall let the live bird fly away over the open **fields.**
14.53 live bird fly away outside the city over the open **fields.**
17. 7 animals in the **fields** as sacrifices to the goat-demons.
19. 9 "When you harvest your **fields,** do not cut the corn at
19. 9 the edges of the **fields,** and do not go back to
19.19 Do not plant two kinds of seed in the same **field.**
23.22 When you harvest your **fields,** do not cut the corn at
23.22 the edges of the **fields,** and do not go back to
23.39 When you have harvested your **fields,** celebrate this festival
25. 3 You shall sow your **fields,** prune your vineyards, and
25. 4 Do not sow your **fields** or prune your vineyards.
25. 7 your domestic animals, and the wild animals in your **fields.**
25.11 You shall not sow your **fields** or harvest the corn that
25.12 you shall eat only what the **fields** produce of themselves.
25.20 seventh year, when no **fields** are sown and no crops gathered.
25.22 When you sow your **fields** in the eighth year, you will
25.31 But houses in unwalled villages are to be treated like **fields;**
27.19 the man who dedicated the **field** wishes to buy it back, he
27.20 If he sells the **field** to someone else without first
27.21 the **field** will become the Lord's permanent property;
27.22 dedicates to the Lord a **field** that he has bought, [23]the
27.24 the Year of Restoration the **field** shall be returned to the

Num 16.14 land or given us **fields** and vineyards as our possession,
20.17 road or go into your **fields** or vineyards, and we will not
21.22 road and go into your **fields** or vineyards, and we will not
22.23 a sword, it left the road and turned into the **fields.**
23.14 He took him to the **field** of Zophim on the top of
24. 7 And plant their seed in well-watered **fields.**

Deut 7.13 he will bless your **fields,** so that you will have corn, wine,
11.10 you sowed seed, you had to work hard to irrigate the **fields;**
14.22 a tithe—a tenth of all that your **fields** produce each year.
21. 1 is found murdered in a **field** in the land that the Lord
22. 9 "Do not plant any crop in the same **field** as your grapevines;
28. 3 "The Lord will bless your towns and your **fields.**
28.16 "The Lord will curse your towns and your **fields.**
29.23 The **fields** will be a barren waste, covered with sulphur and salt;
30. 9 of livestock, and your **fields** will produce abundant crops.
32.13 rule the highlands, and they ate what grew in the **fields.**

Josh 14. 3 cities to live in, with **fields** for their cattle and flocks.
15.18 wedding day Othniel urged her to ask her father for a **field.**
21.12 However, the **fields** of the city, as well as its towns,

Judg 1.14 wedding day Othniel urged her to ask her father for a **field.**
9.32 and your men should move by night and hide in the **fields.**
9.42 to go out into the **fields,** [43]so he took his men,
9.43 divided them into three groups, and hid in the **fields,** waiting.
9.44 attacked the people in the **fields** and killed them all.
13. 9 came back to the woman while she was sitting in the **fields.**
15. 5 was still in the **fields,** and the olive orchards as well.
19.16 came by at the end of a day's work in the **fields.**

Ruth 2. 2 "Let me go to the **fields** to gather the corn that the
2. 3 Ruth went out to the **fields** and walked behind the workers,
2. 3 so happened that she was in a **field** that belonged to Boaz.
2. 8 Don't pick up corn anywhere except in this **field.**
2.17 on gathering corn in the **field** until evening, and when she
2.19 Whose **field** have you been working in?
2.19 had been working in a **field** belonging to a man named Boaz.
2.22 be better for you to work with the women in Boaz' **field.**
2.22 You might be molested if you went to someone else's **field."**
4. 3 to sell the **field** that belonged to our relative Elimelech,
4. 5 but if you buy the **field** from Naomi, then you are also
4. 5 Moabite widow, so that the **field** will stay in the dead man's
4. 6 my right to buy the **field,** because it would mean that my

1 Sam 6.14 The wagon came to a **field** belonging to a man named Joshua,
6.18 The large rock in the **field** of Joshua of Beth Shemesh, on
8.12 will have to plough his **fields,** harvest his crops, and make
8.14 He will take your best **fields,** vineyards, and olive-groves,
11. 5 just coming in from the **field** with his oxen, and he asked,
19. 3 by my father in the **field** where you are hiding, and I
20. 5 go and hide in the **fields** until the evening of the day
20.11 "Let's go out to the **fields,"** Jonathan answered.
20.24 So David hid in the **fields.**
20.35 morning Jonathan went to the **fields** to meet David, as they
22. 7 that David will give **fields** and vineyards to all of you,
25.15 were with them in the **fields,** nothing that belonged to us

2 Sam 1.21 may its **fields** be always barren!
2.16 And so that place in Gibeon is called **"Field** of Swords."
7. 8 looking after sheep in the **fields** and made you the ruler of
14. 6 a quarrel out in the **fields,** where there was no one to
14.30 to his servants, "Look, Joab's **field** is next to mine, and
14.30 So they went and set the **field** on fire.
14.31 demanded, "Why did your servants set fire to my **field?"**
20.12 from the road into the **field** and threw a blanket over it.
23.11 Philistines had gathered at Lehi, where there was a **field** of peas.
23.12 in the **field,** defended it, and killed the Philistines.

1 Kgs 20.21 King Ahab took to the **field,** captured the horses and chariots,
20.24 from their commands and replace them with **field** commanders.

2 Kgs 3.19 all their fertile **fields** by covering them with stones."
3.25 As they passed a fertile **field,** every Israelite would throw
3.25 a stone on it until finally all the **fields** were covered;
4.18 his father, who was in the **field** with the harvest workers.
4.39 One of them went out in the **fields** to get some herbs.
8. 6 all the crops that her **fields** had produced during the seven
9.21 They met him at the **field** which had belonged to Naboth.
9.25 his body and throw it in the **field** that belonged to Naboth.
9.26 I promise that I will punish you here in this same **field.'**
9.26 "and throw it in the **field** that belonged to Naboth, so as
19.26 were like grass in a **field** or weeds growing on a roof
25.12 property, and put them to work in the vineyards and **fields.**

1 Chr 6.56 The **fields** and villages, however, that belonged to the
11.13 was in a **barley-field** when the Israelites started to run away,
11.14 stand in the middle of the **field** and fought the Philistines.
16.32 be glad, **fields,** and everything in you!
17. 7 looking after sheep in the **fields** and made you the ruler of

Neh 5. 3 have had to mortgage our **fields** and vineyards and houses to
5. 4 money to pay the royal tax on our **fields** and vineyards.
5. 5 We are helpless because our **fields** and vineyards have been
5.11 And give them back their **fields,** vineyards, olive-groves,

Job 1.14 "We were ploughing the **fields** with the oxen," he said,
4. 8 I have seen people plough **fields** of evil and sow
5.10 He sends rain on the land and he waters the **fields.**
5.23 The **fields** you plough will be free of rocks;
24. 6 They have to harvest **fields** they don't own, and gather
27.18 web or like the hut of a slave guarding the **fields.**
39.10 Or make him pull a harrow in your **fields?**

Ps 23. 2 He lets me rest in **fields** of green grass and leads me
50.11 wild birds are mine and all living things in the **fields.**
65.10 rain on the ploughed **fields** and soak them with water;
65.13 The **fields** are covered with sheep;
72. 6 like rain on the **fields,** like showers falling on the land.
72.16 May the cities be filled with people, like **fields** full of grass.
78.46 He sent locusts to eat their crops and to destroy their **fields.**
96.12 be glad, **fields,** and everything in you!
105.44 let them take over their **fields,** [45]so that his people
107.37 They sowed the **fields** and planted grapevines
129. 3 deep wounds in my back and made it like a ploughed **field.**
132. 6 the Covenant Box, and we found it in the **fields** of Jearim.
144.13 May the sheep in our **fields** bear young by the tens of

Prov 8.26 made the earth and its **fields** or even the first handful of
13.23 Unused **fields** could yield plenty of food for the poor,
20. 4 too lazy to plough his **fields** at the right time will have
24.27 establish a home until your **fields** are ready, and you are
24.30 I walked through the **fields** and vineyards of a lazy,

Song 2.12 the song of doves is heard in the **fields.**

Is 1. 8 watchman's hut in a vineyard or a shed in a cucumber **field.**
5. 8 You buy more houses and **fields** to add to those you already
16.10 No one is happy now in the fertile **fields.**
17. 5 Israel will be like a **field** where the corn has been cut
17. 5 harvested, as desolate as a **field** in the valley of Rephaim
28.24 ploughing his **fields** and getting them ready for sowing.
28.25 barley, and at the edges of his **fields** he sows other grain.
30.24 and donkeys that plough your **fields** will eat the finest and
32.12 the fertile **fields** and the vineyards have been destroyed,
32.15 and **fields** will produce rich crops.
35. 2 as fertile as the **fields** of Carmel and Sharon.
37.27 were like grass in a **field** or weeds growing on a roof

Jer 4. 3 of Judah and Jerusalem, "Plough up your unploughed **fields;**
4.17 Jerusalem like men guarding a **field,** because her people have
6.12 given to others, and so will their **fields** and their wives.
8.10 So I will give their **fields** to new owners and their
9.22 piles of manure on the **fields,** like corn cut and left behind
10. 5 Such idols are like scarecrows in a **field** of melons;
12. 4 our land be dry, and the grass in every **field** be withered?
12.10 they have trampled down my **fields;**

Jer 13.27 the hills and in the **fields,** like a man lusting after his
14. 5 In the **field** the mother deer abandons her new-born fawn
14.18 I go out into the **fields,** I see the bodies of men
26.18 will be ploughed like a **field,** Jerusalem will become a pile
31.40 is thrown, and all the **fields** above the brook of Kidron as
32. 7 the request to buy his **field** at Anathoth in the territory of
32. 8 me there in the courtyard and asked me to buy the **field.**
32. 9 I bought the **field** from Hanamel and weighed out the money
32.15 Israel, has said that houses, **fields,** and vineyards will
32.25 ordered me to buy the **field** in the presence of witnesses,
32.43 But **fields** will once again be bought in this land.
35. 9 we live in tents—and we own no vineyards, **fields,** or corn.
39.10 owned no property, and he gave them vineyards and **fields.**
41. 8 We have wheat, barley, olive-oil, and honey hidden in the **fields."**
52.16 and he put them to work in the vineyards and **fields.**
Ezek 16. 5 You were thrown out in an open **field.**
17. 5 planted it in a fertile **field,** where there was always water
17. 8 planted in a fertile, well-watered **field** so that it could
34.25 can live safely in the **fields** and sleep in the forests.
34.27 trees will bear fruit, the **fields** will produce crops, and
34.29 I will give them fertile **fields** and put an end to hunger
36.30 of your fruit-trees and your **fields,** so that there will be
36.34 used to walk by your **fields** saw how overgrown and wild they
36.36 I, the Lord, rebuild ruined cities and replant waste **fields.**
39. 5 They will fall dead in the open **field.**
39.10 to gather firewood in the **fields** or cut down trees in the
Dan 4.15 Leave it there in the **field** with the grass.
4.23 round it, and leave it there in the **field** with the grass.
Hos 8. 7 A **field** of corn that doesn't ripen can never produce any bread.
10. 4 growing like poisonous weeds in a ploughed **field.**
12.11 there will become piles of stone in the open **fields."**
Joel 1.10 The **fields** are bare;
2.21 **"Fields,** don't be afraid, but be joyful and glad
Amos 4. 7 Rain fell on one **field,** but another field dried up.
Mic 2. 2 When they want **fields,** they seize them;
3.12 will be ploughed like a **field,** Jerusalem will become a pile
Nah 1. 4 The **fields** of Bashan wither, Mount Carmel turns brown, and
Hab 3.17 the olive-crop fails and the **fields** produce no corn, even
Zeph 2. 6 will become open **fields** with shepherds' huts and sheep pens.
Zech 10. 1 clouds and showers, making the **fields** green for everyone.
12. 6 a forest or in a **field** of ripe corn—they will destroy
Mt 13. 4 scattered the seed in the **field,** some of it fell along the
13.24 A man sowed good seed in his **field.**
13.27 and said, 'Sir, it was good seed you sowed in your **field;**
13.31 A man takes a mustard seed and sows it in his **field.**
13.36 "Tell us what the parable about the weeds in the **field** means."
13.38 the **field** is the world;
13.44 A man happens to find a treasure hidden in a **field.**
13.44 everything he has, and then goes back and buys that **field.**
19.29 or mother or children or **fields** for my sake, will receive a
24.18 man who is in the **field** must not go back to get
24.40 At that time two men will be working in a **field:**
27. 8 that field is called **"Field of Blood"** to this very day.
Mk 4. 4 scattered the seed in the **field,** some of it fell along the
4.26 A man scatters seed in his **field.**
10.29 or father or children or **fields** for me and for the gospel,
10.30 mothers, children and **fields**—and persecutions as well;
11. 8 cut branches in the **fields** and spread them on the road.
13.16 man who is in the **field** must not go back to the
Lk 2. 8 the night in the **fields,** taking care of their flocks.
8. 5 scattered the seed in the **field,** some of it fell along the
13.19 A man takes a mustard seed and sows it in his **field.**
14.18 servant, 'I have bought a **field** and must go and look at
15.25 "In the meantime the elder son was out in the **field.**
17. 7 he comes in from the **field,** do you tell him to hurry
17.31 who is out in the **field** must not go back to the
Jn 4. 5 was not far from the **field** that Jacob had given to his
4.35 But I tell you, take a good look at the **fields;**
4.38 to reap a harvest in a **field** where you did not work;
Acts 1.18 evil act he bought a **field,** where he fell to his death;
1.19 call that **field** Akeldama, which means "Field of Blood.")
4.34 Those who owned **fields** or houses would sell them, bring the
4.37 "One who Encourages"), [37] sold a **field** he owned, brought the money,
28. 7 from that place were some **fields** that belonged to Publius,
1 Cor 3. 9 partners working together for God, and you are God's **field.**
2 Cor 10.16 to boast about work already done in another man's **field.**
Gal 6. 8 If he sows in the **field** of his natural desires, from it
6. 8 if he sows in the **field** of the Spirit, from the Spirit
Jas 5. 4 not paid any wages to the men who work in your **fields.**

FIELD OF BLOOD

Mt 27. 8 that field is called **"Field of Blood"** to this very day.
Acts 1.19 call that field Akeldama, which means **"Field of Blood.")**

FIELD OF SWORDS

2 Sam 2.16 And so that place in Gibeon is called **"Field of Swords."**

FIERCE

Gen 49. 7 anger, because it is so **fierce,** And on their fury, because
49.23 His enemies attack him **fiercely** And pursue him with
Num 32.14 ready to bring down the **fierce** anger of the Lord on Israel
Deut 9.19 was afraid of the Lord's **fierce** anger, because he was
13.17 the Lord will turn from his **fierce** anger and show you mercy.
29.24 What was the reason for his **fierce** anger?'
Judg 15. 8 He attacked them **fiercely** and killed many of them.
1 Sam 4. 2 The Philistines attacked, and after **fierce** fighting they
14.52 lived, Saul had to fight **fiercely** against the Philistines.
2 Sam 17. 8 and that they are as **fierce** as a mother bear robbed of
2 Kgs 23.26 But the Lord's **fierce** anger had been aroused against
1 Chr 12. 8 with shields and spears, as **fierce-looking** as lions and as
Job 28. 8 No lion or other **fierce** beast Ever travels those lonely roads.
41.10 When he is aroused, he is **fierce;**
Ps 22.12 all round me, like **fierce** bulls from the land of Bashan.
58. 6 Break the teeth of these **fierce** lions, O God.
58. 9 in his **fierce** anger God will blow them away while they are
78.49 pouring out his anger and **fierce** rage, which came as
83.15 with your storm and terrify them with your **fierce** winds.
91.13 You will trample down lions and snakes, **fierce** lions
118.13 I was **fiercely** attacked and was being defeated, but the
Prov 1.27 you like a storm, bringing **fierce** winds of trouble, and you
Is 13. 9 Lord is coming—that cruel day of his **fierce** anger and fury.
35. 9 no **fierce** animals will pass that way.
Jer 4. 8 weep and wail because the **fierce** anger of the Lord has not
4.26 its cities were in ruins because of the Lord's **fierce** anger.
6.29 The furnace burns **fiercely,** but the waste metals do not
7.20 Sovereign Lord, will pour out my **fierce** anger on this Temple.
12.13 Because of my **fierce** anger their crops have failed."
25.38 of war and the Lord's **fierce** anger have turned the country
51.45 Run for your life from my **fierce** anger.
Ezek 19. 2 She reared her cubs among the **fierce** male lions.
19. 5 reared another of her cubs, and he grew into a **fierce** lion.
Hab 1. 6 Babylonians to power, those **fierce,** restless people.
1. 8 "Their horses are faster than leopards, **fiercer** than hungry wolves.
Mt 8.24 Suddenly a **fierce** storm hit the lake, and the boat was
8.28 in them and were so **fierce** that no one dared travel on
Acts 15. 2 Barnabas got into a **fierce** argument with them about this,
20.29 know that after I leave, **fierce** wolves will come among you,
2 Tim 3. 3 they will be unkind, merciless, slanderers, violent, and **fierce;**
Heb 10.27 the coming Judgement and the **fierce** fire which will destroy
11.34 mouths of lions, [34] put out **fierce** fires, escaped being
Jas 4. 5 "The spirit that God placed in us is filled with **fierce** desires."
Rev 16. 9 They were burnt by the **fierce** heat, and they cursed the

FIERY see FIRE

FIFTH see FIVE

FIG

Gen 3. 7 so they sewed **fig** leaves together and covered themselves.
Num 13.23 They also brought back some pomegranates and **figs.**
20. 5 There's no corn, no **figs,** no grapes, no pomegranates.
Deut 8. 8 land that produces wheat and barley, grapes, **figs,**
Judg 9.10 the trees said to the **fig-tree,** 'You come and be our king.'
9.11 But the **fig-tree** answered, 'In order to govern you, I
1 Sam 25.18 two hundred cakes of dried **figs,** and loaded them on donkeys.
30.12 and water, [12] some dried **figs,** and two bunches of raisins.
1 Kgs 4.25 each family with its own grapevines and **fig-trees.**
2 Kgs 18.31 from your own vines, and **figs** from your own trees, and to
20. 7 his boil a paste made of **figs,** and he would get well.
1 Chr 12.40 mules, and oxen loaded with food—flour, **figs,** raisins, wine,
Neh 13.15 were loading corn, wine, grapes, **figs,** and other things on
Ps 78.47 killed their grapevines with hail and their **fig-trees** with frost.
105.33 he destroyed their grapevines and **fig-trees**
Prov 27.18 Take care of a **fig-tree**
27.18 and you will have **figs** to eat.
Song 2.13 **Figs** are beginning to ripen;
Is 28. 4 will disappear like the first **figs** of the season, picked and
34. 4 will fall like leaves dropping from a vine or a **fig-tree.**
36.16 from your own vines and **figs** from your own trees, and to
38. 6 put a paste made of **figs** on his boil, and he would
Jer 5.17 flocks and your herds and destroy your vines and **fig-trees.**
8.13 like a vine with no grapes, like a fig-tree with no **figs;**
24. 1 showed me two baskets of **figs** placed in front of the Temple.
24. 2 The first basket contained good **figs,** those that ripen early;
24. 2 the other one contained bad **figs,** too bad to eat.
24. 3 I answered, **"Figs.**
24. 5 Babylonia are like these good **figs,** and I will treat them
24. 8 treat them all like these **figs** that are too bad to be
29.17 I will make them like **figs** that are too rotten to be
Hos 2.12 destroy her grapevines and her **fig-trees,** which she said her
9.10 it was like seeing the first ripe **figs** of the season.
Joel 1. 7 They have destroyed our grapevines and chewed up our **fig-trees.**
1.12 The grapevines and **fig-trees** have withered;
2.22 bear their fruit, and there are plenty of **figs** and grapes.
Amos 4. 9 your gardens and vineyards, your **fig-trees** and olive-trees.
7.14 I am a herdsman, and I take care of **fig-trees.**
Mic 4. 4 among his own vineyards and **fig-trees,** and no one will make
7. 1 All the grapes and all the tasty **figs** have been picked.
Nah 3.12 All your fortresses will be like fig-trees with ripe **figs:**
Hab 3.17 Even though the **fig-trees** have no fruit and no grapes
Hag 2.19 corn left, and the grapevines, **fig-trees,** pomegranates, and
Zech 3.10 and security, surrounded by your vineyards and **fig-trees."**
Mt 7.16 Thorn bushes do not bear grapes, and briars do not bear **figs.**
21.19 He saw a **fig-tree** by the side of the road and went
21.19 At once the **fig-tree** dried up.
21.20 "How did the **fig-tree** dry up so quickly?"
21.21 will be able to do what I have done to this **fig-tree.**
24.32 "Let the **fig-tree** teach you a lesson.
Mk 11.13 saw in the distance a **fig-tree** covered with leaves, so he
11.13 he went to see if he could find any **figs** on it.
11.13 only leaves, because it was not the right time for **figs.**
11.14 Jesus said to the **fig-tree,**
11.14 "No one shall ever eat **figs** from you again!"
11.20 as they walked along the road, they saw the **fig-tree.**

Mk 11.21 Jesus, "Look, Teacher, the **fig-tree** you cursed has died!"
13.28 "Let the **fig-tree** teach you a lesson.
Lk 6.44 you do not pick **figs** from thorn bushes or gather grapes from
13. 6 was once a man who had a **fig-tree** growing in his vineyard.
13. 6 He went looking for **figs** on it but found none.
13. 7 been coming here looking for **figs** on this fig-tree,
13. 9 Then if the tree bears **figs** next year, so much the better;
21.29 "Think of the **fig-tree** and all the other trees.
Jn 1.48 when you were under the **fig-tree** before Philip called you."
1.50 I told you I saw you when you were under the **fig-tree?**
Jas 3.12 A **fig-tree,** my brothers, cannot bear olives;
3.12 a grapevine cannot bear **figs,** nor can a salty spring produce
Rev 6.13 to the earth, like unripe **figs** falling from the tree when a

FIGHT
[FOUGHT]

Gen 14. 8 the Valley of Siddim and **fought** [9]against the kings of Elam,
14.14 he called together all the **fighting** men in his camp, 318 in
30. 8 Rachel said, "I have **fought** a hard fight with my sister,
Ex 1.10 our enemies in order to **fight** against us, and might escape
2.13 The next day he went back and saw two Hebrew men **fighting.**
13.17 Egypt when they see that they are going to have to **fight."**
14.14 The Lord will **fight** for you, and there is no need for
14.25 "The Lord is **fighting** for the Israelites against us.
17. 9 "Pick out some men to go and **fight** the Amalekites tomorrow.
17.10 him and went out to **fight** the Amalekites, while Moses,
17.16 The Lord will continue to **fight** against the Amalekites for ever!"
21.18 "If there is a **fight** and one man hits another
21.22 "If some men are **fighting** and hurt a pregnant woman so
23.22 everything I command, I will **fight** against all your enemies.
23.27 the people against whom you **fight,** and I will make all your
Lev 26.37 you, and you will be unable to **fight** against any enemy.
Num 21.26 king Sihon, who had **fought** against the former king of Moab
22.11 for him, so that he can **fight** them and drive them out."
23.22 He **fights** for them like a wild ox.
24. 8 He **fights** for them like a wild ox.
32.21 All your **fighting** men are to cross the Jordan and under
32.27 We will cross the Jordan and **fight,** just as you have said."
33.55 and thorns in your sides, and they will **fight** against you.
Deut 1.30 lead you, and he will **fight** for you, just as you saw
1.41 of you got ready to **fight,** thinking it would be easy to
2.14 All the **fighting** men of that generation had died, as the
2.32 with all his men to **fight** us near the town of Jahaz,
3. 1 with all his men to **fight** us near the town of Edrei.
3.18 Now arm your **fighting** men and send them across the Jordan
3.22 afraid of them, for the Lord your God will **fight** for you.'
20. 1 "When you go out to **fight** against your enemies and you
20. 2 Before you start **fighting,** a priest is to come forward and
20.12 surrender, but choose to **fight,** surround it with your army.
25.11 two men are having a **fight** and the wife of one tries
29. 7 Heshbon and King Og of Bashan came out to **fight** against us.
32.42 I will spare no one who **fights** against me;
33. 7 **Fight** for them, Lord, And help them against their enemies."
Josh 5. 4 the men who were of **fighting** age when they left Egypt had
7. 3 Don't send the whole army up there to **fight;**
8.14 towards the Jordan Valley to **fight** the Israelites at the
9. 2 joined forces to **fight** against Joshua and the Israelites.
10. 2 it was larger than Ai, and its men were good **fighters.**
10.14 The Lord **fought** on Israel's side!
10.42 because the Lord, Israel's God, was **fighting** for Israel.
11. 5 and set up camp at Merom Brook to **fight** against Israel.
11. 8 The **fight** continued until none of the enemy was left alive.
11.20 had made them determined to **fight** the Israelites, so that
23. 3 The Lord your God has been **fighting** for you.
23.10 the Lord your God is **fighting** for you, just as he promised.
24. 8 They **fought** you, but I gave you victory over them.
24. 9 Then the king of Moab, Balak son of Zippor, **fought** against you.
24.11 The men of Jericho **fought** against you, as did the Amorites,
Judg 1. 3 assigned to us, and we will **fight** the Canaanites together.
1. 5 They found Adonibezek there and **fought** against him.
1. 9 this they went on to **fight** the Canaanites who lived in the
4. 7 of Jabin's army, to **fight** against you at the River Kishon.
5. 2 The Israelites were determined to **fight;**
5.13 the Lord's people came to him ready to **fight.**
5.19 At Taanach, by the stream of Megiddo, the kings came and **fought;**
5.19 the kings of Canaan **fought,** but they took no silver away.
5.20 The stars **fought** from the sky;
5.20 as they moved across the sky, they **fought** against Sisera.
5.23 come to help the Lord, come as soldiers to **fight** for him."
6. 9 from the people who **fought** against you here in this land.
7.24 of Ephraim to say, "Come down and **fight** the Midianites.
8. 1 "Why didn't you call us when you went to **fight** the Midianites?
9.17 Remember that my father **fought** for you.
9.29 to him, 'Reinforce your army, come on out and **fight!' "**
9.38 Go on out now and **fight** them."
9.39 Gaal led the men of Shechem out and **fought** Abimelech.
9.45 The **fighting** continued all day long.
10. 9 even crossed the Jordan to **fight** the tribes of Judah,
10.18 another, "Who will lead the **fight** against the Ammonites?
11. 6 "Come and lead us, so that we can **fight** the Ammonites."
11. 8 to go with us and **fight** the Ammonites and lead all the
11. 9 take me back home to **fight** the Ammonites and the Lord gives
11.32 Jephthah crossed the river to **fight** the Ammonites, and the
12. 1 you cross the border to **fight** the Ammonites without calling
12. 3 and crossed the border to **fight** them, and the Lord gave me
12. 3 So why are you coming to **fight** me now?"
12. 4 men of Gilead together, **fought** the men of Ephraim and defeated
14. 4 the Lord was looking for a chance to **fight** the Philistines.
20.14 came to Gibeah to **fight** against the other people of Israel.
20.27 "Should we go out to **fight** our brothers the Benjaminites again,
Judg 20.27 The Lord answered, **"Fight.**
20.31 The Benjaminites came out to **fight** and were led away
20.34 of all Israel, attacked Gibeah, and the **fighting** was hard.
1 Sam 4. 1 war against Israel, so the Israelites set out to **fight** them.
4. 2 Philistines attacked, and after fierce **fighting** they
4. 9 **Fight** like men, or we will become slaves to the Hebrews,
4. 9 So **fight** like men!"
4.10 The Philistines **fought** hard and defeated the Israelites,
8.20 and to lead us out to war and to **fight** our battles."
12. 9 of Hazor, **fight** against your ancestors and conquer them.
13. 5 The Philistines assembled to **fight** the Israelites;
14.20 who were **fighting** each other in complete confusion.
14.23 the Philistines, [23]**fighting** all the way beyond Bethaven.
14.31 the Israelites defeated the Philistines, **fighting** all the
14.47 Saul became king of Israel, he **fought** against all his enemies
14.47 Wherever he **fought** he was victorious.
14.48 He **fought** heroically and defeated even the people of Amalek.
14.52 lived, Saul had to **fight** fiercely against the Philistines.
15. 7 Saul defeated the Amalekites, **fighting** all the way
15.18 He told you to **fight** until you had killed them all.
17. 2 Valley of Elah, where they got ready to **fight** the Philistines.
17. 8 Choose one of your men to **fight** me.
17.10 I dare you to pick someone to **fight** me!"
17.19 Israelites are in the Valley of Elah **fighting** the Philistines."
17.28 You just came to watch the **fighting!"**
17.32 I will go and **fight** him."
17.33 "How could you **fight** him?
17.39 "I can't **fight** with all this," he said to Saul.
17.48 David ran quickly towards the Philistine battle line to **fight** him.
17.55 saw David going out to **fight** Goliath, he asked Abner, the
18.17 a brave and loyal soldier, and **fight** the Lord's battles."
18.30 Philistine armies would come and **fight,** but in every battle
23.28 So Saul stopped pursuing David and went to **fight** the Philistines.
24. 1 When Saul came back from **fighting** the Philistines, he was
25.28 your descendants also, because you are **fighting** his battles;
28. 1 Philistines gathered their troops to **fight** Israel,
28. 1 understand that you and your men are to **fight** on my side."
29. 4 he might turn against us during the **fighting.**
29. 6 pleased to let you go with me and **fight** in this battle.
29. 8 I go with you, my master and king, and **fight** your enemies?"
30.17 dawn the next day David attacked them and **fought** until evening.
31. 1 The Philistines **fought** a battle against the Israelites on
31. 3 The **fighting** was heavy round Saul, and he himself was hit
2 Sam 2.14 the young men from each side to **fight** an armed contest."
2.15 and the tribe of Benjamin, **fought** twelve of David's men.
2.26 out to Joab, "Do we have to go on **fighting** for ever?
2.28 and so the **fighting** stopped.
3. 1 The **fighting** between the forces supporting Saul's family
3. 6 As the **fighting** continued between David's forces and the
8.10 victory over Hadadezer, against whom Toi had **fought** many times.
10.12 Let's **fight** hard for our people and for the cities of our
10.14 Then Joab turned back from **fighting** the Ammonites and went
10.17 The **fighting** began, [18]and the Israelites drove the Syrian army
11. 7 Joab and the troops were well, and how the **fighting** was going.
11.15 the front line, where the **fighting** is heaviest, then retreat
11.17 enemy troops came out of the city and **fought** Joab's forces;
11.20 you, 'Why did you go so near the city to **fight** them?
11.23 out of the city to **fight** us in the open, but we
17. 8 and his men are hard **fighters** and that they are as fierce
17.10 is a great soldier and that his men are hard **fighters.**
18. 6 out into the countryside and **fought** the Israelites in the forest
18. 8 The **fighting** spread over the countryside, and more men
18.16 be blown to stop the **fighting,** and his troops came back from
21.15 and David and his men went and **fought** the Philistines.
21.20 battle at Gath, where there was a giant who loved to **fight.**
23. 8 **fought** with his spear against eight hundred men and killed them
23.10 he stood his ground and **fought** the Philistines until his hand
23.18 **fought** with his spear against three hundred men and killed them,
1 Kgs 5. 3 my father David had to **fight** against the enemy countries all
14.19 Jeroboam did, the wars he **fought** and how he ruled, are all
20.18 whether they are coming to **fight** or to ask for peace."
20.20 Israelite army, [20]and each one killed the man he **fought.**
20.23 will certainly defeat them if we **fight** them in the plains.
20.25 We will **fight** the Israelites in the plains, and this time we
20.29 the seventh day they started **fighting,** and the Israelites
20.39 said, "Your Majesty, I was **fighting** in the battle when a
22.11 'With these you will **fight** the Syrians and totally defeat them.' "
2 Kgs 3.23 "The three enemy armies must have **fought** and killed each other!
10. 3 descendants, make him king, and **fight** to defend him."
13.17 You will **fight** the Syrians in Aphek until you defeat them."
14. 8 messengers to King Jehoash of Israel, challenging him to **fight.**
14.11 out with his men and **fought** against him at Beth Shemesh in
19. 8 Lachish and was **fighting** against the nearby city of Libnah;
1 Chr 7.40 They were heads of families, famous **fighting** men,
10. 1 The Philistines **fought** a battle against the Israelites on
10. 3 The **fighting** was heavy round Saul, and he was hit by enemy
11.11 **fought** with his spear against three hundred men and killed them
11.13 He **fought** on David's side against the Philistines at the
11.14 stand in the middle of the field and **fought** the Philistines.
11.20 **fought** with his spear against three hundred men and killed them,
12.19 he was marching out with the Philistines to **fight** King Saul.
12.23 Relatives of Zadok, an able young **fighter:**
12.23 and reliable men ready to **fight,** trained to use all kinds of
18.10 victory over Hadadezer, against whom Toi had **fought** many times.
19. 7 too came out from all their cities and got ready to **fight.**
19.13 Let's **fight** hard for our people and for the cities of our
19.17 The **fighting** began, [18]and the Israelites drove the Syrian army
22. 8 that I had killed too many people and **fought** too many wars.
2 Chr 11. 4 They obeyed the Lord's command and did not go to **fight** Jeroboam.
13. 8 Now you propose to **fight** against the royal authority that

2 Chr 13.12 People of Israel, don't **fight** against the Lord, the God of
14.10 Asa went out to **fight** him, and both sides took up their
14.11 your name we have come out to **fight** against this huge army.
14.13 Sudanese were killed that the army was unable to rally and **fight.**
18.10 'With these you will **fight** the Syrians and totally defeat them.' "
20.17 You will not have to **fight** this battle.
20.23 it, and then they turned on each other in savage **fighting.**
25.11 There they **fought** and killed ten thousand Edomite soldiers
25.17 of Jehoahaz and grandson of Jehu, challenging him to **fight.**
26.13 were 307,500 soldiers able to **fight** effectively for the king
27. 5 He **fought** against the king of Ammon and his army and
32. 8 the Lord our God to help us and to **fight** our battles."
35.20 Egypt led an army to **fight** at Carchemish on the River Euphrates.
35.21 "This war I am **fighting** does not concern you, King of
35.21 I have not come to **fight** you, but to fight my enemies,
35.22 But Josiah was determined to **fight.**
Neh 4.14 the Lord is, and **fight** for your fellow-countrymen,
4.20 Our God will **fight** for us."
Esth 8.11 women, the Jews could **fight** back and destroy the attackers;
Job 15.26 he stubbornly holds up his shield and rushes to **fight** against God.
27. 7 who oppose me and **fight** against me be punished like wicked,
41. 8 you'll never forget the **fight!**
Ps 35. 1 who oppose me, Lord, and **fight** those who fight against me!
46.10 "Stop **fighting,**" he says, "and know that I am God,
55.18 back from the battles that I **fight** against so many enemies.
56. 2 There are so many who **fight** against me.
80. 6 You let the surrounding nations **fight** over our land;
110. 3 On the day you **fight** your enemies, your people will volunteer.
Prov 24. 6 make careful plans before you **fight** a battle, and the more
Is 8. 9 Get ready to **fight,** but be afraid!
13. 3 proud and confident soldiers to **fight** a holy war and punish
19. 2 Rival cities will **fight** each other, and rival kings will
22. 2 Your men who died in this war did not die **fighting.**
27. 4 were thorns and briars to **fight** against, then I would burn
28.21 The Lord will **fight** as he did at Mount Perazim and in
30.32 God himself will **fight** against the Assyrians.
33. 3 When you **fight** for us, nations run away from the noise of
37. 8 Lachish and was **fighting** against the nearby city of Libnah;
41.11 Those who **fight** against you will die [12]and will disappear
42.13 The Lord goes out to **fight** like a warrior;
49.25 I will **fight** against whoever fights you, and I will rescue
54.15 whoever **fights** against you will fall.
58. 4 Your fasting makes you violent, and you quarrel and **fight.**
63.10 So the Lord became their enemy and **fought** against them.
Jer 15.20 They will **fight** against you, but they will not defeat you.
21. 4 defeat your army that is **fighting** against the king of
21. 5 I will **fight** against you with all my might, my anger, my
21.13 But I will **fight** against you.
25. 9 going to bring them to **fight** against Judah and its
32. 5 Even if he **fights** the Babylonians, he will not be successful.
33. 5 Some will **fight** against the Babylonians, who will fill the
46.21 They did not stand and **fight;**
50.24 Babylonia, you **fought** against me, and you have been caught
51.30 The Babylonian soldiers have stopped **fighting**
51.46 of violence in the land and of one king **fighting** another.
Ezek 7.15 There is **fighting** in the streets, and sickness and
7.15 country will die in the **fighting,** and anyone in the city
17.17 be able to help him **fight** when the Babylonians build
19. 8 The nations gathered to **fight** him;
26. 8 in the towns on the mainland will be killed in the **fighting.**
32.21 greatest heroes and those who **fought** on the Egyptian side
38. 6 All the **fighting** men of the lands of Gomer and Beth
39.20 of horses and their riders and of soldiers and **fighting** men.
Dan 10.20 I have to go back and **fight** the guardian angel of Persia.
11.15 The soldiers of Egypt will not continue to **fight;**
11.25 Egypt, who will prepare to **fight** back with a huge and
11.32 their religion, but those who follow God will **fight** back.
11.40 the king of Syria will **fight** back with all his power, using
11.44 him, and he will **fight** furiously, killing many people.
Hos 12. 3 when Jacob grew up, he **fought** against God—
12. 4 he **fought** against an angel and won.
Joel 3.10 Even the weak must **fight.**
Amos 1.14 the day of battle, and the **fighting** will rage like a storm.
Obad 9 The **fighting** men of Teman will be terrified, and every
Mic 5. 5 defences, we will send our strongest leaders to **fight** them.
Hab 1. 3 round me, and there is **fighting** and quarrelling everywhere.
Zech 2. 9 "The Lord himself will **fight** against you, and you will be
9.13 men of Zion like a sword, to **fight** the men of Greece."
10. 5 They will **fight** because the Lord is with them, and they will
14. 3 Lord will go out and **fight** against those nations,
14. 3 as he has **fought** in times past.
14.14 The men of Judah will **fight** to defend Jerusalem.
Mt 12.25 divides itself into groups which **fight** each other will not
12.25 itself into groups which **fight** each other will fall apart.
12.26 So if one group is **fighting** another in Satan's kingdom,
24. 7 Countries will **fight** each other, kingdoms will attack one another.
Mk 3.24 divides itself into groups which **fight** each other, that
3.25 divides itself into groups which **fight** each other, that
13. 8 Countries will **fight** each other;
Lk 11.17 divides itself into groups which **fight** each other will not
11.18 Satan's kingdom has groups **fighting** each other, how can it last?
14.31 with ten thousand men to **fight** another king who comes
21.10 He went on to say, "Countries will **fight** each other;
Jn 18.36 this world, my followers would **fight** to keep me from being
Acts 5.39 You could find yourselves **fighting** against God!"
7.26 day he saw two Israelites **fighting,** and he tried to make
7.26 why are you **fighting** like this?'
Rom 1.29 they are full of jealousy, murder, **fighting,** deceit, and
7.23 my body—a law that **fights** against the law which my mind
13.12 dark, and let us take up weapons for **fighting** in the light.
13.13 no immorality or indecency, no **fighting** or jealousy.
1 Cor 15.32 I have, as it were, **fought** "wild beasts" here in Ephesus
2 Cor 10. 3 live in the world, but we do not **fight** from worldly motives.
10. 4 weapons we use in our **fight** are not the world's weapons but
Gal 5.20 People become enemies and they **fight;**
Eph 6.12 For we are not **fighting** against human beings but against
6.13 after **fighting** to the end, you will still hold your ground.
Phil 1.27 only one desire you are **fighting** together for the faith of
1.30 same battle you saw me **fighting** in the past,
1.30 and as you hear, the one I am **fighting** still.
2.25 Epaphroditus, who has worked and **fought** by my side and who
1 Tim 1.18 as weapons in order to **fight** well, [19]and keep your faith
2 Tim 2.14 a solemn warning in God's presence not to **fight** over words.
Tit 3. 9 long lists of ancestors, quarrels, and **fights** about the Law.
Heb 11.33 Through faith they **fought** whole countries and won.
Jas 4. 1 Where do all the **fights** and quarrels among you come from?
4. 1 for pleasure, which are constantly **fighting** within you.
4. 2 things, but you cannot get them, so you quarrel and **fight.**
Jude 3 once to encourage you to **fight** on for the faith which once
Rev 2.16 come to you soon and **fight** against those people with the
11. 7 that comes up out of the abyss will **fight** against them.
12. 7 Michael and his angels **fought** against the dragon,
12. 7 who **fought** back with his angels;
12.17 and went off to **fight** against the rest of her descendants,
13. 4 Who can **fight** against it?"
13. 7 It was allowed to **fight** against God's people and to defeat them,
17.14 They will **fight** against the Lamb;
19.11 it is with justice that he judges and **fights** his battles.
19.19 and their armies gathered to **fight** against the one who was

FIGURE (1)

Ex 26. 1 Embroider them with **figures** of winged creatures.
26.31 Embroider it with **figures** of winged creatures.
36. 8 red wool and embroidered with **figures** of winged creatures.
36.35 wool and embroidered it with **figures** of winged creatures.
1 Kgs 6.29 were all decorated with carved **figures** of winged creatures,
6.32 were decorated with carved **figures** of winged creatures,
6.35 and decorated with carved **figures** of winged creatures,
7.29 with the **figures** of lions, bulls, and winged creatures
7.29 there were spiral **figures** in relief.
7.30 the supports were decorated with spiral **figures** in relief.
7.36 panels were decorated with **figures** of winged creatures, lions,
7.36 with spiral **figures** all round.
10.19 up to it, with the **figure** of a lion at each end
10.19 of the throne was the **figure** of a bull's head,
10.19 beside each of the two arms was the **figure** of a lion.
2 Chr 9.18 of the throne, and the **figure** of a lion stood at each
9.19 Twelve **figures** of lions were on the steps,
Esth 2. 7 she was a beautiful girl, and had a good **figure.**
Ps 68.13 **figures** of doves covered with silver, whose wings glittered
Is 44.13 He outlines a **figure** with chalk, carves it out with his tools,
44.13 a man, a handsome human **figure,** to be placed in his house.
Ezek 1.26 sitting on the throne was a **figure** that looked like a man.
1.27 The **figure** seemed to be shining like bronze in the

FIGURE (2)

Jn 16.25 "I have used **figures** of speech to tell you these things.
16.25 when I will not use **figures** of speech, but will speak to
16.29 "Now you are speaking plainly, without using **figures** of speech.
Rom 5.14 Adam was a **figure** of the one who was to come.
Gal 4.24 These things can be understood as a **figure:**
4.25 Sinai in Arabia, is a **figure** of the present city of Jerusalem,

FIGURE (3)

1 Chr 27.24 this census, so the final **figures** were never recorded

FILL

Gen 1.20 "Let the water be **filled** with many kinds of living beings,
1.20 and let the air be **filled** with birds."
1.22 to reproduce, and to **fill** the sea, and he told the
6. 6 He was so **filled** with regret [7]that he said, "I will wipe
21.19 She went and **filled** the leather bag with water and gave some
24.16 She went down to the well, **filled** her jar, and came back.
26.15 So they **filled** in all the wells which the servants of
42.25 Joseph gave orders to **fill** his brothers' packs with corn,
44. 1 in charge of his house, **"Fill** the men's sacks with as much
Ex 1. 7 so numerous and strong that Egypt was **filled** with them.
2.15 came to draw water and **fill** the troughs for their father's
10. 6 They will **fill** your palaces and the houses of all your
12.34 So the people **filled** their baking-pans with unleavened dough,
31. 3 the tribe of Judah, [3]and I have **filled** him with my power.
35.31 God has **filled** him with his power and given him skill,
40. 7 between the Tent and the altar and **fill** it with water.
40.30 between the Tent and the altar and **filled** it with water.
40.34 Tent and the dazzling light of the Lord's presence **filled** it.
Num 7.84 weighing a total of 1.32 kilogrammes, **filled** with incense
14.21 as surely as my presence **fills** the earth, [22]none of these
Deut 28. 8 your God will bless your work and **fill** your barns with corn.
28.66 and night you will be **filled** with terror, and you will live
33.16 May their land be **filled** with all that is good, Blessed
34. 9 Joshua son of Nun was **filled** with wisdom, because Moses
Josh 9.13 When we **filled** these wineskins, they were new, but look!
Judg 6.38 wrung enough dew out of it to **fill** a bowl with water.
Ruth 2. 9 go and drink from the water jars that they have **filled."**
1 Sam 2. 1 "The Lord has **filled** my heart with joy;
17.42 look at David, he was **filled** with scorn for him because he
2 Sam 5. 9 the place where land was **filled** in on the east side of
13.15 Then Amnon was **filled** with a deep hatred for her;

2 Sam	13.39	Amnon's death, he was **filled** with longing for his son Absalom.
1 Kgs	3.28	they were all **filled** with deep respect for him,
	8.10	the Temple, it was suddenly **filled** with a cloud [11] shining
	9.15	Temple and the palace, to **fill** in land on the east side
	9.24	Solomon **filled** in the land on the east side of the city,
	11.27	Solomon was **filling** in the land on the east side of
	18.33	He said, **"Fill** four jars with water and pour it on the
	18.35	The water ran down round the altar and **filled** the trench.
2 Kgs	3.17	bed will be **filled** with water, and you, your livestock,
	4. 6	When they had **filled** all the jars, she asked if there were
	10.21	into the temple of Baal, **filling** it from one end to the
	11.20	All the people were **filled** with happiness, and the city was quiet,
	12.20	on the land that was **filled** in on the east side of
	14.10	have defeated the Edomites, and you are **filled** with pride.
1 Chr	11. 8	the place where land was **filled** in on the east side of
	16.27	Glory and majesty surround him, power and joy **fill** his Temple.
2 Chr	5.11	the Temple, it was suddenly **filled** with a cloud shining with
	7. 1	the dazzling light of the Lord's presence **filled** the Temple.
	7. 3	from heaven and the light **fill** the Temple, they fell face
	23.21	All the people were **filled** with happiness, and the city was quiet,
	24.10	and they brought their tax money and **filled** the box with it.
	30.26	The city of Jerusalem was **filled** with joy, because
	32. 5	on the land that was **filled** in on the east side of
Ezra	9.11	people who lived in it **filled** it from one end to the
Job	1.10	you have given him enough cattle to **fill** the whole country.
	3.15	like princes who **filled** their houses with gold and silver,
	9.18	he has **filled** my life with bitterness.
	13.11	reprimand you, [11] and his power will **fill** you with terror.
	26. 8	It is God who **fills** the clouds with water and keeps them
	33.19	a man by sending sickness and **filling** his body with pain.
	37.22	in the north, and the glory of God **fills** us with awe.
	41. 7	Can you **fill** his hide with fishing-spears or pierce his
Ps	10. 7	His speech is **filled** with curses, lies, and threats;
	13. 2	How long will sorrow **fill** my heart day and night?
	16.11	your presence **fills** me with joy and brings me pleasure for ever.
	17.15	and when I awake, your presence will **fill** me with joy.
	21. 6	are with him for ever and your presence **fills** him with joy.
	23. 5	me as an honoured guest and **fill** my cup to the brim.
	33. 5	his constant love **fills** the earth.
	38.18	they **fill** me with anxiety.
	45. 1	Beautiful words **fill** my mind, as I compose this song for
	51. 6	**fill** my mind with your wisdom.
	55.10	surrounding it day and night, **filling** it with crime and trouble.
	65. 9	You **fill** the streams with water;
	65.12	The pastures are **filled** with flocks;
	72.16	May the cities be **filled** with people, like fields full of grass.
	72.19	May his glory **fill** the whole world.
	75. 8	a cup in his hand, **filled** with the strong wine of his
	84. 6	the autumn rain **fills** it with pools.
	90.14	**Fill** us each morning with your constant love, so that we
	96. 6	power and beauty **fill** his Temple.
	103. 5	He **fills** my life with good things, so that I stay young
	104.13	on the hills, and the earth is **filled** with your blessings.
	104.24	The earth is **filled** with your creatures.
	105.30	overrun with frogs, even the palace was **filled** with them.
	106.14	They were **filled** with craving in the desert and put God
	107. 9	who are thirsty and **fills** the hungry with good things.
	110. 6	on the nations and **fill** the battlefield with corpses;
	116. 3	I was **filled** with fear and anxiety.
	119.53	I see the wicked breaking your law, I am **filled** with anger.
	119.120	I am **filled** with fear because of your judgements.
	119.143	I am **filled** with trouble and anxiety, but your
	119.158	at those traitors, I am **filled** with disgust, because they do
	144.13	May our barns be **filled** with crops of every kind.
Prov	1.13	We'll find all kinds of riches and **fill** our houses with loot!
	3.10	do, your barns will be **filled** with grain, and you will have
	8.21	wealth to those who love me, **filling** their houses with treasures.
	13.12	heart is crushed, but a wish come true **fills** you with joy.
	26.25	him, because his heart is **filled** to the brim with hate.
Song	1.12	on his couch, and my perfume **filled** the air with fragrance.
	4.16	**fill** the air with fragrance.
Is	1.21	At one time it was **filled** with righteous men, but now only
	6. 1	high and exalted, and his robe **filled** the whole Temple.
	6. 3	His glory **fills** the world."
	6. 4	Temple shake, and the Temple itself was **filled** with smoke.
	21. 3	heard in the vision has **filled** me with terror and pain, pain
	22. 2	The whole city is in an uproar, **filled** with noise and excitement.
	22. 7	The fertile valleys of Judah were **filled** with chariots;
	33. 5	He will **fill** Jerusalem with justice and integrity [6] and give
	35. 7	become a lake, and dry land will be **filled** with springs.
	40. 4	**Fill** every valley;
	41.23	**fill** us with fear and awe!
	42. 1	I have **filled** him with my spirit, and he will bring justice
	54. 3	Cities now deserted will be **filled** with people.
	60. 5	You will see this and be **filled** with joy;
	61. 1	The Sovereign Lord has **filled** me with his spirit.
	65.19	I myself will be **filled** with joy because of Jerusalem
Jer	5.27	Just as a hunter **fills** his cage with birds,
	5.27	they have **filled** their houses with loot.
	9.18	for us, until our eyes **fill** with tears, and our eyelids are
	13.12	of Israel that every wine-jar should be **filled** with wine.
	13.12	that they know every wine-jar should be **filled** with wine.
	13.13	the Lord, am going to **fill** the people in this land with
	15.16	and so your words **filled** my heart with joy and happiness.
	15.17	to your orders I stayed by myself and was **filled** with anger.
	16.18	as corpses, and have **filled** it with their false gods."
	17.18	**Fill** them with terror, but do not terrify me.
	17.25	and the city of Jerusalem will always be **filled** with people.
	19. 4	They have **filled** this place with the blood of innocent people,
	23.16	they are **filling** you with false hopes.
	25.15	said to me, "Here is a wine cup **filled** with my anger.
Jer	31.14	I will **fill** the priests with the richest food and
	31.27	is coming when I will **fill** the land of Israel and Judah
	33. 5	against the Babylonians, who will **fill** the houses with the
	41. 9	Ishmael **filled** the well with the bodies.
	50.31	"Babylonia, you are **filled** with pride,
Lam	3.65	Curse them and **fill** them with despair!
Ezek	3. 3	**fill** your stomach with it."
	7.19	They cannot use it to satisfy their desires or **fill** their stomachs.
	9. 7	**Fill** its courtyards with corpses.
	9. 9	all over the land and have **filled** Jerusalem with crime.
	10. 2	under the creatures and **fill** your hands with burning coals.
	10. 3	Temple when he went in, and a cloud **filled** the inner courtyard.
	10. 4	Then the cloud **filled** the Temple, and the courtyard was
	21. 7	comes, their hearts will be **filled** with fear, their hands
	23.16	she saw them, she was **filled** with lust and sent messengers
	23.20	She was **filled** with lust for oversexed men who had all
	24. 3	Set the pot on the fire and **fill** it up with water.
	24. 4	and the legs— **fill** it with choice bony pieces too.
	27.33	You **filled** the needs of every nation.
	32. 6	until it spreads over the mountains and **fills** the streams.
	43. 5	saw that the Temple was **filled** with the glory of the Lord.
	44. 4	Temple of the Lord was **filled** with the dazzling light of his
Dan	6. 7	this order is to be thrown into a pit **filled** with lions.
	6.12	except you, would be thrown into a pit **filled** with lions."
	6.16	arrested and he was thrown into the pit **filled** with lions.
	6.24	wives and their children, into the pit **filled** with lions.
Amos	3.10	The Lord says, "These people **fill** their mansions with
	4.10	I **filled** your nostrils with the stink of dead bodies in your
Mic	2.12	your land will once again be **filled** with many people."
	3. 8	as for me, the Lord **fills** me with his spirit and power,
Nah	2. 6	the palace is **filled** with terror.
	2.12	he **filled** his den with torn flesh.
Hab	3. 2	heard of what you have done, and I am **filled** with awe.
Zeph	1. 9	and kill in order to **fill** their master's house with loot.
	1.16	and cloudy day, [16] a day **filled** with the sound of
Hag	2. 7	be brought here, and the Temple will be **filled** with wealth.
Zech	7. 7	when Jerusalem was prosperous and **filled** with people and
	10.10	the whole land will be **filled** with people.
	12.10	"I will **fill** the descendants of David and the other
Mt	9.36	the crowds, his heart was **filled** with pity for them, because
	14.14	large crowd, his heart was **filled** with pity for them, and he
	16. 9	How many baskets did you **fill**?
	16.10	How many baskets did you **fill**?
	22.10	and the wedding hall was **filled** with people.
	26. 7	him with an alabaster jar **filled** with an expensive perfume,
	28. 8	a hurry, afraid and yet **filled** with joy, and ran to tell
Mk	1.41	Jesus was **filled** with pity, and stretched out his hand
	4.37	into the boat, so that it was about to **fill** with water.
	6.34	crowd, and his heart was **filled** with pity for them, because
	10.32	Jesus was going ahead of the disciples, who were **filled** with alarm;
Lk	1.15	very birth he will be **filled** with the Holy Spirit, [16] and
	1.41	Elizabeth was **filled** with the Holy Spirit [42] and said in a
	1.53	He has **filled** the hungry with good things, and sent the
	1.65	The neighbours were all **filled** with fear, and the news
	1.67	John's father Zechariah was **filled** with the Holy Spirit,
	3. 5	Every valley must be **filled** up, every hill and mountain levelled off.
	4.28	in the synagogue heard this, they were **filled** with anger.
	5. 7	They came and **filled** both boats so full of fish that the
	6.11	They were **filled** with rage and began to discuss among
	6.21	you will be **filled**!
	7.13	saw her, his heart was **filled** with pity for her, and he
	7.16	They all were **filled** with fear and praised God.
	8.23	and the boat began to **fill** with water, so that they were
	10.21	At that time Jesus was **filled** with joy by the Holy
	10.33	man, and when he saw him, his heart was **filled** with pity.
	15.16	He wished he could **fill** himself with the bean pods the
	15.20	his heart was **filled** with pity, and he ran, threw his arms
	24.52	and went back into Jerusalem, **filled** with great joy, [53] and
Jn	2. 7	Jesus said to the servants, **"Fill** these jars with water."
	2. 7	They **filled** them to the brim, [8] and then he told them, "Now
	6.13	gathered them all up and **filled** twelve baskets with the
	12. 3	The sweet smell of the perfume **filled** the whole house.
	16.22	and your hearts will be **filled** with gladness, the kind of
	20.20	The disciples were **filled** with joy at seeing the Lord.
Acts	1. 8	upon you, you will be **filled** with power, and you will be
	2. 2	strong wind blowing, and it **filled** the whole house where
	2. 4	They were all **filled** with the Holy Spirit and began to
	2.26	And so I am **filled** with gladness, and my words are full
	2.28	that lead to life, and your presence will **fill** me with joy.'
	2.43	done through the apostles, and everyone was **filled** with awe.
	4.31	They were all **filled** with the Holy Spirit and began to
	9.17	you might see again and be **filled** with the Holy Spirit."
	13. 9	Then Saul—also known as Paul—was **filled** with the Holy Spirit;
	13.45	When the Jews saw the crowds, they were **filled** with jealousy;
	14.17	he gives you food and **fills** your hearts with happiness."
	15.31	people read it, they were **filled** with joy by the message of
	16.34	He and his family were **filled** with joy, because they now
	19.17	they were all **filled** with fear, and the name of the Lord
Rom	1.21	nonsense, and their empty minds are **filled** with darkness.
	1.29	They are **filled** with all kinds of wickedness, evil,
	3.14	their speech is **filled** with bitter curses.
	4.20	his faith **filled** him with power, and he gave praise to God.
	15.13	God, the source of hope, **fill** you with all joy and peace
1 Cor	5. 2	the contrary, you should be **filled** with sadness, and the man
2 Cor	11.29	when someone is led into sin, I am **filled** with distress.
Eph	3.19	so be completely **filled** with the very nature of God.
	4.10	the heavens, to **fill** the whole universe with his presence.
	5.18	instead, be **filled** with the Spirit.
Phil	1.11	Your lives will be **filled** with the truly good qualities
	4. 8	In conclusion, my brothers, **fill** your minds with those

Col 1. 9 We ask God to **fill** you with the knowledge of his will,
2. 2 order that they may be **filled** with courage and may be drawn
2. 7 And be **filled** with thanksgiving.
2 Tim 1. 4 see you very much, so that I may be **filled** with joy.
1. 7 his Spirit **fills** us with power, love, and self-control.
Jas 4. 5 "The spirit that God placed in us is **filled** with fierce desires."
1 Pet 1. 3 This **fills** us with a living hope, [4]and so we look forward
Rev 5. 8 a harp and gold bowls **filled** with incense, which are the
8. 5 took the incense-burner, **filled** it with fire from the altar,
11.18 The heathen were **filled** with rage, because the time for
12.12 to you, and he is **filled** with rage, because he knows that
15. 8 The temple was **filled** with smoke from the glory and power
18. 6 **Fill** her cup with a drink twice as strong as the drink

FILTHY

Ezra 9.11 from one end to the other with disgusting, **filthy** actions.
Job 9.31 me into a pit of **filth,** and even my clothes are ashamed
Prov 30.12 they are pure when they are as **filthy** as they can be.
Is 30.22 throw them away like **filth,** shouting, "Out of my sight!"
57.20 whose waves never stop rolling in, bringing **filth** and muck.
64. 6 even our best actions are **filthy** through and through.
Lam 1. 8 Jerusalem made herself **filthy** with terrible sin.
1.17 They treat me like some **filthy** thing.
Ezek 11.18 to get rid of all the **filthy,** disgusting idols they find.
11.21 punish the people who love to worship **filthy,** disgusting idols.
Nah 3. 6 I will treat you with contempt and cover you with **filth.**
Zech 3. 3 Joshua was standing there, wearing **filthy** clothes.
3. 4 "Take away the **filthy** clothes this man is wearing."
Rom 1.24 people over to do the **filthy** things their hearts desire, and
Gal 5.19 It shows itself in immoral, **filthy,** and indecent actions;
Jas 1.21 So get rid of every **filthy** habit and all wicked conduct.
2 Pet 2.10 especially those who follow their **filthy** bodily lusts and despise God's authority.
Rev 17. 4 of obscene and **filthy** things, the result of her immorality.
18. 2 all kinds of **filthy** and hateful birds live in her.
22.11 and whoever is **filthy** must go on being filthy;

FIN

Lev 11. 9 kind of fish that has **fins** and scales, [10]but anything
11.10 water that does not have **fins** and scales must not be eaten.
11.12 that lives in the water and does not have **fins** and scales.
Deut 14. 9 kind of fish that has **fins** and scales, [10]but anything
14.10 water that does not have **fins** and scales may not be eaten;

FINAL

Gen 27. 4 eaten it, I will give you my **final** blessing before I die."
27.33 I gave him my **final** blessing, and so it is his for
Lev 27.12 to its good or bad qualities, and the price will be **final.**
27.14 to its good or bad points, and the price will be **final.**
1 Chr 9.26 chief guards were Levites and had the **final** responsibility.
23.27 On the basis of David's **final** instructions all Levites
27.24 of this census, so the **final** figures were never recorded in
2 Chr 19.11 High Priest will have **final** authority in all religious cases,
19.11 of Judah, will have **final** authority in all civil cases.
Esth 1.22 be the master of his home and speak with **final** authority.
Job 30.12 they prepare their **final** assault.
Ecc 12. 5 We are going to our **final** resting place, and then there
Is 51. 6 my victory will be **final.**
Ezek 21.25 of Israel, your day, the day of your **final** punishment, is
21.29 and your day is coming, the day of your **final** punishment.
35. 5 of her disaster, the time of **final** punishment for her sins.
Dan 11.40 "When the king of Syria's **final** hour has almost come,
Jn 11. 4 heard it, he said, "The **final** result of this illness will
1 Cor 4. 5 **Final** judgement must wait until the Lord comes;
2 Thes 2. 3 will not come until the **final** Rebellion takes place and the
Rev 15. 1 ones, because they are the **final** expression of God's anger.

FINANCE

Acts 6. 2 the preaching of God's word in order to handle **finances.**
2 Cor 12.13 except that I did not bother you for **financial** help?

FIND
[FOUND, FOUND OUT]

Gen 2.12 (Pure gold is **found** there and also rare perfume and precious
4.14 on the earth, and anyone who **finds** me will kill me."
7. 1 I have **found** that you are the only one in all the
8. 9 all the land, the dove did not **find** a place to alight.
16. 4 When she **found out** that she was pregnant, she became proud
16. 5 you, and ever since she **found out** that she was pregnant, she
18.21 I must go down to **find out** whether or not the
18.26 The Lord answered, "If I **find** fifty innocent people in Sodom,
18.28 "I will not destroy the city if I **find** forty-five innocent people."
18.30 He said, "I will not do it if I **find** thirty."
18.31 Suppose that only twenty are **found?"**
18.31 He said, "I will not destroy the city if I **find** twenty."
18.32 What if only ten are **found?"**
19.11 with blindness, so that they couldn't **find** the door.
21.21 His mother **found** an Egyptian wife for him.
24.48 master's relative, where I **found** his daughter for my master's son.
24.57 "Let's call the girl and **find out** what she has to say."
26.19 Isaac's servants dug a well in the valley and **found** water.
26.32 They said, "We have **found** water."
27.12 father will touch me and **find out** that I am deceiving him;
27.20 Isaac said, "How did you **find** it so quickly, my son?"
27.20 Jacob answered, "The Lord your God helped me to **find** it."
28. 6 Jacob and sent him away to Mesopotamia to **find** a wife.
Gen 28. 7 He **found out** that Jacob had obeyed his father and mother
30.14 went into the fields and **found** mandrakes, which he brought to
30.33 the future you can easily **find out** if I have been honest.
31.32 But if you **find** that anyone here has your gods, he will
31.33 tent of the two slave-women, but he did not **find** his gods.
31.34 Laban searched through the whole tent, but did not **find** them.
31.35 Laban searched but did not **find** his household gods.
31.37 what household article have you **found** that belongs to you?
34. 3 But he **found** the girl so attractive that he fell in love
36.24 (This is the Anah who **found** the hot springs in the
37.17 So Joseph went after his brothers and **found** them at Dothan.
37.29 back to the well and **found** that Joseph was not there, he
37.32 took the robe to their father and said, "We **found** this.
38.20 the articles he had pledged, but Hirah could not **find** her.
38.22 He returned to Judah and said, "I couldn't **find** her.
38.23 I did try to pay her, but you couldn't **find** her."
41.38 to them, "We will never **find** a better man than Joseph,
42. 9 you have come to **find out** where our country is weak."
42.12 You have come to **find out** where our country is weak."
42.27 to feed his donkey and **found** his money at the top of
42.33 'This is how I will **find out** if you are honest men:
42.35 out their sacks, every one of them **found** his bag of money;
43.21 our sacks, and each man **found** his money in the top of
44. 8 of Canaan the money we **found** in the top of our sacks.
44. 9 any one of us is **found** to have it, he will be
44.12 with the youngest, and the cup was **found** in Benjamin's sack.
44.15 my position could **find you out** by practising divination?"
44.16 slaves and not just the one with whom the cup was **found."**
Ex 1.10 We must **find** some way to keep them from becoming even more
2.14 said to himself, "People have **found out** what I have done."
5. 7 Make them go and **find** it for themselves.
5.11 for yourselves wherever you can **find** it, but you must still
7.17 Lord says that you will **find out** who he is by what
12.19 days no yeast must be **found** in your houses, for if anyone,
15.22 three days they walked through the desert, but **found** no water.
16. 4 I can test them to **find out** if they will follow my
16.25 the Lord, and you will not **find** any food outside the camp.
16.27 people went out to gather food, but they did not **find** any.
22. 2 donkey, or a sheep, is **found** alive in his possession, he
22. 7 his house, the thief, if he is **found,** shall repay double.
22. 8 if the thief is not **found,** the man who was keeping the
Lev 6. 3 that has been lost and swearing that he did not **find** it.
6. 4 On the day he is **found** guilty, he must repay the owner
13.13 If he **finds** that it actually has covered the whole body, he
13.21 the priest examines it and **finds** that the hairs in it have
13.53 he examines it, the priest **finds** that the mildew has not
14.34 If someone **finds** that the Lord has sent mildew on his house,
14.40 on which the mildew is **found** to be removed and thrown into
Num 10.33 went ahead of them to **find** a place for them to camp.
13.18 **Find out** what kind of country it is, how many people
13.19 **Find out** whether the land is good or bad and whether the
13.20 **Find out** whether the soil is fertile and whether the
13.27 "We explored the land and **found** it to be rich and fertile;
15.32 the wilderness, a man was **found** gathering firewood on the Sabbath.
21.32 and Moses sent men to **find** the best way to attack the
23. 6 went back and **found** Balak still standing by his burnt-offering,
23.17 went back and **found** Balak still standing by his burnt-offering,
35.19 When he **finds** him, he is to kill him.
35.21 When he **finds** him, he is to kill him.
35.27 if the dead man's relative **finds** him and kills him, this act
35.30 accused of murder may be **found** guilty and put to death only
Deut 1.25 us back some fruit they **found** there, and reported that the
1.33 went ahead of you to **find** a place for you to camp.
4.29 you search for him with all your heart, you will **find** him.
12.30 Don't try to **find out** how they worship their gods, so that
21. 1 "Suppose a man is **found** murdered in a field in the land
21. 2 place where the body was **found** to each of the nearby towns.
21. 3 to where the body was **found** are to select a young cow
21. 6 where the murdered man was **found** are to wash their hands
22. 3 the same thing if you **find** a donkey, a piece of clothing,
22. 6 "If you happen to **find** a bird's nest in a tree or
24. 1 doesn't want her, because he **finds** something about her that
28.29 blind man, and you will not be able to **find** your way.
28.65 You will **find** no peace anywhere, no place to call your own;
32.10 "He **found** them wandering through the desert, a desolate,
32.13 They **found** wild honey among the rocks;
Josh 2. 4 I didn't **find out** where they were going, but if you start
2.16 hill-country," she said, "or the king's men will **find** you.
2.22 but they did not **find** them, so they returned to Jericho.
7.15 is then picked out and **found** with the condemned goods will
7.21 You will **find** them buried inside my tent, with the silver at
7.22 ran to the tent and **found** that the condemned things really
8.22 men of Ai **found** themselves completely surrounded by Israelites,
10.17 Someone **found** them, and Joshua was told where they were
10.20 them, although some managed to **find** safety inside their city
20. 9 killed a person accidentally could **find** protection there
Judg 1. 5 They **found** Adonibezek there and fought against him.
2.22 I will use them to **find out** whether or not these
3. 4 a test for Israel, to **find out** whether or not the Israelites
5.30 "They are only **finding** things to capture and divide,
6.28 early the next morning, they **found** that the altar to Baal
6.29 They investigated and **found out** that Gideon son of Joash had
9.42 next day Abimelech **found out** that the people of Shechem were
14. 3 Can't you **find** a girl in our own clan, among all our
14. 8 and he was surprised to **find** a swarm of bees and some
15.15 he **found** the jaw-bone of a donkey that had recently died.
16. 2 The people of Gaza **found out** that Samson was there, so
17. 8 He left Bethlehem to **find** somewhere else to live.
18. 8 and Eshtaol, their countrymen asked them what they had **found out.**

Judg 18.10 you get there, you will **find** that the people don't suspect a
19.27 go on his way, he **found** his concubine lying in front of
21. 8 the gathering at Mizpah, they **found out** that no one from
21.12 the people in Jabesh they **found** four hundred young virgins,
21.17 We must **find** a way for the tribe of Benjamin to survive,
Ruth 2. 2 I am sure to **find** someone who will let me work with
2.17 had beaten it out, she **found** she had nearly ten kilogrammes.
3. 1 said to Ruth, "I must **find** a husband for you, so that
3. 8 over, and was surprised to **find** a woman lying at his feet.
3.13 in the morning we will **find out** whether or not he will
1 Sam 4. 6 When they **found out** that the Lord's Covenant Box had arrived
6. 3 be healed, and you will **find out** why he has kept on
9. 4 Ephraim and the region of Shalishah, but did not **find** them;
9. 4 the territory of Benjamin, but still did not **find** them.
9. 6 and maybe he can tell us where we can **find** the donkeys."
9. 8 that, and then he will tell us where we can **find** them."
9.12 As soon as you go into the town, you will **find** him.
9.12 you go now, you will **find** him before he goes up the
9.20 they have already been **found.**
10. 2 were looking for have been **found,** so that your father isn't
10.14 "When we couldn't **find** them, we went to see Samuel."
10.16 that the animals had been **found,"** Saul answered—but he did
10.21 but when they could not **find** him, [22]they asked the Lord,
12. 5 that you have **found** me to be completely innocent."
13.14 disobeyed him, the Lord will **find** the kind of man he wants
14.17 his men, "Count the soldiers and **find out** who is missing."
14.17 They did so and **found** that Jonathan and the young man who
14.25 They all came into a wooded area and **found** honey everywhere.
14.38 "Come here and **find out** what sin was committed today.
14.52 So whenever he **found** a man who was strong or brave, he
15.12 Early the following morning he went off to **find** Saul.
16.17 Saul ordered them, **"Find** me a man who plays well and
17.18 **Find out** how your brothers are getting on and bring back
17.56 "Then go and **find out,"** Saul ordered.
19. 3 If I **find out** anything, I will let you know."
19.16 They went inside and **found** the household idol in the bed
20.21 Then I will tell my servant to go and **find** them.
20.36 said to him, "Run and **find** the arrows I'm going to shoot."
22. 3 stay with you until I **find out** what God is going to
22. 6 and his men had been **found,** [7]and he said to his officers,
23.14 Saul was always trying to **find** him, but God did not hand
23.22 **find out** for certain where he is and who has seen him
23.23 **Find out** exactly the places where he hides, and be sure
25. 5 to go to Carmel, **find** Nabal, and give him his greetings.
26. 4 he sent spies and **found out** that Saul was indeed there.
26. 7 Abishai entered Saul's camp and **found** Saul sleeping in the
27. 4 David had fled to Gath, he gave up trying to **find** him.
28. 7 Then Saul ordered his officials, **"Find** me a woman who is
29. 3 has done nothing I can **find fault** with since the day he
29. 6 I have not **found any fault** in you from the day you
29. 8 as you say, you haven't **found any fault** in me since the
30. 3 and his men arrived, they **found** that the town had been burnt
30.11 The men with David **found** an Egyptian boy out in the
31. 8 plunder the corpses, and they **found** the bodies of Saul and
2 Sam 2.30 all his men and **found** that nineteen of them were missing,
3. 8 yet today you **find fault** with me about a woman!
3.25 to deceive you and to **find out** everything you do and
11. 3 he sent a messenger to **find out** who she was, and learnt
13. 8 She went there and **found** him in bed.
14.14 the king can at least **find** a way to bring a man
17.12 We will **find** David wherever he is, and attack him before
17.20 for them but could not **find** them, and so they returned to
1 Kgs 1. 2 him, "Your Majesty, let us **find** a young woman to stay with
1. 3 girl, and in Shunem they **found** such a girl named Abishag,
2.40 donkey and went to King Achish in Gath, to **find** his slaves.
2.40 He **found** them and brought them back home.
13.14 the prophet from Judah and **found** him sitting under an oak.
13.28 and he rode off and **found** the prophet's body lying on
18. 5 to see if we can **find** enough grass to keep the horses
18.10 require that ruler to swear that you could not be **found.**
18.12 are here, and he can't **find** you, he will put me to
19.19 Elijah left and **found** Elisha ploughing with a team of oxen;
21.18 You will **find** him in Naboth's vineyard, about to take
22.25 "You will **find out** when you go into some back room to
2 Kgs 1. 2 of Ekron, in order to **find out** whether or not he would
1. 9 The officer **found** him sitting on a hill and said to him,
2.17 high and low for Elijah for three days, but didn't **find** him.
4.26 Hurry to her and **find out** if everything is all right
4.39 He **found** a wild vine, and picked as many gourds as he
6.13 **"Find out** where he is," the king ordered, "and I
7. 8 gold, and clothing they **found,** and went off and hid them;
7.12 will leave the city to **find** food, and then they will take
7.13 that are left, so that we can **find out** what has happened."
7.14 with instructions to go and **find out** what had happened to
8. 4 She **found** the king talking with Gehazi, Elisha's servant;
8. 8 to consult the Lord to **find out** whether or not I am
9. 5 to Ramoth, [5]where he **found** the army officers in a conference.
9.17 replied, "Send a horseman to **find out** if they are friends
9.35 went out to bury her **found** nothing except her skull, and the
14.14 silver and gold he could **find,** all the temple equipment and
18.23 thousand horses if you can **find** that many men to ride them!
22. 8 told him that he had **found** the book of the Law in
23. 2 book of the covenant which had been **found** in the Temple.
23.24 High Priest Hilkiah had **found** in the Temple, King Josiah removed
1 Chr 4.40 **found** plenty of fertile pasture lands there in a stretch of
7.15 Machir **found** a wife for Huppim and one for Shuppim.
10. 8 plunder the corpses, and they **found** the bodies of Saul and
10.13 he tried to **find** guidance by consulting the spirits of the
26.31 belonging to this family were **found** living at Jazer in the
2 Chr 12.14 was evil, because he did not try to **find** the Lord's will.
12.15 and his family records are **found** in The History of Shemaiah
2 Chr 15. 2 him, he will let you **find** him, but if you turn away,
15. 4 They searched for him and **found** him.
18.24 "You will **find out** when you go into some back room to
20.25 take the loot, and they **found** many cattle, supplies, clothing,
22. 9 was made for Ahaziah, and he was **found** hiding in Samaria.
34.14 out of the storeroom, Hilkiah **found** the book of the Law of
34.15 said to Shaphan, "I have **found** the book of the Law here
34.21 **Find out** about the teachings of this book.
34.30 book of the covenant, which had been **found** in the Temple.
35.25 The song is **found** in the collection of laments.
Ezra 2.61 The following priestly clans could **find** no record
4.19 and it has indeed been **found** that from ancient times Jerusalem
5. 8 the province of Judah and **found** that the Temple of the great
5.17 royal records in Babylon to **find** whether or not Cyrus gave
6. 2 province of Media that a scroll was **found,** containing the
8.15 I **found** that there were priests in the group, but no Levites.
9. 9 in ruins, and to **find** safety here in Judah and Jerusalem.
Neh 2.14 I was riding could not **find** any path through the rubble,
4.15 enemies heard that we had **found out** what they were plotting,
5. 8 The leaders were silent and could **find** nothing to say.
7. 5 first returned from captivity, and this is the information I **found:**
7.63 The following priestly clans could **find** no record
9. 8 You **found** that he was faithful to you, and you made a
13. 7 There I was shocked to **find** that Eliashib had allowed Tobiah
Esth 2. 2 "Why don't you make a search to **find** some beautiful young virgins?
2.11 the harem, in order to **find out** how she was getting on
2.22 Queen Esther, who then told the king what Mordecai had **found out.**
3. 7 ("purim," they were called) to **find out** the right day and
3. 8 people scattered all over your empire and **found** in every province.
4. 5 to go to Mordecai and **find out** what was happening and why.
6.10 You will **find** him sitting at the entrance of the palace."
Job 3.17 men stop their evil, and tired workmen **find** rest at last.
4.18 he **finds fault** even with his angels.
5. 4 Their sons can **find** no safety;
5.24 when you look at your sheep, you will **find** them safe.
8.11 they are never **found** outside a swamp.
9.14 So how can I **find** words to answer God?
11.20 look round in despair and **find** that there is no way to
13. 9 If God looks at you closely, will he **find** anything good?
17.10 stood before me, I would not **find** even one of them wise.
22.26 always trust in God and **find** that he is the source of
23. 3 wish I knew where to **find** him, and knew how to go
23. 8 I have not **found** him when I searched in the west.
23.10 if he tests me, he will **find** me pure.
24. 5 nowhere else can they **find** food for their children.
27.19 and when they wake up, they will **find** their wealth gone.
28.12 But where can wisdom be **found?**
28.13 Wisdom is not to be **found** among men;
28.14 of the oceans and seas Say that wisdom is not **found** there.
28.23 the place where wisdom is **found,** [24]Because he sees the ends
29.13 misery praised me, and I helped widows **find** security.
31.19 When I **found** someone in need, too poor to buy clothes,
32. 3 They could **find** no way to answer Job, and this made it
33.10 But God **finds** excuses for attacking me and treats me
38.39 Do you **find** food for lions to eat, and satisfy hungry
Ps 1. 2 Instead, they **find** joy in obeying the Law of the Lord, and
5.11 But all who **find** safety in you will rejoice;
12. 1 honest men can no longer be **found.**
17. 3 have examined me completely and **found** no evil desire in me.
34. 8 **Find out** for yourself how good the Lord is.
34. 8 Happy are those who **find** safety with him.
36. 7 We **find** protection under the shadow of your wings.
37.10 you may look for them, but you won't **find** them;
37.36 I looked for him, but couldn't **find** him.
50.20 to accuse your own brothers and to **find fault** with them.
55. 6 I would fly away and **find** rest.
55. 8 I would quickly **find** myself a shelter from the raging wind
57. 1 shadow of your wings I **find** protection until the raging
59.15 about for food and growling if they do not **find** enough.
61. 4 let me **find** safety under your wings.
64.10 They will **find** safety in him;
69.20 for comfort, but I **found** none.
73.11 the Most High will not **find out."**
73.28 to be near God, to **find** protection with the Sovereign Lord
77. 2 long I lift my hands in prayer, but I cannot **find** comfort.
94.15 Justice will again be **found** in the courts, and all righteous
107. 4 trackless desert and could not **find** their way to a city to
109. 7 May he be tried and **found** guilty;
119.35 obedient to your commandments, because in them I **find** happiness.
119.47 I **find** pleasure in obeying your commands, because I love them.
119.56 I **find** my happiness in obeying your commands.
119.70 These men have no understanding, but I **find** pleasure in your law.
119.162 your promises— as happy as someone who **finds** rich treasure.
119.174 I **find** happiness in your law.
132. 6 the Covenant Box, and we **found** it in the fields of Jearim.
139.17 O God, how difficult I **find** your thoughts;
139.24 **Find out** if there is any evil in me and guide me
Prov 1.11 let's **find** someone to kill!
1.12 alive and well when we **find** them, but they'll be dead when
1.13 We'll **find** all kinds of riches and fill our houses with loot!
1.28 You may look for me everywhere, but you will not **find** me.
2.14 darkness of sin, [14]men who **find** pleasure in doing wrong
5.14 And suddenly I **found** myself publicly disgraced."
5.18 happy with your wife and **find** your joy with the girl you
7.15 I wanted to **find** you, and here you are!
8.17 whoever looks for me can **find** me.
8.35 The man who **finds** me finds life, and the Lord will be

Prov	8.36	The man who does not **find** me hurts himself;
	12.12	wicked people want is to **find** evil things to do, but the
	12.20	surprise, but those who work for good will **find** happiness.
	15.23	a joy it is to **find** just the right word for the
	17.20	speaks evil can expect to **find** nothing good—only disaster.
	18.22	**Find** a wife and you find a good thing;
	19. 4	Rich people are always **finding** new friends, but the poor
	20. 6	faithful he is, but just try to **find** someone who really is!
	20.26	A wise king will **find out** who is doing wrong, and will
	22.21	you are sent to **find it out,** you will bring back the
	28. 9	the law, God will **find** your prayers too hateful to hear.
	30.19	a ship **finding** its way over the sea,
	30.28	hold one in your hand, but you can **find** them in palaces.
	31.10	How hard it is to **find** a capable wife!
Ecc	1.17	But I **found out** that I might as well be chasing the
	2. 1	I decided to enjoy myself and **find out** what happiness is.
	2. 1	But I **found** that this is useless, too.
	3. 6	He sets the time for **finding** and the time for losing, the
	3.16	that in this world you **find** wickedness where justice and
	5.18	This is what I have **found out:**
	6. 5	but at least it has **found** rest—[6] more so than the man
	7.25	I was determined to **find** wisdom and the answers to my questions,
	7.26	I **found** something more bitter than death—woman.
	7.27	said the Philosopher, I **found this out** little by little
	7.28	I have looked for other answers but have **found** none.
	7.28	I **found** one man in a thousand that I could respect, but
	8.17	However hard you try, you will never **find out.**
	10.15	Only someone too stupid to **find** his way home would wear
	12.10	The Philosopher tried to **find** comforting words, but the
Song	1. 8	**find** pasture for your goats near the tents of the shepherds.
	3. 1	I was looking for him, but couldn't **find** him.
	3. 2	I looked, but couldn't **find** him.
	3. 3	I asked them, "Have you **found** my lover?"
	3. 4	As soon as I left them, I **found** him.
	5. 6	I looked for him, but couldn't **find** him;
	5. 7	The watchmen patrolling the city **found** me;
	5. 8	of Jerusalem, that if you **find** my lover, you will tell him
	6. 1	way your lover went, so that we can help you **find** him.
	8.10	My lover knows that with him I **find** contentment and peace.
Is	5.17	lambs will eat grass and young goats will **find** pasture.
	7. 3	You will **find** him on the road where the cloth makers work,
	9.20	of food they can **find,** but their hunger is never satisfied.
	10. 3	Where will you run to **find** help?
	11. 3	have reverence for him, [3]and **find** pleasure in obeying him.
	14.32	Zion and that his suffering people will **find** safety there.
	16. 3	hide us where no one can **find** us.
	22. 9	**found** the places where the walls of Jerusalem needed repair.
	29.19	people will once again **find** the happiness which the Lord,
	32.14	Wild donkeys will roam there, and sheep will **find** pasture there.
	36. 8	thousand horses if you can **find** that many men to ride them.
	40.20	He **finds** a skilful craftsman to make an image that won't
	40.31	in the Lord for help will **find** their strength renewed.
	45.24	that only through me are victory and strength to be **found;**
	48.10	But I have **found** that you are worthless.
	57. 2	Those who live good lives **find** peace and rest in death.
	57. 9	To **find** gods to worship, you send messengers far and wide,
	58.14	that day, [14]then you will **find** the joy that comes from
	59.14	in the public square, and honesty **finds** no place there.
	59.15	who stops doing evil **finds** himself the victim of crime."
	64. 5	You welcome those who **find** joy in doing what is right,
	65. 1	was ready for them to **find** me, but they did not even
	66.16	of the world whom he **finds** guilty—and many will be put
Jer	5. 1	Can you **find** one person who does what is right and tries
	6.27	as you would test metal, and **find out** what they are like.
	13. 7	went back, and when I **found** the place where I had hidden
	14. 3	they go to the cisterns, but **find** no water;
	29.13	seek me, and you will **find** me because you will seek me
	29.14	Yes, I say, you will **find** me, and I will restore you
	31.21	**find** again the way by which you left.
	39.12	"Go and **find** Jeremiah and take good care of him.
	45. 3	I am worn out from groaning, and I can't **find** any rest!'
	48.19	who are running away, **find out** from them what has happened.
	48.45	Helpless refugees try to **find** protection in Heshbon, the
	50. 7	They are attacked by all who **find** them.
	50.20	comes, no sin will be **found** in Israel and no wickedness in
Ezek	7.25	You will look for peace and never **find** it.
	8. 8	I broke through it and **found** a door.
	11.18	to get rid of all the filthy, disgusting idols they **find.**
	17.23	every kind will live there and **find** shelter in its shade.
	22.30	anger is about to destroy it, but I could **find** no one.
	26.21	People may look for you, but you will never be **found."**
	34. 6	earth, and no one looked for them or tried to **find** them.
	34. 8	My shepherds did not try to **find** the sheep.
	34.15	of my sheep, and I will **find** them a place to rest.
	39.14	the land in order to **find** and bury those bodies remaining on
	39.15	the country, every time they **find** a human bone, they will
	40. 8	He measured this room, and **found** it was four metres deep.
	40.14	He measured that room and **found** it was ten metres wide.
Dan	2.25	told the king, "I have **found** one of the Jewish exiles,
	5.16	I have heard that you can **find** hidden meanings
	5.27	have been weighed on the scales and **found** to be too light;
	6. 4	and the governors tried to **find** something wrong with the way
	6. 5	"We are not going to **find** anything of which to accuse
	6.14	upset and did his best to **find** some way to rescue Daniel.
	8. 2	In the vision I suddenly **found** myself in the walled city
Hos	2. 7	She will look for them but will not **find** them.
	5. 6	They cannot **find** him, for he has left them.
	5.15	Perhaps in their suffering they will try to **find** me."
	9.10	Lord says, "When I first **found** Israel,
	9.10	it was like **finding** grapes growing in the desert.
Joel	3.18	covered with vineyards, and cattle will be **found** on every hill;
Amos	3. 4	a lion roar in the forest unless he has **found** a victim?
	4. 8	city where they hoped to **find** water, but there was not
	5. 5	Do not try to **find** me at Bethel—Bethel will come to
	8. 6	We'll **find** a poor man who can't pay his debts, not even
	8.12	for a message from the Lord, but they will not **find** it.
Jon	1. 3	went to Joppa, where he **found** a ship
	1. 6	The captain **found** him there and said to him, "What are
	1. 7	another, "Let's draw lots and **find out** who is to blame for
Mic	2. 3	You are going to **find** yourselves in trouble, and then you
	7. 1	like a hungry man who **finds** no fruit left on the trees
Hag	2.16	heap of corn expecting to **find** two hundred kilogrammes, but
	2.16	a hundred litres of wine from a vat, but **find** only forty.
Zech	1.11	and have **found** that the whole world lies helpless
Mt	1.18	before they were married, she **found out** that she was going
	2. 7	to a secret meeting and **found out** from them the exact time
	2. 8	the child, and when you **find** him, let me know, so that
	7. 7	seek, and you will **find;**
	7. 8	and anyone who seeks will **find,** and the door will be opened
	7.14	to it is hard, and there are few people who **find** it.
	8.10	tell you, I have never **found** anyone in Israel with faith
	9.13	Go and **find out** what is meant by the scripture that says:
	11.29	and you will **find** rest.
	12.43	If it can't **find** one, [44]it says to itself, 'I will go
	12.44	So it goes back and **finds** the house empty, clean, and all
	13.44	A man happens to **find** a treasure hidden in a field.
	13.46	pearls, [46]and when he **finds** one that is unusually fine,
	15.33	asked him, "Where will we **find** enough food in this desert
	16.25	but whoever loses his life for my sake will **find** it.
	17.27	in its mouth you will **find** a coin worth enough for my
	18.13	When he **finds** it, I tell you, he feels far happier over
	21. 2	and at once you will **find** a donkey tied up with her
	21.19	road and went to it, but **found** nothing on it except leaves.
	22. 9	streets and invite to the feast as many people as you **find.'**
	22.10	gathered all the people they could **find,** good and bad alike;
	24.46	servant is if his master **finds** him doing this when he comes
	26.40	Then he returned to the three disciples and **found** them asleep;
	26.43	He returned once more and **found** the disciples asleep;
	26.59	the whole Council tried to **find** some false evidence against
	26.60	but they could not **find** any, even though many people
Mk	1.37	for him, [37]and when they **found** him, they said, "Everyone
	6.38	When they **found out,** they told him, "Five loaves and also
	7.29	back home, where you will **find** that the demon has gone out
	7.30	She went home and **found** her child lying on the bed;
	8. 4	in this desert can anyone **find** enough food to feed all these
	11. 2	you get there, you will **find** a colt tied up that has
	11. 4	So they went and **found** a colt out in the street, tied
	11.13	he went to see if he could **find** any figs on it.
	11.13	he came to it, he **found** only leaves, because it was not
	13.36	If he comes suddenly, he must not **find** you asleep.
	14.16	went to the city, and **found** everything just as Jesus had
	14.37	Then he returned and **found** the three disciples asleep.
	14.40	Then he came back to the disciples and **found** them asleep;
	14.55	the whole Council tried to **find** some evidence against Jesus
	14.55	order to put him to death, but they could not **find** any.
Lk	2.12	you will **find** a baby wrapped in strips of cloth and lying
	2.16	So they hurried off and **found** Mary and Joseph and saw
	2.45	They did not **find** him, so they went back to Jerusalem
	2.46	On the third day they **found** him in the Temple, sitting
	2.48	Your father and I have been terribly worried trying to **find** you."
	4.17	He unrolled the scroll and **found** the place where it is written,
	4.42	for him, and when they **found** him, they tried to keep him
	5.19	the crowd, however, they could **find** no way to take him in.
	7. 9	tell you, I have never **found** faith like this, not even in
	7.10	back to the officer's house and **found** his servant well.
	7.25	who dress like that and live in luxury are **found** in palaces!
	8.17	whatever is covered up will be **found** and brought to light.
	8.35	they came to Jesus, they **found** the man from whom the demons
	8.47	saw that she had been **found out,** so she came trembling and
	9.12	and farms round here and **find** food and lodging, because this
	11. 9	seek, and you will **find;**
	11.10	and he who seeks will **find,** and the door will be opened
	11.24	If it can't **find** one, it says to itself, 'I will go
	11.25	So it goes back and **finds** the house clean and tidy.
	12.37	are those servants whose master **finds** them awake and ready
	12.38	happy they are if he **finds** them ready, even if he should
	12.43	servant is if his master **finds** him doing this when he comes
	13. 6	He went looking for figs on it but **found** none.
	13. 7	looking for figs on this fig-tree, and I haven't **found** any.
	15. 4	goes looking for the one that got lost until he **finds** it.
	15. 5	When he **finds** it, he is so happy that he puts it
	15. 6	says to them, 'I am so happy I **found** my lost sheep.
	15. 8	house, and looks carefully everywhere until she **finds** it.
	15. 9	When she **finds** it, she calls her friends and neighbours together,
	15. 9	to them, 'I am so happy I **found** the coin I lost.
	15.24	he was lost, but now he has been **found.'**
	15.32	he was lost, but now he has been **found.'"**
	18. 8	will the Son of Man **find** faith on earth when he comes?"
	19.15	before him, in order to **find out** how much they had earned.
	19.30	you go in, you will **find** a colt tied up that has
	19.32	went on their way and **found** everything just as Jesus had
	19.48	him, [48]but they could not **find** a way to do it, because
	22. 2	so they were trying to **find** a way of putting Jesus to
	22.13	They went off and **found** everything just as Jesus had told them,
	22.45	back to the disciples and **found** them asleep, worn out by
	23. 4	and the crowds, "I **find** no reason to condemn this man."
	23.14	presence, and I have not **found** him guilty of any of the
	23.15	Nor did Herod **find** him guilty, for he sent him back to
	23.22	I cannot **find** anything he has done to deserve death!
	24. 2	They **found** the stone rolled away from the entrance to the tomb,
	24. 3	but they did not **find** the body of the Lord Jesus.
	24.23	went at dawn to the tomb, [23]but could not **find** his body.

Lk 24.24 went to the tomb and **found** it exactly as the women had
24.33 back to Jerusalem, where they **found** the eleven disciples
Jn 1.41 At once he **found** his brother Simon and told him,
1.41 "We have **found** the Messiah."
1.43 He **found** Philip and said to him, "Come with me!"
1.45 Philip **found** Nathanael and told him,
1.45 "We have **found** the one whom Moses wrote about
2.14 There in the Temple he **found** men selling cattle, sheep,
4.27 were greatly surprised to **find** him talking with a woman.
5.14 Afterwards, Jesus **found** him in the Temple and said,
5.39 Scriptures, because you think that in them you will **find** eternal life.
6.25 When the people **found** Jesus on the other side of the lake,
7.34 me, but you will not **find** me, because you cannot go where
7.35 is he about to go so that we shall not **find** him?
7.36 for him but will not **find** him, and that we cannot go
7.51 a man before hearing him and **finding out** what he has done."
9.35 heard what had happened, he **found** the man and asked him,
10. 9 he will come in and go out and **find** pasture.
11.17 When Jesus arrived, he **found** that Lazarus had been
12.14 Jesus **found** a donkey and rode on it, just as the
18.38 and said to them, "I cannot **find** any reason to condemn him.
19. 4 let you see that I cannot **find** any reason to condemn him."
19. 6 I **find** no reason to condemn him."
19.12 heard this, he tried to **find** a way to set Jesus free.
Acts 4.12 Salvation is to be **found** through him alone;
5.22 officials arrived, they did not **find** the apostles in prison,
5.23 arrived at the jail, we **found** it locked up tight and all
5.23 but when we opened the gates, we **found** no one inside!"
5.39 You could **find** yourselves fighting against God!"
7.11 Our ancestors could not **find** any food, [12]and when Jacob
7.23 years old, he decided to **find out** how his fellow-Israelites
8.40 Philip **found** himself in Azotus;
9. 2 so that if he should **find** there any followers of the Way
9.30 When the believers **found out** about this, they took Saul
10.27 he went into the house, where he **found** many people gathered.
11.26 When he **found** him, he took him to Antioch, and for a
12.19 gave orders to search for him, but they could not **find** him.
13.11 he walked about trying to **find** someone to lead him by the
13.22 'I have **found** that David son of Jesse is the kind of
13.28 And even though they could **find** no reason to pass the
15.36 the Lord, and let us **find out** how they are getting on."
16.37 police officers, "We were not **found** guilty of any crime,
17. 5 Jason, in an attempt to **find** Paul and Silas and bring them
17. 6 But when they did not **find** them, they dragged Jason and
17.23 where you worship, I **found** an altar on which is written,
17.27 look for him, and perhaps **find** him as they felt about for
19. 1 There he **found** some disciples [2]and asked them, "Did you
21. 2 There we **found** a ship that was going to Phoenicia, so we
21. 4 There we **found** some believers and stayed with them a week.
21.34 the commander could not **find out** exactly what had happened,
22.24 whip him in order to **find out** why the Jews were screaming
22.30 The commander wanted to **find out** for certain what the
23. 9 "We cannot **find** anything wrong with this man!
23.29 I **found out** that he had not done anything for which he
23.34 When he **found out** that he was from Cilicia, [35]he said, "I
24. 5 We **found** this man to be a dangerous nuisance;
24.11 As you can **find out** for yourself, it was no more than
24.12 The Jews did not **find** me arguing with anyone in the Temple,
24.12 nor did they **find** me stirring up the people, either
24.18 was doing this that they **found** me in the Temple after I
24.20 here tell what crime they **found** me guilty of when I stood
25.25 But I could not **find** that he had done anything for which
26. 8 do you who are here **find** it impossible to believe that God
27. 6 There the officer **found** a ship from Alexandria that was
27.28 weight tied to it and **found** that the water was forty metres
27.28 they did the same and **found** that it was thirty metres deep.
28.14 We **found** some believers there who asked us to stay with
28.18 to release me, because they **found** that I had done nothing
Rom 6.17 your heart the truths **found** in the teaching you received.
7. 8 means of that commandment sin **found** its chance to stir up
7.11 Sin **found** its chance, and by means of the commandment it
7.21 So I **find** that this law is at work:
9.19 me, "If this is so, how can God **find fault** with anyone?
9.31 law that would put them right with God, did not **find** it.
10.20 when he says, "I was **found** by those who were not looking
11. 7 The people of Israel did not **find** what they were looking for.
11. 7 It was only the small group that God chose who **found** it;
1 Cor 4.19 soon, and then I will **find out** for myself the power which
14.35 If they want to **find out** about something, they should
2 Cor 2. 9 letter because I wanted to **find out** how well you had stood
2.12 Good News about Christ, I **found** that the Lord had opened the
2.13 I was deeply worried, because I could not **find** our brother Titus.
6. 3 do not want anyone to **find fault** with our work, so we
8. 8 help, I am trying to **find out** how real your own love
8.22 him many times and **found** him always very eager to help.
9. 4 should come with me and **find out** that you are not ready,
12.20 I get there I will **find** you different from what I would
12.20 to be and you will **find** me different from what you would
12.20 am afraid that I will **find** quarrelling and jealousy, hot
13. 5 test and judge yourselves, to **find out** whether you are
Gal 2. 4 as spies, in order to **find out** about the freedom we have
2.17 union with Christ, we are **found** to be sinners as much as
Eph 5.17 fools, then, but try to **find out** what the Lord wants you
1 Thes 3. 5 any longer, so I sent him to **find out** about your faith.
1 Tim 1.11 That teaching is **found** in the gospel that was entrusted
5. 7 instructions, so that no one will **find fault** with them.
2 Tim 1.17 in Rome, he started looking for me until he **found** me.
Heb 4. 1 none of you will be **found** to have failed to receive that
4.16 we will receive mercy and **find** grace to help us just when
6.18 So we who have **found** safety with him are greatly encouraged
Heb 8. 8 But God **finds fault** with his people when he says, "The
11. 5 to God, and nobody could **find** him, because God had taken him
12.17 away, because he could not **find** any way to change what he
Jas 2. 8 of the Kingdom, which is **found** in the scripture, "Love your
1 Pet 1.11 They tried to **find out** when the time would be and how
2. 3 the scripture says, "You have **found out** for yourselves how
1 Jn 4. 1 Spirit, but test them to **find out** if the spirit they have
2 Jn 4 How happy I was to **find** that some of your children live
Rev 2. 2 but are not, and have **found out** that they are liars.
3. 2 For I **find** that what you have done is not yet perfect
5. 4 because no one could be **found** who was worthy to open the
9. 6 five months they will seek death, but will not **find** it;
18.14 and glamour are gone, and you will never **find** them again!"
18.22 No workman in any trade will ever be **found** in you again;
18.24 blood of prophets and of God's people was **found** in the city;
22. 3 Nothing that is under God's curse will be **found** in the city.

FINE (1)

Gen 19. 3 to bake some bread and prepare a **fine** meal for the guests.
30.20 She said, "God has given me a **fine** gift.
41.42 He put a **fine** linen robe on him, and placed a gold
Ex 2. 2 When she saw what a **fine** baby he was, she hid him
9. 9 They will spread out like **fine** dust over all the land of
14. 7 the six hundred **finest,** commanded by their officers.
25. 4 **fine** linen;
25. 5 **fine** leather;
26. 1 out of ten pieces of **fine** linen woven with blue, purple, and
26.14 red and the other of **fine** leather, to serve as the outer
26.31 "Make a curtain of **fine** linen woven with blue, purple,
26.36 Tent make a curtain of **fine** linen woven with blue, purple,
27. 9 Tent of my presence make an enclosure out of **fine** linen curtains.
27.16 9 metres long made of **fine** linen woven with blue, purple,
27.18 are to be made of **fine** linen and the bases of bronze.
28. 5 blue, purple, and red wool, gold thread, and **fine** linen.
28. 6 gold thread, and **fine** linen, decorated with embroidery.
28. 8 A **finely** woven belt made of the same materials is to be
28.27 of the ephod near the seam and above the **finely** woven belt.
28.39 "Weave Aaron's shirt of **fine** linen
28.39 and make a turban of **fine** linen and also a sash decorated
29.40 lamb offer one kilogramme of **fine** wheat flour mixed with one
30.23 "Take the **finest** spices—six kilogrammes of liquid myrrh,
30.36 part of it into a **fine** powder, take it into the Tent
32.20 it, ground it into **fine** powder, and mixed it with water.
35. 6 **fine** linen;
35. 7 **fine** leather;
35.23 Everyone who had **fine** linen;
35.23 or **fine** leather, brought it.
35.25 All the skilled women brought **fine** linen thread
35.35 done by engravers, designers, and weavers of **fine** linen;
36. 8 out of ten pieces of **fine** linen woven with blue, purple, and
36.19 red and the other of **fine** leather, to serve as an outer
36.35 They made a curtain of **fine** linen, woven with blue,
36.37 they made a curtain of **fine** linen woven with blue, purple,
38. 9 Lord's presence he made the enclosure out of **fine** linen curtains.
38.16 All the curtains round the enclosure were made of **fine** linen.
38.18 the enclosure was made of **fine** linen woven with blue,
38.23 designer, and a weaver of **fine** linen and of blue, purple,
39. 2 They made the ephod of **fine** linen;
39. 3 to be worked into the **fine** linen and into the blue, purple,
39. 5 The **finely** woven belt, made of the same materials, was
39.20 of the ephod, near the seam and above the **finely** woven belt.
39.24 hem they put pomegranates of **fine** linen and of blue, purple,
39.29 shorts, [29]and the sash of **fine** linen and of blue, purple,
39.34 the covering of **fine** leather;
Lev 8. 7 it by putting its **finely** woven belt round his waist.
16.12 altar and two handfuls of **fine** incense and bring them into
24. 2 Bring pure olive-oil of the **finest** quality for the lamps in
Num 4. 6 They shall put a **fine** leather cover over it, spread a blue
4. 8 over all this, put a **fine** leather cover over it, and then
4.10 all its equipment in a **fine** leather cover and place it on
4.11 the gold altar, put a **fine** leather cover over it, and then
4.12 a blue cloth, put a **fine** leather cover over them, and place
4.14 Then they shall put a **fine** leather cover over it and insert
4.25 cover, its outer cover, the **fine** leather cover on top of it,
Deut 32.14 goats, and cattle, the **finest** wheat, and the choicest wine.
Judg 14.12 of you a piece of **fine** linen
14.12 and a change of **fine** clothes that you can't tell me
14.19 stripped them, and gave their **fine** clothes to the men who
Ruth 3.11 as everyone in town knows, you are a **fine** woman.
2 Sam 15.22 **"Fine!"**
1 Kgs 4.22 were five thousand litres of **fine** flour and ten thousand
5.17 King Solomon's command they quarried **fine** large stones for
7. 9 great court were made of **fine** stones from the foundations to
10.12 It was the **finest** juniper wood ever imported into Israel;
10.18 ivory and the rest of it was covered with the **finest** gold.
2 Kgs 2.19 know, sir, this is a **fine** city, but the water is bad
5. 5 thousand pieces of gold, and ten changes of **fine** clothes.
5.22 pieces of silver and two changes of **fine** clothes."
5.23 them and two changes of **fine** clothes to two of his servants,
8. 9 with all kinds of the **finest** products of Damascus and went
8.12 fortresses on fire, slaughter their **finest** young men, batter
19.23 the tallest cedars and the **finest** cypress-trees and that you
1 Chr 15.27 a robe made of the **finest** linen, and so were the musicians,
29. 4 hundred metric tons of the **finest** gold and almost two
2 Chr 3. 5 with cedar and overlaid with **fine** gold, in which were worked
4.20 lampstands and the lamps of **fine** gold that were to burn in
9. 9 been any other spices as **fine** as those that the queen of
31. 5 Israel brought gifts of their **finest** corn, wine, olive-oil,
Ezra 8.26 2 **fine** bronze bowls, equal in value to gold bowls

Esth 1. 6 curtains, tied by cords of **fine** purple linen to silver rings
8.15 and white, a cloak of **fine** purple linen, and a magnificent
Job 22.24 dump your **finest** gold in the dry stream bed.
26. 1 What a **fine** help you are to me— poor, weak man
28.16 The **finest** gold and jewels Cannot equal its value.
28.17 is worth more than gold, Than a gold vase or **finest** glass.
28.19 The **finest** topaz and the purest gold Cannot compare with
33.20 his appetite, and even the **finest** food looks revolting.
Ps 19.10 They are more desirable than the **finest** gold;
45. 9 throne stands the queen, wearing ornaments of **finest** gold.
68.13 doves covered with silver, whose wings glittered with **fine** gold.
81.16 would feed you with the **finest** wheat and satisfy you with
119.127 I love your commands more than gold, more than the **finest** gold.
147.14 He keeps your borders safe and satisfies you with the **finest** wheat.
Prov 8.10 choose knowledge rather than the **finest** gold.
8.19 better than the **finest** gold, better than the purest silver.
15.17 you love than to eat the **finest** meat where there is hate.
20.17 you may enjoy like the **finest** food, but sooner or later it
23. 3 Don't be greedy for the **fine** food he serves;
23. 6 a stingy man or be greedy for the **fine** food he serves.
25.12 than gold rings or jewellery made of the **finest** gold.
26.23 really thinking is like a **fine** glaze on a cheap clay pot.
26.25 They may sound **fine,** but don't believe him, because his
31.22 She makes bedspreads and wears clothes of **fine** purple linen.
Song 3. 7 sixty soldiers form the bodyguard, the **finest** soldiers in Israel.
3. 9 King Solomon is carried on a throne made of the **finest** wood.
4.13 like an orchard of pomegranate-trees and bear the **finest** fruits.
7. 5 Your braided hair shines like the **finest** satin;
7. 9 fragrance of apples, [9] and your mouth like the **finest** wine.
Is 1.11 you burn as sacrifices and of the fat of your **fine** animals.
3.22 all their **fine** robes, gowns, cloaks, and purses;
3.24 instead of **fine** belts, they will wear coarse ropes;
3.24 instead of **fine** clothes, they will be dressed in rags;
5. 2 he planted the **finest** vines.
5. 9 "All these big, **fine** houses will be empty ruins.
7.23 "When that time comes, the **fine** vineyards, each with a
9.10 cut down, but we will replace them with the **finest** cedar."
10.34 down with an axe, as even the **finest** trees of Lebanon fall!
16. 7 weep when they remember the **fine** food they used to eat in
25. 6 the world—a banquet of the richest food and the **finest** wine.
30.24 that plough your fields will eat the **finest** and best fodder.
37.24 the tallest cedars and the **finest** cypress-trees, and that
47. 2 Strip off your **fine** clothes!
60.13 the cypress, The **finest** wood from the forests of Lebanon,
Jer 22.15 if you build houses of cedar, **finer** than those of others?
48.15 its **finest** young men have been slaughtered.
Lam 4. 5 People who once ate the **finest** foods die starving in the streets;
Ezek 20. 6 for them, a rich and fertile land, the **finest** land of all.
20.15 given them, a rich and fertile land, the **finest** land of all.
24. 5 Use the meat of the **finest** sheep;
25. 9 attacked, including even the **finest** cities—Beth Jeshimoth,
27. 7 Your awnings were made of **finest** cloth, Of purple from the
27.16 gave emeralds, purple cloth, embroidery, **fine** linen, coral,
27.22 Sheba and Raamah exchanged jewels, gold, and the **finest** spices.
34. 3 made from the wool, and kill and eat the **finest** sheep.
Dan 2.32 Its head was made of the **finest** gold;
10. 5 who was wearing linen clothes and a belt of **fine** gold.
Amos 5.11 will not live in the **fine** stone houses you build or drink
6. 6 the bowlful and use the **finest** perfumes, but you do not
Mt 13.45 A man is looking for **fine** pearls, [46] and when he finds one
13.46 finds one that is unusually **fine,** he goes and sells
16. 2 'We are going to have **fine** weather, because the sky is red.'
23.27 like whitewashed tombs, which look **fine** on the outside but
23.29 You make **fine** tombs for the prophets and decorate the
26.10 It is a **fine** and beautiful thing that she has done for
Mk 14. 6 She has done a **fine** and beautiful thing for me.
Lk 11.47 You make **fine** tombs for the prophets—the very prophets your
21. 5 beautiful it looked with its **fine** stones and the gifts
23.11 then they put a **fine** robe on him and sent him back
Rom 16.18 By their **fine** words and flattering speech they deceive innocent people.
Jas 2. 2 wearing a gold ring and **fine** clothes comes to your meeting,

FINE (2)

Ex 21.22 is to be **fined** whatever amount the woman's husband demands,
21.30 is allowed to pay a **fine** to save his life, he must
Deut 22.19 They are also to **fine** him a hundred pieces of silver and
1 Kgs 20.39 life or else pay a **fine** of three thousand pieces of silver.'
Prov 17.26 It is not right to make an innocent person pay a **fine;**
Mt 5.26 I tell you, until you pay the last penny of your **fine.**
Lk 12.59 I tell you, until you pay the last penny of your **fine."**

FINGER

Gen 41.42 The king removed from his **finger** the ring
41.42 engraved with the royal seal and put it on Joseph's **finger.**
Ex 29.12 bull's blood and with your **finger** put it on the projections
Lev 4. 6 He shall dip his **finger** in the blood and sprinkle it in
4.17 into the Tent, [17] dip his **finger** in it, and sprinkle it in
4.25 The priest shall dip his **finger** in the blood of the animal,
4.30 The priest shall dip his **finger** in the blood of the animal,
4.34 The priest shall dip his **finger** in the blood of the animal,
8.15 the blood, and with his **finger** put it on the projections at
9. 9 blood, and he dipped his **finger** in it, put some of it
14.16 own left hand, [16] dip a **finger** of his right hand in it,
14.27 left hand [27] and with a **finger** of his right hand sprinkle
16.14 bull's blood and with his **finger** sprinkle it on the front of
16.19 With his **finger** he must sprinkle some of the blood on
Num 19. 4 its blood and with his **finger** sprinkle it seven times in the
2 Sam 18.12 of silver, I wouldn't lift a **finger** against the king's son.
2 Sam 21.20 He had six **fingers** on each hand and six toes on each
1 Kgs 12.10 'My little **finger** is thicker than my father's waist!'
1 Chr 20. 6 was a giant with six **fingers** on each hand and six toes
2 Chr 10.10 'My little **finger** is thicker than my father's waist.'
Song 5. 5 were covered with myrrh, my **fingers** with liquid myrrh, as I
Is 3.21 the rings they wear on their **fingers** and in their noses;
Mt 23. 4 even to lift a **finger** to help them carry those loads.
Mk 7.33 from the crowd, put his **fingers** in the man's ears, spat, and
Lk 11.46 not stretch out a **finger** to help them carry those loads.
15.22 Put a ring on his **finger** and shoes on his feet.
16.24 send Lazarus to dip his **finger** in some water and cool my
Jn 8. 6 But he bent over and wrote on the ground with his **finger.**
20.25 his hands and put my **finger** on those scars and my hand
20.27 to Thomas, "Put your **finger** here, and look at my hands;

FINGERNAILS see NAIL (2)

FINISH

[UNFINISHED]

Gen 2. 2 By the seventh day God **finished** what he had been doing and
17.22 When God **finished** speaking to Abraham, he left him.
18.33 After he had **finished** speaking with Abraham, the Lord went away,
24.15 Before he had **finished** praying, Rebecca arrived with a
24.19 When he had **finished,** she said, "I will also bring
24.22 When she had **finished,** the man took an expensive gold
24.45 Before I had **finished** my silent prayer, Rebecca came
27.30 Isaac **finished** giving his blessing, and as soon as Jacob left,
38.12 When he had **finished** the time of mourning, he and his friend
49.33 When Jacob had **finished** giving instructions to his sons,
Ex 31.18 When God had **finished** speaking to Moses on Mount Sinai,
34.33 When Moses had **finished** speaking to them, he covered his
36. 7 been brought was more than enough to **finish** all the work.
40.33 So he **finished** all the work.
Lev 9.22 When Aaron had **finished** all the sacrifices, he raised
16.20 When Aaron has **finished** performing the ritual to purify
Num 4.15 Aaron and his sons have **finished** covering them
7. 1 On the day Moses **finished** setting up the Tent of the
16.31 As soon as he had **finished** speaking, the ground under
Deut 20. 9 When the officers have **finished** speaking to the army,
31.25 When he **finished,** he said to the levitical priests, who
32.45 When Moses had **finished** giving God's teachings to the people,
Josh 19.49 When the people of Israel **finished** dividing up the land,
19.51 In this way they **finished** dividing the land.
Ruth 2.21 up corn with his workers until they **finish** the harvest."
3. 3 you are there until he has **finished** eating and drinking.
3. 7 When Boaz had **finished** eating and drinking, he was in a
1 Sam 1. 9 One day, after they had **finished** their meal in the
10.13 When Saul **finished** his ecstatic dancing and shouting, he
13.10 and just as he was **finishing,** Samuel arrived.
18. 1 Saul and David **finished** their conversation.
24.16 When David had **finished** speaking, Saul said, "Is that really you,
2 Sam 6.18 When he had **finished** offering the sacrifices, he blessed
11. 4 (She had just **finished** her monthly ritual of purification.)
13.36 As soon as he **finished** saying this, David's sons came in;
18.15 Joab's soldiers closed in on Absalom and **finished** killing him.
1 Kgs 1.41 his guests were **finishing** the feast, they heard the noise.
1.42 Before he **finished** speaking, Jonathan, the son of the priest
3. 1 David's City until he had **finished** building his palace, the
6. 9 So King Solomon **finished** building the Temple.
6.14 So Solomon **finished** building the Temple.
6.38 Temple was completely **finished** exactly as it had been planned.
7.51 When King Solomon **finished** all the work on the Temple,
8.54 After Solomon had **finished** praying to the Lord, he
9. 1 After King Solomon had **finished** building the Temple and
9.11 After it was **finished,** King Solomon gave Hiram twenty towns
9.25 And so he **finished** building the Temple.
13.23 After they had **finished** eating, the old prophet saddled
21.27 When Elijah **finished** speaking, Ahab tore his clothes,
2 Kgs 6.33 He had hardly **finished** saying this, when the king arrived and said,
16.11 an altar just like it, and **finished** it before Ahaz returned.
16.12 saw that the altar was **finished,** [13] so he burnt animal
1 Chr 16. 2 After David had **finished** offering the sacrifices, he
28.20 stay with you until you **finish** the work to be done on
2 Chr 5. 1 When King Solomon **finished** all the work on the Temple, he
7. 1 When King Solomon **finished** his prayer, fire came down from
7.11 After King Solomon had **finished** the Temple and the palace,
24.14 When the repairs were **finished,** the remaining gold and
29.17 the eighth day they had **finished** it all, including the
29.34 the Levites helped them until the work was **finished.**
Ezra 4.12 They have begun to rebuild the walls and will soon **finish** them.
5.16 until the present, but the Temple is still not **finished.'**
6.15 They **finished** the Temple on the third day of the month
Neh 4. 2 by offering sacrifices they can **finish** the work in one day?
4.13 by clans behind the wall, wherever it was still **unfinished.**
6. 1 enemies heard that we had **finished** building the wall and
6.15 work the entire wall was **finished** on the twenty-fifth day of
12.22 This record was **finished** when Darius was emperor of Persia.
Job 1.16 Before he had **finished** speaking, another servant came and said,
1.17 Before he had **finished** speaking, another servant came and said,
1.18 Before he had **finished** speaking, another servant came and said,
29.22 they had nothing to add when I had **finished.**
32. 4 one there, he had waited until everyone **finished** speaking.
42. 7 After the Lord had **finished** speaking to Job, he said to Eliphaz,
Ps 9. 6 Our enemies are **finished** for ever;
Is 10.12 the Lord says, "When I **finish** what I am doing on Mount
10.25 a little while I will **finish** punishing you, and then I will
65.24 Even before they **finish** praying to me, I will answer
Jer 26. 8 as soon as I had **finished** all that the Lord had commanded

Jer	36.23	As soon as Jehudi **finished** reading three or four columns,
	43. 1	I **finished** telling the people everything that the Lord
	51.63	Seraiah, when you **finish** reading this book to the people,
Ezek	4. 6	When you **finish** that, turn over on your right side and
	7. 6	You are **finished.**
	22.14	enough to lift your hand when I am **finished** with you?
	42.15	When the man had **finished** measuring inside the temple area,
	43.23	When you have **finished** doing that, take a young bull and
Zech	4. 9	foundation of the Temple, and he will **finish** the building.
	5.11	When the temple is **finished,** the basket will be placed there
Mt	7.28	When Jesus **finished** saying these things, the crowd was
	10.23	you that you will not **finish** your work in all the towns
	11. 1	When Jesus **finished** giving these instructions to his twelve disciples,
	13.53	When Jesus **finished** telling these parables, he left that
	19. 1	When Jesus **finished** saying these things, he left Galilee
	23.32	Go on, then, and **finish** what your ancestors started!
	26. 1	When Jesus had **finished** teaching all these things, he said
	27.31	When they had **finished** mocking him, they took the robe
Mk	15.20	When they had **finished** mocking him, they took off the
Lk	2.39	When Joseph and Mary had **finished** doing all that was
	4.13	When the Devil **finished** tempting Jesus in every way, he
	5. 4	When he **finished** speaking, he said to Simon, "Push the
	7. 1	When Jesus had **finished** saying all these things to the people,
	11. 1	When he had **finished,** one of his disciples said to him,
	11.37	When Jesus **finished** speaking, a Pharisee invited him to eat with him;
	13.32	and tomorrow, and on the third day I shall **finish** my work.'
	14.28	cost, to see if he has enough money to **finish** the job.
	14.29	not be able to **finish** the tower after laying the foundation;
	14.30	'This man began to build but can't **finish** the job!'
Jn	4.34	who sent me and to **finish** the work he gave me to
	17. 1	After Jesus **finished** saying this, he looked up to heaven and said,
	17. 4	I have **finished** the work you gave me to do.
	19.30	Jesus drank the wine and said, "It is **finished!"**
Acts	4.31	When they **finished** praying, the place where they were meeting was shaken.
	12.25	Barnabas and Saul **finished** their mission and returned from Jerusalem,
	13.25	as John was about to **finish** his mission, he said to the
	15.13	When they had **finished** speaking, James spoke up:
	20.24	to complete my mission and **finish** the work that the Lord
	20.36	When Paul **finished,** he knelt down with them and prayed.
Rom	15.23	But now that I have **finished** my work in these regions
	15.28	When I have **finished** this task and have handed over to
2 Cor	8.10	is better for you to **finish** now what you began last year.
	8.11	On with it, then, and **finish** the job!
	8.11	Be as eager to **finish** it as you were to plan it,
Gal	3. 3	do you now want to **finish** by your own power?
Phil	1. 6	it on until it is **finished** on the Day of Christ Jesus.
Col	4.17	to Archippus, "Be sure to **finish** the task you were given in
Heb	4. 3	though his work had been **finished** from the time he created
Rev	11. 7	When they **finish** proclaiming their message, the beast that
	22. 8	And when I **finished** hearing and seeing them, I fell down at

FINISHING-LINE

1 Cor	9.26	That is why I run straight for the **finishing-line;**

FIR-TREE

Ps	104.17	the storks nest in the **fir-trees.**
Ezek	27. 5	They used **fir-trees** from Mount Hermon for timber And a
	31. 8	No **fir-tree** ever had such branches, And no plane-tree such boughs.

FIRE

[BONFIRE, FIERY]

Gen	15.17	a smoking **fire-pot** and a flaming torch suddenly appeared
	22. 6	carried a knife and live coals for starting the **fire.**
Ex	3. 2	that the bush was on **fire** but that it was not burning
	13.21	them in a pillar of **fire** to give them light, so that
	13.22	the people during the day, and the pillar of **fire** at night.
	14.24	down from the pillar of **fire** and cloud at the Egyptian army
	19.18	with smoke, because the Lord had come down on it in **fire.**
	22. 6	"If a man starts a **fire** in his field and it spreads
	22. 6	the one who started the **fire** is to pay for the damage.
	24.16	the light looked like a **fire** burning on top of the mountain.
	32.24	I threw the ornaments into the **fire** and out came this bull-calf!"
	35. 3	Do not even light a **fire** in your homes on the Sabbath."
	40.38	the day and a **fire** burning above it during the night.
Lev	1. 7	the priests shall arrange **fire-wood** on the altar and light it.
	1. 8	They shall put on the **fire** the pieces of the animal,
	1.12	priest shall put on the **fire** all the parts, including the
	4.12	poured out, and there he shall burn it on a wood **fire.**
	6. 9	altar all night long, and the **fire** is to be kept burning.
	6.12	The **fire** on the altar must be kept burning and never
	6.12	priest shall put **firewood** on it, arrange the burnt-offering
	6.13	The **fire** must always be kept burning on the altar and
	9.24	Suddenly the Lord sent a **fire,** and it consumed the
	10. 1	But this **fire** was not holy, because the Lord had not
	10. 2	Suddenly the Lord sent **fire,** and it burnt them to death
	10. 6	to mourn this death caused by the **fire** which the Lord sent.
	13.52	it is a spreading mildew which must be destroyed by **fire.**
	16. 1	Aaron who were killed when they offered unholy **fire** to the Lord.
	16.13	put the incense on the **fire,** and the smoke of the incense
Num	3. 4	killed when they offered unholy **fire** to the Lord in the
	6.18	and put it on the **fire** on which the fellowship-offering is
	9.15	At night the cloud looked like **fire.**
	11. 1	Lord heard them, he was angry and sent **fire** on the people.
Num	11. 2	he prayed to the Lord, and the **fire** died down.
	11. 3	because there the **fire** of the Lord burnt among them.
	14.14	pillar of cloud by day and a pillar of **fire** by night.
	15.32	wilderness, a man was found gathering **firewood** on the Sabbath.
	16.35	Then the Lord sent a **fire** that blazed out and burnt up
	19. 6	of hyssop, and a red cord and throw them into the **fire.**
	21.28	this city of Heshbon Sihon's army went forth like a **fire;**
	26.10	with Korah and his followers when **fire** destroyed 250 men;
	26.61	Nadab and Abihu died when they offered unholy **fire** to the Lord.
	31.22	tin, or lead, is to be purified by passing it through **fire.**
Deut	1.33	you in a pillar of **fire** by night and in a pillar
	4.11	thick clouds of dark smoke and **fire** blazing up to the sky.
	4.12	spoke to you from the **fire,** how you heard him speaking but
	4.15	spoke to you from the **fire** on Mount Sinai, you did not
	4.24	idol, [24] because the Lord your God is like a flaming **fire;**
	4.33	hearing a god speak to them from a **fire,** as you have?
	4.36	let you see his holy **fire,** and he spoke to you from
	5. 4	mountain the Lord spoke to you face-to-face from the **fire.**
	5. 5	you were afraid of the **fire** and would not go up the
	5.22	a mighty voice from the **fire** and from the thick clouds, he
	5.23	the whole mountain was on **fire** and you heard the voice from
	5.24	and his glory when we heard him speak from the **fire!**
	5.25	That terrible **fire** will destroy us.
	5.26	ever lived after hearing the living God speak from a **fire?**
	6.15	come against you like **fire** and will destroy you completely,
	9. 3	Lord your God will go ahead of you like a raging **fire.**
	9.10	said to you from the **fire** on the day that you were
	9.15	Flames of **fire** were coming from the mountain.
	9.21	had made—that metal bull-calf—and threw it into the **fire.**
	10. 4	when he spoke from the **fire** on the day you were gathered
	12.31	even sacrifice their children in the **fires** on their altars.
	18.10	Don't sacrifice your children in the **fires** on your altars;
	18.16	again or to see his **fiery** presence any more, because you
	32.22	My anger will flame up like **fire** and burn everything on earth.
	33. 2	angels were with him, a flaming **fire** at his right hand.
Josh	6.24	Then they set **fire** to the city and burnt it to the
	8. 8	the city, set it on **fire,** just as the Lord has commanded.
	8.19	They immediately set the city on **fire.**
	8.21	and that it was on **fire,** they turned round and began killing
Judg	1. 8	They killed its people and set **fire** to the city.
	6.21	**Fire** came out of the rock and burnt up the meat and
	6.26	as an offering, using for **firewood** the symbol of Asherah you
	9.15	If you don't, **fire** will blaze out of my thorny branches and
	9.20	But if not, may **fire** blaze out from Abimelech and burn
	9.20	May **fire** blaze out from the men of Shechem and Bethmillo
	9.49	They set it on **fire,** with the people inside, and all the
	9.52	he went up to the door to set the tower on **fire.**
	14.15	If you don't, we'll set **fire** to your father's house and burn
	15. 5	Then he set **fire** to the torches and turned the foxes loose
	16. 9	the bowstrings just as thread breaks when **fire** touches it.
2 Sam	14.30	Go and set **fire** to it."
	14.30	So they went and set the field on **fire.**
	14.31	demanded, "Why did your servants set **fire** to my field?"
1 Kgs	9.16	it, killing its inhabitants and setting **fire** to the city.
	16.18	fortress, set the palace on **fire,** and died in the flames.
	17.10	to the gate of the town, he saw a widow gathering **firewood.**
	17.12	came here to gather some **firewood** to take back home
	18.23	pieces, and put it on the wood—but don't light the **fire.**
	18.24	the one who answers by sending **fire**—he is God."
	18.25	Pray to your god, but don't set **fire** to the wood."
	18.38	The Lord sent **fire** down, and it burnt up the sacrifice,
	19.12	there was a fire—but the Lord was not in the **fire.**
	19.12	And after the **fire,** there was the soft whisper of a voice.
	19.21	and cooked the meat, using the yoke as fuel for the **fire.**
2 Kgs	1.10	Elijah answered, "may **fire** come down from heaven
	1.10	At once **fire** came down and killed the officer and his men.
	1.12	Elijah answered, "may **fire** come down from heaven
	1.12	At once the **fire** of God came down and killed the officer
	1.14	officers and their men were killed by **fire** from heaven;
	2.11	then suddenly a chariot of **fire** pulled by horses of fire
	4.38	a big pot on the **fire** and make some stew for them.
	6.17	covered with horses and chariots of **fire** all round Elisha.
	8.12	their fortresses on **fire,** slaughter their finest young men,
1 Chr	21.26	Lord answered him by sending **fire** from heaven to burn the
2 Chr	7. 1	King Solomon finished his prayer, **fire** came down from heaven
	7. 3	people of Israel saw the **fire** fall from heaven and the light
	16.14	burial, and they built a huge **bonfire** to mourn his death.
	21.19	subjects did not light a **bonfire** in mourning for him as had
	35.13	Passover sacrifices over the **fire,** according to the regulations,
Neh	2. 3	is in ruins and its gates have been destroyed by **fire?"**
	2.13	of the city and the gates that had been destroyed by **fire.**
	9.12	in day-time, and at night you lighted their way with **fire.**
	9.19	away the cloud or the **fire** that showed them the path by
Job	5. 7	trouble on himself, as surely as sparks fly up from a **fire.**
	15.30	whose branches are burnt by **fire,** whose blossoms are blown
	15.34	descendants for godless men, and **fire** will destroy the homes
	20.26	a **fire** not lit by human hands burns him and all his
	22.20	own is destroyed, and **fire** burns up anything that is left.
	31.12	It would be like a destructive, hellish **fire,**
	41.21	His breath starts **fires** burning;
Ps	18.12	Hailstones and flashes of **fire** came from the lightning
	21. 9	He will destroy them like a blazing **fire** when he appears.
	21. 9	Lord will devour them in his anger, and **fire** will consume them.
	46. 9	he breaks bows, destroys spears, and sets shields on **fire.**
	50. 3	a raging **fire** is in front of him, a furious storm is
	66.10	as silver is purified by **fire** so you have tested us.
	66.12	we went through **fire** and flood, but now you have brought
	68. 2	melts in front of the **fire,** so do the wicked perish in
	69. 9	My devotion to your Temple burns in me like a **fire;**
	74. 7	They wrecked your Temple and set it on **fire;**
	78.14	a cloud and all night long with the light of a **fire.**

Ps	78.21	he attacked his people with **fire,** and his anger against them grew,
	79. 5	Will your anger continue to burn like **fire?**
	80.16	Our enemies have set it on **fire** and cut it down;
	83.14	As **fire** burns the forest, as flames set the hills on fire,
	89.46	How long will your anger burn like **fire?**
	97. 3	**Fire** goes in front of him and burns up his enemies round
	102. 3	my body is burning like **fire.**
	105.39	over his people and a **fire** at night to give them light.
	106.18	**fire** came down on their followers and burnt up those wicked people.
	118.12	bees, but they burnt out as quickly as a **fire** among thorns;
	119.139	me like a **fire,** because my enemies disregard your commands.
Prov	6.27	Can you carry **fire** against your chest without burning
	17. 3	and silver are tested by **fire,** and a person's heart is
	26.20	Without wood, a **fire** goes out;
	26.21	the **fire** burning, and troublemakers keep arguments alive.
	27.21	**Fire** tests gold and silver;
	30.16	and a **fire** burning out of control.
Ecc	7. 6	When a fool laughs, it is like thorns crackling in a **fire.**
Song	8. 6	It bursts into flame and burns like a raging **fire.**
Is	1.31	as straw is set on **fire** by a spark, so powerful men
	5.24	shrivel and burn in the **fire,** your roots will rot and your
	9. 5	all their bloodstained clothing will be destroyed by **fire.**
	9.18	burns like a **fire** that destroys thorn-bushes and thistles.
	9.18	It burns like a forest **fire** that sends up columns of smoke.
	9.19	his punishment burns like a **fire** throughout the land and
	10.16	In their bodies there will be a **fire** that burns and burns.
	10.17	God, the light of Israel, will become a **fire.**
	27.11	are withered and broken, and women gather them for **firewood.**
	29. 6	He will send tempests and raging **fire;**
	30.27	**Fire** and smoke show his anger.
	30.27	He speaks, and his words burn like **fire.**
	30.33	prepared where a huge **fire** will burn the emperor of Assyria.
	30.33	will breathe out a stream of flame to set it on **fire.**
	31. 9	in Jerusalem and whose **fire** burns there for sacrifices.
	33.11	My spirit is like a **fire** that will destroy you.
	33.14	They say, "God's judgement is like a **fire** that burns for ever.
	33.14	Can any of us survive a **fire** like that?"
	40.16	our God, and its trees are too few to kindle the **fire.**
	42.25	Like **fire** his anger burned throughout Israel, but we never
	43. 2	When you pass through **fire,** you will not be burnt;
	44.12	takes a piece of metal and works with it over a **fire.**
	44.15	one part he builds a **fire** to warm himself and bake bread;
	44.16	With some of the wood he makes a **fire;**
	44.16	What a beautiful **fire!"**
	47.14	be like bits of straw, and a **fire** will burn them up!
	47.14	too hot for them, not a cosy **fire** to warm themselves by.
	48.10	have tested you in the **fire** of suffering, as silver is
	54.12	with stones that glow like **fire,** and the wall around you
	54.16	"I create the blacksmith, who builds a **fire** and forges weapons.
	64. 2	They would tremble like water boiling over a hot **fire.**
	64.11	where our ancestors praised you, has been destroyed by **fire.**
	65. 5	my anger against them is like a **fire** that never goes out.
	66.15	The Lord will come with **fire.**
	66.16	By **fire** and sword he will punish all the people of the
	66.24	will never die, and the **fire** that burns them will never be
Jer	4. 4	my anger will burn like **fire** because of the evil things you
	5.13	I will make my words like a **fire** in your mouth.
	5.13	people will be like wood, and the **fire** will burn them up."
	6. 1	trumpet in Tekoa and build a signal **fire** in Beth Haccherem.
	7.18	The children gather **firewood,** the men build fires,
	7.18	gather firewood, the men build **fires,** and the women mix dough
	7.20	anger will be like a **fire** that no one can put out.
	7.31	they can sacrifice their sons and daughters in the **fire.**
	11.16	I will set its leaves on **fire** and break its branches.
	15.14	because my anger is like **fire,** and it will burn for ever."
	17. 4	my anger is like a **fire,** and it will burn for ever."
	17.27	if they do, I will set the gates of Jerusalem on **fire.**
	17.27	**Fire** will burn down the palaces of Jerusalem, and no one
	19. 5	Baal in order to burn their children in the **fire** as sacrifices.
	20. 9	then your message is like a **fire** burning deep within me.
	21.11	make my anger burn like a **fire** that cannot be put out.
	21.14	will set your palace on **fire,**
	21.14	and the **fire** will burn down everything round it.
	22. 7	its beautiful cedar pillars, and throw them into the **fire.**
	23.29	My message is like a **fire,** and like a hammer that breaks
	32.29	they will capture it [29] and set it on **fire.**
	36.22	king was sitting in his winter palace in front of the **fire.**
	36.23	them off with a small knife and threw them into the **fire.**
	43.12	I will set **fire** to the temples of Egypt's gods, and the
	44. 6	and on the streets of Jerusalem, and I set them on **fire.**
	48.45	**Fire** has burnt up the frontiers and the mountain heights of
	49.27	the walls of Damascus on **fire** and will burn down King
	50.32	cities on **fire,** and everything around will be destroyed."
	51.30	The city gates are broken down, and the houses are on **fire.**
	51.32	the river-crossing and have set the fortresses on **fire.**
Lam	1.13	"He sent **fire** from above, a fire that burnt inside me.
	2. 3	He raged against us like **fire,** destroying everything.
	4.11	he lit a **fire** in Zion that burnt it to the ground.
Ezek	1.13	The **fire** would blaze up and shoot out flashes of lightning.
	1.27	seemed to be shining like bronze in the middle of a **fire.**
	4.12	You are to build a **fire** out of dried human excrement,
	4.12	bake bread on the **fire,** and eat it where everyone can
	5. 4	out again, throw them in the **fire,** and let them burn up.
	5. 4	From them **fire** will spread to the whole nation of Israel."
	8. 2	I looked up and saw a vision of a **fiery** human form.
	8. 2	down his body looked like **fire,** and from the waist up he
	10. 6	linen clothes to take some **fire** from between the wheels that
	10. 7	put his hand into the **fire** that was there among them, picked
	11. 3	meat in it, but at least it protects us from the **fire.'**
	15. 4	It is only good for building a **fire.**
Ezek	15. 5	Now that the **fire** has burnt it and charred it, it is
	15. 7	They have escaped one **fire,** but now fire will burn them up.
	19.14	The stem of the vine caught **fire;**
	19.14	**fire** burnt up its branches and fruit.
	20.31	same idols by sacrificing your children to them in the **fire.**
	20.47	I am starting a **fire,** and it will burn up every tree
	20.48	the Lord, set it on **fire** and that no one can put
	21.31	anger when I turn it loose on you like a blazing **fire.**
	21.32	You will be destroyed by **fire.**
	22.20	My anger and rage will melt them just as **fire** melts ore.
	22.21	them in Jerusalem, build a **fire** under them, and melt them
	22.31	on them, and like a **fire** I will destroy them for what
	24. 3	Set the pot on the **fire** and fill it up with water.
	24. 9	I myself will pile up the **firewood.**
	28.18	So I set **fire** to the city and burnt it to the
	30. 8	When I set **fire** to Egypt and all her defenders are killed,
	30.14	southern Egypt desolate and set **fire** to the city of Zoan in
	30.16	I will set **fire** to Egypt, and Pelusium will be in agony.
	38.22	rain and hail, together with **fire** and sulphur, will pour
	39. 6	I will start a **fire** in the land of Magog and along
	39. 9	will go out and collect the abandoned weapons for **firewood.**
	39. 9	They will build **fires** with the shields, bows, arrows, spears,
	39.10	will not have to gather **firewood** in the fields or cut down
Dan	3.23	still tied up, fell into the heart of the blazing **fire.**
	3.25	"Then why do I see four men walking about in the **fire?"**
	3.27	at the three men, who had not been harmed by the **fire.**
	7. 9	His throne, mounted on **fiery** wheels, was blazing with fire,
	7. 9	fiery wheels, was blazing with **fire,**
	7.10	and a stream of **fire** was pouring out from it.
	10. 6	as a flash of lightning, and his eyes blazed like **fire.**
Hos	7. 4	Their hatred smoulders like the **fire** in an oven, which is
	8.14	But I will send **fire** that will burn down their palaces and
Joel	1.19	and trees are dried up, as though a **fire** had burnt them.
	2. 3	Like **fire** they eat up the plants.
	2. 5	they crackle like dry grass on **fire.**
	2.30	there will be bloodshed, **fire,** and clouds of smoke.
Amos	1. 4	So I will send **fire** upon the palace built by King Hazael
	1. 7	So I will send **fire** upon the city walls of Gaza and
	1.10	So I will send **fire** upon the city walls of Tyre and
	1.12	So I will send **fire** upon the city of Teman and burn
	1.14	So I will send **fire** upon the city walls of Rabbah and
	2. 2	I will send **fire** upon the land of Moab and burn down
	2. 5	So I will send **fire** upon Judah and burn down the
	4.11	who survived were like a burning stick saved from a **fire.**
	5. 6	go, he will sweep down like **fire** on the people of Israel.
	5. 6	The **fire** will burn up the people of Bethel, and no one
	7. 4	In it I saw him preparing to punish his people with **fire.**
	7. 4	The **fire** burnt up the great ocean under the earth,
Obad	18	The people of Jacob and of Joseph will be like **fire;**
	18	they will destroy the people of Esau as **fire** burns stubble.
Mic	1. 4	Then the mountains will melt under him like wax in a **fire;**
	1. 7	prostitutes will be destroyed by **fire,** and all its images
Nah	2. 3	Their chariots flash like **fire!**
	3.13	**Fire** will destroy the bars across your gates.
Zeph	1.18	The whole earth will be destroyed by the **fire** of his anger.
	3. 8	The whole earth will be destroyed by the **fire** of my fury.
Zech	2. 5	will be a wall of **fire** round the city to protect it
	3. 2	This man is like a stick snatched from the **fire."**
	11. 1	Lebanon, so that **fire** can burn down your cedar-trees!
	12. 6	clans of Judah like a **fire** in a forest or in a
	13. 9	survives and will purify them as silver is purified by **fire.**
Mal	1.10	as to prevent you from lighting useless **fires** on my altar.
	3. 2	He will be like strong soap, like a **fire** that refines metal.
Mt	3.10	bear good fruit will be cut down and thrown in the **fire.**
	3.11	after me will baptize you with the Holy Spirit and **fire.**
	3.12	he will burn the chaff in a **fire** that never goes out."
	5.22	fool will be in danger of going to the **fire** of hell.
	7.19	not bear good fruit is cut down and thrown in the **fire.**
	13.40	up and burnt in the **fire,** so the same thing will happen
	13.42	will throw them into the **fiery** furnace, where they will cry
	13.50	will throw them into the **fiery** furnace, where they will cry
	17.15	terrible fits that he often falls in the **fire** or into water.
	18. 8	hands and both feet and be thrown into the eternal **fire.**
	18. 9	to keep both eyes and be thrown into the **fire** of hell.
	25.41	Away to the eternal **fire** which has been prepared for the
Mk	9.22	to kill him by throwing him in the **fire** and into water.
	9.43	and go off to hell, to the **fire** that never goes out.
	9.48	them never die, and the **fire** that burns them is never put
	9.49	"Everyone will be purified by **fire** as a sacrifice is
	14.54	sat down with the guards, keeping himself warm by the **fire.**
Lk	3. 9	bear good fruit will be cut down and thrown in the **fire."**
	3.16	He will baptize you with the Holy Spirit and **fire.**
	3.17	he will burn the chaff in a **fire** that never goes out."
	9.54	you want us to call **fire** down from heaven to destroy them?"
	12.49	to set the earth on **fire,** and how I wish it were
	16.24	cool my tongue, because I am in great pain in this **fire!'**
	17.29	the day Lot left Sodom, **fire** and sulphur rained down from
	22.55	A **fire** had been lit in the centre of the courtyard, and
	22.56	him sitting there at the **fire,** she looked straight at him
	24.32	other, "Wasn't it like a **fire** burning in us when he talked
Jn	2.17	devotion to your house, O God, burns in me like a **fire."**
	15. 6	gathered up and thrown into the **fire,** where they are burnt.
	18.18	guards had built a charcoal **fire** and were standing round it,
	21. 9	ashore, they saw a charcoal **fire** there with fish on it and
Acts	2. 3	what looked like tongues of **fire** which spread out and
	2.19	There will be blood, **fire,** and thick smoke;
	28. 2	was cold, so they lit a **fire** and made us all welcome.
	28. 3	was putting them on the **fire** when a snake came out on
	28. 5	the snake off into the **fire** without being harmed at all.
1 Cor	3.13	For on that Day **fire** will reveal everyone's work;
	3.13	the **fire** will test it and show its real quality.

1 Cor 3.14 survives the **fire,** the builder will receive a reward.
3.15 will be saved, as if he had escaped through the **fire.**
2 Thes 1. 8 mighty angels, [8]with a flaming **fire,** to punish those who
Heb 1. 7 "God makes his angels winds, and his servants flames of **fire."**
6. 8 of being cursed by God and will be destroyed by **fire.**
10.27 coming Judgement and the fierce **fire** which will destroy
11.34 put out fierce **fires,** escaped being killed by the sword.
12.18 Mount Sinai with its blazing **fire,** the darkness and the gloom,
12.29 because our God is indeed a destroying **fire.**
Jas 3. 5 large a forest can be set on **fire** by a tiny flame!
3. 6 And the tongue is like a **fire.**
3. 6 It sets on **fire** the entire course of our existence
3. 6 with the **fire** that comes to it from hell
5. 3 a witness against you and will eat up your flesh like **fire.**
1 Pet 1. 7 Even gold, which can be destroyed, is tested by **fire;**
2 Pet 2. 6 and Gomorrah, destroying them with **fire,** and made them an
3. 7 the same command of God, in order to be destroyed by **fire.**
Jude 7 the punishment of eternal **fire** as a plain warning to all.
23 save others by snatching them out of the **fire;**
Rev 1.14 white as wool, or as snow, and his eyes blazed like **fire;**
2.18 God, whose eyes blaze like **fire,** whose feet shine like polished brass.
8. 5 the incense-burner, filled it with **fire** from the altar, and
8. 7 Hail and **fire,** mixed with blood, came pouring down on the earth.
8. 8 looked like a huge mountain on **fire** was thrown into the sea.
9.17 they had breastplates red as **fire,** blue as sapphire, and
9.17 lions' heads, and from their mouths came out **fire,** smoke,
9.18 **fire,** the smoke, and the sulphur coming out of the horses'
10. 1 was like the sun, and his legs were like pillars of **fire.**
11. 5 anyone tries to harm them, **fire** comes out of their mouths
13.13 it made **fire** come down out of heaven to earth in the
14.10 this will be tormented in **fire** and sulphur before the holy
14.11 The smoke of the **fire** that torments them goes up for
14.18 angel, who is in charge of the **fire,** came from the altar.
15. 2 I saw what looked like a sea of glass mixed with **fire.**
16. 8 sun, and it was allowed to burn people with its **fiery** heat.
17.16 they will eat her flesh and destroy her with **fire.**
18. 8 she will be burnt with **fire,** because the Lord God, who
19.12 were like a flame of **fire,** and he wore many crowns on
19.20 thrown alive into the lake of **fire** that burns with sulphur.
20. 9 But **fire** came down from heaven and destroyed them.
20.10 thrown into the lake of **fire** and sulphur, where the beast
20.14 the world of the dead were thrown into the lake of **fire.**
20.14 (This lake of **fire** is the second death.)
20.15 the book of the living was thrown into the lake of **fire.**
21. 8 is the lake burning with **fire** and sulphur, which is the

FIREPAN

see also **PAN**

Ex 27. 3 the greasy ashes, and make shovels, bowls, hooks, and **firepans.**
38. 3 pans, the shovels, the bowls, the hooks, and the **firepans.**
Lev 10. 1 and Abihu, each took his **fire-pan,** put live coals in it,
16.12 he shall take a **fire-pan** full of burning coals from the
Num 4.14 **firepans,** hooks, shovels, and basins.
16. 6 and your followers take **firepans,** put live coals and incense
16.17 of you will take his **firepan,** put incense on it, and then
16.18 So every man took his **firepan,** put live coals and incense
16.37 priest to remove the bronze **firepans** from the remains of the
16.37 scatter the coals from the **firepans** somewhere else,
16.37 because the **firepans** are holy.
16.38 So take the **firepans** of these men who were put to death
16.39 Eleazar the priest took the **firepans** and had them beaten into
16.46 to Aaron, "Take your **firepan,** put live coals from the altar
16.47 Aaron obeyed, took his **firepan** and ran into the middle of

FIREPLACE

Ezek 46.23 stone wall round it, with **fireplaces** built against the wall.

FIRM

1 Kgs 2.12 as king, and his royal power was **firmly** established.
2.24 Lord has **firmly** established me on the throne of my father
2 Kgs 5.14 His flesh became **firm** and healthy, like that of a child.
14. 5 As soon as Amaziah was **firmly** in power, he executed the
1 Chr 16.30 The earth is set **firmly** in place and cannot be moved.
2 Chr 1. 1 of King David, took **firm** control of the kingdom of Israel,
17. 5 Lord gave Jehoshaphat **firm** control over the kingdom of Judah,
20.20 your trust in the Lord your God, and you will stand **firm.**
21. 4 When Jehoram was in **firm** control of the kingdom, he had
25. 3 As soon as he was **firmly** in power, he executed the
Job 11.15 Then face the world again, **firm** and courageous.
18. 7 His steps were **firm,** but now he stumbles;
41.17 are fastened so **firmly** together that nothing can ever pull
Ps 20. 8 will stumble and fall, but we will rise and stand **firm.**
75. 3 earth itself be shaken, I will keep its foundations **firm.**
78. 8 trust in God was never **firm** and who did not remain faithful
78.69 he made it **firm** like the earth itself, secure for all time.
93. 1 The earth is set **firmly** in place and cannot be moved.
93. 2 throne, O Lord, has been **firm** from the beginning, and you
96.10 The earth is set **firmly** in place and cannot be moved;
104. 5 You have set the earth **firmly** on its foundations,
Prov 12. 3 does not give security, but righteous people stand **firm.**
12.12 is to find evil things to do, but the righteous stand **firm.**
Ecc 12.11 and collected proverbs are as lasting as **firmly** driven nails.
Is 22.23 I will fasten him **firmly** in place like a peg, and he
22.25 the peg that was **firmly** fastened will work loose and fall.
26. 3 who keep their purpose **firm** and put their trust in you.
28.16 "I am placing in Zion a foundation that is **firm** and strong.
28.16 are written the words, 'Faith that is **firm** is also patient.'
Is 32. 8 person acts honestly and stands **firm** for what is right.
45.18 formed and made the earth— he made it **firm** and lasting.
Jer 30.20 will restore the nation's ancient power and establish it **firmly**
Ezek 3. 9 I will make you as **firm** as a rock, as hard as
20.37 "I will take **firm** control of you and make you obey my
Dan 9.27 That ruler will have a **firm** agreement with many people
Hos 14. 5 they will be **firmly** rooted like the trees of Lebanon.
Lk 21.19 Stand **firm,** and you will save yourselves.
Rom 14. 5 Each one should **firmly** make up his own mind.
16.25 able to make you stand **firm** in your faith, according to the
1 Cor 1. 6 about Christ has become so **firmly** established in you [7]that
1. 8 He will also keep you **firm** to the end, so that you
7.37 forced to do so, has **firmly** made up his mind not to
10.12 Whoever thinks he is standing **firm** had better be careful
10.13 not allow you to be tested beyond your power to remain **firm;**
15. 1 which you received, and on which your faith stands **firm.**
15. 2 the gospel if you hold **firmly** to it—unless it was for
15.58 So then, my dear brothers, stand **firm** and steady.
16.13 Be alert, stand **firm** in the faith, be brave, be strong.
2 Cor 1.24 we know that you stand **firm** in the faith.
Phil 1. 7 I was free to defend the gospel and establish it **firmly.**
1.27 hear that you are standing **firm** with one common purpose and
4. 1 is how you should stand **firm** in your life in the Lord.
Col 1.23 course, continue faithful on a **firm** and sure foundation, and
2. 5 as I see the resolute **firmness** with which you stand together
4.12 God to make you stand **firm,** as mature and fully convinced Christians,
1 Thes 1. 3 hard, and how your hope in our Lord Jesus Christ is **firm.**
3. 8 really live if you stand **firm** in your life in union with
2 Thes 2.15 So then, our brothers, stand **firm** and hold on to those
2.16 us unfailing courage and a **firm** hope, [17]encourage you and
1 Tim 6.12 God called you when you **firmly** professed your faith before many witnesses.
6.13 Christ Jesus, who **firmly** professed his faith before Pontius Pilate,
2 Tim 1.13 Hold **firmly** to the true words that I taught you, as the
3.14 in the truths that you were taught and **firmly** believe.
Tit 1. 9 He must hold **firmly** to the message which can be trusted
Heb 2. 1 hold on all the more **firmly** to the truths we have heard,
3.14 with Christ if we hold **firmly** to the end the confidence we
4.14 Let us, then, hold **firmly** to the faith we profess.
6.18 encouraged to hold **firmly** to the hope placed before us.
10.23 Let us hold on **firmly** to the hope we profess, because we
1 Pet 5. 9 Be **firm** in your faith and resist him, because you know
5.10 you and give you **firmness,** strength, and a sure foundation.
5.12 Stand **firm** in it.
2 Pet 1.12 already know them and are **firmly** grounded in the truth you
Rev 2.25 But until I come, you must hold **firmly** to what you have.

AV **FIRMAMENT** see **DOME**

FIRST

Gen 1. 5 Evening passed and morning came—that was the **first** day.
2.11 The **first** river is the Pishon;
4. 4 Then Abel brought the **first** lamb born to one of his sheep,
8. 5 going down, and on the **first** day of the tenth month the
8.13 on the first day of the **first** month, the water was gone.
9.20 who was a farmer, was the **first** man to plant a vineyard.
10. 8 named Nimrod, who became the world's **first** great conqueror.
25.25 The **first** one was reddish, and his skin was like a hairy
32. 8 Esau comes and attacks the **first** group, the other may be
32.17 He ordered the **first** servant, "When my brother Esau meets
33. 2 the concubines and their children **first,** then Leah and her
36.15 Esau's **first** son Eliphaz was the ancestor of the following
38. 6 For his **first** son Er, Judah got a wife whose name was
38.28 red thread round it, and said, "This one was born **first."**
38.29 But he pulled his arm back, and his brother was born **first.**
41.51 so he named his **first** son Manasseh.
43.18 of the money that was returned in our sacks the **first** time.
49. 3 are my strength And the **first** child of my manhood,
Ex 4. 8 or be convinced by the **first** miracle, then this one will
12. 2 month is to be the **first** month of the year for you.
12.15 On the **first** day you are to get rid of all the
12.16 On the **first** day and again on the seventh day you are
12.18 the fourteenth day of the **first** month to the evening of the
12.44 that you have bought may eat it if you circumcise him **first.**
12.48 honour the Lord, you must **first** circumcise all the males of
13. 4 Egypt on this day in the **first** month, the month of Abib.
13. 5 celebrate this festival in the **first** month of every year.
19. 1 left Rephidim, and on the **first** day of the third month after
21.10 must continue to give his **first** wife the same amount of food
23.19 house of the Lord your God the **first** corn that you harvest.
26. 5 Put fifty loops on the **first** piece of the first set and
28.17 in the **first** row mount a ruby, a topaz, and a garnet;
29.40 With the **first** lamb offer one kilogramme of fine wheat
34. 1 two stone tablets like the **first** ones, and I will write on
34. 1 the words that were on the **first** tablets, which you broke.
34.22 you begin to harvest the **first** crop of your wheat, and keep
34.26 to the house of the Lord the **first** corn that you harvest.
36.12 put fifty loops on the **first** piece of the first set
39.10 in the **first** row they mounted a ruby, a topaz, and a
40. 2 the first day of the **first** month set up the Tent of
40.17 the first day of the **first** month of the second year after
Lev 2.12 An offering of the **first** corn that you harvest each year
2.14 an offering of the **first** corn harvested, offer roasted grain
19.23 consider the fruit ritually unclean for the **first** three years.
23. 5 begins at sunset on the fourteenth day of the **first** month.
23. 7 On the **first** of these days you shall gather for worship
23. 9 you harvest your corn, take the **first** sheaf to the priest.
23.17 the Lord as an offering of the **first** corn to be harvested.

Lev 23.23 the **first** day of the seventh month observe a special day
23.35 On the **first** of these days come together for worship
23.39 The **first** day shall be a special day of rest.
25.29 buy it back during the **first** full year from the date of
Num 1. 1 On the **first** day of the second month in the second year
1.18 the whole community on the **first** day of the second month and
2. 3 The division of Judah shall march **first.**
2.17 between the **first** two divisions and the last two the Levites
9. 1 the Sinai Desert in the **first** month of the second year after
9. 5 the fourteenth day of the **first** month they did so in the
10.14 tribe of Judah started out **first,** company by company,
15.20 the first loaf of the **first** bread made from the new corn
18.12 all the best of the **first** produce which the Israelites give
20. 1 In the **first** month the whole community of Israel came to
22.15 larger number of leaders, who were more important than the **first.**
22.37 "Why didn't you come when I sent for you the **first** time?
26.64 Aaron had listed in the **first** census in the Sinai Desert.
28. 4 Offer the **first** lamb in the morning, and the second in the
28. 7 the wine-offering with the **first** lamb, pour out at the altar
28.14 the burnt-offering for the **first** day of each month throughout
28.16 is to be held on the fourteenth day of the **first** month.
28.18 On the **first** day of the festival you are to gather for
28.26 On the **first** day of the Harvest Festival, when you present
29. 1 On the **first** day of the seventh month you are to gather
29. 6 the regular burnt-offering for the **first** day of the month
29.13 On this **first** day offer a food-offering to the Lord,
29.18 all the other offerings required for the **first** day.
29.21 all the other offerings required for the **first** day.
29.24 all the other offerings required for the **first** day.
29.27 all the other offerings required for the **first** day.
29.30 all the other offerings required for the **first** day.
29.33 all the other offerings required for the **first** day.
29.37 all the other offerings required for the **first** day.
33. 3 the fifteenth day of the **first** month of the year,
33. 3 the day after the **first** Passover.
33.38 he died there on the **first** day of the fifth month of
Deut 1. 3 On the **first** day of the eleventh month of the fortieth
10. 1 two stone tablets like the **first** ones and make a wooden box
10. 3 two stone tablets like the **first** ones and took them up the
13. 9 Be the **first** to stone him, and then let everyone else stone
16. 4 on the evening of the **first** day must be eaten that same
17. 7 witnesses are to throw the **first** stones, and then the rest
18. 4 They are to receive the **first** share of the corn, wine,
21.15 bear him sons, but the **first** son is not the child of
21.17 of his possessions to his **first** son, even though he is not
21.17 A man must acknowledge his **first** son and give him the share
24. 4 In either case, her **first** husband is not to marry her again;
25. 6 The **first** son that they have will be considered the son of
26. 2 place in a basket the **first** part of each crop that you
26.10 bring to the Lord the **first** part of the harvest that he
Josh 4.19 the tenth day of the **first** month and made camp at Gilgal,
18.11 of the tribe of Benjamin was the **first** to be assigned.
21. 4 Levite clan of Kohath were the **first** to be assigned cities.
21.10 Their assignment was the **first** to be made.
Judg 1. 1 tribes should be the **first** to go and attack the Canaanites?"
1. 2 The Lord answered, "The tribe of Judah will go **first.**
11.31 burn as an offering the **first** person that comes out of my
20.18 asked God, "Which tribe should attack the Benjaminites **first?"**
Ruth 4. 4 right to buy it belongs **first** to you and then to me."
1 Sam 14.14 In that **first** slaughter Jonathan and the young man killed
14.35 built an altar to the Lord, the **first** one that he built.
2 Sam 18.27 said, "I can see that the **first** man runs like Ahimaaz."
19.20 is why I am the **first** one from the northern tribes to
19.43 forget that we were the **first** to talk about bringing the
23. 8 the **first** was Josheb Basshebeth from Tachemon, who was
1 Kgs 3.22 The **first** woman answered, "No!
3.27 Give it to the **first** woman—she is its real mother."
16.23 The **first** six years he ruled in Tirzah,
20. 9 that I agreed to his **first** demand, but I cannot agree to
2 Kgs 4.42 of bread made from the **first** barley harvested that year,
1 Chr 1.10 named Nimrod, who became the world's **first** great conqueror.)
6.33 Heman, the leader of the **first** choir, was the son of Joel.
6.54 received the **first** share of the land assigned to the Levites.
9. 2 The **first** to return to their property in the cities
11. 6 David said, "The **first** man to kill a Jebusite will be
11.11 **First** was Jashobeam of the clan of Hachmon, the leader
12.15 In the **first** month of one year, the time when the River
27. 2 **First** month:
2 Chr 29. 3 In the **first** month of the year after Hezekiah became king,
29.17 work was begun on the **first** day of the first month, and
29.22 The priests killed the bulls **first,** then the sheep,
30. 1 proper time, in the **first** month, because not enough priests
35. 1 the fourteenth day of the **first** month they killed the animals
36.22 In the **first** year that Cyrus of Persia was emperor,
Ezra 1. 1 In the **first** year that Cyrus of Persia was emperor,
3. 6 Temple, they began on the **first** day of the seventh month to
3.12 of clans had seen the **first** Temple, and as they watched the
5.13 Then in the **first** year of the reign of King Cyrus as
6. 3 "In the **first** year of his reign Cyrus the emperor commanded
6.19 the fourteenth day of the **first** month of the following year.
7. 8 They left Babylonia on the **first** day of the first month,
7. 8 arrived in Jerusalem on the **first** day of the fifth month.
8.31 the twelfth day of the **first** month that we left the Ahava
10.16 **first** day of the tenth month they began their investigation,
Neh 7. 5 records of those who had **first** returned from captivity,
8. 1 the **first** day of that month they all assembled in Jerusalem,
8.18 From the **first** day of the festival to the last they read
10. 1 **first** to sign was the governor, Nehemiah son of Hacaliah,
10.35 year an offering of the **first** corn we harvest
10.35 and of the **first** fruit that ripens on our trees.
10.36 The **first** son born to each of us we will take to
Neh 10.36 We will also dedicate the **first** calf born to each
10.36 of our cows, and the **first** lamb or kid born to each
10.37 the dough made from the **first** corn harvested each year
12.31 The **first** group went to the right on top of the wall
12.44 including the tithes and the **first** corn and fruit that ripened
13.31 bring their offerings of the **first** corn and the first fruits
Esth 3. 7 King Xerxes' rule, in the **first** month, the month of Nisan,
3.12 the thirteenth day of the **first** month Haman called the king's
Job 8.12 dries up, they are the **first** to wither, while still too
13.22 Speak **first,** O God, and I will answer.
15. 7 Do you think you were the **first** man born?
40.14 Then I will be the **first** to praise you and admit that
42.12 part of Job's life even more than he had blessed the **first.**
Ps 68.27 **First** comes Benjamin, the smallest tribe, then the leaders
Prov 8.22 "The Lord created me **first** of all, the first of his works,
8.26 the earth and its fields or even the **first** handful of soil.
17.14 start of an argument is like the **first** break in a dam;
18.17 The **first** man to speak in court always seems right until
Is 28. 4 leaders will disappear like the **first** figs of the season,
41.27 I, the Lord, was the **first** to tell Zion the news;
44. 6 "I am the **first,** the last, the only God;
48.12 I am God, the **first,** the last, the only God!
Jer 4.31 in labour, a scream like a woman bearing her **first** child.
7.12 to Shiloh, the **first** place where I chose to be worshipped,
24. 2 **first** basket contained good figs, those that ripen early;
25. 1 was the **first** year that Nebuchadnezzar was king of Babylonia.)
36.28 and write on it everything that had been on the **first** one.
36.32 that had been on the **first** scroll and similar messages that
50. 8 Be the **first** to leave!
Ezek 10.13 were the same as those I had seen in my **first** vision.
10.14 The **first** was the face of a bull, the second a human
17. 9 Won't the **first** eagle pull it up by its roots, pull off
23.13 immoral, that the second sister was as bad as the **first.**
29.17 the **first** day of the first month of the twenty-seventh year
30.20 the seventh day of the **first** month of the eleventh year of
31. 1 On the **first** day of the third month of the eleventh year
32. 1 On the **first** day of the twelfth month of the twelfth year
32.17 the fifteenth day of the **first** month of the twelfth year of
44.30 the best of all the **first** harvest and of everything else
44.30 to give the priests the **first** loaf as an offering, and my
45.18 the first day of the **first** month you are to sacrifice a
45.21 the fourteenth day of the **first** month you will begin the
45.22 the **first** day of the festival the ruling prince must offer
Dan 7. 1 In the **first** year that Belshazzar was king of Babylonia,
7. 4 The **first** one looked like a lion, but had wings like an
8.21 and the prominent horn between his eyes is the **first** king.
8.22 that came up when the **first** horn was broken represent the
8.22 and which will not be as strong as the **first** kingdom.
9. 2 In the **first** year of his reign, I was studying the sacred
10. 4 the twenty-fourth day of the **first** month of the year, I was
10.12 ever since the **first** day you decided to humble yourself
Hos 1. 2 When the Lord **first** spoke to Israel through Hosea, he
1. 3 After the birth of their **first** child, a son, [4]the Lord said
2. 7 am going back to my **first** husband—I was better off then
9.10 The Lord says, "When I **first** found Israel, it was like
9.10 When I **first** saw your ancestors,
9.10 it was like seeing the **first** ripe figs of the season.
Amos 6. 7 So you will be the **first** to go into exile.
Hag 1. 1 emperor of Persia, on the **first** day of the sixth month,
Zech 2. 4 The **first** one said to the other, "Run and tell that young
6. 2 The **first** chariot was pulled by red horses, the second by
Mt 7. 5 **First** take the log out of your own eye, and then you
8.21 was a disciple, said, "Sir, **first** let me go back and bury
10. 2 **first,** Simon (called Peter) and his brother Andrew;
12.29 away his belongings unless he **first** ties up the strong man;
13.30 to pull up the weeds **first,** tie them in bundles and burn
17.10 the teachers of the Law say that Elijah has to come **first?"**
17.11 "Elijah is indeed coming **first,"** answered Jesus, "and
17.25 house, Jesus spoke up **first,** "Simon, what is your opinion?
17.27 Pull up the **first** fish you hook, and in its mouth you
19.30 But many who now are **first** will be last,
19.30 and many who now are last will be **first.**
20. 8 were hired last and ending with those who were hired **first.'**
20.10 the men who were the **first** to be hired came to be
20.16 last will be first, and those who are **first** will be last."
20.27 of you wants to be **first,** he must be your slave—[28]like
21.36 other slaves, more than the **first** time, and the tenants
23.26 what is inside the cup **first,** and then the outside will be
24. 8 All these things are like the **first** pains of childbirth.
26.17 On the **first** day of the Festival of Unleavened Bread the
27.64 This last lie would be even worse than the **first** one."
Mk 3.27 away his belongings unless he **first** ties up the strong man;
4.28 **first** the tender stalk appears, then the ear, and finally
7. 4 that comes from the market unless they wash it **first.**
7.27 But Jesus answered, "Let us **first** feed the children.
9.11 the teachers of the Law say that Elijah has to come **first?"**
9.12 "Elijah is indeed coming **first** in order to get everything ready.
9.35 them, "Whoever wants to be **first** must place himself last of
10.31 But many who now are **first** will be last,
10.31 and many who now are last will be **first."**
10.44 of you wants to be **first,** he must be the slave of
13. 8 These things are like the **first** pains of childbirth.
14.12 On the **first** day of the Festival of Unleavened Bread,
16. 9 early on Sunday, he appeared **first** to Mary Magdalene, from
Lk 2. 2 When this **first** census took place, Quirinius was the governor of
Syria.
2. 7 She gave birth to her **first** son, wrapped him in strips of
6.42 **First** take the log out of your own eye, and then you
9.59 But that man said, "Sir, **first** let me go back and bury
9.61 but **first** let me go and say good-bye to my family."
10. 5 you go into a house, **first** say, 'Peace be with this house.'

Lk 12. 1 on each other, Jesus said **first** to his disciples, "Be on
13.30 are now last will be **first,**
13.30 and those who are now **first** will be last."
14.18 The **first** one told the servant, 'I have bought a field and
14.28 a tower, he sits down **first** and works out what it will
14.31 men, he will sit down **first** and decide if he is strong
16. 5 He asked the **first** one, 'How much do you owe my master?'
17.25 But **first** he must suffer much and be rejected by the
19.16 The **first** one came and said, 'Sir, I have earned ten
21. 9 such things must happen **first,** but they do not mean that the
Jn 2.10 else serves the best wine **first,** and after the guests have
2.11 Jesus performed this **first** miracle in Cana in Galilee;
5. 7 I am trying to get in, somebody else gets there **first."**
8. 7 you has committed no sin may throw the **first** stone at her."
8. 9 heard this, they all left, one by one, the older ones **first.**
15.18 world hates you, just remember that it has hated me **first.**
18.13 Jewish guards arrested Jesus, bound him, [13]and took him **first** to Annas.
19.32 broke the legs of the **first** man and then of the other
19.39 Nicodemus, who at **first** had gone to see Jesus at night,
20. 4 disciple ran faster than Peter and reached the tomb **first.**
20. 8 the other disciple, who had reached the tomb **first,** also
Acts 1. 1 In my **first** book I wrote about all the things that Jesus
3.26 his Servant and sent him **first** to you, to bless you by
7.12 Egypt, he sent his sons, our ancestors, on their **first** visit there.
11.26 It was at Antioch that the believers were **first** called Christians.
12.10 They passed by the **first** guard post and then the second,
12.20 **First** they convinced Blastus, the man in charge of the palace,
13.46 that the word of God should be spoken **first** to you.
15.14 has just explained how God **first** showed his care for the
16.12 to Philippi, a city of the **first** district of Macedonia;
20.18 was with you, from the **first** day I arrived in the province
26. 4 spent my whole life, at **first** in my own country and then
26. 5 testify, that from the very **first** I have lived as a member
26.20 **First** in Damascus and in Jerusalem and then in all
26.23 must suffer and be the **first** one to rise from death, to
27.43 men who could swim to jump overboard **first** and swim ashore;
Rom 1. 8 **First,** I thank my God through Jesus Christ for all of you,
1.16 save all who believe, **first** the Jews and also the Gentiles.
2. 9 what is evil, for the Jews **first** and also for the Gentiles.
2.10 what is good, to the Jews **first** and also to the Gentiles.
3. 2 In the **first** place, God trusted his message to the Jews.
8.23 have the Spirit as the **first** of God's gifts also groan
8.29 Son, so that the Son would be the **first** among many brothers.
10.19 Moses himself is the **first** one to answer:
11.16 If the **first** piece of bread is given to God, then the
13.11 be saved is closer now than it was when we **first** believed.
16. 5 friend Epaenetus, who was the **first** man in the province of
1 Cor 7. 5 to each other, unless you **first** agree to do so for a
9.15 I would rather die **first!**
11.18 In the **first** place, I have been told that there are
11.28 then, everyone should examine himself **first,** and then eat
11.31 If we would examine ourselves **first,** we would not come
12.28 in the **first** place apostles, in the second place prophets,
15.23 Christ, **first** of all;
15.45 For the scripture says, "The **first** man, Adam, was
15.46 not the spiritual that comes **first,** but the physical, and
15.47 The **first** Adam, made of earth, came from the earth;
16.15 they are the **first** Christian converts in Achaia and have
2 Cor 1.15 that I made plans at **first** to visit you, in order that
8. 5 **First** they gave themselves to the Lord;
8.10 You were the **first,** not only to act, but also to be
Gal 4.13 You remember why I preached the gospel to you the **first** time;
Eph 1.12 us, then, who were the **first** to hope in Christ, praise God's
4. 9 It means that **first** he came down to the lowest depths of
6. 2 mother" is the **first** commandment that has a promise added:
Phil 1. 5 the work of the gospel from the very **first** day until now.
Col 1. 5 true message, the Good News, **first** came to you, you heard
1. 6 ever since the day you **first** heard about the grace of God
1.18 that he alone might have the **first** place in all things.
1 Thes 4.16 Those who have died believing in Christ will rise to life **first;**
2 Thes 2.13 God chose you as the **first** to be saved by the Spirit's
1 Tim 2. 1 **First** of all, then, I urge that petitions, prayers,
2.13 For Adam was created **first,** and then Eve.
3.10 They should be tested **first,** and then, if they pass the test,
5. 4 or grandchildren, they should learn **first** to carry out their
2 Tim 2. 6 the hard work should have the **first** share of the harvest.
4.16 No one stood by me the **first** time I defended myself;
Heb 2. 3 The Lord himself **first** announced this salvation, and those
4. 6 Those who **first** heard the Good News did not receive that rest,
5.12 someone to teach you the **first** lessons of God's message.
6. 1 leave behind us the **first** lessons of the Christian message.
7. 2 (The **first** meaning of Melchizedek's name is "King of Righteousness";
7.27 day for his own sins **first** and then for the sins of
8. 7 been nothing wrong with the **first** covenant, there would have
8.13 speaking of a new covenant, God has made the **first** one old;
9. 1 The **first** covenant had rules for worship and a man-made
9.15 the wrongs they did while the **first** covenant was in force.
9.18 That is why even the **first** covenant came into effect
9.19 **First,** Moses proclaimed to the people all the
10. 8 **First** he said, "You neither want nor are you pleased with
10.15 **First** he says, [16]"This is the covenant that I will make
Jas 1.18 so that we should have **first** place among all his creatures.
3.17 But the wisdom from above is pure **first** of all;
1 Pet 4.17 to begin, and God's own people are the **first** to be judged.
2 Pet 3. 3 **First** of all, you must understand that in these last days
1 Jn 4.19 We love because God **first** loved us.
Rev 1. 5 Christ, the faithful witness, the **first** to be raised from
1. 8 "I am the **first** and the last," says the Lord God Almighty,
1.17 I am the **first** and the last.
Rev 2. 4 you do not love me now as you did at **first.**
2. 5 Turn from your sins and do what you did at **first.**
2. 8 the one who is the **first** and the last, who died and
2.19 know that you are doing more now than you did at **first.**
4. 7 The **first** one looked like a lion;
6. 1 the Lamb break open the **first** of the seven seals, and I
8. 7 The **first** angel blew his trumpet.
9.12 The **first** horror is over;
13.12 It used the vast authority of the **first** beast in its presence.
13.12 on it to worship the **first** beast, whose wound had healed.
13.14 was allowed to perform in the presence of the **first** beast.
13.15 into the image of the **first** beast, so that the image could
14. 4 of mankind and are the **first** ones to be offered to God
14. 8 A second angel followed the **first** one, saying, "She has fallen!
14. 9 A third angel followed the **first** two, saying in a loud voice,
16. 2 The **first** angel went and poured out his bowl on the earth.
20. 5 This is the **first** raising of the dead.
20. 6 those who are included in this **first** raising of the dead.
21. 1 The first heaven and the **first** earth disappeared, and the sea vanished.
21. 6 I am the **first** and the last, the beginning and the end.
21.19 The **first** foundation-stone was jasper, the second sapphire, the third agate,
22.13 I am the **first** and the last, the beginning and the end."
also Num 7.12

FIRST-BORN

Gen 22.21 Uz the **first-born,** Buz his brother, Kemuel the father of
25.31 to you if you give me your rights as the **first-born** son."
25.34 was all Esau cared about his rights as the **first-born** son.
27.36 took my rights as the **first-born** son, and now he has taken
49. 3 "Reuben, my **first-born,** you are my strength And the first
Ex 4.22 him that I, the Lord, say, 'Israel is my **first-born** son.
4.23 Now I am going to kill your **first-born** son.'"
6.14 Reuben, Jacob's **first-born,** had four sons:
11. 5 through Egypt, [5]and every **first-born** son in Egypt will die,
11. 5 The **first-born** of all the cattle will die also.
12.12 land of Egypt, killing every **first-born** male, both human and
12.29 Lord killed all the **first-born** sons in Egypt, from the king's
12.29 all the **first-born** of the animals were also killed.
13. 2 "Dedicate all the **first-born** males to me,
13. 2 for every **first-born** male Israelite
13. 2 and every **first-born** male animal belongs to me."
13.12 you must offer every **first-born** male to the Lord.
13.12 Every **first-born** male of your animals belongs to the Lord,
13.13 buy back from him every **first-born** male donkey by offering
13.13 You must buy back every **first-born** male child of yours.
13.15 the Lord killed every **first-born** male in the land of Egypt,
13.15 is why we sacrifice every **first-born** male animal to the Lord,
13.15 but buy back our **first-born** sons.
22.29 "Give me your **first-born** sons.
22.30 Give me the **first-born** of your cattle and your sheep.
22.30 Let the **first-born** male stay with its mother for seven days,
34.19 "Every **first-born** son and first-born male domestic animal belongs to me,
34.20 are to buy back every **first-born** donkey by offering a lamb
34.20 Buy back every **first-born** son.
Lev 27.26 The **first-born** of an animal already belongs to the Lord,
27.27 to the Lord, [27]but the **first-born** of an unclean animal may
Num 3.12 When I killed all the **first-born** of the Egyptians,
3.12 of each Israelite family and the **first-born** of every animal.
3.12 instead of having the **first-born** sons of Israel as my own,
3.40 said to Moses, "All of Israel's **first-born** sons belong to me.
3.40 So register by name every **first-born** male Israelite,
3.40 the Levites in place of all the **first-born** of the livestock."
3.42 registered all the **first-born** males [43]one month old or older;
3.45 in place of all the **first-born** Israelite sons, and dedicate
3.45 in place of the **first-born** of the Israelites' livestock.
3.46 Since the **first-born** Israelite sons outnumber the Levites
8.16 the place of all the **first-born** sons of the Israelites,
8.17 When I killed all the **first-born** in Egypt,
8.17 of each Israelite family and the **first-born** of every animal.
8.18 Levites instead of all the **first-born** of the Israelites,
18.15 "Every **first-born** child or animal that the Israelites present to me
18.15 buy back every **first-born** child, and must also accept payment
18.15 for every **first-born** animal that is ritually unclean.
18.17 But the **first-born** of cows, sheep, and goats are not to
33. 4 were burying the **first-born** sons that the Lord had killed.
Deut 12. 6 offerings, and the **first-born** of your cattle and sheep.
12.17 or your olive-oil, nor the **first-born** of your cattle and sheep,
14.23 and olive-oil, and the **first-born** of your cattle and sheep.
15.19 your God all the **first-born** males of your cattle and sheep;
21.16 by giving him the share that belongs to the **first-born** son.
1 Chr 5. 1 the rights belonging to the **first-born** son,
Ps 78.51 killed the **first-born** sons of all the families of Egypt.
89.27 will make him my **first-born** son, the greatest of all kings.
105.36 He killed the **first-born** sons of all the families of Egypt.
135. 8 In Egypt he killed all the **first-born** of men and animals
136.10 He killed the **first-born** sons of the Egyptians;
Ezek 20.26 own offerings, and I let them sacrifice their **first-born** sons.
Mic 6. 7 Shall I offer him my **first-born** child to pay for my sins?
Zech 12.10 mourn bitterly, like those who have lost their **first-born** son.
Lk 2.23 "Every **first-born** male is to be dedicated to the Lord."
Col 1.15 He is the **first-born** Son, superior to all created things.
1.18 He is the **first-born** Son, who was raised from death, in
Heb 1. 6 was about to send his **first-born** Son into the world, he
11.28 Angel of Death would not kill the **first-born** sons of the Israelites.
12.23 the joyful gathering of God's **first-born** sons, whose names

FISH

Gen 1.26 will have power over the **fish,** the birds, and all animals,
1.28 you in charge of the **fish,** the birds, and all the wild
9. 2 All the animals, birds, and **fish** will live in fear of you.
Ex 7.18 The **fish** will die, and the river will stink so much that
7.21 The **fish** in the river died, and it smelt so bad that
Lev 11. 9 may eat any kind of **fish** that has fins and scales, [10]but
Num 11. 5 used to eat all the **fish** we wanted, and it cost us
11.22 Are all the **fish** in the sea enough for them?"
Deut 4.18 whether man or woman, [17]animal or bird, [18]reptile or **fish.**
14. 9 may eat any kind of **fish** that has fins and scales, [10]but
1 Kgs 4.33 he talked about animals, birds, reptiles, and **fish.**
Neh 13.16 in Jerusalem, and they brought **fish** and all kinds of goods
Job 41. 1 you catch Leviathan with a **fish-hook** or tie his tongue down
41. 7 you fill his hide with **fishing-spears** or pierce his head
Ps 8. 8 the birds and the **fish** and the creatures in the seas.
105.29 He turned their rivers into blood and killed all their **fish.**
Ecc 9.12 caught in a trap, like **fish** caught in a net, we are
Is 19. 8 who earns his living by **fishing** in the Nile will groan and
50. 2 a desert, so that the **fish** in them die for lack of
Ezek 29. 4 your jaw and make the **fish** in your river stick fast to
29. 4 up out of the Nile, with all the **fish** sticking to you.
29. 5 I will throw you and all those **fish** into the desert.
38.20 Every **fish** and bird, every animal large and small,
47. 9 stream flows, there will be all kinds of animals and **fish.**
47.10 as many different kinds of **fish** there as there are in the
Hos 4. 3 All the animals and birds, and even the **fish,** will die."
Amos 4. 2 every one of you will be like a **fish** on a hook.
Jon 1.17 the Lord's command a large **fish** swallowed Jonah,
1.17 and he was inside the **fish** for three days and nights.
2. 1 From deep inside the **fish** Jonah prayed to the Lord his God:
2.10 Then the Lord ordered the **fish** to spew Jonah up on the
Hab 1.14 can you treat people like **fish** or like a swarm of insects
1.15 Babylonians catch people with hooks, as though they were **fish.**
Zeph 1. 3 everything on earth, [3]all human beings and animals, birds and **fish.**
Mt 4.18 his brother Andrew, catching **fish** in the lake with a net.
7.10 would you give him a snake when he asks for a **fish?**
12.40 and nights in the big **fish,** so will the Son of Man
13.47 their net out in the lake and catch all kinds of **fish.**
13.48 they pull it to shore and sit down to divide the **fish:**
14.17 "All we have here are five loaves and two **fish,"** they
14.19 five loaves and the two **fish,** looked up to heaven, and gave
15.34 "Seven loaves," they answered, "and a few small **fish."**
15.36 the seven loaves and the **fish,** gave thanks to God, broke
17.27 Pull up the first **fish** you hook, and in its mouth you
Mk 1.16 Simon and his brother Andrew, catching **fish** with a net.
6.38 found out, they told him, "Five loaves and also two **fish."**
6.41 five loaves and the two **fish,** looked up to heaven, and gave
6.41 He also divided the two **fish** among them all.
6.43 baskets full of what was left of the bread and the **fish.**
8. 7 They also had a few small **fish.**
Lk 5. 6 such a large number of **fish** that the nets were about to
5. 7 both boats so full of **fish** that the boats were about to
5. 9 were all amazed at the large number of **fish** they had caught.
9.13 They answered, "All we have are five loaves and two **fish.**
9.16 the five loaves and two **fish,** looked up to heaven, thanked
11.11 are fathers give your son a snake when he asks for **fish?**
24.42 him a piece of cooked **fish,** [43]which he took and ate in
Jn 6. 9 boy here who has five loaves of barley bread and two **fish.**
6.11 did the same with the **fish,** and they all had as much
21. 3 Simon Peter said to the others, "I am going **fishing."**
21. 6 not pull it back in, because they had caught so many **fish.**
21. 8 came to shore in the boat, pulling the net full of **fish.**
21. 9 saw a charcoal fire there with **fish** on it and some bread.
21.10 to them, "Bring some of the **fish** you have just caught."
21.11 ashore full of big **fish,** a hundred and fifty-three in all;
21.13 he did the same with the **fish.**
Acts 9.18 At once something like **fish** scales fell from Saul's eyes,
1 Cor 15.39 of flesh, animals another, birds another, and **fish** another.
Jas 3. 7 other creatures—wild animals and birds, reptiles and **fish.**

FISH GATE

2 Chr 33.14 of Gihon north to the **Fish Gate** and the area of the
Neh 3. 3 The clan of Hassenaah built the **Fish Gate.**
12.39 Jeshanah Gate, the **Fish Gate,** the Tower of Hananel,
Zeph 1.10 will hear the sound of crying at the **Fish Gate** in Jerusalem.

FISHERMEN

Job 41. 6 Will **fishermen** bargain over him?
Jer 16.16 "I am sending for many **fishermen** to come and catch these people.
Ezek 26. 5 **Fishermen** will dry their nets on it, there where it stands
26.14 leave only a bare rock where **fishermen** can dry their nets.
47.10 Eneglaim, there will be **fishermen** on the shore of the sea,
Mt 4.18 saw two brothers who were **fishermen,** Simon (called Peter)
13.47 Some **fishermen** throw their net out in the lake and catch all
Mk 1.16 Lake Galilee, he saw two **fishermen,** Simon and his brother Andrew,
Lk 5. 2 the **fishermen** had left them and were washing the nets.

FIST

Ex 21.18 a stone or with his **fist,** but does not kill him, he
Num 24.10 Balak clenched his **fists** in anger and said to Balaam,
35.21 by striking him with his **fist,** he is guilty of murder and
Job 15.25 the man who shakes his **fist** at God and defies the Almighty.
Is 10.32 there they are shaking their **fists** at Mount Zion, at the
Ezek 4. 7 Shake your **fist** at the city and prophesy against it.
22.13 "I will bring my **fist** down on your robberies and murders.

FIT (1)
[UNFIT]

Gen 49.20 He will provide food **fit** for a king.
Ex 15.25 and the water became **fit** to drink.
20.25 use a chisel on stones, you make them **unfit** for my use.
Num 1. 3 twenty years old or older who are **fit** for military service.
1.20 old or older who were **fit** for military service were registered
1.49 a census of the men **fit** for military service, do not include
26. 2 years old or older who are **fit** for military service."
Josh 22.19 if your land is not **fit** to worship in, come over into
1 Sam 25.36 Nabal, who was at home having a feast **fit** for a king.
2 Sam 3.29 dreaded skin disease or is **fit** only to do a woman's work
13.27 Absalom prepared a banquet **fit** for a king [28]and instructed
2 Kgs 24.16 the blacksmiths, all of them able-bodied men **fit** for military duty.
Hos 5. 3 She has been unfaithful, and her people are **unfit** to worship me."
Mt 10.37 or mother more than me is not **fit** to be my disciple;
10.37 or daughter more than me is not **fit** to be my disciple.
10.38 and follow in my steps is not **fit** to be my disciple.
Mk 7.19 this, Jesus declared that all foods are **fit** to be eaten.)
Lk 15.19 I am no longer **fit** to be called your son;
15.21 I am no longer **fit** to be called your son.'
Acts 22.22 He's not **fit** to live!"
Eph 5. 4 Nor is it **fitting** for you to use language which is obscene,
Col 1.11 Father, who has made you **fit** to have your share of what
Tit 1.16 They are hateful and disobedient, not **fit** to do anything good.

FIT (2)

Ex 26.29 the frames with gold and **fit** them with gold rings to hold
26.32 of acacia-wood covered with gold, **fitted** with hooks, and set
26.37 posts of acacia-wood covered with gold and **fitted** with gold hooks;
36.34 the frames with gold and **fitted** them with gold rings to hold
36.36 curtain, covered them with gold, and **fitted** them with gold hooks.
36.38 curtain they made five posts **fitted** with hooks, covered
Num 3.36 for the Tent, its bars, posts, bases, and all its **fittings.**
4.26 and all the **fittings** used in setting up these objects.
4.32 the Tent, with all the **fittings** used in setting them up.
Eph 4.16 different parts of the body **fit** together, and the whole body

FIT (3)

Dan 1.10 if you don't look as **fit** as the other young men, he

FIT (4)

Mt 17.15 epileptic and has such terrible **fits** that he often falls in
Mk 9.20 threw the boy into a **fit,** so that he fell on the
9.26 spirit screamed, threw the boy into a bad **fit,** and came out.
Lk 9.39 and throws him into a **fit,** so that he foams at the
9.42 demon knocked him to the ground and threw him into a **fit.**

FIT (5)

Jer 13.11 Just as shorts **fit** tightly round the waist, so I intended

FIVE
[FIFTH, ONE-FIFTH]

Gen 1.23 Evening passed and morning came—that was the **fifth** day.
14. 2 and Tidal of Goiim, [2]went to war against **five** other kings:
14. 3 These **five** kings had formed an alliance and joined forces in
14. 9 of Elam, Goiim, Babylonia, and Ellasar, **five** kings against four.
18.28 Will you destroy the whole city because there are **five** too few?"
30.17 Leah's prayer, and she became pregnant and bore Jacob a **fifth** son.
36.10 Adah bore him one son, Eliphaz, and Eliphaz had **five** sons:
41.34 other officials and take a **fifth** of the crops during the
43.34 table, and Benjamin was served **five** times as much as the
45. 6 there will be **five** more years in which there will be neither
45.11 There will still be **five** years of famine;
45.22 three hundred pieces of silver and **five** changes of clothes.
47. 1 So Joseph took **five** of his brothers and went to the king.
47.24 At the time of harvest you must give **one-fifth** to the king.
47.26 the land of Egypt that **one-fifth** of the harvest should
Ex 22. 1 sells it, he must pay **five** cows for one cow and four
26. 3 Sew **five** of them together in one set,
26. 3 and do the same with the other **five.**
26. 9 Sew **five** of them together in one set, and the other six
26.26 cross-bars of acacia-wood, **five** for the frames on one side
26.27 **five** for the frames on the other
26.27 and **five** for the frames on the west
26.37 For this curtain make **five** posts of acacia-wood covered with
26.37 make **five** bronze bases for these posts.
36.10 They sewed **five** of them together in one set
36.10 and did the same with the other **five.**
36.16 They sewed **five** of them together in one set and the
36.31 cross-bars of acacia-wood, **five** for the frames on one side
36.32 **five** for the frames on the other
36.32 and **five** for the frames on the west
36.38 For this curtain they made **five** posts fitted with hooks,
36.38 rods with gold, and made **five** bronze bases for the posts.
Lev 19.25 But in the **fifth** year you may eat the fruit.
26. 8 **five** of you will be able to defeat a hundred,
27. 3 —young male, **five** to twenty years old:
27. 3 —infant male under **five:**
Num 3.47 For each one pay **five** pieces of silver, according to the
7.12 **five** rams, five goats, and five one-year-old lambs

Num 11.19 one or two days, or **five**, or ten, or even twenty days,
18.16 for the fixed price of **five** pieces of silver, according to
29.26 On the **fifth** day offer nine young bulls, two rams, and
31. 8 and killed all the men, [8] including the **five** kings of Midian:
33.38 the first day of the **fifth** month of the fortieth year after
Josh 10. 5 These **five** Amorite kings, the kings of Jerusalem, Hebron,
10.16 The **five** Amorite kings, however, had escaped and were hiding
10.22 entrance to the cave and bring those **five** kings out to me."
10.26 kings and hanged them on **five** trees, where their bodies stayed
19.24 The **fifth** assignment made was for the families of the
Judg 3. 3 in the land were the **five** Philistine cities, all the Canaanites,
16. 5 The **five** Philistine kings went to her and said, "Trick Samson
16.27 All **five** Philistine kings were there, and there were about three
16.30 the building fell down on the **five** kings and everyone else.
18. 2 the people of Dan chose **five** qualified men out of all the
18. 7 So the **five** men left and went to the town of Laish.
18. 8 When the **five** men returned to Zorah and Eshtaol,
18.14 Then the **five** men who had gone to explore the country
18.17 The **five** spies went straight on into the house and took
19. 8 in the morning of the **fifth** day he started to leave, but
1 Sam 5. 8 messengers and called together all **five** of the Philistine kings
6. 4 They answered, "**Five** gold models of tumours and five gold mice,
6. 4 plague was sent on all of you and on the **five** kings.
6.12 The **five** Philistine kings followed them as far as the border
6.16 The **five** Philistine kings watched them do this and then went
6.17 The Philistines sent the **five** gold tumours to the Lord
6.18 cities ruled by the **five** Philistine kings, both the fortified
7. 7 had gathered at Mizpah, the **five** Philistine kings started out
17.40 stick and then picked up **five** smooth stones from the stream
21. 3 Give me **five** loaves of bread or anything else you have."
25.18 leather bags full of wine, **five** roasted sheep, seventeen
25.42 Accompanied by her **five** maids, she went with David's servants
29. 2 The **five** Philistine kings marched out with their units of
2 Sam 4. 4 Jonathan's son Mephibosheth, who was **five** years old when Saul
21. 8 he also took the **five** sons of Saul's daughter Merab, whom
1 Kgs 7.39 He placed **five** of the carts on the south side
7.39 of the Temple, and the other **five** on the north side;
7.49 Holy Place, five on the south side and **five** on the north;
14.25 In the **fifth** year of Rehoboam's reign King Shishak of
2 Kgs 6.25 two hundred grammes of dove's dung cost **five** pieces of silver.
7.13 let's send some men with **five** of the horses that are left,
8.16 In the **fifth** year of the reign of Joram son of Ahab
13.19 king, "You should have struck **five** or six times, and then
25. 8 the seventh day of the **fifth** month of the nineteenth year of
25.19 in command of the troops, **five** of the king's personal advisers
1 Chr 1.33 Midian had **five** sons:
2. 3 Judah had **five** sons in all.
2. 6 His brother Zerah had **five** sons:
2.25 Jerahmeel, the eldest son of Hezron, had **five** sons:
3.20 He had **five** other sons:
3.22 Shecaniah had one son, Shemaiah, and **five** grandsons:
4.24 Simeon had **five** sons:
4.32 They also lived in **five** other places:
7. 7 Bela had **five** sons:
8. 1 Benjamin had **five** sons.
27. 2 **Fifth** month:
2 Chr 4. 6 They also made ten basins, **five** to be placed on the south
4. 6 side of the Temple and **five** on the north side.
4. 7 of the Temple, five lampstands and **five** tables on each side.
12. 2 In the **fifth** year of Rehoboam's reign their disloyalty to
23. 1 He made a pact with **five** army officers:
Ezra 7. 8 arrived in Jerusalem on the first day of the **fifth** month.
Neh 6. 5 servants to me with a **fifth** message, this one in the form
10.32 year we will each contribute **five** grammes of silver to help
Is 19.18 the Hebrew language will be spoken in **five** Egyptian cities.
30.17 see one enemy soldier, and **five** soldiers will be enough to
Jer 1. 3 In the **fifth** month of that year the people of Jerusalem were
28. 1 That same year, in the **fifth** month of the fourth year that
36. 9 the ninth month of the **fifth** year that Jehoiakim was king of
52.12 the tenth day of the **fifth** month of the nineteenth year of
Ezek 1. 1 On the **fifth** day of the fourth month of the thirtieth year,
1. 2 (It was the **fifth** year since King Jehoiachin had been
8. 1 On the **fifth** day of the sixth month of the sixth year
20. 1 the tenth day of the **fifth** month of the seventh year of
33.21 On the **fifth** day of the tenth month of the twelfth year
40.11 and the space between the open gates was **five** metres.
41. 2 was three metres deep [2] and **five** metres wide, with walls two
42. 4 building was a passage **five** metres wide and fifty metres long,
45. 3 a half kilometres by **five** kilometres, is to be measured off;
48.10 and a half kilometres, and from north to south, **five** kilometres.
48.13 from east to west, by **five** kilometres from north to south.
48.18 south of the holy area—**five** kilometres by two and a half
48.18 kilometres on the east and **five** kilometres by two and a half
Zech 7. 3 Temple, by fasting in the **fifth** month as we have done for
7. 5 fasted and mourned in the **fifth** and seventh months during
8.19 fasts held in the fourth, **fifth**, seventh, and tenth months
Mt 14.17 "All we have here are **five** loaves and two fish," they
14.19 then he took the **five** loaves and the two fish, looked up
16. 9 when I broke the **five** loaves for the five thousand men?
20. 6 It was nearly **five** o'clock when he went to the
20. 9 had begun to work at **five** o'clock were paid a silver coin
25. 2 **Five** of them were foolish, and the other five were wise.
25.10 The **five** girls who were ready went in with him to the
Mk 6.38 found out, they told him, "**Five** loaves and also two fish."
6.41 Then Jesus took the **five** loaves and the two fish, looked
8.19 when I broke the **five** loaves for the five thousand people?
Lk 1.24 Elizabeth became pregnant and did not leave the house for **five** months.
9.13 They answered, "All we have are **five** loaves and two fish.
9.16 done so, [16] Jesus took the **five** loaves and two fish, looked
12. 6 "Aren't **five** sparrows sold for two pennies?

Lk 12.52 now on a family of **five** will be divided, three against two
14.19 one said, 'I have bought **five** pairs of oxen and am on
16.28 Abraham, send Lazarus to my father's house, [28] where I have **five** brothers.
19.18 said, 'Sir, I have earned **five** gold coins with the one you
19.19 this one he said, 'You will be in charge of **five** cities.'
Jn 4.18 You have been married to **five** men, and the man you live
5. 2 Sheep Gate in Jerusalem there is a pool with **five** porches;
6. 9 a boy here who has **five** loaves of barley bread and two
6.13 pieces left over from the **five** barley loaves which the
6.19 The disciples had rowed about **five** or six kilometres
Acts 20. 6 Festival of Unleavened Bread, and **five** days later we joined
24. 1 **Five** days later the High Priest Ananias went to Caesarea
1 Cor 14.19 I would rather speak **five** words that can be understood,
2 Cor 11.24 **Five** times I was given the thirty-nine lashes by the Jews;
Rev 6. 9 Then the Lamb broke open the **fifth** seal.
9. 1 Then the **fifth** angel blew his trumpet.
9. 5 kill these people, but only to torture them for **five** months.
9. 6 During those **five** months they will seek death, but will
9.10 that they have the power to hurt people for **five** months.
16.10 Then the **fifth** angel poured out his bowl on the throne
17.10 **five** of them have fallen, one still rules, and the other
21.20 the fourth emerald, [20] the **fifth** onyx, the sixth carnelian,
also Lev 27.3 Num 7.12 1 Chr 24.7 1 Chr 25.9

Am **FIX** see **TAMPER**

FIX

Gen 41.32 means that the matter is **fixed** by God and that he will
Lev 25.15 The price is to be **fixed** according to the number of
27.12 The priest shall **fix** a price for it, according to its
27.14 the Lord, the priest shall **fix** the price according to its
27.16 Lord, the price shall be **fixed** according to the amount of
27.18 until the next Year of Restoration, and **fix** a reduced price.
27.25 All prices shall be **fixed** according to the official standard.
Num 18.16 of one month for the **fixed** price of five pieces of silver,
Neh 8. 5 above the people, they all kept their eyes **fixed** on him.
Ps 148. 6 by his command they were **fixed** in their places for ever,
Prov 30. 4 Or **fixed** the boundaries of the earth?
Is 51. 7 what is right, who have my teaching **fixed** in your hearts.
Ezek 4. 7 "**Fix** your eyes on the siege of Jerusalem.
Lk 4.20 the synagogue had their eyes **fixed** on him, [21] as he said to
Acts 1.10 They still had their eyes **fixed** on the sky as he went
6.15 those sitting in the Council **fixed** their eyes on Stephen and
17.26 He himself **fixed** beforehand the exact times and the limits
17.31 For he has **fixed** a day in which he will judge the
28.23 So they **fixed** a date with Paul, and a large number of
2 Cor 3. 7 the people of Israel could not keep their eyes **fixed** on him.
4.18 For we **fix** our attention, not on things that are seen,
Col 3. 2 Keep your minds **fixed** on things there, not on things here
Heb 12. 2 Let us keep our eyes **fixed** on Jesus, on whom our faith
1 Pet 1.21 and so your faith and hope are **fixed** on God.

Am **FIXED UP** see **TIDY**

FLAG

Num 2. 2 the banner of his division and the **flag** of his own clan.
Ps 74. 4 they have placed their **flags** there as signs of victory.
Is 11.12 Lord will raise a signal **flag** to show the nations that he
13. 2 On the top of a barren hill raise the battle **flag**!
18. 3 Look for a signal **flag** to be raised on the tops of
31. 9 will be so frightened that they will abandon their battle **flags**."

Am **FLAG POLE** see **FLAGSTAFF**

FLAGSTAFF

Is 30.17 your army except a lonely **flagstaff** on the top of a hill!

FLAKY

Ex 16.14 was something thin and **flaky** on the surface of the desert.

FLAME

Gen 3.24 and a **flaming** sword which turned in all directions.
15.17 a smoking fire-pot and a **flaming** torch suddenly appeared
Ex 3. 2 appeared to him as a **flame** coming from the middle of a
Deut 4.24 because the Lord your God is like a **flaming** fire;
9.15 **Flames** of fire were coming from the mountain.
29.20 the Lord's burning anger will **flame** up against him, and all
32.22 anger will **flame** up like fire and burn everything on earth.
33. 2 angels were with him, a **flaming** fire at his right hand.
Judg 13.20 While the **flames** were going up from the altar, Manoah
13.20 saw the Lord's angel go up towards heaven in the **flames**.
20.40 and were amazed to see the whole city going up in **flames**.
2 Sam 22. 9 a consuming **flame** and burning coals from his mouth.
22.13 burning coals **flamed** up from the lightning before him.
1 Kgs 16.18 fortress, set the palace on fire, and died in the **flames**.
Job 18. 5 its **flame** will never burn again.
41.19 **Flames** blaze from his mouth, and streams of sparks fly out.
41.21 **flames** leap out of his mouth.
Ps 11. 6 He sends down **flaming** coals and burning sulphur on the wicked;
18. 8 a consuming **flame** and burning coals from his mouth.
83.14 fire burns the forest, as **flames** set the hills on fire,
Song 8. 6 It bursts into **flame** and burns like a raging fire.

Is	4. 5	cloud in the daytime and smoke and a bright **flame** at night.
	6. 2	Round him **flaming** creatures were standing, each of which had
	10.17	holy God will become a **flame,** which in a single day will
	30.30	There will be **flames,** cloudbursts, hailstones, and torrents
	30.33	will breathe out a stream of **flame** to set it on fire.
	43.17	fell, never to rise, snuffed out like the **flame** of a lamp!
	47.14	to save themselves— the **flames** will be too hot for them,
Jer	48.45	the city that King Sihon once ruled, but it is in **flames.**
	51.58	their efforts go up in **flames.**
Ezek	20.47	to north, and everyone will feel the heat of the **flames.**
	24.10	Fan the **flames!**
	24.12	although all that corrosion will not disappear in the **flames.**
Dan	3.22	be made extremely hot, the **flames** burnt up the guards who
	7.11	and its body was thrown into the **flames** and destroyed.
Hos	7. 6	their anger smouldered, and in the morning it burst into **flames.**
Nah	1. 6	He pours out his **flaming** anger;
Hab	2.13	useless labour, and all they have built goes up in **flames.**
Acts	7.30	appeared to Moses in the **flames** of a burning bush in the
2 Thes	1. 8	his mighty angels, [8] with a **flaming** fire, to punish those
Heb	1. 7	"God makes his angels winds, and his servants **flames** of fire."
Jas	3. 5	large a forest can be set on fire by a tiny **flame!**
Rev	18. 9	when they see the smoke from the **flames** that consume her.
	18.18	out as they saw the smoke from the **flames** that consumed her:
	19. 3	The smoke from the **flames** that consume the great city goes
	19.12	His eyes were like a **flame** of fire, and he wore many

FLASH

Ex	9.24	The Lord sent [24] a heavy hailstorm, with lightning **flashing**
Deut	32.41	that I will sharpen my **flashing** sword and see that justice
2 Sam	22.15	with **flashes** of lightning he sent them running.
Job	37. 4	majestic sound of thunder, and all the while the lightning **flashes.**
	37.11	Lightning **flashes** from the clouds, [12] as they move at God's
	37.15	God gives the command and makes lightning **flash** from the clouds?
	38.35	you command the lightning to **flash,** will it come to you and
	39.23	weapons which their riders carry rattle and **flash** in the sun.
	41.18	Light **flashes** when he sneezes, and his eyes glow like
Ps	18.12	Hailstones and **flashes** of fire came from the lightning
	18.14	with **flashes** of lightning he sent them running.
	29. 7	The voice of the Lord makes the lightning **flash.**
	77.17	crashed from the sky, and lightning **flashed** in all directions.
	77.18	thunder rolled out, and **flashes** of lightning lit up the world;
	104. 4	as your messengers and **flashes** of lightning as your servants.
	144. 6	Send **flashes** of lightning and scatter your enemies;
Prov	23. 5	can be gone in a **flash,** as if it had grown wings
Jer	10.13	He makes lightning **flash** in the rain and sends the wind from
	51.16	He makes lightning **flash** in the rain and sends the wind from
Ezek	1. 4	Lightning was **flashing** from a huge cloud, and the sky round
	1. 4	Where the lightning was **flashing,** something shone like bronze.
	1.13	The fire would blaze up and shoot out **flashes** of lightning.
	21.10	It is sharpened to kill, polished to **flash** like lightning.
	21.15	city with a sword that **flashes** like lightning and is ready
	21.28	It is polished to kill, to **flash** like lightning.
Dan	10. 6	was as bright as a **flash** of lightning, and his eyes blazed
Nah	2. 3	Their chariots **flash** like fire!
	2. 4	They **flash** like torches and dart about like lightning.
	3. 3	Horsemen charge, swords **flash,** spears gleam!
Hab	3. 4	light **flashes** from his hand, there where his power is hidden.
	3.11	At the **flash** of your speeding arrows and the gleam of
Mt	24.27	come like the lightning which **flashes** across the whole sky
Lk	17.24	As the lightning **flashes** across the sky and lights it up
Acts	9. 3	Damascus, suddenly a light from the sky **flashed** round him.
	22. 6	a bright light from the sky **flashed** suddenly round me.
Rev	4. 5	From the throne came **flashes** of lightning, rumblings, and peals of thunder.
	8. 5	peals of thunder, **flashes** of lightning, and an earthquake.
	11.19	Then there were **flashes** of lightning, rumblings and peals of thunder,
	16.18	There were **flashes** of lightning, rumblings and peals of thunder,

Am **FLAT**
see also **TASTELESS**

FLAT

Num	11. 8	into flour, and then boil it and make it into **flat** cakes.
Judg	7.13	The tent collapsed and lay **flat** on the ground."
Neh	8.16	and built shelters on the **flat** roofs of their houses, in

FLATTER

Job	32.21	I am not going to **flatter** anyone.
	32.22	I don't know how to **flatter,** and God would quickly
Ps	5. 9	Their words are **flattering** and smooth, but full of deadly deceit.
	12. 2	they deceive each other with **flattery.**
	12. 3	Silence those **flattering** tongues, O Lord!
Prov	23. 8	what you have eaten, and all your **flattery** will be wasted.
	26.24	A hypocrite hides his hate behind **flattering** words.
	28.23	and afterwards he will appreciate it more than **flattery.**
	29. 5	If you **flatter** your friends, you set a trap for yourself.
Rom	16.18	By their fine words and **flattering** speech they deceive innocent people.
1 Thes	2. 5	not come to you with **flattering** talk, nor did we use words
Jude	16	they boast about themselves and **flatter** others in order to

Am **FLAVOUR** see **TASTE**

FLAVOUR

Job	6. 6	What **flavour** is there in the white of an egg?
	20.12	him that he keeps some in his mouth to enjoy its **flavour.**
Jer	48.11	Its **flavour** has never been ruined, and it tastes as good as

FLAW

1 Pet	1.19	of Christ, who was like a lamb without defect or **flaw.**

FLAX

A small cultivated plant; the fibres of its stem are spun into thread used in making linen cloth.

Ex	9.31	The **flax** and the barley were ruined,
	9.31	because the barley was ripe, and the **flax** was budding.
Josh	2. 4	them under some stalks of **flax** that she had put there.)

FLEA

1 Sam	24.14	A dead dog, a **flea!**
	26.20	should the king of Israel come to kill a **flea** like me?

FLEE

[FLED, FLIGHT]

Gen	31.22	Three days later Laban was told that Jacob had **fled.**
Ex	2.15	have Moses killed, but Moses **fled** and went to live in the
Num	10.35	scatter your enemies and put to **flight** those who hate you!"
	16.34	of Israel who were there **fled** when they heard their cry.
	35.32	If a man has **fled** to a city of refuge, do not
Judg	4.15	Sisera got down from his chariot and **fled** on foot.
	9.40	Gaal **fled,** and Abimelech pursued him.
	11. 3	Jephthah **fled** from his brothers and lived in the land of Tob.
1 Sam	7.10	They became completely confused and **fled** in panic.
	19. 8	David attacked them and defeated them so thoroughly that they **fled.**
	20. 1	Then David **fled** from Naioth in Ramah and went to Jonathan.
	21.10	So David left, **fleeing** from Saul, and went to King Achish
	22. 1	David **fled** from the city of Gath and went to a cave
	27. 4	Saul heard that David had **fled** to Gath, he gave up trying
	31. 1	the rest of them, including King Saul and his sons, **fled.**
	31. 7	that the Israelite army had **fled** and that Saul and his sons
	31. 7	had been killed, they abandoned their towns and **fled.**
2 Sam	2. 8	Abner son of Ner, had **fled** with Saul's son Ishbosheth across
	4. 3	Its original inhabitants had **fled** to Gittaim, where they have
	4. 4	from the city of Jezreel, his nurse picked him up and **fled;**
	5.21	When the Philistines **fled,** they left their idols behind,
	10.13	Joab and his men advanced to attack, and the Syrians **fled.**
	10.14	the Syrians running away, they **fled** from Abishai and retreated
	13.29	All the rest of David's sons mounted their mules and **fled.**
	13.34	In the meantime Absalom had **fled.**
	13.37	Absalom **fled** and went to the king of Geshur, Talmai
	18.17	All the Israelites **fled,** each man to his own home.
	19. 8	all the Israelites had **fled,** each man to his own home.
	19. 9	but now he has **fled** from Absalom and left the country.
	23.11	The Israelites **fled** from the Philistines, [12] but Shammah stood
1 Kgs	2. 7	kind to me when I was **fleeing** from your brother Absalom.
	2.28	So he **fled** to the Tent of the Lord's presence and took
	2.29	King Solomon that Joab had **fled** to the Tent and was by
	2.29	to Joab to ask him why he had **fled** to the altar.
	2.29	Joab answered that he had **fled** to the Lord because he was
	11.23	Rezon had **fled** from his master, King Hadadezer of Zobah,
	19. 3	Elijah was afraid, and **fled** for his life;
	20.20	The Syrians **fled,** with the Israelites in hot pursuit,
	20.30	survivors **fled** into the city of Aphek, where the city walls
2 Kgs	7. 7	the Syrians had **fled** for their lives, abandoning their tents,
	7.15	clothes and equipment that the Syrians had abandoned as they **fled.**
	9.10	After saying this, the young prophet left the room and **fled.**
	9.23	Joram cried out, as he turned his chariot round and **fled.**
	9.27	saw what happened, so he **fled** in his chariot towards the
	14.12	Amaziah's army was defeated, and all his soldiers **fled** to
	14.19	to assassinate Amaziah, so he **fled** to the city of Lachish,
	25. 4	the two walls, and **fled** in the direction of the Jordan
1 Chr	10. 1	the rest of them, including King Saul and his sons, **fled.**
	10. 7	heard that the army had **fled** and that Saul and his sons
	14.12	When the Philistines **fled,** they left their idols behind,
	19.14	Joab and his men advanced to attack, and the Syrians **fled.**
	19.15	the Syrians running away, they **fled** from Abishai and retreated
2 Chr	13.16	The Israelites **fled** from the Judaeans, and God let the
	14.12	They **fled,** [13] and Asa and his troops pursued them as far as
	25.22	the Judaean army was defeated, and the soldiers **fled** to
	25.27	Finally he **fled** to the city of Lachish, but his enemies
Job	15.28	seized houses whose owners had **fled,** but war will destroy those
Ps	104. 7	When you rebuked the waters, they **fled;**
Is	15. 5	The people have **fled** to the town of Zoar, and to Eglath
	17. 9	the Amorites abandoned as they **fled** from the people of Israel.
	21.15	People are **fleeing** to escape from swords that are ready to
	25. 4	poor and the helpless have **fled** to you and have been safe
Jer	9.10	birds and wild animals have **fled** and gone."
	26.21	so he **fled** in terror and escaped to Egypt.
	49.24	The people of Damascus are weak and have **fled** in terror.
	52. 7	the two walls, and **fled** in the direction of the Jordan
Lam	1. 6	Whose strength is almost gone as they **flee** from the hunters.
Ezek	29.12	They will **flee** to every country and live among other peoples."
Hos	12.12	Our ancestor Jacob had to **flee** to Mesopotamia,
Zech	14. 5	You will **flee** as your ancestors did when the earthquake struck
Acts	7.29	When Moses heard this, he **fled** from Egypt and went to
	14. 6	apostles learnt about it, they **fled** to the cities of Lystra
Rev	9. 6	they will want to die, but death will **flee** from them.

Rev 12. 6 The woman **fled** to the desert, to a place God had prepared
20.11 Earth and heaven **fled** from his presence and were seen no more.

FLEET

1 Kgs 9.26 King Solomon also built a **fleet** of ships at Eziongeber,
9.27 experienced seamen from his **fleet** to serve with Solomon's men.
10.11 (Hiram's **fleet,** which had brought gold from Ophir,
10.22 had a **fleet** of ocean-going ships sailing with Hiram's fleet.
10.22 Every three years his **fleet** would return, bringing gold, silver,
2 Chr 9.21 had a **fleet** of ocean-going ships sailing with King Hiram's fleet.
9.21 Every three years his **fleet** would return, bringing gold, silver,
Ezek 27.25 merchandise was carried in **fleets** of the largest cargo ships.

FLESH

Gen 2.21 took out one of the man's ribs and closed up the **flesh.**
2.23 Bone taken from my bone, and **flesh** from my flesh.
29.14 Laban said, "Yes, indeed, you are my own **flesh and blood."**
37.27 after all, he is our brother, our own **flesh and blood."**
40.19 your body on a pole, and the birds will eat your **flesh."**
Ex 21.28 it is to be stoned, and its **flesh** shall not be eaten;
29.14 burn the bull's **flesh,** its skin, and its intestines outside the
Lev 4.11 take its skin, all its **flesh,** its head, its legs, and its
6.27 or anything that touches the **flesh** of the animal will be
7.15 The **flesh** of the animal must be eaten on the day it
8.17 the bull, including its skin, **flesh,** and intestines, and burnt
13.24 if the raw **flesh** becomes white or reddish-white, [25] the priest
Num 12.12 become like something born dead with half its **flesh** eaten away."
Judg 9. 2 Remember that Abimelech is your own **flesh and blood."**
2 Sam 5. 1 Hebron and said to him, "We are your own **flesh and blood.**
19.12 You are my relatives, my own **flesh and blood;**
2 Kgs 5.14 His **flesh** became firm and healthy, like that of a child.
1 Chr 11. 1 Hebron and said to him, "We are your own **flesh and blood.**
Ps 50.13 Do I eat the **flesh** of bulls or drink the blood of
Prov 5.11 on your deathbed, your **flesh** and muscles being eaten away,
Lam 3. 4 He has left my **flesh** open and raw, and has broken my
Mic 3. 2 You skin my people alive and tear the **flesh** off their bones.
Nah 2.12 he filled his den with torn **flesh.**
Zech 14.12 Their **flesh** will rot away while they are still alive;
Mt 26.41 The spirit is willing, but the **flesh** is weak."
Mk 14.38 The spirit is willing, but the **flesh** is weak."
Lk 24.39 for a ghost doesn't have **flesh** and bones, as you can see
Jn 6.51 will give him is my **flesh,** which I give so that the
6.52 "How can this man give us his **flesh** to eat?"
6.53 you do not eat the **flesh** of the Son of Man and
6.54 Whoever eats my **flesh** and drinks my blood has eternal life,
6.55 For my **flesh** is the real food;
6.56 Whoever eats my **flesh** and drinks my blood lives in me,
Rom 9. 3 pain in my heart [3] for my people, my own **flesh and blood!**
1 Cor 15.39 flesh of living beings is not all the same kind of **flesh;**
15.39 beings have one kind of **flesh,** animals another, birds
15.50 is made of **flesh and blood** cannot share in God's Kingdom,
2 Tim 2.17 Such teaching is like an open sore that eats away the **flesh.**
Heb 2.14 them, are people of **flesh and blood,** Jesus himself became
Jas 5. 3 a witness against you and will eat up your **flesh** like fire.
Rev 17.16 they will eat her **flesh** and destroy her with fire.
19.18 Come and eat the **flesh** of kings, generals, and soldiers, the flesh
19.18 and soldiers, the **flesh** of horses and their riders,
19.18 the **flesh** of all people, slave and free,
19.21 and all the birds ate all they could of their **flesh.**

AV FLESH

see also **BODY, MEAT**

Gen 6. 3 they are **mortal.**
6.13 to Noah, "I have decided to put an end to all **mankind.**
17.13 and this will be a **physical** sign to show that my covenant
Deut 5.26 any **human being** ever lived after hearing the living God speak
2 Chr 32. 8 He has **human** power, but we have the Lord our God to
Neh 5. 5 We are of the same **race** as our fellow-Jews.
Ps 56. 4 What can a mere **human being** do to me?
63. 1 My whole **being** desires you;
78.39 remembered that they were only **mortal** beings, like a wind
84. 2 With my whole **being** I sing for joy to the living God.
145.21 let all his **creatures** praise his holy name for ever.
Is 40. 5 of the Lord will be revealed, and all **mankind** will see it.
40. 6 "Proclaim that all **mankind** are like grass;
49.26 Then all **mankind** will know that I am the Lord, the one
66.24 The sight of them will be disgusting to all **mankind."**
Jer 17. 5 and puts his trust in man, in the strength of **mortal** man.
32.27 said to me, [27] "I am the Lord, the God of all **mankind.**
45. 5 am bringing disaster on all **mankind,** but you will at least
Ezek 32. 5 I will cover mountains and valleys with your rotting **corpse.**
Dan 2.11 except the gods, and they do not live among **human beings."**
Mt 16.17 come to you from any **human being,** but it was given to
Lk 3. 6 All **mankind** will see God's salvation!'"
Jn 1.14 The Word became a **human being** and, full of grace and truth,
3. 6 A person is born **physically**
3. 6 of **human** parents,
6.63 **man's** power is of no use at all.
8.15 You make judgements in a purely **human** way;
17. 2 authority over all **mankind,** so that he might give eternal
Acts 2.26 And I, **mortal** though I am, will rest assured in hope,
Rom 1. 3 as to his **humanity,** he was born a descendant of David;
2.28 Jew on the outside, whose circumcision is a **physical** thing.
4. 1 What shall we say, then, of Abraham, the father of our **race?**
6.19 everyday language because of the weakness of your **natural** selves.)
7. 5 we lived according to our **human nature,** the sinful desires
7.18 good does not live in me—that is, in my **human nature.**
Rom 7.25 with my mind, while my **human nature** serves the law of sin.
8. 3 the Law could not do, because **human nature** was weak, God
8. 3 He condemned sin in **human nature** by sending his own Son,
8. 3 with a nature like man's **sinful** nature, to do away with sin.
8. 4 live according to the Spirit, and not according to **human nature.**
8. 5 Those who live as their **human nature** tells them to,
8. 5 have their minds controlled by what **human nature** wants.
8. 8 Those who obey their **human nature** cannot please God.
8. 9 But you do not live as your **human nature** tells you to;
8.12 it is not to live as our **human nature** wants us to.
8.13 live according to your **human nature,** you are going to die;
9. 5 and Christ, as a **human being,** belongs to their race.
11.14 the people of my own **race** jealous, and so be able to
13.14 attention to your **sinful** nature and satisfying its desires.
1 Cor 1.26 From the **human** point of view few of you were wise or
2 Cor 1.17 do I make them from **selfish** motives,
5.16 No longer, then, do we judge anyone by **human** standards.
5.16 Christ according to **human** standards, we no longer do so.
10. 2 harshly with those who say that we act from **worldly** motives.
10. 3 that we live in the **world,**
10. 3 but we do not fight from **worldly** motives.
11.18 many who boast for merely **human** reasons, I will do the same.
12. 7 I was given a painful **physical** ailment, which acts as Satan's
Gal 4.14 But even though my **physical** condition was a great trial to you,
5.13 become an excuse for letting your **physical** desires control you.
5.16 and you will not satisfy the desires of the **human nature.**
5.17 For what our **human nature** wants is opposed to what the
5.17 the Spirit wants is opposed to what our **human nature** wants.
5.19 What **human nature** does is quite plain.
5.24 have put to death their **human nature** with all its passions
6. 8 in the field of his **natural** desires, from it he will gather
6.12 ones who want to show off and boast about **external** matters.
6.13 they can boast that you submitted to this **physical** ceremony.
Eph 2. 3 lived according to our **natural** desires, doing whatever suited
6. 5 Slaves, obey your **human** masters with fear and trembling;
6.12 we are not fighting against **human beings** but against the wicked
Phil 3. 3 We do not put any trust in **external** ceremonies.
3. 4 thinks he can trust in **external** ceremonies, I have even more
Col 1.22 now, by means of the **physical** death of his Son, God has
1.24 for by means of my **physical** sufferings I am helping to
2. 1 Laodicea and for all others who do not know me **personally.**
2.23 they have no real value in controlling **physical** passions.
3.22 Slaves, obey your **human** masters in all things,
1 Tim 3.16 He appeared in **human** form, was shown to be right by the
Heb 5. 7 In his **life** on earth Jesus made his prayers and requests
12. 9 In the case of our **human** fathers, they punished us and we
1 Pet 1.24 As the scripture says, "All **mankind** are like grass, and all
3.18 He was put to death **physically,** but made alive spiritually,
4. 1 Christ suffered **physically,** you too must strengthen yourselves
4. 1 whoever suffers **physically** is no longer involved with sin.
4. 2 live the rest of your **earthly** lives controlled by God's will
4. 6 had been judged in their **physical** existence as everyone is judged;
1 Jn 2.16 what the **sinful** self desires, what people see
4. 2 Jesus Christ came as a **human being** has the Spirit who comes
2 Jn 7 do not acknowledge that Jesus Christ came as a **human being.**
Jude 7 those angels did and indulged in sexual immorality and **perversion:**
23 but hate their very clothes, stained by their **sinful** lusts.

FLICKERING

Prov 13. 9 the wicked are like a lamp **flickering** out.
Is 42. 3 not break off a bent reed or put out a **flickering** lamp.
Mt 12.20 not break off a bent reed, or put out a **flickering** lamp.

FLIGHT

see also **FLEE, FLY (1)**

Num 10.35 scatter your enemies and put to **flight** those who hate you!"

FLIMSY

Job 41.27 For him iron is as **flimsy** as straw, and bronze as soft

FLING

Ps 24. 7 **Fling** wide the gates, open the ancient doors,
24. 9 **Fling** wide the gates, open the ancient doors,

FLINT

Josh 5. 2 "Make some knives out of **flint** and circumcise the Israelites."
Is 5.28 hooves are as hard as **flint,** and their chariot-wheels turn

FLIRT

Prov 6.25 don't be trapped by their **flirting** eyes.
Is 3.16 They are always **flirting.**

FLIT

Hos 7.11 Israel **flits** about like a silly pigeon;

FLOAT

Gen 7.17 and the water became deep enough for the boat to **float.**
1 Kgs 5. 9 them together in rafts to **float** them down the coast to the
2 Kgs 6. 6 a stick, threw it in the water, and made the axe-head **float.**
2 Chr 2.16 them together in rafts, and **float** them by sea as far as
Job 37.16 Do you know how clouds **float** in the sky, the work of

FLOCK

Gen	12.16	Abram well and gave him **flocks** of sheep and goats, cattle,
	21.28	separated seven lambs from his **flock**, [29]and Abimelech asked
	24.35	He has given him **flocks** of sheep and goats, cattle, silver,
	27. 9	Go to the **flock** and pick out two fat young goats, so
	29. 2	out in the fields with three **flocks** of sheep lying round it.
	29. 2	The **flocks** were watered from this well, which had a large
	29. 3	Whenever all the **flocks** came together there, the shepherds
	29. 6	"Look, here comes his daughter Rachel with his **flock."**
	29. 7	yet time to bring the **flocks** in, why don't you water them
	29. 8	do that until all the **flocks** are here and the stone has
	29. 8	then we will water the **flocks."**
	29. 9	Jacob was still talking to them, Rachel arrived with the **flock.**
	29.10	Rachel with his uncle Laban's **flock,** he went to the well,
	30.29	and how your **flocks** have prospered under my care.
	30.31	to take care of your **flocks** if you agree to this suggestion:
	30.32	me go through all your **flocks** today and take every black
	30.36	away from Jacob with this **flock** as far as he could travel
	30.36	Jacob took care of the rest of Laban's **flocks.**
	30.38	these branches in front of the **flocks** at their drinking-troughs.
	30.40	the direction of the streaked and black animals of Laban's **flock.**
	30.40	he built up his own **flock** and kept it apart from Laban's.
	30.43	He had many **flocks,** slaves, camels, and donkeys.
	31. 4	and Leah to meet him in the field where his **flocks** were.
	31. 8	shall be your wages,' all the **flocks** produced speckled young.
	31. 8	shall be your wages,' all the **flocks** produced striped young.
	31. 9	God has taken **flocks** away from your father and given them
	31.17	and drove all his **flocks** ahead of him, with everything that
	31.38	reproduce, and I have not eaten any rams from your **flocks.**
	31.41	to win your two daughters—and six years for your **flocks.**
	31.43	their children belong to me, and these **flocks** are mine.
	34.28	They took the **flocks,** the cattle, the donkeys,
	37.12	take care of their father's **flock,** [13]Jacob said to Joseph,
	37.13	where your brothers are taking care of the **flock."**
	37.14	if your brothers are safe and if the **flock** is all right;
	37.16	my brothers, who are taking care of their **flock,"** he answered.
	38.17	He answered, "I will send you a young goat from my **flock."**
	46.32	that you have brought your **flocks** and herds and everything else
	47. 1	come from Canaan with their **flocks,** their herds, and all that
	47. 4	famine is so severe that there is no pasture for our **flocks.**
Ex	3. 1	of Midian, he led the **flock** across the desert and came to
	16.13	In the evening a large **flock** of quails flew in, enough
Num	31. 9	took their cattle and their **flocks,** plundered all their wealth,
Josh	14. 3	cities to live in, with fields for their cattle and **flocks.**
Judg	5.16	to listen to shepherds calling the **flocks?**
1 Sam	8.17	He will take a tenth of your **flocks.**
	25.16	the whole time we were with them looking after our **flocks.**
	30.20	He also recovered all the **flocks** and herds;
1 Kgs	20.27	Israelites looked like two small **flocks** of goats compared with
2 Chr	31. 3	From his own **flocks** and herds he provided animals for the
	35. 7	from his own herds and **flocks** thirty thousand sheep, lambs,
Job	24. 2	they steal sheep and put them with their own **flocks.**
	31.20	made of wool that had come from my own **flock** of sheep.
Ps	50. 9	not need bulls from your farms or goats from your **flocks;**
	65.12	The pastures are filled with **flocks;**
	78.48	killed their cattle with hail and their **flocks** with lightning.
	78.71	where he looked after his **flocks,** and he made him king
	79.13	people, the sheep of your **flock,** will thank you for ever
	80. 1	hear us, leader of your **flock.**
	95. 7	the people he cares for, the **flock** for which he provides.
	100. 3	we are his people, we are his **flock.**
	107.41	from their misery and made their families increase like **flocks.**
Song	1. 7	Tell me, my love, Where will you lead your **flock** to graze?
	1. 7	to look for you among the **flocks** of the other shepherds?
	1. 8	Go and follow the **flock;**
	2.16	He feeds his **flock** among the lilies [17]until the morning
	4. 1	Your hair dances, like a **flock** of goats bounding down the
	6. 2	He is feeding his **flock** in the garden and gathering lilies.
	6. 3	he feeds his **flock** among the lilies.
	6. 5	Your hair dances, like a **flock** of goats bounding down the
	6. 6	are as white as a **flock** of sheep that have just been
Is	13.20	tent there, and no shepherd will ever pasture his **flock** there.
	40.11	He will take care of his **flock** like a shepherd;
	61. 5	will take care of your **flocks** And farm your land and tend
Jer	3.24	has made us lose **flocks** and herds, sons and daughters—
	5.17	They will slaughter your **flocks** and your herds and destroy your
	31.10	gather them and guard them as a shepherd guards his **flock.**
	31.24	and there will be farmers, and shepherds with their **flocks.**
	49.29	Seize their tents and their **flocks,** their tent curtains and
	51.23	slaughter shepherds and their **flocks,** to slaughter ploughmen
Ezek	34.17	"Now then, my **flock,** I, the Sovereign Lord, tell you
	34.21	the sick ones aside and butted them away from the **flock.**
	34.31	"You, my sheep, the **flock** that I feed, are my people,
	36.37	I will let them increase in numbers like a **flock** of sheep.
Joel	1.18	the **flocks** of sheep also suffer.
Zeph	2. 7	They will pasture their **flocks** there and sleep in the houses
	2.14	will be a place where **flocks,** herds, and animals of every
Zech	9.16	save his people, as a shepherd saves his **flock** from danger.
	11. 4	of the shepherd of a **flock** of sheep that are going to
	11. 7	And I took care of the **flock.**
	11. 9	Then I said to the **flock,** "I will not be your shepherd
	11.16	shepherd in charge of my **flock,** but he does not help the
	11.17	He has abandoned his **flock.**
Mal	1.14	when he has in his **flock** a good animal that he promised
Mt	26.31	the shepherd, and the sheep of the **flock** will be scattered.'
Mk	10. 1	Crowds came **flocking** to him again, and he taught them, as he
Lk	2. 8	the night in the fields, taking care of their **flocks.**
	12.32	"Do not be afraid, little **flock,** for your Father is
Jn	4.12	he and his sons and his **flocks** all drank from it.
	10.16	my voice, and they will become one **flock** with one shepherd.
Acts	20.28	yourselves and over all the **flock** which the Holy Spirit has
	20.29	will come among you, and they will not spare the **flock.**
1 Pet	5. 2	to be shepherds of the **flock** that God gave you and to
	5. 3	have been put in your care, but be examples to the **flock.**

FLOG

1 Kgs	12.11	I'll **flog** you with a horsewhip!' "
	12.14	I'll **flog** you with a horsewhip!"
2 Chr	10.11	I'll **flog** you with a horsewhip!' "
	10.14	I'll **flog** you with a horsewhip!"

Am **FLOOD**
see also **OVERFLOW**

FLOOD

Gen	6.17	am going to send a **flood** on the earth to destroy every
	7. 6	was six hundred years old when the **flood** came on the earth.
	7. 7	and their wives, went into the boat to escape the **flood.**
	7.10	Seven days later the **flood** came.
	7.17	The **flood** continued for forty days,
	9.11	never again will all living beings be destroyed by a **flood;**
	9.11	never again will a **flood** destroy the earth.
	9.15	the animals that a **flood** will never again destroy all living
	9.28	After the **flood** Noah lived for 350 years [29]and died at
	10. 1	These three had sons after the **flood.**
	10.32	After the **flood** all the nations of the earth were descended
	11.10	Two years after the **flood,** when Shem was 100 years old, he
	49. 4	You are like a raging **flood,** But you will not be the
Josh	3.14	It was harvest time, and the river was in **flood.**
	4.18	the river began flowing once more and **flooded** its banks again.
Judg	5.21	A **flood** in the Kishon swept them away— the onrushing
2 Sam	5.20	He said, "The Lord has broken through my enemies like a **flood."**
1 Chr	14.11	has used me to break through the enemy army like a **flood."**
Job	11.16	fade from your memory, like **floods** that are past and remembered
	12.15	**floods** come when he turns water loose.
	16. 4	shake my head wisely and drown you with a **flood** of words.
	20.28	his wealth will be destroyed in the **flood** of God's anger.
	22.11	so dark that you cannot see, and a **flood** overwhelms you.
	22.16	their time had come, they were washed away by a **flood.**
	24.18	man is swept away by **floods,** and the land he owns is
	27.20	Terror will strike like a sudden **flood;**
	38.36	ibis when the Nile will **flood,** or who tells the cock that
Ps	32. 6	when a great **flood** of trouble comes rushing in, it will
	38. 4	I am drowning in the **flood** of my sins;
	42. 6	roars at me like a **flood,** like waterfalls thundering down to
	66.12	we went through fire and **flood,** but now you have brought
	69.15	Don't let the **flood** come over me;
	88.17	All day long they surround me like a **flood;**
	90. 5	You carry us away like a **flood;**
	124. 4	then the **flood** would have carried us away, the water would
Song	8. 7	no **flood** can drown it.
Is	8. 7	They will advance like the **flood** waters of the River Euphrates,
	8. 8	sweep through Judah in a **flood,** rising shoulder high
	28. 2	like a rushing, overpowering **flood,** and will overwhelm the land.
	28.17	the lies you depend on, and **floods** will destroy your security.
	30.28	in front of him like a **flood** that carries everything away.
	54. 9	the time of Noah I promised never again to **flood** the earth.
Jer	46. 7	that rises like the Nile, like a river **flooding** its banks?
	46. 8	rising like the Nile, like a river **flooding** its banks.
	47. 2	rising in the north and will rush like a river in **flood.**
Ezek	30.16	Thebes will be broken down, and the city will be **flooded.**
Dan	9.26	end will come like a **flood,** bringing the war and destruction
	11.10	will sweep on like a **flood** and attack an enemy fortress.
	11.40	He will invade many countries, like the waters of a **flood.**
Hos	5.10	So I will pour out punishment on them like a **flood.**
Nah	1. 8	Like a great rushing **flood** he completely destroys his enemies;
Mt	24.38	In the days before the **flood** people ate and drank, men
	24.39	was happening until the **flood** came and swept them all away.
Lk	6.49	when the **flood** hit that house it fell at once—and what
	17.27	went into the boat and the **flood** came and killed them all.
2 Cor	11.26	have been in danger from **floods** and from robbers, in danger
2 Pet	2. 5	world, but brought the **flood** on the world of godless people;
	3. 6	the water of the **flood,** that the old world was destroyed.
Rev	12.15	the dragon poured out a **flood** of water after the woman, so
	14.20	of the winepress in a **flood** three hundred kilometres long

FLOODGATES

Gen	7.11	earth burst open, all the **floodgates** of the sky were opened,
	8. 2	beneath the earth and the **floodgates** of the sky were closed.

FLOOR

Num	5.17	earth that is on the **floor** of the Tent of the Lord's
Judg	3.25	And there was their master, lying dead on the **floor.**
2 Sam	12.16	went into his room and spent the night lying on the **floor.**
	12.20	David got up from the **floor,** had a bath, combed his hair,
	22.16	The **floor** of the ocean was laid bare, and the foundations
1 Kgs	6. 6	The temple wall on each **floor**
	6. 6	was thinner than on the **floor** below so that the rooms could
	6.15	cedar panels from the **floor** to the ceiling, and the floor
	6.15	the floor to the ceiling, and the **floor** was made of pine.
	6.16	by cedar boards reaching from the **floor** to the ceiling.
	6.30	Even the **floor** was covered with gold.
	7. 7	had cedar panels from the **floor** to the rafters.
Job	38.16	Have you walked on the **floor** of the ocean?
Ps	18.15	The **floor** of the ocean was laid bare, and the foundations

Ezek 41. 6 rooms were in three storeys, with thirty rooms on each **floor.**
41. 6 Temple's outer wall on each **floor**
41. 6 was thinner than on the **floor** below, so that the rooms could
41.16 were all panelled with wood from the **floor** to the windows.
41.20 all round the wall, [20]from the **floor** to above the doors.
Jas 2. 3 or sit here on the **floor** by my feet," [4]then you are

FLOUR

Gen 18. 6 "Quick, take a sack of your best **flour,** and bake some bread."
Ex 29. 2 Use the best wheat **flour,** but no yeast, and make some
29.40 one kilogramme of fine wheat **flour** mixed with one litre of
29.41 it the same amounts of **flour,** olive-oil, and wine as in the
Lev 2. 1 of grain to the Lord, he must first grind it into **flour.**
2. 2 take a handful of the **flour** and oil and all of the
2. 4 be thick loaves made of **flour** mixed with olive-oil or biscuits
2. 5 to be made of **flour** mixed with olive-oil but without yeast.
2. 7 in a pan, it is to be made of **flour** and olive-oil.
5.11 he shall bring one kilogramme of **flour** as a sin-offering.
5.13 The rest of the **flour** belongs to the priest, just as in
6.15 take a handful of the **flour** and oil, and the incense on
6.20 the Lord one kilogramme of **flour** (the same amount as the
7.12 either thick loaves made of **flour** mixed with olive-oil
7.12 or cakes made of **flour** mixed with olive-oil.
9.17 and took a handful of **flour** and burnt it on the altar.
14.10 three kilogrammes of **flour** mixed with olive-oil,
14.21 one kilogramme of **flour** mixed with olive-oil for a grain-offering
23.13 two kilogrammes of **flour** mixed with olive-oil as a food-offering.
23.17 made of two kilogrammes of **flour** baked with yeast and shall
24. 5 Take twelve kilogrammes of **flour** and bake twelve loaves
Num 5.15 of one kilogramme of barley **flour,** but he shall not pour any
5.18 the woman's hair and put the offering of **flour** in her hands.
5.25 shall take the offering of **flour** out of the woman's hands,
6.15 thick loaves made of **flour** mixed with olive-oil and biscuits
7.12 of them full of **flour** mixed with oil for the grain-offering;
8. 8 a young bull and the required grain-offering of **flour** mixed
11. 8 it or pound it into **flour,** and then boil it and make
15. 4 each animal a kilogramme of **flour** mixed with a litre of
15. 6 is offered, two kilogrammes of **flour** mixed with one and a
15. 9 grain-offering of three kilogrammes of **flour** mixed with two
28. 5 grain-offering of one kilogramme of **flour,** mixed with one litre
28. 9 two kilogrammes of **flour** mixed with olive-oil as a grain-offering,
28.12 As a grain-offering, offer **flour** mixed with olive-oil:
28.12 with each bull, three kilogrammes of **flour;**
28.20 the proper grain-offering of **flour** mixed with olive-oil:
28.28 the proper grain-offering of **flour** mixed with olive-oil:
29. 3 Offer the proper grain-offering of **flour** mixed with olive-oil:
29. 3 three kilogrammes of **flour** with the bull, two kilogrammes with
29. 9 the proper grain-offering of **flour** mixed with olive-oil:
29. 9 three kilogrammes of **flour** with the bull, two kilogrammes with
29.14 the proper grain-offering of **flour** mixed with olive-oil:
29.14 three kilogrammes of **flour** with each bull, two kilogrammes with
Judg 6.19 used ten kilogrammes of **flour** to make bread without any yeast.
1 Sam 1.24 three-year-old bull, ten kilogrammes of **flour,** and a leather bag
28.24 Then she took some **flour,** prepared it, and baked some bread
1 Kgs 4.22 five thousand litres of fine **flour** and ten thousand litres of
17.12 have is a handful of **flour** in a bowl and a drop
17.14 will not run out of **flour** or the jar run out of
17.16 did not run out of **flour** nor did the jar run out
1 Chr 9.29 other sacred equipment, and of the **flour,** wine, olive-oil,
12.40 mules, and oxen loaded with food—**flour,** figs, raisins, wine,
23.29 bread offered to God, the **flour** used in offerings,
23.29 the baked offerings, and the **flour** mixed with olive-oil;
Is 47. 2 Grind the **flour!**
Ezek 16.13 bread made from the best **flour,** and had honey and olive-oil
16.19 gave you food—the best **flour,** olive-oil, and honey—but you
46.14 of two kilogrammes of **flour** is to be made every morning,
46.14 together with one litre of olive-oil for mixing with the **flour.**
46.15 The lamb, the **flour,** and the olive-oil are to be offered
46.20 to bake the offerings of **flour,** so that nothing holy is
Mt 13.33 it with forty litres of **flour** until the whole batch of dough
Lk 13.21 it with forty litres of **flour** until the whole batch of dough
Rev 18.13 **flour** and wheat, cattle and sheep, horses and carriages,

FLOURISH

Deut 32.13 their olive-trees **flourished** in stony ground.
2 Kgs 19.30 in Judah who survive will **flourish** like plants that send roots
Ps 72. 7 May righteousness **flourish** in his lifetime, and may prosperity
92.12 The righteous will **flourish** like palm-trees;
92.13 house of the Lord, that **flourish** in the Temple of our God,
103.15 We grow and **flourish** like a wild flower;
132.18 his enemies with shame, but his kingdom will prosper and **flourish."**
Song 4.13 there the plants **flourish.**
Is 37.31 in Judah who survive will **flourish** like plants that send roots
Ezek 7.10 Violence is **flourishing.**
Hos 13.15 Even though Israel **flourishes** like weeds, I will send a hot
Zech 6.12 is called The Branch will **flourish** where he is and rebuild

FLOW

[DEEP-FLOWING]

Gen 2.10 A stream **flowed** in Eden and watered the garden;
2.11 it **flows** round the country of Havilah.
2.13 it **flows** round the country of Cush.
2.14 river is the Tigris, which **flows** east of Assyria,
Lev 15.25 If a woman has a **flow** of blood for several days outside
15.25 if her **flow** continues beyond her regular period,
15.25 unclean as long as the **flow** continues,
15.28 After her **flow** stops, she must wait seven days,
Deut 8.15 waterless land he made water **flow** out of solid rock for you.
9.21 threw the dust into the stream that **flowed** down the mountain.
Josh 3.13 the Jordan will stop **flowing,** and the water coming downstream
3.16 the water stopped **flowing** and piled up, far upstream at
3.16 The **flow** downstream to the Dead Sea was completely cut off,
4. 7 the Jordan stopped **flowing** when the Lord's Covenant Box crossed
4.18 the river began **flowing** once more and flooded its banks
1 Kgs 18.28 knives and daggers, according to their ritual, until blood **flowed.**
2 Kgs 3.20 morning sacrifice, water came **flowing** from the direction of Edom,
4. 6 And the olive-oil stopped **flowing.**
21.16 that the streets of Jerusalem were **flowing** with blood;
2 Chr 32. 3 all the springs, so that no more water **flowed** out of them.
32.30 and channelled the water to **flow** through a tunnel to a point
Job 20.17 rivers of olive-oil or streams that **flow** with milk and honey.
39.19 who made horses so strong and gave them their **flowing** manes?
Ps 30. 5 Tears may **flow** in the night, but joy comes in the morning.
74.15 You made springs and fountains **flow;**
78.16 come out of the rock and made water **flow** like a river.
78.20 that he struck the rock, and water **flowed** out in a torrent;
79. 3 blood **flowed** like water all through Jerusalem, and no one was
104. 8 They **flowed** over the mountains and into the valleys,
104.10 You make springs **flow** in the valleys, and rivers run between
105.41 and water gushed out, **flowing** through the desert like a river.
107.33 Lord made rivers dry up completely and stopped springs from **flowing.**
107.35 deserts into pools of water and dry land into **flowing** springs.
114. 3 the River Jordan stopped **flowing.**
114. 5 And you, O Jordan, why did you stop **flowing?**
114. 8 rocks into pools of water and solid cliffs into **flowing** springs.
147.18 he sends the wind, and the water **flows.**
Prov 3.20 wisdom caused the rivers to **flow** and the clouds to give rain
18. 4 of wisdom, deep as the ocean, fresh as a **flowing** stream.
Ecc 1. 7 Every river **flows** into the sea, but the sea is not yet
Song 4.15 streams of **flowing** water, brooks gushing down from the
5.12 beautiful as doves by a **flowing** brook, doves washed in milk
7. 9 Then let the wine **flow** straight to my lover,
7. 9 **flowing** over his lips and teeth.
Is 22.11 the city to hold the water **flowing** down from the old pool.
30.25 streams of water will **flow** from every mountain and every hill.
32. 2 They will be like streams **flowing** in a desert, like the
35. 6 Streams of water will **flow** through the desert;
41.18 I will make rivers **flow** among barren hills and springs of
41.18 into pools of water and the dry land into **flowing** springs.
43.20 me when I make rivers **flow** in the desert to give water
44. 3 the thirsty land and make streams **flow** on the dry ground.
48.18 blessings would have **flowed** for you like a stream that never
48.21 he split the rock open, and water **flowed** out.
66.12 wealth of the nations will **flow** to you like a river that
Jer 13.17 and my tears will **flow** because the Lord's people have been
14.17 "May my eyes **flow** with tears day and night, may I never
48.33 I have made the wine stop **flowing** from the winepresses;
Lam 2.18 Let your tears **flow** like rivers night and day;
3.48 My eyes **flow** with rivers of tears at the destruction of
Ezek 28.23 send diseases on you and make blood **flow** in your streets.
31. 7 Its roots reached down to the **deep-flowing** streams.
31.15 hold back the rivers and not let the many streams **flow** out.
47. 1 the entrance and **flowing** east, the direction the Temple faced.
47. 1 It was **flowing** down from under the south part of the temple
47. 2 small stream of water was **flowing** out at the south side of
47. 8 said to me, "This water **flows** through the land to the east
47. 8 When it **flows** into the Dead Sea, it replaces the salt water
47. 9 Wherever the stream **flows,** there will be all kinds of animals
47. 9 Dead Sea fresh, and wherever it **flows,** it will bring life.
47.12 they are watered by the stream that **flows** from the Temple.
Joel 3.18 A stream will **flow** from the Temple of the Lord, and it
Amos 5.24 let justice **flow** like a stream, and righteousness like a river
9.13 will drip with sweet wine, and the hills will **flow** with it.
Mic 2.11 says, 'I prophesy that wine and liquor will **flow** for you.'
Zech 9.15 it will **flow** like the blood of a sacrifice poured on the
14. 8 day comes, fresh water will **flow** from Jerusalem, half of it
14. 8 It will **flow** all the year round, in the dry season as
Rev 22. 2 and of the Lamb [2]and **flowing** down the middle of the city's

FLOWER

Gen 49.26 Blessings of corn and **flowers,** Blessings of ancient mountains,
Ex 25.31 its decorative **flowers,** including buds and petals, are to form
25.33 is to have three decorative **flowers** shaped like almond blossoms
25.34 is to have four decorative **flowers** shaped like almond blossoms
37.17 its decorative **flowers,** including buds and petals, formed one
37.19 six branches had three decorative **flowers** shaped like almond
37.20 the lamp-stand had four decorative **flowers** shaped like almond
1 Kgs 6.18 cedar panels were decorated with carvings of gourds and **flowers;**
6.29 with carved figures of winged creatures, palm-trees, and **flowers.**
6.32 with carved figures of winged creatures, palm-trees, and **flowers.**
6.35 palm-trees, and **flowers,** which were evenly covered with gold.
7.49 the **flowers,** lamps, and tongs;
2 Chr 4. 5 rim of a cup, curving outwards like the petals of a **flower.**
4.21 the **flower** decorations, the lamps, and the tongs;
Job 14. 2 We grow and wither as quickly as **flowers;**
Ps 37.20 the enemies of the Lord will vanish like wild **flowers;**
103.15 We grow and flourish like a wild **flower;**
Song 1.14 lover is like the wild **flowers** that bloom in the vineyards
2. 1 I am only a wild **flower** in Sharon,
2.12 in the countryside the **flowers** are in bloom.
Is 28. 1 fading like the crowns of **flowers** on the heads of its
28. 5 like a glorious crown of **flowers** for his people who survive.
35. 1 desert will rejoice, and **flowers** will bloom in the wilderness.
40. 6 they last no longer than wild **flowers.**
40. 7 Grass withers and **flowers** fade, when the Lord sends the wind

Is 40. 8 Yes, grass withers and **flowers** fade, but the word of our
Hos 14. 5 They will blossom like **flowers;**
Nah 1. 4 Mount Carmel turns brown, and the **flowers** of Lebanon fade.
Mt 6.28 Look how the wild **flowers** grow:
6.29 his wealth had clothes as beautiful as one of these **flowers.**
Lk 12.27 Look how the wild **flowers** grow:
12.27 his wealth had clothes as beautiful as one of these **flowers.**
Acts 14.13 the town, brought bulls and **flowers** to the gate, for he and
Jas 1.10 the rich will pass away like the **flower** of a wild plant.
1.11 its **flower** falls off, and its beauty is destroyed.
1 Pet 1.24 are like grass, and all their glory is like wild **flowers.**
1.24 The grass withers, and the **flowers** fall, [25] but the word of

FLUTE

Gen 4.21 ancestor of all musicians who play the harp and the **flute.**
1 Sam 10. 5 from the altar on the hill, playing harps, drums, **flutes,**
1 Kgs 1.40 shouting for joy and playing **flutes,** making enough noise to
Job 21.12 like lambs [12] and dance to the music of harps and **flutes.**
Ps 150. 4 Praise him with harps and **flutes.**
Is 5.12 your feasts you have harps and tambourines and **flutes**—and wine.
30.29 walk to the music of **flutes** on their way to the Temple
Jer 48.36 song on a **flute,** because everything they owned is gone.
1 Cor 14. 7 lifeless musical instruments as the **flute** or the harp—how
Rev 18.22 voices, of players of the **flute** and the trumpet, will never

FLUTTER

Is 10.14 Not a wing **fluttered** to scare me off;

FLY (1)

[FLEW, FLIGHT, FLOWN]

Gen 8. 7 not come back, but kept **flying** around until the water was
8. 9 It **flew** back to the boat, and Noah reached out and took
Ex 16.13 a large flock of quails **flew** in, enough to cover the camp,
Lev 14. 7 He shall let the live bird **fly** away over the open fields.
14.53 shall let the live bird **fly** away outside the city over the
Num 11.31 brought quails from the sea, **flying** less than a metre above
Deut 32.11 eagle teaching its young to **fly,** catching them safely on its
2 Sam 22.11 He **flew** swiftly on his winged creature;
Job 5. 7 trouble on himself, as surely as sparks **fly** up from a fire.
28. 7 roads to the mines, And no vulture ever **flies** over them.
28.21 No living creature can see it, Not even a bird in **flight.**
39.13 But no ostrich can **fly** like a stork.
39.26 learn from you how to **fly** when it spreads its wings towards
41.19 Flames blaze from his mouth, and streams of sparks **fly** out.
Ps 11. 1 you to say to me, **"Fly** away like a bird to the
18.10 He **flew** swiftly on a winged creature;
55. 6 I would **fly** away and find rest.
55. 7 I would **fly** far away and live in the wilderness.
139. 9 If I **flew** away beyond the east or lived in the farthest
Prov 23. 5 as if it had grown wings and **flown** away like an eagle.
26. 2 They are like birds that **fly** by and never settle.
30.19 an eagle **flying** in the sky,
Is 6. 2 and its body with two, and used the other two for **flying.**
6. 6 Then one of the creatures **flew** down to me, carrying a
14.29 A snake's egg hatches a **flying** dragon.
29. 5 and their terrifying armies will **fly** away like straw.
30. 6 and where there are poisonous snakes and **flying** dragons.
Jer 4.25 even the birds had **flown** away.
Ezek 1.24 I heard the noise their wings made in **flight;**
1.24 When they stopped **flying,** they folded their wings,
10.16 spread their wings to **fly,** the wheels still went with them.
10.17 and when the creatures **flew,** the wheels went with them,
10.19 They spread their wings and **flew** up from the earth while
11.22 living creatures began to **fly,** and the wheels went with them.
17. 3 He **flew** to the Lebanon Mountains and broke off the top of
Dan 2.12 the king **flew** into a rage and ordered the execution
3.13 At that, the king **flew** into a rage and ordered the
9.21 seen in the earlier vision, came **flying** down to where I was.
Hos 9.11 Israel's greatness will **fly** away like a bird,
Nah 3.16 are gone, like locusts that spread their wings and **fly** away.
3.17 the sun comes out, they **fly** away, and no one knows where
Zech 5. 1 again, and this time I saw a scroll **flying** through the air.
5. 2 I answered, "A scroll **flying** through the air;
5. 9 and saw two women **flying** towards me with powerful wings like
5. 9 They picked up the basket and **flew** off with it.
Rev 4. 7 and the fourth looked like an eagle in **flight.**
8.13 heard an eagle that was **flying** high in the air say in
12.14 large eagle in order to **fly** to her place in the desert,
14. 6 Then I saw another angel **flying** high in the air, with an
19.17 shouted in a loud voice to all the birds **flying** in midair:

FLY (2)

Ex 8.21 will punish you by sending **flies** on you, your officials,
8.21 Egyptians will be full of **flies,** and the ground will be
8.22 where my people live, so that there will be no **flies** there.
8.24 Lord sent great swarms of **flies** into the king's palace and
8.24 The whole land of Egypt was brought to ruin by the **flies.**
8.29 the Lord that tomorrow the **flies** will leave you, your officials,
8.31 The **flies** left the king, his officials, and his people;
8.31 not one **fly** remained.
Ps 78.45 He sent **flies** among them, that tormented them, and frogs
105.31 and **flies** and gnats swarmed throughout the whole country.
Ecc 10. 1 Dead **flies** can make a whole bottle of perfume stink,
Is 7.18 the Egyptians to come like **flies** from the farthest branches of
51. 6 like old clothing, and all its people will die like **flies.**
Jer 46.20 a splendid cow, attacked by a stinging **fly** from the north.
Mt 23.24 You strain a **fly** out of your drink, but swallow a camel!

FOAL

Zech 9. 9 on a donkey— on a colt, the **foal** of a donkey.
Mt 21. 5 on a donkey and on a colt, the **foal** of a donkey."

FOAM (1)

Job 41.32 a shining path behind him and turns the sea to white **foam.**
Hab 3.15 trampled the sea with your horses, and the mighty waters **foamed.**
Jude 13 of the sea, with their shameful deeds showing up like **foam.**

FOAM (2)

Mk 9.18 the ground, and he **foams at the mouth,** grits his teeth, and
9.20 fell on the ground and rolled round, **foaming at the mouth.**
Lk 9.39 throws him into a fit, so that he **foams at the mouth;**

FODDER

Gen 24.25 is plenty of straw and **fodder** at our house, and there is
24.32 and Laban unloaded the camels and gave them straw and **fodder.**
Judg 19.19 even though we have **fodder** and straw for our donkeys,
Is 30.24 that plough your fields will eat the finest and best **fodder.**

FOE

Ex 15. 7 In majestic triumph you overthrow your **foes;**
2 Sam 22.49 he subdues the nations under me [49] and saves me from my **foes.**
Neh 9.27 you sent them leaders who rescued them from their **foes.**
Ps 18.48 he subdues the nations under me [48] and saves me from my **foes.**
74.23 shouts of your enemies, the continuous noise made by your **foes.**
76. 4 as you return from the mountains where you defeated your **foes.**
81.14 would quickly defeat their enemies and conquer all their **foes.**
89.23 I will crush his **foes** and kill everyone who hates him.
Lam 1.14 Lord gave me to my **foes,** and I was helpless against them.

FOLD

see also **SHEEPFOLD**

Ex 26. 9 **Fold** the sixth piece double over the front of the Tent.
28.16 is to be square and **folded** double, 22 centimetres long
39. 9 It was square and **folded** double, 22 centimetres long
1 Kgs 6.34 There were two **folding** doors made of pine [35] and decorated
Job 38.14 valleys stand out like the **folds** of a garment, clear as the
Prov 6.10 "I'll **fold** my hands and rest a while."
24.33 **Fold** your hands and rest awhile, [34] but while you are asleep,
Ecc 4. 5 would be a fool to **fold** his hands and let himself starve
Ezek 1.11 and their other two wings were **folded** against their bodies.
1.24 When they stopped flying, they **folded** their wings,
Hag 2.12 from a sacrifice and carries it in a **fold** of his robe.
Heb 1.12 You will **fold** them up like a coat, and they will be

FOLLOW

Gen 33.14 of me, and I will **follow** slowly, going as fast as I
41.31 forgotten, because the famine which **follows** will be so terrible.
Ex 14.28 the Egyptian army that had **followed** the Israelites into the sea;
15.20 and all the women **followed** her, playing tambourines and dancing.
16. 4 test them to find out if they will **follow** my instructions.
23. 2 Do not **follow** the majority when they do wrong or when they
32. 8 They have already left the way that I commanded them to **follow;**
Lev 18. 3 Do not **follow** the practices of the people of Egypt, where
18. 5 **Follow** the practices and the laws that I give you;
18.30 I give and do not **follow** the practices of the people who
22.29 of thanksgiving to the Lord, **follow** the rules so that you
Num 4.34 **Following** the Lord's command, Moses, Aaron,
14.43 not be with you, because you have refused to **follow** him."
15.39 turn away from me and **follow** your own wishes and desires.
25. 8 He took a spear, [8] **followed** the man and the woman into the
31.16 it was the women who **followed** Balaam's instructions and at Peor
32.15 Reuben and Gad refuse to **follow** him now, he will once again
34. 7 northern border will **follow** a line from the Mediterranean
34.10 eastern border will **follow** a line from Hazar Enan to Shepham.
Deut 12.30 make sure that you don't **follow** their religious practices,
13. 4 **Follow** the Lord and honour him;
17.11 their verdict and **follow** their instructions in every detail.
18. 9 don't **follow** the disgusting practices of the nations
18.14 are about to occupy, people **follow** the advice of those who
24. 8 **follow** the instructions that I have given them.
Josh 3. 3 Covenant Box of the Lord your God, break camp and **follow** them.
4. 8 The men **followed** Joshua's orders.
6. 8 who were carrying the Covenant Box, **followed** by a rearguard.
15. 4 went on to Azmon, and **followed** the stream on the border of
20. 5 the man looking for revenge **follows** him there, the people of
22.16 You are no longer **following** him!
22.18 Are you going to refuse to **follow** him now?
22.29 against the Lord or stop **following** him now by building an
24.25 and there at Shechem he gave them laws and rules to **follow.**
Judg 2.22 or not these Israelites will **follow** my ways, as their ancestors
3.28 He said, **"Follow** me!
3.28 they **followed** Ehud down and captured the place where the Moabites
4.10 Zebulun and Naphtali to Kedesh, and ten thousand men **followed** him.
5.15 and Barak too, and they **followed** him into the valley.
6.34 to call the men of the clan of Abiezer to **follow** him.
6.35 of both parts of Manasseh to call them to **follow** him.
9. 3 Shechem decided to **follow** Abimelech because he was their relative.
9.49 then they **followed** Abimelech and piled the wood up against the
13.11 Manoah got up and **followed** his wife.

Ruth 2. 7 asked me to let her **follow** the workers and pick up the
1 Sam 6.12 The five Philistine kings **followed** them as far as the border
8. 3 But they did not **follow** their father's example;
8. 5 you are getting old and your sons don't **follow** your example.
11. 7 "Whoever does not **follow** Saul and Samuel into battle will have
12.14 and obey his commands, and if you and your king **follow** him.
13.15 The rest of the people **followed** Saul as he went to join
14.12 Jonathan said to the young man, **"Follow** me.
14.13 pass on his hands and knees, and the young man **followed** him.
25.19 to the servants, "You go on ahead and I will **follow** you."
30.25 this a rule, and it has been **followed** in Israel ever since.
2 Sam 3.16 Paltiel **followed** her all the way to the town of Bahurim,
13.29 the servants **followed** Absalom's instructions and killed Amnon.
15.18 six hundred soldiers who had **followed** him from Gath also passed
15.23 crossed the brook of Kidron, **followed** by his men, and together
15.30 All who **followed** him covered their heads and wept also.
16.23 both David and Absalom **followed** it.
17. 6 shall we **follow** it?
17.14 good advice would not be **followed,** so that disaster would come
17.23 his advice had not been **followed,** he saddled his donkey and
20. 1 We won't **follow** him!
20. 2 remained loyal and **followed** David from the Jordan to Jerusalem.
20.11 called out, "Everyone who is for Joab and David **follow** Joab!"
20.13 from the road, everyone **followed** Joab in pursuit of Sheba.
20.14 the clan of Bikri assembled and **followed** him into the city.
1 Kgs 1.35 **Follow** him back here when he comes to sit on my throne.
1.40 Then they all **followed** him back, shouting for joy
3. 3 Solomon loved the Lord and **followed** the instructions of his
9. 6 you or your descendants stop **following** me, if you disobey the
13. 2 **Following** the Lord's command, the prophet denounced the altar:
19.21 Then he went and **followed** Elijah as his helper.
20.19 young soldiers led the attack, **followed** by the Israelite army,
20.25 King Benhadad agreed and **followed** their advice.
22.52 He sinned against the Lord, **following** the wicked example
2 Kgs 2. 7 and fifty of the prophets **followed** them to the Jordan.
6.19 **Follow** me, and I will lead you to the man you are
8. 2 had **followed** his instructions, and had gone with her family to
8.18 the family of Ahab he **followed** the evil ways of the kings
10. 6 me, and are ready to **follow** my orders, bring the heads of
10.31 he **followed** the example of Jeroboam, who led Israel into sin.
11.19 from the Temple to the palace, **followed** by all the people.
13.11 against the Lord and **followed** the evil example of King Jeroboam,
13.17 **following** the prophet's instructions, the king opened the window
14. 6 not kill their children but **followed** what the Lord had commanded
14.19 of Lachish, but his enemies **followed** him there and killed him.
14.24 against the Lord, **following** the wicked example of his predecessor
15. 3 **Following** the example of his father, he did what was pleasing
15. 9 He **followed** the wicked example of King Jeroboam son of Nebat,
15.18 day of his death he **followed** the wicked example of King
15.24 against the Lord, **following** the wicked example of King Jeroboam
15.28 against the Lord, **following** the wicked example of King Jeroboam
15.34 **Following** the example of his father Uzziah, Jotham did what
16. 2 He did not **follow** the good example of his ancestor King David;
16. 3 the Lord his God [3] and **followed** the example of the kings of
17. 8 They worshipped other gods, [8] **followed** the customs of the people
17.11 on all the pagan altars, **following** the practice of the people
17.15 and they **followed** the customs of the surrounding nations,
17.22 They **followed** Jeroboam and continued to practise all the
17.40 would not listen, and they continued to **follow** their old customs.
18. 3 **Following** the example of his ancestor King David, he did what
21. 2 **Following** the disgusting practices of the nations whom
22. 2 **followed** the example of his ancestor King David, strictly obeying
23.32 **Following** the example of his ancestors, he sinned against
23.37 **Following** the example of his ancestors, Jehoiakim sinned
24. 9 **Following** the example of his father, Jehoiachin sinned against
2 Chr 2.14 sorts of engraving and can **follow** any design suggested to him.
8.14 **Following** the rules laid down by his father David,
11.16 Lord, the God of Israel, **followed** the Levites to Jerusalem,
17. 3 Lord blessed Jehoshaphat because he **followed** the example of his
19. 3 and you have tried to **follow** God's will."
21. 6 He **followed** the wicked example of King Ahab and the other
21.12 because you did not **follow** the example of your father,
21.13 you have **followed** the example of the kings of Israel
22. 2 Ahaziah also **followed** the example of King Ahab's family,
22. 5 **Following** their advice, he joined King Joram of Israel in
25. 4 however, execute their children, but **followed** what the Lord had
25.27 of Lachish, but his enemies **followed** him there and killed him.
26. 4 **Following** the example of his father, he did what was pleasing
26.17 and courageous priests, **followed** the king [18] to resist him.
28. 1 He did not **follow** the good example of his ancestor King David;
28. 2 pleasing to the Lord [2] and **followed** the example of the kings
29. 2 **Following** the example of his ancestor King David, he did what
29.25 The king **followed** the instructions that the Lord had given
30.12 to obey his will by **following** the commands of the king
33. 2 **Following** the disgusting practices of the nations whom
34. 2 **followed** the example of his ancestor King David, strictly obeying
35. 6 order that your fellow-Israelites may **follow** the instructions
36.14 and the people **followed** the sinful example of the nations
Neh 12.32 behind the singers, **followed** by half the leaders of Judah.
12.36 He was **followed** by other members of his clan—
12.38 the top of the wall, and I **followed** with half the people.
12.42 and they were **followed** by Maaseiah, Shemaiah, Eleazar, Uzzi,
13.27 Are we then to **follow** your example and disobey our God
Esth 2. 4 The king thought this was good advice, so he **followed** it.
9.23 the Jews **followed** Mordecai's instructions, and the celebration
Job 18.11 it **follows** him at every step.
22.15 to walk in the paths that evil men have always **followed?**
23.11 I **follow** faithfully the road he chooses, and never wander
23.12 I **follow** his will, not my own desires.
34. 9 that it never does any good to try to **follow** God's will.
34.27 they have stopped **following** him and ignored all his commands.

Ps 1. 1 evil men, who do not **follow** the example of sinners or join
5. 8 make your way plain for me to **follow.**
17. 4 have obeyed your command and have not **followed** paths of
violence.
25. 8 righteous and good, he teaches sinners the path they should **follow.**
25.12 the Lord will learn from him the path they should **follow.**
45.14 is led to the king, **followed** by her bridesmaids, and they
68.27 of Judah with their group, **followed** by the leaders of Zebulun
119. 2 Happy are those who **follow** his commands, who obey him
119.14 I delight in **following** your commands more than in having
119.31 I have **followed** your instructions, Lord;
119.59 considered my conduct, and I promise to **follow** your instructions.
119.128 And so I **follow** all your instructions;
119.173 be ready to help me, because I **follow** your commands.
Prov 2.20 So you must **follow** the example of good men and live a
4.14 Do not **follow** the example of the wicked.
7. 2 Be as careful to **follow** my teaching as you are to protect
8.20 I **follow** the paths of justice, [21] giving wealth to those who
9. 6 **Follow** the way of knowledge."
13.13 **follow** it and you are safe.
13.21 Trouble **follows** sinners everywhere, but righteous people
28.26 It is foolish to **follow** your own opinions.
28.26 Be safe, and **follow** the teachings of wiser people.
Ecc 11. 9 Do what you want to do, and **follow** your heart's desire.
Song 1. 8 Go and **follow** the flock;
Is 2. 6 The people **follow** foreign customs.
8.11 Lord warned me not to **follow** the path
8.11 which the people were **following.**
26. 8 We **follow** your will and put our hope in you;
30. 1 They **follow** plans that I did not make, and sign treaties
30.21 **Follow** it."
35. 8 no fools will mislead those who **follow** it.
41. 3 He **follows** in pursuit and marches safely on, so fast that
45.14 they will **follow** you in chains.
59. 8 You **follow** a crooked path, and no one who walks that path
59.13 rebelled against you, rejected you, and refused to **follow** you.
Jer 2. 2 you **followed** me through the desert, through a land that had
4.20 One disaster **follows** another;
9. 5 and one deceitful act **follows** another.
10. 2 "Do not **follow** the ways of other nations;
18.15 the way they should go, they no longer **follow** the old ways;
23.12 The paths they **follow** will be slippery and dark;
26. 4 you must obey me by **following** the teaching that I gave you,
35.18 you have **followed** all his instructions, and you have done
42.16 the hunger you dread will **follow** you, and you will die there
Ezek 5. 7 You have **followed** the customs of other nations.
7.26 One disaster will **follow** another, and a steady stream of
9. 5 say to the other men, **"Follow** him through the city, and
16.47 Were you content to **follow** in their footsteps and copy
18.14 the sins his father practised, but does not **follow** his example.
18.19 He kept my laws and **followed** them carefully, and so he will
20.18 do not **follow** their customs or defile yourselves with their
23.31 You **followed** in your sister's footsteps, and so I will give
33.15 if he stops sinning and **follows** the laws that give life,
35. 6 You are guilty of murder, and murder will **follow** you.
36.27 see to it that you **follow** my laws and keep all the
41.18 Palm-trees alternated with creatures, one **following** the other,
Dan 3. 5 the sound of the trumpets, **followed** by the playing of oboes,
4.27 So then, Your Majesty, **follow** my advice.
9.13 you by turning from our sins or by **following** your truth.
11. 2 kings will rule over Persia, **followed** by a fourth, who will
11.20 will be **followed** by another king, who will send an officer
11.30 will **follow** the advice of those who have abandoned that religion.
11.32 already abandoned their religion, but those who **follow** God will
Hos 4.10 because you have turned away from me to **follow** other gods."
10. 6 and put to shame because of the advice she **followed.**
11.10 "My people will **follow** me when I roar like a lion at
14. 9 righteous people live by **following** them, but sinners stumble
Mic 6.16 happen because you have **followed** the evil practices of King Omri
Hab 3. 5 He sends disease before him and commands death to **follow** him.
Zeph 1. 6 turned back and no longer **follow** me, those who do not come
Mt 4.25 Large crowds **followed** him from Galilee and the Ten Towns, from
Jerusalem,
8. 1 When Jesus came down from the hill, large crowds **followed** him.
8.10 and said to the people **following** him, "I tell you, I have
8.22 **"Follow** me," Jesus answered, "and let the dead bury their own
dead."
9. 9 He said to him, **"Follow** me."
9. 9 Matthew got up and **followed** him.
9.19 So Jesus got up and **followed** him, and his disciples went
9.27 and as he walked along, two blind men started **following** him.
10.38 take up his cross and **follow** in my steps is not fit
12.15 and large crowds **followed** him.
14.13 about it, so they left their towns and **followed** him by land.
15. 3 "And why do you disobey God's command and **follow** your own
teaching?
15. 6 God's command, in order to **follow** your own teaching.
15.23 She is **following** us and making all this noise!"
16.24 he must forget self, carry his cross, and **follow** me.
19. 2 Large crowds **followed** him, and he healed them there.
19.21 then come and **follow** me."
19.27 "Look," he said, "we have left everything and **followed** you.
20.29 Jesus and his disciples were leaving Jericho, a large crowd was
following.
20.34 at once they were able to see, and they **followed** him.
23. 3 So you must obey and **follow** everything they tell you to do;
26.58 Peter **followed** from a distance, as far as the courtyard
27.55 who had **followed** Jesus from Galilee and helped him.
Mk 2.14 Jesus said to him, **"Follow** me."
2.14 Levi got up and **followed** him.
2.15 collectors and other outcasts were **following** Jesus, and many

Mk	3. 7	went away to Lake Galilee, and a large crowd **followed** him.
	6. 1	and went back to his home town, **followed** by his disciples.
	7. 3	the rest of the Jews, **follow** the teaching they received from
	7. 4	And they **follow** many other rules which they have received,
	7. 5	that your disciples do not **follow** the teaching handed down
	8.34	"he must forget self, carry his cross, and **follow** me.
	10.21	then come and **follow** me."
	10.28	Then Peter spoke up, "Look, we have left everything and **followed** you."
	10.32	the people who **followed** behind were afraid.
	10.52	once he was able to see and **followed** Jesus on the road.
	11. 9	in front and those who **followed** behind began to shout,
	14.13	**Follow** him [14] to the house he enters, and say to the owner
	14.51	man, dressed only in a linen cloth, was **following** Jesus.
	14.54	Peter **followed** from a distance and went into the
	15.41	They had **followed** Jesus while he was in Galilee and had
Lk	1. 9	According to the custom **followed** by the priests, he was
	5.11	boats up on the beach, left everything, and **followed** Jesus.
	5.27	Jesus said to him, **"Follow** me."
	5.28	Levi got up, left everything, and **followed** him.
	7. 9	and said to the crowd **following** him, "I tell you, I have
	9.11	When the crowds heard about it, they **followed** him.
	9.23	must forget self, take up his cross every day, and **follow** me.
	9.57	a man said to Jesus, "I will **follow** you wherever you go."
	9.59	He said to another man, **"Follow** me."
	9.61	Another man said, "I will **follow** you, sir;
	18.22	then come and **follow** me."
	18.28	We have left our homes to **follow** you."
	18.43	able to see, and he **followed** Jesus, giving thanks to God.
	21. 8	But don't **follow** them.
	22.10	**Follow** him into the house that he enters, [11] and say to the
	22.54	and Peter **followed** at a distance.
	23.27	A large crowd of people **followed** him;
	23.49	including the women who had **followed** him from Galilee, stood
	23.55	The women who had **followed** Jesus from Galilee went with
Jn	1.38	Jesus turned, saw them **following** him, and asked, "What
	6. 2	A large crowd **followed** him, because they had seen his
	8.12	"Whoever **follows** me will have the light of life and will
	8.44	the Devil, and you want to **follow** your father's desires.
	10. 4	them, and the sheep **follow** him, because they know his voice.
	10. 5	They will not **follow** someone else;
	10.27	I know them, and they **follow** me.
	11.31	house with Mary, comforting her, **followed** her when they saw
	12.19	Look, the whole world is **following** him!"
	12.26	wants to serve me must **follow** me, so that my servant will
	13.36	"You cannot **follow** me now where I am going," answered Jesus;
	13.36	"but later you will **follow** me."
	13.37	"Lord, why can't I **follow** you now?"
	18.15	Simon Peter and another disciple **followed** Jesus.
	21.19	Then Jesus said to him, **"Follow** me!"
	21.22	**Follow** me!"
Acts	5.39	The Council **followed** Gamaliel's advice.
	12. 9	Peter **followed** him out of the prison, not knowing,
	13.43	meeting, Paul and Barnabas were **followed** by many Jews and by
	16.17	She **followed** Paul and us, shouting, "These men are
	21.21	to circumcise their children or **follow** the Jewish customs.
	22. 4	I persecuted to the death the people who **followed** this Way.
	24.14	God of our ancestors by **following** that Way which they say is
	27.44	the rest were to **follow,** holding on to the planks or to
Rom	2. 8	and reject what is right, in order to **follow** what is wrong;
	15. 5	among yourselves by **following** the example of Christ Jesus,
1 Cor	1.12	One says, "I **follow** Paul";
	1.12	another, "I **follow** Apollos";
	1.12	another, "I **follow** Peter";
	1.12	and another, "I **follow** Christ."
	3. 4	says, "I **follow** Paul," and another, "I follow Apollos"
	4.16	I beg you, then, to **follow** my example.
	4.17	of the principles which I **follow** in the new life in union
	9. 5	Haven't I the right to **follow** the example of the other
	10. 1	brothers, what happened to our ancestors who **followed** Moses.
	11. 2	you always remember me and **follow** the teachings that I have
	16.16	beg you, my brothers, [16] to **follow** the leadership of such
Gal	6.16	As for those who **follow** this rule in their lives, may
Eph	2. 2	At that time you **followed** the world's evil way;
Phil	3.16	according to the same rules we have **followed** until now.
	3.17	Pay attention to those who **follow** the right example that we
2 Thes	3. 6	and who do not **follow** the instructions that we gave them.
	3. 9	we did it to be an example for you to **follow.**
1 Tim	4. 1	will obey lying spirits and **follow** the teachings of demons.
	4. 6	of faith and of the true teaching which you have **followed.**
	5.15	For some widows have already turned away to **follow** Satan.
2 Tim	1.13	the example for you to **follow,** and remain in the faith and
	3.10	But you have **followed** my teaching, my conduct, and my
	4. 3	to sound doctrine, but will **follow** their own desires and
Heb	2. 2	and anyone who did not **follow** it or obey it received the
	13.17	Obey your leaders and **follow** their orders.
1 Pet	1.11	Christ would have to endure and the glory that would **follow.**
	2.21	left you an example, so that you would **follow** in his steps.
	2.25	have been brought back to **follow** the Shepherd and Keeper of
2 Pet	2. 2	Even so, many will **follow** their immoral ways;
	2.10	of Judgement, [10] especially those who **follow** their filthy
	2.15	they have **followed** the path taken by Balaam son of Beor, who
Jude	11	They have **followed** the way that Cain took.
	16	they **follow** their own evil desires;
	18	mock you, people who **follow** their own godless desires."
Rev	2.14	are some among you who **follow** the teaching of Balaam, who
	2.15	people among you who **follow** the teaching of the Nicolaitans.
	2.24	of you in Thyatira have not **followed** this evil teaching;
	3. 8	you have **followed** my teaching and have been faithful to me.
	6. 8	Its rider was named Death, and Hades **followed** close behind.
	13. 3	The whole earth was amazed and **followed** the beast.
Rev	14. 4	They **follow** the Lamb wherever he goes.
	14. 8	A second angel **followed** the first one, saying, "She has fallen!
	14. 9	A third angel **followed** the first two, saying in a loud voice,
	19.14	The armies of heaven **followed** him, riding on white

FOLLOWER

Num	16. 5	said to Korah and his **followers,** "Tomorrow morning the Lord
	16. 6	Tomorrow morning you and your **followers** take firepans,
	16.11	against the Lord that you and your **followers** are rebelling."
	16.16	"Tomorrow you and your 250 **followers** must come to the Tent
	16.32	together with all of Korah's **followers** and their possessions.
	26. 9	and Aaron and joined the **followers** of Korah when they rebelled
	26.10	died with Korah and his **followers** when fire destroyed 250 men;
	27. 3	He was not among the **followers** of Korah, who rebelled against
Deut	28.13	make you the leader among the nations and not a **follower;**
2 Sam	3. 6	Abner became more and more powerful among Saul's **followers.**
	15.12	gained strength, and Absalom's **followers** grew in number.
	15.23	The people cried loudly as David's **followers** left.
	16.21	as his enemy, and your **followers** will be greatly encouraged."
1 Chr	12.23	**Followers** of Jehoiada, descendant of Aaron:
2 Chr	24. 7	(The **followers** of Athaliah, that corrupt woman, had damaged
Ps	106.18	fire came down on their **followers** and burnt up those wicked
Dan	11.24	he will divide among his **followers** the goods and property
Hab	3.13	the leader of the wicked and completely destroyed his **followers.**
Mt	5.11	kinds of evil lies against you because you are my **followers.**
	9.14	Then the **followers** of John the Baptist came to Jesus,
	10.42	the least of these my **followers** because he is my follower,
	12.27	Well, then, who gives your **followers** the power to drive them out?
	12.27	What your own **followers** do proves that you are wrong!
	19.28	New Age, then you twelve **followers** of mine will also sit on
Mk	2.18	On one occasion the **followers** of John the Baptist and
Lk	11.19	how I drive them out, how do your **followers** drive them out?
	11.19	Your own **followers** prove that you are wrong!
	24.13	same day two of Jesus' **followers** were going to a village
Jn	6.60	Many of his **followers** heard this and said, "This
	6.66	of this, many of Jesus' **followers** turned back and would not
	7. 3	to Judaea, so that your **followers** will see the things that
	18.36	belonged to this world, my **followers** would fight to keep me
	19.38	(Joseph was a **follower** of Jesus, but in secret, because he
	21.23	a report spread among the **followers** of Jesus that this
Acts	5.36	he was killed, all his **followers** were scattered, and his
	5.37	he also was killed, and all his **followers** were scattered.
	9. 1	violent threats of murder against the **followers** of the Lord.
	9. 2	he should find there any **followers** of the Way of the Lord,
	9.25	But one night Saul's **followers** took him and let him down
1 Cor	10. 2	and in the sea they were all baptized as **followers** of Moses.
	15. 6	than five hundred of his **followers** at once, most of whom are
Eph	4.21	about him, and as his **followers** you were taught the truth
1 Pet	3.16	of your good conduct as **followers** of Christ will be ashamed
	4.14	Happy are you if you are insulted because you are Christ's **followers;**
Rev	1. 9	your brother, and as a **follower** of Jesus I am your partner
	2.23	I will also kill her **followers,** and then all the
	17.14	called, chosen, and faithful **followers,** will defeat them,

FOLLY

Mk	7.22	indecency, jealousy, slander, pride, and **folly**—

FOND

1 Sam	19. 1	But Jonathan was very **fond** of David, [2] and so he said to

FOOD

Gen	1.30	provided grass and leafy plants for **food"**—and it was done.
	3.17	hard all your life to make it produce enough **food** for you.
	6.21	Take along all kinds of **food** for you and for them."
	9. 3	I give them all to you for **food.**
	14.11	took everything in Sodom and Gomorrah, including the **food,**
	18. 5	I will also bring a bit of **food;**
	18. 8	some milk, and the meat, and set the **food** before the men.
	21.14	morning Abraham gave Hagar some **food** and a leather bag full
	24.33	When **food** was brought, the man said, "I will not eat
	27. 4	me some of that tasty **food** that I like, and bring it
	27. 9	them and make some of that **food** your father likes so much.
	27.14	her, and she cooked the kind of **food** that his father liked.
	27.17	She handed him the tasty **food,** together with the bread
	27.31	He also cooked some tasty **food** and took it to his father.
	28.20	am making and give me **food** and clothing, [21] and if I return
	39. 6	did not concern himself with anything except the **food** he ate.
	41.35	them to collect all the **food** during the good years that are
	41.36	The **food** will be a reserve supply for the country during
	41.48	In each city he stored the **food** from the fields around it.
	41.54	in every other country, but there was **food** throughout Egypt.
	41.55	began to be hungry, they cried out to the king for **food.**
	42. 7	"We have come from Canaan to buy **food,"** they answered.
	42.10	"We have come as your slaves, to buy **food.**
	42.25	back in his sack, and to give them **food** for the journey.
	43. 2	to his sons, "Go back and buy a little **food** for us."
	43. 4	our brother with us, we will go and buy **food** for you.
	43.20	"If you please, sir, we came here once before to buy **food.**
	43.22	have also brought some more money with us to buy more **food.**
	43.34	**Food** was served to them from Joseph's table,
	44. 1	men's sacks with as much **food** as they can carry, and put
	44.25	Then he told us to return and buy a little **food.**
	45.21	wagons, as the king had ordered, and **food** for the journey.
	45.23	donkeys loaded with corn, bread, and other **food** for the journey.
	47.12	Joseph provided **food** for his father, his brothers, and all
	47.13	severe that there was no **food** anywhere, and the people of

Gen	47.15	the Egyptians came to Joseph and said, "Give us **food!**
	47.16	I will give you **food** in exchange for it if your money
	47.17	Joseph, and he gave them **food** in exchange for their horses,
	47.17	he supplied them with **food** in exchange for all their livestock.
	47.19	Buy us and our land in exchange for **food.**
	47.24	for seed and for **food** for yourselves and your families."
	49.20	"Asher's land will produce rich **food.**
	49.20	He will provide **food** fit for a king.
Ex	12.16	is to be done on those days, but you may prepare **food.**
	12.39	time to get their **food** ready or to prepare leavened dough.
	16. 3	down and eat meat and as much other **food** as we wanted.
	16. 4	I am going to make **food** rain down from the sky for
	16.15	to them, "This is the **food** that the Lord has given you
	16.22	they gathered twice as much **food,** four litres for each person.
	16.25	the Lord, and you will not find any **food** outside the camp.
	16.26	You must gather **food** for six days, but on the seventh day,
	16.27	people went out to gather **food,** but they did not find any.
	16.29	sixth day I will always give you enough **food** for two days.
	16.31	The people of Israel called the **food** manna.
	16.32	that they can see the **food** which he gave us to eat
	21.10	wife the same amount of **food** and clothing and the same
	23.25	I will bless you with **food** and water and take away all
	29.24	Put all this **food** in the hands of Aaron and his sons
	29.33	Only priests may eat this **food,** because it is sacred.
	34.15	will be tempted to eat the **food** they offer to their gods.
Lev	2. 3	holy, since it is taken from the **food** offered to the Lord.
	2.10	holy, since it is taken from the **food** offered to the Lord.
	2.11	must never use yeast or honey in **food** offered to the Lord.
	6.18	as their continuing share of the **food** offered to the Lord.
	7.26	they must never use the blood of birds or animals for **food.**
	7.35	is the part of the **food** offered to the Lord that was
	8.27	He put all this **food** in the hands of Aaron and his
	8.28	Then Moses took the **food** from them and burnt it on the
	10.12	is left over from the **food** offered to the Lord, make
	10.13	to you and your sons from the **food** offered to the Lord.
	11.34	Any **food** which could normally be eaten, but on which water
	21.22	a man may eat the **food** offered to me, both the holy
	22. 7	then he may eat the sacred offerings, which are his **food.**
	22.11	or born in his home, may eat the **food** the priest receives.
	22.13	dependant may eat the **food** her father receives as a priest.
	24. 9	very holy part of the **food** offered to the Lord for the
	25. 6	that year, it will provide **food** for you, your slaves, your
	25.21	year so that it will produce enough **food** for two years.
	25.37	and do not make a profit on the **food** you sell him.
	26.26	I will cut off your **food** supply, so that ten women will
Num	9.12	not leave any of the **food** until the following morning and do
	15.19	When any **food** produced there is eaten, some of it is to
	21. 5	to die in this desert, where there is no **food** or water?
	21. 5	We can't stand any more of this miserable **food!"**
	25. 2	Israelites ate the **food** and worshipped the god [3] Baal of Peor.
	29. 7	eat no **food** and do no work.
Deut	2. 6	You may buy **food** and water from them.'
	2.28	We will pay for the **food** we eat and the water we
	8. 3	gave you manna to eat, **food** that you and your ancestors had
	8.16	you manna to eat, **food** that your ancestors had never eaten.
	10.18	foreigners who live with our people, and gives them **food**
	11.15	You will have all the **food** you want.
	12.16	But you must not use their blood as **food;**
	12.24	Do not use the blood for **food;**
	14.29	This **food** is for the Levites, since they own no property,
	15.23	But do not use their blood for **food;**
	18. 8	receive the same amount of **food** as the other priests, and he
	23. 4	refused to provide you with **food** and water when you were on
	23.19	you lend money or **food** or anything else to a fellow-Israelite,
	24. 6	take away the family's means of preparing **food** to keep alive.
	28. 5	bless your corn crops and the **food** you prepare from them.
	28.17	curse your corn crops and the **food** you prepare from them.
	28.53	will become so desperate for **food** that you will even eat the
	28.54	eat some of his own children because he has no other **food.**
	28.56	will become so desperate for **food** that she will secretly eat
	31.20	they will have all the **food** they want, and they will live
	32.15	they were fat and stuffed with **food.**
Josh	1.11	to the people, "Get some **food** ready, because in three days
	5.11	next day was the first time they ate **food** grown in Canaan:
	5.12	From that time on they ate **food** grown in Canaan.
	9. 4	They went and got some **food** and loaded their donkeys with
	9.11	told us to get some **food** ready for a journey and to
	9.14	men of Israel accepted some **food** from them, but did not
Judg	6.18	Please do not leave until I bring you an offering of **food."**
	8. 6	of Sukkoth said, "Why should we give your army any **food?**
	8.15	that you couldn't give any **food** to my exhausted army because
	13. 4	not to drink any wine or beer, or eat any forbidden **food;**
	13. 7	beer, or eat any forbidden **food,** because the boy is to be
	13.14	must not drink any wine or beer, or eat any forbidden **food.**
	13.15	angel said, "If I do stay, I will not eat your **food.**
	17.10	ten pieces of silver a year, some clothes, and your **food."**
	20.10	men in Israel will provide **food** for the army, and the others
Ruth	2.14	she was satisfied, and she still had some **food** left over.
	2.18	She also gave her the **food** left over from the meal.
1 Sam	1.18	Then she went away, ate some **food,** and was no longer sad.
	2. 5	hire themselves out to get **food,** but the hungry are hungry
	2.36	ask him for money and **food,** and beg to be allowed to
	9. 7	"There is no **food** left in our packs, and we haven't
	14.24	on anyone who eats any **food** today before I take revenge on
	14.28	said, 'A curse be on anyone who eats any **food** today.' "
	14.30	our people had eaten the **food** they took when they defeated
	17.20	of the sheep, took the **food,** and went as Jesse had told
	17.22	David left the **food** with the officer in charge of the
	22.10	then he gave David some **food** and the sword of Goliath the
	22.13	did you give him some **food** and a sword, and consult God
	28.22	Let me prepare some **food** for you.
1 Sam	28.25	She set the **food** before Saul and his officers, and they
	30.11	They gave him some **food** and water, [12] some dried figs, and
2 Sam	6.19	the name of the Lord Almighty [19] and distributed **food** to them
	9.10	Saul's family and bring in the harvest, to provide **food** for them.
	12. 3	with some of his own **food,** let it drink from his cup,
	12.20	the palace, he asked for **food** and ate it as soon as
	13. 5	want her to prepare the **food** here where I can see her,
	13. 7	"Go to Amnon's house and prepare some **food** for him."
	17.28	clay pots, and bedding, and also **food** for David and his men:
	19.32	supplied the king with **food** while he was staying at Mahanaim.
	19.42	He hasn't paid for our **food** nor has he given us anything."
1 Kgs	4. 7	They were to provide **food** from their districts for the king
	4.27	supplied the **food** King Solomon needed for himself and
	5. 9	part, I would like you to supply the **food** for my men."
	10. 5	She saw the **food** that was served at his table, the living
	11.18	gave Hadad some land and a house and provided him with **food.**
	17. 4	and I have commanded ravens to bring you **food** there."
	17.15	told her, and all of them had enough **food** for many days.
	18. 4	two groups of fifty, and provided them with **food** and water.)
	18.13	two groups of fifty, and supplied them with **food** and water?
	19. 8	ate and drank, and the **food** gave him enough strength to walk
	21.27	He refused **food,** slept in the sackcloth, and went about gloomy
2 Kgs	4.44	So the servant set the **food** before them, and, as the
	6.25	result of the siege the **food** shortage in the city was so
	7. 2	but you will never eat any of the **food,"** Elisha replied.
	7.12	leave the city to find **food,** and then they will take us
	7.19	see it happen, but you will never eat any of the **food."**
1 Chr	12.39	feasting on the **food** and drink which their fellow-countrymen had
	12.40	mules, and oxen loaded with **food**—flour, figs, raisins, wine,
	16. 3	in the name of the Lord [3] and distributed **food** to them all.
2 Chr	9. 4	She saw the **food** that was served at his table,
	11.11	he placed supplies of **food,** olive-oil, and wine,
	31.15	They distributed the **food** equally to their fellow-Levites
	31.19	responsible men who distributed the **food** to all the males in
Ezra	2.63	they could not eat the **food** offered to God until there was
	3. 7	and the carpenters and gave **food,** drink, and olive-oil
Neh	5.14	relatives nor I ate the **food** I was entitled to have as
	5.15	and had demanded forty silver coins a day for **food** and wine.
	7.65	they could not eat the **food** offered to God until there was
	8.10	Share your **food** and wine with those who haven't enough.
	9.36	that you gave us, this fertile land which gives us **food.**
	13. 2	and Moab did not give **food** and water to the Israelites on
Esth	9.19	time for feasting and giving gifts of **food** to one another.
	9.22	and parties, giving gifts of **food** to one another and to the
Job	6. 6	But who can eat tasteless, unsalted **food?**
	6. 7	I have no appetite for **food** like that, and everything I
	12.11	just as your tongue enjoys tasting **food,** your ears enjoy hearing
	20.14	But in his stomach the **food** turns bitter, as bitter as
	24. 5	poor, like wild donkeys, search for **food** in the dry wilderness;
	24. 5	nowhere else can they find **food** for their children.
	28. 5	**Food** grows out of the earth, But underneath the same earth
	31. 8	my crops be destroyed, or let others eat the **food** I grow.
	31.10	cook another man's **food** and sleep in another man's bed.
	31.39	if I have eaten the **food** that grew there but let the
	33.20	loses his appetite, and even the finest **food** looks revolting.
	34. 3	You know good **food** when you taste it, but not wise words
	36.16	your table was piled high with **food.**
	36.31	how he feeds the people and provides an abundance of **food.**
	38.39	Do you find **food** for lions to eat, and satisfy hungry
	38.41	wander about hungry, when their young cry to me for **food?**
Ps	34.10	go hungry for lack of **food,** but those who obey the Lord
	35.13	I deprived myself of **food;**
	36. 8	We feast on the abundant **food** you provide;
	37.25	man abandoned by the Lord or his children begging for **food.**
	41. 9	most, the one who shared my **food,** has turned against me.
	42. 3	Day and night I cry, and tears are my only **food;**
	50.12	would not ask you for **food,** for the world and everything in
	59.15	like dogs roaming about for **food** and growling if they do
	78.18	put God to the test by demanding the **food** they wanted.
	78.19	against God and said, "Can God supply **food** in the desert?
	78.25	So they ate the **food** of angels, and God gave them all
	102. 4	I have lost my desire for **food.**
	102. 9	and fury, ashes are my **food,** and my tears are mixed with
	104.21	lions roar while they hunt, looking for the **food** that God
	104.27	them depend on you to give them **food** when they need it.
	104.28	you provide **food,** and they are satisfied.
	105.16	Lord sent famine to their country and took away all their **food.**
	105.40	he gave them **food** from heaven to satisfy them.
	107.18	couldn't stand the sight of **food** and were close to death.
	109.24	My knees are weak from lack of **food;**
	111. 5	He provides **food** for those who honour him;
	132.15	I will satisfy her poor with **food.**
	136.25	He gives **food** to every living creature;
	145.15	hopefully to you, and you give them **food** when they need it.
	146. 7	in favour of the oppressed and gives **food** to the hungry.
	147. 9	He gives animals their **food** and feeds the young ravens when
Prov	4.17	Wickedness and violence are like **food** and drink to them.
	6. 8	but they store up their **food** during the summer, getting ready
	6.30	don't despise a thief if he steals **food** when he is hungry;
	9. 5	she says, [5] "Come, eat my **food** and drink the wine that I
	13.23	fields could yield plenty of **food** for the poor, but unjust
	19.24	Some people are too lazy to put **food** in their own mouths.
	20.17	may enjoy like the finest **food,** but sooner or later it will
	21.17	in luxuries, wine, and rich **food** will never make you wealthy.
	22. 9	Be generous and share your **food** with the poor.
	23. 3	Don't be greedy for the fine **food** he serves;
	23. 6	a stingy man or be greedy for the fine **food** he serves.
	23.20	who drink too much wine or stuff themselves with **food.**
	26.15	Some people are too lazy to put **food** in their own mouths.
	27. 7	but when you are hungry, even bitter **food** tastes sweet.
	30. 8	So give me only as much **food** as I need.

Prov 30.25 they are weak, but they store up their **food** in the summer.
31.14 She brings home **food** from out-of-the-way places, as merchant
31.15 up before daylight to prepare **food** for her family and to
Ecc 9. 7 Go ahead—eat your **food** and be happy;
12. 3 too few to chew your **food,** and your eyes too dim to
Is 3. 1 going to take away their **food** and their water, [2]their heroes
3. 7 I haven't any **food** or clothes either.
9.20 and eat any bit of **food** they can find, but their hunger
16. 7 when they remember the fine **food** they used to eat in the
21.14 You people of the land of Tema, give **food** to the refugees.
23.18 use her money to buy the **food** and the clothing they need.
25. 6 the world—a banquet of the richest **food** and the finest wine.
33.16 You will have **food** to eat and water to drink.
51.14 will live a long life and have all the **food** they need.
55. 2 what I say, and you will enjoy the best **food** of all.
55.10 the crops grow and provide seed for sowing and **food** to eat.
58. 3 Why should we go without **food** if he pays no attention?"
58. 7 Share your **food** with the hungry and open your homes to the
58.10 if you give **food** to the hungry and satisfy those who are
62. 8 corn will no longer be **food** for your enemies, And foreigners
66.17 gardens, and who eat pork and mice and other disgusting **foods.**
Jer 5.17 They will devour your crops and your **food;**
7.33 The corpses will be **food** for the birds and wild animals,
14. 6 their eyesight fails them because they have no **food.**
16. 4 and their bodies will be **food** for the birds and the wild
19. 7 their corpses to the birds and the wild animals as **food.**
31.14 the priests with the richest **food** and satisfy all the needs
31.25 and will satisfy with **food** everyone who is weak from hunger.
38. 9 of starvation, since there is no more **food** in the city."
40. 5 me a present and some **food** to take with me, and let
44.17 Then we had plenty of **food,** we were prosperous, and had no
50.19 They will eat the **food** that grows on Mount Carmel and in
Lam 1.11 exchange their treasures for **food** to keep themselves alive.
1.19 in the city streets, Looking for **food** to keep themselves alive.
3.15 suffering is all he has given me for **food** and drink.
4. 4 children are begging for **food** that no one will give them.
4. 5 People who once ate the finest **foods** die starving in the
4. 5 those raised in luxury are pawing through refuse for **food.**
4. 9 starved slowly to death, with no **food** to keep them alive.
4.10 loving mothers boiled their own children for **food.**
5. 6 To get **food** enough to stay alive, we went begging to Egypt
5. 9 we risk our lives when we look for **food.**
Ezek 4.13 Israelites will have to eat **food** which the Law forbids, when
4.14 I have never eaten any **food** considered unclean."
4.16 as they measure out the **food** they eat and the water they
5.16 I will cut off your supply of **food** and let you starve.
14.13 I will stretch out my hand and destroy its supply of **food.**
16.19 I gave you **food**—the best flour, olive-oil, and honey—
24.17 Don't cover your face or eat the **food** that mourners eat."
24.22 will not cover your faces or eat the **food** that mourners eat.
29. 5 I will give it to the birds and animals for **food.**
39. 4 will let their bodies be **food** for all the birds and wild
44.29 repayment-offerings will be the priests' **food,** and they are to
47.12 of the stream all kinds of trees will grow to provide **food.**
47.12 The trees will provide **food,** and their leaves will be used
Dan 1. 5 to be given the same **food** and wine as the members of
1. 8 ritually unclean by eating the **food** and drinking the wine of
1.13 men who are eating the **food** of the royal court, and base
1.15 stronger than all those who had been eating the royal **food.**
6.18 a sleepless night, without **food** or any form of entertainment.
10. 3 did not eat any rich **food** or any meat, drink any wine,
Hos 2. 4 my lovers—they give me **food** and water, wool and linen,
9. 3 to Egypt and will have to eat forbidden **food** in Assyria.
9. 4 food will defile everyone who eats it, like **food** eaten at funerals.
Mic 5. 8 like a lion hunting for **food** in a forest or a pasture:
Hag 1. 6 You have **food** to eat, but not enough to make you full.
2.12 robe touch any bread, cooked **food,** wine, olive-oil,
2.12 or any kind of **food** at all,
2.12 will it make that **food** consecrated also?"
2.13 touches any of these **foods,** will that make them defiled too?"
Zech 9. 7 longer eat meat with blood in it, or other forbidden **food.**
Mal 1. 7 This is how—by offering worthless **food** on my altar.
1.12 is worthless and when you offer on it **food** that you despise.
3.10 to the Temple, so that there will be plenty of **food** there.
Mt 3. 4 round his waist, and his **food** was locusts and wild honey.
4. 2 After spending forty days and nights without **food,** Jesus was hungry.
6.11 Give us today the **food** we need.
6.17 When you go without **food,** wash your face and comb your hair,
6.25 to be worried about the **food** and drink you need in order
6.25 After all, isn't life worth more than **food?**
6.31 'Where will my **food** come from?
14.15 let them go to the villages to buy **food** for themselves."
15.26 to take the children's **food** and throw it to the dogs."
15.33 "Where will we find enough **food** in this desert to feed this
24.45 other servants to give them their **food** at the proper time.
Mk 1. 6 round his waist, and his **food** was locusts and wild honey.
2.19 you expect the guests at a wedding party to go without **food?**
7. 2 his disciples were eating their **food** with hands that were
7.19 this, Jesus declared that all **foods** are fit to be eaten.)
7.27 to take the children's **food** and throw it to the dogs."
8. 4 can anyone find enough **food** to feed all these people?"
Lk 3.11 the man who has none, and whoever has **food** must share it."
5.34 a wedding party go without **food** as long as the bridegroom is
9. 3 stick, no beggar's bag, no **food,** no money, not even an extra
9.12 farms round here and find **food** and lodging, because this is
9.13 you want us to go and buy **food** for this whole crowd?"
11. 3 Give us day by day the **food** we need.
11. 6 come to my house, and I haven't got any **food** for him!'
12.22 not to worry about the **food** you need to stay alive or
12.23 is much more important than **food,** and the body much more

Lk 12.42 other servants their share of the **food** at the proper time.
16.21 to eat the bits of **food** that fell from the rich man's
Jn 4. 8 (His disciples had gone into town to buy **food.)**
4.32 But he answered, "I have **food** to eat that you know
4.33 among themselves, "Could somebody have brought him **food?"**
4.34 "My **food,"** Jesus said to them, "is to obey the will
6. 5 Philip, "Where can we buy enough **food** to feed all these people?"
6.27 Do not work for **food** that goes bad;
6.27 instead, work for the **food** that lasts for eternal life.
6.27 This is the **food** which the Son of Man will give you,
6.55 For my flesh is the real **food;**
13.18 that says, 'The man who shared my **food** turned against me.'
Acts 7.11 ancestors could not find any **food,** [12]and when Jacob heard
10.10 while the **food** was being prepared, he had a vision.
11. 8 No ritually unclean or defiled **food** has ever entered my mouth.'
12.20 country got its **food** supplies from the king's country.
14.17 he gives you **food** and fills your hearts with happiness."
15.20 them not to eat any **food** that is ritually unclean because it
15.29 eat no **food** that has been offered to idols;
16.34 Silas up into his house and gave them some **food** to eat.
21.25 they must not eat any **food** that has been offered to idols,
27.21 a long time without **food,** Paul stood before them and said,
27.33 Just before dawn, Paul begged them all to eat some **food:**
27.34 I beg you, then, eat some **food;**
27.36 They took heart, and every one of them also ate some **food.**
Rom 14. 6 of the Lord, because he gives thanks to God for the **food.**
14.14 Jesus makes me certain that no **food** is of itself ritually unclean;
14.14 a person believes that some **food** is unclean, then it becomes
14.15 Do not let the **food** that you eat ruin the person for
14.20 Do not, because of **food,** destroy what God has done.
14.20 All **foods** may be eaten, but it is wrong to eat anything
1 Cor 3. 2 you with milk, not solid **food,** because you were not ready
6.13 "Food is for the stomach, and the stomach is for **food."**
8. 1 Now, concerning what you wrote about **food** offered to idols.
8. 4 So then, about eating the **food** offered to idols:
8. 7 day when they eat such **food**
8. 7 they still think of it as **food** that belongs to an idol;
8. 7 is weak, and they feel they are defiled by the **food.**
8. 8 **Food,** however, will not improve our relations with God;
8.10 will not this encourage him to eat **food** offered to idols?
8.13 So then, if **food** makes my brother sin, I will never eat
9. 4 I the right to be given **food** and drink for my work?
9.13 in the Temple get their **food** from the Temple and that those
10.19 that an idol or the **food** offered to it really amounts to
10.28 someone says to you, "This **food** was offered to idols,"
10.28 then do not eat that **food,** for the sake of the one
10.30 I thank God for my **food,** why should anyone criticize me
10.30 anyone criticize me about **food** for which I give thanks?"
2 Cor 6. 5 we have been overworked and have gone without sleep or **food.**
11.27 I have often been without enough **food,** shelter, or clothing.
1 Tim 4. 3 teach that it is wrong to marry and to eat certain **foods.**
4. 3 But God created those **foods** to be eaten, after a prayer of
6. 8 So then, if we have **food** and clothes, that should be
Heb 5.12 Instead of eating solid **food,** you still have to drink milk.
5.14 Solid **food,** on the other hand, is for adults, who
9.10 only with **food,** drink, and various purification ceremonies.
13. 9 from God's grace, and not by obeying rules about **foods;**
Rev 2.14 by persuading them to eat **food** that had been offered to
2.20 immorality and eating **food** that has been offered to idols.

FOOD-OFFERING

Ex 29.18 Burn the whole ram on the altar as a **food offering.**
29.25 on top of the burnt-offering, as a **food-offering** to me.
29.41 This is a **food offering** to me, the Lord, and its odour
30.20 the Tent or approach the altar to offer the **food offering.**
Lev 1. 9 The smell of this **food-offering** is pleasing to the Lord.
1.13 The smell of this **food-offering** is pleasing to the Lord.
1.17 The smell of this **food-offering** is pleasing to the Lord.
2. 2 The smell of this **food-offering** is pleasing to the Lord.
2. 9 The smell of this **food-offering** is pleasing to the Lord.
2.16 and also all the incense, as a **food-offering** to the Lord.
3. 3 following parts of the animal as a **food-offering** to the Lord:
3. 5 The smell of this **food-offering** is pleasing to the Lord.
3. 9 following parts of the animal as a **food-offering** to the Lord:
3.11 burn all this on the altar as a **food-offering** to the Lord.
3.14 present the following parts as a **food-offering** to the Lord:
3.16 this on the altar as a **food-offering** pleasing to the Lord.
4.35 the altar along with the **food-offerings** given to the Lord.
5.12 Lord, and he will burn it on the altar as a **food-offering.**
6.16 given it to the priests as their part of the **food-offerings.**
6.18 Anyone else who touches a **food-offering** will be harmed by the
7. 5 all the fat on the altar as a **food-offering** to the Lord.
7.25 may be offered as a **food-offering** to the Lord will no longer
7.30 Lord, [30]bringing it with his own hands as a **food-offering.**
8.20 This burnt-offering was a **food-offering,** and the smell was
8.28 This was a **food-offering,** and the smell was pleasing to the Lord.
10.15 time the fat is presented as a **food-offering** to the Lord.
21. 6 He offers **food-offerings** to me, and he must be holy.
21. 8 consider the priest holy, because he presents the **food-offerings**
21.17 who has any physical defect may present the **food-offering** to me.
21.21 priest who has any physical defect may present the **food-offering**
21.22 both the holy **food-offering** and the very holy food-offering,
22.22 Do not offer any such animals on the altar as a **food-offering.**
22.25 Do not offer as a **food-offering** any animal obtained from a
22.26 days, but after that it is acceptable as a **food-offering.**
23. 8 Offer your **food-offerings** to the Lord for seven days.
23.13 two kilogrammes of flour mixed with olive-oil as a **food-offering.**
23.25 Present a **food-offering** to the Lord and do none of your
23.26 together for worship, and present a **food-offering** to the Lord.
23.36 Each day for seven days you shall present a **food-offering.**

Lev	23.36	come together again for worship and present a **food-offering.**
	23.37	together for worship and presenting **food-offerings,**
	24. 7	each row, as a token **food-offering** to the Lord to take the
Num	15. 3	the smell of these **food-offerings** is pleasing to the Lord.
	15.13	when he presents a **food-offering,** a smell pleasing to the Lord.
	15.14	a permanent basis, makes a **food-offering,** a smell that pleases
	15.25	they brought their sin-offering as a **food-offering** to the Lord.
	18.17	burn their fat as a **food-offering,** a smell pleasing to me.
	28. 2	at the appointed times the required **food-offerings** that are
	28. 3	are the **food-offerings** that are to be presented to the Lord:
	28. 6	Mount Sinai as a **food-offering,** a smell pleasing to the Lord.
	28. 8	It also is a **food-offering,** a smell pleasing to the Lord.
	28.13	These burnt-offerings are **food-offerings,** a smell pleasing to
	28.19	Offer a burnt-offering as a **food-offering** to the Lord:
	28.24	offer to the Lord a **food-offering,** a smell pleasing to him.
	29. 6	These **food-offerings** are a smell pleasing to the Lord.
	29.13	first day offer a **food-offering** to the Lord, a smell pleasing
	29.36	Offer a burnt-offering as a **food-offering** to the Lord,

FOOL

see also **FOLLY**

Gen	31.28	That was a **foolish** thing to do!
Ex	10. 2	grandchildren how I made **fools** of the Egyptians when I performed
	32.25	out of control and make **fools** of themselves in front of
Num	12.11	do not make us suffer this punishment for our **foolish** sin.
	22.29	Balaam answered, "Because you have made a **fool** of me!
Deut	32. 6	the way you should treat the Lord, you **foolish,** senseless people?
	32.21	I will make them jealous with a nation of **fools.**
Judg	16.10	"Look, you've been making a **fool** of me and not telling me
	16.13	Samson, "You're still making a **fool** of me and not telling
	16.15	You've made a **fool** of me three times, and you still haven't
1 Sam	6. 6	Don't forget how God made **fools** of them until they let the
	13.13	"That was a **foolish** thing to do," Samuel answered.
	25.25	He is exactly what his name means—a **fool!**
	26.21	I have been a **fool!**
2 Sam	3.33	"Why did Abner have to die like a **fool?**
	6.20	exposed himself like a **fool** in the sight of the servant-girls
	24.10	I have acted **foolishly."**
2 Kgs	18.32	Don't let Hezekiah **fool** you into thinking that the Lord will
1 Chr	21. 8	I have acted **foolishly."**
2 Chr	16. 9	You have acted **foolishly,** and so from now on you will always
Job	5. 2	with resentment would be a **foolish,** senseless thing to do.
	5. 3	I have seen **fools** who looked secure, but I called down a
	5. 5	Hungry people will eat the **fool's** crops— even the grain
	12.17	away the wisdom of rulers and makes leaders act like **fools.**
	12.24	He makes their leaders **foolish** and lets them wander confused
	13. 9	Do you think you can **fool** God as you fool men?
	15.31	If he is **foolish** enough to trust in evil, then evil will
	26. 3	good advice and share your knowledge with a **fool** like me!
	39.17	was I who made her **foolish** and did not give her wisdom.
	40. 3	I spoke **foolishly,** Lord.
Ps	11. 1	How **foolish** of you to say to me, "Fly away like a
	14. 1	**Fools** say to themselves, "There is no God."
	38. 5	Because I have been **foolish,** my sores stink and rot.
	39. 8	me from all my sins, and don't let **fools** laugh at me.
	49.10	that even wise men die, as well as **foolish** and stupid men.
	53. 1	**Fools** say to themselves, "There is no God."
	69. 5	you know how **foolish** I have been.
	85. 8	own people, if we do not go back to our **foolish** ways.
	92. 6	This is something a **fool** cannot know;
	94. 8	My people, how can you be such stupid **fools?**
	107.17	Some were **fools,** suffering because of their sins and because
Prov	1.22	**"Foolish** people!
	1.22	How long do you want to be **foolish?**
	7. 7	saw many inexperienced young men, but noticed one **foolish** fellow
	8. 5	Are you **foolish?**
	9. 4	And to the **foolish** man she says, [5] "Come, eat my food and
	9.16	To the **foolish** man she says, [17] "Stolen water is sweeter.
	10. 1	a **foolish** one brings his mother grief.
	10. 8	People who talk **foolishly** will come to ruin.
	10.14	they can, but when **fools** speak, trouble is not far off.
	10.18	Anyone who spreads gossip is a **fool.**
	10.23	It is **foolish** to enjoy doing wrong.
	11.12	It is **foolish** to speak scornfully of others.
	11.29	**Foolish** men will always be servants to the wise.
	12.16	When a **fool** is annoyed, he quickly lets it be known.
	14. 1	by the wisdom of women, but are destroyed by **foolishness.**
	14. 3	A **fool's** pride makes him talk too much;
	14. 7	Stay away from **foolish** people;
	14. 8	Why is a stupid person **foolish?**
	14. 9	**Foolish** people don't care if they sin, but good people
	14.15	A **fool** will believe anything;
	14.17	People with a hot temper do **foolish** things;
	14.18	Ignorant people get what their **foolishness** deserves,
	14.24	are rewarded with wealth, but fools are known by their **foolishness.**
	14.33	**fools** know nothing about wisdom.
	15. 5	It is **foolish** to ignore what your father taught you;
	15. 7	Knowledge is spread by people who are wise, not by **fools.**
	15.20	Only a **fool** despises his mother.
	15.21	people are happy with their **foolishness,** but the wise will do
	17. 7	do not tell lies, and **fools** have nothing worthwhile to say.
	17.10	from one rebuke than a **fool** learns from being beaten a
	17.12	her cubs than to meet some **fool** busy with a stupid project.
	17.16	It does a **fool** no good to spend money on an education,
	17.21	sadness and sorrow for a father whose son does **foolish** things.
	17.24	at wise action, but a **fool** starts off in many directions.
	17.25	A **foolish** son brings grief to his father and bitter regrets
Prov	17.28	After all, even a **fool** may be thought wise and intelligent
	18. 2	A **fool** does not care whether he understands a thing or not;
	18. 6	When some **fool** starts an argument, he is asking for a beating.
	18. 7	When a **fool** speaks, he is ruining himself;
	19. 1	better to be poor but honest than to be a lying **fool.**
	19.10	**Fools** should not live in luxury, and slaves should not rule
	19.29	A conceited **fool** is sure to get a beating.
	20. 1	Drinking too much makes you loud and **foolish.**
	20. 3	Any **fool** can start arguments;
	23. 9	Don't try to talk sense to a **fool;**
	24. 9	Any scheme a **fool** thinks up is sinful.
	26. 1	Praise for a **fool** is out of place, like snow in summer
	26. 3	have to bridle a donkey, and you have to beat a **fool.**
	26. 6	If you let a **fool** deliver a message, you might as well
	26. 7	A **fool** can use a proverb about as well as a crippled
	26. 9	A **fool** quoting a wise saying reminds you of a drunk man
	26.10	An employer who hires any **fool** that comes along is only
	26.11	A **fool** doing some stupid thing a second time is like a
	26.12	The most stupid **fool** is better off than someone who thinks
	27.22	Even if you beat a **fool** until he's half dead,
	27.22	you still can't beat his **foolishness** out of him.
	28.26	It is **foolish** to follow your own opinions.
	29. 3	It is a **foolish** waste to spend money on prostitutes.
	29. 9	brings a lawsuit against a **fool,** the fool only laughs
	29.20	more hope for a stupid **fool** than for someone who speaks
	30.22	a **fool** who has all he wants to eat,
	30.32	you have been **foolish** enough to be arrogant and plan evil,
Ecc	1.17	to learn the difference between knowledge and **foolishness,**
	2. 2	I discovered that laughter is **foolish,** that pleasure does you
	2.12	about what it meant to be wise or reckless or **foolish.**
	2.13	"Wisdom is better than **foolishness,** just as light is better
	2.14	Wise men can see where they are going, and **fools** cannot."
	2.15	I thought to myself, "I will suffer the same fate as **fools.**
	2.16	No one remembers wise men, and no one remembers **fools.**
	2.16	We must all die—wise and **foolish** alike.
	2.19	and he might be wise, or he might be **foolish**—who knows?
	4. 5	a man would be a **fool** to fold his hands and let
	4.13	old age he is too **foolish** to take advice, he is not
	5. 1	to offer sacrifices as **foolish** people do, people who don't know
	5. 3	you talk, the more likely you are to say something **foolish.**
	5. 4	He has no use for a **fool.**
	6. 8	How is a wise man better off than a **fool?**
	7. 4	Someone who is always thinking about happiness is a **fool.**
	7. 6	When a **fool** laughs, it is like thorns crackling in a fire.
	7. 7	When a wise man cheats someone, he is acting like a **fool.**
	7. 9	it is **foolish** to harbour a grudge.
	7.17	be too wicked or too **foolish,** either—why die before you have
	7.25	my questions, and to learn how wicked and **foolish** stupidity is.
	9.17	than to the shouts of a ruler at a council of **fools.**
	10. 2	the right thing and for a **fool** to do the wrong thing.
	10. 3	he lets everyone know that he is a **fool.**
	10.12	brings him honour, but a **fool** is destroyed by his own words.
	10.14	A **fool** talks on and on.
Is	19.11	The leaders of the city of Zoan are **fools!**
	19.13	The leaders of Zoan and Memphis are **fools.**
	29.14	will turn out to be **fools,** and all their cleverness will be
	29.24	**Foolish** people will learn to understand, and those who are
	32. 5	one will think that a **fool** is honourable or say that a
	32. 6	A **fool** speaks foolishly and thinks up evil things to do.
	35. 8	no **fools** will mislead those who follow it.
	36.18	Don't let Hezekiah **fool** you into thinking that the Lord will
	44.20	His **foolish** ideas have so misled him that he is beyond help.
	44.25	I make **fools** of fortune-tellers and frustrate the predictions
	44.25	wise I refute and show that their wisdom is **foolishness.**
Jer	4.22	They are like **foolish** children;
	5. 4	They behave **foolishly;**
	5.21	Pay attention, you **foolish** and stupid people, who have eyes,
	10. 8	All of them are stupid and **foolish.**
	17.11	his riches, and in the end he is nothing but a **fool.**
	50.36	Death to its lying prophets— what **fools** they are!
	50.38	of terrifying idols, that have made **fools** of the people.
Ezek	13. 3	"These **foolish** prophets are doomed!
	28.17	of being handsome, and your fame made you act like a **fool.**
Hos	7. 5	made the king and his officials drunk and **foolish** with wine.
	9. 7	"This prophet," you say, "is a **fool.**
	13.13	to live, but is too **foolish** to take it—like a child
Mic	7. 6	sons treat their fathers like **fools,** daughters oppose their
Mt	5.22	calls his brother a worthless **fool** will be in danger of
	7.26	obey them is like a **foolish** man who built his house on
	23.17	Blind **fools!**
	25. 2	Five of them were **foolish,** and the other five were wise.
	25. 3	The **foolish** ones took their lamps but did not take any
	25. 8	Then the **foolish** ones said to the wise ones, 'Let us have
	25.10	So the **foolish** girls went off to buy some oil;
Lk	11.40	**Fools!**
	12.20	But God said to him, 'You **fool!**
	24.25	Jesus said to them, "How **foolish** you are, how slow you are
Jn	7.47	"Did he **fool** you, too?"
	11.49	Caiaphas, who was High Priest that year, said, "What **fools** you are!
Rom	1.22	They say they are wise, but they are **fools;**
	2.20	an instructor for the **foolish,** and a teacher for the ignorant.
	10.19	means of a nation of **fools** I will make my people angry."
1 Cor	1.20	God has shown that this world's wisdom is **foolishness!**
	1.21	by means of the so-called **"foolish"** message we preach, God
	1.25	seems to be God's **foolishness** is wiser than human wisdom,
	3.18	No one should **fool** himself.
	3.18	he should become a **fool,** in order to be really wise.
	4.10	For Christ's sake we are **fools;**
	6. 9	Do not **fool** yourselves;
	15.33	Do not be **fooled.**

1 Cor	15.36	You **fool!**
2 Cor	11. 1	wish you would tolerate me, even when I am a bit **foolish.**
	11.16	no one should think that I am a **fool.**
	11.16	least accept me as a **fool,** so that I will have a
	11.17	in this matter of boasting I am really talking like a **fool.**
	11.19	You yourselves are so wise, and so you gladly tolerate **fools!**
	11.21	I am talking like a **fool**—I will be just as daring.
	12. 6	I would not be a **fool,** because I would be telling the
	12.11	I am acting like a **fool**—but you have made me do
Gal	3. 1	You **foolish** Galatians!
	3. 3	How can you be so **foolish!**
	6. 7	no one makes a **fool** of God.
Eph	5. 6	Do not let anyone deceive you with **foolish** words;
	5.17	Don't be **fools,** then, but try to find out what the Lord
1 Tim	1. 6	from these and have lost their way in **foolish** discussions.
	6. 9	in the trap of many **foolish** and harmful desires, which pull
	6.20	Avoid the profane talk and **foolish** arguments of what some
2 Tim	2.16	Keep away from profane and **foolish** discussions, which
	2.23	But keep away from **foolish** and ignorant arguments;
Tit	3. 3	For we ourselves were once **foolish,** disobedient, and
Jas	2.20	You **fool!**
1 Pet	2.15	silence the ignorant talk of **foolish** people by the good

FOOT

[FEET, FOUR-FOOTED]
see also **UNDERFOOT**

Gen	18. 4	Let me bring some water for you to wash your **feet;**
	19. 2	You can wash your **feet** and stay the night.
	24.32	water for Abraham's servant and his men to wash their **feet.**
	41.44	so much as lift a hand or a **foot** without your permission."
	43.24	that they could wash their **feet,** and he fed their donkeys.
Ex	4.25	off the foreskin of her son, and touched Moses' **feet** with
	12.11	with your sandals on your **feet** and your stick in your hand.
	12.37	The Israelites set out on **foot** from Rameses for Sukkoth.
	19. 1	set up camp at the **foot** of Mount Sinai, [3] and Moses went
	19.12	If anyone sets **foot** on it, he is to be put to
	19.17	to meet God, and they stood at the **foot** of the mountain.
	21.24	hand for hand, foot for **foot,** [25] burn for burn,
	23. 5	under its load, help him get the donkey to its **feet** again;
	24. 4	built an altar at the **foot** of the mountain and set up
	24.10	Beneath his **feet** was what looked like a pavement of sapphire,
	29.20	their right hands and on the big toes of their right **feet.**
	30.19	to wash their hands and **feet** [20] before they go into the
	30.21	must wash their hands and **feet,** so that they will not die.
	32.19	There at the **foot** of the mountain, he threw down the tablets
	34. 3	sheep or cattle are to graze at the **foot** of the mountain."
	37. 3	attached them to its four **feet,** with two rings on each side.
	40.31	washed their hands and their **feet** there [32] whenever they
Lev	8.23	his right hand, and on the big toe of his right **foot.**
	8.24	their right hands, and on the big toes of their right **feet.**
	11.24	and they chew the cud, and all **four-footed** animals with paws.
	13.12	the person from head to **foot,** [13] the priest shall examine him
	14.14	big toe of the right **foot** of the man who is to
	14.17	big toe of the right **foot** of the man who is to
	14.25	his right hand, and on the big toe of his right **foot.**
	14.28	his right hand, and on the big toe of his right **foot.**
	21.19	no one with a crippled hand or **foot;**
Num	22.25	moved over against the wall and crushed Balaam's **foot** against it.
Deut	3.17	the south and to the **foot** of Mount Pisgah on the east.
	4.11	went and stood at the **foot** of the mountain which was covered
	4.49	as the Dead Sea and east to the **foot** of Mount Pisgah.
	8. 4	clothes have not worn out, nor have your **feet** swollen up.
	19.21	a hand for a hand, and a foot for a **foot.**
	22. 4	help him to get the animal to its **feet** again.
	28.35	boils will cover you from head to **foot.**
	33. 3	So we bow at his **feet** and obey his commands.
Josh	3.13	all the earth put their **feet** in the water, the Jordan will
	10.24	to come and put their **feet** on the necks of the kings.
	11. 3	Hivites who lived at the **foot** of Mount Hermon in the land
	12. 3	of the Dead Sea) and on towards the **foot** of Mount Pisgah.
	18.16	then went down to the **foot** of the mountain that overlooks
Judg	4.15	Sisera got down from his chariot and fled on **foot.**
	5.27	sank to his knees, fell down and lay still at her **feet.**
	5.27	At her **feet** he sank to his knees and fell;
	19.21	His guests washed their **feet** and had a meal.
Ruth	3. 4	asleep, go and lift the covers and lie down at his **feet.**
	3. 7	over quietly, lifted the covers and lay down at his **feet.**
	3. 8	over, and was surprised to find a woman lying at his **feet.**
	3.14	she lay there at his **feet,** but she got up before it
1 Sam	25.24	on the ground [24] at David's **feet,** and said to him,
	25.41	"I am his servant, ready to wash the **feet** of his servants."
2 Sam	3.34	His hands were not tied, And his **feet** were not bound;
	4.12	cut off their hands and **feet,** which they hung up near the
	9.13	who was crippled in both **feet,** lived in Jerusalem, eating
	14.25	he had no defect from head to **foot.**
	19.24	He had not washed his **feet,** trimmed his beard, or washed his
	21.20	had six fingers on each hand and six toes on each **foot.**
	22.10	sky apart and came down, with a dark cloud under his **feet.**
1 Kgs	15.23	But in his old age he was crippled by a **foot** disease.
2 Kgs	4.27	Elisha she bowed down before him and took hold of his **feet.**
	4.37	She fell at Elisha's **feet,** with her face touching the ground;
	9.35	except her skull, and the bones of her hands and **feet.**
	13. 7	and ten thousand men on **foot,** because the king of Syria had
	19.24	foreign lands and that the **feet** of your soldiers tramped the
1 Chr	20. 6	with six fingers on each hand and six toes on each **foot.**
2 Chr	16.12	that Asa was king, he was crippled by a severe **foot** disease;
Neh	9.21	never wore out, and their **feet** were not swollen with pain.
Esth	8. 3	to the king again, throwing herself at his **feet** and crying.
Job	13.27	You bind chains on my **feet;**
	18. 8	He walks into a net, and his **feet** are caught;
Job	28. 4	where anyone lives Or human **feet** ever travel, Men dig the
	29.15	I was eyes for the blind, and **feet** for the lame.
	33.11	He binds chains on my **feet;**
	39.15	She is unaware that a **foot** may crush them or a wild
Ps	18. 9	sky apart and came down with a dark cloud under his **feet.**
	22.16	they tear at my hands and **feet.**
	45. 5	nations fall down at your **feet.**
	66. 6	our ancestors crossed the river on **foot.**
	91.12	hands to keep you from hurting your **feet** on the stones.
	105.18	His **feet** were kept in chains, and an iron collar was
	110. 1	at my right until I put your enemies under your **feet."**
	115. 7	They have hands, but cannot feel, and **feet,** but cannot walk;
Prov	6.16	**feet** that hurry off to do evil,
	6.28	Can you walk on hot coals without burning your **feet?**
	25.19	to chew with a loose tooth or walk with a crippled **foot.**
	26. 6	deliver a message, you might as well cut off your own **feet;**
Ecc	10. 7	seen slaves on horseback while noblemen go on **foot** like slaves.
Song	5. 3	I have washed my **feet;**
	7. 1	How beautiful are your **feet** in sandals.
Is	1. 6	From head to **foot** there is not a healthy spot on your
	26. 6	oppressed walk over it now and trample it under their **feet.**
	37.25	foreign lands, and that the **feet** of your soldiers tramped
	60.14	All who once despised you will worship at your **feet.**
Jer	2.25	Israel, don't wear your **feet** out, or let your throat
	38.22	And now that his **feet** have sunk in the mud, his friends
Ezek	2. 2	and raised me to my **feet,** and I heard the voice continue,
	3.24	but God's spirit entered me and raised me to my **feet.**
	6.11	Stamp your **feet!**
	32. 2	You muddy the water with your **feet** and pollute the rivers.
Dan	2.33	legs of iron, and its **feet** partly of iron and partly of
	2.34	the iron and clay **feet** of the statue, and shattered them.
	2.41	You also saw that the **feet** and the toes were partly clay
	3.24	Suddenly Nebuchadnezzar leapt to his **feet** in amazement.
	8. 5	west, moving so fast that his **feet** didn't touch the ground.
	8.18	me, raised me to my **feet,** [19] and said, "I am showing you
Nah	1. 3	the clouds are the dust raised by his **feet!**
Hab	3.16	My body goes limp, and my **feet** stumble beneath me.
Mal	4. 3	the wicked, and they will be like dust under your **feet.**
Mt	4. 6	so that not even your **feet** will be hurt on the stones.' "
	5.35	nor by earth, for it is the resting place for his **feet;**
	10.14	then leave that place and shake the dust off your **feet.**
	15.25	At this the woman came and fell at his **feet.**
	15.30	and many other sick people, whom they placed at Jesus' **feet;**
	18. 8	"If your hand or your **foot** makes you lose your faith, cut
	18. 8	without a hand or a **foot** than to keep both hands
	18. 8	and both **feet** and be thrown into the eternal
	22.13	'Tie him up hand and **foot,** and throw him outside in the
	22.44	here on my right until I put your enemies under your **feet.'**
	28. 9	came up to him, took hold of his **feet,** and worshipped him.
Mk	5. 4	many times his **feet** and hands had been chained, but every
	5. 4	he broke the chains and smashed the irons on his **feet.**
	5.22	threw himself down at his **feet** [23] and begged him earnestly,
	5.33	with fear, knelt at his **feet,** and told him the whole truth.
	6.11	listen to you, leave it and shake the dust off your **feet.**
	7.25	Jesus and came to him at once and fell at his **feet.**
	9.45	And if your **foot** makes you lose your faith, cut it off!
	9.45	to enter life without a **foot**
	9.45	than to keep both **feet** and be thrown into hell.
	12.36	here on my right until I put your enemies under your **feet.'**
Lk	4.11	so that not even your **feet** will be hurt on the stones.' "
	7.38	stood behind Jesus, by his **feet,**
	7.38	crying and wetting his **feet** with her tears.
	7.38	Then she dried his **feet** with her hair, kissed them, and
	7.44	me no water for my **feet,**
	7.44	but she has washed my **feet** with her tears and dried them
	7.45	but she has not stopped kissing my **feet** since I came.
	7.46	for my head, but she has covered my **feet** with perfume.
	8.28	threw himself down at his **feet,** and shouted, "Jesus, Son of
	8.29	a prisoner, his hands and **feet** fastened with chains, he
	8.35	gone out sitting at the **feet** of Jesus, clothed and in his
	8.41	threw himself down at Jesus' **feet** and begged him to go to
	8.47	so she came trembling and threw herself at Jesus' **feet.**
	9. 5	and shake the dust off your **feet** as a warning to them."
	10.11	that sticks to our **feet** we wipe off against you.
	10.39	who sat down at the **feet** of the Lord and listened to
	15.22	Put a ring on his finger and shoes on his **feet.**
	17.16	He threw himself to the ground at Jesus' **feet** and thanked him.
	20.43	until I put your enemies as a footstool under your **feet.'**
	24.39	at my hands and my **feet,** and see that it is I
	24.40	He said this and showed them his hands and his **feet.**
Jn	11. 2	the perfume on the Lord's **feet** and wiped them with her hair;
	11.32	and as soon as she saw him, she fell at his **feet.**
	11.44	came out, his hands and **feet** wrapped in grave clothes,
	12. 3	poured it on Jesus' **feet,** and wiped them with her hair.
	13. 5	began to wash the disciples' **feet** and dry them with the
	13. 6	who said to him, "Are you going to wash my **feet,** Lord?"
	13. 8	Peter declared, "Never at any time will you wash my **feet!"**
	13. 8	I do not wash your **feet,"** Jesus answered, "you will no
	13. 9	Simon Peter answered, "Lord, do not wash only my **feet,**
	13.10	and does not have to wash himself, except for his **feet.**
	13.12	After Jesus had washed their **feet,** he put his outer
	13.14	I, your Lord and Teacher, have just washed your **feet.**
	13.14	You, then, should wash one another's **feet.**
	20.12	had been, one at the head and the other at the **feet.**
Acts	2.35	until I put your enemies as a footstool under your **feet.'**
	3. 7	At once the man's **feet** and ankles became strong;
	3. 8	he jumped up, stood on his **feet,** and started walking around.
	5.10	At once she fell down at his **feet** and died.
	10.25	Cornelius met him, fell at his **feet,** and bowed down before him.
	13.25	I am not good enough to take his sandals off his **feet.'**
	13.51	shook the dust off their **feet** in protest against them and

Acts 14.10 and said in a loud voice, "Stand up straight on your **feet!**"
16.24 cell and fastened their **feet** between heavy blocks of wood.
16.29 rushed in, and fell trembling at the **feet** of Paul and Silas.
21.11 belt, tied up his own **feet** and hands with it, and said,
26.16 But get up and stand on your **feet.**
Rom 16.20 God, our source of peace, will soon crush Satan under your **feet.**
1 Cor 12.15 If the **foot** were to say, "Because I am not a hand,
12.21 can the head say to the **feet,** "Well, I don't need you!"
15.25 until God defeats all enemies and puts them under his **feet.**
15.27 For the scripture says, "God put all things under his **feet.**"
Eph 1.22 put all things under Christ's **feet** and gave him to the
Heb 1.13 until I put your enemies as a footstool under your **feet.**"
10.13 until God puts his enemies as a footstool under his **feet.**
12.13 paths, so that the lame **foot** may not be disabled, but
Jas 2. 3 on the floor by my **feet,**" [4]then you are guilty of creating
Rev 1.13 robe that reached to his **feet,** and a gold belt round his
1.15 his **feet** shone like brass that has been refined and polished,
1.17 saw him, I fell down at his **feet** like a dead man.
2.18 God, whose eyes blaze like fire, whose **feet** shine like polished brass.
3. 9 not, I will make them come and bow down at your **feet.**
10. 2 He put his right **foot** on the sea
10. 2 and his left **foot** on the land, [3]and called out
12. 1 had the moon under her **feet** and a crown of twelve stars
13. 2 looked like a leopard, with **feet** like a bear's feet
19.10 I fell down at his **feet** to worship him, but he said
22. 8 I fell down at the **feet** of the angel who had shown

FOOT-SOLDIERS see SOLDIER

FOOTHILLS

Josh 9. 1 in the hills, in the **foothills,** and all along the coastal
10.40 eastern slopes, and the western **foothills,** as well as those of
11. 2 Lake Galilee, in the **foothills,** and on the coast near Dor.
11.16 the land—the hill-country and **foothills,** both north and south,
12. 8 the western **foothills,** the Jordan Valley and its foothills,
15.33 The cities in the **foothills** were Eshtaol, Zorah, Ashnah,
Judg 1. 9 in the hill-country, in the **foothills,** and in the dry country
1 Kgs 10.27 was as plentiful as ordinary sycomore in the **foothills** of Judah.
1 Chr 27.25 Olives and sycomore-trees (in the western **foothills):**
2 Chr 9.27 was as plentiful as ordinary sycomore in the **foothills** of Judah.
26.10 had large herds of livestock in the western **foothills** and plains.
28.18 raiding the towns in the western **foothills** and in southern Judah.
Jer 17.26 territory of Benjamin, from the **foothills,** from the mountains,
32.44 in the hill-country, in the **foothills,** and in southern Judah.
33.13 of the hill-country, in the **foothills,** and in southern Judah,
Obad 19 those from the western **foothills** will capture Philistia;
Zech 7. 7 also in the southern region and in the western **foothills.**

FOOTPRINT

Job 13.27 you watch every step I take, and even examine my **footprints.**
Ps 77.19 crossed the deep sea, but your **footprints** could not be seen.

FOOTSTEP

Ezek 16.47 content to follow in their **footsteps** and copy their disgusting
23.31 You followed in your sister's **footsteps,** and so I will give

FOOTSTOOL

1 Chr 28. 2 for the Covenant Box, the **footstool** of the Lord our God.
2 Chr 9.18 and there was a **footstool** attached to it, covered with gold.
Is 66. 1 Lord says, "Heaven is my throne, and the earth is my **footstool.**
Lk 20.43 until I put your enemies as a **footstool** under your feet.'
Acts 2.35 until I put your enemies as a **footstool** under your feet.'
7.49 is my throne, says the Lord, and the earth is my **footstool.**
Heb 1.13 until I put your enemies as a **footstool** under your feet."
10.13 until God puts his enemies as a **footstool** under his feet.

FOR EVER see EVER

FORBID

Gen 9. 4 I **forbid** this because the life is in the blood.
Ex 30. 9 offer on this altar any **forbidden** incense, any animal-offering,
Num 30. 5 But if her father **forbids** her to fulfil the vow when he
30. 8 But if her husband **forbids** her to fulfil the vow when he
30.12 But if her husband **forbids** her to fulfil the vow when he
Deut 22. 9 if you do, you are **forbidden** to use either the grapes or
29.26 gods that the Lord had **forbidden** them to worship.
31.29 have made the Lord angry by doing what he has **forbidden."**
Judg 13. 4 not to drink any wine or beer, or eat any **forbidden** food;
13. 7 or beer, or eat any **forbidden** food, because the boy is to
13.14 must not drink any wine or beer, or eat any **forbidden** food.
1 Sam 12.23 As for me, the Lord **forbid** that I should sin against him
20. 2 Jonathan answered, "God **forbid** that you should die!
26.11 The Lord **forbid** that I should try to harm the one whom
1 Kgs 21. 3 "The Lord **forbid** that I should let you have it!"
1 Chr 28. 3 honour him, [3]but he has **forbidden** me to do it, because I
Ezra 7.24 You are **forbidden** to collect any taxes from the priests,
Is 5. 6 I will even **forbid** the clouds to let rain fall on it."
52.11 Touch no **forbidden** thing;
Lam 1.10 the Temple itself, Where the Lord had **forbidden** Gentiles to go.
Ezek 4.13 food which the Law **forbids,** when I scatter them to foreign
18. 6 or eat the sacrifices offered at **forbidden** shrines.
18.11 He eats sacrifices offered at **forbidden** shrines and seduces
18.15 or eat the sacrifices offered at **forbidden** shrines.
Hos 9. 3 to Egypt and will have to eat **forbidden** food in Assyria.
Jon 3. 7 persons, cattle, and sheep are **forbidden** to eat or drink.
Zech 9. 7 longer eat meat with blood in it, or other **forbidden** food.
Mt 16.22 "God **forbid** it, Lord!"
1 Cor 14.39 God's message, but do not **forbid** the speaking in strange tongues.

FORCE (1)

Gen 47.20 Every Egyptian was **forced** to sell his land, because the famine
49.15 to carry the load And is **forced** to work as a slave.
Ex 1.13 made their lives miserable by **forcing** them into cruel slavery.
2.11 Hebrews, and he saw how they were **forced** to do hard labour.
3.19 will not let you go unless he is **forced** to do so.
5.13 slave-drivers kept trying to **force** them to make the same number
6. 1 I will **force** him to let my people go.
6. 1 In fact, I will **force** him to drive them out of his
Lev 25.25 Israelite becomes poor and is **forced** to sell his land,
26.25 you, and you will be **forced** to surrender to your enemies.
Deut 20.11 are all to become your slaves and do **forced labour** for you.
21.14 Since you **forced** her to have intercourse with you, you cannot
22.29 become his wife, because he **forced** her to have intercourse
26. 6 Egyptians treated us harshly and **forced** us to work as slaves.
Josh 7. 4 Israelites made the attack, but they were **forced** to retreat.
16.10 to this day, but they have been **forced** to work as slaves.
17.13 the Canaanites, but they did **force** them to work for them.
Judg 1.28 Israelites became stronger, they **forced** the Canaanites to work
1.30 to live there with them and were **forced** to work for them.
1.33 with the local Canaanites, but **forced** them to work for them.
1.34 The Amorites **forced** the people of the tribe of Dan into
1.35 them under their rule and **forced** them to work for them.
11. 2 and when they grew up, they **forced** Jephthah to leave home.
11. 7 me so much that you **forced** me to leave my father's house.
21.21 you take a wife by **force** from among the girls and take
1 Sam 2.16 If you don't, I will have to take it by **force!"**
28. 3 Saul had **forced** all the fortune-tellers and mediums to leave
28. 9 how he **forced** the fortune-tellers and mediums to leave
2 Sam 2.22 Why **force** me to kill you?
12.31 and iron axes, and **forced** them to work at making bricks.
13.12 "Don't **force** me to do such a degrading thing!
20.24 Adoniram was in charge of the **forced labour;**
23.16 famous soldiers **forced** their way through the Philistine camp,
1 Kgs 4. 6 Ahishar In charge of the **forced labour:**
5.13 Solomon drafted 30,000 men as **forced labour** from all over Israel,
9.15 King Solomon used **forced labour** to build the Temple
9.17 Using his **forced labour,** Solomon also rebuilt Lower Beth Horon,
9.20 For his **forced labour** Solomon used the descendants of
9.23 officials in charge of the **forced labour** working on Solomon's
11.28 in charge of all the **forced labour** in the territory of the
12.18 was in charge of the **forced labour,** to go to the Israelites,
2 Kgs 3.26 with him and tried to **force** his way through the enemy lines
15.20 rich men of Israel by **forcing** each one to contribute fifty
24. 1 for three years Jehoiakim was **forced** to submit to his rule;
1 Chr 8. 6 in Geba, but which were **forced** out and went to live in
11.18 famous soldiers **forced** their way through the Philistine camp,
2 Chr 8. 7 Solomon employed in **forced labour** all the descendants of
8. 9 Israelites were not used in **forced labour,** but served as
8.10 officials in charge of the **forced labour** working on the various
10.18 was in charge of the **forced labour,** to go to the Israelites,
12. 7 will not feel the full **force** of my anger, [8]but Shishak will
13. 7 of worthless scoundrels, and they **forced** their will on Rehoboam
19.10 and your fellow-citizens will feel the **force** of the Lord's anger.
26.20 king's forehead in horror, and then **forced** him to leave the
27. 5 Then he **forced** the Ammonites to pay him the following tribute
36.13 King Nebuchadnezzar, who had **forced** him to swear in God's name
Ezra 4.23 they hurried to Jerusalem and **forced** the Jews to stop rebuilding
Neh 5. 8 Now you are **forcing** your own brothers to sell themselves to you,
13.21 If you try this again, I'll use **force** against you."
Esth 10. 1 Xerxes imposed **forced labour** on the people of the coastal regions
Job 7. 1 Human life is like **forced** army service, like a life of
9.19 Should I try **force?**
9.19 Try **force** on God?
24. 4 getting their rights and **force** the needy to run and hide.
34.28 They **forced** the poor to cry out to God, and he heard
Is 14. 3 suffering, and from the hard work they were **forced** to do.
30.30 hear his majestic voice and feel the **force** of his anger.
30.31 hear the Lord's voice and feel the **force** of his punishment.
42.25 he made us feel the **force** of his anger and suffer the
51.20 They have felt the **force** of God's anger.
52. 4 Assyria, however, took you away by **force** and paid nothing
Jer 21. 2 one of his miracles for us and **force** Nebuchadnezzar to retreat."
22.26 I am going to **force** you and your mother into exile.
34.11 took them back, and **forced** them to become slaves again.
34.16 as they desired, and you **forced** them into slavery again.
Lam 1. 3 Judah's people are helpless slaves, **forced** away from home.
2. 6 King and priest alike have felt the **force** of his anger.
3. 6 He has **forced** me to live in the stagnant darkness of death.
4.11 The Lord turned loose the full **force** of his fury;
5.11 every Judaean village our daughters have been **forced** to submit.
5.13 Our young men are **forced** to grind corn like slaves;
Ezek 3.14 came on me with great **force,** and as his spirit carried me
5.13 "You will feel all the **force** of my anger and rage until
6.12 They will feel all the **force** of my anger.
7. 8 "Very soon now you will feel all the **force** of my anger.
8.18 They will feel all the **force** of my anger.
13.15 covered it with whitewash will feel the **force** of my anger.
16.34 No one **forced** you to become one.
20. 8 let them feel the full **force** of my anger there in Egypt.
20.13 to let them feel the **force** of my anger there in the
20.21 to let them feel the **force** of my anger there in the
22.10 **force** women to have intercourse with them during their period.

Ezek 24.13 pure again until you have felt the full **force** of my anger.
28.16 So I **forced** you to leave my holy mountain, and the angel
36.18 I let them feel the **force** of my anger because of the
Dan 8. 6 beside the river, and rushed at him with all his **force.**
11. 9 Syria will invade Egypt, but he will be **forced** to retreat.
Mic 5. 6 By **force** of arms they will conquer Assyria, the land of Nimrod,
Hab 2. 6 you go on getting rich by **forcing** your debtors to pay up?"
2. 7 will be in debt yourselves and be **forced** to pay interest.
Zeph 3. 8 kingdoms, in order to let them feel the **force** of my anger.
Mt 5.41 one of the occupation troops **forces** you to carry his pack
27.32 Cyrene named Simon, and the soldiers **forced** him to carry Jesus'
Mk 15.21 the country, and the soldiers **forced** him to carry Jesus'
Lk 3.14 "Don't take money from anyone by **force** or accuse anyone falsely.
16.16 Kingdom of God is being told, and everyone **forces** his way in.
Jn 6.15 come and seize him in order to make him king by **force;**
Acts 5.26 They did not use **force,** however, because they were afraid
7.19 and was cruel to them, **forcing** them to put their babies out
28.19 Jews opposed this, I was **forced** to appeal to the Emperor,
1 Cor 7.37 if a man, without being **forced** to do so, has firmly made
2 Cor 10. 2 I beg you [2]not to **force** me to be harsh when I
Gal 2. 3 he is Greek, was not **forced** to be circumcised, [4]although
2.14 How, then, can you try to **force** Gentiles to live like Jews?"
6.12 people who are trying to **force** you to be circumcised are the
Phil 2. 6 did not think that by **force** he should try to become equal
Col 2.23 in their **forced** worship of angels, and false humility,
Phlm 14 However, I do not want to **force** you to help me;
Rev 13.12 It **forced** the earth and all who live on it to worship
13.16 The beast **forced** all the people, small and great, rich

FORCE (2)

Gen 14. 3 formed an alliance and joined **forces** in the Valley of Siddim,
Josh 9. 2 all came together and joined **forces** to fight against Joshua
10. 5 Jarmuth, Lachish, and Eglon, joined **forces,** surrounded Gibeon,
10. 6 kings in the hill-country have joined **forces** and have attacked
11. 5 these kings joined **forces** and came together and set up camp
1 Sam 15. 4 Saul called his **forces** together and inspected them at Telem:
23. 3 worse if we go to Keilah and attack the Philistine **forces!"**
2 Sam 3. 1 The fighting between the **forces** supporting Saul's family and
3. 6 continued between David's **forces** and the forces loyal to Saul's
11.17 The enemy troops came out of the city and fought Joab's **forces;**
12.28 gather the rest of your **forces,** attack the city and take it
12.29 So David gathered his **forces,** went to Rabbah, attacked it,
1 Kgs 10.26 Solomon built up a **force** of fourteen hundred chariots
20.14 "Who will command the main **force?"**
20.22 back and build up your **forces,** and make careful plans, because
2 Kgs 3.11 officer of King Joram's **forces** answered, "Elisha son of Shaphat
5. 1 through Naaman the Lord had given victory to the Syrian **forces.**
6.14 in Dothan, [14]he sent a large **force** there with horses and
13. 7 Jehoahaz had no armed **forces** left except fifty horsemen,
15.25 officer of Pekahiah's **forces,** Pekah son of Remaliah, plotted
1 Chr 12.22 day new men joined David's **forces,** so that his army was soon
2 Chr 1.14 He built up a **force** of fourteen hundred chariots and twelve
Is 8. 7 the emperor of Assyria and all his **forces** to attack Judah.
36. 2 with a large military **force** to demand that King Hezekiah should
Jer 41.13 and the leaders of the **forces** with him, they were glad,
41.16 and the leaders of the **forces** with him took charge of the
Mic 5. 1 People of Jerusalem, gather your **forces!**
Zech 12. 3 All the nations of the world will join **forces** to attack her.
Eph 6.12 against the wicked spiritual **forces** in the heavenly world,
2 Pet 2.20 have escaped from the corrupting **forces** of the world through

FOREHEAD

Ex 13. 9 like something tied on your hand or on your **forehead;**
13.16 like something tied on our hands or on our **foreheads;**
28.38 to wear it on his **forehead,** so that I, the Lord, will
Deut 6. 8 on your arms and wear them on your **foreheads** as a reminder.
11.18 on your arms and wear them on your **foreheads** as a reminder.
1 Sam 17.49 It hit him on the **forehead** and broke his skull, and Goliath
2 Chr 26.19 and immediately a dreaded skin-disease broke out on his **forehead.**
26.20 priests stared at the king's **forehead** in horror, and then forced
Ezek 9. 4 put a mark on the **forehead** of everyone who is distressed
9. 6 But don't touch anyone who has the mark on his **forehead.**
Mt 23. 5 which they wear on their **foreheads** and arms, and notice how
Rev 7. 3 the servants of our God with a seal on their **foreheads."**
7. 4 who were marked with God's seal on their **foreheads** was 144,000.
9. 4 who did not have the mark of God's seal on their **foreheads.**
13.16 a mark placed on their right hands or on their **foreheads.**
14. 1 his name and his Father's name written on their **foreheads.**
14. 9 receives the mark on his **forehead** or on his hand [10]will
17. 5 On her **forehead** was written a name that has a secret meaning:
20. 4 the mark of the beast on their **foreheads** or their hands.
22. 4 his face, and his name will be written on their **foreheads.**

FOREIGN

Gen 15.13 "Your descendants will be strangers in a **foreign** land;
15.14 when they leave that **foreign** land, they will take great wealth
17. 8 your descendants this land in which you are now a **foreigner.**
17.11 slaves born in your homes and slaves bought from **foreigners.**
19. 9 But they said, "Get out of our way, you **foreigner!**
20.13 from my father's house into **foreign** lands, I said to her,
23. 4 Hittites, and said, [4]"I am a **foreigner** living here among you;
27.46 to Isaac, "I am sick and tired of Esau's **foreign** wives.
31.15 He treats us like **foreigners.**
35. 2 were with him, "Get rid of the **foreign** gods that you have;
35. 4 they gave Jacob all the **foreign** gods that they had and also
Ex 2.22 to himself, "I am a **foreigner** in this land, and so I
6. 4 of Canaan, the land in which they had lived as **foreigners.**
12.19 if anyone, native-born or **foreign,** eats bread made with yeast,
Ex 12.43 No **foreigner** shall eat the Passover meal, [44]but any slave that
12.48 a **foreigner** has settled among you and wants to celebrate Passover
12.49 regulations apply to native-born Israelites and to **foreigners**
18. 3 (Moses had said, "I have been a **foreigner** in a strange land";
20.10 your animals, nor the **foreigners** who live in your country.
21. 8 cannot sell her to **foreigners,** because he has treated her unfairly.
22.21 "Do not ill-treat or oppress a **foreigner;**
22.21 remember that you were **foreigners** in Egypt.
23. 9 "Do not ill-treat a **foreigner;**
23. 9 to be a **foreigner,** because you were foreigners in Egypt.
23.12 that your slaves and the **foreigners** who work for you and
34.16 Your sons might marry those **foreign** women, who would lead
Lev 16.29 the Israelites and the **foreigners** living among them must fast
17. 8 Israelite or any **foreigner** living in the community who offers a
17.10 any Israelite or any **foreigner** living in the community eats meat
17.12 that neither they nor any **foreigner** living among them shall eat
17.13 any Israelite or any **foreigner** living in the community hunts
17.15 Israelite or **foreigner,** who eats meat from an animal that
18.26 whether Israelites or **foreigners** living with you, must keep
19.10 leave them for poor people and **foreigners.**
19.33 "Do not ill-treat **foreigners** who are living in your land.
19.34 Remember that you were once **foreigners** in the land of Egypt.
20. 2 "Any of you or any **foreigner** living among you who gives any
22.18 or any **foreigner** living in Israel presents a burnt-offering,
22.25 not offer as a food-offering any animal obtained from a **foreigner.**
23.22 leave them for poor people and **foreigners.**
24.16 Israelite or any **foreigner** living in Israel who curses the Lord
24.22 to Israelites and to **foreigners** living among you, because I am
25. 6 slaves, your hired men, the **foreigners** living with you,
25.23 and you are like **foreigners** who are allowed to make use
25.45 buy the children of the **foreigners** who are living among you.
25.47 Suppose a **foreigner** living with you becomes rich,
25.47 as a slave to that **foreigner** or to a member of his
26.33 I will bring war on you and scatter you in **foreign** lands.
Num 9.14 "If a **foreigner** living among you wants to keep the Passover,
9.14 The same law applies to everyone, whether native or **foreigner."**
11. 4 There were some **foreigners** travelling with the Israelites.
15.14 if at any time a **foreigner** living among you, whether on a
15.15 are binding on you and on the **foreigners** who live among you.
15.26 of Israel and the **foreigners** living among them will be forgiven,
15.29 whether he is a native Israelite or a resident **foreigner.**
15.30 is a native or a **foreigner,** is guilty of treating the Lord
19.10 for the Israelites and for the **foreigners** living among them.
35.15 refuge for Israelites and for **foreigners** who are temporary or
Deut 1.16 concerns only your own people or involves **foreigners** who live
5.14 your animals, nor the **foreigners** who live in your country.
10.18 he loves the **foreigners** who live with our people, and gives
10.19 for those foreigners, because you were once **foreigners** in Egypt.
14.21 You may let the **foreigners** who live among you eat it,
14.21 or you may sell it to other **foreigners.**
14.29 and for the **foreigners,** orphans, and widows who live in
15. 3 You may collect what a **foreigner** owes you, but you must
16.11 and the Levites, **foreigners,** orphans, and widows who live in
16.14 and the Levites, **foreigners,** orphans, and widows who live in
17.15 do not make a **foreigner** your king.
23.20 what you lend to a **foreigner,** but not on what you lend
24.14 a fellow-Israelite or a **foreigner** living in one of your towns.
24.17 "Do not deprive **foreigners** and orphans of their rights;
24.19 to be left for the **foreigners,** orphans, and widows, so that
24.20 they are for the **foreigners,** orphans, and widows.
24.21 grapes that are left are for the **foreigners,** orphans, and widows.
26.11 let the Levites and the **foreigners** who live among you join
26.12 crops—to the Levites, the **foreigners,** the orphans,
26.13 it to the Levites, the **foreigners,** the orphans, and the widows,
27.19 who deprives **foreigners,** orphans, and widows of their rights.'
28.32 daughters will be given as slaves to **foreigners** while you look
28.33 A **foreign** nation will take all the crops that you have
28.36 your king away to a **foreign** land, where neither you nor your
28.43 **"Foreigners** who live in your land will gain more and more
29.11 women, and children, and the **foreigners** who live among you
29.22 your descendants and **foreigners** from distant lands will see the
29.28 threw them into a **foreign** land, and there they are today.'
31.12 women, and children, and the **foreigners** who live in your towns,
32.12 Lord alone led his people without the help of a **foreign** god.
33.19 They invite **foreigners** to their mountain And offer the right
Josh 8.33 judges, as well as the **foreigners** among them, stood on two
8.35 women and children, as well as the **foreigners** living among them.
20. 9 the people of Israel and for any **foreigner** living among them.
24.20 you leave him to serve **foreign** gods, he will turn against
24.23 "Then get rid of those **foreign** gods that you have,"
Judg 10.16 they got rid of their **foreign** gods and worshipped the Lord;
Ruth 2. 6 man answered, "She is the **foreign** girl who came back from
2.10 Why should you be so kind to a **foreigner?"**
1 Sam 7. 3 get rid of all the **foreign** gods and the images of the
26.19 Lord's land to a country where I can only worship **foreign** gods.
26.20 Don't let me be killed on **foreign** soil, away from the Lord.
2 Sam 15.19 You are a **foreigner,** a refugee away from your own country.
22.45 **Foreigners** bow before me;
1 Kgs 8.41 "When a **foreigner** who lives in a distant land hears
11. 1 Solomon loved many **foreign** women.
11. 4 was old they had led him into the worship of **foreign** gods.
11. 8 where all his **foreign** wives could burn incense and offer
11. 9 commanded him not to worship **foreign** gods, Solomon did not obey
11.33 because Solomon has rejected me and has worshipped **foreign** gods:
2 Kgs 19.24 wells and drank water in **foreign** lands and that the feet of
1 Chr 22. 2 gave orders for all the **foreigners** living in the land of
2 Chr 2.17 a census of all the **foreigners** living in the land of Israel,
2.17 There were 153,600 resident **foreigners.**

2 Chr 6.32 “When a **foreigner** who lives in a distant land hears how
14. 3 He removed the **foreign** altars and the pagan places of worship,
25.15 “Why have you worshipped **foreign** gods that could not even save
28.25 of worship, where incense was to be burnt to **foreign** gods.
30.25 and the **foreigners** who had settled permanently in Israel
33.15 removed from the Temple the **foreign** gods and the image that
Ezra 9. 2 Jewish men were marrying **foreign** women, and so God's holy
9. 7 into the hands of **foreign** kings, and we have been slaughtered,
10. 2 faith with God by marrying **foreign** women, but even so there
10.10 and have brought guilt on Israel by marrying **foreign** women.
10.11 Separate yourselves from the **foreigners** living in our land
10.11 and get rid of your **foreign** wives.”
10.14 let anyone who has a **foreign** wife come at a set time,
10.17 they investigated all the cases of men with **foreign** wives.
10.18 This is the list of the men who had **foreign** wives:
10.44 All these men had **foreign** wives.
Neh 1. 3 and that the **foreigners** who lived near by looked down
4. 4 have, and let them be taken as prisoners to a **foreign** land.
5. 8 back our Jewish brothers who had to sell themselves to **foreigners.**
9. 1 They had already separated themselves from all **foreigners.**
10.28 separated themselves from the **foreigners** living in our land,
10.30 will not intermarry with the **foreigners** living in our land.
10.31 If **foreigners** bring corn or anything else to sell to us
13. 3 Israel heard this law read, they excluded all **foreigners** from
13.25 never again would they or their children intermarry with **foreigners.**
13.26 I said, “It was **foreign** women that made King Solomon sin.
13.27 your example and disobey our God by marrying **foreign** women?”
13.30 I purified the people from everything **foreign;**
Job 15.19 Their land was free from **foreigners;**
19.15 my servant-girls treat me like a stranger and a **foreigner.**
Ps 18.44 **Foreigners** bow before me;
44.11 you scattered us in **foreign** countries.
44.20 prayed to a **foreign** god, [21] you would surely have discovered
69. 8 a stranger to my brothers, like a **foreigner** to my family.
106.27 among the heathen, letting them die in **foreign** countries.
107. 3 has brought you back from **foreign** countries, from east and west,
111. 6 power to his people by giving them the lands of **foreigners.**
114. 1 when Jacob's descendants left that **foreign** land, [2] Judah became
137. 4 can we sing a song to the Lord in a **foreign** land?
144. 7 me from the power of **foreigners,** [8] who never tell the truth
144.11 me from the power of **foreigners,** who never tell the truth
Ecc 11. 1 Invest your money in **foreign** trade, and one of these days
Is 1. 7 While you look on, **foreigners** take over your land and bring
2. 6 The people follow **foreign** customs.
9. 1 and even to Galilee itself, where the **foreigners** live.
13.14 **foreigners** living in Babylon will run away to their own countries,
14. 1 their own land again, and **foreigners** will come and live there
17.10 you plant sacred gardens in order to worship a **foreign** god.
28.11 God will use **foreigners** speaking some strange-sounding language
29. 5 Jerusalem, all the **foreigners** who attack you will be blown
33.18 Your old fears of **foreign** tax-collectors and spies will be
33.19 no longer see any arrogant **foreigners** who speak a language that
37.25 wells and drank water in **foreign** lands, and that the feet of
43.12 No **foreign** god has ever done this;
52. 4 to live in Egypt as **foreigners,** you did so of your own
55. 5 Now you will summon **foreign** nations;
56. 3 A **foreigner** who has joined the Lord's people should not say,
56. 6 Lord says to those **foreigners** who become part of his people,
56. 9 Lord has told the **foreign** nations to come like wild animals
60.10 Lord says to Jerusalem, **“Foreigners** will rebuild your walls,
61. 5 My people, **foreigners** will serve you.
62. 8 for your enemies, And **foreigners** will no longer drink your wine.
Jer 2.25 I have loved **foreign** gods and will go after them.’ ”
3.13 have given your love to **foreign** gods and that you have not
5.19 away from me and served **foreign** gods in their own land, so
8.19 your idols and by bowing down to your useless **foreign** gods?”
12.10 Many **foreign** rulers have destroyed my vineyard;
22. 3 Do not ill-treat or oppress **foreigners,** orphans, or widows;
22. 8 “Afterwards many **foreigners** will pass by and ask one another
25.19 all the Egyptians and all the **foreigners** in Egypt;
30. 8 chains, and they will no longer be the slaves of **foreigners.**
50.16 Every **foreigner** living there will be afraid of the attacking
51. 2 I will send **foreigners** to destroy Babylonia like a wind that
51. 9 **Foreigners** living there said, ‘We tried to help Babylonia,
51.51 helpless because **foreigners** have taken over the holy places
Lam 4.12 not even rulers of **foreign** nations, believed that any invader
5. 2 **foreigners** are living in our homes.
Ezek 3. 5 a nation that speaks a difficult **foreign** language,
4.13 the Law forbids, when I scatter them to **foreign** countries.”
7.21 “I will let **foreigners** rob them,” says the Lord,
11. 9 take you out of the city and hand you over to **foreigners.**
12.15 the other nations and in **foreign** countries, they will know that
14. 7 or one of the **foreigners** who live in the Israelite community
22. 7 You cheat **foreigners** and take advantage of widows and orphans.
22.29 They ill-treat the poor and take advantage of **foreigners.**
28.10 You will die like a dog at the hand of godless **foreigners.**
30.12 **Foreigners** will devastate the whole country.
31.11 I have rejected it and will let a **foreign** ruler have it.
31.12 Ruthless **foreigners** will cut it down and leave it.
34.13 will take them out of **foreign** countries, gather them together,
36.19 lived and acted, and I scattered them through **foreign** countries.
44. 7 my Temple by letting uncircumcised **foreigners,** people who
44. 8 rituals in my Temple, but instead have put **foreigners** in charge.
44. 9 declare that no uncircumcised **foreigner,** no one who disobeys me,
44. 9 my Temple, not even a **foreigner** who lives among the people
47.22 **foreigners** who are living among you and who have had children
47.23 Each **foreign** resident will receive his share with the people
Dan 11.18 But a **foreign** leader will defeat him and put an end to
11.39 his fortresses, he will use people who worship a **foreign** god.
Hos 7. 9 this reliance on **foreigners** has robbed them of their strength.
8. 7 But even if it did, **foreigners** would eat it up.
8.12 for the people, but they reject them as strange and **foreign.**
9. 4 In those **foreign** lands they will not be able to make
Joel 3. 2 have scattered the Israelites in **foreign** countries and divided
3.17 **foreigners** will never conquer it again.
Amos 6.14 I am going to send a **foreign** army to occupy your country.
Zeph 1. 8 the king's sons, and all who practise **foreign** customs.
Zech 7.10 Do not oppress widows, orphans, **foreigners** who live among
7.14 Like a storm I swept them away to live in **foreign** countries.
8.13 In the past **foreigners** have cursed one another by saying,
8.13 save you, and then those **foreigners** will say to one another,
8.23 In those days ten **foreigners** will come to one Jew and say,
10. 3 “I am angry with those **foreigners** who rule my people, and I
Mal 2.11 Men have married women who worship **foreign** gods.
3. 5 advantage of widows, orphans, and **foreigners**—against all who
Mt 17.25 The citizens of the country or the **foreigners?”**
17.26 “The **foreigners,”** answered Peter.
27. 7 money to buy Potter's Field, as a cemetery for **foreigners.**
Lk 17.18 Why is this **foreigner** the only one who came back to give
Acts 7. 6 descendants will live in a **foreign** country, where they will
13.17 nation during the time they lived as **foreigners** in Egypt.
17.18 Others answered, “He seems to be talking about **foreign** gods.”
17.21 citizens of Athens and the **foreigners** who lived there liked
26.11 them that I even went to **foreign** cities to persecute them.
1 Cor 14.11 a foreigner to me and I will be a **foreigner** to him.
14.21 will speak through lips of **foreigners,** but even then my
Eph 2.12 You were **foreigners** and did not belong to God's chosen people.
2.19 So then, you Gentiles are not **foreigners** or strangers any longer;
Heb 11. 9 faith he lived as a **foreigner** in the country that God had
11.13 openly that they were **foreigners** and refugees on earth.
11.34 were mighty in battle and defeated the armies of **foreigners.**

FOREMAN

Ex 5. 6 king commanded the Egyptian slave-drivers and the Israelite **foremen:**
5.10 The slave-drivers and the Israelite **foremen** went out and
5.14 Egyptian slave-drivers beat the Israelite **foremen,** whom they had
5.15 Then the **foremen** went to the king and complained,
5.19 The **foremen** realized that they were in trouble when they
1 Kgs 5.16 and he placed 3,300 **foremen** in charge of them to supervise
Mt 20. 8 came, the owner told his **foreman,** ‘Call the workers and pay

FORESEE

Num 23.21 I **foresee** that Israel's future Will bring her no misfortune
Ezek 7.26 You will beg the prophets to reveal what they **foresee.**

FORESKIN

Ex 4.25 stone, cut off the **foreskin** of her son, and touched Moses'
1 Sam 18.25 for the bride is the **foreskins** of a hundred dead Philistines,
18.27 He took their **foreskins** to the king and counted them all out
2 Sam 3.14 I paid a hundred Philistine **foreskins** in order to marry her.”

FOREST

Deut 19. 5 two men go into the **forest** together to cut wood and if,
Josh 17.15 then go into the **forests** and clear ground for yourselves in
17.18 Even though it is a **forest,** you will clear it and take
1 Sam 22. 5 So David left and went to the **forest** of Hereth.
2 Sam 18. 6 countryside and fought the Israelites in the **forest** of Ephraim.
18. 8 and more men died in the **forest** than were killed in battle.
18.17 a deep pit in the **forest,** and covered it with a huge
1 Kgs 7. 2 The Hall of the **Forest** of Lebanon was 44 metres long,
10.17 these shields placed in the Hall of the **Forest** of Lebanon.
10.21 in the Hall of the **Forest** of Lebanon were of pure gold.
2 Kgs 19.23 and that you reached the deepest parts of the **forests.**
2 Chr 9.16 had them all placed in the Hall of the **Forest** of Lebanon.
9.20 in the Hall of the **Forest** of Lebanon were of pure gold.
27. 4 built cities, and in the **forests** he built forts and towers.
Neh 2. 8 Asaph, keeper of the royal **forests,** instructing him to supply
Ps 50.10 all the animals in the **forest** are mine and the cattle on
83.14 As fire burns the **forest,** as flames set the hills on fire,
148. 9 Praise him, hills and mountains, fruit-trees and **forests;**
Song 2. 3 among the trees of the **forest,** so is my dearest compared
Is 9.18 It burns like a **forest** fire that sends up columns of smoke.
10.18 The rich **forests** and farmlands will be totally destroyed,
10.34 in the heart of the **forest** are cut down with an axe,
29.17 forest will become farmland, and the farmland will go back to **forest.**
32.19 hail will fall on the **forests,** and the city will be torn
33. 9 The **forests** of Lebanon have withered, the fertile valley of
37.24 and that you reached the deepest parts of the **forests.**
40.16 All the animals in the **forests** of Lebanon are not enough
41.19 **Forests** will grow in barren land, forests of pine and juniper
44.14 to use, or choose oak or cypress wood from the **forest.**
44.23 Shout for joy, mountains, and every tree of the **forest!**
60.13 The finest wood from the **forests** of Lebanon, Will be brought
Jer 4.29 Some will run to the **forest,** others will climb up among the
5. 6 That is why lions from the **forest** will kill them;
10. 3 A tree is cut down in the **forest;**
12. 8 like a lion in the **forest** they have roared at me, and
26.18 a pile of ruins, and the Temple hill will become a **forest.’**
46.23 like men cutting down trees [23] and destroying a thick **forest.**
Ezek 15. 2 branch of a grapevine compared with the trees of the **forest?**
15. 6 vine is taken from the **forest** and burnt, so I will take
20.46 against the south and prophesy against the **forest** of the south.
20.47 Tell the southern **forest** to hear what the Sovereign Lord is
31. 4 growing And sent streams to all the trees of the **forest.**

Ezek 31.15 Lebanon Mountains and make all the trees of the **forest** wither.
34.25 can live safely in the fields and sleep in the **forests.**
39.10 cut down trees in the **forest,** because they will have the
Amos 3. 4 a lion roar in the **forest** unless he has found a victim?
Mic 3.12 a pile of ruins, and the Temple hill will become a **forest.**
5. 8 like a lion hunting for food in a **forest** or a pasture:
Hab 2.17 You have cut down the **forests** of Lebanon;
Zech 11. 2 wail, oaks of Bashan— the dense **forest** has been cut down!
11. 3 their **forest** home along the Jordan is destroyed!
12. 6 like a fire in a **forest** or in a field of ripe
Jas 3. 5 Just think how large a **forest** can be set on fire by

FORETELL

Ex 9.35 just as the Lord had **foretold** through Moses, the king would
1 Kgs 16.34 As the Lord had **foretold** through Joshua son of Nun, Hiel
2 Kgs 24.13 As the Lord had **foretold,** Nebuchadnezzar broke up all the gold
2 Chr 36.21 the Lord had **foretold** through the prophet Jeremiah was fulfilled:
Is 43. 9 Which of them **foretold** what is happening now?
46.10 long ago I **foretold** what would happen.
48. 6 "All I **foretold** has now taken place;

FORGE

Is 54.16 the blacksmith, who builds a fire and **forges** weapons.

FORGET

Gen 8. 1 God had not **forgotten** Noah and all the animals with him in
27.45 cools down [45] and he **forgets** what you have done to him.
40.23 never gave Joseph another thought—he **forgot** all about him.
41.30 the good years will be **forgotten,** because the famine will ruin
41.31 of plenty will be entirely **forgotten,** because the famine which
41.51 said, "God has made me **forget** all my sufferings and all my
Deut 4. 9 certain that you do not **forget,** as long as you live, what
4.23 certain that you do not **forget** the covenant that the Lord
4.31 you, and he will not **forget** the covenant that he himself
4.39 So remember today and never **forget:**
6. 6 Never **forget** these commands that I am giving you today.
6.12 certain that you do not **forget** the Lord who rescued you from
7.24 You will kill them, and they will be **forgotten.**
8.11 "Make certain that you do not **forget** the Lord your God;
8.14 do not become proud and **forget** the Lord your God who rescued
8.19 Never **forget** the Lord your God or turn to other gods to
9. 7 "Never **forget** how you made the Lord your God angry in
16.12 do not **forget** that you were slaves in Egypt.
24.22 Never **forget** that you were slaves in Egypt;
25.19 Do not **forget!**
26.13 have not disobeyed or **forgotten** any of your commands concerning
32.18 They **forgot** their God, their mighty saviour,
Judg 2.10 died, and the next generation **forgot** the Lord and what he
3. 7 The people of Israel **forgot** the Lord their God;
1 Sam 1.11 Don't **forget** me!
6. 6 Don't **forget** how God made fools of them until they let the
12. 9 But the people **forgot** the Lord their God, and so he let
24.21 and my family's name will not be completely **forgotten."**
25.31 the Lord has blessed you, sir, please do not **forget** me."
2 Sam 19.19 "Your Majesty, please **forget** the wrong I did that day
19.43 Don't **forget** that we were the first to talk about bringing
2 Kgs 13.23 He has never **forgotten** his people.
17.38 and you shall not **forget** the covenant I made with you.
1 Chr 16.15 Never **forget** God's covenant, which he made to last for ever,
2 Chr 24.22 king **forgot** about the loyal service that Zechariah's father
Neh 4. 5 evil they do and don't **forget** their sins, for they have
9.17 they **forgot** all you did;
9.17 they **forgot** the miracles you had performed.
Job 7. 9 he is **forgotten** by all who knew him.
8.13 their hope is gone, once God is **forgotten.**
9.27 I smile and try to **forget** my pain, all my suffering comes
19.15 Those who were guests in my house have **forgotten** me;
41. 8 you'll never **forget** the fight!
Ps 9. 6 have destroyed their cities, and they are completely **forgotten.**
9.12 he does not **forget** their cry, and he punishes those who
13. 1 How much longer will you **forget** me, Lord?
31.12 Everyone has **forgotten** me, as though I were dead;
34.16 do evil, so that when they die, they are soon **forgotten.**
40.17 am weak and poor, O Lord, but you have not **forgotten** me.
41. 5 They want me to die and be **forgotten.**
42. 9 To God, my defender, I say, "Why have you **forgotten** me?
44.17 even though we have not **forgotten** you or broken the covenant
44.24 Don't **forget** our suffering and trouble!
45.10 to what I say— **forget** your people and your relatives.
59.11 Do not kill them, O God, or my people may **forget.**
69.33 to those in need and does not **forget** his people in prison.
72.17 May the king's name never be **forgotten;**
74.19 don't **forget** your persecuted people!
74.23 Don't **forget** the angry shouts of your enemies,
77. 9 Has God **forgotten** to be merciful?
78. 7 trust in God and not **forget** what he has done, but always
78.11 They **forgot** what he had done, the miracles they had seen
78.42 They **forgot** his great power and the day when he saved
83. 4 us destroy their nation, so that Israel will be **forgotten**
88. 5 those you have **forgotten** completely, who are beyond your help.
88.12 of darkness or your goodness in the land of the **forgotten?**
89.50 Don't **forget** how I, your servant, am insulted, how I endure
103. 2 the Lord, my soul, and do not **forget** how kind he is.
106. 7 they **forgot** the many times he showed them his love, and
106.13 But they quickly **forgot** what he had done and acted without
106.21 They **forgot** the God who had saved them by his mighty
109.13 and may his name be **forgotten** in the next generation.
Ps 109.15 but may they themselves be completely **forgotten!**
111. 4 The Lord does not let us **forget** his wonderful actions;
111. 5 he never **forgets** his covenant.
119.16 your commands I will not **forget.**
119.61 laid a trap for me, but I do not **forget** your law.
119.83 yet I have not **forgotten** your commands.
119.109 I have not **forgotten** your law.
132. 1 Lord, do not **forget** David and all the hardships he endured.
136.23 He did not **forget** us when we were defeated;
137. 5 be able to play the harp again if I **forget** you, Jerusalem!
Prov 2. 1 you, my son, and never **forget** what I tell you to do.
2.17 is faithless to her own husband and **forgets** her sacred vows.
3. 1 Don't **forget** what I teach you, my son.
4. 4 He would say, "Remember what I say and never **forget** it.
4. 5 Do not **forget** or ignore what I say.
5. 7 listen to me, my sons, and never **forget** what I am saying.
6.20 you, my son, and never **forget** what your mother taught you.
7. 1 say, my son, and never **forget** what I tell you to do.
10. 7 as a blessing, but the wicked will soon be **forgotten.**
27.10 Do not **forget** your friends or your father's friends.
31. 5 When they drink, they **forget** the laws and ignore the
31. 7 Let them drink and **forget** their poverty and unhappiness.
Ecc 2.16 In days to come, we will all be **forgotten.**
6. 4 it disappears into darkness, where it is **forgotten.**
9. 5 they are completely **forgotten.**
Is 17.10 Israel, you have **forgotten** the God who rescues you and who
23.15 coming when Tyre will be **forgotten** for seventy years,
23.16 Take your harp, go round the town, you poor **forgotten** whore!
44.21 created you to be my servant, and I will never **forget** you.
49.14 He has **forgotten** us."
49.15 "Can a woman **forget** her own baby and not love the child
49.15 a mother should forget her child, I will never **forget** you.
49.16 Jerusalem, I can never **forget** you!
51.13 Have you **forgotten** the Lord who made you, who stretched out
54. 4 You will **forget** your unfaithfulness as a young wife, and your
56. 5 You will never be **forgotten."**
57.11 afraid, so that you tell me lies and **forget** me completely?
62. 6 the Lord of his promises And never let him **forget** them.
65.16 The troubles of the past will be gone and **forgotten."**
65.17 The events of the past will be completely **forgotten.**
Jer 2.32 Does a young woman **forget** her jewellery, or a bride her
2.32 But my people have **forgotten** me for more days than can be
3.21 have lived sinful lives and have **forgotten** the Lord their God.
13.25 because you have **forgotten** him and have trusted in false
18.15 Yet my people have **forgotten** me;
20. 9 when I say, "I will **forget** the Lord and no longer speak
20.11 Their disgrace will never be **forgotten.**
20.14 **Forget** the day my mother gave me birth!
23.27 forget me, just as their fathers **forgot** me and turned to Baal.
23.40 everlasting shame and disgrace that will never be **forgotten."**
30.14 All your lovers have **forgotten** you;
44. 9 Have you **forgotten** all the wicked things that have been done
44.21 the Lord did not know about them or that he **forgot** them?
50. 6 and they have **forgotten** where their home is.
Lam 3.17 I have **forgotten** what health and peace and happiness are.
Ezek 16.43 You have **forgotten** how I treated you when you were young,
22.12 They have **forgotten** me."
23.35 "Because you **forgot** me and turned your back on me, you will
39.26 they will be able to **forget** how they were disgraced for
Hos 2.13 for the times that she **forgot** me when she burnt incense to
8.14 have built palaces, but they have **forgotten** their own Maker.
13. 6 full and satisfied, and then you grew proud and **forgot** me.
Amos 8. 7 God of Israel, has sworn, "I will never **forget** their evil deeds.
Zeph 3. 7 that they would never **forget** the lesson I taught them.
Mt 16. 5 the other side of the lake, they **forgot** to take any bread.
16.24 come with me, he must **forget** self, carry his cross, and
Mk 8.14 The disciples had **forgotten** to bring enough bread and
8.34 he told them, "he must **forget** self, carry his cross, and
Lk 9.23 come with me, he must **forget** self, take up his cross every
9.44 said to his disciples, [44] "Don't **forget** what I am about to
12. 6 Yet not one sparrow is **forgotten** by God.
Jn 16.21 the baby is born, she **forgets** her suffering, because she is
1 Cor 2. 2 made up my mind to **forget** everything except Jesus Christ and
Phil 3.13 I do, however, is to **forget** what is behind me and do
Col 4.18 Do not **forget** my chains!
Heb 6.10 He will not **forget** the work you did or the love you
12. 5 Have you **forgotten** the encouraging words which God speaks
13.16 Do not **forget** to do good and to help one another,
Jas 1.24 and then goes away and at once **forgets** what he looks like.
1.25 not simply listen and then **forget** it, but puts it into
2 Pet 1. 9 he cannot see and has **forgotten** that he has been purified
3. 8 But do not **forget** one thing, my dear friends!

FORGIVE

Gen 18.27 "Please **forgive** my boldness in continuing to speak to you,
18.31 Abraham said, "Please **forgive** my boldness in continuing to
32.20 gifts, and when I meet him, perhaps he will **forgive** me."
50.17 to ask you, 'Please **forgive** the crime your brothers committed
50.17 Now please **forgive** us the wrong that we, the servants of
Ex 10.17 Now **forgive** my sin this once and pray to the Lord your
29.33 what was used in the ritual of **forgiveness** at their ordination.
29.36 offer a bull as a sacrifice, so that sin may be **forgiven.**
32.30 perhaps I can obtain **forgiveness** for your sin."
32.32 Please **forgive** their sin;
34. 7 my promise for thousands of generations and **forgive** evil and sin;
34. 9 These people are stubborn, but **forgive** our evil and our sin,
Lev 4.20 sacrifice for the people's sin, and they will be **forgiven.**
4.26 for the sin of the ruler, and he will be **forgiven.**
4.31 the sacrifice for the man's sin, and he will be **forgiven.**
4.35 the sacrifice for the man's sin, and he will be **forgiven.**

Lev 5.10 the sacrifice for the man's sin, and he will be **forgiven.**
5.13 the sacrifice for the man's sin, and he will be **forgiven.**
5.16 as a sacrifice for the man's sin, and he will be **forgiven.**
5.18 which the man committed unintentionally, and he will be **forgiven.**
6. 7 the sacrifice for the man's sin, and he will be **forgiven.**
19.22 purification to remove the man's sin, and God will **forgive** him.
Num 14.18 I show great love and faithfulness and **forgive** sin and rebellion.
14.19 greatness of your unchanging love, **forgive,** I pray, the sin of
14.19 just as you have **forgiven** them ever since they left Egypt."
14.20 The Lord answered, "I will **forgive** them, as you have asked.
15.25 and they will be **forgiven,** because the mistake was unintentional
15.26 among them will be **forgiven,** because everyone was involved in
15.28 to purify the man from his sin, and he will be **forgiven.**
25.13 to me and brought about **forgiveness** for the people's sin."
30. 5 The Lord will **forgive** her, because her father refused to let
30. 8 The Lord will **forgive** her.
30.12 The Lord will **forgive** her, because her husband prevented her
Deut 21. 8 Lord, **forgive** your people Israel, whom you rescued from Egypt.
21. 8 **Forgive** us and do not hold us responsible for the murder of
29.20 The Lord will not **forgive** such a man.
32.43 revenge on his enemies and **forgives** the sins of his people."
Josh 24.19 He is a holy God and will not **forgive** your sins.
1 Sam 15.25 But now I beg you, **forgive** my sin and go back with
25.28 Please **forgive** me, sir, for any wrong I have done.
2 Sam 12.13 Nathan replied, "The Lord **forgives** you;
Please **forgive** me.
1 Kgs 8.30 In your home in heaven hear us and **forgive** us.
8.33 humbly praying to you for **forgiveness,** [34] listen to them
8.34 **Forgive** the sins of your people, and bring them back to the
8.36 **Forgive** the sins of the king and of the people of Israel.
8.39 to them in your home in heaven, **forgive** them, and help them.
8.50 **Forgive** all their sins and their rebellion against you,
2 Kgs 5.18 hope that the Lord will **forgive** me when I accompany my king
5.18 Surely the Lord will **forgive** me!"
24. 4 The Lord could not **forgive** Manasseh for that.
1 Chr 6.49 and for the sacrifices by which God **forgives** Israel's sins.
21. 8 Please **forgive** me.
28.11 rooms, and for the Most Holy Place, where sins are **forgiven.**
2 Chr 6.21 In your home in heaven hear us and **forgive** us.
6.24 humbly praying to you for **forgiveness,** [25] listen to them
6.25 **Forgive** the sins of your people and bring them back to the
6.27 to them in heaven and **forgive** the sins of your servants, the
6.30 Listen to them in your home in heaven and **forgive** them.
6.39 merciful to them and **forgive** all the sins of your people.
7.14 hear them in heaven, **forgive** their sins, and make their land
30.19 in your goodness **forgive** those who are worshipping you with
30.20 he **forgave** the people and did not harm them.
Neh 4. 5 Don't **forgive** the evil they do and don't forget their sins,
9.17 But you are a God who **forgives;**
Job 7.21 Can't you ever **forgive** my sin?
10.14 if I would sin, so that you could refuse to **forgive** me.
14.17 You will **forgive** them and put them away;
Ps 25. 7 **Forgive** the sins and errors of my youth.
25.11 Keep your promise, Lord, and **forgive** my sins, for they are
25.18 Consider my distress and suffering and **forgive** all my sins.
32. 1 Happy are those whose sins are **forgiven,** whose wrongs are
32. 5 to confess them to you, and you **forgave** all my sins.
65. 3 Our faults defeat us, but you **forgive** them.
78.38 He **forgave** their sin and did not destroy them.
79. 9 rescue us and **forgive** our sins for the sake of your own
85. 2 have **forgiven** your people's sins and pardoned all their wrongs.
86. 5 are good to us and **forgiving,** full of constant love for all
99. 8 are a God who **forgives,** even though you punished them for
103. 3 He **forgives** all my sins and heals all my diseases.
109.14 the evil of his ancestors and never **forgive** his mother's sins.
130. 4 But you **forgive** us, so that we should stand in awe of
Prov 14. 9 care if they sin, but good people want to be **forgiven.**
16. 6 Be loyal and faithful, and God will **forgive** your sin.
17. 9 want people to like you, **forgive** them when they wrong you.
Is 2. 9 Do not **forgive** them, Lord!
6. 7 and now your guilt is gone, and your sins are **forgiven."**
22.14 "This evil will never be **forgiven** them as long as they live.
27. 9 Israel's sins will be **forgiven** only when the stones of pagan
33.24 again complain of being ill, and all sins will be **forgiven.**
38.17 You **forgive** all my sins.
40. 2 they have suffered long enough and their sins are now **forgiven.**
43.25 I am the God who **forgives** your sins, and I do this
53.10 his death was a sacrifice to bring **forgiveness.**
53.11 punishment of many and for his sake I will **forgive** them.
53.12 of many sinners and prayed that they might be **forgiven."**
55. 7 he is merciful and quick to **forgive.**
Jer 5. 1 If you can, the Lord will **forgive** Jerusalem.
5. 7 The Lord asked, "Why should I **forgive** the sins of my people?
18.23 Do not **forgive** their evil or pardon their sin.
31.34 I will **forgive** their sins and I will no longer remember
33. 8 against me, and I will **forgive** their sins and their rebellion.
36. 3 Then I will **forgive** their wickedness and their sins."
50.20 in Judah, because I will **forgive** those people whose lives I
Lam 3.42 sinned and rebelled, and you, O Lord, have not **forgiven** us.
Ezek 16.63 I will **forgive** all the wrongs you have done, but you
18.22 All his sins will be **forgiven,** and he will live, because
33.16 I will **forgive** the sins he has committed, and he will
45.13 for fellowship-offerings, so that your sins will be **forgiven.**
Dan 9. 9 You are merciful and **forgiving,** although we have rebelled against
9.19 Lord, **forgive** us.
9.24 Sin will be **forgiven** and eternal justice established,
Hos 1. 6 no longer show love to the people of Israel or **forgive** them.
14. 2 **"Forgive** all our sins and accept our prayer, and we will
Joel 2.13 he is always ready to **forgive** and not punish.
Amos 7. 2 and then I said, "Sovereign Lord, **forgive** your people!
Mic 6.11 How can I **forgive** men who use false scales and weights?
7.18 you **forgive** the sins of your people who have survived.
Mt 6.12 **Forgive** us the wrongs we have done,
6.12 as we **forgive** the wrongs that others have done
6.14 "If you **forgive** others the wrongs they have done to you,
6.14 your Father in heaven will also **forgive** you.
6.15 But if you do not **forgive** others,
6.15 then your Father will not **forgive** the wrongs you have done.
9. 2 Your sins are **forgiven."**
9. 5 to say, 'Your sins are **forgiven,'** or to say, 'Get up and
9. 6 the Son of Man has authority on earth to **forgive** sins."
12.31 you that people can be **forgiven** any sin and any evil thing
12.31 evil things against the Holy Spirit will not be **forgiven.**
12.32 Anyone who says something against the Son of Man can be **forgiven;**
12.32 against the Holy Spirit will not be **forgiven**—now or ever.
18.21 sinning against me, how many times do I have to **forgive** him?
18.27 sorry for him, so he **forgave** him the debt and let him
18.32 'I **forgave** you the whole amount you owed me, just because
18.35 of you unless you **forgive** your brother from your heart."
26.28 my blood poured out for many for the **forgiveness** of sins.
Mk 1. 4 he told the people, "and God will **forgive** your sins."
2. 5 Jesus said to the paralysed man, "My son, your sins are **forgiven."**
2. 7 God is the only one who can **forgive** sins!"
2. 9 paralysed man, 'Your sins are **forgiven',** or to say, 'Get up,
2.10 the Son of Man has authority on earth to **forgive** sins."
3.28 you that people can be **forgiven** all their sins and all the
3.29 will never be **forgiven,** because he has committed an eternal
4.12 did, they would turn to God, and he would **forgive** them.'"
11.25 and pray, **forgive** anything you may have against anyone,
11.25 Father in heaven will **forgive** the wrongs you have done."
Lk 1.77 that they will be saved by having their sins **forgiven.**
3. 3 your sins and be baptized, and God will **forgive** your sins."
5.20 had, he said to the man, "Your sins are **forgiven,** my
5.21 God is the only one who can **forgive** sins!"
5.23 to say, 'Your sins are **forgiven** you,' or to say, 'Get up
5.24 the Son of Man has authority on earth to **forgive** sins."
6.37 **forgive** others, and God will forgive you.
7.43 Simon, "that it would be the one who was **forgiven** more."
7.47 she has shown proves that her many sins have been **forgiven.**
7.47 But whoever has been **forgiven** little shows only a little love."
7.48 Then Jesus said to the woman, "Your sins are **forgiven."**
7.49 say to themselves, "Who is this, who even **forgives** sins?"
11. 4 Forgive us our sins, for we **forgive** everyone who does us wrong.
12.10 who says a word against the Son of Man can be **forgiven;**
12.10 evil things against the Holy Spirit will not be **forgiven.**
17. 3 "If your brother sins, rebuke him, and if he repents, **forgive**
17. 4 he comes to you saying, 'I repent,' you must **forgive** him."
23.34 Jesus said, **"Forgive** them, Father!
24.47 message about repentance and the **forgiveness** of sins must be
Jn 20.23 If you **forgive** people's sins, they are forgiven;
20.23 if you do not **forgive** them, they are not forgiven."
Acts 2.38 name of Jesus Christ, so that your sins will be **forgiven;**
3.19 then, and turn to God, so that he will **forgive** your sins.
5.31 Israel the opportunity to repent and have their sins **forgiven.**
8.22 the Lord that he will **forgive** you for thinking such a thing
10.43 will have his sins **forgiven** through the power of his name."
13.38 Jesus that the message about **forgiveness** of sins is preached to you;
15. 9 he **forgave** their sins because they believed.
26.18 they will have their sins **forgiven** and receive their place
Rom 3.25 which people's sins are **forgiven** through their faith in him.
4. 7 "Happy are those whose wrongs are **forgiven,** whose sins are pardoned!
2 Cor 2. 7 Now, however, you should **forgive** him and encourage him, in
2.10 When you **forgive** someone for what he has done, I forgive
2.10 For when I **forgive**—if, indeed, I need to forgive anything—
12.13 Please **forgive** me for being so unfair!
Eph 1. 7 of Christ we are set free, that is, our sins are **forgiven.**
4.32 forgive one another, as God has **forgiven** you through Christ.
Col 1.14 by whom we are set free, that is, our sins are **forgiven.**
2.13 God **forgave** us all our sins;
3.13 tolerant with one another and **forgive** one another whenever
3.13 You must **forgive** one another just as the Lord has forgiven you.
Heb 1. 3 After achieving **forgiveness** for the sins of mankind, he sat
2.17 service to God, so that the people's sins would be **forgiven.**
8.12 I will **forgive** their sins and will no longer remember their wrongs."
9. 5 their wings spread over the place where sins were **forgiven.**
9.22 blood, and sins are **forgiven** only if blood is poured out.
10.18 So when these have been **forgiven,** an offering to take
Jas 5.15 to health, and the sins he has committed will be **forgiven.**
5.20 from death and bring about the **forgiveness** of many sins.
1 Jn 1. 9 he will **forgive** us our sins and purify us from all our
2. 2 by which our sins are **forgiven,** and not our sins only, but
2.12 because your sins are **forgiven** for the sake of Christ.
4.10 his Son to be the means by which our sins are **forgiven.**

FORK (1)

1 Sam 2.13 the priest's servant would come with a three-pronged **fork.**
2.14 cooking, [14] he would stick the **fork** into the cooking-pot,
2.14 and whatever the **fork** brought out belonged to the priest.
1 Chr 28.17 to be used in making **forks,** bowls, and jars, how much silver
2 Chr 4.11 The twelve bulls supporting the tank The pots, shovels, and **forks**

FORK (2)

Ezek 21.19 Put up a signpost where the roads **fork.**
21.21 of Babylonia stands by the signpost at the **fork** of the road.

FORM
[WELL-FORMED]

Gen 1. 2 beginning, when God created the universe, [2]the earth was **formless**
2. 7 some soil from the ground and **formed** a man out of it;
2. 8 in the East, and there he put the man he had **formed.**
2.19 soil from the ground and **formed** all the animals and all the
2.22 He **formed** a woman out of the rib and brought her to
3.19 until you go back to the soil from which you were **formed.**
3.23 made him cultivate the soil from which he had been **formed.**
14. 3 These five kings had **formed** an alliance and joined forces in
37. 7 Yours **formed** a circle round mine and bowed down to it."
Ex 25.19 Make them so that they **form** one piece with the lid.
25.31 flowers, including buds and petals, are to **form** one piece with
26.11 loops to join the two sets so as to **form** one cover.
26.24 The two frames that **form** the two corners are to be made
27. 2 They are to **form** one piece with the altar, and the whole
28. 8 attached to the ephod so as to **form** one piece with it.
29. 2 it, and some in the **form** of biscuits brushed with oil.
30. 2 at the four corners are to **form** one piece with it.
36.18 hooks to join the two sets, so as to **form** one cover.
36.29 The two frames that **formed** the two corners were made in this
37. 8 He made them so that they **formed** one piece with the lid.
37.17 flowers, including buds and petals, **formed** one piece with it.
37.25 Its projections at the four corners **formed** one piece with it.
38. 2 four corners, so that they **formed** one piece with the altar.
39. 5 the ephod so as to **form** one piece with it, as the
Lev 22.23 is stunted or not perfectly **formed,** but it is not acceptable
Num 12. 8 he has even seen my **form!**
31.51 the gold, all of which was in the **form** of ornaments.
Deut 3.16 was the River Jabbok, part of which **formed** the Ammonite border.
4.12 him speaking but did not see him in any **form** at all.
4.15 from the fire on Mount Sinai, you did not see any **form.**
4.16 yourselves an idol in any **form** at all—whether man or woman,
4.25 sin by making for yourselves an idol in any **form** at all.
9.16 making yourselves a metal idol in the **form** of a bull-calf.
32. 2 fall like drops of rain and **form** on the earth like dew.
Josh 15.12 at the Mediterranean Sea, [12]which **formed** the western border.
2 Chr 11.15 demons and the idols he made in the **form** of bull-calves.
Neh 6. 5 fifth message, this one in the **form** of an unsealed letter.
12. 9 The following **formed** the choir that sang the responses:
Job 10. 8 Your hands **formed** and shaped me, and now those same hands
10.11 You **formed** my body with bones and sinews and covered the
33. 6 the same in God's sight, both of us were **formed** from clay.
Ps 33.15 He **forms** all their thoughts and knows everything they do.
83. 5 They agree on their plan and **form** an alliance against you:
95. 5 the land also, which he himself **formed.**
115. 4 Their gods are made of silver and gold, **formed** by human hands.
135.15 they are **formed** by human hands.
139.15 When my bones were being **formed,** carefully put together in
Song 3. 7 sixty soldiers **form** the bodyguard, the finest soldiers in Israel.
5.14 His hands are **well-formed,** and he wears rings set with gems.
Is 18. 4 as quietly as the dew **forms** in the warm nights of harvest
44.13 and makes it in the **form** of a man, a handsome human
45.18 He **formed** and made the earth— he made it firm and
62. 5 a virgin as his bride, He who **formed** you will marry you.
Jer 33. 2 who made the earth, who **formed** it and set it in place,
Ezek 1. 5 four living creatures in human **form,** [6]but each of them had
1. 9 out so that the creatures **formed** a square with their wing
8. 2 I looked up and saw a vision of a fiery human **form.**
16. 7 Your breasts were **well-formed,** and your hair had grown, but
37.10 There were enough of them to **form** an army.
40. 8 It **formed** that end of the gateway which was nearest the Temple,
47.18 with the River Jordan **forming** the boundary between the land of
47.20 "The western boundary is **formed** by the Mediterranean
Dan 6.18 a sleepless night, without food or any **form** of entertainment.
Mt 13.26 the ears of corn began to **form,** then the weeds showed up.
Lk 3.22 Holy Spirit came down upon him in bodily **form** like a dove.
Acts 17. 5 of the worthless loafers from the streets and **formed** a mob.
Gal 4.19 kind of pain for you until Christ's nature is **formed** in you.
Eph 3.10 world might learn of his wisdom in all its different **forms.**
5. 5 greedy (for greed is a **form** of idolatry) will ever receive a
Col 3. 5 evil passions, and greed (for greed is a **form** of idolatry).
1 Tim 3.16 He appeared in human **form,** was shown to be right by the
2 Tim 3. 5 will hold to the outward **form** of our religion, but reject
2 Pet 3. 5 The earth was **formed** out of water and by water, [6]and it

FORMATION

Prov 30.27 they have no king, but they move in **formation.**

FORMER

Heb 13. 7 Remember your **former** leaders, who spoke God's message to you.

FORMULA

Ex 30.32 must not use the same **formula** to make any mixture like it.
30.37 Do not use the same **formula** to make any incense like it

AV FORNICATION
see also **IMMORAL**

2 Chr 21.11 the people of Judah and Jerusalem to **sin** against the Lord.
Is 23.17 old trade, and she will **hire** herself out to all the kingdoms
Ezek 16.15 your beauty and fame to **sleep with** everyone who came along.
16.29 You were also a **prostitute** for the Babylonians,
Mt 5.32 any cause other than her **unfaithfulness,** then he is guilty of
19. 9 any cause other than her **unfaithfulness** commits adultery if he
1 Cor 6. 9 people who are **immoral** or who worship idols or are adulterers

FORSAKE

Neh 9.17 you did not **forsake** them.
9.31 your mercy is great, you did not **forsake** or destroy them.
Job 6.14 I need loyal friends— whether I've **forsaken** God or not.
19.13 God has made my brothers **forsake** me;
Ps 102.17 He will hear his **forsaken** people and listen to their prayer.
Is 1.28 he will kill everyone who **forsakes** him.
2. 6 God, you have **forsaken** your people, the descendants of Jacob!
57. 8 You **forsake** me;
60.15 "You will no longer be **forsaken** and hated, A city deserted
62. 4 longer will you be called **"Forsaken,"** Or your land be called
62.12 "The City That God Loves," "The City That God Did Not **Forsake."**
65.11 be different for you that **forsake** me, who ignore Zion,

FORT

Judg 9.46 the leading men in the **fort** at Shechem heard about this,
9.49 all the people of the **fort** died—about a thousand men and
1 Chr 12. 8 Gad who joined David's troops when he was at the desert **fort.**
12.16 of Benjamin and Judah went out to the **fort** where David was.
2 Chr 27. 4 built cities, and in the forests he built **forts** and towers.
Neh 2. 8 for the gates of the **fort** that guards the Temple,
Ps 89.40 down the walls of his city and left his **forts** in ruins.
Is 30.25 On the day when the **forts** of your enemies are captured
32.14 Homes and the **forts** that guarded them will be in ruins for
Jer 48.18 Moab's destroyer is here and has left its **forts** in ruins.
51.30 Babylonian soldiers have stopped fighting and remain in their **forts.**
Lam 2. 2 in Judah And tore down the **forts** that defended the land.
2. 5 He has left her **forts** and palaces in ruins.
Ezek 19. 7 He wrecked **forts,** he ruined towns.
Acts 21.34 so he ordered his men to take Paul up into the **fort.**
21.37 about to take Paul into the **fort,** he spoke to the commander:
22.24 to take Paul into the **fort,** and he told them to whip
23.10 group, get Paul away from them, and take him into the **fort.**
23.16 so he went to the **fort** and told Paul.
23.32 the foot-soldiers returned to the **fort** and left the horsemen

FORTIFY

Num 13.19 whether the people live in open towns or in **fortified** cities.
13.28 are powerful, and their cities are very large and well **fortified.**
32.16 here for our sheep and **fortified** towns for our dependants.
32.17 can live here in the **fortified** towns, safe from the people
32.34 tribe of Gad rebuilt the **fortified** towns of Dibon, Ataroth,
Deut 3. 5 All these towns were **fortified** with high walls, gates,
28.52 and the high, **fortified** walls in which you trust will
Josh 19.29 border then turned to Ramah, reaching the **fortified** city of Tyre;
19.35 The **fortified** cities were Ziddim, Zer, Hammath, Rakkath,
1 Sam 6.18 both the **fortified** towns and the villages without walls.
23. 7 by going into a walled town with **fortified** gates."
2 Sam 5.17 When David heard of it, he went down to a **fortified** place.
20. 6 he may occupy some **fortified** towns and escape from us."
23.14 time David was on a **fortified** hill, and a group of
24. 7 they went south to the **fortified** city of Tyre, on to all
1 Kgs 4.13 sixty large towns in all, **fortified** with walls and with bronze
12.25 King Jeroboam of Israel **fortified** the town of Shechem in
12.25 Then he left and **fortified** the town of Penuel.
15.17 invaded Judah and started to **fortify** Ramah in order to cut
15.21 heard what had happened, he stopped **fortifying** Ramah and went
15.22 stones and timber that Baasha had been using to **fortify** it.
15.22 With this material Asa **fortified** Mizpah and Geba, a city in
15.23 deeds and the towns he **fortified,** are all recorded in
16.24 Omri **fortified** the hill, built a town there, and named it Samaria,
2 Kgs 3.19 You will conquer all their beautiful **fortified** cities;
10. 2 at your disposal chariots, horses, weapons, and **fortified** cities.
18.13 emperor of Assyria, attacked the **fortified** cities of Judah
19.25 the power to turn **fortified** cities into piles of rubble.
1 Chr 11.16 time David was on a **fortified** hill, and a group of
2 Chr 8. 4 of Hamath and Zobah [4]and **fortified** the city of Palmyra in
8. 5 Horon and Lower Beth Horon (**fortified** cities with gates that
11. 5 remained in Jerusalem and had **fortifications** built for the
11.11 He had them strongly **fortified** and appointed a commander for
11.23 throughout Judah and Benjamin in the **fortified** cities.
12. 4 He captured the **fortified** cities of Judah and advanced as far
14. 6 built **fortifications** for the cities of Judah during this time,
14. 7 people of Judah, "Let us **fortify** the cities by building walls
16. 1 invaded Judah and started to **fortify** Ramah in order to cut
16. 5 was happening, he stopped **fortifying** Ramah and abandoned the work.
16. 6 they used them to **fortify** the cities of Geba and Mizpah.
17. 2 He stationed troops in the **fortified** cities of Judah,
17.12 Throughout Judah he built **fortifications** and cities,
17.19 stationed other soldiers in the other **fortified** cities of Judah.
19. 5 judges in each of the **fortified** cities of Judah [6]and instructed
21. 3 each one in charge of one of the **fortified** cities of Judah.
26. 6 and Ashdod, and built **fortified** cities near Ashdod and in the
26. 9 Uzziah strengthened the **fortifications** of Jerusalem by
26.10 He also built **fortified** towers in the open country and dug
32. 1 He besieged the **fortified** cities and gave orders for his army
33.14 a unit of troops in each of the **fortified** cities of Judah.
Neh 9.25 Your people captured **fortified** cities, fertile land, houses
Ps 60. 9 Who, O God, will take me into the **fortified** city?
108.10 Who, O God, will take me into the **fortified** city?
Is 23.13 up siege-towers, tore down the **fortifications** of Tyre,
25. 2 have turned cities into ruins and destroyed their **fortifications.**
27.10 The **fortified** city lies in ruins.
36. 1 emperor of Assyria, attacked the **fortified** cities of Judah
37.26 the power to turn **fortified** cities into piles of rubble.
Jer 1.18 you will be like a **fortified** city, an iron pillar, and a

Jer 4. 5 people of Judah and Jerusalem to run to the **fortified** cities.
5.17 The **fortified** cities in which you trust will be destroyed by
8.14 "Come on, we will run to the **fortified** cities, and die
34. 7 attacking Lachish and Azekah, the only other **fortified** cities
Ezek 21.20 the other the way to Judah, to the **fortified** city, Jerusalem.
36.35 looted, and left in ruins, are now inhabited and **fortified.**
Dan 11.15 of Syria will lay siege to a **fortified** city and capture it.
Hos 8.14 The people of Judah have built **fortified** cities.
Zeph 1.16 and the battle-cry of soldiers attacking **fortified** cities
Zech 9. 3 Tyre has built **fortifications** for herself and has piled up

FORTRESS

2 Sam 5. 7 David did capture their **fortress** of Zion, and it became known
5. 9 After capturing the **fortress,** David lived in it and named it
22. 2 he is my strong **fortress.**
22.46 lose their courage and come trembling from their **fortresses.**
1 Kgs 16.18 went into the palace's inner **fortress,** set the palace on fire,
2 Kgs 8.12 "You will set their **fortresses** on fire, slaughter their finest
15.25 in the palace's inner **fortress** in Samaria, and succeeded him as
1 Chr 11. 5 but David captured their **fortress** of Zion, and it became known
11. 7 went to live in the **fortress,** it came to be called "David's
Neh 7. 2 Hanani and Hananiah, commanding officer of the **fortress.**
Job 39.28 the highest rocks and makes the sharp peaks its **fortress.**
Ps 18. 2 he is my strong **fortress.**
18.45 lose their courage and come trembling from their **fortresses.**
30. 7 you protected me like a mountain **fortress.**
48. 3 there is safety with him inside the **fortresses** of the city.
48.13 the walls and examine the **fortresses,** so that you may tell
71. 3 Be my secure shelter and a strong **fortress** to protect me;
Is 2.15 and hills, [15] every high tower, and the walls of every **fortress.**
25.12 He will destroy the **fortresses** of Moab with their high walls
33.16 will be as secure as if you were in a strong **fortress.**
Jer 6. 5 we'll destroy the city's **fortresses."**
48. 1 Kiriathaim is captured, its mighty **fortress** torn down,
48.41 and the towns and **fortresses** will be captured.
51.32 captured the river-crossing and have set the **fortresses** on fire.
51.53 sky and build a strong **fortress** there, I would still send
Ezek 30.15 let the city of Pelusium, Egypt's great **fortress,** feel my fury.
Dan 11. 7 of the king of Syria, enter their **fortress,** and defeat them.
11.10 will sweep on like a flood and attack an enemy **fortress.**
11.19 king will return to the **fortresses** of his own land, but he
11.24 will make plans to attack **fortresses,** but his time will soon
11.38 Instead, he will honour the god who protects **fortresses.**
11.39 To defend his **fortresses,** he will use people who worship
Hos 10.14 come to your people, and all your **fortresses** will be destroyed.
Amos 1. 4 and I will burn down the **fortresses** of King Benhadad.
1. 7 upon the city walls of Gaza and burn down its **fortresses.**
1.10 upon the city walls of Tyre and burn down its **fortresses."**
1.12 the city of Teman and burn down the **fortresses** of Bozrah."
1.14 upon the city walls of Rabbah and burn down its **fortresses.**
2. 2 the land of Moab and burn down the **fortresses** of Kerioth.
2. 5 send fire upon Judah and burn down the **fortresses** of Jerusalem."
Obad 3 Your capital is a **fortress** of solid rock;
Mic 7.17 they will come from their **fortresses,** trembling and afraid.
Nah 3.12 All your **fortresses** will be like fig-trees with ripe figs:
3.14 to prepare for a siege, and strengthen your **fortresses!**
Hab 1.10 No **fortress** can stop them—they pile up earth against it and

FORTUNE

Judg 5.24 The most **fortunate** of women is Jael, the wife of Heber
5.24 the Kenite— the most **fortunate** of women who live in tents.
1 Kgs 10. 8 How **fortunate** are your wives!
10. 8 And how **fortunate** your servants, who are always in your presence
2 Chr 9. 7 How **fortunate** are the men who serve you, who are always in
Prov 11.10 when honest people have good **fortune,** and there are joyful
12.27 are after, but if you work hard, you will get a **fortune.**
13. 7 Others pretend to be poor, but own a **fortune.**
20. 7 Children are **fortunate** if they have a father who is honest
Ecc 10.17 But a country is **fortunate** to have a king who makes his
Hos 12. 8 'We've made a **fortune.**
Mt 13.16 "As for you, how **fortunate** you are!
Lk 10.23 said to them privately, "How **fortunate** you are to see the
Acts 26. 2 I consider myself **fortunate** that today I am to defend myself
Jas 1. 2 My brothers, consider yourselves **fortunate** when all kinds

FORTUNE-TELLER

Josh 13.22 the people of Israel killed was the **fortune-teller** Balaam
Judg 9.37 coming along the road from the oak-tree of the **fortune-tellers!"**
1 Sam 28. 3 Saul had forced all the **fortune-tellers** and mediums to leave
28. 9 how he forced the **fortune-tellers** and mediums to leave Israel.
2 Kgs 17.17 they consulted mediums and **fortune-tellers,** and they devoted
21. 6 He practised divination and magic and consulted **fortune-tellers**
23.24 Judah all the mediums and **fortune-tellers,** and all the household
2 Chr 33. 6 He practised divination and magic and consulted **fortune-tellers**
Is 3. 2 and their prophets, their **fortune-tellers** and their statesmen,
8.19 to ask for messages from **fortune-tellers** and mediums, who chirp
44.25 I make fools of **fortune-tellers** and frustrate the predictions
Dan 1.20 more than any **fortune-teller** or magician in his whole kingdom.
2. 2 so he sent for his **fortune-tellers,** magicians, sorcerers,
2.10 made such a demand of his **fortune-tellers,** magicians, and wizards.
2.27 no wizard, magician, **fortune-teller,** or astrologer who can tell
4. 7 **fortune-tellers,** magicians, wizards, and astrologers were brought
4. 9 Belteshazzar, chief of the **fortune-tellers,** I know that the
5.11 your father, made him chief of the **fortune-tellers,** magicians,
Mic 5.12 the magic charms you use and leave you without any **fortune-tellers.**
Zech 10. 2 People consult idols and **fortune-tellers,** but the answers
Acts 16.16 She earned a lot of money for her owners by telling **fortunes.**

FORWARD

Mt 26.60 though many people came **forward** and told lies about him.
Lk 23.10 Law stepped **forward** and made strong accusations against Jesus.
Jn 18. 4 to him, so he stepped **forward** and asked them, "Who is it
Acts 27.40 wind would blow the ship **forward,** and we headed for shore.
Phil 3.16 may be, let us go **forward** according to the same rules we
Heb 6. 1 Let us go **forward,** then, to mature teaching and leave
6. 3 Let us go **forward!**
1 Pet 1. 4 hope, [4] and so we look **forward** to possessing the rich

FOUND
see also **FIND**

Num 13.22 (Hebron was **founded** seven years before Zoan in Egypt.)
Judg 9.28 Be loyal to your ancestor Hamor, who **founded** your clan!
1 Chr 2.24 They had a son named Ashhur, who **founded** the town of Tekoa.
2.49 Shaaph, who **founded** the town of Madmannah;
2.49 and Shevah, who **founded** the towns of Machbenah and Gibea.
2.50 Hur's son Shobal **founded** Kiriath Jearim,
2.51 his second son Salma **founded** Bethlehem,
2.51 and his third son Hareph **founded** Bethgader.
2.52 Shobal, the **founder** of Kiriath Jearim, was the ancestor of
2.54 Salma, the **founder** of Bethlehem, was the ancestor
4. 3 wife Ephrath, and his descendants **founded** the city of Bethlehem.
4. 3 Penuel **founded** the city of Gedor, and Ezer founded Hushah.
4. 5 Ashhur, who **founded** the town of Tekoa, had two wives,
4.12 Tehinnah was the **founder** of the city of Nahash.
4.14 the father of Joab, the **founder** of the Valley of Craftsmen,
4.17 Ishbah **founded** the town of Eshtemoa.
4.17 Jered, who **founded** the town of Gedor;
4.17 Heber, **founder** of the town of Soco;
4.17 and Jekuthiel, **founder** of the town of Zanoah.
4.19 descendants **founded** the clan of Garm, which lived in the town
4.21 His descendants included Er, who **founded** the town of Lecah;
4.21 Laadah, **founder** of the town of Mareshah;
5.12 Joel was the **founder** of the leading clan,
5.12 Janai and Shaphat were **founders** of other clans in Bashan.
7.31 (Malchiel **founded** the city of Birzaith.)
8.29 Jeiel **founded** the city of Gibeon and settled there.
9.35 Jeiel **founded** the city of Gibeon and settled there.
Ps 89.14 Your kingdom is **founded** on righteousness and justice;
Is 23. 7 Can this be the joyful city of Tyre, **founded** so long ago?
Hab 2.12 You **founded** a city on crime and built it up by murder.

FOUNDATION

Josh 6.26 Whoever lays the **foundation** will lose his eldest son;
1 Sam 2. 8 The **foundations** of the earth belong to the Lord;
2 Sam 22. 8 **foundations** of the sky rocked and quivered because God was angry!
22.16 was laid bare, and the **foundations** of the earth were uncovered
1 Kgs 5.17 they quarried fine large stones for the **foundation** of the Temple.
6.37 The **foundation** of the Temple was laid in the second month,
7. 9 were made of fine stones from the **foundations** to the eaves.
7.10 **foundations** were made of large stones prepared at the quarry,
16.34 Abiram when he laid the **foundation** of Jericho, and his youngest
2 Kgs 16.17 twelve bronze bulls, and placed it on a stone **foundation.**
2 Chr 8.16 From the laying of the **foundation** of the Lord's Temple to
Ezra 3.10 men started to lay the **foundation** of the Temple, the priests
3.11 the work on the **foundation** of the Temple had been started.
3.12 and as they watched the **foundation** of this Temple being laid,
5.16 So Sheshbazzar came and laid its **foundation;**
Ps 18. 7 **foundations** of the mountains rocked and quivered,
18.15 was laid bare, and the **foundations** of the earth were uncovered,
24. 2 waters beneath the earth and laid its **foundations** in the ocean
75. 3 the earth itself be shaken, I will keep its **foundations** firm.
104. 5 firmly on its **foundations,** and it will never be moved.
Prov 8.29 I was there when he laid the earth's **foundations.**
24. 3 Homes are built on the **foundation** of wisdom and understanding.
Is 6. 4 of their voices made the **foundation** of the Temple shake,
24.18 rain will pour from the sky, and earth's **foundations** will shake.
28.16 "I am placing in Zion a **foundation** that is firm and strong.
28.17 be the measuring-line for the **foundation,** and honesty will be
44.28 Jerusalem to be rebuilt and the Temple **foundations** to be laid.' "
48.13 My hands made the earth's **foundations** and spread the heavens out.
51.13 who stretched out the heavens and laid the earth's **foundations?**
51.16 I stretched out the heavens and laid the earth's **foundations;**
54.11 I will rebuild your **foundations** with precious stones.
58.12 long been in ruins, building again on the old **foundations.**
Jer 31.37 could be measured and the **foundations** of the earth explored,
Ezek 13.14 to shatter it, and to leave the **foundation** stones bare.
41. 8 it was level with the **foundation** of the rooms by the temple
Mic 1. 6 down into the valley, and will lay bare the city's **foundations.**
3.10 building God's city, Jerusalem, on a **foundation** of murder and
6. 2 mountains, you everlasting **foundations** of the earth, listen to
Hag 2.18 the day that the **foundation** of the Temple has been completed.
Zech 4. 9 "Zerubbabel has laid the **foundation** of the Temple, and he will
8. 9 spoke at the time the **foundation** was being laid for rebuilding
Mt 16.18 rock, and on this rock **foundation** I will build my church,
Lk 6.48 his house, dug deep and laid the **foundation** on rock.
6.49 like a man who built his house without laying a **foundation;**
14.29 not be able to finish the tower after laying the **foundation;**
Acts 16.26 earthquake, which shook the prison to its **foundations.**
Rom 15.20 so as not to build on a **foundation** laid by someone else.
1 Cor 3.10 expert builder and laid the **foundation,** and another man is
3.11 as the one and only **foundation,**

1 Cor 3.11 and no other **foundation** can be laid.
3.12 or silver or precious stones in building on the **foundation;**
3.14 what was built on the **foundation** survives the fire, the
Eph 2.20 built upon the **foundation** laid by the apostles and prophets,
3.17 may have your roots and **foundation** in love, [18] so that you,
Col 1.23 on a firm and sure **foundation,** and must not allow yourselves
1 Tim 6.19 a treasure which will be a solid **foundation** for the future.
2 Tim 2.19 But the solid **foundation** that God has laid cannot be shaken;
Heb 6. 1 should not lay again the **foundation** of turning away from
11.10 God has designed and built, the city with permanent **foundations.**
1 Pet 5.10 you and give you firmness, strength, and a sure **foundation.**
Rev 21.14 wall was built on twelve **foundation-stones,** on which were
21.19 The **foundation-stones** of the city wall were adorned with
21.19 The first **foundation-stone** was jasper, the second sapphire, the third agate,

AV FOUNDATION

Ex 9.18 hailstorm, such as Egypt has never known in all its **history.**
Ezra 3. 6 had not yet started to **rebuild** the Temple, they began on the
Ps 87. 1 The Lord **built** his city on the sacred hill;
102.25 long ago you **created** the earth, and with your own
137. 7 Remember how they kept saying, "Tear it down to the **ground!"**
Prov 10.25 wicked are blown away, but honest people are always **safe.**
Zech 12. 1 who spread out the skies, **created** the earth, and gave life
Mt 13.35 I will tell them things unknown since the **creation** of the world."
25.34 been prepared for you ever since the **creation** of the world.
Lk 11.50 the prophets killed since the **creation** of the world,
Heb 1.10 "You, Lord, in the **beginning** created the earth, and with your
4. 3 work had been finished from the time he **created** the world.
9.26 to suffer many times ever since the **creation** of the world.
1 Pet 1.20 chosen by God before the **creation** of the world and was
Rev 13. 8 names were written before the **creation** of the world in the
17. 8 not been written before the **creation** of the world in the

FOUNDATION GATE

2 Chr 23. 5 palace, and the rest will be stationed at the **Foundation Gate.**

FOUNDRY

1 Kgs 7.46 it all made in the **foundry** between Sukkoth and Zarethan, in
2 Chr 4.17 them all made in the **foundry** between Sukkoth and Zeredah in

FOUNTAIN

Neh 2.13 west and went south past Dragon's **Fountain** to the Rubbish Gate.
Ps 74.15 You made springs and **fountains** flow;
Prov 10.11 good man's words are a **fountain** of life, but a wicked man's
13.14 The teachings of the wise are a **fountain** of life;
14.27 Reverence for the Lord is a **fountain** of life.
16.22 Wisdom is a **fountain** of life to the wise, but trying to
Song 4.15 **Fountains** water the garden, streams of flowing water,
Jer 9. 1 water, and my eyes a **fountain** of tears, so that I could
Zech 13. 1 says the Lord Almighty, "a **fountain** will be opened to purify

FOUNTAIN GATE

Neh 2.14 city I went north to the **Fountain Gate** and the King's Pool.
3.15 ruler of the Mizpah District, rebuilt the **Fountain Gate.**
12.37 At the **Fountain Gate** they went up the steps that led to

FOUR

Gen 1.19 Evening passed and morning came—that was the **fourth** day.
2.10 beyond Eden it divided into **four** rivers.
2.14 flows east of Assyria, and the **fourth** river is the Euphrates.
14. 1 **Four** kings, Amraphel of Babylonia, Arioch of Ellasar,
14. 9 of Elam, Goiim, Babylonia, and Ellasar, five kings against **four.**
14.11 The **four** kings took everything in Sodom and Gomorrah,
14.14 and pursued the **four** kings all the way to Dan.
15.16 will be **four** generations before your descendants come back here,
36.10 Basemath bore him one son, Reuel, and Reuel had **four** sons:
Ex 6.14 Reuben, Jacob's first-born, had **four** sons:
6.18 Kohath had **four** sons:
16.22 they gathered twice as much food, **four** litres for each person.
20. 5 and on their descendants down to the third and **fourth** generation.
22. 1 pay five cows for one cow and **four** sheep for one sheep.
25.12 Make **four** carrying-rings of gold for it
25.12 and attach them to its **four** legs,
25.26 Make **four** carrying-rings of gold for it
25.26 and put them at the **four** corners, where the legs are.
25.34 the lamp-stand is to have **four** decorative flowers shaped like
26.16 Each frame is to be **four** metres long and 66 centimetres wide,
26.32 Hang it on **four** posts of acacia-wood covered with gold,
26.32 fitted with hooks, and set in **four** silver bases.
27. 2 Make projections at the top of the **four** corners.
27. 4 Make a bronze grating and put **four** bronze carrying-rings on
27.16 It is to be supported by **four** posts in four bases.
28.17 Mount **four** rows of precious stones on it;
28.20 and in the **fourth** row, a beryl, a carnelian, and a
29.16 its blood and throw it against all **four** sides of the altar.
29.20 the rest of the blood against all **four** sides of the altar.
30. 2 Its projections at the **four** corners are to form one piece
30. 3 Cover its top, all **four** sides, and its projections with pure
30.10 altar by putting on its **four** projections the blood of the
30.24 Add **four** litres of olive-oil, [25] and make a sacred anointing
34. 7 grandchildren to the third and **fourth** generation for the sins of
36.21 Each frame was **four** metres tall and sixty-six centimetres
36.36 They made **four** posts of acacia-wood to hold the curtain,
36.36 Then they made **four** silver bases to hold the posts.
Ex 37. 3 He made **four** carrying-rings of gold for it
37. 3 and attached them to its **four** feet,
37.13 He made **four** carrying-rings of gold for it
37.13 and put them at the **four** corners, where the legs were.
37.20 shaft of the lamp-stand had **four** decorative flowers shaped
37.25 Its projections at the **four** corners formed one piece with it.
37.26 He covered its top, all **four** sides, and its projections
38. 2 at the top of the **four** corners, so that they formed one
38. 5 He made **four** carrying-rings and put them on the four corners.
38.19 It was supported by **four** posts in four bronze bases.
39.10 They mounted **four** rows of precious stones on it:
39.13 and in the **fourth** row, a beryl, a carnelian, and a
Lev 1. 5 then throw it against all **four** sides of the altar
1.11 shall throw its blood on all **four** sides of the altar.
3. 2 throw the blood against all **four** sides of the altar
3. 8 throw its blood against all **four** sides of the altar
3.13 throw its blood against all **four** sides of the altar
7. 2 blood is to be thrown against all **four** sides of the altar.
8.19 and threw the blood on all **four** sides of the altar.
8.24 the rest of the blood on all **four** sides of the altar.
9.12 blood, and he threw it on all **four** sides of the altar.
9.18 blood, and he threw it on all **four** sides of the altar.
11.24 and they chew the cud, and all **four-footed** animals with paws.
11.42 whether they crawl, or walk on **four** legs, or have many legs.
19.24 In the **fourth** year all the fruit shall be dedicated as
Num 3. 2 Aaron had **four** sons:
3.17 Kohath had **four** sons:
7. 7 He gave two wagons and **four** oxen to the Gershonites,
7. 8 and **four** wagons and eight oxen
14.18 grandchildren to the third and **fourth** generation for the sins of
26.60 Aaron had **four** sons, Nadab, Abihu, Eleazar, and Ithamar.
29.23 On the **fourth** day offer ten young bulls, two rams,
34.12 "These will be the **four** borders of your land."
Deut 3.11 coffin, made of stone, was **four** metres long
5. 9 and on their descendants down to the third and **fourth** generation.
22.12 "Sew tassels on the **four** corners of your clothes.
Josh 19. 7 **four** cities, along with the towns round them.
19.17 The **fourth** assignment made was for the families of the tribe
21.17 From the territory of Benjamin they were given **four** cities:
21.21 They were given **four** cities:
21.23 From the territory of Dan they were given **four** cities:
21.28 From the territory of Issachar they received **four** cities:
21.30 From the territory of Asher they received **four** cities:
21.34 of Merari, received from the territory of Zebulun **four** cities:
21.36 From the territory of Reuben they received **four** cities:
21.38 From the tribe of Gad they received **four** cities:
Judg 9.34 their move at night and hid outside Shechem in **four** groups.
11.40 women would go away for **four** days every year to grieve for
14.15 On the **fourth** day they said to Samson's wife, "Trick your
19. 2 to her father's house in Bethlehem, and stayed there **four** months.
19. 5 On the morning of the **fourth** day they woke up early and
20.47 to the Rock of Rimmon, and they stayed there **four** months.
2 Sam 12. 6 thing, he must pay back **four** times as much as he took."
15. 7 After **four** years Absalom said to King David, "Sir, let me
21.22 These **four** were descendants of the giants of Gath,
1 Kgs 6. 1 Israel left Egypt, during the **fourth** year of Solomon's reign
6.37 the month of Ziv, in the **fourth** year of Solomon's reign.
7.10 three and a half metres long and others **four** metres long.
7.30 Each cart had **four** bronze wheels with bronze axles.
7.30 At the **four** corners were bronze supports for a basin;
7.34 There were **four** supports at the bottom corners of each cart,
18.33 He said, "Fill **four** jars with water and pour it on the
22.41 In the **fourth** year of the reign of King Ahab of Israel,
2 Kgs 7. 3 **Four** men who were suffering from a dreaded skin-disease were
7. 8 When the **four** men reached the edge of the camp, they went
10.30 your descendants, down to the **fourth** generation, will be kings
15.12 "Your descendants, down to the **fourth** generation, will be kings
18. 9 In the **fourth** year of Hezekiah's reign—which was the seventh
25. 3 the ninth day of the **fourth** month of that same year, when
1 Chr 2.43 Hebron had **four** sons:
3. 5 His wife Bathsheba, daughter of Ammiel, bore him **four** sons:
3.15 Josiah had **four** sons:
4. 6 He and Naarah had **four** sons:
4.16 Jehallelel had **four** sons:
4.17 Ezrah had **four** sons:
4.20 Shimon had **four** sons:
5. 3 Reuben, the eldest of Jacob's sons, had **four** sons:
6. 2 Kohath had **four** sons:
6. 3 Aaron had **four** sons:
7. 1 Issachar had **four** sons:
7. 3 Izrahiah and his **four** sons, Michael, Obadiah, Joel, and Isshiah,
7.13 Naphtali had **four** sons:
7.19 (Shemida had **four** sons:
7.30 He had **four** sons:
7.35 His brother Hotham had **four** sons:
8.33 Saul had **four** sons:
8.35 Micah had **four** sons:
9.26 **four** chief guards were Levites and had the final responsibility.
9.39 Saul had **four** sons:
9.41 Micah had **four** sons:
21.20 Araunah and his **four** sons were threshing wheat, and when
23.10 Shimei had **four** sons:
23.12 Kohath had **four** sons:
23.19 Kohath's third son, Hebron, had **four** sons:
23.20 Kohath's **fourth** son, Uzziel, had two sons, Micah and Isshiah.
24. 1 Aaron had **four** sons:
25. 2 The **four** sons of Asaph:
26.10 From the clan of Merari there was Hosah, who had **four** sons:
26.17 duty each day, on the north, **four,** and on the south, four.
26.17 **Four** guards were stationed at the storerooms daily, two at each
26.18 the western pavilion there were **four** guards by the road

1 Chr 27. 2 **Fourth** month:
2 Chr 3. 2 in the second month of the **fourth** year that he was king.
4. 1 was nine metres square and **four** and a half metres high.
11.20 married Maacah, the daughter of Absalom, and they had **four** sons:
20.26 On the **fourth** day they assembled in the Valley of Beracah
28.12 **Four** of the leading men of the Northern Kingdom, Azariah
28.15 their leaders, [15]and the **four** men were appointed to provide
31. 7 month and continued to pile up for the next **four** months.
34. 3 **Four** years later he began to destroy the pagan places of worship,
34.12 They were supervised by **four** Levites:
Ezra 8.33 Then on the **fourth** day we went to the Temple, weighed
Neh 2. 1 One day **four** months later, when Emperor Artaxerxes was dining,
6. 4 sent me the same message **four** times, and each time I sent
Prov 30.15 There are **four** things that are never satisfied:
30.18 are **four** things that are too mysterious for me to understand:
30.21 There are **four** things that the earth itself cannot tolerate:
30.24 There are **four** animals in the world that are small,
30.29 are **four** things that are impressive to watch as they walk:
Is 11.12 Judah and bringing them back from the **four** corners of the earth.
Jer 15. 3 the Lord, have decided that **four** terrible things will happen to
25. 1 In the **fourth** year that Jehoiakim son of Josiah was king
28. 1 the fifth month of the **fourth** year that Zedekiah was king,
36. 1 In the **fourth** year that Jehoiakim son of Josiah was king
36.23 Jehudi finished reading three or **four** columns, the king cut them
39. 2 ninth day of the **fourth** month of Zedekiah's eleventh year as
45. 1 In the **fourth** year that Jehoiakim son of Josiah was king
46. 2 the River Euphrates in the **fourth** year that Jehoiakim was king
51.59 In the **fourth** year that Zedekiah was king of Judah, Seraiah
52. 6 the ninth day of the **fourth** month of that same year, when
Ezek 1. 1 the fifth day of the **fourth** month of the thirtieth year,
1. 5 I saw what looked like **four** living creatures in human form,
1. 6 but each of them had **four** faces and four wings.
1. 8 In addition to their **four** faces and four wings,
1. 8 they each had **four** human hands, one under each wing.
1.10 Each living creature had **four** different faces:
1.12 Each creature faced all **four** directions,
1.15 I was looking at the **four** creatures,
1.15 I saw **four** wheels touching the ground,
1.16 All **four** wheels were alike;
1.17 so that the wheels could move in any of the **four** directions.
10. 9 also saw that there were **four** wheels, all alike,
10.14 Each creature had **four** faces.
10.14 face of a lion, and the **fourth** the face of an eagle.
10.21 Each of them had **four** faces, four wings,
14.21 "I will send my **four** worst punishments on Jerusalem—war, famine,
40. 8 He measured this room, and found it was **four** metres deep.
40.39 this entrance room there were **four** tables, two on each side
40.40 Outside the room there were **four** similar tables, two on
40.41 **four** inside the room and four out in the courtyard.
40.42 The **four** tables in the annexe, used to prepare the offerings
43.15 The projections on the **four** corners were higher than the
45.19 of the Temple, on the **four** corners of the altar, and on
46.21 in each of its **four** corners there was a smaller courtyard,
48.30 Each of the **four** walls measures 2,250 metres and has three
48.35 of the wall on all **four** sides of the city is nine
Dan 1.17 God gave the **four** young men knowledge and skill in
1.20 what problem he raised, these **four** knew ten times more than
2.40 then there will be a **fourth** empire, as strong as iron, which
3.25 "Then why do I see **four** men walking about in the fire?"
3.25 of being hurt—and the **fourth** one looks like an angel."
7. 3 **Four** huge beasts came up out of the ocean, each one
7. 6 on its back there were **four** wings,
7. 6 like the wings of a bird, and it had **four** heads.
7. 7 As I was watching, a **fourth** beast appeared.
7.11 As I watched, the **fourth** beast was killed, and its body was
7.17 "These four huge beasts are **four** empires which will arise on earth.
7.19 to know more about the **fourth** beast, which was not like any
7.23 "The **fourth** beast is a fourth empire
8. 8 In its place **four** prominent horns came up,
8. 9 Out of one of these **four** horns grew a little horn,
8.22 The **four** horns that came up when the first horn was
8.22 represent the **four** kingdoms
11. 2 over Persia, followed by a **fourth,** who will be richer than
11. 4 his empire will break up and be divided into **four** parts.
Zech 1.18 In another vision I saw **four** ox horns.
1.20 Then the Lord showed me **four** workmen with hammers.
5. 2 it is nine metres long and **four** and a half metres wide."
6. 1 This time I saw **four** chariots coming out from between two
6. 3 the third by white horses, and the **fourth** by dappled horses.
6. 5 He answered, "These are the **four** winds;
7. 1 In the **fourth** year that Darius was emperor,
7. 1 on the **fourth** day of the ninth month
8.19 fasts held in the **fourth,** fifth, seventh, and tenth months
Mt 24.31 out his angels to the **four** corners of the earth, and they
Mk 2. 3 the message to them [3]when **four** men arrived, carrying a
13.27 the angels out to the **four** corners of the earth to gather
Lk 19. 8 cheated anyone, I will pay him back **four** times as much."
Jn 1.39 (It was then about **four** o'clock in the afternoon.)
4.35 You have a saying, **'Four** more months and then the harvest.'
11.17 Jesus arrived, he found that Lazarus had been buried **four** days before.
11.39 He has been buried **four** days!"
19.23 and divided them into **four** parts, one part for each soldier.
Acts 10.11 large sheet being lowered by its **four** corners to the earth.
11. 5 sheet being lowered by its **four** corners from heaven, and it
12. 4 over to be guarded by **four** groups of four soldiers each.
21. 9 He had **four** unmarried daughters who proclaimed God's message.
21.23 There are **four** men here who have taken a vow.
27.29 the rocks, so they lowered **four** anchors from the back of the
Heb 7. 1 in which he defeated the **four** kings, Melchizedek met him and
Rev 4. 6 each of its sides, were **four** living creatures covered with
4. 7 and the **fourth** looked like an eagle in flight.
4. 8 Each one of the **four** living creatures had six wings, and
4. 9 The **four** living creatures sing songs of glory and honour
5. 6 surrounded by the **four** living creatures and the elders.
5. 8 As he did so, the **four** living creatures and the
5.11 round the throne, the **four** living creatures, and the elders,
5.14 The **four** living creatures answered, "Amen!"
6. 1 I heard one of the **four** living creatures say in a voice
6. 6 voice coming from among the **four** living creatures, which
6. 7 Then the Lamb broke open the **fourth** seal;
6. 7 and I heard the **fourth** living creature say, "Come!"
7. 1 four angels standing at the **four** corners of the earth,
7. 1 holding back the **four** winds so that no wind should
7. 2 a loud voice to the **four** angels to whom God had given
7.11 round the throne, the elders, and the **four** living creatures.
8.12 Then the **fourth** angel blew his trumpet.
9.13 a voice coming from the **four** corners of the gold altar
9.14 the sixth angel, "Release the **four** angels who are bound at
9.15 The **four** angels were released;
14. 3 the throne, the **four** living creatures, and the elders;
15. 7 Then one of the **four** living creatures gave the seven
16. 8 Then the **fourth** angel poured out his bowl on the sun, and
19. 4 The twenty-four elders and the **four** living creatures fell
21.19 the third agate, the **fourth** emerald, [20]the fifth onyx,
also Num 7.12 1 Chr 24.7 1 Chr 25.9

FOX

Judg 15. 4 So he went and caught three hundred **foxes.**
15. 5 and turned the **foxes** loose in the Philistine cornfields.
Neh 4. 3 Even a **fox** could knock it down!"
Song 2.15 Catch the **foxes,** the little foxes, before they ruin our vineyard
Ezek 13. 4 prophets are as useless as **foxes** living among the ruins of a
Mt 8.20 Jesus answered him, **"Foxes** have holes, and birds have nests,
Lk 9.58 Jesus said to him, **"Foxes** have holes, and birds have nests,
13.32 Jesus answered them, "Go and tell that **fox:**

FRACTURED

Judg 9.53 threw a millstone down on his head and **fractured** his skull.

FRAGRANT

2 Chr 2. 4 by burning incense of **fragrant** spices,
Prov 27. 9 Perfume and **fragrant** oils make you feel happier,
Song 1. 3 There is a **fragrance** about you;
1.12 and my perfume filled the air with **fragrance.**
2.13 the air is **fragrant** with blossoming vines.
3. 6 like a column of smoke, **fragrant** with incense and myrrh,
4.10 your perfume more **fragrant** than any spice.
4.11 Your clothing has all the **fragrance** of Lebanon.
4.14 Myrrh and aloes grow there with all the most **fragrant** perfumes.
4.16 fill the air with **fragrance.**
7. 8 your breath like the **fragrance** of apples,
Hos 14. 6 They will be **fragrant** like the cedars of Lebanon.
2 Cor 2.14 about Christ spread everywhere like a sweet **fragrance.**
2.16 who are being saved, it is a **fragrance** that brings life.

FRAME

[CARRYING-FRAME, DOOR-FRAME]

Ex 26.15 "Make upright **frames** for the Tent out of acacia-wood.
26.16 Each **frame** is to be four metres long and 66 centimetres
26.17 matching projections, so that the **frames** can be joined together.
26.17 All the **frames** are to have these projections.
26.18 Make twenty **frames** for the south side [19]and forty silver
26.19 two bases under each **frame** to hold its two projections.
26.20 Make twenty **frames** for the north side of the Tent
26.21 the Tent [21]and forty silver bases, two under each **frame.**
26.22 the west, make six **frames,** [23]and two frames for the corners.
26.24 These corner **frames** are to be joined at the bottom and
26.24 The two **frames** that form the two corners are to be made
26.25 eight frames with their sixteen silver bases, two under each **frame.**
26.26 of acacia-wood, five for the **frames** on one side of the Tent,
26.27 five for the **frames** on the other side,
26.27 and five for the **frames** on the west end,
26.28 cross-bar, set half-way up the **frames,** is to extend from one
26.29 Cover the **frames** with gold and fit them with gold rings
35.11 covering, its hooks and its **frames,** its cross-bars,
36.20 They made upright **frames** of acacia-wood for the Tent.
36.21 Each **frame** was four metres tall and sixty-six centimetres
36.22 matching projections, so that the **frames** could be joined together.
36.22 All the **frames** had these projections.
36.23 They made twenty **frames** for the south side
36.24 two bases under each **frame** to hold its two projections.
36.25 They made twenty **frames** for the north side of the Tent
36.26 the Tent [26]and forty silver bases, two under each **frame.**
36.27 they made six **frames** [28]and two frames for the corners.
36.29 These corner **frames** were joined at the bottom
36.29 The two **frames** that formed the two corners were made in this
36.30 were eight frames and sixteen silver bases, two under each **frame.**
36.31 of acacia-wood, five for the **frames** on one side of the Tent,
36.32 five for the **frames** on the other side,
36.32 and five for the **frames** on the west end,
36.33 cross-bar, set half-way up the **frames,** extended from one end of
36.34 covered the **frames** with gold and fitted them with gold rings
39.33 its equipment, its hooks, its **frames,** its cross-bars,
40.18 set up its **frames,** attached its cross-bars,
Num 3.36 were assigned responsibility for the **frames** for the Tent,

Num 4.10 in a fine leather cover and place it on a **carrying-frame.**
4.12 leather cover over them, and place them on a **carrying-frame.**
4.31 be responsible for carrying the **frames,** bars, posts,
1 Kgs 6.33 main room a rectangular **door-frame** of olive wood was made.
7. 5 and the windows had rectangular **frames,**
7.28 panels which were set in **frames,** [29] with the figures of lions,
7.29 and on the **frames,** above and underneath the lions and bulls,
7.31 There was a circular **frame** on top for the basin.

FRANK

2 Cor 1.12 have been ruled by God-given **frankness** and sincerity, by the
6.11 We have spoken **frankly** to you;

FRANKINCENSE

A valuable substance made from the sap of a certain tree, probably brought from Arabia. It was burnt to give a pleasant smell.

Ex 30.34 sweet spices—stacte, onycha, galbanum, and pure **frankincense.**
Mt 2.11 out their gifts of gold, **frankincense,** and myrrh, and
Rev 18.13 and cinnamon, spice, incense, myrrh, and **frankincense;**

FRAUD

2 Chr 19. 7 our God does not tolerate **fraud** or partiality or the taking
Ps 55.11 the streets are full of oppression and **fraud.**

FREE

[SET FREE]

Gen 24. 8 to come with you, you will be **free** from this promise.
24.41 is only one way for you to be **free** from your vow:
24.41 my relatives and they refuse you, then you will be **free.'**
26.22 There was no dispute about this one, so he named it **"Freedom."**
26.22 the Lord has given us **freedom** to live in the land,
34.10 may live anywhere you wish, trade **freely,** and own property."
34.21 let them live in the land with us and travel **freely.**
44.10 will become my slave, and the rest of you can go **free."**
44.18 Joseph and said, "Please, sir, allow me to speak with you **freely.**
49.21 "Naphtali is a deer that runs **free,** Who bears lovely fawns.
Ex 6. 6 you and **set you free** from your slavery to the Egyptians.
6. 7 Lord your God when I **set you free** from slavery in Egypt.
6.27 the men who told the king of Egypt to **free** the Israelites.
15.16 have marched past— the people you **set free** from slavery.
21. 2 year he is to be **set free** without having to pay anything.
21. 5 not want to be **set free,** [6] then his master shall take him
21. 7 slave, she is not to be **set free,** as male slaves are.
21.11 to her, he must **set her free** and not receive any payment.
21.26 of it, he is to **free** the slave as payment for the
21.27 a tooth, he is to **free** the slave as payment for the
Lev 19.20 not been paid for and **freed,** then if another man has sexual
25.10 fiftieth year apart and proclaim **freedom** to all the inhabitants
25.49 or if he himself earns enough, he may buy his own **freedom.**
25.54 If he is not **set free** in any of these ways, he
25.54 children must be **set free** in the next Year of Restoration.
27. 2 that person may be **set free** by the payment of the following
Num 5.31 husband shall be **free** of guilt, but the woman, if guilty,
36. 6 the daughters of Zelophehad are **free** to marry anyone they wish
Deut 6.23 He **freed** us from Egypt to bring us here and give us
7. 8 great might and **set you free** from slavery to the king of
7.19 power and strength by which the Lord your God **set you free.**
12.15 "But you are **free** to kill and eat your animals wherever
15.10 Give to him **freely** and unselfishly, and the Lord will bless
15.12 When the seventh year comes, you must let him go **free.**
15.13 When you **set him free,** do not send him away empty-handed.
15.15 were slaves in Egypt and the Lord your God **set you free;**
15.18 Do not be resentful when you set a slave **free;**
21.14 you no longer want her, you are to let her go **free.**
24.18 slaves in Egypt and that the Lord your God **set you free;**
Judg 3. 9 out to the Lord, and he sent a man who **freed** them.
3.15 out to the Lord, and he sent a man to **free** them.
10. 1 the son of Puah and grandson of Dodo, came to **free** Israel.
16.20 woke up and thought, "I'll get loose and go **free,** as
1 Sam 17.26 who kills this Philistine and **frees** Israel from this disgrace?
26.24 Lord do the same to me and **free** me from all troubles!"
2 Sam 7.23 the people whom you **set free** from Egypt to be your own.
1 Kgs 20.34 Ahab replied, "On these terms, then, I will **set you free."**
2 Kgs 13. 5 sent Israel a leader, who **freed** them from the Syrians, and
1 Chr 9.33 the temple buildings and were **free** from other duties, because
Ezra 9. 8 You have **freed** us from slavery and given us new life.
Job 3.18 Even prisoners enjoy peace, **free** from shouts and harsh commands.
3.19 the famous and the unknown, and slaves at last are **free.**
5.23 The fields you plough will be **free** of rocks;
12.14 who can rebuild, and who can **free** the man God imprisons?
15.19 Their land was **free** from foreigners;
33. 9 I am innocent and **free** from sin.
33.24 Here is the ransom to **set him free."**
39. 5 Who gave the wild donkeys their **freedom?**
Ps 2. 3 "Let us **free** ourselves from their rule," they say;
19.13 Then I shall be perfect and **free** from the evil of sin.
31. 8 you have given me **freedom** to go where I wish.
32. 2 not accuse of doing wrong and who is **free** from all deceit.
34. 4 he **freed** me from all my fears.
37.26 At all times he gives **freely** and lends to others, and
54. 1 **set me free** by your might!
68. 6 leads prisoners out into happy **freedom,** but rebels will have to
79.11 by your great power **free** those who are condemned to die.
102.20 of prisoners and **set free** those who were condemned to die.
105.20 the ruler of nations **set him free.**
Ps 111. 9 He set his people **free** and made an eternal covenant with them.
118. 5 he answered me and **set me free.**
119.22 **Free** me from their insults and scorn, because I have kept
119.45 I will live in perfect **freedom,** because I try to obey
119.154 Defend my cause, and **set me free;**
124. 7 the trap is broken, and we are **free!**
129. 4 But the Lord, the righteous one, has **freed** me from slavery."
136.24 he **freed** us from our enemies;
142. 7 **Set me free** from my distress;
146. 7 The Lord sets prisoners **free** [8] and gives sight to the blind.
Prov 11.24 Some people spend their money **freely** and still grow richer.
29. 6 in their own sins, while honest people are happy and **free.**
Is 5.18 You are unable to break **free** from your sins.
5.23 you let guilty men go **free,** and you prevent the innocent
10.27 that time comes, I will **free** you from the power of Assyria,
14.17 this the man who never **freed** his prisoners or let them go
14.25 I will **free** my people from the Assyrian yoke and from the
32. 9 who live an easy life, **free** from worries, listen to what I
32.11 You have been living an easy life, **free** from worries;
32.18 God's people will be **free** from worries, and their homes
35.10 be happy for ever, for ever **free** from sorrow and grief.
42. 7 of the blind and **set free** those who sit in dark prisons.
43. 3 I will give up Egypt to **set you free;**
45. 8 open to receive it and will blossom with **freedom** and justice.
45.13 will rebuild my city, Jerusalem, and set my captive people **free.**
47. 4 God of Israel **sets us free**— his name is the Lord
48.20 Go out from Babylon, go **free!**
49. 9 I will say to the prisoners, 'Go **free!'**
49.26 am the Lord, the one who saves you and **sets you free.**
51.11 be happy for ever, for ever **free** from sorrow and grief.
51.14 Those who are prisoners will soon be **set free;**
52. 2 Shake yourself **free,** Jerusalem!
52. 3 in the same way nothing will be paid to **set you free.**
52. 4 in Egypt as foreigners, you did so of your own **free will;**
58. 6 and the yoke of injustice, and let the oppressed go **free.**
60.16 saved you, That the mighty God of Israel **sets you free.**
61. 1 To announce release to captives And **freedom** to those in prison.
Jer 31.11 I have set Israel's people **free** and have saved them from
34. 8 made an agreement to **set free** [9] their Hebrew slaves, both male
34.10 their leaders agreed to **free** their slaves and never to enslave
34.10 They did **set them free,** [11] but later they changed their minds,
34.13 I rescued them from Egypt and **set them free** from slavery.
34.14 years they were to **set free** any Hebrew slave who had served
34.15 to set your fellow-Israelites **free,** and you made a covenant
34.16 slaves whom you had **set free** as they desired, and you forced
34.17 you have not given your fellow-Israelites their **freedom.**
34.17 Very well, then, I will give you **freedom:**
34.17 the **freedom** to die by war, disease, and starvation.
37. 4 prison and was still moving about **freely** among the people.
40. 1 Nebuzaradan, the commanding officer, had **set me free** at Ramah.
40. 4 I am taking the chains off your wrists and **setting you free.**
Ezek 13.20 arms and **set free** the people that you were controlling.
34.27 chains and **set them free** from those who made them slaves,
37.23 I will **free** them from all the ways in which they sin
Dan 1. 4 well-trained, quick to learn, and **free** from physical defects,
9.24 time God has set for **freeing** your people and your holy city
Mic 2.13 They will break out of the city gates and go **free.**
Zech 9.11 set your people free— **free** from the waterless pit of exile.
Mal 4. 2 You will be as **free** and happy as calves let out of
Mt 27.15 was in the habit of **setting free** any one prisoner the crowd
27.17 them, "Which one do you want me to **set free** for you?
27.20 to ask Pilate to **set Barabbas free** and have Jesus put to
27.21 of these two do you want me to **set free** for you?"
27.26 Then Pilate **set Barabbas free** for them;
Mk 15. 6 was in the habit of **setting free** any one prisoner the people
15. 9 "Do you want me to **set free** for you the king of
15.11 to ask, instead, for Pilate to **set Barabbas free** for them.
15.15 to please the crowd, so he **set Barabbas free** for them.
Lk 1.68 come to the help of his people and has **set them free.**
2.38 to all who were waiting for God to **set Jerusalem free.**
4.18 to **set free** the oppressed [19] and announce that the time has
13.12 out to her, "Woman, you are **free** from your illness!"
23.18 **Set Barabbas free** for us!"
23.20 Pilate wanted to **set Jesus free,** so he appealed to the
23.22 I will have him whipped and **set him free."**
23.25 He **set free** the man they wanted, the one who had been
24.21 he would be the one who was going to **set Israel free!**
Jn 8.32 you will know the truth, and the truth will **set you free."**
8.33 What do you mean, then, by saying, 'You will be **free'?"**
8.36 If the Son **sets you free,** then you will be really free.
10.18 I give it up of my own **free will.**
18.39 custom you have, I always **set free** a prisoner for you during
18.39 Do you want me to **set free** for you the King of
19.10 have the authority to **set you free** and also to have you
19.12 heard this, he tried to find a way to **set Jesus free.**
19.12 shouted back, "If you **set him free,** that means that you are
Acts 2.24 raised him from death, **setting him free** from its power,
3.13 Pilate's presence, even after Pilate had decided to **set him free.**
4.21 Council warned them even more strongly and then **set them free.**
4.23 as Peter and John were **set free,** they returned to their
5.40 and then they **set them free.**
7.25 to use him to **set them free,** but they did not understand.)
7.34 heard their groans, and I have come down to **set them free.**
7.35 rule the people and **set them free** with the help of the
13.38 who believes in him is **set free** from all the sins from
13.38 sins from which the Law of Moses could not **set you free.**
24.23 but to give him some **freedom** and allow his friends to
28.31 Lord Jesus Christ, speaking with all boldness and **freedom.**
Rom 3.24 But by the **free gift** of God's grace all are put right
3.24 put right with him through Christ Jesus, who **sets them free.**
4.16 should be guaranteed as God's **free gift** to all of Abraham's

Rom	5.15	the same, because God's **free gift** is not like Adam's sin.
	5.15	greater, and so is his **free gift** to so many people through
	5.17	God's abundant grace and are **freely** put right with him will
	5.18	one righteous act **sets all mankind free** and gives them life.
	6. 7	a person dies, he is **set free** from the power of sin.
	6.18	You were **set free** from sin and became the slaves of righteousness.
	6.20	When you were the slaves of sin, you were **free** from righteousness.
	6.22	But now you have been **set free** from sin and are the
	6.23	but God's **free gift** is eternal life in union with Christ
	7. 2	he dies, then she is **free** from the law that bound her
	7. 3	dies, she is legally a **free** woman and does not commit
	7. 6	Now, however, we are **free** from the Law, because we died to
	8. 2	with Christ Jesus, has **set me free** from the law of sin
	8.21	itself would one day be **set free** from its slavery to decay
	8.21	and would share the glorious **freedom** of the children of God.
	8.23	God to make us his sons and **set our whole being free.**
	8.32	us his Son—will he not also **freely** give us all things?
	15.26	in Macedonia and Achaia have **freely** decided to give an
1 Cor	1.30	we become God's holy people and are **set free.**
	7.15	Christian partner, whether husband or wife, is **free** to act.
	7.21	if you have a chance to become a **free** man, use it.
	7.22	who has been called by the Lord is the Lord's **free** man;
	7.22	in the same way a **free** man who has been called by
	7.32	I would like you to be **free** from worry.
	7.39	A married woman is not **free** as long as her husband lives;
	7.39	husband dies, then she is **free** to be married to any man
	8. 9	however, not to let your **freedom** of action make those who
	9. 1	Am I not a **free** man?
	9.17	work as a matter of **free** choice, then I could expect to
	9.19	I am a **free** man, nobody's slave;
	10.25	You are **free** to eat anything sold in the meat-market,
	10.29	someone asks, "why should my **freedom** to act be limited by
	12.13	or Gentiles, whether slaves or **free,** have been baptized into
2 Cor	3.17	where the Spirit of the Lord is present, there is **freedom.**
	8. 3	Of their own **free will** [4]they begged us and pleaded for the
	8.17	help that of his own **free will** he decided to go to
Gal	1. 4	In order to **set us free** from this present evil age, Christ
	2. 4	to find out about the **freedom** we have through our union with
	3.28	Jews and Gentiles, between slaves and **free** men, between men and women;
	4.22	two sons, one by a slave-woman, the other by a **free** woman.
	4.23	but his son by the **free** woman was born as a result
	4.26	But the heavenly Jerusalem is **free,** and she is our mother.
	4.30	father's property along with the son of the **free** woman."
	4.31	are not the children of a slave-woman but of a **free** woman.
	5. 1	**Freedom** is what we have—Christ has set us free!
	5. 1	Freedom is what we have—Christ has **set us free!**
	5. 1	Stand, then, as **free** people, and do not allow yourselves to
	5.13	As for you, my brothers, you were called to be **free.**
	5.13	But do not let this **freedom** become an excuse for letting
Eph	1. 6	his glorious grace, for the **free gift** he gave us in his
	1. 7	death of Christ we are **set free,** that is, our sins are
	1.14	us that God will give complete **freedom** to those who are his.
	4.30	guarantee that the Day will come when God will **set you free.**
	6. 8	everyone, whether slave or **free,** for the good work he does.
Phil	1. 7	and also while I was **free** to defend the gospel and establish
	1.10	Then you will be **free** from all impurity and blame on the
	1.19	comes from the Spirit of Jesus Christ I shall be **set free.**
	2. 7	of this, of his own **free will** he gave up all he
Col	1.14	Son, [14]by whom we are **set free,** that is, our sins are
	2.11	Christ, which consists of being **freed** from the power of this
	2.15	And on that cross Christ **freed** himself from the power of
	2.20	died with Christ and are **set free** from the ruling spirits of
	3.11	savages, slaves, and **free** men, but Christ is all,
1 Thes	4. 3	God wants you to be holy and completely **free** from sexual immorality.
	5.23	being—spirit, soul, and body—**free** from every fault at the
Phlm	14	I would like you to do it of your own **free will.**
Heb	2.15	death, [15]and in this way **set free** those who were slaves
	9.15	been a death which **sets people free** from the wrongs they did
	10.19	have, then, my brothers, complete **freedom** to go into the
	11.35	Others, refusing to accept **freedom,** died under torture in
	13. 5	Keep your lives **free** from the love of money, and be
Jas	1.25	the perfect law that **sets people free,** who keeps on paying
	2.12	people who will be judged by the law that **sets us free.**
	3.17	it is **free** from prejudice and hypocrisy.
1 Pet	1.18	what was paid to **set you free** from the worthless manner of
	2.16	Live as **free** people;
	2.16	do not, however, use your **freedom** to cover up any evil, but
2 Pet	2.19	They promise them **freedom** while they themselves are
Rev	1. 5	his sacrificial death he has **freed** us from our sins [6]and
	6.15	all other men, slave and **free,** hid themselves in caves and
	13.16	rich and poor, slave and **free,** to have a mark placed on
	19.18	the flesh of all people, slave and **free,** great and small!"

FREEDMEN

Acts	6. 9	of the synagogue of the **Freedmen** (as it was called), which

FREEWILL

Lev	7.16	vow or as his own **freewill** offering, not all of it has
	22.18	a vow or as a **freewill** offering, the animal must not have
	22.21	a vow or as a **freewill** offering, the animal must be without
	22.23	As a **freewill** offering you may offer an animal that is
	23.38	fulfilment of vows, and your **freewill** offerings that you give
	27.26	so no one may dedicate it to him as a **freewill** offering.
Num	15. 3	a vow or as a **freewill** offering or as an offering at
	29.39	you give in fulfilment of a vow or as **freewill** offerings.
Deut	12. 6	promise to the Lord, your **freewill** offerings, and the first-born
	12.17	you promise to the Lord, your **freewill** offerings, or any other
	16.10	bringing him a **freewill** offering in proportion to the blessing
2 Kgs	12. 4	regular sacrifices and the money given as **free-will** gifts.
Ezra	2.68	leaders of the clans gave **freewill** offerings to help rebuild the
	8.28	silver and gold utensils brought to him as **freewill** offerings.

FREEZE

Job	37.10	The breath of God **freezes** the waters, and turns them to
	38.30	turn the waters to stone and **freeze** the face of the sea?

FREQUENT

Lk	5.33	"The disciples of John fast **frequently** and offer prayers,
Acts	1.14	They gathered **frequently** to pray as a group, together

FRESH

Gen	8.11	him in the evening with a **fresh** olive leaf in its beak.
Lev	14. 5	to be killed over a clay bowl containing **fresh** spring water.
	14.50	of the birds over a clay bowl containing **fresh** spring water.
	14.51	blood of the bird that was killed and in the **fresh** water.
	14.52	with the bird's blood, the **fresh** water, the live bird,
	15.13	his clothes and bathe in **fresh** spring water, and he will be
Num	19.17	shall be taken and put in a pot, and **fresh** water added.
1 Sam	21. 6	removed from the sacred table and replaced by **fresh** bread.
2 Sam	16. 1	a hundred bunches of **fresh** fruit, and a leather bag full
2 Kgs	4.42	barley harvested that year, and some **freshly-cut** ears of corn.
Neh	5.18	and every ten days I provided a **fresh** supply of wine.
Ps	23. 2	of green grass and leads me to quiet pools of **fresh** water.
Prov	18. 4	of wisdom, deep as the ocean, **fresh** as a flowing stream.
Is	12. 3	**fresh** water brings joy to the thirsty, so God's people rejoice
Jer	2.13	me, the spring of **fresh** water, and they have dug cisterns,
	6. 7	keeps its water **fresh,** so Jerusalem keeps its evil fresh.
	17.13	they have abandoned you, the Lord, the spring of **fresh** water.
Lam	3.23	love and mercy still continue, [23]**Fresh** as the morning,
Ezek	47. 8	it replaces the salt water of that sea with **fresh** water.
	47. 9	water of the Dead Sea **fresh,** and wherever it flows, it will
	47.11	marshes and ponds along the shore will not be made **fresh.**
	47.12	They will have **fresh** fruit every month, because they are watered
Zech	14. 8	When that day comes, **fresh** water will flow from Jerusalem,
Mt	9.17	new wine is poured into **fresh** wineskins, and both will keep
Mk	2.22	Instead, new wine must be poured into **fresh** wineskins."
Lk	5.38	Instead, new wine must be poured into **fresh** wineskins!

FRIDAY

see also **PREPARATION DAY**

Neh	13.20	sold all kinds of goods spent **Friday** night outside the city
Lk	23.54	It was **Friday,** and the Sabbath was about to begin.
Jn	19.31	requested this because it was **Friday,** and they did not want

FRIEND

[UNFRIENDLY]

Gen	19. 7	He said to them, **"Friends,** I beg you, don't do such a
	26.27	me, when you were so **unfriendly** to me before and made me
	26.31	Isaac said good-bye to them, and they parted as **friends.**
	29. 4	Jacob asked the shepherds, "My **friends,** where are you from?"
	31. 2	that Laban was no longer as **friendly** as he had been earlier.
	31. 5	your father is not as **friendly** towards me as he used to
	33.10	face of God, now that you have been so **friendly** to me.
	34.21	"These men are **friendly;**
	37. 4	much that they would not speak to him in a **friendly** manner.
	38.12	mourning, he and his **friend** Hirah of Adullam went to Timnah,
	38.20	Judah sent his **friend** Hirah to take the goat and get
Ex	32.27	and kill his brothers, his **friends,** and his neighbours."
	33.11	Moses face to face, just as a man speaks with a **friend.**
Deut	13. 6	or your closest **friend** may secretly encourage you to worship
Josh	9.15	Joshua made a treaty of **friendship** with the people of Gibeon
Judg	5.31	O Lord, but may your **friends** shine like the rising sun!
	7.13	Gideon arrived, he heard a man telling a **friend** about a dream.
	7.14	His **friend** replied, "It's the sword of the Israelite,
	11.37	I can go with my **friends** to wander in the mountains and
	11.38	She and her **friends** went up into the mountains and grieved
	14.16	You asked my **friends** a riddle and didn't tell me what it
	15. 2	thought that you hated her, so I gave her to your **friend.**
	15. 6	from Timnah, had given Samson's wife to a **friend** of Samson's.
	19.23	the old man went outside and said to them, "No, my **friends!**
Ruth	4. 1	Boaz called to him, "Come over here, my **friend,** and sit down."
1 Sam	18. 3	Jonathan swore eternal **friendship** with David because of his
	20.29	then, if you are my **friend,** let me go and see my
	23.18	of them made a sacred promise of **friendship** to each other.
	25. 6	"David sends you greetings, my **friend,** with his best wishes
	25. 8	can to us your servants and to your dear **friend** David."
	27. 5	Achish, "If you are my **friend,** let me have a small town
	30.26	of the loot to his **friends,** the leaders of Judah, with the
2 Sam	3. 8	Saul, his brothers, and his **friends,** and I have saved you
	10. 2	"I must show loyal **friendship** to Hanun, as his father Nahash
	13. 3	But he had a **friend,** a very shrewd man named Jonadab, the
	15.32	place of worship, his trusted **friend** Hushai the Archite met him
	15.37	So Hushai, David's **friend,** returned to the city just as
	16.16	Hushai, David's trusted **friend,** met Absalom, he shouted,
	16.17	"What has happened to your loyalty to your **friend** David?"
	20. 9	Joab said to Amasa, "How are you, my **friend?"**
1 Kgs	2.13	"Is this a **friendly** visit?"
	5. 1	Tyre had always been a **friend** of David's, and when he heard
	11.19	Hadad won the **friendship** of the king, and the king gave
	16.11	Every male relative and **friend** was put to death.
2 Kgs	9.17	"Send a horseman to find out if they are **friends** or enemies."

2 Kgs	9.18	"The king wants to know if you come as a **friend.**"
	10.11	Ahab living in Jezreel, and all his officers, close **friends,**
1 Chr	12.17	"If you are coming as **friends** to help me, you are welcome
	19. 2	"I must show loyal **friendship** to Hanun, as his father Nahash
	27.33	and Hushai the Archite was the king's **friend** and counsellor.
2 Chr	20. 7	the descendants of Abraham, your **friend,** to be theirs for ever.
Esth	5.10	Then he invited his **friends** to his house and asked his wife
	5.14	his wife and all his **friends** suggested, "Why don't you have
	6.13	and all his **friends** everything that had happened to him.
	6.13	Then she and those wise **friends** of his said to him, "You
Job	2.11	Three of Job's **friends** were Eliphaz, from the city of Teman,
	6.14	like this I need loyal **friends**— whether I've forsaken God or
	6.15	But you, my **friends,** you deceive me like streams that go
	6.27	and make yourselves rich off your closest **friends!**
	12. 4	Even my **friends** laugh at me now;
	16.20	My **friends** scorn me;
	16.21	plead with God for me, as a man pleads for his **friend.**
	17. 5	a man betrays his **friends** for money, and his children suffer
	17.12	But my **friends** say night is daylight;
	19.14	my relatives and **friends** are gone.
	19.19	My closest **friends** look at me with disgust;
	19.21	You are my **friends!**
	29. 4	I was prosperous, and the **friendship** of God protected my home.
	32. 3	He was also angry with Job's three **friends.**
	35. 4	I am going to answer you and your **friends** too.
	42. 7	with you and your two **friends,** because you did not speak the
	42.10	had prayed for his three **friends,** the Lord made him prosperous
	42.11	brothers and sisters and former **friends** came to visit him
Ps	7. 3	if I have betrayed a **friend** or without cause done violence
	15. 3	does no wrong to his **friends** nor spreads rumours about his
	25.14	The Lord is the **friend** of those who obey him and he
	28. 3	men whose words are **friendly,** but who have hatred in their
	34.11	Come, my young **friends,** and listen to me, and I will
	35.14	bowed low, [14] as I would pray for a **friend** or a brother.
	35.20	They do not speak in a **friendly** way;
	38.11	My **friends** and neighbours will not come near me, because of
	41. 9	Even my best **friend,** the one I trusted most, the one who
	50.18	You become the **friend** of every thief you see
	55.13	But it is you, my companion, my colleague and close **friend.**
	55.20	My former companion attacked his **friends;**
	88. 8	You have caused my **friends** to abandon me;
	88.18	have made even my closest **friends** abandon me, and darkness
	119.63	I am a **friend** of all who serve you, of all who
	122. 8	sake of my relatives and **friends** I say to Jerusalem, "Peace
Prov	6.16	trouble among **friends.**
	7. 4	Treat wisdom as your sister, and insight as your closest **friend.**
	12.26	is a guide to his **friend,** but the path of the wicked
	13.20	If you make **friends** with stupid people, you will be ruined.
	14.20	likes a poor man, but the rich have many **friends.**
	15.26	Lord hates evil thoughts, but he is pleased with **friendly** words.
	16. 7	When you please the Lord, you can make your enemies into **friends.**
	16.28	they stir up trouble and break up **friendships.**
	16.29	Violent people deceive their **friends** and lead them to disaster.
	17. 9	Remembering wrongs can break up a **friendship.**
	17.17	**Friends** always show their love.
	18.24	Some **friendships** do not last,
	18.24	but some **friends** are more loyal than brothers.
	19. 4	people are always finding new **friends,** but the poor cannot keep
	19. 6	claims the **friendship** of those who give out favours.
	19. 7	no wonder he has no **friends.**
	22.11	and graciousness of speech, the king will be your **friend.**
	22.24	Don't make **friends** with people who have hot, violent tempers.
	24. 1	of evil people, and don't try to make **friends** with them.
	24.26	An honest answer is a sign of true **friendship.**
	27. 6	A **friend** means well, even when he hurts you.
	27.10	Do not forget your **friends** or your father's friends.
	27.14	might as well curse your **friend** as wake him up early in
	28. 7	One who makes **friends** with good-for-nothings is a disgrace to
	29. 5	If you flatter your **friends,** you set a trap for yourself.
Is	1.23	Your leaders are rebels and **friends** of thieves;
	5. 1	sing you this song, a song of my **friend** and his vineyard:
	5. 1	My **friend** had a vineyard on a very fertile hill.
	5. 3	So now my **friend** says, "You people who live in Jerusalem
	41. 8	people that I have chosen, the descendants of Abraham, my **friend.**
Jer	6.21	Fathers and sons will die, and so will **friends** and neighbours."
	9. 4	be on guard against his **friend,** and no one can trust his
	9. 4	is as deceitful as Jacob, and everyone slanders his **friends.**
	9. 5	They all mislead their **friends,** and no one tells the truth;
	9. 8	Everyone speaks **friendly** words to his neighbour, but is really
	9.20	how to mourn, and your **friends** how to sing a funeral song.
	12. 6	Do not trust them, even though they speak **friendly** words."
	13.21	people you thought were your **friends** conquer you and rule over
	20. 4	to yourself and to your **friends,** and you will see them all
	20. 6	buried, along with all your **friends** to whom you have told so
	20.10	Even my close **friends** wait for my downfall.
	22.18	mourn his death or say, 'How terrible, my **friend,** how terrible!'
	23.35	each one should ask his **friends** and his relatives, 'What answer
	38.22	'The king's best **friends** misled him, they overruled him.
	38.22	feet have sunk in the mud, his **friends** have left him.' "
Lam	1. 2	Of all her former **friends,** not one is left to comfort her.
Dan	1.11	Ashpenaz had placed in charge of him and his three **friends.**
	2.13	all of them to be killed, including Daniel and his **friends.**
	2.17	went home and told his **friends** Hananiah, Mishael, and Azariah
Amos	1. 9	and did not keep the treaty of **friendship** they had made.
Obad	7	Those **friends** who ate with you have laid a trap for you;
Mic	7. 5	Don't believe your neighbour or trust your **friend.**
Zech	13. 6	he will answer, 'I got them at a **friend's** house.' "
Mt	5.43	that it was said, 'Love your **friends,** hate your enemies.'
	5.47	you speak only to your **friends,** have you done anything out
	6. 3	a way that even your closest **friend** will not know about it.
Mt	11.19	a drinker, a **friend** of tax collectors and other outcasts!'
	20.13	'Listen, **friend,'** the owner answered one of them, 'I have
	22.12	**'Friend,** how did you get in here without wedding clothes?'
	26.50	Jesus answered, "Be quick about it, **friend!"**
Mk	9.50	"Have the salt of **friendship** among yourselves,
	16. 9	went to Peter and his **friends** and gave them a brief account
Lk	2.44	started looking for him among their relatives and **friends.**
	4.40	After sunset all who had **friends** who were sick with
	5.20	he said to the man, "Your sins are forgiven, my **friend."**
	7. 6	house when the officer sent **friends** to tell him, "Sir,
	7.34	a drinker, a **friend** of tax collectors and other outcasts!'
	11. 5	you should go to a **friend's** house at midnight and say to
	11. 5	midnight and say to him, **'Friend,** let me borrow three loaves
	11. 6	A **friend** of mine who is on a journey has just come
	11. 7	And suppose your **friend** should answer from inside, 'Don't bother me!
	11. 8	bread because you are his **friend,** yet he will get up and
	12. 4	"I tell you, my **friends,** do not be afraid of those who
	12.14	Jesus answered him, "My **friend,** who gave me the right
	14.10	you and say, 'Come on up, my **friend,** to a better place.'
	14.12	dinner, do not invite your **friends** or your brothers or your
	15. 6	Then he calls his **friends** and neighbours together and says to them,
	15. 9	finds it, she calls her **friends** and neighbours together, and
	15.29	even a goat for me to have a feast with my **friends!**
	16. 4	is gone, I shall have **friends** who will welcome me in their
	16. 9	make **friends** for yourselves with worldly wealth, so that
	21.16	parents, your brothers, your relatives, and your **friends;**
	22.25	and the rulers claim the title **'Friends** of the People.'
	23.12	On that very day Herod and Pilate became **friends;**
Jn	3.29	but the bridegroom's **friend,** who stands by and listens, is
	11. 3	"Lord, your dear **friend** is ill."
	11.11	this and then added, "Our **friend** Lazarus has fallen asleep,
	15.13	person can have for his **friends** is to give his life for
	15.14	And you are my **friends** if you do what I command you.
	15.15	Instead, I call you **friends,** because I have told you
	19.12	him free, that means that you are not the Emperor's **friend!**
Acts	10.24	with relatives and close **friends** that he had invited.
	13. 7	He was a **friend** of the governor of the island, Sergius Paulus,
	15.25	will go with our dear **friends** Barnabas and Paul, [26] who
	19.31	provincial authorities, who were his **friends,** also sent him
	24.23	freedom and allow his **friends** to provide for his needs.
	27. 3	to go and see his **friends,** to be given what he needed.
	28. 2	The natives there were very **friendly** to us.
Rom	2. 1	Do you, my **friend,** pass judgement on others?
	2. 3	But you, my **friend,** do those very things for which you
	5.10	but he made us his **friends** through the death of his Son.
	5.10	Now that we are God's **friends,** how much more will we be
	5.11	our Lord Jesus Christ, who has now made us God's **friends.**
	9.20	But who are you, my **friend,** to answer God back?
	11.15	mankind was changed from God's enemies into his **friends.**
	11.28	God's choice, they are his **friends** because of their ancestors.
	12.19	Never take revenge, my **friends,** but instead let God's anger do it.
	16. 2	herself has been a good **friend** to many people and also to
	16. 5	Greetings to my dear **friend** Epaenetus, who was the first
	16. 8	to Ampliatus, my dear **friend** in the fellowship of the Lord.
	16. 9	Urbanus, our fellow-worker in Christ's service, and to Stachys, my dear **friend.**
	16.12	service, and to my dear **friend** Persis, who has done so much
1 Cor	10.14	So then, my dear **friends,** keep away from the worship of idols.
2 Cor	4. 9	there are many enemies, but we are never without a **friend;**
	5.18	us from enemies into his **friends**
	5.18	and gave us the task of making others his **friends** also.
	5.19	that God was making all mankind his **friends** through Christ.
	5.19	us the message which tells how he makes them his **friends.**
	5.20	let God change you from enemies into his **friends!**
	6.11	Dear **friends** in Corinth!
	7. 1	All these promises are made to us, my dear **friends.**
	11.26	dangers on the high seas, and dangers from false **friends.**
	12.19	God, and everything we do, dear **friends,** is done to help you.
Phil	2.12	So then, dear **friends,** as you always obeyed me when I
Col	1.22	God has made you his **friends,** in order to bring you, holy,
Tit	3. 2	but to be peaceful and **friendly,** and always to show a gentle
	3.15	Give our greetings to our **friends** in the faith.
Phlm	1	brother Timothy— To our **friend** and fellow-worker Philemon,
Heb	6. 9	if we speak like this, dear **friends,** we feel sure about you.
	11.31	God, for she gave the Israelite spies a **friendly** welcome.
Jas	2.23	And so Abraham was called God's **friend.**
	3.17	it is also peaceful, gentle, and **friendly;**
	4. 4	know that to be the world's **friend** means to be God's enemy?
	4. 4	Whoever wants to be the world's **friend** makes himself God's enemy.
1 Pet	2.11	I appeal to you, my **friends,** as strangers and refugees
	4.12	My dear **friends,** do not be surprised at the painful test
2 Pet	3. 1	My dear **friends,** this is now the second letter I have
	3. 8	But do not forget one thing, my dear **friends!**
	3.14	And so, my **friends,** as you wait for that Day,
	3.17	But you, my **friends,** already know this.
1 Jn	2. 7	My dear **friends,** this command I am writing to you is not
	3. 2	My dear **friends,** we are now God's children, but it is not
	3.21	And so, my dear **friends,** if our conscience does not condemn us,
	4. 1	My dear **friends,** do not believe all who claim to have the
	4. 7	Dear **friends,** let us love one another,
	4.11	Dear **friends,** if this is how God loved us, then we
3 Jn	2	My dear **friend,** I pray that everything may go well with
	5	My dear **friend,** you are so faithful in the work you do
	11	My dear **friend,** do not imitate what is bad, but imitate
	15	All your **friends** send greetings.
	15	Greet all our **friends** personally.
Jude	3	My dear **friends,** I was doing my best to write to you

Jude 17 But remember, my **friends,** what you were told in the past
20 But you, my **friends,** keep on building yourselves up

FRIGHT

Gen 32. 7 Jacob was **frightened** and worried.
Judg 13. 6 to me, and he looked as **frightening** as the angel of God.
2 Sam 17. 2 He will be **frightened,** and all his men will run away.
2 Kgs 19. 6 not to let the Assyrians **frighten** you with their claims that
19.26 they were **frightened** and stunned.
2 Chr 20. 3 Jehoshaphat was **frightened** and prayed to the Lord for guidance.
29. 8 what he has done to them has shocked and **frightened** everyone.
32.18 in order to **frighten** and discourage the people of Jerusalem
Ezra 4. 4 land tried to discourage and **frighten** the Jews and keep them
9. 4 all those who were **frightened** because of what the God of
Neh 6. 9 They were trying to **frighten** us into stopping work.
6.13 They hired him to **frighten** me into sinning, so that they
6.14 Nodiah and all the other prophets who tried to **frighten** me."
6.19 And he kept sending me letters to try to **frighten** me.
Job 4.15 light breeze touched my face, and my hair bristled with **fright.**
13.25 Are you trying to **frighten** me?
27.23 wind howls at them as they run, **frightening** them with destructive
33.16 to what he says, and they are **frightened** at his warnings.
39.20 make them leap like locusts and **frighten** men with their snorting?
41.25 When he rises up, even the strongest are **frightened;**
Is 7. 4 alert, to stay calm, and not to be **frightened** or disturbed.
31. 9 the officers will be so **frightened** that they will abandon their
33.14 The sinful people of Zion are trembling with **fright.**
37. 6 not to let the Assyrians **frighten** you by their claims that
37.27 they were **frightened** and stunned.
41. 5 they are **frightened** and tremble with fear.
47.12 perhaps you can **frighten** your enemies.
59.11 We are **frightened** and distressed.
Jer 48.41 Moab's soldiers will be as **frightened** as a woman in labour.
49.22 Edom's soldiers will be as **frightened** as a woman in labour."
Ezek 7.16 escape to the mountains like doves **frightened** from the valleys.
32.10 When I swing my sword, kings will shudder with **fright.**
Dan 4. 5 But I had a **frightening** dream and saw terrifying visions
5. 6 pale and was so **frightened** that his knees began to shake.
7.28 I was so **frightened** that I turned pale, and I kept
10.19 "God loves you, so don't let anything worry you or **frighten** you."
11.30 come in ships and oppose him, and he will be **frightened.**
11.44 east and the north will **frighten** him, and he will fight
Mt 8.26 "Why are you so **frightened?"**
Mk 4.40 Then Jesus said to his disciples, "Why are you **frightened?**
9. 6 and the others were so **frightened** that he did not know what
Acts 22.29 the commander was **frightened** when he realized that Paul
2 Cor 10. 9 to appear that I am trying to **frighten** you with my letters.

FROG

Ex 8. 2 I will punish your country by covering it with **frogs.**
8. 3 will be so full of **frogs** that they will leave it and
8. 5 and the pools, and make **frogs** come up and cover the land
8. 6 all the water, and the **frogs** came out and covered the land.
8. 7 used magic, and they too made **frogs** come up on the land.
8. 8 Lord to take away these **frogs,** and I will let your people
8. 9 will be rid of the **frogs,** and there will be none left
8.11 will be rid of the **frogs,** and there will be none left
8.12 Lord to take away the **frogs** which he had brought on the
8.13 as Moses asked, and the **frogs** in the houses, the courtyards,
8.15 the king saw that the **frogs** were dead, he became stubborn
Ps 78.45 that tormented them, and **frogs** that ruined their land.
105.30 Their country was overrun with **frogs,** even the palace was
Rev 16.13 Then I saw three unclean spirits that looked like **frogs.**

FRONT

Ex 25.37 and set them up so that they shine towards the **front.**
26. 9 Fold the sixth piece double over the **front** of the Tent.
28.27 the lower part of the **front** of the two shoulder-straps of
28.37 Tie it to the **front** of the turban with a blue cord.
29.10 "Bring the bull to the **front** of the Tent of my presence
39.20 the lower part of the **front** of the two shoulder straps of
39.31 They tied it to the **front** of the turban with a blue
Lev 8. 9 his head, and on the **front** of it he put the gold
9. 5 They brought to the **front** of the Tent everything that Moses
13.40 at the back or the **front** of his head, this does not
13.55 the object, whether the rot is on the **front** or the back.
16.14 finger sprinkle it on the **front** of the lid and then sprinkle
16.14 some of it seven times in **front** of the Covenant Box.
16.15 the lid and then in **front** of the Covenant Box, as he
19.14 man or put something in **front** of a blind man so as
24. 3 presence outside the curtain in **front** of the Covenant Box,
Num 3.38 sons were to camp in **front** of the Tent on the east.
4. 5 take down the curtain in **front** of the Covenant Box, and
5.16 the woman forward and make her stand in **front** of the altar.
5.29 be made to stand in **front** of the altar, and the priest
8. 2 place them so that the light shines towards the **front."**
8. 3 and placed the lamps facing the **front** of the lamp-stand.
Deut 14. 1 gash yourselves or shave the **front** of your head, as other
2 Sam 11.15 "Put Uriah in the **front** line, where the fighting is heaviest,
2 Kgs 11.11 drawn swords all round the **front** of the Temple, to protect
2 Chr 13.13 from the rear, while the rest faced them from the **front.**
23.10 drawn swords all round the **front** of the Temple, to protect
Is 57. 8 You set up your obscene idols just inside your **front** doors.
Ezek 1.10 a human face in **front,** a lion's face at the right,
41.14 The distance across the **front** of the Temple,
44. 4 took me through the north gate to the **front** of the Temple.
Joel 2.20 Their **front** ranks will be driven into the Dead Sea, their
Mk 3. 3 Jesus said to the man, "Come up here to the **front."**
Lk 6. 8 said to the man, "Stand up and come here to the **front."**
Acts 19.33 was responsible, since the Jews made him go up to the **front.**
27.30 going to put out some anchors from the **front** of the ship.
27.40 raised the sail at the **front** of the ship so that the
27.41 the **front** part of the ship got stuck and could not move,

FRONTIER

Jer 48.45 Fire has burnt up the **frontiers** and the mountain heights of

FROST

Ex 16.14 It was as delicate as **frost.**
Job 38.29 of the ice and the **frost,** [30]which turn the waters to stone
Ps 78.47 killed their grapevines with hail and their fig-trees with **frost.**
147.16 He spreads snow like a blanket and scatters **frost** like dust.
Jer 36.30 to the sun during the day and to the **frost** at night.
Zech 14. 6 there will no longer be cold or **frost,** [7]nor any darkness.

FROWN

Ecc 8. 1 Wisdom makes him smile and makes his **frowns** disappear.

FRUIT

Gen 1.11 that bear grain and those that bear **fruit"**—and it was done.
1.29 kinds of grain and all kinds of **fruit** for you to eat;
2. 9 kinds of beautiful trees grow there and produce good **fruit.**
2.16 him, "You may eat the **fruit** of any tree in the garden,
2.17 You must not eat the **fruit** of that tree;
3. 1 tell you not to eat **fruit** from any tree in the garden?"
3. 2 "We may eat the **fruit** of any tree in the garden," the
3. 3 us not to eat the **fruit** of that tree or even touch
3. 6 how good its **fruit** would be to eat,
3. 6 So she took some of the **fruit** and ate it.
3.11 "Did you eat the **fruit** that I told you not to eat?"
3.12 put here with me gave me the **fruit,** and I ate it."
3.17 your wife and ate the **fruit** which I told you not to
3.22 not be allowed to take **fruit** from the tree that gives life,
Ex 10.15 the hail had left, including all the **fruit** on the trees.
23.16 when you gather the **fruit** from your vineyards and orchards.
34.22 Festival of Shelters in the autumn when you gather your **fruit.**
Lev 19.23 plant any kind of **fruit tree,** consider the fruit ritually unclean
19.24 the fourth year all the **fruit** shall be dedicated as an
19.25 But in the fifth year you may eat the **fruit.**
19.25 If you do all this, your trees will bear more **fruit.**
23.40 take some of the best **fruit** from your trees, take palm
26. 4 the land will produce crops and the trees will bear **fruit.**
26.20 will not produce crops and the trees will not bear **fruit.**
27.30 of the land, whether grain or **fruit,** belongs to the Lord.
Num 13.20 be sure to bring back some of the **fruit** that grows there."
13.26 they had seen and showed them the **fruit** they had brought.
13.27 and here is some of its **fruit.**
Deut 1.25 They brought us back some **fruit** they found there,
20.19 do not cut down its **fruit-trees,** even though the siege lasts
20.19 Eat the **fruit,** but do not destroy the trees;
33.14 fruit, Rich with the best **fruits** of each season.
33.15 May their ancient hills be covered with choice **fruit.**
Judg 9.11 you, I would have to stop producing my good sweet **fruit.'**
2 Sam 16. 1 a hundred bunches of fresh **fruit,** and a leather bag full of
16. 2 ride, the bread and the **fruit** are for the men to eat,
2 Kgs 3.19 will cut down all their **fruit-trees,** stop all their springs,
3.25 also stopped up the springs and cut down the **fruit-trees.**
19.30 that send roots deep into the ground and produce **fruit.**
Neh 9.25 cisterns already dug, olive-trees, **fruit-trees,** and vineyards.
10.35 we harvest and of the first **fruit** that ripens on our trees.
10.37 other offerings of wine, olive-oil, and all kinds of **fruit.**
12.44 tithes and the first corn and **fruit** that ripened each year.
13.31 offerings of the first corn and the first **fruits** that ripened.
Ps 1. 3 beside a stream, that bear **fruit** at the right time, and
72.16 hills be covered with crops, as **fruitful** as those of Lebanon.
92.14 our God, [14]that still bear **fruit** in old age and are always
128. 3 wife will be like a **fruitful** vine in your home,
148. 9 Praise him, hills and mountains, **fruit-trees** and forests;
Ecc 2. 5 gardens and orchards, with all kinds of **fruit-trees** in them;
Song 2. 3 sit in its shadow, and its **fruit** is sweet to my taste.
4.13 like an orchard of pomegranate-trees and bear the finest **fruits.**
4.16 lover come to his garden and eat the best of its **fruits.**
7. 8 I will climb the palm-tree and pick its **fruit.**
7.13 of mandrakes, and all the pleasant **fruits** are near our door.
Is 27. 6 The earth will be covered with the **fruit** they produce.
37.31 that send roots deep into the ground and produce **fruit.**
Jer 11.16 I once called them a leafy olive-tree, full of beautiful **fruit;**
12. 2 they grow and bear **fruit.**
17. 8 it keeps on bearing **fruit.**
40.10 gather and store up wine, **fruit,** and olive-oil, and live in
40.12 and there they gathered in large amounts of wine and **fruit.**
48.32 But now your summer **fruits** and your grapes have been destroyed.
Ezek 19.10 of water, the vine was covered with leaves and **fruit.**
19.12 The east wind dried up its **fruit.**
19.14 fire burnt up its branches and **fruit.**
25. 4 They will eat the **fruit** and drink the milk that should have
34.27 The trees will bear **fruit,** the fields will produce crops,
36. 8 again grow leaves and bear **fruit** for you, my people Israel.
36.30 increase the yield of your **fruit-trees** and your fields, so that
47.12 leaves will never wither, and they will never stop bearing **fruit.**
47.12 They will have fresh **fruit** every month,
Dan 4.12 it was loaded down with **fruit**—enough for the whole world to
4.12 its branches, and every kind of living being ate its **fruit.**

Dan 4.14 strip off its leaves and scatter its **fruit.**
4.21 beautiful, and it had enough **fruit** on it to feed the whole
Hos 9.16 a plant whose roots have dried up and which bears no **fruit.**
10.13 You have eaten the **fruit** produced by your lies.
14. 7 They will grow corn and be **fruitful** like a vineyard.
Joel 1.12 all the **fruit-trees** have wilted and died.
2.22 the trees bear their **fruit,** and there are plenty of figs
Amos 8. 1 In it I saw a basket of **fruit.**
8. 1 "A basket of **fruit,**" I answered.
Mic 7. 1 hungry man who finds no **fruit** left on the trees and no
Nah 3.12 shake the trees, and the **fruit** falls right into your mouth!
Hab 3.17 though the fig-trees have no **fruit** and no grapes grow on the
Mt 3.10 that does not bear good **fruit** will be cut down and thrown
7.17 A healthy tree bears good **fruit,**
7.17 but a poor tree bears bad **fruit.**
7.18 healthy tree cannot bear bad **fruit,**
7.18 and a poor tree cannot bear good **fruit.**
7.19 that does not bear good **fruit** is cut down and thrown in
12.33 "To have good **fruit** you must have a healthy tree;
12.33 if you have a poor tree, you will have bad **fruit.**
12.33 A tree is known by the kind of **fruit** it bears.
13.22 for riches choke the message, and they don't bear **fruit.**
13.23 they bear **fruit,** some as much as a hundred, others sixty,
21.19 So he said to the tree, "You will never again bear **fruit!**"
21.43 given to a people who will produce the proper **fruits.**"
Mk 4.19 crowd in and choke the message, and they don't bear **fruit.**
4.20 They hear the message, accept it, and bear **fruit:**
4.28 The soil itself makes the plants grow and bear **fruit;**
Lk 3. 9 that does not bear good **fruit** will be cut down and thrown
6.43 not bear bad fruit, nor does a poor tree bear good **fruit.**
6.44 Every tree is known by the **fruit** it bears;
8.14 crowd in and choke them, and their **fruit** never ripens.
8.15 and they persist until they bear **fruit.**
Jn 15. 2 me that does not bear **fruit,** and he prunes
15. 2 every branch that does bear **fruit,**
15. 2 so that it will be clean and bear more **fruit.**
15. 4 A branch cannot bear **fruit** by itself;
15. 4 the same way you cannot bear **fruit** unless you remain in me.
15. 5 Whoever remains in me, and I in him, will bear much **fruit;**
15. 8 My Father's glory is shown by your bearing much **fruit;**
15.16 to go and bear much fruit, the kind of **fruit** that endures.
Jude 12 like trees that bear no **fruit,** even in autumn,
Rev 2. 7 the right to eat the **fruit** of the tree of life
22. 2 tree of life, which bears **fruit** twelve times a year,
22.14 the right to eat the **fruit** from the tree of life
22.19 him his share of the **fruit** of the tree of life

AV FRUIT

Ps 104.13 on the hills, and the earth is filled with your **blessings.**
132.11 will make one of your **sons** king, and he will rule after
Prov 31.31 Give her **credit** for all she does.
Hos 10. 1 The more **prosperous** they were, the more altars they built.
14. 8 I am the source of all their **blessings.**"
Acts 2.30 make one of **David's descendants** a king, just as David was.
Rom 1.13 I want to win **converts** among you also, as I have among
7. 4 in order that we might be **useful** in the service of God.
Phil 1.22 live I can do more **worthwhile** work, then I am not sure
4.17 rather, I want to see **profit** added to your account.
Col 1. 6 The gospel keeps bringing **blessings** and is spreading throughout
Heb 12.11 by such punishment reap the peaceful **reward** of a righteous life.
13.15 which is the **offering** presented by lips that confess him

AV FRUIT OF THE WOMB see BABY, CHILD

FRUSTRATE

Ps 14. 6 Evildoers **frustrate** the plans of the humble man, but the Lord
33.10 The Lord **frustrates** the purposes of the nations;
Is 19. 3 I am going to **frustrate** the plans of the Egyptians and
44.25 of fortune-tellers and **frustrate** the predictions of astrologers.
Jer 19. 7 In this place I will **frustrate** all the plans of the people
Mic 7.16 see this and be **frustrated** in spite of all their strength.

FUEL

2 Sam 24.22 are their yokes and the threshing-boards to use as **fuel.**"
1 Kgs 19.21 and cooked the meat, using the yoke as **fuel** for the fire.
1 Chr 21.23 the threshing-boards to use as **fuel,** and wheat to give as
Is 44.15 part of a tree for **fuel** and part of it for making
Lam 5. 4 we must buy the wood we need for **fuel.**

FULFIL

Gen 24.49 if you intend to **fulfil** your responsibility towards my master
38. 8 **Fulfil** your obligation to her as her husband's brother, so that
Ex 21.11 If he does not **fulfil** these duties to her, he must set
Lev 7.16 man brings a fellowship-offering in **fulfilment** of a vow
22.18 presents a burnt-offering, whether in **fulfilment** of a vow or
22.21 to the Lord, whether in **fulfilment** of a vow or
22.23 but it is not acceptable in **fulfilment** of a vow.
23.38 regular gifts, your offerings in **fulfilment** of vows,
27. 2 given to the Lord in **fulfilment** of a special vow, that
Num 6.21 him to give, he must **fulfil** exactly the promise he made.
15. 3 or as a sacrifice in **fulfilment** of a vow or as a
15. 8 or as a sacrifice in **fulfilment** of a vow or as a
18. 3 are to **fulfil** their duties to you and their responsibilities
18. 4 with you and **fulfil** their responsibilities for all the service
18. 5 and your sons alone must **fulfil** the responsibilities for the Holy
18. 7 alone shall **fulfil** all the responsibilities of the priesthood
Num 29.39 the offerings you give in **fulfilment** of a vow or as freewill
30. 5 her father forbids her to **fulfil** the vow when he hears about
30. 8 her husband forbids her to **fulfil** the vow when he hears
30.12 her husband forbids her to **fulfil** the vow when he hears
30.15 must suffer the consequences for the failure to **fulfil** the vow.
32.22 because you will have **fulfilled** your obligation to the Lord
Deut 23.18 the house of the Lord your God in **fulfilment** of a vow.
1 Sam 21. 7 there that day, because he had to **fulfil** a religious obligation.)
2 Sam 7.25 now, Lord God, **fulfil** for all time the promise you made
1 Kgs 8.24 today every word has been **fulfilled.**
2 Kgs 9.26 that belonged to Naboth, so as to **fulfil** the Lord's promise."
15.12 the promise was **fulfilled** which the Lord had made to King
1 Chr 17.23 "And now, O Lord, **fulfil** for all time the promise you
2 Chr 1. 9 O Lord God, **fulfil** the promise you made to my father.
6.15 today every word has been **fulfilled.**
36.21 the Lord had foretold through the prophet Jeremiah was **fulfilled:**
Job 23.14 He will **fulfil** what he has planned for me;
Is 45.13 Cyrus to action to **fulfil** my purpose and put things right.
Jer 33.14 is coming when I will **fulfil** the promise that I made
Lk 9.31 he would soon **fulfil** God's purpose by dying in Jerusalem.
Rom 13. 6 authorities are working for God when they **fulfil** their duties.
1 Cor 7. 3 A man should **fulfil** his duty as a husband,
7. 3 and a woman should **fulfil** her duty as a wife, and
2 Thes 1.11 May he **fulfil** by his power all your desire for goodness

FULL

Gen 37. 3 He made a long robe with **full** sleeves for him.
37.23 brothers, they ripped off his long robe with **full** sleeves.
41. 5 Seven ears of corn, **full** and ripe, were growing on one stalk.
41. 7 and the thin ears of corn swallowed the **full** ones.
41.22 ears of corn which were **full** and ripe, growing on one stalk.
41.24 and the thin ears of corn swallowed the **full** ones.
41.26 seven years, and the seven **full** ears of corn are also seven
Lev 6. 4 repay the owner in **full,** plus an additional twenty per cent.
2 Sam 13.18 wearing a long robe with **full** sleeves, the usual clothing for
2 Kgs 4. 4 Set each one aside as soon as it is **full.**"
2 Chr 24.11 Whenever it was **full,** the royal secretary and the High Priest's
Job 26. 9 He hides the **full moon** behind a cloud.
Ps 22.25 In the **full** assembly I will praise you for what you have
81. 3 festival, when the moon is new and when the moon is **full.**
Prov 27. 7 When you are **full,** you will refuse honey, but when you are
28.20 Honest people will lead a **full,** happy life.
Ecc 1. 7 river flows into the sea, but the sea is not yet **full.**
11. 3 When the clouds are **full,** it rains.
Jer 5. 7 my people until they were **full,** but they committed adultery
22.15 Your father enjoyed a **full** life.
46.10 eat them until it is **full,** and drink their blood until it
Ezek 23.32 the cup is **full.**
Hos 13. 6 the good land, you became **full** and satisfied, and then you
Joel 3.13 are crushed in a **full** winepress until the wine runs over."
Hag 1. 6 You have food to eat, but not enough to make you **full.**
Mt 5. 6 God will satisfy them **fully!**
6. 2 I assure you, they have already been paid in **full.**
6. 5 I assure you, they have already been paid in **full.**
6.16 I assure you, they have already been paid in **full.**
6.22 your eyes are sound, your whole body will be **full of** light;
12.34 For the mouth speaks what the heart is **full of.**
13.48 When the net is **full,** they pull it to shore and sit
14.20 disciples took up twelve baskets **full of** what was left over.
15.37 Then the disciples took up seven baskets **full of** pieces left over.
23.25 plate, while the inside is **full of** what you have obtained by
23.27 on the outside but are **full of** bones and decaying corpses on
23.28 everybody, but inside you are **full of** hypocrisy and sins.
25. 4 while the wise ones took containers **full of** oil for their lamps.
Mk 4.28 appears, then the ear, and finally the ear **full of** corn.
6.43 disciples took up twelve baskets **full of** what was left
8. 8 Then the disciples took up seven baskets **full of** pieces left over.
8.19 How many baskets **full of** leftover pieces did you take up?"
8.20 "how many baskets **full of** leftover pieces did you take
14. 3 with an alabaster jar **full of** a very expensive perfume
Lk 1. 4 you will know the **full** truth about everything which you have
1. 6 and obeyed **fully** all the Lord's laws and commands.
2.40 he was **full of** wisdom, and God's blessings were upon him.
4. 1 Jesus returned from the Jordan **full of** the Holy Spirit
5. 7 and filled both boats so **full of** fish that the boats
5.26 **Full of** fear, they praised God, saying, "What marvellous things
6.25 "How terrible for you who are **full** now;
6.38 Indeed, you will receive a **full** measure, a generous helping,
6.45 For the mouth speaks what the heart is **full of.**
7.37 she brought an alabaster jar **full of** perfume
11.34 When your eyes are sound, your whole body is **full of** light;
11.36 If your whole body is **full of** light, with no part of
11.39 cup and plate, but inside you are **full of** violence and evil.
14.23 and make people come in, so that my house will be **full.**
22.16 until it is given its **full** meaning in the Kingdom of God."
24. 5 **Full of** fear, the women bowed down to the ground,
24.41 could not believe, they were so **full of** joy and wonder;
Jn 1.14 became a human being and, **full of** grace and truth, lived
1.16 Out of the **fullness** of his grace he has blessed us all,
3.34 because God gives him the **fullness** of his Spirit.
5.22 has given his Son the **full** right to judge, [23] so that all
6.12 When they were all **full,** he said to his disciples, "Gather
10.10 in order that you might have life—life in all its **fullness.**
16. 6 now that I have told you, your hearts are **full of** sadness.
17.13 they might have my joy in their hearts in all its **fullness.**
19.29 A bowl was there, **full of** cheap wine;
21. 8 came to shore in the boat, pulling the net **full of** fish.
21.11 and dragged the net ashore **full of** big fish,
Acts 2.26 I am filled with gladness, and my words are **full of** joy.
4. 8 Peter, **full of** the Holy Spirit, answered them,

Acts 5. 8 was this the **full** amount you and your husband received
5. 8 "Yes," she answered, "the **full** amount."
5.21 all the Jewish elders for a **full** meeting of the Council;
6. 3 who are known to be **full of** the Holy Spirit and wisdom,
6. 4 will give our **full** time to prayer and the work
6. 5 they chose Stephen, a man **full of** faith and the Holy Spirit,
6. 8 richly blessed by God and **full of** power,
7.55 But Stephen, **full of** the Holy Spirit, looked up to heaven
8.23 I see that you are **full of** bitter envy
8.39 not see him again, but continued on his way, **full of** joy.
10. 5 to Joppa for a certain man whose **full** name is Simon Peter.
10.32 someone to Joppa for a man whose **full** name is Simon Peter.
11.13 someone to Joppa for a man whose **full** name is Simon Peter.
11.24 Barnabas was a good man, **full of** the Holy Spirit and faith,
13.10 You are **full of** all kinds of evil tricks,
13.52 The believers in Antioch were **full of** joy and the Holy Spirit.
17.16 upset when he noticed how **full of** idols the city was.
Rom 1.29 they are **full of** jealousy, murder, fighting, deceit, and
2.20 you have the **full** content of knowledge and of truth.
3.13 Their words are **full of** deadly deceit;
6.22 Your gain is a life **fully** dedicated to him,
8. 4 of the Law might be **fully** satisfied in us who live according
9.28 the Lord will quickly settle his **full** account with the world."
12.11 Serve the Lord with a heart **full of** devotion.
15.14 feel sure that you are **full of** goodness, that you have all
15.19 I have proclaimed **fully** the Good News about Christ.
15.29 I shall come with a **full** measure of the blessing of Christ.
15.32 I will come to you **full of** joy, if it is God's
1 Cor 7.31 goods, as though they were not **fully** occupied with them.
12. 8 gives one person a message **full of** wisdom,
12. 8 the same Spirit gives a message **full of** knowledge.
15.37 not the **full-bodied** plant that will later grow up.
2 Cor 4. 2 In the **full** light of truth we live in God's sight
5. 6 So we are always **full of** courage.
5. 8 We are **full of** courage and would much prefer to leave our
7. 4 In all our troubles I am still **full of** courage;
11. 3 that you will abandon your **full** and pure devotion to Christ—
Eph 3.19 it can never be **fully** known—and so be completely filled
4.13 reaching to the very height of Christ's **full** stature.
Phil 1.20 just now, I shall be **full of** courage, so that with my
4.12 am content, whether I am **full** or hungry,
Col 1.19 that the Son has in himself the **full** nature of God.
1.25 It is the task of **fully** proclaiming his message,
2. 2 love, and so have the **full** wealth of assurance
2. 9 For the **full** content of divine nature lives in Christ,
2.10 and you have been given **full** life in union with him.
3.10 in order to bring you to a **full** knowledge of himself.
4.12 stand firm, as mature and **fully** convinced Christians,
1 Tim 1.16 Christ Jesus might show his **full** patience in dealing with me,
2 Tim 1.12 But I am still **full of** confidence, because I know whom I
2.15 Do your best to win **full** approval in God's sight, as a
3.17 who serves God may be **fully** qualified and equipped to do
4. 7 race, I have run the **full** distance, and I have kept the
4.17 was able to proclaim the **full** message for all the Gentiles
Tit 2.15 and use your **full** authority as you encourage and rebuke
Heb 10. 1 Jewish Law is not a **full** and faithful model of the real
Jas 3. 8 It is evil and uncontrollable, **full of** deadly poison.
3.17 is **full of** compassion and produces a harvest of good deeds;
5. 5 Your life here on earth has been **full of** luxury and pleasure.
5.11 For the Lord is **full of** mercy and compassion.
1 Pet 1. 2 May grace and peace be yours in **full** measure.
4.13 so that you may be **full of** joy when his glory is
2 Pet 1. 2 peace be yours in **full** measure through your knowledge of God
1.11 you will be given the **full** right to enter the eternal
1 Jn 2.28 he appears we may be **full of** courage and need not hide
2 Jn 8 we have worked for, but will receive your reward in **full.**
Jude 2 May mercy, peace, and love be yours in **full** measure.
Rev 14.10 which he has poured at **full** strength into the cup of his
15. 7 seven angels seven gold bowls **full of** the anger of God,
17. 4 she held a gold cup **full of** obscene and filthy things,
21. 9 who had the seven bowls **full of** the seven last plagues

FULL-BROTHER see **BROTHER**

FULL-GROWN see **GROW**

FUN

Deut 28.37 they will make **fun** of you and ridicule you.
1 Kgs 18.27 At noon Elijah started making **fun** of them:
2 Kgs 2.23 some boys came out of a town and made **fun** of him.
Job 12. 5 You have no troubles, and yet you make **fun** of me;
30. 1 But men younger than I am make **fun** of me now!
Prov 1.11 Let's attack some innocent people for the **fun** of it!
30.17 Anyone who makes **fun** of his father or despises his mother
Is 57. 4 Who are you making **fun** of?
Acts 2.13 But others made **fun** of the believers,
17.32 some of them made **fun** of him, but others said,

FUNCTION

Rom 12. 4 and all these parts have different **functions.**
1 Tim 6. 5 people whose minds do not **function** and who no longer have
2 Tim 3. 8 people whose minds do not **function** and who are failures in

FUNDS

2 Kgs 12.15 there was no need to require them to account for the **funds.**
22. 7 is no need to require them to account for the **funds."**
Ezra 6. 8 out of the royal **funds** received from taxes in West Euphrates,
Acts 6. 1 widows were being neglected in the daily distribution of **funds.**

FUNERAL

Gen 50.14 his brothers and all who had gone with him for the **funeral.**
Lev 21. 1 by taking part in the **funeral** ceremonies when a relative dies,
2 Sam 3.31 And at the **funeral** King David himself walked behind the coffin.
2 Kgs 13.21 Once, during a **funeral,** one of those bands was seen,
Job 21.33 well-guarded tomb, [33]thousands join the **funeral** procession,
Jer 7.29 Sing a **funeral** song on the hill-tops, because I, the Lord,
9.17 mourners to come, for the women who sing **funeral** songs."
9.18 to hurry and sing a **funeral** song for us, until our eyes
9.20 how to mourn, and your friends how to sing a **funeral** song.
22.19 With the **funeral** honours of a donkey, he will be dragged
48.36 Heres, like someone playing a **funeral** song on a flute, because
Ezek 26.17 They will sing this **funeral** song for you:
27. 2 "Mortal man, sing a **funeral** song for Tyre, [3]that city which
27.32 They chant a **funeral** song for you:
32.16 This solemn warning will become a **funeral** song.
Hos 9. 4 defile everyone who eats it, like food eaten at **funerals.**
Amos 5. 1 of Israel, to this **funeral** song which I sing over you:
6.10 one in charge of the **funeral,** will take the body out of
8.10 turn your festivals into **funerals** and change your glad songs into
Mt 9.23 the musicians for the **funeral** and the people all stirred up,
11.17 We sang **funeral** songs, but you wouldn't cry!
Lk 7.12 the gate of the town, a **funeral** procession was coming out.
7.32 We sang **funeral** songs, but you wouldn't cry!'

FURIOUS see **FURY**

FURNACE

Gen 19.28 smoke rising from the land, like smoke from a huge **furnace.**
Ex 9. 8 Moses and Aaron, "Take a few handfuls of ashes from a **furnace;**
19.18 like the smoke of a **furnace,** and all the people trembled
Deut 4.20 you are the people he rescued from Egypt, that blazing **furnace.**
1 Kgs 8.51 own people, whom you brought out of Egypt, that blazing **furnace.**
Ps 12. 6 they are as genuine as silver refined seven times in the **furnace.**
Is 48.10 the fire of suffering, as silver is refined in a **furnace.**
Jer 6.29 The **furnace** burns fiercely, but the waste metals do not melt
11. 4 of Egypt, the land that was like a blazing **furnace** to them.
Ezek 22.18 lead—left over after silver has been refined in a **furnace.**
22.20 copper, iron, lead, and tin is put in a refining **furnace.**
22.22 silver is melted in a **furnace,** and then they will know that
Dan 3. 6 and worship will immediately be thrown into a blazing **furnace."**
3.11 down and worship it is to be thrown into a blazing **furnace.**
3.15 not, you will immediately be thrown into a blazing **furnace.**
3.17 save us from the blazing **furnace** and from your power, then
3.19 his men to heat the **furnace** seven times hotter than usual.
3.20 the three men up and throw them into the blazing **furnace.**
3.21 robes, caps, and all—and threw them into the blazing **furnace.**
3.22 given strict orders for the **furnace** to be made extremely hot,
3.22 flames burnt up the guards who took the men to the **furnace.**
3.24 tie up three men and throw them into the blazing **furnace?"**
3.26 to the door of the blazing **furnace** and called out, "Shadrach!
Mt 13.42 throw them into the fiery **furnace,** where they will cry and
13.50 throw them into the fiery **furnace,** where they will cry and
Rev 9. 2 smoke poured out of it, like the smoke from a large **furnace;**

FURNISH

Ex 25. 9 Make it and all its **furnishings** according to the plan that
31. 7 and its lid, all the **furnishings** of the Tent, [8]the table
1 Kgs 7.48 Solomon also had gold **furnishings** made for the Temple:
7.50 All these **furnishings** were made of gold.
2 Chr 4.19 King Solomon also had gold **furnishings** made for the Temple:
Prov 24. 4 is knowledge, the rooms are **furnished** with valuable, beautiful
Mk 14.15 large upstairs room, prepared and **furnished,**
Lk 22.12 will show you a large **furnished** room upstairs,

FURTHER see **FAR**

FURY
[FURIOUS]

Gen 4. 5 Cain became **furious,** and he scowled in anger.
34. 7 it, they were shocked and **furious** that Shechem had done such
35.22 Jacob heard about it and was **furious.**
39.19 Joseph's master was **furious** [20]and had Joseph arrested
49. 7 is so fierce, And on their **fury,** because it is so cruel.
Ex 32.19 the bull-calf and to see the people dancing, he was **furious.**
Deut 9.19 Lord's fierce anger, because he was **furious** enough to destroy
29.23 Zeboiim, which the Lord destroyed when he was **furiously** angry.
29.28 Lord became **furiously** angry, and in his great anger he uprooted
Josh 7. 1 that order, and so the Lord was **furious** with the Israelites.
7.26 Then the Lord was no longer **furious.**
Judg 2.14 so the Lord became **furious** with Israel and let raiders attack
2.20 Then the Lord would become **furious** with Israel and say,
14.19 he went back home, **furious** about what had happened,
1 Sam 11. 6 spirit of God took control of him, and he became **furious.**
20.30 Saul was **furious** with Jonathan and said to him,
2 Sam 2.17 a **furious** battle broke out, and Abner and the Israelites were
3. 8 This made Abner **furious.**
6. 8 David was **furious** because the Lord had punished Uzzah in anger.
13.21 When King David heard what had happened, he was **furious.**
1 Kgs 19.11 passed by and sent a **furious** wind that split the hills and
1 Chr 13.11 David was **furious** because the Lord had punished Uzzah in anger.
Neh 4. 1 begun rebuilding the wall, he was **furious** and began to ridicule

Neh	13. 8	I was **furious** and threw out all Tobiah's belongings.
Esth	1.12	This made the king **furious.**
	3. 5	Haman was **furious** when he realized that Mordecai was not going
	5. 9	sign of respect as he passed, Haman was **furious** with him.
	7. 7	king got up in a **fury,** left the room, and went outside
Job	20.23	God will punish him in **fury** and anger.
	30.11	and helpless, they turn against me with all their **fury.**
Ps	2. 5	Then he warns them in anger and terrifies them with his **fury.**
	7. 6	Stand up against the **fury** of my enemies;
	48. 7	to bear a child, [7]like ships tossing in a **furious** storm.
	50. 3	fire is in front of him, a **furious** storm is round him.
	78.38	Many times he held back his anger and restrained his **fury.**
	78.58	places of worship, and with their idols they made him **furious.**
	85. 3	stopped being angry with them and held back your **furious** rage.
	88.16	Your **furious** anger crushes me;
	90. 7	we are terrified by your **fury.**
	90.11	Who knows what fear your **fury** can bring?
	102. 9	Because of your anger and **fury,** ashes are my food,
	124. 3	would have swallowed us alive in their **furious** anger against us;
Is	13. 9	Lord is coming—that cruel day of his fierce anger and **fury.**
	51.13	in constant fear of the **fury** of those who oppress you,
	51.13	Their **fury** can no longer touch you.
Jer	21. 5	you with all my might, my anger, my wrath, and my **fury.**
	23.19	anger is a storm, a **furious** wind that will rage over the
	30.23	anger is a storm, a **furious** wind that will rage over the
	32.31	have made me angry and **furious** from the day it was built.
	32.37	them in my anger and **fury,** and I am going to bring
	33. 5	whom I am going to strike down in my anger and **fury.**
	36. 7	Lord has threatened this people with his terrible anger and **fury."**
	37.15	They were **furious** with me and ordered me to be beaten
	42.18	'Just as my anger and **fury** were poured out on the people
	42.18	of Jerusalem, so my **fury** will be poured out on you
	44. 6	poured out my anger and **fury** on the towns of Judah and
Lam	2. 3	In his **fury** he shattered the strength of Israel;
	3.44	anger, [44]By a cloud of **fury** too thick for our prayers to
	4.11	The Lord turned loose the full force of his **fury;**
Ezek	5.15	"When I am angry and **furious** with you and punish you,
	7.19	nor gold can save them when the Lord pours out his **fury.**
	16.38	and in my anger and **fury** I will punish you with death.
	25.14	Edom for me, and they will make Edom feel my **furious** anger.
	30.15	let the city of Pelusium, Egypt's great fortress, feel my **fury.**
	38.18	"On the day when Gog invades Israel, I will be **furious.**
Dan	11.44	will frighten him, and he will fight **furiously,** killing many
Hos	8. 5	I am **furious** with them.
	13.11	given you kings, and in my **fury** I have taken them away.
Nah	1. 6	Who can survive his terrible **fury?**
Hab	2.15	In your **fury** you humiliated and disgraced your neighbours;
	3. 8	Was it the sea that made you **furious?**
	3.12	in **fury** you trampled the nations.
Zeph	1.15	will be a day of **fury,** a day of trouble and distress,
	1.18	when the Lord shows his **fury,** not even all their silver and
	2. 2	Lord comes upon you, before the day when he shows his **fury.**
	3. 8	The whole earth will be destroyed by the fire of my **fury.**
Mt	2.16	the visitors from the east had tricked him, he was **furious.**
Lk	14.21	The master was **furious** and said to his servant, 'Hurry out
Acts	4.25	when he said, 'Why were the Gentiles **furious;**
	5.33	heard this, they were so **furious** that they wanted to have
	7.54	listened to Stephen, they became **furious** and ground their teeth
	19.28	they became **furious** and started shouting, "Great is Artemis
	26.11	I was so **furious** with them that I even went to foreign
Rom	2. 8	on them God will pour out his anger and **fury.**
Rev	12.17	The dragon was **furious** with the woman and went off to
	14.10	wine, the wine of his **fury,** which he has poured at full
	14.19	and threw them into the winepress of God's **furious** anger.
	16.19	drink the wine from his cup—the wine of his **furious** anger.
	19.15	in the winepress of the **furious** anger of the Almighty God.

FUTURE

Gen	17. 7	to your descendants in **future** generations as an everlasting
	17. 9	with me, both you and your descendants in **future** generations.
	30.33	In the **future** you can easily find out if I have been
	41.32	God and that he will make it happen in the near **future.**
	49. 1	I will tell you what will happen to you in the **future:**
Ex	3.15	this is what all **future** generations are to call me.
	13.14	In the **future,** when your son asks what this observance means,
Num	15.23	And suppose that in the **future** the community fails to do
	23.21	I foresee that Israel's **future** Will bring her no misfortune
	24.14	the people of Israel will do to your people in the **future."**
	24.17	I look into the **future,** And I see the nation of Israel.
Deut	29.22	"In **future** generations your descendants and foreigners
Josh	4. 6	In the **future,** when your children ask what these stones mean
	4.21	people of Israel, "In the **future,** when your children ask you
	22.24	afraid that in the **future** your descendants would say to ours,
1 Chr	17.19	to do this for me and to show me my **future** greatness.
Esth	9.28	every Jewish family of every **future** generation in every province
Job	3.23	God keeps their **future** hidden and hems them in on every
	15.23	He knows his **future** is dark;
Ps	16. 5	my **future** is in your hands.
	22.30	**Future** generations will serve him;
Prov	23.18	If it is, you have a bright **future.**
	24.14	Get wisdom and you have a bright **future.**
	24.20	A wicked person has no **future**—nothing to look forward to.
	31.25	She is strong and respected and not afraid of the **future.**
Ecc	3.11	desire to know the **future,** but never gives us the satisfaction
Is	9. 1	once disgraced, but the **future** will bring honour to this region,
	41.23	Tell us what the **future** holds— then we will know that
	43. 9	Which of their gods can predict the **future?**
	45.11	the holy God of Israel, the one who shapes the **future,**
	48. 5	And so I predicted your **future** long ago, announcing events
Jer	27. 9	claims he can predict the **future,** either by dreams or by
Jer	29. 8	you or by any others who claim they can predict the **future.**
	29.11	not disaster, plans to bring about the **future** you hope for.
	31.17	There is hope for your **future;**
Ezek	12.27	think that your visions and prophecies are about the distant **future.**
	37.11	that they are dried up, without any hope and with no **future.**
Dan	2.28	He has informed Your Majesty what will happen in the **future.**
	2.29	"While Your Majesty was sleeping, you dreamt about the **future;**
	2.45	God is telling Your Majesty what will happen in the **future.**
	10.14	understand what will happen to your people in the **future.**
	10.14	This is a vision about the **future."**
Mic	3. 7	who predict the **future** will be disgraced by their failure.
Zech	3. 8	of his, you that are the sign of a good **future:**
Acts	2.31	going to do in the **future,** and so he spoke about the
	16.16	had an evil spirit that enabled her to predict the **future.**
	26.16	of me today and what I will show you in the **future.**
Rom	8.38	neither the present nor the **future,**
1 Cor	3.22	the present and the **future**—all these are yours,
2 Cor	11. 9	As in the past, so in the **future:**
Col	2.17	All such things are only a shadow of things in the **future;**
1 Tim	4. 8	it promises life both for the present and for the **future.**
	6.19	a treasure which will be a solid foundation for the **future.**
Heb	3. 5	he spoke of the things that God would say in the **future.**
	11. 7	warnings about things in the **future** that he could not see.
	11.20	made Isaac promise blessings for the **future** to Jacob and Esau.
	11.26	of Egypt, for he kept his eyes on the **future** reward.

GAAL

Leader of the people of Shechem in their revolt against Abimelech.

Judg	9.26	Then **Gaal** son of Ebed came to Shechem with his brothers,
	9.28	**Gaal** said, "What kind of men are we in Shechem?
	9.30	of the city, became angry when he heard what **Gaal** had said.
	9.31	Abimelech at Arumah to say, **"Gaal** son of Ebed and his brothers
	9.33	Then when **Gaal** and his men come out against you, hit them
	9.35	Abimelech and his men saw **Gaal** come out and stand at the
	9.36	**Gaal** saw them and said to Zebul, "Look!
	9.37	**Gaal** said again, "Look!
	9.39	**Gaal** led the men of Shechem out and fought Abimelech.
	9.40	**Gaal** fled, and Abimelech pursued him.
	9.41	and Zebul drove **Gaal** and his brothers out of Shechem,

GAD (1)

Jacob and Zilpah's son, the tribe descended from him and its territory.

Gen	30.11	so she named him **Gad.**
	35.26	The sons of Leah's slave Zilpah were **Gad** and Asher.
	46.16	**Gad** and his sons:
	49.19	**"Gad** will be attacked by a band of robbers, But he will
Ex	1. 4	Issachar, Zebulun, Benjamin, [4]Dan, Naphtali, **Gad,** and Asher.
Num	10.20	Eliasaph son of Deuel was in command of the tribe of **Gad.**
	26.15	The tribe of **Gad:**
	32. 1	The tribes of Reuben and **Gad** had a lot of livestock.
	32.15	you people of Reuben and **Gad** refuse to follow him now, he
	32.25	The men of **Gad** and Reuben said, "Sir, we will do as
	32.29	"If the men of **Gad** and Reuben cross the Jordan ready
	32.31	The men of **Gad** and Reuben answered, "Sir, we will do as
	32.33	assigned to the tribes of **Gad** and Reuben and to half the
	32.34	The tribe of **Gad** rebuilt the fortified towns of Dibon,
	34.14	tribes of Reuben and **Gad** and the eastern half of Manasseh
Deut	3.12	the tribes of Reuben and **Gad** the territory north of the town
	3.16	tribes of Reuben and **Gad** I assigned the territory from Gilead
	4.43	for the tribe of **Gad** there was Ramoth, in the territory of
	27.13	Reuben, **Gad,** Asher, Zebulun, Dan, and Naphtali.
	29. 8	tribes of Reuben and **Gad,** and half the tribe of Manasseh.
	33.20	About the tribe of **Gad** he said:
	33.20	**Gad** waits like a lion To tear off an arm or a
Josh	1.12	the tribes of Reuben and **Gad** and to half the tribe of
	4.12	the tribes of Reuben and **Gad** and of half the tribe of
	12. 6	the tribes of Reuben and **Gad** and to half the tribe of
	13. 8	The tribes of Reuben and **Gad** and the other half of the
	13.24	to the families of the tribe of **Gad** as their possession.
	13.28	to the families of the tribe of **Gad** as their possession.
	18. 7	the tribes of **Gad,** Reuben, and East Manasseh have already
	20. 8	Ramoth in Gilead, in the territory of **Gad;**
	21. 7	were assigned twelve cities from the territories of Reuben, **Gad,**
	21.38	From the tribe of **Gad** they received four cities:
	22. 1	together the people of the tribes of Reuben, **Gad,** and East
	22. 9	the tribes of Reuben, **Gad,** and East Manasseh went back home.
	22.10	tribes of Reuben, **Gad,** and East Manasseh arrived at Geliloth,
	22.11	of the tribes of Reuben, **Gad,** and East Manasseh have built
	22.13	of the tribes of Reuben, **Gad,** and East Manasseh in the land
	22.15	the people of Reuben, **Gad,** and East Manasseh, [16]and speaking
	22.21	the tribes of Reuben, **Gad,** and East Manasseh answered the heads
	22.25	Jordan a boundary between us and you people of Reuben and **Gad.**
	22.30	of the tribes of Reuben, **Gad,** and East Manasseh had to say,
	22.32	the people of Reuben and **Gad** in the land of Gilead and
	22.33	devastate the land where the people of Reuben and **Gad** had
	22.34	people of Reuben and **Gad** said, "This altar is a witness
Judg	5.17	The tribe of **Gad** stayed east of the Jordan, and the
1 Sam	13. 7	others crossed the River Jordan into the territories of **Gad**
2 Sam	23.24	Nathan from Zobah Bani from **Gad** Zelek from Ammon
	24. 5	city in the middle of the valley, in the territory of **Gad.**
2 Kgs	10.33	Bashan, where the tribes of **Gad,** Reuben, and East Manasseh lived.
1 Chr	2. 2	Dan, Joseph, Benjamin, Naphtali, **Gad,** and Asher.
	5.11	The tribe of **Gad** lived to the north of Reuben in the
	5.18	In the tribes of Reuben, **Gad,** and East Manasseh there were
	5.26	deported the tribes of Reuben, **Gad,** and East Manasseh
	6.63	in the territories of Reuben, **Gad,** and Zebulun were assigned to

1 Chr 6.80 In the territory of **Gad:**
12. 8 soldiers from the tribe of **Gad** who joined David's troops
12.14 men from the tribe of **Gad** were senior officers in command of
12.23 Tribes east of the Jordan—Reuben, **Gad,** and East Manasseh:
26.32 River Jordan—the territories of Reuben, **Gad,** and East Manasseh.
Jer 49. 1 Molech take the territory of the tribe of **Gad** and settle there?
Ezek 48.23 Benjamin Simeon Issachar Zebulun **Gad**
48.28 given to the tribe of **Gad,** the boundary runs south-west from
48.30 those in the west wall are named after **Gad,** Asher, and
Rev 7. 5 Judah, Reuben, **Gad,** Asher, Naphtali, Manasseh, Simeon, Levi,
also Num 1.5 Num 1.20 Num 2.10 Num 7.12 Num 13.3

GAD (2)

Prophet in David's time.

1 Sam 22. 5 the prophet **Gad** came to David and said, "Don't stay here;
2 Sam 24.11 Lord said to **Gad,** David's prophet, "Go and tell David that
24.13 morning, after David got up, [13]**Gad** went to him, told him
24.18 That same day **Gad** went to David and said to him, "Go
24.19 David obeyed the Lord's command and went as **Gad** had told him.
1 Chr 21. 9 the Lord said to **Gad,** David's prophet, [10]"Go and tell David
21.11 **Gad** went to David, told him what the Lord had said,
21.13 David replied to **Gad,** "I am in a desperate situation!
21.18 angel of the Lord told **Gad** to command David to go and
21.19 obeyed the Lord's command and went, as **Gad** had told him to.
29.29 in the records of the three prophets, Samuel, Nathan, and **Gad.**
2 Chr 29.25 given to King David through **Gad,** the king's prophet, and through

GAIN

Gen 32. 5 you word, sir, in the hope of **gaining** your favour."
33. 8 Jacob answered, "It was to **gain** your favour."
33.10 "No, please, if I have **gained** your favour, accept my gift.
33.15 no need for that for I only want to **gain** your favour."
37.26 "What will we **gain** by killing our brother and covering
Ex 14.17 after them, and I will **gain** honour by my victory over the
Deut 28.43 live in your land will **gain** more and more power, while you
1 Sam 2.26 continued to grow and to **gain** favour both with the Lord and
2 Sam 15.12 plot against the king **gained** strength, and Absalom's followers
2 Kgs 15.19 of silver to **gain** his support in strengthening Menahem's power
1 Chr 18. 3 because Hadadezer was trying to **gain** control of the territory
Job 35. 3 What have I **gained** by not sinning?"
Ps 30. 9 "What will you **gain** from my death?
62.10 don't hope to **gain** anything by robbery;
119.104 I **gain** wisdom from your laws, and so I hate all bad
Prov 3.13 Happy is the man who becomes wise—who **gains** understanding.
3.35 Wise men will **gain** an honourable reputation, but stupid men
5. 9 If you do, others will **gain** the respect that you once had,
11.18 Wicked people do not really **gain** anything, but if you do
16. 8 honestly earned, than to have a large income **gained** dishonestly.
17. 2 shrewd servant will **gain** authority over a master's worthless son
19. 6 Everyone tries to **gain** the favour of important people;
Ecc 2.15 So what have I **gained** from being so wise?"
3. 9 What do we **gain** from all our work?
5.11 All you **gain** is the knowledge that you are rich.
Jer 2.18 do you think you will **gain** by going to Egypt to drink
2.18 do you think you will **gain** by going to Assyria to drink
2.37 you will not **gain** anything from them."
36. 9 king of Judah, the people fasted to **gain** the Lord's favour.
43. 3 so that the Babylonians will **gain** power over us and can
Dan 2. 8 You are trying to **gain** time, because you see that I have
10.12 you decided to humble yourself in order to **gain** understanding.
Mt 10.39 Whoever tries to **gain** his own life will lose it;
10.39 but whoever loses his life for my sake will **gain** it.
16.26 Will a person **gain** anything if he wins the whole world
Mk 8.36 Does a person **gain** anything if he wins the whole world
Lk 2.52 in body and in wisdom, **gaining** favour with God and men.
9.25 Will a person **gain** anything if he wins the whole world
Jn 7.18 on his own authority is trying to **gain** glory for himself.
Acts 24.27 Felix wanted to **gain** favour with the Jews so he left Paul
25. 9 But Festus wanted to **gain** favour with the Jews,
Rom 6.21 What did you **gain** from doing the things that you are now
6.22 Your **gain** is a life fully dedicated to him, and the result
1 Cor 8. 8 do not eat, nor shall we **gain** anything if we do eat.
15.32 here in Ephesus simply from human motives, what have I **gained?**
Eph 6. 6 they are watching you, because you want to **gain** their approval;
Phil 3. 8 so that I may **gain** Christ [9]and be completely united with
3. 9 of my own, the kind that is **gained** by obeying the Law.
Col 1.23 shaken from the hope you **gained** when you heard the gospel.
3.22 they are watching you because you want to **gain** their approval;
2 Tim 3. 6 go into people's houses and **gain** control over weak women

GALBANUM

Ex 30.34 each of the following sweet spices—stacte, onycha, **galbanum,**

GALILEE

Region of Israel n. of Jezreel Valley, later ruled by members of Herod's family.
Also Lake Galilee, from which the River Jordan flows to the Dead Sea.
see also TIBERIAS

Num 34.11 eastern shore of Lake **Galilee,** [12]then south along the River
Deut 3.17 the River Jordan, from Lake **Galilee** in the north down to the
33.23 Their land reaches to the south from Lake **Galilee."**
Josh 11. 2 Jordan Valley south of Lake **Galilee,** in the foothills, and on
12. 3 the Jordan Valley from Lake **Galilee** south to Beth Jeshimoth
12.23 Goiim (in **Galilee),** [24]and Tirzah—thirty-one kings in all.
13.27 border was the River Jordan as far north as Lake **Galilee.**
20. 7 set aside Kedesh in **Galilee,** in the hill-country of Naphtali;
Josh 21.32 Kedesh in **Galilee,** with its pasture lands (one of the cities
1 Kgs 9.11 King Solomon gave Hiram twenty towns in the region of **Galilee.**
15.20 the area near Lake **Galilee,** and the whole territory of Naphtali.
2 Kgs 15.29 and the territories of Gilead, **Galilee,** and Naphtali, and took
1 Chr 6.76 Kedesh in **Galilee,** Hammon, and Kiriathaim.
Is 9. 1 and even to **Galilee** itself, where the foreigners live.
Mt 2.22 went to the province of **Galilee** [23]and made his home in a
3.13 that time Jesus arrived from **Galilee** and came to John at the
4.12 that John had been put in prison, he went away to **Galilee.**
4.13 Capernaum, a town by Lake **Galilee,** in the territory of Zebulun
4.15 other side of the Jordan, **Galilee,** land of the Gentiles!
4.18 along the shore of Lake **Galilee,** he saw two brothers who
4.23 Jesus went all over **Galilee,** teaching in the synagogues,
4.25 Large crowds followed him from **Galilee** and the Ten Towns,
14. 1 At that time Herod, the ruler of **Galilee,** heard about Jesus.
15.29 Jesus left there and went along by Lake **Galilee.**
17.22 disciples all came together in **Galilee,** Jesus said to them,
19. 1 saying these things, he left **Galilee** and went to the territory
21.11 "This is the prophet Jesus, from Nazareth in **Galilee,"**
26.32 am raised to life, I will go to **Galilee** ahead of you."
26.69 to him and said, "You, too, were with Jesus of **Galilee."**
27.55 who had followed Jesus from **Galilee** and helped him.
28. 7 from death, and now he is going to **Galilee** ahead of you;
28.10 my brothers to go to **Galilee,** and there they will see me."
28.16 went to the hill in **Galilee** where Jesus had told them to
Mk 1. 9 Nazareth in the province of **Galilee,** and was baptized by John
1.14 Jesus went to **Galilee** and preached the Good News
1.16 along the shore of Lake **Galilee,** he saw two fishermen, Simon
1.28 about Jesus spread quickly everywhere in the province of **Galilee.**
1.39 So he travelled all over **Galilee,** preaching
2.13 Jesus went back again to the shore of Lake **Galilee.**
3. 7 went away to Lake **Galilee,** and a large crowd followed him.
3. 7 They had come from **Galilee,** from Judaea, [8]from Jerusalem,
4. 1 Again Jesus began to teach beside Lake **Galilee.**
5. 1 the other side of Lake **Galilee,** in the territory of Gerasa.
6.21 the military commanders, and the leading citizens of **Galilee.**
7.31 on through Sidon to Lake **Galilee,** going by way of the
9.30 his disciples left that place and went on through **Galilee.**
14.28 am raised to life, I will go to **Galilee** ahead of you."
14.70 you are one of them, because you, too, are from **Galilee."**
15.41 followed Jesus while he was in **Galilee** and had helped him.
16. 7 'He is going to **Galilee** ahead of you;
Lk 1.26 God sent the angel Gabriel to a town in **Galilee** named Nazareth.
2. 4 the town of Nazareth in **Galilee** to the town of Bethlehem
2.39 they returned to their home town of Nazareth in **Galilee.**
3. 1 Herod was ruler of **Galilee,** and his brother Philip was ruler
4.14 Then Jesus returned to **Galilee,**
4.31 to Capernaum, a town in **Galilee,** where he taught the people
5.17 come from every town in **Galilee** and Judaea and from Jerusalem.
8.26 territory of Gerasa, which is across the lake from **Galilee.**
9. 7 When Herod, the ruler of **Galilee,** heard about all the things
13. 1 who told Jesus about the **Galileans** whom Pilate had killed
13. 2 Jesus answered them, "Because those **Galileans** were killed
13. 2 that they were worse sinners than all the other **Galileans?**
17.11 he went along the border between Samaria and **Galilee.**
22.59 this man was with Jesus, because he also is a **Galilean!"**
23. 5 He began in **Galilee** and now has come here."
23. 6 When Pilate heard this, he asked, "Is this man a **Galilean?"**
23.49 followed him from **Galilee,** stood at a distance to watch.
23.55 who had followed Jesus from **Galilee** went with Joseph and saw
24. 6 Remember what he said to you while he was in **Galilee:**
Jn 1.43 The next day Jesus decided to go to **Galilee.**
2. 1 later there was a wedding in the town of Cana in **Galilee.**
2.11 Jesus performed this first miracle in Cana in **Galilee;**
4. 3 was being said, he left Judaea and went back to **Galilee;**
4.43 After spending two days there, Jesus left and went to **Galilee.**
4.45 When he arrived in **Galilee,** the people there welcomed him,
4.46 went back to Cana in **Galilee,** where he had turned the water
4.47 had come from Judaea to **Galilee,** he went to him and asked
4.54 miracle that Jesus performed after coming from Judaea to **Galilee.**
6. 1 Jesus went across Lake **Galilee** (or, Lake Tiberias,
7. 1 After this, Jesus travelled in **Galilee;**
7. 9 He said this, and then stayed on in **Galilee.**
7.41 But others said, "The Messiah will not come from **Galilee!**
7.52 "Well," they answered, "are you also from **Galilee?**
7.52 you will learn that no prophet ever comes from **Galilee."**
12.21 (he was from Bethsaida in **Galilee)** and said, "Sir, we want
21. 2 (the one from Cana in **Galilee),** the sons of Zebedee, and two
Acts 1.11 and said, **"Galileans,** why are you standing there looking
2. 7 "These people who are talking like this are **Galileans!**
5.37 Judas the **Galilean** appeared during the time of the census;
9.31 the church throughout Judaea, **Galilee,** and Samaria
10.37 land of Israel, beginning in **Galilee** after John preached
13.31 those who had travelled with him from **Galilee** to Jerusalem.

Am **GALLERY** see **CORRIDOR**

GALLOP

Judg 5.22 Then the horses came **galloping** on, stamping the ground with
Amos 6.12 Do horses **gallop** on rocks?
Nah 3. 2 rattle of wheels, the **gallop** of horses, the jolting of chariots!

GALLOWS

Esth 2.23 the report was true, so both men were hanged on the **gallows.**
5.14 friends suggested, "Why don't you have a **gallows** built,
5.14 thought this was a good idea, so he had the **gallows** built.
6. 4 to have Mordecai hanged on the **gallows** that was now ready.

Esth 7. 9 far as to build a **gallows** at his house so that he
7.10 Haman was hanged on the **gallows** that he had built for Mordecai.
9.13 bodies of Haman's ten sons to be hung from the **gallows.**"
9.25 for the Jews—he and his sons were hanged from the **gallows.**

GAMBLE

Ps 22.18 They **gamble** for my clothes and divide them among themselves.
Jn 19.24 divided my clothes among themselves and **gambled** for my robe."

GANG

1 Kgs 11.24 Zobah, [24]and had become the leader of a **gang** of outlaws.
Ps 22.16 A **gang** of evil men is round me;
86.14 a **gang** of cruel men is trying to kill me— people
Jer 48.27 them as though they had been caught with a **gang** of robbers.
Hos 6. 9 The priests are like a **gang** of robbers who wait in ambush

GAP

Neh 4. 7 Jerusalem and that the **gaps** in the wall were being closed,
6. 1 and that there were no **gaps** left in it, although we still

GAPE

Is 14.16 "The dead will stare and **gape** at you.

Am **GARBAGE** see **REFUSE (2)**

GARDEN

Gen 2. 8 the Lord God planted a **garden** in Eden, in the East, and
2. 9 In the middle of the **garden** stood the tree that gives life
2.10 A stream flowed in Eden and watered the **garden;**
2.15 placed the man in the **Garden of Eden** to cultivate it and
2.16 any tree in the **garden,** [17]except the tree that gives knowledge
3. 1 tell you not to eat fruit from any tree in the **garden?"**
3. 2 of any tree in the **garden,"** the woman answered, [3]"except the
3. 8 Lord God walking in the **garden,** and they hid from him among
3.10 He answered, "I heard you in the **garden;**
3.23 sent him out of the **Garden of Eden** and made him cultivate
3.24 the east side of the **garden** he put living creatures and a
13.10 plenty of water, like the **Garden of the Lord** or like the
Num 24. 6 long rows of palms Or **gardens** beside a river, Like aloes
1 Kgs 21. 2 palace, and I want to use the land for a vegetable **garden.**
2 Kgs 21.18 was buried in the palace **garden,** the garden of Uzza,
21.26 in the tomb in the **garden** of Uzza, and his son Josiah
25. 4 by way of the royal **garden,** went through the gateway connecting
Neh 3.15 wall next to the royal **garden,** as far as the steps leading
Esth 1. 5 whole week and was held in the **gardens** of the royal palace.
7. 7 fury, left the room, and went outside to the palace **gardens.**
7. 8 when the king came back into the room from the **gardens.**
Job 8.16 in the sun, like weeds that spread all through the **garden.**
Ecc 2. 5 I planted **gardens** and orchards, with all kinds of fruit-trees
Song 4.12 is a secret **garden,** a walled garden, a private spring;
4.15 Fountains water the **garden,** streams of flowing water,
4.16 South Wind, blow on my **garden;**
4.16 my lover come to his **garden** and eat the best of its
5. 1 I have entered my **garden,** my sweetheart, my bride.
5.13 are as lovely as a **garden** that is full of herbs and
6. 2 My lover has gone to his **garden,** where the balsam-trees grow.
6. 2 He is feeding his flock in the **garden** and gathering lilies.
8.13 Let me hear your voice from the **garden,** my love;
Is 1.29 be sorry that you ever worshipped trees and planted sacred **gardens.**
1.30 wither like a dying oak, like a **garden** that no one waters.
17.10 you plant sacred **gardens** in order to worship a foreign god.
51. 3 will make it a garden, like the **garden** I planted in Eden.
58.11 You will be like a **garden** that has plenty of water, like
65. 3 offer pagan sacrifices in sacred **gardens** and burn incense
66.17 go in procession to sacred **gardens,** and who eat pork and
Jer 29. 5 Plant **gardens** and eat what you grow in them.
29.28 houses, settle down, plant **gardens,** and eat what they grow."
31.12 They will be like a well-watered **garden;**
39. 4 by way of the royal **garden,** went through the gateway
52. 7 by way of the royal **garden,** went through the gateway
Ezek 17. 7 water than there was in the **garden** where it was growing.
28.13 You lived in Eden, the **garden** of God, and wore gems of
31. 8 No cedar in God's **garden** could compare with it.
31. 8 No tree in God's own **garden** was so beautiful.
31. 9 was the envy of every tree in Eden, the **garden** of God.
36.35 wilderness, has become like the **Garden of Eden,** and how the
Joel 2. 3 the land is like the **Garden of Eden,** but behind them it
Amos 4. 9 locusts ate up all your **gardens** and vineyards, your fig-trees
9.14 they will plant **gardens** and eat what they grow.
Lk 13. 7 So he said to his **gardener,** 'Look, for three years I have
13. 8 the **gardener** answered, 'Leave it alone, sir, just one more year;
Jn 15. 1 "I am the real vine, and my Father is the **gardener.**
18. 1 There was a **garden** in that place, and Jesus and his
18. 3 So Judas went to the **garden,** taking with him a group of
18.26 "Didn't I see you with him in the **garden?"**
19.41 There was a **garden** in the place where Jesus had been put
20.15 She thought he was the **gardener,** so she said to him,
Rev 2. 7 of the tree of life that grows in the **Garden of God.**

GARLIC

Num 11. 5 the water-melons, the leeks, the onions, and the **garlic** we had?

GARMENT

Ex 28. 2 Make priestly **garments** for your brother Aaron, to provide him
28. 4 make these priestly **garments** for your brother Aaron and his
29. 5 dress Aaron in the priestly **garments**—the shirt, the robe that
29.29 "Aaron's priestly **garments** are to be handed on to his sons
29.30 in the Holy Place is to wear these **garments** for seven days.
31.10 the magnificent priestly **garments** for Aaron and his sons to
35.19 the magnificent **garments** the priests are to wear when they serve
35.21 needed for use in worship and for making the priestly **garments.**
39. 1 made the magnificent **garments** which the priests were to wear
39. 1 made the priestly **garments** for Aaron, as the Lord had commanded
39.41 the magnificent **garments** the priests were to wear in the Holy
40.13 Dress Aaron in the priestly **garments,** anoint him,
Lev 8. 2 presence and bring the priestly **garments,** the anointing oil,
16. 4 Place, he must have a bath and put on the priestly **garments:**
16.23 Tent, take off the priestly **garments** that he had put on
16.32 shall put on the priestly **garments** [33]and perform the ritual
21.10 consecrated to wear the priestly **garments,** so he must not leave
Num 15.38 on the corners of your **garments** and put a blue cord on
Deut 24.10 his house to get the **garment** he is going to give you
24.17 and do not take a widow's **garment** as security for a loan.
1 Kgs 22.30 I will disguise myself, but you wear your royal **garments."**
2 Chr 18.29 I will disguise myself, but you wear your royal **garments."**
Job 38.14 like the folds of a **garment,** clear as the imprint of a
Is 3.23 their revealing **garments,** their linen handkerchiefs,
Zech 13. 4 or wear a prophet's coarse **garment** in order to deceive people.
Jn 13. 4 took off his outer **garment,** and tied a towel round his
13.12 he put his outer **garment** back on and returned to his
21. 7 he wrapped his outer **garment** round him

GARNET

A semi-precious stone, usually red in colour.

Ex 28.17 in the first row mount a ruby, a topaz, and a **garnet;**
39.10 the first row they mounted a ruby, a topaz, and a **garnet;**
Ezek 28.13 sapphires, emeralds, and **garnets.**

GASH

Lev 19.28 or tattoo yourselves or cut **gashes** in your body to mourn
21. 5 trim his beard or cut **gashes** on his body to show that
Deut 14. 1 mourn for the dead, don't **gash** yourselves or shave the front
Jer 16. 6 No one will **gash** himself or shave his head to show his
41. 5 off their beards, torn their clothes, and **gashed** themselves.
48.37 have all made **gashes** on their hands, and everyone is wearing
Hos 7.14 they pray for corn and wine, they **gash** themselves like pagans.

GASP

Jer 4.31 the cry of Jerusalem **gasping** for breath, stretching out her hand
15. 9 who lost her seven children has fainted, **gasping** for breath.

GATE

Gen 19. 1 to Sodom that evening, Lot was sitting at the city **gate.**
23.10 with the other Hittites at the meeting-place at the city **gate;**
28.17 it must be the **gate** that opens into heaven."
34.20 meeting-place at the city **gate** and spoke to their fellow-townsmen:
Ex 32.26 So he stood at the **gate** of the camp and shouted,
32.27 through the camp from this **gate** to the other and kill his
Deut 3. 5 fortified with high walls, **gates,** and bars to lock the gates,
6. 9 Write them on the door-posts of your houses and on your **gates.**
11.20 Write them on the door-posts of your houses and on your **gates.**
20.11 If they open the **gates** and surrender, they are all to
33.25 be protected with iron **gates,** And may he always live secure."
Josh 2. 4 They left at sunset before the city **gate** was closed.
2. 7 The king's men left the city, and then the **gate** was shut.
6. 1 The **gates** of Jericho were kept shut and guarded to keep
6.26 Whoever builds the **gates** will lose his youngest."
7. 5 chased them from the city **gate** as far as some quarries and
8.29 and it was thrown down at the entrance to the city **gate.**
Judg 9.35 and stand at the city **gate,** they got up from their hiding
9.40 Many were wounded, even at the city **gate.**
9.44 forward to guard the city **gate,** the other two companies attacked
16. 2 place and waited for him all night long at the city **gate.**
16. 3 took hold of the city **gate** and pulled it up—doors, posts,
18.16 soldiers from Dan, ready for battle, were standing at the **gate.**
18.17 priest stayed at the **gate** with the six hundred armed men.
Ruth 4. 1 to the meeting place at the town **gate** and sat down there.
1 Sam 4.18 Covenant Box, Eli fell backwards from his seat beside the **gate.**
9.18 Samuel, who was near the **gate,** and asked, "Tell me, where
17.52 them all the way to Gath and to the **gates** of Ekron.
21.13 would scribble on the city **gates** and dribble down his beard.
23. 7 trapped himself by going into a walled town with fortified **gates."**
2 Sam 3.27 took him aside at the **gate,** as though he wanted to speak
11. 9 instead he slept at the palace **gate** with the king's guards.
11.23 in the open, but we drove them back to the city **gate.**
15. 2 early and go and stand by the road at the city **gate.**
18. 4 by the side of the **gate** as his men marched out in
18.24 in the space between the inner and outer **gates** of the city.
18.24 top of the wall and stood on the roof of the **gateway;**
18.26 man running alone, and he called down to the **gatekeeper,** "Look!
18.33 He went up to the room over the **gateway** and wept.
19. 8 the king got up, and went and sat near the city **gate.**
23.15 a drink of water from the well by the **gate** at Bethlehem!"
1 Kgs 4.13 and with bronze bars on the **gates**
14.27 to the officers responsible for guarding the palace **gates.**
16.34 and his youngest son Segub when he built the **gates.**
17.10 as he came to the **gate** of the town, he saw a

1 Kgs 22.10 the threshing-place just outside the **gate** of Samaria, and all
2 Kgs 7. 3 were outside the **gates** of Samaria, and they said to
7.10 back to Samaria and called out to the guards at the **gates:**
7.17 Israel had put the city **gate** under the command of the
7.20 he died, trampled to death by the people at the city **gate.**
9.31 As Jehu came through the **gate,** she called out, "You
10. 8 two heaps at the city **gate** and to be left there until
10. 9 he went out to the **gate** and said to the people who
11. 6 stand guard at the Sur **Gate,** and the other third
11. 6 are to stand guard at the **gate** behind the other guards.
11.16 to the palace, and there at the Horse **Gate** they killed her.
11.19 Joash entered by the Guard **Gate** and took his place on the
14.13 the city wall from Ephraim **Gate** to the Corner Gate,
15.35 It was Jotham who built the North **Gate** of the Temple.
23. 8 to the goat-demons near the **gate** built by Joshua,
23. 8 to the left of the main **gate** as one enters the city.
23.11 the temple courtyard, near the **gate** and not far from
25. 4 went through the **gateway** connecting the two walls, and fled
1 Chr 9.18 had been stationed at the eastern entrance to the King's **Gate.**
9.18 had stood guard at the **gates** to the camps of the Levites.
9.22 212 men were chosen as guards for the entrances and **gates.**
9.23 and their descendants continued to guard the **gates** to the Temple.
9.24 There was a **gate** facing in each direction, north, south,
9.27 their duty to guard it and to open the **gates** every morning.
11.17 a drink of water from the well by the **gate** in Bethlehem!"
16.38 Hosah and Obed Edom were in charge of guarding the **gates.**
16.42 members of Jeduthun's clan were in charge of guarding the **gates.**
22. 3 and clamps for the wooden **gates,** and so much bronze that no
26.13 drew lots to see which **gate** it would be responsible for.
26.14 Shelemiah drew the east **gate,** and his son Zechariah,
26.14 a man who always gave good advice, drew the north **gate.**
26.15 Edom was allotted the south **gate,** and his sons were allotted
26.16 Hosah were allotted the west **gate** and the Shallecheth Gate
2 Chr 4. 9 The doors in the **gates** between the courtyards were covered with
8. 5 Beth Horon (fortified cities with **gates** that could be barred),
8.14 daily duties at each **gate,** in accordance with the commands of
12.10 to the officers responsible for guarding the palace **gates.**
14. 7 walls and towers, and **gates** that can be shut and barred.
18. 9 the threshing-place just outside the **gate** of Samaria, and all
23. 4 will guard the temple **gates,** [5] another third will guard the royal
23. 5 palace, and the rest will be stationed at the Foundation **Gate.**
23.15 to the palace, and there at the Horse **Gate** they killed her.
23.19 on duty at the temple **gates** to keep out anyone who was
23.20 They entered by the main **gate,** and the king took his place
24. 8 a box for contributions and to place it at the temple **gate.**
25.23 the city wall from Ephraim **Gate** to the Corner Gate,
26. 9 building towers at the Corner **Gate,** at the Valley Gate,
27. 3 Jotham who built the North **Gate** of the Temple and did
29. 3 became king, he re-opened the **gates** of the Temple and had
31.14 chief guard at the East **Gate** of the Temple, was in charge
32. 6 them to assemble in the open square at the city **gate.**
33.14 Gihon north to the Fish **Gate** and the area of the city
35.15 The guards at the temple **gates** did not need to leave their
Neh 1. 3 broken down and that the **gates** had not been restored since
2. 3 is in ruins and its **gates** have been destroyed by fire?"
2. 8 me with timber for the **gates** of the fort that guards the
2.13 the city through the Valley **Gate** on the west
2.13 and went south past Dragon's Fountain to the Rubbish **Gate.**
2.13 of the city and the **gates** that had been destroyed by fire.
2.14 city I went north to the Fountain **Gate** and the King's Pool.
2.15 come and went back into the city through the Valley **Gate.**
2.17 because Jerusalem is in ruins and its **gates** are destroyed!
3. 1 his fellow-priests rebuilt the Sheep **Gate,**
3. 1 dedicated it, and put the **gates** in place.
3. 3 The clan of Hassenaah built the Fish **Gate.**
3. 3 put the beams and the **gates** in place,
3. 3 and put in the bolts and bars for locking the **gate.**
3. 6 and Meshullam son of Besodeiah rebuilt Jeshanah **Gate.**
3. 6 put the beams and the **gates** in place,
3. 6 and put in the bolts and bars for locking the **gate.**
3.13 inhabitants of the city of Zanoah rebuilt the Valley **Gate.**
3.13 They put the **gates** in place, put in the bolts and the
3.13 the bars for locking the **gate,**
3.13 the wall for 440 metres, as far as the Rubbish **Gate.**
3.14 ruler of the Beth Haccherem District, rebuilt the Rubbish **Gate.**
3.14 He put the **gates** in place,
3.14 and put in the bolts and the bars for locking the **gate.**
3.15 ruler of the Mizpah District, rebuilt the Fountain **Gate.**
3.15 He covered the **gateway,** put the gates in place,
3.25 east near the Water **Gate** and the tower guarding the Temple.
3.28 going north from the Horse **Gate,** each one building in front
3.29 son of Shecaniah, keeper of the East **Gate,** built the next
3.31 which was by the Miphkad **Gate,** near the room on top of
3.32 from the room at the corner as far as the Sheep **Gate.**
6. 1 although we still had not set up the **gates** in the gateways.
7. 1 wall had been rebuilt, the **gates** had all been put in place,
7. 3 them not to have the **gates** of Jerusalem opened in the
8. 1 assembled in Jerusalem, in the square just inside the Water **Gate.**
8. 3 in the square by the **gate** he read the Law to them
8.16 public squares by the Water **Gate** and by the Ephraim Gate.
12.25 of guarding the storerooms by the **gates** to the Temple:
12.30 ritual purification for themselves, the people, the **gates,**
12.31 to the right on top of the wall towards the Rubbish **Gate.**
12.37 At the Fountain **Gate** they went up the steps that led to
12.37 the wall at the Water **Gate,** on the east side of the
12.39 there we went past Ephraim **Gate,** Jeshanah Gate, the Fish Gate,
12.39 and the Tower of the Hundred, to the Sheep **Gate.**
12.39 We ended our march near the **gate** to the Temple.
13.19 gave orders for the city **gates** to be shut at the beginning
13.19 of my men at the **gates** to make sure that nothing was
13.22 to go and guard the **gates** to make sure that the Sabbath
Job 38. 8 Who closed the **gates** to hold back the sea when it burst
38.10 a boundary for the sea and kept it behind bolted **gates.**
38.17 anyone ever shown you the **gates** that guard the dark world of
Ps 24. 7 Fling wide the **gates,** open the ancient doors,
24. 9 Fling wide the **gates,** open the ancient doors,
84.10 would rather stand at the **gate** of the house of my God
100. 4 Enter the temple **gates** with thanksgiving, go into its courts
118.19 Open to me the **gates** of the Temple;
118.20 This is the **gate** of the Lord;
122. 2 And now we are here, standing inside the **gates** of Jerusalem!
147.13 He keeps your **gates** strong;
Prov 1.21 calling loudly at the city **gates** and wherever people come
8. 3 At the entrance to the city, beside the **gates,** she calls:
Song 7. 4 in the city of Heshbon, near the **gate** of that great city.
8. 9 But if she is a **gate,** we will protect her with panels
Is 3.26 The city **gates** will mourn and cry, and the city itself
13. 2 the signal for them to attack the **gates** of the proud city.
22. 7 soldiers on horseback stood in front of Jerusalem's **gates.**
24.12 The city is in ruins, and its **gates** have been broken down.
26. 2 Open the city **gates** and let the faithful nation enter,
28. 6 and courage to those who defend the city **gates** from attack.
43.14 will break down the city **gates,** and the shouts of her people
45. 1 the Lord will open the **gates** of cities for him.
45. 2 I will break down bronze **gates** and smash their iron bars.
52. 1 The heathen will never enter your **gates** again.
54.12 towers with rubies, your **gates** with stones that glow like fire,
60.11 Day and night your **gates** will be open, So that the kings
Jer 1.15 their thrones at the **gates** of Jerusalem and round its walls,
7. 1 Lord sent me to the **gate** of the Temple where the people
17.19 message at the People's **Gate,** through which the kings of Judah
17.19 then go to all the other **gates** of Jerusalem.
17.20 Jerusalem and enters these **gates,** to listen to what I say.
17.21 carry anything in through the **gates** of Jerusalem [22] or carry
17.24 any load in through the **gates** of this city on the Sabbath.
17.25 and princes will enter the **gates** of Jerusalem and have the
17.27 carry any load through the **gates** of Jerusalem on that day,
17.27 if they do, I will set the **gates** of Jerusalem on fire.
19. 2 and to go through Potsherd **Gate** out to the Valley of Hinnom.
20. 2 placed in chains near the upper Benjamin **Gate** in the Temple.
22. 4 continue to pass through the **gates** of this palace in chariots
22.19 he will be dragged away and thrown outside Jerusalem's **gates."**
26.10 palace to the Temple and took their places at the New **Gate.**
31.38 as my city, from Hananel Tower west to the Corner **Gate.**
31.40 as far as the Horse **Gate** to the east, will be sacred
36.10 court near the entrance of the New **Gate** of the Temple.
37.13 when I reached the Benjamin **Gate,** the officer in charge of
38. 7 At that time the king was holding court at the Benjamin **Gate.**
39. 3 their places at the Middle **Gate,** including Nergal Sarezer,
39. 4 went through the **gateway** connecting the two walls, and escaped
49.31 Their city has no **gates** or locks and is completely unprotected.'
51.30 The city **gates** are broken down, and the houses are on fire.
51.58 be thrown to the ground, and its towering **gates** burnt down.
52. 7 went through the **gateway** connecting the two walls, and fled
Lam 1. 4 The city **gates** stand empty, and Zion is in agony.
2. 9 The **gates** lie buried in rubble, their bars smashed to pieces.
4.12 believed that any invader could enter Jerusalem's **gates.**
5.14 longer sit at the city **gate,** and the young people no longer
Ezek 8. 3 inner entrance of the north **gate** of the Temple, where there
8. 5 by the entrance of the **gateway** I saw the idol that was
8.14 took me to the north **gate** of the Temple and showed me
9. 2 came from the outer north **gate** of the Temple, each one
10.19 They paused at the east **gate** of the Temple, and the dazzling
11. 1 me up and took me to the east **gate** of the Temple.
11. 1 There near the **gate** I saw twenty-five men,
21.22 place battering-rams against the **gates,** to throw up earthworks,
26.10 walls as they pass through the **gates** of the ruined city.
40. 3 and a measuring-rod and was standing by a **gateway.**
40. 6 Then he went to the **gateway** that faced east.
40. 8 formed that end of the **gateway** which was nearest the Temple,
40.11 Next, the man measured the width of the passage in the **gateway.**
40.11 and the space between the open **gates** was five metres.
40.15 The total length of the **gateway** from the outside wall
40.15 outside wall of the **gate** to the far side
40.17 The man took me through the **gateway** into the courtyard.
40.19 There was a **gateway** at a higher level that led to the
40.19 measured the distance between the two **gateways,** and it was
40.20 Then the man measured the **gateway** on the north side
40.21 all had the same measurements as those in the east **gateway.**
40.21 The total length of the **gateway** was twenty-five metres
40.22 and the carved palm-trees were like those in the east **gate.**
40.22 steps led up to the **gate,** and the entrance room was at
40.23 the courtyard from this north **gateway**
40.23 was another **gateway** leading to the inner courtyard,
40.23 measured the distance between these two **gateways,** and it was
40.24 took me to the south side, and there we saw another **gateway.**
40.25 windows in the rooms of this **gateway** just as in the others.
40.25 The total length of the **gateway** was twenty-five metres,
40.27 there was a **gateway** leading to the inner courtyard.
40.27 measured the distance to this second **gateway,** and it was fifty
40.28 man took me through the south **gateway** into the inner courtyard.
40.28 He measured the **gateway,**
40.28 it was the same size as the **gateways** in the outer wall.
40.29 walls were the same size as those in the other **gateways.**
40.29 There were also windows in the rooms of this **gateway.**
40.31 Eight steps led up to this **gate.**
40.32 man took me through the east **gateway** into the inner courtyard.
40.32 He measured the **gateway,** and it was the same size as the
40.33 walls measured the same as those in the other **gateways.**
40.34 Eight steps led up to this **gate.**
40.35 Then the man took me to the north **gateway.**
40.37 Eight steps led up to this **gate.**

Ezek	40.38	an annexe attached to the inner **gateway** on the north side.
	40.40	two on either side of the entrance of the north **gate.**
	40.44	facing south beside the north **gateway**
	40.44	and the other facing north beside the south **gateway.**
	42.15	me out through the east **gate** and then measured the outside
	43. 1	man took me to the **gate** that faces east, [2]and there I
	43. 4	dazzling light passed through the east **gate** and went into the
	44. 1	led me to the outer **gate** at the east side of the
	44. 1	The **gate** was closed, [2]and the Lord said to me,
	44. 2	"This **gate** will stay closed and will never
	44. 3	to enter and leave the **gateway** through the entrance room at
	44. 4	took me through the north **gate** to the front of the Temple.
	44.11	by taking charge of the **gates** and by performing the work of
	44.17	they enter the **gateway** to the inner courtyard of the Temple,
	45.19	and on the posts of the **gateways** to the inner courtyard.
	46. 1	Lord says, "The east **gateway** to the inner courtyard must be
	46. 2	the entrance room by the **gateway** and stand
	46. 2	beside the posts of the **gate** while the priests burn his
	46. 2	There at the **gate** he must worship and then go out again.
	46. 2	The **gate** must not be shut until evening.
	46. 3	to bow down and worship the Lord in front of the **gate.**
	46. 8	the entrance room of the **gateway** and go out by the same
	46. 9	who enter by the north **gate** are to leave
	46. 9	by the south **gate** after they have worshipped, and those
	46. 9	who enter by the south **gate**
	46. 9	are to leave by the north **gate.**
	46. 9	same way as he entered, but must leave by the opposite **gate.**
	46.12	or a fellowship-offering, the east **gate** to the inner courtyard
	46.12	on the Sabbath, and the **gate** is to be closed after he
	46.19	rooms facing north near the **gate** on the south side of the
	47. 2	by way of the north **gate**
	47. 2	and led me round to the **gate** that faces east.
	47. 2	of water was flowing out at the south side of the **gate.**
	48.30	2,250 metres and has three **gates** in it, each named after one
	48.30	The **gates** in the north wall are named after Reuben, Judah,
Hos	11. 6	War will sweep through their cities and break down the city **gates.**
Amos	1. 5	will smash the city **gates** of Damascus and remove the inhabitants
Obad	11	stood aside on that day when enemies broke down their **gates.**
Jon	2. 6	mountains, into the land whose **gates** lock shut for ever.
Mic	1. 9	destruction has reached the **gates** of Jerusalem itself,
	2.13	They will break out of the city **gates** and go free.
Nah	2. 6	The **gates** by the river burst open;
	3.13	Fire will destroy the bars across your **gates.**
Zeph	1.10	will hear the sound of crying at the Fish **Gate** in Jerusalem.
Zech	14.10	will reach from the Benjamin **Gate** to the Corner Gate, where
	14.10	there had been an earlier **gate,**
Mt	7.13	"Go in through the narrow **gate,**
	7.13	because the **gate** to hell is wide
	7.14	But the **gate** to life is narrow
Lk	7.12	as he arrived at the **gate** of the town, a funeral procession
Jn	5. 2	Near the Sheep **Gate** in Jerusalem there is a pool with five
	10. 1	the sheepfold by the **gate,** but climbs in some other way,
	10. 2	who goes in through the **gate** is the shepherd of the sheep.
	10. 3	The gatekeeper opens the **gate** for him;
	10. 7	I am the **gate** for the sheep.
	10. 9	I am the **gate.**
	18.16	while Peter stayed outside by the **gate.**
	18.16	spoke to the girl at the **gate,** and brought Peter inside.
	18.17	The girl at the **gate** said to Peter, "Aren't you also
Acts	3. 2	There at the Beautiful **Gate,** as it was called, was a man
	3. 2	he was carried to the **gate** to beg for money from the
	3.10	had sat at the Beautiful **Gate,** they were all surprised
	5.19	the Lord opened the prison **gates,** led the apostles out,
	5.23	locked up tight and all the guards on watch at the **gates;**
	5.23	but when we opened the **gates,** we found no one inside!"
	9.24	and night they watched the city **gates** in order to kill him.
	10.17	and they were now standing in front of the **gate.**
	12. 6	and there were guards on duty at the prison **gate.**
	12.10	and came at last to the iron **gate** leading into the city.
	12.10	The **gate** opened for them by itself, and they went out.
	14.13	bulls and flowers to the **gate,** for he and the crowds wanted
2 Cor	11.32	King Aretas placed guards at the city **gates** to arrest me.
Rev	21.12	high wall with twelve **gates**
	21.12	and with twelve angels in charge of the **gates.**
	21.12	On the **gates** were written the names of the twelve tribes
	21.13	There were three **gates** on each side:
	21.15	gold measuring-rod to measure the city, its **gates,** and its wall.
	21.21	The twelve **gates** were twelve pearls;
	21.21	each **gate** was made from a single pearl.
	21.25	The **gates** of the city will stand open all day;
	22.14	tree of life and to go through the **gates** into the city.

GATH

One of the five chief cities of the Philistines.
see also MORESHETH GATH

Josh	11.22	a few, however, were left in Gaza, **Gath,** and Ashdod.
	13. 3	kings of the Philistines lived at Gaza, Ashdod, Ashkelon, **Gath,**
1 Sam	5. 8	"Take it over to **Gath,"** they answered;
	5. 8	so they took it to **Gath,** another Philistine city.
	6.17	one each for the cities of Ashdod, Gaza, Ashkelon, **Gath,**
	7.14	had captured between Ekron and **Gath** were returned to Israel,
	17. 4	Goliath, from the city of **Gath,** came out from the Philistine
	17.52	them all the way to **Gath** and to the gates of Ekron.
	17.52	the road that leads to Shaaraim, as far as **Gath** and Ekron.
	21.10	David left, fleeing from Saul, and went to King Achish of **Gath.**
	22. 1	fled from the city of **Gath** and went to a cave near
	27. 2	went over at once to Achish son of Maoch, king of **Gath.**
	27. 3	David and his men settled there in **Gath** with their families.
	27. 4	that David had fled to **Gath,** he gave up trying to find
	27.11	one could go back to **Gath** and report what he and his
2 Sam	1.20	Do not announce it in **Gath** or in the streets of Ashkelon.
	6.10	the house of Obed Edom, a native of the city of **Gath.**
	15.18	who had followed him from **Gath** also passed by, [19]and the
	18. 2	Abishai and Ittai from **Gath,** each in command of a group.
	21.19	from Bethlehem killed Goliath from **Gath,** whose spear had a shaft
	21.20	there was another battle at **Gath,** where there was a giant
	21.22	descendants of the giants of **Gath,** and they were killed by
1 Kgs	2.39	slaves ran away to the king of **Gath,** Achish son of Maacah.
	2.39	heard that they were in **Gath,** [40]he saddled his donkey
	2.40	donkey and went to King Achish in **Gath,** to find his slaves.
2 Kgs	12.17	King Hazael of Syria attacked the city of **Gath** and conquered it;
1 Chr	7.21	to steal the livestock belonging to the native inhabitants of **Gath.**
	8.13	and drove out the people who lived in the city of **Gath.**
	13.13	a man named Obed Edom, a native of the city of **Gath.**
	18. 1	out of their control the city of **Gath** and its surrounding
	20. 5	the brother of Goliath from **Gath,** whose spear had a shaft as
	20. 6	Another battle took place at **Gath,** where there was a giant
	20. 8	David and his men, were descendants of the giants at **Gath.**
2 Chr	11. 8	**Gath,** Mareshah, Ziph,
	26. 6	walls of the cities of **Gath,** Jamnia, and Ashdod, and built
Amos	6. 2	city of Hamath and on down to the Philistine city of **Gath.**
Mic	1.10	Don't tell our enemies in **Gath** about our defeat;
	1.14	people of Judah, say good-bye to the town of Moresheth **Gath.**

GATHER

Gen	31.46	He told his men to **gather** some rocks and pile them up.
Ex	16. 4	people must go out every day and **gather** enough for that day.
	16.16	each of you is to **gather** as much of it as he
	16.17	The Israelites did this, some **gathering** more, others
	16.18	measured it, those who **gathered** much did not have too much,
	16.18	and those who **gathered** less did not have too little.
	16.18	Each had **gathered** just what he needed.
	16.21	Every morning each one **gathered** as much as he needed;
	16.22	On the sixth day they **gathered** twice as much food,
	16.26	You must **gather** food for six days, but on the seventh day,
	16.27	the people went out to **gather** food, but they did not find
	23.10	"For six years sow your field and **gather** in what it produces.
	23.16	in the autumn, when you **gather** the fruit from your vineyards
	34.22	Festival of Shelters in the autumn when you **gather** your fruit.
Lev	19.10	back through your vineyard to **gather** the grapes that were missed
	25. 3	prune your vineyards, and **gather** your crops for six years.
	25. 5	and do not **gather** the grapes from your unpruned vines;
	25.11	grows by itself or **gather** the grapes in your unpruned vineyards.
	25.20	seventh year, when no fields are sown and no crops **gathered.**
Num	11. 8	people would go round and **gather** it, grind it or pound it
	11.32	no one **gathered** less than a thousand kilogrammes.
	15.32	the wilderness, a man was found **gathering** firewood on the Sabbath.
Deut	24.19	"When you **gather** your crops and fail to bring in some
	24.21	When you have **gathered** your grapes once, do not go back
	28.39	them, but you will not **gather** their grapes or drink wine
	30. 4	Lord your God will **gather** you together and bring you back,
Josh	8.35	Joshua to the whole **gathering,** which included women and children,
Judg	20. 2	Israel were present at this **gathering** of God's people, and
	21. 5	not go to the **gathering** in the Lord's presence at Mizpah?"
	21. 8	had not gone to the **gathering** at Mizpah, they found out that
	21.16	So the leaders of the **gathering** said, "There are no
Ruth	2. 2	go to the fields to **gather** the corn that the harvest workers
	2.17	So Ruth went on **gathering** corn in the field until evening,
	2.18	into town and showed her mother-in-law how much she had **gathered.**
	2.19	Naomi asked her, "Where did you **gather** all this?
	2.23	Ruth worked with them and **gathered** corn until all the barley
1 Sam	10.17	people together for a religious **gathering** at Mizpah [18]and said
2 Sam	14.14	like water spilt on the ground, which can't be **gathered** again.
1 Kgs	17.10	to the gate of the town, he saw a widow **gathering** firewood.
	17.12	I came here to **gather** some firewood to take back home and
2 Chr	20.25	They spent three days **gathering** the loot, but there was so
Job	24. 6	they don't own, and **gather** grapes in wicked men's vineyards.
	39.12	your harvest and **gather** the grain from your threshing-place?
Ps	39. 6	he **gathers** wealth, but doesn't know who will get it.
	126. 5	wept as they sowed their seed, **gather** the harvest with joy!
	129. 7	no one **gathers** it up or carries it away in bundles.
Prov	10. 5	A sensible man **gathers** the crops when they are ready;
Song	5. 1	I am **gathering** my spices and myrrh;
	6. 2	He is feeding his flock in the garden and **gathering** lilies.
Is	1.13	New Moon Festivals, your Sabbaths, and your religious **gatherings;**
	10.14	and I gathered their wealth as easily as **gathering** eggs.
	11.12	that he is **gathering** together again the scattered people of
	18. 5	Before the grapes are **gathered,** when the blossoms have all
	27.11	trees are withered and broken, and women **gather** them for firewood.
	27.12	Egyptian border, the Lord will **gather** his people one by one,
	32.10	despair because there will be no grapes for you to **gather.**
	40.11	he will **gather** the lambs together and carry them in his arms;
	62. 9	You that tended and **gathered** the grapes Will drink the wine
	66.18	I am coming to **gather** the people of all the nations.
Jer	6.11	in the streets and on the **gatherings** of the young men.
	7.18	The children **gather** firewood, the men build fires,
	8.13	"I wanted to **gather** my people, as a man gathers his harvest;
	9.22	and left behind by the reapers, corn that no one **gathers.**
	12.13	My people sowed wheat, but **gathered** weeds;
	23. 3	I will **gather** the rest of my people from the countries
	29.14	I will **gather** you from every country and from every place to
	31. 8	them from the north and **gather** them from the ends of the
	31.10	my people, but I will **gather** them and guard them as a
	32.37	I am going to **gather** the people from all the countries

Jer 40.10 But you can **gather** and store up wine, fruit, and olive-oil,
40.12 at Mizpah, and there they **gathered** in large amounts of wine
50.16 seeds be sown in that country or let a harvest be **gathered.**
Ezek 11.17 I will **gather** them out of the countries where I scattered them,
20.34 and my anger when I **gather** you together and bring you back
20.41 you have been scattered and **gather** you together, I will accept
22.21 I will **gather** them in Jerusalem, build a fire under them,
23.23 I will **gather** all those handsome young noblemen and officers,
39.10 They will not have to **gather** firewood in the fields or
39.28 them into captivity and now **gather** them and bring them back
Hos 8.10 But now I am going to **gather** them together and punish them.
9. 6 Egyptians will gather them up—**gather** them for burial there
Joel 3. 2 I will **gather** all the nations and bring them to the Valley
Obad 5 When people **gather** grapes, they always leave a few.
Mic 2.12 "But I will **gather** you together, all you people of Israel
4. 6 the Lord, "when I will **gather** together the people I punished,
Zeph 3. 8 made up my mind to **gather** nations and kingdoms, in order to
Zech 10. 8 "I will call my people and **gather** them together.
Mt 3.12 He will **gather** his wheat into his barn,
5. 1 His disciples **gathered** round him, [2]and he began to teach them:
6.26 they do not sow seeds, **gather** a harvest and put it in
9.37 harvest is large, but there are few workers to **gather** it in.
9.38 that he will send out workers to **gather** in his harvest."
12.30 anyone who does not help me **gather** is really scattering.
13. 2 The crowd that **gathered** round him was so large that he got
13.29 he answered, 'because as you **gather** the weeds you might pull
13.30 burn them, and then to **gather** in the wheat and put it
13.40 Just as the weeds are **gathered** up and burnt in the fire,
13.41 send out his angels to **gather** up out of his Kingdom all
13.49 angels will go out and **gather** up the evil people from among
21.34 When the time came to **gather** the grapes, he sent his
22.10 into the streets and **gathered** all the people they could find,
22.41 When some Pharisees **gathered** together, Jesus asked them,
23.37 just as a hen **gathers** her chicks under her wings,
24.28 "Wherever there is a dead body, the vultures will **gather.**
24.31 the earth, and they will **gather** his chosen people from one
25.24 did not sow, and you **gather** crops where you did not scatter
25.26 I did not sow, and **gather** crops where I did not scatter
25.32 the people of all the nations will be **gathered** before him.
26.57 the teachers of the Law and the elders had **gathered** together.
27.17 So when the crowd **gathered,** Pilate asked them,
27.27 and the whole company **gathered** round him.
Mk 1.33 All the people of the town **gathered** in front of the house.
3.20 Again such a large crowd **gathered** that Jesus and his disciples
4. 1 The crowd that **gathered** round him was so large that he got
5.21 There at the lakeside a large crowd **gathered** round him.
7. 1 teachers of the Law who had come from Jerusalem **gathered** round
12. 2 When the time came to **gather** the grapes, he sent a slave
13.27 corners of the earth to **gather** God's chosen people from one
14.53 the elders, and the teachers of the Law were **gathering.**
15. 8 When the crowd **gathered** and began to ask Pilate for the
Lk 3.17 thresh out all the grain and **gather** the wheat into his barn;
6.44 figs from thorn bushes or **gather** grapes from bramble bushes.
8. 4 and when a great crowd **gathered,** Jesus told this parable:
10. 2 "There is a large harvest, but few workers to **gather** it in.
10. 2 that he will send out workers to **gather** in his harvest.
11.23 anyone who does not help me **gather** is really scattering.
12.24 they don't sow seeds or **gather** a harvest;
13.34 just as a hen **gathers** her chicks under her wings,
17.37 "Wherever there is a dead body, the vultures will **gather.**"
20.10 When the time came to **gather** the grapes, he sent a slave
23.48 When the people who had **gathered** there to watch the spectacle
24.33 found the eleven disciples **gathered** together with the others
Jn 4.36 is being paid and **gathers** the crops for eternal life;
6.12 he said to his disciples, "**Gather** the pieces left over;
6.13 So they **gathered** them all up and filled twelve baskets
8. 2 All the people **gathered** round him, and he sat down and began
10.24 when the people **gathered** round him and asked, "How long
11.56 and as they **gathered** in the Temple, they asked
15. 6 such branches are **gathered** up and thrown into the fire,
20.19 and the disciples were **gathered** together behind locked doors,
Acts 1.14 They **gathered** frequently to pray as a group,
2. 1 Pentecost came, all the believers were **gathered** together
2. 6 When they heard this noise, a large crowd **gathered.**
4. 5 the elders, and the teachers of the Law **gathered** in Jerusalem.
4.28 They **gathered** to do everything that you by your power
10.27 he went into the house, where he found many people **gathered.**
12.12 where many people had **gathered** and were praying.
14.20 But when the believers **gathered** round him, he got up and
14.27 they arrived in Antioch, they **gathered** the people of the church
15.30 Antioch, where they **gathered** the whole group of believers
16.13 thought there would be a place where Jews **gathered** for prayer.
16.13 We sat down and talked to the women who **gathered** there.
17. 5 Jews were jealous and **gathered** some of the worthless loafers
20. 7 we **gathered** together for the fellowship meal.
28. 3 Paul **gathered** up a bundle of sticks
28.17 When they had **gathered,** he said to them, "My fellow-Israelites,
1 Cor 11.33 my brothers, when you **gather** together to eat the Lord's Supper,
2 Cor 8.15 says, "The one who **gathered** much did not have too much,
8.15 and the one who **gathered** little did not have too little."
Gal 6. 8 from it he will **gather** the harvest of death;
6. 8 from the Spirit he will **gather** the harvest of eternal life.
1 Thes 4.17 at that time will be **gathered** up along with them
2 Thes 2. 1 Jesus Christ and our being **gathered** together to be with him:
Heb 12.23 have come to the joyful **gathering** of God's first-born sons,
Jas 5. 4 The cries of those who **gather** in your crops have reached the
Rev 19.17 "Come and **gather** together for God's great feast!
19.19 the earth and their armies **gathered** to fight against the one

GAZA
One of the five chief cities of the Philistines.

Gen 10.19 Sidon southwards to Gerar near **Gaza,** and eastwards to Sodom,
Deut 2.23 over all their land as far south as the city of **Gaza.)**
Josh 10.41 Barnea in the south to **Gaza** near the coast, including all
11.22 a few, however, were left in **Gaza,** Gath, and Ashdod.
13. 3 kings of the Philistines lived at **Gaza,** Ashdod, Ashkelon, Gath,
15.47 There were Ashdod and **Gaza,** with their towns and villages,
Judg 1.18 But they did not capture **Gaza,** Ashkelon, or Ekron, with their
6. 4 and destroy the crops as far south as the area round **Gaza.**
16. 1 to the Philistine city of **Gaza,** where he met a prostitute
16. 2 The people of **Gaza** found out that Samson was there,
16.21 They took him to **Gaza,** chained him with bronze chains, and
1 Sam 6.17 one each for the cities of Ashdod, **Gaza,** Ashkelon, Gath,
1 Kgs 4.24 Tiphsah on the Euphrates as far west as the city of **Gaza.**
2 Kgs 18. 8 the largest city, including **Gaza** and its surrounding territory.
Jer 25.19 Philistine cities of Ashkelon, **Gaza,** Ekron, and what remains
47. 1 the king of Egypt attacked **Gaza,** the Lord spoke to me about
47. 5 to the people of **Gaza,** and Ashkelon's people are silent.
Amos 1. 6 Lord says, "The people of **Gaza** have sinned again and again,
1. 7 upon the city walls of **Gaza** and burn down its fortresses.
Zeph 2. 4 No one will be left in the city of **Gaza.**
Zech 9. 5 The city of **Gaza** will see it and suffer great pain.
9. 5 **Gaza** will lose her king, and Ashkelon will be left deserted.
Acts 8.26 and go south to the road that goes from Jerusalem to **Gaza."**

GAZED

Judg 5.28 she **gazed** from behind the lattice.

GAZELLE
A kind of deer, known for its beauty and gracefulness.

1 Kgs 4.23 pasture-fed cattle, and a hundred sheep, besides deer, **gazelles,**
Song 2. 7 the swift deer and the **gazelles** that you will not interrupt
2. 9 My lover is like a **gazelle,** like a young stag.
2.17 Return, my darling, like a **gazelle,** like a stag on the
3. 5 the swift deer and the **gazelles** that you will not interrupt
4. 5 Your breasts are like **gazelles,** twin deer feeding among lilies.
7. 3 Your breasts are like twin deer, like two **gazelles.**
8.14 my lover, like a **gazelle,** like a young stag on the

GEBA
City in Benjamin.

Josh 18.24 Avvim, Parah, Ophrah, [24]Chepharammoni, Ophni, and **Geba:**
21.17 **Geba,** [18]Anathoth, and Almon, with their pasture lands.
1 Sam 13. 3 killed the Philistine commander in **Geba,** and all the Philistines
13.16 and their men camped in **Geba** in the territory of Benjamin;
14. 5 Michmash, and the other was on the south side, facing **Geba.**
2 Sam 5.25 drive the Philistines back from **Geba** all the way to Gezer.
1 Kgs 15.22 material Asa fortified Mizpah and **Geba,** a city in the territory
1 Chr 6.60 **Geba,** Alemeth, and Anathoth.
8. 6 of families that lived in **Geba,** but which were forced out
2 Chr 16. 6 they used them to fortify the cities of **Geba** and Mizpah.
Ezra 2.21 Ramah and **Geba** - 621
Neh 7.26 Ramah and **Geba** - 621
11.31 tribe of Benjamin lived in **Geba,** Michmash, Ai, Bethel and the
12.29 and from the towns round Netophah, [29]and from Bethgilgal, **Geba,**
Is 10.29 They have crossed the pass and are spending the night at **Geba!**
Zech 14.10 The whole region, from **Geba** in the north to Rimmon in

GEDALIAH (1)
Governor of Judah after the capture of Jerusalem.

2 Kgs 25.22 Nebuchadnezzar of Babylonia made **Gedaliah,** the son of Ahikam
25.23 heard about this, they joined **Gedaliah** at Mizpah.
25.24 **Gedaliah** said to them, "I give you my word that there
25.25 went to Mizpah with ten men, attacked **Gedaliah** and killed him.
Jer 39.14 me under the care of **Gedaliah,** the son of Ahikam and
40. 5 Nebuzaradan said, "Go back to **Gedaliah,** the son of Ahikam
40. 6 I went to stay with **Gedaliah** in Mizpah and lived among the
40. 7 king of Babylonia had made **Gedaliah** governor of the land
40. 8 Jezaniah from Maacah went with their men to **Gedaliah** at Mizpah.
40. 9 **Gedaliah** said to them, "I give you my word that there is
40.11 on in Judah and that he had made **Gedaliah** their governor.
40.12 came to **Gedaliah** at Mizpah, and there they gathered in large
40.13 had not surrendered came to **Gedaliah** at Mizpah [14]and said
40.14 But **Gedaliah** did not believe it.
40.16 But **Gedaliah** answered, "Don't do it!
41. 1 chief officers, went to Mizpah with ten men to see **Gedaliah.**
41. 2 men with him pulled out their swords and killed **Gedaliah.**
41. 3 Israelites who were with **Gedaliah** at Mizpah and the Babylonian
41. 4 before anyone knew about **Gedaliah's** murder, [5]eighty men arrived
41. 6 came to them, he said, "Please come in to see **Gedaliah."**
41.10 the commanding officer had placed under the care of **Gedaliah.**
41.16 prisoners from Mizpah after murdering **Gedaliah**—soldiers, women,
41.17 Babylonians because Ishmael had murdered **Gedaliah,** whom the king
43. 6 officer had left under the care of **Gedaliah,** including Baruch

GEHAZI
Elisha's servant who acted dishonestly concerning the healing of Naaman.

2 Kgs 4.12 He told his servant **Gehazi** to go and call the woman.
4.13 she came, [13]he said to **Gehazi,** "Ask her what I can do

2 Kgs 4.14 Elisha asked **Gehazi**, "What can I do for her then?"
4.25 said to his servant **Gehazi**, "Look—there comes the woman from
4.26 She told **Gehazi** that everything was all right,
4.27 **Gehazi** was about to push her away, but Elisha said, "Leave
4.29 Elisha turned to **Gehazi** and said, "Hurry!
4.31 **Gehazi** went on ahead and held Elisha's stick over the child,
4.36 Elisha called **Gehazi** and told him to call the boy's mother.
5.20 short distance, [20] when Elisha's servant **Gehazi** said to himself,
5.22 "No," **Gehazi** answered.
5.23 to two of his servants, and sent them on ahead of **Gehazi.**
5.24 hill where Elisha lived, **Gehazi** took the two bags and carried
5.27 When **Gehazi** left, he had the disease—his skin was as white
8. 4 She found the king talking with **Gehazi,** Elisha's servant;
8. 5 While **Gehazi** was telling the king how Elisha had brought
8. 5 **Gehazi** said to him, "Your Majesty, here is the woman and
8. 6 she confirmed **Gehazi's** story, and so the king called

GEM

1 Chr 29. 2 iron, timber, precious stones and **gems,** stones for mosaics,
Song 5.14 His hands are well-formed, and he wears rings set with **gems.**
Ezek 28.13 in Eden, the garden of God, and wore **gems** of every kind:
28.14 You lived on my holy mountain and walked among sparkling **gems.**
28.16 who guarded you drove you away from the sparkling **gems.**

GENERAL (1)

Lev 10.10 God and what is for **general** use, between what is ritually
Ezek 48.15 is not holy, but is for the **general** use of the people.

GENERAL (2)

Prov 21.22 A shrewd **general** can take a city defended by strong men,
Dan 11. 5 One of his **generals,** however, will be even stronger and rule
Rev 19.18 eat the flesh of kings, **generals,** and soldiers,

GENERATION

Gen 15.16 will be four **generations** before your descendants come back here,
17. 7 and to your descendants in future **generations** as an everlasting
17. 9 with me, both you and your descendants in future **generations.**
Ex 1. 6 all the rest of that **generation** died, [7] but their descendants,
3.15 this is what all future **generations** are to call me.
20. 5 and on their descendants down to the third and fourth **generation.**
20. 6 my love to thousands of **generations** of those who love me and
34. 7 keep my promise for thousands of **generations** and forgive evil
34. 7 the third and fourth **generation** for the sins of their parents."
Num 14.18 the third and fourth **generation** for the sins of their parents.'
32.13 until that whole **generation** that had displeased him was dead.
32.14 your fathers' place, a new **generation** of sinful men ready to
Deut 1.35 of you from this evil **generation** will enter the fertile land
2.14 the fighting men of that **generation** had died, as the Lord
5. 9 and on their descendants down to the third and fourth **generation.**
5.10 my love to thousands of **generations** of those who love me and
7. 9 constant love to a thousand **generations** of those who love him
17.20 and his descendants will rule Israel for many **generations.**
23. 2 even in the tenth **generation,** may be included among the Lord's
23. 3 even in the tenth **generation**—may be included among the Lord's
23. 8 the third **generation** onward their descendants may be included
29.22 "In future **generations** your descendants and foreigners from
Josh 5. 7 and it was this new **generation** that Joshua circumcised.
22.27 and yours, and for the **generations** after us, that we do
Judg 2.10 That whole **generation** also died, and the next generation
2.17 Lord's commands, but this new **generation** soon stopped doing so.
2.19 to the old ways and behave worse than the previous **generation.**
3. 2 in order to teach each **generation** of Israelites about war,
2 Sam 3.29 In every **generation** may there be some man in his family who
12.10 in every **generation** some of your descendants will die a violent
2 Kgs 10.30 your descendants, down to the fourth **generation,** will be kings
15.12 "Your descendants, down to the fourth **generation,** will be kings
1 Chr 5. 4 the descendants of Joel from **generation to generation:**
6. 4 The descendants of Eleazar from **generation to generation** are as
6.20 the descendants of Gershon from **generation to generation:**
6.22 the descendants of Kohath from **generation to generation:**
6.26 Ahimoth's descendants from **generation to generation:**
6.29 the descendants of Merari from **generation to generation:**
7.20 the descendants of Ephraim from **generation to generation:**
28. 8 you may hand it on to succeeding **generations** for ever."
Esth 9.28 Jewish family of every future **generation** in every province
Ps 22.30 Future **generations** will serve him;
22.30 men will speak of the Lord to the coming **generation.**
48.13 examine the fortresses, so that you may tell the next **generation:**
71.18 I proclaim your power and might to all **generations** to come.
78. 4 we will tell the next **generation** about the Lord's power
78. 6 so that the next **generation** might learn them and in turn
102.12 all **generations** will remember you.
102.18 Write down for the coming **generation** what the Lord has done,
103.17 his goodness endures for all **generations**
105. 8 keep his covenant for ever, his promises for a thousand **generations.**
109.13 and may his name be forgotten in the next **generation.**
135.13 all **generations** will remember you.
145. 4 have done will be praised from one **generation** to the next;
Ecc 1. 4 **Generations** come and generations go, but the world stays just the same.
Ezek 20.21 "But that **generation** also defied me.
44.28 given Israel to be handed down from one **generation** to another.
Joel 1. 3 tell their children, who in turn will tell the next **generation.**
Mt 1.17 So then, there were fourteen **generations** from Abraham to David,
Lk 1.50 from one **generation** to another he shows mercy

AV GENERATION

Deut 32. 5 unworthy to be his people, a sinful and deceitful **nation.**
Ps 112. 2 The good man's **children** will be powerful in the land;
Is 34.10 The land will lie waste **age after age,** and no one will
34.17 will live in the land **age after age,** and it will belong
Mt 1. 1 is the list of the **ancestors** of Jesus Christ, a descendant
3. 7 he said to them, "You **snakes**—who told you that you could
12.34 You **snakes**—how can you say good things when you are evil?
23.33 You **snakes** and sons of snakes!
Mk 8.38 in this godless and wicked **day,** then the Son of Man will
Lk 3. 7 "You **snakes!"**
Acts 8.33 able to tell about his **descendants,** because his life on earth
1 Pet 2. 9 But you are the chosen **race,** the King's priests, the holy nation,

GENEROUS

Deut 15. 8 Instead, be **generous** and lend him as much as he needs.
15.11 in need, and so I command you to be **generous** to them.
15.14 Give to him **generously** from what the Lord has blessed you
1 Kgs 8.56 has kept all the **generous** promises he made through his servant
10.13 all the other customary gifts that he had **generously** given her.
1 Chr 29. 5 else is willing to give a **generous** offering to the Lord?"
2 Chr 11.23 He provided **generously** for them and also secured many wives for
Esth 1. 7 them alike, and the king was **generous** with the royal wine.
Ps 37.21 pays back, but the good man is **generous** with his gifts.
112. 5 is the person who is **generous** with his loans, who runs his
112. 9 He gives **generously** to the needy, and his kindness never fails;
Prov 11.25 Be **generous,** and you will be prosperous.
21.26 A righteous man, however, can give, and give **generously.**
22. 9 Be **generous** and share your food with the poor.
31.20 She is **generous** to the poor and needy.
Mt 20.15 Or are you jealous because I am **generous?"**
Lk 6.38 receive a full measure, a **generous** helping,
Rom 12. 8 Whoever shares with others should do it **generously;**
2 Cor 8. 2 great that they were extremely **generous** in their giving,
8. 7 we want you to be **generous** also in this service of love.
8.20 complaints about the way we handle this **generous** gift.
9. 9 As the scripture says, "He gives **generously** to the needy;
9.10 grow and produce a rich harvest from your **generosity.**
9.11 you rich enough to be **generous** at all times,
9.13 and for your **generosity** in sharing with them and everyone
1 Tim 6.17 God, who **generously** gives us everything for our enjoyment.
6.18 good works, to be **generous** and ready to share with others.
Jas 1. 5 because God gives **generously** and graciously to all.

GENITAL

Num 5.21 May he cause your **genital** organs to shrink and your stomach
5.22 cause it to swell up and your **genital** organs to shrink."
5.27 stomach will swell up and her **genital** organs will shrink.
Deut 25.11 grabbing hold of the other man's **genitals,** [12] show her no mercy;

GENTILE

A person who is not a Jew.

Neh 5. 9 not give our enemies, the **Gentiles,** any reason to ridicule us.
Lam 1.10 the Temple itself, Where the Lord had forbidden **Gentiles** to go.
Mt 4.15 other side of the Jordan, Galilee, land of the **Gentiles!**
10. 5 "Do not go to any **Gentile** territory or any Samaritan towns.
10.18 kings, to tell the Good News to them and to the **Gentiles.**
20.19 hand him over to the **Gentiles,** who will mock him, whip him,
Mk 7.26 The woman was a **Gentile,** born in the region of Phoenicia
10.33 hand him over to the **Gentiles,** [34] who will mock him, spit
Lk 2.32 reveal your will to the **Gentiles** and bring glory to your
18.32 be handed over to the **Gentiles,** who will mock him, insult
Acts 2.11 both Jews and **Gentiles** converted to Judaism,
4.25 when he said, 'Why were the **Gentiles** furious;
4.27 in this city with the **Gentiles** and the people of Israel
6. 5 Nicolaus, a **Gentile** from Antioch
9.15 make my name known to **Gentiles** and kings and to the people
10.28 not allowed by his religion to visit or associate with **Gentiles.**
10.45 poured out his gift of the Holy Spirit on the **Gentiles** also.
11. 1 Judaea heard that the **Gentiles** also had received the word
11. 2 were in favour of circumcising **Gentiles** criticized him, saying,
11. 3 home of uncircumcised **Gentiles,** and you even ate with them!"
11.17 clear that God gave those **Gentiles** the same gift that he
11.18 God has given to the **Gentiles** also the opportunity to repent
11.20 and proclaimed the message to **Gentiles** also,
13.16 "Fellow-Israelites and all **Gentiles** here who worship God:
13.26 descendants of Abraham, and all **Gentiles** here who worship God:
13.43 and by many **Gentiles** who had been converted to Judaism.
13.46 of eternal life, we will leave you and go to the **Gentiles.**
13.47 you a light for the **Gentiles,** so that all the world may
13.48 When the **Gentiles** heard this, they were glad
13.50 and the **Gentile** women of high social standing
14. 1 that a great number of Jews and **Gentiles** became believers.
14. 2 stirred up the **Gentiles** and turned them against the believers.
14. 5 Then some **Gentiles** and Jews, together with their leaders,
14.27 and how he had opened the way for the **Gentiles** to believe.
15. 3 they reported how the **Gentiles** had turned to God;
15. 5 stood up and said, "The **Gentiles** must be circumcised and
15. 7 the Good News to the **Gentiles,** so that they could hear
15. 8 showed his approval of the **Gentiles** by giving the Holy Spirit
15.12 wonders that God had performed through them among the **Gentiles.**
15.14 showed his care for the **Gentiles** by taking from among them a
15.17 come to me, all the **Gentiles** whom I have called to be
15.19 "that we should not trouble the **Gentiles** who are turning to God.
15.23 to all our brothers of **Gentile** birth who live in Antioch,

Acts	17.17	the Jews and with the **Gentiles** who worshipped God, and also
	18. 6	From now on I will go to the **Gentiles."**
	18. 7	the house of a **Gentile** named Titius Justus, who worshipped God;
	19.10	Asia, both Jews and **Gentiles,** heard the word of the Lord.
	19.17	the Jews and **Gentiles** who lived in Ephesus heard about this;
	20.21	To Jews and **Gentiles** alike I gave solemn warning
	21.11	and they will hand him over to the **Gentiles."**
	21.19	that God had done among the **Gentiles** through his work.
	21.21	the Jews who live in **Gentile** countries to abandon the Law of
	21.25	But as for the **Gentiles** who have become believers,
	21.28	he has even brought some **Gentiles** into the Temple
	22.21	'for I will send you far away to the **Gentiles.'"**
	26.17	of Israel and from the **Gentiles** to whom I will send you.
	26.20	and among the **Gentiles,** I preached that they must repent
	26.23	the light of salvation to the Jews and to the **Gentiles."**
	28.28	that God's message of salvation has been sent to the **Gentiles.**
Rom	1.13	win converts among you also, as I have among other **Gentiles.**
	1.16	save all who believe, first the Jews and also the **Gentiles.**
	2. 9	what is evil, for the Jews first and also for the **Gentiles.**
	2.10	what is good, to the Jews first and also to the **Gentiles.**
	2.12	The **Gentiles** do not have the Law of Moses;
	2.14	The **Gentiles** do not have the Law;
	2.24	"Because of you Jews, the **Gentiles** speak evil of God."
	2.26	If the **Gentile,** who is not circumcised, obeys the commands
	2.27	will be condemned by the **Gentiles** because you break the Law,
	3. 1	Have the Jews then any advantage over the **Gentiles?**
	3. 9	Well then, are we Jews in any better condition than the **Gentiles?**
	3. 9	shown that Jews and **Gentiles** alike are all under the power
	3.29	Is he not the God of the **Gentiles** also?
	3.30	and will put the **Gentiles** right through their faith.
	9.24	only from among the Jews but also from among the **Gentiles.**
	9.30	So we say that the **Gentiles,** who were not trying to put
	10.12	because there is no difference between Jews and **Gentiles;**
	11.11	salvation has come to the **Gentiles,** to make the Jews jealous
	11.12	their spiritual poverty brought rich blessings to the **Gentiles.**
	11.13	I am speaking now to you **Gentiles:**
	11.13	am an apostle to the **Gentiles,** I will take pride in my
	11.17	You **Gentiles** are like that wild olive-tree,
	11.24	You **Gentiles** are like the branch of a wild olive-tree
	11.25	last only until the complete number of **Gentiles** comes to God.
	11.28	the Jews are God's enemies for the sake of you **Gentiles.**
	11.30	As for you **Gentiles,** you disobeyed God in the past;
	15. 9	and to enable even the **Gentiles** to praise God for his mercy.
	15. 9	scripture says, "And so I will praise you among the **Gentiles;**
	15.10	Again it says, "Rejoice, **Gentiles,** with God's people!"
	15.11	And again, "Praise the Lord, all **Gentiles;**
	15.12	will come to rule the **Gentiles,** and they will put their hope
	15.16	of being a servant of Christ Jesus to work for the **Gentiles.**
	15.16	in order that the **Gentiles** may be an offering acceptable
	15.18	Christ has done through me to lead the **Gentiles** to obey God.
	15.27	their spiritual blessings with the **Gentiles,**
	15.27	the **Gentiles** ought to use their material blessings
	16. 4	not only I, but all the **Gentile** churches as well.
1 Cor	1.23	offensive to the Jews and nonsense to the **Gentiles;**
	1.24	has called, both Jews and **Gentiles,** this message is Christ,
	9.21	when working with **Gentiles,** I live like a Gentile,
	9.21	outside the Jewish Law, in order to win **Gentiles.**
	10.32	trouble either to Jews or **Gentiles** or to the church of God.
	12.13	of us, whether Jews or **Gentiles,** whether slaves or free,
2 Cor	11.26	in danger from fellow-Jews and from **Gentiles;**
Gal	1.16	News about him to the **Gentiles,** I did not go to anyone
	2. 2	I explained the gospel message that I preach to the **Gentiles.**
	2. 7	preaching the gospel to the **Gentiles,**
	2. 8	made an apostle to the **Gentiles,** just as Peter was made an
	2. 9	and I would work among the **Gentiles** and they among the Jews.
	2.12	Peter had been eating with the **Gentile** brothers.
	2.12	would not eat with the **Gentiles,** because he was afraid
	2.14	yet you have been living like a **Gentile,** not like a Jew.
	2.14	How, then, can you try to force **Gentiles** to live like Jews?"
	2.15	Jews by birth and not **"Gentile** sinners," as they are called.
	2.17	sinners as much as the **Gentiles** are—does this mean that
	3. 8	God would put the **Gentiles** right with himself through faith.
	3.14	might be given to the **Gentiles** by means of Christ Jesus,
	3.28	no difference between Jews and **Gentiles,**
Eph	2.11	You **Gentiles** by birth—called "the uncircumcised"
	2.14	brought us peace by making Jews and **Gentiles** one people.
	2.17	peace to all—to you **Gentiles,** who were far away from God,
	2.18	all of us, Jews and **Gentiles,** are able to come in the
	2.19	So then, you **Gentiles** are not foreigners or strangers
	3. 1	of Christ Jesus for the sake of you **Gentiles,** pray to God.
	3. 6	means of the gospel the **Gentiles** have a part with the Jews
	3. 8	privilege of taking to the **Gentiles** the Good News
Col	2.13	and because you were **Gentiles** without the Law.
	3.11	no longer any distinction between **Gentiles** and Jews,
1 Thes	2.16	us from preaching to the **Gentiles** the message that would bring
1 Tim	2. 7	apostle and teacher of the **Gentiles,** to proclaim the message
2 Tim	4.17	to proclaim the full message for all the **Gentiles** to hear;

GENTLE

Deut	32. 2	like showers on young plants, like **gentle** rain on tender grass.
Ruth	2.13	me feel better by speaking **gently** to me, even though I am
Job	21.33	funeral procession, and even the earth lies **gently** on his body.
Prov	15. 1	A **gentle** answer quietens anger, but a harsh one stirs it up.
	31.26	She speaks with a **gentle** wisdom.
Is	40.11	he will **gently** lead their mothers.
Jer	4.11	It will not be a **gentle** wind that only blows away the
Mt	10.16	You must be as cautious as snakes and as **gentle** as doves.
	11.29	and learn from me, because I am **gentle** and humble in spirit;
1 Cor	4.21	you with a whip, or in a spirit of love and **gentleness?**
2 Cor	10. 1	By the **gentleness** and kindness of Christ I beg you [2] not to
Gal	6. 1	but you must do it in a **gentle** way.
Eph	4. 2	Be always humble, **gentle,** and patient.
Phil	4. 5	Show a **gentle** attitude towards everyone.
Col	3.12	clothe yourselves with compassion, kindness, humility, **gentleness,**
1 Thes	2. 7	But we were **gentle** when we were with you, like a mother
1 Tim	3. 3	not be a drunkard or a violent man, but **gentle** and peaceful;
	6.11	righteousness, godliness, faith, love, endurance, and **gentleness.**
2 Tim	2.25	and patient teacher, [25] who is **gentle** as he corrects his opponents,
Tit	3. 2	and always to show a **gentle** attitude towards everyone.
Heb	5. 2	he is able to be **gentle** with those who are ignorant
Jas	3.17	it is also peaceful, **gentle,** and friendly;
1 Pet	3. 4	the ageless beauty of a **gentle** and quiet spirit,
	3.16	you have in you, [16] but do it with **gentleness** and respect.

GENUINE

Ps	12. 6	as **genuine** as silver refined seven times in the furnace.
Phil	1.15	jealous and quarrelsome, but others from **genuine** goodwill.
1 Tim	1. 5	from a pure heart, a clear conscience, and a **genuine** faith.
Jas	1.27	the Father considers to be pure and **genuine** religion is this:
1 Pet	1. 7	Their purpose is to prove that your faith is **genuine.**

GERAH

One-twentieth of a shekel.

Ezek	45.12	20 **gerahs** = 1 shekel 60 shekels = 1 mina

GERAR

City in s. Canaan where Abraham and Isaac lived.

Gen	10.19	reached from Sidon southwards to **Gerar** near Gaza, and eastwards
	20. 1	while he was living in **Gerar,** [2] he said that his wife Sarah
	20. 2	So King Abimelech of **Gerar** had Sarah brought to him.
	26. 1	Isaac went to Abimelech, king of the Philistines, at **Gerar.**
	26. 6	So Isaac lived at **Gerar.**
	26.17	camp in the Valley of **Gerar,** where he stayed for some time.
	26.20	The shepherds of **Gerar** quarrelled with Isaac's shepherds
	26.26	Abimelech came from **Gerar** with Ahuzzath his adviser
1 Chr	4.39	spread out westwards almost to **Gerar** and pastured their sheep
	4.41	men named above went to **Gerar** and destroyed the tents
2 Chr	14.13	and Asa and his troops pursued them as far as **Gerar.**
	14.14	the area around **Gerar,** because the people there were terrified

GERSHON

Levi's son and the clan descended from him.

Gen	46.11	**Gershon,** Kohath, and Merari.
Ex	6.16	**Gershon,** Kohath, and Merari;
	6.17	**Gershon** had two sons:
Num	3.17	**Gershon,** Kohath, and Merari, who were the ancestors of the clans
	3.17	**Gershon** had two sons:
	3.21	The clan of **Gershon** was composed of the families of Libni
	4.22	of the Levite clan of **Gershon** by sub-clans and families,
	4.27	see to it that the **Gershonites** perform all the duties
	4.28	the responsibilities of the **Gershon** clan in the Tent;
	4.34	a census of the three Levite clans, Kohath, **Gershon,** and Merari.
	4.34	**Gershon** 2,630
	7. 7	four oxen to the **Gershonites,** [8] and four wagons and eight oxen
	10.17	and the clans of **Gershon** and Merari, who carried it, would
	26.57	tribe of Levi consisted of the clans of **Gershon,** Kohath,
Josh	21. 6	The clan of **Gershon** was assigned thirteen cities from the
	21.27	of Levites, the clan of **Gershon,** received from the territory of
	21.33	families of the clan of **Gershon** received a total of thirteen
1 Chr	6. 1	**Gershon,** Kohath, and Merari.
	6.16	**Gershon,** Kohath, and Merari.
	6.17	**Gershon** was the father of Libni and Shimei;
	6.20	the descendants of **Gershon** from generation to generation:
	6.43	Ethan, Zimmah, Shimei, [43] Jahath, **Gershon,** Levi.
	6.62	To the clan of **Gershon,** family by family, were assigned
	6.71	of the clan of **Gershon** were assigned the following towns,
	15. 7	from the clan of **Gershon,** Joel, in charge of 130;
	23. 6	**Gershon,** Kohath, and Merari.
	23. 7	**Gershon** had two sons:
	26.21	one of the sons of **Gershon,** was the ancestor of several
	29. 8	which was administered by Jehiel of the Levite clan of **Gershon.**
2 Chr	29.12	Jehallelel From the clan of **Gershon,** Joah son of Zimnah

GESHUR (1)

Small kingdom n. of Israel.

Deut	3.14	that is, Bashan, as far as the border of **Geshur** and Maacah.
Josh	12. 5	far as the boundaries of **Geshur** and Maacah,
	13.11	included Gilead, the regions of **Geshur** and Maacah,
	13.13	Israelites did not drive out the people of **Geshur** and Maacah;
2 Sam	3. 3	mother was Maacah, the daughter of King Talmai of **Geshur;**
	13.37	went to the king of **Geshur,** Talmai son of Ammihud,
	14.23	up and went to **Geshur** and brought Absalom back to Jerusalem.
	14.32	'Why did I leave **Geshur** and come here?
	15. 8	While I was living in **Geshur** in Syria, I promised the Lord
1 Chr	2.23	But the kingdoms of **Geshur** and Aram conquered sixty towns
	3. 1	daughter of King Talmai of **Geshur**

GESTURE

Prov	6.13	They wink and make **gestures** to deceive you,
Is	58. 9	end to oppression, to every **gesture** of contempt, and to every

GET AWAY

Josh 8.22 No one **got away,** and no one lived through it [23] except the
Judg 3.26 Ehud **got away** while they were waiting.
1 Sam 19.11 warned him, "If you don't **get away** tonight, tomorrow you will
23.26 They were hurrying to **get away** from Saul and his men, who
24.19 a man catch his enemy and then let him **get away** unharmed?
30.17 men who mounted camels and **got away,** none of them escaped.
2 Sam 15.14 him in Jerusalem, "We must **get away** at once if we want
1 Kgs 18.40 don't let any of them **get away!"**
2 Kgs 5.20 "My master has let Naaman **get away** without paying a thing!
Ps 139. 7 Where could I **get away** from your presence?
Prov 3.21 Never let them **get away** from you.
4.21 Never let them **get away** from you.
Ecc 7.26 man who pleases God can **get away,** but she will catch the
Jer 9. 2 stay in the desert where I could **get away** from my people.
35.11 to come to Jerusalem to **get away** from the Babylonian and
41.15 and eight of his men **got away** from Johanan and escaped to
41.17 out for Egypt, in order to **get away** from the Babylonians.
46. 6 Those who run fast cannot **get away;**
Ezek 17.15 Can he **get away** with that?
Amos 2.15 ground, fast runners will not **get away,** and men on horses
9. 1 No one will **get away;**
Jon 1. 3 the opposite direction in order to **get away** from the Lord.
Mal 3.15 God's patience with their evil deeds and **get away** with it.' "
Mt 7.23 **Get away** from me, you wicked people!'
16.23 Jesus turned around and said to Peter, **"Get away** from me,
Mk 8.33 **"Get away** from me, Satan," he said.
Lk 13.27 **Get away** from me, all you wicked people!'

GET BACK

Lk 6.34 Even sinners lend to sinners, to **get back** the same amount!

GET OUT

Gen 12.19 take her and **get out!"**
19. 9 But they said, **"Get out** of our way, you foreigner!
19.14 going to marry, and said, "Hurry up and **get out** of here;
19.15 and your two daughters and **get out,** so that you will not
40.14 to the king and help me to **get out** of this prison.
Ex 10.28 He said to Moses, **"Get out** of my sight!
12.31 Moses and Aaron and said, **"Get out,** you and your Israelites!
14.25 Let's **get out** of here!"
2 Sam 13.15 He said to her, **"Get out!"**
16. 7 Shimei cursed him and said, **"Get out!**
16. 7 **Get out!**
1 Kgs 21. 7 **"Get out** of bed, cheer up and eat.
2 Kgs 2.23 **"Get out** of here, baldy!"
5.26 in spirit when the man **got out** of his chariot to meet
7.12 still night, but the king **got out** of bed and said to
2 Chr 26.20 He hurried to **get out,** because the Lord had punished him.
Ps 140.10 may they be thrown into a pit and never **get out.**
Prov 6. 3 that man's power, but this is how to **get out** of it:
6. 5 **Get out** of the trap like a bird or a deer escaping
26.13 Why doesn't the lazy man ever **get out** of the house?
Is 30.11 **Get out** of our way and stop blocking our path.
Jer 15. 1 make them **get out** of my sight.
Mt 9.24 and the people all stirred up, [24] he said, **"Get out,**
Lk 13.31 said to him, "You must **get out** of here and go somewhere
Acts 9.33 had not been able to **get out** of bed for eight years.
1 Cor 5.10 them you would have to **get out** of the world completely.

GET UP

Gen 19. 1 as he saw them, he **got up** and went to meet them.
19. 2 In the morning you can **get up** early and go on your
21.18 **Get up,** go and pick him up, and comfort him.
24.54 When they **got up** in the morning, he said, "Let me go
25.34 He ate and drank and then **got up** and left.
28.18 Jacob **got up** early next morning, took the stone that was
32.22 That same night Jacob **got up,** took his two wives, his
37. 7 of wheat, when my sheaf **got up** and stood up straight.
Ex 21.18 but later is able to **get up** and walk outside with the
Num 25. 7 Aaron the priest, saw this, he **got up** and left the assembly.
Josh 3. 1 all the people of Israel **got up** early, left the camp at
6.12 Joshua **got up** early the next morning, and for the
6.15 On the seventh day they **got up** at daybreak and marched
7.10 The Lord said to Joshua, **"Get up!**
7.13 **Get up!**
8.10 Joshua **got up** and called the soldiers together.
8.19 men who had been hiding **got up** quickly, ran into the city
Judg 6.28 the people of the town **got up** early the next morning, they
6.38 When Gideon **got up** early the next morning, he squeezed the
7. 1 Gideon and all his men **got up** early and camped beside the
7. 9 the Lord commanded Gideon, **"Get up** and attack the camp;
7.15 Then he went back to the Israelite camp and said, **"Get up!**
9.33 **Get up** tomorrow morning at sunrise and make a sudden attack
9.35 at the city gate, they **got up** from their hiding places.
13.11 Manoah **got up** and followed his wife.
16. 3 Then he **got up** and took hold of the city gate and
19. 7 The Levite **got up** to go, but the father urged him to
19. 9 Tomorrow you can **get up** early for your journey and go home."
19.27 Her husband **got up** that morning, and when he opened the
19.28 He said, **"Get up.**
Ruth 3.14 at his feet, but she **got up** before it was light enough
1 Sam 1. 9 meal in the house of the Lord at Shiloh, Hannah **got up.**
1.19 morning Elkanah and his family **got up** early, and after
3. 6 So he **got up,** went to Eli, and said, "You called me,
3. 8 he **got up,** went to Eli, and said, "You called me, and
3.15 then he **got up** and opened the doors of the house of
1 Sam 9.26 to Saul on the roof, **"Get up,** and I will send you
9.26 Saul **got up,** and he and Samuel went out to the street
17.20 David **got up** early the next morning, left someone else
20.34 Jonathan **got up** from the table in a rage and ate nothing
20.41 the boy had left, David **got up** from behind the pile of
24. 7 Saul **got up,** left the cave, and started on his way.
28.23 He finally gave in, **got up** from the ground, and sat on
29.10 to me will have to **get up** early and leave as soon
2 Sam 11. 2 late in the afternoon, David **got up** from his nap and went
12.17 and tried to make him **get up,** but he refused and would
12.20 David **got up** from the floor, had a bath, combed his hair,
12.21 but as soon as he died, you **got up** and ate!"
14.23 Then he **got up** and went to Geshur and brought Absalom
15. 2 He would **get up** early and go and stand by the road
19. 8 Then the king **got up,** and went and sat near the city
24.11 The next morning, after David **got up,** [11] Gad went to him,
1 Kgs 1.49 were afraid, and they all **got up** and left, each going his
3.20 She **got up** during the night, took my son from my side
19. 7 up a second time, saying, **"Get up** and eat, or the journey
19. 8 Elijah **got up,** ate and drank, and the food gave him enough
2 Kgs 3.22 When they **got up** the following morning, the sun was
4.35 Elisha **got up,** walked about the room, and then went back
6.15 next morning Elisha's servant **got up,** went out of the house,
Ezra 9. 5 for the evening sacrifice, I **got up** from where I had been
Neh 2.12 middle of the night I **got up** and went out, taking a
Esth 7. 7 The king **got up** in a fury, left the room, and went
Job 1. 5 after each feast, Job would **get up** early and offer sacrifices
24.14 At dawn the murderer **gets up** and goes out to kill the
Ps 127. 2 so hard for a living, **getting up** early and going to bed
Prov 6. 9 When is he ever going to **get up?**
24.16 how often an honest man falls, he always **gets up** again;
31.15 She **gets up** before daylight to prepare food for her family
Song 7.12 We will **get up** early and look at the vines to see
Is 5.11 You **get up** early in the morning to start drinking, and you
51.17 Rouse yourself and **get up!**
Jer 25.27 they fall down and cannot **get up,** because of the war that
37.10 tents, those men would still **get up** and burn this city to
Lam 2.19 All through the night **get up** again and again to cry out
Ezek 3.22 heard him say to me, **"Get up** and go out into the
Dan 6.19 At dawn the king **got up** and hurried to the pit.
8.27 Then I **got up** and went back to the work that the
Jon 1. 6 **Get up** and pray to your god for help.
3. 6 Nineveh heard about it, he **got up** from his throne, took off
Mic 2.10 **Get up** and go;
Hab 2.19 or to a block of stone, **"Get up!"**
Mt 2.13 So **get up,** take the child and his mother and escape to
2.14 Joseph **got up,** took the child and his mother, and left
2.20 Joseph in Egypt [20] and said, **"Get up,** take the child and
2.21 So Joseph **got up,** took the child and his mother, and
8.15 fever left her, and she **got up** and began to wait on
8.26 Then he **got up** and ordered the winds and the waves to
9. 5 say, 'Your sins are forgiven,' or to say, **'Get up** and walk'?
9. 6 said to the paralysed man, **"Get up,** pick up your bed,
9. 7 The man **got up** and went home.
9. 9 Matthew **got up** and followed him.
9.19 So Jesus **got up** and followed him, and his disciples went
9.25 girl's room and took hold of her hand, and she **got up.**
17. 7 **"Get up,"** he said.
21.21 to say to this hill, **'Get up** and throw yourself in the
26.46 **Get up,** let us go.
Mk 1.35 morning, long before daylight, Jesus **got up** and left the house.
2. 9 are forgiven', or to say, **'Get up,** pick up your mat,
2.11 paralysed man, [11] "I tell you, **get up,** pick up your mat,
2.12 they all watched, the man **got up,** picked up his mat, and
2.14 Levi **got up** and followed him.
5.41 "Talitha, koum," which means, "Little girl, I tell you to **get up!"**
5.42 She **got up** at once and started walking around.
10.49 **"Get up,** he is calling you."
11.23 whoever tells this hill to **get up** and throw itself in the
14.42 **Get up,** let us go.
Lk 4.39 fever left her, and she **got up** at once and began to
5.23 'Your sins are forgiven you,' or to say, **'Get up** and walk'?
5.24 paralysed man, "I tell you, **get up,** pick up your bed,
5.25 At once the man **got up** in front of them all, took
5.28 Levi **got up,** left everything, and followed him.
6. 8 The man **got up** and stood there.
7.14 **Get up,** I tell you!"
8.24 Jesus **got up** and gave an order to the wind and the
8.54 took her by the hand and called out, **"Get up,** my child!"
8.55 Her life returned, and she **got up** at once, and Jesus
11. 7 I can't **get up** and give you anything.'
11. 8 even if he will not **get up** and give you the bread
11. 8 his friend, yet he will **get up** and give you everything you
13.25 The master of the house will **get up** and close the door;
15.18 I will **get up** and go to my father and say, Father,
15.20 So he **got up** and started back to his father.
17.19 And Jesus said to him, **"Get up** and go;
22.46 **Get up** and pray that you will not fall into temptation."
24.12 But Peter **got up** and ran to the tomb;
24.33 They **got up** at once and went back to Jerusalem, where
Jn 5. 8 Jesus said to him, **"Get up,** pick up your mat, and walk."
11.29 When Mary heard this, she **got up** and hurried out to meet
11.31 followed her when they saw her **get up** and hurry out.
Acts 3. 6 Jesus Christ of Nazareth I order you to **get up** and walk!"
9. 6 "But **get up** and go into the city, where you will be
9. 8 Saul **got up** from the ground and opened his eyes, but could
9.34 **Get up** and make your bed."
9.34 At once Aeneas **got up.**
9.40 then he turned to the body and said, "Tabitha, **get up!"**
9.41 Peter reached over and helped her **get up.**
10.13 A voice said to him, **"Get up,** Peter;

Acts 11. 7 Then I heard a voice saying to me, **'Get up,** Peter;
12. 7 **Get up!"**
14.20 believers gathered round him, he **got up** and went back into
22.10 the Lord said to me, **'Get up** and go into Damascus,
22.16 **Get up** and be baptized and have your sins washed away by
26.16 But **get up** and stand on your feet.
26.30 and all the others **got up,** [31] and after leaving they said

GEZER
Canaanite city-state near Philistine territory which only became Israelite in Solomon's time.

Josh 10.33 King Horam of **Gezer** came to the aid of Lachish,
12.12 Jerusalem, Hebron, [11] Jarmuth, Lachish, [12] Eglon, **Gezer,**
16. 3 on from there to **Gezer** and ended at the Mediterranean Sea.
16.10 the Canaanites who lived in **Gezer,** so the Canaanites have lived
21.21 **Gezer,** [22] Kibzaim, and Beth Horon,
Judg 1.29 living in the city of **Gezer,** and so the Canaanites continued
2 Sam 5.25 drive the Philistines back from Geba all the way to **Gezer.**
1 Kgs 9.15 used it to rebuild the cities of Hazor, Megiddo, and **Gezer.**
9.16 king of Egypt had attacked **Gezer** and captured it,
1 Chr 6.67 in the hills of Ephraim, **Gezer,** [68] Jokmeam, Beth Horon,
7.28 Naaran and as far west as **Gezer** and the towns round it.
14.16 drove the Philistines back from Gibeon all the way to **Gezer.**
20. 4 Later on, war broke out again with the Philistines at **Gezer.**

GHOST

Is 14. 9 The **ghosts** of those who were powerful on earth are stirring about.
14. 9 The **ghosts** of kings are rising from their thrones.
26.14 their **ghosts** will not rise, for you have punished them
29. 4 Jerusalem will be like a **ghost** struggling to speak from under
Mt 14.26 "It's a **ghost!"**
Mk 6.49 "It's a **ghost!"**
Lk 24.37 They were terrified, thinking that they were seeing a **ghost.**
24.39 you will know, for a **ghost** doesn't have flesh and bones,

GIANT

Gen 6. 4 even later, there were **giants** on the earth who were descendants
Num 13.22 the descendants of a race of **giants** called the Anakim, lived.
13.28 Even worse, we saw the descendants of the **giants** there.
13.33 and we even saw **giants** there, the descendants of Anak.
Deut 1.28 They saw **giants** there!'
2.10 (A mighty race of **giants** called the Emim used to live
2.10 They were as tall as the Anakim, another race of **giants.**
9. 2 they are **giants,** and you have heard it said that no one
Josh 11.21 and destroyed the race of **giants** called the Anakim who lived
14.12 then that the race of **giants** called the Anakim were there in
2 Sam 21.16 A **giant** named Ishbibenob, who was carrying a bronze
21.17 came to David's help, attacked the **giant,** and killed him.
21.18 during which Sibbecai from Hushah killed a **giant** named Saph.
21.20 battle at Gath, where there was a **giant** who loved to fight.
21.22 were descendants of the **giants** of Gath, and they were killed
1 Chr 20. 4 Sibbecai from Hushah killed a **giant** named Sippai,
20. 6 Gath, where there was a **giant** with six fingers on each hand
20. 6 He was a descendant of the ancient **giants.**
20. 8 David and his men, were descendants of the **giants** at Gath.
Ps 80.10 its branches overshadowed the **giant** cedars.
Is 32. 2 desert, like the shadow of a **giant** rock in a barren land.
Ezek 17. 3 There was a **giant** eagle with beautiful feathers and huge wings,
17. 7 was another **giant** eagle with huge wings and thick plumage.
Dan 2.31 saw standing before you a **giant** statue, bright and shining,

GIBEAH (1)
City in Benjamin, which later became Saul's capital.

Josh 18.28 Haeleph, Jebus (or Jerusalem), **Gibeah,** and Kiriath Jearim:
Judg 19.12 a little farther and spend the night at **Gibeah** or Ramah."
19.14 sunset when they came to **Gibeah** in the territory of the
19.16 hill-country of Ephraim, but he was now living in **Gibeah.**
20. 4 concubine and I went to **Gibeah** in the territory of Benjamin
20. 5 The men of **Gibeah** came to attack me and surrounded the
20. 9 we will draw lots and choose some men to attack **Gibeah.**
20.10 others will go and punish **Gibeah** for this immoral act that
20.13 hand over those perverts in **Gibeah,** so that we can kill them
20.14 Benjamin they came to **Gibeah** to fight against the other people
20.15 citizens of **Gibeah** gathered seven hundred specially chosen men
20.19 out the next morning and made camp near the city of **Gibeah.**
20.25 the Benjaminites came out of **Gibeah,** and this time they killed
20.29 So the Israelites put some soldiers in hiding round **Gibeah.**
20.30 in battle position facing **Gibeah,** as they had done before.
20.31 country on the road to Bethel and on the road to **Gibeah.**
20.33 the men surrounding **Gibeah** suddenly rushed out of their hiding
20.34 out of all Israel, attacked **Gibeah,** and the fighting was hard.
20.36 relying on the men that they had put in hiding round **Gibeah.**
20.37 These men ran quickly towards **Gibeah;**
20.43 far as a point east of **Gibeah,** killing them as they went.
1 Sam 10. 5 the Hill of God in **Gibeah,** where there is a Philistine camp.
10.10 his servant arrived at **Gibeah,** a group of prophets met him.
10.26 Saul also went back home to **Gibeah.**
11. 4 The messengers arrived at **Gibeah,** where Saul lived,
13. 2 with his son Jonathan to **Gibeah,** in the territory of the
13.15 They went from Gilgal to **Gibeah** in the territory of Benjamin.
14. 2 camping under a pomegranate-tree in Migron, not far from **Gibeah;**
14.16 Saul's men on watch at **Gibeah** in the territory of Benjamin
15.34 Then Samuel went to Ramah, and King Saul went home to **Gibeah.**
22. 6 One day Saul was in **Gibeah,** sitting under a tamarisk-tree
23.19 Ziph went to Saul at **Gibeah** and said, "David is hiding in
26. 1 Ziph came to Saul at **Gibeah** and told him that David was
2 Sam 21. 6 them before the Lord at **Gibeah,** the town of Saul, the Lord's
23.24 Ittai son of Ribai from **Gibeah** in Benjamin
1 Chr 11.26 Ithai son of Ribai from **Gibeah** in Benjamin
12. 3 the command of Ahiezer and Joash, sons of Shemaah, from **Gibeah.**
2 Chr 13. 2 His mother was Micaiah daughter of Uriel, from the city of **Gibeah.**
Is 10.29 and the people in King Saul's town of **Gibeah** have run away.
Hos 5. 8 Blow the war trumpets in **Gibeah!**
9. 9 evil in what they do, just as they were at **Gibeah.**
10. 9 sinning against me since the time of their sin at **Gibeah.**
10. 9 So at **Gibeah** war will catch up with them.

GIBEON
Canaanite city n. of Jerusalem which was later included in Benjamin and became a religious centre.

Josh 9. 3 But the people of **Gibeon,** who were Hivites, heard what Joshua
9.15 friendship with the people of **Gibeon** and allowed them to live.
9.17 **Gibeon,** Chephirah, Beeroth, and Kiriath Jearim.
9.22 Joshua ordered the people of **Gibeon** to be brought to him,
10. 1 that the people of **Gibeon** had made peace with the Israelites
10. 2 greatly alarmed at this because **Gibeon** was as large as any
10. 4 and help me attack **Gibeon,** because its people have made peace
10. 5 and Eglon, joined forces, surrounded **Gibeon,** and attacked it.
10. 6 The men of **Gibeon** sent word to Joshua at the camp in
10. 9 marched from Gilgal to **Gibeon,** and they made a surprise attack
10.10 The Israelites slaughtered them at **Gibeon** and pursued them down
10.12 "Sun, stand still over **Gibeon;**
10.41 all the area of Goshen, and as far north as **Gibeon.**
11.19 people of Israel was **Gibeon,** where some of the Hivites lived.
18.25 There were also **Gibeon,** Ramah, Beeroth,
21.17 **Gibeon,** Geba, [18] Anathoth, and Almon, with their pasture lands.
2 Sam 2.12 officials of Ishbosheth went from Mahanaim to the city of **Gibeon.**
2.16 And so that place in **Gibeon** is called "Field of Swords."
2.24 the east of Giah on the road to the wilderness of **Gibeon.**
3.30 Abner for killing their brother Asahel in the battle at **Gibeon.**
20. 8 When they reached the large rock at **Gibeon,** Amasa met them.
21. 1 he put the people of **Gibeon** to death."
21. 2 (The people of **Gibeon** were not Israelites;
21. 3 David summoned the people of **Gibeon** and said to them,
21. 9 over to the people of **Gibeon,** who hanged them on the
1 Kgs 3. 4 one occasion he went to **Gibeon** to offer sacrifices because that
9. 2 the Lord appeared to him again, as he had in **Gibeon.**
1 Chr 8.29 Jeiel founded the city of **Gibeon** and settled there.
9.35 Jeiel founded the city of **Gibeon** and settled there.
12. 3 Ishmaiah from **Gibeon,** a famous soldier and one of
14.16 drove the Philistines back from **Gibeon** all the way to Gezer.
16.39 the worship of the Lord at the place of worship in **Gibeon.**
21.29 were still at the place of worship at **Gibeon** at this time;
2 Chr 1. 3 them to go with him to the place of worship at **Gibeon.**
1. 5 of Hur, was also in **Gibeon** in front of the Tent of
1.13 the place of worship at **Gibeon,** where the Tent of the Lord's
Neh 3. 7 Melatiah from **Gibeon,** Jadon from Meronoth,
3. 7 and the men of **Gibeon** and Mizpah built the next section,
7. 8 **Gibeon** – 95
Is 28.21 and in the valley of **Gibeon,** in order to do what he
Jer 28. 1 prophet from the town of **Gibeon,** spoke to me in the Temple.
41.12 their men and overtook him near the large pool at **Gibeon.**

GIDEON
Military leader of Israel before the monarchy.

Judg 6.1-40 **Gideon**
7.1-25 **Gideon defeats the Midianites**
8.1-28 **The final defeat of the Midianites**
29-35 **The death of Gideon**
Judg 9. 1 **Gideon's** son Abimelech went to the town of Shechem,
9. 2 governed by all seventy of **Gideon's** sons or by just one man?
9. 5 of a single stone he killed his seventy brothers, **Gideon's** sons.
9. 5 But Jotham, **Gideon's** youngest son, hid and was not killed.
9.16 Did you respect **Gideon's** memory and treat his family properly,
9.19 what you did today to **Gideon** and his family was sincere and
9.24 who encouraged him to murder **Gideon's** seventy sons, would pay
9.28 The son of **Gideon!**
9.57 their wickedness, just as Jotham, **Gideon's** son, said they would
1 Sam 12.11 And the Lord sent **Gideon,** Barak, Jephthah, and finally me.
2 Sam 11.21 Don't you remember how Abimelech son of **Gideon** was killed?
Heb 11.32 for me to speak of **Gideon,** Barak, Samson, Jephthah, David, Samuel,

GIFT

Gen 24.53 He also gave expensive **gifts** to her brother and to her mother.
30.20 She said, "God has given me a fine **gift.**
32.20 win him over with the **gifts,** and when I meet him, perhaps
32.21 He sent the **gifts** on ahead of him and spent that night
33.10 "No, please, if I have gained your favour, accept my **gift.**
33.11 Please accept this **gift** which I have brought for you;
43.15 So the brothers took the **gifts** and twice as much money,
43.25 got their **gifts** ready to present to Joseph when he arrived
43.26 got home, they took the **gifts** into the house to him and
Ex 29.24 and tell them to dedicate it to me as a special **gift.**
29.26 of this ram and dedicate it to me as a special **gift.**
29.27 to me as a special **gift** and set aside for the priests.
29.28 This is the people's **gift** to me, the Lord.
Lev 7.29 of it as a special **gift** to the Lord, [30] bringing it with
7.30 its breast and present it as a special **gift** to the Lord.
7.34 the animal is a special **gift,** and the right hind leg is
8.27 sons, and they presented it as a special **gift** to the Lord.

Lev 8.29 the breast and presented it as a special **gift** to the Lord.
9.21 hind legs as the special **gift** to the Lord for the priests,
10.14 are presented as the special **gift** and the special contribution
14.12 present them as a special **gift** to the Lord for the priest.
14.21 repayment-offering, a special **gift** to the Lord for the priest.
14.24 present them as a special **gift** to the Lord for the priest.
23.17 of bread and present them to the Lord as a special **gift.**
23.20 two lambs as a special **gift** to the Lord for the priests.
23.38 in addition to your regular **gifts,** your offerings in fulfilment
27. 9 to the Lord, then every **gift** made to the Lord is sacred,
Num 6.20 the priest shall present them as a special **gift** to the Lord;
7. 5 said to Moses, [5]"Accept these **gifts** for use in the work to
7.10 ready to present their **gifts** at the altar, [11]the Lord said
7.11 is to present his **gifts** for the dedication of the altar."
8.11 to me as a special **gift** from the Israelites, so that they
8.13 the Levites as a special **gift** to me, and put Aaron and
8.19 and his sons, as a **gift** from the Israelites, to work in
8.21 and Aaron dedicated them as a special **gift** to the Lord.
15.21 time to come, this special **gift** is to be given to the
18. 6 the Levites from among the Israelites as a **gift** to you.
18. 7 because I have given you the **gift** of the priesthood.
18.32 not to profane the sacred **gifts** of the Israelites
18.32 by eating any of the **gifts** before the best part is offered;
Deut 12. 6 and your offerings, the **gifts** that you promise to the Lord,
12.11 your offerings, and those special **gifts** that you have promised
12.17 cattle and sheep, the **gifts** that you promise to the Lord,
12.26 your offerings and the **gifts** that you have promised the Lord.
16.16 man is to bring a **gift** [17]as he is able, in proportion
16.19 not to accept bribes, for **gifts** blind the eyes even of wise
Judg 3.15 Israel sent Ehud to King Eglon of Moab with **gifts** for him.
3.17 Then he took the **gifts** to Eglon, who was a very fat
3.18 Ehud had given him the **gifts,** he told the men who had
1 Sam 6. 3 course, send with it a **gift** to him to pay for your
6. 3 The Covenant Box must not go back without a **gift.**
6. 4 "What **gift** shall we send him?"
6. 8 are sending to him as a **gift** to pay for your sins.
6.17 to the Lord as a **gift** to pay for their sins, one
10.27 They despised Saul and did not bring him any **gifts.**
1 Kgs 10.10 She presented to King Solomon the **gifts** she had brought:
10.13 all the other customary **gifts** that he had generously given her.
10.25 who came brought him a **gift**—articles of silver and gold,
2 Kgs 5.15 so please, sir, accept a **gift** from me."
5.16 whom I serve, I swear that I will not accept a **gift."**
5.17 "If you won't accept my **gift,** then let me have two
8. 8 of his officials, "Take a **gift** to the prophet, and ask him
12. 4 regular sacrifices and the money given as free-will **gifts.**
12.18 sent them all as a **gift** to King Hazael, who then led
1 Chr 26.20 temple treasury and the storerooms for **gifts** dedicated to God.
26.26 in charge of all the **gifts** dedicated to God by King David,
26.28 in the Temple, including the **gifts** brought by the prophet Samuel,
28.12 for the temple equipment and the **gifts** dedicated to the Lord.
29.14 because everything is a **gift** from you, and we have only
2 Chr 9. 9 She presented to King Solomon the **gifts** she had brought:
9.12 he gave her in exchange for the **gifts** she brought to him.
9.24 Each of them brought Solomon **gifts**—articles of silver
17. 5 all the people brought him **gifts,** so that he became wealthy
17.11 amount of silver and other **gifts,** and some Arabs brought him
31. 5 the people of Israel brought **gifts** of their finest corn, wine,
31. 6 large quantities of **gifts,** which they dedicated to the Lord
31. 7 The **gifts** started arriving in the third month and continued
31. 9 the Levites about these **gifts,** [10]and Azariah the High Priest,
31.10 the people started bringing their **gifts** to the Temple,
31.12 and put all the **gifts** and tithes in them for safe-keeping.
31.14 in charge of receiving the **gifts** offered to the Lord and of
32.23 offerings to the Lord and **gifts** to Hezekiah, so that from
Neh 12.47 people of Israel gave daily **gifts** for the support of the
Esth 2.18 for the whole empire and distributed **gifts** worthy of a king.
9.19 time for feasting and giving **gifts** of food to one another.
9.22 with feasts and parties, giving **gifts** of food to one another
Job 6.22 you to give me a **gift** or to bribe someone on my
Ps 16. 6 How wonderful are your **gifts** to me;
37.21 pays back, but the good man is generous with his **gifts.**
45.12 The people of Tyre will bring you **gifts;**
68.18 he receives **gifts** from rebellious men.
68.29 your Temple in Jerusalem, where kings bring **gifts** to you.
72.10 The kings of Spain and of the islands will offer him **gifts;**
76.11 bring **gifts** to him, all you nearby nations.
127. 3 Children are a **gift** from the Lord;
Prov 6.35 no amount of **gifts** will satisfy his anger.
18.16 Take him a **gift** and it will be easy.
21.14 angry with you, a **gift** given secretly will calm him down.
22.16 If you make **gifts** to rich people or oppress the poor to
Ecc 3.13 It is God's **gift.**
5.19 It is a **gift** from God.
Is 1.23 they are always accepting **gifts** and bribes.
30. 6 donkeys and camels with expensive **gifts** for a nation that cannot
66.20 all your fellow-countrymen from the nations as a **gift** to me.
Jer 31.12 with my gifts— **gifts** of corn and wine and olive-oil,
31.12 **gifts** of sheep and cattle.
Ezek 16.41 a prostitute and make you stop giving **gifts** to your lovers.
20.31 you offer the same **gifts** and defile yourselves with the same
20.39 stop dishonouring my holy name by offering **gifts** to your idols.
20.40 bring me your sacrifices, your est offerings, and your holy **gifts.**
Dan 2. 6 its meaning, I will reward you with **gifts** and great honour.
2.48 presented him with many splendid **gifts,** put him in charge of
5.17 Daniel replied, "Keep your **gifts** for yourself or give them
11.38 jewels, and other rich **gifts** to a god his ancestors never
Hos 2. 9 I will take back my **gifts** of corn and wine, and will
3. 5 Then they will fear the Lord and will receive his good **gifts.**
Zech 6.10 He said, "Take the **gifts** given by the exiles Heldai,
Mt 2.11 They brought out their **gifts** of gold, frankincense, and myrrh,
Mt 5.23 are about to offer your **gift** to God at the altar
5.24 leave your **gift** there in front of the altar,
5.24 brother, and then come back and offer your **gift** to God.
23.18 if he swears by the **gift** on the altar, he is bound.'
23.19 important, the gift or the altar which makes the **gift** holy?
23.20 he is swearing by it and by all the **gifts** on it;
Lk 21. 1 saw rich men dropping their **gifts** in the temple treasury,
21. 4 For the others offered their **gifts** from what they had to
21. 5 it looked with its fine stones and the **gifts** offered to God.
Acts 1. 4 but wait for the **gift** I told you about,
1. 4 the **gift** my Father promised.
2.33 see and hear is his **gift** that he has poured out on
2.38 and you will receive God's **gift,** the Holy Spirit.
5.32 the Holy Spirit, who is God's **gift** to those who obey him."
8.20 hell, for thinking that you can buy God's **gift** with money!
10.45 God had poured out his **gift** of the Holy Spirit on the
11.17 gave those Gentiles the same **gift** that he gave us when we
28.10 They gave us many **gifts,** and when we sailed, they put on
Rom 3.24 But by the free **gift** of God's grace all are put right
4. 4 is paid his wages, but they are not regarded as a **gift;**
4.16 guaranteed as God's free **gift** to all of Abraham's descendants—
5. 5 by means of the Holy Spirit, who is God's **gift** to us.
5.15 the same, because God's free **gift** is not like Adam's sin.
5.15 and so is his free **gift** to so many people through the
5.16 is a difference between God's **gift** and the sin of one man.
5.16 after so many sins, comes the undeserved **gift** of "Not guilty!"
6.23 but God's free **gift** is eternal life in union with Christ
8.23 as the first of God's **gifts** also groan within ourselves,
12. 3 And because of God's gracious **gift** to me I say to every
12. 6 are to use our different **gifts** in accordance with the grace
12. 6 If our **gift** is to speak God's message, we should do it
1 Cor 2.14 cannot receive the **gifts** that come from God's Spirit.
3.10 Using the **gift** that God gave me, I did the work of
4. 7 can you boast, as if what you have were not a **gift?**
7. 7 each one has a special **gift** from God,
7. 7 one person this **gift,** another one that gift.
7.17 living according to the Lord's **gift** to him, and as he was
12. 1 concerning what you wrote about the **gifts** from the Holy Spirit.
12. 4 are different kinds of spiritual **gifts,** but the same Spirit
12.10 to another, the **gift** of speaking God's message;
12.10 to tell the difference between **gifts** that come from the Spirit
12.11 as he wishes, he gives a different **gift** to each person.
12.31 Set your hearts, then, on the more important **gifts.**
13. 2 I may have the **gift** of inspired preaching;
13. 8 are **gifts** of speaking in strange tongues, but they will cease;
13. 9 **gifts** of knowledge and of inspired messages are only partial;
14. 1 Set your hearts on spiritual **gifts,**
14. 1 especially the **gift** of proclaiming God's message.
14. 5 rather that you had the **gift** of proclaiming God's message.
14.12 are eager to have the **gifts** of the Spirit, you must try
14.13 then, must pray for the **gift** to explain what he says.
14.22 So then, the **gift** of speaking in strange tongues is proof
14.22 while the **gift** of proclaiming God's message is proof
14.32 The **gift** of proclaiming God's message should be under
14.37 messenger or has a spiritual **gift,** he must realize that what
16. 3 have approved, and send them to take your **gift** to Jerusalem.
2 Cor 8.12 give, God will accept your **gift** on the basis of what you
8.20 any complaints about the way we handle this generous **gift.**
9. 5 me and get ready in advance the **gift** you promised to make.
9.11 will thank God for your **gifts** which they receive from us.
9.15 Let us thank God for his priceless **gift!**
Gal 3.18 For if God's **gift** depends on the Law, then it no longer
3.18 because of his promise that God gave that **gift** to Abraham.
3.22 and so the **gift** which is promised on the basis of faith
Eph 1. 6 glorious grace, for the free **gift** he gave us in his dear
2. 8 your own efforts, but God's **gift,** so that no one can boast
3. 7 the gospel by God's special **gift,** which he gave me through
4. 7 us has received a special **gift** in proportion to what Christ
4. 8 he gave **gifts** to mankind."
4.11 It was he who "gave **gifts** to mankind";
Phil 4.17 It is not that I just want to receive **gifts;**
4.18 I need now that Epaphroditus has brought me all your **gifts.**
1 Tim 4.14 Do not neglect the spiritual **gift** that is in you, which
2 Tim 1. 6 you to keep alive the **gift** that God gave you when I
Heb 2. 4 and by distributing the **gifts** of the Holy Spirit according to
6. 4 they tasted heaven's **gift** and received their share
8. 4 priests who offer the **gifts** required by the Jewish Law.
11. 4 as a righteous man, because God himself approved of his **gifts.**
Jas 1.17 Every good **gift** and every perfect present comes from heaven;
1 Pet 1.10 and they prophesied about this **gift** which God would give you.
3. 7 they also will receive, together with you, God's **gift** of life.
4.10 good manager of God's different **gifts,** must use for the good
4.10 good of others the special **gift** he has received from God.
2 Pet 1. 4 the very great and precious **gifts** he promised,
1. 4 by means of these **gifts** you may escape from the destructive
Rev 22.17 accept the water of life as a **gift,** whoever wants it.

GIGANTIC

1 Chr 11.23 over two metres tall, who was armed with a **gigantic** spear.

GILEAD (1)

General name for much of Israel's territory e. of the R. Jordan.

Gen 31.21 the River Euphrates and started for the hill-country of **Gilead.**
31.23 until he caught up with him in the hill-country of **Gilead.**
31.25 up his camp with his kinsmen in the hill-country of **Gilead.**
37.25 saw a group of Ishmaelites travelling from **Gilead** to Egypt.
Num 32. 1 the land of Jazer and **Gilead** was for cattle, [2]they went to
32.26 cattle and sheep will remain here in the towns of **Gilead.**
32.29 land, then give them the land of **Gilead** as their property.

Num 32.39 Manasseh invaded the land of **Gilead,** occupied it, and drove out
32.40 So Moses gave **Gilead** to the clan of Machir, and they
Deut 2.36 city in the middle of that valley, all the way to **Gilead.**
3.10 the plateau, the regions of **Gilead** and of Bashan, as far
3.12 and part of the hill-country of **Gilead,** along with its towns.
3.13 I assigned the rest of **Gilead** and also all of Bashan, where
3.15 "I assigned **Gilead** to the clan of Machir of the tribe
3.16 Gad I assigned the territory from **Gilead** to the River Arnon.
4.43 tribe of Gad there was Ramoth, in the territory of **Gilead;**
34. 1 the territory of **Gilead** as far north as the town of Dan;
Josh 12. 2 His kingdom included half of **Gilead:**
12. 5 as well as half of **Gilead,** as far as the territory of
13.11 It included **Gilead,** the regions of Geshur and Maacah,
13.25 and all the cities of **Gilead,** half the land of Ammon as
13.31 It included half of **Gilead,** as well as Ashtaroth and Edrei,
17. 1 a military hero, so **Gilead** and Bashan, east of the Jordan,
17. 5 ten shares in addition to **Gilead** and Bashan on the east side
17. 6 The land of **Gilead** was assigned to the rest of the
20. 8 Ramoth in **Gilead,** in the territory of Gad;
21.38 Ramoth in **Gilead,** with its pasture lands (one of the cities
22. 9 own land, the land of **Gilead,** which they had taken as the
22.13 of Reuben, Gad, and East Manasseh in the land of **Gilead.**
22.15 came to the land of **Gilead,** to the people of Reuben, Gad,
22.32 Gad in the land of **Gilead** and went back to Canaan, to
Judg 10. 3 After Tola came Jair from **Gilead.**
10. 4 cities in the land of **Gilead,** which are still called the
10. 8 lived in Amorite country east of the River Jordan in **Gilead.**
10.17 the Ammonite army prepared for battle and made camp in **Gilead.**
10.17 The men of Israel came together and camped at Mizpah in **Gilead.**
10.18 Whoever does will be the leader of everyone in **Gilead."**
11. 1 Jephthah, a brave soldier from **Gilead,** was the son of
11. 5 this happened, the leaders of **Gilead** went to bring Jephthah back
11. 8 fight the Ammonites and lead all the people of **Gilead."**
11.11 went with the leaders of **Gilead,** and the people made him
11.29 He went through **Gilead** and Manasseh
11.29 and returned to Mizpah in **Gilead** and went on to Ammon.
11.40 year to grieve for the daughter of Jephthah of **Gilead.**
12. 4 all the men of **Gilead** together, fought the men of Ephraim
12. 4 (The Ephraimites had said, "You **Gileadites** in Ephraim
12. 5 the **Gileadites** captured the places where the Jordan
12. 5 the men of **Gilead** would ask, "Are you an Ephraimite?"
12. 7 Then he died and was buried in his home town in **Gilead.**
20. 1 as from the land of **Gilead** in the east, answered the call.
21. 8 found out that no one from Jabesh in **Gilead** had been there;
1 Sam 11. 1 town of Jabesh in the territory of **Gilead** and besieged it.
13. 7 crossed the River Jordan into the territories of Gad and **Gilead.**
31.11 the people of Jabesh in **Gilead** heard what the Philistines
2 Sam 2. 4 the people of Jabesh in **Gilead** had buried Saul, [5] he sent
2. 9 king of the territories of **Gilead,** Asher, Jezreel, Ephraim,
17.26 Absalom and his men camped in the land of **Gilead.**
17.27 of Ammiel, from Lodebar, and by Barzillai, from Rogelim in **Gilead.**
19.31 Barzillai, from **Gilead,** had also come down from Rogelim to
21.12 and of his son Jonathan from the people of Jabesh in **Gilead.**
24. 6 and on to **Gilead** and to Kadesh, in Hittite territory.
1 Kgs 2. 7 the sons of Barzillai from **Gilead** and take care of them,
4.13 the city of Ramoth in **Gilead,**
4.13 and the villages in **Gilead** belonging to the clan of Jair,
4.19 the region of **Gilead,** which had been ruled by King Sihon of
17. 1 named Elijah, from Tishbe in **Gilead,** said to King Ahab,
22. 3 to get back Ramoth in **Gilead** from the king of Syria?
22.29 Jehoshaphat of Judah went to attack the city of Ramoth in **Gilead.**
2 Kgs 8.28 armies clashed at Ramoth in **Gilead,** and Joram was wounded
9. 1 and said to him, "Get ready and go to Ramoth in **Gilead.**
10.33 the territories of **Gilead** and Bashan, where the tribes of
15.25 plotted with fifty men from **Gilead,** assassinated Pekahiah in
15.29 and the territories of **Gilead,** Galilee, and Naphtali, and took
1 Chr 2.22 Jair ruled twenty-three cities in the territory of **Gilead.**
5. 9 herds in the land of **Gilead,** and so they occupied the land
5.10 and occupied their land in the eastern part of **Gilead.**
5.16 the territory of Bashan and **Gilead,** in the towns there and
6.80 Ramoth in **Gilead,** Mahanaim, [81] Heshbon, and Jazer.
10.11 people of Jabesh in **Gilead** heard what the Philistines had done
26.31 were found living at Jazer in the territory of **Gilead.**
2 Chr 18. 2 Jehoshaphat to join him in attacking the city of Ramoth in **Gilead.**
18.28 Jehoshaphat of Judah went to attack the city of Ramoth in **Gilead.**
22. 5 armies clashed at Ramoth in **Gilead,** and Joram was wounded
Ezra 2.61 the clan of Barzillai of **Gilead** and had taken the name of
Neh 7.63 the clan of Barzillai of **Gilead** and taken the name of his
Ps 60. 7 **Gilead** is mine, and Manasseh too;
108. 8 **Gilead** is mine, and Manasseh too;
Song 4. 1 like a flock of goats bounding down the hills of **Gilead.**
6. 5 like a flock of goats bounding down the hills of **Gilead.**
Jer 8.22 Is there no medicine in **Gilead?**
22. 6 as the land of **Gilead** and as the Lebanon Mountains;
46.11 People of Egypt, go to **Gilead** and look for medicine!
50.19 crops that grow in the territories of Ephraim and **Gilead.**
Ezek 47.18 Israel on the west and **Gilead** on the east, as far as
Hos 6. 8 **Gilead** is a city full of evil men and murderers.
12.11 Yet idols are worshipped in **Gilead,** and those who worship
Amos 1. 3 They treated the people of **Gilead** with savage cruelty.
1.13 for more territory they even ripped open pregnant women in **Gilead.**
Obad 19 the people of Benjamin will take **Gilead.**
Mic 7.14 rich pastures of Bashan and **Gilead,** as they did long ago.
Zech 10.10 I will settle them in **Gilead** and Lebanon also;

GILEAD (2)

Machir's son.

Num 26.29 Manasseh was the father of **Gilead,**
26.29 and the following clans traced their ancestry to **Gilead:**
27. 1 of Hepher, son of **Gilead,** son of Machir, son of Manasseh,
36. 1 families in the clan of **Gilead,** the son of Machir and
Josh 17. 1 Machir, the father of **Gilead,** was Manasseh's eldest son
17. 3 of Hepher, son of **Gilead,** son of Machir, son of Manasseh,
1 Chr 2.21 he married Machir's daughter, the sister of **Gilead.**
2.23 who lived there were descendants of Machir, the father of **Gilead.**
7.14 Machir was the father of **Gilead.**
7.17 These are all descendants of **Gilead,** the son of Machir
7.18 **Gilead's** sister Hammolecheth had three sons:

GILGAL (1)

Place where the Israelites encamped when they first crossed the Jordan.

Josh 4.19 of the first month and made camp at **Gilgal,** east of Jericho.
5. 9 is why the place was named **Gilgal,** the name it still has.
5.10 the Israelites were camping at **Gilgal** on the plain near Jericho,
9. 6 went to the camp at **Gilgal** and said to Joshua and the
10. 6 men of Gibeon sent word to Joshua at the camp in **Gilgal:**
10. 7 whole army, including the best troops, started out from **Gilgal.**
10. 9 and his army marched from **Gilgal** to Gibeon, and they made a
10.15 this, Joshua and his army went back to the camp at **Gilgal.**
10.43 this, Joshua and his army went back to the camp at **Gilgal.**
14. 6 people from the tribe of Judah came to Joshua at **Gilgal.**
Judg 2. 1 of the Lord went from **Gilgal** to Bochim and said to the
3.19 at the carved stones near **Gilgal,** went back to Eglon, and
1 Sam 7.16 go round to Bethel, **Gilgal,** and Mizpah, and in these places
10. 8 go ahead of me to **Gilgal,** where I will meet you and
11.14 "Let us all go to **Gilgal** and once more proclaim Saul as
11.15 So they all went to **Gilgal,** and there at the holy place
13. 4 So the people answered the call to join Saul at **Gilgal.**
13. 7 Saul was still at **Gilgal,** and the people with him were
13. 8 him to do, but Samuel still had not come to **Gilgal.**
13.12 to attack me here in **Gilgal,** and I have not tried to
13.15 Samuel left **Gilgal** and went on his way.
13.15 They went from **Gilgal** to Gibeah in the territory of Benjamin.
15.12 built a monument to himself, and then had gone on to **Gilgal.**
15.21 they brought them here to **Gilgal** to offer as a sacrifice to
15.33 he cut Agag to pieces in front of the altar in **Gilgal.**
2 Sam 19.15 who had come to **Gilgal** to escort him across the river.
19.40 of Israel, he went on to **Gilgal,** and Chimham went with him.
20. 1 happened to be in **Gilgal** a worthless character named Sheba
Hos 4.15 Don't worship at **Gilgal** or Bethaven, or make promises there in
9.15 The Lord says, "All their evil-doing began in **Gilgal.**
12.11 Bulls are sacrificed in **Gilgal,** and the altars there will become
Amos 4. 4 Go to **Gilgal** and sin with all your might!
5. 5 Do not go to **Gilgal**—her people are doomed to exile."
Mic 6. 5 that happened on the way from the camp at Acacia to **Gilgal.**

GIRL

[SERVANT-GIRL, SLAVE-GIRL]

Gen 6. 1 all over the world, and **girls** were being born, [2] some of the
6. 2 heavenly beings saw that these **girls** were beautiful, so they
16. 1 But she had an Egyptian **slave-girl** named Hagar, [2] and so she
16. 2 Why don't you sleep with my **slave-girl?**
20.17 wife and his **slave-girls,** so that they could have children.
21.10 said to Abraham, "Send this **slave-girl** and her son away.
21.13 to the son of the **slave-girl,** so that they will become a
24. 5 servant asked, "What if the **girl** will not leave home to
24. 8 If the **girl** is not willing to come with you, you will
24.16 She was a very beautiful young **girl** and still a virgin.
24.28 The **girl** ran to her mother's house and told the whole story.
24.37 wife for my son from the **girls** in the land of Canaan.
24.39 asked my master, 'What if the **girl** will not come with me?'
24.55 her mother said, "Let the **girl** stay with us a week or
24.57 They answered, "Let's call the **girl** and find out what she
26.34 he married two Hittite **girls,** Judith the daughter of Beeri,
27.46 marries one of these Hittite **girls,** I might as well die."
28. 1 greeted him, and said to him, "Don't marry a Canaanite **girl.**
28. 2 and marry one of the **girls** there, one of your uncle Laban's
29.24 (Laban gave his **slave-girl** Zilpah to his daughter Leah
29.29 (Laban gave his **slave-girl** Bilhah to his daughter Rachel
30. 3 She said, "Here is my **slave-girl** Bilhah;
30. 9 she gave her **slave-girl** Zilpah to Jacob as his wife.
31.43 Laban answered Jacob, "These **girls** are my daughters;
34. 3 But he found the **girl** so attractive that he fell in love
34. 4 "I want you to get this **girl** for me as my wife."
38. 2 There Judah met a Canaanite **girl** whose father was named Shua.
46.18 of Jacob by Zilpah, the **slave-girl** whom Laban gave to his
46.25 of Jacob by Bilhah, the **slave-girl** whom Laban gave to his
Ex 1.16 but if it is a **girl,** let it live."
1.22 and throw him into the Nile, but let all the **girls** live."
2. 5 basket in the tall grass and sent a **slave-girl** to get it.
2. 8 So the **girl** went and brought the baby's own mother.
21.31 the bull kills a boy or a **girl,** the same rule applies.
Lev 19.20 "If a **slave-girl** is the recognized concubine of a man
Num 31.18 alive for yourselves all the **girls** and all the women who are
Deut 22.13 "Suppose a man marries a **girl** and later he decides he
22.15 this happens, the **girl's** parents are to take the blood-stained
22.15 wedding sheet that proves the **girl** was a virgin, and they
22.16 The **girl's** father will say to them, 'I gave my daughter
22.19 give the money to the **girl's** father,
22.19 because the man has brought disgrace on an Israelite **girl.**
22.20 is no proof that the **girl** was a virgin, [21] then they are
22.23 having intercourse with a **girl** who is engaged to someone else.

Deut 22.24 The **girl** is to die because she did not cry out for
22.24 die because he had intercourse with a **girl** who was engaged.
22.25 the countryside rapes a **girl** who is engaged to someone else.
22.26 to be done to the **girl,** because she has not committed a
22.27 The man raped the engaged **girl** in the countryside,
22.28 "Suppose a man is caught raping a **girl** who is not engaged.
22.29 He is to pay the **girl's** father the bride price of fifty
28.30 will be engaged to a **girl**—but someone else will marry her.
Judg 5.30 to capture and divide, a **girl** or two for every soldier, rich
9.18 Abimelech, his son by his **servant-girl,** is your relative,
12. 9 the clan and brought thirty **girls** from outside the clan for
14. 1 went down to Timnah, where he noticed a certain Philistine **girl.**
14. 2 "There is a Philistine **girl** down at Timnah who has caught
14. 3 Can't you find a **girl** in our own clan, among all our
14. 7 Then he went and talked to the **girl,** and he liked her.
14.10 father went to the **girl's** house, and Samson gave a banquet
19. 1 He took a **girl** from Bethlehem in Judah to be his concubine,
19. 3 The **girl** showed the Levite into the house, and when her
19. 5 the **girl's** father said to the Levite, "Have something to eat
19. 6 the **girl's** father said to him, "Please spend the night here
19. 8 started to leave, but the **girl's** father said, "Eat something,
21.14 other Israelites gave them the **girls** from Jabesh whom they had
21.21 When the **girls** of Shiloh come out to dance during the festival,
21.21 by force from among the **girls** and take her back to the
21.23 chose a wife from the **girls** who were dancing at Shiloh and
Ruth 1. 4 with her two sons, [4] who married Moabite **girls,** Orpah and Ruth.
2. 6 "She is the foreign **girl** who came back from Moab with
1 Sam 9. 9 the town, they met some **girls** who were coming out to draw
9. 9 They asked the **girls,** "Is the seer in town?"
9.12 "Yes, he is," the **girls** answered.
2 Sam 6.20 fool in the sight of the **servant-girls** of his officials!"
6.22 I am nothing, but those **girls** will think highly of me!"
17.17 **servant-girl** would regularly go and tell them what was happening,
1 Kgs 1. 3 over Israel for a beautiful **girl,** and in Shunem
1. 3 they found such a **girl** named Abishag, and brought her to
1.15 very old, and Abishag, the **girl** from Shunem, was taking care
2.17 to let me have Abishag, the **girl** from Shunem, as my wife."
2 Kgs 5. 2 a little Israelite **girl,** who became a servant of Naaman's
5. 4 went to the king and told him what the **girl** had said.
Esth 2. 3 all these beautiful young **girls** to your harem here in Susa,
2. 4 Then take the **girl** you like best and make her queen in
2. 7 she was a beautiful **girl,** and had a good figure.
2. 8 his new proclamation and many **girls** were being brought to Susa,
2. 9 and assigned seven **girls** specially chosen from the royal palace
2.12 After that, each **girl** would be taken in turn to King Xerxes.
2.17 than any of the other **girls,** and more than any of the
2.20 had obeyed him when she was a little **girl** under his care.
4. 4 When Esther's **servant-girls** and eunuchs told her what Mordecai
4.16 My **servant-girls** and I will be doing the same.
Job 19.15 my **servant-girls** treat me like a stranger and a foreigner.
31. 1 made a solemn promise never to look with lust at a **girl.**
41. 5 a pet bird, like something to amuse your **servant-girls?**
Ps 68.25 in between are the **girls** beating the tambourines.
148.12 **girls** and young men, old people and children too.
Prov 5.18 find your joy with the **girl** you married—[19] pretty and graceful
9. 3 She has sent her **servant-girls** to call out from the
27.27 you and your family, and for your **servant-girls** as well.
30.23 and a **servant-girl** who takes the
31.15 for her family and to tell her **servant-girls** what to do.
Song 6.13 Dance, dance, **girl** of Shulam.
7. 1 What a wonderful **girl** you are!
Jer 31.13 Then the **girls** will dance and be happy, and men, young
51.22 to kill boys and **girls,** [23] to slaughter shepherds
Lam 1. 4 **girls** who sang there suffer, and the priests can only groan.
2.10 Young **girls** bow their heads to the ground.
Ezek 23. 8 the time she was a **girl,** men slept with her and treated
23.19 as she did as a **girl,** when she was a prostitute in
23.21 were guilty of as a **girl** in Egypt, where men played with
Hos 1. 6 Gomer had a second child—this time it was a **girl.**
Joel 1. 8 Cry, you people, like a **girl** who mourns the death of the
3. 3 They sold boys and **girls** into slavery to pay for prostitutes
Amos 2. 7 with the same **slave-girl,** and so profane my holy name.
Zech 8. 5 And the streets will again be full of boys and **girls** playing.
Mt 9.24 The little **girl** is not dead—she is only sleeping!"
9.25 Jesus went into the **girl's** room and took hold of her
14.11 dish and given to the **girl,** who took it to her mother.
25. 1 Once there were ten **girls** who took their oil lamps and went
25. 5 late in coming, so the **girls** began to nod and fall asleep.
25. 7 The ten **girls** woke up and trimmed their lamps.
25.10 So the foolish **girls** went off to buy some oil;
25.10 The five **girls** who were ready went in with him
25.11 "Later the other **girls** arrived.
26.69 one of the High Priest's **servant-girls** came to him and said,
26.71 Another **servant-girl** saw him and said to the men there, "He
Mk 5.41 "Talitha, koum," which means, "Little **girl,** I tell you to get up!"
6.22 the king said to the **girl,** "What would you like to have?
6.24 So the **girl** went out and asked her mother, "What shall
6.25 The **girl** hurried back at once to the king and demanded,
6.28 and gave it to the **girl,** who gave it to her mother.
14.66 when one of the High Priest's **servant-girls** came by.
14.69 The **servant-girl** saw him there and began to repeat to the bystanders,
Lk 1.27 had a message for a **girl** promised in marriage to a man
1.27 The **girl's** name was Mary.
22.56 When one of the **servant-girls** saw him sitting there at the fire,
Jn 18.16 back out, spoke to the **girl** at the gate, and brought Peter
18.17 The **girl** at the gate said to Peter, "Aren't you also
Acts 12.13 door, and a **servant-girl** named Rhoda came to answer it.
16.16 we were met by a **slave-girl** who had an evil spirit that
1 Cor 7.36 not acting properly towards the **girl** and if his passions are
7.37 what to do—then he does well not to marry the **girl.**

GIVE

see also **GIVE UP**

Gen 2. 9 garden stood the tree that **gives** life
2. 9 and the tree that **gives** knowledge
2.17 except the tree that **gives** knowledge of what is good and
3. 6 Then she **gave** some to her husband, and he also ate it.
3. 7 had eaten it, they were **given** understanding and realized that
3.12 you put here with me **gave** me the fruit, and I ate
3.22 fruit from the tree that **gives** life, eat it, and live for
3.24 to keep anyone from coming near the tree that **gives** life.
4. 3 some of his harvest and **gave** it as an offering to the
4. 4 his sheep, killed it, and **gave** the best parts of it as
4.25 She said, "God has **given** me a son to replace Abel, whom
9. 3 I **give** them all to you for food.
12. 2 I will **give** you many descendants, and they will become a
12. 7 the country that I am going to **give** to your descendants."
12.16 treated Abram well and **gave** him flocks of sheep and goats,
13.15 I am going to **give** you and your descendants all the land
13.16 I am going to **give** you so many descendants that no one
13.17 whole land, because I am going to **give** it all to you."
14.20 the Most High God, who **gave** you victory over your enemies,
14.20 And Abram **gave** Melchizedek a tenth of all the loot he had
14.21 Abram, "Keep the loot, but **give** me back all my people."
15. 1 I will shield you from danger and **give** you a great reward."
15. 3 You have **given** me no children, and one of my slaves will
15. 7 of Ur in Babylonia, to **give** you this land as your own."
15.18 He said, "I promise to **give** your descendants all this land
16. 3 So she **gave** Hagar to him to be his concubine.
16. 5 I myself **gave** her to you, and ever since she found out
16.10 Then he said, "I will **give** you so many descendants that
17. 2 I will make my covenant with you and **give** you many descendants."
17. 6 I will **give** you many descendants, and some of them will be
17. 8 I will **give** to you and to your descendants this land in
17.16 will bless her, and I will **give** you a son by her.
17.20 I will bless him and **give** him many children and many descendants.
18. 7 was tender and fat, and **gave** it to a servant, who hurried
19.33 That night they **gave** him wine to drink, and the elder
20. 7 But now, **give** the woman back to her husband.
20. 7 But if you do not **give** her back, I warn you that
20.14 Then Abimelech **gave** Sarah back to Abraham,
20.14 and at the same time he **gave** him sheep, cattle, and slaves.
20.16 said to Sarah, "I am **giving** your brother a thousand pieces
21. 8 on the day that he was weaned, Abraham **gave** a great feast.
21.13 I will also **give** many children to the son of the slave-girl,
21.14 the next morning Abraham **gave** Hagar some food and a leather
21.19 filled the leather bag with water and **gave** some to the boy.
21.27 Then Abraham **gave** some sheep and cattle to Abimelech,
22.17 I promise that I will **give** you as many descendants as
23. 6 us would be glad to **give** you a grave, so that you
23.11 I will **give** you the whole field and the cave that is
23.11 my own people, I will **give** it to you, so that you
24. 7 promised me that he would **give** this land to my descendants.
24.17 meet her and said, "Please **give** me a drink of water from
24.21 her in silence, to see if the Lord had **given** him success.
24.32 and Laban unloaded the camels and **gave** them straw and fodder.
24.35 He has **given** him flocks of sheep and goats, cattle, silver,
24.36 was old, and my master has **given** everything he owns to him.
24.43 I will ask her to **give** me a drink of water from
24.45 I said to her, 'Please **give** me a drink.'
24.53 clothing and silver and gold jewellery, and **gave** them to Rebecca.
24.53 He also **gave** expensive gifts to her brother and to her mother.
24.60 And they **gave** Rebecca their blessing in these words:
25. 6 he was still alive, he **gave** presents to the sons his other
25.30 **give** me some of that red stuff."
25.31 Jacob answered, "I will **give** it to you
25.31 if you **give** me your rights as the first-born
25.33 "First make a vow that you will **give** me your rights."
25.33 Esau made the vow and **gave** his rights to Jacob.
25.34 Then Jacob **gave** him some bread and some of the soup.
26. 3 I am going to **give** all this territory to you and to
26. 4 I will **give** you as many descendants as there are stars
26. 4 in the sky, and I will **give** them all this territory.
26.22 said, "Now the Lord has **given** us freedom to live in the
26.24 I will bless you and **give** you many descendants because of my
27.27 him, Isaac smelt his clothes—so he **gave** him his blessing.
27.28 God **give** you dew from heaven and make your fields fertile!
27.28 May he **give** you plenty of corn and wine!
27.33 I **gave** him my final blessing, and so it is his for
27.37 I have **given** him corn and wine.
28. 3 God bless your marriage and **give** you many children, so that
28. 4 in which you have lived and which God **gave** to Abraham!"
28.13 "I will **give** to you and to your descendants this land on
28.20 journey I am making and **give** me food and clothing, [21] and
28.22 and I will give you a tenth of everything you **give** me."
29.19 Laban answered, "I would rather **give** her to you than to
29.24 (Laban **gave** his slave-girl Zilpah to his daughter Leah
29.27 are over, and I will **give** you Rachel, if you will work
29.28 celebrations was over, Laban **gave** him his daughter Rachel as his
29.29 (Laban **gave** his slave-girl Bilhah to his daughter Rachel as
29.33 She said, "The Lord has **given** me this son also, because he
30. 1 and said to Jacob, **"Give** me children, or I will die."
30. 4 So she **gave** Bilhah to her husband, and he had intercourse
30. 6 He has heard my prayer and has **given** me a son";
30. 9 stopped having children, she **gave** her slave-girl Zilpah to Jacob
30.14 said to Leah, "Please **give** me some of your son's mandrakes."

Gen	30.15	Rachel said, "If you will **give** me your son's mandrakes,
	30.18	Leah said, "God has **given** me my reward,
	30.18	because I **gave** my slave to my husband";
	30.20	She said, "God has **given** me a fine gift.
	30.23	said, "God has taken away my disgrace by **giving** me a son.
	30.24	May the Lord **give** me another son";
	30.26	**Give** me my wives and children that I have earned by
	31. 9	taken flocks away from your father and **given** them to me.
	32.12	well for me and to **give** me more descendants than anyone
	33. 5	children whom God has been good enough to **give** me," Jacob
	33.11	God has been kind to me and **given** me everything I need."
	34.11	"Do me this favour, and I will **give** you whatever you want.
	34.12	I will **give** you whatever you ask, if you will only let
	35. 4	So they **gave** Jacob all the foreign gods that they had
	35.12	I will **give** you the land which I gave to Abraham and
	35.12	and I will also **give** it to your descendants after you."
	38.16	She said, "What will you **give** me?"
	38.17	"All right, if you will **give** me something to keep as a
	38.18	"What shall I **give** you as a pledge?"
	38.18	He **gave** them to her.
	38.26	to her—I should have **given** her to my son Shelah in
	40.11	grapes and squeezed them into the cup and **gave** it to him."
	40.13	You will **give** him his cup as you did before when you
	41.43	He **gave** him the second royal chariot to ride in, and his
	41.45	and he **gave** him a wife, Asenath, the daughter
	41.52	He also said, "God has **given** me children in the land of
	42.25	back in his sack, and to **give** them food for the journey.
	42.34	I will **give** your brother back to you, and you can stay
	43.14	you, so that he will **give** Benjamin and your other brother
	43.24	He **gave** them water so that they could wash their feet,
	45.18	I will **give** them the best land in Egypt, and they will
	45.21	Joseph **gave** them wagons, as the king had ordered, and food
	45.22	He also **gave** each of them a change of clothes,
	45.22	but he **gave** Benjamin three hundred pieces of silver
	46.18	by Zilpah, the slave-girl whom Laban **gave** to his daughter Leah.
	46.25	by Bilhah, the slave-girl whom Laban **gave** to his daughter Rachel.
	47. 7	Jacob **gave** the king his blessing, [8]and the king asked him,
	47.10	Jacob **gave** the king a farewell blessing and left.
	47.11	and his brothers in Egypt, **giving** them property in the best
	47.15	the Egyptians came to Joseph and said, "**Give** us food!
	47.16	I will **give** you food in exchange for it if your money
	47.17	livestock to Joseph, and he **gave** them food in exchange for
	47.18	There is nothing left to **give** you except our bodies and our
	47.19	**Give** us corn to keep us alive and seed to sow in
	47.22	lands, because the king **gave** them an allowance to live on.
	47.24	At the time of harvest you must **give** one-fifth to the king.
	48. 4	said to me, 'I will **give** you many children, so that your
	48. 4	I will **give** this land to your descendants as their possession
	48. 9	"These are my sons, whom God has **given** me here in Egypt."
	48.22	your brothers that I am **giving** Shechem, that fertile region
Ex	1.20	he was good to them and **gave** them families of their own.
	2.21	and Jethro **gave** him his daughter Zipporah in marriage,
	4.11	The Lord said to him, "Who **gives** man his mouth?
	4.11	Who **gives** him sight or makes him blind?
	5. 7	"Stop **giving** the people straw for making bricks.
	5.13	every day as they had made when they were **given** straw.
	5.16	We are **given** no straw, but we are still ordered to make
	5.18	You will not be **given** any straw, but you must still make
	6. 4	covenant with them, promising to **give** them the land of Canaan,
	6. 8	land that I solemnly promised to **give** to Abraham, Isaac,
	6. 8	and I will **give** it to you as your own possession.
	12.25	Lord has promised to **give** you, you must perform this ritual.
	12.36	Egyptians respect the people and **give** them what they asked for.
	13. 5	promised your ancestors to **give** you the land of the Canaanites,
	13.11	When he **gives** it to you, [12]you must offer every first-born
	15.25	There the Lord **gave** them laws to live by, and there he
	16. 8	is the Lord who will **give** you meat to eat in the
	16.15	"This is the food that the Lord has **given** you to eat.
	16.29	that I, the Lord, have **given** you a day of rest,
	16.29	sixth day I will always **give** you enough food for two days.
	16.32	see the food which he **gave** us to eat in the desert
	17. 2	They complained to Moses and said, "**Give** us water to drink."
	20.12	live a long time in the land that I am **giving** you.
	21. 4	If his master **gave** him a wife and she bore him sons
	21. 9	buys a female slave to **give** to his son, he is to
	21.10	wife, he must continue to **give** his first wife the same
	21.36	make good the loss by **giving** the other man a live bull,
	22.26	will pay you, you must **give** it back to him before the
	22.29	"**Give** me the offerings from your corn, your wine, and your
	22.29	"**Give** me your first-born sons.
	22.30	**Give** me the first-born of your cattle and your sheep.
	22.31	instead, **give** it to the dogs.
	23.26	I will **give** you long lives.
	24.12	you are here, I will **give** you two stone tablets which
	25. 2	Receive whatever offerings any man wishes to **give.**
	25.16	stone tablets that I will **give** you, on which the commandments
	25.22	two winged creatures I will **give** you all my laws for the
	31. 3	I have **given** him understanding, skill, and ability for every
	31.18	Moses on Mount Sinai, he **gave** him the two stone tablets on
	32.13	you made to them to **give** them as many descendants as there
	32.13	in the sky and to **give** their descendants all that land you
	32.24	those who had any took them off and **gave** them to me.
	32.29	sons and brothers, so the Lord has **given** you his blessing."
	33. 1	land that I promised to **give** to Abraham, Isaac, and Jacob
	34.32	gathered round him, and Moses **gave** them all the laws that
	35.31	with his power and **given** him skill, ability, and understanding
	35.34	The Lord has **given** to him and to Oholiab son of Ahisamach,
	35.35	He has **given** them skill in all kinds of work done by
	36. 1	to whom the Lord has **given** skill and understanding, who know
Lev	4.35	the altar along with the food-offerings **given** to the Lord.
	5.16	He shall **give** it to the priest, and the priest shall offer
Lev	6. 9	Lord commanded Moses [9]to **give** Aaron and his sons the following
	6.16	The Lord has **given** it to the priests as their part of
	6.25	The Lord commanded Moses [25]to **give** Aaron and his sons the
	7.32	of the animal shall be **given** as a special contribution
	7.34	taken from the people of Israel and **given** to the priests.
	7.34	the people of Israel must **give** to the priests for all time
	7.35	to the Lord that was **given** to Aaron and his sons on
	7.36	the people of Israel to **give** them this part of the offering.
	10.11	Israel all the laws which I have **given** to you through Moses."
	10.14	These offerings have been **given** to you and your children as
	10.17	holy, and the Lord has **given** it to you in order to
	14.34	Canaan, which the Lord was going to **give** them as their
	15.14	the Tent of the Lord's presence and **give** them to the priest.
	16. 5	The community of Israel shall **give** Aaron two male goats for
	17. 2	The Lord commanded Moses [2]to **give** Aaron and his sons and
	20. 3	If anyone **gives** one of his children to Molech and makes my
	20.24	fertile land as your possession, and I will **give** it to you.
	22.18	The Lord commanded Moses [18]to **give** Aaron and his sons
	23. 9	land that the Lord is **giving** you and you harvest your corn,
	23.38	and your freewill offerings that you **give** to the Lord.)
	25. 2	land that the Lord is **giving** you, you shall honour the Lord
	25.38	of Egypt in order to **give** you the land of Canaan and
	26. 9	I will bless you and **give** you many children;
	26.34	enjoy the years of complete rest that you would not **give** it;
	26.42	and I will renew my promise to **give** my people the land.
	27. 2	When a person has been **given** to the Lord in fulfilment of
Num	3.48	to the official standard, [48]and **give** this money to Aaron
	3.51	1,365 pieces of silver [51]and **gave** them to Aaron and his sons.
	5. 8	be made, it shall be **given** to the Lord for the priest.
	6.21	his vow requires him to **give,** he must fulfil exactly the
	7. 5	**give** them to the Levites according to the work they have to
	7. 6	So Moses **gave** the wagons and the oxen to the Levites.
	7. 7	He **gave** two wagons and four oxen to the Gershonites,
	7. 9	But Moses **gave** no wagons or oxen to the Kohathites,
	10.29	out for the place which the Lord said he would **give** us.
	10.32	share with you all the blessings that the Lord **gives** us."
	11.17	of the spirit I have **given** you and give it to them.
	11.18	Now the Lord will **give** you meat, and you will have to
	11.21	you say that you will **give** them enough meat for a month?
	11.25	he had given to Moses and **gave** it to the seventy leaders.
	11.29	wish that the Lord would **give** his spirit to all his people
	13. 2	the land of Canaan, which I am **giving** to the Israelites."
	14. 8	will take us there and **give** us that rich and fertile land.
	14.16	able to bring them into the land you promised to **give** them.
	15. 2	to observe in the land that he was going to **give** them.
	15.18	to observe in the land that he was going to **give** them.
	15.21	special gift is to be **given** to the Lord from the bread
	16.14	into a fertile land or **given** us fields and vineyards as our
	17. 2	the people of Israel to **give** you twelve sticks, one from the
	17. 6	and each of their leaders **gave** him a stick, one for each
	18. 7	because I have **given** you the gift of the priesthood.
	18. 8	"Remember that I am **giving** you all the special contributions
	18. 8	I am **giving** them to you and to your descendants as the
	18.11	I am **giving** them to you, your sons, and your daughters for
	18.12	"I am **giving** you all the best of the first produce
	18.12	of the first produce which the Israelites **give** me each year:
	18.19	"I am **giving** to you, to your sons, and to your daughters,
	18.21	The Lord said, "I have **given** to the Levites every tithe
	18.24	in Israel, [24]because I have **given** to them as their possession
	18.26	the tithe that the Lord **gives** you as your possession, you
	18.28	You are to **give** this special contribution for the Lord to
	18.29	**Give** it from the best that you receive.
	19. 3	put to work, [3]and they will **give** it to Eleazar the priest.
	20.12	not lead them into the land that I promised to **give** them."
	20.24	going to enter the land which I promised to **give** to Israel;
	21.16	"Bring the people together, and I will **give** them water."
	22.18	Balaam answered, "Even if Balak **gave** me all the silver and
	22.28	Then the Lord **gave** the donkey the power of speech, and
	22.40	slaughtered cattle and sheep and **gave** some of the meat to
	24.13	me that [13]even if you **gave** me all the silver and gold
	26.62	because they were not **given** any property in Israel.
	27. 4	**Give** us property among our father's relatives."
	27. 7	**give** them property among their father's relatives.
	27.12	look out over the land that I am **giving** to the Israelites.
	29.39	addition to the offerings you **give** in fulfilment of a vow or
	30. 2	man makes a vow to **give** something to the Lord or takes
	30. 3	house makes a vow to **give** something to the Lord or promises
	31.29	**Give** them to Eleazar the priest as a special contribution
	31.30	**Give** them to the Levites who are in charge of the Lord's
	31.41	So Moses **gave** Eleazar the tax as a special contribution to
	31.47	as the Lord had commanded, **gave** them to the Levites who were
	32. 5	Please **give** us this land as our property, and do not make
	32. 7	the Jordan into the land which the Lord has **given** them?
	32. 9	people from entering the land which the Lord had **given** them.
	32.29	to conquer the land, then **give** them the land of Gilead as
	32.40	So Moses **gave** Gilead to the clan of Machir, and they
	33.53	land and settle in it, because I am **giving** it to you.
	33.54	and clans by drawing lots, **giving** a large piece of property
	34. 2	the land which I am **giving** you, the borders of your
	35. 2	property they receive they must **give** the Levites some cities to
	35. 6	You are to **give** the Levites six cities of refuge to which
	35. 6	**give** them forty-two other cities [7]with their pasture land,
	36. 2	commanded you to **give** the property of our relative Zelophehad
Deut	1. 8	I, the Lord, promised to **give** to your ancestors, Abraham, Isaac,
	1.20	the Lord our God, the God of our ancestors, is **giving** us.
	1.25	land which the Lord our God was **giving** us was very fertile.
	1.35	enter the fertile land that I promised to **give** your ancestors.
	1.36	to me, and I will **give** him and his descendants the land
	1.39	I will **give** the land to them, and they will occupy it.
	2. 5	I am not going to **give** you so much as a square
	2. 5	I have **given** Edom to Esau's descendants.

Deut 2. 9 I have **given** them the city of Ar,
2. 9 and I am not going to **give** you any of their land.' "
2.12 their enemies out of the land that the Lord **gave** them.)
2.19 I am not going to **give** you any of the land
2.19 that I have **given** them.' "
2.29 Jordan into the land that the Lord our God is **giving** us.
3. 2 I am going to **give** him, his men, and all his territory
3.18 'The Lord our God has **given** you this land east of the
3.20 land that the Lord is **giving** them west of the Jordan and
4. 1 land which the Lord, the God of your ancestors, is **giving**
4.19 The Lord your God has **given** these to all other peoples for
4.21 River Jordan to enter the fertile land which he is **giving** you.
4.38 might bring you in and **give** you their land, the land which
4.40 the Lord your God is **giving** you to be yours for ever."
5. 1 Israel, listen to all the laws that I am **giving** you today.
5.16 live a long time in the land that I am **giving** you.
5.22 he wrote them on two stone tablets and **gave** them to me.
5.31 they will obey them in the land that I am **giving** them.'
6. 2 his laws that I am **giving** you, so that you may live
6.10 Isaac, and Jacob, he will **give** you a land with large and
6.23 to bring us here and **give** us this land, as he had
7.13 he will bless you by **giving** you a lot of livestock and
7.13 He will **give** you all these blessings in the land
7.13 that he promised your ancestors he would **give** to you.
8. 3 go hungry, and then he **gave** you manna to eat, food that
8.10 Lord your God for the fertile land that he has **given** you.
8.11 to obey any of his laws that I am **giving** you today.
8.16 In the desert he **gave** you manna to eat, food that your
9. 6 that the Lord is not **giving** you this fertile land because
9.10 Then the Lord **gave** me the two stone tablets on which he
9.11 days and nights the Lord **gave** me the two stone tablets on
9.16 the Lord your God had **given** you, and that you had sinned
9.23 the land that he was **giving** you, you rebelled against him;
10. 4 the Ten Commandments that he **gave** you when he spoke from the
10. 4 The Lord **gave** me the tablets, [5]and I turned and went down
10.11 of the land that he had promised to **give** to your ancestors.
10.13 I am **giving** them to you today for your benefit.
10.18 foreigners who live with our people, and **gives** them food
11. 9 land that the Lord promised to **give** your ancestors and their
11.17 even though it is a good land that he is **giving** you.
11.21 that the Lord your God promised to **give** to your ancestors.
11.31 and occupy the land that the Lord your God is **giving** you.
11.32 sure to obey all the laws that I am **giving** you today.
12. 1 land that the Lord, the God of your ancestors, is **giving**
12. 9 the Lord your God is **giving** you, where you can live in
12.15 You may eat as many as the Lord **gives** you.
12.21 sheep that the Lord has **given** you, and you may eat the
13.12 that the Lord your God **gives** you, you may hear [13]that some
15. 4 God will bless you in the land that he is **giving** you.
15. 7 the Lord your God is **giving** you there is a fellow-Israelite
15.10 **Give** to him freely and unselfishly, and the Lord will bless
15.14 **Give** to him generously from what the Lord has blessed you
16. 5 else in the land that the Lord your God will **give** you.
16.18 officials in every town that the Lord your God **gives** you.
16.20 the Lord your God is **giving** you and will continue to live
17.14 your God is going to **give** you and have settled there, then
18. 1 on the offerings and other sacrifices **given** to the Lord.
18. 3 the priests are to be **given** the shoulder, the jaw, and the
18. 9 the Lord your God is **giving** you, don't follow the disgusting
19. 1 people whose land he is **giving** you and after you have taken
19. 8 your ancestors he would, and **gives** you all the land he has
19. 9 (He will **give** you this land if you do everything that I
19.10 them to death in the land that the Lord is **giving** you.
19.14 ago in the land that the Lord your God is **giving** you.
20.14 The Lord has **given** it to you.
20.16 the land that the Lord your God is **giving** you, kill
21. 1 your God is going to **give** you, and you do not know
21.16 of his favourite wife by **giving** him the share that belongs
21.17 He is to **give** a double share of his possessions to his
21.17 acknowledge his first son and **give** him the share he is
21.23 not defile the land that the Lord your God is **giving** you.
22. 2 When its owner comes looking for it, **give** it to him.
22.16 will say to them, 'I **gave** my daughter to this man in
22.19 pieces of silver and **give** the money to the girl's father,
24. 4 sin in the land that the Lord your God is **giving** you.
24.10 to get the garment he is going to **give** you as security;
25.15 time in the land that the Lord your God is **giving** you.
25.19 the Lord your God has **given** you the land and made you
26. 1 the Lord your God is **giving** you and have settled there,
26. 3 the land that he promised our ancestors to **give** us.'
26. 9 He brought us here and **gave** us this rich and fertile land.
26.10 Lord the first part of the harvest that he has **given** me.'
26.11 things that the Lord your God has **given** you and your family;
26.12 "Every third year **give** the tithe—a tenth of your
26.13 I have **given** it to the Levites, the foreigners, the orphans,
26.14 and I have not **given** any of it as an offering for
26.15 land that you have **given** us, as you promised our ancestors.'
27. 2 the Lord your God is **giving** you, you are to set up
27.10 and keep all his laws that I am **giving** you today."
28. 8 He will bless you in the land that he is **giving** you.
28.11 The Lord will **give** you many children, many cattle,
28.11 in the land that he promised your ancestors to **give** you.
28.15 and laws that I am **giving** you today, all these evil things
28.18 Lord will curse you by **giving** you only a few children, poor
28.31 you look on, and they will not be **given** back to you.
28.31 Your sheep will be **given** to your enemies, and there will be
28.45 Lord your God and keep all the laws that he **gave** you.
28.52 the Lord your God is **giving** you, and the high, fortified
28.53 even eat the children that the Lord your God has **given** you.
28.54 He will not even **give** any to his brother or to the
30. 1 God has scattered you, you will remember the choice I **gave** you.

Deut 30. 6 your God will **give** you and your descendants obedient hearts,
30.16 Lord your God, which I **give** you today, if you love him,
30.20 land that he promised to **give** your ancestors, Abraham, Isaac,
31. 9 wrote down God's Law and **gave** it to the levitical priests,
31.21 land that I promised to **give** them, I know what they are
32.14 Their cows and goats **gave** plenty of milk;
32.49 of Canaan that I am about to **give** the people of Israel.
32.52 not enter the land that I am **giving** the people of Israel."
33. 4 obey the Law that Moses **gave** us, our nation's most treasured
34. 4 I promised Abraham, Isaac, and Jacob I would **give** to their

Josh 1. 2 cross the River Jordan into the land that I am **giving** them.
1. 7 that you obey the whole Law that my servant Moses **gave** you.
1.11 to occupy the land that the Lord your God is **giving** you."
1.13 the Lord your God would **give** you this land on the east
1.15 west of the Jordan that the Lord your God has **given** them.
1.15 of the Jordan, which Moses, the Lord's servant, **gave** to you."
2. 9 to them, "I know that the Lord has **given** you this land.
2.14 you that when the Lord **gives** us this land, we will treat
2.24 "We are sure that the Lord has **given** us the whole country.
6.16 to shout, and he said, "The Lord has **given** you the city!
8. 7 The Lord your God will **give** it to you.
8.18 I am **giving** it to you."
8.31 Moses, the Lord's servant, had **given** the Israelites, as it says
9.24 commanded his servant Moses to **give** you the whole land and
10.12 the day that the Lord **gave** the men of Israel victory over
10.30 The Lord also **gave** the Israelites victory over this city
10.32 Lord **gave** the Israelites victory over Lachish on the second day
11. 8 The Lord **gave** the Israelites victory over them;
11.23 Joshua **gave** it to the Israelites as their own and divided it
12. 6 Moses, the Lord's servant, **gave** their land to the tribes of
12. 7 land among the tribes and **gave** it to them as a permanent
13. 8 the land that Moses, the Lord's servant, had **given** them;
13.14 Moses had **given** no land to the tribe of Levi.
13.15 Moses had **given** a part of the land to the families of
13.23 were the cities and towns **given** to the families of the tribe
13.24 Moses had also **given** a part of the land to the families
13.28 were the cities and towns **given** to the families of the tribe
13.29 Moses had **given** a part of the land to the families of
13.31 All this was **given** to half the families descended from Machir
14. 3 However, Moses **gave** the Levites no portion of the territory.
14.12 Now then, **give** me the hill-country that the Lord promised me
14.13 Caleb son of Jephunneh and **gave** him the city of Hebron as
15.13 the territory of Judah was **given** to Caleb son of Jephunneh,
15.17 so Caleb **gave** him his daughter Achsah in marriage.
15.19 The land you have **given** me is in the dry country."
15.19 So Caleb **gave** her the upper and lower springs.
16. 8 This was the land **given** to the families of the tribe of
16. 9 within the borders of Manasseh, but **given** to the Ephraimites.
17. 4 "The Lord commanded Moses to **give** us, as well as our male
17. 4 they were **given** land along with their male relatives.
17.14 to Joshua, "Why have you **given** us only one part of the
18. 3 land that the Lord, the God of your ancestors, has **given**
18. 7 of the Jordan, which Moses, the Lord's servant, **gave** to them."
18. 8 map out the land after Joshua had **given** them these instructions:
19. 9 part of its territory was **given** to the tribe of Simeon.
19.49 dividing up the land, they **gave** Joshua son of Nun a part
19.50 the Lord had commanded, they **gave** him the city he asked for:
20. 4 him into the city and **give** him a place to live in,
21. 2 that we were to be **given** cities to live in, as well
21. 3 the people of Israel **gave** the Levites certain cities and pasture
21. 9 and Simeon which were **given** [10]to the descendants of Aaron
21.11 They were **given** the city of Arba (Arba was Anak's father),
21.12 its towns, had already been **given** to Caleb son of Jephunneh
21.17 From the territory of Benjamin they were **given** four cities:
21.19 with their pasture lands, were **given** to the priests,
21.21 They were **given** four cities:
21.23 From the territory of Dan they were **given** four cities:
21.25 the territory of West Manasseh they were **given** two cities:
21.41 with the pasture lands round them, was **given** to the Levites.
21.43 So the Lord **gave** to Israel all the land
21.43 that he had solemnly promised their ancestors he would **give**
21.44 The Lord **gave** them peace throughout the land, just as he
21.44 because the Lord **gave** the Israelites the victory over all
22. 4 the Lord your God has **given** your fellow-Israelites peace.
22. 4 side of the Jordan, that Moses, the Lord's servant, **gave** you.
22. 6 Moses had **given** land east of the Jordan to one half of
22. 6 the other half Joshua had **given** land west of the Jordan.
23. 1 Much later the Lord **gave** Israel security from their enemies
23.13 in this good land which the Lord your God has **given** you.
23.14 the Lord your God has **given** you all the good things that
23.16 will be left in this good land that he has **given** you."
24. 3 I **gave** him many descendants.
24. 3 I **gave** him Isaac, [4]and to Isaac I gave Jacob and Esau.
24. 4 I **gave** Esau the hill-country of Edom as his possession,
24. 8 They fought you, but I **gave** you victory over them.
24.11 But I **gave** you victory over them all.
24.13 I **gave** you a land that you had never cultivated and
24.25 and there at Shechem he **gave** them laws and rules to follow.
24.33 the hill-country of Ephraim which had been **given** to his son

Judg 1. 4 Lord **gave** them victory over the Canaanites and the Perizzites,
1.13 so Caleb **gave** him his daughter Achsah in marriage.
1.15 The land you have **given** me is in the dry country."
1.15 So Caleb **gave** her the upper and lower springs.
1.20 Moses had commanded, Hebron was **given** to Caleb, who drove out
2.16 Then the Lord **gave** the Israelites leaders who saved them
2.18 Whenever the Lord **gave** Israel a leader, the Lord would help
3.10 to war, and the Lord **gave** him victory over the king of
3.18 When Ehud had **given** him the gifts, he told the men who
4.19 He said to her, "Please **give** me a drink of water;
4.19 a leather bag of milk, **gave** him a drink, and hid him

Judg 4.23 That day God **gave** the Israelites victory over Jabin,
5.25 Sisera asked for water, but she **gave** him milk;
6. 9 drove them out as you advanced, and I **gave** you their land.
6.19 the Lord's angel under the oak-tree, and **gave** them to him.
7.16 men into three groups and **gave** each man a trumpet and a
8. 5 men of the town, "Please **give** my men some loaves of bread.
8. 6 of Sukkoth said, "Why should we **give** your army any food?
8.15 You said that you couldn't **give** any food to my exhausted
8.24 Every one of you **give** me the earrings you took."
8.25 The people answered, "We'll be glad to **give** them to you."
9. 4 They **gave** him seventy pieces of silver from the temple of
11.13 Now you must **give** it back peacefully."
11.21 Lord, the God of Israel, **gave** the Israelites victory over Sihon
11.24 You can keep whatever your god Chemosh has **given** you.
11.24 going to keep everything that the Lord, our God, has **given**
11.32 river to fight the Ammonites, and the Lord **gave** him victory.
12. 3 to fight them, and the Lord **gave** me victory over them.
14. 9 Then he went to his father and mother and **gave** them some.
14.19 thirty men, stripped them, and **gave** their fine clothes to the
15. 2 thought that you hated her, so I **gave** her to your friend.
15.18 to the Lord and said, "You **gave** me this great victory;
16. 5 Each one of us will **give** you eleven hundred pieces of silver."
17. 3 He **gave** the money back to his mother, and she said, "To
17. 3 So now I will **give** the pieces of silver back to you."
17. 4 Then he **gave** them back to his mother.
17. 4 the pieces of silver and **gave** them to a metal-worker, who
17.10 and priest, and I will **give** you ten pieces of silver a
18.10 a person could want, and God has **given** it to you."
19. 3 and when her father saw him, he **gave** him a warm welcome.
20.35 The Lord **gave** Israel victory over the army of Benjamin.
21. 7 the Lord that we will not **give** them any of our daughters."
21.14 and the other Israelites **gave** them the girls from Jabesh
21.22 And since you did not **give** them to us, you are not
Ruth 1. 6 Lord had blessed his people by **giving** them a good harvest;
2.18 She also **gave** her the food left over from the meal.
3.17 back to you empty-handed, so he **gave** me all this barley."
4. 7 seller to take off his sandal and **give** it to the buyer.
4. 8 buy it," he took off his sandal and **gave** it to Boaz.
4.12 children that the Lord will **give** you by this young woman
4.14 He has **given** you a grandson today to take care of you.
4.15 And now she has **given** you a grandson, who will bring new
4.15 new life to you and **give** you security in your old age."
1 Sam 1. 4 offered his sacrifice, he would **give** one share of the meat
1. 5 Hannah very much he would **give** her only one share, because
1.11 If you **give** me a son, I promise that I will dedicate
1.17 may the God of Israel **give** you what you have asked him
1.27 him for this child, and he **gave** me what I asked for.
2.15 man offering the sacrifice, "**Give** me some meat for the priest
2.16 **Give** it to me now!
2.20 Elkanah, "May the Lord **give** you other children by this woman
2.28 And I **gave** them the right to keep a share of the
8.14 vineyards, and olive-groves, and **give** them to his officials.
8.22 Lord answered, "Do what they want and **give** them a king."
9. 7 "If we go to him, what can we **give** him?"
9. 7 in our packs, and we haven't anything to **give** him, have
9. 8 I can **give** him that, and then he will tell us where
9.22 into the large room and **gave** them a place at the head
9.23 the piece of meat I **gave** you, which I told you to
10. 9 When Saul turned to leave Samuel, God **gave** Saul a new nature.
10.19 have rejected me and have asked me to **give** you a king.
12. 1 I have **given** you a king to rule you, [2]and now you
12.13 asked for him, and now the Lord has **given** him to you.
15.28 away from you today and **given** it to someone who is a
17.38 He **gave** his own armour to David for him to wear:
17.44 challenged David, "and I will **give** your body to the birds
17.46 And I will **give** the bodies of the Philistine soldiers to the
18. 4 robe he was wearing and **gave** it to David, together with his
18.21 He said to himself, "I'll **give** Michal to David;
20.40 Jonathan **gave** his weapons to the boy and told him to
21. 3 **Give** me five loaves of bread or anything else you have."
21. 6 the priest **gave** David the sacred bread, because the only bread
21. 8 "Have you got a spear or a sword you can **give** me?
21. 9 "**Give** it to me," David said.
22. 7 you think that David will **give** fields and vineyards to all
22.10 should do, and then he **gave** David some food and the sword
22.13 Why did you **give** him some food and a sword, and consult
25. 8 Please **give** what you can to us your servants and to your
25.11 slaughtered for my shearers, and **give** them to men who come
25.21 is how he pays me back for the help I **gave** him!
25.27 this present I have brought you, and **give** it to your men.
27. 6 So Achish **gave** him the town of Ziklag, and for this reason
28.17 the kingdom away from you and **given** it to David instead.
29. 4 to him, "Send that fellow back to the town you **gave** him.
30. 6 but the Lord his God **gave** him courage.
30.11 They **gave** him some food and water, [12]some dried figs, and
30.22 with us, and so we won't **give** them any of the loot.
30.23 brothers, you can't do this with what the Lord has **given** us!
30.23 He kept us safe and **gave** us victory over the raiders.
2 Sam 3.14 messengers to Ishbosheth to say, "**Give** me back my wife Michal.
3.21 David **gave** Abner a guarantee of safety and sent him on his
4.10 That was the reward I **gave** him for his good news!
6.19 He **gave** each man and woman in Israel a loaf of bread,
9. 7 I will **give** you back all the land that belonged to your
9. 9 and said, "I am **giving** Mephibosheth, your master's grandson,
12. 8 I **gave** you his kingdom and his wives;
12. 8 had not been enough, I would have **given** you twice as much.
12.11 I take your wives from you and **give** them to another man;
13.13 the king, and I'm sure that he will **give** me to you."
14.16 me and so remove us from the land God **gave** his people.
16. 8 The Lord has **given** the kingdom to your son Absalom, and you
18.11 I myself would have **given** you ten pieces of silver

2 Sam 18.12 answered, "Even if you **gave** me a thousand pieces of silver,
19.39 He kissed Barzillai and **gave** him his blessing, and Barzillai
19.42 He hasn't paid for our food nor has he **given** us anything."
22.51 God **gives** great victories to his king;
24.23 Araunah **gave** it all to the king and said to him, "May
1 Kgs 2.22 "Why do you ask me to **give** Abishag to him?"
2.22 "You might as well ask me to **give** him the throne too.
2.24 has kept his promise and **given** the kingdom to me and my
2.33 But the Lord will always **give** success to David's descendants
3. 5 and asked him, "What would you like me to **give** you?"
3. 6 great and constant love by **giving** him a son who today rules
3. 9 So **give** me the wisdom I need to rule your people with
3.12 I will **give** you more wisdom and understanding than anyone has
3.13 I will also **give** you what you have not asked for:
3.14 as your father David did, I will **give** you a long life."
3.25 the living child in two and **give** each woman half of it."
3.26 **Give** it to her!"
3.26 But the other woman said, "Don't **give** it to either of us;
3.27 **Give** it to the first woman—she is its real mother."
3.28 knew then that God had **given** him the wisdom to settle
4.29 God **gave** Solomon unusual wisdom and insight, and knowledge
5. 4 the Lord my God has **given** me peace on all my borders.
5. 7 "Praise the Lord today for **giving** David such a wise son to
5.12 The Lord kept his promise and **gave** Solomon wisdom.
8.34 them back to the land which you **gave** to their ancestors.
8.36 land of yours, which you **gave** to your people as a permanent
8.40 time they live in the land which you **gave** to our ancestors.
8.48 towards this land which you **gave** to our ancestors, this city
8.56 "Praise the Lord who has **given** his people peace,
8.58 and keep all the laws and commands he **gave** our ancestors.
9. 7 my people Israel from the land that I have **given** them.
9.11 was finished, King Solomon **gave** Hiram twenty towns in the region
9.13 "So these, my brother, are the towns you have **given** me!"
9.16 Then he **gave** it as a wedding present to his daughter when
10.10 The amount of spices she **gave** him was by far the greatest
10.13 King Solomon **gave** the queen of Sheba everything she asked
10.13 all the other customary gifts that he had generously **given** her.
10.24 to come and listen to the wisdom that God had **given** him.
11.11 kingdom away from you and **give** it to one of your officials.
11.18 went to the king, who **gave** Hadad some land and a house
11.19 the king, and the king **gave** his sister-in-law, the sister of
11.22 "Have I failed to **give** you something?
11.31 kingdom away from Solomon, and I will **give** you ten tribes.
11.35 from Solomon's son and will **give** you ten tribes, [36]but I
12. 6 "What answer do you advise me to **give** these people?"
13. 8 prophet answered, "Even if you **gave** me half your wealth,
14. 8 the kingdom away from David's descendants and **gave** it to you.
14.15 this good land which he **gave** to their ancestors, and he will
15. 4 sake, the Lord his God **gave** Abijah a son to rule after
16. 7 Baasha and his family was **given** by the prophet Jehu because
17.19 "**Give** the boy to me," Elijah said.
19. 8 and drank, and the food **gave** him enough strength to walk
19.21 He **gave** the meat to the people, and they ate it.
21. 2 I will **give** you a better vineyard for it, or, if you
21. 6 or, if he preferred, to **give** him another one for it,
2 Kgs 3. 4 sheep, and every year he **gave** as tribute to the king of
4.43 Elisha replied, "**Give** it to them to eat, because the Lord
5.22 he would like you to **give** them three thousand pieces of
5.23 the silver in two bags, **gave** them and two changes of fine
6.22 **Give** them something to eat and drink, and let them return to
8. 6 official and told him to **give** back to her everything that
10.22 to bring the robes out and **give** them to the worshippers.
11.10 **gave** the officers the spears and shields that had belonged to
11.12 crown on his head, and **gave** him a copy of the laws
12. 4 the regular sacrifices and the money **given** as free-will gifts.
12. 9 put in the box all the money **given** by the worshippers.
12.16 The money **given** for the repayment offerings and for
15.19 and Menahem **gave** him thirty-four thousand kilogrammes of silver
17.13 contained in the Law I **gave** to your ancestors and which I
18.23 I will **give** you two thousand horses if you can find that
19.25 I **gave** you the power to turn fortified cities into piles of
21. 8 Law that my servant Moses **gave** them, then I will not allow
21. 8 be driven out of the land that I **gave** to their ancestors."
22. 5 Tell him to **give** the money to the men who are in
22. 8 Hilkiah **gave** him the book, and Shaphan read it.
22.10 then he said, "I have here a book that Hilkiah **gave** me."
25.28 Evilmerodach treated him kindly, and **gave** him a position
25.28 of greater honour than he **gave** the other kings who were
25.30 he lived, he was **given** a regular allowance for his needs.
1 Chr 4.10 the God of Israel, "Bless me, God, and **give** me much land.
4.10 And God **gave** him what he prayed for.
5. 1 to the first-born son, and those rights were **given** to Joseph.
11.14 The Lord **gave** him a great victory.
16. 3 He **gave** each man and woman in Israel a loaf of bread,
16.18 "I will **give** you the land of Canaan," he said.
16.40 what was written in the Law which the Lord **gave** to Israel.
17. 9 I promise to defeat all your enemies and to **give** you descendants.
21.22 I'll **give** you the full price."
21.23 to use as fuel, and wheat to **give** as an offering.
21.23 I **give** it all to you."
21.24 I will not **give** as an offering to the Lord something that
22. 9 peace, because I will **give** him peace from all his enemies.
22. 9 Solomon, because during his reign I will **give** Israel peace
22.12 may the Lord your God **give** you insight and wisdom so that
22.13 the laws which the Lord **gave** to Moses for Israel, you will
22.18 God has been with you and **given** you peace on all sides.
23.25 Lord God of Israel has **given** peace to his people, and he
25. 5 God **gave** to Heman, the king's prophet, these fourteen sons
26. 4 Edom, whom God blessed by **giving** him eight sons, listed in
28. 5 He **gave** me many sons, and out of them all he chose

1 Chr 28.11 David **gave** Solomon the plans for all the temple buildings,
28.12 He also **gave** him the plans for all he had in mind
28.13 David also **gave** him the plans for organizing the priests
29. 3 I have provided, I have **given** silver and gold from my
29. 4 I have **given** more than a hundred metric tons of the finest
29. 5 else is willing to **give** a generous offering to the Lord?"
29. 6 volunteered to **give** [7] the following for the work on
29. 8 who had precious stones **gave** them to the temple treasury,
29. 9 The people had **given** willingly to the Lord,
29. 9 and they were happy that so much had been **given.**
29.14 and I cannot really **give** you anything, because everything is
29.14 from you, and we have only **given** back what is yours already.
29.17 and sincerity I have willingly **given** all this to you, and I
29.19 **Give** my son Solomon a wholehearted desire to obey everything
29.21 to the Lord, and then **gave** them to the people to eat.
2 Chr 1. 7 Solomon and asked, "What would you like me to **give** you?"
1.10 they cannot be counted, [10] so **give** me the wisdom and knowledge
1.12 I will **give** you wisdom and knowledge.
1.12 in addition, I will **give** you more wealth, treasure, and fame
2.12 He has **given** King David a wise son, full of understanding
6.25 to the land which you **gave** to them and to their ancestors.
6.27 land of yours, which you **gave** to your people as a permanent
6.31 time they live in the land which you **gave** to our ancestors.
6.38 towards this land which you **gave** to our ancestors, this city
7.10 blessings that the Lord had **given** to his people Israel,
7.20 from the land that I **gave** you, and I will abandon this
8. 2 cities that King Hiram had **given** him, and sent Israelites to
9. 9 fine as those that the queen of Sheba **gave** to King Solomon.
9.12 King Solomon **gave** the queen of Sheba everything she asked
9.12 in addition to what he **gave** her in exchange for the gifts
9.23 consulted him, to hear the wisdom that God had **given** him.
13. 5 covenant with David, **giving** him and his descendants kingship
13. 8 the royal authority that the Lord **gave** to David's descendants.
14. 6 years there was no war, because the Lord **gave** him peace.
14. 7 He has protected us and **given** us security on every side."
15.15 and he accepted them and **gave** them peace on every side.
16. 8 you relied on the Lord, he **gave** you victory over them.
17. 5 Lord **gave** Jehoshaphat firm control over the kingdom of Judah,
20. 7 who were living here and **gave** the land to the descendants of
20.11 come to drive us out of the land that you **gave** us.
20.30 Jehoshaphat ruled in peace, and God **gave** him security on every
21. 3 Their father **gave** them large amounts of gold, silver,
23. 9 Jehoiada **gave** the officers the spears and shields that had
23.11 crown on his head, and **gave** him a copy of the laws
24.12 The king and Jehoiada would **give** the money to those who
24.14 remaining gold and silver was **given** to the king and Jehoiada,
24.22 father Jehoiada had **given** him, and he had Zechariah killed.
25. 9 prophet replied, "The Lord can **give** you back more than that!"
28.15 They **gave** them clothes and sandals to wear,
28.15 **gave** them enough to eat and drink,
28.21 leaders of the people, and **gave** it to the emperor,
30.16 The Levites **gave** the blood of the sacrifices to the priests,
30.24 and the officials **gave** them another thousand bulls and ten
31. 8 saw how much had been **given,** they praised the Lord and
31.16 They **gave** a share to all males thirty years of age or
32.29 Besides all this, God **gave** him sheep and cattle and so
33. 8 be driven out of the land that I **gave** to their ancestors."
34.10 the temple repairs, and they **gave** it to [11] the carpenters and
34.15 He **gave** Shaphan the book, [16] and Shaphan took it to the king.
34.18 Then he added, "I have here a book that Hilkiah **gave** me."
35. 8 High Priest, Zechariah, and Jehiel—**gave** the priests two thousand
Ezra 1. 6 All their neighbours helped them by **giving** them many things:
1. 7 Cyrus **gave** them back the bowls and cups that King
2.68 leaders of the clans **gave** freewill offerings to help rebuild
2.69 They **gave** as much as they could for this work, and the
3. 5 all the offerings that were **given** to the Lord voluntarily.
3. 7 people **gave** money to pay the stonemasons and the carpenters
3. 7 and **gave** food, drink, and olive-oil
6. 9 you are to **give** the priests in Jerusalem whatever they
7. 6 Lord his God, the emperor **gave** him everything he asked for.
7.11 Artaxerxes **gave** the following document to Ezra, the priest
7.15 and my counsellors desire to **give** to the God of Israel,
7.16 Israelite people and their priests **give** for the Temple of their
7.19 the utensils that have been **given** to you for use in the
7.25 wisdom which your God has **given** you, are to appoint
7.28 the Lord my God has **given** me courage, and I have been
8.25 the people of Israel had **given** to be used in the Temple,
8.25 and I **gave** it to the priests.
8.26 This is what I **gave** them:
8.36 the document the emperor had **given** them and gave it to the
8.36 emperor had given them and **gave** it to the governors
9. 8 You have freed us from slavery and **given** us new life.
Neh 2. 7 grant me the favour of **giving** me letters to the governors of
2. 8 The emperor **gave** me all I asked for, because God was with
2. 9 There I **gave** the emperor's letters to the governors.
4.16 And our leaders **gave** their full support to the people
5.11 And **give** them back their fields, vineyards, olive-groves,
5.12 We'll **give** the property back and not try to collect the debts."
8.10 The joy that the Lord **gives** you will make you strong."
9. 6 you **gave** life to all.
9. 8 You promised to **give** him the land of the Canaanites, the
9.13 to your people and **gave** them good laws and sound teachings.
9.15 "When they were hungry, you **gave** them bread from heaven,
9.15 control of the land which you had promised to **give** them.
9.20 you fed them with manna and **gave** them water to drink.
9.23 You **gave** them as many children as there are stars in the
9.23 land that you had promised their ancestors to **give** them.
9.24 You **gave** your people the power to do as they pleased with
9.25 they enjoyed all the good things you **gave** them.
9.35 when they lived in the broad, fertile land you **gave** them;
9.36 the land that you **gave** us,
Neh 9.36 this fertile land which **gives** us food.
12.47 all the people of Israel **gave** daily gifts for the support of
12.47 The people **gave** a sacred offering to the Levites,
12.47 and the Levites **gave** the required portion to the priests.
13. 2 Ammon and Moab did not **give** food and water to the Israelites
13. 5 corn, wine, and olive-oil **given** to the Levites, to the temple
13.10 the people had not been **giving** them enough to live on.
Esth 2. 9 He **gave** her the best place in the harem and assigned seven
3.10 and make them official, and **gave** it to the enemy of the
4. 8 He **gave** Hathach a copy of the proclamation that had been
7. 2 I'll even **give** you half the empire."
8. 1 That same day King Xerxes **gave** Queen Esther all the property
8. 2 (which he had taken back from Haman) and **gave** it to Mordecai.
8. 7 plot against the Jews, and I have **given** Esther his property.
9.19 time for feasting and **giving** gifts of food to one another.
9.22 with feasts and parties, **giving** gifts of food to one another
Job 1.10 he does, and you have **given** him enough cattle to fill the
1.21 The Lord **gave,** and now he has taken away.
3. 9 **give** that night no hope of dawn.
3.20 Why **give** light to men in grief?
5.11 God who raises the humble and **gives** joy to all who mourn.
5.16 He **gives** hope to the poor and silences the wicked.
6. 8 Why won't God **give** me what I ask?
6.22 Have I asked you to **give** me a gift or to bribe
8. 7 will be nothing compared with what God will **give** you then.
9.24 God **gave** the world to the wicked.
10.10 You **gave** my father strength to beget me;
10.12 You have **given** me life and constant love, and your care
27. 3 as long as God **gives** me breath, [4] my lips will never
27.10 They should have desired the joy he **gives;**
28.25 When God **gave** the wind its power And determined the size
29. 3 always with me then and **gave** me light as I walked through
31.20 to buy clothes, [20] I would **give** him clothing made of wool
32. 8 of Almighty God that comes to men and **gives** them wisdom.
33. 4 God's spirit made me and **gave** me life.
33.30 he saves a person's life, and **gives** him the joy of living.
35.10 God, their Creator, who **gives** them hope in their darkest hours.
39. 5 Who **gave** the wild donkeys their freedom?
39. 6 I **gave** them the desert to be their home, and let them
39.17 was I who made her foolish and did not **give** her wisdom.
39.19 who made horses so strong and **gave** them their flowing manes?
42.10 made him prosperous again and **gave** him twice as much as he
42.11 Each of them **gave** him some money and a gold ring.
42.15 Their father **gave** them a share of the inheritance along with
Ps 2. 8 Ask, and I will **give** you all the nations;
4. 7 the joy that you have **given** me is more than they will
12. 5 I will **give** them the security they long for."
16. 5 Lord, are all I have, and you **give** me all I need;
18.28 O Lord, you **give** me light;
18.29 You **give** me strength to attack my enemies and power to
18.39 **give** me strength for the battle and victory over my enemies.
18.47 He **gives** me victory over my enemies;
18.48 O Lord, you **give** me victory over my enemies and protect me
18.50 God **gives** great victories to his king;
19. 7 it **gives** new strength.
19. 7 Lord are trustworthy, **giving** wisdom to those who lack it.
19. 8 commands of the Lord are just and **give** understanding to
19.11 They **give** knowledge to me, your servant;
20. 2 you help from his Temple and **give** you aid from Mount Zion.
20. 4 May he **give** you what you desire and make all your plans
20. 6 Now I know that the Lord **gives** victory to his chosen king;
20. 6 his holy heaven and by his power **gives** him great victories.
20. 9 **Give** victory to the king, O Lord;
21. 1 The king is glad, O Lord, because you **gave** him strength;
21. 2 You have **given** him his heart's desire;
21. 4 asked for life, and you **gave** it, a long and lasting life.
21. 5 you have **given** him fame and majesty.
23. 3 He **gives** me new strength.
28. 4 **give** them what they deserve!
28. 6 **Give** praise to the Lord;
28. 7 He **gives** me help and makes me glad;
29.11 The Lord **gives** strength to his people and blesses them with
31. 8 you have **given** me freedom to go where I wish.
37. 4 in the Lord, and he will **give** you your heart's desire.
37. 5 **Give** yourself to the Lord;
37.26 At all times he **gives** freely and lends to others,
37.34 he will honour you by **giving** you the land, and you will
40. 6 Instead, you have **given** me ears to hear you, [7] and so I
44. 4 you **give** victory to your people, [5] and by your power we
45. 6 The kingdom that God has **given** you will last for ever and
47. 3 He **gave** us victory over the peoples;
48.11 You **give** right judgements;
50.14 sacrifice to God, and **give** the Almighty all that you promised.
51.12 **Give** me again the joy that comes from your salvation,
56.12 I will **give** you my offering of thanksgiving,
61. 5 O God, and you have **given** me what belongs to those who
63.11 Because God **gives** him victory, the king will rejoice.
65. 5 You answer us by **giving** us victory and you do wonderful
66.14 I will **give** you what I said I would when I was
68. 6 He **gives** the lonely a home to live in and leads prisoners
68.35 He **gives** strength and power to his people.
69. 4 They made me **give** back things I did not steal.
69.21 When I was hungry, they **gave** me poison;
72.15 May he be **given** gold from Arabia;
76.11 **Give** the Lord your God what you promised him;
78.15 open in the desert and **gave** them water from the depths.
78.20 he also provide us with bread and **give** his people meat?"
78.24 he **gave** them grain from heaven, by sending down manna for
78.25 ate the food of angels, and God **gave** them all they wanted.
78.29 God **gave** them what they wanted.
78.55 the tribes of Israel and **gave** their homes to his people.

Ps 80. 5 You have **given** us sorrow to eat, a large cup of tears
81. 5 He **gave** it to the people of Israel when he attacked the
85. 7 your constant love, O Lord, and **give** us your saving help.
86.17 when they see that you have **given** me comfort and help.
89.17 You **give** us great victories;
89.18 you, the Holy God of Israel, **gave** us our king.
89.19 I have **given** the throne to one I chose from the people.
90.15 **Give** us now as much happiness
90.15 as the sadness you **gave** us during all our years
90.17 **Give** us success in all we do!
94. 2 rise and **give** the proud what they deserve!
94.13 You **give** him rest from days of trouble until a pit is
95.11 never enter the land where I would have **given** you rest.' "
103. 6 judges in favour of the oppressed and **gives** them their rights.
104.15 olive-oil to make him cheerful, and bread to **give** him strength.
104.27 them depend on you to **give** them food when they need it.
104.28 You **give** it to them, and they eat it;
104.30 But when you **give** them breath, they are created;
104.30 you **give** new life to the earth.
105.11 "I will **give** you the land of Canaan," he said.
105.24 Lord **gave** many children to his people and made them stronger
105.39 over his people and a fire at night to **give** them light.
105.40 he **gave** them food from heaven to satisfy them.
105.44 He **gave** them the lands of other peoples and let them
106.15 so he **gave** them what they asked for, but also sent a
111. 6 power to his people by **giving** them the lands of foreigners.
111. 8 they were **given** in truth and righteousness.
111.10 he **gives** sound judgement to all who obey his commands.
112. 9 He **gives** generously to the needy, and his kindness never fails;
113. 9 he makes her happy by **giving** her children.
115. 1 to us, must glory be **given** because of your constant love and
115.14 May the Lord **give** you children— you and your descendants!
115.16 belongs to the Lord alone, but he **gave** the earth to man.
116.14 of all his people I will **give** him what I have promised.
116.17 I will **give** you a sacrifice of thanksgiving and offer my
116.18 Temple in Jerusalem, I will **give** you what I have promised.
118.21 Lord, because you heard me, because you have **given** me victory.
118.25 **Give** us success, O Lord!
119. 4 Lord, you have **given** us your laws and told us to obey
119.13 I will repeat aloud all the laws you have **given.**
119.32 your commands, because you will **give** me more understanding.
119.36 **Give** me the desire to obey your laws rather than to get
119.40 **give** me new life, for you are righteous.
119.49 it has **given** me hope.
119.50 my suffering I was comforted because your promise **gave** me life.
119.66 **Give** me wisdom and knowledge, because I trust in your
119.72 The law that you **gave** means more to me than all the
119.73 **give** me understanding, so that I may learn your laws.
119.116 **Give** me strength, as you promised, and I shall live;
119.125 **give** me understanding, so that I may know your teachings.
119.138 rules that you have **given** are completely fair and right.
119.144 **give** me understanding, and I shall live.
119.169 **Give** me understanding, as you have promised.
119.175 **Give** me life, so that I may praise you;
135.12 He **gave** their lands to his people;
135.12 he **gave** them to Israel.
136.21 He **gave** their lands to his people;
136.22 he **gave** them to Israel, his servant;
136.25 He **gives** food to every living creature;
140. 8 Lord, don't **give** the wicked what they want;
144.10 You **give** victory to kings and rescue your servant David.
145.15 hopefully to you, and you **give** them food when they need it.
145.16 You **give** them enough and satisfy the needs of all.
146. 7 in favour of the oppressed and **gives** food to the hungry.
146. 8 The Lord sets prisoners free [8] and **gives** sight to the blind.
147. 9 He **gives** animals their food and feeds the young ravens when

Prov 2. 6 It is the Lord who **gives** wisdom;
3. 2 My teaching will **give** you a long and prosperous life.
3.18 wisdom will **give** them life.
3.20 rivers to flow and the clouds to **give** rain to the earth.
4.22 They will **give** life and health to anyone who understands them.
5.15 faithful to your own wife and **give** your love to her alone.
5.20 Why should you **give** your love to another woman, my son?
8.18 I have riches and honour to **give,** prosperity and success.
8.21 the paths of justice, [21] **giving** wealth to those who love me,
11.30 Righteousness **gives** life, but violence takes it away.
19. 6 claims the friendship of those who **give** out favours.
19.14 parents, but only the Lord can **give** him a sensible wife.
19.17 When you **give** to the poor, it is like lending to the
20.12 The Lord has **given** us eyes to see with and ears to
20.27 The Lord **gave** us mind and conscience;
21.14 angry with you, a gift **given** secretly will calm him down.
21.26 A righteous man, however, can **give,** and give generously.
21.31 ready for battle, but it is the Lord who **gives** victory.
23.25 **give** your mother that happiness.
25.14 promise things that they never **give** are like clouds and wind
25.21 if he is thirsty, **give** him a drink.
28.27 **Give** to the poor and you will never be in need.
29.13 have this in common—the Lord **gave** eyes to both of them.
29.21 you **give** your servant everything he wants from childhood on,
30. 8 So **give** me only as much food as I need.
30.15 A leech has two daughters, and both are named **"Give** me!"

Ecc 2.26 God **gives** wisdom, knowledge, and happiness to those who
2.26 that what they get can be **given** to those who please him.
3.11 He has **given** us a desire to know the future, but never
5.18 has worked for during the short life that God has **given** him;
5.19 If God **gives** a man wealth and property and lets him
6. 2 God will **give** someone wealth, honour, and property,
7.12 an inheritance [12] and will **give** you as much security as money
8.15 during the life that God has **given** him in this world.
9. 9 live the useless life that God has **given** you in this world.

Ecc 10. 6 Stupid people are **given** positions of authority while rich men
12. 7 of life will go back to God, who **gave** it to us.
12.11 They have been **given** by God, the one Shepherd of us all.

Song 7.12 There I will **give** you my love.
8. 2 I would **give** you spiced wine, my pomegranate wine to drink.

Is 1.17 help those who are oppressed, **give** orphans their rights,
1.26 I will **give** you rulers and advisers like those you had
2. 5 Jacob, let us walk in the light which the Lord **gives** us!
8.18 Here I am with the children the Lord has **given** me.
9. 3 You have **given** them great joy, Lord;
9. 6 A son is **given** to us!
11. 2 spirit of the Lord will **give** him wisdom, and the knowledge
12. 2 The Lord **gives** me power and strength;
14. 2 the land which the Lord **gave** them, and there the nations
21.14 barren country of Arabia, [14] **give** water to the thirsty people
21.14 You people of the land of Tema, **give** food to the refugees.
26.12 You will **give** us prosperity, Lord;
29.12 If you **give** it to someone who can't read and ask him
29.19 the happiness which the Lord, the holy God of Israel, **gives.**
29.23 the children that I will **give** you, then you will acknowledge
30. 6 expensive gifts for a nation that cannot **give** them any help.
30.23 make them grow and will **give** you a rich harvest, and your
32. 6 never feeds the hungry or **gives** thirsty people anything to drink.
33. 6 with justice and integrity [6] and **give** stability to the nation.
33. 6 always protects his people and **gives** them wisdom and knowledge.
34.17 divide the land among them and **give** each of them a share.
36. 8 I will **give** you two thousand horses if you can find that
37.26 I **gave** you the power to turn fortified cities into piles of
41. 2 Who **gives** him victory over kings and nations?
42. 5 he **gave** life and breath to all its people.
42.24 he wanted us to live or obey the teachings he **gave** us.
43.19 through the wilderness and **give** you streams of water there.
43.20 flow in the desert to **give** water to my chosen people.
44. 3 "I will **give** water to the thirsty land and make streams
45. 3 I will **give** you treasures from dark, secret places;
45. 4 I have **given** you great honour, although you do not know me.
48.15 I led him out and **gave** him success.
49. 5 The Lord **gives** me honour;
50. 5 The Lord has **given** me understanding, and I have not rebelled
50. 7 insults cannot hurt me because the Sovereign Lord **gives** me help.
51. 2 he was childless, but I blessed him and **gave** him children;
51.17 of punishment that the Lord in his anger **gave** you to drink;
51.22 am taking away the cup that I **gave** you in my anger.
51.23 I will **give** it to those who oppressed you, to those who
53.12 And so I will **give** him a place of honour, a place
53.12 He willingly **gave** his life and shared the fate of evil men.
54.13 "I myself will teach your people, and **give** them prosperity
54.17 I will defend my servants and **give** them victory."
55. 3 lasting covenant with you and **give** you the blessings I promised
55. 5 I will **give** you honour and glory."
56. 7 to Zion, my sacred hill, **give** you joy in my house of
57.16 I **gave** my people life, and I will not continue to accuse
58. 2 say they want me to **give** them just laws and that they
58. 7 **Give** clothes to those who have nothing to wear, and do not
58.10 if you **give** food to the hungry and satisfy those who are
58.14 and you will enjoy the land I **gave** to your ancestor, Jacob.
59.21 I have **given** you my power and my teachings to be yours
61. 3 comfort all who mourn, [3] To **give** to those who mourn in Zion
63.11 Where is the Lord, who **gave** his spirit to Moses?
63.14 led into a fertile valley, so the Lord **gave** his people rest.
65.15 But I will **give** a new name to those who obey me.

Jer 1. 5 "I chose you before I **gave** you life, and before you were
1. 9 to me, "Listen, I am **giving** you the words you must speak.
1.18 But today I am **giving** you the strength to resist them;
2. 7 they defiled the country I had **given** them.
3.18 the land that I **gave** your ancestors as a permanent possession."
3.19 you as my son and **give** you a delightful land, the most
5.24 the spring rains and **give** you the harvest season each year.
6.12 Their houses will be **given** to others, and so will their
7. 7 the land which I **gave** your ancestors as a permanent possession.
7.14 in this place that I **gave** to your ancestors and to you,
8.10 So I will **give** their fields to new owners and their
8.14 he has **given** us poison to drink, because we have sinned
9.15 I will **give** my people bitter plants to eat and poison to
11. 5 ancestors that I would **give** them the rich and fertile land
12.14 who have ruined the land I **gave** to my people Israel.
16.15 their own country, to the land that I **gave** their ancestors.
16.19 Lord, you are the one who protects me and **gives** me strength;
17. 4 give up the land I **gave** you, and I will make you
19. 7 I will **give** their corpses to the birds and the wild animals
22.25 would pull you off [25] and **give** you to people you are afraid
22.25 I will **give** you to King Nebuchadnezzar of Babylonia and his
23.15 I will **give** them bitter plants to eat and poison to drink,
23.39 them and the city that I **gave** to them and their ancestors.
24. 7 I will **give** them the desire to know that I am the
24.10 left in the land that I **gave** to them and their ancestors."
25. 5 the land that the Lord **gave** you and your ancestors as a
25.17 cup from the Lord's hand, **gave** it to all the nations to
27. 5 and I **give** it to anyone I choose.
29. 3 I **gave** the letter to Elasah son of Shaphan and to Gemariah
29.15 "You say that the Lord has **given** you prophets in Babylonia.
30. 3 to the land that I **gave** their ancestors, and they will take
32.12 and the open copy—[12] and **gave** them to Baruch, the son of
32.12 I **gave** them to him in the presence of Hanamel and of
32.16 After I had **given** the deed of purchase to Baruch, I
32.22 You **gave** them this rich and fertile land, as you had
32.42 so I am going to **give** them all the good things that
34.17 you have not **given** your fellow-Israelites their freedom.
34.17 Very well, then, I will **give** you freedom:
35.15 on living in the land that I **gave** you and your ancestors.
36.32 I took another scroll and **gave** it to my secretary Baruch,

Jer 37.21 and each day I was **given** a loaf of bread from the
38. 3 said, "I am going to **give** the city to the Babylonian army,
38.16 living God, the God who **gave** us life, that I will not
39.10 who owned no property, and he **gave** them vineyards and fields.
40. 5 Then he **gave** me a present and some food to take with
47. 7 how can it rest, when I have **given** it work to do?
52.34 he lived, he was **given** a regular allowance for his needs.
Lam 1.14 The Lord **gave** me to my foes, and I was helpless against
2.17 He **gave** our enemies victory, gave them joy at our downfall.
3.15 Bitter suffering is all he has **given** me for food and drink.
3.35 He knows when we are denied the rights he **gave** us;
4. 4 children are begging for food that no one will **give** them.
4.17 kept waiting for help from a nation that had none to **give.**
Ezek 2. 8 Open your mouth and eat what I am going to **give** you."
3. 2 I opened my mouth, and he **gave** me the scroll to eat.
3. 3 He said, "Mortal man, eat this scroll that I **give** you;
3.17 You will pass on to them the warnings I **give** you.
11.15 He has **given** us possession of the land.'
11.17 I scattered them, and will **give** the land of Israel back to
11.19 I will **give** them a new heart and a new mind.
11.19 stubborn heart of stone and will **give** them an obedient heart.
16.10 in embroidered gowns and **gave** you shoes of the best leather,
16.12 I **gave** you a nose-ring and earrings and a beautiful crown
16.16 and just like a prostitute, you **gave** yourself to everyone.
16.17 gold jewellery that I had **given** you, used it to make male
16.18 took the embroidered clothes I **gave** you and put them on the
16.18 to the images the olive-oil and incense I had **given** you.
16.19 I **gave** you food—the best flour, olive-oil, and honey—
16.33 prostitute is paid, but you **gave** presents to all your lovers
16.36 and, like a prostitute, you **gave** yourself to your lovers and
16.41 a prostitute and make you stop **giving** gifts to your lovers.
17. 7 the hope that he would **give** it more water than there was
18. 7 He returns what a borrower **gives** him as security;
18. 7 he feeds the hungry and **gives** clothing to the naked.
18.12 he robs, he keeps what a borrower **gives** him as security.
18.16 He returns what a borrower **gives** him as security.
18.16 He feeds the hungry and **gives** clothing to the naked.
20.15 to the land I had **given** them, a rich and fertile land,
20.28 I brought them to the land I had promised to **give** them.
20.42 that I promised I would **give** to your ancestors, then you
21.27 Then I will **give** it to him.
23.31 footsteps, and so I will **give** you the same cup of punishment
23.41 including the incense and the olive-oil that I had **given** them.
27.15 people of many coastal lands **gave** you ivory and ebony in
27.16 They **gave** emeralds, purple cloth, embroidery, fine linen,
28.25 their own land, the land that I **gave** to my servant Jacob.
29. 5 I will **give** it to the birds and animals for food.
29.19 I am **giving** the land of Egypt to King Nebuchadnezzar.
29.20 I am **giving** him Egypt in payment for his services,
30.25 When I **give** him my sword and he points it towards Egypt,
31.11 He will **give** that tree what it deserves for its wickedness.
33.15 took for a loan or **gives** back what he stole—
33.22 next morning, the Lord **gave** me back the power of speech.
33.24 'Abraham was only one man, and he was **given** the whole land.
34.23 I will **give** them a king like my servant David to be
34.29 I will **give** them fertile fields and put an end to hunger
36.26 I will **give** you a new heart and a new mind.
36.26 your stubborn heart of stone and **give** you an obedient heart.
36.28 Then you will live in the land I **gave** your ancestors.
37. 6 I will **give** you sinews and muscles, and cover you with skin.
37.25 live on the land I **gave** to my servant Jacob, the land
39.11 this happens, I will **give** Gog a burial-ground there in Israel,
39.24 I **gave** them what they deserved for their uncleanness
43.19 You will **give** them a young bull to offer as a sacrifice
44.28 share of what I have **given** Israel to be handed down from
44.30 bake bread, they are to **give** the priests the first loaf as
45. 1 the land is divided to **give** each tribe a share, one part
46. 5 with each lamb he is to bring whatever he wants to **give.**
46. 7 the offering is to be whatever the prince wants to **give.**
46.11 and whatever the worshipper wants to **give** with each lamb.
46.16 "If the ruling prince **gives** any of the land he owns to
46.17 But if the ruling prince **gives** any of his land to anyone
46.18 Any land he **gives** to his sons must be from the land
47.14 your ancestors that I would **give** them possession of this land;
48. 8 from east to west as the sections **given** to the tribes.
48.28 south side of the portion **given** to the tribe of Gad, the
Dan 1. 5 day they were to be **given** the same food and wine as
1.12 "**Give** us vegetables to eat and water to drink.
1.17 God **gave** the four young men knowledge and skill in
1.17 In addition, he **gave** Daniel skill in interpreting visions
2.21 it is he who **gives** wisdom and understanding.
2.23 You have **given** me wisdom and strength;
2.37 has made you emperor and **given** you power, might, and honour.
4.17 kingdoms and that he can **give** them to anyone he chooses—even
4.25 kingdoms, and that he can **give** them to anyone he chooses.
4.32 kingdoms and that he can **give** them to anyone he chooses."
4.36 majesty, and the glory of my kingdom were **given** back to me.
4.36 welcomed me, and I was **given** back my royal power, with even
5.17 "Keep your gifts for yourself or **give** them to someone else.
5.18 Nebuchadnezzar a great king and **gave** him dignity and majesty.
5.21 controls all human kingdoms and can **give** them to anyone he
5.28 is divided up and **given** to the Medes and Persians."
7. 4 And then a human mind was **given** to it.
7.14 He was **given** authority, honour, and royal power,
7.27 kingdoms on earth will be **given** to the people of the Supreme
11.39 put them into high offices, and **give** them land as a reward.
Hos 2. 4 go to my lovers—they **give** me food and water, wool and
2. 8 I am the one who **gave** her the corn, the wine, the
2. 9 take away the wool and the linen I **gave** her for clothing.
2.12 fig-trees, which she said her lovers **gave** her for serving them.
2.15 I will **give** back to her the vineyards she had and make
Hos 5.11 insisted on going for help to those who had none to **give.**
13.11 In my anger I have **given** you kings, and in my fury
Joel 2.19 "Now I am going to **give** you corn and wine and olive-oil,
2.23 He has **given** you the right amount of autumn rain;
2.25 I will **give** you back what you lost in the years when
Amos 2.10 desert for forty years, and **gave** you the land of the
6. 8 I will **give** their capital city and everything in it to the
7.17 will be divided up and **given** to others, and you yourself
9.15 people on the land I **gave** them, and they will not be
Obad 15 You will get back what you have **given.**
Jon 4. 6 grow up over Jonah to **give** him some shade, so that he
Mic 1. 7 be smashed to pieces, everything **given** to its temple prostitutes
2. 4 taken our land away And **given** it to those who took us
2. 5 for the land to be **given** back to the Lord's people, there
3. 8 his spirit and power, and **gives** me a sense of justice and
7. 8 We are in darkness now, but the Lord will **give** us light.
Nah 1.15 your festivals and **give** God what you solemnly promised him.
Zeph 3.17 in you, and in his love he will **give** you new life.
Hag 2. 9 and there I will **give** my people prosperity and peace."
Zech 3. 4 away your sin and will **give** you new clothes to wear."
4. 6 angel told me to **give** Zerubbabel this message from the Lord:
6.10 "Take the gifts **given** by the exiles Heldai, Tobijah, and
6.11 silver and gold they have **given,** and put it on the head
8.12 I will **give** all these blessings to the people of my nation
11.12 I said to them, "If you are willing, **give** me my wages.
12. 7 "I, the Lord, will **give** victory to the armies of Judah first,
Mal 1. 8 Try **giving** an animal like that to the governor!
1.14 in his flock a good animal that he promised to **give** me!
2. 4 will know that I have **given** you this command, so that my
2. 5 and this is what I **gave** them, so that they might respect
Mt 2.22 He was **given** more instructions in a dream, so he went to
4. 9 "All this I will **give** you," the Devil said, "if you
5.15 lampstand, where it **gives** light for everyone in the house.
5.31 his wife must **give** her a written notice of divorce.'
5.42 When someone asks you for something, **give** it to him;
5.45 and good people alike, and **gives** rain to those who do good
6. 2 "So when you **give** something to a needy person, do not
6.11 **Give** us today the food we need.
7. 6 "Do not **give** what is holy to dogs—they will only turn
7. 9 of you who are fathers **give** your son a stone when he
7.10 Or would you **give** him a snake when he asks for a
7.11 you are, you know how to **give** good things to your children.
7.11 will your Father in heaven **give** good things to those who ask
9. 8 afraid, and praised God for **giving** such authority to men.
9.34 chief of the demons who **gives** him the power to drive out
10. 1 his twelve disciples together and **gave** them authority to
10. 8 You have received without paying, so **give** without being paid.
10.10 A worker should be **given** what he needs.
10.19 when the time comes, you will be **given** what you will say.
10.42 can be sure that whoever **gives** even a drink of cold water
11. 1 When Jesus finished **giving** these instructions to his twelve disciples,
11.27 "My Father has **given** me all things.
11.28 tired from carrying heavy loads, and I will **give** you rest.
11.30 For the yoke I will **give** you is easy, and the load
12.24 because their ruler Beelzebul **gives** him power to do so."
12.27 out demons because Beelzebul **gives** me the power to do so.
12.27 Well, then, who **gives** your followers the power to drive them out?
12.28 Beelzebul, but God's Spirit, who **gives** me the power to drive
12.36 Day everyone will have to **give** account of every useless word
12.39 only miracle you will be **given** is the miracle of the prophet
13.11 Kingdom of heaven has been **given** to you, but not to them.
13.12 who has something will be **given** more, so that he will have
14. 7 her, "I swear that I will **give** you anything you ask for!"
14. 8 mother's suggestion she asked him, "**Give** me here and now
14.11 in on a dish and **given** to the girl, who took it
14.16 "You yourselves **give** them something to eat!"
14.19 He broke the loaves and **gave** them to the disciples,
14.19 and the disciples **gave** them to the people.
15.36 gave thanks to God, broke them, and **gave** them to the disciples;
15.36 and the disciples **gave** them to the people.
16. 4 The only miracle you will be **given** is the miracle of Jonah."
16.17 human being, but it was **given** to you directly by my Father
16.19 I will **give** you the keys of the Kingdom of heaven;
16.26 There is nothing he can **give** to regain his life.
19. 7 "Why, then, did Moses **give** the law for a man to
19. 8 Jesus answered, "Moses **gave** you permission to divorce
19.11 to everyone, but only to those to whom God has **given** it.
19.21 sell all you have and **give** the money to the poor,
19.29 receive a hundred times more and will be **given** eternal life.
20.10 but they too were **given** a silver coin each.
20.14 I want to **give** this man who was hired last
20.14 as much as I have **given** you.
20.28 but to serve and to **give** his life to redeem many people."
20.33 "Sir," they answered, "we want you to **give** us our sight!"
21.23 Who **gave** you this right?"
21.24 one question, and if you **give** me an answer, I will tell
21.41 to other tenants, who will **give** him his share of the harvest
21.43 taken away from you and **given** to a people who will produce
22.46 No one was able to **give** Jesus any answer, and from that
23.23 You **give** to God a tenth even of the seasoning herbs,
24.45 of the other servants to **give** them their food at the proper
25.15 He **gave** to each one according to his ability:
25.15 to one he **gave** five thousand gold coins,
25.15 to another he **gave** two thousand,
25.15 and to another he **gave** one thousand.
25.20 'You **gave** me five thousand coins, sir,' he said.
25.22 the servant who had been **given** two thousand coins came in
25.22 came in and said, 'You **gave** me two thousand coins, sir.
25.28 money away from him and **give** it to the one who has
25.29 something, even more will be **given,** and he will have more

Mt 25.35 hungry and you fed me, thirsty and you **gave** me a drink;
25.37 you hungry and feed you, or thirsty and **give** you a drink?
25.42 not feed me, thirsty but you would not **give** me a drink;
26. 9 sold for a large amount and the money **given** to the poor!"
26.15 and asked, "What will you **give** me if I betray Jesus to
26.15 They counted out thirty silver coins and **gave** them to him.
26.26 took a piece of bread, **gave** a prayer of thanks,
26.26 broke it, and **gave** it to his disciples.
26.27 took a cup, gave thanks to God, and **gave** it to them.
26.48 The traitor had **given** the crowd a signal:
26.62 Jesus, "Have you no answer to **give** to this accusation against you?"
26.73 "After all, the way you speak **gives** you away!"
27.50 Jesus again **gave** a loud cry and breathed his last.
27.58 Pilate gave orders for the body to be **given** to Joseph.
28.12 they **gave** a large sum of money to the soldiers
28.18 to them, "I have been **given** all authority in heaven and on
Mk 1.26 spirit shook the man hard, **gave** a loud scream, and came out
2.26 bread—but David ate it and even **gave** it to his men."
3.16 Simon (Jesus **gave** him the name Peter);
3.17 the sons of Zebedee (Jesus **gave** them the name Boanerges,
3.22 chief of the demons who **gives** him the power to drive them
4.11 "You have been **given** the secret of the Kingdom of God,"
4.25 who has something will be **given** more, and the person who has
5.43 to tell anyone, and he said, "**Give** her something to eat."
6. 2 "What wisdom is this that has been **given** him?
6. 7 He **gave** them authority over the evil spirits
6.21 on Herod's birthday, when he **gave** a feast for all the chief
6.22 I will **give** you anything you want."
6.23 "I swear that I will **give** you anything you ask for, even
6.25 demanded, "I want you to **give** me here and now the head
6.28 and gave it to the girl, who **gave** it to her mother.
6.37 "You yourselves **give** them something to eat," Jesus answered.
6.41 He broke the loaves and **gave** them to his disciples to
7.34 Jesus looked up to heaven, **gave** a deep groan,
8. 6 broke them, and **gave** them to his disciples to distribute
8.12 But Jesus **gave** a deep groan and said, "Why do the
8.12 No such proof will be **given** to these people!"
8.37 There is nothing he can **give** to regain his life.
9.41 assure you that anyone who **gives** you a drink of water
10. 3 Jesus answered with a question, "What law did Moses **give** you?"
10. 4 Their answer was, "Moses **gave** permission for a man to
10.21 sell all you have and **give** the money to the poor, and
10.40 It is God who will **give** these places to those for whom
10.45 came to serve and to **give** his life to redeem many people."
11.24 received it, and you will be **given** whatever you ask for.
11.28 Who **gave** you this right?"
11.29 one question, and if you **give** me an answer, I will tell
12.28 He saw that Jesus had **given** the Sadducees a good answer, so
12.44 in all she had—she **gave** all she had to live on."
13.11 when the time comes, say whatever is then **given** to you.
13.34 his servants in charge, after **giving** to each one his own
14. 5 hundred silver coins and the money **given** to the poor!"
14.11 hear what he had to say, and promised to **give** him money.
14.22 took a piece of bread, **gave** a prayer of thanks, broke it,
14.22 and **gave** it to his disciples.
14.44 The traitor had **given** the crowd a signal:
15.23 There they tried to **give** him wine mixed with a drug
16. 7 Now go and **give** this message to his disciples, including Peter:
16. 9 Peter and his friends and **gave** them a brief account of all
16.17 Believers will be **given** the power to perform miracles:
Lk 2.21 which the angel had **given** him before he had been conceived.
3.11 "Whoever has two shirts must **give** one to the man who has
4. 6 "I will **give** you all this power and all this wealth,"
4. 6 over to me, and I can **give** it to anyone I choose.
4.20 Jesus rolled up the scroll, **gave** it back to the attendant,
6. 4 offered to God, ate it, and **gave** it also to his men.
6.30 **Give** to everyone who asks you for something,
6.38 **Give** to others, and God will give to you.
7.15 and began to talk, and Jesus **gave** him back to his mother.
7.21 and **gave** sight to many blind people.
7.44 into your home, and you **gave** me no water for my feet,
8.10 Kingdom of God has been **given** to you, but to the rest
8.18 whoever has something will be **given** more, but whoever has
8.28 When he saw Jesus, he **gave** a loud cry, threw himself
8.55 once, and Jesus ordered them to **give** her something to eat.
9. 1 disciples together and **gave** them power and authority
9.13 But Jesus said to them, "You yourselves **give** them something to eat."
9.16 broke them, and **gave** them to the disciples to distribute
9.42 healed the boy, and **gave** him back to his father.
10. 7 they offer you, for a worker should be **given** his pay.
10.19 I have **given** you authority, so that you can walk on snakes
10.22 "My Father has **given** me all things.
10.35 he took out two silver coins and **gave** them to the innkeeper.
11. 3 **Give** us day by day the food we need.
11. 7 I can't get up and **give** you anything.'
11. 8 will not get up and **give** you the bread because you are
11. 8 he will get up and **give** you everything you need because you
11.11 of you who are fathers **give** your son a snake when he
11.12 Or would you **give** him a scorpion when he asks for an
11.13 you are, you know how to **give** good things to your children.
11.13 will the Father in heaven **give** the Holy Spirit to those who
11.15 chief of the demons, who **gives** him the power to drive them
11.18 out demons because Beelzebul **gives** me the power to do so.
11.29 but none will be **given** them except the miracle of Jonah.
11.41 But **give** what is in your cups and plates to the poor,
11.42 You **give** God a tenth of the seasoning herbs, such as mint
12.14 answered him, "My friend, who **gave** me the right to judge
12.20 This very night you will have to **give** up your life;
12.32 flock, for your Father is pleased to **give** you the Kingdom.
Lk 12.33 Sell all your belongings and **give** the money to the poor.
12.42 to run the household and **give** the other servants their share
12.48 Much is required from the person to whom much is **given;**
12.48 is required from the person to whom much more is **given.**
13.15 stall and take it out to **give** it water on the Sabbath.
14.12 to his host, "When you **give** a lunch or a dinner,
14.13 When you **give** a feast, invite the poor, the crippled,
14.16 once a man who was **giving** a great feast to which he
15.12 one said to him, 'Father, **give** me my share of the property
15.16 pods the pigs ate, but no one **gave** him anything to eat.
15.29 What have you **given** me?
16. 9 wealth, so that when it **gives** out, you will be welcomed in
16.12 to someone else, who will **give** you what belongs to you?
16.25 in your lifetime you were **given** all the good things, while
18. 5 the trouble this widow is **giving** me, I will see to it
18.12 days a week, and I **give** you a tenth of all my
18.22 Sell all you have and **give** the money to the poor,
19. 8 I will **give** half my belongings to the poor, and if I
19.13 called his ten servants and **gave** them each a gold coin
19.16 I have earned ten gold coins with the one you **gave** me.'
19.18 I have earned five gold coins with the one you **gave** me.'
19.24 coin away from him and **give** it to the servant who has
19.26 'that to every person who has something, even more will be **given;**
20. 2 Who **gave** you this right?"
21. 4 she, poor as she is, **gave** all she had to live on."
21.15 defend yourselves, [15] because I will **give** you such words
22.16 eat it until it is **given** its full meaning in the Kingdom
22.19 broke it, and **gave** it to them, saying,
22.19 to them, saying, "This is my body, which is **given** for you.
22.20 In the same way, he **gave** them the cup after the supper,
22.29 just as my Father has **given** me the right to rule,
22.29 so I will **give** you the same right.
24.30 then he broke the bread and **gave** it to them.
24.42 They **gave** him a piece of cooked fish, [43] which he took
Jn 1.12 so he **gave** them the right to become God's children.
1.16 he has blessed us all, **giving** us one blessing after another.
1.17 God **gave** the Law through Moses, but grace and truth
1.32 And John **gave** this testimony:
2. 3 When the wine had **given** out, Jesus' mother said to him,
3.16 world so much that he **gave** his only Son, so that everyone
3.27 "No one can have anything unless God **gives** it to him.
3.34 God's words, because God **gives** him the fullness of his Spirit.
4. 5 far from the field that Jacob had **given** to his son Joseph.
4. 7 water, and Jesus said to her, "**Give** me a drink of water."
4.10 only you knew what God **gives** and who it is that is
4.10 would ask him, and he would **give** you life-giving water."
4.12 It was our ancestor Jacob who **gave** us this well;
4.14 the water that I will **give** him will never be thirsty again.
4.14 The water that I will **give** him will become in him a
4.14 provide him with life-giving water and **give** him eternal life."
4.15 "Sir," the woman said, "**give** me that water!
4.34 sent me and to finish the work he **gave** me to do.
5.21 Father raises the dead and **gives** them life,
5.21 the same way the Son **gives** life to those he wants to.
5.22 He has **given** his Son the full right to judge,
5.27 And he has **given** the Son the right to judge,
5.36 which is even greater than the witness that John **gave:**
5.36 is, the deeds my Father **gave** me to do, these speak on
6.27 the Son of Man will **give** you, because God, the Father, has
6.31 scripture says, 'He **gave** them bread from heaven to eat.' "
6.32 "What Moses **gave** you was not the bread from heaven;
6.32 it is my Father who **gives** you the real bread from heaven.
6.33 For the bread that God **gives** is he who comes down
6.33 down from heaven and **gives** life to the world."
6.34 "Sir," they asked him, "**give** us this bread always."
6.37 Everyone whom my Father **gives** me will come to me.
6.39 of all those he has **given** me, but that I should raise
6.51 The bread that I will **give** him is my flesh,
6.51 which I **give** so that the world may live."
6.52 "How can this man **give** us his flesh to eat?"
6.63 What **gives** life is God's Spirit;
6.68 You have the words that **give** eternal life.
7.19 Moses **gave** you the Law, didn't he?
7.39 Spirit had not yet been **given,** because Jesus had not been
9.32 ever heard of anyone **giving** sight to a person born blind.
10.17 because I am willing to **give** up my life, in order that
10.18 I **give** it up of my own free will.
10.18 I have the right to **give** it up, and I have the
10.21 How could a demon **give** sight to blind people?"
10.28 I **give** them eternal life, and they shall never die.
10.29 What my Father has **given** me is greater than everything,
10.32 good deeds in your presence which the Father **gave** me to do;
10.35 those people gods, the people to whom his message was **given.**
11.22 that even now God will **give** you whatever you ask him for."
11.37 some of them said, "He **gave** sight to the blind man, didn't
12. 5 hundred silver coins and the money **given** to the poor?"
13. 3 Jesus knew that the Father had **given** him complete power;
13.26 will dip some bread in the sauce and **give** it to him;
13.26 of bread, dipped it, and **gave** it to Judas, the son of
13.29 needed for the festival, or to **give** something to the poor.
13.34 And now I **give** you a new commandment:
14.16 the Father, and he will **give** you another Helper, who will
14.27 it is my peace that I **give** you.
14.27 I do not **give** it as the world does.
15. 3 been made clean already by the teaching I have **given** you.
15.13 can have for his friends is to **give** his life for them.
15.16 And so the Father will **give** you whatever you ask of him
16.14 He will **give** me glory, because he will take what I say
16.15 Spirit will take what I **give** him and tell it to you.
16.23 the Father will **give** you whatever you ask him for
17. 1 **Give** glory to your Son, so that the Son may give glory

Jn 17. 2 For you **gave** him authority over all mankind,
17. 2 so that he might **give** eternal life
17. 2 to all those you **gave** him.
17. 4 I have finished the work you **gave** me to do.
17. 5 **Give** me glory in your presence now, the same glory I had
17. 6 made you known to those you **gave** me out of the world.
17. 6 They belonged to you, and you **gave** them to me.
17. 7 and now they know that everything you **gave** me comes from you.
17. 8 I **gave** them the message that you gave me,
17. 9 world but for those you **gave** me, for they belong to you.
17.11 your name, the name you **gave** me, so that they may be
17.12 safe by the power of your name, the name you **gave** me.
17.14 I **gave** them your message, and the world hated them,
17.22 I **gave** them the same glory you gave me,
17.24 You have **given** them to me, and I want them to be
17.24 so that they may see my glory, the glory you **gave** me;
18. 9 "Father, I have not lost even one of those you **gave** me.")
18.11 the cup of suffering which my Father has **given** me?"
19.11 authority over me only because it was **given** to you by God.
21.13 So Jesus went over, took the bread, and **gave** it to them;
Acts 1. 4 And when they came together, he **gave** them this order:
1. 6 "Lord, will you at this time **give** the Kingdom back to Israel?"
3. 3 Peter and John going in, he begged them to **give** him something.
3. 6 have no money at all, but I **give** you what I have:
3.13 God of our ancestors, has **given** divine glory to his Servant Jesus.
3.16 the power of his name that **gave** strength to this lame man.
4.12 is no one else whom God has **given** who can save us."
4.33 With great power the apostles **gave** witness to the resurrection
5.31 as Leader and Saviour, to **give** the people of Israel the
6. 4 We ourselves, then, will **give** our full time to prayer and
6.10 But the Spirit **gave** Stephen such wisdom that when he spoke,
7. 5 God did not then **give** Abraham any part of it as his
7. 5 ground, but God promised to **give** it to him, and that it
7. 8 Then God **gave** Abraham the ceremony of circumcision
7.10 God **gave** him a pleasing manner and wisdom,
7.42 away from them and **gave them over** to worship the stars of
8.18 that the Spirit had been **given** to the believers when the
8.19 Peter and John, [19] and said, **"Give** this power to me too,
8.25 After they had **given** their testimony and proclaimed the Lord's message,
11. 4 So Peter **gave** them a complete account of what had happened
11.17 It is clear that God **gave** those Gentiles the same gift
11.17 that he **gave** us when we believed
11.18 God, saying, "Then God has **given** to the Gentiles also the
12.23 Lord struck Herod down, because he did not **give** honour to God.
13.20 "After this he **gave** them judges until the time
13.21 asked for a king, God **gave** them Saul son of Kish from
13.34 'I will **give** you the sacred and sure blessings that I
13.47 For this is the commandment that the Lord has **given** us:
14. 3 his grace was true by **giving** them the power to perform
14.12 They **gave** Barnabas the name Zeus, and Paul the name Hermes,
14.17 But he has always **given** evidence of his existence by the
14.17 he **gives** you rain from heaven and crops at the right times;
14.17 he **gives** you food and fills your hearts with happiness."
15. 8 approval of the Gentiles by **giving** the Holy Spirit to them,
15.30 gathered the whole group of believers and **gave** them the letter.
15.32 a long time with them, **giving** them courage and strength.
16.34 Silas up into his house and **gave** them some food to eat.
17.25 it is he himself who **gives** life and breath and everything
17.31 He has **given** proof of this to everyone by raising that man
18. 5 Paul **gave** his whole time to preaching
19.17 and the name of the Lord Jesus was **given** greater honour.
19.40 we would not be able to **give** a good reason for it."
20.21 Jews and Gentiles alike I **gave** solemn warning
20.24 work that the Lord Jesus **gave** me to do, which is to
20.32 to build you up and **give** you the blessings God has for
20.35 'There is more happiness in **giving** than in receiving.'"
21.19 Paul greeted them and **gave** a complete report of everything
21.26 went into the Temple and **gave** notice of how many days it
21.40 The commander **gave** him permission, so Paul stood on the steps
23.11 You have **given** your witness for me here in Jerusalem, and
24.13 Nor can they **give** you proof of the accusations they now
24.23 him under guard, but to **give** him some freedom and allow his
24.26 same time he was hoping that Paul would **give** him some money;
26.22 and so I stand here **giving** my witness to all, to small
27. 3 to go and see his friends, to be **given** what he needed.
27. 9 So Paul **gave** them this advice:
28.10 They **gave** us many gifts, and when we sailed,
Rom 1. 5 Through him God **gave** me the privilege of being an apostle
1. 7 Father and the Lord Jesus Christ **give** you grace and peace.
1.21 God, but they do not **give** him the honour that belongs to
1.24 And so God has **given those people over** to do the filthy
1.26 God has **given them over** to shameful passions.
1.28 about God, he has **given them over** to corrupted minds, so
2. 7 to them God will **give** eternal life.
2.10 But God will **give** glory, honour, and peace to all who do
3.21 the Law of Moses and the prophets **gave** their witness to it.
4.14 God promises is to be **given** to those who obey the Law,
4.20 his faith filled him with power, and he **gave** praise to God.
5.13 There was sin in the world before the Law was **given;**
5.18 one righteous act sets all mankind free and **gives** them life.
6.13 Instead, **give** yourselves to God, as those who have been
8.11 Christ from death will also **give** life to your mortal bodies
8.15 the Spirit that God has **given** you does not make you slaves
8.32 He **gave** us his Son—
8.32 will he not also freely **give** us all things?
9. 4 he made his covenants with them and **gave** them the Law;
11. 4 What answer did God **give** him?
11.16 first piece of bread is **given** to God, then the whole loaf
11.34 Who is able to **give** him advice?
11.35 Who has ever **given** him anything, so that he had to pay
Rom 12. 3 according to the amount of faith that God has **given** you.
12. 6 gifts in accordance with the grace that God has **given** us.
12.20 if he is thirsty, **give** him a drink;
14.12 us, then, will have to **give** an account of himself to God.
14.17 the righteousness, peace, and joy which the Holy Spirit **gives.**
15. 4 through the patience and encouragement which the Scriptures **give** us.
15.15 of the privilege God has **given** me [16] of being a servant of
15.26 Achaia have freely decided to **give** an offering to help the
15.30 our Lord Jesus Christ and by the love that the Spirit **gives:**
16. 2 as God's people should, and **give** her any help she may need
16.25 Let us **give** glory to God!
1 Cor 1. 3 Father and the Lord Jesus Christ **give** you grace and peace.
1. 4 because of the grace he has **given** you through Christ Jesus.
2.12 God, so that we may know all that God has **given** us.
2.16 Who is able to **give** him advice?"
3. 5 of us does the work which the Lord **gave** him to do:
3.10 Using the gift that God **gave** me, I did the work
4. 7 Didn't God **give** you everything you have?
4. 9 to me that God has **given** the very last place to us
6.19 who lives in you and who was **given** to you by God?
7. 5 you will be kept from **giving** in to Satan's temptation
7.25 from the Lord, but I **give** my opinion as one who by
7.35 right and proper, and to **give** yourselves completely to the
9. 4 I the right to be **given** food and drink for my work?
10.13 to the test, he will **give** you the strength to endure it,
11.15 Her long hair has been **given** her to serve as a covering.
12. 4 kinds of spiritual gifts, but the same Spirit **gives** them.
12. 6 service, but the same God **gives** ability to all for their
12. 8 The Spirit **gives** one person a message full of wisdom,
12. 8 person the same Spirit **gives** a message full of knowledge.
12. 9 One and the same Spirit **gives** faith to one person,
12. 9 while to another person he **gives** the power to heal.
12.10 The Spirit **gives** one person the power to work miracles;
12.10 To one person he **gives** the ability to speak in strange tongues,
12.10 and to another he **gives** the ability to explain what is
12.11 as he wishes, he **gives** a different gift to each person.
12.13 Spirit, and we have all been **given** the one Spirit to drink.
12.24 such a way as to **give** greater honour to those parts that
12.28 followed by those who are **given** the power to heal or to
13. 3 I may **give** away everything I have,
13. 3 and even **give** up my body to be burnt
14. 3 God's message speaks to people and **gives** them help,
14. 9 about if your message **given** in strange tongues is not clear?
14.29 Two or three who are **given** God's message should speak,
15.10 and the grace that he **gave** me was not without effect.
15.38 he **gives** each seed its own proper body.
15.57 thanks be to God who **gives** us the victory through our Lord
16. 3 After I come, I shall **give** letters of introduction to the
16.15 converts in Achaia and have **given** themselves to the service
2 Cor 1. 2 Father and the Lord Jesus Christ **give** you grace and peace.
1. 6 you too are helped and **given** the strength to endure with
1.22 upon us, and who has **given** us the Holy Spirit in our
3. 6 The written law brings death, but the Spirit **gives** life.
3. 7 stone tablets, and God's glory appeared when it was **given.**
4. 1 God in his mercy has **given** us this work to do, and
5. 5 for this change, and he **gave** us his Spirit as the guarantee
5.12 rather, we are trying to **give** you a good reason to be
5.18 enemies into his friends and **gave** us the task of making
5.19 their sins, and he has **given** us the message which tells how
8. 2 generous in their **giving,** even though they are very poor.
8. 3 can assure you that they **gave** as much as they could,
8. 5 First they **gave** themselves to the Lord;
8. 5 and then, by God's will they **gave** themselves to us as well.
8.12 If you are eager to **give,** God will accept your gift on
8.12 basis of what you have to **give,** not on what you haven't.
9. 5 it will show that you **give** because you want to, not because
9. 7 Each one should **give,** then, as he has decided, not with
9. 7 for God loves the one who **gives** gladly.
9. 8 And God is able to **give** you more than you need,
9. 9 As the scripture says, "He **gives** generously to the needy;
9.13 of yours brings, many will **give** glory to God for your
10. 8 that the Lord has **given** us—authority to build you up,
11.24 Five times I was **given** the thirty-nine lashes by the Jews;
12. 1 now talk about visions and revelations **given** me by the Lord.
12. 7 things I saw, I was **given** a painful physical ailment, which
13.10 that the Lord has **given** me—authority to build you up,
Gal 1. 3 Father and the Lord Jesus Christ **give** you grace and peace.
1. 4 this present evil age, Christ **gave** himself for our sins,
2. 5 for you, we did not **give** in to them for a minute.
2. 7 they saw that God had **given** me the task of preaching the
2. 7 Gentiles, just as he had **given** Peter the task of preaching
2. 9 recognized that God had **given** me this special task;
2.20 Son of God, who loved me and **gave** his life for me.
3. 5 Does God **give** you the Spirit and work miracles among you
3.14 promised to Abraham might be **given** to the Gentiles by means
3.17 The Law, which was **given** four hundred and thirty years later,
3.18 because of his promise that God **gave** that gift to Abraham.
3.22 of faith in Jesus Christ is **given** to those who believe.
4. 7 are his son, God will **give** you all that he has for
4.15 out your own eyes, if you could, and **given** them to me.
5.25 The Spirit has **given** us life;
6.17 let no one **give** me any more trouble, because the scars I
Eph 1. 2 Father and the Lord Jesus Christ **give** you grace and peace.
1. 3 he has blessed us by **giving** us every spiritual blessing in
1. 6 for the free gift he **gave** us in his dear Son!
1. 8 grace of God, [8] which he **gave** to us in such large measure!
1.13 of ownership on you by **giving** you the Holy Spirit he had
1.14 assures us that God will **give** complete freedom to those who
1.17 Christ, the glorious Father, to **give** you the Spirit, who
1.22 things under Christ's feet and **gave** him to the church as

Eph 3. 2 God in his grace has **given** me this work to do for
3. 7 God's special gift, which he **gave** me through the working of
3. 8 yet God **gave** me this privilege of taking to the Gentiles the
3.16 wealth of his glory to **give** you power through his Spirit to
4. 3 the unity which the Spirit **gives** by means of the peace that
4. 7 received a special gift in proportion to what Christ has **given.**
4. 8 he **gave** gifts to mankind."
4.11 It was he who **"gave** gifts to mankind";
4.18 in the life that God **gives,** for they are completely ignorant
4.19 they **give themselves over** to vice and do all sorts of
4.27 Don't **give** the Devil a chance.
5. 2 as Christ loved us and **gave** his life for us
5.25 just as Christ loved the church and **gave** his life for it.
6.11 all the armour that God **gives** you, so that you will be
6.17 the word of God as the sword which the Spirit **gives** you.
6.19 for me, that God will **give** me a message when I am
6.21 in the Lord's work, will **give** you all the news about me,
6.23 and the Lord Jesus Christ **give** to all Christian brothers
Phil 1. 2 Father and the Lord Jesus Christ **give** you grace and peace.
1. 7 this privilege that God has **given** me, both now that I am
1.14 my being in prison has **given** most of the brothers more
1.16 they know that God has **given** me the work of defending the
1.28 you will win, because it is God who **gives** you the victory.
1.29 For you have been **given** the privilege of serving Christ,
2. 7 his own free will he **gave** up all he had,
2. 9 the highest place above and **gave** him the name that is
2.30 to give me the help that you yourselves could not **give.**
3. 9 have the righteousness that is **given** through faith in Christ,
4. 9 And the God who **gives** us peace will be with you.
4.13 to face all conditions by the power that Christ **gives** me.
4.18 receipt for everything you have **given** me—and it has been
Col 1. 2 May God our Father **give** you grace and peace.
1. 8 has told us of the love that the Spirit has **given** you.
1. 9 with all the wisdom and understanding that his Spirit **gives.**
1.25 the church by God, who **gave** me this task to perform
2.10 and you have been **given** full life in union with him.
3.15 The peace that Christ **gives** is to guide you in the
3.24 Remember that the Lord will **give** you as a reward what he
4. 3 us, so that God will **give** us a good opportunity to preach
4. 6 you should know how to **give** the right answer to everyone.
4. 7 in the Lord's work, will **give** you all the news about me.
4.15 **Give** our best wishes to the brothers in Laodicea and to
4.17 to finish the task you were **given** in the Lord's service."
1 Thes 2. 2 was much opposition, our God **gave** us courage to tell you the
4. 2 you know the instructions we **gave** you by the authority of
4. 8 not rejecting man, but God, who **gives** you his Holy Spirit.
5.23 May the God who **gives** us peace make you holy in every
2 Thes 1. 2 Father and the Lord Jesus Christ **give** you grace and peace.
1. 7 you suffer, [7]and he will **give** relief to you who suffer and
2.16 us and in his grace **gave** us unfailing courage and a firm
3. 4 And the Lord **gives** us confidence in you, and we are sure
3. 5 God's love and the endurance that is **given** by Christ.
3. 6 who do not follow the instructions that we **gave** them.
3.16 is our source of peace, **give** you peace at all times and
1 Tim 1. 2 Father and Christ Jesus our Lord **give** you grace, mercy, and
1.10 for those who lie and **give** false testimony or who do
1.12 Christ Jesus our Lord, who has **given** me strength for my work.
1.14 abundant grace on me and **gave** me the faith and love which
2. 6 the man Christ Jesus, [6]who **gave** himself to redeem all mankind.
4. 6 If you **give** these instructions to the brothers, you will
4.11 **Give** them these instructions and these teachings.
4.13 Until I come, **give** your time and effort to the public
4.14 is in you, which was **given** to you when the prophets spoke
5. 6 But a widow who **gives** herself to pleasure has already died,
5. 7 **Give** them these instructions, so that no one will find
5.14 their homes, so as to **give** our enemies no chance of speaking
5.18 "A worker should be **given** his pay."
6.13 Before God, who **gives** life to all things, and before Christ Jesus,
6.17 God, who generously **gives** us everything for our enjoyment.
2 Tim 1. 2 Father and Christ Jesus our Lord **give** you grace, mercy, and
1. 6 alive the gift that God **gave** you when I laid my hands
1. 7 the Spirit that God has **given** us does not make us timid;
1. 8 the Good News, as God **gives** you the strength to do it.
1. 9 He **gave** us this grace by means of Christ Jesus
2.14 your people of this, and **give** them a solemn warning in God's
2.25 may be that God will **give** them the opportunity to repent and
3.15 Scriptures, which are able to **give** you the wisdom that leads
3.16 correcting faults, and **giving** instruction for right living,
4. 4 listening to the truth and **give** their attention to legends.
4. 8 Lord, the righteous Judge, will **give** me on that Day—and not
4.17 Lord stayed with me and **gave** me strength, so that I was
Tit 1. 4 Father and Christ Jesus our Saviour **give** you grace and peace.
2.14 He **gave** himself for us, to rescue us from all wickedness
3. 5 through the Holy Spirit, who **gives** us new birth and new life
3. 8 I want you to **give** special emphasis to these matters, so
3. 8 God may be concerned with **giving** their time to doing good deeds,
3.10 **Give** at least two warnings to the person who causes divisions,
3.15 **Give** our greetings to our friends in the faith.
Phlm 3 Father and the Lord Jesus Christ **give** you grace and peace.
22 the prayers of all of you and **give** me back to you.
Heb 1. 4 just as the name that God **gave** him is greater than theirs.
1. 9 has chosen you and has **given** you the joy of an honour
1. 9 far greater than he **gave** to your companions."
2. 2 The message **given** to our ancestors by the angels was shown
2.13 "Here I am with the children that God has **given** me."
3.11 never enter the land where I would have **given** them rest!' "
3.18 land where I would have **given** them rest"—of whom was he
4. 3 never enter the land where I would have **given** them rest!' "
4. 5 never enter that land where I would have **given** them rest."
4. 8 If Joshua had **given** the people the rest that God had promised,
4.13 is to him that we must all **give** an account of ourselves.
Heb 6.10 you gave and are still **giving** to your fellow-Christians.
6.14 you that I will bless you and **give** you many descendants."
7. 2 and blessed him, [2]and Abraham **gave** him a tenth of all he
7. 4 Abraham, our famous ancestor, **gave** him a tenth of all he got
7.11 priesthood that the Law was **given** to the people of Israel.
8. 6 But now, Jesus has been **given** priestly work which is
10.15 And the Holy Spirit also **gives** us his witness.
11. 8 go out to a country which God had promised to **give** him.
11.31 for she **gave** the Israelite spies a friendly welcome.
12.25 to hear the one who **gave** the divine message on earth
13.17 since they must **give** God an account of their service.
13.24 **Give** our greetings to all your leaders and to all God's people.
Jas 1. 5 wisdom, he should pray to God, who will **give** it to him;
1. 5 because God **gives** generously and graciously to all.
2. 7 speak evil of that good name which has been **given** to you.
2.16 if you don't **give** them the necessities of life?
4. 6 But the grace that God **gives** is even stronger.
4. 6 "God resists the proud, but **gives** grace to the humble."
1 Pet 1. 3 of his great mercy he **gave** us new life by raising Jesus
1.10 and they prophesied about this gift which God would **give** you.
1.13 which will be **given** you when Jesus Christ is revealed.
1.21 in God, who raised him from death and **gave** him glory;
2.11 Do not **give** in to bodily passions, which are always at war
3. 9 is what God promised to **give** you when he called you.
4. 5 But they will have to **give** an account of themselves to God,
4.11 with the strength that God **gives** him, so that in all things
4.11 all things praise may be **given** to God through Jesus Christ,
5. 2 of the flock that God **gave** you and to take care
5.10 will himself perfect you and **give** you firmness, strength,
5.12 want to encourage you and **give** my testimony that this is the
2 Pet 1. 1 Saviour Jesus Christ have been **given** a faith as precious as ours:
1. 3 God's divine power has **given** us everything we need
1. 4 In this way he has **given** us the very great and precious
1.11 this way you will be **given** the full right to enter the
1.17 were there when he was **given** honour and glory by God the
2.21 then turn away from the sacred command that was **given** them.
3. 2 the Lord and Saviour which was **given** you by your apostles.
3. 5 fact that long ago God **gave** a command, and the heavens
3.15 as the opportunity he is **giving** you to be saved, just as
3.15 Paul wrote to you, using the wisdom that God **gave** him.
1 Jn 2.25 And this is what Christ himself promised to **give** us—eternal life.
3.16 Christ **gave** his life for us.
3.16 We too, then, ought to **give** our lives for our brothers!
3.24 the Spirit that God has **given** us we know that God lives
4.13 lives in union with us, because he has **given** us his Spirit.
4.21 The command that Christ has **given** us is this:
5. 8 and all three **give** the same testimony.
5. 9 stronger, and he has **given** this testimony about his Son.
5.11 God has **given** us eternal life, and this life has its source
5.15 we know also that he **gives** us what we ask from him.
5.16 to death, you should pray to God, who will **give** him life.
5.20 God has come and has **given** us understanding, so that we know
2 Jn 3 and Jesus Christ, the Father's Son, **give** us grace, mercy,
Jude 3 faith which once and for all God has **given** to his people.
11 they have **given themselves over** to the error that Balaam
21 Lord Jesus Christ in his mercy to **give** you eternal life.
Rev 1. 1 God **gave** him this revelation in order to show his servants
2. 7 win the victory I will **give** the right to eat the fruit
2.10 means death, and I will **give** you life as your prize of
2.17 who win the victory I will **give** some of the hidden manna.
2.17 I will also **give** each of them a white stone on which
2.21 I have **given** her time to repent of her sins,
2.26 what I want, I will **give** the same authority that I received
2.26 I will **give** them authority over the nations, to rule them
2.26 I will also **give** them the morning star.
3.21 win the victory I will **give** the right to sit beside me
4.11 and by your will they were **given** existence and life."
6. 2 Its rider held a bow, and he was **given** a crown.
6. 4 Its rider was **given** the power to bring war on the earth,
6. 4 He was **given** a large sword.
6. 8 They were **given** authority over a quarter of the earth, to
6.11 Each of them was **given** a white robe, and they were told
7. 2 angels to whom God had **given** the power to damage the earth
8. 2 who stand before God, and they were **given** seven trumpets.
8. 3 He was **given** a lot of incense to add to the prayers
9. 1 to the earth, and it was **given** the key to the abyss.
9. 3 the earth, and they were **given** the same kind of power that
10. 9 to the angel and asked him to **give** me the little scroll.
11. 1 I was then **given** a stick that looked like a measuring-rod,
11. 2 because they have been **given** to the heathen, who will trample
12.14 She was **given** the two wings of a large eagle in order
13. 2 The dragon **gave** the beast his own power, his throne,
13. 4 the dragon because he had **given** his authority to the beast.
13. 7 defeat them, and it was **given** authority over every tribe,
15. 2 holding harps that God had **given** them [3]and singing the song
15. 7 four living creatures **gave** the seven angels seven gold bowls
16. 6 of the prophets, and so you have **given** them blood to drink.
17.12 but who will be **given** authority to rule as kings for
17.13 the same purpose, and they **give** their power and authority to
17.17 purpose by acting together and **giving** the beast their power
18. 7 **Give** her as much suffering and grief
18. 7 as the glory and luxury she **gave** herself.
19. 8 She has been **given** clean shining linen to wear."
20. 4 and those who sat on them were **given** the power to judge.
20.13 Then the sea **gave** up its dead.
20.13 the world of the dead also **gave** up the dead they held.
21. 6 who is thirsty I will **give** the right to drink from the
22. 6 And the Lord God, who **gives** his Spirit to the prophets, has
22.12 my rewards with me, to **give** to each one according to what
22.20 He who **gives** his testimony to all this says, "Yes

GIVE UP

Mt 13.21 persecution comes because of the message, they **give up** at once.
24.10 Many will **give up** their faith at that time;
Mk 4.17 persecution comes because of the message, they **give up** at once.
Lk 12.20 This very night you will have to **give up** your life;
14.33 can be my disciple unless he **gives up** everything he has.
Jn 6.61 he said to them, "Does this make you want to **give up?**
10.17 because I am willing to **give up** my life, in order that
10.18 I **give it up** of my own free will.
10.18 have the right to **give it up**, and I have the right
16. 1 told you this, so that you will not **give up** your faith.
Acts 18. 9 on speaking and do not **give up**, [10]for I am with you.
21.14 not convince him, so we **gave up** and said, "May the Lord's
27.15 headed into the wind, we **gave up** trying and let it be
27.20 We finally **gave up** all hope of being saved.
Rom 1.27 the men **give up** natural sexual relations with women
1 Cor 13. 3 everything I have, and even **give up** my body to be burnt
13. 7 Love never **gives up;**
2 Cor 1. 8 and so heavy that we **gave up** all hope of staying alive.
2. 7 to keep him from becoming so sad as to **give up** completely.
Gal 6. 9 for if we do not **give up**, the time will come when
Eph 6.18 For this reason keep alert and never **give up;**
Phil 2. 7 his own free will he **gave up** all he had, and took
1 Tim 1. 4 Tell them to **give up** those legends and those long lists of
Tit 2.12 That grace instructs us to **give up** ungodly living
Heb 10.25 Let us not **give up** the habit of meeting together,
12. 2 He did not **give up** because of the cross!
12. 3 So do not let yourselves become discouraged and **give up.**
Rev 2. 3 you have suffered for my sake, and you have not **given up.**
12.11 and they were willing to **give up** their lives and die.

GLAD

Gen 23. 6 Any of us would be **glad** to give you a grave,
Ex 4.14 now coming to meet you and will be **glad** to see you.
8. 9 Moses replied, "I will be **glad** to pray for you.
Deut 28.47 but you would not serve him with **glad** and joyful hearts.
30. 9 He will be as **glad** to make you prosperous as he was
Judg 5. 2 the people **gladly** volunteered.
5. 9 commanders of Israel, with the people who **gladly** volunteered.
8.25 The people answered, "We'll be **glad** to give them to you."
1 Sam 19. 5 When you saw it, you were **glad.**
2 Sam 1.20 Do not make the women of Philistia **glad;**
1 Chr 16.10 Be **glad** that we belong to him;
16.31 Be **glad**, earth and sky!
16.32 be **glad**, fields, and everything in you!
Job 22.19 Good men are **glad** and innocent men laugh when they see
31.29 I have never been **glad** when my enemies suffered, or pleased
33.32 I would **gladly** admit you are in the right.
Ps 13. 5 I will be **glad**, because you will rescue me.
16. 9 so I am thankful and **glad**, and I feel completely secure,
21. 1 The king is **glad**, O Lord, because you gave him strength;
28. 7 He gives me help and makes me **glad;**
31. 7 I will be **glad** and rejoice because of your constant love.
32.11 You that are righteous, be **glad** and rejoice because of what
33.21 We are **glad** because of him;
34. 2 may all who are oppressed listen and be **glad!**
34. 5 The oppressed look to him and are **glad;**
35. 9 Then I will be **glad** because of the Lord;
35.15 trouble, they were all **glad** and gathered round to mock me;
40.16 May all who come to you be **glad** and joyful.
45.15 With joy and **gladness** they come and enter the king's palace.
48.11 let the people of Zion be **glad!**
51. 8 Let me hear the sounds of joy and **gladness;**
51.14 and save me, and I will **gladly** proclaim your righteousness.
54. 6 I will **gladly** offer you a sacrifice, O Lord;
58.10 The righteous will be **glad** when they see sinners punished;
63. 5 be satisfied, and I will sing **glad** songs of praise to you.
67. 4 May the nations be **glad** and sing for joy, because you
68. 3 But the righteous are **glad** and rejoice in his presence;
68. 4 His name is the Lord—be **glad** in his presence!
69.32 When the oppressed see this, they will be **glad;**
70. 4 May all who come to you be **glad** and joyful.
86. 4 Make your servant **glad**, O Lord, because my prayers go up
90.14 love, so that we may sing and be **glad** all our life.
92. 4 Your mighty deeds, O Lord, make me **glad;**
94. 3 How much longer will the wicked be **glad?**
94.19 I am anxious and worried, you comfort me and make me **glad.**
96.11 Be **glad**, earth and sky!
96.12 be **glad**, fields, and everything in you!
97. 1 Earth, be **glad!**
97. 8 The people of Zion are **glad**, and the cities of Judah
97.11 Light shines on the righteous, and **gladness** on the good.
97.12 you that are righteous be **glad** because of what the Lord has
104.34 he be pleased with my song, for my **gladness** comes from him.
105. 3 Be **glad** that we belong to him;
105.38 Egyptians were afraid of them and were **glad** when they left.
106. 5 of your nation, in the **glad** pride of those who belong to
107.30 They were **glad** because of the calm, and he brought them
107.42 righteous see this and are **glad**, but all the wicked are put
109.28 May my persecutors be defeated, and may I, your servant, be **glad.**
118.15 Listen to the **glad** shouts of victory in the tents of
119.74 who honour you will be **glad** when they see me, because I
122. 1 I was **glad** when they said to me, "Let us go to
149. 2 Be **glad**, Israel, because of your Creator;
Prov 22.18 teachings, [18]and you will be **glad** if you remember them
24.17 Don't be **glad** when your enemy meets disaster,
Ecc 7.14 going well for you, be **glad**, and when trouble comes,
Song 3.11 on his wedding day, on the day of his **gladness** and joy.
Is 14.29 beat you is broken, but you have no reason to be **glad.**
Is 16. 9 because there is no harvest to make the people **glad.**
29.24 those who are always grumbling will be **glad** to be taught."
35.10 reach Jerusalem with **gladness**, singing and shouting for joy.
48.20 Shout the news **gladly;**
51. 3 Joy and **gladness** will be there, and songs of praise and
51.11 reach Jerusalem with **gladness**, singing and shouting for joy.
61. 3 mourn in Zion Joy and **gladness** instead of grief,
65.18 Be **glad** and rejoice for ever in what I create.
66.10 be **glad** for her, all you that love this city!
66.14 When you see this happen, you will be **glad;**
Jer 7.34 the sounds of joy and **gladness** and to the happy sounds of
16. 9 the sounds of joy and **gladness** and the happy sounds of
20.15 man who made my father **glad** when he brought him the news,
25.10 their shouts of joy and **gladness** and the happy sounds of
31.13 and turn their mourning into joy, their sorrow into **gladness.**
33.11 hear again [11]the shouts of **gladness** and joy and the happy
41.13 with him, they were **glad**, [14]and turned and ran to them.
50.11 You are happy and **glad**, going about like a cow threshing
Lam 1.21 My enemies are **glad** that you brought disaster on me.
4.21 be **glad** while you can.
Ezek 25. 4 Because you were **glad**, I will let the tribes from the
Joel 2.21 afraid, but be joyful and **glad** because of all the Lord has
2.23 "Be **glad**, people of Zion, rejoice at what the Lord your
Amos 8.10 into funerals and change your **glad** songs into cries of grief.
Obad 12 You should not have been **glad** on the day of their ruin.
Hab 3.18 will still be joyful and **glad**, because the Lord God is my
Zech 4.10 Zerubbabel continuing to build the Temple, and they will be **glad."**
8.19 become festivals of joy and **gladness** for the people of Judah.
10. 7 remember this victory and be **glad** because of what the Lord
Mt 5.12 Be happy and **glad**, for a great reward is kept for you
13.20 who receive the message **gladly** as soon as they hear it.
Mk 4.16 As soon as they hear the message, they receive it **gladly.**
12.37 A large crowd was listening to Jesus **gladly.**
Lk 1.14 How **glad** and happy you will be, and how happy many
1.44 I heard your greeting, the baby within me jumped with **gladness.**
1.47 my soul is **glad** because of God my Saviour,
6.23 Be **glad** when that happens, and dance for joy,
8.13 stand for those who hear the message and receive it **gladly.**
10.20 But don't be **glad** because the evil spirits obey you;
10.20 rather be **glad** because your names are written in heaven."
Jn 3.29 is **glad** when he hears the bridegroom's voice.
4.36 man who sows and the man who reaps will be **glad** together.
8.56 he saw it and was **glad."**
11.15 for your sake I am **glad** that I was not with him,
14.28 loved me, you would be **glad** that I am going to the
16.20 you will cry and weep, but the world will be **glad;**
16.20 you will be sad, but your sadness will turn into **gladness.**
16.22 hearts will be filled with **gladness,**
16.22 the kind of **gladness** that no one can take away
Acts 2.26 so I am filled with **gladness**, and my words are full of
2.46 eating with **glad** and humble hearts, [47]praising God,
11.23 blessed the people, he was **glad** and urged them all to be
13.48 Gentiles heard this, they were **glad** and praised the Lord's
2 Cor 2. 3 be made sad by the very people who should make me **glad.**
6.10 although saddened, we are always **glad;**
9. 7 for God loves the one who gives **gladly.**
11. 4 For you **gladly** tolerate anyone who comes to you and preaches
11.19 You yourselves are so wise, and so you **gladly** tolerate fools!
12.15 I will be **glad** to spend all I have, and myself as
13. 9 We are **glad** when we are weak but you are strong.
Phil 2.17 that is so, I am **glad** and share my joy with you
2.18 you too must be **glad** and share your joy with me.
2.28 so that you will be **glad** again when you see him,
Col 2. 5 in spirit, and I am **glad** as I see the resolute firmness
Heb 10.34 you endured your loss **gladly**, because you knew that you still
12.11 to us at the time something to make us sad, not **glad.**
13.17 If you obey them, they will do their work **gladly;**
Jas 1. 9 who is poor must be **glad** when God lifts him up,
1.10 and the rich Christian must be **glad** when God brings him down.
1 Pet 1. 6 Be **glad** about this, even though it may now be necessary
4.13 Rather be **glad** that you are sharing Christ's sufferings,
Rev 12.12 And so be **glad**, you heavens, and all you that live there!
18.20 Be **glad**, heaven, because of her destruction!
18.20 Be **glad**, God's people and the apostles and prophets!
19. 7 Let us rejoice and be **glad;**

GLAMOUR

Rev 18.14 and all your wealth and **glamour** are gone, and you will never

GLANCE

Song 2. 9 He looks in through the window and **glances** through the lattice.
6.10 Who is this whose **glance** is like the dawn?
Hab 2. 2 reveal to you, so that it can be read at a **glance.**
3. 6 at his **glance** the nations tremble.

GLARE

2 Kgs 2.24 Elisha turned round, **glared** at them, and cursed them
Job 15.12 But you are excited and **glare** at us in anger.
16. 9 he **glares** at me with hate.
Ps 35.16 men who would mock a cripple, they **glared** at me with hate.
37.12 man plots against the good man and **glares** at him with hate.
112.10 they **glare** in hate and disappear;
Lam 2.16 All your enemies mock you and **glare** at you with hate.

GLASS

Job 28.17 is worth more than gold, Than a gold vase or finest **glass.**
Rev 4. 6 was what looked like a sea of **glass**, clear as crystal.

Rev 15. 2 I saw what looked like a sea of **glass** mixed with fire.
15. 2 standing by the sea of **glass**, holding harps that God had
21.18 the city itself was made of pure gold, as clear as **glass**.
21.21 The street of the city was of pure gold, transparent as **glass**.

GLAZE

Prov 26.23 really thinking is like a fine **glaze** on a cheap clay pot.

GLEAM

Nah 3. 3 Horsemen charge, swords flash, spears **gleam!**
Hab 3.11 your speeding arrows and the **gleam** of your shining spear,
Rev 4. 3 His face **gleamed** like such precious stones as jasper and carnelian,

GLEE

Ezek 36. 5 With **glee** and contempt, they captured my land and took

GLITTER

Ps 68.13 doves covered with silver, whose wings **glittered** with fine gold.
Lam 4. 1 Our **glittering** gold has grown dull;

GLOAT

1 Sam 31. 4 these godless Philistines won't **gloat** over me and kill me."
1 Chr 10. 4 to keep these godless Philistines from **gloating** over me."
Ps 13. 4 Don't let them **gloat** over my downfall.
25. 2 don't let my enemies **gloat** over me!
30. 1 have saved me and kept my enemies from **gloating** over me.
35.19 Don't let my enemies, those liars, **gloat** over my defeat.
35.24 don't let my enemies **gloat** over me.
35.26 May those who **gloat** over my suffering be completely defeated
38.16 Don't let my enemies **gloat** over my distress;
Prov 24.18 will know if you are **gloating**, and he will not like it;
Ezek 36. 2 Israel's enemies **gloated** and said, 'Now those ancient hills are
Obad 12 should not have **gloated** over the misfortune of your brothers
13 city of my people to **gloat** over their suffering and to seize
Mic 7. 8 Our enemies have no reason to **gloat** over us.
Hab 3.14 a storm to scatter us, **gloating** like those who secretly oppress

GLOOM

1 Kgs 21.27 slept in the sackcloth, and went about **gloomy** and depressed.
Job 3. 5 Make it a day of **gloom** and thick darkness;
10.21 land that is dark and **gloomy**, [22] a land of darkness, shadows,
30.28 I go about in **gloom**, without any sunshine;
Ps 107.10 Some were living in **gloom** and darkness, prisoners suffering
107.14 brought them out of their **gloom** and darkness and broke their
Prov 17.22 It is slow death to be **gloomy** all the time.
Joel 2. 2 will be a dark and **gloomy** day, a black and cloudy day.
Amos 5.20 it will be a day of **gloom**, without any brightness.
Zeph 1.15 a day of darkness and **gloom**, a black and cloudy day,
Mk 10.22 When the man heard this, **gloom** spread over his face, and
Heb 12.18 fire, the darkness and the **gloom**, the storm, [19] the blast
Jas 4. 9 change your laughter into crying, your joy into **gloom!**

GLORY

Ex 15. 1 sing to the Lord, because he has won a **glorious** victory;
15.21 "Sing to the Lord, because he has won a **glorious** victory;
Lev 10. 3 I will reveal my **glory** to my people.' "
Deut 5.24 us his greatness and his **glory** when we heard him speak from
1 Sam 4.21 the boy Ichabod, explaining, "God's **glory** has left Israel"—
4.22 "God's **glory** has left Israel," she said, "because God's
1 Chr 16.24 Proclaim his **glory** to the nations, his mighty deeds to all
16.27 **Glory** and majesty surround him, power and joy fill his
16.28 Praise the Lord, all people on earth, praise his **glory**
16.29 Praise the Lord's **glorious** name;
23.30 to praise and **glorify** the Lord every morning and every evening
29.11 You are great and powerful, **glorious**, splendid, and
29.13 God, we give you thanks, and we praise your **glorious** name.
29.25 and he made him more **glorious** than any other king that had
Neh 9. 5 Let everyone praise his **glorious** name, although no human praise
Job 37.22 in the north, and the **glory** of God fills us with awe.
40.10 clothe yourself with majesty and **glory**.
Ps 8. 5 you crowned him with **glory** and honour.
19. 1 How clearly the sky reveals God's **glory!**
21. 5 His **glory** is great because of your help;
26. 8 where you live, O Lord, the place where your **glory** dwells.
29. 1 praise his **glory** and power.
29. 2 Praise the Lord's **glorious** name;
29. 3 **glorious** God thunders, and his voice echoes over the ocean.
29. 9 while everyone in his Temple shouts, **"Glory** to God!"
45. 3 you are **glorious** and majestic.
57. 5 in the sky, O God, and your **glory** over all the earth.
57.11 in the sky, O God, and your **glory** over all the earth.
63. 2 let me see how mighty and **glorious** you are.
66. 2 Sing to the **glory** of his name;
66. 2 offer him **glorious** praise!
71. 8 All day long I praise you and proclaim your **glory**.
72.19 Praise his **glorious** name for ever!
72.19 May his **glory** fill the whole world.
76. 4 How **glorious** you are, O God!
78.61 the Covenant Box, the symbol of his power and **glory**.
84.11 Lord is our protector and **glorious** king, blessing us with
90.16 let our descendants see your **glorious** might.
96. 3 Proclaim his **glory** to the nations, his mighty deeds to all
96. 6 **Glory** and majesty surround him;
Ps 96. 7 praise his **glory** and might.
96. 8 Praise the Lord's **glorious** name;
97. 6 proclaim his righteousness, and all the nations see his **glory**.
104. 1 You are clothed with majesty and **glory;**
104.31 May the **glory** of the Lord last for ever!
106.20 they exchanged the **glory** of God for the image of an
108. 5 in the sky, O God, and your **glory** over all the earth.
113. 4 his **glory** is above the heavens.
115. 1 and not to us, must **glory** be given because of your constant
138. 5 sing about what you have done and about your great **glory**.
145. 5 They will speak of your **glory** and majesty, and I will
145.11 They will speak of the **glory** of your royal power and
145.12 know your mighty deeds and the **glorious** majesty of your kingdom.
148.13 his **glory** is above earth and heaven.
Prov 4. 9 She will be your crowning **glory."**
16.31 grey hair is a **glorious** crown.
Is 2.10 from the Lord's anger and to hide from his power and **glory!**
2.19 hide from his power and **glory**, when he comes to shake the
2.21 escape from his anger and to hide from his power and **glory**.
4. 5 God's **glory** will cover and protect the whole city.
4. 6 His **glory** will shade the city from the heat of the day
6. 3 His **glory** fills the world."
24.23 Mount Zion, and the leaders of the people will see his **glory**.
28. 1 Its **glory** is fading like the crowns of flowers on the heads
28. 4 The fading **glory** of those proud leaders will disappear like
28. 5 Almighty will be like a **glorious** crown of flowers for his
30.27 The Lord's power and **glory** can be seen in the distance.
33.21 The Lord will show us his **glory**.
40. 5 Then the **glory** of the Lord will be revealed, and all
42. 8 No other god may share my **glory;**
42.12 live in distant lands give praise and **glory** to the Lord!
43. 7 are my own people, and I created them to bring me **glory."**
48.11 let anyone else share the **glory** that should be mine and mine
55. 5 I will give you honour and **glory."**
60. 1 The **glory** of the Lord is shining on you!
60. 7 The Lord will make his Temple more **glorious** than ever.
60.13 Jerusalem, To make my Temple beautiful, To make my city **glorious.**
60.19 The light of my **glory** will shine on you.
62. 2 All their kings will see your **glory**.
63.15 us from heaven, where you live in your holiness and **glory**.
Jer 14.21 bring disgrace on Jerusalem, the place of your **glorious** throne.
17.12 Temple is like a **glorious** throne, standing on a high mountain
48.17 its **glory** and might are no more.'
Lam 5.21 Restore our ancient **glory**.
Ezek 3.12 that said, "Praise the **glory** of the Lord in heaven above!"
3.23 and there I saw the **glory** of the Lord, just as I
7.11 remain, nothing of their wealth, their splendour, or their **glory**.
27.10 They are the men who won **glory** for you.
39.21 let the nations see my **glory** and show them how I use
43. 5 saw that the Temple was filled with the **glory** of the Lord.
Dan 4.30 city to display my power and might, my **glory** and majesty."
4.34 God and gave honour and **glory** to the one who lives for
4.36 honour, my majesty, and the **glory** of my kingdom were given
4.37 I, Nebuchadnezzar, praise, honour, and **glorify** the King of Heaven.
Nah 2. 2 is about to restore the **glory** of Israel, as it was before
Hab 2.14 the knowledge of the Lord's **glory** as the seas are full of
Zech 2. 5 protect it and that he will live there in all his **glory."**
11. 2 those **glorious** trees have been destroyed!
11. 3 their **glory** is gone!
Mt 16.27 about to come in the **glory** of his Father with his angels,
19.28 of Man sits on his **glorious** throne in the New Age,
24.30 Man coming on the clouds of heaven with power and great **glory**.
Mk 8.38 when he comes in the **glory** of his Father with the holy
10.37 on your throne in your **glorious** Kingdom, we want you to let
13.26 Man will appear, coming in the clouds with great power and **glory**.
Lk 2. 9 appeared to them, and the **glory** of the Lord shone over them.
2.14 **"Glory** to God in the highest heaven, and peace on earth
2.32 to the Gentiles and bring **glory** to your people Israel."
9.26 when he comes in his **glory**
9.26 and in the **glory** of the Father
9.31 Elijah, [31] who appeared in heavenly **glory** and talked with Jesus
9.32 woke up and saw Jesus' **glory** and the two men who were
19.38 Peace in heaven and **glory** to God!"
21.27 Man will appear, coming in a cloud with great power and **glory**.
24.26 Messiah to suffer these things and then to enter his **glory?"**
Jn 1.14 We saw his **glory**, the glory which he received as the
2.11 he revealed his **glory**, and his disciples believed in him.
7.18 on his own authority is trying to gain **glory** for himself.
7.18 But he who wants **glory** for the one who sent him is
7.39 yet been given, because Jesus had not been raised to **glory**.
11. 4 happened in order to bring **glory** to God, and it will be
11. 4 be the means by which the Son of God will receive **glory."**
11.40 I tell you that you would see God's **glory** if you believed?"
12.16 Jesus had been raised to **glory**, they remembered that the
12.23 has now come for the Son of Man to receive great **glory**.
12.28 Father, bring **glory** to your name!"
12.28 from heaven, "I have brought **glory** to it, and I will do
12.41 Isaiah said this because he saw Jesus' **glory**
13.31 Jesus said, "Now the Son of Man's **glory** is revealed;
13.31 now God's **glory** is revealed through him.
13.32 And if God's **glory** is revealed through him,
13.32 then God will reveal the **glory** of the Son of Man
14.13 so that the Father's **glory** will be shown through the Son.
15. 8 My Father's **glory** is shown by your bearing much fruit;
16.14 He will give me **glory**, because he will take what I say
17. 1 Give **glory** to your Son,
17. 1 so that the Son may give **glory** to you.
17. 4 I have shown your **glory** on earth;
17. 5 Give me **glory** in your presence now,

Jn	17. 5	the same **glory** I had with you before
	17.10	and my **glory** is shown through them.
	17.22	I gave them the same **glory** you gave me,
	17.24	so that they may see my **glory,** the glory you gave me;
	21.19	the way in which Peter would die and bring **glory** to God.)
Acts	2.20	before the great and **glorious** Day of the Lord comes.
	3.13	God of our ancestors, has given divine **glory** to his Servant
	7. 2	in Haran, the God of **glory** appeared to him in Mesopotamia
	7.55	and saw God's **glory** and Jesus standing at the right-hand
Rom	2. 7	keep on doing good, and seek **glory,** honour, and immortal life;
	2.10	But God will give **glory,** honour, and peace to all who do
	3. 7	if my untruth serves God's **glory** by making his truth stand
	5. 2	so we boast of the hope we have of sharing God's **glory!**
	6. 4	raised from death by the **glorious** power of the Father, so
	8.17	we share Christ's suffering, we will also share his **glory.**
	8.18	compared at all with the **glory** that is going to be revealed
	8.21	and would share the **glorious** freedom of the children of God.
	8.30	put right with himself, and he shared his **glory** with them.
	9. 4	he made them his sons and revealed his **glory** to them;
	9.23	wanted to reveal his abundant **glory,** which was poured out on
	9.23	those of us whom he has prepared to receive his **glory.**
	11.36	To God be the **glory** for ever!
	15. 7	one another, then, for the **glory** of God, as Christ has
	16.25	Let us give **glory** to God!
	16.27	who alone is all-wise, be **glory** through Jesus Christ for ever!
1 Cor	2. 7	already chosen for our **glory** even before the world was made.
	2. 8	known it, they would not have crucified the Lord of **glory.**
	6.20	So use your bodies for God's **glory.**
	10.31	do, whether you eat or drink, do it all for God's **glory.**
	11. 7	his head, because he reflects the image and **glory** of God.
	11. 7	But woman reflects the **glory** of man;
2 Cor	1.20	Jesus Christ our "Amen" is said to the **glory** of God.
	3. 7	on stone tablets, and God's **glory** appeared when it was given.
	3. 7	came with such **glory,** [8]how much greater is the glory
	3. 9	The system which brings condemnation was **glorious;**
	3. 9	much more **glorious** is the activity which brings salvation!
	3.10	because of the far brighter **glory** now
	3.10	the **glory** that was so bright
	3.11	For if there was **glory** in that which lasted for a while,
	3.11	how much more **glory** is there in that which lasts
	3.18	reflect the **glory** of the Lord with uncovered faces;
	3.18	that same **glory,** coming from the Lord, who is the Spirit,
	3.18	us into his likeness in an ever greater degree of **glory.**
	4. 4	the Good News about the **glory** of Christ, who is the exact
	4. 6	the knowledge of God's **glory** shining in the face of Christ.
	4.15	offer to the **glory** of God more prayers of thanksgiving.
	4.17	a tremendous and eternal **glory,** much greater than the trouble.
	8.19	the sake of the Lord's **glory,** and in order to show that
	8.23	they represent the churches and bring **glory** to Christ.
	9.13	many will give **glory** to God for your loyalty
Gal	1. 5	To God be the **glory** for ever and ever!
Eph	1. 6	us praise God for his **glorious** grace, for the free gift he
	1.12	who were the first to hope in Christ, praise God's **glory!**
	1.14	Let us praise his **glory!**
	1.17	Lord Jesus Christ, the **glorious** Father, to give you the Spirit,
	3.16	from the wealth of his **glory** to give you power through his
	3.21	to God be the **glory** in the church and in Christ Jesus
Phil	1.11	Jesus Christ can produce, for the **glory** and praise of God.
	2.11	that Jesus Christ is Lord, to the **glory** of God the Father.
	3.21	make them like his own **glorious** body, using that power by
	4.20	To our God and Father be the **glory** for ever and ever!
Col	1.11	strength which comes from his **glorious** power, so that you
	1.27	his people, this rich and **glorious** secret which he has for
	1.27	which means that you will share in the **glory** of God.
	3. 4	then you too will appear with him and share his **glory!**
1 Thes	2.12	God, who calls you to share in his own Kingdom and **glory.**
2 Thes	1. 9	the Lord and from his **glorious** might, [10]when he comes on
	1.10	on that Day to receive **glory** from all his people and honour
	1.12	Lord Jesus will receive **glory** from you, and you from him,
	2.14	to possess your share of the **glory** of our Lord Jesus Christ.
1 Tim	1.11	announce, the Good News from the **glorious** and blessed God.
	1.17	only God—to him be honour and **glory** for ever and ever!
2 Tim	2.10	salvation that comes through Christ Jesus and brings eternal **glory.**
	4.18	To him be the **glory** for ever and ever!
Tit	2.13	we hope for, when the **glory** of our great God and Saviour
Heb	1. 3	reflects the brightness of God's **glory** and is the exact likeness
	2. 7	you crowned him with **glory** and honour, [8]and made him ruler
	2. 9	see him now crowned with **glory** and honour because of the
	2.10	suffering, in order to bring many sons to share his **glory.**
	13.20	And to Christ be the **glory** for ever and ever!
Jas	2. 1	Jesus Christ, the Lord of **glory,** you must never treat people
1 Pet	1. 7	you will receive praise and **glory** and honour on the Day when
	1. 8	rejoice with a great and **glorious** joy which words cannot express,
	1.11	Christ would have to endure and the **glory** that would follow.
	1.21	in God, who raised him from death and gave him **glory;**
	1.24	are like grass, and all their **glory** is like wild flowers.
	4.11	Jesus Christ, to whom belong **glory** and power for ever and ever.
	4.13	that you may be full of joy when his **glory** is revealed.
	4.14	means that the **glorious** Spirit, the Spirit of God, is resting
	5. 1	and I will share in the **glory** that will be revealed.
	5. 4	you will receive the **glorious** crown which will never lose its
	5.10	you to share his eternal **glory** in union with Christ,
2 Pet	1. 3	one who called us to share in his own **glory** and goodness.
	1.17	he was given honour and **glory** by God the Father, when the
	1.17	to him from the Supreme **Glory,** saying, "This is my own dear
	2.10	arrogant, and show no respect for the **glorious** beings above;
	3.18	To him be the **glory,** now and for ever!
Jude	8	despise God's authority and insult the **glorious** beings above.
	24	faultless and joyful before his **glorious** presence—
	25	Jesus Christ our Lord, be **glory,** majesty, might, and authority,
Rev	1. 6	To Jesus Christ be the **glory** and power for ever and ever!
	4. 9	living creatures sing songs of **glory** and honour and thanks
	4.11	You are worthy to receive **glory,** honour, and power.
	5.12	to receive power, wealth, wisdom, and strength, honour, **glory,**
	5.13	Lamb, be praise and honour, **glory** and might, for ever and ever!"
	7.12	Praise, **glory,** wisdom, thanksgiving, honour, power, and might
	15. 8	filled with smoke from the **glory** and power of God,
	18. 7	suffering and grief as the **glory** and luxury she gave herself.
	19. 1	Salvation, **glory,** and power belong to our God!
	21.11	of heaven from God [11]and shining with the **glory** of God.
	21.23	shine on it, because the **glory** of God shines on it,

GLOW

Job	37.22	A golden **glow** is seen in the north, and the glory of
	41.18	when he sneezes, and his eyes **glow** like the rising sun.
Prov	26.21	Charcoal keeps the embers **glowing,** wood keeps the fire
Song	4. 3	Your cheeks **glow** behind your veil.
	6. 7	Your cheeks **glow** behind your veil.
Is	54.12	your gates with stones that **glow** like fire, and the wall
Lam	4. 7	and pure as snow, vigorous and strong, **glowing** with health.
Ezek	1. 4	from a huge cloud, and the sky round it was **glowing.**

GLUTTON

Prov	23.21	Drunkards and **gluttons** will be reduced to poverty.
Mt	11.19	He is a **glutton** and a drinker, a friend of tax collectors
Lk	7.34	He is a **glutton** and a drinker, a friend of tax collectors
Tit	1.12	"Cretans are always liars, wicked beasts, and lazy **gluttons."**

Am **GNASH see GRIND (teeth)**

GNAT

Ex	8.16	over the land of Egypt the dust will change into **gnats."**
	8.17	in Egypt was turned into **gnats,** which covered the people
	8.18	to use their magic to make **gnats** appear, but they failed.
	8.18	were **gnats** everywhere, [19]and the magicians said to the king,
Ps	105.31	and flies and **gnats** swarmed throughout the whole country.

GNAW

Job	30. 3	and hungry that they would **gnaw** dry roots—
	30.17	the pain that **gnaws** me never stops.
Jer	50.17	and then King Nebuchadnezzar of Babylonia **gnawed** their bones.

GO

see also **GO OUT, GO WITHOUT, GO-BETWEEN, LET GO**

Mt	4.10	Then Jesus answered, **"Go** away, Satan!
	4.20	At once they left their nets and **went with** him.
	4.22	they left the boat and their father, and **went with** him.
	6.30	that is here today and **gone** tomorrow, burnt up in the oven.
	7.13	**"Go in** through the narrow gate, because the gate to hell
	8. 4	Don't tell anyone, but **go** straight to the priest and let him
	8. 9	I order this one, **'Go!'**
	8. 9	and he **goes;**
	8.19	he said, "I am ready to **go with** you wherever you go."
	8.23	Jesus got into a boat, and his disciples **went with** him.
	8.32	**"Go,"** Jesus told them;
	10. 5	"Do not **go** to any Gentile territory or any Samaritan towns.
	10. 6	Instead, you are to **go** to the lost sheep of the people
	10.11	to a town or village, **go in** and look for someone who
	16.21	to his disciples, "I must **go** to Jerusalem and suffer much
	17.20	seed, you can say to this hill, **'Go** from here to there!'
	17.20	and it will **go.**
	19.24	than for a camel to **go** through the eye of a needle."
	21. 2	**"Go** to the village there ahead of you, and at once you
	21.30	'Yes, sir,' he answered, but he did not **go.**
	22.11	"The king **went in** to look at the guests and saw a
	23.13	faces, and you yourselves don't **go in,** nor do you allow in
	24.26	don't **go** there;
	25.10	five girls who were ready **went in** with him to the wedding
	26.18	**"Go** to a certain man in the city," he said to them,
	26.36	Then Jesus **went with** his disciples to a place called Gethsemane,
	26.46	Get up, let us **go.**
	28. 7	**Go** quickly now, and tell his disciples, 'He has been
	28.10	**"Go** and tell my brothers to go to Galilee, and there they
	28.16	to the hill in Galilee where Jesus had told them to **go.**
	28.19	**Go,** then, to all peoples everywhere and make them my disciples:
Mk	1.18	At once they left their nets and **went with** him.
	1.20	Zebedee in the boat with the hired men and **went with** Jesus.
	5.18	who had had the demons begged him, "Let me **go with** you!"
	5.19	Instead, he told him, **"Go** back home to your family and tell
	5.34	**Go** in peace, and be healed of your trouble."
	5.39	He **went in** and said to them, "Why all this confusion?
	6.38	**Go** and see."
	10.52	**"Go,"** Jesus told him, "your faith has made you well."
	11. 2	**"Go** to the village there ahead of you.
	13.34	be like a man who **goes away** from home on a journey
	14.13	**"Go** into the city, and a man carrying a jar of water
	14.42	Get up, let us **go.**
	16. 7	'He is **going** to Galilee ahead of you;
	16.15	He said to them, **"Go** throughout the whole world and
Lk	1.17	He will **go** ahead of the Lord, strong and mighty like the
	1.76	You will **go** ahead of the Lord to prepare his road for
	2.15	said to one another, "Let's **go** to Bethlehem and see this
	5. 8	on his knees before Jesus and said, **"Go** away from me, Lord!
	7. 6	So Jesus **went with** them.
	7. 8	I order this one, **'Go!'**
	7. 8	and he **goes;**

Lk 7.50 **go** in peace.”
8. 1 The twelve disciples **went with** him, [2]and so did some women
8.38 demons had gone out begged Jesus, “Let me **go with** you.”
8.48 **Go** in peace.”
8.51 he would not let anyone **go in** with him except Peter, John,
9.57 a man said to Jesus, “I will follow you wherever you **go.”**
10.30 once a man who was **going** down from Jerusalem to Jericho when
10.37 Jesus replied, “You **go,** then, and do the same.”
11.37 so he **went in** and sat down to eat.
11.52 you yourselves will not **go in,** and you stop those who are
11.52 and you stop those who are trying to **go in!”**
12.28 that is here today and **gone** tomorrow, burnt up in the oven.
13.24 them, [24]“Do your best to **go in** through the narrow door;
13.24 people will surely try to **go in** but will not be able.
14.23 master said to the servant, **‘Go** out to the country roads and
15.18 I will get up and **go** to my father and say, Father,
17.19 And Jesus said to him, “Get up and **go;**
19. 7 started grumbling, “This man has **gone** as a guest to the
19.30 **“Go** to the village there ahead of you;
19.30 as you **go in,** you will find a colt tied up that
22.39 and the disciples **went with** him.
23.55 had followed Jesus from Galilee **went with** Joseph and saw the
24. 3 away from the entrance to the tomb, [3]so they **went in;**
24.29 So he **went in** to stay with them.
Jn 1.37 The two disciples heard him say this and **went with** Jesus.
1.39 So they **went with** him and saw where he lived, and spent
1.51 heaven open and God’s angels **going** up and coming down on the
3. 8 do not know where it comes from or where it is **going.**
3.13 And no one has ever **gone** up to heaven except the Son
3.26 Well, he is baptizing now, and everyone is **going** to him!”
4.50 Jesus said to him, **“Go,** your son will live!”
6.22 knew that Jesus had not **gone in** it with his disciples, but
6.66 Jesus’ followers turned back and would not **go with** him any more.
6.68 Simon Peter answered him, “Lord, to whom would we **go?**
8.11 **Go,** but do not sin again.”
8.14 because I know where I came from and where I am **going.**
8.14 do not know where I came from or where I am **going.**
8.21 Again Jesus said to them, “I will **go** away;
8.21 You cannot **go** where I am going.”
8.22 said, “He says that we cannot **go** where he is going.
10. 2 The man who **goes in** through the gate is the shepherd of
11. 7 Then he said to the disciples, “Let us **go** back to Judaea.”
11. 8 and are you planning to **go** back?”
11.15 Let us **go** to him.”
11.16 his fellow-disciples, “Let us all **go with** the Teacher, so
12.35 who walks in the dark does not know where he is **going.**
13. 1 come for him to leave this world and **go** to the Father.
13. 3 knew that he had come from God and was **going** to God.
13.33 I told the Jewish authorities, ‘You cannot **go** where I am going.’
13.36 “Where are you **going,** Lord?”
13.36 “You cannot follow me now where I am **going,”** answered Jesus;
14. 4 know the way that leads to the place where I am **going.”**
14. 5 said to him, “Lord, we do not know where you are **going;**
14. 6 no one **goes** to the Father except by me.
14.12 do even greater things, because I am **going** to the Father.
14.18 “When I **go,** you will not be left all alone;
14.28 me, you would be glad that I am **going** to the Father;
14.31 “Come, let us **go** from this place.
16. 5 But now I am **going** to him who sent me,
16. 5 yet none of you asks me where I am **going.**
16. 7 better for you that I **go** away,
16. 7 because if I do not **go,** the Helper will not come to
16. 7 But if I do **go** away, then I will send him to
16.10 is right, because I am **going** to the Father and you will
16.17 he also says, ‘It is because I am **going** to the Father.’
16.28 and now I am leaving the world and **going** to the Father.”
18. 1 a garden in that place, and Jesus and his disciples **went in.**
18.15 the High Priest, so he **went with** Jesus into the courtyard of
19.39 to see Jesus at night, **went with** Joseph, taking with him
20. 5 over and saw the linen wrappings, but he did not **go in.**
20. 8 disciple, who had reached the tomb first, also **went in;**
20.17 her, “because I have not yet **gone** back up to the Father.
20.17 But **go** to my brothers and tell them that I am returning
21.18 will bind you and take you where you don’t want to **go.”**
Acts 1.11 back in the same way that you saw him **go** to heaven.”
2.34 For it was not David who **went up** into heaven;
3. 3 he saw Peter and John **going in,** he begged them to give
7. 3 your family and country and **go** to the land that I will
7.45 it with them when they **went with** Joshua and took over the
8.29 Holy Spirit said to Philip, **“Go** over to that carriage and
9. 6 “But get up and **go** into the city, where you will be
9.11 to him, “Get ready and **go** to Straight Street, and at the
9.15 The Lord said to him, **“Go,** because I have chosen him to
9.39 So Peter got ready and **went with** them.
10.20 and do not hesitate to **go with** them, for I have sent
10.23 The next day he got ready and **went with** them;
10.25 As Peter was about to **go in,** Cornelius met him, fell at
11.12 The Spirit told me to **go with** them without hesitation.
13.46 of eternal life, we will leave you and **go** to the Gentiles.
15.25 They will **go with** our dear friends Barnabas and Paul,
16.36 You may leave, then, and **go** in peace.”
17.15 men who were taking Paul **went with** him as far as Athens
18. 6 From now on I will **go** to the Gentiles.”
20. 4 Sopater son of Pyrrhus, from Berea, **went with** him;
20.25 “I have **gone** about among all of you, preaching the
20.38 And so they **went with** him to the ship.
21. 5 with their wives and children, **went with** us out of the city
21.16 the disciples from Caesarea also **went with** us and took us to
21.18 The next day Paul **went with** us to see James;
21.24 **Go** along with them and join them in the ceremony of
22.21 **‘Go,’** the Lord said to me, ‘for I will send you far
Acts 23.27 a Roman citizen, so I **went with** my soldiers and rescued him.
25.12 appealed to the Emperor, so to the Emperor you will **go.”**
28.26 For he said, **‘Go** and say to this people:
Rom 3.16 they leave ruin and destruction wherever they **go.**
10. 6 “You are not to ask yourself, Who will **go** up into heaven?”
10. 7 are you to ask, Who will **go** down into the world below?”
1 Cor 10. 4 They drank from the spiritual rock that **went with** them;
16.12 When he gets the chance, however, he will **go.**
2 Cor 3.10 now the glory that was so bright in the past is **gone.**
5.17 the old is **gone,** the new has come.
8.23 the other brothers who are **going with** him, they represent the
12.18 I begged Titus to **go,** and I sent the other Christian
Gal 2. 2 I went because God revealed to me that I should **go.**
Eph 3.12 the boldness to **go** into God’s presence with all confidence.
4. 8 the scripture says, “When he **went up** to the very heights,
4. 9 Now, what does “he **went up”** mean?
4.10 is the same one who **went up,** above and beyond the heavens,
Phil 3.16 that may be, let us **go forward** according to the same rules
1 Thes 2.18 I myself tried to **go** back more than once, but Satan would
2 Thes 2. 4 He will even **go in** and sit down in God’s Temple and
Heb 4.14 great High Priest who has **gone** into the very presence of God
6. 1 Let us **go** forward, then, to mature teaching and leave
6. 3 Let us **go** forward!
6.20 On our behalf Jesus has **gone in** there before us, and has
9.25 But Christ did not **go in** to offer himself many times,
11. 8 when God called him to **go** out to a country which God
Jas 1.24 look at himself and then **goes away** and at once forgets what
3. 4 small rudder, and it goes wherever the pilot wants it to **go.**
1 Pet 3.22 Jesus Christ, [22]who has **gone** to heaven and is at the
1 Jn 2.11 not know where he is **going,** because the darkness has made
2 Jn 9 teaching of Christ, but **goes** beyond it, does not have God.
Rev 8. 4 smoke of the burning incense **went up** with the prayers of
11.12 As their enemies watched, they **went up** into heaven in a cloud.
14. 4 They follow the Lamb wherever he **goes.**
14.13 because the results of their service **go with** them.”
16.14 These three spirits **go** out to all the kings of the world,
18.14 your wealth and glamour are **gone,** and you will never find
20. 8 his prison, [8]and he will **go** out to deceive the nations

GO OUT

Mt 3.12 he will burn the chaff in a fire that never **goes out.”**
25. 8 us have some of your oil, because our lamps are **going out.’**
Mk 9.43 and go off to hell, to the fire that never **goes out.**
Lk 3.17 he will burn the chaff in a fire that never **goes out.”**

GO WITHOUT

Mt 6.17 When you **go without** food, wash your face and comb your hair,
Mk 2.19 you expect the guests at a wedding party to **go without** food?
Lk 5.34 guests at a wedding party **go without** food as long as the
8.27 long time this man had **gone without** clothes and would not
Acts 27.21 After the men had **gone** a long time without food, Paul
2 Cor 6. 5 we have been overworked and have **gone without** sleep or food.
11.27 often I have **gone without** sleep;

GO-BETWEEN

Gal 3.19 handed down by angels, with a man acting as a **go-between.**
3.20 a **go-between** is not needed when only one person is involved;

GOAL

Prov 11.27 If your **goals** are good, you will be respected, but if
Phil 3.14 I run straight towards the **goal** in order to win the prize,

GOAT
[MOUNTAIN-GOATS]

Gen 12.16 gave him flocks of sheep and **goats,** cattle, donkeys, slaves,
13. 2 very rich man, with sheep, **goats,** and cattle, as well as
13. 5 Lot also had sheep, **goats,** and cattle, as well as his own
15. 9 “Bring me a cow, a **goat,** and a ram, each of them
24.35 him flocks of sheep and **goats,** cattle, silver, gold, male
27. 9 pick out two fat young **goats,** so that I can cook them
27.13 do as I say, and go and get the **goats** for me.”
27.16 put the skins of the **goats** on his arms and on the
30.32 every black lamb and every spotted or speckled young **goat.**
30.33 wages, if I have any **goat** that isn’t speckled or spotted or
30.35 day Laban removed the male **goats** that had stripes or spots
30.39 So when the **goats** bred in front of the branches, they
30.40 the sheep separate from the **goats** and made them face in the
31. 8 Whenever Laban said, ‘The speckled **goats** shall be your wages,’
31. 8 When he said, ‘The striped **goats** shall be your wages,’ all
31.10 I saw that the male **goats** that were mating were striped,
31.12 continued, ‘all the male **goats** that are mating are striped,
31.38 your sheep and your **goats** have not failed to reproduce, and
32. 5 I own cattle, donkeys, sheep, **goats,** and slaves.
32. 7 who were with him, and also his sheep, **goats,** cattle, and
32.13 two hundred female **goats** and twenty males, two hundred
37. 2 care of the sheep and **goats** with his brothers, the sons of
37.31 Then they killed a **goat** and dipped Joseph’s robe in its blood.
38.17 He answered, “I will send you a young **goat** from my flock.”
38.17 me something to keep as a pledge until you send the **goat.”**
38.20 friend Hirah to take the **goat** and get back from the woman
45.10 your grandchildren, your sheep, your **goats,** your cattle, and
47.17 them food in exchange for their horses, sheep, **goats,**
50. 8 small children and their sheep, **goats,** and cattle stayed in
Ex 2.15 and fill the troughs for their father’s sheep and **goats.**
3. 1 care of the sheep and **goats** of his father-in-law Jethro, the
9. 3 horses, donkeys, camels, cattle, sheep, and **goats.**

Ex	10. 9	and daughters, our sheep and **goats,** and our cattle, because
	10.24	But your sheep, **goats,** and cattle must stay here."
	12. 3	must choose either a lamb or a young **goat** for his household.
	12. 5	either a sheep or a **goat,** but it must be a one-year-old
	12.21	a lamb or a young **goat** and kill it, so that your
	12.32	Take your sheep, **goats,** and cattle, and leave.
	12.38	and many sheep, **goats,** and cattle also went with them.
	23.19	"Do not cook a young sheep or **goat** in its mother's milk.
	25. 4	cloth made of **goats' hair;**
	26. 7	the Tent out of eleven pieces of cloth made of **goats' hair.**
	34.26	"Do not cook a young sheep or **goat** in its mother's milk."
	35. 6	cloth made of **goats' hair;**
	35.23	cloth of **goats' hair;**
	35.26	They also made thread of **goats' hair.**
	36.14	the Tent out of eleven pieces of cloth made of **goats' hair.**
Lev	1. 2	be one of his cattle or one of his sheep or **goats.**
	1.10	one of his sheep or **goats,** it must be a male without
	3. 6	If a sheep or **goat** is used as a fellowship-offering, it
	3.12	If a man offers a **goat,** [13]he shall put his hand on
	4.23	shall bring as his offering a male **goat** without any defects.
	4.28	bring as his offering a female **goat** without any defects.
	5. 6	bring to the Lord a female sheep or **goat** as an offering.
	5. 7	afford a sheep or a **goat,** he shall bring to the Lord
	5.15	to the Lord a male sheep or **goat** without any defects.
	5.18	repayment-offering a male sheep or **goat** without any defects.
	6. 6	to the Lord a male sheep or **goat** without any defects.
	7.23	No fat of cattle, sheep, or **goats** shall be eaten.
	9. 3	Israel to take a male **goat** for a sin-offering, a one-year-old calf,
	9.15	He took the **goat** that was to be offered for the people's
	10.16	Moses asked about the **goat** for the sin-offering and
	16. 5	shall give Aaron two male **goats** for a sin-offering and a ram
	16. 7	he shall take the two **goats** to the entrance of the Tent
	16. 9	Aaron shall sacrifice the **goat** chosen by lot for the Lord
	16.10	The **goat** chosen for Azazel shall be presented alive to
	16.15	he shall kill the **goat** for the sin-offering for the people,
	16.18	blood and some of the **goat's** blood and put it all over
	16.20	shall present to the Lord the live **goat** chosen for Azazel.
	16.21	both his hands on the **goat's** head and confess over it all
	16.21	people of Israel, and so transfer them to the **goat's** head.
	16.21	Then the **goat** is to be driven off into the desert by
	16.22	The **goat** will carry all their sins away with him into
	16.26	The man who drove the **goat** into the desert to Azazel
	16.27	The bull and the **goat** used for the sin-offering, whose
	17. 3	or a sheep or a **goat** as an offering to the Lord
	17. 7	animals in the fields as sacrifices to the **goat-demons.**
	22.28	and its lamb or a **goat** and its kid on the same
	23.19	Also offer one male **goat** as a sin-offering and two
Num	7.12	one **goat** for the sin-offering;
	7.12	two bulls, five rams, five **goats,** and five one-year-old
	7.84	twelve **goats** for the sin-offerings
	7.84	twenty-four bulls, sixty rams, sixty **goats,**
	15. 3	ram, a sheep, or a **goat** may be presented to the Lord
	15. 4	presents a sheep or a **goat** as a burnt-offering to the Lord
	15.11	what shall be offered with each bull, ram, sheep, or **goat.**
	15.24	In addition, they are to offer a male **goat** as a sin-offering.
	15.27	he is to offer a one-year-old female **goat** as a sin-offering.
	18.17	first-born of cows, sheep, and **goats** are
	28.15	its wine-offering, offer one male **goat** as a sin-offering.
	28.22	Also offer one male **goat** as a sin-offering, and in this
	28.30	Also offer one male **goat** as a sin-offering, and in this
	29. 5	Also offer one male **goat** as a sin-offering, and in this
	29.11	Also offer one male **goat** as a sin-offering,
	29.11	in addition to the **goat** offered in the ritual of purification
	29.16	Also offer one male **goat** as a sin-offering.
	31.20	of clothing and everything made of leather, **goats' hair,**
	31.28	the same proportion of the cattle, donkeys, sheep, and **goats.**
	31.30	the same proportion of the cattle, donkeys, sheep, and **goats.**
	31.32	675,000 sheep and **goats,**
	31.36	337,500 sheep and **goats,**
	31.42	337,500 sheep and **goats,**
Deut	14. 4	cattle, sheep, **goats,** [5]deer, wild sheep, wild goats,
	14.21	"Do not cook a young sheep or **goat** in its mother's milk.
	32.14	Their cows and **goats** gave plenty of milk;
	32.14	they had the best sheep, **goats,** and cattle, the finest wheat,
Judg	6.19	house and cooked a young **goat** and used ten kilogrammes of
	13.15	Let us cook a young **goat** for you."
	13.19	So Manoah took a young **goat** and some grain, and offered
	14. 6	apart with his bare hands, as if it were a young **goat.**
	15. 1	his wife during the wheat harvest and took her a young **goat.**
1 Sam	10. 3	will be leading three young **goats,** another one will be
	16.20	to Saul with a young **goat,** a donkey loaded with bread, and
	19.13	put a pillow made of **goats'-hair** at its head, and put a
	19.16	idol in the bed and the **goats'-hair** pillow at its head.
	24. 2	went looking for David and his men east of Wild **Goat** Rocks.
	25. 2	the owner of three thousand sheep and one thousand **goats.**
1 Kgs	20.27	like two small flocks of **goats** compared with the Syrians,
2 Kgs	23. 8	dedicated to the **goat-demons** near the gate built by Joshua,
1 Chr	27.25	Sheep and **goats:**
2 Chr	17.11	and some Arabs brought him 7,700 sheep and 7,700 **goats.**
	29.21	took seven bulls, seven sheep, seven lambs, and seven **goats.**
	29.23	Finally they took the **goats** to the king and to the other
	29.24	Then the priests killed the **goats** and poured their blood
	35. 6	You are to kill the Passover lambs and **goats.**
	35. 7	sheep, lambs, and young **goats,** and three thousand bulls.
	35. 8	six hundred lambs and young **goats** and three hundred bulls
	35. 9	five thousand lambs and young **goats** and five hundred bulls
	35.11	After the lambs and **goats** had been killed,
Ezra	6.17	lambs as sacrifices, and twelve **goats** as offerings for sin,
	8.35	they also offered 12 **goats** to purify themselves from sin.
Neh	10.36	first lamb or kid born to each of our sheep or **goats.**
Job	29. 6	My cows and **goats** gave plenty of milk, and my olive-trees
Job	39. 1	Do you know when **mountain-goats** are born?
Ps	50. 9	not need bulls from your farms or **goats** from your flocks;
	50.13	I eat the flesh of bulls or drink the blood of **goats?**
	66.15	I will sacrifice bulls and **goats,** and the smoke will go up
	104.18	The wild **goats** live in the high mountains, and the
	114. 4	The mountains skipped like **goats;**
	114. 6	You mountains, why did you skip like **goats?**
Prov	27.26	land with the money you get from selling some of your **goats.**
	27.27	The rest of the **goats** will provide milk for you and your
	30.31	**goats,** strutting cocks, and kings in front of their people.
Song	1. 8	find pasture for your **goats** near the tents of the shepherds.
	4. 1	like a flock of **goats** bounding down the hills of Gilead.
	6. 5	like a flock of **goats** bounding down the hills of Gilead.
Is	1.11	I am tired of the blood of bulls and sheep and **goats.**
	5.17	lambs will eat grass and young **goats** will find pasture.
	7.21	one young cow and two **goats,** [22]they will give so much milk
	11. 6	in peace, and leopards will lie down with young **goats.**
	13.21	and wild **goats** will prance through the ruins.
	34. 6	the blood and fat of lambs and **goats** that are sacrificed.
Jer	51.40	I will take them to be slaughtered, like lambs, **goats,**
Ezek	27.21	Kedar paid for your merchandise with lambs, sheep, and **goats.**
	34.17	separate the good from the bad, the sheep from the **goats.**
	39.18	will be killed like rams or lambs or **goats** or fat bulls.
	43.22	are to take a male **goat** without any defects and offer it
	43.25	you are to offer a **goat,** a bull, and a ram as
	45.23	is also to sacrifice a male **goat** each day as a sin-offering.
Dan	8. 5	what this meant, a **goat** came rushing out of the west,
	8. 8	The **goat** grew more and more arrogant, but at the height
	8.21	The **goat** represents the kingdom of Greece, and the
Mt	25.32	just as a shepherd separates the sheep from the **goats.**
Lk	15.29	Not even a **goat** for me to have a feast with my
Heb	9.12	not take the blood of **goats** and bulls to offer as a
	9.13	The blood of **goats** and bulls and the ashes of a burnt
	9.19	the blood of bulls and **goats,** mixed it with water, and
	10. 4	For the blood of bulls and **goats** can never take away sins.
	11.37	clothed in skins of sheep or **goats**—poor, persecuted,

GOD

for KINGDOM OF GOD see **KINGDOM (1)**
for FALSE GOD(S) see **GOD (2)**
see also **GOD-FEARING, GOD-GIVEN, GOD'S PEOPLE, GODDESS, GODLESS, GODLY, CHILD OF GOD, SON OF GOD, TWIN GODS, UNGODLY**

GOD (1)

[LIVING GOD, LORD GOD]

Gen	1. 1	In the beginning, when **God** created the universe,
	1. 2	darkness, and the power of **God** was moving over the water.
	1. 3	Then **God** commanded, "Let there be light"—and light appeared.
	1. 4	**God** was pleased with what he saw.
	1. 6	Then **God** commanded, "Let there be a dome to divide
	1. 6	So **God** made a dome, and it separated the water under it
	1. 9	Then **God** commanded, "Let the water below the sky come together
	1.10	And **God** was pleased with what he saw.
	1.12	all kinds of plants, and **God** was pleased with what he saw.
	1.14	Then **God** commanded, "Let lights appear in the sky
	1.16	So **God** made the two larger lights,
	1.18	And **God** was pleased with what he saw.
	1.20	Then **God** commanded, "Let the water be filled
	1.21	So **God** created the great sea-monsters,
	1.21	And **God** was pleased with what he saw.
	1.24	**God** commanded, "Let the earth produce all kinds of animal life:
	1.25	So **God** made them all, and he was pleased with what he
	1.26	Then **God** said, "And now we will make human beings;
	1.27	So **God** created human beings, making them to be like himself.
	1.31	**God** looked at everything he had made, and he was very pleased.
	2. 2	By the seventh day **God** finished what he had been doing and
	2. 4	When the **Lord God** made the universe, [5]there were no plants
	2. 7	Then the **Lord God** took some soil from the ground and
	2. 8	Then the **Lord God** planted a garden in Eden, in the East,
	2.15	Then the **Lord God** placed the man in the Garden of Eden
	2.18	Then the **Lord God** said, "It is not good for the man
	2.21	Then the **Lord God** made the man fall into a deep sleep,
	3. 1	was the most cunning animal that the **Lord God** had made.
	3. 1	snake asked the woman, "Did **God** really tell you not to eat
	3. 3	**God** told us not to eat the fruit of that tree or
	3. 5	**God** said that, because he knows that when you eat it
	3. 5	you will be like **God** and know what is good and
	3. 8	That evening they heard the **Lord God** walking in the garden,
	3. 9	But the **Lord God** called out to the man, "Where are you?"
	3.11	**God** asked.
	3.13	The **Lord God** asked the woman, "Why did you do this?"
	3.14	Then the **Lord God** said to the snake, "You will be
	3.21	And the **Lord God** made clothes out of animal skins for
	3.22	Then the **Lord God** said, "Now the man has become like
	3.23	So the **Lord God** sent him out of the Garden of Eden
	4.25	She said, "**God** has given me a son to replace Abel, whom
	5. 1	(When **God** created human beings, he made them like himself.
	5.22	Enoch lived in fellowship with **God** for 300 years
	5.24	his life in fellowship with **God,** and then he disappeared,
	5.24	because **God** took him away.
	6. 9	He lived in fellowship with **God,** [11]but everyone else was evil
	6.11	everyone else was evil in **God's** sight, and violence had spread
	6.12	**God** looked at the world and saw that it was evil,
	6.13	**God** said to Noah, "I have decided to put an end
	6.22	Noah did everything that **God** commanded.
	7. 9	went into the boat with Noah, as **God** had commanded.
	7.16	went into the boat with Noah, [16]as **God** had commanded.

Gen 8. 1 **God** had not forgotten Noah and all the animals with him in
8.15 **God** said to Noah, [16] "Go out of the boat with your wife,
9. 1 **God** blessed Noah and his sons and said, "Have many children,
9. 6 Man was made like **God,** so whoever murders a man will
9. 8 **God** said to Noah and his sons, [9] "I am now making my
9.26 Give praise to the Lord, the **God** of Shem!
9.27 May **God** cause Japheth to increase!
14.18 of the Most High **God,** brought bread and wine to Abram,
14.19 "May the Most High **God,** who made heaven and earth, bless
14.20 May the Most High **God,** who gave you victory over your enemies,
14.22 the Lord, the Most High **God,** Maker of heaven and earth,
15.10 Abram brought the animals to **God,** cut them in half,
16.13 "Have I really seen **God** and lived to tell about it?"
16.13 called the Lord who had spoken to her "A **God** Who Sees."
17. 1 the Lord appeared to him and said, "I am the Almighty **God.**
17. 3 and **God** said, [4] "I make this covenant
17. 7 I will be your **God** and the God of your descendants.
17. 8 to your descendants for ever, and I will be their **God."**
17. 9 **God** said to Abraham, "You also must agree to keep the
17.15 **God** said to Abraham, "You must no longer call your wife Sarai;
17.18 He asked **God,** "Why not let Ishmael be my heir?"
17.19 But **God** said, "No.
17.22 When **God** finished speaking to Abraham, he left him.
17.23 that same day Abraham obeyed **God** and circumcised his son Ishmael
19.29 But when **God** destroyed the cities of the valley where
20. 3 One night **God** appeared to him in a dream and said:
20. 6 **God** replied in the dream, "Yes, I know that you did it
20.11 here who has reverence for **God** and that they would kill me
20.13 So when **God** sent me from my father's house into foreign lands,
20.17 So Abraham prayed for Abimelech, and **God** healed him.
21. 2 was born at the time **God** had said he would be born.
21. 4 Abraham circumcised him, as **God** had commanded.
21. 6 Sarah said, **"God** has brought me joy and laughter.
21.12 But **God** said to Abraham, "Don't be worried about the boy
21.17 **God** heard the boy crying, and from heaven the angel of God
21.17 **God** has heard the boy crying.
21.19 Then **God** opened her eyes, and she saw a well.
21.20 **God** was with the boy as he grew up;
21.22 said to Abraham, **"God** is with you
21.23 in the presence of **God** that you will not deceive me,
21.33 in Beersheba and worshipped the Lord, the Everlasting **God.**
22. 1 Some time later **God** tested Abraham;
22. 2 "Take your son," **God** said, "your only son, Isaac, whom
22. 3 They started out for the place that **God** had told him about.
22. 8 Abraham answered, **"God** himself will provide one."
22. 9 came to the place which **God** had told him about,
22.12 that you honour and obey **God,** because you have not kept back
24. 3 name of the Lord, the **God** of heaven and earth,
24. 7 The Lord, the **God** of heaven, brought me from the home
24.12 He prayed, "Lord, **God** of my master Abraham, give me
24.27 "Praise the Lord, the **God** of my master Abraham,
24.42 I prayed, 'Lord, **God** of my master Abraham,
24.48 I praised the Lord, the **God** of my master Abraham,
25.11 After the death of Abraham, **God** blessed his son Isaac,
26.24 said, "I am the **God** of your father Abraham.
27.20 Jacob answered, "The Lord your **God** helped me to find it."
27.28 May **God** give you dew from heaven and make your fields fertile!
28. 3 May Almighty **God** bless your marriage and give you many children,
28. 4 in which you have lived and which **God** gave to Abraham!"
28.13 "I am the Lord, the **God** of Abraham and Isaac," he said.
28.17 It must be the house of **God;**
28.18 Then he poured olive-oil on it to dedicate it to **God.**
28.21 return safely to my father's home, then you will be my **God.**
30. 2 angry with Rachel and said, "I can't take the place of **God.**
30. 6 Rachel said, **"God** has judged in my favour.
30.17 **God** answered Leah's prayer, and she became pregnant
30.18 Leah said, **"God** has given me my reward,
30.20 She said, **"God** has given me a fine gift.
30.22 Then **God** remembered Rachel;
30.23 She said, **"God** has taken away my disgrace
31. 5 but my father's **God** has been with me.
31. 7 But **God** did not let him harm me.
31. 9 **God** has taken flocks away from your father
31.11 The angel of **God** spoke to me in the dream and said,
31.13 I am the **God** who appeared to you at Bethel,
31.16 All this wealth which **God** has taken from our father
31.16 Do whatever **God** has told you."
31.24 In a dream that night **God** came to Laban and said
31.29 but last night the **God** of your father warned me
31.42 If the **God** of my fathers, the God of Abraham and Isaac,
31.42 But **God** has seen my trouble and the work I have done,
31.50 I don't know about it, remember that **God** is watching us.
31.53 God of Abraham and the **God** of Nahor will judge between us."
31.53 in the name of the **God** whom his father Isaac worshipped,
32. 2 When he saw them, he said, "This is **God's** camp";
32. 9 Then Jacob prayed, **"God** of my grandfather Abraham
32. 9 and **God** of my father Isaac, hear me!
32.28 You have struggled with **God** and with men, and you have won;
32.30 Jacob said, "I have seen **God** face to face,
33. 5 sir, are the children whom **God** has been good enough to give
33.10 like seeing the face of **God,**
33.11 **God** has been kind to me and given me everything I need."
33.20 an altar there and named it after El, the **God** of Israel.
35. 1 **God** said to Jacob, "Go to Bethel at once, and live there.
35. 1 altar there to me, the **God** who appeared to you when you
35. 3 build an altar to the **God** who helped me
35. 7 named the place after the **God** of Bethel,
35. 7 because **God** had revealed himself to him there

Gen 35. 9 When Jacob returned from Mesopotamia, **God** appeared to him again
35.10 **God** said to him, "Your name is Jacob, but from now on
35.10 So **God** named him Israel.
35.11 And **God** said to him, "I am Almighty God.
35.13 Then **God** left him.
35.14 where **God** had spoken to him, Jacob set up a memorial
39. 9 could I do such an immoral thing and sin against **God?"**
40. 8 "It is **God** who gives the ability to interpret dreams,"
41.16 but **God** will give a favourable interpretation."
41.25 **God** has told you what he is going to do.
41.28 just as I told you—**God** has shown you
41.32 the matter is fixed by **God**
41.38 better man than Joseph, a man who has **God's** spirit in him."
41.39 The king said to Joseph, **"God** has shown you all this,
41.51 He said, **"God** has made me forget all my sufferings
41.52 He also said, **"God** has given me children in the land
42.28 fear they asked one another, "What has **God** done to us?"
43.14 May Almighty **God** cause the man to have pity on you,
43.23 Your **God,** the God of your father, must have put the money
43.29 **God** bless you, my son."
44.16 **God** has uncovered our guilt.
45. 5 It was really **God** who sent me ahead of you to save
45. 7 **God** sent me ahead of you to rescue you
45. 8 So it was not really you who sent me here, but **God.**
45. 9 **'God** has made me ruler of all Egypt;
46. 1 where he offered sacrifices to the **God** of his father Isaac.
46. 2 **God** spoke to him in a vision at night and called, "Jacob,
46. 3 "I am God, the **God** of your father," he said.
48. 3 Jacob said to Joseph, "Almighty **God** appeared to me at Luz
48. 9 "These are my sons, whom **God** has given me here in Egypt."
48.11 see you again, and now **God** has even let me see your
48.15 "May the **God** whom my fathers Abraham and Isaac served bless
48.15 May **God,** who has led me to this very day, bless them!
48.20 They will say, 'May **God** make you like Ephraim and Manasseh.' "
48.21 am about to die, but **God** will be with you
49.24 the power of the Mighty **God** of Jacob,
49.25 It is your father's **God** who helps you,
49.25 The Almighty **God** who blesses you
50.17 wrong that we, the servants of your father's **God,** have done."
50.19 I can't put myself in the place of **God.**
50.20 plotted evil against me, but **God** turned it into good,
50.24 am about to die, but **God** will certainly take care of you
50.25 he said, "that when **God** leads you to that land,

Ex 1.17 But the midwives feared **God** and so did not obey the king;
1.20 Because the midwives feared **God,** he was good to them
2.23 Their cry went up to **God,** [24] who heard their groaning and
3. 5 **God** said, "Do not come any closer.
3. 6 the God of your ancestors, the **God** of Abraham, Isaac, and
3. 6 Moses covered his face, because he was afraid to look at **God.**
3.11 But Moses said to **God,** "I am nobody.
3.12 **God** answered, "I will be with you,
3.13 say to them, 'The **God** of your ancestors sent me
3.14 **God** said, "I am who I am.
3.15 that I, the Lord, the **God** of their ancestors,
3.15 the **God** of Abraham, Isaac, and Jacob, have
3.16 that I, the Lord, the **God** of their ancestors,
3.16 the **God** of Abraham, Isaac, and Jacob, appeared
3.18 'The Lord, the **God** of the Hebrews, has revealed himself
3.18 into the desert to offer sacrifices to the Lord, our **God.'**
4. 5 Israelites that the Lord, the **God** of their ancestors,
4. 5 the **God** of Abraham, Isaac, and Jacob,
4.16 Then you will be like **God,** telling him what to say.
4.20 carrying the stick that **God** had told him to take.
5. 1 "The Lord, the **God** of Israel, says, 'Let my people
5. 3 "The **God** of the Hebrews has revealed himself
5. 3 into the desert to offer sacrifices to the Lord our **God.**
5. 8 asking me to let them go and offer sacrifices to their **God!**
6. 2 **God** spoke to Moses and said, "I am the Lord.
6. 3 to Jacob as Almighty **God,** but I did not make myself
6. 7 will make you my own people, and I will be your **God.**
6. 7 I am the Lord your **God** when I set you free
7. 1 going to make you like **God** to the king,
7.16 the king, 'The Lord, the **God** of the Hebrews, sent me
8.10 know that there is no other **god** like the Lord, our God.
8.19 and the magicians said to the king, **"God** has done this!"
8.25 "Go and offer sacrifices to your **God** here in this country."
8.26 sacrificing the animals that we offer to the Lord our **God.**
8.27 sacrifices to the Lord our **God,** just as he commanded us."
8.28 sacrifice to the Lord, your **God,** in the desert,
9. 1 that the Lord, the **God** of the Hebrews, says,
9.13 that the Lord, the **God** of the Hebrews, says,
9.30 that you and your officials do not yet fear the **Lord God."**
10. 3 "The Lord, the **God** of the Hebrews, says 'How much
10. 7 Israelite men go, so that they can worship the Lord their **God.**
10. 8 said to them, "You may go and worship the Lord your **God.**
10.16 "I have sinned against the Lord your **God** and against you.
10.17 pray to the Lord your **God** to take away this fatal punishment
10.25 sacrifices and burnt-offerings to offer to the Lord our **God.**
10.26 select the animals with which to worship the Lord our **God.**
13.17 Egypt let the people go, **God** did not take them by the
13.17 **God** thought, "I do not want the people to change their
13.19 Joseph had said, "When **God** rescues you, you must carry my
14.19 The angel of **God,** who had been in front of the army
15. 2 He is my **God,** and I will praise him, my father's God,
16.12 Then they will know that I, the Lord, am their **God."**
17. 9 holding the stick that **God** told me to carry."
18. 1 Midian, heard about everything that **God** had done for Moses
18. 4 He had also said, "The **God** of my father helped me
18.12 to be burnt whole and other sacrifices to be offered to **God;**
18.15 do this because the people come to me to learn **God's** will.

Ex 18.16 and I tell them **God's** commands and laws."
18.19 give you some good advice, and **God** will be with you.
18.19 the people before **God** and bring their disputes to him.
18.20 You should teach them **God's** commands
18.23 If you do this, as **God** commands, you will not wear
19. 3 and Moses went up the mountain to meet with **God.**
19.17 of the camp to meet **God,** and they stood at the foot
19.19 Moses spoke, and **God** answered him with thunder.
20. 1 **God** spoke, and these were his words:
20. 2 "I am the Lord your **God** who brought you out of Egypt,
20. 5 because I am the Lord your **God** and I tolerate no rivals.
20. 7 for I, the Lord your **God,** will punish anyone who misuses
20.19 we are afraid that if **God** speaks to us, we will die."
20.20 **God** has only come to test you and make you keep on
20.21 and only Moses went near the dark cloud where **God** was.
22. 9 The one whom **God** declares to be guilty shall pay double
22.28 "Do not speak evil of **God,** and do not curse a leader
23.17 all your men must come to worship me, the Lord your **God.**
23.19 house of the Lord your **God** the first corn that you harvest.
23.25 worship me, the Lord your **God,** I will bless you with food
24.10 Israel went up the mountain [10]and they saw the **God** of Israel.
24.11 **God** did not harm these leading men of Israel;
24.11 they saw **God,** and then they ate and drank together.
28.15 for the High Priest to use in determining **God's** will.
29.45 live among the people of Israel, and I will be their **God.**
29.46 I am the Lord their **God** who brought them out of Egypt
29.46 I am the Lord their **God.**
31.18 When **God** had finished speaking to Moses on Mount Sinai,
31.18 tablets on which **God** himself had written the commandments.
32.11 pleaded with the Lord his **God** and said, "Lord, why should
32.16 **God** himself had made the tablets and had engraved the commandments
32.27 he said to them, "The **Lord God** of Israel commands every one
34. 6 "I, the Lord, am a **God** who is full of compassion and
34.23 men must come to worship me, the Lord, the **God** of Israel.
35.13 the bread offered to **God;**
35.31 **God** has filled him with his power and given him skill,
39.36 the table and all its equipment, and the bread offered to **God;**

Lev 2.13 because salt represents the covenant between you and **God.**
7. 9 a griddle belongs to the priest who has offered it to **God.**
7.12 offering as a thank-offering to **God,** he shall present,
7.18 on the third day, **God** will not accept the man's offering.
10.10 between what belongs to **God** and what is for general use,
11.44 I am the Lord your **God,** and you must keep yourselves holy,
11.45 brought you out of Egypt so that I could be your **God.**
18. 2 say to the people of Israel, "I am the Lord your **God.**
18. 4 I am the Lord your **God.**
18.21 because that would bring disgrace on the name of **God,**
18.22 **God** hates that.
18.30 I am the Lord your **God."**
19. 2 of Israel, "Be holy, because I, the Lord your **God,** am holy.
19. 3 I am the Lord your **God.**
19. 4 I am the Lord your **God.**
19.10 I am the Lord your **God.**
19.12 I am the Lord your **God.**
19.14 I am the Lord your **God.**
19.22 purification to remove the man's sin, and **God** will forgive him.
19.25 I am the Lord your **God.**
19.31 I am the Lord your **God.**
19.34 I am the Lord your **God.**
19.36 I am the Lord your **God,** and I brought you out of
20. 7 Keep yourselves holy, because I am the Lord your **God.**
20.24 I am the Lord your **God,** and I have set you apart
22.33 and I brought you out of Egypt to become your **God.**
23.14 into bread, until you have brought this offering to **God.**
23.22 The Lord is your **God.**
23.40 and begin a religious festival to honour the Lord your **God.**
23.43 He is the Lord your **God.**
24.10 During the quarrel he cursed **God,** so they took him to Moses,
24.15 Israel that anyone who curses **God** must suffer the consequences
24.22 foreigners living among you, because I am the Lord your **God."**
25.17 Do not cheat a fellow-Israelite, but obey the Lord your **God.**
25.23 it belongs to **God,** and you are like foreigners who are
25.36 interest, but obey **God** and let your fellow-Israelite live near
25.38 command of the Lord your **God,** who brought you out of Egypt
25.38 to give you the land of Canaan and to be your **God.**
25.43 Do not treat them harshly, but obey your **God.**
25.55 he is the Lord their **God.**
26. 1 I am the Lord your **God.**
26.12 I will be your **God,** and you will be my people.
26.13 I, the Lord your **God,** brought you out of Egypt
26.44 my covenant with them, and I am the Lord their **God.**
26.45 of Egypt, in order that I, the Lord, might be their **God."**

Num 6. 6 sign of his dedication to **God,** and so he must not defile
10. 9 I, the Lord your **God,** will help you and save you
10.10 I am the Lord your **God."**
12.13 So Moses cried out to the Lord, "O **God,** heal her!"
15.41 I am the Lord your **God;**
15.41 I brought you out of Egypt to be your **God.**
16. 9 a small matter that the **God** of Israel has set you apart
16.22 said, "O, **God,** you are the source of all
16.29 death without some punishment from **God,** then the Lord did
21. 5 the people lost their patience [5]and spoke against **God** and Moses.
22. 9 **God** came to Balaam and asked, "Who are these men
22.12 **God** said to Balaam, "Do not go with these men, and do
22.18 the command of the Lord my **God** in even the smallest matter.
22.20 That night **God** came to Balaam and said, "If these men
22.22 **God** was angry that Balaam was going, and as Balaam was
22.38 I can say only what **God** tells me to say."
23. 4 went alone to the top of a hill, [4]and **God** met him.
23. 8 How can I curse what **God** has not cursed,

Num 23.15 "Stand here by your burnt-offering, and I will meet **God** over there."
23.19 **God** is not like men, who lie;
23.20 to bless, And when **God** blesses, I cannot call it back.
23.21 The Lord their **God** is with them;
23.22 **God** has brought them out of Egypt;
23.23 Now people will say about Israel, 'Look what **God** has done!'
23.27 Perhaps **God** will be willing to let you curse them for me
24. 2 The spirit of **God** took control of him, [3]and he uttered this
24. 4 man who can see clearly, [4]Who can hear what **God** is saying.
24. 4 staring eyes I see in a trance A vision from Almighty **God.**
24. 8 **God** brought them out of Egypt;
24.16 Who can hear what **God** is saying And receive the knowledge
24.16 staring eyes I see in a trance A vision from Almighty **God.**
27.16 Moses prayed, [16]"**Lord God,** source of all life,
28. 2 to present to **God** at the appointed times the required

Deut 1. 5 of Moab that Moses began to explain **God's** laws and teachings.
1. 6 Mount Sinai, the Lord our **God** said to us, 'You have stayed
1.10 The Lord your **God** has made you as numerous as the stars
1.11 May the Lord, the **God** of your ancestors, make you increase
1.17 afraid of anyone, for the decisions you make come from **God.**
1.19 "We did what the Lord our **God** commanded us.
1.20 the Lord our God, the **God** of our ancestors, is giving us.
1.25 land which the Lord our **God** was giving us was very fertile.
1.26 command of the Lord your **God,** and you would not enter
1.30 The Lord your **God** will lead you, and he will fight
1.41 now we will attack, just as the Lord our **God** commanded us.'
2. 7 "Remember how the Lord your **God** has blessed you in everything
2.29 Jordan into the land that the Lord our **God** is giving us.
2.30 The Lord your **God** had made him stubborn and rebellious,
2.33 but the Lord our **God** put him in our power,
2.36 The Lord our **God** let us capture all the towns from Aroer,
2.37 place where the Lord our **God** had commanded us not to go.
3.18 'The Lord our **God** has given you this land east of the
3.21 all that the Lord your **God** did to those two kings,
3.22 afraid of them, for the Lord your **God** will fight for you.'
4. 1 land which the Lord, the **God** of your ancestors, is giving
4. 2 the commands of the Lord your **God** that I have given you.
4. 4 were faithful to the Lord your **God** are still alive today.
4. 5 all the laws, as the Lord my **God** told me to do.
4. 7 when they need him as the Lord our **God** is to us.
4.10 presence of the Lord your **God** at Mount Sinai,
4.19 The Lord your **God** has given these to all other peoples
4.21 the Lord your **God** was angry with me
4.23 forget the covenant that the Lord your **God** made with you.
4.24 because the Lord your **God** is like a flaming fire;
4.29 look for the Lord your **God,** and if you search for him
4.31 He is a merciful **God.**
4.32 way back to the time when **God** created man on the earth.
4.34 as the Lord your **God** did for you in Egypt?
4.35 he alone is **God** and that there is no other.
4.39 the Lord is **God** in heaven and on earth.
4.40 land which the Lord your **God** is giving you
4.44 Moses gave **God's** laws and teachings to the people of Israel.
5. 2 Mount Sinai the Lord our **God** made a covenant,
5. 6 'I am the Lord your **God,** who rescued you from Egypt,
5. 9 for I am the Lord your **God** and I tolerate no rivals.
5.11 for I, the Lord your **God,** will punish anyone who misuses
5.12 keep it holy, as I, the Lord your **God,** have commanded you.
5.15 that I, the Lord your **God,** rescued you by my great power
5.16 as I, the Lord your **God,** command you,
5.24 and said, 'The Lord our **God** showed us his greatness
5.24 man to continue to live, even though **God** has spoken to him.
5.25 sure to die if we hear the Lord our **God** speak again.
5.26 ever lived after hearing the **living God** speak from a fire?
5.27 Moses, and listen to everything that the Lord our **God** says.
5.32 you do everything that the Lord your **God** has commanded you.
6. 1 the laws that the Lord your **God** commanded me to teach you.
6. 2 to honour the Lord your **God** and obey all his laws
6. 3 just as the Lord, the **God** of our ancestors, has promised.
6. 4 The Lord—and the Lord alone—is our **God.**
6. 5 Love the Lord your **God** with all your heart,
6.10 "Just as the Lord your **God** promised your ancestors,
6.13 Honour the Lord your **God,** worship only him,
6.15 because the Lord your **God,** who is present with you, tolerates
6.16 not put the Lord your **God** to the test,
6.20 'Why did the Lord our **God** command us to obey
6.24 Then the Lord our **God** commanded us to obey all these
6.25 we faithfully obey everything that **God** has commanded us,
7. 1 "The Lord your **God** will bring you into the land
7. 2 When the Lord your **God** places these people in your power
7. 6 Do this because you belong to the Lord your **God.**
7. 9 Remember that the Lord your **God** is the only God
7.12 then the Lord your **God** will continue to keep his covenant
7.16 nation that the Lord your **God** places in your power,
7.18 remember what the Lord your **God** did to the king of Egypt
7.19 power and strength by which the Lord your **God** set you free.
7.21 The Lord your **God** is with you;
7.21 he is a great **God** and one to be feared.
8. 2 Remember how the Lord your **God** led you on this long
8. 5 Remember that the Lord your **God** corrects and punishes you
8. 7 The Lord your **God** is bringing you into a fertile land—a
8.10 thanks to the Lord your **God** for the fertile land
8.11 "Make certain that you do not forget the Lord your **God;**
8.14 and forget the Lord your **God** who rescued you from Egypt,
8.18 it is the Lord your **God** who gives you the power
8.19 Never forget the Lord your **God** or turn to other gods
9. 3 the Lord your **God** will go ahead of you
9. 4 "After the Lord your **God** has driven them out for you,
9. 7 forget how you made the Lord your **God** angry in the desert.
9.16 command that the Lord your **God** had given you,

Deut 9.22 also made the Lord your **God** angry when you were at Taberah,
10. 9 being the Lord's priests, as the Lord your **God** promised.)
10.12 Israel, listen to what the Lord your **God** demands of you:
10.17 The Lord your **God** is supreme over all gods
10.20 Obey the Lord your **God** and worship only him.
10.21 Praise him—he is your **God**, and you have seen with your
10.22 But now the Lord your **God** has made you as numerous as
11. 1 "Love the Lord your **God** and always obey all his laws.
11.12 The Lord your **God** takes care of this land
11.13 love the Lord your **God** and serve him with all your heart.
11.21 that the Lord your **God** promised to give to your ancestors.
11.22 Love the Lord your **God**, do everything he commands,
11.25 that land, the Lord your **God** will make the people fear you,
11.27 commands of the Lord your **God** that I am giving you today;
11.31 and occupy the land that the Lord your **God** is giving you.
12. 1 land that the Lord, the **God** of your ancestors, is giving
12. 4 not worship the Lord your **God** in the way that these people
12. 7 presence of the Lord your **God**, who has blessed you,
12. 9 land that the Lord your **God** is giving you,
12.18 presence of the Lord your **God**,
12.18 in the one place of worship chosen by the Lord your **God**.
12.20 "When the Lord your **God** enlarges your territory,
12.28 doing what is right and what pleases the Lord your **God**.
12.29 "The Lord your **God** will destroy the nations as you invade
12.31 not worship the Lord your **God** in the way they worship their
13. 3 The Lord your **God** is using him to test you, to see
13.10 away from the Lord your **God**, who rescued you from Egypt,
13.12 towns that the Lord your **God** gives you, you may hear
13.16 and everything in it as an offering to the Lord your **God**.
14. 1 "You are the people of the Lord your **God**.
14. 2 You belong to the Lord your **God**;
14.21 But you belong to the Lord your **God**;
14.23 place where the Lord your **God** has chosen to be worshipped;
14.23 so that you may learn to honour the Lord your **God** always.
14.26 presence of the Lord your **God**, you and your families are to
14.29 and the Lord your **God** will bless you in everything
15. 4 "The Lord your **God** will bless you in the land
15. 7 land that the Lord your **God** is giving you there is a
15.15 were slaves in Egypt and the Lord your **God** set you free;
15.18 and the Lord your **God** will bless you
15.19 aside for the Lord your **God** all the first-born males
15.21 defect, you must not sacrifice them to the Lord your **God**.
16. 1 "Honour the Lord your **God** by celebrating Passover
16. 2 cattle for the Passover meal to honour the Lord your **God**.
16. 5 in the land that the Lord your **God** will give you.
16. 8 to worship the Lord your **God**, and do no work
16.10 honour the Lord your **God**, by bringing him a freewill offering
16.15 Honour the Lord your **God** by celebrating this festival
16.17 to the blessings that the Lord your **God** has given him.
16.18 officials in every town that the Lord your **God** gives you.
16.20 land that the Lord your **God** is giving you
16.21 altar for the Lord your **God**, do not put beside it a
17. 1 sacrifice to the Lord your **God** cattle or sheep that have any
17. 8 chosen by the Lord your **God**, [9] and present your case to the
17.14 land that the Lord your **God** is going to give you
17.18 copy of the book of **God's** laws and teachings
18. 7 priest of the Lord his **God**, like the other Levites
18. 9 land that the Lord your **God** is giving you,
18.12 The Lord your **God** hates people who do these disgusting things,
18.14 omens, but the Lord your **God** does not allow you to do
19. 1 "After the Lord your **God** has destroyed the people whose land
19. 8 "When the Lord your **God** enlarges your territory, as he
19. 9 love the Lord your **God** and live according to his teachings.)
19.14 ago in the land that the Lord your **God** is giving you.
20. 1 The Lord your **God**, who rescued you from Egypt, will be with
20. 4 The Lord your **God** is going with you,
20.13 Then, when the Lord your **God** lets you capture the city,
20.16 the land that the Lord your **God** is giving you, kill
21. 1 land that the Lord your **God** is going to give you,
21. 5 The Lord your **God** has chosen them to serve him
21.10 "When the Lord your **God** gives you victory in battle
21.23 dead body hanging on a post brings **God's** curse on the land.
21.23 not defile the land that the Lord your **God** is giving you.
22. 5 the Lord your **God** hates people who do such things.
23. 5 But the Lord your **God** would not listen to Balaam;
23.14 clean, because the Lord your **God** is with you in your camp
23.18 the house of the Lord your **God** in fulfilment of a vow.
23.20 and the Lord your **God** will bless everything you do
23.21 vow to the Lord your **God**, do not put off doing what
24. 4 sin in the land that the Lord your **God** is giving you.
24. 9 Remember what the Lord your **God** did to Miriam
24.13 grateful, and the Lord your **God** will be pleased with you.
24.18 slaves in Egypt and that the Lord your **God** set you free;
24.19 so that the Lord your **God** will bless you in everything
25.15 in the land that the Lord your **God** is giving you.
25.18 They had no fear of **God**, and so they attacked you
25.19 then, when the Lord your **God** has given you the land
26. 1 land that the Lord your **God** is giving you and have settled
26. 3 acknowledge to the Lord my **God** that I have entered the land
26. 4 and place it before the altar of the Lord your **God**.
26. 7 cried out for help to the Lord, the **God** of our ancestors.
26.11 things that the Lord your **God** has given you and your family;
26.16 "Today the Lord your **God** commands you to obey all his laws;
26.17 Today you have acknowledged the Lord as your **God**;
27. 2 land that the Lord your **God** is giving you,
27. 3 land that the Lord, the **God** of your ancestors, promised you,
27. 6 build for the Lord your **God** must be made of uncut stones.
27. 7 and be grateful in the presence of the Lord your **God**.
27. 8 write clearly every word of **God's** laws."
27. 9 Today you have become the people of the Lord your **God**;
27.15 " '**God's** curse on anyone who makes an idol of stone, wood,

Deut 27.16 " '**God's** curse on anyone who dishonours his father or mother.'
27.17 " '**God's** curse on anyone who moves a neighbour's boundary mark.'
27.18 " '**God's** curse on anyone who leads a blind man in the
27.19 " '**God's** curse on anyone who deprives foreigners, orphans, and widows
27.20 " '**God's** curse on anyone who disgraces his father
27.21 " '**God's** curse on anyone who has sexual relations with an animal.'
27.22 " '**God's** curse on anyone who has intercourse with his sister
27.23 " '**God's** curse on anyone who has intercourse with his mother-in-law.'
27.24 " '**God's** curse on anyone who secretly commits murder.'
27.25 " '**God's** curse on anyone who accepts money to murder an innocent person.'
27.26 " '**God's** curse on anyone who does not obey all of God's
28. 1 obey the Lord your **God** and faithfully keep all his commands
28. 2 Obey the Lord your **God** and all these blessings will be yours:
28. 8 "The Lord your **God** will bless your work and fill your
28. 9 you obey the Lord your **God** and do everything he commands,
28.13 The Lord your **God** will make you the leader among the
28.15 you disobey the Lord your **God** and do not faithfully keep all
28.45 not obey the Lord your **God** and keep all the laws
28.46 the evidence of **God's** judgement on you and your descendants
28.52 land that the Lord your **God** is giving you,
28.53 even eat the children that the Lord your **God** has given you.
28.58 do not obey faithfully all **God's** teachings that are written
28.58 name of the Lord your **God**, [59] he will send on you
28.61 mentioned in this book of **God's** laws and teachings,
28.62 survive, because you did not obey the Lord your **God**.
29. 6 your needs in order to teach you that he is your **God**.
29.10 presence of the Lord your **God**, all of you—your leaders and
29.12 covenant that the Lord your **God** is making with you
29.13 his people and be your **God**, as he promised you
29.18 turns from the Lord our **God** to worship the gods of other
29.25 had made with him, the **God** of their ancestors, when he
29.29 "There are some things that the Lord our **God** has kept secret;
30. 1 nations where the Lord your **God** has scattered you, you will
30. 3 then the Lord your **God** will have mercy on you.
30. 4 the Lord your **God** will gather you together
30. 6 **God** will give you and your descendants obedient hearts,
30.16 commands of the Lord your **God**, which I give you today,
30.16 The Lord your **God** will bless you in the land that you
30.19 between life and death, between **God's** blessing and God's curse,
30.20 Love the Lord your **God**, obey him and be faithful to him,
31. 3 The Lord your **God** himself will go before you
31. 6 Your **God**, the Lord himself, will be with you.
31. 9 So Moses wrote down **God's** Law
31.11 to worship the Lord your **God** at the one place of worship.
31.12 honour the Lord your **God** and to obey his teachings faithfully.
31.13 never heard the Law of the Lord your **God** will hear it.
31.17 to them because I, their **God**, am no longer with them.
31.24 Moses wrote **God's** Law in a book,
31.26 "Take this book of **God's** Law and place it beside the
31.26 Box of the Lord your **God**, so that it will remain there
32. 4 Your **God** is faithful and true;
32.15 They abandoned **God** their Creator and rejected their mighty saviour.
32.18 They forgot their **God**, their mighty saviour,
32.30 The Lord, their **God**, had abandoned them;
32.30 their mighty **God** had given them up.
32.31 that their own gods are weak, not mighty like Israel's **God**.
32.39 'I, and I alone, am **God**;
32.40 surely as I am the **living God**, I raise my hand and
32.45 When Moses had finished giving **God's** teachings to the people,
32.46 so that they may faithfully obey all **God's** teachings.
33. 1 that Moses, the man of **God**, pronounced on the people of
33.20 "Praise **God**, who made their territory large.
33.26 no god is like your **God**, riding in splendour across the sky,
33.27 **God** has always been your defence;

Josh 1. 9 for I, the Lord your **God**, am with you wherever you go."
1.11 to occupy the land that the Lord your **God** is giving you."
1.13 that the Lord your **God** would give you this land
1.15 west of the Jordan that the Lord your **God** has given them.
1.17 and may the Lord your **God** be with you as he was
2.11 The Lord your **God** is God in heaven above and here
2.14 men said to her, "May **God** take our lives if we don't
3. 3 Covenant Box of the Lord your **God**, break camp and follow them.
3. 9 here and listen to what the Lord your **God** has to say.
3.10 You will know that the **living God** is among you [11] when the
4. 5 the Jordan ahead of the Covenant Box of the Lord your **God**.
4.23 them that the Lord your **God** dried up the water
4.24 and you will honour the Lord your **God** for ever."
7.13 ready tomorrow, because I, the **Lord God** of Israel, have this
7.19 here before the Lord, the **God** of Israel, and confess.
7.20 against the Lord, Israel's **God**, and this is what I did.
8. 7 The Lord your **God** will give it to you.
8.30 on Mount Ebal an altar to the Lord, the **God** of Israel.
9. 9 land, sir, because we have heard of the Lord your **God**.
9.18 promise to them in the name of the Lord, Israel's **God**.
9.19 promise to them in the name of the **Lord God** of Israel.
9.20 if we don't, **God** will punish us.
9.23 Because you did this, **God** has condemned you.
9.23 wood and carrying water for the sanctuary of my **God**."
9.24 true that the Lord your **God** had commanded his servant Moses
10.19 The Lord your **God** has given you victory over them."
10.40 This was what the **Lord God** of Israel had commanded.
10.42 because the Lord, Israel's **God**, was fighting for Israel.
13.14 sacrifices burnt on the altar to the **Lord God** of Israel.
13.33 be a share of the offerings to the **Lord God** of Israel.
14. 6 Kadesh Barnea about you and me to Moses, the man of **God**.
14. 8 But I faithfully obeyed the Lord my **God**.

Josh 14.14 because he faithfully obeyed the Lord, the **God** of Israel.
18. 3 land that the Lord, the **God** of your ancestors, has given
18. 6 I will draw lots to consult the Lord our **God** for you.
22. 3 have been careful to obey the commands of the Lord your **God.**
22. 4 the Lord your **God** has given your fellow-Israelites peace.
22. 5 love the Lord your **God,** do his will, obey his commandments,
22.16 "Why have you done this evil thing against the **God** of Israel?
22.19 an altar in addition to the altar of the Lord our **God.**
22.22 "The Mighty One is **God!**
22.22 The Mighty One is **God!**
22.24 do you have to do with the Lord, the **God** of Israel?
22.29 altar of the Lord our **God** that stands in front of the
22.33 The Israelites were satisfied and praised **God.**
22.34 is a witness to all of us that the Lord is **God."**
23. 3 everything that the Lord your **God** has done to all these
23. 3 The Lord your **God** has been fighting for you.
23. 5 The Lord your **God** will make them retreat from you,
23. 5 have their land, as the Lord your **God** has promised you.
23.10 because the Lord your **God** is fighting for you,
23.11 Be careful, then, to love the Lord your **God.**
23.13 the Lord your **God** will no longer drive these nations
23.13 in this good land which the Lord your **God** has given you.
23.14 soul that the Lord your **God** has given you all the good
23.16 covenant which the Lord your **God** commanded you to keep
24. 1 officers of Israel, and they came into the presence of **God.**
24. 2 "This is what the Lord, the **God** of Israel, has to say:
24.17 The Lord our **God** brought our fathers and us out of
24.18 he is our **God."**
24.19 He is a holy **God** and will not forgive your sins.
24.23 "and pledge your loyalty to the Lord, the **God** of Israel."
24.24 then said to Joshua, "We will serve the Lord our **God.**
24.26 Joshua wrote these commands in the book of the Law of **God.**
24.27 against you, to keep you from rebelling against your **God."**
Judg 1. 7 **God** has now done to me what I did to them."
2.12 stopped worshipping the Lord, the **God** of their ancestors,
2.12 the **God** who had brought them out
3. 7 The people of Israel forgot the Lord their **God;**
3.20 and said, "I have a message from **God** for you."
4. 6 "The Lord, the **God** of Israel, has given you this
4.23 **God** gave the Israelites victory over Jabin, the Canaanite king.
5. 3 I will sing, I will play music to Israel's **God,** the Lord.
5. 5 the Lord of Sinai, before the Lord, the **God** of Israel.
6. 8 brought them this message from the Lord, the **God** of Israel:
6.10 I am the Lord your **God** and that you should not worship
6.26 altar to the Lord your **God** on top of this mound.
6.36 Then Gideon said to **God,** "You say that you have decided
6.39 Then Gideon said to **God,** "Don't be angry with me;
6.40 That night **God** did that very thing.
7.14 **God** has given him victory over Midian and our whole army!"
8. 3 through the power of **God** you killed the two Midianite chiefs,
8.27 All the Israelites abandoned **God** and went there to worship the idol.
8.33 Israel were again unfaithful to **God** and worshipped the Baals.
8.34 longer served the Lord their **God,** who had saved them from
9. 7 to me, you men of Shechem, and **God** may listen to you!
9.23 Then **God** made Abimelech and the men of Shechem hostile
9.56 In this way **God** paid Abimelech back for the crime that
9.57 **God** also made the men of Shechem suffer for their wickedness,
10.10 for we left you, our **God,** and worshipped the Baals."
11.21 But the Lord, the **God** of Israel, gave the Israelites victory
11.23 it was the Lord, the **God** of Israel, who drove out the
11.24 to keep everything that the Lord, our **God,** has given us.
13. 5 of his birth he will be dedicated to **God** as a Nazirite.
13. 6 her husband, "A man of **God** has come to me,
13. 6 and he looked as frightening as the angel of **God.**
13. 7 is to be dedicated to **God** as a Nazirite
13. 8 Lord, let the man of **God** that you sent come back
13. 9 **God** did what Manoah asked, and his angel came back
13.22 his wife, "We are sure to die, because we have seen **God!"**
15.19 Then **God** opened a hollow place in the ground there at Lehi,
16.17 "I have been dedicated to **God** as a Nazirite
16.28 please, **God,** give me my strength just once more, so that with this one blow
18. 5 said to him, "Please ask **God** if we are going to be
18.10 a person could want, and **God** has given it to you."
18.31 that the Tent where **God** was worshipped remained at Shiloh.
20.18 they asked **God,** "Which tribe should attack the Benjaminites
20.27 **God's** Covenant Box was there at Bethel in those days,
21. 2 Bethel and sat there in the presence of **God** until evening.
21. 3 **"Lord God** of Israel, why has this happened?
Ruth 1.16 people will be my people, and your **God** will be my God.
1.20 "call me Marah, because Almighty **God** has made my life bitter.
2.12 a full reward from the **Lord God** of Israel, to whom you
2.19 May **God** bless the man who took an interest in you!"
1 Sam 1.17 Eli said, "and may the **God** of Israel give you what you
2. 1 how joyful I am because **God** has helped me!
2. 2 there is none like him, no protector like our **God.**
2. 3 For the Lord is a **God** who knows, and he judges all
2.25 If a man sins against another man, **God** can defend him;
2.30 I, the **Lord God** of Israel, promised in the past that
3.17 **God** will punish you severely if you don't tell me everything he said."
4.11 **God's** Covenant Box was captured,
4.17 and **God's** Covenant Box was captured!"
4.19 When she heard that **God's** Covenant Box had been captured
4.21 Ichabod, explaining, **"God's** glory has left Israel"—
4.22 **"God's** glory has left Israel," she said,
4.22 "because **God's** Covenant Box has been captured."
5. 7 they said, "The **God** of Israel is punishing us
5. 8 shall we do with the Covenant Box of the **God** of Israel?"
5.10 the Covenant Box of the **God** of Israel here, in order to
1 Sam 5.11 panic throughout the city because **God** was punishing them so severely.
6. 3 the Covenant Box of the **God** of Israel, you must, of course,
6. 5 and you must give honour to the **God** of Israel.
6. 6 Don't forget how **God** made fools of them
6. 9 means that it is the **God** of the Israelites who has sent
6.20 Beth Shemesh said, "Who can stand before the Lord, this holy **God?**
7. 8 to the Lord our **God** to save us from the Philistines."
9. 9 whenever someone wanted to ask **God** a question, he would say,
9.27 and I will tell you what **God** has said."
10. 3 on their way to offer a sacrifice to **God** at Bethel.
10. 5 go to the Hill of **God** in Gibeah,
10. 7 When these things happen, do whatever **God** leads you to do.
10. 9 When Saul turned to leave Samuel, **God** gave Saul a new nature.
10.10 Suddenly the spirit of **God** took control of him,
10.18 "The Lord, the **God** of Israel, says, 'I brought you
10.19 I am your **God,** the one who rescues you
10.26 Some powerful men, whose hearts **God** had touched, went with
11. 6 heard this, the spirit of **God** took control of him, and he
12. 9 forgot the Lord their **God,** and so he let the Philistines
12.14 you honour the Lord your **God,** serve him, listen to him,
12.19 pray to the Lord your **God** for us,
13.13 "You have not obeyed the command the Lord your **God** gave you.
14.36 But the priest said, "Let's consult **God** first."
14.37 So Saul asked **God,** "Shall I attack the Philistines?
14.37 But **God** did not answer that day.
14.41 said to the Lord, the **God** of Israel, "Lord, why have you
14.41 Lord, **God** of Israel, answer me by the sacred stones.
14.44 Saul said to him, "May **God** strike me dead if you are
14.45 What he did today was done with **God's** help."
15.15 sacrifice to the Lord your **God,** and the rest we have
15.21 to Gilgal to offer as a sacrifice to the Lord your **God."**
15.29 Israel's majestic **God** does not lie or change his mind.
15.30 back with me so that I can worship the Lord your **God."**
16.15 "We know that an evil spirit sent by **God** is tormenting you.
16.23 the evil spirit sent by **God** came on Saul,
17.26 heathen Philistine to defy the army of the **living God?"**
17.36 Philistine, who has defied the army of the **living God.**
17.45 the Lord Almighty, the **God** of the Israelite armies,
17.46 know that Israel has a **God,** [47] and everyone here will see
18.10 an evil spirit from **God** suddenly took control of Saul,
19.20 Then the spirit of **God** took control of Saul's men,
19.23 the spirit of **God** took control of him also,
20. 2 Jonathan answered, **"God** forbid that you should die!
20.12 said to David, "May the **Lord God** of Israel be our witness!
20.42 Then Jonathan said to David, **"God** be with you.
21. 6 was the loaves offered to **God,** which had been removed from
22. 3 until I find out what **God** is going to do for me."
22.13 give him some food and a sword, and consult **God** for him?
22.15 Yes, I consulted **God** for him, and it wasn't the first time.
23. 7 to Keilah, and he said, **"God** has put him in my power.
23.10 Then David said, "Lord, **God** of Israel, I have heard
23.11 Lord, **God** of Israel, I beg you to answer me!"
23.14 trying to find him, but **God** did not hand David over
23.16 him with assurances of **God's** protection,
25.22 May **God** strike me dead if I don't kill every last one
25.29 the Lord your **God** will keep you safe,
25.32 "Praise the Lord, the **God** of Israel, who sent you today
25.33 Thank **God** for your good sense and for what you have done
25.34 But I swear by the **living God** of Israel that if you
26. 8 Abishai said to David, **"God** has put your enemy in your
26.25 Saul said to David, **"God** bless you, my son!
28.15 The Philistines are at war with me, and **God** has abandoned me.
29. 6 him, "I swear by the **living God** of Israel that you have
29. 9 "I consider you as loyal as an angel of **God.**
30. 6 but the Lord his **God** gave him courage.
30.15 if you promise me in **God's** name that you will not kill
2 Sam 2.27 "I swear by the **living God,"** Joab answered, "that if
3. 9 Now may **God** strike me dead if I don't make this come
3.35 made a solemn promise, "May **God** strike me dead if I eat
3.39 though I am the king chosen by **God,** I feel weak today.
5.10 all the time, because the **Lord God** Almighty was with him.
6. 2 order to bring from there **God's** Covenant Box,
6. 7 At once the **Lord God** became angry with Uzzah and killed
7. 2 house built of cedar, but **God's** Covenant Box is kept
7.17 Nathan told David everything that **God** had revealed to him.
7.22 we have always known that you alone are **God.**
7.24 own people for ever, and you, Lord, have become their **God.**
7.25 "And now, **Lord God,** fulfil for all time the promise
7.26 will for ever say, 'The Lord Almighty is **God** over Israel.'
7.27 Almighty Lord, **God** of Israel!
7.28 "And now, Sovereign Lord, you are **God;**
9. 3 I can show loyalty and kindness, as I promised **God** I would?"
10.12 fight hard for our people and for the cities of our **God.**
12. 7 "And this is what the **Lord God** of Israel says:
12.16 David prayed to **God** that the child would get well.
14.11 pray to the Lord your **God,** so that my relative who is
14.14 Even **God** does not bring the dead back to life,
14.16 and so remove us from the land **God** gave his people.
14.17 because the king is like **God's** angel
14.17 May the Lord your **God** be with you!"
14.20 as the angel of **God** and knows everything that happens."
14.22 David in respect, and said, **"God** bless you, Your Majesty!
16.23 days was accepted as though it were the very word of **God;**
18.28 said, "Praise the Lord your **God,** who has given you victory
19.13 May **God** strike me dead if I don't!"
19.27 but you are like **God's** angel, so do what seems right
21.14 And after that, **God** answered their prayers for the country.
22. 3 My **God** is my protection, and with him I am safe.
22. 7 I called to my **God** for help.

2 Sam 22. 8 the sky rocked and quivered because **God** was angry!
22.14 from the sky, and the voice of Almighty **God** was heard.
22.22 I have not turned away from my **God.**
22.31 This **God**—how perfect are his deeds, how dependable his words!
22.32 The Lord alone is **God;**
22.32 **God** alone is our defence.
22.33 This **God** is my strong refuge;
22.47 Proclaim the greatness of the strong **God** who saves me!
22.51 **God** gives great victories to his king;
23. 1 Jesse was the man whom **God** made great,
23. 1 whom the **God** of Jacob chose to be king,
23. 3 The **God** of Israel has spoken;
23. 3 who rules in obedience to **God,** [4] is like the sun shining
23. 5 And that is how **God** will bless my descendants,
23. 5 that will be my victory, and **God** will surely bring it about.
24. 3 Majesty, may the Lord your **God** make the people of Israel
24.23 to him, "May the Lord your **God** accept your offering."
24.24 to the Lord my **God** sacrifices that have cost me nothing."
1 Kgs 1.17 name of the Lord your **God** that my son Solomon would be
1.30 name of the Lord, the **God** of Israel, that your son Solomon
1.36 answered Benaiah, "and may the Lord your **God** confirm it.
1.47 David, and said, 'May your **God** make Solomon even more famous
1.48 praise the Lord, the **God** of Israel, who has today made
2. 3 and do what the Lord your **God** orders you to do.
2.23 in the Lord's name, "May **God** strike me dead if I don't
3. 7 O **Lord God,** you have let me succeed my father as king,
3.15 woke up and realized that **God** had spoken to him
3.28 because they knew then that **God** had given him the wisdom
4.29 **God** gave Solomon unusual wisdom and insight,
5. 3 worship of the Lord his **God** until the Lord had given him
5. 4 But now the Lord my **God** has given me peace
5. 5 to build that temple for the worship of the Lord my **God.**
7.48 for the bread offered to **God,** [49] the ten lamp-stands that
8.14 Solomon turned to face them, and he asked **God's** blessing on them.
8.15 He said, "Praise the **Lord God** of Israel!
8.17 for the worship of the **Lord God** of Israel, [18] but the Lord
8.20 built the Temple for the worship of the **Lord God** of Israel.
8.23 raised his arms [23] and prayed, **"Lord God** of Israel, there
8.25 And now, **Lord God** of Israel, I pray that you will also
8.26 So now, O **God** of Israel, let everything come true
8.27 "But can you, O **God,** really live on earth?
8.28 Lord my **God,** I am your servant.
8.55 he asked **God's** blessings on all the people assembled
8.57 May the Lord our **God** be with us,
8.59 May the Lord our **God** remember at all times this prayer
8.60 will know that the Lord alone is **God**—there is no other.
8.61 to the Lord our **God,** obeying all his laws and commands,
9. 9 they abandoned the Lord their **God,** who brought their ancestors out
10. 9 Praise the Lord your **God!**
10.24 to come and listen to the wisdom that **God** had given him.
11. 3 made him turn away from **God,**
11. 4 faithful to the Lord his **God,** as his father David had been.
11. 9 the Lord, the **God** of Israel, had appeared to Solomon
11.23 **God** also caused Rezon son of Eliada to turn against Solomon.
11.31 because the Lord, the **God** of Israel, says to you, 'I
12.22 But **God** told the prophet Shemaiah [23] to give this message
13. 6 me to the Lord your **God,** and ask him to heal my
14. 7 this is what the Lord, the **God** of Israel, says to him:
14.13 only one with whom the Lord, the **God** of Israel, is pleased.
15. 3 the Lord his **God,** as his great-grandfather David had been.
15. 4 David's sake, the Lord his **God** gave Abijah a son to rule
15.15 his father had dedicated to **God,** as well as the gold and
15.30 anger of the Lord, the **God** of Israel, by the sins that
16.13 Elah had aroused the anger of the Lord, the **God** of Israel.
16.26 anger of the Lord, the **God** of Israel, by his sins and
16.33 anger of the Lord, the **God** of Israel, than all the kings
17. 1 name of the Lord, the **living God** of Israel, whom I serve,
17.12 "By the living Lord your **God** I swear that I haven't got
17.14 For this is what the Lord, the **God** of Israel, says:
17.18 said to Elijah, "Man of **God,** why did you do this to
17.18 you come here to remind **God** of my sins and so cause
17.20 prayed aloud, "O Lord my **God,** why have you done such a
17.21 and prayed, "O Lord my **God,** restore this child to life!"
17.24 you are a man of **God** and that the Lord really speaks
18.10 By the living Lord, your **God,** I swear that the king has
18.21 If the Lord is **God,** worship him;
18.21 but if Baal is **God,** worship him!"
18.24 Lord, and the one who answers by sending fire—he is **God."**
18.36 and prayed, "O Lord, the **God** of Abraham, Isaac, and Jacob,
18.36 now that you are the **God** of Israel and that I am
18.37 that you, the Lord, are **God,** and that you are bringing them
18.39 themselves on the ground and exclaimed, "The Lord is **God;**
18.39 the Lord alone is **God!"**
19.10 He answered, **"Lord God** Almighty, I have always served you—
19.14 He answered, **"Lord God** Almighty, I have always served you—
21.10 to accuse him to his face of cursing **God** and the king.
21.13 publicly accused him of cursing **God** and the king,
2 Kgs 1. 9 said to him, "Man of **God,** the king orders you to come
1.10 I am a man of **God,"** Elijah answered, "may fire come down
1.11 said to Elijah, "Man of **God,** the king orders you to come
1.12 I am a man of **God,"** Elijah answered, "may fire come down
1.12 At once the fire of **God** came down and killed the officer
1.13 Elijah, and pleaded, "Man of **God,** be merciful to me
2.14 "Where is the Lord, the **God** of Elijah?"
4.16 You are a man of **God!"**
5. 7 he think that I am **God,** with the power of life and
5.11 pray to the Lord his **God,** wave his hand over the diseased
5.15 I know that there is no **god** but the God of Israel;
6.31 "May **God** strike me dead if Elisha is not beheaded
2 Kgs 9. 6 "The Lord, the **God** of Israel, proclaims:
10.31 all his heart the law of the Lord, the **God** of Israel;
14.25 was what the Lord, the **God** of Israel, had promised through
16. 2 pleasing to the Lord his **God** [3] and followed the example of
17. 7 sinned against the Lord their **God,** who had rescued them from
17. 9 The Israelites did things that the Lord their **God** disapproved of.
17.14 their ancestors, who had not trusted in the Lord their **God.**
17.16 laws of the Lord their **God** and made two metal bull-calves to
17.19 of Judah did not obey the laws of the Lord their **God;**
17.39 obey me, the Lord your **God,** and I will rescue you from
18. 5 Hezekiah trusted in the Lord, the **God** of Israel;
18.12 not obey the Lord their **God,** but broke the covenant he had
18.22 you tell me that you are relying on the Lord your **God?**
19. 4 emperor has sent his chief official to insult the **living God.**
19. 4 May the Lord your **God** hear these insults and punish those
19. 4 So pray to **God** for those of our people who survive."
19.10 to say to him, "The **god** you are trusting in has told
19.15 and prayed, "O Lord, the **God** of Israel, enthroned above the
19.15 winged creatures, you alone are **God,** ruling all the kingdoms
19.16 that Sennacherib is saying to insult you, the **living God.**
19.19 Now, Lord our **God,** rescue us from the Assyrians,
19.19 of the world will know that only you, O Lord, are **God."**
19.22 You have been disrespectful to me, the holy **God** of Israel.
20. 5 "I, the Lord, the **God** of your ancestor David, have heard
21.12 So I, the **Lord God** of Israel, will bring such a disaster
21.22 He rejected the Lord, the **God** of his ancestors,
22. 2 ancestor King David, strictly obeying all the laws of **God.**
22.18 king himself, this is what I, the **Lord God** of Israel, say:
23.21 honour of the Lord their **God,** as written in the book of
1 Chr 2. 7 of Israel by keeping loot that had been devoted to **God.**
4.10 But Jabez prayed to the **God** of Israel,
4.10 "Bless me, **God,** and give me much land.
4.10 And **God** gave him what he prayed for.
5.20 They put their trust in **God** and prayed to him for help,
5.20 and **God** answered their prayers and made them
5.22 They killed many of the enemy, because the war was **God's** will.
5.25 people were unfaithful to the **God** of their ancestors and
5.25 gods of the nations whom **God** had driven out of the land.
5.26 So **God** made Emperor Pul of Assyria (also known as Tiglath Pileser)
6.49 and for the sacrifices by which **God** forgives Israel's sins.
6.49 in accordance with the instructions given by Moses, **God's** servant.
11. 2 and the Lord your **God** promised you that you would lead
12.17 tried to hurt you, the **God** of our ancestors will know it
12.18 **God's** spirit took control of one of them, Amasai,
12.18 **God** is on your side."
13. 2 will of the Lord our **God,** let us send messengers to the
13. 3 we will go and fetch **God's** Covenant Box, which was ignored
13. 6 fetch the Covenant Box of **God,** which bears the name of the
13. 8 all the people danced with all their might to honour **God.**
13.10 He died there in **God's** presence,
13.12 Then David was afraid of **God** and said, "How can I take
14.10 David asked **God,** "Shall I attack the Philistines?
14.11 He said, **"God** has used me to break through the enemy army
14.14 David consulted **God,** who answered, "Don't attack them
14.16 David did what **God** had commanded, and so he drove the
15. 1 also prepared a place for **God's** Covenant Box
15.12 the Covenant Box of the **Lord God** of Israel to the place
15.13 the Lord our **God** punished us for not worshipping him
15.14 order to move the Covenant Box of the **Lord God** of Israel.
15.26 to make sure that **God** would help the Levites
16. 1 Then they offered sacrifices and fellowship-offerings to **God.**
16. 4 worship of the Lord, the **God** of Israel,
16.12 You descendants of Jacob, **God's** servant,
16.12 descendants of Israel, whom **God** chose,
16.12 remember the miracles that **God** performed
16.14 The Lord is our **God;**
16.15 Never forget **God's** covenant, which he made to last for ever,
16.21 But **God** let no one oppress them;
16.35 Say to him, "Save us, O **God** our Saviour;
16.36 Praise the Lord, the **God** of Israel!
17. 2 "Do whatever you have in mind, because **God** is with you."
17. 3 that night **God** said to Nathan, [4] "Go and tell my servant
17.15 Nathan told David everything that **God** had revealed to him.
17.16 you have already done for me, **Lord God,** nor is my family.
17.17 years to come, and you, **Lord God,** are already treating me
17.20 we have always known that you alone are **God.**
17.22 own people for ever, and you, Lord, have become their **God.**
17.24 will for ever say, 'The Lord Almighty is **God** over Israel.'
17.25 this prayer to you, my **God,** because you have revealed all
17.26 You, Lord, are **God,** and you have made this wonderful promise
19.13 fight hard for our people and for the cities of our **God.**
21. 7 **God** was displeased with what had been done, so he punished Israel.
21. 8 David said to **God,** "I have committed a terrible sin
21.17 David prayed, "O **God,** I am the one who did wrong.
21.17 my **God,** punish me and my family, and spare your people."
21.30 to go there to worship **God,** because he was afraid
22. 1 said, "This is where the Temple of the **Lord God** will be.
22. 6 him to build a temple for the Lord, the **God** of Israel.
22. 7 I wanted to build a temple to honour the Lord my **God.**
22.11 may the Lord your **God** be with you,
22.12 And may the Lord your **God** give you insight and wisdom
22.18 He said, "The Lord your **God** has been with you
22.19 Now serve the Lord your **God** with all your heart and soul.
23.14 of Moses, the man of **God,** were included among the Levites.)
23.25 David said, "The **Lord God** of Israel has given peace to
23.29 for the bread offered to **God,** the flour used in offerings,
24.19 Aaron in obedience to the commands of the **Lord God** of Israel.
25. 1 They were to proclaim **God's** messages, accompanied by the music

1 Chr	25. 2	who proclaimed **God's** messages whenever the king commanded.
	25. 3	they proclaimed **God's** message, accompanied by the music
	25. 5	**God** gave to Heman, the king's prophet, these fourteen sons
	26. 4	also Obed Edom, whom **God** blessed by giving him eight sons,
	26.20	treasury and the storerooms for gifts dedicated to **God.**
	26.26	all the gifts dedicated to **God** by King David,
	27.24	**God** punished Israel because of this census,
	28. 2	for the Covenant Box, the footstool of the Lord our **God.**
	28. 4	The Lord, the **God** of Israel, chose me and my descendants
	28. 8	in the presence of our **God** and of this assembly
	28. 8	everything that the Lord our **God** has commanded us,
	28. 9	you to acknowledge your father's **God** and to serve him with
	28.16	on which were placed the loaves of bread offered to **God.**
	28.20	The **Lord God,** whom I serve, will be with you.
	29. 1	Solomon is the one whom **God** has chosen,
	29. 1	not a palace for men but a temple for the **Lord God.**
	29. 3	my personal property because of my love for **God's** Temple.
	29.10	He said, **"Lord God** of our ancestor Jacob, may you be
	29.13	Now, our **God,** we give you thanks, and we praise your
	29.16	O Lord, our **God,** we have brought together all this
	29.18	**Lord God** of our ancestors Abraham, Isaac, and Jacob,
	29.20	Then David commanded the people, "Praise the Lord your **God!"**
	29.20	assembly praised the Lord, the **God** of their ancestors,
2 Chr	1. 1	and the Lord his **God** blessed him
	1. 7	That night **God** appeared to Solomon and asked, "What
	1. 9	O **Lord God,** fulfil the promise you made to my father.
	1.11	**God** replied to Solomon, "You have made the right choice.
	2. 4	I am building a temple to honour the Lord my **God.**
	2. 4	and other holy days honouring the Lord our **God.**
	2. 5	great temple, because our **God** is greater than any other god.
	2. 6	really build a temple for **God,** because even all the vastness
	2. 6	would be anything more than a place to burn incense to **God?**
	2.12	Praise the **Lord God** of Israel, Creator of heaven and earth!
	4.19	the altar and the tables for the bread offered to **God;**
	6. 3	The king turned to face them and asked **God's** blessing on them.
	6. 4	He said, "Praise the **Lord God** of Israel!
	6. 7	for the worship of the **Lord God** of Israel, [8] but the Lord
	6.10	built a temple for the worship of the **Lord God** of Israel.
	6.14	He prayed, **"Lord God** of Israel, in all heaven and earth
	6.16	Now, **Lord God** of Israel, keep the other promise you made
	6.17	So now, **Lord God** of Israel, let everything come true
	6.18	"But can you, O **God,** really live on earth among men
	6.19	Lord my **God,** I am your servant.
	6.40	"Now, O my **God,** look on us and listen to the prayers
	6.41	Rise up now, **Lord God,** and with the Covenant Box, the
	6.42	**Lord God,** do not reject the king you have chosen.
	7. 3	downwards on the pavement, worshipping **God** and praising him
	7.22	they abandoned the Lord their **God,** who brought their
	8.14	in accordance with the commands of David, the man of **God.**
	9. 8	Praise the Lord your **God!**
	9.23	consulted him, to hear the wisdom that **God** had given him.
	10.15	was the will of the **Lord God** to bring about what he
	11.16	to worship the Lord, the **God** of Israel, followed the Levites
	11.16	offer sacrifices to the Lord, the **God** of their ancestors.
	13. 5	the Lord, the **God** of Israel, made an unbreakable covenant
	13.10	we still serve the Lord our **God** and have not abandoned him.
	13.12	**God** himself is our leader and his priests are here with trumpets,
	13.12	don't fight against the Lord, the **God** of your ancestors!
	13.15	**God** defeated Jeroboam and the Israelite army.
	13.16	fled from the Judaeans, and **God** let the Judaeans overpower them.
	13.18	they relied on the Lord, the **God** of their ancestors.
	14. 2	Asa pleased the Lord, his **God,** by doing what was right
	14. 4	will of the Lord, the **God** of their ancestors, and to obey
	14. 7	land because we have done the will of the Lord our **God.**
	14.11	prayed to the Lord his **God,** "O Lord, you can help
	14.11	us now, O Lord our **God,** because we are relying on you,
	14.11	Lord, you are our **God;**
	15. 1	The spirit of **God** came upon Azariah son of Oded,
	15. 3	Israel lived without the true **God,** without priests to teach them,
	15. 4	trouble came, they turned to the Lord, the **God** of Israel.
	15. 6	because **God** was bringing trouble and distress
	15.12	to worship the Lord, the **God** of their ancestors,
	15.18	father Abijah had dedicated to **God,**
	16. 7	relying on the Lord your **God,**
	17. 4	He served his father's **God,** obeyed God's commands,
	18. 5	**"God** will give you victory."
	18.13	the living Lord, I will say what my **God** tells me to!"
	18.31	gave a shout, and the **Lord God** rescued him and turned the
	19. 3	and you have tried to follow **God's** will."
	19. 4	the people back to the Lord, the **God** of their ancestors.
	19. 7	because the Lord our **God** does not tolerate fraud or partiality
	20. 6	them [6] and prayed aloud, "O **Lord God** of our ancestors, you
	20. 7	You are our **God.**
	20.12	You are our **God!**
	20.15	The battle depends on **God,** not on you.
	20.19	and with a loud shout praised the Lord, the **God** of Israel.
	20.20	your trust in the Lord your **God,** and you will stand firm.
	20.30	Jehoshaphat ruled in peace, and **God** gave him security
	20.33	to the worship of the **God** of their ancestors.
	21.10	Jehoram had abandoned the Lord, the **God** of his ancestors.
	21.12	"The Lord, the **God** of your ancestor David, condemns you,
	21.13	Jerusalem into being unfaithful to **God,** just as Ahab and his
	22. 7	**God** used this visit to Joram to bring about Ahaziah's downfall.
	22. 8	As Jehu was carrying out **God's** sentence on the dynasty,
	24. 9	the tax which Moses, **God's** servant, had first collected
	24.16	done for the people of Israel, for **God,** and for the Temple.
	24.18	Temple of the Lord, the **God** of their ancestors,
	24.20	Then the spirit of **God** took control of Zechariah
	24.20	him and called out, "The **Lord God** asks why you have
	24.24	people had abandoned him, the **Lord God** of their ancestors.
	25. 8	in battle, but it is **God** who has the power to give
2 Chr	25.16	saying, "Now I know that **God** has decided to destroy you
	25.20	It was **God's** will for Amaziah to be defeated,
	26. 5	he served the Lord faithfully, and **God** blessed him.
	26. 7	**God** helped him to defeat the Philistines,
	26.15	very powerful because of the help he received from **God.**
	26.16	He defied the Lord his **God** by going into the Temple to
	26.18	You have offended the **Lord God,** and you no longer have his
	27. 6	Jotham grew powerful because he faithfully obeyed the Lord his **God.**
	28. 5	Ahaz sinned, the Lord his **God** let the king of Syria defeat
	28. 5	The Lord, the **God** of their ancestors, permitted this to happen,
	28. 9	city, and he said, "The **Lord God** of your ancestors was
	28.10	that you also have committed sins against the Lord your **God?**
	28.25	on himself the anger of the Lord, the **God** of his ancestors.
	29. 5	purify the Temple of the Lord, the **God** of your ancestors.
	29. 6	unfaithful to the Lord our **God** and did what was displeasing
	29. 7	or offer burnt-offerings in the Temple of the **God** of Israel.
	29.10	covenant with the Lord, the **God** of Israel,
	29.19	years he was unfaithful to **God,** and we have rededicated it.
	29.29	Then King Hezekiah and all the people knelt down and worshipped **God.**
	29.30	So everyone sang with great joy as they knelt and worshipped **God.**
	29.36	the people were happy, because **God** had helped them
	30. 1	the Passover in honour of the Lord, the **God** of Israel.
	30. 6	return to the Lord, the **God** of Abraham, Isaac, and Jacob,
	30. 7	fellow-Israelites who were unfaithful to the Lord their **God.**
	30. 8	Jerusalem, which the Lord your **God** has made holy for ever,
	30. 9	The Lord your **God** is kind and merciful, and if you return
	30.12	**God** was also at work in Judah and united the people
	30.16	to the instructions in the Law of Moses, the man of **God.**
	30.19	"O Lord, the **God** of our ancestors, in your goodness
	30.22	praise of the Lord, the **God** of their ancestors,
	30.27	In his home in heaven **God** heard their prayers and accepted them.
	31. 6	of gifts, which they dedicated to the Lord their **God.**
	31.20	what was right and what was pleasing to the Lord his **God.**
	31.21	in a spirit of complete loyalty and devotion to his **God.**
	32. 8	we have the Lord our **God** to help us and to fight
	32.11	you that the Lord your **God** will save you from our power,
	32.14	Then what makes you think that your **god** can save you?
	32.15	So certainly this **god** of yours can't save you!"
	32.16	things about the **Lord God** and Hezekiah, the Lord's servant.
	32.17	that the emperor wrote defied the Lord, the **God** of Israel.
	32.17	and neither will Hezekiah's **god** save his people from me."
	32.19	They talked about the **God** of Jerusalem in the same way
	32.20	son of Amoz prayed to **God** and cried out to him for
	32.29	Besides all this, **God** gave him sheep and cattle and so
	32.31	had happened in the land, **God** let Hezekiah go his own way
	33. 7	Temple, the place about which **God** had said to David and his
	33.12	humble, turned to the Lord his **God,** and begged him for help.
	33.13	**God** accepted Manasseh's prayer and answered it by
	33.13	This convinced Manasseh that the Lord was **God.**
	33.16	the people of Judah to worship the Lord, the **God** of Israel.
	33.18	prayer he made to his **God,** and the messages of the prophets
	33.18	name of the Lord, the **God** of Israel, are all recorded in
	33.19	The king's prayer and **God's** answer to it,
	34. 2	ancestor King David, strictly obeying all the laws of **God.**
	34. 3	he began to worship the **God** of his ancestor King David.
	34. 8	Josiah sent three men to repair the Temple of the **Lord God:**
	34.14	Law of the Lord, the Law that **God** had given to Moses.
	34.26	king himself, this is what I, the **Lord God** of Israel, say:
	34.32	the covenant they had made with the **God** of their ancestors.
	34.33	the people to serve the Lord, the **God** of their ancestors.
	35. 3	you are to serve the Lord your **God** and his people Israel.
	35.21	but to fight my enemies, and **God** has told me to hurry.
	35.21	**God** is on my side, so don't oppose me, or he will
	35.22	refused to listen to what **God** was saying through King Neco,
	36. 5	He sinned against the Lord his **God.**
	36.13	forced him to swear in **God's** name that he would be loyal.
	36.13	refused to repent and return to the Lord, the **God** of Israel.
	36.15	The Lord, the **God** of their ancestors, had continued to
	36.16	But they ridiculed **God's** messengers,
	36.17	**God** handed them all over to him.
	36.23	The Lord, the **God** of Heaven, has made me ruler over the
	36.23	people, go there, and may the Lord your **God** be with you."
Ezra	1. 2	The Lord, the **God** of Heaven, has made me ruler over the
	1. 3	May **God** be with all of you who are his people.
	1. 3	Temple of the Lord, the **God** of Israel,
	1. 3	the **God** who is worshipped in Jerusalem.
	1. 4	offerings to present in the Temple of **God** in Jerusalem."
	1. 5	and everyone else whose heart **God** had moved got ready to go
	2.63	eat the food offered to **God** until there was a priest who
	3. 2	rebuilt the altar of the **God** of Israel,
	3. 2	instructions written in the Law of Moses, the man of **God.**
	4. 1	were rebuilding the Temple of the Lord, the **God** of Israel.
	4. 2	We worship the same **God** you worship,
	4. 3	need your help to build a temple for the Lord our **God.**
	5. 1	in the name of the **God** of Israel
	5. 5	But **God** was watching over the Jewish leaders,
	5. 8	the Temple of the great **God** is being rebuilt
	5.11	'We are servants of the **God** of heaven and earth,
	5.12	because our ancestors made the **God** of Heaven angry,
	6. 7	Jewish leaders rebuild the Temple of **God** where it stood before.
	6. 9	burnt as offerings to the **God** of Heaven,
	6.10	that are acceptable to the **God** of Heaven
	6.12	May the **God** who chose Jerusalem as the place where he is
	6.14	had been commanded by the **God** of Israel and by Cyrus,
	6.21	land and who had come to worship the **Lord God** of Israel.
	6.22	their work of rebuilding the Temple of the **God** of Israel.
	7. 6	Law which the Lord, the **God** of Israel, had given to Moses.
	7. 6	blessing of the Lord his **God,** the emperor gave him everything

Ezra 7. 8 and with **God's** help they arrived in Jerusalem
7.12 Ezra the priest, scholar in the Law of the **God** of Heaven.
7.14 the Law of your **God,** which has been entrusted to you,
7.15 desire to give to the **God** of Israel, whose Temple is in
7.16 priests give for the Temple of their **God** in Jerusalem.
7.18 desire, in accordance with the will of your **God.**
7.19 You are to present to **God** in Jerusalem all the utensils
7.21 in the Law of the **God** of Heaven, everything he asks you
7.23 everything which the **God** of Heaven requires for his Temple,
7.25 using the wisdom which your **God** has given you, are to
7.25 people in West Euphrates who live by the Law of your **God.**
7.26 disobeys the laws of your **God** or the laws of the empire,
7.27 Ezra said, "Praise the Lord, the **God** of our ancestors!
7.28 By **God's** grace I have won the favour of the emperor,
7.28 the Lord my **God** has given me courage,
8.17 workmen, to send us people to serve **God** in the Temple.
8.18 Through **God's** grace they sent us Sherebiah, an able man,
8.21 and humble ourselves before our **God** and to ask him to lead
8.22 had told him that our **God** blesses everyone who trusts him,
8.23 we fasted and prayed for **God** to protect us, and he answered
8.28 sacred to the Lord, the **God** of your ancestors,
8.31 Our **God** was with us and protected us from enemy attacks
8.35 offerings to be burnt as sacrifices to the **God** of Israel.
9. 4 frightened because of what the **God** of Israel had said
9. 5 in prayer and stretched out my hands to the Lord my **God.**
9. 6 I said, "O **God,** I am too ashamed to raise my head
9. 8 O Lord our **God,** you have been gracious to us
9.10 "But now, O **God,** what can we say
9.13 we know that you, our **God,** have punished us less than we
9.15 **Lord God** of Israel, you are just, but you have let us
10. 2 "We have broken faith with **God** by marrying foreign women,
10. 3 a solemn promise to our **God** that we will send these women
10. 3 and the others who honour **God's** commands advise us to do.
10. 3 We will do what **God's** Law demands.
10.11 sins to the Lord, the **God** of your ancestors, and do what
10.14 In this way **God's** anger over this situation will be turned away."
Neh 1. 5 I prayed to God, [5]"**Lord God** of Heaven!
2. 4 I prayed to the **God** of Heaven, [5]and then I said
2. 8 emperor gave me all I asked for, because **God** was with me.
2.12 did not tell anyone what **God** had inspired me to do
2.18 And I told them how **God** had been with me and helped
2.20 I answered, "The **God** of Heaven will give us success.
4. 4 I prayed, "Listen to them mocking us, O **God!**
4. 9 but we prayed to our **God** and kept men on guard
4.15 and they realized that **God** had defeated their plans.
4.20 Our **God** will fight for us."
5. 9 You ought to obey **God** and do what's right.
5.13 "This is how **God** will shake any of you who don't keep
5.13 "**God** will take away your houses and everything you own,
5.15 But I acted differently, because I honoured **God.**
5.19 I pray you, O **God,** remember to my credit everything that
6. 9 I prayed, "But now, **God,** make me strong!"
6.12 I realized that **God** had not spoken to Shemaiah,
6.14 I prayed, "**God,** remember what Tobiah and Sanballat have
6.16 everyone knew that the work had been done with **God's** help.
7. 5 **God** inspired me to assemble the people and their leaders
7.65 eat the food offered to **God** until there was a priest who
8. 6 Ezra said, "Praise the Lord, the great **God!"**
8. 8 gave an oral translation of **God's** Law and explained it
8. 9 holy to the Lord your **God,** so you are not to mourn
8.18 they read a part of **God's** Law every day.
9. 3 Law of the Lord their **God** was read to them,
9. 3 they confessed their sins and worshipped the Lord their **God.**
9. 4 They prayed aloud to the Lord their **God.**
9. 5 "Stand up and praise the Lord your **God;**
9. 7 You, **Lord God,** chose Abram and led him out of Ur in
9.17 But you are a **God** who forgives;
9.31 You are a gracious and merciful **God!**
9.32 "O **God,** our God, how great you are!
10.28 who in obedience to **God's** Law have separated themselves
10.29 we will live according to **God's** Law, which God gave
10.34 offered to the Lord our **God,** according to the requirements
10.36 Temple and there, as required by the Law, dedicate him to **God.**
10.39 We will not neglect the house of our **God.**
12.24 at a time praised **God** responsively and gave thanks to him,
12.24 the instructions given by King David, the man of **God.**
12.31 large groups to march round the city, giving thanks to **God.**
12.36 of the kind played by King David, the man of **God.**
12.40 that were giving thanks to **God** reached the temple area.
12.43 were full of joy because **God** had made them very happy.
12.45 purification and the other rituals that **God** had commanded.
12.46 the musicians have led songs of praise and thanksgiving to **God.**
13. 2 curse Israel, but our **God** turned the curse into a blessing.
13.14 Remember, my **God,** all these things that I have done
13.18 This is exactly why **God** punished your ancestors
13.18 bringing more of **God's** anger down on Israel by profaning
13.22 Remember me, O **God,** for this also, and spare me
13.25 them take an oath in **God's** name that never again would they
13.26 **God** loved him and made him king over all Israel,
13.27 example and disobey our **God** by marrying foreign women?"
13.29 Remember, O **God,** how those people defiled both the
13.31 Remember all this, O **God,** and give me credit for it.
Job 1. 1 the land of Uz, who worshipped **God** and was faithful to him.
1. 5 one of them might have sinned by insulting **God** unintentionally.
1.22 Job did not sin by blaming **God.**
2. 9 Why don't you curse **God** and die?"
2.10 When **God** sends us something good, we welcome it.
2.10 In spite of everything he suffered, Job said nothing against **God.**
3. 2 O **God,** put a curse on the day I was born;
3. 4 Turn that day into darkness, **God.**
3.23 **God** keeps their future hidden and hems them in on every side.

Job 4. 6 You worshipped **God,** and your life was blameless;
4. 9 Like a storm, **God** destroys them in his anger.
4.10 growl like lions, but **God** silences them and breaks their teeth.
4.17 in the sight of **God** or be pure before his Creator?
4.18 **God** does not trust his heavenly servants;
5. 8 I would turn to **God** and present my case to him.
5.11 Yes, it is **God** who raises the humble and gives joy to
5.15 But **God** saves the poor from death;
5.17 Happy is the person whom **God** corrects!
5.18 **God** bandages the wounds he makes;
5.21 **God** will rescue you from slander;
6. 4 Almighty **God** has pierced me with arrows,
6. 4 **God** has lined up his terrors against me.
6. 8 Why won't **God** give me what I ask?
6.10 I know that **God** is holy;
6.14 I need loyal friends— whether I've forsaken **God** or not.
7. 7 Remember, O **God,** my life is only a breath;
8. 3 **God** never twists justice;
8. 4 children must have sinned against **God,** and so he punished them
8. 5 But turn now and plead with Almighty **God;**
8. 6 so honest and pure, then **God** will come and help you
8. 7 will be nothing compared with what **God** will give you then.
8.13 their hope is gone, once **God** is forgotten.
8.20 But **God** will never abandon the faithful
9. 1 But how can a man win his case against **God?**
9. 4 **God** is so wise and powerful;
9. 6 **God** sends earthquakes and shakes the ground;
9. 8 No one helped **God** spread out the heavens
9. 9 **God** hung the stars in the sky—the Great Bear, Orion,
9.11 **God** passes by, but I cannot see him.
9.13 **God's** anger is constant.
9.14 So how can I find words to answer **God?**
9.15 all I can do is beg for mercy from **God** my judge.
9.19 Try force on **God?**
9.21 innocent or guilty, **God** will destroy us.
9.23 When an innocent man suddenly dies, **God** laughs.
9.24 **God** gave the world to the wicked.
9.24 And if **God** didn't do it, who did?
9.27 I know that **God** does hold me guilty.
9.31 **God** throws me into a pit of filth,
9.32 If **God** were human, I could answer him;
9.33 step between us— no one to judge both **God** and me.
9.34 Stop punishing me, **God!**
10. 2 Don't condemn me, **God.**
10.18 Why, **God,** did you let me be born?
11. 4 you claim you are pure in the sight of **God.**
11. 5 How I wish **God** would answer you!
11. 6 **God** is punishing you less than you deserve.
11. 7 the limits and bounds of the greatness and power of **God?**
11. 8 sky is no limit for **God,** but it lies beyond your reach.
11. 8 **God** knows the world of the dead, but you do not know
11. 9 **God's** greatness is broader than the earth, wider than the sea.
11.10 If **God** arrests you and brings you to trial, who is there
11.11 **God** knows which men are worthless;
11.13 Reach out to **God.**
11.18 **God** will protect you and give you rest.
12. 4 but there was a time when **God** answered my prayers.
12.10 It is **God** who directs the lives of his creatures;
12.12 Old men have wisdom, but **God** has wisdom and power.
12.12 **God** has insight and power to act.
12.14 When **God** tears down, who can rebuild,
12.14 and who can free the man **God** imprisons?
12.15 Drought comes when **God** withholds rain;
12.16 **God** is strong and always victorious;
13. 3 But my dispute is with **God,** not you;
13. 7 Do you think your lies will benefit **God?**
13. 9 If **God** looks at you closely, will he find anything good?
13. 9 Do you think you can fool **God** as you fool men?
13.15 I've lost all hope, so what if **God** kills me?
13.16 since no wicked man would dare to face **God.**
13.19 Are you coming to accuse me, **God?**
13.22 Speak first, O **God,** and I will answer.
14. 3 you even look at me, **God,** or put me on trial
15. 4 If you had your way, no one would fear **God;**
15. 7 Were you there when **God** made the mountains?
15. 8 Did you overhear the plans **God** made?
15.11 **God** offers you comfort;
15.13 You are angry with **God** and denounce him.
15.14 Can anyone be right with **God?**
15.15 Why, **God** does not trust even his angels;
15.19 there was no one to lead them away from **God.**
15.25 the man who shakes his fist at **God** and defies the Almighty.
15.26 he stubbornly holds up his shield and rushes to fight against **God.**
16. 7 You have worn me out, **God;**
16. 9 In anger **God** tears me limb from limb;
16.11 **God** has handed me over to evil men.
16.12 was living in peace, but **God** took me by the throat
16.12 **God** uses me for target-practice [13]and shoots arrows at me
16.17 guilty of any violence, and my prayer to **God** is sincere.
16.20 my eyes pour out tears to **God.**
16.21 want someone to plead with **God** for me, as a man pleads
17. 3 I am being honest, **God.**
18. 4 Will **God** move mountains to satisfy you?
18.21 of evil men, the fate of those who care nothing for **God.**
19. 6 Can't you see it is **God** who has done this?
19. 8 **God** has blocked the way, and I can't get through;
19.11 **God** is angry and rages against me;
19.13 **God** has made my brothers forsake me;
19.21 The hand of **God** has struck me down.
19.22 Why must you persecute me as **God** does?
19.26 eaten by disease, while still in this body I will see **God.**

Job 19.29 the sword that brings **God's** wrath on
20.15 **God** takes it back, even out of his stomach.
20.23 **God** will punish him in fury and anger.
20.28 All his wealth will be destroyed in the flood of **God's** anger.
20.29 the fate of wicked men, the fate that **God** assigns to them.
21. 7 Why does **God** let evil men live, let them grow old
21. 9 **God** does not bring disaster on their homes;
21.14 The wicked tell **God** to leave them alone;
21.15 no need to serve **God** nor any advantage in praying
21.17 Did **God** ever punish the wicked in anger [18]and blow them
21.19 You claim **God** punishes a child for the sins of his father.
21.19 Let **God** punish the sinners themselves;
21.20 let them feel the wrath of Almighty **God.**
21.22 Can a man teach **God,** who judges even those in high places?
21.30 On the day **God** is angry and punishes, it is the wicked
22. 1 man, even the wisest, who could ever be of use to **God?**
22. 3 Does your doing right benefit **God,** or does your being good
22. 4 you stand in awe of **God** that he reprimands you
22.12 Doesn't **God** live in the highest heavens
22.13 And yet you ask, "What does **God** know?
22.17 are the men who rejected **God** and believed that he could do
22.18 And yet it was **God** who made them prosperous—
22.21 Now, Job, make peace with **God**
22.23 you must humbly return to **God**
22.25 Let Almighty **God** be your gold, and let him be silver,
22.26 you will always trust in **God**
22.29 **God** brings down the proud and saves the humble.
23. 1 I still rebel and complain against **God;**
23. 6 Would **God** use all his strength against me?
23. 7 I could reason with **God;**
23. 8 I have searched in the east, but **God** is not there;
23. 9 **God** has been at work in the north and the south,
23.10 Yet **God** knows every step I take;
23.12 I always do what **God** commands;
23.16 Almighty **God** has destroyed my courage.
23.16 It is **God,** not the dark, that makes me afraid—
24. 1 Why doesn't **God** set a time for judging, a day of justice
24.12 the wounded and dying cry out, but **God** ignores their prayers.
24.18 away by floods, and the land he owns is under **God's** curse;
24.22 **God,** in his strength, destroys the mighty;
24.22 **God** acts—and the wicked man dies.
24.23 **God** may let him live secure, but keeps an eye on him
25. 1 **God** is powerful;
25. 3 Is there any place where **God's** light does not shine?
25. 4 Can anyone be righteous or pure in **God's** sight?
25. 6 What is man worth in **God's** eyes?
26. 6 The world of the dead lies open to **God;**
26. 7 **God** stretched out the northern sky and hung the earth
26. 8 It is **God** who fills the clouds with water and keeps them
26.14 Who can know how truly great **God** is?
27. 1 swear by the living Almighty **God,** who refuses me justice
27. 3 as long as **God** gives me breath,
27. 8 for godless men in the hour when **God** demands their life?
27. 9 When trouble comes, will **God** hear their cries?
27.11 is God's power, and explain what Almighty **God** has planned.
27.13 This is how Almighty **God** punishes wicked, violent men.
28.23 **God** alone knows the way, Knows the place where wisdom is found,
28.25 When **God** gave the wind its power
28.26 When **God** decided where the rain would fall,
28.28 **God** said to men, "To be wise, you must have reverence
29. 2 could once again be as it was when **God** watched over me.
29. 3 **God** was always with me then and gave me light
29. 4 I was prosperous, and the friendship of **God** protected my home.
29. 5 Almighty **God** was with me then, and I was surrounded
30.11 Because **God** has made me weak and helpless, they turn
30.18 **God** seizes me by my collar and twists my clothes
30.20 I call to you, O **God,** but you never answer;
31. 2 What does Almighty **God** do to us?
31. 4 **God** knows everything I do;
31. 6 Let **God** weigh me on honest scales, and he will see how
31.14 If I did not, how could I then face **God?**
31.14 What could I say when **God** came to judge me?
31.15 The same **God** who created me created my servants also.
31.23 Because I fear **God's** punishment, I could never do such a thing.
31.28 it denies Almighty **God.**
31.35 Let Almighty **God** answer me.
31.37 I would tell **God** everything I have done,
32. 2 longer, because Job was justifying himself and blaming **God.**
32. 3 and this made it appear that **God** was in the wrong.
32. 8 is the spirit of Almighty **God** that comes to men
32.13 **God** must answer Job, for you have failed.
32.22 know how to flatter, and **God** would quickly punish me
33. 4 **God's** spirit made me and gave me life.
33. 6 are the same in **God's** sight, both of us were formed
33.10 But **God** finds excuses for attacking me
33.12 **God** is greater than any man.
33.13 Why do you accuse **God** of never answering a man's complaints?
33.14 Although **God** speaks again and again, no one pays attention
33.15 At night when men are asleep, **God** speaks in dreams and visions.
33.17 **God** speaks to make them stop their sinning and to save
33.19 **God** corrects a man by sending sickness
33.23 his aid— one of **God's** thousands of angels, who remind men
33.26 when he prays, **God** will answer him;
33.26 he will worship **God** with joy;
33.26 **God** will set things right for him again.
33.27 I have not done right, but **God** spared me.
33.29 **God** does all this again and again;
34. 5 that he is innocent, that **God** refuses to give him justice.
34. 7 He never shows respect for **God.**
34. 9 that it never does any good to try to follow **God's** will.

Job 34.10 Will Almighty **God** do what is wrong?
34.12 Almighty **God** does not do evil;
34.13 Did **God** get his power from someone else?
34.14 If **God** took back the breath of life, [15]then everyone living
34.17 Are you condemning the righteous **God?**
34.18 **God** condemns kings and rulers when they are worthless or wicked.
34.20 **God** strikes men down and they perish;
34.22 There is no darkness dark enough to hide a sinner from **God.**
34.23 **God** does not need to set a time for men to go
34.28 poor to cry out to **God,** and he heard their calls
34.29 If **God** decided to do nothing at all, no one could
34.31 confessed your sins to **God** and promised not to sin again?
34.32 Have you asked **God** to show you your faults,
34.33 Since you object to what **God** does, can you expect
34.37 in front of us all he mocks **God.**
35. 1 that you are innocent in **God's** sight,
35. 3 God's sight, [3]or to ask **God,** "How does my sin affect you?
35. 6 If you sin, that does no harm to **God.**
35. 7 Do you help **God** by being so righteous?
35. 7 There is nothing **God** needs from you.
35.10 But they don't turn to **God,** their Creator,
35.11 They don't turn to **God,** who makes us wise,
35.12 They cry for help, but **God** doesn't answer,
35.13 Almighty **God** does not see or hear them.
35.14 Job, you say you can't see **God;**
35.15 You think that **God** does not punish,
36. 1 listen a little longer to what I am saying on **God's** behalf.
36. 3 use what I know to show that **God,** my Creator, is just.
36. 5 How strong **God** is!
36. 9 for what they have done, [9]**God** shows them their sins
36.11 If they obey **God** and serve him, they live out their
36.15 But **God** teaches men through suffering
36.16 **God** brought you out of trouble, and let you enjoy security;
36.22 Remember how great is **God's** power;
36.23 No one can tell **God** what to do or accuse him
36.27 It is **God** who takes water from the earth
36.29 or how the thunder roars through the sky, where **God** dwells.
37. 2 to the voice of **God,** to the thunder
37. 5 At **God's** command amazing things happen,
37.10 The breath of **God** freezes the waters,
37.12 Lightning flashes from the clouds, [12]as they move at **God's** will.
37.12 They do all that **God** commands, everywhere throughout the world.
37.13 **God** sends rain to water the earth;
37.14 consider the wonderful things **God** does.
37.15 Do you know how **God** gives the command and makes lightning
37.16 clouds float in the sky, the work of **God's** amazing skill?
37.18 Can you help **God** stretch out the sky
37.19 Teach us what to say to **God;**
37.20 I won't ask to speak with **God;**
37.22 and the glory of **God** fills us with awe.
37.23 **God's** power is so great that we cannot come near him;
40. 1 Job, you challenged Almighty **God;**

Ps 1. 1 example of sinners or join those who have no use for **God.**
1. 5 Sinners will be condemned by **God**
3. 2 They talk about me and say, **"God** will not help him."
3. 7 Save me, my **God!**
4. 1 Answer me when I pray, O **God,** my defender!
5. 2 Listen to my cry for help, my **God** and king!
5. 4 You are not a **God** who is pleased with wrongdoing;
5.10 Condemn and punish them, O **God;**
7. 1 O Lord, my **God,** I come to you for protection;
7. 3 O Lord, my **God,** if I have wronged anyone,
7. 9 You are a righteous **God** and judge our thoughts and desires.
7.10 **God** is my protector;
7.11 **God** is a righteous judge and always condemns the wicked.
7.12 If they do not change their ways, **God** will sharpen his sword.
9. 2 I will sing praise to you, Almighty **God.**
9.12 **God** remembers those who suffer;
9.17 the destiny of all the wicked, of all those who reject **God.**
10. 4 in his pride he thinks that **God** doesn't matter.
10. 5 He cannot understand **God's** judgements;
10.11 The wicked man says to himself, **"God** doesn't care!
10.13 can a wicked man despise **God** and say to himself, "He will
13. 3 Look at me, O Lord my **God,** and answer me.
14. 1 Fools say to themselves, "There is no **God."**
14. 5 they will be terrified, for **God** is with those who obey him.
15. 2 A person who obeys **God** in everything and always does what
15. 4 He despises those whom **God** rejects, but honours those who obey
16. 1 Protect me, O **God;**
17. 6 I pray to you, O **God,** because you answer me;
18. 2 My **God** is my protection, and with him I am safe.
18. 6 I called to my **God** for help.
18. 7 the mountains rocked and quivered, because **God** was angry.
18.21 I have not turned away from my **God.**
18.30 This **God**—how perfect are his deeds!
18.31 The Lord alone is **God;**
18.31 **God** alone is our defence.
18.32 He is the **God** who makes me strong,
18.46 Proclaim the greatness of the **God** who saves me.
18.50 **God** gives great victories to his king;
19. 1 How clearly the sky reveals **God's** glory!
19. 4 **God** made a home in the sky for the sun;
20. 1 May the **God** of Jacob protect you!
20. 5 celebrate your triumph by praising our **God.**
20. 7 but we trust in the power of the Lord our **God.**
22. 1 My **God,** my **God,** why have you abandoned me?
22. 2 I call to you, my **God,** but you do not answer;
22.10 the day I was born, and you have always been my **God.**
24. 5 **God** will declare them innocent.

Ps 24. 6 the people who come to **God,**
24. 6 who come into the presence of the **God** of Jacob.
25. 2 in you, my **God,** I trust.
25. 5 for you are my **God,** who saves me.
25.22 From all their troubles, O **God,** save your people Israel!
27. 3 even if enemies attack me, I will still trust **God.**
27. 9 don't leave me, don't abandon me, O **God,** my saviour.
29. 3 the glorious **God** thunders, and his voice echoes over the ocean.
29. 9 while everyone in his Temple shouts, "Glory to **God!"**
30. 2 to you for help, O Lord my **God,** and you healed me;
30.12 Lord, you are my **God,** I will give you thanks for ever.
31. 1 You are a righteous **God;**
31. 5 you are a faithful **God.**
31.14 you are my **God.**
33.12 Happy is the nation whose **God** is the Lord;
35.23 rise up, my **God,** and plead my cause.
36. 1 he rejects **God** and has no reverence for him.
36. 2 he thinks that **God** will not discover his sin
36. 7 How precious, O **God,** is your constant love!
37.31 keeps the law of his **God** in his heart and never departs
38.15 and you, O Lord my **God,** will answer me.
38.21 do not stay away, my **God!**
40. 3 to sing a new song, a song of praise to our **God.**
40. 5 You have done many things for us, O Lord our **God;**
40. 8 How I love to do your will, my **God!**
40.17 You are my saviour and my **God**— hurry to my aid!
41.13 Praise the Lord, the **God** of Israel!
42. 1 a stream of cool water, so I long for you, O **God.**
42. 2 I thirst for you, the **living God;**
42. 3 all the time my enemies ask me, "Where is your **God?"**
42. 4 crowds to the house of **God** and led them as they walked
42. 4 along, a happy crowd, singing and shouting praise to **God.**
42. 5 will put my hope in **God,**
42. 5 and once again I will praise him, my saviour and my **God.**
42. 8 a song at night, a prayer to the **God** of my life.
42. 9 To **God,** my defender, I say, "Why have you forgotten me?
42.10 insults, as they keep on asking me, "Where is your **God?"**
42.11 will put my hope in **God,**
42.11 and once again I will praise him, my saviour and my **God.**
43. 1 O **God,** declare me innocent, and defend my cause against the ungodly;
43. 4 Then I will go to your altar, O **God;**
43. 4 play my harp and sing praise to you, O **God,** my God.
43. 5 will put my hope in **God,**
43. 5 and once again I will praise him, my saviour and my **God.**
44. 1 we have heard it, O **God**— our ancestors have told us
44. 4 You are my king and my **God;**
44.20 had stopped worshipping our **God** and prayed to a foreign god,
45. 2 **God** has always blessed you.
45. 6 The kingdom that **God** has given you will last for ever and
45. 7 That is why **God,** your God, has chosen you
46. 1 **God** is our shelter and strength, always ready to help
46. 4 joy to the city of **God,** to the sacred house
46. 5 **God** is in that city, and it will never be destroyed;
46. 6 **God** thunders, and the earth dissolves.
46. 7 the **God** of Jacob is our refuge.
46.10 "and know that I am **God,** supreme among the nations,
46.11 the **God** of Jacob is our refuge.
47. 1 Praise **God** with loud songs!
47. 5 **God** goes up to his throne.
47. 6 Sing praise to **God;**
47. 7 **God** is king over all the world;
47. 8 **God** sits on his sacred throne;
47. 9 the nations assemble with the people of the **God** of Abraham.
48. 1 highly praised in the city of our **God,** on his sacred hill.
48. 2 Zion, the mountain of **God,** is high and beautiful;
48. 3 **God** has shown that there is safety with him
48. 8 We have heard what **God** has done,
48. 8 have seen it in the city of our **God,** the Lord Almighty;
48. 9 Inside your Temple, O **God,** we think of your constant love.
48.12 People of **God,** walk round Zion and count the towers;
48.14 "This **God** is our God for ever and ever;
49. 7 he cannot pay **God** the price for his life,
49.15 But **God** will rescue me;
50. 1 The Almighty **God,** the Lord, speaks;
50. 2 **God** shines from Zion, the city perfect in its beauty.
50. 3 Our **God** is coming, but not in silence;
50. 6 The heavens proclaim that **God** is righteous, that he himself is judge.
50. 7 I am **God,** your God.
50.14 thanks be your sacrifice to **God,**
50.16 **God** says to the wicked, "Why should you recite my commandments?
51. 1 Be merciful to me, O **God,** because of your constant love.
51.10 pure heart in me, O **God,** and put a new and loyal
51.14 Spare my life, O **God,** and save me,
51.17 My sacrifice is a humble spirit, O **God;**
51.18 O **God,** be kind to Zion and help her;
52. 1 **God's** faithfulness is eternal.
52. 5 So **God** will ruin you for ever;
52. 7 who did not depend on **God** for safety, but trusted instead
52. 8 But I am like an olive-tree growing in the house of **God;**
52. 9 I will always thank you, **God,** for what you have done;
53. 1 Fools say to themselves, "There is no **God."**
53. 2 **God** looks down from heaven at mankind
53. 4 **God** asks.
53. 5 have never been before, for **God** will scatter the bones of
53. 5 **God** has rejected them, and so Israel will totally defeat them.
53. 6 of Israel will be when **God** makes them prosperous again!
54. 1 Save me by your power, O **God;**
54. 2 Hear my prayer, O **God;**

Ps 54. 3 trying to kill me— men who do not care about **God.**
54. 4 But **God** is my helper.
54. 5 May **God** use their own evil to punish my enemies.
55. 1 Hear my prayer, O **God;**
55.16 But I call to the **Lord God** for help, and he will
55.19 **God,** who has ruled from eternity, will hear me and defeat them;
55.23 But you, O **God,** will bring those murderers and liars to
56. 1 Be merciful to me, O **God,** because I am under attack;
56. 4 I trust in **God** and am not afraid;
56. 7 Punish them, O **God,** for their evil;
56. 9 **God** is on my side— [10] the Lord, whose promises I praise.
56.12 O **God,** I will offer you what I have promised;
56.13 walk in the presence of **God,** in the light that shines
57. 1 Be merciful to me, O **God,** be merciful,
57. 2 I call to **God,** the Most High,
57. 2 to **God,** who supplies my every need.
57. 3 **God** will show me his constant love and faithfulness.
57. 5 greatness in the sky, O **God,** and your glory over all the
57. 7 I have complete confidence, O **God;**
57.11 greatness in the sky, O **God,** and your glory over all the
58. 6 Break the teeth of these fierce lions, O **God.**
58. 9 in his fierce anger **God** will blow them away
58.11 there is indeed a **God** who judges the world."
59. 1 Save me from my enemies, my **God;**
59. 5 Rise, **Lord God** Almighty, and come to my aid;
59. 5 see for yourself, **God** of Israel!
59. 9 you are my refuge, O **God.**
59.10 My **God** loves me and will come to me;
59.11 Do not kill them, O **God,** or my people may forget.
59.13 Then everyone will know that **God** rules in Israel,
59.17 My refuge is **God,** the God who loves me.
60. 1 You have rejected us, **God,** and defeated us;
60. 6 **God** has said, "In triumph I will divide Shechem
60. 9 Who, O **God,** will take me into the fortified city?
60.12 With **God** on our side we will win;
61. 1 Hear my cry, O **God;**
61. 5 have heard my promises, O **God,** and you have given me what
61. 7 May he rule for ever in your presence, O **God;**
62. 1 I wait patiently for **God** to save me;
62. 5 I depend on **God** alone;
62. 7 My salvation and honour depend on **God;**
62. 8 Trust in **God** at all times, my people.
62.11 I have heard **God** say that power belongs to him
63. 1 O **God,** you are my God, and I long for you.
63.11 Because **God** gives him victory, the king will rejoice.
63.11 Those who make promises in **God's** name will praise him,
64. 1 I am in trouble, **God**—listen to my prayer!
64. 7 But **God** shoots his arrows at them, and suddenly they are wounded.
64. 9 they will think about what **God** has done
65. 1 O **God,** it is right for us to praise you in Zion
66. 1 Praise **God** with shouts of joy, all people!
66. 3 Say to **God,** "How wonderful are the things you do!
66. 5 Come and see what **God** has done, his wonderful acts among men.
66. 8 Praise our **God,** all nations;
66.10 You have put us to the test, **God;**
66.16 listen, all who honour **God,** and I will tell you what
66.19 But **God** has indeed heard me;
66.20 I praise **God,** because he did not reject my prayer
67. 1 **God,** be merciful to us and bless us;
67. 3 May the peoples praise you, O **God;**
67. 5 May the peoples praise you, O **God;**
67. 6 **God,** our God, has blessed us.
67. 7 **God** has blessed us;
68. 1 **God** rises up and scatters his enemies.
68. 2 so do the wicked perish in **God's** presence.
68. 4 Sing to **God,** sing praises to his name;
68. 5 **God,** who lives in his sacred Temple, cares for orphans
68. 7 O **God,** when you led your people,
68. 8 of the coming of the **God** of Sinai,
68. 8 the coming of the **God** of Israel.
68.14 When Almighty **God** scattered the kings on Mount Zalmon,
68.16 look with scorn on the mountain on which **God** chose to live?
68.18 The **Lord God** will live there.
68.19 he is the **God** who saves us.
68.20 Our **God** is a God who saves;
68.21 **God** will surely break the heads of his enemies,
68.24 O **God,** your march of triumph is seen by all,
68.24 the procession of **God,** my king, into his sanctuary.
68.26 "Praise **God** in the meeting of his people;
68.28 Show your power, O **God,** the power you have used
68.31 the Sudanese will raise their hands in prayer to **God.**
68.32 Sing to **God,** kingdoms of the world, sing praise to the Lord,
68.34 Proclaim **God's** power;
68.35 How awesome is **God** as he comes from his sanctuary—
68.35 the **God** of Israel!
68.35 Praise **God!**
69. 1 Save me, O **God!**
69. 5 My sins, O **God,** are not hidden from you;
69. 6 bring disgrace to those who worship you, O **God** of Israel!
69.13 answer me, **God,** at a time you choose.
69.29 lift me up, O **God,** and save me!
69.30 I will praise **God** with a song;
69.32 those who worship **God** will be encouraged.
69.34 Praise **God,** O heaven and earth, seas and all creatures in them.
70. 1 Save me, O **God!**
70. 4 for your salvation always say, "How great is **God!"**
70. 5 come to me quickly, O **God.**
71. 4 My **God,** rescue me from wicked men,
71.11 They say, **"God** has abandoned him;
71.12 Don't stay so far away, O **God;**

Ps 71.12 my **God,** hurry to my aid!
71.18 old and my hair is grey, do not abandon me, O **God!**
71.19 Your righteousness, **God,** reaches the skies.
71.22 I will praise your faithfulness, my **God.**
72. 1 Teach the king to judge with your righteousness, O **God;**
72.15 may **God's** blessings be on him always!
72.17 May all nations ask **God** to bless them
72.18 Praise the Lord, the **God** of Israel!
73. 1 **God** is indeed good to Israel, to those who have pure hearts.
73. 9 They speak evil of **God** in heaven and give arrogant orders
73.11 They say, **"God** will not know;
73.14 O **God,** you have made me suffer all day long;
73.26 mind and my body may grow weak, but **God** is my strength;
73.28 how wonderful to be near **God,** to find protection
74. 1 Why have you abandoned us like this, O **God?**
74.10 How long, O **God,** will our enemies laugh at you?
74.12 But you have been our king from the beginning, O **God;**
74.22 Rouse yourself, **God,** and defend your cause!
75. 1 We give thanks to you, O **God,** we give thanks to you!
75. 2 judgement," says **God,** "and I will judge with fairness.
75. 7 it is **God** who is the judge, condemning some and acquitting others.
75. 9 never stop speaking of the **God** of Jacob or singing praises
76. 1 **God** is known in Judah;
76. 4 How glorious you are, O **God!**
76. 6 When you threatened them, O **God** of Jacob, the horses and
76.11 Give the Lord your **God** what you promised him;
76.11 **God** makes men fear him;
77. 1 I cry aloud to **God;**
77. 3 When I think of **God,** I sigh;
77. 9 Has **God** forgotten to be merciful?
77.10 hurts me most is this— that **God** is no longer powerful."
77.13 Everything you do, O **God,** is holy.
77.14 You are the **God** who works miracles;
77.16 the waters saw you, O **God,** they were afraid,
78. 7 would put their trust in **God** and not forget
78. 8 disobedient people, whose trust in **God** was never firm
78.10 They did not keep their covenant with **God;**
78.12 While their ancestors watched, **God** performed miracles
78.17 they continued to sin against **God,**
78.18 They deliberately put **God** to the test
78.19 They spoke against **God** and said,
78.19 "Can **God** supply food in the desert?
78.25 ate the food of angels, and **God** gave them all they wanted.
78.29 **God** gave them what they wanted.
78.31 and were still eating, [31] when **God** became angry with them
78.35 They remembered that **God** was their protector,
78.38 But **God** was merciful to his people.
78.41 Again and again they put **God** to the test
78.41 and brought pain to the Holy **God** of Israel.
78.56 But they rebelled against Almighty **God** and put him to the test.
78.59 **God** was angry when he saw it, so he rejected his people
78.71 made him king of Israel, the shepherd of the people of **God.**
79. 1 O **God,** the heathen have invaded your land.
79. 9 Help us, O **God,** and save us;
79.10 Why should the nations ask us, "Where is your **God?"**
80. 3 Bring us back, O **God!**
80. 4 How much longer, **Lord God** Almighty, will you be angry with
80. 7 Bring us back, Almighty **God!**
80.14 Turn to us, Almighty **God!**
80.19 Bring us back, **Lord God** Almighty.
81. 1 Shout for joy to **God** our defender;
81. 1 sing praise to the **God** of Jacob!
81. 4 is the law in Israel, an order from the **God** of Jacob.
81.10 I am the Lord your **God,** who brought you out of Egypt.
82. 1 **God** presides in the heavenly council;
82. 8 Come, O **God,** and rule the world;
83. 1 O **God,** do not keep silent;
83.12 "We will take for our own the land that belongs to **God."**
83.13 Scatter them like dust, O **God,** like straw blown away
84. 2 With my whole being I sing for joy to the **living God.**
84. 3 young near your altars, Lord Almighty, my king and my **God.**
84. 7 they will see the **God** of gods on Zion.
84. 8 Hear my prayer, **Lord God** Almighty.
84. 8 Listen, O **God** of Jacob!
84. 9 Bless our king, O **God,** the king you have chosen.
84.10 of the house of my **God** than live in the homes of
85. 4 Bring us back, O **God** our saviour, and stop being displeased
85. 8 I am listening to what the **Lord God** is saying;
85.11 and **God's** righteousness will look down from heaven.
86. 3 You are my **God,** so be merciful to me;
86.10 you alone are **God.**
86.12 I will praise you with all my heart, O Lord my **God;**
86.14 Proud men are coming against me, O **God;**
86.15 a merciful and loving **God,** always patient, always kind and faithful.
87. 3 Listen, city of **God,** to the wonderful things he says about you:
88. 1 **Lord God,** my saviour, I cry out all day, and at night
89. 8 **Lord God** Almighty, none is as mighty as you;
89.18 you, the Holy **God** of Israel, gave us our king.
89.26 He will say to me, 'You are my father and my **God;**
90. 2 you were eternally **God,** and will be God for ever.
90.17 Lord our **God,** may your blessings be with us.
91. 2 You are my **God;**
91.11 **God** will put his angels in charge of you to protect you
91.14 **God** says, "I will save those who love me
92. 1 your honour, O Most High **God,** [2] to proclaim your constant love
92.13 in the Temple of our **God,** [14] that still bear fruit
94. 1 Lord, you are a **God** who punishes;
94. 7 the **God** of Israel does not notice."
94. 9 **God** made our ears—can't he hear?
94.22 my **God** protects me.

Ps 94.23 the Lord our **God** will destroy them.
95. 1 Let us sing for joy to **God,** who protects us!
95. 3 the Lord is a mighty **God,** a mighty king
95. 7 He is our **God;**
97.12 Remember what the holy **God** has done, and give thanks to him.
98. 3 All people everywhere have seen the victory of our **God.**
99. 5 Praise the Lord our **God;**
99. 8 O Lord, our **God,** you answered your people;
99. 8 you are a **God** who forgives, even though you punished
99. 9 Praise the Lord our **God,** and worship at his sacred hill!
99. 9 The Lord our **God** is holy.
100. 3 Acknowledge that the Lord is **God.**
101. 3 I hate the actions of those who turn away from **God;**
101. 6 those who are faithful to **God** and will let them live
102.24 O **God,** do not take me away now before I grow old.
104. 1 O Lord, my **God,** how great you are!
104.21 while they hunt, looking for the food that **God** provides.
104.33 as long as I live I will sing praises to my **God.**
105. 5 that **God** performed
105. 7 The Lord is our **God;**
105.14 But **God** let no one oppress them;
105.27 They did **God's** mighty acts and performed miracles in Egypt.
105.28 **God** sent darkness on the country,
105.31 **God** commanded, and flies and gnats swarmed
105.39 **God** put a cloud over his people and a fire at night
106. 7 Our ancestors in Egypt did not understand **God's** wonderful acts;
106.14 filled with craving in the desert and put **God** to the test;
106.20 they exchanged the glory of **God** for the image of an
106.21 They forgot the **God** who had saved them by his mighty
106.23 When **God** said that he would destroy his people, his chosen servant,
106.23 Moses, stood up against **God** and prevented his anger from destroying
106.24 pleasant land, because they did not believe **God's** promise.
106.39 made themselves impure by their actions and were unfaithful to **God.**
106.47 Save us, O Lord our **God,** and bring us back
106.48 Praise the Lord, the **God** of Israel;
107.11 commands of Almighty **God**
108. 1 I have complete confidence, O **God!**
108. 5 greatness in the sky, O **God,** and your glory over all the
108. 7 **God** has said, "In triumph I will divide Shechem
108.10 Who, O **God,** will take me into the fortified city?
108.13 With **God** on our side we will win;
109. 1 I praise you, **God;**
109.26 Help me, O Lord my **God;**
113. 5 There is no one like the Lord our **God.**
114. 7 at the presence of the **God** of Jacob, [8] who changes rocks
115. 2 Why should the nations ask us, "Where is your **God?"**
115. 3 Our **God** is in heaven;
115.10 Trust in the Lord, you priests of **God.**
115.12 will bless the people of Israel and all the priests of **God.**
116. 5 our **God** is compassionate.
118. 3 Let the priests of **God** say, "His love is eternal."
118.26 May **God** bless the one who comes in the name of the
118.27 The Lord is **God;**
118.28 You are my **God,** and I give you thanks;
119.115 I will obey the commands of my **God.**
120. 3 You liars, what will **God** do to you?
122. 9 the house of the Lord our **God** I pray for your prosperity.
123. 2 to you, O Lord our **God,** until you have mercy on us.
132. 2 the vow he made to you, the Mighty **God** of Jacob:
132. 5 place for the Lord, a home for the Mighty **God** of Jacob."
135. 2 who stand in the Lord's house, in the Temple of our **God.**
135.13 Lord, you will always be proclaimed as **God;**
135.19 praise him, you priests of **God!**
136.26 Give thanks to the **God** of heaven;
139.17 O **God,** how difficult I find your thoughts;
139.19 O **God,** how I wish you would kill the wicked!
139.23 Examine me, O **God,** and know my mind;
140. 6 I say to the Lord, "You are my **God."**
143.10 You are my **God;**
144. 9 I will sing you a new song, O **God;**
144.15 happy are the people whose **God** is the Lord!
145. 1 I will proclaim your greatness, my **God** and king;
146. 2 I will sing to my **God** all my life.
146. 5 the man who has the **God** of Jacob to help him
146. 5 depends on the Lord his **God,** [6] the Creator of heaven, earth,
146.10 Your **God,** O Zion, will reign for all time.
147. 1 It is good to sing praise to our **God;**
147. 7 play music on the harp to our **God.**
147.12 Praise your **God,** O Zion!
149. 6 shout aloud as they praise **God,** with their sharp swords
149. 9 to punish the nations as **God** has commanded.
150. 1 Praise **God** in his Temple!

Prov 2. 5 to fear the Lord and you will succeed in learning about **God.**
2.22 But **God** will snatch wicked men from the land
3. 4 If you do this, both **God** and man will be pleased
8.26 were set in place, [26] before **God** made the earth and its
14.31 If you oppress poor people, you insult the **God** who made them;
15.11 how then can a man hide his thoughts from **God?**
16. 1 We may make our plans, but **God** has the last word.
16. 6 Be loyal and faithful, and **God** will forgive your sin.
16. 9 You may make your plans, but **God** directs your actions.
16.33 Men cast lots to learn **God's** will,
16.33 but **God** himself determines the answer.
17. 5 you laugh at poor people, you insult the **God** who made them.
19.16 Keep **God's** laws and you will live longer;
20.25 Think carefully before you promise an offering to **God.**
21.12 **God,** the righteous one, knows what goes on
24.12 none of your business, but **God** knows and judges your motives.

Prov 24.22 Do you realize the disaster that **God** or the king can cause?
25. 2 We honour **God** for what he conceals;
28. 9 not obey the law, **God** will find your prayers too hateful
28.13 then **God** will show mercy to you.
29.18 A nation without **God's** guidance is a nation without order.
29.18 Happy is the man who keeps **God's** law!
29.24 the truth in court, and **God** will curse him if he doesn't.
30. 1 **"God** is not with me, God is not with me,
30. 3 learned any wisdom, and I know nothing at all about **God.**
30. 5 **"God** keeps every promise he makes.
30. 7 I ask you, **God,** to let me have two things
30. 9 I am poor, I might steal and bring disgrace on my **God.**
Ecc 1.13 **God** has laid a miserable fate upon us.
2.24 And yet, I realized that even this comes from **God.**
2.26 **God** gives wisdom, knowledge, and happiness to those who please him,
3. 1 Everything that happens in this world happens at the time **God** chooses.
3.10 I know the heavy burdens that **God** has laid on us.
3.13 It is **God's** gift.
3.14 I know that everything **God** does will last for ever.
3.14 And one thing **God** does is to make us stand in awe
3.15 **God** makes the same thing happen again and again.
3.17 I told myself, **"God** is going to judge the righteous
3.18 I concluded that **God** is testing us,
5. 2 Think before you speak, and don't make any rash promises to **God.**
5. 4 you make a promise to **God,** keep it as quickly as possible.
5. 6 that you have to tell **God's** priest that you didn't mean it.
5. 6 Why make **God** angry with you?
5. 7 how much you talk, you must still stand in awe of **God.**
5.18 has worked for during the short life that **God** has given him;
5.19 If **God** gives a man wealth and property
5.19 It is a gift from **God.**
5.20 Since **God** has allowed him to be happy, he will not worry
6. 2 **God** will give someone wealth, honour, and property,
7.13 Think about what **God** has done.
7.13 How can anyone straighten out what **God** has made crooked?
7.14 **God** sends both happiness and trouble;
7.18 If you have reverence for **God,** you will be successful anyway.
7.26 A man who pleases **God** can get away,
7.29 **God** made us plain and simple,
8. 2 don't make any rash promises to **God.**
8.12 "If you obey **God,** everything will be all right,
8.13 they will die young, because they do not obey **God."**
8.15 during the life that **God** has given him in this world.
8.17 and never be able to understand what **God** is doing.
9. 1 and saw that **God** controls the actions of wise
9. 7 It's all right with **God.**
9. 9 live the useless life that **God** has given you in this world.
11. 5 **God** made everything, and you can no more understand what
11. 9 But remember that **God** is going to judge you
12. 7 of life will go back to **God,** who gave it to us.
12.11 They have been given by **God,** the one Shepherd of us all.
12.13 Have reverence for **God,** and obey his commands,
12.14 **God** is going to judge everything we do, whether good or bad,
Is 1. 1 about Judah and Jerusalem which **God** revealed to Isaiah
1. 4 rejected the Lord, the holy **God** of Israel,
1.10 Pay attention to what our **God** is teaching you.
1.24 listen to what the Lord Almighty, Israel's powerful **God,** is saying:
2. 1 This is the message which **God** gave to Isaiah son of Amoz
2. 3 up the hill of the Lord, to the Temple of Israel's **God.**
2. 6 O **God,** you have forsaken your people, the descendants of Jacob!
3. 8 they openly insult **God** himself.
4. 3 left in Jerusalem, whom **God** has chosen for survival,
4. 5 **God's** glory will cover and protect the whole city.
5.19 Let Israel's holy **God** carry out his plans;
5.24 rejected what the Lord Almighty, Israel's holy **God,** has taught us.
7.11 "Ask the Lord your **God** to give you a sign.
7.13 the patience of men—must you wear out **God's** patience too?
8. 8 **God** is with us!
8.10 But it is all useless, because **God** is with us.
8.16 to guard and preserve the messages that **God** has given me.
8.21 and their anger they will curse their king and their **God.**
9. 6 will be called, "Wonderful Counsellor," "Mighty **God,"**
10. 3 What will you do when **God** punishes you?
10.17 **God,** the light of Israel, will become a fire.
10.17 Israel's holy **God** will become a flame,
10.20 They will truly put their trust in the Lord, Israel's holy **God.**
10.21 of the people of Israel will come back to their mighty **God.**
11. 9 On Zion, **God's** sacred hill, there will be nothing harmful or evil.
12. 2 **God** is my saviour;
12. 6 Israel's holy **God** is great, and he lives among his people."
13. 1 about Babylon, which Isaiah son of Amoz received from **God.**
15. 9 is red with blood, and **God** has something even worse in store
17. 6 I, the **Lord God** of Israel, have spoken."
17. 7 will turn for help to their Creator, the holy **God** of Israel.
17.10 Israel, you have forgotten the **God** who rescues you
17.13 advance like rushing waves, but **God** reprimands them and they retreat,
21. 2 **God** will put an end to the suffering which Babylon has caused.
21.10 I have heard from the Lord Almighty, the **God** of Israel.
21.17 I, the **Lord God** of Israel, have spoken."
22.11 you paid no attention to **God,** who planned all this long ago
24. 5 defiled the earth by breaking **God's** laws and by violating
24. 6 So **God** has pronounced a curse on the earth.
24.15 live along the sea will praise the Lord, the **God** of Israel.
24.22 **God** will crowd kings together like prisoners in a pit.
25. 1 Lord, you are my **God;**
25. 9 When it happens, everyone will say, "He is our **God!**
25.11 were trying to swim, but **God** will humiliate them,
26. 1 **God** himself defends its walls!
Is 26.13 Lord our **God,** we have been ruled by others,
26.20 Hide yourselves for a little while until **God's** anger is over.
27.11 understood nothing, **God** their Creator will not pity them
28. 7 to understand the visions that **God** sends,
28.11 won't listen to me, then **God** will use foreigners
28.19 Each new message from **God** will bring new terror!
28.26 He knows how to do his work, because **God** has taught him.
28.29 The plans **God** makes are wise, and they always succeed!
29. 1 **God's** altar, Jerusalem itself, is doomed!
29. 2 God will bring disaster on the city that is called **"God's** altar."
29. 3 **God** will attack the city, surround it, and besiege it.
29. 7 nations attacking the city of **God's** altar,
29.10 be the eyes of the people, but **God** has blindfolded them.
29.19 find the happiness which the Lord, the holy **God** of Israel,
29.20 end of those who oppress others and show contempt for **God.**
29.21 **God** will destroy those who slander others,
29.22 So now the Lord, the **God** of Israel, who rescued Abraham
29.23 then you will acknowledge that I am the holy **God** of Israel.
30. 6 This is **God's** message about the animals of the southern desert:
30. 8 **God** told me to write down in a book what the people
30. 9 They are always rebelling against **God,** always lying,
30.11 We don't want to hear about your holy **God** of Israel."
30.12 But this is what the holy **God** of Israel says:
30.15 The Sovereign Lord, the holy **God** of Israel, says to the people,
30.32 **God** himself will fight against the Assyrians.
31. 1 on the Lord, the holy **God** of Israel, or ask him for
32.15 But once more **God** will send us his spirit.
33.14 They say, **"God's** judgement is like a fire that burns for ever.
35. 4 **God** is coming to your rescue, coming to punish your enemies."
36. 7 you tell me that you are relying on the Lord your **God?**
37. 4 emperor has sent his chief official to insult the **living God.**
37. 4 May the Lord your **God** hear these insults and punish those
37. 4 So pray to **God** for those of our people who survive."
37.10 to say to him, "The **god** you are trusting in has told
37.16 "Almighty Lord, **God** of Israel, enthroned above the
37.16 winged creatures, you alone are **God,** ruling all the kingdoms
37.17 that Sennacherib is saying to insult you, the **living God.**
37.20 Now, Lord our **God,** rescue us from the Assyrians,
37.20 nations of the world will know that you alone are **God."**
37.23 You have been disrespectful to me, the holy **God** of Israel.
38. 5 "I, the Lord, the **God** of your ancestor David, have heard
38.12 I thought that **God** was ending my life.
38.13 I thought that **God** was ending my life.
40. 1 "Comfort my people," says our **God.**
40. 3 Clear the way in the desert for our **God!**
40. 8 flowers fade, but the word of our **God** endures for ever."
40. 9 Tell the towns of Judah that their **God** is coming!
40.14 With whom does **God** consult in order to know and understand
40.16 for a sacrifice to our **God,** and its trees are too few
40.18 To whom can **God** be compared?
40.25 To whom can the holy **God** be compared?
40.28 The Lord is the everlasting **God;**
41. 1 **God** says,
41.10 I am your **God**—let nothing terrify you!
41.13 I am the Lord your **God;**
41.14 I, the holy **God** of Israel, am the one who saves you.
41.16 Then you will be happy because I am your **God;**
41.16 you will praise me, the holy **God** of Israel.
41.17 I, the **God** of Israel, will never abandon them.
41.20 to understand that Israel's holy **God** has made it happen."
42. 5 **God** created the heavens and stretched them out;
42. 5 And now the **Lord God** says to his servant, [6] "I, the Lord,
42. 8 "I alone am the Lord your **God.**
42.11 Let the desert and its towns praise **God;**
42.14 **God** says,
42.21 The Lord is a **God** who is eager to save,
43. 3 I am the Lord your **God,**
43. 3 the holy **God** of Israel, who saves you.
43. 8 **God says,**
43.10 and believe in me and understand that I am the only **God.**
43.13 I am **God** and always will be.
43.14 Israel's holy **God,** the Lord who saves you, says,
43.15 I am the Lord, your holy **God.**
43.25 And yet, I am the **God** who forgives your sins,
44. 6 "I am the first, the last, the only **God;**
45. 3 the Lord, and that the **God** of Israel has called you
45.11 The Lord, the holy **God** of Israel, the one who shapes
45.14 confess, 'God is with you—he alone is **God.**
45.15 The **God** of Israel, who saves his people,
45.15 is a **God** who conceals himself.
45.18 Lord created the heavens— he is the one who is **God!**
45.21 Was it not I, the Lord, the **God** who saves his people?
45.22 I am the only **God** there is.
46. 4 I am your **God** and will take care of you
46. 9 acknowledge that I alone am **God** and that there is no one
47. 4 The holy **God** of Israel sets us free—
47. 8 you are as great as **God**— that there is no one
47.10 said to yourself, 'I am **God**— there is no one else
48. 1 and claim to worship the **God** of Israel— but you don't
48. 2 depend on Israel's **God,** whose name is the Lord Almighty.
48.12 I am **God,** the first, the last, the only God!
48.17 The holy **God** of Israel, the Lord who saves you, says:
48.17 "I am the Lord your **God,** the one who wants to teach
49. 7 Israel's holy **God** and saviour says to the one who is
49. 7 the holy **God** of Israel keeps his promises.
49.18 surely as I am the **living God,** you will be proud of
49.26 They will know that I am Israel's powerful **God."**
50. 8 will not be disgraced, [8] for **God** is near,
50.10 be dark indeed, but trust in the Lord, rely on your **God.**
51.15 "I am the Lord your **God;**
51.20 They have felt the force of **God's** anger.

Is 51.22 the Lord your **God** defends you and says, "I am
52. 1 Holy city of **God**, clothe yourself with splendour!
52. 6 will acknowledge that I am **God** and that I have spoken
52. 7 He announces victory and says to Zion, "Your **God** is king!"
52.12 The Lord your **God** will lead you and protect you
53. 4 while we thought that his suffering was punishment sent by **God.**
54. 5 The holy **God** of Israel will save you—
55. 5 Lord your God, the holy **God** of Israel, will make all this
55. 7 Let them turn to the Lord, our **God;**
57.15 "I am the high and holy **God,** who lives for ever.
59. 2 sins that separate you from **God** when you try to worship him.
59. 9 say, "Now we know why **God** does not save us
59.11 We long for **God** to save us from oppression and wrong,
60. 9 of the Lord, The holy **God** of Israel, Who has made all
60.14 'The City of the Lord,' 'Zion, the City of Israel's Holy **God.'**
60.16 saved you, That the mighty **God** of Israel sets you free.
61. 3 do what is right, And **God** will be praised
61. 6 known as the priests of the Lord, The servants of our **God.**
61.10 **God** has clothed her with salvation and victory.
62. 4 Your new name will be **"God** Is Pleased with Her."
62. 5 delighted with his bride, So your **God** will delight in you.
62.12 "The City That God Loves," "The City That **God** Did Not Forsake."
64. 4 seen or heard of a **God** like you, who does such deeds
65.16 for a blessing will ask to be blessed by the Faithful **God.**
65.16 takes an oath will swear by the name of the Faithful **God.**
Jer 2.11 people have exchanged me, the **God** who has brought them honour,
2.17 deserted me, the Lord your **God,** while I was leading you
2.19 abandon me, the Lord your **God,** and no longer to remain loyal
3.13 and that you have rebelled against the Lord, your **God.**
3.21 lived sinful lives and have forgotten the Lord their **God.**
3.22 "Yes, we are coming to the Lord, because he is our **God.**
3.23 Help for Israel comes only from the Lord our **God.**
3.25 We and our ancestors have always sinned against the Lord our **God;**
5. 1 who does what is right and tries to be faithful to **God?**
5. 4 they don't know what their **God** requires, what the Lord wants
5. 5 Surely they know what their **God** requires, what the Lord wants
5. 6 are numerous and time after time they have turned from **God.**
5.13 The **Lord God** Almighty said to me, "Jeremiah, because these
7. 1 what the Lord Almighty, the **God** of Israel, had to say
7.23 that I would be their **God** and they would be my people.
7.28 obey me, the Lord their **God,** or learn from their punishment.
8.14 The Lord our **God** has condemned us to die;
9. 3 and do not acknowledge me as their **God."**
9.15 to what I, the Lord Almighty, the **God** of Israel, will do:
10.10 you, Lord, are the true **God,**
10.10 you are the **living God** and the eternal king.
10.16 The **God** of Jacob is not like them;
11. 3 of Jerusalem [3]that I, the **Lord God** of Israel, have placed a
11. 4 obeyed, they would be my people and I would be their **God.**
12. 4 people who say, **'God** doesn't see what we are doing.' "
13.12 The **Lord God** said to me, "Jeremiah, tell the people of
13.16 Honour the Lord, your **God,** before he brings darkness,
14.22 in you, O Lord our **God,** because you are the one
15.16 I belong to you, **Lord God** Almighty, and so your words filled
16. 9 what I, the Lord Almighty, the **God** of Israel, have to say.
16.10 what sin they have committed against the Lord their **God.**
16.14 swear by me as the **living God** who brought the people of
16.15 swear by me as the **living God** who brought the people of
18.18 and prophets to proclaim **God's** message.
19. 3 what I, the Lord Almighty, the **God** of Israel, have to say.
19.15 that the Lord Almighty, the **God** of Israel, had said,
21. 4 that the Lord, the **God** of Israel, had said, "Zedekiah,
22. 9 your covenant with me, your **God,** and have worshipped and
22.24 surely as I am the **living God,** even if you were the
23. 2 is what the Lord, the **God** of Israel, says about the rulers
23. 7 swear by me as the **living God** who brought the people of
23. 8 swear by me as the **living God** who brought the people of
23.23 "I am a **God** who is everywhere and not in one place
23.36 the words of their God, the **living God,** the Lord Almighty.
24. 5 "I, the Lord, the **God** of Israel, consider that the people
24. 7 and I will be their **God,** because they will return to me
25.15 The Lord, the **God** of Israel, said to me, "Here is a
25.27 I, the Lord Almighty, the **God** of Israel, am commanding them
26.13 the things you are doing, and must obey the Lord your **God.**
26.16 man spoke to us in the name of the Lord our **God;**
27. 4 The Lord Almighty, the **God** of Israel, told me to command
27.21 I, the Lord Almighty, the **God** of Israel, say about the
28. 2 told me [2]that the Lord Almighty, the **God** of Israel, had
28.14 The Lord Almighty, the **God** of Israel, has said that he
29. 4 "The Lord Almighty, the **God** of Israel, says to all those
29. 8 I, the Lord, the **God** of Israel, warn you not to let
29.21 "The Lord Almighty, the **God** of Israel, has spoken about Ahab
29.24 The Lord Almighty, the **God** of Israel, gave me a message
30. 1 The Lord, the **God** of Israel, [2]said to me:
30. 9 serve me, the Lord their **God,** and a descendant of David,
30.21 They will be my people, and I will be their **God.**
31. 1 when I will be the **God** of all the tribes of Israel,
31. 6 'Let's go up to Zion, to the Lord our **God.'** "
31.18 we are ready to return to you, the Lord our **God.**
31.23 The Lord Almighty, the **God** of Israel, says, "When I restore
31.33 I will be their **God,** and they will be my people.
32.14 Baruch, [14]"The Lord Almighty, the **God** of Israel, has ordered you
32.15 The Lord Almighty, the **God** of Israel, has said that houses,
32.18 You are a great and powerful **God;**
32.27 said to me, [27]"I am the Lord, the **God** of all mankind.
32.36 The Lord, the **God** of Israel, said to me, "Jeremiah,
32.38 Then they will be my people, and I will be their **God.**
33. 4 I, the Lord, the **God** of Israel, say that the houses
34. 2 The Lord, the **God** of Israel, told me to go and say

Jer 34.13 Then the Lord, [13]the **God** of Israel, told me to say
35.12 Then the Lord Almighty, the **God** of Israel, told me
35.17 I, the Lord Almighty, the **God** of Israel, will bring on you
35.18 that the Lord Almighty, the **God** of Israel, had said, "You
35.19 I, the Lord Almighty, the **God** of Israel, promise that Jonadab
37. 3 to pray to the Lord our **God** on behalf of our nation.
37. 6 Then the Lord, the **God** of Israel, told me [7]to say
38.16 secret, "I swear by the **living God,** the God who gave us
38.17 that the Lord Almighty, the **God** of Israel, had said, "If
39.16 that the Lord Almighty, the **God** of Israel, had said, "Just
40. 2 "The Lord your **God** threatened this land with destruction,
42. 2 Pray to the Lord our **God** for us.
42. 3 Pray that the Lord our **God** will show us the way
42. 4 pray to the Lord our **God,** just as you have asked,
42. 5 all the commands that the Lord our **God** gives you for us.
42. 6 will obey the Lord our **God,** to whom we are asking you
42. 9 to them, "The Lord, the **God** of Israel, to whom you sent
42.13 not disobey the Lord your **God** and refuse to live in this
42.13 then the Lord Almighty, the **God** of Israel, says, 'If you are
42.18 "The Lord, the **God** of Israel, says, 'Just as my anger
42.20 pray to the Lord our **God** for you, and you promised
42.21 everything that the Lord our **God** sent me to tell you.
43. 1 everything that the Lord their **God** had sent me to tell them.
43. 2 The Lord our **God** did not send you to tell us not
43.10 I, the Lord Almighty, the **God** of Israel, am going to bring
44. 2 The Lord Almighty, the **God** of Israel, said, "You
44. 7 I, the Lord Almighty, the **God** of Israel, now ask why you
44.11 I, the Lord Almighty, the **God** of Israel, will turn against
44.24 what the Lord Almighty, the **God** of Israel, was saying
45. 2 that the Lord, the **God** of Israel, had said, "Baruch,
46.18 I am the **living God.**
46.25 The Lord Almighty, the **God** of Israel, says,
50. 4 Israel and Judah will come weeping, looking for me, their **God.**
50.18 I, the Lord Almighty, the **God** of Israel, will punish King
50.28 tell how the Lord our **God** took revenge for what the
51. 5 I, the **Lord God** Almighty, have not abandoned Israel and Judah,
51. 9 **God** has punished Babylonia with all his might and has destroyed
51.10 the people in Jerusalem what the Lord our **God** has done.' "
51.19 The **God** of Jacob is not like them;
51.33 I, the Lord Almighty, the **God** of Israel, have spoken."
51.56 I am a **God** who punishes evil, and I will treat Babylon
Lam 3. 1 am one who knows what it is to be punished by **God.**
3. 8 I cry aloud for help, but **God** refuses to listen;
3.41 open our hearts to **God** in heaven and pray,
4. 6 which met with a sudden downfall at the hands of **God.**
Ezek 1. 1 The sky opened, and I saw a vision of **God.**
1.24 the noise of a huge army, like the voice of Almighty **God.**
2. 2 While the voice was speaking, **God's** spirit entered me
3. 1 **God** said, "Mortal man, eat this scroll;
3. 4 Then **God** said, "Mortal man, go to the people of Israel
3.10 **God** continued, "Mortal man, pay close attention
3.12 Then **God's** spirit lifted me up,
3.24 but **God's** spirit entered me and raised me
4. 1 **God** said, "Mortal man, get a brick, put it in front of
4.15 So **God** said, "Very well.
5.11 "Therefore, as I am the **living God**—this is the word of
7.12 because **God's** punishment will fall on everyone alike.
7.13 what he has lost, because **God's** anger is on everyone.
7.14 war, for **God's** anger will fall on everyone alike.
8. 3 Then in this vision **God's** spirit lifted me high in the air
8. 3 Temple, where there was an idol that was an outrage to **God.**
8. 4 shows the presence of Israel's **God,** just as I had seen it
8. 5 **God** said to me, "Mortal man, look towards the north."
8. 5 the gateway I saw the idol that was an outrage to **God.**
8. 6 **God** said to me, "Mortal man, do you see what is happening?
8.12 **God** asked me, "Mortal man, do you see what the Israelite
9. 1 Then I heard **God** shout, "Come here,
9. 3 of the presence of the **God** of Israel rose up
9. 5 And I heard **God** say to the other men, "Follow him through
9. 7 **God** said to them, "Defile the Temple.
9. 9 **God** answered, "The people of Israel and Judah are guilty
10. 2 **God** said to the man wearing linen clothes, "Go between
10. 5 It sounded like the voice of Almighty **God.**
10.20 I had seen beneath the **God** of Israel at the River Chebar.
11. 1 **God's** spirit lifted me up and took me to the east gate
11. 2 **God** said to me, "Mortal man, these men make evil plans
11.20 They will be my people, and I will be their **God.**
11.22 light of the presence of the **God** of Israel was over them.
11.24 the vision the spirit of **God** lifted me up and brought me
14.11 They are to be my people, and I will be their **God."**
14.16 the Sovereign Lord, am the **living God**—they would not be able
14.18 the Sovereign Lord, am the **living God**—they would not be able
14.20 the Sovereign Lord, am the **living God**—they would not be able
16.48 sure as I am the **living God,"** the Sovereign Lord says,
17.16 surely as I am the **living God,"** says the Sovereign Lord,
17.19 surely as I am the **living God,** I will punish him for
18. 3 surely as I am the **living God,"** says the Sovereign Lord,
20. 3 surely as I am the **living God,** I will not let you
20. 5 I am the Lord your **God.**
20. 7 the false gods of Egypt, because I am the Lord their **God.**
20.19 I am the Lord your **God.**
20.20 and will remind you that I am the Lord your **God.**
20.31 the Sovereign Lord, am the **living God,** I will not let you
20.33 the Sovereign Lord, am the **living God,** I warn you that in
28.13 in Eden, the garden of **God,** and wore gems of every kind:
28.26 Then they will know that I am the Lord their **God."**
31. 3 No cedar in **God's** garden could compare with it.
31. 8 No tree in **God's** own garden was so beautiful.
31. 9 was the envy of every tree in Eden, the garden of **God.**
33.11 the Sovereign Lord, am the **living God,** I do not enjoy seeing
33.27 surely as I am the **living God,** the people who live in

Ezek	34. 8	surely as I am the **living God,** you had better listen to
	34.24	the Lord, will be their **God,** and a king like my servant
	34.31	my people, and I am your **God,"** says the Sovereign Lord.
	35. 6	the Sovereign Lord, am the **living God**—death is your fate,
	35.10	would possess them, even though I, the Lord, was their **God.**
	35.11	the Sovereign Lord, am the **living God,** I will pay you back
	36.28	You will be my people, and I will be your **God.**
	37. 9	**God** said to me, "Mortal man, prophesy to the wind.
	37.11	**God** said to me, "Mortal man, the people of Israel are
	37.23	they will be my people, and I will be their **God.**
	37.27	I will be their **God,** and they will be my people.
	39. 7	will know that I, the Lord, am the Holy **God** of Israel."
	39.22	will know from then on that I am the Lord their **God.**
	39.28	Then my people will know that I am the Lord their **God.**
	40. 2	In a vision **God** took me to the land of Israel
	43. 2	the dazzling light of the presence of the **God** of Israel.
	43. 2	**God's** voice sounded like the roar of the sea,
	43. 3	one I had seen when **God** came to destroy Jerusalem,
	44. 2	use it, because I, the **Lord God** of Israel, have entered
Dan	1. 9	and **God** made Ashpenaz sympathetic to Daniel.
	1.17	**God** gave the four young men knowledge and skill in literature
	2.18	them to pray to the **God** of heaven for mercy
	2.19	to Daniel in a vision, and he praised the **God** of heaven:
	2.20	**"God** is wise and powerful!
	2.23	I praise you and honour you, **God** of my ancestors.
	2.28	But there is a **God** in heaven, who reveals mysteries.
	2.29	**God,** who reveals mysteries, showed you what is going to happen.
	2.37	The **God** of heaven has made you emperor and given you power,
	2.44	the **God** of heaven will establish a kingdom
	2.45	The great **God** is telling Your Majesty what will happen
	2.47	The king said, "Your **God** is the greatest of all gods,
	3.17	If the **God** whom we serve is able to save us
	3.26	Servants of the Supreme **God!**
	3.28	The king said, "Praise the **God** of Shadrach, Meshach,
	3.29	speaks disrespectfully of the **God** of Shadrach, Meshach, and Abednego,
	4. 2	the wonders and miracles which the Supreme **God** has shown me.
	4. 3	"How great are the wonders **God** shows us!
	4. 3	**God** is king for ever;
	4.17	know that the Supreme **God** has power over human kingdoms
	4.24	is what the Supreme **God** has declared will happen to you.
	4.25	will admit that the Supreme **God** controls all human kingdoms,
	4.26	again when you acknowledge that **God** rules all the world.
	4.32	acknowledge that the Supreme **God** has power over human kingdoms
	4.34	I praised the Supreme **God** and gave honour and glory
	5.18	"The Supreme **God** made your father Nebuchadnezzar a great king
	5.21	he admitted that the Supreme **God** controls all human kingdoms
	5.23	you did not honour the **God** who determines whether you live
	5.24	That is why **God** has sent the hand to write these words.
	5.26	number, **God** has numbered the days of your kingdom
	6.10	at the open windows and prayed to **God** three times a day.
	6.11	enemies observed him praying to **God,** [12]all of them went together
	6.16	Daniel, "May your **God,** whom you serve so loyally, rescue
	6.20	called out anxiously, "Daniel, servant of the **living God!**
	6.20	Was the **God** you serve so loyally able to save you
	6.22	**God** sent his angel to shut the mouths of the lions
	6.23	that he had not been hurt at all, for he trusted **God.**
	6.26	throughout my empire everyone should fear and respect Daniel's **God.**
	6.26	"He is a **living God,** and he will rule for ever.
	7.18	the people of the Supreme **God** will receive royal power
	7.22	pronounced judgement in favour of the people of the Supreme **God.**
	7.25	He will speak against the Supreme **God** and oppress God's people.
	7.27	on earth will be given to the people of the Supreme **God.**
	8.19	"I am showing you what the result of **God's** anger will be.
	9. 3	I prayed earnestly to the **Lord God,** pleading with him,
	9. 4	prayed to the Lord my **God** and confessed the sins
	9. 4	I said, **"Lord God,** you are great, and we honour you.
	9.10	to you, O Lord our **God,** when you told us to live
	9.13	even now, O Lord our **God,** we have not tried to please
	9.14	You, O Lord our **God,** were prepared to punish us,
	9.15	"O Lord our **God,** you showed your power by bringing
	9.17	O **God,** hear my prayer and pleading.
	9.17	restore it so that everyone will know that you are **God.**
	9.18	Listen to us, O **God;**
	9.19	that everyone will know that you are **God,** do not delay!
	9.20	pleading with the Lord my **God** to restore his holy Temple.
	9.23	When you began to plead with **God,** he answered you.
	9.24	the length of time **God** has set for freeing your people
	9.25	given to rebuild Jerusalem, until **God's** chosen leader comes,
	9.26	**God's** chosen leader will be killed unjustly.
	9.26	bringing the war and destruction which **God** has prepared.
	9.27	meets the end which **God** has prepared for him."
	10.11	The angel said to me, "Daniel, **God** loves you.
	10.12	**God** has heard your prayers ever since the first day
	10.19	He said, **"God** loves you, so don't let anything worry you
	11.22	Anyone who opposes him, even **God's** High Priest,
	11.32	but those who follow **God** will fight back.
	11.35	until the end comes, the time that **God** has set.
	11.36	is greater than any god, superior even to the Supreme **God.**
	11.36	be able to do this until the time when **God** punishes him.
	11.36	**God** will do exactly what he has planned.
	12. 1	whose names are written in **God's** book will be saved.
	12. 7	made a solemn promise in the name of the Eternal **God.**
Hos	1. 7	I, the Lord their **God,** will save them,
	1. 9	Israel are not my people, and I am not their **God."**
	1.10	Now **God** says to them, "You are not my people,"
	1.10	say to them, "You are the children of the **living God!"**
	2.23	"You are my people," and they will answer, "You are our **God."**
Hos	3. 5	turn to the Lord their **God,** and to a descendant of David
	4. 1	and the people do not acknowledge me as **God.**
	5. 4	the people have done prevents them from returning to their **God.**
	7.10	they have not returned to me, the Lord their **God.**
	8. 2	though they call me their **God**
	9. 1	turned away from your **God** and have been unfaithful to him.
	9. 8	**God** has sent me as a prophet to warn his people Israel.
	9. 8	Even in **God's** Temple the people are the prophet's enemies.
	9. 9	**God** will remember their sin and punish them for it.
	9.17	The **God** I serve will reject his people,
	10. 2	**God** will break down their altars and destroy their sacred pillars.
	11. 9	For I am **God** and not man.
	11.12	Judah are still rebelling against me, the faithful and holy **God.**
	12. 3	grew up, he fought against **God**—[4]he fought against an angel
	12. 4	And at Bethel **God** came to our ancestor Jacob
	12. 5	This was the **Lord God** Almighty—the Lord is the name by
	12. 6	descendants of Jacob, trust in your **God** and return to him.
	12. 6	Be loyal and just, and wait patiently for your **God** to act.
	12. 9	But I, the Lord your **God** who led you out of Egypt,
	13. 4	"I am the Lord your **God,** who led you out of Egypt.
	13. 4	You have no **God** but me.
	14. 1	Return to the Lord your **God,** people of Israel.
	14. 3	will never again say to our idols that they are our **God.**
Joel	1.13	There is no corn or wine to offer your **God.**
	1.14	the Temple of the Lord your **God** and cry out to him.
	1.16	There is no joy in the Temple of our **God.**
	2. 1	sound the alarm on Zion, **God's** sacred hill.
	2.13	Come back to the Lord your **God.**
	2.14	Perhaps the Lord your **God** will change his mind and bless
	2.17	despise us and mock us by saying, 'Where is your **God?'**
	2.23	Zion, rejoice at what the Lord your **God** has done for you.
	2.26	will praise the Lord your **God,** who has done wonderful things
	2.27	that I, the Lord, am your **God** and there is no other.
	3.17	"Then, Israel, you will know that I am the Lord your **God.**
Amos	1. 1	Jehoash was king of Israel, **God** revealed to Amos
	2. 8	In the temple of their **God** they drink wine
	4. 5	in thanksgiving to **God,** and boast about the extra offerings
	4.13	**God** is the one who made the mountains and created the winds.
	4.13	the **Lord God** Almighty!
	5.14	Then the **Lord God** Almighty really will be with you, as you
	5.27	Damascus," says the Lord, whose name is Almighty **God.**
	6.14	The **Lord God** Almighty himself says, "People of Israel,
	8. 7	The Lord, the **God** of Israel, has sworn, "I will never
	9.10	all those who say, **'God** will not let any harm come
	9.15	The Lord your **God** has spoken.
Jon	1. 9	"I worship the Lord, the **God** of heaven,
	2. 1	From deep inside the fish Jonah prayed to the Lord his **God:**
	2. 6	But you, O Lord my **God,** brought me back from the depths
	3. 5	The people of Nineveh believed **God's** message.
	3. 8	Everyone must pray earnestly to **God**
	3. 9	Perhaps **God** will change his mind;
	3.10	**God** saw what they did;
	4. 2	a loving and merciful **God,** always patient, always kind,
	4. 6	Then the **Lord God** made a plant grow up over Jonah to
	4. 7	the next day, at **God's** command, a worm attacked the plant,
	4. 8	After the sun had risen, **God** sent a hot east wind,
	4. 9	But **God** said to him, "What right have you to be angry
Mic	1. 5	because the people of Israel have sinned and rebelled against **God.**
	2. 6	**God** is not going to disgrace us.
	2.13	**God** will open the way for them and lead them out
	3. 7	They will all be humiliated because **God** does not answer them.
	3.10	You are building **God's** city, Jerusalem, on a foundation of murder
	4. 2	up the hill of the Lord, to the Temple of Israel's **God.**
	4. 5	will worship and obey the Lord our **God** for ever and ever.
	4. 8	Jerusalem, where **God,** like a shepherd, watches over his people,
	5. 4	from the Lord and with the majesty of the **Lord God** himself.
	5. 7	They will depend on **God,** not man.
	6. 6	bring to the Lord, the **God** of heaven, when I come
	6. 8	love, and to live in humble fellowship with our **God.**
	7. 2	an honest person left in the land, no one loyal to **God.**
	7. 4	The day has come when **God** will punish the people,
	7. 7	I will wait confidently for **God,** who will save me.
	7. 7	My **God** will hear me.
	7.10	who taunted us by asking, "Where is the Lord your **God?"**
	7.17	They will turn in fear to the Lord our **God.**
Nah	1. 2	The **Lord God** tolerates no rivals;
	1.15	your festivals and give **God** what you solemnly promised him.
Hab	1.12	Lord, from the very beginning you are **God.**
	1.12	You are my **God,** holy and eternal.
	1.12	Lord, my **God** and protector, you have chosen the Babylonians
	2. 4	righteous will live because they are faithful to **God.' "**
	3. 3	**God** is coming again from Edom;
	3. 3	the holy **God** is coming from the hills of Paran.
	3.16	the time to come when **God** will punish those who attack us.
	3.18	be joyful and glad, because the **Lord God** is my saviour.
Zeph	2. 7	The Lord their **God** will be with them and make them prosper
	2. 9	am the living Lord, the **God** of Israel, I swear that Moab
	3. 4	and twist the law of **God** to their own advantage.
	3.17	The Lord your **God** is with you;
Hag	1.12	in Babylonia, did what the Lord their **God** told them to do.
	1.14	of the Lord Almighty, their **God,** [15]on the twenty-fourth day
Zech	4.14	are the two men whom **God** has chosen and anointed to serve
	6.15	happen if you fully obey the commands of the Lord your **God.**
	8. 8	I will be their **God,** ruling over them faithfully and justly.
	8.23	destiny, because we have heard that **God** is with you.' "
	10. 6	I am the Lord their **God;**
	11. 4	The Lord my **God** said to me, "Act the part of the
	12. 5	will say to themselves, 'The **Lord God** Almighty gives
	12. 8	will lead them like the angel of the Lord, like **God** himself.
	13. 9	are my people, and they will confess that I am their **God."**
	14. 5	The Lord my **God** will come, bringing all the angels with him.

Zech	14. 9	everyone will worship him as **God** and know him
Mal	1. 9	Now, you priests, try asking **God** to be good to us.
	2. 7	is the duty of priests to teach the true knowledge of **God.**
	2.10	Didn't the same **God** create us all?
	2.10	do we despise the covenant that **God** made with our ancestors?
	2.11	have broken their promise to **God** and done a horrible thing
	2.14	although you promised before **God** that you would be faithful
	2.15	Didn't **God** make you one body and spirit with her?
	2.16	"I hate divorce," says the **Lord God** of Israel.
	2.17	by asking, "Where is the **God** who is supposed to be just?"
	3. 8	I ask you, is it right for a person to cheat **God?**
	3.14	You have said, 'It's useless to serve **God.**
	3.15	but they test **God's** patience with their evil deeds
Mt	1.23	he will be called Immanuel" (which means, **"God** is with us").
	2.12	country by another road, since **God** had warned them in a
	3. 7	you could escape from the punishment **God** is about to send?
	3. 9	I tell you that **God** can take these stones and make
	3.15	For in this way we shall do all that **God** requires."
	3.16	he saw the Spirit of **God** coming down like a dove and
	4. 4	on bread alone, but needs every word that **God** speaks.' "
	4. 6	for the scripture says, **'God** will give orders to his angels
	4. 7	also says, 'Do not put the Lord your **God** to the test.' "
	4.10	scripture says, 'Worship the Lord your **God** and serve only him!' "
	5. 4	**God** will comfort them!
	5. 5	they will receive what **God** has promised!
	5. 6	"Happy are those whose greatest desire is to do what **God** requires;
	5. 6	**God** will satisfy them fully!
	5. 7	**God** will be merciful to them!
	5. 8	they will see **God!**
	5. 9	**God** will call them his children!
	5.10	"Happy are those who are persecuted because they do what **God** requires;
	5.20	of the Law and the Pharisees in doing what **God** requires.
	5.23	to offer your gift to **God** at the altar and there you
	5.24	brother, and then come back and offer your gift to **God.**
	5.34	Do not swear by heaven, for it is **God's** throne;
	5.46	Why should **God** reward you if you love only the people
	6.24	You cannot serve both **God** and money.
	6.30	It is **God** who clothes the wild grass—grass that is here
	7. 1	not judge others, so that **God** will not judge you,
	7. 2	for **God** will judge you in the same
	7.22	In your name we spoke **God's** message, by your name we drove
	9. 8	afraid, and praised **God** for giving such authority to men.
	10.15	that on the Judgement Day **God** will show more mercy to the
	10.28	rather be afraid of **God,** who can destroy both body and soul
	10.41	Whoever welcomes **God's** messenger because he is God's messenger,
	11.10	**'God** said, I will send my messenger ahead of you to open
	11.19	**God's** wisdom, however, is shown to be true by its results."
	11.22	that on the Judgement Day **God** will show more mercy to the
	11.24	that on the Judgement Day **God** will show more mercy to Sodom
	12. 4	ate the bread offered to **God,** even though it was against the
	12.17	so as to make what **God** had said through the prophet Isaiah
	13.15	they would turn to me, says **God,** and I would heal them.'
	14.19	the two fish, looked up to heaven, and gave thanks to **God.**
	15. 3	"And why do you disobey **God's** command and follow your own teaching?
	15. 4	For **God** said, 'Respect your father and your mother,'
	15. 5	but says, 'This belongs to **God,'** [6] he does not need to
	15. 6	In this way you disregard **God's** command, in order to follow
	15. 8	'These people, says **God,** honour me with their words,
	15.31	and they praised the **God** of Israel.
	15.36	the fish, gave thanks to **God,** broke them, and gave them to
	16. 1	a miracle for them, to show that **God** approved of him.
	16.16	Peter answered, "You are the Messiah, the Son of the **living God."**
	16.22	**"God** forbid it, Lord!"
	16.23	these thoughts of yours don't come from **God,** but from man."
	19. 5	And **God** said, 'For this reason a man will leave his father
	19. 6	Man must not separate, then, what **God** has joined together."
	19.11	to everyone, but only to those to whom **God** has given it.
	19.26	"This is impossible for man, but for **God** everything is possible."
	21. 9	**God** bless him who comes in the name of the Lord!
	21. 9	Praise **God!"**
	21.13	written in the Scriptures that **God** said, 'My Temple will be
	21.25	was it from **God** or from man?"
	21.25	If we answer, 'From **God,'** he will say to us, 'Why, then,
	22.16	You teach the truth about **God's** will for man, without worrying
	22.21	belongs to the Emperor, and pay **God** what belongs to God."
	22.29	It is because you don't know the Scriptures or **God's** power.
	22.31	haven't you ever read what **God** has told you?
	22.32	He said, [32] 'I am the **God** of Abraham,
	22.32	the God of Isaac, and the **God** of Jacob.'
	22.32	He is the **God** of the living, not of the dead."
	22.37	answered, " 'Love the Lord your **God** with all your heart,
	23.21	Temple, he is swearing by it and by **God,** who lives there;
	23.22	heaven, he is swearing by **God's** throne and by him who sits
	23.23	You give to **God** a tenth even of the seasoning herbs, such
	23.37	You kill the prophets and stone the messengers **God** has sent you!
	23.39	me again until you say, **'God** bless him who comes in the
	24.20	Pray to **God** that you will not have to run away during
	24.22	But **God** has already reduced the number of days;
	24.22	of his chosen people, however, **God** will reduce the days.
	25.41	on his left, 'Away from me, you that are under **God's** curse!
	26.27	took a cup, gave thanks to **God,** and gave it to them.
	26.28	is my blood, which seals **God's** covenant, my blood poured out
	26.31	me, for the scripture says, **'God** will kill the shepherd, and
	26.61	am able to tear down **God's** Temple and three days later build
	26.63	"In the name of the **living God** I now put you on
	26.74	May **God** punish me if I am not!
	27.43	He trusts in **God** and claims to be God's Son.
Mt	27.43	Well, then, let us see if **God** wants to save him now!"
	27.46	which means, "My **God,** my God, why did you abandon me?"
Mk	1. 2	**"God** said, 'I will send my messenger ahead of you to clear
	1. 4	baptized," he told the people, "and **God** will forgive your sins."
	1.14	Jesus went to Galilee and preached the Good News from **God.**
	1.24	I know who you are—you are **God's** holy messenger!"
	2. 7	**God** is the only one who can forgive sins!"
	2.12	completely amazed and praised **God,** saying, "We have never seen
	2.26	into the house of God and ate the bread offered to **God.**
	3.35	Whoever does what **God** wants him to do is my brother, my
	4.12	did, they would turn to **God,** and he would forgive them.' "
	4.14	The sower sows **God's** message.
	4.24	others will be used by **God** to judge you—but with even
	5. 7	For **God's** sake, I beg you, don't punish me!"
	6.41	the two fish, looked up to heaven, and gave thanks to **God.**
	7. 6	'These people, says **God,** honour me with their words,
	7. 7	because they teach man-made rules as though they were **God's** laws!'
	7. 8	"You put aside **God's** command and obey the teachings of men."
	7. 9	a clever way of rejecting **God's** law in order to uphold your
	7.11	(which means, it belongs to **God),** [12] he is excused from helping
	8. 6	seven loaves, gave thanks to **God,** broke them, and gave them
	8.11	him to perform a miracle to show that **God** approved of him.
	8.33	"Your thoughts don't come from **God** but from man!"
	10. 6	at the time of creation, **'God** made them male and female,' as
	10. 9	Man must not separate, then, what **God** has joined together."
	10.18	"No one is good except **God** alone.
	10.27	and answered, "This is impossible for man, but not for **God;**
	10.27	everything is possible for **God."**
	10.40	It is **God** who will give these places to those for whom
	11. 9	and those who followed behind began to shout, "Praise **God!**
	11. 9	**God** bless him who comes in the name of the Lord!
	11.10	**God** bless the coming kingdom of King David, our father!
	11.10	Praise **God!"**
	11.17	written in the Scriptures that **God** said, 'My Temple will be
	11.22	Jesus answered them, "Have faith in **God.**
	11.30	was it from **God** or from man?"
	11.31	If we answer, 'From **God,'** he will say, 'Why, then, did you
	12.14	man's status, but teach the truth about **God's** will for man.
	12.17	belongs to the Emperor, and pay **God** what belongs to God."
	12.24	It is because you don't know the Scriptures or **God's** power.
	12.26	There it is written that **God** said to Moses, 'I am the
	12.26	God of Abraham, the God of Isaac, and the **God** of Jacob.'
	12.27	He is the **God** of the living, not of the dead.
	12.29	The Lord our **God** is the only Lord.
	12.30	Love the Lord your **God** with all your heart, with all
	12.32	Lord is God and that there is no other **god** but he.
	12.33	And man must love **God** with all his heart and with all
	12.33	than to offer animals and other sacrifices to **God."**
	13.18	Pray to **God** that these things will not happen in the winter!
	13.19	from the very beginning when **God** created the world
	14.23	took a cup, gave thanks to **God,** and handed it to them;
	14.24	is poured out for many, my blood which seals **God's** covenant.
	14.27	for the scripture says, **'God** will kill the shepherd,
	14.71	May **God** punish me if I am not!
	15.34	which means, "My **God,** my God, why did you abandon me?"
	16.19	taken up to heaven and sat at the right side of **God.**
Lk	1. 6	both lived good lives in **God's** sight and obeyed fully all
	1.13	**God** has heard your prayer, and your wife Elizabeth will bear
	1.16	back many of the people of Israel to the Lord their **God.**
	1.19	stand in the presence of **God,** who sent me to speak to
	1.26	sixth month of Elizabeth's pregnancy **God** sent the angel Gabriel
	1.30	**God** has been gracious to you.
	1.32	The Lord **God** will make him a king, as his ancestor David
	1.35	Spirit will come on you, and **God's** power will rest upon you.
	1.37	For there is nothing that **God** cannot do."
	1.47	soul is glad because of **God** my Saviour, [48] for he has
	1.49	because of the great things the Mighty **God** has done for me.
	1.64	Zechariah was able to speak again, and he started praising **God.**
	1.67	Zechariah was filled with the Holy Spirit, and he spoke **God's** message:
	1.68	"Let us praise the Lord, the **God** of Israel!
	1.76	my child, will be called a prophet of the Most High **God.**
	1.78	Our **God** is merciful and tender.
	2.13	heaven's angels appeared with the angel, singing praises to **God:**
	2.14	"Glory to **God** in the highest heaven, and peace on earth
	2.20	went back, singing praises to **God** for all they had heard and
	2.28	Simeon took the child in his arms and gave thanks to **God:**
	2.34	"This child is chosen by **God** for the destruction and the
	2.34	will be a sign from **God** which many people will speak against
	2.36	day and night she worshipped **God,** fasting and praying.
	2.38	arrived and gave thanks to **God** and spoke about the child to
	2.38	to all who were waiting for **God** to set Jerusalem free.
	2.40	he was full of wisdom, and **God's** blessings were upon him.
	2.52	in body and in wisdom, gaining favour with **God** and men.
	3. 3	your sins and be baptized, and **God** will forgive your sins."
	3. 6	All mankind will see **God's** salvation!' "
	3. 7	you could escape from the punishment **God** is about to send?
	3. 8	I tell you that **God** can take these stones and make
	3.38	the son of Seth, the son of Adam, the son of **God.**
	4. 8	'Worship the Lord your **God** and serve only him!' "
	4.10	For the scripture says, **'God** will order his angels to
	4.12	says, 'Do not put the Lord your **God** to the test.' "
	4.34	you are **God's** holy messenger!"
	4.43	other towns also, because that is what **God** sent me to do."
	5.21	**God** is the only one who can forgive sins!"
	5.25	the bed he had been lying on, and went home, praising **God.**
	5.26	Full of fear, they praised **God,** saying, "What marvellous things
	6. 4	took the bread offered to **God,** ate it, and gave it also
	6.12	hill to pray and spent the whole night there praying to **God.**
	6.35	great reward, and you will be sons of the Most High **God.**

Lk 6.37 “Do not judge others, and **God** will not judge you;
6.37 do not condemn others, and **God** will not condemn you;
6.37 forgive others, and **God** will forgive you.
6.38 Give to others, and **God** will give to you.
6.38 use for others is the one that **God** will use for you.”
7.16 They all were filled with fear and praised **God.**
7.16 **“God** has come to save his people!”
7.27 **‘God** said, I will send my messenger ahead of you to open
7.29 the ones who had obeyed **God’s** righteous demands and had been
7.30 teachers of the Law rejected **God’s** purpose for themselves
7.35 **God’s** wisdom, however, is shown to be true by all who
8.39 “Go back home and tell what **God** has done for you.”
9.16 looked up to heaven, thanked **God** for them, broke them, and
9.20 Peter answered, “You are **God’s** Messiah.”
9.31 he would soon fulfil **God’s** purpose by dying in Jerusalem.
10.12 you that on Judgement Day **God** will show more mercy to Sodom
10.14 **God** will show more mercy on Judgement Day to Tyre and
10.27 answered, “ ‘Love the Lord your **God** with all your heart,
11.16 him to perform a miracle to show that **God** approved of him.
11.20 is rather by means of **God’s** power that I drive out demons,
11.40 Did not **God,** who made the outside, also make the inside?
11.42 You give **God** a tenth of the seasoning herbs, such as mint
11.42 the other herbs, but you neglect justice and love for **God.**
11.49 this reason the Wisdom of **God** said, ‘I will send them
12. 5 **God,** who, after killing, has the authority to throw into hell.
12. 6 Yet not one sparrow is forgotten by **God.**
12. 8 Man will do the same for him before the angels of **God.**
12. 9 Son of Man will also reject him before the angels of **God.**
12.20 But **God** said to him, ‘You fool!
12.21 up riches for themselves but are not rich in **God’s** sight.”
12.24 **God** feeds them!
12.28 It is **God** who clothes the wild grass—grass that is here
13. 1 whom Pilate had killed while they were offering sacrifices to **God.**
13.13 and at once she straightened herself up and praised **God.**
13.34 You kill the prophets, you stone the messengers **God** has sent you!
13.35 time comes when you say, **‘God** bless him who comes in the
14.14 **God** will repay you on the day the good people rise from
15.10 the angels of **God** rejoice over one sinner who repents.”
15.18 Father, I have sinned against **God** and against you.
15.21 the son said, ‘I have sinned against **God** and against you.
16.13 You cannot serve both **God** and money.”
16.15 look right in other people’s sight, but **God** knows your hearts.
16.15 of great value by man are worth nothing in **God’s** sight.
17.15 he was healed, he came back, praising **God** in a loud voice.
17.18 the only one who came back to give thanks to **God?”**
18. 2 there was a judge who neither feared **God** nor respected man.
18. 4 ‘Even though I don’t fear **God** or respect man, [5]yet because
18. 7 Now, will **God** not judge in favour of his own people who
18.11 and prayed, ‘I thank you, **God,** that I am not greedy,
18.13 on his breast and said, **‘God,** have pity on me, a sinner!’
18.14 was in the right with **God** when he went home.
18.19 “No one is good except **God** alone.
18.27 “What is impossible for man is possible for **God.”**
18.43 able to see, and he followed Jesus, giving thanks to **God.**
18.43 When the crowd saw it, they all praised **God.**
19.37 his disciples began to thank **God** and praise him in loud
19.38 **“God** bless the king who comes in the name of the Lord!
19.38 Peace in heaven and glory to **God!”**
19.44 you did not recognize the time when **God** came to save you!”
19.46 written in the Scriptures that **God** said, ‘My Temple will be
20. 4 did John’s right to baptize come from **God** or from man?”
20. 5 If we say, ‘From **God,’** he will say, ‘Why, then, did you
20.21 man’s status, but teach the truth about **God’s** will for man.
20.25 belongs to the Emperor, and pay **God** what belongs to God.”
20.36 They are the sons of **God,** because they have risen from death.
20.37 God of Abraham, the God of Isaac, and the **God** of Jacob.’
20.38 He is the **God** of the living, not of the dead,
21. 5 it looked with its fine stones and the gifts offered to **God.**
21.23 upon this land, and **God’s** punishment will fall on this people.
22.17 a cup, gave thanks to **God,** and said, “Take this and share
22.19 of bread, gave thanks to **God,** broke it, and gave it to
22.20 saying, “This cup is **God’s** new covenant sealed with my blood,
22.22 of Man will die as **God** has decided, but how terrible for
22.69 Son of Man will be seated on the right of Almighty **God.”**
23.35 him save himself if he is the Messiah whom **God** has chosen!”
23.40 The other one, however, rebuked him, saying, “Don’t you fear **God?**
23.47 happened, and he praised **God,** saying, “Certainly he was a good
24.19 prophet and was considered by **God** and by all the people to
24.53 and spent all their time in the Temple giving thanks to **God.**
Jn 1. 1 he was with **God,** and he was the same as God.
1. 2 From the very beginning the Word was with **God.**
1. 3 Through him **God** made all things;
1. 6 **God** sent his messenger, a man named John, [7]who came to
1.10 in the world, and though **God** made the world through him, yet
1.13 **God** himself was their Father.
1.17 **God** gave the Law through Moses, but grace and truth came
1.18 No one has ever seen **God.**
1.18 who is the same as **God** and is at the Father’s side,
1.33 he was the one, but **God,** who sent me to baptize with
1.51 will see heaven open and **God’s** angels going up and coming
2.17 devotion to your house, O **God,** burns in me like a fire.”
3. 2 him, “Rabbi, we know that you are a teacher sent by **God.**
3. 2 the miracles you are doing unless **God** were with him.”
3.16 For **God** loved the world so much that he gave his only
3.17 For **God** did not send his Son into the world to be
3.21 light may show that what he did was in obedience to **God.**
3.27 “No one can have anything unless **God** gives it to him.
3.33 whoever accepts his message confirms by this that **God** is truthful.
3.34 The one whom **God** has sent speaks God’s words,
3.34 because **God** gives him the fullness

Jn 3.36 will not have life, but will remain under **God’s** punishment.
4.10 “If only you knew what **God** gives and who it is that
4.20 “My Samaritan ancestors worshipped **God** on this mountain,
4.20 Jews say that Jerusalem is the place where we should worship **God.”**
4.24 **God** is Spirit, and only by the power of his Spirit can
5.18 but he had said that **God** was his own Father
5.18 and in this way had made himself equal with **God.**
5.30 I judge only as **God** tells me, so my judgement is right,
5.42 I know that you have no love for **God** in your hearts.
5.44 not try to win praise from the one who alone is **God;**
6.11 the bread, gave thanks to **God,** and distributed it to the
6.27 will give you, because **God, the Father,** has put his mark of
6.28 we do in order to do what **God** wants us to do?”
6.29 Jesus answered, “What **God** wants you to do is to believe
6.33 For the bread that **God** gives is he who comes down from
6.45 The prophets wrote, ‘Everyone will be taught by **God.’**
6.46 he who is from **God** is the only one who has seen
6.63 The words I have spoken to you bring **God’s** life-giving Spirit.
6.69 know that you are the Holy One who has come from **God.”**
7.16 not my own teaching, but it comes from **God,** who sent me.
7.17 is willing to do what **God** wants will know whether what I
7.17 what I teach comes from **God** or whether I speak on my
7.49 not know the Law of Moses, so they are under **God’s** curse!”
8.40 the truth I heard from **God,** yet you are trying to kill
8.41 **“God** himself is the only Father we have,” they answered,
8.42 Jesus said to them, “If **God** really were your Father,
8.42 love me, because I came from **God** and now I am here.
8.47 He who comes from **God** listens to God’s words.
8.47 You, however, are not from **God,** and that is why you will
8.54 me is my Father—the very one you say is your **God.**
9. 3 He is blind so that **God’s** power might be seen at work
9.16 did this cannot be from **God,** for he does not obey the
9.24 to him, “Promise before **God** that you will tell the truth!
9.29 We know that **God** spoke to Moses;
9.31 We know that **God** does not listen to sinners;
9.33 Unless this man came from **God,** he would not be able to
10.33 are only a man, but you are trying to make yourself **God!”**
10.34 is written in your own Law that **God** said, ‘You are gods.’
10.35 and **God** called those people gods, the people to whom his
11. 4 order to bring glory to **God,** and it will be the means
11.22 I know that even now **God** will give you whatever you ask
11.40 I tell you that you would see **God’s** glory if you believed?”
11.52 together into one body all the scattered people of **God.**
12.13 of palm-trees and went out to meet him, shouting, “Praise **God!**
12.13 **God** bless him who comes in the name of the Lord!
12.13 **God** bless the King of Israel!”
12.40 Isaiah also said, [40]**“God** has blinded their eyes and closed
12.40 would not turn to me, says **God,** for me to heal them.”
12.43 They loved the approval of men rather than the approval of **God.**
13. 3 knew that he had come from **God** and was going to God.
13.31 now **God’s** glory is revealed through him.
13.32 And if **God’s** glory is revealed through him,
13.32 then **God** will reveal the glory of the
14. 1 “Believe in **God** and believe also in me.
14.17 He is the Spirit who reveals the truth about **God.**
15.26 reveals the truth about **God** and who comes from the Father.
16. 2 kills you will think that by doing this he is serving **God.**
16. 8 about sin and about what is right and about **God’s** judgement.
16.13 who reveals the truth about **God,** he will lead you into all
16.27 because you love me and have believed that I came from **God.**
16.30 This makes us believe that you came from **God.”**
17. 3 knowing you, the only true **God,** and knowing Jesus Christ,
19.11 authority over me only because it was given to you by **God.**
20.17 who is my Father and their Father, my **God** and their God.”
20.28 Thomas answered him, “My Lord and my **God!”**
21.19 the way in which Peter would die and bring glory to **God.)**
Acts 2.11 own languages about the great things that **God** has done!”
2.17 ‘This is what I will do in the last days, **God** says:
2.22 by all the miracles and wonders which **God** performed through him.
2.23 accordance with his own plan **God** had already decided that Jesus
2.24 But **God** raised him from death, setting him free from its power,
2.30 He was a prophet, and he knew what **God** had promised him:
2.30 **God** had made a vow that he would make one of David’s
2.31 David saw what **God** was going to do in the future, and
2.32 **God** has raised this very Jesus from death, and we are
2.33 to the right-hand side of **God,** his Father, and has received
2.36 crucified, is the one that **God** has made Lord and Messiah!”
2.38 and you will receive **God’s** gift, the Holy Spirit.
2.39 For **God’s** promise was made to you and your children, and
2.39 are far away—all whom the Lord our **God** calls to himself.”
2.47 humble hearts, [47]praising **God,** and enjoying the good will
3. 8 into the Temple with them, walking and jumping and praising **God.**
3. 9 saw him walking and praising **God,** [10]and when they recognized him
3.13 The **God** of Abraham, Isaac, and Jacob, the God of our ancestors,
3.15 who leads to life, but **God** raised him from death—and we
3.18 **God** announced long ago through all the prophets that his Messiah
3.19 Repent, then, and turn to **God,** so that he will forgive
3.21 to be made new, as **God** announced through his holy prophets
3.22 Moses said, ‘The Lord your **God** will send you a prophet, just
3.25 The promises of **God** through his prophets are for you,
3.25 share in the covenant which **God** made with your ancestors.
3.26 And so **God** chose his Servant and sent him first to you,
4.10 Christ of Nazareth—whom you crucified and whom **God** raised
4.12 is no one else whom **God** has given who can save us.”
4.19 judge which is right in **God’s** sight—
4.19 to obey you or to obey **God.**
4.21 because the people were all praising **God** for what had happened.
4.24 heard it, they all joined together in prayer to **God:**

Acts	4.31	the Holy Spirit and began to proclaim **God's** message with boldness.
	4.33	the Lord Jesus, and **God** poured rich blessings on them all.
	5. 4	You have not lied to men—you have lied to **God!"**
	5.29	Peter and the other apostles replied, "We must obey **God,**
	5.30	The **God** of our ancestors raised Jesus from death,
	5.31	**God** raised him to his right-hand side as Leader and Saviour,
	5.32	the Holy Spirit, who is **God's** gift to those who obey him."
	5.39	but if it comes from **God,** you cannot possibly defeat them.
	5.39	You could find yourselves fighting against **God!"**
	5.41	they were happy, because **God** had considered them worthy to suffer
	6. 2	neglect the preaching of **God's** word in order to handle finances.
	6. 8	a man richly blessed by **God** and full of power, performed
	6.11	"We heard him speaking against Moses and against **God!"**
	7. 2	to live in Haran, the **God** of glory appeared to him in
	7. 4	After Abraham's father died, **God** made him move to this land
	7. 5	**God** did not then give Abraham any part of it as his
	7. 5	square metre of ground, but **God** promised to give it to him,
	7. 5	At the time **God** made this promise, Abraham had no children.
	7. 6	This is what **God** said to him:
	7. 8	Then **God** gave Abraham the ceremony of circumcision as a
	7. 9	But **God** was with him [10] and brought him safely through all
	7.10	before the king of Egypt, **God** gave him a pleasing manner and
	7.17	the time drew near for **God** to keep the promise he had
	7.25	own people would understand that **God** was going to use him to
	7.32	the God of your ancestors, the **God** of Abraham, Isaac, and
	7.35	He is the one whom **God** sent to rule the people and
	7.37	to the people of Israel, **'God** will send you a prophet, just
	7.38	Mount Sinai, and he received **God's** living messages to pass on
	7.42	So **God** turned away from them and gave them over to
	7.44	had the Tent of **God's** presence with them in the desert.
	7.44	It had been made as **God** had told Moses to make it,
	7.45	land from the nations that **God** drove out as they advanced.
	7.46	He won **God's** favour and asked God to allow him to
	7.46	provide a dwelling place for the **God** of Jacob.
	7.48	"But the Most High **God** does not live in houses built by
	7.51	"How heathen your hearts, how deaf you are to **God's** message!
	7.52	They killed **God's** messengers, who long ago announced the coming
	7.53	are the ones who received **God's** law, that was handed down by
	7.55	God's glory and Jesus standing at the right-hand side of **God.**
	7.56	and the Son of Man standing at the right-hand side of **God!"**
	8.20	hell, for thinking that you can buy **God's** gift with money!
	8.21	in our work, because your heart is not right in **God's** sight.
	8.27	been to Jerusalem to worship **God** and was going back home in
	10. 2	he and his whole family worshipped **God.**
	10. 2	the Jewish poor people and was constantly praying to **God.**
	10. 3	clearly saw an angel of **God** come in and say to him,
	10. 4	The angel answered, **"God** is pleased with your prayers
	10.15	"Do not consider anything unclean that **God** has declared clean."
	10.22	a good man who worships **God** and is highly respected by all
	10.22	An angel of **God** told him to invite you to his house,
	10.28	But **God** has shown me that I must not consider any person
	10.31	**God** has heard your prayer and has taken notice of your works
	10.33	here in the presence of **God,** waiting to hear anything that
	10.34	that it is true that **God** treats everyone on the same basis.
	10.38	Jesus of Nazareth and how **God** poured out on him the Holy
	10.38	were under the power of the Devil, for **God** was with him.
	10.40	But **God** raised him from death three days later and
	10.41	only to the witnesses that **God** had already chosen, that is,
	10.42	he is the one whom **God** has appointed judge of the living
	10.45	with Peter were amazed that **God** had poured out his gift of
	10.46	speaking in strange tongues and praising **God's** greatness.
	11. 9	'Do not consider anything unclean that **God** has declared clean.'
	11.17	It is clear that **God** gave those Gentiles the same gift
	11.17	who was I, then, to try to stop **God!"**
	11.18	stopped their criticism and praised **God,**
	11.18	saying, "Then **God** has given to the Gentiles also
	11.23	he arrived and saw how **God** had blessed the people, he was
	12. 5	people of the church were praying earnestly to **God** for him.
	12.23	Lord struck Herod down, because he did not give honour to **God.**
	13.16	"Fellow-Israelites and all Gentiles here who worship **God:**
	13.17	The **God** of the people of Israel chose our ancestors and
	13.17	**God** brought them out of Egypt by his great power, [18] and
	13.21	they asked for a king, **God** gave them Saul son of Kish
	13.22	After removing him, **God** made David their king.
	13.22	This is what **God** said about him:
	13.23	a descendant of David, whom **God** made the Saviour of the
	13.26	descendants of Abraham, and all Gentiles here who worship **God:**
	13.30	But **God** raised him from death, [31] and for many days he
	13.32	what **God** promised our ancestors he would do, he has now done
	13.34	And this is what **God** said about raising him from death,
	13.36	For David served **God's** purposes in his own time, and
	13.37	this did not happen to the one whom **God** raised from death.
	13.43	and encouraged them to keep on living in the grace of **God.**
	13.50	the Gentile women of high social standing who worshipped **God.**
	14.15	these worthless things to the **living God,** who made heaven,
	14.26	commended to the care of **God's** grace for the work they had
	14.27	told them about all that **God** had done with them and how
	15. 3	they reported how the Gentiles had turned to **God;**
	15. 4	to whom they told all that **God** had done through them.
	15. 7	that a long time ago **God** chose me from among you to
	15. 8	And **God,** who knows the thoughts of everyone, showed his approval
	15.10	you now want to put **God** to the test by laying a
	15.12	the miracles and wonders that **God** had performed through them
	15.14	Simon has just explained how **God** first showed his care
	15.19	"that we should not trouble the Gentiles who are turning to **God.**
	16.10	Macedonia, because we decided that **God** had called us to preach
	16.14	was a woman who worshipped **God,** and the Lord opened her mind
Acts	16.17	us, shouting, "These men are servants of the Most High **God!**
	16.25	and singing hymns to **God,** and the other prisoners were listening
	16.34	were filled with joy, because they now believed in **God.**
	17. 4	women and a large group of Greeks who worshipped **God.**
	17.17	the Gentiles who worshipped **God,** and also in the public square
	17.24	**God,** who made the world and everything in it, is Lord of
	17.27	Yet **God** is actually not far from any one of us;
	17.30	**God** has overlooked the times when people did not know him,
	18. 7	house of a Gentile named Titius Justus, who worshipped **God;**
	18.13	to persuade people to worship **God** in a way that is against
	18.21	it is the will of **God,** I will come back to you."
	18.26	them and explained to him more correctly the Way of **God.**
	18.27	great help to those who through **God's** grace had become believers.
	19. 6	spoke in strange tongues and also proclaimed **God's** message.
	19.11	**God** was performing unusual miracles through Paul.
	20.21	turn from their sins to **God** and believe in our Lord Jesus.
	20.24	which is to declare the Good News about the grace of **God.**
	20.27	held back from announcing to you the whole purpose of **God.**
	20.28	shepherds of the church of **God,** which he made his own
	20.32	you to the care of **God** and to the message of his
	20.32	up and give you the blessings **God** has for all his people.
	21. 9	He had four unmarried daughters who proclaimed **God's** message.
	21.19	report of everything that **God** had done among the Gentiles
	21.20	After hearing him, they all praised **God.**
	22. 3	was just as dedicated to **God** as are all of you who
	22.10	be told everything that **God** has determined for you to do.'
	22.14	He said, 'The **God** of our ancestors has chosen you to
	23. 1	way in which I have lived before **God** to this very day."
	23. 3	Paul said to him, **"God** will certainly strike you—
	23. 4	to Paul said to him, "You are insulting **God's** High Priest!"
	24.14	I worship the **God** of our ancestors by following that Way
	24.15	have the same hope in **God** that these themselves have,
	24.16	best always to have a clear conscience before **God** and man.
	26. 6	have in the promise that **God** made to our ancestors— [7] the
	26. 7	people hope to receive, as they worship **God** day and night.
	26. 8	find it impossible to believe that **God** raises the dead?
	26.18	the power of Satan to **God,** so that through their faith in
	26.20	their sins and turn to **God** and do the things that would
	26.22	I have been helped by **God,** and so I stand here giving
	26.29	Paul answered, "my prayer to **God** is that you and all the
	27.23	night an angel of the **God** to whom I belong and whom
	27.24	And **God** in his goodness to you has spared the lives of
	27.25	For I trust in **God** that it will be just as I
	27.35	some bread, gave thanks to **God** before them all, broke it,
	28.15	When Paul saw them, he thanked **God** and was greatly encouraged.
	28.27	they would turn to me, says **God,** and I would heal them.'"
	28.28	are to know, then, that **God's** message of salvation has been
Rom	1. 1	apostle chosen and called by **God** to preach his Good News.
	1. 2	was promised long ago by **God** through his prophets, as
	1. 5	Through him **God** gave me the privilege of being an apostle
	1. 6	who are in Rome, whom **God** has called to belong to Jesus
	1. 7	of you in Rome whom **God** loves and has called to be
	1. 7	May **God** our Father and the Lord Jesus Christ give you grace
	1. 8	First, I thank my **God** through Jesus Christ for all of you,
	1. 9	**God** is my witness that what I say is true—the God
	1. 9	**God** knows that I remember you [10] every time I pray.
	1.10	I ask that **God** in his good will may at last make
	1.16	it is **God's** power to save all who believe, first the Jews
	1.17	For the gospel reveals how **God** puts people right with himself:
	1.17	"The person who is put right with **God** through faith shall live."
	1.18	**God's** anger is revealed from heaven against all the sin
	1.19	**God** punishes them, because
	1.19	what can be known about **God** is plain to them,
	1.19	for **God** himself made it plain.
	1.20	Ever since **God** created the world, his invisible qualities,
	1.20	they are perceived in the things that **God** has made.
	1.21	They know **God,** but they do not give him the honour that
	1.23	instead of worshipping the immortal **God,** they worship images
	1.24	And so **God** has given those people over to do the filthy
	1.25	They exchange the truth about **God** for a lie;
	1.25	they worship and serve what **God** has created instead of the
	1.26	**God** has given them over to shameful passions.
	1.28	mind the true knowledge about **God,** he has given them over to
	1.30	they are hateful to **God,** insolent, proud, and boastful;
	1.32	They know that **God's** law says that people who live in
	2. 2	We know that **God** is right when he judges the people who
	2. 3	Do you think you will escape **God's** judgement?
	2. 4	Surely you know that **God** is kind, because he is trying to
	2. 5	greater on the Day when **God's** anger and righteous judgements
	2. 6	For **God** will reward every person according to what he has done.
	2. 7	to them **God** will give eternal life.
	2. 8	on them **God** will pour out his anger and fury.
	2.10	But **God** will give glory, honour, and peace to all who do
	2.11	For **God** judges everyone by the same standard.
	2.13	people are put right with **God,** but by doing what the Law
	2.16	be on that Day when **God** through Jesus Christ will judge the
	2.17	you depend on the Law and boast about **God;**
	2.18	you know what **God** wants you to do, and you have learnt
	2.23	You boast about having **God's** law—
	2.23	but do you bring shame on **God** by breaking his law?
	2.24	"Because of you Jews, the Gentiles speak evil of **God."**
	2.26	commands of the Law, will **God** not regard him as though he
	2.29	Such a person receives his praise from **God,** not from man.
	3. 2	In the first place, **God** trusted his message to the Jews.
	3. 3	Does this mean that **God** will not be faithful?
	3. 4	**God** must be true, even though every man is a liar.
	3. 5	wrong serves to show up more clearly **God's** doing right?
	3. 5	Can we say that **God** does wrong when he punishes us?
	3. 6	If **God** is not just, how can he judge the world?

Rom 3. 7 what if my untruth serves **God's** glory by making his truth
3.11 no one who is wise or who worships **God.**
3.12 All have turned away from **God;**
3.18 nor have they learnt reverence for **God."**
3.19 human excuses and bring the whole world under **God's** judgement.
3.20 one is put right in **God's** sight by doing what the Law
3.21 But now **God's** way of putting people right with himself
3.22 **God** puts people right through their faith in Jesus Christ.
3.22 **God** does this to all who believe in Christ, because there is
3.23 everyone has sinned and is far away from **God's** saving presence.
3.24 by the free gift of **God's** grace all are put right with
3.25 **God** offered him, so that by his sacrificial death
3.25 **God** did this in order to demonstrate that he is righteous.
3.25 In this way **God** shows that he himself is righteous and that
3.28 person is put right with **God** only through faith, and not by
3.29 Or is **God** the God of the Jews only?
3.29 Is he not the **God** of the Gentiles also?
3.30 **God** is one, and he will put the Jews right with himself
4. 2 he was put right with **God** by the things he did,
4. 2 would have something to boast about—but not in **God's** sight.
4. 3 scripture says, "Abraham believed **God,**
4. 3 and because of his faith **God** accepted him as righteous."
4. 5 and who believes in the **God** who declares the guilty to be
4. 5 it is his faith that **God** takes into account in order to
4. 6 happiness of the person whom **God** accepts as righteous,
4. 9 "Abraham believed **God,**
4. 9 and because of his faith **God** accepted him as righteous."
4.11 that because of his faith **God** had accepted him as righteous
4.11 of all who believe in **God** and are accepted as righteous by
4.13 When **God** promised Abraham and his descendants that the world
4.13 because he believed and was accepted as righteous by **God.**
4.14 For if what **God** promises is to be given to those who
4.14 then man's faith means nothing and **God's** promise is worthless.
4.15 The Law brings down **God's** anger;
4.16 should be guaranteed as **God's** free gift to all of Abraham's
4.17 good in the sight of **God,** in whom Abraham believed—
4.17 the **God** who brings the dead to life
4.20 faith did not leave him, and he did not doubt **God's** promise;
4.20 his faith filled him with power, and he gave praise to **God.**
4.21 He was absolutely sure that **God** would be able to do what
4.22 Abraham, through faith, "was accepted as righteous by **God."**
4.25 was raised to life in order to put us right with **God.**
5. 1 have been put right with **God** through faith,
5. 1 we have peace with **God** through our Lord Jesus Christ.
5. 2 into this experience of **God's** grace, in which we now live.
5. 2 so we boast of the hope we have of sharing **God's** glory!
5. 4 endurance brings **God's** approval, and his approval creates hope.
5. 5 does not disappoint us, for **God** has poured out his love into
5. 5 by means of the Holy Spirit, who is **God's** gift to us.
5. 6 Christ died for the wicked at the time that **God** chose.
5. 8 But **God** has shown us how much he loves us—
5. 9 By his sacrificial death we are now put right with **God;**
5. 9 much more, then, will we be saved by him from **God's** anger!
5.10 We were **God's** enemies, but he made us his friends
5.10 Now that we are **God's** friends, how much more will we be
5.11 we rejoice because of what **God** has done through our Lord
5.11 our Lord Jesus Christ, who has now made us **God's** friends.
5.14 the same way that Adam did when he disobeyed **God's** command.
5.15 are not the same, because **God's** free gift is not like Adam's
5.15 But **God's** grace is much greater, and so is his free gift
5.16 there is a difference between **God's** gift and the sin of one
5.17 All who receive **God's** abundant grace and are freely put right
5.19 all be put right with **God** as the result of the obedience
5.20 but where sin increased, **God's** grace increased much more.
5.21 of death, so also **God's** grace rules by means of righteousness,
6. 1 continue to live in sin so that **God's** grace will increase?
6.10 and now he lives his life in fellowship with **God.**
6.11 but living in fellowship with **God** through Christ Jesus.
6.13 Instead, give yourselves to **God,** as those who have been brought
6.14 for you do not live under law but under **God's** grace.
6.15 we sin, because we are not under law but under **God's** grace?
6.16 or of obedience, which results in being put right with **God.**
6.17 But thanks be to **God!**
6.22 have been set free from sin and are the slaves of **God.**
6.23 but **God's** free gift is eternal life in union with Christ
7. 4 in order that we might be useful in the service of **God.**
7.22 My inner being delights in the law of **God.**
7.25 Thanks be to **God,** who does this through our Lord Jesus Christ!
7.25 my own I can serve **God's** law only with my mind, while
8. 3 Law could not do, because human nature was weak, **God** did.
8. 4 **God** did this so that the righteous demands of the Law
8. 7 person becomes an enemy of **God** when he is controlled by his
8. 7 for he does not obey **God's** law, and in fact he cannot
8. 8 Those who obey their human nature cannot please **God.**
8.10 have been put right with **God,** even though your bodies are
8.11 If the Spirit of **God,** who raised Jesus from death, lives
8.14 Those who are led by God's Spirit are **God's** sons.
8.15 For the Spirit that **God** has given you does not make you
8.15 children, and by the Spirit's power we cry out to **God,**
8.17 we will also possess with Christ what **God** has kept for him;
8.19 waits with eager longing for **God** to reveal his sons.
8.20 of its own will, but because **God** willed it to be so.
8.23 Spirit as the first of **God's** gifts also groan within ourselves,
8.23 as we wait for **God** to make us his sons
8.26 the Spirit himself pleads with **God** for us in groans that
8.27 And **God,** who sees into our hearts, knows what the
8.27 because the Spirit pleads with **God** on behalf of his people
8.28 know that in all things **God** works for good with those who
8.29 Those whom **God** had already chosen he also set apart to
8.30 And so those whom **God** set apart, he called;
8.31 If **God** is for us, who can be against us?

Rom 8.32 Certainly not **God,** who did not even keep back his own Son,
8.33 **God** himself declares them not guilty!
8.34 is at the right-hand side of **God,** pleading with him for us!
8.39 us from the love of **God** which is ours through Christ Jesus
9. 3 that I myself were under **God's** curse and separated from Christ.
9. 4 they have received **God's** promises;
9. 5 May **God,** who rules over all, be praised for ever!
9. 6 I am not saying that the promise of **God** has failed;
9. 6 for not all the people of Israel are the people of **God.**
9. 7 **God** said to Abraham, "It is through Isaac that you will
9. 8 born as a result of **God's** promise are regarded as the true
9. 9 For **God's** promise was made in these words:
9.11 completely the result of **God's** own purpose, God said to her,
9.11 so **God's** choice was based on his call, and not on anything
9.14 Shall we say, then, that **God** is unjust?
9.16 not on what man wants or does, but only on **God's** mercy.
9.18 So then, **God** has mercy on anyone he wishes, and he makes
9.19 "If this is so, how can **God** find fault with anyone?
9.19 Who can resist **God's** will?"
9.20 But who are you, my friend, to answer **God** back?
9.22 And the same is true of what **God** has done.
9.26 there they will be called the sons of the **living God."**
9.30 to put themselves right with **God,** were put right with him
9.31 law that would put them right with **God,** did not find it.
10. 1 How I pray to **God** for them!
10. 2 I can assure you that they are deeply devoted to **God;**
10. 3 known the way in which **God** puts people right with himself,
10. 3 did not submit themselves to **God's** way of putting people right.
10. 4 so that everyone who believes is put right with **God.**
10. 5 this about being put right with **God** by obeying the Law:
10. 6 scripture says about being put right with **God** through faith
10. 8 **"God's** message is near you, on your lips and in your heart"
10. 9 is Lord and believe that **God** raised him from death, you will
10.10 it is by our faith that we are put right with **God;**
10.12 **God** is the same Lord of all and richly blesses all who
11. 1 Did **God** reject his own people?
11. 2 **God** has not rejected his people, whom he chose from the beginning.
11. 2 in the passage where Elijah pleads with **God** against Israel:
11. 4 What answer did **God** give him?
11. 5 left of those whom **God** has chosen because of his grace.
11. 6 For if **God's** choice were based on what people do, then his
11. 7 It was only the small group that **God** chose who found it;
11. 7 the rest grew deaf to **God's** call.
11. 8 As the scripture says, **"God** made their minds and hearts dull;
11.15 mankind was changed from **God's** enemies into his friends.
11.16 of bread is given to **God,** then the whole loaf is his
11.16 of a tree are offered to **God,** the branches are his also.
11.21 **God** did not spare the Jews, who are like natural branches;
11.22 Here we see how kind and how severe **God** is.
11.23 for **God** is able to do that.
11.24 will be much easier for **God** to join these broken-off
11.25 only until the complete number of Gentiles comes to **God.**
11.28 Good News, the Jews are **God's** enemies for the sake of you
11.28 But because of **God's** choice, they are his friends
11.29 For **God** does not change his mind about whom he chooses
11.30 As for you Gentiles, you disobeyed **God** in the past;
11.30 you have received **God's** mercy because the Jews were disobedient.
11.31 received, the Jews now disobey **God,**
11.31 in order that they also may now receive **God's** mercy.
11.32 For **God** has made all people prisoners of disobedience,
11.33 How great are **God's** riches!
11.36 To **God** be the glory for ever!
12. 1 then, my brothers, because of **God's** great mercy to us I
12. 1 as a living sacrifice to **God,** dedicated to his service and
12. 2 of this world, but let **God** transform you inwardly by a
12. 2 to know the will of **God**—what is good and is pleasing
12. 3 And because of **God's** gracious gift to me I say to every
12. 3 according to the amount of faith that **God** has given you.
12. 6 gifts in accordance with the grace that **God** has given us.
12. 6 our gift is to speak **God's** message, we should do it
12.14 Ask **God** to bless those who persecute you—
12.19 Never take revenge, my friends, but instead let **God's** anger do it.
13. 1 no authority exists without **God's** permission,
13. 1 and the existing authorities have been put there by **God.**
13. 2 Whoever opposes the existing authority opposes what **God** has ordered;
13. 4 because he is **God's** servant working for your own good.
13. 4 He is **God's** servant
13. 4 and carries out **God's** punishment on those who do evil.
13. 5 authorities—not just because of **God's** punishment, but also
13. 6 the authorities are working for **God** when they fulfil their duties.
14. 3 for **God** has accepted him.
14. 6 because he gives thanks to **God** for the food.
14. 6 so in honour of the Lord, and he gives thanks to **God.**
14.10 All of us will stand before **God** to be judged by him.
14.11 surely as I am the **living God,** says the Lord, everyone will
14.11 kneel before me, and everyone will confess that I am **God."**
14.12 will have to give an account of himself to **God.**
14.18 in this way, he pleases **God** and is approved by others.
14.20 Do not, because of food, destroy what **God** has done.
14.22 Keep what you believe about this matter, then, between yourself and **God.**
14.23 doubts about what he eats, **God** condemns him when he eats it,
15. 5 may **God,** the source of patience and encouragement, enable you to
15. 6 praise with one voice the **God** and Father of our Lord Jesus
15. 7 for the glory of **God,** as Christ has accepted you.
15. 8 the Jews, to show that **God** is faithful, to make his promises
15. 9 and to enable even the Gentiles to praise **God** for his mercy.

Rom 15.13 May **God,** the source of hope, fill you with all joy and
15.15 bold because of the privilege **God** has given me [16]of being
15.16 preaching the Good News from **God,** in order that the Gentiles
15.16 be an offering acceptable to **God,** dedicated to him by the
15.17 Christ Jesus, then, I can be proud of my service for **God.**
15.18 Christ has done through me to lead the Gentiles to obey **God.**
15.19 miracles and wonders, and by the power of the Spirit of **God.**
15.30 join me in praying fervently to **God** for me.
15.32 of joy, if it is **God's** will, and enjoy a refreshing visit
15.33 May **God,** our source of peace, be with all of you.
16.20 And **God,** our source of peace, will soon crush Satan
16.25 Let us give glory to **God!**
16.26 the command of the eternal **God** it is made known to all
16.27 To the only **God,** who alone is all-wise, be glory through
1 Cor 1. 1 called by the will of **God** to be an apostle of Christ
1. 2 To the church of **God** which is in Corinth, to all
1. 3 May **God** our Father and the Lord Jesus Christ give you
1. 4 always give thanks to my **God** for you because of the grace
1. 9 **God** is to be trusted, the God who called you to have
1.14 I thank **God** that I did not baptize any of you except
1.18 but for us who are being saved it is **God's** power.
1.20 **God** has shown that this world's wisdom is foolishness!
1.21 For **God** in his wisdom made it impossible for people to
1.21 **God** decided to save those who believe.
1.24 but for those whom **God** has called, both Jews and Gentiles,
1.24 Christ, who is the power of **God** and the wisdom of God.
1.25 For what seems to be **God's** foolishness is wiser than human wisdom,
1.25 seems to be **God's** weakness is stronger than human strength.
1.26 Now remember what you were, my brothers, when **God** called you.
1.27 **God** purposely chose what the world considers nonsense
1.29 This means that no one can boast in **God's** presence.
1.30 But **God** has brought you into union with Christ Jesus,
1.30 and **God** has made Christ to be our
1.30 By him we are put right with **God;**
2. 1 you, my brothers, to preach **God's** secret truth, I did not
2. 5 then, does not rest on human wisdom but on **God's** power.
2. 7 The wisdom I proclaim is **God's** secret wisdom, which is hidden
2. 9 is the very thing **God** prepared for those who love him."
2.10 it was to us that **God** made known his secret by means
2.10 The Spirit searches everything, even the hidden depths of **God's** purposes.
2.11 in the same way, only God's Spirit knows all about **God.**
2.12 received the Spirit sent by **God,**
2.12 so that we may know all that **God** has given us.
3. 5 We are simply **God's** servants, by whom you were led to believe.
3. 6 watered the plant, but it was **God** who made the plant grow.
3. 7 It is **God** who matters, because he makes the plant grow.
3. 8 **God** will reward each one according to the work he has done.
3. 9 partners working together for God, and you are **God's** field.
3. 9 You are also **God's** building.
3.10 Using the gift that **God** gave me, I did the work of
3.11 For **God** has already placed Jesus Christ as the one and
3.16 you are God's temple and that **God's** Spirit lives in you!
3.17 So if anyone destroys **God's** temple, God will destroy him.
3.17 For **God's** temple is holy, and you yourselves are his temple.
3.19 world considers to be wisdom is nonsense in **God's** sight.
3.19 As the scripture says, **"God** traps the wise in their cleverness";
3.23 and you belong to Christ, and Christ belongs to **God.**
4. 1 servants, who have been put in charge of **God's** secret truths.
4. 5 And then everyone will receive from **God** the praise he deserves.
4. 7 Didn't **God** give you everything you have?
4. 9 it seems to me that **God** has given the very last place
5.12 **God** will judge them.
6.11 you have been dedicated to **God;**
6.11 have been put right with **God** by the Lord Jesus Christ
6.11 and by the Spirit of our **God.**
6.13 but **God** will put an end to both.
6.14 **God** raised the Lord from death, and he will also raise
6.19 who lives in you and who was given to you by **God?**
6.19 You do not belong to yourselves but to **God;**
6.20 So use your bodies for **God's** glory.
7. 7 has a special gift from **God,** one person this gift, another
7.14 is made acceptable to **God** by being united to his wife,
7.14 wife is made acceptable to **God** by being united to her
7.14 but as it is, they are acceptable to **God.**
7.15 **God** has called you to live in peace.
7.17 Lord's gift to him, and as he was when **God** called him.
7.18 a circumcised man has accepted **God's** call, he should not try
7.18 uncircumcised man has accepted **God's** call, he should not get
7.19 what matters is to obey **God's** commandments.
7.20 Everyone should remain as he was when he accepted **God's** call.
7.21 Were you a slave when **God** called you?
7.23 **God** bought you for a price;
7.24 should remain in fellowship with **God** in the same condition
8. 3 But the person who loves **God** is known by him.
8. 4 we know that there is only the one **God.**
8. 6 for us only one **God, the Father,** who is the Creator of
8. 8 Food, however, will not improve our relations with **God;**
9. 9 Now, is **God** concerned about oxen?
9.17 matter of duty, because **God** has entrusted me with this task.
9.21 This does not mean that I don't obey **God's** law;
10. 5 But even then **God** was not pleased with most of them, and
10.13 But **God** keeps his promise, and he will not allow you to
10.16 in the Lord's Supper and for which we give thanks to **God:**
10.18 is offered in sacrifice share in the altar's service to **God.**
10.20 sacrificed on pagan altars is offered to demons, not to **God.**
10.30 If I thank **God** for my food, why should anyone criticize
10.31 do, whether you eat or drink, do it all for **God's** glory.
10.32 trouble either to Jews or Gentiles or to the church of **God.**
11. 3 is supreme over his wife, and **God** is supreme over Christ.
1 Cor 11. 4 man who prays or proclaims **God's** message in public worship
11. 5 woman who prays or proclaims **God's** message in public worship
11. 7 his head, because he reflects the image and glory of **God.**
11.12 and it is **God** who brings everything into existence.
11.13 a woman to pray to **God** in public worship with nothing on
11.16 nor the churches of **God** have any other custom in worship.
11.22 rather despise the church of **God** and put to shame the people
11.24 of bread, [24]gave thanks to **God,** broke it, and said, "This
11.25 "This cup is **God's** new covenant, sealed with my blood.
11.31 examine ourselves first, we would not come under **God's** judgement.
11.34 will not come under **God's** judgement as you meet together.
12. 6 perform service, but the same **God** gives ability to all for
12.10 to another, the gift of speaking **God's** message;
12.18 As it is, however, **God** put every different part in the
12.24 **God** himself has put the body together in such a way as
12.28 In the church **God** has put all in place:
13.12 it will be complete—as complete as **God's** knowledge of me.
14. 1 spiritual gifts, especially the gift of proclaiming **God's** message.
14. 2 speak to others but to **God,** because no one understands him.
14. 3 the one who proclaims **God's** message speaks to people and gives
14. 4 but the one who proclaims **God's** message helps the whole church.
14. 5 I would rather that you had the gift of proclaiming **God's** message.
14. 5 For the person who proclaims **God's** message is of greater value
14. 6 bring you some revelation from **God** or some knowledge
14.16 When you give thanks to **God** in spirit only, how can an
14.17 your prayer of thanks to **God** is quite good, the other person
14.18 I thank **God** that I speak in strange tongues much more
14.22 while the gift of proclaiming **God's** message is proof for believers,
14.24 But if everyone is proclaiming **God's** message when some unbeliever
14.25 and worship God, confessing, "Truly **God** is here among you!"
14.26 another a revelation from **God,** another a message in strange tongues,
14.28 tongues must be quiet and speak only to himself and to **God.**
14.29 or three who are given **God's** message should speak,
14.30 receives a message from **God,** the one who is speaking should
14.31 All of you may proclaim **God's** message, one by one, so
14.32 gift of proclaiming **God's** message should be under the speaker's
14.33 under the speaker's control, [33]because **God** does not want us to
14.37 If anyone supposes he is **God's** messenger or has a spiritual gift,
14.39 set your heart on proclaiming **God's** message, but do not forbid
15. 9 deserve to be called an apostle, because I persecuted **God's** church.
15.10 But by **God's** grace I am what I am, and the grace
15.10 not really my own doing, but **God's** grace working with me.
15.15 shown to be lying about **God,** because we said that he raised
15.24 powers, and will hand over the Kingdom to **God the Father.**
15.25 For Christ must rule until **God** defeats all enemies
15.27 For the scripture says, **"God** put all things under his feet."
15.27 "all things" do not include **God** himself, who puts all things
15.28 will place himself under **God,** who placed all things under him;
15.28 and **God** will rule completely over all.
15.34 declare to your shame that some of you do not know **God.**
15.38 **God** provides that seed with the body he wishes;
15.57 But thanks be to **God** who gives us the victory through
2 Cor 1. 1 apostle of Christ Jesus by **God's** will, and from our brother
1. 1 To the church of **God** in Corinth, and to all God's
1. 2 May **God** our Father and the Lord Jesus Christ give you
1. 3 us give thanks to the **God** and Father of our Lord Jesus
1. 3 the merciful Father, the **God** from whom all help comes!
1. 4 using the same help that we ourselves have received from **God.**
1. 5 so also through Christ we share in **God's** great help.
1. 9 not on ourselves, but only on **God,** who raises the dead.
1.11 many prayers for us will be answered, and **God** will bless us;
1.12 by the power of **God's** grace, and not by human wisdom.
1.18 As surely as **God** speaks the truth, my promise to you was
1.19 On the contrary, he is **God's** "Yes";
1.20 for it is he who is the "Yes" to all **God's** promises.
1.20 Jesus Christ our "Amen" is said to the glory of **God.**
1.21 It is **God** himself who makes us, together with you, sure
1.21 it is **God** himself who has set us apart, [22]who has placed
1.23 I call **God** as my witness—he knows my heart!
2.14 But thanks be to **God!**
2.14 led by **God** as prisoners in Christ's victory procession.
2.14 **God** uses us to make the knowledge about Christ spread everywhere
2.15 incense offered by Christ to **God,** which spreads among those who
2.17 so many others, who handle **God's** message as if it were cheap
2.17 but because **God** has sent us, we speak with sincerity in his
3. 3 with the Spirit of the **living God,** and not on stone tablets
3. 4 We say this because we have confidence in **God** through Christ.
3. 5 The capacity we have comes from **God;**
3. 7 letters on stone tablets, and **God's** glory appeared
4. 1 **God** in his mercy has given us this work to do,
4. 2 of truth we live in **God's** sight and try to commend ourselves
4. 4 about the glory of Christ, who is the exact likeness of **God.**
4. 6 The **God** who said, "Out of darkness the light shall shine!"
4. 6 is the same **God** who made his light shine in our hearts,
4. 6 bring us the knowledge of **God's** glory shining in the face of
4. 7 to show that the supreme power belongs to **God,** not to us.
4.14 We know that **God,** who raised the Lord Jesus to life,
4.15 and as **God's** grace reaches more and more people, they will
4.15 offer to the glory of **God** more prayers of thanksgiving.
5. 1 on earth—is torn down, **God** will have a house in heaven
5. 5 **God** is the one who has prepared us for this change, and
5.11 **God** knows us completely, and I hope that in your hearts you
5.13 It is for **God's** sake.
5.18 All this is done by **God,** who through Christ changed us
5.19 Our message is that **God** was making all mankind his friends
5.19 **God** did not keep an account of their sins, and he has

2 Cor 5.20 speaking for Christ, as though **God** himself were making his appeal
5.20 let **God** change you from enemies into his friends!
5.21 but for our sake **God** made him share our sin
5.21 in union with him we might share the righteousness of **God.**
6. 1 In our work together with **God,** then, we beg you
6. 1 you who have received **God's** grace not to let it be
6. 2 Hear what **God** says:
6. 2 This is the hour to receive **God's** favour;
6. 4 we show that we are **God's** servants by patiently enduring troubles,
6. 6 have shown ourselves to be **God's** servants—by the Holy Spirit,
6.16 How can **God's** temple come to terms with pagan idols?
6.16 For we are the temple of the **living God!**
6.16 As **God** himself has said, "I will make my home with my
6.16 I will be their **God,** and they shall be my people."
7. 1 and let us be completely holy by living in awe of **God.**
7. 6 But **God,** who encourages the downhearted, encouraged us
7. 9 That sadness was used by **God,**
7.10 sadness that is used by **God** brings a change of heart
7.11 See what **God** did with this sadness of yours:
7.12 make plain to you, in **God's** sight, how deep your devotion to
8. 1 you to know what **God's** grace has accomplished in the churches
8. 5 and then, by **God's** will they gave themselves to us as well.
8.12 you are eager to give, **God** will accept your gift
8.16 How we thank **God** for making Titus as eager as we are
9. 7 for **God** loves the one who gives gladly.
9. 8 And **God** is able to give you more than you need,
9.10 And **God,** who supplies seed to sow and bread to eat, will
9.11 so that many will thank **God** for your gifts which they
9.12 but also produces an outpouring of gratitude to **God.**
9.13 many will give glory to **God** for your loyalty to the gospel
9.14 you because of the extraordinary grace **God** has shown you.
9.15 Let us thank **God** for his priceless gift!
10. 4 not the world's weapons but **God's** powerful weapons,
10. 5 every proud obstacle that is raised against the knowledge of **God;**
10.13 limits of the work which **God** has set for us, and this
10.15 work that others have done beyond the limits **God** set for us.
10.15 work among you, always within the limits that **God** has set.
11. 2 I am jealous for you, just as **God** is;
11. 7 a thing when I preached the Good News of **God** to you;
11.11 **God** knows I love you!
11.31 The **God** and Father of the Lord Jesus—blessed be his name
12. 2 happened or whether he had a vision—only **God** knows).
12. 3 it was a vision—only **God** knows), and there he heard things
12.19 speak in the presence of **God,** and everything we do, dear
12.21 next time I come my **God** will humiliate me in your presence,
13. 4 death on the cross, it is by **God's** power that he lives.
13. 4 relations with you we shall share **God's** power in his life.
13. 7 We pray to **God** that you will do no wrong—not in
13.11 And the **God** of love and peace will be with you.
13.13 Jesus Christ, the love of **God,** and the fellowship of the

Gal 1. 1 Jesus Christ and **God the Father,** who raised him from death.
1. 3 May **God** our Father and the Lord Jesus Christ give you
1. 4 our sins, in obedience to the will of our **God** and Father.
1. 5 To **God** be the glory for ever and ever!
1.10 What I want is **God's** approval!
1.13 without mercy the church of **God** and did my best to destroy
1.15 But **God** in his grace chose me even before I was born,
1.20 **God** knows that I am not lying!
1.24 And so they praised **God** because of me.
2. 2 I went because **God** revealed to me that I should go.
2. 6 **God** does not judge by outward appearances—
2. 7 the contrary, they saw that **God** had given me the task of
2. 8 For by **God's** power I was made an apostle to the Gentiles,
2. 9 recognized that **God** had given me this special task;
2.16 is put right with **God** only through faith in Jesus Christ,
2.16 to be put right with **God** through our faith in Christ, and
2.16 one is put right with **God** by doing what the Law requires.
2.17 to be put right with **God** by our union with Christ, we
2.19 by the Law itself—in order that I might live for **God.**
2.21 I refuse to reject the grace of **God.**
2.21 person is put right with **God** through the Law, it means that
3. 5 Does **God** give you the Spirit and work miracles among you
3. 6 the scripture says, "He believed **God,**
3. 6 and because of his faith **God** accepted him as righteous."
3. 8 The scripture predicted that **God** would put the Gentiles
3. 8 "Through you **God** will bless all mankind."
3.10 is written in the book of the Law is under **God's** curse!"
3.11 put right with **God** by means of the Law,
3.11 person who is put right with **God** through faith shall live."
3.13 "Anyone who is hanged on a tree is under **God's** curse."
3.14 that the blessing which **God** promised to Abraham might be given
3.14 through faith we might receive the Spirit promised by **God.**
3.16 Now, **God** made his promises to Abraham and to his descendant.
3.17 What I mean is that **God** made a covenant with Abraham and
3.17 cannot break that covenant and cancel **God's** promise.
3.18 For if **God's** gift depends on the Law, then it no longer
3.18 because of his promise that **God** gave that gift to Abraham.
3.20 and **God** is one.
3.21 Does this mean that the Law is against **God's** promises?
3.21 then everyone could be put right with **God** by obeying it.
3.24 that we might then be put right with **God** through faith.
3.26 that all of you are **God's** sons in union with Christ Jesus.
3.29 descendants of Abraham and will receive what **God** has promised.
4. 4 But when the right time finally came, **God** sent his own Son.
4. 5 who were under the Law, so that we might become **God's** sons.
4. 6 that you are his sons, **God** sent the Spirit of his Son
4. 7 since you are his son, **God** will give you all that he
4. 8 past you did not know **God,** and so you were slaves of
4. 9 But now that you know **God**—or, I should say,

Gal 4. 9 now that **God** knows you—how is it that
4.23 by the free woman was born as a result of **God's** promise.
5. 4 to be put right with **God** by obeying the Law have cut
5. 4 You are outside **God's** grace.
5. 5 us, our hope is that **God** will put us right with him;
5. 8 It was not done by **God,** who calls you.
5.10 is upsetting you, whoever he is, will be punished by **God.**
6. 7 no one makes a fool of **God.**

Eph 1. 1 From Paul, who by **God's** will is an apostle of Christ Jesus
1. 2 May **God** our Father and the Lord Jesus Christ give you
1. 3 us give thanks to the **God** and Father of our Lord Jesus
1. 4 before the world was made, **God** had already chosen us to be
1. 5 **God** had already decided that through Jesus Christ
1. 6 Let us praise **God** for his glorious grace, for the free
1. 7 great is the grace of **God,** [8] which he gave to us in
1. 9 all his wisdom and insight [9] **God** did what he had purposed,
1.10 This plan, which **God** will complete when the time is right,
1.11 All things are done according to **God's** plan and decision;
1.11 and **God** chose us to be his own people in union with
1.12 who were the first to hope in Christ, praise **God's** glory!
1.13 You believed in Christ, and **God** put his stamp of ownership
1.14 that we shall receive what **God** has promised his people,
1.14 this assures us that **God** will give complete freedom to those
1.16 I have not stopped giving thanks to **God** for you.
1.17 my prayers [17] and ask the **God** of our Lord Jesus Christ,
1.17 make you wise and reveal **God** to you, so that you will
1.22 **God** put all things under Christ's feet and gave him to
2. 2 the spirit who now controls the people who disobey **God.**
2. 3 like everyone else, were destined to suffer **God's** anger.
2. 4 But **God's** mercy is so abundant, and his love for us is
2. 5 It is by **God's** grace that you have been saved.
2. 8 For it is by **God's** grace that you have been saved
2. 8 of your own efforts, but **God's** gift, so that no one can
2.10 **God** has made us what we are, and in our union with
2.12 covenants, which were based on **God's** promises to his people,
2.12 you lived in this world without hope and without **God.**
2.16 both races into one body and brought them back to **God.**
2.17 who were far away from **God,** and to the Jews, who were
2.19 fellow-citizens with God's people and members of the family of **God.**
2.22 the others into a place where **God** lives through his Spirit.
3. 1 of Christ Jesus for the sake of you Gentiles, pray to **God.**
3. 2 Surely you have heard that **God** in his grace has given me
3. 3 **God** revealed his secret plan and made it known to me.
3. 5 not told this secret, but **God** has revealed it now by the
3. 6 the Gentiles have a part with the Jews in **God's** blessings;
3. 6 share in the promise that **God** made through Christ Jesus.
3. 7 servant of the gospel by **God's** special gift, which he gave
3. 8 yet **God** gave me this privilege of taking to the Gentiles the
3. 9 making all people see how **God's** secret plan is to be put
3. 9 **God,** who is the Creator of all things, kept his secret
3.11 **God** did this according to his eternal purpose, which he achieved
3.12 the boldness to go into **God's** presence with all confidence.
3.16 I ask **God** from the wealth of his glory to give you
3.19 so be completely filled with the very nature of **God.**
3.21 to **God** be the glory in the church and in Christ Jesus
4. 1 that measures up to the standard **God** set when he called you.
4. 4 just as there is one hope to which **God** has called you.
4. 6 there is one **God** and Father of all mankind, who is Lord
4.18 part in the life that **God** gives, for they are completely
4.24 self, which is created in **God's** likeness and reveals itself in
4.30 for the Spirit is **God's** mark of ownership on you, a
4.30 guarantee that the Day will come when **God** will set you free.
4.32 and forgive one another, as **God** has forgiven you through Christ.
5. 2 as a sweet-smelling offering and sacrifice that pleases **God.**
5. 4 Rather you should give thanks to **God.**
5. 5 ever receive a share in the Kingdom of Christ and of **God.**
5. 6 of these very things that **God's** anger will come upon those
5.20 Jesus Christ, always give thanks for everything to **God the Father.**
5.26 to dedicate the church to **God** by his word, after making it
6. 6 with all your heart do what **God** wants, as slaves of Christ.
6.11 on all the armour that **God** gives you, so that you will
6.13 So put on **God's** armour now!
6.18 Do all this in prayer, asking for **God's** help.
6.19 pray also for me, that **God** will give me a message when
6.23 May **God the Father** and the Lord Jesus Christ give to all
6.24 May **God's** grace be with all those who love our Lord

Phil 1. 2 May **God** our Father and the Lord Jesus Christ give you
1. 3 I thank my **God** for you every time I think of you;
1. 6 so I am sure that **God,** who began this good work in
1. 7 me in this privilege that **God** has given me, both now that
1. 8 **God** is my witness that I am telling the truth when I
1.11 Jesus Christ can produce, for the glory and praise of **God.**
1.16 love, because they know that **God** has given me the work of
1.28 you will win, because it is **God** who gives you the victory.
2. 6 always had the nature of **God,** but he did not think that
2. 6 think that by force he should try to become equal with **God.**
2. 9 For this reason **God** raised him to the highest place above
2.11 that Jesus Christ is Lord, to the glory of **God the Father.**
2.13 complete your salvation, [13] because **God** is always at work
2.17 an offering on the sacrifice that your faith offers to **God.**
2.27 But **God** had pity on him, and not only on him but
3. 3 true circumcision, for we worship **God** by means of his Spirit
3. 9 the righteousness that comes from **God** and is based on faith.
3.14 win the prize, which is **God's** call through Christ Jesus to
3.15 have a different attitude, **God** will make this clear to you.
4. 3 other fellow-workers, whose names are in **God's** book of the living.
4. 6 in all your prayers ask **God** for what you need, always asking
4. 7 And **God's** peace, which is far beyond human understanding,
4. 9 And the **God** who gives us peace will be with you.
4.18 a sweet-smelling offering to **God,** a sacrifice which is acceptable

Phil	4.19	through Christ Jesus, my **God** will supply all your needs.
	4.20	To our **God** and Father be the glory for ever and ever!
Col	1. 1	From Paul, who by **God's** will is an apostle of Christ Jesus,
	1. 2	May **God** our Father give you grace and peace.
	1. 3	We always give thanks to **God,** the Father of our Lord Jesus
	1. 6	heard about the grace of **God** and came to know it as
	1. 7	You learnt of **God's** grace from Epaphras, our dear fellow-servant,
	1. 9	We ask **God** to fill you with the knowledge of his will,
	1.10	of good deeds, and you will grow in your knowledge of **God.**
	1.11	have your share of what **God** has reserved for his people in
	1.15	Christ is the visible likeness of the invisible **God.**
	1.16	For through him **God** created everything in heaven and on earth,
	1.16	**God** created the whole universe through him and for him.
	1.19	For it was by **God's** own decision
	1.19	that the Son has in himself the full nature of **God.**
	1.20	Through the Son, then, **God** decided to bring the whole
	1.20	**God** made peace through his Son's sacrificial death on the cross
	1.21	you were far away from **God** and were his enemies
	1.22	physical death of his Son, **God** has made you his friends,
	1.25	servant of the church by **God,** who gave me this task
	1.27	**God's** plan is to make known his secret to his people,
	1.27	which means that you will share in the glory of **God.**
	1.28	to bring each one into **God's** presence as a mature individual
	2. 2	In this way they will know **God's** secret, which is Christ himself.
	2. 3	key that opens all the hidden treasures of **God's** wisdom
	2.13	But **God** has now brought you to life with Christ.
	2.13	**God** forgave us all our sins;
	2.19	joints and ligaments, and it grows as **God** wants it to grow.
	3. 1	Christ sits on his throne at the right-hand side of **God.**
	3. 3	you have died, and your life is hidden with Christ in **God.**
	3. 6	Because of such things **God's** anger will come upon those
	3.10	the new being which **God,** its Creator, is constantly renewing
	3.12	You are the people of **God;**
	3.15	to this peace that **God** has called you together
	3.16	sing to **God** with thanksgiving in your hearts.
	3.17	Lord Jesus, as you give thanks through him to **God the Father.**
	3.20	to obey your parents always, for that is what pleases **God.**
	3.25	because **God** judges everyone by the same standard.
	4. 2	and keep alert as you pray, giving thanks to **God.**
	4. 3	also for us, so that **God** will give us a good opportunity
	4.12	prays fervently for you, asking **God** to make you stand firm,
	4.12	fully convinced Christians, in complete obedience to **God's** will.
	4.18	May **God's** grace be with you.
1 Thes	1. 1	Thessalonica, who belong to **God the Father** and the Lord Jesus
	1. 2	We always thank **God** for you all and always mention you
	1. 3	For we remember before our **God** and Father how you put your
	1. 4	Our brothers, we know that **God** loves you and has chosen
	1. 8	but the news about your faith in **God** has gone everywhere.
	1. 9	turned away from idols to **God,** to serve the true and living
	1. 9	to serve the true and **living God** [10] and to wait for his
	1.10	death and who rescues us from **God's** anger that is coming.
	2. 2	there was much opposition, our **God** gave us courage to tell
	2. 4	Instead, we always speak as **God** wants us to,
	2. 4	try to please men, but to please **God,** who tests our motives.
	2. 5	did we use words to cover up greed—**God** is our witness!
	2. 8	not only the Good News from **God** but even our own lives.
	2. 9	as we preached to you the Good News from **God.**
	2.10	our witnesses, and so is **God,** that our conduct towards you
	2.12	kind of life that pleases **God,** who calls you to share in
	2.13	And there is another reason why we always give thanks to **God.**
	2.13	When we brought you **God's** message, you heard it and accepted it,
	2.13	as man's message but as **God's** message, which indeed it is.
	2.13	For **God** is at work in you who believe.
	2.14	happened to the churches of **God** in Judaea, to the people
	2.15	How displeasing they are to **God!**
	2.16	And now **God's** anger has at last come down on them!
	3. 2	who works with us for **God** in preaching the Good News
	3. 3	know that such persecutions are part of **God's** will for us.
	3. 9	Now we can give thanks to our **God** for you.
	3.11	May our **God** and Father himself and our Lord Jesus
	3.13	in the presence of our **God** and Father when our Lord Jesus
	4. 1	learnt from us how you should live in order to please **God.**
	4. 3	**God** wants you to be holy and completely free from sexual immorality.
	4. 5	with a lustful desire, like the heathen who do not know **God.**
	4. 7	**God** did not call us to live in immorality, but in holiness.
	4. 8	not rejecting man, but **God,** who gives you his Holy Spirit.
	4. 9	have been taught by **God** how you should love one another.
	4.14	and so we believe that **God** will take back with Jesus those
	4.16	archangel's voice, the sound of **God's** trumpet, and the Lord
	5. 9	**God** did not choose us to suffer his anger, but to possess
	5.18	This is what **God** wants from you in your life in union
	5.23	May the **God** who gives us peace make you holy in every
2 Thes	1. 1	in Thessalonica, who belong to **God** our Father and the Lord
	1. 2	May **God** our Father and the Lord Jesus Christ give you
	1. 3	Our brothers, we must thank **God** at all times for you.
	1. 4	is why we ourselves boast about you in the churches of **God.**
	1. 5	All of this proves that **God's** judgement is just and as a
	1. 6	**God** will do what is right:
	1. 8	to punish those who reject **God** and who do not obey the
	1.11	We ask our **God** to make you worthy of the life he
	1.12	by the grace of our **God** and of the Lord Jesus Christ.
	2. 4	in and sit down in **God's** Temple and claim to be God.
	2.11	And so **God** sends the power of error to work in them
	2.13	We must thank **God** at all times for you, brothers, you
	2.13	For **God** chose you as the first to be saved by the
	2.14	**God** called you to this through the Good News we preached
	2.16	Lord Jesus Christ himself and **God** our Father, who loved us
	3. 2	Pray also that **God** will rescue us from wicked and evil people;
	3. 5	a greater understanding of **God's** love and the endurance that is
1 Tim	1. 1	Christ Jesus by order of **God** our Saviour and Christ Jesus
	1. 2	May **God the Father** and Christ Jesus our Lord give you grace,
	1. 4	they do not serve **God's** plan, which is known by faith.
	1. 7	want to be teachers of **God's** law, but they do not understand
	1.11	to announce, the Good News from the glorious and blessed **God.**
	1.13	But **God** was merciful to me because I did not yet have
	1.16	the worst of them, [16] but **God** was merciful to me in order
	1.17	immortal and invisible, the only **God**—to him be honour and
	2. 1	requests, and thanksgivings be offered to **God** for all people;
	2. 2	with all reverence towards **God** and with proper conduct.
	2. 3	is good and it pleases **God** our Saviour, [4] who wants everyone
	2. 5	For there is one **God,**
	2. 5	there is one who brings **God** and mankind together, the man
	2. 6	at the right time that **God** wants everyone to be saved,
	2. 8	men who are dedicated to **God** and can lift up their hands
	2.14	it was the woman who was deceived and broke **God's** law.
	3. 5	own family, how can he take care of the church of **God?**
	3.15	should conduct ourselves in **God's** household, which is the church
	3.15	is the church of the **living God,** the pillar and support of
	4. 3	But **God** created those foods to be eaten, after a prayer of
	4. 4	Everything that **God** has created is good;
	4. 5	the word of God and the prayer make it acceptable to **God.**
	4.10	placed our hope in the **living God,** who is the Saviour of
	5. 4	repay their parents and grandparents, because that is what pleases **God.**
	5. 5	has placed her hope in **God** and continues to pray and ask
	5.21	In the presence of **God** and of Christ Jesus and of the
	6. 1	will speak evil of the name of **God** and of our teaching.
	6.11	But you, man of **God,** avoid all these things.
	6.12	was to this life that **God** called you when you firmly
	6.13	Before **God,** who gives life to all things, and before Christ
	6.15	at the right time by **God,** the blessed and only Ruler,
	6.17	thing as riches, but in **God,** who generously gives us everything
	6.21	**God's** grace be with you all.
2 Tim	1. 1	apostle of Christ Jesus by **God's** will, sent to proclaim
	1. 2	May **God the Father** and Christ Jesus our Lord give you grace,
	1. 3	I give thanks to **God,** whom I serve with a clear conscience,
	1. 6	keep alive the gift that **God** gave you when I laid my
	1. 7	For the Spirit that **God** has given us does not make us
	1. 8	for the Good News, as **God** gives you the strength to do
	1.11	**God** has appointed me as an apostle and teacher to proclaim
	2.14	a solemn warning in **God's** presence not to fight over words.
	2.15	to win full approval in **God's** sight, as a worker who is
	2.15	one who correctly teaches the message of **God's** truth.
	2.16	foolish discussions, which only drive people further away from **God.**
	2.19	But the solid foundation that **God** has laid cannot be shaken;
	2.25	for it may be that **God** will give them the opportunity to
	3. 4	they will love pleasure rather than **God;**
	3.16	All Scripture is inspired by **God** and is useful for
	3.17	that the person who serves **God** may be fully qualified and
	4. 1	In the presence of **God** and of Christ Jesus, who will judge
	4. 5	Good News, and perform your whole duty as a servant of **God.**
	4. 8	put right with **God,** which the Lord, the righteous Judge,
	4.16	May **God** not count it against them!
	4.22	**God's** grace be with you all.
Tit	1. 1	From Paul, a servant of **God** and an apostle of Jesus Christ.
	1. 2	**God,** who does not lie, promised us this life before the
	1. 3	and I proclaim it by order of **God** our Saviour.
	1. 4	May **God the Father** and Christ Jesus our Saviour give you
	1. 7	leader is in charge of **God's** work, he should be blameless.
	1.16	They claim that they know **God,** but their actions deny it.
	2. 5	no one will speak evil of the message that comes from **God.**
	2.10	to the teaching about **God** our Saviour in all they do.
	2.11	For **God** has revealed his grace for the salvation of all mankind.
	2.13	glory of our great **God** and Saviour Jesus Christ will appear.
	3. 4	the kindness and love of **God** our Saviour was revealed, [5] he
	3. 6	**God** poured out the Holy Spirit abundantly on us through Jesus
	3. 7	might be put right with **God** and come into possession of the
	3. 8	that those who believe in **God** may be concerned with giving
	3.15	**God's** grace be with you all.
Phlm	3	May **God** our Father and the Lord Jesus Christ give you
	4	time I pray, I mention you and give thanks to my **God.**
	22	because I hope that **God** will answer the prayers
Heb	1. 1	In the past, **God** spoke to our ancestors many times
	1. 2	is the one through whom **God** created the universe,
	1. 2	the one whom **God** has chosen to possess all things
	1. 3	He reflects the brightness of **God's** glory
	1. 3	is the exact likeness of **God's** own being, sustaining the universe
	1. 3	in heaven at the right-hand side of **God,** the Supreme Power.
	1. 4	just as the name that **God** gave him is greater than theirs.
	1. 5	For **God** never said to any of his angels, "You are my
	1. 5	Nor did **God** say about any angel, "I will be his Father,
	1. 6	But when **God** was about to send his first-born Son
	1. 6	Son into the world, he said, "All **God's** angels must worship him."
	1. 7	But about the angels **God** said, "God makes his angels winds,
	1. 8	About the Son, however, **God** said:
	1. 8	"Your kingdom, O **God,** will last for ever and ever!
	1. 9	That is why **God,** your God, has chosen you and has given
	1.13	**God** never said to any of his angels:
	1.14	They are spirits who serve **God** and are sent by him
	2. 4	At the same time **God** added his witness to theirs
	2. 5	**God** has not placed the angels as rulers over the new world
	2. 6	"What is man, O **God,** that you should think of him;
	2. 8	It says that **God** made man "ruler over all things";
	2. 9	so that through **God's** grace he should die for everyone.
	2.10	It was only right that **God,** who creates and preserves all things,
	2.12	He says to **God,** "I will tell my brothers what you have
	2.13	He also says, "I will put my trust in **God.**"
	2.13	"Here I am with the children that **God** has given me."
	2.17	Priest in his service to **God,** so that the people's sins
	3. 1	My Christian brothers, who also have been called by **God!**

Heb 3. 1 Think of Jesus, whom **God** sent to be the High Priest
3. 2 He was faithful to **God,** who chose him to do this work,
3. 2 just as Moses was faithful in his work in **God's** house.
3. 4 is built by someone—and **God** is the one who has built
3. 5 Moses was faithful in **God's** house as a servant,
3. 5 he spoke of the things that **God** would say in the future.
3. 6 But Christ is faithful as the Son in charge of **God's** house.
3. 7 Spirit says, "If you hear **God's** voice today, [8] do not be stubborn,
3. 8 were when they rebelled against **God,** as they were that day
3. 9 test and tried me, says **God,** although they had seen what I
3.12 and unbelieving that he will turn away from the **living God.**
3.15 "If you hear **God's** voice today, do not be stubborn,
3.15 as your ancestors were when they rebelled against **God."**
3.16 Who were the people who heard **God's** voice and rebelled against him?
3.17 With whom was **God** angry for forty years?
3.18 **God** made his solemn promise, "They will never enter the land
4. 1 Now, **God** has offered us the promise that we may receive
4. 3 We who believe, then, do receive that rest which **God** promised.
4. 4 **"God** rested on the seventh day from all his work."
4. 7 shown by the fact that **God** sets another day,
4. 7 "If you hear **God's** voice today, do not be stubborn."
4. 8 rest that God had promised, **God** would not have spoken later
4. 9 God's people a rest like **God's** resting on the seventh day.
4.10 whoever receives that rest which **God** promised
4.10 will rest from his own work, just as **God** rested from his.
4.13 There is nothing that can be hidden from **God;**
4.14 gone into the very presence of **God**—Jesus, the Son of God.
4.16 confidence, then, and approach **God's** throne, where there is grace.
5. 1 appointed to serve **God** on their behalf, to offer sacrifices
5. 4 It is only by **God's** call that a man is made a
5. 5 Instead, **God** said to him, "You are my Son;
5. 7 loud cries and tears to **God,** who could save him from death.
5. 7 Because he was humble and devoted, **God** heard him.
5.10 who obey him, [10] and **God** declared him to be high priest,
5.12 need someone to teach you the first lessons of **God's** message.
6. 1 foundation of turning away from useless works and believing in **God;**
6. 3 And this is what we will do, if **God** allows.
6. 4 They were once in **God's** light;
6. 5 they knew from experience that **God's** word is good, and
6. 7 **God** blesses the soil which drinks in the rain that often
6. 8 of being cursed by **God** and will be destroyed by fire.
6.10 **God** is not unfair.
6.12 and are patient, and so receive what **God** has promised.
6.13 When **God** made his promise to Abraham, he made a vow
6.15 Abraham was patient, and so he received what **God** had promised.
6.17 to receive what he promised, **God** wanted to make it very
6.18 then, that cannot change and about which **God** cannot lie.
7. 1 was king of Salem and a priest of the Most High **God.**
7. 6 Abraham and blessed him, the man who received **God's** promises.
7.19 hope has been provided through which we come near to **God.**
7.20 In addition, there is also **God's** vow.
7.21 means of a vow when **God** said to him, "The Lord has
7.25 save those who come to **God** through him,
7.25 because he lives for ever to plead with **God** for them.
7.28 but **God's** promise made with the vow, which came later than
8. 3 offerings and animal sacrifices to **God,** and so our High Priest
8. 5 to build the Covenant Tent, **God** said to him, "Be sure to
8. 6 covenant which he arranged between **God** and his people is a
8. 8 But **God** finds fault with his people when he says, "The
8.10 I will be their **God,** and they will be my people.
8.13 speaking of a new covenant, **God** has made the first one old;
9. 2 lampstand and the table with the bread offered to **God.**
9. 5 the winged creatures representing **God's** presence, with their wings
9. 7 blood which he offers to **God** on behalf of himself and for
9. 9 presented to **God** cannot make the worshipper's heart perfect,
9.10 only until the time when **God** will establish the new order.
9.14 he offered himself as a perfect sacrifice to **God.**
9.14 from useless rituals, so that we may serve the **living God.**
9.15 who have been called by **God**
9.15 may receive the eternal blessings that **God** has promised.
9.20 seals the covenant that **God** has commanded you to obey."
9.24 he now appears on our behalf in the presence of **God.**
9.27 Everyone must die once, and after that be judged by **God.**
10. 1 these sacrifices make perfect the people who come to **God?**
10. 2 If the people worshipping **God** had really been purified
10. 5 Christ was about to come into the world, he said to **God:**
10. 7 to do your will, O **God,** just as it is written
10. 9 Then he said, "Here I am, O **God,** to do your will."
10. 9 So **God** does away with all the old sacrifices
10.10 Because Jesus Christ did what **God** wanted him to do,
10.12 and then he sat down at the right-hand side of **God.**
10.13 There he now waits until **God** puts his enemies as a
10.22 let us come near to **God** with a sincere heart
10.23 because we can trust **God** to keep his promise.
10.27 the fierce fire which will destroy those who oppose **God!**
10.29 the blood of **God's** covenant which purified him from sin?
10.31 terrifying thing to fall into the hands of the **living God!**
10.32 In those days, after **God's** light had shone on you, you
10.36 order to do the will of **God** and receive what he promises.
11. 2 by their faith that people of ancient times won **God's** approval.
11. 3 the universe was created by **God's** word, so that what can be
11. 4 that made Abel offer to **God** a better sacrifice than Cain's.
11. 4 Through his faith he won **God's** approval as a righteous man,
11. 4 because **God** himself approved of his gifts.
11. 5 he was taken up to **God,**
11. 5 and nobody could find him, because **God** had taken him up.
11. 5 before Enoch was taken up, he had pleased **God.**

Heb 11. 6 No one can please **God** without faith,
11. 6 for whoever comes to **God** must have faith that God exists
11. 7 faith that made Noah hear **God's** warnings about things in the
11. 7 He obeyed **God** and built a boat
11. 7 and Noah received from **God** the righteousness that comes by faith.
11. 8 that made Abraham obey when **God** called him to go out
11. 8 to a country which **God** had promised to give him.
11. 9 as a foreigner in the country that **God** had promised him.
11. 9 Isaac and Jacob, who received the same promise from **God.**
11.10 waiting for the city which **God** has designed and built,
11.11 He trusted **God** to keep his promise.
11.13 did not receive the things **God** had promised,
11.16 And so **God** is not ashamed for them to call him
11.16 to call him their **God,** because he has prepared a city
11.17 son Isaac as a sacrifice when **God** put Abraham to the test.
11.17 was the one to whom **God** had made the promise,
11.18 **God** had said to him, "It is through Isaac that you will
11.19 Abraham reckoned that **God** was able to raise Isaac from death—
11.21 He leaned on the top of his walking-stick and worshipped **God.**
11.27 As though he saw the invisible **God,** he refused to turn back.
11.31 with those who disobeyed **God,** for she gave the Israelite spies
11.33 They did what was right and received what **God** had promised.
11.39 they did not receive what **God** had promised,
12. 2 he is now seated at the right-hand side of **God's** throne.
12. 5 the encouraging words which **God** speaks to you as his sons?
12. 7 your suffering shows that **God** is treating you as his sons.
12.10 but **God** does it for our own good, so that we may
12.15 Guard against turning back from the grace of **God.**
12.22 to the city of the **living God,** the heavenly Jerusalem,
12.23 to the joyful gathering of **God's** first-born sons, whose
12.23 You have come to **God,** who is the judge of all mankind,
12.28 be grateful and worship **God** in a way that will please
12.29 because our **God** is indeed a destroying fire.
13. 4 **God** will judge those who are immoral and those who commit adultery.
13. 5 For **God** has said, "I will never leave you;
13. 7 Remember your former leaders, who spoke **God's** message to you.
13. 9 receive inner strength from **God's** grace, and not by obeying rules
13.15 always offer praise to **God** as our sacrifice through Jesus,
13.16 because these are the sacrifices that please **God.**
13.17 since they must give **God** an account of their service.
13.19 more earnestly to pray that **God** will send me back to you
13.20 **God** has raised from death our Lord Jesus, who is
13.20 May the **God** of peace provide you with every good thing
13.25 May **God's** grace be with you all.

Jas 1. 1 From James, a servant of **God** and of the Lord Jesus Christ:
1. 5 wisdom, he should pray to **God,** who will give it to him;
1. 5 because **God** gives generously and graciously to all.
1. 9 poor must be glad when **God** lifts him up,
1.10 and the rich Christian must be glad when **God** brings him down.
1.12 his reward the life which **God** has promised to those who love
1.13 he must not say, "This temptation comes from **God."**
1.13 For **God** cannot be tempted by evil, and he himself tempts no
1.17 it comes down from **God,** the Creator of the heavenly lights,
1.20 Man's anger does not achieve **God's** righteous purpose.
1.21 Submit to **God** and accept the word that he plants
1.25 that person will be blessed by **God** in what he does.
1.27 What **God the Father** considers to be pure and genuine
2. 5 **God** chose the poor people of this world to be rich
2.13 For **God** will not show mercy when he judges the person
2.16 What good is there in your saying to them, **"God** bless you!
2.19 Do you believe that there is only one **God?**
2.21 How was our ancestor Abraham put right with **God?**
2.23 that said, "Abraham believed **God,**
2.23 and because of his faith **God** accepted him as righteous."
2.23 And so Abraham was called **God's** friend.
2.24 person is put right with **God,** and not by his faith alone.
2.25 She was put right with **God** through her actions, by welcoming
3. 9 curse our fellow-man, who is created in the likeness of **God.**
4. 2 have what you want because you do not ask **God** for it.
4. 4 know that to be the world's friend means to be **God's** enemy?
4. 4 Whoever wants to be the world's friend makes himself **God's** enemy.
4. 5 that says, "The spirit that **God** placed in us is filled with
4. 6 But the grace that **God** gives is even stronger.
4. 6 As the scripture says, **"God** resists the proud, but gives grace
4. 7 So then, submit to **God.**
4. 8 Come near to **God,** and he will come near to you.
4.12 **God** is the only lawgiver and judge.
5. 4 your crops have reached the ears of **God,** the Lord Almighty.
5. 9 one another, my brothers, so that **God** will not judge you.
5.12 mean no, and then you will not come under **God's** judgement.

1 Pet 1. 2 to the purpose of **God the Father** and were made a holy
1. 3 us give thanks to the **God** and Father of our Lord Jesus
1. 4 possessing the rich blessings that **God** keeps for his people.
1. 5 faith are kept safe by **God's** power for the salvation which
1.10 and they prophesied about this gift which **God** would give you.
1.12 **God** revealed to these prophets that their work was not
1.14 Be obedient to **God,** and do not allow your lives to be
1.15 all that you do, just as **God** who called you is holy.
1.17 Father, when you pray to **God,** who judges all people by the
1.20 He had been chosen by **God** before the creation of the
1.21 Through him you believe in **God,** who raised him from death
1.21 and so your faith and hope are fixed on **God.**
2. 4 rejected by man as worthless but chosen by **God** as valuable.
2. 5 spiritual and acceptable sacrifices to **God** through Jesus Christ.
2. 8 such was **God's** will for them.
2. 9 proclaim the wonderful acts of **God,** who called you out of
2.10 time you did not know **God's** mercy, but now you have received
2.12 good deeds and so praise **God** on the Day of his coming.

1 Pet 2.15 For **God** wants you to silence the ignorant talk of
2.16 your freedom to cover up any evil, but live as **God's** slaves.
2.17 love your fellow-believers, honour **God,** and respect the Emperor.
2.19 **God** will bless you for this, if you endure the pain
2.20 even when you have done right, **God** will bless you for it.
2.21 It was to this that **God** called you, for Christ himself
2.23 not threaten, but placed his hopes in **God,** the righteous Judge.
3. 1 of them do not believe **God's** word, your conduct will win
3. 4 quiet spirit, which is of the greatest value in **God's** sight.
3. 5 who placed their hope in **God** used to make themselves beautiful
3. 7 they also will receive, together with you, **God's** gift of life.
3. 9 because a blessing is what **God** promised to give you
3.17 good, if this should be **God's** will, than for doing evil.
3.18 on behalf of sinners, in order to lead you to **God.**
3.20 those who had not obeyed **God** when he waited patiently
3.21 but the promise made to **God** from a good conscience.
3.22 at the right-hand side of **God,** ruling over all angels
4. 2 earthly lives controlled by **God's** will and not by human desires.
4. 5 an account of themselves to **God,** who is ready to judge
4. 6 in their spiritual existence they may live as **God** lives.
4.10 as a good manager of **God's** different gifts, must use for the
4.10 good of others the special gift he has received from **God.**
4.11 Whoever preaches must preach **God's** messages;
4.11 serve with the strength that **God** gives him,
4.11 praise may be given to **God** through Jesus Christ,
4.14 the glorious Spirit, the Spirit of **God,** is resting on you.
4.16 ashamed of it, but thank **God** that you bear Christ's name.
4.17 end with those who do not believe the Good News from **God?**
4.19 who suffer because it is **God's** will for them, should by
5. 2 shepherds of the flock that **God** gave you and to take care
5. 2 of it willingly, as **God** wants you to, and not unwillingly.
5. 5 for the scripture says, "**God** resists the proud, but shows favour
5. 6 Humble yourselves, then, under **God's** mighty hand,
5.10 for a little while, the **God** of all grace, who calls you
5.12 and give my testimony that this is the true grace of **God.**
5.13 in Babylon, also chosen by **God,** sends you greetings,
2 Pet 1. 1 through the righteousness of our **God** and Saviour Jesus Christ
1. 2 through your knowledge of **God** and of Jesus our Lord.
1. 3 **God's** divine power has given us everything we need to live
1.10 try even harder to make **God's** call and his choice of you
1.17 honour and glory by **God the Father,** when the voice came to
1.21 Holy Spirit as they spoke the message that came from **God.**
2. 4 **God** did not spare the angels who sinned,
2. 5 **God** did not spare the ancient world, but brought the flood
2. 6 **God** condemned the cities of Sodom and Gomorrah,
2.10 who follow their filthy bodily lusts and despise **God's** authority.
2.14 They are under **God's** curse!
2.17 **God** has reserved a place for them in the deepest darkness.
3. 5 the fact that long ago **God** gave a command,
3. 7 by the same command of **God,** in order to be destroyed
3.11 be holy and dedicated to **God,** [12]as you wait for the Day
3.12 wait for the Day of **God** and do your best to make
3.13 But we wait for what **God** has promised:
3.14 be pure and faultless in **God's** sight and to be at peace
3.15 Paul wrote to you, using the wisdom that **God** gave him.
1 Jn 1. 5 **God** is light, and there is no darkness at all in him.
1. 9 we confess our sins to **God,** he will keep his promise
1.10 have not sinned, we make **God** out to be a liar,
2. 3 If we obey **God's** commands, then we are sure that we know
2. 5 is the one whose love for **God** has really been made perfect.
2. 5 how we can be sure that we are in union with **God:**
2. 6 he remains in union with **God** should live just as Jesus
2.17 but he who does the will of **God** lives for ever.
3. 1 it has not known **God.**
3. 4 sins is guilty of breaking **God's** law, because sin is a
3. 9 Whoever is a child of **God** does not continue to sin,
3. 9 for **God's** very nature is in him;
3. 9 and because **God** is his Father, he cannot continue to sin.
3.17 against his brother, how can he claim that he loves **God?**
3.19 this is how we will be confident in **God's** presence.
3.20 we know that **God** is greater than our conscience
3.21 conscience does not condemn us, we have courage in **God's** presence.
3.24 Whoever obeys **God's** commands lives in union with God
3.24 and **God** lives in union with him.
3.24 because of the Spirit that **God** has given us
3.24 we know that **God** lives in union with us.
4. 1 to find out if the spirit they have comes from **God.**
4. 2 came as a human being has the Spirit who comes from **God.**
4. 3 denies this about Jesus does not have the Spirit from **God.**
4. 4 But you belong to **God,** my children, and have defeated the
4. 6 But we belong to **God.**
4. 6 Whoever knows **God** listens to us;
4. 6 whoever does not belong to **God** does not listen to us.
4. 7 let us love one another, because love comes from **God.**
4. 7 Whoever loves is a child of **God** and knows God.
4. 8 Whoever does not love does not know **God,** for God is love.
4. 9 And **God** showed his love for us by sending his only Son
4.10 not that we have loved **God,** but that he loved us
4.11 friends, if this is how **God** loved us, then we should love
4.12 No one has ever seen **God,**
4.12 if we love one another, **God** lives in union with us,
4.13 we live in union with **God** and that he lives in union
4.15 lives in union with God and **God** lives in union with him.
4.16 ourselves know and believe the love which **God** has for us.
4.16 **God** is love, and whoever lives in love
4.16 lives in union with God and **God** lives in union with him.
4.19 We love because **God** first loved us.
4.20 If someone says he loves **God,** but hates his brother,
4.20 For he cannot love **God,** whom he has not seen,
4.21 whoever loves **God** must love his brother also.

1 Jn 5. 2 it is by loving **God** and obeying his commands.
5. 3 For our love for **God** means that we obey his commands.
5. 9 but **God's** testimony is much stronger, and he has given
5.10 but whoever does not believe **God,** has made him out to be
5.10 because he has not believed what **God** has said about his Son.
5.11 **God** has given us eternal life, and this life has its source
5.14 We have courage in **God's** presence, because we are sure
5.16 to death, you should pray to **God,** who will give him life.
5.16 I do not say that you should pray to **God** about that.
5.19 know that we belong to **God** even though the whole world is
5.20 given us understanding, so that we know the true **God.**
5.20 in union with the true **God**—in union with his Son Jesus
5.20 This is the true **God,** and this is eternal life.
2 Jn 3 May **God the Father** and Jesus Christ, the Father's Son,
6 means that we must live in obedience to **God's** commands.
9 but goes beyond it, does not have **God.**
3 Jn 6 continue their journey in a way that will please **God.**
11 Whoever does good belongs to **God;**
11 whoever does what is bad has not seen **God.**
Jude 1 who have been called by **God,**
1 in the love of **God the Father** and the protection of Jesus
3 faith which once and for all **God** has given to his people.
4 about the grace of our **God** in order to excuse their immoral
6 in the darkness below, where **God** is keeping them for that
8 **God's** authority and insult the glorious beings above.
13 like wandering stars, for whom **God** has reserved a place for
21 yourselves in the love of **God,** as you wait for our Lord
25 to the only **God** our Saviour, through Jesus Christ
Rev 1. 1 **God** gave him this revelation in order to show his servants
1. 2 concerning the message from **God** and the truth revealed by Jesus
1. 4 and peace be yours from **God,** who is, who was,
1. 6 made us a kingdom of priests to serve his **God** and Father.
1. 8 the last," says the Lord **God Almighty,** who is, who was,
1. 9 Patmos because I had proclaimed **God's** word and the truth
2. 7 of the tree of life that grows in the Garden of **God.**
2.20 that woman Jezebel, who calls herself a messenger of **God.**
3. 1 one who has the seven spirits of **God** and the seven stars.
3. 2 have done is not yet perfect in the sight of my **God.**
3.12 in the temple of my **God,** and he will never leave it.
3.12 him the name of my **God** and the name of the city
3.12 of the city of my **God,** the new Jerusalem,
3.12 which will come down out of heaven from my **God.**
3.14 true witness, who is the origin of all that **God** has created.
4. 5 lighted torches were burning, which are the seven spirits of **God.**
4. 8 holy, holy, is the Lord **God Almighty,** who was, who is,
4.11 in front of the throne and say, [11]"Our Lord and **God!**
5. 6 are the seven spirits of **God** that have been sent throughout
5. 9 you bought for **God** people from every tribe, language, nation,
5.10 of priests to serve our **God,** and they shall rule on earth."
6. 9 because they had proclaimed **God's** word and had been faithful
7. 2 coming up from the east with the seal of the **living God.**
7. 2 the four angels to whom **God** had given the power to damage
7. 3 the servants of our **God** with a seal on their foreheads."
7. 4 who were marked with **God's** seal on their foreheads was 144,000.
7.10 "Salvation comes from our **God,** who sits on the throne,
7.11 in front of the throne and worshipped **God,** [12]saying, "Amen!
7.12 power, and might belong to our **God** for ever and ever!
7.15 is why they stand before **God's** throne and serve him day and
7.17 And **God** will wipe away every tear from their eyes."
8. 2 angels who stand before **God,** and they were given seven trumpets.
8. 4 from the hands of the angel standing before **God.**
9. 4 who did not have the mark of **God's** seal on their foreheads.
9.13 from the four corners of the gold altar standing before **God.**
10. 6 vow in the name of **God,** who lives for ever and ever,
10. 7 angel blows his trumpet, then **God** will accomplish his secret plan,
10.11 "Once again you must proclaim **God's** message about many nations,
11. 1 and measure the temple of **God** and the altar,
11. 3 and they will proclaim **God's** message during those 1,260 days."
11. 6 will be no rain during the time they proclaim **God's** message.
11.11 a life-giving breath came from **God** and entered them,
11.13 were terrified and praised the greatness of the **God** of heaven.
11.16 their thrones in front of **God**
11.16 threw themselves face downwards and worshipped **God,** [17]saying:
11.17 "Lord **God Almighty,** the one who is and who was!
11.19 **God's** temple in heaven was opened, and the Covenant Box
12. 5 the child was snatched away and taken to **God** and his throne.
12. 6 the desert, to a place **God** had prepared for her, where she
12.10 a loud voice in heaven saying, "Now **God's** salvation has come!
12.10 Now **God** has shown his power as King!
12.10 one who stood before our **God** and accused our brothers day
12.17 all those who obey **God's** commandments and are faithful
13. 1 there was a name that was insulting to **God.**
13. 5 claims which were insulting to **God,** and it was permitted to
13. 6 It began to curse **God,** his name, the place where he lives,
14. 4 the first ones to be offered to **God** and to the Lamb.
14. 7 He said in a loud voice, "Honour **God** and praise his greatness!
14.10 will himself drink **God's** wine, the wine of his fury,
14.12 those who obey **God's** commandments and are faithful to Jesus.
14.19 and threw them into the winepress of **God's** furious anger.
15. 1 last ones, because they are the final expression of **God's** anger.
15. 2 holding harps that **God** had given them [3]and singing
15. 3 of Moses, the servant of **God,** and the song of the Lamb:
15. 3 "Lord **God Almighty,** how great and wonderful are your deeds!
15. 5 in heaven open, with the Tent of **God's** presence in it.
15. 7 full of the anger of **God,** who lives for ever and ever.
16. 1 and pour out the seven bowls of **God's** anger on the earth!"
16. 7 Then I heard a voice from the altar saying, "Lord **God Almighty!**
16. 9 the name of **God,** who has authority over these plagues.
16.11 and they cursed the **God** of heaven for their pains
16.14 together for the battle on the great Day of Almighty **God.**

Rev 16.19 **God** remembered great Babylon and made her drink the wine
16.21 people, who cursed **God** on account of the plague
17. 3 beast that had names insulting to **God** written all over it;
17.17 For **God** has placed in their hearts the will to carry out
17.17 the beast their power to rule until **God's** words come true.
18. 5 up as high as heaven, and **God** remembers her wicked ways.
18. 8 burnt with fire, because the Lord **God,** who judges her, is
18.20 For **God** has condemned her for what she did to you!
19. 1 a large crowd of people in heaven, saying, "Praise **God!**
19. 1 Salvation, glory, and power belong to our **God!**
19. 2 **God** has punished her because she killed his servants."
19. 3 Again they shouted, "Praise **God!**
19. 4 fell down and worshipped **God,** who was seated on the throne.
19. 4 Praise **God!"**
19. 5 saying, "Praise our **God,** all his servants and all people,
19. 6 I heard them say, "Praise **God!**
19. 6 For the Lord, our Almighty **God,** is King!
19.10 Worship **God!"**
19.15 in the winepress of the furious anger of the Almighty **God.**
19.17 "Come and gather together for **God's** great feast!
20. 6 they shall be priests of **God** and of Christ,
21. 2 down out of heaven from **God,** prepared and ready, like a
21. 3 "Now **God's** home is with mankind!
21. 3 **God** himself will be with them, and he will be their God.
21. 7 I will be his **God,** and he will be my son.
21.11 of heaven from God [11] and shining with the glory of **God.**
21.22 because its temple is the Lord **God Almighty** and the Lamb.
21.23 because the glory of **God** shines on it, and the Lamb
22. 1 coming from the throne of **God** and of the Lamb [2] and flowing
22. 3 Nothing that is under **God's** curse will be found in the city.
22. 3 The throne of **God** and of the Lamb will be in the
22. 5 or sunlight, because the Lord **God** will be their light,
22. 6 And the Lord **God,** who gives his Spirit to the prophets,
22. 9 Worship **God!"**
22.18 anyone adds anything to them, **God** will add to his punishment
22.19 prophetic words of this book, **God** will take away from him

GOD (2) (OTHER GODS)

[FALSE GODS]
see also **GODDESS**

Gen 31.19 Rachel stole the household **gods** that belonged to her father.
31.30 get back home, but why did you steal my household **gods?"**
31.32 that anyone here has your **gods,** he will be put to death.
31.32 Jacob did not know that Rachel had stolen Laban's **gods.**
31.33 tent of the two slave-women, but he did not find his **gods.**
31.34 Rachel had taken the household **gods** and put them in a
31.35 Laban searched but did not find his household **gods.**
35. 2 were with him, "Get rid of the foreign **gods** that you have;
35. 4 gave Jacob all the foreign **gods** that they had and also the
Ex 8.10 know that there is no other **god** like the Lord, our God.
12.12 both human and animal, and punishing all the **gods** of Egypt.
15.11 "Lord, who among the **gods** is like you?
18.11 is greater than all the **gods,** because he did this when the
20. 3 "Worship no **god** but me.
20.23 Do not make for yourselves **gods** of silver or gold to be
22.20 anyone who offers sacrifices to any **god** except to me,
23.13 Do not pray to other **gods;**
23.24 not bow down to their **gods** or worship them,
23.24 Destroy their **gods** and break down their sacred stone pillars.
23.32 Do not make any agreement with them or with their **gods.**
23.33 If you worship their **gods,** it will be a fatal trap for
32. 1 so make us a **god** to lead us."
32. 4 said, "Israel, this is our **god,** who led us out of Egypt!"
32. 8 saying that this is their **god,** who led them out of Egypt.
32.23 so make us a **god** to lead us.'
32.31 They have made a **god** out of gold and worshipped it.
34.14 "Do not worship any other **god,** because I, the Lord,
34.15 when they worship their pagan **gods** and sacrifice to them,
34.15 will be tempted to eat the food they offer to their **gods.**
34.16 to be unfaithful to me and to worship their pagan **gods.**
34.17 "Do not make and worship **gods** of metal.
Lev 18.21 in the worship of the **god Molech,** because that would bring
19. 4 do not make **gods** of metal and worship them.
19.29 you will turn to other **gods** and the land will be full
20. 2 in the worship of the **god Molech** shall be stoned to death
Num 14. 9 Lord is with us and has defeated the **gods** who protected them;
21.29 Your **god** let the men become refugees,
25. 2 to sacrificial feasts, where the **god of Moab** was worshipped.
25. 2 The Israelites ate the food and worshipped the **god** [3] **Baal** of Peor.
25.11 tolerate the worship of any **god** but me, and that is why
33. 4 Lord showed that he was more powerful than the **gods** of Egypt.
Deut 3.24 There is no **god** in heaven or on earth who can do
4. 7 matter how great, has a **god** who is so near
4.28 There you will serve **gods** made by human hands,
4.28 gods of wood and stone, **gods** that cannot see or hear,
4.33 ever lived after hearing a **god** speak to them from a fire,
4.34 Has any **god** ever dared to go and take a people from
4.39 There is no other **god.**
5. 7 " 'Worship no **god** but me.
6.14 Do not worship other **gods,**
6.14 any of the **gods** of the peoples around you.
6.15 If you do worship other **gods,** the Lord's anger will come
7. 4 lead your children away from the Lord to worship other **gods.**
7.16 Do not worship their **gods,** for that would be fatal.
8.19 your God or turn to other **gods** to worship and serve them.
10.17 Lord your God is supreme over all **gods** and over all powers.
11.16 be led away from the Lord to worship and serve other **gods.**
11.28 to worship other **gods** that you have never worshipped before.
12. 2 where the people worship their **gods** on high mountains, on
12. 4 Lord your God in the way that these people worship their **gods.**
12.30 out how they worship their **gods,** so that you can worship in

Deut 12.31 the way they worship their **gods,**
12.31 in the worship of their **gods** they do all the disgusting
13. 2 worship and serve **gods** that you have not worshipped before.
13. 6 encourage you to worship other **gods,** gods that you and your
13. 7 encourage you to worship the **gods** of the people
13. 7 live near you or the **gods** of those who live far away.
13.13 town to worship **gods** that you have never worshipped before.
17. 3 by worshipping and serving other **gods** or the sun or the
18.20 so must any prophet who speaks in the name of other **gods.'**
20.18 things that they do in the worship of their **gods.**
28.14 disobey them in any way, or worship and serve other **gods.**
28.36 there you will serve **gods** made of wood and stone.
28.64 and there you will serve **gods** made of wood and stone,
28.64 **gods** that neither you nor your ancestors
29.18 from the Lord our God to worship the **gods** of other nations.
29.26 They served other **gods** that they had never worshipped before,
29.26 **gods** that the Lord had forbidden them
30.17 led away to worship other **gods,** [18] you will be destroyed—I
31.16 me and worship the pagan **gods** of the land they are about
31.18 because they have done evil and worshipped other **gods.**
31.20 But they will turn away and worship other **gods.**
32. 8 assigned to each nation a **god,**
32.12 Lord alone led his people without the help of a foreign **god.**
32.17 They sacrificed to **gods** that are not real,
32.17 new **gods** their ancestors had never known,
32.17 **gods** that Israel had never obeyed,
32.21 with their so-called **gods,** gods that are really not gods.
32.31 enemies know that their own **gods** are weak, not mighty like
32.37 Lord will ask his people, 'Where are those mighty **gods** you
32.39 no other **god** is real.
33.26 People of Israel, no **god** is like your God,
Josh 23. 7 speak the names of their **gods** or use those names
23. 7 in taking vows or worship those **gods** or bow down to them.
23.16 you serve and worship other **gods,** then in his anger he will
24. 2 other side of the River Euphrates and worshipped other **gods.**
24.14 Get rid of the **gods** which your ancestors used to worship
24.15 the **gods** your ancestors worshipped in Mesopotamia
24.15 or the **gods** of the Amorites, in whose land
24.16 "We would never leave the Lord to serve other **gods!**
24.20 leave him to serve foreign **gods,** he will turn against you
24.23 get rid of those foreign **gods** that you have," he demanded,
Judg 2. 3 and you will be trapped by the worship of their **gods."**
2.12 to worship other gods, the **gods** of the peoples round them.
2.17 Israel was unfaithful to the Lord and worshipped other **gods.**
2.19 would serve and worship other **gods,** and refused to give up
3. 6 They intermarried with them and worshipped their **gods.**
5. 8 was war in the land when the Israelites chose new **gods.**
6.10 you should not worship the **gods** of the Amorites, whose land
6.31 If Baal is a **god,** let him defend himself.
8.33 They made Baal-of-the-Covenant their **god,**
9. 9 producing my oil, which is used to honour **gods** and men.'
9.13 to stop producing my wine, that makes **gods** and men happy.'
9.27 into the temple of their **god,** where they ate and drank
10. 6 Astartes, as well as the **gods** of Syria, of Sidon, of Moab,
10.13 left me and worshipped other **gods,** so I am not going to
10.14 Go and cry out to the **gods** you have chosen.
10.16 So they got rid of their foreign **gods** and worshipped the Lord;
11.24 You can keep whatever your **god Chemosh** has given you.
16.23 to celebrate and offer a great sacrifice to their **god Dagon.**
16.23 They sang, "Our **god** has given us victory over our enemy Samson!"
16.24 When the people saw him, they sang praise to their **god:**
16.24 "Our **god** has given us victory over our enemy, who
18.24 take my priest and the **gods** that I made, and walk off!
Ruth 1.15 sister-in-law has gone back to her people and to her **god.**
1 Sam 4. 7 they were afraid, and said, "A **god** has come into their camp!
4. 8 Who can save us from those powerful **gods?**
4. 8 They are the **gods** who slaughtered the Egyptians in the desert!
5. 2 into the temple of their **god Dagon,** and set it up beside
5. 7 said, "The God of Israel is punishing us and our **god Dagon.**
5.12 tumours and the people cried out to their **gods** for help.
6. 5 Perhaps he will stop punishing you, your **gods,** and your
7. 3 rid of all the foreign **gods** and the images of the goddess
8. 8 they have turned away from me and worshipped other **gods;**
12.21 Don't go after **false gods;**
17.43 And he called down curses from his **god** on David.
26.19 Lord's land to a country where I can only worship foreign **gods.**
2 Sam 7.23 out other nations and their **gods** as your people advanced,
12.30 the idol of the Ammonite **god Molech** David took a gold crown
1 Kgs 8.23 there is no **god** like you in heaven above or
9. 6 given you, and worship other **gods,** [7] then I will remove my
9. 9 They gave their allegiance to other **gods** and worshipped them.
11. 2 cause the Israelites to give their loyalty to other **gods.**
11. 4 was old they had led him into the worship of foreign **gods.**
11. 5 Astarte the goddess of Sidon, and Molech the disgusting **god of Ammon.**
11. 7 worship Chemosh, the disgusting **god of Moab,** and a place to
11. 7 and a place to worship Molech, the disgusting **god of Ammon.**
11. 8 could burn incense and offer sacrifices to their own **gods.**
11. 9 not to worship foreign **gods,** Solomon did not obey the Lord,
11.33 Solomon has rejected me and has worshipped foreign **gods:**
11.33 Chemosh, the **god of Moab;**
11.33 and Molech, the **god of Ammon.**
12.28 Israel, here are your **gods** who brought you out of Egypt!"
14.23 built places of worship for **false gods,** and put up stone
18.24 of Baal pray to their **god,** and I will pray to the
18.25 Pray to your **god,** but don't set fire to the wood."
18.27 He is a **god!**
19. 2 "May the **gods** strike me dead if by this time tomorrow I
20.10 May the **gods** strike me dead if I don't!"
20.23 said to him, "The **gods** of Israel are mountain gods,
20.28 say that I am a **god** of the hills and not of

2 Kgs 1. 2 consult Baalzebub, the **god** of the Philistine city of Ekron,
1. 3 "Why are you going to consult Baalzebub, the **god of Ekron?**
1. 3 Is it because you think there is no **god** in Israel?
1. 6 'Why are you sending messengers to consult Baalzebub, the **god of Ekron?**
1. 6 Is it because you think there is no **god** in Israel?
1.16 to consult Baalzebub, the **god of Ekron**—as if there were no
1.16 as if there were no **god** in Israel to consult—
3.27 on the city wall as a sacrifice to the **god of Moab.**
5.15 I know that there is no **god** but the God of Israel;
5.17 sacrifices or burnt-offerings to any **god** except the Lord.
5.18 to the temple of Rimmon, the **god of Syria,** and worship him.
10.18 said, "King Ahab served the **god Baal** a little, but I will
17. 7 They worshipped other **gods,** [8] followed the customs of the
17.16 goddess Asherah, worshipped the stars, and served the **god Baal.**
17.17 sacrificed their sons and daughters as burnt-offerings to pagan **gods;**
17.26 know the law of the **god** of that land,
17.26 and so the **god** had sent lions, which were killing
17.27 to teach the people the law of the **god** of that land."
17.30 The people of Babylon made idols of the **god** Succoth Benoth;
17.31 sacrificed their children as burnt-offerings to their **gods**
17.33 they also worshipped their own **gods** according to the customs
17.35 "Do not worship other **gods;**
17.37 You shall not obey other **gods,** [38] and you shall not forget
18.33 Did the **gods** of any other nations save their countries
18.34 Where are they now, the **gods** of Hamath and Arpad?
18.34 Where are the **gods** of Sepharvaim, Hena, and Ivvah?
18.35 When did any of the **gods** of all these countries ever
19.12 lived in Telassar, and none of their **gods** could save them.
19.18 their gods—which were no **gods** at all, only images of wood
19.37 in the temple of his **god Nisroch,** two of his sons,
22.17 have offered sacrifices to other **gods,** and so have stirred
23.10 his son or daughter as a burnt-offering to the **god Molech.**
23.13 Chemosh the **god of Moab,**
23.13 and Molech the **god of Ammon.**
23.24 fortune-tellers, and all the household **gods,** idols, and all
1 Chr 5.25 deserted him to worship the **gods** of the nations whom God had
10.10 temples and hung his head in the temple of their **god Dagon.**
16.25 he is to be honoured more than all the **gods.**
16.26 The **gods** of all other nations are only idols, but the
2 Chr 2. 5 great temple, because our God is greater than any other **god.**
6.14 in all heaven and earth there is no **god** like you.
7.19 given you, and worship other **gods,** [20] then I will remove
7.22 They gave their allegiance to other **gods** and worshipped them.
13. 8 you the gold bull-calves that Jeroboam made to be your **gods.**
13. 9 consecrated as a priest of those so-called **gods** of yours.
25.15 "Why have you worshipped foreign **gods** that could not even
28.25 of worship, where incense was to be burnt to foreign **gods.**
32.13 Did the **gods** of any other nation save their people from the
32.14 When did any of the **gods** of all those countries ever
32.15 No **god** of any nation has ever been able to save his
32.17 It said, "The **gods** of the nations have not saved their
32.19 that they talked about the **gods** of the other peoples, idols
32.21 in the temple of his **god,** some of his sons killed him
33.15 from the Temple the foreign **gods** and the image that he had
34.25 have offered sacrifices to other **gods,** and so have stirred
Ezra 1. 7 Temple in Jerusalem and had put in the temple of his **gods.**
Neh 9.18 bull-calf and said it was the **god** who led them from Egypt!
Job 12. 6 live in peace, though their only **god** is their own strength.
Ps 10.16 Those who worship other **gods** will vanish from his land.
16. 4 Those who rush to other **gods** bring many troubles on themselves.
16. 4 I will not worship their **gods.**
31. 6 You hate those who worship **false gods,** but I trust in you.
40. 4 do not turn to idols or join those who worship **false gods.**
44.20 prayed to a foreign **god,** [21] you would surely have discovered it,
77.13 No **god** is as great as you.
81. 9 You must never worship another **god.**
82. 1 in the assembly of the **gods** he gives his decision:
82. 6 'You are **gods,'** I said;
84. 7 they will see the God of **gods** on Zion.
86. 8 There is no **god** like you, O Lord, not one has done
95. 3 Lord is a mighty God, a mighty king over all the **gods.**
96. 4 he is to be honoured more than all the **gods.**
96. 5 The **gods** of all other nations are only idols, but the Lord
97. 7 all the **gods** bow down before the Lord.
97. 9 you are much greater than all the **gods.**
106.28 of Baal, and ate sacrifices offered to lifeless **gods.**
115. 4 Their **gods** are made of silver and gold, formed by human hands.
135. 5 I know that our Lord is great, greater than all the **gods.**
135.15 The **gods** of the nations are made of silver and gold;
136. 2 Give thanks to the greatest of all **gods;**
138. 1 I sing praise to you before the **gods.**
Is 14.13 king on that mountain in the north where the **gods** assemble.
17.10 you plant sacred gardens in order to worship a foreign **god.**
31. 3 The Egyptians are not **gods**—they are only human.
36.18 Did the **gods** of any other nations save their countries from
36.19 Where are they now, the **gods** of Hamath and Arpad?
36.19 Where are the **gods** of Sepharvaim?
36.20 When did any of the **gods** of all these countries ever
37.12 lived in Telassar, and none of their **gods** could save them.
37.19 their gods—which were no **gods** at all, only images of wood
37.38 in the temple of his **god Nisroch,** two of his sons,
41.21 "You **gods** of the nations, present your case.
41.23 the future holds— then we will know that you are **gods!**
41.28 When I looked among the **gods,** none of them had a thing
41.29 All these **gods** are useless;
42. 8 No other **god** may share my glory;
42.17 call images their **gods,** will be humiliated and disgraced."
43. 9 Which of their **gods** can predict the future?
43. 9 Let these **gods** bring in their witnesses to prove that they

Is 43.10 Besides me there is no other **god;**
43.12 No foreign **god** has ever done this;
44. 6 there is no other **god** but me.
44. 8 Is there any other **god?**
44. 8 Is there some powerful **god** I never heard of?"
44. 9 worthless, and the **gods** they prize so highly are useless.
44. 9 Those who worship these **gods** are blind and ignorant—
44.10 It's no good making a metal image to worship as a **god!**
44.15 with the other part he makes a **god** and worships it.
44.17 He prays to it and says, "You are my **god**—save me!"
44.20 idol he holds in his hand is not a **god** at all.
45. 5 there is no other **god.**
45. 6 that I am the Lord and that there is no other **god.**
45.18 who says, "I am the Lord, and there is no other **god.**
45.20 and pray to **gods** that cannot save them—
45.21 There is no other **god.**
46. 1 "This is the end for Babylon's **gods!**
46. 2 This is the end for Babylon's **gods!**
46. 6 They hire a goldsmith to make a **god;**
48.14 None of the **gods** could predict that the man I have chosen
57. 5 You worship the fertility **gods** by having sex under those
57. 6 You take smooth stones from there and worship them as **gods.**
57. 9 perfumes and ointments and go to worship the **god Molech.**
57. 9 To find **gods** to worship, you send messengers far and wide,
57.10 out looking for other **gods,** but you never give up.
57.11 Lord says, "Who are these **gods** that make you afraid, so
65.11 hill, and worship Gad and Meni, the **gods** of luck and fate.
Jer 1.16 have offered sacrifices to other **gods,** and have made idols
2.11 has ever changed its **gods,** even though they were not real.
2.11 **gods** that can do nothing for them.
2.20 and under every green tree you worshipped fertility **gods.**
2.25 or let your throat become dry from chasing after other **gods.**
2.25 I have loved foreign **gods** and will go after them.' "
2.28 "Where are the **gods** that you made for yourselves?
2.28 Judah, you have as many **gods** as you have cities.
2.36 You have cheapened yourself by turning to the **gods** of other nations.
3.13 given your love to foreign **gods** and that you have not obeyed
3.24 the worship of Baal, the **god** of shame, has made us lose
5. 7 They have abandoned me and have worshipped **gods** that are not real.
5.19 from me and served foreign **gods** in their own land, so they
7. 6 Stop worshipping other **gods,** for that will destroy you.
7. 9 to Baal, and worship **gods** that you had not known before.
7.18 pour out wine-offerings to other **gods,** in order to hurt me.
8.19 idols and by bowing down to your useless foreign **gods?"**
10.11 must tell them that the **gods** who did not make the earth
10.14 because the **gods** they make are false and lifeless.
11.10 they have worshipped other **gods.**
11.12 Jerusalem will go to the **gods** to whom they offer sacrifices
11.12 But those **gods** will not be able to save them
11.13 of Judah have as many **gods** as they have cities, and the
11.13 for sacrifices to that disgusting **god Baal** as there are
13.10 wicked as ever, and have worshipped and served other **gods.**
13.25 you have forgotten him and have trusted in **false gods.**
13.27 seen you go after pagan **gods** on the hills and in the
16.11 ancestors turned away from me and worshipped and served other **gods.**
16.13 there you will serve other **gods** day and night, and I will
16.18 as corpses, and have filled it with their **false gods."**
16.19 "Our ancestors had nothing but **false gods,**
16.20 Can a man make his own **gods?**
16.20 No, if he did, they would not really be **gods."**
19. 4 sacrifices here to other gods—**gods** that neither they nor
19.13 as an offering to other **gods**—they will all be as unclean
22. 9 me, your God, and have worshipped and served other **gods."**
25. 6 to worship and serve other **gods** and not to make the Lord
32.29 and by pouring out wine-offerings to other **gods.**
32.35 to sacrifice their sons and daughters to the **god Molech.**
35.15 to worship and serve other **gods,** so that you could go on
43.12 to the temples of Egypt's **gods,**
43.12 of Babylonia will either burn their **gods** or carry them off.
43.13 Egypt and will burn down the temples of the Egyptian **gods."**
44. 3 They offered sacrifices to other **gods** and served gods
44. 5 not give up your evil practice of sacrificing to other **gods.**
44. 8 and by sacrificing to other **gods** here in Egypt, where you
44.15 wives offered sacrifices to other **gods,** and all the women
44.23 you offered sacrifices to other **gods** and sinned against the
46.15 Why has your mighty **god Apis** fallen?
46.25 to punish Amon, the **god of Thebes,**
46.25 together with Egypt and its **gods** and kings.
48. 7 your **god Chemosh** will go into exile, along with his princes
48.13 will be disillusioned with their **god Chemosh,** just as the
48.13 Israelites were disillusioned with Bethel, a **god** in whom they trusted.
48.35 of worship and from offering sacrifices to their **gods.**
49. 3 Your **god Molech** will be taken into exile, together with his
50. 2 Her **god Marduk** has been shattered!
51.17 because the **gods** they make are false and lifeless.
51.44 will punish Bel, the **god of Babylonia,** and make him give up
Ezek 8.14 showed me women weeping over the death of the **god Tammuz.**
20. 7 make themselves unclean with the **false gods** of Egypt,
20. 8 away their disgusting idols or give up the Egyptian **gods.**
28. 2 Puffed up with pride, you claim to be a **god.**
28. 2 You say that like a **god** you sit on a throne, surrounded
28. 2 may pretend to be a **god,** but, no, you are mortal,
28. 6 are as wise as a **god,** [7] I will bring ruthless enemies
28. 9 to kill you, will you still claim that you are a **god?**
30.13 "I will destroy the idols and the **false gods** in Memphis.
43. 7 holy name by worshipping other **gods** or by burying the
43. 9 they must stop worshipping other **gods** and remove the corpses

Dan 1. 2 to the temple of his **gods** in Babylon, and put the captured
2.11 it for you except the **gods,** and they do not live among
2.47 is the greatest of all **gods,** the Lord over kings, and the
3.12 They do not worship your **god** or bow down to the statue
3.14 you refuse to worship my **god** and to bow down
3.15 Do you think there is any **god** who can save you?"
3.18 we will not worship your **god,** and we will not bow down
3.28 rather than bow down and worship any **god** except their own.
3.29 There is no other **god** who can rescue like this."
4. 8 (He is also called Belteshazzar, after the name of my **god.)**
4. 8 The spirit of the holy **gods** is in him, so I told
4. 9 the spirit of the holy **gods** is in you, and that you
4.18 you can, because the spirit of the holy **gods** is in you."
5. 4 out of them [4]and praised **gods** made of gold, silver, bronze,
5.11 who has the spirit of the holy **gods** in him.
5.11 knowledge, and wisdom like the wisdom of the **gods.**
5.14 the spirit of the holy **gods** is in you and that you
5.23 praised **gods** made of gold, silver, bronze, iron,
5.23 wood, and stone—**gods** that cannot see or hear
6. 7 to request anything from any **god** or from any man except from
6.12 requested anything from any **god** or from any man except you,
11. 8 the images of their **gods**
11. 8 and the articles of gold and silver dedicated to those **gods.**
11.36 he is greater than any **god,**
11.37 The king will ignore the **god** his ancestors served,
11.37 and also the **god** that women love.
11.37 he will ignore every **god,**
11.38 Instead, he will honour the **god** who protects fortresses.
11.38 other rich gifts to a **god** his ancestors never worshipped.
11.39 he will use people who worship a foreign **god.**
Hos 3. 1 though they turn to other **gods** and like to take offerings of
4.10 You will worship the fertility **gods,** but still have no children,
4.10 because you have turned away from me to follow other **gods."**
4.12 a prostitute, they have given themselves to other **gods.**
7.16 keep on turning away from me to a **god** that is powerless.
8. 6 craftsman made the idol, and it is not a **god** at all!
9. 1 yourselves like prostitutes to the **god Baal** and have loved
9.10 Baal, and soon became as disgusting as the **gods** they loved.
Amos 2. 4 astray by the same **false gods** that their ancestors served.
5.26 of Sakkuth, your king **god,** and of Kaiwan, your star god,
8.14 who say, 'By the **god of Dan,'**
8.14 or, 'By the **god of Beersheba'**—those people will fall and
Jon 1. 5 terrified and cried out for help, each one to his own **god.**
1. 6 Get up and pray to your **god** for help.
Mic 4. 5 worships and obeys its own **god,**
7.18 There is no other **god** like you, O Lord;
Nah 1.14 destroy the idols that are in the temples of their **gods.**
Hab 1.11 these men whose power is their **god."**
2.18 for its maker to trust it—a **god** that can't even talk!
Zeph 1. 5 me, but then take oaths in the name of the **god Molech.**
2.11 He will reduce the **gods** of the earth to nothing, and then
3. 9 and they will pray to me alone and not to other **gods.**
Mal 2.11 Men have married women who worship foreign **gods.**
Mt 6. 7 who think that their **gods** will hear them because their prayers
Jn 10.34 is written in your own Law that God said, 'You are **gods.'**
10.35 and God called those people **gods,** the people to whom his
Acts 7.40 they said to Aaron, 'Make us some **gods** who will lead us.
7.43 was the tent of the **god Molech** that you carried, and the
12.22 "It isn't a man speaking, but a **god!"**
14.11 their own Lycaonian language, "The **gods** have become like men
14.13 The priest of the **god Zeus,** whose temple stood just
17.18 Others answered, "He seems to be talking about foreign **gods."**
19.26 He says that man-made **gods** are not gods at all, and he
28. 6 to him, they changed their minds and said, "He is a **god!"**
Rom 11. 4 seven thousand men who have not worshipped the false **god Baal."**
1 Cor 8. 5 if there are so-called **"gods,"** whether in heaven or on earth,
8. 5 there are many of these **"gods"** and "lords," [6]yet there is
2 Cor 4. 4 been kept in the dark by the evil **god of this world.**
Gal 4. 8 God, and so you were slaves of beings who are not **gods.**
Phil 3.19 end up in hell, because their **god** is their bodily desires.
2 Thes 2. 4 He will oppose every so-called **god** or object of worship
1 Jn 5.21 My children, keep yourselves safe from **false gods!**

GOD-FEARING

Gen 42.18 to them, "I am a **God-fearing** man, and I will spare your
Ex 18.21 They must be **God-fearing** men who can be trusted and who
2 Kgs 4. 1 you know, he was a **God-fearing** man, but now a man he
Neh 7. 2 Hananiah was a reliable and **God-fearing** man without an equal.
Lk 2.25 He was a good, **God-fearing** man and was waiting for Israel to

GOD-GIVEN

2 Cor 1.12 you, have been ruled by **God-given** frankness and sincerity,

GOD'S ALTAR see **ALTAR**

GOD'S ANGEL see **ANGEL**

GOD'S ANGER see **ANGER**

GOD'S CHILDREN see **CHILD OF GOD**

GOD'S KINGDOM see **KINGDOM (1)**

GOD'S PEOPLE

[CHOSEN PEOPLE, HIS PEOPLE, HOLY PEOPLE, LORD'S PEOPLE, MY PEOPLE, PEOPLE OF GOD]

Gen 17.14 longer be considered one of **my people,** because he has not
Ex 3. 7 "I have seen how cruelly **my people** are being treated in Egypt;
3. 9 indeed heard the cry of **my people,** and I see how the
3.10 Egypt so that you can lead **my people** out of his country."
3.18 **"My people** will listen to what you say to them.
3.21 respect you so that when **my people** leave, they will not go
5. 1 God of Israel, says, 'Let **my people** go, so that they can
6. 1 I will force him to let **my people** go.
6. 7 I will make you **my own people,** and I will be your
7. 3 Egypt and lead the tribes of **my people** out of the land.
7.16 to tell you to let **his people** go, so that they can
8. 1 that the Lord says, 'Let **my people** go, so that they can
8.20 that the Lord says, 'Let **my people** go, so that they can
8.22 the region of Goshen, where **my people** live, so that there
8.23 I will make a distinction between **my people** and your people.
9. 1 of the Hebrews, says, 'Let **my people** go, so that they may
9.13 of the Hebrews, says, 'Let **my people** go, so that they may
9.17 Yet you are still arrogant and refuse to let **my people** go.
10. 3 Let **my people** go, so that they may worship me.
11. 8 they will beg me to take all **my people** and go away.
12.15 yeast, he shall no longer be considered one of **my people.**
12.19 yeast, he shall no longer be considered one of **my people."**
12.41 430 years ended, all the tribes of the **Lord's people** left Egypt.
18.10 Praise the Lord, who saved **his people** from slavery!
19. 5 obey me and keep my covenant, you will be **my own people.**
19. 5 but you will be my **chosen people,** [6]a people dedicated to me
22.25 lend money to any of **my people** who are poor, do not
22.31 "You are **my people,** so you must not eat the meat of
28.12 so that I, the Lord, will always remember **my people.**
28.29 Israel, so that I, the Lord, will always remember **my people.**
29.28 that when **my people** make their fellowship-offerings,
29.42 That is where I will meet **my people** and speak to you.
30.33 a priest will no longer be considered one of **my people.' "**
30.38 he will no longer be considered one of **my people."**
31.13 to show that I, the Lord, have made you **my own people.**
32.14 did not bring on **his people** the disaster he had threatened.
34. 9 our evil and our sin, and accept us as your **own people."**
Lev 7.20 he shall no longer be considered one of **God's people.**
7.21 he shall no longer be considered one of **God's people.**
7.25 will no longer be considered one of **God's people.**
7.27 will no longer be considered one of **God's people.**
10. 3 I will reveal my glory to **my people.' "**
17. 3 blood and shall no longer be considered one of **God's people.**
17. 9 shall no longer be considered one of **God's people.**
17.10 against him and no longer consider him one of **his people.**
17.14 who does so will no longer be considered one of **his people.**
18.29 will no longer be considered one of **God's people.**
19. 8 me, and he will no longer be considered one of **my people.**
20. 3 him and will no longer consider him one of **my people.**
20. 5 I will no longer consider them **my people.**
20. 6 him and will no longer consider him one of **my people.**
21. 8 I am holy and I make **my people** holy.
23.29 that day will no longer be considered one of **God's people.**
26.12 I will be your God, and you will be **my people.**
26.42 and I will renew my promise to give **my people** the land.
26.45 nations my power by bringing **my people** out of Egypt, in
Num 5. 3 will not defile the camp, where I live among **my people."**
9.13 longer be considered one of **my people,** because he did not
11.29 give his spirit to all **his people** and make all of them
12. 7 I have put him in charge of all **my people** Israel.
16.41 Aaron and said, "You have killed some of the **Lord's people."**
19.13 and he will no longer be considered one of **God's people.**
19.20 Lord's Tent and will no longer be considered one of **God's people.**
23.10 Let me end my days like one of **God's people;**
31.16 That was what brought the epidemic on the **Lord's people.**
Deut 4.20 you out to make you his **own people,** as you are today.
9.26 'Sovereign Lord, don't destroy your **own people,** the people
10.15 of any other people, and you are still his **chosen people.**
14. 2 chosen you to be his **own people** from among all the peoples
14.21 you are **his people.**
17.16 the Lord has said that **his people** are never to return there.
23. 1 has been cut off may be included among the **Lord's people.**
23. 2 tenth generation, may be included among the **Lord's people.**
23. 3 tenth generation—may be included among the **Lord's people.**
23. 8 their descendants may be included among the **Lord's people.**
26.18 Lord has accepted you as his **own people,** as he promised you;
26.19 You will be his **own people,** as he promised."
28. 9 he will make you his **own people,** as he has promised.
28.10 chosen you to be his **own people,** and they will be afraid
29.13 may now confirm you as **his people** and be your God,
29.25 be, 'It is because the **Lord's people** broke the covenant they
29.27 Lord became angry with **his people** and brought on their land
31.26 that it will remain there as a witness against **his people.**
32. 3 of the Lord, and **his people** will tell of his greatness.
32. 5 unworthy to be **his people,** a sinful and deceitful nation.
32.12 Lord alone led **his people** without the help of a foreign
32.15 "The **Lord's people** grew rich, but rebellious;
32.27 boast that they had defeated **my people,** when it was I myself
32.36 Lord will rescue **his people** when he sees that their strength
32.37 the Lord will ask **his people,** 'Where are those mighty gods
32.43 "Nations, you must praise the **Lord's people**— he
32.43 revenge on his enemies and forgives the sins of **his people."**
33. 2 the sun over Edom and shone on **his people** from Mount Paran.
33. 3 Lord loves **his people** and protects those who belong to him.
33. 5 The Lord became king of **his people** Israel when their tribes
Josh 1. 3 have given you and all **my people** the entire land that you
22.17 when the Lord punished his **own people** with an epidemic?

Judg	5.11	Then the **Lord's people** marched down from their cities.
	5.13	the **Lord's people** came to him ready to fight.
	11.23	who drove out the Amorites for **his people,** the Israelites.
	20. 2	of **God's people,** and there were 400,000 foot-soldiers.
Ruth	1. 6	that the Lord had blessed **his people** by giving them a good
1 Sam	2.29	the sacrifices and offerings which I require from **my people?**
	2.29	the best parts of all the sacrifices **my people** offer to me?
	9.16	anoint him as ruler of **my people** Israel, and he will rescue
	9.16	have seen the suffering of **my people** and have heard their
	9.17	He will rule **my people."**
	10. 1	said, "The Lord anoints you as ruler of **his people** Israel.
	10. 1	You will rule **his people** and protect them from all their
	10. 1	the Lord has chosen you to be the ruler of **his people:**
	12.22	abandon you, for he has decided to make you his **own people.**
	13.14	kind of man he wants and make him ruler of **his people."**
	15. 1	whom the Lord sent to anoint you king of **his people** Israel.
	17.47	the Lord does not need swords or spears to save **his people.**
2 Sam	3.18	my servant David to rescue **my people** Israel from the
	5. 2	you that you would lead **his people** and be their ruler."
	5.12	making his kingdom prosperous for the sake of **his people.**
	6.21	and his family to make me the leader of **his people** Israel.
	7. 8	in the fields and made you the ruler of **my people** Israel.
	7.10	have chosen a place for **my people** Israel and have settled
	7.23	whom you rescued from slavery to make them your **own people.**
	7.24	You have made Israel your **own people** for ever, and you,
	14.13	to him, "Why have you done such a wrong to **God's people?**
	14.16	and so remove us from the land God gave **his people.**
	21. 3	done to you, so that you will bless the **Lord's people."**
1 Kgs	6.13	I will live among **my people** Israel in this Temple that
	8.16	'From the time I brought **my people** out of Egypt, I have
	8.16	But I chose you, David, to rule **my people.' "**
	8.51	They are your **own people,** whom you brought out of Egypt,
	8.53	the peoples to be your **own people,** as you told them through
	8.56	the Lord who has given **his people** peace, as he promised he
	8.61	May you, **his people,** always be faithful to the Lord
	8.66	the Lord had given his servant David and **his people** Israel.
	9. 7	gods, [7] then I will remove **my people** Israel from the land
	14. 7	among the people and made you the ruler of **my people** Israel.
	16. 2	a nobody, but I made you the leader of **my people** Israel.
	16. 2	have sinned like Jeroboam and have led **my people** into sin.
2 Kgs	9. 6	'I anoint you king of **my people** Israel.
	11.17	covenant with the Lord that they would be the **Lord's people;**
	13.23	He has never forgotten **his people.**
	17. 8	Lord had driven out as **his people** advanced, and adopted
	20. 5	to Hezekiah, ruler of the **Lord's people,** and say to him,
	21. 2	out of the land as **his people** advanced, Manasseh sinned
	21. 9	the Lord had driven out of the land as **his people** advanced.
	21.15	I will do this to **my people** because they have sinned
1 Chr	11. 2	you that you would lead **his people** and be their ruler."
	14. 2	making his kingdom prosperous for the sake of **his people.**
	16.19	**God's people** were few in number, strangers in the land of Canaan.
	17. 7	in the fields and made you the ruler of **my people** Israel.
	17. 9	have chosen a place for **my people** Israel and have settled
	17.14	put him in charge of **my people** and my kingdom for ever.
	17.21	whom you rescued from slavery to make them your **own people.**
	17.22	You have made Israel your **own people** for ever, and you,
	23.25	Israel has given peace to **his people,** and he himself will
	28. 8	assembly of all Israel, the **Lord's people,** I charge you to
2 Chr	1.11	so that you can rule **my people,** over whom I have made
	2.11	"Because the Lord loves **his people,** he has made you their
	6. 5	'From the time I brought **my people** out of Egypt until now,
	6. 5	and I did not choose anyone to lead **my people** Israel.
	6. 6	I will be worshipped, and you, David, to rule **my people.' "**
	7.10	the Lord had given to **his people** Israel, to David, and to
	7.13	or send an epidemic on **my people,** [14] if they pray to me
	9. 8	Because he loves **his people** Israel and wants to preserve them
	23.16	in making a covenant that they would be the **Lord's people.**
	31. 8	they praised the Lord and praised **his people** Israel.
	31.10	We have all this because the Lord has blessed **his people."**
	32.17	and neither will Hezekiah's god save **his people** from me."
	33. 2	out of the land as **his people** advanced, Manasseh sinned
	33. 9	the Lord had driven out of the land as **his people** advanced.
	35. 3	you are to serve the Lord your God and **his people** Israel.
	36.15	send prophets to warn **his people,** because he wanted to spare
	36.16	the Lord's anger against **his people** was so great that there
	36.23	all of you who are **God's people,** go there,
Ezra	1. 3	May God be with all of you who are **his people.**
	1. 4	If any of **his people** in exile need help to return,
	9. 2	women, and so **God's holy people** had become contaminated.
Neh	1.10	"Lord, these are your servants, your **own people.**
	13. 1	Ammonite or Moabite was ever to be permitted to join **God's people.**
Ps	1. 5	be condemned by God and kept apart from **God's own people.**
	3. 8	Victory comes from the Lord— may he bless **his people.**
	14. 4	They live by robbing **my people,** and they never pray to me."
	22.31	"The Lord saved **his people."**
	26.12	in the assembly of **his people** I praise the Lord.
	28. 8	The Lord protects **his people;**
	29.11	The Lord gives strength to **his people** and blesses them
	34. 9	Honour the Lord, all **his people;**
	34.22	The Lord will save **his people;**
	44.12	You sold your **own people** for a small price as though
	47. 4	the proud possession of **his people,** whom he loves.
	48.12	**People of God,** walk round Zion and count the towers;
	50. 4	heaven and earth as witnesses to see him judge **his people.**
	50. 7	"Listen, **my people,** and I will speak;
	53. 4	They live by robbing **my people,** and they never pray to me."
	53. 5	God will scatter the bones of the enemies of **his people.**
	60. 6	Shechem and distribute the Valley of Sukkoth to **my people.**
	68.26	"Praise God in the meeting of **his people;**
	68.35	He gives strength and power to **his people.**
Ps	69.33	to those in need and does not forget **his people** in prison.
	69.35	**His people** will live there and possess the land;
	73.10	on earth, [10] so that even **God's people** turn to them and
	74. 1	Will you be angry with your **own people** for ever?
	78.20	he also provide us with bread and give **his people** meat?"
	78.21	attacked **his people** with fire, and his anger against them grew,
	78.27	and to **his people** he sent down birds, as many as the
	78.38	But God was merciful to **his people.**
	78.52	Then he led **his people** out like a shepherd and guided
	78.55	He drove out the inhabitants as **his people** advanced;
	78.55	the tribes of Israel and gave their homes to **his people.**
	78.59	angry when he saw it, so he rejected **his people** completely.
	78.62	He was angry with his **own people** and let them be killed
	78.71	made him king of Israel, the shepherd of the **people of God.**
	81. 8	Listen, **my people,** to my warning;
	81.11	"But **my people** would not listen to me;
	81.13	How I wish **my people** would listen to me;
	85. 8	promises peace to us, his **own people,** if we do not go
	94.14	The Lord will not abandon **his people;**
	97.10	he protects the lives of **his people;**
	100. 3	we are **his people,** we are his flock.
	105.12	**God's people** were few in number, strangers in the land of Canaan.
	105.24	Lord gave many children to **his people** and made them stronger
	105.25	He made the Egyptians hate **his people** and treat his
	105.39	God put a cloud over **his people** and a fire at night
	105.43	So he led his **chosen people** out, and they sang and
	105.45	over their fields, [45] so that **his people** would obey his laws
	106. 9	he led **his people** across on dry land.
	106.12	**his people** believed his promises and sang praises to him.
	106.23	said that he would destroy **his people,** his chosen servant,
	106.28	Then at Peor, **God's people** joined in the worship of Baal,
	106.36	**God's people** worshipped idols, and this caused their destruction.
	106.40	So the Lord was angry with **his people;**
	106.43	Many times the Lord rescued **his people,** but they chose to
	107.38	He blessed **his people,** and they had many children;
	107.39	When **God's people** were defeated and humiliated
	108. 7	Shechem and distribute the Valley of Sukkoth to **my people.**
	111. 1	heart I will thank the Lord in the assembly of **his people.**
	111. 6	has shown his power to **his people** by giving them the lands
	111. 9	set **his people** free and made an eternal covenant with them.
	113. 8	makes them companions of princes, the princes of **his people.**
	114. 2	Judah became the Lord's **holy people,** Israel became his own possession.
	116.14	In the assembly of all **his people** I will give him what
	116.15	painful it is to the Lord when one of **his people** dies!
	118.15	to the glad shouts of victory in the tents of **God's people:**
	125. 2	so the Lord surrounds **his people** now and for ever.
	130. 8	He will save **his people** Israel from all their sins.
	133. 1	how pleasant, for **God's people** to live together in harmony!
	135.12	He gave their lands to **his people;**
	135.14	The Lord will defend **his people;**
	136.14	he led **his people** through it;
	136.16	He led **his people** through the desert;
	136.21	He gave their lands to **his people;**
	147.19	He gives his message to **his people,** his instructions and
	148.14	nation strong, so that all **his people** praise him— the people
	149. 4	The Lord takes pleasure in **his people;**
	149. 5	Let **God's people** rejoice in their triumph and sing
	149. 9	This is the victory of **God's people.**
Is	1. 3	But that is more than **my people** Israel know.
	2. 3	from Zion he speaks to **his people."**
	3.12	Money-lenders oppress **my people,** and their creditors cheat
	3.12	**My people,** your leaders are misleading you, so that you do
	3.13	he is ready to judge **his people.**
	3.14	bringing the elders and leaders of **his people** to judgement.
	3.15	have no right to crush **my people** and take advantage of the
	5.16	is right, and he reveals his holiness by judging **his people.**
	5.25	The Lord is angry with **his people** and has stretched out
	6.13	(The stump represents a new beginning for **God's people.)**
	8.17	Lord has hidden himself from **his people,** but I trust him and
	10. 1	You make unjust laws that oppress **my people.**
	10.24	Sovereign Lord Almighty says to **his people** who live in Zion,
	11.11	bring back home those of **his people** who are left in Assyria
	11.16	of Assyria for those of **his people** Israel who have survived
	12. 3	the thirsty, so **God's people** rejoice when he saves them."
	12. 6	Israel's holy God is great, and he lives among **his people."**
	14. 1	once again be merciful to **his people** Israel and choose them
	14.25	I will free **my people** from the Assyrian yoke and from the
	14.30	shepherd to the poor of **his people** and will let them live
	19.25	bless them and say, "I will bless you, Egypt, **my people;**
	19.25	and you, Israel, my **chosen people."**
	21.10	**My people** Israel, you have been threshed like wheat, but
	22. 4	to weep bitterly over all those of **my people** who have died.
	25. 8	and take away the disgrace **his people** have suffered
	26.20	Go into your houses, **my people,** and shut the door behind you.
	27. 5	But if the enemies of **my people** want my protection, let
	27. 8	The Lord punished **his people** by sending them into exile.
	27.12	the Lord will gather **his people** one by one, like someone
	28. 5	like a glorious crown of flowers for **his people** who survive.
	29.22	rescued Abraham from trouble, says, **"My people,** you will
	30.26	Lord bandages and heals the wounds he has given **his people.**
	30.29	But you, **God's people,** will be happy and sing as you do
	30.32	strikes them again and again, **his people** will keep time with
	32.13	and thorn-bushes and briars are growing on **my people's** land.
	32.18	**God's people** will be free from worries, and their homes
	33. 6	He always protects **his people** and gives them wisdom
	40. 1	"Comfort **my people,"** says our God.
	41.17	"When **my people** in their need look for water, when
	42.14	I did not answer **my people.**
	42.21	laws and teachings, and he wanted **his people** to honour them.
	42.22	But now **his people** have been plundered;

Is 43. 6 Let **my people** return from distant lands, from every part of
43. 7 They are **my own people,** and I created them to bring me
43. 8 "Summon **my people** to court.
43.20 flow in the desert to give water to my **chosen people.**
43.28 I let **my own people** be insulted."
44. 1 "Listen now, Israel, my servant, my **chosen people,**
44. 2 you are my servant, my **chosen people** whom I love.
44. 5 the Lord on his arm and call himself one of **God's people."**
44. 8 Do not be afraid, **my people!**
44.23 The Lord has shown his greatness by saving **his people** Israel.
45.15 God of Israel, who saves **his people,** is a God who conceals
45.21 Was it not I, the Lord, the God who saves **his people?**
46. 3 to me, descendants of Jacob, all who are left of **my people.**
47. 6 I was angry with **my people;**
48.21 When the Lord led **his people** through a hot, dry desert,
49. 5 his servant to bring back **his people,** to bring back the
49. 8 The Lord says to **his people,**
49.11 the mountains and prepare a road for **my people** to travel.
49.12 **My people** will come from far away, from the north and
49.13 The Lord will comfort **his people;**
49.22 The Sovereign Lord says to **his people:**
50. 1 "Do you think I sent **my people** away like a man who
50. 2 "Why did **my people** fail to respond when I went to them
51. 4 "Listen to me, **my people,** listen to what I say:
51.16 I say to Jerusalem, 'You are **my people!**
52. 3 Sovereign Lord says to **his people,** "When you became slaves,
52. 9 The Lord will rescue his city and comfort **his people.**
52.10 he will save **his people,** and all the world will see it.
55. 3 "Listen now, **my people,** and come to me;
56. 1 The Lord says to **his people,** "Do what is just and right,
56. 3 who has joined the **Lord's people** should not say,
56. 3 "The Lord will not let me worship with **his people."**
56. 3 cannot have children, he can never be part of **God's people.**
56. 5 in my Temple and among **my people** longer than if you had
56. 6 foreigners who become part of **his people,** who love him
56. 8 Lord, who has brought **his people** Israel home from exile,
56. 9 foreign nations to come like wild animals and devour **his people.**
56.10 "All the leaders, who are supposed to warn **my people,** are
57.14 The Lord says, "Let **my people** return to me.
57.16 I gave **my people** life, and I will not continue to accuse
57.19 I will heal **my people.**
58. 1 Tell **my people** Israel about their sins!
59.20 The Lord says to **his people,** "I will come to Jerusalem
60. 9 ships coming from distant lands, Bringing **God's people** home.
60. 9 God of Israel, Who has made all nations honour **his people.**
61. 2 When the Lord will save **his people** And defeat their enemies.
61. 5 **My people,** foreigners will serve you.
61. 8 I will faithfully reward **my people** And make an eternal
61.11 The Sovereign Lord will save **his people,** And all the nations
62.12 You will be called **"God's Holy People,"** "The People
63. 4 I decided that the time to save **my people** had come;
63. 8 The Lord said, "They are **my people;**
63.11 the Lord, who saved the leaders of **his people** from the sea?
63.12 of the sea and leading **his people** through the deep water,
63.14 led into a fertile valley, so the Lord gave **his people** rest.
63.14 He led **his people** and brought honour to his name.
63.18 We, your **holy people,** were driven out by our enemies for
65. 1 "I was ready to answer **my people's** prayers, but they did
65. 2 always been ready to welcome **my people,** who stubbornly do
65. 8 Neither will I destroy all **my people—**I will save those who
65. 9 My **chosen people,** who serve me, will live there.
65.15 My **chosen people** will use your name as a curse.
65.21 Like trees, **my people** will live long lives.
66. 9 think that I will bring **my people** to the point of birth

Jer 1.16 I will punish **my people** because they have sinned;
2. 9 so I, the Lord, will state my case against **my people** again.
2.11 But **my people** have exchanged me, the God who has brought
2.13 and astonished, [13] for **my people** have committed two sins:
2.32 But **my people** have forgotten me for more days than can be
4.12 It is the Lord himself who is pronouncing judgement on **his people.**
4.22 The Lord says, **"My people** are stupid;
5. 7 The Lord asked, "Why should I forgive the sins of **my people?**
5. 7 I fed **my people** until they were full, but they committed
5.10 send enemies to cut down **my people's** vineyards, but not to
5.12 The **Lord's people** have denied him and have said, "He
5.18 "Yet even in those days I will not completely destroy **my people.**
5.26 "Evil men live among **my people;**
5.31 as the prophets command, and **my people** offer no objections.
6.14 They act as if **my people's** wounds were only scratches.
6.16 Lord said to **his people,** "Stand at the crossroads and look.
6.18 you nations, and learn what is going to happen to **my people.**
6.26 The Lord says to **his people,** "Put on sackcloth and roll
6.27 Jeremiah, test **my people,** as you would test metal, and
6.29 useless to go on refining **my people,** because those who are
7.12 I did to it because of the sins of **my people** Israel.
7.21 **"My people,** some sacrifices you burn completely on the altar,
7.23 that I would be their God and they would be **my people.**
7.27 speak all these words to **my people,** but they will not listen
7.29 because I, the Lord, am angry, and have rejected **my people.**
8. 4 told me to say to **his people,** "When someone falls down,
8. 5 Why then, **my people,** do you turn away from me without ever
8. 7 But, **my people,** you do not know the laws by which I
8.11 They act as if **my people's** wounds were only scratches.
8.12 **My people,** were you ashamed because you did these disgusting
8.13 "I wanted to gather **my people,** as a man gathers his harvest;
8.14 **God's people** ask.
8.19 Throughout the land I hear **my people** crying out, "Is the
8.21 My heart has been crushed because **my people** are crushed;
8.22 Why, then, have **my people** not been healed?
9. 1 could cry day and night for **my people** who have been killed.
9. 2 stay in the desert where I could get away from **my people.**

Jer 9. 3 **"My people** do one evil thing after another, and do not
9. 5 The Lord says that **his people** reject him.
9. 7 Almighty says, "I will refine **my people** like metal and put
9. 7 **My people** have done evil— what else can I do with
9.13 answered, "This has happened because **my people** have
9.15 I will give **my people** bitter plants to eat and poison to
10.16 and he has chosen Israel to be his very **own people.**
11. 4 they obeyed, they would be **my people** and I would be their
12. 8 My **chosen people** have turned against me;
12. 9 My **chosen people** are like a bird attacked from all sides
12.13 **My people** sowed wheat, but gathered weeds;
12.14 who have ruined the land I gave to **my people** Israel.
12.16 will accept the religion of **my people** and will swear, 'As
12.16 lives'—as they once taught **my people** to swear by Baal—then
12.16 they will also be a part of **my people** and will prosper.
13.11 so that they would be **my people** and would bring praise and
13.17 tears will flow because the **Lord's people** have been taken
14. 7 **My people** cry out to me, 'Even though our sins accuse us,
14.17 I never stop weeping, for **my people** are deeply wounded and
15. 7 I destroyed you, **my people,** I killed your children because
15.13 the wealth and treasures of **my people,** in order to punish
16. 5 I will no longer bless **my people** with peace or show them
18.15 Yet **my people** have forgotten me;
18.17 I will scatter **my people** before their enemies, like dust
23. 1 judgement on those rulers who destroy and scatter **his people!**
23. 2 the rulers who were supposed to take care of **his people:**
23. 2 "You have not taken care of **my people;**
23. 3 will gather the rest of **my people** from the countries where I
23. 4 **My people** will no longer be afraid or terrified, and I will
23.13 spoken in the name of Baal and have led **my people** astray.
23.20 In days to come **his people** will understand this clearly."
23.22 have proclaimed my message to **my people** and could have made
23.26 longer will those prophets mislead **my people** with the lies
23.27 dreams they tell will make **my people** forget me, just as
23.32 tell these dreams and lead **my people** astray with their lies
23.33 me, "Jeremiah, when one of **my people** or a prophet or a
23.34 If one of **my people** or a prophet or a priest even
24. 7 Then they will be **my people,** and I will be their God,
25.30 He will roar against **his people;**
25.34 Cry, you leaders, you shepherds of **my people,** cry out
25.38 The Lord has abandoned **his people** like a lion that leaves
29.31 am going to do for **my people,** because he told them to
30. 3 is coming when I will restore **my people,** Israel and Judah.
30. 7 a time of distress for **my people,** but they will survive."
30.10 **"My people,** do not be afraid;
30.12 The Lord says to **his people,**
30.18 "I will restore **my people** to their land and have mercy on
30.21 They will be **my people,** and I will be their God.
30.23 In days to come **his people** will understand this clearly.
31. 1 of all the tribes of Israel, and they will be **my people.**
31. 7 Sing your song of praise, 'The Lord has saved **his people;**
31. 9 **My people** will return weeping, praying as I lead them back.
31.10 I scattered **my people,** but I will gather them and guard them
31.14 the richest food and satisfy all the needs of **my people.**
31.33 I will be their God, and they will be **my people.**
32.38 Then they will be **my people,** and I will be their God.
33.24 they look with contempt on **my people** and no longer consider
33.26 I will be merciful to **my people** and make them prosperous again."
46.27 **"My people,** do not be afraid, people of Israel, do not
50. 6 **"My people** are like sheep whose shepherds have let them
51.10 The Lord says, **"My people** shout, 'The Lord has shown
51.19 and he has chosen Israel to be his very **own people.**
51.50 The Lord says to **his people** in Babylonia:

Lam 1.15 He crushed **my people** like grapes in a winepress.
1.16 **my people** have nothing left.
2.11 I am exhausted with grief at the destruction of **my people.**
3.48 flow with rivers of tears at the destruction of **my people.**
4. 3 will nurse her cubs, but **my people** are like ostriches, cruel
4. 6 **My people** have been punished even more than the inhabitants
4.10 The disaster that came to **my people** brought horror;

Ezek 11.20 They will be **my people,** and I will be their God.
13. 9 You will not be there when **my people** gather to make decisions;
13.10 "The prophets mislead **my people** by saying that all is well.
13.10 **My people** have put up a wall of loose stones, and then
13.18 of life and death over **my people** and to use it for
13.19 dishonour me in front of **my people** in order to get a
13.19 So you tell lies to **my people,** and they believe you."
13.21 off your scarves and let **my people** escape from your power
13.23 I am rescuing **my people** from your power, so that you will
14. 8 him from the community of **my people,** so that you will know
14.11 They are to be **my people,** and I will be their God."
21.10 can be no rejoicing, for **my people** have disregarded every
21.12 this sword is meant for **my people** and for all the leaders
21.12 are going to be killed with all the rest of **my people.**
21.13 I am testing **my people,** and if they refuse to repent,
21.15 It makes **my people** lose courage and stumble.
25.14 **My people** Israel will take revenge on Edom for me, and
30. 5 Libya, Arabia, Kub, and even from among **my own people."**
33.31 So **my people** crowd in to hear what you have to say,
34.27 When I break **my people's** chains and set them free from those
34.30 will know that I protect Israel and that they are **my people.**
34.31 flock that I feed, are **my people,** and I am your God,"
35.11 anger, your jealousy, and your hatred towards **my people.**
36. 8 again grow leaves and bear fruit for you, **my people** Israel.
36.12 I will bring you, **my people** Israel, back to live again
36.28 You will be **my people,** and I will be your God.
37.12 So prophesy to **my people** Israel and tell them that I,
37.13 I open the graves where **my people** are buried and bring them
37.21 am going to take all **my people** out of the nations where
37.23 they will be **my people,** and I will be their God.
37.27 I will be their God, and they will be **my people.**

Ezek	37.28	that I, the Lord, have chosen Israel to be **my own people."**
	38.14	"Now while **my people** Israel live in security, you will set
	38.16	You will attack **my people** Israel like a storm moving
	39. 7	I will make sure that **my people** Israel know my holy name,
	39.27	am holy, I will bring **my people** back from all the countries
	39.28	Then **my people** will know that I am the Lord their God.
	44. 7	So **my people** have broken my covenant by all the disgusting
	44.23	"The priests are to teach **my people** the difference
	45. 9	You must never again drive **my people** off their land.
	46.18	will not oppress any of **my people** by taking their land."
Dan	7.21	that horn made war on **God's people** and conquered them.
	7.22	The time had arrived for **God's people** to receive royal power.
	7.25	He will speak against the Supreme God and oppress **God's people.**
	7.25	and **God's people** will be under his power
	8.24	He will bring destruction on powerful men and on **God's own people.**
	9. 4	to the Lord my God and confessed the sins of **my people.**
	9.20	sins and the sins of **my people** Israel, and pleading with the
	11.28	determined to destroy the religion of **God's people.**
	11.30	in a rage and try to destroy the religion of **God's people.**
	11.34	**God's people** will receive a little help,
	12. 7	When the persecution of **God's people** ends, all these things
Hos	1. 2	In the same way, **my people** have left me and become unfaithful."
	1. 9	people of Israel are not **my people,** and I am not their
	1.10	to them, "You are not **my people,"** but the day is coming
	2. 1	So call your fellow-Israelites **"God's People"**
	2.18	animals and birds, so that they will not harm **my people.**
	2.18	and bows, and will let **my people** live in peace and safety.
	2.21	At that time I will answer the prayers of **my people** Israel.
	2.23	I will establish **my people** in the land and make them prosper.
	2.23	I will say, "You are **my people,"** and they will answer,
	4. 6	**My people** are doomed because they do not acknowledge me.
	4. 8	rich from the sins of **my people,** and so you want them
	4.11	"Wine, both old and new, is robbing **my people** of their senses!
	5.15	"I will abandon **my people** until they have suffered
	6. 6	I would rather have **my people** know me than burn offerings to
	6.10	**my people** have defiled themselves by worshipping idols.
	7. 1	"Whenever I want to heal **my people** Israel and make them
	8. 1	**My people** have broken the covenant I made with them and have
	8. 2	and claim that they are **my people** and that they know me,
	8. 4	**"My people** chose kings, but they did it on their own.
	9. 8	God has sent me as a prophet to warn **his people** Israel.
	9.17	God I serve will reject **his people,** because they have not
	11. 2	**My people** sacrificed to Baal;
	11. 3	I took **my people** up in my arms, but they did not
	11. 6	It will destroy **my people** because they do what they
	11.10	**"My people** will follow me when I roar like a lion at
	12.10	visions, and through the prophets I gave **my people** warnings.
	14. 4	"I will bring **my people** back to me.
Joel	2.18	he had mercy on **his people.**
	2.26	**My people** will never be despised again.
	2.27	**My people** will never be despised again.
	3. 2	I will judge them for all they have done to **my people.**
	3.16	But he will defend **his people.**
Amos	2. 9	"And yet, **my people,** it was for your sake that I totally
	7. 4	In it I saw him preparing to punish **his people** with fire.
	7. 8	using it to show that **my people** are like a wall that
	7.15	and ordered me to come and prophesy to **his people** Israel.
	8. 1	Lord said to me, "The end has come for **my people** Israel.
	9.10	The sinners among **my people** will be killed in war—all
	9.14	I will bring **my people** back to their land.
	9.15	I will plant **my people** on the land I gave them, and
Obad	13	have entered the city of **my people** to gloat over their
	16	**My people** have drunk a bitter cup of punishment on my
Mic	1. 9	the gates of Jerusalem itself, where **my people** live."
	2. 5	be given back to the **Lord's people,** there will be no share
	2. 8	The Lord replies, "You attack **my people** like enemies.
	2. 9	You drive the women of **my people** out of the homes they
	3. 2	You skin **my people** alive and tear the flesh off their bones.
	3. 3	You eat **my people** up.
	3. 5	**My people** are deceived by prophets who promise peace to
	3. 6	you mislead **my people,** you will have no more prophetic visions,
	4. 2	from Zion he speaks to **his people."**
	4. 8	like a shepherd, watches over **his people,** will once again be
	5. 3	So the Lord will abandon **his people** to their enemies until
	5. 4	he will rule **his people** with the strength that comes
	5. 4	**His people** will live in safety because people all over the
	6. 2	The Lord has a case against **his people.**
	6. 3	The Lord says, **"My people,** what have I done to you?
	6. 5	**My people,** remember what King Balak of Moab planned to do
Nah	1. 7	he protects **his people** in times of trouble;
	1.12	This is what the Lord says to **his people** Israel:
	1.12	**My people,** I made you suffer, but I will not do it
Hab	1. 5	the Lord said to **his people,** "Keep watching the nations
Zeph	1. 7	Lord is preparing to sacrifice **his people** and has invited
	2. 8	and Ammon insulting and taunting **my people,** and boasting
	2. 9	Those of **my people** who survive will plunder them and take
	3. 5	Every morning without fail, he brings justice to **his people.**
	3. 7	I thought that then **my people** would have reverence for me
	3.11	At that time you, **my people,** will no longer need to be
Hag	1. 4	**"My people,** why should you be living in well-built houses
	2. 9	one, and there I will give **my people** prosperity and peace."
Zech	1.15	holding back my anger against **my people,**
	1.15	those nations made the sufferings of **my people** worse.
	2. 6	Lord said to **his people,** "I scattered you in all directions.
	2. 8	with this message for the nations that had plundered **his people:**
	2.11	many nations will come to the Lord and become **his people.**
	4. 9	When this happens, **my people** will know that it is I who
	7. 9	"Long ago I gave these commands to **my people:**
	7.11	"But **my people** stubbornly refused to listen.
	8. 7	I will rescue **my people** from the lands where they have
Zech	8. 8	They will be **my people,** and I will be their God, ruling
	9. 7	survivors will become part of **my people** and be like a clan
	9. 7	Ekron will become part of **my people,** as the Jebusites did.
	9. 8	I will not allow tyrants to oppress **my people** any more.
	9. 8	I have seen how **my people** have suffered."
	9.14	The Lord will appear above **his people;**
	9.15	The Lord Almighty will protect **his people,** and they will
	9.16	the Lord will save **his people,** as a shepherd saves his
	10. 3	with those foreigners who rule **my people,** and I am going to
	10. 4	come rulers, leaders, and commanders to govern **my people.**
	10. 8	"I will call **my people** and gather them together.
	10.12	I will make **my people** strong;
	12. 5	Lord God Almighty gives strength to **his people** who live in
	13. 7	I will attack **my people** [8]and throughout the land two-thirds
	13. 9	tell them that they are **my people,** and they will confess
Mal	1. 2	The Lord says to **his people,** "I have always loved you."
	2. 9	will, and when you teach **my people,** you do not treat
	2.15	It was that you should have children who are truly **God's people.**
	3.17	"They will be **my people,"** says the Lord Almighty.
	3.18	Once again **my people** will see the difference between
Mt	1.21	him Jesus—because he will save **his people** from their sins."
	2. 6	you will come a leader who will guide **my people** Israel.'"
	13.17	many prophets and many of **God's people** wanted very much to
	13.43	Then **God's people** will shine like the sun in their Father's
	24.22	For the sake of his **chosen people,** however, God will reduce
	24.24	in order to deceive even God's **chosen people,** if possible.
	24.31	and they will gather his **chosen people** from one end of the
	27.52	broke open, and many of **God's people** who had died were
Mk	13.20	For the sake of his **chosen people,** however, he has reduced
	13.22	in order to deceive even God's **chosen people,** if possible.
	13.27	the earth to gather God's **chosen people** from one end of the
Lk	1.68	come to the help of **his people** and has set them free.
	1.77	road for him, [77]to tell **his people** that they will be saved
	4.19	that the time has come when the Lord will save **his people."**
	7.16	"God has come to save **his people!"**
	18. 7	judge in favour of his **own people** who cry to him day
Jn	1.11	to his own country, but his **own people** did not receive him.
	11.52	together into one body all the scattered **people of God.**
Acts	3.23	that prophet shall be separated from **God's people** and destroyed.'
	7.34	I have seen the cruel suffering of **my people** in Egypt.
	9.32	occasion he went to visit **God's people** who lived in Lydda.
	13.19	land of Canaan and made **his people** the owners of the land.
	18.10	able to harm you, for many in this city are **my people."**
	20.32	up and give you the blessings God has for all **his people.**
	26.10	the chief priests and put many of **God's people** in prison;
	26.18	sins forgiven and receive their place among God's **chosen people.'**
Rom	1. 7	Rome whom God loves and has called to be his **own people:**
	8.17	the blessings he keeps for **his people,** and we will also
	8.27	with God on behalf of **his people** and in accordance with his
	8.33	Who will accuse God's **chosen people?**
	9. 4	They are **God's people;**
	9. 6	for not all the people of Israel are the **people of God.**
	9.25	"The people who were not mine I will call **'My People.'**
	9.26	were told, 'You are not **my people,'** there they will be
	9.31	while **God's people,** who were seeking a law that would
	10.19	"I will use a so-called nation to make **my people** jealous;
	10.19	means of a nation of fools I will make **my people** angry."
	11. 1	Did God reject his **own people?**
	11. 2	God has not rejected **his people,** whom he chose from the beginning.
	15.10	Again it says, "Rejoice, Gentiles, with **God's people!"**
	15.25	I am going to Jerusalem in the service of **God's people** there.
	15.26	offering to help the poor among **God's people** in Jerusalem.
	15.31	my service in Jerusalem may be acceptable to **God's people** there.
	16. 2	in the Lord's name, as **God's people** should, and give her any
	16.15	to Olympas and to all of **God's people** who are with them.
1 Cor	1. 2	are called to be God's **holy people,** who belong to him in
	1.30	we become God's **holy people** and are set free.
	6. 1	heathen judges instead of letting **God's people** settle the matter?
	6. 2	Don't you know that **God's people** will judge the world?
	14.21	strange languages I will speak to **my people,** says the Lord.
	14.21	foreigners, but even then **my people** will not listen to me."
	14.33	all the churches of **God's people,** [34]the women should keep quiet
	16. 1	about the money to be raised to help **God's people** in Judaea.
	16.15	Achaia and have given themselves to the service of **God's people.**
2 Cor	1. 1	of God in Corinth, and to all **God's people** throughout Achaia:
	6.16	"I will make my home with **my people** and live among them;
	6.16	I will be their God, and they shall be **my people."**
	8. 4	of having a part in helping **God's people** in Judaea.
	9. 1	to you about the help being sent to **God's people** in Judaea.
	9.12	meets the needs of **God's people,** but also produces an outpouring
	13.12	All **God's people** send you their greetings.
Gal	6.16	and mercy be with them—with them and with all **God's people!**
Eph	1. 1	of Christ Jesus— To **God's people** in Ephesus, who are
	1.11	chose us to be his **own people** in union with Christ because
	1.13	you also became **God's people** when you heard the true message,
	1.14	receive what God has promised **his people,** and this assures
	1.15	and your love for all **God's people,** [16]I have not stopped
	1.18	wonderful blessings he promises **his people,** [19]and how very great
	2.12	You were foreigners and did not belong to God's **chosen people.**
	2.12	based on God's promises to **his people,** and you lived in this
	2.19	now fellow-citizens with **God's people** and members of the family
	3. 8	I am less than the least of all **God's people;**
	3.18	that you, together with all **God's people,** may have the power
	4.12	did this to prepare all **God's people** for the work of
	5. 3	Since you are **God's people,** it is not right that any
	6.18	pray always for all **God's people.**
Phil	1. 1	Christ Jesus— To all **God's people** in Philippi who are in
	4.21	Greetings to each one of **God's people** who belong to Christ Jesus.
	4.22	All **God's people** here send greetings, especially those who belong
Col	1. 2	our brother Timothy— [2]To **God's people** in Colossae, who are

Col 1. 4 faith in Christ Jesus and of your love for all **God's people.**
1.11 God has reserved for **his people** in the kingdom of light.
1.26 ages from all mankind but has now revealed to **his people.**
1.27 make known his secret to **his people,** this rich and glorious
3.12 You are the **people of God;**
3.24 give you as a reward what he has kept for **his people.**
2 Thes 1.10 to receive glory from all **his people** and honour from all who
2.13 power to make you his **holy people** and by your faith in
2 Tim 1. 9 called us to be his **own people,** not because of what we
2.10 for the sake of God's **chosen people,** in order that they too
Tit 1. 1 help the faith of God's **chosen people** and to lead them to
Phlm 5 of your love for all **God's people** and the faith you have
7 You have cheered the hearts of all **God's people.**
Heb 4. 9 there still remains for **God's people** a rest like God's resting
8. 6 he arranged between God and **his people** is a better one,
8. 8 But God finds fault with **his people** when he says, "The
8.10 I will be their God, and they will be **my people.**
10.30 and who also said, "The Lord will judge **his people."**
11.25 He preferred to suffer with **God's people** rather than to
13.24 Give our greetings to all your leaders and to all **God's people.**
Jas 1. 1 Greetings to all **God's people** scattered over the whole world.
1 Pet 1. 1 To God's **chosen people** who live as refugees scattered
1. 4 possessing the rich blessings that God keeps for **his people.**
2. 9 holy nation, **God's own people,** chosen to proclaim the wonderful
2.10 time you were not God's people, but now you are **his people;**
4.17 judgement to begin, and **God's own people** are the first to be
Jude 3 faith which once and for all God has given to **his people.**
Rev 5. 8 bowls filled with incense, which are the prayers of **God's people.**
8. 3 to the prayers of all **God's people** and to offer it on
8. 4 up with the prayers of **God's people** from the hands of the
13. 7 was allowed to fight against **God's people** and to defeat them,
13.10 This calls for endurance and faith on the part of **God's people."**
14.12 endurance on the part of **God's people,** those who obey God's
16. 6 poured out the blood of **God's people** and of the prophets,
17. 6 drunk with the blood of **God's people** and the blood of those
18. 4 I heard another voice from heaven, saying, "Come out, **my people!**
18.20 Be glad, **God's people** and the apostles and prophets!
18.24 blood of prophets and of **God's people** was found in the city;
19. 8 (The linen is the good deeds of **God's people.)**
20. 9 and surrounded the camp of **God's people** and the city that he
21. 3 He will live with them, and they shall be **his people.**

GOD'S POWER see **POWER**

GOD'S SON see **SON OF GOD**

GOD'S SONS see **CHILD OF GOD**

GOD'S SPIRIT see **SPIRIT (1)**

GOD'S WILL see **WILL (1)**

GOD'S WORD see **WORD (1)**

GODDESS

Ex 34.13 pillars, and cut down the symbols of their **goddess** Asherah.
Deut 7. 5 the symbols of their **goddess** Asherah, and burn their idols.
12. 3 Burn their symbols of the **goddess** Asherah and chop down their idols,
16.21 do not put beside it a wooden symbol of the **goddess** Asherah.
Judg 6.25 down the symbol of the **goddess** Asherah, which is beside it.
1 Sam 7. 3 all the foreign gods and the images of the **goddess** Astarte.
31.10 in the temple of the **goddess** Astarte, and they nailed his
1 Kgs 11. 5 He worshipped Astarte the **goddess** of Sidon,
11.33 Astarte, the **goddess** of Sidon;
14.15 aroused his anger by making idols of the **goddess** Asherah.
15.13 had made an obscene idol of the fertility **goddess** Asherah.
16.33 He also put up an image of the **goddess** Asherah.
18.19 the 400 prophets of the **goddess** Asherah who are supported by
2 Kgs 13. 6 and the image of the **goddess** Asherah remained in Samaria.
17.10 pillars and images of the **goddess** Asherah, [11]and they
17.16 made an image of the **goddess** Asherah, worshipped the stars,
18. 4 pillars, and cut down the images of the **goddess** Asherah.
21. 3 made an image of the **goddess** Asherah, as King Ahab of Israel
21. 7 placed the symbol of the **goddess** Asherah in the Temple, the
23. 4 worship of Baal, of the **goddess** Asherah, and of the stars.
23. 6 Temple the symbol of the **goddess** Asherah, took it out of the
23.13 idols—Astarte the **goddess** of Sidon, Chemosh the god
23.14 down the symbols of the **goddess** Asherah, and the ground
2 Chr 14. 3 columns, and cut down the symbols of the **goddess** Asherah.
15.16 had made an obscene idol of the fertility **goddess** Asherah.
17. 6 of worship and the symbols of the **goddess** Asherah in Judah.
19. 3 the symbols of the **goddess** Asherah which people worshipped,
24.18 to worship idols and the images of the **goddess** Asherah.
31. 1 down the symbols of the **goddess** Asherah, and destroyed the
33. 3 images of the **goddess** Asherah, and worshipped the stars.
33.19 and the symbols of the **goddess** Asherah that he made and the
34. 3 the symbols of the **goddess** Asherah, and all the other idols.
Is 17. 8 of the **goddess** Asherah and altars for burning incense.
27. 9 incense-altars or symbols of the **goddess** Asherah are left.
Jer 7.18 to bake cakes for the **goddess** they call the Queen of Heaven.
17. 2 been set up for the **goddess** Asherah by every green tree, on
44.17 will offer sacrifices to our **goddess,** the Queen of Heaven,
Mic 5.14 down the images of the **goddess** Asherah in your land and
Acts 19.24 of the temple of the **goddess** Artemis, and his business
19.27 the temple of the great **goddess** Artemis will come to mean
19.27 will be destroyed—the **goddess** worshipped by everyone in Asia
19.37 not robbed temples or said evil things about our **goddess.**

GODLESS

1 Sam 31. 4 kill me, so that these **godless** Philistines won't gloat over
2 Sam 23. 6 But **godless** men are like thorns that are thrown away;
1 Chr 10. 4 to keep these **godless** Philistines from gloating over me."
Job 8.13 **Godless** men are like those reeds;
12. 6 But thieves and **godless** men live in peace, though their only god
15.34 will be no descendants for **godless** men, and fire will
17. 8 be honest are shocked, and they all condemn me as **godless.**
27. 8 What hope is there for **godless** men in the hour when God
34.30 could do to keep **godless** oppressors from ruling them.
36.13 Those who are **godless** keep on being angry, and even when punished,
Ps 74.18 laugh at you, that they are **godless** and despise you.
74.22 Remember that **godless** people laugh at you all day long.
Prov 11. 9 ruined by the talk of **godless** people, but the wisdom of the
Is 9.17 because all the people are **godless** and wicked and everything
10. 6 sent Assyria to attack a **godless** nation, people who have
Jer 23.11 "The prophets and the priests are **godless;**
Ezek 28.10 You will die like a dog at the hand of **godless** foreigners.
Mt 12.39 "How evil and **godless** are the people of this day!"
16. 4 How evil and **godless** are the people of this day!
Mk 8.38 of my teaching in this **godless** and wicked day, then the Son
1 Tim 1. 9 lawbreakers and criminals, for the **godless** and sinful,
4. 7 keep away from those **godless** legends, which are not worth telling.
1 Pet 4.18 what, then, will become of **godless** sinners?"
2 Pet 2. 5 world, but brought the flood on the world of **godless** people;
2. 6 and made them an example of what will happen to the **godless.**
3. 7 the day when **godless** people will be judged and destroyed.
Jude 4 For some **godless** people have slipped in unnoticed among us,
15 condemn them all for the **godless** deeds they have performed
15 the terrible words that **godless** sinners have spoken against him!"
18 who will mock you, people who follow their own **godless** desires."

GODLY

Acts 3.12 of our own power or **godliness** that we made this man walk?
1 Tim 4. 7 Keep yourself in training for a **godly** life.
6.11 Strive for righteousness, **godliness,** faith, love, endurance, and gentleness.
2 Tim 3.12 who wants to live a **godly** life in union with Christ Jesus
Tit 2.12 to live self-controlled, upright, and **godly** lives in this world,
2 Pet 1. 6 to your endurance add **godliness;**
1. 7 to your **godliness** add brotherly affection;
2. 9 Lord knows how to rescue **godly** people from their trials and

GOG (1)

Warrior, otherwise unidentified.

Ezek 38. 2 "Mortal man," he said, "denounce **Gog,** chief ruler
38.10 This is what the Sovereign Lord says to **Gog:**
38.14 Lord sent me to tell **Gog** what he was saying to him:
38.18 "On the day when **Gog** invades Israel, I will be furious.
38.21 I will terrify **Gog** with all sorts of calamities.
39. 1 Lord said, "Mortal man, denounce **Gog,** the chief ruler
39. 4 **Gog** and his army and his allies will fall dead
39.11 happens, I will give **Gog** a burial-ground there in Israel,
39.11 **Gog** and all his army will be buried there,
39.11 and the valley will be called 'The Valley of **Gog's** Army.'
39.15 can come and bury it in the Valley of **Gog's** Army.
Rev 20. 8 nations scattered over the whole world, that is, **Gog** and Magog.

GOLD

Gen 2.12 (Pure **gold** is found there and also rare perfume
13. 2 with sheep, goats, and cattle, as well as silver and **gold.**
24.22 the man took an expensive **gold** ring and put it
24.22 in her nose and put two large **gold** bracelets on her arms.
24.35 and goats, cattle, silver, **gold,** male and female slaves,
24.53 and silver and **gold** jewellery, and gave them to Rebecca.
41.42 linen robe on him, and placed a **gold** chain round his neck.
44. 8 Why then should we steal silver or **gold** from your master's house?
Ex 3.22 and will ask for clothing and for **gold** and silver jewellery.
11. 2 to ask their neighbours for **gold** and silver jewellery."
12.35 Egyptians for **gold** and silver jewellery and for clothing.
20.23 yourselves gods of silver or **gold** to be worshipped in
25. 3 **gold,** silver, and bronze;
25.11 Cover it with pure **gold** inside and out
25.11 and put a **gold** border all round it.
25.12 Make four carrying-rings of **gold** for it and attach them
25.13 acacia-wood and cover them with **gold** [14]and put them
25.17 "Make a lid of pure **gold,** 110 centimetres long
25.18 two winged creatures of hammered **gold,** [19]one for each end
25.24 Cover it with pure **gold** and put a gold border round it.
25.25 75 millimetres wide round it and a **gold** border round the rim.
25.26 Make four carrying-rings of **gold** for it and put them at
25.28 Make the poles of acacia-wood and cover them with **gold.**
25.29 All of these are to be made of pure **gold.**
25.31 "Make a lamp-stand of pure **gold.**
25.31 Make its base and its shaft of hammered **gold;**
25.36 lamp-stand are to be a single piece of pure hammered **gold.**
25.38 Make its tongs and trays of pure **gold.**
25.39 Use thirty-five kilogrammes of pure **gold** to make the
26. 6 Make fifty **gold** hooks with which to join the two sets into
26.29 Cover the frames with **gold** and fit them with gold rings

Ex 26.29 hold the cross-bars, which are also to be covered with **gold.**
26.32 posts of acacia-wood covered with **gold,** fitted with hooks,
26.37 of acacia-wood covered with **gold** and fitted with gold hooks;
28. 5 blue, purple, and red wool, **gold** thread, and fine linen.
28. 6 blue, purple, and red wool, **gold** thread, and fine linen,
28.11 of the sons of Jacob, and mount the stones in **gold** settings.
28.13 Make two **gold** settings [14]and two chains of pure gold
28.20 These are to be mounted in **gold** settings.
28.22 For the breast-piece make chains of pure **gold,** twisted like cords.
28.23 Make two **gold** rings and attach them to the upper corners
28.24 and fasten the two **gold** cords to the two rings.
28.26 Then make two rings of **gold** and attach them to the lower
28.27 Make two more **gold** rings and attach them to the lower
28.33 of blue, purple, and red wool, alternating with **gold** bells.
28.36 "Make an ornament of pure **gold** and engrave on it
30. 3 projections with pure gold, and put a **gold** border round it.
30. 4 Make two **gold** carrying-rings for it and attach them below
30. 5 Make these poles of acacia-wood and cover them with **gold.**
31. 4 for planning skilful designs and working them in **gold,**
31. 8 the lamp-stand of pure **gold** and all its equipment,
32. 2 to them, "Take off the **gold** earrings which your wives, your
32. 3 took off their **gold** earrings and brought them to Aaron.
32. 4 poured the gold into a mould, and made a **gold** bull-calf.
32. 5 altar in front of the **gold** bull and announced, "Tomorrow
32. 8 a bull-calf out of melted **gold** and have worshipped it and
32.24 them to bring me their **gold** ornaments, and those who had any
32.31 They have made a god out of **gold** and worshipped it.
32.35 because they had caused Aaron to make the **gold** bull-calf.
35. 5 do so is to bring an offering of **gold,** silver, or bronze;
35.22 necklaces, and all kinds of **gold** jewellery and dedicated
35.32 for planning skilful designs and working them in **gold,**
36.13 They made fifty **gold** hooks, with which to join the two
36.34 They covered the frames with **gold** and fitted them with gold
36.34 to hold the cross-bars, which were also covered with **gold.**
36.36 covered them with **gold,** and fitted them with gold hooks.
36.38 tops and their rods with **gold,** and made five bronze bases
37. 2 He covered it with pure **gold** inside and out
37. 2 and put a **gold** border all round it.
37. 3 He made four carrying-rings of **gold** for it and attached
37. 4 of acacia-wood, covered them with **gold,** [5]and put them
37. 6 made a lid of pure **gold,** 110 centimetres long and 66
37. 7 two winged creatures of hammered **gold,** [8]one for each end of
37.11 covered it with pure gold and put a **gold** border round it.
37.12 wide round it and put a **gold** border round the rim.
37.13 He made four carrying-rings of **gold** for it and put them
37.15 He made the poles of acacia-wood and covered them with **gold.**
37.16 He made the dishes of pure **gold** for the table:
37.17 He made the lamp-stand of pure **gold.**
37.17 He made its base and its shaft of hammered **gold;**
37.22 the lamp-stand were a single piece of pure hammered **gold.**
37.23 lamp-stand, and he made its tongs and trays of pure **gold.**
37.24 used 35 kilogrammes of pure **gold** to make the lamp-stand and
37.26 projections with pure gold and put a **gold** border round it.
37.27 He made two **gold** carrying-rings for it and attached them
37.28 He made the poles of acacia-wood and covered them with **gold.**
38.24 All the **gold** that had been dedicated to the Lord for the
39. 2 and **gold** thread.
39. 3 They hammered out sheets of **gold** and cut them into thin
39. 6 They prepared the carnelians and mounted them in **gold** settings;
39.13 These were mounted in **gold** settings.
39.15 For the breast-piece they made chains of pure **gold,**
39.16 They made two **gold** settings and two gold rings
39.17 They fastened the two **gold** cords to the two rings
39.19 They made two rings of **gold** and attached them
39.20 They made two more **gold** rings and attached them
39.24 alternating with bells of pure **gold,** just as the Lord had
39.30 of dedication, out of pure **gold,** and they engraved on it
39.37 the lamp-stand of pure **gold,** its lamps, all its equipment,
39.38 the **gold** altar;
40. 5 Put the **gold** altar for burning incense in front of the
40.26 He put the **gold** altar in the Tent, in front of the
Lev 8. 9 it he put the **gold** ornament, the sacred sign of dedication,
24. 4 on the lampstand of pure **gold** and must see that they burn
24. 6 covered with pure **gold,** which is in the Lord's presence.
Num 4.11 a blue cloth over the **gold** altar, put a fine leather cover
7.12 one **gold** dish weighing 110 grammes, full of incense;
7.84 **gold** dishes weighing a total of 1.32 kilogrammes,
8. 4 lamp-stand was made of hammered **gold,** according to the
22.18 me all the silver and **gold** in his palace, I could not
24.13 me all the silver and **gold** in your palace, I could not
31.22 will not burn, such as **gold,** silver, bronze, iron, tin, or
31.50 So we are bringing the **gold** ornaments, armlets,
31.51 Moses and Eleazar received the **gold,** all of which was in
31.54 Moses and Eleazar took the **gold** to the Tent, so that the
Deut 7.25 not desire the silver or **gold** that is on them, and do
8.13 and sheep, your silver and **gold,** and all your other
17.17 and he is not to make himself rich with silver and **gold.**
29.17 You saw their disgusting idols made of wood, stone, silver, and **gold.**
Josh 6.19 Everything made of silver, **gold,** bronze, or iron is set
6.24 except the things made of **gold,** silver, bronze, and iron,
7.21 silver, and a bar of **gold** weighing over half a kilogramme.
7.24 the bar of **gold,** together with Achan's sons and daughters,
22. 6 of livestock, silver, **gold,** bronze, iron, and many clothes.
Judg 8.24 (The Midianites, like other desert people, wore **gold** earrings.)
8.26 **gold** earrings that Gideon received weighed nearly twenty kilogrammes,
8.27 made an idol from the **gold** and put it in his home
1 Sam 6. 4 They answered, "Five **gold** models of tumours and five gold mice,
6. 8 a box beside it the **gold** models that you are sending to
6.11 with the box containing the **gold** models of the mice and of

1 Sam 6.15 and the box with the **gold** models in it, and placed them
6.17 The Philistines sent the five **gold** tumours to the Lord
6.18 They also sent **gold** mice, one for each of the cities
2 Sam 1.24 rich scarlet dresses and adorned you with jewels and **gold.**
8. 7 David captured the **gold** shields carried by Hadadezer's
8.10 Joram took David presents made of **gold,** silver, and bronze.
8.11 along with the silver and **gold** he took from the nations he
12.30 god Molech David took a **gold** crown which weighed about
21. 4 be settled with silver or **gold,** nor do we want to kill
1 Kgs 6.20 wide, and nine metres high, all covered with pure **gold.**
6.21 the Temple was covered with **gold,**
6.21 and **gold** chains were placed across the entrance
6.21 of the inner room, which was also covered with **gold.**
6.22 the Temple was covered with **gold,** as well as the altar in
6.28 The two winged creatures were covered with **gold.**
6.30 Even the floor was covered with **gold.**
6.32 the winged creatures, and the palm-trees were covered with **gold.**
6.35 and flowers, which were evenly covered with **gold.**
7.48 Solomon also had **gold** furnishings made for the Temple:
7.50 All these furnishings were made of **gold.**
7.51 dedicated to the Lord—the silver, **gold,** and other articles.
9.11 and pine and with all the **gold** he wanted for this work.
9.14 Hiram had sent Solomon more than four thousand kilogrammes of **gold.**
9.28 to Solomon more than fourteen thousand kilogrammes of **gold.**
10. 2 loaded with spices, jewels, and a large amount of **gold.**
10.10 four thousand kilogrammes of **gold** and a very large amount
10.11 (Hiram's fleet, which had brought **gold** from Ophir, also
10.14 almost twenty-three thousand kilogrammes of **gold**
10.16 had each one overlaid with almost seven kilogrammes of **gold.**
10.17 each one of them with almost two kilogrammes of **gold.**
10.18 ivory and the rest of it was covered with the finest **gold.**
10.21 drinking cups were made of **gold,** and all the utensils
10.21 in the Hall of the Forest of Lebanon were of pure **gold.**
10.22 years his fleet would return, bringing **gold,** silver, ivory,
10.25 gift—articles of silver and **gold,** robes, weapons, spices,
12.28 he made two bull-calves of **gold** and said to his people,
12.29 He placed one of the **gold** bull-calves in Bethel and the
12.32 he offered sacrifices to the **gold** bull-calves he had made,
14.26 including the **gold** shields Solomon had made.
15.15 God, as well as the **gold** and silver objects that he himself
15.18 took all the silver and **gold** that was left in the Temple
15.19 This silver and **gold** is a present for you.
20. 3 to him your silver and **gold,** your women and the strongest of
20. 5 to me your silver and **gold,** your women and your children.
20. 7 my wives and children, my silver and **gold,** and I agreed."
22.48 ocean-going ships to sail to the land of Ophir for **gold;**
2 Kgs 5. 5 thousand pieces of **gold,** and ten changes of fine clothes.
7. 8 there, grabbed the silver, **gold,** and clothing they found,
10.29 the sin of worshipping the **gold** bull-calves he set up in
12.13 the lamps, or any other article of silver or of **gold.**
12.18 own offerings and all the **gold** in the treasuries of the
14.14 took all the silver and **gold** he could find, all the temple
16. 8 Ahaz took the silver and **gold** from the Temple and the
18.14 kilogrammes of silver and a thousand kilogrammes of **gold.**
18.16 he also stripped the **gold** from the temple doors
18.16 and the **gold** with which he himself had covered
20.13 his wealth—his silver and **gold,** his spices and perfumes, and
23.33 thirty-four kilogrammes of **gold** as tribute.
24.13 Nebuchadnezzar broke up all the **gold** utensils
25.15 everything that was made of **gold** or silver, including the
1 Chr 18. 7 David captured the **gold** shields carried by Hadadezer's
18.10 Joram brought David presents made of **gold,** silver, and
18.11 along with the silver and **gold** he took from the nations he
20. 2 Ammonite idol Molech had a **gold** crown
21.25 he paid Araunah six hundred **gold** coins for the threshing-place.
22.14 than 3,400 metric tons of **gold** and over 34,000 metric tons
22.16 of every sort who can work [16]with **gold,** silver, bronze,
28.14 to how much silver and **gold** was to be used for making
28.16 silver tables, and for each **gold** table on which were placed
28.17 as to how much pure **gold** was to be used in making
28.17 jars, how much silver and **gold** in making dishes,
28.18 and how much pure **gold** in making the altar
29. 2 prepare materials for the Temple—**gold,** silver, bronze, iron,
29. 3 I have given silver and **gold** from my personal property
29. 4 metric tons of the finest **gold** and almost two hundred and
29. 7 170 metric tons of **gold,** over 340 metric tons of silver,
2 Chr 1.15 During his reign silver and **gold** became as common in
2. 7 skill in engraving, in working **gold,** silver, bronze, and
2.14 to make things out of **gold,** silver, bronze, iron, stone, and
3. 4 The inside of the room was overlaid with pure **gold.**
3. 5 cedar and overlaid with fine **gold,** in which were worked
3. 6 stones and with **gold** imported from the land of Parvaim.
3. 7 He used the **gold** to overlay the temple walls, the rafters,
3. 8 Over twenty metric tons of **gold** were used to cover the walls
3. 9 570 grammes of **gold** were used for making nails,
3. 9 the walls of the upper rooms were also covered with **gold.**
3.10 of metal, cover them with **gold,** and place them in the Most
4. 7 They made ten **gold** lampstands according to the usual pattern,
4. 7 They also made a hundred **gold** bowls.
4.19 King Solomon also had **gold** furnishings made for the Temple:
4.20 and the lamps of fine **gold** that were to burn in front
4.22 All these objects were made of pure **gold.**
4.22 the doors to the Most Holy Place were overlaid with **gold.**
5. 1 dedicated to the Lord—the silver, **gold,** and other articles.
8.18 to Solomon more than fifteen thousand kilogrammes of **gold.**
9. 1 loaded with spices, jewels, and a large amount of **gold.**
9. 9 than four thousand kilogrammes of **gold** and a very large
9.10 of King Solomon who brought **gold** from Ophir also brought
9.13 almost twenty-three thousand kilogrammes of **gold,**
9.14 of the Israelite districts also brought him silver and **gold.**

2 Chr	9.15	about seven kilogrammes of beaten **gold,**
	9.16	each covered with about three kilogrammes of beaten **gold.**
	9.17	with ivory and the rest of it was covered with pure **gold.**
	9.18	and there was a footstool attached to it, covered with **gold.**
	9.20	Solomon's cups were made of **gold,** and all the utensils
	9.20	in the Hall of the Forest of Lebanon were of pure **gold.**
	9.21	years his fleet would return, bringing **gold,** silver, ivory,
	9.24	gifts—articles of silver and **gold,** robes, weapons, spices,
	12. 9	including the **gold** shields that King Solomon had made.
	13. 8	and have with you the **gold** bull-calves that Jeroboam made to
	13.11	every evening they light the lamps on the **gold** lampstand.
	15.18	God, as well as the **gold** and silver objects that he himself
	16. 2	So Asa took silver and **gold** from the treasuries of the
	16. 3	This silver and **gold** is a present for you.
	21. 3	amounts of **gold,** silver, and other valuable possessions,
	24.14	repairs were finished, the remaining **gold** and silver was
	25.24	Samaria as loot all the **gold** and silver in the Temple, the
	28.21	So Ahaz took the **gold** from the Temple, the palace, and
	32.27	had storerooms built for his **gold,** silver, precious stones,
	36. 3	34 kilogrammes of **gold** as tribute.
Ezra	1. 4	them with silver and **gold,** supplies and pack animals,
	1. 6	utensils, **gold,** supplies, pack animals, other valuables,
	1. 9	**gold** bowls for offerings 30
	1. 9	small **gold** bowls 30
	1.11	In all there were 5,400 **gold** and silver bowls
	2.69	to 500 kilogrammes of **gold,**
	5.14	He restored the **gold** and silver temple utensils
	6. 5	Also the **gold** and silver utensils which King Nebuchadnezzar
	7.15	to take with you the **gold** and silver offerings which I and
	7.16	take all the silver and **gold** which you collect throughout
	7.18	may use the silver and **gold** that is left over for whatever
	8.25	the silver, the **gold,** and the utensils which the emperor,
	8.26	**gold** - 3,400 kilogrammes
	8.26	20 **gold** bowls - 8.4 kilogrammes
	8.26	2 fine bronze bowls, equal in value to **gold** bowls
	8.28	are all the silver and **gold** utensils brought to him as
	8.30	charge of the silver, the **gold,** and the utensils, to take
	8.33	Temple, weighed the silver, the **gold,** and the utensils, and
Neh	3. 8	Uzziel son of Harhaiah, a **goldsmith,** built the next section.
	3.31	Malchijah, a **goldsmith,** built the next section, as far
	3.32	The **goldsmiths** and the merchants built the last section,
	7.70	The governor 8 kilogrammes of **gold**
	7.70	Heads of clans 168 kilogrammes of **gold**
	7.70	The rest of the people 168 kilogrammes of **gold**
Esth	1. 6	Couches made of **gold** and silver had been placed in the courtyard,
	1. 7	Drinks were served in **gold** cups, no two of them alike, and
	4.11	the king holds out his **gold** sceptre to someone, then that
	5. 2	won his favour, and he held out to her the **gold** sceptre.
	8. 4	The king held out the **gold** sceptre to her, so she stood
	8.15	a cloak of fine purple linen, and a magnificent **gold** crown.
Job	3.15	who filled their houses with **gold** and silver,
	22.24	Throw away your **gold;**
	22.24	dump your finest **gold** in the dry stream bed.
	22.25	Let Almighty God be your **gold,** and let him be silver,
	28. 1	There are places where **gold** is refined.
	28. 6	The stones of the earth contain sapphires, And its dust contains **gold.**
	28.15	It cannot be bought with silver or **gold.**
	28.16	The finest **gold** and jewels Cannot equal its value.
	28.17	It is worth more than **gold,** Than a gold vase
	28.19	finest topaz and the purest **gold** Cannot compare with the
	37.22	A **golden** glow is seen in the north, and the glory of
	42.11	Each of them gave him some money and a **gold** ring.
Ps	19.10	They are more desirable than the finest **gold;**
	21. 3	with great blessings and set a crown of **gold** on his head.
	45. 9	throne stands the queen, wearing ornaments of finest **gold.**
	45.13	Her gown is made of **gold** thread.
	68.13	doves covered with silver, whose wings glittered with fine **gold.**
	72.15	May he be given **gold** from Arabia;
	105.37	they carried silver and **gold,** and all of them were healthy
	106.19	They made a **gold** bull-calf at Sinai and worshipped that idol;
	115. 4	Their gods are made of silver and **gold,** formed by human hands.
	119.127	I love your commands more than **gold,** more than the finest gold.
	135.15	The gods of the nations are made of silver and **gold;**
Prov	3.14	it is worth more to you than **gold.**
	8.10	choose knowledge rather than the finest **gold.**
	8.19	better than the finest **gold,** better than the purest silver.
	11.22	good judgement is like a **gold** ring in a pig's snout.
	16.16	better—to have wisdom and knowledge than **gold** and silver.
	17. 3	**Gold** and silver are tested by fire, and a person's heart
	20.15	you have something more valuable than **gold** or jewels.
	25.11	An idea well-expressed is like a design of **gold,** set in silver.
	25.12	than gold rings or jewellery made of the finest **gold.**
	27.21	Fire tests **gold** and silver;
Ecc	2. 8	also piled up silver and **gold** from the royal treasuries of
	12. 6	chain will snap, and the **golden** lamp will fall and break;
Song	1.11	will make for you a chain of **gold** with ornaments of silver.
	3.10	over it is cloth embroidered with **gold.**
	5.15	His thighs are columns of alabaster set in sockets of **gold.**
Is	2. 7	is full of silver and **gold,** and there is no end to
	2.20	will throw away the **gold** and silver idols they have made,
	13.12	Those who survive will be scarcer than **gold.**
	13.17	They care nothing for silver and are not tempted by **gold.**
	30.22	and your idols covered with **gold,** and will throw them away
	31. 7	throw away the sinful idols you made out of silver and **gold.**
	39. 2	his wealth—his silver and **gold,** his spices and perfumes, and
	40.19	make, that metalworkers cover with **gold** and set in a base of
	40.20	afford silver or **gold** chooses wood that will not rot.
	41. 7	The carpenter says to the **goldsmith,** 'Well done!'
	46. 6	People open their purses and pour out **gold;**
	46. 6	They hire a **goldsmith** to make a god;
Is	60. 6	They will come from Sheba, bringing **gold** and incense.
	60. 9	bring with them silver and **gold** To honour the name of the
	60.17	"I will bring you **gold** instead of bronze, Silver and
Jer	10. 4	of the woodcarver, [4]and decorated with silver and **gold.**
	10. 9	silver from Spain and with **gold** from Uphaz, all the work of
	51. 7	Babylonia was like a **gold** cup in my hand, making the whole
	52.19	They took away everything that was made of **gold** or silver:
Lam	4. 1	Our glittering **gold** has grown dull;
	4. 2	as precious to us as **gold,** but now they are treated like
Ezek	7.19	They will throw their **gold** and silver away in the
	7.19	refuse, because neither silver nor **gold** can save them when
	7.19	**Gold** and silver led them into sin.
	16.13	You had ornaments of **gold** and silver, and you always
	16.17	You took the silver and **gold** jewellery that I had given you,
	27.22	Sheba and Raamah exchanged jewels, **gold,** and the finest spices.
	28. 4	and skill made you rich with treasures of **gold** and silver.
	28.13	You had ornaments of **gold.**
	38.13	intend to get silver and **gold,** livestock and property, and
Dan	2.32	Its head was made of the finest **gold;**
	2.35	iron, clay, bronze, silver, and **gold** crumbled and became
	2.38	You are the head of **gold.**
	2.45	the statue made of iron, bronze, clay, silver, and **gold.**
	3. 1	King Nebuchadnezzar had a **gold** statue made, twenty-seven
	3. 5	bow down and worship the **gold** statue that King
	3. 7	bowed down and worshipped the **gold** statue which King
	3.10	bow down and worship the **gold** statue, [11]and that anyone
	3.14	and to bow down to the **gold** statue I have set up?
	3.18	not bow down to the **gold** statue that you have set up."
	5. 2	orders to bring in the **gold** and silver cups and bowls which
	5. 3	At once the **gold** cups and bowls were brought in, and they
	5. 4	and praised gods made of **gold,** silver, bronze, iron, wood,
	5. 7	of royal purple, wear a **gold** chain of honour round his neck,
	5.16	royal purple, wear a **gold** chain of honour round your neck,
	5.23	and praised gods made of **gold,** silver, bronze, iron, wood,
	5.29	purple and to hang a **gold** chain of honour round his neck.
	10. 5	who was wearing linen clothes and a belt of fine **gold.**
	11. 8	and the articles of **gold** and silver dedicated to those gods.
	11.38	He will offer **gold,** silver, jewels, and other rich gifts to
	11.43	away Egypt's hidden treasures of **gold** and silver and its
Hos	2. 8	and all the silver and **gold** that she used in the worship
	8. 4	They took their silver and **gold** and made idols—for their own
	8. 5	I hate the **gold** bull worshipped by the people of the city
	8. 6	The **gold** bull worshipped in Samaria will be smashed to pieces!
	10. 5	afraid and will mourn the loss of the **gold** bull at Bethel.
	10. 5	They will wail when it is stripped of its **golden** splendour.
Joel	3. 5	have taken my silver and **gold** and carried my rich treasures
Nah	2. 9	Plunder the **gold!**
Hab	2.19	be covered with silver and **gold,** but there is no life in
Zeph	1.18	his fury, not even all their silver and **gold** will save them.
Hag	2. 8	All the silver and **gold** of the world is mine.
Zech	4. 2	"A lamp-stand made of **gold,"** I answered.
	4.12	beside the two **gold** pipes from which the olive-oil pours?"
	6.11	out of the silver and **gold** they have given, and put it
	9. 3	up so much silver and **gold** that it is as common as
	13. 9	I will test them as **gold** is tested.
	14.14	the nations—**gold,** silver, and clothing in great abundance.
Mal	3. 3	a metal-worker refines silver and **gold,** so the Lord's
Mt	2.11	brought out their gifts of **gold,** frankincense, and myrrh,
	10. 9	Do not carry any **gold,** silver, or copper money in your pockets;
	23.16	if he swears by the **gold** in the Temple, he is bound.'
	23.17	important, the gold or the Temple which makes the **gold** holy?
	25.15	one he gave five thousand **gold coins,** to another he gave two
Lk	19.13	and gave them each a **gold coin** and told them, 'See what
	19.16	'Sir, I have earned ten **gold coins** with the one you gave
	19.18	'Sir, I have earned five **gold coins** with the one you gave
	19.20	"Another servant came and said, 'Sir, here is your **gold coin;**
	19.24	were standing there, 'Take the **gold coin** away from him and
Acts	17.29	anything like an image of **gold** or silver or stone, shaped by
	20.33	I have not wanted anyone's silver or **gold** or clothing.
1 Cor	3.12	Some will use **gold** or silver or precious stones in
1 Tim	2. 9	fancy hair styles or with **gold** ornaments or pearls
2 Tim	2.20	some are made of silver and **gold,** others of wood and clay;
Heb	9. 4	In it were the **gold** altar for the burning of incense and
	9. 4	Covenant Box all covered with **gold** and containing the **gold** jar
Jas	2. 2	a rich man wearing a **gold** ring and fine clothes comes to
	5. 3	Your **gold** and silver are covered with rust, and this rust
1 Pet	1. 7	Even **gold,** which can be destroyed, is tested by fire;
	1. 7	is much more precious than **gold,** must also be tested, so
	1.18	not something that can be destroyed, such as silver or **gold;**
Rev	1.12	and I saw seven **gold** lamp-stands, [13]and among them there was
	1.13	that reached to his feet, and a **gold** belt round his chest.
	1.20	you see in my right hand, and of the seven **gold** lamp-stands:
	2. 1	right hand and who walks among the seven **gold** lamp-stands.
	3.18	to buy gold from me, pure **gold,** in order to be rich.
	4. 4	twenty-four elders dressed in white and wearing crowns of **gold.**
	5. 8	Each had a harp and **gold** bowls filled with incense, which
	8. 3	Another angel, who had a **gold** incense-burner, came and stood
	8. 3	to offer it on the **gold** altar that stands before the throne.
	9. 7	seemed to be crowns of **gold,** and their faces were like men's
	9.13	from the four corners of the **gold** altar standing before God.
	9.20	demons, nor the idols of **gold,** silver, bronze, stone, and wood,
	14.14	being, with a crown of **gold** on his head and a sharp
	15. 6	clean shining linen and with **gold** belts tied around their chests.
	15. 7	gave the seven angels seven **gold** bowls full of the anger of
	17. 4	and covered with **gold** ornaments, precious stones, and pearls.
	17. 4	her hand she held a **gold** cup full of obscene and filthy
	18.12	no one buys their **gold,** silver, precious stones, and
	18.16	cover herself with **gold** ornaments, precious stones, and pearls!
	21.15	spoke to me had a **gold** measuring-rod to measure the city,
	21.18	the city itself was made of pure **gold,** as clear as glass.
	21.21	The street of the city was of pure **gold,** transparent as glass.

GOLIATH
Philistine giant defeated by David (or Elhanan).

1 Sam 17. 4 A man named **Goliath,** from the city of Gath, came out
17. 8 **Goliath** stood and shouted at the Israelites, "What are you doing there,
17.16 **Goliath** challenged the Israelites every morning and evening
17.23 he was talking to them, **Goliath** came forward and challenged
17.24 When the Israelites saw **Goliath,** they ran away in terror.
17.27 told him what would be done for the man who killed **Goliath.**
17.40 With his catapult ready, he went out to meet **Goliath.**
17.48 **Goliath** started walking towards David again,
17.49 his bag and took out a stone, which he slung at **Goliath.**
17.49 broke his skull, and **Goliath** fell face downwards on the ground.
17.50 David defeated and killed **Goliath** with a catapult and a stone!
17.51 him, stood over him, took **Goliath's** sword out of its sheath,
17.54 David picked up **Goliath's** head and took it to Jerusalem,
17.54 but he kept **Goliath's** weapons in his own tent.
17.55 David going out to fight **Goliath,** he asked Abner, the
17.57 David returned to camp after killing **Goliath,**
17.57 David was still carrying **Goliath's** head.
18. 6 David was returning after killing **Goliath** and as the
19. 5 his life when he killed **Goliath,** and the Lord won a great
21. 9 "I have the sword of **Goliath** the Philistine,
22.10 David some food and the sword of **Goliath** the Philistine."
2 Sam 21.19 of Jair from Bethlehem killed **Goliath** from Gath, whose spear
1 Chr 20. 5 killed Lahmi, the brother of **Goliath** from Gath, whose spear

GOMORRAH
One of the "cities of the plain" destroyed at the same time as Sodom.

Gen 10.19 eastwards to Sodom, **Gomorrah,** Admah, and Zeboiim near Lasha.
13.10 the Lord had destroyed the cities of Sodom and **Gomorrah.)**
14. 2 Birsha of **Gomorrah,**
14. 8 Then the kings of Sodom, **Gomorrah,** Admah, Zeboiim, and
14.10 the kings of Sodom and **Gomorrah** tried to run away from the
14.11 took everything in Sodom and **Gomorrah,** including the food,
18.20 against Sodom and **Gomorrah,** and their sin is very great.
19.24 the cities of Sodom and **Gomorrah** [25] and destroyed them
19.28 looked down at Sodom and **Gomorrah** and the whole valley
Deut 29.23 the cities of Sodom and **Gomorrah,** of Admah and Zeboiim,
32.32 enemies, corrupt as Sodom and **Gomorrah,** are like vines that
Is 1. 9 totally destroyed, just as Sodom and **Gomorrah** were.
1.10 rulers and your people are like those of Sodom and **Gomorrah.**
13.19 Lord, will overthrow Babylon as I did Sodom and **Gomorrah!**
Jer 23.14 they are all as bad as the people of Sodom and **Gomorrah.**
49.18 as happened to Sodom and **Gomorrah,** when they and the near-by
50.40 as happened to Sodom and **Gomorrah,** when I destroyed them and
Amos 4.11 "I destroyed some of you as I destroyed Sodom and **Gomorrah.**
Zeph 2. 9 Moab and Ammon are going to be destroyed like Sodom and **Gomorrah.**
Mt 10.15 the people of Sodom and **Gomorrah** than to the people of that
Rom 9.29 have become like Sodom, we would have been like **Gomorrah."**
2 Pet 2. 6 the cities of Sodom and **Gomorrah,** destroying them with fire,
Jude 7 Remember Sodom and **Gomorrah,** and the nearby towns,

GONG

1 Cor 13. 1 speech is no more than a noisy **gong** or a clanging bell.

GONORRHOEA

2 Sam 3.29 in his family who has **gonorrhoea** or a dreaded skin disease

GOOD
[FOR YOUR OWN GOOD]

Gen 2. 9 kinds of beautiful trees grow there and produce **good** fruit.
2. 9 tree that gives knowledge of what is **good** and what is bad.
2.17 tree that gives knowledge of what is **good** and what is bad.
2.18 God said, "It is not **good** for the man to live alone.
3. 5 be like God and know what is **good** and what is bad."
3. 6 the tree was and how **good** its fruit would be to eat,
3.22 us and has knowledge of what is **good** and what is bad.
6. 9 had no faults and was the only **good** man of his time.
6.14 Build a boat for yourself out of **good** timber;
15. 2 Abram answered, "Sovereign Lord, what **good** will your reward do me,
25.32 what **good** will my rights do me then?"
31.39 You demanded that I make **good** anything that was stolen
33. 5 whom God has been **good** enough to give me," Jacob answered.
41.30 of famine, and all the **good** years will be forgotten, because
41.35 all the food during the **good** years that are coming, and give
44. 4 with them, ask them, 'Why have you paid back evil for **good?**
47.25 you have been **good** to us, sir, and we will be the
49.15 the resting-place is **good** And that the land is delightful.
50.20 but God turned it into **good,** in order to preserve the lives
Ex 1.20 midwives feared God, he was **good** to them and gave them
4.10 I have never been a **good** speaker, and I haven't become one
18.19 let me give you some **good** advice, and God will be with
21.36 penned up, he must make **good** the loss by giving the other
22. 5 man's field, he must make **good** the loss with the crops from
Lev 26.16 it will do you no **good,** because your enemies will conquer
26.20 work will do you no **good,** because your land will not produce
27.12 for it, according to its **good** or bad qualities, and the
27.14 the price according to its **good** or bad points, and the price
Num 13.19 out whether the land is **good** or bad and whether the people
32. 3 Sibmah, Nebo, and Beon—is **good** land for livestock, and we
Deut 1.14 And you agreed that this was a **good** thing to do.
1.23 "That seemed a **good** thing to do, so I selected twelve men,
Deut 4.15 **For your own good,** then, make certain [16] that you do not
6.11 houses will be full of **good** things which you did not put
6.18 Lord says is right and **good,** and all will go well with
8.12 to eat and have built **good** houses to live in [13] and when
8.16 so that in the end he could bless you with **good** things.
9. 5 is not because you are **good** and do what is right that
11.17 even though it is a **good** land that he is giving you.
12. 7 eat and enjoy the **good** things that you have worked for.
26.11 Be grateful for the **good** things that the Lord your God
29.19 That would destroy all of you, **good** and evil alike.
30.15 you a choice between **good** and evil, between life and death.
33.16 filled with all that is **good,** Blessed by the goodness of the
33.16 is good, Blessed by the **goodness** of the Lord, Who spoke from
33.23 "Naphtali is richly blessed by the Lord's **good** favour;
34. 7 he was as strong as ever, and his eyesight was still **good.**
Josh 23.13 you are left in this **good** land which the Lord your God
23.14 your God has given you all the **good** things that he promised.
23.16 will be left in this **good** land that he has given you."
24.20 He will destroy you, even though he was **good** to you before."
Judg 9.11 you, I would have to stop producing my **good** sweet fruit.'
18. 9 We saw the land, and it's very **good.**
19. 5 It will do you **good.**
19. 9 stay here and have a **good** time.
Ruth 1. 6 Lord had blessed his people by giving them a **good** harvest;
1. 8 May the Lord be as **good** to you as you have been
3. 7 Boaz had finished eating and drinking, he was in a **good** mood.
1 Sam 10.27 people said, "How can this fellow do us any **good?"**
12.23 will teach you what is **good** and right for you to do.
15. 9 the best calves and lambs, or anything else that was **good;**
20.12 If his attitude towards you is **good,** I will send you word.
24.17 You have been so **good** to me, while I have done such
24.18 Today you have shown how **good** you are to me, because you
25.15 Yet they were very **good** to us;
25.30 Lord has done all the **good** things he has promised you and
25.36 was drunk and in a **good** mood, so she did not tell
2 Sam 9. 8 Why should you be so **good** to me?"
14.17 is like God's angel and can distinguish **good** from evil.
17. 4 This seemed like **good** advice to Absalom
17. 7 "The advice Ahithophel gave you this time is no **good.**
17.14 Lord had decided that Ahithophel's **good** advice would not be followed,
18.27 "He's a **good** man," the king said,
22.26 to you, and completely **good** to those who are perfect.
1 Kgs 1.42 "You're a **good** man—you must be bringing good news."
3. 6 your servant, and he was **good,** loyal, and honest in his
3. 9 justice and to know the difference between **good** and evil.
14.15 people of Israel from this **good** land which he gave to their
20.33 watching for a **good** sign, and when Ahab said "brother,"
22. 8 But I hate him, because he never prophesies anything **good** for me;
22.18 "Didn't I tell you that he never prophesies anything **good** for me?
2 Kgs 16. 2 He did not follow the **good** example of his ancestor King David;
20.19 "The message you have given me from the Lord is **good."**
1 Chr 16.34 Give thanks to the Lord, because he is **good;**
26.14 a man who always gave **good** advice, drew the north gate.
28. 8 may continue to possess this **good** land and so that you may
2 Chr 5.11 "Praise the Lord, because he is **good,** And his love is eternal."
6.41 all your people be happy because of your **goodness** to them.
7. 3 God and praising him for his **goodness** and his eternal love.
14. 2 pleased the Lord, his God, by doing what was right and **good.**
18. 7 But I hate him because he never prophesies anything **good** for me;
18.17 "I told you that he never prophesies anything **good** for me;
19. 3 But even so, there is some **good** in you.
28. 1 He did not follow the **good** example of his ancestor King David;
30.19 of our ancestors, in your **goodness** forgive those who are
Ezra 3.11 "The Lord is **good,** and his love for Israel is eternal."
Neh 2.10 come to work for the **good** of the people of Israel, and
5. 5 Aren't our children just as **good** as theirs?
6.19 of me about all the **good** deeds Tobiah had done and would
9.13 to your people and gave them **good** laws and sound teachings.
9.20 In your **goodness** you told them what they should do;
9.25 they enjoyed all the **good** things you gave them.
Esth 2. 4 The king thought this was **good** advice, so he followed it.
5. 9 Haman left the banquet he was happy and in a **good** mood.
5.14 Haman thought this was a **good** idea, so he had the gallows
10. 3 He worked for the **good** of his people and for the security
Job 1. 1 He was a **good** man, careful not to do anything evil.
1. 8 is no one on earth as faithful and **good** as he is.
2. 3 is no one on earth as faithful and **good** as he is.
2.10 When God sends us something **good,** we welcome it.
9.25 My days race by, not one of them **good.**
13. 9 If God looks at you closely, will he find anything **good?**
20.12 Evil tastes so **good** to him that he keeps some in
22. 3 right benefit God, or does your being **good** help him at all?
22.19 **Good** men are glad and innocent men laugh when they see
26. 3 You give such **good** advice and share your knowledge with a
27.17 but some **good** man will wear the clothes, and some honest
29.11 or heard of me had **good** things to say about what I
30.10 they think they are too **good** for me, and even come and
34. 3 You know **good** food when you taste it, but not wise words
34. 9 that it never does any **good** to try to follow God's will.
35. 8 who suffers from your sins, and the **good** you do helps him.
36.19 It will do you no **good** to cry out for help;
Ps 7. 9 Stop the wickedness of evil men and reward those who are **good.**
11. 2 aimed their arrows to shoot from the shadows at **good** men.
11. 3 There is nothing a **good** man can do when everything falls apart."
11. 5 He examines the **good** and the wicked alike;
11. 7 The Lord is righteous and loves **good** deeds;
12. 1 There is not a **good** man left;
13. 6 sing to you, O Lord, because you have been **good** to me.
16. 2 all the **good** things I have come from you."
16. 6 how **good** they are!

Ps 18.25 completely **good** to those who are perfect.
19. 9 Reverence for the Lord is **good;**
23. 6 I know that your **goodness** and love will be with me all
25. 7 In your constant love and **goodness,** remember me, Lord!
25. 8 the Lord is righteous and **good,** he teaches sinners the path
25.21 May my **goodness** and honesty preserve me, because I trust in you.
27. 4 marvel there at his **goodness,** and to ask for his guidance.
27.13 I will live to see the Lord's **goodness** in this present life.
30. 5 His anger lasts only a moment, his **goodness** for a lifetime.
30. 7 You were **good** to me, Lord;
30. 9 Can they proclaim your unfailing **goodness?**
31.19 How wonderful are the **good** things you keep for those who
31.19 Everyone knows how **good** you are, how securely you protect
34. 8 Find out for yourself how **good** the Lord is.
34.10 of food, but those who obey the Lord lack nothing **good.**
34.14 Turn away from evil and do **good;**
34.19 The **good** man suffers many troubles, but the Lord saves
35.12 They pay me back evil for **good,** and I sink in despair.
36. 3 he no longer does what is wise and **good.**
36. 4 nothing he does is **good,** and he never rejects anything evil.
36. 8 you let us drink from the river of your **goodness.**
36.10 who know you and to do **good** to those who are righteous.
37. 3 Trust in the Lord and do **good;**
37.12 wicked man plots against the **good** man and glares at him with
37.16 The little that a **good** man owns is worth more than the
37.17 the strength of the wicked, but protect those who are **good.**
37.21 pays back, but the **good** man is generous with his gifts.
37.25 I have never seen a **good** man abandoned by the Lord or
37.27 away from evil and do **good,** and your descendants will always
37.30 A **good** man's words are wise, and he is always fair.
37.32 A wicked man watches a **good** man and tries to kill him;
37.37 Notice the **good** man, observe the righteous man;
38.20 who pay back evil for **good** are against me because I try
39. 2 I kept quiet, not saying a word, not even about anything **good!**
52. 3 You love evil more than **good** and falsehood more than truth.
52. 9 presence of your people I will proclaim that you are **good.**
54. 6 I will give you thanks because you are **good.**
64. 4 they destroy **good** men with cowardly slander.
64.10 all **good** people will praise him.
65. 4 shall be satisfied with the **good** things of your house,
65.11 What a rich harvest your **goodness** provides!
68.10 in your **goodness** you provided for the poor.
69.16 Answer me, Lord, in the **goodness** of your constant love;
71.15 I will tell of your **goodness;**
71.16 I will proclaim your **goodness,** yours alone.
73. 1 God is indeed **good** to Israel, to those who have pure hearts.
84.11 He does not refuse any **good** thing to those who do what
86. 5 You are **good** to us and forgiving, full of constant love
86.17 Show me proof of your **goodness,** Lord;
88.12 of darkness or your **goodness** in the land of the forgotten?
89.16 all day long, and they praise you for your **goodness.**
92. 1 How **good** it is to give thanks to you, O Lord, to
94.21 who plot against **good** men and sentence the innocent
97.11 Light shines on the righteous, and gladness on the **good.**
100. 5 The Lord is **good;**
103. 5 He fills my life with **good** things, so that I stay young
103.17 lasts for ever, and his **goodness** endures for all generations
106. 1 Give thanks to the Lord, because he is **good;**
107. 1 "Give thanks to the Lord, because he is **good;**
107. 9 who are thirsty and fills the hungry with **good** things.
109. 5 They pay me back evil for **good** and hatred for love.
109.21 and rescue me because of the **goodness** of your love.
112. 2 The **good** man's children will be powerful in the land;
112. 4 in the darkness for **good** men, for those who are merciful,
112. 6 A **good** person will never fail;
116. 5 The Lord is merciful and **good;**
116. 7 Be confident, my heart, because the Lord has been **good** to me.
116.12 What can I offer the Lord for all his **goodness** to me?
118. 1 to the Lord, because he is **good,** and his love is eternal.
118.27 he has been **good** to us.
118.29 to the Lord, because he is **good,** and his love is eternal.
119.17 Be **good** to me, your servant, so that I may live and
119.29 the wrong way, and in your **goodness** teach me your law.
119.37 be **good** to me, as you have promised.
119.65 kept your promise, Lord, and you are **good** to me,
119.68 How **good** you are—how kind!
119.71 My punishment was **good** for me, because it made me learn
119.88 of your constant love be **good** to me, so that I may
119.121 I have done what is right and **good;**
125. 4 Lord, do **good** to those who are good, to those who obey
135. 3 Praise the Lord, because he is **good;**
136. 1 Give thanks to the Lord, because he is **good;**
141. 5 A **good** man may punish me and rebuke me in kindness, but
142. 7 people I will praise you because of your **goodness** to me.
143.10 Be **good** to me, and guide me on a safe path.
143.11 in your **goodness** save me from my troubles!
145. 7 They will tell about all your **goodness**
145. 9 He is **good** to everyone and has compassion on all he made.
147. 1 It is **good** to sing praise to our God;
Prov 1. 2 you to recognize wisdom and **good** advice, and understand
1.17 It does no **good** to spread a net when the bird you
1.23 I will give you **good** advice and share my knowledge with you.
2.20 follow the example of **good** men and live a righteous life.
3. 8 it will be like **good** medicine, healing your wounds
3.27 Whenever you possibly can, do **good** to those who need it.
4. 2 What I am teaching you is **good,** so remember it all.
5.16 Children that you have by other women will do you no **good.**
8.15 I help kings to govern and rulers to make **good** laws.
10. 2 will do you no **good,** but honesty can save your life.
10. 3 The Lord will not let **good** people go hungry, but he will
10. 6 A **good** man will receive blessings.
Prov 10. 7 **Good** people will be remembered as a blessing, but the
10. 8 Sensible people accept **good** advice.
10.11 A **good** man's words are a fountain of life, but a wicked
10.16 The reward for doing **good** is life, but sin leads only to
10.20 A **good** man's words are like pure silver;
10.21 A **good** man's words will benefit many people, but you can
10.28 The hopes of **good** men lead to joy, but wicked people can
11. 3 If you are **good,** you are guided by honesty.
11. 4 Riches will do you no **good** on the day you face death,
11. 5 Honesty makes a **good** man's life easier, but a wicked man
11.23 What **good** people want always results in good;
11.27 If your goals are **good,** you will be respected, but if
11.31 Those who are **good** are rewarded here on earth, so you
12. 2 The Lord is pleased with **good** people, but condemns those
12. 4 A **good** wife is her husband's pride and joy;
12.10 A **good** man takes care of his animals, but wicked men are
12.20 surprise, but those who work for **good** will find happiness.
13. 2 **Good** people will be rewarded for what they say, but those
13.13 If you refuse **good** advice, you are asking for trouble;
13.19 How **good** it is to get what you want!
13.21 but righteous people will be rewarded with **good** things.
13.22 A **good** man will have wealth to leave to his grandchildren,
14. 9 care if they sin, but **good** people want to be forgiven.
14.11 A **good** man's house will still be standing after an evil
14.14 **Good** people will be rewarded for their deeds.
14.22 earn the trust and respect of others if you work for **good;**
14.32 deeds, but **good** people are protected by their integrity.
15. 3 he is watching us, whether we do **good** or evil.
15. 8 The Lord is pleased when **good** men pray, but hates the
15.28 **Good** people think before they answer.
15.29 When **good** people pray, the Lord listens, but he ignores
16.17 Those who are **good** travel a road that avoids evil;
16.24 are like honey—sweet to the taste and **good** for your health.
17.13 If you repay **good** with evil, you will never get evil out
17.16 It does a fool no **good** to spend money on an education,
17.20 speaks evil can expect to find nothing **good**—only disaster.
17.26 justice is perverted when **good** people are punished.
18.22 Find a wife and you find a **good** thing;
18.22 it shows that the Lord is **good** to you.
19. 2 Enthusiasm without knowledge is not **good;**
20.11 you can tell if he is honest and **good.**
20.18 Get **good** advice and you will succeed;
20.21 easily you get your wealth, the less **good** it will do you.
21.15 When justice is done, **good** people are happy, but evil
21.18 on themselves the suffering they try to cause **good** people.
22. 1 have to choose between a **good** reputation and great wealth,
22. 1 choose a **good** reputation.
22.20 They contain knowledge and **good** advice, [21] and will teach
22.29 a man who does a **good** job, and I will show you
24. 6 a battle, and the more **good** advice you get, the more likely
24.13 it is **good.**
24.14 you may be sure that wisdom is **good** for the soul.
24.25 however, will be prosperous and enjoy a **good** reputation.
25.26 A **good** person who gives in to someone who is evil
28.12 When **good** men come to power, everybody celebrates, but
29. 7 A **good** person knows the rights of the poor, but wicked
29.15 Correction and discipline are **good** for children.
29.26 Everybody wants the **good** will of the ruler, but only
30.13 think they are so good—oh, how **good** they think they are!
31.12 As long as she lives, she does him **good** and never harm.
31.29 He says, "Many women are **good** wives, but you are the
Ecc 2. 2 I discovered that laughter is foolish, that pleasure does you no **good.**
2. 3 decided to cheer myself up with wine and have a **good** time.
6. 4 It does that baby no **good** to be born;
6. 8 What **good** does it do a poor man to know how to
7. 1 A **good** reputation is better than expensive perfume;
7.11 it is as **good** as receiving an inheritance [12] and will give
7.15 A **good** man may die while another man lives on, even though
7.16 So don't be too **good** or too wise—why kill yourself?
9. 2 and the wicked, to the **good** and the bad, to those who
9. 2 A **good** man is no better off than a sinner;
9.18 Wisdom does more **good** than weapons,
9.18 but one sinner can undo a lot of **good.**
11. 7 It is **good** to be able to enjoy the pleasant light of
12.14 judge everything we do, whether **good** or bad,
Is 1.19 obey me, you will eat the **good** things the land produces.
1.22 you were like **good** wine, but now you are only water.
5. 4 it produce sour grapes and not the **good** grapes I expected?
5. 7 to do what was **good,** but instead they committed murder.
5.20 You call evil **good** and call good evil.
8.20 listen to mediums—what they tell you will do you no **good."**
16.12 to their temples to pray, but it will do them no **good.**
26. 7 Lord, you make the path smooth for **good** men;
28. 9 It's only **good** for babies that have just been weaned!
39. 8 "The message you have given me from the Lord is **good."**
41. 7 They say, 'The soldering is **good'**— and they fasten the idol
41.23 Do something **good** or bring some disaster;
44.10 It's no **good** making a metal image to worship as a god!
47.15 That is all the **good** they will do you— those astrologers
48.17 wants to teach you **for your own good** and direct you in
57. 1 **Good** people die, and no one understands or even cares.
57. 2 Those who live **good** lives find peace and rest in death.
58.11 And I will always guide you and satisfy you with **good** things.
59. 5 plots will do you no **good**—they are as useless as clothing
65. 8 The Lord says, "No one destroys **good** grapes;
Jer 2. 7 land, to enjoy its harvests and its other **good** things.
2.30 I punished you, but it did no **good;**
4.22 doing what is evil, but failures at doing what is **good."**
5.25 Instead, your sins have kept these **good** things from you.
10. 5 can cause you no harm, and they can do you no **good."**

Jer 13. 7 I saw that they were ruined and were no longer any **good.**
13.10 will become like these shorts that are no longer any **good.**
14.19 We looked for peace, but nothing **good** happened;
17. 6 Nothing **good** ever happens to him.
18.20 Is evil the payment for **good?**
23.28 What **good** is straw compared with wheat?
24. 2 The first basket contained **good** figs, those that ripen early;
24. 3 The **good** ones are very good, and the bad ones are very
24. 5 to Babylonia are like these **good** figs, and I will treat them
29. 7 Work for the **good** of the cities where I have made you
29.31 not live to see the **good** things that I am going to
32.39 time, for their own **good** and the good of their descendants.
32.40 I will never stop doing **good** things for them, and I will
32.41 will take pleasure in doing **good** things for them, and I will
32.42 going to give them all the **good** things that I have promised.
33. 9 when they hear about the **good** things that I do for the
33.11 Lord Almighty, because he is **good** and his love is eternal.'
48.11 has never been ruined, and it tastes as **good** as ever.
Lam 3.25 The Lord is **good** to everyone who trusts in him, [26]So
3.38 **Good** and evil alike take place at his command.
Ezek 3.20 "If a truly **good** man starts doing evil and I put him
3.20 I will not remember the **good** he did—and I will hold
3.21 If you do warn a **good** man not to sin and he
13.12 and everyone will ask you what **good** the whitewash did."
13.22 "By your lies you discourage **good** people, whom I do not
14.14 their **goodness** would save only their own lives."
14.20 Their **goodness** would save only their own lives."
18. 5 "Suppose there is a truly **good** man, righteous and honest.
18.19 The answer is that the son did what was right and **good.**
18.20 A **good** man will be rewarded for doing good,
18.21 if he does what is right and **good,** he will not die;
18.24 man stops doing **good** and starts doing all the evil,
18.24 None of the **good** he did will be remembered.
18.26 a righteous man stops doing **good** and starts doing evil and
18.27 sinning and does what is right and **good,** he saves his life.
20.25 them laws that are not **good** and commands that do not bring
21. 3 draw my sword and kill all of you, **good** and evil alike.
23.41 have a table covered with **good** things, including the incense
30.22 break both his arms—the **good** one and the one already broken
33.12 a good man sins, the **good** he has done will not save
33.12 be punished, and if a **good** man starts sinning, his life will
33.13 may promise life to a **good** man, but if he starts thinking
33.13 thinking that his past **goodness** is enough and begins to sin,
33.13 to sin, I will not remember any of the **good** he did.
33.14 does what is right and **good**—[15]for example, if he returns
33.16 he will live because he has done what is right and **good.**
33.18 a righteous man stops doing **good** and starts doing evil, he
33.19 and does what is right and **good,** he has saved his life.
34.17 of you and separate the **good** from the bad, the sheep from
34.22 judge each of my sheep and separate the **good** from the bad.
Hos 3. 5 Then they will fear the Lord and will receive his **good** gifts.
5. 6 offer as sacrifices to the Lord, but it does them no **good.**
8. 3 and that they know me, [3]they have rejected what is **good.**
13. 6 But when you entered the **good** land, you became full and satisfied,
Amos 5.12 You persecute **good** men, take bribes, and prevent the poor
Mic 3. 2 yet you hate what is **good** and you love what is evil.
6. 8 No, the Lord has told us what is **good.**
Nah 1. 7 The Lord is **good;**
Zech 3. 8 of his, you that are the sign of a **good** future:
7.14 This **good** land was left a desolate place, with no one living
9.17 How **good** and beautiful the land will be!
Mal 1. 9 Now, you priests, try asking God to be **good** to us.
1.14 has in his flock a **good** animal that he promised to give
2.17 By saying, "The Lord Almighty thinks all evildoers are **good;**
3.10 and pour out on you in abundance all kinds of **good** things.
3.12 happy, because your land will be a **good** place to live in.
Mt 3.10 tree that does not bear **good** fruit will be cut down and
3.11 and I am not **good** enough even to carry his sandals.
5.16 that they will see the **good** things you do and praise your
5.45 to shine on bad and **good** people alike, and gives rain to
5.45 rain to those who do **good** and to those who do evil.
6.23 if your eyes are no **good,** your body will be in darkness.
7.11 you are, you know how to give **good** things to your children.
7.11 Father in heaven give **good** things to those who ask him!
7.17 A healthy tree bears **good** fruit, but a poor tree bears
7.18 bear bad fruit, and a poor tree cannot bear **good** fruit.
7.19 tree that does not bear **good** fruit is cut down and thrown
9.17 into fresh wineskins, and both will keep in **good** condition."
10.41 And whoever welcomes a **good** man because he is good, will
12.33 "To have **good** fruit you must have a healthy tree;
12.34 You snakes—how can you say **good** things when you are evil?
12.35 good person brings good things out of his treasure of **good** things;
13. 8 But some seeds fell in **good** soil, and the plants produced corn;
13.23 the seeds sown in the **good** soil stand for those who hear
13.24 A man sowed **good** seed in his field.
13.27 and said, 'Sir, it was **good** seed you sowed in your field;
13.37 "The man who sowed the **good** seed is the Son of Man;
13.38 the **good** seed is the people who belong to the Kingdom;
13.48 the **good** ones go into their buckets, the worthless ones
13.49 evil people from among the **good** [50]and will throw them into
17. 4 said to Jesus, "Lord, how **good** it is that we are here!
19.16 "Teacher," he asked, "what **good** thing must I do to receive
19.17 "Why do you ask me concerning what is **good?"**
19.17 "There is only One who is **good.**
22.10 gathered all the people they could find, **good** and bad alike;
23.28 on the outside you appear **good** to everybody, but inside you
23.29 prophets and decorate the monuments of those who lived **good** lives;
25.21 'Well done, you **good** and faithful servant!'
25.23 'Well done, you **good** and faithful servant!'
26.16 Judas was looking for a **good** chance to hand Jesus over to
Mk 1. 7 I am not **good** enough even to bend down and untie his
2.27 Jesus concluded, "The Sabbath was made for the **good** of man;
4. 8 But some seeds fell in **good** soil, and the plants sprouted,
4.20 But other people are like the seeds sown in **good** soil.
6.20 knew that John was a **good** and holy man, and so he
9. 5 said to Jesus, "Teacher, how **good** it is that we are here!
9.50 "Salt is **good;**
10.17 before him, and asked him, **"Good** Teacher, what must I do to
10.18 "Why do you call me **good?"**
10.18 "No one is **good** except God alone.
12.28 had given the Sadducees a **good** answer, so he came to him
14.11 Judas started looking for a **good** chance to hand Jesus over
Lk 1. 3 I thought it would be **good** to write an orderly account for
1. 6 They both lived **good** lives in God's sight and obeyed fully
1.53 has filled the hungry with **good** things, and sent the rich
1.58 relatives heard how wonderfully **good** the Lord had been to her,
2.25 He was a **good,** God-fearing man and was waiting for Israel to
3. 9 tree that does not bear **good** fruit will be cut down and
3.16 I am not **good** enough even to untie his sandals.
4.10 says, 'God will order his angels to take **good** care of you.'
6.27 Love your enemies, do **good** to those who hate you, [28]bless
6.33 And if you do **good** only to those who do good to
6.35 Love your enemies and do **good** to them;
6.35 For he is **good** to the ungrateful and the wicked.
6.43 not bear bad fruit, nor does a poor tree bear **good** fruit.
6.45 A **good** person brings good out of the treasure of good
8. 8 And some seeds fell in **good** soil;
8.15 The seeds that fell in **good** soil stand for those who
8.15 and retain it in a **good** and obedient heart, and they persist
9.33 said to him, "Master, how **good** it is that we are here!
11.13 you are, you know how to give **good** things to your children.
11.34 when your eyes are no **good,** your whole body will be in
12.16 was once a rich man who had land which bore **good** crops.
12.19 You have all the **good** things you need for many years.
14.14 will repay you on the day the **good** people rise from death."
14.34 "Salt is **good,** but if it loses its saltiness, there is
14.35 It is no **good** for the soil or for the manure heap;
16.25 you were given all the **good** things, while Lazarus got all
18. 9 people who were sure of their own **goodness** and despised everybody
18.18 A Jewish leader asked Jesus, **"Good** Teacher, what must I
18.19 "Why do you call me **good?"**
18.19 "No one is **good** except God alone.
19.17 'you are a **good** servant!
20.39 of the teachers of the Law spoke up, "A **good** answer,
22. 6 and started looking for a **good** chance to hand Jesus over to
22.31 of you, to separate the **good** from the bad, as a farmer
23.47 and he praised God, saying, "Certainly he was a **good** man!"
23.50 He was a **good** and honourable man, who was waiting for the
Jn 1.27 me, but I am not **good** enough even to untie his sandals."
1.46 "Can anything **good** come from Nazareth?"
4.35 But I tell you, take a **good** look at the fields;
5.29 those who have done **good** will rise and live, and those who
7.12 "He is a **good** man," some people said.
10.11 "I am the **good** shepherd, who is willing to die for the
10.14 I am the **good** shepherd.
10.32 them, "I have done many **good** deeds in your presence which
10.33 because of any **good** deeds, but because of your blasphemy!
Acts 2.47 praising God, and enjoying the **good** will of all the people.
3.14 He was holy and **good,** but you rejected him, and instead
4. 9 being questioned today about the **good** deed done to the lame
9.36 She spent all her time doing **good** and helping the poor.
10.22 "He is a **good** man who worships God and is highly respected
10.33 for you at once, and you have been **good** enough to come.
10.38 He went everywhere, doing **good** and healing all who were
11.24 Barnabas was a **good** man, full of the Holy Spirit and faith,
13.10 You are the enemy of everything that is **good.**
13.25 me, and I am not **good** enough to take his sandals off
14.17 given evidence of his existence by the **good** things he does:
19.40 we would not be able to give a **good** reason for it."
24. 2 reforms are being made for the **good** of our country.
24.15 that all people, both the **good** and the bad, will rise from
24.25 Paul went on discussing about **goodness,** self-control,
27.12 The harbour was not a **good** one to spend the winter in;
27.24 And God in his **goodness** to you has spared the lives of
Rom 1.10 ask that God in his **good** will may at last make it
2. 7 Some people keep on doing **good,** and seek glory, honour,
2.10 all who do what is **good,** to the Jews first and also
3. 8 not say, then, "Let us do evil so that **good** may come"?
4.17 So the promise is **good** in the sight of God, in whom
5. 7 even be that someone might dare to die for a **good** person.
7.12 Law itself is holy, and the commandment is holy, right, and **good.**
7.13 But does this mean that what is **good** caused my death?
7.13 by using what is **good,** sin brought death to me, in order
7.18 I know that **good** does not live in me—that is, in
7.18 though the desire to do **good** is in me, I am not
7.19 I don't do the **good** I want to do;
7.21 want to do what is **good,** what is evil is the only
8.28 all things God works for **good** with those who love him, those
9.11 were born, before they had done anything either **good** or bad;
12. 2 will of God—what is **good** and is pleasing to him and
12. 9 Hate what is evil, hold on to what is **good.**
12.17 Try to do what everyone considers to be **good.**
12.21 instead, conquer evil with **good.**
13. 3 feared by those who do **good,** but by those who do evil.
13. 3 Then do what is **good,** and he will praise you, [4]because he
13. 4 because he is God's servant working for your own **good.**
14.16 Do not let what you regard as **good** get a bad name.
15. 2 our brothers for their own **good,** in order to build them up
15.14 that you are full of **goodness,** that you have all knowledge,
16. 2 she herself has been a **good** friend to many people and also

Rom	16.19	be wise about what is **good,** but innocent in what is evil.
1 Cor	6.12	but not everything is **good** for you.
	10.23	That is true, but not everything is **good.**
	10.33	not thinking of my own **good,** but of the good of all,
	11.17	because your meetings for worship actually do more harm than **good.**
	12. 7	shown in some way in each person for the **good** of all.
	13. 3	—but if I have no love, this does me no **good.**
	14.17	thanks to God is quite **good,** the other person is not helped
	15.19	our hope in Christ is **good** for this life only and no
	15.33	"Bad companions ruin **good** character."
2 Cor	4. 2	and try to commend ourselves to everyone's **good** conscience.
	5.10	to everything he has done, **good** or bad, in his bodily life.
	5.12	trying to give you a **good** reason to be proud of us,
	9. 8	for yourselves and more than enough for every **good** cause.
	12. 1	I have to boast, even though it doesn't do any **good.**
Gal	4.17	a deep interest in you, but their intentions are not **good.**
	4.18	Now, it is **good** to have such a deep interest
	4.18	if the purpose is **good**—this is true always, and not
	5.22	love, joy, peace, patience, kindness, **goodness,** faithfulness,
	6. 4	If it is **good,** then he can be proud of what he
	6. 6	should share all the **good** things he has with his teacher.
	6. 9	So let us not become tired of doing **good;**
	6.10	chance, we should do **good** to everyone, and especially to those
Eph	2.10	us for a life of **good** deeds, which he has already prepared
	3. 2	his grace has given me this work to do for your **good.**
	4.29	that what you say will do **good** to those who hear you.
	5. 9	rich harvest of every kind of **goodness,** righteousness, and truth.
	5.16	Make **good** use of every opportunity you have,
	6. 8	everyone, whether slave or free, for the **good** work he does.
Phil	1. 6	that God, who began this **good** work in you, will carry it
	1.11	be filled with the truly **good** qualities which only Jesus Christ
	4. 8	minds with those things that are **good** and that deserve praise:
	4.14	But it was very **good** of you to help me in my
Col	1.10	will produce all kinds of **good** deeds, and you will grow in
	1.25	by God, who gave me this task to perform for your **good.**
	2. 4	with false arguments, no matter how **good** they seem to be.
	4. 3	God will give us a **good** opportunity to preach his message
	4. 5	are not believers, making **good** use of every opportunity you have.
1 Thes	1. 5	it was for your own **good.**
	5.15	it your aim to do **good** to one another and to all
	5.21	keep what is **good** [22] and avoid every kind of evil.
2 Thes	1.11	your desire for **goodness** and complete your work of faith.
	2.17	you and strengthen you to always do and say what is **good.**
	3.13	But you, brothers, must not get tired of doing **good.**
1 Tim	1. 8	know that the Law is **good** if it is used as it
	1. 9	laws are made, not for **good** people, but for lawbreakers
	2. 3	This is **good** and it pleases God our Saviour, [4] who wants
	2.10	expensive dresses, [10] but with **good** deeds, as is proper for women
	3. 8	Church helpers must also have a **good** character and be sincere;
	3.11	Their wives also must be of **good** character and must not gossip;
	3.13	well win for themselves a **good** standing and are able to
	4. 4	Everything that God has created is **good;**
	4. 6	brothers, you will be a **good** servant of Christ Jesus, as you
	5.10	been married only once [10] and have a reputation for **good** deeds:
	5.10	helped people in trouble, and devoted herself to doing **good.**
	5.17	elders who do **good** work as leaders should be considered worthy
	5.25	In the same way **good** deeds are plainly seen, and even
	6.18	Command them to do **good,** to be rich in good works, to
2 Tim	1.14	lives in us, keep the **good** things that have been entrusted
	2.14	It does no **good,** but only ruins the people who listen.
	2.21	useful to his Master, ready to be used for every **good** deed.
	2.24	be kind towards all, a **good** and patient teacher,
	3. 3	they will hate the **good;**
	3.17	fully qualified and equipped to do every kind of **good** deed.
Tit	1. 8	He must be hospitable and love what is **good.**
	1.16	They are hateful and disobedient, not fit to do anything **good.**
	2. 3	They must teach what is **good,** [4] in order to train the
	2. 5	and to be **good** housewives who submit to their husbands,
	2. 7	In all things you yourself must be an example of **good** behaviour.
	2.10	show that they are always **good** and faithful, so as to bring
	2.14	people who belong to him alone and are eager to do **good.**
	3. 1	obey them, and to be ready to do **good** in every way.
	3. 5	not because of any **good** deeds that we ourselves had done,
	3. 8	to doing good deeds, which are **good** and useful for everyone.
	3.14	to spend their time doing **good,** in order to provide for real
Heb	4. 2	but it did them no **good,** because when they heard it, they
	5.14	who through practice are able to distinguish between **good** and evil.
	6. 5	experience that God's word is **good,** and they had felt the
	9.11	as the High Priest of the **good** things that are already here.
	10. 1	it is only a faint outline of the **good** things to come.
	10.24	another, to help one another to show love and to do **good.**
	11.38	The world was not **good** enough for them!
	12.10	does it for our own **good,** so that we may share his
	12.23	all mankind, and to the spirits of **good** people made perfect.
	13. 9	It is **good** to receive inner strength from God's grace, and
	13.16	Do not forget to do **good** and to help one another,
	13.20	peace provide you with every **good** thing you need in order to
Jas	1.17	Every **good** gift and every perfect present comes from heaven;
	1.24	He takes a **good** look at himself and then goes away and
	2. 7	who speak evil of that **good** name which has been given to
	2.14	My brothers, what **good** is it for someone to say that he
	2.16	What **good** is there in your saying to them, "God bless you!
	2.19	**Good!**
	3.13	to prove it by his **good** life, by his good deeds performed
	3.17	is full of compassion and produces a harvest of **good** deeds;
	3.18	And **goodness** is the harvest that is produced from the seeds
	4.17	who does not do the **good** he knows he should do is
	5.16	The prayer of a **good** person has a powerful effect.
1 Pet	2.12	the heathen should be so **good** that when they accuse you of
1 Pet	2.12	will have to recognize your **good** deeds and so praise God on
	2.14	him to punish the evildoers and to praise those who do **good.**
	2.15	ignorant talk of foolish people by the **good** things you do.
	3. 6	daughters if you do **good** and are not afraid of anything.
	3.10	life and wishes to see **good** times, must keep from speaking
	3.11	He must turn away from evil and do **good;**
	3.13	will harm you if you are eager to do what is **good?**
	3.16	who speak evil of your **good** conduct as followers of Christ
	3.17	to suffer for doing **good,** if this should be God's will,
	3.18	once and for all, a **good** man on behalf of sinners, in
	3.21	dirt, but the promise made to God from a **good** conscience.
	4.10	Each one, as a **good** manager of God's different gifts,
	4.10	must use for the **good** of others the special gift he
	4.18	scripture says, "It is difficult for **good** people to be saved;
	4.19	should by their **good** actions trust themselves completely to their
2 Pet	1. 3	one who called us to share in his own glory and **goodness.**
	1. 5	this very reason do your best to add **goodness** to your faith;
	1. 5	to your **goodness** add knowledge;
	2. 7	He rescued Lot, a **good** man, who was distressed by the
	2. 8	That **good** man lived among them, and day after day he
3 Jn	2	that you may be in **good** health—as I know you are
	11	do not imitate what is bad, but imitate what is **good.**
	11	Whoever does **good** belongs to God;
Rev	18.14	say to her, "All the **good** things you longed to own have
	19. 8	(The linen is the **good** deeds of God's people.)
	22.11	whoever is **good** must go on doing good, and whoever is holy

GOOD NEWS

1 Sam	31. 9	throughout Philistia to tell the **good news** to their idols
2 Sam	4.10	told me of Saul's death thought he was bringing **good news.**
	4.10	That was the reward I gave him for his **good news!**
	18.19	to the king with the **good news** that the Lord has saved
	18.20	"No," Joab said, "today you will not take any **good news.**
	18.25	the king said, "If he is alone, he is bringing **good news."**
	18.26	The king answered, "This one also is bringing **good news."**
	18.27	good man," the king said, "and he is bringing **good news."**
	18.31	and said to the king, "I have **good news** for Your Majesty!
1 Kgs	1.42	"You're a good man—you must be bringing **good news."**
2 Kgs	7. 9	We have **good news** and we shouldn't keep it to ourselves.
1 Chr	10. 9	throughout Philistia to tell the **good news** to their idols
	16.23	Proclaim every day the **good news** that he has saved us.
Ps	40. 9	your people, Lord, I told the **good news** that you save us.
	96. 2	Proclaim every day the **good news** that he has saved us.
Prov	15.30	Smiling faces make you happy, and **good news** makes you feel better.
	25.25	Finally, hearing **good news** from a distant land is like a
Is	21.10	have announced to you the **good news** that I have heard from
	40. 9	Jerusalem, go up on a high mountain and proclaim the **good news!**
	40. 9	announce the **good news!**
	52. 7	the mountains, bringing **good news,** the news of peace!
	60. 6	People will tell the **good news** of what the Lord has done!
	61. 1	and sent me To bring **good news** to the poor, To heal
Nah	1.15	Look, a messenger is coming over the mountains with **good news!**
Mt	4.23	in the synagogues, preaching the **Good News** about the Kingdom,
	9.35	in the synagogues, preached the **Good News** about the Kingdom,
	10.18	and kings, to tell the **Good News** to them and to the
	11. 5	back to life, and the **Good News** is preached to the poor.
	24.14	And this **Good News** about the Kingdom will be preached through
Mk	1. 1	This is the **Good News** about Jesus Christ, the Son of God.
	1.14	Jesus went to Galilee and preached the **Good News** from God.
	1.15	Turn away from your sins and believe the **Good News!"**
	13. 9	rulers and kings for my sake to tell them the **Good News.**
Lk	1.19	sent me to speak to you and tell you this **good news.**
	2.10	I am here with **good news** for you, which will bring great
	3.18	different ways John preached the **Good News** to the people
	4.18	because he has chosen me to bring **good news** to the poor.
	4.43	them, "I must preach the **Good News** about the Kingdom of God
	7.22	raised to life, and the **Good News** is preached to the poor.
	8. 1	villages, preaching the **Good News** about the Kingdom of God.
	9. 6	villages, preaching the **Good News** and healing people everywhere.
	16.16	since then the **Good News** about the Kingdom of God is being
	20. 1	the people and preaching the **Good News,** the chief priests
	21.13	This will be your chance to tell the **Good News.**
Acts	5.42	to teach and preach the **Good News** about Jesus the Messiah.
	8.12	Philip's message about the **good news** of the Kingdom of God
	8.25	they preached the **Good News** in many villages of Samaria.
	8.35	passage of scripture, he told him the **Good News** about Jesus.
	8.40	and on the way he preached the **Good News** in every town.
	10.36	people of Israel, proclaiming the **Good News** of peace through Jesus
	11.20	Gentiles also, telling them the **Good News** about the Lord Jesus.
	13.32	And we are here to bring the **Good News** to you:
	14. 7	There they preached the **Good News.**
	14.15	are here to announce the **Good News,** to turn you away from
	14.21	Paul and Barnabas preached the **Good News** in Derbe and
	15. 7	among you to preach the **Good News** to the Gentiles, so that
	16.10	had called us to preach the **Good News** to the people there.
	20.24	which is to declare the **Good News** about the grace of God.
Rom	1. 1	apostle chosen and called by God to preach his **Good News.**
	1. 2	The **Good News** was promised long ago by God through his prophets,
	1. 9	with all my heart by preaching the **Good News** about his Son.
	1.15	am eager to preach the **Good News** to you also who live
	2.16	And so, according to the **Good News** I preach, this is how
	10.15	"How wonderful is the coming of messengers who bring **good news!"**
	10.16	But not all have accepted the **Good News.**
	11.28	Because they reject the **Good News,** the Jews are God's enemies
	15.16	a priest in preaching the **Good News** from God, in order that

Rom 15.19 to Illyricum, I have proclaimed fully the **Good News** about Christ.
15.20 always been to proclaim the **Good News** in places where Christ
16.25 your faith, according to the **Good News** I preach about Jesus
1 Cor 1.17 sent me to tell the **Good News,** and to tell it without
4.15 I have become your father by bringing the **Good News** to you.
9.12 put any obstacle in the way of the **Good News** about Christ.
9.18 the privilege of preaching the **Good News** without charging for it,
15. 1 you, my brothers, of the **Good News** which I preached to you,
2 Cor 2.12 in Troas to preach the **Good News** about Christ, I found that
4. 4 that comes from the **Good News** about the glory of Christ,
10.14 when we came to you, bringing the **Good News** about Christ.
10.16 Then we can preach the **Good News** in other countries
11. 7 a thing when I preached the **Good News** of God to you;
Gal 1.16 that I might preach the **Good News** about him to the Gentiles,
3. 8 And so the scripture announced the **Good News** to Abraham:
Eph 1.13 heard the true message, the **Good News** that brought you salvation.
2.17 Christ came and preached the **Good News** of peace to all—to
3. 8 taking to the Gentiles the **Good News** about the infinite riches
6.15 your shoes the readiness to announce the **Good News** of peace.
Phil 4.15 early days of preaching the **Good News,** you were the only
Col 1. 5 When the true message, the **Good News,** first came to you,
1 Thes 1. 5 For we brought the **Good News** to you, not with words only,
2. 2 us courage to tell you the **Good News** that comes from him.
2. 4 he has judged us worthy to be entrusted with the **Good News.**
2. 8 with you not only the **Good News** from God but even our
2. 9 to you as we preached to you the **Good News** from God.
3. 2 with us for God in preaching the **Good News** about Christ.
2 Thes 1. 8 and who do not obey the **Good News** about our Lord Jesus.
2.14 called you to this through the **Good News** we preached to you;
1 Tim 1.11 to me to announce, the **Good News** from the glorious and
2 Tim 1. 8 part in suffering for the **Good News,** as God gives you the
1.11 and teacher to proclaim the **Good News,** [12]and it is for
2. 8 descendant of David, as is taught in the **Good News** I preach.
2. 9 Because I preach the **Good News,** I suffer and I am even
4. 5 of a preacher of the **Good News,** and perform your whole duty
Heb 4. 2 For we have heard the **Good News,** just as they did.
4. 6 Those who first heard the **Good News** did not receive that rest,
1 Pet 1.12 the messengers who announced the **Good News** by the power of
1.25 This word is the **Good News** that was proclaimed to you.
4. 6 That is why the **Good News** was preached also to the dead,
4.17 end with those who do not believe the **Good News** from God?
Rev 14. 6 with an eternal message of **Good News** to announce to the

GOOD-BYE

Gen 26.31 Isaac said **good-bye** to them, and they parted as friends.
31.28 even let me kiss my grandchildren and my daughters **good-bye.**
31.55 and his daughters **good-bye,** and left to go back home.
Ex 4.18 Jethro agreed and said **good-bye** to him.
18.27 Then Moses said **good-bye** to Jethro, and Jethro went back home.
Ruth 1. 9 So Naomi kissed them **good-bye.**
1.14 Then Orpah kissed her mother-in-law **good-bye** and went back home,
1 Kgs 19.20 kiss my father and mother **good-bye,** and then I will go with
Mic 1.14 people of Judah, say **good-bye** to the town of Moresheth Gath.
Mk 6.46 After saying **good-bye** to the people he went away to a
Lk 9.61 but first let me go and say **good-bye** to my family."
Acts 20. 1 believers and with words of encouragement said **goodbye** to them.
20.37 They were all crying as they hugged him and kissed him **good-bye.**
21. 1 We said **good-bye** to them and left.
21. 6 Then we said **good-bye** to one another, and we went on board
2 Cor 2.13 So I said **good-bye** to the people there and went on to
13.11 And now, my brothers, **good-bye!**

GOOD-FOR-NOTHING

1 Sam 25.25 Please, don't pay any attention to Nabal, that **good-for-nothing!**
Prov 28. 7 One who makes friends with **good-for-nothings** is a disgrace
Mt 5.22 brought to trial, whoever calls his brother 'You **good-for-nothing!**'

GOOD-LOOKING

Gen 39. 6 Joseph was well-built and **good-looking,**
1 Sam 17.42 scorn for him because he was just a nice, **good-looking** boy.

GOODS

Gen 45.23 the best Egyptian **goods** and ten donkeys loaded with corn,
Josh 7.15 and found with the condemned **goods** will be burnt, along with
8. 2 time you may keep its **goods** and livestock for yourselves.
8.27 for themselves the livestock and **goods** captured in the city,
Neh 13.16 fish and all kinds of **goods** into the city to sell to
13.20 who sold all kinds of **goods** spent Friday night outside the
Jer 51.44 the god of Babylonia, and make him give up his stolen **goods;**
Ezek 27.12 iron, tin, and lead in payment for your abundant **goods.**
27.13 and Meshech and traded your **goods** for slaves and for
27.14 You sold your **goods** for draught-horses, war-horses, and mules
27.15 lands gave you ivory and ebony in exchange for your **goods.**
27.17 and Israel paid for your **goods** with wheat, honey, olive-oil,
27.18 They exchanged wrought iron and spices for your **goods.**
27.20 The people of Dedan exchanged saddle-cloths for your **goods.**
27.22 For your **goods** the merchants of Sheba and Raamah exchanged jewels,
27.33 Kings were made rich By the wealth of your **goods.**
27.34 Your **goods** and all who worked for you Have vanished with you
Dan 11.24 divide among his followers the **goods** and property he has
Lk 12.18 ones, where I will store my corn and all my other **goods.**
1 Cor 7.31 those who deal in material **goods,** as though they were
Rev 18.11 mourn for her, because no one buys their **goods** any longer;
18.12 their **goods** of linen, purple cloth, silk, and scarlet cloth;

GOODWILL

Phil 1.15 they are jealous and quarrelsome, but others from genuine **goodwill.**

GORE

Ex 21.28 "If a bull **gores** someone to death, it is to be stoned,
21.29 penned up—then if it **gores** someone to death, it is to
Deut 33.17 With them he **gores** the nations And pushes them to the ends

GORGE

Ezek 6. 3 the mountains, the hills, the **gorges,** and the valleys:

GOSHEN (1)

Area in Egypt where the Israelites lived before the Exodus.

Gen 45.10 live in the region of **Goshen,** where you can be near me
45.11 If you are in **Goshen,** I can take care of you.
46.28 Jacob sent Judah ahead to ask Joseph to meet them in **Goshen.**
46.29 got in his chariot and went to **Goshen** to meet his father.
46.34 this way he will let you live in the region of **Goshen."**
47. 1 They are now in the region of **Goshen."**
47. 4 Please give us permission to live in the region of **Goshen."**
47. 6 settle in the region of **Goshen,** the best part of the land.
47.27 Egypt in the region of **Goshen,** where they became rich and
50. 8 sheep, goats, and cattle stayed in the region of **Goshen.**
Ex 8.22 will spare the region of **Goshen,** where my people live, so
9.26 The region of **Goshen,** where the Israelites lived, was

GOSPEL

see also **GOOD NEWS**

Mt 26.13 that wherever this **gospel** is preached all over the world,
Mk 8.35 loses his life for me and for the **gospel** will save it.
10.29 for me and for the **gospel,** [30]will receive much more in
13.10 the end comes, the **gospel** must be preached to all peoples.
14. 9 that wherever the **gospel** is preached all over the world,
16.15 "Go throughout the whole world and preach the **gospel** to all mankind.
Acts 10.42 commanded us to preach the **gospel** to the people and to
Rom 1.16 I have complete confidence in the **gospel;**
1.17 For the **gospel** reveals how God puts people right with himself:
16.19 of your loyalty to the **gospel,** and for this reason I am
1 Cor 9.14 who preach the **gospel** should get their living from it.
9.16 I have no right to boast just because I preach the **gospel.**
9.16 it would be for me if I did not preach the **gospel!**
9.18 it, without claiming my rights in my work for the **gospel.**
9.23 this I do for the **gospel's** sake, in order to share in
15. 2 That is the **gospel,** the message that I preached to you.
15. 2 You are saved by the **gospel** if you hold firmly to it
2 Cor 4. 3 For if the **gospel** we preach is hidden, it is hidden only
8.18 in all the churches for his work in preaching the **gospel.**
9.13 for your loyalty to the **gospel** of Christ, which you profess,
11. 4 accept a spirit and a **gospel** completely different
11. 4 from the Spirit and the **gospel** you received from us!
Gal 1. 6 by the grace of Christ, and are accepting another **gospel.**
1. 7 Actually, there is no "other **gospel,"** but I say this because
1. 7 are upsetting you and trying to change the **gospel** of Christ.
1. 8 should preach to you a **gospel** that is different from the one
1. 9 anyone preaches to you a **gospel** that is different from the
1.11 my brothers, that the **gospel** I preach is not of human
2. 2 the leaders I explained the **gospel** message that I preach to
2. 5 keep the truth of the **gospel** safe for you, we did not
2. 7 the task of preaching the **gospel** to the Gentiles, just as he
2. 7 given Peter the task of preaching the **gospel** to the Jews.
2.14 with the truth of the **gospel,** I said to Peter in front
3. 2 the Law requires or by hearing the **gospel** and believing it?
3. 5 Law requires or because you hear the **gospel** and believe it?
4.13 You remember why I preached the **gospel** to you the first time;
Eph 3. 6 that by means of the **gospel** the Gentiles have a part with
3. 7 made a servant of the **gospel** by God's special gift, which he
6.19 that I may speak boldly and make known the **gospel's** secret.
6.20 For the sake of this **gospel** I am an ambassador, though
6.20 I may be bold in speaking about the **gospel** as I should.
Phil 1. 5 in the work of the **gospel** from the very first day until
1. 7 I was free to defend the **gospel** and establish it firmly.
1.12 to me have really helped the progress of the **gospel.**
1.16 know that God has given me the work of defending the **gospel.**
1.27 life should be as the **gospel** of Christ requires, so that,
1.27 you are fighting together for the faith of the **gospel.**
2.22 his father, have worked together for the sake of the **gospel.**
4. 3 with me to spread the **gospel,** together with Clement and all
Col 1. 6 The **gospel** keeps bringing blessings and is spreading throughout
1.23 shaken from the hope you gained when you heard the **gospel.**
1.23 It is of this **gospel** that I, Paul, became a servant—
1.23 this **gospel** which has been preached to everybody
1 Tim 1.11 teaching is found in the **gospel** that was entrusted to me to
2 Tim 1.10 power of death and through the **gospel** has revealed immortal life.
Phlm 13 am in prison for the **gospel's** sake, so that he could help

GOSSIP

Prov 10.18 Anyone who spreads **gossip** is a fool.
11.13 No one who **gossips** can be trusted with a secret,
16.28 **Gossip** is spread by wicked people;
18. 8 **Gossip** is so tasty—how we love to swallow it!
20.19 A **gossip** can never keep a secret.
25.23 **Gossip** brings anger just as surely as the north wind brings rain.
26.20 without **gossip,** quarrelling stops.

Prov 26.22 **Gossip** is so tasty!
Jer 6.28 They are all corrupt, going round and spreading **gossip.**
Ezek 23.10 Women everywhere **gossiped** about her fate.
Rom 1.29 They **gossip** [30] and speak evil of one another;
2 Cor 12.20 tempers and selfishness, insults and **gossip,** pride and disorder.
1 Tim 3.11 Their wives also must be of good character and must not **gossip;**
5.13 they learn to be **gossips** and busybodies, talking of things they

GOURD

1 Kgs 6.18 The cedar panels were decorated with carvings of **gourds**
7.24 were two rows of bronze **gourds,** which had been cast all in
2 Kgs 4.39 a wild vine, and picked as many **gourds** as he could carry.

GOVERN

Gen 41.41 I now appoint you **governor** over all Egypt."
41.43 And so Joseph was appointed **governor** over all Egypt.
42. 6 Joseph, as **governor** of the land of Egypt, was selling corn
42.30 "The **governor** of Egypt spoke harshly to us and accused
43.11 of the land in your packs as a present for the **governor:**
Judg 9. 2 To be **governed** by all seventy of Gideon's sons or by just
9. 9 olive-tree answered, 'In order to **govern** you, I would have
9.11 fig-tree answered, 'In order to **govern** you, I would have to
9.13 vine answered, 'In order to **govern** you, I would have to stop
1 Kgs 4. 5 Chief of the district **governors:** Azariah
4. 7 Solomon appointed twelve men as district **governors** in Israel.
4.19 there was one **governor** over the whole land.
4.27 His twelve **governors,** each one in the month assigned to him,
4.28 Each **governor** also supplied his share of barley and straw,
10.15 Arabian kings and the **governors** of the Israelite districts.
20.14 under the command of the district **governors** are to do it."
22.26 take him to Amon, the **governor** of the city, and to Prince
2 Kgs 11.12 head, and gave him a copy of the laws **governing** kingship.
15. 5 of all duties, while his son Jotham **governed** the country.
23. 8 built by Joshua, the city **governor,** which was to the left of
25.22 Ahikam and grandson of Shaphan, **governor** of Judah, and
1 Chr 22.12 wisdom so that you may **govern** Israel according to his Law.
2 Chr 1. 2 all the **government** officials, all the heads of families,
9.14 kings of Arabia and the **governors** of the Israelite districts
18.25 take him to Amon, the **governor** of the city, and to Prince
19.11 and Zebadiah son of Ishmael, **governor** of Judah, will have
23.11 head, and gave him a copy of the laws **governing** kingship.
26.21 of all duties, while his son Jotham **governed** the country.
34. 8 son of Azaliah, Maaseiah, the **governor** of Jerusalem, and
Ezra 1. 8 for Sheshbazzar, the **governor** of Judah, [9-10] as follows:
2.63 The Jewish **governor** told them that they could not eat
4. 5 They also bribed Persian **government** officials to work against them.
4. 8 Also Rehum, the **governor,** and Shimshai, the secretary
4. 9 "From Rehum, the **governor,** from Shimshai, secretary of the province,
4.15 Its people have always been hard to **govern.**
4.17 "To Rehum, the **governor,** to Shimshai, secretary of the province,
5. 3 Almost at once Tattenai, **governor** of West Euphrates,
5.14 man named Sheshbazzar, whom he appointed **governor** of Judah.
6. 6 "To Tattenai, **governor** of West Euphrates, Shethar Bozenai,
6. 7 Let the **governor** of Judah and the Jewish leaders rebuild the
6.13 Then Tattenai the **governor,** Shethar Bozenai, and their
7.25 appoint administrators and judges to **govern** all the people
8.36 and gave it to the **governors** and officials of the province
Neh 2. 7 me letters to the **governors** of West Euphrates Province,
2. 9 There I gave the emperor's letters to the **governors.**
3. 7 as far as the residence of the **governor** of West Euphrates.
5.14 twelve years that I was **governor** of the land of Judah, from
5.14 nor I ate the food I was entitled to have as **governor.**
5.15 Every **governor** who had been in office before me had been
5.18 I did not claim the allowance that the **governor** is entitled to.
7. 2 I put two men in charge of **governing** the city of Jerusalem:
7.65 The Jewish **governor** told them that they could not eat
7.70 The **governor** 8 kilogrammes of gold
8. 9 So Nehemiah, who was the **governor,** Ezra, the priest and
10. 1 first to sign was the **governor,** Nehemiah son of Hacaliah,
12.26 the time of Nehemiah the **governor,** and the time of Ezra, the
Esth 1. 3 as well as the **governors** and noblemen of the provinces.
3.12 empire and to be sent to all the rulers, **governors,** and
8. 9 the Jews and to the **governors,** administrators, and officials
9. 3 all the provincial officials—**governors,** administrators,
Job 38.33 you know the laws that **govern** the skies, and can you make
Ps 72. 2 with justice and **govern** the oppressed with righteousness.
105.21 him in charge of his **government** and made him ruler over all
Prov 8.15 I help kings to **govern** and rulers to make good laws.
8.16 Every ruler on earth **governs** with my help,
16.12 justice is what makes a **government** strong.
25. 5 the king and his **government** will be known for its justice.
Ecc 5. 8 when you see that the **government** oppresses the poor and
Is 3. 4 The Lord will let the people be **governed** by immature boys.
32. 1 integrity, and national leaders who **govern** with justice.
Jer 40. 5 king of Babylonia has made **governor** of the towns of Judah.
40. 7 of Babylonia had made Gedaliah **governor** of the land and had
40.11 on in Judah and that he had made Gedaliah their **governor.**
41.17 whom the king of Babylonia had made **governor** of the land.
43. 9 of the entrance to the **government** building here in the city,
Ezek 22.27 The **government** officials are like wolves tearing apart
Dan 3. 2 come together—the princes, **governors,** lieutenant-governors,
3.27 All the princes, **governors,** lieutenant-governors, and
6. 1 and twenty **governors** to hold office throughout his empire.
6. 2 two others to supervise the **governors** and to look after the
6. 3 do better work than the other supervisors or the **governors.**
6. 4 supervisors and the **governors** tried to find something wrong
6. 7 supervisors, the **governors,** the lieutenant-governors,
Mic 3.11 The city's rulers **govern** for bribes, the priests
Nah 3.18 Emperor of Assyria, your **governors** are dead,
Hag 1. 1 The message was for the **governor** of Judah, Zerubbabel
1.14 Zerubbabel, the **governor** of Judah;
2. 2 to speak to Zerubbabel, the **governor** of Judah, to Joshua,
2.21 Lord gave Haggai a second message [21] for Zerubbabel, the **governor**
Zech 10. 4 come rulers, leaders, and commanders to **govern** my people.
Mal 1. 8 Try giving an animal like that to the **governor!**
Mt 27. 2 him off, and handed him over to Pilate, the Roman **governor.**
27.11 Jesus stood before the Roman **governor,** who questioned him.
27.14 with the result that the **Governor** was greatly surprised.
27.15 every Passover Festival the Roman **governor** was in the habit
27.27 took Jesus into the **governor's** palace, and the whole company
28.14 And if the **Governor** should hear of this, we will
Mk 6.21 for all the chief **government** officials, the military commanders,
15.16 to the courtyard of the **governor's** palace and called together
Lk 2. 2 this first census took place, Quirinius was the **governor** of Syria.
3. 1 Pontius Pilate was **governor** of Judaea, Herod was ruler of Galilee,
3.19 John reprimanded Herod, the **governor,** because he had married Herodias, his
12.11 the synagogues or before **governors** or rulers, do not be worried
20.20 him over to the authority and power of the Roman **Governor.**
Jn 4.46 A **government** official was there whose son was ill in Capernaum.
18.28 Jesus was taken from Caiaphas' house to the **governor's** palace.
Acts 7.10 and the king made Joseph **governor** over the country and the
13. 1 Manaen (who had been brought up with Herod the **governor),**
13. 7 was a friend of the **governor** of the island, Sergius Paulus,
13. 7 The **governor** called Barnabas and Saul before him
13. 8 Greek), who tried to turn the **governor** away from the faith.
13.12 When the **governor** saw what had happened, he believed;
18.12 Gallio was made the Roman **governor** of Achaia, the Jews got
23.24 Paul to ride and get him safely through to the **governor** Felix."
23.26 "Claudius Lysias to His Excellency, the **governor** Felix:
23.33 the letter to the **governor,** and handed Paul over to him.
23.34 The **governor** read the letter and asked Paul what
23.35 for Paul to be kept under guard in the **governor's** headquarters.
24.10 The **governor** then motioned to Paul to speak, and Paul said,
24.27 two years had passed, Porcius Festus succeeded Felix as **governor.**
26.30 Then the king, the **governor,** Bernice, and all the others got up,
2 Cor 11.32 I was in Damascus, the **governor** under King Aretas placed guards
1 Pet 2.14 authority, [14] and to the **governors,** who have been appointed

GOWN

Ps 45.13 Her **gown** is made of gold thread.
45.14 In her colourful **gown** she is led to the king, followed
Is 3.22 all their fine robes, **gowns,** cloaks, and purses;
Ezek 16.10 I dressed you in embroidered **gowns** and gave you shoes of

Am

GRAB

see also **SEIZE**

GRAB

Deut 25.11 her husband by **grabbing** hold of the other man's genitals,
1 Sam 17.35 bear turns on me, I **grab** it by the throat and beat
2 Sam 13.11 offered them to him, he **grabbed** her and said, "Come to bed
2 Kgs 7. 8 and drank what was there, **grabbed** the silver, gold, and
Job 8.15 If they **grab** for a thread, will it help them stand?"
Prov 26.17 like going down the street and **grabbing** a dog by the ears.
Is 4. 1 time comes, seven women will **grab** hold of one man and say,
Mt 14.31 once Jesus reached out and **grabbed** hold of him and said,
18.28 He **grabbed** him and started choking him.
22. 6 to his shop, [6] while others **grabbed** the servants, beat them,

GRACE

Num 6.25 May the Lord be kind and **gracious** to you;
Ezra 7.28 By God's **grace** I have won the favour of the emperor, of
8.18 Through God's **grace** they sent us Sherebiah, an able man,
9. 8 our God, you have been **gracious** to us and have let some
Neh 9.17 you are **gracious** and loving, slow to be angry.
9.31 You are a **gracious** and merciful God!
Prov 5.19 with the girl you married—[19] pretty and **graceful** as a deer.
11.16 A **gracious** lady is respected, but a woman without virtue
22.11 love purity of heart and **graciousness** of speech, the king
Song 7. 7 You are as **graceful** as a palm-tree, and your breasts are
Lk 1.30 God has been **gracious** to you.
Jn 1.14 a human being and, full of **grace** and truth, lived among us.
1.16 of the fullness of his **grace** he has blessed us all, giving
1.17 the Law through Moses, but **grace** and truth came through Jesus
Acts 13.43 and encouraged them to keep on living in the **grace** of God.
14. 3 that their message about his **grace** was true by giving them
14.26 to the care of God's **grace** for the work they had now
15.11 and are saved by the **grace** of the Lord Jesus, just as
15.40 commended by the believers to the care of the Lord's **grace.**
18.27 great help to those who through God's **grace** had become believers.
20.24 which is to declare the Good News about the **grace** of God.
20.32 to the message of his **grace,** which is able to build you
Rom 1. 7 Father and the Lord Jesus Christ give you **grace** and peace.
3.24 the free gift of God's **grace** all are put right with him
5. 2 into this experience of God's **grace,** in which we now live.
5.15 But God's **grace** is much greater, and so is his free gift
5.15 so many people through the **grace** of the one man, Jesus
5.17 All who receive God's abundant **grace** and are freely put right

Rom	5.20	but where sin increased, God's **grace** increased much more.
	5.21	so also God's **grace** rules by means of righteousness, leading
	6. 1	continue to live in sin so that God's **grace** will increase?
	6.14	for you do not live under law but under God's **grace.**
	6.15	we sin, because we are not under law but under God's **grace?**
	11. 5	left of those whom God has chosen because of his **grace.**
	11. 6	choice is based on his **grace,** not on what they have done.
	11. 6	on what people do, then his **grace** would not be real grace.
	12. 3	And because of God's **gracious** gift to me I say to every
	12. 6	gifts in accordance with the **grace** that God has given us.
	16.20	The **grace** of our Lord Jesus be with you.
1 Cor	1. 3	Father and the Lord Jesus Christ give you **grace** and peace.
	1. 4	for you because of the **grace** he has given you through Christ
	15.10	But by God's **grace** I am what I am,
	15.10	and the **grace** that he gave me was not
	15.10	not really my own doing, but God's **grace** working with me.
	16.23	The **grace** of the Lord Jesus be with you.
2 Cor	1. 2	Father and the Lord Jesus Christ give you **grace** and peace.
	1.12	by the power of God's **grace,** and not by human wisdom.
	4.15	and as God's **grace** reaches more and more people, they will
	6. 1	you who have received God's **grace** not to let it be wasted.
	8. 1	you to know what God's **grace** has accomplished in the
	8. 9	You know the **grace** of our Lord Jesus Christ;
	9.14	you because of the extraordinary **grace** God has shown you.
	12. 9	"My **grace** is all you need, for my power is greatest when
	13.13	The **grace** of the Lord Jesus Christ, the love of God,
Gal	1. 3	Father and the Lord Jesus Christ give you **grace** and peace.
	1. 6	who called you by the **grace** of Christ, and are accepting
	1.15	But God in his **grace** chose me even before I was born,
	2.21	I refuse to reject the **grace** of God.
	5. 4	You are outside God's **grace.**
	6.18	May the **grace** of our Lord Jesus Christ be with you all,
Eph	1. 2	Father and the Lord Jesus Christ give you **grace** and peace.
	1. 6	praise God for his glorious **grace,** for the free gift he gave
	1. 7	How great is the **grace** of God, [8] which he gave to us
	2. 5	It is by God's **grace** that you have been saved.
	2. 7	the extraordinary greatness of his **grace** in the love he
	2. 8	For it is by God's **grace** that you have been saved
	3. 2	heard that God in his **grace** has given me this work to
	6.24	May God's **grace** be with all those who love our Lord
Phil	1. 2	Father and the Lord Jesus Christ give you **grace** and peace.
	4.23	May the **grace** of the Lord Jesus Christ be with you all.
Col	1. 2	May God our Father give you **grace** and peace.
	1. 6	you first heard about the **grace** of God and came to know
	1. 7	You learnt of God's **grace** from Epaphras, our dear fellow-servant,
	4.18	May God's **grace** be with you.
1 Thes	1. 1	May **grace** and peace be yours.
	5.28	The **grace** of our Lord Jesus Christ be with you.
2 Thes	1. 2	Father and the Lord Jesus Christ give you **grace** and peace.
	1.12	you from him, by the **grace** of our God and of the
	2.16	loved us and in his **grace** gave us unfailing courage and a
	3.18	May the **grace** of our Lord Jesus Christ be with you all.
1 Tim	1. 2	Father and Christ Jesus our Lord give you **grace,** mercy, and
	1.14	Lord poured out his abundant **grace** on me and gave me the
	6.21	God's **grace** be with you all.
2 Tim	1. 2	Father and Christ Jesus our Lord give you **grace,** mercy, and
	1. 9	what we have done, but because of his own purpose and **grace.**
	1. 9	He gave us this **grace** by means of Christ Jesus before the
	2. 1	son, be strong through the **grace** that is ours in union with
	4.22	God's **grace** be with you all.
Tit	1. 4	Father and Christ Jesus our Saviour give you **grace** and peace.
	2.11	For God has revealed his **grace** for the salvation of all mankind.
	2.12	That **grace** instructs us to give up ungodly living and worldly passions,
	3. 7	Saviour, [7] so that by his **grace** we might be put right with
	3.15	God's **grace** be with you all.
Phlm	3	Father and the Lord Jesus Christ give you **grace** and peace.
	25	May the **grace** of the Lord Jesus Christ be with you all.
Heb	2. 9	angels, so that through God's **grace** he should die for everyone.
	4.16	confidence, then, and approach God's throne, where there is **grace.**
	4.16	will receive mercy and find **grace** to help us just when we
	10.29	who insults the Spirit of **grace?**
	12.15	Guard against turning back from the **grace** of God.
	13. 9	receive inner strength from God's **grace,** and not by obeying rules
	13.25	May God's **grace** be with you all.
Jas	1. 5	because God gives generously and **graciously** to all.
	4. 6	But the **grace** that God gives is even stronger.
	4. 6	"God resists the proud, but gives **grace** to the humble."
1 Pet	1. 2	May **grace** and peace be yours in full measure.
	5.10	while, the God of all **grace,** who calls you to share his
	5.12	and give my testimony that this is the true **grace** of God.
2 Pet	1. 2	May **grace** and peace be yours in full measure
	3.18	continue to grow in the **grace** and knowledge of our Lord and
2 Jn	3	and Jesus Christ, the Father's Son, give us **grace,** mercy,
Jude	4	distort the message about the **grace** of our God in order to
Rev	1. 4	**Grace** and peace be yours from God, who is, who was, and
	22.21	May the **grace** of the Lord Jesus be with everyone.

GRAIN

Gen	1.11	of plants, those that bear **grain** and those that bear
	1.29	have provided all kinds of **grain** and all kinds of fruit for
Lev	2. 1	anyone presents an offering of **grain** to the Lord, he must
	2.14	first corn harvested, offer roasted **grain** or ground meal.
	27.30	of the land, whether **grain** or fruit, belongs to the Lord.
Josh	5.11	roasted **grain** and bread made without yeast.
Judg	13.19	a young goat and some **grain,** and offered them on the rock
Ruth	2.14	with the workers, and Boaz passed some roasted **grain** to her.
1 Sam	17.17	of this roasted **grain** and these ten loaves of bread,
	25.18	kilogrammes of roasted **grain,** a hundred bunches of raisins,
2 Sam	17.19	of the well and scattered **grain** over it, so that no one
	17.28	wheat, barley, meal, roasted **grain,** beans, peas, honey,
2 Kgs	7. 2	not even if the Lord himself were to send **grain** at once!"
	7.19	not even if the Lord himself were to send **grain** at once!"
	19.29	you will have only wild **grain** to eat, but the following year
Job	5. 5	fool's crops— even the **grain** growing among thorns— and
	39.12	harvest and gather the **grain** from your threshing-place?
Ps	78.24	he gave them **grain** from heaven, by sending down manna
Prov	3.10	barns will be filled with **grain,** and you will have too much
	11.26	curse a man who hoards **grain,** waiting for a higher price,
Is	28.25	barley, and at the edges of his fields he sows other **grain.**
	28.28	it by driving a cart over it without bruising the **grains.**
	37.30	you will have only wild **grain** to eat, but the following year
Jer	50.26	side and break open the places where its **grain** is stored!
	50.26	Pile up the loot like piles of **grain!**
Hos	10.11	a well-trained young cow, ready and willing to thresh **grain.**
Joel	1.17	There is no **grain** to be stored, and so the empty granaries
Amos	5.11	You have oppressed the poor and robbed them of their **grain.**
Mt	3.12	his winnowing shovel with him to thresh out all the **grain.**
	12. 1	so they began to pick ears of corn and eat the **grain.**
	13. 8	a hundred **grains,** others sixty, and others thirty."
Mk	4. 8	had thirty **grains,** others sixty, and others a hundred."
Lk	3.17	to thresh out all the **grain** and gather the wheat into his
	6. 1	ears of corn, rub them in their hands, and eat the **grain.**
	8. 8	the plants grew and produced corn, a hundred **grains** each."
Jn	12.24	a **grain** of wheat remains no more than a single grain unless
	12.24	If it does die, then it produces many **grains.**
1 Cor	15.37	a bare seed, perhaps a **grain** of wheat or some other grain,

GRAIN-OFFERING

Ex	30. 9	incense, any animal-offering, or any **grain-offering,**
	40.29	and the **grain-offering,** just as the Lord had commanded.
Lev	2. 3	The rest of the **grain-offering** belongs to the priests;
	2.11	None of the **grain-offerings** which you present to the
	2.13	Put salt on every **grain-offering,** because salt
	5.11	on it, because it is a sin-offering, not a **grain-offering.**
	5.13	to the priest, just as in the case of a **grain-offering.**
	6.14	The following are the regulations for **grain-offerings.**
	6.14	Aaronite priest shall present the **grain-offering** to the Lord
	6.20	same amount as the daily **grain-offering),** half in the
	6.21	presented as a **grain-offering,** a smell pleasing to the Lord.
	6.23	No part of a **grain-offering** that a priest makes may be eaten;
	7. 9	Every **grain-offering** that has been baked in an oven or
	7.10	But all uncooked **grain-offerings,** whether mixed with oil or dry,
	7.37	**grain-offerings,** the sin-offerings, the repayment-offerings, the ordination-offerings,
	9. 4	them to the Lord with the **grain-offering** mixed with oil.
	9.17	He presented the **grain-offering** and took a handful of
	10.12	Eleazar and Ithamar, "Take the **grain-offering** that is left
	14.20	and offer it with the **grain-offering** on the altar.
	14.21	mixed with olive-oil for a **grain-offering** and a third of a
	14.31	the other as the burnt-offering with the **grain-offering.**
	23.18	Lord, together with a **grain-offering** and a wine-offering.
	23.37	**grain-offerings,** sacrifices, and wine-offerings,
Num	4.16	lamps, the incense, the **grain-offerings,** the anointing oil,
	7.12	of them full of flour mixed with oil for the **grain-offering;**
	7.84	lambs, together with the **grain-offerings** that go with them,
	8. 8	the required **grain-offering** of flour mixed with olive-oil;
	15. 4	as a **grain-offering,** together with a litre of wine.
	15. 6	to be presented as a **grain-offering,** [7] together with one and
	15. 9	or as a fellowship-offering, [9] a **grain-offering** of three
	15.24	the Lord, with the proper **grain-offering** and wine-offering.
	18. 9	**grain-offerings,** the sin-offerings, and the repayment offerings.
	28. 5	each with a **grain-offering** of one kilogramme of flour,
	28. 9	with olive-oil as a **grain-offering,** and the wine-offering.
	28.12	As a **grain-offering,** offer flour mixed with olive-oil:
	28.20	Offer the proper **grain-offering** of flour mixed with olive-oil:
	28.28	Offer the proper **grain-offering** of flour mixed with olive-oil:
	28.31	in addition to the daily burnt-offering and **grain-offering.**
	29. 3	Offer the proper **grain-offering** of flour mixed with olive-oil:
	29. 6	the month with its **grain-offering,**
	29. 6	and the daily burnt-offering with its **grain-offering**
	29. 9	Offer the proper **grain-offering** of flour mixed with olive-oil:
	29.11	burnt-offering with its **grain-offering** and wine-offering.
	29.14	Offer the proper **grain-offering** of flour mixed with olive-oil:
	29.16	burnt-offering with its **grain-offering** and wine-offering.
	29.39	the burnt-offerings, **grain-offerings,** wine-offerings,
Josh	22.23	on or to use for **grain-offerings** or fellowship-offerings,
	22.29	to burn offerings on or for **grain-offerings** or sacrifices.
1 Kgs	8.64	the sacrifices burnt whole, the **grain-offerings,** and the fat
2 Kgs	16.13	he burnt animal sacrifices and **grain-offerings** on it, and
	16.15	morning burnt-offerings and the evening **grain-offerings,**
	16.15	for the burnt-offerings and **grain-offerings** of the king
2 Chr	7. 7	**grain-offerings,** and the fat from the fellowship-offerings.
Neh	10.33	the sacred bread, the daily **grain-offering,** the animals to
	13. 9	**grain-offerings,** and incense to be put back.
Is	57. 6	You pour out wine as offerings to them and bring them **grain-offerings.**
	66. 3	whether they present a **grain-offering** or offer pigs' blood;
	66.20	just as Israelites bring **grain-offerings** to the Temple
Jer	14.12	they offer me burnt-offerings and **grain-offerings,**
	17.26	**grain-offerings** and incense, as well as thank-offerings.
	33.18	to offer burnt-offerings, **grain-offerings,** and sacrifices."
Ezek	42.13	**grain-offerings** and the sacrifices offered for sin
	44.29	The **grain-offerings,** the sin-offerings
	45.13	"You are to bring **grain-offerings,** animals to be burnt whole,
	45.17	the **grain-offerings,** and the wine-offerings
	45.17	the sin-offerings, the **grain-offerings,**
	46. 5	For each such **grain-offering** he is to bring three litres
	46. 7	are to be offered with each such **grain-offering** of corn.

Ezek 46.11 and at the festivals the **grain-offering** will be seventeen
46.11 olive-oil are to be offered with each such **grain-offering.**
Amos 5.22 When you bring me burnt-offerings and **grain-offerings,**

GRAINS OF SAND

Gen 22.17 are stars in the sky or **grains of sand** along the seashore.
32.12 count, as many as the **grains of sand** along the seashore."
Josh 11. 4 as many men as there are **grains of sand** on the seashore.
Judg 7.12 many camels as there were **grains of sand** on the seashore.
1 Sam 13. 5 many soldiers as there are **grains of sand** on the seashore.
2 Sam 17.11 other, as many as the **grains of sand** on the sea-shore, and
1 Kgs 4.20 Israel were as numerous as the **grains of sand** on the seashore;
Ps 78.27 down birds, as many as the **grains of sand** on the shore;
139.18 I counted them, they would be more than the **grains of sand.**
Is 10.22 of Israel as there are **grains of sand** by the sea, only
48.19 would be as numerous as **grains of sand,** and I would have
Jer 15. 8 more widows in your land than **grains of sand** by the sea.
33.22 stars in the sky or the **grains of sand** on the sea-shore."
Hab 1. 9 Their captives are as numerous as **grains of sand.**
Rom 9.27 as many as the **grains of sand** by the sea, yet only
Heb 11.12 as many as the numberless **grains of sand** on the sea-shore.
Rev 20. 8 for battle, as many as the **grains of sand** on the sea-shore.

GRAMME

also Num 7.12 Num 7.12 2 Kgs 6.25 2 Chr 3.9 Neh 10.32 Ezek 4.10

GRANARY

Joel 1.17 grain to be stored, and so the empty **granaries** are in ruins.

GRANDCHILDREN

Gen 31.28 even let me kiss my **grandchildren** and my daughters good-bye.
31.55 Laban kissed his **grandchildren** and his daughters good-bye,
45.10 me—you, your children, your **grandchildren,** your sheep, your
50.23 He lived to see Ephraim's children and **grandchildren.**
Ex 10. 2 to tell your children and **grandchildren** how I made fools of
34. 7 fail to punish children and **grandchildren** to the third and
Num 14.18 fail to punish children and **grandchildren** to the third and
Deut 4. 9 Tell your children and your **grandchildren** [10] about the day
4.25 time and have children and **grandchildren,** do not sin by
Job 21. 8 They have children and **grandchildren,** and live to watch
42.16 enough to see his **grandchildren** and great-grandchildren.
Ps 128. 6 May you live to see your **grandchildren!**
Prov 13.22 wealth to leave to his **grandchildren,** but the wealth of
17. 6 men are proud of their **grandchildren,** just as boys are proud
1 Tim 5. 4 a widow has children or **grandchildren,** they should learn first

GRANDDAUGHTER

Gen 46. 7 his sons, his grandsons, his daughters, and his **granddaughters.**
Lev 18.10 Do not have intercourse with your **granddaughter;**
18.17 intercourse with the daughter or **granddaughter** of a woman
2 Chr 22. 2 daughter of King Ahab and **granddaughter** of King Omri of

GRANDFATHER

Gen 28. 2 to the home of your **grandfather** Bethuel, and marry one of
32. 9 Jacob prayed, "God of my **grandfather** Abraham and God of my
2 Sam 9. 7 land that belonged to your **grandfather** Saul, and you will
16. 3 restore to him the kingdom of his **grandfather** Saul."
1 Chr 2.44 Shema was the father of Raham and the **grandfather** of Jorkeam.
2 Chr 21.12 your father, King Jehoshaphat, or that of your **grandfather,**
22. 9 out of respect for his **grandfather** King Jehoshaphat, who had

GRANDMOTHER

1 Kgs 15.10 His **grandmother** was Maacah, the daughter of Absalom.
15.13 He removed his **grandmother** Maacah from her position
2 Chr 15.16 King Asa removed his **grandmother** Maacah from her position
2 Tim 1. 5 kind of faith that your **grandmother** Lois and your mother Eunice

GRANDPARENTS

1 Tim 5. 4 their parents and **grandparents,** because that is what pleases God.

GRANDSON

Gen 11.31 took his son Abram, his **grandson** Lot, who was the son of
46. 7 his sons, his **grandsons,** his daughters, and his granddaughters.
Judg 12.14 He had forty sons and thirty **grandsons,** who rode on seventy donkeys.
Ruth 4.14 He has given you a **grandson** today to take care of you.
4.15 she has given you a **grandson,** who will bring new life to
2 Sam 9. 9 am giving Mephibosheth, your master's **grandson,** everything
16. 3 "Where is Mephibosheth, the **grandson** of your master Saul?"
19.24 Then Mephibosheth, Saul's **grandson,** came down to meet the king.
21. 7 David spared Jonathan's son Mephibosheth, the **grandson** of Saul.
1 Chr 3.22 Shecaniah had one son, Shemaiah, and five **grandsons:**
8.40 He had a hundred and fifty sons and **grandsons** in all.
Neh 12.23 only until the time of Jonathan, the **grandson** of Eliashib.
Jer 27. 7 serve his son and his **grandson** until the time comes for his

GRANT

2 Sam 14.22 are pleased with me, because you have **granted** my request."
1 Kgs 8.28 Listen to my prayer, and **grant** the requests I make to you
2 Kgs 2.10 "That is a difficult request to **grant,**" Elijah replied.
2 Chr 6.19 Listen to my prayer and **grant** the requests I make to you.
Neh 2. 5 me and is willing to **grant** my request, let me go to
2. 7 Then I asked him to **grant** me the favour of giving me
Esth 5. 6 I will **grant** your request, even if you ask for half my
5. 8 Majesty is kind enough to **grant** my request, I would like you
7. 3 it please Your Majesty to **grant** my humble request, my wish
Mal 1. 8 Would he be pleased with you or **grant** you any favours?"
Mt 14. 9 of all his guests he gave orders that her wish be **granted.**
Acts 4.30 your hand to heal, and **grant** that wonders and miracles may
2 Tim 1.18 May the Lord **grant** him his mercy on that Day!

GRAPE

Gen 40. 9 my dream there was a **grapevine** in front of me [10] with three
40.10 came out, the blossoms appeared, and the **grapes** ripened.
40.11 so I took the **grapes** and squeezed them into the cup and
49.11 his young donkey to a **grapevine,** To the very best of the
Lev 19.10 your vineyard to gather the **grapes** that were missed
19.10 or to pick up the **grapes** that have fallen;
25. 5 sown, and do not gather the **grapes** from your unpruned vines;
25.11 by itself or gather the **grapes** in your unpruned vineyards.
26. 5 it is time to pick **grapes,**
26. 5 you will still be picking **grapes** when it is time to sow
Num 6. 3 drink made from **grapes** or eat any grapes or raisins.
6. 4 anything that comes from a **grapevine,**
6. 4 not even the seeds or skins of **grapes.**
13.20 (It was the season when **grapes** were beginning to ripen.)
13.23 which had one bunch of **grapes** on it so heavy that it
13.24 because of the bunch of **grapes** the Israelites cut off there.)
20. 5 There's no corn, no figs, no **grapes,** no pomegranates.
Deut 8. 8 land that produces wheat and barley, **grapes,** figs,
16.13 corn and pressed all your **grapes,** celebrate the Festival of
20. 6 but has not yet had the chance to harvest its **grapes?**
22. 9 "Do not plant any crop in the same field as your **grapevines;**
22. 9 forbidden to use either the **grapes** or the produce of the
23.24 you may eat all the **grapes** you want, but you must not
24.21 When you have gathered your **grapes** once, do not go back
24.21 the **grapes** that are left are for the foreigners, orphans,
28.30 You will plant a vineyard—but never eat its **grapes.**
28.39 you will not gather their **grapes** or drink wine from them,
32.32 that bear bitter and poisonous **grapes,** [33] like wine made
Josh 24.13 are living there and eating **grapes** from vines that you did
Judg 9.12 then said to the **grapevine,** 'You come and be our king.'
9.27 their vineyards and picked the **grapes,** made wine from them,
13.14 She must not eat anything that comes from the **grapevine;**
1 Sam 8.15 your corn and of your **grapes** for his court officers and
1 Kgs 4.25 each family with its own **grapevines** and fig-trees.
2 Kgs 18.31 all be allowed to eat **grapes** from your own vines, and figs
19.29 your corn and harvest it, and plant vines and eat **grapes.**
Neh 13.15 I saw people in Judah pressing juice from **grapes** on the Sabbath.
13.15 Others were loading corn, wine, **grapes,** figs, and other
Job 15.33 He will be like a vine that loses its unripe **grapes;**
24. 6 don't own, and gather **grapes** in wicked men's vineyards.
24.11 press olives for oil, and **grapes** for wine, but they
Ps 78.47 killed their **grapevines** with hail and their fig-trees with frost.
80. 8 You brought a **grapevine** out of Egypt;
80.12 Now anyone passing by can steal its **grapes;**
80.15 Come and save this **grapevine** that you planted, this
105.33 he destroyed their **grapevines** and fig-trees
107.37 They sowed the fields and planted **grapevines** and reaped
Song 7. 8 breasts are like bunches of **grapes,** your breath like the
Is 5. 2 a tower to guard them, dug a pit for treading the **grapes.**
5. 2 He waited for the grapes to ripen, but every **grape** was sour.
5. 4 it produce sour grapes and not the good **grapes** I expected?
5.10 The **grapevines** growing on ten hectares of land will
16.10 No one tramples **grapes** to make wine;
18. 5 Before the **grapes** are gathered, when the blossoms have all fallen
18. 5 and the **grapes** are ripening, the enemy will destroy
24. 7 The **grapevines** wither, and wine is becoming scarce.
24.13 off every tree and the last **grapes** picked from the vines.
32.10 despair because there will be no **grapes** for you to gather.
36.16 all be allowed to eat **grapes** from your own vines and figs
37.30 your corn and harvest it, and plant vines and eat **grapes.**
62. 9 that tended and gathered the **grapes** Will drink the wine in
63. 2 red, like that of a man who tramples **grapes** to make wine?"
63. 3 have trampled the nations like **grapes,** and no one came to
65. 8 The Lord says, "No one destroys good **grapes;**
Jer 6. 9 like a vineyard from which every **grape** has been picked.
8.13 like a vine with no **grapes,** like a fig-tree with no figs;
25.30 he will shout like a man treading **grapes.**
31.29 'The parents ate the sour **grapes,** But the children got the
31.30 Instead, whoever eats sour **grapes** will have his own
48.32 But now your summer fruits and your **grapes** have been destroyed.
49. 9 When men pick **grapes,** they leave a few on the vines, and
Lam 1.15 He crushed my people like **grapes** in a winepress.
Ezek 15. 2 is a branch of a **grapevine** compared with the trees of the
17. 6 The plant sprouted and became a low, wide-spreading **grapevine.**
17. 8 grow leaves and bear **grapes** and be a magnificent vine.
17. 9 its roots, pull off the **grapes,** and break off the branches
18. 2 'The parents ate the sour **grapes,** But the children got the
19.10 Your mother was like a **grapevine** planted near a stream.
Hos 2.12 I will destroy her **grapevines** and her fig-trees, which
2.21 and the earth will produce corn and **grapes** and olives.
9.10 Israel, it was like finding **grapes** growing in the desert.
10. 1 of Israel were like a grapevine that was full of **grapes.**
Joel 1. 5 the **grapes** for making new wine have been destroyed.
1. 7 They have destroyed our **grapevines** and chewed up our fig-trees.
1.10 the corn is destroyed, the **grapes** are dried up, and the
1.12 The **grapevines** and fig-trees have withered;
2.22 bear their fruit, and there are plenty of figs and **grapes.**
3.13 crush them as **grapes** are crushed in a full winepress until
Amos 9.13 it can be harvested, and **grapes** will grow faster than the

Obad 5 When people gather **grapes,** they always leave a few.
Mic 1. 6 ruins in the open country, a place for planting **grapevines.**
7. 1 no fruit left on the trees and no **grapes** on the vines.
7. 1 All the **grapes** and all the tasty figs have been picked.
Hab 3.17 have no fruit and no **grapes** grow on the vines, even though
Hag 2.19 no corn left, and the **grapevines,** fig-trees, pomegranates,
Zech 8.12 Their vines will bear **grapes,** the earth will produce crops,
Mal 3.11 your crops, and your grapevines will be loaded with **grapes.**
Mt 7.16 Thorn bushes do not bear **grapes,** and briars do not bear figs.
21.34 time came to gather the **grapes,** he sent his slaves to the
Mk 12. 2 time came to gather the **grapes,** he sent a slave to the
Lk 6.44 not pick figs from thorn bushes or gather **grapes** from bramble
20.10 time came to gather the **grapes,** he sent a slave to the
1 Cor 9. 7 What farmer does not eat the **grapes** from his own vineyard?
Jas 3.12 a **grapevine** cannot bear figs, nor can a salty spring produce
Rev 14.18 sickle, and cut the **grapes** from the vineyard of the earth,
14.18 because the **grapes** are ripe!"
14.19 on the earth, cut the **grapes** from the vine, and threw them
14.20 The **grapes** were squeezed out in the winepress outside the city,

GRASP

Song 5. 5 with liquid myrrh, as I **grasped** the handle of the door.
Mk 6.52 their minds could not **grasp** it.

GRASS

Gen 1.30 the birds I have provided **grass** and leafy plants for
41. 2 up out of the river and began to feed on the **grass.**
41.18 came up out of the river and began feeding on the **grass.**
Ex 2. 3 placed it in the tall **grass** at the edge of the river.
2. 5 the basket in the tall **grass** and sent a slave-girl to get
Num 22. 4 round us, like a bull eating the **grass** in a pasture."
Deut 11.15 and olive-oil for you, [15]and **grass** for your livestock.
32. 2 showers on young plants, like gentle rain on tender **grass.**
2 Sam 23. 4 dawn, the sun that makes the **grass** sparkle after rain."
1 Kgs 18. 5 if we can find enough **grass** to keep the horses and mules
2 Kgs 19.26 They were like **grass** in a field or weeds growing on a
Job 5.25 as many children as there are blades of **grass** in a pasture.
6. 5 donkey is content when eating **grass,** and a cow is quiet when
38.27 Who waters the dry and thirsty land, so that **grass** springs up?
40.15 He eats **grass** like a cow, [16]but what strength there is in
40.20 **Grass** to feed him grows on the hills where wild beasts play.
Ps 23. 2 rest in fields of green **grass** and leads me to quiet pools
37. 2 They will soon disappear like **grass** that dries up;
72.16 May the cities be filled with people, like fields full of **grass.**
102. 4 I am beaten down like dry **grass;**
102.11 I am like dry **grass.**
103.15 As for us, our life is like **grass.**
104.14 You make **grass** grow for the cattle and plants for man to
106.20 glory of God for the image of an animal that eats **grass.**
129. 6 May they all be like **grass** growing on the house-tops,
147. 8 rain for the earth and makes **grass** grow on the hills.
Prov 27.25 hay and then cut the **grass** on the hillsides while the next
Song 1.16 The green **grass** will be our bed;
Is 5.17 lambs will eat **grass** and young goats will find pasture.
5.24 just as straw and dry **grass** shrivel and burn in the fire,
15. 6 of Nimrim is dry, the **grass** beside it has withered, and
35. 7 Where jackals used to live, marsh **grass** and reeds will grow.
37.27 They were like **grass** in a field or weeds growing on a
40. 6 "Proclaim that all mankind are like **grass;**
40. 7 **Grass** withers and flowers fade, when the Lord sends the
40. 7 People are no more enduring than **grass.**
40. 8 Yes, **grass** withers and flowers fade, but the word of our
42.15 the hills and mountains and dry up the **grass** and trees.
44. 4 They will thrive like well-watered **grass,** like willows by
51.12 you fear mortal man, who is no more enduring than **grass?**
58. 5 low like a blade of **grass,** and spread out sackcloth and
Jer 12. 4 our land be dry, and the **grass** in every field be withered?
14. 5 deer abandons her new-born fawn because there is no **grass.**
Ezek 34.18 Some of you are nct satisfied with eating the best **grass;**
34.19 sheep have to eat the **grass** you trample down and drink the
Dan 4.15 Leave it there in the field with the **grass.**
4.23 round it, and leave it there in the field with the **grass.**
4.25 seven years you will eat **grass** like an ox, and sleep in
4.32 with wild animals, and eat **grass** like an ox for seven years.
4.33 was driven out of human society and ate **grass** like an ox.
5.21 lived with wild donkeys, ate **grass** like an ox, and slept in
Joel 2. 5 they crackle like dry **grass** on fire.
Amos 1. 2 The pastures dry up, and the **grass** on Mount Carmel turns brown."
7. 1 hay had been cut and the **grass** was starting to grow again.
Mt 6.30 God who clothes the wild **grass**—
6.30 **grass** that is here today and gone
11. 7 A blade of **grass** bending in the wind?
14.19 He ordered the people to sit down on the **grass;**
Mk 6.39 people divide into groups and sit down on the green **grass.**
Lk 7.24 A blade of **grass** bending in the wind?
12.28 God who clothes the wild **grass**—
12.28 **grass** that is here today and gone
Jn 6.10 (There was a lot of **grass** there.)
1 Cor 3.12 others will use wood or **grass** or straw.
1 Pet 1.24 says, "All mankind are like **grass,** and all their glory is
1.24 The **grass** withers, and the flowers fall, [25]but the word of
Rev 8. 7 up, a third of the trees, and every blade of green **grass.**
9. 4 told not to harm the **grass** or the trees or any other

GRASSHOPPER

Lev 11.22 You may eat locusts, crickets, or **grasshoppers.**
Num 13.33 We felt as small as **grasshoppers,** and that is how we must

GRATEFUL
[UNGRATEFUL]

Lev 19.24 dedicated as an offering to show your **gratitude** to me, the
Deut 24.13 Then he will be **grateful,** and the Lord your God will be
26.11 Be **grateful** for the good things that the Lord your God
27. 7 eat your fellowship-offerings and be **grateful** in the
Judg 8.35 They were not **grateful** to the family of Gideon for all
2 Chr 32.25 was too proud to show **gratitude** for what the Lord had done
Ecc 4.16 is gone, no one will be **grateful** for what he has done.
5.19 enjoy them, he should be **grateful** and enjoy what he has
11. 8 Be **grateful** for every year you live.
Lk 6.35 For he is good to the **ungrateful** and the wicked.
Acts 24. 3 and at all times, and we are deeply **grateful** to you.
Rom 16. 4 I am **grateful** to them—not only I, but all the Gentile
2 Cor 9.12 God's people, but also produces an outpouring of **gratitude** to God.
2 Tim 3. 2 they will be insulting, disobedient to their parents, **ungrateful,** and
Heb 12.28 Let us be **grateful** and worship God in a way that will

GRATING

Ex 27. 4 Make a bronze **grating** and put four bronze carrying-rings
27. 5 Put the **grating** under the rim of the altar, so that it
35.16 burn offerings, with its bronze **grating** attached, its poles,
38. 4 He made a bronze **grating** and put it under the rim of
38.30 with its bronze **grating,** all the equipment for the altar,
39.39 with its bronze **grating,** its poles, and all its equipment;
2 Kgs 25.17 bronze **grating** decorated with pomegranates made of bronze.
Jer 52.21 all round it was a **grating** decorated with pomegranates, all
52.23 On the **grating** of each column there were a hundred

GRAVE

Gen 23. 6 bury your wife in the best **grave** that we have.
23. 6 glad to give you a **grave,** so that you can bury her."
35.20 stone there, and it still marks Rachel's **grave** to this day.
Ex 14.11 They said to Moses, "Weren't there any **graves** in Egypt?
Num 11.34 named Kibroth Hattaavah (which means **"Graves** of Craving"),
19.16 a human bone or a **grave,** he becomes unclean for seven days.
19.18 had touched the human bone or the dead body or the **grave.**
33.15 Sinai Desert, Kibroth Hattaavah (or **"Graves** of Craving"),
2 Sam 3.32 king wept aloud at the **grave,** and so did all the people.
17.23 He was buried in the family **grave.**
19.37 Then let me go back home and die near my parents' **grave.**
21.14 Saul and Jonathan in the **grave** of Saul's father Kish, in
22. 6 death was round me, and the **grave** set its trap for me.
1 Kgs 13.22 and your body will not be buried in your family **grave."**
13.30 it in his own family **grave,** and he and his sons mourned
13.31 die, bury me in this **grave** and lay my body next to
2 Chr 34. 4 scattered the dust on the **graves** of the people who had
Job 3.17 In the **grave** wicked men stop their evil, and tired
3.21 they prefer a **grave** to any treasure.
7.21 I will be in my **grave,** and I'll be gone when you
10.19 the womb straight to the **grave** would have been as good as
17. 1 there is nothing left for me but the **grave.**
17.14 I will call the **grave** my father, and the worms that eat
21.32 he is carried to the **graveyard,** to his well-guarded tomb,
Ps 18. 5 death was round me, and the **grave** set its trap for me.
30. 3 you kept me from the **grave.**
30. 9 What profit from my going to the **grave?**
49. 9 to keep him from the **grave,** to let him live for ever.
49.11 Their **graves** are their homes for ever;
49.17 his wealth will not go with him to the **grave.**
55.23 and liars to their **graves** before half their life is over.
69.15 don't let me drown in the depths or sink into the **grave.**
71.20 you will keep me from the **grave.**
86.13 You have saved me from the **grave** itself.
88. 5 lying in their **graves,** those you have forgotten completely,
88.11 love spoken of in the **grave** or your faithfulness in the
89.48 How can man keep himself from the **grave?**
103. 4 He keeps me from the **grave** and blesses me with love and
107.20 He healed them with his command and saved them from the **grave.**
116. 3 the horrors of the **grave** closed in on me;
141. 7 so their bones are scattered at the edge of the **grave.**
Prov 5.23 His utter stupidity will send him to his **grave.**
28.17 of murder is digging his own **grave** as fast as he can.
Ecc 8.10 men buried and in their **graves,** but on the way back from
Is 26.19 All those sleeping in their **graves** will wake up and sing for
53. 9 He was placed in a **grave** with evil men, he was buried
Jer 8. 1 who lived in Jerusalem, will be taken out of their **graves.**
20.17 Then my mother's womb would have been my **grave.**
Ezek 28. 8 They will kill you and send you to a watery **grave.**
32.22 "Assyria is there, with the **graves** of her soldiers all around.
32.23 killed in battle, [23]and their **graves** are in the deepest
32.23 her soldiers fell in battle, and their **graves** surround her tomb.
32.24 "Elam is there, with the **graves** of her soldiers all around.
32.25 killed in battle, and the **graves** of her soldiers are all
32.26 Tubal are there, with the **graves** of their soldiers all around.
37.12 that I, the Sovereign Lord, am going to open their **graves.**
37.13 When I open the **graves** where my people are buried and
39.15 beside it so that the **grave-diggers** can come and bury it in
Nah 1.14 I am preparing a **grave** for the Assyrians—they don't deserve
Mt 27.52 rocks split apart, [52]the **graves** broke open, and many of God's
27.53 They left the **graves,** and after Jesus rose from death,
Lk 11.44 You are like unmarked **graves** which people walk on without knowing it."
Jn 5.29 dead will hear his voice [29]and come out of their **graves:**
11.31 They thought that she was going to the **grave** to weep there.
11.44 hands and feet wrapped in **grave** clothes, and with a cloth
12.17 called Lazarus out of the **grave** and raised him from death

Acts 2.27 you will not allow your faithful servant to rot in the **grave.**
2.29 and was buried, and his **grave** is here with us to this
2.31 his body did not rot in the **grave.'**
7.16 they were buried in the **grave** which Abraham had bought from
13.34 raising him from death, never to rot away in the **grave:**
13.35 'You will not allow your devoted servant to rot in the **grave.'**
13.36 buried with his ancestors, and his body rotted in the **grave.**

GRAVEL

Ps 147.17 He sends hail like **gravel;**
Lam 3.16 my face in the ground and broke my teeth on the **gravel.**

GRAZE

Ex 22. 5 a man lets his animals **graze** in a field or a vineyard
34. 3 sheep or cattle are to **graze** at the foot of the mountain."
Song 1. 7 Tell me, my love, Where will you lead your flock to **graze?**
Is 7.25 It will be a place where cattle and sheep **graze."**
27.10 become a pasture for cattle, where they can rest and **graze.**
49. 9 They will be like sheep that **graze** on the hills;
Ezek 34.14 I will let them **graze** in safety in the mountain meadows
Mt 18.12 will leave the other ninety-nine **grazing** on the hillside and go

GREASY

Ex 27. 3 Make pans for the **greasy** ashes, and make shovels, bowls,
Lev 6.10 linen shorts, shall remove the **greasy** ashes left on the
Num 4.13 They shall remove the **greasy** ashes from the altar and

GREAT

Gen 1.21 So God created the **great** sea-monsters,
6. 4 They were the **great** heroes and famous men of long ago.
10. 8 named Nimrod, who became the world's first **great** conqueror.
10. 9 Lord's help he was a **great** hunter, and that is why people
10. 9 say, "May the Lord make you as **great** a hunter as Nimrod!"
10.12 and Resen, which is between Nineveh and the **great** city of Calah.
12. 2 you many descendants, and they will become a **great** nation.
15. 1 I will shield you from danger and give you a **great** reward."
15.14 that foreign land, they will take **great** wealth with them.
17.20 princes, and I will make a **great** nation of his descendants.
18.18 His descendants will become a **great** and mighty nation,
18.20 against Sodom and Gomorrah, and their sin is very **great.**
19.19 You have done me a **great** favour and saved my life.
21. 8 on the day that he was weaned, Abraham gave a **great** feast.
21.18 I will make a **great** nation out of his descendants."
24.35 "The Lord has **greatly** blessed my master and made him a
35. 5 his sons started to leave, **great** fear fell on the people of
41.29 will be seven years of **great** plenty in all the land of
41.39 that you have **greater** wisdom and insight than anyone else.
42.21 we saw the **great** trouble he was in when he begged for
46. 3 I will make your descendants a **great** nation there.
48. 7 To my **great** sorrow she died in the land of Canaan, not
48.19 Manasseh's descendants will also become a **great** people.
48.19 his younger brother will be **greater** than he,
48.19 and his descendants will become **great** nations."
Ex 8.14 Egyptians piled them up in **great** heaps, until the land stank
8.24 The Lord sent **great** swarms of flies into the king's
11. 3 and all the people considered Moses to be a very **great** man.
11. 8 Then in **great** anger Moses left the king.
13. 3 is the day the Lord brought you out by his **great** power.
13. 9 the Lord brought you out of Egypt by his **great** power.
13.14 will answer him, 'By using **great** power the Lord brought us
13.16 the Lord brought us out of Egypt by his **great** power.' "
14.25 get stuck, so that they moved with **great** difficulty.
14.31 When the Israelites saw the **great** power with which the
15. 2 him, my father's God, and I will sing about his **greatness.**
18.11 know that the Lord is **greater** than all the gods, because he
31. 6 also given **great** ability to all the other skilful craftsmen,
32.10 Then I will make you and your descendants into a **great** nation."
32.11 whom you rescued from Egypt with **great** might and power?
34. 6 easily angered and who shows **great** love and faithfulness.
34.10 their presence I will do **great** things such as have never
34.10 the people will see what **great** things I, the Lord, can do,
Lev 26.29 Your hunger will be so **great** that you will eat your own
Num 14.18 easily angered, and I show **great** love and faithfulness and
14.19 Lord, according to the **greatness** of your unchanging love,
20.11 twice with it, and a **great** stream of water gushed out, and
24. 7 Their king shall be **greater** than Agag, And his rule shall be
Deut 1. 7 the Lebanon Mountains as far as the **great** River Euphrates.
3.24 only the beginning of the **great** and wonderful things you are
4. 6 say, 'What wisdom and understanding this **great** nation has!'
4. 7 other nation, no matter how **great,** has a god who is so
4. 8 other nation, no matter how **great,** has laws so just as those
4.32 Has anything as **great** as this ever happened before?
4.34 Before your very eyes he used his **great** power and strength;
4.37 chose you, and by his **great** power he himself brought you out
4.38 he drove out nations **greater** and more powerful than you,
5.15 Lord your God, rescued you by my **great** power and strength.
5.24 our God showed us his **greatness** and his glory when we heard
6.21 king of Egypt, and the Lord rescued us by his **great** power.
7. 8 he saved you by his **great** might and set you free from
7.19 miracles and wonders, and the **great** power and strength by
7.21 he is a **great** God and one to be feared.
9. 1 belonging to nations **greater** and more powerful than you.
9.26 and brought out of Egypt by your **great** strength and power.
9.29 you brought out of Egypt by your **great** power and might.'
10.17 He is **great** and mighty, and he is to be feared.
10.21 with your own eyes the **great** and astounding things that he
11. 2 You saw the Lord's **greatness,** his power, his might,

Deut 11. 7 have seen all these **great** things that the Lord has done.
11.23 belonging to nations **greater** and more powerful than you.
19. 6 to it might be too **great,** and the relative who is
26. 8 By his **great** power and strength he rescued us from Egypt.
26.19 He will make you **greater** than any other nation that he
28. 1 he will make you **greater** than any other nation on earth.
29. 3 the miracles, and the **great** wonders that the Lord performed.
29.28 furiously angry, and in his **great** anger he uprooted them
32. 3 of the Lord, and his people will tell of his **greatness.**
33. 9 They showed **greater** loyalty to you Than to parents,
34.12 been able to do the **great** and terrifying things that Moses
Josh 1. 4 **great** River Euphrates in the east, through the Hittite country,
3. 7 to honour you as a **great** man, and they will realize that
4.14 day made the people of Israel consider Joshua a **great** man.
4.24 on earth will know how **great** the Lord's power is, and you
10. 2 The people of Jerusalem were **greatly** alarmed at this
14.15 (Arba had been the **greatest** of the Anakim.)
23. 9 The Lord has driven **great** and powerful nations out as you
24. 5 I sent Moses and Aaron, and I brought **great** trouble on Egypt.
Judg 2. 7 seen for themselves all the **great** things that the Lord had
2.15 They were in **great** distress.
6.14 him, "Go with all your **great** strength and rescue Israel
10. 9 Israel was in **great** distress.
11.33 There was a **great** slaughter, and the Ammonites were defeated
15.18 to the Lord and said, "You gave me this **great** victory;
16.23 to celebrate and offer a **great** sacrifice to their god Dagon.
Ruth 3.10 "You are showing even **greater** family loyalty in what you
1 Sam 2. 7 he humbles some and makes others **great.**
4.10 There was a **great** slaughter:
5. 9 the Lord punished that city too and caused a **great** panic.
6.19 the Lord had caused such a **great** slaughter among them.
12.16 and you will see the **great** thing which the Lord is going
12.17 realize that you committed a **great** sin against the Lord when
12.24 Remember the **great** things he has done for you.
14.15 the earth shook, and there was **great** panic.
14.45 "Will Jonathan, who won this **great** victory for Israel, be
18.23 "It's a **great** honour to become the king's son-in-law,
18.23 too **great** for someone poor and insignificant
19. 4 everything he has done has been a **great** help to you.
19. 5 killed Goliath, and the Lord won a **great** victory for Israel.
20.41 David's grief was even **greater** than Jonathan's.
26.15 answered, "Abner, aren't you the **greatest** man in Israel?
28.15 Saul answered, "I am in **great** trouble!
30. 6 David was now in **great** trouble, because his men were all
2 Sam 3.38 you realize that this day a **great** leader in Israel has died?
6.12 Obed's house to take it to Jerusalem with a **great** celebration.
7. 9 make you as famous as the **greatest** leaders in the world.
7.21 you have done all these **great** things in order to teach me.
7.22 How **great** you are, Sovereign Lord!
7.23 The **great** and wonderful things you did for them have spread
7.26 Your fame will be **great,** and people will for ever say,
8. 8 He also took a **great** quantity of bronze from Betah and Berothai,
13.16 away like this is a **greater** crime than what you just did!"
14.11 will not commit a **greater** crime by killing my other son."
16.21 his enemy, and your followers will be **greatly** encouraged."
17.10 that your father is a **great** soldier and that his men are
18.29 sent me, I saw a **great** commotion, but I couldn't tell what
19.36 I don't deserve such a **great** reward.
20.19 Ours is a **great** city, one of the most peaceful and loyal
22.36 your help has made me **great.**
22.47 Proclaim the **greatness** of the strong God who saves me!
22.51 God gives **great** victories to his king;
23. 1 the man whom God made **great,** whom the God of Jacob chose
23.10 The Lord won a **great** victory that day.
23.12 The Lord won a **great** victory that day.
23.20 brave deeds, including killing two **great** Moabite warriors.
1 Kgs 1.50 Adonijah, in **great** fear of Solomon, went to the Tent of
3. 6 Solomon answered, "You always showed **great** love for my father
3. 6 continued to show him your **great** and constant love
3. 9 would I ever be able to rule this **great** people of yours?"
4.29 wisdom and insight, and knowledge too **great** to be measured.
5. 7 a wise son to succeed him as king of that **great** nation!"
7. 9 All these buildings and the **great** court were made of fine
8.41 your fame and of the **great** things you have done for your
10. 7 wisdom and wealth are much **greater** than what I was told.
10.10 him was by far the **greatest** that he ever received at any
14. 9 committed far **greater** sins than those who ruled before you.
2 Kgs 5. 1 a **great** soldier, but he suffered from a dreaded skin-disease.
6.11 The Syrian king became **greatly** upset over this;
6.23 So the king of Israel provided a **great** feast for them;
10.19 am going to offer a **great** sacrifice to Baal, and whoever is
17.36 who brought you out of Egypt with **great** power and strength;
21. 6 He sinned **greatly** against the Lord and stirred up his anger.
21. 9 led them to commit even **greater** sins than those committed by
25.28 gave him a position of **greater** honour than he gave the other
1 Chr 1.10 named Nimrod, who became the world's first **great** conqueror.)
5.23 Baal Hermon, Senir, and Mount Hermon, and their population increased **greatly.**
11.14 The Lord gave him a **great** victory.
11.22 brave deeds, including killing two **great** Moabite warriors.
15.25 Edom to fetch the Covenant Box, and they had a **great** celebration.
16. 8 Give thanks to the Lord, proclaim his **greatness;**
16.25 The Lord is **great** and is to be highly praised;
17. 8 make you as famous as the **greatest** leaders in the world.
17.17 you, Lord God, are already treating me like a **great** man.
17.19 to do this for me and to show me my future **greatness.**
17.21 The **great** and wonderful things you did for them spread your
17.24 Your fame will be **great,** and people will for ever say,
18. 8 He also took a **great** quantity of bronze from Tibhath and Kun,
26. 6 important men in their clan because of their **great** ability;
29.11 You are **great** and powerful, glorious, splendid, and

1 Chr 29.12 and you are able to make anyone **great** and strong.
2 Chr 1. 8 Solomon answered, "You always showed **great** love for my father
1.10 would I ever be able to rule this **great** people of yours?"
2. 5 I intend to build a **great** temple,
2. 5 because our God is **greater** than any other god.
6.32 a distant land hears how **great** and powerful you are and how
7.21 "The Temple is now **greatly** honoured, but then everyone
29.30 So everyone sang with **great** joy as they knelt and worshipped God.
30.13 A **great** number of people gathered in Jerusalem in the
30.21 Festival of Unleavened Bread with **great** joy, and day after
32.33 of Judah and Jerusalem paid him **great** honour at his death.
33. 6 He sinned **greatly** against the Lord and stirred up his anger.
33. 9 of Judah to commit even **greater** sins than those committed by
36.16 against his people was so **great** that there was no escape.
Ezra 4.10 the other peoples whom the **great** and powerful Ashurbanipal
5. 8 that the Temple of the **great** God is being rebuilt with large
5. 8 is being done with **great** care and is moving ahead steadily.
9. 7 ancestors until now, we, your people, have sinned **greatly.**
Neh 1. 3 in the homeland were in **great** difficulty and that the
1. 5 You are **great,** and we stand in fear of you.
1.10 You rescued them by your **great** power and strength.
4.14 Remember how **great** and terrifying the Lord is, and fight for
8. 6 Ezra said, "Praise the Lord, the **great** God!"
9. 5 glorious name, although no human praise is **great** enough."
9.17 Your mercy is **great;**
9.19 abandon them there in the desert, for your mercy is **great.**
9.27 In your **great** mercy you sent them leaders who rescued them
9.28 and time after time you rescued them in your **great** mercy.
9.31 yet, because your mercy is **great,** you did not forsake or
9.32 "O God, our God, how **great** you are!
13.22 for this also, and spare me because of your **great** love.
13.26 was a man who was **greater** than any of the kings of
Esth 2.18 Then the king gave a **great** banquet in Esther's honour
10. 2 All the **great** and wonderful things he did, as well as the
Job 5. 9 We cannot understand the **great** things he does, and to his
6.10 would, I would leap for joy, no matter how **great** my pain.
7.20 Am I so **great** a burden to you?
9. 9 stars in the sky—the **Great** Bear, Orion, the Pleiades, and
9.10 We cannot understand the **great** things he does, and to
11. 7 the limits and bounds of the **greatness** and power of God?
11. 9 God's **greatness** is broader than the earth, wider than the sea.
12.23 He makes nations strong and **great,** but then he defeats
20. 6 He may grow **great,** towering to the sky,
20. 6 so **great** that his head reaches the clouds,
21.28 is the house of the **great** man now, the man who practised
26.14 Who can know how truly **great** God is?
27.11 Let me teach you how **great** is God's power, and explain
33.12 God is **greater** than any man.
36.22 Remember how **great** is God's power;
36.22 he is the **greatest** teacher of all.
36.26 We cannot fully know his **greatness** or count the number
37.23 God's power is so **great** that we cannot come near him;
38.32 season by season and direct the **Great** and the Little Bear?
39.11 Can you rely on his **great** strength and expect him to do
41.12 Leviathan's legs and describe how **great** and strong he is.
42. 3 I did not understand, about marvels too **great** for me to know.
42.17 And then he died at a very **great** age.
Ps 5. 7 But because of your **great** love I can come into your house;
8. 1 O Lord, our Lord, your **greatness** is seen in all the world!
8. 9 O Lord, our Lord, your **greatness** is seen in all the world!
16. 3 My **greatest** pleasure is to be with them.
18.35 your care has made me **great,** and your power has kept me
18.46 Proclaim the **greatness** of the God who saves me.
18.50 God gives **great** victories to his king;
20. 6 his holy heaven and by his power gives him **great** victories.
21. 3 You came to him with **great** blessings and set a crown of
21. 5 His glory is **great** because of your help;
21.13 We praise you, Lord, for your **great** strength!
24. 7 open the ancient doors, and the **great** king will come in.
24. 8 Who is this **great** king?
24. 9 open the ancient doors, and the **great** king will come in.
24.10 Who is this **great** king?
24.10 The triumphant Lord—he is the **great** king!
32. 6 when a **great** flood of trouble comes rushing in, it will
33.17 their **great** strength cannot save.
34. 3 Proclaim with me the Lord's **greatness;**
35.27 for joy and say again and again, "How **great** is the Lord!
38. 3 Because of your anger, I am in **great** pain;
40. 5 could never speak of them all— their number is so **great!**
40.16 for your salvation always say, "How **great** is the Lord!"
44. 1 us about it, about the **great** things you did in their time,
45. 4 Your strength will win you **great** victories!
47. 2 he is a **great** king, ruling over all the world.
48. 1 The Lord is **great** and is to be highly praised in the
48. 2 the city of the **great** king brings joy to all the world.
49. 2 **great** and small alike, rich and poor together.
49. 6 who trust in their riches and boast of their **great** wealth.
49. 8 life, [8]because the payment for a human life is too **great.**
49.12 A man's **greatness** cannot save him from death;
49.16 a man becomes rich, when his wealth grows even **greater;**
49.20 A man's **greatness** cannot save him from death;
51. 1 Because of your **great** mercy wipe away my sins!
52. 1 Why do you boast, **great** man, of your evil?
52. 7 but trusted instead in his **great** wealth and looked for
57. 5 Show your **greatness** in the sky, O God, and your glory over
57.11 Show your **greatness** in the sky, O God, and your glory
60. 3 You have made your people suffer **greatly;**
62. 9 **great** and small alike are worthless.
65. 8 world stands in awe of the **great** things that you have done.
66. 3 Your power is so **great** that your enemies bow down in fear
69.13 Answer me because of your **great** love, because you keep your
Ps 69.16 in your **great** compassion turn to me!
69.17 I am in **great** trouble—answer me now!
69.30 I will proclaim his **greatness** by giving him thanks.
70. 4 for your salvation always say, "How **great** is God!"
71.19 You have done **great** things;
71.21 You will make me **greater** than ever;
75. 1 We proclaim how **great** you are and tell of the wonderful
76.12 he humbles proud princes and terrifies **great** kings.
77.11 I will remember your **great** deeds, Lord;
77.13 No god is as **great** as you.
78. 4 the Lord's power and his **great** deeds and the wonderful
78.42 They forgot his **great** power and the day when he saved
78.49 He caused them **great** distress by pouring out his anger
79.11 the prisoners, and by your **great** power free those who are
86. 9 they will praise your **greatness.**
86.12 I will proclaim your **greatness** for ever.
86.13 How **great** is your constant love for me!
89.13 How **great** is your strength!
89.17 You give us **great** victories;
89.27 I will make him my first-born son, the **greatest** of all kings.
92. 5 How **great** are your actions, Lord!
93. 4 Lord rules supreme in heaven, **greater** than the roar of the ocean,
96. 4 The Lord is **great** and is to be highly praised;
97. 9 you are much **greater** than all the gods.
99. 3 Everyone will praise his **great** and majestic name.
102.16 When the Lord rebuilds Zion, he will reveal his **greatness.**
103.11 is above the earth, so **great** is his love for those who
104. 1 O Lord, my God, how **great** you are!
105. 1 Give thanks to the Lord, proclaim his **greatness;**
106. 2 Who can tell all the **great** things he has done?
106. 8 them, as he had promised, in order to show his **great** power.
106.45 his covenant, and because of his **great** love he relented.
107.32 They must proclaim his **greatness** in the assembly of the
108. 5 Show your **greatness** in the sky, O God, and your glory over
115.13 everyone who honours him, the **great** and the small alike.
118.28 I will proclaim your **greatness.**
119.14 in following your commands more than in having **great** wealth.
119.100 I have **greater** wisdom than old men, because I obey your
commands.
119.156 But your compassion, Lord, is **great;**
126. 2 said about us, "The Lord did **great** things for them."
126. 3 Indeed he did **great** things for us;
131. 1 I am not concerned with **great** matters or with subjects too
132.17 Here I will make one of David's descendants a **great** king;
135. 5 I know that our Lord is **great,** greater than all the gods.
136. 2 Give thanks to the **greatest** of all gods;
136. 4 He alone performs **great** miracles;
137. 6 you, if I do not think of you as my **greatest** joy!
138. 5 sing about what you have done and about your **great** glory.
145. 1 I will proclaim your **greatness,** my God and king;
145. 3 The Lord is **great** and is to be highly praised;
145. 3 his **greatness** is beyond understanding.
145. 6 of your mighty deeds, and I will proclaim your **greatness.**
147. 5 **Great** and mighty is our Lord;
148.13 His name is **greater** than all others;
150. 2 Praise his supreme **greatness.**
Prov 4. 8 Love wisdom, and she will make you **great.**
11.11 A city becomes **great** when righteous men give it their blessing;
12. 9 than to play the part of a **great** man but go hungry.
14.28 A king's **greatness** depends on how many people he rules;
14.34 Righteousness makes a nation **great;**
19.11 When someone wrongs you, it is a **great** virtue to ignore it.
22. 1 good reputation and **great** wealth, choose a good reputation.
Ecc 1. 8 Everything leads to weariness—a weariness too **great** for words.
1.16 myself, "I have become a **great** man, far wiser than anyone
2. 4 I accomplished **great** things.
2. 9 Yes, I was **great,** greater than anyone else who had ever
10. 1 and a little stupidity can cancel out the **greatest** wisdom.
Song 6. 4 the city of Tirzah, as breathtaking as these **great** cities.
7. 4 in the city of Heshbon, near the gate of that **great** city.
Is 2. 4 He will settle disputes among **great** nations.
5.16 Lord Almighty shows his **greatness** by doing what is right,
8.11 With his **great** power the Lord warned me not to follow
9. 2 The people who walked in darkness have seen a **great** light.
9. 3 You have given them **great** joy, Lord;
10.15 an axe claim to be **greater** than the man who uses it?
12. 4 Tell them how **great** he is!
12. 5 Sing to the Lord because of the **great** things he has done.
12. 6 Israel's holy God is **great,** and he lives among his people."
13. 4 mountains—the sound of a **great** crowd of people, the sound of
16.14 "In exactly three years Moab's **great** wealth will disappear.
17. 4 day is coming when Israel's **greatness** will come to an end,
21.16 "In exactly one year the **greatness** of the tribes of Kedar
23. 4 The sea and the **great** ocean depths disown you and say, "I
24.14 the west will tell how **great** the Lord is, [15]and those in
26.10 they refuse to recognize your **greatness.**
33. 5 How **great** the Lord is!
33. 6 Their **greatest** treasure is their reverence for the Lord.
34. 6 he will make this a **great** slaughter in the land of Edom.
35. 2 Everyone will see the Lord's splendour, see his **greatness**
40.26 His power is so **great**— not one of them is ever
44.23 The Lord has shown his **greatness** by saving his people Israel.
45. 4 I have given you **great** honour, although you do not know me.
47. 8 You claim you are as **great** as God— that there is
49. 6 "I have a **greater** task for you, my servant.
49. 6 only will you restore to **greatness** the people of Israel who
52. 1 Jerusalem, be strong and **great** again!
53.12 a place of honour, a place among **great** and powerful men.
59.19 From east to west everyone will fear him and his **great** power.
60. 6 **Great** caravans of camels will come, from Midian and Ephah.
60.15 I will make you **great** and beautiful, A place of joy for

Is 60.21 I planted them, I made them, To reveal my **greatness** to all.
60.22 humblest family Will become as **great** as a powerful nation.
63.12 who by his power did **great** things through Moses, dividing
63.15 Where is your **great** concern for us?
64. 5 in spite of your **great** anger we have continued to do wrong
66. 5 'Let the Lord show his **greatness** and save you, so that we
66.19 have not heard of my fame or seen my **greatness** and power:
66.19 Among these nations they will proclaim my **greatness.**
Jer 4. 6 Lord is bringing disaster and **great** destruction from the north.
6.13 Everyone, **great** and small, tries to make money dishonestly;
8.10 Everyone, **great** and small, tries to make money dishonestly.
10. 6 you are mighty, and your name is **great** and powerful.
10.22 There is a **great** commotion in a nation to the north;
13. 9 destroy the pride of Judah and the **great** pride of Jerusalem.
22. 8 I, the Lord, have done such a thing to this **great** city.
25.14 many nations and **great** kings will make slaves of them.' "
25.32 nation after another, and a **great** storm is gathering at the
27. 5 "By my **great** power and strength I created the world,
27. 7 Then his nation will serve powerful nations and **great** kings.
30.14 because your sins are many and your wickedness is **great.**
30.15 because your sins are many and your wickedness is **great.**
31. 7 "Sing with joy for Israel, the **greatest** of the nations.
31. 8 They will come back a **great** nation.
31.34 because all will know me, from the least to the **greatest.**
32.17 made the earth and the sky by your **great** power and might;
32.18 You are a **great** and powerful God;
42.10 The destruction I brought on you has caused me **great** sorrow.
44.12 All of them, **great** and small, will die in Egypt, either in
47. 5 **Great** sorrow has come to the people of Gaza, and
49.37 In my **great** anger I will destroy the people of Elam and
50.12 but your own **great** city will be humiliated and disgraced.
50.22 battle is heard in the land, and there is **great** destruction.
52.32 gave him a position of **greater** honour than he gave the other
Ezek 3. 6 If I sent you to **great** nations that spoke difficult
3.14 Lord came on me with **great** force, and as his spirit carried
23.40 invite men to come from a **great** distance, and the men came.
26. 7 am going to bring the **greatest** king of all—King
30. 4 There will be war in Egypt And **great** distress in Sudan.
30.15 will let the city of Pelusium, Egypt's **great** fortress, feel
32.21 The **greatest** heroes and those who fought on the Egyptian
36.23 nations the holiness of my **great** name—the name you disgraced
38.23 all the nations that I am **great** and that I am holy.
Dan 2. 6 its meaning, I will reward you with gifts and **great** honour.
2.10 No king, not even the **greatest** and most powerful, has ever
2.34 were looking at it, a **great** stone broke loose from a cliff
2.37 Your Majesty, you are the **greatest** of all kings.
2.39 be another empire, not as **great** as yours, and after that a
2.45 The **great** God is telling Your Majesty what will happen in
2.47 said, "Your God is the **greatest** of all gods, the Lord over
4. 3 "How **great** are the wonders God shows us!
4. 4 living comfortably in my palace, enjoying **great** prosperity.
4.22 You have grown so **great** that you reach the sky, and your
4.30 palace in Babylon, [30]he said, "Look how **great** Babylon is!
4.36 back my royal power, with even **greater** honour than before.
5. 1 noblemen to a **great** banquet, and they drank wine together.
5.18 made your father Nebuchadnezzar a **great** king and gave him
5.19 He was so **great** that people of all nations, races, and
7.27 The power and **greatness** of all the kingdoms on earth
8.25 He will even defy the **greatest** King of all, but he will
9. 4 I said, "Lord God, you are **great,** and we honour you.
10. 6 and his voice sounded like the roar of a **great** crowd.
11. 5 however, will be even stronger and rule a **greater** kingdom.
11.36 will boast that he is **greater** than any god, superior even to
11.37 god, because he will think he is **greater** than any of them.
11.39 He will give **great** honour to those who accept him as ruler,
12. 1 "At that time the **great** angel Michael, who guards your people,
Hos 1.11 Yes, the day of Jezreel will be a **great** day!
5.13 to Assyria to ask the **great** emperor for help, but he could
9. 7 You people hate me so much because your sin is so **great.**
9.11 Israel's **greatness** will fly away like a bird, and there
10. 6 be carried off to Assyria as tribute to the **great** emperor.
Joel 2. 2 The **great** army of locusts advances like darkness spreading
2. 5 They are lined up like a **great** army ready for battle.
2.31 red as blood before the **great** and terrible day of the Lord
Amos 3. 9 surrounding Samaria and see the **great** disorder and the
6. 1 safe in Samaria—you **great** men of this great nation Israel,
6. 2 Then go on to the **great** city of Hamath and on down
7. 4 The fire burnt up the **great** ocean under the earth, and
Jon 1. 2 "Go to Nineveh, that **great** city, and speak out against it;
3. 2 said, "Go to Nineveh, that **great** city, and proclaim to the
3. 5 all the people, from the **greatest** to the least, put on
4.11 more, then, should I have pity on Nineveh, that **great** city.
Mic 4. 3 among the nations, among the **great** powers near and far.
4. 7 those who are left, and they will become a **great** nation.
5. 4 will acknowledge his **greatness,** [5]and he will bring peace.
5.15 And in my **great** anger I will take revenge on all nations
Nah 1. 8 Like a **great** rushing flood he completely destroys his enemies;
Hab 3. 2 do again in our times the **great** deeds you used to do.
Zeph 1.10 part of the city and a **great** crashing sound in the hills.
1.14 The **great** day of the Lord is near—very near and coming
2.15 Its people think that their city is the **greatest** in the world.
Zech 4. 7 Obstacles as **great** as mountains will disappear before you.
9. 5 The city of Gaza will see it and suffer **great** pain.
12. 7 will receive will be no **greater** than that of the rest of
12.11 in Jerusalem will be as **great** as the mourning for
14.14 the nations—gold, silver, and clothing in **great** abundance.
Mal 1.14 For I am a **great** king, and people of all nations fear
4. 5 "But before the **great** and terrible day of the Lord comes,
Mt 3.11 He is much **greater** than I am;
4. 8 him all the kingdoms of the world in all their **greatness.**
4.16 The people who live in darkness will see a **great** light.
Mt 5. 6 "Happy are those whose **greatest** desire is to do what God requires;
5.12 happy and glad, for a **great** reward is kept for you in
5.19 to do the same, will be **great** in the Kingdom of heaven.
5.35 nor by Jerusalem, for it is the city of the **great** King.
8.26 winds and the waves to stop, and there was a **great** calm.
10.24 "No pupil is **greater** than his teacher;
10.24 no slave is **greater** than his master.
11.11 that John the Baptist is **greater** than any man who has ever
11.11 who is least in the Kingdom of heaven is **greater** than John.
12. 6 I tell you that there is something here **greater** than the Temple.
12.41 I tell you that there is something here **greater** than Jonah!
12.42 I assure you that there is something here **greater** than Solomon!
15.28 So Jesus answered her, "You are a woman of **great** faith!
18. 1 Jesus, asking, "Who is the **greatest** in the Kingdom of heaven?"
18. 4 The **greatest** in the Kingdom of heaven is the one who
20.26 of you wants to be **great,** he must be the servant of
22.36 he asked, "which is the **greatest** commandment in the Law?"
22.38 This is the **greatest** and the most important commandment.
23.11 The **greatest** one among you must be your servant.
23.12 Whoever makes himself **great** will be humbled,
23.12 and whoever humbles himself will be made **great.**
24.24 they will perform **great** miracles and wonders in order to deceive
24.30 Man coming on the clouds of heaven with power and **great** glory.
24.31 The **great** trumpet will sound, and he will send out his
26.38 sorrow in my heart is so **great** that it almost crushes me.
27.14 with the result that the Governor was **greatly** surprised.
Mk 1. 7 man who will come after me is much **greater** than I am.
4.24 be used by God to judge you—but with even **greater** severity.
4.39 The wind died down, and there was a **great** calm.
6. 6 He was **greatly** surprised, because the people did not have faith.
6.20 even though he became **greatly** disturbed every time he heard him.
9.15 people saw Jesus, they were **greatly** surprised, and ran to him
9.34 they had been arguing among themselves about who was the **greatest.**
10.43 of you wants to be **great,** he must be the servant of
13. 2 Jesus answered, "You see these **great** buildings?
13.26 Man will appear, coming in the clouds with **great** power and glory.
14.34 sorrow in my heart is so **great** that it almost crushes me.
Lk 1.15 He will be a **great** man in the Lord's sight.
1.28 The Lord is with you and has **greatly** blessed you!"
1.32 He will be **great** and will be called the Son of the
1.43 Why should this **great** thing happen to me, that my Lord's
1.49 because of the **great** things the Mighty God has done
2.10 news for you, which will bring **great** joy to all the people.
2.13 Suddenly a **great** army of heaven's angels appeared with the angel,
3.16 water, but someone is coming who is much **greater** than I am.
6.23 dance for joy, because a **great** reward is kept for you in
6.35 You will then have a **great** reward, and you will be sons
6.40 No pupil is **greater** than his teacher;
7.16 "A **great** prophet has appeared among us!"
7.28 you," Jesus added, "John is **greater** than any man who has
7.28 who is least in the Kingdom of God is **greater** than John."
7.47 I tell you, then, the **great** love she has shown proves
8. 4 and when a **great** crowd gathered, Jesus told this parable:
8.23 to fill with water, so that they were all in **great** danger.
8.24 they died down, and there was a **great** calm.
9.46 the disciples as to which one of them was the **greatest.**
9.48 For he who is least among you all is the **greatest."**
10.17 The seventy-two men came back in **great** joy.
11.31 and I tell you there is something here **greater** than Solomon.
11.32 I assure you that there is something here **greater** than Jonah!
14.11 For everyone who makes himself **great** will be humbled,
14.11 and everyone who humbles himself will be made **great."**
14.16 man who was giving a **great** feast to which he invited many
16.15 things that are considered of **great** value by man are worth
16.19 most expensive clothes and lived in **great** luxury every day.
16.23 Hades, where he was in **great** pain, he looked up and saw
16.24 cool my tongue, because I am in **great** pain in this fire!'
17. 5 The apostles said to the Lord, "Make our faith **greater."**
18.14 For everyone who makes himself **great** will be humbled,
18.14 and everyone who humbles himself will be made **great."**
19. 6 Zacchaeus hurried down and welcomed him with **great** joy.
19.37 in loud voices for all the **great** things that they had seen:
21.27 Man will appear, coming in a cloud with **great** power and glory.
22.24 to which one of them should be thought of as the **greatest.**
22.26 rather, the **greatest** one among you must be like the youngest,
22.27 Who is **greater,** the one who sits down to eat or the
22.44 In **great** anguish he prayed even more fervently;
24.52 Jerusalem, filled with **great** joy, [53]and spent all their time
Jn 1.15 after me, but he is **greater** than I am, because he existed
1.30 after me, but he is **greater** than I am, because he existed
1.50 You will see much **greater** things than this!"
3.10 Jesus answered, "You are a **great** teacher in Israel,
3.31 He who comes from above is **greater** than all.
4.12 You don't claim to be **greater** than Jacob, do you?"
4.27 disciples returned, and they were **greatly** surprised to find him
5.20 He will show him even **greater** things to do than this, and
5.36 which is even **greater** than the witness that John gave:
7.15 The Jewish authorities were **greatly** surprised and said,
8.53 you do not claim to be **greater** than Abraham, do you?
10.29 Father has given me is **greater** than everything, and no one
12.23 has now come for the Son of Man to receive **great** glory.
13.16 no slave is **greater** than his master,
13.16 and no messenger is **greater** than the one who sent him.
14.12 yes, he will do even **greater** things, because I am going to
14.28 for he is **greater** than I.
15.13 The **greatest** love a person can have for his friends is
15.20 'No slave is **greater** than his master.'

Acts 2.11 own languages about the **great** things that God has done!"
2.20 red as blood, before the **great** and glorious Day of the Lord
4.33 With **great** power the apostles gave witness to the resurrection
5.36 claiming to be somebody **great,** and about four hundred men joined
6. 7 larger, and a **great** number of priests accepted the faith.
6. 8 power, performed **great** miracles and wonders among the people.
7.22 of the Egyptians and became a **great** man in words and deeds.
8. 8 So there was **great** joy in that city.
8. 9 claimed that he was someone **great,** [10]and everyone in the city,
8.10 is that power of God known as 'The **Great** Power'," they
8.13 astounded when he saw the **great** wonders and miracles that were
10.37 You know of the **great** event that took place throughout
10.46 heard them speaking in strange tongues and praising God's **greatness.**
11.21 was with them, and a **great** number of people believed and
13.12 for he was **greatly** amazed at the teaching about the Lord.
13.17 and made the people a **great** nation during the time they
13.17 out of Egypt by his **great** power, [18]and for forty years he
14. 1 such a way that a **great** number of Jews and Gentiles became
15. 3 this news brought **great** joy to all the believers.
17.11 listened to the message with **great** eagerness, and every day they
17.16 Silas and Timothy, he was **greatly** upset when he noticed how
18.25 of the Lord, and with **great** enthusiasm he proclaimed and taught
18.27 he arrived, he was a **great** help to those who through God's
19.17 and the name of the Lord Jesus was given **greater** honour.
19.24 his business brought a **great** deal of profit to the workers.
19.27 that the temple of the **great** goddess Artemis will come to
19.27 and that her **greatness** will be destroyed—the goddess worshipped
19.28 became furious and started shouting, **"Great** is Artemis of Ephesus!"
19.34 **"Great** is Artemis of Ephesus!"
19.35 of the temple of the **great** Artemis and of the sacred stone
20.12 They took the young man home alive and were **greatly** comforted.
25.23 Agrippa and Bernice came with **great** pomp and ceremony and entered
26.22 here giving my witness to all, to small and **great** alike.
26.24 Your **great** learning is driving you mad!"
27. 7 for several days and with **great** difficulty finally arrived
27. 8 to the coast and with **great** difficulty came to a place
27.10 there will be **great** damage to the cargo and to the ship,
28.15 When Paul saw them, he thanked God and was **greatly** encouraged.

Rom 1. 4 holiness, he was shown with **great** power to be the Son of
2. 4 perhaps you despise his **great** kindness, tolerance, and patience.
2. 5 making your own punishment even **greater** on the Day when God's
5.15 But God's grace is much **greater,** and so is his free gift
5.17 But how much **greater** is the result of what was done by
9. 2 lying [2]when I say how **great** is my sorrow, how endless the
11.12 Then, how much **greater** the blessings will be when the complete
11.33 How **great** are God's riches!
12. 1 my brothers, because of God's **great** mercy to us I appeal to

1 Cor 2. 1 God's secret truth, I did not use big words and **great** learning.
9.12 to expect this from you, haven't we an even **greater** right?
12.23 very much are the ones which we treat with **greater** care;
12.24 a way as to give **greater** honour to those parts that need
13.13 and the **greatest** of these is love.
14. 5 proclaims God's message is of **greater** value than the one who
14.12 above everything else to make **greater** use of those which
15. 3 to you what I received, which is of the **greatest** importance:
16. 9 a real opportunity here for **great** and worthwhile work,

2 Cor 1. 5 so also through Christ we share in God's **great** help.
1. 8 laid upon us were so **great** and so heavy that we gave
2. 4 wrote to you with a **greatly** troubled and distressed heart
3. 8 with such glory, [8]how much **greater** is the glory that
3.18 us into his likeness in an ever **greater** degree of glory.
4.17 a tremendous and eternal glory, much **greater** than the trouble.
5. 2 And now we sigh, so **great** is our desire that our home
8. 2 but their joy was so **great** that they were extremely generous
10.15 able to do a much **greater** work among you, always within the
11.15 So it is no **great** thing if his servants disguise
12. 9 all you need, for my power is **greatest** when you are weak."

Gal 4.14 my physical condition was a **great** trial to you, you did not

Eph 1. 7 How **great** is the grace of God, [8]which he gave to us
1.19 his people, [19]and how very **great** is his power at work in
2. 4 love for us is so **great,** [5]that while we were spiritually
2. 7 time to come the extraordinary **greatness** of his grace in the

Phil 2. 9 and gave him the name that is **greater** than any other name.
2.27 him but on me, too, and spared me an even **greater** sorrow.
4.10 the Lord it is a **great** joy to me that after so

Col 4.11 Kingdom of God, and they have been a **great** help to me.

1 Thes 3.12 more and more and become as **great** as our love for you.
5.13 Treat them with the **greatest** respect and love because of

2 Thes 1. 3 the love each of you has for the others is becoming **greater.**
3. 5 Lord lead you into a **greater** understanding of God's love and

1 Tim 3.16 No one can deny how **great** is the secret of our religion:

Tit 2.13 when the glory of our **great** God and Saviour Jesus Christ

Phlm 7 Your love, dear brother, has brought me **great** joy and much encouragement!

Heb 1. 4 The Son was made **greater** than the angels,
1. 4 just as the name that God gave him is **greater** than theirs.
1. 9 of an honour far **greater** than he gave to your companions."
2. 3 we escape if we pay no attention to such a **great** salvation?
3. 3 same way Jesus is worthy of much **greater** honour than Moses.
4.14 For we have a **great** High Priest who has gone into the
6.11 Our **great** desire is that each one of you keep up his
6.13 Since there was no one **greater** than himself, he used his own
6.16 uses the name of someone **greater** than himself, and the vow
6.18 found safety with him are **greatly** encouraged to hold firmly
7. 4 You see, then, how **great** he was.
7. 7 the one who blesses is **greater** than the one who is blessed.
8.11 For they will all know me, from the least to the **greatest.**
9.11 The tent in which he serves is **greater** and more perfect;
10.21 We have a **great** priest in charge of the house of God.
10.35 courage, then, because it brings with it a **great** reward.
13.20 Lord Jesus, who is the **Great** Shepherd of the sheep as the

Jas 3. 1 we teachers will be judged with **greater** strictness than others.
3. 5 small as it is, it can boast about **great** things.

1 Pet 1. 3 Because of his **great** mercy he gave us new life by raising
1. 8 So you rejoice with a **great** and glorious joy which words
2. 7 This stone is of **great** value for you that believe;
3. 4 quiet spirit, which is of the **greatest** value in God's sight.

2 Pet 1. 4 has given us the very **great** and precious gifts he promised,
1.16 With our own eyes we saw his **greatness.**

1 Jn 3. 1 His love is so **great** that we are called God's children—and
3.20 we know that God is **greater** than our conscience and that he

Jude 6 is keeping them for that **great** Day on which they will be

Rev 5. 5 Lion from Judah's tribe, the **great** descendant of David, has won
9.14 "Release the four angels who are bound at the **great** river Euphrates!"
11. 8 street of the **great** city, where their Lord was crucified.
11.13 were terrified and praised the **greatness** of the God of heaven.
11.17 you have taken your **great** power and have begun to rule!
11.18 all who have reverence for you, **great** and small alike.
12. 1 Then a **great** and mysterious sight appeared in the sky.
13.13 This second beast performed **great** miracles;
13.16 the people, small and **great,** rich and poor, slave and free,
14. 7 He said in a loud voice, "Honour God and praise his **greatness!**
14. 8 **Great** Babylon has fallen!
15. 1 I saw in the sky another mysterious sight, **great** and amazing.
15. 3 "Lord God Almighty, how **great** and wonderful are your deeds!
15. 4 Who will refuse to declare your **greatness?**
16. 9 But they would not turn from their sins and praise his **greatness.**
16.12 angel poured out his bowl on the **great** river Euphrates.
16.14 together for the battle on the **great** Day of Almighty God.
16.19 The **great** city was split into three parts, and the
16.19 God remembered **great** Babylon and made her drink the wine
17. 1 is to be punished, that **great** city that is built near many
17. 5 **"Great** Babylon, the mother of all the prostitutes and perverts
17.18 woman you saw is the **great** city that rules over the kings
18. 1 He had **great** authority, and his splendour
18. 2 **Great** Babylon has fallen!
18.10 This **great** and mighty city Babylon!
18.16 How awful for the **great** city!
18.18 "There never has been another city like this **great** city!"
18.19 How awful for the **great** city!
18.21 "This is how the **great** city Babylon will be violently thrown
19. 3 the flames that consume the **great** city goes up for ever and
19. 5 servants and all people, both **great** and small, who have reverence
19. 7 let us praise his **greatness!**
19.17 "Come and gather together for God's **great** feast!
19.18 the flesh of all people, slave and free, **great** and small!"
20. 6 Happy and **greatly** blessed are those who are included
20.11 Then I saw a **great** white throne and the one who sits
20.12 And I saw the dead, **great** and small alike, standing
21.12 It had a **great,** high wall with twelve gates and with
21.26 The **greatness** and the wealth of the nations will be brought

GREAT-GRANDCHILDREN

Job 42.16 long enough to see his grandchildren and **great-grandchildren.**

GREAT-GRANDFATHER

1 Kgs 15. 3 loyal to the Lord his God, as his **great-grandfather** David

GREECE

Modern term generally used to translate the Hebrew word JAVAN, and the Roman province of Achaia.

Is 66.19 and Lydia, with its skilled bowmen, and to Tubal and **Greece.**

Ezek 27.13 You did business in **Greece,** Tubal, and Meshech and

Dan 8.21 goat represents the kingdom of **Greece,** and the prominent
10.20 After that, the guardian angel of **Greece** will appear.
11. 2 power and wealth he will challenge the kingdom of **Greece.**

Joel 3. 6 Jerusalem far from their own country and sold them to the **Greeks.**

Zech 9.13 men of Zion like a sword, to fight the men of **Greece."**

Jn 7.35 Will he go to the **Greek** cities where our people live,
7.35 and teach the **Greeks?**
12.20 Some **Greeks** were among those who had gone to Jerusalem
19.20 The notice was written in Hebrew, Latin, and **Greek.**

Acts 6. 1 was a quarrel between the **Greek-speaking** Jews and the native Jews.
6. 1 The **Greek-speaking** Jews claimed that their widows were being
9.29 disputed with the **Greek-speaking** Jews, but they tried to kill
9.36 (Her name in **Greek** is Dorcas, meaning "a deer.")
13. 8 (that is his name in **Greek),** who tried to turn the governor
16. 1 also a Christian, was Jewish, but his father was a **Greek.**
16. 3 Jews who lived in those places knew that Timothy's father was **Greek.**
17. 4 women and a large group of **Greeks** who worshipped God.
17.12 and many **Greek** women of high social standing
17.12 and many **Greek** men also believed.
18. 4 synagogue every Sabbath, trying to convince both Jews and **Greeks.**
21.37 "You speak **Greek,** do you?"

1 Cor 1.22 Jews want miracles for proof, and **Greeks** look for wisdom.

Gal 2. 3 Titus, even though he is **Greek,** was not forced to be circumcised,

Rev 9.11 in **Greek** the name is Apollyon (meaning "The Destroyer").

GREED

1 Sam 2.29 then, do you look with **greed** at the sacrifices and offerings
Job 20.20 His **greed** is never satisfied.
Ps 10. 3 the **greedy** man curses and rejects the Lord.
Prov 11. 6 someone who can't be trusted is trapped by his own **greed.**
19.22 It is a disgrace to be **greedy;**
23. 3 Don't be **greedy** for the fine food he serves;
23. 6 a stingy man or be **greedy** for the fine food he serves.
Is 56.11 They are like **greedy** dogs that never get enough.
57.17 because of their sin and **greed,** and so I punished them and
Jer 51.39 Are they **greedy?**
Ezek 33.31 but they continue their **greedy** ways.
Hab 2. 5 **Greedy** men are proud and restless—like death itself they are
Zeph 3. 3 hungry wolves, too **greedy** to leave a bone until morning.
Mk 7.22 kill, [22] commit adultery, be **greedy,** and do all sorts of evil
Lk 12.15 "Watch out and guard yourselves from every kind of **greed;**
18.11 that I am not **greedy,** dishonest, or an adulterer, like everybody
Rom 1.29 are filled with all kinds of wickedness, evil, **greed,** and vice;
1 Cor 5.10 pagans who are immoral or **greedy** or are thieves or who
5.11 brother but is immoral or **greedy** or worships idols or is a
6.10 or who steal or are **greedy** or are drunkards or who
Eph 5. 3 or indecency or **greed** should even be mentioned among you.
5. 5 indecent, or greedy (for **greed** is a form of idolatry) will
Col 3. 5 evil passions, and greed (for **greed** is a form of idolatry).
1 Thes 2. 5 did we use words to cover up **greed**—God is our witness!
1 Tim 3. 8 they must not drink too much wine or be **greedy** for money;
2 Tim 3. 2 People will be selfish, **greedy,** boastful, and conceited;
Tit 1. 7 or quick-tempered, or a drunkard or violent or **greedy** for money.
2 Pet 2. 3 In their **greed** these false teachers will make a profit out
2.14 Their hearts are trained to be **greedy.**

GREEK see GREECE

GREEN

Gen 9. 3 Now you can eat them, as well as **green** plants;
30.37 Jacob got **green** branches of poplar, almond, and plane
Ex 10.15 Not a **green** thing was left on any tree or plant in
Lev 13.49 made of leather, [49] if it is **greenish** or reddish, it is a
14.37 If there are **greenish** or reddish spots that appear to be
Deut 12. 2 gods on high mountains, on hills, and under **green** trees.
Job 15.32 will wither, wither like a branch and never be **green** again.
39. 8 they feed, where they search for anything **green** to eat.
Ps 23. 2 me rest in fields of **green** grass and leads me to quiet
92.14 bear fruit in old age and are always **green** and strong.
Song 1.16 The **green** grass will be our bed;
Is 15. 6 the grass beside it has withered, and nothing **green** is left.
Jer 2.20 and under every **green** tree you worshipped fertility gods.
3. 6 high hill and under every **green** tree she has acted like a
3.13 Confess that under every **green** tree you have given your love
17. 2 the goddess Asherah by every **green** tree, on the hill-tops
17. 8 when hot weather comes, because its leaves stay **green;**
49.19 the Jordan up to the **green** pasture land, I will come and
50.44 the Jordan up to the **green** pasture land, I, the Lord, will
Ezek 6.13 every mountain, under every **green** tree and every large oak,
17.24 up the green trees and make the dry trees become **green.**
20.28 saw the high hills and **green** trees, they offered sacrifices
20.47 it will burn up every tree in you, whether **green** or dry.
34.14 valleys and in all the **green** pastures of the land of Israel.
Joel 2.22 The pastures are **green;**
Amos 7. 2 the locusts eat up every **green** thing in the land, and then
Zech 10. 1 clouds and showers, making the fields **green** for everyone.
Mt 24.32 When its branches become **green** and tender and it starts putting
Mk 6.39 people divide into groups and sit down on the **green** grass.
13.28 When its branches become **green** and tender and it starts putting
Lk 23.31 done when the wood is **green,** what will happen when it is
Rev 8. 7 up, a third of the trees, and every blade of **green** grass.

GREET

Gen 28. 1 Isaac called Jacob, **greeted** him, and said to him, "Don't
Num 21.17 And we will **greet** it with a song—
Ruth 2. 4 Boaz himself arrived from Bethlehem and **greeted** the workers.
1 Sam 10. 4 They will **greet** you and offer you two of the loaves, which
15.13 up to Saul, who **greeted** him, saying, "The Lord bless you,
25. 5 to go to Carmel, find Nabal, and give him his **greetings.**
25. 6 "David sends you **greetings,** my friend, with his best wishes
25.14 from the wilderness with **greetings** for our master,
30.21 his men, and David went up to them and **greeted** them warmly.
2 Sam 6.20 when David went home to **greet** his family, Michal came out to
8.10 sent his son Joram to **greet** King David and congratulate him
18.28 Ahimaaz called out a **greeting** to the king, threw
1 Kgs 2.19 The king stood up to **greet** his mother and bowed to her.
2 Kgs 4.29 Don't stop to **greet** anyone you meet, and if anyone greets you,
10.15 Jehu **greeted** him and said, "You and I think alike.
1 Chr 18.10 sent his son Joram to **greet** King David and congratulate him
Ezra 4.17 in Samaria and in the rest of West Euphrates, **greetings.**
Prov 27.14 as wake him up early in the morning with a loud **greeting.**
Dan 4. 1 **"Greetings!**
6.25 **"Greetings!**
Mt 10.13 in that house welcome you, let your **greeting** of peace remain;
10.13 if they do not welcome you, then take back your **greeting.**
23. 7 they love to be **greeted** with respect in the market-places
Mk 9.15 they were greatly surprised, and ran to him and **greeted** him.
12.38 their long robes and be **greeted** with respect in the market-place,
Lk 1.40 She went into Zechariah's house and **greeted** Elizabeth.
1.41 When Elizabeth heard Mary's **greeting,** the baby moved within her.
1.44 soon as I heard your **greeting,** the baby within me jumped
Lk 10. 4 don't stop to **greet** anyone on the road.
10. 6 man lives there, let your **greeting** of peace remain on him;
10. 6 if not, take back your **greeting** of peace.
11.43 synagogues and to be **greeted** with respect in the market-places.
20.46 and love to be **greeted** with respect in the market-place;
Acts 15.23 the elders, your brothers, send **greetings** to all our brothers
18.22 he went to Jerusalem and **greeted** the church, and then went
21. 7 Tyre to Ptolemais, where we **greeted** the believers and stayed
21.19 Paul **greeted** them and gave a complete report of everything
23.26 **Greetings.**
Rom 16. 3 I send **greetings** to Priscilla and Aquila, my fellow-workers
16. 5 **Greetings** also to the church that meets in their house.
16. 5 **Greetings** to my dear friend Epaenetus, who was the first
16. 6 **Greetings** to Mary, who has worked so hard for you.
16. 7 **Greetings** also to Andronicus and Junias, fellow-Jews who were in
16. 8 My **greetings** to Ampliatus, my dear friend in the fellowship
16. 9 **Greetings** also to Urbanus, our fellow-worker in Christ's service,
16.10 **Greetings** to Apelles, whose loyalty to Christ has been proved.
16.10 **Greetings** to those who belong to the family of Aristobulus.
16.11 **Greetings** to Herodion, a fellow-Jew, and to the Christian
16.12 My **greetings** to Tryphaena and Tryphosa, who work in the Lord's
16.13 I send **greetings** to Rufus, that outstanding worker in the Lord's
16.14 My **greetings** to Asyncritus, Phlegon, Hermes, Patrobas, Hermas,
16.15 **Greetings** to Philologus and Julia, to Nereus and his sister,
16.16 **Greet** one another with a brotherly kiss.
16.16 All the churches of Christ send you their **greetings.**
16.21 Timothy, my fellow-worker, sends you his **greetings;**
16.22 I, Tertius, the writer of this letter, send you Christian **greetings.**
16.23 Gaius, in whose house the church meets, sends you his **greetings;**
16.23 city treasurer, and our brother Quartus send you their **greetings.**
1 Cor 16.19 The churches in the province of Asia send you their **greetings;**
16.19 the church that meets in their house send warm Christian **greetings.**
16.20 All the brothers here send **greetings.**
16.20 **Greet** one another with a brotherly kiss.
16.21 **Greetings** from Paul.
2 Cor 13.12 **Greet** one another with a brotherly kiss.
13.12 All God's people send you their **greetings.**
Gal 1. 2 join me in sending **greetings** to the churches of Galatia:
Phil 4.21 **Greetings** to each one of God's people who belong to Christ Jesus.
4.21 The brothers here with me send you their **greetings.**
4.22 All God's people here send **greetings,** especially those who
Col 4.10 prison with me, sends you **greetings,** and so does Mark, the
4.11 Joshua, also called Justus, sends **greetings** too.
4.12 **Greetings** from Epaphras, another member of your group
4.14 Luke, our dear doctor, and Demas send you their **greetings.**
4.18 **Greetings** from Paul.
1 Thes 5.26 **Greet** all the believers with a brotherly kiss.
2 Thes 3.17 **Greetings** from Paul.
2 Tim 4.19 I send **greetings** to Priscilla and Aquila and to the
4.21 Linus, and Claudia send their **greetings,** and so do all the
Tit 3.15 All who are with me send you **greetings.**
3.15 Give our **greetings** to our friends in the faith.
Phlm 23 Jesus, sends you his **greetings,** [24] and so do my fellow-workers
Heb 13.24 Give our **greetings** to all your leaders and to all God's people.
13.24 The brothers from Italy send you their **greetings.**
Jas 1. 1 **Greetings** to all God's people scattered over the whole world.
1 Pet 5.13 chosen by God, sends you **greetings,** and so does my son Mark.
5.14 **Greet** one another with the kiss of Christian love.
2 Jn 13 The children of your dear Sister send you their **greetings.**
3 Jn 15 All your friends send **greetings.**
15 **Greet** all our friends personally.

GREY

1 Sam 12. 2 me, I am old and **grey,** and my sons are with you.
Job 15.10 We learnt our wisdom from **grey-haired** men— men born
Ps 71.18 old and my hair is **grey,** do not abandon me, O God!
Prov 16.31 **grey** hair is a glorious crown.
20.29 the strength of youth and respect the **grey** hair of age.
Is 46. 4 care of you until you are old and your hair is **grey.**

GRIDDLE

Lev 2. 5 is bread cooked on a **griddle,** it is to be made of
6.21 oil and cooked on a **griddle** and then crumbled and presented
7. 9 a pan or on a **griddle** belongs to the priest who has

GRIEF

Josh 7. 6 Israel tore their clothes in **grief,** threw themselves to the
Judg 11.37 in the mountains and **grieve** that I must die a virgin."
11.38 up into the mountains and **grieved** because she was going to
11.40 four days every year to **grieve** for the daughter of Jephthah
1 Sam 4.12 To show his **grief,** he had torn his clothes and put earth
15.35 but he **grieved** over him.
16. 1 to Samuel, "How long will you go on **grieving** over Saul?
20.41 David's **grief** was even greater than Jonathan's.
2 Sam 1. 2 To show his **grief,** he had torn his clothes and put earth
1.12 They **grieved** and mourned and fasted until evening for
1.26 "I **grieve** for you, my brother Jonathan;
15.30 was barefoot and had his head covered as a sign of **grief.**
18.33 The king was overcome with **grief.**
2 Kgs 2.12 In **grief,** Elisha tore his cloak in two.
18.37 Joah tore their clothes in **grief,** and went and reported to
19. 1 he tore his clothes in **grief,** put on sackcloth, and went to
Ezra 9. 3 tore my hair and my beard, and sat down crushed with **grief.**
9. 4 I sat there **grieving** until the time for the evening
9. 5 I had been **grieving,** and still wearing my torn clothes,
10. 6 night there **grieving** over the unfaithfulness of the exiles.
Neh 9. 1 sackcloth and put dust on their heads as signs of **grief.**

Esth 9.22 turned from a time of **grief** and despair into a time of
Job 1.20 Then Job stood up and tore his clothes in **grief.**
2.12 wail, tearing their clothes in **grief** and throwing dust into
3.10 letting me be born, for exposing me to trouble and **grief.**
3.20 Why give light to men in **grief?**
6. 1 If my troubles and **griefs** were weighed on scales,
7. 3 night after night brings me **grief.**
14.22 pain of his own body and the **grief** of his own mind.
17. 7 My **grief** has almost made me blind;
Ps 6. 6 I am worn out with **grief;**
Prov 10. 1 a foolish one brings his mother **grief.**
17.25 A foolish son brings **grief** to his father and bitter
Ecc 5.17 to live our lives in darkness and **grief,** worried, angry, and
Is 15. 2 people of Moab wail in **grief** over the cities of Nebo and
15. 2 they have shaved their heads and their beards in **grief.**
15. 5 some escape to Horonaim, **grieving** loudly.
16.11 I groan with sadness for Moab, with **grief** for Kir Heres.
23. 1 Howl with **grief,** you sailors out on the ocean!
23. 6 Howl with **grief,** you people of Phoenicia!
23.14 Howl with **grief,** you sailors out on the ocean!
32.12 Beat your breasts in **grief** because the fertile fields
35.10 be happy for ever, for ever free from sorrow and **grief.**
36.22 Joah tore their clothes in **grief** and went and reported to
37. 1 he tore his clothes in **grief,** put on sackcloth, and went to
51.11 be happy for ever, for ever free from sorrow and **grief.**
60.20 Your days of **grief** will come to an end.
61. 3 Joy and gladness instead of **grief,** A song of praise instead
Jer 15. 5 you, people of Jerusalem, and who will **grieve** over you?
16. 5 Do not **grieve** for anyone.
16. 6 one will gash himself or shave his head to show his **grief.**
31.18 people of Israel say in **grief,** 'Lord, we were like an
31.19 After you had punished us, we hung our heads in **grief.**
Lam 2.11 I am exhausted with **grief** at the destruction of my people.
2.18 Wear yourself out with weeping and **grief!**
3.33 He takes no pleasure in causing us **grief** or pain.
3.51 My heart is **grieved** when I see what has happened to
5.15 **grief** has taken the place of our dances.
Ezek 2.10 on both sides—cries of **grief** were written there, and wails
21.12 Howl in **grief,** mortal man;
28.12 "Mortal man," he said, **"grieve** for the fate that is
Joel 1.11 **Grieve,** you farmers;
Amos 8.10 funerals and change your glad songs into cries of **grief.**
Zech 11. 3 The rulers cry out in **grief;**
Mt 26.37 **Grief** and anguish came over him, [38] and he said to them,
Lk 22.45 disciples and found them asleep, worn out by their **grief.**
Rev 18. 7 her as much suffering and **grief** as the glory and luxury she
18. 7 I am no widow, I will never know **grief!'**
18. 8 day she will be struck with plagues— disease, **grief,** and
21. 4 will be no more death, no more **grief** or crying or pain.

GRILLWORK see GRATING

GRIN

Prov 16.30 Watch out for people who **grin** and wink at you;

GRIND (1)
[GROUND]

Ex 11. 5 the throne, to the son of the slave-woman who **grinds** corn.
32.20 they had made, melted it, **ground** it into fine powder, and
Lev 2. 1 of grain to the Lord, he must first **grind** it into flour.
2.14 first corn harvested, offer roasted grain or **ground** meal.
Num 11. 8 go round and gather it, **grind** it or pound it into flour,
Deut 9.21 I broke it in pieces, **ground** it to dust, and threw the
24. 6 take as security his millstones used for **grinding** his corn.
Judg 16.21 and put him to work **grinding** at the mill in the prison.
2 Chr 34. 4 They **ground** to dust the images of Asherah and all the other
34. 7 and the symbols of Asherah, **ground** the idols to dust, and
Ecc 12. 4 hear the mill as it **grinds** or music as it plays, but
Is 27. 9 stones of pagan altars are **ground** up like chalk, and no more
47. 2 **Grind** the flour!
Lam 5.13 Our young men are forced to **grind** corn like slaves;
Mt 24.41 Two women will be at a mill **grinding** meal:
Lk 17.35 Two women will be **grinding** corn together:

GRIND (2)
[GROUND]

Mt 8.12 the darkness, where they will cry and **grind** their teeth."
13.42 the fiery furnace, where they will cry and **grind** their teeth.
13.50 the fiery furnace, where they will cry and **grind** their teeth.
22.13 There he will cry and **grind** his teeth.' "
24.51 There he will cry and **grind** his teeth.
25.30 there he will cry and **grind** his teeth.'
Lk 13.28 How you will cry and **grind** your teeth when you see Abraham,
Acts 7.54 they became furious and **ground** their teeth at him in anger.

GRIP

Job 20.25 its shiny point drips with his blood, and terror **grips** his heart.
Ps 55. 5 I am **gripped** by fear and trembling;

GRIT

Mk 9.18 he foams at the mouth, **grits** his teeth, and becomes stiff

GROAN

Ex 2.23 but the Israelites were still **groaning** under their slavery
2.24 heard their **groaning** and remembered his covenant with Abraham,
6. 5 Now I have heard the **groaning** of the Israelites, whom the
Judg 2.18 because they **groaned** under their suffering and oppression.
Job 3.24 Instead of eating, I mourn, and I can never stop **groaning.**
23. 1 I can't hold back my **groaning.**
35. 9 When men are oppressed, they **groan;**
Ps 12. 5 the needy are oppressed and the persecuted **groan** in pain.
38. 8 my heart is troubled, and I **groan** with pain.
38. 9 you hear all my **groans.**
55.17 and night my complaints and **groans** go up to him, and he
79.11 Listen to the **groans** of the prisoners, and by your great
102. 5 I **groan** aloud;
102.20 He heard the **groans** of prisoners and set free those who
Prov 5.11 You will lie **groaning** on your deathbed, your flesh and
Is 16.11 I **groan** with sadness for Moab, with grief for Kir Heres.
19. 8 earns his living by fishing in the Nile will **groan** and cry;
Jer 45. 3 I am worn out from **groaning,** and I can't find any rest!'
51.52 and the wounded will **groan** throughout the country.
Lam 1. 4 The girls who sang there suffer, and the priests can only **groan.**
1. 8 She **groans** and hides her face in shame.
1.11 Her people **groan** as they look for something to eat;
1.21 "Listen to my **groans;**
1.22 I **groan** in misery, and I am sick at heart."
Ezek 2.10 of grief were written there, and wails and **groans.**
21. 6 "Mortal man, **groan** as if your heart is breaking with despair.
21. 6 **Groan** in sorrow where everyone can watch you.
21. 7 ask you why you are **groaning,** tell them it is because of
24.23 because of your sins, and you will **groan** to one another.
30.24 of Egypt, and he will **groan** and die in front of his
Amos 2.13 the ground, and you will **groan** like a cart loaded with corn.
Mic 4.10 Twist and **groan,** people of Jerusalem, like a woman giving birth,
Mk 7.34 to heaven, gave a deep **groan,** and said to the man,
8.12 But Jesus gave a deep **groan** and said, "Why do the
Acts 7.34 I have heard their **groans,** and I have come down to set
Rom 8.22 present time all of creation **groans** with pain, like the pain
8.23 But it is not just creation alone which **groans;**
8.23 first of God's gifts also **groan** within ourselves, as we wait
8.26 pleads with God for us in **groans** that words cannot express.
2 Cor 5. 4 in this earthly tent, we **groan** with a feeling of oppression;

GROOM see BRIDEGROOM

GROPE

Deut 28.29 You will **grope** about in broad daylight like a blind man,
Job 5.14 even at noon they **grope** in darkness.
12.25 they **grope** in the dark and stagger like drunkards.
Is 59.10 is only darkness, [10] and we **grope** about like blind people.
Zeph 1.17 on mankind that everyone will **grope** about like a blind man.

GROUND
see also **GRIND (1), GRIND (2), UNDERGROUND**

Gen 2. 6 come up from beneath the surface and water the **ground.**
2. 7 took some soil from the **ground** and formed a man out of
2.19 took some soil from the **ground** and formed all the animals
3.17 of what you have done, the **ground** will be under a curse.
4.10 out to me from the **ground,** like a voice calling for revenge.
5.29 and said, "From the very **ground** on which the Lord put a
8.13 boat, looked round, and saw that the **ground** was getting dry.
17. 3 with his face touching the **ground,** and God said, [4] "I make
17.17 with his face touching the **ground,** but he began to laugh
18. 2 with his face touching the **ground,** [3] he said, "Sirs, please
33. 3 and bowed down to the **ground** seven times as he approached
38. 9 the semen spill on the **ground,** so that there would be no
42. 6 and bowed down before him with their faces to the **ground.**
43.26 the house to him and bowed down to the **ground** before him.
44.11 their sacks to the **ground,** and each man opened his sack.
48.12 lap and bowed down before him with his face to the **ground.**
49.25 deep waters from beneath the **ground,**
Ex 3. 5 Take off your sandals, because you are standing on holy **ground.**
4. 3 The Lord said, "Throw it on the **ground."**
4. 9 take some water from the Nile and pour it on the **ground.**
8.16 "Tell Aaron to strike the **ground** with his stick, and all
8.17 So Aaron struck the **ground** with his stick, and all the
8.21 be full of flies, and the **ground** will be covered with them.
9.23 Lord sent thunder and hail, and lightning struck the **ground.**
10. 5 There will be so many that they will completely cover the **ground.**
10.15 They covered the **ground** until it was black with them;
14.13 Stand your **ground,** and you will see what the Lord will do
14.16 Israelites will be able to walk through the sea on dry **ground.**
14.22 through the sea on dry **ground,** with walls of water on both
14.29 through the sea on dry **ground,** with walls of water on both
15.19 The Israelites walked through the sea on dry **ground.**
16.21 when the sun grew hot, what was left on the **ground** melted.
34. 8 Moses quickly bowed down to the **ground** and worshipped.
Lev 9.24 all shouted and bowed down with their faces to the **ground.**
11.41 animals that move on the **ground,** [42] whether they crawl, or
11.46 lives in the water, and everything that moves on the **ground.**
17.13 pour out its blood on the **ground** and cover it with earth.
Num 11.31 from the sea, flying less than a metre above the **ground.**
14. 5 and Aaron bowed to the **ground** in front of all the people.
16. 4 When Moses heard this, he threw himself on the **ground** and prayed.
16.22 with their faces to the **ground** and said, "O, God, you are
16.31 he had finished speaking, the **ground** under Dathan and Abiram

Num 16.45 with their faces to the **ground,** [46]and Moses said to Aaron,
20. 6 with their faces to the **ground,** and the dazzling light of
22.31 and Balaam threw himself face downwards on the **ground.**
26.10 The **ground** opened and swallowed them, and they died with
Deut 11.17 back the rain, and your **ground** will become too dry for crops
11.24 All the **ground** that you march over will be yours.
12.16 you must pour it out on the **ground** like water.
12.24 instead pour it out on the **ground** like water.
15.23 instead, you must pour it out on the **ground** like water.
21. 4 dry and where the **ground** has never been ploughed or planted,
22. 6 a tree or on the **ground** with the mother bird sitting either
28.23 rain will fall, and your **ground** will become as hard as iron.
32.13 their olive-trees flourished in stony **ground.**
33.28 of corn and wine, where dew from the sky waters the **ground.**
Josh 3.17 people walked across on dry **ground,** the priests carrying the
3.17 Covenant Box stood on dry **ground** in the middle of the Jordan
4.22 about the time when Israel crossed the Jordan on dry **ground.**
5.14 Joshua threw himself on the **ground** in worship and said, "I
5.15 you are standing on holy **ground."**
6.24 and burnt it to the **ground,** along with everything in it,
7. 6 themselves to the **ground** before the Lord's Covenant Box,
7.10 Why are you lying on the **ground** like this?
17.15 into the forests and clear **ground** for yourselves in the land
Judg 4.21 peg right through the side of his head and into the **ground.**
4.22 there was Sisera on the **ground,** dead, with the tent-peg
5.22 Then the horses came galloping on, stamping the **ground**
5.27 he fell to the **ground,** dead.
6.37 putting some wool on the **ground** where we thresh the wheat.
6.37 wool but not on the **ground,** then I will know that you
6.39 This time let the wool be dry, and the **ground** be wet."
6.40 morning the wool was dry, but the **ground** was wet with dew.
7.13 The tent collapsed and lay flat on the **ground."**
9.45 its people, tore it down, and covered the **ground** with salt.
13.20 and his wife threw themselves face downwards on the **ground.**
15.19 a hollow place in the **ground** there at Lehi, and water came
Ruth 2.10 with her face touching the **ground,** and said to Boaz, "Why
1 Sam 5. 3 fallen face downwards on the **ground** in front of the Lord's
17.49 his skull, and Goliath fell face downwards on the **ground.**
20.41 his knees and bowed with his face to the **ground** three times.
24. 8 David bowed down to the **ground** in respect [9]and said, "Why
25.23 and threw herself on the **ground** [24]at David's feet, and said,
25.41 Abigail bowed down to the **ground** and said, "I am his servant,
26. 7 the camp with his spear stuck in the **ground** near his head.
26. 8 and pin him to the **ground** with just one blow—I won't
28.14 that it was Samuel, and he bowed to the **ground** in respect.
28.20 out on the **ground,** terrified by what Samuel had said.
28.23 gave in, got up from the **ground,** and sat on the bed.
2 Sam 1. 2 He went to David and bowed to the **ground** in respect.
2.23 Asahel dropped to the **ground** dead, and everyone who came to
8. 2 prisoners lie down on the **ground** and put two out of every
13.31 tore his clothes in sorrow, and threw himself to the **ground.**
14. 4 king, bowed down to the **ground** in respect, and said, "Help
14.14 water spilt on the **ground,** which can't be gathered again.
14.22 Joab threw himself to the **ground** in front of David in respect,
14.33 to him and bowed down to the **ground** in front of him.
18.28 threw himself down to the **ground** before him, and said,
20.10 him in the belly, and his entrails spilt out on the **ground.**
23.10 back, [10]but he stood his **ground** and fought the Philistines
23.12 Philistines, [12]but Shammah stood his **ground** in the field,
24.20 He threw himself on the **ground** in front of David [21]and asked,
1 Kgs 1.40 playing flutes, making enough noise to shake the **ground.**
13. 5 the ashes spilt to the **ground,** as the prophet had predicted
18.39 themselves on the **ground** and exclaimed, "The Lord is God;
18.42 bowed down to the **ground,** with his head between his knees.
2 Kgs 2. 8 and he and Elisha crossed to the other side on dry **ground.**
3.20 flowing from the direction of Edom, and covered the **ground.**
4.37 She fell at Elisha's feet, with her face touching the **ground;**
13.18 to take the other arrows and strike the **ground** with them.
13.18 The king struck the **ground** three times, and then stopped.
15. 7 buried in the royal burial **ground** in David's City, and his
19.30 that send roots deep into the **ground** and produce fruit.
23.14 the goddess Asherah, and the **ground** where they had stood he
1 Chr 21.16 sackcloth—bowed low, with their faces touching the **ground.**
21.21 and bowed low, with his face touching the **ground.**
2 Chr 20.18 with his face touching the **ground,** and all the people bowed
20.24 enemy and saw that they were all lying on the **ground,** dead.
Neh 8. 6 They knelt in worship, with their faces to the **ground.**
9.11 a path for your people and led them through on dry **ground.**
Job 1.20 He shaved his head and threw himself face downwards on the **ground.**
2.13 they sat there on the **ground** with him for seven days and
5. 6 grow in the soil, nor does trouble grow out of the **ground.**
9. 6 God sends earthquakes and shakes the **ground;**
14. 8 its stump dies in the **ground,** [9]with water it will sprout
18.10 On the **ground** a snare is hidden;
28. 2 dig iron out of the **ground** And melt copper out of the
39.14 leaves her eggs on the **ground** for the heat in the soil
39.21 They eagerly paw the **ground** in the valley;
40.13 Bury them all in the **ground;**
41. 9 Anyone who sees Leviathan loses courage and falls to the **ground.**
41.30 they tear up the muddy **ground** like a threshing-sledge.
Ps 7. 5 me down and kill me and leave me lifeless on the **ground!**
22.14 My strength is gone, gone like water spilt on the **ground.**
44.25 We fall crushed to the **ground;**
69. 2 I am sinking in deep mud, and there is no solid **ground;**
72. 9 his enemies will throw themselves to the **ground.**
83.10 You defeated them at Endor, and their bodies rotted on the **ground.**
89.44 away his royal sceptre and hurled his throne to the **ground.**
137. 7 Remember how they kept saying, "Tear it down to the **ground!"**
143. 6 like dry **ground** my soul is thirsty for you.
Ps 147. 6 He raises the humble, but crushes the wicked to the **ground.**
Prov 2.22 and pull sinners out of it like plants from the **ground.**
30.16 dry **ground** that needs rain,
Ecc 3.21 upwards while an animal's spirit goes down into the **ground?**
Is 1. 7 devastated, and your cities have been burnt to the **ground.**
2.10 or dig holes in the **ground** to try to escape from the
2.19 or dig holes in the **ground** to try to escape from the
3.26 will be like a woman sitting on the **ground,** stripped naked.
5. 6 I will not prune the vines or hoe the **ground;**
8.22 sky [22]or stare at the **ground,** but they will see nothing
14.12 nations, but now you have been thrown to the **ground.**
21. 9 All the idols they worshipped lie shattered on the **ground."**
26.21 will be revealed, and the **ground** will no longer hide those
29. 4 to speak from under the **ground,** a muffled voice coming from
37.31 that send roots deep into the **ground** and produce fruit.
41. 3 safely on, so fast that he hardly touches the **ground!**
44. 3 the thirsty land and make streams flow on the dry **ground.**
47. 1 down from your throne, and sit in the dust on the **ground.**
53. 2 servant should grow like a plant taking root in dry **ground.**
63. 6 I poured out their life-blood on the **ground."**
Jer 8. 2 buried, their bones will be like manure lying on the **ground.**
14. 2 its people lie on the **ground** in sorrow, and Jerusalem cries
14. 4 is no rain and the **ground** is dried up, the farmers are
16. 4 Their bodies will lie like piles of manure on the **ground.**
17. 6 the dry wilderness, on salty **ground** where nothing else grows.
21.10 the king of Babylonia and he will burn it to the **ground.**
25.33 They will lie on the **ground** like piles of manure.
37.10 men would still get up and burn this city to the **ground."**
38.23 of Babylonia, and this city will be burnt to the **ground."**
46.12 trips over another, and both of them fall to the **ground.**
48.18 your place of honour and sit on the **ground** in the dust;
49. 2 will be left in ruins and its villages burnt to the **ground.**
51.25 of you, level you to the **ground,** and leave you in ashes.
51.58 be thrown to the **ground,** and its towering gates burnt down.
52.23 all, and ninety-six of these were visible from the **ground.**
Lam 1.13 He set a trap for me and brought me to the **ground.**
2.10 old men sit on the **ground** in silence, With dust on their
2.10 Young girls bow their heads to the **ground.**
3.16 rubbed my face in the **ground** and broke my teeth on the
4.11 he lit a fire in Zion that burnt it to the **ground.**
Ezek 1.15 I saw four wheels touching the **ground,** one beside each of them.
1.28 When I saw this, I fell face downwards on the **ground.**
3.23 fell face downwards on the **ground,** [24]but God's spirit
9. 8 face downwards on the **ground** and shouted, "Sovereign Lord,
11.13 downwards on the **ground** and shouted, "No, Sovereign Lord!
19.12 pulled it up by the roots and threw it to the **ground.**
24. 7 was not spilt on the **ground** where the dust could hide it;
26.11 Your mighty pillars will be thrown to the **ground.**
26.16 their embroidered clothes and sit trembling on the **ground.**
28.17 I hurled you to the **ground** and left you as a warning
28.18 I set fire to the city and burnt it to the **ground.**
29. 5 Your body will fall on the **ground** and be left unburied.
32. 4 throw you out on the **ground** and bring all the birds and
37. 1 me down in a valley where the **ground** was covered with bones.
39.14 those bodies remaining on the **ground,** so that they can make
41. 8 was three metres above the **ground** and it was level with the
43. 3 Then I threw myself face downwards on the **ground.**
44. 4 face downwards on the **ground,** [5]and the Lord said to me,
Dan 2.46 King Nebuchadnezzar bowed to the **ground** and gave orders for
4.15 leave the stump in the **ground** with a band of iron and
4.23 tree down and destroy it, but leave the stump in the **ground.**
4.26 The angel ordered the stump to be left in the **ground.**
8. 5 west, moving so fast that his feet didn't touch the **ground.**
8. 7 He was thrown to the **ground** and trampled on, and there was
8.10 it threw some of them to the **ground** and trampled on them.
8.12 sacrifices, and true religion was thrown to the **ground.**
8.17 me, and I was so terrified that I fell to the **ground.**
8.18 While he was talking, I fell to the **ground** unconscious.
10. 9 I fell to the **ground** unconscious and lay there face downwards.
10.15 When he said this, I stared at the **ground,** speechless.
Hos 10.12 I said, 'Plough new **ground** for yourselves, plant righteousness,
13.16 will be dashed to the **ground,** and pregnant women will be
Joel 1.10 the **ground** mourns because the corn is destroyed, the grapes
Amos 2.13 will crush you to the **ground,** and you will groan like a
2.15 Bowmen will not stand their **ground,** fast runners will not
3.14 every altar will be broken off and will fall to the **ground.**
5. 2 She lies abandoned on the **ground,** And no one helps her up.
Hab 1. 8 their horses paw the **ground.**
Zeph 1.17 and their dead bodies will lie rotting on the **ground."**
Hag 1.11 every crop the **ground** produces, on men and animals,
Zech 9. 4 into the sea, and the city will be burnt to the **ground.**
Mt 10.29 not one sparrow falls to the **ground** without your Father's consent.
13. 5 Some of it fell on rocky **ground,** where there was little soil.
13.20 seeds that fell on rocky **ground** stand for those who receive
15.35 So Jesus ordered the crowd to sit down on the **ground.**
17. 6 terrified that they threw themselves face downwards on the **ground.**
25.18 off, dug a hole in the **ground,** and hid his master's money.
25.25 afraid, so I went off and hid your money in the **ground.**
26.39 face downwards on the **ground,** and prayed, "My Father, if it
Mk 4. 5 Some of it fell on rocky **ground,** where there was little soil.
4.16 Other people are like the seeds that fall on rocky **ground.**
4.31 the smallest seed in the world, and plants it in the **ground.**
8. 6 He ordered the crowd to sit down on the **ground.**
9.18 it throws him to the **ground,** and he foams at the mouth,
9.20 that he fell on the **ground** and rolled round, foaming at the
14.35 threw himself on the **ground,** and prayed that, if possible,
Lk 8. 6 of it fell on rocky **ground,** and when the plants sprouted,
8.13 seeds that fell on rocky **ground** stand for those who hear the
9.42 demon knocked him to the **ground** and threw him into a fit.
17.16 He threw himself to the **ground** at Jesus' feet and thanked him.

Lk 22.44 his sweat was like drops of blood falling to the **ground.**
24. 5 women bowed down to the **ground,** as the men said to them,
Jn 8. 6 But he bent over and wrote on the **ground** with his finger.
8. 8 Then he bent over again and wrote on the **ground.**
9. 6 this, Jesus spat on the **ground** and made some mud with the
12.24 single grain unless it is dropped into the **ground** and dies.
18. 6 them, "I am he," they moved back and fell to the **ground.**
Acts 7. 5 even a square metre of **ground,** but God promised to give it
7.33 off, for the place where you are standing is holy **ground.**
9. 4 He fell to the **ground** and heard a voice saying to him,
9. 8 Saul got up from the **ground** and opened his eyes,
20. 9 sound asleep and fell from the third storey to the **ground.**
22. 7 I fell to the **ground** and heard a voice saying to me,
26.14 of us fell to the **ground,** and I heard a voice say
1 Cor 15.36 sow a seed in the **ground,** it does not sprout to life
Eph 6.13 after fighting to the end, you will still hold your **ground.**
Heb 11.38 deserts and hills, living in caves and holes in the **ground.**

GROUNDED

2 Pet 1.12 them and are firmly **grounded** in the truth you have received.

GROUP

Gen 8.19 birds went out of the boat in **groups** of their own kind.
10. 5 tribes and countries, each **group** speaking its own language.
10.20 tribes and countries, each **group** speaking its own language.
10.31 tribes and countries, each **group** speaking its own language.
14.15 he divided his men into **groups,** attacked the enemy by night,
32. 7 He divided into two **groups** the people who were with him, and
32. 8 comes and attacks the first **group,** the other may be able to
32.10 and now I have come back with these two **groups.**
33. 8 Esau asked, "What about that other **group** I met?
37.25 eating, they suddenly saw a **group** of Ishmaelites travelling
50. 9 it was a huge **group.**
Num 1.52 each man with his own **group** and under his own banner.
2. 3 of Judah shall camp in their **groups,** under their leaders, as
2.10 of Reuben shall camp in their **groups,** under their leaders,
2.18 of Ephraim shall camp in their **groups,** under their leaders,
2.25 of Dan shall camp in their **groups,** under their leaders, as
2.32 people of Israel enrolled in the divisions, **group by group,**
11.10 they stood about in **groups** at the entrances of their tents.
25.15 Zur, her father, was chief of a **group** of Midianite clans.
26. 3 Eleazar obeyed, and called together all the men of that age **group.**
Josh 6.11 So he told this **group** of men to take the Lord's Covenant
21.27 Another **group** of Levites, the clan of Gershon, received
Judg 7.16 three hundred men into three **groups** and gave each man a
7.18 When my **group** and I blow our trumpets, then you blow
7.20 were holding, [20] and the other two **groups** did the same.
9.34 their move at night and hid outside Shechem in four **groups.**
9.37 of the mountain and one **group** is coming along the road from
9.43 men, divided them into three **groups,** and hid in the fields,
9.44 Abimelech and his **group** hurried forward to guard the city gate,
11. 3 There he attracted a **group** of worthless men, and they went
21. 5 They asked, "Is there any **group** out of all the tribes of
21. 8 asked if there was some **group** out of the tribes of Israel
1 Sam 10. 5 you will meet a **group of prophets** coming down from the altar
10.10 his servant arrived at Gibeah, a **group of prophets** met him.
11.11 divided his men into three **groups,** and at dawn they rushed
13.17 soldiers went out on raids from their camp in three **groups:**
13.17 one **group** went towards Ophrah in the territory of Shual,
13.23 The Philistines sent a **group** of soldiers to defend the
19.20 They saw the **group of prophets** dancing and shouting, with
2 Sam 2.13 they all sat down, one **group** on one side of the pool
2.13 and the other **group** on the opposite side.
18. 2 sent them out in three **groups,** with Joab and Joab's brother
18. 2 Abishai and Ittai from Gath, each in command of a **group.**
21. 2 they were a small **group** of Amorites whom the Israelites had
23.14 hill, and a **group** of Philistines had occupied Bethlehem.
1 Kgs 5.14 He divided them into three **groups** of 10,000 men,
5.14 and each **group** spent one month in Lebanon and
10. 2 brought with her a large **group** of attendants, as well as
18. 4 them in caves in two **groups** of fifty, and provided them with
18.13 them in caves, in two **groups** of fifty, and supplied them
20.17 reported to him that a **group** of soldiers was coming out of
20.27 marched out and camped in two **groups** facing the Syrians.
20.35 a member of a **group of prophets** ordered a fellow-prophet to
2 Kgs 2. 3 A **group of prophets** who lived there went to Elisha and
2. 5 A **group of prophets** who lived there went to Elisha and
4. 1 a member of a **group of prophets** went to Elisha and said,
4.38 he was teaching a **group of prophets,** he told his servant to
4.42 feed the **group of prophets** with this, [43] but he answered,
5.22 two members of the **group of prophets** in the hill-country of
6. 1 One day the **group of prophets** that Elisha was in charge of
9.18 the messenger had reached the **group** but was not returning.
9.20 the messenger had reached the **group** but was not returning.
9.20 added, "The leader of the **group** is driving his chariot like
11. 7 The two **groups** that go off duty on the Sabbath are to
17.29 Each different **group** made idols in the cities they were living in:
1 Chr 11.16 hill, and a **group** of Philistines had occupied Bethlehem.
11.42 of Reuben, with his own **group** of thirty soldiers) Hanan son
12.16 Once a **group** of men from the tribes of Benjamin and
23. 6 David divided the Levites into three **groups,**
24. 1 These are the **groups** to which the descendants of Aaron belong.
24. 3 David organized the descendants of Aaron into **groups**
24. 4 Eleazar were organized into sixteen **groups,** while the
24. 7 the twenty-four family **groups** were given their assignments:
25. 1 with the type of service that each **group** performed:
25. 9 according to families into twenty-four **groups** of twelve,
25. 9 with a leader in charge of each **group.**
26.12 guards were divided into **groups,** according to families,
1 Chr 26.21 the ancestor of several family **groups,** including the family
26.26 of families, leaders of clan **groups,** and army officers.
27. 1 of the year a different **group** of twenty-four thousand men
27. 2 (his son Amizzabad succeeded him as commander of this **group)**
2 Chr 5.11 present, regardless of the **group** to which they belonged,
9. 1 brought with her a large **group** of attendants, as well as
13. 7 Later he gathered together a **group** of worthless scoundrels,
22. 8 dynasty, he came across a **group** made up of Judaean leaders
29. 4 He assembled a **group** of priests and Levites in the east
31.17 years of age or older were assigned theirs by work **groups.**
35.12 people, by family **groups,** the animals for burnt-offerings,
Ezra 7. 6 Babylonia for Jerusalem with a **group** of Israelites
8.15 I assembled the entire **group** by the canal that runs to
8.15 I found that there were priests in the **group,** but no Levites.
10. 1 confessing these sins, a large **group** of Israelites—men,
Neh 1. 2 arrived from Judah with a **group** of other men, and I asked
3.28 A **group** of priests built the next section, going north
11.36 Some **groups** of Levites that had lived in the territory
12.24 Binnui, and Kadmiel, the Levites were organized into **groups.**
12.24 Two **groups** at a time praised God responsively and gave
12.31 in charge of two large **groups** to march round the city,
12.31 The first **group** went to the right on top of the wall
12.36 Ezra the scholar led this **group** in the procession.
12.38 The other **group** of those who gave thanks went to the
12.40 So both the **groups** that were giving thanks to God
12.41 my **group** included the following priests, blowing trumpets:
Esth 2. 6 along with a **group** of captives, Mordecai was among them.
Ps 68.27 leaders of Judah with their **group,** followed by the leaders
Jer 41. 8 were ten men in the **group** who said to Ishmael, "Please
50. 9 going to stir up a **group** of strong nations in the north
Ezek 1. 9 they moved as a **group** without turning their bodies.
1.12 directions, and so the **group** could go wherever they wished,
23.42 crowd could be heard, a **group** of men brought in from the
40. 2 in front of me a **group** of buildings that looked like a
Mt 11.16 One **group** shouts to the other, [17] 'We played wedding music
12.25 country that divides itself into **groups** which fight each other
12.25 family that divides itself into **groups** which fight each other
12.26 So if one **group** is fighting another in Satan's kingdom,
12.26 it is already divided into **groups** and will soon fall apart!
14. 6 the daughter of Herodias danced in front of the whole **group.**
25.32 will divide them into two **groups,** just as a shepherd separates
Mk 3.24 a country divides itself into **groups** which fight each other,
3.25 a family divides itself into **groups** which fight each other,
3.26 if Satan's kingdom divides into **groups,** it cannot last,
6.39 all the people divide into **groups** and sit down on the green
6.40 down in rows, in groups of a hundred and **groups** of fifty.
9.38 told him to stop, because he doesn't belong to our **group."**
Lk 2.44 that he was with the **group,** so they travelled a whole day
5.19 his bed into the middle of the **group** in front of Jesus.
5.30 Law who belonged to their **group** complained to Jesus' disciples.
7.32 One **group** shouts to the other, 'We played wedding music for you,
9.14 "Make the people sit down in **groups** of about fifty each."
9.49 told him to stop, because he doesn't belong to our **group."**
11.17 country that divides itself into **groups** which fight each other
11.18 So if Satan's kingdom has **groups** fighting each other,
23. 1 The whole **group** rose up and took Jesus before Pilate,
24.22 Some of the women of our **group** surprised us;
24.24 Some of our **group** went to the tomb and found it exactly
Jn 18. 3 garden, taking with him a **group** of Roman soldiers, and some
Acts 1.14 frequently to pray as a **group,** together with the women and
1.17 was a member of our **group,** for he had been chosen to
1.21 men who were in our **group** during the whole time that the
1.26 Matthias, who was added to the **group** of eleven apostles.
2.41 about three thousand people were added to the **group** that day.
2.46 day they met as a **group** in the Temple, and they had
2.47 the Lord added to their **group** those who were being saved.
4.23 free, they returned to their **group** and told them what the
4.32 The **group** of believers was one in mind and heart.
4.34 There was no one in the **group** who was in need.
5.13 Nobody outside the **group** dared to join them, even though the
5.14 people were added to the **group**—a crowd of men and women
6. 2 twelve apostles called the whole **group** of believers together
6. 5 The whole **group** was pleased with the apostles' proposal,
6. 6 The **group** presented them to the apostles, who prayed
11.26 met with the people of the church and taught a large **group.**
12. 4 over to be guarded by four **groups** of four soldiers each.
12.20 Tyre and Sidon, so they went in a **group** to see him.
15.12 The whole **group** was silent as they heard Barnabas and Paul
15.22 choose some men from the **group** and send them to Antioch with
15.24 men who went from our **group** have troubled and upset you by
15.30 where they gathered the whole **group** of believers and gave them
17. 4 women and a large **group** of Greeks who worshipped God.
19. 9 and before the whole **group** they said evil things about the
20.30 some men from your own **group** will tell lies to lead the
23. 6 saw that some of the **group** were Sadducees and the others
23. 7 and Sadducees started to quarrel, and the **group** was divided.
23.10 to go down into the **group,** get Paul away from them, and
Rom 11. 7 It was only the small **group** that God chose who found it;
1 Cor 1.13 Christ has been divided into **groups!**
5.12 As the scripture says, "Remove the evil man from your **group."**
11.18 I have been told that there are opposing **groups** in your meetings;
11.20 you meet together as a **group,** it is not the Lord's Supper
Gal 2. 4 these men slipped into our **group** as spies, in order to find
2.10 remember the needy in their **group,** which is the very thing I
5.20 They separate into parties and **groups;**
Col 4. 9 Onesimus, that dear and faithful brother, who belongs to your **group.**
4.12 Epaphras, another member of your **group** and a servant of Christ
Rev 2. 9 they are a **group** that belongs to Satan!
3. 9 As for that **group** that belongs to Satan, those liars who

GROW

[FULL-GROWN, GREW]

Gen 2. 9 kinds of beautiful trees **grow** there and produce good fruit.
4.12 If you try to **grow** crops, the soil will not produce anything;
19.25 all the people there and everything that **grew** on the land.
21. 8 The child **grew,** and on the day that he was weaned, Abraham
21.20 God was with the boy as he **grew** up;
25.27 The boys **grew** up, and Esau became a skilled hunter, a
30.30 had before I came has **grown** enormously, and the Lord has
38.11 house and remain a widow until my son Shelah **grows** up."
38.14 youngest son Shelah had now **grown** up, and yet she had not
41. 5 Seven ears of corn, full and ripe, were **growing** on one stalk.
41.22 ears of corn which were full and ripe, **growing** on one stalk.
Ex 2.11 When Moses had **grown** up, he went out to visit his people,
10.12 that **grows,** everything that has survived the hail."
22. 5 and eat up the crops **growing** in another man's field, he must
22. 6 burns up corn that is **growing** or that has been cut and
23.11 let it rest, and do not harvest anything that **grows** on it.
23.11 The poor may eat what **grows** there, and the wild animals can
Lev 13.37 and healthy hairs are **growing** in it, the sore has healed,
25. 5 harvest the corn that **grows** by itself without being sown,
25.11 or harvest the corn that **grows** by itself or gather the
26.16 your enemies will conquer you and eat what you have **grown.**
Num 6. 5 to the Lord, and he shall let his hair and beard **grow.**
13.20 be sure to bring back some of the fruit that **grows** there."
20. 5 out of Egypt into this miserable place where nothing will **grow?**
Deut 11.17 rain, and your ground will become too dry for crops to **grow.**
28.33 have worked so hard to **grow,** while you receive nothing
28.40 Olive-trees will **grow** everywhere in your land,
29.18 be like a root that **grows** to be a bitter and poisonous
29.23 nothing will be planted, and not even weeds will **grow** there.
32.13 rule the highlands, and they ate what **grew** in the fields.
Josh 5.11 next day was the first time they ate food **grown** in Canaan:
5.12 From that time on they ate food **grown** in Canaan.
Judg 11. 2 his wife, and when they **grew** up, they forced Jephthah to
13.24 The child **grew** and the Lord blessed him.
16.22 But his hair started **growing** again.
Ruth 1.13 and had sons, [13] would you wait until they had **grown** up?
1 Sam 2.21 The boy Samuel **grew** up in the service of the Lord.
2.26 The boy Samuel continued to **grow** and to gain favour
3.19 As Samuel **grew** up, the Lord was with him and made
2 Sam 10. 5 Jericho and not return until their beards had **grown** again.
12. 3 care of it, and it **grew** up in his home with his
14.26 cut it once a year, when it **grew** too long and heavy.
14.30 field is next to mine, and it has barley **growing** in it.
15.12 gained strength, and Absalom's followers **grew** in number.
1 Kgs 4.33 from the Lebanon cedars to the hyssop that **grows** on walls;
12. 8 the young men who had **grown** up with him and who were
2 Kgs 19.26 in a field or weeds **growing** on a roof when the hot
1 Chr 4.27 tribe of Simeon did not **grow** as much as the tribe of
4.34 Because their families continued to **grow,** [39] they spread
19. 5 Jericho and not return until their beards had **grown** again.
2 Chr 10. 8 the young men who had **grown** up with him and who were
Neh 10.37 villages, the tithes from the crops that **grow** on our land.
Job 5. 5 crops— even the grain **growing** among thorns— and thirsty
5. 6 Evil does not **grow** in the soil,
5. 6 nor does trouble **grow** out of the ground.
8.11 "Reeds can't **grow** where there is no water;
10.10 you made me **grow** in my mother's womb.
10.17 your anger towards me **grows** and grows;
14. 2 We **grow** and wither as quickly as flowers;
14. 8 Even though its roots **grow** old, and its stump dies in the
20. 6 He may **grow** great, towering to the sky, so great that his
21. 8 and grandchildren, and live to watch them all **grow** up.
28. 5 Food **grows** out of the earth, But underneath the same earth
29. 6 of milk, and my olive-trees **grew** in the rockiest soil.
31. 8 my crops be destroyed, or let others eat the food I **grow.**
31.39 have eaten the food that **grew** there
31.39 but let the farmers that **grew** it starve— [40] then instead of
31.40 then instead of wheat and barley, may weeds and thistles **grow.**
40.20 Grass to feed him **grows** on the hills where wild beasts play.
Ps 1. 3 They are like trees that **grow** beside a stream, that bear
49.16 a man becomes rich, when his wealth **grows** even greater;
52. 8 But I am like an olive-tree **growing** in the house of God;
65.10 the soil with showers and cause the young plants to **grow.**
69.31 offering him cattle, more than sacrificing a **full-grown** bull.
80. 9 You cleared a place for it to **grow;**
80.15 that you planted, this young vine you made **grow** so strong!
90. 6 sprout in the morning, [6] that **grow** and burst into bloom,
92. 7 the wicked may **grow** like weeds, those who do wrong may prosper;
92.12 they will **grow** like the cedars of Lebanon.
103.15 We **grow** and flourish like a wild flower;
104.14 You make grass **grow** for the cattle and plants for man to
104.14 so that he can **grow** his crops [15] and produce wine
129. 6 they all be like grass **growing** on the house-tops,
129. 6 which dries up before it can **grow;**
139.15 mother's womb, when I was **growing** there in secret, you knew
144.12 our sons in their youth be like plants that **grow** up strong.
147. 8 rain for the earth and makes grass **grow** on the hills.
Prov 5.17 Your children should **grow** up to help you, not strangers.
23. 5 flash, as if it had **grown** wings and flown away like an
27.25 on the hillsides while the next crop of hay is **growing.**
Ecc 11. 6 know whether it will all **grow** well or whether one sowing
Song 4.13 They **grow** like an orchard of pomegranate-trees
4.14 Myrrh and aloes **grow** there with all the most fragrant perfumes.
6. 2 My lover has gone to his garden, where the balsam-trees **grow.**
7.12 whether they've started to **grow,** whether the blossoms are opening
8.14 like a young stag on the mountains where spices **grow.**
Is 4. 2 every plant and tree in the land **grow** large and beautiful.
5.10 The grapevines **growing** on ten hectares of land will yield
7.25 where crops used to **grow** will be so overgrown with thorns
23. 3 and sell the corn that **grew** in Egypt and to do business
26.15 made our nation **grow,** enlarging its territory on every side,
30.23 send rain to make them **grow** and will give you a rich
32.13 and thorn-bushes and briars are **growing** on my people's land.
34.13 Thorns and thistles will **grow** up in all the palaces
35. 7 Where jackals used to live, marsh grass and reeds will **grow.**
37.27 in a field or weeds **growing** on a roof when the hot
41.19 I will make cedars **grow** in the desert,
41.19 Forests will **grow** in barren land, forests of pine and juniper
44.14 plant a laurel-tree and wait for the rain to make it **grow.**
53. 2 Lord that his servant should **grow** like a plant taking root
55.10 They make the crops **grow** and provide seed for sowing and
55.13 Cypress-trees will **grow** where now there are briars;
61.11 surely as seeds sprout and **grow,** The Sovereign Lord will
Jer 6. 4 is almost over, and the evening shadows are **growing** long.
12. 2 they **grow** and bear fruit.
17. 6 bush in the desert, which **grows** in the dry wilderness,
17. 6 on salty ground where nothing else **grows.**
17. 8 He is like a tree **growing** near a stream
29. 5 Plant gardens and eat what you **grow** in them.
29.28 settle down, plant gardens, and eat what they **grow."**
50.19 will eat the food that **grows** on Mount Carmel
50.19 of the crops that **grow** in the territories of Ephraim
Ezek 16. 7 I made you **grow** like a healthy plant.
16. 7 You **grew** strong and tall and became a young woman.
16. 7 breasts were well-formed, and your hair had **grown,**
17. 5 fertile field, where there was always water to make it **grow.**
17. 6 branches **grew** upward towards the eagle, and the roots grew deep.
17. 7 water than there was in the garden where it was **growing.**
17. 8 field so that it could **grow** leaves and bear grapes
17. 9 Will this vine live and **grow?**
17.10 Yes, it is planted, but will it live and **grow?**
17.10 Won't it wither there where it is **growing?"**
17.23 It will **grow** branches and bear seed
17.24 cut down the tall trees and make the small trees **grow** tall.
19. 5 reared another of her cubs, and he **grew** into a fierce lion.
19. 6 When he was **full-grown,** he prowled with the other lions.
19.11 Its branches were strong, and **grew** to be royal sceptres.
19.11 The vine **grew** tall enough to reach the clouds;
31. 4 water to make it **grow,** And underground rivers to feed it.
31. 4 place where the tree was **growing** And sent streams to all the
31. 5 Because it was well-watered, It **grew** taller than other trees.
31. 5 Its branches **grew** thick and long.
31.10 happen to that tree that **grew** until it reached the clouds.
31.10 As it **grew** taller it grew proud;
31.14 how well-watered it is, will **grow** as tall as that again
36. 8 Israel the trees will again **grow** leaves and bear fruit for you,
36.10 I will make your population **grow.**
44.20 must neither shave their heads nor let their hair **grow** long.
47.12 of the stream all kinds of trees will **grow** to provide food.
Dan 2.35 But the stone **grew** to be a mountain that covered the whole
4.11 It **grew** bigger and bigger until it reached the sky and
4.22 You have **grown** so great that you reach the sky,
4.33 his body, and his hair **grew** as long as eagles' feathers and
8. 9 one of these four horns **grew** a little horn, whose power
8.10 It **grew** strong enough to attack the army of heaven, the
Hos 1.11 and once again they will **grow** and prosper in their land.
9.10 found Israel, it was like finding grapes **growing** in the desert.
10. 4 Justice has become injustice, **growing** like poisonous weeds
10. 8 Thorns and weeds will **grow** up over their altars.
12. 3 when Jacob **grew** up, he fought against God— [4] he fought
14. 6 They will be alive with new **growth,** and beautiful
14. 7 They will **grow** corn and be fruitful like a vineyard.
Amos 4. 1 you women of Samaria, who **grow** fat like the well-fed cows of
7. 1 hay had been cut and the grass was starting to **grow** again.
9.13 "when corn will **grow** faster than it can be harvested,
9.13 and grapes will **grow** faster than the wine can be
9.14 they will plant gardens and eat what they **grow.**
Jon 4. 6 Lord God made a plant **grow** up over Jonah to give him
4.10 said to him, "This plant **grew** up in one night and
4.10 you didn't make it **grow**—yet you feel sorry for it!
Mic 5. 7 by the Lord for many nations, like showers on **growing** plants.
Hab 3.17 no fruit and no grapes **grow** on the vines,
Hag 1.10 That is why there is no rain and nothing can **grow.**
1.11 on men and animals, on everything you try to **grow."**
2.17 everything you tried to **grow,** but still you did not repent.
Zech 9.17 The young people will **grow** strong on its corn and wine.
Mt 6.28 Look how the wild flowers **grow:**
13. 6 because the roots had not **grown** deep enough, the plants soon
13. 7 among thorn bushes, which **grew** up and choked the plants.
13.26 When the plants **grew** and the ears of corn began to form,
13.30 Let the wheat and the weeds both **grow** together until harvest.
13.32 all seeds, but when it **grows** up, it is the biggest of
24.12 the spread of evil that many people's love will **grow** cold.
24.29 those days, the sun will **grow** dark, the moon will no longer
Mk 4. 6 because the roots had not **grown** deep enough, the plants soon
4. 7 fell among thorn bushes, which **grew** up and choked the plants,
4. 8 in good soil, and the plants sprouted, **grew,** and produced corn:
4.27 day, and all the while the seeds are sprouting and **growing.**
4.28 The soil itself makes the plants **grow** and bear fruit;
4.32 After a while it **grows** up and becomes the biggest of all
13.24 of trouble the sun will **grow** dark, the moon will no longer
Lk 1.80 The child **grew** and developed in body and spirit.
2.40 The child **grew** and became strong;
2.52 Jesus **grew** both in body and in wisdom, gaining favour
8. 7 fell among thorn bushes, which **grew** up with the plants and
8. 8 the plants **grew** and produced corn, a hundred grains each."

Lk 12.27 Look how the wild flowers **grow:**
13. 6 was once a man who had a fig-tree **growing** in his vineyard.
13.19 The plant **grows** and becomes a tree, and the birds make their
Jn 3. 4 "How can a **grown** man be born again?"
Acts 4. 4 and the number of men **grew** to about five thousand.
6. 1 the number of disciples kept **growing,** there was a quarrel between
6. 7 number of disciples in Jerusalem **grew** larger and larger,
7.17 Abraham, the number of our people in Egypt had **grown** much larger.
9.31 Spirit it was strengthened and **grew** in numbers, as it lived
12.24 Meanwhile the word of God continued to spread and **grow.**
16. 5 made stronger in the faith and **grew** in numbers every day.
19.20 the word of the Lord kept spreading and **growing** stronger.
Rom 11. 7 the rest **grew** deaf to God's call.
15.13 your hope will continue to **grow** by the power of the Holy
1 Cor 3. 6 watered the plant, but it was God who made the plant **grow.**
3. 7 It is God who matters, because he makes the plant **grow.**
14.20 far as evil is concerned, but be **grown-up** in your thinking.
15.37 other grain, not the full-bodied plant that will later **grow** up.
2 Cor 7.15 so his love for you **grows** stronger, as he remembers how all
9.10 need and will make it **grow** and produce a rich harvest from
10.15 hope that your faith may **grow** and that we may be able
Eph 2.21 building together and makes it **grow** into a sacred temple dedicated
4.15 spirit of love, we must **grow** up in every way to Christ,
4.16 the whole body **grows** and builds itself up through love.
Phil 1. 9 your love will keep on **growing** more and more, together with
1.14 the Lord, so that they **grow** bolder all the time to preach
Col 1.10 of good deeds, and you will **grow** in your knowledge of God.
2.19 joints and ligaments, and it **grows** as God wants it to grow.
1 Thes 3.12 another and for all people **grow** more and more and become as
2 Thes 1. 3 so, because your faith is **growing** so much and the love each
Heb 6. 7 falls on it and which **grows** plants that are useful to those
6. 8 But if it **grows** thorns and weeds, it is worth nothing;
11.24 made Moses, when he had **grown** up, refuse to be called the
12.15 like a bitter plant that **grows** up and causes many troubles
Jas 1.15 and sin, when it is **full-grown,** gives birth to death.
1 Pet 2. 2 so that by drinking it you may **grow** up and be saved.
2 Pet 3.18 But continue to **grow** in the grace and knowledge of our
Rev 2. 7 of the tree of life that **grows** in the Garden of God.
18. 3 businessmen of the world **grew** rich from her unrestrained lust."

GROWL

Job 4.10 The wicked roar and **growl** like lions, but God silences
Ps 59.15 about for food and **growling** if they do not find enough.
Prov 20. 2 Fear an angry king as you would a **growling** lion;
28.15 he is as dangerous as a **growling** lion or a prowling bear.
Jer 51.38 The Babylonians all roar like lions and **growl** like lion cubs.
Amos 3. 4 Does a young lion **growl** in his den unless he has caught

GRUDGE

Lev 19.17 "Do not bear a **grudge** against anyone, but settle your
Ecc 7. 9 it is foolish to harbour a **grudge.**
Mk 6.19 So Herodias held a **grudge** against John and wanted to kill him,

GRUMBLE

Deut 1.27 You **grumbled** to one another:
Ps 106.25 stayed in their tents and **grumbled** and would not listen to
Is 29.24 those who are always **grumbling** will be glad to be taught."
Mt 20.11 They took their money and started **grumbling** against the employer.
Lk 15. 2 teachers of the Law started **grumbling,** "This man welcomes outcasts
19. 7 people who saw it started **grumbling,** "This man has gone as
Jn 6.41 The people started **grumbling** about him, because he said,
6.43 Jesus answered, "Stop **grumbling** among yourselves.
6.61 Jesus knew that they were **grumbling** about this, so he said
Jude 16 These people are always **grumbling** and blaming others;

GUARANTEE

2 Sam 3.21 David gave Abner a **guarantee** of safety and sent him on his
3.22 because David had sent him away with a **guarantee** of safety.
3.23 King David and had been sent away with a **guarantee** of safety.
Esth 3. 9 If you do, I **guarantee** that I will be able to put
Prov 20.16 ought to have his own property held to **guarantee** payment.
27.13 to have his own property held to **guarantee** payment.
Ezek 34.25 I will make a covenant with them that **guarantees** their security.
37.26 covenant with them that **guarantees** their security for ever.
Rom 4.16 that the promise should be **guaranteed** as God's free gift to
1 Cor 15.20 raised from death, as the **guarantee** that those who sleep in
2 Cor 1.22 in our hearts as the **guarantee** of all that he has in
5. 5 us his Spirit as the **guarantee** of all that he has in
Eph 1.14 The Spirit is the **guarantee** that we shall receive what
4.30 of ownership on you, a **guarantee** that the Day will come when
Heb 7.22 also makes Jesus the **guarantee** of a better covenant.

GUARD

[REARGUARD, WELL-GUARDED]
see also **BODYGUARD**

Gen 2.15 man in the Garden of Eden to cultivate it and **guard** it.
37.36 king's officers, who was the captain of the palace **guard.**
39. 1 king's officers, who was the captain of the palace **guard.**
40. 3 of the captain of the **guard,** in the same place where Joseph
41.10 us in prison in the house of the captain of the **guard.**
41.12 was there with us, a slave of the captain of the **guard.**
Gen 41.35 them authority to store up corn in the cities and **guard** it.
41.43 to ride in, and his **guard** of honour went ahead of him
42.16 you will be kept under **guard** until the truth of what you
Lev 24.12 to Moses, [12] put him under **guard,** and waited for the Lord
Num 1.53 camp round the Tent to **guard** it, so that no one may
10.25 of Dan, serving as the **rearguard** of all the divisions, would
15.34 community, [34] and was put under **guard,** because it was not
Deut 4. 9 Be on your **guard!**
33.12 He **guards** them all the day long, And he dwells in their
Josh 6. 1 Jericho were kept shut and **guarded** to keep the Israelites out.
6. 7 the city, with an advance **guard** going on ahead of the Lord's
6. 8 Joshua had ordered, an advance **guard** started out ahead of
6. 8 who were carrying the Covenant Box, followed by a **rearguard.**
6.12 first, the advance **guard;**
6.12 and finally, the **rearguard.**
10.18 Place some **guards** there, [19] but don't stay there yourselves.
Judg 7.19 before midnight, just after the **guard** had been changed.
9.44 his group hurried forward to **guard** the city gate, the other
1 Sam 22.17 Then he said to the **guards** standing near him, "Kill
22.17 But the **guards** refused to lift a hand to kill the Lord's
25.29 God will keep you safe, as a man **guards** a precious treasure.
2 Sam 11. 9 instead he slept at the palace gate with the king's **guards.**
20. 3 left to take care of the palace, and put them under **guard.**
20.10 Amasa was not on **guard** against the sword that Joab was
1 Kgs 14.27 to the officers responsible for **guarding** the palace gates.
14.28 went to the Temple, the **guards** carried the shields, and then
20.39 brought a captured enemy to me and said, **'Guard** this man;
2 Kgs 6.10 the men who lived in that place, and they were on **guard.**
7.10 back to Samaria and called out to the **guards** at the gates:
7.11 The **guards** announced the news, and it was reported in the palace.
9.17 A **guard** on duty in the watch-tower at Jezreel saw Jehu
9.18 The **guard** on the watch-tower reported that the messenger
9.20 Once more the **guard** reported that the messenger had
10.25 offerings, he said to the **guards** and officers, "Go in and
11. 4 bodyguard and of the palace **guards,** and told them to come to
11. 5 on the Sabbath, one third of you are to **guard** the palace;
11. 6 another third are to stand **guard** at the Sur Gate, and the
11. 6 other third are to stand **guard** at the gate behind the other
11. 6 are to stand guard at the gate behind the other **guards.**
11. 7 the Sabbath are to stand **guard** at the Temple to protect the
11. 8 You are to **guard** King Joash with drawn swords and stay
11.13 noise being made by the **guards** and the people, so she
11.15 out between the rows of **guards,** and kill anyone who tries to
11.18 Jehoiada put **guards** on duty at the Temple,
11.19 and the palace **guards** escorted the king from the Temple
23. 4 his assistant priests, and the **guards** on duty at the
1 Chr 9.17 The following temple **guards** lived in Jerusalem:
9.18 Formerly they had stood **guard** at the gates to the camps of
9.19 of Korah, was responsible for **guarding** the entrance to the
9.21 of Meshelemiah was also a **guard** at the entrance to the Tent
9.22 212 men were chosen as **guards** for the entrances and gates.
9.23 They and their descendants continued to **guard** the gates
9.24 north, south, east, and west, and each had a chief **guard.**
9.25 These **guards** were assisted by their relatives, who lived
9.25 had to take turns at **guard** duty for seven days at a
9.26 four chief **guards** were Levites and had the final responsibility.
9.27 it was their duty to **guard** it and to open the gates
15.17 Azaziah, and the temple **guards,** Obed Edom and Jeiel.
15.23 Obed Edom and Jehiah, were chosen as **guards** for the Covenant Box.
16.38 Hosah and Obed Edom were in charge of **guarding** the gates.
16.42 Jeduthun's clan were in charge of **guarding** the gates.
23. 5 disputes, [5] four thousand to do **guard** duty, and four
26. 1 of work for the Levites who served as temple **guards.**
26.11 thirteen members of Hosah's family who were temple **guards.**
26.12 The temple **guards** were divided into groups,
26.15 gate, and his sons were allotted to **guard** the storerooms.
26.16 **Guard** duty was divided into assigned periods, one after another.
26.17 On the east, six **guards** were on duty each day,
26.17 Four **guards** were stationed at the storerooms daily,
26.18 western pavilion there were four **guards** by the road
26.19 This is the assignment of **guard** duty to the clan of
2 Chr 8.14 He also organized the temple **guards** in sections
12.10 to the officers responsible for **guarding** the palace gates.
12.11 the **guards** carried the shields and then returned
23. 4 one third of them will **guard** the temple gates,
23. 5 another third will **guard** the royal palace, and the rest
23. 7 The Levites are to stand **guard** round the king, with their
23.14 out between the rows of **guards,** and kill anyone who tries to
23.19 Jehoiada also put **guards** on duty at the temple gates
25.24 temple equipment **guarded** by the descendants of Obed Edom,
31.14 a Levite who was chief **guard** at the East Gate of the
34. 9 The money that the Levite **guards** had collected in the Temple
34.13 and others kept records or served as **guards.**
35.15 The **guards** at the temple gates did not need to leave
Ezra 2.40 Temple **guards** (descendants of Shallum, Ater, Talmon, Akkub,
2.70 the musicians, the temple **guards,** and the temple workmen
7. 6 which included priests, Levites, temple musicians, temple **guards,**
7.24 musicians, **guards,** workmen, or anyone else connected with
8.22 a troop of cavalry to **guard** us from any enemies during our
8.29 **Guard** them carefully until you reach the Temple.
10.24 Temple **guards:**
Neh 2. 8 gates of the fort that **guards** the Temple,
3.25 the tower of the upper palace near the court of the **guard;**
3.25 east near the Water Gate and the tower **guarding** the Temple.
3.27 point opposite the large tower **guarding** the Temple as far as
4. 9 our God and kept men on **guard** against them day and night.
4.16 men worked and half stood **guard,** wearing coats of armour and
4.21 on the wall, while the other half stood **guard** with spears.
4.22 night, so that we could **guard** the city at night as well

Neh 7. 1 and the temple **guards,** the members of the sacred choir,
7. 3 closed and barred before the **guards** went off duty at sunset.
7. 3 told them to appoint **guards** from among the people
7.43 Temple **guards**
7.73 priests, the Levites, the temple **guards,** the musicians,
10.28 priests, the Levites, the temple **guards,** the temple musicians,
10.39 are on duty, the temple **guards,** and the members of the
11.19 Temple **guards:**
12.25 The following temple **guards** were in charge
12.25 of **guarding** the storerooms
12.45 musicians and the temple **guards** also performed their duties
12.47 for the support of the temple musicians and the temple **guards.**
13. 5 to the temple musicians, and to the temple **guards.**
13.22 themselves and to go and **guard** the gates to make sure that
Esth 2.21 palace eunuchs who **guarded** the entrance to the king's rooms,
6. 2 the two palace eunuchs who had **guarded** the king's rooms.
Job 7.12 Why do you keep me under **guard?**
21.32 **well-guarded** tomb, [33]thousands join the funeral procession,
27.18 web or like the hut of a slave **guarding** the fields.
30. 1 that I wouldn't let them help my dogs **guard** sheep.
38.17 shown you the gates that **guard** the dark world of the dead?
Ps 34. 7 His angel **guards** those who honour the Lord and rescues them
121. 5 The Lord will **guard** you;
127. 1 the city, it is useless for the sentries to stand **guard.**
141. 3 Lord, place a **guard** at my mouth, a sentry at the door
Prov 2. 8 and **guards** those who are devoted to him.
4.13 Your education is your life—**guard** it well.
Song 3. 8 is armed with a sword, on **guard** against a night attack.
5. 7 the **guards** at the city wall tore off my cape.
7. 4 as the tower of Lebanon that stands **guard** at Damascus.
Is 5. 2 He built a tower to **guard** them, dug a pit for treading
8.16 You, my disciples are to **guard** and preserve the messages
21. 8 "Sir, I have been standing **guard** at my post day and night."
27. 3 I **guard** it night and day so that no one will harm
32.14 Homes and the forts that **guarded** them will be in ruins for
49. 8 I will **guard** and protect you and through you make a covenant
52. 8 Those who **guard** the city are shouting, shouting together for joy!
Jer 4.17 will surround Jerusalem like men **guarding** a field, because
9. 4 Everyone must be on **guard** against his friend, and no one
12. 3 **guard** them until it is time for them to be slaughtered.
31.10 I will gather them and **guard** them
31.10 as a shepherd **guards** his flock.
50.33 All who captured them are **guarding** them closely and will not
51.12 Strengthen the **guard!**
Ezek 13. 5 They don't **guard** the places where the walls have crumbled,
19. 9 They kept him under **guard,** so that his roar would never be
27.11 Soldiers from Arvad **guarded** your walls,
27.11 and men from Gamad **guarded** your towers.
28.14 I put a terrifying angel there to **guard** you.
28.16 mountain, and the angel who **guarded** you drove you away from
Dan 1.11 So Daniel went to the **guard** whom Ashpenaz had placed in
1.16 So from then on the **guard** let them continue to eat
3.22 the flames burnt up the **guards** who took the men
12. 1 the great angel Michael, who **guards** your people, will appear.
Nah 2. 1 **Guard** the road!
Zech 9. 8 I will **guard** my land and keep armies from passing through it.
Mt 7.15 "Be on your **guard** against false prophets;
16. 6 on your **guard** against the yeast of the Pharisees and Sadducees."
16.11 **Guard** yourselves from the yeast of the Pharisees and Sadducees!"
16.12 was not warning them to **guard** themselves from the yeast used
24. 4 Jesus answered, "Be on your **guard,** and do not let anyone
24.42 "Be on your **guard,** then, because you do not know what
25.13 Jesus concluded, "Be on your **guard,** then, because you do
26.58 and sat down with the **guards** to see how it would all
27.64 his tomb to be carefully **guarded** until the third day, so
27.65 "Take a **guard,"** Pilate told them;
27.66 putting a seal on the stone and leaving the **guard** on watch.
28. 4 The **guards** were so afraid that they trembled and became
28.11 way, some of the soldiers **guarding** the tomb went back to the
28.15 The **guards** took the money and did what they were told to
Mk 6.27 So he sent off a **guard** at once with orders to bring
6.27 The **guard** left, went to the prison, and cut John's head off;
8.15 them, "and be on your **guard** against the yeast of the
13. 5 to them, "Be on **guard,** and don't let anyone deceive you.
13. 9 "You yourselves must be on **guard.**
13.23 Be on your **guard!**
13.35 Be on **guard,** then, because you do not know when the
14.44 Arrest him and take him away under **guard."**
14.54 sat down with the **guards,** keeping himself warm by the fire.
14.65 And the **guards** took him and slapped him.
Lk 11.21 all his weapons ready, **guards** his own house, all his belongings
12. 1 his disciples, "Be on **guard** against the yeast of the Pharisees
12.15 "Watch out and **guard** yourselves from every kind of greed;
20.46 "Be on your **guard** against the teachers of the Law,
21. 8 Jesus said, "Be on **guard;**
21.34 "Be on your **guard!**
22. 4 the officers of the temple **guard** about how he could betray
22.52 the officers of the temple **guard** and the elders who had come
22.63 The men who were **guarding** Jesus mocked him and beat him.
Jn 7.32 they and the chief priests sent some **guards** to arrest him.
7.45 When the **guards** went back, the chief priests and Pharisees
7.46 The **guards** answered, "Nobody has ever talked like this man!"
18. 3 Roman soldiers, and some temple **guards** sent by the chief priests
18.12 commanding officer and the Jewish **guards** arrested Jesus, bound him,
18.18 cold, so the servants and **guards** had built a charcoal fire
18.22 said this, one of the **guards** there slapped him and said,
19. 6 priests and the temple **guards** saw him, they shouted, "Crucify him!
Acts 4. 1 officer in charge of the temple **guards,** and some Sadducees arrived.
Acts 5.23 locked up tight and all the **guards** on watch at the gates;
5.24 in charge of the temple **guards** heard this, they wondered
12. 4 was handed over to be **guarded** by four groups of four
12. 6 out to the people, Peter was sleeping between two **guards.**
12. 6 chains, and there were **guards** on duty at the prison gate.
12.10 They passed by the first **guard** post and then the second,
12.18 tremendous confusion among the **guards**—what had happened to Peter?
12.19 So he had the **guards** questioned and ordered them to be put
23.35 Paul to be kept under **guard** in the governor's headquarters.
24.23 Paul to keep him under **guard,** but to give him some freedom
25.21 asked to be kept under **guard** and to let the Emperor decide
25.21 him to be kept under **guard** until I could send him to
28.16 Paul was allowed to live by himself with a soldier **guarding** him.
2 Cor 11.32 under King Aretas placed **guards** at the city gates to arrest
Phil 1.13 a result, the whole palace **guard** and all the others here
2 Tim 4.15 Be on your **guard** against him yourself, because he was violently
Heb 12.15 **Guard** against turning back from the grace of God.
2 Pet 3.17 Be on your **guard,** then, so that you will not be led
2 Jn 8 Be on your **guard,** then, so that you will not lose what
Rev 16.15 he who stays awake and **guards** his clothes, so that he will

GUARD GATE

2 Kgs 11.19 Joash entered by the **Guard Gate** and took his place on the

GUARDIAN

2 Kgs 10. 1 citizens, and to the **guardians** of Ahab's descendants.
10. 5 citizens and the **guardians,** sent this message to Jehu:
Dan 10.20 I have to go back and fight the **guardian angel** of Persia.
10.20 After that, the **guardian angel** of Greece will appear.
10.20 no one to help me except Michael, Israel's **guardian angel.**
1 Cor 4.15 if you have ten thousand **guardians** in your Christian life,

GUARDROOM

2 Sam 11.13 instead he slept on his blanket in the palace **guardroom.**
1 Kgs 14.28 carried the shields, and then returned them to the **guard-room.**
2 Chr 12.11 carried the shields and then returned them to the **guardroom.**
Ezek 40. 7 was a passage, which had three **guardrooms** on each side.
40. 7 Beyond the **guardrooms** there was a passage three metres long
40.10 (These **guardrooms** on each side of the passage were all
40.12 front of each of the **guardrooms** there was a low wall fifty
40.21 The three **guardrooms** on each side of the passage, the
40.29 Its **guardrooms,** its entrance room, and its inner
40.33 Its **guardrooms,** its entrance room, and its inner walls
40.36 Like them, it also had **guardrooms,** decorated inner walls,

GUEST

Gen 19. 3 to bake some bread and prepare a fine meal for the **guests.**
19. 4 Before the **guests** went to bed, the men of Sodom surrounded
19. 8 they are **guests** in my house, and I must protect them."
Judg 19.21 His **guests** washed their feet and had a meal.
19.23 This man is my **guest.**
1 Sam 9.22 of the table where the **guests,** about thirty in all, were
2 Sam 9.10 But Mephibosheth himself will always be a **guest** at my table."
12. 4 took the poor man's lamb and cooked a meal for his **guest."**
1 Kgs 1.41 As Adonijah and all his **guests** were finishing the feast,
1.49 Then Adonijah's **guests** were afraid, and they all got up and left,
Esth 1.11 to show off her beauty to the officials and all his **guests.**
5. 4 and Haman to be my **guests** tonight at a banquet I am
5. 5 Haman to come quickly, so that they could be Esther's **guests.**
5. 8 and Haman to be my **guests** tomorrow at another banquet that I
Job 19.15 Those who were **guests** in my house have forgotten me;
Ps 23. 5 welcome me as an honoured **guest** and fill my cup to the
39.12 all my ancestors I am only your **guest** for a little while.
Is 21. 5 rugs are spread for the **guests** to sit on.
Mt 9.15 answered, "Do you expect the **guests** at a wedding party to
14. 9 in front of all his **guests** he gave orders that her wish
22. 3 servants to tell the invited **guests** to come to the feast,
22. 4 So he sent other servants with this message for the **guests:**
22. 5 But the invited **guests** paid no attention and went about their business:
22.11 in to look at the **guests** and saw a man who was
Mk 2.19 answered, "Do you expect the **guests** at a wedding party to
6.22 Herodias came in and danced, and pleased Herod and his **guests.**
6.26 of the vows he had made in front of all his **guests.**
Lk 5.29 for Jesus, and among the **guests** was a large number of tax
5.34 think you can make the **guests** at a wedding party go without
14. 7 noticed how some of the **guests** were choosing the best places,
14.10 bring you honour in the presence of all the other **guests.**
14.17 sent his servant to tell his **guests,** 'Come, everything is ready!'
19. 7 man has gone as a **guest** to the home of a sinner!"
Jn 2.10 wine first, and after the **guests** have had plenty to drink,
Acts 10. 6 He is a **guest** in the home of a tanner of leather
10.18 and asked, "Is there a **guest** here by the name of Simon
10.32 He is a **guest** in the home of Simon the tanner of
11. 3 saying, [3]"You were a **guest** in the home of uncircumcised Gentiles,
28. 7 He welcomed us kindly and for three days we were his **guests.**

GUIDE

Ex 15.13 by your strength you **guided** them to your sacred land.
32.34 Remember that my angel will **guide** you, but the time is
33. 2 will send an angel to **guide** you, and I will drive out
Num 10.31 we can camp in the wilderness, and you can be our **guide.**
2 Sam 6. 3 Ahio, sons of Abinadab, were **guiding** the cart, [4]with Ahio
1 Chr 10.13 he tried to find **guidance** by consulting the spirits of the
13. 7 Uzzah and Ahio **guided** the cart, [8]while David and all the

2 Chr 20. 3 Jehoshaphat was frightened and prayed to the Lord for **guidance.**
20. 4 to ask the Lord for **guidance,** [5] and they and the people of
Job 38.32 Can you **guide** the stars season by season and direct the
Ps 1. 6 The righteous are **guided** and protected by the Lord, but
16. 7 praise the Lord, because he **guides** me, and in the night my
23. 3 He **guides** me in the right paths, as he has promised.
26. 3 Your constant love is my **guide;**
27. 4 marvel there at his goodness, and to ask for his **guidance.**
31. 3 **guide** me and lead me as you have promised.
37.23 The Lord **guides** a man in the way he should go and
67. 4 the peoples with justice and **guide** every nation on earth.
73.24 You **guide** me with your instruction and at the end you
78.52 out like a shepherd and **guided** them through the desert.
119.105 word is a lamp to **guide** me and a light for my
139.24 is any evil in me and **guide** me in the everlasting way.
143.10 Be good to me, and **guide** me on a safe path.
Prov 1. 5 of wise men and give **guidance** to the educated, [6] so that
11. 3 If you are good, you are **guided** by honesty.
11.14 A nation will fall if it has no **guidance.**
12.26 The righteous man is a **guide** to his friend, but the path
29.18 A nation without God's **guidance** is a nation without order.
Ecc 12.11 sticks that shepherds use to **guide** sheep, and collected
Is 58.11 And I will always **guide** you and satisfy you with good things.
Jer 10.21 they do not ask the Lord for **guidance.**
31. 9 I will **guide** them to streams of water, on a smooth road
Zeph 1. 6 who do not come to me or ask me to **guide** them."
Mt 2. 6 you will come a leader who will **guide** my people Israel.'"
23.16 "How terrible for you, blind **guides!**
23.24 Blind **guides!**
Lk 1.79 dark shadow of death, to **guide** our steps into the path of
Acts 1.16 about Judas, who was the **guide** for those who arrested Jesus.
Rom 2.19 sure that you are a **guide** for the blind, a light for
1 Cor 12. 3 "Jesus is Lord," unless he is **guided** by the Holy Spirit.
Col 3.15 that Christ gives is to **guide** you in the decisions you make;
1 Thes 5.12 who work among you, who **guide** and instruct you in the
Rev 7.17 shepherd, and he will **guide** them to springs of life-giving water.

GUILTY

Gen 18.23 "Are you really going to destroy the innocent with the **guilty?**
18.25 Surely you won't kill the innocent with the **guilty.**
18.25 If you did, the innocent would be punished along with the **guilty.**
26.10 wife, and you would have been responsible for our **guilt."**
44.16 God has uncovered our **guilt.**
Ex 22. 2 is killed, the one who killed him is not **guilty** of murder.
22. 2 But if it happens during the day, he is **guilty** of murder.
22. 9 whom God declares to be **guilty** shall pay double to the other
23. 1 and do not help a **guilty** man by giving false evidence.
Lev 4. 3 who sins and so brings **guilt** on the people, he shall present
4.13 Israel that sins and becomes **guilty** of breaking one of the
4.22 ruler who sins and becomes **guilty** of breaking one of the
4.27 people who sins and becomes **guilty** of breaking one of the
5. 2 he is unclean and **guilty** as soon as he realizes what
5. 3 it may be, he is **guilty** as soon as he realizes what
5. 4 it is about, he is **guilty** as soon as he realizes what
5. 5 When a person is **guilty,** he must confess the sin, [6] and as
5.17 the Lord's commands, he is **guilty** and must pay the penalty.
6. 4 the day he is found **guilty,** he must repay the owner in
19. 8 who eats it will be **guilty** of treating as ordinary what is
22. 9 Otherwise, they will be **guilty** and die, because they have
22.16 this would bring **guilt** and punishment on such a person.
24.14 to testify that he is **guilty,** and then the whole community
Num 5. 8 to perform the ritual of purification for the **guilty** person.
5.31 husband shall be free of **guilt,**
5.31 but the woman, if **guilty,** must suffer the consequences.
15.30 a foreigner, is **guilty** of treating the Lord with contempt,
18. 1 suffer the consequences of any **guilt** connected with serving
18.32 You will not become **guilty** when you eat it, as long as
35.16 to kill someone, he is **guilty** of murder and is to be
35.21 with his fist, he is **guilty** of murder and is to be
35.25 is to rescue the man **guilty** of manslaughter from the dead
35.26 If the man **guilty** of manslaughter leaves the city of
35.28 The man **guilty** of manslaughter must remain in the city
35.30 of murder may be found **guilty** and put to death only on
Deut 15. 9 out to the Lord against you, and you will be held **guilty.**
19.10 that you will not be **guilty** of putting them to death in
19.15 two witnesses are necessary to prove that a man is **guilty.**
24.15 against you to the Lord, and you will be **guilty** of sin.
25. 1 dispute, and one is declared innocent and the other **guilty.**
25. 2 If the **guilty** man is sentenced to be beaten, the judge is
Judg 21.22 to us, you are not **guilty** of breaking your promise.'"
1 Sam 14.39 Israel victory, that the **guilty** one will be put to death,
14.41 If the **guilt** is Jonathan's or mine, answer by the Urim;
20. 8 But if I'm **guilty,** kill me yourself!
2 Sam 14.32 the king, and if I'm **guilty,** then let him put me to
21. 1 the Lord said, "Saul and his family are **guilty** of murder;
24.17 the people, and said to the Lord, "I am the **guilty** one.
1 Kgs 8.32 Punish the **guilty** one as he deserves, and acquit the one who
1 Chr 21. 3 do you want to do this and make the whole nation **guilty?"**
2 Chr 6.23 Punish the **guilty** one as he deserves and acquit the one who
19.10 that they do not become **guilty** of sinning against the Lord.
19.10 But if you do your duty, you will not be **guilty.**
24.18 Their **guilt** for these sins brought the Lord's anger on Judah
28.13 Now you want to do something that will increase our **guilt."**
Ezra 9.15 We confess our **guilt** to you;
10.10 and have brought **guilt** on Israel by marrying foreign women.
Job 9.20 faithful, but my words sound **guilty,** and everything I say
9.21 innocent or **guilty,** God will destroy us.
9.27 I know that God does hold me **guilty.**
9.29 Since I am held **guilty,** why should I bother?
10. 7 know that I am not **guilty,** that no one can save me
Job 16. 8 skin and bones, and people take that as proof of my **guilt.**
16.17 shadows, [17] but I am not **guilty** of any violence, and my
19. 5 than I am, and regard my troubles as proof of my **guilt.**
33. 9 "I am not **guilty;**
Ps 106.30 Phinehas stood up and punished the **guilty,**
109. 7 May he be tried and found **guilty;**
Prov 18. 5 not right to favour the **guilty** and prevent the innocent from
21. 8 **Guilty** people walk a crooked path;
24.24 If he pronounces a **guilty** person innocent, he will be
24.25 Judges who punish the **guilty,** however, will be
28.17 A man **guilty** of murder is digging his own grave as fast
Is 4. 4 nation and wash away the **guilt** of Jerusalem and the blood
5.23 just a bribe you let **guilty** men go free, and you prevent
6. 7 your lips, and now your **guilt** is gone, and your sins are
30.13 You are **guilty.**
50. 9 Sovereign Lord himself defends me— who, then, can prove me **guilty?**
59. 3 You are **guilty** of lying, violence, and murder.
66.16 the world whom he finds **guilty**—and many will be put to
Jer 2.22 strongest soap, I would still see the stain of your **guilt.**
3.13 Only admit that you are **guilty** and that you have
16.10 ask what crime they are **guilty** of and what sin they have
26.15 of this city will be **guilty** of killing an innocent man,
29.23 their fate because they are **guilty** of terrible sins—they
Lam 4.13 sinned and her priests were **guilty** of causing the death of
4.22 he will expose your **guilty** deeds.
Ezek 4. 4 I will place on you the **guilt** of the nation of Israel.
4. 4 390 days you will stay there and suffer because of their **guilt.**
4. 6 side and suffer for the **guilt** of Judah for forty days—one
9. 9 "The people of Israel and Judah are **guilty** of terrible sins.
21.24 Everyone knows how **guilty** you are.
22. 4 You are **guilty** of those murders and are defiled by the
23.21 repeat the immorality you were **guilty** of as a girl in Egypt,
25.12 Judah, and that revenge has brought lasting **guilt** on Edom.
35. 6 You are **guilty** of murder, and murder will follow you.
Hos 4.15 unfaithful to me, may Judah not be **guilty** of the same thing.
13.12 "Israel's sin and **guilt** are on record, and the records
Joel 3.20 I will not spare the **guilty.**
Mic 1. 5 Who is **guilty** of idolatry in Judah?
Nah 1. 3 but he is powerful and never lets the **guilty** go unpunished.
Mt 5.28 wants to possess her is **guilty** of committing adultery with her
5.32 unfaithfulness, then he is **guilty** of making her commit adultery
12. 5 Temple actually break the Sabbath law, yet they are not **guilty?**
12. 7 this means, you would not condemn people who are not **guilty;**
12.37 to judge you—to declare you either innocent or **guilty."**
26.66 They answered, "He is **guilty** and must die."
Mk 14.64 he was **guilty** and should be put to death.
Lk 23.14 I have not found him **guilty** of any of the crimes you
23.15 Nor did Herod find him **guilty,** for he sent him back to
Jn 8.46 Which one of you can prove that I am **guilty** of sin?
9.41 Jesus answered, "If you were blind, then you would not be **guilty;**
9.41 that you can see, this means that you are still **guilty."**
15.22 They would not have been **guilty** of sin if I had not
15.24 They would not have been **guilty** of sin if I had not
19.11 who handed me over to you is **guilty** of a worse sin."
Acts 16.37 "We were not found **guilty** of any crime, yet they whipped
24.20 what crime they found me **guilty** of when I stood before the
Rom 4. 5 the God who declares the **guilty** to be innocent, it is his
5.16 After the one sin, came the judgement of **"Guilty";**
5.16 after so many sins, comes the undeserved gift of "Not **guilty!"**
8.33 God himself declares them not **guilty!**
14.22 person who does not feel **guilty** when he does something he
1 Cor 5. 1 so terrible that not even the heathen would be **guilty** of it.
6.18 but the man who is **guilty** of sexual immorality sins against
10. 8 We must not be **guilty** of sexual immorality, as some of
11.27 that dishonours him, he is **guilty** of sin against the Lord's
1 Tim 5.12 and so become **guilty** of breaking their earlier promise to
2 Tim 3. 6 who are burdened by the **guilt** of their sins and driven by
Heb 10. 2 sins, they would not feel **guilty** of sin any more, and all
10.22 been purified from a **guilty** conscience and with bodies washed
10.28 without any mercy when judged **guilty** on the evidence of two
Jas 2. 4 then you are **guilty** of creating distinctions among yourselves
2. 9 their outward appearance, you are **guilty** of sin, and the Law
2.10 Whoever breaks one commandment is **guilty** of breaking them all.
4.17 do the good he knows he should do is **guilty** of sin.
1 Jn 3. 4 Whoever sins is **guilty** of breaking God's law, because sin is

GULF

Ex 10.19 picked up the locusts and blew them into the **Gulf of Suez.**
23.31 land extend from the **Gulf of Aqaba** to the Mediterranean Sea
Num 14.25 the wilderness in the direction of the **Gulf of Aqaba."**
21. 4 that leads to the **Gulf of Aqaba,** in order to go round
33.10 They left Elim and camped near the **Gulf of Suez.**
Deut 1.40 back into the desert along the road to the **Gulf of Aqaba.'**
2. 1 the road to the **Gulf of Aqaba,** as the Lord had commanded,
Judg 11.16 through the desert to the **Gulf of Aqaba** and came to Kadesh.
1 Kgs 9.26 the shore of the **Gulf of Aqaba,** in the land of Edom.
2 Chr 8.17 the shore of the **Gulf of Aqaba,** in the land of Edom.
Is 11.15 will dry up the **Gulf of Suez,**
Jer 49.21 alarm will be heard as far away as the **Gulf of Aqaba.**

GULP

Is 5.14 It **gulps** down the nobles of Jerusalem along with the noisy

GUSH

Num 20. 8 to that rock over there, and water will **gush** out of it.
20.11 a great stream of water **gushed** out, and all the people and
Deut 8. 7 underground streams **gushing** out into the valleys and hills;

Ps 105.41 opened a rock, and water **gushed** out, flowing through the
Song 4.15 water, brooks **gushing** down from the Lebanon Mountains.

GUTTER

Ezek 43.13 the altar there was a **gutter** fifty centimetres deep and
43.17 (The **gutter** was fifty centimetres wide.)

HABIT

Prov 22.25 You might learn their **habits** and not be able to change.
Mt 27.15 Roman governor was in the **habit** of setting free any one
Mk 15. 6 Festival Pilate was in the **habit** of setting free any one
Acts 17. 2 According to his usual **habit** Paul went to the synagogue.
25.16 Romans are not in the **habit** of handing over any man accused
Col 3. 9 the old self with its **habits** [10] and have put on the new
Heb 10.25 us not give up the **habit** of meeting together, as some are
Jas 1.21 So get rid of every filthy **habit** and all wicked conduct.
2 Pet 2.19 are slaves of destructive **habits**—for a person is a slave

AV HABITATION

Ex 15.13 by your strength you guided them to your sacred **land.**
Lev 13.46 and he must **live** outside the camp, away from others.
Deut 12. 5 the people are to come into his **presence** and worship him.
26.15 Look down from your holy **place** in heaven and bless your
2 Sam 15.25 me come back to see it and the **place** where it stays.
2 Chr 6. 2 majestic temple for you, a **place** for you to live in for
29. 6 him and turned their backs on the **place** where he dwells.
Ezra 7.15 to give to the God of Israel, whose **Temple** is in Jerusalem.
Job 5. 3 secure, but I called down a sudden curse on their **homes.**
8. 6 come and help you and restore your **household** as your reward.
Ps 26. 8 I love the **house** where you live, O Lord, the place where
68. 5 his sacred **Temple,** cares for orphans and protects widows.
69.25 May their **camps** be left deserted;
71. 3 Be my secure **shelter** and a strong fortress to protect me;
104.12 In the trees near by, the birds make their **nests** and sing.
107. 7 them by a straight road to a city where they could **live.**
107.36 people settle there, and they built a city to **live** in.
132. 5 place for the Lord, a **home** for the Mighty God of Jacob."
132.13 he wants to make it his **home:**
Prov 3.33 but blesses the **homes** of the righteous.
Is 22.16 have you to carve a **tomb** for yourself out of the rocky
32.18 will be free from worries, and their **homes** peaceful and safe.
33.20 What a safe place it will be to **live** in!
34.13 and walled towns, and jackals and owls will **live** in them.
35. 7 Where jackals used to **live,** marsh grass and reeds will grow.
63.15 us from heaven, where you **live** in your holiness and glory.
Jer 10.25 they have destroyed us completely and left our **country** in ruins.
25.30 Lord will roar from heaven and thunder from the heights of **heaven.**
31.23 sacred hill of Jerusalem, the holy place where he **lives.'**
33.12 where no people or animals **live,** there will once again be
49.19 Jordan up to the green **pasture** land, I will come and make
50.19 I will restore the people of Israel to their **land.**
50.44 Jordan up to the green **pasture** land, I, the Lord, will come
Ezek 29.14 I will let them live in southern Egypt, their original **home.**
Obad 3 your **home** is high in the mountains, and so you say to
Zech 2.13 for he is coming from his holy **dwelling-place.**
Acts 1.20 written in the book of Psalms, 'May his **house** become empty;
17.26 times and the limits of the places where they would **live.**
Eph 2.22 the others into a **place** where God lives through his Spirit.
Jude 6 of their proper authority, but abandoned their own **dwelling place:**
Rev 18. 2 all kinds of filthy and hateful birds **live** in her.

HADAD (1)

Member of the Edomite royal family in David and Solomon's time.

1 Kgs 11.14 So the Lord caused **Hadad,** of the royal family of Edom,
11.17 every male in Edom [17] except **Hadad** and some of his father's
11.17 (At that time **Hadad** was just a child.)
11.18 to the king, who gave **Hadad** some land and a house and
11.19 **Hadad** won the friendship of the king, and the king
11.19 the sister of Queen Tahpenes, to **Hadad** in marriage.
11.21 When the news reached **Hadad** in Egypt that David had died
11.21 of the army was dead, **Hadad** said to the king, "Let me
11.21 "Just let me go," **Hadad** answered the king.
11.21 As king of Edom, **Hadad** was an evil, bitter enemy of Israel.

HADADEZER

King of Zobah (Syria) in David's time.

2 Sam 8. 3 Hadadezer son of Rehob, as **Hadadezer** was on his way to
8. 5 an army to help King **Hadadezer,** David attacked it and killed
8. 7 carried by **Hadadezer's** officials and took them to Jerusalem.
8. 8 bronze from Betah and Berothai, cities ruled by **Hadadezer.**
8. 9 heard that David had defeated all of **Hadadezer's** army.
8.10 him on his victory over **Hadadezer,** against whom Toi had
8.12 as well as part of the loot he had taken from **Hadadezer.**
10.16 King **Hadadezer** sent for the Syrians who were on the east
10.16 Shobach, commander of the army of King **Hadadezer** of Zobah.
10.19 kings who were subject to **Hadadezer** realized that they had
1 Kgs 11.23 fled from his master, King **Hadadezer** of Zobah, [24] and had
11.24 David had defeated **Hadadezer**
1 Chr 18. 3 David attacked King **Hadadezer** of the Syrian state of Zobah,
18. 3 the territory of Hamath, because **Hadadezer** was trying to
18. 5 an army to help King **Hadadezer,** David attacked it and killed
18. 7 carried by **Hadadezer's** officials and took them to Jerusalem.
18. 8 of bronze from Tibhath and Kun, cities ruled by **Hadadezer.**
18. 9 heard that David had defeated **Hadadezer's** entire army.
1 Chr 18.10 him for his victory over **Hadadezer,** against whom Toi had
19.16 Shobach, commander of the army of King **Hadadezer** of Zobah.
19.19 kings who were subject to **Hadadezer** realized that they had

HADES

see also **HELL, WORLD OF THE DEAD**

Lk 16.23 was buried, [23] and in **Hades,** where he was in great pain,
Rev 6. 8 Its rider was named Death, and **Hades** followed close behind.

HAGAR

Sarah's Egyptian slave-girl, and mother of Abraham's son Ishmael.

Gen 16. 1 Egyptian slave-girl named **Hagar,** [2] and so she said to Abram,
16. 3 So she gave **Hagar** to him to be his concubine.
16. 4 Abram had intercourse with **Hagar,** and she became pregnant.
16. 5 Sarai said to Abram, "It's your fault that **Hagar** despises me.
16. 6 Then Sarai treated **Hagar** so cruelly that she ran away.
16. 7 angel of the Lord met **Hagar** at a spring in the desert
16. 8 road to Shur [8] and said, **"Hagar,** slave of Sarai, where have
16.13 **Hagar** asked herself, "Have I really seen God and lived
16.15 **Hagar** bore Abram a son, and he named him Ishmael.
21. 9 One day Ishmael, whom **Hagar** the Egyptian had borne to Abraham,
21.12 "Don't be worried about the boy and your slave **Hagar.**
21.14 the next morning Abraham gave **Hagar** some food and a leather
21.17 of God spoke to **Hagar,** "What are you troubled about, Hagar?
25.12 whom **Hagar,** the Egyptian slave of Sarah, bore to Abraham,
Gal 4.24 are born in slavery is **Hagar,** and she represents the covenant
4.25 **Hagar,** who stands for Mount Sinai in Arabia, is a figure

HAGGAI

Prophet who encouraged the people in rebuilding the Temple.

Ezra 5. 1 At that time two prophets, **Haggai** and Zechariah son of Iddo,
6.14 the Temple, encouraged by the prophets **Haggai** and Zechariah.
Hag 1. 1 the sixth month, the Lord spoke through the prophet **Haggai.**
1. 2 The Lord Almighty said to **Haggai,** "These people say that
1. 3 gave this message to the people through the prophet **Haggai:**
1.12 were afraid and obeyed the prophet **Haggai,** the Lord's messenger.
1.13 Then **Haggai** gave the Lord's message to the people:
2. 1 same year, the Lord spoke again through the prophet **Haggai.**
2. 2 He told **Haggai** to speak to Zerubbabel, the governor of Judah,
2.10 the Lord Almighty spoke again to the prophet **Haggai.**
2.13 Then **Haggai** asked, "Suppose a man is defiled because he
2.14 Then **Haggai** said, "The Lord says that the same thing
2.20 the Lord gave **Haggai** a second message [21] for Zerubbabel,

HAIL

Ex 9.18 I will cause a heavy **hailstorm,** such as Egypt has never
9.19 **Hail** will fall on the people and animals left outside unprotected,
9.22 hand towards the sky, and **hail** will fall over the whole land
9.23 Lord sent thunder and **hail,** and lightning struck the ground.
9.24 The Lord sent [24] a heavy **hailstorm,** with lightning flashing
9.25 All over Egypt the **hail** struck down everything in the open,
9.26 Israelites lived, was the only place where there was no **hail.**
9.28 We have had enough of this thunder and **hail!**
9.29 there will be no more **hail,** so that you may know that
9.33 The thunder, the **hail,** and the rain all stopped.
10. 5 will eat everything that the **hail** did not destroy, even the
10.12 that grows, everything that has survived the **hail."**
10.15 they ate everything that the **hail** had left, including all
Josh 10.11 army, the Lord made large **hailstones** fall down on them all
10.11 More were killed by the **hailstones** than by the Israelites.
Job 38.22 visited the storerooms, where I keep the snow and the **hail?**
Ps 18.12 **Hailstones** and flashes of fire came from the lightning
78.47 He killed their grapevines with **hail** and their fig-trees
78.48 He killed their cattle with **hail** and their flocks with lightning.
105.32 He sent **hail** and lightning on their land instead of rain;
147.17 He sends **hail** like gravel;
148. 8 lightning and **hail,** snow and clouds, strong winds
Is 28. 2 who will come like a **hailstorm,** like a torrent of rain, like
28.17 **Hailstorms** will sweep away all the lies you depend on, and
30.30 will be flames, cloudbursts, **hailstones,** and torrents of rain.
32.19 ([19] But **hail** will fall on the forests, and the city will be
Ezek 13.11 **Hailstones** will fall on it, and a strong wind will blow
13.13 wind, pouring rain, and **hailstones** to destroy the wall.
38.22 Torrents of rain and **hail,** together with fire and sulphur,
Hag 2.17 I sent scorching winds and **hail** to ruin everything you
Rev 8. 7 **Hail** and fire, mixed with blood, came pouring down on the earth.
11.19 rumblings and peals of thunder, an earthquake, and heavy **hail.**
16.21 Huge **hailstones,** each weighing as much as fifty kilogrammes,
16.21 account of the plague of **hail,** because it was such a

HAIR

[GREY-HAIRED]

Gen 25.25 his skin was like a **hairy** robe, so he was named Esau.
27.11 know that Esau is a **hairy** man, but I have smooth skin.
27.16 goats on his arms and on the **hairless** part of his neck.
27.23 did not recognize Jacob, because his arms were **hairy** like Esau's.
Lev 10. 6 Ithamar, "Do not leave your **hair** uncombed or tear your
13. 3 the sore, and if the **hairs** in it have turned white and
13. 4 skin round it and the **hairs** have not turned white, the
13.10 his skin which turns the **hairs** white and is full of pus,
13.20 the surrounding skin and the **hairs** in it have turned white,
13.21 it and finds that the **hairs** in it have not turned white
13.25 If the **hairs** in the spot have turned white and it appears
13.26 But if the **hairs** in it have not turned white and it

Lev 13.30 surrounding skin and the **hairs** in it are yellowish and thin,
13.31 there are still no healthy **hairs** in it, he shall isolate him
13.32 and there are no yellowish **hairs** in it and it does not
13.36 If the sore has spread, he need not look for yellowish **hairs;**
13.37 has not spread and healthy **hairs** are growing in it, the sore
13.40 If a man loses his **hair** at the back or the front
13.45 wear torn clothes, leave his **hair** uncombed, cover the lower
14. 8 wash his clothes, shave off all his **hair,** and have a bath;
14. 9 his eyebrows, and all the rest of the **hair** on his body;
19.27 Do not cut the **hair** on the sides of your head or
21.10 he must not leave his **hair** uncombed or tear his clothes to
Num 5.18 he shall loosen the woman's **hair** and put the offering of
6. 5 under the Nazirite vow, he must not cut his **hair** or shave.
6. 5 to the Lord, and he shall let his **hair** and beard grow.
6. 6 His **hair** is the sign of his dedication to God, and so
6. 9 If the consecrated **hair** of a Nazirite is defiled because
6. 9 must wait seven days and then shave off his **hair** and beard;
6.11 the man shall reconsecrate his **hair** [12] and rededicate to
6.12 doesn't count, because his consecrated **hair** was defiled.
6.18 Nazirite shall shave off his **hair** and put it on the fire
Judg 13. 5 you must never cut his **hair,** because from the day of his
16.13 weave my seven locks of **hair** into a loom, and make it
16.14 took his seven locks of **hair,** and wove them into the loom.
16.14 But he woke up and pulled his **hair** loose from the loom.
16.17 "My **hair** has never been cut," he said.
16.17 If my **hair** were cut, I would lose my strength
16.19 then called a man, who cut off Samson's seven locks of **hair.**
16.22 But his **hair** started growing again.
20.15 could sling a stone at a strand of **hair** and never miss.
1 Sam 1.11 his whole life and that he will never have his **hair** cut."
14.45 Lord that he will not lose even a **hair** from his head.
2 Sam 12.20 floor, had a bath, combed his **hair,** and changed his clothes.
14. 2 put on your mourning clothes, and don't comb your **hair.**
14.26 His **hair** was very thick, and he had to cut it once
1 Kgs 1.52 is loyal, not even a **hair** on his head will be touched;
2 Kgs 9.30 put on eyeshadow, arranged her **hair,** and stood looking down
Ezra 9. 3 clothes in despair, tore my **hair** and my beard, and sat down
Neh 13.25 down curses on them, beat them, and pulled out their **hair.**
Job 4.15 breeze touched my face, and my **hair** bristled with fright.
15.10 We learnt our wisdom from **grey-haired** men— men born
Ps 40.12 they are more than the **hairs** of my head, and I have
69. 4 for no reason are more numerous than the **hairs** of my head.
71.18 I am old and my **hair** is grey, do not abandon me,
Prov 16.31 grey **hair** is a glorious crown.
20.29 the strength of youth and respect the grey **hair** of age.
Ecc 12. 5 Your **hair** will turn white;
Song 1.10 Your **hair** is beautiful upon your cheeks and falls along
4. 1 Your **hair** dances, like a flock of goats bounding down the
5. 2 is wet with dew, and my **hair** is damp from the mist.
5.11 his **hair** is wavy, black as a raven.
6. 5 Your **hair** dances, like a flock of goats bounding down the
7. 5 Your braided **hair** shines like the finest satin;
Is 3.24 instead of having beautiful **hair,** they will be bald;
7.20 your beards, and the **hair** on your heads and your bodies.
46. 4 care of you until you are old and your **hair** is grey.
50. 6 when they pulled out the **hairs** of my beard and spat in
Jer 7.29 cut off your **hair** and throw it away.
9.25 Moab, and the desert people, who have their **hair** cut short.
25.19 all the people who cut their **hair** short;
49.32 those people who cut their **hair** short, and I will bring
Ezek 5. 1 and use it to shave off your beard and all your **hair.**
5. 1 Then weigh the **hair** on scales and divide it into three parts.
5. 3 Keep back a few **hairs** and wrap them in the hem of
8. 3 what seemed to be a hand and seized me by the **hair.**
16. 7 well-formed, and your **hair** had grown, but you were naked.
44.20 must neither shave their heads nor let their **hair** grow long.
Dan 3.27 Their **hair** was not singed, their clothes were not burnt, and
4.33 on his body, and his **hair** grew as long as eagles' feathers
7. 9 clothes were white as snow, and his **hair** was like pure wool.
10. 3 any wine, or comb my **hair** until the three weeks were past.
Mic 1.16 of Judah, cut off your **hair** in mourning for the children you
Mt 3. 4 John's clothes were made of camel's **hair;**
5.36 head, because you cannot make a single **hair** white or black.
6.17 your face and comb your **hair,** [18] so that others cannot know
10.30 As for you, even the **hairs** of your head have all been
Mk 1. 6 wore clothes made of camel's **hair,** with a leather belt round
Lk 7.38 dried his feet with her **hair,** kissed them, and poured the
7.44 washed my feet with her tears and dried them with her **hair.**
12. 7 Even the **hairs** of your head have all been counted.
21.18 But not a single **hair** from your heads will be lost.
Jn 11. 2 the perfume on the Lord's feet and wiped them with her **hair;**
12. 3 poured it on Jesus' feet, and wiped them with her **hair.**
Acts 27.34 Not even a **hair** of your heads will be lost."
1 Cor 11. 6 does not cover her head, she might as well cut her **hair.**
11. 6 shave her head or cut her **hair,** she should cover her head.
11.14 itself teaches you that long **hair** on a man is a disgrace,
11.15 Her long **hair** has been given her to serve as a covering.
1 Tim 2. 9 not with fancy **hair** styles or with gold ornaments or pearls
1 Pet 3. 3 the way you do your **hair,** or the jewellery you put on,
Rev 1.14 His **hair** was white as wool, or as snow, and his eyes
9. 8 Their **hair** was like women's hair, their teeth were like lions'

HALF

[HALVES]

Gen 15.10 to God, cut them in **half,** and placed the halves opposite
Ex 24. 6 Moses took **half** the blood of the animals
24. 6 and the other **half** he threw against the altar.
26.12 Hang the extra **half-piece** over the back of the Tent.
26.28 The middle cross-bar, set **half-way** up the frames, is to
27. 5 rim of the altar, so that it reaches **half-way** up the altar.
Ex 36.33 The middle cross-bar, set **half-way** up the frames,
38. 4 rim of the altar, so that it reached **half-way** up the altar.
Lev 6.20 half in the morning and **half** in the evening.
Num 12.12 like something born dead with **half** its flesh eaten away."
31.36 The **half-share** of the soldiers was 337,500 sheep and goats,
32.33 Gad and Reuben and to **half** the tribe of Manasseh all the
34.13 that the Lord has assigned to the nine and a **half** tribes.
34.14 and the eastern **half** of Manasseh have received their property,
Deut 3.13 To **half** the tribe of Manasseh I assigned the rest of
15.18 you for six years at **half** the cost of a hired servant.
29. 8 tribes of Reuben and Gad, and **half** the tribe of Manasseh.
Josh 1.12 Reuben and Gad and to **half** the tribe of Manasseh,
4.12 Reuben and Gad and of **half** the tribe of Manasseh,
8.33 **Half** the people stood with their backs to Mount Gerizim
8.33 and the other **half** with their backs to Mount Ebal.
12. 2 His kingdom included **half** of Gilead:
12. 5 and Maacah, as well as **half** of Gilead, as far as the
12. 6 Reuben and Gad and to **half** the tribe of Manasseh,
13. 7 the other nine tribes and **half** of the tribe of Manasseh,
13. 8 and Gad and the other **half** of the tribe of Manasseh
13.25 all the cities of Gilead, **half** the land of Ammon
13.29 land to the families of **half** the tribe of Manasseh
13.31 It included **half** of Gilead, as well as Ashtaroth and Edrei,
13.31 All this was given to **half** the families descended from Machir
14. 2 the nine and a **half** tribes west of the Jordan
14. 3 east of the Jordan to the other two and a **half** tribes.
22. 6 of the Jordan to one **half** of the tribe of Manasseh,
22. 6 but to the other **half** Joshua had given land west
2 Sam 2.11 he ruled in Hebron over Judah for seven and a **half** years.
5. 5 Judah for seven and a **half** years, and in Jerusalem over all
18. 3 turn and run, or even if **half** of us are killed;
19.40 the men of Judah and **half** the men of Israel,
1 Kgs 3.25 the living child in two and give each woman **half** of it."
10. 7 But I didn't hear even **half** of it;
13. 8 "Even if you gave me **half** your wealth, I would not go
16. 9 in charge of **half** the king's chariots, plotted against him.
1 Chr 2.52 the people of Haroeh, of **half** the inhabitants of Menuhoth,
3. 4 Hebron during the seven and a **half** years that David ruled there.
2 Chr 9. 6 I had not heard of even **half** your wisdom.
13.17 a crushing defeat—**half** a million of Israel's best soldiers
Neh 3. 9 ruler of **half** the Jerusalem District, built the next
3.12 ruler of the other **half** of the Jerusalem District, built the
3.16 ruler of **half** the Bethzur District, built the next
3.17 Hashabiah, ruler of **half** the Keilah District, built the next
3.18 Henadad, ruler of the other **half** of the Keilah District,
4. 6 and soon it was **half** its full height, because the people
4.16 half my men worked and **half** stood guard, wearing coats of
4.21 stars came out at night, **half** of us worked on the wall,
4.21 while the other **half** stood guard with spears.
12.32 behind the singers, followed by **half** the leaders of Judah.
12.38 the top of the wall, and I followed with **half** the people.
13.24 **Half** their children spoke the language of Ashdod
Esth 5. 3 and you shall have it—even if it is **half** my empire."
5. 6 grant your request, even if you ask for **half** my empire."
7. 2 I'll even give you **half** the empire."
Ps 55.23 liars to their graves before **half** their life is over.
Prov 27.22 beat a fool until he's **half** dead, you still can't beat his
Jer 34.18 by walking between the two **halves** of a bull that they had
Ezek 16.51 "Samaria did not sin **half** as much as you have.
42. 7 building was solid for twenty-five metres, **half** its length;
45. 3 **Half** of this area,
45. 5 The other **half** of the area is to be set aside as
Dan 7.25 people will be under his power for three and a **half** years.
9.27 for seven years, and when **half** this time is past, he will
12. 7 I heard him say, "It will be three and a **half** years.
Hos 7. 8 "The people of Israel are like a **half-baked** loaf of bread.
Zeph 2. 4 will be driven out in **half** a day,
Zech 14. 2 **Half** the people will go into exile,
14. 4 **Half** the mountain will move northwards and half of it southwards.
14. 8 water will flow from Jerusalem, **half** of it to the Dead Sea
14. 8 and the other **half** to the Mediterranean.
Mk 6.23 you anything you ask for, even as much as **half** my kingdom!"
Lk 4.25 rain for three and a **half** years and a severe famine spread
10.30 stripped him, and beat him up, leaving him **half** dead.
19. 8 I will give **half** my belongings to the poor, and if I
Jn 7.14 The festival was nearly **half** over when Jesus went to the
12. 3 Then Mary took **half** a litre of a very expensive perfume
Acts 18.11 for a year and a **half,** teaching the people the word of
Jas 5.17 no rain fell on the land for three and a **half** years.
Rev 8. 1 there was silence in heaven for about **half** an hour.
11. 9 bodies for three and a **half** days and will not allow them
11.11 After three and a **half** days a life-giving breath came
12.14 for three and a **half** years, safe from the dragon's attack.

HALF-BROTHER

Gen 42. 3 So Joseph's ten **half-brothers** went to buy corn in Egypt,
2 Sam 13. 4 in love with Tamar, the sister of my **half-brother** Absalom,"
13.20 He is your **half-brother,** so don't tell anyone about it."
1 Kgs 1.10 not invite his **half brother** Solomon or Nathan the prophet,

HALF-SISTER

Lev 18.11 Do not have intercourse with a **half-sister;**
20.17 man marries his sister or **half-sister,** they shall be
Deut 27.22 anyone who has intercourse with his sister or **half sister.'**
2 Kgs 11. 2 who was King Jehoram's daughter and Ahaziah's **half-sister.**
2 Chr 22.11 Ahaziah had a **half-sister,** Jehosheba, who was married to
Ezek 22.11 and others seduce their daughters-in-law or their **half-sisters.**

HALL

1 Kgs	7. 2	The **Hall** of the Forest of Lebanon was 44 metres long,
	7. 6	The **Hall** of Columns was 22 metres long and 13.5 metres wide.
	7. 7	also called the **Hall** of Judgement, where Solomon decided cases,
	7. 8	in another court behind the **Hall** of Judgement, were made
	10.17	these shields placed in the **Hall** of the Forest of Lebanon.
	10.21	all the utensils in the **Hall** of the Forest of Lebanon were
2 Chr	9.16	had them all placed in the **Hall** of the Forest of Lebanon.
	9.20	all the utensils in the **Hall** of the Forest of Lebanon were
Song	2. 4	brought me to his banqueting **hall** and raised the banner of
Mt	22.10	and the wedding **hall** was filled with people.
	27.19	sitting in the judgement **hall**, his wife sent him a message:
Acts	19. 9	every day he held discussions in the lecture **hall** of Tyrannus.
	25.23	ceremony and entered the audience **hall** with the military chiefs

HAM (1)
Noah's son and Canaan's father

Gen	5.32	was 500 years old, he had three sons, Shem, **Ham,** and
	6. 9	He had three sons, Shem, **Ham,** and Japheth.
	7.13	their three sons, Shem, **Ham,** and Japheth, and their wives.
	9.18	Noah who went out of the boat were Shem, **Ham,** and Japheth.
	9.18	**(Ham** was the father of Canaan.)
	9.22	When **Ham,** the father of Canaan, saw that his father was naked,
	10. 1	These are the descendants of Noah's sons, Shem, **Ham,** and
	10. 6	The sons of **Ham**—Cush, Egypt, Libya and Canaan—were the
	10.20	These are the descendants of **Ham,** living in their
1 Chr	1. 4	Shem, **Ham,** and Japheth.
	1. 8	The sons of **Ham**—Cush, Egypt, Libya, and Canaan—
	4.40	The people who had lived there before were **Hamites.**

HAMAN
Chief enemy of the Jews in Esther's time.

Esth	3.1-15	**Haman plots to destroy the Jews**
	4.1-17	**Mordecai asks for Esther's help**
	5.1-8	**Esther invites the king and Haman to a banquet**
	9-14	**Haman plots to kill Mordecai**
	6.1-13	**The king honours Mordecai**
	6.14–7.10	**Haman is put to death**
	8.1-17	**The Jews are told to fight back**
	9.1-19	**The Jews destroy their enemies**
	20-32	**The Festival of Purim**

HAMATH
City at northernmost limit of Israel in Solomon's time.

Num	13.21	south all the way to Rehob, near **Hamath** Pass in the north.
	34. 8	Mediterranean to Mount Hor [8] and from there to **Hamath** Pass.
Josh	13. 5	Baalgad, which is south of Mount Hermon, to **Hamath** Pass.
Judg	3. 3	Lebanon Mountains from Mount Baal Hermon as far as **Hamath** Pass.
2 Sam	8. 9	King Toi of **Hamath** heard that David had defeated all of
1 Kgs	8.65	from as far away as **Hamath** Pass in the north and the
2 Kgs	14.25	had belonged to Israel, from **Hamath** Pass in the north to the
	14.28	how he restored Damascus and **Hamath** to Israel, are all
	17.24	cities of Babylon, Cuth, Ivvah, **Hamath,** and Sepharvaim, and
	17.30	the people of **Hamath,** idols of Ashima;
	18.34	Where are they now, the gods of **Hamath** and Arpad?
	19.13	the kings of the cities of **Hamath,** Arpad, Sepharvaim, Hena,
	23.33	Riblah, in the land of **Hamath,** and made Judah pay 3,400
	25.21	was in the city of Riblah [21] in the territory of **Hamath.**
1 Chr	13. 5	border in the south to **Hamath** Pass in the north, in order
	18. 3	Zobah, near the territory of **Hamath,** because Hadadezer was
	18. 9	King Toi of **Hamath** heard that David had defeated Hadadezer's
2 Chr	7. 8	from as far away as **Hamath** Pass in the north and the
	8. 3	He captured the territory of **Hamath** and Zobah [4] and
	8. 4	the cities in **Hamath** that were centres for storing supplies.
Is	10. 9	of Calno and Carchemish, the cities of **Hamath** and Arpad.
	11.11	Pathros, Sudan, Elam, Babylonia, and **Hamath,** and in the
	36.19	Where are they now, the gods of **Hamath** and Arpad?
	37.13	the kings of the cities of **Hamath,** Arpad, Sepharvaim, Hena,
Jer	39. 5	Riblah in the territory of **Hamath,** and there Nebuchadnezzar
	49.23	people in the cities of **Hamath** and Arpad are worried and
	52. 9	Riblah in the territory of **Hamath,** and there Nebuchadnezzar
	52.27	was in the city of Riblah [27] in the territory of **Hamath.**
Ezek	47.15	the city of Hethlon, to **Hamath** Pass, to the city of Zedad,
	47.16	that of the kingdom of **Hamath),** and to the city of Ticon
	47.17	border regions of Damascus and **Hamath** to the north of it.
	47.20	Mediterranean and runs north to a point west of **Hamath** Pass.
	48. 1	the city of Hethlon, to **Hamath** Pass, to the city of Enon,
	48. 1	to the boundary between the kingdoms of Damascus and **Hamath.**
Amos	6. 2	to the great city of **Hamath** and on down to the Philistine
	6.14	It will oppress you from **Hamath** Pass in the north to the
Zech	9. 2	**Hamath,** which borders on Hadrach, also belongs to him, and

HAMMER
[SLEDGE-HAMMERS]

Ex	25.18	Make two winged creatures of **hammered** gold, [19] one for
	25.31	Make its base and its shaft of **hammered** gold;
	25.36	lamp-stand are to be a single piece of pure **hammered** gold.
	37. 7	made two winged creatures of **hammered** gold, [8] one for each
	37.17	He made its base and its shaft of **hammered** gold;
	37.22	the lamp-stand were a single piece of pure **hammered** gold.
	39. 3	They **hammered** out sheets of gold and cut them into thin
Num	8. 4	the lamp-stand was made of **hammered** gold, according to the
	10. 2	Moses, [2] "Make two trumpets of **hammered** silver to use for
Judg	4.21	Then Jael took a **hammer** and a tent-peg, went up to him
	5.26	a tent peg in one hand, a workman's **hammer** in the other;
1 Kgs	6. 7	was no noise made by **hammers,** axes, or any other iron tools
Ps	74. 6	smashed all the wooden panels with their axes and **sledge-hammers.**
Is	2. 4	They will **hammer** their swords into ploughs
	44.12	His strong arm swings a **hammer** to pound the metal into shape.
Jer	23.29	like a fire, and like a **hammer** that breaks rocks in pieces.
	50.23	Babylonia **hammered** the whole world to pieces,
	50.23	and now that **hammer** is shattered!
	51.20	"Babylonia, you are my **hammer,** my weapon of war.
Joel	3.10	**Hammer** the points of your ploughs into swords and your
Mic	4. 3	They will **hammer** their swords into ploughs
Zech	1.20	Then the Lord showed me four workmen with **hammers.**

HAMOR
Ancestor of the tribe of Shechem.

Gen	33.19	field from the descendants of **Hamor** father of Shechem for a
	34. 2	When Shechem son of **Hamor** the Hivite, who was chief of
	34. 6	Shechem's father **Hamor** went out to talk with Jacob,
	34. 8	**Hamor** said to him, "My son Shechem has fallen in love
	34.13	answered Shechem and his father **Hamor** in a deceitful way.
	34.18	These terms seemed fair to **Hamor** and his son Shechem,
	34.20	**Hamor** and his son Shechem went to the meeting-place
	34.24	the city agreed with what **Hamor** and Shechem proposed,
	34.26	killed all the men, [26] including **Hamor** and his son Shechem.
Josh	24.32	bought from the sons of **Hamor,** the father of Shechem,
Judg	9.28	Be loyal to your ancestor **Hamor,** who founded your clan!
Acts	7.16	had bought from the clan of **Hamor** for a sum of money.

HAND (1)
[EMPTY-HANDED, LEFT HAND, LEFT-HANDED, RIGHT HAND, RIGHT-HANDED]

Gen	19.16	his two daughters by the **hand** and led them out of the
	24. 2	that he had, "Place your **hand** between my thighs and make a
	24. 9	So the servant put his **hand** between the thighs of Abraham,
	31.42	with me, you would have already sent me away **empty-handed.**
	39.12	But he escaped and ran outside, leaving his robe in her **hand.**
	41.44	so much as lift a **hand** or a foot without your permission."
	47.29	said to him, "Place your **hand** between my thighs and make a
	48.14	But Jacob crossed his **hands,**
	48.14	and put his **right hand** on the head of Ephraim,
	48.14	was the younger, and his **left hand** on the head of Manasseh,
	48.17	that his father had put his **right hand** on Ephraim's head;
	48.17	so he took his father's **hand** to move it from Ephraim's head
	48.18	put your **right hand** on his head."
Ex	3.21	so that when my people leave, they will not go **empty-handed.**
	4. 6	Lord spoke to Moses again, "Put your **hand** inside your robe."
	4. 6	and when he took his **hand** out, it was diseased,
	4. 7	Then the Lord said, "Put your **hand** inside your robe again."
	7. 5	Lord, when I raise my **hand** against them and bring the
	9. 8	Moses and Aaron, "Take a few **handfuls** of ashes from a furnace;
	9.15	If I had raised my **hand** to strike you and your people
	9.22	said to Moses, "Raise your **hand** towards the sky, and hail
	9.29	city, I will lift up my **hands** in prayer to the Lord.
	9.33	the city, and lifted up his **hands** in prayer to the Lord.
	10.12	said to Moses, "Raise your **hand** over the land of Egypt to
	10.21	said to Moses, "Raise your **hand** towards the sky, and a
	10.22	Moses raised his **hand** towards the sky, and there was
	12.11	with your sandals on your feet and your stick in your **hand.**
	13. 9	like something tied on your **hand** or on your forehead;
	13.16	like something tied on our **hands** or on our foreheads;
	14.21	Moses held out his **hand** over the sea, and the Lord drove
	14.26	to Moses, "Hold out your **hand** over the sea, and the water
	14.27	So Moses held out his **hand** over the sea, and at daybreak
	15. 6	"Your **right hand,** Lord, is awesome in power;
	15.12	You stretched out your **right hand,** and the earth swallowed our enemies.
	21.24	**hand for hand,** foot for foot,
	29.10	tell Aaron and his sons to put their **hands** on its head.
	29.15	tell Aaron and his sons to put their **hands** on its head.
	29.19	tell Aaron and his sons to put their **hands** on its head.
	29.20	the thumbs of their **right hands** and on the big toes of
	29.24	all this food in the **hands** of Aaron and his sons and
	30.19	the water to wash their **hands** and feet [20] before they go
	30.21	They must wash their **hands** and feet, so that they will
	33.22	rock and cover you with my **hand** until I have passed by.
	33.23	Then I will take my **hand** away, and you will see my
	40.31	and his sons washed their **hands** and their feet there
Lev	1. 4	The man shall put his **hand** on its head, and it will
	2. 2	officiating priest shall take a **handful** of the flour and oil
	3. 2	The man shall put his **hand** on the head of the animal
	3. 8	sheep, [8] he shall put his **hand** on its head and kill it
	3.13	goat, [13] he shall put his **hand** on its head and kill it
	4. 4	of the Tent, put his **hand** on its head, and kill it
	4.15	the community shall put their **hands** on its head, and it
	4.24	He shall put his **hand** on its head and kill it on
	4.29	He shall put his **hand** on its head and kill it on
	4.33	He shall put his **hand** on its head and kill it on
	5.12	priest, who will take a **handful** of it as a token that
	6.15	Then he shall take a **handful** of the flour and oil, and
	7.30	Lord, [30] bringing it with his own **hands** as a food-offering.
	8.14	and Aaron and his sons put their **hands** on its head.
	8.18	and Aaron and his sons put their **hands** on its head.
	8.22	priests, and Aaron and his sons put their **hands** on its head.
	8.23	the thumb of his **right hand,** and on the big toe of
	8.24	the thumbs of their **right hands,** and on the big toes of
	8.27	all this food in the **hands** of Aaron and his sons, and
	9.17	the grain-offering and took a **handful** of flour and burnt it
	9.22	he raised his **hands** over the people and blessed them,
	14.14	the thumb of the **right hand,** and on the big toe of

Lev	14.15	the palm of his own **left hand,** [16]dip a finger of his
	14.16	a finger of his **right hand** in it, and sprinkle some of
	14.17	in the palm of his **hand** and some of the blood of
	14.17	the thumb of the **right hand,** and on the big toe of
	14.18	that is in the palm of his **hand** on the man's head.
	14.25	the thumb of his **right hand,** and on the big toe of
	14.26	the palm of his own **left hand** [27]and with a finger of
	14.27	of his **right hand** sprinkle some of it seven times
	14.28	the thumb of his **right hand,** and on the big toe of
	15.11	without first having washed his **hands,** that person must wash
	16.12	from the altar and two **handfuls** of fine incense and bring
	16.21	He shall put both his **hands** on the goat's head and
	21.19	no one with a crippled **hand** or foot;
	24.14	him curse shall put his **hands** on the man's head to testify
Num	5.18	the woman's hair and put the offering of flour in her **hands.**
	5.18	In his **hands** the priest shall hold the bowl containing the
	5.25	flour out of the woman's **hands,** hold it out in dedication to
	5.26	Then he shall take a **handful** of it as a token offering
	6.19	one biscuit from the basket, into the **hands** of the Nazirite.
	8.10	Israel are to place their **hands** on the heads of the Levites,
	8.12	Levites shall then put their **hands** on the heads of the two
	27.18	of Nun, a capable man, and place your **hands** on his head.
	27.23	had commanded, Moses put his **hands** on Joshua's head and
Deut	4.28	serve gods made by human **hands,** gods of wood and stone, gods
	9.10	had written with his own **hand** what he had said to you
	15.13	When you set him free, do not send him away **empty-handed.**
	19.21	a **hand for a hand,** and a foot for a foot.
	21. 6	found are to wash their **hands** over the cow [7]and say, 'We
	23.25	can pull off with your **hands,** but you must not cut any
	25.12	cut off her **hand.**
	32.40	living God, I raise my **hand** and I vow [41]that I will
	33. 2	angels were with him, a flaming fire at his **right hand.**
Josh	6. 2	"I am putting into your **hands** Jericho, with its king and
	8.19	soon as he lifted his **hand,** the men who had been hiding
Judg	3.15	This was Ehud, a **left-handed** man, who was the son of Gera,
	3.21	With his **left hand** Ehud took the sword from his right
	5.26	a tent peg in one **hand,** a workman's hammer in the other;
	7. 6	men who scooped up water in their **hands** and lapped it;
	7.20	torches in their **left hands,** the trumpets in their right,
	14. 6	lion apart with his bare **hands,** as if it were a young
	14. 9	the honey out into his **hands** and ate it as he walked
	15.14	ropes round his arms and **hands** as if they were burnt thread.
	16.26	was leading him by the **hand,** "Let me touch the pillars that
	16.29	Putting one **hand** on each pillar, he pushed against them
	19.27	in front of the house with her **hands** reaching for the door.
	20.15	Gibeah gathered seven hundred specially chosen men who were **left-handed.**
Ruth	3.17	not come back to you **empty-handed,** so he gave me all this
1 Sam	14.13	of the pass on his **hands** and knees, and the young man
	17.49	He put his **hand** into his bag and took out a stone,
	19. 9	with his spear in his **hand,** and David was there,
	22. 6	with his spear in his **hand,** and all his officers were
	22.17	guards refused to lift a **hand** to kill the Lord's priests.
2 Sam	3.34	His **hands** were not tied, And his feet were not bound;
	4.12	Baanah and cut off their **hands** and feet, which they hung up
	13.19	and with her face buried in her **hands** went away crying.
	20. 9	of his beard with his **right hand** in order to kiss him.
	20.10	was holding in his other **hand,** and Joab stabbed him in the
	21.20	had six fingers on each **hand** and six toes on each foot.
	23. 6	no one can touch them with bare **hands.**
	23.10	fought the Philistines until his **hand** was so stiff that he
	23.21	the spear from the Egyptian's **hand,** and killed him with it.
1 Kgs	8.38	stretch out their **hands** in prayer towards this Temple,
	8.54	the altar, where he had been kneeling with uplifted **hands.**
	17.12	All I have is a **handful** of flour in a bowl and
	18.44	no bigger than a man's **hand,** coming up from the sea."
	20.10	this city of yours and carry off the rubble in their **hands.**
2 Kgs	4.34	mouth, eyes, and hands on the boy's mouth, eyes, and **hands.**
	5.11	Lord his God, wave his **hand** over the diseased spot, and cure
	9.35	except her skull, and the bones of her **hands** and feet.
	10.15	"Give me your **hand,** then," Jehu replied.
	10.15	They clasped **hands,** and Jehu helped him up into the chariot,
	11.12	people clapped their **hands** and shouted, "Long live the king!"
	13.16	did so, and Elisha placed his **hands** on the king's hands.
	18.21	a reed as a walking-stick—it would break and jab your **hand.**
	19.10	will not fall into my **hands,** but don't let that deceive you.
	19.18	at all, only images of wood and stone made by human **hands.**
1 Chr	11.23	the spear from the Egyptian's **hand,** and killed him with it.
	12. 2	They could shoot arrows and sling stones either **right-handed** or left-handed.
	13. 9	and Uzzah stretched out his **hand** and took hold of the
	20. 6	with six fingers on each **hand** and six toes on each foot.
	21.16	holding his sword in his **hand,** ready to destroy Jerusalem.
2 Chr	6.13	could see him, and raised his **hands** towards heaven.)
	6.29	stretch out their **hands** in prayer towards this Temple,
	22.11	hidden, she saved him from death at the **hands** of Athaliah.
	29.23	and to the other worshippers, who laid their **hands** on them.
	32.19	the gods of the other peoples, idols made by human **hands.**
Ezra	3.10	places with trumpets in their **hands,** and the Levites of the
	9. 5	in prayer and stretched out my **hands** to the Lord my God.
	9. 7	priests have fallen into the **hands** of foreign kings, and we
Neh	4.17	building materials worked with one **hand** and kept a weapon in
	4.23	And we all kept our weapons to **hand.**
Job	4. 3	You have taught many people and given strength to feeble **hands.**
	5.18	his **hand** hurts you, and his hand heals.
	10. 8	Your **hands** formed and shaped me,
	10. 8	and now those same **hands** destroy me.
	12. 9	All of them know that the Lord's **hand** made them.
	19.21	The **hand** of God has struck me down.
	20.26	fire not lit by human **hands** burns him and all his family.
	26.13	sky clear, and his **hand** that killed the escaping monster.
Job	31. 7	attracted to evil, if my **hands** are stained with sin, [8]then
	31.27	to honour them by kissing my **hand** in reverence to them.
	36.32	seizes the lightning with his **hands** and commands it to hit
Ps	16. 5	my future is in your **hands.**
	22.16	they tear at my **hands** and feet.
	26. 6	Lord, I wash my **hands** to show that I am innocent and
	28. 2	for help, when I lift my **hands** towards your holy Temple.
	47. 1	Clap your **hands** for joy, all peoples!
	63. 4	I will raise my **hands** to you in prayer.
	63. 8	I cling to you, and your **hand** keeps me safe.
	68.31	the Sudanese will raise their **hands** in prayer to God.
	73.23	always stay close to you, and you hold me by the **hand.**
	74.11	Why do you keep your **hands** behind you?
	75. 8	holds a cup in his **hand,** filled with the strong wine of
	77. 2	night long I lift my **hands** in prayer, but I cannot find
	88. 9	I call to you and lift my **hands** to you in prayer.
	91.12	hold you up with their **hands** to keep you from hurting your
	98. 8	Clap your **hands,** you rivers;
	102.25	the earth, and with your own **hands** you made the heavens.
	115. 4	Their gods are made of silver and gold, formed by human **hands.**
	115. 7	They have **hands,** but cannot feel, and feet, but cannot walk;
	118.27	With branches in your **hands,** start the festival and march
	127. 4	has when he is young are like arrows in a soldier's **hand.**
	134. 2	Raise your **hands** in prayer in the Temple, and praise the Lord!
	135.15	they are formed by human **hands.**
	136.12	with his strong **hand,** his powerful arm;
	141. 2	my prayer as incense, my uplifted **hands** as an evening sacrifice.
	143. 6	I lift up my **hands** to you in prayer;
	149. 6	their sharp swords in their **hands** [7]to defeat the nations
Prov	5. 9	had, and you will die young at the **hands** of merciless men.
	6.10	"I'll fold my **hands** and rest a while."
	6.16	**hands** that kill innocent people,
	8.26	the earth and its fields or even the first **handful** of soil.
	24.33	Fold your **hands** and rest awhile, [34]but while you are asleep,
	26. 9	a drunk man trying to pick a thorn out of his **hand.**
	27.16	stop the wind or ever tried to hold a **handful** of oil?
	30. 4	Who has ever caught the wind in his **hand?**
	30.28	can hold one in your **hand,** but you can find them in
Ecc	4. 5	a fool to fold his **hands** and let himself starve to death.
	4. 6	all the time with both **hands,** trying to catch the wind.
Song	2. 6	His left **hand** is under my head, and his right hand
	5. 4	My lover put his **hand** to the door, and I was thrilled
	5. 5	My **hands** were covered with myrrh, my fingers with liquid myrrh,
	5.14	His **hands** are well-formed, and he wears rings set with gems.
	8. 3	Your left **hand** is under my head, and your right hand
Is	1.15	"When you lift your **hands** in prayer, I will not look at
	1.15	I will not listen, for your **hands** are covered with blood.
	2. 8	worship objects that they have made with their own **hands.**
	5.25	his people and has stretched out his **hand** to punish them.
	5.25	not be ended, but his **hand** will still be stretched out to
	9.12	his **hand** is still stretched out to punish.
	9.17	not be ended, but his **hand** will still be stretched out to
	9.21	his **hand** is still stretched out to punish.
	10. 4	his **hand** will still be stretched out to punish.
	10.10	I stretched out my **hand** to punish those kingdoms that worship
	13. 7	Everyone's **hands** will hang limp,
	17. 8	made with their own **hands,** or trust in their own handiwork
	19.16	the Lord Almighty has stretched out his **hand** to punish them.
	23.11	Lord has stretched out his **hand** over the sea and overthrown
	25.11	They will stretch out their **hands** as if they were trying
	25.11	God will humiliate them, and their **hands** will sink helplessly.
	35. 3	Give strength to **hands** that are tired and to knees that
	36. 6	a reed as a walking-stick—it would break and jab your **hand.**
	37.10	will not fall into my **hands,** but don't let that deceive you.
	37.19	at all, only images of wood and stone made by human **hands.**
	40.12	anyone measure the ocean by **handfuls**
	40.12	or measure the sky with his **hands?**
	44.20	idol he holds in his **hand** is not a god at all.
	48.13	My **hands** made the earth's foundations and spread the heavens out.
	49. 2	With his own **hand** he protected me.
	49.16	I have written your name on the palms of my **hands.**
	51.16	given you my teaching, and I protect you with my **hand.'"**
	51.18	you, no one among your people to take you by the **hand.**
	53. 1	Who could have seen the Lord's **hand** in this?
Jer	1. 9	the Lord stretched out his **hand,** touched my lips, and said
	4.31	breath, stretching out her **hand** and saying, "I am doomed!
	6.24	say the people of Jerusalem, "and our **hands** hang limp;
	11.20	I have placed my cause in your **hands;**
	15. 6	So I stretched out my **hand** and crushed you because I was
	18. 6	You are in my **hands** just like clay in the potter's hands.
	20.12	on my enemies, for I have placed my cause in your **hands.**
	22.24	the signet-ring on my **right hand,** I would pull you off
	25.17	the cup from the Lord's **hand,** gave it to all the nations
	25.28	take the cup from your **hand** and drink from it, then tell
	30. 6	see every man with his **hands** on his stomach like a woman
	31.32	I took them by the **hand** and led them out of Egypt.
	32.24	and disease will make the city fall into their **hands.**
	32.36	make this city fall into the **hands** of the king of Babylonia.
	47. 3	their **hands** will hang limp at their sides.
	48.37	gashes on their **hands,** and everyone is wearing sackcloth.
	50.43	The king of Babylonia hears the news, and his **hands** hang limp.
	51. 7	like a gold cup in my **hand,** making the whole world drunk.
Lam	1.17	"I stretch out my **hands,** but no one will help me.
	4. 6	which met with a sudden downfall at the **hands** of God.
	5. 2	Our property is in the **hands** of strangers;
Ezek	1. 8	wings, they each had four human **hands,** one under each wing.
	2. 9	I saw a **hand** stretched out towards me, and it was holding
	2.10	The **hand** unrolled the scroll, and I saw that there was
	6.11	The Sovereign Lord said, "Wring your **hands!**

Ezek 6.14 Yes, I will stretch out my **hand** and destroy their country.
7.17 Everyone's **hands** will be weak, and their knees will shake.
8. 3 what seemed to be a **hand** and seized me by the hair.
10. 2 under the creatures and fill your **hands** with burning coals.
10. 7 of the creatures put his **hand** into the fire that was there
10. 7 coals, and put them in the **hands** of the man in linen.
10. 8 had what looked like a human **hand** under each of its wings.
10.12 bodies, backs, **hands,** wings, and wheels were covered with eyes.
10.21 wings, and what looked like a human **hand** under each wing.
12. 7 dug a hole in the wall with my **hands** and went out.
13.19 order to get a few **handfuls** of barley and a few pieces
14.13 I will stretch out my **hand** and destroy its supply of food.
16.27 "Now I have raised my **hand** to punish you and to take
19.12 But angry **hands** pulled it up by the roots and threw it
20.33 will rule over you with a strong **hand,** with all my power.
21. 7 be filled with fear, their **hands** will hang limp, their
21.11 sharpened and polished, to be put in the **hands** of a killer.
21.14 Clap your **hands,** and the sword will strike again and again.
21.17 I also will clap my **hands,** and my anger will be over.
21.22 His **right hand** holds the arrow marked 'Jerusalem'!
22.14 enough to lift your **hand** when I am finished with you?
23.45 practise adultery and their **hands** are stained with blood."
25. 6 You clapped your **hands** and jumped for joy.
28.10 You will die like a dog at the **hand** of godless foreigners.
30.22 one already broken—and the sword will fall from his **hand.**
30.24 the king of Babylonia strong and put my sword in his **hands.**
37.17 end to end in your **hand** so that they look like one
37.19 two I will make one stick and hold it in my **hand.**
37.20 "Hold in your **hand** the two sticks and let the people
39. 3 his bow out of his **left hand**
39. 3 and his arrows out of his **right hand.**
Dan 5. 5 Suddenly a human **hand** appeared and began writing on the
5. 5 And the king saw the **hand** as it was writing.
5.24 That is why God has sent the **hand** to write these words.
10.10 Then a **hand** took hold of me
10.10 and raised me to my **hands** and knees;
10.16 like a man, stretched out his **hand** and touched my lips.
12. 7 The angel raised both **hands** towards the sky and made a
Hos 13. 2 of silver, designed by human minds, made by human **hands.**
Amos 5.19 comes home and puts his **hand** on the wall—only to be
7. 7 of a plumb-line, and there was a plumb-line in his **hand.**
Nah 3.19 hear the news of your destruction clap their **hands** for joy.
Hab 3. 4 light flashes from his **hand,** there where his power is hidden.
Zeph 3.16 Do not let your **hands** hang limp!
Zech 2. 1 vision I saw a man with a measuring-line in his **hand.**
Mt 4. 6 hold you up with their **hands,** so that not even your feet
5.30 If your **right hand** causes you to sin, cut it off
8. 3 Jesus stretched out his **hand** and touched him.
8.15 He touched her **hand;**
9.18 but come and place your **hands** on her, and she will live."
9.25 girl's room and took hold of her **hand,** and she got up.
12.10 where there was a man who had a paralysed **hand.**
12.13 the man with the paralysed **hand,** "Stretch out your hand."
15. 2 They don't wash their **hands** in the proper way before they eat!"
15.20 to eat without washing your **hands** as they say you
18. 8 "If your **hand** or your foot makes you lose your faith, cut
18. 8 to enter life without a **hand** or a foot
18. 8 than to keep both **hands** and both feet and be thrown
19.13 for him to place his **hands** on them and to pray for
19.15 He placed his **hands** on them and then went away.
22.13 the servants, 'Tie him up **hand** and foot, and throw him
27.24 took some water, washed his **hands** in front of the crowd, and
27.29 it on his head, and put a stick in his **right hand;**
Mk 1.31 went to her, took her by the **hand,** and helped her up.
1.41 with pity, and stretched out his **hand** and touched him.
3. 1 synagogue, where there was a man who had a paralysed **hand.**
3. 5 Then he said to the man, "Stretch out your **hand."**
5. 4 many times his feet and **hands** had been chained, but every
5.23 Please come and place your **hands** on her, so that she will
5.41 He took her by the **hand** and said to her, "Talitha,
6. 5 except that he placed his **hands** on a few sick people and
7. 2 eating their food with **hands** that were ritually unclean—that is,
7. 3 do not eat unless they wash their **hands** in the proper way;
7. 5 but instead eat with ritually unclean **hands?"**
7.32 speak, and they begged Jesus to place his **hands** on him.
8.23 the blind man by the **hand** and led him out of the
8.23 man's eyes, Jesus placed his **hands** on him and asked him,
8.25 Jesus again placed his **hands** on the man's eyes.
9.27 took the boy by the **hand** and helped him to rise, and
9.43 So if your **hand** makes you lose your faith, cut it off!
9.43 to enter life without a **hand** than to keep both hands and
10.13 for him to place his **hands** on them, but the disciples
10.16 in his arms, placed his **hands** on each of them, and blessed
16.18 will place their **hands** on sick people, who will get well."
Lk 1.22 to say a word, he made signs to them with his **hands.**
1.53 with good things, and sent the rich away with empty **hands.**
4.11 hold you up with their **hands** so that not even your feet
4.40 he placed his **hands** on every one of them and healed them
5.13 Jesus stretched out his **hand** and touched him.
6. 1 ears of corn, rub them in their **hands,** and eat the grain.
6. 6 A man was there whose **right hand** was paralysed.
6.10 then he said to the man, "Stretch out your **hand."**
6.10 He did so, and his **hand** became well again.
6.38 helping, poured into your **hands**—all that you can hold.
8.29 was kept a prisoner, his **hands** and feet fastened with chains,
8.54 Jesus took her by the **hand** and called out, "Get up,
13.13 He placed his **hands** on her, and at once she straightened
18.15 their babies to Jesus for him to place his **hands** on them.
23.46 In your **hands** I place my spirit!"
24.39 Look at my **hands** and my feet, and see that it is
24.40 He said this and showed them his **hands** and his feet.
Lk 24.50 far as Bethany, where he raised his **hands** and blessed them.
Jn 7.30 but no one laid a **hand** on him, because his hour had
7.44 wanted to seize him, but no one laid a **hand** on him.
10.39 tried to seize Jesus, but he slipped out of their **hands.**
11.44 He came out, his **hands** and feet wrapped in grave clothes,
13. 9 Wash my **hands** and head, too!"
20.20 After saying this, he showed them his **hands** and his side.
20.25 of the nails in his **hands** and put my finger on those
20.25 on those scars and my **hand** in his side, I will not
20.27 to Thomas, "Put your finger here, and look at my **hands;**
20.27 then stretch out your **hand** and put it in my side.
21.18 you will stretch out your **hands** and someone else will bind
Acts 3. 7 Then he took him by his **right hand** and helped him up.
4.30 Stretch out your **hand** to heal, and grant that wonders
6. 6 to the apostles, who prayed and placed their **hands** on them.
7.57 members of the Council covered their ears with their **hands.**
8.17 Peter and John placed their **hands** on them, and they received
8.18 the believers when the apostles placed their **hands** on them.
8.19 anyone I place my **hands** on will receive the Holy Spirit."
9. 8 So they took him by the **hand** and led him into Damascus.
9.12 come in and place his **hands** on him so that he might
9.17 the house where Saul was, and placed his **hands** on him.
12. 7 At once the chains fell off Peter's **hands.**
12.17 He motioned with his **hand** for them to be quiet, and he
13. 3 and prayed, placed their **hands** on them, and sent them off.
13.11 The Lord's **hand** will come down on you now;
13.11 trying to find someone to lead him by the **hand.**
13.16 Paul stood up, motioned with his **hand,** and began to speak:
19. 6 Paul placed his **hands** on them, and the Holy Spirit came
19.33 Alexander motioned with his **hand** for the people to be silent,
20.34 I have worked with these **hands** of mine to provide everything
21.11 up his own feet and **hands** with it, and said, "This is
21.40 and motioned with his **hand** for the people to be silent.
22.11 my companions took me by the **hand** and led me into Damascus.
23.19 commander took him by the **hand,** led him off by himself, and
26. 1 Paul stretched out his **hand** and defended himself as follows:
28. 3 out on account of the heat and fastened itself to his **hand.**
28. 4 the snake hanging on Paul's **hand** and said to one another,
28. 8 his room, prayed, placed his **hands** on him, and healed him.
Rom 10.21 long I held out my **hands** to welcome a disobedient and
1 Cor 12.15 "Because I am not a **hand,** I don't belong to the body,"
12.21 then, the eye cannot say to the **hand,** "I don't need you!"
16.21 With my own **hand** I write this:
2 Cor 2.11 in order to keep Satan from getting the upper **hand** of us;
Gal 2. 9 so they shook **hands** with Barnabas and me, as a sign that
6.11 I make as I write to you now with my own **hand!**
Col 4.18 With my own **hand** I write this:
2 Thes 3.17 With my own **hand** I write this:
1 Tim 2. 8 can lift up their **hands** in prayer without anger or argument.
4.14 the prophets spoke and the elders laid their **hands** on you.
5.22 in no hurry to lay **hands** on someone to dedicate him to
2 Tim 1. 6 gift that God gave you when I laid my **hands** on you.
Phlm 19 Here, I will write this with my own **hand:**
Heb 1.10 the earth, and with your own **hands** you made the heavens.
6. 2 of the teaching about baptisms and the laying on of **hands;**
8. 9 I took them by the **hand** and led them out of Egypt.
10.31 terrifying thing to fall into the **hands** of the living God!
12.12 Lift up your tired **hands,** then, and strengthen your trembling knees!
Jas 4. 8 Wash your **hands,** you sinners!
1 Pet 5. 6 then, under God's mighty **hand,** so that he will lift you
1 Jn 1. 1 yes, we have seen it, and our **hands** have touched it.
Rev 1.16 held seven stars in his **right hand,** and a sharp two-edged
1.17 He placed his **right hand** on me and said, "Don't be afraid!
1.20 that you see in my **right hand,** and of the seven gold
2. 1 the seven stars in his **right hand** and who walks among the
5. 1 saw a scroll in the **right hand** of the one who sits
5. 7 took the scroll from the **right hand** of the one who sits
6. 5 Its rider held a pair of scales in his **hand.**
7. 9 dressed in white robes and holding palm branches in their **hands.**
8. 4 God's people from the **hands** of the angel standing before God.
10. 2 He had a small scroll open in his **hand.**
10. 5 on the land raised his **right hand** to heaven [6] and took a
10. 8 scroll which is in the **hand** of the angel standing on the
10.10 the little scroll from his **hand** and ate it, and it tasted
13.16 a mark placed on their **right hands** or on their foreheads.
14. 9 his forehead or on his **hand** [10] will himself drink God's wine,
14.14 of gold on his head and a sharp sickle in his **hand.**
17. 4 In her **hand** she held a gold cup full of obscene and
20. 1 holding in his **hand** the key of the abyss and
20. 4 the mark of the beast on their foreheads or their **hands.**

HAND (2)

Gen 27.17 She **handed** him the tasty food, together with the bread
39. 6 Potiphar **handed over** everything he had to the care of
Ex 29.29 priestly garments are to be **handed** on to his sons after his
Lev 5.15 sins unintentionally by failing to **hand over** the payments
5.16 payments he has failed to **hand over** and must pay an
9.13 They **handed** him the head and the other pieces of the animal,
18.21 Do not **hand over** any of your children to be used in
Deut 1.27 of Egypt just to **hand us over** to these Amorites, so that
19.12 send for him and **hand him over** to the relative responsible
Josh 7. 7 To **hand us over** to the Amorites?
20. 5 the people of the city must not **hand him over** to him.
Judg 4. 9 because the Lord will **hand Sisera over** to a woman."
8. 7 When the Lord has **handed** Zebah and Zalmunna over to me, I
15.12 tie you up, so that we can **hand you over** to them."
15.13 only going to tie you up and **hand you over** to them.
20.13 Now **hand over** those perverts in Gibeah, so that we can
1 Sam 11.12 **Hand them over** to us, and we will kill them!"

1 Sam	23.11	Will the citizens of Keilah **hand me over** to Saul?
	23.12	will the citizens of Keilah **hand** my men and me over to
	23.14	to find him, but God did not **hand David over** to him.
	28.19	He will **hand you and Israel over** to the Philistines.
	28.19	and the Lord will also **hand the army of Israel over** to
	30.15	you will not kill me or **hand me over** to my master."
2 Sam	14. 7	are demanding that I **hand my son over** to them, so that
	20.21	**Hand over** this one man, and I will withdraw from the city."
	21. 6	So **hand over** seven of his male descendants, and we will hang
	21. 6	"I will **hand them over,"** the king answered.
	21. 9	David **handed them over** to the people of Gibeon, who hanged
1 Kgs	20. 5	word that you were to **hand over** to me your silver and
2 Kgs	12. 7	you must **hand it over,** so that the repairs can be made."
	12.11	exact amount, they would **hand the silver over** to the men in
	17.13	your ancestors and which I **handed** on to you through my
	17.20	the Israelites, punishing them and **handing them over** to
	21.14	who survive, and will **hand them over** to their enemies, who
	22. 9	in the Temple and have **handed it over** to the men in
1 Chr	28. 8	and so that you may **hand** it on to succeeding generations for
2 Chr	28.14	So then the army **handed** the prisoners and the loot over
	34. 9	in the Temple was **handed over** to Hilkiah the High Priest.
	34.10	This money was then **handed over** to the three men in
	34.17	kept in the Temple and **handed it over** to the workmen and
	36.17	God **handed them all over** to him.
Ezra	1. 8	He **handed them over** to Mithredath, chief of the royal treasury,
	3.10	Lord according to the instructions **handed** down from the time
	5.14	Cyrus **handed** these utensils over to a man named Sheshbazzar,
	8.29	room weigh them and **hand them over** to the leaders of the
	8.33	the utensils, and **handed them over** to Meremoth the priest,
Job	16.11	God has **handed me over** to evil men.
Is	19. 4	I will **hand the Egyptians over** to a tyrant, to a cruel
Jer	26.24	of Shaphan, I was not **handed over** to the people and killed.
	29.21	said that he will **hand them over** to the power of King
	32. 4	He will be **handed over** to the king of Babylonia;
	34. 2	"I, the Lord, will **hand this city over** to the king of
	34. 3	you will be captured and **handed over** to him.
	34.20	I will **hand them over** to their enemies, who want to kill
	34.21	I will also **hand over** King Zedekiah of Judah and his
	34.21	I will **hand them over** to the Babylonian army, which has
	37.17	added, "You will be **handed over** to the king of Babylonia."
	38.16	you to death or **hand you over** to the men who want
	38.18	then this city will be **handed over** to the Babylonians, who
	38.19	I may be **handed over** to them and tortured."
	38.20	I said, "You will not be **handed over** to them.
	39.17	and you will not be **handed over** to the men you are
	44.30	I will **hand over** King Hophra of Egypt to his enemies who
	44.30	kill him, just as I **handed over** King Zedekiah of Judah to
	46.26	trust in him, [26] and **hand them over** to those who want to
Ezek	11. 9	take you out of the city and **hand you over** to foreigners.
	16.27	I have **handed you over** to the Philistines, who hate you and
	21.24	You stand condemned, and I will **hand you over** to your enemies.
	21.31	And I will **hand you over** to brutal men, experts at destruction.
	23. 9	So I **handed her over** to her Assyrian lovers whom she
	23.24	I will **hand you over** to them, and they will judge you
	23.28	"I will **hand you over** to people you hate and are disgusted
	25. 7	you did, I will **hand you over** to other nations who will
	44.28	Israel to be **handed** down from one generation to another.
Obad	14	You should not have **handed them over** to the enemy on the
Mic	1.15	Mareshah, the Lord will **hand you over** to an enemy, who is
Mt	5.25	he will **hand you over** to the judge,
	5.25	who will **hand you over** to the police,
	10.21	"Men will **hand over** their own brothers to be put to death,
	15. 2	your disciples disobey the teaching **handed** down by our ancestors?
	17.22	Man is about to be **handed over** to men [23] who will kill
	19. 7	law for a man to **hand** his wife a divorce notice and
	20.18	Son of Man will be **handed over** to the chief priests and
	20.19	to death [19] and then **hand him over** to the Gentiles, who
	24. 9	you will be arrested and **handed over** to be punished and be
	25.20	coins came in and **handed over** the other five thousand.
	26. 2	and the Son of Man will be **handed over** to be crucified."
	26.16	was looking for a good chance to **hand Jesus over** to them.
	26.45	Son of Man to be **handed over** to the power of sinful
	27. 2	chains, led him off, and **handed him over** to Pilate, the
	27.18	the Jewish authorities had **handed Jesus over** to him because they
	27.26	he had Jesus whipped, he **handed him over** to be crucified.
Mk	7. 5	do not follow the teaching **handed** down by our ancestors,
	9.31	Son of Man will be **handed over** to men who will kill
	10.33	Son of Man will be **handed over** to the chief priests and
	10.33	to death and then **hand him over** to the Gentiles, [34] who
	12. 9	kill those men and **hand the vineyard over** to other tenants.
	13.12	Men will **hand over** their own brothers to be put to death,
	14.11	looking for a good chance to **hand Jesus over** to them.
	14.23	took a cup, gave thanks to God, and **handed** it to them;
	14.41	of Man is now being **handed over** to the power of sinful
	15. 1	Jesus in chains, led him away, and **handed him over** to Pilate.
	15.10	that the chief priests had **handed Jesus over** to him because
	15.15	Then he had Jesus whipped and **handed him over** to be crucified.
Lk	4. 6	"It has all been **handed over** to me, and I can give
	4.17	the Scriptures [17] and was **handed** the book of the prophet Isaiah.
	9.44	Man is going to be **handed over** to the power of men."
	12.58	the judge, who will **hand you over** to the police, and you
	16. 2	**Hand** in a complete account of your handling of my property,
	18.32	He will be **handed over** to the Gentiles, who will mock him,
	20.16	those men, and **hand the vineyard over** to other tenants."
	20.20	so that they could **hand him over** to the authority and power
	21.12	you will be **handed over** to be tried in synagogues and be
	21.16	You will be **handed over** by your parents, your brothers,
	22. 6	for a good chance to **hand Jesus over** to them without the
	23.25	riot and murder, and he **handed Jesus over** for them to do
	24. 7	Son of Man must be **handed over** to sinful men, be crucified,
Lk	24.20	Our chief priests and rulers **handed him over** to be sentenced
Jn	18.35	own people and the chief priests who **handed you over** to me.
	18.36	to keep me from being **handed over** to the Jewish authorities.
	19.11	So the man who **handed me over** to you is guilty of
	19.16	Then Pilate **handed Jesus over** to them to be crucified.
Acts	2.23	God had already decided that Jesus would be **handed over** to you;
	3.13	But you **handed him over** to the authorities, and you rejected
	4.35	from the sale, [35] and **hand it over** to the apostles;
	4.37	brought the money, and **handed it over** to the apostles.
	5. 2	money for himself and **handed the rest over** to the apostles.
	7.53	received God's law, that was **handed** down by angels—yet you
	12. 4	in jail, where he was **handed over** to be guarded by four
	21.11	Jews in Jerusalem, and they will **hand him over** to the Gentiles."
	23.33	the letter to the governor, and **handed Paul over** to him.
	25.11	they bring against me, no one can **hand me over** to them.
	27. 1	should sail to Italy, they **handed** Paul and some other prisoners
	28.17	made a prisoner in Jerusalem and **handed over** to the Romans.
Rom	4.25	of our sins he was **handed over** to die, and he was
	15.28	finished this task and have **handed over** to them all the
1 Cor	5. 5	us, [5] you are to **hand this man over** to Satan for his
	11. 2	me and follow the teachings that I have **handed** on to you.
	15.24	authorities, and powers, and will **hand over** the Kingdom to God
Gal	3.19	The Law was **handed** down by angels, with a man acting as
Col	2. 8	which comes from the teachings **handed** down by men and from
1 Pet	1.18	the worthless manner of life **handed** down by your ancestors.

HANDIWORK

Is	17. 8	or trust in their own **handiwork**—symbols of the goddess

HANDKERCHIEF

Is	3.23	their revealing garments, their linen **handkerchiefs,** and
Lk	19.20	I kept it hidden in a **handkerchief.**
Acts	19.12	Even **handkerchiefs** and aprons he had used were taken to those

HANDLE (1)

Deut	19. 5	the axe comes off the **handle** and kills the other, he can
Judg	3.22	The whole sword went in, **handle** and all, and the fat
Song	5. 5	with liquid myrrh, as I grasped the **handle** of the door.

HANDLE (2)

Lk	16. 2	a complete account of your **handling** of my property,
	16. 8	are much more shrewd in **handling** their affairs than the
	16.11	have not been faithful in **handling** worldly wealth, how can
Acts	6. 2	neglect the preaching of God's word in order to **handle** finances.
2 Cor	2.17	like so many others, who **handle** God's message as if it were
	8.20	any complaints about the way we **handle** this generous gift.
Col	2.21	obey such rules as [21] "Don't **handle** this," "Don't taste that,"

HANDSOME

1 Sam	9. 2	a son named Saul, a **handsome** man in the prime of life.
	9. 2	than anyone else in Israel and more **handsome** as well.
	16. 7	to him, "Pay no attention to how tall and **handsome** he is.
	16.12	He was a **handsome,** healthy young man, and his eyes sparkled.
	16.18	is also a brave and **handsome** man, a good soldier, and an
1 Kgs	1. 5	He was a very **handsome** man.
Ps	45. 2	You are the most **handsome** of men;
Prov	1. 9	improve your character as a **handsome** turban or a necklace
Song	1.16	How **handsome** you are, my dearest;
	5.10	My lover is **handsome** and strong;
Is	44.13	form of a man, a **handsome** human figure, to be placed in
Ezek	23. 6	all of them were **handsome** young cavalry officers.
	23.12	for the cavalry officers, all those **handsome** young men.
	23.23	I will gather all those **handsome** young noblemen and officers,
	28.12	How wise and **handsome** you were!
	28.17	You were proud of being **handsome,** and your fame made you
Dan	1. 4	They had to be **handsome,** intelligent, well-trained,

HANG (1)

[HUNG]

Ex	26.12	**Hang** the extra half-piece over the back of the Tent.
	26.13	of the length is to **hang** over the sides of the Tent
	26.32	**Hang** it on four posts of acacia-wood covered with gold,
	30. 6	the curtain which **hangs** in front of the Covenant Box.
	40. 5	of the Covenant Box and **hang** the curtain at the entrance of
	40. 8	the surrounding enclosure and **hang** the curtain at its entrance.
	40.21	he put the box in the Tent and **hung** up the curtain.
	40.28	He **hung** the curtain at the entrance of the Tent,
	40.33	Tent and the altar and **hung** the curtain at the entrance of
2 Sam	4.12	hands and feet, which they **hung** up near the pool in Hebron.
	18. 9	The mule ran on and Absalom was left **hanging** in mid air.
	18.10	to Joab, "Sir, I saw Absalom **hanging** in an oak-tree!"
	18.14	Absalom's chest while he was still alive, **hanging** in the oak-tree.
1 Chr	10.10	one of their temples and **hung** his head in the temple of
Job	9. 9	God **hung** the stars in the sky—the Great Bear, Orion, the
	19.20	My skin **hangs** loose on my bones;
	26. 7	out the northern sky and **hung** the earth in empty space.
Ps	137. 2	On the willows near by we **hung** up our harps.
Prov	4.25	don't **hang** your head in shame.
Song	4. 4	with a necklace like a thousand shields **hung** round it.
Is	13. 7	Everyone's hands will **hang** limp,
	22.24	will hang on him like pots and bowls **hanging** from a peg!
	22.25	that will be the end of everything that was **hanging** on it."
	25. 7	cloud of sorrow that has been **hanging** over all the nations.
Jer	2.37	You will turn away from Egypt, **hanging** your head in shame.
	6.24	say the people of Jerusalem, "and our hands **hang** limp;

Jer 10.20 there is no one to **hang** their curtains."
31.19 After you had punished us, we **hung** our heads in grief.
47. 3 their hands will **hang** limp at their sides.
50.43 The king of Babylonia hears the news, and his hands **hang** limp.
Lam 1.14 He **hung** them round my neck, and I grew weak beneath the
Ezek 15. 3 you even make a peg out of it to **hang** things on?
21. 7 fear, their hands will **hang** limp, their courage will fail,
27.10 They **hung** their shields and their helmets in your barracks.
27.11 They **hung** their shields on your walls.
Dan 5.29 of royal purple and to **hang** a gold chain of honour round
Zeph 3.16 Do not let your hands **hang** limp!
Mt 27.51 Then the curtain **hanging** in the Temple was torn in two
Mk 15.38 The curtain **hanging** in the Temple was torn in two, from
Lk 23.45 and the curtain **hanging** in the Temple was torn in two.
Acts 28. 4 The natives saw the snake **hanging** on Paul's hand and said

HANG (2)

[HUNG]

Gen 40.19 Then he will **hang** your body on a pole, and the birds
Deut 21.22 crime and his body is **hung** on a post, [23] it is not
21.23 because a dead body **hanging** on a post brings God's curse
Josh 8.29 He **hanged** the king of Ai from a tree and left his
10.26 Joshua killed the kings and **hanged** them on five trees, where
2 Sam 17.23 After putting his affairs in order, he **hanged** himself.
21. 6 and we will **hang** them before the Lord at Gibeah,
21. 9 the people of Gibeon, who **hanged** them on the mountain before
21.12 Shan, where the Philistines had **hanged** the bodies on the day
21.13 gathered up the bones of the seven men who had been **hanged.**
Esth 2.23 the report was true, so both men were **hanged** on the gallows.
5.14 the king to have Mordecai **hanged** on it, and then you can
6. 4 the king to have Mordecai **hanged** on the gallows that was now
7. 9 that he could **hang** Mordecai, who saved Your Majesty's life.
7. 9 **"Hang** Haman on it!"
7.10 So Haman was **hanged** on the gallows that he had built for
8. 7 the Jew, "Look, I have **hanged** Haman for his plot against
9.13 bodies of Haman's ten sons to be **hung** from the gallows."
9.25 for the Jews—he and his sons were **hanged** from the gallows.
Lam 5.12 Our leaders have been taken and **hanged;**
Mt 27. 5 then he went off and **hanged** himself.
Lk 23.39 One of the criminals **hanging** there hurled insults at him:
Gal 3.13 scripture says, "Anyone who is **hanged** on a tree is under

HANNAH

Samuel's mother and wife of Elkanah (1).

1 Sam 1. 2 Elkanah had two wives, **Hannah** and Peninnah.
1. 2 Peninnah had children, but **Hannah** had none.
1. 5 And even though he loved **Hannah** very much he would give
1. 7 Peninnah would upset **Hannah** so much that she would cry
1. 8 Her husband Elkanah would ask her, **"Hannah,** why are you crying?
1. 9 meal in the house of the Lord at Shiloh, **Hannah** got up.
1.11 **Hannah** made a solemn promise:
1.12 **Hannah** continued to pray to the Lord for a long time,
1.19 with his wife **Hannah,** and the Lord answered her prayer.
1.22 But this time **Hannah** did not go.
1.23 So **Hannah** stayed at home and nursed her child.
1.26 **Hannah** said to him, "Excuse me, sir.
2. 1 **Hannah** prayed:
2.21 The Lord did bless **Hannah,** and she had three more sons

HAPPEN

Mt 1.22 Now all this **happened** in order to make what the Lord had
8.33 story and what had **happened** to the men with the demons.
9.29 eyes and said, "Let it **happen,** then, just as you believe!"
11.26 Yes, Father, this was how you wanted it to **happen.**
12.45 This is what will **happen** to the evil people of this day."
13.40 so the same thing will **happen** at the end of the age:
13.44 A man **happens** to find a treasure hidden in a field.
16.22 "That must never **happen** to you!"
18. 7 Such things will always **happen—**but how terrible for the one
18.31 other servants saw what had **happened,** they were very upset
21. 4 This **happened** in order to make what the prophet had said
22.26 The same thing **happened** to the second brother, to the third,
24. 3 they asked, "and what will **happen** to show that it is the
24. 6 Such things must **happen,** but they do not mean that the end
24.34 all these things will **happen** before the people now living have
24.37 of Man will be like what **happened** in the time of Noah.
24.39 did not realize what was **happening** until the flood came and
26.54 Scriptures come true which say that this is what must **happen?"**
26.56 But all this has **happened** in order to make what the
27.54 earthquake and everything else that **happened,** they were terrified
28.11 the city and told the chief priests everything that had **happened.**
Mk 2.26 This **happened** when Abiathar was the High Priest.
4.27 Yet he does not know how it **happens.**
5.14 to see what had **happened,** [15] and when they came to Jesus,
5.16 the people what had **happened** to the man with the demons,
5.33 The woman realized what had **happened** to her, so she came,
5.42 When this **happened,** they were completely amazed.
10.32 and spoke of the things that were going to **happen** to him.
11.21 Peter remembered what had **happened** and said to Jesus, "Look,
11.23 that what he says will **happen,** it will be done for him.
12.21 The same thing **happened** to the third brother, [22] and then
13. 4 "and tell us what will **happen** to show that the time has
13. 7 Such things must **happen,** but they do not mean that the end
13.18 Pray to God that these things will not **happen** in the winter!
13.29 when you see these things **happening,** you will know that the
13.30 all these things will **happen** before the people now living have

Lk 1.38 "may it **happen** to me as you have said."
1.43 Why should this great thing **happen** to me, that my Lord's
2.15 this thing that has **happened,** which the Lord has told us."
5. 8 Simon Peter saw what had **happened,** he fell on his knees
6.23 Be glad when that **happens,** and dance for joy, because a
8.34 of the pigs saw what **happened,** so they ran off and spread
8.35 out to see what had **happened,** and when they came to Jesus,
8.56 but Jesus commanded them not to tell anyone what had **happened.**
9. 7 all the things that were **happening,** he was very confused,
10.21 Yes, Father, this was how you wanted it to **happen.**
10.31 It so **happened** that a priest was going down that road;
14. 5 son or an ox that **happened** to fall in a well on
14. 8 It could **happen** that someone more important than you has been
14.29 and all who see what **happened** will laugh at him.
17. 1 into sin are bound to **happen,**
17. 1 but how terrible for the one who makes them **happen!**
20.31 The same thing **happened** to all seven—they died without having children.
21. 7 And what will **happen** in order to show that the time has
21. 9 such things must **happen** first, but they do not mean that the
21.25 "There will be strange things **happening** to the sun, the moon,
21.28 When these things begin to **happen,** stand up and raise your heads,
21.31 you see these things **happening,** you will know that the Kingdom
21.36 all those things that will **happen** and to stand before the
22.49 saw what was going to **happen,** they asked, "Shall we use our
23.31 when the wood is green, what will **happen** when it is dry?"
23.47 army officer saw what had **happened,** and he praised God, saying,
23.48 watch the spectacle saw what **happened,** they all went back home,
24.12 Then he went back home amazed at what had **happened.**
24.14 to each other about all the things that had **happened.**
24.18 the things that have been **happening** there these last few days?"
24.19 "The things that **happened** to Jesus of Nazareth," they
24.21 Besides all that, this is now the third day since it **happened.**
24.35 explained to them what had **happened** on the road, and how
Jn 1.28 All this **happened** in Bethany on the east side of the
5. 9 The day this **happened** was a Sabbath, [10] so the Jewish authorities
5.14 so stop sinning or something worse may **happen** to you."
9.35 When Jesus heard what had **happened,** he found the man and
11. 4 this has **happened** in order to bring glory to God, and it
12.17 and raised him from death had reported what had **happened.**
13.19 you this now before it **happens,** so that when it does happen,
14.29 this now before it all **happens,** so that when it does happen,
15.25 This, however, was bound to **happen** so that what is
18. 4 everything that was going to **happen** to him, so he stepped
18.32 (This **happened** in order to make the words of Jesus come true,
19.24 This **happened** in order to make the scripture come true:
19.35 (The one who saw this **happen** has spoken of it, so that
21. 1 This is how it **happened.**
Acts 2.22 You yourselves know this, for it **happened** here among you.
3.10 were all surprised and amazed at what had **happened** to him.
3.24 also announced what has been **happening** these days.
4.21 because the people were all praising God for what had **happened.**
4.28 you by your power and will had already decided would **happen.**
5. 7 three hours later his wife, not knowing what had **happened,**
5.24 guards heard this, they wondered what had **happened** to the apostles.
7.40 do not know what has **happened** to that man Moses, who brought
8.24 that none of these things you spoke of will **happen** to me."
10. 8 He told them what had **happened** and sent them off to Joppa.
10.16 This **happened** three times, and then the thing was taken back
11. 4 a complete account of what had **happened** from the very beginning:
11.10 This **happened** three times, and finally the whole thing was drawn
12. 3 (This **happened** during the time of the Festival of Unleavened Bread.)
12.11 Then Peter realized what had **happened** to him, and said,
12.11 power and from everything the Jewish people expected to **happen."**
12.18 tremendous confusion among the guards—what had **happened** to Peter?
13.12 When the governor saw what had **happened,** he believed;
13.37 But this did not **happen** to the one whom God raised from
13.40 then, so that what the prophets said may not **happen** to you:
14. 1 The same thing **happened** in Iconium:
17.17 square every day with the people who **happened** to pass by.
19.21 After these things had **happened,** Paul made up his mind
19.40 For after what has **happened** today, there is the danger
20.22 to Jerusalem, not knowing what will **happen** to me there.
21.34 find out exactly what had **happened,** so he ordered his men to
26.22 thing which the prophets and Moses said was going to **happen:**
26.26 for this thing has not **happened** hidden away in a corner.
28. 6 not seeing anything unusual **happening** to him, they changed their
28. 9 When this **happened,** all the other sick people on the
1 Cor 2. 9 no one ever thought could **happen,** is the very thing God
10. 1 brothers, what **happened** to our ancestors who followed Moses.
10.11 All these things **happened** to them as examples for others,
2 Cor 1. 9 But this **happened** so that we should rely, not on ourselves,
12. 2 not know whether this actually **happened** or whether he had a
12. 3 not know whether this actually **happened** or whether it was a
Gal 4.15 What has **happened?**
Phil 1.12 that the things that have **happened** to me have really helped
Col 4. 9 They will tell you everything that is **happening** here.
1 Thes 2.14 Our brothers, the same things **happened** to you
2.14 that **happened** to the churches of God in
3. 4 and as you well know, that is exactly what **happened.**
5. 1 about the times and occasions when these things will **happen.**
2 Thes 2. 6 something that keeps this from **happening** now, and you know what
2. 7 but what is going to **happen** will not happen until the one
2 Tim 3. 9 That is just what **happened** to Jannes and Jambres.

2 Tim 3.11 You know all that **happened** to me in Antioch, Iconium, and
Jas 3.10 My brothers, this should not **happen!**
1 Pet 4.12 suffering, as though something unusual were **happening** to you.
2 Pet 2. 6 and made them an example of what will **happen** to the godless.
2.22 What **happened** to them shows that the proverbs are true:
Rev 1. 1 in order to show his servants what must **happen** very soon.
1. 3 For the time is near when all these things will **happen.**
1.19 things that are now and the things that will **happen** afterwards.
4. 1 up here, and I will show you what must **happen** after this."
22. 6 his angel to show his servants what must **happen** very soon."
22.10 secret, because the time is near when all this will **happen.**

HAPPILY MARRIED

Is 62. 4 Your land will be called **"Happily Married,"** Because the

HAPPY

Am see also **MERRY**

HAPPY
[UNHAPPY]

Gen 30.13 bore Jacob another son, [13]and Leah said, "How **happy** I am!
30.13 Now women will call me **happy";**
Ex 18. 9 all this, he was **happy** [10]and said, "Praise the Lord,
Deut 12.18 And you are to be **happy** there over everything that you have
24. 5 so that he can stay at home and make his wife **happy.**
33.29 Israel, how **happy** you are!
Judg 9.13 to stop producing my wine, that makes gods and men **happy.'**
9.19 then be happy with Abimelech and let him be **happy** with you.
18.20 This made the priest very **happy,** so he took the sacred
1 Sam 2. 1 how **happy** I am because of what he has done!
2 Sam 19. 6 that you would be quite **happy** if Absalom were alive today
1 Kgs 4.20 they ate and drank, and were **happy.**
8.66 praised him and went home **happy** because of all the blessings
2 Kgs 11.20 people were filled with **happiness,** and the city was quiet,
1 Chr 29. 9 the Lord, and they were **happy** that so much had been given.
29. 9 King David also was extremely **happy.**
29.17 are gathered here have been **happy** to bring offerings to you.
29.22 that day they were very **happy** as they ate and drank in
2 Chr 6.41 all your people be **happy** because of your goodness to them.
7.10 They were **happy** about all the blessings that the Lord had
15.15 the people of Judah were **happy** because they had made this
23.21 people were filled with **happiness,** and the city was quiet,
29.36 Hezekiah and the people were **happy,** because God had helped
30.25 So everyone was **happy**—the people of Judah, the priests,
Neh 2. 2 You aren't ill, so it must be that you're **unhappy."**
8.17 of Joshua son of Nun, and everybody was excited and **happy.**
12.43 were full of joy because God had made them very **happy.**
Esth 5. 9 Haman left the banquet he was **happy** and in a good mood.
5.14 hanged on it, and then you can go to the banquet **happy."**
8.16 Jews there was joy and relief, **happiness** and a sense of victory.
8.17 the Jews held a joyful holiday with feasting and **happiness.**
9.22 time of grief and despair into a time of joy and **happiness.**
Job 3.22 They are not **happy** till they are dead and buried;
5.17 **Happy** is the person whom God corrects!
7. 7 my **happiness** has already ended.
20. 5 placed on earth, [5]no wicked man has been **happy** for long.
21.21 over, does he really care whether his children are **happy?**
21.23 they die **happy** and at ease, their bodies well-nourished.
21.25 Others have no **happiness** at all;
30.26 I hoped for **happiness** and light, but trouble and darkness came instead.
Ps 1. 1 **Happy** are those who reject the advice of evil men, who do
2.12 **Happy** are all who go to him for protection.
5.11 because of you they are truly **happy.**
14. 7 How **happy** the people of Israel will be when the Lord makes
19. 5 in the morning like a **happy** bridegroom, like an athlete
19. 8 of the Lord are right, and those who obey them are **happy.**
32. 1 **Happy** are those whose sins are forgiven, whose wrongs are pardoned.
32. 2 **Happy** is the man whom the Lord does not accuse of doing
33.12 **Happy** is the nation whose God is the Lord;
33.12 **happy** are the people he has chosen for his own!
34. 8 **Happy** are those who find safety with him.
34.12 Do you want long life and **happiness?**
35. 9 I will be **happy** because he saved me.
37. 4 Seek your **happiness** in the Lord, and he will give you your
39.13 that I may have some **happiness** before I go away and am
40. 4 **Happy** are those who trust the Lord, who do not turn to
40.14 May those who are **happy** because of my troubles be turned
41. 1 **Happy** are those who are concerned for the poor;
41. 2 he will make them **happy** in the land;
42. 4 as they walked along, a **happy** crowd, singing and shouting
43. 4 you are the source of my **happiness.**
45. 7 and has poured out more **happiness** on you than on any other
51. 8 have crushed me and broken me, I will be **happy** once again.
53. 6 How **happy** the people of Israel will be when God makes them
65. 4 **Happy** are those whom you choose, whom you bring to live in
68. 3 they are **happy** and shout for joy.
68. 6 and leads prisoners out into **happy** freedom, but rebels will
70. 2 May those who are **happy** because of my troubles be turned
84. 4 How **happy** are those who live in your Temple, always
84. 5 How **happy** are those whose strength comes from you, who are
84.12 Lord Almighty, how **happy** are those who trust in you!
89.15 How **happy** are the people who worship you with songs, who
89.42 you have made them all **happy.**
90.15 Give us now as much **happiness** as the sadness you gave us
92.10 you have blessed me with **happiness.**
94.12 Lord, how **happy** is the person you instruct, the one to
Ps 100. 2 come before him with **happy** songs!
104.15 wine to make him **happy,** olive-oil to make him cheerful,
104.31 May the Lord be **happy** with what he has made!
106. 3 **Happy** are those who obey his commands, who always do what
106. 5 people and share in the **happiness** of your nation, in the
112. 1 **Happy** is the person who honours the Lord, who takes pleasure
112. 5 **Happy** is the person who is generous with his loans, who
113. 9 he makes her **happy** by giving her children.
118.24 let us be **happy,** let us celebrate!
119. 1 **Happy** are those whose lives are faultless, who live
119. 2 **Happy** are those who follow his commands, who obey him with
119.35 obedient to your commandments, because in them I find **happiness.**
119.56 I find my **happiness** in obeying your commands.
119.162 How **happy** I am because of your promises—
119.162 as **happy** as someone who finds rich treasure.
119.174 I find **happiness** in your law.
126. 3 how **happy** we were!
127. 5 **Happy** is the man who has many such arrows.
128. 1 **Happy** are those who obey the Lord, who live by his commands.
128. 2 you will be **happy** and prosperous.
137. 8 **Happy** is the man who pays you back for what you have
144.15 **Happy** is the nation of whom this is true;
144.15 **happy** are the people whose God is the Lord!
146. 5 **Happy** is the man who has the God of Jacob to help
Prov 3.13 **Happy** is the man who becomes wise—who gains understanding.
3.18 Those who become wise are **happy;**
3.22 They will provide you with life—a pleasant and **happy** life.
5.18 So be **happy** with your wife and find your joy with the
5.19 Let her charms keep you **happy;**
7.18 We'll be **happy** in each other's arms.
8.31 happy in his presence— [31]**happy** with the world
8.32 Do as I say, and you will be **happy.**
8.34 listens to me will be **happy**— the man who stays at
11. 1 He is **happy** with honest weights.
11.10 A city is **happy** when honest people have good fortune,
12.20 surprise, but those who work for good will find **happiness.**
12.25 Worry can rob you of **happiness,** but kind words will
14.13 When **happiness** is gone, sorrow is always there.
14.21 If you want to be **happy,** be kind to the poor;
15.13 When people are **happy,** they smile, but when they are sad,
15.15 is a constant struggle, but **happy** people always enjoy life.
15.20 A wise son makes his father **happy.**
15.21 Stupid people are **happy** with their foolishness, but the
15.30 Smiling faces make you **happy,** and good news makes you feel better.
16.14 A wise man will try to keep the king **happy;**
16.20 trust in the Lord and you will be **happy.**
21.15 is done, good people are **happy,** but evil people are brought
23.15 Son, if you become wise, I will be very **happy.**
23.24 A righteous man's father has good reason to be **happy.**
23.25 give your mother that **happiness.**
27. 9 fragrant oils make you feel **happier,** but trouble shatters
27.11 Be wise, my son, and I will be **happy;**
28.14 Always obey the Lord and you will be **happy.**
28.20 Honest people will lead a full, **happy** life.
29. 2 me a righteous ruler and I will show you a **happy** people.
29. 6 in their own sins, while honest people are **happy** and free.
29.18 **Happy** is the man who keeps God's law!
31. 7 Let them drink and forget their poverty and **unhappiness.**
Ecc 2. 1 I decided to enjoy myself and find out what **happiness** is.
2.26 God gives wisdom, knowledge, and **happiness** to those who please
3.12 can do is to be **happy** and do the best we can
5.20 has allowed him to be **happy,** he will not worry too much
6. 3 not get his share of **happiness** and does not receive a decent
7. 4 Someone who is always thinking about **happiness** is a fool.
7.14 God sends both **happiness** and trouble;
9. 7 Go ahead—eat your food and be **happy;**
9. 8 Always look **happy** and cheerful.
10.19 Feasting makes you **happy** and wine cheers you up, but you
11. 9 Be **happy** while you are still young.
Song 1. 4 We will be **happy** together, drink deep, and lose ourselves in love.
Is 3.10 Righteous men will be **happy,** and things will go well for them.
9. 3 you have made them **happy.**
16.10 No one is **happy** now in the fertile fields.
23.12 City of Sidon, your **happiness** has ended,
24. 7 Everyone who was once **happy** is now sad, [8]and the joyful
24. 9 There is no more **happy** singing over wine;
24.11 **Happiness** is gone for ever;
25. 9 him, and now we are **happy** and joyful because he has saved
29.19 will once again find the **happiness** which the Lord, the holy
30.18 **Happy** are those who put their trust in the Lord.
30.29 you, God's people, will be **happy** and sing as you do on
30.29 You will be as **happy** as those who walk to the music
32.13 the houses where people were **happy** and for the city that was
32.20 How **happy** everyone will be with plenty of water for the
35.10 They will be **happy** for ever, for ever free from sorrow and
41.16 Then you will be **happy** because I am your God;
51.11 They will be **happy** for ever, for ever free from sorrow and
65.13 They will be **happy,** but you will be disgraced.
65.18 make will be full of joy, and her people will be **happy.**
Jer 7.34 joy and gladness and to the **happy** sounds of wedding feasts.
11.15 Will that make them **happy?**
15.10 What an **unhappy** man I am!
15.16 and so your words filled my heart with joy and **happiness.**
16. 9 of joy and gladness and the **happy** sounds of wedding feasts.
25.10 of joy and gladness and the **happy** sounds of wedding feasts.
31.13 girls will dance and be **happy,** and men, young and old, will
33.11 of gladness and joy and the **happy** sounds of wedding feasts.
48.33 **Happiness** and joy have been taken away from the fertile
49.25 The famous city that used to be **happy** is completely deserted.

Jer	50.11	You are **happy** and glad, going about like a cow threshing
	51.39	I will prepare them a feast and make them drunk and **happy.**
Lam	3.17	I have forgotten what health and peace and **happiness** are.
	5.15	**Happiness** has gone out of our lives;
Dan	12.12	**Happy** are those who remain faithful until 1,335 days are over!
Jon	4. 1	Jonah was very **unhappy** about this and became angry.
Zech	10. 7	will be strong like soldiers, **happy** like men who have been
Mal	3.12	all nations will call you **happy,** because your land will be a
	3.15	As we see it, proud people are the ones who are **happy.**
	4. 2	will be as free and **happy** as calves let out of a
Mt	2. 9	When they saw it, how **happy** they were, what joy was theirs!
	5. 3	**"Happy** are those who know they are spiritually poor;
	5. 4	**"Happy** are those who mourn;
	5. 5	**"Happy** are those who are humble;
	5. 6	**"Happy** are those whose greatest desire is to do what God requires;
	5. 7	**"Happy** are those who are merciful to others;
	5. 8	**"Happy** are the pure in heart;
	5. 9	**"Happy** are those who work for peace;
	5.10	**"Happy** are those who are persecuted because they do what God requires;
	5.11	**"Happy** are you when people insult you and persecute you
	5.12	Be **happy** and glad, for a great reward is kept for you
	11. 6	How **happy** are those who have no doubts about me!"
	13.44	up again, and is so **happy** that he goes and sells everything
	18.13	tell you, he feels far **happier** over this one sheep than over
	24.46	How **happy** that servant is if his master finds him doing
	25.21	Come on in and share my **happiness!'**
	25.23	Come on in and share my **happiness!'**
Lk	1.14	How glad and **happy** you will be,
	1.14	and how **happy** many others will be when he
	1.45	How **happy** you are to believe that the Lord's message to
	1.48	all people will call me **happy,** [49] because of the great things
	6.20	Jesus looked at his disciples and said, **"Happy** are you poor;
	6.21	**"Happy** are you who are hungry now;
	6.21	**"Happy** are you who weep now;
	6.22	**"Happy** are you when people hate you, reject you, insult you,
	7.23	How **happy** are those who have no doubts about me!"
	11.27	and said to him, "How **happy** is the woman who bore you
	11.28	Jesus answered, "Rather, how **happy** are those who hear the word
	12.37	How **happy** are those servants whose master finds them awake
	12.38	How **happy** they are if he finds them ready, even if he
	12.43	How **happy** that servant is if his master finds him doing
	14.15	he said to Jesus, "How **happy** are those who will sit down
	15. 5	finds it, he is so **happy** that he puts it on his
	15. 6	says to them, 'I am so **happy** I found my lost sheep.
	15. 9	to them, 'I am so **happy** I found the coin I lost.
	15.32	had to celebrate and be **happy,** because your brother was dead,
Jn	3.29	This is how my own **happiness** is made complete.
	13.17	you know this truth, how **happy** you will be if you put
	16.21	her suffering, because she is **happy** that a baby has been
	16.24	you will receive, so that your **happiness** may be complete.
	20.29	How **happy** are those who believe without seeing me!"
Acts	5.41	they were **happy,** because God had considered them worthy
	12.14	Peter's voice and was so **happy** that she ran back in without
	14.17	he gives you food and fills your hearts with **happiness."**
	20.35	'There is more **happiness** in giving than in receiving.'"
	24.10	many years, and so I am **happy** to defend myself before you.
Rom	4. 6	when he spoke of the **happiness** of the person whom God
	4. 7	**"Happy** are those whose wrongs are forgiven,
	4. 8	**Happy** is the person whose sins the Lord will not keep
	4. 9	Does this **happiness** that David spoke of belong only to those
	7.24	What an **unhappy** man I am!
	12.15	Be **happy** with those who are happy, weep with those who weep.
	14.22	**Happy** is the person who does not feel guilty when he does
	16.19	to the gospel, and for this reason I am **happy** about you.
1 Cor	7.30	those who laugh, as though they were not **happy;**
	7.40	She will be **happier,** however, if she stays as she is.
	12.26	part is praised, all the other parts share its **happiness.**
	13. 6	love is not **happy** with evil, but is happy with the truth.
	16.17	I am **happy** about the coming of Stephanas, Fortunatus,
2 Cor	1.24	Instead, we are working with you for your own **happiness.**
	2. 3	convinced that when I am **happy,**
	2. 3	then all of you are **happy** too.
	7. 7	and so I am even **happier** now.
	7. 9	But now I am **happy**—not because I made you sad, but
	7.13	how **happy** Titus made us with his happiness over the way in
	7.16	How **happy** I am that I can depend on you completely!
	12. 9	I am most **happy,** then, to be proud of my weaknesses, in
Gal	4.15	You were so **happy!**
	4.27	For the scripture says, "Be **happy,** you childless woman!
Phil	1.18	I am **happy** about it—so long as Christ is preached in
	1.18	I will continue to be **happy,** [19] because I know that by
	2. 2	to make me completely **happy** by having the same thoughts,
	4. 1	How **happy** you make me, and how proud I am of you!
Col	1.24	And now I am **happy** about my sufferings for you, for by
Jas	1.12	**Happy** is the person who remains faithful under trials,
	5.11	We call them **happy** because they endured.
	5.13	Is anyone **happy?**
1 Pet	3.14	should suffer for doing what is right, how **happy** you are!
	4.14	**Happy** are you if you are insulted because you are Christ's followers;
2 Jn	4	How **happy** I was to find that some of your children live
	12	talk with you personally, so that we shall be completely **happy.**
3 Jn	3	I was so **happy** when some Christian brothers arrived and
	4	Nothing makes me **happier** than to hear that my children
Rev	1. 3	**Happy** is the one who reads this book,
	1. 3	and **happy** are those who listen to the
	11.10	of the earth will be **happy** because of the death of these
	14.13	**Happy** are those who from now on die in the service of
	16.15	**Happy** is he who stays awake and guards his clothes, so that
Rev	19. 9	**Happy** are those who have been invited to the wedding-feast
	20. 6	**Happy** and greatly blessed are those who are included in
	22. 7	**Happy** are those who obey the prophetic words in this book!"
	22.14	**Happy** are those who wash their robes clean and so have

HARAN (1)

City in Mesopotamia from which Abraham set out for Canaan.

Gen	11.31	They went as far as **Haran** and settled there.
	12. 4	old, he started out from **Haran,** as the Lord had told him
	12. 5	slaves they had acquired in **Haran,** and they started out for
	27.43	to my brother Laban in **Haran,** [44] and stay with him for a
	28.10	Jacob left Beersheba and started towards **Haran.**
	29. 4	"From **Haran,"** they answered.
2 Kgs	19.12	destroyed the cities of Gozan, **Haran,** and Rezeph, and killed
Is	37.12	destroyed the cities of Gozan, **Haran,** and Rezeph, and killed
Ezek	27.23	The cities of **Haran,** Canneh, and Eden, the merchants of Sheba,
Acts	7. 2	had gone to live in **Haran,** the God of glory appeared to
	7. 4	And so he left his country and went to live in **Haran.**

HARBOUR

see also **SAFE HARBOURS**

Is	23. 1	its houses and its **harbour** are in ruins.
Acts	27.12	The **harbour** was not a good one to spend the winter in;
	27.12	Phoenix is a **harbour** in Crete that faces south-west and north-west.

HARD

Gen	3.17	You will have to work **hard** all your life to make it
	3.19	You will have to work **hard** and sweat to make the soil
	4.13	to the Lord, "This punishment is too **hard** for me to bear.
	5.29	this child will bring us relief from all our **hard work";**
	11. 3	Let's make bricks and bake them **hard."**
	18.14	Is anything too **hard** for the Lord?
	30. 8	said, "I have fought a **hard** fight with my sister, but I
	33.13	If they are driven **hard** for even one day, the whole herd
Ex	1.11	slave-drivers over them to crush their spirits with **hard** labour.
	2.11	Hebrews, and he saw how they were forced to do **hard** labour.
	5. 9	Make these men work **harder** and keep them busy, so that
Lev	26.19	rain, and your land will be dry and as **hard** as iron.
	26.20	All your **hard work** will do you no good, because your
	26.24	turn on you and punish you seven times **harder** than before.
Deut	11.10	you sowed seed, you had to work **hard** to irrigate the fields;
	28.23	rain will fall, and your ground will become as **hard** as iron.
	28.33	that you have worked so **hard** to grow, while you receive
Judg	4.24	pressed **harder** and harder against him until they destroyed him.
	9.33	men come out against you, hit them as **hard** as you can!"
	20.34	of all Israel, attacked Gibeah, and the fighting was **hard.**
1 Sam	4.10	The Philistines fought **hard** and defeated the Israelites,
2 Sam	10.12	Let's fight **hard** for our people and for the cities of our
	17. 8	David and his men are **hard** fighters and that they are as
	17.10	is a great soldier and that his men are **hard** fighters.
1 Kgs	11.28	and when Solomon noticed how **hard** he worked, he put him in
	20.37	he hit him a **hard** blow and hurt him.
1 Chr	19.13	Let's fight **hard** for our people and for the cities of our
2 Chr	24.13	All the workmen worked **hard,** and they restored the
Ezra	4.15	Its people have always been **hard** to govern.
	10. 9	It was raining **hard,** and because of the weather and the
	10.13	But they added, "The crowd is too big, and it's raining **hard.**
Job	7. 1	service, like a life of **hard** manual labour, [2] like a slave
	14. 6	let him enjoy his **hard** life—if he can.
	28. 9	Men dig the **hardest** rocks, Dig mountains away at their base.
	37.18	stretch out the sky and make it as **hard** as polished metal?
	38.38	out the rain, [38] rain that **hardens** the dust into lumps?
	41.15	of rows of shields, fastened together and **hard** as stone.
	41.23	it is as **hard** and unyielding as iron.
	41.24	is without fear, as unyielding and **hard** as a millstone.
Ps	107.12	They were worn out from **hard work;**
	127. 2	is useless to work so **hard** for a living, getting up early
Prov	2. 4	Look for it as **hard** as you would for silver or some
	10. 4	lazy will make you poor, but **hard work** will make you rich.
	10.22	**Hard work** can make you no richer.
	12.11	A **hard-working** farmer has plenty to eat, but it is
	12.24	**Hard work** will give you power;
	12.27	are after, but if you work **hard,** you will get a fortune.
	13. 4	A **hard worker** will get everything he wants.
	13.11	The **harder** it is to earn, the more you will have.
	15. 6	wealth, but wicked men lose theirs when **hard** times come.
	16.26	labourer's appetite makes him work **harder,** because he wants
	19. 7	No matter how **hard** he tries, he cannot win any.
	28.19	A **hard-working** farmer has plenty to eat.
	31.10	How **hard** it is to find a capable wife!
	31.17	She is a **hard worker,** strong and industrious.
Ecc	2.11	I had done and how **hard** I had worked doing it, and
	2.20	So I came to regret that I had worked so **hard.**
	4. 4	I have also learnt why people work so **hard** to succeed:
	4. 8	For whom is he working so **hard** and denying himself any pleasure?
	4.12	A rope made of three cords is **hard** to break.
	7.24	It is too deep for us, too **hard** to understand.
	8.17	However **hard** you try, you will never find out.
	9. 1	I thought long and **hard** about all this and saw that God
	9.10	Work **hard** at whatever you do, because there will be no action,
	10.10	you don't sharpen it, you have to work **harder** to use it.
Is	5.28	Their horses' hooves are as **hard** as flint, and their
	14. 3	suffering, and from the **hard work** they were forced to do.
	28.22	If you do, it will be even **harder** for you to escape.
	30.20	will make you go through **hard** times, but he himself will be
	43. 2	the **hard** trials that come will not hurt you.
Jer	5.12	We won't have **hard** times;

Jer 6.28 They are all stubborn rebels, **hard** as bronze and iron.
10.24 but do not be too **hard** on us or punish us when
12.13 they have worked **hard,** but got nothing for it.
Lam 5. 5 Driven **hard** like donkeys or camels, we are tired, but are
Ezek 3. 9 make you as firm as a rock, as **hard** as a diamond;
Dan 10. 1 The message was true but extremely **hard** to understand.
Hos 10.11 on her beautiful neck and to harness her for **harder** work.
Amos 9. 1 the temple columns so **hard** that the whole porch will shake.
Zech 7.12 They closed their minds [12]and made their hearts as **hard** as rock.
Mt 6.13 Do not bring us to **hard** testing, but keep us safe from
7.14 that leads to it is **hard,** and there are few people who
7.25 the rivers overflowed, and the wind blew **hard** against that house.
7.27 the wind blew **hard** against that house, and it fell.
19. 8 to divorce your wives because you are so **hard** to teach.
19.23 it will be very **hard** for rich people to enter the Kingdom
19.24 it is much **harder** for a rich person to enter the Kingdom
23. 4 loads that are heavy and **hard** to carry, yet they aren't
25.24 came in and said, 'Sir, I know you are a **hard** man;
Mk 1.26 evil spirit shook the man **hard,** gave a loud scream, and came
10. 5 wrote this law for you because you are so **hard** to teach.
10.23 and said to them, "How **hard** it will be for rich people
10.24 to say, "My children, how **hard** it is to enter the Kingdom
10.25 It is much **harder** for a rich person to enter the Kingdom
Lk 5. 5 Simon answered, "we worked **hard** all night long and caught nothing.
11. 4 And do not bring us to **hard** testing.'"
11.46 on people's backs which are **hard** to carry, but you yourselves
18.24 was sad and said, "How **hard** it is for rich people to
18.25 It is much **harder** for a rich person to enter the Kingdom
19.21 I was afraid of you, because you are a **hard** man.
19.22 know that I am a **hard** man, taking what is not mine
Jn 6.60 followers heard this and said, "This teaching is too **hard.**
Acts 20.19 the Lord's servant during the **hard** times that came to me
20.35 all things that by working **hard** in this way we must help
27.20 sun or the stars, and the wind kept on blowing very **hard.**
Rom 2. 5 But you have a **hard** and stubborn heart, and so you are
12. 8 whoever has authority should work **hard;**
12.11 Work **hard** and do not be lazy.
16. 6 Greetings to Mary, who has worked so **hard** for you.
1 Cor 4.12 we wear ourselves out with **hard work.**
9.27 I **harden** my body with blows and bring it under complete control,
15.10 I have worked **harder** than any of the other apostles,
2 Cor 2. 5 this because I do not want to be too **hard** on him.)
11.23 I have worked much **harder,** I have been in prison more times,
Phil 4. 3 for they have worked **hard** with me to spread the gospel,
Col 2. 1 Let me tell you how **hard** I have worked for you
4.13 can personally testify to his **hard work** for you
1 Thes 1. 3 love made you work so **hard,** and how your hope in our
2.17 we missed you and how **hard** we tried to see you again!
1 Tim 4.10 We struggle and work **hard,** because we have placed our hope
5.17 especially those who work **hard** at preaching and teaching.
2 Tim 2. 6 farmer who has done the **hard work** should have the first
Heb 5.11 this matter, but it is **hard** to explain to you,
2 Pet 1.10 then, my brothers, try even **harder** to make God's call
1 Jn 5. 3 his commands are not too **hard** for us,
Rev 2. 2 I know how **hard** you have worked and how patient you have
14.13 enjoy rest from their **hard work,** because the results of their

HARDSHIP

Ex 18. 8 also told him about the **hardships** the people had faced on
Num 20.14 You know the **hardships** we have suffered, [15]how our
Deut 8. 2 these past forty years, sending **hardships** to test you,
8.16 He sent **hardships** on you to test you,
26. 7 He heard us and saw our suffering, **hardship,** and misery.
Ps 132. 1 Lord, do not forget David and all the **hardships** he endured.
Rom 8.35 Can trouble do it, or **hardship** or persecution or hunger
2 Cor 6. 4 by patiently enduring troubles, **hardships,** and difficulties.
12.10 am content with weaknesses, insults, **hardships,** persecutions,

HAREM

Esth 2. 3 young girls to your **harem** here in Susa, the capital city.
2. 8 palace in the care of Hegai, who had charge of the **harem.**
2. 9 the best place in the **harem** and assigned seven girls
2.11 of the courtyard of the **harem,** in order to find out how
2.13 When she went from the **harem** to the palace,
2.14 would be taken to another **harem** and put in the care of
2.15 the eunuch in charge of the **harem,** advised her to wear.

AV **HARLOT** see **PROSTITUTE, WHORE**

HARM
[UNHARMED]

Gen 26.29 promise [29]that you will not **harm** us,
26.29 just as we did not **harm** you.
31. 7 But God did not let him **harm** me.
31.29 the power to do you **harm,** but last night the God of
42.22 "I told you not to **harm** the boy, but you wouldn't listen.
48.16 May the angel, who has rescued me from all **harm,** bless
50.15 to pay us back for all the **harm** we did to him?"
Ex 12.13 over you and will not **harm** you when I punish the Egyptians.
24.11 God did not **harm** these leading men of Israel;
29.37 touches it will be **harmed** by the power of its holiness.
30.29 touches them will be **harmed** by the power of its holiness.
Lev 6.18 food-offering will be **harmed** by the power of its holiness.
6.27 of the animal will be **harmed** by the power of its holiness.
Num 5.19 adultery, you will not be **harmed** by the curse that this
5.28 innocent, she will not be **harmed** and will be able to bear
Deut 19.16 If one man tries to **harm** another by falsely accusing him
Josh 2.19 the house with you is **harmed,** then we will be responsible.
9.19 Now we cannot **harm** them.
1 Sam 20. 7 angry, you will know that he is determined to **harm** me.
20. 9 father was determined to **harm** you, wouldn't I tell you?"
20.13 If he intends to **harm** you, may the Lord strike me dead
23.17 My father Saul won't be able to **harm** you.
24. 6 keep me from doing any **harm** to my master, whom the Lord
24. 6 I must not **harm** him in the least, because he is the
24. 9 listen to people who say that I am trying to **harm** you?
24.10 said that I would not **harm** you in the least, because you
24.11 I have no thought of rebelling against you or of **harming** you.
24.12 action against me, for I will not **harm** you in the least.
24.13 And so I will not **harm** you.
24.19 a man catch his enemy and then let him get away **unharmed?**
25. 7 your shepherds have been with us and we did not **harm** them.
25.26 and all who want to **harm** you will be punished like Nabal.
25.34 The Lord has kept me from **harming** you.
26. 9 But David said, "You must not **harm** him!
26. 9 The Lord will certainly punish whoever **harms** his chosen king.
26.11 that I should try to **harm** the one whom the Lord has
26.21 I will never **harm** you again, because you have spared my life
26.23 power, but I did not **harm** you, whom the Lord made king.
2 Sam 12.18 He might do himself some **harm!"**
14.11 David replied, "that your son will not be **harmed** in the least."
18. 5 "For my sake don't **harm** the young man Absalom."
18.12 'For my sake don't **harm** the young man Absalom.'
1 Chr 16.22 "Don't **harm** my chosen servants;
2 Chr 30.20 he forgave the people and did not **harm** them.
Ezra 4.22 once, so that no more **harm** may be done to my interests."
Neh 6. 2 This was a trick of theirs to try to **harm** me.
Esth 9. 2 organized themselves to attack anyone who tried to **harm** them.
Job 5.19 Time after time he will save you from **harm;**
7.20 Are you **harmed** by my sin, you jailer?
10.13 that all that time you were secretly planning to **harm** me.
35. 6 If you sin, that does no **harm** to God.
41.26 no spear or arrow or lance that can **harm** him.
Ps 3. 7 You punish all my enemies and leave them powerless to **harm** me.
71.24 those who tried to **harm** me have been defeated and disgraced.
91. 7 ten thousand all round you, but you will not be **harmed.**
105.15 "Don't **harm** my chosen servants;
141.10 wicked fall into their own traps while I go by **unharmed.**
Prov 3.30 someone for no reason when he has never done you any **harm.**
16.27 Evil people look for ways to **harm** others;
19.23 and you will live a long life, content and safe from **harm.**
31.12 As long as she lives, she does him good and never **harm.**
Is 11. 8 a baby will not be **harmed** if it plays near a poisonous
11. 9 On Zion, God's sacred hill, there will be nothing **harmful** or evil.
27. 3 guard it night and day so that no one will **harm** it.
65.25 On Zion, my sacred hill, there will be nothing **harmful** or evil."
Jer 10. 5 they can cause you no **harm,** and they can do you no
39.12 Do not **harm** him, but do for him whatever he wants."
Ezek 44.19 in order to keep their sacred clothing from **harming** the people.
46.20 to the outer courtyard, where it might **harm** the people."
Dan 3.27 at the three men, who had not been **harmed** by the fire.
Hos 2.18 animals and birds, so that they will not **harm** my people.
Amos 9.10 those who say, 'God will not let any **harm** come near us.'
Mic 3.11 "No **harm** will come to us," they say.
Hab 2. 9 have tried to make your own home safe from **harm** and danger!
Zech 7.10 And do not plan ways of **harming** one another.'
8.17 Do not plan ways of **harming** one another.
Mk 3. 4 To help or to **harm?**
16.18 pick up snakes or drink any poison, they will not be **harmed;**
Lk 4.35 of them and went out of him without doing him any **harm.**
6. 9 To help or to **harm?**
Acts 16.28 But Paul shouted at the top of his voice, "Don't **harm** yourself!
18.10 one will be able to **harm** you, for many in this city
28. 5 the snake off into the fire without being **harmed** at all.
1 Cor 11.17 because your meetings for worship actually do more **harm** than good.
2 Cor 7. 9 sadness was used by God, and so we caused you no **harm.**
Gal 5.15 like wild animals, hurting and **harming** each other, then watch out,
Eph 4.29 Do not use **harmful** words, but only helpful words, the
1 Tim 6. 9 trap of many foolish and **harmful** desires, which pull them down
2 Tim 4.14 Alexander the metal-worker did me much **harm;**
1 Pet 3.13 Who will **harm** you if you are eager to do what is
1 Jn 5.18 of God keeps him safe, and the Evil One cannot **harm** him.
Rev 7. 3 The angel said, "Do not **harm** the earth, the sea, or the
9. 4 They were told not to **harm** the grass or the trees or
9. 4 they could **harm** only the people who did not have the mark
11. 5 If anyone tries to **harm** them, fire comes out of their
11. 5 and in this way, whoever tries to **harm** them will be killed.

HARMLESS DRAGON

Is 30. 7 So I have nicknamed Egypt, 'The **Harmless Dragon.'** "

HARMONY

2 Chr 5.11 singers were accompanied in perfect **harmony** by trumpets, cymbals,
Ps 122. 3 Jerusalem is a city restored in beautiful order and **harmony.**
133. 1 how pleasant, for God's people to live together in **harmony!**
Zech 6.13 throne, and they will work together in peace and **harmony.'**
Mal 2. 6 They lived in **harmony** with me;
1 Cor 14.33 not want us to be in disorder but in **harmony** and peace.

HARNESS

Jer	46. 4	**Harness** your horses and mount them!
Hos	10.11	on her beautiful neck and to **harness** her for harder work.
Zech	14.20	At that time even the **harness** bells of the horses will

HARP

Gen	4.21	ancestor of all musicians who play the **harp** and the flute.
	31.27	with rejoicing and singing to the music of tambourines and **harps.**
1 Sam	10. 5	from the altar on the hill, playing **harps,** drums, flutes,
	16.16	will look for a man who knows how to play the **harp.**
	16.16	the man can play his **harp,** and you will be all right
	16.23	God came on Saul, David would get his **harp** and play it.
	18.10	David was playing the **harp,** as he did every day, and Saul
	19. 9	spear in his hand, and David was there, playing his **harp.**
2 Sam	6. 5	They were playing **harps,** lyres, drums, rattles, and
1 Kgs	10.12	palace, and also to make **harps** and lyres for the musicians.
2 Kgs	3.15	As the musician played his **harp,** the power of the Lord came
1 Chr	13. 8	They sang and played musical instruments—**harps,** drums, cymbals,
	15.16	Levites to sing and to play joyful music on **harps** and cymbals.
	15.17	they chose the following Levites to play the high-pitched **harps:**
	15.17	To play the low-pitched **harps** they chose the following Levites:
	15.28	of trumpets, horns, and cymbals, and the music of **harps.**
	16. 5	Eliab, Benaiah, Obed Edom, and Jeiel were to play **harps.**
	25. 1	to proclaim God's messages, accompanied by the music of **harps**
	25. 3	accompanied by the music of **harps,** and sang praise and thanks
	25. 6	sons played cymbals and **harps** under their father's direction,
2 Chr	5.11	the altar with cymbals and **harps,** and with them were a
	9.11	his palace, and to make **harps** and lyres for the musicians.
	20.28	marched to the Temple, to the music of **harps** and trumpets.
	29.25	Levites in the Temple, with **harps** and cymbals,
Neh	12.27	of thanksgiving and with the music of cymbals and **harps.**
Job	21.12	like lambs [12] and dance to the music of **harps** and flutes.
Ps	33. 2	to the Lord with **harps,** sing to him with stringed instruments.
	33. 3	song to him, play the **harp** with skill, and shout for joy!
	43. 4	I will play my **harp** and sing praise to you, O God,
	49. 4	to proverbs and explain their meaning as I play the **harp.**
	57. 8	Wake up, my **harp** and lyre!
	71.22	I will indeed praise you with the **harp;**
	71.22	On my **harp** I will play hymns to you, the Holy One
	81. 2	play pleasant music on the **harps** and the lyres.
	92. 3	the music of stringed instruments and with melody on the **harp.**
	98. 5	Play music on the **harps!**
	108. 2	Wake up, my **harp** and lyre!
	137. 2	On the willows near by we hung up our **harps.**
	137. 5	be able to play the **harp** again if I forget you, Jerusalem!
	144. 9	I will play the **harp** and sing to you.
	147. 7	play music on the **harp** to our God.
	149. 3	play drums and **harps** in praise of him.
	150. 3	Praise him with **harps** and lyres.
	150. 4	Praise him with **harps** and flutes.
Is	5.12	At your feasts you have **harps** and tambourines and flutes—
	14.11	honoured with the music of **harps,** but now here you are in
	23.16	Take your **harp,** go round the town, you poor forgotten whore!
	24. 8	and the joyful music of their **harps** and drums has ceased.
	30.32	his people will keep time with the music of drums and **harps.**
	38.20	We will play **harps** and sing your praise, Sing praise in your
Ezek	26.13	all your songs, and I will silence the music of your **harps.**
	33.32	an entertainer singing love songs or playing a **harp.**
Dan	3. 5	followed by the playing of oboes, lyres, zithers, and **harps;**
	3.15	oboes, lyres, zithers, **harps,** and all the other instruments,
Amos	5.23	I do not want to listen to your **harps.**
	6. 5	like to compose songs, as David did, and play them on **harps.**
1 Cor	14. 7	as the flute or the **harp**—how will anyone know the tune
Rev	5. 8	Each had a **harp** and gold bowls filled with incense, which
	14. 2	It sounded like the music made by musicians playing their **harps.**
	15. 2	the sea of glass, holding **harps** that God had given them
	18.22	The music of **harps** and of human voices, of players of

HARPOON

Job	41. 7	hide with fishing-spears or pierce his head with a **harpoon?**

HARROW

A metal frame used to break up the ground and level it after it has been ploughed.

Job	39.10	Or make him pull a **harrow** in your fields?
Hos	10.11	I made Judah pull the plough and Israel pull the **harrow.**

HARSH

Gen	42. 7	He asked them **harshly,** "Where do you come from?"
	42.30	"The governor of Egypt spoke **harshly** to us and accused us
Lev	25.43	Do not treat them **harshly,** but obey your God.
	25.46	But you must not treat any of your fellow-Israelites **harshly.**
	25.53	His master must not treat him **harshly.**
Deut	23.16	that he chooses, and you are not to treat him **harshly.**
	26. 6	Egyptians treated us **harshly** and forced us to work as slaves.
	28.33	receive nothing but constant oppression and **harsh** treatment.
	28.48	The Lord will oppress you **harshly** until you are destroyed.
1 Kgs	12. 4	Solomon treated us **harshly** and placed heavy burdens on us.
	12.13	the older men and spoke **harshly** to the people,
2 Kgs	13. 4	and the Lord, seeing how **harshly** the king of Syria was
2 Chr	10.13	the older men and spoke **harshly** to the people,
Job	3.18	prisoners enjoy peace, free from shouts and **harsh** commands.
Prov	15. 1	A gentle answer quietens anger, but a **harsh** one stirs it up.
Is	47. 6	even the aged you treated **harshly.**
	53. 7	"He was treated **harshly,** but endured it humbly;
Jer	16.10	will ask you why I have decided to punish them so **harshly.**
	30.14	your punishment has been **harsh** because your sins are many
Dan	2.15	he asked Arioch why the king had issued such a **harsh** order.
Mk	14. 5	And they criticized her **harshly.**
2 Cor	10. 1	I am with you, but **harsh** with you when I am away.
	10. 2	beg you [2] not to force me to be **harsh** when I come;
	10. 2	am sure I can deal **harshly** with those who say that we
	13.10	will not have to deal **harshly** with you in using the
Col	3.19	Husbands, love your wives and do not be **harsh** with them.
1 Pet	2.18	are kind and considerate, but also to those who are **harsh.**

HARVEST

[NEWLY-HARVESTED, WHEAT-HARVEST]

The Israelite festival celebrating the wheat harvest was held in the latter part of May, fifty days after Passover. The Jewish name for this festival is Shavuoth (the Feast of Weeks). It has also been called Pentecost.

Gen	4. 3	Cain brought some of his **harvest** and gave it as an offering
	8.22	there will be a time for planting and a time for **harvest.**
	26.12	land, and that year he **harvested** a hundred times as much as
	30.14	During the **wheat-harvest** Reuben went into the fields
	47.24	At the time of **harvest** you must give one-fifth to the king.
	47.26	Egypt that one-fifth of the **harvest** should belong to the king.
Ex	23.11	let it rest, and do not **harvest** anything that grows on it.
	23.16	"Celebrate the **Harvest** Festival
	23.16	when you begin to **harvest** your crops.
	23.19	house of the Lord your God the first corn that you **harvest.**
	34.21	the seventh day, not even during ploughing time or **harvest.**
	34.22	"Keep the **Harvest** Festival
	34.22	when you begin to **harvest** the first crop of your wheat,
	34.26	to the house of the Lord the first corn that you **harvest.**
Lev	2.12	the first corn that you **harvest** each year shall be brought
	2.14	offering of the first corn **harvested,** offer roasted grain
	19. 9	"When you **harvest** your fields, do not cut the corn at the
	23. 9	is giving you and you **harvest** your corn, take the first
	23.17	the Lord as an offering of the first corn to be **harvested.**
	23.22	When you **harvest** your fields, do not cut the corn at the
	23.39	When you have **harvested** your fields, celebrate this festival
	25. 5	Do not even **harvest** the corn that grows by itself without
	25.11	not sow your fields or **harvest** the corn that grows by itself
	25.22	still be eating what you **harvested** during the sixth year,
	25.22	to eat until the crops you plant that year are **harvested.**
	26. 5	that you will still be **harvesting** corn when it is time to
	26.10	Your **harvests** will be so plentiful that they will last for
	26.10	is left of the old **harvest** to make room for the new.
Num	28.26	the first day of the **Harvest** Festival, when you present the
Deut	16. 9	time that you begin to **harvest** the corn,
	16.10	and then celebrate the **Harvest** Festival, to honour the Lord
	16.15	Be joyful, because the Lord has blessed your **harvest**
	16.16	at Passover, **Harvest** Festival, and the Festival of Shelters.
	20. 6	but has not yet had the chance to **harvest** its grapes?
	26. 2	of each crop that you **harvest** and you must take it with
	26.10	Lord the first part of the **harvest** that he has given me.'
	28.38	but reap only a small **harvest,** because the locusts will eat
Josh	3.14	It was **harvest** time, and the river was in flood.
Judg	15. 1	his wife during the wheat **harvest** and took her a young goat.
	15. 5	the corn that had been **harvested** but also the corn that was
Ruth	1. 6	Lord had blessed his people by giving them a good **harvest;**
	1.22	The barley **harvest** was just beginning when they arrived
	2. 2	fields to gather the corn that the **harvest** workers leave.
	2.21	up corn with his workers until they finish the **harvest."**
	2.23	gathered corn until all the barley and wheat had been **harvested.**
1 Sam	6.13	people of Beth Shemesh were **harvesting** wheat in the valley,
	8.12	to plough his fields, **harvest** his crops, and make his weapons
	23. 1	town of Keilah and were stealing the **newly-harvested** corn.
2 Sam	9.10	Saul's family and bring in the **harvest,** to provide food for them.
	21. 9	beginning of the barley **harvest,** when they were put to death.
	21.10	stayed there from the beginning of **harvest** until the autumn rains
	23.13	Near the beginning of **harvest** time three of "The Thirty"
2 Kgs	4.18	Some years later, at **harvest** time, the boy went out
	4.18	his father, who was in the field with the **harvest** workers.
	4.42	made from the first barley **harvested** that year,
	19.29	to sow your corn and **harvest** it, and plant vines and eat
2 Chr	8.13	Festival of Unleavened Bread, the **Harvest** Festival,
Neh	10.35	of the first corn we **harvest** and of the first fruit that
	10.37	made from the first corn **harvested** each year
Job	4. 8	now they **harvest** wickedness and evil.
	5.26	Like wheat that ripens till **harvest** time, you will live to
	24. 6	They have to **harvest** fields they don't own, and gather grapes
	24.10	they must go hungry while **harvesting** wheat.
	39.12	to bring in your **harvest** and gather the grain from your
Ps	65.11	What a rich **harvest** your goodness provides!
	67. 6	The land has produced its **harvest;**
	85.12	will make us prosperous, and our land will produce rich **harvests.**
	107.37	and planted grapevines and reaped an abundant **harvest.**
	126. 5	wept as they sowed their seed, gather the **harvest** with joy!
	126. 6	come back singing for joy, as they bring in the **harvest.**
Prov	10. 5	it is a disgrace to sleep through the time of **harvest.**
	20. 4	his fields at the right time will have nothing to **harvest.**
	25.13	who sends him, like cold water in the heat of **harvest** time.
	26. 1	out of place, like snow in summer or rain at **harvest** time.
Ecc	5. 9	Even a king depends on the **harvest.**
	11. 4	you will never sow anything and never **harvest** anything.
Is	9. 3	people rejoice when they **harvest** their corn or when they divide
	16. 9	because there is no **harvest** to make the people glad.
	17. 5	corn has been cut and **harvested,** as desolate as a field in
	17.11	morning you planted them, there would still be no **harvest.**
	18. 4	in the warm nights of **harvest** time, as serenely as the sun
	24.13	be like the end of **harvest,** when the olives have been beaten
	30.23	will give you a rich **harvest,** and your livestock will have

Is 37.30 to sow your corn and **harvest** it, and plant vines and eat
62. 9 But you that sowed and **harvested** the corn Will eat the
Jer 2. 7 land, to enjoy its **harvests** and its other good things.
5.24 the spring rains and give you the **harvest** season each year.
8.13 "I wanted to gather my people, as a man gathers his **harvest;**
8.20 "The summer is gone, the **harvest** is over, but we have not
50.16 seeds be sown in that country or let a **harvest** be gathered.
Ezek 44.30 best of all the first **harvest** and of everything else that is
45.13 **Wheat: 1/60th of your harvest**
45.13 **Barley: 1/60th of your harvest**
Hos 2. 9 So at **harvest** time I will take back my gifts of corn
10.13 But instead you planted evil and reaped its **harvest.**
Joel 3.13 cut them down like corn at **harvest** time;
Amos 9.13 faster than it can be **harvested,** and grapes will grow faster
Mic 6.15 You will sow corn, but not **harvest** the crop.
Hag 1. 6 You have sown much corn, but have **harvested** very little.
1. 9 "You hoped for large **harvests,** but they turned out to be small.
1. 9 And when you brought the **harvest** home, I blew it away.
Mt 6.26 do not sow seeds, gather a **harvest** and put it in barns;
9.37 said to his disciples, "The **harvest** is large, but there are
9.38 to the owner of the **harvest**
9.38 that he will send out workers to gather in his **harvest."**
13.30 Let the wheat and the weeds both grow together until **harvest.**
13.30 Then I will tell the **harvest** workers to pull up the weeds
13.39 The **harvest** is the end of the age,
13.39 and the **harvest** workers are angels.
21.34 slaves to the tenants to receive his share of the **harvest.**
21.41 will give him his share of the **harvest** at the right time."
25.24 you reap **harvests** where you did not sow, and you gather
25.26 did you, that I reap **harvests** where I did not sow, and
Mk 4.29 cutting it with his sickle, because **harvest** time has come.
12. 2 the tenants to receive from them his share of the **harvest.**
Lk 10. 2 "There is a large **harvest,** but few workers to gather it
10. 2 to the owner of the **harvest** that he will send out workers
10. 2 to gather in his **harvest.**
12.24 they don't sow seeds or gather a **harvest;**
20.10 the tenants to receive from them his share of the **harvest.**
Jn 4.35 You have a saying, 'Four more months and then the **harvest.'**
4.35 the crops are now ripe and ready to be **harvested!**
4.36 The man who reaps the **harvest** is being paid and gathers
4.38 sent you to reap a **harvest** in a field where you did
2 Cor 9.10 it grow and produce a rich **harvest** from your generosity.
Gal 6. 8 desires, from it he will gather the **harvest** of death;
6. 8 from the Spirit he will gather the **harvest** of eternal life.
6. 9 give up, the time will come when we will reap the **harvest.**
Eph 5. 9 light that brings a rich **harvest** of every kind of goodness,
2 Tim 2. 6 the hard work should have the first share of the **harvest.**
Jas 3.17 is full of compassion and produces a **harvest** of good deeds;
3.18 And goodness is the **harvest** that is produced from the
Rev 14.15 "Use your sickle and reap the **harvest,** because the time has come;
14.15 the earth is ripe for the **harvest!"**
14.16 sickle on the earth, and the earth's **harvest** was reaped.

HAT

Is 3.20 He will take away their veils [20] and their **hats;**

HATCH

Is 14.29 A snake's egg **hatches** a flying dragon.
34.15 build their nests, lay eggs, **hatch** their young, and care for
Jer 17.11 is like a bird that **hatches** eggs it didn't lay.

HATE
[HATRED]

Gen 3.15 I will make you and the woman **hate** each other;
27.41 Esau **hated** Jacob, because his father had given Jacob
34.30 the Perizzites, and everybody else in the land will **hate** me.
37. 4 than he loved them, they **hated** their brother so much that
37. 5 he told his brothers about it, they **hated** him even more.
37. 8 So they **hated** him even more because of his dreams and
50.15 said, "What if Joseph still **hates** us and plans to pay us
Ex 5.21 punish you for making the king and his officers **hate** us.
20. 5 bring punishment on those who **hate** me and on their descendants
Lev 18.22 God **hates** that.
19.18 on anyone or continue to **hate** him, but love your neighbour
26.17 will be defeated, and those who **hate** you will rule over you;
Num 10.35 scatter your enemies and put to flight those who **hate** you!"
35.20 "If a man **hates** someone and kills him by pushing him
35.22 kills someone he does not **hate,** whether by pushing him down
Deut 1.27 'The Lord **hates** us.
5. 9 bring punishment on those who **hate** me and on their descendants
7.10 but he will not hesitate to punish those who **hate** him.
7.25 If you do, that will be fatal, because the Lord **hates** idolatry.
7.26 You must **hate** and despise these idols, because they are under
9.28 out into the desert to kill them, because you **hated** them.
12.31 gods they do all the disgusting things that the Lord **hates.**
16.22 the Lord **hates** them.
17. 1 the Lord **hates** this.
18.12 Lord your God **hates** people who do these disgusting things,
22. 5 the Lord your God **hates** people who do such things.
23.18 The Lord **hates** temple prostitutes.
25.16 The Lord **hates** people who cheat.
27.15 the Lord **hates** idolatry.'
30. 7 curses against your enemies, who **hated** you and oppressed you,
32.41 take revenge on my enemies and punish those who **hate** me.
Judg 11. 7 But Jephthah answered, "You **hated** me so much that you forced
14.16 You just **hate** me!
15. 2 "I really thought that you **hated** her, so I gave her to
1 Sam 13. 4 and that the Philistines **hated** them.
1 Sam 27.12 said to himself, "He is **hated** so much by his own people
2 Sam 5. 8 his men, "Does anybody here **hate** the Jebusites as much as I
13.15 Then Amnon was filled with a deep **hatred** for her;
13.15 he **hated** her now even more than he had loved her before.
13.22 Absalom **hated** Amnon so much for having raped his sister Tamar
19. 6 You oppose those who love you and support those who **hate** you!
22.18 and from all those who **hate** me— they were too strong
22.41 I destroy those who **hate** me.
1 Kgs 22. 8 I **hate** him, because he never prophesies anything good for me;
2 Chr 18. 7 I **hate** him because he never prophesies anything good for me;
19. 2 wicked and to take the side of those who **hate** the Lord?
Esth 9.16 by killing seventy-five thousand people who **hated** them.
Job 8.22 bring disgrace on those who **hate** you, and the homes of the
16. 9 he glares at me with **hate.**
16.14 he attacks like a soldier gone mad with **hate.**
34.17 Do you think that he **hates** justice?
Ps 5. 5 you **hate** all wicked people.
10. 7 he is quick to speak **hateful,** evil words.
11. 5 the lawless he **hates** with all his heart.
18.17 and from all those who **hate** me— they were too strong
18.40 I destroy those who **hate** me.
21. 8 he will capture everyone who **hates** him.
25.19 see how much they **hate** me.
26. 5 I **hate** the company of evil men and avoid the wicked.
28. 3 whose words are friendly, but who have **hatred** in their hearts.
31. 6 You **hate** those who worship false gods, but I trust in you.
34.21 those who **hate** the righteous will be punished.
35.16 men who would mock a cripple, they glared at me with **hate.**
35.19 Don't let those who **hate** me for no reason smirk with delight
37.12 man plots against the good man and glares at him with **hate.**
38.19 there are many who **hate** me for no reason.
41. 7 All who **hate** me whisper to each other about me, they
44. 7 saved us from our enemies and defeated those who **hate** us.
44.16 the sneers and insults of my enemies and those who **hate** me.
45. 7 you love what is right and **hate** what is evil.
55. 3 they are angry with me and **hate** me.
55.21 smoother than cream, but there was **hatred** in his heart;
68. 1 Those who **hate** him run away in defeat.
69. 4 Those who **hate** me for no reason are more numerous than the
81.15 Those who **hate** me would bow in fear before me;
83. 2 Your enemies are in revolt, and those who **hate** you are rebelling.
86.17 those who **hate** me will be ashamed when they see that you
89.23 I will crush his foes and kill everyone who **hates** him.
97.10 The Lord loves those who **hate** evil;
101. 3 I **hate** the actions of those who turn away from God;
105.25 He made the Egyptians **hate** his people and treat his servants
106.10 He saved them from those who **hated** them;
109. 5 They pay me back evil for good and **hatred** for love.
109.17 He **hated** to give blessings—may no one bless him!
112.10 they glare in **hate** and disappear;
119.104 gain wisdom from your laws, and so I **hate** all bad conduct.
119.113 I **hate** those who are not completely loyal to you,
119.128 I **hate** all wrong ways.
119.163 I **hate** and detest all lies, but I love your law.
120. 6 I have lived too long with people who **hate** peace!
129. 5 May everyone who **hates** Zion be defeated and driven back.
139.21 O Lord, how I **hate** those who hate you!
139.22 I **hate** them with a total hatred;
Prov 3.32 they do, [32] because the Lord **hates** people who do evil, but
6.16 are seven things that the Lord **hates** and cannot tolerate:
8. 7 lies are **hateful** to me.
8.13 To honour the Lord is to **hate** evil;
8.13 I **hate** pride and arrogance, evil ways and false words.
8.36 anyone who **hates** me loves death."
9. 8 he will **hate** you for it.
10.12 **Hate** stirs up trouble, but love overlooks all offences.
10.18 A man who hides his **hatred** is a liar.
11. 1 The Lord **hates** people who use dishonest scales.
11.20 Lord **hates** evil-minded people, but loves those who do right.
12. 1 It is stupid to **hate** being corrected.
12.22 The Lord **hates** liars, but is pleased with those who keep
13. 5 Honest people **hate** lies, but the words of wicked people are
15. 8 when good men pray, but **hates** the sacrifices that wicked men
15. 9 The Lord **hates** the ways of evil people, but loves those
15.17 you love than to eat the finest meat where there is **hate.**
15.26 Lord **hates** evil thoughts, but he is pleased with friendly words.
16. 5 The Lord **hates** everyone who is arrogant;
17.15 or letting the wicked go—both are **hateful** to the Lord.
20.10 The Lord **hates** people who use dishonest weights and measures.
20.23 The Lord **hates** people who use dishonest scales and weights.
21.27 The Lord **hates** it when wicked men offer him sacrifices,
24. 9 People **hate** a person who has nothing but scorn for others.
24.24 person innocent, he will be cursed and **hated** by everyone.
25.17 he may get tired of you and come to **hate** you.
26.24 A hypocrite hides his **hate** behind flattering words.
26.25 him, because his heart is filled to the brim with **hate.**
26.26 He may disguise his **hatred,** but everyone will see the evil
26.28 You have to **hate** someone to want to hurt him with lies.
28. 9 the law, God will find your prayers too **hateful** to hear.
28.16 One who **hates** dishonesty will rule a long time.
29.10 Bloodthirsty people **hate** anyone who's honest,
29.27 The righteous **hate** the wicked, and the wicked hate the righteous.
30.23 a **hateful** woman who gets married,
Ecc 3. 8 the time for **hate,** the time for war
9. 1 of wise and righteous men, even their love and their **hate.**
9. 6 Their loves, their **hates,** their passions, all died with them.
Is 1.14 I **hate** your New Moon Festivals and holy days;
45.24 but all who **hate** me will suffer disgrace.
49. 7 is deeply despised, who is **hated** by the nations
60.15 no longer be forsaken and **hated,** A city deserted and desolate.
61. 8 "I love justice and I **hate** oppression and crime.

Is	66. 5	some of your own people **hate** you and will have nothing to
Jer	4. 1	and remove the idols I **hate,** [2]it will be right for you
	7.10	You do these things I **hate,** and then you come and stand
	7.30	placed their idols, which I **hate,** in my Temple and have
	12. 8	the forest they have roared at me, and so I **hate** them.
	13.27	He has seen you do the things he **hates.**
	14.19	Do you **hate** the people of Zion?
	44. 4	who told you not to do this terrible thing that I **hate.**
Lam	2.16	All your enemies mock you and glare at you with **hate.**
	3.52	like a bird by enemies who had no cause to **hate** me.
	3.60	You know how my enemies **hate** me and how they plot
Ezek	5. 9	things you do that I **hate,** I will punish Jerusalem as I
	13.20	"I **hate** the wristbands that you use in your attempt to
	16.27	over to the Philistines, who **hate** you and are disgusted with
	16.37	lovers together—the ones you liked and the ones you **hated.**
	16.45	like your sisters, who **hated** their husbands and their children.
	16.50	did the things that I **hate,** so I destroyed them, as you
	16.57	the Philistines, and your other neighbours who **hate** you.
	23.28	hand you over to people you **hate** and are disgusted with.
	23.29	And because they **hate** you, they will take away everything
	25.15	revenge on their age-long enemies and destroyed them in their **hate.**
	35.11	your anger, your jealousy, and your **hatred** towards my people.
Hos	7. 4	Their **hatred** smoulders like the fire in an oven, which is
	8. 5	I **hate** the gold bull worshipped by the people of the city
	9. 7	You people **hate** me so much because your sin is so great.
	9.15	It was there that I began to **hate** them.
Amos	5.10	You people **hate** anyone who challenges injustice
	5.15	**Hate** what is evil, love what is right, and see that
	5.21	The Lord says, "I **hate** your religious festivals;
	6. 8	"I **hate** the pride of the people of Israel;
Mic	3. 2	concerned about justice, [2]yet you **hate** what is good
	3. 9	of Israel, you that **hate** justice and turn right into wrong.
	6.10	They use false measures, a thing that I **hate.**
Zech	8.17	I **hate** lying, injustice, and violence."
	11. 8	with three other shepherds, who **hated** me, and I got rid of
Mal	1. 3	and have **hated** Esau and his descendants.
	2.16	"I **hate** divorce," says the Lord God of Israel.
	2.16	"I **hate** it when one of you does such a cruel thing
Mt	5.43	heard that it was said, 'Love your friends, **hate** your enemies.'
	6.24	he will **hate** one and love the other;
	10.22	Everyone will **hate** you because of me.
	24. 9	All mankind will **hate** you because of me.
	24.10	they will betray one another and **hate** one another.
Mk	13.13	Everyone will **hate** you because of me.
Lk	1.71	from our enemies, from the power of all those who **hate** us.
	6.22	"Happy are you when people **hate** you, reject you, insult you,
	6.27	good to those who **hate** you, [28]bless those who curse you,
	16.13	he will **hate** one and love the other;
	19.14	Now, his countrymen **hated** him, and so they sent messengers
	21.17	Everyone will **hate** you because of me.
Jn	3.20	Anyone who does evil things **hates** the light and will not
	7. 7	The world cannot **hate** you, but it hates me, because I keep
	12.25	whoever **hates** his own life in this world will keep it for
	15.18	world hates you, just remember that it has **hated** me first.
	15.19	that is why the world **hates** you.
	15.23	Whoever **hates** me hates my Father also.
	15.24	seen what I did, and they **hate** both me and my Father.
	15.25	'They **hated** me for no reason at all.'
	17.14	your message, and the world **hated** them, because they do not
Rom	1.30	they are **hateful** to God, insolent, proud, and boastful;
	7.15	I would like to do, but instead I do what I **hate.**
	9.13	As the scripture says, "I loved Jacob, but I **hated** Esau."
	12. 9	**Hate** what is evil, hold on to what is good.
Eph	4.31	No more shouting or insults, no more **hateful** feelings of any sort.
	5.29	(No one ever **hates** his own body.
Col	3. 8	anger, passion, and **hateful** feelings.
2 Tim	3. 3	they will **hate** the good;
Tit	1.16	They are **hateful** and disobedient, not fit to do anything good.
	3. 3	others **hated** us and we hated them.
Heb	1. 9	You love what is right and **hate** what is wrong.
	12. 3	how he put up with so much **hatred** from sinners!
1 Jn	2. 9	is in the light, yet **hates** his brother, is in the darkness
	2.11	But whoever **hates** his brother is in the darkness;
	3.13	surprised, my brothers, if the people of the world **hate** you.
	3.15	Whoever **hates** his brother is a murderer, and you know
	4.20	says he loves God, but **hates** his brother, he is a liar.
Jude	23	mercy mixed with fear, but **hate** their very clothes, stained
Rev	2. 6	you **hate** what the Nicolaitans do, as much as I do.
	17.16	The ten horns you saw, and the beast, will **hate** the prostitute;
	18. 2	all kinds of filthy and **hateful** birds live in her.

HATRED see **HATE**

HAUNT

Job	9.27	to forget my pain, all my suffering comes back to **haunt** me;
Jer	50.39	"And so Babylon will be **haunted** by demons and evil spirits,
Rev	18. 2	She is now **haunted** by demons and unclean spirits;

HAVE

Mt	8.26	"How little faith you **have!"**
	13.12	For the person who **has** something will be given more, so
	13.12	but the person who **has** nothing
	13.12	will have taken away from him even the little he **has.**
	13.44	goes and sells everything he **has,** and then goes back and
	13.46	he goes and sells everything he **has,** and buys that pearl.
	18.25	children and all that he **had,** in order to pay the debt.
	19.27	What will we **have?"**
Mt	25.29	For to every person who **has** something, even more will be given,
	25.29	even the little that he **has** will be taken away from him.
	26.11	have poor people with you, but you will not always **have** me.
Mk	4.25	The person who **has** something will be given more, and the
	4.25	will have taken away from him even the little he **has."**
	6.22	the king said to the girl, "What would you like to **have?**
	6.42	Everyone ate and **had** enough.
	7.11	teach that if a person **has** something he could use to help
	8. 8	Everybody ate and **had** enough—there were about four thousand people.
	9.24	Help me to **have** more!"
	12.44	is, put in all she **had**—she gave all she had to
	14. 7	But you will not always **have** me.
Lk	1.62	father, asking him what name he would like the boy to **have.**
	3.11	one to the man who **has** none, and whoever has food must
	8.18	because whoever **has** something will be given more,
	8.18	have taken away from him even the little he thinks he **has."**
	8.43	she had spent all she **had** on doctors, but no one had
	9.13	They answered, "All we **have** are five loaves and two fish.
	9.17	They all ate and **had** enough, and the disciples took up
	12.28	How little faith you **have!**
	14.33	can be my disciple unless he gives up everything he **has.**
	15.14	He spent everything he **had.**
	15.17	'All my father's hired workers **have** more than they can eat,
	15.31	'you are always here with me, and everything I **have** is yours.
	16. 4	job is gone, I shall **have** friends who will welcome me in
	19.26	'that to every person who **has** something, even more will be given;
	19.26	but the person who **has** nothing,
	19.26	even the little that he **has** will be taken away from him.
	24.39	ghost doesn't have flesh and bones, as you can see I **have."**
	24.41	so he asked them, **"Have** you anything here to eat?"
Jn	3.27	John answered, "No one can **have** anything unless God gives it
	5. 7	sick man answered, "Sir, I **have** no one here to put me
	6. 7	Philip answered, "For everyone to **have** even a little, it would
	6.11	with the fish, and they all **had** as much as they wanted.
	6.26	you ate the bread and **had** all you wanted, not because you
	12. 8	have poor people with you, but you will not always **have** me."
	15. 7	you will ask for anything you wish, and you shall **have** it.
	16.15	All that my Father **has** is mine;
	17. 5	now, the same glory I **had** with you before the world was
	17.10	All I **have** is yours, and all you have is mine;
Acts	3. 6	have no money at all, but I give you what I **have:**
	4.32	but they all shared with one another everything they **had.**
	20.32	up and give you the blessings God **has** for all his people.
1 Cor	4. 7	Didn't God give you everything you **have?**
	13. 3	may give away everything I **have,** and even give up my body
	15.35	What kind of body will they **have?"**
2 Cor	5. 5	as the guarantee of all that he **has** in store for us.
	8. 7	You are so rich in all you **have:**
	8.11	were to plan it, and do it with what you now **have.**
	8.12	basis of what you have to give, not on what you **haven't.**
	8.13	but since you **have** plenty at this time, it is only fair
	8.13	you are in need and they **have** plenty, they will help you.
	8.15	who gathered much did not **have** too much,
	8.15	and the one who gathered little did not **have** too little."
	12.15	glad to spend all I **have,** and myself as well, in order
Gal	5. 1	Freedom is what we **have**—Christ has set us free!
	6. 6	should share all the good things he **has** with his teacher.
Phil	2. 5	The attitude you should have is the one that Christ Jesus **had:**
	2. 6	He always **had** the nature of God, but he did not think
	2. 7	he gave up all he **had,** and took the nature of a
	4.11	for I have learnt to be satisfied with what I **have.**
	4.12	be in need and what it is to **have** more than enough.
	4.12	am full or hungry, whether I **have** too much or too little.
	4.18	I **have** all I need now that Epaphroditus has brought me all
Col	1.19	own decision that the Son **has** in himself the full nature of
	1.27	this rich and glorious secret which he **has** for all peoples.
1 Tim	6. 6	a person very rich, if he is satisfied with what he **has.**
Heb	13. 5	from the love of money, and be satisfied with what you **have.**
Jas	2. 3	man and say to him, **"Have** this best seat here," but say
1 Pet	3.15	to explain the hope you **have** in you,
	4. 1	strengthen yourselves with the same way of thinking that he **had;**
1 Jn	2. 7	old command, the one you have **had** from the very beginning.
	2.23	whoever accepts the Son **has** the Father also.
	4. 3	denies this about Jesus does not **have** the Spirit from God.
	4. 3	The spirit that he **has** is from the Enemy of Christ;
	4. 9	Son into the world, so that we might **have** life through him.
	4.16	ourselves know and believe the love which God **has** for us.
	5.12	Whoever **has** the Son has this life;
	5.12	whoever does not **have** the Son of God does not have life.
	5.13	you may know that you **have** eternal life—you that believe in
2 Jn	5	it is the command which we have **had** from the beginning.
	9	teaching of Christ, but goes beyond it, does not **have** God.
Jude	19	controlled by their natural desires, who do not **have** the Spirit.
Rev	2. 4	But this is what I **have** against you:
	2. 6	But this is what you **have** in your favour:
	2.14	But there are a few things I **have** against you:
	2.20	But this is what I **have** against you:
	2.25	But until I come, you must hold firmly to what you **have.**
	3. 2	and strengthen what you still **have** before it dies completely.
	3.11	Keep safe what you **have,** so that no one will rob you
	3.17	I **have** all I need.'
	17.16	they will take away everything she **has** and leave her naked;

HAVE TO

Mt	12.36	on Judgement Day everyone will **have to** give account of every
	14.16	"They don't **have to** leave," answered Jesus.
	17.10	the teachers of the Law say that Elijah **has to** come first?"
	17.17	How long do I **have to** put up with you?
	17.26	"that means that the citizens don't **have to** pay.

Mt 18.21 sinning against me, how many times do I **have to** forgive him?
24.20 God that you will not **have to** run away during the winter
26.35 will never say that, even if I **have to** die with you!"
26.55 to the crowd, "Did you **have to** come with swords and clubs
Mk 1.38 I **have to** preach in them also, because that is why I
9.11 the teachers of the Law say that Elijah **has to** come first?"
9.19 How long do I **have to** put up with you?
14.31 will never say that, even if I **have to** die with you!"
14.35 if possible, he might not **have to** go through that time
14.48 "Did you **have to** come with swords and clubs
Lk 2.49 He answered them, "Why did you **have to** look for me?
2.49 Didn't you know that I **had to** be in my Father's house?"
9.41 How long do I **have to** put up with you?"
10.40 over all the work she **had to** do, so she came and
12.20 This very night you will **have to** give up your life;
14. 9 invited both of you, would **have to** come and say to you,
14. 9 would be embarrassed and **have to** sit in the lowest place.
15.32 But we **had to** celebrate and be happy, because your brother
22.52 "Did you **have to** come with swords and clubs,
24.44 writings of the prophets, and the Psalms **had to** come true."
Jn 1.22 "We **have to** take an answer back to those who sent us.
4. 4 on his way there he **had to** go through Samaria.
4.15 thirsty again, nor will I **have to** come here to draw water."
13.10 clean and does not **have to** wash himself, except for his
Acts 1.16 brothers," he said, "the scripture **had to** come true in which
3.18 ago through all the prophets that his Messiah **had to** suffer;
17. 3 them that the Messiah **had to** suffer and rise from death.
19.39 that you want, it will **have to** be settled in a legal
21.35 him, and then the soldiers **had to** carry him because the mob
Rom 11.35 ever given him anything, so that he **had to** pay it back?"
14.12 one of us, then, will **have to** give an account of himself
1 Cor 3. 1 I **had to** talk to you as though you belonged to this
3. 2 I **had to** feed you with milk, not solid food, because you
5.10 To avoid them you would **have to** get out of the world
9. 6 the only ones who **have to** work for our living?
9. 7 What soldier ever **has to** pay his own expenses in the army?
9. 8 I don't **have to** limit myself to these everyday examples,
15.44 a physical body, so there **has to** be a spiritual body.
16. 5 I have gone through Macedonia—for I **have to** go through Macedonia.
2 Cor 3.13 are not like Moses, who **had to** put a veil over his
9. 5 that you give because you want to, not because you **have to.**
10.16 and shall not **have to** boast about work already done
12. 1 I **have to** boast, even though it doesn't do any good.
12.14 After all, children should not **have to** provide for their parents,
13.10 I will not **have to** deal harshly with you
Gal 6. 4 himself has done, without **having to** compare it with what someone
6. 5 For everyone **has to** carry his own load.
1 Thes 3. 5 That is why I **had to** send Timothy.
4.12 and you will not **have to** depend on anyone
Phlm 19 (I should not **have to** remind you, of course, that you owe
Heb 2.17 This means that he **had to** become like his brothers in
5.12 Instead of eating solid food, you still **have to** drink milk.
5.13 Anyone who **has to** drink milk is still a child, without
7.12 priesthood is changed, there also **has to** be a change in the
8.11 None of them will **have to** teach his fellow-citizen
9.23 of the heavenly originals, **had to** be purified in that way.
9.26 for then he would have **had to** suffer many times ever
12. 4 sin you have not yet **had to** resist to the point of
1 Pet 1.11 the sufferings that Christ would **have to** endure and the
2.12 they will **have to** recognize your good deeds
4. 5 But they will **have to** give an account of themselves to God,

HAVEN

Gen 49.13 His shore will be a **haven** for ships.

HAWK

Lev 11.13 eagles, owls, **hawks,** falcons;
Deut 14.12 eagles, owls, **hawks,** falcons;
Job 28. 7 No **hawk** sees the roads to the mines, And no vulture ever
39.26 Does a **hawk** learn from you how to fly when it spreads
Is 46.11 swoop down like a **hawk** and accomplish what I have planned.
Jer 12. 9 people are like a bird attacked from all sides by **hawks.**

HAY

Job 6. 5 when eating grass, and a cow is quiet when eating **hay.**
Prov 27.25 You cut the **hay** and then cut the grass on the hillsides
27.25 while the next crop of **hay** is growing.
Amos 7. 1 the king's share of the **hay** had been cut and the grass

HAZAEL

King of Syria in Elisha's time who murdered his predecessor.

1 Kgs 19.15 then enter the city and anoint **Hazael** as king of Syria;
19.17 being put to death by **Hazael** will be killed by Jehu,
2 Kgs 8. 8 was there, [8] he said to **Hazael,** one of his officials, "Take
8. 9 **Hazael** loaded forty camels with all kinds of the finest products
8. 9 **Hazael** met him, he said, "Your servant King Benhadad has sent
8.11 horrified look on his face until **Hazael** became ill at ease.
8.12 "Why are you crying, sir?" **Hazael** asked.
8.13 "How could I ever be that powerful?" **Hazael** asked.
8.14 **Hazael** went back to Benhadad, who asked him,
8.14 that you would certainly get well," **Hazael** answered.
8.15 But on the following day **Hazael** took a blanket, soaked it
8.15 And **Hazael** succeeded Benhadad as king of Syria.
8.28 King Joram of Israel in a war against King **Hazael** of Syria.
9.14 received in the battle at Ramoth against King **Hazael** of Syria.
10.32 King **Hazael** of Syria conquered all the Israelite territory
2 Kgs 12.17 At that time King **Hazael** of Syria attacked the city of
12.18 as a gift to King **Hazael,** who then led his army away
13. 3 and he allowed King **Hazael** of Syria and his son Benhadad
13.22 King **Hazael** of Syria oppressed the Israelites during all
13.24 At the death of King **Hazael** of Syria his son Benhadad
2 Chr 22. 5 King Joram of Israel in a war against King **Hazael** of Syria.
Amos 1. 4 the palace built by King **Hazael** and I will burn down

HAZOR (1)

Important city in the n. of Palestine, conquered by Joshua.

Josh 11. 1 reached King Jabin of **Hazor,** he sent word to King Jobab
11.10 Joshua then turned back, captured **Hazor** and killed its king.
11.10 (At that time **Hazor** was the most powerful of all those kingdoms.)
11.13 cities built on mounds, except **Hazor,** which Joshua did burn.
12.19 Tappuah, Hepher, [18] Aphek, Lasharon, [19] Madon, **Hazor,**
19.36 Hammath, Rakkath, Chinnereth, [36] Adamah, Ramah, **Hazor,**
Judg 4. 2 by Jabin, a Canaanite king who ruled in the city of **Hazor.**
4.17 because King Jabin of **Hazor** was at peace with Heber's family.
1 Sam 12. 9 army of the city of **Hazor,** fight against your ancestors and
1 Kgs 9.15 also used it to rebuild the cities of **Hazor,** Megiddo, and
2 Kgs 15.29 Kedesh, and **Hazor,** and the territories of Gilead, Galilee,

Am **HEAD (of wheat)** see **EAR OF CORN**

HEAD (1)

Gen 3.15 Her offspring will crush your **head,** and you will bite their heel."
28.11 He lay down to sleep, resting his **head** on a stone.
28.18 stone that was under his **head,** and set it up as a
40.16 I was carrying three bread-baskets on my **head.**
40.19 the king will release you—and have your **head** cut off!
48.14 his right hand on the **head** of Ephraim, even though he was
48.14 his left hand on the **head** of Manasseh, who was the elder.
48.17 that his father had put his right hand on Ephraim's **head;**
48.17 hand to move it from Ephraim's **head** to the head of Manasseh.
48.18 put your right hand on his **head."**
49.26 these blessings rest on the **head** of Joseph,
Ex 6.25 These were the **heads** of the families and the clans of the
12. 9 it roasted whole, including the **head,** the legs, and the internal
28.32 have a hole for the **head,** and this hole is to be
29. 7 the anointing oil, pour it on his **head,** and anoint him.
29. 9 put sashes round their waists and tie caps on their **heads.**
29.10 tell Aaron and his sons to put their hands on its **head.**
29.15 tell Aaron and his sons to put their hands on its **head.**
29.17 and put them on top of the **head** and the other pieces.
29.19 tell Aaron and his sons to put their hands on its **head.**
39.23 The hole for the **head** was reinforced with a woven binding
Lev 1. 4 put his hand on its **head,** and it will be accepted as
1. 8 the pieces of the animal, including the **head** and the fat.
1.12 on the fire all the parts, including the **head** and the fat.
1.15 wring its neck, and burn its **head** on the altar.
3. 2 put his hand on the **head** of the animal and kill it
3. 8 put his hand on its **head** and kill it in front of
3.13 put his hand on its **head** and kill it in front of
4. 4 put his hand on its **head,** and kill it there in the
4.11 all its flesh, its **head,** its legs, and its internal organs
4.15 put their hands on its **head,** and it shall be killed there.
4.24 put his hand on its **head** and kill it on the north
4.29 put his hand on its **head** and kill it on the north
4.33 put his hand on its **head** and kill it on the north
5. 8 neck without pulling off its **head** [9] and sprinkle some of its
8. 9 placed the turban on his **head,** and on the front of it
8.12 Aaron by pouring some of the anointing oil on his **head.**
8.13 tied caps on their **heads,** just as the Lord had commanded.
8.14 and Aaron and his sons put their hands on its **head.**
8.18 and Aaron and his sons put their hands on its **head.**
8.20 with water, and burnt the **head,** the fat, and all the rest
8.22 priests, and Aaron and his sons put their hands on its **head.**
9.13 They handed him the **head** and the other pieces of the animal,
13.12 and covers the person from **head** to foot,
13.29 has a sore on the **head** or the chin, [30] the priest shall
13.33 person shall shave the **head** except the area round the sore.
13.40 or the front of his **head,** this does not make him unclean.
13.44 unclean, because of the dreaded skin-disease on his **head.**
14. 9 he shall again shave his **head,** his beard, his eyebrows,
14.18 that is in the palm of his hand on the man's **head.**
14.29 shall put on the man's **head** and in this way perform the
16.21 his hands on the goat's **head** and confess over it all the
16.21 people of Israel, and so transfer them to the goat's **head.**
19.27 on the sides of your **head** or trim your beard [28] or tattoo
21. 5 shave any part of his **head** or trim his beard or cut
21.10 anointing oil poured on his **head** and has been consecrated
24.14 his hands on the man's **head** to testify that he is guilty,
26.13 and I let you walk with your **head** held high."
Num 8.10 place their hands on the **heads** of the Levites,
8.12 shall then put their hands on the **heads** of the two bulls;
25.14 Zimri son of Salu, the **head** of a family in the tribe
27.18 a capable man, and place your hands on his **head.**
27.23 his hands on Joshua's **head** and proclaimed him as his successor.
36. 1 The **heads** of the families in the clan of Gilead,
Deut 14. 1 or shave the front of your **head,** as other people do.
19. 5 chopping down a tree, the **head** of the axe comes off the
21.12 where she will shave her **head,** cut her fingernails,
28.35 boils will cover you from **head** to foot.
Josh 7. 6 till evening, with dust on their **heads** to show their sorrow.
17. 2 of Manasseh son of Joseph, and they were **heads** of families.
21. 1 of Nun, and to the **heads** of the families of all
22.14 tribes and each one the **head** of a family among the clans.
22.21 East Manasseh answered the **heads** of the families of the western

Josh 22.30 were with him, the **heads** of families of the western tribes,
Judg 4.21 peg right through the side of his **head** and into the ground.
4.22 Sisera on the ground, dead, with the tent-peg through his **head.**
5.26 she pierced him through the **head.**
7.25 Midianites and brought the **heads** of Oreb and Zeeb to Gideon,
9.53 threw a millstone down on his **head** and fractured his skull.
12. 1 We'll burn the house down over your **head!"**
1 Sam 4.12 he had torn his clothes and put earth on his **head.**
5. 4 This time its **head** and both its arms were broken off
9. 2 Saul was a **head** taller than anyone else in Israel and more
9.22 them a place at the **head** of the table where the guests,
10. 1 and poured it on Saul's **head,** kissed him, and said, "The
10.23 they could see that he was a **head** taller than anyone else.
14.45 that he will not lose even a hair from his **head.**
17. 7 and its iron **head** weighed about seven kilogrammes.
17.38 helmet, which he put on David's **head,** and a coat of armour.
17.46 I will defeat you and cut off your **head.**
17.51 out of its sheath, and cut off his **head** and killed him.
17.54 David picked up Goliath's **head** and took it to Jerusalem,
17.57 David was still carrying Goliath's **head.**
19.13 made of goats'-hair at its **head,** and put a cover over it.
19.16 idol in the bed and the goats'-hair pillow at its **head.**
26. 7 the camp with his spear stuck in the ground near his **head.**
26.12 jar from just beside Saul's **head,** and he and Abishai left.
26.16 Where is the water jar that was beside his **head?"**
31. 9 They cut off Saul's **head,** stripped off his armour, and sent
2 Sam 1. 2 he had torn his clothes and put earth on his **head.**
1.10 took the crown from his **head** and the bracelet from his arm,
2.16 caught his opponent by the **head** and plunged his sword into
4. 7 Then they cut off his **head,** took it with them, and walked
4. 8 They presented the **head** to King David at Hebron and said
4. 8 to him, "Here is the **head** of Ishbosheth, the son of your
4.12 They took Ishbosheth's **head** and buried it in Abner's tomb there
12.30 From the **head** of the idol of the Ammonite god Molech
13.13 How could I ever hold up my **head** in public again?
13.19 She sprinkled ashes on her **head,** tore her robe,
14.25 he had no defect from **head** to foot.
15.30 was barefoot and had his **head** covered as a sign of grief.
15.30 All who followed him covered their **heads** and wept also.
15.32 met him with his clothes torn and with earth on his **head.**
16. 9 Let me go over there and cut off his **head!"**
18. 9 a large oak-tree, Absalom's **head** got caught in the branches.
20.21 "We will throw his **head** over the wall to you," she said.
20.22 and they cut off Sheba's **head** and threw it over the wall
1 Kgs 1.52 is loyal, not even a hair on his **head** will be touched;
10.19 the figure of a bull's **head,** and beside each of the two
18.42 bowed down to the ground, with his **head** between his knees.
19. 6 a loaf of bread and a jar of water near his **head.**
2 Kgs 4.19 Suddenly he cried out to his father, "My **head** hurts!
4.19 My **head** hurts!"
6.25 so severe that a donkey's **head** cost eighty pieces of silver,
9. 3 pour this olive-oil on his **head,** and say, 'The Lord proclaims
9. 6 poured the olive-oil on Jehu's **head** and said to him,
10. 6 bring the **heads** of King Ahab's descendants to me
10. 7 of Ahab's descendants, put their **heads** in baskets, and sent
10. 8 was told that the **heads** of Ahab's descendants had been brought,
11.12 placed the crown on his **head,** and gave him a copy of
1 Chr 1.29 The sons of Ishmael became the **heads** of twelve tribes:
4.34 The following men were the **heads** of their clans:
5.15 son of Abdiel and grandson of Guni, was **head** of these clans.
5.24 The following were the **heads** of their clans:
7. 2 They were **heads** of families of the clan of Tola
7. 3 Michael, Obadiah, Joel, and Isshiah, were all **heads** of families.
7. 7 They were **heads** of families in the clan and were all famous
7.11 They were **heads** of families in the clan and were all
7.40 They were **heads** of families, famous fighting men, outstanding
8. 6 They were **heads** of families that lived in Geba, but which
8.10 His sons all became **heads** of families.
8.13 Beriah and Shema were **heads** of families that settled in
8.28 the ancestral **heads** of families and their principal descendants
9. 4 had as their leader Asaiah, who was the **head** of his family.
9. 9 All the men named above were **heads** of families.
9.13 The priests who were **heads** of families totalled 1,760.
9.33 The **heads** of these families lived in some of the temple
9.34 The men named above were **heads** of Levite families,
10. 9 They cut off Saul's **head,** stripped off his armour, and sent
10.10 and hung his **head** in the temple of their god
23. 9 who were the **heads** of the clans descended from Ladan.
23.18 son, Izhar, had a son, Shelomith, the **head** of the clan.
24. 4 there were more male **heads** of families among the descendants of
24. 6 son of Abiathar, and the **heads** of the priestly families
24.20 These are other **heads** of families descended from Levi:
24.31 The **head** of each family and one of his younger brothers
24.31 Zadok, Ahimelech, and the **heads** of families of the priests
26.26 by King David, the **heads** of families, leaders of clan groups,
26.32 outstanding **heads** of families from Jeriah's relatives and
27. 1 the list of the Israelite **heads** of families and clan leaders
29. 6 Then the **heads** of the clans, the officials of the tribes,
2 Chr 1. 2 officials, all the **heads** of families, and all the rest
23. 2 to Jerusalem the Levites and all the **heads** of the clans.
23.11 placed the crown on his **head,** and gave him a copy of
Ezra 1. 5 Then the **heads** of the clans of the tribes of Judah
3.12 older priests, Levites, and **heads** of clans had seen the first
4. 2 to see Zerubbabel and the **heads** of the clans and said,
4. 3 Zerubbabel, Joshua, and the **heads** of the clans said to them,
7.28 to persuade many of the **heads** of the clans of Israel
8. 1 is the list of the **heads** of the clans who had been
8.17 I sent them to Iddo, **head** of the community at Casiphia,
9. 6 God, I am too ashamed to raise my **head** in your presence.
9. 6 Our sins pile up, high above our **heads;**
10.16 appointed men from among the **heads** of the clans and recorded

Neh 4. 4 Let their ridicule fall on their own **heads.**
7.70 **Heads** of clans 168 kilogrammes of gold
8.13 next day the **heads** of the clans, together with the priests
9. 1 sackcloth and put dust on their **heads** as signs of grief.
11.13 In all, 242 members of this clan were **heads** of families.
12.12 the following priests were the **heads** of the priestly clans:
12.22 record was kept of the **heads** of the Levite families and of
12.23 The **heads** of the Levite families, however, were recorded
Esth 2.17 the royal crown on her **head** and made her queen in place
4. 1 dressed in sackcloth, covered his **head** with ashes,
7. 8 no sooner said this than the eunuchs covered Haman's **head.**
Job 1.20 shaved his **head** and threw himself face downwards on the ground.
2.12 in grief and throwing dust into the air and on their **heads.**
16. 4 I could shake my **head** wisely and drown you with a flood
20. 6 so great that his **head** reaches the clouds,
31.36 on my shoulder and place them on my **head** like a crown.
31.37 I have done, and hold my **head** high in his presence.
41. 7 his hide with fishing-spears or pierce his **head** with a harpoon?
Ps 21. 3 with great blessings and set a crown of gold on his **head.**
22. 7 they stick out their tongues and shake their **heads.**
35.13 I prayed with my **head** bowed low, [14]as I would pray for
40.12 than the hairs of my **head,** and I have lost my courage.
44.14 they shake their **heads** at us in scorn.
64. 8 all who see them will shake their **heads.**
68.21 God will surely break the **heads** of his enemies,
69. 4 for no reason are more numerous than the hairs of my **head.**
74.13 you divided the sea and smashed the **heads** of the sea-monsters;
74.14 you crushed the **heads** of the monster Leviathan
109.25 they shake their **heads** in scorn.
133. 2 oil running down from Aaron's **head** and beard, down to the
Prov 4.25 don't hang your **head** in shame.
Song 2. 6 left hand is under my **head,** and his right hand caresses me.
3.11 his mother placed on his **head** on his wedding day,
5. 2 My **head** is wet with dew, and my hair is damp from
7. 5 Your **head** is held high like Mount Carmel.
8. 3 hand is under my **head,** and your right hand caresses me.
Is 1. 5 Israel, your **head** is already covered with wounds,
1. 6 From **head** to foot there is not a healthy spot
3.17 punish them—I will shave their **heads** and leave them bald."
3.18 on their ankles, on their **heads,** on their necks,
3.23 and the scarves and long veils they wear on their **heads.**
7.20 your beards, and the hair on your **heads** and your bodies.
9.14 he will cut them off, **head** and tail.
9.15 and honourable men are the **head**—and the tail is the prophets
15. 2 they have shaved their **heads** and their beards in grief.
21. 4 My **head** is spinning, and I am trembling with fear.
22.12 to weep and mourn, to shave your **heads** and wear sackcloth.
28. 1 the crowns of flowers on the **heads** of its drunken leaders.
28. 1 Their proud **heads** are well perfumed, but there they lie,
58. 5 you bow your **heads** low like a blade of grass, and spread
Jer 2.37 You will turn away from Egypt, hanging your **head** in shame.
9. 1 I wish my **head** were a well of water, and my eyes
13.18 because their beautiful crowns have fallen from their **heads.**
16. 6 will gash himself or shave his **head** to show his grief.
18.16 they will shake their **heads** in amazement.
23.19 that will rage over the **heads** of the wicked,
30.23 a furious wind that will rage over the **heads** of the wicked.
31.19 After you had punished us, we hung our **heads** in grief.
48.37 All of them have shaved their **heads** and cut off their beards.
Lam 2.10 With dust on their **heads** and sackcloth on their bodies.
2.10 Young girls bow their **heads** to the ground.
2.15 They shake their **heads** and laugh at the ruins of Jerusalem.
Ezek 1.22 Above the **heads** of the creatures there was something that
1.25 still a sound coming from above the dome over their **heads.**
7.18 Their **heads** will be shaved, and they will all be disgraced.
10. 1 at the dome over the **heads** of the living creatures and above
13.18 everyone to wear on their **heads,** so that they can have power
23.14 with sashes round their waists and fancy turbans on their **heads.**
23.42 bracelets on the women's arms and beautiful crowns on their **heads.**
27.30 for you, Throwing dust on their **heads** and rolling in ashes.
27.31 shave their **heads** for you And dress themselves in sackcloth.
29.18 such heavy loads that their **heads** were rubbed bald
32.27 their swords placed under their **heads** and their shields over
44.20 "Priests must neither shave their **heads** nor let their hair
Dan 2.32 Its **head** was made of the finest gold;
2.38 You are the **head** of gold.
2.48 of Babylon, and made him the **head** of all the royal advisers.
7. 6 wings, like the wings of a bird, and it had four **heads.**
7.20 the ten horns on its **head** and the horn that had come
Hos 7. 2 It never enters their **heads** that I will remember all this evil;
Amos 8.10 will make you shave your **heads** and wear sackcloth,
9. 1 them off and let them fall on the **heads** of the people.
Jon 2. 5 sea covered me completely, and seaweed was wrapped round my **head.**
4. 8 faint from the heat of the sun beating down on his **head.**
Zech 3. 5 commanded the attendants to put a clean turban on Joshua's **head.**
6.11 and put it on the **head** of the High Priest, Joshua
Mt 5.36 not even swear by your **head,** because you cannot make a
10.25 If the **head** of the family is called Beelzebul, the members
10.30 for you, even the hairs of your **head** have all been counted.
14. 8 me here and now the **head** of John the Baptist on a
14.11 The **head** was brought in on a dish and given to the
26. 7 with an expensive perfume, which she poured on his **head.**
27.29 and placed it on his **head,** and put a stick in his
27.30 on him, and took the stick and hit him over the **head.**
27.37 Above his **head** they put the written notice of the accusation
27.39 People passing by shook their **heads** and hurled insults at Jesus:
Mk 4.38 the back of the boat, sleeping with his **head** on a pillow.
6.16 I had his **head** cut off, but he has come back to
6.24 "The **head** of John the Baptist," she answered.

Mk 6.25 me here and now the **head** of John the Baptist on a
6.27 sent off a guard at once with orders to bring John's **head.**
6.27 The guard left, went to the prison, and cut John's **head** off;
12. 4 tenants beat him over the **head** and treated him shamefully.
14. 3 She broke the jar and poured the perfume on Jesus' **head.**
15.17 a crown out of thorny branches, and put it on his **head.**
15.19 They beat him over the **head** with a stick, spat on him,
15.29 People passing by shook their **heads** and hurled insults at Jesus:
Lk 7.46 provided no olive-oil for my **head,** but she has covered my
9. 9 Herod said, "I had John's **head** cut off;
12. 7 Even the hairs of your **head** have all been counted.
21.18 But not a single hair from your **heads** will be lost.
21.28 stand up and raise your **heads,** because your salvation is near."
Jn 13. 9 Wash my hands and **head,** too!"
19. 2 a crown out of thorny branches and put it on his **head;**
19.30 Then he bowed his **head** and died.
20. 7 lying there [7] and the cloth which had been round Jesus' **head.**
20.12 had been, one at the **head** and the other at the feet.
Acts 18.18 from Cenchreae he had his **head** shaved because of a vow he
21.24 then they will be able to shave their **heads.**
27.34 Not even a hair of your **heads** will be lost."
1 Cor 11. 4 message in public worship with his **head** covered disgraces Christ.
11. 5 in public worship with nothing on her **head** disgraces her husband;
11. 5 between her and a woman whose **head** has been shaved.
11. 6 woman does not cover her **head,** she might as well cut her
11. 6 a woman to shave her **head** or cut her hair,
11. 6 she should cover her **head.**
11. 7 no need to cover his **head,** because he reflects the image
11.10 have a covering over her **head** to show that she is under
11.13 to pray to God in public worship with nothing on her **head.**
12.21 Nor can the **head** say to the feet, "Well, I don't need
Eph 1.10 everything in heaven and on earth, with Christ as **head.**
4.15 must grow up in every way to Christ, who is the **head.**
Col 1.18 He is the **head** of his body, the church;
2.19 stopped holding on to Christ, who is the **head** of the body.
Rev 9. 7 on their **heads** they had what seemed to be crowns of gold,
9.17 The horses' **heads** were like lions' heads, and from their mouths
9.19 tails are like snakes with **heads,** and they use them to hurt
10. 1 was wrapped in a cloud and had a rainbow round his **head;**
12. 1 under her feet and a crown of twelve stars on her **head.**
12. 3 huge red dragon with seven **heads** and ten horns
12. 3 and a crown on each of his **heads.**
13. 1 It had ten horns and seven **heads;**
13. 1 and on each of its **heads** there was a name that was
13. 3 One of the **heads** of the beast seemed to have been fatally
14.14 crown of gold on his **head** and a sharp sickle in his
17. 3 the beast had seven **heads** and ten horns.
17. 7 that carries her, the beast with seven **heads** and ten horns.
17. 9 The seven **heads** are seven hills, on which the woman sits.
18.19 They threw dust on their **heads,** they cried and mourned,
19.12 a flame of fire, and he wore many crowns on his **head.**

HEAD (2)

Jn 6.21 the boat reached land at the place they were **heading** for.
Acts 27.15 impossible to keep the ship **headed** into the wind, we gave up
27.40 wind would blow the ship forward, and we **headed** for shore.

HEADBAND

Ezek 16.10 of the best leather, a linen **headband,** and a silk cloak.

HEADQUARTERS

Acts 23.35 Paul to be kept under guard in the governor's **headquarters.**

HEAL

Gen 20.17 So Abraham prayed for Abimelech, and God **healed** him.
20.17 He also **healed** his wife and his slave-girls, so that they
Ex 15.26 I am the Lord, the one who **heals** you."
Lev 13.16 But when the sore **heals** and becomes white again, the person
13.18 a boil that has **healed** [19] and if afterwards a white swelling
13.37 in it, the sore has **healed,** and the priest shall pronounce
14. 3 If the disease is **healed,** [4] the priest shall order two ritually
Num 12.13 So Moses cried out to the Lord, "O God, **heal** her!"
21. 8 that anyone who was bitten could look at it and be **healed.**
21. 9 been bitten would look at the bronze snake and be **healed.**
Deut 32.39 I wound and I **heal,** and no one can oppose what
Josh 5. 8 whole nation stayed in the camp until the wounds had **healed.**
1 Sam 6. 3 this way you will be **healed,** and you will find out why
1 Kgs 13. 6 to the Lord your God, and ask him to **heal** my arm!"
13. 6 The prophet prayed to the Lord, and the king's arm was **healed.**
2 Kgs 20. 5 I will **heal** you, and in three days you will go to
20. 8 prove that the Lord will **heal** me and that three days later
Job 5.18 his hand hurts you, and his hand **heals.**
13. 4 you are like doctors who can't **heal** anyone.
Ps 30. 2 to you for help, O Lord my God, and you **healed** me;
41. 4 be merciful to me and **heal** me."
60. 2 now **heal** its wounds, because it is falling apart.
103. 3 He forgives all my sins and **heals** all my diseases.
107.20 He **healed** them with his command and saved them from the grave.
147. 3 He **heals** the broken-hearted and bandages their wounds.
Prov 3. 8 like good medicine, **healing** your wounds and easing your pains.
12.18 as deeply as any sword, but wisely spoken words can **heal.**
Ecc 3. 3 killing and the time for **healing,** the time for tearing down
Is 6.10 If they did, they might turn to me and be **healed."**
19.22 Lord will punish the Egyptians, but then he will **heal** them.
19.22 turn to him, and he will hear their prayers and **heal** them.
30.26 when the Lord bandages and **heals** the wounds he has given his
Is 38.16 **Heal** me and let me live.
38.20 Lord, you have **healed** me.
53. 5 We are **healed** by the punishment he suffered, made whole by
57.18 "I have seen how they acted, but I will **heal** them.
57.19 I will **heal** my people.
58. 8 the morning sun, and your wounds will be quickly **healed.**
61. 1 news to the poor, To **heal** the broken-hearted, To announce
Jer 3.22 he will **heal** you and make you faithful.
8.15 for peace and a time of **healing,** but it was no use;
8.18 My sorrow cannot be **healed;**
8.22 Why, then, have my people not been **healed?**
10.19 Our wounds will not **heal.**
14.19 Why have you hurt us so badly that we cannot be **healed?**
14.19 we hoped for **healing,** but terror came instead.
15.18 Why won't they **heal?**
17. 9 it is too sick to be **healed.**
17.14 Lord, **heal** me and I will be completely well;
30.12 "Your wounds are incurable, your injuries cannot be **healed.**
30.13 no remedy for your sores, no hope of **healing** for you.
30.17 I will **heal** your wounds, though your enemies say, 'Zion is
33. 6 But I will **heal** this city and its people and restore them
46.11 nothing can **heal** you.
51. 8 Get medicine for its wounds, and perhaps it can be **healed.**
Ezek 30.21 sling so that it could **heal** and be strong enough to hold
34. 4 care of the weak ones, **healed** those that are sick,
34.16 bandage those that are hurt, and **heal** those that are sick;
47.12 provide food, and their leaves will be used for **healing** people."
Hos 5.13 for help, but he could not cure them or **heal** their wounds.
6. 1 He has hurt us, but he will be sure to **heal** us;
7. 1 "Whenever I want to **heal** my people Israel and make them
Mic 1. 9 Samaria's wounds cannot be **healed,** and Judah is about to suffer
Nah 3.19 remedy for your injuries, and your wounds cannot be **healed.**
Zech 11.16 look for the lost, or **heal** those that are hurt,
Mal 4. 2 on you like the sun and bring **healing** like the sun's rays.
Mt 4.23 News about the Kingdom, and **healing** people who had all kinds
4.24 and epileptics, and paralytics—and Jesus **healed** them all.
8. 3 At once the man was **healed** of his disease.
8.13 And the officer's servant was **healed** that very moment.
8.16 the evil spirits with a word and **healed** all who were sick.
9.28 he asked them, "Do you believe that I can **heal** you?"
9.35 about the Kingdom, and **healed** people with every kind of disease
10. 1 drive out evil spirits and to **heal** every disease
10. 8 **Heal** the sick, bring the dead back to life,
10. 8 **heal** those who suffer from dreaded skin-diseases,
12.10 asked him, "Is it against our Law to **heal** on the Sabbath?"
12.15 He **healed** all those who were ill [16] and gave them orders
12.22 Jesus **healed** the man, so that he was able to talk
13.15 they would turn to me, says God, and I would **heal** them.'
14.14 with pity for them, and he **healed** those who were ill.
15.28 And at that very moment her daughter was **healed.**
15.30 and he **healed** them.
17.16 I brought him to your disciples, but they could not **heal** him."
17.18 out of the boy, and at that very moment he was **healed.**
19. 2 Large crowds followed him, and he **healed** them there.
21.14 the crippled came to him in the Temple, and he **healed** them.
Mk 1.34 Jesus **healed** many who were sick with all kinds of diseases
3. 2 closely to see whether he would **heal** the man on the Sabbath.
3.10 He had **healed** many people, and all those who were ill
5.29 the feeling inside herself that she was **healed** of her trouble.
5.34 Go in peace, and be **healed** of your trouble."
6. 5 he placed his hands on a few sick people and **healed** them.
6.13 and rubbed olive-oil on many sick people and **healed** them.
Lk 4.23 will quote this proverb to me, 'Doctor, **heal** yourself.'
4.27 not one of them was **healed,** but only Naaman the Syrian."
4.40 placed his hands on every one of them and **healed** them all.
5.15 people came to hear him and be **healed** from their diseases.
5.17 power of the Lord was present for Jesus to **heal** the sick.
6. 7 watched him closely to see if he would **heal** on the Sabbath.
6.18 had come to hear him and to be **healed** of their diseases.
6.18 Those who were troubled by evil spirits also came and were **healed.**
6.19 him, for power was going out from him and **healing** them all.
7. 3 some Jewish elders to ask him to come and **heal** his servant.
8. 2 some women who had been **healed** of evil spirits and diseases:
8.47 she had touched him and how she had been **healed** at once.
9. 2 Kingdom of God and to **heal** the sick, [3] after saying to them,
9. 6 preaching the Good News and **healing** people everywhere.
9.11 about the Kingdom of God, and **healed** those who needed it.
9.42 command to the evil spirit, **healed** the boy, and gave him
10. 9 what is set before you, [9] **heal** the sick in that town,
13.14 was angry that Jesus had **healed** on the Sabbath, so he spoke
13.14 during those days and be **healed,** but not on the Sabbath!"
14. 3 "Does our Law allow **healing** on the Sabbath or not?"
14. 4 Jesus took the man, **healed** him, and sent him away.
17.15 them saw that he was **healed,** he came back, praising God in
17.17 Jesus said, "There were ten men who were **healed;**
22.51 He touched the man's ear and **healed** him.
Jn 4.47 to go to Capernaum and **heal** his son, who was about to
5.10 the man who had been **healed,** "This is a Sabbath, and it
5.13 the man who had been **healed** did not know who Jesus was,
5.15 the Jewish authorities that it was Jesus who had **healed** him.
5.16 Jesus, because he had done this **healing** on a Sabbath.
6. 2 they had seen his miracles of **healing** those who were ill.
12.40 would not turn to me, says God, for me to **heal** them."
Acts 4. 9 man and how he was **healed,** [10] then you should all know,
4.14 man who had been **healed** standing there with Peter and John.
4.22 on whom this miracle of **healing** had been performed was over
4.30 Stretch out your hand to **heal,** and grant that wonders
5.16 and they were all **healed.**
8. 7 a loud cry, and many paralysed and lame people were **healed.**
10.38 everywhere, doing good and **healing** all who were under the power

Acts 14. 9 he believed and could be **healed,** so he looked straight at
28. 8 his room, prayed, placed his hands on him, and **healed** him.
28. 9 the other sick people on the island came and were **healed.**
28.27 they would turn to me, says God, and I would **heal** them.'"
1 Cor 12. 9 person, while to another person he gives the power to **heal.**
12.28 are given the power to **heal** or to help others or to
12.30 to work miracles [30] or to **heal** diseases or to speak in
Heb 12.13 the lame foot may not be disabled, but instead be **healed.**
Jas 5.15 This prayer made in faith will **heal** the sick person;
5.16 and pray for one another, so that you will be **healed.**
1 Pet 2.24 It is by his wounds that you have been **healed.**
Rev 13. 3 to have been fatally wounded, but the wound had **healed.**
13.12 on it to worship the first beast, whose wound had **healed.**
22. 2 and its leaves are for the **healing** of the nations.

HEALTH
[UNHEALTHY]

Gen 30.41 When the **healthy** animals were mating, Jacob put the branches
30.42 Laban had all the weak animals, and Jacob all the **healthy** ones.
43.27 He asked about their **health** and then said, "You told me
Ex 4. 7 out this time, it was **healthy,** just like the rest of his
18. 7 asked about each other's **health** and then went into Moses' tent.
Lev 13.31 but there are still no **healthy** hairs in it, he shall isolate
13.37 sore has not spread and **healthy** hairs are growing in it,
1 Sam 16.12 He was a handsome, **healthy** young man, and his eyes sparkled.
2 Kgs 5.14 His flesh became firm and **healthy,** like that of a child.
2 Chr 36.17 on anyone, young or old, man or woman, sick or **healthy.**
Job 21.23 Some men stay **healthy** till the day they die;
Ps 38.19 My enemies are **healthy** and strong;
41. 3 them when they are sick and will restore them to **health.**
41.10 me, Lord, and restore my **health,** and I will pay my enemies
73. 4 they are strong and **healthy.**
105.37 silver and gold, and all of them were **healthy** and strong.
Prov 4.22 They will give life and **health** to anyone who understands
14.30 mind makes the body **healthy,** but jealousy is like a cancer.
16.24 are like honey—sweet to the taste and good for your **health.**
17.22 Being cheerful keeps you **healthy.**
Is 1. 6 head to foot there is not a **healthy** spot on your body.
66.14 it will make you strong and **healthy.**
Jer 11.19 saying, "Let's chop down the tree while it is still **healthy;**
33. 6 heal this city and its people and restore them to **health.**
Lam 3.17 I have forgotten what **health** and peace and happiness are.
4. 7 and pure as snow, vigorous and strong, glowing with **health.**
Ezek 16. 7 I made you grow like a **healthy** plant.
Dan 1.15 time was up, they looked **healthier** and stronger than all those
Amos 8.13 On that day even **healthy** young men and women will collapse
Zech 11.16 the lost, or heal those that are hurt, or feed the **healthy.**
Mt 7.17 A **healthy** tree bears good fruit, but a poor tree bears
7.18 A **healthy** tree cannot bear bad fruit, and a poor tree
12.33 "To have good fruit you must have a **healthy** tree;
Lk 6.43 "A **healthy** tree does not bear bad fruit, nor does a
1 Tim 6. 4 He has an **unhealthy** desire to argue and quarrel about words,
Tit 1.12 that they may have a **healthy** faith [14] and no longer hold on
Jas 5.15 Lord will restore him to **health,** and the sins he has
3 Jn 2 you may be in good **health**—as I know you are well

HEAP

Ex 8.14 them up in great **heaps,** until the land stank with them.
2 Kgs 10. 8 be piled up in two **heaps** at the city gate
Ezra 6.11 And his house is to be made a rubbish **heap.**
Neh 4. 2 Can they make building-stones out of **heaps** of burnt rubble?"
Job 2. 8 and sat by the rubbish **heap** and took a piece of broken
Lam 3.45 You have made us the refuse **heap** of the world.
Mic 1. 7 by fire, and all its images will become a desolate **heap.**
Hag 2.16 you would go to a **heap** of corn expecting to find two
Lk 14.35 It is no good for the soil or for the manure **heap;**

HEAR
[OVERHEAR, UNHEARD]

Gen 3. 8 That evening they **heard** the Lord God walking in the garden,
3.10 He answered, "I **heard** you in the garden;
14.14 When Abram **heard** that his nephew had been captured,
15. 1 Abram had a vision and **heard** the Lord say to him,
15. 4 Then he **heard** the Lord speaking to him again:
16.11 Ishmael, because the Lord has **heard** your cry of distress.
17.20 I have **heard** your request about Ishmael,
18.21 whether or not the accusations which I have **heard** are true."
19.13 The Lord has **heard** the terrible accusations against these people
21. 6 Everyone who **hears** about it will laugh with me."
21.17 God **heard** the boy crying, and from heaven the angel of
21.17 God has **heard** the boy crying.
21.26 and this is the first I have **heard** of it."
23.10 answered in the **hearing** of everyone there, [11] "Listen, sir;
23.13 Ephron, so that everyone could **hear,** "May I ask you, please,
23.16 Ephron had mentioned in the **hearing** of the people—
24.30 his sister's arms and had **heard** her say what the man had
24.52 the servant of Abraham **heard** this, he bowed down and worshipped
27. 6 to Jacob, "I have just **heard** your father say to Esau,
27.34 When Esau **heard** this, he cried out loudly and bitterly
27.42 But when Rebecca **heard** about Esau's plan, she sent for Jacob
29.13 and when he **heard** the news about his nephew Jacob, he
29.33 me this son also, because he **heard** that I was not loved";
30. 6 He has **heard** my prayer and has given me a son";
31. 1 Jacob **heard** that Laban's sons were saying, "Jacob has taken
32. 9 of my grandfather Abraham and God of my father Isaac, **hear**
34. 7 When they **heard** about it, they were shocked and furious
35.22 Jacob **heard** about it and was furious.
Gen 37.17 I **heard** them say that they were going to Dothan."
37.21 Reuben **heard** them and tried to save Joseph.
39.15 When he **heard** me scream, he ran outside, leaving his robe
42. 2 I **hear** that there is corn in Egypt;
45. 2 loud sobs that the Egyptians **heard** it, and the news was
45. 3 But when his brothers **heard** this, they were so terrified that
Ex 2.15 the king **heard** about what had happened, he tried to have
2.24 to God, [24] who **heard** their groaning and remembered his covenant
3. 7 I have **heard** them cry out to be rescued
3. 9 I have indeed **heard** the cry of my people, and I see
4.31 They believed, and when they **heard** that the Lord had come
6. 5 Now I have **heard** the groaning of the Israelites,
15.14 The nations have **heard,** and they tremble with fear;
16. 7 He has **heard** your complaints against him—yes, against him,
16. 8 because he has **heard** how much you have complained against
16. 9 stand before the Lord, because he has **heard** their complaints."
16.12 Lord said to Moses, [12] "I have **heard** the complaints of the
18. 1 the priest of Midian, **heard** about everything that God had done
18. 9 When Jethro **heard** all this, he was happy [10] and said,
19. 9 so that the people will **hear** me speaking with you and will
19.16 on the mountain, and a very loud trumpet blast was **heard.**
20.18 When the people **heard** the thunder and the trumpet blast
28.35 of the bells will be **heard,** and he will not be killed.
32.17 Joshua **heard** the people shouting
32.17 and said to Moses, "I **hear** the sound of battle
33. 4 When the people **heard** this, they began to mourn and did
Lev 5. 1 something he has seen or **heard,** he must suffer the consequences.
10.20 When Moses **heard** this, he was satisfied.
24.14 Everyone who **heard** him curse shall put his hands on the
Num 7.89 talk with the Lord, he **heard** the Lord speaking to him from
11. 1 When the Lord **heard** them, he was angry and sent fire on
11.10 Moses **heard** all the people complaining as they stood about
11.18 The Lord has **heard** you whining and saying that you wished
12. 2 The Lord **heard** what they said.
12. 6 forward, [6] and the Lord said, "Now **hear** what I have to say!
14.13 When the Egyptians **hear** what you have done to your people,
14.14 These people have already **heard** that you, Lord, are with us,
14.15 the nations who have **heard** of your fame will say
14.27 I have **heard** enough of these complaints!
16. 4 Moses **heard** this, he threw himself on the ground and prayed.
16.30 if the Lord does something **unheard** of, and the earth opens
16.34 of Israel who were there fled when they **heard** their cry.
20.16 He **heard** our cry and sent an angel, who led us out
21. 1 southern part of Canaan **heard** that the Israelites were coming
21. 3 The Lord **heard** them and helped them to conquer the Canaanites.
22. 2 Moab, Balak son of Zippor, **heard** what the Israelites had done
22.36 When Balak **heard** that Balaam was coming, he went to meet
24. 4 man who can see clearly, [4] Who can **hear** what God is saying.
24.16 Who can **hear** what God is saying And receive
30. 4 unless her father raises an objection when he **hears** about it.
30. 5 fulfil the vow when he **hears** about it, she is not required
30. 7 unless her husband raises an objection when he **hears** about it.
30. 8 fulfil the vow when he **hears** about it, she is not required
30.11 unless her husband raises an objection when he **hears** about it.
30.12 fulfil the vow when he **hears** about it, she is not required
30.14 by the day after he **hears** of the vow, he has raised
30.14 the vow by not objecting on the day he **heard** of it.
33.40 king of Arad in southern Canaan **heard** that the Israelites were
Deut 1.34 "The Lord **heard** your complaints and became angry,
4. 6 When they **hear** of all these laws, they will say, 'What
4.10 I want them to **hear** what I have to say, so that
4.12 from the fire, how you **heard** him speaking but did not see
4.28 wood and stone, gods that cannot see or **hear,** eat or smell.
4.32 Has anyone ever **heard** of anything like this?
4.33 any people ever lived after **hearing** a god speak to them from
4.36 He let you **hear** his voice from heaven so that he could
5.23 was on fire and you **heard** the voice from the darkness,
5.24 and his glory when we **heard** him speak from the fire!
5.25 sure to die if we **hear** the Lord our God speak again.
5.26 human being ever lived after **hearing** the living God speak from
5.28 "When the Lord **heard** this, he said to me,
5.28 'I have **heard** what these people said,
9. 2 are giants, and you have **heard** it said that no one can
13.11 Then all the people of Israel will **hear** what happened;
13.12 God gives you, you may **hear** [13] that some worthless men of
13.14 If you **hear** such a rumour, investigate it thoroughly;
17. 2 "Suppose you **hear** that in one of your towns some man
17. 4 If you **hear** such a report, then investigate it thoroughly.
17.13 Then everyone will **hear** of it and be afraid,
18.16 Sinai, you begged not to **hear** the Lord speak again
19.20 Then everyone else will **hear** what happened;
21.21 Everyone in Israel will **hear** what has happened and be afraid.
22.24 although she was in a town, where she could have been **heard.**
26. 7 He **heard** us and saw our suffering, hardship, and misery.
29.19 no one here today who **hears** these solemn demands and yet
30.12 down for us, so that we can **hear** it and obey it?'
30.13 it to us, so that we may **hear** it and obey it?'
31.12 towns, so that everyone may **hear** it and learn to honour the
31.13 never heard the Law of the Lord your God will **hear** it.
32. 1 "Earth and sky, **hear** my words, listen closely to what I say.
32.44 this song, so that the people of Israel could **hear** it.
Josh 2. 2 king of Jericho **heard** that some Israelites had come that night
2.10 We have **heard** how the Lord dried up the Red Sea
2.10 We have also **heard** how you killed Sihon and Og, the two
2.11 We were afraid as soon as we **heard** about it;
5. 1 kings along the Mediterranean Sea **heard** that the Lord had
6. 5 As soon as you **hear** it, all the men are to give
6.20 As soon as the men **heard** it, they gave a loud shout,
7. 9 Canaanites and everyone else in the country will **hear** about it.
9. 3 who were Hivites, **heard** what Joshua had done to Jericho
9. 9 land, sir, because we have **heard** of the Lord your God.

Josh 9. 9 We have **heard** about everything that he did in Egypt
10. 1 the king of Jerusalem, **heard** that Joshua had captured
10. 1 He also **heard** that the people of Gibeon had made peace
22.12 When the people of Israel **heard** this, the whole community
22.30 of the western tribes, **heard** what the people of the tribes
24.27 It has **heard** all the words that the Lord has spoken
Judg 7.11 You will **hear** what they are saying, and then you will
7.13 When Gideon arrived, he **heard** a man telling a friend about
7.15 When Gideon **heard** about the man's dream and what it meant,
9. 7 When Jotham **heard** about this, he went and stood on top of
9.30 of the city, became angry when he **heard** what Gaal had said.
9.46 in the fort at Shechem **heard** about this, they sought safety
14. 5 through the vineyards there, he **heard** a young lion roaring.
14.12 "Let's **hear** it."
17. 2 I **heard** you do it.
19.30 who saw it said, "We have never **heard** of such a thing!
20. 3 the people of Benjamin **heard** that all the other Israelites had
Ruth 1. 6 later Naomi **heard** that the Lord had blessed his people
2.11 Boaz answered, "I have **heard** about everything that you
1 Sam 2.22 **hearing** about everything his sons were doing to the Israelites
3.11 so terrible that everyone who **hears** about it will be stunned.
4. 6 The Philistines **heard** the shouting and said, "Listen to all
4.14 Eli **heard** the noise and asked, "What is all this noise
4.19 When she **heard** that God's Covenant Box had been captured
7. 7 Philistines **heard** that the Israelites had gathered at Mizpah,
7. 7 The Israelites **heard** about it and were afraid,
9.16 of my people and have **heard** their cries for help."
11. 6 When Saul **heard** this, the spirit of God took control of him,
13. 3 commander in Geba, and all the Philistines **heard** about it.
14.22 hills of Ephraim, **heard** that the Philistines were running away,
14.27 But Jonathan had not **heard** his father threaten the people
15.12 He **heard** that Saul had gone to the town of Carmel,
15.14 "Why, then, do I **hear** cattle mooing and sheep bleating?"
16. 2 "If Saul **hears** about it, he will kill me!"
17.11 When Saul and his men **heard** this, they were terrified.
17.23 And David **heard** him.
17.28 David's eldest brother, **heard** David talking to the men.
17.31 Some men **heard** what David had said, and they told Saul,
18.20 with David, and when Saul **heard** of this, he was pleased.
19.21 When Saul **heard** of this, he sent more messengers,
22. 1 the rest of the family **heard** that he was there, they joined
23. 1 David **heard** that the Philistines were attacking the town
23. 9 When David **heard** that Saul was planning to attack him,
23.10 God of Israel, I have **heard** that Saul is planning to come
23.11 Will Saul really come, as I have **heard?**
23.13 When Saul **heard** that David had escaped from Keilah, he gave
23.22 I **hear** that he is very cunning.
23.25 look for David, but he **heard** about it and went to
23.25 When Saul **heard** about this, he went after David.
25. 4 who was in the wilderness, **heard** about it, [5] so he sent ten
25. 7 He **heard** that you were shearing your sheep, and he wants
25.10 I've never **heard** of him!
25.14 Nabal's servants said to Nabal's wife Abigail, "Have you **heard?**
25.39 David **heard** that Nabal had died, he said, "Praise the Lord!
26.14 Can you **hear** me?"
27. 4 When Saul **heard** that David had fled to Gath, he gave up
31. 7 east of the River Jordan **heard** that the Israelite army had
31.11 people of Jabesh in Gilead **heard** what the Philistines had done
2 Sam 2. 4 When David **heard** that the people of Jabesh in Gilead had
3.28 When David **heard** the news, he said, "The Lord knows that
4. 1 When Saul's son Ishbosheth **heard** that Abner had been killed
5.17 When David **heard** of it, he went down to a fortified place.
5.24 When you **hear** the sound of marching in the tree-tops,
6.12 King David **heard** that because of the Covenant Box the Lord
8. 9 Toi of Hamath **heard** that David had defeated all of Hadadezer's
10. 5 When David **heard** about what had happened, he sent word
10. 7 David **heard** of it and sent Joab against them with the
10.17 When David **heard** of it, he gathered the Israelite troops,
11.10 When David **heard** that Uriah had not gone home, he asked
11.26 When Bathsheba **heard** that her husband had been killed,
13.21 When King David **heard** what had happened, he was furious.
15. 3 there is no representative of the king to **hear** your case."
15.10 to say, "When you **hear** the sound of trumpets, shout, 'Absalom
15.35 tell them everything you **hear** in the king's palace.
17. 5 "Now call Hushai, and let us **hear** what he has to say."
17. 9 David attacks your men, whoever **hears** about it will say that
18. 5 all the troops **heard** David give this command to his officers.
18.12 We all **heard** the king command you and Abishai and Ittai,
18.13 the king would have **heard** about it—he hears about everything
19. 2 troops that day, because they **heard** that the king was mourning
19. 8 His men **heard** that he was there, and they all gathered round
19.35 I eat and drink, and I can't **hear** the voices of singers.
20.15 Joab's men **heard** that Sheba was there, and so they went
21.11 When David **heard** what Rizpah had done, [12] he went and got
22. 7 In his temple he **heard** my voice;
22.14 from the sky, and the voice of Almighty God was **heard.**
22.45 when they **hear** me, they obey.
1 Kgs 1.11 "Haven't you **heard** that Haggith's son Adonijah has made
1.41 all his guests were finishing the feast, they **heard** the noise.
1.41 when Joab **heard** the trumpet, he asked, "What's the meaning of
1.45 That's the noise you just **heard.**
2.28 Joab **heard** what had happened.
2.39 Shimei **heard** that they were in Gath, [40] he saddled his donkey
2.41 When Solomon **heard** what Shimei had done, [42] he sent for him
3.28 When the people of Israel **heard** of Solomon's decision,
4.34 Kings all over the world **heard** of his wisdom and sent
5. 1 and when he **heard** that Solomon had succeeded his father
8.29 **Hear** me when I face this Temple and pray.
8.30 **Hear** my prayers and the prayers of your people when they
8.30 In your home in heaven **hear** us and forgive us.
8.39 hands in prayer towards this Temple, [39] **hear** their prayer.
1 Kgs 8.41 lives in a distant land **hears** of your fame and of the
8.43 In heaven, where you live, **hear** him and do what he asks
8.45 **Hear** them in heaven, and give them victory.
8.47 sinful and wicked they have been, **hear** their prayers O Lord.
8.49 In your home in heaven **hear** them and be merciful to them.
8.52 Israel and their king, and **hear** their prayer whenever they call
9. 3 The Lord said to him, "I have **heard** your prayer.
10. 1 The queen of Sheba **heard** of Solomon's fame, and she travelled
10. 4 The queen of Sheba **heard** Solomon's wisdom and saw the palace
10. 6 to King Solomon, "What I **heard** in my own country about you
10. 7 But I didn't **hear** even half of it;
10. 8 and are privileged to **hear** your wise sayings!
12. 2 from King Solomon, **heard** this news, he returned from Egypt.
12.20 people of Israel **heard** that Jeroboam had returned from Egypt,
13. 4 When King Jeroboam **heard** this, he pointed at him and ordered,
13.26 When the old prophet **heard** about it, he said, "That is
14. 6 But when Ahijah **heard** her coming in the door, he said,
15.21 King Baasha **heard** what had happened, he stopped fortifying Ramah
16.16 and when they **heard** that Zimri had plotted against the
18.13 Haven't you **heard** that when Jezebel was killing the prophets
18.29 but no answer came, not a sound was **heard.**
18.41 I **hear** the roar of rain approaching."
19.13 When Elijah **heard** it, he covered his face with his cloak
20.31 and said, "We have **heard** that the Israelite kings are merciful.
2 Kgs 3.21 the Moabites **heard** that the three kings had come to attack
5. 4 When Naaman **heard** of this, he went to the king and told
5. 8 When the prophet Elisha **heard** what had happened, he sent word
6.30 **Hearing** this, the king tore his clothes in dismay,
7. 6 Lord had made the Syrians **hear** what sounded like the advance
7.10 "We went to the Syrian camp and didn't see or **hear** anybody;
9.30 Jezebel, having **heard** what had happened, put on eyeshadow,
11.13 Queen Athaliah **heard** the noise being made by the guards
19. 1 soon as King Hezekiah **heard** their report, he tore his clothes
19. 4 May the Lord your God **hear** these insults and punish those
19. 7 will cause the emperor to **hear** a rumour that will make him
19. 9 When the emperor **heard** this, he sent a letter to King
19.11 You have **heard** what an Assyrian emperor does to any country
19.25 "Have you never **heard** that I planned all this long ago?
20. 5 ancestor David, have **heard** your prayer and seen your tears.
20.12 the son of Baladan, **heard** that King Hezekiah had been ill,
21.12 that everyone who **hears** about it will be stunned.
22.11 the king **heard** the book being read, he tore his clothes
22.19 weeping, when you **heard** how I threatened to punish Jerusalem
22.19 But I have **heard** your prayer, [20] and the punishment which I
25.23 soldiers who had not surrendered **heard** about this, they joined
1 Chr 10. 7 in the Valley of Jezreel **heard** that the army had fled
10.11 people of Jabesh in Gilead **heard** what the Philistines had done
14. 8 When the Philistines **heard** that David had now been made king
14.15 When you **hear** the sound of marching in the tree-tops,
18. 9 King Toi of Hamath **heard** that David had defeated Hadadezer's
19. 5 When David **heard** what had happened, he sent word for them to
19. 8 When David **heard** what was happening, he sent out Joab
19.17 When David **heard** of it, he gathered the Israelite troops,
2 Chr 6.20 you will be worshipped, so **hear** me when I face this Temple
6.21 **Hear** my prayers and the prayers of your people Israel
6.21 In your home in heaven **hear** us and forgive us.
6.30 their hands in prayer towards this Temple, [30] **hear** their prayer.
6.32 lives in a distant land **hears** how great and powerful you are
6.33 In heaven, where you live, **hear** him and do what he asks
6.35 **Hear** them in heaven and give them victory.
6.37 sinful and wicked they have been, **hear** their prayers, O Lord.
6.39 In your home in heaven **hear** them and be merciful to them
7.12 said to him, "I have **heard** your prayer, and I accept this
7.14 then I will **hear** them in heaven, forgive their sins,
7.15 Temple and be ready to **hear** all the prayers that are offered
9. 1 queen of Sheba **heard** of King Solomon's fame, and she travelled
9. 3 The queen of Sheba **heard** Solomon's wisdom and saw the palace
9. 5 to the king, "What I **heard** in my own country about you
9. 6 I had not **heard** of even half your wisdom.
9. 7 and are privileged to **hear** your wise sayings!
9.23 They all consulted him, to **hear** the wisdom that God had
10. 2 to escape from King Solomon, **heard** this news, he returned home.
15. 8 Asa **heard** the prophecy that Azariah son of Oded had spoken,
16. 5 King Baasha **heard** what was happening, he stopped fortifying
20. 9 in their trouble, and you would **hear** them and rescue them.
20.29 that **heard** how the Lord had defeated Israel's enemies
23.12 Athaliah **heard** the people cheering for the king,
28. 9 but now he has **heard** of the vicious way you slaughtered
30.27 In his home in heaven God **heard** their prayers and accepted them.
34.19 the king **heard** the book being read, he tore his clothes
34.27 weeping, when you **heard** how I threatened to punish Jerusalem
34.27 I have **heard** your prayer, [28] and the punishment which I am
Ezra 3.13 was so loud that it could be **heard** far and wide.
4. 1 people of Judah and Benjamin **heard** that those who had returned
5. 2 and Joshua son of Jehozadak **heard** their messages, they began
9. 3 When I **heard** this, I tore my clothes in despair,
Neh 1. 4 When I **heard** all this, I sat down and wept.
1. 6 Look at me, Lord, and **hear** my prayer,
2.10 in the province of Ammon, **heard** that someone had come to
2.19 and an Arab named Geshem **heard** what we were planning to do,
4. 1 Sanballat **heard** that we Jews had begun rebuilding the wall,
4. 7 Arabia, Ammon, and Ashdod **heard** that we were making progress
4.15 enemies **heard** that we had found out what they were plotting,
4.20 If you **hear** the bugle, gather round me.
5. 6 I **heard** their complaints, I was angry [7] and decided to act.
6. 1 the rest of our enemies **heard** that we had finished building
6. 7 His Majesty is certain to **hear** about this, so I suggest that
6.16 enemies in the surrounding nations **heard** this, they realized
8. 9 the people **heard** what the Law required, they were so moved

Neh 9. 9 you **heard** their call for help at the Red Sea.
9.28 in heaven you **heard,** and time after time you rescued
12.43 and the noise they all made could be **heard** far and wide.
13. 3 When the people of Israel **heard** this law read, they excluded
Esth 1.17 her husband as soon as she **hears** what the queen has done.
1.18 officials of Persia and Media **hear** about the queen's behaviour
Job 2.11 When they **heard** how much Job had been suffering, they decided
4.12 a message came quietly, so quietly I could hardly **hear** it.
4.16 Then I **heard** a voice out of the silence:
9. 1 Yes, I've **heard** all that before.
12.11 your tongue enjoys tasting food, your ears enjoy **hearing** words.
13. 1 Everything you say, I have **heard** before.
15. 8 Did you **overhear** the plans God made?
16. 1 I have **heard** words like that before;
18.20 east to west, all who **hear** of his fate shudder and tremble
19. 7 no one **hears** my cry for justice.
26. 4 Who do you think will **hear** all your words?
26.14 hints of his power, only the whispers that we have **heard.**
27. 9 When trouble comes, will God **hear** their cries?
28.22 death and destruction Admit they have **heard** only rumours.
29.11 Everyone who saw me or **heard** of me had good things to
30.31 Where once I **heard** joyful music, now I hear only mourning
32.12 I paid close attention and **heard** you fail;
33. 8 Now this is what I **heard** you say:
33.32 But if you have something to say, let me **hear** it;
34. 3 when you taste it, but not wise words when you **hear** them.
34.28 to cry out to God, and he **heard** their calls for help.
34.34 any wise man who **hears** me will say [35]that Job is
35.13 Almighty God does not see or **hear** them.
37. 4 roar of his voice is **heard,** the majestic sound of thunder,
39.25 and they **hear** the officers shouting commands.
Ps 4. 1 Be kind to me now and **hear** my prayer.
4. 3 for his own, and he **hears** me when I call to him.
5. 1 Listen to my words, O Lord, and **hear** my sighs.
5. 3 you **hear** my voice in the morning;
6. 8 The Lord **hears** my weeping;
10.18 You will **hear** the cries of the oppressed and the orphans;
18. 6 In his temple he **heard** my voice;
18.13 and the voice of the Most High was **heard.**
18.44 when they **hear** me, they obey.
19. 3 No speech or words are used, no sound is **heard;**
19. 4 all the world and is **heard** to the ends of the earth.
27. 7 **Hear** me, Lord, when I call to you!
28. 2 **Hear** me when I cry to you for help, when I lift
28. 6 he has **heard** my cry for help.
29. 3 The voice of the Lord is **heard** on the seas;
29. 4 voice of the Lord is **heard** in all its might and majesty.
30.10 **Hear** me, Lord, and be merciful!
31. 2 **Hear** me!
31.13 I **hear** many enemies whispering;
31.22 But he **heard** my cry, when I called to him for help.
38. 9 you **hear** all my groans.
38.13 a deaf man and cannot **hear,** like a dumb man and cannot
38.14 am like a man who does not answer, because he cannot **hear.**
39.12 **Hear** my prayer, Lord, and listen to my cry;
40. 1 then he listened to me and **heard** my cry.
40. 6 have given me ears to **hear** you, [7]and so I answered,
44. 1 our own ears we have **heard** it, O God— our ancestors
44.16 am covered with shame [16]from **hearing** the sneers and insults
48. 8 We have **heard** what God has done, and now we have seen
49. 1 **Hear** this, everyone!
51. 8 Let me **hear** the sounds of joy and gladness;
54. 2 **Hear** my prayer, O God;
55. 1 **Hear** my prayer, O God;
55.17 and groans go up to him, and he will **hear** my voice.
55.19 God, who has ruled from eternity, will **hear** me and defeat
58. 5 deaf cobra, [5]which does not **hear** the voice of the snake-charmer,
59. 7 in their mouths, yet they think that no one **hears** them.
61. 1 **Hear** my cry, O God;
61. 5 You have **heard** my promises, O God, and you have given me
62.11 More than once I have **heard** God say that power belongs
66. 8 let your praise be **heard.**
66.19 But God has indeed **heard** me;
77. 1 I cry aloud, and he **hears** me.
78. 3 things we have **heard** and known, things that our fathers
78.21 And so the Lord was angry when he **heard** them;
80. 1 **hear** us, leader of your flock.
81. 5 I **hear** an unknown voice saying, [6]"I took the burdens off
84. 8 **Hear** my prayer, Lord God Almighty.
86. 6 **hear** my cries for help.
88. 2 **Hear** my prayer;
92.11 the defeat of my enemies and **heard** the cries of the wicked.
94. 9 God made our ears—can't he **hear?**
102. 1 Listen to my prayer, O Lord, and **hear** my cry for help!
102.17 He will **hear** his forsaken people and listen to their prayer.
102.20 He **heard** the groans of prisoners and set free those who
104. 7 they rushed away when they **heard** your shout of command.
106.44 Yet the Lord **heard** them when they cried out, and he took
115. 6 They have ears, but cannot **hear,** and noses, but cannot smell.
116. 1 I love the Lord, because he **hears** me;
118.21 praise you, Lord, because you **heard** me, because you have given
119.149 Because your love is constant, **hear** me, O Lord;
130. 2 **Hear** my cry, O Lord;
132. 6 In Bethlehem we **heard** about the Covenant Box, and we found
135.17 They have ears, but cannot **hear;**
138. 4 will praise you, Lord, because they have **heard** your promises.
140. 6 **Hear** my cry for help, Lord!
143. 1 Lord, **hear** my prayer!
145.19 he **hears** their cries and saves them.
Prov 8. 1 Reason is making herself **heard.**
16.13 A king wants to **hear** the truth and will favour those
Prov 21.13 of the poor, your own cry for help will not be **heard.**
23.16 I will be proud when I **hear** you speaking words of wisdom.
25.25 **hearing** good news from a distant land is like a drink
28. 9 God will find your prayers too hateful to **hear.**
Ecc 1. 8 our ears can never **hear** enough.
7.21 everything people say—you may **hear** your servant insulting you,
12. 4 will barely be able to **hear** the mill as it grinds or
Song 2. 8 I **hear** my lover's voice.
2.12 the song of doves is **heard** in the fields.
2.14 Let me see your lovely face and **hear** your enchanting voice.
5. 6 How I wanted to **hear** his voice!
5. 6 I called to him, but **heard** no answer.
8.13 Let me **hear** your voice from the garden, my love;
8.13 my companions are waiting to **hear** you speak.
Is 5. 9 **heard** the Lord Almighty say, "All these big, fine houses
6. 8 Then I **heard** the Lord say, "Whom shall I send?
6.10 eyes blind, so that they cannot see or **hear** or understand.
12. 5 Let the whole world **hear** the news.
15. 4 and their cry can be **heard** as far away as Jahaz.
15. 8 Everywhere at Moab's borders the sound of crying is **heard.**
15. 8 It is **heard** at the towns of Eglaim and Beerelim.
16. 6 of Judah say, "We have **heard** how proud the people of Moab
18. 1 Sudan there is a land where the sound of wings is **heard.**
19.22 turn to him, and he will **hear** their prayers and heal them.
21. 3 What I saw and **heard** in the vision has filled me with
21.10 good news that I have **heard** from the Lord Almighty, the God
24.16 of the world we will **hear** songs in praise of Israel,
28.22 **heard** the Lord Almighty's decision to destroy the whole country.
29.18 deaf will be able to **hear** a book being read aloud,
30.10 Tell us what we want to **hear.**
30.11 We don't want to **hear** about your holy God of Israel."
30.21 or the left, you will **hear** his voice behind you saying,
30.30 The Lord will let everyone **hear** his majestic voice and feel
30.31 will be terrified when they **hear** the Lord's voice and feel
33.13 Let everyone near and far **hear** what I have done
35. 5 The blind will be able to see, and the deaf will **hear.**
37. 1 soon as King Hezekiah **heard** their report, he tore his clothes
37. 4 May the Lord your God **hear** these insults and punish those
37. 7 will cause the emperor to **hear** a rumour that will make him
37. 9 When the emperor **heard** this, he sent a letter to King
37.11 You have **heard** what an Assyrian emperor does to any country
37.17 Now, Lord, **hear** us and look at what is happening to us.
37.26 "Have you never **heard** that I planned all this long ago?
38. 5 ancestor David, have **heard** your prayer and seen your tears;
39. 1 son of Baladan, **heard** that King Hezekiah had been ill,
40.21 Have you not **heard** how the world began?
40.28 Haven't you **heard?**
41.26 no one **heard** you say a thing!
42.20 You have ears to **hear** with, but what have you really heard?"
44. 8 Is there some powerful god I never **heard** of?"
48. 8 That is why you never **heard** of this at all,
48.16 "Now come close to me and **hear** what I say.
50. 4 he makes me eager to **hear** what he is going to teach
59. 1 to save you or too deaf to **hear** your call for help!
59. 2 It is because of your sins that he doesn't **hear** you.
60.18 The sounds of violence will be **heard** no more;
64. 4 has ever seen or **heard** of a God like you,
66. 8 Has anyone ever seen or **heard** of such a thing?
66.19 distant lands that have not **heard** of my fame or seen my
Jer 3.21 A noise is **heard** on the hill-tops:
4.19 I **hear** the trumpets and the shouts of battle.
4.21 I see the battle raging and **hear** the blasts of trumpets?
4.31 I **heard** a cry, like a woman in labour, a scream like
5.21 have eyes, but cannot see, and have ears, but cannot **hear.**
6. 7 I **hear** violence and destruction in the city;
6.24 "We have **heard** the news," say the people of Jerusalem,
8.16 we **hear** the snorting of their horses.
8.19 Throughout the land I **hear** my people crying out, "Is the
9.10 The sound of livestock is no longer **heard;**
9.16 they nor their ancestors have **heard** about, and I will send
18.19 So I prayed, "Lord, **hear** what I am saying and listen
19. 3 this place that everyone who **hears** about it will be stunned.
20. 1 chief officer of the Temple, **heard** me proclaim these things,
20.10 I **hear** everybody whispering, "Terror is everywhere!
20.16 May he **hear** cries of pain in the morning and the battle
23.18 None of them has ever **heard** or understood his message,
23.28 prophet who has **heard** my message should proclaim that message
25.30 Everyone on earth will **hear** him, [31]and the sound will echo
26. 7 and all the people **heard** me saying these things in the
26.10 the leaders of Judah **heard** what had happened, they hurried from
26.11 You **heard** him with your own ears."
26.12 proclaim everything that you **heard** me say against this Temple
26.21 and his soldiers and officials **heard** what Uriah had said,
26.21 But Uriah **heard** about it;
30. 5 "I **heard** a cry of terror, a cry of fear and not
31.15 "A sound is **heard** in Ramah, the sound of bitter weeping.
31.18 "I **hear** the people of Israel say in grief, 'Lord, we
33. 9 fear and tremble when they **hear** about the good things that I
33.10 in these places you will **hear** again [11]the shouts of gladness
33.11 You will **hear** people sing as they bring thank-offerings
36. 3 when the people of Judah **hear** about all the destruction that
36. 6 aloud, so that they will **hear** everything that the Lord has
36. 6 this where everyone can **hear** you, including the people of Judah
36.11 and grandson of Shaphan, **heard** Baruch read from the scroll
36.13 told them everything that he had **heard** Baruch read
36.24 any of his officials who **heard** all this was afraid or showed
37. 5 but when they **heard** that the Egyptian army had crossed
38. 1 and Pashhur son of Malchiah **heard** that I was telling the
38. 7 worked in the royal palace, **heard** that they had put me in
38.25 If the officials **hear** that I have talked with you,
38.27 could do, because no one had **overheard** the conversation.

Jer 40. 7 They **heard** that the king of Babylonia had made Gedaliah governor
40.11 Edom, and other countries, **heard** that the king of Babylonia
41.11 the army leaders with him **heard** of the crime that Ishmael
42.13 face war any more or **hear** the call to battle or go
46.12 Nations have **heard** of your shame;
46.12 everyone has **heard** you cry.
47. 3 They will **hear** the hoof beats of horses, the clatter
48. 5 **Hear** the sound of their sobs along the road up to Luhith,
48.29 I have **heard** how proud, arrogant, and conceited the people are,
48.34 cry out, and their cry can be **heard** as far as Jahaz;
48.34 it can be **heard** by the people in Zoar,
48.34 and it is **heard** as far as Horonaim and Eglath
49. 2 the capital city of Rabbah **hear** the noise of battle,
49.21 cries of alarm will be **heard** as far away as the Gulf
49.23 are worried and troubled because they have **heard** bad news.
50.22 The noise of battle is **heard** in the land, and there is
50.43 king of Babylonia **hears** the news, and his hands hang limp.
50.46 the cries of alarm will be **heard** by the other nations."
51.27 Blow the trumpet so that the nations can **hear!**
51.46 lose courage or be afraid because of the rumours you **hear.**
Lam 3.56 And when I begged you to listen to my cry, you **heard.**
3.61 "You have **heard** them insult me, O Lord;
Ezek 1. 3 beside the River Chebar, I **heard** the Lord speak to me
1.24 I **heard** the noise their wings made in flight;
1.28 Then I **heard** a voice [1] saying, "Mortal man, stand up.
2. 2 to my feet, and I **heard** the voice continue, [3] "Mortal man,
3.12 lifted me up, and I **heard** behind me the loud roar of
3.13 **heard** the wings of the creatures beating together in the air,
3.15 I stayed there, overcome by what I had seen and **heard.**
3.22 presence of the Lord and **heard** him say to me, "Get up
6. 3 the mountains of Israel to **hear** the word of the Lord—
6. 3 to **hear** what I, the Sovereign Lord, am
9. 1 Then I **heard** God shout, "Come here, you men who are going
9. 5 And I **heard** God say to the other men, "Follow him through
10. 5 by the creatures' wings was **heard** even in the outer courtyard.
12. 2 have ears, but they **hear** nothing, because they are rebellious.
16.35 **Hear** what the Lord is saying.
19. 4 The nations **heard** about him and trapped him in a pit.
19. 9 his roar would never be **heard** again on the hills of Israel.
20.47 the southern forest to **hear** what the Sovereign Lord is saying:
23.42 a carefree crowd could be **heard,** a group of men brought in
24.17 Don't let your sobbing be **heard.**
29.21 speak out where everyone can **hear** you, so that they will
32. 9 news of your destruction through countries you never **heard** of.
33. 4 someone **hears** it but pays no attention and the enemy comes
33.30 one another, 'Let's go and **hear** what word has come from the
33.31 my people crowd in to **hear** what you have to say,
35.12 know that I, the Lord, **heard** you say with contempt that the
35.13 have **heard** the wild, boastful way you have talked against me."
37. 7 While I was speaking, I **heard** a rattling noise, and the
43. 6 beside me there, and I **heard** the Lord speak to me
44. 5 "Mortal man, pay attention to everything you see and **hear.**
Dan 3. 5 You will **hear** the sound of the trumpets,
3. 7 so, as soon as they **heard** the sound of the instruments,
3.15 then, as soon as you **hear** the sound of the trumpets, oboes,
5.10 The queen mother **heard** the noise made by the king and
5.14 I have **heard** that the spirit of the holy gods is in
5.16 I have **heard** that you can find hidden meanings and explain
5.23 gods that cannot see or **hear** and that do not know anything.
6.14 When the king **heard** this, he was upset and did his best
7.11 I could still **hear** the little horn bragging and boasting.
8.13 I **heard** one angel ask another, "How long will these things
8.14 **heard** the other angel answer, "It will continue for 1,150 days,
8.16 **heard** a voice call out over the River Ulai, "Gabriel, explain
9.17 O God, **hear** my prayer and pleading.
9.19 Lord, **hear** us.
10. 9 When I **heard** his voice, I fell to the ground unconscious
10.12 God has **heard** your prayers ever since the first day you
12. 7 I **heard** him say, "It will be three and a half years.
12. 8 I **heard** what he said, but I did not understand it.
Obad 15 his messenger to the nations, and we have **heard** his message:
Jon 2. 2 world of the dead I cried for help, and you **heard** me.
2. 7 I prayed to you, and in your holy Temple you **heard** me.
3. 6 When the king of Nineveh **heard** about it, he got up from
Mic 1. 2 **Hear** this, all you nations;
1.11 When you **hear** the people of Bethezel mourn, you will know
6. 1 let the mountains and the hills **hear** what you say.
7. 7 My God will **hear** me.
Nah 2.13 The demands of your envoys will no longer be **heard."**
3.19 All those who **hear** the news of your destruction clap their
Hab 1. 5 something that you will not believe when you **hear** about it.
3. 2 O Lord, I have **heard** of what you have done,
3.16 I **hear** all this, and I tremble;
Zeph 1.10 says the Lord, "you will **hear** the sound of crying
1.10 You will **hear** wailing in the newer part of the city
1.11 Wail and cry when you **hear** this, you that live in
2. 8 Lord Almighty says, "I have **heard** the people of Moab and
Zech 3. 7 and I will **hear** your prayers,
3. 7 just as I **hear** the prayers of the angels
8. 9 You are now **hearing** the same words the prophets spoke at the
8.23 destiny, because we have **heard** that God is with you.' "
Mal 3.16 one another, and the Lord listened and **heard** what they said.
Mt 2. 3 When King Herod **heard** about this, he was very upset, and
2.18 "A sound is **heard** in Ramah, the sound of bitter weeping.
2.22 when Joseph **heard** that Archelaus had succeeded his father Herod
4.12 When Jesus **heard** that John had been put in prison, he
5.21 "You have **heard** that people were told in the past, 'Do
5.27 "You have **heard** that it was said, 'Do not commit adultery.'
5.33 "You have also **heard** that people were told in the past,
Mt 5.38 "You have **heard** that it was said, 'An eye for an eye,
5.43 "You have **heard** that it was said, 'Love your friends,
6. 7 that their gods will **hear** them because their prayers are long.
7.24 "So then, anyone who **hears** these words of mine and
7.26 "But anyone who **hears** these words of mine and does not
8.10 When Jesus **heard** this, he was surprised and said to the
9.12 Jesus **heard** them and answered, "People who are well do not
10.27 and what you have **heard** in private you must announce from
11. 2 When John the Baptist **heard** in prison about the things
11. 4 "Go back and tell John what you are **hearing** and seeing:
11. 5 are made clean, the deaf **hear,** the dead are brought back to
12.15 When Jesus **heard** about the plot against him, he went
12.24 When the Pharisees **heard** this, they replied, "He drives out
12.41 because they turned from their sins when they **heard** Jonah preach;
13.13 do not see, and they listen, but do not **hear** or understand.
13.15 would see, their ears would **hear,** their minds would understand,
13.16 Your eyes see and your ears **hear.**
13.17 could not, and to hear what you **hear,** but they did not.
13.19 Those who **hear** the message about the Kingdom
13.20 who receive the message gladly as soon as they **hear** it.
13.22 fell among thorn bushes stand for those who **hear** the message;
13.23 soil stand for those who **hear** the message and understand it:
13.54 He taught in the synagogue, and those who **heard** him were amazed.
14. 1 At that time Herod, the ruler of Galilee, **heard** about Jesus.
14.13 When Jesus **heard** the news about John, he left there in a
14.13 The people **heard** about it, so they left their towns and
17. 6 When the disciples **heard** the voice, they were so terrified
19.22 When the young man **heard** this, he went away sad, because
19.25 When the disciples **heard** this, they were completely amazed.
20.24 When the other ten disciples **heard** about this, they became angry
20.30 were sitting by the road **heard** that Jesus was passing by,
21.16 So they asked Jesus, "Do you **hear** what they are saying?"
21.45 chief priests and the Pharisees **heard** Jesus' parables and knew
22.22 When they **heard** this, they were amazed;
22.33 When the crowds **heard** this, they were amazed at his teaching.
22.34 When the Pharisees **heard** that Jesus had silenced the Sadducees,
24. 6 You are going to **hear** the noise of battles close by and
26.65 You have just **heard** his blasphemy!
27.13 said to him, "Don't you **hear** all these things they accuse
27.47 of the people standing there **heard** him and said, "He is
28.14 And if the Governor should **hear** of this, we will
Mk 1. 5 of Judaea and the city of Jerusalem went out to **hear** John.
1.22 The people who **heard** him were amazed at the way he taught,
2.17 Jesus **heard** them and answered, "People who are well
3. 8 to Jesus because they had **heard** of the things he was doing.
3.21 When his family **heard** about it, they set out to take
4.10 some of those who had **heard** him came to him with the
4.11 are on the outside, **hear** all things by means of parables,
4.15 as soon as they **hear** the message, Satan comes and takes it
4.16 As soon as they **hear** the message, they receive it gladly.
4.18 These are the ones who **hear** the message, [19] but the worries
4.20 They **hear** the message, accept it, and bear fruit:
4.24 He also said to them, "Pay attention to what you **hear!**
5.20 And all who **heard** it were amazed.
5.27 She had **heard** about Jesus, so she came in the crowd
5.38 Jesus saw the confusion and **heard** all the loud crying
6. 2 and when they **heard** him, they were all amazed.
6.14 Now King Herod **heard** about all this, because Jesus' reputation
6.16 When Herod **heard** it, he said, "He is John the Baptist!
6.20 even though he became greatly disturbed every time he **heard** him.
6.29 When John's disciples **heard** about this, they came and took away
6.55 and wherever they **heard** he was, they brought to him sick
7.25 an evil spirit in her, **heard** about Jesus and came to him
7.35 the man was able to **hear,** his speech impediment was removed,
7.37 And all who **heard** were completely amazed.
7.37 "He even causes the deaf to **hear** and the dumb to speak!"
8.18 You have ears—can't you **hear?**
10.22 When the man **heard** this, gloom spread over his face, and
10.41 When the other ten disciples **heard** about it, they became angry
10.47 When he **heard** that it was Jesus of Nazareth, he began to
11.14 And his disciples **heard** him.
11.18 the teachers of the Law **heard** of this, so they began looking
12.28 A teacher of the Law was there who **heard** the discussion.
13. 7 don't be troubled when you **hear** the noise of battles close
14.11 They were pleased to **hear** what he had to say, and
14.58 "We **heard** him say, 'I will tear down this Temple which
14.64 You **heard** his blasphemy.
15.35 Some of the people there **heard** him and said, "Listen, he
15.44 Pilate was surprised to **hear** that Jesus was already dead.
15.45 After **hearing** the officer's report, Pilate told Joseph
16.11 and when they **heard** her say that Jesus was alive and
Lk 1.13 God has **heard** your prayer, and your wife Elizabeth will bear
1.41 When Elizabeth **heard** Mary's greeting, the baby moved within her.
1.44 For as soon as I **heard** your greeting, the baby within me
1.58 Her neighbours and relatives **heard** how wonderfully good the Lord
1.66 Everyone who **heard** of it thought about it and asked,
2.18 All who **heard** it were amazed at what the shepherds said.
2.20 singing praises to God for all they had **heard** and seen;
2.47 All who **heard** him were amazed at his intelligent answers.
4.21 scripture has come true today, as you **heard** it being read."
4.23 home town the same things you **heard** were done in Capernaum.
4.28 people in the synagogue **heard** this, they were filled with anger.
5.15 crowds of people came to **hear** him and be healed from their
6.18 they had come to **hear** him and to be healed of their
6.27 "But I tell you who **hear** me:
6.49 But anyone who **hears** my words and does not obey them is

Lk	7. 3	When the officer **heard** about Jesus, he sent some Jewish elders
	7. 9	Jesus was surprised when he **heard** this;
	7.22	"Go back and tell John what you have seen and **heard:**
	7.22	the deaf can **hear,** the dead are raised to life,
	7.29	All the people **heard** him;
	7.37	She **heard** that Jesus was eating in the Pharisee's house, so
	8.12	The seeds that fell along the path stand for those who **hear;**
	8.13	stand for those who **hear** the message and receive it gladly.
	8.14	The seeds that fell among thorn bushes stand for those who **hear;**
	8.15	soil stand for those who **hear** the message and retain it in
	8.21	and brothers are those who **hear** the word of God and obey
	8.50	But Jesus **heard** it and said to Jairus, "Don't be afraid;
	9. 7	Herod, the ruler of Galilee, **heard** about all the things that
	9. 9	but who is this man I **hear** these things about?"
	9.11	When the crowds **heard** about it, they followed him.
	10.24	could not, and to hear what you **hear,** but they did not."
	11.28	how happy are those who **hear** the word of God and obey
	11.32	because they turned from their sins when they **heard** Jonah preach;
	12. 3	in the dark will be **heard** in broad daylight, and whatever
	14.15	the men sitting at table **heard** this, he said to Jesus,
	15.25	he came close to the house, he **heard** the music and dancing.
	16. 2	called him in and said, 'What is this I **hear** about you?
	16.14	When the Pharisees **heard** all this, they sneered at Jesus,
	18.22	When Jesus **heard** this, he said to him, "There is still
	18.23	But when the man **heard** this, he became very sad, because
	18.26	The people who **heard** him asked, "Who, then, can be saved?"
	18.36	When he **heard** the crowd passing by, he asked, "What is this?"
	20.16	When the people **heard** this, they said, "Surely not!"
	21. 9	Don't be afraid when you **hear** of wars and revolutions;
	22.71	We ourselves have **heard** what he said!"
	23. 6	When Pilate **heard** this, he asked, "Is this man a Galilean?"
	23. 8	saw Jesus, because he had **heard** about him and had been
Jn	1. 7	the light, so that all should **hear** the message and believe.
	1.37	The two disciples **heard** him say this and went with Jesus.
	3. 8	you **hear** the sound it makes, but you do not know where
	3.29	and listens, is glad when he **hears** the bridegroom's voice.
	3.32	what he has seen and **heard,** yet no one accepts his message.
	4. 1	The Pharisees **heard** that Jesus was winning and baptizing
	4. 3	So when Jesus **heard** what was being said, he left Judaea
	4.42	but because we ourselves have **heard** him, and we know that he
	4.47	When he **heard** that Jesus had come from Judaea to Galilee,
	5.24	whoever **hears** my words and believes in him who sent me has
	5.25	come—when the dead will **hear** the voice of the
	5.25	Son of God, and those who **hear** it will come to life.
	5.28	when all the dead will **hear** his voice [29] and come out of
	5.37	You have never **heard** his voice or seen his face, [38] and you
	6.45	Anyone who **hears** the Father and learns from him comes to me.
	6.60	Many of his followers **heard** this and said, "This teaching
	7.32	Pharisees **heard** the crowd whispering these things about Jesus,
	7.40	the people in the crowd **heard** him say this and said,
	7.51	cannot condemn a man before **hearing** him and finding out what
	8. 9	When they **heard** this, they all left, one by one, the older
	8.26	and I tell the world only what I have **heard** from him."
	8.30	Many who **heard** Jesus say these things believed in him.
	8.40	tell you the truth I **heard** from God, yet you are trying
	9.27	Why do you want to **hear** it again?
	9.32	the world nobody has ever **heard** of anyone giving sight to a
	9.35	When Jesus **heard** what had happened, he found the man and
	9.40	who were there with him **heard** him say this and asked him,
	10. 3	the sheep **hear** his voice as he calls his own sheep by
	11. 4	When Jesus **heard** it, he said, "The final result of this
	11.20	When Martha **heard** that Jesus was coming, she went out to
	11.29	When Mary **heard** this, she got up and hurried out to meet
	12. 9	A large number of people **heard** that Jesus was in Bethany,
	12.12	the Passover Festival **heard** that Jesus was coming to Jerusalem.
	12.18	met him—because they **heard** that he had performed this miracle.
	12.29	The crowd standing there **heard** the voice, and some of
	12.47	If anyone **hears** my message and does not obey it, I will
	14.24	And the teaching you have **heard** is not mine, but comes from
	14.28	You **heard** me say to you, 'I am leaving, but I will
	15.15	I have told you everything I have **heard** from my Father.
	16.13	will speak of what he **hears,** and will tell you of things
	18.21	Question the people who **heard** me.
	19. 8	When Pilate **heard** this, he was even more afraid.
	19.12	When Pilate **heard** this, he tried to find a way to set
	19.13	When Pilate **heard** these words, he took Jesus outside
	21. 7	When Peter **heard** that it was the Lord, he wrapped his outer
Acts	1.19	the people living in Jerusalem **heard** about it, and so in
	2. 6	When they **heard** this noise, a large crowd gathered.
	2. 6	because each one of them **heard** the believers speaking in his
	2. 8	then, that all of us **hear** them speaking in our own native
	2.11	Arabia—yet all of us **hear** them speaking in our own languages
	2.33	What you now see and **hear** is his gift that he has
	2.37	When the people **heard** this, they were deeply troubled
	4. 4	But many who **heard** the message believed;
	4.20	stop speaking of what we ourselves have seen and **heard."**
	4.24	When the believers **heard** it, they all joined together in prayer
	5. 5	As soon as Ananias **heard** this, he fell down dead;
	5. 5	and all who **heard** about it were terrified.
	5.11	church and all the others who **heard** of this were terrified.
	5.24	the temple guards **heard** this, they wondered what had happened
	5.33	the members of the Council **heard** this, they were so furious
	6.11	some men to say, "We **heard** him speaking against Moses
	6.14	We **heard** him say that this Jesus of Nazareth will tear
	7.12	food, [12] and when Jacob **heard** that there was corn in Egypt,
	7.29	When Moses **heard** this, he fled from Egypt and went to
	7.31	But he **heard** the Lord's voice:
	7.34	I have **heard** their groans, and I have come down to set
	8.14	The apostles in Jerusalem **heard** that the people of Samaria
	8.30	Philip ran over and **heard** him reading from the book of
Acts	9. 4	fell to the ground and **heard** a voice saying to him, "Saul,
	9. 7	they **heard** the voice but could not see anyone.
	9.21	All who **heard** him were amazed and asked, "Isn't he the
	9.38	when the believers in Joppa **heard** that Peter was in Lydda,
	10.22	his house, so that he could **hear** what you have to say."
	10.31	God has **heard** your prayer and has taken notice of your works
	10.33	waiting to **hear** anything that the Lord has instructed
	10.46	For they **heard** them speaking in strange tongues and praising
	11. 1	believers throughout Judaea **heard** that the Gentiles also had
	11. 7	Then I **heard** a voice saying to me, 'Get up, Peter;
	11.18	When they **heard** this, they stopped their criticism and praised
	13. 7	Saul before him because he wanted to **hear** the word of God.
	13.16	**hear** me!
	13.44	everyone in the town came to **hear** the word of the Lord.
	13.48	When the Gentiles **heard** this, they were glad and praised
	14.14	When Barnabas and Paul **heard** what they were about to do,
	15. 7	Good News to the Gentiles, so that they could **hear** and believe.
	15.12	group was silent as they **heard** Barnabas and Paul report all
	15.24	We have **heard** that some men who went from our group have
	16.14	One of those who **heard** us was Lydia from Thyatira, who
	16.38	when they **heard** that Paul and Silas were Roman citizens, they
	17.13	the Jews in Thessalonica **heard** that Paul had preached the word
	17.20	Some of the things we **hear** you say sound strange to us,
	17.21	all their time telling and **hearing** the latest new thing.)
	17.32	When they **heard** Paul speak about a raising from death,
	17.32	others said, "We want to **hear** you speak about this again."
	18. 8	people in Corinth **heard** the message, believed, and were baptized.
	18.26	When Priscilla and Aquila **heard** him, they took him home with
	19. 2	"We have not even **heard** that there is a Holy Spirit,"
	19. 5	When they **heard** this, they were baptized in the name of
	19.10	Asia, both Jews and Gentiles, **heard** the word of the Lord.
	19.17	All the Jews and Gentiles who lived in Ephesus **heard** about this;
	19.26	Now, you can see and **hear** for yourselves what this
	19.28	As the crowd **heard** these words, they became furious
	21.12	When we **heard** this, we and the others there begged Paul
	21.20	After **hearing** him, they all praised God.
	21.22	They are sure to **hear** that you have arrived.
	22. 2	When they **heard** him speaking to them in Hebrew, they
	22. 7	fell to the ground and **heard** a voice saying to me, 'Saul,
	22. 9	the light, but did not **hear** the voice of the one who
	22.14	righteous Servant, and to **hear** him speaking with his own voice.
	22.15	for him to tell everyone what you have seen and **heard.**
	22.26	When the officer **heard** this, he went to the commander
	23.16	But the son of Paul's sister **heard** about the plot;
	23.35	he said, "I will **hear** you when your accusers arrive."
	24.22	well informed about the Way, brought the **hearing** to a close.
	25.22	Agrippa said to Festus, "I would like to **hear** this man myself."
	25.22	"You will **hear** him tomorrow," Festus answered.
	26.14	to the ground, and I **heard** a voice say to me in
	28.15	The believers in Rome **heard** about us and came as far as
	28.22	But we would like to **hear** your ideas, because we know
	28.27	would see, their ears would **hear,** their minds would understand,
Rom	1. 8	of you, because the whole world is **hearing** about your faith.
	2.13	For it is not by **hearing** the Law that people are put
	10.14	And how can they believe if they have not **heard** the message?
	10.14	And how can they **hear** if the message is not proclaimed?
	10.17	So then, faith comes from **hearing** the message,
	10.18	Is it true that they did not **hear** the message?
	11. 8	to this very day they cannot see or **hear."**
	15.20	where Christ has not been **heard** of, so as not to build
	15.21	will see, and those who have not **heard** will understand."
	16.19	Everyone has **heard** of your loyalty to the gospel, and
1 Cor	2. 9	no one ever saw or **heard,** what no one ever thought could
	12.17	If the whole body were just an eye, how could it **hear?**
	14.24	in, he will be convinced of his sin by what he **hears.**
	14.24	judged by all he **hears,** [25] his secret thoughts will be brought
2 Cor	6. 2	**Hear** what God says:
	6. 2	the time came for me to show you favour I **heard** you;
	12. 3	God knows), and there he **heard** things which cannot be put
	12. 6	result of what he has seen me do and **heard** me say.
Gal	3. 2	the Law requires or by **hearing** the gospel and believing it?
	3. 5	Law requires or because you **hear** the gospel and believe it?
	4.21	do you not **hear** what the Law says?
Eph	1.13	became God's people when you **heard** the true message, the
	1.15	this reason, ever since I **heard** of your faith in the Lord
	3. 2	Surely you have **heard** that God in his grace has given me
	4.21	You certainly **heard** about him, and as his followers
	4.29	that what you say will do good to those who **hear** you.
Phil	1.27	and see you, I will **hear** that you are standing firm with
	1.30	the past, and as you **hear,** the one I am fighting still.
	2.26	and is very upset because you had **heard** that he was ill.
Col	1. 4	For we have **heard** of your faith in Christ Jesus and of
	1. 5	News, first came to you, you **heard** about the hope it offers.
	1. 6	since the day you first **heard** about the grace of God and
	1. 9	have always prayed for you, ever since we **heard** about you.
	1.23	shaken from the hope you gained when you **heard** the gospel.
1 Thes	2.13	brought you God's message, you **heard** it and accepted it, not
2 Thes	3.11	We say this because we **hear** that there are some people
1 Tim	4.16	you do, you will save both yourself and those who **hear** you.
2 Tim	2. 2	Take the teachings that you **heard** me proclaim in the
	4. 3	teachers who will tell them what they are itching to **hear.**
	4.17	to proclaim the full message for all the Gentiles to **hear;**
Tit	2.15	use your full authority as you encourage and rebuke your **hearers.**
Phlm	5	For I **hear** of your love for all God's people and the
Heb	2. 1	to the truths we have **heard,** so that we will not be
	2. 3	this salvation, and those who **heard** him proved to us that it
	3. 7	Holy Spirit says, "If you **hear** God's voice today, [8] do not
	3.15	"If you **hear** God's voice today, do not be stubborn, as
	3.16	Who were the people who **heard** God's voice and rebelled against him?
	4. 2	For we have **heard** the Good News, just as they did.

Heb 4. 2 They **heard** the message, but it did them no good,
4. 2 because when they **heard** it, they did not accept it
4. 6 Those who first **heard** the Good News did not receive that rest,
4. 7 "If you **hear** God's voice today, do not be stubborn."
5. 7 Because he was humble and devoted, God **heard** him.
11. 7 was faith that made Noah **hear** God's warnings about things in
12.19 When the people **heard** the voice, they begged not to hear
12.19 they begged not to **hear** another word, [20]because they could not
12.25 Be careful, then, and do not refuse to **hear** him who speaks.
12.25 Those who refused to **hear** the one who gave the divine
Jas 5.11 You have **heard** of Job's patience, and you know how the Lord
1 Pet 1.12 things which you have now **heard** from the messengers who announced
2.22 sin, and no one ever **heard** a lie come from his lips.
2 Pet 1.18 We ourselves **heard** this voice coming from heaven, when we were
2. 8 he suffered agony as he saw and **heard** their evil actions.
1 Jn 1. 1 We have **heard** it, and we have seen it with our eyes;
1. 3 What we have seen and **heard** we announce to you also, so
1. 5 the message that we have **heard** from his Son and announce is
2. 7 The old command is the message you have already **heard.**
2.24 in your hearts the message you **heard** from the beginning.
3.11 The message you **heard** from the very beginning is this:
4. 3 you **heard** that it would come, and now it is here in
5.14 we are sure that he **hears** us if we ask him for
5.15 He **hears** us whenever we ask him;
2 Jn 6 command, as you have all **heard** from the beginning, is that
3 Jn 4 makes me happier than to **hear** that my children live in the
Rev 1.10 control of me, and I **heard** a loud voice, that sounded like
3. 3 Remember, then, what you were taught and what you **heard;**
3.20 if anyone **hears** my voice and opens the door, I will come
4. 1 a trumpet, which I had **heard** speaking to me before, said,
5.11 Again I looked, and I **heard** angels, thousands and millions
5.13 And I **heard** every creature in heaven, on earth, in the
6. 1 the seven seals, and I **heard** one of the four living
6. 3 and I **heard** the second living creature say, "Come!"
6. 5 and I **heard** the third living creature say, "Come!"
6. 6 I **heard** what sounded like a voice coming from among the
6. 7 and I **heard** the fourth living creature say, "Come!"
8.13 Then I looked, and I **heard** an eagle that was flying high
9.13 I **heard** a voice coming from the four corners of the gold
9.20 silver, bronze, stone, and wood, which cannot see, **hear,** or walk.
10. 4 But I **heard** a voice speak from heaven, "Keep secret what
10. 8 the voice that I had **heard** speaking from heaven spoke to me
11.12 Then the two prophets **heard** a loud voice say to them
12.10 I **heard** a loud voice in heaven saying, "Now God's
14. 2 And I **heard** a voice from heaven that sounded like a
14.13 Then I **heard** a voice from heaven saying, "Write this:
16. 1 Then I **heard** a loud voice speaking from the temple to the
16. 5 I **heard** the angel in charge of the waters say, "The
16. 7 Then I **heard** a voice from the altar saying, "Lord God Almighty!
18. 4 Then I **heard** another voice from heaven, saying, "Come out,
18.22 the flute and the trumpet, will never be **heard** in you again!
18.22 and the sound of the millstone will be **heard** no more!
18.23 more will the voices of brides and grooms be **heard** in you.
19. 1 After this I **heard** what sounded like the roar of a large
19. 6 Then I **heard** what sounded like a large crowd,
19. 6 I **heard** them say, "Praise God!
21. 3 I **heard** a loud voice speaking from the throne:
22. 8 I, John, have **heard** and seen all these things.
22. 8 And when I finished **hearing** and seeing them, I fell down at
22.17 Everyone who **hears** this must also say, "Come!"
22.18 solemnly warn everyone who **hears** the prophetic words of this book:

HEARSAY

Is 11. 3 He will not judge by appearance or **hearsay;**

HEART

[BROKEN-HEARTED, WHOLE-HEARTED]

Gen 42.28 Their **hearts** sank, and in fear they asked one another,
43.30 Joseph left suddenly, because his **heart** was full of tender
50.21 So he reassured them with kind words that touched their **hearts.**
Deut 4.29 you search for him **with all your heart,** you will find him.
6. 5 the Lord your God **with all your heart,** with all your soul,
10.12 Love him, serve him **with all your heart,** [13]and obey all
11.13 love the Lord your God and serve him **with all your heart.**
13. 3 you, to see if you love the Lord **with all your heart.**
26.16 so obey them faithfully **with all your heart.**
28.47 but you would not serve him with glad and joyful **hearts.**
28.67 Your **hearts** will pound with fear at everything you see.
30. 2 to the Lord and **with all your heart** obey his commands that
30. 6 you and your descendants obedient **hearts,** so that you will
30. 6 you will love him **with all your heart,** and you will continue
30.10 You will have to turn to him **with all your heart.**
Josh 22. 5 to him, and serve him **with all your heart** and soul."
23.14 of you knows in his **heart** and soul that the Lord your
Judg 5. 9 My **heart** is with the commanders of Israel, with the people
11.35 You are breaking my **heart!**
1 Sam 2. 1 "The Lord has filled my **heart** with joy;
7. 3 turn to the Lord **with all your hearts,** you must get rid
10.26 Some powerful men, whose **hearts** God had touched, went with
12.20 turn away from the Lord, but serve him **with all your heart.**
12.24 Obey the Lord and serve him faithfully **with all your heart.**
16. 7 Man looks at the outward appearance, but I look at the **heart."**
1 Kgs 2. 4 obey his commands faithfully **with all their heart** and soul.
3.26 The real mother, her **heart** full of love for her son,
8.23 your love when they live in **whole-hearted** obedience to you.
8.38 Israel, out of **heartfelt** sorrow, stretch out their hands in
1 Kgs 8.39 You alone know the thoughts of the human **heart.**
2 Kgs 9.24 arrow that struck Joram in the back and pierced his **heart.**
10.31 Jehu did not obey **with all his heart** the law of the
23. 3 his laws and commands **with all his heart** and soul, and to
23.25 who served the Lord **with all his heart,** mind, and strength,
1 Chr 22.19 Now serve the Lord your God **with all your heart** and soul.
28. 9 and to serve him with an undivided **heart** and a willing mind.
29.17 know that you test everyone's **heart** and are pleased with
29.18 strong in your people's **hearts** and keep them always faithful
29.19 Give my son Solomon a **wholehearted** desire to obey
2 Chr 6.14 your love when they live in **wholehearted** obedience to you.
6.29 Israel, out of **heartfelt** sorrow, stretch out their hands in
6.30 You alone know the thoughts of the human **heart.**
15.12 the God of their ancestors, **with all their heart** and soul.
15.15 because they had made this covenant **with all their heart.**
16. 9 to give strength to those whose **hearts** are loyal to him.
20.33 people still did not turn **wholeheartedly** to the worship of
30.19 who are worshipping you **with all their heart,** even though
34.31 his laws and commands **with all his heart** and soul, and to
Ezra 1. 5 Levites, and everyone else whose **heart** God had moved got ready
Job 9.35 I am going to talk because I know my own **heart.**
11.13 Put your **heart** right, Job.
15.35 their **hearts** are always full of deceit.
20.25 shiny point drips with his blood, and terror grips his **heart.**
21.25 they live and die with bitter **hearts.**
22.22 keep his words in your **heart.**
31.20 Then he would praise me **with all his heart.**
37. 1 The storm makes my **heart** beat wildly.
41.24 His stony **heart** is without fear, as unyielding and hard as
Ps 9. 1 I will praise you, Lord, **with all my heart;**
11. 5 the lawless he hates **with all his heart.**
13. 2 How long will sorrow fill my **heart** day and night?
17. 3 You know my **heart.**
21. 2 You have given him his **heart's** desire;
22.14 my **heart** is like melted wax.
28. 3 whose words are friendly, but who have hatred in their **hearts.**
34.14 strive for peace **with all your heart.**
35.10 **With all my heart** I will say to the Lord, "There is
36. 1 Sin speaks to the wicked man deep in his **heart;**
37. 4 in the Lord, and he will give you your **heart's** desire.
37.31 law of his God in his **heart** and never departs from it.
38. 8 my **heart** is troubled, and I groan with pain.
38.10 My **heart** is pounding, my strength is gone, and my eyes
40. 8 I keep your teaching in my **heart."**
42. 4 My **heart** breaks when I remember the past, when I went with
42. 6 Here in exile my **heart** is breaking, and so I turn my
45. 5 arrows are sharp, they pierce the **hearts** of your enemies;
51.10 Create a pure **heart** in me, O God, and put a new
51.17 you will not reject a humble and repentant **heart.**
55.15 Evil is in their homes and in their **hearts.**
55.21 smoother than cream, but there was hatred in his **heart;**
62. 4 You speak words of blessing, but in your **heart** you curse him.
64. 6 The **heart** and mind of man are a mystery.
69.20 Insults have broken my **heart,** and I am in despair.
73. 1 God is indeed good to Israel, to those who have pure **hearts.**
73. 7 their **hearts** pour out evil, and their minds are busy with
86.12 I will praise you **with all my heart,** O Lord my God;
109.22 I am hurt to the depths of my **heart.**
111. 1 **With all my heart** I will thank the Lord in the assembly
116. 7 Be confident, my **heart,** because the Lord has been good to me.
119. 2 who follow his commands, who obey him **with all their heart.**
119. 7 your righteous judgements, I will praise you with a pure **heart.**
119.10 **With all my heart** I try to serve you;
119.11 keep your law in my **heart,** so that I will not sin
119.20 My **heart** aches with longing;
119.34 I will keep it **with all my heart.**
119.58 I ask you **with all my heart** to have mercy on me,
119.69 about me, but **with all my heart** I obey your instructions.
119.111 they are the joy of my **heart.**
119.129 I obey them **with all my heart.**
119.145 **With all my heart** I call to you;
119.160 The **heart** of your law is truth, and all your righteous
119.167 I love them **with all my heart.**
131. 2 in its mother's arms, so my **heart** is quiet within me.
138. 1 I thank you, Lord, **with all my heart;**
139.14 I know it **with all my heart.**
147. 3 He heals the **broken-hearted** and bandages their wounds.
Prov 3. 3 write them on your **heart.**
3. 5 Trust in the Lord **with all your heart.**
4.21 Remember them and keep them in your **heart.**
6.21 Keep their words with you always, locked in your **heart.**
7. 3 write it on your **heart.**
7.23 prancing into a trap [23]where an arrow would pierce its **heart.**
7.25 Do not let such a woman win your **heart;**
13.12 When hope is crushed, the **heart** is crushed,
17. 3 tested by fire, and a person's **heart** is tested by the Lord.
22.11 If you love purity of **heart** and graciousness of speech,
26.25 don't believe him, because his **heart** is filled to the brim
27.19 and it is your own self that you see in your **heart.**
Ecc 2.23 everything you do brings nothing but worry and **heartache.**
11. 9 Do what you want to do, and follow your **heart's** desire.
Song 4. 9 and the necklace you are wearing have stolen my **heart.**
5. 2 While I slept, my **heart** was awake.
8. 6 Close your **heart** to every love but mine;
Is 1. 5 already covered with wounds, and your **heart** and mind are sick.
10.34 down as trees in the **heart** of the forest are cut down
15. 5 My **heart** cries out for Moab!
26. 9 At night I long for you **with all my heart;**
29.13 words are meaningless, and their **hearts** are somewhere else.
38.15 My **heart** is bitter, and I cannot sleep.
47. 7 not take these things to **heart** or think how it all would

Is 51. 7 what is right, who have my teaching fixed in your **hearts.**
61. 1 the poor, To heal the **broken-hearted,** To announce release to
65.14 will sing for joy, but you will cry with a broken **heart.**
Jer 3.17 no longer do what their stubborn and evil **hearts** tell them.
4.14 wash the evil from your **heart,** so that you may be saved.
4.18 it has stabbed you through the **heart.**
4.19 My **heart!**
4.19 My **heart** is beating wildly!
7.24 whatever their stubborn and evil **hearts** told them to do,
8.18 I am sick at **heart.**
8.21 My **heart** has been crushed because my people are crushed;
12.16 If **with all their hearts** they will accept the religion
14. 4 and the ground is dried up, the farmers are sick at **heart;**
15. 9 she is disgraced and sick at **heart.**
15.16 and so your words filled my **heart** with joy and happiness.
17. 1 it is engraved on your **hearts** with a diamond point and
17. 9 "Who can understand the human **heart?**
17.10 I, the Lord, search the minds and test the **hearts** of men.
20.12 you know what is in their **hearts** and minds.
23. 9 My **heart** is crushed, and I am trembling.
24. 7 God, because they will return to me **with all their heart.**
29.13 will find me because you will seek me **with all your heart.**
31.20 My **heart** goes out to you;
31.33 will put my law within them and write it on their **hearts.**
32.40 make them fear me **with all their heart,** so that they will
48.10 man who does not do the Lord's work **with all his heart!**
48.36 "So my **heart** mourns for Moab and for the people of Kir
Lam 1.20 My **heart** is broken in sorrow for my sins.
1.22 I groan in misery, and I am sick at **heart."**
2.19 Pour out your **heart** and beg him for mercy on your children
3.41 Let us open our **hearts** to God in heaven and pray,
3.51 My **heart** is grieved when I see what has happened to
5.17 are sick at our very **hearts** and can hardly see through our
Ezek 6. 9 disgraced them, because their faithless **hearts** deserted me
11.19 I will give them a new **heart** and a new mind.
11.19 will take away their stubborn **heart** of stone
11.19 and will give them an obedient **heart.**
14. 3 "these men have given their **hearts** to idols and are letting
14. 4 Israelite who has given his **heart** to idols and lets them
18.31 have been doing, and get yourselves new minds and **hearts.**
21. 6 "Mortal man, groan as if your **heart** is breaking with despair.
21. 7 When it comes, their **hearts** will be filled with fear,
27.31 Their **hearts** are bitter as they weep.
36.26 I will give you a new **heart** and a new mind.
36.26 will take away your stubborn **heart** of stone
36.26 and give you an obedient **heart.**
Dan 3.23 still tied up, fell into the **heart** of the blazing fire.
Hos 10. 2 The people whose **hearts** are deceitful must now suffer for
11. 8 My **heart** will not let me do it!
14. 4 I will love them **with all my heart;**
14. 9 what is written here, and may they take it to **heart.**
Joel 2.13 Let your broken **heart** show your sorrow;
Nah 2.10 **Hearts** melt with fear;
Zeph 3.14 Rejoice **with all your heart,** Jerusalem!
Zech 7.12 closed their minds [12] and made their **hearts** as hard as rock.
Mt 5. 8 "Happy are the pure in **heart;**
5.28 her is guilty of committing adultery with her in his **heart.**
6.21 For your **heart** will always be where your riches are.
9.36 he saw the crowds, his **heart** was filled with pity for them,
12.34 For the mouth speaks what the **heart** is full of.
14.14 the large crowd, his **heart** was filled with pity for them,
15. 8 their words, but their **heart** is really far away from me.
15.18 the mouth come from the **heart,** and these are the things that
15.19 For from his **heart** come the evil ideas which lead him to
18.35 of you unless you forgive your brother from your **heart."**
22.37 Lord your God **with all your heart,** with all your soul,
26.38 them, "The sorrow in my **heart** is so great that it almost
Mk 6.34 large crowd, and his **heart** was filled with pity for them,
7. 6 their words, but their **heart** is really far away from me.
7.19 does not go into his **heart** but into his stomach and then
7.21 the inside, from a person's **heart,** come the evil ideas which
11.23 does not doubt in his **heart,** but believes that what he says
12.30 your God **with all your heart,** with all your soul, with all
12.33 love God **with all his heart** and with all his mind and
14.34 them, "The sorrow in my **heart** is so great that it almost
Lk 1.46 Mary said, "My **heart** praises the Lord;
2.35 And sorrow, like a sharp sword, will break your own **heart."**
2.51 His mother treasured all these things in her **heart.**
6.45 brings good out of the treasure of good things in his **heart;**
6.45 For the mouth speaks what the **heart** is full of.
7.13 the Lord saw her, his **heart** was filled with pity for her,
8.12 the message away from their **hearts** in order to keep them
8.15 in a good and obedient **heart,** and they persist until they
10.27 Lord your God **with all your heart,** with all your soul, with
10.33 man, and when he saw him, his **heart** was filled with pity.
12.34 For your **heart** will always be where your riches are.
15.20 his **heart** was filled with pity, and he ran, threw his arms
16.15 look right in other people's sight, but God knows your **hearts.**
Jn 2.25 them, because he himself knew what was in their **hearts.**
5.38 keep his message in your **hearts,** for you do not believe in
5.42 I know that you have no love for God in your **hearts.**
7.38 of life-giving water will pour out from his **heart.' "**
11.33 his **heart** was touched, and he was deeply moved.
12.27 "Now my **heart** is troubled—and what shall I say?
13. 2 had already put into the **heart** of Judas, the son of Simon
16. 6 now that I have told you, your **hearts** are full of sadness.
16.22 see you again, and your **hearts** will be filled with gladness,
17.13 they might have my joy in their **hearts** in all its fullness.
Acts 2.46 eating with glad and humble **hearts,** [47] praising God, and enjoying
4.32 The group of believers was one in mind and **heart.**
7.51 "How heathen your **hearts,** how deaf you are to God's message!
Acts 8.21 in our work, because your **heart** is not right in God's sight.
11.23 to be faithful and true to the Lord **with all their hearts.**
14.17 he gives you food and fills your **hearts** with happiness."
21.13 "What are you doing, crying like this and breaking my **heart?**
27.22 But now I beg you, take **heart!**
27.25 So take **heart,** men!
27.36 They took **heart,** and every one of them also ate some food.
Rom 1. 9 I serve **with all my heart** by preaching the Good News about
1.24 the filthy things their **hearts** desire, and they do shameful things
2. 5 have a hard and stubborn **heart,** and so you are making your
2.15 shows that what the Law commands is written in their **hearts.**
2.29 the inside, that is, whose **heart** has been circumcised,
5. 5 out his love into our **hearts** by means of the Holy Spirit,
6.17 have obeyed **with all your heart** the truths found in the
8.27 God, who sees into our **hearts,** knows what the thought of the
9. 2 endless the pain in my **heart** [3] for my people, my own flesh
10. 1 I wish **with all my heart** that my own people might be
10. 8 your lips and in your **heart"**—that is, the message of faith
11. 8 As the scripture says, "God made their minds and **hearts** dull;
12.11 Serve the Lord with a **heart** full of devotion.
1 Cor 12.31 Set your **hearts,** then, on the more important gifts.
14. 1 Set your **hearts** on spiritual gifts, especially the gift
14.39 then, my brothers, set your **heart** on proclaiming God's message,
2 Cor 1.22 the Holy Spirit in our **hearts** as the guarantee of all that
1.23 I call God as my witness—he knows my **heart!**
2. 4 with a greatly troubled and distressed **heart** and with many tears;
3. 2 have, written on our **hearts** for everyone to know and read.
3. 3 living God, and not on stone tablets but on human **hearts.**
4. 6 his light shine in our **hearts,** to bring us the knowledge of
5.11 and I hope that in your **hearts** you know me as well.
6.11 we have opened our **hearts** wide.
6.12 It is not we who have closed our **hearts** to you;
6.12 it is you who have closed your **hearts** to us.
6.13 Open your **hearts** wide!
7. 2 Make room for us in your **hearts.**
7. 5 troubles everywhere, quarrels with others, fears in our **hearts.**
7.10 God brings a change of **heart** that leads to salvation—and
Gal 4. 6 of his Son into our **hearts,** the Spirit who cries out,
Eph 3.17 that Christ will make his home in your **hearts** through faith.
4.23 Your **hearts** and minds must be made completely new,
5.19 hymns and psalms to the Lord with praise in your **hearts.**
6. 5 it with a sincere **heart,** as though you were serving Christ.
6. 6 but **with all your heart** do what God wants, as slaves of
Phil 1. 7 You are always in my **heart!**
1. 8 for you all comes from the **heart** of Christ Jesus himself.
4. 6 God for what you need, always asking him with a thankful **heart.**
4. 7 human understanding, will keep your **hearts** and minds safe in union
Col 3. 1 with Christ, so set your **hearts** on the things that are in
3.16 Christ's message in all its richness must live in your **hearts.**
3.16 sing to God with thanksgiving in your **hearts.**
3.22 do it with a sincere **heart** because of your reverence for the
3.23 at it **with all your heart,** as though you were working for
1 Thes 3.10 ask him **with all our heart** to let us see you personally
1 Tim 1. 5 that comes from a pure **heart,** a clear conscience, and a
6.10 from the faith and have broken their **hearts** with many sorrows.
2 Tim 2.22 those who with a pure **heart** call out to the Lord for
Phlm 7 You have cheered the **hearts** of all God's people.
12 sending him back to you now, and with him goes my **heart.**
Heb 3.12 one among you has a **heart** so evil and unbelieving that he
4.12 It judges the desires and thoughts of man's **heart.**
8.10 put my laws in their minds and write them on their **hearts.**
9. 9 God cannot make the worshipper's **heart** perfect, [10] since they
10.16 put my laws in their **hearts** and write them on their minds."
10.22 to God with a sincere **heart** and a sure faith,
10.22 with **hearts** that have been purified from a
Jas 1.21 that he plants in your **hearts,** which is able to save you.
3.14 But if in your **heart** you are jealous, bitter, and selfish,
4. 8 Purify your **hearts,** you hypocrites!
1 Pet 1.22 love one another earnestly **with all your heart.**
3.11 he must strive for peace **with all his heart.**
3.15 reverence for Christ in your **hearts,** and honour him as Lord.
2 Pet 1.19 and the light of the morning star shines in your **hearts.**
2.14 Their **hearts** are trained to be greedy.
1 Jn 2.24 then, to keep in your **hearts** the message you heard from the
3.17 in need, yet closes his **heart** against his brother, how can
5.10 in the Son of God has this testimony in his own **heart;**
Rev 17.17 God has placed in their **hearts** the will to carry out his

HEAT (1)

Gen 8.22 be cold and **heat,** summer and winter, day and night."
31.40 times I suffered from the **heat** during the day and from the
Job 6.17 but in the **heat** they disappear, and the stream beds
24.19 As snow vanishes in **heat** and drought, so a sinner vanishes
37.17 can only suffer in the **heat** when the south wind oppresses
39.14 on the ground for the **heat** in the soil to warm them.
Ps 19. 6 Nothing can hide from its **heat.**
32. 4 completely drained, as moisture is dried up by the summer **heat.**
Prov 25.13 who sends him, like cold water in the **heat** of harvest time.
Is 4. 6 shade the city from the **heat** of the day and make it
16. 3 a cool shadow in the **heat** of noon, and let us rest
18. 4 as serenely as the sun shines in the **heat** of the day.
25. 4 You give them shelter from storms and shade from the burning **heat.**
49.10 Sun and desert **heat** will not hurt them, for they will be
Ezek 20.47 to north, and everyone will feel the **heat** of the flames.
36. 5 spoken out in the **heat** of my anger against the surrounding
38.19 I declare in the **heat** of my anger that on that day
Dan 3.19 he ordered his men to **heat** the furnace seven times hotter
Hos 7. 7 "In the **heat** of their anger they murdered their rulers.

Jon 4. 8 about to faint from the **heat** of the sun beating down on
Acts 28. 3 out on account of the **heat** and fastened itself to his hand.
Jas 1.11 The sun rises with its blazing **heat** and burns the plant;
2 Pet 3.12 and the heavenly bodies will be melted by the **heat.**
Rev 7.16 neither sun nor any scorching **heat** will burn them,
16. 8 sun, and it was allowed to burn people with its fiery **heat.**
16. 9 were burnt by the fierce **heat,** and they cursed the name of

HEAT (2)

Jer 2.23 like a wild camel on **heat,** running about loose,
2.24 When she is on **heat,** who can control her?

HEATHEN

Judg 14. 3 you have to go to those **heathen** Philistines to get a wife?
15.18 die of thirst and be captured by these **heathen** Philistines?"
1 Sam 14. 6 "Let's cross over to the camp of those **heathen** Philistines.
17.26 After all, who is this **heathen** Philistine to defy the army
17.36 the same to this **heathen** Philistine, who has defied the army
Ps 9. 5 You have condemned the **heathen** and destroyed the wicked;
9.15 The **heathen** have dug a pit and fallen in;
9.19 Bring the **heathen** before you and pronounce judgement on them.
44. 2 you yourself drove out the **heathen** and established your people
59. 5 Wake up and punish the **heathen;**
59. 8 you mock all the **heathen.**
78.58 They angered him with their **heathen** places of worship,
79. 1 O God, the **heathen** have invaded your land.
89.50 am insulted, how I endure all the curses of the **heathen.**
106.27 scatter their descendants among the **heathen,** letting them die
106.34 They did not kill the **heathen,** as the Lord had commanded
106.41 the power of the **heathen,** and their enemies ruled over them.
Is 52. 1 The **heathen** will never enter your gates again.
Ezek 34.28 The **heathen** nations will not plunder them any more,
Hos 7.14 instead they throw themselves down and wail as the **heathen** do.
Amos 7.17 and you yourself will die in a **heathen** country.
Mt 20.25 that the rulers of the **heathen** have power over them, and the
Mk 10.42 are considered rulers of the **heathen** have power over them,
Lk 21.24 **heathen** will trample over Jerusalem until their time is up.
Acts 7.51 "How **heathen** your hearts, how deaf you are to God's message!
1 Cor 5. 1 so terrible that not even the **heathen** would be guilty of it.
6. 1 how dare he go before **heathen** judges instead of letting God's
12. 2 that while you were still **heathen,** you were led astray in
Eph 4.17 continue to live like the **heathen,** whose thoughts are worthless
1 Thes 4. 5 with a lustful desire, like the **heathen** who do not know God.
1 Pet 2.12 Your conduct among the **heathen** should be so good that
4. 3 enough time in the past doing what the **heathen** like to do.
4. 4 And now the **heathen** are surprised when you do not join
Rev 11. 2 have been given to the **heathen,** who will trample on the Holy
11.18 The **heathen** were filled with rage, because the time for

HEAVEN

[EARTH AND HEAVEN, QUEEN OF HEAVEN]
see also **KINGDOM (1)**

Gen 6. 2 some of the **heavenly** beings saw that these girls were
6. 4 who were descendants of human women and the **heavenly** beings.
14.19 the Most High God, who made **heaven and earth,** bless Abram!
14.22 High God, Maker of **heaven and earth,** [23] that I will not
21.17 the boy crying, and from **heaven** the angel of God spoke to
22.11 the angel of the Lord called to him from **heaven,** "Abraham,
22.15 Lord called to Abraham from **heaven** a second time,
24. 3 Lord, the God of **heaven and earth,** that you will not choose
24. 7 The Lord, the God of **heaven,** brought me from the home of
27.28 God give you dew from **heaven** and make your fields fertile!
27.39 "No dew from **heaven** for you, No fertile fields for you.
28.12 stairway reaching from earth to **heaven,** with angels going up
28.17 it must be the gate that opens into **heaven."**
Ex 20. 4 yourselves images of anything in **heaven** or on earth or in
20.22 have seen how I, the Lord, have spoken to you from **heaven.**
31.17 I, the Lord, made **heaven and earth** in six days,
Deut 3.24 There is no god in **heaven** or on earth who can do
4.26 I call **heaven and earth** as witnesses against you today
4.36 hear his voice from **heaven** so that he could instruct you;
4.39 the Lord is God in **heaven and on earth.**
5. 8 yourselves images of anything in **heaven** or on earth or in
10.14 To the Lord belong even the highest **heavens;**
26.15 down from your holy place in **heaven** and bless your people
30.19 curse, and I call **heaven and earth** to witness the choice you
31.28 I will call **heaven and earth** to be my witnesses against them.
Josh 2.11 Lord your God is God in **heaven** above and here on earth.
Judg 13.20 saw the Lord's angel go up towards **heaven** in the flames.
1 Sam 2.10 he will thunder against them from **heaven.**
7.10 but just then the Lord thundered from **heaven** against them.
1 Kgs 8.23 is no god like you in **heaven** above or on earth below!
8.27 Not even all **heaven** is large enough to hold you,
8.30 In your home in **heaven** hear us and forgive us.
8.32 O Lord, listen in **heaven** and judge your servants.
8.34 praying to you for forgiveness, [34] listen to them in **heaven.**
8.36 humbly praying to you, [36] listen to them in **heaven.**
8.39 to them in your home in **heaven,** forgive them, and help them.
8.43 In **heaven,** where you live, hear him and do what he asks
8.45 Hear them in **heaven,** and give them victory.
8.49 In your home in **heaven** hear them and be merciful to them.
22.19 sitting on his throne in **heaven,** with all his angels standing
2 Kgs 1.10 "may fire come down from **heaven** and kill you and your men!"
1.12 "may fire come down from **heaven** and kill you and your men!"
1.14 officers and their men were killed by fire from **heaven;**
2. 1 for the Lord to take Elijah up to **heaven** in a whirlwind.
2.11 them, and Elijah was taken up to **heaven** by a whirlwind.
1 Chr 16.26 other nations are only idols, but the Lord created the **heavens.**
1 Chr 21.26 by sending fire from **heaven** to burn the sacrifices on the
29.11 Everything in **heaven and earth** is yours, and you are king,
2 Chr 2. 6 because even all the vastness of **heaven** cannot contain him.
2.12 Praise the Lord God of Israel, Creator of **heaven and earth!**
6.13 everyone could see him, and raised his hands towards **heaven.)**
6.14 of Israel, in all **heaven and earth** there is no god like
6.18 Not even all **heaven** is large enough to hold you,
6.21 In your home in **heaven** hear us and forgive us.
6.23 O Lord, listen in **heaven** and judge your servants.
6.25 praying to you for forgiveness, [25] listen to them in **heaven.**
6.27 Lord, listen to them in **heaven** and forgive the sins of your
6.30 Listen to them in your home in **heaven** and forgive them.
6.33 In **heaven,** where you live, hear him and do what he asks
6.35 Hear them in **heaven** and give them victory.
6.39 In your home in **heaven** hear them and be merciful to them
7. 1 fire came down from **heaven** and burnt up the sacrifices that
7. 3 saw the fire fall from **heaven** and the light fill the Temple,
7.14 I will hear them in **heaven,** forgive their sins, and make
18.18 sitting on his throne in **heaven,** with all his angels standing
20. 6 you rule in **heaven** over all the nations of the
30.27 In his home in **heaven** God heard their prayers and accepted
36.23 The Lord, the God of **Heaven,** has made me ruler over the
Ezra 1. 2 The Lord, the God of **Heaven,** has made me ruler over the
5.11 of the God of **heaven and earth,** and we are rebuilding the
5.12 made the God of **Heaven** angry, he let them be conquered
6. 9 offerings to the God of **Heaven,** or wheat, salt, wine,
6.10 acceptable to the God of **Heaven** and pray for his blessing on
7.12 Ezra the priest, scholar in the Law of the God of **Heaven.**
7.21 Law of the God of **Heaven,** everything he asks you for,
7.23 everything which the God of **Heaven** requires for his Temple,
9. 6 they reach as high as the **heavens.**
Neh 1. 5 I prayed to God, [5] "Lord God of **Heaven!**
2. 4 prayed to the God of **Heaven,** [5] and then I said to the
2.20 I answered, "The God of **Heaven** will give us success.
9. 6 you made the **heavens** and the stars of the sky.
9. 6 The **heavenly** powers bow down and worship you.
9.13 At Mount Sinai you came down from **heaven;**
9.15 you gave them bread from **heaven,** and water from a rock when
9.27 called to you for help, and you answered them from **heaven.**
9.28 you to save them, in **heaven** you heard, and time after time
Esth 4.14 help will come from **heaven** to the Jews, and they will
Job 1. 6 day came for the **heavenly** beings to appear before the Lord,
2. 1 day came for the **heavenly** beings to appear before the Lord
4.18 God does not trust his **heavenly** servants;
9. 8 helped God spread out the **heavens** or trample the sea-monster's
16.19 There is someone in **heaven** to stand up for me and take
19.25 know there is someone in **heaven** who will come at last to
20.27 **Heaven** reveals this man's sin, and the earth gives testimony
22.12 God live in the highest **heavens** and look down on the stars,
25. 1 he keeps his **heavenly** kingdom in peace.
38. 7 stars sang together, and the **heavenly** beings shouted for joy.
Ps 2. 4 From his throne in **heaven** the Lord laughs and mocks their
8. 1 Your praise reaches up to the **heavens;**
11. 4 he has his throne in **heaven.**
14. 2 The Lord looks down from **heaven** at mankind to see if there
20. 6 answers him from his holy **heaven** and by his power gives him
29. 1 Praise the Lord, you **heavenly** beings;
33. 6 The Lord created the **heavens** by his command, the sun, moon,
33.13 The Lord looks down from **heaven** and sees all mankind.
36. 5 Lord, your constant love reaches the **heavens;**
50. 4 He calls **heaven and earth** as witnesses to see him judge
50. 6 **heavens** proclaim that God is righteous, that he himself is judge.
53. 2 God looks down from **heaven** at mankind to see if there are
57. 3 He will answer from **heaven** and save me;
57.10 Your constant love reaches the **heavens;**
69.34 Praise God, O **heaven and earth,** seas and all creatures
73. 9 speak evil of God in **heaven** and give arrogant orders to men
73.25 What else have I in **heaven** but you?
76. 8 You made your judgement known from **heaven;**
78.24 gave them grain from **heaven,** by sending down manna for them
78.69 There he built his Temple like his home in **heaven;**
80.14 Look down from **heaven** at us;
82. 1 God presides in the **heavenly** council;
85.11 and God's righteousness will look down from **heaven.**
89. 5 The **heavens** sing of the wonderful things you do;
89. 6 No one in **heaven** is like you, Lord;
89. 6 none of the **heavenly** beings is your equal.
89.11 **Heaven** is yours, the earth also;
93. 4 The Lord rules supreme in **heaven,** greater than the roar of
96. 5 other nations are only idols, but the Lord created the **heavens.**
97. 6 The **heavens** proclaim his righteousness, and all the nations
102.19 holy place on high, he looked down from **heaven** to earth.
102.25 the earth, and with your own hands you made the **heavens.**
103.19 The Lord placed his throne in **heaven;**
103.21 Praise the Lord, all you **heavenly** powers, you servants of
104. 2 You have spread out the **heavens** like a tent [3] and built your
105.40 he gave them food from **heaven** to satisfy them.
108. 4 Your constant love reaches above the **heavens;**
113. 4 his glory is above the **heavens.**
113. 6 but he bends down to see the **heavens and the earth.**
115. 3 Our God is in **heaven;**
115.15 May you be blessed by the Lord, who made **heaven and earth!**
115.16 **Heaven** belongs to the Lord alone, but he gave the earth
119.89 it is eternal in **heaven.**
121. 2 My help will come from the Lord, who made **heaven and earth.**
123. 1 Lord, I look up to you, up to **heaven,** where you rule.
124. 8 Our help comes from the Lord, who made **heaven and earth.**
134. 3 the Lord, who made **heaven and earth,** bless you from Zion!
135. 6 whatever he wishes in **heaven and on earth,** in the seas and
136. 5 By his wisdom he made the **heavens;**
136.26 Give thanks to the God of **heaven;**

Ps 139. 8 If I went up to **heaven,** you would be there;
146. 6 his God, [6]the Creator of **heaven,** earth, and sea, and all
148. 1 Praise the Lord from **heaven,** you that live in the heights above.
148. 2 Praise him, all his angels, all his **heavenly** armies.
148. 4 Praise him, highest **heavens,** and the waters above the sky.
148.13 his glory is above **earth and heaven.**
150. 1 Praise his strength in **heaven!**
Prov 30. 4 Who has ever mastered **heavenly** knowledge?
Ecc 5. 2 He is in **heaven** and you are on earth, so don't say
Is 7.11 in the world of the dead or from high up in **heaven."**
13.13 I will make the **heavens** tremble, and the earth will be
14.12 of Babylonia, bright morning star, you have fallen from **heaven!**
14.13 determined to climb up to **heaven** and to place your
18. 4 "I will look down from **heaven** as quietly as the dew forms
26.21 Lord is coming from his **heavenly** dwelling-place to punish
34. 5 prepared his sword in **heaven,** and now it will strike Edom,
38.14 My eyes grew tired from looking to **heaven.**
42. 5 God created the **heavens** and stretched them out;
44.23 Shout for joy, you **heavens!**
44.24 I alone stretched out the **heavens;**
45.12 By my power I stretched out the **heavens;**
45.18 The Lord created the **heavens**— he is the one who is
47.13 out the zones of the **heavens** and tell you from month to
48.13 My hands made the earth's foundations and spread the **heavens** out.
49.13 Sing, **heavens!**
51. 6 Look up at the **heavens;**
51. 6 The **heavens** will disappear like smoke;
51.13 who stretched out the **heavens** and laid the earth's
51.16 I stretched out the **heavens** and laid the earth's
55. 9 As high as the **heavens** are above the earth, so high are
63.15 look upon us from **heaven,** where you live in your holiness
65.17 The Lord says, "I am making a new earth and new **heavens.**
66. 1 The Lord says, **"Heaven** is my throne, and the earth is my
66.22 new earth and the new **heavens** will endure by my power,
Jer 7.18 to bake cakes for the goddess they call the **Queen of Heaven.**
10.12 his wisdom he created the world and stretched out the **heavens.**
23.24 you not know that I am everywhere in **heaven and on earth?**
25.30 Lord will roar from heaven and thunder from the heights of **heaven.**
44.17 to our goddess, the **Queen of Heaven,** and we will pour out
44.18 stopped sacrificing to the **Queen of Heaven** and stopped
44.19 shaped like the **Queen of Heaven,** offered sacrifices to her,
44.24 your wives have made solemn promises to the **Queen of Heaven.**
51.15 his wisdom he created the world and stretched out the **heavens.**
Lam 2. 1 Its **heavenly** splendour he has turned into ruins.
3.41 our hearts to God in **heaven** and pray, [42]"We have sinned
3.50 Until the Lord looks down from **heaven** and sees us.
Ezek 3.12 that said, "Praise the glory of the Lord in **heaven** above!"
32. 8 all the lights of **heaven** and plunge your world into darkness.
Dan 2.18 pray to the God of **heaven** for mercy and to ask him
2.19 to Daniel in a vision, and he praised the God of **heaven:**
2.28 But there is a God in **heaven,** who reveals mysteries.
2.37 The God of **heaven** has made you emperor and given you power,
2.44 the God of **heaven** will establish a kingdom that will
4.13 I saw coming down from **heaven** an angel, alert and watchful.
4.23 an angel came down from **heaven** and said, 'Cut the tree down
4.31 a voice spoke from **heaven,** "King Nebuchadnezzar, listen to
4.35 angels in **heaven** and people on earth are under his control.
4.37 I, Nebuchadnezzar, praise, honour, and glorify the King of **Heaven.**
5.23 acted against the Lord of **heaven** and brought in the cups and
6.27 he performs wonders and miracles in **heaven and on earth.**
7.26 the **heavenly** court will sit in judgement, take away his power,
8.10 to attack the army of **heaven,** the stars themselves,
8.11 defied the Prince of the **heavenly** army, stopped the daily
8.13 will the army of **heaven** and the Temple be trampled on?"
Amos 9. 2 Even if they climb up to **heaven,** I will bring them down.
9. 6 builds his home in the **heavens,** and over the earth he puts
Jon 1. 9 the Lord, the God of **heaven,** who made land and sea."
Mic 1. 2 He speaks from his **heavenly** temple.
6. 6 the Lord, the God of **heaven,** when I come to worship him?
Hab 3. 3 His splendour covers the **heavens;**
Hag 2. 6 "Before long I will shake **heaven and earth,** land and sea.
2.21 am about to shake **heaven and earth** [22]and overthrow kingdoms
Zech 3. 4 angel said to his **heavenly** attendants, "Take away the filthy
Mal 3.10 will open the windows of **heaven** and pour out on you in
Mt 3.16 Then **heaven** was opened to him, and he saw the Spirit of
3.17 Then a voice said from **heaven,** "This is my own dear Son,
5.12 and glad, for a great reward is kept for you in **heaven.**
5.16 the good things you do and praise your Father in **heaven.**
5.18 that as long as **heaven and earth** last, not the least point
5.34 Do not swear by **heaven,** for it is God's throne;
5.45 so that you may become the sons of your Father in **heaven.**
5.48 You must be perfect—just as your Father in **heaven** is perfect!
6. 1 you will not have any reward from your Father in **heaven.**
6. 9 'Our Father in **heaven:**
6.10 may your will be done on earth as it is in **heaven.**
6.14 done to you, your Father in **heaven** will also forgive you.
6.20 up riches for yourselves in **heaven,** where moths and rust cannot
6.26 yet your Father in **heaven** takes care of them!
6.32 Your Father in **heaven** knows that you need all these things.
7.11 then, will your Father in **heaven** give good things to those
7.21 those who do what my Father in **heaven** wants them to do.
10.32 I will do the same for him before my Father in **heaven.**
10.33 me publicly, I will reject him before my Father in **heaven.**
11.23 Did you want to lift yourself up to **heaven?**
11.25 At that time Jesus said, "Father, Lord of **heaven and earth!**
12.50 does what my Father in **heaven** wants him to do is my
14.19 the two fish, looked up to **heaven,** and gave thanks to God.
15.13 plant which my Father in **heaven** did not plant will be pulled
16.17 but it was given to you directly by my Father in **heaven.**
Mt 16.19 earth will be prohibited in **heaven,**
16.19 and what you permit on earth will be permitted in **heaven."**
18.10 Their angels in **heaven,** I tell you,
18.10 are always in the presence of my Father in **heaven.**
18.14 same way your Father in **heaven** does not want any of these
18.18 earth will be prohibited in **heaven,**
18.18 and what you permit on earth will be permitted in **heaven.**
18.19 for, it will be done for you by my Father in **heaven.**
18.35 is how my Father in **heaven** will treat every one of you
19.21 the money to the poor, and you will have riches in **heaven;**
22.30 they will be like the angels in **heaven** and will not marry.
23. 9 'Father', because you have only the one Father in **heaven.**
23.22 when someone swears by **heaven,** he is swearing by God's throne
24.29 the stars will fall from **heaven,** and the powers in space
24.30 Man coming on the clouds of **heaven** with power and great glory.
24.35 **Heaven and earth** will pass away, but my words will never
24.36 and hour will come—neither the angels in **heaven** nor the Son;
26.64 right of the Almighty and coming on the clouds of **heaven!"**
28. 2 the Lord came down from **heaven,** rolled the stone away, and
28.18 "I have been given all authority in **heaven and on earth.**
Mk 1.10 of the water, he saw **heaven** opening and the Spirit coming
1.11 And a voice came from **heaven,** "You are my own dear Son.
6.41 the two fish, looked up to **heaven,** and gave thanks to God.
7.34 Then Jesus looked up to **heaven,** gave a deep groan, and
10.21 the money to the poor, and you will have riches in **heaven;**
11.25 so that your Father in **heaven** will forgive the wrongs you
12.25 they will be like the angels in **heaven** and will not marry.
13.25 the stars will fall from **heaven,** and the powers in space
13.31 **Heaven and earth** will pass away, but my words will never
13.32 or hour will come—neither the angels in **heaven,** nor the Son;
14.62 of the Almighty and coming with the clouds of **heaven!"**
16.19 he was taken up to **heaven** and sat at the right side
Lk 1.79 and to shine from **heaven** on all those who live in
2.13 Suddenly a great army of **heaven's** angels appeared with the angel,
2.14 to God in the highest **heaven,** and peace on earth to those
2.15 from them back into **heaven,** the shepherds said to one another,
3.21 While he was praying, **heaven** was opened, [22]and the Holy Spirit
3.22 And a voice came from **heaven,** "You are my own dear Son.
6.23 because a great reward is kept for you in **heaven.**
9.16 two fish, looked up to **heaven,** thanked God for them, broke
9.31 Elijah, [31]who appeared in **heavenly** glory and talked with Jesus
9.51 would be taken up to **heaven,** he made up his mind and
9.54 you want us to call fire down from **heaven** to destroy them?"
10.15 Did you want to lift yourself up to **heaven?**
10.18 Jesus answered them, "I saw Satan fall like lightning from **heaven.**
10.20 rather be glad because your names are written in **heaven."**
10.21 Holy Spirit and said, "Father, Lord of **heaven and earth!**
11.13 then, will the Father in **heaven** give the Holy Spirit to
12.33 and save your riches in **heaven,** where they will never decrease,
15. 7 will be more joy in **heaven** over one sinner who repents than
16.17 it is easier for **heaven and earth** to disappear than for the
16.22 by the angels to sit beside Abraham at the feast in **heaven.**
17.29 fire and sulphur rained down from **heaven** and killed them all.
18.13 even raise his face to **heaven,** but beat on his breast and
18.22 the money to the poor, and you will have riches in **heaven;**
19.38 Peace in **heaven** and glory to God!"
21.33 **Heaven and earth** will pass away, but my words will never
22.43 An angel from **heaven** appeared to him and strengthened him.
24.51 them, he departed from them and was taken up into **heaven.**
Jn 1.32 Spirit come down like a dove from **heaven** and stay on him.
1.51 you will see **heaven** open and God's angels going up and
3.12 me, then, when I tell you about the things of **heaven?**
3.13 has ever gone up to **heaven** except the Son of Man,
3.13 who came down from **heaven."**
3.31 earthly matters, but he who comes from **heaven** is above all.
6.31 scripture says, 'He gave them bread from **heaven** to eat.' "
6.32 "What Moses gave you was not the bread from **heaven;**
6.32 it is my Father who gives you the real bread from **heaven.**
6.33 he who comes down from **heaven** and gives life to the world."
6.38 I have come down from **heaven** to do not my own will
6.41 he said, "I am the bread that came down from **heaven."**
6.42 How, then, does he now say he came down from **heaven?"**
6.50 bread that comes down from **heaven** is of such a kind that
6.51 I am the living bread that came down from **heaven.**
6.58 This, then, is the bread that came down from **heaven;**
12.28 Then a voice spoke from **heaven,** "I have brought glory to it,
17. 1 this, he looked up to **heaven** and said, "Father, the hour
Acts 1. 2 began his work [2]until the day he was taken up to **heaven.**
1. 9 he was taken up to **heaven** as they watched him, and a
1.11 was taken from you into **heaven,** will come back
1.11 in the same way that you saw him go to **heaven."**
1.21 until the day Jesus was taken up from us to **heaven."**
2.34 For it was not David who went up into **heaven;**
3.21 He must remain in **heaven** until the time comes for all
4.24 "Master and Creator of **heaven,** earth, and sea, and all that
7.42 to worship the stars of **heaven,** as it is written in the
7.49 as the prophet says, [49]**'Heaven** is my throne, says the Lord,
7.55 Holy Spirit, looked up to **heaven** and saw God's glory and
7.56 "I see **heaven** opened and the Son of Man standing at the
10.11 He saw **heaven** opened and something coming down that
10.16 times, and then the thing was taken back up into **heaven.**
11. 5 by its four corners from **heaven,** and it stopped next to me.
11. 9 The voice spoke again from **heaven,** 'Do not consider anything
11.10 and finally the whole thing was drawn back up into **heaven.**
14.15 the living God, who made **heaven,** earth, sea, and all that is
14.17 he gives you rain from **heaven** and crops at the right times;
17.24 it, is Lord of **heaven and earth** and does not live in
19.35 Artemis and of the sacred stone that fell down from **heaven.**
26.19 King Agrippa, I did not disobey the vision I had from **heaven.**
Rom 1.18 God's anger is revealed from **heaven** against all the sin

Rom 8.38 neither angels nor other **heavenly rulers** or powers,
10. 6 "You are not to ask yourself, Who will go up into **heaven?"**
1 Cor 8. 5 so-called "gods," whether in **heaven** or on earth, and even
15.40 And there are **heavenly bodies** and earthly bodies;
15.40 the beauty that belongs to **heavenly bodies** is different from
15.47 the second Adam came from **heaven.**
15.48 those who are of **heaven** are like the one
15.48 who came from **heaven.**
15.49 earth, so we will wear the likeness of the Man from **heaven.**
2 Cor 5. 1 will have a house in **heaven** for us to live in, a
5. 2 our home which comes from **heaven** should be put on over us;
5. 4 we want to have the **heavenly** one put on over us, so
12. 2 snatched up to the highest **heaven** (I do not know whether
Gal 1. 8 we or an angel from **heaven** should preach to you a gospel
4.14 Instead, you received me as you would an angel from **heaven;**
4.26 But the **heavenly Jerusalem** is free, and she is our mother.
Eph 1. 3 by giving us every spiritual blessing in the **heavenly world.**
1.10 together, everything in **heaven and on earth,** with Christ as head.
1.20 and seated him at his right side in the **heavenly world.**
1.21 Christ rules there above all **heavenly rulers,** authorities, powers,
2. 6 us up with him to rule with him in the **heavenly world.**
3.10 rulers and powers in the **heavenly world** might learn of his
3.15 every family in **heaven and on earth** receives its true name.
4.10 above and beyond the **heavens,** to fill the whole universe with
6. 9 to the same Master in **heaven,** who judges everyone by the
6.12 wicked spiritual forces in the **heavenly world,** the rulers,
Phil 2.10 of Jesus all beings in **heaven,** on earth, and in the world
3.20 We, however, are citizens of **heaven,** and we eagerly wait for
3.20 for our Saviour, the Lord Jesus Christ, to come from **heaven.**
Col 1. 5 what you hope for, which is kept safe for you in **heaven.**
1.16 God created everything in **heaven and on earth,** the seen and
1.20 back to himself all things, both on earth and in **heaven.**
3. 1 the things that are in **heaven,** where Christ sits on his
4. 1 Remember that you too have a Master in **heaven.**
1 Thes 1.10 his Son to come from **heaven**—his Son Jesus, whom he raised
4.16 God's trumpet, and the Lord himself will come down from **heaven.**
2 Thes 1. 7 the Lord Jesus appears from **heaven** with his mighty angels,
1 Tim 3.16 in throughout the world, and was taken up to **heaven.**
2 Tim 4.18 from all evil and take me safely into his **heavenly Kingdom.**
Heb 1. 3 he sat down in **heaven** at the right-hand side of God,
1.10 the earth, and with your own hands you made the **heavens.**
6. 4 tasted **heaven's** gift and received their share of the Holy
6.19 the curtain of the **heavenly** temple into the inner sanctuary.
7.26 he has been set apart from sinners and raised above the **heavens.**
8. 1 at the right of the throne of the Divine Majesty in **heaven.**
8. 5 really only a copy and a shadow of what is in **heaven.**
9.23 which are copies of the **heavenly** originals, had to be purified
9.23 But the **heavenly** things themselves require much better sacrifices.
9.24 He went into **heaven** itself, where he now appears on our
11.16 it was a better country they longed for, the **heavenly** country.
12.22 living God, the **heavenly Jerusalem,** with its thousands of angels.
12.23 God's first-born sons, whose names are written in **heaven.**
12.25 then, if we turn away from the one who speaks from **heaven!**
12.26 once more shake not only the earth but **heaven** as well."
Jas 1.17 Every good gift and every perfect present comes from **heaven;**
1.17 God, the Creator of the **heavenly** lights, who does not change
3.15 Such wisdom does not come down from **heaven;**
5.12 Do not swear by **heaven** or by earth or by anything else.
1 Pet 1. 4 keeps them for you in **heaven,** where they cannot decay or
1.12 Good News by the power of the Holy Spirit sent from **heaven.**
3.22 Christ, [22] who has gone to **heaven** and is at the right-hand
3.22 ruling over all angels and **heavenly** authorities and powers.
2 Pet 1.18 heard this voice coming from **heaven,** when we were with him
3. 5 God gave a command, and the **heavens** and earth were created.
3. 7 But the **heavens** and the earth that now exist are being
3.10 On that Day the **heavens** will disappear with a shrill noise,
3.10 the **heavenly bodies** will burn up
3.12 soon—the Day when the **heavens** will burn up and be destroyed,
3.12 and the **heavenly bodies** will be melted
3.13 **heavens** and a new earth, where righteousness will be at home.
Rev 3.12 Jerusalem, which will come down out of **heaven** from my God.
4. 1 point I had another vision and saw an open door in **heaven.**
4. 2 There in **heaven** was a throne with someone sitting on it.
5. 3 there was no one in **heaven** or on earth or in the
5.13 I heard every creature in **heaven,** on earth, in the world below,
8. 1 seal, there was silence in **heaven** for about half an hour.
10. 1 Then I saw another mighty angel coming down out of **heaven.**
10. 4 heard a voice speak from **heaven,** "Keep secret what the seven
10. 5 raised his right hand to **heaven** [6] and took a vow in the
10. 6 and ever, who created **heaven,** earth, and the sea, and everything
10. 8 I had heard speaking from **heaven** spoke to me again, saying,
11.12 a loud voice say to them from **heaven,** "Come up here!"
11.12 As their enemies watched, they went up into **heaven** in a cloud.
11.13 terrified and praised the greatness of the God of **heaven.**
11.15 there were loud voices in **heaven,** saying, "The power to
11.19 God's temple in **heaven** was opened, and the Covenant Box
12. 7 Then war broke out in **heaven.**
12. 8 his angels were not allowed to stay in **heaven** any longer.
12.10 a loud voice in **heaven** saying, "Now God's salvation has come!
12.10 our brothers day and night has been thrown out of **heaven.**
12.12 And so be glad, you **heavens,** and all you that live there!
13. 6 the place where he lives, and all those who live in **heaven.**
13.13 fire come down out of **heaven** to earth in the sight of
14. 2 I heard a voice from **heaven** that sounded like a roaring waterfall,
14. 7 Worship him who made **heaven,** earth, sea, and the springs of water!"
14.13 Then I heard a voice from **heaven** saying, "Write this:
14.17 out of the temple in **heaven,** and he also had a sharp
15. 5 I saw the temple in **heaven** open, with the Tent of God's
16.11 and they cursed the God of **heaven** for their pains and sores.
Rev 18. 1 After this I saw another angel coming down out of **heaven.**
18. 4 Then I heard another voice from **heaven,** saying, "Come out,
18. 5 up as high as **heaven,** and God remembers her wicked ways.
18.20 Be glad, **heaven,** because of her destruction!
19. 1 roar of a large crowd of people in **heaven,** saying, "Praise
19.11 Then I saw **heaven** open, and there was a white horse.
19.14 The armies of **heaven** followed him, riding on white horses
20. 1 an angel coming down from **heaven,** holding in his hand the
20. 9 But fire came down from **heaven** and destroyed them.
20.11 Earth and **heaven** fled from his presence and were seen no more.
21. 1 Then I saw a new **heaven** and a new earth.
21. 1 The first **heaven** and the first earth disappeared, and the sea
21. 2 Jerusalem, coming down out of **heaven** from God, prepared and ready,
21.10 City, coming down out of **heaven** from God [11] and shining

HEAVENLY KINGDOM see KINGDOM (1)

HEAVENLY WORLD see WORLD ABOVE

HEAVY

Ex 9.18 I will cause a **heavy** hailstorm, such as Egypt has never
9.24 The Lord sent [24] a **heavy** hailstorm, with lightning flashing
Num 13.23 of grapes on it so **heavy** that it took two men to
Deut 1.12 how can I alone bear the **heavy** responsibility for settling
1 Sam 26.12 because the Lord had sent a **heavy** sleep on them all.
31. 3 The fighting was **heavy** round Saul, and he himself was hit
2 Sam 11.15 line, where the fighting is **heaviest,** then retreat and let him
14.26 cut it once a year, when it grew too long and **heavy.**
1 Kgs 12. 4 Solomon treated us harshly and placed **heavy** burdens on us.
12.11 Tell them, 'My father placed **heavy** burdens on you;
12.11 I will make them even **heavier.**
12.14 He said, "My father placed **heavy** burdens on you;
12.14 I will make them even **heavier.**
18.45 the wind began to blow, and **heavy** rain began to fall.
2 Kgs 25.16 the carts, and the large tank—were too **heavy** to weigh.
1 Chr 10. 3 The fighting was **heavy** round Saul, and he was hit by enemy
2 Chr 10. 4 and said to him, [4] "Your father placed **heavy** burdens on us.
10.11 Tell them, 'My father placed **heavy** burdens on you;
10.11 I will make them even **heavier.**
10.14 He said, "My father placed **heavy** burdens on you;
10.14 I will make them even **heavier.**
Neh 5.18 But I knew what **heavy** burdens the people had to bear,
Job 14.19 wear down rocks, and **heavy** rain will wash away the soil;
39.11 on his great strength and expect him to do your **heavy** work?
Ps 38. 4 they are a burden too **heavy** to bear.
66.11 us fall into a trap and placed **heavy** burdens on our backs.
88. 7 Your anger lies **heavy** on me, and I am crushed beneath its
Ecc 3.10 I know the **heavy** burdens that God has laid on us.
Is 28.27 He never uses a **heavy** club to beat out dill seeds
Jer 52.20 the twelve bulls that supported it—were too **heavy** to weigh.
Lam 5.13 boys go staggering under **heavy** loads of wood.
Ezek 27.25 You were like a ship at sea Loaded with **heavy** cargo.
29.18 made his soldiers carry such **heavy** loads that their heads
Zech 12. 3 will make Jerusalem like a **heavy** stone—any nation that tries
Mt 11.28 who are tired from carrying **heavy** loads, and I will give you
23. 4 people's backs loads that are **heavy** and hard to carry, yet
Lk 12.47 ready and do it, will be punished with a **heavy** whipping.
Acts 16.24 inner cell and fastened their feet between **heavy** blocks of wood.
2 Cor 1. 8 were so great and so **heavy** that we gave up all hope
Rev 11.19 rumblings and peals of thunder, an earthquake, and **heavy** hail.
20. 1 in his hand the key of the abyss and a **heavy** chain.

HEBREW

[FELLOW-HEBREW]

Word used to describe the people of Israel, usually by foreigners. Also their language.

Gen 10.21 elder brother of Japheth, was the ancestor of all the **Hebrews.**
14.13 all this to Abram, the **Hebrew,** who was living near the
39.14 This **Hebrew** that my husband brought to the house is insulting
39.17 "That **Hebrew** slave that you brought here came into my room
40.15 from the land of the **Hebrews,** and even here in Egypt
41.12 A young **Hebrew** was there with us, a slave of the captain
43.32 they considered it beneath their dignity to eat with **Hebrews.**
Ex 1.15 the two midwives who helped the **Hebrew** women.
1.16 "When you help the **Hebrew** women give birth," he said
1.19 answered, "The **Hebrew** women are not like Egyptian women;
1.22 "Take every new-born **Hebrew** boy and throw him into the Nile,
2. 6 "This is one of the **Hebrew** babies," she said.
2. 7 I go and call a **Hebrew** woman to act as a wet-nurse?"
2.11 to visit his people, the **Hebrews,** and he saw how they were
2.11 even saw an Egyptian kill a **Hebrew,** one of Moses' own
2.13 The next day he went back and saw two **Hebrew** men fighting.
2.13 in the wrong, "Why are you beating up a **fellow-Hebrew?"**
3.18 'The Lord, the God of the **Hebrews,** has revealed himself to us.
5. 3 Aaron replied, "The God of the **Hebrews** has revealed himself
7.16 Lord, the God of the **Hebrews,** sent me to tell you to
9. 1 Lord, the God of the **Hebrews,** says, 'Let my people go,
9.13 Lord, the God of the **Hebrews,** says, 'Let my people go,
10. 3 Lord, the God of the **Hebrews,** says 'How much longer will you
21. 2 If you buy a **Hebrew** slave, he shall serve you for six
1 Sam 4. 6 and said, "Listen to all that shouting in the **Hebrew** camp!
4. 6 Box had arrived in the **Hebrew** camp, [7] they were afraid,
4. 9 become slaves to the **Hebrews,** just as they were our slaves.
13. 3 messengers to call the **Hebrews** to war by blowing a trumpet
13.19 determined to keep the **Hebrews** from making swords and spears.
14.11 Some **Hebrews** are coming out of the holes they have been

1 Sam 14.21 Some **Hebrews,** who had been on the Philistine side
29. 3 saw them and asked, "What are these **Hebrews** doing here?"
2 Kgs 18.26 Don't speak **Hebrew;**
18.28 stood up and shouted in **Hebrew,** "Listen to what the emperor
2 Chr 32.18 The officials shouted this in **Hebrew** in order to frighten
Esth 2. 7 He had a cousin, Esther, whose **Hebrew** name was Hadassah;
Is 19.18 When that time comes, the **Hebrew** language will be spoken
36.11 Don't speak **Hebrew;**
36.13 stood up and shouted in **Hebrew,** "Listen to what the emperor
Jer 34. 9 agreement to set free [9]their **Hebrew** slaves, both male and
34.14 were to set free any **Hebrew** slave who had served them for
Jon 1. 9 "I am a **Hebrew,**" Jonah answered.
Jn 5. 2 in **Hebrew** it is called Bethzatha.
19.13 (In **Hebrew** the name is "Gabbatha.")
19.17 (In **Hebrew** it is called "Golgotha.")
19.20 The notice was written in **Hebrew,** Latin, and Greek.
20.16 She turned towards him and said in **Hebrew,** "Rabboni!"
Acts 21.40 When they were quiet, Paul spoke to them in **Hebrew:**
22. 2 heard him speaking to them in **Hebrew,** they became even quieter;
26.14 and I heard a voice say to me in **Hebrew,** 'Saul, Saul!
Rom 9. 5 they are descended from the famous **Hebrew** ancestors;
2 Cor 11.22 Are they **Hebrews?**
Phil 3. 5 Israelite by birth, of the tribe of Benjamin, a pure-blooded **Hebrew.**
Rev 9.11 His name in **Hebrew** is Abaddon;
16.16 kings together in the place that in **Hebrew** is called Armageddon.

HEBRON (1)

Important city in Judah, at one time David's capital.

Gen 13.18 sacred trees of Mamre at **Hebron,** and there he built an altar
23. 2 died in **Hebron** in the land of Canaan, and Abraham mourned
35.27 Isaac at Mamre, near **Hebron,** where Abraham and Isaac had lived.
37.14 his father sent him on his way from the Valley of **Hebron.**
Num 13.22 the land and came to **Hebron,** where the clans of Ahiman,
13.22 (**Hebron** was founded seven years before Zoan in Egypt.)
Josh 10. 3 message to King Hoham of **Hebron,** King Piram of Jarmuth,
10. 5 Jerusalem, **Hebron,** Jarmuth, Lachish, and Eglon, joined forces,
10.23 of Jerusalem, **Hebron,** Jarmuth, Lachish, and Eglon were brought
10.36 into the hills to **Hebron,** attacked it [37]and captured it.
10.39 what he had done to **Hebron** and to Libnah and its king.
11.21 lived in the hill-country—in **Hebron,** Debir, Anab, and in all
12.10 Jericho, Ai (near Bethel), [10]Jerusalem, **Hebron,**
14.13 Jephunneh and gave him the city of **Hebron** as his possession.
14.14 **Hebron** still belongs to the descendants of Caleb
14.15 Before this, **Hebron** was called the city of Arba.
15.13 He received **Hebron,** the city belonging to Arba, father of Anak.
15.54 Beth Tappuah, Aphekah, [54]Humtah, **Hebron,** and Zior:
20. 7 and **Hebron,** in the hill-country of Judah.
21.11 now called **Hebron,** in the hill-country of Judah,
21.13 In addition to **Hebron** (one of the cities of refuge),
Judg 1.10 living in the city of **Hebron,** which used to be called
1.20 As Moses had commanded, **Hebron** was given to Caleb,
16. 3 them all the way to the top of the hill overlooking **Hebron.**
1 Sam 30.31 people in the towns of Hormah, Borashan, Athach, [31]and **Hebron.**
2 Sam 2. 1 **"Hebron,"** the Lord said.
2. 2 So David went to **Hebron,** taking with him his two wives:
2. 3 and their families, and they settled in the towns round **Hebron.**
2. 4 men of Judah came to **Hebron** and anointed David as king of
2.11 David, [11]and he ruled in **Hebron** over Judah for seven and a
2.32 Then they marched all night and at dawn arrived back at **Hebron.**
3. 2 in the order of their birth, were born to David at **Hebron:**
3. 5 All of these sons were born in **Hebron.**
3.12 at that time was at **Hebron,** to say, "Who is going to
3.19 Benjamin and then went to **Hebron** to tell David what the
3.20 Abner came to David at **Hebron** with twenty men, David gave a
3.22 no longer there at **Hebron** with David, because David had sent
3.27 Abner arrived in **Hebron,** Joab took him aside at the gate,
3.32 Abner was buried at **Hebron,** and the king wept aloud
4. 1 Abner had been killed in **Hebron,** he was afraid, and all the
4. 8 head to King David at **Hebron** and said to him, "Here is
4.12 hands and feet, which they hung up near the pool in **Hebron.**
4.12 Ishbosheth's head and buried it in Abner's tomb there at **Hebron.**
5. 1 Israel came to David at **Hebron** and said to him, "We are
5. 3 So all the leaders of Israel came to King David at **Hebron.**
5. 5 He ruled in **Hebron** over Judah for seven and a half years,
5.13 moving from **Hebron** to Jerusalem, David took more concubines
15. 7 "Sir, let me go to **Hebron** and keep a promise I made
15. 8 take me back to Jerusalem, I would worship him in **Hebron."**
15. 9 So Absalom went to **Hebron.**
15.10 sound of trumpets, shout, 'Absalom has become king at **Hebron!'** "
1 Kgs 2.11 forty years, ruling seven years in **Hebron** and thirty-three
1 Chr 3. 1 are David's sons who were born while he was in **Hebron:**
3. 4 All six were born in **Hebron** during the seven and a half
6.55 This included **Hebron** in the territory of Judah
6.57 **Hebron,** a city of refuge, Jattir, and the towns of Libnah,
11. 1 Israel went to David at **Hebron** and said to him, "We are
11. 3 So all the leaders of Israel came to King David at **Hebron.**
12.23 David was at **Hebron,** many trained soldiers joined his army
12.38 went to **Hebron,** determined to make David king over
29.27 He ruled in **Hebron** for seven years and in Jerusalem for
2 Chr 11.10 Ziph, [9]Adoraim, Lachish, Azekah, [10]Zorah, Aijalon, and **Hebron.**

HEDGE

Is 5. 5 I will take away the **hedge** round it, break down the wall

HEEL

Gen 3.15 Her offspring will crush your head, and you will bite their **heel."**
25.26 holding on tightly to the **heel** of Esau, so he was named
49.17 That strikes at the horse's **heel,** So that the rider is
Job 18. 9 a trap catches his **heels** and holds him.

HEIGHT see HIGH

HEIR

Gen 15. 2 My only **heir** is Eliezer of Damascus.
15. 4 your own son will be your **heir."**
17.18 He asked God, "Why not let Ishmael be my **heir?"**
Ex 11. 5 the king's son, who is **heir** to the throne, to the son
12.29 the king's son, who was **heir** to the throne, to the son

HELL

see also **HADES, WORLD OF THE DEAD**

Job 31.12 like a destructive, **hellish** fire, consuming everything I have.
Mt 5.22 fool will be in danger of going to the fire of **hell.**
5.29 of your body than to have your whole body thrown into **hell.**
5.30 of your limbs than for your whole body to go to **hell.**
7.13 gate, because the gate to **hell** is wide and the road that
10.28 afraid of God, who can destroy both body and soul in **hell.**
11.23 You will be thrown down to **hell!**
18. 9 to keep both eyes and be thrown into the fire of **hell.**
23.15 twice as deserving of going to **hell** as you yourselves are!
23.33 How do you expect to escape from being condemned to **hell?**
Mk 9.43 hands and go off to **hell,** to the fire that never goes
9.45 a foot than to keep both feet and be thrown into **hell.**
9.47 one eye than to keep both eyes and be thrown into **hell.**
Lk 10.15 You will be thrown down to **hell!"**
12. 5 who, after killing, has the authority to throw into **hell.**
Acts 8.20 and your money go to **hell,** for thinking that you can buy
Gal 1. 8 the one we preached to you, may he be condemned to **hell!**
1. 9 from the one you accepted, may he be condemned to **hell!**
Phil 3.19 going to end up in **hell,** because their god is their bodily
2 Thes 2. 3 place and the Wicked One appears, who is destined for **hell.**
Jas 3. 6 existence with the fire that comes to it from **hell** itself.
2 Pet 2. 4 sinned, but threw them into **hell,** where they are kept

HELMET

1 Sam 17. 5 weighed about fifty-seven kilogrammes and a bronze **helmet.**
17.38 a bronze **helmet,** which he put on David's head, and a coat
2 Chr 26.14 the army with shields, spears, **helmets,** coats of armour,
Ps 60. 7 Ephraim is my **helmet** and Judah my royal sceptre.
108. 8 Ephraim is my **helmet** and Judah my royal sceptre.
Is 59.17 like a coat of armour and saving power like a **helmet.**
Jer 46. 4 Fall in line and put on your **helmets!**
Ezek 23.24 Protected by shields and **helmets,** they will surround you.
27.10 They hung their shields and their **helmets** in your barracks.
38. 5 and Libya are with him, and all have shields and **helmets.**
Eph 6.17 And accept salvation as a **helmet,** and the word of God as
1 Thes 5. 8 as a breastplate, and our hope of salvation as a **helmet.**

HELP

see also **HELPER, HELPLESS**

Gen 2.18 I will make a suitable companion to **help** him."
2.20 but not one of them was a suitable companion to **help** him.
4. 1 and said, "By the Lord's **help** I have acquired a son."
10. 9 By the Lord's **help** he was a great hunter, and that is
27.20 Jacob answered, "The Lord your God **helped** me to find it."
35. 3 altar to the God who **helped** me in the time of my
40.14 me to the king and **help** me to get out of this
42.21 was in when he begged for **help,** but we would not listen.
49.25 your father's God who **helps** you, The Almighty God who blesses
Ex 1.15 the two midwives who **helped** the Hebrew women.
1.16 "When you **help** the Hebrew women give birth," he said
2.23 were still groaning under their slavery and cried out for **help.**
4.12 I will **help** you to speak, and I will tell you what
4.15 I will **help** both of you to speak, and I will tell
5.23 And you have done nothing to **help** them!"
14.10 they were terrified and cried out to the Lord for **help.**
14.15 The Lord said to Moses, "Why are you crying out for **help?**
18. 4 "The God of my father **helped** me and saved me from being
21.18 and walk outside with the **help** of a stick, the man who
22.23 cry out to me for **help,** [24]and I will be angry
22.27 cries out to me for **help,** I will answer him because I
23. 1 false rumours, and do not **help** a guilty man by giving false
23. 5 has fallen under its load, **help** him get the donkey to its
24.13 Moses and his **helper** Joshua got ready, and Moses began to
33.11 young man who was his **helper,** Joshua son of Nun, stayed in
36. 2 and who were willing to **help,** and Moses told them to start
38.23 His **helper,** Oholiab son of Ahisamach, from the tribe of Dan,
Lev 19.16 for his life, speak out if your testimony can **help** him.
Num 1. 4 Ask one clan chief from each tribe to **help** you."
1.17 With the **help** of these twelve men Moses and Aaron
8.26 he may **help** his fellow-Levites in performing their duties in
10. 9 the Lord your God, will **help** you and save you from your
10.10 Then I will **help** you.
11. 2 The people cried out to Moses for **help;**
11.17 they can **help** you to bear the responsibility for these people,
11.28 who had been Moses' **helper** since he was a young man,
18. 2 to work with you and **help** you while you and your sons
20.16 our ancestors and us, [16]and we cried to the Lord for **help.**
21. 3 Lord heard them and **helped** them to conquer the Canaanites.
32. 3 region which the Lord has **helped** the Israelites to occupy—
32.29 command and if with their **help** you are able to conquer the
34.18 Take also one leader from each tribe to **help** them divide
Deut 1.38 But strengthen the determination of your **helper,** Joshua

Deut 1.45 out to the Lord for **help,** but he would not listen to
3.18 other tribes of Israel, to **help** them to occupy their land.
3.20 **Help** your fellow-Israelites until they occupy the land
4. 7 He answers us whenever we call for **help.**
15. 7 in need, then do not be selfish and refuse to **help** him.
22. 4 **help** him to get the animal to its feet again.
22.24 did not cry out for **help,** although she was in a town,
22.27 although she cried for help, there was no one to **help** her.
23. 6 never do anything to **help** these nations or to make them
25.11 wife of one tries to **help** her husband by grabbing hold of
26. 7 Then we cried out for **help** to the Lord, the God of
28.29 oppressed and robbed, and there will be no one to **help** you.
28.31 to your enemies, and there will be no one to **help** you.
31.18 And I will refuse to **help** them then, because they have
32.12 Lord alone led his people without the **help** of a foreign god.
32.20 'I will no longer **help** them,' he said;
32.38 Let them come and **help** you now;
33. 7 "Lord, listen to their cry for **help;**
33. 7 Fight for them, Lord, And **help** them against their enemies."
33.11 Lord, **help** their tribe to grow strong;
Josh 1. 1 the Lord spoke to Moses' **helper,** Joshua son of Nun.
1.14 their fellow-Israelites in order to **help** them [15]until they
10. 4 and **help** me attack Gibeon, because its people have made peace
10. 6 Come at once and **help** us!
24. 7 cried out to me for **help,** and I put darkness between them
Judg 1.18 Lord **helped** the people of Judah, and they took possession of
1.22 The Lord **helped** them.
2.18 a leader, the Lord would **help** him and would save the people
4. 3 Then the people of Israel cried out to the Lord for **help.**
5.23 They did not come to **help** the Lord, come as soldiers to
6. 7 out to the Lord for **help** against the Midianites, [8]and he
6.16 Lord answered, "You can do it because I will **help** you.
8.15 of Sukkoth and said, "Remember when you refused to **help** me?
Ruth 3.15 twenty kilogrammes of barley and **helped** her to lift it on
1 Sam 2. 1 how joyful I am because God has **helped** me!
2.36 beg to be allowed to **help** the priests, in order to have
4.20 she was dying, the women **helping** her said to her, "Be
5.12 tumours and the people cried out to their gods for **help.**
7. 2 During this time all the Israelites cried to the Lord for **help.**
7. 9 prayed to the Lord to **help** Israel, and the Lord answered his
7.12 and said, "The Lord has **helped** us all the way"—
7.12 and he named it "Stone of **Help."**
9.16 of my people and have heard their cries for **help."**
11. 3 If no one will **help** us, then we will surrender to you."
12. 8 cried to the Lord for **help,** and he sent Moses and Aaron,
12.10 cried to the Lord for **help** and said, 'We have sinned,
12.21 they cannot **help** you or save you, for they are not real.
14. 6 Maybe the Lord will **help** us;
14.45 What he did today was done with God's **help."**
19. 4 everything he has done has been a great **help** to you.
19.17 said he would kill me if I didn't **help** him to escape."
25.21 is how he pays me back for the **help** I gave him!
2 Sam 3.12 with me, and I will **help** you win all Israel over to
8. 5 Damascus sent an army to **help** King Hadadezer, David attacked
10.11 are defeating me, come and **help** me,
10.11 if the Ammonites are defeating you, I will go and **help** you.
10.19 And the Syrians were afraid to **help** the Ammonites any more.
14. 4 to the ground in respect, and said, **"Help** me, Your Majesty!"
15.33 "You will be of no **help** to me if you come with
15.34 with me, [34]but you can **help** me by returning to the city
18. 3 better if you stay here in the city and send us **help."**
19.11 you be the last to **help** bring the king back to his
21.17 came to David's **help,** attacked the giant, and killed him.
22. 7 I called to my God for **help.**
22. 7 he listened to my cry for **help.**
22.20 He **helped** me out of danger;
22.36 your **help** has made me great.
22.42 They look for **help,** but no one saves them;
1 Kgs 8.39 to them in your home in heaven, forgive them, and **help** them.
8.52 and hear their prayer whenever they call to you for **help.**
15.22 without exception, to **help** carry away from Ramah the stones
19.21 Then he went and followed Elijah as his **helper.**
2 Kgs 3.13 "Why should I **help** you?"
6.26 city wall when a woman cried out, **"Help** me, Your Majesty!"
6.27 "If the Lord won't **help** you, what help can I provide?"
10.15 They clasped hands, and Jehu **helped** him up into the chariot,
13.23 them be destroyed, but **helped** them, because of his covenant
14.26 there was no one at all to **help** them.
17. 4 of Egypt, asking for his **help,** and stopped paying the annual
18.20 Who do you think will **help** you rebel against Assyria?
18.21 You are expecting Egypt to **help** you, but that would be
18.25 attacked your country and destroyed it without the Lord's **help?**
23.29 army to the River Euphrates to **help** the emperor of Assyria.
1 Chr 5.20 and prayed to him for **help,** and God answered their prayers
11.10 the people of Israel, they **helped** him to become king, as the
12.17 you are coming as friends to **help** me, you are welcome here.
12.18 Success to you and those who **help** you!
12.19 he did not **help** the Philistines, for their kings were afraid
12.23 soldiers joined his army to **help** make him king in place of
15.26 make sure that God would **help** the Levites who were carrying
16.11 Go to the Lord for **help,** and worship him continually.
18. 5 Damascus sent an army to **help** King Hadadezer, David attacked
19. 9 kings who had come to **help** took up their position in the
19.12 are defeating me, come and **help** me,
19.12 if the Ammonites are defeating you, I will go and **help** you.
19.19 The Syrians were never again willing to **help** the Ammonites.
22.17 David commanded all the leaders of Israel to **help** Solomon.
23.28 **help** the priests descended from Aaron with the temple worship,
28.21 of skill are eager to **help** you, and all the people and
2 Chr 13.14 to the Lord for **help,** and the priests blew the trumpets.
14.11 "O Lord, you can **help** a weak army as easily as

2 Chr 14.11 **Help** us now, O Lord our God, because we are relying on
16.12 he did not turn to the Lord for **help,** but to doctors.
19. 2 think it is right to **help** those who are wicked and to
20.12 not know what to do, but we look to you for **help."**
26. 7 God **helped** him to defeat the Philistines, the Arabs living
26.15 became very powerful because of the **help** he received from God.
28.16 Ahaz asked Tiglath Pileser, the emperor of Assyria, to send **help.**
28.20 Assyrian emperor, instead of **helping** Ahaz, opposed him
28.21 and gave it to the emperor, but even this did not **help.**
28.23 He said, "The Syrian gods **helped** the kings of Syria,
28.23 so if I sacrifice to them, they may **help** me too."
29.34 the Levites **helped** them until the work was finished.
29.36 were happy, because God had **helped** them to do all this so
32. 8 the Lord our God to **help** us and to fight our battles."
32.20 of Amoz prayed to God and cried out to him for **help.**
33.12 humble, turned to the Lord his God, and begged him for **help.**
35. 5 you will be available to **help** each family of the people of
Ezra 1. 4 his people in exile need **help** to return,
1. 4 their neighbours are to give them this **help.**
1. 6 All their neighbours **helped** them by giving them many things:
2.68 gave freewill offerings to **help** rebuild the Temple on its old
3. 9 (They were **helped** by the Levites of the clan of Henadad.)
4. 3 "We don't need your **help** to build a temple for the
5. 2 the Temple in Jerusalem, and the two prophets **helped** them.
5. 4 names of all the men who were **helping** to build the Temple.
6. 8 I hereby command you to **help** them rebuild it.
7. 8 first month, and with God's **help** they arrived in Jerusalem on
9.12 those people and never to **help** them prosper or succeed if we
Neh 2.18 had been with me and **helped** me, and what the emperor had
3.12 (His daughters **helped** with the work.)
4.22 that they and all their **helpers** had to stay in Jerusalem at
6.16 everyone knew that the work had been done with God's **help.**
7.70 the people contributed to **help** pay the cost of restoring the
9. 9 you heard their call for **help** at the Red Sea.
9.27 called to you for **help,** and you answered them from heaven.
10.32 grammes of silver to **help** pay the expenses of the Temple.
Esth 4.14 at a time like this, **help** will come from heaven to the
9. 3 administrators, and royal representatives—**helped** the Jews
Job 6.13 there is nowhere I can turn for **help.**
8. 6 then God will come and **help** you and restore your household
8.15 If they grab for a thread, will it **help** them stand?"
8.20 never abandon the faithful or ever give **help** to evil men.
9. 8 No one **helped** God spread out the heavens or trample
9.13 He crushed his enemies who **helped** Rahab, the
11.19 many people will ask you for **help.**
16. 6 But nothing I say **helps,** and being silent does not calm my
19.16 he doesn't answer— even when I beg him to **help** me.
22. 3 right benefit God, or does your being good **help** him at all?
22. 9 You not only refused to **help** widows, but you also robbed
26. 1 What a fine **help** you are to me— poor, weak man
29.12 When the poor cried out, I **helped** them;
29.12 I gave **help** to orphans who had nowhere to turn.
29.13 praised me, and I **helped** widows find security.
30. 1 that I wouldn't let them **help** my dogs guard sheep.
30.28 I stand up in public and plead for **help.**
31.16 I have never refused to **help** the poor;
32. 9 that makes men wise or **helps** them to know what is right.
34.28 to cry out to God, and he heard their calls for **help.**
35. 7 Do you **help** God by being so righteous?
35. 8 who suffers from your sins, and the good you do **helps** him.
35.12 They cry for **help,** but God doesn't answer, for they are
36.13 being angry, and even when punished, they don't pray for **help.**
36.19 It will do you no good to cry out for **help;**
36.19 all your strength can't **help** you now.
37.18 Can you **help** God stretch out the sky and make it as
Ps 3. 2 They talk about me and say, "God will not **help** him."
3. 4 call to the Lord for **help,** and from his sacred hill he
4. 1 When I was in trouble, you **helped** me.
5. 2 Listen to my cry for **help,** my God and king!
6. 3 How long, O Lord, will you wait to **help** me?
6. 9 he listens to my cry for **help** and will answer my prayer.
7. 6 rouse yourself and **help** me!
10.14 notice of trouble and suffering and are always ready to **help.**
10.14 you have always **helped** the needy.
12. 1 **Help** us, Lord!
17. 1 pay attention to my cry for **help!**
18. 6 I called to my God for **help.**
18. 6 he listened to my cry for **help.**
18.19 He **helped** me out of danger;
18.41 They cry for **help,** but no one saves them;
20. 2 May he send you **help** from his Temple and give you aid
21. 5 His glory is great because of your **help;**
22. 1 I have cried desperately for **help,** but still it does not come.
22. 8 If the Lord likes you, why doesn't he **help** you?"
22.11 Trouble is near, and there is no one to **help.**
22.24 turn away from them, but answers when they call for **help."**
25.15 look to the Lord for **help** at all times, and he rescues
27. 9 You have been my **help;**
28. 2 I cry to you for **help,** when I lift my hands towards
28. 6 he has heard my cry for **help.**
28. 7 He gives me **help** and makes me glad;
30. 2 I cried to you for **help,** O Lord my God, and you
30. 8 I begged for your **help:**
30.10 **Help** me, Lord!"
31.22 But he heard my cry, when I called to him for **help.**
33.20 he is our protector and our **help.**
37. 5 trust in him, and he will **help** you;
37.24 will not stay down, because the Lord will **help** them up.
37.40 He **helps** them and rescues them;
38.22 **Help** me now, O Lord my saviour!
40. 1 I waited patiently for the Lord's **help;**

Ps 40.10 I have always spoken of your faithfulness and **help**.
40.13 **Help** me now!
41. 1 the Lord will **help** them when they are in trouble.
41. 3 The Lord will **help** them when they are sick and will
41.12 You will **help** me, because I do what is right;
46. 1 and strength, always ready to **help** in times of trouble.
51.15 **Help** me to speak, Lord, and I will praise you.
51.18 O God, be kind to Zion and **help** her;
54. 4 But God is my **helper.**
55.16 call to the Lord God for **help,** and he will save me.
60.11 **Help** us against the enemy;
60.11 human **help** is worthless.
63. 7 I think of you, [7]because you have always been my **help.**
66.17 I cried to him for **help;**
69. 3 am worn out from calling for **help,** and my throat is aching.
69. 3 I have strained my eyes, looking for your **help.**
70. 1 Lord, **help** me now!
71. 2 Because you are righteous, **help** me and rescue me.
72. 4 may he **help** the needy and defeat their oppressors.
74.11 Why have you refused to **help** us?
79. 9 **Help** us, O God, and save us;
85. 7 your constant love, O Lord, and give us your saving **help.**
86. 6 hear my cries for **help.**
86.17 when they see that you have given me comfort and **help.**
88. 2 listen to my cry for **help!**
88. 5 those you have forgotten completely, who are beyond your **help.**
88.13 Lord, I call to you for **help;**
89.19 "I have given **help** to a famous soldier;
94.17 If the Lord had not **helped** me, I would have gone quickly
102. 1 Listen to my prayer, O Lord, and hear my cry for **help!**
105. 4 Go to the Lord for **help;**
106. 4 Remember me, Lord, when you **help** your people;
107.12 they would fall down, and no one would **help.**
108.12 **Help** us against the enemy;
108.12 human **help** is worthless.
109.21 But my Sovereign Lord, **help** me as you have promised,
109.26 **Help** me, O Lord my God;
115. 9 He **helps** you and protects you.
115.10 He **helps** you and protects you.
115.11 He **helps** you and protects you.
118. 7 It is the Lord who **helps** me, and I will see my
118.13 attacked and was being defeated, but the Lord **helped** me.
119.27 **Help** me to understand your laws, and I will meditate on
119.82 what you promised, while I ask, "When will you **help** me?"
119.86 men persecute me with lies—**help** me!
119.122 Promise that you will **help** your servant;
119.123 tired from watching for your saving **help,** for the deliverance
119.147 Before sunrise I call to you for **help;**
119.169 Let my cry for **help** reach you, Lord!
119.173 be ready to **help** me, because I follow your commands.
119.174 How I long for your saving **help,** O Lord!
119.175 may your instructions **help** me.
121. 1 where will my **help** come from?
121. 2 My **help** will come from the Lord, who made heaven and earth.
124. 8 Our **help** comes from the Lord, who made heaven and earth.
130. 2 listen to my call for **help!**
130. 5 wait eagerly for the Lord's **help,** and in his word I trust.
139.10 be there to lead me, you would be there to **help** me.
140. 6 Hear my cry for **help,** Lord!
141. 1 **help** me now!
142. 1 I call to the Lord for **help;**
142. 4 there is no one to **help** me, no one to protect me.
142. 5 Lord, I cry to you for **help;**
142. 6 Listen to my cry for **help,** for I am sunk in despair.
145.14 He **helps** those who are in trouble;
146. 5 the God of Jacob to **help** him and who depends on the
146. 9 **helps** widows and orphans, but takes the wicked to their ruin.
Prov 1. 2 Here are proverbs that will **help** you to recognize wisdom
2. 7 He provides **help** and protection for righteous, honest men.
3.28 neighbour to wait until tomorrow if you can **help** him now.
5.17 Your children should grow up to **help** you, not strangers.
8.15 I **help** kings to govern and rulers to make good laws.
8.16 Every ruler on earth governs with my **help,**
11.25 **Help** others, and you will be helped.
13.14 they will **help** you escape when your life is in danger.
18.19 **Help** your brother and he will protect you like a strong
19.18 If you don't, you are **helping** them to destroy themselves.
21.13 of the poor, your own cry for **help** will not be heard.
21.30 insight—they are of no **help** if the Lord is against you.
27.10 If you are in trouble, don't ask your brother for **help;**
27.10 a neighbour near by can **help** you more than a brother who
Ecc 4. 1 The oppressed were weeping, and no one would **help** them.
4. 1 No one would **help** them, because their oppressors had power on
4.10 If one of them falls down, the other can **help** him up.
4.10 it's just too bad, because there is no one to **help** him.
Song 6. 1 way your lover went, so that we can **help** you find him.
Is 1.17 See that justice is done—**help** those who are oppressed,
3. 7 I can't **help** you.
10. 3 Where will you run to find **help?**
12. 4 Call for him to **help** you!
14. 2 Many nations will **help** the people of Israel to return to
14.31 Howl and cry for **help,** all you Philistine cities!
17. 7 people will turn for **help** to their Creator, the holy God
19. 3 will ask their idols to **help** them, and they will go and
19.15 Egypt, rich or poor, important or unknown, can offer **help.**
19.20 out to the Lord for **help,** he will send someone to rescue
22. 5 battered down, and cries for **help** have echoed among the hills.
30. 2 They go to Egypt for **help** without asking for my advice.
30. 3 king will be powerless to **help** them, and Egypt's protection
30. 5 a nation that fails them when they expect **help."**
30. 6 expensive gifts for a nation that cannot give them any **help.**
Is 30. 7 The **help** that Egypt gives is useless.
30.19 and when you cry to him for **help,** he will answer you.
31. 1 Those who go to Egypt for **help** are doomed!
31. 1 the Lord, the holy God of Israel, or ask him for **help.**
31. 3 nation will crumble, and the weak nation it **helped** will fall.
33. 7 Brave men are calling for **help.**
36. 5 Who do you think will **help** you rebel against Assyria?
36. 6 You are expecting Egypt to **help** you, but that would be
36.10 attacked your country and destroyed it without the Lord's **help?**
40.31 trust in the Lord for **help** will find their strength renewed.
41. 6 The craftsmen **help** and encourage one another.
41.10 I will make you strong and **help** you;
41.13 I will **help** you.' "
41.14 I will **help** you.
44. 2 from the time you were born, I have **helped** you.
44.20 His foolish ideas have so misled him that he is beyond **help.**
44.24 when I made the earth, no one **helped** me.
45. 4 I appoint you to **help** my servant Israel, the people that I
46. 4 I will give you **help** and rescue you.
47.12 Perhaps they will be of some **help** to you;
49. 8 I will show you favour and answer your cries for **help.**
49.23 no one who waits for my **help** will be disappointed."
50. 7 insults cannot hurt me because the Sovereign Lord gives me **help.**
51. 1 that want to be saved, you that come to me for **help.**
51. 9 Wake up, Lord, and **help** us!
57.12 your conduct, and your idols will not be able to **help** you.
57.13 When you cry for **help,** let those idols of yours save you!
57.18 I will lead them and **help** them, and I will comfort those
58. 7 to wear, and do not refuse to **help** your own relatives.
59. 1 to save you or too deaf to hear your call for **help!**
59.16 to see that there is no one to **help** the oppressed.
63. 3 the nations like grapes, and no one came to **help** me.
63. 5 I looked and saw that there was no one to **help** me.
64. 7 no one goes to you for **help.**
65. 1 I will **help** you.'
65.19 There will be no weeping there, no calling for **help.**
66.14 know that I, the Lord, **help** those who obey me, and I
Jer 3.23 We were not **helped** at all by our pagan worship on the
3.23 **Help** for Israel comes only from the Lord our God.
11.11 cry out to me for **help,** I will not listen to them.
11.12 they offer sacrifices and will cry out to them for **help.**
11.14 and call to me for **help,** I will not listen to them."
14. 2 on the ground in sorrow, and Jerusalem cries out for **help.**
14. 7 our sins accuse us, **help** us, Lord, as you have promised.
14. 9 a man taken by surprise, like a soldier powerless to **help?**
14.11 Lord said to me, "Do not ask me to **help** these people.
14.12 if they fast, I will not listen to their cry for **help;**
15.15 Remember me and **help** me.
16.19 you **help** me in times of trouble.
18.17 I will not **help** them when the disaster comes."
23.14 they **help** people to do wrong, so that no one stops doing
23.32 and they are of no **help** at all to the people.
37. 7 is on its way to **help** you, but it will return home.
38. 4 He is not trying to **help** the people;
47. 2 People will call out for **help;**
47. 4 to cut off from Tyre and Sidon all the **help** that remains.
50.32 nation will stumble and fall, and no one will **help** you up.
51. 9 said, 'We tried to **help** Babylonia, but it was too late.
Lam 1. 7 she fell to the enemy, there was no one to **help** her;
1.17 "I stretch out my hands, but no one will **help** me.
1.19 "I called to my allies, but they refused to **help** me.
2. 3 He refused to **help** us when the enemy came.
3. 8 I cry aloud for **help,** but God refuses to listen;
4.17 until we could look no longer for **help** that never came.
4.17 We kept waiting for **help** from a nation that had none to
Ezek 17.17 will not be able to **help** him fight when the Babylonians
29.16 Israel will never again depend on them for **help.**
36.37 the Israelites ask me for **help,** and I will let them increase
39.13 Everyone in the land will **help** to bury them,
Dan 1. 8 so he asked Ashpenaz to **help** him, [9]and God made Ashpenaz
9.22 "Daniel, I have come here to **help** you understand the prophecy.
10.13 the chief angels, came to **help** me, because I had been left
10.20 is no one to **help** me except Michael, Israel's guardian angel.
11. 1 He is responsible for **helping** and defending me.
11.34 people will receive a little **help,** even though many who join
11.45 But he will die, with no one there to **help** him."
Hos 5.11 she insisted on going for **help** to those who had none to
5.13 ask the great emperor for **help,** but he could not cure them
7. 7 one after another, but no one prays to me for **help."**
7.11 people call on Egypt for **help,** and then they run to Assyria!
8. 9 have gone off to seek **help** from Assyria, and have paid other
13. 9 Then who can **help** you?
Joel 2.32 But all who ask the Lord for **help** will be saved.
Amos 5. 2 She lies abandoned on the ground, And no one **helps** her up.
6. 1 great nation Israel, you to whom the people go for **help!**
7. 7 had been built with the **help** of a plumb-line, and there was
9. 4 I am determined to destroy them, not to **help** them."
Jon 1. 5 terrified and cried out for **help,** each one to his own god.
1. 6 Get up and pray to your god for **help.**
2. 2 world of the dead I cried for **help,** and you heard me.
Mic 1.14 kings of Israel will get no **help** from the town of Achzib.
Hab 1. 2 long must I call for **help** before you listen, before you save
Zeph 3. 2 not put its trust in the Lord or asked for his **help.**
3.12 a humble and lowly people, who will come to me for **help.**
Zech 1.17 that he will once again **help** Jerusalem and claim the city as
6.15 far away will come and **help** to rebuild the Temple of the
8. 2 "I have longed to **help** Jerusalem because of my deep love
11.16 flock, but he does not **help** the sheep that are threatened by
Mal 2. 6 but they also **helped** many others to stop doing evil.
Mt 4.11 and angels came and **helped** him.
6. 3 But when you **help** a needy person, do it in such a

Mt 8. 5 entered Capernaum, a Roman officer met him and begged for **help:**
12.12 our Law does allow us to **help** someone on the Sabbath."
12.30 anyone who does not **help** me gather is really scattering.
15. 5 something he could use to **help** his father or mother, but
15.25 **"Help** me, sir!"
23. 4 even to lift a finger to **help** them carry those loads.
25.44 or naked or sick or in prison, and would not **help** you?'
25.45 whenever you refused to **help** one of these least important ones,
25.45 you refused to **help** me.'
26.53 call on my Father for **help,** and at once he would send
27.55 a distance, who had followed Jesus from Galilee and **helped** him.
Mk 1.13 Wild animals were there also, but angels came and **helped** him.
1.31 went to her, took her by the hand, and **helped** her up.
1.40 skin-disease came to Jesus, knelt down, and begged him for **help.**
3. 4 To **help** or to harm?
7.11 something he could use to **help** his father or mother, but
7.12 he is excused from **helping** his father or mother.
9.22 Have pity on us and **help** us, if you possibly can!"
9.24 **Help** me to have more!"
9.27 boy by the hand and **helped** him to rise, and he stood
14. 7 with you, and any time you want to, you can **help** them.
15.41 followed Jesus while he was in Galilee and had **helped** him.
Lk 1.25 "Now at last the Lord has **helped** me," she said.
1.54 ancestors, and has come to the **help** of his servant Israel.
1.68 He has come to the **help** of his people and has set
5. 7 to their partners in the other boat to come and **help** them.
6. 9 To **help** or to harm?
6.38 a full measure, a generous **helping,** poured into your hands—all
7. 4 begged him earnestly, "This man really deserves your **help.**
8. 3 who used their own resources to **help** Jesus and his disciples.
10.40 Tell her to come and **help** me!"
11.23 anyone who does not **help** me gather is really scattering.
11.46 not stretch out a finger to **help** them carry those loads.
18. 3 pleading for her rights, saying, **'Help** me against my opponent!'
18. 7 his own people who cry to him day and night for **help?**
18. 7 Will he be slow to **help** them?
19.35 threw their cloaks over the animal and **helped** Jesus get on.
Jn 12. 2 prepared a dinner for him there, which Martha **helped** to serve;
12. 6 He carried the money bag and would **help** himself from it.
Acts 2.21 then, whoever calls out to the Lord for **help** will be saved.'
3. 7 Then he took him by his right hand and **helped** him up.
7.24 so he went to his **help** and took revenge on the Egyptian
7.35 set them free with the **help** of the angel who appeared to
9.27 Then Barnabas came to his **help** and took him to the apostles.
9.31 Through the **help** of the Holy Spirit it was strengthened and
9.36 She spent all her time doing good and **helping** the poor.
9.41 Peter reached over and **helped** her get up.
10. 2 He also did much to **help** the Jewish poor people and was
11.29 as he could to **help** their fellow-believers who lived in Judaea.
12.20 the man in charge of the palace, that he should **help** them.
13. 5 They had John Mark with them to **help** in the work.
16. 9 and begging him, "Come over to Macedonia and **help** us!"
18.27 the believers in Ephesus **helped** him by writing to the believers
18.27 arrived, he was a great **help** to those who through God's
19.22 Erastus, two of his **helpers,** to Macedonia, while he spent more
20.20 anything that would be of **help** to you as I preached and
20.35 in this way we must **help** the weak, remembering the words
21.28 **"Help!**
26.22 very day I have been **helped** by God, and so I stand
Rom 1.12 you and I will be **helped** at the same time, you by
8.26 way the Spirit also comes to **help** us, weak as we are.
10.13 "Everyone who calls out to the Lord for **help** will be saved."
10.14 can they call to him for **help** if they have not believed?
14.19 things that bring peace and that **help** to strengthen one another.
15. 1 in the faith ought to **help** the weak to carry their burdens.
15.24 way to Spain, and be **helped** by you to go there, after
15.26 to give an offering to **help** the poor among God's people in
15.27 as a matter of fact, they have an obligation to **help** them.
15.27 Gentiles ought to use their material blessings to **help** the Jews.
16. 2 people should, and give her any **help** she may need from you;
1 Cor 7.35 I am saying this because I want to **help** you.
10.23 "We are allowed to do anything"—but not everything is **helpful.**
12.28 power to heal or to **help** others or to direct them or
14. 3 speaks to people and gives them **help,** encouragement, and comfort.
14. 4 who speaks in strange tongues **helps** only himself,
14. 4 but the one who proclaims God's message **helps** the whole church.
14. 5 what he says, so that the whole church may be **helped.**
14.12 greater use of those which **help** to build up the church.
14.17 God is quite good, the other person is not **helped** at all.
14.26 Everything must be of **help** to the church.
16. 1 about the money to be raised to **help** God's people in Judaea.
16. 6 winter, and then you can **help** me to continue my journey,
16.11 on him, but you must **help** him to continue his trip in
2 Cor 1. 3 the merciful Father, the God from whom all **help** comes!
1. 4 He **helps** us in all our troubles,
1. 4 we are able to **help** others
1. 4 using the same **help** that we ourselves have received
1. 5 so also through Christ we share in God's great **help.**
1. 6 If we suffer, it is for your **help** and salvation;
1. 6 if we are **helped,** then you too are helped
1. 7 in our sufferings, you also share in the **help** we receive.
1.11 save us again, [11] as you **help** us by means of your prayers
1.16 back, in order to get **help** from you for my journey to
6. 2 when the day arrived for me to save you I **helped** you."
7.13 the way in which all of you **helped** to cheer him up!
8. 4 of having a part in **helping** God's people in Judaea.
8. 6 work, to continue it and **help** you complete this special service
8. 7 in your eagerness to **help** and in your love for us.
8. 8 how eager others are to **help,** I am trying to find out
2 Cor 8.13 is only fair that you should **help** those who are in need.
8.13 you are in need and they have plenty, they will **help** you.
8.16 God for making Titus as eager as we are to **help** you!
8.17 he was so eager to **help** that of his own free will
8.19 Lord's glory, and in order to show that we want to **help.**
8.22 him many times and found him always very eager to **help.**
8.22 much confidence in you, he is all the more eager to **help.**
8.23 Titus, he is my partner and works with me to **help** you;
9. 1 write to you about the **help** being sent to God's people in
9. 2 that you are willing to **help,** and I have boasted of you
9. 2 Achaia," I said, "have been ready to **help** since last year."
9. 3 But, just as I said, you will be ready with your **help.**
11. 8 I was robbing them, so to speak, in order to **help** you.
11. 9 you I did not bother you for **help** when I needed money;
12.13 except that I did not bother you for financial **help?**
12.15 all I have, and myself as well, in order to **help** you.
12.19 God, and everything we do, dear friends, is done to **help** you.
Gal 6. 2 **Help** to carry one another's burdens, and in this way you
Eph 4.28 honest living for himself and to be able to **help** the poor.
4.29 use harmful words, but only **helpful** words, the kind that build
6.18 Do all this in prayer, asking for God's **help.**
Phil 1. 5 way in which you have **helped** me in the work of the
1.12 happened to me have really **helped** the progress of the gospel.
1.19 of your prayers and the **help** which comes from the Spirit of
2.25 my side and who has served as your messenger in **helping** me.
2.30 to give me the **help** that you yourselves could not give.
4. 3 too, my faithful partner, I want you to **help** these women;
4.14 it was very good of you to **help** me in my troubles.
4.15 the Good News, you were the only church to **help** me;
4.16 than once when I needed **help** in Thessalonica, you sent it to
Col 1.24 physical sufferings I am **helping** to complete what still remains
4.11 Kingdom of God, and they have been a great **help** to me.
1 Thes 3. 2 him to strengthen you and **help** your faith, [3] so that none of
5.11 so encourage one another and **help** one another, just as you
5.14 encourage the timid, **help** the weak, be patient with everyone.
1 Tim 5. 5 continues to pray and ask him for his **help** night and day.
5.10 humble duties for fellow-Christians, **helped** people in trouble,
5.23 take a little wine to **help** your digestion, since you are ill
2 Tim 2.22 who with a pure heart call out to the Lord for **help.**
4.11 bring him with you, because he can **help** me in the work.
Tit 1. 1 was chosen and sent to **help** the faith of God's chosen people
3.13 Do your best to **help** Zenas the lawyer and Apollos to get
Phlm 13 the gospel's sake, so that he could **help** me in your place.
14 However, I do not want to force you to **help** me;
Heb 1.14 are sent by him to **help** those who are to receive salvation.
2.16 it is clear that it is not the angels that he **helps.**
2.16 as the scripture says, "He **helps** the descendants of Abraham."
2.18 And now he can **help** those who are tempted, because he
3.13 become stubborn, you must **help** one another every day, as long
4.16 mercy and find grace to **help** us just when we need it.
6.10 showed for him in the **help** you gave and are still giving
10.24 concerned for one another, to **help** one another to show love
13. 6 and say, "The Lord is my **helper,** I will not be afraid.
13. 9 those who obey these rules have not been **helped** by them.
13.16 to do good and to **help** one another, because these are the
13.17 it with sadness, and that would be of no **help** to you.
Jas 2.25 the Israelite spies and **helping** them to escape by a different
1 Pet 5.12 this brief letter with the **help** of Silas, whom I regard as
3 Jn 6 Please **help** them to continue their journey in a way that
7 the service of Christ without accepting any **help** from unbelievers.
8 We Christians, then, must **help** these people, so that we
Rev 12.16 But the earth **helped** the woman;

HELPER (1)

Acts 21. 8 the seven men who had been chosen as **helpers** in Jerusalem.
Phil 1. 1 union with Christ Jesus, including the church leaders and **helpers:**
1 Tim 3. 8 Church **helpers** must also have a good character and be sincere;
3.12 A church **helper** must have only one wife, and be able to
3.13 Those **helpers** who do their work well win for themselves

HELPER (2)

Jn 14.16 he will give you another **Helper,** who will stay with you for
14.26 The **Helper,** the Holy Spirit, whom the Father will send
15.26 "The **Helper** will come—the Spirit, who reveals the truth
16. 7 if I do not go, the **Helper** will not come to you.

HELPLESS

Ex 15.16 O Lord, and stand **helpless** with fear until your people have
Deut 2.31 I have made King Sihon and his land **helpless** before you;
32.36 on those who serve him, when he sees how **helpless** they are.
Judg 6. 6 devastated the land, [6] and Israel was **helpless** against them.
16. 5 how we can overpower him, tie him up, and make him **helpless.**
16. 6 tie you up and make you **helpless,** how could he do it?"
2 Chr 20.12 Punish them, for we are **helpless** in the face of this large
Neh 5. 5 are **helpless** because our fields and vineyards have been taken
Job 14. 1 We are all born weak and **helpless.**
30.11 has made me weak and **helpless,** they turn against me with all
34.29 If he hid his face, men would be **helpless.**
41.25 they are **helpless** with fear.
Ps 10. 8 He spies on his **helpless** victims;
10.10 The **helpless** victims lie crushed;
10.14 The **helpless** man commits himself to you;
22.21 I am **helpless** before these wild bulls.
34. 6 The **helpless** call to him, and he answers;
44.19 Yet you left us **helpless** among wild animals;
74.19 Don't abandon your **helpless** people to their cruel enemies;
82. 3 be fair to the needy and the **helpless.**
86. 1 to me, Lord, and answer me, for I am **helpless** and weak.

Ps 109.16 he persecuted and killed the poor, the needy, and the **helpless.**
116. 6 The Lord protects the **helpless;**
Prov 22.22 don't take advantage of those who stand **helpless** in court.
25.28 your anger, you are as **helpless** as a city without walls,
28.15 Poor people are **helpless** against a wicked ruler;
30. 1 not with me, God is not with me, and I am **helpless.**
31. 8 Protect the rights of all who are **helpless.**
Is 11. 4 the poor fairly and defend the rights of the **helpless.**
13.16 they look on **helplessly,** their babies will be battered
25. 4 The poor and the **helpless** have fled to you and have been
25.11 God will humiliate them, and their hands will sink **helplessly.**
54.11 "O Jerusalem, you suffering, **helpless** city, with no one to
Jer 46.21 Even her hired soldiers are **helpless** as calves.
48.45 **Helpless** refugees try to find protection in Heshbon,
51.51 we feel completely **helpless** because foreigners have taken over
Lam 1. 3 Judah's people are **helpless** slaves, forced away from home.
1.14 Lord gave me to my foes, and I was **helpless** against them.
Ezek 38.11 decide to invade a **helpless** country where the people live in
Joel 1.16 We look on **helpless** as our crops are destroyed.
Amos 2. 7 trample down the weak and **helpless** and push the poor out of
Zech 1.11 and have found that the whole world lies **helpless** and subdued."
Mt 9.36 they were worried and **helpless,** like sheep without a shepherd.
Rom 5. 6 For when we were still **helpless,** Christ died for the

HEM

Ex 28.33 All round its lower **hem** put pomegranates of blue,
39.24 All round its lower **hem** they put pomegranates of
Job 3.23 God keeps their future hidden and **hems** them in on every
Ezek 5. 3 a few hairs and wrap them in the **hem** of your clothes.

HEN

Mt 23.37 people, just as a **hen** gathers her chicks under her wings,
Lk 13.34 people, just as a **hen** gathers her chicks under her wings,

HENNA

Song 4.13 There is no lack of **henna** and nard, [14]of saffron, calamus,

HERALD

Dan 3. 4 front of the statue, [4]a **herald** announced in a loud voice,

HERBS

Ex 12. 8 and eaten with bitter **herbs** and with bread made without yeast.
Num 9.11 Celebrate it with unleavened bread and bitter **herbs.**
2 Kgs 4.39 One of them went out in the fields to get some **herbs.**
Song 5.13 as lovely as a garden that is full of **herbs** and spices.
Is 28.25 soil, he sows the seeds of **herbs** such as dill and cumin.
Mt 23.23 tenth even of the seasoning **herbs,** such as mint, dill, and
Lk 11.42 a tenth of the seasoning **herbs,** such as mint and rue
11.42 and all the other **herbs,** but you neglect justice and love

HERD

Gen 18. 7 Then he ran to the **herd** and picked out a calf that
26.14 he had many **herds** of sheep and cattle and many servants,
32.16 He divided them into **herds**
32.16 and put one of his servants in charge of each **herd.**
32.16 and leave a space between each **herd** and the one behind it."
32.19 and to all the others who were in charge of the **herds:**
33.13 are driven hard for even one day, the whole **herd** will die.
46.32 have brought your flocks and **herds** and everything else that
47. 1 from Canaan with their flocks, their **herds,** and all that they
1 Sam 30.20 He also recovered all the flocks and **herds;**
1 Chr 5. 9 They had large **herds** in the land of Gilead, and so they
2 Chr 26.10 he had large **herds** of livestock in the western foothills
31. 3 From his own flocks and **herds** he provided animals for the
35. 7 Josiah contributed from his own **herds** and flocks
Ps 68.30 rebuke the nations, that **herd** of bulls with their calves,
107.38 he kept their **herds** of cattle from decreasing.
Jer 3.24 made us lose flocks and **herds,** sons and daughters—everything
5.17 slaughter your flocks and your **herds** and destroy your vines
Zeph 2.14 be a place where flocks, **herds,** and animals of every kind
Mt 8.30 Not far away there was a large **herd** of pigs feeding.
8.31 going to drive us out, send us into that **herd** of pigs."
8.32 The whole **herd** rushed down the side of the cliff into the
Mk 5.11 There was a large **herd** of pigs near by, feeding on a
5.13 The whole **herd**—about two thousand pigs in all—rushed down
Lk 8.32 There was a large **herd** of pigs near by, feeding on a
8.33 The whole **herd** rushed down the side of the cliff into the

HERDSMAN

1 Sam 21. 7 (Saul's chief **herdsman,** Doeg, who was from Edom, happened
Amos 7.14 I am a **herdsman,** and I take care of fig-trees.

AV HERESY

Acts 24.14 our ancestors by following that Way which they say is **false.**
1 Cor 11.19 (No doubt there must be **divisions** among you so that the
Gal 5.20 They separate into **parties** and groups;
Tit 3.10 the person who causes **divisions,** and then have nothing more to
2 Pet 2. 1 bring in destructive, untrue **doctrines,** and will deny the Master

HERMON

Mountain to the n. of Palestine.
see also BAAL HERMON, SENIR, SIRION

Deut 3. 8 of the River Jordan, from the River Arnon to Mount **Hermon.**
3. 9 (Mount **Hermon** is called Sirion by the Sidonians, and Senir
4.48 all the way north to Mount Sirion, that is, Mount **Hermon.**
Josh 11. 3 lived at the foot of Mount **Hermon** in the land of Mizpah.
11.17 the north, in the valley of Lebanon south of Mount **Hermon.**
12. 1 Valley up the Jordan Valley and as far north as Mount **Hermon.**
12. 5 His kingdom included Mount **Hermon,** Salecah, and all of Bashan
13. 5 from Baalgad, which is south of Mount **Hermon,** to Hamath Pass.
13.11 Geshur and Maacah, all Mount **Hermon,** and all of Bashan as
1 Chr 5.23 as far north as Baal Hermon, Senir, and Mount **Hermon,**
Ps 29. 6 like calves and makes Mount **Hermon** leap like a young bull.
42. 6 waterfalls thundering down to the Jordan from Mount **Hermon**
89.12 Mount Tabor and Mount **Hermon** sing to you for joy.
133. 3 like the dew on Mount **Hermon,** falling on the hills of Zion.
Song 4. 8 Senir and Mount **Hermon,** where the lions and leopards live.
Ezek 27. 5 They used fir-trees from Mount **Hermon** for timber

HERO

Gen 6. 4 They were the great **heroes** and famous men of long ago.
Josh 17. 1 eldest son and a military **hero,** so Gilead and Bashan, east
1 Sam 14.48 fought **heroically** and defeated even the people of Amalek.
17.51 the Philistines saw that their **hero** was dead, they ran away.
Is 3. 2 food and their water, [2]their **heroes** and their soldiers,
5.22 **Heroes** of the wine bottle!
Jer 48.14 do you claim to be **heroes,** brave soldiers tested in war?
Ezek 32.21 greatest **heroes** and those who fought on the Egyptian side
32.27 given honourable burial like the **heroes** of ancient times,
32.27 These **heroes** were once powerful enough to terrify the living.
Dan 11. 3 "Then a **heroic** king will appear.

HEROD (1)

Herod the Great, ruler of Judaea 37-4 B.C., builder of the Temple in Jerusalem.

Mt 2. 1 of Bethlehem in Judaea, during the time when **Herod** was king.
2. 3 When King **Herod** heard about this, he was very upset, and
2. 7 So **Herod** called the visitors from the east to a secret
2.12 had warned them in a dream not to go back to **Herod.**
2.13 dream to Joseph and said, "**Herod** will be looking for the
2.15 during the night for Egypt, [15]where he stayed until **Herod** died.
2.16 When **Herod** realized that the visitors from the east
2.19 After **Herod** died, an angel of the Lord appeared in a
2.22 Archelaus had succeeded his father **Herod** as king of Judaea,
Lk 1. 5 During the time when **Herod** was king of Judaea,

HEROD (2)

Herod Antipas, ruler of Galilee 4 B.C. - 39 A.D., husband of Herodias.

Mt 14. 1 At that time **Herod,** the ruler of Galilee, heard about Jesus.
14. 3 For **Herod** had earlier ordered John's arrest, and he had him
14. 4 John the Baptist had told **Herod,** "It isn't right for you to
14. 5 **Herod** wanted to kill him, but he was afraid of the Jewish
14. 6 On **Herod's** birthday the daughter of Herodias danced in front of
14. 6 **Herod** was so pleased [7]that he promised her, "I swear that
22.16 some of their disciples and some members of **Herod's party.**
Mk 3. 6 once with some members of **Herod's party,** and they made plans
6.14 Now King **Herod** heard about all this, because Jesus' reputation
6.16 When **Herod** heard it, he said, "He is John the Baptist!
6.17 **Herod** himself had ordered John's arrest, and he had him chained
6.17 **Herod** did this because of Herodias, whom he had married, even
6.18 John the Baptist kept telling **Herod,** "It isn't right for you
6.19 and wanted to kill him, but she could not because of **Herod.**
6.20 **Herod** was afraid of John because he knew that John was a
6.21 It was on **Herod's** birthday, when he gave a feast for all
6.22 Herodias came in and danced, and pleased **Herod** and his guests.
8.15 against the yeast of the Pharisees and the yeast of **Herod."**
12.13 Pharisees and some members of **Herod's party** were sent to
Lk 3. 1 Pilate was governor of Judaea, **Herod** was ruler of Galilee,
3.19 But John reprimanded **Herod,** the governor, because he had married
3.20 Then **Herod** did an even worse thing by putting John in prison.
8. 3 Joanna, whose husband Chuza was an officer in **Herod's** court;
9. 7 When **Herod,** the ruler of Galilee, heard about all the things
9. 9 **Herod** said, "I had John's head cut off;
13.31 and go somewhere else, because **Herod** wants to kill you."
23. 7 from the region ruled by **Herod,**
23. 7 he sent him to **Herod,** who was also in Jerusalem
23. 8 **Herod** was very pleased when he saw Jesus,
23. 9 So **Herod** asked Jesus many questions, but Jesus made no answer.
23.11 **Herod** and his soldiers mocked Jesus and treated him with contempt;
23.12 On that very day **Herod** and Pilate became friends;
23.15 Nor did **Herod** find him guilty, for he sent him back
Acts 4.27 For indeed **Herod** and Pontius Pilate met together in this city
13. 1 Manaen (who had been brought up with **Herod** the governor),

HEROD (3)

Herod Agrippa I, ruler of Palestine 41-44 A.D.

Acts 12. 1 About this time King **Herod** began to persecute some members
12. 4 **Herod** planned to put him on trial in public after Passover.
12. 6 The night before **Herod** was going to bring him out to the
12.11 to rescue me from **Herod's** power and from everything the Jewish
12.19 **Herod** gave orders to search for him, but they could not
12.19 After this, **Herod** left Judaea and spent some time in Caesarea.

Acts	12.20	**Herod** was very angry with the people of Tyre and Sidon,
	12.20	Then they went to **Herod** and asked him for peace, because
	12.21	On a chosen day **Herod** put on his royal robes, sat on
	12.23	angel of the Lord struck **Herod** down, because he did not give

HERON

Lev	11.13	seagulls, storks, **herons,** pelicans, cormorants;
Deut	14.12	sea-gulls, storks, **herons,** pelicans, cormorants;

HESHBON

City e. of R. Jordan in Reuben or Moab.

Num	21.25	the Amorite cities, including **Heshbon** and all the surrounding
	21.26	**Heshbon** was the capital city of the Amorite king Sihon,
	21.27	"Come to **Heshbon,** to King Sihon's city!
	21.28	Once from this city of **Heshbon** Sihon's army went forth
	21.30	destroyed, All the way from **Heshbon** to Dibon,
	21.34	you did to Sihon, the Amorite king who ruled at **Heshbon."**
	32. 3	of Ataroth, Dibon, Jazer, Nimrah, **Heshbon,** Elealeh, Sibmah,
	32.37	The tribe of Reuben rebuilt **Heshbon,** Elealeh, Kiriathaim,
Deut	1. 4	ruled in the town of **Heshbon,** and King Og of Bashan,
	2.24	Sihon, the Amorite king of **Heshbon,** along with his land.
	2.26	to King Sihon of **Heshbon** with the following offer of peace:
	3. 2	as you did to Sihon the Amorite king who ruled in **Heshbon.'**
	3. 6	we did in the towns that belonged to King Sihon of **Heshbon.**
	4.45	Sihon of the Amorites, who had ruled in the town of **Heshbon.**
	29. 7	this place, King Sihon of **Heshbon** and King Og of Bashan came
Josh	9.10	King Sihon of **Heshbon** and King Og of Bashan,
	12. 2	One was Sihon, the Amorite king who ruled at **Heshbon.**
	12. 5	Gilead, as far as the territory of King Sihon of **Heshbon.**
	13.10	ruled by the Amorite king Sihon, who had ruled at **Heshbon.**
	13.17	It included **Heshbon** and all the cities on the plateau:
	13.21	kingdom of the Amorite king Sihon, who had ruled at **Heshbon.**
	13.26	their land extended from **Heshbon** to Ramath Mizpeh
	13.27	Zaphon, the rest of the kingdom of King Sihon of **Heshbon.**
	21.39	Mahanaim, [39] **Heshbon,** and Jazer, with their pasture lands.
Judg	11.19	Sihon, the Amorite king of **Heshbon,** and asked him for
	11.26	hundred years Israel has occupied **Heshbon** and Aroer,
1 Chr	6.81	Ramoth in Gilead, Mahanaim, [81] **Heshbon,** and Jazer.
Neh	9.22	They conquered the land of **Heshbon,** where Sihon ruled,
Song	7. 4	pools in the city of **Heshbon,** near the gate of that great
Is	15. 4	The people of **Heshbon** and Elealeh cry out, and their cry
	16. 8	farms near **Heshbon** and the vineyards of Sibmah are destroyed—
	16. 9	My tears fall for **Heshbon** and Elealeh, because there is no
Jer	48. 2	enemy have captured **Heshbon** and plot to destroy the nation of
	48.34	"The people of **Heshbon** and Elealeh cry out, and their cry
	48.45	try to find protection in **Heshbon,** the city that King Sihon
	49. 3	People of **Heshbon,** cry out!

HESITATE

Gen	19.16	Lot **hesitated.**
Ex	4.10	I am a poor speaker, slow and **hesitant."**
Deut	1.20	Do not **hesitate** or be afraid.'
	7.10	but he will not **hesitate** to punish those who hate him.
Judg	8.20	He **hesitated,** because he was still only a boy.
2 Sam	13.28	Be brave and don't **hesitate!"**
2 Chr	20.17	People of Judah and Jerusalem, do not **hesitate** or be afraid.
Ps	50.19	you never **hesitate** to tell lies.
Prov	23.13	Don't **hesitate** to discipline a child.
	24.11	Don't **hesitate** to rescue someone who is about to be executed unjustly.
Is	59. 7	You never **hesitate** to murder innocent people.
Jer	31.22	How long will you **hesitate,** faithless people?
Acts	10.20	go down, and do not **hesitate** to go with them, for I
	11.12	The Spirit told me to go with them without **hesitation.**

HEZEKIAH (1)

King of Judah who reformed the worship in Jerusalem.

2 Kgs	18.1-12	**King Hezekiah of Judah**
	13-37	**The Assyrians threaten Jerusalem**
	19.1-7	**The king asks Isaiah's advice**
	8-19	**The Assyrians send another threat**
	20-37	**Isaiah's message to the king**
	20.1-11	**King Hezekiah's illness and recovery**
	12-19	**Messengers from Babylonia**
	20-21	**The end of Hezekiah's reign**
1 Chr	3.10-16	**The descendants of King Solomon**
2 Chr	29.1-2	**King Hezekiah of Judah**
	3-17	**The purification of the Temple**
	18-36	**The Temple is rededicated**
	30.1-12	**Preparations for Passover**
	13-22a	**Passover is celebrated**
	22b-27	**A second celebration**
	31.1-21	**Hezekiah reforms religious life**
	32.1-23	**The Assyrians threaten Jerusalem**
	24-26	**Hezekiah's illness and pride**
	27-31	**Hezekiah's wealth and splendour**
	32-33	**The end of Hezekiah's reign**
Is	36.1-22	**The Assyrians threaten Jerusalem**
	37.1-7	**The king asks Isaiah's advice**
	8-20	**The Assyrians send another threat**
	21-38	**Isaiah's message to the king**
	38.1-20	**King Hezekiah's illness and recovery**
	39.1-8	**Messengers from Babylonia**

2 Kgs	16.20	in David's City, and his son **Hezekiah** succeeded him as king.
	21. 3	pagan places of worship that his father **Hezekiah** had destroyed;
1 Chr	4.41	In the time of King **Hezekiah** of Judah, the men named
2 Chr	28.27	His son **Hezekiah** succeeded him as king.
	33. 3	pagan places of worship that his father **Hezekiah** had destroyed.
Prov	25. 1	proverbs, copied by men at the court of King **Hezekiah**
Is	1. 1	when Uzziah, Jotham, Ahaz, and **Hezekiah** were kings of Judah.
Jer	15. 4	because of what **Hezekiah's** son Manasseh did in Jerusalem when
	26.18	"When **Hezekiah** was king of Judah, the prophet
	26.19	King **Hezekiah** and the people of Judah did not put Micah
	26.19	**Hezekiah** honoured the Lord and tried to win his favour.
Hos	1. 1	that Uzziah, Jotham, Ahaz, and **Hezekiah** were kings of Judah,
Mic	1. 1	time that Jotham, Ahaz, and **Hezekiah** were kings of Judah,
Zeph	1. 1	(Zephaniah was descended from King **Hezekiah** through Amariah,
Mt	1. 6	Jehoram, Uzziah, Jotham, Ahaz, **Hezekiah,** Manasseh, Amon, Josiah,

HIDE (1)

Gen	3. 8	in the garden, and they **hid** from him among the trees.
	3.10	I was afraid and **hid** from you, because I was naked."
	18.17	to himself, "I will not **hide** from Abraham what I am going
	47.18	and said, "We will not **hide** the fact from you, sir, that
Ex	2. 2	what a fine baby he was, she **hid** him for three months.
	2. 3	But when she could not **hide** him any longer, she took a
	2.12	he killed the Egyptian and **hid** his body in the sand.
Lev	16.13	smoke of the incense will **hide** the lid of the Covenant Box
Deut	7.20	them and will destroy those who escape and go into **hiding.**
Josh	2. 4	up on the roof and **hidden** them under some stalks of flax
	2.16	**Hide** there for three days until they come back.
	2.22	The spies went into the hills and **hid.**
	6.17	and her household will be spared, because she **hid** our spies.
	6.25	her relatives, because she had **hidden** the two spies that he
	7.19	Don't try to **hide** it from me."
	8. 4	**"Hide** on the other side of the city, but not too far
	8. 7	Then you will come out of **hiding** and capture the city.
	8. 9	and they went to their **hiding place** and waited there, west
	8.12	men and put them in **hiding** west of the city, between Ai
	8.19	the men who had been **hiding** got up quickly, ran into the
	10.16	kings, however, had escaped and were **hiding** in the cave
	10.17	found them, and Joshua was told where they were **hiding.**
	10.27	and thrown into the same cave where they had **hidden** earlier.
Judg	4.18	So he went in, and she **hid** him behind a curtain.
	4.19	leather bag of milk, gave him a drink, and **hid** him again.
	6. 2	and the people of Israel **hid** from them in caves and other
	9. 5	But Jotham, Gideon's youngest son, **hid** and was not killed.
	9.32	and your men should move by night and **hide** in the fields.
	9.34	made their move at night and **hid** outside Shechem
	9.35	at the city gate, they got up from their **hiding places.**
	9.43	divided them into three groups, and **hid** in the fields, waiting.
	9.43	out of the city, he came out of **hiding** to kill them.
	20.29	the Israelites put some soldiers in **hiding** round Gibeah.
	20.33	rushed out of their **hiding places** in the rocky country
	20.36	relying on the men that they had put in **hiding** round Gibeah.
	20.38	Israelite army and the men in **hiding** had arranged a signal.
	21.20	said to the Benjaminites, "Go and **hide** in the vineyards
1 Sam	10.22	answered, "Saul is over there, **hiding** behind the supplies."
	13. 6	Some of the Israelites **hid** in caves and holes or among the
	14.11	Hebrews are coming out of the holes they have been **hiding** in!"
	14.22	Others, who had been **hiding** in the hills of Ephraim, heard
	19. 2	**hide** in some secret place and stay there.
	19. 3	the field where you are **hiding,** and I will speak to him
	20. 2	does, important or not, and he would not **hide** this from me.
	20. 5	you, I will go and **hide** in the fields until the evening
	20.19	to the place where you **hid** the other time,
	20.19	and **hide** behind the pile of stones there.
	20.24	So David **hid** in the fields.
	22. 4	they stayed there as long as David was **hiding** in the cave.
	23.14	David stayed in **hiding** in the hill-country,
	23.19	Gibeah and said, "David is **hiding** in our territory at Horesh
	23.23	exactly the places where he **hides,** and be sure to bring back
	23.29	went to the region of Engedi, where he stayed in **hiding.**
	24. 3	which David and his men were **hiding** far back in the cave.
	24.22	and David and his men went back to their **hiding place.**
	26. 1	told him that David was **hiding** on Mount Hachilah at the edge
2 Sam	17. 9	Just now he is probably **hiding** in a cave or some other
	17.18	so they hurried off to **hide** in the house of a certain
1 Kgs	17. 3	and go east and **hide** yourself near the brook of Cherith,
	18. 4	took a hundred of them, **hid** them in caves in two groups
	18.13	prophets of the Lord I **hid** a hundred of them in caves,
	22.25	when you go into some back room to **hide,"** Micaiah replied.
2 Kgs	6.29	her that we would eat her son, but she had **hidden** him!"
	7. 8	gold, and clothing they found, and went off and **hid** them;
	7.12	they have left their camp to go and **hide** in the countryside.
	11. 2	bedroom in the Temple and **hid** him from Athaliah, so that he
	11. 3	and kept him **hidden** in the Temple, while Athaliah ruled
1 Chr	21.20	wheat, and when they saw the angel, the sons ran and **hid.**
2 Chr	18.24	when you go into some back room to **hide,"** Micaiah replied.
	22. 9	was made for Ahaziah, and he was found **hiding** in Samaria.
	22.11	about to be murdered and **hid** him and a nurse in
	22.11	By keeping him **hidden,** she saved him from death at the hands
	22.12	he remained there in **hiding,** while Athaliah ruled as queen.
Neh	6.10	and I must go and **hide** together in the Holy Place of
	6.11	I answered, "I'm not the kind of man that runs and **hides.**
	6.11	I would try to save my life by **hiding** in the Temple?
Job	3.23	God keeps their future **hidden** and hems them in on every
	13.10	Even though your prejudice is **hidden,** he will reprimand
	13.20	agree to them, and I will not try to **hide** from you;
	14.13	I wish you would **hide** me in the world of the dead;
	14.13	let me be **hidden** until your anger is over, and then set
	15. 5	you are trying to **hide** behind clever words.
	15.18	they learnt from their fathers, and they kept no secrets **hidden.**
	16.18	O Earth, don't **hide** the wrongs done to me!
	18.10	On the ground a snare is **hidden;**
	19. 8	he has **hidden** my path in darkness.

Job 22.13 He is **hidden** by clouds—how can he judge us?"
24. 4 getting their rights and force the needy to run and **hide.**
24.16 into houses, but by day they **hide** and avoid the light.
26. 9 He **hides** the full moon behind a cloud.
28.11 to the sources of rivers And bring to light what is **hidden.**
31. 9 my neighbour's wife, and waited, **hidden,** outside her door,
31.33 Other men try to **hide** their sins, but I have never
34.22 There is no darkness dark enough to **hide** a sinner from God.
34.29 If he **hid** his face, men would be helpless.
38.13 seize the earth and shake the wicked from their **hiding places?**
38.40 hungry young lions [40] when they **hide** in their caves, or lie
40.21 the thorn-bushes, and **hides** among the reeds in the swamp.
Ps 10. 1 Why do you **hide** yourself when we are in trouble?
10. 8 **hides** himself in the villages, waiting to murder innocent people.
10. 9 he waits in his **hiding place** like a lion.
13. 1 How much longer will you **hide** yourself from me?
17. 8 **hide** me in the shadow of your wings [9] from the attacks of
19. 6 Nothing can **hide** from its heat.
19.12 deliver me, Lord, from **hidden** faults!
27. 9 don't **hide** yourself from me!"
30. 7 But then you **hid** yourself from me, and I was afraid.
31.20 You **hide** them in the safety of your presence from the
31.20 in a safe shelter you **hide** them from the insults of their
32. 7 You are my **hiding place;**
44.24 Why are you **hiding** from us?
55.12 an opponent boasting over me, I could **hide** myself from him.
56. 6 They gather in **hiding-places** and watch everything I do,
69. 5 My sins, O God, are not **hidden** from you;
69.17 Don't **hide** yourself from your servant;
81. 7 From my **hiding-place** in the storm, I answered you.
89.46 Lord, will you **hide** yourself for ever?
91. 3 keep you safe from all **hidden** dangers and from all deadly
104.18 the high mountains, and the rock-badgers **hide** in the cliffs.
119.19 do not **hide** your commands from me.
138. 6 you care for the lowly, and the proud cannot **hide** from you.
139.11 could ask the darkness to **hide** me or the light round me
142. 3 path where I walk, my enemies have **hidden** a trap for me.
143. 7 Don't **hide** yourself from me, or I will be among those who
Prov 1. 6 that they can understand the **hidden** meanings of proverbs
2. 4 it as hard as you would for silver or some **hidden** treasure.
10. 6 A wicked man's words **hide** a violent nature.
10.11 but a wicked man's words **hide** a violent nature.
10.18 A man who **hides** his hatred is a liar.
14.13 Laughter may **hide** sadness.
15.11 how then can a man **hide** his thoughts from God?
20.27 we cannot **hide** from ourselves.
26.23 Insincere talk that **hides** what you are really thinking
26.24 A hypocrite **hides** his hate behind flattering words.
28.12 but when bad men rule, people stay in **hiding.**
28.13 will never succeed in life if you try to **hide** your sins.
28.28 People stay in **hiding** when bad men come to power.
Song 2.14 are like a dove that **hides** in the crevice of a rock.
Is 2.10 They will **hide** in caves in the rocky hills or dig holes
2.10 from the Lord's anger and to **hide** from his power and glory!
2.19 People will **hide** in caves in the rocky hills or dig
2.19 the Lord's anger and to **hide** from his power and glory, when
2.21 shake the earth, people will **hide** in holes and caves in the
2.21 escape from his anger and to **hide** from his power and glory.
8.17 Lord has **hidden** himself from his people, but I trust him
10. 3 Where will you **hide** your wealth?
16. 3 **hide** us where no one can find us.
26.20 **Hide** yourselves for a little while until God's anger is over.
26.21 the ground will no longer **hide** those who have been killed.
29.11 meaning of every prophetic vision will be **hidden** from you;
29.15 who try to **hide** their plans from the Lord are doomed!
32. 2 a shelter from the wind and a place to **hide** from storms.
42.22 they are locked up in dungeons and **hidden** away in prisons.
45.19 I have not spoken in secret or kept my purpose **hidden.**
64. 7 You have **hidden** yourself from us and have abandoned us
Jer 4. 7 a lion coming from its **hiding place,** a destroyer of nations
7.11 Do you think that my Temple is a **hiding place** for robbers?
13. 4 to the River Euphrates and **hide** the shorts in a hole in
13. 5 So I went and **hid** them near the Euphrates.
13. 7 the place where I had **hidden** them, I saw that they were
14. 3 Discouraged and confused, they **hide** their faces.
14. 4 they **hide** their faces.
16.17 Nothing is **hidden** from me;
23.24 No one can **hide** where I cannot see him.
36.19 Then they said to him, "You and Jeremiah must go and **hide.**
36.26 But the Lord had **hidden** us.
41. 8 have wheat, barley, olive-oil, and honey **hidden** in the fields."
49. 8 **Hide!**
49.10 uncovered their hiding places, so that they can no longer **hide.**
49.30 Hazor, I, the Lord, warn you to run far away and **hide.**
Lam 1. 8 She groans and **hides** her face in shame.
3.43 your mercy was **hidden** by your anger, [44] By a cloud of fury
Ezek 22.28 prophets have **hidden** these sins like men covering a wall with
24. 7 was not spilt on the ground where the dust could **hide** it;
24. 8 blood there, where it cannot be **hidden,** where it demands angry
32. 7 The sun will **hide** behind the clouds, and the moon will give
33.27 Those **hiding** in the mountains and in caves will die of disease.
Dan 2.22 he knows what is **hidden** in darkness, and he himself is
5.16 I have heard that you can find **hidden** meanings and explain
10. 7 not see anything, but they were terrified and ran and **hid.**
11.43 He will take away Egypt's **hidden** treasures of gold
12. 9 words are to be kept secret and **hidden** until the end comes.
Hos 5. 3 I know what Israel is like—she cannot **hide** from me.
10. 8 The people will call out to the mountains, **"Hide** us!"
Amos 9. 3 If they **hide** on the top of Mount Carmel, I will search
9. 3 If they **hide** from me at the bottom of the sea,
Mic 1.15 leaders of Israel will go and **hide** in the cave at Adullam.
Hab 3. 4 light flashes from his hand, there where his power is **hidden.**
Mt 5.14 A city built on a hill cannot be **hidden.**
11.25 unlearned what you have **hidden** from the wise and learned.
13.44 A man happens to find a treasure **hidden** in a field.
21.13 But you are making it a **hideout** for thieves!"
24.26 or if they say, 'Look, he is **hiding** here!'
25.18 dug a hole in the ground, and **hid** his master's money.
25.25 afraid, so I went off and **hid** your money in the ground.
Mk 4.22 Whatever is **hidden** away will be brought out into the open,
7.24 anyone to know he was there, but he could not stay **hidden.**
11.17 But you have turned it into a **hideout** for thieves!"
Lk 8.17 "Whatever is **hidden** away will be brought out into the open,
9.45 It had been **hidden** from them so that they could not
10.21 unlearned what you have **hidden** from the wise and learned.
11.33 lights a lamp and then **hides** it or puts it under a
18.34 meaning of the words was **hidden** from them, and they did not
19.20 I kept it **hidden** in a handkerchief.
19.46 But you have turned it into a **hideout** for thieves!"
23.30 and to the hills, **'Hide** us!'
Jn 7. 4 No one **hides** what he is doing if he wants to be
8.59 to throw at him, but Jesus **hid** himself and left the Temple.
12.36 After Jesus said this, he went off and **hid** himself from them.
Acts 1. 9 as they watched him, and a cloud **hid** him from their sight.
23.21 more than forty men who will be **hiding** and waiting for him.
26.26 for this thing has not happened **hidden** away in a corner.
Rom 16.25 the secret truth which was **hidden** for long ages in the past.
1 Cor 2. 7 God's secret wisdom, which is **hidden** from mankind, but which
2.10 The Spirit searches everything, even the **hidden** depths of God's purposes.
4. 5 the dark secrets and expose the **hidden** purposes of people's minds.
2 Cor 4. 3 the gospel we preach is **hidden,**
4. 3 it is **hidden** only from those who are being
Eph 3. 9 all things, kept his secret **hidden** through all the past ages,
Col 1.26 which is the secret he **hid** through all past ages from
2. 3 key that opens all the **hidden** treasures of God's wisdom
3. 3 you have died, and your life is **hidden** with Christ in God.
1 Tim 5.25 and even those that are not so plain cannot be **hidden.**
Heb 4.13 There is nothing that can be **hidden** from God;
11.23 made the parents of Moses **hide** him for three months after he
1 Jn 2.28 of courage and need not **hide** in shame from him on the
Rev 2.17 who win the victory I will give some of the **hidden** manna.
6.15 men, slave and free, **hid** themselves in caves and under rocks
6.16 rocks, "Fall on us and **hide** us from the eyes of the

HIDE (2)

Job 41. 7 Can you fill his **hide** with fishing-spears or pierce his head

HIDING-PLACE see HIDE (1), PLACE (1)

HIGH
[HEIGHT]

Gen 7.19 It became so deep that it covered the **highest** mountains;
34.12 and set the payment for the bride as **high** as you wish;
45. 8 He has made me the king's **highest** official.
Ex 15. 8 You blew on the sea and the water piled up **high;**
17.16 He said, "Hold **high** the banner of the Lord!
Lev 25.16 years, the price shall be **higher,** but if there are only a
26.13 you down and I let you walk with your head held **high."**
Num 23. 9 From the **high** rocks I can see them;
24.21 Safe as a nest set **high** on a cliff, [22] But you Kenites
Deut 3. 5 these towns were fortified with **high** walls, gates, and bars
10.14 To the Lord belong even the **highest heavens;**
12. 2 people worship their gods on **high** mountains, on hills,
28.52 giving you, and the **high,** fortified walls in which you trust
2 Sam 6.22 I am nothing, but those girls will think **highly** of me!"
1 Kgs 4. 2 was king of all Israel, [2] and these were his **high** officials:
2 Kgs 2.17 of them went and looked **high** and low for Elijah for three
18.17 it was commanded by his three **highest** officials.
19.23 you had conquered the **highest** mountains of Lebanon.
23.11 from the living-quarters of Nathan Melech, a **high** official.)
1 Chr 15.17 chose the following Levites to play the **high-pitched** harps:
18.17 and King David's sons held **high** positions in his service.
2 Chr 17. 5 him gifts, so that he became wealthy and **highly** honoured.
33.14 Manasseh increased the **height** of the outer wall on the
34. 8 governor of Jerusalem, and Joah son of Joahaz, a **high** official.
Ezra 9. 6 Our sins pile up, **high** above our heads;
9. 6 they reach as **high** as the heavens.
Neh 4. 6 it was half its full **height,** because the people were eager
8. 5 stood there on the platform **high** above the people,
Esth 1.14 Persia and Media who held the **highest** offices in the kingdom.
5.11 had promoted him to **high** office, and how much more important
6. 9 Then get one of your **highest** noblemen to dress the man in
10. 2 how he promoted Mordecai to **high** office, are recorded in
Job 21.22 Can a man teach God, who judges even those in **high** places?
22.12 Doesn't God live in the **highest heavens**
22.12 and look down on the stars, even though they are **high?**
22.25 be your gold, and let him be silver, piled **high** for you.
31.37 I have done, and hold my head **high** in his presence.
35. 5 See how **high** the clouds are!
36.16 your table was piled **high** with food.
39.27 for your command to build its nest **high** in the mountains?
39.28 makes its home on the **highest** rocks and makes the sharp
Ps 27. 5 safe in his Temple and make me secure on a **high** rock.
36. 2 Because he thinks so **highly** of himself, he thinks that God
48. 2 Zion, the mountain of God, is **high** and beautiful;
68.18 He goes up to the **heights,** taking many captives with him;
95. 4 the whole earth, from the deepest caves to the **highest** hills.

Ps	102.19	from his holy place on **high,** he looked down from heaven to
	103.11	As **high** as the sky is above the earth, so great is
	104.18	wild goats live in the **high** mountains, and the rock-badgers
	107.26	The ships were lifted **high** in the air and plunged down
	113. 5	He lives in the **heights** above, [6]but he bends down to see
	138. 6	Even though you are so **high** above, you care for the lowly,
	148. 1	Praise the Lord from heaven, you that live in the **heights**
	148. 4	Praise him, **highest heavens,** and the waters above the sky.
Prov	9. 3	servant-girls to call out from the **highest** place in the town:
	9.14	on a seat in the **highest** part of the town, [15]and calls
	11.26	hoards grain, waiting for a **higher** price, but they praise the
	18.11	wealth protects them like **high,** strong walls round a city.
	20.14	that the price is too **high,** but then he goes off and
	23.34	on the ocean, sea-sick, swinging **high** up in the rigging of a
	25. 3	are beyond us, like the **heights** of the sky or the depths
	25. 7	be asked to take a **higher** position than to be told to
Ecc	5. 8	over him, and both are protected by still **higher** officials.
	9.11	and capable men do not always rise to **high** positions.
	12. 5	will be afraid of **high** places, and walking will be dangerous.
Song	7. 5	Your head is held **high** like Mount Carmel.
Is	2. 2	Temple stands will be the **highest** one of all, towering above
	2.14	He will level the **high** mountains and hills,
	2.15	every **high** tower, and the walls of every
	6. 1	sitting on his throne, **high** and exalted, and his robe filled
	7.11	in the world of the dead or from **high** up in heaven."
	8. 8	sweep through Judah in a flood, rising shoulder **high**
	10.33	proudest and **highest** of them will be cut down and humiliated.
	14.13	to heaven and to place your throne above the **highest** stars.
	22.19	you from office and bring you down from your **high** position."
	25.12	fortresses of Moab with their **high** walls and bring them
	30.13	You are like a **high** wall with a crack running down it;
	30.33	It is deep and wide, and piled **high** with wood.
	37.24	you had conquered the **highest** mountains of Lebanon.
	40. 9	Jerusalem, go up on a **high** mountain and proclaim the good news!
	44. 9	are worthless, and the gods they prize so **highly** are useless.
	52.13	he will be **highly** honoured.
	55. 9	As **high** as the heavens are above the earth,
	55. 9	so **high** are my ways and thoughts above
	57. 7	You go to the **high** mountains to offer sacrifices
	57.15	"I am the **high** and holy God, who lives for ever.
	57.15	I live in a **high** and holy place, but I also live
Jer	2.20	On every **high** hill and under every green tree you worshipped
	3. 6	from me, and on every **high** hill and under every green tree
	17.12	like a glorious throne, standing on a **high** mountain
	18.14	Are Lebanon's rocky **heights** ever without snow?
	21.13	You, Jerusalem, are sitting **high** above the valleys,
	25.30	will roar from heaven and thunder from the **heights** of heaven.
	39. 3	Jerusalem was captured, all the **high** officials of the king of
	39.13	So Nebuzaradan, together with the **high** officials
	46.18	mountains and Mount Carmel stands **high** above the sea,
	48.45	and the mountain **heights** of the war-loving people of Moab.
	49.16	You live on the rocky cliffs, **high** on top of the mountain;
	49.16	even though you live as **high** up as an eagle, the Lord
	51.23	to crush rulers and **high** officials."
Ezek	6.13	the altars, scattered on every **high** hill, on the top of
	8. 3	vision God's spirit lifted me **high** in the air and took me
	17.22	I will plant it on a **high** mountain, [23]on Israel's highest mountain.
	20.28	When they saw the **high** hills and green trees, they offered
	20.29	What are these **high** places where you go?
	20.29	So they have been called **'High Places'** ever since.
	20.40	on my holy mountain, the **high** mountain of Israel, all you
	23. 6	in uniforms of purple, noblemen and **high-ranking** officers;
	23.14	attracted by the images of **high** Babylonian officials carved
	23.23	those important officials and **high-ranking** cavalry officers.
	31.14	or push its top through the clouds and reach such a **height.**
	34. 6	So my sheep wandered over the **high** hills and the mountains.
	40. 2	to the land of Israel and put me on a **high** mountain.
	40.19	was a gateway at a **higher** level that led to the inner
	41.17	of the Temple, up as **high** as above the doors, were
	43.15	on the four corners were **higher** than the rest of the top.
Dan	2.48	Then he gave Daniel a **high** position, presented him with
	3.30	and Abednego to **higher** positions in the province of Babylon.
	9.27	will be placed on the **highest** point of the Temple and will
	11.39	as ruler, put them into **high** offices, and give them land as
Amos	4.13	He walks on the **heights** of the earth.
	8. 6	We can sell worthless wheat at a **high** price.
Obad	3	your home is **high** in the mountains, and so you say to
	4	you make your home as **high** as an eagle's nest, so that
Mic	4. 1	Temple stands will be the **highest** one of all, towering above
Nah	3. 3	Corpses are piled **high,** dead bodies without number—
Hab	1.10	They treat kings with contempt and laugh at **high** officials.
	3.10	The waters under the earth roared, and their waves rose **high.**
Zeph	1.16	of soldiers attacking fortified cities and **high** towers.
Mt	4. 5	City, set him on the **highest** point of the Temple, [6]and said
	4. 8	took Jesus to a very **high** mountain and showed him all the
	17. 1	John and led them up a **high** mountain where they were alone.
Mk	9. 2	John, and led them up a **high** mountain, where they were alone.
Lk	2.14	"Glory to God in the **highest heaven,** and peace on earth
	4. 9	and set him on the **highest** point of the Temple, and said
	4.38	mother-in-law was sick with a **high** fever, and they spoke to
	19.12	was once a man of **high** rank who was going to a
Acts	5.13	to join them, even though the people spoke **highly** of them.
	5.34	of the Law and was **highly** respected by all the people, stood
	10.22	God and is **highly** respected by all the Jewish people.
	13.50	the Gentile women of **high** social standing who worshipped God.
	15.22	chose two men who were **highly** respected by the believers, Judas,
	17.12	and many Greek women of **high** social standing and many Greek
	22.12	obeyed our Law and was **highly** respected by all the Jews
Rom	12. 3	Do not think of yourself more **highly** than you should.
	14. 6	Whoever thinks **highly** of a certain day does so in honour
1 Cor	1.26	few of you were wise or powerful or of **high** social standing.
2 Cor	8.18	sending the brother who is **highly** respected in all the churches
	10.12	or compare ourselves with those who rate themselves so **highly.**
	11.26	wilds, dangers on the **high seas,** and dangers from false friends.
	12. 2	was snatched up to the **highest heaven** (I do not know whether
	12. 6	want anyone to have a **higher** opinion of me than he has
Eph	3.18	how broad and long, how **high** and deep, is Christ's love.
	4. 8	up to the very **heights,** he took many captives with him;
	4.13	reaching to the very **height** of Christ's full stature.
Phil	2. 9	God raised him to the **highest** place above and gave him the
Jas	5. 8	Keep your hopes **high,** for the day of the Lord's coming is
Rev	8.13	an eagle that was flying **high** in the air say in a
	14. 6	I saw another angel flying **high** in the air, with an eternal
	18. 5	sins are piled up as **high** as heaven, and God remembers her
	21.10	the angel carried me to the top of a very **high** mountain.
	21.12	It had a great, **high** wall with twelve gates and with
	21.16	long and was as wide and as **high** as it was long.
	21.17	and it was sixty metres **high,** according to the standard unit

HIGH PRIEST

The chief Jewish priest and president of their supreme Council. Once a year (on the Day of Atonement) he would enter the Most Holy Place in the Temple and offer a sacrifice for himself and for the sins of the people of Israel.

Ex	25. 7	set in the ephod of the **High Priest** and in his breast-piece.
	28.15	"Make a breast-piece for the **High Priest** to use in
	35. 9	be set in the **High Priest's** ephod and in his breast-piece.
Lev	4. 3	If it is the **High Priest** who sins and so brings guilt
	4. 5	Then the **High Priest** shall take some of the bull's blood
	4.16	The **High Priest** shall take some of the bull's blood into
	6.22	by every descendant of Aaron who is serving as **High Priest.**
	16.32	**High Priest,** properly ordained and consecrated to succeed his
	21.10	**High Priest** has had the anointing oil poured on his head
	21.15	and I have set him apart as the **High Priest."**
Num	35.25	there until the death of the man who is then **High Priest.**
	35.28	until the death of the **High Priest,** but after that he may
	35.32	in order to return home before the death of the **High Priest.**
Josh	20. 6	until the death of the man who is then the **High Priest.**
2 Kgs	12.10	the royal secretary and the **High Priest** would come, melt down
	22. 4	"Go to the **High Priest** Hilkiah and get a report on the
	23. 4	Josiah ordered the **High Priest** Hilkiah, his assistant priests,
	23.24	in the book that the **High Priest** Hilkiah had found in the
	25.18	away as prisoners Seraiah the **High Priest,** Zephaniah
2 Chr	19.11	**High Priest** will have final authority in all religious cases,
	24.11	and the **High Priest's** representative would take the money
	31.10	and Azariah the **High Priest,** a descendant of Zadok, said
	31.13	under the authority of King Hezekiah and Azariah the **High Priest.**
	34. 9	in the Temple was handed over to Hilkiah the **High Priest.**
	35. 8	of the Temple—Hilkiah, the **High Priest,** Zechariah, and Jehiel—
Ezra	7. 1	He traced his ancestors back to Aaron, the **High Priest,**
Neh	3. 1	The **High Priest** Eliashib and his fellow-priests rebuilt
	3.20	as the entrance to the house of the **High Priest** Eliashib;
	11.11	included Zadok, Meraioth, and Ahitub, who was the **High Priest.**
	12. 1	exile with Zerubbabel son of Shealtiel and with the **High Priest**
	12.12	When Joiakim was **High Priest,** the following priests
	12.22	families during the lifetimes of the following **High Priests:**
	13.28	the son of Eliashib the **High Priest,** but one of Joiada's
Jer	52.24	away as prisoners Seraiah the **High Priest,** Zephaniah
Dan	11.22	who opposes him, even God's **High Priest,** will be swept away
Hag	1. 1	and for the **High Priest,** Joshua son of Jehozadak.
	1.14	Joshua, the **High Priest,** and all the people who had returned
	2. 2	of Judah, to Joshua, the **High Priest,** and to the people,
Zech	3. 1	Lord showed me the **High Priest** Joshua standing before the angel
	3. 8	Listen then, Joshua, you who are the **High Priest;**
	6.11	it on the head of the **High Priest,** Joshua son of Jehozadak.
Mt	26. 3	palace of Caiaphas, the **High Priest,** [4]and made plans to arrest
	26.51	and struck at the **High Priest's** slave, cutting off his ear.
	26.57	the house of Caiaphas, the **High Priest,** where the teachers
	26.58	as far as the courtyard of the **High Priest's** house.
	26.62	The **High Priest** stood up and said to Jesus, "Have you
	26.63	Again the **High Priest** spoke to him, "In the name of the
	26.65	At this the **High Priest** tore his clothes and said,
	26.69	courtyard when one of the **High Priest's** servant-girls came to him
Mk	2.26	This happened when Abiathar was the **High Priest.**
	14.47	and struck at the **High Priest's** slave, cutting off his ear.
	14.53	Jesus was taken to the **High Priest's** house, where all the
	14.54	and went into the courtyard of the **High Priest's** house.
	14.60	The **High Priest** stood up in front of them all and
	14.61	Again the **High Priest** questioned him, "Are you the Messiah,
	14.63	The **High Priest** tore his robes and said, "We don't need
	14.66	the courtyard when one of the **High Priest's** servant-girls came by.
Lk	3. 2	ruler of Abilene, [2]and Annas and Caiaphas were **high priests.**
	22.50	one of them struck the **High Priest's** slave and cut off his
	22.54	Jesus and took him away into the house of the **High Priest;**
Jn	11.49	them, named Caiaphas, who was **High Priest** that year, said,
	11.51	rather, as he was **High Priest** that year, he was prophesying
	18.10	drew it and struck the **High Priest's** slave, cutting off his
	18.13	was the father-in-law of Caiaphas, who was **High Priest** that year.
	18.15	was well known to the **High Priest,** so he went with Jesus
	18.15	into the courtyard of the **High Priest's** house, [16]while Peter
	18.19	The **High Priest** questioned Jesus about his disciples
	18.22	said, "How dare you talk like that to the **High Priest!"**
	18.24	Then Annas sent him, still bound, to Caiaphas the **High Priest.**
	18.26	One of the **High Priest's** slaves, a relative of the man
Acts	4. 6	They met with the **High Priest** Annas and with Caiaphas, John,
	4. 6	Alexander, and the others who belonged to the **High Priest's** family.
	5.17	Then the **High Priest** and all his companions, members

Acts	5.21	The **High Priest** and his companions called together all the Jewish
	5.27	stand before the Council, and the **High Priest** questioned them.
	7. 1	The **High Priest** asked Stephen, "Is this true?"
	9. 1	He went to the **High Priest** [2]and asked for letters of
	19.14	sons of a Jewish **High Priest** named Sceva, were doing this.
	22. 5	The **High Priest** and the whole Council can prove that I am
	23. 2	The **High Priest** Ananias ordered those who were standing close
	23. 4	Paul said to him, "You are insulting God's **High Priest!"**
	23. 5	"My fellow-Israelites, I did not know that he was the **High Priest.**
	24. 1	Five days later the **High Priest** Ananias went to Caesarea
Heb	2.17	faithful and merciful **High Priest** in his service to God,
	3. 1	God sent to be the **High Priest** of the faith we profess.
	4.14	For we have a great **High Priest** who has gone into the
	4.15	Our **High Priest** is not one who cannot feel sympathy for
	4.15	the contrary, we have a **High Priest** who was tempted in every
	5. 1	Every **high priest** is chosen from his fellow-men and appointed
	5. 4	No one chooses for himself the honour of being a **high priest.**
	5. 4	that a man is made a **high priest**—just as Aaron was.
	5. 5	did not take upon himself the honour of being a **high priest.**
	5.10	God declared him to be **high priest,** in the priestly order of
	6.20	us, and has become a **high priest** for ever, in the priestly
	7.26	Jesus, then, is the **High Priest** that meets our needs.
	7.27	He is not like other **high priests;**
	7.28	Law of Moses appoints men who are imperfect to be **high priests;**
	8. 1	that we have such a **High Priest,** who sits at the right
	8. 2	He serves as **High Priest** in the Most Holy Place, that is,
	8. 3	**High Priest** is appointed to present offerings and animal
	8. 3	to God, and so our **High Priest** must also have something to
	9. 7	duties, [7]but only the **High Priest** goes into the inner Tent,
	9.11	has already come as the **High Priest** of the good things that
	9.25	The Jewish **High Priest** goes into the Most Holy Place
	13.11	The Jewish **High Priest** brings the blood of the animals

HIGHLANDS

Deut	32.13	"He let them rule the **highlands,** and they ate what grew
2 Chr	21.11	worship in the Judaean **highlands** and led the people of Judah
Jer	12.12	Across all the desert **highlands** men have come to plunder.

HIGHWAY

Is	11.16	There will be a **highway** out of Assyria for those of his
	19.23	time comes, there will be a **highway** between Egypt and Assyria.
	33. 8	The **highways** are so dangerous that no one travels on them.
	35. 8	will be a **highway** there, called "The Road of Holiness."
	49.11	"I will make a **highway** across the mountains and prepare
	62.10	Prepare a **highway;**

HILKIAH (1)

High priest in King Josiah's reign.

2 Kgs	22. 4	"Go to the High Priest **Hilkiah** and get a report on the
	22. 8	delivered the king's order to **Hilkiah,**
	22. 8	and **Hilkiah** told him that he had found
	22. 8	**Hilkiah** gave him the book, and Shaphan read it.
	22.10	then he said, "I have here a book that **Hilkiah** gave me."
	22.12	gave the following order to **Hilkiah** the priest, to Ahikam
	22.14	**Hilkiah,** Ahikam, Achbor, Shaphan, and Asaiah went to
	23. 4	Josiah ordered the High Priest **Hilkiah,** his assistant priests,
	23.24	book that the High Priest **Hilkiah** had found in the Temple,
1 Chr	6.13	Amariah, Ahitub, [12]Zadok, Shallum, [13]**Hilkiah,** Azariah,
	9.10	Azariah son of **Hilkiah** (the chief official in the Temple),
2 Chr	34. 9	collected in the Temple was handed over to **Hilkiah** the High
	34.14	taken out of the storeroom, **Hilkiah** found the book of the
	34.18	Then he added, "I have here a book that **Hilkiah** gave me."
	34.20	gave the following order to **Hilkiah,** to Ahikam son of Shaphan,
	34.22	the king's command, **Hilkiah** and the others went to consult a
	35. 8	in charge of the Temple—**Hilkiah,** the High Priest, Zechariah,
Ezra	7. 1	son of Azariah, son of **Hilkiah,** [2]son of Shallum, son of
Neh	11.11	Seraiah, the son of **Hilkiah** and grandson of Meshullam.

HILL

[SEPARATION HILL]
see also **FOOTHILLS**

Gen	19.17	Run to the **hills,** so that you won't be killed."
	19.19	But the **hills** are too far away;
	19.30	two daughters moved up into the **hills** and lived in a cave.
	49.22	a wild donkey by a spring, A wild colt on a **hillside.**
	49.26	Delightful things from everlasting **hills.**
Ex	17. 9	stand on top of the **hill** holding the stick that God told
	17.10	Moses, Aaron, and Hur went up to the top of the **hill.**
Lev	26.30	places of worship on the **hills,** tear down your incense-altars,
Num	21.28	of Ar in Moab And devoured the **hills** of the upper Arnon.
	23. 3	went alone to the top of a **hill,** [4]and God met him.
	23. 9	I can watch them from the **hills.**
	34.11	Ain, and on to the **hills** on the eastern shore of Lake
Deut	1.44	Amorites who lived in those **hills** came out against you like
	2. 3	wandering about in those **hills** and that we should go north.
	8. 7	and underground streams gushing out into the valleys and **hills;**
	8. 9	have iron in them, and from its **hills** you can mine copper.
	12. 2	worship their gods on high mountains, on **hills,**
	33.15	May their ancient **hills** be covered with choice fruit.
Josh	2.22	The spies went into the **hills** and hid.
	2.23	spies came down from the **hills,** crossed the river, and went
	5. 3	circumcised the Israelites at a place called Circumcision **Hill.**
	6.20	went straight up the **hill** into the city and captured it.
	7. 5	killed about thirty-six of them on the way down the **hill.**
	9. 1	of the Jordan—in the **hills,** in the foothills, and all along
	10.36	from Eglon up into the **hills** to Hebron, attacked it
Josh	13.19	Sibmah, Zereth-shahar on the **hill** in the valley,
	15. 8	south side of the **hill** where the Jebusite city of Jerusalem
	15. 8	to the top of the **hill** on the west side of the
	15.11	went out to the **hill** north of Ekron, turned towards Shikkeron,
Judg	3.27	then he led them down from the **hills.**
	6. 2	hid from them in caves and other safe places in the **hills.**
	7. 1	was in the valley to the north of them by Moreh **Hill.**
	16. 3	them all the way to the top of the **hill** overlooking Hebron.
1 Sam	7. 1	the house of a man named Abinadab, who lived on a **hill.**
	9. 9	they were going up the **hill** to the town, they met some
	9.12	are going to offer a sacrifice on the altar on the **hill.**
	9.12	you will find him before he goes up the **hill** to eat."
	10. 5	you will go to the **Hill of God** in Gibeah, where there
	10. 5	from the altar on the **hill,** playing harps, drums, flutes,
	10.13	dancing and shouting, he went to the altar on the **hill.**
	14.22	hiding in the **hills** of Ephraim, heard that the Philistines
	17. 3	Philistines lined up on one **hill** and the Israelites on another,
	22. 6	under a tamarisk-tree on a **hill,** with his spear in his hand,
	23.25	and went to a rocky **hill** in the wilderness of Maon and
	23.26	on one side of the **hill,** separated from David and his men,
	23.28	That is why that place is called **Separation Hill.**
	25.20	round a bend on a **hillside** when suddenly she met David and
	26.13	to the top of the **hill,** a safe distance away, [14]and
2 Sam	1.19	"On the **hills** of Israel our leaders are dead!
	1.21	"May no rain or dew fall on Gilboa's **hills;**
	1.25	Jonathan lies dead in the **hills.**
	2.24	sunset they came to the **hill** of Ammah, which is to the
	2.25	Abner again and took their stand on the top of a **hill.**
	5. 9	where land was filled in on the east side of the **hill.**
	6. 3	from Abinadab's home on the **hill** and placed it on a new
	13.34	large crowd coming down the **hill** on the road from Horonaim.
	15.32	reached the top of the **hill,** where there was a place of
	16. 1	beyond the top of the **hill,** he was suddenly met by Ziba,
	16.13	Shimei kept up with them, walking on the **hillside;**
	17.13	a single stone will be left there on top of the **hill."**
	23.14	David was on a fortified **hill,** and a group of Philistines
1 Kgs	12.31	built places of worship on **hilltops,** and he chose priests
	14.23	symbols of Asherah to worship on the **hills** and under shady
	16.24	and then he bought the **hill** of Samaria for six thousand
	16.24	Omri fortified the **hill,** built a town there,
	16.24	it Samaria, after Shemer, the former owner of the **hill.**
	19.11	furious wind that split the **hills** and shattered the rocks—
	20.28	am a god of the **hills** and not of the plains,
	22.17	army of Israel scattered over the **hills** like sheep
2 Kgs	1. 9	found him sitting on a **hill** and said to him, "Man of
	1.13	He went up the **hill,** fell on his knees in front of
	5.24	When they reached the **hill** where Elisha lived,
	6.17	and saw the **hillside** covered with horses and chariots
	16. 4	places of worship, on the **hills,** and under every shady tree,
	17.10	On all the **hills** and under every shady tree they put up
	23.16	Josiah looked round and saw some tombs there on the **hill;**
1 Chr	6.67	city of refuge in the **hills** of Ephraim, Gezer,
	11. 8	the east side of the **hill,** and Joab restored the rest of
	11.16	David was on a fortified **hill,** and a group of Philistines
2 Chr	18.16	army of Israel scattered over the **hills** like sheep
	28. 4	places of worship, on the **hills,** and under every shady tree
	33.15	altars that were on the **hill** where the Temple stood and in
Neh	8.15	"Go out to the **hills** and get branches from pines, olives,
Job	38.14	Daylight makes the **hills** and valleys stand out like the
	40.20	Grass to feed him grows on the **hills** where wild beasts play.
Ps	2. 6	"On Zion, my sacred **hill,"** he says, "I have installed my king."
	3. 4	the Lord for help, and from his sacred **hill** he answers me.
	15. 1	Who may worship on Zion, your sacred **hill?**
	24. 3	Who has the right to go up the Lord's **hill?**
	43. 3	back to Zion, your sacred **hill,** and to your Temple, where
	46. 3	roar and rage, and the **hills** are shaken by the violence.
	48. 1	highly praised in the city of our God, on his sacred **hill.**
	50.10	the forest are mine and the cattle on thousands of **hills.**
	65.12	the **hillsides** are full of joy.
	72.16	may the **hills** be covered with crops, as fruitful as those
	80.10	It covered the **hills** with its shade;
	83.14	forest, as flames set the **hills** on fire, [15]chase them away
	87. 1	The Lord built his city on the sacred **hill;**
	90. 2	Before you created the **hills** or brought the world into being,
	95. 4	the whole earth, from the deepest caves to the highest **hills.**
	97. 5	The **hills** melt like wax before the Lord, before the Lord
	98. 8	you **hills,** sing together with joy before the Lord,
	99. 9	Praise the Lord our God, and worship at his sacred **hill!**
	104.10	springs flow in the valleys, and rivers run between the **hills.**
	104.13	you send rain on the **hills,** and the earth is filled with
	110. 3	your young men will come to you on the sacred **hills.**
	114. 4	the **hills** jumped about like lambs.
	114. 6	You **hills,** why did you jump about like lambs?
	133. 3	like the dew on Mount Hermon, falling on the **hills** of Zion.
	147. 8	rain for the earth and makes grass grow on the **hills.**
	148. 9	Praise him, **hills** and mountains, fruit-trees and forests;
Prov	8. 2	On the **hilltops** near the road and at the cross-roads
	8.25	before the mountains, before the **hills** were set in place,
	27.25	cut the grass on the **hillsides** while the next crop of hay
Song	2. 8	He comes running over the mountains, racing across the **hills**
	4. 1	like a flock of goats bounding down the **hills** of Gilead.
	4. 6	I will stay on the **hill** of myrrh, the hill of incense,
	6. 5	like a flock of goats bounding down the **hills** of Gilead.
Is	2. 2	be the highest one of all, towering above all the **hills.**
	2. 3	"Let us go up the **hill** of the Lord, to the Temple
	2.10	in caves in the rocky **hills** or dig holes in the ground
	2.14	level the high mountains and **hills,** [15]every high tower,
	2.19	in caves in the rocky **hills** or dig holes in the ground
	2.21	and caves in the rocky **hills** to try to escape from his
	5. 1	My friend had a vineyard on a very fertile **hill.**
	7.25	the **hills** where crops used to grow will be so overgrown

Is 11. 9 On Zion, God's sacred **hill,** there will be nothing harmful
13. 2 On the top of a barren **hill** raise the battle flag!
15. 2 The people of Dibon climb the **hill** to weep at the shrine.
17.13 away like dust on a **hillside,** like straw in a whirlwind.
22. 5 battered down, and cries for help have echoed among the **hills.**
22.16 you to carve a tomb for yourself out of the rocky **hillside?**
27.13 come and worship the Lord in Jerusalem, on his sacred **hill.**
30.17 your army except a lonely flagstaff on the top of a **hill!**
30.25 streams of water will flow from every mountain and every **hill.**
40. 4 The **hills** will become a plain, and the rough country will be
40.12 earth in a cup or weigh the mountains and **hills** on scales?
41.15 **hills** will crumble into dust.
41.18 make rivers flow among barren **hills** and springs of water run
42.15 I will destroy the **hills** and mountains and dry up the
45. 2 "I myself will prepare your way, levelling mountains and **hills.**
49. 9 They will be like sheep that graze on the **hills;**
54.10 The mountains and **hills** may crumble, but my love for you
55.12 The mountains and **hills** will burst into singing,
56. 7 you to Zion, my sacred **hill,** give you joy in my house
65. 7 burnt incense at pagan **hill shrines** and spoken evil of me.
65.11 who ignore Zion, my sacred **hill,** and worship Gad and Meni,
65.25 On Zion, my sacred **hill,** there will be nothing harmful
66.20 bring them to my sacred **hill** in Jerusalem on horses, mules,
Jer 2.20 On every high **hill** and under every green tree you worshipped
3. 2 Look up at the **hill-tops.**
3. 6 and on every high **hill** and under every green tree she
3.21 A noise is heard on the **hill-tops:**
3.23 not helped at all by our pagan worship on the **hill-tops.**
4.15 of Dan and from the **hills** of Ephraim announce the bad news.
4.24 they were shaking, and the **hills** were rocking to and fro.
7.29 funeral song on the **hill-tops,** because I, the Lord, am angry,
13.27 after pagan gods on the **hills** and in the fields, like a
14. 6 wild donkeys stand on the **hill-tops** and pant for breath
16.16 down on every mountain and **hill** and in the caves among the
17. 2 every green tree, on the **hill-tops** [3] and on the mountains
26.18 a pile of ruins, and the Temple **hill** will become a forest.'
31. 5 will plant vineyards on the **hills** of Samaria, and those who
31. 6 will call out on the **hills** of Ephraim, 'Let's go up to
31.23 the Lord bless the sacred **hill** of Jerusalem, the holy place
31.39 on the west to the **hill** of Gareb and then round to
Lam 4.19 They tracked us down in the **hills;**
Ezek 6. 3 Lord, am telling the mountains, the **hills,** the gorges,
6.13 scattered on every high **hill,** on the top of every mountain,
19. 9 his roar would never be heard again on the **hills** of Israel.
20.28 When they saw the high **hills** and green trees, they offered
34. 6 So my sheep wandered over the high **hills** and the mountains.
34.26 "I will bless them and let them live round my sacred **hill.**
35. 8 who are killed in battle will cover the **hills** and valleys.
36. 2 enemies gloated and said, 'Now those ancient **hills** are ours!'
36. 4 say to you mountains and **hills,** to you brooks and valleys,
36. 6 tell the mountains, **hills,** brooks, and valleys what I,
Dan 9.16 It is your city, your sacred **hill.**
Hos 4.13 offer sacrifices, and on the **hills** they burn incense
10. 8 **hilltop shrines** of Aven, where the people of Israel worship
10. 8 and to the **hills,** "Cover us!"
Joel 2. 1 sound the alarm on Zion, God's sacred **hill.**
3.17 I live on Zion, my sacred **hill.**
3.18 covered with vineyards, and cattle will be found on every **hill;**
Amos 3. 9 "Gather together in the **hills** surrounding Samaria and see
9.13 will drip with sweet wine, and the **hills** will flow with it.
Obad 16 have drunk a bitter cup of punishment on my sacred **hill.**
Mic 1. 4 pour down into the valleys like water pouring down a **hill.**
3.12 a pile of ruins, and the Temple **hill** will become a forest.
4. 1 be the highest one of all, towering above all the **hills.**
4. 2 "Let us go up the **hill** of the Lord, to the Temple
6. 1 let the mountains and the **hills** hear what you say.
Nah 1. 5 **hills** melt before him.
Hab 3. 3 the holy God is coming from the **hills** of Paran.
3. 6 the everlasting **hills** sink down,
3. 6 the **hills** where he walked in ancient times.
Zeph 1.10 part of the city and a great crashing sound in the **hills.**
3.11 you will never again rebel against me on my sacred **hill.**
Hag 1. 8 go up into the **hills,** get timber, and rebuild the Temple;
1.11 on the land—on its **hills,** cornfields, vineyards,
Zech 8. 3 hill of the Lord Almighty will be called the sacred **hill.**
Mt 5. 1 saw the crowds and went up a **hill,** where he sat down.
5.14 A city built on a **hill** cannot be hidden.
8. 1 When Jesus came down from the **hill,** large crowds followed him.
14.23 the people away, he went up a **hill** by himself to pray.
15.29 He climbed a **hill** and sat down.
17.20 seed, you can say to this **hill,** 'Go from here to there!'
18.12 other ninety-nine grazing on the **hillside** and go and look
21.21 able to say to this **hill,** 'Get up and throw yourself in
24.16 "Then those who are in Judaea must run away to the **hills.**
28.16 eleven disciples went to the **hill** in Galilee where Jesus had
Mk 3.13 Then Jesus went up a **hill** and called to himself the men
5. 5 the tombs and through the **hills,** screaming and cutting himself
5.11 was a large herd of pigs near by, feeding on a **hillside.**
6.46 good-bye to the people he went away to a **hill** to pray.
11.23 you that whoever tells this **hill** to get up and throw itself
13.14 "Then those who are in Judaea must run away to the **hills.**
Lk 3. 5 Every valley must be filled up, every **hill** and mountain levelled
4.29 to the top of the **hill** on which their town was built.
6.12 time Jesus went up a **hill** to pray and spent the whole
6.17 had come down from the **hill** with the apostles, he stood on
8.32 was a large herd of pigs near by, feeding on a **hillside.**
9.28 John, and James with him and went up a **hill** to pray.
9.37 went down from the **hill,** and a large crowd met Jesus.
21.21 Then those who are in Judaea must run away to the **hills;**
23.30 and to the **hills,** 'Hide us!'
Jn 6. 3 Jesus went up a **hill** and sat down with his disciples.
Jn 6.15 so he went off again to the **hills** by himself.
Heb 11.38 refugees in the deserts and **hills,** living in caves and holes
Rev 17. 9 The seven heads are seven **hills,** on which the woman sits.

HILL-COUNTRY

Gen 10.30 extended from Mesha to Sephar in the eastern **hill-country.**
12. 8 moved on south to the **hill-country** east of the city of
31.21 River Euphrates and started for the **hill-country** of Gilead.
31.23 until he caught up with him in the **hill-country** of Gilead.
31.25 his camp with his kinsmen in the **hill-country** of Gilead.
36. 8 So Esau lived in the **hill-country** of Edom.
Num 13.17 of the land of Canaan and then on into the **hill-country.**
13.29 Hittites, Jebusites, and Amorites live in the **hill-country;**
14.40 started out to invade the **hill-country,** saying,
14.44 go up into the **hill-country,** even though neither the Lord's
Deut 1. 2 Mount Sinai to Kadesh Barnea by way of the **hill-country** of Edom.)
1. 7 Go to the **hill-country** of the Amorites and to all the
1. 7 the Jordan Valley, to the **hill-country** and the lowlands,
1.19 fearful desert on the way to the **hill-country** of the Amorites.
1.20 have now come to the **hill-country** of the Amorites,
1.24 went into the **hill-country** as far as the Valley of Eshcol
1.41 to fight, thinking it would be easy to invade the **hill-country.**
1.43 against him, and in your pride you marched into the **hill-country.**
1.44 as Hormah and defeated you there in the **hill-country** of Edom.
2. 1 spent a long time wandering about in the **hill-country** of Edom.
2. 4 about to go through the **hill-country** of Edom, the territory
2.22 the descendants of Esau, who live in the **hill-country** of Edom.
2.37 to the towns of the **hill-country** or to any other place where
3.12 and part of the **hill-country** of Gilead, along with its towns.
3.25 the beautiful **hill-country** and the Lebanon Mountains.'
Josh 2.16 "Go into the **hill-country,**" she said, "or the king's
10. 6 the Amorite kings in the **hill-country** have joined forces
10.40 defeated the kings of the **hill-country,** the eastern slopes,
11. 2 to the kings in the **hill-country** in the north, in the Jordan
11. 3 the Jebusites in the **hill-country,** as well as to the Hivites
11.16 captured all the land—the **hill-country** and foothills,
11.21 Anakim who lived in the **hill-country**—in Hebron, Debir, Anab,
11.21 and in all the **hill-country** of Judah and Israel.
12. 8 portion included the **hill-country,** the western foothills,
13. 6 Sidonians, who live in the **hill-country** between the Lebanon
14.12 Now then, give me the **hill-country** that the Lord promised
15.10 west of Baalah towards the **hill-country** of Edom,
15.48 In the **hill-country** there were Shamir, Jattir, Socoh,
16. 1 It went from Jericho up into the **hill-country** as far as Bethel.
17.15 many of you and the **hill-country** of Ephraim is too small
17.16 They replied, "The **hill-country** is not big enough for us,
17.18 The **hill-country** will be yours.
18.12 and westwards through the **hill-country** as far as the desert
19.50 Timnath Serah, in the **hill-country** of Ephraim.
20. 7 set aside Kedesh in Galilee, in the **hill-country** of Naphtali;
20. 7 Shechem, in the **hill-country** of Ephraim;
20. 7 and Hebron, in the **hill-country** of Judah.
21.11 now called Hebron, in the **hill-country** of Judah,
21.21 its pasture lands in the **hill-country** of Ephraim
24. 4 I gave Esau the **hill-country** of Edom as his possession,
24.30 Timnath Serah in the **hill-country** of Ephraim north of Mount
24.33 Gibeah, the town in the **hill-country** of Ephraim
Judg 1. 9 Canaanites who lived in the **hill-country,** in the foothills,
1.18 people of Judah, and they took possession of the **hill-country.**
1.34 tribe of Dan into the **hill-country** and did not let them come
2. 9 Timnath Serah in the **hill-country** of Ephraim north of Mount
3.27 he arrived there in the **hill-country** of Ephraim,
4. 5 Ramah and Bethel in the **hill-country** of Ephraim,
7.24 messengers through all the **hill-country** of Ephraim to say,
10. 1 and lived at Shamir in the **hill-country** of Ephraim.
12.15 territory of Ephraim in the **hill-country** of the Amalekites.
17. 1 a man named Micah, who lived in the **hill-country** of Ephraim.
17. 8 he came to Micah's house in the **hill-country** of Ephraim.
18. 2 arrived in the **hill-country** of Ephraim, they stayed at Micah's
18.13 and came to Micah's house in the **hill-country** of Ephraim.
19. 1 was a Levite living far back in the **hill-country** of Ephraim.
19.16 He was originally from the **hill-country** of Ephraim,
19.18 we are on our way home deep in the **hill-country** of Ephraim.
1 Sam 1. 1 lived in the town of Ramah in the **hill-country** of Ephraim.
9. 4 went through the **hill-country** of Ephraim and the region of
13. 2 in Michmash and in the **hill-country** of Bethel and sending one
23.14 David stayed in hiding in the **hill-country,**
2 Sam 20.21 Bikri, who is from the **hill-country** of Ephraim,
1 Kgs 4. 8 the **hill-country** of Ephraim
5.15 had 80,000 men in the **hill-country** quarrying stone,
12.25 town of Shechem in the **hill-country** of Ephraim and lived there
2 Kgs 5.22 group of prophets in the **hill-country** of Ephraim arrived,
2 Chr 13. 4 The armies met in the **hill-country** of Ephraim.
15. 8 in the cities he had captured in the **hill-country** of Ephraim.
19. 4 to the edge of the **hill-country** of Ephraim in the north,
26.10 plant vineyards in the **hill-country** and to farm the fertile
Jer 32.44 in the towns in the **hill-country,** in the foothills,
33.13 In the towns of the **hill-country,** in the foothills,
Ezek 35. 7 I will make the **hill-country** of Edom a waste and kill
Mal 1. 3 I have devastated Esau's **hill-country** and abandoned the land
Lk 1.39 and hurried off to a town in the **hill-country** of Judaea.
1.65 these things spread through all the **hill-country** of Judaea.

HIND LEG

Ex 29.17 its internal organs and its **hind legs,** and put them on top
Lev 1. 9 internal organs and the **hind legs,** and the officiating priest
1.13 internal organs and the **hind legs,** and the priest will present
7.32 The right **hind leg** of the animal shall be given as a

Lev 7.34 and the right **hind leg** is a special contribution
8.20 the internal organs and the **hind legs** with water, and burnt
8.25 the kidneys with the fat on them, and the right **hind leg.**
8.26 put them on top of the fat and the right **hind leg.**
9.14 the internal organs and the **hind legs** and burnt them
9.21 the breasts and the right **hind legs** as the special gift
10.14 eat the breast and the **hind leg** that are presented
10.15 They shall bring the **hind leg** and the breast
Num 18.18 the breast and the right **hind leg** of the special offering.
Dan 7. 5 The second beast looked like a bear standing on its **hind legs.**

HINGES

1 Kgs 7.50 and the **hinges** for the doors of the Most Holy Place
Prov 26.14 He gets no farther than a door swinging on its **hinges.**

HINNOM

Valley near Jerusalem where pagan worship took place.
see also TOPHETH, **(Valley of) SLAUGHTER**

Josh 15. 8 up through the Valley of **Hinnom** on the south side
15. 8 side of the Valley of **Hinnom,** at the northern end
18.16 that overlooks the Valley of **Hinnom,** at the north end of the
18.16 south through the Valley of **Hinnom,** south of the Jebusite
2 Kgs 23.10 worship in the Valley of **Hinnom,** so that no one could
2 Chr 28. 3 incense in the Valley of **Hinnom,** and even sacrificed his own
33. 6 He sacrificed his sons in the Valley of **Hinnom**
Neh 11.30 Beersheba in the south and the Valley of **Hinnom** in the north.
Jer 7.31 In the Valley of **Hinnom** they have built an altar
7.32 called Topheth or the Valley of **Hinnom,** but the Valley of Slaughter.
19. 2 and to go through Potsherd Gate out to the Valley of **Hinnom.**
19. 6 will no longer be called Topheth or the Valley of **Hinnom.**
32.35 in the Valley of **Hinnom,** to sacrifice their sons and daughters

HINT

Job 26.14 But these are only **hints** of his power, only the whispers

HIP

Gen 32.25 he struck Jacob on the **hip,** and it was thrown out of
32.31 Jacob was leaving Peniel, and he was limping because of his **hip.**
32.32 muscle which is on the **hip-joint,** because it was on this
2 Sam 10. 4 cut off their clothes at the **hips,** and sent them away.
1 Chr 19. 4 cut off their clothes at the **hips,** and sent them away.
Dan 2.32 its waist and **hips** of bronze;

HIRAM

King of Tyre in Solomon's time.
see also **HURAM (1)**

2 Sam 5.11 King **Hiram** of Tyre sent a trade mission to David;
1 Kgs 5. 1 King **Hiram** of Tyre had always been a friend of David's,
5. 2 Solomon sent back this message to **Hiram:**
5. 7 **Hiram** was extremely pleased when he received Solomon's message,
5. 8 Then **Hiram** sent Solomon the following message:
5.10 So **Hiram** supplied Solomon with all the cedar and pine
5.11 and Solomon provided **Hiram** with two thousand metric tons
5.12 There was peace between **Hiram** and Solomon, and they made a
5.18 and **Hiram's** workmen and men from the city of Byblos prepared
9.11 King **Hiram** of Tyre had provided him with all the cedar
9.11 King Solomon gave **Hiram** twenty towns in the region of
9.12 **Hiram** went to see them, and he did not like them.
9.14 **Hiram** had sent Solomon more than four thousand kilogrammes
9.27 King **Hiram** sent some experienced seamen from his fleet
10.11 **(Hiram's** fleet, which had brought gold from Ophir,
10.22 had a fleet of ocean-going ships sailing with **Hiram's** fleet.
1 Chr 14. 1 King **Hiram** of Tyre sent a trade mission to David;
2 Chr 2. 3 Solomon sent a message to King **Hiram** of Tyre:
2.11 King **Hiram** sent Solomon a letter in reply.
8. 2 rebuilt the cities that King **Hiram** had given him,
8.18 **Hiram** sent him ships under the command of his own officers
9.10 (The men of King **Hiram** and of King Solomon who brought gold
9.21 a fleet of ocean-going ships sailing with King **Hiram's** fleet.

HIRE

Ex 12.45 No temporary resident or **hired worker** may eat it.
22.15 If it is a **hired** animal,
22.15 the loss is covered by the **hiring** charge.
Lev 19.13 the wages of someone you have **hired,** not even for one night.
22.10 them—not even someone staying with a priest or **hired** by him.
25. 6 for you, your slaves, your **hired men,** the foreigners living
25.35 as you would for a **hired man,** so that he can continue
25.40 stay with you as a **hired man** and serve you
25.50 release on the basis of the wages paid to a **hired man.**
25.53 years left, [53] as if he had been **hired** on an annual basis.
Deut 15.18 you for six years at half the cost of a **hired** servant.
23. 4 and they **hired** Balaam son of Beor,
24.14 poor and needy **hired** servant, whether he is a fellow-Israelite
Judg 9. 4 and with this money he **hired** a bunch of worthless scoundrels
1 Sam 2. 5 once were well fed now **hire** themselves out to get food,
2 Sam 10. 6 so they **hired** twenty thousand Syrian soldiers from Bethrehob
2 Kgs 7. 6 the king of Israel had **hired** Hittite and Egyptian kings and
1 Chr 19. 6 silver to **hire** chariots and charioteers from Upper Mesopotamia
19. 7 The thirty-two thousand chariots they **hired** and the army of
2 Chr 24.12 repairing the Temple, and they **hired** stonemasons, carpenters,
25. 6 In addition, he **hired** 100,000 soldiers from Israel at a cost
25.10 So Amaziah sent the **hired** troops away and told them to go
Neh 6.13 They **hired** him to frighten me into sinning, so that they
Prov 6.26 A man can **hire** a prostitute for the price of a loaf
26.10 An employer who **hires** any fool that comes along is only
Is 7.20 the Lord will **hire** a barber from across the Euphrates
23.17 old trade, and she will **hire** herself out to all the kingdoms
45.13 No one has **hired** him or bribed him to do this."
46. 6 They **hire** a goldsmith to make a god;
Jer 46.21 Even her **hired** soldiers are helpless as calves.
50.37 Death to its **hired** soldiers— how weak they are!
Ezek 30. 5 will also kill the soldiers **hired** from Sudan, Lydia, Libya,
Zech 8.10 no one could afford to **hire** either men or animals, and no
11. 7 bought and sold the sheep **hired** me, and I became the
Mt 20. 1 early in the morning to **hire** some men to work in his
20. 7 'No one **hired** us,' they answered.
20. 8 starting with those who were **hired** last
20. 8 and ending with those who were **hired** first.'
20.10 were the first to be **hired** came to be paid, they thought
20.12 'These men who were **hired** last worked only one hour,'
20.14 give this man who was **hired** last as much as I have
Mk 1.20 Zebedee in the boat with the **hired men** and went with Jesus.
Lk 15.17 said, 'All my father's **hired workers** have more than they can
15.19 treat me as one of your **hired workers.'**
Jn 10.12 When the **hired man,** who is not a shepherd
10.13 The **hired man** runs away because he is only a hired man

HISS

Jer 46.22 Egypt runs away, **hissing** like a snake,

HISTORY

Ex 9.18 hailstorm, such as Egypt has never known in all its **history.**
9.24 worst storm that Egypt had ever known in all its **history.**
1 Kgs 11.41 and his wisdom, are all recorded in The **History** of Solomon.
14.19 are all recorded in The **History** of the Kings of Israel.
14.29 Rehoboam did is recorded in The **History** of the Kings of Judah.
15. 7 Abijah did is recorded in The **History** of the Kings of Judah.
15.23 are all recorded in The **History** of the Kings of Judah.
15.31 Nadab did is recorded in The **History** of the Kings of Israel.
16. 5 deeds are recorded in The **History** of the Kings of Israel.
16.14 Elah did is recorded in The **History** of the Kings of Israel.
16.20 conspiracy, is recorded in The **History** of the Kings of Israel.
16.27 are recorded in The **History** of the Kings of Israel.
22.39 he built, is recorded in The **History** of the Kings of Israel.
22.45 battles, are recorded in The **History** of the Kings of Judah.
2 Kgs 1.18 Ahaziah did is recorded in The **History** of the Kings of Israel.
8.23 Jehoram did is recorded in The **History** of the Kings of Judah.
10.34 deeds, is recorded in The **History** of the Kings of Israel.
12.19 Joash did is recorded in The **History** of the Kings of Judah.
13. 8 deeds are recorded in The **History** of the Kings of Israel.
13.12 of Judah, is recorded in The **History** of the Kings of Israel.
14.15 of Judah, is recorded in The **History** of the Kings of Israel.
14.18 Amaziah did is recorded in The **History** of the Kings of Judah.
14.28 are all recorded in The **History** of the Kings of Israel.
15. 6 Uzziah did is recorded in The **History** of the Kings of Judah.
15.11 is recorded in The **History** of the Kings of Israel.
15.15 is recorded in The **History** of the Kings of Israel.
15.21 Menahem did is recorded in The **History** of the Kings of Israel.
15.26 Pekahiah did is recorded in The **History** of the Kings of Israel.
15.31 Pekah did is recorded in The **History** of the Kings of Israel.
15.36 Jotham did is recorded in The **History** of the Kings of Judah.
16.19 Ahaz did is recorded in The **History** of the Kings of Judah.
20.20 city, are all recorded in The **History** of the Kings of Judah.
21.17 committed, is recorded in The **History** of the Kings of Judah.
21.25 Amon did is recorded in The **History** of the Kings of Judah.
23.28 Josiah did is recorded in The **History** of the Kings of Judah.
24. 5 Jehoiakim did is recorded in The **History** of the Kings of Judah.
1 Chr 29.29 **history** of King David from beginning to end is recorded in
2 Chr 9.29 The rest of the **history** of Solomon from beginning to end
9.29 is recorded in The **History** of Nathan the Prophet,
12.15 records are found in The **History** of Shemaiah the Prophet
12.15 and The **History** of Iddo the Prophet.
13.22 The rest of the **history** of Abijah, what he said and
13.22 what he did, is written in The **History** of Iddo the Prophet.
16.11 end are recorded in The **History** of the Kings of Judah and
20.34 end, is recorded in The **History** of Jehu Son of Hanani,
20.34 which is a part of The **History** of the Kings of Israel.
25.26 reign are recorded in The **History** of the Kings of Judah and
27. 7 are all recorded in The **History** of the Kings of Israel and
28.26 end, are recorded in The **History** of the Kings of Judah and
32.32 of Amoz and in The **History** of the Kings of Judah and
33.18 are all recorded in The **History** of the Kings of Israel.
33.19 he worshipped—are all recorded in The **History** of the Prophets.
35.27 to the Law, [27] and his **history** from beginning to end—
35.27 is all recorded in The **History** of the Kings of Israel
36. 8 committed, is recorded in The **History** of the Kings of Israel
Is 41. 4 Who has determined the course of **history?**
Jer 32.30 the very beginning of their **history** the people of Israel and

HIT

Ex 21.12 "Whoever **hits** a man and kills him is to be put to
21.15 "Whoever **hits** his father or his mother is to be put to
21.18 a fight and one man **hits** another with a stone or with
21.18 If the man who was **hit** has to stay in bed,
21.18 a stick, the man who **hit** him is to pay for his
21.26 "If a man **hits** his male or female slave in the eye
Judg 7.13 loaf of barley bread rolled into our camp and **hit** a tent.
9.33 men come out against you, **hit** them as hard as you can!"
1 Sam 17.49 It **hit** him on the forehead and broke his skull, and Goliath
31. 3 and he himself was **hit** by enemy arrows and badly wounded.

1 Kgs 20.35 of a group of prophets ordered a fellow-prophet to **hit** him.
20.37 this same prophet went to another man and said, **"Hit** me!"
20.37 he **hit** him a hard blow and hurt him.
1 Chr 10. 3 Saul, and he was **hit** by enemy arrows and badly wounded.
Job 12. 5 you **hit** a man who is about to fall.
36.32 lightning with his hands and commands it to **hit** the mark.
Prov 23.35 "I must have been **hit,"** you will say;
30.33 If you **hit** someone's nose, it bleeds.
Mt 8.24 Suddenly a fierce storm **hit** the lake, and the boat was
26.68 Guess who **hit** you!"
27.30 on him, and took the stick and **hit** him over the head.
Mk 14.65 to spit on Jesus, and they blindfolded him and **hit** him.
14.65 "Guess who **hit** you!"
Lk 6.29 If anyone **hits** you on one cheek,
6.29 let him **hit** the other one too;
6.48 The river overflowed and **hit** that house but could not shake it,
6.49 when the flood **hit** that house it fell at once—and what
22.64 They blindfolded him and asked him, "Who **hit** you?
Jn 18.23 am right in what I have said, why do you **hit** me?"
Acts 26.14 You are hurting yourself by **hitting** back, like an ox kicking
27.15 It **hit** the ship, and since it was impossible to keep the
27.41 But the ship **hit** a sandbank and went aground;
1 Thes 5. 3 then suddenly destruction will **hit** them!

HITCH

Deut 22.10 "Do not **hitch** an ox and a donkey together for ploughing.
1 Sam 6. 7 **hitch** them to the wagon and drive their calves back to the
6.10 they took two cows and **hitched** them to the wagon,
Mic 1.13 You that live in Lachish, **hitch** the horses to the chariots.

HITTITES

Inhabitants of Canaan before its conquest by Israel.

Gen 15.20 the Kenizzites, the Kadmonites, [20]the **Hittites,**
23. 3 went to the **Hittites,** and said, [4]"I am a foreigner
23.10 was sitting with the other **Hittites** at the meeting-place
23.12 Abraham bowed before the **Hittites** [13]and said to Ephron,
23.18 Abraham's property by all the **Hittites** who were there at the
23.20 which had belonged to the **Hittites,** and the cave in it,
25. 9 Mamre that had belonged to Ephron son of Zohar the **Hittite.**
25.10 It was the field that Abraham had bought from the **Hittites;**
26.34 he married two **Hittite** girls, Judith the daughter of Beeri,
27.46 marries one of these **Hittite** girls, I might as well die."
36. 2 Adah, the daughter of Elon the **Hittite;**
49.29 field of Ephron the **Hittite,** [30]at Machpelah, east of Mamre,
49.32 The field and the cave in it were bought from the **Hittites.**
50.13 field which Abraham had bought from Ephron the **Hittite**
Ex 3. 8 in which the Canaanites, the **Hittites,** the Amorites,
3.17 land of the Canaanites, the **Hittites,** the Amorites,
13. 5 land of the Canaanites, the **Hittites,** the Amorites,
23.23 land of the Amorites, the **Hittites,** the Perizzites,
23.28 drive out the Hivites, the Canaanites, and the **Hittites** as you
33. 2 the Canaanites, the Amorites, the **Hittites,** the Perizzites,
34.11 the Amorites, the Canaanites, the **Hittites,** the Perizzites,
Num 13.29 **Hittites,** Jebusites, and Amorites live in the hill-country;
Deut 7. 1 the **Hittites,** the Girgashites, the Amorites, the Canaanites,
20.17 the **Hittites,** the Amorites, the Canaanites, the Perizzites,
Josh 1. 4 the east, through the **Hittite** country, to the Mediterranean
3.10 drive out the Canaanites, the **Hittites,** the Hivites,
9. 1 were the kings of the **Hittites,** the Amorites, the Canaanites,
11. 3 Jordan, to the Amorites, the **Hittites,** the Perizzites,
12. 8 been the home of the **Hittites,** the Amorites, the Canaanites,
24.11 the Perizzites, the Canaanites, the **Hittites,** the Girgashites,
Judg 1.26 to the land of the **Hittites,** built a city there, and named
3. 5 down among the Canaanites, the **Hittites,** the Amorites,
1 Sam 26. 6 Then David asked Ahimelech the **Hittite,** and Abishai
2 Sam 11. 3 the daughter of Eliam and the wife of Uriah the **Hittite.**
11. 6 "Send me Uriah the **Hittite."**
23.24 Uriah the **Hittite.**
24. 6 and on to Gilead and to Kadesh, in **Hittite** territory.
1 Kgs 9.20 These included Amorites, **Hittites,** Perizzites, Hivites,
10.29 They supplied the **Hittite** and Syrian kings with horses and
11. 1 he married **Hittite** women and women from Moab, Ammon,
15. 5 of his commands, except in the case of Uriah the **Hittite.**
2 Kgs 7. 6 king of Israel had hired **Hittite** and Egyptian kings and their
1 Chr 11.26 Uriah the **Hittite**
2 Chr 1.17 They supplied the **Hittite** and Syrian kings with horses and
8. 7 These included **Hittites,** Amorites, Perizzites, Hivites,
Ezra 9. 1 Moab, and Egypt or from the Canaanites, **Hittites,** Perizzites,
Neh 9. 8 the land of the **Hittites** and the Amorites, the land of
Ezek 16. 3 Your father was an Amorite, and your mother was a **Hittite.**
16.45 your sister cities had a **Hittite** mother and an Amorite father.

HIVITES

Inhabitants of Canaan before its conquest by Israel.

Gen 10.17 the Amorites, the Girgashites, [17]the **Hivites,** the Arkites,
34. 2 Shechem son of Hamor the **Hivite,** who was chief of that region,
36. 2 Oholibamah, the daughter of Anah son of Zibeon the **Hivite;**
Ex 3. 8 the Perizzites, the **Hivites,** and the Jebusites now live.
3.17 the Amorites, the Perizzites, the **Hivites,** and the Jebusites.
13. 5 the Hittites, the Amorites, the **Hivites,** and the Jebusites.
23.23 Perizzites, the Canaanites, the **Hivites,** and the Jebusites,
23.28 I will drive out the **Hivites,** the Canaanites, and the Hittites
33. 2 the Hittites, the Perizzites, the **Hivites,** and the Jebusites.
34.11 Perizzites, the **Hivites,** and the Jebusites, as you advance.
Deut 7. 1 the Perizzites, the **Hivites,** and the Jebusites.
20.17 the Canaanites, the Perizzites, the **Hivites,** and the Jebusites,
Josh 3.10 the Canaanites, the Hittites, the **Hivites,** the Perizzites,
9. 1 the Perizzites, the **Hivites,** and the Jebusites.
Josh 9. 3 people of Gibeon, who were **Hivites,** heard what Joshua had done
11. 3 as well as to the **Hivites** who lived at the foot of
11.19 was Gibeon, where some of the **Hivites** lived.
12. 8 the Perizzites, the **Hivites,** and the Jebusites.
24.11 the Girgashites, the **Hivites,** and the Jebusites.
Judg 3. 3 and the **Hivites** who lived in the Lebanon Mountains
3. 5 the Perizzites, the **Hivites,** and the Jebusites.
2 Sam 24. 7 all the cities of the **Hivites** and the Canaanites, and finally
1 Kgs 9.20 These included Amorites, Hittites, Perizzites, **Hivites,**
1 Chr 1.15 the Jebusites, the Amorites, Girgashites, [15]**Hivites,**
2 Chr 8. 7 These included Hittites, Amorites, Perizzites, **Hivites,**
Is 17. 9 like the cities that the **Hivites** and the Amorites abandoned

HOARD

Prov 11.26 People curse a man who **hoards** grain, waiting for a higher

HOE

1 Sam 13.20 to get their ploughs, **hoes,** axes, and sickles sharpened;
13.21 and two coins for sharpening ploughs or **hoes.)**
2 Sam 12.31 to work with saws, iron **hoes,** and iron axes, and forced them
1 Chr 20. 3 and put them to work with saws, iron **hoes,** and axes.
Is 5. 6 I will not prune the vines or **hoe** the ground;

Am **HOG** see **PIG**

HOLD (1)

[HELD]

Gen 9.23 took a robe and **held** it behind them on their shoulders.
11. 3 they had bricks to build with and tar to **hold** them together.
24.18 her jar from her shoulder and **held** it while he drank.
25.26 The second one was born **holding** on tightly to the heel
40.11 I was **holding** the king's cup;
49. 8 You **hold** your enemies by the neck.
49.10 Judah will **hold** the royal sceptre, And his descendants
Ex 4. 2 So the Lord asked him, "What are you **holding?"**
7.19 to take his stick and **hold** it out over all the rivers,
8. 5 Moses, "Tell Aaron to **hold** out his stick over the rivers,
8. 6 So Aaron **held** it out over all the water, and the frogs
14.16 Lift up your stick and **hold** it out over the sea.
14.21 Moses **held** out his hand over the sea, and the Lord drove
14.26 The Lord said to Moses, **"Hold** out your hand over the sea,
14.27 So Moses **held** out his hand over the sea, and at daybreak
17. 9 on top of the hill **holding** the stick that God told me
17.11 As long as Moses **held** up his arms, the Israelites won,
17.12 stood beside him and **held** up his arms, holding them steady
17.16 He said, **"Hold** high the banner of the Lord!
25.27 The rings to **hold** the poles for carrying the table are
26.19 two bases under each frame to **hold** its two projections.
26.29 them with gold rings to **hold** the cross-bars, which are also
30. 4 border on two sides to **hold** the poles with which it is
36.24 two bases under each frame to **hold** its two projections.
36.34 gold rings to **hold** the cross-bars, which were also covered
36.36 four posts of acacia-wood to **hold** the curtain, covered them
36.36 Then they made four silver bases to **hold** the posts.
37.14 The rings to **hold** the poles for carrying the table were
37.27 on the two sides, to **hold** the poles with which it was
Lev 1.17 He shall take **hold** of its wings and tear its body open,
10. 5 So they came and took **hold** of the clothing on the corpses
26.13 I broke the power that **held** you down
26.13 and I let you walk with your head **held** high."
Num 5.18 the priest shall **hold** the bowl containing the bitter water
5.25 out of the woman's hands, **hold** it out in dedication to the
22.23 saw the angel standing there **holding** a sword, it left the
Deut 25.11 help her husband by grabbing **hold** of the other man's genitals,
Josh 5.13 saw a man standing in front of him, **holding** a sword.
Judg 6.21 and the bread with the end of the stick he was **holding.**
7.19 broke the jars they were **holding,** [20]and the other two
7.20 They all **held** the torches in their left hands, the trumpets
7.24 **Hold** the River Jordan and the streams as far as Bethbarah,
7.24 and they **held** the River Jordan and the streams
16. 3 he got up and took **hold** of the city gate and pulled
16.26 "Let me touch the pillars that **hold** up the building.
16.29 Samson took hold of the two middle pillars **holding** up the building.
Ruth 1.14 good-bye and went back home, but Ruth **held** on to her.
4.16 Naomi took the child, **held** him close, and took care of him.
1 Sam 14.43 "I ate a little honey with the stick I was **holding.**
15.27 to leave, but Saul caught **hold** of his cloak, and it tore.
18.10 harp, as he did every day, and Saul was **holding** a spear.
24.11 my father, look at the piece of your robe I am **holding!**
2 Sam 6. 6 and Uzzah reached out and took **hold** of the Covenant Box.
12. 3 let it drink from his cup, and **hold** it in his lap.
13.13 How could I ever **hold** up my head in public again?
15. 5 Absalom would reach out, take **hold** of him, and kiss him.
20. 9 and took **hold** of his beard with his right hand in order
20.10 the sword that Joab was **holding** in his other hand, and Joab
22.17 The Lord reached down from above and took **hold** of me;
1 Kgs 1.50 Lord's presence and took **hold** of the corners of the altar.
1.51 him and that he was **holding** on to the corners of the
2.28 Lord's presence and took **hold** of the corners of the altar.
7.26 The tank **held** about forty thousand litres.
7.38 basin was 1.8 metres in diameter, and **held** about 800 litres.
8.27 heaven is large enough to **hold** you, so how can this Temple
18.32 trench round it, large enough to **hold** almost fourteen litres
2 Kgs 4.16 time next year you will be **holding** a son in your arms."
4.20 back to his mother, who **held** him in her lap until noon,
4.27 Elisha she bowed down before him and took **hold** of his feet.
4.29 Go straight to the house and **hold** my stick over the boy."

2 Kgs 4.31 Gehazi went on ahead and **held** Elisha's stick over the child,
1 Chr 13. 9 Uzzah stretched out his hand and took **hold** of the Covenant Box.
21.16 angel standing in mid air, **holding** his sword in his hand,
2 Chr 4. 5 The tank **held** about sixty thousand litres.
6.18 heaven is large enough to **hold** you, so how can this Temple
7.13 Whenever I **hold** back the rain or send locusts to eat up
26.19 beside the incense altar and was **holding** an incense burner.
Esth 4.11 if the king **holds** out his gold sceptre to someone, then that
5. 2 won his favour, and he **held** out to her the gold sceptre.
8. 4 The king **held** out the gold sceptre to her, so she stood
Job 3.12 Why did my mother **hold** me on her knees?
8.15 If they lean on a web, will it **hold** them up?
8.17 roots wrap round the stones and **hold** fast to every rock.
15.26 he stubbornly **holds** up his shield and rushes to fight
18. 9 a trap catches his heels and **holds** him.
26.11 he threatens the pillars that **hold** up the sky, they shake
31.37 I have done, and **hold** my head high in his presence.
38. 6 What **holds** up the pillars that support the earth?
38. 8 Who closed the gates to **hold** back the sea when it burst
38.31 tie the Pleiades together or loosen the bonds that **hold** Orion?
39.10 Can you **hold** one with a rope and make him plough?
Ps 18.16 The Lord reached down from above and took **hold** of me;
52. 5 he will take **hold** of you and snatch you from your home;
73.23 always stay close to you, and you **hold** me by the hand.
75. 8 The Lord **holds** a cup in his hand, filled with the strong
91.12 They will **hold** you up with their hands to keep you from
94.18 but your constant love, O Lord, **held** me up.
119.117 **Hold** me, and I will be safe, and I will always pay
Prov 20.16 ought to have his own property **held** to guarantee payment.
27.13 deserves to have his own property **held** to guarantee payment.
27.16 stop the wind or ever tried to **hold** a handful of oil?
30.28 you can **hold** one in your hand, but you can find them
Ecc 7.26 and her arms round you will **hold** you like a chain.
Song 3. 4 I **held** him and wouldn't let him go until I took him
7. 5 Your head is **held** high like Mount Carmel.
8. 6 **hold** no one in your arms but me.
Is 4. 1 comes, seven women will grab **hold** of one man and say,
22.11 reservoir inside the city to **hold** the water flowing down from
40.12 Can anyone **hold** the soil of the earth in a cup
44.20 himself that the idol he **holds** in his hand is not a
56.12 some wine,' these drunkards say, 'and drink all we can **hold!**
Jer 2.13 dug cisterns, cracked cisterns that can **hold** no water at all.
10.20 the ropes that **held** them have broken.
13.11 all the people of Israel and Judah to **hold** tightly to me.
51.25 I will take **hold** of you, level you to the ground, and
52.19 the bowls for **holding** the blood from the sacrifices,
Lam 1. 5 they **hold** her in their power.
Ezek 2. 9 hand stretched out towards me, and it was **holding** a scroll.
8.11 Each one was **holding** an incense-burner, and smoke was rising
21.22 His right hand **holds** the arrow marked 'Jerusalem'!
30.21 it could heal and be strong enough to **hold** a sword again.
37.17 Then **hold** the two sticks end to end in your hand so
37.19 two I will make one stick and **hold** it in my hand.
37.20 "**Hold** in your hand the two sticks and let the people
39.19 all the fat they can **hold** and to drink blood until they
39.20 will eat all they can **hold** of horses and their riders and
40. 3 He was **holding** a linen tape-measure and a measuring-rod
Dan 7. 5 It was **holding** three ribs between its teeth, and a voice
8.18 But he took **hold** of me, raised me to my feet, [19] and
10.10 Then a hand took **hold** of me and raised me to my
10.18 Once more he took **hold** of me, and I felt stronger.
Hos 5. 4 Idolatry has a powerful **hold** on them, and they do not
11. 4 I picked them up and **held** them to my cheek;
Mt 4. 6 they will **hold** you up with their hands, so that not even
9.25 the girl's room and took **hold** of her hand, and she got
10.22 But whoever **holds** out to the end will be saved.
12.11 Will he not take **hold** of it and lift it out?
14.31 Jesus reached out and grabbed **hold** of him and said, "How
24.13 But whoever **holds** out to the end will be saved.
26.50 Then they came up, arrested Jesus, and **held** him tight.
28. 9 came up to him, took **hold** of his feet, and worshipped him.
Mk 13.13 But whoever **holds** out to the end will be saved.
14.46 So they arrested Jesus and **held** him tight.
15.36 Then he **held** it up to Jesus' lips and said, "Wait!
Lk 4.11 It also says, 'They will **hold** you up with their hands so
6.38 helping, poured into your hands—all that you can **hold.**
24.29 but they **held** him back, saying, "Stay with us;
Jn 2. 6 there, each one large enough to **hold** about a hundred litres.
20.17 "Do not **hold** on to me," Jesus told her, "because I
21.25 whole world could not **hold** the books that would be written.
Acts 2.24 because it was impossible that death should **hold** him prisoner.
3.11 As the man **held** on to Peter and John in Solomon's Porch,
20.20 know that I did not **hold** back anything that would be of
20.27 For I have not **held** back from announcing to you the
27.32 soldiers cut the ropes that **held** the boat and let it go.
27.40 same time they untied the ropes that **held** the steering oars.
27.44 the rest were to follow, **holding** on to the planks or to
Rom 7. 6 Law, because we died to that which once **held** us prisoners.
10.21 says, "All day long I **held** out my hands to welcome a
12. 9 Hate what is evil, **hold** on to what is good.
1 Cor 15. 2 by the gospel if you **hold** firmly to it—unless it was
Eph 2.21 He is the one who **holds** the whole building together and
4.16 and the whole body is **held** together by every joint with
6.13 after fighting to the end, you will still **hold** your ground.
Col 2.19 of thinking [19] and has stopped **holding** on to Christ, who is
2.19 body is nourished and **held** together by its joints and ligaments,
2 Thes 2. 7 happen until the one who **holds** it back is taken out of
2.15 our brothers, stand firm and **hold** on to those truths which
1 Tim 3. 9 they should **hold** to the revealed truth of the faith with a
2 Tim 1.13 **Hold** firmly to the true words that I taught you, as the
3. 5 they will **hold** to the outward form of our religion, but
Tit 1. 9 He must **hold** firmly to the message which can be trusted
1.14 healthy faith [14] and no longer **hold** on to Jewish legends
Heb 2. 1 That is why we must **hold** on all the more firmly to
3.14 partners with Christ if we **hold** firmly to the end the
4.14 Let us, then, **hold** firmly to the faith we profess.
6.18 him are greatly encouraged to **hold** firmly to the hope placed
10.23 Let us **hold** on firmly to the hope we profess, because we
12. 1 and of the sin which **holds** on to us so tightly, and
Rev 1.16 He **held** seven stars in his right hand, and a sharp
2. 1 message from the one who **holds** the seven stars in his right
2.25 But until I come, you must **hold** firmly to what you have.
6. 2 Its rider **held** a bow, and he was given a crown.
6. 5 Its rider **held** a pair of scales in his hand.
7. 1 four corners of the earth, **holding** back the four winds so
7. 9 dressed in white robes and **holding** palm branches in their hands.
15. 2 by the sea of glass, **holding** harps that God had given them
17. 4 In her hand she **held** a gold cup full of obscene and
19.10 brothers, all those who **hold** to the truth that Jesus revealed.
20. 1 angel coming down from heaven, **holding** in his hand the key
20.13 the world of the dead also gave up the dead they **held.**

HOLD (2)

Jon 1. 5 had gone below and was lying in the ship's **hold,** sound

HOLE

Ex 28.32 It is to have a **hole** for the head,
28.32 and this **hole** is to be reinforced with a
39.23 The **hole** for the head was reinforced with a woven binding
Deut 23.13 a bowel movement you can dig a **hole** and cover it up.
1 Sam 13. 6 Israelites hid in caves and **holes** or among the rocks or in
14.11 Hebrews are coming out of the **holes** they have been hiding in!"
2 Kgs 12. 9 took a box, made a **hole** in the lid, and placed the
Job 30. 6 to live in caves, in **holes** dug in the sides of cliffs.
30.14 They pour through the **holes** in my defences and come
Ps 35. 7 a trap for me and dug a deep **hole** to catch me.
Is 2.10 the rocky hills or dig **holes** in the ground to try to
2.19 the rocky hills or dig **holes** in the ground to try to
2.21 earth, people will hide in **holes** and caves in the rocky
Jer 13. 4 River Euphrates and hide the shorts in a **hole** in the rocks."
Ezek 8. 7 of the outer courtyard and showed me a **hole** in the wall.
12. 5 they are watching, break a **hole** through the wall of your
12. 7 getting dark I dug a **hole** in the wall with my hands
12.12 dark and escape through a **hole** that they dig for him in
Mt 8.20 Jesus answered him, "Foxes have **holes,** and birds have nests,
9.16 patch will shrink and make an even bigger **hole** in the coat.
12.11 a sheep and it falls into a deep **hole** on the Sabbath?
21.33 fence around it, dug a **hole** for the winepress, and built a
25.18 coins went off, dug a **hole** in the ground, and hid his
Mk 2. 4 So they made a **hole** in the roof right above the place
2.21 tear off some of the old cloth, making an even bigger **hole.**
12. 1 fence round it, dug a **hole** for the winepress, and built a
Lk 9.58 said to him, "Foxes have **holes,** and birds have nests, but
Heb 11.38 deserts and hills, living in caves and **holes** in the ground.

HOLIDAY

Esth 2.18 He proclaimed a **holiday** for the whole empire and distributed
8.17 the Jews held a joyful **holiday** with feasting and happiness.
9.18 made the fifteenth a **holiday,** since they had slaughtered their
9.19 of Adar as a joyous **holiday,** a time for feasting and giving
9.21 observe the fourteenth and fifteenth days of Adar as **holidays**
9.26 That is why the **holidays** are called Purim.

HOLIEST see HOLY

HOLINESS see HOLY

HOLLOW

Ex 27. 8 of boards and leave it **hollow,** according to the plan that I
38. 7 The altar was made of boards and was **hollow.**
Judg 15.19 Then God opened a **hollow** place in the ground there at Lehi,
Jer 52.21 They were **hollow,** and the metal was 75 millimetres thick.

HOLY

[HOLIEST, HOLINESS]

Gen 4.26 then that people began using the Lord's **holy name** in worship.
12. 6 came to the sacred tree of Moreh, the **holy** place at Shechem.
28.11 At sunset he came to a **holy** place and camped there.
Ex 3. 1 flock across the desert and came to Sinai, the **holy** mountain.
3. 5 Take off your sandals, because you are standing on **holy** ground.
4.27 So he went to meet him at the **holy** mountain;
6. 3 not make myself known to them by my **holy name,** the Lord.
15.11 Who is like you, wonderful in **holiness?**
16.23 that tomorrow is a **holy** day of rest, dedicated to him.
18. 5 into the desert where Moses was camped at the **holy** mountain.
20. 8 "Observe the Sabbath and keep it **holy.**
20.11 is why I, the Lord, blessed the Sabbath and made it **holy.**
24.13 Joshua got ready, and Moses began to go up the **holy** mountain.
28.30 Aaron will carry them when he comes into my **holy** presence.
29.11 the bull there in my **holy** presence at the entrance of the
29.31 of Aaron and his sons and boil it in a **holy** place.
29.36 Then anoint it with olive-oil to make it **holy.**
29.37 the altar will be completely **holy,** and anyone or anything
29.37 touches it will be harmed by the power of its **holiness.**
29.43 the dazzling light of my presence will make the place **holy.**

Ex	29.44	the Tent and the altar **holy,** and I will set Aaron and
	30.10	altar is to be completely **holy,** dedicated to me, the Lord."
	30.29	and they will be completely **holy,** and anyone or anything that
	30.29	touches them will be harmed by the power of its **holiness.**
	30.31	the people of Israel, 'This **holy** anointing oil is to be used
	30.32	It is **holy,** and you must treat it as holy.
	30.35	Add salt to keep it pure and **holy.**
	30.36	Treat this incense as completely **holy.**
	30.37	Treat it as a **holy** thing dedicated to me.
	34. 5	stood with him there, and pronounced his **holy name,** the Lord.
	40. 9	by anointing it with the sacred oil, and it will be **holy.**
	40.10	its equipment by anointing it, and it will be completely **holy.**
Lev	2. 3	it is very **holy,** since it is taken from the food offered
	2.10	it is very **holy,** since it is taken from the food offered
	6.16	yeast and eaten in a **holy** place, the courtyard of the Tent
	6.16	very **holy,** like the sin-offerings and the repayment-offerings.
	6.18	will be harmed by the power of its **holiness.**
	6.25	This is a very **holy** offering.
	6.26	shall eat it in a **holy** place, the courtyard of the Tent
	6.27	of the animal will be harmed by the power of its **holiness.**
	6.27	with the animal's blood, it must be washed in a **holy** place.
	6.29	it is very **holy.**
	7. 1	the regulations for repayment-offerings, which are very **holy.**
	7. 6	must be eaten in a **holy** place, because it is very holy.
	10. 1	this fire was not **holy,** because the Lord had not commanded
	10. 3	when he said, 'All who serve me must respect my **holiness;**
	10.12	eat it beside the altar, because this offering is very **holy.**
	10.13	Eat it in a **holy** place;
	10.17	It is very **holy,** and the Lord has given it to you
	11.44	and you must keep yourselves **holy,** because I am holy.
	11.45	You must be holy, because I am **holy.**
	12. 4	not touch anything that is **holy** or enter the sacred Tent
	14.13	like the sin-offering, belongs to the priest and is very **holy.**
	16.19	from the sins of the people of Israel and make it **holy.**
	16.24	He must bathe in a **holy** place and put on his own
	16.31	is to be a very **holy** day, one on which they fast
	19. 2	of Israel, "Be holy, because I, the Lord your God, am **holy.**
	20. 3	unclean and disgraces my **holy name,** I will turn against him
	20. 7	Keep yourselves **holy,** because I am the Lord your God.
	20. 8	my laws, because I am the Lord and I make you **holy."**
	20.26	You shall be **holy** and belong only to me,
	20.26	because I am the Lord and I am **holy.**
	21. 6	He must be **holy** and must not disgrace my name.
	21. 6	He offers food-offerings to me, and he must be **holy.**
	21. 7	he is **holy.**
	21. 8	people must consider the priest **holy,** because he presents the
	21. 8	I am **holy** and I make my people holy.
	21.15	his children, who ought to be **holy,** will be ritually unclean.
	21.22	both the **holy** food-offering and the very holy food-offering,
	21.23	He must not profane these **holy** things,
	21.23	because I am the Lord and I make them **holy."**
	22. 2	not bring disgrace on my **holy name,** so treat with respect
	22. 9	I am the Lord and I make them **holy.**
	22.16	I am the Lord and I make the offerings **holy."**
	22.32	Do not bring disgrace on my **holy name;**
	22.32	all the people of Israel must acknowledge me to be **holy.**
	22.32	I am the Lord and I make you **holy;**
	23.20	These offerings are **holy.**
	24. 9	shall eat it in a **holy** place,
	24. 9	because this is a very **holy** part of the food offered to
Num	4. 4	Their service involves the most **holy** things.
	5.17	He shall pour some **holy** water into a clay bowl and take
	10.33	the people left Sinai, the **holy** mountain, they travelled for
	16.37	from the firepans somewhere else, because the firepans are **holy.**
	16.38	became **holy** when they were presented at the Lord's altar.
	18.10	eat these things in a **holy** place, and only males may eat
	18.10	consider them **holy.**
	20.12	enough faith to acknowledge my **holy** power before the people
	20.13	against the Lord and where he showed them that he was **holy.**
	27.14	you refused to acknowledge my **holy** power before them."
Deut	4.36	he let you see his **holy** fire, and he spoke to you
	5.12	the Sabbath and keep it **holy,** as I, the Lord your God,
	26.15	Look down from your **holy** place in heaven and bless your
Josh	5.15	you are standing on **holy** ground."
	24.19	He is a **holy** God and will not forgive your sins.
1 Sam	2. 2	"No one is **holy** like the Lord;
	6.20	"Who can stand before the Lord, this **holy** God?
	9. 6	this town there is a **holy** man who is highly respected
	9. 9	So they went to the town where the **holy** man lived.
	10.25	wrote them in a book, which he deposited in a **holy** place.
	11.15	Gilgal, and there at the **holy** place they proclaimed Saul king.
1 Kgs	19. 8	strength to walk forty days to Sinai, the **holy** mountain.
2 Kgs	4. 9	that this man who comes here so often is a **holy** man.
	19.22	You have been disrespectful to me, the **holy** God of Israel.
1 Chr	16.29	Bow down before the **Holy One** when he appears;
	16.35	so that we may be thankful and praise your **holy name."**
	28.10	that the Lord has chosen you to build his **holy** Temple.
	29.16	a temple to honour your **holy name,** but it all came from
2 Chr	2. 4	It will be a **holy** place where my people and I will
	2. 4	New Moon Festivals, and other **holy** days honouring the Lord
	8.11	because any place where the Covenant Box has been is **holy."**
	8.13	to the requirements of the Law of Moses for each **holy** day:
	26.18	Leave this **holy** place.
	30. 8	Lord your God has made **holy** for ever, and worship him so
	36.14	defiled the Temple, which the Lord himself had made **holy.**
Ezra	9. 2	and so God's **holy** people had become contaminated.
	9. 8	escape from slavery and live in safety in this **holy** place.
Neh	8. 9	the people, "This day is **holy** to the Lord your God, so
	8.10	Today is **holy** to our Lord, so don't be sad.
	8.11	and telling them not to be sad on such a **holy** day.
	9.14	to keep your Sabbaths **holy,** and through your servant Moses
Neh	10.31	Sabbath or on any other **holy** day, we will not buy from
	11. 1	go and live in the **holy city** of Jerusalem, while the rest
	11.18	In all, 284 Levites lived in the **holy city** of Jerusalem.
	13.22	the gates to make sure that the Sabbath was kept **holy.**
Job	6.10	I know that God is **holy;**
Ps	5. 7	I can worship in your **holy** Temple and bow down to you
	11. 4	The Lord is in his **holy** temple;
	20. 6	he answers him from his **holy** heaven and by his power gives
	22. 3	are enthroned as the **Holy One,** the one whom Israel praises.
	24. 3	Who may enter his **holy** Temple?
	28. 2	for help, when I lift my hands towards your **holy** Temple.
	29. 2	bow down before the **Holy One** when he appears.
	30. 4	Remember what the **Holy One** has done, and give him thanks!
	33.21	we trust in his **holy name.**
	51.11	do not take your **holy** spirit away from me.
	68.17	the Lord comes from Sinai into the **holy** place.
	71.22	harp I will play hymns to you, the **Holy One** of Israel.
	74. 8	they burnt down every **holy** place in the land.
	77.13	Everything you do, O God, is **holy.**
	78.41	to the test and brought pain to the **Holy** God of Israel.
	78.54	He brought them to his **holy** land, to the mountains which
	79. 1	have desecrated your **holy** Temple and left Jerusalem in ruins.
	89. 5	the **holy ones** sing of your faithfulness, Lord.
	89. 7	You are feared in the council of the **holy ones;**
	89.18	you, the **Holy** God of Israel, gave us our king.
	89.20	made my servant David king by anointing him with **holy** oil.
	89.35	"Once and for all I have promised by my **holy name:**
	93. 5	eternal, Lord, and your Temple is **holy** indeed, for ever
	96. 9	Bow down before the **Holy One** when he appears;
	97.12	Remember what the **holy** God has done, and give thanks to him.
	98. 1	By his own power and **holy** strength he has won the victory.
	99. 3	**Holy** is he!
	99. 5	**Holy** is he!
	99. 9	The Lord our God is **holy.**
	102.19	Lord looked down from his **holy** place on high, he looked down
	103. 1	All my being, praise his **holy name!**
	106.16	were jealous of Moses and of Aaron, the Lord's **holy** servant.
	106.47	so that we may be thankful and praise your **holy name.**
	111. 9	**Holy** and mighty is he!
	114. 2	Judah became the Lord's **holy** people, Israel became his own
	138. 2	I face your **holy** Temple, bow down, and praise your name
	145.21	let all his creatures praise his **holy name** for ever.
Prov	9.10	If you know the **Holy One,** you have understanding.
Is	1. 4	rejected the Lord, the **holy** God of Israel, and have turned
	1.14	I hate your New Moon Festivals and **holy** days;
	4. 3	whom God has chosen for survival, will be called **holy.**
	5.16	and he reveals his **holiness** by judging his people.
	5.19	Let Israel's **holy** God carry out his plans;
	5.24	rejected what the Lord Almighty, Israel's **holy** God, has taught
	6. 3	**"Holy, holy, holy!**
	6. 3	The Lord Almighty is **holy!**
	8.13	Remember that I, the Lord Almighty, am **holy;**
	8.14	Because of my awesome **holiness** I am like a stone that
	10.17	Israel's **holy** God will become a flame, which in a single day
	10.20	will truly put their trust in the Lord, Israel's **holy** God.
	12. 6	Israel's **holy** God is great, and he lives among his people."
	13. 3	confident soldiers to fight a **holy** war and punish those he
	17. 7	will turn for help to their Creator, the **holy** God of Israel.
	29.19	the happiness which the Lord, the **holy** God of Israel, gives.
	29.23	then you will acknowledge that I am the **holy** God of Israel.
	30.11	We don't want to hear about your **holy** God of Israel."
	30.12	But this is what the **holy** God of Israel says:
	30.15	Sovereign Lord, the **holy** God of Israel, says to the people,
	31. 1	rely on the Lord, the **holy** God of Israel, or ask him
	35. 8	There will be a highway there, called "The Road of **Holiness."**
	37.23	You have been disrespectful to me, the **holy** God of Israel.
	40.25	To whom can the **holy** God be compared?
	41.14	I, the **holy** God of Israel, am the one who saves you.
	41.16	you will praise me, the **holy** God of Israel.
	41.20	to understand that Israel's **holy** God has made it happen."
	43. 3	the Lord your God, the **holy** God of Israel, who saves you.
	43.14	Israel's **holy** God, the Lord who saves you, says,
	43.15	I am the Lord, your **holy** God.
	45.11	The Lord, the **holy** God of Israel, the one who shapes the
	47. 4	The **holy** God of Israel sets us free— his name is
	48. 2	you are citizens of the **holy city** and that you depend on
	48.17	The **holy** God of Israel, the Lord who saves you, says:
	49. 7	Israel's **holy** God and saviour says to the one who is
	49. 7	the **holy** God of Israel keeps his promises.
	52. 1	**Holy city** of God, clothe yourself with splendour!
	52.10	The Lord will use his **holy** power;
	52.11	keep yourselves **holy** and leave.
	54. 5	The **holy** God of Israel will save you— he is the
	55. 5	the Lord your God, the **holy** God of Israel, will make all
	57.15	"I am the high and **holy** God, who lives for ever.
	57.15	live in a high and **holy** place, but I also live with
	58.13	if you value my **holy** day and honour it by not travelling,
	60. 9	name of the Lord, The **holy** God of Israel, Who has made
	60.14	'The City of the Lord,' 'Zion, the City of Israel's **Holy** God.'
	62.12	You will be called "God's **Holy** People,"
	63.10	they rebelled against him and made his **holy** spirit sad.
	63.15	from heaven, where you live in your **holiness** and glory.
	63.18	We, your **holy** people, were driven out by our enemies
	65. 5	we are too **holy** for you to touch!'
	66. 7	"My **holy city** is like a woman who suddenly gives birth to
Jer	22. 3	and do not kill innocent people in this **holy** place.
	23. 9	the Lord, because of his **holy** words, I am like a man
	31.23	the sacred hill of Jerusalem, the **holy** place where he lives.'
	50.29	it acted with pride against me, the **Holy One** of Israel.
	51. 5	though they have sinned against me, the **Holy One** of Israel.
	51.51	foreigners have taken over the **holy** places in the Temple.'

Lam	1. 4	one comes to the Temple now to worship on the **holy** days.
	2. 6	He has put an end to **holy** days and Sabbaths.
	2. 7	The Lord rejected his altar and deserted his **holy** Temple;
Ezek	8. 6	driving me farther and farther away from my **holy** place.
	20.12	between us, to remind them that I, the Lord, make them **holy.**
	20.20	Make the Sabbath a **holy** day, so that it will be a
	20.39	and stop dishonouring my **holy name** by offering gifts to your
	20.40	the land, on my **holy** mountain, the high mountain of Israel,
	20.40	your sacrifices, your best offerings, and your **holy** gifts.
	20.41	that you burn, and the nations will see that I am **holy.**
	22. 8	have no respect for the **holy** places, and you don't keep the
	22.26	priests break my law and have no respect for what is **holy.**
	22.26	They make no distinction between what is **holy** and what is not.
	28.14	You lived on my **holy** mountain and walked among sparkling gems.
	28.16	forced you to leave my **holy** mountain, and the angel who
	28.22	when I show how **holy** I am by punishing those who
	28.25	and all the nations will know that I am **holy.**
	36.20	brought disgrace on my **holy name,** because people would say,
	36.21	made me concerned for my **holy name,** since the Israelites
	36.22	for the sake of my **holy name,** which you have disgraced in
	36.23	demonstrate to the nations the **holiness** of my great name—
	36.23	I will use you to show the nations that I am **holy.**
	38.16	I am, to show my **holiness** by what I do through you.
	38.23	all the nations that I am great and that I am **holy.**
	39. 7	my people Israel know my **holy name,** and I will not let
	39. 7	will know that I, the Lord, am the **Holy** God of Israel."
	39.25	I will protect my **holy name.**
	39.27	many nations that I am **holy,** I will bring my people back
	42.13	The man said to me, "Both these buildings are **holy.**
	42.13	who enter the Lord's presence eat the **holiest** offerings.
	42.13	Because the rooms are **holy,**
	42.13	the priests will place the **holiest** offerings there:
	42.14	leave in these rooms the **holy** clothing they wore while serving
	42.20	The wall served to separate what was **holy** from what was not.
	43. 7	ever again disgrace my **holy name** by worshipping other gods
	43. 8	disgraced my **holy name** by all the disgusting things they did,
	43.12	it on the top of the mountain is sacred and **holy."**
	44. 3	however, may go there to eat a **holy** meal in my presence.
	44.13	go near anything that is **holy** to me or to enter the
	44.19	on duty in the Temple and leave them in the **holy** rooms.
	44.23	the difference between what is **holy** and what is not,
	44.24	and regulations, and they are to keep the Sabbaths **holy.**
	45. 1	The entire area will be **holy.**
	45. 3	it will contain the Temple, the **holiest** place of all.
	45. 4	It will be a **holy** part of the country, set aside for
	45. 6	Next to the **holy** area, another section, twelve and a half
	45. 7	the western boundary of the **holy** area it will extend west to
	45.20	In this way, you will keep the Temple **holy.**
	46.19	These are **holy** rooms for the priests.
	46.20	so that nothing **holy** is carried to the outer courtyard,
	48.10	The priests are to have a portion of this **holy** area.
	48.11	This **holy** area is to be for the priests who are
	48.12	belonging to the Levites, and it will be the **holiest** of all.
	48.14	It is **holy** and belongs to the Lord.
	48.15	a half kilometres, is not **holy,** but is for the general use
	48.18	to the south of the **holy** area—five kilometres by two and
Dan	4. 8	The spirit of the **holy** gods is in him, so I told
	4. 9	that the spirit of the **holy** gods is in you, and that
	4.18	you can, because the spirit of the **holy** gods is in you."
	5.11	your kingdom who has the spirit of the **holy** gods in him.
	5.14	that the spirit of the **holy** gods is in you and that
	9.20	pleading with the Lord my God to restore his **holy** Temple.
	9.24	freeing your people and your **holy city** from sin and evil.
	9.24	will come true, and the **holy** Temple will be rededicated.
Hos	6. 9	on the road to the **holy** place at Shechem they commit murder.
	11. 9	I, the **Holy One,** am with you.
	11.12	are still rebelling against me, the faithful and **holy** God.
Amos	2. 7	with the same slave-girl, and so profane my **holy name.**
	4. 2	As the Sovereign Lord is **holy,** he has promised, "The days
	4. 4	of Israel, go to the **holy** place in Bethel and sin,
	7. 9	The **holy** places of Israel will be left in ruins.
	8. 5	can hardly wait for the **holy** days to be over so that
Jon	2. 4	from your presence and would never see your **holy** Temple again.
	2. 7	I prayed to you, and in your **holy** Temple you heard me.
Mic	1. 3	The Lord is coming from his **holy** place;
Hab	1.12	You are my God, **holy** and eternal.
	1.13	Your eyes are too **holy** to look at evil, and you cannot
	2.20	The Lord is in his **holy** Temple;
	3. 3	the **holy** God is coming from the hills of Paran.
Zech	1.14	concern for Jerusalem, my **holy city,** [15]and I am very angry
	2.13	of the Lord, for he is coming from his **holy** dwelling-place.
	8. 3	I will return to Jerusalem, my **holy city,** and live there.
Mt	4. 5	took Jesus to Jerusalem, the **Holy City,** set him on the
	6. 9	May your **holy name** be honoured;
	7. 6	"Do not give what is **holy** to dogs—they will only turn
	23.17	important, the gold or the Temple which makes the gold **holy?**
	23.19	important, the gift or the altar which makes the gift **holy?**
	27.53	they went into the **Holy City,** where many people saw them.
Mk	1.24	I know who you are—you are God's **holy** messenger!"
	6.20	John was a good and **holy** man, and so he kept him
	8.38	he comes in the glory of his Father with the **holy** angels."
Lk	1.35	For this reason the **holy** child will be called the Son of
	1.49	His name is **holy;**
	1.70	He promised through his **holy** prophets long ago
	1.75	so that we might be **holy** and righteous before him all
	4.34	you are God's **holy** messenger!"
	9.26	and in the glory of the Father and of the **holy** angels.
	11. 2	May your **holy name** be honoured;
Jn	6.69	know that you are the **Holy One** who has come from God."
	17.11	**Holy** Father!
Jn	19.31	crosses on the Sabbath, since the coming Sabbath was especially **holy.**
Acts	3.14	He was **holy** and good, but you rejected him,
	3.21	as God announced through his **holy** prophets who lived long ago.
	4.27	Israel against Jesus, your **holy** Servant, whom you made Messiah.
	4.30	may be performed through the name of your **holy** Servant Jesus."
	7.33	off, for the place where you are standing is **holy** ground.
Rom	1. 2	by God through his prophets, as written in the **Holy Scriptures.**
	1. 4	as to his divine **holiness,** he was shown with great power
	6.19	yourselves entirely as slaves of righteousness for **holy** purposes.
	7.12	then, the Law itself is **holy,**
	7.12	and the commandment is **holy,** right, and good.
1 Cor	3.17	For God's temple is **holy,** and you yourselves are his temple.
2 Cor	7. 1	and let us be completely **holy** by living in awe of God.
Eph	1. 4	Christ, so that we would be **holy** and without fault before him.
	3. 5	it now by the Spirit to his **holy** apostles and prophets.
	4.24	reveals itself in the true life that is upright and **holy.**
Col	1.22	to bring you, **holy,** pure, and faultless, into his presence.
	2.16	eat or drink or about **holy** days or the New Moon Festival
1 Thes	3.13	you will be perfect and **holy** in the presence of our God
	4. 3	wants you to be **holy** and completely free from sexual immorality.
	4. 4	with his wife in a **holy** and honourable way, [5]not with a
	4. 7	God did not call us to live in immorality, but in **holiness.**
	5.23	gives us peace make you **holy** in every way and keep your
1 Tim	2.15	if she perseveres in faith and love and **holiness,** with modesty.
	5.21	Christ Jesus and of the **holy** angels I solemnly call upon you
2 Tim	3.15	child, you have known the **Holy Scriptures,** which are able to
Tit	1. 8	He must be self-controlled, upright, **holy,** and disciplined.
	2. 3	older women to behave as women should who live a **holy** life.
Heb	7.26	He is **holy;**
	12.10	it for our own good, so that we may share his **holiness.**
	12.14	and try to live a **holy** life, because no one will see
1 Pet	1. 2	Father and were made a **holy** people by his Spirit, to obey
	1.15	Instead, be **holy** in all that you do,
	1.15	just as God who called you is **holy.**
	1.16	The scripture says, "Be **holy** because I am holy."
	2. 5	you will serve as **holy** priests to offer spiritual and acceptable
	2. 9	the King's priests, the **holy** nation, God's own people, chosen to
2 Pet	1.18	from heaven, when we were with him on the **holy** mountain.
	3. 2	spoken long ago by the **holy** prophets, and the command from
	3.11	Your lives should be **holy** and dedicated to God, [12]as you
Jude	14	thousands of his **holy** angels [15]to bring judgement on all,
Rev	3. 7	"This is the message from the one who is **holy** and true.
	4. 8	**"Holy, holy, holy,** is the Lord God Almighty, who was, who
	6.10	They shouted in a loud voice, "Almighty Lord, **holy** and
	11. 2	who will trample on the **Holy City** for forty-two months.
	14.10	in fire and sulphur before the **holy** angels and the Lamb.
	15. 4	You alone are **holy.**
	16. 5	have made are just, O **Holy One,** you who are and who
	21. 2	And I saw the **Holy City,** the new Jerusalem, coming down
	21.10	He showed me Jerusalem, the **Holy City,** coming down out of
	22.11	on doing good, and whoever is **holy** must go on being holy."
	22.19	of life and of the **Holy City,** which are described in this

AV **HOLY OF HOLIES** see **(Most) HOLY PLACE**

HOLY PEOPLE see **GOD'S PEOPLE**

HOLY PLACE

[MOST HOLY PLACE]

Ex	26.33	The curtain will separate the **Holy Place**
	26.33	from the **Most Holy Place.**
	26.35	Outside the **Most Holy Place** put the table against the
	28.29	"When Aaron enters the **Holy Place,** he will wear this
	28.35	into my presence in the **Holy Place** or when he leaves it,
	28.43	serve as priests in the **Holy Place,** so that they will not
	29.30	presence to serve in the **Holy Place** is to wear these
	31.11	anointing oil, and the sweet-smelling incense for the **Holy Place.**
	35.19	when they serve in the **Holy Place**—the sacred clothes for
	39. 1	the priests were to wear when they served in the **Holy Place.**
	39.41	were to wear in the **Holy Place**—the sacred clothes for Aaron
Lev	16. 2	the curtain into the **Most Holy Place,** because that is where
	16. 3	He may enter the **Most Holy Place** only after he has brought
	16. 4	Aaron goes into the **Most Holy Place,** he must have a bath
	16.12	of fine incense and bring them into the **Most Holy Place.**
	16.15	its blood into the **Most Holy Place,** and sprinkle it on the
	16.16	ritual to purify the **Most Holy Place** from the uncleanness of
	16.17	time Aaron enters the **Most Holy Place** to perform the ritual
	16.20	ritual to purify the **Most Holy Place,** the rest of the Tent
	16.23	before entering the **Most Holy Place,** and leave them there.
	16.27	was brought into the **Most Holy Place** to take away sin, shall
	16.33	ritual to purify the **Most Holy Place,** the rest of the Tent
	24. 3	front of the Covenant Box, which is in the **Most Holy Place.**
Num	3.31	the priests use in the **Holy Place,**
	3.31	and the curtain at the entrance to the **Most Holy Place.**
	3.32	of those who carried out the duties in the **Holy Place.**
	3.38	services performed in the **Holy Place** for the people of Israel.
	4.12	the utensils used in the **Holy Place,** wrap them in a blue
	8.19	would strike them if they came too near the **Holy Place."**
	18. 3	contact with sacred objects in the **Holy Place** or with
	18. 5	fulfil the responsibilities for the **Holy Place** and the altar,
	18. 7	that concern the altar and what is in the **Most Holy Place.**
1 Kgs	6.16	inner room, called the **Most Holy Place,** was built in the
	6.17	in front of the **Most Holy Place** was eighteen metres long.
	6.22	with gold, as well as the altar in the **Most Holy Place.**
	6.23	and placed in the **Most Holy Place,** each one 4.4 metres tall.
	6.27	by side in the **Most Holy Place,** so that two of their
	6.31	was set in place at the entrance of the **Most Holy Place;**

1 Kgs 7.49 in front of the **Most Holy Place,** five on the south side
7.50 the doors of the **Most Holy Place** and of the outer doors
8. 6 put it in the **Most Holy Place,** beneath the winged creatures.
8. 8 in front of the **Most Holy Place,** but from nowhere else.
1 Chr 6.49 the worship in the **Most Holy Place** and for the sacrifices by
28.11 rooms, and for the **Most Holy Place,** where sins are forgiven.
2 Chr 3. 8 inner room, called the **Most Holy Place,** was nine metres long
3. 8 gold were used to cover the walls of the **Most Holy Place;**
3.10 place them in the **Most Holy Place,** [11-13] where they
3.14 A curtain for the **Most Holy Place** was made of linen and
4.20 to burn in front of the **Most Holy Place,** according to plan;
4.22 the doors to the **Most Holy Place** were overlaid with gold.
5. 7 put it in the **Most Holy Place,** beneath the winged creatures.
5. 9 in front of the **Most Holy Place,** but from nowhere else.
Neh 6.10 and hide together in the **Holy Place** of the Temple and lock
Ezek 41. 1 Next, the man took me into the central room, the **Holy Place.**
41. 4 Then he said to me, "This is the **Most Holy Place."**
41.15 room of the Temple, the **Holy Place,** and the Most Holy Place
41.15 Holy Place, and the **Most Holy Place** [16] were all panelled
41.21 The door-posts of the **Holy Place** were square.
41.21 the entrance of the **Most Holy Place** there was something that
41.23 the passage leading to the **Holy Place**
41.23 at the end of the passage leading to the **Most Holy Place.**
41.25 on the doors of the **Holy Place,** just as there were on
44.13 that is holy to me or to enter the **Most Holy Place.**
Mt 24.15 It will be standing in the **holy place."**
Lk 11.51 Zechariah, who was killed between the altar and the **Holy Place.**
Acts 21.28 brought some Gentiles into the Temple and defiled this **holy place!"**
Heb 8. 2 High Priest in the **Most Holy Place,** that is, in the real
9. 2 was put up, the outer one, which was called the **Holy Place.**
9. 3 Behind the second curtain was the Tent called the **Most Holy Place.**
9. 8 the way into the **Most Holy Place** has not yet been opened
9.12 for all into the **Most Holy Place,** he did not take the
9.24 not go into a man-made **Holy Place,** which was a copy of
9.25 Priest goes into the **Most Holy Place** every year with the
10.19 to go into the **Most Holy Place** by means of the death
13.11 the animals into the **Most Holy Place** to offer it as a

HOLY SPIRIT see SPIRIT (1)

HOME

Gen 4.12 you will be a **homeless** wanderer on the earth."
4.14 I will be a **homeless** wanderer on the earth, and anyone who
12. 1 your relatives, and your father's **home,** and go to a land
17.11 including slaves born in your **homes** and slaves bought from
17.23 the slaves born in his **home** and those he had bought.
18. 3 "Sirs, please do not pass by my **home** without stopping;
18. 5 honoured me by coming to my **home,** so let me serve you."
18.33 the Lord went away, and Abraham returned **home.**
24. 5 the girl will not leave **home** to come with me to this
24. 7 brought me from the **home** of my father and from the
24.31 his camels at the well, [31] and said, "Come **home** with me.
25.27 outdoor life, but Jacob was a quiet man who stayed at **home.**
28. 2 to Mesopotamia, to the **home** of your grandfather Bethuel,
28.21 return safely to my father's **home,** then you will be my God.
30.25 said to Laban, "Let me go, so that I can return **home.**
31.30 so anxious to get back **home,** but why did you steal my
31.55 and his daughters good-bye, and left to go back **home.**
38.11 So Tamar went back **home.**
38.19 Tamar went **home,** took off her veil, and put her widow's
39.16 She kept his robe with her until Joseph's master came **home.**
43.21 up camp on the way **home,** we opened our sacks, and each
43.26 When Joseph got **home,** they took the gifts into the house
45.25 Egypt and went back **home** to their father Jacob in Canaan.
Ex 12.30 because there was not one **home** in which there was not a
15.17 Lord, have chosen for your **home,** the Temple that you yourself
16.29 where he is on the seventh day and not leave his **home."**
18.23 and all these people can go **home** with their disputes settled."
18.27 Then Moses said good-bye to Jethro, and Jethro went back **home.**
35. 3 Do not even light a fire in your **homes** on the Sabbath."
Lev 22.11 money or born in his **home,** may eat the food the priest
Num 14.31 into the land that you rejected, and it will be their **home.**
22.13 Balaam went to Balak's messengers and said, "Go back **home;**
22.34 it is wrong for me to go on, I will return **home."**
24.11 Now go off **home!**
24.25 got ready and went back **home,** and Balak went on his way.
32.18 will not return to our **homes** until all the other Israelites
35.28 death of the High Priest, but after that he may return **home.**
35.32 payment in order to return **home** before the death of the High
Deut 6. 7 them when you are at **home** and when you are away,
7.26 of these idols into your **homes,** or the same curse will be
11.19 them when you are at **home** and when you are away,
12.21 you may eat the meat at **home,** as I have told you.
14.24 is too far from your **home** for you to carry there the
15.22 You may eat such animals at **home.**
16. 7 and the next morning return **home.**
20. 5 If so, he is to go **home.**
20. 6 If so, he is to go **home.**
20. 7 If so, he is to go **home.**
20. 8 If so, he is to go **home.**
21.12 Take her to your **home,** where she will shave her head,
21.13 is to stay in your **home** and mourn for her parents for
22. 2 you don't know who owns it, then take it **home** with you.
24. 1 papers, gives them to her, and sends her away from his **home.**
24. 3 papers, gives them to her, and sends her away from his **home.**
24. 5 so that he can stay at **home** and make his wife happy.
32.25 terrors will strike in the **homes.**
Deut 33.18 trade on the sea, And may Issachar's wealth increase at **home.**
Josh 1.13 this land on the east side of the Jordan as your **home.**
9.12 When we left **home** with it and started out to meet you,
12. 8 This land had been the **home** of the Hittites, the Amorites,
20. 6 the man may go back **home** to his own town, from which
22. 4 So go back **home** to the land which you claimed for your
22. 6 Joshua sent them **home** with his blessing and with these
22. 6 "You are going back **home** very rich, with a lot of livestock,
22. 6 Then they left for **home.**
22. 9 the tribes of Reuben, Gad, and East Manasseh went back **home.**
Judg 3.18 he told the men who had carried them to go back **home.**
7. 3 is afraid should go back **home,** and we will stay here at
7. 7 Tell everyone else to go **home."**
7. 8 Gideon sent all the Israelites **home,** except the three hundred,
8.27 idol from the gold and put it in his **home** town, Ophrah.
8.29 Gideon went back to his own **home** and lived there.
9.55 the Israelites saw that Abimelech was dead, they all went **home.**
11. 2 and when they grew up, they forced Jephthah to leave **home.**
11. 9 "If you take me back **home** to fight the Ammonites and the
11.34 Jephthah went back **home** to Mizpah, there was his daughter
12. 7 Then he died and was buried in his **home** town in Gilead.
14. 2 He went back **home** and said to his father and mother,
14.19 After that, he went back **home,** furious about what had happened,
17.12 appointed him as his priest, and he lived in Micah's **home.**
18.26 were too strong for him, so he turned and went back **home.**
19. 9 Tomorrow you can get up early for your journey and go **home."**
19.15 square, but no one offered to take them **home** for the night.
19.18 we are on our way **home** deep in the hill-country of Ephraim.
19.20 The old man said, "You are welcome in my **home!**
19.21 So he took them **home** with him and fed their donkeys.
19.22 the old man, "Bring out that man that came **home** with you!
19.28 put her body across the donkey and started on his way **home.**
20. 8 he lives in a tent or in a house, will go **home.**
Ruth 1. 8 she said to them, "Go back **home** and stay with your mothers.
1. 9 possible for each of you to marry again and have a **home."**
1.12 Go back **home,** for I am too old to get married again.
1.14 mother-in-law good-bye and went back **home,** but Ruth held on
1.15 Go back **home** with her."
3. 1 for you, so that you will have a **home** of your own.
3.16 When she arrived **home,** her mother-in-law asked her,
4.13 So Boaz took Ruth **home** as his wife.
1 Sam 1.19 and after worshipping the Lord, they went back **home** to Ramah.
1.23 stay at **home** until you have weaned him.
1.23 So Hannah stayed at **home** and nursed her child.
2.11 Elkanah went back **home** to Ramah, but the boy Samuel stayed
2.20 After that they would go back **home.**
4.10 and defeated the Israelites, who went running to their **homes.**
7.17 would go back to his **home** in Ramah, where also he would
8.22 Then Samuel told all the men of Israel to go back **home.**
9. 5 "Let's go back **home,** or my father might stop thinking
10.25 Then he sent everyone **home.**
10.26 Saul also went back **home** to Gibeah.
13. 2 The rest of the men Saul sent **home.**
15.34 Samuel went to Ramah, and King Saul went **home** to Gibeah.
18. 2 from that day on and did not let him go back **home.**
18. 6 the soldiers were coming back **home,** women from every town
20. 6 begged your permission to hurry **home** to Bethlehem, since it's
23.18 David stayed at Horesh, and Jonathan went **home.**
24.22 Then Saul went back **home,** and David and his men went back
25. 1 Then they buried him at his **home** in Ramah.
25.35 brought him and said to her, "Go back **home** and don't worry.
25.36 to Nabal, who was at **home** having a feast fit for a
26.25 So David went on his way, and Saul returned **home.**
29. 7 So go back **home** in peace, and don't do anything that would
2 Sam 3.16 But when Abner said, "Go back **home,"** he did.
6. 3 They took it from Abinadab's **home** on the hill and placed
6.19 Then everyone went **home.**
6.20 Afterwards, when David went **home** to greet his family,
9. 4 the **home** of Machir son of Ammiel in Lodebar," Ziba answered.
10. 5 They were too ashamed to return **home.**
11. 4 Then she went back **home.**
11. 8 Then he said to Uriah, "Go **home** and rest a while."
11. 8 Uriah left, and David sent a present to his **home.**
11. 9 But Uriah did not go **home;**
11.10 that Uriah had not gone **home,** he asked him, "You have just
11.10 why didn't you go **home?"**
11.11 How could I go **home,** eat and drink, and sleep with my
11.13 But again that night Uriah did not go **home;**
12. 3 of it, and it grew up in his **home** with his children.
12. 4 One day a visitor arrived at the rich man's **home.**
12.15 Then Nathan went **home.**
13.30 While they were on their way **home,** David was told:
14. 8 "Go back **home,"** the king answered, "and I will take care
18.17 All the Israelites fled, each man to his own **home.**
19. 8 Meanwhile all the Israelites had fled, each man to his own **home.**
19.30 "It's enough for me that Your Majesty has come **home** safely."
19.37 Then let me go back **home** and die near my parents' grave.
19.39 and gave him his blessing, and Barzillai went back **home.**
20. 1 Men of Israel, let's go **home!"**
20.22 for his men to leave the city, and they went back **home.**
23.15 David felt **homesick** and said, "How I wish someone would
1 Kgs 1.53 before him, and the king said to him, "You may go **home."**
2.26 Abiathar the priest, "Go to your country **home** in Anathoth.
2.34 Joab, and he was buried at his **home** in the open country.
2.40 He found them and brought them back **home.**
3.17 gave birth to a baby boy at **home** while she was there.
5.14 group spent one month in Lebanon and two months back **home.**
8.30 In your **home** in heaven hear us and forgive us.
8.39 Listen to them in your **home** in heaven, forgive them, and
8.49 In your **home** in heaven hear them and be merciful to them.
8.66 On the eighth day Solomon sent the people **home.**

1 Kgs	8.66	praised him and went **home** happy because of all the blessings
	11.22	Is that why you want to go back **home?"**
	12.16	Men of Israel, let's go **home!**
	12.24	Go **home,** all of you.
	12.24	They all obeyed the Lord's command and went back **home.**
	13. 7	said to the prophet, "Come **home** with me and have something
	13. 9	a thing, and not to return **home** the same way I came."
	13.15	"Come **home** and have a meal with me," he said.
	13.16	"I can't go **home** with you or accept your hospitality.
	13.17	a thing, and not to return **home** the same way I came."
	13.18	told me to take you **home** with me and offer you my
	13.19	the prophet from Judah went **home** with the old prophet and
	14. 4	So she went to Ahijah's **home** in Shiloh.
	14.12	Ahijah went on to say to Jeroboam's wife, "Now go back **home.**
	14.17	Just as she entered her **home,** the child died.
	16. 9	was getting drunk in the **home** of Arza, who was in charge
	17.12	some firewood to take back **home** and prepare what little I
	18.44	his chariot and go back **home** before the rain stops him."
	20. 6	search your palace and the **homes** of your officials,
	20.43	The king went back **home** to Samaria, worried and depressed.
	21. 4	Ahab went **home,** depressed and angry over what Naboth had
	22.17	let them go **home** in peace.' "
2 Kgs	4. 2	"Tell me, what have you got at **home?"**
	5.17	mule-loads of earth to take **home** with me, because from now
	6.32	Elisha was at **home** with some elders who were visiting him.
	8.21	break out and escape, and his soldiers scattered to their **homes.**
	14.10	Be satisfied with your fame and stay at **home.**
	14.12	army was defeated, and all his soldiers fled to their **homes.**
1 Chr	11.17	David got **homesick** and said, "How I wish someone would
	16.43	Then everyone went **home,** and David went home to spend
	19. 5	They were too ashamed to return **home.**
	28. 2	wanted to build a permanent **home** for the Covenant Box,
2 Chr	6.21	In your **home** in heaven hear us and forgive us.
	6.30	Listen to them in your **home** in heaven and forgive them.
	6.39	In your **home** in heaven hear them and be merciful to them
	7.10	of the seventh month, Solomon sent the people **home.**
	10. 2	to escape from King Solomon, heard this news, he returned **home.**
	10.16	Men of Israel, let's go **home!**
	11. 4	Go **home,** all of you.
	18.16	let them go **home** in peace.' "
	25.10	Amaziah sent the hired troops away and told them to go **home.**
	25.10	they went **home,** bitterly angry with the people of Judah.
	25.19	defeated the Edomites, but I advise you to stay at **home.**
	25.22	Judaean army was defeated, and the soldiers fled to their **homes.**
	28.15	Then the Israelites returned **home** to Samaria.
	28.21	the palace, and the **homes** of the leaders of the people,
	30. 9	will take pity on them and let them come back **home.**
	30.27	In his **home** in heaven God heard their prayers and accepted
	31. 1	then they all returned **home.**
Ezra	4.10	moved from their **homes** and settled in the city of
Neh	1. 3	and were back in the **homeland** were in great difficulty
	4.14	fellow-countrymen, your children, your wives, and your **homes."**
	8.10	Now go **home** and have a feast.
	8.12	So all the people went **home** and ate and drank joyfully
Esth	1.22	be the master of his **home** and speak with final authority.
	5.10	But he controlled himself and went **home.**
	6.12	while Haman hurried **home,** covering his face in embarrassment.
Job	1.13	having a feast at the **home** of their eldest brother,
	1.18	having a feast at the **home** of your eldest son, [19] when a
	5. 3	secure, but I called down a sudden curse on their **homes.**
	8.22	who hate you, and the **homes** of the wicked will vanish.
	11.14	Put away evil and wrong from your **home.**
	15.34	and fire will destroy the **homes** built by bribery.
	18.17	His fame is ended at **home** and abroad;
	21. 9	God does not bring disaster on their **homes;**
	27.21	the east wind will sweep them from their **homes;**
	29. 4	I was prosperous, and the friendship of God protected my **home.**
	29.18	to live a long life and to die at **home** in comfort.
	31.32	I invited travellers into my **home** and never let them sleep
	39. 6	the desert to be their **home,** and let them live on the
	39.28	It makes its **home** on the highest rocks and makes the
Ps	19. 4	God made a **home** in the sky for the sun;
	23. 6	and your house will be my **home** as long as I live.
	49.11	Their graves are their **homes** for ever;
	49.14	decay in the world of the dead far from their **homes.**
	52. 5	he will take hold of you and snatch you from your **home:**
	55.15	Evil is in their **homes** and in their hearts.
	61. 2	In despair and far from **home** I call to you!
	68. 6	He gives the lonely a **home** to live in and leads prisoners
	68.10	your people made their **home** there;
	68.12	The women at **home** divided what was captured:
	76. 2	He has his **home** in Jerusalem;
	78.55	the tribes of Israel and gave their **homes** to his people.
	78.60	his tent in Shiloh, the **home** where he had lived among us.
	78.69	There he built his Temple like his **home** in heaven;
	84. 3	have built a nest, and the swallows have their own **home;**
	84.10	house of my God than live in the **homes** of the wicked.
	90. 1	O Lord, you have always been our **home.**
	91.10	will strike you, no violence will come near your **home.**
	104. 3	like a tent [3] and built your **home** on the waters above.
	109.10	May his children be **homeless** beggars;
	113. 9	He honours the childless wife in her **home;**
	128. 3	a fruitful vine in your **home,** and your sons will be like
	132. 3	"I will not go **home** or go to bed;
	132. 5	place for the Lord, a **home** for the Mighty God of Jacob."
	132.13	he wants to make it his **home:**
	135.21	Praise the Lord in Zion, in Jerusalem, his **home.**
Prov	3.33	puts a curse on the **homes** of wicked men,
	3.33	but blesses the **homes** of the righteous.
	7.19	My husband isn't at **home.**
	8.34	at my door every day, waiting at the entrance to my **home.**
Prov	14. 1	**Homes** are made by the wisdom of women, but are destroyed
	15.25	The Lord will destroy the **homes** of arrogant men,
	19.26	ill-treat his father or turn his mother away from his **home.**
	21.12	what goes on in the **homes** of the wicked, and he will
	22.13	The lazy man stays at **home;**
	24. 3	**Homes** are built on the foundation of wisdom
	24.15	scheme to rob an honest man or to take away his **home.**
	24.27	your house and establish a **home** until your fields are ready,
	27. 8	A man away from **home** is like a bird away from its
	30.26	not strong either, but they make their **homes** among the rocks.
	31.14	She brings **home** food from out-of-the-way places,
Ecc	7. 2	better to go to a **home** where there is mourning than to
	10.15	to find his way **home** would wear himself out with work.
Is	11.11	his power and bring back **home** those of his people who are
	14.17	the man who never freed his prisoners or let them go **home?'**
	18. 2	Go back **home,** swift messengers!
	23. 1	Your **home** port of Tyre has been destroyed;
	32.14	**Homes** and the forts that guarded them will be in ruins for
	32.18	will be free from worries, and their **homes** peaceful and safe.
	35. 9	Those whom the Lord has rescued will travel **home** by that road.
	41.27	They are coming **home!'**
	43. 5	east and the farthest west, I will bring your people **home.**
	49.18	Your people are assembling—they are coming **home!**
	49.22	signal to the nations, and they will bring your children **home.**
	56. 8	has brought his people Israel **home** from exile, has promised
	58. 7	with the hungry and open your **homes** to the homeless poor.
	60. 4	Your people are gathering to come **home!**
	60. 8	ships that skim along like clouds, Like doves returning **home?**
	60. 9	ships coming from distant lands, Bringing God's people **home.**
Jer	9.19	our **homes** have been torn down."
	18.22	Send a mob to plunder their **homes** without warning;
	23. 3	scattered them, and I will bring them back to their **homeland.**
	29.10	concern for you and keep my promise to bring you back **home.**
	30.10	You will come back **home** and live in peace;
	31.17	your children will come back **home.**
	31.21	Come back, people of Israel, come **home** to the towns you left.
	35. 9	do not build houses for **homes**—we live in tents—and we
	37. 7	is on its way to help you, but it will return **home.**
	39.14	grandson of Shaphan, who was to see that I got **home** safely.
	42.12	make him have mercy on you and let you go back **home.**
	46.16	Let's go **home** to our people and escape the enemy's sword!'
	46.27	You will come back **home** and live in peace;
	50. 6	to another, and they have forgotten where their **home** is.
	50.16	be afraid of the attacking army and will go back **home."**
	51. 9	Let's leave her now and go back **home.**
	51.50	Though you are far from **home,** think about me, your Lord, and
Lam	1. 3	Judah's people are helpless slaves, forced away from **home.**
	3.19	The thought of my pain, my **homelessness,** is bitter poison;
	5. 2	foreigners are living in our **homes.**
Ezek	3.24	Lord said to me, "Go **home** and shut yourself up in the
	7.24	the most evil nations here and let them have your **homes.**
	27. 4	Your **home** is the sea.
	29.14	I will let them live in southern Egypt, their original **home.**
	36. 8	You are going to come **home** soon.
	44.30	as an offering, and my blessing will rest on their **homes.**
Dan	2.17	Then Daniel went **home** and told his friends Hananiah,
	6.10	Daniel learnt that the order had been signed, he went **home.**
	11.28	king of Syria will return **home** with all the loot he has
Hos	9. 6	and the places where their **homes** once stood will be overgrown
	11.11	I will bring them to their **homes** again.
Amos	5.19	like a man who comes **home** and puts his hand on the
	9. 6	The Lord builds his **home** in the heavens, and over the
Obad	3	your **home** is high in the mountains, and so you say to
	4	Even though you make your **home** as high as an eagle's nest,
Jon	4. 2	I say before I left **home** that this is just what you
Mic	2. 8	thinking they are safe at **home,** but there you are, waiting
	2. 9	my people out of the **homes** they love, and you have robbed
	4. 7	are crippled and far from **home,** but I will make a new
Nah	3.18	the mountains, and there is no one to bring them **home** again.
Hab	2. 9	have tried to make your own **home** safe from harm and danger!
Zeph	3.19	I will rescue all the lame and bring the exiles **home.**
	3.20	I will bring your scattered people **home;**
Hag	1. 9	And when you brought the harvest **home,** I blew it away.
Zech	6.10	and go at once to the **home** of Josiah son of Zephaniah.
	10. 6	I will have compassion on them and bring them all back **home.**
	10. 9	They and their children will survive and return **home** together.
	10.10	Assyria I will bring them **home** and settle them in their own
	11. 3	their forest **home** along the Jordan is destroyed!
Mt	2.23	of Galilee [23] and made his **home** in a town named Nazareth.
	8. 6	in bed at **home,** unable to move and suffering terribly."
	8.13	said to the officer, "Go **home,** and what you believe will be
	8.14	went to Peter's **home,** and there he saw Peter's mother-in-law sick
	9. 6	paralysed man, "Get up, pick up your bed, and go **home!"**
	9. 7	The man got up and went **home.**
	10.14	And if some **home** or town will not welcome you or listen
	13.54	he left that place [54] and went back to his **home town.**
	13.57	everywhere except in his **home town** and by his own family."
	15.32	feeding them, for they might faint on their way **home."**
	20.14	Now take your pay and go **home.**
	24.46	is if his master finds him doing this when he comes **home!**
	25.35	you received me in your **homes,** [36] naked and you clothed me;
	25.38	and welcome you in our **homes,** or naked and clothe you?
	25.43	not welcome me in your **homes,** naked but you would not clothe
Mk	1.29	synagogue and went straight to the **home** of Simon and Andrew.
	2. 1	back to Capernaum, and the news spread that he was at **home.**
	2.11	"I tell you, get up, pick up your mat, and go **home!"**
	3.20	Then Jesus went **home.**
	5.19	he told him, "Go back **home** to your family and tell them
	6. 1	and went back to his **home town,** followed by his disciples.
	6. 4	everywhere except in his own **home town** and by his relatives
	7.29	of that answer, go back **home,** where you will find that the

Mk 7.30 She went **home** and found her child lying on the bed;
8. 3 If I send them **home** without feeding them, they will faint
8.26 Jesus then sent him **home** with the order, "Don't go back
10.29 you that anyone who leaves **home** or brothers or sisters or
12. 1 let out the vineyard to tenants and left **home** on a journey.
12.40 and rob them of their **homes,** and then make a show of
13.34 man who goes away from **home** on a journey and leaves his
Lk 1.23 of service in the Temple was over, Zechariah went back **home.**
1.56 stayed about three months with Elizabeth and then went back **home.**
2.39 Lord, they returned to their **home town** of Nazareth in Galilee.
2.43 was over, they started back **home,** but the boy Jesus stayed
4.23 to do here in my **home town** the same things you heard
4.24 Jesus added, "a prophet is never welcomed in his **home town.**
5.24 "I tell you, get up, pick up your bed, and go **home!"**
5.25 the bed he had been lying on, and went **home,** praising God.
7.44 I came into your **home,** and you gave me no water for
8.27 and would not stay at **home,** but spent his time in the
8.39 him away, saying, [39] "Go back **home** and tell what God has
8.41 him to go to his **home,** [42] because his only daughter, who
10.38 village where a woman named Martha welcomed him in her **home.**
12.43 is if his master finds him doing this when he comes **home!**
14. 1 eat a meal at the **home** of one of the leading Pharisees;
15. 6 that he puts it on his shoulders [6] and carries it back **home.**
15.13 sold his part of the property and left **home** with the money.
15.20 was still a long way from **home** when his father saw him;
15.27 'Your brother has come back **home,'** the servant answered,
15.30 and when he comes back **home,** you kill the prize calf for
16. 4 I shall have friends who will welcome me in their **homes.'**
16. 9 when it gives out, you will be welcomed in the eternal **home.**
18.14 the Pharisee, was in the right with God when he went **home.**
18.28 We have left our **homes** to follow you."
18.29 you that anyone who leaves **home** or wife or brothers or
19. 7 man has gone as a guest to the **home** of a sinner!"
19.12 to be made king, after which he planned to come back **home.**
20. 9 it out to tenants, and then left **home** for a long time.
20.47 and rob them of their **homes,** and then make a show of
23.48 they all went back **home,** beating their breasts in sorrow.
23.56 Then they went back **home** and prepared the spices and
24.12 Then he went back **home** amazed at what had happened.
Jn 4.51 On his way **home** his servants met him with the news,
8. 1 Then everyone went **home,** but Jesus went to the Mount of Olives.
12. 1 Jesus went to Bethany, the **home** of Lazarus, the man he had
16.32 each one to his own **home,** and I will be left all
19.27 From that time the disciple took her to live in his **home.**
20.10 Then the disciples went back **home.**
Acts 2.46 meals together in their **homes,** eating with glad and humble hearts,
5.42 the Temple and in people's **homes** they continued to teach
7.19 put their babies out of their **homes,** so that they would die.
7.20 He was cared for at **home** for three months, [21] and when he
7.21 was put out of his **home,** the king's daughter adopted him and
8.27 the treasury of the queen of Ethiopia, was on his way **home.**
8.27 Jerusalem to worship God and was going back **home** in his carriage.
10. 6 is a guest in the **home** of a tanner of leather named
10.32 is a guest in the **home** of Simon the tanner of leather,
11. 3 were a guest in the **home** of uncircumcised Gentiles, and you
12.12 situation, he went to the **home** of Mary, the mother of John
17. 5 an uproar and attacked the **home** of a man called Jason, in
18.26 heard him, they took him **home** with them and explained to him
20.12 They took the young man **home** alive and were greatly comforted.
20.20 you as I preached and taught in public and in your **homes.**
21. 6 and we went on board the ship while they went back **home.**
Rom 12.13 with your needy fellow-Christians, and open your **homes** to strangers.
1 Cor 11.22 Haven't you got your own **homes** in which to eat and drink?
11.34 hungry, he should eat at **home,** so that you will not come
14.35 find out about something, they should ask their husbands at **home.**
2 Cor 5. 1 us to live in, a **home** he himself has made, which will
5. 2 is our desire that our **home** which comes from heaven should
5. 6 at home in the body we are away from the Lord's **home.**
5. 8 much prefer to leave our **home** in the body
5. 8 and be at **home** with the Lord.
5. 9 we want to please him, whether in our **home** here or there.
6.16 said, "I will make my **home** with my people and live among
Eph 3.17 that Christ will make his **home** in your hearts through faith.
1 Tim 3. 2 he must welcome strangers in his **home;**
5.10 received strangers in her **home,** performed humble duties
5.14 and take care of their **homes,** so as to give our enemies
Heb 13. 2 Remember to welcome strangers in your **homes.**
1 Pet 4. 9 Open your **homes** to each other without complaining.
2 Pet 3.13 and a new earth, where righteousness will be at **home.**
2 Jn 10 not bring this teaching, do not welcome him in your **homes;**
Rev 21. 3 "Now God's **home** is with mankind!

Am **HOMELAND** see **COUNTRY**

Am **HOMEOWNER** see **OWNER (of a house)**

HOMER

Measure equal to ten ephahs, about 175 litres.

Ezek 45.11 The standard is the **homer.**
45.11 1 **homer** = 10 ephahs = 10 baths
45.13 10 baths = 1 **homer** = 1 kor.)

Am **HOMETOWN** see **TOWN**

HOMICIDE

2 Chr 19.10 before you a case of **homicide** or any other violation of a

HOMOSEXUAL

1 Cor 6. 9 idols or are adulterers or **homosexual** perverts [10] or who steal

HONEST

Gen 30.33 the future you can easily find out if I have been **honest.**
42.11 We are not spies, sir, we are **honest** men."
42.19 To prove that you are **honest,** one of you will stay in
42.31 'We are not spies,' we answered, 'we are **honest** men.
42.33 'This is how I will find out if you are **honest** men:
42.34 Then I will know that you are not spies, but **honest** men;
Lev 19.15 "Be **honest** and just when you make decisions in legal
19.36 Use **honest** scales, honest weights, and honest measures.
Deut 16.19 eyes even of wise and **honest** men, and cause them to give
25.15 Use true and **honest** weights and measures, so that you may
Josh 14. 7 I brought an **honest** report back to him.
Judg 9.16 "were you really **honest** and sincere when you made Abimelech
9.19 family was sincere and **honest,** then be happy with Abimelech
1 Sam 8. 3 so they accepted bribes and did not decide cases **honestly.**
1 Kgs 3. 6 he was good, loyal, and **honest** in his relations with you.
9. 4 will serve me in **honesty** and integrity, as your father David
2 Kgs 12.15 of the work were thoroughly **honest,** so there was no need to
22. 7 of the work are thoroughly **honest,** so there is no need to
1 Chr 29.17 In **honesty** and sincerity I have willingly given all this
2 Chr 34.12 The men who did the work were thoroughly **honest.**
Neh 13.13 trust these men to be **honest** in distributing the supplies to
Job 6.25 **Honest** words are convincing, but you are talking nonsense.
8. 6 if you are so **honest** and pure, then God will come and
17. 3 I am being **honest,** God.
17. 8 Those who claim to be **honest** are shocked,
23. 7 I am **honest;**
27.17 wear the clothes, and some **honest** man will get the silver.
31. 6 Let God weigh me on **honest** scales, and he will see how
Ps 9. 4 You are fair and **honest** in your judgements, and you have
12. 1 **honest** men can no longer be found.
17. 1 Listen to my **honest** prayer.
25.21 May my goodness and **honesty** preserve me, because I trust
55.22 he never lets **honest** men be defeated.
101. 6 Those who are completely **honest** will be allowed to serve me.
112. 5 who is generous with his loans, who runs his business **honestly.**
Prov 1. 3 to live intelligently and how to be **honest,** just, and fair.
2. 7 He provides help and protection for righteous, **honest** men.
4.25 Look straight ahead with **honest** confidence;
10. 2 will do you no good, but **honesty** can save your life.
10. 9 **Honest** people are safe and secure, but the dishonest will
10.25 the wicked are blown away, but **honest** people are always safe.
10.29 The Lord protects **honest** people, but destroys those who
11. 1 He is happy with **honest** weights.
11. 3 If you are good, you are guided by **honesty.**
11. 4 on the day you face death, but **honesty** can save your life.
11. 5 **Honesty** makes a good man's life easier, but a wicked man
11. 6 Righteousness rescues the **honest** man, but someone who can't
11.10 A city is happy when **honest** people have good fortune,
12. 5 **Honest** people will treat you fairly;
12.13 own words, but an **honest** man gets himself out of trouble.
13. 5 **Honest** people hate lies, but the words of wicked people are
14. 2 Be **honest** and you show that you have reverence for the Lord;
15.19 but if you are **honest,** you will have no trouble.
16. 8 better to have a little, **honestly** earned, than to have
16.11 and measures to be **honest** and every sale to be fair.
19. 1 better to be poor but **honest** than to be a lying fool.
20. 7 they have a father who is **honest** and does what is right.
20.11 you can tell if he is **honest** and good.
20.28 in power as long as his rule is **honest,** just, and fair.
21.21 Be kind and **honest** and you will live a long life;
24.15 who scheme to rob an **honest** man or to take away his
24.16 No matter how often an **honest** man falls, he always gets
24.26 An **honest** answer is a sign of true friendship.
28. 1 is chasing them, but an **honest** person is as brave as a
28. 6 Better to be poor and **honest** than rich and dishonest.
28.10 If you trick an **honest** person into doing evil,
28.18 Be **honest** and you will be safe.
28.20 **Honest** people will lead a full, happy life.
29. 6 in their own sins, while **honest** people are happy and free.
29.10 Bloodthirsty people hate anyone who's **honest,**
Ecc 12. 9 He studied proverbs and **honestly** tested their truth.
12.10 to find comforting words, but the words he wrote were **honest.**
Is 28.17 for the foundation, and **honesty** will be its plumb-line."
29.21 those who tell lies to keep **honest** men from getting justice.
32. 5 that a fool is honourable or say that a scoundrel is **honest.**
32. 8 But an honourable person acts **honestly** and stands firm
59.14 in the public square, and **honesty** finds no place there.
59.15 is so little **honesty** that anyone who stops doing evil finds
Ezek 18. 5 "Suppose there is a truly good man, righteous and **honest.**
18. 8 to do evil and gives an **honest** decision in any dispute.
45.10 "Everyone must use **honest** weights and measures:
Amos 2. 6 They sell into slavery **honest** men who cannot pay their debts,
3.10 They don't even know how to be **honest.**
Mic 7. 2 There is not an **honest** person left in the land, no one
7. 4 Even the best and most **honest** of them are as worthless as
Mt 23.23 teachings of the Law, such as justice and mercy and **honesty.**
Jn 7.18 one who sent him is **honest,** and there is nothing false in

Eph	4.28	in order to earn an **honest** living for himself and to be
1 Tim	3.11	they must be sober and **honest** in everything.

HONEY

Gen	43.11	a little resin, a little **honey,** spices, pistachio nuts,
Ex	16.31	a small white seed, and tasted like biscuits made with **honey.**
Lev	2.11	must never use yeast or **honey** in food offered to the Lord.
Deut	8. 8	wheat and barley, grapes, figs, pomegranates, olives, and **honey.**
	32.13	They found wild **honey** among the rocks;
Judg	14. 8	find a swarm of bees and some **honey** inside the dead body.
	14. 9	He scraped the **honey** out into his hands and ate it as
	14. 9	that he had taken the **honey** from the dead body of a
	14.18	"What could be sweeter than **honey?**
1 Sam	14.25	all came into a wooded area and found **honey** everywhere.
	14.26	The woods were full of **honey,** but no one ate any of
	14.27	was carrying, dipped it in a honeycomb, and ate some **honey.**
	14.29	See how much better I feel because I ate some **honey!**
	14.43	"I ate a little **honey** with the stick I was holding.
2 Sam	17.28	beans, peas, **honey,** cheese, cream, and some sheep.
1 Kgs	14. 3	him ten loaves of bread, some cakes, and a jar of **honey.**
2 Kgs	18.32	it is a land of olives, olive-oil, and **honey.**
2 Chr	31. 5	finest corn, wine, olive-oil, **honey,** and other farm produce,
Job	20.17	of olive-oil or streams that flow with milk and **honey.**
Ps	19.10	they are sweeter than the purest **honey.**
	81.16	with the finest wheat and satisfy you with wild **honey."**
	119.103	is the taste of your instructions— sweeter even than **honey!**
Prov	5. 3	may be as sweet as **honey** and her kisses as smooth as
	16.24	Kind words are like **honey**—sweet to the taste and good
	24.13	Son, eat **honey;**
	24.13	And just as **honey** from the comb is sweet on your tongue,
	25.16	Never eat more **honey** than you need;
	25.27	Too much **honey** is bad for you, and so is trying to
	27. 7	are full, you will refuse **honey,** but when you are hungry,
Song	4.11	The taste of **honey** is on your lips, my darling;
	4.11	your tongue is milk and **honey** for me.
	5. 1	I am eating my **honey** and honeycomb;
Is	7.15	his own decisions, people will be drinking milk and eating **honey.**
	7.22	survivors left in the land will have milk and **honey** to eat.
Jer	41. 8	wheat, barley, olive-oil, and **honey** hidden in the fields."
Ezek	3. 3	I ate it, and it tasted as sweet as **honey.**
	16.13	from the best flour, and had **honey** and olive-oil to eat.
	16.19	the best flour, olive-oil, and **honey**—but you offered it as a
	27.17	and Israel paid for your goods with wheat, **honey,** olive-oil,
Mt	3. 4	round his waist, and his food was locusts and wild **honey.**
Mk	1. 6	round his waist, and his food was locusts and wild **honey.**
Rev	10. 9	your stomach, but in your mouth it will be sweet as **honey."**
	10.10	and ate it, and it tasted sweet as **honey** in my mouth.

HONOUR

Gen	18. 5	You have **honoured** me by coming to my home, so let me
	22.12	"Now I know that you **honour** and obey God, because you have
	41.43	in, and his guard of **honour** went ahead of him and cried
Ex	5. 1	they can hold a festival in the desert to **honour** me.' "
	10. 9	because we must hold a festival to **honour** the Lord."
	12.11	It is the Passover Festival to **honour** me, the Lord.
	12.27	the sacrifice of Passover to **honour** the Lord,
	12.48	wants to celebrate Passover to **honour** the Lord, you must first
	13. 6	seventh day there is to be a festival to **honour** the Lord.
	14. 4	my victory over the king and his army will bring me **honour.**
	14.17	them, and I will gain **honour** by my victory over the king,
	23.14	"Celebrate three festivals a year to **honour** me.
	32. 5	"Tomorrow there will be a festival to **honour** the Lord."
Lev	19.30	the Sabbath, and **honour** the place where I am worshipped.
	19.32	"Show respect for old people and **honour** them.
	23. 5	Passover, celebrated to **honour** the Lord, begins at sunset on
	23.37	religious festivals on which you **honour** the Lord by gathering
	23.40	and begin a religious festival to **honour** the Lord your God.
	23.44	for observing the religious festivals to **honour** the Lord.
	25. 2	is giving you, you shall **honour** the Lord by not cultivating
	26. 2	festivals and **honour** the place where I am worshipped.
Num	16.10	the other Levites have this **honour**—and now you are trying to
	28.16	The Passover Festival in **honour** of the Lord is to be
	29.12	Celebrate this festival in **honour** of the Lord for seven days
Deut	5.29	If only they would always **honour** me and obey all my commands,
	6. 2	and your descendants are to **honour** the Lord your God and
	6.13	**Honour** the Lord your God, worship only him, and make your
	6.24	God commanded us to obey all these laws and to **honour** him.
	13. 4	Follow the Lord and **honour** him;
	14.23	so that you may learn to **honour** the Lord your God always.
	16. 1	**"Honour** the Lord your God by celebrating Passover in the
	16. 2	or cattle for the Passover meal to **honour** the Lord your God.
	16.10	celebrate the Harvest Festival, to **honour** the Lord your God,
	16.15	**Honour** the Lord your God by celebrating this festival for
	17.19	that he will learn to **honour** the Lord and to obey faithfully
	26.19	created, and you will bring praise and **honour** to his name.
	28.58	and if you do not **honour** the wonderful and awesome name of
	31.12	hear it and learn to **honour** the Lord your God and to
Josh	3. 7	people of Israel begin to **honour** you as a great man, and
	4.14	**honoured** him all his life, just as they had honoured Moses.
	4.24	power is, and you will **honour** the Lord your God for ever."
	7. 9	And then what will you do to protect your **honour?"**
	24.14	Joshua continued, **"honour** the Lord and serve him sincerely
Judg	9. 9	producing my oil, which is used to **honour** gods and men.'
	13.17	so that we can **honour** you when your words come true."
1 Sam	2. 8	them companions of princes and puts them in places of **honour.**
	2.29	Why, Eli, do you **honour** your sons more than me by letting
	2.30	Instead, I will **honour** those who honour me, and I will treat
	6. 5	your country, and you must give **honour** to the God of Israel.
	12.14	well with you if you **honour** the Lord your God, serve him,
1 Sam	18.23	"It's a great **honour** to become the king's son-in-law,
2 Sam	6. 5	dancing and singing with all their might to **honour** the Lord.
	6.14	his waist, danced with all his might to **honour** the Lord.
	6.21	answered, "I was dancing to **honour** the Lord, who chose me
	6.21	go on dancing to **honour** the Lord, [22]and will disgrace myself
	10. 3	it is in your father's **honour** that David has sent these men
1 Kgs	3.13	you will have wealth and **honour,** more than that of any other
	21. 9	call the people together, and give Naboth the place of **honour.**
	21.12	called the people together, and gave Naboth the place of **honour.**
2 Kgs	10.20	Jehu ordered, "Proclaim a day of worship in **honour** of Baal!"
	18. 4	time the people of Israel had burnt incense in its **honour.**
	19.34	the sake of my own **honour** and because of the promise I
	20. 6	the sake of my own **honour** and because of the promise I
	23.21	to celebrate the Passover in **honour** of the Lord their God,
	25.28	him a position of greater **honour** than he gave the other
1 Chr	13. 8	all the people danced with all their might to **honour** God.
	16.25	he is to be **honoured** more than all the gods.
	17.18	You know me well, and yet you **honour** me, your servant.
	19. 3	it is in your father's **honour** that David has sent these men
	22. 7	I wanted to build a temple to **honour** the Lord my God.
	28. 2	for building a temple to **honour** him, [3]but he has forbidden
	29.16	to build a temple to **honour** your holy name, but it all
	29.20	they bowed low and gave **honour** to the Lord and also to
2 Chr	2. 4	I am building a temple to **honour** the Lord my God.
	2. 4	Festivals, and other holy days **honouring** the Lord our God.
	6.31	so that your people may **honour** you and obey you all the
	7.21	"The Temple is now greatly **honoured,** but then everyone
	17. 5	brought him gifts, so that he became wealthy and highly **honoured.**
	18. 2	To **honour** Jehoshaphat and those with him, Ahab had a large
	19. 7	**Honour** the Lord and act carefully, because the Lord our God
	20. 8	built a temple to **honour** you, knowing [9]that if any disaster
	30. 1	to celebrate the Passover in **honour** of the Lord, the God of
	32.23	that from then on all the nations held Hezekiah in **honour.**
	32.27	Hezekiah became very wealthy, and everyone held him in **honour.**
	32.33	of Judah and Jerusalem paid him great **honour** at his death.
	35. 1	celebrated the Passover at Jerusalem in **honour** of the Lord;
Ezra	7.27	made the emperor willing to **honour** in this way the Temple
	10. 3	and the others who **honour** God's commands advise us to do.
Neh	1.11	prayers of all your other servants who want to **honour** you.
	5.15	But I acted differently, because I **honoured** God.
Esth	2.18	great banquet in Esther's **honour** and invited all his officials
	6. 3	"How have we **honoured** and rewarded Mordecai for this?"
	6. 6	said to him, "There is someone I wish very much to **honour.**
	6. 6	to himself, "Now who could the king want to **honour** so much?
	6. 9	'See how the king rewards a man he wishes to **honour!' "**
	6.10	and provide these **honours** for Mordecai the Jew.
	6.11	"See how the king rewards a man he wishes to **honour!"**
	10. 3	He was **honoured** and well-liked by his fellow-Jews.
Job	14.21	His sons win **honour,** but he never knows it, nor is he
	31.27	not been led astray to **honour** them by kissing my hand in
	36. 7	them to rule like kings and lets them be **honoured** for ever.
	40.10	If so, stand up in your **honour** and pride;
Ps	8. 5	you crowned him with glory and **honour.**
	15. 4	those whom God rejects, but **honours** those who obey the Lord.
	22.23	**Honour** him, you descendants of Jacob!
	23. 5	you welcome me as an **honoured** guest and fill my cup to
	31.19	are the good things you keep for those who **honour** you!
	33. 8	**Honour** him, all peoples of the world!
	34. 7	His angel guards those who **honour** the Lord and rescues them
	34. 9	**Honour** the Lord, all his people;
	34.11	listen to me, and I will teach you to **honour** the Lord.
	37.34	he will **honour** you by giving you the land, and you will
	50.23	thanks is the sacrifice that **honours** me, and I will surely
	61. 5	and you have given me what belongs to those who **honour** you.
	62. 4	You only want to bring him down from his place of **honour;**
	62. 7	My salvation and **honour** depend on God;
	66.16	Come and listen, all who **honour** God, and I will tell you
	67. 7	may all people everywhere **honour** him.
	73.24	instruction and at the end you will receive me with **honour.**
	76. 1	his name is **honoured** in Israel.
	79. 9	us and forgive our sins for the sake of your own **honour.**
	84.11	and glorious king, blessing us with kindness and **honour.**
	85. 9	ready to save those who **honour** him, and his saving presence
	91.15	I will rescue them and **honour** them.
	92. 1	Lord, to sing in your **honour,** O Most High God, [2]to proclaim
	96. 4	he is to be **honoured** more than all the gods.
	103.11	the earth, so great is his love for those who **honour** him.
	103.13	his children, so the Lord is kind to those who **honour** him.
	103.17	for those who **honour** the Lord, his love lasts for ever,
	111. 3	All he does is full of **honour** and majesty;
	111. 5	He provides food for those who **honour** him;
	111.10	The way to become wise is to **honour** the Lord;
	112. 1	Happy is the person who **honours** the Lord, who takes pleasure
	113. 9	He **honours** the childless wife in her home;
	115.13	will bless everyone who **honours** him, the great and the small
	119.74	Those who **honour** you will be glad when they see me,
	119.79	May those who **honour** you come to me— all those who
	141. 5	but I will never accept **honour** from evil men, because I am
	145.19	He supplies the needs of those who **honour** him;
	147.11	takes pleasure in those who **honour** him, in those who trust
	149. 4	he **honours** the humble with victory.
Prov	3. 9	**Honour** the Lord by making him an offering from the best of
	3.16	Wisdom offers you long life, as well as wealth and **honour.**
	3.35	Wise men will gain an **honourable** reputation,
	4. 8	Embrace her, and she will bring you **honour.**
	8.13	To **honour** the Lord is to hate evil;
	8.18	I have riches and **honour** to give, prosperity and success.
	15.33	You must be humble before you can ever receive **honours.**
	18. 3	Lose your **honour,** and you will get scorn in its place.
	20. 3	the **honourable** thing is to stay out of them.
	22. 4	humble, and you will get riches, **honour,** and a long life.

Prov 24.21 Have reverence for the Lord, my son, and **honour** the king.
25. 2 We **honour** God for what he conceals;
25. 2 we **honour** kings for what they explain.
27.18 A servant who takes care of his master will be **honoured.**
31.30 but a woman who **honours** the Lord should be praised.
Ecc 6. 2 God will give someone wealth, **honour,** and property,
10.12 wise man says brings him **honour,** but a fool is destroyed by
Is 9. 1 but the future will bring **honour** to this region,
9.15 The old and **honourable** men are the head—and the tail is
11.10 They will gather in his royal city and give him **honour.**
14.11 You used to be **honoured** with the music of harps, but now
22.23 and he will be a source of **honour** to his whole family.
23. 8 whose merchant princes were the most **honoured** men on earth?
23. 9 in what they had done and to humiliate their **honoured** men.
25. 1 I will **honour** you and praise your name.
26.15 its territory on every side, and this has brought you **honour.**
29.23 You will **honour** me and stand in awe of me.
32. 5 think that a fool is **honourable** or say that a scoundrel is
32. 8 But an **honourable** person acts honestly and stands firm
37.35 the sake of my own **honour** and because of the promise I
42.21 laws and teachings, and he wanted his people to **honour** them.
43. 4 precious to me and because I love you and give you **honour.**
43.20 Even the wild animals will **honour** me;
43.23 you did not **honour** me with your sacrifices.
45. 4 I have given you great **honour,** although you do not know me.
46.13 I will save Jerusalem and bring **honour** to Israel there."
49. 5 The Lord gives me **honour;**
49. 7 also will see it, and they will bow low to **honour** you."
49.23 They will bow low before you and **honour** you;
50.10 All of you that **honour** the Lord and obey the words of
52.13 he will be highly **honoured.**
53.12 give him a place of **honour,** a place among great and powerful
55. 5 I will give you **honour** and glory."
56. 4 such a man, "If you **honour** me by observing the Sabbath and
57.11 Have you stopped **honouring** me because I have kept silent for
58.13 value my holy day and **honour** it by not travelling, working,
58.14 I will make you **honoured** all over the world, and you will
60. 9 them silver and gold To **honour** the name of the Lord, The
60. 9 God of Israel, Who has made all nations **honour** his people.
63.14 He led his people and brought **honour** to his name.
Jer 2.11 God who has brought them **honour,** for gods that can do
5.24 You never thought to **honour** me, even though I send the
10. 7 Who would not **honour** you, the king of all nations?
10. 7 You deserve to be **honoured.**
13.11 be my people and would bring praise and **honour** to my name;
13.16 **Honour** the Lord, your God, before he brings darkness,
22.19 With the funeral **honours** of a donkey, he will be dragged
26.19 Hezekiah **honoured** the Lord and tried to win his favour.
30.19 my blessing will bring them **honour.**
32.39 to **honour** me for all time, for their own good and the
33. 9 Jerusalem will be a source of joy, **honour,** and pride to me;
44.10 You have not **honoured** me or lived according to all the laws
48.18 down from your place of **honour** and sit on the ground in
52.32 him a position of greater **honour** than he gave the other
Lam 1. 1 Once **honoured** by the world, she is now like a widow;
1. 8 Her **honour** is gone;
Ezek 16.60 But I will **honour** the covenant I made with you when you
20.44 I act to protect my **honour,** you Israelites will know that I
22. 7 No one in the city **honours** his parents.
32.27 not given **honourable** burial like the heroes of ancient times,
39.13 them, and they will be **honoured** for this on the day of
Dan 2. 6 its meaning, I will reward you with gifts and great **honour.**
2.23 I praise you and **honour** you, God of my ancestors.
2.37 has made you emperor and given you power, might, and **honour.**
4.34 the Supreme God and gave **honour** and glory to the one who
4.36 "When my sanity returned, my **honour,** my majesty,
4.36 back my royal power, with even greater **honour** than before.
4.37 I, Nebuchadnezzar, praise, **honour,** and glorify the King of Heaven.
5. 7 wear a gold chain of **honour** round his neck,
5.16 wear a gold chain of **honour** round your neck,
5.19 He **honoured** or disgraced anyone he wanted to.
5.20 removed from his royal throne and lost his place of **honour.**
5.23 you did not **honour** the God who determines whether you live
5.29 purple and to hang a gold chain of **honour** round his neck.
7.14 He was given authority, **honour,** and royal power,
9. 4 I said, "Lord God, you are great, and we **honour** you.
11.38 Instead, he will **honour** the god who protects fortresses.
11.39 He will give great **honour** to those who accept him as ruler,
Hos 4. 7 against me, and so I will turn your **honour** into disgrace.
4.18 delight in their prostitution, preferring disgrace to **honour.**
9. 5 for the appointed festivals in **honour** of the Lord, what will
Hab 2.16 You in turn will be covered with shame instead of **honour.**
2.16 cup of punishment, and your **honour** will be turned to disgrace.
Zeph 3.19 turn their shame to **honour,** and all the world will praise
Zech 6.13 build it and receive the **honour** due to a king, and he
6.14 in the Lord's Temple in **honour** of Heldai, Tobijah, Jedaiah,
7. 5 during these seventy years, it was not in **honour** of me.
12. 7 so that the **honour** which the descendants of David
Mal 1. 6 "A son honours his father, and a servant **honours** his master.
1. 6 I am your father—why don't you **honour** me?
1.11 People from one end of the world to the other **honour** me.
1.11 All of them **honour** me!
2. 2 You must **honour** me by what you do.
Mt 6. 9 May your holy name be **honoured;**
15. 6 'This belongs to God,' [6] he does not need to **honour** his father.
15. 8 'These people, says God, **honour** me with their words,
Mk 7. 6 'These people, says God, **honour** me with their words,
Lk 1.50 to another he shows mercy to those who **honour** him.
11. 2 May your holy name be **honoured;**
14.10 This will bring you **honour** in the presence of all the other
23.50 He was a good and **honourable** man, who was waiting for the
Jn 5.23 honour the Son in the same way as they **honour** the Father.
5.23 Whoever does not **honour** the Son does not honour the Father
8.49 "I **honour** my Father, but you dishonour me.
8.50 I am not seeking **honour** for myself.
8.54 "If I were to honour myself, that **honour** would be worth nothing.
8.54 The one who **honours** me is my Father—the very one you
12.26 And my Father will **honour** anyone who serves me.
Acts 7.41 and had a feast in **honour** of what they themselves had made.
12.23 Lord struck Herod down, because he did not give **honour** to God.
19.17 and the name of the Lord Jesus was given greater **honour.**
Rom 1.21 do not give him the **honour** that belongs to him, nor do
2. 7 keep on doing good, and seek glory, **honour,** and immortal life;
2.10 But God will give glory, **honour,** and peace to all who do
13. 7 property taxes, and show respect and **honour** for them all.
14. 6 of a certain day does so in **honour** of the Lord;
14. 6 eat anything does so in **honour** of the Lord, because he gives
14. 6 certain things does so in **honour** of the Lord, and he gives
1 Cor 4.10 We are despised, but you are **honoured!**
12.24 way as to give greater **honour** to those parts that need it.
2 Cor 6. 8 We are **honoured** and disgraced;
Phil 1.20 whole being I shall bring **honour** to Christ, whether I live
2.10 And so, in **honour** of the name of Jesus all beings in
4. 8 that are true, noble, right, pure, lovely, and **honourable.**
1 Thes 4. 4 in a holy and **honourable** way, [5] not with a lustful desire,
2 Thes 1.10 glory from all his people and **honour** from all who believe.
3. 1 and be received with **honour,** just as it was among you.
1 Tim 1.17 only God—to him be **honour** and glory for ever and ever!
6.16 To him be **honour** and eternal dominion!
Heb 1. 9 you the joy of an **honour** far greater than he gave to
2. 7 crowned him with glory and **honour,** [8] and made him ruler over
2. 9 crowned with glory and **honour** because of the death he suffered.
3. 3 builds a house receives more **honour** than the house itself.
3. 3 same way Jesus is worthy of much greater **honour** than Moses.
5. 4 No one chooses for himself the **honour** of being a high priest.
5. 5 did not take upon himself the **honour** of being a high priest.
13. 4 Marriage is to be **honoured** by all, and husbands and wives
1 Pet 1. 7 receive praise and glory and **honour** on the Day when Jesus
2.17 love your fellow-believers, **honour** God, and respect the Emperor.
3.15 reverence for Christ in your hearts, and **honour** him as Lord.
2 Pet 1.17 there when he was given **honour** and glory by God the Father,
Rev 4. 9 sing songs of glory and **honour** and thanks to the one who
4.11 You are worthy to receive glory, **honour,** and power.
5.12 power, wealth, wisdom, and strength, **honour,** glory, and praise!"
5.13 the Lamb, be praise and **honour,** glory and might, for ever
7.12 wisdom, thanksgiving, **honour,** power, and might
13.14 to build an image in **honour** of the beast that had been
14. 7 He said in a loud voice, **"Honour** God and praise his greatness!

HOOF

[HOOVES]

Lev 11. 3 animal [3] that has divided **hoofs** and that also chews the cud,
11. 4 they chew the cud, but do not have divided **hoofs.**
11. 7 they have divided **hoofs,** but do not chew the cud.
11.24 animals with hoofs, unless their **hoofs** are divided and they
Deut 14. 6 animals that have divided **hoofs** and that also chew the cud.
14. 7 eaten unless they have divided **hoofs** and also chew the cud.
14. 7 they chew the cud but do not have divided **hoofs.**
14. 8 they have divided **hoofs** but do not chew the cud.
Judg 5.22 horses came galloping on, stamping the ground with their **hooves.**
Is 5.28 Their horses' **hooves** are as hard as flint,
Jer 47. 3 They will hear the **hoof** beats of horses, the clatter of
Ezek 1. 7 legs were straight, and they had **hoofs** like those of a bull.
Mic 4.13 you as strong as a bull with iron horns and bronze **hoofs.**
Zech 11.16 the meat of the fattest sheep and tears off their **hoofs.**

HOOK

[FISH-HOOK]

Ex 26. 6 Make fifty gold **hooks** with which to join the two sets into
26.11 Make fifty bronze **hooks** and put them in the loops to
26.32 with gold, fitted with **hooks,** and set in four silver bases.
26.33 curtain under the row of **hooks** in the roof of the Tent,
26.37 of acacia-wood covered with gold and fitted with gold **hooks;**
27. 3 pans for the greasy ashes, and make shovels, bowls, **hooks,**
27.10 in twenty bronze bases, with **hooks** and rods made of silver.
27.17 with silver rods, and their **hooks** are to be made of silver
35.11 its outer covering, its **hooks** and its frames, its cross-bars,
36.13 They made fifty gold **hooks,** with which to join the two
36.18 They made fifty bronze **hooks** to join the two sets,
36.36 curtain, covered them with gold, and fitted them with gold **hooks.**
36.38 made five posts fitted with **hooks,** covered their tops
38. 3 pans, the shovels, the bowls, the **hooks,** and the firepans.
38.10 in twenty bronze bases, with **hooks** and rods made of silver.
38.12 posts and ten bases and with **hooks** and rods made of silver.
38.17 made of bronze, and the **hooks,** the rods, and the covering of
38.19 Their **hooks,** the covering of their tops, and their rods were
38.28 Bezalel made the rods, the **hooks** for the posts,
39.33 and all its equipment, its **hooks,** its frames, its cross-bars,
Num 4.14 firepans, **hooks,** shovels, and basins.
2 Kgs 19.28 now I will put a **hook** through your nose and a bit
2 Chr 33.11 They captured Manasseh, stuck **hooks** in him, put him in chains,
Job 41. 1 you catch Leviathan with a **fish-hook** or tie his tongue down
41. 2 a rope through his snout or put a **hook** through his jaws?
Is 19. 8 their **hooks** and their nets will be useless.
37.29 now I will put a **hook** through your nose and a bit
Ezek 19. 4 With **hooks** they dragged him off to Egypt.
29. 4 am going to put a **hook** through your jaw and make the
38. 4 will turn him round, put **hooks** in his jaws, and drag him
Amos 4. 2 "The days will come when they will drag you away with **hooks;**
4. 2 every one of you will be like a fish on a **hook.**

Hab 1.15 Babylonians catch people with **hooks,** as though they were fish.
Mt 17.27 up the first fish you **hook,** and in its mouth you will

HOOPOE

Lev 11.13 **hoopoes;**
Deut 14.12 **hoopoes;**

HOOT

Zeph 2.14 Owls will live among its ruins and **hoot** from the windows.

HOP

Lev 11.21 All winged insects are unclean, [21] except those that **hop.**

HOPE

Gen 32. 5 you word, sir, in the **hope** of gaining your favour."
Deut 28.65 the Lord will overwhelm you with anxiety, **hopelessness,**
Ruth 1.12 I thought there was still **hope,** and so got married tonight
1 Sam 2.33 become blind and lose all **hope,** and all your other descendants
2 Sam 14. 7 They will destroy my last **hope** and leave my husband without
14.15 speak to you in the **hope** that you would do what I
21.17 "You are the **hope** of Israel, and we don't want to lose
2 Kgs 4.28 Didn't I tell you not to raise my **hopes?"**
5.18 So I **hope** that the Lord will forgive me when I accompany
2 Chr 14.11 no one can **hope** to defeat you."
Ezra 10. 2 foreign women, but even so there is still **hope** for Israel.
Esth 9. 1 enemies of the Jews were **hoping** to get them in their power.
Job 3. 9 give that night no **hope** of dawn.
4. 6 and so you should have confidence and **hope.**
5.16 He gives **hope** to the poor and silences the wicked.
6.11 Why go on living when I have no **hope?**
6.20 search, [20] but their **hope** dies beside dry streams.
7. 6 My days pass by without **hope,** pass faster than a weaver's
8.13 their **hope** is gone, once God is forgotten.
11.18 You will live secure and full of **hope;**
11.20 Their one **hope** is that death will come.
13.15 I've lost all **hope,** so what if God kills me?
14. 7 There is **hope** for a tree that has been cut down;
14.19 so you destroy man's **hope** for life.
15.22 He has no **hope** of escaping from darkness, for somewhere
17.11 my **hope** is gone.
17.13 My only **hope** is the world of the dead, where I will
17.15 Where is there any **hope** for me?
17.16 **Hope** will not go with me when I go down to the
19.10 He uproots my **hope** and leaves me to wither and die.
27. 8 What **hope** is there for godless men in the hour when God
30.26 **hoped** for happiness and light, but trouble and darkness came
35.10 their Creator, who gives them **hope** in their darkest hours.
Ps 9.18 the **hope** of the poor will not be crushed for ever.
31.24 Be strong, be courageous, all you that **hope** in the Lord.
33.20 We put our **hope** in the Lord;
33.22 love be with us, Lord, as we put our **hope** in you.
34.18 he saves those who have lost all **hope.**
37.34 Put your **hope** in the Lord and obey his commands;
39. 7 What, then, can I **hope** for, Lord?
39. 7 I put my **hope** in you.
42. 5 I will put my **hope** in God, and once again I will
42.11 I will put my **hope** in God, and once again I will
43. 5 I will put my **hope** in God, and once again I will
56. 6 in hiding-places and watch everything I do, **hoping** to kill me.
62. 5 I put my **hope** in him.
62.10 don't **hope** to gain anything by robbery;
69.20 I had **hoped** for sympathy, but there was none;
71. 5 Sovereign Lord, I put my **hope** in you;
71.14 I will always put my **hope** in you;
79. 8 we have lost all **hope.**
107. 5 They were hungry and thirsty and had given up all **hope.**
112.10 their **hopes** are gone for ever.
119. 5 I **hope** that I shall be faithful in keeping your instructions!
119.43 truth at all times, because my **hope** is in your judgements.
119.49 it has given me **hope.**
119.114 I put my **hope** in your promise.
119.116 don't let me be disappointed in my **hope!**
119.147 I place my **hope** in your promise.
143. 7 I have lost all **hope.**
145.15 All living things look **hopefully** to you, and you give
Prov 10.28 The **hopes** of good men lead to joy, but wicked people can
11. 7 When a wicked man dies, his **hope** dies with him.
13.12 When **hope** is crushed, the heart is crushed, but a wish
18.14 are sick, but if you lose it, your last **hope** is gone.
29.20 There is more **hope** for a stupid fool than for someone
Ecc 9. 4 who is alive in the world of the living has some **hope;**
Is 6. 5 I said, "There is no **hope** for me!
8.17 his people, but I trust him and place my **hope** in him.
20. 5 about Egypt will be disillusioned, their **hopes** shattered.
24.16 But there is no **hope** for me!
26. 8 We follow your will and put our **hope** in you;
33. 2 We have put our **hope** in you.
42. 4 He will not lose **hope** or courage;
49. 4 I said, "I have worked, but how **hopeless** it is!
51. 5 they wait with **hope** for me to save them.
57.15 and repentant, so that I can restore their confidence and **hope.**
59. 9 We **hope** for light to walk by, but there is only darkness,
64. 4 who does such deeds for those who put their **hope** in him.
Jer 8.15 We **hoped** for peace and a time of healing, but it was
13.16 before he turns into deep darkness the light you **hoped** for.
14. 8 You are Israel's only **hope;**
14.19 we **hoped** for healing, but terror came instead.
Jer 14.22 We have put our **hope** in you, O Lord our God, because
17.13 Lord, you are Israel's **hope;**
23.16 they are filling you with false **hopes.**
28. 6 I **hope** the Lord will do this!
28. 6 I certainly **hope** he will make your prophecy come true
29.11 not disaster, plans to bring about the future you **hope** for.
30.13 you, no remedy for your sores, no **hope** of healing for you.
31.17 There is **hope** for your future;
Lam 2.13 there is no possible **hope.**
3. 7 I am a prisoner with no **hope** of escape.
3.18 my **hope** in the Lord is gone.
3.21 Yet **hope** returns when I remember this one thing:
3.24 is all I have, and so I put my **hope** in him.
3.29 We should bow in submission, for there may still be **hope.**
Ezek 7.27 the prince will give up **hope,** and the people will shake with
14. 5 me, but by my answer I **hope** to win back their loyalty.
17. 7 leaves towards him, in the **hope** that he would give it more
19. 5 She waited until she saw all **hope** was gone.
37.11 that they are dried up, without any **hope** and with no future.
Dan 2. 9 me lies because you **hope** that in time things will change.
Hos 2.15 vineyards she had and make Trouble Valley a door of **hope.**
9. 9 They are **hopelessly** evil in what they do, just as they
Amos 4. 8 to a city where they **hoped** to find water, but there was
Mic 5. 8 and tears them to pieces—and there is no **hope** of rescue.
7. 1 It's **hopeless!**
Hag 1. 9 **hoped** for large harvests, but they turned out to be small.
Zech 9. 5 So will Ekron, and her **hopes** will be shattered.
9.12 Return, you exiles who now have **hope;**
Mt 12.21 triumph, [21] and in him all peoples will put their **hope."**
Lk 3.15 People's **hopes** began to rise, and they began to wonder whether
6.34 to those from whom you **hope** to get it back, why should
16.21 to the rich man's door, [21] **hoping** to eat the bits of food
23. 8 He was **hoping** to see Jesus perform some miracle.
24.21 And we had **hoped** that he would be the one who was
Jn 5.45 whom you have put your **hope,** is the very one who will
Acts 2.26 will rest assured in **hope,** [27] because you will not abandon me
23. 6 trial here because of the **hope** I have that the dead will
24.15 I have the same **hope** in God that these themselves have,
24.26 the same time he was **hoping** that Paul would give him some
26. 6 be tried because of the **hope** I have in the promise that
26. 7 twelve tribes of our people **hope** to receive, as they worship
26. 7 it is because of this **hope,** Your Majesty, that I am being
27.20 We finally gave up all **hope** of being saved.
27.31 don't stay on board, you have no **hope** of being saved."
28.20 for the sake of him for whom the people of Israel **hope."**
Rom 4.18 Abraham believed and **hoped,**
4.18 there was no reason for **hoping,** and so became "the father
5. 2 so we boast of the **hope** we have of sharing God's glory!
5. 4 endurance brings God's approval, and his approval creates **hope.**
5. 5 This **hope** does not disappoint us, for God has poured out
8.20 Yet there was the **hope** [21] that creation itself would one
8.24 For it was by **hope** that we were saved;
8.24 if we see what we **hope** for, then
8.24 it is not really **hope.**
8.24 For who **hopes** for something he sees?
8.25 But if we **hope** for what we do not see, we wait
12.12 Let your **hope** keep you joyful, be patient in your troubles,
15. 4 we might have **hope** through the patience and encouragement
15.12 to rule the Gentiles, and they will put their **hope** in him."
15.13 May God, the source of **hope,** fill you with all joy and
15.13 in him, so that your **hope** will continue to grow by the
15.24 years to come to see you, [24] I **hope** to do so now.
1 Cor 9.10 do their work in the **hope** of getting a share of the
13. 7 and its faith, **hope,** and patience never fail.
13.13 faith, **hope,** and love;
15.19 If our **hope** in Christ is good for this life only and
15.29 What do they **hope** to accomplish?
16. 7 I **hope** to spend quite a long time with you, if the
2 Cor 1. 7 So our **hope** in you is never shaken;
1. 8 and so heavy that we gave up all **hope** of staying alive.
1.10 and we have placed our **hope** in him that he will save
1.13 us only in part, I **hope** that you will come to understand
3.12 Because we have this **hope,** we are very bold.
5.11 knows us completely, and I **hope** that in your hearts you know
8. 5 It was more than we could have **hoped** for!
10.15 Instead, we **hope** that your faith may grow and that we may
Gal 5. 5 As for us, our **hope** is that God will put us right
Eph 1.12 who were the first to **hope** in Christ, praise God's glory!
1.18 will know what is the **hope** to which he has called you,
2.12 and you lived in this world without **hope** and without God.
4. 4 just as there is one **hope** to which God has called you.
Phil 1.20 My deep desire and **hope** is that I shall never fail in
2.19 is the Lord's will, I **hope** that I will be able to
2.23 So I **hope** to send him to you as soon as I
3.11 in his death, [11] in the **hope** that I myself will be raised
Col 1. 5 News, first came to you, you heard about the **hope** it offers.
1. 5 are based on what you **hope** for, which is kept safe for
1.23 to be shaken from the **hope** you gained when you heard the
1 Thes 1. 3 so hard, and how your **hope** in our Lord Jesus Christ is
2.19 who are our **hope,** our joy, and our reason for boasting of
4.13 you will not be sad, as are those who have no **hope.**
5. 8 as a breastplate, and our **hope** of salvation as a helmet.
2 Thes 2.16 unfailing courage and a firm **hope,** [17] encourage you
1 Tim 1. 1 Saviour and Christ Jesus our **hope**— [2] To Timothy, my true son
3.14 this letter to you, I **hope** to come and see you soon.
4.10 because we have placed our **hope** in the living God, who is
5. 5 of her, has placed her **hope** in God and continues to pray
6.17 proud, but to place their **hope,** not in such an uncertain
Tit 1. 2 our religion, [2] which is based on the **hope** for eternal life.
2.13 for the blessed Day we **hope** for, when the glory of our
3. 7 God and come into possession of the eternal life we **hope** for.

Phlm	22	ready for me, because I **hope** that God will answer the
Heb	3. 6	keep up our courage and our confidence in what we **hope** for.
	6.11	the end, so that the things you **hope** for will come true.
	6.18	greatly encouraged to hold firmly to the **hope** placed before us.
	6.19	We have this **hope** as an anchor for our lives.
	7.19	And now a better **hope** has been provided through which we
	10.23	hold on firmly to the **hope** we profess, because we can trust
	11. 1	sure of the things we **hope** for, to be certain of the
Jas	5. 8	Keep your **hopes** high, for the day of the Lord's coming is
1 Pet	1. 3	fills us with a living **hope,** [4] and so we look forward to
	1.13	Keep alert and set your **hope** completely on the blessing
	1.21	and so your faith and **hope** are fixed on God.
	2.23	not threaten, but placed his **hopes** in God, the righteous Judge.
	3. 5	the past who placed their **hope** in God used to make
	3.15	asks you to explain the **hope** you have in you, [16] but do
1 Jn	3. 3	Everyone who has this **hope** in Christ keeps himself pure,
2 Jn	12	instead, I **hope** to visit you and talk with you personally,
3 Jn	14	I **hope** to see you soon, and then we will talk personally.

HOR (1)

Mountain on border of Edom on which Aaron died.

Num	20.22	Kadesh and arrived at Mount **Hor,** [23] on the border of Edom.
	20.25	his son Eleazar up Mount **Hor,** [26] and there remove Aaron's
	20.27	They went up Mount **Hor** in the sight of the whole community,
	21. 4	The Israelites left Mount **Hor** by the road that leads to
	33.15	From Rephidim to Mount **Hor** they set up camp at the
	33.15	(that is, Kadesh), and Mount **Hor,** at the edge of the land
	33.38	the command of the Lord, Aaron the priest climbed Mount **Hor.**
	33.41	From Mount **Hor** to the plains of Moab the Israelites
Deut	32.50	brother Aaron died on Mount **Hor,** [51] because both of you were

HORDE

Num	22. 4	"This **horde** will soon destroy everything round us,

HORIZON

Prov	8.27	when he stretched the **horizon** across the ocean,

HORN

Gen	22.13	round and saw a ram caught in a bush by its **horns.**
Deut	33.17	has the strength of a bull, The **horns** of a wild ox.
	33.17	His **horns** are Manasseh's thousands And Ephraim's ten thousands.
1 Kgs	22.11	son of Chenaanah, made iron **horns** and said to Ahab, "This
1 Chr	15.28	joy, the sound of trumpets, **horns,** and cymbals, and the
2 Chr	18.10	son of Chenaanah, made iron **horns** and said to Ahab, "This
Ps	98. 6	Blow trumpets and **horns,** and shout for joy to the Lord,
Dan	7. 7	Unlike the other beasts, it had ten **horns.**
	7. 8	I was staring at the **horns,**
	7. 8	I saw a little **horn** coming up among the others.
	7. 8	It tore out three of the **horns** that were already there.
	7. 8	This **horn** had human eyes and a mouth that was boasting proudly.
	7.11	I could still hear the little **horn** bragging and boasting.
	7.20	to know about the ten **horns** on its head
	7.20	and the **horn** that had come up afterwards
	7.20	and had made three of the **horns** fall.
	7.21	While I was looking, that **horn** made war on God's people
	7.24	The ten **horns** are ten kings who will rule that empire.
	8. 3	ram that had two long **horns,** one of which was longer and
	8. 4	the ram butting with his **horns** to the west, the north, and
	8. 5	He had one prominent **horn** between his eyes.
	8. 7	so angry that he smashed into him and broke the two **horns.**
	8. 8	but at the height of his power his **horn** was broken.
	8. 8	In its place four prominent **horns** came up, each pointing in
	8. 9	of one of these four **horns** grew a little horn, whose power
	8.12	The **horn** was successful in everything it did.
	8.20	you saw that had two **horns** represents the kingdoms of Media
	8.21	Greece, and the prominent **horn** between his eyes is the first
	8.22	The four **horns** that came up when the first horn was
Mic	4.13	you as strong as a bull with iron **horns** and bronze hoofs.
Zech	1.18	In another vision I saw four ox **horns.**
	1.19	that had been speaking to me, "What do these **horns** mean?"
Rev	5. 6	It had seven **horns** and seven eyes, which are the seven
	12. 3	with seven heads and ten **horns** and a crown on each of
	13. 1	It had ten **horns** and seven heads;
	13. 1	on each of its **horns** there was a crown, and on each
	13.11	It had two **horns** like a lamb's horns,
	17. 3	the beast had seven heads and ten **horns.**
	17. 7	that carries her, the beast with seven heads and ten **horns.**
	17.12	"The ten **horns** you saw are ten kings who have not yet
	17.16	The ten **horns** you saw, and the beast, will hate the prostitute;

AV **HORNS (OF THE ALTAR)** see **CORNER**

HORROR

see also **AWFUL HORROR**

Deut	28.59	diseases and **horrible** epidemics that can never be stopped.
2 Kgs	8.11	stared at him with a **horrified** look on his face until Hazael
	8.12	I know the **horrible** things you will do against the people
2 Chr	26.20	the king's forehead in **horror,** and then forced him to leave
Ps	55. 5	I am overcome with **horror.**
	73.19	they go down to a **horrible** end.
	116. 3	the **horrors** of the grave closed in on me;
Jer	2.12	the sky to shake with **horror,** to be amazed and astonished,
	15. 4	the people of the world **horrified** at them because of what
	18.16	made this land a thing of **horror,** to be despised for ever.
	25.38	The **horrors** of war and the Lord's fierce anger have turned
Jer	29.18	the nations of the world will be **horrified** at what they see.
	34.17	every nation in the world **horrified** at what I do to you.
	42.18	You will be a **horrifying** sight;
	44. 6	in ruins and became a **horrifying** sight, as they are today.
	44.12	They will be a **horrifying** sight;
	44.22	It has become a **horrifying** sight, and people use its name as
	49.13	city of Bozrah will become a **horrifying** sight and a desert;
	49.20	children will be dragged off, and everyone will be **horrified.**
	50.45	children will be dragged off, and everyone will be **horrified.**
	51.37	It will be a **horrible** sight;
	51.41	What a **horrifying** sight Babylon has become to the nations!
	51.43	towns have become a **horrifying** sight and are like a waterless
Lam	4.10	The disaster that came to my people brought **horror;**
Dan	7. 7	It was powerful, **horrible,** terrifying.
Hos	6.10	I have seen a **horrible** thing in Israel:
Nah	3. 6	People will stare at you in **horror.**
Zeph	2.15	Everyone who passes by will shrink back in **horror.**
Mal	2.11	to God and done a **horrible** thing in Jerusalem and all over
Rev	8.13	flying high in the air say in a loud voice, "O **horror!**
	8.13	**horror!**
	8.13	How **horrible** it will be for all who live on earth when
	9.12	The first **horror** is over;
	9.12	after this there are still two more **horrors** to come.
	11.14	The second horror is over, but the third **horror** will come soon!

HORSE

[CHARIOT-HORSES, DRAUGHT-HORSES, WAR-HORSES]

Gen	47.17	them food in exchange for their **horses,** sheep, goats, cattle,
	49.17	path, That strikes at the **horse's** heel, So that the rider is
	50. 9	Men in chariots and men on **horseback** also went with him;
Ex	9. 3	on all your animals—your **horses,** donkeys, camels, cattle,
	14. 9	Egyptian army, with all the **horses,** chariots, and drivers,
	14.23	after them into the sea with all their **horses,** chariots,
	15. 1	he has thrown the **horses** and their riders into the sea.
	15.19	the Egyptian chariots with their **horses** and drivers went into
	15.21	he has thrown the **horses** and their riders into the sea."
Deut	11. 4	army, along with their **horses** and chariots, by drowning them
	17.16	have a large number of **horses** for his army, and he is
	17.16	people to Egypt to buy **horses,** because the Lord has said
	20. 1	you see chariots and **horses** and an army that outnumbers yours,
Josh	11. 4	They also had many **horses** and chariots.
	11. 6	You are to cripple their **horses** and burn their chariots."
	11. 9	he crippled their **horses** and burnt their chariots.
Judg	5.22	**horses** came galloping on, stamping the ground with their hooves.
	5.28	"Why are his **horses** so slow to return?"
2 Sam	8. 4	He kept enough **horses** for a hundred chariots and crippled all
	15. 1	Absalom provided a chariot and **horses** for himself,
1 Kgs	1. 5	provided for himself chariots, **horses,** and an escort of fifty
	4.26	had forty thousand stalls for his **chariot-horses**
	4.26	and twelve thousand cavalry **horses.**
	4.28	was needed, for the **chariot-horses** and the draught animals.
	9.19	kept, the cities for his **horses** and chariots, and everything
	10.25	of silver and gold, robes, weapons, spices, **horses,**
	10.26	hundred chariots and twelve thousand cavalry **horses.**
	10.28	controlled the export of **horses** from Musri and Cilicia,
	10.29	Hittite and Syrian kings with **horses** and chariots, selling
	10.29	for 600 pieces of silver each and **horses** for 150 each.
	18. 5	we can find enough grass to keep the **horses** and mules alive.
	20. 1	thirty-two other rulers with their **horses** and chariots,
	20.20	but Benhadad escaped on **horseback,** accompanied by some of the
	20.21	to the field, captured the **horses** and chariots, and inflicted
	20.25	deserted you, with the same number of **horses** and chariots.
2 Kgs	2.11	chariot of fire pulled by **horses** of fire came between them,
	3. 7	am at your disposal, and so are my men and my **horses.**
	5. 9	So Naaman went with his **horses** and chariot, and stopped at
	6.14	he sent a large force there with **horses** and chariots.
	6.15	Syrian troops with their **horses** and chariots surrounding the
	6.17	hillside covered with **horses** and chariots of fire all round
	7. 6	large army, with **horses** and chariots, and the Syrians thought
	7. 7	abandoning their tents, **horses,** and donkeys, and leaving
	7.10	the **horses** and donkeys have not been untied, and the tents
	7.13	men with five of the **horses** that are left, so that we
	9.33	her down, and her blood spattered the wall and the **horses.**
	9.33	Jehu drove his **horses** and chariot over her body, [34] entered
	10. 2	and you have at your disposal chariots, **horses,** weapons,
	14.20	back to Jerusalem on a **horse** and was buried in the royal
	18.23	will give you two thousand **horses** if you can find that many
	23.11	He also removed the **horses** that the kings of Judah had
1 Chr	18. 4	He kept enough **horses** for a hundred chariots and crippled all
2 Chr	1.14	of fourteen hundred chariots and twelve thousand cavalry **horses.**
	1.16	agents controlled the export of **horses** from Musri and Cilicia,
	1.17	Hittite and Syrian kings with **horses** and chariots, selling
	1.17	of silver each and **horses** for a hundred and fifty each.
	8. 6	and the cities where his **horses** and chariots were stationed.
	9.24	silver and gold, robes, weapons, spices, **horses,** and mules.
	9.25	stalls for his chariots and **horses,**
	9.25	and had twelve thousand cavalry **horses.**
	9.28	Solomon imported **horses** from Musri and from every other
	25.28	carried to Jerusalem on a **horse,** and he was buried in the
Ezra	2.64	**Horses** - 736
Neh	7.66	**Horses** - 736
Esth	6. 7	Order a royal ornament to be put on your own **horse.**
	6. 9	and lead him, mounted on the **horse,** through the city square.
	6.10	robes and the **horse,** and provide these honours for Mordecai
	6.11	got the robes and the **horse,** and he put the robes on
	6.11	Mordecai got on the **horse,** and Haman led him through the
	8.10	delivered by riders mounted on fast **horses** from the royal
	8.14	the riders mounted royal **horses** and rode off at top speed.
Job	39.18	she begins to run, she can laugh at any **horse** and rider.
	39.19	it you, Job, who made **horses** so strong and gave them their

Job 39.24 Trembling with excitement, the **horses** race ahead;
Ps 20. 7 and others in their **horses,** but we trust in the power
32. 9 Don't be stupid like a **horse** or a mule, which must be
33.17 **War-horses** are useless for victory;
76. 6 O God of Jacob, the **horses** and their riders fell dead.
147.10 pleasure is not in strong **horses,** nor his delight in brave
Prov 21.31 You can get **horses** ready for battle, but it is the Lord
26. 3 You have to whip a **horse,** you have to bridle a donkey,
Ecc 10. 7 I have seen slaves on **horseback** while noblemen go on foot
Is 2. 7 Their land is full of **horses,** and there is no end to
5.28 **horses'** hooves are as hard as flint, and their chariot-wheels
21. 7 he sees men coming on **horseback,** two by two, and men riding
21. 9 Men on **horseback,** two by two.
22. 6 land of Elam came riding on **horseback,** armed with bows
22. 7 soldiers on **horseback** stood in front of Jerusalem's gates.
30.16 you plan to escape from your enemies by riding fast **horses.**
30.16 You think your **horses** are fast enough, but those who pursue
31. 1 relying on Egypt's vast military strength—**horses,** chariots,
31. 3 Their **horses** are not supernatural.
36. 8 will give you two thousand **horses** if you can find that many
43.17 mighty army to destruction, an army of chariots and **horses.**
63.12 they were as sure-footed as wild **horses,** and never stumbled.
66.20 sacred hill in Jerusalem on **horses,** mules, and camels,
Jer 4.13 are like a whirlwind, and his **horses** are faster than eagles.
6.23 They sound like the roaring sea, as they ride their **horses.**
8. 6 on going his own way, like a **horse** rushing into battle.
8.16 we hear the snorting of their **horses.**
8.16 The whole land trembles when their **horses** neigh.
12. 5 get tired racing against men, how can you race against **horses?**
17.25 ride in chariots and on **horses,** and the city of Jerusalem
22. 4 through the gates of this palace in chariots and on **horses.**
46. 4 Harness your **horses** and mount them!
46. 9 Command the **horses** to go and the chariots to roll!
47. 3 hear the hoof beats of **horses,** the clatter of chariots,
50.11 corn or like a neighing **horse,** [12]but your own great city
50.37 Destroy its **horses** and chariots!
50.42 They sound like the roaring sea, as they ride their **horses.**
51.21 to shatter **horses** and riders, to shatter chariots and
51.23 to slaughter ploughmen and their **horses,** to crush rulers
51.27 Bring up the **horses** like a swarm of locusts.
Ezek 17.15 and sent agents to Egypt to get **horses** and a large army.
26. 7 with a huge army, with **horses** and chariots and with cavalry.
26.10 The clouds of dust raised by their **horses** will cover you.
26.10 The noise of their **horses** pulling wagons and chariots will
27.14 You sold your goods for **draught-horses,**
27.14 **war-horses,** and mules
38. 4 His army, with its **horses** and uniformed riders, is enormous,
38.15 army of soldiers from many nations, all of them on **horseback.**
39.20 all they can hold of **horses** and their riders and of soldiers
Dan 11.40 fight back with all his power, using chariots, **horses,**
Hos 1. 7 with swords or bows and arrows or with **horses** and horsemen."
14. 3 Assyria can never save us, and **war-horses** cannot protect us.
Joel 2. 4 They look like **horses;**
2. 4 they run like **war-horses.**
Amos 2.15 away, and men on **horses** will not escape with their lives.
4.10 I killed your young men in battle and took your **horses** away.
6.12 Do **horses** gallop on rocks?
Mic 1.13 You that live in Lachish, hitch the **horses** to the chariots.
5.10 I will take away your **horses** and destroy your chariots.
Nah 2. 3 Their **horses** prance!
3. 2 the rattle of wheels, the gallop of **horses,** the jolting of
Hab 1. 8 "Their **horses** are faster than leopards, fiercer than hungry
1. 8 their **horses** paw the ground.
3.15 trampled the sea with your **horses,** and the mighty waters
Hag 2.22 the **horses** will die, and their riders will kill one another.
Zech 1. 8 I saw an angel of the Lord riding a red **horse.**
1. 8 and behind him were other **horses**—red, dappled, and white.
1. 9 I asked him, "Sir, what do these **horses** mean?"
6. 2 chariot was pulled by red **horses,** the second by black horses,
6. 3 the third by white horses, and the fourth by dappled **horses.**
6. 6 chariot pulled by the black **horses** was going north to Babylonia,
6. 6 the white **horses** were going to the west,
6. 6 and the dappled **horses** were going to the country in
6. 7 As the dappled **horses** came out, they were impatient to go
6. 8 cried out to me, "The **horses** that went north to Babylonia
9.10 remove the war-chariots from Israel and take the **horses** from
10. 3 They will be my powerful **war-horses.**
12. 4 I will terrify all their **horses** and make all their riders go
12. 4 of Judah, but I will make the **horses** of their enemies blind.
14.15 will also fall on the **horses,** the mules, the camels, and the
14.20 harness bells of the **horses** will be inscribed with the words
Acts 23.24 Provide some **horses** for Paul to ride and get him safely
Jas 3. 3 into the mouth of a **horse** to make it obey us, and
Rev 6. 2 I looked, and there was a white **horse.**
6. 4 Another **horse** came out, a red one.
6. 5 I looked, and there was a black **horse.**
6. 8 I looked, and there was a pale-coloured **horse.**
9. 7 The locusts looked like **horses** ready for battle;
9. 9 like the noise of many **horse-drawn** chariots rushing into battle.
9.17 And in my vision I saw the **horses** and their riders:
9.17 The **horses'** heads were like lions' heads, and from their mouths
9.18 the smoke, and the sulphur coming out of the **horses'** mouths.
9.19 For the power of the **horses** is in their mouths and also
18.13 cattle and sheep, **horses** and carriages, slaves, and even human
19.11 Then I saw heaven open, and there was a white **horse.**
19.14 riding on white **horses** and dressed in clean white linen.
19.18 and soldiers, the flesh of **horses** and their riders, the
19.19 the one who was riding the **horse** and against his army.
19.21 out of the mouth of the one who was riding the **horse;**

HORSE GATE

2 Kgs 11.16 to the palace, and there at the **Horse Gate** they killed her.
2 Chr 23.15 to the palace, and there at the **Horse Gate** they killed her.
Neh 3.28 going north from the **Horse Gate,** each one building in front
Jer 31.40 Kidron as far as the **Horse Gate** to the east,

HORSEMAN

1 Sam 13. 5 war chariots, six thousand **horsemen,** and as many soldiers as
2 Sam 1. 6 that the chariots and **horsemen** of the enemy were closing in
8. 4 captured seventeen hundred of his **horsemen** and twenty thousand
10.18 chariot drivers and forty thousand **horsemen,** and they wounded
1 Kgs 9.22 soldiers, officers, commanders, chariot captains, and **horsemen.**
2 Kgs 9.17 replied, "Send a **horseman** to find out if they are friends
13. 7 armed forces left except fifty **horsemen,** ten chariots,
18.24 yet you expect the Egyptians to send you chariots and **horsemen!**
1 Chr 18. 4 thousand of his chariots, seven thousand **horsemen,** and twenty
2 Chr 8. 9 served as soldiers, officers, chariot commanders, and **horsemen.**
12. 3 twelve hundred chariots, sixty thousand **horsemen,**
16. 8 the Libyans have large armies with many chariots and **horsemen?**
Neh 2. 9 officers and a troop of **horsemen** with me, and I made the
Jer 4.29 At the noise of the **horsemen** and bowmen everyone will run
Ezek 26.11 Their **horsemen** will storm through your streets, killing
Hos 1. 7 swords or bows and arrows or with horses and **horsemen."**
Nah 3. 3 **Horsemen** charge, swords flash, spears gleam!
Hab 1. 8 Their **horsemen** come riding from distant lands;
Zech 10. 5 Lord is with them, and they will defeat even the enemy **horsemen.**
Acts 23.23 Caesarea, together with seventy **horsemen** and two hundred spearmen,
23.32 to the fort and left the **horsemen** to go on with him.

HORSEWHIP see WHIP

HOSHEA (1)

Last king of the n. kingdom (Israel).

2 Kgs 15.30 Uzziah as king of Judah, **Hoshea** son of Elah plotted against
17. 1 of King Ahaz of Judah, **Hoshea** son of Elah became king of
17. 3 **Hoshea** surrendered to Shalmaneser and paid him tribute every
17. 4 But one year **Hoshea** sent messengers to So, king of Egypt,
17. 4 Shalmaneser learnt of this, he had **Hoshea** arrested and put in
17. 6 year of the reign of **Hoshea,** the Assyrian emperor captured
18. 1 year of the reign of **Hoshea** son of Elah as king of
18. 9 the seventh year of King **Hoshea's** reign over Israel—Emperor
18.10 year of Hezekiah's reign, and the ninth year of **Hoshea's** reign.

HOSPITALITY

1 Kgs 13.16 answered, "I can't go home with you or accept your **hospitality.**
13.18 me to take you home with me and offer you my **hospitality."**
Tit 1. 8 He must be **hospitable** and love what is good.

HOST

Lk 14. 9 has been invited, [9]and your **host,** who invited both of you,
14.10 lowest place, so that your **host** will come to you and say,
14.12 Then Jesus said to his **host,** "When you give a lunch or
Rom 16.23 My **host** Gaius, in whose house the church meets, sends

AV HOST see ARMY

HOSTAGE

2 Kgs 14.14 He also took **hostages** with him.
2 Chr 25.24 He also took **hostages** with him.
Ezek 17.13 He took important men as **hostages** [14]to keep the nation from

HOSTILE

Judg 9.23 the men of Shechem **hostile** to each other, and they rebelled
2 Sam 22.27 to those who are pure, but **hostile** to those who are wicked.
Esth 2.21 the king's rooms, became **hostile** to King Xerxes and plotted
Ps 18.26 to those who are pure, but **hostile** to those who are wicked.
Is 33.21 and streams, but **hostile** ships will not sail on them.
1 Thes 2.15 How **hostile** they are to everyone!

AV HOSTS, LORD OF see ALMIGHTY

HOT

[RED-HOT]

Gen 18. 1 of his tent during the **hottest** part of the day, [2]he looked
36.24 the Anah who found the **hot** springs in the wilderness when he
Ex 16.21 and when the sun grew **hot,** what was left on the ground
2 Kgs 19.26 weeds growing on a roof when the **hot** east wind blasts them.
Ps 120. 4 With a soldier's sharp arrows, with **red-hot** charcoal!
140.10 May **red-hot** coals fall on them;
Prov 6.28 Can you walk on **hot** coals without burning your feet?
Is 11.15 and he will bring a **hot** wind to dry up the Euphrates,
25. 5 the shouts of cruel men, as a cloud cools a **hot** day.
30.14 big enough to pick up **hot** coals with, or to scoop water
37.27 weeds growing on a roof when the **hot** east wind blasts them.
47.14 the flames will be too **hot** for them, not a cosy fire
48.21 led his people through a **hot,** dry desert, they did not
64. 2 They would tremble like water boiling over a **hot** fire.
Jer 17. 8 It is not afraid when **hot** weather comes, because its leaves

Lam 5.10 burn with fever, until our skin is as **hot** as an oven.
Ezek 24.11 the empty bronze pot on the coals and let it get **red-hot.**
Dan 3.19 his men to heat the furnace seven times **hotter** than usual.
3.22 furnace to be made extremely **hot,** the flames burnt up the
Hos 13.15 weeds, I will send a **hot** east wind from the desert, and
Jon 4. 8 had risen, God sent a **hot** east wind, and Jonah was about
Mt 20.12 whole day's work in the **hot** sun—yet you paid them the
Lk 12.55 you say that it is going to get **hot**—and it does.
2 Cor 12.20 will find quarrelling and jealousy, **hot** tempers and selfishness,
1 Tim 4. 2 whose consciences are dead, as if burnt with a **hot** iron.
Rev 3.15 I know that you are neither cold nor **hot.**
3.16 because you are lukewarm, neither **hot** nor cold, I am going

HOUR

1 Kgs 18.36 At the **hour** of the afternoon sacrifice the prophet Elijah
Neh 9. 3 For about three **hours** the Law of the Lord their God was
9. 3 the next three **hours** they confessed their sins and worshipped
Job 7. 4 When I lie down to sleep, the **hours** drag;
11.17 and life's darkest **hours** will shine like the dawn.
27. 8 for godless men in the **hour** when God demands their life?
35.10 God, their Creator, who gives them hope in their darkest **hours.**
Ps 90. 4 like yesterday, already gone, like a short **hour** in the night.
Dan 11.40 the king of Syria's final **hour** has almost come,
Mt 20.12 hired last worked only one **hour,'** they said, 'while we put
24.36 however, when that day and **hour** will come—neither the angels
24.44 Man will come at an **hour** when you are not expecting him.
25.13 guard, then, because you do not know the day or the **hour.**
26.18 'The Teacher says, My **hour** has come;
26.40 were not able to keep watch with me even for one **hour?**
26.45 The **hour** has come for the Son of Man to be handed
27.45 country was covered with darkness, which lasted for three **hours.**
Mk 13.32 however, when that day or **hour** will come—neither the angels
14.37 Weren't you able to stay awake even for one **hour?"**
14.41 The **hour** has come!
15.33 country was covered with darkness, which lasted for three **hours.**
Lk 1.10 people outside prayed during the **hour** when the incense was burnt.
2.38 That very same **hour** she arrived and gave thanks to God
12.40 Man will come at an **hour** when you are not expecting him."
22.14 When the **hour** came, Jesus took his place at the table
22.53 But this is your **hour** to act, when the power of darkness
22.59 And about an **hour** later another man insisted strongly,
Jn 4.53 it was at that very **hour** when Jesus had told him, "Your
7.30 laid a hand on him, because his **hour** had not yet come.
8.20 And no one arrested him, because his **hour** had not come.
11. 9 Jesus said, "A day has twelve **hours,** hasn't it?
12.23 Jesus answered them, "The **hour** has now come for the Son
12.27 Shall I say, 'Father, do not let this **hour** come upon me'?
12.27 I came—so that I might go through this **hour** of suffering.
13. 1 Jesus knew that the **hour** had come for him to leave this
16.21 birth, she is sad because her **hour** of suffering has come;
17. 1 looked up to heaven and said, "Father, the **hour** has come.
Acts 3. 1 Temple at three o'clock in the afternoon, the **hour** for prayer.
5. 7 About three **hours** later his wife, not knowing what had happened,
16.33 At that very **hour** of the night the jailer took them and
19.34 Jew, they all shouted together the same thing for two **hours:**
1 Cor 15.30 for us—why would we run the risk of danger every **hour?**
2 Cor 6. 2 This is the **hour** to receive God's favour;
11.25 three shipwrecks, and once I spent twenty-four **hours** in the water.
2 Tim 4. 6 As for me, the **hour** has come for me to be sacrificed;
1 Jn 2. 9 yet hates his brother, is in the darkness to this very **hour.**
Rev 8. 1 seal, there was silence in heaven for about half an **hour.**
9.15 for this very **hour** of this very day of this very month
17.12 authority to rule as kings for one **hour** with the beast.
18.10 In just one **hour** you have been punished!"
18.17 And in one **hour** she has lost all this wealth!"
18.19 And in one **hour** she has lost everything!"

HOUSE

Gen 19. 2 Please come to my **house.**
19. 3 on urging them, and finally they went with him to his **house.**
19. 4 guests went to bed, the men of Sodom surrounded the **house.**
19. 8 they are guests in my **house,** and I must protect them."
19.10 pulled Lot back into the **house,** and shut the door.
20.13 sent me from my father's **house** into foreign lands, I said to
24.23 Is there room in his **house** for my men and me to
24.25 straw and fodder at our **house,** and there is a place for
24.28 girl ran to her mother's **house** and told the whole story.
24.31 ready for you in my **house,** and there is a place for
24.32 the man went into the **house,** and Laban unloaded the camels
27.15 clothes, which she kept in the **house,** and put them on Jacob.
28.17 It must be the **house** of God;
29.13 hugged him and kissed him, and brought him into the **house.**
33.17 Sukkoth, where he built a **house** for himself and shelters for
34.26 Then they took Dinah from Shechem's **house** and left.
34.29 women and children, and carried off everything in the **houses.**
36. 6 all the people of his **house,** together with all his livestock
38.11 Tamar, "Return to your father's **house** and remain a widow
39. 2 He lived in the **house** of his Egyptian master, [3] who saw that
39. 4 he put him in charge of his **house** and everything he owned.
39. 5 and everything that he had in his **house** and in his fields.
39. 8 concern himself with anything in the **house,** because I am here.
39. 9 as much authority in this **house** as he has, and he has
39.11 when Joseph went into the **house** to do his work,
39.11 none of the **house** servants was there.
39.13 had run out of the **house,** [14] she called to her house
39.14 Hebrew that my husband brought to the **house** is insulting us.
40. 3 them in prison in the **house** of the captain of the guard,
41.10 us in prison in the **house** of the captain of the guard.
Gen 43.16 in charge of his **house,** "Take these men to my house.
43.17 he was commanded and took the brothers to Joseph's **house.**
43.18 were being brought to the **house,** they were afraid and thought,
43.19 at the door of the **house,** they said to the servant in
43.24 The servant took the brothers into the **house.**
43.26 took the gifts into the **house** to him and bowed down to
44. 1 servant in charge of his **house,** "Fill the men's sacks with
44. 4 the servant in charge of his **house,** "Hurry after those men.
44. 8 Why then should we steal silver or gold from your master's **house?**
44.14 Judah and his brothers came to Joseph's **house,** he was still
Ex 3.22 Egyptian woman living in her **house** and will ask for clothing
8. 3 your bedroom, your bed, the **houses** of your officials and your
8.13 the frogs in the **houses,** the courtyards, and the fields died.
8.21 The **houses** of the Egyptians will be full of flies, and the
8.24 flies into the king's palace and the **houses** of his officials.
10. 6 fill your palaces and the **houses** of all your officials
10.23 see each other, and no one left his **house** during that time.
12. 7 above the doors of the **houses** in which the animals are to
12.13 will be a sign to mark the **houses** in which you live.
12.15 all the yeast in your **houses,** for if anyone during those
12.19 must be found in your **houses,** for if anyone, native-born or
12.22 on the door-posts and the beam above the door of your **house.**
12.22 Not one of you is to leave the **house** until morning.
12.23 not let the Angel of Death enter your **houses** and kill you.
12.27 because he passed over the **houses** of the Israelites in Egypt.
12.46 meal must be eaten in the **house** in which it was prepared;
20.17 "Do not desire another man's **house;**
22. 2 is caught breaking into a **house** at night and is killed, the
22. 7 they are stolen from his **house,** the thief, if he is found,
23.19 "Each year bring to the **house** of the Lord your God the
34.26 "Each year bring to the **house** of the Lord the first
Lev 14.34 regulations about **houses** affected by spreading mildew.
14.34 has sent mildew on his **house,** then he must go and tell
14.36 be moved out of the **house** before he goes to examine the
14.36 otherwise everything in the **house** will be declared unclean.
14.36 Then he shall go to the **house** [37] and examine the mildew.
14.38 wall, [38] he shall leave the **house** and lock it up for seven
14.43 breaks out again in the **house** after the stones have been
14.43 been removed and the **house** has been scraped and plastered,
14.44 If it has spread, the **house** is unclean.
14.46 Anyone who enters the **house** while it is locked up will
14.47 who lies down or eats in the **house** must wash his clothes.
14.48 has not reappeared after the **house** has been replastered,
14.48 shall pronounce the **house** ritually clean, because the mildew
14.49 To purify the **house,** he shall take two birds,
14.51 And he shall sprinkle the **house** seven times.
14.52 he shall purify the **house** with the bird's blood, the fresh
14.53 ritual of purification for the **house,** and it will be ritually
14.55 and about mildew in clothes or **houses.**
18. 9 or not she was brought up in the same **house** with you.
21. 3 daughter, brother, [3] or unmarried sister living in his **house.**
21.11 it and entering a **house** where there is a dead person,
22.13 to live in her father's **house** as a dependant may eat the
25.29 If a man sells a **house** in a walled city, he has
25.30 of repurchase, and the **house** becomes the permanent property
25.31 **houses** in unwalled villages are to be treated like fields;
25.33 If a **house** in one of these cities is sold by a
25.33 Year of Restoration, because the **houses** which the Levites own
27.14 When someone dedicates his **house** to the Lord, the priest
27.15 the one who dedicated the **house** wishes to buy it back, he
Num 30. 3 still living in her father's **house** makes a vow to give
30.16 unmarried woman living in her father's **house** or by a married
Deut 5.21 do not desire his **house,** his land, his slaves, his cattle,
6. 9 Write them on the door-posts of your **houses** and on your
6.11 The **houses** will be full of good things which you did not
8.12 eat and have built good **houses** to live in [13] and when your
11.20 Write them on the door-posts of your **houses** and on your
15.17 him to the door of your **house** and there pierce his ear;
16. 4 one in your land is to have any yeast in his **house;**
19. 1 have taken their cities and **houses** and settled there,
20. 5 who has just built a **house,** but has not yet dedicated it?
20. 5 is killed in battle, someone else will dedicate his **house.**
22. 8 "When you build a new **house,** be sure to put a railing
22.21 the entrance of her father's **house,** where the men of her
22.21 was married, while she was still living in her father's **house.**
23.18 may be brought into the **house** of the Lord your God in
24.10 do not go into his **house** to get the garment he is
26.13 the Lord, 'None of the sacred tithe is left in my **house;**
26.14 any of it out of my **house** when I was ritually unclean;
28.30 You will build a **house**—but never live in it.
Josh 2. 1 to spend the night in the **house** of a prostitute named Rahab.
2. 3 "The men in your **house** have come to spy out the whole
2. 4 men did come to my **house,"** she answered, "but I don't know
2.15 Rahab lived in a **house** built into the city wall, so she
2.18 and all your father's family together in your **house.**
2.19 anyone goes out of the **house,** his death will be his own
2.19 but if anyone in the **house** with you is harmed, then we
6.22 "Go into the prostitute's **house** and bring her and her family
Judg 6.19 So Gideon went into his **house** and cooked a young goat
9. 5 He went to his father's **house** at Ophrah, and there on the
11. 7 me so much that you forced me to leave my father's **house.**
11.31 that comes out of my **house** to meet me, when I come
12. 1 We'll burn the **house** down over your head!"
14.10 father went to the girl's **house,** and Samson gave a banquet
14.15 we'll set fire to your father's **house** and burn you with it.
15. 6 burnt the woman to death and burnt down her father's **house.**
17. 4 It was placed in Micah's **house.**
17. 8 he came to Micah's **house** in the hill-country of Ephraim.
18. 2 in the hill-country of Ephraim, they stayed at Micah's **house.**
18.13 and came to Micah's **house** in the hill-country of Ephraim.
18.14 here in one of these **houses** there is a wooden idol covered

Judg	18.15	they went into Micah's **house,** where the young Levite lived,
	18.17	went straight on into the **house** and took the wooden idol
	18.18	the men went into Micah's **house** and took the sacred objects,
	18.22	good distance from the **house** when Micah called his neighbours
	19. 2	went back to her father's **house** in Bethlehem, and stayed
	19. 3	the Levite into the **house,** and when her father saw him,
	19.22	from the town surrounded the **house** and started beating on the
	19.26	at the door of the old man's **house,** where her husband was.
	19.27	lying in front of the **house** with her hands reaching for the
	19.29	When he arrived, he went into the **house** and got a knife.
	20. 5	Gibeah came to attack me and surrounded the **house** at night.
	20. 8	he lives in a tent or in a **house,** will go home.
1 Sam	1. 7	whenever they went to the **house** of the Lord, Peninnah would
	1. 9	finished their meal in the **house** of the Lord at Shiloh,
	1.22	will take him to the **house** of the Lord, where he will
	1.24	young as he was, to the **house** of the Lord at Shiloh.
	3.15	got up and opened the doors of the **house** of the Lord.
	7. 1	and took it to the **house** of a man named Abinadab, who
	18.10	control of Saul, and he raved in his **house** like a madman.
	19. 9	He was sitting in his **house** with his spear in his hand,
	19.11	men to watch David's **house** and kill him the next morning.
	21.15	me with his daft actions right here in my own **house?"**
2 Sam	4. 5	Baanah set out for Ishbosheth's **house** and arrived there about
	4.11	evil men who murder an innocent man asleep in his own **house!**
	5. 8	"The blind and the crippled cannot enter the Lord's **house.")**
	6.10	and took it to the **house** of Obed Edom, a native of
	6.12	the Covenant Box from Obed's **house** to take it to Jerusalem
	7. 2	I am living in a **house** built of cedar, but God's Covenant
	12.20	Then he went and worshipped in the **house** of the Lord.
	13. 7	"Go to Amnon's **house** and prepare some food for him."
	13.20	So Tamar lived in Absalom's **house,** sad and lonely.
	14.24	Absalom lived in his own **house** and did not appear before the
	14.31	Joab went to Absalom's **house** and demanded,
	15.17	men were leaving the city, they stopped at the last **house.**
	17.18	off to hide in the **house** of a certain man in Bahurim.
	17.18	had a well near his **house,** and they got down into it.
	17.20	Absalom's officials came to the **house** and asked the woman,
	19. 5	Joab went to the king's **house** and said to him, "Today
1 Kgs	2.36	said to him, "Build a **house** for yourself here in Jerusalem.
	3.17	I live in the same **house,** and I gave birth to a
	3.18	of us were there in the **house**—no one else was present.
	7. 8	built the same kind of **house** for his wife, the daughter of
	11.18	gave Hadad some land and a **house** and provided him with food.
	16.10	Zimri entered the **house,** assassinated Elah,
	20.30	the city and took refuge in the back room of a **house.**
2 Kgs	4. 4	sons go into the **house,** close the door, and start pouring
	4. 5	woman went into her **house** with her sons, closed the door,
	4. 8	he went to Shunem he would have his meals at her **house.**
	4.29	Go straight to the **house** and hold my stick over the boy."
	5. 9	and chariot, and stopped at the entrance to Elisha's **house.**
	5.24	Gehazi took the two bags and carried them into the **house.**
	5.25	He went back into the **house,** and Elisha asked him,
	6.15	up, went out of the **house,** and saw the Syrian troops with
	8. 3	king to ask for her **house** and her land to be restored
	12.20	Shomer, killed him at the **house** built on the land that was
	15. 5	He lived in a **house** on his own, relieved of all duties,
	25. 9	Temple, the palace, and the **houses** of all the important people
1 Chr	13. 7	At Abinadab's **house** they brought out the Covenant Box
	13.13	he left it at the **house** of a man named Obed Edom,
	15. 1	For his own use, David built **houses** in David's City.
	15.25	military commanders went to the **house** of Obed Edom to fetch
	17. 1	I am living in a **house** built of cedar, but the Lord's
2 Chr	8.11	of Egypt, from David's City to a **house** he built for her.
	26.21	he lived in his own **house,** relieved of all duties, while his
Ezra	6.11	be torn out of his **house,** sharpened at one end, and then
	6.11	And his **house** is to be made a rubbish heap.
Neh	2. 8	the city walls, and for the **house** I was to live in.
	3.10	Harumaph built the next section, which was near his own **house.**
	3.20	as the entrance to the **house** of the High Priest Eliashib;
	3.21	the next section, up to the far end of Eliashib's **house.**
	3.23	built the next section, which was in front of their **houses;**
	3.23	built the next section, which was in front of his **house;**
	3.24	next section, from Azariah's **house** to the corner of the wall;
	3.28	Horse Gate, each one building in front of his own **house.**
	3.29	Immer built the next section, which was in front of his **house.**
	3.30	Berechiah built the next section, which was in front of his **house.**
	5. 3	fields and vineyards and **houses** to get enough corn to keep
	5.11	give them back their fields, vineyards, olive-groves, and **houses**
	5.13	"God will take away your **houses** and everything you own,
	6.10	and grandson of Mehetabel, who was unable to leave his **house.**
	7. 3	and others to patrol the area round their own **houses.**
	7. 4	were living in it, and not many **houses** had been built yet.
	8.16	the flat roofs of their **houses,** in their yards, in the
	9.25	captured fortified cities, fertile land, **houses** full of wealth,
	10.39	We will not neglect the **house** of our God.
Esth	5.10	invited his friends to his **house** and asked his wife Zeresh
	7. 9	build a gallows at his **house** so that he could hang Mordecai,
Job	1.19	It blew the **house** down and killed them all.
	3.15	like princes who filled their **houses** with gold and silver,
	15.28	who captured cities and seized **houses** whose owners had fled,
	15.28	but war will destroy those cities and **houses.**
	19.15	Those who were guests in my **house** have forgotten me;
	20.19	neglected the poor and seized **houses** someone else had built.
	21.28	You ask, "Where is the **house** of the great man now, the
	22.23	an end to all the evil that is done in your **house.**
	24.16	At night thieves break into **houses,** but by day they hide
	27.18	The wicked build **houses** like a spider's web or like
	42.11	friends came to visit him and feasted with him in his **house.**
Ps	5. 7	But because of your great love I can come into your **house;**
	23. 6	and your **house** will be my home as long as I live.
	26. 8	I love the **house** where you live, O Lord, the place where
Ps	27. 4	to live in the Lord's **house** all my life, to marvel there
	42. 4	with the crowds to the **house** of God and led them as
	46. 4	the city of God, to the sacred **house** of the Most High.
	52. 8	But I am like an olive-tree growing in the **house** of God;
	65. 4	good things of your **house,** the blessings of your sacred Temple.
	66.13	I will bring burnt-offerings to your **house;**
	84.10	at the gate of the **house** of my God than live in
	92.13	like trees planted in the **house** of the Lord, that flourish
	101. 2	a pure life in my **house,** [3]and will never tolerate evil.
	122. 1	when they said to me, "Let us go to the Lord's **house."**
	122. 9	For the sake of the **house** of the Lord our God I
	127. 1	Lord does not build the **house,** the work of the builders is
	132. 7	We said, "Let us go to the Lord's **house;**
	135. 2	who stand in the Lord's **house,** in the Temple of our God.
Prov	1.13	find all kinds of riches and fill our **houses** with loot!
	2.18	If you go to her **house,** you are travelling the road to
	7. 6	the window of my **house,** [7]and I saw many inexperienced young
	7. 8	He was passing near her **house** [9]in the evening after it was
	7.27	If you go to her **house,** you are on the way to
	8.21	to those who love me, filling their **houses** with treasures.
	9. 1	Wisdom has built her **house** and made seven pillars for it.
	9.14	at the door of her **house** or on a seat in the
	9.18	die who go to her **house,** that those who have already entered
	14.11	A good man's **house** will still be standing
	14.11	after an evil man's **house** has been destroyed.
	17. 1	mind than to have a banquet in a **house** full of trouble.
	17.13	good with evil, you will never get evil out of your **house.**
	19.14	A man can inherit a **house** and money from his parents,
	21. 9	live on the roof than share the **house** with a nagging wife.
	24.27	Don't build your **house** and establish a home until your
	25.24	live on the roof than share the **house** with a nagging wife.
	26.13	Why doesn't the lazy man ever get out of the **house?**
Ecc	2. 4	I built myself **houses** and planted vineyards.
	10.18	repair his roof, it will leak, and the **house** will fall in.
Song	1.17	be the beams of our **house,** and the cypress-trees the ceiling.
	3. 4	took him to my mother's **house,** to the room where I was
	8. 2	you to my mother's **house,** where you could teach me love.
Is	3.14	have plundered vineyards, and your **houses** are full of what
	5. 8	You buy more **houses** and fields to add to those you already
	5. 9	Almighty say, "All these big, fine **houses** will be empty ruins.
	6.11	ruined and empty—until the **houses** are uninhabited—
	13.16	be battered to death, their **houses** will be looted,
	22. 1	people of the city celebrating on the roofs of the **houses?**
	22. 9	You inspected all the **houses** in Jerusalem and tore some of
	23. 1	its **houses** and its harbour are in ruins.
	24.10	chaos, and people lock themselves in their **houses** for safety.
	26.20	Go into your **houses,** my people, and shut the door behind
	32.13	Weep for all the **houses** where people were happy and for the
	44.13	a man, a handsome human figure, to be placed in his **house.**
	56. 7	give you joy in my **house** of prayer, and accept the
	56. 7	Temple will be called a **house** of prayer for the people of
	58.12	people who rebuilt the walls, who restored the ruined **houses."**
	65.21	People will build **houses** and live in them themselves—
	66. 1	What kind of **house,** then, could you build for me, what kind
Jer	5.27	his cage with birds, they have filled their **houses** with loot.
	6.12	Their **houses** will be given to others, and so will their
	16. 5	"You must not enter a **house** where there is mourning.
	16. 8	"Do not enter a **house** where people are feasting.
	17.22	or carry anything out of their **houses** on the Sabbath.
	18. 2	"Go down to the potter's **house,** where I will give you my
	19.13	The **houses** of Jerusalem, the houses of the kings of Judah,
	19.13	and indeed all the **houses** on whose roofs incense has been
	21.11	message to the royal **house** of Judah, the descendants of David:
	22.13	the man who builds his **house** by injustice and enlarges it by
	22.14	he puts windows in his **house,** panels it with cedar, and
	22.15	better king if you build **houses** of cedar, finer than those
	29. 5	'Build **houses** and settle down.
	29.28	long time and should build **houses,** settle down, plant gardens,
	32.15	of Israel, has said that **houses,** fields, and vineyards will
	32.29	together with the **houses** where people have made me angry
	33. 4	say that the **houses** of Jerusalem and the royal palace
	33. 5	Babylonians, who will fill the **houses** with the corpses of
	35. 7	told us not to build **houses** or farm the land, and not
	35. 9	We do not build **houses** for homes—we live in
	37.15	and locked up in the **house** of Jonathan,
	37.15	the court secretary, whose **house** had been made into a prison.
	37.20	Please do not send me back to the prison in Jonathan's **house.**
	39. 8	the royal palace and the **houses** of the people and tore down
	51.30	The city gates are broken down, and the **houses** are on fire.
	52.13	Temple, the palace, and the **houses** of all the important people
Ezek	3.24	said to me, "Go home and shut yourself up in the **house.**
	7.15	fighting in the streets, and sickness and hunger in the **houses.**
	8. 1	of the exiles from Judah were sitting in my **house** with me.
	11. 3	They say, 'We will soon be building **houses** again.
	12. 5	through the wall of your **house** and take your pack out
	16.41	They will burn your **houses** down and let crowds of women
	23.47	with swords, kill their children, and burn down their **houses.**
	26.12	They will pull down your walls and shatter your luxurious **houses.**
	28.26	They will build **houses** and plant vineyards.
	33.30	meet by the city walls or in the doorways of their **houses.**
	45. 4	It will contain their **houses** and the section of land for the
Dan	2. 5	torn limb from limb and make your **houses** a pile of ruins.
	3.29	limb from limb, and his **house** is to be made a pile
	6.10	an upstairs room of his **house** there were windows that faced
Hos	7. 1	they break into **houses** and steal;
Joel	2. 9	they climb up the **houses** and go in through the windows
Amos	3.15	I will destroy winter **houses** and summer houses.
	3.15	The **houses** decorated with ivory will fall in ruins;
	3.15	every large **house** will be destroyed."
	5.11	live in the fine stone **houses** you build or drink wine from
	6.10	charge of the funeral, will take the body out of the **house.**

Amos 6.10 still left in the **house,** "Is anyone else there with you?"
6.11 Lord gives the command, **houses** large and small will be smashed
9.11 kingdom of David, which is like a **house** fallen into ruins.
Mic 2. 2 when they want **houses,** they take them.
6.10 In the **houses** of evil men are treasures which they got
Zeph 1. 9 and kill in order to fill their master's **house** with loot.
1.13 Their wealth will be looted and their **houses** destroyed.
1.13 will never live in the **houses** they are building or drink
2. 7 their flocks there and sleep in the **houses** of Ashkelon.
Hag 1. 4 living in well-built **houses** while my Temple lies in ruins?
1. 9 while every one of you is busy working on his own **house.**
Zech 5. 4 and it will enter the **house** of every thief
5. 4 and the **house** of everyone who tells lies under
5. 4 It will remain in their **houses** and leave them in ruins."
13. 6 he will answer, 'I got them at a friend's **house.'** "
14. 2 city will be taken, the **houses** looted, and the women raped.
Mt 2.11 They went into the **house,** and when they saw the child
5.15 lampstand, where it gives light for everyone in the **house.**
6. 2 hypocrites do in the **houses of worship** and on the streets.
6. 5 and pray in the **houses of worship** and on the street corners,
7.24 them is like a wise man who built his **house** on rock.
7.25 the rivers overflowed, and the wind blew hard against that **house.**
7.26 them is like a foolish man who built his **house** on sand.
7.27 the wind blew hard against that **house,** and it fell.
8. 8 "I do not deserve to have you come into my **house.**
9.10 a meal in Matthew's **house,** many tax collectors and other outcasts
9.23 Then Jesus went into the official's **house.**
10.12 When you go into a **house,** say, 'Peace be with you.'
10.13 If the people in that **house** welcome you, let your
12. 4 He went into the **house of God,** and he and his men
12.29 break into a strong man's **house** and take away his belongings
12.29 then he can plunder his **house.**
12.44 one, [44]it says to itself, 'I will go back to my **house.'**
12.44 it goes back and finds the **house** empty, clean, and all tidy.
13. 1 same day Jesus left the **house** and went to the lake-side,
13.52 like the owner of a **house** who takes new and old things
17.25 When Peter went into the **house,** Jesus spoke up first,
19.29 And everyone who has left **houses** or brothers or sisters
21.13 that God said, 'My Temple will be called a **house of prayer.'**
24.17 on the roof of his **house** must not take
24.17 the time to go down and get his belongings from the **house.**
24.43 If the owner of a **house** knew the time when the thief
24.43 would stay awake and not let the thief break into his **house.**
26. 6 was in Bethany at the **house** of Simon, a man who had
26.18 and I will celebrate the Passover at your **house.'** "
26.57 Jesus took him to the **house** of Caiaphas, the High Priest,
26.58 as far as the courtyard of the High Priest's **house.**
Mk 1.33 All the people of the town gathered in front of the **house.**
1.35 morning, long before daylight, Jesus got up and left the **house.**
2.15 Later on Jesus was having a meal in Levi's **house.**
2.26 he went into the **house of God** and ate the bread offered
3.27 break into a strong man's **house** and take away his belongings
3.27 then he can plunder his **house.**
3.31 They stood outside the **house** and sent in a message, asking
5.35 some messengers came from Jairus' **house** and told him,
5.38 They arrived at Jairus' **house,** where Jesus saw the confusion
6.10 welcomed, stay in the same **house** until you leave that place.
7.17 crowd and went into the **house,** his disciples asked him to
7.24 He went into a **house** and did not want anyone to know
10.10 they went back into the **house,** the disciples asked Jesus about
10.30 receive a hundred times more **houses,** brothers, sisters, mothers,
11. 4 colt out in the street, tied to the door of a **house.**
11.17 will be called a **house of prayer** for the people of all
13.15 on the roof of his **house** must not lose time
13.15 by going down into the **house** to get anything to take with
13.16 the field must not go back to the **house** for his cloak.
13.35 when the master of the **house** is coming—it might be in
14. 3 was in Bethany at the **house** of Simon, a man who had
14.14 Follow him [14]to the **house** he enters,
14.14 and say to the owner of the **house:**
14.53 taken to the High Priest's **house,** where all the chief priests,
14.54 and went into the courtyard of the High Priest's **house.**
Lk 1.24 Elizabeth became pregnant and did not leave the **house** for five months.
1.40 She went into Zechariah's **house** and greeted Elizabeth.
2.49 Didn't you know that I had to be in my Father's **house?"**
4.38 Jesus left the synagogue and went to Simon's **house.**
5.18 to take him into the **house** and put him in front of
5.29 a big feast in his **house** for Jesus, and among the guests
6. 4 He went into the **house of God,** took the bread offered to
6.48 man who, in building his **house,** dug deep and laid the
6.48 river overflowed and hit that **house** but could not shake it,
6.49 like a man who built his **house** without laying a foundation;
6.49 when the flood hit that **house** it fell at once—and what
7. 6 was not far from the **house** when the officer sent friends to
7. 6 have you come into my **house,** [7]neither do I consider myself
7.10 went back to the officer's **house** and found his servant well.
7.36 him, and Jesus went to his **house** and sat down to eat.
7.37 eating in the Pharisee's **house,** so she brought an alabaster jar
8.49 Jesus was saying this, a messenger came from the official's **house.**
8.51 When he arrived at the **house,** he would not let anyone go
9. 4 welcomed, stay in the same **house** until you leave that town;
10. 5 Whenever you go into a **house,**
10. 5 'Peace be with this **house.'**
10. 7 Stay in that same **house,** eating and drinking whatever they offer
10. 7 Don't move round from one **house** to another.
11. 5 should go to a friend's **house** at midnight and say to him,
11. 6 has just come to my **house,** and I haven't got any food
11.21 weapons ready, guards his own **house,** all his belongings are safe.
11.24 one, it says to itself, 'I will go back to my **house.'**
11.25 So it goes back and finds the **house** clean and tidy.
Lk 11.52 kept the key that opens the door to the **house** of knowledge;
12.39 if the owner of a **house** knew the time when the thief
12.39 would come, he would not let the thief break into his **house.**
13.25 The master of the **house** will get up and close the door;
14.23 and make people come in, so that my **house** will be full.
15. 8 lights a lamp, sweeps her **house,** and looks carefully everywhere
15.25 he came close to the **house,** he heard the music and dancing.
15.28 brother was so angry that he would not go into the **house;**
16.27 send Lazarus to my father's **house,** [28]where I have five brothers.
17.31 on the roof of his **house** must not go down
17.31 into the **house** to get his belongings;
17.31 is out in the field must not go back to the **house.**
19. 5 "Hurry down, Zacchaeus, because I must stay in your **house** today."
19. 9 "Salvation has come to this **house** today, for this man, also,
19.46 that God said, 'My Temple will be called a **house of prayer.'**
22.10 Follow him into the **house** that he enters,
22.11 and say to the owner of the **house:**
22.54 Jesus and took him away into the **house** of the High Priest;
Jn 2.16 Stop making my Father's **house** a market-place!"
2.17 says, "My devotion to your **house,** O God, burns in me like
11.20 she went out to meet him, but Mary stayed in the **house.**
11.31 people who were in the **house** with Mary, comforting her,
12. 3 The sweet smell of the perfume filled the whole **house.**
14. 2 many rooms in my Father's **house,** and I am going to prepare
18.15 courtyard of the High Priest's **house,** [16]while Peter stayed outside
18.28 Jesus was taken from Caiaphas' **house** to the governor's palace.
Acts 1.20 written in the book of Psalms, 'May his **house** become empty;
2. 2 blowing, and it filled the whole **house** where they were sitting.
4.34 Those who owned fields or **houses** would sell them, bring the
7.47 But it was Solomon who built him a **house.**
7.48 the Most High God does not live in **houses** built by men;
7.49 What kind of **house** would you build for me?
8. 3 going from house to **house,** he dragged out the believers,
9.11 Straight Street, and at the **house** of Judas ask for a man
9.17 So Ananias went, entered the **house** where Saul was,
10. 7 Cornelius called two of his **house** servants and a soldier,
10. 9 on the roof of the **house** about noon in order to pray.
10.17 Cornelius had learnt where Simon's **house** was, and they were now
10.22 to invite you to his **house,** so that he could hear what
10.27 he went into the **house,** where he found many people gathered.
10.30 I was praying in my **house** at three o'clock in the afternoon.
11.11 me from Caesarea arrived at the **house** where I was staying.
11.12 me to Caesarea, and we all went into the **house** of Cornelius.
11.13 an angel standing in his **house,** who said to him, 'Send
16.15 the people of her **house** had been baptized, she invited us,
16.15 "Come and stay in my **house** if you have decided that I
16.32 the Lord to him and to all the others in his **house.**
16.34 and Silas up into his **house** and gave them some food to
16.40 Paul and Silas left the prison and went to Lydia's **house.**
17. 7 come to our city, [7]and Jason has kept them in his **house.**
18. 7 went to live in the **house** of a Gentile named Titius Justus,
18. 7 his **house** was next to the synagogue.
19.16 They ran away from his **house,** wounded and with their clothes
21. 8 There we stayed at the **house** of Philip the evangelist, one
21.16 and took us to the **house** of the man we were going
Rom 16. 5 Greetings also to the church that meets in their **house.**
16.23 My host Gaius, in whose **house** the church meets, sends
1 Cor 16.19 church that meets in their **house** send warm Christian greetings.
2 Cor 5. 1 God will have a **house** in heaven for us to live
Col 4.15 Laodicea and to Nympha and the church that meets in her **house.**
1 Tim 5.13 to waste their time in going round from house to **house;**
2 Tim 2.20 In a large **house** there are dishes and bowls of all kinds:
3. 6 of them go into people's **houses** and gain control over weak
Phlm 2 church that meets in your **house,** and our sister Apphia, and
Heb 3. 2 work, just as Moses was faithful in his work in God's **house.**
3. 3 builds a house receives more honour than the **house** itself.
3. 4 Every **house,** of course, is built by someone—and God is the
3. 5 Moses was faithful in God's **house** as a servant, and he
3. 6 But Christ is faithful as the Son in charge of God's **house.**
3. 6 We are his **house** if we keep up our courage and our
10.21 We have a great priest in charge of the **house of God.**
Rev 3.20 I will come into his **house** and eat with him, and he

HOUSE-TOP

Ps 102. 7 I am like a lonely bird on a **house-top.**
129. 6 like grass growing on the **house-tops,** which dries up before
Is 15. 3 the city squares and on the **house-tops** people mourn and cry.
Jer 48.38 all the **house-tops** of Moab and in all its public squares
Mt 10.27 have heard in private you must announce from the **housetops.**
Lk 12. 3 in a closed room will be shouted from the **housetops.**

HOUSEHOLD

Gen 17.23 the other males in his **household,** including the slaves born
31.19 Rachel stole the **household** gods that belonged to her father.
31.30 get back home, but why did you steal my **household** gods?"
31.34 Rachel had taken the **household** gods and put them in
31.35 Laban searched but did not find his **household** gods.
31.37 what **household** article have you found that belongs
39. 5 the Lord blessed the **household** of the Egyptian and everything
Ex 12. 3 must choose either a lamb or a young goat for his **household.**
12.48 you must first circumcise all the males of his **household.**
16.16 as he needs, two litres for each member of his **household."**
Josh 6.17 the prostitute Rahab and her **household** will be spared,
1 Sam 19.13 Then she took the **household** idol, laid it on the bed,
19.16 went inside and found the **household** idol in the bed and the
1 Kgs 4. 7 for the king and his **household,** each man being responsible
2 Kgs 23.24 and fortune-tellers, and all the **household** gods, idols,

Job 8. 6 come and help you and restore your **household** as your reward.
Ecc 2. 7 bought many slaves, and there were slaves born in my **household.**
Is 22.15 the manager of the royal **household,** and say to him,
22.18 You are a disgrace to your master's **household.**
Lk 12.42 in charge, to run the **household** and give the other servants
Acts 7.10 king made Joseph governor over the country and the royal **household.**
1 Tim 3.15 should conduct ourselves in God's **household,** which is the church

HOUSEWIFE see WIFE

HOVER

Is 31. 5 Just as a bird **hovers** over its nest to protect its young,

HOWL

Job 27.23 The wind **howls** at them as they run, frightening them with
30. 7 Out in the wilds they **howled** like animals and huddled
Is 13. 6 **Howl** in pain!
14.31 **Howl** and cry for help, all you Philistine cities!
23. 1 **Howl** with grief, you sailors out on the ocean!
23. 6 **Howl** with grief, you people of Phoenicia!
23.14 **Howl** with grief, you sailors out on the ocean!
Ezek 21.12 **Howl** in grief, mortal man;
Mic 1. 8 I will **howl** like a jackal and wail like an ostrich.

HUB

1 Kgs 7.33 their axles, rims, spokes, and **hubs** were all of bronze.

HUDDLE

Job 24. 8 falls on the mountains, and they **huddle** beside the rocks for
30. 7 howled like animals and **huddled** together under the bushes.

HUG

Gen 29.13 he ran to meet him, **hugged** him and kissed him, and brought
45.14 Benjamin also cried as he **hugged** him.
48.10 brought the boys to him, and he **hugged** them and kissed them.
Acts 20.10 But Paul went down and threw himself on him and **hugged** him.
20.37 They were all crying as they **hugged** him and kissed him good-bye.

HUGE

Gen 19.28 smoke rising from the land, like smoke from a **huge** furnace.
50. 9 it was a **huge** group.
Josh 7.26 They put a **huge** pile of stones over him, which is there
8.29 They covered it with a **huge** pile of stones, which is still
2 Sam 18.17 in the forest, and covered it with a **huge** pile of stones.
23.21 also killed an Egyptian, a **huge** man who was armed with a
1 Kgs 8.65 There was a **huge** crowd of people from as far away as
20.13 said, "The Lord says, 'Don't be afraid of that **huge** army!
20.28 give you victory over their **huge** army, and you and your
1 Chr 11.23 also killed an Egyptian, a **huge** man over two metres tall,
2 Chr 7. 8 There was a **huge** crowd of people from as far away as
13. 8 You have a **huge** army and have with you the gold bull-calves
14.11 your name we have come out to fight against this **huge** army.
16.14 burial, and they built a **huge** bonfire to mourn his death.
17.13 and cities, [13]where supplies were stored in **huge** amounts.
Esth 1.20 made known all over this **huge** empire, every woman will treat
Is 17.12 like the roar of the sea, like the crashing of **huge** waves.
30.33 place was prepared where a **huge** fire will burn the emperor
Ezek 1. 4 Lightning was flashing from a **huge** cloud, and the sky round
1.24 like the noise of a **huge** army, like the voice of Almighty
17. 3 was a giant eagle with beautiful feathers and **huge** wings,
17. 7 was another giant eagle with **huge** wings and thick plumage.
26. 7 from the north with a **huge** army, with horses and chariots
39.17 It will be a **huge** feast on the mountains of Israel, where
Dan 4.10 had a vision of a **huge** tree in the middle of the
7. 3 Four **huge** beasts came up out of the ocean, each one
7. 7 With its **huge** iron teeth it crushed its victims, and then it
7.17 "These four **huge** beasts are four empires which will arise
11. 3 He will rule over a **huge** empire and do whatever he wants.
11.11 to war against the king of Syria and capture his **huge** army.
11.25 will prepare to fight back with a **huge** and powerful army.
11.45 will even set up his **huge** royal tents between the sea and
Rev 8. 8 Something that looked like a **huge** mountain on fire was thrown
12. 3 There was a **huge** red dragon with seven heads and ten horns
12. 9 **huge** dragon was thrown out—that ancient serpent, called the Devil,
16.21 **Huge** hailstones, each weighing as much as fifty kilogrammes,

HUMAN

Gen 1.26 Then God said, "And now we will make **human beings;**
1.27 God created **human beings,** making them to be like himself.
3.20 wife Eve, because she was the mother of all **human beings.**
5. 1 (When God created **human beings,** he made them like himself.
6. 4 who were descendants of **human** women and the heavenly beings.
7.23 destroyed all living beings on the earth—**human beings,** animals,
9. 5 If anyone takes **human** life, he will be punished.
9. 5 I will punish with death any animal that takes a **human** life.
Ex 12.12 killing every first-born male, both **human** and animal,
13.15 first-born male in the land of Egypt, both **human** and animal.
Lev 5. 3 touches anything of **human** origin that is unclean, whatever it
27.28 whether it is a **human being,** an animal, or land.
27.29 even a **human being** who has been unconditionally dedicated
Num 19.16 or if someone touches a **human** bone or a grave, he becomes
Num 19.18 man who had touched the **human** bone or the dead body or
23.19 He is not a **human** who changes his mind.
Deut 4.28 will serve gods made by **human** hands, gods of wood and stone,
5.26 any **human being** ever lived after hearing the living God speak
Josh 10.14 been a day like it, when the Lord obeyed a **human being.**
1 Kgs 8.39 You alone know the thoughts of the **human** heart.
13. 2 sacrifices on you, and he will burn **human** bones on you."
2 Kgs 19.18 at all, only images of wood and stone made by **human** hands.
23.14 the ground where they had stood he covered with **human** bones.
23.20 where they served, and he burnt **human** bones on every altar.
2 Chr 6.30 You alone know the thoughts of the **human** heart.
19. 6 you are not acting on **human** authority, but on the authority
32. 8 He has **human** power, but we have the Lord our God to
32.19 the gods of the other peoples, idols made by **human** hands.
Neh 9. 5 although no **human** praise is great enough."
Job 7. 1 **Human** life is like forced army service,
9.32 If God were **human,** I could answer him;
11. 6 there are things too deep for **human** knowledge.
15. 8 Does **human** wisdom belong to you alone?
20.26 a fire not lit by **human** hands burns him and all his
28. 4 from where anyone lives Or **human** feet ever travel, Men dig
31. 2 How does he repay **human** deeds?
Ps 49. 8 life, [8]because the payment for a **human** life is too great.
56. 4 What can a mere **human being** do to me?
56.11 What can a mere **human being** do to me?
60.11 **human** help is worthless.
108.12 **human** help is worthless.
115. 4 gods are made of silver and gold, formed by **human** hands.
118. 9 to trust in the Lord than to depend on **human** leaders.
135.15 they are formed by **human** hands.
146. 3 Don't put your trust in **human** leaders;
146. 3 no **human being** can save you.
Prov 8.31 happy with the world and pleased with the **human** race.
21.30 **Human** wisdom, brilliance, insight—they are of no help if
27.20 **Human** desires are like the world of the dead—there is
Ecc 3.19 A **human being** is no better off than an animal, because life
Is 2.11 when human pride will be ended and **human** arrogance destroyed.
2.17 **Human** pride will be ended, and human arrogance will be destroyed.
29.13 Their religion is nothing but **human** rules and traditions,
31. 3 The Egyptians are not gods—they are only **human.**
31. 8 Assyria will be destroyed in war, but not by **human** power.
37.19 at all, only images of wood and stone made by **human** hands.
44.11 The people who make idols are **human beings** and nothing more.
44.13 of a man, a handsome **human** figure, to be placed in his
52.14 he was so disfigured that he hardly looked **human.**
66. 3 they kill a bull as a sacrifice or sacrifice a **human being;**
Jer 17. 9 "Who can understand the **human** heart?
Ezek 1. 5 like four living creatures in **human** form, [6]but each of them
1. 8 they each had four **human** hands, one under each wing.
1.10 a **human** face in front, a lion's face at the right, a
4.12 a fire out of dried **human** excrement, bake bread on the fire,
8. 2 I looked up and saw a vision of a fiery **human** form.
10. 8 had what looked like a **human** hand under each of its wings.
10.14 a bull, the second a **human** face, the third the face of
10.21 wings, and what looked like a **human** hand under each wing.
29.11 No **human being** or animal will walk through it.
38.20 large and small, and every **human being** on the face of the
39.15 every time they find a **human** bone, they will put a marker
41.19 **human** face that was turned towards the palm-tree on one side,
44. 2 No **human being** is allowed to use it, because I, the Lord
Dan 2.11 except the gods, and they do not live among **human beings."**
4.16 he will not have a **human** mind, but the mind of an
4.17 Supreme God has power over **human** kingdoms and that he can
4.25 driven away from **human** society and will live with wild
4.25 the Supreme God controls all **human** kingdoms, and that he can
4.32 driven away from **human** society, live with wild animals,
4.32 Supreme God has power over **human** kingdoms and that he can
4.33 Nebuchadnezzar was driven out of **human** society and ate grass
5. 5 a **human** hand appeared and began writing on the plaster wall
5.21 He was driven away from **human** society, and his mind became
5.21 the Supreme God controls all **human** kingdoms and can give them
7. 4 And then a **human** mind was given to it.
7. 8 This horn had **human** eyes and a mouth that was boasting
7.13 vision in the night, I saw what looked like a **human being.**
8.25 but he will be destroyed without the use of any **human** power.
Hos 13. 2 idols of silver, designed by **human** minds, made by human hands.
Zeph 1. 3 destroy everything on earth, [3]all **human beings** and animals,
Mt 16.17 come to you from any **human being,** but it was given to
Jn 1.13 that is, by being born as the children of a **human** father;
1.14 The Word became a **human being** and, full of grace and truth,
3. 6 born physically of **human** parents, but he is born spiritually
5.41 "I am not looking for **human** praise.
8.15 You make judgements in a purely **human** way;
Acts 5.38 planned and done is of **human** origin, it will disappear,
14.15 We ourselves are only **human beings** like you!
Rom 1. 3 as to his **humanity,** he was born a descendant of David;
3.19 in order to stop all **human** excuses and bring the whole world
5.12 spread to the whole **human** race because everyone has sinned.
7. 5 we lived according to our **human nature,** the sinful desires
7.18 good does not live in me—that is, in my **human nature.**
7.25 with my mind, while my **human nature** serves the law of sin.
8. 3 the Law could not do, because **human nature** was weak, God
8. 3 He condemned sin in **human nature** by sending his own Son,
8. 4 live according to the Spirit, and not according to **human nature.**
8. 5 Those who live as their **human nature** tells them to,
8. 5 have their minds controlled by what **human nature** wants.
8. 6 To be controlled by **human nature** results in death;
8. 7 an enemy of God when he is controlled by his **human nature;**
8. 8 Those who obey their **human nature** cannot please God.
8. 9 But you do not live as your **human nature** tells you to;

Rom 8.12 it is not to live as our **human nature** wants us to.
8.13 live according to your **human nature,** you are going to die;
9. 5 and Christ, as a **human being,** belongs to their race.
1 Cor 1.17 without using the language of **human** wisdom, in order to make
1.25 God's foolishness is wiser than **human** wisdom, and
1.25 what seems to be God's weakness is stronger than **human** strength.
1.26 From the **human** point of view few of you were wise or
2. 4 delivered with skilful words of **human** wisdom, but with convincing
2. 5 then, does not rest on **human** wisdom but on God's power.
2.13 speak in words taught by **human** wisdom, but in words taught
4. 3 about being judged by you or by any **human** standard;
15.32 here in Ephesus simply from **human** motives, what have I gained?
15.39 **human beings** have one kind of flesh, animals another,
2 Cor 1.12 by the power of God's grace, and not by **human** wisdom.
3. 3 living God, and not on stone tablets but on **human** hearts.
5.16 No longer, then, do we judge anyone by **human** standards.
5.16 Christ according to **human** standards, we no longer do so.
7.10 But sadness that is merely **human** causes death.
11.18 many who boast for merely **human** reasons, I will do the same.
12. 3 be put into words, things that **human** lips may not speak.
Gal 1.11 brothers, that the gospel I preach is not of **human** origin.
4. 4 as the son of a **human** mother and lived under the Jewish
5.16 and you will not satisfy the desires of the **human nature.**
5.17 For what our **human nature** wants is opposed to what the
5.17 the Spirit wants is opposed to what our **human nature** wants.
5.19 What **human nature** does is quite plain.
5.24 have put to death their **human nature** with all its passions
Eph 6. 5 Slaves, obey your **human** masters with fear and trembling;
6.12 we are not fighting against **human beings** but against the wicked
Phil 2. 7 He became like man and appeared in **human** likeness.
4. 7 peace, which is far beyond **human** understanding, will keep
Col 2. 8 worthless deceit of **human** wisdom, which comes from the teachings
2. 9 lives in Christ, in his **humanity,** [10]and you have been given
2.18 all puffed up by his **human** way of thinking [19]and has
3.22 Slaves, obey your **human** masters in all things,
1 Tim 3.16 He appeared in **human** form, was shown to be right by the
Tit 1.14 Jewish legends and to **human** commandments which come from people
Heb 2.14 Jesus himself became like them and shared their **human nature.**
7.16 made a priest, not by **human** rules and regulations, but through
12. 9 In the case of our **human** fathers, they punished us and we
12.10 Our **human** fathers punished us for a short time, as it
1 Pet 2.13 For the sake of the Lord submit to every **human** authority:
4. 2 earthly lives controlled by God's will and not by **human** desires.
2 Pet 2.16 His donkey spoke with a **human** voice and stopped the prophet's
1 Jn 4. 2 Jesus Christ came as a **human being** has the Spirit who comes
2 Jn 7 do not acknowledge that Jesus Christ came as a **human being.**
Rev 1.13 was what looked like a **human being,** wearing a robe that
14.14 was what looked like a **human being,** with a crown of gold
18.13 and sheep, horses and carriages, slaves, and even **human** lives.
18.22 music of harps and of **human** voices, of players of the flute

HUMBLE
[HUMILITY]

Gen 43.28 "Your **humble** servant, our father, is still alive and well."
Lev 26.41 last, when your descendants are **humbled** and they have paid
Num 12. 3 (Moses was a **humble** man, more humble than anyone else
1 Sam 2. 7 he **humbles** some and makes others great.
2 Sam 22.28 You save those who are **humble,**
22.28 but you **humble** those who are proud.
1 Kgs 8.33 come to this Temple, **humbly** praying to you for forgiveness,
8.35 repent and face this Temple, **humbly** praying to you,
21.29 "Have you noticed how Ahab has **humbled** himself before me?
2 Kgs 22.19 and you repented and **humbled** yourself before me,
2 Chr 6.24 come to this Temple, **humbly** praying to you for forgiveness,
6.26 repent and face this Temple, **humbly** praying to you,
32.26 the people of Jerusalem **humbled** themselves, and so the Lord
33.12 In his suffering he became **humble,** turned to the Lord
33.23 his father, he did not become **humble** and turn to the Lord;
34.27 and you repented and **humbled** yourself before me,
36.12 and did not listen **humbly** to the prophet Jeremiah, who spoke
Ezra 8.21 us all to fast and **humble** ourselves before our God and to
Esth 7. 3 Your Majesty to grant my **humble** request, my wish is that I
Job 5.11 is God who raises the **humble** and gives joy to all who
12.19 he **humbles** priests and men of power.
22.23 Yes, you must **humbly** return to God and put an end to
22.29 God brings down the proud and saves the **humble.**
40.11 pour out your anger and **humble** them.
Ps 14. 6 frustrate the plans of the **humble** man, but the Lord is his
18.27 You save those who are **humble,**
18.27 but you **humble** those who are proud.
25. 9 He leads the **humble** in the right way and teaches them his
37.11 the **humble** will possess the land and enjoy prosperity
51.17 My sacrifice is a **humble** spirit, O God;
51.17 you will not reject a **humble** and repentant heart.
69.10 I **humble** myself by fasting, and people insult me;
76.12 he **humbles** proud princes and terrifies great kings.
147. 6 He raises the **humble,** but crushes the wicked to the ground.
149. 4 he honours the **humble** with victory.
Prov 3.34 for conceited people, but shows favour to those who are **humble.**
14.19 to bow down to the righteous and **humbly** beg their favour.
15.33 You must be **humble** before you can ever receive honours.
16.19 It is better to be **humble** and stay poor than to be
18.12 No one is respected unless he is **humble;**
22. 4 Obey the Lord, be **humble,** and you will get riches, honour,
29.23 but if you are **humble,** you will be respected.
Is 2.12 day the Lord Almighty will **humble** everyone who is powerful,
5.15 will be disgraced, and all who are proud will be **humbled.**
13.11 I will **humble** everyone who is proud and punish everyone who
26. 5 He has **humbled** those who were proud;
29.19 Poor and **humble** people will once again find the happiness
47. 3 they will see you **humbled** and shamed.
49.23 they will **humbly** show their respect for you.
53. 7 "He was treated harshly, but endured it **humbly;**
57.15 live with people who are **humble** and repentant, so that I can
60.22 your smallest and **humblest** family Will become as great as
66. 2 pleased with those who are **humble** and repentant, who fear me
Jer 13.15 Be **humble** and listen to him.
44.10 But to this day you have not **humbled** yourselves.
Dan 4.37 right and just, and he can **humble** anyone who acts proudly."
5.22 you, his son, have not **humbled** yourself, even though you knew
10.12 you decided to **humble** yourself in order to gain understanding.
Mic 6. 8 constant love, and to live in **humble** fellowship with our God.
Zeph 2. 3 to the Lord, all you **humble** people of the land, who obey
2. 3 Do what is right, and **humble** yourselves before the Lord.
3.12 I will leave there a **humble** and lowly people, who will
Zech 9. 6 The Lord says, "I will **humble** all these proud Philistines.
9. 9 triumphant and victorious, but **humble** and riding on a donkey—
10.11 Proud Assyria will be **humbled,** and mighty Egypt will lose her
Mt 5. 5 "Happy are those who are **humble;**
11.29 and learn from me, because I am gentle and **humble** in spirit;
18. 4 is the one who **humbles** himself and becomes like this child.
21. 5 He is **humble** and rides on a donkey and on a colt,
23.12 makes himself great will be **humbled,**
23.12 and whoever **humbles** himself will be made great.
Lk 14.11 makes himself great will be **humbled,**
14.11 and everyone who **humbles** himself will be made great."
18.14 makes himself great will be **humbled,**
18.14 and everyone who **humbles** himself will be made great."
Acts 2.46 eating with glad and **humble** hearts, [47]praising God,
20.19 With all **humility** and many tears I did my work as the
Rom 12.16 Do not be proud, but accept **humble** duties.
2 Cor 11. 7 I **humbled** myself in order to make you important.
Gal 5.23 kindness, goodness, faithfulness, [23]**humility,** and self-control.
Eph 4. 2 Be always **humble,** gentle, and patient.
Phil 2. 3 but be **humble** towards one another, always considering others
2. 8 He was **humble** and walked the path of obedience all the way
Col 2.18 and who insists on false **humility** and the worship of angels.
2.23 and false **humility,** and severe treatment of the body;
3.12 you must clothe yourselves with compassion, kindness, **humility,**
1 Tim 2.11 Women should learn in silence and all **humility.**
5.10 performed **humble** duties for fellow-Christians, helped people in
Heb 5. 7 Because he was **humble** and devoted, God heard him.
Jas 3.13 good life, by his good deeds performed with **humility** and wisdom.
4. 6 "God resists the proud, but gives grace to the **humble."**
4.10 **Humble** yourselves before the Lord, and he will lift you up.
1 Pet 3. 8 as brothers, and be kind and **humble** with one another.
5. 5 you must put on the apron of **humility,** to serve one another;
5. 5 "God resists the proud, but shows favour to the **humble."**
5. 6 **Humble** yourselves, then, under God's mighty hand,

HUMILIATE

Deut 25. 3 more than that would **humiliate** him publicly.
1 Sam 1. 6 her rival, would torment and **humiliate** her, because the Lord
2 Sam 19. 5 "Today you have **humiliated** your men—the men who saved
Neh 6.13 so that they could ruin my reputation and **humiliate** me.
Ps 107.39 God's people were defeated and **humiliated** by cruel oppression
Is 2. 9 Everyone will be **humiliated** and disgraced.
10.33 The proudest and highest of them will be cut down and **humiliated.**
23. 9 pride in what they had done and to **humiliate** their honoured
25.11 swim, but God will **humiliate** them, and their hands will sink
42.17 who call images their gods, will be **humiliated** and disgraced."
44.11 Everyone who worships it will be **humiliated.**
54. 4 you will not be **humiliated.**
Jer 50.12 but your own great city will be **humiliated** and disgraced.
Ezek 36. 6 the way the nations have insulted and **humiliated** them.
36. 7 solemnly promise that the surrounding nations will be **humiliated.**
Mic 3. 7 They will all be **humiliated** because God does not answer them.
Hab 2.15 In your fury you **humiliated** and disgraced your neighbours;
Acts 8.33 He was **humiliated,** and justice was denied him.
2 Cor 12.21 I come my God will **humiliate** me in your presence, and I

HUMILITY see HUMBLE

HUNCHBACK

Lev 21.20 no one who is a **hunchback** or a dwarf;

HUNDRED

Gen 11.10 the flood, when Shem was **100** years old, he had a son,
17.17 a man have a child when he is a **hundred** years old?
21. 5 Abraham was a **hundred** years old when Isaac was born.
21.16 under a bush [16]and sat down about a **hundred** metres away.
26.12 that year he harvested a **hundred** times as much as he had
33.19 of Hamor father of Shechem for a **hundred** pieces of silver.
Ex 18.21 leaders of thousands, **hundreds,** fifties, and tens.
18.25 He appointed them as leaders of thousands, **hundreds,** fifties,
38.27 were used to make the **hundred** bases for the sacred Tent and
Lev 26. 8 be able to defeat a **hundred,**
26. 8 and a **hundred** will be able to defeat ten
Deut 1.15 thousand people, some for a **hundred,** some for fifty, and some
22.19 also to fine him a **hundred** pieces of silver and give the
Josh 24.32 Hamor, the father of Shechem, for a **hundred** pieces of silver.
Judg 7.19 Gideon and his **hundred** men came to the edge of the camp
1 Sam 18.25 is the foreskins of a **hundred** dead Philistines, as revenge on

1 Sam 25.18 kilogrammes of roasted grain, a **hundred** bunches of raisins,
29. 2 out with their units of a **hundred** and of a thousand men;
2 Sam 3.14 I paid a **hundred** Philistine foreskins in order to marry her."
8. 4 kept enough horses for a **hundred** chariots and crippled all
16. 1 loaves of bread, a **hundred** bunches of raisins,
16. 1 a **hundred** bunches of fresh fruit,
18. 1 a thousand and of a **hundred**, and placed officers in command
18. 4 men marched out in units of a thousand and of a **hundred.**
24. 3 people of Israel a **hundred** times more numerous than they are
1 Kgs 3. 4 He had offered **hundreds** of burnt-offerings there in the past.
4.23 twenty pasture-fed cattle, and a **hundred** sheep, besides deer,
7.40 in two rows of a **hundred** each round the design on each
18. 4 Lord's prophets, Obadiah took a **hundred** of them, hid them in
18.13 the Lord I hid a **hundred** of them in caves, in two
2 Kgs 4.43 "Do you think this is enough for a **hundred** men?"
1 Chr 12.14 and others were junior officers in command of a **hundred.**
13. 1 of units of a thousand men and units of a **hundred** men.
18. 4 kept enough horses for a **hundred** chariots and crippled all
21. 3 people of Israel a **hundred** times more numerous than they are
29. 4 have given more than a **hundred** metric tons of the finest
2 Chr 1. 2 and of a **hundred** men, all the government officials, all
3.16 of interwoven chains and one **hundred** bronze pomegranates.
4. 7 They also made a **hundred** gold bowls.
25. 5 of units of a thousand men and units of a **hundred** men.
29.32 They brought seventy bulls, a **hundred** sheep,
Ezra 2.69 2,800 kilogrammes of silver, and **100** robes for priests.
6.17 dedication they offered a **hundred** bulls, two hundred sheep,
8.26 silver - 22 metric tons **100** silver utensils - 70 kilogrammes
Neh 3. 1 far as the Tower of the **Hundred** and the Tower of Hananel.
12.39 of Hananel, and the Tower of the **Hundred,** to the Sheep Gate.
Prov 17.10 rebuke than a fool learns from being beaten a **hundred** times.
Ecc 6. 3 A man may have a **hundred** children and live a long time,
8.12 A sinner may commit a **hundred** crimes and still live.
Is 65.20 Those who live to be a **hundred** will be considered young.
Jer 52.23 each column there were a **hundred** pomegranates in all,
Amos 5. 3 sends out a thousand soldiers, but only a **hundred** return;
5. 3 another city sends out a **hundred,** but only ten come back."
Hag 2.16 find two hundred kilogrammes, but there would be only a **hundred.**
2.16 would go to draw a **hundred** litres of wine from a vat,
Mt 13. 8 a **hundred** grains, others sixty, and others thirty."
13.23 as much as a **hundred,** others sixty, and others thirty."
18.12 man does who has a **hundred** sheep and one of them gets
19.29 my sake, will receive a **hundred** times more and will be given
Mk 4. 8 had thirty grains, others sixty, and others a **hundred."**
4.20 some thirty, some sixty, and some a **hundred."**
6.40 down in rows, in groups of a **hundred** and groups of fifty.
10.30 He will receive a **hundred** times more houses, brothers, sisters,
Lk 8. 8 the plants grew and produced corn, a **hundred** grains each."
15. 4 one of you has a **hundred** sheep and loses one of them
16. 6 'One **hundred** barrels of olive-oil,' he answered.
Jn 2. 6 each one large enough to hold about a **hundred** litres.
21. 8 They were not very far from land, about a **hundred** metres away.
Rom 4.19 He was then almost one **hundred** years old;

HUNGER

Gen 25.29 He was **hungry** [30] and said to Jacob, "I'm starving;
41.55 the Egyptians began to be **hungry,** they cried out to the king
47.13 and the people of Egypt and Canaan became weak with **hunger.**
Lev 26.26 and when you have eaten it all, you will still be **hungry.**
26.29 Your **hunger** will be so great that you will eat your own
Deut 8. 3 He made you go **hungry,** and then he gave you manna to
8. 9 There you will never go **hungry** or ever be in need.
28.48 You will be **hungry,** thirsty, and naked—in need of everything.
32.24 They will die from **hunger** and fever;
1 Sam 2. 5 out to get food, but the **hungry** are hungry no more.
14.24 The Israelites were weak with **hunger** that day, because
14.28 "We are all weak with **hunger,** but your father threatened us
14.31 Israelites were very weak with **hunger,** [32] and so they rushed
2 Sam 17.28 his men would be **hungry,** thirsty, and tired in the wilderness.
2 Chr 32.11 is deceiving you and will let you die of **hunger** and thirst.
Neh 9.15 "When they were **hungry,** you gave them bread from heaven,
Job 5. 5 **Hungry** people will eat the fool's crops— even the
5.22 will laugh at violence and **hunger** and not be afraid of wild
18.12 He used to be rich, but now he goes **hungry;**
22. 7 who were tired, and refused to feed those who were **hungry.**
24.10 they must go **hungry** while harvesting wheat.
30. 3 They were so poor and **hungry** that they would gnaw dry
31.17 live in despair [17] or let orphans go **hungry** while I ate.
38.39 lions to eat, and satisfy **hungry** young lions
38.41 ravens when they wander about **hungry,** when their young cry to
Ps 34.10 Even lions go **hungry** for lack of food, but those who
50.12 "If I were **hungry,** I would not ask you for food, for
69.21 When I was **hungry,** they gave me poison;
107. 5 They were **hungry** and thirsty and had given up all hope.
107. 9 those who are thirsty and fills the **hungry** with good things.
107.36 He let **hungry** people settle there, and they built a city
146. 7 in favour of the oppressed and gives food to the **hungry.**
Prov 6.30 don't despise a thief if he steals food when he is **hungry;**
10. 3 not let good people go **hungry,** but he will keep the wicked
12. 9 than to play the part of a great man but go **hungry.**
13. 2 but those who are deceitful are **hungry** for violence.
13.25 righteous have enough to eat, but the wicked are always **hungry.**
16.26 makes him work harder, because he wants to satisfy his **hunger.**
19.15 sleep on, but you will go **hungry.**
21.10 Wicked people are always **hungry** for evil;
25.21 If your enemy is **hungry,** feed him;
27. 7 but when you are **hungry,** even bitter food tastes sweet.
Is 5.14 world of the dead is **hungry** for them, and it opens its
8.21 people will wander through the land, discouraged and **hungry.**
8.21 In their **hunger** and their anger they will curse their king
Is 9.20 of food they can find, but their **hunger** is never satisfied.
29. 8 is eating and wakes up **hungry,** or like a man dying of
32. 6 he never feeds the **hungry** or gives thirsty people anything to
44.12 As he works, he gets **hungry,** thirsty, and tired.
49.10 they will never be **hungry** or thirsty.
55. 2 Why spend your wages and still be **hungry?**
58. 7 Share your food with the **hungry** and open your homes to the
58.10 you give food to the **hungry** and satisfy those who are in
65.13 plenty to eat and drink, but you will be **hungry** and thirsty.
Jer 31.25 and will satisfy with food everyone who is weak from **hunger.**
42.13 war any more or hear the call to battle or go **hungry.'**
42.16 will overtake you, and the **hunger** you dread will follow you,
Lam 1. 6 deer that are weak from **hunger,** Whose strength is almost gone
2.12 **Hungry** and thirsty, they cry to their mothers;
4. 4 They let their babies die of **hunger** and thirst;
5.10 **Hunger** has made us burn with fever, until our skin is as
Ezek 5.12 your people will die from sickness and **hunger** in the city;
5.16 will feel the pains of **hunger** like sharp arrows sent to
5.17 I will send **hunger** and wild animals to kill your children,
7.15 in the streets, and sickness and **hunger** in the houses.
7.15 anyone in the city will be a victim of sickness and **hunger.**
18. 7 he feeds the **hungry** and gives clothing to the naked.
18.16 He feeds the **hungry** and gives clothing to the naked.
34.29 them fertile fields and put an end to **hunger** in the land.
Hos 4.10 will eat your share of the sacrifices, but still be **hungry.**
9. 4 It will be used only to satisfy their **hunger;**
Amos 8.11 People will be **hungry,** but not for bread;
8.11 They will **hunger** and thirst for a message from the Lord.
Mic 6.14 eat, but not be satisfied—in fact you will still be **hungry.**
7. 1 I am like a **hungry** man who finds no fruit left on
Hab 1. 8 horses are faster than leopards, fiercer than **hungry** wolves.
Zeph 3. 3 its judges are like **hungry** wolves, too greedy to leave a
Mt 4. 2 spending forty days and nights without food, Jesus was **hungry.**
12. 1 His disciples were **hungry,** so they began to pick ears of
12. 3 what David did that time when he and his men were **hungry?**
21.18 way back to the city early next morning, Jesus was **hungry.**
25.35 I was **hungry** and you fed me, thirsty and you gave me
25.37 did we ever see you **hungry** and feed you, or thirsty and
25.42 I was **hungry** but you would not feed me, thirsty but you
25.44 did we ever see you **hungry** or thirsty or a stranger or
Mk 2.25 He and his men were **hungry,** [26] so he went into the house
11.12 as they were coming back from Bethany, Jesus was **hungry.**
Lk 1.53 He has filled the **hungry** with good things, and sent the
4. 2 he ate nothing, so that he was **hungry** when it was over.
6. 3 you read what David did when he and his men were **hungry?**
6.21 "Happy are you who are **hungry** now;
6.25 you will go **hungry!**
Jn 6.35 "He who comes to me will never be **hungry;**
Acts 10.10 He became **hungry** and wanted something to eat;
Rom 8.35 hardship or persecution or **hunger** or poverty or danger or death?
12.20 "If your enemy is **hungry,** feed him;
1 Cor 4.11 To this very moment we go **hungry** and thirsty;
11.21 own meal, so that some are **hungry** while others get drunk.
11.34 And if anyone is **hungry,** he should eat at home, so that
2 Cor 11.27 I have been **hungry** and thirsty;
Phil 4.12 whether I am full or **hungry,** whether I have too much or
Rev 7.16 Never again will they **hunger** or thirst;

HUNT

Gen 10. 9 he was a great **hunter,** and that is why people say,
10. 9 "May the Lord make you as great a **hunter** as Nimrod!"
21.20 in the wilderness of Paran and became a skilful **hunter.**
25.27 and Esau became a skilled **hunter,** a man who loved the
25.29 Jacob was cooking some bean soup, Esau came in from **hunting.**
27. 5 when Esau went out to **hunt,** [6] she said to Jacob, "I have
27.30 soon as Jacob left, his brother Esau came in from **hunting.**
31.36 have I broken that gives you the right to **hunt** me down?
Lev 17.13 foreigner living in the community **hunts** an animal or a bird
1 Sam 23.23 in the region, I will **hunt** him down, even if I have
24.11 You are **hunting** me down to kill me, even though I have
26.20 Why should he **hunt** me down like a wild bird?"
Job 10. 6 track down all my sins and **hunt** down every fault I have?
10.16 have any success at all, you **hunt** me down like a lion;
Ps 104.21 young lions roar while they **hunt,** looking for the food that
124. 7 We have escaped like a bird from a **hunter's** trap;
143. 3 My enemy has **hunted** me down and completely defeated me.
Prov 6. 5 the trap like a bird or a deer escaping from a **hunter.**
Is 7.24 People will go **hunting** there with bows and arrows.
13.14 countries, scattering like deer escaping from **hunters,**
51.20 they are like deer caught in a **hunter's** net.
Jer 2.14 Why then do his enemies **hunt** him down?
5.27 Just as a **hunter** fills his cage with birds, they have
16.16 I will send for many **hunters**
16.16 to **hunt** them down on every mountain
50. 9 They are skilful **hunters,** shooting arrows that never miss
Lam 1. 6 Whose strength is almost gone as they flee from the **hunters.**
3.66 **Hunt** them down and wipe them off the earth!"
Ezek 17.20 I will spread out a **hunter's** net and catch him in it.
19. 3 She reared a cub and taught him to **hunt;**
19. 6 He too learnt to **hunt** and became a man-eater.
19. 8 They spread their **hunting** nets and caught him in their trap.
Hos 9.13 I can see their children being **hunted** down and killed.
Amos 1.11 They **hunted** down their brothers, the Israelites, and showed
Mic 5. 8 will be like a lion **hunting** for food in a forest or
7. 2 Everyone **hunts** down his fellow-countryman.

HURAM (1)

Craftsman mainly responsible for the bronze work in Solomon's Temple.

1 Kgs 7.13 sent for a man named **Huram,** a craftsman living in the city
7.14 **Huram** was an intelligent and experienced craftsman.
7.15 **Huram** cast two bronze columns, each one 8 metres tall
7.21 **Huram** placed these two bronze columns in front of the
7.23 **Huram** made a round tank of bronze, 2.2 metres deep,
7.27 **Huram** also made ten bronze carts;
7.38 **Huram** also made ten basins, one for each cart.
7.40 **Huram** also made pots, shovels, and bowls.
7.40 equipment for the Temple, which **Huram** made for King Solomon,
2 Chr 2.13 am sending you a wise and skilful master craftsman named **Huram.**
4.11 **Huram** also made pots, shovels, and bowls.
4.11 **Huram** the master craftsman made all these objects

HURL

1 Sam 25.29 throw them away, as a man **hurls** stones with his catapult.
Ps 69. 9 the insults which are **hurled** at you fall on me.
79.12 seven times for all the insults they have **hurled** at you.
89.44 away his royal sceptre and **hurled** his throne to the ground.
Ezek 28.17 Because of this I **hurled** you to the ground and left you
Mt 27.39 People passing by shook their heads and **hurled** insults at Jesus:
Mk 15.29 People passing by shook their heads and **hurled** insults at Jesus:
Lk 23.39 One of the criminals hanging there **hurled** insults at him:
Rom 15. 3 "The insults which are **hurled** at you have fallen on me."

HURRY

Gen 18. 6 Abraham **hurried** into the tent and said to Sarah, "Quick,
18. 7 and gave it to a servant, who **hurried** to get it ready.
19.14 going to marry, and said, **"Hurry** up and get out of here;
19.15 At dawn the angels tried to make Lot **hurry.**
19.22 **Hurry!**
19.27 Early the next morning Abraham **hurried** to the place where
31.21 He took everything he owned and left in a **hurry.**
44. 4 the servant in charge of his house, **"Hurry** after those men.
45. 9 "Now **hurry** back to my father and tell him that this is
45.13 Then **hurry** and bring him here."
Ex 10.16 Then the king **hurriedly** called Moses and Aaron and said,
12.33 Egyptians urged the people to **hurry** and leave the country;
Num 16.46 Then **hurry** with it to the people and perform the ritual of
16.46 **Hurry!**
Deut 16. 3 you did when you had to leave Egypt in such a **hurry.**
Josh 4.10 The people **hurried** across the river.
Judg 9.44 Abimelech and his group **hurried** forward to guard the city gate,
18. 9 **hurry!**
1 Sam 4.14 The man **hurried** to Eli to tell him the news.
9.12 If you **hurry,** you will catch up with him.
17.17 ten loaves of bread, and **hurry** with them to your brothers in
20. 6 I begged your permission to **hurry** home to Bethlehem,
20.38 **Hurry** up!"
21. 8 me leave in such a **hurry** that I didn't have time to
23.26 They were **hurrying** to get away from Saul and his men, who
25.34 that if you had not **hurried** to meet me, all of Nabal's
2 Sam 4. 4 she was in such a **hurry** that she dropped him, and he
15.14 **Hurry!**
17.18 so they **hurried** off to hide in the house of a certain
17.21 planned against him and said, **"Hurry** up and cross the river."
19.16 son of Gera from Bahurim **hurried** to the Jordan to meet King
1 Kgs 12.18 At this, Rehoboam **hurriedly** got into his chariot and escaped
2 Kgs 4.26 **Hurry** to her and find out if everything is all right
4.29 Elisha turned to Gehazi and said, **"Hurry!**
11.13 and the people, so she **hurried** to the Temple, where the
2 Chr 10.18 At this, Rehoboam **hurriedly** got into his chariot and escaped
20. 4 city of Judah people **hurried** to Jerusalem to ask the Lord
23.12 for the king, so she **hurried** to the Temple, where the crowd
26.20 He **hurried** to get out, because the Lord had punished him.
35.21 but to fight my enemies, and God has told me to **hurry.**
Ezra 4.23 they **hurried** to Jerusalem and forced the Jews
Esth 6.10 the king said to Haman, **"Hurry** and get the robes and the
6.12 while Haman **hurried** home, covering his face in embarrassment.
6.14 eunuchs arrived in a **hurry** to take Haman to Esther's banquet.
Ps 40.17 You are my saviour and my God— **hurry** to my aid!
59. 4 any fault of mine, O Lord, that they **hurry** to their places.
70. 5 You are my saviour, O Lord— **hurry** to my aid!
71.12 my God, **hurry** to my aid!
119.60 Without delay I **hurry** to obey your commands.
Prov 6. 3 **hurry** to him, and beg him to release you.
6.16 feet that **hurry** off to do evil,
28.20 if you are in a **hurry** to get rich, you are going
28.22 people are in such a **hurry** to get rich that they do
Is 5.19 You say, "Let the Lord **hurry** up and do what he says
52.12 This time you will not have to leave in a **hurry;**
Jer 9.18 "Tell them to **hurry** and sing a funeral song for us, until
26.10 heard what had happened, they **hurried** from the royal palace
46.16 each one says to the other, **'Hurry!**
Dan 6.19 At dawn the king got up and **hurried** to the pit.
Hos 11.10 They will **hurry** to me from the west.
Joel 3.11 **Hurry** and come, all you surrounding nations, and gather
Mt 28. 8 left the tomb in a **hurry,** afraid and yet filled with joy,
Mk 2.12 the man got up, picked up his mat, and **hurried** away.
6.25 The girl **hurried** back at once to the king and demanded,
15. 1 the chief priests met **hurriedly** with the elders, the teachers of
Lk 1.39 afterwards Mary got ready and **hurried** off to a town in the
2.16 So they **hurried** off and found Mary and Joseph and saw
14.21 and said to his servant, **'Hurry** out to the streets and
15.22 **'Hurry!'**
Lk 17. 7 the field, do you tell him to **hurry** and eat his meal?
19. 5 said to Zacchaeus, **"Hurry** down, Zacchaeus, because I must stay
19. 6 Zacchaeus **hurried** down and welcomed him with great joy.
Jn 11.29 Mary heard this, she got up and **hurried** out to meet him.
11.31 followed her when they saw her get up and **hurry** out.
Acts 9.38 to him with the message, "Please **hurry** and come to us."
12. 7 shook Peter by the shoulder, woke him up, and said, **"Hurry!**
20.16 He was in a **hurry** to arrive in Jerusalem by the day
22.18 as he said to me, **'Hurry** and leave Jerusalem quickly,
1 Tim 5.22 Be in no **hurry** to lay hands on someone to dedicate him

HURT

Gen 22.12 "Don't **hurt** the boy or do anything to him," he said.
37.22 him into this well in the wilderness, but don't **hurt** him."
37.27 Then we won't have to **hurt** him;
Ex 21.22 some men are fighting and **hurt** a pregnant woman so that she
21.22 other way, the one who **hurt** her is to be fined whatever
Num 35.23 he did not intend to **hurt** and who was not his enemy.
Judg 1.24 us how to get into the city, and we won't **hurt** you."
1 Sam 20. 3 know what he plans to do, because you would be deeply **hurt.**
1 Kgs 20.37 he hit him a hard blow and **hurt** him.
2 Kgs 4.19 Suddenly he cried out to his father, "My head **hurts!**
4.19 My head **hurts!"**
1 Chr 12.17 I have not tried to **hurt** you, the God of our ancestors
2 Chr 35.23 I'm badly **hurt!"**
Job 1.12 has is in your power, but you must not **hurt** Job himself."
2. 5 But now suppose you **hurt** his body—he will curse you to
5.18 his hand **hurts** you, and his hand heals.
10.16 to **hurt** me you even work miracles.
18. 4 You are only **hurting** yourself with your anger.
19. 4 Even if I have done wrong, how does that **hurt** you?
Ps 7.16 by their own evil and are **hurt** by their own violence.
38.12 me, and those who want to **hurt** me threaten to ruin me;
52. 4 You love to **hurt** people with your words, you liar!
56. 5 they are always planning how to **hurt** me!
71.13 May those who try to **hurt** me be shamed and disgraced.
73.21 bitter and my feelings were **hurt,** [22] I was as stupid as an
77.10 Then I said, "What **hurts** me most is this— that God
91.12 hands to keep you from **hurting** your feet on the stones.
109.22 I am **hurt** to the depths of my heart.
121. 6 The sun will not **hurt** you during the day, nor the moon
Prov 3.29 Don't plan anything that will **hurt** your neighbour;
4.16 They lie awake unless they have **hurt** someone.
8.36 The man who does not find me **hurts** himself;
9. 7 If you reprimand an evil man, you will only get **hurt.**
10.32 to say, but the wicked are always saying things that **hurt.**
11.17 If you are cruel, you only **hurt** yourself.
15.32 If you refuse to learn, you are **hurting** yourself.
19.28 There is no justice where a witness is determined to **hurt**
24. 2 time they open their mouth someone is going to be **hurt.**
26. 2 Curses cannot **hurt** you unless you deserve them.
26.10 who hires any fool that comes along is only **hurting** everybody
26.28 You have to hate someone to want to **hurt** him with lies.
27. 6 A friend means well, even when he **hurts** you.
Ecc 1.18 the more you know, the more it **hurts.**
10. 9 If you work in a stone quarry, you get **hurt** by stones.
10. 9 If you split wood, you get **hurt** doing it.
Is 43. 2 the hard trials that come will not **hurt** you.
49.10 and desert heat will not **hurt** them, for they will be led
50. 7 But their insults cannot **hurt** me because the Sovereign Lord
54.17 But no weapon will be able to **hurt** you;
57. 1 But when they die, no calamity can **hurt** them.
59. 4 You carry out your plans to **hurt** others.
Jer 2. 3 I sent suffering and disaster on everyone who **hurt** you.
7.18 pour out wine-offerings to other gods, in order to **hurt** me.
7.19 But am I really the one they are **hurting?**
7.19 they are **hurting** themselves and bringing shame on themselves.
10.19 "How badly we are **hurt!**
14.17 for my people are deeply wounded and are badly **hurt.**
14.19 Why have you **hurt** us so badly that we cannot be healed?
38. 4 he only wants to **hurt** them."
38.12 the rags under my arms, so that the ropes wouldn't **hurt** me.
Ezek 13.22 lies you discourage good people, whom I do not wish to **hurt.**
28.24 will ever again be like thorns and briars to **hurt** Israel.
34. 4 bandaged those that are **hurt,** brought back those that
34.16 bandage those that are **hurt,** and heal those that are sick;
Dan 3.25 show no sign of being **hurt**—and the fourth one looks like
6.22 the mouths of the lions so that they would not **hurt** me.
6.23 that he had not been **hurt** at all, for he trusted God.
Hos 6. 1 He has **hurt** us, but he will be sure to heal us;
Zech 11.16 the lost, or heal those that are **hurt,** or feed the healthy.
12. 3 heavy stone—any nation that tries to lift it will be **hurt.**
Mt 4. 6 so that not even your feet will be **hurt** on the stones.' "
15.12 that the Pharisees had their feelings **hurt** by what you said?"
Lk 4.11 so that not even your feet will be **hurt** on the stones.' "
9.39 it keeps on **hurting** him and will hardly let him go!
10.19 all the power of the Enemy, and nothing will **hurt** you.
Acts 26.14 You are **hurting** yourself by hitting back, like an ox kicking
Rom 3.15 They are quick to **hurt** and kill;
14.15 If you **hurt** your brother because of something you eat,
1 Cor 15.55 Where, Death, is your power to **hurt?"**
15.56 Death gets its power to **hurt** from sin, and sin gets its
2 Cor 4. 9 and though badly **hurt** at times, we are not destroyed.
Gal 5.15 you act like wild animals, **hurting** and harming each other,
Rev 2.11 who win the victory will not be **hurt** by the second death.
9.10 that they have the power to **hurt** people for five months.
9.19 like snakes with heads, and they use them to **hurt** people.

HUSBAND

Gen 3. 6 Then she gave some to her **husband,** and he also ate it.
3.16 still have desire for your **husband,** yet you will be subject
18.12 And besides, my **husband** is old too."
20. 7 But now, give the woman back to her **husband.**
29.32 Lord has seen my trouble, and now my **husband** will love me";
29.34 She said, "Now my **husband** will be bound more tightly to me,
30. 4 she gave Bilhah to her **husband,** and he had intercourse with
30.15 answered, "Isn't it enough that you have taken away my **husband?**
30.18 given me my reward, because I gave my slave to my **husband";**
30.20 Now my **husband** will accept me, because I have borne him six
38. 8 obligation to her as her **husband's** brother, so that your
39.14 This Hebrew that my **husband** brought to the house is insulting
Ex 4.25 she said to Moses, "You are a **husband** of blood to me."
21.22 fined whatever amount the woman's **husband** demands, subject to
Num 5.12 But the **husband** may not be certain, for his wife may have
5.12 it may happen that a **husband** becomes suspicious of his wife,
5.15 offering from a suspicious **husband,** made to bring the truth
5.31 The **husband** shall be free of guilt, but the woman,
30. 7 vowed or promised unless her **husband** raises an objection
30. 8 But if her **husband** forbids her to fulfil the vow when he
30.11 vowed or promised unless her **husband** raises an objection when
30.12 But if her **husband** forbids her to fulfil the vow when he
30.12 because her **husband** prevented her from keeping her vow.
30.13 Her **husband** has the right to affirm or to annul any vow
Deut 22.18 the town leaders are to take the **husband** and beat him.
24. 3 Or suppose her second **husband** dies.
24. 4 In either case, her first **husband** is not to marry her again;
25. 7 leaders and say, 'My **husband's** brother will not do his duty;
25.11 one tries to help her **husband** by grabbing hold of the other
28.56 not share them with the **husband** she loves or with any of
Judg 13. 6 went and said to her **husband,** "A man of God has come
13. 9 Her **husband** Manoah was not with her, [10]so she ran at once
14.15 to Samson's wife, "Trick your **husband** into telling us what
19.26 at the door of the old man's house, where her **husband** was.
19.27 Her **husband** got up that morning, and when he opened the
Ruth 1. 5 and Naomi was left all alone, without **husband** or sons.
2. 1 man who belonged to the family of her **husband** Elimelech.
2.11 you have done for your mother-in-law since your **husband** died.
3. 1 Ruth, "I must find a **husband** for you, so that you will
1 Sam 1. 8 **husband** Elkanah would ask her, "Hannah, why are you crying?
1.22 She told her **husband,** "As soon as the child is weaned, I
2.19 she accompanied her **husband** to offer the yearly sacrifice.
4.19 that her father-in-law and her **husband** were dead, she suddenly
4.21 Covenant Box and the death of her father-in-law and her **husband.**
25.19 But she said nothing to her **husband.**
2 Sam 3.15 So Ishbosheth took her away from her **husband** Paltiel
11.26 When Bathsheba heard that her **husband** had been killed,
14. 5 "My **husband** is dead.
14. 7 last hope and leave my **husband** without a son to keep his
17. 3 all his men to you, like a bride returning to her **husband.**
2 Kgs 4. 1 went to Elisha and said, "Sir, my **husband** has died!
4. 1 my two sons as slaves in payment for my **husband's** debt."
4. 9 She said to her **husband,** "I am sure that this man who
4.14 "Well, she has no son, and her **husband** is an old man."
4.22 she called her **husband** and said to him, "Send a servant
4.23 her **husband** asked.
4.26 is all right with her, her **husband,** and her son."
22.14 (Her **husband** Shallum, the son of Tikvah and grandson of
2 Chr 34.22 (Her **husband** Shallum, the son of Tikvah and grandson of
Esth 1.17 to look down on her **husband** as soon as she hears what
1.18 they will be telling their **husbands** about it before the day
1.18 have no respect for their **husbands,**
1.18 and **husbands** will be angry with their wives.
1.20 every woman will treat her **husband** with proper respect,
1.22 saying that every **husband** should be the master of his
Prov 2.17 is faithless to her own **husband** and forgets her sacred vows.
6.34 A **husband** is never angrier than when he is jealous;
7.19 My **husband** isn't at home.
12. 4 A good wife is her **husband's** pride and joy;
12. 4 who brings shame on her **husband** is like a cancer in his
31.11 Her **husband** puts his confidence in her, and he will never
31.23 Her **husband** is well known, one of the leading citizens.
31.28 children show their appreciation, and her **husband** praises her.
Is 4. 1 us say you are our **husband,** so that we won't have to
47. 9 the magic you use, you will lose your **husband** and children.
54. 1 have more children than a woman whose **husband** never left her!
54. 5 Creator will be like a **husband** to you— the Lord Almighty
54. 6 a young wife, deserted by her **husband** and deeply distressed.
62. 4 pleased with you And will be like a **husband** to your land.
Jer 6.11 **Husbands** and wives will be taken away, and even the very old
18.21 Let the women lose their **husbands** and children;
31.32 Although I was like a **husband** to them, they did not keep
44.19 wine-offerings to her, our **husbands** approved of what we were
Ezek 16.32 commits adultery with strangers instead of loving her **husband.**
16.45 She detested her **husband** and her children.
16.45 like your sisters, who hated their **husbands** and their children.
Dan 11. 6 not last, and she, her **husband,** her child, and the servants
Hos 2. 2 longer a wife to me, and I am no longer her **husband.**
2. 7 going back to my first **husband**—I was better off then than
2.16 she will call me her **husband**—she will no longer call me
Amos 4. 1 and demand that your **husbands** keep you supplied with liquor!
Mk 10.12 a woman who divorces her **husband** and marries another man commits
Lk 8. 3 Joanna, whose **husband** Chuza was an officer in Herod's court;
Jn 4.16 "Go and call your **husband,"** Jesus told her, "and come back."
4.17 "I haven't got a **husband,"** she answered.
4.17 "You are right when you say you haven't got a **husband.**
4.18 and the man you live with now is not really your **husband.**
Acts 5. 8 the full amount you and your **husband** received for your property?"
5. 9 "Why did you and your **husband** decide to put the Lord's
5. 9 The men who buried your **husband** are now at the door,
5.10 so they carried her out and buried her beside her **husband.**
Rom 7. 2 bound by the law to her **husband** as long as he lives;
7. 3 with another man while her **husband** is alive, she will be
7. 3 but if her **husband** dies, she is legally a free woman
1 Cor 7. 2 his own wife, and every woman should have her own **husband.**
7. 3 fulfil his duty as a **husband,** and a woman should fulfil her
7. 4 is not the master of her own body, but her **husband** is;
7. 4 in the same way a **husband** is not the master of his
7.10 a wife must not leave her **husband;**
7.11 she must remain single or else be reconciled to her **husband;**
7.11 and a **husband** must not divorce his wife.
7.14 the unbelieving **husband** is made acceptable to God by being united
7.14 acceptable to God by being united to her Christian **husband.**
7.15 the Christian partner, whether **husband** or wife, is free to act.
7.16 sure, Christian wife, that you will not save your **husband?**
7.16 can you be sure, Christian **husband,** that you will not save
7.34 with worldly matters, because she wants to please her **husband.**
7.39 A married woman is not free as long as her **husband** lives;
7.39 but if her **husband** dies, then she is free to be married
11. 3 supreme over every man, the **husband** is supreme over his wife,
11. 5 in public worship with nothing on her head disgraces her **husband;**
11.10 her head to show that she is under her **husband's** authority.
14.35 find out about something, they should ask their **husbands** at home.
Gal 4.27 have more children than the woman whose **husband** never left her."
Eph 5.22 Wives, submit to your **husbands** as to the Lord.
5.23 For a **husband** has authority over his wife just as Christ
5.24 submit completely to their **husbands** just as the church submits
5.25 **Husbands,** love your wives just as Christ loved the church
5.33 every **husband** must love his wife as himself,
5.33 and every wife must respect her **husband.**
Col 3.18 Wives, submit to your **husbands,** for that is what you
3.19 **Husbands,** love your wives and do not be harsh with them.
Tit 2. 4 younger women to love their **husbands** and children,
2. 5 housewives who submit to their **husbands,** so that no one will
Heb 13. 4 be honoured by all, and **husbands** and wives must be faithful
1 Pet 3. 1 wives must submit to your **husbands,** so that if any of them
3. 5 used to make themselves beautiful by submitting to their **husbands.**
3. 7 In the same way you **husbands** must live with your wives
Rev 21. 2 prepared and ready, like a bride dressed to meet her **husband.**

HUSHAI

David's friend, who gave unsuitable advice to Absalom.

2 Sam 15.32 his trusted friend **Hushai** the Archite met him with his
15.37 So **Hushai,** David's friend, returned to the city just as
16.16 **Hushai,** David's trusted friend, met Absalom, he shouted,
16.18 **Hushai** answered, "How could I?
17. 5 Absalom said, "Now call **Hushai,** and let us hear what he
17. 6 **Hushai** arrived, Absalom said to him, "This is the advice that
17. 7 **Hushai** answered, "The advice Ahithophel gave you
17.14 **"Hushai's** advice is better than Ahithophel's."
17.15 Then **Hushai** told the priests Zadok and Abiathar what
17.16 **Hushai** added, "Quick, now!
1 Kgs 4.16 the territory of Naphtali [16] Baana son of **Hushai:**
1 Chr 27.33 to the king, and **Hushai** the Archite was the king's friend

HUT

1 Chr 4.41 destroyed the tents and **huts** of the people who lived there.
Job 27.18 web or like the **hut** of a slave guarding the fields.
Is 1. 8 as defenceless as a watchman's **hut** in a vineyard or a shed
24.20 like a drunken man and sway like a **hut** in a storm.
Zeph 2. 6 sea will become open fields with shepherds' **huts** and sheep

HYENA

Is 13.22 and palaces will echo with the cries of **hyenas** and jackals.

HYMN

2 Chr 7. 6 had provided and singing the **hymn,** "His Love Is Eternal!"
8.14 assisted the priests in singing **hymns** and in doing their work.
Neh 12. 8 were in charge of the singing of **hymns** of thanksgiving:
Ps 26. 7 I sing a **hymn** of thanksgiving and tell of all your
71.22 my harp I will play **hymns** to you, the Holy One of
147. 7 Sing **hymns** of praise to the Lord;
Mt 26.30 Then they sang a **hymn** and went out to the Mount of
Mk 14.26 Then they sang a **hymn** and went out to the Mount of
Acts 16.25 were praying and singing **hymns** to God, and the other prisoners
1 Cor 14.26 one person has a **hymn,** another a teaching, another a revelation
Eph 5.19 another with the words of psalms, **hymns,** and sacred songs;
5.19 **hymns** and psalms to the Lord with praise in your hearts.
Col 3.16 Sing psalms, **hymns,** and sacred songs;

HYPOCRITE

Ps 26. 4 I have nothing to do with **hypocrites.**
101. 7 no **hypocrite** will remain in my presence.
Prov 26.24 A **hypocrite** hides his hate behind flattering words.
Mt 6. 2 show of it, as the **hypocrites** do in the houses of worship
6. 5 "When you pray, do not be like the **hypocrites!**
6.16 fast, do not put on a sad face as the **hypocrites** do.
7. 5 You **hypocrite!**
15. 7 You **hypocrites!**

Mt 22.18 aware of their evil plan, and so he said, "You **hypocrites!**
23.13 You **hypocrites!**
23.15 You **hypocrites!**
23.23 You **hypocrites!**
23.25 You **hypocrites!**
23.27 You **hypocrites!**
23.28 everybody, but inside you are full of **hypocrisy** and sins.
23.29 You **hypocrites!**
24.51 him in pieces and make him share the fate of the **hypocrites.**
Mk 7. 6 You are **hypocrites,** just as he wrote:
Lk 6.42 You **hypocrite!**
12. 1 against the yeast of the Pharisees—I mean their **hypocrisy.**
12.56 **Hypocrites!**
13.15 The Lord answered him, "You **hypocrites!**
Jas 3.17 it is free from prejudice and **hypocrisy.**
4. 8 Purify your hearts, you **hypocrites!**
1 Pet 2. 1 more lying or **hypocrisy** or jealousy or insulting language.

HYSSOP

A small bushy plant used in religious ceremonies to sprinkle liquids.

Ex 12.22 Take a sprig of **hyssop,** dip it in the bowl containing
Lev 14. 4 a piece of cedar-wood, a red cord, and a sprig of **hyssop.**
14. 6 the red cord, and the **hyssop,** in the blood of the bird
14.49 birds, some cedar-wood, a red cord, and a sprig of **hyssop.**
14.51 shall take the cedar-wood, the **hyssop,** the red cord,
14.52 the live bird, the cedar-wood, the **hyssop,** and the red cord.
Num 19. 6 some cedar-wood, a sprig of **hyssop,** and a red cord and throw
19.18 to take a sprig of **hyssop,** dip it in the water, and
1 Kgs 4.33 from the Lebanon cedars to the **hyssop** that grows on walls;
Jn 19.29 put on a stalk of **hyssop,** and lifted up to his lips.
Heb 9.19 all the people, using a sprig of **hyssop** and some red wool.

I AM

Ex 3.14 God said, **"I am who I am.**
3.14 'The one who is called **I AM** has sent me to you.'
Mt 22.32 He said, [32]**'I am** the God of Abraham, the God of Isaac,
Mk 12.26 God said to Moses, **'I am** the God of Abraham, the God
Jn 5.45 not think, however, that **I am** the one who will accuse you
6.35 **"I am** the bread of life," Jesus told them.
6.41 because he said, **"I am** the bread that came down from
6.48 **I am** the bread of life.
6.51 **I am** the living bread that came down from heaven.
8.12 **"I am** the light of the world," he said.
8.24 sins if you do not believe that **'I Am Who I Am'."**
8.28 Son of Man, you will know that **'I Am Who I Am';**
9. 5 I am in the world, **I am** the light for the world."
10. 7 **I am** the gate for the sheep.
10. 9 **I am** the gate.
10.11 **"I am** the good shepherd, who is willing to die for the
10.14 **I am** the good shepherd.
10.36 I blaspheme because I said that **I am** the Son of God?
11.25 Jesus said to her, **"I am** the resurrection and the life.
13.19 it does happen, you will believe that **'I Am Who I Am.'**
14. 6 Jesus answered him, **"I am** the way, the truth, and the life;
15. 1 **"I am** the real vine, and my Father is the gardener.
15. 5 **"I am** the vine, and you are the branches.
19.21 but rather, 'This man said, **I am** the King of the Jews.' "
Acts 7.32 **'I am** the God of your ancestors, the God of Abraham,
10.21 said to the men, **"I am** the man you are looking for.
Rom 14.11 says, "As surely as **I am** the living God, says the Lord,
Rev 1. 8 **"I am** the first and the last," says the Lord God Almighty,
1.17 **I am** the first and the last.
1.18 **I am** the living one!
2.23 will know that **I am** the one who knows everyone's thoughts
3.11 **I am coming soon.**
21. 6 **I am** the first and the last, the beginning and the end.
22. 7 **"I am coming soon!**
22.12 **"I am coming soon!**
22.13 **I am** the first and the last, the beginning and the end."
22.16 **I am** the bright morning star."
22.20 **I am coming soon!"**

IBIS

Job 38.36 Who tells the **ibis** when the Nile will flood, or who

ICE

Job 6.16 choked with snow and **ice,** [17] but in the heat they disappear,
37.10 of God freezes the waters, and turns them to solid **ice.**
38.29 is the mother of the **ice** and the frost, [30] which turn the
Ps 147.18 Then he gives a command, and the **ice** melts;

IDEA

Josh 22.28 It was our **idea** that, if this should ever happen,
1 Sam 9. 9 Saul replied, "A good **idea!**
17.55 "I have no **idea,** Your Majesty," Abner answered.
Esth 1.21 and his officials liked this **idea,** and the king did what
5.14 thought this was a good **idea,** so he had the gallows built.
Job 38.18 Have you any **idea** how big the world is?
Prov 10.20 a wicked man's **ideas** are worthless.
17. 4 Evil people listen to evil **ideas,** and liars listen to lies.
25.11 **idea** well-expressed is like a design of gold, set in silver.
Is 44.20 His foolish **ideas** have so misled him that he is beyond help.
Dan 5. 9 grew even paler, and his noblemen had no **idea** what to do.
Mt 15.19 his heart come the evil **ideas** which lead him to kill, commit
Mk 7.21 person's heart, come the evil **ideas** which lead him to do
Acts 28.22 would like to hear your **ideas,** because we know that everywhere

IDENTICAL

Num 7.12 The offerings each one brought were **identical:**
2 Kgs 25.17 The two columns were **identical:**
Jer 52.21 The two columns were **identical:**
Ezek 42. 9 the Temple there was an **identical** building not far from the

IDENTIFY

2 Kgs 9.37 dung, so that no one will be able to **identify** them.' "

IDLE

[IDLY]

Is 33. 9 The land lies **idle** and deserted.
58.13 not travelling, working, or talking **idly** on that day,
1 Thes 5.14 brothers, to warn the **idle,** encourage the timid, help the weak,

IDOL

Ex 20. 5 not bow down to any **idol** or worship it, because I am
Lev 19. 4 "Do not abandon me and worship **idols;**
26. 1 Lord said, "Do not make **idols** or set up statues, stone
26.30 and throw your dead bodies on your fallen **idols.**
Num 33.52 their stone and metal **idols** and all their places of worship.
Deut 4.16 by making for yourselves an **idol** in any form at all—whether
4.23 make yourselves any kind of **idol,** [24] because the Lord
4.25 sin by making for yourselves an **idol** in any form at all.
5. 9 not bow down to any **idol** or worship it, for I am
7. 5 down the symbols of their goddess Asherah, and burn their **idols.**
7.25 Burn their **idols.**
7.25 If you do, that will be fatal, because the Lord hates **idolatry.**
7.26 not bring any of these **idols** into your homes, or the same
7.26 must hate and despise these **idols,** because they are under the
9.12 and they have made an **idol** for themselves.'
9.16 making yourselves a metal **idol** in the form of a bull-calf.
12. 3 Asherah and chop down their **idols,** so that they will never
16.22 And do not set up any stone pillar for **idol** worship;
27.15 on anyone who makes an **idol** of stone, wood, or metal and
27.15 the Lord hates **idolatry.'**
29.17 You saw their disgusting **idols** made of wood, stone,
32.16 Their **idolatry** made the Lord jealous;
32.21 With their **idols** they have made me angry, jealous with
Judg 3. 7 against him and worshipped the **idols** of Baal and Asherah.
8.27 Gideon made an **idol** from the gold and put it in his
8.27 the Israelites abandoned God and went there to worship the **idol.**
17. 3 It will be used to make a wooden **idol** covered with silver.
17. 4 a metal-worker, who made an **idol,** carving it from wood
17. 5 He made some **idols** and an ephod, and appointed one of his
18.14 of these houses there is a wooden **idol** covered with silver?
18.14 There are also other **idols** and an ephod.
18.17 house and took the wooden **idol** covered with silver,
18.17 the other **idols,** and the ephod,
18.30 from Dan set up the **idol** to be worshipped, and Jonathan,
18.31 Micah's **idol** remained there all the time that the Tent
1 Sam 7. 4 Israelites got rid of their **idols** of Baal and Astarte,
12.10 you, Lord, and worshipped the **idols** of Baal and Astarte.
15.23 bad as witchcraft, and arrogance is as sinful as **idolatry.**
19.13 Then she took the household **idol,** laid it on the bed,
19.16 and found the household **idol** in the bed and the goats'-hair
31. 9 to tell the good news to their **idols** and to their people.
2 Sam 5.21 Philistines fled, they left their **idols** behind, and David
12.30 From the head of the **idol** of the Ammonite god Molech
1 Kgs 14. 9 aroused my anger by making **idols** and metal images to worship.
14.15 have aroused his anger by making **idols** of the goddess Asherah.
15.12 and he removed all the **idols** his predecessors had made.
15.13 she had made an obscene **idol** of the fertility goddess Asherah.
15.13 Asa cut down the **idol** and burnt it in the valley of
16.13 Because of their **idolatry** and because they led Israel
16.26 by his sins and by leading the people into sin and **idolatry.**
18.18 You are disobeying the Lord's commands and worshipping the **idols**
19.18 to me and have not bowed to Baal or kissed his **idol."**
21.26 shameful sins by worshipping **idols,** as the Amorites had done,
2 Kgs 9.22 the witchcraft and **idolatry** that your mother Jezebel started?"
11.18 smashed the altars and the **idols,** and killed Mattan,
16. 3 son as a burnt-offering to **idols,** imitating the disgusting
17.12 and disobeyed the Lord's command not to worship **idols.**
17.15 worshipped worthless **idols** and became worthless themselves,
17.29 continued to make their own **idols,** and they placed them in
17.29 Each different group made **idols** in the cities they were
17.30 people of Babylon made **idols** of the god Succoth Benoth;
17.30 the people of Cuth, **idols** of Nergal;
17.30 the people of Hamath, **idols** of Ashima;
17.31 the people of Ivvah, **idols** of Nibhaz and Tartak;
17.41 people worshipped the Lord, but they also worshipped their **idols;**
21.11 and with his **idols** he has led the people of Judah into
21.16 the people of Judah into **idolatry,** causing them to sin
21.21 and he worshipped the **idols** that his father had worshipped.
23.13 the worship of disgusting **idols**—Astarte the goddess of Sidon,
23.24 all the household gods, **idols,** and all other pagan objects of
1 Chr 10. 9 to tell the good news to their **idols** and to their people.
14.12 Philistines fled, they left their **idols** behind, and David
16.26 other nations are only **idols,** but the Lord created the heavens.
20. 2 The Ammonite **idol** Molech had a gold crown which weighed
2 Chr 11.15 to worship demons and the **idols** he made in the form of
15. 8 did away with all the **idols** in the land of Judah
15. 8 and Benjamin and all the **idols** in the cities he had captured

2 Chr 15.16 she had made an obscene **idol** of the fertility goddess Asherah.
15.16 Asa cut down the **idol,** chopped it up, and burnt the pieces
23.17 They smashed the altars and **idols** there and killed Mattan,
24.18 and began to worship **idols** and the images of the goddess
25.14 Edomites, he brought their **idols** back with him, set them up,
25.20 to be defeated, because he had worshipped the Edomite **idols.**
28. 3 own sons as burnt-offerings to **idols,** imitating the disgusting
32.19 the gods of the other peoples, **idols** made by human hands.
33.19 he made and the **idols** that he worshipped—are all recorded
33.22 and he worshipped the **idols** that his father had worshipped.
34. 3 the symbols of the goddess Asherah, and all the other **idols.**
34. 4 Asherah and all the other **idols** and then scattered the dust
34. 7 symbols of Asherah, ground the **idols** to dust, and broke in
34.33 Josiah destroyed all the disgusting **idols** that were in the
36.14 nations round them in worshipping **idols,** and so they defiled
Neh 9.18 They made an **idol** in the shape of a bull-calf and said
Ps 24. 4 in thought, who do not worship **idols** or make false promises.
40. 4 who do not turn to **idols** or join those who worship false
78.58 places of worship, and with their **idols** they made him furious.
96. 5 other nations are only **idols,** but the Lord created the heavens.
97. 7 Everyone who worships **idols** is put to shame;
106.19 They made a gold bull-calf at Sinai and worshipped that **idol;**
106.36 God's people worshipped **idols,** and this caused their
106.37 own sons and daughters as sacrifices to the **idols** of Canaan.
115. 8 and who trust in them become like the **idols** they have made.
135.18 and who trust in them become like the **idols** they have made!
Is 2. 8 Their land is full of **idols,** and they worship objects that
2.17 **Idols** will completely disappear, and the Lord alone will be
2.20 away the gold and silver **idols** they have made, and abandon
10.10 punish those kingdoms that worship **idols,**
10.10 **idols** more numerous than those of Jerusalem
10.11 destroyed Samaria and all its **idols,** and I will do the same
19. 1 Egyptian **idols** tremble before him, and the people of Egypt
19. 3 They will ask their **idols** to help them, and they will go
21. 9 All the **idols** they worshipped lie shattered on the ground."
30.22 You will take your **idols** plated with silver
30.22 and your **idols** covered with gold, and will throw
31. 7 will throw away the sinful **idols** you made out of silver and
40.19 He is not like an **idol** that workmen make,
41. 7 The man who beats the **idol** smooth encourages the one who
41.29 do nothing at all— these **idols** are weak and powerless."
42. 8 I will not let **idols** share my praise.
42.17 All who trust in **idols,** who call images their gods,
44. 9 All those who make **idols** are worthless, and the gods they
44.11 The people who make **idols** are human beings and nothing more.
44.15 a tree for fuel and part of it for making an **idol.**
44.17 wood he makes into an **idol,** and then he bows down and
44.19 The maker of **idols** hasn't the wit or the sense to say,
44.19 And the rest of the wood I made into an **idol.**
44.20 admit to himself that the **idol** he holds in his hand is
45.16 Those who make **idols** will all be ashamed;
45.20 people who parade with their **idols** of wood and pray to gods
46. 2 The **idols** cannot save themselves;
48. 5 from claiming that your **idols** and images made them happen.
57. 8 You set up your obscene **idols** just inside your front doors.
57.10 You think your obscene **idols** give you strength, and so you
57.12 expose your conduct, and your **idols** will not be able to help
57.13 When you cry for help, let those **idols** of yours save you!
66. 3 whether they offer incense or pray to an **idol.**
Jer 1.16 to other gods, and have made **idols** and worshipped them.
2. 5 worshipped worthless **idols** and became worthless themselves.
2. 8 the prophets spoke in the name of Baal and worshipped useless **idols.**
4. 1 to me and remove the **idols** I hate, [2]it will be right
7.30 They have placed their **idols,** which I hate, in my Temple and
8. 5 You cling to your **idols** and refuse to return to me.
8.19 me angry by worshipping your **idols** and by bowing down to
9.14 and have worshipped the **idols** of Baal as their fathers taught
10. 5 Such **idols** are like scarecrows in a field of melons;
10. 8 What can they learn from wooden **idols?**
10. 9 Their **idols** are covered with silver from Spain and with
10.14 those who make **idols** are disillusioned, because the gods
14.22 None of the **idols** of the nations can send rain;
16.18 defiled my land with **idols** that are as lifeless as corpses,
16.19 ancestors had nothing but false gods, nothing but useless **idols.**
18.15 they burn incense to **idols.**
25. 6 make the Lord angry by worshipping the **idols** you had made.
25. 7 him angry with your **idols** and have brought his punishment on
32.34 They even placed their disgusting **idols** in the Temple
44. 8 make me angry by worshipping **idols** and by sacrificing to
50. 2 Babylon's **idols** are put to shame, her disgusting images are
50.38 is a land of terrifying **idols,** that have made fools of the
51.17 those who make **idols** are disillusioned because the gods
51.47 the time is coming when I will deal with Babylonia's **idols.**
51.52 I will deal with Babylon's **idols,** and the wounded will groan
Ezek 6. 3 send a sword to destroy the places where people worship **idols.**
6. 4 All the people there will be killed in front of their **idols.**
6. 6 all their altars and their **idols** will be smashed to pieces,
6. 9 faithless hearts deserted me and they preferred **idols** to me.
6.13 will be scattered among the **idols** and round the altars,
6.13 in every place where they burnt sacrifices to their **idols.**
7.20 beautiful jewels, but they used them to make disgusting **idols.**
8. 3 Temple, where there was an **idol** that was an outrage to God.
8. 5 the gateway I saw the **idol** that was an outrage to God.
11.18 to get rid of all the filthy, disgusting **idols** they find.
11.21 punish the people who love to worship filthy, disgusting **idols.**
14. 3 have given their hearts to **idols**
14. 3 and are letting **idols** lead them into sin.
14. 4 has given his heart to **idols** and lets them lead him into
14. 4 an answer from me—the answer that his many **idols** deserve!
14. 5 All those **idols** have turned the Israelites away from me,

Ezek 14. 6 Turn back and leave your disgusting **idols.**
14. 7 away from me and worships **idols,** and then goes to consult a
16.19 you offered it as a sacrifice to win the favour of **idols."**
16.20 you had borne me and offered them as sacrifices to **idols.**
16.21 without taking my children and sacrificing them to **idols?**
16.24 you built places to worship **idols** and practise prostitution.
16.31 On every street you built places to worship **idols**
16.36 and to all your disgusting **idols,**
16.36 and you killed your children as sacrifices to **idols.**
16.39 the places where you engage in prostitution and worship **idols.**
18. 6 He doesn't worship the **idols** of the Israelites or eat the
18.12 goes to pagan shrines, worships disgusting **idols,**
18.15 He doesn't worship the **idols** of the Israelites or eat the
20. 7 to throw away the disgusting **idols** they loved and not to
20. 8 not throw away their disgusting **idols** or give up the Egyptian
20.16 and profaned the Sabbath—they preferred to worship their **idols.**
20.18 not follow their customs or defile yourselves with their **idols.**
20.24 and worshipped the same **idols** their ancestors had served.
20.30 same sins your fathers did and go running after their **idols?**
20.31 defile yourselves with the same **idols** by sacrificing your
20.39 Go on and serve your **idols!**
20.39 stop dishonouring my holy name by offering gifts to your **idols.**
21.21 he consults his **idols;**
22. 3 people and have defiled yourself by worshipping **idols,**
22. 4 and are defiled by the **idols** you made, and so your day
22. 9 Some of them eat sacrifices offered to **idols.**
23. 7 her lust led her to defile herself by worshipping Assyrian **idols.**
23.27 look at any more **idols** or think about Egypt any more."
23.30 prostitute for the nations and defiled yourself with their **idols.**
23.37 adultery and murder—adultery with **idols** and murder of the
23.37 They sacrificed my sons to their **idols.**
23.39 my children as sacrifices to **idols,** they came to my Temple
23.49 punish you for your immorality and your sin of worshipping **idols.**
30.13 "I will destroy the **idols** and the false gods in Memphis.
33.25 You worship **idols.**
36.18 land and because of the **idols** by which they had defiled it.
36.25 you clean from all your **idols** and everything else that has
37.23 not defile themselves with disgusting **idols** any more
44.10 rest of the people of Israel, deserted me and worshipped **idols.**
44.12 they conducted the worship of **idols** for the people of Israel
Hos 3. 1 gods and like to take offerings of raisins to **idols."**
3. 4 stone pillars, without **idols** or images to use for divination.
4.17 The people of Israel are under the spell of **idols.**
5. 4 **Idolatry** has a powerful hold on them, and they do not
6.10 my people have defiled themselves by worshipping **idols.**
8. 4 silver and gold and made **idols**—for their own destruction.
8. 5 How long will it be before they give up their **idolatry?**
8. 6 An Israelite craftsman made the **idol,** and it is not a god
10. 5 They and the priests who serve the **idol** will weep over it.
10. 6 The **idol** will be carried off to Assyria as tribute to the
10. 8 where the people of Israel worship **idols,** will be destroyed.
11. 2 they burnt incense to **idols.**
12.11 Yet **idols** are worshipped in Gilead, and those who worship
13. 2 images to worship—**idols** of silver, designed by human minds,
13. 2 How can men kiss those **idols**—idols in the shape of bulls!
14. 3 will never again say to our **idols** that they are our God.
14. 8 The people of Israel will have nothing more to do with **idols;**
Amos 8.14 Those who swear by the **idols** of Samaria, who say,
Jon 2. 8 Those who worship worthless **idols** have abandoned their
Mic 1. 5 Who is guilty of **idolatry** in Judah?
1. 7 All its precious **idols** will be smashed to pieces,
5.13 I will destroy your **idols** and sacred stone pillars;
Nah 1.14 I will destroy the **idols** that are in the temples of their
Hab 2.18 What's the use of an **idol?**
2.19 Can an **idol** reveal anything to you?
Zech 10. 2 People consult **idols** and fortune-tellers, but the answers
13. 1 David and the people of Jerusalem from their sin and **idolatry.**
13. 2 remove the names of the **idols** from the land, and no one
13. 2 be a prophet and will take away the desire to worship **idols.**
Acts 7.41 that they made an **idol** in the shape of a bull,
7.43 they were **idols** that you had made to worship.
15.20 is ritually unclean because it has been offered to **idols;**
15.29 eat no food that has been offered to **idols;**
17.16 upset when he noticed how full of **idols** the city was.
21.25 that has been offered to **idols,** or any blood, or any animal
Rom 2.22 You detest **idols**—but do you rob temples?
1 Cor 5.10 are immoral or greedy or are thieves or who worship **idols.**
5.11 immoral or greedy or worships **idols** or is a slanderer or a
6. 9 are immoral or who worship **idols** or are adulterers
8. 1 Now, concerning what you wrote about food offered to **idols.**
8. 4 So then, about eating the food offered to **idols:**
8. 4 we know that an **idol** stands for something that does not
8. 7 have been so used to **idols** that to this day when they
8. 7 they still think of it as food that belongs to an **idol;**
8.10 who have so-called "knowledge," eating in the temple of an **idol;**
8.10 will not this encourage him to eat food offered to **idols?**
10. 7 as they did, [7] nor to worship **idols,** as some of them did.
10.14 So then, my dear friends, keep away from the worship of **idols.**
10.19 I imply, then, that an **idol** or the food offered to it
10.28 "This food was offered to **idols,"** then do not eat that food,
12. 2 led astray in many ways to the worship of lifeless **idols.**
2 Cor 6.16 How can God's temple come to terms with pagan **idols?**
Gal 5.20 in worship of **idols** and witchcraft.
Eph 5. 5 greed is a form of **idolatry**) will ever receive a share in
Col 3. 5 evil passions, and greed (for greed is a form of **idolatry**).
1 Thes 1. 9 how you turned away from **idols** to God, to serve the true
1 Pet 4. 3 orgies, drinking parties, and the disgusting worship of **idols.**
Rev 2.14 food that had been offered to **idols** and to practise sexual
2.20 sexual immorality and eating food that has been offered to **idols.**
9.20 stop worshipping demons, nor the **idols** of gold, silver, bronze,

Rev 21. 8 practise magic, those who worship **idols,** and all liars—
22.15 murderers, those who worship **idols** and those who are liars

IGNORANT

Num 15.24 was made because of the **ignorance** of the community, they are
Job 13. 4 You cover up your **ignorance** with lies;
34.35 that Job is speaking from **ignorance** and that nothing he
36.12 not, they will die in **ignorance** and cross the stream into
38. 2 are you to question my wisdom with your **ignorant,** empty words?
42. 3 how I dare question your wisdom when I am so very **ignorant.**
Ps 14. 4 "Are all these evildoers **ignorant?**
53. 4 "Are these evildoers **ignorant?**
82. 5 "How **ignorant** you are!
119.130 of your teachings gives light and brings wisdom to the **ignorant.**
Prov 9. 4 "Come in, **ignorant** people!"
9. 6 Leave the company of **ignorant** people, and live.
9.13 Stupidity is like a loud, **ignorant,** shameless woman.
9.16 "Come in, **ignorant** people!"
12.23 what they know, but stupid people advertise their **ignorance.**
13.16 before they act, but stupid people advertise their **ignorance.**
14.18 **Ignorant** people get what their foolishness deserves,
15.14 want to learn, but stupid people are satisfied with **ignorance.**
Is 44. 9 worship these gods are blind and **ignorant**—and they will be
Jer 5. 4 Then I thought, "These are only the poor and **ignorant.**
Ezek 45.20 behalf of anyone who sins unintentionally or through **ignorance.**
Acts 3.17 you and your leaders did to Jesus was due to your **ignorance.**
17.18 "What is this **ignorant** show-off trying to say?"
Rom 1.14 and to the savage, to the educated and to the **ignorant.**
2.20 an instructor for the foolish, and a teacher for the **ignorant.**
Eph 4.18 that God gives, for they are completely **ignorant** and stubborn.
5.15 Don't live like **ignorant** people, but like wise people.
2 Tim 2.23 But keep away from foolish and **ignorant** arguments;
Heb 5. 2 to be gentle with those who are **ignorant** and make mistakes.
1 Pet 1.14 shaped by those desires you had when you were still **ignorant.**
2.15 wants you to silence the **ignorant** talk of foolish people by
2 Pet 3.16 in his letters which **ignorant** and unstable people explain falsely,

IGNORE

Lev 20. 4 But if the community **ignores** what he has done and does not
Deut 22. 1 cow or sheep running loose, do not **ignore** it;
22. 4 donkey or cow has fallen down, don't **ignore** it;
1 Kgs 12. 8 he **ignored** the advice of the older men and went instead
12.13 The king **ignored** the advice of the older men and spoke
1 Chr 13. 3 God's Covenant Box, which was **ignored** while Saul was king."
2 Chr 10. 8 he **ignored** the advice of the older men and went instead
10.13 The king **ignored** the advice of the older men and spoke
25.16 because you have done all this and have **ignored** my advice."
36.16 But they ridiculed God's messengers, **ignoring** his words
Ezra 9.14 how can we **ignore** your commandments again and intermarry with
Job 24.12 the wounded and dying cry out, but God **ignores** their prayers.
34.27 they have stopped following him and **ignored** all his commands.
37.24 of him, and that he **ignores** those who claim to be wise.
Ps 22.24 He does not neglect the poor or **ignore** their suffering;
50.22 "Listen to this, you that **ignore** me, or I will destroy
66.18 If I had **ignored** my sins, the Lord would not have
Prov 1.25 You have **ignored** all my advice and have not been willing
4. 5 Do not forget or **ignore** what I say.
12.16 Sensible people will **ignore** an insult.
15. 5 It is foolish to **ignore** what your father taught you;
15.29 pray, the Lord listens, but he **ignores** those who are evil.
19.11 When someone wrongs you, it is a great virtue to **ignore** it.
19.16 if you **ignore** them, you will die.
31. 5 forget the laws and **ignore** the rights of people in need.
Ecc 10. 6 are given positions of authority while rich men are **ignored.**
Is 30.12 "You **ignore** what I tell you and rely on violence and deceit.
53. 3 look at him— we **ignored** him as if he were nothing.
63.15 Do not **ignore** us.
65.11 you that forsake me, who **ignore** Zion, my sacred hill,
Ezek 3.27 will listen, but some will **ignore** you, for they are a nation
16.59 because you **ignored** your promises and broke the covenant.
22.26 between clean and unclean things, and they **ignore** the Sabbath.
24.14 I will not **ignore** your sins or show pity or be merciful.
Dan 11.37 The king will **ignore** the god his ancestors served,
11.37 In fact, he will **ignore** every god, because he will think he
Hos 14. 9 but sinners stumble and fall because they **ignore** them.
2 Pet 3. 5 They purposely **ignore** the fact that long ago God gave a command,

ILL

Gen 48. 1 Some time later Joseph was told that his father was **ill.**
Ex 23.25 you with food and water and take away all your **illnesses.**
1 Sam 19.14 men came to get David, Michal told them that he was **ill.**
30.13 "My master left me behind three days ago because I was **ill.**
2 Sam 12.15 that Uriah's wife had borne to David to become very **ill.**
13. 2 with her that he became **ill,** because it seemed impossible for
13. 5 said to him, "Pretend that you are **ill** and go to bed.
13. 6 So Amnon pretended that he was **ill** and went to bed.
1 Kgs 14. 1 At that time King Jeroboam's son Abijah fell **ill.**
14. 5 wife was coming to ask him about her son, who was **ill.**
17.17 Some time later the widow's son fell **ill;**
2 Kgs 8. 7 to Damascus at a time when King Benhadad of Syria was **ill.**
8. 9 ask you whether or not he will recover from his **illness."**
8.11 horrified look on his face until Hazael became **ill** at ease.
13.14 The prophet Elisha fell **ill** with a fatal disease,
20. 1 About this time King Hezekiah fell **ill** and almost died.
20.12 that King Hezekiah had been **ill,** so he sent him a letter
2 Chr 32.24 About this time King Hezekiah fell **ill** and almost died.
Neh 2. 2 You aren't **ill,** so it must be that you're unhappy."
Ps 41. 8 They say, "He is fatally **ill;**
Is 33.24 ever again complain of being **ill,** and all sins will be
38. 1 About this time King Hezekiah fell **ill** and almost died.
38. 9 Hezekiah recovered from his **illness,** he wrote this song of
39. 1 that King Hezekiah had been **ill,** so he sent him a letter
Ezek 6.12 Those far away will fall **ill** and die;
Dan 8.27 I was depressed and **ill** for several days.
Mt 12.15 healed all those who were **ill** [16]and gave them orders not
14.14 with pity for them, and he healed those who were **ill.**
14.36 to let those who were **ill** at least touch the edge of
Mk 3.10 and all those who were **ill** kept pushing their way to him
5.23 and begged him earnestly, "My little daughter is very **ill.**
6.56 would take those who were **ill** to the market-places and beg
Lk 13.11 had an evil spirit that had made her **ill** for eighteen years;
13.12 out to her, "Woman, you are free from your **illness!"**
Jn 4.46 A government official was there whose son was **ill** in Capernaum.
5. 5 A man was there who had been **ill** for thirty-eight years.
5. 6 knew that the man had been **ill** for such a long time;
6. 2 they had seen his miracles of healing those who were **ill.**
11. 1 A man named Lazarus, who lived in Bethany, was **ill.**
11. 2 it was her brother Lazarus who was **ill.)**
11. 3 "Lord, your dear friend is **ill."**
11. 4 "The final result of this **illness** will not be the death of
11. 6 the news that Lazarus was **ill,** he stayed where he was for
Acts 5.16 Jerusalem, bringing those who were **ill** or who had evil spirits
9.37 At that time she became **ill** and died.
19.12 to those who were **ill,** and their diseases were driven away,
1 Cor 11.30 why many of you are weak and **ill,** and several have died.
Gal 4.13 it was because I was **ill.**
Phil 2.26 and is very upset because you had heard that he was **ill.**
2.27 Indeed he was **ill** and almost died.
1 Tim 5.23 wine to help your digestion, since you are **ill** so often.
2 Tim 4.20 Corinth, and I left Trophimus in Miletus, because he was **ill.**
Jas 5.14 Is there anyone who is **ill?**

ILL-MANNERED

1 Cor 13. 5 love is not **ill-mannered** or selfish or irritable;

ILL-TREAT

Gen 26.11 "Anyone who **ill-treats** this man or his wife will be put to
31.50 Laban went on, "If you **ill-treat** my daughters or if you
Ex 5.22 Lord again and said, "Lord, why do you **ill-treat** your people?
22.21 "Do not **ill-treat** or oppress a foreigner;
22.22 Do not **ill-treat** any widow or orphan.
23. 9 "Do not **ill-treat** a foreigner;
Lev 19.33 "Do not **ill-treat** foreigners who are living in your land.
Num 20.15 The Egyptians **ill-treated** our ancestors and us,
Job 22. 9 to help widows, but you also robbed and **ill-treated** orphans.
24.21 happens because he **ill-treated** widows and showed no kindness
Prov 19.26 a shameful, disgraceful person would **ill-treat** his father or
Jer 22. 3 Do not **ill-treat** or oppress foreigners, orphans, or widows;
Ezek 22.29 They **ill-treat** the poor and take advantage of foreigners.
34.22 rescue my sheep and not let them be **ill-treated** any more.
Amos 4. 1 well-fed cows of Bashan, who **ill-treat** the weak, oppress the
Mt 17.12 In the same way they will also **ill-treat** the Son of Man."
Lk 6.28 bless those who curse you, and pray for those who **ill-treat** you.
Acts 7.24 saw one of them being **ill-treated** by an Egyptian, so he went
7.27 But the one who was **ill-treating** the other pushed Moses aside.
14. 5 together with their leaders, decided to **ill-treat** the apostles
1 Thes 2. 2 how we had already been **ill-treated** and insulted in Philippi
Heb 10.33 at times publicly insulted and **ill-treated,** and at other times
11.37 in skins of sheep or goats—poor, persecuted, and **ill-treated.**

ILLUSION

Is 30.10 Let us keep our **illusions.**

ILLUSTRATION

Heb 9. 9 This is an **illustration** which points to the present time.

IMAGE

Ex 20. 4 "Do not make for yourselves **images** of anything in heaven
Deut 5. 8 " 'Do not make for yourselves **images** of anything in heaven
1 Sam 7. 3 all the foreign gods and the **images** of the goddess Astarte.
1 Kgs 14. 9 aroused my anger by making idols and metal **images** to worship.
16.33 He also put up an **image** of the goddess Asherah.
2 Kgs 3. 2 he pulled down the **image** his father had made for the worship
13. 6 and the **image** of the goddess Asherah remained in Samaria.
17.10 put up stone pillars and **images** of the goddess Asherah,
17.16 they also made an **image** of the goddess Asherah, worshipped
18. 4 stone pillars, and cut down the **images** of the goddess Asherah.
19.18 no gods at all, only **images** of wood and stone made by
21. 3 of Baal and made an **image** of the goddess Asherah, as King
23.15 he also burnt the **image** of Asherah.
2 Chr 24.18 began to worship idols and the **images** of the goddess Asherah.
28. 2 He had metal **images** of Baal made, [3]burnt incense in the
33. 3 the worship of Baal, made **images** of the goddess Asherah,
33. 7 He placed an **image** in the Temple, the place about which
33.15 the foreign gods and the **image** that he had placed there, and
34. 4 They ground to dust the **images** of Asherah and all the other
Ps 106.20 glory of God for the **image** of an animal that eats grass.
Is 10.11 same to Jerusalem and the **images** that are worshipped there."
37.19 no gods at all, only **images** of wood and stone made by
40.20 a skilful craftsman to make an **image** that won't fall down.
42.17 in idols, who call **images** their gods, will be humiliated and
44.10 It's no good making a metal **image** to worship as a god!

Is 48. 5 from claiming that your idols and **images** made them happen.
Jer 50. 2 Babylon's idols are put to shame, her disgusting **images** are
Ezek 8.12 They are all worshipping in a room full of **images.**
16.17 used it to make male **images,** and committed adultery with them.
16.18 and put them on the **images,** and you offered to the images
23.14 She was attracted by the **images** of high Babylonian officials
Dan 11. 8 carry back to Egypt the **images** of their gods and the
Hos 3. 4 stone pillars, without idols or **images** to use for divination.
13. 2 on sinning by making metal **images** to worship—idols of silver,
Amos 5.26 because you have worshipped **images** of Sakkuth, your king god,
5.26 have to carry those **images** [27] when I take you into exile
Mic 1. 7 by fire, and all its **images** will become a desolate heap.
5.14 I will pull down the **images** of the goddess Asherah in
Acts 7.43 Molech that you carried, and the **image** of Rephan, your star god;
17.29 nature is anything like an **image** of gold or silver or stone,
Rom 1.23 immortal God, they worship **images** made to look like mortal man
1 Cor 11. 7 his head, because he reflects the **image** and glory of God.
13.12 What we see now is like a dim **image** in a mirror;
Col 3.10 constantly renewing in his own **image,** in order to bring you
Rev 13.14 told them to build an **image** in honour of the beast that
13.15 to breathe life into the **image** of the first beast,
13.15 so that the **image** could talk and put to death
14. 9 worships the beast and its **image** and receives the mark on
14.11 worship the beast and its **image,** for anyone who has the mark
15. 2 over the beast and its **image** and over the one whose name
16. 2 of the beast and on those who had worshipped its **image.**
19.20 beast and those who had worshipped the **image** of the beast.)
20. 4 worshipped the beast or its **image,** nor had they received the

AV IMAGE
see also **IDOL**

Lev 26. 1 set up statues, stone **pillars,** or carved stones to worship.
Deut 16.22 And do not set up any stone **pillar** for idol worship;
2 Kgs 10.27 So they destroyed the sacred **pillar** and the temple, and
21. 7 He placed the **symbol** of the goddess Asherah in the Temple,
Dan 2.31 standing before you a giant **statue,** bright and shining, and
3. 1 King Nebuchadnezzar had a gold **statue** made, twenty-seven
3. 2 of the **statue** which King Nebuchadnezzar had set up.
3. 3 stood in front of the **statue,** [4] a herald announced in a loud
3. 5 worship the gold **statue** that King Nebuchadnezzar has set up.
3. 7 the gold **statue** which King Nebuchadnezzar had set up.
3.10 down and worship the gold **statue,** [11] and that anyone who
3.12 worship your god or bow down to the **statue** you set up."
3.14 and to bow down to the gold **statue** I have set up?
3.15 all the other instruments, bow down and worship the **statue.**
3.18 not bow down to the gold **statue** that you have set up."
Mt 22.20 and he asked them, "Whose **face** and name are these?"
Mk 12.16 him one, and he asked, "Whose **face** and name are these?"
Lk 20.24 Whose **face** and name are these on it?"
Acts 19.35 Artemis and of the sacred **stone** that fell down from heaven.
1 Cor 15.49 Just as we wear the **likeness** of the man made of earth,
15.49 so we will wear the **likeness** of the Man from heaven.
2 Cor 3.18 Spirit, transforms us into his **likeness** in an ever greater degree
4. 4 about the glory of Christ, who is the exact **likeness** of God.
Col 1.15 Christ is the visible **likeness** of the invisible God.
Heb 1. 3 glory and is the exact **likeness** of God's own being, sustaining
10. 1 Law is not a full and faithful **model** of the real things;

IMAGINE

Esth 4.13 "Don't **imagine** that you are safer than any other Jew just
Ps 41. 7 to each other about me, they **imagine** the worst about me.
Prov 18.11 Rich people, however, **imagine** that their wealth protects
Is 29. 7 vanish like a dream, like something **imagined** in the night.
Jer 14.14 predictions are worthless things that they have **imagined.**
23.16 tell you what they have **imagined** and not what I have said.

IMITATE

2 Kgs 10.29 But he **imitated** the sin of King Jeroboam, who led Israel
16. 3 burnt-offering to idols, **imitating** the disgusting practice of
17.15 disobeying the Lord's command not to **imitate** them.
17.19 they **imitated** the customs adopted by the people of Israel.
21.21 **imitated** his father's actions, and he worshipped the idols that
2 Chr 28. 3 burnt-offerings to idols, **imitating** the disgusting practice of
Mic 1.13 You **imitated** the sins of Israel and so caused Jerusalem to sin.
Mt 23. 3 do not, however, **imitate** their actions, because they don't
1 Cor 11. 1 **Imitate** me, then, just as I imitate Christ.
Phil 3.17 Keep on **imitating** me, my brothers.
1 Thes 1. 6 You **imitated** us and the Lord;
Heb 13. 7 Think back on how they lived and died, and **imitate** their faith.
3 Jn 11 do not imitate what is bad, but **imitate** what is good.

IMMANUEL

Is 7.14 is pregnant will have a son and will name him **'Immanuel.'**
Mt 1.23 be called **Immanuel"** (which means, "God is with us").

IMMATURE

Prov 8. 5 Are you **immature?**
Is 3. 4 The Lord will let the people be governed by **immature** boys.

IMMORAL

Gen 39. 9 then could I do such an **immoral** thing and sin against God?"
Lev 19.29 turn to other gods and the land will be full of **immorality.**
Judg 19.23 Don't do such an evil, **immoral** thing!
20. 6 These people have committed an evil and **immoral** act among us.
20.10 punish Gibeah for this **immoral** act that they have committed in
Prov 2.16 be able to resist any **immoral** woman who tries to seduce you
23.27 Prostitutes and **immoral** women are a deadly trap.
Ezek 16.27 who hate you and are disgusted with your **immoral** actions.
16.43 Why did you add sexual **immorality** to all the other disgusting
23.13 saw that she was completely **immoral,** that the second sister
23.14 "She sank deeper and deeper in her **immorality.**
23.21 you wanted to repeat the **immorality** you were guilty of as a
23.44 They went back to Oholah and Oholibah, those **immoral** women.
23.48 will put a stop to **immorality,** as a warning to every woman
23.49 will punish you for your **immorality** and your sin
24.13 Jerusalem, your **immoral** actions have defiled you.
Mt 15.19 lead him to kill, commit adultery, and do other **immoral** things;
Mk 7.21 lead him to do **immoral** things, to rob, kill, [22] commit adultery,
Acts 15.20 to keep themselves from sexual **immorality;**
15.29 and keep yourselves from sexual **immorality.**
21.25 and that they must keep themselves from sexual **immorality."**
Rom 13.13 no orgies or drunkenness, no **immorality** or indecency, no fighting
1 Cor 5. 1 said that there is sexual **immorality** among you so terrible
5. 9 I wrote you I told you not to associate with **immoral** people.
5.10 not mean pagans who are **immoral** or greedy or are thieves or
5.11 himself a brother but is **immoral** or greedy or worships idols
6. 9 people who are **immoral** or who worship idols or are adulterers
6.13 not to be used for sexual **immorality,** but to serve the Lord;
6.18 Avoid **immorality.**
6.18 is guilty of sexual **immorality** sins against his own body.
7. 2 because there is so much **immorality,** every man should have
10. 8 not be guilty of sexual **immorality,** as some of them were—
2 Cor 12.21 have not repented of the **immoral** things they have done—
Gal 5.19 It shows itself in **immoral,** filthy, and indecent actions;
Eph 5. 3 that any matters of sexual **immorality** or indecency or greed
5. 5 that no one who is **immoral,** indecent, or greedy
Col 3. 5 such as sexual **immorality,** indecency, lust, evil passions,
1 Thes 4. 3 God wants you to be holy and completely free from sexual **immorality.**
4. 7 God did not call us to live in **immorality,** but in holiness.
1 Tim 1.10 for murderers, [10] for the **immoral,** for sexual perverts,
Heb 12.16 Let no one become **immoral** or unspiritual like Esau,
13. 4 God will judge those who are **immoral** and those who commit
2 Pet 2. 2 Even so, many will follow their **immoral** ways;
2. 7 who was distressed by the **immoral** conduct of lawless people.
2.14 They want to look at nothing but **immoral** women;
2.18 stupid statements, and use **immoral** bodily lusts to trap those who
Jude 4 in order to excuse their **immoral** ways, and who reject Jesus
7 those angels did and indulged in sexual **immorality** and perversion:
Rev 2.14 that had been offered to idols and to practise sexual **immorality.**
2.20 my servants into practising sexual **immorality** and eating food
2.21 her sins, but she does not want to turn from her **immorality.**
9.21 repent of their murders, their magic, their sexual **immorality,**
14. 8 drink her wine—the strong wine of her **immoral** lust!"
17. 2 of the earth practised sexual **immorality** with her, and the people
17. 2 became drunk from drinking the wine of her **immorality."**
17. 4 of obscene and filthy things, the result of her **immorality.**
18. 3 have drunk her wine—the strong wine of her **immoral** lust.
18. 3 of the earth practised sexual **immorality** with her,
18. 9 who took part in her **immorality** and lust will cry and weep
19. 2 the prostitute who was corrupting the earth with her **immorality.**
21. 8 perverts, murderers, the **immoral,** those who practise magic,
22.15 those who practise magic, the **immoral** and the murderers,

IMMORTAL

Rom 1.23 instead of worshipping the **immortal** God, they worship images
2. 7 keep on doing good, and seek glory, honour, and **immortal** life;
1 Cor 15.42 when raised, it will be **immortal.**
15.50 and what is mortal cannot possess **immortality.**
15.53 For what is mortal must be changed into what is **immortal;**
15.54 been changed into the **immortal,** then the scripture will come true:
1 Tim 1.17 To the eternal King, **immortal** and invisible, the only God—
6.16 He alone is **immortal;**
2 Tim 1.10 power of death and through the gospel has revealed **immortal** life.
1 Pet 1.23 again as the children of a parent who is **immortal,** not

IMPARTIAL

Deut 16.18 These men are to judge the people **impartially.**

IMPATIENT

Job 20. 1 Now I'm **impatient** to answer.
21. 4 I have good reason to be **impatient.**
Prov 19. 2 **impatience** will get you into trouble.
Is 32. 4 They will not be **impatient** any longer, but they will act
Zech 6. 7 they were **impatient** to go and inspect the earth.

IMPEDIMENT

Mk 7.35 able to hear, his speech **impediment** was removed, and he

IMPERFECT

Jer 18. 4 piece of pottery turned out **imperfect,** he would take the clay
Eph 5.27 faultless, without spot or wrinkle or any other **imperfection.**
Heb 7.28 Law of Moses appoints men who are **imperfect** to be high priests;

IMPERIAL

Esth 1. 4 of the riches of the **imperial** court with all its splendour
Is 23. 8 all this on Tyre, that **imperial** city, whose merchant princes

IMPLY

1 Cor 10.19 Do I **imply,** then, that an idol or the food offered to

IMPORT

1 Kgs 10.12 It was the finest juniper wood ever **imported** into Israel;
2 Chr 3. 6 stones and with gold **imported** from the land of Parvaim.
9.28 Solomon **imported** horses from Musri and from every other

IMPORTANT
[UNIMPORTANT]

Gen 34.19 He was the most **important** member of his family.
49. 4 not be the most **important,** For you slept with my concubine
Num 22.15 number of leaders, who were more **important** than the first.
Judg 6.15 and I am the least **important** member of my family."
1 Sam 9.21 and my family is the least **important** one in the tribe.
15.17 you consider yourself of no **importance,** you are the leader of
20. 2 tells me everything he does, **important** or not, and he would
2 Kgs 24.16 deported all the **important** men to Babylonia, seven thousand in
25. 9 the houses of all the **important** people in Jerusalem,
25.18 next in rank, and the three other **important** temple officials.
25.19 in charge of military records, and sixty other **important** men.
1 Chr 5.12 leading clan, and Shapham of the second most **important** clan.
26. 6 **important** men in their clan because of their great ability;
28. 1 leading soldiers, and **important** men—gathered in Jerusalem.
Ezra 10. 9 and the **importance** of the meeting everyone was trembling.
Neh 6. 3 them, "I am doing **important** work and can't go down there.
Esth 5.11 office, and how much more **important** he was than any of the
Job 7.17 Why is man so **important** to you?
29.10 even the most **important** men kept silent.
Ps 118.22 as worthless turned out to be the most **important** of all.
119.141 I am **unimportant** and despised,
Prov 4. 7 Getting wisdom is the most **important** thing you can do.
18.16 Do you want to meet an **important** person?
19. 6 Everyone tries to gain the favour of **important** people;
23. 1 down to eat with an **important** man, keep in mind who he
24. 5 yes, knowledge is more **important** than strength.
24. 7 has nothing to say when **important** matters are being discussed.
25. 6 king, don't try to impress him and pretend to be **important.**
25. 7 to be told to give your place to someone more **important.**
Is 10.15 Is a saw more **important** than the man who saws with it?
19.15 in Egypt, rich or poor, **important** or unknown, can offer help.
22.17 You may be **important,** but the Lord will pick you up and
29.16 Which is more **important,** the potter or the clay?
Jer 35. 4 Maaseiah son of Shallum, an **important** official in the Temple,
50.12 Babylonia will be the least **important** nation of all;
52.13 and the houses of all the **important** people in Jerusalem;
52.24 next in rank, and the three other **important** temple officials.
52.25 in charge of military records, and sixty other **important** men.
Ezek 17.13 He took **important** men as hostages [14] to keep the nation from
23.23 young noblemen and officers, all those **important** officials
29.15 I will make them so **unimportant** that they will not be able
Dan 4.17 to anyone he chooses—even to the least **important** of men.'
Mt 5.19 whoever disobeys even the least **important** of the commandments
21.42 as worthless turned out to be the most **important** of all.
22.38 This is the greatest and the most **important** commandment.
22.39 The second most **important** commandment is like it:
23.17 Which is more **important,** the gold or the Temple which makes
23.19 Which is the more **important,** the gift or the altar which
23.23 neglect to obey the really **important** teachings of the Law,
25.40 for one of the least **important** of these brothers of mine,
25.45 one of these least **important** ones, you refused to help me.'
Mk 12.10 as worthless turned out to be the most **important** of all.
12.28 "Which commandment is the most **important** of all?"
12.29 Jesus replied, "The most **important** one is this:
12.31 The second most **important** commandment is this:
12.31 There is no other commandment more **important** than these two."
12.33 It is more **important** to obey these two commandments than to
Lk 12.23 Life is much more **important** than food,
12.23 and the body much more **important** than clothes.
14. 8 happen that someone more **important** than you has been invited,
20.17 as worthless turned out to be the most **important** of all.'
Jn 3.30 He must become more **important** while I become less important."
7.37 On the last and most **important** day of the festival Jesus
Acts 4.11 despised turned out to be the most **important** of all.'
8.27 eunuch, who was an **important** official in charge of the treasury
21.39 Jew, born in Tarsus in Cilicia, a citizen of an **important** city.
Rom 14. 5 certain day is more **important** than other days, while someone else
1 Cor 1.28 in order to destroy what the world thinks is **important.**
12.31 Set your hearts, then, on the more **important** gifts.
15. 3 to you what I received, which is of the greatest **importance:**
2 Cor 11. 7 I humbled myself in order to make you **important.**
Phil 1.24 for your sake it is much more **important** that I remain alive.
1.27 Now, the **important** thing is that your way of life should
2.12 it is even more **important** that you obey me now while
1 Pet 2. 7 as worthless turned out to be the most **important** of all."

IMPOSE

Esth 10. 1 Xerxes **imposed** forced labour on the people of the coastal

IMPOSSIBLE

Gen 18.25 That's **impossible!**
18.25 That is **impossible.**
20.17 the Lord had made it **impossible** for any woman in Abimelech's
Ruth 1.13 No, my daughters, you know that's **impossible.**
2 Sam 13. 2 became ill, because it seemed **impossible** for him to have her;
Jer 33.22 that it will be as **impossible** to count them as it is
Zech 8. 6 "This may seem **impossible** to those of the nation
8. 6 who are now left, but it's not **impossible** for me.
Mt 19.26 answered, "This is **impossible** for man, but for God everything
Mk 10.27 answered, "This is **impossible** for man, but not for God;
Lk 18.27 answered, "What is **impossible** for man is possible for God."
Acts 2.24 because it was **impossible** that death should hold him prisoner.
4.21 saw that it was **impossible** to punish them, because the people
26. 8 who are here find it **impossible** to believe that God raises
27.15 and since it was **impossible** to keep the ship headed into
1 Cor 1.21 in his wisdom made it **impossible** for people to know him by
6.15 **Impossible!**
Heb 6. 6 It is **impossible** to bring them back to repent again,

IMPOSTOR

2 Tim 3.13 and evil persons and **impostors** will keep on going from

IMPRESS

Josh 22.10 they built a large, **impressive** altar there by the river.
1 Sam 21.12 Their words made a deep **impression** on David, and he
Prov 25. 6 king, don't try to **impress** him and pretend to be important.
30.29 are four things that are **impressive** to watch as they walk:
Ezek 31.18 Not even the trees in Eden were so tall and **impressive.**
Dan 1.19 Daniel, Hananiah, Mishael, and Azariah **impressed** him more than
Lk 4.22 They were all well **impressed** with him and marvelled

IMPRINT

Job 38.14 of a garment, clear as the **imprint** of a seal on clay.

IMPRISON see PRISON

IMPROPER

2 Chr 30.18 of purification, and so they were observing Passover **improperly.**

IMPROVE

Prov 1. 9 Their teaching will **improve** your character
1. 9 as a handsome turban or a necklace **improves** your appearance.
1 Cor 8. 8 Food, however, will not **improve** our relations with God;

IMPURE

Lev 12. 7 to take away her **impurity,** and she will be ritually clean.
12. 8 to take away her **impurity,** and she will be ritually clean.
15.24 he is contaminated by her **impurity** and remains unclean for
Ezra 9.11 going to occupy was an **impure** land because the people who
Ps 106.39 They made themselves **impure** by their actions and were
Prov 25. 4 Take the **impurities** out of silver and the artist can
Is 1.25 just as metal is refined, and will remove all your **impurity.**
Rom 6.19 surrendered yourselves entirely as slaves to **impurity**
Phil 1.10 will be free from all **impurity** and blame on the Day of
1 Thes 2. 3 not based on error or **impure** motives, nor do we try to
Heb 9.13 and this purifies them by taking away their ritual **impurity.**
Rev 21.27 But nothing that is **impure** will enter the city, nor anyone

IN PERSON see PERSONALLY

IN THE NAME OF see NAME (2)

INCENSE

Material which is burnt in order to produce a pleasant smell. The Israelites used it in their worship.

Ex 25. 6 for the anointing oil and for the sweet-smelling **incense;**
30. 1 "Make an altar out of acacia-wood, for burning **incense.**
30. 7 get the lamps ready, he is to burn sweet-smelling **incense** on
30. 8 This offering of **incense** is to continue without interruption
30. 9 on this altar any forbidden **incense,**
30.27 equipment, the altar for burning **incense,**
30.35 Use them to make **incense,** mixed like perfume.
30.36 Treat this **incense** as completely holy.
30.37 the same formula to make any **incense** like it for yourselves.
31. 8 equipment, the altar for burning **incense,** [9] the altar for
31.11 oil, and the sweet-smelling **incense** for the Holy Place.
35. 8 for the anointing oil and for the sweet-smelling **incense;**
35.15 the altar for burning **incense** and its poles;
35.15 the sweet-smelling **incense;**
35.28 lamps, for the anointing oil, and for the sweet-smelling **incense.**
37.25 He made an altar out of acacia-wood, for burning **incense.**
37.29 the sacred anointing oil and the pure sweet-smelling **incense,**
39.38 the sweet-smelling **incense;**
40. 5 gold altar for burning **incense** in front of the Covenant Box
40.27 and burnt the sweet-smelling **incense,** just as the Lord
Lev 2. 1 He must put olive-oil and **incense** on it [2] and bring it to
2. 2 oil and all of the **incense** and burn it on the altar
2.15 Add olive-oil and put **incense** on it.
2.16 and also all the **incense,** as a food-offering to the Lord.
4. 7 projections at the corners of the **incense-altar** in the Tent.
4.18 the corners of the **incense-altar** inside the Tent and pour out
5.11 put any olive-oil or any **incense** on it, because it is a
6.15 flour and oil, and the **incense** on it, and burn it on
10. 1 coals in it, added **incense,** and presented it to the Lord.
16.12 and two handfuls of fine **incense** and bring them into the

Lev 16.13 presence he shall put the **incense** on the fire,
16.13 and the smoke of the **incense** will hide the lid of the
24. 7 Put some pure **incense** on each row, as a token food-offering
26.30 tear down your **incense-altars,** and throw your dead bodies on
Num 4. 7 on it the dishes, the **incense** bowls, the offering bowls,
4.16 oil for the lamps, the **incense,** the grain-offerings,
5.15 on it or put any **incense** on it, because it is an
7.12 one gold dish weighing 110 grammes, full of **incense;**
7.84 dishes weighing a total of 1.32 kilogrammes, filled with **incense**
16. 6 firepans, put live coals and **incense** on them, and take them
16.17 will take his firepan, put **incense** on it, and then present
16.18 firepan, put live coals and **incense** on it, and stood at the
16.35 out and burnt up the 250 men who had presented the **incense.**
16.40 Aaron should come to the altar to burn **incense** for the Lord.
16.46 from the altar in it, and put some **incense** on the coals.
16.47 already begun, he put the **incense** on the coals and performed
1 Sam 2.28 the altar, to burn the **incense,** and to wear the ephod to
1 Kgs 7.50 lamp snuffers, bowls, dishes for **incense,** and the pans used
9.25 He also burnt **incense** to the Lord.
11. 8 his foreign wives could burn **incense** and offer sacrifices to
22.43 people continued to offer sacrifices and burn **incense** there.
2 Kgs 12. 3 people continued to offer sacrifices and burn **incense** there.
14. 4 and the people continued to offer sacrifices and burn **incense**
15. 4 people continued to offer sacrifices and burn **incense** there.
15.35 people continued to offer sacrifices and burn **incense** there.
16. 4 every shady tree, Ahaz offered sacrifices and burnt **incense.**
17.11 and they burnt **incense** on all the pagan altars, following
18. 4 time the people of Israel had burnt **incense** in its honour.
25.14 the bowls used for burning **incense,** and all the other bronze
1 Chr 6.49 descendants presented the offerings of **incense** and offered
9.29 sacred equipment, and of the flour, wine, olive-oil, **incense,**
23.13 for ever, to burn **incense** in the worship of the Lord,
28.18 making the altar on which **incense** was burnt and in making
2 Chr 2. 4 will worship him by burning **incense** of fragrant spices,
2. 6 would be anything more than a place to burn **incense** to God?
4.22 the bowls, the dishes for **incense,** and the pans used for
13.11 every evening they offer him **incense** and animal sacrifices
14. 5 places of worship and the **incense-altars** from all the cities
25.14 set them up, worshipped them, and burnt **incense** to them.
26.16 into the Temple to burn **incense** on the altar of incense.
26.18 You have no right to burn **incense** to the Lord.
26.19 in the Temple beside the **incense altar**
26.19 and was holding an **incense burner.**
27. 2 his father he did not sin by burning **incense** in the Temple.
28. 3 images of Baal made, [3] burnt **incense** in the Valley of Hinnom,
28. 4 under every shady tree Ahaz offered sacrifices and burnt **incense.**
28.25 places of worship, where **incense** was to be burnt to foreign
29. 7 failed to burn **incense** or offer burnt-offerings in the Temple
29.11 Lord has chosen to burn **incense** to him and to lead the
30.14 for offering sacrifices and burning **incense** and threw them
32.12 Judah and Jerusalem to worship and burn **incense** at one altar
34. 4 where Baal was worshipped and tore down the **incense-altars**
34. 7 the idols to dust, and broke in pieces all the **incense-altars.**
Neh 13. 5 storing offerings of corn and **incense,** the equipment used in
13. 9 temple equipment, grain-offerings, and **incense** to be put back.
Ps 141. 2 Receive my prayer as **incense,** my uplifted hands as
Song 3. 6 column of smoke, fragrant with **incense** and myrrh,
3. 6 the **incense** sold by the traders?
4. 6 of myrrh, the hill of **incense,** until the morning breezes blow
4.14 saffron, calamus, and cinnamon, or **incense** of every kind.
Is 1.13 I am disgusted with the smell of the **incense** you burn.
17. 8 symbols of the goddess Asherah and altars for burning **incense.**
27. 9 and no more **incense-altars** or symbols of the goddess Asherah
43.23 by demanding offerings or wear you out by asking for **incense.**
43.24 You didn't buy **incense** for me or satisfy me with the fat
60. 6 They will come from Sheba, bringing gold and **incense.**
65. 3 sacrifices in sacred gardens and burn **incense** on pagan altars.
65. 7 They have burnt **incense** at pagan hill shrines and spoken evil
66. 3 whether they offer **incense** or pray to an idol.
Jer 6.20 do I care about the **incense** they bring me from Sheba, or
17.26 grain-offerings and **incense,** as well as thank-offerings.
18.15 they burn **incense** to idols.
19.13 the houses on whose roofs **incense** has been burnt to the
32.29 made me angry by burning **incense** to Baal on the roof-tops
34. 5 and as people burnt **incense** when they buried your ancestors,
34. 5 before you, in the same way they will burn **incense** for you.
41. 5 They were taking corn and **incense** to offer in the Temple.
52.18 the bowls used for burning **incense,** and all the other bronze
52.19 lampstands, the bowls used for **incense,** and the bowls used
Ezek 6. 4 The altars will be torn down and the **incense-altars** broken.
6. 6 be smashed to pieces, their **incense-altars** will be shattered,
8.11 Each one was holding an **incense-burner,**
8.11 and smoke was rising from the **incense.**
16.18 offered to the images the olive-oil and **incense** I had given
23.41 with good things, including the **incense** and the olive-oil
Hos 2.13 forgot me when she burnt **incense** to Baal and put on her
4.13 on the hills they burn **incense** under tall, spreading trees,
11. 2 they burnt **incense** to idols.
Mal 1.11 they burn **incense** to me and offer acceptable sacrifices.
Lk 1. 9 priests, he was chosen by lot to burn **incense** on the altar.
1.10 people outside prayed during the hour when the **incense** was burnt.
1.11 on the right of the altar where the **incense** was burnt.
2 Cor 2.15 we are like a sweet-smelling **incense** offered by Christ to God,
Heb 9. 4 altar for the burning of **incense** and the Covenant Box all
Rev 5. 8 gold bowls filled with **incense,** which are the prayers of God's
8. 3 who had a gold **incense-burner,** came and stood at the altar.
8. 3 was given a lot of **incense** to add to the prayers of
8. 4 The smoke of the burning **incense** went up with the prayers
8. 5 Then the angel took the **incense-burner,** filled it with fire
18.13 and cinnamon, spice, **incense,** myrrh, and frankincense;

INCEST

Lev 18.17 they may be related to you, and that would be **incest.**
20.12 have committed **incest** and are responsible for their own death.
20.19 his aunt, both of them must suffer the consequences for **incest.**

INCITE

2 Chr 21.16 The Lord **incited** them to go to war against Jehoram.

INCLUDE

Acts 6. 9 Freedmen (as it was called), which **included** Jews from Cyrene
Rom 1. 6 This also **includes** you who are in Rome, whom God has
10.12 This **includes** everyone, because there is no difference between
11.12 blessings will be when the complete number of Jews is **included!**
1 Cor 15.27 "all things" do not **include** God himself, who puts all things
2 Cor 10.13 God has set for us, and this **includes** our work among you.
1 Tim 5.11 But do not **include** younger widows in the list;
Heb 2. 8 this clearly **includes** everything.
Jas 2.17 if it is alone and **includes** no actions, then it is dead.
Rev 20. 6 blessed are those who are **included** in this first raising of

INCOME

Prov 16. 8 a little, honestly earned, than to have a large **income** gained
Lk 18.12 a week, and I give you a tenth of all my **income.'**

INCONSIDERATE

Prov 21.24 will show you someone who is arrogant, proud, and **inconsiderate.**

AV INCORRUPTIBLE

1 Cor 9.25 but we do it for one that will last **for ever.**
15.51 will be raised, never to **die** again, and we shall all be
1 Pet 1. 4 in heaven, where they cannot **decay** or spoil or fade away.
1.23 again as the children of a parent who is **immortal,** not

INCREASE

Gen 1.22 fill the sea, and he told the birds to **increase** in number.
3.16 to the woman, "I will **increase** your trouble in pregnancy and
9.27 May God cause Japheth to **increase!**
Ex 1.12 the Israelites, the more they **increased** in number and the
1.20 And the Israelites continued to **increase** and become strong.
Lev 26.18 do not obey me, I will **increase** your punishment seven times.
26.21 to obey me, I will again **increase** your punishment seven times.
Num 15.12 the accompanying offering is to be **increased** proportionately.
Deut 1.11 of your ancestors, make you **increase** a thousand times more
7.13 so that you will **increase** in number and have many children;
7.22 of wild animals would **increase** and be a threat to you.
8. 1 so that you may live, **increase** in number, and occupy the
8.13 all your other possessions have **increased,** [14] make sure that
28.63 prosper and in making you **increase** in number, so he will
33.18 trade on the sea, And may Issachar's wealth **increase** at home.
1 Chr 5.23 and Mount Hermon, and their population **increased** greatly.
2 Chr 12.13 Rehoboam ruled in Jerusalem and **increased** his power as
28.13 Now you want to do something that will **increase** our guilt."
33.14 Manasseh **increased** the height of the outer wall on the
Ps 62.10 even if your riches **increase,** don't depend on them.
75.10 wicked, but the power of the righteous will be **increased.**
107.41 the needy from their misery and made their families **increase**
Prov 29.16 When evil men are in power, crime **increases.**
Jer 23. 3 They will have many children and **increase** in number.
29. 6 You must **increase** in numbers and not decrease.
30.19 By my blessing they will **increase** in numbers;
33.22 will **increase** the number of descendants of my servant David
Ezek 36.11 I will make people and cattle **increase** in number.
36.30 will **increase** the yield of your fruit-trees and your fields,
36.37 and I will let them **increase** in numbers like a flock of
37.26 I will establish them and **increase** their population, and put
Dan 11.20 with taxes in order to **increase** the wealth of his kingdom.
Hos 4. 2 Crimes **increase,** and there is one murder after another.
12. 1 Treachery and acts of violence **increase** among them.
Rom 5.20 Law was introduced in order to **increase** wrongdoing;
5.20 but where sin **increased,** God's grace increased much more.
6. 1 continue to live in sin so that God's grace will **increase?**

INCURABLE

Lev 26.16 will bring disaster on you—**incurable** diseases and fevers that
26.25 for safety, I will send **incurable** diseases among you, and you
Deut 28.35 Lord will cover your legs with **incurable,** painful sores;
28.59 you and on your descendants **incurable** diseases and horrible
Is 17.11 There would be only trouble and **incurable** pain.
Jer 15.18 Why are my wounds **incurable?**
30.12 "Your wounds are **incurable,** your injuries cannot be healed.

INDECENT

Deut 23.14 Do not do anything **indecent** that would cause the Lord to
Mk 7.22 deceit, **indecency,** jealousy, slander, pride, and folly—
Rom 13.13 no orgies or drunkenness, no immorality or **indecency,** no fighting
Gal 5.19 It shows itself in immoral, filthy, and **indecent** actions;
Eph 4.19 to vice and do all sorts of **indecent** things without restraint.
5. 3 matters of sexual immorality or **indecency** or greed should even
5. 5 no one who is immoral, **indecent,** or greedy (for greed is
Col 3. 5 such as sexual immorality, **indecency,** lust, evil passions,
1 Pet 4. 3 Your lives were spent in **indecency,** lust, drunkenness, orgies,

INDEPENDENT

2 Kgs 8.20 Edom revolted against Judah and became an **independent** kingdom.
8.22 Edom has been **independent** of Judah ever since.
2 Chr 21. 8 Edom revolted against Judah and became an **independent** kingdom.
21.10 Edom has been **independent** of Judah ever since.
Is 17. 3 will be defenceless, and Damascus will lose its **independence.**
1 Cor 11.11 is not independent of man, nor is man **independent** of woman.

INDICATE

Jn 12.33 (In saying this he **indicated** the kind of death he was
18.32 words he used when he **indicated** the kind of death he would
21.19 (In saying this, Jesus was **indicating** the way in which Peter
Acts 25.27 send a prisoner without clearly **indicating** the charges against

INDIGNATION

Neh 2.10 good of the people of Israel, and they were highly **indignant.**
Ps 69.24 let your **indignation** overtake them.
2 Cor 7.11 Such **indignation,** such alarm, such feelings, such devotion,

INDIVIDUAL

Col 1.28 into God's presence as a mature **individual** in union with Christ.

INDOORS

Ex 9.20 and they brought their slaves and animals **indoors** for shelter.
2 Kgs 9. 6 the two of them went **indoors,** and the young prophet poured
Job 31.34 have never kept quiet or stayed **indoors** because I feared
Lam 1.20 even **indoors** there is death.
Mt 9.28 When Jesus had gone **indoors,** the two blind men came to him,
13.36 left the crowd and gone **indoors,** his disciples came to him
Mk 9.28 Jesus had gone **indoors,** his disciples asked him privately,
9.33 to Capernaum, and after going **indoors** Jesus asked his disciples,
Jn 20.26 disciples were together again **indoors,** and Thomas was with them.

INDULGE

Prov 21.17 **Indulging** in luxuries, wine, and rich food will never
Jude 7 acted as those angels did and **indulged** in sexual immorality

INDUSTRIOUS

Prov 31.17 She is a hard worker, strong and **industrious.**

INEXPERIENCED

1 Chr 22. 5 he is young and **inexperienced,** so I must make preparations
2 Chr 13. 7 son of Solomon, who was too young and **inexperienced** to resist
Prov 1. 4 They can make an **inexperienced** person clever and teach
1.32 **Inexperienced** people die because they reject wisdom.
7. 7 I saw many **inexperienced** young men, but noticed one foolish

INFANT

Lev 27. 3 **—infant** male under five:
27. 3 **—infant** female:
Job 24. 9 men make slaves of fatherless **infants** and take the poor man's
Is 65.20 will no longer die in **infancy,** and all people will live out

INFECTIOUS

Deut 28.22 The Lord will strike you with **infectious** diseases,

INFERIOR

Job 12. 3 I am in no way **inferior** to you;
13. 1 I'm not your **inferior.**
Ps 8. 5 Yet you made him **inferior** only to yourself;
2 Cor 11. 5 the least bit **inferior** to those very special so-called "apostles"
12.11 I am in no way **inferior** to those very special "apostles"

INFINITE

Eph 3. 8 the Good News about the **infinite** riches of Christ,

INFLAMMATION

Lev 13. 2 a boil or an **inflammation** which could develop into a dreaded
14.55 sores, boils, or **inflammations;**

INFLICTED

1 Kgs 20.21 and chariots, and **inflicted** a severe defeat on the Syrians.

INFLUENTIAL

Ruth 2. 1 named Boaz, a rich and **influential** man who belonged to the
1 Sam 9. 1 There was a wealthy and **influential** man named Kish, from
Mic 7. 3 **influential** man tells them what he wants, and so they scheme

INFORM
[WELL-INFORMED]

Lev 5. 1 and does not give **information** about something he has seen or
2 Sam 15.36 can send them to me with all the **information** you gather."
1 Chr 9. 1 their families, and this **information** was recorded in The Book
Ezra 5.10 names so that we could **inform** you who the leaders of this
5.17 to be rebuilt, and then **inform** us what your will is in
Neh 7. 5 returned from captivity, and this is the **information** I found:
Prov 8. 9 to the **well-informed,** it is all plain.
29.12 ruler pays attention to false **information,** all his officials
Jer 11.18 Lord **informed** me of the plots that my enemies were making
Dan 2.28 He has **informed** Your Majesty what will happen in the future.
Acts 23.15 pretending that you want to get more accurate **information**
23.20 the Council wants to get more accurate **information** about him.
23.30 And when I was **informed** that there was a plot against him,
24.22 Felix, who was well **informed** about the Way, brought the hearing
25.20 about how I could get **information** on these matters, so I
Gal 1.18 went to Jerusalem to obtain **information** from Peter, and I stayed

INHABIT
[UNINHABITED]

Gen 36.20 original **inhabitants** of the land of Edom were divided into
Ex 23.31 give you power over the **inhabitants** of the land, and you
Lev 16.22 all their sins away with him into some **uninhabited** land.
25.10 proclaim freedom to all the **inhabitants** of the land.
Num 33.52 you must drive out all the **inhabitants** of the land.
33.55 do not drive out the **inhabitants** of the land, those that are
Deut 2.23 destroyed the Avvim, the original **inhabitants,** and had taken
Judg 18.27 They killed the **inhabitants** and burnt the town.
1 Sam 22.19 ordered all the other **inhabitants** of Nob, the city of priests,
2 Sam 4. 3 Its original **inhabitants** had fled to Gittaim, where they
1 Kgs 9.16 and captured it, killing its **inhabitants** and setting fire to
2 Kgs 15.16 Tappuah, its **inhabitants,** and the surrounding territory,
1 Chr 1.38 The original **inhabitants** of Edom were descended
2.52 of Haroeh, of half the **inhabitants** of Menuhoth,
7.21 tried to steal the livestock belonging to the native **inhabitants**
11. 4 and the Jebusites, the original **inhabitants** of the land, were
2 Chr 19. 8 legal disputes between **inhabitants** of the city.
Neh 3.13 and the **inhabitants** of the city of Zanoah rebuilt the Valley
Ps 78.55 He drove out the **inhabitants** as his people advanced;
87. 4 among the **inhabitants** of Jerusalem the people of Philistia,
Is 6.11 empty—until the houses are **uninhabited**—until the land itself
Jer 11.13 they have cities, and the **inhabitants** of Jerusalem have set
19.12 that I will make this city and its **inhabitants** like Topheth.
25. 9 fight against Judah and its **inhabitants** and against all the
Lam 4. 6 punished even more than the **inhabitants** of Sodom, which met
Ezek 26.20 you will never again be **inhabited** and take your place in the
36.35 torn down, looted, and left in ruins, are now **inhabited**
Dan 2.38 you ruler of all the **inhabited** earth and ruler over all the
Joel 3.20 Judah and Jerusalem will be **inhabited** for ever,
Amos 1. 5 of Damascus and remove the **inhabitants** of the Valley of Aven

INHERIT

Gen 15. 3 no children, and one of my slaves will **inherit** my property."
15. 4 "This slave Eliezer will not **inherit** your property;
21.10 part of your wealth, which my son Isaac should **inherit."**
31.14 "There is nothing left for us to **inherit** from our father.
48. 6 **inheritance** they get will come through Ephraim and Manasseh.
Lev 25.46 may leave them as an **inheritance** to your sons, whom they
Num 18.20 any property that can be **inherited,** and no part of the land
27. 7 Let his **inheritance** pass on to them.
27. 8 dies without leaving a son, his daughter is to **inherit** his
27. 9 If he has no daughter, his brothers are to **inherit** it.
27.10 he has no brothers, his father's brothers are to **inherit** it.
27.11 his nearest relative is to **inherit** it and hold it as his
36. 8 Every woman who **inherits** property in an Israelite tribe
36. 8 way each Israelite will **inherit** the property of his ancestors,
Josh 24.32 This land was **inherited** by Joseph's descendants.
Judg 11. 2 said to him, "You will not **inherit** anything from our father;
Ruth 4. 6 it would mean that my own children would not **inherit** it.
1 Kgs 21. 3 "I **inherited** this vineyard from my ancestors," Naboth
Job 42.15 father gave them a share of the **inheritance** along with their
Ps 69.36 descendants of his servants will **inherit** it, and those who
Prov 17. 2 a master's worthless son and receive a part of the **inheritance.**
19.14 A man can **inherit** a house and money from his parents,
Ecc 7.11 as good as receiving an **inheritance** [12] and will give you as

INIQUITY

Ezek 36.31 with yourselves because of your sins and your **iniquities.**

AV INIQUITY
see also **EVIL, SIN**

Gen 15.16 Amorites until they become so **wicked** that they must be punished."
44.16 God has uncovered our **guilt.**
Ex 20. 5 I bring **punishment** on those who hate me and on their
34. 7 I will not fail to **punish** children and grandchildren to the
Lev 5.17 the Lord's commands, he is guilty and must pay the **penalty.**
18.25 and so the Lord is **punishing** the land and making it reject
19. 8 who eats it will be **guilty** of treating as ordinary what is
22.16 this would bring guilt and **punishment** on such a person.
Num 5.31 but the woman, if **guilty,** must suffer the consequences.
15.31 He is responsible for his own **death.**
23.21 I foresee that Israel's future Will bring her no **misfortune**
Deut 5. 9 I bring **punishment** on those who hate me and on their
19.15 "One witness is not enough to convict a man of a **crime;**
1 Sam 20. 1 "What **crime** have I committed?
20. 8 But if I'm **guilty,** kill me yourself!
25.24 Let me take the **blame.**
2 Sam 7.14 When he does **wrong,** I will punish him as a father punishes
14. 9 "whatever you do, my family and I will take the **blame;**
14.32 the king, and if I'm **guilty,** then let him put me to

2 Sam	19.19	“Your Majesty, please forget the **wrong** I did that day you
	22.24	I am faultless, that I have kept myself from doing **wrong.**
Job	4. 8	people plough fields of **evil** and sow wickedness like seed;
	5.16	He gives hope to the poor and silences the **wicked.**
	6.30	I am lying— you think I can't tell right from **wrong.**
	11. 6	God is **punishing** you less than you deserve.
	14.17	you will wipe out all the **wrongs** I have done.
	15. 5	Your **wickedness** is evident by what you say;
	31. 3	He sends disaster and ruin to those who do **wrong.**
	31.11	Such **wickedness** should be punished by death.
	34.10	Will Almighty God do what is **wrong?**
Ps	5. 5	you hate all **wicked** people.
	7. 3	my God, if I have **wronged** anyone, if I have betrayed a
	18.23	I am faultless, that I have kept myself from doing **wrong.**
	32. 2	does not accuse of doing **wrong** and who is free from all
	36. 3	His speech is **wicked** and full of lies;
	37. 1	Don't be worried on account of the **wicked;**
	41. 6	they gather **bad** news about me and then go out and tell
	49. 5	when I am surrounded by **enemies,** [6] by evil men who trust in
	53. 1	They are all corrupt, and they have done **terrible** things;
	55. 3	They bring **trouble** on me;
	92. 7	the wicked may grow like weeds, those who do **wrong** may prosper;
	92. 9	your enemies will die, and all the **wicked** will be defeated.
	94. 4	and boast about their **crimes?**
	94.20	nothing to do with **corrupt** judges, who make injustice legal,
	107.42	this and are glad, but all the **wicked** are put to silence.
	119. 3	They never do **wrong;**
	125. 5	But when you punish the **wicked,** punish also those who
Prov	10.29	The Lord protects honest people, but destroys those who do **wrong.**
	22. 8	you sow the seeds of **injustice,** disaster will spring up,
Ecc	3.16	in this world you find **wickedness** where justice and right
Is	6. 7	your lips, and now your **guilt** is gone, and your sins are
	30.13	You are **guilty.**
	53. 6	the **punishment** all of us deserved.
	53.11	am pleased, will bear the **punishment** of many and for his
	59. 3	You are **guilty** of lying, violence, and murder.
Jer	2. 5	“What **accusation** did your ancestors bring against me?
	2.22	strongest soap, I would still see the stain of your **guilt.**
	3.13	Only admit that you are **guilty** and that you have
	14.10	I will remember the **wrongs** they have done and punish them
	36. 3	Then I will forgive their **wickedness** and their sins.”
Lam	4. 6	people have been **punished** even more than the inhabitants of Sodom,
	4.22	he will expose your **guilty** deeds.
Ezek	3.18	he will die, still a **sinner,** and I will hold you responsible
	3.19	and he doesn't stop sinning, he will die, still a **sinner,**
	4. 4	I will place on you the **guilt** of the nation of Israel.
	4. 4	390 days you will stay there and suffer because of their **guilt.**
	4. 4	you to one day for each year their **punishment** will last.
	4. 6	side and suffer for the **guilt** of Judah for forty days—one
	14.10	and the one who consults him will get the same **punishment.**
	21.25	of Israel, your day, the day of your final **punishment,** is
	21.29	and your day is coming, the day of your final **punishment.**
	29.16	fate will remind Israel how **wrong** it was to rely on them.
	35. 5	of her disaster, the time of final **punishment** for her sins.
	44.10	said to me, “I am **punishing** those Levites who, together
	44.12	Sovereign Lord, solemnly swear that they must be **punished.**
Hos	12. 8	And no one can accuse us of getting rich **dishonestly.**’
Mic	3.10	God's city, Jerusalem, on a foundation of murder and **injustice.**
Hab	1. 3	How can you endure to look on such **wrongdoing?**
	2.12	You founded a city on **crime** and built it up by murder.
Zeph	3. 5	he does what is right and never what is **wrong.**
	3.13	who survive will do no **wrong** to anyone, tell no lies, nor
Mt	7.23	Get away from me, you **wicked** people!'
Lk	13.27	Get away from me, all you **wicked** people!'
Rom	6.19	as slaves to impurity and wickedness for **wicked** purposes.
2 Thes	2. 7	The **Mysterious Wickedness** is already at work, but what is
2 Tim	2.19	he belongs to the Lord must turn away from **wrongdoing.”**
Tit	2.14	to rescue us from all **wickedness** and to make us a pure
Heb	1. 9	You love what is right and hate what is **wrong.**
Jas	3. 6	It is a world of **wrong,** occupying its place in our bodies

INJURE

Ex	21.22	child, but she is not **injured** in any other way, the one
	21.23	if the woman herself is **injured,** the punishment shall be life
	22.10	the animal dies or is **injured** or is carried off in a
	22.14	another man and it is **injured** or dies when its owner is
Lev	24.19	“If anyone **injures** another person, whatever he has done
	24.20	Whatever **injury** he causes another person shall be done to him
Deut	17. 8	property rights or of bodily **injury** or those cases that
2 Kgs	1. 2	the roof of his palace in Samaria and was seriously **injured.**
	1. 4	that the Lord says, ‘You will not recover from your **injuries;**
	1. 6	You will not recover from your **injuries;**
Jer	30.12	“Your wounds are incurable, your **injuries** cannot be healed.
	30.15	Complain no more about your **injuries;**
Nah	3.19	no remedy for your **injuries,** and your wounds cannot be healed.

INJUSTICE

Ps	94.20	with corrupt judges, who make **injustice** legal, [21] who plot
Prov	12.17	the truth, justice is done, but lies lead to **injustice.**
	22. 8	you sow the seeds of **injustice,** disaster will spring up,
Ecc	4. 1	again at all the **injustice** that goes on in this world.
	4. 3	have never seen the **injustice** that goes on in this world.
	6. 1	have noticed that in this world a serious **injustice** is done.
	10. 5	Here is an **injustice** I have seen in the world—
	10. 5	an **injustice** caused by rulers.
Is	40.27	Lord doesn't know your troubles or care if you suffer **injustice?**
	58. 6	and the yoke of **injustice,** and let the oppressed go free.
Jer	22.13	builds his house by **injustice** and enlarges it by dishonesty;
Hos	10. 4	Justice has become **injustice,** growing like poisonous weeds
Amos	5.10	people hate anyone who challenges **injustice** and speaks the
Mic	3.10	God's city, Jerusalem, on a foundation of murder and **injustice.**
Zech	8.17	I hate lying, **injustice,** and violence.”

INK

Jer	36.18	to me, and I wrote it down in **ink** on this scroll.”
2 Cor	3. 3	It is written, not with **ink** but with the Spirit of the
2 Jn	12	but I would rather not do it with paper and **ink;**
3 Jn	13	but I do not want to do it with pen and **ink.**

INLAID

Ezek	27. 6	your deck out of pine from Cyprus And **inlaid** it with ivory.

INLAND

Acts	16.12	From there we went **inland** to Philippi, a city of the

INLET

Josh	15. 5	the way up to the **inlet** where the Jordan empties into it.
	18.19	and ended at the northern **inlet** on the Dead Sea, where the

INN

see also **THREE INNS**

Lk	2. 7	manger—there was no room for them to stay in the **inn.**
	10.34	and took him to an **inn,** where he took care of him.
	10.35	he took out two silver coins and gave them to the **innkeeper.**
	10.35	of him,' he told the **innkeeper,** ‘and when I come back this

INNER

Num	3.25	responsible for the Tent, its **inner** cover, its outer cover,
	4.25	the Tent, its **inner** cover, its outer cover, the fine
2 Sam	18.24	in the space between the **inner** and outer gates of the city.
1 Kgs	6.16	An **inner** room, called the Most Holy Place, was built in
	6.19	rear of the Temple an **inner** room was built, where the Lord's
	6.20	This **inner** room was nine metres long, nine metres wide,
	6.21	across the entrance of the **inner** room, which was also covered
	6.29	main room and of the **inner** room were all decorated with
	6.36	An **inner** court was built in front of the Temple,
	7. 9	cut to measure, with their **inner** and outer sides trimmed with
	7.12	The palace court, the **inner** court of the Temple, and the
	16.18	went into the palace's **inner** fortress, set the palace on fire,
2 Kgs	10.25	they went on into the **inner** sanctuary of the temple,
	15.25	assassinated Pekahiah in the palace's **inner** fortress in
2 Chr	3. 8	The **inner** room, called the Most Holy Place, was nine metres
	4. 9	They made an **inner** courtyard for the priests, and also
Esth	4.11	goes to the **inner** courtyard and sees the king without
	5. 1	went and stood in the **inner** courtyard of the palace, facing
Ezek	8. 3	He took me to the **inner** entrance of the north gate of
	8.16	So he took me to the **inner** courtyard of the Temple.
	10. 3	Temple when he went in, and a cloud filled the **inner** courtyard.
	40.16	all the rooms and also in the **inner** walls between the rooms.
	40.16	palm-trees carved on the **inner** walls that faced the passage.
	40.18	outer courtyard was at a lower level than the **inner** courtyard.
	40.19	a gateway at a higher level that led to the **inner** courtyard.
	40.23	another gateway leading to the **inner** courtyard, just as there
	40.24	He measured its **inner** walls and its entrance room, and they
	40.26	palm-trees carved on the **inner** walls that faced the passage.
	40.27	there was a gateway leading to the **inner** courtyard.
	40.28	took me through the south gateway into the **inner** courtyard.
	40.29	its entrance room, and its **inner** walls were the same size as
	40.32	man took me through the east gateway into the **inner** courtyard.
	40.33	its entrance room, and its **inner** walls measured the same as
	40.36	also had guardrooms, decorated **inner** walls, an entrance room,
	40.38	an annexe attached to the **inner** gateway on the north side.
	40.44	Then he brought me into the **inner** courtyard.
	40.44	two rooms opening on the **inner** courtyard, one facing south
	40.47	The man measured the **inner** courtyard, and it was fifty
	41. 3	Then he went to the **innermost** room.
	41. 5	the thickness of the **inner** wall of the temple building, and
	43. 5	and took me into the **inner** courtyard, where I saw that the
	44. 3	leave the gateway through the entrance room at the **inner** end.”
	44.17	enter the gateway to the **inner** courtyard of the Temple,
	44.17	they are on duty in the **inner** courtyard or in the Temple.
	44.21	must not drink any wine before going into the **inner** courtyard.
	44.27	then go into the **inner** courtyard of the Temple and offer
	45.19	and on the posts of the gateways to the **inner** courtyard.
	46. 1	“The east gateway to the **inner** courtyard must be kept closed
	46.12	the east gate to the **inner** courtyard will be opened for him.
	46.19	near the gate on the south side of the **inner** courtyard.
Acts	16.24	jailer threw them into the **inner** cell and fastened their feet
Rom	7.22	My **inner** being delights in the law of God.
Eph	3.16	to be strong in your **inner** selves, [17] and I pray that
Heb	6.19	through the curtain of the heavenly temple into the **inner** sanctuary.
	9. 7	High Priest goes into the **inner** Tent, and he does so only
	13. 9	It is good to receive **inner** strength from God's grace, and
1 Pet	3. 4	should consist of your true **inner** self, the ageless beauty of

INNOCENT

Gen	18.23	“Are you really going to destroy the **innocent** with the guilty?
	18.24	If there are fifty **innocent** people in the city, will you
	18.25	Surely you won't kill the **innocent** with the guilty.
	18.25	you did, the **innocent** would be punished along with the guilty.

Gen 18.26 "If I find fifty **innocent** people in Sodom, I will spare
18.28 But perhaps there will be only forty-five **innocent** people
18.28 not destroy the city if I find forty-five **innocent** people."
20. 4 had not come near her, and he said, "Lord, I am **innocent!**
20.16 as proof to all who are with you that you are **innocent;**
Ex 23. 7 and do not put an **innocent** person to death, for I will
23. 8 is right and ruins the cause of those who are **innocent.**
Num 5.28 But if she is **innocent,** she will not be harmed and will
Deut 19. 6 might catch him and in his anger kill an **innocent** man.
19.10 Do this, so that **innocent** people will not die and so
21. 8 not hold us responsible for the murder of an **innocent** man.'
25. 1 a dispute, and one is declared **innocent** and the other guilty.
27.25 on anyone who accepts money to murder an **innocent** person.'
1 Sam 12. 5 witnesses today that you have found me to be completely **innocent."**
19. 5 to do wrong to an **innocent** man and kill David for no
2 Sam 3.28 subjects and I are completely **innocent** of the murder of Abner.
4.11 evil men who murder an **innocent** man asleep in his own house!
14. 9 you and the royal family are **innocent."**
22.21 he blesses me because I am **innocent.**
22.25 I do what is right, because he knows that I am **innocent.**
1 Kgs 2. 5 He killed **innocent** men and now I bear the responsibility for
2.31 responsible for what Joab did when he killed **innocent** men.
2.32 Joab killed two **innocent** men who were better men than he:
8.31 an oath that he is **innocent,** [32]O Lord, listen in heaven
8.32 one as he deserves, and acquit the one who is **innocent.**
2 Kgs 21.16 Manasseh killed so many **innocent** people that the streets
24. 4 especially because of all the **innocent** people he had killed.
2 Chr 6.22 an oath that he is **innocent,** [23]O Lord, listen in heaven
6.23 one as he deserves and acquit the one who is **innocent.**
Job 9.15 Though I am **innocent,** all I can do is beg for mercy
9.20 I am **innocent** and faithful, but my words sound guilty,
9.21 I am **innocent,** but I no longer care.
9.21 **innocent** or guilty, God will destroy us.
9.23 When an **innocent** man suddenly dies, God laughs.
22.19 Good men are glad and **innocent** men laugh when they see
22.30 rescue you if you are **innocent,** if what you do is right.
23. 7 he would declare me **innocent** once and for all.
27. 5 I will insist on my **innocence** to my dying day.
31. 6 me on honest scales, and he will see how **innocent** I am.
32. 1 was convinced of his own **innocence,** the three men gave up
33. 9 I am **innocent** and free from sin.
34. 5 Job claims that he is **innocent,** that God refuses to give
35. 1 to say that you are **innocent** in God's sight, [3]or to ask
Ps 7. 8 you know that I am **innocent.**
10. 8 himself in the villages, waiting to murder **innocent** people.
15. 5 and cannot be bribed to testify against the **innocent.**
18.20 he blesses me because I am **innocent.**
18.24 I do what is right, because he knows that I am **innocent.**
24. 5 God will declare them **innocent.**
26. 1 Declare me **innocent,** O Lord, because I do what is right
26. 6 to show that I am **innocent** and march in worship round your
35.24 You are righteous, O Lord, so declare me **innocent;**
43. 1 O God, declare me **innocent,** and defend my cause against
94.21 plot against good men and sentence the **innocent** to death.
106.38 killed those **innocent** children, and the land was defiled by
143. 2 no one is **innocent** in your sight.
Prov 1.11 Let's attack some **innocent** people for the fun of it!
6.16 hands that kill **innocent** people,
13. 6 Righteousness protects the **innocent;**
17.15 Condemning the **innocent** or letting the wicked go—both are
17.26 It is not right to make an **innocent** person pay a fine;
18. 5 the guilty and prevent the **innocent** from receiving justice.
21. 8 the **innocent** do what is right.
24.24 he pronounces a guilty person **innocent,** he will be cursed
28.10 The **innocent** will be well rewarded.
Is 5.23 go free, and you prevent the **innocent** from getting justice.
50. 8 for God is near, and he will prove me **innocent.**
59. 7 You never hesitate to murder **innocent** people.
Jer 2.34 of the poor and **innocent,** not with the blood of burglars.
2.35 "But in spite of all this, [35]you say, 'I am **innocent;**
7. 6 Stop killing **innocent** people in this land.
19. 4 place with the blood of **innocent** people, [5]and they have
22. 3 and do not kill **innocent** people in this holy place.
22.17 you kill the **innocent** and violently oppress your people.
26.15 be guilty of killing an **innocent** man, because it is the Lord
Lam 4.13 priests were guilty of causing the death of **innocent** people.
Ezek 16.51 corruption makes your sisters look **innocent** by comparison.
16.52 than those of your sisters that they look **innocent** beside you.
Dan 6.22 he knew that I was **innocent** and because I have not wronged
Joel 3.19 attacked the land of Judah and killed its **innocent** people.
Jon 4.11 it has more than 120,000 **innocent** children in it, as well as
Mt 12.37 to judge you—to declare you either **innocent** or guilty."
23.35 for the murder of all **innocent** men will fall on you,
23.35 from the murder of **innocent** Abel to the murder of Zachariah
27. 4 "I have sinned by betraying an **innocent** man to death!"
27.19 nothing to do with that **innocent** man, because in a dream
28.14 convince him that you are **innocent,** and you will have
Rom 4. 5 declares the guilty to be **innocent,** it is his faith that God
16.18 fine words and flattering speech they deceive **innocent** people.
16.19 be wise about what is good, but **innocent** in what is evil.
1 Cor 4. 4 is clear, but that does not prove that I am really **innocent.**
2 Cor 7.11 earnest it has made you, how eager to prove your **innocence!**
Phil 2.15 so that you may be **innocent** and pure as God's perfect children,
Jas 5. 6 You have condemned and murdered **innocent** people,

INQUIRE

2 Chr 32.31 the Babylonian ambassadors came to **inquire** about the unusual

INSANE

1 Sam 21.13 around, David pretended to be **insane** and acted like a madman
Hos 9. 7 This inspired man is **insane."**
2 Cor 5.13 Are we really **insane?**
2 Pet 2.16 spoke with a human voice and stopped the prophet's **insane** action.

INSCRIBE

Zech 3. 9 I will engrave an **inscription** on it, and in a single day
14.20 of the horses will be **inscribed** with the words "Dedicated to

INSECT

Lev 11.20 All winged **insects** are unclean, [21]except those that hop.
Deut 14.19 "All winged **insects** are unclean;
14.20 You may eat any clean **insect.**
28.42 All your trees and crops will be devoured by **insects.**
Job 25. 6 Then what about man, that worm, that **insect?**
Ps 109.23 I am blown away like an **insect.**
Hab 1.14 or like a swarm of **insects** that have no ruler to direct
Mal 3.11 I will not let **insects** destroy your crops, and your

INSERT

Num 4. 6 a blue cloth on top, and then **insert** the carrying-poles.
4. 8 leather cover over it, and then **insert** the carrying-poles.
4.11 leather cover over it, and then **insert** the carrying-poles.
4.14 a fine leather cover over it and **insert** the carrying-poles.

INSIDE

Gen 6.14 make rooms in it and cover it with tar **inside** and out.
19.10 But the two men **inside** reached out, pulled Lot back into
Ex 4. 6 Lord spoke to Moses again, "Put your hand **inside** your robe."
4. 7 Then the Lord said, "Put your hand **inside** your robe again."
25.11 Cover it with pure gold **inside** and out and put a gold
25.21 Put the two stone tablets **inside** the box and put the lid
28.26 of the breast-piece on the **inside** edge next to the ephod.
37. 2 covered it with pure gold **inside** and out and put a gold
39.19 of the breast-piece, on the **inside** edge next to the ephod.
Lev 4.18 the corners of the incense-altar **inside** the Tent and pour out
Josh 7.21 You will find them buried **inside** my tent, with the silver at
10.20 some managed to find safety **inside** their city walls and were
Judg 3.24 they only thought that the king was **inside,** relieving himself.
7.16 each man a trumpet and a jar with a torch **inside** it.
9.49 on fire, with the people **inside,** and all the people of the
14. 8 find a swarm of bees and some honey **inside** the dead body.
1 Sam 6.19 of Beth Shemesh because they looked **inside** the Covenant Box.
19.16 They went **inside** and found the household idol in the bed
26. 5 Saul slept **inside** the camp, and his men camped round him.
2 Sam 4. 7 Once **inside,** they went to Ishbosheth's bedroom, where he
1 Kgs 6. 2 **Inside** it was 27 metres long, 9 metres wide,
6. 4 openings in them, narrower on the outside than on the **inside.**
6.15 The **inside** walls were covered with cedar panels from the
6.21 The **inside** of the Temple was covered with gold,
8. 9 nothing **inside** the Covenant Box except the two stone tablets
2 Kgs 6.20 their sight, and they saw that they were **inside** Samaria.
1 Chr 11. 5 David he would never get **inside** the city, but David captured
16. 1 the tent which David had prepared for it and put it **inside.**
2 Chr 3. 4 The **inside** of the room was overlaid with pure gold.
5.10 nothing **inside** the Covenant Box except the two stone tablets
29.16 The priests went **inside** the Temple to purify it, and they
32.30 through a tunnel to a point **inside** the walls of Jerusalem.
Neh 8. 1 in Jerusalem, in the square just **inside** the Water Gate.
Esth 1. 9 **inside** the royal palace Queen Vashti was giving a banquet for
4. 2 not go in because no one wearing sackcloth was allowed **inside.**
5. 1 The king was **inside,** seated on the royal throne, facing the
Ps 48. 3 there is safety with him **inside** the fortresses of the city.
48. 9 **Inside** your Temple, O God, we think of your constant love.
122. 2 And now we are here, standing **inside** the gates of Jerusalem!
122. 7 there be peace **inside** your walls and safety in your palaces."
Is 22.11 you built a reservoir **inside** the city to hold the water
57. 8 You set up your obscene idols just **inside** your front doors.
Jer 19. 9 terrible that the people **inside** the city will eat one another
41. 7 As soon as they were **inside** the city, Ishmael and his men
Lam 1.13 "He sent fire from above, a fire that burnt **inside** me.
Ezek 40.41 four **inside** the room and four out in the courtyard.
41.17 The **inside** walls of the Temple, up as high as above the
42.15 man had finished measuring **inside** the temple area, he took me
Jon 1.17 swallowed Jonah, and he was **inside** the fish for three days
2. 1 From deep **inside** the fish Jonah prayed to the Lord his God:
Mt 7.15 outside, but on the **inside** they are really like wild wolves.
23.25 cup and plate, while the **inside** is full of what you have
23.26 Clean what is **inside** the cup first, and then the outside
23.27 but are full of bones and decaying corpses on the **inside.**
23.28 appear good to everybody, but **inside** you are full of hypocrisy
Mk 5.29 and she had the feeling **inside** herself that she was healed
7.21 from the **inside,** from a person's heart, come the evil ideas
7.23 things come from **inside** a person and make him unclean."
15.16 soldiers took Jesus **inside** to the courtyard of the governor's
Lk 11. 7 suppose your friend should answer from **inside,** 'Don't bother me!
11.39 your cup and plate, but **inside** you are full of violence and
11.40 Did not God, who made the outside, also make the **inside?**
Jn 18.16 spoke to the girl at the gate, and brought Peter **inside.**
18.28 Jewish authorities did not go **inside** the palace, for they wanted
Acts 5.23 but when we opened the gates, we found no one **inside!"**
11. 6 I looked closely **inside** and saw domesticated and wild animals,
Rom 2.29 is a Jew on the **inside,** that is, whose heart has been
Rev 4. 8 six wings, and they were covered with eyes, **inside** and out.

Rev 5. 3 world below who could open the scroll and look **inside** it.
5. 4 found who was worthy to open the scroll or look **inside** it.

Am **INSIDES** see **BOWELS**

INSIGHT

Gen 41.33 some man with wisdom and **insight** and put him in charge of
41.39 that you have greater wisdom and **insight** than anyone else.
1 Kgs 4.29 gave Solomon unusual wisdom and **insight,** and knowledge too
1 Chr 22.12 Lord your God give you **insight** and wisdom so that you may
Job 12.12 Old men have **insight;**
12.12 God has **insight** and power to act.
Prov 2. 3 plead for **insight.**
2.11 Your **insight** and understanding will protect you
3.21 Hold on to your wisdom and **insight,** my son.
4. 5 Get wisdom and **insight!**
4. 7 Whatever else you get, get **insight.**
5. 1 Pay attention, my son, and listen to my wisdom and **insight.**
7. 4 Treat wisdom as your sister, and **insight** as your closest friend.
8. 9 To the man with **insight,** it is all clear;
8.12 I am Wisdom, and I have **insight;**
17.27 People who stay calm have real **insight.**
20. 5 in a deep well, but someone with **insight** can draw them out.
21.30 Human wisdom, brilliance, **insight**—they are of no help if
28.11 but a poor person who has **insight** into character knows better.
Eph 1. 8 In all his wisdom and **insight** [9] God did what he had purposed,

INSIGNIFICANT

1 Sam 18.23 too great for someone poor and **insignificant** like me."

INSINCERE

Prov 26.23 **Insincere** talk that hides what you are really thinking is
26.28 **Insincere** talk brings nothing but ruin.

INSIST

Judg 19. 4 The father **insisted** that he stay, and so he stayed for
2 Sam 13.25 Absalom **insisted,** but the king would not give in, and he
13.27 Absalom kept on **insisting** until David finally let Amnon and
18.22 Ahimaaz **insisted,** "I don't care what happens;
2 Kgs 2.17 But they **insisted** until he gave in and let them go.
5.16 Naaman **insisted** that he accept it, but he would not.
5.23 He **insisted** on it, tied up the silver in two bags, gave
Neh 13.18 And yet you **insist** on bringing more of God's anger down on
Job 27. 5 I will **insist** on my innocence to my dying day.
Prov 11.19 will live, but anyone who **insists** on doing wrong will die.
Hos 5.11 was rightfully hers, because she **insisted** on going for help
11. 7 They **insist** on turning away from me.
Zech 13. 3 Then if anyone still **insists** on prophesying, his own father
Lk 22.59 hour later another man **insisted** strongly, "There isn't any doubt
23. 5 But they **insisted** even more strongly, "With his teaching he is
Acts 12.15 But she **insisted** that it was true.
Phil 3. 2 those dogs, those men who **insist** on cutting the body.
Col 2.18 special visions and who **insists** on false humility and the worship
2 Tim 4. 2 to preach the message, to **insist** upon proclaiming it

INSOLENT

Rom 1.30 they are hateful to God, **insolent,** proud, and boastful;

INSPECT

1 Sam 13.15 Saul **inspected** his troops, about six hundred men.
15. 4 Saul called his forces together and **inspected** them at
Neh 2.13 As I went, I **inspected** the broken walls of the city
Job 7.18 You **inspect** him every morning and test him every minute.
Is 22. 9 You **inspected** all the houses in Jerusalem and tore some of
Zech 1.10 The Lord sent them to go and **inspect** the earth."
6. 7 came out, they were impatient to go and **inspect** the earth.
6. 7 The angel said, "Go and **inspect** the earth!"—

INSPIRE

Neh 2.12 tell anyone what God had **inspired** me to do for Jerusalem.
7. 5 God **inspired** me to assemble the people and their leaders
9.30 **inspired** your prophets to speak, but your people were deaf, so
Job 26. 4 Who **inspired** you to speak like this?
Ezek 13. 3 provide their own **inspiration** and invent their own visions.
Hos 9. 7 This **inspired** man is insane."
Hag 1.14 The Lord **inspired** everyone to work on the Temple:
Mt 22.43 Jesus asked, "did the Spirit **inspire** David to call him 'Lord'?
Mk 12.36 The Holy Spirit **inspired** David to say:
1 Cor 13. 2 I may have the gift of **inspired** preaching;
13. 8 There are **inspired** messages, but they are temporary;
13. 9 our gifts of knowledge and of **inspired** messages are only partial;
14. 6 God or some knowledge or some **inspired** message, or some teaching.
1 Thes 5.20 do not despise **inspired** messages.
2 Tim 3.16 All Scripture is **inspired** by God and is useful for teaching
Rev 19.10 For the truth that Jesus revealed is what **inspires** the prophets.

INSTALL

Ps 2. 6 Zion, my sacred hill," he says, "I have **installed** my king."

INSTANT

Ps 73.19 They are **instantly** destroyed;
1 Cor 15.51 all be changed in an **instant,** as quickly as the blinking of

INSTINCT

Rom 2.14 but whenever they do by **instinct** what the Law commands, they
2 Pet 2.12 But these men act by **instinct,** like wild animals born to
Jude 10 things that they know by **instinct,** like wild animals,

INSTITUTE

1 Kgs 12.32 Jeroboam also **instituted** a religious festival on the
12.33 celebration of the festival he had **instituted** for the people

INSTRUCT

Gen 32. 4 He **instructed** them to say:
49.33 When Jacob had finished giving **instructions** to his sons,
Ex 12. 3 Give these **instructions** to the whole community of Israel:
16. 4 test them to find out if they will follow my **instructions.**
16. 7 against him, because we are only carrying out his **instructions."**
24.12 laws that I have written for the **instruction** of the people."
Lev 16. 4 Then the Lord gave the following **instructions.**
Num 2. 1 The Lord gave Moses and Aaron the following **instructions.**
4. 5 The Lord gave Moses the following **instructions.**
5. 6 Lord gave Moses [6] the following **instructions** for the people
5.12 to give the Israelites the following **instructions.**
6. 2 commanded Moses [2] to give the following **instructions** to the
9. 8 Moses answered, "Wait until I receive **instructions** from
23.20 I have been **instructed** to bless, And when God blesses,
28. 2 The Lord commanded Moses [2] to **instruct** the Israelites to
30. 1 Moses gave the following **instructions** to the leaders of
31.16 the women who followed Balaam's **instructions** and at Peor led
33.51 the Lord gave Moses [51] the following **instructions** for Israel:
34. 2 Lord gave Moses [2] the following **instructions** for the people
Deut 1.16 I **instructed** them, 'Listen to the disputes that come
1.18 same time I gave you **instructions** for everything else you
2. 4 He told me to give you the following **instructions:**
3.18 "At the same time, I gave them the following **instructions:**
3.21 "Then I **instructed** Joshua:
3.28 Give Joshua his **instructions.**
4.36 hear his voice from heaven so that he could **instruct** you;
17.11 Accept their verdict and follow their **instructions** in
24. 8 follow the **instructions** that I have given them.
27. 1 the people, "Obey all the **instructions** that I am giving you
27. 4 Mount Ebal, as I am **instructing** you today, and cover them
31.14 him to the Tent, so that I may give him his **instructions."**
Josh 8.31 made it according to the **instructions** that Moses, the Lord's
18. 8 map out the land after Joshua had given them these **instructions:**
Judg 18. 2 of Zorah and Eshtaol with **instructions** to explore the land.
1 Sam 13. 8 as Samuel had **instructed** him to do, but Samuel still
15.24 "I disobeyed the Lord's command and your **instructions.**
25. 6 He **instructed** them to say to Nabal:
2 Sam 11.19 and he **instructed** the messenger, "After you have told
13.28 a banquet fit for a king [28] and **instructed** his servants:
13.29 the servants followed Absalom's **instructions** and killed Amnon.
1 Kgs 2. 1 he called his son Solomon and gave him his last **instructions:**
3. 3 the Lord and followed the **instructions** of his father David,
12.12 all the people returned to King Rehoboam, as he had **instructed**
2 Kgs 5.14 times, as Elisha had **instructed,** and he was completely cured.
7.14 in two chariots with **instructions** to go and find out what
8. 2 had followed his **instructions,** and had gone with her family
10.24 eighty men outside the temple and had **instructed** them:
11. 9 officers obeyed Jehoiada's **instructions** and brought their men
12. 2 pleased the Lord, because Jehoiada the priest **instructed** him.
13.17 following the prophet's **instructions,** the king opened the
17.15 They refused to obey his **instructions,** they did not keep
1 Chr 6.49 all this in accordance with the **instructions** given by Moses,
23.27 the basis of David's final **instructions** all Levites were
28.14 He gave **instructions** as to how much silver and gold was
28.17 He also gave **instructions** as to how much pure gold was
28.19 plan written according to the **instructions** which the Lord
2 Chr 8.15 The **instructions** which David had given the priests and
10.12 all the people returned to King Rehoboam, as he had **instructed**
19. 6 judges in each of the fortified cities of Judah [6] and **instructed**
19. 9 He gave them the following **instructions:**
19.10 you must **instruct** them carefully how to conduct themselves
19.11 courageous and carry out these **instructions,** and may the Lord
23. 6 rest of the people must obey the Lord's **instructions** and stay
23. 8 and the people of Judah carried out Jehoiada's **instructions.**
29.25 king followed the **instructions** that the Lord had given to King
30.16 the Temple according to the **instructions** in the Law of Moses,
35. 3 also gave these **instructions** to the Levites, the teachers of
35. 6 fellow-Israelites may follow the **instructions** which the Lord
35.12 offer them according to the **instructions** in the Law of Moses.
35.15 were in the places assigned to them by King David's **instructions:**
Ezra 3. 2 according to the **instructions** written in the Law of Moses,
3.10 the Lord according to the **instructions** handed down from the
6.18 according to the **instructions** contained in the book of Moses.
Neh 2. 7 governors of West Euphrates Province, **instructing** them to let
2. 8 keeper of the royal forests, **instructing** him to supply me
8.15 So they gave the following **instructions** and sent them all
8.15 trees to make shelters according to the **instructions** written
12.24 him, in accordance with the **instructions** given by King David,
Esth 3.13 It contained the **instructions** that on a single day,
9.23 Jews followed Mordecai's **instructions,** and the celebration
9.27 would be regularly observed according to Mordecai's **instructions.**
Ps 32. 8 I will **instruct** you and advise you.
40. 7 your **instructions** for me are in the book of the Law.

Ps 73.24 You guide me with your **instruction** and at the end you
78. 5 **instructed** our ancestors to teach his laws to their children,
89.31 if they disregard my **instructions** and do not keep my
94.12 happy is the person you **instruct,** the one to whom you teach
105.22 the king's officials and authority to **instruct** his advisers.
107.11 the commands of Almighty God and had rejected his **instructions.**
119. 5 I hope that I shall be faithful in keeping your **instructions!**
119.15 I study your **instructions;**
119.24 Your **instructions** give me pleasure;
119.31 I have followed your **instructions,** Lord;
119.48 I will meditate on your **instructions.**
119.59 considered my conduct, and I promise to follow your **instructions.**
119.69 about me, but with all my heart I obey your **instructions.**
119.78 as for me, I will meditate on your **instructions.**
119.93 I will never neglect your **instructions,** because by them
119.99 than all my teachers, because I meditate on your **instructions.**
119.102 I have not neglected your **instructions,** for you
119.103 sweet is the taste of your **instructions**— sweeter even than
119.106 will keep my solemn promise to obey your just **instructions.**
119.119 all the wicked like rubbish, and so I love your **instructions.**
119.128 And so I follow all your **instructions;**
119.144 Your **instructions** are always just;
119.148 night long I lie awake, to meditate on your **instructions.**
119.152 Long ago I learnt about your **instructions;**
119.159 See how I love your **instructions,** Lord.
119.168 I obey your commands and your **instructions;**
119.175 may your **instructions** help me.
147.19 message to his people, his **instructions** and laws to Israel.
Prov 6.23 Their **instructions** are a shining light;
8.10 Choose my **instruction** instead of silver;
Jer 18.18 will always be priests to **instruct** us, wise men to give us
35. 8 We have obeyed all the **instructions** that Jonadab gave us.
35.12 why you refuse to listen to me and to obey my **instructions.**
35.18 you have followed all his **instructions,** and you have done
36. 5 Then I gave Baruch the following **instructions:**
51.59 going to Babylonia with him, and I gave him some **instructions.**
Mt 2. 8 Then he sent them to Bethlehem with these **instructions:**
2.22 He was given more **instructions** in a dream, so he went to
10. 5 twelve men were sent out by Jesus with the following **instructions:**
11. 1 Jesus finished giving these **instructions** to his twelve disciples,
21. 2 Jesus sent two of the disciples on ahead [2] with these **instructions:**
Mk 11. 2 Jesus sent two of his disciples on ahead [2] with these **instructions:**
14.13 Then Jesus sent two of them with these **instructions:**
Lk 19.30 he sent two disciples ahead [30] with these **instructions:**
22. 8 Jesus sent off Peter and John with these **instructions:**
Jn 8.28 but I say only what the Father has **instructed** me to say.
Acts 1. 2 was taken up, he gave **instructions** by the power of the Holy
10.33 to hear anything that the Lord has **instructed** you to say."
15.24 they had not, however, received any **instruction** from us.
17.15 then returned to Berea with **instructions** from Paul that Silas and
18.25 He had been **instructed** in the Way of the Lord, and with
22. 3 I received strict **instruction** in the Law of our ancestors
Rom 2.20 in darkness, [20] an **instructor** for the foolish, and a teacher
1 Cor 4.14 feel ashamed, but to **instruct** you as my own dear children.
11.17 In the following **instructions,** however, I do not praise you,
2 Cor 2. 9 and whether you are always ready to obey my **instructions.**
7.15 ready to obey his **instructions,** how you welcomed him with fear
Eph 6. 4 Instead, bring them up with Christian discipline and **instruction.**
Col 3.16 Teach and **instruct** each other with all wisdom.
4.10 (You have already received **instructions** to welcome Mark
1 Thes 4. 2 For you know the **instructions** we gave you by the authority
5.12 among you, who guide and **instruct** you in the Christian life.
2 Thes 3. 6 and who do not follow the **instructions** that we gave them.
1 Tim 4. 6 If you give these **instructions** to the brothers, you will
4.11 Give them these **instructions** and these teachings.
5. 7 Give them these **instructions,** so that no one will find fault
5.21 upon you to obey these **instructions** without showing any prejudice
2 Tim 3.16 correcting faults, and giving **instruction** for right living,
Tit 1. 5 Remember my **instructions:**
2. 2 **Instruct** the older men to be sober, sensible, and self-controlled;
2. 3 In the same way **instruct** the older women to behave as
2.12 That grace **instructs** us to give up ungodly living and worldly
Heb 11.22 Israelites from Egypt, and leave **instructions** about what should

INSTRUMENT

1 Chr 13. 8 They sang and played musical **instruments**—harps, drums, cymbals,
16.42 and the other **instruments** which were played when the songs
23. 5 the Lord, using the musical **instruments** provided by the king
2 Chr 5.11 by trumpets, cymbals, and other **instruments,** as they praised
7. 6 the Lord with the musical **instruments** that King David had
23.13 musicians with their **instruments** were leading the celebration.
29.26 harps and cymbals, [26] **instruments** like those that King David
29.27 began to play the trumpets and all the other **instruments.**
Neh 12.36 all of whom carried musical **instruments** of the kind played by
Ps 33. 2 to the Lord with harps, sing to him with stringed **instruments.**
92. 3 the music of stringed **instruments** and with melody on the harp.
Dan 3. 5 and then all the other **instruments** will join in.
3. 7 heard the sound of the **instruments,** the people of all the
3.15 harps, and all the other **instruments,** bow down and worship
1 Cor 14. 7 Take such lifeless musical **instruments** as the flute or the harp—

INSULT

Gen 34. 7 such a thing and had **insulted** the people of Israel by raping
39.14 Hebrew that my husband brought to the house is **insulting** us.
39.17 that you brought here came into my room and **insulted** me.
1 Sam 20.34 deeply distressed about David, because Saul had **insulted** him.
25.14 with greetings for our master, but he **insulted** them.
1 Sam 25.39 taken revenge on Nabal for **insulting** me and has kept me his
2 Kgs 19. 4 emperor has sent his chief official to **insult** the living God.
19. 4 your God hear these **insults** and punish those who spoke them.
19.16 the things that Sennacherib is saying to **insult** you,
19.22 Whom do you think you have been **insulting** and ridiculing?
Neh 4. 5 don't forget their sins, for they have **insulted** us who are
9.18 How much they **insulted** you, Lord!
9.26 **insulted** you time after time, [27] so you let their enemies
Esth 1.16 Vashti has **insulted** not only the king but also his officials
Job 1. 5 of them might have sinned by **insulting** God unintentionally.
19. 3 Time after time you **insult** me and show no shame for the
20. 3 you have said is an **insult,** but I know how to reply
Ps 4. 2 How long will you people **insult** me?
31.20 safe shelter you hide them from the **insults** of their enemies.
42.10 I am crushed by their **insults,** as they keep on asking me,
44.16 from hearing the sneers and **insults** of my enemies and
59. 7 Listen to their **insults** and threats.
69. 7 sake that I have been **insulted** and that I am covered with
69. 9 the **insults** which are hurled at you fall on me.
69.10 I humble myself by fasting, and people **insult** me;
69.19 You know how I am **insulted,** how I am disgraced and
69.20 **Insults** have broken my heart, and I am in despair.
74.10 Will they **insult** your name for ever?
79. 4 The surrounding nations **insult** us;
79.12 seven times for all the **insults** they have hurled at you.
80. 6 our enemies **insult** us.
89.50 how I, your servant, am **insulted,** how I endure all the
89.51 Your enemies **insult** your chosen king, O Lord!
89.51 They **insult** him wherever he goes.
102. 8 All day long my enemies **insult** me;
119.22 Free me from their **insults** and scorn, because I have kept
119.39 Save me from the **insults** I fear;
119.42 I can answer those who **insult** me because I trust in your
Prov 9. 7 If you correct a conceited man, you will only be **insulted.**
12.16 Sensible people will ignore an **insult.**
14.31 you oppress poor people, you **insult** the God who made them;
17. 5 you laugh at poor people, you **insult** the God who made them.
18.13 If you don't you are being stupid and **insulting.**
Ecc 7.21 you may hear your servant **insulting** you,
7.22 and you know yourself that you have **insulted** other people
Is 3. 8 they openly **insult** God himself.
32. 6 what he says are an **insult** to the Lord, and he never
37. 4 emperor has sent his chief official to **insult** the living God.
37. 4 your God hear these **insults** and punish those who spoke them.
37.17 the things that Sennacherib is saying to **insult** you,
37.23 Whom do you think you have been **insulting** and ridiculing?
43.28 I let my own people be **insulted."**
50. 6 not stop them when they **insulted** me, when they pulled out
50. 7 But their **insults** cannot hurt me because the Sovereign Lord
51. 7 Do not be afraid when people taunt and **insult** you;
Jer 15.15 Remember that it is for your sake that I am **insulted.**
Lam 3.30 Though beaten and **insulted,** we should accept it all.
3.46 "We are **insulted** and mocked by all our enemies.
3.61 "You have heard them **insult** me, O Lord;
Ezek 8.17 Look how they **insult** me in the most offensive way possible!
20.27 another way their fathers **insulted** me by their unfaithfulness.
21.28 Lord, am saying to the Ammonites, who are **insulting** Israel.
36. 3 the mountains of Israel, all of them **insulted** Israel.
36. 6 of the way the nations have **insulted** and humiliated them.
Zeph 2. 8 people of Moab and Ammon **insulting** and taunting my people,
2.10 pride and arrogance and for **insulting** the people of the Lord
Mt 5.11 "Happy are you when people **insult** you and persecute you
27.39 People passing by shook their heads and hurled **insults** at Jesus:
27.44 had been crucified with him **insulted** him in the same way.
Mk 15.29 People passing by shook their heads and hurled **insults** at Jesus:
15.32 And the two who were crucified with Jesus **insulted** him also.
Lk 6.22 people hate you, reject you, **insult** you, and say that you
11.45 to him, "Teacher, when you say this, you **insult** us too!"
18.32 Gentiles, who will mock him, **insult** him, and spit on him.
22.65 And they said many other **insulting** things to him.
23.39 One of the criminals hanging there hurled **insults** at him:
Acts 13.45 they disputed what Paul was saying and **insulted** him.
23. 4 Paul said to him, "You are **insulting** God's High Priest!"
Rom 3. 8 Some people, indeed, have **insulted** me by accusing me of saying
15. 3 as the scripture says, "The **insults** which are hurled at you
1 Cor 4.13 when we are **insulted,** we answer with kind words.
2 Cor 6. 8 we are **insulted** and praised.
12.10 I am content with weaknesses, **insults,** hardships, persecutions,
12.20 tempers and selfishness, **insults** and gossip, pride and disorder.
Eph 4.31 No more shouting or **insults,** no more hateful feelings of any sort.
Col 3. 8 No **insults** or obscene talk must ever come from your lips.
1 Thes 2. 2 had already been ill-treated and **insulted** in Philippi before we
1 Tim 1.13 past I spoke evil of him and persecuted and **insulted** him.
6. 4 this brings on jealousy, disputes, **insults,** evil suspicions,
2 Tim 3. 2 they will be **insulting,** disobedient to their parents, ungrateful,
Heb 10.29 who **insults** the Spirit of grace?
10.33 You were at times publicly **insulted** and ill-treated,
1 Pet 2. 1 more lying or hypocrisy or jealousy or **insulting** language.
2.23 When he was insulted, he did not answer back with an **insult;**
3.16 so that when you are **insulted,** those who speak evil of your
4. 4 in the same wild and reckless living, and so they **insult** you.
4.14 Happy are you if you are **insulted** because you are Christ's
2 Pet 2.10 instead, they **insult** them.
2.11 do not accuse them with **insults** in the presence of the Lord.
2.12 they attack with **insults** anything they do not understand.
Jude 8 God's authority and **insult** the glorious beings above.
9 to condemn the Devil with **insulting** words, but said,
10 these people attack with **insults** anything they do not understand;
Rev 13. 1 of its heads there was a name that was **insulting** to God.
13. 5 make proud claims which were **insulting** to God,
17. 3 beast that had names **insulting** to God written all over it;

INTEGRITY

1 Kgs 9. 4 serve me in honesty and **integrity,** as your father David did,
1 Chr 29.17 test everyone's heart and are pleased with people of **integrity.**
Prov 2.21 Righteous men—men of **integrity**—will live in this land
14.32 evil deeds, but good people are protected by their **integrity.**
Is 11. 5 He will rule his people with justice and **integrity.**
32. 1 king who rules with **integrity,** and national leaders who govern
33. 5 fill Jerusalem with justice and **integrity** [6] and give stability

INTELLIGENT

1 Sam 25. 2 wife Abigail was beautiful and **intelligent,** but he was a mean,
1 Kgs 7.14 Huram was an **intelligent** and experienced craftsman.
Prov 1. 3 teach you how to live **intelligently** and how to be honest,
10.13 **Intelligent** people talk sense, but stupid people need to
10.23 **Intelligent** people take pleasure in wisdom.
12. 8 If you are **intelligent,** you will be praised;
13.15 **Intelligence** wins respect, but those who can't be trusted
14. 6 can never become wise, but **intelligent** people learn easily.
14.33 Wisdom is in every thought of an **intelligent** man;
15.14 **Intelligent** people want to learn, but stupid people are
16.23 **Intelligent** people think before they speak;
17.10 An **intelligent** person learns more from one rebuke than
17.24 An **intelligent** person aims at wise action, but a fool
17.28 be thought wise and **intelligent** if he stays quiet and keeps
18.15 **Intelligent** people are always eager and ready to learn.
26.16 will think he is more **intelligent** than seven men who can
28. 2 strong and endure when it has **intelligent,** sensible leaders.
28. 7 A young man who obeys the law is **intelligent.**
29. 9 When an **intelligent** man brings a lawsuit against a fool,
Ecc 4.13 as well off as a young man who is poor but **intelligent.**
7.10 It's not an **intelligent** question.
9.11 earn a living, **intelligent** men do not always get rich,
Dan 1. 4 They had to be handsome, **intelligent,** well-trained, quick
Mt 15.16 them, "You are still no more **intelligent** than the others.
Mk 7.18 "You are no more **intelligent** than the others," Jesus said
Lk 2.47 All who heard him were amazed at his **intelligent** answers.
Acts 13. 7 governor of the island, Sergius Paulus, who was an **intelligent** man.
Rev 13.18 Whoever is **intelligent** can work out the meaning of the

INTEND

Gen 24.49 if you **intend** to fulfil your responsibility towards my master
Ex 21. 8 is sold to someone who **intends** to make her his wife, but
Lev 4. 2 of the Lord's commands without **intending** to, would have to
4.13 of the Lord's commands without **intending** to, [14] then as soon
4.22 of the Lord's commands without **intending** to, [23] then as soon
4.27 of the Lord's commands without **intending** to, [28] then as soon
19.12 promise in my name if you do not **intend** to keep it;
22.14 of the sacred offerings without **intending** to, he must repay
Num 35.23 someone whom he did not **intend** to hurt and who was not
Deut 8. 2 he might know what you **intended** to do and whether you would
9. 5 are wicked and because he **intends** to keep the promise that
9.14 I **intend** to destroy them so that no one will remember them
Judg 20. 5 They **intended** to kill me;
1 Sam 20.13 If he **intends** to harm you, may the Lord strike me dead
1 Kgs 12.21 He **intended** to go to war and restore his control over the
1 Chr 12.17 But if you **intend** to betray me to my enemies, even though
2 Chr 2. 5 I **intend** to build a great temple, because our God is
2. 9 timber, because this temple I **intend** to build will be large
11. 1 He **intended** to go to war and restore his control over the
28.10 And now you **intend** to make the men and women of
32. 2 Hezekiah saw that Sennacherib **intended** to attack Jerusalem
Neh 4. 2 Do they **intend** to rebuild the city?
6. 6 you and the Jewish people **intend** to revolt and that this is
13. 5 a large room that was **intended** only for storing offerings of
Is 7. 6 They **intend** to invade Judah, terrify the people into
28.21 order to do what he **intends** to do—strange as his actions
46.10 never fail, that I would do everything I **intended** to do.
Jer 13.11 round the waist, so I **intended** all the people of Israel and
15.18 Do you **intend** to disappoint me like a stream that goes dry
23.20 will not end until he has done everything he **intends** to do.
30.23 not end until he has done all that he **intends** to do.
36. 3 all the destruction that I **intend** to bring on them, they
49.20 Edom, and to what I **intend** to do to the people of
50.45 of Babylon and to what I **intend** to do to its people.
51.11 the kings of Media, because he **intends** to destroy Babylonia.
Ezek 13.14 I **intend** to break down the wall they whitewashed,
38.13 Do you **intend** to get silver and gold, livestock and property,
Gal 4.17 a deep interest in you, but their **intentions** are not good.

INTENTLY

Mk 8.25 This time the man looked **intently,** his eyesight returned,

INTERCOURSE

Gen 4. 1 Adam had **intercourse** with his wife, and she became pregnant.
16. 4 Abram had **intercourse** with Hagar, and she became pregnant.
19.33 wine to drink, and the elder daughter had **intercourse** with
19.35 they made him drunk, and the younger daughter had **intercourse** with
29.23 he took Leah to Jacob, and Jacob had **intercourse** with her.
29.30 Jacob had **intercourse** with Rachel also, and he loved her
30. 4 gave Bilhah to her husband, and he had **intercourse** with her.
30.16 So he had **intercourse** with her that night.
35.22 Reuben had sexual **intercourse** with Bilhah, one of his father's
38. 9 him, so whenever he had **intercourse** with his brother's widow,
38.18 Then they had **intercourse,** and she became pregnant.
Gen 38.26 And Judah never had **intercourse** with her again.
Ex 19.15 tomorrow and don't have sexual **intercourse** in the meantime."
Lev 15.18 After sexual **intercourse** both the man and the woman must
15.24 a man has sexual **intercourse** with her during her period, he
15.33 a man who has sexual **intercourse** with a woman who is
18. 6 Do not have sexual **intercourse** with any of your relatives.
18. 7 disgrace your father by having **intercourse** with your mother.
18. 8 disgrace your father by having **intercourse** with any of his
18. 9 Do not have **intercourse** with your sister or your stepsister,
18.10 Do not have **intercourse** with your granddaughter;
18.11 Do not have **intercourse** with a half-sister;
18.12 Do not have **intercourse** with an aunt, whether she
18.14 Do not have **intercourse** with your uncle's wife;
18.15 Do not have **intercourse** with your daughter-in-law
18.17 Do not have **intercourse** with the daughter or granddaughter
18.17 of a woman with whom you have had **intercourse;**
18.19 not have **intercourse** with a woman during her monthly period,
18.20 Do not have **intercourse** with another man's wife;
20.11 A man who has **intercourse** with one of his father's wives
20.12 If a man has **intercourse** with his daughter-in-law, they
20.17 He has had **intercourse** with his sister and must suffer the
20.18 a man has **intercourse** with a woman during her monthly period,
20.19 If a man has **intercourse** with his aunt, both of them
20.20 a man has **intercourse** with his uncle's wife, he disgraces his
Num 5.12 has defiled herself by having **intercourse** with another man.
25. 1 men began to have sexual **intercourse** with the Moabite women
31.17 woman who has had sexual **intercourse,** [18] but keep alive for
Deut 21.14 forced her to have **intercourse** with you, you cannot treat her
22.21 among our people by having **intercourse** before she was married,
22.22 a man is caught having **intercourse** with another man's wife,
22.23 in a town having **intercourse** with a girl who is engaged
22.24 die because he had **intercourse** with a girl who was engaged.
22.29 become his wife, because he forced her to have **intercourse**
22.30 by having **intercourse** with any of his father's wives.
27.20 by having **intercourse** with any of his father's wives.'
27.22 on anyone who has **intercourse** with his sister or half sister.'
27.23 curse on anyone who has **intercourse** with his mother-in-law.'
1 Sam 1.19 Elkanah had **intercourse** with his wife Hannah, and the Lord
2 Sam 12.11 and he will have **intercourse** with them in broad daylight.
12.24 He had **intercourse** with her, and she bore a son, whom David
16.21 "Go and have **intercourse** with your father's concubines whom
16.22 went in and had **intercourse** with his father's concubines.
20. 3 provided for their needs, but did not have **intercourse** with
1 Kgs 1. 4 took care of him, but he did not have **intercourse** with her.
1 Chr 5. 1 he had **intercourse** with one of his father's concubines,
7.23 had **intercourse** with his wife again, and she became pregnant
Ezek 18. 6 man's wife or have **intercourse** with a woman during her period.
22.10 force women to have **intercourse** with them during their period.
Amos 2. 7 man and his father have **intercourse** with the same slave-girl,

INTEREST (1)

Gen 30.30 it is time for me to look out for my own **interests."**
Num 11.29 Moses answered, "Are you concerned about my **interests?**
Ruth 2.19 May God bless the man who took an **interest** in you!"
1 Sam 8. 3 were **interested** only in making money, so they accepted bribes
Ezra 4.22 once, so that no more harm may be done to my **interests."**
Esth 3. 8 so it is not in your best **interests** to tolerate them.
Prov 18. 1 not get along with others are **interested** only in themselves;
Is 58. 3 you pursue your own **interests** and oppress your workers.
58.13 as sacred and do not pursue your own **interests** on that day;
Jer 22.17 But you can only see your selfish **interests;**
Dan 6. 2 supervise the governors and to look after the king's **interests.**
1 Cor 10.24 to his own **interests,** but to the interests of others.
Gal 4.17 other people show a deep **interest** in you, but their intentions
4.17 you will have the same **interest** in them as they have in
4.18 to have such a deep **interest** if the purpose is good—
Phil 2. 4 And look out for one another's **interests,** not just for your own.
Col 4. 6 should always be pleasant and **interesting,** and you should know

INTEREST (2)

Ex 22.25 not act like a money-lender and require him to pay **interest.**
Lev 25.36 Do not charge him any **interest,** but obey God and let
25.37 Do not make him pay **interest** on the money you lend him,
Deut 23.19 anything else to a fellow-Israelite, do not charge him **interest.**
23.20 You may charge **interest** on what you lend to a foreigner,
Ps 15. 5 makes loans without charging **interest** and cannot be bribed to
Prov 28. 8 get rich by charging **interest** and taking advantage of people,
Ezek 22.12 Some charge **interest** on the loans they make to their
Hab 2. 7 will be in debt yourselves and be forced to pay **interest.**
Mt 25.27 I would have received it all back with **interest** when I returned.
Lk 19.23 Then I would have received it back with **interest** when I returned.'

INTERFERE

Ezra 6. 7 from the Temple [7] and do not **interfere** with its construction.
Ezek 7.22 I will not **interfere** when my treasured Temple is profaned,
1 Pet 3. 7 Do this so that nothing will **interfere** with your prayers.

INTERIOR

Ex 26. 1 "Make the **interior** of the sacred Tent, the Tent of my
Lev 14.41 he must have all the **interior** walls scraped and the plaster
1 Kgs 6.18 the whole **interior** was covered with cedar, so that the stones
6.22 The whole **interior** of the Temple was covered with gold,
Esth 10. 1 regions of his empire as well as on those of the **interior.**
Acts 19. 1 Corinth, Paul travelled through the **interior** of the province

INTERMARRY see **MARRY**

INTERNAL ORGANS

Ex 12. 9 including the head, the legs, and the **internal organs.**
29.13 the fat which covers the **internal organs,** the best part of
29.17 wash its **internal organs** and its hind legs, and put them on
29.22 tail, the fat covering the **internal organs,** the best part of
Lev 1. 9 The man must wash the **internal organs** and the hind legs,
1.13 The man must wash the **internal organs** and the hind legs,
3. 3 all the fat on the **internal organs,** [4]the kidneys and the
3. 9 all the fat covering the **internal organs,** [10]the kidneys
3.14 all the fat on the **internal organs,** [15]the kidneys and the
4. 8 the fat on the **internal organs,** [9]the kidneys and the fat
4.11 its legs, and its **internal organs** including the intestines,
7. 3 tail, the fat covering the **internal organs,** [4]the kidneys and
8.16 all the fat on the **internal organs,** the best part of the
8.20 ram in pieces, washed the **internal organs** and the hind legs
8.25 all the fat covering the **internal organs,** the best part of
9.14 he washed the **internal organs** and the hind legs and burnt

INTERPRET

Gen 40. 8 God who gives the ability to **interpret** dreams," Joseph said.
40.16 baker saw that the **interpretation** of the wine steward's dream
41.12 We told him our dreams, and he **interpreted** them for us.
41.15 I have been told that you can **interpret** dreams."
41.16 Your Majesty, but God will give a favourable **interpretation."**
42.23 because they had been speaking to him through an **interpreter.**
Deut 13. 1 prophet or an **interpreter** of dreams may promise a miracle or
13. 5 put to death any **interpreter** of dreams or prophet that tells
Dan 1.17 he gave Daniel skill in **interpreting** visions and dreams.
5.12 is wise and skilful in **interpreting** dreams, solving riddles,
Mic 3.11 govern for bribes, the priests **interpret** the Law for pay,
Zech 10. 2 Some **interpret** dreams, but only mislead you;
Mt 16. 3 but you cannot **interpret** the signs concerning these times!
Lk 10.26 How do you **interpret** them?"

INTERRUPT

Ex 30. 8 of incense is to continue without **interruption** for all time
2 Chr 25.16 Amaziah **interrupted,** "have we made you adviser to the king?
Ezra 6. 8 taxes in West Euphrates, so that the work is not **interrupted.**
Song 2. 7 deer and the gazelles that you will not **interrupt** our love.
3. 5 deer and the gazelles that you will not **interrupt** our love.
8. 4 women of Jerusalem, that you will not **interrupt** our love.

INTERSECT

Ezek 1.16 and each had another wheel **intersecting** it at right angles,
10. 9 had another wheel which **intersected** it at right angles.

INTERWOVEN see WEAVE

INTESTINES

Ex 29.14 bull's flesh, its skin, and its **intestines** outside the camp.
Lev 4.11 its internal organs including the **intestines,** [12]carry it
8.17 skin, flesh, and **intestines,** and burnt it outside the camp,
16.27 Skin, meat, and **intestines** shall all be burnt.
Num 19. 5 including skin, meat, blood, and **intestines,** is to be burnt
2 Chr 21.15 a painful disease of the **intestines** that will grow worse
21.18 Lord brought on the king a painful disease of the **intestines.**

INTIMATE

Ps 55.14 We had **intimate** talks with each other and worshipped

INTRODUCE

2 Kgs 5. 6 "This letter will **introduce** my officer Naaman.
17. 8 and adopted customs **introduced** by the kings of Israel.
Acts 9. 2 asked for letters of **introduction** to the synagogues in Damascus,
Rom 5.20 Law was **introduced** in order to increase wrongdoing;
1 Cor 16. 3 I shall give letters of **introduction** to the men you have approved,

INVADE

Num 14.40 morning they started out to **invade** the hill-country, saying,
24.24 **Invaders** will sail from Cyprus;
32.39 of Machir son of Manasseh **invaded** the land of Gilead,
Deut 1.41 fight, thinking it would be easy to **invade** the hill-country.
3.21 he will do the same to everyone else whose land you **invade.**
4. 5 them in the land that you are about to **invade** and occupy.
4.14 obey in the land that you are about to **invade** and occupy.
12.29 destroy the nations as you **invade** their land, and you will
Josh 2.18 When we **invade** your land, tie this red cord to the window
Judg 11.12 Why have you **invaded** my country?"
1 Sam 7.13 the Lord prevented them from **invading** Israel's territory as
23.27 The Philistines are **invading** the country!"
1 Kgs 15.17 Baasha **invaded** Judah and started to fortify Ramah
2 Kgs 13.20 year bands of Moabites used to **invade** the land of Israel.
15.19 Pileser, the emperor of Assyria, **invaded** Israel, and Menahem
17. 5 Then Shalmaneser **invaded** Israel and besieged Samaria.
18. 9 Shalmaneser of Assyria **invaded** Israel and besieged Samaria.
24. 1 King Nebuchadnezzar of Babylonia **invaded** Judah,
1 Chr 5.26 (also known as Tiglath Pileser) **invade** their country.
20. 1 war, Joab led out the army and **invaded** the land of Ammon;
2 Chr 14. 9 Sudanese named Zerah **invaded** Judah with an army of a million
16. 1 King Baasha of Israel **invaded** Judah and started to fortify
20. 1 together with their allies, the Meunites, **invaded** Judah.
20.22 the Lord threw the **invading** armies into a panic.
2 Chr 21. 9 Jehoram and his officers set out with chariots and **invaded** Edom.
21.17 They **invaded** Judah, looted the royal palace, and carried
32. 1 Sennacherib, the emperor of Assyria, **invaded** Judah.
33.11 Lord let the commanders of the Assyrian army **invade** Judah.
36. 6 Nebuchadnezzar of Babylonia **invaded** Judah, captured Jehoiakim,
Ps 79. 1 O God, the heathen have **invaded** your land.
Is 7. 6 They intend to **invade** Judah, terrify the people into
9. 5 The boots of the **invading** army and all their bloodstained
Jer 35.11 when King Nebuchadnezzar **invaded** the country, we decided to
Lam 4.12 believed that any **invader** could enter Jerusalem's gates.
4.20 the one we had trusted to protect us from every **invader.**
Ezek 38. 8 I will order him to **invade** a country where the people were
38. 8 He will **invade** the mountains of Israel, which were desolate
38.11 You will decide to **invade** a helpless country where the
38.16 I will send you to **invade** my land in order to show
38.18 "On the day when Gog **invades** Israel, I will be furious.
Dan 9.26 Temple will be destroyed by the **invading** army of a powerful
11. 9 the king of Syria will **invade** Egypt, but he will be forced
11.16 The Syrian **invader** will do with them as he pleases,
11.24 He will **invade** a wealthy province without warning
11.29 "Later on he will **invade** Egypt again, but this time
11.40 He will **invade** many countries, like the waters of a flood.
11.41 will even **invade** the Promised Land and kill tens of thousands,
11.42 he **invades** all those countries, even Egypt will not be spared.
Hos 5.10 leaders of Judah have **invaded** Israel and stolen land from her.
Mic 5. 5 When the Assyrians **invade** our country and break through our
5. 6 save us from the Assyrians when they **invade** our territory.
Nah 1.15 The wicked will never **invade** your land again.

INVENT

2 Chr 26.15 In Jerusalem his **inventors** made equipment for shooting
Ps 35.20 they **invent** all kinds of lies about peace-loving people.
52. 2 You are always **inventing** lies.
Jer 23.26 prophets mislead my people with the lies they have **invented?**
Ezek 13. 3 provide their own inspiration and **invent** their own visions.
Eph 4.14 men, who lead others into error by the tricks they **invent.**

INVENTORY

Ezra 1. 8 royal treasury, who made an **inventory** of them for Sheshbazzar,

INVEST

Ecc 11. 1 **Invest** your money in foreign trade, and one of these days
11. 2 Put your **investments** in several places—many places, in fact—
Mt 25.16 went at once and **invested** his money and earned another five

INVESTIGATE

Deut 13.14 If you hear such a rumour, **investigate** it thoroughly;
17. 4 If you hear such a report, then **investigate** it thoroughly.
19.18 The judges will **investigate** the case thoroughly;
Judg 6.29 They **investigated** and found out that Gideon son of Joash had
1 Chr 26.31 David was king, an **investigation** was made of the family line
Ezra 4.19 I gave orders for an **investigation** to be made, and it
7.14 send you to **investigate** the conditions in Jerusalem and Judah
10.16 tenth month they began their **investigation,** [17]and within the
10.17 next three months they **investigated** all the cases of men with
Esth 2.23 There was an **investigation,** and it was discovered that
Job 34.24 He does not need an **investigation** to remove leaders and
Acts 25.26 after **investigating** his case, I may have something to write.
1 Pet 1.10 made careful search and **investigation,** and they prophesied about

INVISIBLE

Rom 1.20 God created the world, his **invisible** qualities, both his eternal
Col 1.15 Christ is the visible likeness of the **invisible** God.
1 Tim 1.17 the eternal King, immortal and **invisible,** the only God—to
Heb 11.27 As though he saw the **invisible** God, he refused to turn back.

INVITE

Gen 29.22 So Laban gave a wedding-feast and **invited** everyone.
31.54 on the mountain, and he **invited** his men to the meal.
Ex 2.20 Go and **invite** him to eat with us."
34.15 sacrifice to them, they will **invite** you to join them, and
Num 25. 2 These women **invited** them to sacrificial feasts, where the
Deut 33.19 They **invite** foreigners to their mountain And offer the
Judg 14.15 You two **invited** us so that you could rob us, didn't you?"
1 Sam 9.12 people who are **invited** won't start eating until he gets there,
9.24 for you to eat at this time with the people I **invited."**
16. 3 **Invite** Jesse to the sacrifice, and I will tell you what to
16. 5 to purify themselves, and he **invited** them to the sacrifice.
2 Sam 11.13 David **invited** him to supper and made him drunk.
13.23 town of Ephraim, and he **invited** all the king's sons to be
15.11 who at Absalom's **invitation** had gone from Jerusalem with him;
1 Kgs 1. 9 **invited** the other sons of King David and the king's officials
1.10 but he did not **invite** his half brother Solomon or Nathan
1.19 and fattened calves, and he **invited** your sons, and Abiathar
1.19 army to the feast, but he did not **invite** your son Solomon.
1.25 He **invited** all your sons, Joab the commander of your army,
1.26 But he did not **invite** me, sir, or Zadok the priest, or
7.14 He accepted King Solomon's **invitation** to be in charge of all
12.20 had returned from Egypt, they **invited** him to a meeting of
20.33 When Benhadad arrived, Ahab **invited** him to get in the chariot
2 Kgs 4. 8 She **invited** him to a meal, and from then on every time
2 Chr 30. 1 of Ephraim and Manasseh, **inviting** them to come to the Temple
30. 5 with their plan, [5]so they **invited** all the Israelites,

2 Chr 30. 6 through all Judah and Israel with the following **invitation:**
Esth 2.18 banquet in Esther's honour and **invited** all his officials
5.10 Then he **invited** his friends to his house and asked his wife
5.12 one but the king and me, and we are **invited** back tomorrow.
Job 1. 4 and they always **invited** their three sisters to join them.
31.32 I **invited** travellers into my home and never let them
Prov 1.24 I have been calling you, **inviting** you to come, but you
Jer 30.21 will approach me when I **invite** him, for who would dare come
Lam 2.22 You **invited** my enemies to hold a carnival of terror
Ezek 23.40 again they sent messengers to **invite** men to come from a
Dan 5. 1 Belshazzar **invited** a thousand noblemen to a great banquet,
Zeph 1. 7 sacrifice his people and has **invited** enemies to plunder Judah.
Zech 3.10 each of you will **invite** his neighbour to come and enjoy
Mt 22. 3 servants to tell the **invited** guests to come to the feast,
22. 5 **invited** guests paid no attention and went about their business:
22. 8 feast is ready, but the people I **invited** did not deserve it.
22. 9 to the main streets and **invite** to the feast as many people
22.14 And Jesus concluded, "Many are **invited,** but few are chosen."
Lk 7.36 Pharisee **invited** Jesus to have dinner with him, and Jesus went
11.37 Jesus finished speaking, a Pharisee **invited** him to eat with him;
14. 8 "When someone **invites** you to a wedding feast, do not sit
14. 8 important than you has been **invited,**
14. 9 and your host, who **invited** both of you, would have to
14.10 Instead, when you are **invited,** go and sit in the lowest place,
14.12 or a dinner, do not **invite** your friends or your brothers or
14.12 rich neighbours—for they will **invite** you back, and in this
14.13 When you give a feast, **invite** the poor, the crippled,
14.16 was giving a great feast to which he **invited** many people.
14.24 none of those men who were **invited** will taste my dinner!' "
Jn 2. 2 Jesus and his disciples had also been **invited** to the wedding.
Acts 8.31 And he **invited** Philip to climb up and sit in the carriage
10.22 of God told him to **invite** you to his house, so that
10.23 Peter **invited** the men in and persuaded them to spend the
10.24 together with relatives and close friends that he had **invited.**
13.42 leaving the synagogue, the people **invited** them to come back
16.15 had been baptized, she **invited** us, "Come and stay in my
1 Cor 10.27 If an unbeliever **invites** you to a meal and you decide to
Rev 19. 9 those who have been **invited** to the wedding-feast of the Lamb."

INVOLVE

Ex 22. 9 dispute about property, whether it **involves** cattle, donkeys,
Num 4. 4 Their service **involves** the most holy things.
15.26 be forgiven, because everyone was **involved** in the mistake.
Deut 1.16 only your own people or **involves** foreigners who live among you.
17. 8 that **involve** a distinction between murder and manslaughter.
21. 5 they are to decide every legal case **involving** violence.
2 Chr 19. 8 citizens as judges in cases **involving** a violation of the Law
Ezra 10.13 two days, because so many of us are **involved** in this sin.
Prov 11.15 You are better off if you don't get **involved.**
26.17 Getting **involved** in an argument that is none of your
Gal 3.20 But a go-between is not needed when only one person is **involved;**
1 Pet 4. 1 whoever suffers physically is no longer **involved** with sin.

INWARDLY

Rom 12. 2 but let God transform you **inwardly** by a complete change of

IRON

Gen 4.22 Cain, who made all kinds of tools out of bronze and **iron.**
Lev 26.19 rain, and your land will be dry and as hard as **iron.**
Num 31.22 such as gold, silver, bronze, **iron,** tin, or lead, is to be
35.16 man uses a weapon of **iron** or stone or wood to kill
Deut 8. 9 Its rocks have **iron** in them, and from its hills you can
27. 5 stones that have had no **iron** tools used on them, [6]because
28.23 rain will fall, and your ground will become as hard as **iron.**
33.25 his towns be protected with **iron** gates, And may he always
Josh 6.19 of silver, gold, bronze, or **iron** is set apart for the Lord.
6.24 of gold, silver, bronze, and **iron,** which they took and put
8.31 made of stones which have not been cut with **iron** tools."
17.16 Canaanites in the plains have **iron** chariots, both those who
17.18 though they do have **iron** chariots and are a strong people."
22. 6 with a lot of livestock, silver, gold, bronze, **iron,** and many
Judg 1.18 living along the coast had **iron** chariots, and so the people
4. 3 Jabin had nine hundred **iron** chariots, and he ruled the
4.13 called out his nine hundred **iron** chariots and all his men,
1 Sam 17. 7 loom, and its **iron** head weighed about seven kilogrammes.
2 Sam 12.31 to work with saws, **iron** hoes, and iron axes, and forced
23. 7 You must use an **iron** tool or a spear;
1 Kgs 6. 7 axes, or any other **iron** tools as the Temple was being
22.11 Zedekiah son of Chenaanah, made **iron** horns and said to Ahab,
2 Kgs 6. 5 down a tree, suddenly his **iron** axe-head fell in the water.
1 Chr 20. 3 city and put them to work with saws, **iron** hoes, and axes.
22. 3 supplied a large amount of **iron** for making nails and clamps
22.14 Besides that, there is an unlimited supply of bronze and **iron.**
22.16 every sort who can work [16]with gold, silver, bronze, and **iron.**
29. 2 the Temple—gold, silver, bronze, **iron,** timber, precious
29. 7 tons of bronze, and more than 3,400 metric tons of **iron.**
2 Chr 2. 7 working gold, silver, bronze, and **iron,** and in making blue,
2.14 to make things out of gold, silver, bronze, **iron,** stone,
18.10 Zedekiah son of Chenaanah, made **iron** horns and said to Ahab,
Job 20.24 tries to escape from an **iron** sword, a bronze bow will shoot
28. 2 Men dig **iron** out of the ground And melt copper out of
40.18 are as strong as bronze, and his legs are like **iron** bars.
41.23 it is as hard and unyielding as **iron.**
41.27 For him **iron** is as flimsy as straw, and bronze as soft
Ps 2. 9 You will break them with an **iron** rod;
105.18 kept in chains, and an **iron** collar was round his neck,
107.16 He breaks down doors of bronze and smashes **iron** bars.
149. 8 bind their kings in chains, their leaders in chains of **iron;**
Prov 27.17 People learn from one another, just as **iron** sharpens iron.
Is 45. 2 I will break down bronze gates and smash their **iron** bars.
48. 4 to be stubborn, as rigid as **iron** and unyielding as bronze.
60.17 Silver and bronze instead of **iron** and wood,
60.17 And **iron** instead of stone.
Jer 1.18 be like a fortified city, an **iron** pillar, and a bronze wall.
6.28 They are all stubborn rebels, hard as bronze and **iron.**
15.12 (No one can break **iron,** especially the iron from the north
17. 1 "People of Judah, your sin is written with an **iron** pen;
28.13 a wooden yoke, but he will replace it with an **iron** yoke.
28.14 that he will put an **iron** yoke on all these nations and
29.26 is placed in chains with an **iron** collar round his neck.
Ezek 4. 3 Take an **iron** pan and set it up like a wall between
22.18 the waste metal—copper, tin, **iron,** and lead—left over after
22.20 the ore of silver, copper, **iron,** lead, and tin is put in
26. 9 with battering-rams and tear down your towers with **iron** bars.
27.12 in Spain and took silver, **iron,** tin, and lead in payment for
27.18 They exchanged wrought **iron** and spices for your goods.
Dan 2.33 its legs of **iron,**
2.33 and its feet partly of **iron** and partly of clay.
2.34 touching it, struck the **iron** and clay feet of the statue,
2.35 At once the **iron,** clay, bronze, silver, and gold crumbled
2.40 as strong as **iron,** which shatters and breaks everything.
2.40 And just as **iron** shatters everything, it will shatter and crush
2.41 that the feet and the toes were partly clay and partly **iron.**
2.41 something of the strength of **iron,**
2.41 because there was **iron** mixed with the clay.
2.42 The toes—partly **iron** and partly clay—mean that part of
2.43 You also saw that the **iron** was mixed with the clay.
2.43 not be able to, any more than **iron** can mix with clay.
2.45 it struck the statue made of **iron,** bronze, clay, silver,
4.15 in the ground with a band of **iron** and bronze round it.
4.23 Wrap a band of **iron** and bronze round it, and leave it
5. 4 and praised gods made of gold, silver, bronze, **iron,** wood,
5.23 made of gold, silver, bronze, **iron,** wood, and stone—gods that
7. 7 With its huge **iron** teeth it crushed its victims, and then it
7.19 with its bronze claws and **iron** teeth and then trampled on
Mic 4.13 you as strong as a bull with **iron** horns and bronze hoofs.
Mk 5. 4 time he broke the chains and smashed the **irons** on his feet.
Acts 12.10 and came at last to the **iron** gate leading into the city.
1 Tim 4. 2 whose consciences are dead, as if burnt with a hot **iron.**
Rev 2.26 to rule them with an **iron** rod and to break them to
9. 9 covered with what looked like **iron** breastplates, and the sound
12. 5 a son, who will rule over all nations with an **iron** rod.
18.12 made of ivory and of expensive wood, of bronze, **iron,** and
19.15 them with a rod of **iron,** and he will trample out the

IRRELIGIOUS

2 Tim 3. 2 disobedient to their parents, ungrateful, and **irreligious;**

IRRESPONSIBLE

Zeph 3. 4 The prophets are **irresponsible** and treacherous;

IRREVERENCE

2 Sam 6. 7 angry with Uzzah and killed him because of his **irreverence.**

IRRIGATE

Deut 11.10 you sowed seed, you had to work hard to **irrigate** the fields;
Ecc 2. 6 I dug ponds to **irrigate** them.

IRRITATE

Prov 10.26 he will be as **irritating** as vinegar on your teeth or smoke
1 Cor 13. 5 love is not ill-mannered or selfish or **irritable;**
Gal 5.26 must not be proud or **irritate** one another or be jealous of
Col 3.21 do not **irritate** your children, or they will become discouraged.

ISAAC

Abraham and Sarah's son and Esau and Jacob's father.

Gen 21.1-8 **The birth of Isaac**
9-21 **Hagar and Ishmael are sent away**
22.1-19 **God commands Abraham to offer Isaac**
24.1-67 **A wife for Isaac**
25.1-6 **Other descendants of Abraham**
7-11 **The death and burial of Abraham**
19-26 **The birth of Esau and Jacob**
27-34 **Esau sells his rights as the first-born son**
26.1-25 **Isaac lives at Gerar**
26-33 **The agreement between Isaac and Abimelech**
34-35 **Esau's foreign wives**
27.1-29 **Isaac blesses Jacob**
30-45 **Esau begs for Isaac's blessing**
27.46–28.5 **Isaac sends Jacob to Laban**
28.6-9 **Esau takes another wife**
35.27-29 **The death of Isaac**

Gen 17.19 Sarah will bear you a son and you will name him **Isaac.**
17.21 my covenant with your son **Isaac,** who will be born to Sarah
28.13 "I am the Lord, the God of Abraham and **Isaac,"** he said.
31.42 the God of Abraham and **Isaac,** had not been with me, you
31.53 God whom his father **Isaac** worshipped, Jacob solemnly vowed to
32. 9 of my grandfather Abraham and God of my father **Isaac,** hear
35.12 gave to Abraham and to **Isaac,** and I will also give it
46. 1 where he offered sacrifices to the God of his father **Isaac.**
48.15 God whom my fathers Abraham and **Isaac** served bless these boys!
48.16 name of my fathers Abraham and **Isaac** live on through these
49.31 that is where they buried **Isaac** and his wife Rebecca;

Gen	50.24	the land he solemnly promised to Abraham, **Isaac,** and Jacob."
Ex	2.24	and remembered his covenant with Abraham, **Isaac,** and Jacob.
	3. 6	God of your ancestors, the God of Abraham, **Isaac,** and Jacob."
	3.15	ancestors, the God of Abraham, **Isaac,** and Jacob, have sent
	3.16	the God of Abraham, **Isaac,** and Jacob, appeared to you.
	4. 5	the God of Abraham, **Isaac,** and Jacob, has appeared to you."
	6. 3	appeared to Abraham, to **Isaac,** and to Jacob as Almighty God,
	6. 8	land that I solemnly promised to give to Abraham, **Isaac,** and.
	32.13	Remember your servants Abraham, **Isaac,** and Jacob.
	33. 1	promised to give to Abraham, **Isaac,** and Jacob and to their
Lev	26.42	covenant with Jacob and with **Isaac** and with Abraham,
Num	32.11	enter the land that I promised to Abraham, **Isaac,** and Jacob.'
Deut	1. 8	give to your ancestors, Abraham, **Isaac,** and Jacob, and to
	6.10	God promised your ancestors, Abraham, **Isaac,** and Jacob,
	9. 5	the promise that he made to your ancestors, Abraham, **Isaac,**
	9.27	Remember your servants, Abraham, **Isaac,** and Jacob,
	29.13	God, as he promised you and your ancestors, Abraham, **Isaac,**
	30.20	land that he promised to give your ancestors, Abraham, **Isaac,**
	34. 4	land that I promised Abraham, **Isaac,** and Jacob I would give
Josh	24. 3	I gave him **Isaac,** [4]and to Isaac I gave Jacob and Esau.
1 Kgs	18.36	Lord, the God of Abraham, **Isaac,** and Jacob, prove now that
2 Kgs	13.23	but helped them, because of his covenant with Abraham, **Isaac,**
1 Chr	1.28	Abraham had two sons, **Isaac** and Ishmael.
	1.34	Abraham's son **Isaac** had two sons, Esau and Jacob.
	16.16	covenant he made with Abraham, the promise he made to **Isaac.**
	29.18	God of our ancestors Abraham, **Isaac,** and Jacob, keep such
2 Chr	30. 6	Lord, the God of Abraham, **Isaac,** and Jacob, and he will
Ps	105. 9	agreement he made with Abraham and his promise to **Isaac.**
Jer	33.26	descendants to rule over the descendants of Abraham, **Isaac,**
Amos	7. 9	places where **Isaac's** descendants worship will be destroyed.
Mt	1. 2	Abraham, **Isaac,** Jacob, Judah and his brothers;
	8.11	and sit down with Abraham, **Isaac,** and Jacob at the feast in
	22.32	God of Abraham, the God of **Isaac,** and the God of Jacob.'
Mk	12.26	God of Abraham, the God of **Isaac,** and the God of Jacob.'
Lk	3.34	of Jacob, the son of **Isaac,** the son of Abraham, the son
	13.28	when you see Abraham, **Isaac,** and Jacob, and all the prophets
	20.37	God of Abraham, the God of **Isaac,** and the God of Jacob.'
Acts	3.13	The God of Abraham, **Isaac,** and Jacob, the God of our ancestors,
	7. 8	So Abraham circumcised **Isaac** a week after he was born;
	7. 8	**Isaac** circumcised his son Jacob, and Jacob circumcised his twelve
	7.32	the God of your ancestors, the God of Abraham, **Isaac,** and
Rom	9. 7	"It is through **Isaac** that you will have the descendants
	9.10	For Rebecca's two sons had the same father, our ancestor **Isaac.**
Gal	4.28	God's children as a result of his promise, just as **Isaac** was.
Heb	11. 9	lived in tents, as did **Isaac** and Jacob, who received the
	11.17	made Abraham offer his son **Isaac** as a sacrifice when God put
	11.18	to him, "It is through **Isaac** that you will have the
	11.19	God was able to raise **Isaac** from death—
	11.19	and, so to speak, Abraham did receive **Isaac** back from death.
	11.20	It was faith that made **Isaac** promise blessings for the future
Jas	2.21	his actions, when he offered his son **Isaac** on the altar.

ISAIAH
Prophet who lived in Jerusalem in the eighth century B.C.

2 Kgs	19. 2	and the senior priests to the prophet **Isaiah** son of Amoz.
	19. 3	This is the message which he told them to give **Isaiah:**
	19. 5	**Isaiah** received King Hezekiah's message, [6]he sent back
	19.20	Then **Isaiah** sent a message telling King Hezekiah that in
	19.29	Then **Isaiah** said to King Hezekiah, "This is a sign of
	20. 1	The prophet **Isaiah** son of Amoz went to see him and said
	20. 4	**Isaiah** left the king, but before he had passed through the
	20. 7	Then **Isaiah** told the king's attendants to put on his boil
	20. 9	**Isaiah** replied, "The Lord will give you a sign to prove
	20.11	**Isaiah** prayed to the Lord, and the Lord made the shadow
	20.14	Then the prophet **Isaiah** went to King Hezekiah and asked,
	20.16	**Isaiah** then said to the king, "The Lord Almighty says
2 Chr	26.22	prophet **Isaiah** son of Amoz recorded all the other things that
	32.20	Hezekiah and the prophet **Isaiah** son of Amoz prayed to God
	32.32	The Vision of the Prophet **Isaiah** Son of Amoz and in
Is	1. 1	Jerusalem which God revealed to **Isaiah** son of Amoz during the
	2. 1	message which God gave to **Isaiah** son of Amoz about Judah and
	7. 3	The Lord said to **Isaiah,** "Take your son Shear Jashub, and
	7.13	**Isaiah** replied, "Listen, now, descendants of King David.
	13. 1	a message about Babylon, which **Isaiah** son of Amoz received
	20. 2	earlier the Lord had told **Isaiah** son of Amoz to take off
	20. 3	the Lord said, "My servant **Isaiah** has been going about naked
	37. 2	and the senior priests to the prophet **Isaiah** son of Amoz.
	37. 3	This is the message which he told them to give to **Isaiah:**
	37. 5	When **Isaiah** received King Hezekiah's message, [6]he sent
	37.21	Then **Isaiah** sent a message telling King Hezekiah that in
	37.30	Then **Isaiah** said to King Hezekiah, "This is a sign of
	38. 1	The prophet **Isaiah** son of Amoz went to see him and said
	38. 4	the Lord commanded **Isaiah** [5]to go back to Hezekiah and say
	38. 6	**Isaiah** told the king to put a paste made of figs on
	38. 7	**Isaiah** replied, "The Lord will give you a sign to prove
	39. 3	Then the prophet **Isaiah** went to King Hezekiah and asked,
	39. 5	**Isaiah** then told the king, "The Lord Almighty says that
Mt	3. 3	the man the prophet **Isaiah** was talking about when he said,
	4.14	to make what the prophet **Isaiah** had said come true,
	8.17	to make what the prophet **Isaiah** had said come true, "He
	12.17	what God had said through the prophet **Isaiah** come true:
	13.14	So the prophecy of **Isaiah** applies to them:
	15. 7	How right **Isaiah** was when he prophesied about you!
Mk	1. 2	It began as the prophet **Isaiah** had written:
	7. 6	Jesus answered them, "How right **Isaiah** was when he prophesied
Lk	3. 4	As it is written in the book of the prophet **Isaiah:**
	4.17	and was handed the book of the prophet **Isaiah.**
Jn	1.23	John answered by quoting the prophet **Isaiah:**
	12.38	so that what the prophet **Isaiah** had said might come true:
Jn	12.39	not able to believe, because **Isaiah** also said, [40]"God has
	12.41	**Isaiah** said this because he saw Jesus' glory and spoke about
Acts	8.27	along, he was reading from the book of the prophet **Isaiah.**
	8.30	and heard him reading from the book of the prophet **Isaiah.**
	28.25	Holy Spirit spoke through the prophet **Isaiah** to your ancestors!
Rom	9.27	And **Isaiah** exclaims about Israel:
	9.29	It is as **Isaiah** had said before, "If the Lord Almighty
	10.16	**Isaiah** himself said, "Lord, who believed our message?"
	10.20	And **Isaiah** is even bolder when he says, "I was found by
	15.12	And again, **Isaiah** says, "A descendant of Jesse will appear;

ISHBOSHETH
Saul's son, king of Israel.
see also ESHBAAL

2 Sam	2. 8	fled with Saul's son **Ishbosheth** across the Jordan to Mahanaim.
	2. 9	Abner made **Ishbosheth** king of the territories of Gilead,
	2.12	the officials of **Ishbosheth** went from Mahanaim to the city
	2.15	twelve men, representing **Ishbosheth** and the tribe of Benjamin,
	3. 7	**Ishbosheth** son of Saul accused Abner of sleeping with Saul's
	3.11	**Ishbosheth** was so afraid of Abner that he could not say
	3.14	David also sent messengers to **Ishbosheth** to say, "Give me
	3.15	So **Ishbosheth** took her away from her husband Paltiel
	4. 1	When Saul's son **Ishbosheth** heard that Abner had been killed
	4. 2	**Ishbosheth** had two officers who were leaders of raiding
	4. 5	Baanah set out for **Ishbosheth's** house and arrived there about
	4. 7	they went to **Ishbosheth's** bedroom, where he was sound asleep,
	4. 8	"Here is the head of **Ishbosheth,** the son of your enemy Saul,
	4.12	They took **Ishbosheth's** head and buried it in Abner's tomb

ISHMAEL (1)
Abraham and Hagar's son and the people descended from him.

Gen	16.11	and you will name him **Ishmael,** because the Lord has heard
	16.15	Hagar bore Abram a son, and he named him **Ishmael.**
	17.18	He asked God, "Why not let **Ishmael** be my heir?"
	17.20	have heard your request about **Ishmael,** so I will bless him
	17.23	God and circumcised his son **Ishmael** and all the other males
	17.25	when he was circumcised, [25]and his son **Ishmael** was thirteen.
	21. 9	**Ishmael,** whom Hagar the Egyptian had borne to Abraham, was
	21.11	troubled Abraham very much, because **Ishmael** was also his son.
	25. 9	His sons Isaac and **Ishmael** buried him in Machpelah Cave,
	25.12	**Ishmael,** whom Hagar, the Egyptian slave of Sarah, bore to
	25.17	**Ishmael** was a hundred and thirty-seven years old when he
	25.18	descendants of **Ishmael** lived in the territory between Havilah
	28. 9	he went to **Ishmael** son of Abraham and married his daughter
	36. 3	Basemath, the daughter of **Ishmael** and sister of Nebaioth.
	37.25	saw a group of **Ishmaelites** travelling from Gilead to Egypt.
	37.27	Let's sell him to these **Ishmaelites.**
	37.28	pieces of silver to the **Ishmaelites,** who took him to Egypt.
	39. 1	Now the **Ishmaelites** had taken Joseph to Egypt and sold him
2 Sam	17.25	Amasa was the son of Jether the **Ishmaelite;**
1 Chr	1.28	Abraham had two sons, Isaac and **Ishmael.**
	1.29	The sons of **Ishmael** became the heads of twelve tribes:
	1.29	Nebaioth (from the name of **Ishmael's** eldest son), Kedar,
	2.17	married Jether, a descendant of **Ishmael,** and they had a son
	27.25	Obil, an **Ishmaelite**
Ps	83. 6	the people of Edom and the **Ishmaelites;**

ISHMAEL (2)
A Judaean officer.

2 Kgs	25.23	These officers were **Ishmael** son of Nethaniah, Johanan
	25.25	seventh month of that year, **Ishmael,** the son of Nethaniah
Jer	40. 8	So **Ishmael** son of Nethaniah, Johanan son of Kareah, Seraiah
	40.14	that King Baalis of Ammon has sent **Ishmael** to murder you?"
	40.15	"Let me go and kill **Ishmael,** and no one will know who
	40.16	What you are saying about **Ishmael** is not true!"
	41. 1	seventh month of that year, **Ishmael,** the son of Nethaniah
	41. 2	eating a meal together, [2]**Ishmael** and the ten men with him
	41. 3	**Ishmael** also killed all the Israelites who were with
	41. 6	So **Ishmael** went out from Mizpah to meet them, weeping as
	41. 7	they were inside the city, **Ishmael** and his men killed them
	41. 8	in the group who said to **Ishmael,** "Please don't kill us!
	41. 9	The well into which **Ishmael** threw the bodies of the men he
	41. 9	**Ishmael** filled the well with the bodies.
	41.10	**Ishmael** took them prisoner and started off in the direction
	41.11	with him heard of the crime that **Ishmael** had committed.
	41.13	When **Ishmael's** prisoners saw Johanan and the leaders of
	41.15	But **Ishmael** and eight of his men got away from Johanan
	41.16	charge of the people whom **Ishmael** had taken away as prisoners
	41.17	of the Babylonians because **Ishmael** had murdered Gedaliah,

ISLAND

Gen	10. 5	of the people who live along the coast and on the **islands.**
Deut	2.23	coast had been settled by people from the **island** of Crete.
Ps	72.10	kings of Spain and of the **islands** will offer him gifts;
	97. 1	Rejoice, you **islands** of the seas!
Is	11.11	Hamath, and in the coastlands and on the **islands** of the sea.
	40.15	the distant **islands** are as light as dust.
Jer	2.10	Go west to the **island** of Cyprus, and send someone
Ezek	26.18	it has fallen, The **islands** are trembling, And their people
	27. 7	made of finest cloth, Of purple from the **island** of Cyprus.
Acts	13. 4	to Seleucia and sailed from there to the **island** of Cyprus.
	13. 6	all the way across the **island** to Paphos, where they met a
	13. 7	governor of the **island,** Sergius Paulus, who was an intelligent
	27. 4	we sailed on the sheltered side of the **island** of Cyprus.
	27. 7	sheltered side of the **island** of Crete, passing by Cape Salmone.
	27.14	wind—the one called "North-easter"—blew down from the **island.**
	27.16	when we passed to the south of the little **island** of Cauda.

Acts	27.26	But we will be driven ashore on some **island."**
	28. 1	were safely ashore, we learnt that the **island** was called Malta.
	28. 7	fields that belonged to Publius, the chief official of the **island.**
	28. 9	the other sick people on the **island** came and were healed.
	28.11	"The Twin Gods," which had spent the winter in the **island.**
Rev	1. 9	I was put on the **island** of Patmos because I had proclaimed
	6.14	and every mountain and **island** was moved from its place.
	16.20	All the **islands** disappeared, all the mountains vanished.

ISOLATE

Lev	13. 4	not turned white, the priest shall **isolate** the person for
	13. 5	has not spread, he shall **isolate** him for another seven days.
	13.11	is no need to **isolate** him, because he is obviously unclean.
	13.21	light in colour, the priest shall **isolate** him for seven days.
	13.26	light in colour, the priest shall **isolate** him for seven days.
	13.31	no healthy hairs in it, he shall **isolate** him for seven days.
	13.33	The priest shall then **isolate** him for another seven days.

ISRAEL (1)

Another name for Jacob.

Gen	32.28	so your name will be **Israel."**
	32.32	Even today the descendants of **Israel** do not eat the
	33.20	an altar there and named it after El, the God of **Israel.**
	35.10	"Your name is Jacob, but from now on it will be **Israel."**
	35.10	So God named him **Israel.**
	49. 2	Listen to your father **Israel.**
	49.24	Mighty God of Jacob, By the Shepherd, the Protector of **Israel.**
1 Kgs	18.31	Jacob, the man to whom the Lord had given the name **Israel.**
2 Kgs	17.34	he gave to the descendants of Jacob, whom he named **Israel.**

ISRAEL (2)

[FELLOW-ISRAELITE, JUDAH AND ISRAEL, KING OF ISRAEL, PEOPLE OF ISRAEL]

Nation descended from Jacob/Israel. Also used to describe the n. Kingdom as distinct from Judah after their division.

Gen	34. 7	insulted the **people of Israel** by raping Jacob's daughter.
	36.31	there were any kings in **Israel,** the following kings
	47.27	The **Israelites** lived in Egypt in the region of Goshen,
	48.20	them that day, saying, "The **Israelites** will use your names
	49. 7	I will scatter them throughout the land of **Israel.**
	49.16	They will be like the other tribes of **Israel.**
	49.28	the twelve tribes of **Israel,** and this is what their father
Ex	1. 7	but their descendants, the **Israelites,** had many children
	1. 9	said to his people, "These **Israelites** are so numerous and
	1.11	**Israelites** built the cities of Pithom and Rameses to serve as
	1.12	more the Egyptians oppressed the **Israelites,** the more they
	1.12	Egyptians came to fear the **Israelites** [13-14]and made
	1.20	And the **Israelites** continued to increase and become strong.
	2.23	but the **Israelites** were still groaning under their slavery
	2.25	He saw the slavery of the **Israelites** and was concerned
	3.11	I go to the king and bring the **Israelites** out of Egypt?"
	3.13	"When I go to the **Israelites** and say to them, 'The God
	3.15	Tell the **Israelites** that I, the Lord, the God of their
	3.16	and gather the leaders of **Israel** together and tell them that
	3.18	go with the leaders of **Israel** to the king of Egypt and
	3.22	Every **Israelite** woman will go to her Egyptian neighbours
	3.22	**Israelites** will put these things on their sons and daughters and
	4. 1	the Lord, "But suppose the **Israelites** do not believe me and
	4. 5	this to prove to the **Israelites** that the Lord, the God of
	4.22	him that I, the Lord, say, '**Israel** is my first-born son.
	4.29	went to Egypt and gathered all the **Israelite** leaders together.
	5. 1	"The Lord, the God of **Israel,** says, 'Let my people go, so
	5. 2	"Why should I listen to him and let **Israel** go?
	5. 2	and I will not let **Israel** go."
	5. 6	the Egyptian slave-drivers and the **Israelite** foremen:
	5.10	The slave-drivers and the **Israelite** foremen went out and
	5.10	out and said to the **Israelites,** "The king has said that he
	5.14	The Egyptian slave-drivers beat the **Israelite** foremen,
	6. 5	groaning of the **Israelites,** whom the Egyptians have enslaved,
	6. 6	So tell the **Israelites** that I say to them, 'I am the
	6. 9	Moses told this to the **Israelites,** but they would not listen
	6.11	of Egypt that he must let the **Israelites** leave his land."
	6.12	But Moses replied, "Even the **Israelites** will not listen
	6.13	"Tell the **Israelites** and the king of Egypt
	6.13	I have ordered you to lead the **Israelites** out of Egypt."
	6.26	the Lord said, "Lead the tribes of **Israel** out of Egypt."
	6.27	the men who told the king of Egypt to free the **Israelites.**
	7. 2	will tell the king to let the **Israelites** leave his country.
	7. 5	my hand against them and bring the **Israelites** out of their
	9. 4	the animals of the **Israelites** and those of the Egyptians,
	9. 4	and no animal that belongs to the **Israelites** will die.
	9. 6	but not one of the animals of the **Israelites** died.
	9. 7	told that none of the animals of the **Israelites** had died.
	9.26	Goshen, where the **Israelites** lived, was the only place where
	9.35	foretold through Moses, the king would not let the **Israelites**
	10. 7	Let the **Israelite** men go, so that they can worship the Lord
	10.20	the king stubborn, and he did not let the **Israelites** go.
	10.23	But the **Israelites** had light where they were living.
	11. 2	Now speak to the **people of Israel** and tell all of them
	11. 3	The Lord made the Egyptians respect the **Israelites.**
	11. 7	not even a dog will bark at the **Israelites** or their animals.
	11. 7	make a distinction between the Egyptians and the **Israelites.'"**
	11.10	and he would not let the **Israelites** leave his country.
	12. 3	Give these instructions to the whole community of **Israel:**
	12. 6	month, the whole community of **Israel** will kill the animals.
	12.21	for all the leaders of **Israel** and said to them, "Each of
	12.27	because he passed over the houses of the **Israelites** in Egypt.
	12.27	The **Israelites** knelt down and worshipped.
Ex	12.31	Moses and Aaron and said, "Get out, you and your **Israelites!**
	12.35	The **Israelites** had done as Moses had said, and had asked
	12.36	way the **Israelites** carried away the wealth of the Egyptians.
	12.37	The **Israelites** set out on foot from Rameses for Sukkoth.
	12.40	The **Israelites** had lived in Egypt for 430 years.
	12.42	to come as a night when the **Israelites** must keep watch.
	12.47	whole community of **Israel** must celebrate this festival,
	12.48	be treated like a native-born **Israelite** and may join in the
	12.49	same regulations apply to native-born **Israelites** and to
	12.50	All the **Israelites** obeyed and did what the Lord had
	12.51	that day the Lord brought the **Israelite** tribes out of Egypt.
	13. 2	for every first-born male **Israelite** and every first-born male
	13.18	The **Israelites** were armed for battle.
	13.19	as Joseph had made the **Israelites** solemnly promise to do.
	13.20	The **Israelites** left Sukkoth and camped at Etham on the
	14. 2	said to Moses, [2]"Tell the **Israelites** to turn back and camp
	14. 3	king will think that the **Israelites** are wandering about in
	14. 4	The **Israelites** did as they were told.
	14. 5	We have let the **Israelites** escape, and we have lost them as
	14. 8	and he pursued the **Israelites,** who were leaving triumphantly.
	14.10	When the **Israelites** saw the king and his army marching
	14.16	water will divide, and the **Israelites** will be able to walk
	14.19	front of the army of **Israel,** moved and went to the rear.
	14.20	moved until it was [20]between the Egyptians and the **Israelites.**
	14.20	gave light to the **people of Israel,** and so the armies could
	14.22	divided, [22]and the **Israelites** went through the sea on dry
	14.25	The Egyptians said, "The Lord is fighting for the **Israelites**
	14.28	Egyptian army that had followed the **Israelites** into the sea;
	14.29	But the **Israelites** walked through the sea on dry ground,
	14.30	the Lord saved the **people of Israel** from the Egyptians, and
	14.30	from the Egyptians, and the **Israelites** saw them lying dead
	14.31	the **Israelites** saw the great power with which the Lord had
	15. 1	Then Moses and the **Israelites** sang this song to the Lord:
	15.19	The **Israelites** walked through the sea on dry ground.
	15.22	Then Moses led the **people of Israel** away from the Red
	16. 1	The whole **Israelite** community set out from Elim, and on the
	16. 6	Aaron said to all the **Israelites,** "This evening you will know
	16.12	"I have heard the complaints of the **Israelites.**
	16.15	When the **Israelites** saw it, they didn't know what it was
	16.17	The **Israelites** did this, some gathering more, others
	16.31	The **people of Israel** called the food manna.
	16.35	The **Israelites** ate manna for the next forty years,
	17. 1	The whole **Israelite** community left the desert of Sin,
	17. 5	some of the leaders of **Israel** with you, and go on ahead
	17. 6	Moses did so in the presence of the leaders of **Israel.**
	17. 7	Massah and Meribah, because the **Israelites** complained and put
	17. 8	The Amalekites came and attacked the **Israelites** at Rephidim.
	17.11	held up his arms, the **Israelites** won, but when he put his
	18. 1	for Moses and the **people of Israel** when he led them out
	18. 8	and the people of Egypt in order to rescue the **Israelites.**
	18.11	the Egyptians treated the **Israelites** with such contempt."
	18.12	and all the leaders of **Israel** went with him to eat the
	18.25	and chose capable men from among all the **Israelites.**
	19. 1	The **people of Israel** left Rephidim, and on the first
	19. 3	and told him to say to the **Israelites,** Jacob's descendants:
	20.22	The Lord commanded Moses to say to the **Israelites:**
	21. 1	"Give the **Israelites** the following laws:
	24. 1	and Aaron, Nadab, Abihu, and seventy of the leaders of **Israel;**
	24. 4	twelve stones, one for each of the twelve tribes of **Israel.**
	24. 9	seventy of the leaders of **Israel** went up the mountain
	24.10	and they saw the God of **Israel.**
	24.11	God did not harm these leading men of **Israel;**
	24.16	To the **Israelites** the light looked like a fire burning on
	25. 2	said to Moses, [2]"Tell the **Israelites** to make an offering to
	25.22	I will give you all my laws for the **people of Israel.**
	27.20	"Command the **people of Israel** to bring you the best
	27.21	to be kept for ever by the **Israelites** and their descendants.
	28. 1	Separate them from the **people of Israel,** so that they may
	28.12	of the ephod to represent the twelve tribes of **Israel.**
	28.21	one of the sons of Jacob, to represent the tribes of **Israel.**
	28.29	names of the tribes of **Israel,** so that I, the Lord, will
	28.30	so that he can determine my will for the **people of Israel.**
	28.38	all the offerings that the **Israelites** dedicate to me, even if
	29.43	I will meet the **people of Israel,** and the dazzling light of
	29.45	will live among the **people of Israel,** and I will be their
	30.12	a census of the **people of Israel,** each man is to pay
	30.16	this money from the **people of Israel** and spend it for the
	30.31	Say to the **people of Israel,** 'This holy anointing oil is
	31.13	to say to the **people of Israel,** "Keep the Sabbath, my
	31.16	The **people of Israel** are to keep this day as a sign
	31.17	permanent sign between the **people of Israel** and me, because
	32. 4	The people said, **"Israel,** this is our god, who led us out
	32.20	Then he made the **people of Israel** drink it.
	32.27	them, "The Lord God of **Israel** commands every one of you to
	33. 6	Mount Sinai, the **people of Israel** no longer wore jewellery.
	33. 7	Whenever the **people of Israel** set up camp, Moses would
	34.10	to Moses, "I now make a covenant with the **people of Israel.**
	34.23	men must come to worship me, the Lord, the God of **Israel.**
	34.27	that I am making a covenant with you and with **Israel."**
	34.32	After that, all the **people of Israel** gathered round him,
	34.34	he would tell the **people of Israel** everything that he had
	35. 1	whole community of the **people of Israel** and said to them,
	35. 4	said to all the **people of Israel,** "This is what the Lord
	35.20	All the **people of Israel** left, [21]and everyone who
	35.29	All the **people of Israel** who wanted to brought their
	35.30	said to the **Israelites,** "The Lord has chosen Bezalel,
	36. 3	offerings which the **Israelites** had brought for constructing
	36. 3	But the **people of Israel** continued to bring Moses their
	39. 7	represent the twelve tribes of **Israel,** just as the Lord had
	39.14	of Jacob, in order to represent the twelve tribes of **Israel.**

Ex	39.32	**Israelites** made everything just as the Lord had commanded Moses.
	39.42	The **Israelites** had done all the work just as the Lord
	40.36	**Israelites** moved their camp to another place only when the cloud
Lev	1. 2	rules [2]for the **Israelites** to observe when they offer their
	3.17	No **Israelite** may eat any fat or any blood;
	3.17	to be kept for ever by all **Israelites** wherever they live.
	4. 2	Moses [2]to tell the **people of Israel** that anyone who sinned
	4.13	is the whole community of **Israel** that sins and becomes guilty
	6. 2	refusing to return what a **fellow-Israelite** has left as a
	7.23	the following regulations [23]for the **people of Israel.**
	7.26	where the **Israelites** live, they must never use the blood
	7.29	the following regulations [29]for the **people of Israel.**
	7.34	taken from the **people of Israel** and given to the priests.
	7.34	This is what the **people of Israel** must give to the priests
	7.36	the Lord commanded the **people of Israel** to give them this
	7.36	a regulation that the **people of Israel** must obey for all
	7.38	day he told the **people of Israel** to make their offerings.
	9. 1	Moses called Aaron and his sons and the leaders of **Israel.**
	9. 3	Then tell the **people of Israel** to take a male goat for
	10. 6	But all your **fellow-Israelites** are allowed to mourn this
	10.11	You must teach the **people of Israel** all the laws which I
	10.14	you from the fellowship-offerings of the **people of Israel.**
	11. 2	the following regulations [2]for the **people of Israel.**
	12. 2	the following regulations [2]for the **people of Israel.**
	14.34	apply after the **people of Israel** entered the land of Canaan,
	15. 2	the following regulations [2]for the **people of Israel.**
	15.31	Moses to warn the **people of Israel** about their uncleanness,
	16. 5	The community of **Israel** shall give Aaron two male goats for
	16.16	uncleanness of the **people of Israel** and from all their sins.
	16.19	from the sins of the **people of Israel** and make it holy.
	16.21	and rebellions of the **people of Israel,** and so transfer them
	16.29	of the seventh month the **Israelites** and the foreigners living
	16.34	a year to purify the **people of Israel** from all their sins.
	17. 2	sons and all the **people of Israel** the following regulations.
	17. 3	An **Israelite** who kills a cow or a sheep or a goat
	17. 5	command is that the **people of Israel** shall now bring to the
	17. 7	The **people of Israel** must no longer be unfaithful to the
	17. 7	The **people of Israel** must keep this regulation for all time
	17. 8	Any **Israelite** or any foreigner living in the community who
	17.10	any **Israelite** or any foreigner living in the community eats
	17.12	Lord has told the **people of Israel** that neither they nor any
	17.13	any **Israelite** or any foreigner living in the community hunts
	17.14	Lord has told the **people of Israel** that they shall not eat
	17.15	Any person, **Israelite** or foreigner, who eats meat from
	18. 2	to say to the **people of Israel,** "I am the Lord your
	18.26	whether **Israelites** or foreigners living with you, must keep
	19. 2	to the community of **Israel,** "Be holy, because I, the Lord
	19.34	them as you would a **fellow-Israelite,** and love them as you
	20. 2	to say to the **people of Israel,** "Any of you or any
	20.10	with the wife of a **fellow-Israelite,** both he and the woman
	21.24	Aaron, the sons of Aaron, and to all the **people of Israel.**
	22. 2	sacred offerings that the **people of Israel** dedicate to me.
	22. 3	offerings which the **people of Israel** have dedicated to me,
	22.18	sons and all the **people of Israel** the following regulations.
	22.18	When any **Israelite** or any foreigner living in Israel presents
	22.32	all the **people of Israel** must acknowledge me to be holy.
	23. 2	when the **people of Israel** are to gather for worship.
	23.42	All the **people of Israel** shall live in shelters for seven days,
	23.43	the Lord made the **people of Israel** live in simple shelters
	23.44	way Moses gave the **people of Israel** the regulations for
	24. 2	Moses [2]to give the following orders to the **people of Israel:**
	24. 8	This is **Israel's** duty for ever.
	24.10	and whose mother was an **Israelite** named Shelomith,
	24.10	There in the camp this man quarrelled with an **Israelite.**
	24.15	Then tell the **people of Israel** that anyone who curses
	24.16	**Israelite** or any foreigner living in Israel who curses the Lord
	24.16	or any foreigner living in **Israel** who curses the Lord shall
	24.22	all of you, to **Israelites** and to foreigners living among you,
	24.23	said this to the **people of Israel,** they took the man outside
	24.23	In this way the **people of Israel** did what the Lord had
	25. 2	to give the following regulations to the **people of Israel.**
	25.14	you sell land to your **fellow-Israelite** or buy land from him,
	25.17	Do not cheat a **fellow-Israelite,** but obey the Lord your God.
	25.25	an **Israelite** becomes poor and is forced to sell his land,
	25.33	are their permanent property among the **people of Israel.**
	25.35	If a **fellow-Israelite** living near you becomes poor
	25.36	but obey God and let your **fellow-Israelite** live near you.
	25.39	If a **fellow-Israelite** living near you becomes so poor
	25.42	The **people of Israel** are the Lord's slaves, and he
	25.46	But you must not treat any of your **fellow-Israelites** harshly.
	25.47	you becomes rich, while a **fellow-Israelite** becomes poor and
	25.55	An **Israelite** cannot be a permanent slave, because the
	25.55	slave, because the **people of Israel** are the Lord's slaves.
	26.46	Lord gave to Moses on Mount Sinai for the **people of Israel.**
	27. 2	the following regulations for the **people of Israel.**
	27.34	Lord gave Moses on Mount Sinai for the **people of Israel.**
Num	1. 1	second year after the **people of Israel** left Egypt, the Lord
	1. 2	take a census of the **people of Israel** by clans and families.
	1.52	rest of the **Israelites** shall set up camp, company by company,
	1.53	near and cause my anger to strike the community of **Israel."**
	1.54	So the **people of Israel** did everything that the Lord had
	2. 2	When the **Israelites** set up camp, each man will camp under
	2.32	number of the **people of Israel** enrolled in the divisions,
	2.33	the Levites were not registered with the rest of the **Israelites.**
	2.34	So the **people of Israel** did everything the Lord had commanded
	3. 8	Tent and perform the duties for the rest of the **Israelites.**
	3.12	the eldest son of each **Israelite** family and the first-born of
	3.12	having the first-born sons of **Israel** as my own, I have the
	3.38	performed in the Holy Place for the **people of Israel.**
	3.40	Lord said to Moses, "All of **Israel's** first-born sons belong
Num	3.40	register by name every first-born male **Israelite,** one month
	3.45	place of all the first-born **Israelite** sons, and dedicate the
	3.45	in place of the first-born of the **Israelites'** livestock.
	3.46	Since the first-born **Israelite** sons outnumber the Levites
	5. 2	to Moses, [2]"Command the **people of Israel** to expel from the
	5. 4	The **Israelites** obeyed and expelled them all from the camp.
	5. 6	the following instructions for the **people of Israel.**
	5. 9	special contribution which the **Israelites** offer to the Lord
	5.12	The Lord commanded Moses [12-14]to give the **Israelites**
	6. 2	Moses [2]to give the following instructions to the **people of Israel.**
	6.23	use the following words in blessing the **people of Israel:**
	6.27	a blessing upon the **people of Israel,** I will bless them."
	7. 2	leaders in the tribes of **Israel,** the same men who were in
	8. 6	the rest of the **people of Israel** and purify them [7]in the
	8. 9	assemble the whole community of **Israel** and make the Levites
	8.10	The **people of Israel** are to place their hands on the
	8.11	a special gift from the **Israelites,** so that they may do my
	8.14	from the rest of the **Israelites,** so that they will belong to
	8.16	the first-born sons of the **Israelites,** and they belong to me
	8.17	the eldest son of each **Israelite** family and the first-born of
	8.18	all the first-born of the **Israelites,** [19]and I assign the
	8.19	as a gift from the **Israelites,** to work in the Tent for
	8.19	the Tent for the **people of Israel** and to protect the
	8.19	to protect the **Israelites** from the disaster that would strike
	8.20	Aaron, and all the **people of Israel** dedicated the Levites,
	9. 1	the second year after the **people of Israel** had left Egypt.
	9. 2	beginning at sunset, the **people of Israel** are to observe the
	9. 7	presenting the Lord's offering with the rest of the **Israelites?"**
	9.10	to say to the **people of Israel,** "When any of you or
	9.17	the cloud lifted, the **people of Israel** broke camp, and they
	10.12	Lord's presence lifted, [12]and the **Israelites** started on
	10.28	march, company by company, whenever the **Israelites** broke camp
	10.29	He has promised to make **Israel** prosperous, so come with us,
	10.36	"Return, Lord, to the thousands of families of **Israel."**
	11. 4	There were some foreigners travelling with the **Israelites.**
	11. 4	and even the **Israelites** themselves began to complain:
	11.30	Moses and the seventy leaders of **Israel** went back to camp.
	12. 7	I have put him in charge of all my people **Israel.**
	13. 2	the land of Canaan, which I am giving to the **Israelites."**
	13.24	because of the bunch of grapes the **Israelites** cut off there.)
	13.26	and the whole community of **Israel** at Kadesh in the wilderness
	13.32	a false report among the **Israelites** about the land they had
	14.39	When Moses told the **Israelites** what the Lord had said,
	15. 2	following regulations for the **people of Israel** to observe in
	15.13	Every native **Israelite** is to do this when he presents
	15.18	following regulations for the **people of Israel** to observe in
	15.26	whole community of **Israel** and the foreigners living among them
	15.29	sin, whether he is a native **Israelite** or a resident foreigner.
	15.32	Once, while the **Israelites** were still in the wilderness,
	15.38	The Lord commanded Moses [38]to say to the **people of Israel:**
	16. 1	and by 250 other **Israelites,** well-known leaders chosen by
	16. 9	matter that the God of **Israel** has set you apart from the
	16.25	Moses, accompanied by the leaders of **Israel,** went to Dathan
	16.34	All the **people of Israel** who were there fled when they
	16.38	It will be a warning to the **people of Israel."**
	16.40	was a warning to the **Israelites** that no one who was not
	17. 2	"Tell the **people of Israel** to give you twelve sticks,
	17. 5	put a stop to the constant complaining of these **Israelites**
	17. 6	So Moses spoke to the **Israelites,** and each of their leaders
	17. 9	Moses took all the sticks and showed them to the **Israelites.**
	17.10	a warning to the rebel **Israelites** that they will die unless
	17.12	The **people of Israel** said to Moses, "Then that's the
	18. 5	anger will not again break out against the **people of Israel.**
	18. 6	relatives the Levites from among the **Israelites** as a gift to
	18.11	other special contributions that the **Israelites** present to me
	18.12	best of the first produce which the **Israelites** give me each
	18.14	"Everything in **Israel** that has been unconditionally
	18.15	child or animal that the **Israelites** present to me belongs to
	18.19	the special contributions which the **Israelites** present to me.
	18.20	no part of the land of **Israel** will be assigned to you.
	18.21	Levites every tithe that the **people of Israel** present to me.
	18.22	The other **Israelites** must no longer approach the Tent and
	18.23	no permanent property in **Israel,** [24]because I have given
	18.24	the tithe which the **Israelites** present to me as a special
	18.24	told them that they would have no permanent property in **Israel."**
	18.26	you receive from the **Israelites** the tithe that the Lord gives
	18.28	Lord from all the tithes which you receive from the **Israelites.**
	18.32	the sacred gifts of the **Israelites** by eating any of the
	19. 2	Lord commanded Moses and Aaron [2]to give the **Israelites** the
	19. 9	to be kept for the **Israelite** community to use in preparing
	19.10	both for the **Israelites** and for the foreigners living among
	20. 1	the whole community of **Israel** came to the wilderness of Zin
	20. 3	front of the Lord's Tent along with our **fellow-Israelites.**
	20.12	holy power before the **people of Israel,** you will not lead
	20.13	at Meribah, where the **people of Israel** complained against
	20.14	said, "This message is from your kinsmen, the tribes of **Israel.**
	20.19	The **people of Israel** said, "We will stay on the main road,
	20.20	out with a powerful army to attack the **people of Israel.**
	20.21	would not let the **Israelites** pass through their territory,
	20.21	the **Israelites** turned and went another way.
	20.22	The whole community of **Israel** left Kadesh and arrived at
	20.24	going to enter the land which I promised to give to **Israel;**
	21. 1	heard that the **Israelites** were coming by way of Atharim,
	21. 2	Then the **Israelites** made a vow to the Lord:
	21. 3	So the **Israelites** completely destroyed them and their cities,
	21. 4	The **Israelites** left Mount Hor by the road that leads to
	21. 6	snakes among the people, and many **Israelites** were bitten and died.
	21.10	The **Israelites** moved on and camped at Oboth.
	21.17	At that time the **people of Israel** sang this song:

Num	21.21	Then the **people of Israel** sent messengers to the Amorite
	21.23	permit the **people of Israel** to pass through his territory.
	21.23	went out to Jahaz in the wilderness and attacked the **Israelites.**
	21.24	But the **Israelites** killed many of the enemy in battle and
	21.25	So the **people of Israel** captured all the Amorite cities,
	21.31	So the **people of Israel** settled in the territory of the Amorites,
	21.32	**Israelites** captured it and its surrounding towns and drove
	21.33	Then the **Israelites** turned and took the road to Bashan,
	21.35	So the **Israelites** killed Og, his sons, and all his people,
	22. 1	The **Israelites** moved on and set up camp in the plains of
	22. 2	of Zippor, heard what the **Israelites** had done to the Amorites
	22. 2	and how many **Israelites** there were, [3]he and all his
	22.12	on the **people of Israel,** because they have my blessing."
	22.41	from where Balaam could see a part of the **people of Israel.**
	23. 7	'Put a curse on the **people of Israel.'**
	23.10	The descendants of **Israel** are like the dust— There are
	23.13	place from which you can see only some of the **Israelites.**
	23.21	foresee that **Israel's** future Will bring her no misfortune
	23.23	no witchcraft, That can be used against the nation of **Israel.**
	23.23	Now people will say about **Israel,** 'Look what God has done!'
	23.24	The nation of **Israel** is like a mighty lion:
	23.25	refuse to curse the **people of Israel,** but at least don't
	24. 1	him to bless the **people of Israel,** so he did not go
	24. 2	desert [2]and saw the **people of Israel** camped tribe by tribe.
	24. 5	The tents of **Israel** are beautiful, [6]Like long rows of palms
	24. 9	Whoever blesses **Israel** will be blessed,
	24. 9	And whoever curses **Israel** will be cursed."
	24.14	warning you what the **people of Israel** will do to your people
	24.17	I look into the future, And I see the nation of **Israel.**
	24.17	Like a comet he will come from **Israel.**
	24.18	their land his property, While **Israel** continues victorious.
	24.19	The nation of **Israel** will trample them down And wipe out
	25. 1	When the **Israelites** were camped in the Valley of Acacia,
	25. 2	**Israelites** ate the food and worshipped the god [3]Baal of Peor.
	25. 4	"Take all the leaders of **Israel** and, in obedience to me,
	25. 6	One of the **Israelites** took a Midianite woman into his tent
	25. 8	the epidemic that was destroying **Israel** was stopped, [9]but it
	25.11	has done, I am no longer angry with the **people of Israel.**
	25.14	name of the **Israelite** who was killed with the Midianite woman
	26. 2	of the whole community of **Israel,** of all men twenty years
	26. 3	These were the **Israelites** who came out of Egypt:
	26.51	The total number of the **Israelite** men was 601,730.
	26.62	from the rest of the **Israelites,** because they were not given
	26.62	because they were not given any property in **Israel.**
	26.63	took a census of the **Israelites** in the plains of Moab across
	27. 4	had no sons, why should our father's name disappear from **Israel?**
	27. 8	Tell the **people of Israel** that whenever a man dies without
	27.11	The **people of Israel** are to observe this as a legal requirement,
	27.12	look out over the land that I am giving to the **Israelites.**
	27.20	so that the whole community of **Israel** will obey him.
	27.21	direct Joshua and the whole community of **Israel** in all their
	28. 2	Moses [2]to instruct the **Israelites** to present to God at the
	29.40	So Moses told the **people of Israel** everything that the
	30. 1	following instructions to the leaders of the tribes of **Israel.**
	31. 2	"Punish the Midianites for what they did to the **people of Israel.**
	31. 4	From each tribe of **Israel** send a thousand men to war."
	31. 9	The **people of Israel** captured the Midianite women and children,
	31.12	the community of the **people of Israel,** who were at the camp
	31.54	Tent, so that the Lord would protect the **people of Israel.**
	32. 3	Lord has helped the **Israelites** to occupy—the towns of Ataroth,
	32. 6	"Do you want to stay here while your **fellow-Israelites** go to war?
	32. 7	try to discourage the **people of Israel** from crossing the
	32.14	to bring down the fierce anger of the Lord on **Israel** again.
	32.17	ready to go with our **fellow-Israelites** into battle and lead
	32.18	homes until all the other **Israelites** have taken possession of
	32.22	your obligation to the Lord and to your **fellow-Israelites.**
	32.28	commands to Eleazar, Joshua, and the other leaders of **Israel:**
	33. 1	the places where the **Israelites** set up camp after they left
	33. 3	The **people of Israel** left Egypt on the fifteenth day of
	33. 5	The **people of Israel** left Rameses and set up camp at Sukkoth.
	33.38	of the fortieth year after the **Israelites** had left Egypt.
	33.40	Arad in southern Canaan heard that the **Israelites** were coming.
	33.41	the plains of Moab the **Israelites** set up camp at the
	33.51	the Lord gave Moses [51]the following instructions for **Israel:**
	34. 2	the following instructions for the **people of Israel:**
	34.13	So Moses said to the **Israelites,** "This is the land that
	34.29	property for the **people of Israel** in the land of Canaan.
	35. 2	said to Moses, [2]"Tell the **Israelites** that from the property
	35.10	The Lord told Moses [10]to say to the **people of Israel:**
	35.15	as cities of refuge for **Israelites** and for foreigners who are
	35.34	I am the Lord and I live among the **people of Israel."**
	36. 2	distribute the land to the **people of Israel** by drawing lots.
	36. 5	So Moses gave the **people of Israel** the following command
	36. 7	property of every **Israelite** will remain attached to his tribe.
	36. 8	who inherits property in an **Israelite** tribe must marry a man
	36. 8	way each **Israelite** will inherit the property of his ancestors,
	36.13	that the Lord gave the **Israelites** through Moses in the plains
Deut	1. 1	Moses spoke to the **people of Israel** when they were in the
	1.38	He will lead **Israel** to occupy the land.'
	2.12	just as the **Israelites** later chased their enemies out of
	3.18	of the other tribes of **Israel,** to help them to occupy their
	3.20	Help your **fellow-Israelites** until they occupy the land
	4.44	Moses gave God's laws and teachings to the **people of Israel.**
	4.45	Moses and the **people of Israel** defeated him when they came
	5. 1	called together all the **people of Israel** and said to them,
	5. 1	**"People of Israel,** listen to all the laws
	5.32	**"People of Israel,** be sure that you do everything that
	6. 3	Listen to them, **people of Israel,** and obey them!
	6. 4	**"Israel,** remember this!
	9. 1	"Listen, **people of Israel!**
	10. 6	**Israelites** set out from the wells that belonged to the people
Deut	10.12	"Now, **people of Israel,** listen to what the Lord your
	13.11	Then all the **people of Israel** will hear what happened;
	15. 2	has lent money to a **fellow-Israelite** is to cancel the debt;
	15. 7	giving you there is a **fellow-Israelite** in need, then do not
	15.11	will always be some **Israelites** who are poor and in need,
	15.12	"If a **fellow-Israelite,** man or woman, sells himself to
	17. 4	evil thing has happened in **Israel,** [5]then take that person
	17.12	in this way you will remove this evil from **Israel.**
	17.20	he is better than his **fellow-Israelites** and from disobeying
	17.20	and his descendants will rule **Israel** for many generations.
	18. 1	of Levi is not to receive any share of land in **Israel;**
	18. 6	come from any town in **Israel** to the one place of worship
	19.13	Rid **Israel** of this murderer, so that all will go well with
	19.18	a false accusation against his **fellow-Israelite,** [19]he is
	20. 3	come forward and say to the army, [3]'Men of **Israel,** listen!
	21. 8	forgive your people **Israel,** whom you rescued from Egypt.
	21.21	Everyone in **Israel** will hear what has happened and be afraid.
	22. 1	"If you see a **fellow-Israelite's** cow or sheep running loose,
	22. 3	or anything else that your **fellow-Israelite** may have lost.
	22. 4	"If a **fellow-Israelite's** donkey or cow has fallen down,
	22.19	because the man has brought disgrace on an **Israelite** girl.
	23.17	"No **Israelite,** man or woman, is to become a temple prostitute.
	23.19	else to a **fellow-Israelite,** do not charge him interest.
	23.20	a foreigner, but not on what you lend to a **fellow-Israelite.**
	24. 7	"Whoever kidnaps a **fellow-Israelite** and makes him his
	24.14	servant, whether he is a **fellow-Israelite** or a foreigner
	25. 1	"Suppose two **Israelites** go to court to settle a dispute,
	25. 6	dead man, so that his family line will continue in **Israel.**
	25. 7	give his brother a descendant among the **people of Israel.'**
	25.10	family will be known in **Israel** as 'the family of the man
	26.15	from your holy place in heaven and bless your people **Israel;**
	27. 1	together with the leaders of **Israel,** said to the people,
	27. 9	said to all the **people of Israel,**
	27. 9	"Give me your attention, **people of Israel,** and listen to me.
	27.11	Moses said to the **people of Israel,** [12]"After you have
	29. 1	to make with the **people of Israel** in the land of Moab;
	29. 2	called together all the **people of Israel** and said to them,
	29.21	before all the tribes of **Israel** and will bring disaster on
	31. 1	continued speaking to the **people of Israel,** [2]and said, "I
	31. 7	of all the **people of Israel,** "Be determined and confident;
	31. 9	of the Lord's Covenant Box, and to the leaders of **Israel.**
	31.11	Read it to the **people of Israel** when they come to
	31.19	Teach it to the **people of Israel,** so that it will stand
	31.22	wrote down the song and taught it to the **people of Israel.**
	31.23	You will lead the **people of Israel** into the land that I
	31.30	recited the entire song while all the **people of Israel** listened.
	32.11	on its spreading wings, the Lord kept **Israel** from falling.
	32.17	had never known, gods that **Israel** had never obeyed,
	32.28	**"Israel** is a nation without sense;
	32.31	that their own gods are weak, not mighty like **Israel's** God.
	32.44	this song, so that the **people of Israel** could hear it.
	32.49	of Canaan that I am about to give the **people of Israel.**
	32.51	unfaithful to me in the presence of the **people of Israel.**
	32.52	not enter the land that I am giving the **people of Israel."**
	33. 1	of God, pronounced on the **people of Israel** before he died.
	33. 5	became king of his people **Israel** when their tribes and leaders
	33.21	and laws When the leaders of **Israel** were gathered together."
	33.26	**People of Israel,** no god is like your God, riding in
	33.29	**Israel,** how happy you are!
	34. 8	The **people of Israel** mourned for him for thirty days in
	34. 9	The **people of Israel** obeyed Joshua and kept the commands
	34.10	There has never been a prophet in **Israel** like Moses;
	34.12	things that Moses did in the sight of all **Israel.**
Josh	1. 2	you and all the **people of Israel,** and cross the River Jordan
	1.14	cross over ahead of their **fellow-Israelites** in order to help
	1.15	to all the tribes of **Israel,** then you may come back and
	2. 2	Jericho heard that some **Israelites** had come that night to spy
	2. 7	They went looking for the **Israelite** spies as far as the
	3. 1	Joshua and all the **people of Israel** got up early, left the
	3. 7	will make all the **people of Israel** begin to honour you as
	3.12	Now choose twelve men, one from each of the tribes of **Israel.**
	4. 5	on your shoulder, one for each of the tribes of **Israel.**
	4. 7	always remind the **people of Israel** of what happened here."
	4. 8	of the tribes of **Israel,** carried them to the camping place,
	4.14	day made the **people of Israel** consider Joshua a great man.
	4.21	He said to the **people of Israel,** "In the future, when
	4.22	about the time when **Israel** crossed the Jordan on dry ground.
	5. 1	up the Jordan until the **people of Israel** had crossed it.
	5. 1	became afraid and lost their courage because of the **Israelites.**
	5. 2	"Make some knives out of flint and circumcise the **Israelites."**
	5. 3	circumcised the **Israelites** at a place called Circumcision Hill.
	5. 4	When the **people of Israel** left Egypt, all the males
	5.10	While the **Israelites** were camping at Gilgal on the plain
	5.12	manna stopped falling then, and the **Israelites** no longer had
	6. 1	Jericho were kept shut and guarded to keep the **Israelites** out.
	6.18	you will bring trouble and destruction on the **Israelite** camp.
	6.23	all, family and slaves, to safety near the **Israelite** camp.
	6.25	(Her descendants have lived in **Israel** to this day.)
	7. 1	The Lord's command to **Israel** not to take from Jericho
	7. 1	that order, and so the Lord was furious with the **Israelites.**
	7. 4	So about three thousand **Israelites** made the attack,
	7. 5	Then the **Israelites** lost their courage and were afraid.
	7. 6	Joshua and the leaders of **Israel** tore their clothes in grief,
	7. 8	I say, O Lord, now that **Israel** has retreated from the enemy?
	7.11	**Israel** has sinned!
	7.12	is why the **Israelites** cannot stand against their enemies.
	7.13	because I, the Lord God of **Israel,** have this to say:
	7.13	**'Israel,** you have in your possession some things that I
	7.15	brought terrible shame on **Israel** and has broken my covenant."
	7.16	next morning Joshua brought **Israel** forward, tribe by tribe,
	7.19	truth here before the Lord, the God of **Israel,** and confess.

Josh 7.20 have sinned against the Lord, **Israel's** God, and this is what
7.23 to Joshua and all the **Israelites,** and laid them down in the
7.24 along with all the **people of Israel,** seized Achan, the
8.10 Then he and the leaders of **Israel** led them to Ai.
8.14 Valley to fight the **Israelites** at the same place as before,
8.17 in Ai went after the **Israelites,** and the city was left wide
8.20 them to escape, because the **Israelites** who had run towards
8.22 **Israelites** in the city now came down to join the battle.
8.22 Ai found themselves completely surrounded by **Israelites,**
8.24 **Israelites** killed every one of the enemy in the barren country
8.27 **Israelites** kept for themselves the livestock and goods captured
8.30 on Mount Ebal an altar to the Lord, the God of **Israel.**
8.31 Lord's servant, had given the **Israelites,** as it says in the
8.32 with the **Israelites** looking on, Joshua made on the stones
8.33 The **Israelites,** with their leaders, officers, and judges,
9. 1 The victories of **Israel** became known to all the kings west
9. 2 and joined forces to fight against Joshua and the **Israelites.**
9. 6 Joshua and the men of **Israel,** "We have come from a distant
9. 7 But the men of **Israel** said, "Why should we make a treaty
9.14 The men of **Israel** accepted some food from them, but did
9.15 leaders of the community of **Israel** gave their solemn promise
9.16 treaty had been made, the **Israelites** learnt that these people
9.17 So the **people of Israel** started out and three days later
9.18 **Israelites** could not kill them, because their leaders had made
9.18 solemn promise to them in the name of the Lord, **Israel's**
9.19 promise to them in the name of the Lord God of **Israel.**
9.26 them and did not allow the **people of Israel** to kill them.
9.27 water for the **people of Israel** and for the Lord's altar.
10. 1 Gibeon had made peace with the **Israelites** and were living
10. 4 its people have made peace with Joshua and the **Israelites."**
10.10 Lord made the Amorites panic at the sight of **Israel's** army.
10.10 The **Israelites** slaughtered them at Gibeon and pursued them
10.11 down the pass from the **Israelite** army, the Lord made large
10.11 More were killed by the hailstones than by the **Israelites.**
10.12 Lord gave the men of **Israel** victory over the Amorites, Joshua
10.12 In the presence of the **Israelites** he said,
10.14 The Lord fought on **Israel's** side!
10.20 Joshua and the men of **Israel** slaughtered them, although
10.21 No one in the land dared even to speak against the **Israelites.**
10.24 called all the men of **Israel** to him and ordered the officers
10.30 The Lord also gave the **Israelites** victory over this city
10.32 The Lord gave the **Israelites** victory over Lachish on the
10.40 This was what the Lord God of **Israel** had commanded.
10.42 because the Lord, **Israel's** God, was fighting for Israel.
10.42 campaign because the Lord, Israel's God, was fighting for **Israel.**
11. 1 the news of **Israel's** victories reached King Jabin of Hazor,
11. 5 and set up camp at Merom Brook to fight against **Israel.**
11. 6 time tomorrow I will have killed all of them for **Israel.**
11. 8 The Lord gave the **Israelites** victory over them;
11. 8 the **Israelites** attacked and pursued them as far north
11.13 the **Israelites** did not burn any of the cities built on
11.14 The **people of Israel** took all the valuables and
11.19 made peace with the **people of Israel** was Gibeon, where some
11.20 them determined to fight the **Israelites,** so that they would
11.21 and in all the hill-country of **Judah and Israel.**
11.22 None of the Anakim were left in the land of **Israel;**
11.23 Joshua gave it to the **Israelites** as their own and divided it
12. 1 The **people of Israel** had already conquered and occupied
12. 6 These two kings were defeated by Moses and the **people of Israel.**
12. 7 Joshua and the **people of Israel** defeated all the kings in
12. 9 The **people of Israel** defeated the kings of the following cities:
13. 6 drive all these peoples out as the **people of Israel** advance.
13. 6 divide the land among the **Israelites,** just as I have
13.13 the **Israelites** did not drive out the people of Geshur and
13.13 they still live in **Israel.**
13.14 sacrifices burnt on the altar to the Lord God of **Israel.**
13.22 Among those whom the **people of Israel** killed was the
13.33 be a share of the offerings to the Lord God of **Israel.**
14. 1 Canaan west of the Jordan was divided among the **people of Israel.**
14. 1 of the families of the **Israelite** tribes divided it among the
14. 5 The **people of Israel** divided the land as the Lord had
14.10 was when **Israel** was going through the desert, and the Lord,
14.14 because he faithfully obeyed the Lord, the God of **Israel.**
17.13 when the **Israelites** became stronger, they did not drive out
18. 1 the entire community of **Israel** assembled at Shiloh and set up
18. 2 seven tribes of the **people of Israel** who had not yet been
18. 3 Joshua said to the **people of Israel,** "How long are you
18.10 the remaining tribes of **Israel** a certain part of the land.
19.49 When the **people of Israel** finished dividing up the land,
19.51 families of the tribes of **Israel** assigned these parts of the
20. 2 to say to the **people of Israel,** "Choose the cities of
20. 9 chosen for all the **people of Israel** and for any foreigner
21. 1 to the heads of the families of all the tribes of **Israel.**
21. 3 the Lord's command the **people of Israel** gave the Levites
21. 8 By drawing lots, the **people of Israel** assigned these
21.41 the land that the **people of Israel** possessed, a total of
21.43 So the Lord gave to **Israel** all the land that he had
21.44 Lord gave the **Israelites** the victory over all their enemies.
21.45 of the promises that he had made to the **people of Israel.**
22. 3 All this time you have never once deserted your **fellow-Israelites.**
22. 4 the Lord your God has given your **fellow-Israelites** peace.
22. 9 the rest of the **people of Israel** at Shiloh in the land
22.11 The rest of the **people of Israel** were told, "Listen!
22.12 When the **people of Israel** heard this, the whole
22.13 Then the **people of Israel** sent Phinehas, the son of
22.16 "Why have you done this evil thing against the God of **Israel?**
22.18 Lord today, he will be angry with everyone in **Israel** tomorrow.
22.20 the whole community of **Israel** was punished for that.
22.24 do you have to do with the Lord, the God of **Israel?**
22.31 saved the **people of Israel** from the Lord's punishment."

Josh 22.32 to Canaan, to the **people of Israel,** and reported to them.
22.33 The **Israelites** were satisfied and praised God.
23. 1 the Lord gave **Israel** security from their enemies around them.
23. 2 so he called all **Israel,** the elders, leaders, judges,
24. 1 Joshua gathered all the tribes of **Israel** together at Shechem.
24. 1 and the officers of **Israel,** and they came into the presence
24. 2 "This is what the Lord, the God of **Israel,** has to say:
24.23 "and pledge your loyalty to the Lord, the God of **Israel."**
24.31 as Joshua lived, the **people of Israel** served the Lord, and
24.31 seen for themselves everything that the Lord had done for **Israel.**
24.32 Joseph, which the **people of Israel** had brought from Egypt,
Judg 1. 1 After Joshua's death the **people of Israel** asked the Lord,
1.28 **Israelites** became stronger, they forced the Canaanites to work
2. 1 Bochim and said to the **Israelites,** "I took you out of Egypt
2. 4 said this, all the **people of Israel** began to cry, [5] and that
2. 6 Joshua sent the **people of Israel** on their way, and each
2. 7 as Joshua lived, the **people of Israel** served the Lord, and
2. 7 all the great things that the Lord had done for **Israel.**
2.10 generation forgot the Lord and what he had done for **Israel.**
2.11 Then the **people of Israel** sinned against the Lord and
2.14 the Lord became furious with **Israel** and let raiders attack
2.14 overpower them, and the **Israelites** could no longer protect
2.16 Then the Lord gave the **Israelites** leaders who saved them
2.17 But the **Israelites** paid no attention to their leaders.
2.17 **Israel** was unfaithful to the Lord and worshipped other gods.
2.18 Whenever the Lord gave **Israel** a leader, the Lord would
2.20 Lord would become furious with **Israel** and say, "This nation
2.22 whether or not these **Israelites** will follow my ways, as their
3. 1 the land to test the **Israelites** who had not been through the
3. 2 to teach each generation of **Israelites** about war, especially
3. 4 to be a test for **Israel,** to find out whether or not
3. 4 whether or not the **Israelites** would obey the commands that
3. 5 And so the **people of Israel** settled down among the Canaanites,
3. 7 The **people of Israel** forgot the Lord their God;
3. 8 the Lord became angry with **Israel** and let King Cushan
3. 9 Then the **Israelites** cried out to the Lord, and he sent a
3.10 of the Lord came upon him, and he became **Israel's** leader.
3.12 The **people of Israel** sinned against the Lord again.
3.12 this the Lord made King Eglon of Moab stronger than **Israel.**
3.13 defeated **Israel** and captured Jericho, the city of palm-trees.
3.14 The **Israelites** were subject to Eglon for eighteen years.
3.15 Then the **Israelites** cried out to the Lord, and he sent
3.15 The **people of Israel** sent Ehud to King Eglon of Moab with
3.27 he blew a trumpet to call the men of **Israel** to battle;
3.30 That day the **Israelites** defeated Moab, and there was peace
3.31 rescued **Israel,** and did so by killing six hundred Philistines
4. 1 After Ehud died, the **people of Israel** sinned against the Lord
4. 3 and he ruled the **people of Israel** with cruelty and violence
4. 3 Then the **people of Israel** cried out to the Lord for help.
4. 4 she was serving as a judge for the **Israelites** at that time.
4. 5 of Ephraim, and the **people of Israel** would go there for her
4. 6 "The Lord, the God of **Israel,** has given you this command:
4.23 That day God gave the **Israelites** victory over Jabin,
5. 2 The **Israelites** were determined to fight;
5. 3 I will sing, I will play music to **Israel's** God, the Lord.
5. 5 the Lord of Sinai, before the Lord, the God of **Israel.**
5. 7 The towns of **Israel** stood abandoned, Deborah;
5. 7 they stood empty until you came, came like a mother for **Israel.**
5. 8 was war in the land when the **Israelites** chose new gods.
5. 8 the forty thousand men in **Israel,** did anyone carry shield or
5. 9 commanders of **Israel,** with the people who gladly volunteered.
5.11 of the Lord's victories, the victories of **Israel's** people!
6. 1 Once again the **people of Israel** sinned against the Lord,
6. 2 The Midianites were stronger than **Israel,**
6. 2 than Israel, and the **people of Israel** hid from them in caves
6. 3 Whenever the **Israelites** sowed any seed, the Midianites
6. 4 and donkeys, and leave nothing for the **Israelites** to live on.
6. 6 They came and devastated the land, [6] and **Israel** was helpless
6. 7 Then the **people of Israel** cried out to the Lord for help
6. 8 brought them this message from the Lord, the God of **Israel:**
6.14 "Go with all your great strength and rescue **Israel** from the
6.15 Gideon replied, "But Lord, how can I rescue **Israel?**
6.36 "You say that you have decided to use me to rescue **Israel.**
6.37 will know that you are going to use me to rescue **Israel."**
7. 8 Gideon sent all the **Israelites** home, except the three hundred,
7.14 "It's the sword of the **Israelite,** Gideon son of Joash!
7.15 Then he went back to the **Israelite** camp and said, "Get up!
8.22 After that, the **Israelites** said to Gideon, "Be our ruler—
8.27 **Israelites** abandoned God and went there to worship the idol.
8.28 Midian was defeated by the **Israelites** and was no longer
8.33 After Gideon's death the **people of Israel** were again
8.35 of Gideon for all the good that he had done for **Israel.**
9.22 Abimelech ruled **Israel** for three years.
9.55 **Israelites** saw that Abimelech was dead, they all went home.
10. 1 the son of Puah and grandson of Dodo, came to free **Israel.**
10. 2 He was **Israel's** leader for twenty-three years.
10. 3 He led **Israel** for twenty-two years.
10. 6 **Israelites** sinned against the Lord by worshipping the Baals
10. 7 Lord became angry with the **Israelites,** and let the Philistines
10. 8 persecuted all the **Israelites** who lived in Amorite country
10. 9 **Israel** was in great distress.
10.10 Then the **Israelites** cried out to the Lord and said,
10.15 But the **people of Israel** said to the Lord, "We have sinned.
10.16 and he became troubled over **Israel's** distress.
10.17 men of **Israel** came together and camped at Mizpah in Gilead.
10.18 and the leaders of the **Israelite** tribes asked one another,
11. 4 some time later that the Ammonites went to war against **Israel.**
11.13 answered Jephthah's messengers, "When the **Israelites** came out
11.15 "It is not true that **Israel** took away the land of Moab
11.16 when the **Israelites** left Egypt, they went through the desert
11.17 So the **Israelites** stayed at Kadesh.

Judg 11.19 **Israelites** sent messengers to Sihon, the Amorite king of Heshbon,
11.20 But Sihon would not let **Israel** do it.
11.20 his whole army together, made camp at Jahaz, and attacked **Israel.**
11.21 the God of **Israel,** gave the Israelites victory over Sihon
11.21 God of Israel, gave the **Israelites** victory over Sihon and his
11.21 **Israelites** took possession of all the territory of the Amorites
11.23 the Lord, the God of **Israel,** who drove out the Amorites for
11.23 who drove out the Amorites for his people, the **Israelites.**
11.25 He never challenged **Israel,** did he?
11.26 For three hundred years **Israel** has occupied Heshbon and
11.27 He will decide today between the **Israelites** and the Ammonites."
11.33 was a great slaughter, and the Ammonites were defeated by **Israel.**
11.39 origin of the custom in **Israel** [40] that the young women would
12. 7 Jephthah led **Israel** for six years.
12. 8 After Jephthah, Ibzan from Bethlehem led **Israel.**
12. 9 Ibzan led **Israel** for seven years, [10] then he died and was
12.11 After Ibzan, Elon from Zebulun led **Israel** for ten years.
12.13 After Elon, Abdon son of Hillel from Pirathon led **Israel.**
12.14 Abdon led **Israel** for eight years, [15] then he died and was
13. 1 The **Israelites** sinned against the Lord again, and he let
13. 5 will begin the work of rescuing **Israel** from the Philistines."
14. 4 At this time the Philistines were ruling **Israel.**
15.20 Samson led **Israel** for twenty years while the Philistines
16.31 He had been **Israel's** leader for twenty years.
17. 6 There was no king in **Israel** at that time;
18. 1 There was no king in **Israel** at that time.
18. 1 received any land of their own among the tribes of **Israel.**
18.19 a priest for a whole **Israelite** tribe than for the family of
19. 1 In those days, before **Israel** had a king, there was a
19.12 going to stop in a city where the people are not **Israelites.**
19.29 and sent one piece to each of the twelve tribes of **Israel.**
19.30 like this has ever happened since the **Israelites** left Egypt!
20. 1 All the **people of Israel** from Dan in the north to
20. 2 of all the tribes of **Israel** were present at this gathering
20. 3 of Benjamin heard that all the other **Israelites** had gathered
20. 3 **Israelites** asked, "Tell us, how was this crime committed?"
20. 6 and sent one piece to each of the twelve tribes of **Israel.**
20. 7 All of you here are **Israelites.**
20.10 tenth of the men in **Israel** will provide food for the army,
20.10 Gibeah for this immoral act that they have committed in **Israel."**
20.11 all the men in **Israel** assembled with one purpose—to attack
20.12 **Israelite** tribes sent messengers all through the territory of
20.13 so that we can kill them and remove this evil from **Israel."**
20.13 the people of Benjamin paid no attention to the other **Israelites.**
20.14 came to Gibeah to fight against the other people of **Israel.**
20.17 of the **Israelite** tribes gathered 400,000 trained soldiers.
20.18 The **Israelites** went to the place of worship at Bethel,
20.19 **Israelites** started out the next morning and made camp near
20.21 they had killed twenty-two thousand **Israelite** soldiers.
20.22 the **Israelites** went to the place of worship and mourned in
20.22 **Israelite** army was encouraged, and they placed their soldiers in
20.25 they killed eighteen thousand trained **Israelite** soldiers.
20.26 Then all the **people of Israel** went up to Bethel and mourned.
20.29 the **Israelites** put some soldiers in hiding round Gibeah.
20.31 they began killing some **Israelites** in the open country on the
20.31 They killed about thirty **Israelites.**
20.32 But the **Israelites** had planned to retreat and lead them away
20.33 the main army of the **Israelites** pulled back and regrouped at
20.34 specially chosen out of all **Israel,** attacked Gibeah, and the
20.35 The Lord gave **Israel** victory over the army of Benjamin.
20.35 The **Israelites** killed 25,100 of the enemy that day,
20.36 The main body of the **Israelite** army had retreated from the
20.38 main **Israelite** army and the men in hiding had arranged a
20.39 up from the town, [39] the **Israelites** out on the battlefield
20.39 the Benjaminites had already killed the thirty **Israelites.**
20.41 the **Israelites** turned round, and the Benjaminites were thrown
20.42 They retreated from the **Israelites** and ran towards the
20.43 **Israelites** had the enemy trapped, and without stopping they
20.45 The **Israelites** continued to pursue the rest to Gidom, killing
20.48 **Israelites** turned back against the rest of the Benjaminites and
21. 1 the **Israelites** had gathered at Mizpah, they had made a solemn
21. 2 So now the **people of Israel** went to Bethel and sat there
21. 3 "Lord God of **Israel,** why has this happened?
21. 3 Why is the tribe of Benjamin about to disappear from **Israel?"**
21. 5 of all the tribes of **Israel** that did not go to the
21. 6 The **people of Israel** felt sorry for their brothers the
21. 6 and said, "Today **Israel** has lost one of its tribes.
21. 8 out of the tribes of **Israel** that had not gone to the
21.14 and the other **Israelites** gave them the girls from Jabesh
21.15 the Lord had broken the unity of the tribes of **Israel.**
21.17 **Israel** must not lose one of its twelve tribes.
21.24 time the rest of the **Israelites** left, and every man went
21.25 There was no king in **Israel** at that time.
Ruth 1. 1 ago, in the days before **Israel** had a king, there was a
2.12 from the Lord God of **Israel,** to whom you have come for
4. 7 In this way the **Israelites** showed that the matter was settled.
4.14 May the boy become famous in **Israel!**
1 Sam 1.17 "and may the God of **Israel** give you what you have asked
2.14 **Israelites** who came to Shiloh to offer sacrifices were treated
2.22 sons were doing to the **Israelites** and that they were even
2.28 From all the tribes of **Israel** I chose his family to be
2.30 I, the Lord God of **Israel,** promised in the past that
2.32 to the other people of **Israel,** but no one in your family
3.11 do something to the **people of Israel** that is so terrible
3.20 So all the **people of Israel,** from one end of the country
3.21 And when Samuel spoke, all **Israel** listened.
4. 1 to go to war against **Israel,** so the Israelites set out to
4. 1 war against Israel, so the **Israelites** set out to fight them.
4. 1 The **Israelites** set up their camp at Ebenezer

1 Sam 4. 2 fierce fighting they defeated the **Israelites** and killed about
4. 3 to camp, the leaders of **Israel** said, "Why did the Lord let
4. 5 the Covenant Box arrived, the **Israelites** gave such a loud
4.10 defeated the **Israelites,** who went running to their homes.
4.10 thirty thousand **Israelite** soldiers were killed.
4.17 messenger answered, **"Israel** ran away from the Philistines;
4.18 He had been a leader in **Israel** for forty years.
4.21 named the boy Ichabod, explaining, "God's glory has left **Israel"**
4.22 "God's glory has left **Israel,"** she said,
5. 7 they said, "The God of **Israel** is punishing us and our god
5. 8 shall we do with the Covenant Box of the God of **Israel?"**
5.10 Box of the God of **Israel** here, in order to kill us
5.11 "Send the Covenant Box of **Israel** back to its own place, so
6. 3 Box of the God of **Israel,** you must, of course, send with
6. 5 your country, and you must give honour to the God of **Israel.**
6. 6 God made fools of them until they let the **Israelites** leave Egypt.
6. 9 is the God of the **Israelites** who has sent this terrible
7. 2 During this time all the **Israelites** cried to the Lord for help.
7. 3 Samuel said to the **people of Israel,** "If you are going
7. 4 So the **Israelites** got rid of their idols of Baal and Astarte,
7. 5 Samuel sent for all the **Israelites** to meet at Mizpah,
7. 6 (It was at Mizpah that Samuel settled disputes among the **Israelites.)**
7. 7 Philistines heard that the **Israelites** had gathered at Mizpah,
7. 7 The **Israelites** heard about it and were afraid,
7. 9 the Lord to help **Israel,** and the Lord answered his prayer.
7.11 The **Israelites** marched out from Mizpah and pursued the
7.13 Lord prevented them from invading **Israel's** territory as long
7.14 and Gath were returned to **Israel,**
7.14 and so **Israel** got back all its territory.
7.14 there was peace also between the **Israelites** and the Canaanites.
7.15 Samuel ruled **Israel** as long as he lived.
8. 1 When Samuel grew old, he made his sons judges in **Israel.**
8. 4 all the leaders of **Israel** met together, went to Samuel in
8.22 Then Samuel told all the men of **Israel** to go back home.
9. 2 taller than anyone else in **Israel** and more handsome as well.
9.16 as ruler of my people **Israel,** and he will rescue them from
9.20 But who is it that the **people of Israel** want so much?
9.21 the smallest tribe in **Israel,** and my family is the least
10. 1 said, "The Lord anoints you as ruler of his people **Israel.**
10.18 "The Lord, the God of **Israel,** says, 'I brought you out of
11. 2 out everyone's right eye and so bring disgrace on all **Israel."**
11. 3 us seven days to send messengers throughout the land of **Israel.**
11. 7 the pieces throughout the land of **Israel** with this warning:
11. 7 The **people of Israel** were afraid of what the Lord might do,
11. 8 there were 300,000 from **Israel** and 30,000 from Judah.
11.12 Then the **people of Israel** said to Samuel, "Where are the people
11.13 death today, for this is the day the Lord rescued **Israel."**
11.15 and Saul and all the **people of Israel** celebrated the event.
12. 1 Samuel said to the **people of Israel,** "I have done what you
13. 4 All the **Israelites** were told that Saul had killed the
13. 5 The Philistines assembled to fight the **Israelites;**
13. 6 the **Israelites,** putting them in a desperate situation.
13. 6 Some of the **Israelites** hid in caves and holes or among the
13.13 have let you and your descendants rule over **Israel** for ever.
13.19 were no blacksmiths in **Israel** because the Philistines were
13.20 (The **Israelites** had to go to the Philistines to get their ploughs,
13.22 battle none of the **Israelite** soldiers except Saul and his son
14.12 The Lord has given **Israel** victory over them."
14.18 Ahijah was carrying it in front of the **people of Israel.)**
14.23 The Lord saved **Israel** that day.
14.24 The **Israelites** were weak with hunger that day, because
14.31 That day the **Israelites** defeated the Philistines,
14.31 By this time the **Israelites** were very weak with hunger,
14.39 living Lord, who gives **Israel** victory, that the guilty one
14.41 Lord, the God of **Israel,** "Lord, why have you not answered
14.41 Lord, God of **Israel,** answer me by the sacred stones.
14.41 if it belongs to your people **Israel,** answer by the Thummim."
14.45 Jonathan, who won this great victory for **Israel,** be put to
14.47 After Saul became **king of Israel,** he fought against all
14.48 He saved the **Israelites** from all attacks.
15. 1 whom the Lord sent to anoint you king of his people **Israel.**
15. 2 because their ancestors opposed the **Israelites** when they were
15. 4 were 200,000 soldiers from **Israel** and 10,000 from Judah.
15. 6 ancestors had been kind to the **Israelites** when they came from
15.17 no importance, you are the leader of the tribes of **Israel.**
15.17 The Lord anointed you **king of Israel,**
15.26 and he has rejected you as **king of Israel."**
15.28 has torn the kingdom of **Israel** away from you today and given
15.29 **Israel's** majestic God does not lie or change his mind.
15.30 respect in front of the leaders of my people and all **Israel.**
15.35 The Lord was sorry that he had made Saul **king of Israel.**
16. 1 I have rejected him as **king of Israel.**
17. 2 Saul and the **Israelites** assembled and camped in the Valley
17. 3 on one hill and the **Israelites** on another, with a valley
17. 4 came out from the Philistine camp to challenge the **Israelites.**
17. 8 and shouted at the **Israelites,** "What are you doing there,
17.10 Here and now I challenge the **Israelite** army.
17.16 Goliath challenged the **Israelites** every morning and evening
17.19 and all the other **Israelites** are in the Valley of Elah
17.20 camp just as the **Israelites** were going out to their battle
17.21 The Philistine and the **Israelite** armies took up positions
17.23 Goliath came forward and challenged the **Israelites** as he had
17.24 When the **Israelites** saw Goliath, they ran away in terror.
17.26 who kills this Philistine and frees **Israel** from this disgrace?
17.45 the God of the **Israelite** armies, which you have defied.
17.46 whole world will know that **Israel** has a God, [47] and everyone
17.52 The men of **Israel and Judah** shouted and ran after them,
17.53 the **Israelites** came back from pursuing the Philistines,
18. 6 women from every town in **Israel** came out to meet King Saul.
18.16 But everyone in **Israel and Judah** loved David because he

1 Sam 19. 5 killed Goliath, and the Lord won a great victory for **Israel.**
20.12 said to David, "May the Lord God of **Israel** be our witness!
23.10 David said, "Lord, God of **Israel,** I have heard that Saul is
23.11 Lord, God of **Israel,** I beg you to answer me!"
23.17 who will be the **king of Israel**
24. 2 of the best soldiers in **Israel** and went looking for David
24.14 Look at what the **king of Israel** is trying to kill!
24.20 that you will be **king of Israel**
25. 1 Samuel died, and all the **Israelites** came together and mourned
25.30 and has made you **king of Israel,**
25.32 the Lord, the God of **Israel,** who sent you today to meet
25.34 by the living God of **Israel** that if you had not hurried
26. 2 of the best soldiers in **Israel** to the wilderness of Ziph to
26.15 answered, "Abner, aren't you the greatest man in **Israel?**
26.20 Why should the **king of Israel** come to kill a flea
27. 1 give up looking for me in **Israel,** and I will be safe."
27.12 by his own people the **Israelites** that he will have to serve
28. 1 gathered their troops to fight **Israel,** and Achish said
28. 3 had died, and all the **Israelites** had mourned for him and had
28. 3 had forced all the fortune-tellers and mediums to leave **Israel.**
28. 4 Saul gathered the **Israelites** and camped at Mount Gilboa.
28. 9 how he forced the fortune-tellers and mediums to leave **Israel.**
28.19 He will hand you and **Israel** over to the Philistines.
28.19 will also hand the army of **Israel** over to the Philistines."
29. 1 together at Aphek, while the **Israelites** camped at the spring
29. 6 by the living God of **Israel** that you have been loyal to
30.25 this a rule, and it has been followed in **Israel** ever since.
31. 1 The Philistines fought a battle against the **Israelites** on
31. 1 Many **Israelites** were killed there, and the rest of them,
31. 7 the **Israelites** on the other side of the Valley of Jezreel
31. 7 heard that the **Israelite** army had fled and that Saul
2 Sam 1. 3 "I have escaped from the **Israelite** camp," he answered.
1.12 Saul and Jonathan and for **Israel,** the people of the Lord,
1.19 "On the hills of **Israel** our leaders are dead!
1.24 "Women of **Israel,** mourn for Saul!
2. 9 Jezreel, Ephraim, and Benjamin, and indeed over all **Israel.**
2.10 when he was made **king of Israel,** and he ruled for two
2.17 and Abner and the **Israelites** were defeated by David's men.
2.28 as a signal for his men to stop pursuing the **Israelites;**
3. 9 David king of both **Israel and Judah,** from one end of the
3.12 and I will help you win all **Israel** over to your side."
3.17 went to the leaders of **Israel** and said to them, "For a
3.18 David to rescue my people **Israel** from the Philistines and
3.19 what the people of Benjamin and of **Israel** had agreed to do.
3.21 "I will go now and win all **Israel** over to Your Majesty.
3.37 and all the people in **Israel** understood that the king had no
3.38 you realize that this day a great leader in **Israel** has died?
4. 1 he was afraid, and all the **people of Israel** were alarmed.
5. 1 Then all the tribes of **Israel** came to David at Hebron and
5. 2 king, you led the **people of Israel** in battle, and the Lord
5. 3 So all the leaders of **Israel** came to King David at Hebron.
5. 3 they anointed him, and he became **king of Israel.**
5. 5 in Jerusalem over all **Israel and Judah** for thirty-three years.
5.12 had established him as **king of Israel**
5.17 David had been made **king of Israel,** so their army set out
6. 1 the best soldiers in **Israel,** a total of thirty thousand men,
6. 5 David and all the **Israelites** were dancing and singing with
6.15 so he and all the **Israelites** took the Covenant Box up to
6.19 each man and woman in **Israel** a loaf of bread, a piece
6.20 "The **king of Israel** made a big name for himself today!"
6.21 and his family to make me the leader of his people **Israel.**
7. 6 time I rescued the **people of Israel** from Egypt until now, I
7. 7 my travelling with the **people of Israel** I never asked any of
7. 8 in the fields and made you the ruler of my people **Israel.**
7.10 a place for my people **Israel** and have settled them there,
7.23 nation on earth like **Israel,** whom you rescued from slavery to
7.24 You have made **Israel** your own people for ever, and you,
7.26 will for ever say, 'The Lord Almighty is God over **Israel.'**
7.27 Almighty Lord, God of **Israel!**
8.15 David ruled over all **Israel** and made sure that his
10. 9 chose the best of **Israel's** soldiers and put them in position
10.15 defeated by the **Israelites,** so they called all their troops
10.17 he gathered the **Israelite** troops, crossed the River Jordan,
10.18 The fighting began, [18]and the **Israelites** drove the Syrian
10.19 had been defeated by the **Israelites,** they made peace with
11. 1 David sent out Joab with his officers and the **Israelite** army;
11.11 answered, "The men of **Israel and Judah** are away at the war,
12. 7 "And this is what the Lord God of **Israel** says:
12. 7 'I made you **king of Israel** and rescued you from Saul.
12. 8 I made you king over **Israel and Judah.**
12.12 make this happen in broad daylight for all **Israel** to see.' "
13.13 And you—you would be completely disgraced in **Israel.**
14.25 There was no one in **Israel** as famous for his good looks
15. 6 Absalom did this with every **Israelite** who came to the king
15.10 to all the tribes of **Israel** to say, "When you hear the
15.13 "The **Israelites** are pledging their loyalty to Absalom."
16. 3 he is convinced that the **Israelites** will now restore to him
16.15 Absalom and all the **Israelites** with him entered Jerusalem,
16.18 by the Lord, by these people, and by all the **Israelites.**
16.21 Then everyone in **Israel** will know that your father regards
17. 4 like good advice to Absalom and all the **Israelite** leaders.
17.10 be afraid because everyone in **Israel** knows that your father
17.11 that you bring all the **Israelites** together from one end of
17.14 Absalom and all the **Israelites** said, "Hushai's advice
17.15 given to Absalom and the **Israelite** leaders and what advice
17.24 by the time Absalom and the **Israelites** had crossed the Jordan.
18. 6 into the countryside and fought the **Israelites** in the forest
18. 7 The **Israelites** were defeated by David's men;
18.16 and his troops came back from pursuing the **Israelites.**
18.17 All the **Israelites** fled, each man to his own home.
19. 8 Meanwhile all the **Israelites** had fled, each man to his own
2 Sam 19.11 news of what the **Israelites** were saying reached King David.
19.22 the one who is **king of Israel** now,
19.22 Israel now, and no **Israelite** will be put to death today."
19.40 and half the men of **Israel,** he went on to Gilgal, and
19.41 Then all the **Israelites** went to the king and said to him,
19.43 **Israelites** replied, "We have ten times as many claims on King
19.43 more violent in making their claims than the men of **Israel.**
20. 1 Men of **Israel,** let's go home!"
20. 2 So the **Israelites** deserted David and went with Sheba,
20.14 of all the tribes of **Israel** and came to the city of
20.19 a great city, one of the most peaceful and loyal in **Israel.**
20.23 Joab was in command of the army of **Israel;**
21. 2 (The people of Gibeon were not **Israelites;**
21. 2 group of Amorites whom the **Israelites** had promised to protect,
21. 2 because of his zeal for the people of **Israel and Judah.)**
21. 4 silver or gold, nor do we want to kill any **Israelite."**
21. 5 to destroy us and leave none of us alive anywhere in **Israel.**
21.15 war between the Philistines and **Israel,** and David and his men
21.17 "You are the hope of **Israel,** and we don't want to lose
21.21 He defied the **Israelites,** and Jonathan, the son of David's
23. 1 and who was the composer of beautiful songs for **Israel.**
23. 3 The God of **Israel** has spoken;
23. 3 the protector of **Israel** said to me:
23. 9 **Israelites** fell back, [10]but he stood his ground and fought the
23.10 After it was over, the **Israelites** returned to where Eleazar
23.11 **Israelites** fled from the Philistines, [12]but Shammah stood his
24. 1 The Lord was angry with **Israel** once more, and he made
24. 1 to him, "Go and count the people of **Israel and Judah."**
24. 2 through all the tribes of **Israel** from one end of the country
24. 3 your God make the **people of Israel** a hundred times more
24. 4 his presence and went out to count the **people of Israel.**
24. 9 800,000 in **Israel** and 500,000 in Judah.
24.15 sent an epidemic on **Israel,** which lasted from that morning
24.15 of the country to the other seventy thousand **Israelites** died.
24.25 answered his prayer, and the epidemic in **Israel** was stopped.
1 Kgs 1. 3 search was made all over **Israel** for a beautiful girl, and in
1.20 Your Majesty, all the **people of Israel** are looking to
1.30 the Lord, the God of **Israel,** that your son Solomon would
1.34 where Zadok and Nathan are to anoint him as **king of Israel.**
1.35 one I have chosen to be the ruler of **Israel and Judah."**
1.48 the Lord, the God of **Israel,** who has today made one of
2. 4 my descendants would rule **Israel** as long as they were careful
2. 5 killing the two commanders of **Israel's** armies, Abner son of
2.11 He had been **king of Israel** for forty years,
2.15 I should have become king and that everyone in **Israel** expected
2.32 commander of the army of **Israel,** and Amasa, commander of the
3.28 When the **people of Israel** heard of Solomon's decision,
4. 1 Solomon was king of all **Israel,** [2]and these were his high
4. 7 Solomon appointed twelve men as district governors in **Israel.**
4.20 people of **Judah and Israel** were as numerous as the grains
4.25 the people throughout **Judah and Israel** lived in safety,
5.13 forced labour from all over **Israel,** [14]and put Adoniram in
6. 1 eighty years after the **people of Israel** left Egypt, during
6. 1 year of Solomon's reign over **Israel,** in the second month,
6.13 will live among my people **Israel** in this Temple that you are
8. 1 the tribes and clans of **Israel** to come to him in Jerusalem
8. 5 Solomon and all the **people of Israel** assembled in front of
8. 9 a covenant with the **people of Israel** as they were coming
8.15 He said, "Praise the Lord God of **Israel!**
8.16 in all the land of **Israel** in which a temple should be
8.17 of the Lord God of **Israel,** [18]but the Lord said to him,
8.20 succeeded my father as **king of Israel,**
8.20 built the Temple for the worship of the Lord God of **Israel.**
8.23 prayed, "Lord God of **Israel,** there is no god like you
8.25 And now, Lord God of **Israel,** I pray that you will also
8.25 his descendants ruling as **king of Israel,**
8.26 So now, O God of **Israel,** let everything come true that
8.33 "When your people **Israel** are defeated by their enemies
8.36 Forgive the sins of the king and of the **people of Israel.**
8.38 any of your people **Israel,** out of heartfelt sorrow, stretch
8.43 world may know you and obey you, as your people **Israel** do.
8.52 with favour on your people **Israel** and their king, and hear
8.59 be merciful to the **people of Israel** and to their king,
8.65 Solomon and all the **people of Israel** celebrated the Festival
8.66 the Lord had given his servant David and his people **Israel.**
9. 5 when I told him that **Israel** would always be ruled by his
9. 7 I will remove my people **Israel** from the land that I have
9. 7 People everywhere will ridicule **Israel** and treat her with
9.20 people of Canaan whom the **Israelites** had not killed when they
9.22 Solomon did not make slaves of **Israelites;**
10. 9 how pleased he is with you by making you **king of Israel.**
10. 9 Because his love for **Israel** is eternal, he has made you
10.12 It was the finest juniper wood ever imported into **Israel;**
10.15 Arabian kings and the governors of the **Israelite** districts.
11. 2 commanded the **Israelites** not to intermarry with these people,
11. 2 they would cause the **Israelites** to give their loyalty to other
11. 9 the Lord, the God of **Israel,** had appeared to Solomon twice
11.21 As king of Edom, Hadad was an evil, bitter enemy of **Israel.**
11.25 He was an enemy of **Israel** during the lifetime of Solomon.
11.31 the Lord, the God of **Israel,** says to you, 'I am going
11.32 have chosen to be my own from the whole land of **Israel.**
11.37 I will make you **king of Israel,** and you will rule
11.38 I will make you **king of Israel** and will make sure
11.42 He was king in Jerusalem over all **Israel** for forty years.
12. 1 the people of northern **Israel** had gathered to make him king.
12.16 Men of **Israel,** let's go home!
12.16 So the **people of Israel** rebelled, [17]leaving Rehoboam as
12.18 to go to the **Israelites,** but they stoned him to death.
12.19 of the northern kingdom of **Israel** have been in rebellion
12.20 the **people of Israel** heard that Jeroboam had returned
12.20 to a meeting of the people and made him **king of Israel.**

1 Kgs 12.21 war and restore his control over the northern tribes of **Israel.**
12.24 "Do not attack your own brothers, the **people of Israel.**
12.25 King Jeroboam of **Israel** fortified the town of Shechem
12.28 **People of Israel,** here are your gods who brought you out of
12.33 of the festival he had instituted for the **people of Israel.**
13.33 King Jeroboam of **Israel** still did not turn from his evil
14. 2 Ahijah lives, the one who said I would be **king of Israel.**
14. 7 this is what the Lord, the God of **Israel,** says to him:
14. 7 among the people and made you the ruler of my people **Israel.**
14.13 All the **people of Israel** will mourn for him and bury him.
14.13 only one with whom the Lord, the God of **Israel,** is pleased.
14.14 to place a king over **Israel** who will put an end to
14.15 The Lord will punish **Israel,** and she will shake like a
14.15 He will uproot the **people of Israel** from this good land
14.16 The Lord will abandon **Israel** because Jeroboam sinned
14.16 Jeroboam sinned and led the **people of Israel** into sin."
14.18 The **people of Israel** mourned for him and buried him, as
14.19 are all recorded in The History of the **Kings of Israel.**
14.21 from all the territory of **Israel** as the place where he was
14.24 driven out of the land as the **Israelites** advanced into the
15. 1 reign of King Jeroboam of **Israel,** Abijah became king of Judah,
15. 9 reign of King Jeroboam of **Israel,** Asa became king of Judah,
15.16 Judah and King Baasha of **Israel** were constantly at war with
15.19 alliance with King Baasha of **Israel,** so that he will have to
15.20 officers and their armies to attack the cities of **Israel.**
15.25 Jeroboam's son Nadab became **king of Israel,**
15.26 he sinned against the Lord and led **Israel** into sin.
15.28 And so Baasha succeeded Nadab as **king of Israel.**
15.30 the Lord, the God of **Israel,** by the sins that he committed
15.30 and that he caused **Israel** to commit.
15.31 Nadab did is recorded in The History of the **Kings of Israel.**
15.32 Judah and King Baasha of **Israel** were constantly at war with
15.33 Ahijah became king of all **Israel,** and he ruled in Tirzah for
15.34 he sinned against the Lord and led **Israel** into sin.
16. 2 a nobody, but I made you the leader of my people **Israel.**
16. 5 deeds are recorded in The History of the **Kings of Israel.**
16. 8 son of Baasha became **king of Israel,** and he ruled in Tirzah
16.13 idolatry and because they led **Israel** into sin, Baasha and his
16.13 Elah had aroused the anger of the Lord, the God of **Israel.**
16.14 Elah did is recorded in The History of the **Kings of Israel.**
16.15 of Judah, Zimri ruled in Tirzah over **Israel** for seven days.
16.15 The **Israelite** troops were besieging the city of Gibbethon in
16.16 they all proclaimed their commander Omri **king of Israel.**
16.19 the Lord by his own sins and by leading **Israel** into sin.
16.20 conspiracy, is recorded in The History of the **Kings of Israel.**
16.21 The **people of Israel** were divided:
16.23 Omri became **king of Israel,**
16.26 the Lord, the God of **Israel,** by his sins and by leading
16.27 accomplishments are recorded in The History of the **Kings of Israel.**
16.29 son of Omri became **king of Israel,** and he ruled in Samaria
16.33 the God of Israel, than all the **kings of Israel** before him.
17. 1 Lord, the living God of **Israel,** whom I serve, I tell you
17.14 For this is what the Lord, the God of **Israel,** says:
18.17 he said, "So there you are—the worst troublemaker in **Israel!"**
18.19 Now order all the **people of Israel** to meet me at Mount
18.20 Ahab summoned all the **Israelites** and the prophets of Baal to
18.36 you are the God of **Israel** and that I am your servant
19.10 But the **people of Israel** have broken their covenant with you,
19.14 But the **people of Israel** have broken their covenant with you,
19.16 son of Nimshi as **king of Israel,** and anoint Elisha son of
19.18 seven thousand people alive in **Israel**—all those who are loyal
20. 2 city to King Ahab of **Israel** to say, "King Benhadad demands
20.15 he called out the **Israelite** army, a total of seven thousand
20.19 the attack, followed by the **Israelite** army, [20] and each one
20.20 The Syrians fled, with the **Israelites** in hot pursuit,
20.23 to him, "The gods of **Israel** are mountain gods,
20.23 and that is why the **Israelites** defeated us.
20.25 We will fight the **Israelites** in the plains, and this time we
20.26 with them to the city of Aphek to attack the **Israelites.**
20.27 The **Israelites** were called up and equipped;
20.27 **Israelites** looked like two small flocks of goats compared with
20.29 Syrians and the **Israelites** stayed in their camps, facing each
20.29 fighting, and the **Israelites** killed a hundred thousand Syrians.
20.31 said, "We have heard that the **Israelite kings** are merciful.
20.31 to go to the **king of Israel** with sackcloth round our waists
20.38 stood by the road, waiting for the **king of Israel** to pass.
21.22 you have stirred up my anger by leading **Israel** into sin.'
21.26 driven out of the land as the **people of Israel** advanced.)
22. 1 was peace between **Israel** and Syria for the next two years,
22. 2 King Jehoshaphat of Judah went to see King Ahab of **Israel.**
22.17 see the army of **Israel** scattered over the hills like sheep
22.29 King Ahab of **Israel** and King Jehoshaphat of Judah went to
22.30 So the **king of Israel** went into battle in disguise.
22.31 commanders to attack no one else except the **king of Israel.**
22.32 that he was the **king of Israel,** and they turned to attack
22.33 was not the **king of Israel,** and they stopped their attack.
22.36 Near sunset the order went out through the **Israelite** ranks:
22.39 he built, is recorded in The History of the **Kings of Israel.**
22.41 reign of King Ahab of **Israel,** Jehoshaphat son of Asa became
22.44 Jehoshaphat made peace with the **king of Israel.**
22.49 Then King Ahaziah of **Israel** offered to let his men sail
22.51 son of Ahab became **king of Israel,** and he ruled in Samaria
22.52 Jezebel, and King Jeroboam, who had led **Israel** into sin.
22.53 him, he aroused the anger of the Lord, the God of **Israel.**

2 Kgs 1. 1 death of King Ahab of **Israel,**
1. 1 the country of Moab rebelled against **Israel.**
1. 2 King Ahaziah of **Israel** fell off the balcony on the roof
1. 3 Is it because you think there is no god in **Israel?**
1. 6 Is it because you think there is no god in **Israel?**
1.16 there were no god in **Israel** to consult—you will not get

2 Kgs 1.18 Ahaziah did is recorded in The History of the **Kings of Israel.**
2.12 Mighty defender of **Israel!**
3. 1 son of Ahab became **king of Israel,** and he ruled in Samaria
3. 3 Nebat before him, he led **Israel** into sin, and would not stop.
3. 4 as tribute to the **king of Israel** 100,000 lambs,
3. 5 when King Ahab of Israel died, Mesha rebelled against **Israel.**
3.13 Elisha said to the **king of Israel.**
3.24 the camp, the **Israelites** attacked them and drove them back.
3.24 The **Israelites** kept up the pursuit, slaughtering the Moabites
3.25 passed a fertile field, every **Israelite** would throw a stone
3.27 **Israelites** were terrified and so they drew back from the city
5. 2 one of their raids against **Israel,** the Syrians had carried
5. 2 had carried off a little **Israelite** girl, who became a servant
5. 5 said, "Go to the **king of Israel** and take this letter
5. 7 When the **king of Israel** read the letter, he tore his
5. 8 me, and I'll show him that there is a prophet in **Israel!"**
5.12 and Pharpar, back in Damascus, better than any river in **Israel?**
5.15 I know that there is no god but the God of **Israel;**
6. 8 The king of Syria was at war with **Israel.**
6. 9 sent word to the **king of Israel,** warning him not to go
6.10 So the **king of Israel** warned the men who lived in that
6.11 one of you is on the side of the **king of Israel?"**
6.12 prophet Elisha tells the **king of Israel** what you say
6.21 When the **king of Israel** saw the Syrians, he asked Elisha,
6.23 So the **king of Israel** provided a great feast for them;
6.23 From then on the Syrians stopped raiding the land of **Israel.**
6.24 led his entire army against **Israel** and laid siege to the
6.26 The **king of Israel** was walking by on the city wall
7. 6 Syrians thought that the **king of Israel** had hired Hittite
7.17 so happened that the **king of Israel** had put the city gate
8. 3 seven years, she returned to **Israel** and went to the king to
8.12 you will do against the **people of Israel,"** Elisha answered.
8.16 son of Ahab as **king of Israel,** Jehoram son of Jehoshaphat
8.18 of Ahab he followed the evil ways of the **kings of Israel.**
8.25 son of Ahab as **king of Israel,** Ahaziah son of Jehoram became
8.26 daughter of King Ahab and granddaughter of King Omri of **Israel.**
8.28 joined King Joram of **Israel** in a war against King Hazael
9. 3 'The Lord proclaims that he anoints you **king of Israel.'**
9. 6 head and said to him, "The Lord, the God of **Israel,**
9. 6 'I anoint you king of my people **Israel.**
9. 9 of King Jeroboam of Israel and of King Baasha of **Israel.**
9.12 'I anoint you **king of Israel.' "**
9.29 eleventh year that Joram son of Ahab was **king of Israel.**
10.21 and Jehu sent word throughout all the land of **Israel.**
10.28 That was how Jehu wiped out the worship of Baal in **Israel.**
10.29 of King Jeroboam, who led **Israel** into the sin of worshipping
10.30 descendants, down to the fourth generation, will be **kings of Israel."**
10.31 all his heart the law of the Lord, the God of **Israel;**
10.31 he followed the example of Jeroboam, who led **Israel** into sin.
10.32 the Lord began to reduce the size of **Israel's** territory.
10.32 of Syria conquered all the **Israelite** territory [33] east of
10.34 deeds, is recorded in The History of the **Kings of Israel.**
10.36 Jehu had ruled in Samaria as **king of Israel**
12. 1 reign of King Jehu of **Israel,** Joash became king of Judah,
13. 1 son of Jehu became **king of Israel,** and he ruled in Samaria
13. 2 him he sinned against the Lord and led **Israel** into sin;
13. 3 the Lord was angry with **Israel,** and he allowed King Hazael
13. 3 and his son Benhadad to defeat **Israel** time after time.
13. 4 harshly the king of Syria was oppressing the **Israelites,**
13. 5 Lord sent **Israel** a leader, who freed them from the Syrians,
13. 5 the Syrians, and so the **Israelites** lived in peace, as before.
13. 6 into which King Jeroboam had led **Israel,** but kept on
13. 8 deeds are recorded in The History of the **Kings of Israel.**
13.10 son of Jehoahaz became **king of Israel,** and he ruled in
13.11 evil example of King Jeroboam, who had led **Israel** into sin.
13.12 of Judah, is recorded in The History of the **Kings of Israel.**
13.14 as he lay dying King Jehoash of **Israel** went to visit him.
13.14 "You have been the mighty defender of **Israel!"**
13.20 Every year bands of Moabites used to invade the land of **Israel.**
13.22 Syria oppressed the **Israelites** during all of Jehoahaz' reign,
13.25 Then King Jehoash of **Israel** defeated Benhadad three times
14. 1 son of Jehoahaz as **king of Israel,** Amaziah son of Joash
14. 8 sent messengers to King Jehoash of **Israel,** challenging him
14.15 of Judah, is recorded in The History of the **Kings of Israel.**
14.17 lived fifteen years after the death of King Jehoash of **Israel.**
14.23 son of Jehoash became **king of Israel,** and he ruled in
14.24 King Jeroboam son of Nebat, who led **Israel** into sin.
14.25 territory that had belonged to **Israel,** from Hamath Pass in
14.25 the Lord, the God of **Israel,** had promised through his servant
14.26 The Lord saw the terrible suffering of the **Israelites;**
14.27 the Lord's purpose to destroy **Israel** completely and for ever,
14.28 restored Damascus and Hamath to **Israel,**
14.28 are all recorded in The History of the **Kings of Israel.**
15. 1 of King Jeroboam II of **Israel,** Uzziah son of Amaziah became
15. 8 of Jeroboam II became **king of Israel,** and he ruled in
15. 9 of King Jeroboam son of Nebat, who led **Israel** into sin.
15.11 Zechariah did is recorded in The History of the **Kings of Israel.**
15.12 descendants, down to the fourth generation, will be **kings of Israel."**
15.13 son of Jabesh became **king of Israel,** and he ruled in Samaria
15.15 conspiracy, is recorded in The History of the **Kings of Israel.**
15.17 son of Gadi became **king of Israel,** and he ruled in Samaria
15.18 son of Nebat, who led **Israel** into sin till the day of
15.19 the emperor of Assyria, invaded **Israel,** and Menahem gave him
15.20 from the rich men of **Israel** by forcing each one to
15.21 Menahem did is recorded in The History of the **Kings of Israel.**
15.23 son of Menahem became **king of Israel,** and he ruled in
15.24 of King Jeroboam son of Nebat, who led **Israel** into sin.
15.26 Pekahiah did is recorded in The History of the **Kings of Israel.**
15.27 son of Remaliah became **king of Israel,** and he ruled in

2 Kgs 15.28 of King Jeroboam son of Nebat, who led **Israel** into sin.
15.31 Pekah did is recorded in The History of the **Kings of Israel.**
15.32 son of Remaliah as **king of Israel,** Jotham son of Uzziah
15.37 King Rezin of Syria and King Pekah of **Israel** to attack Judah.
16. 1 son of Remaliah as **king of Israel,** Ahaz son of Jotham became
16. 3 Lord his God [3]and followed the example of the **kings of Israel.**
16. 3 Lord had driven out of the land as the **Israelites** advanced.
16. 5 and King Pekah of **Israel** attacked Jerusalem and besieged it,
16. 7 the kings of Syria and of **Israel,** who are attacking me."
17. 1 son of Elah became **king of Israel,** and he ruled in Samaria
17. 2 not as much as the kings who had ruled **Israel** before him.
17. 5 Then Shalmaneser invaded **Israel** and besieged Samaria.
17. 6 captured Samaria, took the **Israelites** to Assyria as prisoners,
17. 7 Samaria fell because the **Israelites** sinned against the
17. 8 adopted customs introduced by the **kings of Israel.**
17. 9 **Israelites** did things that the Lord their God disapproved of.
17.13 had sent his messengers and prophets to warn **Israel and Judah:**
17.18 Lord was angry with the **Israelites** and banished them from
17.19 they imitated the customs adopted by the **people of Israel.**
17.20 The Lord rejected all the **Israelites,** punishing them and
17.21 separated Israel from Judah, the **Israelites** made Jeroboam
17.23 So the **people of Israel** were taken into exile to Assyria,
17.24 in the cities of Samaria, in place of the exiled **Israelites.**
17.28 So an **Israelite** priest who had been deported from Samaria
17.29 placed them in the shrines that the **Israelites** had built.
18. 1 of Elah as king of **Israel,** Hezekiah son of Ahaz became king
18. 4 to that time the **people of Israel** had burnt incense in its
18. 5 Hezekiah trusted in the Lord, the God of **Israel;**
18. 9 of King Hoshea's reign over **Israel—**
18. 9 Emperor Shalmaneser of Assyria invaded **Israel**
18.11 Assyrian emperor took the **Israelites** to Assyria as prisoners
18.12 Samaria fell because the **Israelites** did not obey the
19.15 Lord, the God of **Israel,** enthroned above the winged creatures,
19.22 You have been disrespectful to me, the holy God of **Israel.**
21. 3 of the goddess Asherah, as King Ahab of **Israel** had done.
21. 7 of the twelve tribes of **Israel** as the place where I am
21. 8 And if the **people of Israel** will obey all my commands and
21.12 I, the Lord God of **Israel,** will bring such a disaster on
21.13 Samaria, as I did King Ahab of **Israel** and his descendants.
22.18 king himself, this is what I, the Lord God of **Israel,** say:
23.15 by King Jeroboam son of Nebat, who led **Israel** into sin.
23.19 every city of **Israel** King Josiah tore down all the pagan
23.19 built by the **kings of Israel,** who thereby aroused the Lord's
23.22 by any of the **kings of Israel** or of Judah,
23.27 said, "I will do to Judah what I have done to **Israel:**
25.25 He also killed the **Israelites** and Babylonians who were there
25.26 Then all the **Israelites,** rich and poor alike, together
1 Chr 1.43 other, in the time before there were any kings in **Israel:**
2. 7 brought disaster on the **people of Israel** by keeping loot
4.10 prayed to the God of **Israel,** "Bless me, God, and give me
5.17 of King Jotham of Judah and King Jeroboam II of **Israel.)**
6.49 and for the sacrifices by which God forgives **Israel's** sins.
6.64 In this way the **people of Israel** assigned towns for the
9. 1 All the **people of Israel** were listed according to their families,
9. 1 was recorded in The Book of the **Kings of Israel.**
9. 2 property in the cities included **Israelite** laymen, priests,
10. 1 The Philistines fought a battle against the **Israelites**
10. 1 Many **Israelites** were killed there, and the rest of them,
10. 7 the **Israelites** who lived in the Valley of Jezreel heard that
11. 1 All the **people of Israel** went to David at Hebron and said
11. 2 king, you led the **people of Israel** in battle, and the Lord
11. 3 So all the leaders of **Israel** came to King David at Hebron.
11. 3 and he became **king of Israel,**
11. 4 David and all the **Israelites** went and attacked the city of
11.10 the rest of the **people of Israel,** they helped him to become
11.13 in a barley-field when the **Israelites** started to run away,
12.21 Later they were officers in the **Israelite** army.
12.23 (these leaders knew what **Israel** should do and the best time
12.38 went to Hebron, determined to make David king over all **Israel.**
12.38 the rest of the **people of Israel** were united in the same
13. 2 announced to all the **people of Israel,** "If you give your
13. 5 So David assembled the **people of Israel** from all over the country,
14. 2 established him as **king of Israel** and was making his kingdom
14. 8 the whole country of **Israel,** their army went out to capture
15. 3 David summoned all the **people of Israel** to Jerusalem in
15.12 of the Lord God of **Israel** to the place I have prepared
15.14 order to move the Covenant Box of the Lord God of **Israel.**
15.25 David, the leaders of **Israel,** and the military commanders went
15.28 the **Israelites** accompanied the Covenant Box up to Jerusalem
16. 3 each man and woman in **Israel** a loaf of bread, a piece
16. 4 the Lord, the God of **Israel,** in front of the Covenant Box,
16.12 Jacob, God's servant, descendants of **Israel,** whom God chose,
16.36 Praise the Lord, the God of **Israel!**
16.40 what was written in the Law which the Lord gave to **Israel.**
17. 5 time I rescued the **people of Israel** from Egypt until now, I
17. 6 my travelling with the **people of Israel** I never asked any of
17. 7 in the fields and made you the ruler of my people **Israel.**
17. 9 a place for my people **Israel** and have settled them there,
17.21 nation on earth like **Israel,** whom you rescued from slavery
17.22 You have made **Israel** your own people for ever, and you,
17.24 will for ever say, 'The Lord Almighty is God over **Israel.'**
18.14 David ruled over all **Israel** and made sure that his people
19.10 chose the best of **Israel's** soldiers and put them in position
19.16 had been defeated by the **Israelites,** so they brought troops
19.17 of it, he gathered the **Israelite** troops, crossed the Jordan,
19.18 The fighting began, [18]and the **Israelites** drove the Syrian
19.19 they had been defeated by **Israel,** they made peace with David
20. 7 He defied the **Israelites,** and Jonathan, the son of David's
21. 1 bring trouble on the **people of Israel,** so he made David
21. 2 officers, "Go through **Israel,** from one end of the country
21. 3 the Lord make the **people of Israel** a hundred times more
1 Chr 21. 4 travelled through the whole country of **Israel,** and then
21. 5 1,100,000 in **Israel,** and 470,000 in Judah.
21. 7 God was displeased with what had been done, so he punished **Israel.**
21.12 on your land, using his angel to bring death throughout **Israel?**
21.14 an epidemic on the **people of Israel,** and seventy thousand of
22. 1 where the **people of Israel** are to offer burnt-offerings."
22. 2 living in the land of **Israel** to assemble, and he put them
22. 6 him to build a temple for the Lord, the God of **Israel.**
22. 9 Solomon, because during his reign I will give **Israel** peace
22.10 His dynasty will rule **Israel** for ever.' "
22.12 wisdom so that you may govern **Israel** according to his Law.
22.13 the Lord gave to Moses for **Israel,** you will be successful.
22.17 David commanded all the leaders of **Israel** to help Solomon.
23. 1 David was very old, he made his son Solomon **king of Israel.**
23. 2 David brought together all the **Israelite** leaders and all the
23.25 "The Lord God of **Israel** has given peace to his people,
24.19 Aaron in obedience to the commands of the Lord God of **Israel.**
26.29 records and settling disputes for the **people of Israel.**
26.30 all religious and civil matters in **Israel** west of the River
26.32 religious and civil matters in **Israel** east of the River
27. 1 the list of the **Israelite** heads of families and clan leaders
27.16 is the list of the administrators of the tribes of **Israel:**
27.23 promise to make the **people of Israel** as numerous as the
27.24 God punished **Israel** because of this census, so the final
28. 1 David commanded all the officials of **Israel** to assemble in
28. 4 The Lord, the God of **Israel,** chose me
28. 4 chose me and my descendants to rule **Israel** for ever.
28. 4 his pleasure to take me and make me king over all **Israel.**
28. 5 he chose Solomon to rule over **Israel,** the Lord's kingdom.
28. 8 of this assembly of all **Israel,** the Lord's people, I charge
29.23 a successful king, and the whole nation of **Israel** obeyed him.
29.25 more glorious than any other king that had ruled **Israel.**
29.26 David son of Jesse ruled over all **Israel** [27]for forty
29.30 happened to him, to **Israel,** and to the surrounding kingdoms.
2 Chr 1. 1 control of the kingdom of **Israel,** and the Lord his God
1.13 There he ruled over **Israel.**
2. 4 He has commanded **Israel** to do this for ever.
2.12 Praise the Lord God of **Israel,** Creator of heaven and
2.17 in the land of **Israel,** similar to the census his father
5. 2 the tribes and clans of **Israel** to assemble in Jerusalem,
5. 6 Solomon and all the **people of Israel** assembled in front of
5.10 a covenant with the **people of Israel** as they were coming
6. 3 All the **people of Israel** were standing there.
6. 4 He said, "Praise the Lord God of **Israel!**
6. 5 city in the land of **Israel** as the place to build a
6. 5 and I did not choose anyone to lead my people **Israel.**
6. 7 of the Lord God of **Israel,** [8]but the Lord said to him,
6.10 succeeded my father as **king of Israel,**
6.10 built a temple for the worship of the Lord God of **Israel.**
6.11 covenant which the Lord made with the **people of Israel."**
6.14 He prayed, "Lord God of **Israel,** in all heaven and earth
6.16 Now, Lord God of **Israel,** keep the other promise you made
6.16 his descendants ruling as **king of Israel,**
6.17 So now, Lord God of **Israel,** let everything come true that
6.21 the prayers of your people **Israel** when they face this place
6.24 "When your people **Israel** are defeated by their enemies
6.27 of your servants, the **people of Israel,** and teach them to do
6.29 any of your people **Israel,** out of heartfelt sorrow, stretch
6.33 world may know you and obey you, as your people **Israel** do.
7. 3 When the **people of Israel** saw the fire fall from heaven
7. 8 Solomon and all the **people of Israel** celebrated the
7.10 Lord had given to his people **Israel,** to David, and to Solomon.
7.18 when I told him that **Israel** would always be ruled by his
8. 2 Hiram had given him, and sent **Israelites** to settle in them.
8. 7 people of Canaan whom the **Israelites** had not killed when they
8. 9 **Israelites** were not used in forced labour, but served as
8.11 palace of King David of **Israel,** because any place where the
9. 8 Because he loves his people **Israel** and wants to preserve them
9.14 governors of the **Israelite** districts also brought him silver
9.29 which also deal with the reign of King Jeroboam of **Israel.**
9.30 Solomon ruled in Jerusalem over all **Israel** for forty
10. 1 the people of northern **Israel** had gathered to make him king.
10.16 Men of **Israel,** let's go home!
10.16 So the **people of Israel** rebelled, [17]leaving Rehoboam as
10.18 to go to the **Israelites,** but they stoned him to death.
10.19 of the northern kingdom of **Israel** have been in rebellion
11. 1 war and restore his control over the northern tribes of **Israel.**
11. 4 "Do not attack your **fellow-Israelites.**
11.13 From all the territory of **Israel** priests and Levites came
11.14 because King Jeroboam of **Israel** and his successors would not
11.16 the tribes of **Israel** people who sincerely wanted to worship
11.16 the Lord, the God of **Israel,** followed the Levites to Jerusalem,
12.13 from all the territory of **Israel** as the place where he was
13. 1 reign of King Jeroboam of **Israel,** Abijah became king of Judah,
13. 4 up Mount Zemaraim and called out to Jeroboam and the **Israelites:**
13. 5 the God of **Israel,** made an unbreakable covenant with David,
13. 5 giving him and his descendants kingship over **Israel** for ever?
13.12 **People of Israel,** don't fight against the Lord, the God of
13.15 God defeated Jeroboam and the **Israelite** army.
13.16 The **Israelites** fled from the Judaeans, and God let the
13.17 and his army dealt the **Israelites** a crushing defeat—
13.17 defeat—half a million of **Israel's** best soldiers were killed.
13.18 of Judah were victorious over **Israel,** because they relied on
15. 3 For a long time **Israel** lived without the true God, without
15. 4 trouble came, they turned to the Lord, the God of **Israel.**
16. 1 King Baasha of **Israel** invaded Judah and started to fortify
16. 3 alliance with King Baasha of **Israel** so that he will have to
16. 4 officers and their armies to attack the cities of **Israel.**
16. 7 the army of the **king of Israel** has escaped from you.

2 Chr 16.11 recorded in The History of the **Kings of Judah and Israel.**
17. 1 father Asa as king and strengthened his position against **Israel.**
17. 4 and did not act in the way the **kings of Israel** did.
18. 1 member of his family and the family of King Ahab of **Israel.**
18.16 see the army of **Israel** scattered over the hills like sheep
18.28 King Ahab of **Israel** and King Jehoshaphat of Judah went to
18.29 So the **king of Israel** went into battle in disguise.
18.30 commanders to attack no one else except the **king of Israel.**
18.31 that he was the **king of Israel,** and they turned to attack
18.32 he was not the **king of Israel,** so they stopped pursuing him.
20. 7 When your people **Israel** moved into this land, you drove out
20.19 and with a loud shout praised the Lord, the God of **Israel.**
20.29 how the Lord had defeated **Israel's** enemies was terrified,
20.34 which is a part of The History of the **Kings of Israel.**
20.35 an alliance with King Ahaziah of **Israel,** who did many wicked
21. 4 all his brothers killed, and also some **Israelite** officials.
21. 6 Ahab and the other **kings of Israel,** because he had married
21.13 the example of the **kings of Israel** and have led the people
21.13 as Ahab and his successors led **Israel** into unfaithfulness.
22. 2 granddaughter of King Omri of **Israel**—gave him advice that led
22. 5 he joined King Joram of **Israel** in a war against King Hazael
24.16 had done for the **people of Israel,** for God, and for the
25. 6 he hired 100,000 soldiers from **Israel** at a cost of about
25. 7 king and said to him, "Don't take these **Israelite** soldiers
25.13 the **Israelite** soldiers that Amaziah had not allowed to go
25.17 Amaziah of Judah and his advisers plotted against **Israel.**
25.17 message to King Jehoash of **Israel,** who was the son of
25.21 King Jehoash of **Israel** went into battle against King Amaziah
25.25 King Amaziah of Judah outlived King Jehoash of **Israel**
25.26 recorded in The History of the **Kings of Judah and Israel.**
27. 7 recorded in The History of the **Kings of Israel and Judah.**
28. 2 the Lord [2]and followed the example of the **kings of Israel.**
28. 3 Lord had driven out of the land as the **Israelites** advanced.
28. 5 Lord also let the **king of Israel,** Pekah son of Remaliah,
28. 7 An **Israelite** soldier named Zichri killed King Ahaz' son
28. 8 the **Israelite** army captured 200,000 women and children
28. 9 met the returning **Israelite** army with its Judaean prisoners
28.15 Then the **Israelites** returned home to Samaria.
28.26 recorded in The History of the Kings of **Judah and Israel.**
29. 7 or offer burnt-offerings in the Temple of the God of **Israel.**
29.10 the Lord, the God of **Israel,** so that he will no longer
29.24 burnt-offerings and sin-offerings to be made for all **Israel.**
30. 1 the king sent word to all the people of **Israel and Judah.**
30. 1 the Passover in honour of the Lord, the God of **Israel.**
30. 5 so they invited all the **Israelites,** from Dan in the north
30. 6 through all **Judah and Israel** with the following invitation:
30. 6 **"People of Israel,** You have survived the Assyrian conquest
30. 7 like your ancestors and your **fellow-Israelites** who were
30.25 the foreigners who had settled permanently in **Israel and Judah.**
31. 1 festival ended, all the **people of Israel** went to every city
31. 5 order was given, the **people of Israel** brought gifts of their
31. 8 been given, they praised the Lord and praised his people **Israel.**
32.17 that the emperor wrote defied the Lord, the God of **Israel.**
32.32 Amoz and in The History of the **Kings of Judah and Israel.**
33. 7 of the twelve tribes of **Israel** as the place where I am
33. 8 And if the **people of Israel** will obey all my commands and
33.16 the people of Judah to worship the Lord, the God of **Israel.**
33.18 the Lord, the God of **Israel,**
33.18 are all recorded in The History of the **Kings of Israel.**
34.21 me and for the people who still remain in **Israel and Judah.**
34.26 king himself, this is what I, the Lord God of **Israel,** say:
34.33 territory belonging to the **people of Israel,** and as long as
35. 3 the teachers of **Israel,** who were dedicated to the Lord:
35. 3 you are to serve the Lord your God and his people **Israel.**
35. 5 be available to help each family of the **people of Israel.**
35. 6 sacrifices in order that your **fellow-Israelites** may follow
35.17 seven days all the **people of Israel** who were present
35.18 and the people of Judah, **Israel,** and Jerusalem [19]in the
35.25 has become a custom in **Israel** for the singers, both men and
35.27 recorded in The History of the **Kings of Israel and Judah.**
36. 8 is recorded in The History of the **Kings of Israel and Judah.**
36.13 refused to repent and return to the Lord, the God of **Israel.**
Ezra 1. 3 the Lord, the God of **Israel,** the God who is worshipped in
2. 2 list of the clans of **Israel,** with the number of those from
2.59 they could not prove that they were descendants of **Israelites.**
2.70 and the rest of the **Israelites** settled in the towns where
3. 1 the seventh month the **people of Israel** were all settled in
3. 2 altar of the God of **Israel,** so that they could burn
3.11 "The Lord is good, and his love for **Israel** is eternal."
4. 1 were rebuilding the Temple of the Lord, the God of **Israel.**
5. 1 name of the God of **Israel** to the Jews who lived in
5.11 and equipped many years ago by a powerful **king of Israel.**
6.14 commanded by the God of **Israel** and by Cyrus, Darius,
6.16 Then the **people of Israel**—the priests, the Levites, and
6.17 goats as offerings for sin, one for each tribe of **Israel.**
6.21 were eaten by all the **Israelites** who had returned from exile
6.21 land and who had come to worship the Lord God of **Israel.**
6.22 their work of rebuilding the Temple of the God of **Israel.**
7. 6 Law which the Lord, the God of **Israel,** had given to Moses.
7. 6 Jerusalem with a group of **Israelites** which included priests,
7.10 all its laws and regulations to the **people of Israel.**
7.11 the laws and commands which the Lord had given to **Israel:**
7.13 throughout my empire all the **Israelite** people, priests,
7.15 to give to the God of **Israel,** whose Temple is in Jerusalem.
7.16 offerings which the **Israelite** people and their priests give
7.28 of the heads of the clans of **Israel** to return with me."
8.25 and officials, and the **people of Israel** had given to be used
8.29 and to the leaders of the **people of Israel** in Jerusalem."
8.35 offerings to be burnt as sacrifices to the God of **Israel.**
8.35 They offered 12 bulls for all **Israel,** 96 rams, and 77 lambs;
9. 1 the leaders of the **people of Israel** came and told me that

Ezra 9. 4 of what the God of **Israel** had said about the sins of
9.15 Lord God of **Israel,** you are just, but you have let us
10. 1 a large group of **Israelites**—men, women, and children—gathered
10. 2 foreign women, but even so there is still hope for **Israel.**
10.10 and have brought guilt on **Israel** by marrying foreign women.
Neh 1. 6 I pray day and night for your servants, the **people of Israel.**
1. 6 I confess that we, the **people of Israel,** have sinned.
1. 8 'If you **people of Israel** are unfaithful to me, I will
2.10 of the **people of Israel,** and they were highly indignant.
7. 8 list of the clans of **Israel,** with the number of those from
7.61 they could not prove that they were descendants of **Israelites.**
7.73 temple workmen—all the **people of Israel**—settled in the towns
8. 1 the seventh month the **people of Israel** were all settled in
8. 1 the Lord had given **Israel** through Moses, to get the book
8.14 through Moses, ordered the **people of Israel** to live in
9. 1 the same month the **people of Israel** assembled to fast in
9. 6 And then the **people of Israel** prayed this prayer:
9.38 has happened, we, the **people of Israel,** hereby make a solemn
10.28 We, the **people of Israel,** the priests, the Levites,
10.33 take away the sins of **Israel,** and anything else needed for
10.39 The **people of Israel** and the Levites are to take the
11. 3 towns and cities the **people of Israel,** the priests, the
11.20 The rest of the **people of Israel** and the remaining
11.24 represented the **people of Israel** at the Persian court.
12.47 of Nehemiah, all the **people of Israel** gave daily gifts for
13. 2 food and water to the **Israelites** on their way out of Egypt.
13. 2 money to Balaam to curse **Israel,** but our God turned the
13. 3 When the **people of Israel** heard this law read, they
13.12 Then all the **people of Israel** again started bringing to
13.18 more of God's anger down on **Israel** by profaning the Sabbath."
13.26 made him king over all **Israel,** and yet he fell into this
Ps 14. 7 How I pray that victory will come to **Israel** from Zion.
14. 7 How happy the **people of Israel** will be when the Lord makes
22. 3 are enthroned as the Holy One, the one whom **Israel** praises.
22.23 Worship him, you **people of Israel!**
25.22 From all their troubles, O God, save your people **Israel!**
41.13 Praise the Lord, the God of **Israel!**
50. 7 I will testify against you, **Israel.**
53. 5 God has rejected them, and so **Israel** will totally defeat them.
53. 6 How I pray that victory will come to **Israel** from Zion.
53. 6 How happy the **people of Israel** will be when God makes them
59. 5 see for yourself, God of **Israel!**
59.13 know that God rules in **Israel,** that his rule extends over
68. 8 of the God of Sinai, the coming of the God of **Israel.**
68.34 his majesty is over **Israel,** his might is in the skies.
68.35 God as he comes from his sanctuary— the God of **Israel!**
69. 6 bring disgrace to those who worship you, O God of **Israel!**
71.22 harp I will play hymns to you, the Holy One of **Israel.**
72.18 Praise the Lord, the God of **Israel!**
73. 1 God is indeed good to **Israel,** to those who have pure hearts.
76. 1 his name is honoured in **Israel.**
78. 5 gave laws to the **people of Israel** and commandments to the
78.31 and killed their strongest men, the best young men of **Israel.**
78.41 to the test and brought pain to the Holy God of **Israel.**
78.55 land among the tribes of **Israel** and gave their homes to his
78.71 and he made him **king of Israel,** the shepherd of the people
80. 1 Listen to us, O Shepherd of **Israel;**
81. 4 This is the law in **Israel,** an order from the God of
81. 5 gave it to the **people of Israel** when he attacked the land
81. 8 **Israel,** how I wish you would listen to me!
81.11 **Israel** would not obey me.
83. 4 destroy their nation, so that **Israel** will be forgotten
85. 1 you have made **Israel** prosperous again.
87. 2 any other place in **Israel** he loves the city of Jerusalem.
89.18 you, the Holy God of **Israel,** gave us our king.
94. 7 the God of **Israel** does not notice."
98. 3 his promise to the **people of Israel** with loyalty and
99. 4 you have established justice in **Israel;**
103. 7 to Moses and let the **people of Israel** see his mighty deeds.
105.37 Then he led the **Israelites** out;
106.48 Praise the Lord, the God of **Israel;**
114. 1 When the **people of Israel** left Egypt, when Jacob's
114. 2 the Lord's holy people, **Israel** became his own possession.
115. 9 Trust in the Lord, you **people of Israel.**
115.12 he will bless the **people of Israel** and all the priests of
118. 2 Let the **people of Israel** say, "His love is eternal."
121. 4 The protector of **Israel** never dozes or sleeps.
122. 4 tribes come, the tribes of **Israel,** to give thanks to the
122. 5 Here the **kings of Israel** sat to judge their people.
124. 1 Answer, O **Israel!**
125. 5 Peace be with **Israel!**
128. 6 Peace be with **Israel!**
129. 1 **Israel,** tell us how your enemies have persecuted you ever
130. 7 **Israel,** trust in the Lord, because his love is constant and
130. 8 He will save his people **Israel** from all their sins.
131. 3 **Israel,** trust in the Lord now and for ever!
135. 4 He chose Jacob for himself, the **people of Israel** for his own.
135.12 he gave them to **Israel.**
135.19 Praise the Lord, **people of Israel;**
136.11 He led the **people of Israel** out of Egypt;
136.22 he gave them to **Israel,** his servant;
147.19 his message to his people, his instructions and laws to **Israel.**
148.14 people praise him— the **people of Israel,** so dear to him.
149. 2 Be glad, **Israel,** because of your Creator;
Prov 1. 1 The proverbs of Solomon, son of David and **king of Israel.**
Ecc 1.12 I, the Philosopher, have been king over **Israel** in Jerusalem.
Song 3. 7 soldiers form the bodyguard, the finest soldiers in **Israel.**
Is 1. 3 But that is more than my people **Israel** know.
1. 4 Lord, the holy God of **Israel,** and have turned your backs on
1. 5 **Israel,** your head is already covered with wounds, and your
1.24 now, listen to what the Lord Almighty, **Israel's** powerful God,

Is 2. 3 up the hill of the Lord, to the Temple of **Israel's** God.
4. 2 All the **people of Israel** who survive will take delight and
5. 7 **Israel** is the vineyard of the Lord Almighty;
5.19 Let **Israel's** holy God carry out his plans;
5.24 have rejected what the Lord Almighty, **Israel's** holy God, has
5.30 day comes, they will roar over **Israel** as loudly as the sea.
7. 1 Pekah son of Remaliah, **king of Israel,** attacked Jerusalem,
7. 2 already in the territory of **Israel,** he and all his people
7. 5 Syria, together with **Israel** and its king, has made a plot.
7. 8 for **Israel,** within sixty-five years it will be too shattered
7. 9 **Israel** is no stronger than Samaria, its capital city,
7.17 come since the kingdom of **Israel** separated from Judah—he is
8.14 the kingdoms of **Judah and Israel** and the people of Jerusalem.
8.18 has sent us as living messages to the **people of Israel.**
9. 8 pronounced judgement on the kingdom of **Israel,**
9. 9 All the **people of Israel,** everyone who lives in the city
9.12 Philistia on the west have opened their mouths to devour **Israel.**
9.13 The **people of Israel** have not repented;
9.14 day the Lord will punish **Israel's** leaders and its people;
10.17 God, the light of **Israel,** will become a fire.
10.17 **Israel's** holy God will become a flame, which in a single day
10.20 is coming when the **people of Israel** who have survived will
10.20 will truly put their trust in the Lord, **Israel's** holy God.
10.21 A few of the **people of Israel** will come back to their
10.22 there are as many **people of Israel** as there are grains of
11.12 the scattered people of **Israel and Judah** and bringing them
11.13 kingdom of **Israel** will not be jealous of Judah any more,
11.13 and Judah will not be the enemy of **Israel.**
11.16 for those of his people **Israel** who have survived there,
12. 6 **Israel's** holy God is great, and he lives among his people."
14. 1 be merciful to his people **Israel** and choose them as his own.
14. 2 nations will help the **people of Israel** to return to the land
14. 2 Lord gave them, and there the nations will serve **Israel** as
14. 2 Those who once captured **Israel** will now be captured by Israel,
14. 2 and the **people of Israel** will rule
14. 3 Lord will give the **people of Israel** relief from their pain
14.25 Assyrians in my land of **Israel** and trample upon them on my
17. 3 **Israel** will be defenceless, and Damascus will lose its
17. 3 Syrians who survive will be in disgrace like the **people of Israel.**
17. 4 "A day is coming when **Israel's** greatness will come to an end,
17. 5 **Israel** will be like a field where the corn has been cut
17. 6 few people will survive, and **Israel** will be like an olive-tree
17. 6 I, the Lord God of **Israel,** have spoken."
17. 7 will turn for help to their Creator, the holy God of **Israel.**
17. 9 Amorites abandoned as they fled from the **people of Israel.**
17.10 **Israel,** you have forgotten the God who rescues you and
19.24 When that time comes, **Israel** will rank with Egypt and
19.25 and you, **Israel,** my chosen people."
21.10 My people **Israel,** you have been threshed like wheat,
21.10 I have heard from the Lord Almighty, the God of **Israel.**
21.17 I, the Lord God of **Israel,** have spoken."
24.15 live along the sea will praise the Lord, the God of **Israel.**
24.16 we will hear songs in praise of **Israel,** the righteous nation.
27. 6 days to come the **people of Israel,** the descendants of Jacob,
27. 7 **Israel** has not been punished by the Lord as severely as
27. 9 But **Israel's** sins will be forgiven only when the stones of
27.13 from Assyria and Egypt all the **Israelites** who are in exile
28. 1 The kingdom of **Israel** is doomed!
29.19 the happiness which the Lord, the holy God of **Israel,** gives.
29.22 the Lord, the God of **Israel,** who rescued Abraham from trouble,
29.23 then you will acknowledge that I am the holy God of **Israel.**
30.11 We don't want to hear about your holy God of **Israel."**
30.12 But this is what the holy God of **Israel** says:
30.15 Lord, the holy God of **Israel,** says to the people, "Come
30.29 way to the Temple of the Lord, the defender of **Israel.**
31. 1 the Lord, the holy God of **Israel,** or ask him for help.
31. 6 The Lord said, **"People of Israel,** you have sinned against
37.16 prayed, [16]"Almighty Lord, God of **Israel,** enthroned above
37.23 You have been disrespectful to me, the holy God of **Israel.**
40.27 **Israel,** why then do you complain that the Lord doesn't
41. 8 "But you, **Israel** my servant, you are the people that I
41.14 "Small and weak as you are, **Israel,** don't be afraid;
41.14 I, the holy God of **Israel,** am the one who saves you.
41.16 you will praise me, the holy God of **Israel.**
41.17 I, the God of **Israel,** will never abandon them.
41.20 come to understand that **Israel's** holy God has made it happen."
41.21 The Lord, the **king of Israel,** has this to say:
42.20 **Israel,** you have seen so much, but what has it meant to
42.24 Who gave **Israel** up to the looters?
42.25 his anger burned throughout **Israel,** but we never knew what
43. 1 **Israel,** the Lord who created you says,
43. 3 the Lord your God, the holy God of **Israel,** who saves you.
43.10 **"People of Israel,** you are my witnesses;
43.14 **Israel's** holy God, the Lord who saves you, says,
43.15 I created you, **Israel,** and I am your king."
43.22 "But you were tired of me, **Israel;**
43.28 So I brought destruction on **Israel;**
44. 1 "Listen now, **Israel,** my servant, my chosen people,
44. 5 They will come to join the **people of Israel.**
44. 6 Lord, who rules and protects **Israel,** the Lord Almighty, has
44.21 **"Israel,** remember this;
44.23 The Lord has shown his greatness by saving his people **Israel.**
45. 3 Lord, and that the God of **Israel** has called you by name.
45. 4 to help my servant **Israel,** the people that I have chosen.
45.11 Lord, the holy God of **Israel,** the one who shapes the future,
45.14 The Lord says to **Israel,**
45.15 The God of **Israel,** who saves his people, is a God who
45.17 But **Israel** is saved by the Lord, and her victory lasts
45.19 did not require the **people of Israel** to look for me in
46.13 I will save Jerusalem and bring honour to **Israel** there."
47. 4 The holy God of **Israel** sets us free— his name is

Is 48. 1 Listen to this, **people of Israel,**
48. 1 to worship the God of **Israel—** but you don't mean a
48. 2 and that you depend on **Israel's** God, whose name is the Lord
48. 3 The Lord says to **Israel,**
48.12 "Listen to me, **Israel,** the people I have called!
48.17 The holy God of **Israel,** the Lord who saves you, says:
48.20 "The Lord has saved his servant **Israel!"**
49. 3 He said to me, **"Israel,** you are my servant;
49. 5 his people, to bring back the scattered **people of Israel.**
49. 6 restore to greatness the **people of Israel** who have survived,
49. 7 **Israel's** holy God and saviour says to the one who is
49. 7 the holy God of **Israel** keeps his promises.
49.26 They will know that I am **Israel's** powerful God."
54. 5 The holy God of **Israel** will save you— he is the
54. 6 **Israel,** you are like a young wife, deserted by her husband
55. 5 God, the holy God of **Israel,** will make all this happen;
56. 8 has brought his people **Israel** home from exile, has promised
58. 1 Tell my people **Israel** about their sins!
60. 9 Lord, The holy God of **Israel,** Who has made all nations
60.14 'The City of the Lord,' 'Zion, the City of **Israel's** Holy God.'
60.16 saved you, That the mighty God of **Israel** sets you free.
63. 7 has richly blessed the **people of Israel** because of his mercy
65. 9 will bless the **Israelites** who belong to the tribe of Judah,
66.20 chariots and wagons, just as **Israelites** bring grain-offerings

Jer 2. 3 **Israel,** you belonged to me alone;
2. 4 Lord's message, you descendants of Jacob, you tribes of **Israel.**
2.14 **"Israel** is not a slave;
2.17 **Israel,** you brought this on yourself!
2.20 **"Israel,** long ago you rejected my authority;
2.25 **Israel,** don't wear your feet out, or let your throat
2.26 caught, so all you **people of Israel** will be disgraced—your
2.31 **People of Israel,** listen to what I am saying.
3. 1 But, **Israel,** you have had many lovers, and now you want to
3. 5 **Israel,** that is what you said, but you did all the evil
3. 6 "Have you seen what **Israel,** that unfaithful woman, has done?
3. 8 also saw that I divorced **Israel** and sent her away because
3. 8 But Judah, **Israel's** unfaithful sister, was not afraid.
3.10 Judah, **Israel's** unfaithful sister, only pretended to return
3.11 told me that, even though **Israel** had turned away from him,
3.12 go and say to **Israel,** "Unfaithful Israel, come back to me.
3.18 **Israel** will join with Judah, and together they will come
3.19 **"Israel,** I wanted to accept you as my son and give you
3.21 it is the **people of Israel** crying and pleading, because
3.23 Help for **Israel** comes only from the Lord our God.
4. 1 The Lord says, **"People of Israel,** if you want to turn,
5.11 people of **Israel and Judah** have betrayed me completely.
5.15 **People of Israel,** the Lord is bringing a nation from
6. 9 Lord Almighty said to me, **"Israel** will be stripped clean
7. 1 the Lord Almighty, the God of **Israel,** had to say to them:
7.12 I did to it because of the sins of my people **Israel.**
7.15 sight as I drove out your relatives, the **people of Israel.**
9.15 to what I, the Lord Almighty, the God of **Israel,** will do:
9.25 none of the **people of Israel** have kept my covenant."
10. 1 **People of Israel,** listen to the message that the Lord has
10.16 and he has chosen **Israel** to be his very own people.
11. 3 I, the Lord God of **Israel,** have placed a curse on everyone
11.10 Both **Israel and Judah** have broken the covenant that I made
11.17 "I, the Lord Almighty, planted **Israel and Judah;**
12. 7 "I have abandoned **Israel;**
12.14 to say about **Israel's** neighbours
12.14 who have ruined the land I gave to my people **Israel.**
13.11 all the people of **Israel and Judah** to hold tightly to me.
13.12 me, "Jeremiah, tell the **people of Israel** that every
13.15 **People of Israel,** the Lord has spoken!
14. 8 You are **Israel's** only hope;
16. 9 what I, the Lord Almighty, the God of **Israel,** have to say.
16.14 God who brought the **people of Israel** out of the land of
16.15 God who brought the **people of Israel** out of a northern land
17.13 Lord, you are **Israel's** hope;
18. 6 to do with you **people of Israel** what the potter did with
18.13 The **people of Israel** have done a terrible thing!
19. 3 what I, the Lord Almighty, the God of **Israel,** have to say.
19.15 Lord Almighty, the God of **Israel,** had said, "I am going to
21. 4 the Lord, the God of **Israel,** had said, "Zedekiah, I am
23. 2 the Lord, the God of **Israel,** says about the rulers who were
23. 6 will be safe, and the **people of Israel** will live in peace.
23. 7 God who brought the **people of Israel** out of the land of
23. 8 God who brought the **people of Israel** out of a northern land
24. 5 Lord, the God of **Israel,** consider that the people who were
25.15 The Lord, the God of **Israel,** said to me, "Here is a
25.27 Lord Almighty, the God of **Israel,** am commanding them to drink
27. 4 Lord Almighty, the God of **Israel,** told me to command them to
27.21 Lord Almighty, the God of **Israel,** say about the treasures
28. 2 told me [2]that the Lord Almighty, the God of **Israel,** had
28.14 Lord Almighty, the God of **Israel,** has said that he will put
29. 4 Lord Almighty, the God of **Israel,** says to all those people
29. 8 the Lord, the God of **Israel,** warn you not to let yourselves
29.21 Lord Almighty, the God of **Israel,** has spoken about Ahab
29.24 Almighty, the God of **Israel,** gave me a message for Shemaiah
30. 1 The Lord, the God of **Israel,** [2]said to me:
30. 3 is coming when I will restore my people, **Israel and Judah.**
30. 4 The Lord says to the people of **Israel and Judah:**
30.10 **people of Israel,** do not be terrified.
31. 1 of all the tribes of **Israel,** and they will be my people.
31. 2 When the **people of Israel** longed for rest, [3]I appeared to
31. 3 **People of Israel,** I have always loved you, so I continue to
31. 7 "Sing with joy for **Israel,** the greatest of the nations.
31. 9 am like a father to **Israel,** and Ephraim is my eldest son."
31.11 I have set **Israel's** people free and have saved them from
31.18 "I hear the **people of Israel** say in grief, 'Lord, we
31.20 **"Israel,** you are my dearest son, the child I love best.

Jer 31.21 Come back, **people of Israel,** come home to the towns you left.
31.23 Lord Almighty, the God of **Israel,** says, "When I restore the
31.27 fill the land of **Israel and Judah** with people and animals.
31.31 new covenant with the **people of Israel** and with the people
31.33 that I will make with the **people of Israel** will be this:
31.36 the natural order lasts, so long will **Israel** be a nation.
31.37 would he reject the **people of Israel** because of all they
32.14 Lord Almighty, the God of **Israel,** has ordered you to take
32.15 Almighty, the God of **Israel,** has said that houses, fields,
32.20 to this day, both in **Israel** and among all the other nations,
32.21 power and might to bring your people **Israel** out of Egypt.
32.30 of their history the **people of Israel** and the people of
32.36 Lord, the God of **Israel,** said to me, "Jeremiah, the people
33. 4 Lord, the God of **Israel,** say that the houses of Jerusalem
33. 7 I will make **Judah and Israel** prosperous,
33.14 the promise that I made to the people of **Israel and Judah.**
33.17 of David to be **king of Israel** [18]and that there will always
33.24 that I have rejected **Israel and Judah,** the two families that
34. 2 The Lord, the God of **Israel,** told me to go and say
34. 9 so that no one would have a **fellow-Israelite** as a slave.
34.13 the Lord, [13]the God of **Israel,** told me to say to the
34.15 you agreed to set your **fellow-Israelites** free, and you made
34.17 you have not given your **fellow-Israelites** their freedom.
35.12 Lord Almighty, the God of **Israel,** told me to go and say
35.17 Lord Almighty, the God of **Israel,** will bring on you people
35.18 Lord Almighty, the God of **Israel,** had said, "You have obeyed
35.19 Lord Almighty, the God of **Israel,** promise that Jonadab
36. 2 I have told you about **Israel and Judah** and all the nations.
37. 6 the Lord, the God of **Israel,** told me [7]to say to Zedekiah,
38.17 Almighty, the God of **Israel,** had said, "If you surrender to
39.16 Lord Almighty, the God of **Israel,** had said, "Just as I said
40.11 Meanwhile, all the **Israelites** who were in Moab, Ammon,
40.11 of Babylonia had allowed some **Israelites** to stay on in Judah
41. 3 Ishmael also killed all the **Israelites** who were with
41. 9 had dug when he was being attacked by King Baasha of **Israel.**
42. 9 "The Lord, the God of **Israel,** to whom you sent me with
42.13 Almighty, the God of **Israel,** says, 'If you are determined to
42.18 "The Lord, the God of **Israel,** says, 'Just as my anger
43. 9 the city, and let some of the **Israelites** see you do it.
43.10 Almighty, the God of **Israel,** am going to bring my servant
44. 1 to me concerning all the **Israelites** living in Egypt, in the
44. 2 Almighty, the God of **Israel,** said, "You yourselves have seen
44. 7 Lord Almighty, the God of **Israel,** now ask why you are doing
44.11 Lord Almighty, the God of **Israel,** will turn against you and
44.15 there, including the **Israelites** who lived in southern Egypt—
44.24 Lord Almighty, the God of **Israel,** was saying to the people
44.26 have made in my mighty name to all you **Israelites** in Egypt:
45. 2 Lord, the God of **Israel,** had said, "Baruch, [3]you are saying,
46.25 Almighty, the God of **Israel,** says, "I am going to punish
46.27 do not be afraid, **people of Israel,** do not be terrified.
48.13 just as the **Israelites** were disillusioned with Bethel, a god
48.27 Moab, remember how you jeered at the **people of Israel?**
49. 1 "Where are the men of **Israel?**
49. 2 Then **Israel** will take its land back from those who took it
50. 4 the people of both **Israel and Judah** will come weeping,
50. 8 **"People of Israel,** run away from Babylonia!
50.17 The Lord says, "The **people of Israel** are like sheep,
50.18 Almighty, the God of **Israel,** will punish King Nebuchadnezzar
50.19 I will restore the **people of Israel** to their land.
50.20 sin will be found in **Israel** and no wickedness in Judah,
50.29 it acted with pride against me, the Holy One of **Israel.**
50.33 "The **people of Israel** and of Judah are oppressed.
51. 5 not abandoned **Israel and Judah,** even though they have sinned
51. 5 they have sinned against me, the Holy One of **Israel.**
51.19 and he has chosen **Israel** to be his very own people.
51.33 I, the Lord Almighty, the God of **Israel,** have spoken."
51.45 **People of Israel,** run away from there!
51.49 will fall because it caused the death of so many **Israelites.**
Lam 2. 3 In his fury he shattered the strength of **Israel;**
2. 5 Like an enemy, the Lord has destroyed **Israel;**
Ezek 2. 3 "Mortal man, I am sending you to the **people of Israel.**
3. 1 then go and speak to the **people of Israel."**
3. 4 man, go to the **people of Israel** and say to them whatever
3. 5 that speaks a difficult foreign language, but to the **Israelites.**
3. 7 But none of the **people of Israel** will be willing to listen;
3.17 said, "I am making you a watchman for the nation of **Israel.**
4. 3 This will be a sign to the nation of **Israel.**
4. 4 I will place on you the guilt of the nation of **Israel.**
4.13 "This represents the way the **Israelites** will have to eat
5. 4 From them fire will spread to the whole nation of **Israel."**
6. 2 "look towards the mountains of **Israel** and give them my message.
6. 3 Tell the mountains of **Israel** to hear the word of the Lord
6. 5 I will scatter the corpses of the **people of Israel;**
6. 6 All the cities of **Israel** will be destroyed, so that all
6.11 of all the evil, disgusting things the **Israelites** have done.
6.14 the north, not sparing any place where the **Israelites** live.
7. 2 what I, the Sovereign Lord, am saying to the land of **Israel:**
7. 3 **"Israel,** the end has come.
7.10 The day of disaster is coming for **Israel.**
8. 4 that shows the presence of **Israel's** God, just as I had seen
8. 6 the disgusting things the **people of Israel** are doing here,
8.10 of the other things which the **Israelites** were worshipping.
8.11 Seventy **Israelite** leaders were there, including Jaazaniah
8.12 do you see what the **Israelite** leaders are doing in secret?
9. 3 presence of the God of **Israel** rose up from the winged
9. 8 that you are going to kill everyone left in **Israel?"**
9. 9 "The people of **Israel and Judah** are guilty of terrible sins.
10.20 I had seen beneath the God of **Israel** at the River Chebar.
11. 5 **"People of Israel,** I know what you are saying and what you
11.11 will punish you wherever you may be in the land of **Israel.**
11.13 Are you going to kill everyone left in **Israel?"**
Ezek 11.15 talking about you and your **fellow-Israelites** who are in exile.
11.17 them, and will give the land of **Israel** back to them.
11.22 light of the presence of the God of **Israel** was over them.
12. 6 What you do will be a warning to the **Israelites."**
12. 9 "now that those **Israelite** rebels are asking you what you're
12.22 he said, "why do the **people of Israel** repeat this proverb:
12.23 It won't be repeated in **Israel** any more.
12.24 "Among the **people of Israel** there will be no more false
12.27 "Mortal man, the **Israelites** think that your visions and
13. 2 "denounce the prophets of **Israel** who make up their own
13. 4 **People of Israel,** your prophets are as useless as foxes
13. 5 rebuild the walls, and so **Israel** cannot be defended when war
13. 9 will not be included in the list of the citizens of **Israel;**
14. 1 of the leaders of the **Israelites** came to consult me about
14. 4 Every **Israelite** who has given his heart to idols and lets
14. 5 those idols have turned the **Israelites** away from me,
14. 6 tell the **Israelites** what I, the Sovereign Lord, am saying:
14. 7 "Whenever one of the **Israelites** or one of the foreigners
14. 7 foreigners who live in the **Israelite** community turns away
14. 9 I will remove him from the **people of Israel.**
14.11 do this to keep the **Israelites** from deserting me and defiling
17. 2 he said, "tell the **Israelites** a parable [3]to let them know
17. 5 plant from the land of **Israel** and planted it in a fertile
17.23 plant it on a high mountain, [23]on **Israel's** highest mountain.
18. 2 is this proverb people keep repeating in the land of **Israel?**
18. 3 Lord, "you will not repeat this proverb in **Israel** any more.
18. 6 worship the idols of the **Israelites** or eat the sacrifices
18.15 worship the idols of the **Israelites** or eat the sacrifices
18.25 Listen to me, you **Israelites.**
18.29 And you **Israelites** say, 'What the Lord does isn't right.'
18.30 Sovereign Lord, am telling you **Israelites** that I will judge
18.31 Why do you **Israelites** want to die?
19. 1 me to sing this song of sorrow for two princes of **Israel:**
19. 9 his roar would never be heard again on the hills of **Israel.**
20. 1 of the leaders of the **Israelite** community came to consult me
20. 5 When I chose **Israel,** I made them a promise.
20. 9 living I had announced to **Israel** that I was going to lead
20.14 the nations which had seen me lead **Israel** out of Egypt.
20.22 the nations which had seen me bring **Israel** out of Egypt.
20.27 mortal man, tell the **Israelites** what I, the Sovereign Lord,
20.30 tell the **Israelites** what I, the Sovereign Lord, am saying:
20.31 And then you **Israelites** still come to ask what my will is!
20.38 but I will not let them return to the land of **Israel.**
20.39 Lord said, "And now, all you **Israelites,** please yourselves!
20.40 mountain, the high mountain of **Israel,**
20.40 all you **people of Israel** will worship me.
20.42 I bring you back to **Israel,** the land that I promised I
20.44 to protect my honour, you **Israelites** will know that I am the
21. 2 Warn the land of **Israel** [3]that I, the Lord, am saying:
21.12 is meant for my people and for all the leaders of **Israel.**
21.25 "You wicked, unholy ruler of **Israel,** your day, the day
21.28 Lord, am saying to the Ammonites, who are insulting **Israel.**
22. 6 **Israel's** leaders trust in their own strength and commit murder.
22.12 loans they make to their **fellow-Israelites** and get rich by
22.18 to me, [18]"Mortal man, the **Israelites** are of no use to me.
22.24 he said, "tell the **Israelites** that their land is unholy,
22.26 As a result the **people of Israel** do not respect me.
24.21 to me and told me [21]to give you **Israelites** this message:
25. 3 to see the land of **Israel** devastated, to see the people of
25. 6 You despised the land of **Israel.**
25.14 My people **Israel** will take revenge on Edom for me,
27.17 **Judah and Israel** paid for your goods with wheat, honey,
28.24 the surrounding nations that treated **Israel** with scorn
28.24 will ever again be like thorns and briars to hurt **Israel.**
28.25 will bring back the **people of Israel** from the nations where
28.25 The **people of Israel** will live in their own land, the land
28.26 who treated them with scorn, and **Israel** will be secure.
29. 6 The Lord says, "The **Israelites** relied on you Egyptians for
29.16 **Israel** will never again depend on them for help.
29.16 Egypt's fate will remind **Israel** how wrong it was to rely on
29.16 Then **Israel** will know that I am the Sovereign Lord."
29.21 I will make the **people of Israel** strong and let you,
33. 7 I am making you a watchman for the nation of **Israel.**
33.10 "Mortal man," he said, "repeat to the **Israelites** what they
33.11 **Israel,** stop the evil you are doing.
33.12 mortal man, tell the **Israelites** that when a good man sins,
33.20 But **Israel,** you say that what I do isn't right.
33.24 in the ruined cities of the land of **Israel** are saying:
33.28 The mountains of **Israel** will be so wild that no one will
34. 2 "Mortal man," he said, "denounce the rulers of **Israel.**
34. 2 You are doomed, you shepherds of **Israel!**
34.13 mountains and the streams of **Israel** and will feed them in
34.14 valleys and in all the green pastures of the land of **Israel.**
34.30 will know that I protect **Israel** and that they are my people.
35. 5 "You were **Israel's** constant enemy and let her people be
35.10 the two nations, **Judah and Israel,** together with their lands,
35.12 contempt that the mountains of **Israel** were desolate and that
35.15 you rejoiced at the devastation of **Israel,** my own possession.
36. 1 speak to the mountains of **Israel** and tell them to listen to
36. 2 **Israel's** enemies gloated and said, 'Now those ancient hills
36. 3 captured and plundered the mountains of **Israel,**
36. 3 all of them insulted **Israel.**
36. 6 "So prophesy to the land of **Israel;**
36. 8 But on the mountains of **Israel** the trees will again grow
36. 8 again grow leaves and bear fruit for you, my people **Israel.**
36.12 will bring you, my people **Israel,** back to live again in the
36.17 he said, "when the **Israelites** were living in their land,
36.21 my holy name, since the **Israelites** brought disgrace on it
36.22 give the **Israelites** the message that I, the Sovereign Lord,
36.22 for the sake of you **Israelites,** but for the sake of my
36.32 **Israel,** I want you to know that I am not doing all

Ezek	36.37	will once again let the **Israelites** ask me for help, and I
	37.11	me, "Mortal man, the **people of Israel** are like these bones.
	37.12	So prophesy to my people **Israel** and tell them that I,
	37.12	take them out and bring them back to the land of **Israel.**
	37.16	stick and write on it the words, 'The kingdom of **Israel.'**
	37.19	to take the stick representing **Israel** and put it with the
	37.22	into one nation in the land, on the mountains of **Israel.**
	37.28	that I, the Lord, have chosen **Israel** to be my own people."
	38. 8	will invade the mountains of **Israel,** which were desolate and
	38.14	while my people **Israel** live in security, you will set out
	38.16	You will attack my people **Israel** like a storm moving
	38.17	my servants, the prophets of **Israel,** that in days to come
	38.17	I would bring someone to attack **Israel."**
	38.18	"On the day when Gog invades **Israel,** I will be furious.
	38.19	day there will be a severe earthquake in the land of **Israel.**
	39. 2	of the far north until he comes to the mountains of **Israel.**
	39. 4	dead on the mountains of **Israel,** and I will let their bodies
	39. 7	make sure that my people **Israel** know my holy name,
	39. 7	will know that I, the Lord, am the Holy God of **Israel."**
	39. 9	live in the cities of **Israel** will go out and collect the
	39.11	Gog a burial-ground there in **Israel,** in Travellers' Valley,
	39.12	will take the **Israelites** seven months to bury all the corpses
	39.17	feast on the mountains of **Israel,** where they can eat meat
	39.22	The **Israelites** will know from then on that I am the Lord
	39.23	nations will know that the **Israelites** went into exile because
	39.25	the **people of Israel,** and make them prosperous again.
	39.29	my spirit on the **people of Israel** and never again turn away
	40. 2	me to the land of **Israel** and put me on a high
	40. 4	You are to tell the **people of Israel** everything you see."
	43. 2	the dazzling light of the presence of the God of **Israel.**
	43. 7	live here among the **people of Israel** and rule over them for
	43. 7	Neither the **people of Israel** nor their kings will ever again
	43.10	"Mortal man, tell the **people of Israel** about the Temple,
	44. 2	because I, the Lord God of **Israel,** have entered through it.
	44. 6	"Tell those rebellious **people of Israel** that I, the Sovereign Lord,
	44. 9	even a foreigner who lives among the **people of Israel."**
	44.10	of the **people of Israel,** deserted me and worshipped idols.
	44.12	of idols for the **people of Israel** and in this way led
	44.15	when the rest of the **people of Israel** turned away from me.
	44.22	is to marry only an **Israelite** virgin or the widow of another
	44.28	of what I have given **Israel** to be handed down from one
	44.28	They are not to hold property in **Israel;**
	44.29	to receive everything in **Israel** that is set apart for me.
	45. 6	for a city where any of the **people of Israel** may live.
	45. 7	length of one of the areas allotted to the tribes of **Israel.**
	45. 8	have in the land of **Israel,** so that he will no longer
	45. 8	let the rest of the country belong to the tribes of **Israel.**
	45. 9	Lord said, "You have sinned too long, you rulers of **Israel!**
	45.13	1 sheep out of every 200 from the meadows of **Israel**
	45.16	must take these offerings to the ruling prince of **Israel.**
	45.17	for the whole nation of **Israel** at the New Moon Festivals,
	45.17	to take away the sins of the **people of Israel."**
	47.18	boundary between the land of **Israel** on the west and Gilead
	47.22	be treated like full **Israelite** citizens and are to draw lots
	47.22	for shares of the land along with the tribes of **Israel.**
	48.11	join the rest of the **Israelites** in doing wrong, as the other
	48.29	divided into sections for the tribes of **Israel** to possess."
Dan	1. 3	to select from among the **Israelite** exiles some young men of
	9. 7	and of all the **Israelites** whom you scattered in countries near
	9.11	All **Israel** broke your laws and refused to listen to what
	9.20	the sins of my people **Israel,** and pleading with the Lord my
	10.20	no one to help me except Michael, **Israel's** guardian angel.
Hos	1. 1	kings of Judah, and Jeroboam son of Jehoash was **king of Israel.**
	1. 2	Lord first spoke to **Israel** through Hosea, he said to Hosea,
	1. 4	before I punish the **king of Israel** for the murders that his
	1. 5	I will at that time destroy **Israel's** military power."
	1. 6	no longer show love to the **people of Israel** or forgive them.
	1. 9	'Not-My-People,' because the **people of Israel** are not my people,
	1.10	The **people of Israel** will become like the sand of the sea,
	1.11	The people of Judah and the **people of Israel** will be reunited.
	2. 1	So call your **fellow-Israelites** "God's People"
	2.19	**Israel,** I will make you my wife;
	2.21	that time I will answer the prayers of my people **Israel.**
	3. 1	I still love the **people of Israel,** even though they turn to
	3. 4	just this way the **people of Israel** will have to live for
	3. 5	will come when the **people of Israel** will once again turn to
	4. 1	Listen, **Israel,** to what he says:
	4. 5	I am going to destroy **Israel,** your mother.
	4.15	"Even though you **people of Israel** are unfaithful to me,
	4.16	The **people of Israel** are as stubborn as mules.
	4.17	The **people of Israel** are under the spell of idols.
	5. 1	Pay attention, **people of Israel!**
	5. 3	I know what **Israel** is like—she cannot hide from me.
	5. 5	The arrogance of the **people of Israel** cries out against them.
	5. 9	The day of punishment is coming, and **Israel** will be ruined.
	5. 9	**People of Israel,** this will surely happen!
	5.10	leaders of Judah have invaded **Israel** and stolen land from her.
	5.11	**Israel** is suffering oppression;
	5.12	I will bring destruction on **Israel** and ruin on the people
	5.13	"When **Israel** saw how sick she was and when Judah saw
	5.13	saw her own wounds, then **Israel** went to Assyria to ask the
	5.14	I will attack the people of **Israel and Judah** like a lion.
	6. 4	But the Lord says, **"Israel and Judah,** what am I going to
	6.10	I have seen a horrible thing in **Israel:**
	7. 1	want to heal my people **Israel** and make them prosperous again,
	7. 8	The Lord says, "The **people of Israel** are like a
	7.10	The arrogance of the **people of Israel** cries out against them.
	7.11	**Israel** flits about like a silly pigeon;
	8. 6	An **Israelite** craftsman made the idol, and it is not a god
	8. 8	**Israel** has become like any other nation and is as useless
	8. 9	Stubborn as wild donkeys, the **people of Israel** go their own way.
Hos	8.11	"The more altars the **people of Israel** build for removing sin,
	8.14	"The **people of Israel** have built palaces, but they
	9. 1	**People of Israel,** stop celebrating your festivals like pagans.
	9. 3	The **people of Israel** will not remain in the Lord's land,
	9. 7	When that happens, **Israel** will know it!
	9. 8	God has sent me as a prophet to warn his people **Israel.**
	9.10	"When I first found **Israel,** it was like finding grapes growing
	9.11	**Israel's** greatness will fly away like a bird,
	9.16	The **people of Israel** are like a plant whose roots have
	10. 1	The **people of Israei** were like a grapevine that was full
	10. 6	**Israel** will be disgraced and put to shame because of the
	10. 8	where the **people of Israel** worship idols, will be destroyed.
	10. 9	The Lord says, "The **people of Israel** have not stopped
	10.11	**"Israel** was once like a well-trained young cow, ready
	10.11	I made Judah pull the plough and **Israel** pull the harrow.
	10.15	As soon as the battle begins, the **king of Israel** will die."
	11. 1	"When **Israel** was a child, I loved him and called him out
	11. 3	Yet I was the one who taught **Israel** to walk.
	11. 8	"How can I give you up, **Israel?**
	11. 9	I will not destroy **Israel** again.
	11.12	The Lord says, "The **people of Israel** have surrounded
	12. 1	Everything that the **people of Israel** do from morning to
	12. 2	is also going to punish **Israel** for the way her people act.
	12. 7	The Lord says, "The **people of Israel** are as dishonest as
	12.13	prophet to rescue the **people of Israel** from slavery in Egypt
	12.14	The **people of Israel** have made the Lord bitterly angry;
	13. 1	of Ephraim spoke, the other tribes of **Israel** were afraid;
	13. 9	"I will destroy you, **people of Israel!**
	13.12	**"Israel's** sin and guilt are on record, and the records
	13.13	**Israel** has a chance to live, but is too foolish to take
	13.15	Even though **Israel** flourishes like weeds, I will send a
	14. 1	Return to the Lord your God, **people of Israel.**
	14. 5	will be to the **people of Israel** like rain in a dry
	14. 8	The **people of Israel** will have nothing more to do with idols;
Joel	2.27	Then, **Israel,** you will know that I am among you, and
	3. 2	They have scattered the **Israelites** in foreign countries
	3. 2	and divided up **Israel,**
	3.17	"Then, **Israel,** you will know that I am the Lord your God.
Amos	1. 1	son of Jehoash was **king of Israel,**
	1. 1	God revealed to Amos all these things about **Israel.**
	1.11	hunted down their brothers, the **Israelites,** and showed them
	2. 6	The Lord says, "The **people of Israel** have sinned again and again,
	2.11	Isn't this true, **people of Israel?**
	3. 1	**People of Israel,** listen to this message which the Lord
	3.14	when I punish the **people of Israel** for their sins, I will
	4. 4	The Sovereign Lord says, **"People of Israel,** go to the
	4.12	"So then, **people of Israel,** I am going to punish you.
	5. 1	Listen, **people of Israel,** to this funeral song which I
	5. 2	Virgin **Israel** has fallen, Never to rise again!
	5. 3	Lord says, "A city in **Israel** sends out a thousand soldiers,
	5. 4	Lord says to the **people of Israel,** "Come to me, and you
	5. 6	go, he will sweep down like fire on the **people of Israel.**
	5.25	**"People of Israel,** I did not demand sacrifices and
	6. 1	men of this great nation **Israel,** you to whom the people go
	6. 2	Were they any better than the kingdoms of **Judah and Israel?**
	6. 6	perfumes, but you do not mourn over the ruin of **Israel.**
	6. 8	"I hate the pride of the **people of Israel;**
	6.14	God Almighty himself says, **"People of Israel,** I am going to
	7. 9	The holy places of **Israel** will be left in ruins.
	7.10	of Bethel, then sent a report to King Jeroboam of **Israel:**
	7.11	in battle, and the **people of Israel** will be taken away from
	7.15	and ordered me to come and prophesy to his people **Israel.**
	7.16	prophesying, to stop raving against the **people of Israel.**
	7.17	And the **people of Israel** will certainly be taken away from
	8. 1	Lord said to me, "The end has come for my people **Israel.**
	8. 7	Lord, the God of **Israel,** has sworn, "I will never forget
	9. 7	The Lord says, **"People of Israel,** I think as much of the
	9. 8	watching this sinful kingdom of **Israel,** and I will destroy it
	9. 9	command and shake the **people of Israel** like corn in a sieve.
	9.12	And so the **people of Israel** will conquer what is left of
Obad	19	**Israelites** will possess the territory of Ephraim and Samaria;
	20	exiles from northern **Israel** will return and conquer Phoenicia
Mic	1. 5	will happen because the **people of Israel** have sinned and
	1. 5	Who is to blame for **Israel's** rebellion?
	1.13	imitated the sins of **Israel** and so caused Jerusalem to sin.
	1.14	The **kings of Israel** will get no help from the town of
	1.15	The leaders of **Israel** will go and hide in the cave at
	2. 7	Do you think the **people of Israel** are under a curse?
	2.12	gather you together, all you **people of Israel** that are left.
	3. 1	Listen, you rulers of **Israel!**
	3. 8	courage to tell the **people of Israel** what their sins are.
	3. 9	to me, you rulers of **Israel,** you that hate justice and turn
	4. 2	up the hill of the Lord, to the Temple of **Israel's** God.
	5. 1	They are attacking the leader of **Israel!**
	5. 2	bring a ruler for **Israel,** whose family line goes back to
	5. 7	The **people of Israel** who survive will be like refreshing
	5. 9	**Israel** will conquer her enemies and destroy them all.
	6. 1	Listen to the Lord's case against **Israel.**
	6. 2	He is going to bring an accusation against **Israel.**
Nah	1.12	This is what the Lord says to his people **Israel:**
	2. 2	to restore the glory of **Israel,** as it was before her enemies
Zeph	2. 9	living Lord, the God of **Israel,** I swear that Moab and Ammon
	3.13	The **people of Israel** who survive will do no wrong to anyone,
	3.14	Sing and shout for joy, **people of Israel!**
	3.15	The Lord, the **king of Israel,** is with you;
Zech	1.19	world powers that have scattered the people of Judah, **Israel,**
	8.13	People of **Judah and Israel!**
	8.13	same disasters fall on you that fell on **Judah and Israel!'**
	8.13	'May you receive the same blessings that came to **Judah and Israel!'**
	9. 1	Not only the tribes of **Israel,** but also the capital of Syria

Zech 9.10 will remove the war-chariots from **Israel** and take the horses
9.13 use Judah like a soldier's bow and **Israel** like the arrows.
10. 6 I will rescue the **people of Israel.**
10. 7 The **people of Israel** will be strong like soldiers, happy
11.14 and the unity of **Judah and Israel** was shattered.
12. 1 This is a message about **Israel** from the Lord, the Lord who
Mal 1. 1 that the Lord gave Malachi to tell the **people of Israel.**
1. 5 The **people of Israel** are going to see this with their own
1. 5 say, "The Lord is mighty even outside the land of **Israel!"**
2. 9 turn, will make the **people of Israel** despise you because you
2.12 remove from the community of **Israel** those who did this,
2.16 "I hate divorce," says the Lord God of **Israel.**
4. 4 him at Mount Sinai for all the **people of Israel** to obey.
Mt 1. 6 the time when the **people of Israel** were taken into exile in
2. 6 you will come a leader who will guide my people **Israel.'"**
2.20 back to the land of **Israel,** because those who tried to kill
2.21 took the child and his mother, and went back to **Israel.**
8.10 I have never found anyone in **Israel** with faith like this.
9.33 "We have never seen anything like this in **Israel!"**
10. 6 are to go to the lost sheep of the **people of Israel.**
10.23 in all the towns of **Israel** before the Son of Man comes.
15.24 been sent only to the lost sheep of the **people of Israel."**
15.31 and they praised the God of **Israel.**
19.28 also sit on thrones, to rule the twelve tribes of **Israel.**
27. 9 coins, the amount the **people of Israel** had agreed to pay for
27.42 Isn't he the **king of Israel?**
Mk 12.29 'Listen, **Israel!**
15.32 see the Messiah, the **king of Israel,** come down from the
Lk 1.16 back many of the **people of Israel** to the Lord their God.
1.54 ancestors, and has come to the help of his servant **Israel.**
1.68 "Let us praise the Lord, the God of **Israel!**
1.80 the day when he appeared publicly to the **people of Israel.**
2.25 God-fearing man and was waiting for **Israel** to be saved.
2.32 to the Gentiles and bring glory to your people **Israel."**
2.34 God for the destruction and the salvation of many in **Israel.**
4.25 there were many widows in **Israel** during the time of Elijah,
4.26 not sent to anyone in **Israel,** but only to a widow living
4.27 skin-disease who lived in **Israel** during the time of the prophet
7. 9 I have never found faith like this, not even in **Israel!"**
22.30 sit on thrones to rule over the twelve tribes of **Israel.**
24.21 he would be the one who was going to set **Israel** free!
Jn 1.31 water in order to make him known to the **people of Israel."**
1.47 to him, he said about him, "Here is a real **Israelite;**
1.49 You are the **King of Israel!"**
3.10 "You are a great teacher in **Israel,** and you don't know this?
12.13 God bless the **King of Israel!"**
Acts 1. 6 "Lord, will you at this time give the Kingdom back to **Israel?"**
2.22 "Listen to these words, **fellow-Israelites!**
2.36 "All the **people of Israel,** then, are to know for sure
3.12 to them, **"Fellow-Israelites,** why are you surprised at this,
4.10 know, and all the **people of Israel** should know, that this
4.27 the Gentiles and the **people of Israel** against Jesus, your holy
5.31 Saviour, to give the **people of Israel** the opportunity to repent
5.35 he said to the Council, **"Fellow-Israelites,** be careful what
7.23 to find out how his **fellow-Israelites** were being treated.
7.26 next day he saw two **Israelites** fighting, and he tried to
7.26 'Listen, men,' he said, 'you are **fellow-Israelites;**
7.35 "Moses is the one who was rejected by the **people of Israel.**
7.37 who said to the **people of Israel,** 'God will send you a
7.38 who was with the **people of Israel** assembled in the desert;
7.42 **'People of Israel!**
9.15 known to Gentiles and kings and to the **people of Israel.**
10.36 he sent to the **people of Israel,** proclaiming the Good News
10.37 throughout the land of **Israel,** beginning in Galilee after John
10.39 that he did in the land of **Israel** and in Jerusalem.
13.16 **"Fellow-Israelites** and all Gentiles here who worship God:
13.17 The God of the **people of Israel** chose our ancestors and
13.23 the Saviour of the **people of Israel,** as he had promised.
13.24 preached to all the **people of Israel** that they should turn
13.26 "My **fellow-Israelites,** descendants of Abraham, and all Gentiles here who worship God:
13.31 They are now witnesses for him to the **people of Israel.**
13.38 want you to know, my **fellow-Israelites,** that it is through
19. 4 and he told the **people of Israel** to believe in the one
21.28 "Men of **Israel!"**
21.28 teaching everyone against the **people of Israel,** the Law of Moses,
22. 1 "My **fellow-Israelites,** listen to me as I make my defence before you!"
23. 1 Paul looked straight at the Council and said, "My **fellow-Israelites!**
23. 5 Paul answered, "My **fellow-Israelites,** I did not know that
23. 6 Pharisees, he called out in the Council, **"Fellow-Israelites!**
26.17 rescue you from the **people of Israel** and from the Gentiles
28.17 he said to them, "My **fellow-Israelites,** even though I did
28.20 for the sake of him for whom the **people of Israel** hope."
Rom 9. 6 for not all the **people of Israel** are the people of God.
9.27 And Isaiah exclaims about **Israel:**
9.27 "Even if the **people of Israel** are as many as the grains
10.19 Did the **people of Israel** not understand?
10.21 But concerning **Israel** he says, "All day long I held out
11. 1 I myself am an **Israelite,** a descendant of Abraham, a member
11. 2 says in the passage where Elijah pleads with God against **Israel:**
11. 7 The **people of Israel** did not find what they were looking for.
11.25 the stubbornness of the **people of Israel** is not permanent,
11.26 And this is how all **Israel** will be saved.
1 Cor 10.18 Consider the **people of Israel;**
2 Cor 3. 7 so strong that the **people of Israel** could not keep their
3.13 face so that the **people of Israel** would not see the
11.22 Are they **Israelites?**
Phil 3. 5 I am an **Israelite** by birth, of the tribe of Benjamin,
Heb 7. 5 a tenth from the **people of Israel,** that is, from their own
7.11 priesthood that the Law was given to the **people of Israel.**
Heb 8. 8 new covenant with the **people of Israel** and with the people
8.10 will make with the **people of Israel** in the days to come,
11.22 departure of the **Israelites** from Egypt, and leave instructions
11.28 Angel of Death would not kill the first-born sons of the **Israelites.**
11.29 was faith that made the **Israelites** able to cross the Red Sea
11.30 Jericho fall down after the **Israelites** had marched round them
11.31 for she gave the **Israelite** spies a friendly welcome.
12.18 not come, as the **people of Israel** came, to what you can
Jas 2.25 by welcoming the **Israelite** spies and helping them to escape
Jude 5 Lord once rescued the **people of Israel** from Egypt, but afterwards
Rev 2.14 how to lead the **people of Israel** into sin by persuading them
7. 4 from the twelve tribes of **Israel,** [5-8]twelve thousand from each
21.12 the names of the twelve tribes of the **people of Israel.**

ISRAELITE see **ISRAEL (2)**

ISSACHAR (1)

Jacob and Leah's son, the tribe descended from him, and its territory.

Gen 30.18 so she named her son **Issachar.**
35.23 were Reuben (Jacob's eldest son), Simeon, Levi, Judah, **Issachar,**
46.13 **Issachar** and his sons:
49.14 **"Issachar** is no better than a donkey That lies stretched
Ex 1. 3 Reuben, Simeon, Levi, Judah, [3]**Issachar,** Zebulun, Benjamin,
Num 10.15 command of the tribe of **Issachar,** [16]and Eliab son of Helon
Deut 27.12 Simeon, Levi, Judah, **Issachar,** Joseph, and Benjamin.
33.18 About the tribes of Zebulun and **Issachar** he said:
33.18 trade on the sea, And may **Issachar's** wealth increase at home.
Josh 17.10 Asher was to the north-west, and **Issachar** to the north-east.
17.11 Within the territories of **Issachar** and Asher, Manasseh
19.17 assignment made was for the families of the tribe of **Issachar.**
19.23 which the families of the tribe of **Issachar** received as their
21. 6 thirteen cities from the territories of **Issachar,** Asher,
21.28 From the territory of **Issachar** they received four cities:
Judg 5.15 The leaders of **Issachar** came with Deborah;
5.15 yes, **Issachar** came and Barak too, and they followed him
10. 1 was from the tribe of **Issachar** and lived at Shamir in the
1 Kgs 4.17 the territory of **Issachar** [18]Shimei son of Ela:
15.27 Ahijah, of the tribe of **Issachar,** plotted against Nadab and
1 Chr 2. 1 Reuben, Simeon, Levi, Judah, **Issachar,** Zebulun,
6.62 towns in the territories of **Issachar,** Asher, Naphtali, and
6.72 In the territory of **Issachar:**
7. 1 **Issachar** had four sons:
7. 5 families of the tribe of **Issachar** listed 87,000 men eligible
12.40 as the northern tribes of **Issachar,** Zebulun, and Naphtali,
2 Chr 30.18 Manasseh, **Issachar,** and Zebulun had not performed the
Ezek 48.23 Benjamin Simeon **Issachar** Zebulun Gad
48.30 those in the south wall, after Simeon, **Issachar,** and
Rev 7. 5 Manasseh, Simeon, Levi, **Issachar,** Zebulun, Joseph, and Benjamin.
also Num 1.5 Num 1.20 Num 2.3 Num 7.12 Num 13.3 Num 26.23 Num 34.19 1 Chr 12.23 1 Chr 27.16

ISSUE

2 Chr 36.22 He prompted Cyrus to **issue** the following command and send it
Ezra 1. 1 He prompted Cyrus to **issue** the following command and send it
4.21 you are to **issue** orders that those men are to stop
Esth 1.19 If it please Your Majesty, **issue** a royal proclamation
3. 9 If it please Your Majesty, **issue** a decree that they are to
8. 5 seems right to you, please **issue** a proclamation to prevent
Dan 6. 7 Your Majesty should **issue** an order and enforce it strictly.
6. 8 So let Your Majesty **issue** this order and sign it,

ITALIAN REGIMENT

Acts 10. 1 a captain in the Roman regiment called "The **Italian Regiment."**

ITCH

Deut 28.27 with scabs, and you will **itch,** but there will be no cure.
2 Tim 4. 3 teachers who will tell them what they are **itching** to hear.

ITHAMAR

Aaron's son, ancestor of many priests at Jerusalem.

Ex 6.23 she bore him Nadab, Abihu, Eleazar, and **Ithamar.**
28. 1 brother Aaron and his sons, Nadab, Abihu, Eleazar, and **Ithamar.**
38.21 worked under the direction of **Ithamar** son of Aaron the priest.
Lev 10. 6 sons Eleazar and **Ithamar,** "Do not leave your hair uncombed
10.12 sons, Eleazar and **Ithamar,** "Take the grain-offering that is
10.16 him angry with Eleazar and **Ithamar,** and he demanded,
Num 3. 2 Nadab, the eldest, Abihu, Eleazar, and **Ithamar.**
3. 4 Eleazar and **Ithamar** served as priests during Aaron's lifetime.
4.28 them out under the direction of **Ithamar** son of Aaron
4.33 them out under the direction of **Ithamar** son of Aaron
7. 8 was to be done under the direction of **Ithamar** son of Aaron.
26.60 Aaron had four sons, Nadab, Abihu, Eleazar, and **Ithamar.**
1 Chr 6. 3 Nadab, Abihu, Eleazar, and **Ithamar.**
24. 1 Nadab, Abihu, Eleazar, and **Ithamar.**
24. 2 so their brothers Eleazar and **Ithamar** became priests.
24. 3 of Eleazar, and by Ahimelech, a descendant of **Ithamar.**
24. 4 while the descendants of **Ithamar** were organized into eight;
24. 5 of both Eleazar and **Ithamar,** assignments were made by drawing
24. 6 descendants of Eleazar and of **Ithamar** took turns in drawing
Ezra 8. 2 Daniel, of the clan of **Ithamar** Hattush son of Shecaniah,

IVORY

1 Kgs 10.18 of it was covered with **ivory** and the rest of it was
10.22 years his fleet would return, bringing gold, silver, **ivory,**
22.39 his palace decorated with **ivory** and all the cities he built,
2 Chr 9.17 of it was covered with **ivory** and the rest of it was
9.21 years his fleet would return, bringing gold, silver, **ivory,**
Ps 45. 8 musicians entertain you in palaces decorated with **ivory.**
Song 5.14 His body is like smooth **ivory,** with sapphires set in it.
7. 4 Your neck is like a tower of **ivory.**
Ezek 27. 6 your deck out of pine from Cyprus And inlaid it with **ivory.**
27.15 many coastal lands gave you **ivory** and ebony in exchange for
Amos 3.15 The houses decorated with **ivory** will fall in ruins;
Rev 18.12 kinds of objects made of **ivory** and of expensive wood, of

JAB

2 Kgs 18.21 a reed as a walking-stick—it would break and **jab** your hand.
Is 36. 6 a reed as a walking-stick—it would break and **jab** your hand.

JABESH (1)

Town in Gilead, e. of R. Jordan.

Judg 21. 8 found out that no one from **Jabesh** in Gilead had been there;
21. 9 the roll call of the army no one from **Jabesh** had responded.
21.10 and kill everyone in **Jabesh,** including the women and children.
21.12 Among the people in **Jabesh** they found four hundred young
21.14 gave them the girls from **Jabesh** whom they had not killed.
1 Sam 11. 1 army against the town of **Jabesh** in the territory of Gilead
11. 1 The men of **Jabesh** said to Nahash, "Make a treaty with us,
11. 3 The leaders of **Jabesh** said, "Give us seven days to send
11. 5 They told him what the messengers from **Jabesh** had reported.
11. 9 said to the messengers from **Jabesh,** "Tell your people that
11. 9 people of **Jabesh** received the message, they were overjoyed
31.11 the people of **Jabesh** in Gilead heard what the Philistines
31.12 from the wall, brought them back to **Jabesh,** and burnt them
2 Sam 2. 4 heard that the people of **Jabesh** in Gilead had buried Saul,
21.12 and of his son Jonathan from the people of **Jabesh** in Gilead.
1 Chr 10.11 the people of **Jabesh** in Gilead heard what the Philistines
10.12 the bodies of Saul and his sons and took them to **Jabesh.**

JACKAL

A small wild animal like a fox.

Job 30.29 sad and lonely as the cries of a **jackal** or an ostrich.
Is 13.22 and palaces will echo with the cries of hyenas and **jackals.**
34.13 and walled towns, and **jackals** and owls will live in them.
35. 7 Where **jackals** used to live, marsh grass and reeds will grow.
43.20 **jackals** and ostriches will praise me when I make rivers flow
Jer 9.11 make Jerusalem a pile of ruins, a place where **jackals** live;
10.22 cities of Judah into a desert, a place where **jackals** live."
14. 6 donkeys stand on the hill-tops and pant for breath like **jackals;**
49.33 be made a desert for ever, a place where only **jackals** live.
Lam 5.18 Zion lies lonely and deserted, and wild **jackals** prowl through
Mic 1. 8 I will howl like a **jackal** and wail like an ostrich.
Mal 1. 3 Esau's hill-country and abandoned the land to **jackals."**

JACOB (1)

Isaac and Rebecca's son, also known as Israel, ancestor of the Israelites.

Gen 25.19-26 **The birth of Esau and Jacob**
27-34 **Esau sells his rights as the first-born son**
27.1-29 **Isaac blesses Jacob**
30-45 **Esau begs for Isaac's blessing**
27.46–28.5 **Isaac sends Jacob to Laban**
28.6-9 **Esau takes another wife**
10-22 **Jacob's dream at Bethel**
29.1-14 **Jacob arrives at Laban's home**
15-30 **Jacob serves Laban for Rachel and Leah**
29.31–30.24 **The children born to Jacob**
30.25-43 **Jacob's bargain with Laban**
31.1-21 **Jacob flees from Laban**
22-42 **Laban pursues Jacob**
43-55 **The agreement between Jacob and Laban**
32.1-21 **Jacob prepares to meet Esau**
22-32 **Jacob wrestles at Peniel**
33.1-20 **Jacob meets Esau**
34.1-31 **The rape of Dinah**
35.1-15 **God blesses Jacob at Bethel**
16-21 **The death of Rachel**
22-26 **The sons of Jacob**
27-29 **The death of Isaac**
36.1-19 **The descendants of Esau**
37.1-11 **Joseph and his brothers**
12-36 **Joseph is sold and taken to Egypt**
42.1-24 **Joseph's brothers go to Egypt to buy corn**
25-38 **Joseph's brothers return to Canaan**
43.1-34 **Joseph's brothers return to Egypt with Benjamin**
45.1-28 **Joseph tells his brothers who he is**
46.1-27 **Jacob and his family go to Egypt**
46.28–47.12 **Jacob and his family in Egypt**
47.27-31 **Jacob's last request**
48.1-22 **Jacob blesses Ephraim and Manasseh**
49.1-28 **The last words of Jacob**
49.29–50.14 **The death and burial of Jacob**

Gen 50.12 So **Jacob's** sons did as he had commanded them;
50.24 land he solemnly promised to Abraham, Isaac, and **Jacob."**
Ex 1. 1 The sons of **Jacob** who went to Egypt with him, each with
1. 5 number of these people directly descended from **Jacob** was seventy.
Ex 2.24 and remembered his covenant with Abraham, Isaac, and **Jacob.**
3. 6 God of your ancestors, the God of Abraham, Isaac, and **Jacob."**
3.15 the God of Abraham, Isaac, and **Jacob,** have sent you to them.
3.16 the God of Abraham, Isaac, and **Jacob,** appeared to you.
4. 5 God of Abraham, Isaac, and **Jacob,** has appeared to you."
6. 3 Abraham, to Isaac, and to **Jacob** as Almighty God, but I did
6. 8 I solemnly promised to give to Abraham, Isaac, and **Jacob;**
6.14 Reuben, **Jacob's** first-born, had four sons:
19. 3 and told him to say to the Israelites, **Jacob's** descendants:
28. 9 the twelve sons of **Jacob,** [10] in the order of their birth,
28.11 names of the sons of **Jacob,** and mount the stones in gold
28.21 one of the sons of **Jacob,** to represent the tribes of Israel.
32.13 Remember your servants Abraham, Isaac, and **Jacob.**
33. 1 give to Abraham, Isaac, and **Jacob** and to their descendants.
39. 6 engraved with the names of the twelve sons of **Jacob.**
39.14 one of the sons of **Jacob,** in order to represent the twelve
Lev 26.42 my covenant with **Jacob** and with Isaac and with Abraham,
Num 1.20 beginning with the tribe of Reuben, **Jacob's** eldest son.
26. 5 The tribe of Reuben (Reuben was the eldest son of **Jacob):**
32.11 the land that I promised to Abraham, Isaac, and **Jacob.'**
Deut 1. 8 Abraham, Isaac, and **Jacob,** and to their descendants.
6.10 your ancestors, Abraham, Isaac, and **Jacob,** he will give you
9. 5 that he made to your ancestors, Abraham, Isaac, and **Jacob.**
9.27 your servants, Abraham, Isaac, and **Jacob,** and do not pay any
29.13 promised you and your ancestors, Abraham, Isaac, and **Jacob.**
30.20 to give your ancestors, Abraham, Isaac, and **Jacob."**
32. 9 nation a god, [9] but **Jacob's** descendants he chose for himself.
33.28 So **Jacob's** descendants live in peace, secure in a land
34. 4 I promised Abraham, Isaac, and **Jacob** I would give
Josh 24. 4 I gave him Isaac, [4] and to Isaac I gave **Jacob** and Esau.
24. 4 his possession, but your ancestor **Jacob** and his children
24.32 the piece of land that **Jacob** had bought from the sons of
Judg 18.29 Laish to Dan, after their ancestor Dan, the son of **Jacob.**
Ruth 4.11 like Rachel and Leah, who bore many children to **Jacob.**
1 Sam 12. 8 When **Jacob** and his family went to Egypt and the Egyptians
2 Sam 23. 1 great, whom the God of **Jacob** chose to be king, and who
1 Kgs 18.31 named after the sons of **Jacob,** the man to whom the Lord
18.36 God of Abraham, Isaac, and **Jacob,** prove now that you are the
2 Kgs 13.23 because of his covenant with Abraham, Isaac, and **Jacob.**
17.34 he gave to the descendants of **Jacob,** whom he named Israel.
1 Chr 1.34 Abraham's son Isaac had two sons, Esau and **Jacob.**
2. 1 **Jacob** had twelve sons:
5. 1 are the descendants of Reuben, the eldest of **Jacob's** sons.
5. 3 Reuben, the eldest of **Jacob's** sons, had four sons:
6.33 His family line went back to **Jacob** as follows:
6.38 Assir, Ebiasaph, Korah, [38] Izhar, Kohath, Levi, **Jacob.**
7.29 places where the descendants of Joseph son of **Jacob** lived.
16.12 descendants of **Jacob,** God's servant, descendants of Israel,
16.17 Lord made a covenant with **Jacob,** one that will last for ever.
29.10 "Lord God of our ancestor **Jacob,** may you be praised for
29.18 our ancestors Abraham, Isaac, and **Jacob,** keep such devotion
2 Chr 30. 6 God of Abraham, Isaac, and **Jacob,** and he will return to you.
Ps 20. 1 May the God of **Jacob** protect you!
22.23 Honour him, you descendants of **Jacob!**
24. 6 to God, who come into the presence of the God of **Jacob.**
46. 7 the God of **Jacob** is our refuge.
46.11 the God of **Jacob** is our refuge.
68.26 praise the Lord, all you descendants of **Jacob!"**
75. 9 speaking of the God of **Jacob** or singing praises to him.
76. 6 threatened them, O God of **Jacob,** the horses and their riders
77.15 saved your people, the descendants of **Jacob** and of Joseph.
78. 5 of Israel and commandments to the descendants of **Jacob.**
81. 1 sing praise to the God of **Jacob!**
81. 4 is the law in Israel, an order from the God of **Jacob.**
84. 8 Listen, O God of **Jacob!**
105. 5 you descendants of **Jacob,** the man he chose:
105.10 Lord made a covenant with **Jacob,** one that will last for ever.
105.23 Then **Jacob** went to Egypt and settled in that country.
114. 1 left Egypt, when **Jacob's** descendants left that foreign land,
114. 7 presence of the God of **Jacob,** [8] who changes rocks into pools
132. 2 promised, the vow he made to you, the Mighty God of **Jacob:**
132. 5 place for the Lord, a home for the Mighty God of **Jacob."**
135. 4 He chose **Jacob** for himself, the people of Israel for his own.
146. 5 who has the God of **Jacob** to help him and who depends
Is 2. 5 Now, descendants of **Jacob,** let us walk in the light which
2. 6 O God, you have forsaken your people, the descendants of **Jacob!**
9. 8 on the kingdom of Israel, on the descendants of **Jacob.**
27. 6 the descendants of **Jacob,** will take root like a tree,
44. 1 Israel, my servant, my chosen people, the descendants of **Jacob.**
45.25 all the descendants of **Jacob,** and they will give me praise.
46. 3 "Listen to me, descendants of **Jacob,** all who are left of
58.14 and you will enjoy the land I gave to your ancestor, **Jacob.**
63.16 Our ancestors Abraham and **Jacob** do not acknowledge us, but
Jer 2. 4 Lord's message, you descendants of **Jacob,** you tribes of Israel.
5.20 "Tell the descendants of **Jacob,** tell the people of Judah:
9. 4 as deceitful as **Jacob,** and everyone slanders his friends.
10.16 The God of **Jacob** is not like them;
33.26 will maintain my covenant with **Jacob's** descendants and with
33.26 to rule over the descendants of Abraham, Isaac, and **Jacob.**
51.19 The God of **Jacob** is not like them;
Ezek 28.25 their own land, the land that I gave to my servant **Jacob.**
37.25 I gave to my servant **Jacob,** the land where their ancestors lived.
39.25 will be merciful to **Jacob's** descendants, the people of Israel,
Hos 12. 3 Their ancestor **Jacob** struggled with his twin brother Esau
12. 3 when **Jacob** grew up, he fought against God—[4] he fought
12. 4 Bethel God came to our ancestor **Jacob** and spoke with him.
12. 6 So now, descendants of **Jacob,** trust in your God and return
12.12 Our ancestor **Jacob** had to flee to Mesopotamia, where,
Amos 3.13 descendants of **Jacob,"** says the Sovereign Lord Almighty.
9. 8 But I will not destroy all the descendants of **Jacob.**
Obad 10 your brothers, the descendants of **Jacob,** you will be

Obad 17 The people of **Jacob** will possess the land that is theirs by
18 The people of **Jacob** and of Joseph will be like fire;
Mic 7.20 descendants of Abraham and of **Jacob,** as you promised our
Mal 1. 2 The Lord answers, "Esau and **Jacob** were brothers,
1. 2 but I have loved **Jacob** and his descendants, [3]and have hated
3. 6 so you, the descendants of **Jacob,** are not yet completely lost.
Mt 1. 2 Abraham, Isaac, **Jacob,** Judah and his brothers;
8.11 down with Abraham, Isaac, and **Jacob** at the feast in the
22.32 God of Abraham, the God of Isaac, and the God of **Jacob.'**
Mk 12.26 God of Abraham, the God of Isaac, and the God of **Jacob.'**
Lk 1.33 he will be the king of the descendants of **Jacob** for ever;
3.34 of Judah, [34]the son of **Jacob,** the son of Isaac, the son
13.28 you see Abraham, Isaac, and **Jacob,** and all the prophets in
20.37 God of Abraham, the God of Isaac, and the God of **Jacob.'**
Jn 4. 5 far from the field that **Jacob** had given to his son Joseph.
4. 6 **Jacob's** well was there, and Jesus, tired out by the journey,
4.12 It was our ancestor **Jacob** who gave us this well;
4.12 You don't claim to be greater than **Jacob,** do you?"
Acts 3.13 God of Abraham, Isaac, and **Jacob,** the God of our ancestors,
7. 8 Isaac circumcised his son **Jacob,**
7. 8 and **Jacob** circumcised his twelve sons,
7. 9 **"Jacob's** sons became jealous of their brother Joseph and sold him
7.12 find any food, [12]and when **Jacob** heard that there was corn
7.14 to his father **Jacob,** telling him and the whole family,
7.15 Then **Jacob** went to Egypt, where he and his sons died.
7.32 God of your ancestors, the God of Abraham, Isaac, and **Jacob.'**
7.46 allow him to provide a dwelling place for the God of **Jacob.**
Rom 9.13 As the scripture says, "I loved **Jacob,** but I hated Esau."
11.26 from Zion and remove all wickedness from the descendants of **Jacob.**
Heb 11. 9 tents, as did Isaac and **Jacob,** who received the same promise
11.20 made Isaac promise blessings for the future to **Jacob** and Esau.
11.21 It was faith that made **Jacob** bless each of the sons of

JAGGED

1 Sam 14. 4 camp, there were two large **jagged** rocks, one on each side of
Job 41.30 The scales on his belly are like **jagged** pieces of pottery;

JAIL

Gen 39.21 Joseph and blessed him, so that the **jailer** was pleased with
39.23 **jailer** did not have to look after anything for which Joseph
Job 7.20 Are you harmed by my sin, you **jailer?**
Mt 5.25 you over to the police, and you will be put in **jail.**
18.30 he had him thrown into **jail** until he should pay the debt.
18.34 he sent the servant to **jail** to be punished until he should
Lk 12.58 you over to the police, and you will be put in **jail.**
Acts 4. 3 and put them in **jail** until the next day, since it
5.18 They arrested the apostles and put them in the public **jail.**
5.23 "When we arrived at the **jail,** we found it locked up
8. 3 believers, both men and women, and threw them into **jail.**
12. 4 arrest Peter was put in **jail,** where he was handed over to
12. 5 So Peter was kept in **jail,** but the people of the church
16.23 thrown into jail, and the **jailer** was ordered to lock them up
16.24 receiving this order, the **jailer** threw them into the inner cell
16.27 The **jailer** woke up, and when he saw the prison doors open,
16.29 The **jailer** called for a light, rushed in, and fell trembling
16.33 of the night the **jailer** took them and washed their wounds;
16.36 So the **jailer** told Paul, "The officials have sent an order

JAIR (1)

Member of Manasseh's tribe, after whom the "Villages of Jair" were named.

Num 32.41 **Jair,** of the tribe of Manasseh, attacked
32.41 and captured some villages and named them "Villages of **Jair."**
Deut 3.14 **Jair,** from the tribe of Manasseh, took the entire region
3.14 himself, and they are still known as the villages of **Jair.)**
Josh 13.30 as well as all sixty of the villages of **Jair** in Bashan.
1 Kgs 4.13 belonging to the clan of **Jair,** a descendant of Manasseh,
1 Chr 2.22 had a son named Segub, [22]and Segub had a son named **Jair.**
2.22 **Jair** ruled twenty-three cities in the territory of Gilead.
2.23 including the villages of **Jair** and Kenath, and the towns near

JAMES (1)

Zebedee's son and John's brother.

Mt 4.21 saw two other brothers, **James** and John, the sons of Zebedee.
10. 2 **James** and his brother John, the sons of Zebedee;
17. 1 Peter and the brothers **James** and John and led them up
Mk 1.19 saw two other brothers, **James** and John, the sons of Zebedee.
1.29 and his disciples, including **James** and John, left the synagogue
3.17 **James** and his brother John, the sons of Zebedee
5.37 go on with him except Peter and **James** and his brother John.
9. 2 Jesus took with him Peter, **James,** and John, and led them up
10.35 Then **James** and John, the sons of Zebedee, came to Jesus.
10.41 disciples heard about it, they became angry with **James** and John.
13. 3 from the Temple, when Peter, **James,** John, and Andrew came to
14.33 He took Peter, **James,** and John with him.
Lk 5.10 of Simon's partners, **James** and John, the sons of Zebedee.
6.14 **James** and John, Philip and Bartholomew,
8.51 except Peter, John, and **James,** and the child's father and mother.
9.28 Jesus took Peter, John, and **James** with him and went up a
9.54 When the disciples **James** and John saw this, they said,
Acts 1.13 Peter, John, **James** and Andrew, Philip and Thomas,
12. 2 He had **James,** the brother of John, put to death by the

JAMES (2)

Son of Alphaeus, also called "the younger James".

Mt 10. 3 **James** son of Alphaeus, and Thaddaeus;
Mk 3.18 Bartholomew, Matthew, Thomas, **James** son of Alphaeus, Thaddaeus,
Lk 6.15 Matthew and Thomas, **James** son of Alphaeus, and Simon
Acts 1.13 Bartholomew and Matthew, **James** son of Alphaeus,

JAMES (3)

Son of Mary (perhaps the same as (2)).

Mt 27.56 Mary the mother of **James** and Joseph, and the wife of
Mk 15.40 Mary the mother of the younger **James** and of Joseph, and
16. 1 Mary the mother of **James,** and Salome bought spices to go
Lk 24.10 women were Mary Magdalene, Joanna, and Mary the mother of **James;**

JAMES (4)

Jesus' brother who became a leader of the early Church.

Mt 13.55 and aren't **James,** Joseph, Simon, and Judas his brothers?
Mk 6. 3 son of Mary, and the brother of **James,** Joseph, Judas, and
Acts 12.17 "Tell this to **James** and the rest of the believers," he
15.13 When they had finished speaking, **James** spoke up:
15.19 is my opinion," **James** went on, "that we should not trouble
21.18 The next day Paul went with us to see **James;**
1 Cor 15. 7 Then he appeared to **James,** and afterwards to all the apostles.
Gal 1.19 did not see any other apostle except **James,** the Lord's brother.
2. 9 **James,** Peter, and John, who seemed to be the leaders, recognized
2.12 who had been sent by **James** arrived there, Peter had been

JAMES (5)

Judas' father.

Lk 6.16 Judas son of **James,** and Judas Iscariot, who became the
Acts 1.13 Simon the Patriot, and Judas son of **James.**

JAMES (6)

Writer of "The Letter from James" (perhaps the same as (4)).

Jas 1. 1 From **James,** a servant of God and of the Lord Jesus Christ:

JAMES (7)

Jude's brother (perhaps the same as (4).

Jude 1 Jesus Christ, and brother of **James**— To those who have been

JAPHETH

Noah's son.

Gen 5.32 500 years old, he had three sons, Shem, Ham, and **Japheth.**
6. 9 He had three sons, Shem, Ham, and **Japheth.**
7.13 boat with their three sons, Shem, Ham, and **Japheth,** and their
9.18 Noah who went out of the boat were Shem, Ham, and **Japheth.**
9.23 Then Shem and **Japheth** took a robe and held it behind
9.27 May God cause **Japheth** to increase!
9.27 Canaan will be the slave of **Japheth."**
10. 1 are the descendants of Noah's sons, Shem, Ham, and **Japheth.**
10. 2 The sons of **Japheth**—Gomer, Magog, Madai, Javan, Tubal,
10. 5 the descendants of **Japheth,** living in their different tribes
10.21 Shem, the elder brother of **Japheth,** was the ancestor of
1 Chr 1. 4 Shem, Ham, and **Japheth.**
1. 5 The sons of **Japheth**—Gomer, Magog, Madai, Javan, Tubal,

JAR

[WATER-JAR, WINE-JAR]

Gen 24.14 of them, 'Please, lower your **jar** and let me have a drink.'
24.15 praying, Rebecca arrived with a **water-jar** on her shoulder.
24.16 She went down to the well, filled her **jar,** and came back.
24.17 said, "Please give me a drink of water from your **jar."**
24.18 and quickly lowered her **jar** from her shoulder and held it
24.20 quickly emptied her **jar** into the animals' drinking-trough
24.43 ask her to give me a drink of water from her **jar.**
24.45 prayer, Rebecca came with a **water-jar** on her shoulder and
24.46 She quickly lowered her **jar** from her shoulder and said,
Ex 7.19 will be blood, even in the wooden tubs and stone **jars."**
16.33 said to Aaron, "Take a **jar,** put two litres of manna in
25.29 Make plates, cups, **jars,** and bowls to be used for the
37.16 the plates, the cups, the **jars,** and the bowls to be used
Num 4. 7 the offering bowls, and the **jars** for the wine-offering.
19.15 Every **jar** and pot in the tent that has no lid on
Judg 7.16 each man a trumpet and a **jar** with a torch inside it.
7.19 the trumpets and broke the **jars** they were holding,
Ruth 2. 9 go and drink from the **water jars** that they have filled."
1 Sam 10. 1 Samuel took a **jar** of olive-oil and poured it on Saul's
26.11 Let's take his spear and his **water jar,** and go."
26.12 the spear and the **water jar** from just beside Saul's head,
26.16 Where is the **water jar** that was beside his head?"
1 Kgs 14. 3 him ten loaves of bread, some cakes, and a **jar** of honey.
17.12 flour in a bowl and a drop of olive-oil in a **jar.**
17.14 out of flour or the **jar** run out of oil before the
17.16 run out of flour nor did the **jar** run out of oil.
18.33 He said, "Fill four **jars** with water and pour it on the
19. 6 a loaf of bread and a **jar** of water near his head.
2 Kgs 4. 2 "Nothing at all, except a small **jar** of olive-oil," she
4. 3 and borrow as many empty **jars** as you can," Elisha told her.
4. 4 house, close the door, and start pouring oil into the **jars.**
4. 5 the door, took the small **jar** of olive-oil,
4. 5 and poured oil into the **jars** as her sons brought them to

2 Kgs 4. 6 they had filled all the **jars,** she asked if there were any
9. 1 Take this **jar** of olive-oil with you, [2]and when you get
1 Chr 28.17 in making forks, bowls, and **jars,** how much silver and gold
Ecc 12. 6 at the well will break, and the **water jar** will be shattered.
Jer 13.12 of Israel that every **wine-jar** should be filled with wine.
13.12 that they know every **wine-jar** should be filled with wine.
13.14 I will smash them like **jars** against one another, old and
14. 3 they come back with their **jars** empty.
19. 1 The Lord told me to go and buy a clay **jar.**
19.10 told me to break the **jar** in front of the men who
19.11 like this broken clay **jar** that cannot be put together again.
22.28 Jehoiachin become like a broken **jar** that is thrown away and
32.14 place them in a clay **jar,** so that they may be preserved
48.11 left to settle undisturbed and never poured from **jar to jar.**
48.12 They will empty its **wine-jars** and break them in pieces.
48.38 because I have broken Moab like a **jar** that no one wants.
51.34 He emptied the city like a **jar;**
Mt 26. 7 to him with an alabaster **jar** filled with an expensive perfume,
Mk 14. 3 came in with an alabaster **jar** full of a very expensive
14. 3 She broke the **jar** and poured the perfume on Jesus' head.
14.13 city, and a man carrying a **jar** of water will meet you.
Lk 7.37 she brought an alabaster **jar** full of perfume [38]and stood behind
22.10 the city, a man carrying a **jar** of water will meet you.
Jn 2. 6 for this purpose six stone **water jars** were there, each one
2. 7 Jesus said to the servants, "Fill these **jars** with water."
4.28 Then the woman left her **water jar,** went back to the town,
Heb 9. 4 gold and containing the gold **jar** with the manna in it,

JASPER

A semi-precious stone of various colours. The jasper mentioned in the Bible was probably green, or else clear.

Ex 28.20 and in the fourth row, a beryl, a carnelian, and a **jasper.**
39.13 and in the fourth row, a beryl, a carnelian, and a **jasper.**
Ezek 28.13 topaz, beryl, carnelian, and **jasper;**
Rev 4. 3 like such precious stones as **jasper** and carnelian, and all round
21.11 like a precious stone, like a **jasper,** clear as crystal.
21.18 The wall was made of **jasper,** and the city itself was
21.19 The first foundation-stone was **jasper,** the second sapphire,

JAVELIN

1 Sam 17. 6 and he carried a bronze **javelin** slung over his shoulder.
17.45 me with sword, spear, and **javelin,** but I come against you in

JAW

Deut 18. 3 priests are to be given the shoulder, the **jaw,** and the
Judg 15.15 he found the **jaw-bone** of a donkey that had recently died.
15.16 "With the **jaw-bone** of a donkey I killed a thousand men;
15.16 With the **jaw-bone** of a donkey I piled them up in piles."
15.17 After that, he threw the **jaw-bone** away.
Job 41. 2 a rope through his snout or put a hook through his **jaws?**
41.14 Who can make him open his **jaws,** ringed with those
Prov 21. 6 but not before they lead you into the **jaws** of death.
Ezek 29. 4 put a hook through your **jaw** and make the fish in your
38. 4 round, put hooks in his **jaws,** and drag him and all his

JAZER

City in Gilead.

Num 21.32 men to find the best way to attack the city of **Jazer.**
32. 1 how suitable the land of **Jazer** and Gilead was for cattle,
32. 3 the towns of Ataroth, Dibon, **Jazer,** Nimrah, Heshbon, Elealeh,
32.35 Dibon, Ataroth, Aroer, [35]Atroth Shophan, **Jazer,** Jogbehah,
Josh 13.25 territory included **Jazer** and all the cities of Gilead,
21.39 Mahanaim, [39]Heshbon, and **Jazer,** with their pasture lands.
2 Sam 24. 5 there they went north to **Jazer,** [6]and on to Gilead and to
1 Chr 6.81 Ramoth in Gilead, Mahanaim, [81]Heshbon, and **Jazer.**
26.31 family were found living at **Jazer** in the territory of Gilead.
Is 16. 8 far as the city of **Jazer,** and eastwards into the desert,
16. 9 Now I weep for Sibmah's vines as I weep for **Jazer.**
Jer 48.32 people of Sibmah, even more than for the people of **Jazer.**
48.32 branches reach across the Dead Sea and go as far as **Jazer.**

JEALOUS

Gen 26.14 cattle and many servants, the Philistines were **jealous** of him.
30. 1 children, and so she became **jealous** of her sister and said
37.11 Joseph's brothers were **jealous** of him, but his father
Num 5.29 where a man is **jealous** and becomes suspicious that his wife
Deut 32.16 Their idolatry made the Lord **jealous;**
32.21 they have made me angry, **jealous** with their so-called gods,
32.21 I will make them **jealous** with a nation of fools.
1 Sam 18. 9 And so he was **jealous** and suspicious of David from that
Ps 37. 1 don't be **jealous** of those who do wrong.
73. 3 almost gone [3]because I was **jealous** of the proud when I saw
106.16 in the desert they were **jealous** of Moses and of Aaron,
Prov 3.31 Don't be **jealous** of violent people or decide to act as
6.34 A husband is never angrier than when he is **jealous;**
14.30 mind makes the body healthy, but **jealousy** is like a cancer.
27. 4 Anger is cruel and destructive, but it is nothing compared to **jealousy.**
Is 11.13 of Israel will not be **jealous** of Judah any more, and Judah
Ezek 16.42 I will not be angry or **jealous** any more.
35.11 your **jealousy,** and your hatred towards my people.
36. 6 Sovereign Lord, am saying in **jealous** anger because of the way
Mt 20.15 Or are you **jealous** because I am generous?' "
27.18 authorities had handed Jesus over to him because they were **jealous.**
Mk 7.22 **jealousy,** slander, pride, and folly—[23]all these evil things
15.10 priests had handed Jesus over to him because they were **jealous.**
Acts 5.17 party of the Sadducees, became extremely **jealous** of the apostles;
7. 9 "Jacob's sons became **jealous** of their brother Joseph and sold
13.45 When the Jews saw the crowds, they were filled with **jealousy;**
17. 5 the Jews were **jealous** and gathered some of the worthless loafers
Rom 1.29 they are full of **jealousy,** murder, fighting, deceit, and
10.19 "I will use a so-called nation to make my people **jealous;**
11.11 has come to the Gentiles, to make the Jews **jealous** of them.
11.14 people of my own race **jealous,** and so be able to save
13.13 no immorality or indecency, no fighting or **jealousy.**
1 Cor 3. 3 When there is **jealousy** among you and you quarrel with one another,
10.22 Or do we want to make the Lord **jealous?**
13. 4 it is not **jealous** or conceited or proud;
2 Cor 11. 2 I am **jealous** for you, just as God is;
12.20 I will find quarrelling and **jealousy,** hot tempers and selfishness,
Gal 5.20 they become **jealous,** angry, and ambitious.
5.26 proud or irritate one another or be **jealous** of one another.
Phil 1.15 preach Christ because they are **jealous** and quarrelsome,
1 Tim 6. 4 and this brings on **jealousy,** disputes, insults, evil suspicions,
Jas 3.14 in your heart you are **jealous,** bitter, and selfish, don't sin
3.16 Where there is **jealousy** and selfishness, there is also disorder
1 Pet 2. 1 more lying or hypocrisy or **jealousy** or insulting language.

JEBUSITES

Inhabitants of Jerusalem before its conquest by Israel.
see also **JERUSALEM**

Gen 10.16 also the ancestor of the **Jebusites,** the Amorites,
15.21 Amorites, the Canaanites, the Girgashites, and the **Jebusites."**
Ex 3. 8 the Perizzites, the Hivites, and the **Jebusites** now live.
3.17 the Amorites, the Perizzites, the Hivites, and the **Jebusites.**
13. 5 the Hittites, the Amorites, the Hivites, and the **Jebusites.**
23.23 the Hivites, and the **Jebusites,** and I will destroy them.
33. 2 the Hittites, the Perizzites, the Hivites, and the **Jebusites.**
34.11 Perizzites, the Hivites, and the **Jebusites,** as you advance.
Num 13.29 Hittites, **Jebusites,** and Amorites live in the hill-country;
Deut 7. 1 the Canaanites, the Perizzites, the Hivites, and the **Jebusites.**
20.17 the Hivites, and the **Jebusites,** as the Lord ordered you to
Josh 3.10 the Perizzites, the Girgashites, the Amorites, and the **Jebusites.**
9. 1 the Canaanites, the Perizzites, the Hivites, and the **Jebusites.**
11. 3 Perizzites, and the **Jebusites** in the hill-country, as well as
12. 8 the Canaanites, the Perizzites, the Hivites, and the **Jebusites.**
15. 8 side of the hill where the **Jebusite** city of Jerusalem was
15.63 not able to drive out the **Jebusites,** who lived in Jerusalem.
15.63 The **Jebusites** still live there with the people of Judah.
18.16 through the Valley of Hinnom, south of the **Jebusite** ridge,
18.28 Haeleph, **Jebus** (or Jerusalem), Gibeah, and Kiriath Jearim:
24.11 the Hittites, the Girgashites, the Hivites, and the **Jebusites.**
Judg 1.21 did not drive out the **Jebusites** living in Jerusalem,
1.21 and the **Jebusites** have continued to live there with
3. 5 the Amorites, the Perizzites, the Hivites, and the **Jebusites.**
19.10 day when they came near **Jebus** (that is, Jerusalem),
19.10 we stop and spend the night here in this **Jebusite** city?"
19.14 So they went past **Jebus** and continued on their way.
2 Sam 5. 6 The **Jebusites,** who lived there, thought that David would not
5. 8 "Does anybody here hate the **Jebusites** as much as I do?
24.16 The angel was by the threshing-place of Araunah, a **Jebusite.**
1 Kgs 9.20 and **Jebusites,** whose descendants continue to be slaves
1 Chr 1.14 also the ancestor of the **Jebusites,** the Amorites,
11. 4 It was then known as **Jebus,** and the Jebusites, the original
11. 4 and the **Jebusites,** the original inhabitants of the land,
11. 5 **Jebusites** told David he would never get inside the city,
11. 6 man to kill a **Jebusite** will be commander of the army!"
21.15 angel was standing by the threshing-place of Araunah, a **Jebusite.**
2 Chr 3. 1 which Araunah the **Jebusite** had used as a threshing-place.
8. 7 and **Jebusites,** whose descendants continue to be slaves
Ezra 9. 1 Egypt or from the Canaanites, Hittites, Perizzites, **Jebusites,**
Neh 9. 8 land of the Perizzites, the **Jebusites,** and the Girgashites,
Zech 9. 7 Ekron will become part of my people, as the **Jebusites** did.

JEDUTHUN

Father of Obed Edom (2).

1 Chr 9.14 whose ancestors included Galal and **Jeduthun** Berechiah,
16.38 Obed Edom son of **Jeduthun** and sixty-eight men of his clan
16.41 with them were Heman and **Jeduthun** and the others who were
16.42 Heman and **Jeduthun** also had charge of the trumpets and
16.42 of **Jeduthun's** clan were in charge of guarding the gates.
25. 1 Asaph, Heman, and **Jeduthun.**
25. 3 The six sons of **Jeduthun:**
25. 6 Asaph, **Jeduthun,** and Heman were under orders from the king.
2 Chr 5.11 Levite musicians—Asaph, Heman, and **Jeduthun,** and the members
29.12 From the clan of **Jeduthun,** Shemaiah and Uzziel
35.15 Asaph, Heman, and **Jeduthun,** the king's prophet.
Neh 11.17 son of Shammua and grandson of Galal, a descendant of **Jeduthun.**

JEER

Ps 22. 7 All who see me **jeer** at me;
40.15 May those who **jeer** at me be dismayed by their defeat.
70. 3 May those who **jeer** at me be dismayed by their defeat.
Is 57. 4 Who are you liars **jeering** at?
Jer 20. 7 Everyone **jeers** at me;
48.27 Moab, remember how you **jeered** at the people of Israel?
48.39 It is in ruins, and all the surrounding nations **jeer** at it.
49.13 people will **jeer** at it and use its name as a curse.
Lam 1.15 "The Lord **jeered** at all my strongest soldiers;
3.63 From morning till night they **jeer** at me.
Mt 27.41 and the teachers of the Law and the elders **jeered** at him:

Mk 15.31 teachers of the Law **jeered** at Jesus, saying to each other,
Lk 23.35 stood there watching while the Jewish leaders **jeered** at him:

JEHOAHAZ
King of Israel. (The name is written in this way to distinguish this king from Joahaz, king of Judah.)

2 Kgs 10.35 buried in Samaria, and his son **Jehoahaz** succeeded him as king.
13. 1 Ahaziah as king of Judah, **Jehoahaz** son of Jehu became king
13. 4 Then **Jehoahaz** prayed to the Lord, and the Lord, seeing how
13. 7 **Jehoahaz** had no armed forces left except fifty horsemen,
13. 8 Everything else that **Jehoahaz** did and all his brave deeds
13.10 of Judah, Jehoash son of **Jehoahaz** became king of Israel,
13.22 the Israelites during all of **Jehoahaz'** reign, [23] but the
13.25 taken by Benhadad during the reign of **Jehoahaz,** the father
14. 1 reign of Jehoash son of **Jehoahaz** as king of Israel, Amaziah
2 Chr 25.17 was the son of **Jehoahaz** and grandson of Jehu, challenging him

JEHOASH
King of Israel. (The name is written in this way to distinguish this king from Joash, king of Judah.)

2 Kgs 13. 9 buried in Samaria, and his son **Jehoash** succeeded him as king.
13.10 of King Joash of Judah, **Jehoash** son of Jehoahaz became king
13.12 Everything else that **Jehoash** did, including his bravery
13.13 **Jehoash** died and was buried in the royal tombs in Samaria,
13.14 as he lay dying King **Jehoash** of Israel went to visit him.
13.15 **Jehoash** got them, [16] and Elisha told him to get ready
13.25 King **Jehoash** of Israel defeated Benhadad three times
13.25 by Benhadad during the reign of Jehoahaz, the father of **Jehoash.**
14. 1 year of the reign of **Jehoash** son of Jehoahaz as king of
14. 8 sent messengers to King **Jehoash** of Israel, challenging him to
14. 9 But King **Jehoash** sent back the following reply:
14.11 refused to listen, so King **Jehoash** marched out with his men
14.13 **Jehoash** took Amaziah prisoner, advanced on Jerusalem,
14.15 Everything else that **Jehoash** did, including his bravery
14.16 **Jehoash** died and was buried in the royal tombs in Samaria,
14.17 lived fifteen years after the death of King **Jehoash** of Israel.
14.23 Jeroboam son of **Jehoash** became king of Israel, and he
2 Chr 25.17 sent a message to King **Jehoash** of Israel, who was the son
25.18 **Jehoash** sent this answer to Amaziah:
25.21 King **Jehoash** of Israel went into battle against King Amaziah
25.23 **Jehoash** captured Amaziah and took him to Jerusalem.
25.25 King Amaziah of Judah outlived King **Jehoash** of Israel
Hos 1. 1 of Judah, and Jeroboam son of **Jehoash** was king of Israel.
Amos 1. 1 and Jeroboam son of **Jehoash** was king of Israel, God revealed

JEHOIACHIN
King of Judah.

2 Kgs 24. 6 and his son **Jehoiachin** succeeded him as king.
24. 8 **Jehoiachin** was eighteen years old when he became king
24. 9 the example of his father, **Jehoiachin** sinned against the Lord.
24.12 to Jerusalem, [12] and King **Jehoiachin,** along with his mother,
24.12 of Nebuchadnezzar's reign he took **Jehoiachin** prisoner
24.15 Nebuchadnezzar took **Jehoiachin** to Babylon as a prisoner,
24.15 together with **Jehoiachin's** mother, his wives, his officials,
24.17 Nebuchadnezzar made **Jehoiachin's** uncle Mattaniah king
25.27 showed kindness to King **Jehoiachin** of Judah by releasing him
25.27 the thirty-seventh year after **Jehoiachin** had been taken away
25.29 **Jehoiachin** was permitted to change from his prison clothes
1 Chr 3.16 **Jehoiachin** and Zedekiah.
3.17 descendants of King **Jehoiachin,** who was taken prisoner by the
3.17 **Jehoiachin** had seven sons:
2 Chr 36. 8 His son **Jehoiachin** succeeded him as king.
36. 9 **Jehoiachin** was eighteen years old when he became king
36.10 spring came, King Nebuchadnezzar took **Jehoiachin** to Babylonia
36.10 Nebuchadnezzar made **Jehoiachin's** uncle Zedekiah king of Judah
Esth 2. 6 of Babylon took King **Jehoiachin** of Judah into exile
Jer 22.24 Lord said to King **Jehoiachin,** son of King Jehoiakim of Judah,
22.28 I said, "Has King **Jehoiachin** become like a broken jar
24. 1 taken away Jehoiakim's son, King **Jehoiachin** of Judah,
27.19 Babylonia the king of Judah, **Jehoiachin** son of Jehoiakim,
28. 4 back the king of Judah, **Jehoiachin** son of Jehoiakim, along
29. 2 I wrote it after King **Jehoiachin,** his mother, the palace
37. 1 Josiah king of Judah in the place of **Jehoiachin**
52.31 showed kindness to King **Jehoiachin** of Judah by releasing him
52.31 the thirty-seventh year after **Jehoiachin** had been taken away
52.33 **Jehoiachin** was permitted to change from his prison clothes
Ezek 1. 2 fifth year since King **Jehoiachin** had been taken into exile.)
Mt 1. 6 Manasseh, Amon, Josiah, and **Jehoiachin** and his brothers.
1.12 **Jehoiachin,** Shealtiel, Zerubbabel, Abiud, Eliakim, Azor, Zadok,

JEHOIADA (1)
Father of Benaiah.

2 Sam 8.18 Benaiah son of **Jehoiada** was in charge of David's
20.23 Benaiah son of **Jehoiada** was in charge of David's bodyguard;
23.20 Benaiah son of **Jehoiada,** from Kabzeel, was another
1 Kgs 1. 8 the priest, Benaiah son of **Jehoiada,** Nathan the prophet,
4. 4 Benaiah son of **Jehoiada**
1 Chr 11.22 Benaiah son of **Jehoiada** from Kabzeel was a famous soldier;
12.23 Followers of **Jehoiada,** descendant of Aaron:
18.17 Benaiah son of **Jehoiada** was in charge of David's
27. 2 Benaiah son of **Jehoiada** the priest;

JEHOIADA (2)
Priest in Jerusalem in Athaliah and Joash's time.

2 Kgs 11. 4 in the seventh year **Jehoiada** the priest sent for the officers
11. 9 officers obeyed **Jehoiada's** instructions and brought their men
11.12 **Jehoiada** led Joash out, placed the crown on his head,
11.15 **Jehoiada** did not want Athaliah killed in the temple area,
11.17 priest **Jehoiada** made King Joash and the people enter into
11.18 **Jehoiada** put guards on duty at the Temple, [19] and then he,
12. 2 pleased the Lord, because **Jehoiada** the priest instructed him.
12. 7 So he called in **Jehoiada** and the other priests and asked
12. 9 Then **Jehoiada** took a box, made a hole in the lid,
2 Chr 22.11 Jehosheba, who was married to a priest named **Jehoiada.**
23. 1 After waiting six years **Jehoiada** the priest decided that
23. 3 **Jehoiada** said to them, "Here is the son of the late king!
23. 8 and the people of Judah carried out **Jehoiada's** instructions.
23. 9 **Jehoiada** gave the officers the spears and shields that had
23.11 **Jehoiada** led Joash out, placed the crown on his head,
23.11 **Jehoiada** the priest and his sons anointed Joash,
23.14 **Jehoiada** did not want Athaliah killed in the temple area,
23.16 priest **Jehoiada** got King Joash and the people to join him
23.18 **Jehoiada** put the priests and Levites in charge of the
23.19 **Jehoiada** also put guards on duty at the temple gates
23.20 the people joined **Jehoiada** in a procession that brought the
24. 2 to the Lord as long as **Jehoiada** the priest was alive.
24. 3 **Jehoiada** chose two wives for King Joash, and they bore him
24. 6 delayed, [6] so he called in **Jehoiada,** their leader,
24.12 The king and **Jehoiada** would give the money to those who
24.14 given to the king and **Jehoiada,** who used it to have bowls
24.14 As long as **Jehoiada** was alive, sacrifices were offered
24.17 **Jehoiada** was dead, the leaders of Judah persuaded King Joash
24.20 spirit of God took control of Zechariah son of **Jehoiada**
24.22 loyal service that Zechariah's father **Jehoiada** had given him,
24.25 bed to avenge the murder of the son of **Jehoiada** the priest.
Jer 29.26 a priest in place of **Jehoiada,** and you are now the chief

JEHOIAKIM
King of Judah who opposed and ill-treated Jeremiah.
see also ELIAKIM (2)

2 Kgs 23.34 as successor to Josiah, and changed his name to **Jehoiakim.**
23.35 **Jehoiakim** collected a tax from the people in proportion to
23.36 **Jehoiakim** was twenty-five years old when he became king
23.37 example of his ancestors, **Jehoiakim** sinned against the Lord.
24. 1 **Jehoiakim** was king, King Nebuchadnezzar of Babylonia invaded
24. 1 Judah, and for three years **Jehoiakim** was forced to submit to
24. 2 Moabites, and Ammonites against **Jehoiakim** to destroy Judah,
24. 5 Everything else that **Jehoiakim** did is recorded in
24. 6 **Jehoiakim** died, and his son Jehoiachin succeeded him
24.19 Zedekiah sinned against the Lord, just as King **Jehoiakim** had
1 Chr 3.15 Johanan, **Jehoiakim,** Zedekiah, and Joahaz.
3.16 **Jehoiakim** had two sons:
2 Chr 36. 4 brother Eliakim king of Judah and changed his name to **Jehoiakim.**
36. 5 **Jehoiakim** was twenty-five years old when he became king
36. 6 invaded Judah, captured **Jehoiakim,** and took him to Babylonia
36. 8 Everything that **Jehoiakim** did, including his disgusting
Jer 1. 3 he spoke to him again when Josiah's son **Jehoiakim** was king.
22.18 the Lord says about Josiah's son **Jehoiakim,** king of Judah,
22.24 Jehoiachin, son of King **Jehoiakim** of Judah, "As surely as I
24. 1 of Babylonia had taken away **Jehoiakim's** son, King Jehoiachin
25. 1 In the fourth year that **Jehoiakim** son of Josiah was king
26. 1 Soon after **Jehoiakim** son of Josiah became king of Judah,
26.21 When King **Jehoiakim** and his soldiers and officials heard
26.22 King **Jehoiakim,** however, sent Elnathan son of Achbor
26.23 brought him back to King **Jehoiakim,** who had him killed
27.19 Jehoiachin son of **Jehoiakim,** and the leading men of Judah
28. 4 Jehoiachin son of **Jehoiakim,** along with all the people of
35. 1 **Jehoiakim** son of Josiah was king of Judah, the Lord said
36. 1 In the fourth year that **Jehoiakim** son of Josiah was king
36. 9 the fifth year that **Jehoiakim** was king of Judah, the people
36.27 King **Jehoiakim** had burnt the scroll that I had dictated to
36.30 Lord, say to you, King **Jehoiakim,** that no descendant of yours
37. 1 Josiah king of Judah in the place of Jehoiachin son of **Jehoiakim.**
45. 1 In the fourth year that **Jehoiakim** son of Josiah was king
46. 2 River Euphrates in the fourth year that **Jehoiakim** was king
52. 2 Zedekiah sinned against the Lord, just as King **Jehoiakim** had
Dan 1. 1 In the third year that **Jehoiakim** was king of Judah,
1. 2 Lord let him capture King **Jehoiakim** and seize some of the

JEHORAM (1)
King of Judah. (The name is written in this way to distinguish this king from Joram, king of Israel.)

1 Kgs 22.50 in David's City, and his son **Jehoram** succeeded him as king.
2 Kgs 1.17 of the reign of **Jehoram** son of Jehoshaphat, king of Judah.
8.16 as king of Israel, **Jehoram** son of Jehoshaphat became king of
8.20 During **Jehoram's** reign Edom revolted against Judah
8.21 So **Jehoram** set out with all his chariots for Zair,
8.23 Everything else that **Jehoram** did is recorded in
8.24 **Jehoram** died and was buried in the royal tombs
8.25 of Israel, Ahaziah son of **Jehoram** became king of Judah
11. 2 by his aunt Jehosheba, who was King **Jehoram's** daughter
12.18 predecessors Jehoshaphat, **Jehoram,** and Ahaziah had dedicated
1 Chr 3.11 **Jehoram,** Ahaziah, Joash, [12] Amaziah, Uzziah, Jotham, [13] Ahaz,
2 Chr 21. 1 in David's City and his son **Jehoram** succeeded him as king.
21. 2 **Jehoram** son of King Jehoshaphat of Judah had six brothers:
21. 3 **Jehoram** was the eldest, Jehoshaphat made him his successor.
21. 4 When **Jehoram** was in firm control of the kingdom, he had
21. 5 **Jehoram** became king at the age of thirty-two, and he ruled
21. 8 During **Jehoram's** reign Edom revolted against Judah
21. 9 **Jehoram** and his officers set out with chariots and invaded Edom.
21.10 Libnah also revolted, because **Jehoram** had abandoned the Lord,
21.12 prophet Elijah sent **Jehoram** a letter, which read as follows:
21.16 The Lord incited them to go to war against **Jehoram.**
21.20 **Jehoram** had become king at the age of thirty-two

2 Chr 22. 1 a raid and killed all King **Jehoram's** sons except Ahaziah,
Mt 1. 6 Asa, Jehoshaphat, **Jehoram,** Uzziah, Jotham, Ahaz, Hezekiah,

JEHOSHAPHAT (1)
King of Judah.

1 Kgs 22.1-28 **The prophet Micaiah warns Ahab**
29-40 **The death of Ahab**
41-50 **King Jehoshaphat of Judah**
2 Kgs 3.1-27 **War between Israel and Moab**
1 Chr 3.10-16 **The descendants of King Solomon**
2 Chr 17.1-9 **Jehoshaphat becomes king**
10-19 **Jehoshaphat's greatness**
18.1-27 **The prophet Micaiah warns Ahab**
28-34 **The death of Ahab**
19.1-3 **A prophet reprimands Jehoshaphat**
4-11 **Jehoshaphat's reforms**
20.1-30 **War against Edom**
20.31-21.1 **The end of Jehoshaphat's reign**

1 Kgs 15.24 in David's City, and his son **Jehoshaphat** succeeded him as king.
22.51 the reign of King **Jehoshaphat** of Judah, Ahaziah son of Ahab
2 Kgs 1.17 of the reign of Jehoram son of **Jehoshaphat,** king of Judah.
8.16 of Israel, Jehoram son of **Jehoshaphat** became king of Judah
12.18 the offerings that his predecessors **Jehoshaphat,** Jehoram,
2 Chr 21. 2 Jehoram son of King **Jehoshaphat** of Judah had six brothers:
21. 3 Jehoram was the eldest, **Jehoshaphat** made him his successor.
21.12 example of your father, King **Jehoshaphat,** or that of your
22. 9 respect for his grandfather King **Jehoshaphat,** who had done
Mt 1. 6 Rehoboam, Abijah, Asa, **Jehoshaphat,** Jehoram, Uzziah, Jotham,

JEHU (1)
King of Israel, who assassinated King Joram.

2 Kgs 9.1-13 **Jehu is anointed king of Israel**
14-26 **King Joram of Israel is killed**
27-29 **King Ahaziah of Judah is killed**
30-37 **Queen Jezebel is killed**
10.1-11 **The descendants of Ahab are killed**
12-14 **The relatives of King Ahaziah are killed**
15-17 **All remaining relatives of Ahab are killed**
18-31 **The worshippers of Baal are killed**
32-36 **The death of Jehu**
2 Chr 22.1-9 **King Ahaziah of Judah**

1 Kgs 19.16 anoint **Jehu** son of Nimshi as king of Israel, and anoint
19.17 Hazael will be killed by **Jehu,**
19.17 and anyone who escapes **Jehu** will be killed by Elisha.
2 Kgs 12. 1 of the reign of King **Jehu** of Israel, Joash became king of
13. 1 of Judah, Jehoahaz son of **Jehu** became king of Israel,
15.12 promise was fulfilled which the Lord had made to King **Jehu:**
2 Chr 25.17 the son of Jehoahaz and grandson of **Jehu,** challenging him to
Hos 1. 4 for the murders that his ancestor **Jehu** committed at Jezreel.
1. 4 I am going to put an end to **Jehu's** dynasty.

JEPHTHAH
Leader of Israel before the monarchy.

Judg 11. 1 **Jephthah,** a brave soldier from Gilead, was the son of
11. 2 and when they grew up, they forced **Jephthah** to leave home.
11. 3 **Jephthah** fled from his brothers and lived in the land of Tob.
11. 5 of Gilead went to bring **Jephthah** back from the land of Tob.
11. 7 **Jephthah** answered, "You hated me so much that you forced me
11. 8 They said to **Jephthah,** "We are turning to you now because
11. 9 **Jephthah** said to them, "If you take me back home to
11.11 **Jephthah** went with the leaders of Gilead, and the people made
11.11 **Jephthah** stated his terms at Mizpah in the presence of
11.12 **Jephthah** sent messengers to the king of Ammon to say,
11.13 The king of Ammon answered **Jephthah's** messengers,
11.14 **Jephthah** sent messengers back to the king of Ammon
11.28 king of Ammon paid no attention to this message from **Jephthah.**
11.29 Then the spirit of the Lord came upon **Jephthah.**
11.30 **Jephthah** promised the Lord:
11.32 So **Jephthah** crossed the river to fight the Ammonites,
11.34 **Jephthah** went back home to Mizpah, there was his daughter
11.40 every year to grieve for the daughter of **Jephthah** of Gilead.
12. 1 Zaphon and said to **Jephthah,** "Why did you cross the border
12. 2 But **Jephthah** said to them, "My people and I had a
12. 4 **Jephthah** brought all the men of Gilead together, fought
12. 7 **Jephthah** led Israel for six years.
12. 8 After **Jephthah,** Ibzan from Bethlehem led Israel.
1 Sam 12.11 And the Lord sent Gideon, Barak, **Jephthah,** and finally me.
Heb 11.32 to speak of Gideon, Barak, Samson, **Jephthah,** David, Samuel,

JEREMIAH (1)
Prophet from Anathoth.

2 Chr 35.25 The prophet **Jeremiah** composed a lament for King Josiah.
36.12 listen humbly to the prophet **Jeremiah,** who spoke the word of
36.21 Lord had foretold through the prophet **Jeremiah** was fulfilled:
36.22 made what he had said through the prophet **Jeremiah** come true.
Ezra 1. 1 made what he had said through the prophet **Jeremiah** come true.
Jer 1. 1 of what was said by **Jeremiah** son of Hilkiah, one of the
1. 2 Lord spoke to **Jeremiah** in the thirteenth year that Josiah son
1.11 The Lord asked me, **"Jeremiah,** what do you see?"
1.17 Get ready, **Jeremiah;**
1.18 Listen, **Jeremiah!**
5.13 God Almighty said to me, **"Jeremiah,** because these people
5.19 tell them, **Jeremiah,** that just as they turned away
6.27 **Jeremiah,** test my people, as you would test metal,
7.16 The Lord said, **"Jeremiah,** do not pray for these people.
7.27 **Jeremiah,** you will speak all these words to my people,
11.14 **Jeremiah,** don't pray to me or plead with me on behalf of
Jer 12. 5 **"Jeremiah,** if you get tired racing against men, how can you
13.12 Lord God said to me, **"Jeremiah,** tell the people of Israel
17.19 Lord said to me, **"Jeremiah,** go and announce my message at
18.18 Then the people said, "Let's do something about **Jeremiah!**
23.33 The Lord said to me, **"Jeremiah,** when one of my people
23.37 **Jeremiah,** ask the prophets, 'What answer did the Lord
24. 3 Then the Lord said to me, **"Jeremiah,** what do you see?"
25.13 when I spoke through **Jeremiah**—all the disasters recorded in
25.30 "You, **Jeremiah,** must proclaim everything I have said.
26.20 the Lord against this city and nation just as **Jeremiah** did.
29.27 haven't you done this to **Jeremiah** of Anathoth, who has been
32.36 said to me, **"Jeremiah,** the people are saying that war,
35. 3 Jaazaniah (the son of another **Jeremiah,** who was Habazziniah's
36.17 Did **Jeremiah** dictate it to you?"
36.18 Baruch answered, **"Jeremiah** dictated every word of it to
36.19 they said to him, "You and **Jeremiah** must go and hide.
36.29 and you have asked **Jeremiah** why he wrote that the king
38. 9 They have put **Jeremiah** in the well, where he is sure to
39.12 "Go and find **Jeremiah** and take good care of him.
51.64 The words of **Jeremiah** end here.
Dan 9. 2 ruins, according to what the Lord had told the prophet **Jeremiah.**
Mt 2.17 In this way what the prophet **Jeremiah** had said came true:
16.14 say Elijah, while others say **Jeremiah** or some other prophet."
27. 9 Then what the prophet **Jeremiah** had said came true:

JERICHO
Important city in the Jordan Valley, captured by Joshua.

Num 22. 1 the plains of Moab east of the Jordan and opposite **Jericho.**
26. 3 in the plains of Moab across the River Jordan from **Jericho.**
26.63 in the plains of Moab across the River Jordan from **Jericho.**
31.12 camp on the plains of Moab across the Jordan from **Jericho.**
33.41 across the River Jordan from **Jericho,** between Beth Jeshimoth
33.50 Moab across the Jordan from **Jericho** the Lord gave Moses
34.15 on the eastern side of the Jordan, opposite **Jericho."**
35. 1 Moab across the Jordan from **Jericho** the Lord said to Moses,
36.13 Moses in the plains of Moab across the River Jordan from **Jericho.**
Deut 32.49 Mountains in the land of Moab opposite the city of **Jericho;**
34. 1 Mount Pisgah east of **Jericho,** and there the Lord showed him
34. 3 that reaches from Zoar to **Jericho,** the city of palm-trees.
Josh 2. 1 explore the land of Canaan, especially the city of **Jericho.**
2. 2 The king of **Jericho** heard that some Israelites had come
2.22 but they did not find them, so they returned to **Jericho.**
3.16 off, and the people were able to cross over near **Jericho.**
4.13 men ready for war crossed over to the plain near **Jericho.**
4.19 of the first month and made camp at Gilgal, east of **Jericho.**
5.10 Gilgal on the plain near **Jericho,** they observed Passover on
5.13 Joshua was near **Jericho,** he suddenly saw a man standing in
6. 1 The gates of **Jericho** were kept shut and guarded to keep
6. 2 am putting into your hands **Jericho,** with its king and all
6.25 she had hidden the two spies that he had sent to **Jericho.**
6.26 rebuild the city of **Jericho** will be under the Lord's curse.
7. 1 not to take from **Jericho** anything that was to be destroyed
7. 2 Joshua sent some men from **Jericho** to Ai, a city east of
8. 2 king what you did to **Jericho** and its king, but this time
9. 3 what Joshua had done to **Jericho** and Ai, [4] and they decided
10. 1 its king, just as he had done to **Jericho** and its king.
10.28 king of Makkedah what he had done to the king of **Jericho.**
10.30 to the king what they had done to the king of **Jericho.**
12. 9 **Jericho,** Ai (near Bethel), [10] Jerusalem, Hebron,
13.32 divided the land east of **Jericho** and the Jordan when he was
16. 1 started from the Jordan near **Jericho,** at a point
16. 1 east of the springs of **Jericho,** and went into the desert.
16. 1 went from **Jericho** up into the hill-country as far as Bethel.
16. 7 and Naarah, reaching **Jericho** and ending at the Jordan.
18.12 up the slope north of **Jericho** and westwards through the
18.21 the tribe of Benjamin were **Jericho,** Beth Hoglah, Emek Keziz,
20. 8 the desert plateau east of **Jericho,** they chose Bezer in the
24.11 You crossed the Jordan and came to **Jericho.**
24.11 The men of **Jericho** fought against you, as did the Amorites,
Judg 1.16 the people of Judah from **Jericho,** the city of palm-trees,
3.13 defeated Israel and captured **Jericho,** the city of palm-trees.
2 Sam 10. 5 they should stay in **Jericho** and not return until their beards
1 Kgs 16.34 During his reign Hiel from Bethel rebuilt **Jericho.**
16.34 he laid the foundation of **Jericho,** and his youngest son Segub
2 Kgs 2. 4 the Lord has ordered me to go to **Jericho."**
2. 4 So they went on to **Jericho.**
2.15 The fifty prophets from **Jericho** saw him and said,
2.18 Elisha, who had waited at **Jericho,** and he said to them,
2.19 Some men from **Jericho** went to Elisha and said,
2.23 Elisha left **Jericho** to go to Bethel, and on the way
25. 5 in the plains near **Jericho,** and all his soldiers deserted him.
1 Chr 6.78 territory of Reuben, east of the River Jordan beyond **Jericho:**
19. 5 for them to stay in **Jericho** and not return until their
2 Chr 28.15 back to Judaean territory at **Jericho,** the city of palm-trees.
Ezra 2.21 **Jericho** - 345
Neh 3. 2 The men of **Jericho** built the next section.
7.26 **Jericho** - 345
Jer 39. 5 pursued them and captured Zedekiah in the plains near **Jericho.**
52. 8 in the plains near **Jericho,** and all his soldiers deserted him.
Mt 20.29 Jesus and his disciples were leaving **Jericho,** a large crowd was
Mk 10.46 came to **Jericho,** and as Jesus was leaving with his disciples
Lk 10.30 going down from Jerusalem to **Jericho** when robbers attacked him,
18.35 Jesus was coming near **Jericho,** there was a blind man sitting
19. 1 Jesus went on into **Jericho** and was passing through.
Heb 11.30 that made the walls of **Jericho** fall down after the

JEROBOAM (1)

First king of the n. kingdom (Israel).

1 Kgs 11.26-40 **God's promise to Jeroboam**
12.1-20 **The Northern tribes revolt**
25-31 **Jeroboam turns away from the LORD**
12.32-13.10 **Worship at Bethel is condemned**
13.11-32 **The old prophet of Bethel**
33-34 **Jeroboam's fatal sin**
14.1-18 **The death of Jeroboam's son**
19-20 **The death of Jeroboam**
2 Kgs 17.5-23 **The fall of Samaria**
2 Chr 10.1-19 **The Northern tribes revolt**
11.1-4 **Shemaiah's prophecy**
13-17 **Priests and Levites come to Judah**
12.13-16 **Summary of Rehoboam's reign**
13.1-22 **Abijah's war with Jeroboam**

1 Kgs 14.30 all this time Rehoboam and **Jeroboam** were constantly at war
15. 1 the reign of King **Jeroboam** of Israel, Abijah became king of
15. 6 war which had begun between Rehoboam and **Jeroboam** continued
15. 9 of the reign of King **Jeroboam** of Israel, Asa became king of
15.25 King **Jeroboam's** son Nadab became king of Israel,
15.29 he began killing all the members of **Jeroboam's** family.
15.29 prophet Ahijah from Shiloh, all **Jeroboam's** family were killed;
15.30 happened because **Jeroboam** aroused the anger of the Lord,
15.34 Like King **Jeroboam** before him, he sinned against the Lord
16. 2 now you have sinned like **Jeroboam** and have led my people
16. 3 away with you and your family, just as I did with **Jeroboam.**
16. 7 he did, just as King **Jeroboam** had done before him,
16. 7 but also because he killed all **Jeroboam's** family.
16.19 Like his predecessor **Jeroboam** he displeased the Lord by his
16.26 Like **Jeroboam** before him, he aroused the anger of the Lord,
16.31 It was not enough for him to sin like King **Jeroboam;**
21.22 like the family of King **Jeroboam** son of Nebat and like the
22.52 mother Jezebel, and King **Jeroboam,** who had led Israel into
2 Kgs 3. 3 Yet, like King **Jeroboam** son of Nebat before him, he led
9. 9 the families of King **Jeroboam** of Israel and of King Baasha
10.29 imitated the sin of King **Jeroboam,** who led Israel into the
10.31 he followed the example of **Jeroboam,** who led Israel into sin.
13. 2 Like King **Jeroboam** before him he sinned against the Lord
13. 6 the sins into which King **Jeroboam** had led Israel, but kept
13.11 evil example of King **Jeroboam,** who had led Israel into sin.
14.24 example of his predecessor King **Jeroboam** son of Nebat,
15. 9 wicked example of King **Jeroboam** son of Nebat, who led Israel
15.18 wicked example of King **Jeroboam** son of Nebat, who led Israel
15.24 wicked example of King **Jeroboam** son of Nebat, who led Israel
15.28 wicked example of King **Jeroboam** son of Nebat, who led Israel
23.15 had been built by King **Jeroboam** son of Nebat, who led Israel
23.16 during the festival as King **Jeroboam** was standing by the altar.
2 Chr 9.29 which also deal with the reign of King **Jeroboam** of Israel.

JEROBOAM (2)

Later king of Israel.

2 Kgs 13.13 in Samaria, and his son **Jeroboam** II succeeded him as king.
14.16 in Samaria, and his son **Jeroboam** II succeeded him as king.
14.23 as king of Judah, **Jeroboam** son of Jehoash became king of
14.27 and for ever, so he rescued them through King **Jeroboam** II.
14.28 Everything else that **Jeroboam** II did, his brave battles,
14.29 **Jeroboam** died and was buried in the royal tombs, and his
15. 1 of the reign of King **Jeroboam** II of Israel, Uzziah son of
15. 8 of Judah, Zechariah son of **Jeroboam** II became king of Israel,
1 Chr 5.17 of King Jotham of Judah and King **Jeroboam** II of Israel.)
Hos 1. 1 were kings of Judah, and **Jeroboam** son of Jehoash was king of
Amos 1. 1 was king of Judah and **Jeroboam** son of Jehoash was king of
7. 9 I will bring the dynasty of King **Jeroboam** to an end."
7.10 of Bethel, then sent a report to King **Jeroboam** of Israel:
7.11 '**Jeroboam** will die in battle, and the people of Israel will

JERUSALEM

City captured by David which became his capital and the site of the Temple.

see also **(David's) CITY, (Holy) CITY**

Josh 10. 1 Adonizedek, the king of **Jerusalem,** heard that Joshua had
10. 2 The people of **Jerusalem** were greatly alarmed at this
10. 5 Amorite kings, the kings of **Jerusalem,** Hebron, Jarmuth,
10.23 opened, and the kings of **Jerusalem,** Hebron, Jarmuth, Lachish,
12.10 Jericho, Ai (near Bethel), [10]**Jerusalem,** Hebron,
15. 8 side of the hill where the Jebusite city of **Jerusalem** was
15.63 not able to drive out the Jebusites, who lived in **Jerusalem.**
18.28 Haeleph, Jebus (or **Jerusalem**), Gibeah, and Kiriath Jearim:
Judg 1. 7 He was taken to **Jerusalem,** where he died.
1. 8 The men of Judah attacked **Jerusalem** and captured it.
1.21 out the Jebusites living in **Jerusalem,** and the Jebusites have
19.10 came near Jebus (that is, **Jerusalem**), so the servant said to
1 Sam 17.54 head and took it to **Jerusalem,** but he kept Goliath's weapons
2 Sam 5. 5 a half years, and in **Jerusalem** over all Israel and Judah for
5. 6 when King David and his men set out to attack **Jerusalem.**
5.13 moving from Hebron to **Jerusalem,** David took more concubines
5.14 The following children were born to him in **Jerusalem:**
6.10 So he decided not to take it with him to **Jerusalem;**
6.12 from Obed's house to take it to **Jerusalem** with a great
6.15 the Covenant Box up to **Jerusalem** with shouts of joy and the
8. 7 carried by Hadadezer's officials and took them to **Jerusalem.**
9.13 in both feet, lived in **Jerusalem,** eating all his meals at
10.14 back from fighting the Ammonites and went back to **Jerusalem.**
11. 1 But David himself stayed in **Jerusalem.**
11.12 So Uriah stayed in **Jerusalem** that day and the next.
12.31 Then he and his men returned to **Jerusalem.**
2 Sam 14.23 up and went to Geshur and brought Absalom back to **Jerusalem.**
14.28 Absalom lived two years in **Jerusalem** without seeing the
15. 8 take me back to **Jerusalem,** I would worship him in Hebron."
15.11 who at Absalom's invitation had gone from **Jerusalem** with him;
15.14 who were with him in **Jerusalem,** "We must get away at once
15.29 took the Covenant Box back into **Jerusalem** and stayed there.
16. 3 "He is staying in **Jerusalem,**" Ziba answered, "because he
16.15 all the Israelites with him entered **Jerusalem,** and Ahithophel
17.17 on the outskirts of **Jerusalem,** because they did not dare to
17.20 but could not find them, and so they returned to **Jerusalem.**
19.19 please forget the wrong I did that day you left **Jerusalem.**
19.24 the time the king left **Jerusalem** until he returned victorious.
19.25 When Mephibosheth arrived from **Jerusalem** to meet the king,
19.33 "Come with me to **Jerusalem,** and I will take care of
19.34 why should I go with Your Majesty to **Jerusalem?**
20. 2 remained loyal and followed David from the Jordan to **Jerusalem.**
20. 3 at his palace in **Jerusalem,** he took the ten concubines he
20. 7 other soldiers left **Jerusalem** with Abishai to go after Sheba.
20.22 And Joab returned to **Jerusalem** to the king.
24. 8 returned to **Jerusalem,** having travelled through the whole
24.16 angel was about to destroy **Jerusalem,** the Lord changed his
1 Kgs 2.11 ruling seven years in Hebron and thirty-three years in **Jerusalem.**
2.36 said to him, "Build a house for yourself here in **Jerusalem.**
2.38 So he lived in **Jerusalem** a long time.
2.42 "I made you promise in the Lord's name not to leave **Jerusalem.**
3. 1 building his palace, the Temple, and the wall round **Jerusalem.**
3.15 Then he went to **Jerusalem** and stood in front of the Lord's
8. 1 to come to him in **Jerusalem** in order to take the Lord's
9.19 he wanted to build in **Jerusalem,** in Lebanon, and elsewhere in
10. 1 travelled to **Jerusalem** to test him with difficult questions.
10.26 of them he kept in **Jerusalem** and the rest he stationed in
10.27 silver was as common in **Jerusalem** as stone, and cedar was as
11. 7 the mountain east of **Jerusalem** he built a place to worship
11.13 and for the sake of **Jerusalem,** the city I have made my
11.27 on the east side of **Jerusalem** and repairing the city walls.
11.29 as Jeroboam was travelling from **Jerusalem,** the prophet Ahijah,
11.32 and for the sake of **Jerusalem,** the city I have chosen to
11.36 my servant David ruling in **Jerusalem,** the city I have chosen
11.42 He was king in **Jerusalem** over all Israel for forty years.
12.18 Rehoboam hurriedly got into his chariot and escaped to **Jerusalem.**
12.21 When Rehoboam arrived in **Jerusalem,** he called together
12.26 if my people go to **Jerusalem** and offer sacrifices to the
12.28 "You have been going long enough to **Jerusalem** to worship.
14.21 ruled for seventeen years in **Jerusalem,** the city which the
14.25 of Rehoboam's reign King Shishak of Egypt attacked **Jerusalem.**
15. 2 king of Judah, [2]and he ruled for three years in **Jerusalem.**
15. 4 to rule after him in **Jerusalem** and to keep Jerusalem secure.
15.10 of Judah, [10]and he ruled for forty-one years in **Jerusalem.**
22.42 the age of thirty-five, and he ruled in **Jerusalem** for
2 Kgs 8.17 age of thirty-two, and he ruled in **Jerusalem** for eight years.
8.26 age of twenty-two, and he ruled in **Jerusalem** for one year.
9.28 took his body back to **Jerusalem** in a chariot and buried him
12. 1 king of Judah, and he ruled in **Jerusalem** for forty years.
12.17 then he decided to attack **Jerusalem.**
12.18 to King Hazael, who then led his army away from **Jerusalem.**
12.20 on the east side of **Jerusalem,** on the road that goes down
14. 2 the age of twenty-five, and he ruled in **Jerusalem** for
14. 2 His mother was Jehoaddin, from **Jerusalem.**
14.13 took Amaziah prisoner, advanced on **Jerusalem,** and tore down
14.19 There was a plot in **Jerusalem** to assassinate Amaziah,
14.20 body was carried back to **Jerusalem** on a horse and was buried
15. 2 the age of sixteen, and he ruled in **Jerusalem** for fifty-two
15. 2 His mother was Jecoliah from **Jerusalem.**
15.33 of twenty-five, and he ruled in **Jerusalem** for sixteen years.
16. 2 age of twenty, and he ruled in **Jerusalem** for sixteen years.
16. 5 King Pekah of Israel attacked **Jerusalem** and besieged it,
18. 2 the age of twenty-five, and he ruled in **Jerusalem** for
18.17 sent a large army from Lachish to attack Hezekiah at **Jerusalem;**
18.17 When they arrived at **Jerusalem,** they occupied the road where
18.22 Judah and Jerusalem to worship only at the altar in **Jerusalem.**
18.35 Then what makes you think the Lord can save **Jerusalem?"**
19.21 had said, "The city of **Jerusalem** laughs at you, Sennacherib,
19.31 There will be people in **Jerusalem** and on Mount Zion who
20. 6 rescue you and this city of **Jerusalem** from the emperor
21. 1 became king of Judah, and he ruled in **Jerusalem** for
21. 7 "Here in **Jerusalem,** in this Temple, is the place that I
21.12 bring such a disaster on **Jerusalem** and Judah that everyone
21.13 I will punish **Jerusalem** as I did Samaria, as I did King
21.13 I will wipe **Jerusalem** clean of its people, as clean as a
21.16 that the streets of **Jerusalem** were flowing with blood;
21.19 became king of Judah, and he ruled in **Jerusalem** for two
22. 1 became king of Judah, and he ruled in **Jerusalem** for
22.14 Huldah, a prophet who lived in the newer part of **Jerusalem.**
22.16 "I am going to punish **Jerusalem** and all its people,
22.17 My anger is aroused against **Jerusalem,** and it will not die
22.19 you heard how I threatened to punish **Jerusalem** and its people.
22.20 am going to bring on **Jerusalem** will not come until after
23. 1 the leaders of Judah and **Jerusalem,** [2]and together they went
23. 5 and in places near **Jerusalem**—all the priests who offered
23. 8 He brought to **Jerusalem** the priests who were in the cities
23.13 Solomon had built east of **Jerusalem,** south of the Mount of
23.20 Then he returned to **Jerusalem.**
23.23 of the reign of Josiah, the Passover was celebrated in **Jerusalem.**
23.24 King Josiah removed from **Jerusalem** and the rest of Judah all
23.27 sight, and I will reject **Jerusalem,** the city I chose,
23.30 and took it back to **Jerusalem,** where he was buried in the
23.31 king of Judah, and he ruled in **Jerusalem** for three months.
23.36 king of Judah, and he ruled in **Jerusalem** for eleven years.
24. 8 king of Judah, and he ruled in **Jerusalem** for three months.
24. 8 mother was Nehushta, the daughter of Elnathan from **Jerusalem.**

2 Kgs	24.10	officers, marched against **Jerusalem** and besieged it.
	24.11	siege Nebuchadnezzar himself came to **Jerusalem,**
	24.14	as prisoners the people of **Jerusalem,** all the royal princes,
	24.18	king of Judah, and he ruled in **Jerusalem** for eleven years.
	24.20	angry with the people of **Jerusalem** and Judah that he banished
	25. 1	all his army and attacked **Jerusalem** on the tenth day of the
	25. 8	adviser to the king and commander of his army, entered **Jerusalem.**
	25. 9	important people in **Jerusalem,** [10] and his soldiers tore down
1 Chr	3. 4	In **Jerusalem** he ruled as king for thirty-three years,
	6.10	which King Solomon built in **Jerusalem),** [11] Amariah, Ahitub,
	6.15	people of Judah and **Jerusalem** whom the Lord sent into exile.
	6.31	the place of worship in **Jerusalem** after the Covenant Box was
	8.28	families and their principal descendants who lived in **Jerusalem.**
	8.32	Their descendants lived in **Jerusalem** near other families of
	9. 3	Benjamin, Ephraim, and Manasseh went to live in **Jerusalem.**
	9. 4	690 families of the tribe of Judah who lived in **Jerusalem.**
	9. 7	following members of the tribe of Benjamin lived in **Jerusalem:**
	9.10	The following priests lived in **Jerusalem:**
	9.14	The following Levites lived in **Jerusalem:**
	9.17	The following temple guards lived in **Jerusalem:**
	9.34	They were the leaders who lived in **Jerusalem.**
	9.38	Their descendants lived in **Jerusalem** near other families of
	11. 4	and all the Israelites went and attacked the city of **Jerusalem.**
	13. 5	to bring the Covenant Box from Kiriath Jearim to **Jerusalem.**
	13.13	So David did not take it with him to **Jerusalem.**
	14. 3	There in **Jerusalem,** David married more wives and had more
	14. 4	The following children were born to him in **Jerusalem:**
	15. 3	people of Israel to **Jerusalem** in order to bring the Covenant
	15.28	the Covenant Box up to **Jerusalem** with shouts of joy,
	18. 7	shields carried by Hadadezer's officials and took them to **Jerusalem.**
	19.15	Then Joab went back to **Jerusalem.**
	20. 1	King David, however, stayed in **Jerusalem.**
	20. 3	Then he and his men returned to **Jerusalem.**
	21. 4	the whole country of Israel, and then returned to **Jerusalem.**
	21.15	sent an angel to destroy **Jerusalem,** but he changed his mind
	21.16	holding his sword in his hand, ready to destroy **Jerusalem.**
	23.25	his people, and he himself will live in **Jerusalem** for ever.
	28. 1	commanded all the officials of Israel to assemble in **Jerusalem.**
	28. 1	leading soldiers, and important men—gathered in **Jerusalem.**
	29.27	He ruled in Hebron for seven years and in **Jerusalem** for
2 Chr	1. 4	Covenant Box, however, was in **Jerusalem,** kept in a tent which
	1.13	the Tent of the Lord's presence was, and returned to **Jerusalem.**
	1.14	of them he kept in **Jerusalem,** and the rest he stationed in
	1.15	gold became as common in **Jerusalem** as stone, and cedar was
	2. 7	the craftsmen of Judah and **Jerusalem** whom my father David
	2.16	From there you can take them to **Jerusalem."**
	3. 1	It was in **Jerusalem,** on Mount Moriah, where the Lord appeared
	5. 2	Israel to assemble in **Jerusalem,** in order to take the Lord's
	6. 6	But now I have chosen **Jerusalem** as the place where I will
	8. 6	his plans for building in **Jerusalem,** in Lebanon,
	9. 1	travelled to **Jerusalem** to test him with difficult questions.
	9.25	of them he kept in **Jerusalem** and the rest he stationed in
	9.27	silver was as common in **Jerusalem** as stone, and cedar was as
	9.30	Solomon ruled in **Jerusalem** over all Israel for forty years.
	10.18	Rehoboam hurriedly got into his chariot and escaped to **Jerusalem.**
	11. 1	When King Rehoboam arrived in **Jerusalem,** he called together
	11. 5	Rehoboam remained in **Jerusalem** and had fortifications built
	11.14	moved to Judah and **Jerusalem,** because King Jeroboam of Israel
	11.16	followed the Levites to **Jerusalem,** so that they could offer
	12. 2	King Shishak of Egypt attacked **Jerusalem** [3] with an army of
	12. 4	the fortified cities of Judah and advanced as far as **Jerusalem.**
	12. 5	leaders who had gathered in **Jerusalem** to escape Shishak.
	12. 7	**Jerusalem** will not feel the full force of my anger,
	12. 9	King Shishak came to **Jerusalem** and took the treasures from
	12.13	Rehoboam ruled in **Jerusalem** and increased his power
	12.13	ruled for seventeen years in **Jerusalem,** the city which
	13. 2	king of Judah, [2] and he ruled for three years in **Jerusalem.**
	14.15	Then they returned to **Jerusalem.**
	15.10	They assembled in **Jerusalem** in the third month of the
	17.13	In **Jerusalem** he stationed outstanding officers,
	17.19	served the king in **Jerusalem,** and in addition he stationed
	19. 1	Jehoshaphat of Judah returned safely to his palace in **Jerusalem.**
	19. 4	though King Jehoshaphat lived in **Jerusalem,** he travelled
	19. 8	In **Jerusalem** Jehoshaphat appointed Levites, priests,
	20. 4	people hurried to **Jerusalem** to ask the Lord for guidance,
	20. 5	and the people of **Jerusalem** gathered in the new courtyard of
	20.15	people of Judah and **Jerusalem,** the Lord says that you must
	20.17	People of Judah and **Jerusalem,** do not hesitate or be afraid.
	20.20	"Men of Judah and **Jerusalem!**
	20.27	led his troops back to **Jerusalem** in triumph, because the Lord
	20.31	thirty-five and had ruled in **Jerusalem** for twenty-five years.
	21. 5	age of thirty-two, and he ruled in **Jerusalem** for eight years.
	21.11	the people of Judah and **Jerusalem** to sin against the Lord.
	21.13	people of Judah and **Jerusalem** into being unfaithful to God,
	21.20	age of thirty-two and had ruled in **Jerusalem** for eight years.
	22. 1	now the people of **Jerusalem** made Ahaziah king as his father's
	22. 2	age of twenty-two, and he ruled in **Jerusalem** for one year.
	23. 2	brought back with them to **Jerusalem** the Levites and all the
	24. 1	the age of seven, and he ruled in **Jerusalem** for forty years.
	24. 6	Levites collect from Judah and **Jerusalem** the tax which Moses,
	24. 9	They sent word throughout **Jerusalem** and Judah for everyone
	24.18	for these sins brought the Lord's anger on Judah and **Jerusalem.**
	24.23	Syrian army attacked Judah and **Jerusalem,** killed all the
	25. 1	the age of twenty-five, and he ruled in **Jerusalem** for
	25. 1	His mother was Jehoaddin from **Jerusalem.**
	25.23	Jehoash captured Amaziah and took him to **Jerusalem.**
	25.27	the Lord, there had been a plot against him in **Jerusalem.**
	25.28	His body was carried to **Jerusalem** on a horse, and he was
2 Chr	26. 3	the age of sixteen, and he ruled in **Jerusalem** for
	26. 3	His mother was Jecoliah from **Jerusalem.**
	26. 9	Uzziah strengthened the fortifications of **Jerusalem**
	26.15	In **Jerusalem** his inventors made equipment for shooting
	27. 1	the age of twenty-five, and he ruled in **Jerusalem** for
	27. 3	work on the city wall in the area of **Jerusalem** called Ophel.
	27. 8	he became king, and he ruled in **Jerusalem** for sixteen years.
	28. 1	age of twenty, and he ruled in **Jerusalem** for sixteen years.
	28.10	make the men and women of **Jerusalem** and Judah your slaves.
	28.24	the Temple and set up altars in every part of **Jerusalem.**
	28.27	and was buried in **Jerusalem,** but not in the royal tombs.
	29. 1	twenty-five, and he ruled in **Jerusalem** for twenty-nine years.
	29. 8	been angry with Judah and **Jerusalem,** and what he has done to
	30. 1	and not many people had assembled in **Jerusalem.**
	30. 1	and the people of **Jerusalem** agreed to celebrate it in the
	30. 1	come to the Temple in **Jerusalem** to celebrate the Passover
	30. 5	to come together in **Jerusalem** and celebrate the Passover
	30. 8	Come to the Temple in **Jerusalem,** which the Lord your God has
	30.11	Manasseh, and Zebulun who were willing to come to **Jerusalem.**
	30.13	people gathered in **Jerusalem** in the second month to celebrate
	30.14	that had been used in **Jerusalem** for offering sacrifices
	30.21	people who had gathered in **Jerusalem** celebrated the Festival
	30.26	The city of **Jerusalem** was filled with joy,
	31. 4	king told the people of **Jerusalem** to bring the offerings to
	32. 2	that Sennacherib intended to attack **Jerusalem** also,
	32. 3	Assyrians from having any water when they got near **Jerusalem.**
	32. 5	filled in on the east side of the old part of **Jerusalem.**
	32. 9	Hezekiah and the people of Judah who were with him in **Jerusalem:**
	32.10	you people the confidence to remain in **Jerusalem** under siege.
	32.12	people of Judah and **Jerusalem** to worship and burn incense at
	32.18	discourage the people of **Jerusalem** who were on the city wall,
	32.19	talked about the God of **Jerusalem** in the same way that they
	32.22	and the people of **Jerusalem** from the power of Sennacherib,
	32.23	Many people came to **Jerusalem,** bringing offerings to
	32.25	Lord had done for him, and Judah and **Jerusalem** suffered for
	32.26	Hezekiah and the people of **Jerusalem** humbled themselves,
	32.30	through a tunnel to a point inside the walls of **Jerusalem.**
	32.33	the people of Judah and **Jerusalem** paid him great honour at
	33. 1	became king of Judah, and he ruled in **Jerusalem** for
	33. 7	"Here in **Jerusalem,** in this Temple, is the place that I
	33.13	answered it by letting him go back to **Jerusalem** and rule
	33.15	hill where the Temple stood and in other places in **Jerusalem;**
	33.21	king of Judah, and he ruled in **Jerusalem** for two years.
	34. 1	king of Judah, and he ruled in **Jerusalem** for thirty-one years.
	34. 5	By doing all this, he made Judah and **Jerusalem** ritually clean
	34. 7	Then he returned to **Jerusalem.**
	34. 8	Azaliah, Maaseiah, the governor of **Jerusalem,** and Joah
	34. 9	and from the people of Judah, Benjamin, and **Jerusalem.)**
	34.22	Huldah, a prophet who lived in the newer part of **Jerusalem.**
	34.24	"I am going to punish **Jerusalem** and all its people with the
	34.25	My anger is aroused against **Jerusalem,** and it will not die
	34.27	you heard how I threatened to punish **Jerusalem** and its people.
	34.28	am going to bring on **Jerusalem** will not come until after
	34.29	leaders of Judah and **Jerusalem,** [30] and together they went
	34.32	and everyone else present in **Jerusalem** promise to keep the
	34.32	people of **Jerusalem** obeyed the requirements of the covenant
	35. 1	King Josiah celebrated the Passover at **Jerusalem** in honour
	35.18	Judah, Israel, and **Jerusalem** [19] in the eighteenth year of
	35.24	chariot which he had there, and took him to **Jerusalem.**
	35.24	All the people of Judah and **Jerusalem** mourned his death.
	36. 1	chose Josiah's son Joahaz and anointed him king in **Jerusalem.**
	36. 2	king of Judah, and he ruled in **Jerusalem** for three months.
	36. 5	king of Judah, and he ruled in **Jerusalem** for eleven years.
	36. 9	and he ruled in **Jerusalem** for three months and ten days.
	36.10	made Jehoiachin's uncle Zedekiah king of Judah and **Jerusalem.**
	36.11	became king of Judah, and he ruled in **Jerusalem** for eleven
	36.23	the responsibility of building a temple for him in **Jerusalem**
Ezra	1. 2	the responsibility of building a temple for him in **Jerusalem**
	1. 3	You are to go to **Jerusalem** and rebuild the Temple of the
	1. 3	the God of Israel, the God who is worshipped in **Jerusalem.**
	1. 4	offerings to present in the Temple of God in **Jerusalem."**
	1. 5	got ready to go and rebuild the Lord's Temple in **Jerusalem.**
	1. 7	taken from the Temple in **Jerusalem** and had put in the temple
	1.11	he and the other exiles went from Babylon to **Jerusalem.**
	2. 1	Babylon and returned to **Jerusalem** and Judah, each to his own
	2.68	at the Lord's Temple in **Jerusalem,** some of the leaders of
	2.70	Levites, and some of the people settled in or near **Jerusalem;**
	3. 1	Then they all assembled in **Jerusalem,** [2] and Joshua son of
	3. 8	to the site of the Temple in **Jerusalem,** they began work.
	3. 8	exiles who had come back to **Jerusalem,** joined in the work.
	4. 6	people living in Judah and **Jerusalem** brought written charges
	4. 8	wrote the following letter to Artaxerxes about **Jerusalem:**
	4.12	have settled in **Jerusalem** and are rebuilding that evil and
	4.19	that from ancient times **Jerusalem** has revolted against royal
	4.23	they hurried to **Jerusalem** and forced the Jews to stop
	5. 1	God of Israel to the Jews who lived in Judah and **Jerusalem.**
	5. 2	to rebuild the Temple in **Jerusalem,** and the two prophets
	5. 3	and their fellow-officials came to **Jerusalem** and demanded:
	5.14	taken from the Temple in **Jerusalem** and had placed in the
	5.15	to the Temple in **Jerusalem,** and to rebuild the Temple where
	5.17	orders for this Temple in **Jerusalem** to be rebuilt, and then
	6. 3	that the Temple in **Jerusalem** be rebuilt as a place where
	6. 5	Babylon from the Temple in **Jerusalem** are to be returned
	6. 5	returned to their proper place in the **Jerusalem** Temple."
	6. 9	to give the priests in **Jerusalem** whatever they tell you they
	6.12	May the God who chose **Jerusalem** as the place where he is
	6.18	for the temple services in **Jerusalem,** according to the
	7. 6	out from Babylonia for **Jerusalem** with a group of Israelites
	7. 8	God's help they arrived in **Jerusalem** on the first day of the
	7.13	Levites that so desire be permitted to go with you to **Jerusalem.**

Ezra 7.14 investigate the conditions in **Jerusalem** and Judah in order to
7.15 to give to the God of Israel, whose Temple is in **Jerusalem.**
7.16 priests give for the Temple of their God in **Jerusalem.**
7.17 wine and offer them on the altar of the Temple in **Jerusalem.**
7.19 present to God in **Jerusalem** all the utensils that have been
7.27 to honour in this way the Temple of the Lord in **Jerusalem.**
8. 1 returned with Ezra to **Jerusalem** when Artaxerxes was emperor:
8.29 and to the leaders of the people of Israel in **Jerusalem."**
8.30 and the utensils, to take them to the Temple in **Jerusalem.**
8.31 first month that we left the Ahava Canal to go to **Jerusalem.**
8.32 When we reached **Jerusalem,** we rested for three days.
9. 9 in ruins, and to find safety here in Judah and **Jerusalem.**
10. 7 A message was sent throughout **Jerusalem** and Judah that all
10. 7 exile were to meet in **Jerusalem** [8] by order of the leaders of
10. 9 Judah and Benjamin came to **Jerusalem** and assembled in the
10.14 Let our officials stay in **Jerusalem** and take charge of
Neh 1. 2 and I asked them about **Jerusalem** and about our fellow-Jews
1. 3 that the walls of **Jerusalem** were still broken down and that
2.11 I went on to **Jerusalem,** and for three days [12] I did not
2.12 tell anyone what God had inspired me to do for **Jerusalem.**
2.17 trouble we are in because **Jerusalem** is in ruins and its
2.20 right to any property in **Jerusalem,** and you have no share in
3. 9 ruler of half the **Jerusalem** District, built the next section.
3.12 other half of the **Jerusalem** District, built the next section.
3.22 Priests from the area around **Jerusalem** built the next
4. 7 in rebuilding the wall of **Jerusalem** and that the gaps in the
4. 8 together to come and attack **Jerusalem** and create confusion,
4.22 helpers had to stay in **Jerusalem** at night, so that we could
6. 7 some prophets to proclaim in **Jerusalem** that you are the king
7. 2 I put two men in charge of governing the city of **Jerusalem:**
7. 3 to have the gates of **Jerusalem** opened in the morning until
7. 3 the people who lived in **Jerusalem** and to assign some of them
7. 4 **Jerusalem** was a large city, but not many people were living
7. 6 Babylon and returned to **Jerusalem** and Judah, each to his own
8. 1 they all assembled in **Jerusalem,** in the square just inside
8.15 and sent them all through **Jerusalem** and the other cities and
11. 1 leaders settled in **Jerusalem,** and the rest of the people drew
11. 1 in the holy city of **Jerusalem,** while the rest were to live
11. 2 people praised anyone else who volunteered to live in **Jerusalem.**
11. 3 citizens of the province of Judah who lived in **Jerusalem:**
11. 6 descendants of Perez, 468 outstanding men lived in **Jerusalem.**
11. 8 In all, 928 Benjaminites lived in **Jerusalem.**
11.18 In all, 284 Levites lived in the holy city of **Jerusalem.**
11.21 lived in the part of **Jerusalem** called Ophel and worked under
11.22 the Levites who lived in **Jerusalem** was Uzzi, the son of Bani
12.27 the city wall of **Jerusalem** was dedicated, the Levites were
12.28 where they had settled round **Jerusalem** and from the towns
13. 6 I was not in **Jerusalem,** because in the thirty-second year
13. 7 some time I received his permission [7] and returned to **Jerusalem.**
13.10 other Levites had left **Jerusalem** and gone back to their farms,
13.15 other things on their donkeys and taking them into **Jerusalem;**
13.16 of Tyre were living in **Jerusalem,** and they brought fish
13.28 the town of Beth Horon, so I made Joiada leave **Jerusalem.**
Esth 2. 6 into exile from **Jerusalem,** along with a group of captives,
Ps 9.14 stand before the people of **Jerusalem** and tell them all the
51.18 rebuild the walls of **Jerusalem.**
68.29 from your Temple in **Jerusalem,** where kings bring gifts to
69.35 He will save **Jerusalem** and rebuild the towns of Judah.
76. 2 He has his home in **Jerusalem;**
79. 1 desecrated your holy Temple and left **Jerusalem** in ruins.
79. 3 flowed like water all through **Jerusalem,** and no one was left
87. 2 any other place in Israel he loves the city of **Jerusalem.**
87. 4 among the inhabitants of **Jerusalem** the people of Philistia,
87. 6 of the peoples and include them all as citizens of **Jerusalem.**
102.21 he will be praised in **Jerusalem** [22] when nations and kingdoms
116.18 sanctuary of your Temple in **Jerusalem,** I will give you what
122. 2 And now we are here, standing inside the gates of **Jerusalem!**
122. 3 **Jerusalem** is a city restored in beautiful order and harmony.
122. 6 Pray for the peace of **Jerusalem:**
122. 8 and friends I say to **Jerusalem,** "Peace be with you!"
125. 2 As the mountains surround **Jerusalem,** so the Lord surrounds
126. 1 the Lord brought us back to **Jerusalem,** it was like a dream!
128. 5 May you see **Jerusalem** prosper all the days of your life!
135.21 Praise the Lord in Zion, in **Jerusalem,** his home.
137. 5 be able to play the harp again if I forget you, **Jerusalem!**
137. 7 what the Edomites did the day **Jerusalem** was captured.
147. 2 The Lord is restoring **Jerusalem;**
147.12 Praise the Lord, O **Jerusalem!**
Ecc 1. 1 of the Philosopher, David's son, who was king in **Jerusalem.**
1.12 I, the Philosopher, have been king over Israel in **Jerusalem.**
1.16 a great man, far wiser than anyone who ruled **Jerusalem** before
2. 7 more livestock than anyone else who had ever lived in **Jerusalem.**
2. 9 who had ever lived in **Jerusalem,** and my wisdom never failed
Song 1. 5 Women of **Jerusalem,** I am dark but beautiful, dark as
2. 7 Promise me, women of **Jerusalem;**
3. 5 Promise me, women of **Jerusalem;**
3.10 with purple cloth, lovingly woven by the women of **Jerusalem.**
5. 8 Promise me, women of **Jerusalem,** that if you find my lover,
5.16 This is what my lover is like, women of **Jerusalem.**
6. 4 you are as beautiful as **Jerusalem,** as lovely as the city of
8. 4 Promise me, women of **Jerusalem,** that you will not interrupt
Is 1. 1 the messages about Judah and **Jerusalem** which God revealed to
1. 8 **Jerusalem** alone is left, a city under siege—as defenceless
1. 9 **Jerusalem** would have been totally destroyed,
1.10 **Jerusalem,** your rulers and your people are like those of
1.22 **Jerusalem,** you were once like silver, but now you are
1.26 Then **Jerusalem** will be called the righteous, faithful city."
1.27 he will save **Jerusalem** and everyone there who repents.
2. 1 God gave to Isaiah son of Amoz about Judah and **Jerusalem:**
2. 3 For the Lord's teaching comes from **Jerusalem;**
3. 1 to take away from **Jerusalem** and Judah everything and everyone
Is 3. 8 Yes, **Jerusalem** is doomed!
3.16 Lord said, "Look how proud the women of **Jerusalem** are!
3.18 from the women of **Jerusalem** everything they are so proud of
4. 3 who is left in **Jerusalem,** whom God has chosen for survival,
4. 4 wash away the guilt of **Jerusalem** and the blood that has been
5. 3 "You people who live in **Jerusalem** and Judah, judge between
5.14 gulps down the nobles of **Jerusalem** along with the noisy crowd
7. 1 Remaliah, king of Israel, attacked **Jerusalem,** but were unable
8.14 kingdoms of Judah and Israel and the people of **Jerusalem.**
10.10 that worship idols, idols more numerous than those of **Jerusalem**
10.11 do the same to **Jerusalem** and the images that are worshipped
10.12 on Mount Zion and in **Jerusalem,** I will punish the emperor of
10.32 their fists at Mount Zion, at the city of **Jerusalem.**
16. 1 a lamb as a present to the one who rules in **Jerusalem.**
22. 7 soldiers on horseback stood in front of **Jerusalem's** gates.
22. 9 found the places where the walls of **Jerusalem** needed repair.
22. 9 inspected all the houses in **Jerusalem** and tore some of them
22.21 will be like a father to the people of **Jerusalem** and Judah.
24.23 He will rule in **Jerusalem** on Mount Zion, and the leaders of
27.13 come and worship the Lord in **Jerusalem,** on his sacred hill.
28.14 men who rule here in **Jerusalem** over this people, listen to
29. 1 God's altar, **Jerusalem** itself, is doomed!
29. 4 **Jerusalem** will be like a ghost struggling to speak from
29. 5 **Jerusalem,** all the foreigners who attack you will be blown
29. 8 that assemble to attack **Jerusalem** will be like a starving man
30.19 You people who live in **Jerusalem** will not weep any more.
31. 5 the Lord Almighty, will protect **Jerusalem** and defend it."
31. 9 Lord who is worshipped in **Jerusalem** and whose fire burns there
33. 5 He will fill **Jerusalem** with justice and integrity
33.20 Look at **Jerusalem!**
35.10 They will reach **Jerusalem** with gladness, singing and
36. 2 to go from Lachish to **Jerusalem** with a large military force
36. 7 people of Judah and **Jerusalem** to worship at one altar only.
36.20 Then what makes you think the Lord can save **Jerusalem?"**
37.22 had said, "The city of **Jerusalem** laughs at you, Sennacherib,
37.32 There will be people in **Jerusalem** and on Mount Zion who
38. 6 you and this city of **Jerusalem** from the emperor of Assyria,
40. 2 Encourage the people of **Jerusalem.**
40. 9 **Jerusalem,** go up on a high mountain and proclaim the good
41.27 a messenger to **Jerusalem** to say, 'Your people are coming!
44.26 I tell **Jerusalem** that people will live there again,
44.28 order **Jerusalem** to be rebuilt and the Temple foundations to
45.13 He will rebuild my city, **Jerusalem,** and set my captive
46.13 I will save **Jerusalem** and bring honour to Israel there."
49.14 But the people of **Jerusalem** said,
49.16 **Jerusalem,** I can never forget you!
51. 3 "I will show compassion to **Jerusalem,** to all who live in
51.11 you have rescued will reach **Jerusalem** with gladness, singing
51.16 I say to **Jerusalem,** 'You are my people!
51.17 **Jerusalem,** wake up!
51.21 You suffering people of **Jerusalem,** you that stagger as
52. 1 **Jerusalem,** be strong and great again!
52. 2 Shake yourself free, **Jerusalem!**
52. 9 Break into shouts of joy, you ruins of **Jerusalem!**
54. 1 **Jerusalem,** you have been like a childless woman, but now
54.11 "O **Jerusalem,** you suffering, helpless city, with no one to
59.20 people, "I will come to **Jerusalem** to defend you and to save
60. 1 Arise, **Jerusalem,** and shine like the sun;
60.10 Lord says to **Jerusalem,** "Foreigners will rebuild your walls,
60.13 to rebuild you, **Jerusalem,** To make my Temple beautiful,
61.10 **Jerusalem** rejoices because of what the Lord has done.
62. 1 I will speak out to encourage **Jerusalem;**
62. 2 **Jerusalem,** the nations will see you victorious!
62. 6 On your walls, **Jerusalem,** I have placed sentries;
62. 7 no rest until he restores **Jerusalem** And makes it a city the
62.10 People of **Jerusalem,** go out of the city And build a road
62.11 "Tell the people of **Jerusalem** That the Lord is coming to
62.12 **Jerusalem** will be called "The City That God Loves,"
64.10 **Jerusalem** is a deserted ruin, [11] and our Temple, the sacred
65.18 The new **Jerusalem** I make will be full of joy, and her
65.19 will be filled with joy because of **Jerusalem** and her people.
66.10 Rejoice with **Jerusalem;**
66.13 I will comfort you in **Jerusalem,** as a mother comforts her
66.20 to my sacred hill in **Jerusalem** on horses, mules, and camels,
66.23 will come to worship me here in **Jerusalem,"** says the Lord.
Jer 1. 3 of that year the people of **Jerusalem** were taken into exile.
1.15 thrones at the gates of **Jerusalem** and round its walls,
2. 2 told me [2] to proclaim this message to everyone in **Jerusalem.**
3.17 that time comes, **Jerusalem** will be called 'The Throne of the
4. 3 to the people of Judah and **Jerusalem,** "Plough up your
4. 4 dedicate yourselves to me, you people of Judah and **Jerusalem.**
4. 5 people of Judah and **Jerusalem** to run to the fortified cities.
4.10 Lord, you have completely deceived the people of **Jerusalem!**
4.11 when the people of **Jerusalem** will be told that a scorching
4.14 **Jerusalem,** wash the evil from your heart, so that you may
4.16 the nations and to tell **Jerusalem** that enemies are coming
4.17 and will surround **Jerusalem** like men guarding a
4.30 **Jerusalem,** you are doomed!
4.31 It was the cry of **Jerusalem** gasping for breath, stretching
5. 1 People of **Jerusalem,** run through your streets!
5. 1 If you can, the Lord will forgive **Jerusalem.**
6. 1 Escape from **Jerusalem!**
6. 4 They will say, "Prepare to attack **Jerusalem!**
6. 6 down trees and build mounds in order to besiege **Jerusalem.**
6. 7 well keeps its water fresh, so **Jerusalem** keeps its evil fresh.
6. 8 People of **Jerusalem,** let these troubles be a warning to you,
6.23 They are ready for battle against **Jerusalem."**
6.24 the news," say the people of **Jerusalem,** "and our hands hang
7.17 in the cities of Judah and in the streets of **Jerusalem?**
7.29 "Mourn, people of **Jerusalem;**
7.34 and in the streets of **Jerusalem** I will put an end to

Jer 8. 1 other people who lived in **Jerusalem,** will be taken out of
9.11 Lord says, "I will make **Jerusalem** a pile of ruins, a place
10.17 People of **Jerusalem,** you are under siege!
10.19 The people of **Jerusalem** cried out,
11. 2 people of Judah and of **Jerusalem** [3]that I, the Lord God of
11. 6 "Go to the cities of Judah and to the streets of **Jerusalem.**
11. 9 people of Judah and of **Jerusalem** are plotting against me.
11.12 people of Judah and of **Jerusalem** will go to the gods to
11.13 and the inhabitants of **Jerusalem** have set up as many altars
13. 9 destroy the pride of Judah and the great pride of **Jerusalem.**
13.13 the priests, the prophets, and all the people of **Jerusalem.**
13.20 **Jerusalem,** look!
13.27 People of **Jerusalem,** you are doomed!
14. 2 on the ground in sorrow, and **Jerusalem** cries out for help.
14.16 out into the streets of **Jerusalem,** and there will be no one
14.21 not bring disgrace on **Jerusalem,** the place of your glorious
15. 4 Manasseh did in **Jerusalem** when he was king of Judah."
15. 5 pity you, people of **Jerusalem,** and who will grieve over you?
17.19 then go to all the other gates of **Jerusalem.**
17.20 and everyone who lives in **Jerusalem** and enters these gates,
17.21 in through the gates of **Jerusalem** [22]or carry anything out
17.25 will enter the gates of **Jerusalem** and have the same royal
17.25 people of Judah and of **Jerusalem,** they will ride in chariots
17.25 and the city of **Jerusalem** will always be filled with people.
17.26 from the towns of Judah and from the villages round **Jerusalem;**
17.27 load through the gates of **Jerusalem** on that day, for
17.27 if they do, I will set the gates of **Jerusalem** on fire.
17.27 burn down the palaces of **Jerusalem,** and no one will be able
18.11 people of Judah and of **Jerusalem** that I am making plans
19. 3 of Judah and people of **Jerusalem,** listen to what I, the Lord
19. 7 frustrate all the plans of the people of Judah and **Jerusalem.**
19.13 The houses of **Jerusalem,** the houses of the kings of Judah,
21.13 You, **Jerusalem,** are sitting high above the valleys,
22. 1 and the people of **Jerusalem** to listen to what the Lord
22.19 will be dragged away and thrown outside **Jerusalem's** gates."
22.20 People of **Jerusalem,** go to Lebanon and shout, go to
23.14 But I have seen the prophets in **Jerusalem** do even worse:
23.15 what I, the Lord Almighty, say about the prophets of **Jerusalem:**
23.16 said to the people of **Jerusalem,** "Do not listen to what the
24. 1 as a prisoner from **Jerusalem** to Babylonia, together with
24. 8 rest of the people of **Jerusalem** who have stayed in this land
25. 2 people of Judah and of **Jerusalem,** [3]"For twenty-three years,
25.18 **Jerusalem** and all the towns of Judah, together with its
26.18 ploughed like a field, **Jerusalem** will become a pile of ruins,
27. 3 ambassadors who had come to **Jerusalem** to see King Zedekiah.
27.19 leading men of Judah and **Jerusalem,** he left the columns,
27.21 are left in the Temple and in the royal palace in **Jerusalem:**
29. 1 had taken away as prisoners from **Jerusalem** to Babylonia.
29. 2 leaders of Judah and of **Jerusalem,** the craftsmen, and the
29. 4 to take away as prisoners from **Jerusalem** to Babylonia:
29.22 taken away as prisoners from **Jerusalem** to Babylonia want to
29.24 to all the people of **Jerusalem** and to the priest Zephaniah
30.18 **Jerusalem** will be rebuilt, and its palace restored.
31.23 bless the sacred hill of **Jerusalem,** the holy place where he
31.38 the Lord, "when all **Jerusalem** will be rebuilt as my city,
32. 2 king of Babylonia was attacking **Jerusalem,** and I was locked up
32.32 the people of Judah and **Jerusalem,** together with their kings
32.44 in the villages round **Jerusalem,** in the towns of Judah,
33. 4 say that the houses of **Jerusalem** and the royal palace of
33. 9 **Jerusalem** will be a source of joy, honour, and pride to me;
33. 9 do for the people of **Jerusalem** and about the prosperity that
33.10 the towns of Judah and the streets of **Jerusalem** are empty;
33.13 in the villages round **Jerusalem,** and in the towns of Judah,
33.16 people of Judah and of **Jerusalem** will be rescued and will
34. 1 subject to him, were attacking **Jerusalem** and its nearby towns.
34. 6 message to King Zedekiah in **Jerusalem** [7]while the army of
34. 8 Zedekiah and the people of **Jerusalem** had made an agreement
34.18 officials of Judah and of **Jerusalem,** together with the palace
35.11 decided to come to **Jerusalem** to get away from the Babylonian
35.11 That is why we are living in **Jerusalem."**
35.12 the people of Judah and **Jerusalem,** "I, the Lord, ask you
35.17 people of Judah and of **Jerusalem** all the destruction that I
36. 9 by all who lived in **Jerusalem** and by all who came there
36.31 you nor the people of **Jerusalem** and of Judah have paid any
37. 5 Babylonian army had been besieging **Jerusalem,** but when they
37.11 Babylonian army retreated from **Jerusalem** because the Egyptian
37.12 So I started to leave **Jerusalem** and go to the territory
38.28 in the palace courtyard until the day **Jerusalem** was captured.
39. 1 of Babylonia came with his whole army and attacked **Jerusalem.**
39. 3 (When **Jerusalem** was captured, all the high officials of
39. 8 houses of the people and tore down the walls of **Jerusalem.**
40. 1 other people from **Jerusalem** and Judah who were being taken
42.18 out on the people of **Jerusalem,** so my fury will be poured
44. 2 destruction I brought on **Jerusalem** and all the other cities
44. 6 and on the streets of **Jerusalem,** and I set them on fire.
44. 9 in the streets of **Jerusalem** by your ancestors, by the kings
44.13 in Egypt, just as I punished **Jerusalem**—with war, starvation,
44.17 do in the towns of Judah and in the streets of **Jerusalem.**
44.21 and in the streets of **Jerusalem**—do you think that the Lord
50.28 Babylonia and come to **Jerusalem,** and they tell how the Lord
51.10 and tell the people in **Jerusalem** what the Lord our God has
51.24 Babylonia and its people for all the evil they did to **Jerusalem.**
51.34 The king of Babylonia cut **Jerusalem** up and ate it.
51.35 people of **Jerusalem** say, "May Babylonia be held responsible
51.36 said to the people of **Jerusalem,** "I will take up your cause
51.50 far from home, think about me, your Lord, and remember **Jerusalem.**
52. 1 became king of Judah, and he ruled in **Jerusalem** for eleven
52. 3 angry with the people of **Jerusalem** and Judah that he banished
52. 4 all his army and attacked **Jerusalem** on the tenth day of the

Jer 52.12 adviser to the king and commander of his army, entered **Jerusalem.**
52.13 palace, and the houses of all the important people in **Jerusalem;**
52.29 in his eighteenth year, 832 from **Jerusalem;**
Lam 1. 1 How lonely lies **Jerusalem,** once so full of people!
1. 6 The splendour of **Jerusalem** is a thing of the past.
1. 7 A lonely ruin now, **Jerusalem** recalls her ancient splendour.
1. 8 **Jerusalem** made herself filthy with terrible sin.
2. 4 Here in **Jerusalem** we felt his burning anger.
2.10 **Jerusalem's** old men sit on the ground in silence,
2.13 O **Jerusalem,** beloved Jerusalem, what can I say?
2.15 They shake their heads and laugh at the ruins of **Jerusalem.**
2.18 O **Jerusalem,** let your very walls cry out to the Lord!
4.12 believed that any invader could enter **Jerusalem's** gates.
Ezek 4. 1 and scratch lines on it to represent the city of **Jerusalem.**
4. 7 "Fix your eyes on the siege of **Jerusalem.**
4.16 I am going to cut off the supply of bread for **Jerusalem.**
5. 5 The Sovereign Lord said, "Look at **Jerusalem.**
5. 6 But **Jerusalem** rebelled against my commands
5. 6 **Jerusalem** rejected my commands and refused to keep my laws.
5. 7 listen, **Jerusalem,** to what I, the Sovereign Lord, am saying.
5. 9 I hate, I will punish **Jerusalem** as I have never done before
5.10 As a result, parents in **Jerusalem** will eat their children,
8. 3 spirit lifted me high in the air and took me to **Jerusalem.**
9. 4 through the whole city of **Jerusalem** and put a mark on the
9. 8 are you so angry with **Jerusalem** that you are going to kill
9. 9 murder all over the land and have filled **Jerusalem** with crime.
11.15 "the people who live in **Jerusalem** are talking about you
12.10 for the prince ruling in **Jerusalem** and for all the people
12.19 Lord to the people of **Jerusalem** who are still living in
13.16 those prophets who assured **Jerusalem** that all was
14.21 my four worst punishments on **Jerusalem**—war, famine, wild
14.22 that the punishment I am bringing on **Jerusalem** is justified;
15. 6 take the people who live in **Jerusalem** [7]and will punish them.
16. 2 "point out to **Jerusalem** what disgusting things she has done.
16. 3 Tell **Jerusalem** what the Sovereign Lord is saying to her:
16.35 Now then, **Jerusalem,** you whore!
16.44 Lord said, "People will use this proverb about you, **Jerusalem:**
16.53 Lord said to **Jerusalem,** "I will make them prosperous again—
17.12 king of Babylonia came to **Jerusalem** and took the king and
21. 2 "Mortal man," he said, "denounce **Jerusalem.**
21.20 the other the way to Judah, to the fortified city, **Jerusalem.**
21.22 His right hand holds the arrow marked **'Jerusalem'!**
21.23 The people of **Jerusalem** won't believe this, because of
22.19 bring them all together in **Jerusalem** [20]in the same way that
22.21 I will gather them in **Jerusalem,** build a fire under them,
22.22 They will be melted in **Jerusalem** just as silver is melted
23. 4 the younger one was named Oholibah (she represents **Jerusalem).**
24. 2 that the king of Babylonia is beginning the siege of **Jerusalem.**
24.13 **Jerusalem,** your immoral actions have defiled you.
24.21 families who are left in **Jerusalem** will be killed in war.
26. 2 They shout, **'Jerusalem** is shattered!
33.21 man who had escaped from **Jerusalem** came and told me that the
36.38 as full of people as **Jerusalem** was once full of the sheep
40. 1 and the fourteenth year after **Jerusalem** was captured.
43. 3 when God came to destroy **Jerusalem,** and the one I saw by
48.30 There are twelve entrances to the city of **Jerusalem.**
Dan 1. 1 King Nebuchadnezzar of Babylonia attacked **Jerusalem** and surrounded
5. 2 Nebuchadnezzar had carried off from the Temple in **Jerusalem.**
6.10 of his house there were windows that faced towards **Jerusalem.**
9. 2 about the seventy years that **Jerusalem** would be in ruins,
9. 7 live in Judaea and in **Jerusalem** and of all the Israelites
9.12 You punished **Jerusalem** more severely than any other city
9.16 in the past, so do not be angry with **Jerusalem** any longer.
9.16 neighbouring countries look down on **Jerusalem** and on your
9.25 command is given to rebuild **Jerusalem,** until God's chosen
9.25 **Jerusalem** will be rebuilt with streets and strong defences,
Joel 2.32 As the Lord has said, 'Some in **Jerusalem** will escape;
3. 1 that time I will restore the prosperity of Judah and **Jerusalem.**
3. 6 the people of Judah and **Jerusalem** far from their own country
3.16 his voice thunders from **Jerusalem;**
3.17 **Jerusalem** will be a sacred city;
3.20 But Judah and **Jerusalem** will be inhabited for ever,
Amos 1. 2 his voice thunders from **Jerusalem.**
2. 5 fire upon Judah and burn down the fortresses of **Jerusalem."**
Obad 11 strangers who carried off **Jerusalem's** wealth and divided it
20 The exiles from **Jerusalem** who are in Sardis will capture the
21 The victorious men of **Jerusalem** will attack Edom and rule
Mic 1. 1 revealed to Micah all these things about Samaria and **Jerusalem.**
1. 5 **Jerusalem** itself!
1. 9 destruction has reached the gates of **Jerusalem** itself,
1.12 because the Lord has brought disaster close to **Jerusalem.**
1.13 imitated the sins of Israel and so caused **Jerusalem** to sin.
3.10 building God's city, **Jerusalem,** on a foundation of murder and
3.12 ploughed like a field, **Jerusalem** will become a pile of ruins,
4. 2 For the Lord's teaching comes from **Jerusalem;**
4. 8 **Jerusalem,** where God, like a shepherd, watches over his people,
4.10 and groan, people of **Jerusalem,** like a woman giving birth,
4.11 They say, **"Jerusalem** must be destroyed!
4.13 Lord says, "People of **Jerusalem,** go and punish your enemies!
5. 1 People of **Jerusalem,** gather your forces!
7.11 People of **Jerusalem,** the time to rebuild the city walls
Zeph 1. 4 "I will punish the people of **Jerusalem** and of all Judah.
1.10 will hear the sound of crying at the Fish Gate in **Jerusalem.**
1.12 "At that time I will take a lamp and search **Jerusalem.**
3. 1 **Jerusalem** is doomed, that corrupt, rebellious city that
3.14 Rejoice with all your heart, **Jerusalem!**
3.16 when they will say to **Jerusalem,** "Do not be afraid, city of
Zech 1.12 you have been angry with **Jerusalem** and the cities of Judah
1.14 deep love and concern for **Jerusalem,** my holy city,

Zech 1.16 I have come back to **Jerusalem** to show mercy to the city.
1.17 he will once again help **Jerusalem** and claim the city as his
1.19 have scattered the people of Judah, Israel, and **Jerusalem."**
2. 2 "To measure **Jerusalem,"** he answered, "to see how long and
2. 4 and so much livestock in **Jerusalem** that it will be too big
2. 6 now, you exiles, escape from Babylonia and return to **Jerusalem.**
2.10 The Lord said, "Sing for joy, people of **Jerusalem!**
2.12 in his sacred land, and **Jerusalem** will be the city he loves
3. 2 May the Lord, who loves **Jerusalem,** condemn you.
7. 7 prophets at the time when **Jerusalem** was prosperous and filled
8. 2 "I have longed to help **Jerusalem** because of my deep love
8. 3 I will return to **Jerusalem,** my holy city, and live there.
8. 8 bring them back from east and west to live in **Jerusalem.**
8.15 I am planning to bless the people of **Jerusalem** and Judah.
8.20 is coming when people from many cities will come to **Jerusalem.**
8.22 powerful nations will come to **Jerusalem** to worship the Lord
9. 9 Shout for joy, you people of **Jerusalem!**
9.10 war-chariots from Israel and take the horses from **Jerusalem;**
12. 2 He says, [2]"I will make **Jerusalem** like a cup of wine;
12. 2 when they besiege **Jerusalem,** the cities of the rest of Judah
12. 3 time comes, I will make **Jerusalem** like a heavy stone—
12. 5 Almighty gives strength to his people who live in **Jerusalem.'**
12. 6 The people of **Jerusalem** will remain safe in the city.
12. 7 and the people of **Jerusalem** will receive will be no greater
12. 8 protect those who live in **Jerusalem,** and even the weakest
12. 9 I will destroy every nation that tries to attack **Jerusalem.**
12.10 and the other people of **Jerusalem** with the spirit of mercy
12.11 that time the mourning in **Jerusalem** will be as great as the
13. 1 and the people of **Jerusalem** from their sin and idolatry.
14. 1 Then **Jerusalem** will be looted, and the loot will be divided
14. 2 will bring all the nations together to make war on **Jerusalem.**
14. 4 will stand on the Mount of Olives, to the east of **Jerusalem.**
14. 8 fresh water will flow from **Jerusalem,** half of it to the Dead
14.10 **Jerusalem** will tower above the land round it;
14.12 terrible disease on all the nations that make war on **Jerusalem.**
14.14 The men of Judah will fight to defend **Jerusalem.**
14.16 nations that have attacked **Jerusalem** will go there each year
14.21 Every cooking-pot in **Jerusalem** and in all Judah will be

Mal 2.11 done a horrible thing in **Jerusalem** and all over the country.
3. 4 the people of Judah and **Jerusalem** bring to the Lord will be

Mt 2. 1 came from the east to **Jerusalem** [2]and asked, "Where is the
2. 3 he was very upset, and so was everyone else in **Jerusalem.**
3. 5 People came to him from **Jerusalem,** from the whole province of
4. 5 the Devil took Jesus to **Jerusalem,** the Holy City, set him on
4.25 and the Ten Towns, from **Jerusalem,** Judaea, and the land on
5.35 nor by **Jerusalem,** for it is the city of the great King.
15. 1 of the Law came from **Jerusalem** to Jesus and asked him,
16.21 "I must go to **Jerusalem** and suffer much from the elders,
20.17 Jesus was going up to **Jerusalem,** he took the twelve disciples
20.18 "we are going up to **Jerusalem,** where the Son of Man will
21. 1 Jesus and his disciples approached **Jerusalem,** they came to
21.10 When Jesus entered **Jerusalem,** the whole city was thrown into an uproar.
23.37 "Jerusalem, **Jerusalem!**

Mk 1. 5 of Judaea and the city of **Jerusalem** went out to hear John.
3. 8 from Judaea, [8]from **Jerusalem,** from the territory of Idumea,
3.22 who had come from **Jerusalem** were saying, "He has Beelzebul in
7. 1 of the Law who had come from **Jerusalem** gathered round Jesus.
10.32 his disciples were now on the road going up to **Jerusalem.**
10.33 "we are going up to **Jerusalem** where the Son of Man will
11. 1 As they approached **Jerusalem,** near the towns of Bethphage and
11.11 Jesus entered **Jerusalem,** went into the Temple, and looked
11.15 When they arrived in **Jerusalem,** Jesus went to the Temple
11.27 They arrived once again in **Jerusalem.**
15.41 women who had come to **Jerusalem** with him were there also.

Lk 2.22 they took the child to **Jerusalem** to present him to the Lord,
2.25 At that time there was a man named Simeon living in **Jerusalem.**
2.38 to all who were waiting for God to set **Jerusalem** free.
2.41 the parents of Jesus went to **Jerusalem** for the Passover Festival.
2.43 they started back home, but the boy Jesus stayed in **Jerusalem.**
2.45 find him, so they went back to **Jerusalem** looking for him.
4. 9 the Devil took him to **Jerusalem** and set him on the highest
5.17 from every town in Galilee and Judaea and from **Jerusalem.**
6.17 all over Judaea and from **Jerusalem** and from the coastal cities
9.31 he would soon fulfil God's purpose by dying in **Jerusalem.**
9.51 made up his mind and set out on his way to **Jerusalem.**
9.53 because it was clear that he was on his way to **Jerusalem.**
10.30 going down from **Jerusalem** to Jericho when robbers attacked him,
13. 4 were worse than all the other people living in **Jerusalem?**
13.22 teaching the people and making his way towards **Jerusalem.**
13.33 for a prophet to be killed anywhere except in **Jerusalem.**
13.34 **"Jerusalem, Jerusalem!**
17.11 Jesus made his way to **Jerusalem,** he went along the border
18.31 We are going to **Jerusalem** where everything the prophets wrote
19.11 was now almost at **Jerusalem,** and they supposed that the Kingdom
19.28 Jesus said this and then went on to **Jerusalem** ahead of them.
19.37 When he came near **Jerusalem,** at the place where the road
21.20 "When you see **Jerusalem** surrounded by armies, then you will
21.24 the heathen will trample over **Jerusalem** until their time is up.
23. 7 sent him to Herod, who was also in **Jerusalem** at that time.
23.28 Jesus turned to them and said, "Women of **Jerusalem!**
24.13 Emmaus, about eleven kilometres from **Jerusalem,** [14]and they were
24.18 the only visitor in **Jerusalem** who doesn't know the things that
24.33 and went back to **Jerusalem,** where they found the eleven disciples
24.47 must be preached to all nations, beginning in **Jerusalem.**
24.52 went back into **Jerusalem,** filled with great joy, [53]and spent

Jn 1.19 authorities in **Jerusalem** sent some priests and Levites to John,
2.13 almost time for the Passover Festival, so Jesus went to **Jerusalem.**
2.23 While Jesus was in **Jerusalem** during the Passover Festival,
4.20 but you Jews say that **Jerusalem** is the place where we should
4.21 not worship the Father either on this mountain or in **Jerusalem.**
4.45 to the Passover Festival in **Jerusalem** and had seen everything
5. 1 After this, Jesus went to **Jerusalem** for a religious festival.
5. 2 Near the Sheep Gate in **Jerusalem** there is a pool with five
7.25 Some of the people of **Jerusalem** said, "Isn't this the man
10.22 of the Dedication of the Temple was being celebrated in **Jerusalem.**
11.18 less than three kilometres from **Jerusalem,** [19]and many Judaeans
11.55 the country to **Jerusalem** to perform the ritual of purification
12.12 to the Passover Festival heard that Jesus was coming to **Jerusalem.**
12.20 those who had gone to **Jerusalem** to worship during the festival.

Acts 1. 4 "Do not leave **Jerusalem,** but wait for the gift I told you
1. 8 be witnesses for me in **Jerusalem,** in all Judaea and Samaria,
1.12 the apostles went back to **Jerusalem** from the Mount of Olives,
1.19 All the people living in **Jerusalem** heard about it,
2. 5 There were Jews living in **Jerusalem,** religious men who had come
2.14 of you who live in **Jerusalem,** listen to me and let me
4. 5 the elders, and the teachers of the Law gathered in **Jerusalem.**
4.16 "Everyone in **Jerusalem** knows that this extraordinary miracle has
5.16 in from the towns around **Jerusalem,** bringing those who were ill
5.28 spread your teaching all over **Jerusalem,** and you want to
6. 7 The number of disciples in **Jerusalem** grew larger and larger,
8. 1 day the church in **Jerusalem** began to suffer cruel persecution.
8.14 The apostles in **Jerusalem** heard that the people of Samaria had
8.25 the Lord's message, Peter and John went back to **Jerusalem.**
8.26 and go south to the road that goes from **Jerusalem** to Gaza."
8.27 He had been to **Jerusalem** to worship God and was going back
9. 2 them, both men and women, and bring them back to **Jerusalem.**
9.13 the terrible things he has done to your people in **Jerusalem.**
9.21 the one who in **Jerusalem** was killing those who worship that
9.26 Saul went to **Jerusalem** and tried to join the disciples.
9.28 and went all over **Jerusalem,** preaching boldly in the name of
10.39 that he did in the land of Israel and in **Jerusalem.**
11. 2 Peter went to **Jerusalem,** those who were in favour of circumcising
11.22 reached the church in **Jerusalem,** so they sent Barnabas to Antioch.
11.27 About that time some prophets went from **Jerusalem** to Antioch.
12.25 their mission and returned from **Jerusalem,** taking John Mark
13.13 Pamphylia, where John Mark left them and went back to **Jerusalem.**
13.27 the people who live in **Jerusalem** and their leaders did not
13.31 to those who had travelled with him from Galilee to **Jerusalem.**
15. 2 in Antioch should go to **Jerusalem** and see the apostles and
15. 4 they arrived in **Jerusalem,** they were welcomed by the church,
16. 4 the apostles and elders in **Jerusalem,** and told them to obey
18.22 at Caesarea, he went to **Jerusalem** and greeted the church,
19.21 travel through Macedonia and Achaia and go on to **Jerusalem.**
20.16 a hurry to arrive in **Jerusalem** by the day of Pentecost,
20.22 I am going to **Jerusalem,** not knowing what will happen to
21. 4 power of the Spirit they told Paul not to go to **Jerusalem.**
21. 8 the seven men who had been chosen as helpers in **Jerusalem.**
21.11 way by the Jews in **Jerusalem,** and they will hand him over
21.12 we and the others there begged Paul not to go to **Jerusalem.**
21.13 to be tied up in **Jerusalem** but even to die there for
21.15 time there, we got our things ready and left for **Jerusalem.**
21.17 When we arrived in **Jerusalem,** the believers welcomed us warmly.
21.31 the commander of the Roman troops that all **Jerusalem** was rioting.
22. 3 but brought up here in **Jerusalem** as a student of Gamaliel.
22. 5 and bring them back in chains to **Jerusalem** to be punished.
22.17 "I went back to **Jerusalem,** and while I was praying in
22.18 'Hurry and leave **Jerusalem** quickly, because the people here will
23.11 witness for me here in **Jerusalem,** and you must also do the
24.11 than twelve days ago that I went to **Jerusalem** to worship.
24.17 "After being away from **Jerusalem** for several years, I went
25. 1 he went from Caesarea to **Jerusalem,** [2]where the chief priests
25. 3 favour of bringing Paul to **Jerusalem,** for they had made a
25. 7 Jews who had come from **Jerusalem** stood round him and started
25. 9 be willing to go to **Jerusalem** and be tried on these charges
25.15 when I went to **Jerusalem,** the Jewish chief priests and elders
25.20 be willing to go to **Jerusalem** and be tried there on these
25.24 people, both here and in **Jerusalem,** have brought complaints to me.
26. 4 life, at first in my own country and then in **Jerusalem.**
26.10 That is what I did in **Jerusalem.**
26.20 First in Damascus and in **Jerusalem** and then in all Judaea
28.17 made a prisoner in **Jerusalem** and handed over to the Romans.

Rom 15.19 all the way from **Jerusalem** to Illyricum, I have proclaimed fully
15.25 however, I am going to **Jerusalem** in the service of God's
15.26 offering to help the poor among God's people in **Jerusalem.**
15.31 that my service in **Jerusalem** may be acceptable to God's people

1 Cor 16. 3 have approved, and send them to take your gift to **Jerusalem.**

Gal 1.17 nor did I go to **Jerusalem** to see those who were apostles
1.18 later that I went to **Jerusalem** to obtain information from Peter,
2. 1 later I went back to **Jerusalem** with Barnabas, taking Titus along
4.25 present city of **Jerusalem,** in slavery with all its people.
4.26 But the heavenly **Jerusalem** is free, and she is our mother.

Heb 12.22 the heavenly **Jerusalem,** with its thousands of angels.

Rev 3.12 of my God, the new **Jerusalem,** which will come down out of
21. 2 the Holy City, the new **Jerusalem,** coming down out of heaven
21.10 He showed me **Jerusalem,** the Holy City, coming down out of

JESHANAH GATE

Neh 3. 6 Joiada son of Paseah and Meshullam son of Besodeiah rebuilt **Jeshanah Gate.**
12.39 we went past Ephraim Gate, **Jeshanah Gate,** the Fish Gate, the

JESSE

David's father.

Ruth 4.17 Obed became the father of **Jesse,** who was the father of David.
4.18 Ram, Amminadab, Nahshon, Salmon, Boaz, Obed, **Jesse,** David.
1 Sam 16. 1 Bethlehem, to a man named **Jesse,** because I have chosen one
16. 3 Invite **Jesse** to the sacrifice, and I will tell you what to
16. 5 He also told **Jesse** and his sons to purify themselves, and he
16. 6 Samuel saw **Jesse's** son Eliab and said to himself,
16. 8 **Jesse** called his son Abinadab and brought him to Samuel.
16. 9 **Jesse** then brought Shammah.
16.10 In this way **Jesse** brought seven of his sons to Samuel.
16.11 **Jesse** answered, "There is still the youngest, but he is out
16.12 So **Jesse** sent for him.
16.18 his attendants said, "**Jesse,** of the town of Bethlehem, has
16.19 Saul sent messengers to **Jesse** to say, "Send me your son
16.20 **Jesse** sent David to Saul with a young goat, a donkey
16.22 Then Saul sent a message to **Jesse:**
17.12 David was the son of **Jesse,** who was an Ephrathite
17.12 **Jesse** had eight sons, and at the time Saul was king,
17.17 One day **Jesse** said to David, "Take ten kilogrammes of
17.20 took the food, and went as **Jesse** had told him to.
17.58 son of your servant **Jesse** from Bethlehem," David answered.
2 Sam 23. 1 David son of **Jesse** was the man whom God made great,
1 Chr 2.10 The family line from Ram to **Jesse** is as follows:
2.12 Salmon, Boaz, [12]Obed, and **Jesse.**
2.13 **Jesse** had seven sons.
2.16 **Jesse's** daughter Zeruiah had three sons:
10.14 him and gave control of the kingdom to David son of **Jesse.**
12.18 "David son of **Jesse,** we are yours!
29.26 David son of **Jesse** ruled over all Israel
2 Chr 11.18 was Abihail, the daughter of Eliab and granddaughter of **Jesse.**
Ps 72.20 This is the end of the prayers of David son of **Jesse.**
Mt 1. 2 Obed (his mother was Ruth), **Jesse,** and King David.
Lk 3.32 of David, [32]the son of **Jesse,** the son of Obed,
Acts 13.22 found that David son of **Jesse** is the kind of man I
Rom 15.12 And again, Isaiah says, "A descendant of **Jesse** will appear;

JESUS

[CHRIST JESUS]
see also **CHRIST**
For sayings of Jesus see **JESUS SAID**

Mt 1. 1 list of the ancestors of **Jesus Christ,** a descendant of David,
1.12 Babylon to the birth of **Jesus,** the following ancestors are listed:
1.12 Mary, the mother of **Jesus,** who was called the Messiah.
1.18 This was how the birth of **Jesus Christ** took place.
1.21 and you will name him **Jesus**—because he will save his people
1.25 And Joseph named him **Jesus.**
2. 1 **Jesus** was born in the town of Bethlehem in Judaea, during
3.13 At that time **Jesus** arrived from Galilee and came to John
3.16 As soon as **Jesus** was baptized, he came up out of the
4. 1 Then the Spirit led **Jesus** into the desert to be tempted
4. 2 spending forty days and nights without food, **Jesus** was hungry.
4. 5 Then the Devil took **Jesus** to Jerusalem, the Holy City, set
4. 8 Then the Devil took **Jesus** to a very high mountain and
4.11 Then the Devil left **Jesus;**
4.12 When **Jesus** heard that John had been put in prison, he
4.17 From that time **Jesus** began to preach his message:
4.18 As **Jesus** walked along the shore of Lake Galilee, he saw
4.21 **Jesus** called them, [22]and at once they left the boat and
4.23 **Jesus** went all over Galilee, teaching in the synagogues,
4.24 and epileptics, and paralytics—and **Jesus** healed them all.
5. 1 **Jesus** saw the crowds and went up a hill, where he sat
7.28 When **Jesus** finished saying these things, the crowd was amazed
8. 1 When **Jesus** came down from the hill, large crowds followed him.
8. 3 **Jesus** stretched out his hand and touched him.
8. 5 When **Jesus** entered Capernaum, a Roman officer met him
8.10 **Jesus** heard this, he was surprised and said to the people
8.14 **Jesus** went to Peter's home, and there he saw Peter's
8.16 came, people brought to **Jesus** many who had demons in them.
8.16 **Jesus** drove out the evil spirits with a word and healed all
8.18 **Jesus** noticed the crowd round him, he ordered his disciples
8.23 **Jesus** got into a boat, and his disciples went with him.
8.24 But **Jesus** was asleep.
8.28 When **Jesus** came to the territory of Gadara on the other
8.31 So the demons begged **Jesus,** "If you are going to drive
8.32 "Go," **Jesus** told them;
8.34 So everyone from the town went out to meet **Jesus;**
9. 1 **Jesus** got into the boat and went back across the lake to
9. 2 When **Jesus** saw how much faith they had, he said to the
9. 4 **Jesus** perceived what they were thinking, so he said, "Why are
9. 9 **Jesus** left that place, and as he walked along, he saw
9.10 **Jesus** was having a meal in Matthew's house, many tax collectors
9.10 outcasts came and joined **Jesus** and his disciples at the table.
9.12 **Jesus** heard them and answered, "People who are well do
9.14 John the Baptist came to **Jesus,** asking, "Why is it that we
9.18 While **Jesus** was saying this, a Jewish official came to him,
9.19 **Jesus** got up and followed him, and his disciples went along
9.20 came up behind **Jesus** and touched the edge of his
9.22 **Jesus** turned round and saw her, and said, "Courage, my
9.23 Then **Jesus** went into the official's house.
9.25 people had been put out, **Jesus** went into the girl's room
9.27 **Jesus** left that place, and as he walked along, two blind
9.28 When **Jesus** had gone indoors, the two blind men came to him,
Mt 9.29 Then **Jesus** touched their eyes and said, "Let it happen, then,
9.30 **Jesus** spoke sternly to them, "Don't tell this to anyone!"
9.31 and spread the news about **Jesus** all over that part of the
9.32 leaving, some people brought to **Jesus** a man who could not
9.35 **Jesus** went round visiting all the towns and villages.
10. 1 **Jesus** called his twelve disciples together and gave them authority
10. 4 Simon the Patriot, and Judas Iscariot, who betrayed **Jesus.**
10. 5 These twelve men were sent out by **Jesus** with the following
11. 1 **Jesus** finished giving these instructions to his twelve disciples,
11. 3 "Tell us," they asked **Jesus,** "are you the one John said
11. 7 While John's disciples were leaving, **Jesus** spoke about him to
11.20 in the towns where **Jesus** had performed most of his miracles
12. 1 **Jesus** was walking through some cornfields on the Sabbath.
12. 2 saw this, they said to **Jesus,** "Look, it is against our Law
12. 9 **Jesus** left that place and went to a synagogue, [10]where
12.10 there who wanted to accuse **Jesus** of doing wrong, so they
12.14 Then the Pharisees left and made plans to kill **Jesus.**
12.15 When **Jesus** heard about the plot against him, he went away
12.22 Then some people brought to **Jesus** a man who was blind
12.22 **Jesus** healed the man, so that he was able to talk and
12.23 The crowds were all amazed at what **Jesus** had done.
12.25 **Jesus** knew what they were thinking, so he said to them,
12.46 **Jesus** was still talking to the people when his mother and
13. 1 That same day **Jesus** left the house and went to the lake-side,
13.10 Then the disciples came to **Jesus** and asked him, "Why do
13.24 **Jesus** told them another parable:
13.31 **Jesus** told them another parable:
13.33 **Jesus** told them still another parable:
13.34 **Jesus** used parables to tell all these things to the crowds;
13.36 **Jesus** had left the crowd and gone indoors, his disciples came
13.53 When **Jesus** finished telling these parables, he left that place
14. 1 At that time Herod, the ruler of Galilee, heard about **Jesus.**
14.12 then they went and told **Jesus.**
14.13 When **Jesus** heard the news about John, he left there in a
14.14 **Jesus** got out of the boat, and when he saw the large
14.22 Then **Jesus** made the disciples get into the boat and go
14.23 When evening came, **Jesus** was there alone;
14.25 six o'clock in the morning **Jesus** came to the disciples, walking
14.27 **Jesus** spoke to them at once.
14.29 out of the boat and started walking on the water to **Jesus.**
14.31 At once **Jesus** reached out and grabbed hold of him and said,
14.33 Then the disciples in the boat worshipped **Jesus.**
14.35 came to land at Gennesaret, [35]where the people recognized **Jesus.**
14.35 people in all the surrounding country and brought them to **Jesus.**
15. 1 Law came from Jerusalem to **Jesus** and asked him, [2]"Why is
15.10 Then **Jesus** called the crowd to him and said to them,
15.21 **Jesus** left that place and went off to the territory near
15.23 But **Jesus** did not say a word to her.
15.29 **Jesus** left there and went along by Lake Galilee.
15.30 and many other sick people, whom they placed at **Jesus'** feet;
15.32 **Jesus** called his disciples to him and said, "I feel
15.35 So **Jesus** ordered the crowd to sit down on the ground.
15.39 Then **Jesus** sent the people away, got into a boat, and
16. 1 and Sadducees who came to **Jesus** wanted to trap him, so they
16. 8 **Jesus** knew what they were saying, so he asked them, "Why
16.13 **Jesus** went to the territory near the town of Caesarea Philippi,
16.20 **Jesus** ordered his disciples not to tell anyone that he was
16.21 From that time on **Jesus** began to say plainly to his disciples,
16.23 **Jesus** turned around and said to Peter, "Get away from me,
17. 1 Six days later **Jesus** took with him Peter and the brothers
17. 2 As they looked on, a change came over **Jesus:**
17. 3 Then the three disciples saw Moses and Elijah talking with **Jesus.**
17. 4 spoke up and said to **Jesus,** "Lord, how good it is that
17. 7 **Jesus** came to them and touched them.
17. 8 So they looked up and saw no one there but **Jesus.**
17. 9 came down the mountain, **Jesus** ordered them, "Don't tell anyone
17.10 the disciples asked **Jesus,** "Why do the teachers of the Law
17.14 a man came to **Jesus,** knelt before him, [15]and said, "Sir,
17.18 **Jesus** gave a command to the demon, and it went out of
17.19 Then the disciples came to **Jesus** in private and asked him,
17.20 "It was because you haven't enough faith," answered **Jesus.**
17.24 **Jesus** and his disciples came to Capernaum, the collectors of the
17.25 Peter went into the house, **Jesus** spoke up first, "Simon,
18. 1 the disciples came to **Jesus,** asking, "Who is the greatest in
18. 2 So **Jesus** called a child, made him stand in front of them,
18.21 Peter came to **Jesus** and asked, "Lord, if my brother keeps
19. 1 When **Jesus** finished saying these things, he left Galilee
19.13 people brought children to **Jesus** for him to place his hands
19.16 Once a man came to **Jesus.**
19.26 **Jesus** looked straight at them and answered, "This is impossible
20.17 **Jesus** was going up to Jerusalem, he took the twelve disciples
20.20 wife of Zebedee came to **Jesus** with her two sons, bowed
20.25 So **Jesus** called them all together and said, "You know that
20.29 **Jesus** and his disciples were leaving Jericho, a large crowd was
20.30 by the road heard that **Jesus** was passing by, so they began
20.32 **Jesus** stopped and called them.
20.34 **Jesus** had pity on them and touched their eyes;
21. 1 As **Jesus** and his disciples approached Jerusalem, they came to
21. 1 **Jesus** sent two of the disciples on ahead [2]with these instructions:
21. 6 the disciples went and did what **Jesus** had told them to do:
21. 7 the colt, threw their cloaks over them, and **Jesus** got on.
21. 9 crowds walking in front of **Jesus** and those walking behind began
21.10 **Jesus** entered Jerusalem, the whole city was thrown into an uproar.
21.11 prophet **Jesus,** from Nazareth in Galilee," the crowds answered.
21.12 **Jesus** went into the Temple and drove out all those who
21.16 So they asked **Jesus,** "Do you hear what they are saying?"
21.17 **Jesus** left them and went out of the city to Bethany,
21.18 way back to the city early next morning, **Jesus** was hungry.
21.23 **Jesus** came back to the Temple;
21.27 So they answered **Jesus,** "We don't know."

Mt 21.45 priests and the Pharisees heard **Jesus'** parables and knew that he
21.46 afraid of the crowds, who considered **Jesus** to be a prophet.
22. 1 **Jesus** again used parables in talking to the people.
22.15 Pharisees went off and made a plan to trap **Jesus** with questions.
22.18 **Jesus,** however, was aware of their evil plan, and so he said,
22.23 some Sadducees came to **Jesus** and claimed that people will not
22.34 the Pharisees heard that **Jesus** had silenced the Sadducees,
22.41 When some Pharisees gathered together, **Jesus** asked them,
22.43 "Why, then," **Jesus** asked, "did the Spirit inspire David
22.46 one was able to give **Jesus** any answer, and from that day
23. 1 Then **Jesus** spoke to the crowds and to his disciples.
24. 1 **Jesus** left and was going away from the Temple when his
24. 3 As **Jesus** sat on the Mount of Olives, the disciples came to
26. 1 When **Jesus** had finished teaching all these things, he said to
26. 4 and made plans to arrest **Jesus** secretly and put him to death.
26. 6 **Jesus** was in Bethany at the house of Simon, a man who
26. 7 While **Jesus** was eating, a woman came to him with an
26.10 **Jesus** knew what they were saying, so he said to them,
26.15 asked, "What will you give me if I betray **Jesus** to you?"
26.16 was looking for a good chance to hand **Jesus** over to them.
26.17 the disciples came to **Jesus** and asked him, "Where do you
26.19 disciples did as **Jesus** had told them and prepared the Passover
26.20 When it was evening, **Jesus** and the twelve disciples sat down
26.26 While they were eating, **Jesus** took a piece of bread,
26.33 spoke up and said to **Jesus,** "I will never leave you, even
26.36 **Jesus** went with his disciples to a place called Gethsemane,
26.42 Once more **Jesus** went away and prayed, "My Father, if
26.44 Again **Jesus** left them, went away, and prayed the third time,
26.47 **Jesus** was still speaking when Judas, one of the twelve disciples,
26.49 Judas went straight to **Jesus** and said, "Peace be with you,
26.50 Then they came up, arrested **Jesus,** and held him tight.
26.51 of those who were with **Jesus** drew his sword and struck at
26.55 Then **Jesus** spoke to the crowd, "Did you have to come
26.57 who had arrested **Jesus** took him to the house of Caiaphas,
26.59 find some false evidence against **Jesus** to put him to death;
26.62 stood up and said to **Jesus,** "Have you no answer to give
26.63 But **Jesus** kept quiet.
26.69 to him and said, "You, too, were with **Jesus** of Galilee."
26.71 said to the men there, "He was with **Jesus of Nazareth."**
26.75 a cock crowed, [75]and Peter remembered what **Jesus** had told him:
27. 1 elders made their plans against **Jesus** to put him to death.
27. 3 Judas, the traitor, learnt that **Jesus** had been condemned,
27.11 **Jesus** stood before the Roman governor, who questioned him.
27.14 But **Jesus** refused to answer a single word, with the result
27.17 Jesus Barabbas or **Jesus** called the Messiah?"
27.18 Jewish authorities had handed **Jesus** over to him because they were
27.20 ask Pilate to set Barabbas free and have **Jesus** put to death.
27.22 "What, then, shall I do with **Jesus** called the Messiah?"
27.26 and after he had **Jesus** whipped, he handed him over to be
27.27 Then Pilate's soldiers took **Jesus** into the governor's palace,
27.32 named Simon, and the soldiers forced him to carry **Jesus'** cross.
27.34 There they offered **Jesus** wine mixed with a bitter substance;
27.37 "This is **Jesus,** the King of the Jews."
27.38 they crucified two bandits with **Jesus,** one on his right and
27.39 People passing by shook their heads and hurled insults at **Jesus:**
27.46 At about three o'clock **Jesus** cried out with a loud shout,
27.50 **Jesus** again gave a loud cry and breathed his last.
27.53 left the graves, and after **Jesus** rose from death, they went
27.54 who were watching **Jesus** saw the earthquake and everything else
27.55 who had followed **Jesus** from Galilee and helped him.
27.57 his name was Joseph, and he also was a disciple of **Jesus.**
27.58 into the presence of Pilate and asked for the body of **Jesus.**
28. 5 "I know you are looking for **Jesus,** who was crucified.
28. 9 Suddenly **Jesus** met them and said, "Peace be with you."
28.16 to the hill in Galilee where **Jesus** had told them to go.
28.18 **Jesus** drew near and said to them, "I have been given

Mk 1. 1 This is the Good News about **Jesus Christ,** the Son of God.
1. 9 Not long afterwards **Jesus** came from Nazareth in the province
1.10 As soon as **Jesus** came up out of the water, he saw
1.14 had been put in prison, **Jesus** went to Galilee and preached
1.16 As **Jesus** walked along the shore of Lake Galilee, he saw
1.20 As soon as **Jesus** saw them, he called them;
1.20 Zebedee in the boat with the hired men and went with **Jesus.**
1.21 **Jesus** and his disciples came to the town of Capernaum,
1.21 and on the next Sabbath **Jesus** went to the synagogue and
1.24 and screamed, [24]"What do you want with us, **Jesus of Nazareth?**
1.25 **Jesus** ordered the spirit, "Be quiet, and come out of the man!"
1.28 so the news about **Jesus** spread quickly everywhere in the province
1.29 **Jesus** and his disciples, including James and John, left the
1.30 fever, and as soon as **Jesus** arrived, he was told about her.
1.32 people brought to **Jesus** all the sick and those who
1.34 **Jesus** healed many who were sick with all kinds of diseases
1.35 long before daylight, **Jesus** got up and left the house.
1.40 dreaded skin-disease came to **Jesus,** knelt down, and begged him
1.41 **Jesus** was filled with pity, and stretched out his hand
1.43 Then **Jesus** spoke sternly to him and sent him away at once,
1.45 he talked so much that **Jesus** could not go into a town
2. 1 A few days later **Jesus** went back to Capernaum, and the
2. 2 **Jesus** was preaching the message to them [3]when four men arrived,
2. 3 carrying a paralysed man to **Jesus.**
2. 4 a hole in the roof right above the place where **Jesus** was.
2. 8 At once **Jesus** knew what they were thinking, so he said to
2.13 **Jesus** went back again to the shore of Lake Galilee.
2.15 Later on **Jesus** was having a meal in Levi's house.
2.15 and other outcasts were following **Jesus,** and many of them joined
2.16 who were Pharisees, saw that **Jesus** was eating with these outcasts
2.17 **Jesus** heard them and answered, "People who are well do
2.18 Some people came to **Jesus** and asked him, "Why is it that
2.23 **Jesus** was walking through some cornfields on the Sabbath.
2.24 So the Pharisees said to **Jesus,** "Look, it is against
3. 1 Then **Jesus** went back to the synagogue, where there was a
3. 2 people were there who wanted to accuse **Jesus** of doing wrong;
3. 5 **Jesus** was angry as he looked round at them, but at the
3. 6 of Herod's party, and they made plans to kill **Jesus.**
3. 7 **Jesus** and his disciples went away to Lake Galilee, and a
3. 8 All these people came to **Jesus** because they had heard of the
3. 9 crowd was so large that **Jesus** told his disciples to get
3.12 **Jesus** sternly ordered the evil spirits not to tell anyone who
3.13 Then **Jesus** went up a hill and called to himself the men
3.16 Simon **(Jesus** gave him the name Peter);
3.17 the sons of Zebedee **(Jesus** gave them the name Boanerges,
3.19 and Judas Iscariot, who betrayed **Jesus.**
3.20 Then **Jesus** went home.
3.20 a large crowd gathered that **Jesus** and his disciples had no
3.23 So **Jesus** called them to him and spoke to them in parables:
3.31 Then **Jesus'** mother and brothers arrived.
3.32 A crowd was sitting round **Jesus,** and they said to him,
4. 1 Again **Jesus** began to teach beside Lake Galilee.
4.10 When **Jesus** was alone, some of those who had heard him
4.13 Then **Jesus** asked them, "Don't you understand this parable?
4.33 **Jesus** preached his message to the people, using many other
4.36 into the boat in which **Jesus** was already sitting, and they
4.38 **Jesus** was in the back of the boat, sleeping with his
4.39 **Jesus** stood up and commanded the wind, "Be quiet!"
5. 1 **Jesus** and his disciples arrived on the other side of Lake Galilee,
5. 2 As soon as **Jesus** got out of the boat, he was met
5. 6 He was some distance away when he saw **Jesus;**
5. 7 screamed in a loud voice, **"Jesus,** Son of the Most High God!
5.10 And he kept begging **Jesus** not to send the evil spirits
5.12 So the spirits begged **Jesus,** "Send us to the pigs, and
5.15 and when they came to **Jesus,** they saw the man who used
5.17 So they asked **Jesus** to leave their territory.
5.18 As **Jesus** was getting into the boat, the man who had
5.19 But **Jesus** would not let him.
5.20 through the Ten Towns, telling what **Jesus** had done for him.
5.21 **Jesus** went back across to the other side of the lake.
5.22 arrived, and when he saw **Jesus,** he threw himself down at his
5.24 Then **Jesus** started off with him.
5.24 people were going along with **Jesus** that they were crowding him
5.27 She had heard about **Jesus,** so she came in the crowd
5.30 At once **Jesus** knew that power had gone out of him,
5.32 But **Jesus** kept looking round to see who had done it.
5.36 **Jesus** paid no attention to what they said, but told him,
5.38 arrived at Jairus' house, where **Jesus** saw the confusion and heard
5.43 But **Jesus** gave them strict orders not to tell anyone,
6. 1 **Jesus** left that place and went back to his home town,
6. 6 Then **Jesus** went to the villages round there, teaching the people.
6.14 Herod heard about all this, because **Jesus'** reputation had spread
6.30 apostles returned and met with **Jesus,** and told him all they
6.31 people coming and going that **Jesus** and his disciples didn't even
6.33 and arrived at the place ahead of **Jesus** and his disciples.
6.34 When **Jesus** got out of the boat, he saw this large crowd,
6.38 So **Jesus** asked them, "How much bread have you got?
6.39 **Jesus** then told his disciples to make all the people
6.41 Then **Jesus** took the five loaves and the two fish, looked
6.45 At once **Jesus** made his disciples get into the boat and
6.47 in the middle of the lake, while **Jesus** was alone on land.
6.54 As they left the boat, people recognized **Jesus** at once.
6.56 everywhere **Jesus** went, to villages, towns, or farms, people would
7. 1 of the Law who had come from Jerusalem gathered round **Jesus.**
7. 5 teachers of the Law asked **Jesus,** "Why is it that your
7.14 Then **Jesus** called the crowd to him once more and said to
7.19 (In saying this, **Jesus** declared that all foods are fit to be
7.24 Then **Jesus** left and went away to the territory near the
7.25 spirit in her, heard about **Jesus** and came to him at once
7.26 She begged **Jesus** to drive the demon out of her daughter.
7.31 **Jesus** then left the neighbourhood of Tyre and went on through
7.32 speak, and they begged **Jesus** to place his hands on him.
7.33 So **Jesus** took him off alone, away from the crowd, put
7.34 Then **Jesus** looked up to heaven, gave a deep groan, and
7.36 Then **Jesus** ordered the people not to speak of it to anyone;
8. 1 had nothing left to eat, **Jesus** called the disciples to him
8. 7 **Jesus** gave thanks for these and told the disciples to distribute
8. 8 **Jesus** sent the people away [10]and at once got into a boat
8.11 Some Pharisees came to **Jesus** and started to argue with him.
8.12 But **Jesus** gave a deep groan and said, "Why do the
8.17 **Jesus** knew what they were saying, so he asked them,
8.20 four thousand people," asked **Jesus,** "how many baskets full of
8.22 brought a blind man to **Jesus** and begged him to touch him.
8.23 **Jesus** took the blind man by the hand and led him out
8.23 spitting on the man's eyes, **Jesus** placed his hands on him
8.25 **Jesus** again placed his hands on the man's eyes.
8.26 **Jesus** then sent him home with the order, "Don't go back
8.27 **Jesus** and his disciples went away to the villages near Caesarea
8.30 Then **Jesus** ordered them, "Do not tell anyone about me."
8.31 Then **Jesus** began to teach his disciples:
8.33 **Jesus** turned round, looked at his disciples, and rebuked Peter.
8.34 Then **Jesus** called the crowd and his disciples to him.
9. 2 Six days later **Jesus** took with him Peter, James, and John,
9. 2 a change came over **Jesus,** [3]and his clothes became shining white
9. 4 Then the three disciples saw Elijah and Moses talking with **Jesus.**
9. 5 spoke up and said to **Jesus,** "Teacher, how good it is that
9. 8 only **Jesus** was with them.
9. 9 came down the mountain, **Jesus** ordered them, "Don't tell anyone
9.11 And they asked **Jesus,** "Why do the teachers of the Law
9.15 When the people saw **Jesus,** they were greatly surprised, and ran
9.16 **Jesus** asked his disciples, "What are you arguing with them
9.20 They brought him to **Jesus.**

Mk 9.20 soon as the spirit saw **Jesus,** it threw the boy into
9.21 **Jesus** asked the father.
9.25 **Jesus** noticed that the crowd was closing in on them,
9.27 But **Jesus** took the boy by the hand and helped him to
9.28 **Jesus** had gone indoors, his disciples asked him privately,
9.30 **Jesus** and his disciples left that place and went on through
9.30 **Jesus** did not want anyone to know where he was, [31] because
9.33 after going indoors **Jesus** asked his disciples, "What were you
9.35 **Jesus** sat down, called the twelve disciples, and said to them,
10. 1 Then **Jesus** left that place, went to the province of Judaea,
10.10 back into the house, the disciples asked **Jesus** about this matter.
10.13 people brought children to **Jesus** for him to place his hands
10.14 **Jesus** noticed this, he was angry and said to his disciples,
10.17 As **Jesus** was starting on his way again, a man ran up,
10.21 **Jesus** looked straight at him with love and said, "You need
10.23 **Jesus** looked round at his disciples and said to them,
10.32 **Jesus** and his disciples were now on the road going up to
10.32 **Jesus** was going ahead of the disciples, who were filled with alarm;
10.32 Once again **Jesus** took the twelve disciples aside and spoke of
10.35 Then James and John, the sons of Zebedee, came to **Jesus.**
10.36 **Jesus** asked them.
10.42 So **Jesus** called them all together to him and said, "You
10.46 came to Jericho, and as **Jesus** was leaving with his disciples
10.47 that it was Jesus of Nazareth, he began to shout, **"Jesus!**
10.50 He threw off his cloak, jumped up, and came to **Jesus.**
10.52 once he was able to see and followed **Jesus** on the road.
11. 1 **Jesus** sent two of his disciples on ahead [2] with these instructions:
11. 6 They answered just as **Jesus** had told them, and the men let
11. 7 They brought the colt to **Jesus,**
11. 7 threw their cloaks over the animal, and **Jesus** got on.
11.11 **Jesus** entered Jerusalem, went into the Temple, and looked round
11.12 as they were coming back from Bethany, **Jesus** was hungry.
11.15 they arrived in Jerusalem, **Jesus** went to the Temple and began
11.18 so they began looking for some way to kill **Jesus.**
11.19 When evening came, **Jesus** and his disciples left the city.
11.21 and said to **Jesus,** "Look, Teacher, the fig-tree you cursed
11.27 **Jesus** was walking in the Temple, the chief priests, the teachers
11.33 So their answer to **Jesus** was, "We don't know."
12. 1 Then **Jesus** spoke to them in parables:
12.12 Jewish leaders tried to arrest **Jesus,** because they knew that he
12.13 Herod's party were sent to **Jesus** to trap him with questions.
12.15 **Jesus** saw through their trick and answered, "Why are you trying
12.17 And they were amazed at **Jesus.**
12.18 came to **Jesus** and said, [19] "Teacher, Moses wrote this
12.28 He saw that **Jesus** had given the Sadducees a good answer,
12.32 The teacher of the Law said to **Jesus,** "Well done,
12.34 **Jesus** noticed how wise his answer was, and so he told him,
12.34 After this nobody dared to ask **Jesus** any more questions.
12.35 As **Jesus** was teaching in the Temple, he asked the question,
12.37 A large crowd was listening to **Jesus** gladly.
12.41 As **Jesus** sat near the temple treasury, he watched the people
13. 1 As **Jesus** was leaving the Temple, one of his disciples said,
13. 3 **Jesus** was sitting on the Mount of Olives, across from the Temple,
14. 1 for a way to arrest **Jesus** secretly and put him to death.
14. 3 **Jesus** was in Bethany at the house of Simon, a man who
14. 3 While **Jesus** was eating, a woman came in with an alabaster
14. 3 She broke the jar and poured the perfume on **Jesus'** head.
14.10 off to the chief priests in order to betray **Jesus** to them.
14.11 looking for a good chance to hand **Jesus** over to them.
14.12 Passover meal were killed, **Jesus'** disciples asked him, "Where do
14.13 Then **Jesus** sent two of them with these instructions:
14.16 the city, and found everything just as **Jesus** had told them;
14.17 When it was evening, **Jesus** came with the twelve disciples.
14.22 While they were eating, **Jesus** took a piece of bread,
14.43 **Jesus** was still speaking when Judas, one of the twelve
14.45 soon as Judas arrived, he went up to **Jesus** and said,
14.46 So they arrested **Jesus** and held him tight.
14.51 young man, dressed only in a linen cloth, was following **Jesus.**
14.53 Then **Jesus** was taken to the High Priest's house,
14.55 to find some evidence against **Jesus** in order to put him to
14.56 Many witnesses told lies against **Jesus,** but their stories
14.57 Then some men stood up and told this lie against **Jesus:**
14.60 of them all and questioned **Jesus,** "Have you no answer to
14.61 But **Jesus** kept quiet and would not say a word.
14.65 began to spit on **Jesus,** and they blindfolded him and hit
14.67 at him and said, "You, too, were with **Jesus of Nazareth."**
14.72 and Peter remembered how **Jesus** had said to him, "Before the
15. 1 They put **Jesus** in chains, led him away, and handed him over
15. 3 chief priests were accusing **Jesus** of many things, [4] so Pilate
15. 5 Again **Jesus** refused to say a word, and Pilate was amazed.
15.10 the chief priests had handed **Jesus** over to him because they
15.15 Then he had **Jesus** whipped and handed him over to be crucified.
15.16 soldiers took **Jesus** inside to the courtyard of the governor's
15.17 put a purple robe on **Jesus,** made a crown out of thorny
15.21 the country, and the soldiers forced him to carry **Jesus'** cross.
15.22 They took **Jesus** to a place called Golgotha, which means
15.23 with a drug called myrrh, but **Jesus** would not drink it.
15.27 also crucified two bandits with **Jesus,** one on his right and
15.29 People passing by shook their heads and hurled insults at **Jesus:**
15.31 of the Law jeered at **Jesus,** saying to each other, "He saved
15.32 And the two who were crucified with **Jesus** insulted him also.
15.34 At three o'clock **Jesus** cried out with a loud shout,
15.36 Then he held it up to **Jesus'** lips and said, "Wait!
15.37 With a loud cry **Jesus** died.
15.39 standing there in front of the cross saw how **Jesus** had died.
15.41 They had followed **Jesus** while he was in Galilee and had
15.42 the presence of Pilate and asked him for the body of **Jesus.**
15.44 Pilate was surprised to hear that **Jesus** was already dead.
15.44 officer and asked him if **Jesus** had been dead a long time.
15.47 Joseph were watching and saw where the body of **Jesus** was placed.

Mk 16. 1 and Salome bought spices to go and anoint the body of **Jesus.**
16. 6 "I know you are looking for **Jesus of Nazareth,** who was crucified.
16. 9 After **Jesus** rose from death early on Sunday, he appeared first
16.10 After this, **Jesus** himself sent out through his disciples
16.11 they heard her say that **Jesus** was alive and that she had
16.12 After this, **Jesus** appeared in a different manner to two of
16.14 Last of all, **Jesus** appeared to the eleven disciples as they
16.19 After the Lord **Jesus** had talked with them, he was taken

Lk 1.31 and give birth to a son, and you will name him **Jesus.**
2.21 be circumcised, he was named **Jesus,** the name which the angel
2.27 the parents brought the child **Jesus** into the Temple to do
2.41 the parents of **Jesus** went to Jerusalem for the Passover
2.42 When **Jesus** was twelve years old, they went to the
2.43 they started back home, but the boy **Jesus** stayed in Jerusalem.
2.51 **Jesus** went back with them to Nazareth, where he was obedient
2.52 **Jesus** grew both in body and in wisdom, gaining favour
3.21 After all the people had been baptized, **Jesus** also was baptized.
3.23 When **Jesus** began his work, he was about thirty years old.
4. 1 **Jesus** returned from the Jordan full of the Holy Spirit and
4.13 When the Devil finished tempting **Jesus** in every way, he left
4.14 **Jesus** returned to Galilee, and the power of the Holy Spirit
4.16 Then **Jesus** went to Nazareth, where he had been brought up,
4.20 **Jesus** rolled up the scroll, gave it back to the attendant,
4.29 They rose up, dragged **Jesus** out of the town, and took
4.31 **Jesus** went to Capernaum, a town in Galilee, where he taught
4.34 What do you want with us, **Jesus of Nazareth?**
4.35 **Jesus** ordered the spirit, "Be quiet and come out of the man!"
4.37 And the report about **Jesus** spread everywhere in that region.
4.38 **Jesus** left the synagogue and went to Simon's house.
4.38 sick with a high fever, and they spoke to **Jesus** about her.
4.40 friends who were sick with various diseases brought them to **Jesus;**
4.41 **Jesus** gave the demons an order and would not let them speak,
4.42 At daybreak **Jesus** left the town and went off to a lonely
5. 1 One day **Jesus** was standing on the shore of Lake Gennesaret
5. 3 **Jesus** got into one of the boats—it belonged to Simon—
5. 3 **Jesus** sat in the boat and taught the crowd.
5. 8 fell on his knees before **Jesus** and said, "Go away from me,
5.11 the boats up on the beach, left everything, and followed **Jesus.**
5.12 Once **Jesus** was in a town where there was a man who
5.12 When he saw **Jesus,** he threw himself down and begged him,
5.13 **Jesus** stretched out his hand and touched him.
5.14 **Jesus** ordered him, "Don't tell anyone, but go straight to the
5.15 the news about **Jesus** spread all the more widely, and crowds
5.17 One day when **Jesus** was teaching, some Pharisees and teachers
5.17 power of the Lord was present for **Jesus** to heal the sick.
5.18 take him into the house and put him in front of **Jesus.**
5.19 his bed into the middle of the group in front of **Jesus.**
5.20 When **Jesus** saw how much faith they had, he said to the
5.22 **Jesus** knew their thoughts and said to them, "Why do you
5.27 After this, **Jesus** went out and saw a tax collector named Levi,
5.29 feast in his house for **Jesus,** and among the guests was
5.30 Law who belonged to their group complained to **Jesus'** disciples.
5.33 people said to **Jesus,** "The disciples of John fast frequently
5.36 **Jesus** also told them this parable:
6. 1 **Jesus** was walking through some cornfields on the Sabbath.
6. 6 On another Sabbath **Jesus** went into a synagogue and taught.
6. 7 wanted a reason to accuse **Jesus** of doing wrong, so they
6. 8 But **Jesus** knew their thoughts and said to the man, "Stand
6.11 to discuss among themselves what they could do to **Jesus.**
6.12 At that time **Jesus** went up a hill to pray and spent
6.17 When **Jesus** had come down from the hill with the apostles,
6.20 **Jesus** looked at his disciples and said, "Happy are you poor;
6.39 And **Jesus** told them this parable:
7. 1 When **Jesus** had finished saying all these things to the people,
7. 3 When the officer heard about **Jesus,** he sent some Jewish elders
7. 4 They came to **Jesus** and begged him earnestly, "This man really
7. 6 So **Jesus** went with them.
7. 9 **Jesus** was surprised when he heard this;
7.11 Soon afterwards **Jesus** went to a town called Nain, accompanied
7.15 and began to talk, and **Jesus** gave him back to his mother.
7.17 This news about **Jesus** went out through all the country
7.20 When they came to **Jesus,** they said, "John the Baptist
7.21 At that very time **Jesus** cured many people of their sicknesses,
7.24 John's messengers had left, **Jesus** began to speak about him to
7.36 A Pharisee invited **Jesus** to have dinner with him,
7.36 and **Jesus** went to his house and sat
7.37 She heard that **Jesus** was eating in the Pharisee's house, so
7.38 and stood behind **Jesus,** by his feet, crying and wetting
8. 1 **Jesus** travelled through towns and villages, preaching the Good
8. 3 who used their own resources to help **Jesus** and his disciples.
8. 4 People kept coming to **Jesus** from one town after another;
8. 4 and when a great crowd gathered, **Jesus** told this parable:
8. 9 His disciples asked **Jesus** what this parable meant,
8.19 **Jesus'** mother and brothers came to him, but were unable
8.20 Someone said to **Jesus,** "Your mother and brothers are standing
8.22 One day **Jesus** got into a boat with his disciples and
8.23 As they were sailing, **Jesus** fell asleep.
8.24 The disciples went to **Jesus** and woke him up, saying, "Master,
8.24 **Jesus** got up and gave an order to the wind and the
8.26 **Jesus** and his disciples sailed on over to the territory of
8.27 As **Jesus** stepped ashore, he was met by a man from the
8.28 When he saw **Jesus,** he gave a loud cry, threw himself
8.28 at his feet, and shouted, **"Jesus,** Son of the Most High God!
8.29 He said this because **Jesus** had ordered the evil spirit
8.30 **Jesus** asked him, "What is your name?"
8.31 The demons begged **Jesus** not to send them into the abyss.
8.32 So the demons begged **Jesus** to let them go into the pigs,
8.35 and when they came to **Jesus,** they found the man from whom
8.35 sitting at the feet of **Jesus,** clothed and in his right mind;
8.37 people from that territory asked **Jesus** to go away, because they

Lk 8.37 So **Jesus** got into the boat and left.
8.38 demons had gone out begged **Jesus,** "Let me go with you."
8.38 But **Jesus** sent him away, saying, [39] "Go back home and
8.39 went through the town, telling what **Jesus** had done for him.
8.40 When **Jesus** returned to the other side of the lake, the
8.41 He threw himself down at **Jesus'** feet and begged him to go
8.42 **Jesus** went along, the people were crowding him from every side.
8.44 up in the crowd behind **Jesus** and touched the edge of his
8.45 **Jesus** asked, "Who touched me?"
8.47 so she came trembling and threw herself at **Jesus'** feet.
8.49 **Jesus** was saying this, a messenger came from the official's house.
8.50 But **Jesus** heard it and said to Jairus, "Don't be afraid;
8.54 But **Jesus** took her by the hand and called out, "Get up,
8.55 got up at once, and **Jesus** ordered them to give her something
8.56 parents were astounded, but **Jesus** commanded them not to tell
9. 1 **Jesus** called the twelve disciples together and gave them power
9. 9 And he kept trying to see **Jesus.**
9.10 The apostles came back and told **Jesus** everything they had done.
9.16 the disciples had done so, [16] **Jesus** took the five loaves
9.18 when **Jesus** was praying alone, the disciples came to him.
9.21 Then **Jesus** gave them strict orders not to tell this to anyone.
9.28 he had said these things, **Jesus** took Peter, John, and James
9.31 heavenly glory and talked with **Jesus** about the way in which
9.32 they woke up and saw **Jesus'** glory and the two men who
9.33 As the men were leaving **Jesus,** Peter said to him, "Master,
9.36 When the voice stopped, there was **Jesus** all alone.
9.37 The next day **Jesus** and the three disciples went down
9.37 from the hill, and a large crowd met **Jesus.**
9.42 **Jesus** gave a command to the evil spirit, healed the boy,
9.43 were still marvelling at everything **Jesus** was doing, when he said
9.47 **Jesus** knew what they were thinking, so he took a child,
9.51 the time drew near when **Jesus** would be taken up to heaven,
9.55 **Jesus** turned and rebuked them.
9.56 Then **Jesus** and his disciples went on to another village.
9.57 a man said to **Jesus,** "I will follow you wherever you
10.21 At that time **Jesus** was filled with joy by the Holy
10.23 Then **Jesus** turned to the disciples and said to them privately,
10.25 A teacher of the Law came up and tried to trap **Jesus.**
10.29 to justify himself, so he asked **Jesus,** "Who is my neighbour?"
10.38 As **Jesus** and his disciples went on their way, he came to
11. 1 One day **Jesus** was praying in a certain place.
11.14 **Jesus** was driving out a demon that could not talk;
11.16 Others wanted to trap **Jesus,** so they asked him to
11.17 But **Jesus** knew what they were thinking, so he said to them,
11.27 When **Jesus** had said this, a woman spoke up from the
11.37 **Jesus** finished speaking, a Pharisee invited him to eat with him;
11.38 surprised when he noticed that **Jesus** had not washed before eating.
11.53 When **Jesus** left that place, the teachers of the Law and
12.13 in the crowd said to **Jesus,** "Teacher, tell my brother to
12.16 Then **Jesus** told them this parable:
13. 1 people were there who told **Jesus** about the Galileans whom Pilate
13. 6 Then **Jesus** told them this parable:
13.10 One Sabbath **Jesus** was teaching in a synagogue.
13.12 When **Jesus** saw her, he called out to her, "Woman, you
13.14 synagogue was angry that **Jesus** had healed on the Sabbath,
13.18 **Jesus** asked, "What is the Kingdom of God like?
13.20 Again **Jesus** asked, "What shall I compare the Kingdom of God
13.22 **Jesus** went through towns and villages, teaching the people
13.31 some Pharisees came to **Jesus** and said to him, "You must
14. 1 One Sabbath **Jesus** went to eat a meal at the home of
14. 1 and people were watching **Jesus** closely.
14. 2 arms were swollen came to **Jesus,** [3] and Jesus asked the teachers
14. 4 **Jesus** took the man, healed him, and sent him away.
14. 7 **Jesus** noticed how some of the guests were choosing the best places,
14.15 heard this, he said to **Jesus,** "How happy are those who will
14.25 were going along with **Jesus,** he turned and said to them,
15. 1 outcasts came to listen to **Jesus,** [2] the Pharisees and the
15. 3 So **Jesus** told them this parable:
16.14 heard all this, they sneered at **Jesus,** because they loved money.
17.11 As **Jesus** made his way to Jerusalem, he went along the
17.13 They stood at a distance [13] and shouted, **"Jesus!**
17.16 He threw himself to the ground at **Jesus'** feet and thanked him.
17.20 Some Pharisees asked **Jesus** when the Kingdom of God would come.
18. 1 Then **Jesus** told his disciples a parable to teach them that
18. 9 **Jesus** also told this parable to people who were sure of
18.15 people brought their babies to **Jesus** for him to place his
18.16 them for doing so, [16] but **Jesus** called the children to him
18.18 A Jewish leader asked **Jesus,** "Good Teacher, what must I
18.22 When **Jesus** heard this, he said to him, "There is still
18.24 **Jesus** saw that he was sad and said, "How hard it is
18.31 **Jesus** took the twelve disciples aside and said to them, "Listen!
18.34 them, and they did not know what **Jesus** was talking about.
18.35 As **Jesus** was coming near Jericho, there was a blind man
18.37 **"Jesus of Nazareth** is passing by," they told him.
18.38 He cried out, **"Jesus!**
18.40 So **Jesus** stopped and ordered the blind man to be brought
18.40 When he came near, **Jesus** asked him, [41] "What do you want
18.43 able to see, and he followed **Jesus,** giving thanks to God.
19. 1 **Jesus** went on into Jericho and was passing through.
19. 3 was trying to see who **Jesus** was, but he was
19. 3 a little man and could not see **Jesus** because of the crowd.
19. 4 a sycomore tree to see **Jesus,** who was going to pass that
19. 5 When **Jesus** came to that place, he looked up and said to
19.11 were listening to this, **Jesus** continued and told them a parable.
19.32 their way and found everything just as **Jesus** had told them.
19.35 needs it," they answered, [35] and they took the colt to **Jesus.**
19.35 threw their cloaks over the animal and helped **Jesus** get on.

Lk 19.39 Then some of the Pharisees in the crowd spoke to **Jesus.**
19.45 Then **Jesus** went into the Temple and began to drive out
19.47 Every day **Jesus** taught in the Temple.
20. 1 One day when **Jesus** was in the Temple teaching the people
20. 9 Then **Jesus** told the people this parable:
20.17 **Jesus** looked at them and asked, "What, then, does this
20.19 priests tried to arrest **Jesus** on the spot, because they knew
20.20 they sent them to trap **Jesus** with questions, so that they
20.21 spies said to **Jesus,** "Teacher, we know that what you say
20.23 **Jesus** saw through their trick and said to them, [24] "Show me
20.27 came to **Jesus** and said, [28] "Teacher, Moses wrote this
20.41 **Jesus** asked them, "How can it be said that the Messiah
21. 1 **Jesus** looked round and saw rich men dropping their gifts
21.29 Then **Jesus** told them this parable:
21.37 **Jesus** spent those days teaching in the Temple, and when evening
22. 2 trying to find a way of putting **Jesus** to death secretly.
22. 4 of the temple guard about how he could betray **Jesus** to them.
22. 6 a good chance to hand **Jesus** over to them without the people
22. 8 **Jesus** sent off Peter and John with these instructions:
22.13 found everything just as **Jesus** had told them, and they prepared
22.14 When the hour came, **Jesus** took his place at the table
22.17 Then **Jesus** took a cup, gave thanks to God, and said,
22.35 **Jesus** asked his disciples, "When I sent you out that time
22.39 **Jesus** left the city and went, as he usually did, to the
22.47 **Jesus** was still speaking when a crowd arrived, led by Judas,
22.47 He came up to **Jesus** to kiss him.
22.49 disciples who were with **Jesus** saw what was going to happen,
22.54 They arrested **Jesus** and took him away into the house of
22.56 straight at him and said, "This man too was with **Jesus!"**
22.59 this man was with **Jesus,** because he also is a Galilean!"
22.63 The men who were guarding **Jesus** mocked him and beat him.
22.66 the Law met together, and **Jesus** was brought before the Council.
23. 1 group rose up and took **Jesus** before Pilate, [2] where they
23. 7 When he learnt that **Jesus** was from the region ruled by Herod,
23. 8 very pleased when he saw **Jesus,** because he had heard about
23. 8 He was hoping to see **Jesus** perform some miracle.
23. 9 So Herod asked **Jesus** many questions, but Jesus made no answer.
23.10 the Law stepped forward and made strong accusations against **Jesus.**
23.11 Herod and his soldiers mocked **Jesus** and treated him with contempt;
23.20 Pilate wanted to set **Jesus** free, so he appealed to the
23.23 top of their voices that **Jesus** should be crucified, and finally
23.24 Pilate passed the sentence on **Jesus** that they were asking for.
23.25 and murder, and he handed **Jesus** over for them to do as
23.26 The soldiers led **Jesus** away, and as they were going,
23.26 put the cross on him, and made him carry it behind **Jesus.**
23.32 criminals, were also led out to be put to death with **Jesus.**
23.33 "The Skull," they crucified **Jesus** there, and the two criminals,
23.42 to Jesus, "Remember me, **Jesus,** when you come as King!"
23.46 **Jesus** cried out in a loud voice, "Father!
23.49 All those who knew **Jesus** personally, including the women who
23.52 into the presence of Pilate and asked for the body of **Jesus.**
23.55 women who had followed **Jesus** from Galilee went with Joseph
23.55 and saw the tomb and how **Jesus'** body was placed in it.
24. 3 but they did not find the body of the Lord **Jesus.**
24.13 that same day two of **Jesus'** followers were going to a
24.15 As they talked and discussed, **Jesus** himself drew near
24.19 "The things that happened to **Jesus of Nazareth,"** they
24.27 And **Jesus** explained to them what was said about himself
24.28 to which they were going, **Jesus** acted as if he were going

Jn 1.17 Law through Moses, but grace and truth came through **Jesus Christ.**
1.29 The next day John saw **Jesus** coming to him, and said,
1.36 with two of his disciples, [36] when he saw **Jesus** walking by.
1.37 The two disciples heard him say this and went with **Jesus.**
1.38 **Jesus** turned, saw them following him, and asked, "What are you
1.42 Then he took Simon to **Jesus.**
1.43 The next day **Jesus** decided to go to Galilee.
1.45 He is **Jesus** son of Joseph, from Nazareth."
1.47 When **Jesus** saw Nathanael coming to him, he said about him,
2. 1 **Jesus'** mother was there,
2. 2 and **Jesus** and his disciples had also been
2. 3 the wine had given out, **Jesus'** mother said to him, "They
2. 5 **Jesus'** mother then told the servants, "Do whatever he tells you."
2.11 **Jesus** performed this first miracle in Cana in Galilee;
2.12 **Jesus** and his mother, brothers, and disciples went to Capernaum
2.13 almost time for the Passover Festival, so **Jesus** went to Jerusalem.
2.21 But the temple **Jesus** was speaking about was his body.
2.22 and they believed the scripture and what **Jesus** had said.
2.23 While **Jesus** was in Jerusalem during the Passover Festival,
2.24 But **Jesus** did not trust himself to them, because he knew
3. 2 One night he went to **Jesus** and said to him, "Rabbi, we
3.22 **Jesus** and his disciples went to the province of Judaea,
4. 1 The Pharisees heard that **Jesus** was winning and baptizing more
4. 2 (Actually, **Jesus** himself did not baptize anyone;
4. 3 So when **Jesus** heard what was being said, he left Judaea
4. 6 Jacob's well was there, and **Jesus,** tired out by the journey,
4.27 moment **Jesus'** disciples returned, and they were greatly surprised
4.30 So they left the town and went to **Jesus.**
4.31 disciples were begging **Jesus,** "Teacher, have something to eat!"
4.39 in that town believed in **Jesus** because the woman had said,
4.40 him to stay with them, and **Jesus** stayed there two days.
4.43 After spending two days there, **Jesus** left and went to Galilee.
4.46 Then **Jesus** went back to Cana in Galilee, where he had
4.47 When he heard that **Jesus** had come from Judaea to Galilee,
4.50 The man believed **Jesus'** words and went.
4.53 at that very hour when **Jesus** had told him, "Your son will
4.54 the second miracle that **Jesus** performed after coming from Judaea

Jn 5. 1 After this, **Jesus** went to Jerusalem for a religious festival.
5. 6 **Jesus** saw him lying there, and he knew that the man had
5.13 healed did not know who **Jesus** was, for there was
5.13 a crowd in that place, and **Jesus** had slipped away.
5.14 Afterwards, **Jesus** found him in the Temple and said, "Listen,
5.15 the Jewish authorities that it was **Jesus** who had healed him.
5.16 they began to persecute **Jesus**, because he had done this healing
6. 1 After this, **Jesus** went across Lake Galilee (or, Lake Tiberias,
6. 3 **Jesus** went up a hill and sat down with his disciples.
6. 5 **Jesus** looked round and saw that a large crowd was coming
6.11 **Jesus** took the bread, gave thanks to God, and
6.14 Seeing this miracle that **Jesus** had performed, the people
6.15 **Jesus** knew that they were about to come and seize him in
6.16 When evening came, **Jesus'** disciples went down to the lake,
6.17 Night came on, and **Jesus** still had not come to them.
6.19 kilometres when they saw **Jesus** walking on the water, coming near
6.22 They knew that **Jesus** had not gone in it with his disciples,
6.24 When the crowd saw that **Jesus** was not there, nor his disciples,
6.25 When the people found **Jesus** on the other side of the lake,
6.42 So they said, "This man is **Jesus** son of Joseph, isn't
6.61 Without being told, **Jesus** knew that they were grumbling about
6.64 **(Jesus** knew from the very beginning who were the ones that
6.66 Because of this, many of **Jesus'** followers turned back
7. 1 After this, **Jesus** travelled in Galilee;
7. 3 Shelters was near, [3]so **Jesus'** brothers said to him, "Leave this
7.10 After his brothers had gone to the festival, **Jesus** also went;
7.14 was nearly half over when **Jesus** went to the Temple and began
7.28 As **Jesus** taught in the Temple, he said in a loud voice,
7.32 crowd whispering these things about **Jesus**, so they and the chief
7.37 important day of the festival **Jesus** stood up and said in a
7.39 yet been given, because **Jesus** had not been raised to glory.
7.43 So there was a division in the crowd because of **Jesus.**
7.50 was Nicodemus, the man who had gone to see **Jesus** before.
8. 1 Then everyone went home, but **Jesus** went to the Mount of Olives.
8. 4 "Teacher," they said to **Jesus**, "this woman was caught in the
8. 6 They said this to trap **Jesus**, so that they could accuse him.
8. 9 **Jesus** was left alone, with the woman still standing there.
8.12 **Jesus** spoke to the Pharisees again.
8.27 They did not understand that **Jesus** was talking to them about
8.30 Many who heard **Jesus** say these things believed in him.
8.48 They asked **Jesus**, "Were we not right in saying that you
8.59 to throw at him, but **Jesus** hid himself and left the Temple.
9. 1 As **Jesus** was walking along, he saw a man who had been
9. 6 After he said this, **Jesus** spat on the ground and made some
9.11 He answered, "The man called **Jesus** made some mud, rubbed it
9.14 The day that **Jesus** made the mud and cured him of his
9.22 who said he believed that **Jesus** was the Messiah would be
9.35 When **Jesus** heard what had happened, he found the man and
9.38 the man said, and knelt down before **Jesus.**
10. 6 **Jesus** told them this parable, but they did not understand
10.23 **Jesus** was walking in Solomon's Porch in the Temple,
10.39 more they tried to seize **Jesus**, but he slipped out of their
10.40 **Jesus** then went back again across the River Jordan to
11. 3 The sisters sent **Jesus** a message:
11. 5 **Jesus** loved Martha and her sister and Lazarus.
11.13 **Jesus** meant that Lazarus had died, but they thought he meant
11.17 When **Jesus** arrived, he found that Lazarus had been buried
11.20 When Martha heard that **Jesus** was coming, she went out to
11.21 Martha said to **Jesus**, "If you had been here, Lord, my
11.30 **(Jesus** had not yet arrived in the village, but was still
11.32 Mary arrived where **Jesus** was, and as soon as she saw him,
11.33 **Jesus** saw her weeping, and he saw how the people who
11.35 **Jesus** wept.
11.38 Deeply moved once more, **Jesus** went to the tomb, which
11.45 to visit Mary saw what **Jesus** did, and they believed in him.
11.46 returned to the Pharisees and told them what **Jesus** had done.
11.51 he was prophesying that **Jesus** was going to die for the
11.53 From that day on the Jewish authorities made plans to kill **Jesus.**
11.54 So **Jesus** did not travel openly in Judaea, but left and
11.56 were looking for **Jesus**, and as they gathered in the Temple,
11.57 that if anyone knew where **Jesus** was, he must report it,
12. 1 Six days before the Passover, **Jesus** went to Bethany, the
12. 2 was one of those who were sitting at the table with **Jesus.**
12. 3 pure nard, poured it on **Jesus'** feet, and wiped them with her
12. 4 One of **Jesus'** disciples, Judas Iscariot—the one who was going
12. 9 number of people heard that **Jesus** was in Bethany, so they
12. 9 there, not only because of **Jesus** but also to see Lazarus,
12. 9 Lazarus, whom **Jesus** had raised from death.
12.11 many Jews were rejecting them and believing in **Jesus.**
12.12 to the Passover Festival heard that **Jesus** was coming to Jerusalem.
12.14 **Jesus** found a donkey and rode on it, just as the
12.16 but when **Jesus** had been raised to glory, they remembered that
12.17 people who had been with **Jesus** when he called Lazarus out of
12.21 Bethsaida in Galilee) and said, "Sir, we want to see **Jesus."**
12.22 and told Andrew, and the two of them went and told **Jesus.**
12.41 Isaiah said this because he saw **Jesus'** glory and spoke about
12.42 Even then, many of the Jewish authorities believed in **Jesus;**
13. 1 **Jesus** knew that the hour had come for him to leave this
13. 2 **Jesus** and his disciples were at supper.
13. 2 Judas, the son of Simon Iscariot, the thought of betraying **Jesus.**
13. 3 **Jesus** knew that the Father had given him complete power;
13.11 **(Jesus** already knew who was going to betray him;
13.12 After **Jesus** had washed their feet, he put his outer garment
13.21 **Jesus** had said this, he was deeply troubled and declared openly,
13.23 the one whom **Jesus** loved, was sitting next to Jesus.
13.25 that disciple moved closer to **Jesus'** side and asked, "Who
13.29 of the disciples thought that **Jesus** had told him to go and
16.19 **Jesus** knew that they wanted to question him, so he said
17. 1 **Jesus** finished saying this, he looked up to heaven and said,

Jn 17. 3 you, the only true God, and knowing **Jesus Christ**, whom you
18. 1 After **Jesus** had said this prayer, he left with his disciples
18. 1 a garden in that place, and **Jesus** and his disciples went in.
18. 2 because many times **Jesus** had met there with his disciples.
18. 4 **Jesus** knew everything that was going to happen to him, so
18. 5 **"Jesus of Nazareth,"** they answered.
18. 7 Again **Jesus** asked them, "Who is it you are looking for?"
18. 7 **"Jesus of Nazareth,"** they said.
18.12 and the Jewish guards arrested **Jesus**, bound him, [13]and took him
18.15 Simon Peter and another disciple followed **Jesus.**
18.15 Priest, so he went with **Jesus** into the courtyard of the High
18.19 The High Priest questioned **Jesus** about his disciples and about
18.28 Early in the morning **Jesus** was taken from Caiaphas' house
18.32 to make the words of **Jesus** come true, the words he used
18.33 Pilate went back into the palace and called **Jesus.**
19. 1 Then Pilate took **Jesus** and had him whipped.
19. 5 So **Jesus** came out, wearing the crown of thorns and the
19. 9 into the palace and asked **Jesus**, "Where do you come from?"
19. 9 But **Jesus** did not answer.
19.12 heard this, he tried to find a way to set **Jesus** free.
19.13 heard these words, he took **Jesus** outside and sat down on the
19.16 Then Pilate handed **Jesus** over to them to be crucified.
19.16 So they took charge of **Jesus.**
19.18 crucified two other men, one on each side, with **Jesus** between
19.19 **"Jesus of Nazareth,** the King of the Jews," is what he wrote.
19.20 because the place where **Jesus** was crucified was not far from
19.23 soldiers had crucified **Jesus**, they took his clothes and divided
19.25 Standing close to **Jesus'** cross were his mother, his mother's
19.26 **Jesus** saw his mother and the disciple he loved standing there;
19.28 **Jesus** knew that by now everything had been completed;
19.30 **Jesus** drank the wine and said, "It is finished!"
19.32 and then of the other man who had been crucified with **Jesus.**
19.33 But when they came to **Jesus**, they saw that he was
19.34 plunged his spear into **Jesus'** side, and at once blood and
19.38 of Arimathea, asked Pilate if he could take **Jesus'** body.
19.38 (Joseph was a follower of **Jesus**, but in secret, because he
19.39 first had gone to see **Jesus** at night, went with Joseph,
19.40 The two men took **Jesus'** body and wrapped it in linen
19.41 garden in the place where **Jesus** had been put to death,
19.42 and because the tomb was close by, they placed **Jesus'** body
20. 2 the other disciple, whom **Jesus** loved, and told them, "They have
20. 7 lying there [7]and the cloth which had been round **Jesus'** head.
20.12 sitting where the body of **Jesus** had been, one at the head
20.14 Then she turned round and saw **Jesus** standing there;
20.14 but she did not know that it was **Jesus.**
20.17 not hold on to me," **Jesus** told her, "because I have not
20.19 Then **Jesus** came and stood among them.
20.24 Thomas (called the Twin), was not with them when **Jesus** came.
20.26 The doors were locked, but **Jesus** came and stood among them
20.30 In his disciples' presence **Jesus** performed many other miracles
20.31 that you may believe that **Jesus** is the Messiah, the Son of
21. 1 **Jesus** appeared once more to his disciples at Lake Tiberias.
21. 2 of Zebedee, and two other disciples of **Jesus** were all together.
21. 4 As the sun was rising, **Jesus** stood at the water's edge,
21. 4 but the disciples did not know that it was **Jesus.**
21. 7 The disciple whom **Jesus** loved said to Peter, "It is the Lord!"
21.13 So **Jesus** went over, took the bread, and gave it to them;
21.14 was the third time **Jesus** appeared to the disciples after he
21.17 Peter was sad because **Jesus** asked him the third time, "Do
21.19 (In saying this, **Jesus** was indicating the way in which Peter
21.20 that other disciple, whom **Jesus** loved—the one who
21.20 had leaned close to **Jesus** at the meal and had asked,
21.21 Peter saw him, he asked **Jesus**, "Lord, what about this man?"
21.23 among the followers of **Jesus** that this disciple would not die.
21.23 But **Jesus** did not say that he would not die;
21.25 Now, there are many other things that **Jesus** did.
Acts 1. 1 about all the things that **Jesus** did and taught from the time
1. 6 the apostles met together with **Jesus**, they asked him, "Lord,
1.11 This **Jesus**, who was taken from you into heaven, will come
1.14 and with Mary the mother of **Jesus** and with his brothers.
1.16 about Judas, who was the guide for those who arrested **Jesus.**
1.21 join us as a witness to the resurrection of the Lord **Jesus.**
1.21 whole time that the Lord **Jesus** travelled about with us, beginning
1.21 of baptism until the day **Jesus** was taken up from us to
2.22 **Jesus of Nazareth** was a man whose divine authority was clearly
2.23 God had already decided that **Jesus** would be handed over to you;
2.32 God has raised this very **Jesus** from death, and we are
2.36 know for sure that this **Jesus**, whom you crucified, is the
2.38 baptized in the name of **Jesus Christ**, so that your sins will
3. 6 in the name of **Jesus Christ** of Nazareth I order you to
3.13 God of our ancestors, has given divine glory to his Servant **Jesus.**
3.16 it was faith in **Jesus** that has made him well, as you
3.17 you and your leaders did to **Jesus** was due to your ignorance.
3.20 Lord, and he will send **Jesus**, who is the Messiah he has
4. 2 teaching the people that **Jesus** had risen from death, which proved
4.10 power of the name of **Jesus Christ** of Nazareth—whom you
4.11 **Jesus** is the one of whom the scripture says, 'The stone
4.13 They realized then that they had been companions of **Jesus.**
4.17 men never again to speak to anyone in the name of **Jesus."**
4.18 were they to speak or to teach in the name of **Jesus.**
4.27 people of Israel against **Jesus**, your holy Servant, whom you made
4.30 may be performed through the name of your holy Servant **Jesus."**
4.33 resurrection of the Lord **Jesus**, and God poured rich blessings on
5.30 God of our ancestors raised **Jesus** from death, after you had
5.40 and ordered them never again to speak in the name of **Jesus;**
5.41 considered them worthy to suffer disgrace for the sake of **Jesus.**
5.42 continued to teach and preach the Good News about **Jesus**
6.14 say that this **Jesus of Nazareth** will tear down the Temple
7.55 and saw God's glory and **Jesus** standing at the right-hand
7.59 called out to the Lord, "Lord **Jesus**, receive my spirit!"
8.12 Kingdom of God and about **Jesus Christ**, they were baptized,

Acts	8.16	they had only been baptized in the name of the Lord **Jesus.**
	8.35	passage of scripture, he told him the Good News about **Jesus.**
	9. 5	"I am **Jesus,** whom you persecute," the voice said.
	9.17	"the Lord has sent me—**Jesus** himself, who appeared to you on
	9.20	and began to preach that **Jesus** was the Son of God.
	9.21	in Jerusalem was killing those who worship that man **Jesus?**
	9.22	and his proofs that **Jesus** was the Messiah were so convincing
	9.27	boldly Saul had preached in the name of **Jesus** in Damascus.
	9.34	"Aeneas," Peter said to him, **"Jesus Christ** makes you well.
	10.36	Good News of peace through **Jesus Christ,** who is Lord of all.
	10.38	You know about **Jesus of Nazareth** and how God poured out
	10.48	he ordered them to be baptized in the name of **Jesus Christ.**
	11.17	that he gave us when we believed in the Lord **Jesus Christ;**
	11.20	Gentiles also, telling them the Good News about the Lord **Jesus.**
	13.23	It was **Jesus,** a descendant of David, whom God made the
	13.24	Before **Jesus** began his work, John preached to all the people
	13.27	Yet they made the prophets' words come true by condemning **Jesus.**
	13.32	for us, who are their descendants, by raising **Jesus** to life.
	13.38	that it is through **Jesus** that the message about forgiveness of
	15.11	saved by the grace of the Lord **Jesus,** just as they are."
	15.26	risked their lives in the service of our Lord **Jesus Christ.**
	16. 7	of Bithynia, but the Spirit of **Jesus** did not allow them.
	16.18	spirit, "In the name of **Jesus Christ** I order you to come
	16.31	answered, "Believe in the Lord **Jesus,** and you will be saved—
	17. 3	"This **Jesus** whom I announce to you," Paul said, "is the Messiah."
	17. 7	saying that there is another king, whose name is **Jesus."**
	17.18	because Paul was preaching about **Jesus** and the resurrection.
	18. 5	the message, testifying to the Jews that **Jesus** is the Messiah.
	18.25	enthusiasm he proclaimed and taught correctly the facts about **Jesus.**
	18.28	debates by proving from the Scriptures that **Jesus** is the Messiah.
	19. 4	in the one who was coming after him—that is, in **Jesus."**
	19. 5	this, they were baptized in the name of the Lord **Jesus.**
	19.13	tried to use the name of the Lord **Jesus** to do this.
	19.13	"I command you in the name of **Jesus,** whom Paul preaches."
	19.15	spirit said to them, "I know **Jesus,** and I know about Paul;
	19.17	and the name of the Lord **Jesus** was given greater honour.
	20.21	turn from their sins to God and believe in our Lord **Jesus.**
	20.24	the work that the Lord **Jesus** gave me to do, which is
	20.35	words that the Lord **Jesus** himself said, 'There is more happiness
	21.13	but even to die there for the sake of the Lord **Jesus."**
	22. 8	'I am **Jesus of Nazareth,** whom you persecute,' he said to me.
	24.24	listened to him as he talked about faith in **Christ Jesus.**
	25.19	their own religion and about a man named **Jesus,** who has
	26. 9	everything I could against the cause of **Jesus of Nazareth.**
	26.15	And the Lord answered, 'I am **Jesus,** whom you persecute.
	28.23	tried to convince them about **Jesus** by quoting from the Law
	28.31	taught about the Lord **Jesus Christ,** speaking with all boldness
Rom	1. 1	From Paul, a servant of **Christ Jesus** and an apostle chosen
	1. 3	It is about his Son, our Lord **Jesus Christ:**
	1. 6	are in Rome, whom God has called to belong to **Jesus Christ.**
	1. 7	Father and the Lord **Jesus Christ** give you grace and peace.
	1. 8	I thank my God through **Jesus Christ** for all of you, because
	2.16	Day when God through **Jesus Christ** will judge the secret thoughts
	3.22	God puts people right through their faith in **Jesus Christ.**
	3.24	put right with him through **Christ Jesus,** who sets them free.
	3.25	and that he puts right everyone who believes in **Jesus.**
	4.24	who believe in him who raised **Jesus** our Lord from death.
	5. 1	we have peace with God through our Lord **Jesus Christ.**
	5.11	has done through our Lord **Jesus Christ,** who has now made us
	5.15	many people through the grace of the one man, **Jesus Christ.**
	5.17	the result of what was done by the one man, **Jesus Christ!**
	5.21	leading us to eternal life through **Jesus Christ** our Lord.
	6. 3	baptized into union with **Christ Jesus,** we were baptized
	6.11	but living in fellowship with God through **Christ Jesus.**
	6.23	gift is eternal life in union with **Christ Jesus** our Lord.
	7.25	Thanks be to God, who does this through our Lord **Jesus Christ!**
	8. 1	now for those who live in union with **Christ Jesus.**
	8. 2	life in union with **Christ Jesus,** has set me free from
	8.11	Spirit of God, who raised **Jesus** from death, lives in you,
	8.34	Not **Christ Jesus,** who died, or rather, who was raised to
	8.39	love of God which is ours through **Christ Jesus** our Lord.
	10. 9	If you confess that **Jesus** is Lord and believe that God
	13.14	weapons of the Lord **Jesus Christ,** and stop paying attention to
	14.14	My union with the Lord **Jesus** makes me certain that no
	15. 5	by following the example of **Christ Jesus,** [6] so that all of
	15. 6	with one voice the God and Father of our Lord **Jesus Christ.**
	15.16	of being a servant of **Christ Jesus** to work for the Gentiles.
	15.17	In union with **Christ Jesus,** then, I can be proud of my
	15.30	you, brothers, by our Lord **Jesus Christ** and by the love that
	16. 3	and Aquila, my fellow-workers in the service of **Christ Jesus;**
	16.20	The grace of our Lord **Jesus** be with you.
	16.25	News I preach about **Jesus Christ** and according to the revelation
	16.27	God, who alone is all-wise, be glory through **Jesus Christ** for ever!
1 Cor	1. 1	to be an apostle of **Christ Jesus,** and from our brother
	1. 2	in union with **Christ Jesus,** together with all people everywhere
	1. 2	who worship our Lord **Jesus Christ,** their Lord and ours:
	1. 3	Father and the Lord **Jesus Christ** give you grace and peace.
	1. 4	because of the grace he has given you through **Christ Jesus.**
	1. 7	as you wait for our Lord **Jesus Christ** to be revealed.
	1. 8	you will be faultless on the Day of our Lord **Jesus Christ.**
	1. 9	called you to have fellowship with his Son **Jesus Christ,** our
	1.10	the authority of our Lord **Jesus Christ** I appeal to all of
	1.30	brought you into union with **Christ Jesus,** and God has made
	2. 2	forget everything except **Jesus Christ** and especially his death on
	3.11	For God has already placed **Jesus Christ** as the one and
	4.15	your life in union with **Christ Jesus** I have become your
	4.17	new life in union with **Christ Jesus** and which I teach in
	5. 3	the name of our Lord **Jesus** already passed judgement on the
	5. 3	the power of our Lord **Jesus** present with us, [5] you are to
1 Cor	6.11	with God by the Lord **Jesus Christ** and by the Spirit of
	8. 6	there is only one Lord, **Jesus Christ,** through whom all things
	9. 1	Haven't I seen **Jesus** our Lord?
	11.23	that the Lord **Jesus,** on the night he was betrayed, took a
	12. 3	who is led by God's Spirit can say "A curse on **Jesus!"**
	12. 3	and no one can confess **"Jesus** is Lord," unless he is
	15.31	our life in union with **Christ Jesus** our Lord, makes me
	15.57	God who gives us the victory through our Lord **Jesus Christ!**
	16.23	The grace of the Lord **Jesus** be with you.
	16.24	My love be with you all in **Christ Jesus.**
2 Cor	1. 1	From Paul, an apostle of **Christ Jesus** by God's will, and
	1. 2	Father and the Lord **Jesus Christ** give you grace and peace.
	1. 3	and Father of our Lord **Jesus Christ,** the merciful Father,
	1.13	the Day of our Lord **Jesus** you can be as proud of
	1.19	For **Jesus Christ,** the Son of God, who was preached among
	1.20	This is why through **Jesus Christ** our "Amen" is said to the
	4. 5	we preach **Jesus Christ** as Lord,
	4. 5	and ourselves as your servants for **Jesus'** sake.
	4.10	mortal bodies the death of **Jesus,** so that his life also may
	4.11	in danger of death for **Jesus'** sake, in order that his life
	4.14	God, who raised the Lord **Jesus** to life, will also
	4.14	raise us up with **Jesus** and take us, together with you,
	8. 9	You know the grace of our Lord **Jesus Christ;**
	11. 4	you and preaches a different **Jesus,** not the one we preached;
	11.31	and Father of the Lord **Jesus**—blessed be his name for ever!
	13. 5	Surely you know that **Christ Jesus** is in you?
	13.13	The grace of the Lord **Jesus Christ,** the love of God,
Gal	1. 1	means of man, but from **Jesus Christ** and God the Father, who
	1. 3	Father and the Lord **Jesus Christ** give you grace and peace.
	1.12	It was **Jesus Christ** himself who revealed it to me.
	2. 4	about the freedom we have through our union with **Christ Jesus.**
	2.16	God only through faith in **Jesus Christ,** never by doing what
	2.16	We, too, have believed in **Christ Jesus** in order to be put
	3. 1	clear description of the death of **Jesus Christ** on the cross!
	3.14	the Gentiles by means of **Christ Jesus,** so that through faith
	3.22	the basis of faith in **Jesus Christ** is given to those who
	3.26	that all of you are God's sons in union with **Christ Jesus.**
	3.28	you are all one in union with **Christ Jesus.**
	4.14	you received me as you would **Christ Jesus.**
	5. 6	in union with **Christ Jesus,** neither circumcision nor the lack
	5.24	And those who belong to **Christ Jesus** have put to death
	6.14	I will boast only about the cross of our Lord **Jesus Christ;**
	6.17	have on my body show that I am the slave of **Jesus.**
	6.18	the grace of our Lord **Jesus Christ** be with you all,
Eph	1. 1	an apostle of **Christ Jesus**— To God's people in
	1. 1	Ephesus, who are faithful in their life in union with **Christ Jesus:**
	1. 2	Father and the Lord **Jesus Christ** give you grace and peace.
	1. 3	give thanks to the God and Father of our Lord **Jesus Christ!**
	1. 5	already decided that through **Jesus Christ** he would make us his
	1.15	your faith in the Lord **Jesus** and your love for all God's
	1.17	the God of our Lord **Jesus Christ,** the glorious Father, to
	2. 6	In our union with **Christ Jesus** he raised us up with him
	2. 7	of his grace in the love he showed us in **Christ Jesus.**
	2.10	and in our union with **Christ Jesus** he has created us for
	2.13	But now, in union with **Christ Jesus,** you who used to be
	2.20	apostles and prophets, the cornerstone being **Christ Jesus** himself.
	3. 1	I, Paul, the prisoner of **Christ Jesus** for the sake of you
	3. 6	and share in the promise that God made through **Christ Jesus.**
	3.11	eternal purpose, which he achieved through **Christ Jesus** our Lord.
	3.21	in the church and in **Christ Jesus** for all time, for ever
	4.21	as his followers you were taught the truth that is in **Jesus.**
	5.20	name of our Lord **Jesus Christ,** always give thanks for everything
	6.23	Father and the Lord **Jesus Christ** give to all Christian brothers
	6.24	all those who love our Lord **Jesus Christ** with undying love.
Phil	1. 1	Paul and Timothy, servants of **Christ Jesus**— To all God's
	1. 1	who are in union with **Christ Jesus,** including the church leaders
	1. 2	Father and the Lord **Jesus Christ** give you grace and peace.
	1. 6	until it is finished on the Day of **Christ Jesus.**
	1. 8	for you all comes from the heart of **Christ Jesus** himself.
	1.11	truly good qualities which only **Jesus Christ** can produce,
	1.19	comes from the Spirit of **Jesus Christ** I shall be set free.
	1.26	be proud of me in your life in union with **Christ Jesus.**
	2. 5	The attitude you should have is the one that **Christ Jesus** had:
	2.10	honour of the name of **Jesus** all beings in heaven, on earth,
	2.11	all will openly proclaim that **Jesus Christ** is Lord, to the
	2.21	with his own affairs, not with the cause of **Jesus Christ.**
	3. 3	Spirit and rejoice in our life in union with **Christ Jesus.**
	3. 8	much more valuable, the knowledge of **Christ Jesus** my Lord.
	3.12	win the prize for which **Christ Jesus** has already won me to
	3.14	which is God's call through **Christ Jesus** to the life above.
	3.20	for our Saviour, the Lord **Jesus Christ,** to come from heaven.
	4. 7	keep your hearts and minds safe in union with **Christ Jesus.**
	4.19	all his abundant wealth through **Christ Jesus,** my God will supply
	4.21	Greetings to each one of God's people who belong to **Christ Jesus.**
	4.23	May the grace of the Lord **Jesus Christ** be with you all.
Col	1. 1	an apostle of **Christ Jesus,** and from our brother Timothy
	1. 3	the Father of our Lord **Jesus Christ,** when we pray for you.
	1. 4	heard of your faith in **Christ Jesus** and of your love for
	2. 6	Since you have accepted **Christ Jesus** as Lord, live in
	3.17	the name of the Lord **Jesus,** as you give thanks through him
	4.12	Epaphras, another member of your group and a servant of **Christ Jesus.**
1 Thes	1. 1	who belong to God the Father and the Lord **Jesus Christ:**
	1. 3	and how your hope in our Lord **Jesus Christ** is firm.
	1.10	come from heaven—his Son **Jesus,** whom he raised from death
	2.14	in Judaea, to the people there who belong to **Christ Jesus.**
	2.15	who killed the Lord **Jesus** and the prophets, and persecuted us.
	2.19	our victory in the presence of our Lord **Jesus** when he comes.
	3.11	Father himself and our Lord **Jesus** prepare the way for us to
	3.13	and Father when our Lord **Jesus** comes with all who belong to
	4. 1	you in the name of the Lord **Jesus** to do even more.

1 Thes	4. 2	instructions we gave you by the authority of the Lord **Jesus.**
	4.14	We believe that **Jesus** died and rose again, and so we
	4.14	God will take back with **Jesus** those who have died believing
	5. 9	possess salvation through our Lord **Jesus Christ,** [10] who died for
	5.18	God wants from you in your life in union with **Christ Jesus.**
	5.23	from every fault at the coming of our Lord **Jesus Christ.**
	5.28	The grace of our Lord **Jesus Christ** be with you.
2 Thes	1. 1	who belong to God our Father and the Lord **Jesus Christ:**
	1. 2	Father and the Lord **Jesus Christ** give you grace and peace.
	1. 7	do this when the Lord **Jesus** appears from heaven with his
	1. 8	and who do not obey the Good News about our Lord **Jesus.**
	1.12	the name of our Lord **Jesus** will receive glory from you,
	1.12	by the grace of our God and of the Lord **Jesus Christ.**
	2. 1	coming of our Lord **Jesus Christ** and our being gathered together
	2. 8	but when the Lord **Jesus** comes, he will kill him with
	2.14	to possess your share of the glory of our Lord **Jesus Christ.**
	2.16	May our Lord **Jesus Christ** himself and God our Father,
	3. 6	the name of our Lord **Jesus Christ** to keep away from all
	3.12	the name of the Lord **Jesus Christ** we command these people
	3.18	May the grace of our Lord **Jesus Christ** be with you all.
1 Tim	1. 1	From Paul, an apostle of **Christ Jesus** by order of God
	1. 1	God our Saviour and **Christ Jesus** our hope— [2] To Timothy,
	1. 2	May God the Father and **Christ Jesus** our Lord give you grace,
	1.12	I give thanks to **Christ Jesus** our Lord, who has given me
	1.14	faith and love which are ours in union with **Christ Jesus.**
	1.15	**Christ Jesus** came into the world to save sinners.
	1.16	in order that **Christ Jesus** might show his full patience
	2. 5	mankind together, the man **Christ Jesus,** [6] who gave himself to redeem
	3.13	are able to speak boldly about their faith in **Christ Jesus.**
	4. 6	be a good servant of **Christ Jesus,** as you feed yourself
	5.21	presence of God and of **Christ Jesus** and of the holy angels
	6. 3	true words of our Lord **Jesus Christ** and with the teaching of
	6.13	and before **Christ Jesus,** who firmly professed his faith
	6.14	faithfully until the Day when our Lord **Jesus Christ** will appear.
2 Tim	1. 1	From Paul, an apostle of **Christ Jesus** by God's will, sent
	1. 1	we have in union with **Christ Jesus**— [2] To Timothy, my dear
	1. 2	May God the Father and **Christ Jesus** our Lord give you grace,
	1. 9	grace by means of **Christ Jesus** before the beginning of time,
	1.10	revealed to us through the coming of our Saviour, **Christ Jesus.**
	1.13	the faith and love that are ours in union with **Christ Jesus.**
	2. 1	through the grace that is ours in union with **Christ Jesus.**
	2. 3	Take your part in suffering, as a loyal soldier of **Christ Jesus.**
	2. 8	Remember **Jesus Christ,** who was raised from death, who was
	2.10	obtain the salvation that comes through **Christ Jesus** and brings
	3.12	a godly life in union with **Christ Jesus** will be persecuted;
	3.15	the wisdom that leads to salvation through faith in **Christ Jesus.**
	4. 1	presence of God and of **Christ Jesus,** who will judge the
Tit	1. 1	From Paul, a servant of God and an apostle of **Jesus Christ.**
	1. 4	May God the Father and **Christ Jesus** our Saviour give you
	2.13	glory of our great God and Saviour **Jesus Christ** will appear.
	3. 6	Spirit abundantly on us through **Jesus Christ** our Saviour,
Phlm	3	Father and the Lord **Jesus Christ** give you grace and peace.
	5	all God's people and the faith you have in the Lord **Jesus.**
	9	Paul, the ambassador of **Christ Jesus,** and at present also a
	15	prisoner for the sake of **Christ Jesus,** and from our brother
	23	for the sake of **Christ Jesus,** sends you his greetings,
	25	May the grace of the Lord **Jesus Christ** be with you all.
Heb	2. 9	But we do see **Jesus,** who for a little while was made
	2.10	preserves all things, should make **Jesus** perfect through suffering,
	2.10	For **Jesus** is the one who leads them to salvation.
	2.11	That is why **Jesus** is not ashamed to call them his brothers.
	2.14	people of flesh and blood, **Jesus** himself became like them
	3. 1	Think of **Jesus,** whom God sent to be the High Priest of
	3. 3	In the same way **Jesus** is worthy of much greater honour than
	4.14	gone into the very presence of God—**Jesus,** the Son of God.
	5. 7	In his life on earth **Jesus** made his prayers and requests
	6.20	On our behalf **Jesus** has gone in there before us, and has
	7.21	But **Jesus** became a priest by means of a vow when God
	7.22	then, also makes **Jesus** the guarantee of a better covenant.
	7.24	But **Jesus** lives on for ever, and his work as priest does
	7.26	**Jesus,** then, is the High Priest that meets our needs.
	8. 6	But now, **Jesus** has been given priestly work which is superior
	10.10	Because **Jesus Christ** did what God wanted him to do, we
	10.19	into the Most Holy Place by means of the death of **Jesus.**
	12. 2	keep our eyes fixed on **Jesus,** on whom our faith depends from
	12.24	You have come to **Jesus,** who arranged the new covenant,
	13. 8	**Jesus Christ** is the same yesterday, today, and for ever.
	13.12	For this reason **Jesus** also died outside the city, in
	13.15	as our sacrifice through **Jesus,** which is the offering presented
	13.20	raised from death our Lord **Jesus,** who is the Great Shepherd
	13.20	and may he, through **Jesus Christ,** do in us what pleases
Jas	1. 1	From James, a servant of God and of the Lord **Jesus Christ:**
	2. 1	as believers in our Lord **Jesus Christ,** the Lord of glory,
1 Pet	1. 1	From Peter, apostle of **Jesus Christ**— To God's chosen
	1. 2	by his Spirit, to obey **Jesus Christ** and be purified by his
	1. 3	give thanks to the God and Father of our Lord **Jesus Christ!**
	1. 3	he gave us new life by raising **Jesus Christ** from death.
	1. 7	glory and honour on the Day when **Jesus Christ** is revealed.
	1.13	blessing which will be given you when **Jesus Christ** is revealed.
	2. 5	spiritual and acceptable sacrifices to God through **Jesus Christ.**
	3.21	the resurrection of **Jesus Christ,** [22] who has gone to heaven
	4.11	be given to God through **Jesus Christ,** to whom belong glory
2 Pet	1. 1	a servant and apostle of **Jesus Christ**— To those who through
	1. 1	of our God and Saviour **Jesus Christ** have been given a faith
	1. 2	through your knowledge of God and of **Jesus** our Lord.
	1. 8	active and effective in your knowledge of our Lord **Jesus Christ.**
	1.11	the eternal Kingdom of our Lord and Saviour **Jesus Christ.**
	1.14	this mortal body, as our Lord **Jesus Christ** plainly told me.
	1.16	known to you the mighty coming of our Lord **Jesus Christ.**
	2.20	of our Lord and Saviour **Jesus Christ,** and then are again
2 Pet	3.18	grace and knowledge of our Lord and Saviour **Jesus Christ.**
1 Jn	1. 3	that we have with the Father and with his Son **Jesus Christ.**
	1. 7	and the blood of **Jesus,** his Son, purifies us from every
	2. 1	with the Father on our behalf—**Jesus Christ,** the righteous one.
	2. 6	in union with God should live just as **Jesus Christ** did.
	2.22	It is anyone who says that **Jesus** is not the Messiah.
	3.23	we believe in his Son **Jesus Christ** and love one another,
	4. 2	anyone who acknowledges that **Jesus Christ** came as a human being
	4. 3	anyone who denies this about **Jesus** does not have the Spirit
	4.15	If anyone declares that **Jesus** is the Son of God, he
	5. 1	Whoever believes that **Jesus** is the Messiah is a child of God;
	5. 5	Only the person who believes that **Jesus** is the Son of God.
	5. 6	**Jesus Christ** is the one who came with the water of his
	5.20	union with the true God—in union with his Son **Jesus Christ.**
2 Jn	3	May God the Father and **Jesus Christ,** the Father's Son,
	7	do not acknowledge that **Jesus Christ** came as a human being.
Jude	1	From Jude, servant of **Jesus Christ,** and brother of James—
	1	love of God the Father and the protection of **Jesus Christ:**
	4	and who reject **Jesus Christ,** our only Master and Lord.
	17	told in the past by the apostles of our Lord **Jesus Christ.**
	21	you wait for our Lord **Jesus Christ** in his mercy to give
	25	God our Saviour, through **Jesus Christ** our Lord, be glory, majesty,
Rev	1. 1	This book is the record of the events that **Jesus Christ** revealed.
	1. 2	the message from God and the truth revealed by **Jesus Christ.**
	1. 5	and from **Jesus Christ,** the faithful witness, the first
	1. 6	To **Jesus Christ** be the glory and power for ever and ever!
	1. 9	and as a follower of **Jesus** I am your partner in patiently
	1. 9	I had proclaimed God's word and the truth that **Jesus** revealed.
	12.17	God's commandments and are faithful to the truth revealed by **Jesus.**
	14.12	those who obey God's commandments and are faithful to **Jesus.**
	17. 6	those who were killed because they had been loyal to **Jesus.**
	19.10	brothers, all those who hold to the truth that **Jesus** revealed.
	19.10	For the truth that **Jesus** revealed is what inspires the prophets.
	20. 4	the truth that **Jesus** revealed and the word of God.
	22.16	"I, **Jesus,** have sent my angel to announce these things
	22.20	Come, Lord **Jesus!**
	22.21	May the grace of the Lord **Jesus** be with everyone.

JESUS SAID

Mt	3.15	But **Jesus answered** him, "Let it be so for now.
	4. 4	**Jesus answered,** "The scripture says, 'Man cannot live on bread
	4. 7	**Jesus answered,** "But the scripture also says, 'Do not put the
	4.10	Then **Jesus answered,** "Go away, Satan!
	4.19	**Jesus said** to them, "Come with me, and I will teach you
	8. 4	Then **Jesus said** to him, "Listen!
	8. 7	"I will go and make him well," **Jesus said.**
	8.13	**Jesus said** to the officer, "Go home, and what you believe
	8.20	**Jesus answered** him, "Foxes have holes, and birds have nests,
	8.22	"Follow me," **Jesus answered,** "and let the dead bury their
	9.15	**Jesus answered,** "Do you expect the guests at a wedding party
	11. 4	**Jesus answered,** "Go back and tell John what you are
	11.25	At that time **Jesus said,** "Father, Lord of heaven and earth!
	12. 3	**Jesus answered,** "Have you never read what David did that time
	12.11	**Jesus answered,** "What if one of you has a sheep and it
	12.48	**Jesus answered,** "Who is my mother?
	13. 9	And **Jesus** concluded, "Listen, then, if you have ears!"
	13.11	**Jesus answered,** "The knowledge about the secrets of the Kingdom
	13.37	**Jesus answered,** "The man who sowed the good seed is the
	13.57	**Jesus said** to them, "A prophet is respected everywhere except in
	14.16	"They don't have to leave," answered **Jesus.**
	14.18	"Then bring them here to me," **Jesus said.**
	15. 3	**Jesus answered,** "And why do you disobey God's command and follow
	15.13	Father in heaven did not plant will be pulled up," answered **Jesus.**
	15.16	**Jesus said** to them, "You are still no more intelligent
	15.24	Then **Jesus** replied, "I have been sent only to the lost
	15.26	**Jesus answered,** "It isn't right to take the children's food
	15.28	So **Jesus answered** her, "You are a woman of great faith!
	16. 2	But **Jesus answered,** "When the sun is setting, you say,
	16. 6	**Jesus said** to them, "Take care;
	16.24	Then **Jesus said** to his disciples, "If anyone wants to come
	17.11	is indeed coming first," answered **Jesus,** "and he will get
	17.17	**Jesus answered,** "How unbelieving and wrong you people are!
	17.22	all came together in Galilee, **Jesus said** to them, "The Son
	17.26	"Well, then," replied **Jesus,** "that means that the citizens
	18.22	not seven times," answered **Jesus,** "but seventy times seven,
	18.35	**Jesus** concluded, "That is how my Father in heaven will treat
	19. 4	**Jesus answered,** "Haven't you read the scripture that says that
	19. 8	**Jesus answered,** "Moses gave you permission to divorce your wives
	19.11	**Jesus answered,** "This teaching does not apply to everyone,
	19.14	**Jesus said,** "Let the children come to me and do not
	19.18	**Jesus answered,** "Do not commit murder;
	19.21	**Jesus said** to him, "If you want to be perfect, go and
	19.23	**Jesus** then said to his disciples, "I assure you:
	19.28	**Jesus said** to them, "You can be sure that when the Son
	20.16	And **Jesus** concluded, "So those who are last will be first,
	20.22	don't know what you are asking for," **Jesus answered** the sons.
	20.23	indeed drink from my cup," **Jesus** told them, "but I do not
	21.16	"Indeed I do," answered **Jesus.**
	21.21	**Jesus answered,** "I assure you that if you believe and
	21.24	**Jesus answered** them, "I will ask you just one question,
	21.31	So **Jesus said** to them, "I tell you:
	21.33	"Listen to another parable," **Jesus said.**
	21.42	**Jesus said** to them, "Haven't you ever read what the Scriptures
	21.43	so I tell you," added **Jesus,** "the Kingdom of God will be
	22.14	And **Jesus** concluded, "Many are invited, but few are chosen."

Mt	22.21	**Jesus said** to them, "Well, then, pay the Emperor what belongs
	22.29	**Jesus answered** them, "How wrong you are!
	22.37	**Jesus answered,** " 'Love the Lord your God with all your heart,
	24. 4	**Jesus answered,** "Be on your guard, and do not let anyone
	25.13	**Jesus** concluded, "Be on your guard, then, because you do not
	26.21	During the meal **Jesus said,** "I tell you, one of you
	26.23	**Jesus answered,** "One who dips his bread in the dish
	26.25	**Jesus answered,** "So you say."
	26.31	Then **Jesus said** to them, "This very night all of you
	26.34	**Jesus said** to Peter, "I tell you that before the cock
	26.50	**Jesus answered,** "Be quick about it, friend!"
	26.52	"Put your sword back in its place," **Jesus said** to him.
	26.64	**Jesus answered** him, "So you say.
	27.11	"So you say," answered **Jesus.**
	28.10	"Do not be afraid," **Jesus said** to them.
Mk	1.17	**Jesus said** to them, "Come with me, and I will teach you
	1.38	But **Jesus answered,** "We must go on to the other villages
	2. 5	how much faith they had, **Jesus said** to the paralysed man,
	2.14	**Jesus said** to him, "Follow me."
	2.19	**Jesus answered,** "Do you expect the guests at a wedding party
	2.25	**Jesus answered,** "Have you never read what David did that time
	2.27	**Jesus** concluded, "The Sabbath was made for the good of man;
	3. 3	**Jesus said** to the man, "Come up here to the front."
	3.30	**(Jesus said** this because some people were saying, "He has
	3.33	**Jesus answered,** "Who is my mother?
	4. 9	And **Jesus** concluded, "Listen, then, if you have ears!"
	4.11	given the secret of the Kingdom of God," **Jesus answered.**
	4.21	**Jesus** continued, "Does anyone ever bring in a lamp and
	4.26	**Jesus** went on to say, "The Kingdom of God is like this.
	4.35	evening of that same day **Jesus said** to his disciples, "Let
	4.40	Then **Jesus said** to his disciples, "Why are you frightened?
	5. 8	(He said this because **Jesus** was saying, "Evil spirit, come out
	5. 9	So **Jesus** asked him, "What is your name?"
	5.34	**Jesus said** to her, "My daughter, your faith has made you well.
	5.35	**Jesus** was saying this, some messengers came from Jairus' house
	6. 4	**Jesus said** to them, "A prophet is respected everywhere except in
	6.37	"You yourselves give them something to eat," **Jesus answered.**
	6.50	**Jesus** spoke to them at once, "Courage!"
	7. 6	**Jesus answered** them, "How right Isaiah was when he prophesied
	7. 9	**Jesus** continued, "You have a clever way of rejecting God's law
	7.18	"You are no more intelligent than the others," **Jesus said**
	7.27	But **Jesus answered,** "Let us first feed the children.
	7.29	So **Jesus said** to her, "Because of that answer, go back
	8.15	"Take care," **Jesus** warned them, "and be on your guard
	9.19	**Jesus said** to them, "How unbelieving you people are!
	9.23	"Yes," said **Jesus,** "if you yourself can!
	9.29	"Only prayer can drive this kind out," answered **Jesus;**
	9.39	not try to stop him," **Jesus** told them, "because no one who
	10. 3	**Jesus answered** with a question, "What law did Moses give you?"
	10. 5	**Jesus said** to them, "Moses wrote this law for you because
	10.24	shocked at these words, but **Jesus** went on to say, "My
	10.27	**Jesus** looked straight at them and answered, "This is impossible
	10.29	"Yes," **Jesus said** to them, "and I tell you that
	10.38	**Jesus said** to them, "You don't know what you are asking for.
	10.39	**Jesus said** to them, "You will indeed drink the cup I must
	10.49	**Jesus** stopped and said, "Call him."
	10.52	"Go," **Jesus** told him, "your faith has made you well."
	11.14	**Jesus said** to the fig-tree, "No one shall ever eat figs
	11.22	**Jesus answered** them, "Have faith in God.
	11.29	**Jesus answered** them, "I will ask you just one question,
	11.33	**Jesus said** to them, "Neither will I tell you, then, by
	12.17	So **Jesus said,** "Well, then, pay the Emperor what belongs to
	12.24	**Jesus answered** them, "How wrong you are!
	12.29	**Jesus** replied, "The most important one is this:
	13. 2	**Jesus answered,** "You see these great buildings?
	13. 5	**Jesus said** to them, "Be on guard, and don't let anyone
	14. 6	But **Jesus said,** "Leave her alone!
	14.18	were at the table eating, **Jesus said,** "I tell you that one
	14.20	**Jesus answered,** "It will be one of you twelve, one who
	14.24	**Jesus said,** "This is my blood which is poured out for many,
	14.27	**Jesus said** to them, "All of you will run away and leave
	14.30	**Jesus said** to Peter, "I tell you that before the cock
	14.32	called Gethsemane, and **Jesus said** to his disciples, "Sit here
	14.48	Then **Jesus** spoke up and said to them, "Did you have to
	14.62	"I am," answered **Jesus,** "and you will all see the Son
	15. 2	**Jesus answered,** "So you say."
Lk	4. 4	**Jesus answered,** "The scripture says, 'Man cannot live on bread
	4. 8	**Jesus answered,** "The scripture says, 'Worship the Lord your God
	4.12	But **Jesus answered,** "The scripture says, 'Do not put the Lord
	4.24	I tell you this," **Jesus** added, "a prophet is never welcomed
	5.10	**Jesus said** to Simon, "Don't be afraid;
	5.27	**Jesus said** to him, "Follow me."
	5.31	**Jesus answered** them, "People who are well do not need a doctor,
	5.34	**Jesus answered,** "Do you think you can make the guests
	6. 3	**Jesus answered** them, "Haven't you read what David did when he
	6. 5	And **Jesus** concluded, "The Son of Man is Lord of the Sabbath."
	6. 9	Then **Jesus said** to them, "I ask you:
	7.14	**Jesus said,** "Young man!
	7.28	I tell you," **Jesus** added, "John is greater than any
	7.31	**Jesus** continued, "Now to what can I compare the people
	7.40	**Jesus** spoke up and said to him, "Simon, I have
	7.41	were two men who owed money to a money-lender," **Jesus** began.
	7.43	"You are right," said **Jesus.**
	7.48	Then **Jesus said** to the woman, "Your sins are forgiven."
	7.50	But **Jesus said** to the woman, "Your faith has saved you;
	8. 8	And **Jesus** concluded, "Listen, then, if you have ears!"
	8.21	**Jesus said** to them all, "My mother and brothers are
	8.46	But **Jesus said,** "Someone touched me, for I knew it when
	8.48	**Jesus said** to her, "My daughter, your faith has made you well.
	8.52	**Jesus said,** "Don't cry;
	9.13	**Jesus said** to them, "You yourselves give them something to eat."
Lk	9.14	**Jesus said** to his disciples, "Make the people sit down in
	9.41	**Jesus answered,** "How unbelieving and wrong you people are!
	9.50	not try to stop him," **Jesus said** to him and to the
	9.58	**Jesus said** to him, "Foxes have holes, and birds have nests,
	9.60	**Jesus answered,** "Let the dead bury their own dead.
	9.62	**Jesus said** to him, "Anyone who starts to plough and
	10.16	**Jesus said** to his disciples, "Whoever listens to you listens to me;
	10.18	**Jesus answered** them, "I saw Satan fall like lightning from heaven.
	10.26	**Jesus answered** him, "What do the Scriptures say?
	10.28	"You are right," **Jesus** replied;
	10.30	**Jesus answered,** "There was once a man who was going
	10.36	**Jesus** concluded, "In your opinion, which one of these three acted
	10.37	**Jesus** replied, "You go, then, and do the same."
	11. 2	**Jesus said** to them, "When you pray, say this:
	11. 5	And **Jesus said** to his disciples, "Suppose one of you
	11.28	**Jesus answered,** "Rather, how happy are those who hear the word
	11.29	As the people crowded round **Jesus,** he went on to say,
	11.46	**Jesus answered,** "How terrible also for you teachers of the Law!
	12. 1	were stepping on each other, **Jesus said** first to his disciples,
	12.14	**Jesus answered** him, "My friend, who gave me the right
	12.21	And **Jesus** concluded, "This is how it is with those who
	12.22	Then **Jesus said** to the disciples, "And so I tell you
	12.54	**Jesus said** also to the people, "When you see a cloud
	13. 2	**Jesus answered** them, "Because those Galileans were killed in
	13.23	**Jesus answered** them, [24]"Do your best to go in through
	13.32	**Jesus answered** them, "Go and tell that fox:
	14.12	Then **Jesus said** to his host, "When you give a lunch or
	14.16	**Jesus said** to him, "There was once a man who was giving
	14.33	In the same way," concluded **Jesus,** "none of you can be
	15.11	**Jesus** went on to say, "There was once a man who had
	16. 1	**Jesus said** to his disciples, "There was once a rich man
	16. 9	And **Jesus** went on to say, "And so I tell you:
	16.15	**Jesus said** to them, "You are the ones who make
	17. 1	**Jesus said** to his disciples, "Things that make people fall into
	17.14	**Jesus** saw them and said to them, "Go and let the
	17.17	**Jesus said,** "There were ten men who were healed;
	17.19	And **Jesus said** to him, "Get up and go;
	17.37	**Jesus answered,** "Wherever there is a dead body, the vultures will
	18.14	tell you," said **Jesus,** "the tax collector, and not the Pharisee,
	18.27	**Jesus answered,** "What is impossible for man is possible for God."
	18.29	"Yes," **Jesus said** to them, "and I assure you that anyone
	18.42	**Jesus said** to him, "Then see!
	19. 9	**Jesus said** to him, "Salvation has come to this house today,
	19.28	**Jesus said** this and then went on to Jerusalem ahead of them.
	19.40	**Jesus answered,** "I tell you that if they keep quiet,
	20. 3	**Jesus answered** them, "Now let me ask you a question.
	20. 8	And **Jesus said** to them, "Neither will I tell you, then,
	20.25	So **Jesus said,** "Well, then, pay the Emperor what belongs to
	20.34	**Jesus answered** them, "The men and women of this age marry,
	20.45	people listened to him, **Jesus said** to his disciples, [46]"Be on
	21. 5	**Jesus said,** [6]"All this you see—the time will come when not
	21. 8	**Jesus said,** "Be on guard;
	22.25	**Jesus said** to them, "The kings of the pagans have power
	22.34	tell you, Peter," **Jesus said,** "the cock will not crow tonight
	22.36	"But now," **Jesus said,** "whoever has a purse or a bag
	22.48	But **Jesus said,** "Judas, is it with a kiss that you
	22.51	But **Jesus said,** "Enough of this!"
	22.52	Then **Jesus said** to the chief priests and the officers of
	23. 3	"So you say," answered **Jesus.**
	23.28	**Jesus** turned to them and said, "Women of Jerusalem!
	23.34	**Jesus said,** "Forgive them, Father!
	23.43	**Jesus said** to him, "I promise you that today you will
	24.17	**Jesus said** to them, "What are you talking about to each other,
	24.25	Then **Jesus said** to them, "How foolish you are, how slow
Jn	1.42	**Jesus** looked at him and said, "Your name is Simon son of
	1.48	**Jesus answered,** "I saw you when you were under the
	1.50	**Jesus said,** "Do you believe just because I told you I
	2. 4	"You must not tell me what to do," **Jesus** replied.
	2. 7	**Jesus said** to the servants, "Fill these jars with water."
	2.19	**Jesus answered,** "Tear down this Temple, and in three
	3. 3	**Jesus answered,** "I am telling you the truth:
	3. 5	"I am telling you the truth," replied **Jesus.**
	3.10	**Jesus answered,** "You are a great teacher in Israel, and you
	4. 7	to draw some water, and **Jesus said** to her, "Give me a
	4.10	**Jesus answered,** "If only you knew what God gives and
	4.13	**Jesus answered,** "Whoever drinks this water will be thirsty
	4.16	"Go and call your husband," **Jesus** told her, "and come back."
	4.17	**Jesus** replied, "You are right when you say you haven't got
	4.21	**Jesus said** to her, "Believe me, woman, the time will
	4.26	**Jesus answered,** "I am he, I who am talking with you."
	4.34	"My food," **Jesus said** to them, "is to obey the will
	4.48	**Jesus said** to him, "None of you will ever believe
	4.50	**Jesus said** to him, "Go, your son will live!"
	5. 8	**Jesus said** to him, "Get up, pick up your mat, and walk."
	5.17	**Jesus answered** them, "My Father is always working, and I too
	5.19	So **Jesus answered** them, "I am telling you the truth:
	6.10	"Make the people sit down," **Jesus** told them.
	6.20	"Don't be afraid," **Jesus** told them, "it is I!"
	6.26	**Jesus answered,** "I am telling you the truth:
	6.29	**Jesus answered,** "What God wants you to do is to believe
	6.32	"I am telling you the truth," **Jesus said.**
	6.35	"I am the bread of life," **Jesus** told them.
	6.43	**Jesus answered,** "Stop grumbling among yourselves.
	6.53	**Jesus said** to them, "I am telling you the truth:
	6.59	**Jesus said** this as he taught in the synagogue in Capernaum.
	6.70	**Jesus** replied, "I chose the twelve of you, didn't I?
	7. 6	**Jesus said** to them, "The right time for me has not yet
	7.16	**Jesus answered,** "What I teach is not my own teaching,
	7.21	**Jesus answered,** "I performed one miracle, and you were all surprised.
	7.33	**Jesus said,** "I shall be with you a little while longer,

Jn 7.39 **Jesus said** this about the Spirit, which those who believed
8.11 "Well, then," **Jesus said,** "I do not condemn you either.
8.14 **Jesus answered,** "even though I do testify on my own behalf,
8.19 "You know neither me nor my Father," **Jesus answered.**
8.20 **Jesus said** all this as he taught in the Temple,
8.21 Again **Jesus said** to them, "I will go away;
8.23 **Jesus answered,** "You belong to this world here below, but I
8.25 **Jesus answered,** "What I have told you from the very beginning.
8.31 So **Jesus said** to those who believed in him, "If you
8.34 **Jesus said** to them, "I am telling you the truth:
8.39 were Abraham's children," **Jesus** replied, "you would do the same
8.42 **Jesus said** to them, "If God really were your Father,
8.49 "I have no demon," **Jesus answered.**
8.54 **Jesus answered,** "If I were to honour myself, that honour would
8.58 "I am telling you the truth," **Jesus** replied.
9. 3 **Jesus answered,** "His blindness has nothing to do with his sins
9.37 **Jesus said** to him, "You have already seen him, and he
9.39 **Jesus said,** "I came to this world to judge, so that the
9.41 **Jesus answered,** "If you were blind, then you would not be guilty;
10. 1 **Jesus said,** "I am telling you the truth:
10. 7 So **Jesus said** again, "I am telling you the truth:
10.25 **Jesus answered,** "I have already told you, but you would not
10.32 **Jesus said** to them, "I have done many good deeds in
10.34 **Jesus answered,** "It is written in your own Law that God said,
11. 4 When **Jesus** heard it, he said, "The final result of this
11. 9 **Jesus said,** "A day has twelve hours, hasn't it?
11.11 **Jesus said** this and then added, "Our friend Lazarus has fallen
11.14 **Jesus** told them plainly, "Lazarus is dead, [15] but for your sake
11.23 "Your brother will rise to life," **Jesus** told her.
11.25 **Jesus said** to her, "I am the resurrection and the life.
11.40 **Jesus said** to her, "Didn't I tell you that you would
11.41 **Jesus** looked up and said, "I thank you, Father, that you
11.44 "Untie him," **Jesus** told them, "and let him go."
12. 7 But **Jesus said,** "Leave her alone!
12.23 **Jesus answered** them, "The hour has now come for the Son
12.30 But **Jesus said** to them, "It was not for my sake that
12.35 **Jesus answered,** "The light will be among you a little longer.
12.36 After **Jesus said** this, he went off and hid himself from them.
12.44 **Jesus said** in a loud voice, "Whoever believes in me believes
13. 7 **Jesus answered** him, "You do not understand now what I am doing,
13. 8 do not wash your feet," **Jesus answered,** "you will no
13.10 **Jesus said,** "Anyone who has had a bath is completely
13.26 **Jesus answered,** "I will dip some bread in the sauce and
13.27 **Jesus said** to him, "Be quick about what you are doing!"
13.28 others at the table understood why **Jesus said** this to him.
13.31 After Judas had left, **Jesus said,** "Now the Son of Man's
13.36 "You cannot follow me now where I am going," answered **Jesus;**
13.38 **Jesus answered,** "Are you really ready to die for me?
14. 1 "Do not be worried and upset," **Jesus** told them.
14. 6 **Jesus answered** him, "I am the way, the truth, and the
14. 9 **Jesus answered,** "For a long time I have been with you all;
14.10 I have spoken to you," **Jesus said** to his disciples, "do
14.23 **Jesus answered** him, "Whoever loves me will obey my teaching.
16.31 **Jesus answered** them, "Do you believe now?
18. 6 When **Jesus said** to them, "I am he," they moved back
18. 8 "I have already told you that I am he," **Jesus said.**
18.11 **Jesus said** to Peter, "Put your sword back in its place!
18.20 **Jesus answered,** "I have always spoken publicly to everyone;
18.22 When **Jesus said** this, one of the guards there slapped him
18.23 **Jesus answered** him, "If I have said anything wrong, tell
18.34 **Jesus answered,** "Does this question come from you or have
18.36 **Jesus said,** "My kingdom does not belong to this world;
18.37 **Jesus answered,** "You say that I am a king.
19.11 **Jesus answered,** "You have authority over me only because it was
20.16 **Jesus said** to her, "Mary!"
20.21 **Jesus said** to them again, "Peace be with you.
20.29 **Jesus said** to him, "Do you believe because you see me?
21.10 Then **Jesus said** to them, "Bring some of the fish you
21.12 **Jesus said** to them, "Come and eat."
21.15 After they had eaten, **Jesus said** to Simon Peter, "Simon son
21.15 **Jesus said** to him, "Take care of my lambs."
21.16 A second time **Jesus said** to him, "Simon son of John, do
21.16 **Jesus said** to him, "Take care of my sheep."
21.17 A third time **Jesus said,** "Simon son of John, do you
21.17 **Jesus said** to him, "Take care of my sheep.
21.19 Then **Jesus said** to him, "Follow me!"
21.22 **Jesus answered** him, "If I want him to live until I come,
Acts 1. 7 **Jesus said** to them, "The times and occasions are set by
also Mt 8.26 Mt 12.39 Mt 13.51 Mt 15.34 Mt 20.21 Mk 10.18 Mk 10.51 Mk 12.9 Lk 18.19 Lk 20.15 Jn 11.39 Jn 20.15 Rev 22.7 Rev 22.12

JETHRO

Moses' father-in-law.

Ex 2.15 a well, seven daughters of **Jethro,** the priest of Midian, came
2.17 But some shepherds drove **Jethro's** daughters away.
2.21 agreed to live there, and **Jethro** gave him his daughter
3. 1 and goats of his father-in-law **Jethro,** the priest of Midian,
4.18 Moses went back to **Jethro,** his father-in-law, and said
4.18 **Jethro** agreed and said good-bye to him.
18. 1 Moses' father-in-law **Jethro,** the priest of Midian, heard
18. 5 **Jethro** came with Moses' wife and her two sons into the
18. 8 Moses told **Jethro** everything that the Lord had done to the
18. 9 When **Jethro** heard all this, he was happy [10] and said,
18.12 Then **Jethro** brought an offering to be burnt whole
18.14 When **Jethro** saw everything that Moses had to do, he asked,
18.17 Then **Jethro** said, "You are not doing it the right way.
18.24 Moses took **Jethro's** advice [25] and chose capable men
Ex 18.27 Moses said good-bye to **Jethro,** and Jethro went back home.
Num 10.29 his brother-in-law Hobab son of **Jethro** the Midianite,

JEW

[FELLOW-JEW, KING OF THE JEWS]

The word refers to the Israelites of the s. kingdom (Judah), or to the community in and around Jerusalem after the Exile, as well as their contemporaries outside Palestine. In the N.T. the term JEWS is often used to distinguish the followers of the Jewish religion from the Gentiles.

see also **JUDAISM**

Ezra 2.63 The **Jewish** governor told them that they could not eat
4. 4 discourage and frighten the **Jews** and keep them from building.
4.12 Majesty to know that the **Jews** who came here from your other
4.23 hurried to Jerusalem and forced the **Jews** to stop rebuilding
5. 1 God of Israel to the **Jews** who lived in Judah and Jerusalem.
5. 5 God was watching over the **Jewish** leaders, and the Persian
6. 7 governor of Judah and the **Jewish** leaders rebuild the Temple
6.14 The **Jewish** leaders made good progress with the building
9. 2 **Jewish** men were marrying foreign women, and so God's holy
Neh 1. 2 about Jerusalem and about our **fellow-Jews** who had returned
2.16 anything to any of my **fellow-Jews**—the priests, the leaders,
4. 1 Sanballat heard that we **Jews** had begun rebuilding the wall,
4. 2 he said, "What do these miserable **Jews** think they're doing?
4.12 time after time **Jews** who were living among our enemies came
5. 1 men and women, began to complain against their **fellow-Jews.**
5. 5 We are of the same race as our **fellow-Jews.**
5. 8 buying back our **Jewish** brothers who had to sell themselves
5. 8 own brothers to sell themselves to you, their **fellow-Jews!"**
5.17 hundred and fifty of the **Jewish** people and their leaders,
6. 6 that you and the **Jewish** people intend to revolt and that
6.17 all this time the **Jewish** leaders had been in correspondence
6.18 on his side because of his **Jewish** father-in-law, Shecaniah
7.65 The **Jewish** governor told them that they could not eat
13.17 reprimanded the **Jewish** leaders and said, "Look at the evil
13.23 that many of the **Jewish** men had married women from Ashdod,
Esth 2. 5 There in Susa lived a **Jew** named Mordecai son of Jair;
2.10 of Mordecai, Esther had kept it secret that she was **Jewish.**
2.20 she had still not let it be known that she was **Jewish.**
3. 4 "I am a **Jew,"** he explained, "and I cannot bow to Haman."
3. 6 learnt that Mordecai was a **Jew,** he decided to do more than
3. 6 He made plans to kill every **Jew** in the whole Persian Empire.
3.10 to the enemy of the **Jewish** people, Haman son of Hammedatha,
3.13 thirteenth day of Adar, all **Jews**—young and old, women and
4. 3 was made known, there was loud mourning among the **Jews.**
4. 7 to put into the royal treasury if all the **Jews** were killed.
4. 8 had been issued in Susa, ordering the destruction of the **Jews.**
4.13 are safer than any other **Jew** just because you are in the
4.14 come from heaven to the **Jews,** and they will be saved,
4.16 "Go and gather all the **Jews** in Susa together;
5.13 long as I see that **Jew** Mordecai sitting at the entrance of
6.10 and the horse, and provide these honours for Mordecai the **Jew.**
6.13 He is a **Jew,** and you cannot overcome him.
8. 1 Queen Esther all the property of Haman, the enemy of the **Jews.**
8. 3 that Haman, the descendant of Agag, had made against the **Jews.**
8. 5 Agag gave for the destruction of all the **Jews** in the empire.
8. 7 Esther and Mordecai, the **Jew,** "Look, I have hanged Haman for
8. 7 for his plot against the **Jews,** and I have given Esther his
8. 8 You may, however, write to the **Jews** whatever you wish;
8. 9 and dictated letters to the **Jews** and to the governors,
8. 9 of writing and to the **Jews** in their language and system of
8.11 the king would allow the **Jews** in every city to organize
8.11 in any province attacked the **Jewish** men, their children or
8.11 children or their women, the **Jews** could fight back
8.12 for the slaughter of the **Jews,** the thirteenth of Adar,
8.13 province, so that the **Jews** would be ready to take revenge
8.16 For the **Jews** there was joy and relief, happiness and
8.17 king's proclamation was read, the **Jews** held a joyful holiday
8.17 many other people became **Jews,** because they were afraid of
9. 1 when the enemies of the **Jews** were hoping to get them in
9. 1 But instead, the **Jews** triumphed over them.
9. 2 In the **Jewish** quarter of every city in the empire the Jews
9. 2 city in the empire the **Jews** organized themselves to attack
9. 3 and royal representatives—helped the **Jews** because they were
9. 5 So the **Jews** could do what they wanted with their enemies.
9. 6 Susa, the capital city itself, the **Jews** killed five hundred
9. 7 ten sons of Haman son of Hammedatha, the enemy of the **Jews:**
9.12 Esther, "In Susa alone the **Jews** have killed five hundred men,
9.13 please Your Majesty, let the **Jews** in Susa do again tomorrow
9.15 fourteenth day of Adar the **Jews** of Susa got together again
9.16 **Jews** in the provinces also organized and defended themselves.
9.18 The **Jews** of Susa, however, made the fifteenth a holiday,
9.19 is why **Jews** who live in small towns observe the fourteenth
9.20 letters to all the **Jews,** near and far, throughout the Persian
9.22 days on which the **Jews** had rid themselves of their enemies;
9.23 the **Jews** followed Mordecai's instructions, and the celebration
9.24 the enemy of the **Jewish** people—had cast lots (or "purim,"
9.24 to determine the day for destroying the **Jews;**
9.25 he had planned for the **Jews**—he and his sons were hanged
9.27 happened to them, [27] the **Jews** made it a rule for themselves,
9.27 anyone who might become a **Jew,** that at the proper time each
9.28 resolved that every **Jewish** family of every future generation
9.30 was addressed to all the **Jews,** and copies were sent to all
9.30 It wished the **Jews** peace and security [31] and directed them
10. 3 Mordecai the **Jew** was second in rank only to King Xerxes
10. 3 He was honoured and well-liked by his **fellow-Jews.**
Jer 40.15 That would cause all the **Jews** who have gathered round you to
Ezek 1. 1 Buzi, was living with the **Jewish** exiles by the River Chebar
Dan 2.25 found one of the **Jewish** exiles, who can tell Your Majesty
3. 8 that some Babylonians took the opportunity to denounce the **Jews.**

Dan	3.12	There are some **Jews** whom you put in charge of the
	5.13	"Are you Daniel, that **Jewish** exile whom my father the king
Zech	8.23	foreigners will come to one **Jew** and say, 'We want to share
Mt	2. 2	"Where is the baby born to be the **king of the Jews?**
	9.18	Jesus was saying this, a **Jewish** official came to him, knelt
	14. 5	he was afraid of the **Jewish** people, because they considered John
	27.11	"Are you the **king of the Jews?"**
	27.18	knew very well that the **Jewish** authorities had handed Jesus over
	27.29	"Long live the **King of the Jews!"**
	27.37	"This is Jesus, the **King of the Jews."**
	28.15	is the report spread round by the **Jews** to this very day.
Mk	7. 3	as the rest of the **Jews,** follow the teaching they received
	12.12	The **Jewish** leaders tried to arrest Jesus, because they knew
	15. 2	Pilate questioned him, "Are you the **king of the Jews?"**
	15. 9	want me to set free for you the **king of the Jews?"**
	15.12	to do with the one you call the **king of the Jews?"**
	15.18	"Long live the **King of the Jews!"**
	15.26	"The **King of the Jews."**
Lk	2.46	the Temple, sitting with the **Jewish** teachers, listening to them
	7. 3	about Jesus, he sent some **Jewish** elders to ask him to come
	18.18	A **Jewish** leader asked Jesus, "Good Teacher, what must I
	23. 3	Pilate asked him, "Are you the **king of the Jews?"**
	23.35	stood there watching while the **Jewish** leaders jeered at him:
	23.37	and said, "Save yourself if you are the **king of the Jews!"**
	23.38	"This is the **King of the Jews."**
Jn	1.19	The **Jewish** authorities in Jerusalem sent some priests and
	2. 6	The **Jews** have rules about ritual washing, and for this purpose
	2.18	**Jewish** authorities replied with a question, "What miracle can you
	3. 1	There was a **Jewish** leader named Nicodemus, who belonged to the
	3.25	began arguing with a **Jew** about the matter of ritual washing.
	4. 9	woman answered, "You are a **Jew,** and I am a Samaritan—so
	4. 9	**(Jews** will not use the same cups and bowls that Samaritans use.)
	4.20	on this mountain, but you **Jews** say that Jerusalem is the
	4.22	but we **Jews** know whom we worship,
	4.22	because it is from the **Jews** that salvation comes.
	5.10	was a Sabbath, [10] so the **Jewish** authorities told the man
	5.15	man left and told the **Jewish** authorities that it was Jesus
	5.18	made the **Jewish** authorities all the more determined to kill
	7. 1	Judaea, because the **Jewish** authorities there were wanting to kill
	7.11	The **Jewish** authorities were looking for him at the festival.
	7.13	because they were afraid of the **Jewish** authorities.
	7.15	**Jewish** authorities were greatly surprised and said, "How does this
	7.35	**Jewish** authorities said among themselves, "Where is he about to go
	8.22	So the **Jewish** authorities said, "He says that we cannot go
	9.18	The **Jewish** authorities, however, were not willing to believe
	9.22	were afraid of the **Jewish** authorities, who had already agreed
	11.51	to die for the **Jewish** people, [52] and not only for them,
	11.53	that day on the **Jewish** authorities made plans to kill Jesus.
	12.11	on his account many **Jews** were rejecting them and believing in
	12.42	Even then, many of the **Jewish** authorities believed in Jesus;
	13.33	now what I told the **Jewish** authorities, 'You cannot go where
	18.12	their commanding officer and the **Jewish** guards arrested Jesus,
	18.14	Caiaphas who had advised the **Jewish** authorities that it was
	18.28	**Jewish** authorities did not go inside the palace, for they wanted
	18.33	"Are you the **King of the Jews?"**
	18.35	Pilate replied, "Do you think I am a **Jew?**
	18.36	to keep me from being handed over to the **Jewish** authorities.
	18.39	want me to set free for you the **King of the Jews?"**
	19. 3	came to him and said, "Long live the **King of the Jews!"**
	19.19	"Jesus of Nazareth, the **King of the Jews,"** is what he wrote.
	19.21	"Do not write 'The **King of the Jews,'**
	19.21	but rather, 'This man said, I am the **King of the Jews.'** "
	19.31	the **Jewish** authorities asked Pilate to allow them to break the
	19.38	but in secret, because he was afraid of the **Jewish** authorities.)
	19.40	the spices according to the **Jewish** custom of preparing a
	20.19	locked doors, because they were afraid of the **Jewish** authorities.
Acts	2. 5	There were **Jews** living in Jerusalem, religious men who had come
	2.11	from Rome, [11] both **Jews** and Gentiles converted to Judaism,
	2.14	**"Fellow-Jews** and all of you who live in Jerusalem, listen
	4. 5	The next day the **Jewish** leaders, the elders, and the teachers
	5.21	called together all the **Jewish** elders for a full meeting of
	6. 1	was a quarrel between the Greek-speaking Jews and the native **Jews.**
	6. 1	The Greek-speaking **Jews** claimed that their widows were being
	6. 9	which included **Jews** from Cyrene and Alexandria.
	6. 9	They and other **Jews** from the provinces of Cilicia and Asia
	9.22	were so convincing that the **Jews** who lived in Damascus could
	9.23	days had gone by, the **Jews** met together and made plans to
	9.29	disputed with the Greek-speaking **Jews,** but they tried to kill him.
	10. 2	much to help the **Jewish** poor people and was constantly praying
	10.22	worships God and is highly respected by all the **Jewish** people.
	10.28	know very well that a **Jew** is not allowed by his religion
	10.45	**Jewish** believers who had come from Joppa with Peter were amazed
	11.19	Phoenicia, Cyprus, and Antioch, telling the message to **Jews** only.
	12. 3	saw that this pleased the **Jews,** he went on to arrest Peter.
	12.11	and from everything the **Jewish** people expected to happen."
	13. 6	magician named Bar-Jesus, a **Jew** who claimed to be a prophet.
	13.43	Barnabas were followed by many **Jews** and by many Gentiles who
	13.45	When the **Jews** saw the crowds, they were filled with jealousy;
	13.50	But the **Jews** stirred up the leading men of the city and
	14. 1	that a great number of **Jews** and Gentiles became believers.
	14. 2	But the **Jews** who would not believe stirred up the Gentiles
	14. 4	some were for the **Jews,** others for the apostles.
	14. 5	and **Jews,** together with their leaders, decided to ill-treat
	14.19	Some **Jews** came from Antioch in Pisidia and from Iconium;
	16. 1	also a Christian, was **Jewish,** but his father was a Greek.
Acts	16. 3	did so because all the **Jews** who lived in those places knew
	16.13	there would be a place where **Jews** gathered for prayer.
	16.20	and said, "These men are **Jews,** and they are causing trouble
	17. 5	the **Jews** were jealous and gathered some of the worthless loafers
	17.13	But when the **Jews** in Thessalonica heard that Paul had preached
	17.17	the synagogue with the **Jews** and with the Gentiles who worshipped
	18. 2	There he met a **Jew** named Aquila, born in Pontus, who had
	18. 2	the Emperor Claudius had ordered all the **Jews** to leave Rome.
	18. 4	synagogue every Sabbath, trying to convince both **Jews** and Greeks.
	18. 5	the message, testifying to the **Jews** that Jesus is the Messiah.
	18.12	the **Jews** got together, seized Paul, and took
	18.14	when Gallio said to the **Jews,** "If this were a matter of
	18.14	it would be reasonable for me to be patient with you **Jews.**
	18.19	He went into the synagogue and held discussions with the **Jews.**
	18.24	At that time a **Jew** named Apollos, who had been born in
	18.28	strong arguments he defeated the **Jews** in public debates
	19.10	the province of Asia, both **Jews** and Gentiles, heard the word
	19.13	Some **Jews** who travelled round and drove out evil spirits
	19.14	were the sons of a **Jewish** High Priest named Sceva, were
	19.17	All the **Jews** and Gentiles who lived in Ephesus heard about this;
	19.33	Alexander was responsible, since the **Jews** made him go up to
	19.34	recognized that he was a **Jew,** they all shouted together the
	20. 3	Syria when he discovered that the **Jews** were plotting against him;
	20.19	times that came to me because of the plots of the **Jews.**
	20.21	To **Jews** and Gentiles alike I gave solemn warning that
	21.11	in this way by the **Jews** in Jerusalem, and they will hand
	21.20	how many thousands of **Jews** have become believers, and how devoted
	21.21	have been teaching all the **Jews** who live in Gentile countries
	21.21	not to circumcise their children or follow the **Jewish** customs.
	21.27	come to an end, some **Jews** from the province of Asia saw
	21.39	Paul answered, "I am a **Jew,** born in Tarsus in Cilicia,
	22. 3	"I am a **Jew,** born in Tarsus in Cilicia, but brought up
	22. 5	from them letters written to **fellow-Jews** in Damascus, so I
	22.12	Law and was highly respected by all the **Jews** living there.
	22.24	find out why the **Jews** were screaming like this against him.
	22.30	to find out for certain what the **Jews** were accusing Paul of;
	23.12	The next morning some **Jews** met together and made a plan.
	23.20	He said, "The **Jewish** authorities have agreed to ask you
	23.27	The **Jews** seized this man and were about to kill him.
	24. 5	he starts riots among the **Jews** all over the world and is
	24. 9	The **Jews** joined in the accusation and said that all this
	24.12	The **Jews** did not find me arguing with anyone in the Temple,
	24.19	But some **Jews** from the province of Asia were there;
	24.24	Felix came with his wife Drusilla, who was **Jewish.**
	24.27	to gain favour with the **Jews** so he left Paul in prison.
	25. 2	priests and the **Jewish** leaders brought their charges against Paul.
	25. 7	When Paul arrived, the **Jews** who had come from Jerusalem stood
	25. 8	against the Law of the **Jews** or against the Temple or against
	25. 9	to gain favour with the **Jews,** so he asked Paul, "Would you
	25.10	have done no wrong to the **Jews,** as you yourself well know.
	25.15	to Jerusalem, the **Jewish** chief priests and elders brought charges
	25.24	against whom all the **Jewish** people, both here and in Jerusalem,
	26. 2	from all the things the **Jews** accuse me of, [3] particularly since
	26. 3	since you know so well all the **Jewish** customs and disputes.
	26. 4	"All the **Jews** know how I have lived ever since I was
	26. 7	hope, Your Majesty, that I am being accused by the **Jews!**
	26.21	for this reason that the **Jews** seized me while I was in
	26.23	the light of salvation to the **Jews** and to the Gentiles."
	28.17	Paul called the local **Jewish** leaders to a meeting.
	28.19	But when the **Jews** opposed this, I was forced to appeal
Rom	1.16	save all who believe, first the **Jews** and also the Gentiles.
	2. 9	what is evil, for the **Jews** first and also for the Gentiles.
	2.10	what is good, to the **Jews** first and also to the Gentiles.
	2.12	The **Jews** have the Law;
	2.17	You call yourself a **Jew;**
	2.24	says, "Because of you **Jews,** the Gentiles speak evil of God."
	2.27	And so you **Jews** will be condemned by the Gentiles
	2.28	After all, who is a real **Jew,** truly circumcised?
	2.28	the man who is a **Jew** on the outside, whose circumcision is
	2.29	Rather, the real **Jew** is the person
	2.29	the person who is a **Jew** on the inside, that is, whose
	3. 1	Have the **Jews** then any advantage over the Gentiles?
	3. 2	In the first place, God trusted his message to the **Jews.**
	3. 9	Well then, are we **Jews** in any better condition than the Gentiles?
	3. 9	I have already shown that **Jews** and Gentiles alike are all
	3.29	Or is God the God of the **Jews** only?
	3.30	and he will put the **Jews** right with himself on the basis
	9.24	only from among the **Jews** but also from among the Gentiles.
	10.12	because there is no difference between **Jews** and Gentiles;
	11.11	When the **Jews** stumbled, did they fall to their ruin?
	11.11	has come to the Gentiles, to make the **Jews** jealous of them.
	11.12	The sin of the **Jews** brought rich blessings to the world,
	11.12	blessings will be when the complete number of **Jews** is included!
	11.17	and now you share the strong spiritual life of the **Jews.**
	11.21	God did not spare the **Jews,** who are like natural branches;
	11.23	And if the **Jews** abandon their unbelief, they will be put
	11.24	The **Jews** are like this cultivated tree;
	11.28	reject the Good News, the **Jews** are God's enemies for the
	11.30	you have received God's mercy because the **Jews** were disobedient.
	11.31	that you have received, the **Jews** now disobey God, in order
	15. 8	was on behalf of the **Jews,** to show that God is faithful,
	15.27	Since the **Jews** shared their spiritual blessings with the Gentiles,
	15.27	Gentiles ought to use their material blessings to help the **Jews.**
	16. 7	Andronicus and Junias, **fellow-Jews** who were in prison with me;
	16.11	Greetings to Herodion, a **fellow-Jew,** and to the
	16.21	and so do Lucius, Jason, and Sosipater, **fellow-Jews.**
1 Cor	1.22	**Jews** want miracles for proof, and Greeks look for wisdom.

1 Cor 1.23 that is offensive to the **Jews** and nonsense to the Gentiles;
1.24 God has called, both **Jews** and Gentiles, this message is Christ,
9.20 While working with the **Jews,**
9.20 I live like a **Jew** in order to win them;
10.32 cause no trouble either to **Jews** or Gentiles or to the church
12.13 all of us, whether **Jews** or Gentiles, whether slaves or free,
2 Cor 11.24 Five times I was given the thirty-nine lashes by the **Jews;**
11.26 from robbers, in danger from **fellow-Jews** and from Gentiles;
Gal 1.13 I was devoted to the **Jewish** religion, how I persecuted without
1.14 I was ahead of most **fellow-Jews** of my age
1.14 in my practice of the **Jewish** religion,
2. 7 given Peter the task of preaching the gospel to the **Jews.**
2. 8 the Gentiles, just as Peter was made an apostle to the **Jews.**
2. 9 and I would work among the Gentiles and they among the **Jews.**
2.13 **Jewish** brothers also started acting like cowards along with Peter;
2.14 "You are a **Jew,**
2.14 yet you have been living like a Gentile, not like a **Jew.**
2.14 How, then, can you try to force Gentiles to live like **Jews?"**
2.15 Indeed, we are **Jews** by birth and not "Gentile sinners,"
3.28 there is no difference between **Jews** and Gentiles, between slaves
Eph 2.11 called "the uncircumcised" by the **Jews,** who call themselves
2.14 has brought us peace by making **Jews** and Gentiles one people.
2.17 away from God, and to the **Jews,** who were near to him.
2.18 Christ that all of us, **Jews** and Gentiles, are able to come
3. 6 the Gentiles have a part with the **Jews** in God's blessings;
Col 3.11 any distinction between Gentiles and **Jews,** circumcised
4.11 These three are the only **Jewish** believers who work with me
1 Thes 2.14 that they suffered from the **Jews,** [15] who killed the Lord Jesus
Tit 1.14 no longer hold on to **Jewish** legends and to human commandments
Heb 9.25 **Jewish** High Priest goes into the Most Holy Place every year
10.11 Every **Jewish** priest performs his services every day and offers
13.10 priests who serve in the **Jewish** place of worship have no
13.11 The **Jewish** High Priest brings the blood of the animals into
Rev 2. 9 against you by those who claim to be **Jews** but are not;
3. 9 who claim that they are **Jews** but are not, I will make

JEWEL

Gen 24.53 and silver and gold **jewellery,** and gave them to Rebecca.
Ex 3.22 and will ask for clothing and for gold and silver **jewellery.**
11. 2 of them to ask their neighbours for gold and silver **jewellery."**
12.35 had asked the Egyptians for gold and silver **jewellery**
25. 7 carnelians and other **jewels** to be set in the ephod of the
28.11 Get a skilful **jeweller** to engrave on the two stones
31. 5 for cutting **jewels** to be set;
33. 4 they began to mourn and did not wear **jewellery** any more.
33. 5 Now take off your **jewellery,** and I will decide what to do
33. 6 left Mount Sinai, the people of Israel no longer wore **jewellery.**
35. 9 and other **jewels** to be set in the High Priest's ephod
35.22 all kinds of gold **jewellery** and dedicated them to the Lord.
35.27 brought carnelians and other **jewels** to be set in the ephod
35.33 for cutting **jewels** to be set;
2 Sam 1.24 rich scarlet dresses and adorned you with **jewels** and gold.
12.30 which weighed about thirty-five kilogrammes and had a **jewel**
12.30 David took the **jewel** and put it in his own crown.
1 Kgs 10. 2 camels loaded with spices, **jewels,** and a large amount of gold.
10.10 of gold and a very large amount of spices and **jewels.**
10.11 brought from there a large amount of juniper wood and **jewels.**
1 Chr 20. 2 In it there was a **jewel,** which David took and put in
2 Chr 9. 1 camels loaded with spices, **jewels,** and a large amount of gold.
9. 9 of gold and a very large amount of spices and **jewels.**
9.10 brought gold from Ophir also brought juniper wood and **jewels.**
Job 28.16 The finest gold and **jewels** Cannot equal its value.
Prov 3.15 Wisdom is more valuable than **jewels;**
8.11 "I am Wisdom, I am better than **jewels;**
20.15 you have something more valuable than gold or **jewels.**
25.12 more valuable than gold rings or **jewellery** made of the finest
31.10 She is worth far more than **jewels!**
Song 1.10 upon your cheeks and falls along your neck like **jewels.**
Is 49.18 of your people, as proud as a bride is of her **jewels.**
54.12 that glow like fire, and the wall around you with **jewels.**
Jer 2.32 Does a young woman forget her **jewellery,** or a bride her
4.30 Why do you put on **jewellery** and paint your eyes?
Ezek 7.20 proud of their beautiful **jewels,** but they used them to make
16.11 I put **jewels** on you—bracelets and necklaces.
16.17 took the silver and gold **jewellery** that I had given you,
16.39 away your clothes and **jewels** and leave you completely naked.
23.26 They will tear off your clothes and take your **jewels.**
23.40 The two sisters would bathe and put on eye-shadow and **jewellery.**
27.22 merchants of Sheba and Raamah exchanged **jewels,** gold,
Dan 10. 6 His body shone like a **jewel.**
11.38 He will offer gold, silver, **jewels,** and other rich gifts
Hos 2.13 Baal and put on her **jewellery** to go chasing after her lovers.
Zech 9.16 They will shine in his land like the **jewels** of a crown.
1 Pet 3. 3 do your hair, or the **jewellery** you put on, or the dresses

JEZEBEL (1)

King Ahab's wife.

1 Kgs 16.31 further and married **Jezebel,** the daughter of King Ethbaal
18. 4 and when **Jezebel** was killing the Lord's prophets, Obadiah
18.13 you heard that when **Jezebel** was killing the prophets of the
18.19 of the goddess Asherah who are supported by Queen **Jezebel."**
19. 1 King Ahab told his wife **Jezebel** everything that Elijah had
21. 5 His wife **Jezebel** went to him and asked, "Why are you so
21. 7 **Jezebel** replied.
21.11 leading citizens of Jezreel did what **Jezebel** had commanded.
21.14 The message was sent to **Jezebel:**
21.15 soon as **Jezebel** received the message, she said to Ahab,
21.23 concerning **Jezebel,** the Lord says that dogs will eat her body
21.25 Lord's sight as Ahab—all at the urging of his wife **Jezebel.**
22.52 his father Ahab, his mother **Jezebel,** and King Jeroboam,
2 Kgs 3. 2 he was not as bad as his father or his mother **Jezebel;**
9. 7 so that I may punish **Jezebel** for murdering my prophets and
9.10 **Jezebel** will not be buried;
9.22 witchcraft and idolatry that your mother **Jezebel** started?"
9.30 **Jezebel,** having heard what had happened, put on eyeshadow,
9.36 'Dogs will eat **Jezebel's** body in the territory of Jezreel.
10.13 to the children of Queen **Jezebel** and to the rest of the

JEZEBEL (2)

Symbolic name probably based on Jezebel (1).

Rev 2.20 that woman **Jezebel,** who calls herself a messenger of God.

JEZREEL (1)

City in Judah.

Josh 17.16 surrounding towns and those who live in the Valley of **Jezreel."**
19.18 Its area included **Jezreel,** Chesulloth, Shunem,
Judg 6.33 crossed the River Jordan, and camped in the Valley of **Jezreel.**
1 Sam 25.43 David had married Ahinoam from **Jezreel,** and now Abigail
27. 3 wives with him, Ahinoam from **Jezreel,** and Abigail,
29. 1 the Israelites camped at the spring in the Valley of **Jezreel.**
29.11 back to Philistia, and the Philistines went on to **Jezreel.**
31. 7 side of the Valley of **Jezreel** and east of the River Jordan
2 Sam 2. 2 Ahinoam, who was from **Jezreel,** and Abigail, Nabal's widow,
2. 9 the territories of Gilead, Asher, **Jezreel,** Ephraim,
3. 2 Amnon, whose mother was Ahinoam, from **Jezreel;**
4. 4 came from the city of **Jezreel,** his nurse picked him up and
1 Kgs 4.12 south of the town of **Jezreel,** as far as the city of
18.45 Ahab got into his chariot and started back to **Jezreel.**
18.46 his waist and ran ahead of Ahab all the way to **Jezreel.**
21. 1 Near King Ahab's palace in **Jezreel** there was a vineyard
21. 8 and sent them to the officials and leading citizens of **Jezreel.**
21.11 leading citizens of **Jezreel** did what Jezebel had commanded.
21.23 says that dogs will eat her body in the city of **Jezreel.**
2 Kgs 8.29 returned to the city of **Jezreel** to recover from his wounds,
9.10 body will be eaten by dogs in the territory of **Jezreel.' "**
9.14 King Joram, who was in **Jezreel,** where he had gone to recover
9.14 slips out of Ramoth to go and warn the people in **Jezreel."**
9.16 Then he got into his chariot and set off for **Jezreel.**
9.17 duty in the watch-tower at **Jezreel** saw Jehu and his men
9.30 Jehu arrived in **Jezreel.**
9.36 'Dogs will eat Jezebel's body in the territory of **Jezreel.**
10. 6 Ahab's descendants to me at **Jezreel** by this time tomorrow."
10. 7 their heads in baskets, and sent them to Jehu at **Jezreel.**
10.11 relatives of Ahab living in **Jezreel,** and all his officers,
10.12 Jehu left **Jezreel** to go to Samaria.
10.13 "We are going to **Jezreel** to pay our respects to the
1 Chr 3. 1 whose mother was Ahinoam from **Jezreel**
10. 7 lived in the Valley of **Jezreel** heard that the army had fled
2 Chr 22. 6 returned to the city of **Jezreel** to recover from his wounds,
Hos 1. 4 for the murders that his ancestor Jehu committed at **Jezreel.**
1. 5 And in the Valley of **Jezreel** I will at that time destroy
1.11 Yes, the day of **Jezreel** will be a great day!

JINGLE

Is 3.16 dainty little steps, and the bracelets on their ankles **jingle.**

JOAB (1)

Commander of David's army.

1 Sam 26.1-25 **David spares Saul's life again**
2 Sam 2.12-3.1 **War between Israel and Judah**
3.22-30 **Abner is murdered**
31-39 **Abner is buried**
8.1-18 **David's military victories**
10.1-19 **David defeats the Ammonites and the Syrians**
11.1-27 **David and Bathsheba**
12.26-31 **David captures Rabbah**
14.1-24 **Joab arranges for Absalom's return**
25-33 **Absalom is reconciled to David**
17.15-29 **David is warned and escapes**
18.1-18 **Absalom is defeated and killed**
19-33 **David is told of Absalom's death**
19.1-8a **Joab reprimands David**
8b-18a **David starts back to Jerusalem**
20.1-22 **Sheba's rebellion**
23-26 **David's officials**
23.8-39 **David's famous soldiers**
24.1-25 **David takes a census**
1 Kgs 1.5-10 **Adonijah claims the throne**
11-53 **Solomon is made king**
2.1-9 **David's last instructions to Solomon**
13-25 **The death of Adonijah**
26-35 **Abiathar's banishment and Joab's death**
11.14-25 **Solomon's enemies**
1 Chr 2.9-17 **The family tree of King David**
11.1-9 **David becomes king of Israel and Judah**
10-47 **David's famous soldiers**
18.1-17 **David's military victories**
19.1-19 **David defeats the Ammonites and the Syrians**
20.1-3 **David captures Rabbah**
21.1-22.1 **David takes a census**
26.20-28 **Other Temple duties**
27.1-15 **Military and civil organization**
16-24 **Administration of the tribes of Israel**
32-34 **David's personal advisers**

also 2 Sam 16.10 2 Sam 19.22

JOAHAZ (1)

King of Judah. (The name is written in this way to distinguish this king from King Jehoahaz of Israel.)

2 Kgs	23.30	of Judah chose Josiah's son **Joahaz** and anointed him king.
	23.31	**Joahaz** was twenty-three years old when he became king of
	23.34	**Joahaz** was taken to Egypt by King Neco, and there he died.
1 Chr	3.15	Johanan, Jehoiakim, Zedekiah, and **Joahaz.**
2 Chr	36. 1	chose Josiah's son **Joahaz** and anointed him king in Jerusalem.
	36. 2	**Joahaz** was twenty-three years old when he became king of
	36. 4	Neco made **Joahaz'** brother Eliakim king of Judah
	36. 4	**Joahaz** was taken to Egypt by Neco.
Jer	22.10	But weep bitterly for **Joahaz,** his son;
	22.11	Lord says concerning Josiah's son **Joahaz,** who succeeded his

JOASH (1)

King of Judah. (The name is written in this way to distinguish this king from King Jehoash of Israel).

2 Kgs	11. 2	Only Ahaziah's son **Joash** escaped.
	11. 4	showed them King Ahaziah's son **Joash** [5]and gave them
	11. 8	You are to guard King **Joash** with drawn swords and stay
	11.12	Jehoiada led **Joash** out, placed the crown on his head,
	11.12	Then **Joash** was anointed and proclaimed king.
	11.17	priest Jehoiada made King **Joash** and the people enter into a
	11.19	**Joash** entered by the Guard Gate and took his place on the
	11.21	**Joash** became king of Judah at the age of seven.
	12. 1	of King Jehu of Israel, **Joash** became king of Judah, and he
	12. 4	**Joash** called the priests and ordered them to save up the
	12. 6	twenty-third year of **Joash's** reign the priests still had not
	12.18	**Joash** of Judah took all the offerings that his predecessors
	12.19	Everything else that King **Joash** did is recorded in
	12.20	**Joash's** officials plotted against him, and two of them,
	12.20	**Joash** was buried in the royal tombs in David's City,
	13. 1	year of the reign of **Joash** son of Ahaziah as king of
	13.10	of the reign of King **Joash** of Judah, Jehoash son of Jehoahaz
	14. 1	of Israel, Amaziah son of **Joash** became king of Judah
	14. 3	instead, he did what his father **Joash** had done.
	14.23	reign of Amaziah son of **Joash** as king of Judah, Jeroboam
1 Chr	3.11	Abijah, Asa, Jehoshaphat, [11] Jehoram, Ahaziah, **Joash,**
	7. 8	Zemirah, **Joash,** Eliezer, Eleoenai, Omri, Jeremoth, Abijah,
	27.25	**Joash** Cattle in the Plain of Sharon:
2 Chr	22.11	rescued one of Ahaziah's sons, **Joash,** took him away from the
	23. 3	and there they made a covenant with **Joash,** the king's son.
	23.11	Jehoiada led **Joash** out, placed the crown on his head,
	23.11	priest and his sons anointed **Joash,** and everyone shouted,
	23.16	priest Jehoiada got King **Joash** and the people to join him
	24. 1	**Joash** became king of Judah at the age of seven,
	24. 3	chose two wives for King **Joash,** and they bore him sons and
	24. 4	king for a while, **Joash** decided to have the Temple repaired.
	24.17	the leaders of Judah persuaded King **Joash** to listen to them
	24.21	King **Joash** joined in a conspiracy against Zechariah,
	24.24	In this way King **Joash** was punished.
	24.27	stories of the sons of **Joash,** the prophecies spoken against

JOB (1)

Judg	8.21	It takes a man to do a man's **job."**
2 Chr	34.13	supervising the workmen on various **jobs,** and others kept
Ps	109. 8	may another man take his **job!**
Prov	22.29	man who does a good **job,** and I will show you a
Lk	14.28	cost, to see if he has enough money to finish the **job.**
	14.30	'This man began to build but can't finish the **job!'**
	16. 3	to himself, 'My master is going to dismiss me from my **job.**
	16. 4	Then when my **job** is gone, I shall have friends who will
2 Cor	8.11	On with it, then, and finish the **job!**

JOB (2)

Hero of the book of Job.

Job	1. 1	There was a man named **Job,** living in the land of Uz,
	1. 4	**Job's** sons used to take it in turns to give a feast,
	1. 5	The morning after each feast, **Job** would get up early
	1. 8	"Did you notice my servant **Job?"**
	1. 9	Satan replied, "Would **Job** worship you if he got nothing
	1.12	has is in your power, but you must not hurt **Job** himself."
	1.13	One day when **Job's** children were having a feast at the
	1.14	of their eldest brother, [14]a messenger came running to **Job.**
	1.20	Then **Job** stood up and tore his clothes in grief.
	1.22	everything that had happened, **Job** did not sin by blaming God.
	2. 3	"Did you notice my servant **Job?"**
	2. 3	no reason at all, but **Job** is still as faithful as ever."
	2. 7	Lord's presence and made sores break out all over **Job's** body.
	2. 8	**Job** went and sat by the rubbish heap and took a piece
	2.10	**Job** answered, "You are talking nonsense!
	2.10	of everything he suffered, **Job** said nothing against God.
	2.11	Three of **Job's** friends were Eliphaz, from the city of
	2.11	When they heard how much **Job** had been suffering, they decided
	2.12	a long way off they saw **Job,** but did not recognize him.
	3. 1	Finally **Job** broke the silence and cursed the day on which
	4. 1	**Job,** will you be annoyed if I speak?
	5. 1	Call out, **Job.**
	5.27	**Job,** we have learnt this by long study.
	11. 3	**Job,** do you think we can't answer you?
	11.13	Put your heart right, **Job.**
	15. 1	Empty words, **Job!**
	15.17	Now listen, **Job,** to what I know.
	18. 1	**Job,** can't people like you ever be quiet?
	20. 1	**Job,** you upset me.
	22.21	Now, **Job,** make peace with God and stop treating him like
	29. 1	**Job** began speaking again.
Job	31.40	The words of **Job** are ended.
	32. 1	Because **Job** was convinced of his own innocence, the three
	32. 2	because **Job** was justifying himself and blaming God.
	32. 3	He was also angry with **Job's** three friends.
	32. 3	find no way to answer **Job,** and this made it appear that
	32. 5	three men could not answer **Job,** he was angry [6]and began to
	32.12	you have not disproved what **Job** has said.
	32.13	God must answer **Job,** for you have failed.
	32.14	**Job** was speaking to you, not to me, but I would never
	32.15	Words have failed them, **Job;**
	33. 1	And now, **Job,** listen carefully to all that I have to say.
	33.12	But I tell you, **Job,** you are wrong.
	33.31	Now, **Job,** listen to what I am saying;
	34. 5	**Job** claims that he is innocent, that God refuses to give
	34. 7	Have you ever seen anyone like this man **Job?**
	34.31	**Job,** have you confessed your sins to God and promised not
	34.35	hears me will say [35] that **Job** is speaking from ignorance and
	34.36	Think through everything that **Job** says;
	35. 1	It is not right, **Job,** for you to say that you are
	35.14	**Job,** you say you can't see God;
	37.14	Pause a moment, **Job,** and listen;
	38. 1	Then out of the storm the Lord spoke to **Job.**
	38.12	**Job,** have you ever in all your life commanded a day to
	39.19	Was it you, **Job,** who made horses so strong and gave them
	40. 1	**Job,** you challenged Almighty God;
	40. 6	Then out of the storm the Lord spoke to **Job** once again.
	42. 1	Then **Job** answered the Lord.
	42. 7	Lord had finished speaking to **Job,** he said to Eliphaz, "I
	42. 7	did not speak the truth about me, as my servant **Job** did.
	42. 8	bulls and seven rams to **Job** and offer them as a sacrifice
	42. 8	**Job** will pray for you, and I will answer his prayer and
	42. 9	Lord had told them to do, and the Lord answered **Job's** prayer.
	42.10	after **Job** had prayed for his three friends, the Lord made
	42.11	All **Job's** brothers and sisters and former friends came
	42.12	blessed the last part of **Job's** life even more than he had
	42.12	**Job** owned fourteen thousand sheep, six thousand camels,
	42.15	women in the whole world as beautiful as **Job's** daughters.
	42.16	**Job** lived a hundred and forty years after this,
Jas	5.11	You have heard of **Job's** patience, and you know how the Lord

JOHN (1)

John the Baptist, who called the Jews to repentance, and baptized them in the River Jordan.

Mt	3. 1	At that time **John the Baptist** came to the desert of Judaea
	3. 3	**John** was the man the prophet Isaiah was talking about when
	3. 4	**John's** clothes were made of camel's hair;
	3. 7	When **John** saw many Pharisees and Sadducees coming to him
	3.13	from Galilee and came to **John** at the Jordan to be baptized
	3.14	But **John** tried to make him change his mind.
	3.14	to be baptized by you," **John** said, "and yet you have come
	3.15	So **John** agreed.
	4.12	When Jesus heard that **John** had been put in prison, he
	9.14	Then the followers of **John the Baptist** came to Jesus, asking,
	11. 2	**John the Baptist** heard in prison about the things that Christ
	11. 3	Jesus, "are you the one **John** said was going to come, or
	11. 4	"Go back and tell **John** what you are hearing and seeing:
	11. 7	While **John's** disciples were leaving, Jesus spoke about him
	11. 7	"When you went out to **John** in the desert, what did you
	11.10	For **John** is the one of whom the scripture says:
	11.11	I assure you that **John the Baptist** is greater than any
	11.11	who is least in the Kingdom of heaven is greater than **John.**
	11.12	From the time **John** preached his message until this very day
	11.13	Until the time of **John** all the prophets and the Law of
	11.14	willing to believe their message, **John** is Elijah, whose coming
	11.18	When **John** came, he fasted and drank no wine, and everyone said,
	14. 2	"He is really **John the Baptist,** who has come back to life,"
	14. 3	Herod had earlier ordered **John's** arrest, and he had him chained
	14. 4	For some time **John the Baptist** had told Herod, "It isn't
	14. 5	the Jewish people, because they considered **John** to be a prophet.
	14. 8	here and now the head of **John the Baptist** on a dish!"
	14.10	So he had **John** beheaded in prison.
	14.12	**John's** disciples came, carried away his body, and buried
	14.13	Jesus heard the news about **John,** he left there in a boat
	16.14	"Some say **John the Baptist,"** they answered.
	17.13	understood that he was talking to them about **John the Baptist.**
	21.25	Where did **John's** right to baptize come from:
	21.25	he will say to us, 'Why, then, did you not believe **John?'**
	21.26	because they are all convinced that **John** was a prophet."
	21.32	For **John the Baptist** came to you showing you the right
Mk	1. 4	So **John** appeared in the desert, baptizing and preaching.
	1. 5	of Judaea and the city of Jerusalem went out to hear **John.**
	1. 6	**John** wore clothes made of camel's hair, with a leather
	1. 9	province of Galilee, and was baptized by **John** in the Jordan.
	1.14	After **John** had been put in prison, Jesus went to Galilee
	2.18	the followers of **John the Baptist** and the Pharisees were fasting.
	2.18	that the disciples of **John the Baptist** and the disciples of
	6.14	Some people were saying, **"John the Baptist** has come back to life!
	6.16	When Herod heard it, he said, "He is **John the Baptist!**
	6.17	Herod himself had ordered **John's** arrest, and he had him chained
	6.18	**John the Baptist** kept telling Herod, "It isn't right
	6.19	Herodias held a grudge against **John** and wanted to kill him,
	6.20	Herod was afraid of **John**
	6.20	because he knew that **John** was a good and holy man,
	6.24	"The head of **John the Baptist,"** she answered.
	6.25	here and now the head of **John the Baptist** on a dish!"
	6.27	sent off a guard at once with orders to bring **John's** head.
	6.27	The guard left, went to the prison, and cut **John's** head off;
	6.29	**John's** disciples heard about this, they came and took away his
	8.28	"Some say that you are **John the Baptist,"** they
	11.30	Tell me, where did **John's** right to baptize come from:

Mk 11.31 'From God,' he will say, 'Why, then, did you not believe **John?'**
11.32 because everyone was convinced that **John** had been a prophet.)
Lk 1.13 You are to name him **John.**
1.60 His name is to be **John."**
1.63 asked for a writing tablet and wrote, "His name is **John."**
1.67 **John's** father Zechariah was filled with the Holy Spirit,
3. 2 word of God came to **John** son of Zechariah in the desert.
3. 3 So **John** went throughout the whole territory of the River Jordan,
3. 7 Crowds of people came out to **John** to be baptized by him.
3.15 they began to wonder whether **John** perhaps might be the Messiah.
3.16 So **John** said to all of them, "I baptize you with water,
3.18 In many different ways **John** preached the Good News to the
3.19 **John** reprimanded Herod, the governor, because he had married
3.20 Then Herod did an even worse thing by putting **John** in prison.
5.33 "The disciples of **John** fast frequently and offer prayers,
7.18 When **John's** disciples told him about all these things,
7.19 "Are you the one **John** said was going to come, or
7.20 to Jesus, they said, **"John the Baptist** sent us to ask
7.22 He answered **John's** messengers,
7.22 "Go back and tell **John** what you have seen and heard:
7.24 **John's** messengers had left, Jesus began to speak about him to
7.24 "When you went out to **John** in the desert, what did you
7.27 For **John** is the one of whom the scripture says:
7.28 I tell you," Jesus added, **"John** is greater than any
7.28 who is least in the Kingdom of God is greater than **John."**
7.29 had obeyed God's righteous demands and had been baptized by **John.**
7.30 God's purpose for themselves and refused to be baptized by **John.**
7.33 **John the Baptist** came, and he fasted and drank no wine,
9. 7 were saying that **John the Baptist** had come back to life.
9. 9 Herod said, "I had **John's** head cut off;
9.19 "Some say that you are **John the Baptist,"** they
11. 1 "Lord, teach us to pray, just as **John** taught his disciples."
16.16 prophets were in effect up to the time of **John the Baptist;**
20. 4 Tell me, [4] did **John's** right to baptize come from God or from
20. 5 'From God,' he will say, 'Why, then, did you not believe **John?'**
20. 6 stone us, because they are convinced that **John** was a prophet."
Jn 1. 6 his messenger, a man named **John,** [7] who came to tell people
1.15 **John** spoke about him.
1.19 priests and Levites to **John,** to ask him, "Who are you?"
1.20 **John** did not refuse to answer, but spoke out openly and clearly,
1.21 "No, I am not," **John** answered.
1.23 **John** answered by quoting the prophet Isaiah:
1.25 the Pharisees, [25] then asked **John,** "If you are not the Messiah
1.26 **John** answered, "I baptize with water, but among you stands
1.28 east side of the River Jordan, where **John** was baptizing.
1.29 The next day **John** saw Jesus coming to him, and said,
1.32 And **John** gave this testimony:
1.34 I have seen it," said **John,** "and I tell you that he
1.35 The next day **John** was standing there again with two of
3.23 **John** also was baptizing in Aenon, not far from Salim,
3.24 (This was before **John** had been put in prison.)
3.25 Some of **John's** disciples began arguing with a Jew about
3.26 So they went to **John** and said, "Teacher, you remember
3.27 **John** answered, "No one can have anything unless God gives it
4. 1 heard that Jesus was winning and baptizing more disciples than **John.**
5.33 **John** is the one to whom you sent your messengers,
5.35 **John** was like a lamp, burning and shining, and you were
5.36 which is even greater than the witness that **John** gave:
10.40 Jordan to the place where **John** had been baptizing, and he
10.41 **"John** performed no miracles," they said, "but everything he said
Acts 1. 5 **John** baptized with water, but in a few days you will be
1.21 beginning from the time **John** preached his message of baptism
10.37 beginning in Galilee after **John** preached his message of baptism.
11.16 **'John** baptized with water, but you will be baptized with the
13.24 Before Jesus began his work, **John** preached to all the people
13.25 And as **John** was about to finish his mission, he said to
18.25 However, he knew only the baptism of **John.**
19. 3 "The baptism of **John,"** they answered.
19. 4 Paul said, "The baptism of **John** was for those who turned

JOHN (2)
The son of Zebedee and brother of James.

Mt 4.21 saw two other brothers, James and **John,** the sons of Zebedee.
10. 2 James and his brother **John,** the sons of Zebedee;
17. 1 and the brothers James and **John** and led them up a high
Mk 1.19 saw two other brothers, James and **John,** the sons of Zebedee.
1.29 his disciples, including James and **John,** left the synagogue
3.17 James and his brother **John,** the sons of Zebedee (Jesus gave
5.37 go on with him except Peter and James and his brother **John.**
9. 2 with him Peter, James, and **John,** and led them up a high
9.38 **John** said to him, "Teacher, we saw a man who was
10.35 Then James and **John,** the sons of Zebedee, came to Jesus.
10.41 heard about it, they became angry with James and **John.**
13. 3 the Temple, when Peter, James, **John,** and Andrew came to him
14.33 He took Peter, James, and **John** with him.
Lk 5.10 of Simon's partners, James and **John,** the sons of Zebedee.
6.14 James and **John,** Philip and Bartholomew, [15] Matthew and Thomas,
8.51 in with him except Peter, **John,** and James, and the child's
9.28 Jesus took Peter, **John,** and James with him and went
9.49 **John** spoke up, "Master, we saw a man driving out demons
9.54 When the disciples James and **John** saw this, they said, "Lord,
22. 8 Jesus sent off Peter and **John** with these instructions:
Acts 1.13 Peter, **John,** James and Andrew, Philip and Thomas, Bartholomew
3. 1 One day Peter and **John** went to the Temple at three o'clock
3. 3 When he saw Peter and **John** going in, he begged them to
Acts 3.11 held on to Peter and **John** in Solomon's Porch, as it was
4. 1 Peter and **John** were still speaking to the people when some
4.13 see how bold Peter and **John** were and to learn that they
4.14 man who had been healed standing there with Peter and **John.**
4.19 But Peter and **John** answered them, "You yourselves judge which
4.23 As soon as Peter and **John** were set free, they returned
8.14 the word of God, so they sent Peter and **John** to them.
8.17 Peter and **John** placed their hands on them, and they received
8.18 offered money to Peter and **John,** [19] and said, "Give this power
8.24 Simon said to Peter and **John,** "Please pray to the Lord
8.25 the Lord's message, Peter and **John** went back to Jerusalem.
12. 2 had James, the brother of **John,** put to death by the sword.
Gal 2. 9 James, Peter, and **John,** who seemed to be the leaders, recognized

JOHN (3)
Writer of The Revelation.

Rev 1. 1 known to his servant **John** by sending his angel to him,
1. 2 and **John** has told all that he has
1. 4 From **John** to the seven churches in the province of Asia:
1. 9 I am **John,** your brother, and as a follower of Jesus I
22. 8 I, **John,** have heard and seen all these things.
22.18 I, **John,** solemnly warn everyone who hears the prophetic words

JOHN (4)
Simon Peter's father.

Mt 16.17 "Good for you, Simon son of **John!"**
Jn 1.42 name is Simon son of **John,** but you will be called Cephas."
21.15 Simon Peter, "Simon son of **John,** do you love me more than
21.16 Jesus said to him, "Simon son of **John,** do you love me?"
21.17 time Jesus said, "Simon son of **John,** do you love me?"

JOHN (5)
Member of the High Priest's family.

Acts 4. 6 and with Caiaphas, **John,** Alexander, and the others who belonged

JOHN (6)
John Mark, Paul's companion on his first missionary journey and Barnabas' cousin.

Acts 12.12 of Mary, the mother of **John Mark,** where many people had
12.25 and returned from Jerusalem, taking **John Mark** with them.
13. 5 They had **John Mark** with them to help in the work.
13.13 a city in Pamphylia, where **John Mark** left them and went back
15.37 Barnabas wanted to take **John Mark** with them,

JOIN

Gen 14. 3 formed an alliance and **joined** forces in the Valley of Siddim,
49. 6 I will not **join** in their secret talks, Nor will I take
49.29 that I am going to **join** my people in death, bury me
Ex 1.10 case of war they might **join** our enemies in order to fight
12.48 like a native-born Israelite and may **join** in the festival.
26. 6 gold hooks with which to **join** the two sets into one piece.
26.11 them in the loops to **join** the two sets so as to
26.17 projections, so that the frames can be **joined** together.
26.24 corner frames are to be **joined** at the bottom and connected
34.15 they will invite you to **join** them, and you will be tempted
36.13 gold hooks, with which to **join** the two sets into one piece.
36.18 made fifty bronze hooks to **join** the two sets, so as to
36.22 projections, so that the frames could be **joined** together.
36.29 corner frames were **joined** at the bottom and connected all the
Lev 20. 5 family and against all who **join** him in being unfaithful to
Num 16. 1 He was **joined** by three members of the tribe of Reuben—
26. 9 defied Moses and Aaron and **joined** the followers of Korah when
Deut 26.11 the foreigners who live among you **join** in the celebration.
Josh 8.22 Israelites in the city now came down to **join** the battle.
9. 2 all came together and **joined** forces to fight against Joshua
10. 5 Lachish, and Eglon, **joined** forces, surrounded Gibeon, and attacked it.
10. 6 Amorite kings in the hill-country have **joined** forces and have
11. 5 these kings **joined** forces and came together and set up camp
23.12 If you are disloyal and **join** with the nations that are
Judg 3.13 Eglon **joined** the Ammonites and the Amalekites;
6.35 Zebulun, and Naphtali, and they also came to **join** him.
9. 4 money he hired a bunch of worthless scoundrels to **join** him.
1 Sam 10. 6 and you will **join** in their religious dancing and shouting
10.10 control of him, and he **joined** in their ecstatic dancing
13. 4 So the people answered the call to **join** Saul at Gilgal.
13.15 of the people followed Saul as he went to **join** his soldiers.
14.21 to the camp, changed sides again and **joined** Saul and Jonathan.
14.22 so they also **joined** in and attacked the Philistines,
22. 1 rest of the family heard that he was there, they **joined** him.
22.20 one of Ahimelech's sons, escaped, and went and **joined** David.
23. 6 son of Ahimelech escaped and **joined** David in Keilah, he took
28.19 you and your sons will **join** me, and the Lord will also
2 Sam 15.31 was told that Ahithophel had **joined** Absalom's rebellion,
1 Kgs 6.10 walls of the Temple, and was **joined** to them by cedar beams.
11.18 Midian and went to Paran, where some other men **joined** them.
2 Kgs 3. 7 will you **join** me in war against him?"
4.18 went out one morning to **join** his father, who was in the
8.28 Ahaziah **joined** King Joram of Israel in a war against King
25.23 had not surrendered heard about this, they **joined** Gedaliah
1 Chr 12. 1 There he was **joined** by many experienced, reliable soldiers,
12. 8 the tribe of Gad who **joined** David's troops when he was at
12.17 **Join** us!
12.22 Almost every day new men **joined** David's forces,
12.23 at Hebron, many trained soldiers **joined** his army to help make
2 Chr 18. 2 tried to persuade Jehoshaphat to **join** him in attacking the

2 Chr 18. 3 We will **join** you."
22. 5 their advice, he **joined** King Joram of Israel in a war
23.16 Joash and the people to **join** him in making a covenant that
23.20 the rest of the people **joined** Jehoiada in a procession that
24.21 King Joash **joined** in a conspiracy against Zechariah,
29.28 Everyone who was there **joined** in worship, and the singing
Ezra 3. 8 exiles who had come back to Jerusalem, **joined** in the work.
3. 9 sons (the clan of Hodaviah) **joined** together in taking charge
4. 2 clans and said, "Let us **join** you in building the Temple.
Neh 5.16 Everyone who worked for me **joined** in the rebuilding.
10.29 understand, [29]do hereby **join** with our leaders in an oath,
12.27 living, so that they could **join** in celebrating the dedication
12.43 The women and the children **joined** in the celebration,
13. 1 or Moabite was ever to be permitted to **join** God's people.
Esth 5.10 friends to his house and asked his wife Zeresh to **join** them.
Job 1. 4 and they always invited their three sisters to **join** them.
21.33 well-guarded tomb, [33]thousands **join** the funeral procession,
41.16 Each one is **joined** so tight to the next, not even a
Ps 1. 1 the example of sinners or **join** those who have no use for
40. 4 do not turn to idols or **join** those who worship false gods.
49.19 is successful, [19]he will **join** all his ancestors in death,
83. 8 Assyria has also **joined** them as a strong ally of the
106.28 Then at Peor, God's people **joined** in the worship of Baal,
141. 4 to do wrong and from **joining** evil men in their wickedness.
Prov 1.14 Come and **join** us, and we'll all share what we steal."
Is 7. 6 Judah, terrify the people into **joining** their side, and then
8.12 He said, [12]"Do not **join** in the schemes of the people and
33.15 Don't **join** with those who plan to commit murder or to do
44. 5 They will come to **join** the people of Israel.
55. 5 not know you, but now they will come running to **join** you!
56. 3 A foreigner who has **joined** the Lord's people should not say,
56. 8 promised that he will bring still other people to **join** them.
Jer 3.18 Israel will **join** with Judah, and together they will come
12. 6 they **join** in the attacks against you.
12. 9 Call the wild animals to come and **join** in the feast!
Ezek 26.20 world of the dead to **join** the people who lived in ancient
31.14 like mortal men, doomed to **join** those who go down to the
31.17 world of the dead to **join** those that have already fallen.
31.18 world of the dead and **join** the ungodly and those killed in
37. 7 heard a rattling noise, and the bones began to **join** together.
48.11 me faithfully and did not **join** the rest of the Israelites in
Dan 3. 5 and then all the other instruments will **join** in.
11.34 help, even though many who **join** them will do so for selfish
Hos 10.10 Nations will **join** together against them, and they will be
Zech 12. 3 All the nations of the world will **join** forces to attack her.
Mt 9.10 and other outcasts came and **joined** Jesus and his disciples
19. 6 Man must not separate, then, what God has **joined** together."
Mk 2.15 Jesus, and many of them **joined** him and his disciples at the
9.14 When they **joined** the rest of the disciples, they saw a
10. 9 Man must not separate, then, what God has **joined** together."
Lk 8.19 to him, but were unable to **join** him because of the crowd.
22.55 the courtyard, and Peter **joined** those who were sitting round it.
Acts 1.21 then, someone must **join** us as a witness to the resurrection
4.24 believers heard it, they all **joined** together in prayer to God:
5.13 outside the group dared to **join** them, even though the people
5.36 to be somebody great, and about four hundred men **joined** him.
9.26 Saul went to Jerusalem and tried to **join** the disciples.
16.22 And the crowd **joined** in the attack against Paul and Silas.
17. 4 Some of them were convinced and **joined** Paul and Silas;
17.15 Paul that Silas and Timothy should **join** him as soon as possible.
17.34 Some men **joined** him and believed, among whom was Dionysius,
20. 6 and five days later we **joined** them in Troas, where we spent
21.24 along with them and **join** them in the ceremony of purification
24. 9 The Jews **joined** in the accusation and said that all this
Rom 8.16 God's Spirit **joins** himself to our spirits to declare that we
11.17 and a branch of a wild olive-tree has been **joined** to it.
11.24 then, contrary to nature, is **joined** to a cultivated olive-tree.
11.24 much easier for God to **join** these broken-off branches to their
12. 5 Christ, and we are all **joined** to each other as different
15.30 **join** me in praying fervently to God for me.
1 Cor 6.16 know that the man who **joins** his body to a prostitute becomes
6.17 But he who **joins** himself to the Lord becomes spiritually one
2 Cor 3.14 The veil is removed only when a person is **joined** to Christ.
5.17 When anyone is **joined** to Christ, he is a new being;
Gal 1. 2 the brothers who are here **join** me in sending greetings to
Heb 10.33 times you were ready to **join** those who were being treated in
1 Pet 4. 4 surprised when you do not **join** them in the same wild and
2 Pet 2.13 and a disgrace as they **join** you in your meals, all the
1 Jn 1. 3 also, so that you will **join** with us in the fellowship that

JOINT
[HIP-JOINT]

Gen 32.25 struck Jacob on the hip, and it was thrown out of **joint.**
32.32 muscle which is on the **hip-joint,** because it was on this
1 Kgs 22.34 arrow which struck King Ahab between the **joints** of his armour.
2 Chr 18.33 arrow which struck King Ahab between the **joints** of his armour.
Ps 22.14 All my bones are out of **joint;**
Eph 4.16 is held together by every **joint** with which it is provided.
Col 2.19 and held together by its **joints** and ligaments, and it grows
Heb 4.12 soul and spirit meet, to where **joints** and marrow come together.

Am **JOKE** see **CONTEMPT**

JOKE

Gen 19.14 But they thought he was **joking.**
Job 30. 9 I am nothing but a **joke** to them.
Prov 26.18 claims that he was only **joking** is like a madman playing with
Jer 24. 9 People will mock them, make **jokes** about them, ridicule them,
Lam 3.14 I am a **joke** to them all.
Ezek 16.56 Didn't you **joke** about Sodom in those days when you were
16.57 are just like her—a **joke** to the Edomites, the Philistines,

JOLT

Nah 3. 2 of wheels, the gallop of horses, the **jolting** of chariots!

JONAH
Prophet who gave his name to a book in the Old Testament.

2 Kgs 14.25 servant the prophet **Jonah** son of Amittai, from Gath Hepher.
Jon 1. 1 One day, the Lord spoke to **Jonah** son of Amittai.
1. 3 **Jonah,** however, set out in the opposite direction in order
1. 5 **Jonah** had gone below and was lying in the ship's hold,
1. 7 They did so, and **Jonah's** name was drawn.
1. 9 "I am a Hebrew," **Jonah** answered.
1.10 **Jonah** went on to tell them that he was running away from
1.12 **Jonah** answered, "Throw me into the sea, and it will calm down.
1.15 Then they picked **Jonah** up and threw him into the sea,
1.17 command a large fish swallowed **Jonah,** and he was inside the
2. 1 From deep inside the fish **Jonah** prayed to the Lord his God:
2.10 ordered the fish to spew **Jonah** up on the beach, and it
3. 1 Once again the Lord spoke to **Jonah.**
3. 3 So **Jonah** obeyed the Lord and went to Nineveh, a city so
3. 4 **Jonah** started through the city, and after walking a whole day,
4. 1 **Jonah** was very unhappy about this and became angry.
4. 5 **Jonah** went out east of the city and sat down.
4. 6 a plant grow up over **Jonah** to give him some shade, so
4. 6 **Jonah** was extremely pleased with the plant.
4. 8 a hot east wind, and **Jonah** was about to faint from the
4. 9 **Jonah** replied, "I have every right to be angry—angry
Mt 12.39 you will be given is the miracle of the prophet **Jonah.**
12.40 In the same way that **Jonah** spent three days and nights
12.41 because they turned from their sins when they heard **Jonah** preach;
12.41 I tell you that there is something here greater than **Jonah!**
16. 4 The only miracle you will be given is the miracle of **Jonah."**
Lk 11.29 but none will be given them except the miracle of **Jonah.**
11.30 same way that the prophet **Jonah** was a sign for the people
11.32 because they turned from their sins when they heard **Jonah** preach;
11.32 I assure you that there is something here greater than **Jonah!**

JONATHAN (1)
Saul's son and close friend of David.

1 Sam 13.2-23 **War against the Philistines**
14.1-15 **Jonathan's daring deed**
16-23 **The defeat of the Philistines**
24-46 **Events after the battle**
47-52 **Saul's reign and family**
17.55–18.5 **David is presented to Saul**
19.1-24 **David is persecuted by Saul**
20.1-42 **Jonathan helps David**
23.14-29 **David in the hill-country**
31.1-13 **The death of Saul and his sons**
2 Sam 1.1-16 **David learns of Saul's death**
17-27 **David's lament for Saul and Jonathan**
1 Chr 8.33-40 **The family of King Saul**
9.35-44 **The ancestors and descendants of King Saul**
10.1-14 **The death of King Saul**

2 Sam 4. 4 Another descendant of Saul was **Jonathan's** son Mephibosheth,
4. 4 who was five years old when Saul and **Jonathan** were killed.
9. 1 I would like to show him kindness for **Jonathan's** sake."
9. 3 Ziba answered, "There is still one of **Jonathan's** sons.
9. 6 When Mephibosheth, the son of **Jonathan** and grandson of Saul,
9. 7 will be kind to you for the sake of your father **Jonathan.**
21. 7 sacred promise that he and **Jonathan** had made to each other,
21. 7 David spared **Jonathan's** son Mephibosheth, the grandson of Saul.
21.12 Saul and of his son **Jonathan** from the people of Jabesh in
21.13 the bones of Saul and **Jonathan** and also gathered up the
21.14 the bones of Saul and **Jonathan** in the grave of Saul's father

JOPPA
Seaport on the Mediterranean coast.

Josh 19.46 Mejarkon, and Rakkon, as well as the territory round **Joppa.**
2 Chr 2.16 together in rafts, and float them by sea as far as **Joppa.**
Ezra 3. 7 from Lebanon, which were to be brought by sea to **Joppa.**
Jon 1. 3 He went to **Joppa,** where he found a ship about to go
Acts 9.36 In **Joppa** there was a woman named Tabitha, who was a believer.
9.38 **Joppa** was not very far from Lydda,
9.38 when the believers in **Joppa** heard that Peter was in Lydda,
9.42 about this spread all over **Joppa,** and many people believed
9.43 Peter stayed on in **Joppa** for many days with a tanner of
10. 5 now send some men to **Joppa** for a certain man whose full
10. 8 He told them what had happened and sent them off to **Joppa.**
10. 9 their way and coming near **Joppa,** Peter went up on the roof
10.23 and some of the believers from **Joppa** went along with him.
10.32 Send someone to **Joppa** for a man whose full name is Simon
10.45 believers who had come from **Joppa** with Peter were amazed
11. 5 I was praying in the city of **Joppa,** I had a vision.
11.12 These six fellow-believers from **Joppa** accompanied me to Caesarea,
11.13 to him, 'Send someone to **Joppa** for a man whose full name

JORAM (1)

King of Israel. (The name is written in this way to distinguish this king from King Jehoram of Judah.)

2 Kgs 1.17 no sons, so his brother **Joram** succeeded him as king in the
3. 1 of King Jehoshaphat of Judah, **Joram** son of Ahab became king
3. 6 At once King **Joram** left Samaria and gathered all his troops.
3. 8 long way, through the wilderness of Edom," **Joram** answered.
3. 9 So King **Joram** and the kings of Judah and Edom set out.
3.10 King **Joram** exclaimed.
3.11 An officer of King **Joram's** forces answered, "Elisha son of
3.13 **Joram** replied.
8.16 year of the reign of **Joram** son of Ahab as king of
8.25 year of the reign of **Joram** son of Ahab as king of
8.28 King Ahaziah joined King **Joram** of Israel in a war
8.28 at Ramoth in Gilead, and **Joram** was wounded in battle.
9.14 Then Jehu plotted against King **Joram,** who was in Jezreel,
9.16 **Joram** had still not recovered, and King Ahaziah of Judah was there,
9.17 **Joram** replied, "Send a horseman to find out if they are
9.21 "Get my chariot ready," King **Joram** ordered.
9.22 **Joram** asked him.
9.23 **Joram** cried out, as he turned his chariot round and fled.
9.24 shot an arrow that struck **Joram** in the back and pierced his
9.24 **Joram** fell dead in his chariot,
9.25 were riding together behind King **Joram's** father Ahab, the
9.26 So take **Joram's** body," Jehu ordered his aide, "and throw
9.29 in the eleventh year that **Joram** son of Ahab was king of
10. 4 said, "when neither King **Joram** nor King Ahaziah could?"
10. 9 "I was the one who plotted against King **Joram** and killed him;
2 Chr 22. 5 their advice, he joined King **Joram** of Israel in a war
22. 5 at Ramoth in Gilead, and **Joram** was wounded in battle.
22. 7 God used this visit to **Joram** to bring about Ahaziah's downfall.
22. 7 he and **Joram** were confronted by a man

JORDAN

River which runs from n. Palestine into the Dead Sea, crossed by the Israelites when they invaded Canaan.
see also **EAST (of the Jordan)**

Gen 13.10 and saw that the whole **Jordan** Valley, all the way to Zoar,
13.11 So Lot chose the whole **Jordan** Valley for himself and
32.10 I crossed the **Jordan** with nothing but a walking-stick, and
Num 13.29 Canaanites live by the Mediterranean Sea and along the River **Jordan."**
26. 3 in the plains of Moab across the River **Jordan** from Jericho.
26.63 in the plains of Moab across the River **Jordan** from Jericho.
31.12 camp on the plains of Moab across the **Jordan** from Jericho.
32. 5 do not make us cross the River **Jordan** and settle there."
32. 7 of Israel from crossing the **Jordan** into the land which the
32.19 the other side of the **Jordan,**
32.19 because we have received our share here east of the **Jordan."**
32.21 men are to cross the **Jordan** and under the command of the
32.27 We will cross the **Jordan** and fight, just as you have said."
32.29 Gad and Reuben cross the **Jordan** ready for battle at the
32.30 they do not cross the **Jordan** and go into battle with you,
33.41 of Moab across the River **Jordan** from Jericho, between Beth
33.50 plains of Moab across the **Jordan** from Jericho the Lord gave
33.51 "When you cross the **Jordan** into the land of Canaan, [52]you
34.12 then south along the River **Jordan** to the Dead Sea.
34.15 on the eastern side of the **Jordan,** opposite Jericho."
35. 1 plains of Moab across the **Jordan** from Jericho the Lord said
35.10 "When you cross the River **Jordan** and enter the land of Canaan,
36.13 Moses in the plains of Moab across the River **Jordan** from Jericho.
Deut 1. 1 They were in the **Jordan** Valley near Suph, between the town
1. 7 the surrounding regions—to the **Jordan** Valley, to the
2.29 until we cross the River **Jordan** into the land that the
3.17 territory extended to the River **Jordan,** from Lake Galilee in
3.18 and send them across the **Jordan** ahead of the other tribes of
3.20 giving them west of the **Jordan** and until the Lord lets them
3.25 Let me cross the River **Jordan,** Lord, and see the fertile
3.27 what you see, because you will never go across the **Jordan.**
4.21 would not cross the River **Jordan** to enter the fertile land
4.26 in the land across the **Jordan** that you are about to occupy.
9. 1 about to cross the River **Jordan** and occupy the land
11.30 are west of the River **Jordan**
11.30 territory of the Canaanites who live in the **Jordan** Valley.
11.31 about to cross the River **Jordan** and occupy the land that the
12.10 When you cross the River **Jordan,** the Lord will let you
27. 2 day you cross the River **Jordan** and enter the land that the
27. 4 the other side of the **Jordan,** set up these stones on Mount
27.12 "After you have crossed the **Jordan,** the following
30.18 in that land across the **Jordan** that you are about to occupy.
31. 2 the Lord has told me that I will not cross the **Jordan.**
31.13 the land that you are about to occupy across the **Jordan."**
32.47 that land across the **Jordan** that you are about to occupy."
Josh 1. 2 Israel, and cross the River **Jordan** into the land that I am
1.11 going to cross the River **Jordan** to occupy the land that the
1.15 the land west of the **Jordan** that the Lord your God has
2. 7 as far as the place where the road crosses the **Jordan.**
3. 1 Acacia, and went to the **Jordan,** where they camped while
3.11 the Lord of all the earth crosses the **Jordan** ahead of you.
3.13 feet in the water, the **Jordan** will stop flowing, and the
3.14 camp to cross the **Jordan,** the priests went ahead of them,
3.17 in the middle of the **Jordan** until all the people had crossed
4. 1 nation had crossed the **Jordan,** the Lord said to Joshua,
4. 3 of the middle of the **Jordan,** from the very place where the
4. 5 and said, "Go into the **Jordan** ahead of the Covenant Box
4. 7 that the water of the **Jordan** stopped flowing when the Lord's
4. 8 from the middle of the **Jordan,** one for each of the tribes
4. 9 in the middle of the **Jordan,** where the priests carrying the
Josh 4.10 in the middle of the **Jordan** until everything had been done
4.16 carrying the Covenant Box to come up out of the **Jordan.**
4.19 The people crossed the **Jordan** on the tenth day of the
4.20 There Joshua set up the twelve stones taken from the **Jordan.**
4.22 about the time when Israel crossed the **Jordan** on dry ground.
4.23 up the water of the **Jordan** for you until you had crossed,
5. 1 Amorite kings west of the **Jordan** and all the Canaanite kings
5. 1 Lord had dried up the **Jordan** until the people of Israel had
7. 7 Why did you bring us across the **Jordan** at all?
7. 7 Why didn't we just stay on the other side of the **Jordan?**
8.14 men went out towards the **Jordan** Valley to fight the
9. 1 the kings west of the **Jordan**—in the hills, in the foothills,
11. 2 in the north, in the **Jordan** Valley south of Lake Galilee, in
11. 3 on both sides of the **Jordan,** to the Amorites, the Hittites,
11.16 the dry country south of it, as well as the **Jordan** Valley.
12. 1 the land east of the **Jordan,** from the Arnon Valley
12. 1 up the **Jordan** Valley and as far north
12. 3 it included the **Jordan** Valley from Lake Galilee south to
12. 7 the territory west of the **Jordan,** from Baalgad in the valley
12. 8 the western foothills, the **Jordan** Valley and its foothills,
13.23 The **Jordan** was the western border of the tribe of Reuben.
13.27 In the **Jordan** Valley it included Beth Haram, Bethnimrah,
13.27 border was the River **Jordan** as far north as Lake Galilee.
13.32 east of Jericho and the **Jordan** when he was in the plains
14. 1 of Canaan west of the **Jordan** was divided among the people of
14. 2 tribes west of the **Jordan** were determined by drawing lots.
15. 5 the way up to the inlet where the **Jordan** empties into it.
15. 6 and went north of the ridge overlooking the **Jordan** Valley.
16. 1 of Joseph started from the **Jordan** near Jericho, at a point
16. 7 reaching Jericho and ending at the **Jordan.**
17. 1 the land west of the **Jordan** was assigned to some of the
17. 2 Land west of the **Jordan** was assigned to the rest of the
18.12 their border began at the **Jordan** and then went up the slope
18.18 and passed north of the ridge overlooking the **Jordan** Valley.
18.19 on the Dead Sea, where the River **Jordan** empties into it.
18.20 The **Jordan** was the eastern border.
19.22 Tabor, Shahazumah, and Beth Shemesh, ending at the **Jordan.**
19.33 and to Jamnia, as far as Lakkum, and ended at the **Jordan.**
19.34 the south, Asher on the west, and the **Jordan** on the east.
20. 7 west side of the **Jordan** they set aside Kedesh in Galilee,
22. 6 given land west of the **Jordan,** along with the other tribes.
22.10 the west side of the **Jordan,** they built a large, impressive
22.11 built an altar at Geliloth, on our side of the **Jordan!"**
22.25 He made the **Jordan** a boundary between us and you people
23. 4 already conquered, from the River **Jordan** in the east to the
24.11 You crossed the **Jordan** and came to Jericho.
Judg 3.28 the place where the Moabites were to cross the **Jordan;**
6.33 tribes assembled, crossed the River **Jordan,** and camped in
7.24 Hold the River **Jordan** and the streams as far as Bethbarah,
7.24 and they held the River **Jordan** and the streams as far as
8. 4 hundred men had come to the River **Jordan** and had crossed it.
10. 9 The Ammonites even crossed the **Jordan** to fight the tribes of Judah,
11.13 the River Arnon to the River Jabbok and the River **Jordan.**
11.22 from the desert on the east to the **Jordan** on the west.
12. 1 crossed the River **Jordan** to Zaphon and said to Jephthah,
12. 5 Gileadites captured the places where the **Jordan** could be crossed.
12. 6 and kill him there at one of the crossings of the **Jordan.**
1 Sam 13. 7 crossed the River **Jordan** into the territories of Gad and Gilead.
2 Sam 2. 8 with Saul's son Ishbosheth across the **Jordan** to Mahanaim.
2.29 Abner and his men marched through the **Jordan** Valley
2.29 the River **Jordan,** and after marching all the next morning,
4. 7 with them, and walked all night through the **Jordan** Valley.
10.17 Israelite troops, crossed the River **Jordan,** and marched to Helam,
16.14 worn out when they reached the **Jordan,** and there they rested.
17.16 wilderness, but to cross the **Jordan** at once, so that he and
17.22 his men started crossing the **Jordan,** and by daybreak they
17.24 by the time Absalom and the Israelites had crossed the **Jordan.**
18.23 down the road through the **Jordan** Valley, and soon he passed
19.15 was met at the River **Jordan** by the men of Judah, who
19.16 Gera from Bahurim hurried to the **Jordan** to meet King David.
19.17 servants, and they arrived at the **Jordan** before the king.
19.31 come down from Rogelim to escort the king across the **Jordan.**
19.36 I will go just a little way with you beyond the **Jordan.**
19.39 Then David and all his men crossed the **Jordan.**
19.41 escort you, your family, and your men across the **Jordan?"**
20. 2 Judah remained loyal and followed David from the **Jordan** to Jerusalem.
24. 5 They crossed the **Jordan** and camped south of Aroer, the
1 Kgs 2. 8 met me at the River **Jordan,** I gave him my solemn promise
7.46 foundry between Sukkoth and Zarethan, in the **Jordan** Valley.
17. 3 hide yourself near the brook of Cherith, east of the **Jordan.**
2 Kgs 2. 6 the Lord has ordered me to go to the River **Jordan."**
2. 7 on, [7]and fifty of the prophets followed them to the **Jordan.**
2.13 him, and went back and stood on the bank of the **Jordan.**
5.10 seven times in the River **Jordan,** and he would be completely
5.14 Naaman went down to the **Jordan,** dipped himself in it seven times,
6. 2 permission to go to the **Jordan** and cut down some trees, so
6. 4 When they arrived at the **Jordan,** they began to work.
7.15 went as far as the **Jordan,** and all along the road they
25. 4 two walls, and fled in the direction of the **Jordan** Valley.
1 Chr 12.15 the time when the River **Jordan** overflowed its banks, they
19.17 the Israelite troops, crossed the **Jordan,** and put them in
26.30 and civil matters in Israel west of the River **Jordan.**
2 Chr 4.17 foundry between Sukkoth and Zeredah in the **Jordan** Valley.
Job 40.23 he is calm when the **Jordan** dashes in his face.
Ps 42. 6 down to the **Jordan** from Mount Hermon and Mount Mizar.
114. 3 the River **Jordan** stopped flowing.
114. 5 And you, O **Jordan,** why did you stop flowing?
Is 9. 1 the other side of the **Jordan,** and even to Galilee itself,

Jer 12. 5 country, how will you manage in the jungle by the **Jordan?**
39. 4 walls, and escaped in the direction of the **Jordan** Valley.
49.19 thick woods along the **Jordan** up to the green pasture land,
50.44 thick woods along the **Jordan** up to the green pasture land,
52. 7 two walls, and fled in the direction of the **Jordan** Valley.
Ezek 47. 8 east and down into the **Jordan** Valley and to the Dead Sea.
47.18 of Hauran, with the River **Jordan** forming the boundary
Zech 11. 3 their forest home along the **Jordan** is destroyed!
Mt 3. 5 of Judaea, and from all the country near the River **Jordan.**
3. 6 They confessed their sins, and he baptized them in the **Jordan.**
3.13 and came to John at the **Jordan** to be baptized by him.
4.15 other side of the **Jordan,** Galilee, land of the Gentiles!
4.25 Jerusalem, Judaea, and the land on the other side of the **Jordan.**
19. 1 territory of Judaea on the other side of the River **Jordan.**
Mk 1. 5 They confessed their sins, and he baptized them in the River **Jordan.**
1. 9 province of Galilee, and was baptized by John in the **Jordan.**
3. 8 the east side of the **Jordan,** and from the region round the
10. 1 went to the province of Judaea, and crossed the River **Jordan.**
Lk 3. 3 territory of the River **Jordan,** preaching, "Turn away from your
4. 1 Jesus returned from the **Jordan** full of the Holy Spirit and
Jn 1.28 east side of the River **Jordan,** where John was baptizing.
3.26 on the east side of the **Jordan,** the one you spoke about?
10.40 back again across the River **Jordan** to the place where John

JOSEPH (1)

Jacob and Rachel's son and Manasseh and Ephraim's father.

Gen 29.31–30.24 **The children born to Jacob**
30.25-43 **Jacob's bargain with Laban**
33.1-20 **Jacob meets Esau**
35.22-26 **The sons of Jacob**
37.1-11 **Joseph and his brothers**
12-36 **Joseph is sold and taken to Egypt**
39.1-23 **Joseph and Potiphar's wife**
40.1-23 **Joseph interprets the prisoners' dreams**
41.1-36 **Joseph interprets the king's dreams**
37-57 **Joseph is made governor over Egypt**
42.1-24 **Joseph's brothers go to Egypt to buy corn**
25-38 **Joseph's brothers return to Canaan**
43.1-34 **Joseph's brothers return to Egypt with Benjamin**
44.1-17 **The missing cup**
18-34 **Judah pleads for Benjamin**
45.1-28 **Joseph tells his brothers who he is**
46.1-27 **Jacob and his family go to Egypt**
46.28–47.12 **Jacob and his family in Egypt**
47.13-26 **The famine**
27-31 **Jacob's last request**
48.1-22 **Jacob blesses Ephraim and Manasseh**
49.1-28 **The last words of Jacob**
49.29–50.14 **The death and burial of Jacob**
50.15-21 **Joseph reassures his brothers**
22-26 **The death of Joseph**
Ex 1.1-22 **The Israelites are treated cruelly in Egypt**

Ex 13.19 Moses took the body of **Joseph** with him,
13.19 as **Joseph** had made the Israelites solemnly promise
13.19 **Joseph** had said, "When God rescues you, you must carry my
Num 26.28 The tribes of **Joseph,** who was the father of two sons,
26.37 These are the clans descended from **Joseph.**
27. 1 of Gilead, son of Machir, son of Manasseh, son of **Joseph,**
36. 1 grandson of Manasseh son of **Joseph,** went to Moses and the
36.12 tribe of Manasseh son of **Joseph,** and their property remained
Deut 27.12 Simeon, Levi, Judah, Issachar, **Joseph,** and Benjamin.
33.13 About the tribe of **Joseph** he said:
33.16 come to the tribe of **Joseph,** Because he was the leader among
33.17 **Joseph** has the strength of a bull, The horns of a wild
Josh 14. 3 (The descendants of **Joseph** were divided into two tribes:
16. 1 descendants of **Joseph** started from the Jordan near Jericho,
16. 4 The descendants of **Joseph,** the tribes of Ephraim and West Manasseh,
17. 1 of the families descended from **Joseph's** elder son Manasseh.
17. 2 of Manasseh son of **Joseph,** and they were heads of families.
17.14 The descendants of **Joseph** said to Joshua, "Why have you
18. 5 in the south, and **Joseph** in its territory in the north.
18.11 Their land lay between the tribes of Judah and **Joseph.**
24.32 The body of **Joseph,** which the people of Israel had
24.32 This land was inherited by **Joseph's** descendants.
1 Chr 2. 2 Simeon, Levi, Judah, Issachar, Zebulun, [2] Dan, **Joseph,**
5. 1 the first-born son, and those rights were given to **Joseph.**
7.29 places where the descendants of **Joseph** son of Jacob lived.
Ps 77.15 saved your people, the descendants of Jacob and of **Joseph.**
78.67 But he rejected the descendants of **Joseph;**
105.17 a man ahead of them, **Joseph,** who had been sold as a
Ezek 47.13 tribes, with the tribe of **Joseph** receiving two sections.
48.30 those in the east wall, after **Joseph,** Benjamin, and Dan;
Obad 18 The people of Jacob and of **Joseph** will be like fire;
Jn 4. 5 far from the field that Jacob had given to his son **Joseph.**
Acts 7. 9 became jealous of their brother **Joseph** and sold him to be a
7.10 When **Joseph** appeared before the king of Egypt, God gave him
7.10 and the king made **Joseph** governor over the country and the
7.13 On the second visit **Joseph** made himself known to his brothers,
7.13 and the king of Egypt came to know about **Joseph's** family.
7.14 So **Joseph** sent a message to his father Jacob, telling him
7.18 king who did not know about **Joseph** began to rule in Egypt.
Heb 11.21 Jacob bless each of the sons of **Joseph** just before he died.
11.22 It was faith that made **Joseph,** when he was about to die,
Rev 7. 5 Manasseh, Simeon, Levi, Issachar, Zebulun, **Joseph,** and Benjamin.

JOSEPH (2)

An ancestor of Jesus.

Lk 3.30 of Judah, the son of **Joseph,** the son of Jonam, the son

JOSEPH (3)

An ancestor of Jesus.

Lk 3.24 of Jannai, the son of **Joseph,** [25] the son of Mattathias, the

JOSEPH (4)

Mary's husband.

Mt 1.12 Matthan, Jacob, and **Joseph,** who married Mary, the mother of
1.18 mother Mary was engaged to **Joseph,** but before they were married,
1.19 **Joseph** was a man who always did what was right,
1.20 in a dream and said, **"Joseph,** descendant of David, do not
1.24 So when **Joseph** woke up, he married Mary, as the angel
1.25 And **Joseph** named him Jesus.
2.13 appeared in a dream to **Joseph** and said, "Herod will be
2.14 **Joseph** got up, took the child and his mother, and left
2.19 appeared in a dream to **Joseph** in Egypt [20] and said, "Get
2.21 So **Joseph** got up, took the child and his mother, and
2.22 when **Joseph** heard that Archelaus had succeeded his father Herod
Lk 1.27 marriage to a man named **Joseph,** who was a descendant of King
2. 4 **Joseph** went from the town of Nazareth in Galilee to the
2. 4 **Joseph** went there because he was a descendant of David.
2.16 and found Mary and **Joseph** and saw the baby lying in
2.22 The time came for **Joseph** and Mary to perform the
2.39 When **Joseph** and Mary had finished doing all that was required
3.23 son, so people thought, of **Joseph,** who was the son of Heli,
4.22 They said, "Isn't he the son of **Joseph?"**
Jn 1.45 He is Jesus son of **Joseph,** from Nazareth."
6.42 So they said, "This man is Jesus son of **Joseph,**

JOSEPH (5)

Jesus' brother.

Mt 13.55 and aren't James, **Joseph,** Simon, and Judas his brothers?
Mk 6. 3 son of Mary, and the brother of James, **Joseph,** Judas,

JOSEPH (6)

Joseph of Arimathea, in whose tomb Jesus was buried.

Mt 27.57 his name was **Joseph,** and he also was a disciple of Jesus.
27.58 Pilate gave orders for the body to be given to **Joseph.**
27.59 So **Joseph** took it, wrapped it in a new linen sheet,
Mk 15.42 It was towards evening when **Joseph** of Arimathea arrived.
15.42 day before the Sabbath), so **Joseph** went boldly into the presence
15.45 the officer's report, Pilate told **Joseph** he could have the body.
15.46 **Joseph** bought a linen sheet, took the body down, wrapped
Lk 23.50 was a man named **Joseph** from Arimathea, a town in Judaea.
23.55 Jesus from Galilee went with **Joseph** and saw the tomb and how
Jn 19.38 **Joseph,** who was from the town of Arimathea, asked Pilate
19.38 **(Joseph** was a follower of Jesus, but in secret, because he
19.38 he could have the body, so **Joseph** went and took it away.
19.39 went with **Joseph,** taking with him about thirty kilogrammes

JOSEPH (7)

see also **BARNABAS**

Acts 4.36 And so it was that **Joseph,** a Levite born in Cyprus, whom

JOSEPH (8)

A follower of Jesus.

Acts 1.23 **Joseph,** who was called Barsabbas (also known as Justus), and

JOSEPH (9)

Mary's son and James' brother.

Mt 27.56 Mary the mother of James and **Joseph,** and the wife of Zebedee.
Mk 15.40 Mary the mother of the younger James and of **Joseph,** and
15.47 and Mary the mother of **Joseph** were watching and saw where

JOSHUA (1)

Moses' successor as leader of the Israelites into Canaan.
see also HOSHEA (2).

Ex 17.8-16 **War with the Amalekites**
24.12-18 **Moses on Mount Sinai**
32.1-35 **The gold bull-calf**
33.7-11 **The Tent of the LORD's presence**
Num 11.4-30 **Moses chooses seventy leaders**
13.1-33 **The spies**
14.1-10 **The people complain**
26-38 **The LORD punishes the people for complaining**
26.1-65 **The second census**
27.12-23 **Joshua is chosen as successor to Moses**
32.1-42 **The tribes east of the Jordan**
34.16-29 **The leaders responsible for dividing the land**
Deut 1.34-45 **The LORD punishes Israel**
3.12-22 **The tribes that settled east of the Jordan**
23-29 **Moses is not permitted to enter Canaan**
31.1-8 **Joshua becomes Moses' successor**
14-29 **The LORD's last instruction to Moses**

Deut 31.30–32.44 **The song of Moses**
34.1-12 **The death of Moses**
Josh 1.1-9 **God commands Joshua to conquer Canaan**
10-18 **Joshua gives orders to the people**
2.1-24 **Joshua sends spies into Jericho**
3.1-17 **The people of Israel cross the Jordan**
4.1–5.1 **Memorial stones are set up**
5.2-12 **The circumcision at Gilgal**
13-15 **Joshua and the man with a sword**
6.1-27 **The fall of Jericho**
7.1-26 **Achan's sin**
8.1-29 **The capture and destruction of Ai**
30-35 **The Law is read at Mount Ebal**
9.1-27 **The Gideonites deceive Joshua**
10.1-15 **The Amorites are defeated**
16-27 **Joshua captures the five Amorite kings**
28-43 **Joshua captures more Amorite territory**
11.1-15 **Joshua defeats Jabin and his allies**
16-23 **The territory taken by Joshua**
12.7-24 **The kings defeated by Joshua**
13.1-7 **The land still to be taken**
14.1-5 **The division of the territory west of the Jordan**
6-15 **Hebron is given to Caleb**
15.13-19 **Caleb conquers Hebron and Debir**
17.1-13 **West Manasseh**
14-18 **Ephraim and West Manasseh request more land**
18.1-10 **The division of the rest of the land**
19.49-51 **The final assignment of the land**
20.1-9 **The cities of refuge**
21.1-42 **The cities of the Levites**
22.1-9 **Joshua sends the eastern tribes home**
23.1-16 **Joshua's farewell address**
24.1-28 **Joshua speaks to the people at Shechem**
29-33 **Joshua and Eleazar die**
Judg 2.6-10 **The death of Joshua**

Judg 1. 1 After **Joshua's** death the people of Israel asked the Lord,
2.21 of the nations that were still in the land when **Joshua** died.
2.23 he did not give **Joshua** victory over them,
2.23 nor did he drive them out soon after **Joshua's** death.
1 Kgs 16.34 the Lord had foretold through **Joshua** son of Nun, Hiel lost
1 Chr 7.27 Tahan, [26] Ladan, Ammihud, Elishama, [27] Nun, **Joshua.**
Neh 8.17 done since the days of **Joshua** son of Nun, and everybody was
Acts 7.45 when they went with **Joshua** and took over the land from
Heb 4. 8 If **Joshua** had given the people the rest that God had promised,

JOSHUA (2)

A leading priest in rebuilding the Temple after the exile.

Ezra 2. 2 Their leaders were Zerubbabel, **Joshua,** Nehemiah, Seraiah,
3. 2 and **Joshua** son of Jehozadak, his fellow-priests,
3. 8 Zerubbabel, **Joshua,** and the rest of their fellow-countrymen,
4. 3 Zerubbabel, **Joshua,** and the heads of the clans said to them,
5. 2 Zerubbabel son of Shealtiel and **Joshua** son of Jehozadak heard their messages,
10.18 Clan of **Joshua** and his brothers, sons of Jehozadak:
Neh 7. 7 Their leaders were Zerubbabel, **Joshua,** Nehemiah, Azariah,
12. 1 Zerubbabel son of Shealtiel and with the High Priest **Joshua:**
12. 2 among all their fellow-priests in the days of **Joshua.**
12.10 **Joshua** was the father of Joiakim;
12.26 of Joiakim, the son of **Joshua** and grandson of Jehozadak, and
Hag 1. 1 and for the High Priest, **Joshua** son of Jehozadak.
1.12 Then Zerubbabel and **Joshua** and all the people who had
1.14 **Joshua,** the High Priest, and all the people who had returned
2. 2 the governor of Judah, to **Joshua,** the High Priest, and to
Zech 3. 1 showed me the High Priest **Joshua** standing before the angel
3. 1 And there beside **Joshua** stood Satan, ready to bring an
3. 3 **Joshua** was standing there, wearing filthy clothes.
3. 4 Then he said to **Joshua,** "I have taken away your sin and
3. 5 He commanded the attendants to put a clean turban on **Joshua's** head.
3. 6 Then the angel told **Joshua** that [7] the Lord Almighty had said:
3. 8 Listen then, **Joshua,** you who are the High Priest;
3. 9 placing in front of **Joshua** a single stone with seven facets.
6.11 it on the head of the High Priest, **Joshua** son of Jehozadak.

JOSIAH (1)

King of Judah.

1 Kgs 13. 2 child, whose name will be **Josiah,** will be born to the family
2 Kgs 21.24 Judah killed Amon's assassins and made his son **Josiah** king.
21.26 garden of Uzza, and his son **Josiah** succeeded him as king.
22. 1 **Josiah** was eight years old when he became king of Judah,
22. 2 **Josiah** did what was pleasing to the Lord;
22. 3 of his reign, King **Josiah** sent the court secretary Shaphan,
22.20 The men returned to King **Josiah** with this message.
23. 1 King **Josiah** summoned all the leaders of Judah and Jerusalem,
23. 4 Then **Josiah** ordered the High Priest Hilkiah, his assistant priests,
23.10 King **Josiah** also desecrated Topheth, the pagan place of
23.12 above King Ahaz' quarters, King **Josiah** tore down, along with
23.13 **Josiah** desecrated the altars that King Solomon had built east of Jerusalem,
23.14 King **Josiah** broke the stone pillars to pieces, cut down
23.15 **Josiah** also tore down the place of worship in Bethel
23.15 **Josiah** pulled down the altar, broke its stones into pieces,
23.16 Then **Josiah** looked round and saw some tombs there on the hill;
23.16 King **Josiah** looked round and saw the tomb of the prophet who
23.18 "Leave it as it is," **Josiah** ordered.
23.19 every city of Israel King **Josiah** tore down all the pagan
23.21 King **Josiah** ordered the people to celebrate the
23.23 reign of **Josiah,** the Passover was celebrated in Jerusalem.
2 Kgs 23.24 found in the Temple, King **Josiah** removed from Jerusalem and
23.28 Everything else that King **Josiah** did is recorded in The
23.29 While **Josiah** was king, King Neco of Egypt led an army to
23.29 King **Josiah** tried to stop the Egyptian army at Megiddo and
23.30 The people of Judah chose **Josiah's** son Joahaz and anointed him king.
23.34 King Neco made **Josiah's** son Eliakim king of Judah
23.34 as successor to **Josiah,** and changed his name to Jehoiakim.
1 Chr 3.14 Jehoram, Ahaziah, Joash, [12] Amaziah, Uzziah, Jotham, [13] Ahaz, Hezekiah, Manasseh, [14] Amon, and **Josiah.**
3.15 **Josiah** had four sons:
2 Chr 33.25 Judah killed Amon's assassins and made his son **Josiah** king.
34. 1 **Josiah** was eight years old when he became king of Judah,
34. 3 In the eighth year that **Josiah** was king, while he was
34. 8 by ending pagan worship, King **Josiah** sent three men to
34.28 The men returned to King **Josiah** with this message.
34.29 King **Josiah** summoned all the leaders of Judah and Jerusalem,
34.33 King **Josiah** destroyed all the disgusting idols that were
35. 1 King **Josiah** celebrated the Passover at Jerusalem
35. 7 people at the Passover, King **Josiah** contributed from his own
35.16 So, as King **Josiah** had commanded, everything was done
35.18 this one celebrated by King **Josiah,** the priests, the
35.19 and Jerusalem [19] in the eighteenth year of **Josiah's** reign.
35.20 After King **Josiah** had done all this for the Temple,
35.20 **Josiah** tried to stop him, [21] but Neco sent Josiah this message:
35.22 But **Josiah** was determined to fight.
35.23 During the battle King **Josiah** was struck by Egyptian arrows.
35.25 The prophet Jeremiah composed a lament for King **Josiah.**
35.26 Everything that **Josiah** did—his devotion to the Lord, his
36. 1 The people of Judah chose **Josiah's** son Joahaz and anointed
Jer 1. 2 in the thirteenth year that **Josiah** son of Amon was king of
1. 3 and he spoke to him again when **Josiah's** son Jehoiakim was king.
1. 3 the eleventh year of the reign of Zedekiah son of **Josiah.**
3. 6 When **Josiah** was king, the Lord said to me, "Have you seen
22.10 People of Judah, do not weep for King **Josiah;**
22.11 The Lord says concerning **Josiah's** son Joahaz, who
22.18 So then, the Lord says about **Josiah's** son Jehoiakim, king of Judah,
25. 1 year that Jehoiakim son of **Josiah** was king of Judah, I
25. 3 from the thirteenth year that **Josiah** son of Amon was king of
26. 1 Soon after Jehoiakim son of **Josiah** became king of Judah,
27. 1 Soon after **Josiah's** son Zedekiah became king of Judah, the
35. 1 When Jehoiakim son of **Josiah** was king of Judah, the Lord
36. 1 year that Jehoiakim son of **Josiah** was king of Judah, the
36. 2 first spoke to you, when **Josiah** was king, up to the present.
37. 1 Babylonia made Zedekiah son of **Josiah** king of Judah in the
45. 1 year that Jehoiakim son of **Josiah** was king of Judah, Baruch
Zeph 1. 1 Zephaniah during the time that **Josiah** son of Amon was king
Mt 1. 6 Manasseh, Amon, **Josiah,** and Jehoiachin and his brothers.

JOTHAM (1)

King of Judah.

2 Kgs 15. 5 of all duties, while his son **Jotham** governed the country.
15. 7 in David's City, and his son **Jotham** succeeded him as king.
15.30 year of the reign of **Jotham** son of Uzziah as king of
15.32 Remaliah as king of Israel, **Jotham** son of Uzziah became king
15.34 example of his father Uzziah, **Jotham** did what was pleasing
15.35 It was **Jotham** who built the North Gate of the Temple.
15.36 Everything else that **Jotham** did is recorded in The
15.38 **Jotham** died and was buried in the royal tombs in David's City,
16. 1 of Israel, Ahaz son of **Jotham** became king of Judah [2] at the
1 Chr 3.12 Jehoram, Ahaziah, Joash, [12] Amaziah, Uzziah, **Jotham,**
5.17 in the days of King **Jotham** of Judah and King Jeroboam II
2 Chr 26.21 of all duties, while his son **Jotham** governed the country.
26.23 His son **Jotham** succeeded him as king.
27. 1 **Jotham** became king at the age of twenty-five, and he ruled
27. 3 It was **Jotham** who built the North Gate of the Temple and
27. 6 **Jotham** grew powerful because he faithfully obeyed the Lord his God.
27. 7 The other events of **Jotham's** reign, his wars, and his policies,
27. 8 **Jotham** was twenty-five years old when he became king, and
Is 1. 1 during the time when Uzziah, **Jotham,** Ahaz, and Hezekiah were
7. 1 King Ahaz, the son of **Jotham** and grandson of Uzziah, ruled
Hos 1. 1 during the time that Uzziah, **Jotham,** Ahaz, and Hezekiah were
Mic 1. 1 During the time that **Jotham,** Ahaz, and Hezekiah were kings of Judah,
Mt 1. 6 Abijah, Asa, Jehoshaphat, Jehoram, Uzziah, **Jotham,** Ahaz, Hezekiah,

JOURNEY

Gen 18. 5 it will give you strength to continue your **journey.**
24.56 The Lord has made my **journey** a success;
28.20 and protect me on the **journey** I am making and give me
42.25 back in his sack, and to give them food for the **journey.**
45.21 wagons, as the king had ordered, and food for the **journey.**
45.23 loaded with corn, bread, and other food for the **journey.**
Num 9.10 are far away on a **journey,** but still want to keep the
9.13 and not away on a **journey** and who does not observe the
10.12 the Israelites started on their **journey** out of the Sinai Desert.
22.32 your way, because you should not be making this **journey.**
Deut 8. 2 led you on this long **journey** through the desert these past
Josh 9.11 some food ready for a **journey** and to go and meet you.
9.13 Our clothes and sandals are worn out from the long **journey."**
Judg 18. 5 ask God if we are going to be successful on our **journey."**
18. 6 The Lord is taking care of you on this **journey."**
19. 9 Tomorrow you can get up early for your **journey** and go home."
1 Kgs 18.27 or relieving himself, or perhaps he's gone on a **journey!**
19. 7 up and eat, or the **journey** will be too much for you."
Ezra 8.21 to lead us on our **journey** and protect us and our children
8.22 from any enemies during our **journey,** because I had told him

Neh 2. 9 horsemen with me, and I made the **journey** to West Euphrates.
Prov 7.19 He's gone away on a long **journey.**
Mt 10.10 a beggar's bag for the **journey** or an extra shirt or shoes
21.33 he let out the vineyard to tenants and went on a **journey.**
25.14 there was a man who was about to go on a **journey;**
25.15 Then he left on his **journey.**
Mk 6. 8 anything with you on your **journey** except a stick—no bread,
12. 1 let out the vineyard to tenants and left home on a **journey.**
13.34 from home on a **journey** and leaves his servants in charge,
Lk 9. 3 after saying to them, "Take nothing with you for the **journey:**
11. 6 mine who is on a **journey** has just come to my house,
Jn 4. 6 and Jesus, tired out by the **journey,** sat down by the well.
1 Cor 16. 6 help me to continue my **journey,** wherever it is I shall go
2 Cor 1.16 in order to get help from you for my **journey** to Judaea.
3 Jn 6 help them to continue their **journey** in a way that will
7 they set out on their **journey** in the service of Christ

JOY
[OVERJOYED]

Gen 21. 6 Sarah said, "God has brought me **joy** and laughter.
29.11 Then he kissed her and began to cry for **joy.**
Num 10.10 Also on **joyful** occasions—at your New Moon Festivals and
Deut 12.12 Be **joyful** there in his presence,
16.11 Be **joyful** in the Lord's presence,
16.15 Be **joyful,** because the Lord has blessed your harvest
28.47 but you would not serve him with glad and **joyful** hearts.
1 Sam 2. 1 "The Lord has filled my heart with **joy;**
2. 1 how **joyful** I am because God has helped me!
4. 5 Israelites gave such a loud shout of **joy** that the earth shook.
6.13 They were **overjoyed** at the sight.
11. 9 the message, they were **overjoyed** [10]and said to Nahash,
18. 6 singing **joyful** songs, dancing, and playing tambourines and
2 Sam 6.15 to Jerusalem with shouts of **joy** and the sound of trumpets.
19. 2 And so the **joy** of victory was turned into sadness for all
1 Kgs 1.40 followed him back, shouting for **joy** and playing flutes,
1.45 into the city, shouting for **joy,** and the people are now in
2 Kgs 11.14 the people were all shouting **joyfully** and blowing trumpets.
1 Chr 12.40 an expression of the **joy** that was felt throughout the whole
15.16 Levites to sing and to play **joyful** music on harps and cymbals.
15.28 to Jerusalem with shouts of **joy,** the sound of trumpets, horns,
15.29 David dancing and leaping for **joy,** and she was disgusted
16.27 Glory and majesty surround him, power and **joy** fill his Temple.
16.33 the woods will shout for **joy** when the Lord comes to rule
2 Chr 23.13 All the people were shouting **joyfully** and blowing trumpets,
29.30 everyone sang with great **joy** as they knelt and worshipped God.
30.21 Unleavened Bread with great **joy,** and day after day the Levites
30.23 So they celebrated with **joy.**
30.26 Jerusalem was filled with **joy,** because nothing like this
Ezra 3.12 But the others who were there shouted for **joy.**
3.13 could distinguish between the **joyful** shouts and the crying,
6.16 who had returned from exile—**joyfully** dedicated the Temple.
6.22 they **joyfully** celebrated the Festival of Unleavened Bread.
6.22 They were full of **joy** because the Lord had made the emperor
Neh 8.10 The **joy** that the Lord gives you will make you strong."
8.12 ate and drank **joyfully** and shared what they had
12.43 the people were full of **joy** because God had made them very
Esth 8.15 Then the streets of Susa rang with cheers and **joyful** shouts.
8.16 For the Jews there was **joy** and relief, happiness
8.17 the Jews held a **joyful** holiday with feasting and happiness.
9.17 no more killing, and they made it a **joyful** day of feasting.
9.19 month of Adar as a **joyous** holiday, a time for feasting
9.22 time of grief and despair into a time of **joy** and happiness.
Job 3. 7 make it a barren, **joyless** night.
5.11 God who raises the humble and gives **joy** to all who mourn.
6.10 would, I would leap for **joy,** no matter how great my pain.
8.19 Yes, that's all the **joy** evil men have;
22.26 in God and find that he is the source of your **joy.**
27.10 They should have desired the **joy** he gives;
30.31 Where once I heard **joyful** music, now I hear only mourning
33.26 he will worship God with **joy;**
33.30 he saves a person's life, and gives him the **joy** of living.
38. 7 the stars sang together, and the heavenly beings shouted for **joy.**
Ps 1. 2 Instead, they find **joy** in obeying the Law of the Lord, and
4. 7 But the **joy** that you have given me is more than they
5.11 they can always sing for **joy.**
9. 2 I will sing with **joy** because of you.
16.11 your presence fills me with **joy** and brings me pleasure
17.15 and when I awake, your presence will fill me with **joy.**
20. 5 Then we will shout for **joy** over your victory and celebrate
21. 6 are with him for ever and your presence fills him with **joy.**
27. 6 With shouts of **joy** I will offer sacrifices in his Temple;
28. 7 I praise him with **joyful** songs.
30. 5 Tears may flow in the night, but **joy** comes in the morning.
30.11 You have changed my sadness into a **joyful** dance;
30.11 you have taken away my sorrow and surrounded me with **joy.**
32.11 You that obey him, shout for **joy!**
33. 1 are righteous, shout for **joy** for what the Lord has done;
33. 3 song to him, play the harp with skill, and shout for **joy!**
35.27 see me acquitted shout for **joy** and be glad and say again and again,
40.16 May all who come to you be glad and **joyful.**
45.15 With **joy** and gladness they come and enter the king's palace.
46. 4 is a river that brings **joy** to the city of God, to
47. 1 Clap your hands for **joy,** all peoples!
47. 5 There are shouts of **joy** and the blast of trumpets, as the
48. 2 the city of the great king brings **joy** to all the world.
48.11 let there be **joy** in the cities of Judah!
51. 8 Let me hear the sounds of **joy** and gladness;
51.12 Give me again the **joy** that comes from your salvation,
63. 7 In the shadow of your wings I sing for **joy.**
65. 8 Your deeds bring shouts of **joy** from one end of the earth
Ps 65.12 the hillsides are full of **joy.**
65.13 Everything shouts and sings for **joy.**
66. 1 Praise God with shouts of **joy,** all people!
67. 4 be glad and sing for **joy,** because you judge the peoples with
68. 3 they are happy and shout for **joy.**
70. 4 May all who come to you be glad and **joyful.**
71.23 I will shout for **joy** as I play for you;
81. 1 Shout for **joy** to God our defender;
84. 2 With my whole being I sing for **joy** to the living God.
89.12 Mount Tabor and Mount Hermon sing to you for **joy.**
92. 4 because of what you have done, I sing for **joy.**
95. 1 Let us sing for **joy** to God, who protects us!
95. 2 before him with thanksgiving and sing **joyful** songs of praise.
96.12 the woods will shout for **joy** [13]when the Lord comes to rule
98. 4 Sing for **joy** to the Lord, all the earth;
98. 4 praise him with songs and shouts of **joy!**
98. 6 trumpets and horns, and shout for **joy** to the Lord, our
98. 8 you hills, sing together with **joy** before the Lord,
100. 2 Worship the Lord with **joy;**
105.43 his chosen people out, and they sang and shouted for **joy.**
107.22 sacrifices, and with songs of **joy** must tell all that he has
119.92 been the source of my **joy,** I would have died from my
119.111 they are the **joy** of my heart.
119.143 trouble and anxiety, but your commandments bring me **joy.**
126. 2 How we laughed, how we sang for **joy!**
126. 5 wept as they sowed their seed, gather the harvest with **joy!**
126. 6 come back singing for **joy,** as they bring in the harvest.
132. 9 may your people shout for **joy!**
132.16 all they do, and her people will sing and shout for **joy.**
137. 6 you, if I do not think of you as my greatest **joy!**
149. 5 God's people rejoice in their triumph and sing **joyfully**
Prov 5.18 and find your **joy** with the girl you married—
8.30 was his daily source of **joy,** always happy in his presence—
10.28 of good men lead to **joy,** but wicked people can look forward
11.10 and there are **joyful** shouts when wicked men die.
12. 4 A good wife is her husband's pride and **joy;**
13.12 heart is crushed, but a wish come true fills you with **joy.**
14.10 Your **joy** is your own;
15.23 What a **joy** it is to find just the right word for
Ecc 3. 4 sorrow and the time for **joy,** the time for mourning and the
Song 3.11 on his wedding day, on the day of his gladness and **joy.**
Is 9. 3 You have given them great **joy,** Lord;
12. 3 As fresh water brings **joy** to the thirsty,
14. 7 world enjoys rest and peace, and everyone sings for **joy.**
16.10 the shouts of **joy** are ended.
23. 7 Can this be the **joyful** city of Tyre, founded so long ago?
24. 8 is now sad, [8]and the **joyful** music of their harps and drums
24.14 Those who survive will sing for **joy.**
25. 9 and now we are happy and **joyful** because he has saved us."
26.19 sleeping in their graves will wake up and sing for **joy.**
35. 2 The desert will sing and shout for **joy;**
35. 6 and dance, and those who cannot speak will shout for **joy.**
35.10 will reach Jerusalem with gladness, singing and shouting for **joy.**
42.11 city of Sela shout for **joy** from the tops of the mountains!
44.23 Shout for **joy,** you heavens!
44.23 Shout for **joy,** mountains, and every tree of the forest!
49.13 Shout for **joy,** earth!
51. 3 **Joy** and gladness will be there, and songs of praise and
51.11 will reach Jerusalem with gladness, singing and shouting for **joy.**
52. 8 who guard the city are shouting, shouting together for **joy!**
52. 9 Break into shouts of **joy,** you ruins of Jerusalem!
53.11 After a life of suffering, he will again have **joy;**
54. 1 a childless woman, but now you can sing and shout for **joy.**
55.12 "You will leave Babylon with **joy;**
55.12 will burst into singing, and the trees will shout for **joy.**
56. 7 my sacred hill, give you **joy** in my house of prayer, and
58.14 then you will find the **joy** that comes from serving me.
60. 5 You will see this and be filled with **joy;**
60.15 you great and beautiful, A place of **joy** for ever and ever.
61. 3 those who mourn in Zion **Joy** and gladness instead of grief,
61. 7 Your **joy** will last for ever.
64. 5 You welcome those who find **joy** in doing what is right,
65.14 They will sing for **joy,** but you will cry with a broken
65.18 make will be full of **joy,** and her people will be happy.
65.19 will be filled with **joy** because of Jerusalem and her people.
Jer 7.34 end to the sounds of **joy** and gladness and to the happy
15.16 and so your words filled my heart with **joy** and happiness.
16. 9 will silence the sounds of **joy** and gladness
25.10 will silence their shouts of **joy** and gladness
30.19 they will shout for **joy.**
31. 4 Once again you will take up your tambourines and dance **joyfully.**
31. 7 "Sing with **joy** for Israel, the greatest of the nations.
31.12 will come and sing for **joy** on Mount Zion and be delighted
31.13 comfort them and turn their mourning into **joy,**
33. 9 Jerusalem will be a source of **joy,** honour, and pride to me;
33.11 the shouts of gladness and **joy** and the happy sounds
48.33 Happiness and **joy** have been taken away from the fertile land
48.33 there is no one to make the wine and shout for **joy.**
51.48 the sky will shout for **joy** when Babylonia falls to the
Lam 2. 4 He killed all those who were our **joy** and delight.
2. 7 They shouted in victory where once we had worshipped in **joy.**
2.17 He gave our enemies victory, gave them **joy** at our downfall.
Ezek 24.25 that was their pride and **joy,** which they liked to look at
25. 6 You clapped your hands and jumped for **joy.**
Dan 6.23 The king was **overjoyed** and gave orders for Daniel to be
Joel 1.12 The **joy** of the people is gone.
1.16 There is no **joy** in the Temple of our God.
2.21 don't be afraid, but be **joyful** and glad because of all the
Nah 3.19 hear the news of your destruction clap their hands for **joy.**
Hab 1.15 drag them off in nets and shout for **joy** over their catch!
3.18 I will still be **joyful** and glad, because the Lord God

Zeph 3.14 Sing and shout for **joy,** people of Israel!
3.17 He will sing and be **joyful** over you,
3.18 as **joyful** as people at a festival."
Zech 2.10 The Lord said, "Sing for **joy,** people of Jerusalem!
8.19 will become festivals of **joy** and gladness for the people
9. 9 Shout for **joy,** you people of Jerusalem!
Mt 2. 9 When they saw it, how happy they were, what **joy** was theirs!
28. 8 and yet filled with **joy,** and ran to tell his disciples.
Lk 2.10 news for you, which will bring great **joy** to all the people.
6.23 that happens, and dance for **joy,** because a great reward is
10.17 The seventy-two men came back in great **joy.**
10.21 Jesus was filled with **joy** by the Holy Spirit and said,
15. 7 there will be more **joy** in heaven over one sinner who
19. 6 Zacchaeus hurried down and welcomed him with great **joy.**
24.41 could not believe, they were so full of **joy** and wonder;
24.52 Jerusalem, filled with great **joy,** [53] and spent all their time
Jn 15.11 you this so that my **joy** may be in you
15.11 and that your **joy** may be complete.
17.13 that they might have my **joy** in their hearts in all its
20.20 The disciples were filled with **joy** at seeing the Lord.
Acts 2.26 I am filled with gladness, and my words are full of **joy.**
2.28 that lead to life, and your presence will fill me with **joy.'**
8. 8 So there was great **joy** in that city.
8.39 not see him again, but continued on his way, full of **joy.**
13.52 The believers in Antioch were full of **joy** and the Holy Spirit.
15. 3 this news brought great **joy** to all the believers.
15.31 they were filled with **joy** by the message of encouragement.
16.34 were filled with **joy,** because they now believed in God.
Rom 12.12 Let your hope keep you **joyful,** be patient in your troubles,
14.17 of the righteousness, peace, and **joy** which the Holy Spirit gives.
15.13 fill you with all **joy** and peace by means of your
15.32 come to you full of **joy,** if it is God's will,
2 Cor 7. 4 I am running over with **joy.**
8. 2 but their **joy** was so great that they were extremely generous
Gal 4.27 Shout and cry with **joy,** you who never felt the pains of
5.22 But the Spirit produces love, **joy,** peace, patience, kindness,
Phil 1. 4 you all, I pray with **joy** [5] because of the way in which
1.25 add to your progress and **joy** in the faith, [26] so that when
2.17 is so, I am glad and share my **joy** with you all.
2.18 you too must be glad and share your **joy** with me.
2.29 Receive him, then, with **joy,** as a brother in the Lord.
3. 1 my brothers, be **joyful** in your union with the Lord.
4. 4 May you always be **joyful** in your union with the Lord.
4.10 Lord it is a great **joy** to me that after so long
Col 1.11 And with **joy** give thanks to the Father, who has made you
1 Thes 1. 6 the message with the **joy** that comes from the Holy Spirit.
2.19 who are our hope, our **joy,** and our reason for boasting of
2.20 Indeed, you are our pride and our **joy!**
3. 9 We thank him for the **joy** we have in his presence because
5.16 Be **joyful** always, [17] pray at all times, [18] be thankful
2 Tim 1. 4 see you very much, so that I may be filled with **joy.**
Phlm 7 Your love, dear brother, has brought me great **joy** and much
Heb 1. 9 and has given you the **joy** of an honour far greater than
12. 2 the contrary, because of the **joy** that was waiting for him,
12.23 You have come to the **joyful** gathering of God's first-born sons,
Jas 4. 9 change your laughter into crying, your **joy** into gloom!
1 Pet 1. 8 with a great and glorious **joy** which words cannot express,
4.13 that you may be full of **joy** when his glory is revealed.
1 Jn 1. 4 We write this in order that our **joy** may be complete.
Jude 24 to bring you faultless and **joyful** before his glorious presence—

JUDAEA

The territory of Judah, sometimes including a larger area.

1 Sam 23.19 Mount Hachilah, in the southern part of the **Judaean** wilderness.
23.24 desolate valley in the southern part of the **Judaean** wilderness.
26. 1 Mount Hachilah at the edge of the **Judaean** wilderness.
2 Kgs 16. 6 city of Elath, and drove out the **Judaeans** who lived there.
25.23 the **Judaean** officers and soldiers who had not surrendered
2 Chr 12. 5 Rehoboam and the **Judaean** leaders who had gathered in Jerusalem
13.13 his troops to ambush the **Judaean** army from the rear,
13.14 **Judaeans** looked round and saw that they were surrounded.
13.15 **Judaeans** gave a loud shout, and led by Abijah, they attacked;
13.16 The Israelites fled from the **Judaeans,**
13.16 and God let the **Judaeans** overpower them.
14.12 the Sudanese army when Asa and the **Judaean** army attacked them.
17. 2 cities of Judah, in the **Judaean** countryside, and in the cities
20.24 the **Judaean** army reached a tower that was in the desert,
21.11 places of worship in the **Judaean** highlands
22. 8 a group made up of **Judaean** leaders and of Ahaziah's nephews
24.24 defeat a much larger **Judaean** army because the people
25.13 attacked the **Judaean** cities between Samaria and Beth Horon,
25.22 Beth Shemesh in Judah, [22] the **Judaean** army was defeated,
28. 5 take a large number of **Judaeans** back to Damascus as prisoners.
28. 5 and kill 120,000 of the bravest **Judaean** soldiers in one day.
28. 8 Even though the **Judaeans** were their fellow-countrymen,
28. 9 returning Israelite army with its **Judaean** prisoners
28.15 prisoners were taken back to **Judaean** territory at Jericho,
Is 36. 3 Three **Judaeans** came out to meet him:
Jer 40. 7 the **Judaean** officers and soldiers had not surrendered.
Lam 5.11 in every **Judaean** village our daughters have been forced to submit.
Dan 9. 7 of us who live in **Judaea** and in Jerusalem and of all
Mt 2. 1 the town of Bethlehem in **Judaea,** during the time when Herod
2. 5 "In the town of Bethlehem in **Judaea,"** they answered.
2.22 father Herod as king of **Judaea,** he was afraid to go there.
3. 1 the Baptist came to the desert of **Judaea** and started preaching.
3. 5 from the whole province of **Judaea,** and from all the country
4.25 the Ten Towns, from Jerusalem, **Judaea,** and the land on the
Mt 19. 1 went to the territory of **Judaea** on the other side of the
24.16 "Then those who are in **Judaea** must run away to the hills.
Mk 1. 5 people from the province of **Judaea** and the city of Jerusalem
3. 7 had come from Galilee, from **Judaea,** [8] from Jerusalem,
10. 1 went to the province of **Judaea,** and crossed the River Jordan.
13.14 "Then those who are in **Judaea** must run away to the hills.
Lk 1. 5 Herod was king of **Judaea,** there was a priest named Zechariah,
1.39 and hurried off to a town in the hill-country of **Judaea.**
1.65 about these things spread through all the hill-country of **Judaea.**
2. 4 town of Bethlehem in **Judaea,** the birthplace of King David.
3. 1 Pilate was governor of **Judaea,** Herod was ruler of Galilee,
5.17 come from every town in Galilee and **Judaea** and from Jerusalem.
6.17 was there from all over **Judaea** and from Jerusalem and from
21.21 Then those who are in **Judaea** must run away to the hills;
23. 5 he is starting a riot among the people all through **Judaea.**
23.50 was a man named Joseph from Arimathea, a town in **Judaea.**
Jn 3.22 went to the province of **Judaea,** where he spent some time
4. 3 was being said, he left **Judaea** and went back to Galilee;
4.47 that Jesus had come from **Judaea** to Galilee, he went to him
4.54 the second miracle that Jesus performed after coming from **Judaea**
7. 1 not want to travel in **Judaea,** because the Jewish authorities
7. 3 this place and go to **Judaea,** so that your followers will see
11. 7 Then he said to the disciples, "Let us go back to **Judaea."**
11.19 from Jerusalem, [19] and many **Judaeans** had come to see Martha
11.54 did not travel openly in **Judaea,** but left and went to a
Acts 1. 8 me in Jerusalem, in all **Judaea** and Samaria, and to the ends
2. 9 from Mesopotamia, **Judaea,** and Cappadocia;
8. 1 were scattered throughout the provinces of **Judaea** and Samaria.
9.31 the church throughout **Judaea,** Galilee, and Samaria had a time
11. 1 other believers throughout **Judaea** heard that the Gentiles also
11.29 he could to help their fellow-believers who lived in **Judaea.**
12.19 After this, Herod left **Judaea** and spent some time in Caesarea.
15. 1 came from **Judaea** to Antioch and started teaching the believers,
21.10 for several days when a prophet named Agabus arrived from **Judaea.**
26.20 and then in all **Judaea** and among the Gentiles, I preached
28.21 not received any letters from **Judaea** about you, nor have any
Rom 15.31 safe from the unbelievers in **Judaea** and that my service in
1 Cor 16. 1 about the money to be raised to help God's people in **Judaea.**
2 Cor 1.16 in order to get help from you for my journey to **Judaea.**
8. 4 of having a part in helping God's people in **Judaea.**
9. 1 to you about the help being sent to God's people in **Judaea.**
Gal 1.22 of the churches in **Judaea** did not know me personally.
1 Thes 2.14 the churches of God in **Judaea,** to the people there who

JUDAH (1)

Jacob and Leah's son.

Gen 29.35 so she named him **Judah.**
35.23 Reuben (Jacob's eldest son), Simeon, Levi, **Judah,** Issachar,
37.26 **Judah** said to his brothers, "What will we gain by killing
38. 1 About that time **Judah** left his brothers
38. 2 There **Judah** met a Canaanite girl whose father was named Shua.
38. 5 **Judah** was at Achzib when the boy was born.
38. 6 For his first son Er, **Judah** got a wife
38. 8 Then **Judah** said to Er's brother Onan, "Go and sleep with
38.11 Then **Judah** said to his daughter-in-law Tamar,
38.12 After some time **Judah's** wife died.
38.14 As she well knew, **Judah's** youngest son Shelah had now grown up,
38.15 When **Judah** saw her, he thought that she was a prostitute,
38.20 **Judah** sent his friend Hirah to take the goat
38.22 He returned to **Judah** and said, "I couldn't find her.
38.23 **Judah** said, "Let her keep the things.
38.24 later someone said to **Judah,** "Your daughter-in-law Tamar
38.24 **Judah** ordered, "Take her out and burn her to death."
38.26 **Judah** recognized them and said, "She is in the right.
38.26 And **Judah** never had intercourse with her again.
43. 3 **Judah** said to him, "The man sternly warned us
43. 8 **Judah** said to his father, "Send the boy with me,
44.14 When **Judah** and his brothers came to Joseph's house,
44.16 **Judah** answered.
44.18 **Judah** went up to Joseph and said, "Please, sir, allow me
44.30 "And now, sir," **Judah** continued, "if I go back
46.12 **(Judah's** other sons, Er and Onan, had died in Canaan.)
46.28 Jacob sent **Judah** ahead to ask Joseph to meet them in Goshen.
49. 8 **"Judah,** your brothers will praise you.
49. 9 **Judah** is like a lion, Killing his victim and returning
49.10 **Judah** will hold the royal sceptre, And his descendants
Ex 1. 2 family, were [2] Reuben, Simeon, Levi, **Judah,** [3] Issachar,
Num 26.19 (Two of **Judah's** sons, Er and Onan, had died in the land
Josh 19. 9 Since **Judah's** assignment was larger than was needed,
Ruth 4.12 like the family of Perez, the son of **Judah** and Tamar."
1 Chr 2. 1 Reuben, Simeon, Levi, **Judah,** Issachar, Zebulun,
2. 3 **Judah** had five sons in all.
2. 4 By his daughter-in-law Tamar, **Judah** had two more sons,
4. 1 These are some of the descendants of **Judah:**
4.21 Shelah was one of **Judah's** sons.
9. 4 descendants of **Judah's** son Perez had as their leader Uthai,
9. 4 descendants of **Judah's** son Shelah had as their leader Asaiah,
9. 4 descendants of **Judah's** son Zerah had Jeuel as their leader.
Neh 11. 4 Shephatiah, and Mahalalel, descendants of **Judah's** son Perez.
11. 5 Joiarib, and Zechariah, descendants of **Judah's** son Shelah.
Mt 1. 2 Abraham, Isaac, Jacob, **Judah** and his brothers;
Lk 3.33 of Perez, the son of **Judah,** [34] the son of Jacob, the son
also Gen 46.12

JUDAH (2)

[ISRAEL AND JUDAH, KING OF JUDAH]

The tribe descended from Judah, and its territory, which later became the s. kingdom, as distinct from the n. kingdom (Israel).

Ex 31. 2 Hur, from the tribe of **Judah,** [3]and I have filled him with
35.30 son of Uri and grandson of Hur, from the tribe of **Judah.**
38.22 Hur, from the tribe of **Judah,** made everything that the Lord
Num 2. 3 banner of the division of **Judah** shall camp in their groups,
2. 3 The division of **Judah** shall march first.
10.14 by the tribe of **Judah** started out first, company by company,
Deut 33. 7 About the tribe of **Judah** he said:
34. 2 the territory of **Judah** as far west as the Mediterranean Sea;
34. 3 the southern part of **Judah;**
Josh 7. 1 to the clan of Zerah, a part of the tribe of **Judah.)**
7.16 tribe by tribe, and the tribe of **Judah** was picked out.
7.17 He brought the tribe of **Judah** forward, clan by clan, and
11.21 and in all the hill-country of **Judah and Israel.**
14. 6 people from the tribe of **Judah** came to Joshua at Gilgal.
15. 1 families of the tribe of **Judah** received a part of the land
15. 4 That was the southern border of **Judah.**
15.12 Within these borders lived the people of the families of **Judah.**
15.13 part of the territory of **Judah**
15.13 given to Caleb son of Jephunneh, from the tribe of **Judah.**
15.20 families of the tribe of **Judah** received as their possession.
15.63 But the people of **Judah** were not able to drive out
15.63 The Jebusites still live there with the people of **Judah.**
18. 5 **Judah** will stay in its territory in the south,
18.11 Their land lay between the tribes of **Judah** and Joseph.
18.14 (or Kiriath Jearim), which belongs to the tribe of **Judah.**
19. 1 Its territory extended into the land assigned to the tribe of **Judah.**
20. 7 Hebron, in the hill-country of **Judah.**
21. 4 were assigned thirteen cities from the territories of **Judah,**
21. 9 cities from the territories of **Judah** and Simeon
21.11 Hebron, in the hill-country of **Judah,** along with the pasture
21.16 nine cities from the tribes of **Judah** and Simeon.
Judg 1. 2 The Lord answered, "The tribe of **Judah** will go first.
1. 3 The people of **Judah** said to the people of Simeon, "Go
1. 4 So the tribes of Simeon [4]and **Judah** went into battle together.
1. 8 The men of **Judah** attacked Jerusalem and captured it.
1.11 the men of **Judah** marched against the city of Debir,
1.16 with the people of **Judah** from Jericho, the city of palm-trees,
1.16 into the barren country south of Arad in **Judah.**
1.17 The people of **Judah** went with the people of Simeon,
1.18 Lord helped the people of **Judah,** and they took possession
1.18 and so the people of **Judah** were not able to drive them
10. 9 crossed the Jordan to fight the tribes of **Judah,** Benjamin, and
15. 9 came and made camp in **Judah,** and attacked the town of Lehi.
15.10 The men of **Judah** asked them, "Why are you attacking us?"
15.11 So three thousand men of **Judah** went to the cave in the
17. 7 Levite who had been living in the town of Bethlehem in **Judah.**
17. 9 He answered, "I am a Levite from Bethlehem in **Judah.**
18.12 They went up and made camp west of Kiriath Jearim in **Judah.**
19. 1 a girl from Bethlehem in **Judah** to be his concubine,
19.18 have been to Bethlehem in **Judah,** and now we are on our
20.18 The Lord answered, "The tribe of **Judah.**"
Ruth 1. 1 who lived in Bethlehem in **Judah,** went with his wife Naomi
1. 7 together to go back to **Judah,** but on the way [8]she said
1 Sam 11. 8 there were 300,000 from Israel and 30,000 from **Judah.**
15. 4 were 200,000 soldiers from Israel and 10,000 from **Judah.**
17. 1 The Philistines gathered for battle in Socoh, a town in **Judah;**
17.12 son of Jesse, who was an Ephrathite from Bethlehem in **Judah.**
17.52 The men of **Israel and Judah** shouted and ran after them,
18.16 But everyone in **Israel and Judah** loved David because he
22. 5 go at once to the land of **Judah."**
23. 3 to him, "We have enough to be afraid of here in **Judah;**
23.23 down, even if I have to search the whole land of **Judah."**
27. 6 Ziklag has belonged to the **kings of Judah** ever since.
27.10 to the southern part of **Judah** or to the territory of the
30. 1 The Amalekites had raided southern **Judah** and attacked Ziklag.
30.14 in the southern part of **Judah** and the territory of the clan
30.16 amount of loot they had captured from Philistia and **Judah.**
30.26 his friends, the leaders of **Judah,** with the message, "Here is
30.27 in the southern part of **Judah,** and to the people in the
2 Sam 1.18 and ordered it to be taught to the people of **Judah.**
2. 1 I go and take control of one of the towns of **Judah?"**
2. 4 Then the men of **Judah** came to Hebron
2. 4 and anointed David as **king of Judah.**
2. 7 and the people of **Judah** have anointed me as their king."
2.10 But the tribe of **Judah** was loyal to David,
2.11 he ruled in Hebron over **Judah** for seven and a half years.
3. 8 Do you really think I'm serving **Judah?"**
3. 9 David king of both **Israel and Judah,** from one end of the
5. 5 He ruled in Hebron over **Judah** for seven and a half years,
5. 5 in Jerusalem over all **Israel and Judah** for thirty-three years.
6. 2 led them to Baalah in **Judah,** in order to bring from there
11.11 answered, "The men of **Israel and Judah** are away at the war,
12. 8 I made you king over **Israel and Judah.**
19.11 to ask the leaders of **Judah,** "Why should you be the last
19.14 of all the men of **Judah,** and they sent him word to
19.15 Jordan by the men of **Judah,** who had come to Gilgal to
19.40 by all the men of **Judah** and half the men of Israel,
19.41 our brothers, the men of **Judah,** think they had the right to
19.42 The men of **Judah** answered, "We did it because the king
19.43 But the men of **Judah** were more violent in making their
20. 2 but the men of **Judah** remained loyal and followed David
20. 4 Amasa, "Call the men of **Judah** together and be back here
21. 2 because of his zeal for the people of **Israel and Judah.)**
24. 1 to him, "Go and count the people of **Israel and Judah."**
24. 7 and finally to Beersheba, in the southern part of **Judah.**
24. 9 800,000 in Israel and 500,000 in **Judah.**
1 Kgs 1. 9 officials who were from **Judah** to come to this sacrificial feast,
1.35 one I have chosen to be the ruler of **Israel and Judah."**
2.32 army of Israel, and Amasa, commander of the army of **Judah.**
4.20 people of **Judah and Israel** were as numerous as the grains
4.25 the people throughout **Judah and Israel** lived in safety,
9.18 Tamar in the wilderness of **Judah,**
10.27 was as plentiful as ordinary sycomore in the foothills of **Judah.**
12.17 only of the people who lived in the territory of **Judah.**
12.20 Only the tribe of **Judah** remained loyal to David's descendants.
12.21 of the best soldiers from the tribes of **Judah** and Benjamin.
12.23 and to all the people of the tribes of **Judah** and Benjamin:
12.32 day of the eighth month, like the festival in **Judah.**
13. 1 Lord's command a prophet from **Judah** went to Bethel
13.11 what the prophet from **Judah** had done in Bethel that day
13.14 road after the prophet from **Judah** and found him sitting under
13.14 "Are you the prophet from **Judah?"**
13.16 the prophet from **Judah** answered, "I can't go home with you
13.19 So the prophet from **Judah** went home with the old prophet
13.21 to the prophet from **Judah,** "The Lord says that you disobeyed
13.23 prophet saddled the donkey for the prophet from **Judah,**
14.22 The people of **Judah** sinned against the Lord
14.24 The people of **Judah** practised all the shameful things
14.29 Rehoboam did is recorded in The History of the **Kings of Judah.**
15. 7 Abijah did is recorded in The History of the **Kings of Judah.**
15.17 Baasha invaded **Judah** and started to fortify Ramah
15.17 in order to cut off all traffic in and out of **Judah.**
15.22 all **Judah** requiring everyone, without exception, to help
15.23 are all recorded in The History of the **Kings of Judah.**
19. 3 he took his servant and went to Beersheba in **Judah.**
22.45 battles, are recorded in The History of the **Kings of Judah.**
22.47 it was ruled by a deputy appointed by the **king of Judah.**
2 Kgs 1.17 of the reign of Jehoram son of Jehoshaphat, **king of Judah.**
3. 9 So King Joram and the kings of **Judah** and Edom set out.
8.19 was not willing to destroy **Judah,** because he had promised
8.20 During Jehoram's reign Edom revolted against **Judah**
8.22 Edom has been independent of **Judah** ever since.
8.23 Jehoram did is recorded in The History of the **Kings of Judah.**
12.19 Joash did is recorded in The History of the **Kings of Judah.**
14.11 his men and fought against him at Beth Shemesh in **Judah.**
14.18 Amaziah did is recorded in The History of the **Kings of Judah.**
14.21 The people of **Judah** then crowned his sixteen-year-old son Uzziah
15. 6 Uzziah did is recorded in The History of the **Kings of Judah.**
15.36 Jotham did is recorded in The History of the **Kings of Judah.**
15.37 King Rezin of Syria and King Pekah of Israel to attack **Judah.**
16.19 Ahaz did is recorded in The History of the **Kings of Judah.**
17.13 had sent his messengers and prophets to warn **Israel and Judah:**
17.18 them from his sight, leaving only the kingdom of **Judah.**
17.19 But even the people of **Judah** did not obey the laws of
17.21 Lord had separated Israel from **Judah,** the Israelites made
18. 5 **Judah** never had another king like him, either before or
18.13 attacked the fortified cities of **Judah** and conquered them.
18.22 he told the people of **Judah** and Jerusalem to worship only at
19.30 Those in **Judah** who survive will flourish like plants
20.20 city, are all recorded in The History of the **Kings of Judah.**
21. 9 But the people of **Judah** did not obey the Lord, and
21.11 with his idols he has led the people of **Judah** into sin.
21.12 a disaster on Jerusalem and **Judah** that everyone who hears
21.16 to leading the people of **Judah** into idolatry, causing them
21.17 committed, is recorded in The History of the **Kings of Judah.**
21.24 The people of **Judah** killed Amon's assassins and made his
21.25 Amon did is recorded in The History of the **Kings of Judah.**
22.13 all the people of **Judah** about the teachings of this book.
23. 1 summoned all the leaders of **Judah** and Jerusalem, [2]and
23. 5 the priests that the **kings of Judah** had ordained
23. 5 altars in the cities of **Judah** and in places near Jerusalem—
23. 8 were in the cities of **Judah,** and throughout the whole
23.11 the horses that the **kings of Judah** had dedicated
23.12 The altars which the **kings of Judah** had built
23.17 the prophet who came from **Judah** and predicted these things
23.22 kings of Israel or of **Judah,** since the time when judges
23.24 Jerusalem and the rest of **Judah** all the mediums and fortune-tellers,
23.26 been aroused against **Judah** by what King Manasseh had done,
23.27 said, "I will do to **Judah** what I have done to Israel:
23.27 will banish the people of **Judah** from my sight,
23.28 Josiah did is recorded in The History of the **Kings of Judah.**
23.30 The people of **Judah** chose Josiah's son Joahaz and anointed him
23.33 land of Hamath, and made **Judah** pay 3,400 kilogrammes of
24. 1 King Nebuchadnezzar of Babylonia invaded **Judah,** and for
24. 2 Ammonites against Jehoiakim to destroy **Judah,** as the Lord
24. 3 to banish the people of **Judah** from his sight because of all
24. 5 Jehoiakim did is recorded in The History of the **Kings of Judah.**
24.14 leaving only the poorest of the people behind in **Judah.**
24.15 his wives, his officials, and the leading men of **Judah.**
24.20 the people of Jerusalem and **Judah** that he banished them from
25.12 But he left in **Judah** some of the poorest people, who
25.21 So the people of **Judah** were carried away from their land
25.22 grandson of Shaphan, governor of **Judah,** and placed him in
1 Chr 2.10 prominent man of the tribe of **Judah),** [11]Salmon, Boaz,
4.17 a woman from the tribe of **Judah,** and they had three sons:
4.27 Simeon did not grow as much as the tribe of **Judah** did.
5. 2 It was the tribe of **Judah,** however, that became the
6.15 with the other people of **Judah** and Jerusalem whom the Lord
6.55 Hebron in the territory of **Judah** and the pasture lands round it.
6.65 territories of **Judah,** Simeon, and Benjamin, mentioned above,
9. 1 The people of **Judah** had been deported to Babylon as
9. 3 People from the tribes of **Judah,** Benjamin, Ephraim, and
9. 4 690 families of the tribe of **Judah** who lived in Jerusalem.
12.16 the tribes of Benjamin and **Judah** went out to the fort where
13. 6 Jearim, in the territory of **Judah,** to fetch the Covenant Box
21. 5 1,100,000 in Israel, and 470,000 in **Judah.**

1 Chr 27. 2 clan of Perez, a part of the tribe of **Judah)**
27. 2 clan of Zerah, a part of the tribe of **Judah)**
28. 4 He chose the tribe of **Judah** to provide leadership,
28. 4 and out of **Judah** he chose my father's family.
2 Chr 2. 7 work with the craftsmen of **Judah** and Jerusalem whom my
9.11 like that had ever been seen before in the land of **Judah.)**
9.27 as plentiful as ordinary sycomore in the foothills of **Judah.**
10.17 only of the people who lived in the territory of **Judah.**
11. 1 of the best soldiers from the tribes of Benjamin and **Judah.**
11. 3 and to all the people of the tribes of **Judah** and Benjamin:
11. 5 built for the following cities of **Judah** and Benjamin:
11.12 In this way he kept **Judah** and Benjamin under his control.
11.13 territory of Israel priests and Levites came south to **Judah.**
11.14 other land and moved to **Judah** and Jerusalem, because King
11.17 This strengthened the kingdom of **Judah,** and for three
11.23 them throughout **Judah** and Benjamin in the fortified cities.
12. 4 fortified cities of **Judah** and advanced as far as Jerusalem.
12.12 not completely destroy him, and things went well for **Judah.**
13.18 And so the people of **Judah** were victorious over Israel,
14. 4 He commanded the people of **Judah** to do the will of the
14. 5 from all the cities of **Judah,** the kingdom was at peace under
14. 6 fortifications for the cities of **Judah** during this time, and
14. 7 said to the people of **Judah,** "Let us fortify the cities by
14. 8 of 300,000 men from **Judah,** armed with shields and spears,
14. 9 A Sudanese named Zerah invaded **Judah** with an army of a
15. 2 to me, King Asa, and all you people of **Judah** and Benjamin!
15. 8 idols in the land of **Judah** and Benjamin and all the idols
15. 9 Asa summoned all of them and the people of **Judah** and Benjamin.
15.15 All the people of **Judah** were happy because they had made
16. 1 in order to cut off all traffic in and out of **Judah.**
16. 6 Asa gathered men from throughout **Judah** and ordered them to
16.11 recorded in The History of the Kings of **Judah and Israel.**
17. 2 the fortified cities of **Judah,** in the Judaean countryside,
17. 5 control over the kingdom of **Judah,** and all the people
17. 6 of worship and the symbols of the goddess Asherah in **Judah.**
17. 7 out the following officials to teach in the cities of **Judah:**
17. 9 through all the towns of **Judah,** teaching it to the people.
17.12 Throughout **Judah** he built fortifications and cities,
17.14 troops from the clans of **Judah,** and he had 300,000 soldiers
17.19 other soldiers in the other fortified cities of **Judah.**
19. 5 judges in each of the fortified cities of **Judah**
19.11 son of Ishmael, governor of **Judah,** will have final authority
20. 1 Moab and Ammon, together with their allies, the Meunites, invaded **Judah.**
20. 4 From every city of **Judah** people hurried to Jerusalem to
20.13 All the men of **Judah,** with their wives and children,
20.15 and all you people of **Judah** and Jerusalem, the Lord says
20.17 People of **Judah** and Jerusalem, do not hesitate or be afraid.
20.20 "Men of **Judah** and Jerusalem!
21. 3 each one in charge of one of the fortified cities of **Judah.**
21. 8 During Jehoram's reign Edom revolted against **Judah**
21.10 Edom has been independent of **Judah** ever since.
21.11 and led the people of **Judah** and Jerusalem to sin against the
21.13 have led the people of **Judah** and Jerusalem into being
21.17 They invaded **Judah,** looted the royal palace, and carried
22.10 all the members of the royal family of **Judah** to be killed.
23. 2 to all the cities of **Judah** and brought back with them to
23. 8 the people of **Judah** carried out Jehoiada's instructions.
24. 5 go to the cities of **Judah** and collect from all the people
24. 6 Levites collect from **Judah** and Jerusalem the tax which Moses,
24. 9 sent word throughout Jerusalem and **Judah** for everyone to
24.17 was dead, the leaders of **Judah** persuaded King Joash to
24.18 these sins brought the Lord's anger on **Judah** and Jerusalem.
24.23 Syrian army attacked **Judah** and Jerusalem, killed all the leaders,
25. 5 men of the tribes of **Judah** and Benjamin into army units,
25.10 At this they went home, bitterly angry with the people of **Judah.**
25.21 met at Beth Shemesh in **Judah,** [22] the Judaean army was defeated,
25.26 recorded in The History of the Kings of **Judah and Israel.**
26. 1 All the people of **Judah** chose Amaziah's sixteen-year-old
27. 4 In the mountains of **Judah** he built cities, and in the
27. 7 recorded in The History of the Kings of **Israel and Judah.**
28. 5 to happen, because the people of **Judah** had abandoned him.
28. 9 your ancestors was angry with **Judah** and let you defeat them,
28.10 make the men and women of Jerusalem and **Judah** your slaves.
28.16 The Edomites began to raid **Judah** again and captured many prisoners,
28.18 the towns in the western foothills and in southern **Judah.**
28.19 and had defied the Lord, the Lord brought troubles on **Judah.**
28.25 city and town in **Judah,** he built pagan places of worship,
28.26 recorded in The History of the Kings of **Judah and Israel.**
29. 8 Lord has been angry with **Judah** and Jerusalem, and what he
29.21 and of the people of **Judah** and to purify the Temple, they
30. 1 the king sent word to all the people of **Israel and Judah.**
30. 6 through all **Judah and Israel** with the following invitation:
30.12 was also at work in **Judah** and united the people in their
30.25 was happy—the people of **Judah,** the priests, the Levites,
30.25 the foreigners who had settled permanently in **Israel and Judah.**
31. 1 went to every city in **Judah** and broke the stone pillars,
31. 1 throughout the rest of **Judah,** and the territories of Benjamin,
31. 6 lived in the cities of **Judah** brought tithes of their cattle
31.20 Throughout all **Judah,** King Hezekiah did what was right
32. 1 Sennacherib, the emperor of Assyria, invaded **Judah.**
32. 9 Hezekiah and the people of **Judah** who were with him in Jerusalem:
32.12 then told the people of **Judah** and Jerusalem to worship and
32.25 Lord had done for him, and **Judah** and Jerusalem suffered for it.
32.32 Amoz and in The History of the Kings of **Judah and Israel.**
32.33 All the people of **Judah** and Jerusalem paid him great honour
33. 9 Manasseh led the people of **Judah** to commit even greater
33.11 So the Lord let the commanders of the Assyrian army invade **Judah.**
2 Chr 33.14 a unit of troops in each of the fortified cities of **Judah.**
33.16 commanded all the people of **Judah** to worship the Lord, the
33.25 The people of **Judah** killed Amon's assassins and made his
34. 5 he made **Judah** and Jerusalem ritually clean again.
34. 9 and from the people of **Judah,** Benjamin, and Jerusalem.)
34.11 the buildings that the **kings of Judah** had allowed to decay.
34.21 me and for the people who still remain in **Israel and Judah.**
34.29 summoned all the leaders of **Judah** and Jerusalem,
35.18 Levites, and the people of **Judah,** Israel, and Jerusalem
35.21 "This war I am fighting does not concern you, **King of Judah.**
35.24 All the people of **Judah** and Jerusalem mourned his death.
35.27 recorded in The History of the Kings of **Israel and Judah.**
36. 1 The people of **Judah** chose Josiah's son Joahaz
36. 2 when he became **king of Judah,** and he ruled in Jerusalem
36. 3 prisoner and made **Judah** pay 3,400 kilogrammes of silver
36. 4 Eliakim **king of Judah** and changed his name to Jehoiakim.
36. 5 when he became **king of Judah,** and he ruled in Jerusalem for
36. 6 King Nebuchadnezzar of Babylonia invaded **Judah,**
36. 8 is recorded in The History of the Kings of **Israel and Judah.**
36. 9 when he became **king of Judah,** and he ruled in Jerusalem
36.10 Nebuchadnezzar made Jehoiachin's uncle Zedekiah **king of Judah**
36.11 when he became **king of Judah,** and he ruled in Jerusalem for
36.14 In addition, the leaders of **Judah,** the priests,
36.17 The king killed the young men of **Judah,** even in the Temple.
36.23 responsibility of building a temple for him in Jerusalem in **Judah.**
Ezra 1. 2 responsibility of building a temple for him in Jerusalem in **Judah.**
1. 5 clans of the tribes of **Judah** and Benjamin,
1. 8 an inventory of them for Sheshbazzar, the governor of **Judah,**
2. 1 and returned to Jerusalem and **Judah,** each to his own city.
4. 1 enemies of the people of **Judah** and Benjamin heard that those
4. 6 people living in **Judah** and Jerusalem brought written charges
5. 1 God of Israel to the Jews who lived in **Judah** and Jerusalem.
5. 8 went to the province of **Judah** and found that the Temple of
5.14 a man named Sheshbazzar, whom he appointed governor of **Judah.**
6. 7 governor of **Judah** and the Jewish leaders rebuild the Temple
7.14 conditions in Jerusalem and **Judah** in order to see how well
9. 9 and to find safety here in **Judah** and Jerusalem.
10. 7 throughout Jerusalem and **Judah** that all those who had returned
10. 9 in the territory of **Judah** and Benjamin came to Jerusalem
Neh 1. 2 my brothers, arrived from **Judah** with a group of other men,
2. 5 go to the land of **Judah,** to the city where my ancestors
2. 7 instructing them to let me travel to **Judah.**
4.10 The people of **Judah** had a song they sang:
5.14 governor of the land of **Judah,** from the twentieth year that
6. 7 to proclaim in Jerusalem that you are the **king of Judah.**
6.18 people in **Judah** were on his side because of his Jewish
7. 6 returned to Jerusalem and **Judah,** each to his own city.
7.73 people of Israel—settled in the towns and cities of **Judah.**
11. 3 the leading citizens of the province of **Judah**
11. 4 Members of the tribe of **Judah:**
11.20 their own property in the other cities and towns of **Judah.**
11.24 Zerah and the tribe of **Judah,** represented the people of Israel
11.25 were of the tribe of **Judah** lived in Kiriath Arba, Dibon, and
11.30 the people of **Judah** lived in the territory between Beersheba
11.36 lived in the territory of **Judah** were assigned to live with
12.31 I assembled the leaders of **Judah** on top of the wall
12.32 marched behind the singers, followed by half the leaders of **Judah.**
12.33 Meshullam, **Judah,** Benjamin, Shemaiah, and Jeremiah.
12.44 All the people of **Judah** were pleased with the priests
13.15 I saw people in **Judah** pressing juice from grapes
Esth 2. 6 took King Jehoiachin of **Judah** into exile from Jerusalem,
Ps 48.11 let there be joy in the cities of **Judah!**
60. 7 Ephraim is my helmet and **Judah** my royal sceptre.
68.27 then the leaders of **Judah** with their group,
69.35 He will save Jerusalem and rebuild the towns of **Judah.**
76. 1 God is known in **Judah;**
78.68 he chose the tribe of **Judah** and Mount Zion,
97. 8 and the cities of **Judah** rejoice because of your judgements,
108. 8 Ephraim is my helmet and **Judah** my royal sceptre.
114. 2 **Judah** became the Lord's holy people,
Prov 25. 1 copied by men at the court of King Hezekiah of **Judah.**
Is 1. 1 the messages about **Judah** and Jerusalem which God revealed
1. 1 when Uzziah, Jotham, Ahaz, and Hezekiah were **kings of Judah.**
2. 1 God gave to Isaiah son of Amoz about **Judah** and Jerusalem:
3. 1 take away from Jerusalem and **Judah** everything and everyone
3. 8 **Judah** is collapsing!
5. 3 Jerusalem and **Judah,** judge between my vineyard and me.
5. 7 the people of **Judah** are the vines he planted.
7. 1 grandson of Uzziah, ruled **Judah,** war broke out.
7. 2 word reached the **king of Judah** that the armies of Syria
7. 6 They intend to invade **Judah,** terrify the people
7.17 kingdom of Israel separated from **Judah**—he is going to bring
8. 7 the emperor of Assyria and all his forces to attack **Judah.**
8. 8 They will sweep through **Judah** in a flood,
8.14 the kingdoms of **Judah and Israel** and the people of Jerusalem.
9.21 Ephraim attack each other, and together they attack **Judah.**
11.12 the scattered people of **Israel and Judah** and bringing them
11.13 will not be jealous of **Judah** any more, and Judah will not
16. 3 They say to the people of **Judah,** "Tell us what to do.
16. 6 The people of **Judah** say, "We have heard how proud
19.17 Egypt will be terrified of **Judah** every time they are reminded
22. 7 The fertile valleys of **Judah** were filled with chariots;
22. 8 All **Judah's** defences crumbled.
22.21 will be like a father to the people of Jerusalem and **Judah.**
26. 1 when the people will sing this song in the land of **Judah:**
30. 1 "Those who rule **Judah** are doomed because they rebel against
30. 5 the people of **Judah** will regret that they ever trusted
36. 1 Hezekiah was **king of Judah,** Sennacherib, the emperor of Assyria,
36. 1 attacked the fortified cities of **Judah** and captured them.
36. 7 he told the people of **Judah** and Jerusalem to worship at one

Is 37.10 letter to King Hezekiah [10] of **Judah** to say to him, "The
37.31 Those in **Judah** who survive will flourish like plants
40. 9 Tell the towns of **Judah** that their God is coming!
44.26 and the cities of **Judah** that they will be rebuilt.
48. 1 you that are descended from **Judah:**
65. 9 to the tribe of **Judah,** and their descendants will possess my
Jer 1. 2 of Amon was **king of Judah,** [3] and he spoke to him again
1.15 round its walls, and also round the other cities of **Judah.**
1.18 the **kings of Judah,** the officials, the priests,
2.28 **Judah,** you have as many gods as you have cities.
3. 7 did not return, and her unfaithful sister **Judah** saw it all.
3. 8 **Judah** also saw that I divorced Israel and sent her away
3. 8 But **Judah,** Israel's unfaithful sister, was not afraid.
3.10 And after all this, **Judah,** Israel's unfaithful sister,
3.11 she had proved to be better than unfaithful **Judah.**
3.18 Israel will join with **Judah,** and together they will come
4. 3 people of **Judah** and Jerusalem, "Plough up your unploughed
4. 4 dedicate yourselves to me, you people of **Judah** and Jerusalem.
4. 5 Tell the people of **Judah** and Jerusalem to run to the
4. 7 He is coming to destroy **Judah.**
4. 7 The cities of **Judah** will be left in ruins,
4. 8 fierce anger of the Lord has not turned away from **Judah.**
4.16 against the cities of **Judah** [17] and will surround Jerusalem
4.18 **Judah,** you have brought this on yourself
5.11 people of **Israel and Judah** have betrayed me completely.
5.20 "Tell the descendants of Jacob, tell the people of **Judah:**
7. 1 of the Temple where the people of **Judah** went in to worship.
7.17 in the cities of **Judah** and in the streets of Jerusalem?
7.30 "The people of **Judah** have done an evil thing.
7.34 In the cities of **Judah** and in the streets of Jerusalem I
8. 1 and of the officials of **Judah,** as well as the bones of
9.11 the cities of **Judah** will become a desert, a place where no
9.25 punish the people of Egypt, **Judah,** Edom, Ammon, Moab,
10.22 will turn the cities of **Judah** into a desert,
11. 2 Tell the people of **Judah** and of Jerusalem [3] that I, the Lord
11. 6 "Go to the cities of **Judah** and to the streets of Jerusalem.
11. 9 "The people of **Judah** and of Jerusalem are plotting
11.10 Both **Israel and Judah** have broken the covenant that I made
11.12 Then the people of **Judah** and of Jerusalem will go to the
11.13 The people of **Judah** have as many gods as they have cities,
11.17 "I, the Lord Almighty, planted **Israel and Judah;**
12.14 like an uprooted plant, and I will rescue **Judah** from them.
13. 9 destroy the pride of **Judah** and the great pride of Jerusalem.
13.11 all the people of **Israel and Judah** to hold tightly to me.
13.19 The towns of southern **Judah** are under siege;
13.19 All the people of **Judah** have been taken away into exile."
14. 2 **"Judah** is in mourning;
14.19 Lord, have you completely rejected **Judah?**
15. 4 Hezekiah's son Manasseh did in Jerusalem when he was **king of Judah."**
17. 1 The Lord says, "People of **Judah,** your sin is written
17.19 through which the **kings of Judah** enter and leave the city;
17.20 the people of **Judah** and everyone who lives in Jerusalem
17.25 with the people of **Judah** and of Jerusalem, they will ride
17.26 from the towns of **Judah** and from the villages round Jerusalem;
17.26 from the foothills, from the mountains, and from southern **Judah.**
18.11 then, tell the people of **Judah** and of Jerusalem that I am
19. 3 **"Kings of Judah** and people of Jerusalem, listen
19. 4 ancestors nor the **kings of Judah** have known anything about.
19. 7 frustrate all the plans of the people of **Judah** and Jerusalem.
19.13 the houses of the **kings of Judah,** and indeed all the houses
20. 4 put all the people of **Judah** under the power of the king
20. 5 the treasures of the **kings of Judah,** and carry everything off
21. 1 King Zedekiah of **Judah** sent Pashhur son of Malchiah
21.11 message to the royal house of **Judah,** the descendants of David:
22. 1 the palace of the **king of Judah,** the descendant of David,
22. 6 "To me, **Judah's** royal palace is as beautiful as the land
22.10 People of **Judah,** do not weep for King Josiah;
22.11 succeeded his father as **king of Judah,** "He has gone away
22.18 the Lord says about Josiah's son Jehoiakim, **king of Judah,**
22.24 son of King Jehoiakim of **Judah,** "As surely as I am the
22.30 no descendants who will rule in **Judah** as David's successors.
23. 6 is king, the people of **Judah** will be safe, and the people
24. 1 Jehoiakim's son, King Jehoiachin of **Judah,** as a prisoner
24. 1 the leaders of **Judah,** the craftsmen, and the skilled workers.)
24. 8 "As for King Zedekiah of **Judah,** the politicians round him,
25. 1 Josiah was **king of Judah,** I received a message
25. 1 from the Lord concerning all the people of **Judah.**
25. 2 people of **Judah** and of Jerusalem, [3] "For twenty-three years,
25. 3 of Amon was **king of Judah** until this very day, the Lord
25. 9 bring them to fight against **Judah** and its inhabitants
25.18 all the towns of **Judah,** together with its kings and leaders,
26. 1 of Josiah became **king of Judah,** [2] the Lord said to me,
26. 2 people who come from the towns of **Judah** to worship there.
26.10 When the leaders of **Judah** heard what had happened,
26.18 "When Hezekiah was **king of Judah,** the prophet Micah
26.19 Hezekiah and the people of **Judah** did not put Micah to death.
27. 1 son Zedekiah became **king of Judah,** the Lord told me [2] to
27.12 to King Zedekiah of **Judah,** "Submit to the king of Babylonia.
27.19 to Babylonia the **king of Judah,** Jehoiachin son of Jehoiakim,
27.19 and the leading men of **Judah** and Jerusalem,
28. 4 bring back the **king of Judah,** Jehoiachin son of Jehoiakim,
28. 4 all the people of **Judah** who went into exile in Babylonia.
29. 2 the leaders of **Judah** and of Jerusalem, the craftsmen,
29. 3 Hilkiah, whom King Zedekiah of **Judah** was sending
30. 3 is coming when I will restore my people, **Israel and Judah.**
30. 4 The Lord says to the people of **Israel and Judah:**
31.23 once again say in the land of **Judah** and in its towns,
31.24 People will live in **Judah** and in all its towns,
31.27 fill the land of **Israel and Judah** with people and animals.
31.31 with the people of Israel and with the people of **Judah.**
Jer 32. 1 Zedekiah was **king of Judah,** which was also the eighteenth
32.30 Israel and the people of **Judah** have displeased me and made
32.32 the people of **Judah** and Jerusalem, together with their kings
32.35 would do such a thing and make the people of **Judah** sin."
32.44 Jerusalem, in the towns of **Judah,** and in the towns
32.44 in the hill-country, in the foothills, and in southern **Judah.**
33. 4 and the royal palace of **Judah** will be torn down
33. 7 I will make **Judah and Israel** prosperous,
33.10 the towns of **Judah** and the streets of Jerusalem are empty;
33.13 foothills, and in southern **Judah,** in the territory of Benjamin,
33.13 in the towns of **Judah,** shepherds will once again
33.14 the promise that I made to the people of **Israel and Judah.**
33.16 The people of **Judah** and of Jerusalem will be rescued
33.24 that I have rejected **Israel and Judah,** the two families that
34. 2 say to King Zedekiah of **Judah,** "I, the Lord, will hand this
34. 7 Lachish and Azekah, the only other fortified cities left in **Judah.**
34.18 The officials of **Judah** and of Jerusalem,
34.21 hand over King Zedekiah of **Judah** and his officials
34.22 will make the towns of **Judah** like a desert
35. 1 of Josiah was **king of Judah,** the Lord said to me, [2] "Go
35.12 say to the people of **Judah** and Jerusalem, "I, the Lord, ask
35.17 on you people of **Judah** and of Jerusalem all the destruction
36. 1 of Josiah was **king of Judah,** the Lord said to me, [2] "Get
36. 2 I have told you about **Israel and Judah** and all the nations.
36. 3 when the people of **Judah** hear about all the destruction
36. 6 including the people of **Judah** who have come in from their
36. 9 year that Jehoiakim was **king of Judah,** the people fasted
36. 9 Jerusalem and by all who came there from the towns of **Judah.**
36.31 people of Jerusalem and of **Judah** have paid any attention
37. 1 son of Josiah **king of Judah** in the place of Jehoiachin
38.22 all the women left in **Judah's** royal palace being led out
39. 1 Zedekiah was **king of Judah,** King Nebuchadnezzar of Babylonia
39. 6 and he also executed the officials of **Judah.**
39.10 left in the land of **Judah** some of the poorest people,
40. 1 people from Jerusalem and **Judah** who were being taken away
40. 5 king of Babylonia has made governor of the towns of **Judah.**
40.11 Israelites to stay on in **Judah** and that he had made Gedaliah
40.12 the places where they had been scattered, and returned to **Judah.**
40.15 bring disaster on all the people who are left in **Judah."**
42.13 people who are left in **Judah** must not disobey the Lord
42.19 you people who are left in **Judah** not to go to Egypt.
43. 4 obey the Lord's command to remain in the land of **Judah.**
43. 5 officers took everybody left in **Judah** away to Egypt,
44. 2 I brought on Jerusalem and all the other cities of **Judah.**
44. 6 fury on the towns of **Judah** and on the streets of Jerusalem,
44. 9 done in the towns of **Judah** and in the streets of Jerusalem
44. 9 your ancestors, by the **kings of Judah** and their wives,
44.11 God of Israel, will turn against you and destroy all **Judah.**
44.12 As for the people of **Judah** who are left
44.14 None of the people of **Judah** who are left
44.14 will return to **Judah,** where they long to live
44.17 do in the towns of **Judah** and in the streets of Jerusalem.
44.21 offered in the towns of **Judah** and in the streets of
44.24 Israel, was saying to the people of **Judah** living in Egypt:
44.28 few of you will escape death and return from Egypt to **Judah.**
44.30 handed over King Zedekiah of **Judah** to King Nebuchadnezzar
45. 1 of Josiah was **king of Judah,** Baruch wrote down what I had
46. 2 Euphrates in the fourth year that Jehoiakim was **king of Judah:**
49.34 after Zedekiah became **king of Judah,** the Lord Almighty spoke
50. 4 the people of both **Israel and Judah** will come weeping,
50.20 no wickedness in **Judah,** because I will forgive
50.33 "The people of Israel and of **Judah** are oppressed.
51. 5 not abandoned **Israel and Judah,** even though they have sinned
51.59 Zedekiah was **king of Judah,** Seraiah was going to Babylonia
52. 1 when he became **king of Judah,** and he ruled in Jerusalem
52. 3 the people of Jerusalem and **Judah** that he banished them
52.10 and he also had the officials of **Judah** executed.
52.16 But he left in **Judah** some of the poorest people,
52.27 So the people of **Judah** were carried away from their land
52.31 showed kindness to King Jehoiachin of **Judah** by releasing him
Lam 1. 3 **Judah's** people are helpless slaves, forced away from home.
2. 2 without mercy every village in **Judah** And tore down the forts
2. 5 He has brought on the people of **Judah** unending sorrow.
Ezek 4. 6 suffer for the guilt of **Judah** for forty days—
8. 1 leaders of the exiles from **Judah** were sitting in my house
8.17 These people of **Judah** are not satisfied with merely doing all
9. 9 "The people of **Israel and Judah** are guilty of terrible sins.
17.15 But the **king of Judah** rebelled and sent agents to Egypt
21.20 other the way to **Judah,** to the fortified city, Jerusalem.
25. 3 Israel devastated, to see the people of **Judah** go into exile.
25. 8 Moab has said that **Judah** is like all the other nations,
25.12 Edom took cruel revenge on **Judah,**
27.17 **Judah and Israel** paid for your goods with wheat, honey,
35.10 the two nations, **Judah and Israel,** together with their lands,
37.16 stick and write on it the words, 'The kingdom of **Judah.'**
37.19 Israel and put it with the one that represents **Judah.**
48. 1 Dan Asher Naphtali Manasseh Ephraim Reuben **Judah**
48.21 by the section belonging to **Judah**
48.30 gates in the north wall are named after Reuben, **Judah,**
Dan 1. 1 Jehoiakim was **king of Judah,** King Nebuchadnezzar of Babylonia
1. 6 and Azariah, all of whom were from the tribe of **Judah.**
5.13 Jewish exile whom my father the king brought here from **Judah?**
6.13 one of the exiles from **Judah,** does not respect Your Majesty
Hos 1. 1 Ahaz, and Hezekiah were **kings of Judah,** and Jeroboam son of
1. 7 But to the people of **Judah** I will show love.
1.11 people of **Judah** and the people of Israel will be reunited.
4.15 are unfaithful to me, may **Judah** not be guilty of the same
5. 5 stumble and fall, and the people of **Judah** fall with them.
5.10 angry because the leaders of **Judah** have invaded Israel
5.12 destruction on Israel and ruin on the people of **Judah.**
5.13 sick she was and when **Judah** saw her own wounds, then Israel

Hos 5.14 I will attack the people of **Israel and Judah** like a lion.
6. 4 But the Lord says, **"Israel and Judah,** what am I going to
6.11 as for you, people of **Judah,** I have set a time to
8.14 The people of **Judah** have built fortified cities.
10.11 I made **Judah** pull the plough and Israel pull the harrow.
11.12 and the people of **Judah** are still rebelling against me,
12. 2 Lord has an accusation to bring against the people of **Judah;**
Joel 1. 2 everyone in **Judah,** listen.
1.14 and all the people of **Judah** into the Temple of the Lord
2. 1 Tremble, people of **Judah!**
3. 1 "At that time I will restore the prosperity of **Judah**
3. 6 taken the people of **Judah** and Jerusalem far from their own
3. 8 let your sons and daughters be sold to the people of **Judah;**
3.18 there will be plenty of water for all the streams of **Judah.**
3.19 attacked the land of **Judah** and killed its innocent people.
3.20 But **Judah** and Jerusalem will be inhabited for ever,
Amos 1. 1 earthquake, when Uzziah was **king of Judah** and Jeroboam son of
2. 4 Lord says, "The people of **Judah** have sinned again and again,
2. 5 I will send fire upon **Judah** and burn down the fortresses of
6. 2 Were they any better than the kingdoms of **Judah and Israel?**
7.12 Go on back to **Judah** and do your preaching there.
Obad 12 not have gloated over the misfortune of your brothers in **Judah.**
19 "People from southern **Judah** will occupy Edom;
20 will capture the towns of southern **Judah.**
Mic 1. 1 and Hezekiah were **kings of Judah,** the Lord gave this message
1. 5 Who is guilty of idolatry in **Judah?**
1. 9 wounds cannot be healed, and **Judah** is about to suffer
1.14 people of **Judah,** say good-bye to the town of Moresheth
1.16 People of **Judah,** cut off your hair in mourning
5. 2 of the smallest towns in **Judah,** but out of you I will
Nah 1.15 People of **Judah,** celebrate your festivals
Zeph 1. 1 during the time that Josiah son of Amon was **king of Judah.**
1. 4 "I will punish the people of Jerusalem and of all **Judah.**
1. 7 sacrifice his people and has invited enemies to plunder **Judah.**
2. 7 The people of **Judah** who survive will occupy your land.
Hag 1. 1 was for the governor of **Judah,** Zerubbabel son of Shealtiel,
1.14 Zerubbabel, the governor of **Judah;**
2. 2 to Zerubbabel, the governor of **Judah,**
2.21 a second message [21] for Zerubbabel, the governor of **Judah:**
Zech 1.12 angry with Jerusalem and the cities of **Judah** for seventy years
1.19 world powers that have scattered the people of **Judah,**
1.21 nations that completely crushed the land of **Judah**
2.12 again **Judah** will be the special possession of the Lord
8.13 People of **Judah and Israel!**
8.13 same disasters fall on you that fell on **Judah and Israel!'**
8.13 'May you receive the same blessings that came to **Judah and Israel!'**
8.15 I am planning to bless the people of Jerusalem and **Judah.**
8.19 become festivals of joy and gladness for the people of **Judah.**
9. 7 my people and be like a clan in the tribe of **Judah.**
9.13 I will use **Judah** like a soldier's bow
10. 3 The people of **Judah** are mine, and I, the Lord Almighty,
10. 5 The people of **Judah** will be victorious like soldiers
10. 6 "I will make the people of **Judah** strong;
11.14 and the unity of **Judah and Israel** was shattered.
12. 2 the cities of the rest of **Judah** will also be besieged.
12. 4 watch over the people of **Judah,** but I will make the horses
12. 5 Then the clans of **Judah** will say to themselves, 'The Lord
12. 6 will make the clans of **Judah** like a fire in a forest
12. 7 victory to the armies of **Judah** first, so that the honour
12. 7 receive will be no greater than that of the rest of **Judah.**
14. 5 the earthquake struck in the time of King Uzziah of **Judah.**
14.14 The men of **Judah** will fight to defend Jerusalem.
14.21 in Jerusalem and in all **Judah** will be set apart for use
Mal 2.11 The people of **Judah** have broken their promise to God
3. 4 offerings which the people of **Judah** and Jerusalem bring
Mt 2. 6 'Bethlehem in the land of **Judah,** you are by no means
2. 6 the least of the leading cities of **Judah;**
Heb 7.14 known that he was born a member of the tribe of **Judah;**
8. 8 with the people of Israel and with the people of **Judah.**
Rev 5. 5 The Lion from **Judah's** tribe, the great descendant of David,
7. 5 **Judah,** Reuben, Gad, Asher, Naphtali, Manasseh, Simeon, Levi,
also Num 1.5 Num 1.20 Num 2.3 Num 7.12 Num 13.3 Num 26.19 Num 34.19 Deut 27.12 1 Chr 12.23 1 Chr 27.16

JUDAISM

Acts 2.11 Jews and Gentiles converted to **Judaism,** and some of us are
6. 5 Nicolaus, a Gentile from Antioch who had earlier been converted to **Judaism.**
13.43 Jews and by many Gentiles who had been converted to **Judaism.**
Tit 1.10 especially converts from **Judaism,** who rebel and deceive others

JUDAS (1)
Judas Iscariot, the disciple who betrayed Jesus.

Mt 10. 4 Simon the Patriot, and **Judas Iscariot,** who betrayed Jesus.
26.14 the one named **Judas Iscariot**—went to the chief priests
26.16 From then on **Judas** was looking for a good chance to hand
26.25 **Judas,** the traitor, spoke up.
26.47 still speaking when **Judas,** one of the twelve disciples, arrived.
26.49 **Judas** went straight to Jesus and said, "Peace be with you,
27. 3 When **Judas,** the traitor, learnt that Jesus had been condemned,
27. 5 **Judas** threw the coins down in the Temple and left;
Mk 3.19 Simon the Patriot, [19] and **Judas Iscariot,** who betrayed Jesus.
14.10 Then **Judas Iscariot,** one of the twelve disciples, went off
14.11 So **Judas** started looking for a good chance to hand Jesus
14.43 still speaking when **Judas,** one of the twelve disciples, arrived.
14.45 As soon as **Judas** arrived, he went up to Jesus and said,
Lk 6.16 Judas son of James, and **Judas Iscariot,** who became the traitor.
22. 3 Satan entered **Judas, called Iscariot,** who was one of the twelve
Lk 22. 4 So **Judas** went off and spoke with the chief priests and the
22. 6 **Judas** agreed to it and started looking for a good chance
22.47 a crowd arrived, led by **Judas,** one of the twelve disciples.
22.48 But Jesus said, **"Judas,** is it with a kiss that you
Jn 6.71 He was talking about **Judas,** the son of Simon Iscariot.
6.71 For **Judas,** even though he was one of the twelve disciples,
12. 4 One of Jesus' disciples, **Judas Iscariot**—the one who was going
13. 2 put into the heart of **Judas,** the son of Simon Iscariot,
13.26 dipped it, and gave it to **Judas,** the son of Simon Iscariot.
13.27 As soon as **Judas** took the bread, Satan entered him.
13.29 Since **Judas** was in charge of the money bag, some of the
13.30 **Judas** accepted the bread and went out at once.
13.31 After **Judas** had left, Jesus said, "Now the Son of Man's
14.22 Judas (not **Judas Iscariot**) said, "Lord, how can it be that
18. 2 **Judas,** the traitor, knew where it was, because many times Jesus
18. 3 So **Judas** went to the garden, taking with him a group of
18. 5 **Judas,** the traitor, was standing there with them.
Acts 1.16 made a prediction about **Judas,** who was the guide for those
1.17 **Judas** was a member of our group, for he had been chosen
1.18 (With the money that **Judas** got for his evil act he
1.25 apostle in the place of **Judas,** who left to go to the

JUDAS (2)
Jesus' brother.

Mt 13.55 and aren't James, Joseph, Simon, and **Judas** his brothers?
Mk 6. 3 son of Mary, and the brother of James, Joseph, **Judas,** and

JUDAS (3)
One of the twelve disciples, James' son.

Lk 6.16 (who was called the Patriot), [16] **Judas** son of James,
Jn 14.22 **Judas** (not Judas Iscariot) said, "Lord, how can it be
Acts 1.13 James son of Alphaeus, Simon the Patriot, and **Judas** son of James.

JUDAS (4)
Judas the Galilean, the leader of a revolt.

Acts 5.37 **Judas the Galilean** appeared during the time of the census;

JUDAS (5)
Jew in Damascus at whose house Paul stayed.

Acts 9.11 and at the house of **Judas** ask for a man from Tarsus

JUDAS (6)
Church leader in Jerusalem, also known as Barsabbas.

Acts 15.22 highly respected by the believers, **Judas, called Barsabbas,**
15.27 We send you, then, **Judas** and Silas, who will tell you in
15.32 **Judas** and Silas, who were themselves prophets, spoke a long time

JUDGE
[HALL OF JUDGEMENT, VALLEY OF JUDGEMENT]
see also **DAY OF JUDGEMENT**

Gen 16. 5 May the Lord **judge** which of us is right, you or me!"
18.25 The **judge** of all the earth has to act justly."
30. 6 Rachel said, "God has **judged** in my favour.
31.42 work I have done, and last night he gave his **judgement."**
31.53 God of Abraham and the God of Nahor will **judge** between us."
Ex 2.14 The man answered, "Who made you our ruler and **judge?**
18.22 Let them serve as **judges** for the people
18.26 They served as **judges** for the people on a permanent basis,
21.22 husband demands, subject to the approval of the **judges.**
Num 35.24 such cases the community shall **judge** in favour of the man
Deut 1.16 **Judge** every dispute fairly,
1.17 **judge** everyone on the same basis, no matter who he is.
16.18 "Appoint **judges** and other officials in every town
16.18 These men are to **judge** the people impartially.
16.19 not to be unjust or show partiality in their **judgements;**
17. 8 too difficult for the local **judges** to decide,
17. 9 levitical priests and to the **judge** who is in office at that
17.12 dares to disobey either the **judge** or the priest on duty is
19.17 place of worship and be **judged** by the priests and judges
19.17 be judged by the priests and **judges** who are then in office.
19.18 The **judges** will investigate the case thoroughly;
21. 2 Your leaders and **judges** are to go out and measure the
25. 2 sentenced to be beaten, the **judge** is to make him lie face
28.46 be the evidence of God's **judgement** on you and your descendants
Josh 8.33 with their leaders, officers, and **judges,**
20. 4 go to the place of **judgement** at the entrance to the city,
23. 2 all Israel, the elders, leaders, **judges,**
24. 1 elders, the leaders, the **judges,** and the officers of Israel,
Judg 4. 4 she was serving as a **judge** for the Israelites at that time.
11.27 The Lord is the **judge.**
1 Sam 2. 3 is a God who knows, and he **judges** all that people do.
2.10 The Lord will **judge** the whole world;
7.17 to his home in Ramah, where also he would serve as **judge.**
8. 1 When Samuel grew old, he made his sons **judges** in Israel.
8. 2 they were **judges** in Beersheba.
16. 7 I have rejected him, because I do not **judge** as man judges.
24.12 May the Lord **judge** which one of us is wrong!
24.15 The Lord will **judge,** and he will decide which one of us
2 Sam 15. 4 And he would add, "How I wish I were a **judge!**
1 Kgs 7. 7 called the **Hall of Judgement,** where Solomon decided cases,
7. 8 court behind the **Hall of Judgement,**
8.32 O Lord, listen in heaven and **judge** your servants.
2 Kgs 23.22 since the time when **judges** ruled the nation.
1 Chr 16.12 the miracles that God performed and the **judgements** that he gave.

2 Chr 6.23 O Lord, listen in heaven and **judge** your servants.
19. 5 He appointed **judges** in each of the fortified cities of Judah
19. 6 "Be careful in pronouncing **judgement;**
19. 8 leading citizens as **judges** in cases involving a violation
Ezra 4. 9 their associates, the **judges,** and from all the other officials,
7.25 to appoint administrators and **judges** to govern all the people
10.14 together with the leaders and the **judges** of his city.
Job 9.15 all I can do is beg for mercy from God my **judge.**
9.24 He made all the **judges** blind.
9.33 step between us— no one to **judge** both God and me.
14. 3 look at me, God, or put me on trial and **judge** me?
19.29 on sin, so that you will know there is one who **judges.**
21.22 Can a man teach God, who **judges** even those in high places?
22.13 He is hidden by clouds—how can he **judge** us?"
24. 1 God set a time for **judging,** a day of justice
31.14 What could I say when God came to **judge** me?
34.23 set a time for men to go and be **judged** by him.
Ps 7. 8 You are the **judge** of all mankind.
7. 8 **Judge** in my favour, O Lord;
7. 9 You are a righteous God and **judge** our thoughts and desires.
7.11 God is a righteous **judge** and always condemns the wicked.
9. 4 honest in your judgements, and you have **judged** in my favour.
9. 7 he has set up his throne for **judgement.**
9. 8 he **judges** the nations with justice.
9.16 revealed himself by his righteous **judgements,**
9.19 Bring the heathen before you and pronounce **judgement** on them.
10. 5 He cannot understand God's **judgements;**
10.18 you will **judge** in their favour, so that mortal men may
17. 2 You will **judge** in my favour, because you know what is right.
19. 9 The **judgements** of the Lord are just;
26. 2 **judge** my desires and thoughts.
48.11 You give right **judgements;**
50. 4 heaven and earth as witnesses to see him **judge** his people.
50. 6 The heavens proclaim that God is righteous, that he himself is **judge.**
51. 4 So you are right in **judging** me;
58. 1 Do you **judge** all men fairly?
58.11 there is indeed a God who **judges** the world."
67. 4 sing for joy, because you **judge** the peoples with justice
72. 1 Teach the king to **judge** with your righteousness, O God;
72. 4 May the king **judge** the poor fairly;
75. 2 set a time for **judgement,"** says God, "and I will judge
75. 2 says God, "and I will **judge** with fairness.
75. 6 **Judgement** does not come from the east or from the west,
75. 7 it is God who is the **judge,** condemning some and acquitting
76. 8 You made your **judgement** known from heaven;
76. 9 you rose up to pronounce **judgement,** to save all the oppressed
82. 2 "You must stop **judging** unjustly;
94. 2 You are the **judge** of all men;
94.20 nothing to do with corrupt **judges,** who make injustice legal,
96.10 he will **judge** the peoples with justice."
97. 8 cities of Judah rejoice because of your **judgements,** O Lord.
103. 6 The Lord **judges** in favour of the oppressed
105. 5 the miracles that God performed and the **judgements** that he gave.
109. 6 Choose some corrupt **judge** to try my enemy,
110. 6 He will pass **judgement** on the nations
111.10 he gives sound **judgement** to all who obey his commands.
119. 7 As I learn your righteous **judgements,** I will praise you
119.20 I want to know your **judgements** at all times.
119.30 I have paid attention to your **judgements.**
119.39 how wonderful are your **judgements!**
119.43 truth at all times, because my hope is in your **judgements.**
119.52 I remember your **judgements** of long ago,
119.62 I wake up to praise you for your righteous **judgements.**
119.75 I know that your **judgements** are righteous, Lord,
119.120 I am filled with fear because of your **judgements.**
119.160 and all your righteous **judgements** are eternal.
119.164 I thank you for your righteous **judgements.**
122. 5 Here the kings of Israel sat to **judge** their people.
127. 5 when he meets his enemies in the place of **judgement.**
146. 7 he **judges** in favour of the oppressed and gives food
Prov 8.12 I have knowledge and sound **judgement.**
11.22 in a woman without good **judgement** is like a gold ring in
16. 2 but the Lord **judges** your motives.
17.23 Corrupt **judges** accept secret bribes, and then justice is not done.
20. 8 The king sits in **judgement** and knows evil when he sees it.
21. 2 but remember that the Lord **judges** your motives.
24.12 none of your business, but God knows and **judges** your motives.
24.23 It is wrong for a **judge** to be prejudiced.
24.25 **Judges** who punish the guilty, however, will be prosperous
28.21 But some **judges** will do wrong to get even the smallest bribe.
31. 9 Speak for them and be a righteous **judge.**
Ecc 3.17 "God is going to **judge** the righteous and the evil alike,
11. 9 that God is going to **judge** you for whatever you do.
12.14 God is going to **judge** everything we do,
Is 3. 2 heroes and their soldiers, their **judges** and their prophets,
3.13 he is ready to **judge** his people.
3.14 Lord is bringing the elders and leaders of his people to **judgement.**
4. 4 the Lord will **judge** and purify the nation
5. 3 **judge** between my vineyard and me.
5.16 and he reveals his holiness by **judging** his people.
9. 8 The Lord has pronounced **judgement** on the kingdom of Israel,
11. 3 He will not **judge** by appearance or hearsay;
11. 4 he will **judge** the poor fairly
26. 9 when you **judge** the earth and its people, they will all
28. 6 to those who serve as **judges,** and courage to those who
33.14 They say, "God's **judgement** is like a fire that burns for ever.
57. 3 Come here to be **judged,** you sinners!
Jer 4.12 the Lord himself who is pronouncing **judgement** on his people.
11.20 Then I prayed, "Almighty Lord, you are a just **judge;**
Jer 23. 1 terrible will be the Lord's **judgement** on those rulers
48.21 **"Judgement** has come on the cities of the plateau:
48.24 **Judgement** has come on all the cities of Moab, far and near.
49. 7 "Have the people of Edom lost their good **judgement?**
Lam 3.59 **Judge** in my favour;
Ezek 5. 8 I will pass **judgement** on you where all the nations can see
7. 3 my anger, because I am **judging** you for what you have done.
7. 8 I am **judging** you for what you have done,
7.27 will judge you in the same way as you have **judged** others.
18.30 you Israelites that I will **judge** each of you
21.30 I will **judge** you in the place where you were created,
22. 2 said, "are you ready to **judge** the city
23.24 over to them, and they will **judge** you by their own laws.
23.36 "Mortal man, are you ready to **judge** Oholah and Oholibah?
33.20 I am going to **judge** you by what you do."
34.17 tell you that I will **judge** each of you
34.20 tell you that I will **judge** between you strong sheep
34.22 I will **judge** each of my sheep and separate the good from
Dan 3. 2 commissioners, treasurers, **judges,** magistrates,
7.22 for ever came and pronounced **judgement** in favour of the people
7.26 heavenly court will sit in **judgement,** take away his power,
Hos 5. 1 You are supposed to **judge** with justice—
5. 1 so **judgement** will fall on you!
6. 5 sent my prophets to you with my message of **judgement**
Joel 3. 2 all the nations and bring them to the **Valley of Judgement.**
3. 2 There I will **judge** them for all they have done
3.12 nations must get ready and come to the **Valley of Judgement.**
3.12 I, the Lord, will sit to **judge** all the surrounding nations.
3.14 Thousands and thousands are in the **Valley of Judgement.**
Amos 4.12 I am going to do this, get ready to face my **judgement!"**
Obad 15 "The day is near when I, the Lord, will **judge** all nations.
Mic 7. 3 Officials and **judges** ask for bribes.
Zeph 1. 7 The day is near when the Lord will sit in **judgement;**
3. 3 its **judges** are like hungry wolves,
Zech 14. 1 The day when the Lord will sit in **judgement** is near.
Mal 3. 3 He will come to **judge** like one who refines and purifies silver.
3. 5 will appear among you to **judge,**
Mt 5.25 hand you over to the **judge,** who will hand you over to
7. 1 "Do not **judge** others, so that God will not judge you,
7. 2 for God will **judge** you in the
7. 2 same way as you **judge** others, and he will apply to
12.18 Spirit upon him, and he will announce my **judgement** to the nations.
12.37 words will be used to **judge** you—to declare you either
27.19 Pilate was sitting in the **judgement** hall, his wife sent him
Mk 4.24 same rules you use to **judge** others will be
4.24 used by God to **judge** you—but with even greater severity.
Lk 6.37 "Do not **judge** others, and God will not judge you;
12.14 gave me the right to **judge** or to divide the property between
12.57 "Why do you not **judge** for yourselves the right thing to do?
12.58 will drag you before the **judge,** who will hand you over to
18. 2 town there was a **judge** who neither feared God nor respected
18. 4 For a long time the **judge** refused to act, but at last
18. 6 the Lord continued, "Listen to what that corrupt **judge** said.
18. 7 Now, will God not **judge** in favour of his own people who
18. 8 I tell you, he will **judge** in their favour and do it
Jn 3.17 into the world to be its **judge,** but to be its saviour.
3.18 Whoever believes in the Son is not **judged;**
3.18 not believe has already been **judged,** because he has not believed
3.19 This is how the **judgement** works:
5.22 Nor does the Father himself **judge** anyone.
5.22 Son the full right to **judge,** [23] so that all will honour the
5.24 He will not be **judged,** but has already passed from death to
5.27 the Son the right to **judge,** because he is the Son of
5.30 I **judge** only as God tells me,
5.30 so my **judgement** is right,
7.24 Stop **judging** by external standards,
7.24 and **judge** by true standards."
8.15 You make **judgements** in a purely human way;
8.16 were to do so, my **judgement** would be true, because I am
8.50 is one who is seeking it and who **judges** in my favour.
9.39 came to this world to **judge,** so that the blind should see
12.31 Now is the time for this world to be **judged;**
12.47 my message and does not obey it, I will not **judge** him.
12.47 I came, not to **judge** the world, but to save it.
12.48 and does not accept my message has one who will **judge** him.
12.48 words I have spoken will be his **judge** on the last day!
16. 8 about sin and about what is right and about God's **judgement.**
16.11 they are wrong about **judgement,**
16.11 because the ruler of this world has already been **judged.**
19.13 and sat down on the **judge's** seat in the place called
Acts 4.19 John answered them, "You yourselves **judge** which is right in God's
7.27 'Who made you ruler and **judge** over us?'
7.35 'Who made you ruler and **judge** over us?'
10.42 one whom God has appointed **judge** of the living and the dead.
13.20 "After this he gave them **judges** until the time of the
17.31 day in which he will **judge** the whole world with justice by
18.15 I will not be the **judge** of such things!"
23. 3 You sit there to **judge** me according to the Law, yet you
24.10 that you have been a **judge** over this nation for many years,
25. 6 down in the court of **judgement** and ordered Paul to be
25.10 the Emperor's own court of **judgement,** where I should be tried.
Rom 2. 1 For when you **judge** others and then do the same things which
2. 2 God is right when he **judges** the people who do such things
2. 3 Do you think you will escape God's **judgement?**
2. 5 Day when God's anger and righteous **judgements** will be revealed.
2.11 For God **judges** everyone by the same standard.
2.12 they sin and are **judged** by the Law.
2.16 God through Jesus Christ will **judge** the secret thoughts of all.
3. 6 If God is not just, how can he **judge** the world?

Rom 3.19 all human excuses and bring the whole world under God's **judgement.**
5.16 After the one sin, came the **judgement** of "Guilty";
12. 3 modest in your thinking, and **judge** yourself according to the
13. 2 and anyone who does so will bring **judgement** on himself.
14. 4 Who are you to **judge** the servant of someone else?
14.10 All of us will stand before God to be **judged** by him.
14.13 So then, let us stop **judging** one another.
14.22 not feel guilty when he does something he **judges** is right!
1 Cor 2.14 because their value can be **judged** only on a spiritual basis.
2.15 Spirit, however, is able to **judge** the value of everything,
2.15 but no one is able to **judge** him.
4. 3 at all concerned about being **judged** by you or by any human
4. 5 Final **judgement** must wait until the Lord comes;
5.12 After all, it is none of my business to **judge** outsiders.
5.12 God will **judge** them.
5.12 But should you not **judge** the members of your own fellowship?
6. 1 dare he go before heathen **judges** instead of letting God's people
6. 2 Don't you know that God's people will **judge** the world?
6. 2 then, if you are to **judge** the world,
6. 2 aren't you capable of **judging** small matters?
6. 3 Do you not know that we shall **judge** the angels?
6. 6 goes to court against another and lets unbelievers **judge** the case!
10.15 **judge** for yourselves what I say.
11.13 **Judge** for yourselves whether it is proper for a woman to
11.29 from the cup, he brings **judgement** on himself as he eats and
11.31 examine ourselves first, we would not come under God's **judgement.**
11.32 But we are **judged** and punished by the Lord, so that we
11.34 you will not come under God's **judgement** as you meet together.
14.24 He will be **judged** by all he hears, [25] his secret thoughts
14.29 should speak, while the others are to **judge** what they say.
2 Cor 5.10 all of us must appear before Christ, to be **judged** by him.
5.16 No longer, then, do we **judge** anyone by human standards.
5.16 if at one time we **judged** Christ according to human standards,
10.12 and they **judge** themselves by their own standards!
13. 5 yourselves to the test and **judge** yourselves, to find out whether
Gal 2. 6 God does not **judge** by outward appearances—those leaders, I say,
6. 4 Each one should **judge** his own conduct.
Eph 6. 9 same Master in heaven, who **judges** everyone by the same standard.
Phil 1. 9 with true knowledge and perfect **judgement,** [10] so that you will
Col 3.25 things he does, because God **judges** everyone by the same standard.
1 Thes 2. 4 because he has **judged** us worthy to be entrusted with
2 Thes 1. 5 of this proves that God's **judgement** is just and as a result
1 Tim 5.24 plain to see, and their sins go ahead of them to **judgement;**
2 Tim 4. 1 of Christ Jesus, who will **judge** the living and the dead,
4. 8 which the Lord, the righteous **Judge,** will give me on that
Heb 4.12 It **judges** the desires and thoughts of man's heart.
6. 2 of the resurrection of the dead and the eternal **judgement.**
9.27 Everyone must die once, and after that be **judged** by God.
10.27 in fear for the coming **Judgement** and the fierce fire which
10.28 death without any mercy when **judged** guilty on the evidence
10.30 and who also said, "The Lord will **judge** his people."
12.23 to God, who is the **judge** of all mankind, and to the
13. 4 God will **judge** those who are immoral and those who commit
Jas 2. 4 among yourselves and of making **judgements** based on evil motives.
2. 6 are the ones who oppress you and drag you before the **judges?**
2.12 as people who will be **judged** by the law that sets us
2.13 not show mercy when he **judges** the person who has not been
2.13 but mercy triumphs over **judgement.**
3. 1 we teachers will be **judged** with greater strictness than others.
4.11 criticizes a Christian brother or **judges** him,
4.11 criticizes the Law and **judges** it.
4.11 If you **judge** the Law, then you are no longer one who
4.11 who obeys the Law, but one who **judges** it.
4.12 God is the only lawgiver and **judge.**
4.12 Who do you think you are, to **judge** your fellow-man?
5. 9 one another, my brothers, so that God will not **judge** you.
5. 9 The **Judge** is near, ready to appear.
5.12 mean no, and then you will not come under God's **judgement.**
1 Pet 1.17 you pray to God, who **judges** all people by the same standard,
2.23 threaten, but placed his hopes in God, the righteous **Judge.**
4. 5 to God, who is ready to **judge** the living and the dead.
4. 6 to those who had been **judged** in their physical existence
4. 6 as everyone is **judged;**
4.17 The time has come for **judgement** to begin,
4.17 and God's own people are the first to be **judged.**
2 Pet 2. 3 a long time now their **Judge** has been ready, and their
3. 7 for the day when godless people will be **judged** and destroyed.
Jude 15 his holy angels [15] to bring **judgement** on all, to condemn them
Rev 6.10 will it be until you **judge** the people on earth and punish
11.18 your anger has come, the time for the dead to be **judged.**
14. 7 For the time has come for him to **judge** mankind.
16. 5 of the waters say, "The **judgements** you have made are just,
16. 7 True and just indeed are your **judgements!"**
18. 8 burnt with fire, because the Lord God, who **judges** her, is
19. 2 True and just are his **judgements!**
19.11 it is with justice that he **judges** and fights his battles.
20. 4 and those who sat on them were given the power to **judge.**
20.12 The dead were **judged** according to what they had done,
20.13 And all were **judged** according to what they had done.

JUDGEMENT DAY see DAY OF JUDGEMENT

JUICE

Neh 13.15 I saw people in Judah pressing **juice** from grapes on the Sabbath.

JUMP

Ex 8. 4 They will **jump** up on you, your people, and all your officials.' "
2 Sam 6.16 King David dancing and **jumping** around in the sacred dance,
Ps 29. 6 makes the mountains of Lebanon **jump** like calves
114. 4 the hills **jumped** about like lambs.
114. 6 You hills, why did you **jump** about like lambs?
Ezek 25. 6 You clapped your hands and **jumped** for joy.
Mk 10.50 He threw off his cloak, **jumped** up, and came to Jesus.
Lk 1.44 I heard your greeting, the baby within me **jumped** with gladness.
Jn 21. 7 (for he had taken his clothes off) and **jumped** into the water.
Acts 3. 8 he **jumped** up, stood on his feet, and started walking around.
3. 8 into the Temple with them, walking and **jumping** and praising God.
14.10 The man **jumped** up and started walking around.
27.43 men who could swim to **jump** overboard first and swim ashore;

JUNGLE

Jer 12. 5 how will you manage in the **jungle** by the Jordan?

JUNIOR OFFICERS

1 Chr 12.14 and others were **junior officers** in command of a hundred.

JUNIPER

1 Kgs 10.11 brought from there a large amount of **juniper** wood and jewels.
10.12 It was the finest **juniper** wood ever imported into Israel;
2 Chr 2. 8 so send me cedar, cypress, and **juniper** logs from Lebanon.
9.10 Solomon who brought gold from Ophir also brought **juniper** wood
Is 41.19 grow in barren land, forests of pine and **juniper** and cypress.
60.13 the pine, the **juniper,** and the cypress, The finest wood

JUSTICE

see also **INJUSTICE, UNJUST**

Gen 18.19 descendants to obey me and to do what is right and **just.**
18.25 The judge of all the earth has to act **justly."**
Ex 23. 2 when they give evidence that perverts **justice.**
23. 6 "Do not deny **justice** to a poor man when he appears in
Lev 19.15 "Be honest and **just** when you make decisions in legal cases;
Deut 4. 8 Laws so **just** as those that I have taught you
16.20 Always be fair and **just,** so that you will occupy the
32. 4 Lord is your mighty defender, perfect and **just** in all his ways;
32.41 I will sharpen my flashing sword and see that **justice** is done.
2 Sam 8.15 made sure that his people were always treated fairly and **justly.**
15. 4 a claim could come to me, and I would give him **justice."**
15. 6 came to the king for **justice,** and so he won their loyalty.
23. 3 "The king who rules with **justice,** who rules in obedience to God,
1 Kgs 3. 9 to rule your people with **justice**
3.11 the wisdom to rule **justly,** instead of long life for yourself
10. 9 you their king so that you can maintain law and **justice."**
1 Chr 18.14 made sure that his people were always treated fairly and **justly.**
2 Chr 9. 8 you their king so that you can maintain law and **justice."**
12. 6 sinned, and they said, "What the Lord is doing is **just."**
Ezra 9.15 God of Israel, you are **just,** but you have let us survive.
Job 8. 3 God never twists **justice;**
16.18 Don't let my call for **justice** be silenced!
19. 7 no one hears my cry for **justice.**
24. 1 time for judging, a day of **justice** for those who serve him?
27. 1 Almighty God, who refuses me **justice** and makes my life bitter—
29.14 I have always acted **justly** and fairly.
34. 5 that he is innocent, that God refuses to give him **justice.**
34.17 Do you think that he hates **justice?**
36. 3 use what I know to show that God, my Creator, is **just.**
36. 6 live on, and he always treats the poor with **justice.**
37.23 he is righteous and **just** in his dealings with men.
Ps 7. 6 **Justice** is what you demand,
7.17 thank the Lord for his **justice,** I sing praises to the Lord,
9. 8 he judges the nations with **justice.**
17. 1 Listen, O Lord, to my plea for **justice;**
19. 8 commands of the Lord are **just** and give understanding
19. 9 The judgements of the Lord are **just;**
33. 5 The Lord loves what is righteous and **just;**
36. 6 your **justice** is like the depths of the sea.
45. 4 in majesty to victory for the defence of truth and **justice!**
45. 6 You rule over your people with **justice;**
48.10 You rule with **justice;**
58. 1 Do you rulers ever give a **just** decision?
67. 4 you judge the peoples with **justice**
72. 1 share with him your own **justice,** [2] so that he will rule
72. 2 rule over your people with **justice** and govern the oppressed
82. 5 **justice** has disappeared from the world.
89.14 Your kingdom is founded on righteousness and **justice;**
92.15 shows that the Lord is **just,** that there is no wrong
94.15 **Justice** will again be found in the courts,
96.10 he will judge the peoples with **justice."**
96.13 He will rule the peoples of the world with **justice**
97. 2 he rules with righteousness and **justice.**
98. 9 He will rule the peoples of the world with **justice**
99. 4 you have established **justice** in Israel;
101. 1 song is about loyalty and **justice,** and I sing it to you,
111. 7 In all he does he is faithful and **just;**
112. 4 for good men, for those who are merciful, kind, and **just.**
119.106 I will keep my solemn promise to obey your **just** instructions.
119.137 You are righteous, Lord, and your laws are **just.**
119.144 Your instructions are always **just;**
119.172 I will sing about your law, because your commands are **just.**
Prov 1. 3 how to live intelligently and how to be honest, **just,** and
2. 9 listen to me, you will know what is right, **just,** and fair.

Prov 8.20 I follow the paths of **justice,**
12.17 When you tell the truth, **justice** is done,
16.12 because **justice** is what makes a government strong.
17.23 judges accept secret bribes, and then **justice** is not done.
17.26 **justice** is perverted when good people are punished.
18. 5 favour the guilty and prevent the innocent from receiving **justice.**
19.28 There is no **justice** where a witness is determined to hurt someone.
20.28 in power as long as his rule is honest, **just,** and fair.
21.15 When **justice** is done, good people are happy,
25. 5 the king and his government will be known for its **justice.**
28. 5 people do not know what **justice** is, but those who worship
29. 4 the king is concerned with **justice,** the nation will be strong,
29.26 of the ruler, but only from the Lord can you get **justice.**
Ecc 3.16 you find wickedness where **justice** and right ought to be.
5. 8 the government oppresses the poor and denies them **justice**
Is 1.17 See that **justice** is done—help those who are oppressed,
5. 7 but their victims cried out for **justice.**
5.23 and you prevent the innocent from getting **justice.**
9. 7 his power on right and **justice,** from now until the end of
10. 2 prevent the poor from having their rights and from getting **justice.**
11. 5 He will rule his people with **justice** and integrity.
16. 5 do what is right, and he will see that **justice** is done.)
26. 9 earth and its people, they will all learn what **justice** is.
28. 6 will give a sense of **justice** to those who serve as judges,
28.17 **Justice** will be the measuring-line for the foundation,
29.21 who tell lies to keep honest men from getting **justice.**
32. 1 rules with integrity, and national leaders who govern with **justice.**
32.16 Everywhere in the land righteousness and **justice** will be done.
33. 5 He will fill Jerusalem with **justice** and integrity
42. 1 with my spirit, and he will bring **justice** to every nation.
42. 3 He will bring lasting **justice** to all.
42. 4 he will establish **justice** on the earth.
42. 6 and given you power to see that **justice** is done on earth.
45. 8 to receive it and will blossom with freedom and **justice.**
54.14 **Justice** and right will make you strong.
56. 1 "Do what is **just** and right,
58. 2 want me to give them **just** laws and that they take pleasure
59. 4 You go to court, but you haven't got **justice** on your side.
59.14 **Justice** is driven away, and right cannot come near.
59.15 seen this, and he is displeased that there is no **justice.**
59.17 He will wear **justice** like a coat of armour
60.17 I will make them rule with **justice** and peace.
61. 8 "I love **justice** and I hate oppression and crime.
Jer 5.28 not give orphans their rights or show **justice** to the oppressed.
9.24 my love is constant, and I do what is **just** and right.
11.20 Then I prayed, "Almighty Lord, you are a **just** judge;
12. 1 Yet I must question you about matters of **justice.**
20.12 But, Almighty Lord, you test men **justly;**
21.11 See that **justice** is done every day.
22. 3 "I, the Lord, command you to do what is **just** and right.
22.15 He was always **just** and fair, and he prospered in everything
23. 5 wisely and do what is right and **just** throughout the land.
33.15 That king will do what is right and **just** throughout the land.
Lam 1.18 "But the Lord is **just,** for I have disobeyed him.
3.36 When **justice** is perverted in court, he knows.
Ezek 39.21 how I use my power to carry out my **just** decisions.
45. 9 Do what is right and **just.**
Dan 4.37 he does is right and **just,** and he can humble anyone
9.24 will be forgiven and eternal **justice** established,
Hos 5. 1 supposed to judge with **justice**—so judgement will fall on you!
10. 4 **Justice** has become injustice, growing like poisonous weeds
12. 6 Be loyal and **just,** and wait patiently for your God to act.
Amos 5. 7 are doomed, you that twist **justice** and cheat people out of
5.12 take bribes, and prevent the poor from getting **justice**
5.15 what is right, and see that **justice** prevails in the courts.
5.24 Instead, let **justice** flow like a stream,
6.12 Yet you have turned **justice** into poison, and right into wrong.
Mic 3. 1 concerned about **justice,** [2] yet you hate what is good
3. 8 gives me a sense of **justice** and the courage to tell
3. 9 you that hate **justice** and turn right into wrong.
6. 8 to do what is **just,** to show constant love,
Hab 1. 4 The law is weak and useless, and **justice** is never done.
1. 4 get the better of the righteous, and so **justice** is perverted.
Zeph 3. 5 Every morning without fail, he brings **justice** to his people.
Zech 7. 9 'You must see that **justice** is done, and must show kindness
8. 8 I will be their God, ruling over them faithfully and **justly.**
8.16 In the courts, give real **justice**—the kind that brings peace.
Mal 2.17 by asking, "Where is the God who is supposed to be **just?"**
Mt 12.20 will persist until he causes **justice** to triumph,
23.23 important teachings of the Law, such as **justice** and mercy
Lk 11.42 the other herbs, but you neglect **justice** and love for God.
Acts 8.33 He was humiliated, and **justice** was denied him.
17.31 judge the whole world with **justice** by means of a man he
Rom 3. 6 If God is not **just,** how can he judge the world?
Col 4. 1 Masters, be fair and **just** in the way you treat your slaves.
2 Thes 1. 5 proves that God's judgement is **just** and as a result you will
Heb 1. 8 You rule over your people with **justice.**
Rev 15. 4 worship you, because your **just** actions are seen by all."
16. 5 judgements you have made are **just,** O Holy One, you who are
16. 7 True and **just** indeed are your judgements!"
19. 2 True and **just** are his judgements!
19.11 it is with **justice** that he judges and fights his battles.

AV **JUSTIFICATION**
see also **INNOCENT, RIGHT (1), RIGHT WITH GOD**

Ex 23. 7 to death, for I will **condemn** anyone who does such an evil
1 Kgs 8.32 one as he deserves, and **acquit** the one who is innocent.
2 Chr 6.23 one as he deserves and **acquit** the one who is innocent.
Job 25. 4 Can anyone be **righteous** or pure in God's sight?
Is 45.25 I, the Lord, will **rescue** all the descendants of Jacob,
53.11 punishment of many and for his sake I will **forgive** them.
Jer 3.11 from him, she had proved to be **better** than unfaithful Judah.
Mt 11.19 God's wisdom, however, is shown to be **true** by its results."
Lk 7.29 ones who had obeyed God's **righteous** demands and had been baptized
7.35 wisdom, however, is shown to be **true** by all who accept it."
Acts 13.38 who believes in him is **set free** from all the sins from
13.38 sins from which the Law of Moses could not **set you free.**
Rom 5.16 after so many sins, comes the undeserved gift of **"Not guilty!"**
5.18 one righteous act **sets all mankind free** and gives them life.
8.33 God himself declares them not **guilty!**

JUSTIFY

Job 32. 2 because Job was **justifying** himself and blaming God.
Ps 51. 4 you are **justified** in condemning me.
Ezek 14.22 the punishment I am bringing on Jerusalem is **justified;**
Lk 10.29 of the Law wanted to **justify** himself, so he asked Jesus,

KADESH (1)
Place where the Israelites encamped on the way to Canaan.
see also ENMISHPAT

Gen 14. 7 turned round and came back to **Kadesh** (then known as Enmishpat).
16.14 people call the well between **Kadesh** and Bered
20. 1 southern part of Canaan and lived between **Kadesh** and Shur.
Num 13.26 community of Israel at **Kadesh** in the wilderness of Paran.
20. 1 Israel came to the wilderness of Zin and camped at **Kadesh.**
20.14 Moses sent messengers from **Kadesh** to the king of Edom.
20.16 Now we are at **Kadesh,** a town at the border of your
20.22 community of Israel left **Kadesh** and arrived at Mount Hor,
27.14 (Meribah is the spring at **Kadesh** in the wilderness of Zin.)
32. 8 did when I sent them from **Kadesh Barnea** to explore the land.
33.15 wilderness of Zin (that is, **Kadesh),**
34. 4 continue on through Zin as far south as **Kadesh Barnea.**
Deut 1. 2 from Mount Sinai to **Kadesh Barnea** by way of the hill-country
1.19 When we reached **Kadesh Barnea,**
1.46 after we had stayed at **Kadesh** for a long time,
2.14 thirty-eight years after we had left **Kadesh Barnea.**
9.23 when he sent you from **Kadesh Barnea**
32.51 Meribah, near the town of **Kadesh** in the wilderness of Zin,
Josh 10.41 Joshua's campaign took him from **Kadesh Barnea** in the south
14. 6 what the Lord said in **Kadesh Barnea** about you and me
14. 7 Moses sent me from **Kadesh Barnea** to spy out this land.
15. 3 It ran south of **Kadesh Barnea,** past Hezron and up to Addar,
Judg 11.16 through the desert to the Gulf of Aqaba and came to **Kadesh.**
11.17 So the Israelites stayed at **Kadesh.**
Ps 29. 8 he shakes the desert of **Kadesh.**
Ezek 48.28 Tamar to the oasis of **Kadesh,** and then north-west

KEDAR
Tribe of desert people descended from Ishmael.

Gen 25.13 Nebaioth, **Kedar,** Adbeel, Mibsam,
1 Chr 1.29 **Kedar,** Adbeel, Mibsam,
Ps 120. 5 as bad as living in Meshech or among the people of **Kedar.**
Song 1. 5 as the desert tents of **Kedar,** but beautiful as the curtains
Is 21.16 the greatness of the tribes of **Kedar** will be at an end.
21.17 are the bravest men of **Kedar,** but few of them will be
42.11 let the people of **Kedar** praise him!
60. 7 All the sheep of **Kedar** and Nebaioth Will be brought to you
Jer 2.10 of Cyprus, and send someone eastwards to the land of **Kedar.**
49.28 the tribe of **Kedar** and the districts controlled by Hazor,
49.28 "Attack the people of **Kedar**
Ezek 27.21 rulers of the land of **Kedar** paid for your merchandise

Am **KEEP**
see also **PREVENT, SAVE**

KEEP
[KEPT]
see also **KEEP FROM, KEEP SAFE**

Gen 1. 6 divide the water and to **keep** it in two separate places"—
6.19 and of every kind of bird, in order to **keep** them alive.
7. 3 animal and bird will be **kept** alive to reproduce again on the
14.21 of Sodom said to Abram, **"Keep** the loot, but give me back
14.23 earth, [23] that I will not **keep** anything of yours, not even
22.12 because you have not **kept** back your only son from me."
22.16 did this and did not **keep** back your only son from me,
26. 5 because Abraham obeyed me and **kept** all my laws and commands."
27.15 Esau's best clothes, which she **kept** in the house,
30.40 Jacob **kept** the sheep separate from the goats
30.40 he built up his own flock and **kept** it apart from Laban's.
31.43 I can do nothing to **keep** my daughters and their children,
33. 9 **keep** what you have."
38.17 will give me something to **keep** as a pledge until you send
38.23 Judah said, "Let her **keep** the things.
39. 9 and he has not **kept** back anything from me except you.
39.16 She **kept** his robe with her until Joseph's master came home.
39.20 the prison where the king's prisoners were **kept,**
40. 3 of the guard, in the same place where Joseph was being **kept.**
42.16 rest of you will be **kept** under guard until the truth of
42.19 of you will stay in the prison where you have been **kept;**
47.19 Give us corn to **keep** us alive and seed to sow in
Ex 12.17 **Keep** this festival, because it was on this day
15.26 I consider right and by **keeping** my commands, I will not

Ex 16.19 to them, "No one is to **keep** any of it for tomorrow."
16.23 Whatever is left should be put aside and **kept** for tomorrow."
16.24 As Moses had commanded, they **kept** what was left
16.32 save some manna, to be **kept** for our descendants,
16.33 it in the Lord's presence to be **kept** for our descendants."
16.34 in front of the Covenant Box, so that it could be **kept.**
20. 8 "Observe the Sabbath and **keep** it holy.
21.16 to sell him or to **keep** him as a slave, is to
21.34 pay the money to the owner and may **keep** the dead animal.
21.36 other man a live bull, but he may **keep** the dead animal.
22. 7 "If a man agrees to **keep** another man's money
22. 8 found, the man who was **keeping** the valuables is to be
22.10 "If a man agrees to **keep** another man's donkey,
27.21 This command is to be **kept** for ever by the Israelites
30.35 Add salt to **keep** it pure and holy.
31.13 to the people of Israel, **"Keep** the Sabbath, my day of rest,
31.14 You must **keep** the day of rest, because it is sacred.
31.14 Whoever does not **keep** it, but works on that day, is to
31.16 people of Israel are to **keep** this day as a sign of
34.18 **"Keep** the Festival of Unleavened Bread.
34.22 **"Keep** the Harvest Festival when you begin to harvest
34.22 and **keep** the Festival of Shelters
34.25 Do not **keep** until the following morning any part of the
38.21 the two stone tablets were **kept** on which the Ten Commandments
Lev 3.17 is a rule to be **kept** for ever by all Israelites
10. 9 This is a law to be **kept** by all your descendants.
11.44 God, and you must **keep** yourselves holy, because I am holy.
17. 7 The people of Israel must **keep** this regulation for all time
18.26 foreigners living with you, must **keep** the Lord's laws
19. 3 his father, and must **keep** the Sabbath, as I have commanded.
19. 5 for a fellowship-offering, **keep** the regulations that I have given
19.12 promise in my name if you do not intend to **keep** it;
19.30 **Keep** the Sabbath, and honour the place where I am worshipped.
20. 7 **Keep** yourselves holy, because I am the Lord your God.
20.22 The Lord said, **"Keep** all my laws and commands, so that
23.41 This regulation is to be **kept** by your descendants for all
26. 2 **Keep** the religious festivals and honour the place
Num 5.10 Each priest shall **keep** the offerings presented to him.
9. 6 and they were not able to **keep** the Passover on that day.
9.10 journey, but still want to **keep** the Passover,
9.14 living among you wants to **keep** the Passover, he must observe
15.22 someone unintentionally fails to **keep** some of these regulations
15.40 tassels will remind you to **keep** all my commands,
17.10 It is to be **kept** as a warning to the rebel Israelites
18.30 the best part, you may **keep** the rest,
18.30 just as the farmer **keeps** what is left
19. 9 where they are to be **kept** for the Israelite community
30. 5 when he hears about it, she is not required to **keep** it.
30. 5 forgive her, because her father refused to let her **keep** it.
30. 8 when he hears about it, she is not required to **keep** it.
30. 9 or a divorced woman must **keep** every vow she makes and every
30.12 when he hears about it, she is not required to **keep** it.
30.12 because her husband prevented her from **keeping** her vow.
31.15 He asked them, "Why have you **kept** all the women alive?
31.18 but **keep** alive for yourselves all the girls
31.32 captured by the soldiers, in addition to what they **kept**
31.53 Those who were not officers **kept** the loot they had taken.
Deut 5.12 "'Observe the Sabbath and **keep** it holy,
6.24 he will always watch over our nation and **keep** it prosperous.
13. 4 obey him and **keep** his commands;
13.17 Do not **keep** for yourselves anything that was condemned
17.18 made from the original copy **kept** by the levitical priests.
17.19 He is to **keep** this book near him and read from it
18. 8 and he may **keep** whatever his family sends him.
23.14 **Keep** your camp ritually clean,
23.21 your vow, and it is a sin not to **keep** it.
23.23 but if you make one voluntarily, be sure that you **keep** it.
24.12 If he is a poor man, do not **keep** it overnight;
26.17 promised to obey him, to **keep** all his laws, and to do
27.10 so obey him and **keep** all his laws that I am giving
28. 1 Lord your God and faithfully **keep** all his commands
28.15 God and do not faithfully **keep** all his commands and laws
28.45 the Lord your God and **keep** all the laws that he gave
29.29 some things that the Lord our God has **kept** secret;
30. 8 will again obey him and **keep** all his commands
30.10 have to obey him and **keep** all his laws that are written
30.16 love him, obey him, and **keep** all his laws,
34. 9 of Israel obeyed Joshua and **kept** the commands that the Lord
Josh 7.11 broken the agreement with me that I ordered them to **keep.**
8. 2 this time you may **keep** its goods and livestock for yourselves.
8.27 The Israelites **kept** for themselves the livestock and goods
9.15 Israel gave their solemn promise to **keep** the treaty.
11.14 livestock from these cities and **kept** them for themselves.
14.10 and the Lord, as he promised, has **kept** me alive ever since.
22.22 we rebelled and did not **keep** faith with the Lord,
23.16 If you do not **keep** the covenant
23.16 your God commanded you to **keep** and if you serve and worship
Judg 1.35 tribes of Ephraim and Manasseh **kept** them under their rule
2.20 broken the covenant that I commanded their ancestors to **keep.**
7. 8 the three hundred, who **kept** all the supplies and trumpets.
11.24 You can **keep** whatever your god Chemosh has given you.
11.24 But we are going to **keep** everything that the Lord,
21.22 can say, 'Please let us **keep** them, because we did not take
Ruth 4.10 This will **keep** the property in the dead man's family,
1 Sam 2.28 gave them the right to **keep** a share of the sacrifices burnt
3.18 he did not **keep** anything back.
9.24 Samuel said, "Look, here is the piece that was **kept** for you.
15.15 They **kept** the best sheep and cattle to offer as a sacrifice
17.54 but he **kept** Goliath's weapons in his own tent.
18. 2 Saul **kept** David with him from that day on
20.23 the Lord will make sure that we will **keep** it for ever."
2 Sam 7. 2 built of cedar, but God's Covenant Box is **kept** in a tent!"
7.12 make one of your sons king and will **keep** his kingdom strong.
8. 4 He **kept** enough horses for a hundred chariots and crippled
14. 7 leave my husband without a son to **keep** his name alive."
18.18 King's Valley, because he had no son to **keep** his name alive.
20. 3 They were **kept** confined for the rest of their lives,
1 Kgs 3.14 if you obey me and **keep** my laws and commands, as your
8.58 wants us to live, and **keep** all the laws and commands he
9.19 cities where his supplies were **kept,** the cities for his horses
10.26 Some of them he **kept** in Jerusalem and the rest he stationed
11.32 Solomon will **keep** one tribe, for the sake of my servant
11.33 done wrong, and has not **kept** my laws and commands as his
11.34 from Solomon, and I will **keep** him in power
11.36 I will let Solomon's son **keep** one tribe,
15. 4 to rule after him in Jerusalem and to **keep** Jerusalem secure.
18. 5 we can find enough grass to **keep** the horses and mules alive.
2 Kgs 7. 9 We have good news and we shouldn't **keep** it to ourselves.
11. 3 care of the boy and **kept** him hidden in the Temple, while
11.10 King David and had been **kept** in the Temple,
12. 7 From now on you are not to **keep** the money you receive;
16.15 But **keep** the bronze altar for me to use for divination."
18. 6 never disobeyed him, but carefully **kept** all the commands
21. 8 obey all my commands and **keep** the whole Law that my servant
23. 3 Lord to obey him, to **keep** his laws and commands with all
23.11 (These were **kept** in the temple courtyard, near the gate
1 Chr 2. 7 the people of Israel by **keeping** loot that had been devoted
4.33 are the records which they **kept** of their families
9.26 for the rooms in the Temple and for the supplies **kept** there.
16.37 that was held at the place where the Covenant Box was **kept.**
17. 1 of cedar, but the Lord's Covenant Box is **kept** in a tent!"
17.11 make one of your sons king and will **keep** his kingdom strong.
18. 4 He **kept** enough horses for a hundred chariots
23. 4 six thousand to **keep** records and decide disputes,
23.28 and to **keep** undefiled everything that is sacred;
26.29 **keeping** records and settling disputes for the people of Israel.
29.18 ancestors Abraham, Isaac, and Jacob, **keep** such devotion
29.18 strong in your people's hearts and **keep** them always faithful
2 Chr 1. 4 Box, however, was in Jerusalem, **kept** in a tent
1.14 Some of them he **kept** in Jerusalem, and the rest he stationed
9.25 Some of them he **kept** in Jerusalem and the rest he stationed
22.11 By **keeping** him hidden, she saved him from death at the hands
23. 9 had belonged to King David and had been **kept** in the Temple.
26.11 Its records were **kept** by his secretaries Jeiel and Maaseiah
29.34 Levites were more faithful in **keeping** ritually clean
33. 8 obey all my commands and **keep** the whole Law
34.13 workmen on various jobs, and others **kept** records
34.17 taken the money that was **kept** in the Temple and handed it
34.31 Lord to obey him, to **keep** his laws and commands
35.16 worship of the Lord, the **keeping** of the Passover Festival,
Ezra 4.15 a search to be made in the records your ancestors **kept.**
6. 1 to be made in the royal records that were **kept** in Babylon.
9. 1 Levites had not **kept** themselves separate from the people
Neh 1. 7 We have not **kept** the laws which you gave us through Moses,
2. 8 a letter to Asaph, **keeper** of the royal forests,
3.29 Shemaiah son of Shecaniah, **keeper** of the East Gate,
4.17 worked with one hand and **kept** a weapon in the other,
4.18 everyone who was building **kept** a sword strapped to his waist.
4.23 And we all **kept** our weapons to hand.
5. 2 "We have large families, we need corn to **keep** us alive."
9.14 You taught them to **keep** your Sabbaths holy,
9.29 they rejected your laws, although **keeping** your Law is the way
9.34 our kings, leaders, and priests have not **kept** your Law.
10.29 and that we will **keep** all his laws and requirements.
10.39 utensils for the Temple are **kept** and where the priests who
12.22 A record was **kept** of the heads of the Levite families
12.44 contributions for the Temple were **kept,** including the tithes
13.22 the gates to make sure that the Sabbath was **kept** holy.
Job 3.23 God **keeps** their future hidden and hems them in
5.20 when famine comes, he will **keep** you alive,
7.12 Why do you **keep** me under guard?
9.34 **Keep** your terrors away!
10.12 me life and constant love, and your care has **kept** me alive.
20.12 good to him that he **keeps** some in his mouth to enjoy
22.22 **keep** his words in your heart.
22.27 he will answer you, and you will **keep** the vows you made.
24. 3 that belong to orphans, and **keep** a widow's ox till she pays
25. 1 he **keeps** his heavenly kingdom in peace.
38.10 a boundary for the sea and **kept** it behind bolted gates.
38.22 visited the storerooms, where I **keep** the snow and the hail?
38.23 I **keep** them ready for times of trouble, for days of
Ps 31.19 the good things you **keep** for those who honour you!
33.19 he **keeps** them alive in times of famine.
37.31 He **keeps** the law of his God in his heart
40. 8 I **keep** your teaching in my heart."
40.10 I have not **kept** the news of salvation to myself;
41.12 you will **keep** me in your presence for ever.
56. 8 you have **kept** a record of my tears.
66. 9 He has **kept** us alive and has not allowed us to fall.
66.20 reject my prayer or **keep** back his constant love from me.
69.27 **Keep** a record of all their sins;
75. 3 the earth itself be shaken, I will **keep** its foundations firm.
76.10 those who survive the wars will **keep** your festivals.
80.18 **keep** us alive, and we will praise you.
84. 3 they **keep** their young near your altars, Lord Almighty, my king
89.31 and do not **keep** my commandments, [32] then I will punish
105. 9 He will **keep** the agreement he made with Abraham
105.45 his people would obey his laws and **keep** all his commands.
119. 5 I hope that I shall be faithful in **keeping** your instructions!
119. 9 How can a young man **keep** his life pure?
119.11 I **keep** your law in my heart,
119.22 from their insults and scorn, because I have **kept** your laws.

Ps	119.34	I will **keep** it with all my heart.
	119.35	**Keep** me obedient to your commandments,
	119.93	your instructions, because by them you have **kept** me alive.
	119.107	**keep** me alive, as you have promised.
	119.146	save me, and I will **keep** your laws.
	119.150	persecutors are coming closer, people who never **keep** your law.
	119.158	filled with disgust, because they do not **keep** your commands.
	130. 3	If you **kept** a record of our sins, who could escape being
	147.14	He **keeps** your borders safe and satisfies you
Prov	2.12	They will **keep** you away from people who stir up trouble by
	4.21	Remember them and **keep** them in your heart.
	6.21	**Keep** their words with you always, locked in your heart.
	7. 3	**Keep** my teaching with you all the time;
	12.22	Lord hates liars, but is pleased with those who **keep** their word.
	15. 6	Righteous men **keep** their wealth, but wicked men lose theirs
	19. 4	new friends, but the poor cannot **keep** the few they have.
	19.16	**Keep** God's laws and you will live longer;
	20.19	A gossip can never **keep** a secret.
	25.10	will learn that you can't **keep** a secret, and you will never
	29.18	Happy is the man who **keeps** God's law!
Song	7.13	Darling, I have **kept** for you the old delights and the new.
Is	30.10	Let us **keep** our illusions.
	47.12	**Keep** all your magic spells and charms;
	48. 9	I am **keeping** it back and will not destroy you.
	58.11	I will **keep** you strong and well.
Jer	6. 7	well keeps its water fresh, so Jerusalem **keeps** its evil fresh.
	20. 9	best to hold it in, but can no longer **keep** it back.
	36. 9	The fast was **kept** by all who lived in Jerusalem
	37.16	was put in an underground cell and **kept** there a long time.
	38.13	After that I was **kept** in the courtyard.
	38.28	And I was **kept** in the palace courtyard until the day
	42. 4	I will not **keep** back anything from you."
	52. 5	walls round it, [5]and **kept** it under siege until Zedekiah's
Lam	4.22	the Lord will not **keep** us in exile any longer.
Ezek	5. 3	**Keep** back a few hairs and wrap them in the hem
	5. 6	Jerusalem rejected my commands and refused to **keep** my laws.
	5. 7	not obeying my laws or **keeping** my commands,
	11.12	while you were **keeping** the laws of the neighbouring nations,
	11.20	they will **keep** my laws and faithfully obey all my commands.
	13.19	deserve to die, and you **keep** people alive who don't deserve
	17.14	rising again and to make sure that the treaty would be **kept.**
	17.19	for breaking the treaty which he swore in my name to **keep.**
	18. 9	Such a man obeys my commands and carefully **keeps** my laws.
	18.12	he robs, he **keeps** what a borrower gives him
	18.17	He **keeps** my laws and obeys my commands.
	18.19	He **kept** my laws and followed them carefully,
	18.21	evil man stops sinning and **keeps** my laws, if he does what
	19. 9	They **kept** him under guard, so that his roar would never be
	20.12	I made the **keeping** of the Sabbath a sign of the
	20.18	Do not **keep** the laws your ancestors made;
	20.21	and did not **keep** my commands, which bring life
	22. 8	respect for the holy places, and you don't **keep** the Sabbath.
	22.14	I, the Lord, have spoken, and I **keep** my word.
	25. 5	Rabbah into a place to **keep** camels, and the whole country
	25. 5	Ammon into a place to **keep** sheep, so that you will know
	28. 3	are wiser than Danel, that no secret can be **kept** from you.
	36.27	you follow my laws and **keep** all the commands I have given
	40.42	used in killing the sacrificial animals was **kept** on these tables.
	44.20	They are to **keep** it a proper length.
	44.24	They are to **keep** the religious festivals according to my rules
	44.24	and they are to **keep** the Sabbaths holy.
	45.20	In this way, you will **keep** the Temple holy.
Dan	5.17	Daniel replied, **"Keep** your gifts for yourself
	5.19	if he wanted to **keep** someone alive, he did.
	7.18	God will receive royal power and **keep** it for ever and ever."
	7.28	frightened that I turned pale, and I **kept** everything to myself.
Amos	1. 9	of Edom, and did not **keep** the treaty of friendship they had
	2. 4	They have despised my teachings and have not **kept** my commands.
Zech	11.12	But if not, **keep** them."
Mal	3. 7	you, have turned away from my laws and have not **kept** them.
Mt	5.12	and glad, for a great reward is **kept** for you in heaven.
	9.17	into fresh wineskins, and both will **keep** in good condition."
	18. 8	or a foot than to **keep** both hands and both feet and
	18. 9	only one eye than to **keep** both eyes and be thrown into
	19.17	**Keep** the commandments if you want to enter life."
	26.38	Stay here and **keep watch** with me."
	26.40	three were not able to **keep watch** with me even for one
	26.41	**Keep watch** and pray that you will not fall into temptation.
	26.43	they could not **keep** their eyes open.
Mk	5. 3	Nobody could **keep** him chained up any more;
	9.43	without a hand than to **keep** both hands and go off to
	9.45	without a foot than to **keep** both feet and be thrown into
	9.47	only one eye than to **keep** both eyes and be thrown into
	13.34	work to do and after telling the doorkeeper to **keep watch.**
	14.34	Stay here and **keep watch."**
	14.38	And he said to them, **"Keep watch,** and pray that you
	14.40	they could not **keep** their eyes open.
	14.54	sat down with the guards, **keeping** himself warm by the fire.
Lk	1.54	He has **kept** the promise he made to our ancestors, and
	2.29	"Now, Lord, you have **kept** your promise, and you may let
	6.23	for joy, because a great reward is **kept** for you in heaven.
	8.29	and even though he was **kept** a prisoner, his hands and feet
	11.52	You have **kept** the key that opens the door to the house
	12.17	think to himself, 'I haven't anywhere to **keep** all my crops.
	12.20	who will get all these things you have **kept** for yourself?' "
	13.16	descendant of Abraham whom Satan has **kept** bound up for eighteen
	19.20	I **kept** it hidden in a handkerchief.
Jn	2.10	But you have **kept** the best wine until now!"
	5.38	and you do not **keep** his message in your hearts, for
Jn	11.37	Could he not have **kept** Lazarus from dying?"
	12. 7	Let her **keep** what she has for the day of my burial.
	12.25	his own life in this world will **keep** it for life eternal.
	18.25	Peter was still standing there **keeping** himself warm.
	18.28	for they wanted to **keep** themselves ritually clean, in order to
Acts	5. 2	with his wife's agreement he **kept** part of the money for
	5. 3	to the Holy Spirit by **keeping** part of the money you received
	7.17	drew near for God to **keep** the promise he had made to
	17. 7	come to our city, [7]and Jason has **kept** them in his house.
	19.35	city of Ephesus is the **keeper** of the temple of the great
	20.28	So **keep watch** over yourselves and over all the flock which
	23.35	for Paul to be **kept** under guard in the governor's headquarters.
	24.23	in charge of Paul to **keep** him under guard, but to give
	25. 4	Festus answered, "Paul is being **kept** a prisoner in Caesarea,
	25.21	he asked to be **kept** under guard and to let the Emperor
	25.21	orders for him to be **kept** under guard until I could send
	27.15	it was impossible to **keep** the ship headed into the wind,
Rom	1.28	Because those people refuse to **keep** in mind the true knowledge
	1.31	they do not **keep** their promises, and they show no kindness
	8.17	will possess the blessings he **keeps** for his people, and we
	8.17	we will also possess with Christ what God has **kept** for him;
	8.32	God, who did not even **keep** back his own Son, but offered
	11. 4	"I have **kept** for myself seven thousand men who have not
	12.12	Let your hope **keep** you joyful, be patient in your troubles,
	14.22	**Keep** what you believe about this matter, then, between yourself
1 Cor	1. 8	He will also **keep** you firm to the end, so that you
	10.13	But God **keeps** his promise, and he will not allow you to
2 Cor	3. 7	the people of Israel could not **keep** their eyes fixed on him.
Gal	2. 5	but in order to **keep** the truth of the gospel safe
	3.17	God made a covenant with Abraham and promised to **keep** it.
	3.23	for faith came, the Law **kept** us all locked up as prisoners
Phil	3. 5	As far as **keeping** the Jewish Law is concerned, I was
	4. 7	beyond human understanding, will **keep** your hearts and minds safe
Col	2. 7	**Keep** your roots deep in him, build your lives on him,
	3. 2	**Keep** your minds fixed on things there, not on things here
	3.24	give you as a reward what he has **kept** for his people.
1 Thes	5.21	**keep** what is good [22]and avoid every kind of evil.
	5.23	holy in every way and **keep** your whole being—spirit, soul,
1 Tim	1.19	to fight well, [19]and **keep** your faith and a clear conscience.
	4. 7	**Keep** yourself in training for a godly life.
	6.14	to obey your orders and **keep** them faithfully until the Day
2 Tim	1.14	Spirit, who lives in us, **keep** the good things that have been
	4. 7	I have run the full distance, and I have **kept** the faith.
Phlm	13	I would like to **keep** him here with me, while I am
Heb	10.23	we profess, because we can trust God to **keep** his promise.
	11.11	He trusted God to **keep** his promise.
	11.26	of Egypt, for he **kept** his eyes on the future reward.
	11.31	It was faith that **kept** the prostitute Rahab from being killed
1 Pet	1. 4	to possessing the rich blessings that God **keeps** for his people.
	1. 4	He **keeps** them for you in heaven, where they cannot decay or
	2.25	brought back to follow the Shepherd and **Keeper** of your souls.
	4.19	completely to their Creator, who always **keeps** his promise.
2 Pet	2. 4	into hell, where they are **kept** chained in darkness, waiting for
	2. 9	their trials and how to **keep** the wicked under punishment for
	3. 7	They are being **kept** for the day when godless people will be
1 Jn	1. 9	sins to God, he will **keep** his promise and do what is
	2.24	Be sure, then, to **keep** in your hearts the message you
	2.24	If you **keep** that message, then you will always live in union
	3. 3	has this hope in Christ **keeps** himself pure, just as Christ
Jude	6	darkness below, where God is **keeping** them for that great Day
Rev	3.10	Because you have **kept** my command to endure, I will also

KEEP FROM

[KEPT FROM]

Gen	3.24	This was to **keep anyone from** coming near the tree that gives
	16. 2	said to Abram, "The Lord has **kept me from** having children.
	20. 6	so I **kept you from** sinning against me and did not let
	30. 2	He is the one who **keeps you from** having children."
	42. 2	go there and buy some to **keep us from** starving to death."
Ex	1.10	find some way to **keep them from** becoming even more numerous."
	28.32	be reinforced with a woven binding to **keep it from** tearing.
	39.23	reinforced with a woven binding to **keep it from** tearing.
Num	24.11	you, but the Lord has **kept you from** getting the reward."
Deut	17.20	This will **keep him from** thinking that he is better than
	32.11	the Lord **kept Israel from** falling.
Josh	22.27	This was to **keep your descendants from** saying that ours have
	24.27	to **keep you from** rebelling against your God."
Judg	7.24	to **keep the Midianites from** crossing them."
	12. 5	In order to **keep the Ephraimites from** escaping,
Ruth	1.13	Would this **keep you from** marrying someone else?
1 Sam	1. 5	because the Lord had **kept her from** having children.
	3.17	"Don't **keep anything from** me.
	13.19	determined to **keep the Hebrews from** making swords and spears.
	14. 6	he does, nothing can **keep him from** giving us the victory, no
	24. 6	men, "May the Lord **keep me from** doing any harm to my
	25.26	the Lord who has **kept you from** taking revenge and killing
	25.33	have done today in **keeping me from** the crime of murder
	25.34	The Lord has **kept me from** harming you.
	25.39	insulting me and has **kept me his servant from** doing wrong.
2 Sam	13. 2	as a virgin, she was **kept from** meeting men.
	22.24	I am faultless, that I have **kept myself from** doing wrong.
	22.37	You have **kept me from** being captured,
1 Chr	4.10	Be with me and **keep me from** anything evil that might cause
	10. 4	to **keep these godless Philistines from** gloating over me."
Ezra	4. 4	discourage and frighten the Jews and **keep them from** building.
Neh	5. 3	to get enough corn to **keep us from** starving."
Job	3. 9	**Keep the morning star from** shining;
	9. 7	He can **keep the sun from** rising, and the stars from

Job 22.14 think the thick clouds **keep him from** seeing, as he walks on
24. 7 nothing to cover them, nothing to **keep them from** the cold.
26. 8 clouds with water and **keeps them from** bursting with the weight.
33.28 He **kept me from** going to the world of the dead, and
34.30 to **keep godless oppressors from** ruling them.
36.21 your suffering was sent to **keep you from** it.
Ps 18.23 I am faultless, that I have **kept myself from** doing wrong.
18.36 You have **kept me from** being captured,
25.20 **keep me from** defeat.
30. 1 have saved me and **kept my enemies from** gloating over me.
30. 3 you **kept me from** the grave.
33.10 he **keeps them from** carrying out their plans.
39. 3 I could not **keep from** asking:
49. 9 never be enough [9] to **keep him from** the grave, to let him
56.13 you have rescued me from death and **kept me from** defeat.
71.20 you will **keep me from** the grave.
78. 4 We will not **keep them from** our children;
89.48 How can man **keep himself from** the grave?
91.12 with their hands to **keep you from** hurting your feet on the
103. 4 He **keeps me from** the grave and blesses me with love
104. 9 to **keep them from** covering the earth again.
116. 8 he stopped my tears and **kept me from** defeat.
119.10 **keep me from** disobeying your commandments.
119.29 **Keep me from** going the wrong way,
119.37 **Keep me from** paying attention to what is worthless;
119.133 As you have promised, **keep me from** falling;
141. 4 **Keep me from** wanting to do wrong and from joining evil men
Prov 10. 3 but he will **keep the wicked from** getting what they want.
13.23 for the poor, but unjust men **keep them from** being farmed.
15.11 of the dead can **keep the Lord from** knowing what is there;
30. 8 **keep me from** lying, and let me be neither rich nor poor.
Ecc 8. 8 No one can **keep himself from** dying or put off the day
Is 29.21 those who tell lies to **keep honest men from** getting justice.
Jer 5.25 Instead, your sins have **kept these good things from** you.
10. 4 It is fastened down with nails to **keep it from** falling over.
Ezek 14.11 will do this to **keep the Israelites from** deserting me
17.14 men as hostages [14] to **keep the nation from** rising again
44.19 to **keep their sacred clothing from** harming the people.
Lk 4.42 when they found him, they tried to **keep him from** leaving.
8.12 hearts in order to **keep them from** believing and being saved.
Jn 18.36 followers would fight to **keep me from** being handed over to
Acts 4.17 to **keep this matter from** spreading any further among the people,
8.36 What is to **keep me from** being baptized?"
14.18 apostles could hardly **keep the crowd from** offering a sacrifice
15.20 to **keep themselves from** sexual immorality;
15.29 and **keep yourselves from** sexual immorality.
21.25 and that they must **keep themselves from** sexual immorality."
27.42 the prisoners, in order to **keep them from** swimming ashore
Rom 1.13 visit you, but something has always **kept me from** doing so.
11.25 for it will **keep you from** thinking how wise you are.
14.21 thing to do is to **keep from** eating meat, drinking wine, or
16.17 **Keep away** from them!
1 Cor 7. 5 this way you will be **kept from** giving in to Satan's
9.27 to **keep myself from** being disqualified after having called
10.14 So then, my dear friends, **keep away from** the worship of idols.
12.15 that would not **keep it from** being a part of the
12.16 that would not **keep it from** being a part of the
2 Cor 2. 7 encourage him, in order to **keep him from** becoming so sad as
2.11 in order to **keep Satan from** getting the upper hand
4. 4 He **keeps them from** seeing the light shining on them, the
11.12 in order to **keep** those other "apostles" **from** having any
12. 7 But to **keep me from** being puffed up with pride because of
12. 7 Satan's messenger to beat me and **keep me from** being proud.
2 Thes 2. 6 is something that **keeps this from** happening now, and you know
3. 6 our Lord Jesus Christ to **keep away from** all brothers who are
1 Tim 4. 7 **keep away from** those godless legends, which are not worth telling.
2 Tim 2.16 **Keep away from** profane and foolish discussions,
2.23 But **keep away from** foolish and ignorant arguments;
3. 5 **Keep away from** such people.
Heb 11. 5 It was faith that **kept Enoch from** dying.
Jas 1.27 and to **keep oneself from** being corrupted by the world.
1 Pet 3.10 to see good times, must **keep from** speaking evil and stop
Jude 24 who is able to **keep you from** falling, and to bring you

KEEP SAFE

[KEPT SAFE, SAFE-KEEPING]

Deut 12.10 He will **keep you safe** from all your enemies,
Josh 24.17 He **kept us safe** wherever we went among all the nations
1 Sam 25.29 Lord your God will **keep you safe,**
30.23 He **kept us safe** and gave us victory over the raiders.
2 Sam 7. 1 his palace, and the Lord **kept him safe** from all his enemies.
7.10 I promise to **keep you safe** from all your enemies
22. 3 he defends me and **keeps me safe.**
22.34 he **keeps me safe** on the mountains.
2 Chr 31.12 and put all the gifts and tithes in them for **safe-keeping.**
Ps 4. 8 you alone, O Lord, **keep me perfectly safe.**
12. 7 **Keep us always safe,** O Lord, and preserve us from such people.
18. 2 he defends me and **keeps me safe.**
18.33 he **keeps me safe** on the mountains.
18.35 care has made me great, and your power has **kept me safe.**
19.13 **Keep me safe,** also, from wilful sins;
22. 9 through birth, and when I was a baby, you **kept me safe.**
27. 5 he will **keep me safe** in his Temple and make me secure
31. 4 **Keep me safe** from the trap that has been set for me;
40.11 Your love and loyalty will always **keep me safe.**
48. 8 he will **keep the city safe** for ever.
63. 8 I cling to you, and your hand **keeps me safe.**
69.14 **keep me safe** from my enemies, safe from the deep water.
91. 3 He will **keep you safe** from all hidden dangers
119.73 You created me, and you **keep me safe;**
121. 7 he will **keep you safe.**
138. 7 When I am surrounded by troubles, you **keep me safe.**
140. 1 **keep me safe** from violent men.
140. 4 **keep me safe** from violent men who plot my downfall.
Prov 3.26 The Lord will **keep you safe.**
4. 6 love her, and she will **keep you safe.**
22.12 to it that truth is **kept safe** by disproving the words of
Ecc 7.12 Wisdom **keeps you safe**—this is the advantage of knowledge.
Is 28.15 because you depend on lies and deceit to **keep you safe.**
Jer 15.20 I will be with you to protect you and **keep you safe.**
39.18 I will **keep you safe,** and you will not be put to
Hab 3.19 sure-footed as a deer, and **keeps me safe** on the mountains.
Mt 6.13 us to hard testing, but **keep us safe** from the Evil One.'
Mk 6.20 was a good and holy man, and so he **kept him safe.**
Jn 17.11 **Keep them safe** by the power of your name, the name you
17.12 was with them, I **kept them safe** by the power of your
17.15 I do ask you to **keep them safe** from the Evil One.
Rom 15.31 Pray that I may be **kept safe** from the unbelievers in
Col 1. 5 what you hope for, which is **kept safe** for you in heaven.
2 Thes 3. 3 he will strengthen you and **keep you safe** from the Evil One.
1 Tim 6.20 Timothy, **keep safe** what has been entrusted to your care.
2 Tim 1.12 that he is able to **keep safe** until that Day what he
1 Pet 1. 5 you, who through faith are **kept safe** by God's power for the
1 Jn 5.18 the Son of God **keeps him safe,** and the Evil One cannot
5.21 My children, **keep yourselves safe** from false gods!
Rev 3.10 I will also **keep you safe** from the time of trouble
3.11 **Keep safe** what you have, so that no one will rob you

KEILAH

City in Judah occupied by David when he was an outlaw.

Josh 15.44 Iphtah, Ashnah, Nezib, [44] **Keilah,** Achzib, and Mareshah:
1 Sam 23. 1 were attacking the town of **Keilah** and were stealing
23. 2 "Attack them and save **Keilah."**
23. 3 worse if we go to **Keilah** and attack the Philistine forces!"
23. 4 to him, "Go and attack **Keilah,** because I will give you
23. 5 David and his men went to **Keilah** and attacked the Philistines;
23. 6 and joined David in **Keilah,** he took the ephod with him.
23. 7 that David had gone to **Keilah,** and he said, "God has put
23. 8 war, to march against **Keilah** and besiege David and his men.
23.10 is planning to come to **Keilah** and destroy it
23.11 Will the citizens of **Keilah** hand me over to Saul?
23.12 "And will the citizens of **Keilah** hand my men and me
23.13 six hundred in all—left **Keilah** at once
23.13 that David had escaped from **Keilah,** he gave up his plan.
1 Chr 4.19 lived in the town of **Keilah,** and the clan of Maacath,
Neh 3.17 Hashabiah, ruler of half the **Keilah** District, built the next
3.18 of the other half of the **Keilah** District, built the next

KENITES

Inhabitants of Canaan, related to the Midianites, before its conquest by Israel.

Gen 15.19 including the lands of the **Kenites,** the Kenizzites,
Num 24.21 In his vision he saw the **Kenites,** and uttered this prophecy:
24.22 But you **Kenites** will be destroyed When Assyria takes
Judg 1.16 descendants of Moses' father-in-law, the **Kenite,**
4.11 In the meantime Heber the **Kenite** had set up his tent
4.11 moved away from the other **Kenites,** the descendants of Hobab,
4.17 the wife of Heber the **Kenite,**
5.24 the wife of Heber the **Kenite**— the most fortunate of women
1 Sam 15. 6 sent a warning to the **Kenites,** a people whose ancestors
15. 6 So the **Kenites** left.
27.10 or to the territory where the **Kenites** lived.
30.29 clan of Jerahmeel, to the **Kenites,** [30] and to the people in
1 Chr 2.55 They were **Kenites** who had intermarried with the Rechabites.)

KEY

Judg 3.25 did not open the door, they took the **key** and opened it.
Is 22.22 He will have the **keys** of office;
Mt 16.19 I will give you the **keys** of the Kingdom of heaven;
Lk 11.52 You have kept the **key** that opens the door to the house
Col 2. 3 He is the **key** that opens all the hidden treasures of God's
Rev 3. 7 He has the **key** that belonged to David, and when he opens
9. 1 to the earth, and it was given the **key** to the abyss.
20. 1 holding in his hand the **key** of the abyss and a heavy

KICK

Acts 26.14 by hitting back, like an ox **kicking** against its owner's stick.'

KID

Lev 22.26 or a lamb or a **kid** is born, it must not be
22.28 its lamb or a goat and its **kid** on the same day.
27.26 calf, a lamb, or a **kid** belongs to the Lord, [27] but the
Neh 10.36 and the first lamb or **kid** born to each of our sheep

KIDNAP

Gen 40.15 After all, I was **kidnapped** from the land of the Hebrews,
Ex 21.16 "Whoever **kidnaps** a man, either to sell him or to keep
Deut 24. 7 "Whoever **kidnaps** a fellow-Israelite and makes him his slave
1 Tim 1.10 for sexual perverts, for **kidnappers,** for those who lie and give

KIDNEYS

Ex 29.13 the liver, and the two **kidneys** with the fat on them
29.22 of the liver, the two **kidneys** with the fat on them,

Lev 3. 4 on the internal organs, [4]the **kidneys** and the fat on them,
3.10 the internal organs, [10]the **kidneys** and the fat on them,
3.15 on the internal organs, [15]the **kidneys** and the fat on them,
4. 9 on the internal organs, [9]the **kidneys** and the fat on them,
7. 4 the internal organs, [4]the **kidneys** and the fat on them,
8.16 of the liver, and the **kidneys** with the fat on them,
8.25 part of the liver, the **kidneys** with the fat on them,
9.10 the altar the fat, the **kidneys,** and the best part of the

KIDRON

Brook near Jerusalem.

2 Sam 15.23 king crossed the brook of **Kidron,** followed by his men,
1 Kgs 2.37 go beyond the brook of **Kidron,** you will certainly die—
15.13 down the idol and burnt it in the valley of the **Kidron.**
2 Kgs 23. 4 near the valley of the **Kidron,** and then had the ashes taken
23. 6 to the valley of the **Kidron,** burnt it, pounded its ashes to
23.12 altars to bits and threw them into the valley of the **Kidron.**
2 Chr 15.16 it up, and burnt the pieces in the valley of the **Kidron.**
29.16 took it all outside the city to the valley of the **Kidron.**
30.14 incense and threw them into the valley of the **Kidron.**
Neh 2.15 into the valley of the **Kidron** and rode along, looking at the
Jer 31.40 fields above the brook of **Kidron** as far as the Horse Gate
Jn 18. 1 with his disciples and went across the brook called **Kidron.**

KILL

Gen 4. 4 to one of his sheep, **killed** it, and gave the best parts
4. 8 in the fields, Cain turned on his brother and **killed** him.
4.11 it had opened its mouth to receive it when you **killed** him.
4.14 on the earth, and anyone who finds me will **kill** me."
4.15 If anyone **kills** you, seven lives will be taken in revenge."
4.15 on Cain to warn anyone who met him not to **kill** him.
4.23 I have **killed** a young man because he struck me.
4.24 taken to pay for **killing** Cain,
4.24 Seventy-seven will be taken if anyone **kills** me."
4.25 "God has given me a son to replace Abel, whom Cain **killed."**
9. 6 so whoever murders a man will himself be **killed**
12.12 my wife, and so they will **kill** me and let you live.
18.25 Surely you won't **kill** the innocent with the guilty.
19.17 Run to the hills, so that you won't be **killed."**
20.11 for God and that they would **kill** me to get my wife.
22.10 Then he picked up the knife to **kill** him.
25.28 because he enjoyed eating the animals Esau **killed,**
26. 7 that the men there would **kill** him to get Rebecca, who was
26. 9 "I thought I would be **killed** if I said she was
27. 3 arrows, go out into the country, and **kill** an animal for me.
27.33 "Who was it, then, who **killed** an animal and brought it
27.41 then I will **kill** Jacob."
27.42 brother Esau is planning to get even with you and **kill** you.
31.39 Whenever a sheep was **killed** by wild animals, I always
31.54 He **killed** an animal, which he offered as a sacrifice
34.25 city without arousing suspicion, and **killed** all the men,
37.18 they plotted against him and decided to **kill** him.
37.20 Come on now, let's **kill** him and throw his body into one
37.20 We can say that a wild animal **killed** him.
37.21 "Let's not **kill** him," he said.
37.26 "What will we gain by **killing** our brother
37.31 Then they **killed** a goat and dipped Joseph's robe in its blood.
37.33 Some wild animal has **killed** him.
38. 7 and it displeased the Lord, so the Lord **killed** him.
38.10 What he did displeased the Lord, and the Lord **killed** him
38.11 afraid that Shelah would be **killed,** as his brothers had been.
42.37 not bring Benjamin back to you, you can **kill** my two sons.
42.38 old man, and the sorrow you would cause me would **kill** me."
43.16 eat with me at noon, so **kill** an animal and prepare it."
44.29 sorrow you would cause me would **kill** me, old as I am.'
44.30 so old that the sorrow we would cause him would **kill** him.
49. 6 in their meetings, For they **killed** men in anger
49. 9 Judah is like a lion, **Killing** his victim
49.27 Morning and evening he **kills** and devours."
Ex 1.16 birth," he said to them, **"kill** the baby if it is a
2.11 He even saw an Egyptian **kill** a Hebrew, one of Moses' own
2.12 no one was watching, he **killed** the Egyptian and hid his body
2.14 Are you going to **kill** me just as you killed that Egyptian?"
2.15 he tried to have Moses **killed,** but Moses fled
4.19 to Egypt, for all those who wanted to **kill** you are dead."
4.23 Now I am going to **kill** your first-born son.' "
4.24 way to Egypt, the Lord met Moses and tried to **kill** him.
5. 3 don't do so, he will **kill** us with disease or by war."
5.21 You have given them an excuse to **kill** us."
12. 6 the whole community of Israel will **kill** the animals.
12.12 through the land of Egypt, **killing** every first-born male,
12.21 or a young goat and **kill** it, so that your families can
12.23 Lord goes through Egypt to **kill** the Egyptians, he will see
12.23 not let the Angel of Death enter your houses and **kill** you.
12.27 He **killed** the Egyptians, but spared us.' "
12.29 the Lord **killed** all the first-born sons in Egypt,
12.29 all the first-born of the animals were also **killed.**
13.15 the Lord **killed** every first-born male in the land
16. 3 "We wish that the Lord had **killed** us in Egypt.
17. 3 To **kill** us and our children and our livestock with thirst?"
18. 4 and saved me from being **killed** by the king of Egypt";
21.12 "Whoever hits a man and **kills** him is to be put to
21.13 he did not mean to **kill** the man, he can escape to
21.14 man gets angry and deliberately **kills** another man,
21.18 his fist, but does not **kill** him, he is not to be
21.31 If the bull **kills** a boy or a girl, the same rule
21.32 If the bull **kills** a male or female slave,
21.35 If one man's bull **kills** another man's bull,
22. 1 cow or a sheep and **kills** it or sells it,

Ex 22. 2 is killed, the one who **killed** him is not guilty of murder.
22.13 If it was **killed** by wild animals, the man is to bring
22.13 he need not pay for what has been **killed** by wild animals.
22.24 for help, [24]and I will be angry and **kill** you in war.
22.31 the meat of any animal that has been **killed** by wild animals;
28.35 of the bells will be heard, and he will not be **killed.**
28.43 so that they will not be **killed** for exposing themselves.
29.11 **Kill** the bull there in my holy presence at the entrance
29.16 **Kill** it, and take its blood and throw it against all
29.20 **Kill** it, and take some of its blood and put it on
30.20 Then they will not be **killed.**
32.12 out of Egypt, planning to **kill** them in the mountains and
32.27 gate to the other and **kill** his brothers, his friends, and
32.28 The Levites obeyed, and **killed** about three thousand men
32.29 service of the Lord by **killing** your sons and brothers,
34.25 any part of the animal **killed** at the Passover Festival.
Lev 1. 5 He shall **kill** the bull there, and the Aaronite priests shall
1.11 He shall **kill** it on the north side of the altar, and
3. 2 head of the animal and **kill** it at the entrance of the
3. 8 hand on its head and **kill** it in front of the Tent.
3.13 hand on its head and **kill** it in front of the Tent.
4. 4 hand on its head, and **kill** it there in the Lord's presence.
4.10 the fat from the animal **killed** for the fellowship-offering.
4.15 put their hands on its head, and it shall be **killed** there.
4.24 hand on its head and **kill** it on the north side of
4.24 the altar, where the animals for the burnt-offerings are **killed.**
4.26 the fat of the animals **killed** for the fellowship-offerings.
4.29 hand on its head and **kill** it on the north side of
4.29 altar, where the animals for the burnt-offerings are **killed.**
4.31 removed from the animals **killed** for the fellowship-offerings,
4.33 hand on its head and **kill** it on the north side of
4.33 the altar, where the animals for the burnt-offerings are **killed.**
4.35 removed from the sheep **killed** for the fellowship-offerings,
6.25 for a sin-offering shall be **killed** on the north side
6.25 altar, where the animals for the burnt offerings are **killed.**
7. 2 this offering is to be **killed** on the north side
7. 2 animals for the burnt-offerings are **killed,**
7.24 natural death or has been **killed** by a wild animal must not
8.15 Moses **killed** it and took some of the blood,
8.19 Moses **killed** it and threw the blood on all four sides
8.23 Moses **killed** it and took some of the blood and put it
9. 8 went to the altar and **killed** the young bull
9.12 He **killed** the animal which was for his own burnt-offering.
9.15 offered for the people's sins, **killed** it, and offered it,
9.18 He **killed** the bull and the ram as a fellowship-offering
14. 5 of the birds to be **killed** over a clay bowl containing fresh
14. 6 and the hyssop, in the blood of the bird that was **killed.**
14.13 He shall **kill** the lamb in the place where the animals
14.13 animals for the sin-offerings and the burnt-offerings are **killed.**
14.19 After that, he shall **kill** the animal for the burnt-offering
14.25 He shall **kill** the lamb and take some of the blood and
14.50 He shall **kill** one of the birds over a clay bowl
14.51 blood of the bird that was **killed** and in the fresh water.
15.31 If they did, they would be **killed.**
16. 1 sons of Aaron who were **killed** when they offered unholy fire
16. 2 If he disobeys, he will be **killed.**
16.15 After that, he shall **kill** the goat for the sin-offering
17. 3 An Israelite who **kills** a cow or a sheep or a goat
17. 5 Lord the animals which they used to **kill** in the open country.
17. 5 the entrance of the Tent and **kill** them as fellowship-offerings.
17. 7 unfaithful to the Lord by **killing** their animals in the fields
17.15 natural death or has been **killed** by wild animals must wash
19. 5 "When you **kill** an animal for a fellowship-offering,
19. 6 on the day the animal is **killed** or on the next day.
22. 8 has died a natural death or has been **killed** by wild animals;
24.18 anyone who **kills** an animal belonging to someone else
24.21 Whoever **kills** an animal shall replace it, but whoever kills
26.22 and they will **kill** your children, destroy your livestock,
Num 3. 4 but Nadab and Abihu were **killed** when they offered unholy fire
3.12 When I **killed** all the first-born of the Egyptians,
4.19 the clan of Kohath [19]be **killed** by coming near
8.17 When I **killed** all the first-born in Egypt,
11.15 take pity on me and **kill** me, so that I won't have
11.22 Could enough cattle and sheep be **killed** to satisfy them?
14. 3 We will be **killed** in battle, and our wives and children will
14.15 Now if you **kill** all your people, the nations who have
14.16 will say [16]that you **killed** your people in the wilderness
16.13 the fertile land of Egypt to **kill** us here in the wilderness?
16.41 Aaron and said, "You have **killed** some of the Lord's people."
19. 3 is to be taken outside the camp and **killed** in his presence.
19.16 a person who has been **killed** or has died a natural death
21.24 But the Israelites **killed** many of the enemy in battle
21.35 So the Israelites **killed** Og, his sons, and all his people,
22.29 If I had a sword, I would **kill** you."
22.33 If it hadn't, I would have **killed** you and spared the donkey."
23.24 Until it has drunk the blood of those it has **killed."**
25. 5 "Each of you is to **kill** every man in your tribe who
25. 9 but it had already **killed** twenty-four thousand people.
25.14 Israelite who was **killed** with the Midianite woman was Zimri
25.18 because of Cozbi, who was **killed** at the time of the epidemic
26.11 But the sons of Korah were not **killed.)**
31. 7 Lord had commanded Moses, and **killed** all the men,
31. 8 They also **killed** Balaam son of Beor.
31.17 now kill every boy and **kill** every woman who has had sexual
31.19 all of you who have **killed** anyone or have touched a corpse
33. 4 were burying the first-born sons that the Lord had **killed.**
35. 6 to which a man can escape if he **kills** someone accidentally.
35.11 to which a man can escape if he **kills** someone accidentally.
35.15 Anyone who **kills** someone accidentally can escape to one of them.
35.16 or stone or wood to **kill** someone, he is guilty of murder
35.19 When he finds him, he is to **kill** him.

Num	35.20	a man hates someone and **kills** him by pushing him down
	35.21	When he finds him, he is to **kill** him.
	35.22	"But suppose a man accidentally **kills** someone
	35.23	man throws a stone that **kills** someone whom he did not intend
	35.27	man's relative finds him and **kills** him, this act of revenge
Deut	1.27	hand us over to these Amorites, so that they could **kill** us.
	2.33	in our power, and we **killed** him, his sons, and all his
	4.42	safe if he had accidentally **killed** someone who had not been
	7.24	You will **kill** them, and they will be forgotten.
	9.20	angry enough with Aaron to **kill** him, so I prayed for Aaron
	9.28	out into the desert to **kill** them, because you hated them.
	12.15	"But you are free to **kill** and eat your animals
	12.21	whenever you wish, you may **kill** any of the cattle or sheep
	13. 9	**Kill** him!
	13.15	then **kill** all the people in that town
	16. 4	the meat of the animal **killed** on the evening of the first
	19. 2	Then a man who **kills** someone will be able to escape
	19. 4	If a man accidentally **kills** someone who is not his enemy,
	19. 5	comes off the handle and **kills** the other, he can run to
	19. 6	for taking revenge for the **killing** might catch him
	19. 6	and in his anger **kill** an innocent man.
	19. 6	was by accident that he **killed** a man who was not his
	20. 5	if he is **killed** in battle, someone else will dedicate his
	20. 6	if he is **killed** in battle, someone else will enjoy
	20. 7	if he is **killed** in battle, someone else will marry
	20.13	your God lets you capture the city, **kill** every man in it.
	20.16	the land that the Lord your God is giving you, **kill**
	20.18	**Kill** them, so that they will not make you sin against
	21. 1	going to give you, and you do not know who **killed** him.
	22. 8	will not be responsible if someone falls off and is **killed.**
	25.18	tired and exhausted, and **killed** all who were straggling behind.
	25.19	around you, be sure to **kill** all the Amalekites, so that no
	32.39	I **kill** and I give life, I wound and I heal, and
	32.42	with their blood, and my sword will **kill** all who oppose me.
	32.43	praise the Lord's people— he punishes all who **kill** them.
Josh	2.10	have also heard how you **killed** Sihon and Og, the two Amorite
	2.13	Don't let us be **killed!"**
	6.21	With their swords they **killed** everyone in the city,
	6.21	They also **killed** the cattle, sheep, and donkeys.
	7. 5	far as some quarries and **killed** about thirty-six of them on
	7. 9	They will surround us and **kill** every one of us!
	8.21	they turned round and began **killing** the men of Ai.
	8.22	completely surrounded by Israelites, and they were all **killed.**
	8.24	The Israelites **killed** every one of the enemy
	8.24	Then they went back to Ai and **killed** everyone there.
	8.25	not put it down until every person there had been **killed.**
	8.25	whole population of Ai was **killed** that day—
	9.18	But the Israelites could not **kill** them,
	9.24	the whole land and to **kill** the people living in it as
	9.26	them and did not allow the people of Israel to **kill** them.
	10. 1	totally destroyed Ai and had **killed** its king, just as he had
	10.11	More were **killed** by the hailstones than by the Israelites.
	10.20	find safety inside their city walls and were not **killed.**
	10.26	Joshua **killed** the kings and hanged them on five trees,
	10.30	They spared no one, but **killed** every person in it.
	10.32	they spared no one, but **killed** every person in the city.
	10.37	They **killed** the king and everyone else in the city as well
	11. 6	time tomorrow I will have **killed** all of them for Israel.
	11.10	Joshua then turned back, captured Hazor and **killed** its king.
	11.20	condemned to total destruction and all be **killed** without mercy.
	13.22	the people of Israel **killed** was the fortune-teller Balaam
	19.47	They captured it, **killed** its people, and claimed it
	20. 3	A person who **kills** someone accidentally can go there
	20. 5	must protect him because he **killed** the person accidentally
	20. 9	Anyone who **killed** a person accidentally could find protection
	20. 9	he could not be **killed** unless he had first received a public
Judg	1. 8	They **killed** its people and set fire to the city.
	1.25	people of Ephraim and Manasseh **killed** everyone in the city,
	3.29	they **killed** about ten thousand of the best Moabite soldiers;
	3.31	did so by **killing** six hundred Philistines with an ox-goad.
	4.16	and Sisera's whole army was **killed.**
	4.21	up to him quietly, and **killed** him by driving the peg
	6.30	Joash, "Bring your son out here, so that we can **kill** him!
	6.31	Anyone who stands up for him will be **killed** before morning.
	7.25	they **killed** Oreb at Oreb Rock, and Zeeb at the Winepress of
	8. 3	the power of God you **killed** the two Midianite chiefs,
	8.10	120,000 soldiers had been **killed.**
	8.17	down the tower at Penuel and **killed** the men of that city.
	8.18	Zebah and Zalmunna, "What about the men you **killed** at Tabor?"
	8.19	that if you had not **killed** them, I would not kill you."
	8.20	he said to Jether, his eldest son, "Go ahead, **kill** them!"
	8.21	Zebah and Zalmunna said to Gideon, "Come on, **kill** us yourself.
	8.21	So Gideon **killed** them and took the ornaments that were on
	9. 5	a single stone he **killed** his seventy brothers, Gideon's sons.
	9. 5	But Jotham, Gideon's youngest son, hid and was not **killed.**
	9.18	You **killed** his sons—seventy men on a single stone—and just
	9.43	out of the city, he came out of hiding to **kill** them.
	9.44	attacked the people in the fields and **killed** them all.
	9.45	Abimelech captured the city, **killed** its people, tore it down,
	9.54	ordered, "Draw your sword and **kill** me.
	9.54	I don't want it said that a woman **killed** me."
	9.56	committed against his father in **killing** his seventy brothers.
	12. 6	they would seize him and **kill** him there
	12. 6	At that time forty-two thousand of the Ephraimites were **killed.**
	13.23	the Lord had wanted to **kill** us, he would not have accepted
	14. 8	at the lion he had **killed,** and he was surprised to find
	14.19	to Ashkelon, where he **killed** thirty men, stripped them,
	15. 8	He attacked them fiercely and **killed** many of them.
	15.12	Samson said, "Give me your word that you won't **kill** me
	15.13	We won't **kill** you."
	15.15	down and picked it up, and **killed** a thousand men with it.
Judg	15.16	"With the jaw-bone of a donkey I **killed** a thousand men;
	16. 2	"We'll wait until daybreak, and then we'll **kill** him."
	16.24	enemy, who devastated our land and **killed** so many of us!"
	16.30	Samson **killed** more people at his death
	16.30	than he had **killed** during his life.
	18.27	They **killed** the inhabitants and burnt the town.
	20. 5	They intended to **kill** me;
	20.13	Gibeah, so that we can **kill** them and remove this evil
	20.21	they had **killed** twenty-two thousand Israelite soldiers.
	20.25	they **killed** eighteen thousand trained Israelite soldiers.
	20.31	they began **killing** some Israelites in the open country
	20.31	They **killed** about thirty Israelites.
	20.35	The Israelites **killed** 25,100 of the enemy that day,
	20.37	they spread out in the city and **killed** everyone there.
	20.39	the Benjaminites had already **killed** the thirty Israelites.
	20.43	far as a point east of Gibeah, **killing** them as they went.
	20.44	Eighteen thousand of the best Benjaminite soldiers were **killed.**
	20.45	Five thousand of them were **killed** along the road.
	20.45	The Israelites continued to pursue the rest to Gidom, **killing** two thousand.
	20.46	twenty-five thousand Benjaminites were **killed** that day—
	20.48	Benjaminites and **killed** them all—men, women, and children,
	21.10	"Go and **kill** everyone in Jabesh, including the women
	21.11	**Kill** all the males, and also every woman who is not a
	21.14	Israelites gave them the girls from Jabesh whom they had not **killed.**
1 Sam	1.25	After they had **killed** the bull, they took the child to Eli.
	2. 6	The Lord **kills** and restores to life;
	2.25	to their father, for the Lord had decided to **kill** them.
	2.31	is coming when I will **kill** all the young men in your
	4. 2	they defeated the Israelites and **killed** about four thousand
	4.10	thirty thousand Israelite soldiers were **killed.**
	4.11	and Eli's sons, Hophni and Phinehas, were both **killed.**
	4.17	Hophni and Phinehas were **killed,**
	5.10	of the God of Israel here, in order to **kill** us all!"
	5.11	its own place, so that it won't **kill** us and our families."
	6.14	up the wooden wagon and **killed** the cows and offered them
	6.19	The Lord **killed** seventy of the men of Beth Shemesh
	7. 9	Samuel **killed** a young lamb and burnt it whole as a
	7.11	**killing** them along the way.
	11.12	Hand them over to us, and we will **kill** them!"
	13. 3	Jonathan **killed** the Philistine commander in Geba,
	13. 4	were told that Saul had **killed** the Philistine commander
	14.13	knocked them down, and the young man **killed** them.
	14.14	Jonathan and the young man **killed** about twenty men
	14.30	Just think how many more Philistines they would have **killed!"**
	14.36	plunder them until dawn, and **kill** them all."
	15. 3	**kill** all the men, women, children, and babies;
	15. 6	the Amalekites, so that I won't **kill** you along with them."
	15. 8	captured King Agag of Amalek alive and **killed** all the people.
	15. 9	Agag's life and did not **kill** the best sheep and cattle,
	15.18	He told you to fight until you had **killed** them all.
	15.20	brought back King Agag, and **killed** all the Amalekites.
	15.21	But my men did not **kill** the best sheep and cattle that
	16. 2	"If Saul hears about it, he will **kill** me!"
	17. 9	If he wins and **kills** me, we will be your slaves;
	17. 9	but if I win and **kill** him, you will be our slaves.
	17.25	promised to give a big reward to the man who **kills** him;
	17.26	will the man get who **kills** this Philistine and frees Israel
	17.27	told him what would be done for the man who **killed** Goliath.
	17.36	I have **killed** lions and bears, and I will do the same
	17.50	David defeated and **killed** Goliath with a catapult
	17.51	out of its sheath, and cut off his head and **killed** him.
	17.57	David returned to camp after **killing** Goliath,
	18. 6	As David was returning after **killing** Goliath
	18. 7	"Saul has **killed** thousands, but David tens of thousands."
	18.17	this way the Philistines would **kill** David,
	18.21	her to trap him, and he will be **killed** by the Philistines."
	18.25	(This was how Saul planned to have David **killed** by the Philistines.)
	18.27	David and his men went and **killed** two hundred Philistines.
	19. 1	Jonathan and all his officials that he planned to **kill** David.
	19. 2	so he said to him, "My father is trying to **kill** you.
	19. 5	risked his life when he **killed** Goliath,
	19. 5	to an innocent man and **kill** David for no reason at all?"
	19. 6	a vow in the Lord's name that he would not **kill** David.
	19.11	men to watch David's house and **kill** him the next morning.
	19.15	them, "Carry him here in his bed, and I will **kill** him."
	19.17	answered, "He said he would **kill** me if I didn't help him
	20. 1	I done to your father to make him want to **kill** me?"
	20. 8	But if I'm guilty, **kill** me yourself!
	20. 8	Why take me to your father to be **killed?"**
	20.33	his spear at Jonathan to **kill** him,
	20.33	Jonathan realized that his father was really determined to **kill** David.
	21. 9	Goliath the Philistine, whom you **killed** in the Valley of Elah;
	21.11	as they danced, 'Saul has **killed** thousands,
	21.11	but David has **killed** tens of thousands.'
	22. 8	looking for a chance to **kill** me,
	22.13	turned against me and is waiting for a chance to **kill** me!"
	22.17	said to the guards standing near him, **"Kill** the Lord's priests!
	22.17	guards refused to lift a hand to **kill** the Lord's priests.
	22.18	So Saul said to Doeg, "You **kill** them!"—
	22.18	and Doeg **killed** them all.
	22.18	On that day he **killed** eighty-five priests
	22.19	babies, cattle, donkeys, and sheep—they were all **killed.**
	22.23	Saul wants to **kill** both you and me, but you will be
	23. 5	they **killed** many of them and took their livestock.
	23.15	David saw that Saul was out to **kill** him.
	24.10	my men told me to **kill** you, but I felt sorry for
	24.11	I could have **killed** you, but instead I only cut this off.

1 Sam	24.11	are hunting me down to **kill** me, even though I have not
	24.14	Look at what the king of Israel is trying to **kill!**
	24.18	me, because you did not **kill** me, even though the Lord put
	25.22	me dead if I don't **kill** every last one of those men
	25.26	Lord who has kept you from taking revenge and **killing** your enemies.
	25.29	attack you and try to **kill** you, the Lord your God will
	25.31	or remorse, sir, for having **killed** without cause
	26.10	that the Lord himself will **kill** Saul,
	26.15	Just now someone entered the camp to **kill** your master.
	26.20	Don't let me be **killed** on foreign soil, away from the Lord.
	26.20	should the king of Israel come to **kill** a flea like me?
	27. 1	David said to himself, "One of these days Saul will **kill** me.
	27. 9	to Egypt, [9]**killing** all the men and women
	27.11	David would **kill** everyone, men and women,
	28. 9	Why, then, are you trying to trap me and get me **killed?"**
	28.24	The woman quickly **killed** a calf which she had been fattening.
	29. 5	as they danced, 'Saul has **killed** thousands,
	29. 5	but David has **killed** tens of thousands.' "
	30. 2	they had not **killed** anyone, but had taken everyone with them
	30.15	that you will not **kill** me or hand me over
	31. 1	Many Israelites were **killed** there, and the rest of them,
	31. 2	caught up with them and **killed** three of Saul's sons,
	31. 4	"Draw your sword and **kill** me,
	31. 4	these godless Philistines won't gloat over me and **kill** me."
	31. 7	and his sons had been **killed,** they abandoned their towns
2 Sam	1. 4	the battle," he replied, "and many of our men were **killed.**
	1. 4	Saul and his son Jonathan were also **killed."**
	1. 9	Then he said, 'Come here and **kill** me!
	1.10	went up to him and **killed** him, because I knew that he
	1.12	of the Lord, because so many had been **killed** in battle.
	1.14	"How is it that you dared to **kill** the Lord's chosen king?"
	1.15	Then David called one of his men and said, **"Kill** him!"
	1.16	when you admitted that you **killed** the one whom the Lord
	1.22	Saul was merciless, striking down the mighty, **killing** the enemy.
	1.25	"The brave soldiers have fallen, they were **killed** in battle.
	2.22	Why force me to **kill** you?
	2.31	David's men had **killed** 360 of Abner's men
	3.27	Abner was murdered because he had **killed** Joab's brother Asahel.
	3.29	a woman's work or is **killed** in battle or hasn't enough
	3.30	took revenge on Abner for **killing** their brother Asahel
	3.34	He died like someone **killed** by criminals!"
	4. 1	heard that Abner had been **killed** in Hebron, he was afraid,
	4. 4	who was five years old when Saul and Jonathan were **killed.**
	4. 7	Ishbosheth's bedroom, where he was sound asleep, and **killed** him.
	4. 8	the son of your enemy Saul, who tried to **kill** you.
	4.12	and his soldiers **killed** Rechab and Baanah
	5. 8	Enough to **kill** them?
	6. 7	God became angry with Uzzah and **killed** him
	8. 5	David attacked it and **killed** twenty-two thousand men.
	8.13	when he returned from **killing** eighteen thousand Edomites
	10.18	David and his men **killed** seven hundred Syrian chariot drivers
	11.15	the fighting is heaviest, then retreat and let him be **killed."**
	11.17	some of David's officers were **killed,** and so was Uriah.
	11.21	Don't you remember how Abimelech son of Gideon was **killed?**
	11.21	a woman threw a millstone down from the wall and **killed** him.
	11.21	tell him, 'Your officer Uriah was also **killed.' "**
	11.24	from the wall, and some of Your Majesty's officers were **killed;**
	11.24	your officer Uriah was also **killed."**
	11.26	Bathsheba heard that her husband had been **killed,**
	12. 4	rich man didn't want to **kill** one of his own animals to
	12. 9	You had Uriah **killed** in battle;
	12. 9	you let the Ammonites **kill** him, and then you took his wife!
	13.28	much to drink, and then when I give the order, **kill** him.
	13.29	the servants followed Absalom's instructions and **killed** Amnon.
	13.30	"Absalom has **killed** all your sons—not one of them is left!"
	13.32	"Your Majesty, they haven't **killed** all your sons.
	13.33	only Amnon was **killed."**
	14. 6	no one to separate them, and one of them **killed** the other.
	14. 7	them, so that they can **kill** him for murdering his brother.
	14.11	will not commit a greater crime by **killing** my other son."
	14.16	one who is trying to **kill** my son and me and so
	15.14	soon be here and defeat us and **kill** everyone in the city!"
	16.11	to all his officials, "My own son is trying to **kill** me;
	17. 2	I will **kill** only the king [3]and then bring back all his
	17. 3	You want to **kill** only one man;
	17.16	so that he and his men won't all be caught and **killed."**
	18. 3	us turn and run, or even if half of us are **killed;**
	18. 7	it was a terrible defeat, with twenty thousand men **killed**
	18. 8	and more men died in the forest than were **killed** in battle.
	18.11	"If you saw him, why didn't you **kill** him on the spot?
	18.13	had disobeyed the king and **killed** Absalom,
	18.15	Joab's soldiers closed in on Absalom and finished **killing** him.
	19.10	Absalom as our king, but he has been **killed** in battle.
	21. 4	silver or gold, nor do we want to **kill** any Israelite."
	21.12	the bodies on the day they **killed** Saul on Mount Gilboa.)
	21.16	who was wearing a new sword, thought he could **kill** David.
	21.17	came to David's help, attacked the giant, and **killed** him.
	21.18	Sibbecai from Hushah **killed** a giant named Saph.
	21.19	son of Jair from Bethlehem **killed** Goliath from Gath,
	21.21	Jonathan, the son of David's brother Shammah, **killed** him.
	21.22	giants of Gath, and they were **killed** by David and his men.
	23. 8	against eight hundred men and **killed** them all in one battle.
	23.12	defended it, and **killed** the Philistines.
	23.18	against three hundred men and **killed** them, and became famous
	23.20	brave deeds, including **killing** two great Moabite warriors.
	23.20	down into a pit on a snowy day and **killed** a lion.
	23.21	He also **killed** an Egyptian, a huge man who was armed
	23.21	snatched the spear from the Egyptian's hand, and **killed** him
	24.16	said to the angel who was **killing** them, "Stop!
	24.17	saw the angel who was **killing** the people,
1 Kgs	2. 5	Joab did to me by **killing** the two commanders of Israel's armies,
	2. 5	He **killed** innocent men and now I bear the responsibility
	2. 8	the name of the Lord that I would not have him **killed.**
	2.25	Solomon gave orders to Benaiah, who went out and **killed** Adonijah.
	2.29	So King Solomon sent Benaiah to **kill** Joab.
	2.31	**"Kill** him and bury him.
	2.31	responsible for what Joab did when he **killed** innocent men.
	2.32	Joab **killed** two innocent men who were better men than he:
	2.34	of the Lord's presence and **killed** Joab, and he was buried
	2.46	king gave orders to Benaiah, who went out and **killed** Shimei.
	3.26	"Please, Your Majesty, don't **kill** the child!
	3.27	Then Solomon said, "Don't **kill** the child!
	9.16	attacked Gezer and captured it, **killing** its inhabitants
	9.20	whom the Israelites had not **killed** when they took possession
	11.15	and during that time they **killed** every male in Edom
	11.40	And so Solomon tried to **kill** Jeroboam,
	12.26	allegiance to King Rehoboam of Judah and will **kill** me."
	13.22	of this you will be **killed,** and your body will not be
	13.24	On the way, a lion met him and **killed** him.
	13.26	the lion to attack and **kill** him, just as the Lord said
	14.10	on your dynasty and will **kill** all your male descendants,
	15.27	plotted against Nadab and **killed** him
	15.29	he began **killing** all the members of Jeroboam's family.
	15.29	all Jeroboam's family were **killed;**
	16. 7	but also because he **killed** all Jeroboam's family.
	16.11	as Zimri became king he **killed** off all the members of
	16.12	Zimri **killed** all the family of Baasha.
	17.20	enough to take care of me, and now you **kill** her son!"
	18. 4	and when Jezebel was **killing** the Lord's prophets,
	18. 5	Maybe we won't have to **kill** any of our animals."
	18. 9	want to put me in danger of being **killed** by King Ahab?
	18.13	heard that when Jezebel was **killing** the prophets of the Lord
	18.14	He will **kill** me!"
	18.23	prophets of Baal take one, **kill** it, cut it in pieces,
	18.40	Elijah led them down to the River Kishon and **killed** them.
	19.10	torn down your altars, and **killed** all your prophets.
	19.10	am the only one left—and they are trying to **kill** me!"
	19.14	torn down your altars, and **killed** all your prophets.
	19.14	am the only one left—and they are trying to **kill** me."
	19.17	death by Hazael will be **killed** by Jehu,
	19.17	and anyone who escapes Jehu will be **killed** by Elisha.
	19.21	to his team of oxen, **killed** them, and cooked the meat, using
	20.20	and each one **killed** the man he fought.
	20.29	and the Israelites **killed** a hundred thousand Syrians.
	20.36	Lord's command, a lion will **kill** you as soon as you leave
	20.36	as soon as he left, a lion came along and **killed** him.
	20.42	I had ordered to be **killed,** you will pay for it with
	22.20	deceive Ahab so that he will go and be **killed** at Ramoth?'
2 Kgs	1.10	"may fire come down from heaven and **kill** you and your men!"
	1.10	At once fire came down and **killed** the officer and his men.
	1.12	"may fire come down from heaven and **kill** you and your men!"
	1.12	fire of God came down and **killed** the officer and his men.
	1.14	officers and their men were **killed** by fire from heaven;
	3.23	"The three enemy armies must have fought and **killed** each other!
	6.21	saw the Syrians, he asked Elisha, "Shall I **kill** them, sir?
	6.21	Shall I **kill** them?"
	6.32	"That murderer is sending someone to **kill** me!
	7. 4	worst they can do is **kill** us, but maybe they will spare
	9. 7	You are to **kill** your master the king, that son of Ahab,
	9.27	**"Kill** him too!"
	10. 7	the leaders of Samaria **killed** all seventy of Ahab's descendants,
	10. 9	"I was the one who plotted against King Joram and **killed** him;
	10. 9	But who **killed** all these?
	10.17	Jehu **killed** all of Ahab's relatives,
	10.19	Jehu by which he meant to **kill** all the worshippers of Baal.)
	10.24	"You are to **kill** all these people;
	10.25	said to the guards and officers, "Go in and **kill** them all;
	10.25	with drawn swords, **killed** them all, and dragged the bodies
	11. 1	orders for all the members of the royal family to be **killed.**
	11. 2	He was about to be **killed** with the others, but was rescued
	11. 2	Temple and hid him from Athaliah, so that he was not **killed.**
	11. 8	Anyone who comes near you is to be **killed."**
	11.15	Jehoiada did not want Athaliah **killed** in the temple area,
	11.15	rows of guards, and **kill** anyone who tries to rescue her."
	11.16	to the palace, and there at the Horse Gate they **killed** her.
	11.18	altars and the idols, and **killed** Mattan, the priest of Baal,
	11.20	now that Athaliah had been **killed** in the palace.
	12.20	and Jehozabad son of Shomer, **killed** him at the house
	14. 5	he executed the officials who had **killed** his father, the king.
	14. 6	However, he did not **kill** their children
	14. 7	Amaziah **killed** ten thousand Edomite soldiers in Salt Valley;
	14.19	Lachish, but his enemies followed him there and **killed** him.
	16. 9	army against Damascus, captured it, **killed** King Rezin,
	17.25	the Lord, and so he sent lions, which **killed** some of them.
	17.26	and so the god had sent lions, which were **killing** them.
	19. 7	his own country, and the Lord will have him **killed** there."
	19.12	Gozan, Haran, and Rezeph, and **killed** the people of Betheden
	19.35	went to the Assyrian camp and **killed** 185,000 soldiers.
	19.37	sons, Adrammelech and Sharezer, **killed** him with their swords,
	21.16	Manasseh **killed** so many innocent people
	21.24	The people of Judah **killed** Amon's assassins
	23.20	He **killed** all the pagan priests on the altars
	23.29	stop the Egyptian army at Megiddo and was **killed** in battle.
	24. 4	especially because of all the innocent people he had **killed.**
	25.25	went to Mizpah with ten men, attacked Gedaliah and **killed** him.
	25.25	He also **killed** the Israelites and Babylonians who were there
1 Chr	2. 3	His eldest son, Er, was so evil that the Lord **killed** him.
	4.43	There they **killed** the surviving Amalekites,
	5.10	of Reuben attacked the Hagrites, **killed** them in battle,
	5.22	**killed** many of the enemy, because the war was God's will.

1 Chr 7.21 Ezer and Elead, who were **killed** when they tried to steal
10. 1 Many Israelites were **killed** there,
10. 2 caught up with them and **killed** three of Saul's sons,
10. 4 "Draw your sword and **kill** me, to keep these godless
10.14 So the Lord **killed** him and gave control of the kingdom
11. 6 said, "The first man to **kill** a Jebusite will be commander
11.11 against three hundred men and **killed** them all in one battle.
11.20 against three hundred men and **killed** them, and became famous
11.22 brave deeds, including **killing** two great Moabite warriors.
11.22 down into a pit on a snowy day and **killed** a lion.
11.23 He also **killed** an Egyptian, a huge man
11.23 snatched the spear from the Egyptian's hand, and **killed** him
12.40 They also brought cattle and sheep to **kill** and eat.
13.10 Lord became angry with Uzzah and **killed** him
18. 5 David attacked it and **killed** twenty-two thousand men.
18.12 Edomites in the Valley of Salt and **killed** eighteen thousand
19.18 David and his men **killed** seven thousand Syrian chariot drivers
19.18 They also **killed** the Syrian commander, Shobach.
20. 4 Sibbecai from Hushah **killed** a giant named Sippai,
20. 5 Elhanan son of Jair **killed** Lahmi, the brother of Goliath
20. 7 Jonathan, the son of David's brother Shammah, **killed** him.
20. 8 These three, who were **killed** by David and his men,
22. 8 told me that I had **killed** too many people
29.21 The following day they **killed** animals as sacrifices,
2 Chr 1. 6 he had a thousand animals **killed** and burnt whole on it.
8. 7 whom the Israelites had not **killed** when they took possession
13.17 half a million of Israel's best soldiers were **killed.**
14.13 many of the Sudanese were **killed**
18.19 deceive Ahab so that he will go and get **killed** at Ramoth?'
21. 4 he had all his brothers **killed,** and also some Israelite officials.
22. 1 **killed** all King Jehoram's sons except Ahaziah,
22. 8 Jehu **killed** them all.
22.10 all the members of the royal family of Judah to be **killed.**
23. 7 Anyone who tries to enter the Temple is to be **killed."**
23.14 Jehoiada did not want Athaliah **killed** in the temple area,
23.14 rows of guards, and **kill** anyone who tries to rescue her."
23.15 to the palace, and there at the Horse Gate they **killed** her.
23.17 altars and idols there and **killed** Mattan, the priest of Baal,
23.21 and the city was quiet, now that Athaliah had been **killed.**
24.22 and he had Zechariah **killed.**
24.23 army attacked Judah and Jerusalem, **killed** all the leaders,
24.25 officials plotted against him and **killed** him in his bed
25.11 There they fought and **killed** ten thousand Edomite soldiers
25.12 them off, so that they were **killed** on the rocks below.
25.13 between Samaria and Beth Horon, **killed** three thousand men,
25.16 Stop talking, or I'll have you **killed!"**
25.27 Lachish, but his enemies followed him there and **killed** him.
28. 5 defeat Ahaz and **kill** 120,000 of the bravest Judaean soldiers
28. 7 An Israelite soldier named Zichri **killed** King Ahaz' son
29. 9 Our fathers were **killed** in battle,
29.22 The priests **killed** the bulls first, then the sheep,
29.24 Then the priests **killed** the goats and poured their blood
29.34 were not enough priests to **kill** all these animals,
30.15 they **killed** the lambs for the Passover sacrifice.
30.17 they could not **kill** the Passover lambs, so the Levites
30.24 sheep for the people to **kill** and eat, and the officials gave
32.21 Lord sent an angel that **killed** the soldiers and officers
32.21 some of his sons **killed** him with their swords.
33.25 The people of Judah **killed** Amon's assassins
35. 1 of the first month they **killed** the animals for the festival.
35. 6 You are to **kill** the Passover lambs and goats.
35.11 lambs and goats had been **killed,** the Levites skinned them,
36.17 The king **killed** the young men of Judah, even in the Temple.
Ezra 6.20 The Levites **killed** the animals for the Passover sacrifices
Neh 4.11 they were already upon us, **killing** us and putting an end
6.10 lock the doors, because they are coming to **kill** you.
6.10 Any night now they will come to **kill** you."
9.26 They **killed** the prophets who warned them,
Esth 3. 6 He made plans to **kill** every Jew in the whole Persian Empire.
3.13 Jews—young and old, women and children—were to be **killed.**
4. 7 to put into the royal treasury if all the Jews were **killed.**
8. 6 disaster comes on my people, and my own relatives are **killed?"**
9. 6 In Susa, the capital city itself, the Jews **killed** five hundred men.
9.11 the number of people **killed** in Susa was reported
9.12 Susa alone the Jews have **killed** five hundred men,
9.15 got together again and **killed** three hundred more men
9.16 their enemies by **killing** seventy-five thousand people
9.17 there was no more **killing,**
Job 1.15 They **killed** every one of your servants except me.
1.16 "Lightning struck the sheep and the shepherds and **killed** them
1.17 took away the camels, and **killed** all your servants except me.
1.19 It blew the house down and **killed** them all.
2. 6 he is in your power, but you are not to **kill** him."
4.11 Like lions with nothing to **kill** and eat, they die,
6. 9 If only he would go ahead and **kill** me!
13.15 I've lost all hope, so what if God **kills** me?
15.22 a sword is waiting to **kill** him, [23] and vultures are waiting
16. 7 you have let my family be **killed.**
20.16 it **kills** him like the bite of a deadly snake.
24.14 up and goes out to **kill** the poor, and at night he
26.13 and his hand that **killed** the escaping monster.
27.14 They may have many sons, but all will be **killed** in war;
34.20 he **kills** the mighty with no effort at all.
39.29 it watches near and far for something to **kill** and eat.
Ps 7. 5 them cut me down and **kill** me and leave me lifeless on
21.10 the king will **kill** them all.
27. 2 men attack me and try to **kill** me, they stumble and fall.
31.13 They are making plans against me, plotting to **kill** me.
34.21 Evil will **kill** the wicked;
35. 4 May those who try to **kill** me be defeated and disgraced!
37.14 and bend their bows to **kill** the poor and needy, to slaughter

Ps 37.15 but they will be **killed** by their own swords,
37.32 A wicked man watches a good man and tries to **kill** him;
38.12 Those who want to **kill** me lay traps for me, and those
40.14 May those who try to **kill** me be completely defeated
44.22 account that we are being **killed** all the time,
54. 3 cruel men are trying to **kill** me— men who do not
56. 6 and watch everything I do, hoping to **kill** me.
59. 3 They are waiting to **kill** me;
59.11 Do not **kill** them, O God, or my people may forget.
63. 9 Those who are trying to **kill** me will go down into the
63.10 They will be **killed** in battle, and their bodies eaten
69. 4 they are strong and want to **kill** me.
70. 2 May those who try to **kill** me be defeated and confused.
71.10 My enemies want to **kill** me;
78.31 became angry with them and **killed** their strongest men,
78.34 Whenever he **killed** some of them, the rest would turn to him;
78.47 He **killed** their grapevines with hail and their fig-trees with frost.
78.48 He **killed** their cattle with hail and their flocks with lightning.
78.50 anger or spare their lives, but **killed** them with a plague.
78.51 He **killed** the first-born sons of all the families of Egypt.
78.62 his own people and let them be **killed** by their enemies.
78.63 Young men were **killed** in war, and young women had no one
79. 7 For they have **killed** your people;
86.14 cruel men is trying to **kill** me— people who pay no
89.10 You crushed the monster Rahab and **killed** it;
89.23 I will crush his foes and **kill** everyone who hates him.
91. 6 that strike in the dark or the evils that **kill** in daylight.
94. 6 They **kill** widows and orphans, and murder the strangers
105.29 He turned their rivers into blood and **killed** all their fish.
105.36 He **killed** the first-born sons of all the families of Egypt.
106.34 They did not **kill** the heathen, as the Lord had commanded
106.38 They **killed** those innocent children,
109.16 he persecuted and **killed** the poor, the needy,
119.87 They have almost succeeded in **killing** me,
119.95 Wicked men are waiting to **kill** me, but I will meditate
135. 8 In Egypt he **killed** all the first-born of men and animals
135.10 He destroyed many nations and **killed** powerful kings:
136.10 He **killed** the first-born sons of the Egyptians;
136.17 He **killed** powerful kings;
136.18 he **killed** famous kings;
139.19 O God, how I wish you would **kill** the wicked!
143.12 of your love for me, **kill** my enemies and destroy all my
Prov 1.11 let's find someone to **kill!**
1.16 They're always ready to **kill.**
6.16 hands that **kill** innocent people,
9. 2 She has had an animal **killed** for a feast,
10.21 but you can **kill** yourself with stupidity.
21.25 A lazy man who refuses to work is only **killing** himself;
23.13 A good spanking won't **kill** him.
Ecc 3. 3 the time for **killing** and the time for healing,
7.16 So don't be too good or too wise—why **kill** yourself?
Is 1.28 he will **kill** everyone who forsakes him.
3.25 yes, even the strongest men, will be **killed** in war.
5.29 roar like lions that have **killed** an animal and are carrying
10. 4 You will be **killed** in battle or dragged off as prisoners.
13.18 With their bows and arrows they will **kill** the young men.
14.19 by the bodies of soldiers **killed** in battle,
14.20 you ruined your country and **killed** your own people,
21.15 swords that are ready to **kill** them, from bows that are ready
22.13 You **killed** sheep and cattle to eat, and you drank wine.
26.21 the ground will no longer hide those who have been **killed.**
27. 1 wriggling, twisting dragon, and to **kill** the monster
30.25 and their people are **killed,** streams of water will flow
31. 4 can't scare away a lion from an animal that it has **killed;**
37. 7 his own country, and the Lord will have him **killed** there."
37.12 Gozan, Haran, and Rezeph, and **killed** the people of Betheden
37.36 of the Lord went to the Assyrian camp and **killed** 185,000
37.38 sons, Adrammelech and Sharezer, **killed** him with their swords
49.26 I will make your oppressors **kill** each other;
54.16 I also create the soldier, who uses the weapons to **kill.**
66. 3 same to them whether they **kill** a bull as a sacrifice or
Jer 4.30 Your lovers have rejected you and want to **kill** you.
4.31 They are coming to **kill** me!"
5. 6 That is why lions from the forest will **kill** them;
5.16 Their bowmen are mighty soldiers who **kill** without mercy.
5.17 they will **kill** your sons and your daughters.
7. 6 Stop **killing** innocent people in this land.
9. 1 could cry day and night for my people who have been **killed.**
10.25 They have **killed** your people;
11.19 lamb taken out to be **killed,** and I did not know that
11.19 let's **kill** him so that no one will remember him any more."
11.21 men of Anathoth wanted me **killed,**
11.21 told me that they would **kill** me if I kept on proclaiming
11.22 Their young men will be **killed** in war;
13.14 No pity, compassion, or mercy will stop me from **killing** them."
14.12 I will **kill** them in war and by starvation and disease."
14.15 strike this land—I will **kill** them in war and by starvation.
14.16 they have said these things will be **killed** in the same way.
14.18 into the fields, I see the bodies of men **killed** in war;
15. 3 they will be **killed** in war;
15. 7 destroyed you, my people, I **killed** your children
15. 8 I **killed** your young men in their prime
15. 9 I will let your enemies **kill** those of you who are still
15.15 not be so patient with them that they succeed in **killing** me.
16. 4 They will be **killed** in war or die of starvation,
18.21 let them be **killed** in war.
18.21 men die of disease and the young men be **killed** in battle.
18.23 But, Lord, you know all their plots to **kill** me.
19. 7 let their enemies triumph over them and **kill** them in battle.
19. 9 The enemy will surround the city and try to **kill** its people.
20. 4 you will see them all **killed** by the swords of their enemies.

Jer 20.17 because he didn't **kill** me before I was born.
21. 6 I will **kill** everyone living in this city;
21. 7 King Nebuchadnezzar and by your enemies, who want to **kill** you.
21. 9 in the city will be **killed** in war or by starvation
21. 9 Babylonians, who are now attacking the city, will not be **killed;**
22. 3 and do not **kill** innocent people in this holy place.
22.17 you **kill** the innocent and violently oppress your people.
22.25 to people you are afraid of, people who want to **kill** you.
25.33 those whom the Lord has **killed** will lie scattered from one
26. 8 seized me and shouted, "You ought to be **killed** for this!
26.15 if you **kill** me, you and the people of this city
26.15 will be guilty of **killing** an innocent man,
26.21 what Uriah had said, the king tried to have him **killed.**
26.23 King Jehoiakim, who had him **killed** and his body thrown
26.24 I was not handed over to the people and **killed.**
27.15 and you will be **killed,** you and the prophets
34. 4 You will not be **killed** in battle.
34.20 enemies, who want to **kill** them, and their corpses will be
34.21 of Judah and his officials to those who want to **kill** them.
36.29 and destroy this land and **kill** its people and its animals.
38. 2 out and surrenders to the Babylonians will not be **killed;**
38.16 or hand you over to the men who want to **kill** you."
40.15 him, "Let me go and **kill** Ishmael, and no one will know
41. 2 men with him pulled out their swords and **killed** Gedaliah.
41. 3 Ishmael also **killed** all the Israelites who were with Gedaliah
41. 7 Ishmael and his men **killed** them
41. 8 in the group who said to Ishmael, "Please don't **kill** us!
41. 9 of the men he had **killed** was the large one that King
43. 3 over us and can either **kill** us or take us away to
43.11 those doomed to be killed in war will be **killed** in war.
44.30 his enemies who want to **kill** him, just as I handed over
44.30 who was his enemy and wanted to **kill** him."
46.26 those who want to **kill** them, to King Nebuchadnezzar
48.10 Curse the man who does not slash and **kill!)**
49.26 her young men will be **killed** in the city streets,
49.35 He said, "I will **kill** all the bowmen who have made Elam
49.37 of Elam afraid of their enemies, who want to **kill** them.
50.21 **Kill** and destroy them.
50.27 **Kill** all their soldiers!
50.30 its young men will be **killed** in the city streets,
51. 6 Do not be **killed** because of Babylonia's sin.
51.22 chariots and their drivers, [22]to **kill** men and women,
51.22 slay old and young, to **kill** boys and girls,
51.47 will be put to shame, and all its people will be **killed.**

Lam 2. 4 He **killed** all those who were our joy and delight.
2.20 Priests and prophets are being **killed** in the Temple itself!
2.21 Young men and women, **killed** by enemy swords.
3.43 "You pursued us and **killed** us;
5. 3 Our fathers have been **killed** by the enemy,

Ezek 4.14 that died a natural death or was **killed** by wild animals.
5.17 hunger and wild animals to **kill** your children,
5.17 and will send sickness, violence, and war to **kill** you.
6. 4 All the people there will be **killed** in front of their idols.
6. 7 People will be **killed** everywhere, and those who survive
6.12 those near by will be **killed** in war;
9. 5 to the other men, "Follow him through the city, and **kill.**
9. 6 **Kill** the old men, young men, young women, mothers,
9. 7 So they began to **kill** the people in the city.
9. 8 While the **killing** was going on, I was there alone.
9. 8 that you are going to **kill** everyone left in Israel?"
11. 7 The corpses of those you have **killed!**
11.10 and you will be **killed** in battle in your own country.
11.13 Are you going to **kill** everyone left in Israel?"
12.14 and people will search for them to **kill** them.
13.14 It will collapse and **kill** you all.
13.19 You **kill** people who don't deserve to die, and you keep
14.13 I will send a famine and **kill** people and animals alike.
14.15 might send wild animals to **kill** the people, making the land
14.19 my anger take many lives, **killing** people and animals,
16.36 and you **killed** your children as sacrifices to idols.
17.17 earthworks and dig trenches in order to **kill** many people.
17.21 His best soldiers will be **killed** in battle,
18.10 a son who robs and **kills,** who does any of these things
20.17 I decided not to **kill** them there in the desert.
20.21 force of my anger there in the desert and **kill** them all.
21. 3 will draw my sword and **kill** all of you, good and evil
21.10 It is sharpened to **kill,** polished to flash like lightning.
21.11 sharpened and polished, to be put in the hands of a **killer.**
21.12 They are going to be **killed** with all the rest
21.14 It is a sword that **kills,** a sword that terrifies
21.15 a sword that flashes like lightning and is ready to **kill.**
21.28 It is polished to **kill,** to flash like lightning.
22.25 leaders are like lions roaring over the animals they have **killed.**
22.25 They **kill** the people, take all the money and property they
22.27 officials are like wolves tearing apart the animals they have **killed.**
23.10 her sons and daughters, and then **killed** her with a sword.
23.25 will cut off your nose and your ears and **kill** your children.
23.39 they **killed** my children as sacrifices to idols,
23.47 and attack them with swords, **kill** their children,
24.21 families who are left in Jerusalem will be **killed** in war.
25.13 that I will punish Edom and **kill** every man and animal there.
25.13 the city of Dedan, and the people will be **killed** in battle.
26. 6 with their swords they will **kill** those who live in her towns
26. 8 in the towns on the mainland will be **killed** in the fighting.
26.11 horsemen will storm through your streets, **killing** your people
28. 8 They will **kill** you and send you to a watery grave.
28. 9 When they come to **kill** you, will you still claim that you
28.23 be attacked from every side, and your people will be **killed.**
29. 8 and they will **kill** your people and your animals.
30. 4 Many in Egypt will be **killed;**
30. 5 "That war will also **kill** the soldiers hired from Sudan,
30. 6 all Egypt's defenders will be **killed** in battle.
30. 8 and all her defenders are **killed,** then they will know that I
31.18 of the dead and join the ungodly and those **killed** in battle.
32.12 cruel nations draw their swords and **kill** all your people.
32.20 of Egypt will fall with those who are **killed** in battle.
32.20 A sword is ready to **kill** them all.
32.21 'The ungodly who were **killed** in battle have come down here,
32.22 They were all **killed** in battle,
32.24 They were all **killed** in battle,
32.25 Elam lies down among those **killed** in battle,
32.25 They are all uncircumcised, all **killed** in battle.
32.25 disgraced, sharing the fate of those **killed** in battle.
32.26 They are all uncircumcised, all **killed** in battle.
32.28 Egyptians will lie crushed among the uncircumcised who were **killed**
32.29 with the uncircumcised who were **killed** in battle.
32.30 down in disgrace with those **killed** in battle
32.31 of all these who were **killed** in battle will be a comfort
32.32 all his army will be **killed** and laid to rest
33. 4 and the enemy comes and **kills** him, then he is to blame
33. 6 the enemy will come and **kill** those sinners,
33.27 the people who live in the ruined cities will be **killed.**
34. 3 made from the wool, and **kill** and eat the finest sheep.
34. 5 they were scattered, and wild animals **killed** and ate them.
34. 8 attacked by wild animals that **killed** and ate them
34.28 any more, and the wild animals will not **kill** and eat them.
35. 7 Edom a waste and **kill** everyone who travels through it.
35. 8 bodies of those who are **killed** in battle will cover the
39.18 all of whom will be **killed** like rams or lambs or goats
39.19 When I **kill** these people like sacrifices,
39.23 and let their enemies defeat them and **kill** them in battle.
40.39 on these tables that they **killed** the animals to be offered
40.41 tables on which the animals to be sacrificed were **killed:**
40.42 All the equipment used in **killing** the sacrificial animals
44.11 They may **kill** the animals which the people offer
44.31 dies a natural death or is **killed** by another animal."

Dan 1.10 look as fit as the other young men, he may **kill** me."
2.13 all of them to be **killed,** including Daniel and his friends.
2.18 that they would not be **killed** along with the other advisers
5.19 If he wanted to **kill** someone, he did;
5.30 That same night Belshazzar, the king of Babylonia, was **killed;**
6.27 He saved Daniel from being **killed** by the lions."
7.11 the fourth beast was **killed,** and its body was thrown into
9.26 God's chosen leader will be **killed** unjustly.
11. 6 and the servants who went with her will all be **killed.**
11.12 the many soldiers he has **killed,** but he will not continue
11.20 time that king will be **killed,** but not publicly
11.26 of his soldiers will be **killed,** and his army will be wiped
11.33 some of them will be **killed** in battle or be burnt
11.34 While the **killing** is going on, God's people will receive
11.35 those wise leaders will be **killed,** but as a result of this
11.41 invade the Promised Land and **kill** tens of thousands,
11.44 and he will fight furiously, **killing** many people.

Hos 9.13 Lord, I can see their children being hunted down and **killed.**
9.16 if they did, I would **kill** the children so dear to them."

Joel 3.19 attacked the land of Judah and **killed** its innocent people.
3.20 I will avenge those who were **killed;**

Amos 2. 3 I will **kill** the ruler of Moab and all the leaders of
4.10 I **killed** your young men in battle and took your horses away.
7.17 and your children will be **killed** in war.
9. 1 I will **kill** the rest of the people in war.
9.10 among my people will be **killed** in war—all those who say,

Obad 9 Teman will be terrified, and every soldier in Edom will be **killed.**
10 "Because you robbed and **killed** your brothers,

Nah 2.12 The lion **killed** his prey and tore it to pieces
2.13 Your soldiers will be **killed** in war,
3.15 you will still be burnt to death or **killed** in battle.

Hab 2.17 You **killed** its animals;

Zeph 1. 9 pagans and who steal and **kill** in order to fill their

Hag 2.22 the horses will die, and their riders will **kill** one another.

Zech 11. 5 Their owners **kill** them and go unpunished.
13. 7 **Kill** him, and the sheep will be scattered.

Mt 2.13 "Herod will be looking for the child in order to **kill** him.
2.16 He gave orders to **kill** all the boys in Bethlehem and its
2.20 Israel, because those who tried to **kill** the child are dead."
10.28 afraid of those who kill the body but cannot **kill** the soul;
12.14 Then the Pharisees left and made plans to **kill** Jesus.
14. 5 Herod wanted to **kill** him, but he was afraid of the Jewish
15.19 ideas which lead him to **kill,** commit adultery, and do other
17.23 is about to be handed over to men [23]who will **kill** him;
21.35 The tenants seized his slaves, beat one, **killed** another,
21.38 Come on, let's **kill** him, and we will get his property!'
21.39 seized him, threw him out of the vineyard, and **killed** him.
21.41 "He will certainly **kill** those evil men," they answered,
22. 6 while others grabbed the servants, beat them, and **killed** them.
22. 7 he sent his soldiers, who **killed** those murderers and burnt down
23.30 would not have done what they did and **killed** the prophets.
23.34 you will **kill** some of them, crucify others, and whip others
23.37 You **kill** the prophets and stone the messengers God has sent you!
26.31 the scripture says, 'God will **kill** the shepherd, and the sheep

Mk 3. 6 of Herod's party, and they made plans to **kill** Jesus.
6.19 against John and wanted to **kill** him, but she could not
7.21 do immoral things, to rob, **kill,** [22]commit adultery, be greedy,
9.22 evil spirit has tried to **kill** him by throwing him in the
9.31 of Man will be handed over to men who will **kill** him.
10.34 who will mock him, spit on him, whip him, and **kill** him;
11.18 so they began looking for some way to **kill** Jesus.
12. 5 The owner sent another slave, and they **killed** him;
12. 5 treated many others the same way, beating some and **killing** others.
12. 7 Come on, let's **kill** him, and his property will be ours!'

Mk 12. 8 they seized the son and **killed** him and threw his body out
12. 9 "He will come and **kill** those men and hand the vineyard over
14.12 for the Passover meal were **killed,** Jesus' disciples asked him,
14.27 scripture says, 'God will **kill** the shepherd, and the sheep will
Lk 11.49 they will **kill** some of them and persecute others.'
11.50 of all the prophets **killed** since the creation of the world,
11.51 of Zechariah, who was **killed** between the altar and the Holy
12. 4 be afraid of those who **kill** the body but cannot afterwards
12. 5 God, who, after **killing,** has the authority to throw into hell.
13. 1 the Galileans whom Pilate had **killed** while they were offering
13. 2 "Because those Galileans were **killed** in that way, do you think
13. 4 in Siloam who were **killed** when the tower fell on them?
13.31 and go somewhere else, because Herod wants to **kill** you."
13.33 for a prophet to be **killed** anywhere except in Jerusalem.
13.34 You **kill** the prophets, you stone the messengers God has sent you!
15.23 get the prize calf and **kill** it, and let us celebrate with
15.27 'and your father has **killed** the prize calf, because he got
15.30 when he comes back home, you **kill** the prize calf for him!'
17.27 went into the boat and the flood came and **killed** them all.
17.29 fire and sulphur rained down from heaven and **killed** them all.
18.33 They will whip him and **kill** him, but three days later he
19.27 their king, bring them here and **kill** them in my presence!'"
19.47 of the people wanted to **kill** him, [48]but they could not
20.14 Let's **kill** him, and his property will be ours!'
20.15 So they threw him out of the vineyard and **killed** him.
20.16 "He will come and **kill** those men, and hand the vineyard
21.24 Some will be **killed** by the sword, and others will be
22. 7 when the lambs for the Passover meal were to be **killed.**
23.18 The whole crowd cried out, **"Kill** him!
Jn 5.18 made the Jewish authorities all the more determined to **kill** him;
7. 1 because the Jewish authorities there were wanting to **kill** him.
7.19 Why are you trying to **kill** me?"
7.20 "Who is trying to **kill** you?"
7.25 said, "Isn't this the man the authorities are trying to **kill?**
8.22 Does this mean that he will **kill** himself?"
8.37 Yet you are trying to **kill** me, because you will not accept
8.40 truth I heard from God, yet you are trying to **kill** me.
10.10 The thief comes only in order to steal, **kill,** and
11.53 that day on the Jewish authorities made plans to **kill** Jesus.
12.10 chief priests made plans to **kill** Lazarus too, [11]because on his
16. 2 will come when anyone who **kills** you will think that by doing
19.15 They shouted back, **"Kill** him!
19.15 **Kill** him!
Acts 2.23 and you **killed** him by letting sinful men crucify him.
3.15 You **killed** the one who leads to life, but God raised him
5.30 from death, after you had **killed** him by nailing him to a
5.36 But he was **killed,** all his followers were scattered,
5.37 but he also was **killed,** and all his followers were scattered.
7.24 to his help and took revenge on the Egyptian by **killing** him.
7.28 'Do you want to **kill** me, just as you killed that
7.52 They **killed** God's messengers, who long ago announced the coming
9.21 who in Jerusalem was **killing** those who worship that man Jesus?
9.23 together and made plans to **kill** Saul, [24]but he was told of
9.24 and night they watched the city gates in order to **kill** him.
9.29 with the Greek-speaking Jews, but they tried to **kill** him.
10.13 **kill** and eat!"
11. 7 **kill** and eat!'
11.19 took place when Stephen was **killed** went as far as Phoenicia,
16.27 so he pulled out his sword and was about to **kill** himself.
21.31 The mob was trying to **kill** Paul, when a report was sent
21.36 They were all coming after him and screaming, **"Kill**
22.22 **Kill** him!
23.12 would not eat or drink anything until they had **killed** Paul.
23.14 vow together not to eat a thing until we have **killed** Paul.
23.15 we will be ready to **kill** him before he ever gets here."
23.21 a vow not to eat or drink until they have **killed** him.
23.27 The Jews seized this man and were about to **kill** him.
25. 3 for they had made a plot to **kill** him on the way.
26.21 while I was in the Temple, and they tried to **kill** me.
27.42 soldiers made a plan to **kill** all the prisoners, in order to
Rom 3.15 They are quick to hurt and **kill;**
7.11 by means of the commandment it deceived me and **killed** me.
11. 3 "Lord, they have **killed** your prophets and torn down your altars;
11. 3 am the only one left, and they are trying to **kill** me."
1 Cor 10. 9 test, as some of them did—and they were **killed** by snakes.
2 Cor 2.16 those who are being lost, it is a deadly stench that **kills;**
6. 9 Although punished, we are not **killed;**
Gal 2.19 however, I am dead—**killed** by the Law itself—in order
1 Thes 2.15 from the Jews, [15]who **killed** the Lord Jesus and the prophets,
2 Thes 2. 8 Lord Jesus comes, he will **kill** him with the breath from his
1 Tim 1. 9 for those who **kill** their fathers or mothers, for murderers,
Heb 11.28 Angel of Death would not **kill** the first-born sons of the Israelites.
11.31 prostitute Rahab from being **killed** with those who disobeyed God,
11.34 put out fierce fires, escaped being **killed** by the sword.
11.37 they were sawn in two, they were **killed** by the sword.
12. 4 have not yet had to resist to the point of being **killed.**
Jas 4. 2 things, but you cannot have them, so you are ready to **kill;**
2 Pet 2.12 instinct, like wild animals born to be captured and **killed;**
Rev 2.13 Antipas, my faithful witness, was **killed** there where Satan lives.
2.23 I will also **kill** her followers, and then all the churches
5. 6 The Lamb appeared to have been **killed.**
5. 9 For you were **killed,** and by your sacrificial death you
5.12 "The Lamb who was **killed** is worthy to receive power, wealth,
6. 4 bring war on the earth, so that men should **kill** each other.
6. 8 quarter of the earth, to **kill** by means of war, famine,
6. 9 those who had been **killed** because they had proclaimed God's word
6.10 judge the people on earth and punish them for **killing** us?"
6.11 fellow-servants and brothers had been **killed,** as they had been.
9. 5 locusts were not allowed to **kill** these people, but only to
Rev 9.15 they had been kept ready to **kill** a third of all mankind.
9.18 A third of mankind was **killed** by those three plagues:
9.20 those who had not been **killed** by these plagues, did not turn
11. 5 and in this way, whoever tries to harm them will be **killed.**
11. 7 He will defeat them and **kill** them, [8]and their bodies will
11.13 of the city was destroyed, and seven thousand people were **killed.**
13. 8 of the living which belongs to the Lamb that was **killed.**
13.10 whoever is meant to be **killed** by the sword
13.10 will surely be **killed** by the sword.
17. 6 blood of those who were **killed** because they had been loyal
18.24 yes, the blood of all those who have been **killed** on earth.
19. 2 God has punished her because she **killed** his servants."
19.21 Their armies were **killed** by the sword that comes out of

KILOGRAMME

Ex 25.39 Ex 29.40 Ex 30.23 Ex 30.23 Ex 30.23 Ex 30.24 Ex 37.24 Ex 38.24 Ex 38.24 Ex 38.27 Ex 38.28 Ex 38.29 Lev 5.11 Lev 6.20 Lev 14.10 Lev 14.21 Lev 23.13 Lev 23.17 Lev 24.5 Lev 27.16 Num 5.15 Num 7.12 Num 7.84 Num 7.84 Num 11.32 Num 15.4 Num 15.6 Num 15.9 Num 28.5 Num 28.9 Num 28.12 Num 28.12 Num 28.13 Num 28.20 Num 28.20 Num 28.21 Num 28.28 Num 28.28 Num 28.29 Num 29.3 Num 29.3 Num 29.4 Num 29.9 Num 29.9 Num 29.10 Num 29.14 Num 29.14 Num 29.15 Num 31.52 Josh 7.21 Josh 7.21 Judg 6.19 Judg 8.26 Ruth 2.17 Ruth 3.15 1 Sam 1.24 1 Sam 17.5 1 Sam 17.7 1 Sam 17.17 1 Sam 25.18 2 Sam 12.30 2 Sam 14.26 2 Sam 21.16 1 Kgs 9.14 1 Kgs 9.28 1 Kgs 10.10 1 Kgs 10.14 1 Kgs 10.16 1 Kgs 10.17 2 Kgs 7.1 2 Kgs 7.1 2 Kgs 7.16 2 Kgs 7.18 2 Kgs 7.18 2 Kgs 15.19 2 Kgs 18.14 2 Kgs 18.14 2 Kgs 23.33 2 Kgs 23.33 1 Chr 19.6 1 Chr 20.2 2 Chr 8.18 2 Chr 9.9 2 Chr 9.13 2 Chr 9.15 2 Chr 9.16 2 Chr 25.6 2 Chr 27.5 2 Chr 36.3 2 Chr 36.3 Ezra 2.69 Ezra 2.69 Ezra 7.22 Ezra 7.22 Ezra 8.26 Ezra 8.26 Ezra 8.26 Neh 7.70 Neh 7.70 Neh 7.70 Neh 7.70 Neh 7.70 Esth 3.9 Ezek 46.14 Hos 3.2 Hag 2.16 Jn 19.39 Rev 16.21

KILOMETRE

Num 11.31 Josh 3.4 Ezek 45.1 Ezek 45.1 Ezek 45.3 Ezek 45.3 Ezek 45.6 Ezek 45.6 Ezek 48.8 Ezek 48.9 Ezek 48.9 Ezek 48.10 Ezek 48.10 Ezek 48.13 Ezek 48.13 Ezek 48.15 Ezek 48.15 Ezek 48.18 Ezek 48.18 Ezek 48.18 Ezek 48.18 Ezek 48.20 Mt 5.41 Mt 5.41 Lk 24.13 Jn 6.19 Jn 11.18 Acts 1.12 Rev 14.20 Rev 21.16

KIND

Gen 26.29 We were **kind** to you and let you leave peacefully.
32.10 am not worth all the **kindness** and faithfulness that you have
33.11 God has been **kind** to me and given me everything I need."
40.14 for you, and please be **kind** enough to mention me to the
50.21 So he reassured them with **kind** words that touched their hearts.
Num 6.25 May the Lord be **kind** and gracious to you;
Josh 2.12 will treat my family as **kindly** as I have treated you, and
Ruth 2.10 Why should you be so **kind** to a foreigner?"
2.13 Ruth answered, "You are very **kind** to me, sir.
1 Sam 1.18 "May you always think **kindly** of me," she replied.
15. 6 people whose ancestors had been **kind** to the Israelites
23.21 answered, "May the Lord bless you for being so **kind** to me!
25. 8 on a feast day, and David asks you to receive us **kindly.**
2 Sam 2. 6 And now may the Lord be **kind** and faithful to you.
9. 1 I would like to show him **kindness** for Jonathan's sake."
9. 3 I can show loyalty and **kindness,** as I promised God I would?"
9. 7 "I will be **kind** to you for the sake of your father
15.20 with you—and may the Lord be **kind** and faithful to you."
1 Kgs 2. 7 "But show **kindness** to the sons of Barzillai from Gilead
2. 7 of them, because they were **kind** to me when I was fleeing
8.50 and make their enemies treat them with **kindness.**
17.20 She has been **kind** enough to take care of me, and now
2 Kgs 13.23 but the Lord was **kind** and merciful to them.
25.27 he showed **kindness** to King Jehoiachin of Judah
25.28 Evilmerodach treated him **kindly,**
2 Chr 10. 7 They replied, "If you are **kind** to these people and try
30. 9 The Lord your God is **kind** and merciful, and if you return
Esth 5. 8 "If Your Majesty is **kind** enough to grant my request,
Job 24.21 ill-treated widows and showed no **kindness** to childless women.
Ps 4. 1 Be **kind** to me now and hear my prayer.
4. 6 Look on us with **kindness!"**
25. 6 Remember, O Lord, your **kindness** and constant love
31.16 Look on your servant with **kindness;**
51.18 O God, be **kind** to Zion and help her;
67. 1 look on us with **kindness,**
84.11 glorious king, blessing us with **kindness** and honour.
86.15 loving God, always patient, always **kind** and faithful.
89.15 you with songs, who live in the light of your **kindness!**
103. 2 the Lord, my soul, and do not forget how **kind** he is.
103.13 As a father is **kind** to his children,
103.13 so the Lord is **kind** to those who honour him.
109.12 May no one ever be **kind** to him or care for the
109.16 That man never thought of being **kind;**
111. 4 he is **kind** and merciful.
112. 4 for those who are merciful, **kind,** and just.
112. 9 gives generously to the needy, and his **kindness** never fails;
119.68 How good you are—how **kind!**
135. 3 sing praises to his name, because he is **kind.**
141. 5 rebuke me in **kindness,** but I will never accept honour
145. 7 tell about all your goodness and sing about your **kindness.**
Prov 10.32 Righteous people know the **kind** thing to say,
11.17 You do yourself a favour when you are **kind.**
12.25 can rob you of happiness, but **kind** words will cheer you up.
14.21 If you want to be happy, be **kind** to the poor;
14.31 but **kindness** shown to the poor is an act of worship.

Prov 15. 4 **Kind** words bring life, but cruel words crush your spirit.
16.24 **Kind** words are like honey—sweet to the taste and good
21.21 Be **kind** and honest and you will live a long life;
28. 8 your wealth will go to someone who is **kind** to the poor.
Is 26.10 Even though you are **kind** to wicked men, they never learn
Jer 24. 5 like these good figs, and I will treat them with **kindness.**
52.31 he showed **kindness** to King Jehoiachin of Judah
52.32 Evilmerodach treated him **kindly**
Joel 2.13 He is **kind** and full of mercy;
Jon 4. 2 merciful God, always patient, always **kind,**
Mic 2. 7 Doesn't he speak **kindly** to those who do right?"
Zech 7. 9 and must show **kindness** and mercy to one another.
Mt 9.13 'It is **kindness** that I want, not animal sacrifices.'
12. 7 says, 'It is **kindness** that I want, not animal sacrifices.'
Mk 5.19 has done for you and how **kind** he has been to you."
Lk 10.37 of the Law answered, "The one who was **kind** to him."
Acts 24. 4 I beg you to be **kind** and listen to our brief account.
27. 3 Julius was **kind** to Paul and allowed him to go and see
28. 7 He welcomed us **kindly** and for three days we were his guests.
Rom 1.31 promises, and they show no **kindness** or pity for others.
2. 4 perhaps you despise his great **kindness,** tolerance, and patience.
2. 4 you know that God is **kind,** because he is trying to lead
11.22 Here we see how **kind** and how severe God is.
11.22 those who have fallen, but **kind** to you—
11.22 if you continue in his **kindness.**
12. 8 whoever shows **kindness** to others should do it cheerfully.
1 Cor 4.13 when we are insulted, we answer with **kind** words.
13. 4 Love is patient and **kind;**
2 Cor 6. 6 our purity, knowledge, patience, and **kindness** we have shown
9. 9 his **kindness** lasts for ever."
10. 1 By the gentleness and **kindness** of Christ I beg you [2]not to
Gal 5.22 Spirit produces love, joy, peace, patience, **kindness,** goodness,
Eph 4.32 Instead, be **kind** and tender-hearted to one another,
Phil 2. 1 the Spirit, and you have **kindness** and compassion for one another.
Col 3.12 you must clothe yourselves with compassion, **kindness,** humility,
2 Tim 2.24 He must be **kind** towards all, a good and patient teacher,
Tit 3. 4 But when the **kindness** and love of God our Saviour was revealed,
1 Pet 2. 3 "You have found out for yourselves how **kind** the Lord is."
2.18 to those who are **kind** and considerate, but also to those
3. 8 as brothers, and be **kind** and humble with one another.

KINDLE

Is 40.16 our God, and its trees are too few to **kindle** the fire.
Lk 12.49 the earth on fire, and how I wish it were already **kindled!**

KING

[BOOK OF KINGS, EGYPT'S KING, SYRIA'S KING, SYRIAN KING]
see also **DAVID, SAUL, SOLOMON**
For KING - OF ISRAEL see also ISRAEL (2), JEROBOAM (1), NADAB, BAASHA, ELAH, ZIMRI, OMRI, AHAB, AHAZIAH (1), JORAM, JEHU, JEHOAHAZ, JEHOASH, JEROBOAM (2), ZECHARIAH, SHALLUM, MENAHEM, PEKAHIAH, PEKAH, HOSHEA
For KING - OF JUDAH see also JUDAH (2), REHOBOAM, ABIJAH, ASA (1), JEHOSHAPHAT, JEHORAM, AHAZIAH (2), ATHALIAH, JOASH, AMAZIAH (1), UZZIAH, JOTHAM, AHAZ, HEZEKIAH, MANASSEH, AMON, JOSIAH, JOAHAZ, JEHOIAKIM, JEHOIACHIN, ZEDEKIAH

Gen 12.15 officials saw her and told the **king** how beautiful she was;
12.16 Because of her the **king** treated Abram well
12.17 But because the **king** had taken Sarai,
12.18 Then the **king** sent for Abram and asked him,
12.20 The **king** gave orders to his men, so they took Abram and
14. 1 Four **kings,** Amraphel of Babylonia, Arioch of Ellasar,
14. 2 went to war against five other **kings:**
14. 2 Admah, Shemeber of Zeboiim, and the **king** of Bela (or Zoar).
14. 3 These five **kings** had formed an alliance
14. 8 Then the **kings** of Sodom, Gomorrah, Admah, Zeboiim, and Bela
14. 9 and fought [9]against the **kings** of Elam, Goiim,
14. 9 Babylonia, and Ellasar, five **kings** against four.
14.10 tar pits, and when the **kings** of Sodom and Gomorrah tried to
14.10 but the other three **kings** escaped to the mountains.
14.11 The four **kings** took everything in Sodom and Gomorrah,
14.14 and pursued the four **kings** all the way to Dan.
14.17 over Chedorlaomer and the other **kings,** the king of Sodom went
14.18 And Melchizedek, who was **king** of Salem and also a priest
14.21 The **king** of Sodom said to Abram, "Keep the loot, but
17. 6 give you many descendants, and some of them will be **kings.**
17.16 nations, and there will be **kings** among her descendants."
20. 2 So **King** Abimelech of Gerar had Sarah brought to him.
26. 1 Isaac went to Abimelech, **king** of the Philistines, at Gerar.
26. 8 **King** Abimelech looked down from his window
35.11 descended from you, and you will be the ancestor of **kings.**
36.31 Before there were any **kings** in Israel, the following kings
37. 8 think you are going to be a **king** and rule over us?"
37.36 Potiphar, one of the **king's** officers,
39. 1 Potiphar, one of the **king's** officers,
39.20 in the prison where the **king's** prisoners were kept,
40. 1 Some time later the **king of Egypt's** wine steward
40. 1 and his chief baker offended the **king.**
40.11 I was holding the **king's** cup;
40.13 In three days the **king** will release you, pardon you,
40.14 to mention me to the **king** and help me to get out
40.17 pastries for the **king,** and the birds were eating them."
40.19 In three days the **king** will release you—and have your
40.20 birthday three days later the **king** gave a banquet for all
41. 1 the **king of Egypt** dreamt that he was standing
41. 4 Then the **king** woke up.
41. 7 The **king** woke up and realized that he had been dreaming.
41. 9 wine steward said to the **king,** "I must confess today that I

Gen 41.14 The **king** sent for Joseph, and he was immediately brought
41.14 changed his clothes, he came into the **king's** presence.
41.15 The **king** said to him, "I have had a dream, and no
41.17 The **king** said, "I dreamt that I was standing on the
41.25 Joseph said to the **king,** "The two dreams mean the same
41.37 The **king** and his officials approved this plan,
41.39 The **king** said to Joseph, "God has shown you all this,
41.42 The **king** removed from his finger the ring engraved with
41.44 The **king** said to him, "I am the king—
41.45 thirty years old when he began to serve the **king of Egypt.**
41.45 He left the **king's** court and travelled all over the land.
41.55 began to be hungry, they cried out to the **king** for food.
42.15 by the name of the **king** that you will never leave unless
42.16 Otherwise, as sure as the **king** lives, you are spies."
44.18 you are like the **king** himself.
45. 2 and the news was taken to the **king's** palace.
45. 8 He has made me the **king's** highest official.
45.16 brothers had come, the **king** and his officials were pleased.
45.21 gave them wagons, as the **king** had ordered, and food
46. 5 their wives in the wagons which the **king of Egypt** had sent.
46.31 must go and tell the **king** that my brothers and all my
46.33 When the **king** calls for you and asks what your occupation
47. 1 So Joseph took five of his brothers and went to the **king.**
47. 2 He then presented his brothers to the **king.**
47. 3 The **king** asked them, "What is your occupation?"
47. 5 The **king** said to Joseph, "Now that your father and your
47. 7 Joseph brought his father Jacob and presented him to the **king.**
47. 7 Jacob gave the **king** his blessing,
47. 8 and the **king** asked him, "How old are you?"
47.10 Jacob gave the **king** a farewell blessing and left.
47.11 land near the city of Rameses, as the **king** had commanded.
47.19 We will be the **king's** slaves, and he will own our land.
47.20 Joseph bought all the land in Egypt for the **king.**
47.20 and all the land became the **king's** property.
47.22 sell their lands, because the **king** gave them an allowance
47.23 see, I have now bought you and your lands for the **king.**
47.24 At the time of harvest you must give one-fifth to the **king.**
47.25 been good to us, sir, and we will be the **king's** slaves."
47.26 Egypt that one-fifth of the harvest should belong to the **king.**
47.26 the lands of the priests did not become the **king's** property.
49.20 He will provide food fit for a **king.**
50. 4 Joseph said to the **king's** officials,
50. 4 "Please take this message to the **king:**
50. 6 The **king** answered, "Go and bury your father,
50. 7 All the **king's** officials, the senior men of his court,
Ex 1. 8 a new **king,** who knew nothing about Joseph, came to power
1.11 Pithom and Rameses to serve as supply centres for the **king.**
1.15 Then the **king of Egypt** spoke to Shiphrah and Puah,
1.17 But the midwives feared God and so did not obey the **king;**
1.18 So the **king** sent for the midwives and asked them,
1.22 Finally the **king** issued a command to all his people:
2. 5 The **king's** daughter came down to the river to bathe,
2.10 she took him to the **king's** daughter, who adopted him
2.15 When the **king** heard about what had happened,
2.23 Years later the **king of Egypt** died,
3.10 sending you to the **king of Egypt** so that you can lead
3.11 can I go to the **king** and bring the Israelites out
3.18 Israel to the **king of Egypt** and say to him,
3.19 I know that the **king of Egypt** will not let you go
4.21 sure to perform before the **king** all the miracles
4.21 But I will make the **king** stubborn, and he will not let
5. 1 Aaron went to the **king of Egypt** and said, "The Lord,
5. 2 the **king** demanded.
5. 4 The **king** said to Moses and Aaron, "What do you mean
5. 6 That same day the **king** commanded the Egyptian slave-drivers
5.10 said to the Israelites, "The **king** has said that he will not
5.15 the foremen went to the **king** and complained, "Why do you do
5.17 The **king** answered, "You are lazy and don't want to work,
5.21 punish you for making the **king** and his officers hate us.
5.23 since I went to the **king** to speak for you, he has
6. 1 you are going to see what I will do to the **king.**
6.11 "Go and tell the **king of Egypt** that he must let
6.12 Israelites will not listen to me, so why should the **king?**
6.13 the Israelites and the **king of Egypt** that I have ordered you
6.27 the men who told the **king of Egypt** to free the Israelites.
6.29 Tell the **king of Egypt** everything I tell you."
6.30 why should the **king** listen to me?"
7. 1 you like God to the **king,** and your brother Aaron will speak
7. 2 and he will tell the **king** to let the Israelites leave his
7. 3 I will make the **king** stubborn, and he will not listen
7. 7 when they spoke to the **king,** Moses was eighty years old,
7. 9 "If the **king** demands that you prove yourselves
7. 9 down in front of the **king,** and it will turn into a
7.10 and Aaron went to the **king** and did as the Lord had
7.10 down in front of the **king** and his officers, and it turned
7.11 Then the **king** called for his wise men and magicians,
7.13 The **king,** however, remained stubborn
7.13 the **king** would not listen to Moses and
7.14 Lord said to Moses, "The **king** is very stubborn and refuses
7.16 Then say to the **king,** 'The Lord, the God of the Hebrews,
7.20 In the presence of the **king** and his officers, Aaron raised
7.22 Then the **king's** magicians did the same thing
7.22 means of their magic, and the **king** was as stubborn as ever.
7.22 the **king** refused to listen to Moses
8. 1 to Moses, "Go to the **king** and tell him that the Lord
8. 8 The **king** called for Moses and Aaron and said, "Pray to
8.10 The **king** answered, "Pray for me tomorrow."
8.12 Moses and Aaron left the **king,** and Moses prayed to the Lord
8.12 to take away the frogs which he had brought on the **king.**
8.15 When the **king** saw that the frogs were dead, he became
8.15 the **king** would not listen to Moses

Ex 8.19 and the magicians said to the **king,** "God has done this!"
8.19 But the **king** was stubborn and, just as the Lord had said,
8.19 the **king** would not listen to Moses
8.20 morning go and meet the **king** as he goes to the river,
8.24 swarms of flies into the **king's** palace
8.25 Then the **king** called for Moses and Aaron and said, "Go
8.28 The **king** said, "I will let you go to sacrifice to the
8.30 Moses left the **king** and prayed to the Lord,
8.31 The flies left the **king,** his officials, and his people;
8.32 But even this time the **king** became stubborn,
9. 1 to Moses, "Go to the **king** and tell him that the Lord,
9. 7 The **king** asked what had happened and was told that none of
9. 8 Moses shall throw them into the air in front of the **king.**
9.10 So they got some ashes and stood before the **king;**
9.12 But the Lord made the **king** stubborn
9.12 the **king** would not listen to Moses
9.13 morning meet with the **king** and tell him that the Lord,
9.20 Some of the **king's** officials were afraid
9.27 The **king** sent for Moses and Aaron and said, "This time
9.33 Moses left the **king,** went out of the city, and lifted up
9.34 When the **king** saw what had happened, he sinned again.
9.35 the **king** would not let the Israelites go.
10. 1 Then the Lord said to Moses, "Go and see the **king.**
10. 3 and Aaron went to the **king** and said to him, "The Lord,
10. 7 The **king's** officials said to him, "How long
10. 8 were brought back to the **king,** and he said to them, "You
10.10 The **king** said, "I swear by the Lord that I will never
10.11 Moses and Aaron were driven out of the **king's** presence.
10.16 Then the **king** hurriedly called Moses and Aaron
10.18 Moses left the **king** and prayed to the Lord.
10.20 But the Lord made the **king** stubborn, and he did not let
10.24 The **king** called Moses and said, "You may go and worship
10.27 The Lord made the **king** stubborn, and he would not let
11. 1 one more punishment on the **king of Egypt** and his people.
11. 4 Moses then said to the **king,** "The Lord says, 'At about
11. 5 Egypt will die, from the **king's** son, who is heir
11. 8 Then in great anger Moses left the **king.**
11. 9 "The **king** will continue to refuse to listen
11.10 miracles before the **king,** but the Lord made him stubborn,
12.29 sons in Egypt, from the **king's** son, who was heir
12.30 the **king,** his officials, and all the other Egyptians
12.31 That same night the **king** sent for Moses and Aaron and said,
13.15 When the **king of Egypt** was stubborn and refused to let
13.17 When the **king of Egypt** let the people go,
14. 3 The **king** will think that the Israelites are wandering about
14. 4 and my victory over the **king** and his army will bring me
14. 5 When the **king of Egypt** was told that the people had escaped,
14. 6 The **king** got his war chariot and his army ready.
14. 8 The Lord made the **king** stubborn, and he pursued the Israelites,
14.10 When the Israelites saw the **king** and his army
14.17 my victory over the **king,** his army, his chariots,
15.18 You, Lord, will be **king** for ever and ever."
18. 4 saved me from being killed by the **king of Egypt";**
18. 8 Lord had done to the **king** and the people of Egypt
18.10 Lord, who saved you from the **king** and the people of Egypt!
Num 20.14 Moses sent messengers from Kadesh to the **king** of Edom.
21. 1 When the Canaanite **king** of Arad in the southern part of
21.21 people of Israel sent messengers to the Amorite **king** Sihon
21.26 capital city of the Amorite **king** Sihon, who had fought
21.26 against the former **king** of Moab
21.27 "Come to Heshbon, to **King** Sihon's city!
21.29 And the women became captives of the Amorite **king.**
21.33 the road to Bashan, and **King** Og of Bashan marched out
21.34 you did to Sihon, the Amorite **king** who ruled at Heshbon."
22. 2 When the **king** of Moab, Balak son of Zippor, heard
22. 4 So **King** Balak [5] sent messengers to summon Balaam son of Beor,
22.10 He answered, **"King** Balak of Moab has sent them to tell
23. 7 "Balak **king** of Moab has brought me From Syria,
23.21 They proclaim that he is their **king.**
24. 7 Their **king** shall be greater than Agag,
24.17 A **king,** like a bright star, will arise in that nation.
31. 8 killed all the men, [8] including the five **kings** of Midian:
32.33 all the territory of **King** Sihon of the Amorites
32.33 and **King** Og of Bashan,
33.40 **king** of Arad in southern Canaan heard that the Israelites
Deut 1. 4 after the Lord had defeated **King** Sihon of the Amorites,
1. 4 the town of Heshbon, and **King** Og of Bashan,
2.24 Sihon, the Amorite **king** of Heshbon, along with his land.
2.26 desert of Kedemoth to **King** Sihon of Heshbon with the following
2.30 "But **King** Sihon would not let us pass through his country.
2.31 'Look, I have made **King** Sihon and his land helpless
3. 1 the region of Bashan, and **King** Og came out
3. 2 as you did to Sihon the Amorite **king** who ruled in Heshbon.'
3. 3 "So the Lord also placed **King** Og and his people in our
3. 4 the whole region of Argob, where **King** Og of Bashan ruled.
3. 6 we did in the towns that belonged to **King** Sihon of Heshbon.
3. 8 took from those two Amorite **kings** the land east of the River
3.10 We took all the territory of **King** Og of Bashan:
3.11 **(King** Og was the last of the Rephaim.
3.21 the Lord your God did to those two **kings,** Sihon and Og;
4.45 territory that had belonged to **King** Sihon of the Amorites,
4.47 and the land of **King** Og of Bashan,
4.47 the other Amorite **king** who lived east of the Jordan.
6.21 were slaves of the **king of Egypt,** and the Lord rescued us
6.22 to the Egyptians and to their **king** and to all his officials.
7. 8 and set you free from slavery to the **king of Egypt.**
7.18 God did to the **king of Egypt** and to all his people.
7.24 He will put their **kings** in your power.
11. 3 he did to the **king of Egypt** and to his entire country.
17.14 will decide you need a **king** like all the nations round you.
17.15 man you choose to be **king** is the one whom the Lord

Deut 17.15 do not make a foreigner your **king.**
17.16 The **king** is not to have a large number of horses
17.17 The **king** is not to have many wives,
17.18 When he becomes **king,** he is to have a copy
28.36 will take you and your **king** away to a foreign land,
29. 2 Lord did to the **king of Egypt,** to his officials,
29. 7 we came to this place, **King** Sihon of Heshbon
29. 7 and **King** Og of Bashan came out
31. 4 he defeated Sihon and Og, **kings** of the Amorites,
33. 5 The Lord became **king** of his people Israel when their tribes
34.11 to perform against the **king of Egypt,** his officials,
Josh 2. 2 The **king** of Jericho heard that some Israelites had come
2. 7 The **king's** men left the city, and then the gate was shut.
2.10 Sihon and Og, the two Amorite **kings** east of the Jordan.
2.16 hill-country," she said, "or the **king's** men will find you.
2.22 The **king's** men looked for them all over the countryside
5. 1 All the Amorite **kings** west of the Jordan
5. 1 and all the Canaanite **kings** along the Mediterranean Sea
6. 2 Jericho, with its **king** and all its brave soldiers.
8. 1 I will give you victory over the **king** of Ai;
8. 2 do to Ai and its **king** what you did
8. 2 to Jericho and its **king,**
8.14 When the **king** of Ai saw Joshua's men, he acted quickly.
8.23 and no one lived through it [23] except the **king** of Ai.
8.29 He hanged the **king** of Ai from a tree
9. 1 became known to all the **kings** west of the Jordan—
9. 1 these were the **kings** of the Hittites, the Amorites,
9.10 what he did to the two Amorite **kings** east of the Jordan:
9.10 **King** Sihon of Heshbon and King Og of Bashan,
10. 1 Adonizedek, the **king** of Jerusalem, heard that Joshua had
10. 1 its king, just as he had done to Jericho and its **king.**
10. 2 was as large as any of the cities that had a **king;**
10. 3 sent the following message to **King** Hoham of Hebron,
10. 3 **King** Piram of Jarmuth,
10. 3 King Japhia of Lachish, and to **King** Debir of Eglon:
10. 5 These five Amorite **kings,** the kings of Jerusalem, Hebron,
10. 6 All the Amorite **kings** in the hill-country have joined forces
10.16 The five Amorite **kings,** however, had escaped
10.22 entrance to the cave and bring those five **kings** out to me."
10.23 cave was opened, and the **kings** of Jerusalem, Hebron, Jarmuth,
10.24 to come and put their feet on the necks of the **kings.**
10.26 Joshua killed the **kings** and hanged them on five trees,
10.28 Joshua attacked and captured Makkedah and its **king** that day.
10.28 He did to the **king** of Makkedah
10.28 what he had done to the **king** of Jericho.
10.30 Lord also gave the Israelites victory over this city and its **king.**
10.30 They did to the **king**
10.30 what they had done to the **king** of Jericho.
10.33 **King** Horam of Gezer came to the aid of Lachish, but
10.37 They killed the **king** and everyone else in the city as well
10.39 He captured it, with its **king** and all the nearby towns.
10.39 did to Debir and its **king**
10.39 what he had done to Hebron and to Libnah and its **king.**
10.40 He defeated the **kings** of the hill-country,
10.42 Joshua conquered all these **kings** and their territory
11. 1 news of Israel's victories reached **King** Jabin of Hazor,
11. 1 he sent word to **King** Jobab of Madon,
11. 1 Jobab of Madon, to the **kings** of Shimron and Achshaph,
11. 2 and to the **kings** in the hill-country in the north,
11. 5 All these **kings** joined forces and came together
11.10 Joshua then turned back, captured Hazor and killed its **king.**
11.12 all these cities and their **kings,** putting everyone to death,
11.17 was at war with the **kings** of this territory for a long
12. 1 They defeated two **kings.**
12. 2 One was Sihon, the Amorite **king** who ruled at Heshbon.
12. 4 They also defeated **King** Og of Bashan, who was one of the
12. 5 Gilead, as far as the territory of **King** Sihon of Heshbon.
12. 6 These two **kings** were defeated by Moses
12. 7 Israel defeated all the **kings** in the territory west
12. 9 Israel defeated the **kings** of the following cities:
12.24 Goiim (in Galilee), [24] and Tirzah—thirty-one **kings** in all.
13. 3 the **kings** of the Philistines lived at Gaza, Ashdod, Ashkelon,
13.10 ruled by the Amorite **king** Sihon, who had ruled at Heshbon.
13.21 kingdom of the Amorite **king** Sihon, who had ruled at Heshbon.
13.21 All of them had ruled the land for **King** Sihon.
13.27 Zaphon, the rest of the kingdom of **King** Sihon of Heshbon.
13.30 whole kingdom of Og, the **king** of Bashan, as well as all
24. 9 the **king** of Moab, Balak son of Zippor, fought against you.
24.12 them into panic in order to drive out the two Amorite **kings.**
Judg 1. 7 "Seventy **kings** with their thumbs and big toes cut off
3. 8 and let **King** Cushan Rishathaim of Mesopotamia conquer them,
3.10 and the Lord gave him victory over the **king** of Mesopotamia.
3.12 this the Lord made **King** Eglon of Moab stronger than Israel.
3.15 of Israel sent Ehud to **King** Eglon of Moab with gifts for
3.19 So the **king** ordered his servants, "Leave us alone!"
3.20 as the **king** was sitting there alone in his cool room
3.20 The **king** stood up.
3.21 from his right side and plunged it into the **king's** belly.
3.22 pull it out of the **king's** belly, and it stuck out behind,
3.24 they only thought that the **king** was inside, relieving himself.
4. 2 conquered by Jabin, a Canaanite **king** who ruled in the city
4.17 of Heber the Kenite, because **King** Jabin of Hazor was at
4.23 God gave the Israelites victory over Jabin, the Canaanite **king.**
5. 3 Listen, you **kings!**
5.19 by the stream of Megiddo, the **kings** came and fought;
5.19 the **kings** of Canaan fought, but they took no silver away.
8. 5 and I am pursuing Zebah and Zalmunna, the Midianite **kings."**
8.12 The two Midianite **kings,** Zebah and Zalmunna, ran away,
8.18 every one of them like the son of a **king."**
8.26 and purple clothes that the **kings** of Midian wore,

Judg 9. 6 to the sacred oak-tree at Shechem, where they made Abimelech **king.**
9. 8 time the trees got together to choose a **king** for themselves.
9. 8 They said to the olive-tree, 'Be our **king.'**
9.10 the trees said to the fig-tree, 'You come and be our **king.'**
9.12 then said to the grapevine, 'You come and be our **king.'**
9.14 trees said to the thorn-bush, 'You come and be our **king.'**
9.15 want to make me your **king,** then come and take shelter
9.16 "were you really honest and sincere when you made Abimelech **king?**
9.18 is your relative, you have made him **king** of Shechem.
11.12 Jephthah sent messengers to the **king** of Ammon
11.13 The **king** of Ammon answered Jephthah's messengers,
11.14 Jephthah sent messengers back to the **king** of Ammon
11.17 they sent messengers to the **king** of Edom to ask permission
11.17 But the **king** of Edom would not let them.
11.17 They also asked the **king** of Moab, but neither would he let
11.19 messengers to Sihon, the Amorite **king** of Heshbon, and asked
11.25 you are any better than Balak son of Zippor, **king** of Moab?
11.28 But the **king** of Ammon paid no attention to this message
16. 5 The five Philistine **kings** went to her and said, "Trick
16. 8 the Philistine **kings** brought Delilah seven new bowstrings
16.18 message to the Philistine **kings** and said, "Come back
16.23 The Philistine **kings** met together to celebrate
16.27 All five Philistine **kings** were there,
16.30 the building fell down on the five **kings** and everyone else.
17. 6 There was no **king** in Israel at that time;
18. 1 There was no **king** in Israel at that time.
19. 1 before Israel had a **king,** there was a Levite living far
21.25 There was no **king** in Israel at that time.
Ruth 1. 1 days before Israel had a **king,** there was a famine in the
1 Sam 2.10 power to his king, he will make his chosen **king** victorious."
2.27 slaves of the **king of Egypt,** I revealed myself to Aaron.
2.35 who will always serve in the presence of my chosen **king.**
5. 8 all five of the Philistine **kings** and asked them, "What shall
5.11 all the Philistine **kings** and said, "Send the Covenant Box
6. 4 and five gold mice, one of each for each Philistine **king.**
6. 4 plague was sent on all of you and on the five **kings.**
6. 6 stubborn, as the **king of Egypt** and the Egyptians were?
6.12 The five Philistine **kings** followed them as far as the border
6.16 The five Philistine **kings** watched them do this
6.18 ruled by the five Philistine **kings,** both the fortified towns
7. 7 the five Philistine **kings** started out
8. 5 So then, appoint a **king** to rule over us,
8. 5 so that we will have a **king,** as other countries have."
8. 6 Samuel was displeased with their request for a **king;**
8. 7 I am the one they have rejected as their **king.**
8. 9 and explain how their **kings** will treat them."
8.10 were asking him for a **king** everything that the Lord had said
8.11 "This is how your **king** will treat you," Samuel explained.
8.18 complain bitterly because of your **king,** whom you yourselves chose,
8.19 We want a **king,** [20] so that we will be like other nations,
8.20 with our own **king** to rule us
8.22 The Lord answered, "Do what they want and give them a **king."**
10.16 his uncle what Samuel had said about his becoming **king.**
10.19 have rejected me and have asked me to give you a **king.**
10.24 All the people shouted, "Long live the **king!"**
10.25 rights and duties of a **king,** and then wrote them
11. 1 About a month later **King** Nahash of Ammon led his army
11.12 are the people who said that Saul should not be our **king?**
11.14 all go to Gilgal and once more proclaim Saul as our **king."**
11.15 and there at the holy place they proclaimed Saul **king.**
12. 1 I have given you a **king** to rule you,
12. 3 in the presence of the Lord and the **king** he has chosen.
12. 5 replied, "The Lord and the **king** he has chosen are witnesses
12. 9 let the Philistines and the **king** of Moab and Sisera,
12.12 But when you saw that **King** Nahash of Ammon was about to
12.12 rejected the Lord as your **king**
12.12 and said to me, 'We want a **king** to rule us.'
12.13 "Now here is the **king** you chose;
12.14 and obey his commands, and if you and your **king** follow him.
12.15 disobey his commands, he will be against you and your **king.**
12.17 great sin against the Lord when you asked him for a **king."**
12.19 all our other sins, we have sinned by asking for a **king."**
12.25 you continue to sin, you and your **king** will be destroyed."
14.47 After Saul became **king of Israel,** he fought against all
14.47 Ammon, and of Edom, the **kings** of Zobah, and the Philistines.
15. 1 whom the Lord sent to anoint you **king** of his people Israel.
15. 8 captured **King** Agag of Amalek alive and killed all the people.
15.11 Lord said to Samuel, [11] "I am sorry that I made Saul **king;**
15.17 The Lord anointed you **king of Israel,**
15.20 to, brought back **King** Agag, and killed all the Amalekites.
15.23 you rejected the Lord's command, he has rejected you as **king."**
15.26 and he has rejected you as **king of Israel."**
15.32 "Bring **King** Agag here to me," Samuel ordered.
15.35 As long as Samuel lived, he never again saw the **king;**
15.35 The Lord was sorry that he had made Saul **king of Israel.**
16. 1 I have rejected him as **king of Israel.**
16. 1 Jesse, because I have chosen one of his sons to be **king."**
16. 3 You will anoint as **king** the man I tell you to."
17.12 at the time Saul was **king,** he was already a very old
17.25 the **king** will also give him his daughter to marry
18. 8 They will be making him **king** next!"
18.18 what is my family that I should become the **king's** son-in-law?"
18.22 David and tell him, "The **king** is pleased with you and all
18.23 great honour to become the **king's** son-in-law,
18.25 "All the **king** wants from you as payment for the bride is
18.26 David was delighted with the thought of becoming the **king's** son-in-law.
18.27 took their foreskins to the **king** and counted them all out to
1 Sam 19. 7 him to Saul, and David served the **king** as he had before.
20. 5 David replied, "and I am supposed to eat with the **king.**
20.31 as David is alive, you will never be **king** of this country?
21. 2 "I am here on the **king's** business," David answered.
21. 8 The **king's** orders made me leave in such a hurry
21.10 David left, fleeing from Saul, and went to **King** Achish of Gath.
21.11 The **king's** officials said to Achish,
21.11 "Isn't this David, the **king** of his country?
21.12 on David, and he became very much afraid of **King** Achish.
22. 3 Moab and said to the **king** of Moab, "Please let my father
22. 4 left his parents with the **king** of Moab, and they stayed
22.16 The **king** said, "Ahimelech, you and all your relatives
23.17 who will be the **king of Israel**
24. 6 doing any harm to my master, whom the Lord chose as **king!**
24. 6 because he is the **king** chosen by the Lord!"
24.10 because you are the one whom the Lord chose to be **king.**
24.14 Look at what the **king of Israel** is trying to kill!
24.20 that you will be **king of Israel**
25.28 The Lord will make you **king,** and your descendants also,
25.30 and has made you **king of Israel,**
25.36 Nabal, who was at home having a feast fit for a **king.**
26. 9 The Lord will certainly punish whoever harms his chosen **king.**
26.11 should try to harm the one whom the Lord has made **king!**
26.14 "Who is that shouting and waking up the **king?"**
26.15 So why aren't you protecting your master, the **king?**
26.16 you have not protected your master, whom the Lord made **king.**
26.16 Where is the **king's** spear?
26.20 Why should the **king of Israel** come to kill a flea
26.23 power, but I did not harm you, whom the Lord made **king.**
27. 2 went over at once to Achish son of Maoch, **king** of Gath.
27. 6 Ziklag has belonged to the **kings of Judah** ever since.
28.13 the **king** said to her.
29. 2 The five Philistine **kings** marched out with their units
29. 2 David and his men marched in the rear with **King** Achish.
29. 6 But the other **kings** don't approve of you.
29. 8 I go with you, my master and **king,** and fight your enemies?"
29. 9 But the other **kings** have said that you can't go with us
2 Sam 1.14 "How is it that you dared to kill the Lord's chosen **king?"**
1.16 that you killed the one whom the Lord chose to be **king."**
2. 4 Judah came to Hebron and anointed David as **king of Judah.**
2. 5 you for showing your loyalty to your **king** by burying him.
2. 7 Saul your **king** is dead,
2. 7 and the people of Judah have anointed me as their **king."**
2. 9 There Abner made Ishbosheth **king** of the territories
2.10 when he was made **king of Israel,** and he ruled for two
3. 3 Absalom, whose mother was Maacah, the daughter of **King** Talmai
3. 9 and would make David **king** of both Israel and Judah,
3.17 "For a long time you have wanted David to be your **king.**
3.21 They will accept you as **king,** and then you will get what
3.24 So Joab went to the **king** and said to him, "What have
3.32 buried at Hebron, and the **king** wept aloud at the grave, and
3.36 Indeed, everything the **king** did pleased the people.
3.37 in Israel understood that the **king** had no part in the murder
3.38 The **king** said to his officials, "Don't you realize
3.39 Even though I am the **king** chosen by God, I feel weak
5. 2 when Saul was still our **king,** you led the people of Israel
5. 3 they anointed him, and he became **king of Israel.**
5. 4 years old when he became **king,** and he ruled for forty years.
5.11 **King** Hiram of Tyre sent a trade mission to David;
5.12 had established him as **king of Israel**
5.17 David had been made **king of Israel,** so their army set out
6.20 "The **king of Israel** made a big name for himself today!"
7. 2 Then the **king** said to the prophet Nathan, "Here I am
7.12 make one of your sons **king** and will keep his kingdom strong.
7.15 did from Saul, whom I removed so that you could be **king.**
7.27 and have told me that you will make my descendants **kings.**
8. 3 Then he defeated the **king** of the Syrian state of Zobah,
8. 5 sent an army to help **King** Hadadezer, David attacked it
8. 9 **King** Toi of Hamath heard that David had defeated all of
9. 2 "Are you Ziba?" the **king** asked.
9. 3 The **king** asked him, "Is there anyone left of Saul's family
9. 4 "Where is he?" the **king** asked.
9. 9 Then the **king** called Ziba, Saul's servant, and said,
9.11 So Mephibosheth ate at the **king's** table,
9.11 just like one of the **king's** sons.
9.13 lived in Jerusalem, eating all his meals at the **king's** table.
10. 1 Some time later **King** Nahash of Ammon died,
10. 1 and his son Hanun became **king.**
10. 3 Ammonite leaders said to the **king,** "Do you think that it is
10. 6 men from Tob, and the **king** of Maacah with a thousand men.
10.16 **King** Hadadezer sent for the Syrians
10.16 Shobach, commander of the army of **King** Hadadezer of Zobah.
10.19 When the **kings** who were subject to Hadadezer realized
11. 1 time of the year when **kings** usually go to war,
11. 9 instead he slept at the palace gate with the **king's** guards.
11.19 "After you have told the **king** all about the battle,
11.21 If the **king** asks you this, tell him, 'Your officer Uriah was
12. 7 'I made you **king of Israel** and rescued you from Saul.
12. 8 I made you **king** over Israel and Judah.
13. 4 to Amnon, "You are the **king's** son, yet day after day
13.13 Please, speak to the **king,** and I'm sure that he will give
13.23 and he invited all the **king's** sons to be there.
13.25 "No, my son," the **king** answered.
13.25 Absalom insisted, but the **king** would not give in,
13.26 the **king** asked.
13.27 Absalom prepared a banquet fit for a **king**
13.31 The **king** stood up, tore his clothes in sorrow,
13.34 He went to the **king** and reported what he had seen.
13.37 fled and went to the **king** of Geshur, Talmai son of Ammihud,
14. 3 Then go to the **king** and say to him what I tell

2 Sam 14. 4 The woman went to the **king,** bowed down to the ground in
14. 8 "Go back home," the **king** answered, "and I will take care
14.10 The **king** replied, "If anyone threatens you, bring him
14.14 back to life, but the **king** can at least find a way
14.17 make me safe, because the **king** is like God's angel
14.18 The **king** answered, "I'm going to ask you a question,
14.21 Later on the **king** said to Joab, "I have decided to do
14.24 The **king,** however, gave orders that Absalom should not
14.24 "I don't want to see him," the **king** said.
14.24 lived in his own house and did not appear before the **king.**
14.28 Absalom lived two years in Jerusalem without seeing the **king.**
14.29 for Joab, to ask him to go to the **king** for him;
14.32 wanted you to go to the **king** and ask him from me:
14.32 for me to see the **king,** and if I'm guilty,
14.33 The **king** sent for Absalom, who went to him and bowed down
14.33 The **king** welcomed him with a kiss.
15. 2 dispute that he wanted the **king** to settle, Absalom would call
15. 3 there is no representative of the **king** to hear your case."
15. 6 Israelite who came to the **king** for justice, and so he won
15. 9 "Go in peace," the **king** said.
15.10 shout, 'Absalom has become **king** at Hebron!' "
15.12 The plot against the **king** gained strength,
15.16 So the **king** left, accompanied by all his family
15.17 As the **king** and all his men were leaving the city,
15.19 also passed by, [19]and the **king** said to Ittai, their leader,
15.19 Go back and stay with the new **king.**
15.23 The **king** crossed the brook of Kidron, followed by his men,
15.25 Then the **king** said to Zadok, "Take the Covenant Box back
15.35 tell them everything you hear in the **king's** palace.
16. 3 the **king** asked him.
16. 4 The **king** said to Ziba, "Everything that belonged to Mephibosheth is yours."
16. 9 Zeruiah, said to the **king,** "Your Majesty, why do you let
16.10 none of your business," the **king** said to Abishai
16.14 The **king** and all his men were worn out
16.16 David's trusted friend, met Absalom, he shouted, "Long live the **king!**
16.16 Long live the **king!"**
17. 2 I will kill only the **king**
18. 2 And the **king** said to his men, "I will go with you
18. 4 "I will do whatever you think best," the **king** answered.
18.12 I wouldn't lift a finger against the **king's** son.
18.12 We all heard the **king** command you and Abishai and Ittai,
18.13 if I had disobeyed the **king** and killed Absalom,
18.13 the **king** would have heard about it—
18.19 "Let me run to the **king** with the good news
18.20 may do so, but not today, for the **king's** son is dead."
18.21 Sudanese slave, "Go and tell the **king** what you have seen."
18.25 told the king, and the **king** said, "If he is alone,
18.26 The **king** answered, "This one also is bringing good news."
18.27 "He's a good man," the **king** said, "and he is bringing
18.28 a greeting to the **king,** threw himself down to the ground
18.29 the **king** asked.
18.30 "Stand over there," the **king** said;
18.31 arrived and said to the **king,** "I have good news for Your
18.32 the **king** asked.
18.33 The **king** was overcome with grief.
19. 2 because they heard that the **king** was mourning for his son.
19. 4 The **king** covered his face and cried loudly, "O my son!
19. 5 Joab went to the **king's** house and said to him,
19. 8 Then the **king** got up, and went and sat near the city
19.10 We anointed Absalom as our **king,** but he has been killed
19.11 be the last to help bring the **king** back to his palace?
19.15 On his way back the **king** was met at the River Jordan
19.17 servants, and they arrived at the Jordan before the **king.**
19.18 the royal party across and to do whatever the **king** wanted.
19.18 As the **king** was getting ready to cross, Shimei threw
19.21 because he cursed the one whom the Lord chose as **king."**
19.22 the one who is **king of Israel** now,
19.24 Mephibosheth, Saul's grandson, came down to meet the **king.**
19.24 from the time the **king** left Jerusalem until he returned
19.25 Jerusalem to meet the **king,** the king said to him, "Mephibosheth,
19.29 The **king** answered, "You don't have to say anything more.
19.31 come down from Rogelim to escort the **king** across the Jordan.
19.32 rich and had supplied the **king** with food while he was
19.33 The **king** said to him, "Come with me to Jerusalem,
19.38 The **king** answered, "I will take him with me
19.40 the **king** had crossed, escorted by all the men of Judah
19.41 Israelites went to the **king** and said to him, "Your Majesty,
19.42 answered, "We did it because the **king** is one of us.
19.43 we were the first to talk about bringing the **king** back!"
20. 4 The **king** said to Amasa, "Call the men of Judah together
20. 5 he did not get back by the time the **king** had set.
20. 6 the **king** said to Abishai, "Sheba will give us more trouble
20.22 And Joab returned to Jerusalem to the **king.**
21. 6 Lord at Gibeah, the town of Saul, the Lord's chosen **king."**
21. 6 "I will hand them over," the **king** answered.
21.14 territory of Benjamin, doing all that the **king** had commanded.
22.51 God gives great victories to his **king;**
23. 1 of Jacob chose to be **king,** and who was the composer of
23. 3 "The **king** who rules with justice, who rules in obedience to God,
24. 3 But Joab answered the **king,** "Your Majesty,
24. 4 But the **king** made Joab and his officers obey his order;
24. 9 They reported to the **king** the total number of men capable
24.20 looked down and saw the **king** and his officials coming up
24.23 gave it all to the **king** and said to him, "May the
24.24 But the **king** answered, "No, I will pay you for it.

1 Kgs 1. 3 such a girl named Abishag, and brought her to the **king.**
1. 4 beautiful, and waited on the **king** and took care of him,
1. 5 him about anything, and he was ambitious to be **king.**
1. 9 King David and the **king's** officials who were from Judah
1.10 Nathan the prophet, or Benaiah, or the **king's** bodyguard.
1.11 "Haven't you heard that Haggith's son Adonijah has made himself **king?**
1.13 promise me that my son Solomon would succeed you as **king?**
1.13 How is it, then, that Adonijah has become **king?' "**
1.15 So Bathsheba went to see the **king** in his bedroom.
1.16 Bathsheba bowed low before the **king,**
1.17 that my son Solomon would be **king** after you.
1.18 But Adonijah has already become **king,**
1.20 to tell them who is to succeed you as **king.**
1.23 The **king** was told that the prophet was there,
1.23 and Nathan went in and bowed low before the **king.**
1.24 have you announced that Adonijah would succeed you as **king?**
1.25 they are feasting with him and shouting, 'Long live **King** Adonijah!'
1.27 even tell your officials who is to succeed you as **king?"**
1.30 that your son Solomon would succeed me as **king."**
1.31 bowed low and said, "May my lord the **king** live for ever!"
1.34 where Zadok and Nathan are to anoint him as **king of Israel.**
1.35 He will succeed me as **king,** because he is the one I
1.43 "His Majesty King David has made Solomon **king.**
1.44 made him ride on the **king's** mule,
1.45 Zadok and Nathan anointed him as **king** at the spring of Gihon.
1.46 Solomon is now the **king.**
1.48 my descendants succeed me as **king,** and has let me live to
1.53 Adonijah went to the **king** and bowed low before him,
1.53 and the **king** said to him, "You may go
2.11 He had been **king of Israel** for forty years,
2.12 succeeded his father David as **king,** and his royal power was
2.15 that I should have become **king** and that everyone in Israel
2.15 my brother became **king,** because it was the Lord's will.
2.18 "I will speak to the **king** for you."
2.19 So Bathsheba went to the **king** to speak to him
2.19 The **king** stood up to greet his mother and bowed to her.
2.22 the **king** asked.
2.30 said to Joab, "The **king** orders you to come out."
2.30 Benaiah went back to the **king** and told him what Joab
2.35 The **king** made Benaiah commander of the army in Joab's place
2.36 Then the **king** sent for Shimei and said to him,
2.39 slaves ran away to the **king** of Gath, Achish son of Maacah.
2.40 his donkey and went to **King** Achish in Gath,
2.46 Then the **king** gave orders to Benaiah,
3. 1 alliance with the **king of Egypt** by marrying his daughter.
3. 7 succeed my father as **king,** even though I am very young
3.13 have wealth and honour, more than that of any other **king.**
3.22 And so they argued before the **king.**
3.26 said to the **king,** "Please, Your Majesty, don't kill the
4. 1 Solomon was **king** of all Israel, [2]and these were his high officials:
4. 7 from their districts for the **king** and his household,
4.19 which had been ruled by **King** Sihon of the Amorites
4.19 and **King** Og of Bashan
4.24 All the **kings** west of the Euphrates were subject to him,
4.34 **Kings** all over the world heard of his wisdom
5. 1 **King** Hiram of Tyre had always been a friend of David's,
5. 1 succeeded his father David as **king** he sent ambassadors to him.
5. 5 son, whom I will make **king** after you, will build a temple
5. 7 a wise son to succeed him as **king** of that great nation!"
7. 8 for his wife, the daughter of the **king of Egypt.**
7.46 The **king** had it all made in the foundry
8.20 succeeded my father as **king of Israel,**
8.25 his descendants ruling as **king of Israel,**
8.36 Forgive the sins of the **king** and of the people of Israel.
8.52 your people Israel and their **king,** and hear their prayer
8.59 Israel and to their **king,** according to their daily needs.
8.63 And so the **king** and all the people dedicated the Temple.
9.11 **King** Hiram of Tyre had provided him with all the cedar
9.16 (The **king of Egypt** had attacked Gezer and captured it,
9.24 daughter of the **king of Egypt,** had moved from David's City
9.27 **King** Hiram sent some experienced seamen from his fleet
10. 9 how pleased he is with you by making you **king of Israel.**
10. 9 he has made you their **king** so that you can maintain law
10.15 tribute paid by the Arabian **kings**
10.23 **King** Solomon was richer and wiser than any other king,
10.28 The **king's** agents controlled the export of horses
10.29 supplied the Hittite and Syrian **kings** with horses and chariots,
11. 1 the daughter of the **king of Egypt** he married Hittite women
11.18 Egypt and went to the **king,** who gave Hadad some land
11.19 friendship of the **king,** and the king gave his sister-in-law,
11.20 the palace, where he lived with the **king's** sons.
11.21 Hadad said to the **king,** "Let me go back
11.22 "Why?" the **king** asked.
11.22 "Just let me go," Hadad answered the **king.**
11.22 As **king** of Edom, Hadad was an evil, bitter enemy of Israel.
11.23 had fled from his master, **King** Hadadezer of Zobah,
11.24 and lived in Damascus, where his men made him **king of Syria.**
11.37 I will make you **king of Israel,** and you will rule
11.38 I will make you **king of Israel** and will make sure
11.40 but he escaped to **King** Shishak of Egypt and stayed there
11.42 He was **king** in Jerusalem over all Israel for forty years.
11.43 and his son Rehoboam succeeded him as **king.**
12. 1 the people of northern Israel had gathered to make him **king.**
12.13 The **king** ignored the advice of the older men and spoke
12.15 This is why the **king** did not pay any attention
12.16 the people saw that the **king** would not listen to them,
12.17 Israel rebelled, [17]leaving Rehoboam as **king** only of the people
12.20 to a meeting of the people and made him **king of Israel.**
13. 4 At once the **king's** arm became paralysed
13. 6 The prophet prayed to the Lord, and the **king's** arm was healed.
13. 7 Then the **king** said to the prophet, "Come home with me
14. 2 Ahijah lives, the one who said I would be **king of Israel.**
14.14 is going to place a **king** over Israel
14.19 are all recorded in The History of the **Kings of Israel.**

1 Kgs 14.20 Jeroboam ruled as **king** for twenty-two years.
14.20 and his son Nadab succeeded him as **king.**
14.25 **King** Shishak of Egypt attacked Jerusalem.
14.28 Every time the **king** went to the Temple, the guards carried
14.29 Rehoboam did is recorded in The History of the **Kings of Judah.**
14.31 and his son Abijah succeeded him as **king.**
15. 7 Abijah did is recorded in The History of the **Kings of Judah.**
15. 8 and his son Asa succeeded him as **king.**
15.18 his officials to Damascus, to **King** Benhadad of Syria,
15.20 **King** Benhadad agreed to Asa's proposal
15.23 are all recorded in The History of the **Kings of Judah.**
15.24 and his son Jehoshaphat succeeded him as **king.**
15.25 Jeroboam's son Nadab became **king of Israel,**
15.28 And so Baasha succeeded Nadab as **king of Israel.**
15.31 Nadab did is recorded in The History of the **Kings of Israel.**
15.33 Baasha son of Ahijah became **king** of all Israel,
16. 5 deeds are recorded in The History of the **Kings of Israel.**
16. 6 and his son Elah succeeded him as **king.**
16. 8 son of Baasha became **king of Israel,** and he ruled in Tirzah
16. 9 who was in charge of half the **king's** chariots,
16.10 Zimri entered the house, assassinated Elah, and succeeded him as **king.**
16.11 As soon as Zimri became **king** he killed off
16.14 Elah did is recorded in The History of the **Kings of Israel.**
16.16 Zimri had plotted against the **king** and assassinated him,
16.16 they all proclaimed their commander Omri **king of Israel.**
16.20 conspiracy, is recorded in The History of the **Kings of Israel.**
16.21 make Tibni son of Ginath **king,**
16.22 Tibni died and Omri became **king.**
16.23 Omri became **king of Israel,**
16.27 accomplishments are recorded in The History of the **Kings of Israel.**
16.28 and his son Ahab succeeded him as **king.**
16.29 son of Omri became **king of Israel,** and he ruled in Samaria
16.31 married Jezebel, the daughter of **King** Ethbaal of Sidon,
16.33 the God of Israel, than all the **kings of Israel** before him.
18. 8 "Go and tell your master the **king** that I am here."
18.10 I swear that the **king** has made a search for you
18.14 order me to go and tell the **king** that you are here?
18.15 I promise that I will present myself to the **king** today."
19.15 then enter the city and anoint Hazael as **king of Syria;**
19.16 son of Nimshi as **king of Israel,** and anoint Elisha son of
20. 1 **King** Benhadad of Syria gathered all his troops,
20. 2 to say, "**King** Benhadad demands that [3]you surrender
20. 4 "Tell my lord, **King** Benhadad, that I agree;
20. 9 "Tell my lord the **king** that I agreed to his first
20.11 King Ahab answered, "Tell **King** Benhadad that a real
20.14 the **king** asked.
20.15 So the **king** called out the young soldiers who were under
20.22 the **king of Syria** will attack again next spring."
20.23 **King** Benhadad's officials said to him, "The gods of Israel
20.25 **King** Benhadad agreed and followed their advice.
20.31 said, "We have heard that the Israelite **kings** are merciful.
20.31 to go to the **king of Israel** with sackcloth round our waists
20.38 stood by the road, waiting for the **king of Israel** to pass.
20.39 As the **king** was passing by, the prophet called out to
20.40 The **king** answered, "You have pronounced your own sentence,
20.41 face, and at once the **king** recognized him as one of the
20.42 prophet then said to the **king,** "This is the word of the
20.43 The **king** went back home to Samaria, worried and depressed.
21. 7 "Well, are you the **king** or aren't you?"
21.10 to accuse him to his face of cursing God and the **king.**
21.13 of cursing God and the **king,** and so he was taken outside
22. 3 to get back Ramoth in Gilead from the **king of Syria?**
22.10 The two **kings,** dressed in their royal robes,
22.13 have prophesied success for the **king,** and you had better do
22.15 before King Ahab, the **king** asked him, "Micaiah, should King
22.30 So the **king of Israel** went into battle in disguise.
22.31 The **king of Syria** had ordered his thirty-two chariot
22.31 commanders to attack no one else except the **king of Israel.**
22.32 that he was the **king of Israel,** and they turned to attack
22.33 was not the **king of Israel,** and they stopped their attack.
22.39 he built, is recorded in The History of the **Kings of Israel.**
22.40 At his death his son Ahaziah succeeded him as **king.**
22.44 Jehoshaphat made peace with the **king of Israel.**
22.45 battles, are recorded in The History of the **Kings of Judah.**
22.47 The land of Edom had no **king;**
22.47 it was ruled by a deputy appointed by the **king of Judah.**
22.50 in David's City, and his son Jehoram succeeded him as **king.**
22.51 son of Ahab became **king of Israel,** and he ruled in Samaria

2 Kgs 1. 4 Tell the **king** that the Lord says, 'You will not recover
1. 5 as the Lord commanded, [5]and the messengers returned to the **king.**
1. 7 the **king** asked.
1. 8 the **king** exclaimed.
1. 9 to him, "Man of God, the **king** orders you to come down."
1.11 The **king** sent another officer with fifty men,
1.11 Elijah, "Man of God, the **king** orders you to come down at
1.13 Once more the **king** sent an officer with fifty men.
1.15 with the officer to the **king** [16]and said to him, "This is
1.17 brother Joram succeeded him as **king** in the second year
1.17 of the reign of Jehoram son of Jehoshaphat, **king of Judah.**
1.18 Ahaziah did is recorded in The History of the **Kings of Israel.**
3. 1 son of Ahab became **king of Israel,** and he ruled in Samaria
3. 4 **King** Mesha of Moab bred sheep, and every year he gave
3. 4 as tribute to the **king of Israel** 100,000 lambs,
3. 7 "The **king** of Moab has rebelled against me;
3. 9 So King Joram and the **kings** of Judah and Edom set out.
3.10 the three of us at the mercy of the **king** of Moab!"
3.12 So the three **kings** went to Elisha.
3.13 Elisha said to the **king of Israel.**

2 Kgs 3.13 put us three kings at the mercy of the **king** of Moab."
3.21 Moabites heard that the three **kings** had come to attack them,
3.26 the **king** of Moab realized that he was losing the battle,
3.26 escape to the **king of Syria,** but he failed.
3.27 was to succeed him as **king,** and offered him on the city
4.13 me to go to the **king** or the army commander and put
5. 1 esteemed by the **king of Syria,** because through Naaman
5. 4 this, he went to the **king** and told him what the girl
5. 5 The **king** said, "Go to the king of Israel
5. 5 "Go to the **king of Israel** and take this letter
5. 7 When the **king of Israel** read the letter, he tore his
5. 7 "How can the **king of Syria** expect me to cure this
5. 8 Elisha heard what had happened, he sent word to the **king:**
5.18 me when I accompany my **king** to the temple of Rimmon, the
6. 8 The **king of Syria** was at war with Israel.
6. 9 sent word to the **king of Israel,** warning him not to go
6.10 So the **king of Israel** warned the men who lived in that
6.11 The **Syrian king** became greatly upset over this;
6.11 one of you is on the side of the **king of Israel?"**
6.12 prophet Elisha tells the **king of Israel** what you say
6.13 he is," the **king** ordered, "and I will capture him."
6.21 When the **king of Israel** saw the Syrians, he asked Elisha,
6.22 to eat and drink, and let them return to their **king."**
6.23 So the **king of Israel** provided a great feast for them;
6.23 eaten and drunk, he sent them back to the **king of Syria.**
6.24 Some time later **King** Benhadad of Syria led his entire army
6.26 The **king of Israel** was walking by on the city wall
6.30 Hearing this, the **king** tore his clothes in dismay,
6.32 Before the **king's** messenger arrived, Elisha said to the elders,
6.32 The **king** himself will be just behind him."
6.33 saying this, when the **king** arrived and said, "It's the Lord
7. 2 attendant of the **king** said to Elisha, "That can't happen
7. 6 Syrians thought that the **king of Israel** had hired
7. 6 Hittite and Egyptian **kings** and their armies to attack them.
7. 9 Let's go at once and tell the **king's** officers!"
7.12 was still night, but the **king** got out of bed and said
7.14 chose some men, and the **king** sent them in two chariots
7.15 Then they returned and reported to the **king.**
7.17 so happened that the **king of Israel** had put the city gate
7.17 died, as Elisha had predicted when the **king** went to see him.
7.18 Elisha had told the **king** that by that time the following
8. 3 went to the **king** to ask for her house
8. 4 She found the **king** talking with Gehazi, Elisha's servant;
8. 4 the **king** wanted to know about Elisha's miracles.
8. 5 Gehazi was telling the **king** how Elisha had brought a dead
8. 5 person back to life, the woman made her appeal to the **king.**
8. 6 In answer to the **king's** question, she confirmed Gehazi's story,
8. 6 and so the **king** called an official
8. 7 to Damascus at a time when **King** Benhadad of Syria was ill.
8. 7 When the **king** was told that Elisha was there, [8]he said to
8. 9 he said, "Your servant **King** Benhadad has sent me to ask
8.13 shown me that you will be **king of Syria,"** Elisha replied.
8.15 Hazael took a blanket, soaked it in water, and smothered the **king.**
8.15 And Hazael succeeded Benhadad as **king of Syria.**
8.16 son of Ahab as **king of Israel,** Jehoram son of Jehoshaphat
8.18 of Ahab he followed the evil ways of the **kings of Israel.**
8.23 Jehoram did is recorded in The History of the **Kings of Judah.**
8.24 and his son Ahaziah succeeded him as **king.**
8.25 son of Ahab as **king of Israel,** Ahaziah son of Jehoram became
8.28 King Ahaziah joined **King** Joram of Israel
8.28 in a war against **King** Hazael of Syria.
9. 3 'The Lord proclaims that he anoints you **king of Israel.'**
9. 6 'I anoint you **king** of my people Israel.
9. 7 to kill your master the **king,** that son of Ahab,
9.12 'I anoint you **king of Israel.'** "
9.13 Jehu to stand on, blew trumpets, and shouted, "Jehu is **king!"**
9.14 in the battle at Ramoth against **King** Hazael of Syria.
9.18 and said to him, "The **king** wants to know if you come
9.29 eleventh year that Joram son of Ahab was **king of Israel.**
9.34 she is a **king's** daughter."
10. 2 are in charge of the **king's** descendants and you have at your
10. 3 the best qualified of the **king's** descendants,
10. 3 make him **king,** and fight to defend him."
10. 5 But we will not make anyone **king;**
10.30 descendants, down to the fourth generation, will be **kings of Israel."**
10.32 **King** Hazael of Syria conquered all the Israelite territory
10.34 deeds, is recorded in The History of the **Kings of Israel.**
10.35 and his son Jehoahaz succeeded him as **king.**
10.36 Jehu had ruled in Samaria as **king of Israel**
11. 7 Sabbath are to stand guard at the Temple to protect the **king.**
11.11 all round the front of the Temple, to protect the **king.**
11.12 and gave him a copy of the laws governing **kingship.**
11.12 Then Joash was anointed and proclaimed **king.**
11.12 The people clapped their hands and shouted, "Long live the **king!"**
11.14 There she saw the new **king** standing by the column at the
11.17 he also made a covenant between the **king** and the people.
11.19 palace guards escorted the **king** from the Temple to the palace,
12.17 At that time **King** Hazael of Syria attacked the city of
12.18 all as a gift to **King** Hazael, who then led his army
12.19 Joash did is recorded in The History of the **Kings of Judah.**
12.20 in David's City, and his son Amaziah succeeded him as **king.**
13. 1 son of Jehu became **king of Israel,** and he ruled in Samaria
13. 3 with Israel, and he allowed **King** Hazael of Syria and his son
13. 4 how harshly the **king of Syria** was oppressing the Israelites,
13. 7 because the **king of Syria** had destroyed the rest,
13. 8 deeds are recorded in The History of the **Kings of Israel.**
13. 9 in Samaria, and his son Jehoash succeeded him as **king.**
13.10 son of Jehoahaz became **king of Israel,** and he ruled in
13.12 of Judah, is recorded in The History of the **Kings of Israel.**
13.13 in Samaria, and his son Jeroboam II succeeded him as **king.**

2 Kgs 13.16 king did so, and Elisha placed his hands on the **king's** hands.
13.17 following the prophet's instructions, the **king** opened the window
13.17 As soon as the **king** shot the arrow,
13.18 Then Elisha told the **king** to take the other arrows
13.18 The **king** struck the ground three times, and then stopped.
13.19 and he said to the **king**, "You should have struck five or
13.22 **King** Hazael of Syria oppressed the Israelites
13.24 At the death of **King** Hazael of Syria
13.24 his son Benhadad became **king.**
14. 1 son of Jehoahaz as **king of Israel,** Amaziah son of Joash
14. 5 he executed the officials who had killed his father, the **king.**
14.15 of Judah, is recorded in The History of the **Kings of Israel.**
14.16 and his son Jeroboam II succeeded him as **king.**
14.18 Amaziah did is recorded in The History of the **Kings of Judah.**
14.21 people of Judah then crowned his sixteen-year-old son Uzziah as **king.**
14.23 son of Jehoash became **king of Israel,** and he ruled in
14.28 are all recorded in The History of the **Kings of Israel.**
14.29 and his son Zechariah succeeded him as **king.**
15. 6 Uzziah did is recorded in The History of the **Kings of Judah.**
15. 7 and his son Jotham succeeded him as **king.**
15. 8 of Jeroboam II became **king of Israel,** and he ruled in
15.10 assassinated him at Ibleam, and succeeded him as **king.**
15.11 Zechariah did is recorded in The History of the **Kings of Israel.**
15.12 descendants, down to the fourth generation, will be **kings of Israel."**
15.13 son of Jabesh became **king of Israel,** and he ruled in Samaria
15.14 assassinated Shallum, and succeeded him as **king.**
15.15 conspiracy, is recorded in The History of the **Kings of Israel.**
15.17 son of Gadi became **king of Israel,** and he ruled in Samaria
15.21 Menahem did is recorded in The History of the **Kings of Israel.**
15.22 and was buried, and his son Pekahiah succeeded him as **king.**
15.23 son of Menahem became **king of Israel,** and he ruled in
15.25 palace's inner fortress in Samaria, and succeeded him as **king.**
15.26 Pekahiah did is recorded in The History of the **Kings of Israel.**
15.27 son of Remaliah became **king of Israel,** and he ruled in
15.29 It was while Pekah was **king** that Tiglath Pileser,
15.30 against King Pekah, assassinated him, and succeeded him as **king.**
15.31 Pekah did is recorded in The History of the **Kings of Israel.**
15.32 son of Remaliah as **king of Israel,** Jotham son of Uzziah
15.36 Jotham did is recorded in The History of the **Kings of Judah.**
15.37 It was while he was **king**
15.37 that the Lord first sent **King** Rezin of Syria and King Pekah
15.38 and his son Ahaz succeeded him as **king.**
16. 1 son of Remaliah as **king of Israel,** Ahaz son of Jotham became
16. 3 Lord his God [3]and followed the example of the **kings of Israel.**
16. 5 **King** Rezin of Syria and King Pekah of Israel attacked Jerusalem
16. 6 (At the same time, the **king** of Edom regained control
16. 7 and rescue me from the **kings** of Syria and of Israel,
16. 9 against Damascus, captured it, killed **King** Rezin, and took
16.15 burnt-offerings and grain-offerings of the **king** and the people,
16.16 Uriah did as the **king** commanded.
16.18 and closed up the **king's** private entrance to the Temple.
16.19 Ahaz did is recorded in The History of the **Kings of Judah.**
16.20 and his son Hezekiah succeeded him as **king.**
17. 1 son of Elah became **king of Israel,** and he ruled in Samaria
17. 2 not as much as the **kings** who had ruled Israel before him.
17. 4 sent messengers to So, **king of Egypt,** asking for his help,
17. 7 rescued them from the **king of Egypt** and had led them out
17. 8 adopted customs introduced by the **kings of Israel.**
17.21 the Israelites made Jeroboam son of Nebat their **king.**
18. 1 son of Elah as **king of Israel,** Hezekiah son of Ahaz became
18. 5 Judah never had another **king** like him, either before or after
18.21 That is what the **king of Egypt** is like when anyone relies
18.27 you think you and the **king** are the only ones the emperor
18.37 reported to the **king** what the Assyrian official had said.
19. 9 the Egyptian army, led by **King** Tirhakah of Sudan, was coming
19.13 Where are the **kings** of the cities of Hamath, Arpad,
19.20 that in answer to the **king's** prayer [21]the Lord had said,
20. 4 Isaiah left the **king,** but before he had passed through
20. 7 Then Isaiah told the **king's** attendants to put on his boil
20.12 that same time the **king of Babylonia,** Merodach Baladan,
20.16 Isaiah then said to the **king,** "The Lord Almighty says
20.18 eunuchs to serve in the palace of the **king of Babylonia."**
20.20 city, are all recorded in The History of the **Kings of Judah.**
20.21 Hezekiah died, and his son Manasseh succeeded him as **king.**
21.17 committed, is recorded in The History of the **Kings of Judah.**
21.18 and his son Amon succeeded him as **king.**
21.24 Judah killed Amon's assassins and made his son Josiah **king.**
21.25 Amon did is recorded in The History of the **Kings of Judah.**
21.26 and his son Josiah succeeded him as **king.**
22. 8 Shaphan delivered the **king's** order to Hilkiah,
22. 9 Then he went back to the **king** and reported:
22.10 And he read it aloud to the **king.**
22.11 When the **king** heard the book being read, he tore his
22.12 and to Asaiah, the **king's** attendant:
22.15 go back to the **king** and give him [16]the following message
22.16 as written in the book that the **king** has read.
22.18 As for the **king** himself, this is what I, the Lord God
23. 2 Before them all, the **king** read aloud the whole book
23. 4 The **king** burnt all these objects outside the city
23. 5 the priests that the **kings of Judah** had ordained
23.11 the horses that the **kings of Judah** had dedicated
23.12 The altars which the **kings of Judah** had built
23.19 built by the **kings of Israel,** who thereby aroused the Lord's
23.22 celebrated by any of the **kings** of Israel or of Judah,
23.25 There had never been a **king** like him before,
23.25 nor has there been a **king** like him since.
23.28 Josiah did is recorded in The History of the **Kings of Judah.**
23.29 While Josiah was **king,** King Neco of Egypt led an army
23.30 people of Judah chose Josiah's son Joahaz and anointed him **king.**

2 Kgs 23.33 His reign ended when **King** Neco of Egypt took him prisoner
23.34 **King** Neco made Josiah's son Eliakim king of Judah
23.34 Joahaz was taken to Egypt by **King** Neco, and there he died.
23.35 needed to pay the tribute demanded by the **king of Egypt.**
24. 1 Jehoiakim was **king,**
24. 1 **King Nebuchadnezzar of Babylonia** invaded Judah,
24. 5 Jehoiakim did is recorded in The History of the **Kings of Judah.**
24. 6 Jehoiakim died, and his son Jehoiachin succeeded him as **king.**
24. 7 The **king of Egypt** and his army never marched out of Egypt
24. 7 because the **king of Babylonia** now controlled all the territory
25. 1 Zedekiah rebelled against **King Nebuchadnezzar of Babylonia,**
25. 8 the nineteenth year of **King Nebuchadnezzar of Babylonia,**
25. 8 Nebuzaradan, adviser to the **king** and commander of his army,
25.19 five of the **king's** personal advisers
25.20 took them to the **king of Babylonia,** who was in the city
25.21 There the **king** had them beaten and put to death.
25.22 **King Nebuchadnezzar of Babylonia** made Gedaliah, the son
25.24 this land, serve the **king of Babylonia,** and all will go well
25.27 Evilmerodach became **king of Babylonia,** he showed kindness
25.28 than he gave the other **kings** who were exiles with him
25.29 and to dine at the **king's** table
1 Chr 1.43 The following **kings** ruled the land of Edom
1.43 in the time before there were any **kings** in Israel:
3. 1 mother was Maacah, daughter of **King** Talmai of Geshur
3. 4 In Jerusalem he ruled as **king** for thirty-three years,
4.17 a daughter of the **king of Egypt,** and they had a daughter,
4.23 in the service of the **king** and lived in the towns
9. 1 was recorded in The Book of the **Kings of Israel.**
11. 2 when Saul was still our **king,** you led the people of Israel
11. 3 and he became **king of Israel,**
11.10 they helped him to become **king,** as the Lord had promised,
12.19 help the Philistines, for their **kings** were afraid that he
12.23 army to help make him **king** in place of Saul,
12.23 18,000 men chosen to go and make David **king;**
12.38 went to Hebron, determined to make David **king** over all Israel.
13. 3 God's Covenant Box, which was ignored while Saul was **king."**
14. 1 **King** Hiram of Tyre sent a trade mission to David;
14. 2 established him as **king of Israel** and was making his kingdom
14. 8 David had now been made **king** over the whole country of Israel,
16.21 to protect them, he warned the **kings:**
16.31 Tell the nations that the Lord is **king.**
17.11 make one of your sons **king** and will keep his kingdom strong.
17.13 Saul, whom I removed so that you could be **king.**
17.25 and have told me that you will make my descendants **kings.**
18. 3 David attacked **King** Hadadezer of the Syrian state of Zobah,
18. 5 sent an army to help **King** Hadadezer, David attacked it
18. 9 **King** Toi of Hamath heard that David had defeated Hadadezer's entire army.
19. 1 Some time later **King** Nahash of Ammon died,
19. 1 and his son Hanun became **king.**
19. 2 in Ammon and called on **King** Hanun, [3]the Ammonite leaders
19. 3 said to the **king,** "Do you think that it is
19. 6 **King** Hanun and the Ammonites realized that they had made David
19. 7 and the army of the **king** of Maacah came and camped
19. 9 their capital city, and the **kings** who had come to help took
19.16 Shobach, commander of the army of **King** Hadadezer of Zobah.
19.19 When the **kings** who were subject to Hadadezer realized
20. 1 time of the year when **kings** usually go to war, Joab led
21. 4 But the **king** made Joab obey the order.
21. 6 Because Joab disapproved of the **king's** command,
21.24 the **king** answered, "No, I will pay you the full price.
23. 1 David was very old, he made his son Solomon **king of Israel.**
23. 4 The **king** assigned twenty-four thousand to administer the work
23. 5 using the musical instruments provided by the **king**
24. 6 The **king,** his officials, the priest Zadok, Ahimelech
25. 2 Asaph, who proclaimed God's messages whenever the **king** commanded.
25. 5 God gave to Heman, the **king's** prophet, these fourteen sons
25. 6 And Asaph, Jeduthun, and Heman were under orders from the **king.**
26.31 fortieth year that David was **king,** an investigation was made
27.32 in charge of the education of the **king's** sons.
27.33 Ahithophel was adviser to the **king,**
27.33 Hushai the Archite was the **king's** friend and counsellor.
28. 1 livestock that belonged to the **king** and his sons—
28. 4 his pleasure to take me and make me **king** over all Israel.
29.11 earth is yours, and you are **king,** supreme ruler over all.
29.20 gave honour to the Lord and also to the **king.**
29.22 For a second time they proclaimed Solomon **king.**
29.23 He was a successful **king,** and the whole nation of Israel
29.24 David's other sons promised to be loyal to Solomon as **king.**
29.25 more glorious than any other **king** that had ruled Israel.
29.28 and his son Solomon succeeded him as **king.**
2 Chr 1. 6 the **king** worshipped the Lord by offering sacrifices
1. 8 and now you have let me succeed him as **king.**
1. 9 You have made me **king** over a people who are so many
1.11 you can rule my people, over whom I have made you **king.**
1.12 treasure, and fame than any **king** has ever had before
1.16 The **king's** agents controlled the export of horses
1.17 supplied the Hittite and Syrian **kings** with horses and chariots,
2. 3 Solomon sent a message to **King** Hiram of Tyre:
2.11 **King** Hiram sent Solomon a letter in reply.
2.11 "Because the Lord loves his people, he has made you their **king.**
3. 2 in the second month of the fourth year that he was **king.**
3. 6 The **king** decorated the Temple with beautiful precious stones
3.10 The **king** also ordered his workmen to make two winged creatures
3.15 The **king** made two columns,
4.17 The **king** had them all made in the foundry
6. 3 The **king** turned to face them and asked God's blessing on them.

2 Chr 6.10 succeeded my father as **king of Israel,**
6.16 his descendants ruling as **king of Israel,**
6.42 Lord God, do not reject the **king** you have chosen.
8. 2 also rebuilt the cities that **King** Hiram had given him,
8.11 the daughter of the **king of Egypt,** from David's City
8.18 **King** Hiram sent him ships under the command of his own
9. 5 She said to the **king,** "What I heard in my own country
9. 8 is with you by making you **king,** to rule in his name.
9. 8 he has made you their **king** so that you can maintain law
9.10 (The men of **King** Hiram and of King Solomon who brought
9.14 The **kings** of Arabia and the governors of the Israelite
9.17 The **king** also had a large throne made.
9.21 a fleet of ocean-going ships sailing with **King** Hiram's fleet.
9.22 Solomon was richer and wiser than any other **king** in the world.
9.26 supreme ruler of all the **kings** in the territory
9.31 and his son Rehoboam succeeded him as **king.**
10. 1 the people of northern Israel had gathered to make him **king.**
10.13 The **king** ignored the advice of the older men and spoke
10.15 This is why the **king** did not pay any attention
10.16 the people saw that the **king** would not listen to them,
10.17 Israel rebelled, [17]leaving Rehoboam as **king** only of the
11.22 children, choosing him as the one to succeed him as **king.**
12. 1 established his authority as **king,** he and all his people abandoned
12. 2 **King** Shishak of Egypt attacked Jerusalem
12. 6 The **king** and the leaders admitted that they had sinned,
12. 9 **King** Shishak came to Jerusalem and took the treasures
12.11 Every time the **king** went to the Temple, the guards carried
12.13 Rehoboam ruled in Jerusalem and increased his power as **king.**
12.13 when he became **king,** and he ruled for seventeen years
12.16 and his son Abijah succeeded him as **king.**
13. 5 David, giving him and his descendants **kingship** over Israel
13. 6 Jeroboam son of Nebat rebelled against Solomon, his **king.**
14. 1 son Asa succeeded him as **king,** and under Asa the land
15.10 in the third month of the fifteenth year that Asa was **king.**
16. 2 to Damascus, to **King** Benhadad of Syria, with this message:
16. 7 you relied on the **king of Syria**
16. 7 the army of the **king of Israel** has escaped from you.
16.11 recorded in The History of the **Kings of Judah** and Israel.
16.12 thirty-ninth year that Asa was **king,** he was crippled
17. 1 succeeded his father Asa as **king** and strengthened his position
17. 4 and did not act in the way the **kings of Israel** did.
17.19 These men served the **king** in Jerusalem,
18. 9 The two **kings,** dressed in their royal
18.12 have prophesied success for the **king,**
18.14 the **king** asked him, "Micaiah, should King Jehoshaphat
18.29 So the **king of Israel** went into battle in disguise.
18.30 The **king of Syria** had ordered his chariot commanders
18.30 to attack no one else except the **king of Israel.**
18.31 that he was the **king of Israel,** and they turned to attack
18.32 he was not the **king of Israel,** so they stopped pursuing him.
19. 2 Hanani, went to meet the **king** and said to him, "Do you
20.21 consulting with the people, the **king** ordered some musicians
20.34 which is a part of The History of the **Kings of Israel.**
21. 1 and his son Jehoram succeeded him as **king.**
21. 5 Jehoram became **king** at the age of thirty-two,
21. 6 Ahab and the other **kings of Israel,** because he had married
21.13 the example of the **kings of Israel** and have led the people
21.17 as prisoners all the **king's** wives and sons except Ahaziah,
21.18 Lord brought on the **king** a painful disease of the intestines.
21.19 it grew steadily worse until finally the **king** died in agony.
21.20 Jehoram had become **king** at the age of thirty-two
22. 1 people of Jerusalem made Ahaziah **king** as his father's successor.
22. 2 Ahaziah became **king** at the age of twenty-two,
22. 5 King Joram of Israel in a war against **King** Hazael of Syria.
23. 3 they made a covenant with Joash, the **king's** son.
23. 3 Jehoiada said to them, "Here is the son of the late **king!**
23. 3 He is now to be **king,** as the Lord promised
23. 7 to stand guard round the **king,** with their swords drawn,
23. 7 and are to stay with the **king** wherever he goes.
23.10 all round the front of the Temple, to protect the **king.**
23.11 and gave him a copy of the laws governing **kingship.**
23.11 And so he was made **king.**
23.11 his sons anointed Joash, and everyone shouted, "Long live the **king!"**
23.12 people cheering for the **king,** so she hurried to the Temple,
23.13 There she saw the new **king** at the temple entrance,
23.13 by the column reserved for **kings** and surrounded by the army
23.20 procession that brought the **king** from the Temple to the palace.
23.20 and the **king** took his place on the throne.
24. 4 After he had been **king** for a while, Joash decided
24. 8 The **king** ordered the Levites to make a box for contributions
24.12 The **king** and Jehoiada would give the money to those
24.14 silver was given to the **king** and Jehoiada,
24.21 and on the **king's** orders the people stoned Zechariah
24.22 The **king** forgot about the loyal service that Zechariah's father
24.27 Commentary on the **Book of Kings** contains the stories of the
24.27 His son Amaziah succeeded him as **king.**
25. 1 Amaziah became **king** at the age of twenty-five,
25. 7 a prophet went to the **king** and said to him, "Don't take
25.16 Amaziah interrupted, "have we made you adviser to the **king?**
25.26 recorded in The History of the **Kings of Judah** and Israel.
26. 1 Amaziah's sixteen-year-old son Uzziah to succeed his father as **king.**
26. 3 Uzziah became **king** at the age of sixteen,
26.11 under the supervision of Hananiah, a member of the **king's** staff.
26.13 307,500 soldiers able to fight effectively for the **king**
26.17 courageous priests, followed the **king** [18]to resist him.
26.20 other priests stared at the **king's** forehead in horror,
26.23 His son Jotham succeeded him as **king.**
27. 1 Jotham became **king** at the age of twenty-five,
27. 5 He fought against the **king** of Ammon and his army

2 Chr 27. 7 recorded in The History of the **Kings of Israel** and Judah.
27. 8 when he became **king,** and he ruled in Jerusalem
27. 9 and his son Ahaz succeeded him as **king.**
28. 1 Ahaz became **king** at the age of twenty,
28. 2 the Lord [2]and followed the example of the **kings of Israel.**
28. 5 his God let the **king of Syria** defeat him
28. 5 Lord also let the **king of Israel,** Pekah son of Remaliah,
28. 7 Elkanah, who was second in command to the **king.**
28.23 Syrian gods helped the **kings of Syria,** so if I sacrifice
28.26 recorded in The History of the **Kings of Judah** and Israel.
28.27 His son Hezekiah succeeded him as **king.**
29. 3 the year after Hezekiah became **king,** he re-opened the gates
29.15 Then, as the **king** had commanded them to do, they began to
29.21 The **king** told the priests, who were descendants of Aaron,
29.23 took the goats to the **king** and to the other worshippers,
29.24 for the **king** had commanded burnt-offerings and sin-offerings
29.25 The **king** followed the instructions that the Lord had given
29.25 Gad, the **king's** prophet, and through the prophet Nathan;
29.30 The **king** and the leaders of the nation told the Levites
30. 1 and the **king** sent word to all the people
30. 4 The **king** and the people were pleased with their plan,
30. 6 at the command of the **king** and his officials through all
30.12 by following the commands of the **king** and his officials.
31. 4 In addition, the **king** told the people of Jerusalem to bring
31. 9 **king** spoke to the priests and the Levites about these gifts,
31.11 On the **king's** orders they prepared storerooms
32. 5 The **king** strengthened the city's defences
32. 8 The people were encouraged by these words of their **king.**
32.32 Amoz and in The History of the **Kings of Judah** and Israel.
32.33 His son Manasseh succeeded him as **king.**
33.18 are all recorded in The History of the **Kings of Israel.**
33.19 The **king's** prayer and God's answer to it,
33.20 and his son Amon succeeded him as **king.**
33.25 killed Amon's assassins and made his son Josiah **king.**
34. 3 year that Josiah was **king,** while he was still very young,
34.11 the buildings that the **kings of Judah** had allowed to decay.
34.16 He gave Shaphan the book, [16]and Shaphan took it to the **king.**
34.18 And he read it aloud to the **king.**
34.19 When the **king** heard the book being read, he tore his
34.20 and to Asaiah, the **king's** attendant:
34.22 At the **king's** command, Hilkiah and the others went
34.23 go back to the **king** and give him [24]the following message
34.24 the curses written in the book that was read to the **king.**
34.26 As for the **king** himself, this is what I, the Lord God
34.30 Before them all, the **king** read aloud the whole book
35.10 Levites took their places, as commanded by the **king.**
35.15 Asaph, Heman, and Jeduthun, the **king's** prophet.
35.18 None of the former **kings** had ever celebrated a Passover like
35.20 **King** Neco of Egypt led an army
35.21 "This war I am fighting does not concern you, **King of Judah.**
35.22 what God was saying through **King** Neco, so he disguised himself
35.27 recorded in The History of the **Kings of Israel** and Judah.
36. 1 chose Josiah's son Joahaz and anointed him **king** in Jerusalem.
36. 3 **King** Neco of Egypt took him prisoner
36. 6 **King Nebuchadnezzar of Babylonia** invaded Judah,
36. 8 is recorded in The History of the **Kings of Israel** and Judah.
36. 8 His son Jehoiachin succeeded him as **king.**
36.10 Nebuchadnezzar made Jehoiachin's uncle Zedekiah **king of Judah** and
36.17 So the Lord brought the **king of Babylonia** to attack them.
36.17 The **king** killed the young men of Judah, even in the Temple.
36.18 The **king of Babylonia** looted the Temple,
36.18 wealth of the **king** and his officials, and took everything
Ezra 4.15 it has given trouble to **kings** and to rulers of provinces.
4.20 Powerful **kings** have reigned there and have ruled
5.11 and equipped many years ago by a powerful **king of Israel.**
5.12 King Nebuchadnezzar of Babylonia, a **king** of the Chaldean dynasty.
5.13 the reign of **King** Cyrus as emperor of Babylonia,
6.12 overthrow any **king** or nation that defies this command
9. 7 of our sins we, our **kings,** and our priests have fallen
9. 7 into the hands of foreign **kings,** and we have been slaughtered,
Neh 6. 6 you plan to make yourself **king**
6. 7 to proclaim in Jerusalem that you are the **king of Judah.**
9.10 worked amazing miracles against the **king,**
9.22 Sihon ruled, and the land of Bashan, where Og was **king.**
9.24 to do as they pleased with the people and **kings** of Canaan.
9.32 From the time when Assyrian **kings** oppressed us, even till now,
9.32 Our **kings,** our leaders, our priests and prophets,
9.34 Our ancestors, our **kings,** leaders, and priests have not
9.35 With your blessing, **kings** ruled your people
9.37 land produces goes to the **kings** that you put over us
13. 6 thirty-second year that Artaxerxes was **king** of Babylon
13.26 man who was greater than any of the **kings** of other nations.
13.26 loved him and made him **king** over all Israel,
Esth 1. 1 **King** Xerxes ruled over 127 provinces,
1. 5 After that, the **king** gave a banquet for all the men
1. 7 and the **king** was generous with the royal wine.
1. 8 the **king** had given orders to the palace servants
1.10 the **king** was drinking and feeling merry,
1.11 a beautiful woman, and the **king** wanted to show off her
1.12 servants told Queen Vashti of the **king's** command,
1.12 This made the **king** furious.
1.13 Now it was the **king's** custom to ask for expert opinion
1.15 said to these men, "I, **King** Xerxes, sent my servants to
1.16 Then Memucan declared to the **king** and his officials:
1.16 has insulted not only the **king** but also his officials—
1.17 They'll say, **'King** Xerxes commanded Queen Vashti to come
1.19 proclamation that Vashti may never again appear before the **king.**
1.21 The **king** and his officials liked this idea,
1.21 and the **king** did what Memucan suggested.

Esth 2. 1 Later, even after the **king's** anger had cooled down,
2. 2 the **king's** advisers who were close to him suggested,
2. 4 The **king** thought this was good advice, so he followed it.
2. 6 When **King Nebuchadnezzar of Babylon** took King Jehoiachin
2. 8 When the **king** had issued his new proclamation
2.12 After that, each girl would be taken in turn to **King** Xerxes.
2.14 Shaashgaz, the eunuch in charge of the **king's** concubines.
2.14 would not go to the **king** again unless he liked her enough
2.15 The time came for Esther to go to the **king.**
2.16 in Xerxes' seventh year as **king,** in the tenth month,
2.16 Esther was brought to **King** Xerxes in the royal palace.
2.17 The **king** liked her more than any of the other girls,
2.18 Then the **king** gave a great banquet in Esther's honour
2.18 distributed gifts worthy of a **king.**
2.19 Mordecai had been appointed by the **king** to an administrative position.
2.21 guarded the entrance to the **king's** rooms,
2.21 became hostile to **King** Xerxes and plotted to assassinate him.
2.22 Esther, who then told the **king** what Mordecai had found out.
2.23 The **king** ordered an account of this to be written down
3. 1 Some time later **King** Xerxes promoted a man named Haman
3. 2 The **king** ordered all the officials in his service to show
3. 3 asked him why he was disobeying the **king's** command;
3. 7 In the twelfth year of **King** Xerxes' rule,
3. 8 So Haman told the **king,** "There is a certain race of
3.10 The **king** took off his ring,
3.11 The **king** told him, "The people and their money are yours;
3.12 Haman called the **king's** secretaries and dictated a proclamation
3.12 issued in the name of **King** Xerxes and stamped with his ring.
3.15 At the **king's** command the decree was made public
3.15 The **king** and Haman sat down and had a drink
4. 3 wherever the **king's** proclamation was made known,
4. 5 as her servant by the **king,** and told him to go
4. 8 go and plead with the **king** and beg him to have mercy
4.11 inner courtyard and sees the **king** without being summoned,
4.11 everyone, from the **king's** advisers to the people
4.11 if the **king** holds out his gold sceptre to someone,
4.11 But it has been a month since the **king** sent for me."
4.16 I will go to the **king,** even though it is against the
5. 1 The **king** was inside, seated on the royal throne,
5. 2 When the **king** saw Queen Esther standing outside,
5. 3 the **king** asked.
5. 5 The **king** then ordered Haman to come quickly,
5. 5 So the **king** and Haman went to Esther's banquet.
5. 6 Over the wine the **king** asked her, "Tell me what you want,
5.11 how the **king** had promoted him to high office,
5.11 more important he was than any of the **king's** other officials.
5.12 for no one but the **king** and me, and we are invited
5.14 you can ask the **king** to have Mordecai hanged on it,
6. 1 That same night the **king** could not get to sleep,
6. 2 a plot to assassinate the **king**—the plot made by Bigthana
6. 2 the two palace eunuchs who had guarded the **king's** rooms.
6. 3 The **king** asked, "How have we honoured and rewarded Mordecai
6. 4 the **king** asked.
6. 4 had come to ask the **king** to have Mordecai hanged
6. 5 "Show him in," said the **king.**
6. 6 Haman came in, and the **king** said to him, "There is someone
6. 6 to himself, "Now who could the **king** want to honour so much?
6. 7 So he answered the **king,** "Order royal robes
6. 9 'See how the **king** rewards a man he wishes to honour!' "
6.10 Then the **king** said to Haman, "Hurry and get the robes
6.11 "See how the **king** rewards a man he wishes to honour!"
7. 1 And so the **king** and Haman went to eat with Esther
7. 2 Over the wine the **king** asked her again, "Now, Queen Esther,
7. 5 Then **King** Xerxes asked Queen Esther, "Who dares to do such
7. 6 Haman stared at the **king** and queen in terror.
7. 7 The **king** got up in a fury, left the room, and went
7. 7 Haman could see that the **king** was determined to punish him
7. 8 beg for mercy, when the **king** came back into the room
7. 8 Seeing this, the **king** cried out, "Is this man going to rape
7. 8 The **king** had no sooner said this than the eunuchs covered
7. 9 the **king** commanded.
7.10 Then the **king's** anger cooled down.
8. 1 **King** Xerxes gave Queen Esther all the property
8. 1 Esther told the **king** that Mordecai was related to her,
8. 1 Mordecai was allowed to enter the **king's** presence.
8. 2 The **king** took off his ring with his seal on it
8. 3 Then Esther spoke to the **king** again,
8. 4 The **king** held out the gold sceptre to her, so she stood
8. 7 **King** Xerxes then said to Queen Esther and Mordecai,
8. 8 a proclamation issued in the **king's** name
8. 9 Mordecai called the **king's** secretaries and dictated letters
8.10 written in the name of **King** Xerxes, and he stamped them with
8.11 These letters explained that the **king** would allow the Jews
8.14 At the **king's** command the riders mounted royal horses
8.17 wherever the **king's** proclamation was read,
9.11 number of people killed in Susa was reported to the **king.**
9.14 The **king** ordered this to be done,
9.25 But Esther went to the **king,** and the king issued written
10. 1 **King** Xerxes imposed forced labour on the people
10. 2 in the official records of the **kings** of Persia and Media.
10. 3 Mordecai the Jew was second in rank only to **King** Xerxes

Job 3.14 sleeping like the **kings** and rulers who rebuilt ancient palaces.
12.18 He dethrones **kings** and makes them prisoners;
15.24 disaster, like a powerful **king,** is waiting to attack him.
18.14 he lived secure, and is dragged off to face **King** Death.
29.25 I led them as a **king** leads his troops,
34.18 God condemns **kings** and rulers when they are worthless
36. 7 allows them to rule like **kings** and lets them be honoured
41.34 he is **king** of all wild beasts.

Ps 2. 2 Their **kings** revolt, their rulers plot together
2. 2 against the Lord and against the **king**
2. 6 "On Zion, my sacred hill," he says, "I have installed my **king.**"
2. 7 "I will announce," says the **king,** "what the Lord has declared.
2.10 Now listen to this warning, you **kings;**
5. 2 Listen to my cry for help, my God and **king!**
9. 7 But the Lord is **king** for ever;
10.16 The Lord is **king** for ever and ever.
18.50 God gives great victories to his **king;**
20. 6 Now I know that the Lord gives victory to his chosen **king;**
20. 9 Give victory to the **king,** O Lord;
21. 1 The **king** is glad, O Lord, because you gave him strength;
21. 7 The **king** trusts in the Lord Almighty;
21. 8 The **king** will capture all his enemies;
21.10 the **king** will kill them all.
22.28 The Lord is **king,** and he rules the nations.
24. 7 open the ancient doors, and the great **king** will come in.
24. 8 Who is this great **king?**
24. 9 open the ancient doors, and the great **king** will come in.
24.10 Who is this great **king?**
24.10 The triumphant Lord—he is the great **king!**
28. 8 he defends and saves his chosen **king.**
29.10 he rules as **king** for ever.
33.16 A **king** does not win because of his powerful army;
44. 4 You are my **king** and my God;
45. 1 words fill my mind, as I compose this song for the **king.**
45. 3 Buckle on your sword, mighty **king;**
45. 7 poured out more happiness on you than on any other **king.**
45. 9 your court are daughters of **kings,** and on the right of your
45.10 Bride of the **king,** listen to what I say—
45.11 Your beauty will make the **king** desire you;
45.14 she is led to the **king,** followed by her bridesmaids,
45.15 With joy and gladness they come and enter the **king's** palace.
45.16 You, my **king,** will have many sons
45.16 to succeed your ancestors as **kings,**
47. 2 he is a great **king,** ruling over all the world.
47. 6 sing praise to our **king!**
47. 7 God is **king** over all the world;
48. 2 the city of the great **king** brings joy to all the world.
48. 4 The **kings** gathered together and came to attack Mount Zion.
61. 6 Add many years to the **king's** life;
63.11 Because God gives him victory, the **king** will rejoice.
68.12 **"Kings** and their armies are running away!"
68.14 When Almighty God scattered the **kings** on Mount Zalmon,
68.24 the procession of God, my **king,** into his sanctuary.
68.29 from your Temple in Jerusalem, where **kings** bring gifts to you.
72. 1 Teach the **king** to judge with your righteousness, O God;
72. 4 May the **king** judge the poor fairly;
72. 6 May the **king** be like rain on the fields,
72.10 The **kings** of Spain and of the islands will offer him gifts;
72.10 the **kings** of Sheba and Seba will bring him offerings.
72.11 All **kings** will bow down before him;
72.15 Long live the **king!**
72.17 May the **king's** name never be forgotten;
72.17 nations ask God to bless them as he has blessed the **king.**
74.12 But you have been our **king** from the beginning, O God;
76.12 he humbles proud princes and terrifies great **kings.**
78.71 flocks, and he made him **king** of Israel, the shepherd
78.71 and he made him **king of Israel,** the shepherd of the people
84. 3 near your altars, Lord Almighty, my **king** and my God.
84. 9 Bless our **king,** O God, the king you have chosen.
84.11 our protector and glorious **king,** blessing us with kindness
89. 4 David, "'A descendant of yours will always be **king;**
89.18 you, the Holy God of Israel, gave us our **king.**
89.20 made my servant David **king** by anointing him with holy oil.
89.27 I will make him my first-born son, the greatest of all **kings.**
89.29 a descendant of his will always be **king.**
89.38 But you are angry with your chosen **king;**
89.51 Your enemies insult your chosen **king,** O Lord!
93. 1 The Lord is **king.**
95. 3 Lord is a mighty God, a mighty **king** over all the gods.
96.10 Say to all the nations, "The Lord is **king!**
97. 1 The Lord is **king!**
98. 6 and horns, and shout for joy to the Lord, our **king.**
99. 1 The Lord is **king;**
99. 4 Mighty **king,** you love what is right;
102.12 But you, O Lord, are **king** for ever;
102.15 all the **kings** of the earth will fear his power.
103.19 he is **king** over all.
105.14 to protect them, he warned the **kings:**
105.20 Then the **king of Egypt** had him released;
105.22 with power over the **king's** officials and authority
110. 1 said to my lord, the **king,** "Sit here at my right
110. 5 when he becomes angry, he will defeat **kings.**
110. 6 he will defeat **kings** all over the earth.
110. 7 The **king** will drink from the stream by the road,
119.46 announce your commands to **kings** and I will not be ashamed.
122. 5 Here the **kings of Israel** sat to judge their people.
132.10 do not reject your chosen **king,** Lord.
132.11 make one of your sons **king,** and he will rule after you.
132.12 their sons, also, will succeed you for all time as **kings."**
132.17 Here I will make one of David's descendants a great **king;**
132.17 here I will preserve the rule of my chosen **king.**
135. 9 performed miracles and wonders to punish the **king**
135.10 He destroyed many nations and killed powerful **kings:**
135.11 Sihon, **king** of the Amorites,
135.11 Og, **king** of Bashan,
135.11 and all the **kings** in Canaan.
136.15 but he drowned the **king of Egypt** and his army;
136.17 He killed powerful **kings;**
136.18 he killed famous **kings;**
136.19 Sihon, **king** of the Amorites;

Ps 136.20 and Og, **king** of Bashan;
138. 4 All the **kings** in the world will praise you, Lord,
144.10 You give victory to **kings** and rescue your servant David.
145. 1 I will proclaim your greatness, my God and **king**;
145.13 Your rule is eternal, and you are **king** for ever.
146.10 The Lord is **king** for ever.
148.11 Praise him, **kings** and all peoples,
149. 2 rejoice, people of Zion, because of your **king!**
149. 8 to bind their **kings** in chains, their leaders in chains of iron;
Prov 1. 1 The proverbs of Solomon, son of David and **king of Israel.**
8.15 I help **kings** to govern and rulers to make good laws.
14.28 A **king's** greatness depends on how many people he rules;
14.35 **Kings** are pleased with competent officials,
16.10 The **king** speaks with divine authority;
16.12 **Kings** cannot tolerate evil,
16.13 A **king** wants to hear the truth
16.14 A wise man will try to keep the **king** happy;
16.14 if the **king** becomes angry, someone may die.
16.15 The **king's** favour is like the clouds that bring rain
19.12 The **king's** anger is like the roar of a lion,
20. 2 Fear an angry **king** as you would a growling lion;
20. 8 The **king** sits in judgement and knows evil when he sees it.
20.26 A wise **king** will find out who is doing wrong,
20.28 A **king** will remain in power as long as his rule is
21. 1 controls the mind of a **king** as easily as he directs
22.11 graciousness of speech, the **king** will be your friend.
22.29 who is better than most and worthy of the company of **kings.**
24.21 Have reverence for the Lord, my son, and honour the **king.**
24.22 Do you realize the disaster that God or the **king** can cause?
25. 1 copied by men at the court of **King** Hezekiah of Judah.
25. 2 we honour **kings** for what they explain.
25. 3 You never know what a **king** is thinking;
25. 5 evil advisers away from the **king** and his government will be
25. 6 When you stand before the **king,** don't try to impress him
29. 4 When the **king** is concerned with justice, the nation will be strong,
29.14 If a **king** defends the rights of the poor, he will rule
30.22 a slave who becomes a **king,**
30.27 they have no **king,** but they move in formation.
30.31 goats, strutting cocks, and **kings** in front of their people.
31. 1 These are the solemn words which **King** Lemuel's mother said
31. 3 they have destroyed **kings.**
31. 4 **Kings** should not drink wine or have a craving for alcohol.
Ecc 1. 1 the Philosopher, David's son, who was **king** in Jerusalem.
1.12 I, the Philosopher, have been **king** over Israel
2.12 a **king** can only do what previous kings have done.
4.13 rise from poverty to become **king** of his country,
4.15 there is a young man who will take the **king's** place.
4.16 may be no limit to the number of people a **king** rules;
5. 9 Even a **king** depends on the harvest.
8. 2 Do what the **king** says, and don't make any rash promises
8. 3 The **king** can do anything he likes,
8. 4 The **king** acts with authority, and no one can challenge
9.14 A powerful **king** attacked it.
10.16 is in trouble when its **king** is a youth
10.17 is fortunate to have a **king** who makes his own decisions
10.20 Don't criticize the **king,** even silently,
Song 1. 4 be my **king** and take me to your room.
1.12 My **king** was lying on his couch,
6. 8 Let the **king** have sixty queens, eighty concubines,
7. 5 its beauty could hold a **king** captive.
Is 1. 1 when Uzziah, Jotham, Ahaz, and Hezekiah were **kings of Judah.**
6. 5 my own eyes, I have seen the **King,** the Lord Almighty!"
7. 1 **king of Syria,** and Pekah son of Remaliah, king of Israel,
7. 2 word reached the **king of Judah** that the armies of Syria
7. 4 The anger of **King** Rezin and his Syrians and of King Pekah
7. 5 Syria, together with Israel and its **king,** has made a plot.
7. 8 and Damascus is no stronger than **King** Rezin.
7. 9 and Samaria is no stronger than **King** Pekah.
7.16 lands of those two **kings** who terrify you will be deserted.
7.17 from Judah—he is going to bring the **king** of Assyria.
8. 4 of Samaria will be carried off by the **king** of Assyria."
8. 6 and tremble before **King** Rezin and King Pekah,
8.21 they will curse their **king** and their God.
10. 8 He boasts, "Every one of my commanders is a **king!**
11. 1 so a new **king** will arise from among David's descendants.
11.10 is coming when the new **king** from the royal line of David
14. 4 they are to mock the **king of Babylonia** and say:
14. 4 "The cruel **king** has fallen!
14. 8 Lebanon rejoice over the fallen **king,**
14. 9 the dead is getting ready to welcome the **king of Babylonia.**
14. 9 The ghosts of **kings** are rising from their thrones.
14.12 **"King of Babylonia,** bright morning star,
14.13 you would sit like a **king** on that mountain in the north
14.18 All the **kings** of the earth lie in their magnificent tombs,
14.20 your own people, you will not be buried like other **kings.**
14.21 The sons of this **king** will die because of their ancestors'
16. 5 of David's descendants will be **king,** and he will rule
19. 2 and rival **kings** will struggle for power.
19. 4 over to a tyrant, to a cruel **king** who will rule them.
19.11 How dare they tell the **king** that they are successors
19.11 successors to the ancient scholars and **kings?**
19.12 **King of Egypt,** where are those clever advisers of yours?
22.22 complete authority under the **king,** the descendant of David.
23.15 Tyre will be forgotten for seventy years, the lifetime of a **king.**
24.22 God will crowd **kings** together like prisoners in a pit.
24.23 will no longer shine, for the Lord Almighty will be **king.**
30. 2 Egypt to protect them, so they put their trust in **Egypt's king.**
30. 3 But the **king** will be powerless to help them,
32. 1 day there will be a **king** who rules with integrity,
33.17 again you will see a **king** ruling in splendour over a land
33.22 The Lord himself will be our **king;**
Is 34.12 There will be no **king** to rule the country,
36. 1 Hezekiah was **king of Judah,** Sennacherib, the emperor of Assyria,
36. 6 That is what the **king of Egypt** is like when anyone relies
36.12 you think you and the **king** are the only ones the emperor
36.22 reported to the **king** what the Assyrian official had said.
37. 1 As soon as **King** Hezekiah heard their report, he tore his
37. 5 When Isaiah received **King** Hezekiah's message,
37. 9 the Egyptian army, led by **King** Tirhakah of Sudan, was coming
37.13 Where are the **kings** of the cities of Hamath, Arpad,
37.21 that in answer to the **king's** prayer [22] the Lord had said,
38. 6 Isaiah told the **king** to put a paste made of figs
39. 1 the **king of Babylonia,** Merodach Baladan, son of Baladan,
39. 5 Isaiah then told the **king,** "The Lord Almighty says
39. 7 eunuchs to serve in the palace of the **king of Babylonia."**
41. 2 Who gives him victory over **kings** and nations?
41.21 The Lord, the **king of Israel,** has this to say:
43.15 I created you, Israel, and I am your **king."**
45. 1 The Lord has chosen Cyrus to be **king!**
45. 1 he sends him to strip **kings** of their power;
49. 7 **"Kings** will see you released and will rise to show their respect;
49.23 **Kings** will be like fathers to you;
52. 7 He announces victory and says to Zion, "Your God is **king!"**
52.15 and **kings** will be speechless with amazement.
60. 3 drawn to your light, And **kings** to the dawning of your new
60.10 "Foreigners will rebuild your walls, And their **kings** will serve you.
60.11 So that the **kings** of the nations May bring you
60.16 Nations and **kings** will care for you
62. 2 All their **kings** will see your glory.
Jer 1. 3 and he spoke to him again when Josiah's son Jehoiakim was **king.**
1.15 Their **kings** will set up their thrones at the gates of
1.18 the **kings of Judah,** the officials, the priests,
2.26 Israel will be disgraced—your **kings** and officials,
3. 6 When Josiah was **king,** the Lord said to me, "Have you seen
4. 9 "On that day **kings** and officials will lose their courage;
6. 3 **kings** will camp there with their armies.
6. 6 Lord Almighty has ordered these **kings** to cut down trees
8. 1 the bones of the **kings** and of the officials of Judah,
8.19 Is Zion's **king** no longer there?"
8.19 The Lord, their **king,** replies, "Why have you made me angry
10. 7 Who would not honour you, the **king** of all nations?
10. 7 the wise men of the nations or among any of their **kings.**
10.10 the true God, you are the living God and the eternal **king.**
13.13 the **kings,** who are David's descendants, the priests,
13.18 said to me, "Tell the **king** and his mother to come down
15. 4 Hezekiah's son Manasseh did in Jerusalem when he was **king of Judah."**
17.19 through which the **kings of Judah** enter and leave the city;
17.20 Tell the **kings** and all the people of Judah
17.25 Then their **kings** and princes will enter the gates
19. 3 **"Kings of Judah** and people of Jerusalem, listen
19. 4 ancestors nor the **kings of Judah** have known anything about.
19.13 the houses of the **kings of Judah,** and indeed all the houses
20. 4 people of Judah under the power of the **king of Babylonia;**
20. 5 the treasures of the **kings of Judah,** and carry everything off
21. 2 because **King Nebuchadnezzar of Babylonia** and his army are
21. 4 fighting against the **king of Babylonia** and his army.
21.10 given over to the **king of Babylonia** and he will burn it
22. 1 the palace of the **king of Judah,** the descendant of David,
22. 1 and there tell the **king,** his officials, and the people
22. 4 then David's descendants will continue to be **kings.**
22.11 succeeded his father as **king of Judah,** "He has gone away
22.15 it make you a better **king** if you build houses of cedar,
22.18 the Lord says about Josiah's son Jehoiakim, **king of Judah,**
22.18 **My king!"**
22.25 I will give you to **King Nebuchadnezzar of Babylonia**
23. 5 I will choose as **king** a righteous descendant of David.
23. 5 That **king** will rule wisely and do what is right and just
23. 6 When he is **king,** the people of Judah will be safe,
24. 1 **King Nebuchadnezzar of Babylonia** had taken away Jehoiakim's son,
25. 1 (This was the first year that Nebuchadnezzar was **king of Babylonia.)**
25. 9 and for my servant, **King Nebuchadnezzar of Babylonia.**
25.11 the neighbouring nations will serve the **king of Babylonia**
25.12 I will punish Babylonia and its **king** for their sin.
25.14 many nations and great **kings** will make slaves of them.' "
25.18 Judah, together with its **kings** and leaders, were made to drink
25.19 the **king of Egypt,** his officials and leaders;
25.19 all the **kings** of the land of Uz;
25.19 all the **kings** of the Philistine cities of Ashkelon, Gaza,
25.19 all the **kings** of Tyre and Sidon;
25.19 all the **kings** of the Mediterranean lands;
25.19 all the **kings** of Arabia;
25.19 all the **kings** of the desert tribes;
25.19 all the **kings** of Zimri, Elam, and Media;
25.19 the **kings** of the north, far and near, one after another.
25.19 Last of all, the **king of Babylonia** will drink from it.
26.18 "When Hezekiah was **king of Judah,** the prophet Micah
26.21 what Uriah had said, the **king** tried to have him killed.
27. 3 send a message to the **kings** of Edom, Moab, Ammon, Tyre,
27. 4 to command them to tell their **kings** that the Lord had said:
27. 6 power of my servant, **King Nebuchadnezzar of Babylonia,**
27. 7 Then his nation will serve powerful nations and great **kings.**
27. 9 They all tell you not to submit to the **king of Babylonia.**
27.11 nation submits to the **king of Babylonia** and serves him,
27.12 to King Zedekiah of Judah, "Submit to the **king of Babylonia.**
27.13 to any nation that does not submit to the **king of Babylonia.**
27.17 Submit to the **king of Babylonia** and you will live!
27.19 to Babylonia the **king of Judah,** Jehoiachin son of Jehoiakim,
28. 1 fourth year that Zedekiah was **king,** Hananiah son of Azzur,
28. 2 "I have broken the power of the **king of Babylonia.**

Jer 28. 4 bring back the **king of Judah,** Jehoiachin son of Jehoiakim,
28. 4 Yes, I will break the power of the **king of Babylonia.**
28.14 they will serve **King Nebuchadnezzar of Babylonia.**
29. 3 Zedekiah of Judah was sending to **King Nebuchadnezzar of Babylonia.**
29.16 the Lord says about the **king** who rules the kingdom that
29.21 to the power of **King Nebuchadnezzar of Babylonia,**
29.22 Zedekiah and Ahab, whom the **king of Babylonia** roasted alive!'
30. 9 and a descendant of David, whom I will enthrone as **king.**
32. 1 the eighteenth year of **King Nebuchadnezzar of Babylonia.**
32. 2 the army of the **king of Babylonia** was attacking Jerusalem,
32. 3 going to let the **king of Babylonia** capture this city,
32. 4 He will be handed over to the **king of Babylonia;**
32.28 give this city over to **King Nebuchadnezzar of Babylonia**
32.32 Jerusalem, together with their **kings** and leaders,
32.36 make this city fall into the hands of the **king of Babylonia.**
33.15 I will choose as **king** a righteous descendant of David.
33.15 That **king** will do what is right and just throughout the land.
33.17 of David to be **king of Israel** [18] and that there will always
33.21 have a descendant to be **king,** and I have made a covenant
34. 1 spoke to me when **King Nebuchadnezzar of Babylonia** and his army,
34. 2 city over to the **king of Babylonia,** and he will burn it
34. 5 buried your ancestors, who were **kings** before you,
34. 5 They will mourn over you and say, 'Our **king** is dead!'
34. 7 the army of the **king of Babylonia** was attacking the city.
36. 2 first spoke to you, when Josiah was **king,** up to the present.
36. 9 year that Jehoiakim was **king of Judah,** the people fasted
36.16 and said to Baruch, "We must report this to the **king."**
36.20 the king's court, where they reported everything to the **king.**
36.21 Then the **king** sent Jehudi to get the scroll.
36.21 and read it to the **king** and all the officials
36.22 It was winter and the **king** was sitting in his winter
36.23 the **king** cut them off
36.24 But neither the **king** nor any of his officials
36.25 Gemariah begged the **king** not to burn the scroll,
36.29 say to the **king,** "You have burnt the scroll,
36.29 he wrote that the **king of Babylonia** would come and destroy
37. 1 **King Nebuchadnezzar of Babylonia** made Zedekiah son of Josiah
37.17 added, "You will be handed over to the **king of Babylonia."**
37.19 told you that the **king of Babylonia** would not attack you
38. 4 the officials went to the **king** and said, "This man must be
38. 7 At that time the **king** was holding court at the Benjamin Gate.
38. 8 and said to the **king,** [9] "Your Majesty, what these men have
38.10 the **king** ordered Ebedmelech to take with him three men
38.17 you surrender to the **king of Babylonia's** officers,
38.19 But the **king** answered, "I am afraid of our countrymen
38.22 being led out to the **king of Babylonia's** officers.
38.22 'The **king's** best friends misled him, they overruled him.
38.23 taken prisoner by the **king of Babylonia,**
38.27 I told them exactly what the **king** had told me to say.
39. 1 Zedekiah was **king of Judah,**
39. 1 **King Nebuchadnezzar of Babylonia** came with his whole
39. 2 Zedekiah's eleventh year as **king,** the city walls were broken
39. 3 officials of the **king of Babylonia** came and took their places
39.13 other officers of the **king of Babylonia,**
40. 5 of Shaphan, whom the **king of Babylonia** has made governor
40. 7 heard that the **king of Babylonia** had made Gedaliah governor
40. 9 serve the **king of Babylonia,** and all will go well
40.11 heard that the **king of Babylonia** had allowed some Israelites
40.14 "Don't you know that **King** Baalis of Ammon has sent Ishmael
41. 1 one of the **king's** chief officers, went to Mizpah
41.10 he made prisoners of the **king's** daughters
41.17 Gedaliah, whom the **king of Babylonia** had made governor
42.11 Stop being afraid of the **king of Babylonia.**
43. 6 the men, the women, the children, and the **king's** daughters.
43.10 bring my servant **King Nebuchadnezzar of Babylonia** to this place,
43.12 and the **king of Babylonia** will either burn their gods
43.12 of lice, so the **king of Babylonia** will pick the land
44. 9 your ancestors, by the **kings of Judah** and their wives,
44.17 we and our ancestors, our **king** and our leaders, used to do
44.21 you and your ancestors, your **kings** and your leaders,
44.30 I will hand over **King** Hophra of Egypt to his enemies
44.30 to **King Nebuchadnezzar of Babylonia,** who was his enemy
46. 2 said about the army of **King** Neco of Egypt,
46. 2 which **King Nebuchadnezzar of Babylonia** defeated at Carchemish
46. 2 Euphrates in the fourth year that Jehoiakim was **king of Judah:**
46.13 When **King Nebuchadnezzar of Babylonia** came to attack Egypt,
46.17 "Give the **king of Egypt** a new name— 'Noisy
46.18 I, the Lord Almighty, am **king.**
46.25 god of Thebes, together with Egypt and its gods and **kings.**
46.25 going to take the **king of Egypt** and all who put their
46.26 to **King Nebuchadnezzar of Babylonia** and his army.
47. 1 Before the **king of Egypt** attacked Gaza, the Lord spoke to
48.15 I am the **king,** the Lord Almighty, and I have spoken.
48.45 in Heshbon, the city that **King** Sihon once ruled,
49.27 Damascus on fire and will burn down **King** Benhadad's palaces.
49.28 which were conquered by **King Nebuchadnezzar of Babylonia:**
49.30 **King Nebuchadnezzar of Babylonia** has plotted against you,
49.34 after Zedekiah became **king of Judah,** the Lord Almighty spoke
49.38 I will destroy their **kings** and leaders,
50.17 and then **King Nebuchadnezzar of Babylonia** gnawed their bones.
50.41 many **kings** are preparing for war.
50.43 The **king of Babylonia** hears the news, and his hands hang limp.
51.11 Lord has stirred up the **kings** of Media,
51.28 Send for the **kings** of Media, their leaders and officials,
51.31 runs to tell the **king of Babylonia** that his city
51.34 The **king of Babylonia** cut Jerusalem up and ate it.
51.46 violence in the land and of one **king** fighting another.

Jer 51.57 I, the **king,** have spoken, I am the Lord Almighty.
51.59 Zedekiah was **king of Judah,** Seraiah was going to Babylonia
52. 3 Zedekiah rebelled against **King Nebuchadnezzar of Babylonia.**
52.12 the nineteenth year of **King Nebuchadnezzar of Babylonia,**
52.12 Nebuzaradan, adviser to the **king** and commander of his army,
52.25 the troops, seven of the **king's** personal advisers who were
52.26 took them to the **king of Babylonia,** who was in the city
52.27 There the **king** had them beaten and put to death.
52.28 in his seventh year as **king** he carried away 3,023;
52.31 year that Evilmerodach became **king of Babylonia,**
52.32 than he gave the other **kings** who were exiles with him
52.33 and to dine at the **king's** table

Lam 2. 6 **King** and priest alike have felt the force of his anger.
2. 9 The **king** and the noblemen now are in exile.
4.20 source of our life, the **king** the Lord had chosen,
5.19 But you, O Lord, are **king** for ever,

Ezek 7.27 The **king** will mourn, the prince will give up hope,
17.12 Tell them that the **king of Babylonia** came to Jerusalem
17.12 and took the **king** and his officials back with him
17.13 He took one of the **king's** family, made a treaty with him,
17.15 But the **king of Judah** rebelled and sent agents to Egypt
17.16 says the Sovereign Lord, "this **king** will die in Babylonia
17.16 had made with the **king of Babylonia,** who put him on the
17.17 powerful army of the **king of Egypt** will not be able
19. 9 him in a cage and took him to the **king of Babylonia.**
21.19 by which the **king of Babylonia** can come with his sword.
21.20 One will show the **king** the way to the Ammonite city
21.21 The **king of Babylonia** stands by the signpost
24. 2 the day that the **king of Babylonia** is beginning the siege
26. 7 the greatest king of all—**King Nebuchadnezzar of Babylonia**—
26.16 All the **kings** of the seafaring nations will come down
27.33 **Kings** were made rich By the wealth of your goods.
27.35 their **kings** are terrified, and fear is written on their faces.
28.12 "grieve for the fate that is waiting for the **king** of Tyre.
28.17 to the ground and left you as a warning to other **kings.**
29. 2 "Mortal man," he said, "denounce the **king of Egypt.**
29. 3 is what the Sovereign Lord is telling the **king of Egypt:**
29.18 "Mortal man," he said, **"King Nebuchadnezzar of Babylonia**
29.18 worn raw, but neither the **king** nor his army got anything
30.10 "I will use **King Nebuchadnezzar of Babylonia** to put an end
30.21 he said, "I have broken the arm of the **king of Egypt.**
30.22 I am the enemy of the **king of Egypt.**
30.24 the arms of the **king of Babylonia** strong
30.24 the arms of the **king of Egypt,** and he will groan
30.25 Yes, I will weaken him and strengthen the **king of Babylonia.**
31. 2 he said, "say to the **king of Egypt** and all his people:
31.18 "The tree is the **king of Egypt** and all his people.
32. 2 he said, "give a solemn warning to the **king of Egypt.**
32.10 When I swing my sword, **kings** will shudder with fright.
32.11 Lord says to the **king of Egypt,**
32.11 "You will face the sword of the **king of Babylonia.**
32.29 "Edom is there with her **kings** and rulers.
32.31 a comfort to the **king of Egypt** and his army,"
32.32 "I made the **king of Egypt** terrorize the living,
34.23 I will give them a **king** like my servant David
34.24 be their God, and a **king** like my servant David will be
37.22 They will have one **king** to rule over them,
37.24 A **king** like my servant David will be their king.
37.25 A **king** like my servant David will rule over them for ever.
43. 7 Israel nor their **kings** will ever again disgrace my holy
43. 7 or by burying the corpses of their **kings** in this place.
43. 8 The **kings** built the thresholds and door-posts of their palace
43. 9 stop worshipping other gods and remove the corpses of their **kings.**

Dan 1. 1 Jehoiakim was **king of Judah,**
1. 1 **King Nebuchadnezzar of Babylonia** attacked Jerusalem
1. 3 The **king** ordered Ashpenaz, his chief official, to select
1. 5 The **king** also gave orders that every day they were to be
1. 5 years of this training they were to appear before the **king.**
1.10 was afraid of the **king,** so he said to Daniel,
1.10 "The **king** has decided what you are to
1.16 continue to eat vegetables instead of what the **king** provided.
1.18 three years set by the **king,** Ashpenaz took all the young men
1.19 The **king** talked with them all, and Daniel, Hananiah,
1.19 So they became members of the **king's** court.
1.20 No matter what question the **king** asked,
2. 1 In the second year that Nebuchadnezzar was **king,** he had a dream.
2. 2 came and stood before the **king,**
2. 4 They answered the **king** in Aramaic, "May Your Majesty live
2. 5 The **king** said to them, "I have made up my mind
2. 7 answered the **king** again, "If Your Majesty will only tell us
2. 8 At that, the **king** exclaimed, "Just as I thought!
2.10 No **king,** not even the greatest and most powerful,
2.12 the **king** flew into a rage and ordered the execution
2.14 Arioch, commander of the **king's** bodyguard,
2.15 he asked Arioch why the **king** had issued such a harsh order.
2.16 so that he could tell the **king** what the dream meant.
2.21 he makes and unmakes **kings;**
2.23 answered my prayer and shown us what to tell the **king."**
2.24 went to Arioch, whom the **king** had commanded to execute
2.24 Take me to the **king,** and I will tell him
2.25 and told the **king,** "I have found one of the
2.26 The **king** said to Daniel (who was also called Belteshazzar),
2.37 Your Majesty, you are the greatest of all **kings.**
2.47 The **king** said, "Your God is the greatest of all gods,
2.47 the Lord over **kings,** and the one who reveals mysteries.
2.49 the **king** put Shadrach, Meshach, and Abednego in charge
3. 2 the **king** gave orders for all his officials to come together
3.13 At that, the **king** flew into a rage and ordered the
3.22 the **king** had given strict orders for the furnace to

Dan 3.27 and other officials of the **king** gathered to look at the
3.28 The **king** said, "Praise the God of Shadrach, Meshach,
3.30 And the **king** promoted Shadrach, Meshach, and Abednego
4. 3 God is **king** for ever;
4.19 The **king** said to him, "Belteshazzar, don't let the dream
4.26 you will become **king** again when you acknowledge that God
4.34 years had passed," said the **king,** "I looked up at the sky,
4.37 I, Nebuchadnezzar, praise, honour, and glorify the **King** of Heaven.
5. 1 **King** Belshazzar invited a thousand noblemen to a great banquet,
5. 2 The **king** sent for them so that he, his noblemen, his wives,
5. 5 And the **king** saw the hand as it was writing.
5. 7 When they came in, the **king** said to them, "Anyone who can
5. 8 read the writing or tell the **king** what it meant.
5. 9 In his distress **King** Belshazzar grew even paler,
5.10 the noise made by the **king** and his noblemen
5.11 When your father was **king,** this man showed good sense,
5.12 this man Daniel, whom the **king** named Belteshazzar,
5.13 brought at once into the **king's** presence,
5.13 and the **king** said to him, "Are you Daniel,
5.13 Jewish exile whom my father the **king** brought here from Judah?
5.18 your father Nebuchadnezzar a great **king** and gave him dignity
5.30 Belshazzar, the **king of Babylonia,** was killed;
6. 2 to supervise the governors and to look after the **king's** interests.
6. 3 so outstanding, the **king** considered putting him in charge of
6. 6 they went to see the **king** and said, "King Darius, may Your
6. 9 And so **King** Darius signed the order.
6.12 all of them went together to the **king** to accuse Daniel.
6.12 The **king** replied, "Yes, a strict order, a law of the Medes
6.13 Then they said to the **king,** "Daniel, one of the exiles
6.14 When the **king** heard this, he was upset and did his best
6.15 men came back to the **king** and said to him, "Your Majesty
6.15 no order which the **king** issues can be changed."
6.16 So the **king** gave orders for Daniel to be arrested
6.17 of the pit, and the **king** placed his own royal seal
6.18 the **king** returned to the palace and spent a sleepless night,
6.19 At dawn the **king** got up and hurried to the pit.
6.23 The **king** was overjoyed and gave orders for Daniel to be
6.24 Then the **king** gave orders to arrest all the men
6.25 Then **King** Darius wrote to the people of all nations,
7. 1 year that Belshazzar was **king of Babylonia,** I had a dream
7.24 The ten horns are ten **kings** who will rule that empire.
7.24 Then another **king** will appear;
7.24 different from the earlier ones and will overthrow three **kings.**
8. 1 third year that Belshazzar was **king,** I saw a second vision.
8.21 and the prominent horn between his eyes is the first **king.**
8.23 there will be a stubborn, vicious, and deceitful **king.**
8.25 will even defy the greatest **King** of all,
8.27 to the work that the **king** had assigned to me,
9. 6 in your name to our **kings,** our rulers, our ancestors,
9. 8 **kings,** our rulers, and our ancestors have acted shamefully
11. 2 The angel said, "Three more **kings** will rule over Persia,
11. 3 "Then a heroic **king** will appear.
11. 4 **Kings** not descended from him will rule in his place,
11. 5 "The **king of Egypt** will be strong.
11. 6 number of years the **king of Egypt** will make an alliance
11. 6 with the **king of Syria** and give him his daughter
11. 7 Soon afterwards, one of her relatives will become **king.**
11. 7 the army of the **king of Syria,** enter their fortress,
11. 9 the **king of Syria** will invade Egypt,
11.10 "The sons of the **king of Syria** will prepare for war
11.11 In his anger the **king of Egypt** will go to war
11.11 to war against the **king of Syria** and capture his huge army.
11.13 "The **king of Syria** will go back and gather a larger
11.14 Then many people will rebel against the **king of Egypt.**
11.15 So the **king of Syria** will lay siege to a fortified city
11.17 "The **king of Syria** will plan an expedition,
11.18 he will turn the arrogance of **Syria's king** back on him.
11.19 The **king** will return to the fortresses of his own land,
11.20 will be followed by another **king,** who will send an officer
11.20 In a short time that **king** will be killed, but not publicly
11.21 "The next **king of Syria** will be an evil man
11.21 has no right to be **king,** but he will come unexpectedly
11.25 army to attack the **king of Egypt,** who will prepare to fight
11.25 But the **king of Egypt** will be deceived
11.27 Then the two **kings** will sit down to eat at the same
11.28 The **king of Syria** will return home with all the loot
11.32 By deceit the **king** will win the support of those
11.36 "The **king of Syria** will do as he pleases.
11.37 The **king** will ignore the god his ancestors served,
11.40 "When the **king of Syria's** final hour has almost come,
11.40 the **king of Egypt** will attack him,
11.40 and the **king of Syria** will fight back
Hos 1. 1 Ahaz, and Hezekiah were **kings of Judah,**
1. 1 and Jeroboam son of Jehoash was **king of Israel.**
1. 4 before I punish the **king of Israel** for the murders that his
3. 4 for a long time without **kings** or leaders, without sacrifices
3. 5 the Lord their God, and to a descendant of David their **king.**
7. 3 Lord says, "People deceive the **king** and his officers
7. 5 On the day of the **king's** celebration
7. 5 they made the **king** and his officials drunk and foolish
7. 7 Their **kings** have been assassinated one after another,
8. 4 "My people chose **kings,** but they did it on their own.
10. 3 be saying, "We have no **king**
10. 3 But what could a **king** do for us anyway?"
10. 7 Her **king** will be carried off, like a chip of wood
10.14 like the day when **King** Shalman destroyed the city of Betharbel
10.15 As soon as the battle begins, the **king of Israel** will die."
13.10 You asked for a **king** and for leaders,
13.11 anger I have given you **kings,** and in my fury I have
Amos 1. 1 earthquake, when Uzziah was **king of Judah** and Jeroboam
1. 1 son of Jehoash was **king of Israel,** God revealed to Amos all

Amos 1. 4 and I will burn down the fortresses of **King** Benhadad.
1.15 Their **king** and his officers will go into exile."
2. 1 dishonoured the bones of the **king** of Edom by burning them
5.26 worshipped images of Sakkuth, your **king** god,
7. 1 of locusts just after the **king's** share of the hay had been
7.13 This is the **king's** place of worship, the national temple."
Obad 21 And the Lord himself will be **King."**
Jon 3. 6 When the **king** of Nineveh heard about it, he got up
3. 7 "This is an order from the **king** and his officials:
Mic 1. 1 and Hezekiah were **kings of Judah,** the Lord gave this message
1.14 The **kings of Israel** will get no help from the town of
2.13 Their **king,** the Lord himself, will lead them out.
4. 9 Is it because you have no **king,** and your counsellors are dead?
6. 5 My people, remember what **King** Balak of Moab planned to do
Hab 1.10 They treat **kings** with contempt and laugh at high officials.
3.13 You went out to save your people, to save your chosen **king.**
Zeph 1. 1 during the time that Josiah son of Amon was **king of Judah.**
1. 8 will punish the officials, the **king's** sons,
3.15 The Lord, the **king of Israel,** is with you;
Zech 6.13 the honour due to a **king,** and he will rule his people.
9. 5 Gaza will lose her **king,** and Ashkelon will be left deserted.
9. 9 Look, your **king** is coming to you!
9.10 Your **king** will make peace among the nations;
14. 9 Then the Lord will be **king** over all the earth;
14.16 worship the Lord Almighty as **king,**
14.17 worship the Lord Almighty as **king,** then rain will not fall
Mal 1.14 For I am a great **king,** and people of all nations fear
Mt 1. 2 Abraham to **King** David, the following ancestors are listed:
1. 2 Obed (his mother was Ruth), Jesse, and **King** David.
2. 1 of Bethlehem in Judaea, during the time when Herod was **king.**
2. 2 "Where is the baby born to be the **king of the Jews?**
2. 3 When **King** Herod heard about this, he was very upset, and
2.22 succeeded his father Herod as **king** of Judaea, he was afraid
5.35 nor by Jerusalem, for it is the city of the great **King.**
6.29 tell you that not even **King** Solomon with all his wealth had
10.18 to trial before rulers and **kings,** to tell the Good News to
12.42 from her country to listen to **King** Solomon's wise teaching;
14. 9 The **king** was sad, but because of the promise he had made
16.28 die until they have seen the Son of Man come as **King."**
17.25 Who pays duties or taxes to the **kings** of this world?
18.23 Once there was a **king** who decided to check on his servants'
18.25 pay his debt, so the **king** ordered him to be sold as
18.26 The servant fell on his knees before the **king.**
18.27 The **king** felt sorry for him, so he forgave him the debt
18.31 very upset and went to the **king** and told him everything.
18.34 The **king** was very angry, and he sent the servant to jail
20.21 will sit at your right and your left when you are **King."**
21. 5 "Tell the city of Zion, Look, your **king** is coming to you!
22. 2 Once there was a **king** who prepared a wedding feast for his
22. 7 The **king** was very angry;
22.11 "The **king** went in to look at the guests and saw
22.12 the **king** asked him.
22.13 Then the **king** told the servants, 'Tie him up hand and foot,
25.31 Son of Man comes as **King** and all the angels with him,
25.34 Then the **King** will say to the people on his right,
25.40 The **King** will reply, 'I tell you, whenever you did this
25.45 The **King** will reply, 'I tell you, whenever you refused
27.11 "Are you the **king of the Jews?"**
27.29 "Long live the **King of the Jews!"**
27.37 "This is Jesus, the **King of the Jews."**
27.42 Isn't he the **king of Israel?**
Mk 6.14 Now **King** Herod heard about all this, because Jesus' reputation
6.22 So the **king** said to the girl, "What would you like to
6.25 back at once to the **king** and demanded, "I want you to
6.26 This made the **king** very sad, but he could not refuse her
11.10 God bless the coming kingdom of **King** David, our father!
13. 9 will stand before rulers and **kings** for my sake to tell them
15. 2 Pilate questioned him, "Are you the **king of the Jews?"**
15. 9 want me to set free for you the **king of the Jews?"**
15.12 to do with the one you call the **king of the Jews?"**
15.18 "Long live the **King of the Jews!"**
15.26 "The **King of the Jews."**
15.32 see the Messiah, the **king of Israel,** come down from the
Lk 1. 5 the time when Herod was **king** of Judaea, there was a priest
1.27 to a man named Joseph, who was a descendant of **King** David.
1.32 God will make him a **king,** as his ancestor David was,
1.33 and he will be the **king** of the descendants of Jacob for
1.52 He has brought down mighty **kings** from their thrones,
2. 4 town of Bethlehem in Judaea, the birthplace of **King** David.
10.24 that many prophets and **kings** wanted to see what you see,
11.31 from her country to listen to **King** Solomon's wise teaching;
12.27 tell you that not even **King** Solomon with all his wealth had
14.31 "If a **king** goes out with ten thousand men
14.31 to fight another **king** who comes against him with twenty
14.31 and decide if he is strong enough to face that other **king.**
14.32 messengers to meet the other **king,** to ask for terms of peace
19.12 far away to be made **king,** after which he planned to come
19.14 to say, 'We don't want this man to be our **king.'**
19.15 "The man was made **king** and came back.
19.27 want me to be their **king,** bring them here and kill them
19.38 "God bless the **king** who comes in the name of the Lord!
21.12 you will be brought before **kings** and rulers for my sake.
22.25 Jesus said to them, "The **kings** of the pagans have power
23. 2 Emperor and claiming that he himself is the Messiah, a **king."**
23. 3 Pilate asked him, "Are you the **king of the Jews?"**
23.37 and said, "Save yourself if you are the **king of the Jews!"**
23.38 "This is the **King of the Jews."**
23.42 to Jesus, "Remember me, Jesus, when you come as **King!"**
Jn 1.49 You are the **King of Israel!"**
6.15 come and seize him in order to make him **king** by force;
7.42 will be a descendant of **King** David and will be born in

Jn 12.13 God bless the **King of Israel!"**
12.15 Here comes your **king**, riding on a young donkey."
18.33 "Are you the **King of the Jews?"**
18.37 So Pilate asked him, "Are you a **king**, then?"
18.37 Jesus answered, "You say that I am a **king.**
18.39 want me to set free for you the **King of the Jews?"**
19. 3 came to him and said, "Long live the **King of the Jews!"**
19.12 who claims to be a **king** is a rebel against the Emperor!"
19.14 Pilate said to the people, "Here is your **king!"**
19.15 Pilate asked them, "Do you want me to crucify your **king?"**
19.15 chief priests answered, "The only **king** we have is the Emperor!"
19.19 "Jesus of Nazareth, the **King of the Jews,"** is what he wrote.
19.21 "Do not write 'The **King of the Jews,'**
19.21 but rather, 'This man said, I am the **King of the Jews.' "**
Acts 2.29 I must speak to you plainly about our famous ancestor **King** David.
2.30 make one of David's descendants a **king**, just as David was.
4.26 The **kings** of the earth prepared themselves, and the rulers
7.10 Joseph appeared before the **king of Egypt,** God gave him a
7.10 and wisdom, and the **king** made Joseph governor over the country
7.13 his brothers, and the **king of Egypt** came to know about
7.18 At last a **king** who did not know about Joseph began to
7.21 out of his home, the **king's** daughter adopted him and brought
9.15 known to Gentiles and **kings** and to the people of Israel.
12. 1 About this time **King** Herod began to persecute some members of
12.20 their country got its food supplies from the **king's** country.
13.21 when they asked for a **king,** God gave them Saul son of
13.21 the tribe of Benjamin, to be their **king** for forty years.
13.22 After removing him, God made David their **king.**
17. 7 saying that there is another **king,** whose name is Jesus."
25.13 Some time later **King** Agrippa and Bernice came to Caesarea
25.14 there several days, Festus explained Paul's situation to the **king:**
25.24 Festus said, **"King** Agrippa and all who are here with us:
25.26 him here before you—and especially before you, **King** Agrippa!
26. 2 **"King** Agrippa!
26.19 "And so, **King** Agrippa, I did not disobey the vision I
26.26 **King** Agrippa!
26.27 **King** Agrippa, do you believe the prophets?
26.30 the **king,** the governor, Bernice, and all the others got up,
Rom 9.17 scripture says to the **king of Egypt,**
9.17 "I made you **king** in order to use you
1 Cor 4. 8 Have you become **kings,** even though we are not?
4. 8 I wish you really were **kings,**
4. 8 so that we could be **kings** together with you.
2 Cor 11.32 the governor under **King** Aretas placed guards at the city
1 Tim 1.17 To the eternal **King,** immortal and invisible, the only God—
2. 2 for **kings** and all others who are in authority, that we may
6.15 blessed and only Ruler, the **King of kings**
2 Tim 4. 1 is coming to rule as **King,** I solemnly urge you [2] to preach
Heb 7. 1 This Melchizedek was **king** of Salem and a priest of the
7. 1 he defeated the four **kings,** Melchizedek met him and blessed him,
7. 2 first meaning of Melchizedek's name is **"King** of Righteousness";
7. 2 and because he was **king** of Salem,
7. 2 his name also means **"King** of Peace.")
11.23 and they were not afraid to disobey the **king's** order.
11.24 up, refuse to be called the son of the **king's** daughter.
11.27 made Moses leave Egypt without being afraid of the **king's** anger.
1 Pet 2. 9 are the chosen race, the **King's** priests, the holy nation,
Rev 1. 5 and who is also the ruler of the **kings** of the world.
6.15 the **kings** of the earth, the rulers and the military chiefs,
9.11 They have a **king** ruling over them, who is the angel in
10.11 God's message about many nations, races, languages, and **kings."**
12.10 Now God has shown his power as **King!**
15. 3 **King** of the nations, how right and true are your ways!
16.12 to provide a way for the **kings** who come from the east.
16.14 go out to all the **kings** of the world, to bring them
16.16 Then the spirits brought the **kings** together in the place that
17. 2 The **kings** of the earth practised sexual immorality with her,
17. 9 They are also seven **kings:**
17.11 is itself an eighth **king** who is one of the seven
17.12 horns you saw are ten **kings** who have not yet begun to
17.12 authority to rule as **kings** for one hour with the beast.
17.14 them, because he is Lord of lords and **King of kings."**
17.18 is the great city that rules over the **kings** of the earth."
18. 3 The **kings** of the earth practised sexual immorality with her,
18. 9 The **kings** of the earth who took part in her immorality and
19. 6 For the Lord, our Almighty God, is **King!**
19.16 **"King of kings** and Lord of lords."
19.18 and eat the flesh of **kings,** generals, and soldiers, the
19.19 saw the beast and the **kings** of the earth and their armies
20. 4 to life and ruled as **kings** with Christ for a thousand years.
21.24 by its light, and the **kings** of the earth will bring their
22. 5 their light, and they will rule as **kings** for ever and ever.

KING'S GATE

1 Chr 9.18 stationed at the eastern entrance to the **King's Gate.**

KING'S POOL

Neh 2.14 I went north to the Fountain Gate and the **King's Pool.**

KING'S VALLEY

see also SHAVEH

Gen 14.17 the Valley of Shaveh (also called the **King's Valley).**
2 Sam 18.18 monument for himself in **King's Valley,** because he had no son

KINGDOM (1) (OF GOD, OF HEAVEN)

[GOD'S KINGDOM, HEAVENLY KINGDOM, LORD'S KINGDOM]

1 Chr 28. 5 he chose Solomon to rule over Israel, the **Lord's kingdom.**
Job 25. 1 he keeps his heavenly **kingdom** in peace.
Ps 45. 6 The **kingdom** that God has given you will last for ever
89.14 Your **kingdom** is founded on righteousness and justice;
145.12 your mighty deeds and the glorious majesty of your **kingdom.**
Is 9. 7 his **kingdom** will always be at peace.
Dan 2.44 God of heaven will establish a **kingdom** that will never end.
4.34 will rule for ever, and his **kingdom** will last for all time.
6.26 His **kingdom** will never be destroyed,
7.14 and his **kingdom** would never end.
Mt 3. 2 your sins," he said, "because the **Kingdom of heaven** is near!"
4.17 "Turn away from your sins, because the **Kingdom of heaven** is near!"
4.23 the Good News about the **Kingdom,** and healing people who had
5. 3 the **Kingdom of heaven** belongs to them!
5.10 the **Kingdom of heaven** belongs to them!
5.19 to do the same, will be least in the **Kingdom of heaven.**
5.19 to do the same, will be great in the **Kingdom of heaven.**
5.20 able to enter the **Kingdom of heaven** only if you are more
6.10 may your **Kingdom** come;
6.33 everything else with the **Kingdom of God** and with what he
7.21 Lord' will enter the **Kingdom of heaven,** but only those who
8.11 Abraham, Isaac, and Jacob at the feast in the **Kingdom of heaven.**
8.12 who should be in the **Kingdom** will be thrown out into the
9.35 Good News about the **Kingdom,** and healed people with every kind
10. 7 Go and preach, 'The **Kingdom of heaven** is near!'
11.11 who is least in the **Kingdom of heaven** is greater than John.
11.12 this very day the **Kingdom of heaven** has suffered violent attacks,
11.13 the prophets and the Law of Moses spoke about the **Kingdom;**
12.28 proves that the **Kingdom of God** has already come upon you.
13.11 the secrets of the **Kingdom of heaven** has been given to you,
13.19 hear the message about the **Kingdom** but do not understand it
13.24 "The **Kingdom of heaven** is like this.
13.31 "The **Kingdom of heaven** is like this.
13.33 "The **Kingdom of heaven** is like this.
13.38 the good seed is the people who belong to the **Kingdom;**
13.41 gather up out of his **Kingdom** all those who cause people to
13.43 God's people will shine like the sun in their Father's **Kingdom.**
13.44 "The **Kingdom of heaven** is like this.
13.45 "Also, the **Kingdom of heaven** is like this.
13.47 "Also, the **Kingdom of heaven** is like this.
13.52 a disciple in the **Kingdom of heaven** is like the owner of
16.19 I will give you the keys of the **Kingdom of heaven;**
18. 1 Jesus, asking, "Who is the greatest in the **Kingdom of heaven?"**
18. 3 become like children, you will never enter the **Kingdom of heaven.**
18. 4 The greatest in the **Kingdom of heaven** is the one who
18.23 seventy times seven, [23] because the **Kingdom of heaven** is like
19.12 others do not marry for the sake of the **Kingdom of heaven.**
19.14 because the **Kingdom of heaven** belongs to such as these."
19.23 be very hard for rich people to enter the **Kingdom of heaven.**
19.24 person to enter the **Kingdom of God** than for a camel to
20. 1 "The **Kingdom of heaven** is like this.
21.31 prostitutes are going into the **Kingdom of God** ahead of you.
21.43 added Jesus, "the **Kingdom of God** will be taken away from
22. 2 "The **Kingdom of heaven** is like this.
23.13 the door to the **Kingdom of heaven** in people's faces,
24.14 this Good News about the **Kingdom** will be preached through
25. 1 "At that time the **Kingdom of heaven** will be like this.
25.14 "At that time the **Kingdom of heaven** will be like this.
25.34 Come and possess the **kingdom** which has been prepared for you
26.29 day I drink the new wine with you in my Father's **Kingdom."**
Mk 1.15 time has come," he said, "and the **Kingdom of God** is near!
4.11 been given the secret of the **Kingdom of God,"** Jesus answered.
4.26 Jesus went on to say, "The **Kingdom of God** is like this.
4.30 "What shall we say the **Kingdom of God** is like?"
9. 1 until they have seen the **Kingdom of God** come with power."
9.47 you to enter the **Kingdom of God** with only one eye than
10.14 because the **Kingdom of God** belongs to such as these.
10.15 does not receive the **Kingdom of God** like a child will never
10.23 it will be for rich people to enter the **Kingdom of God!"**
10.24 "My children, how hard it is to enter the **Kingdom of God!**
10.25 person to enter the **Kingdom of God** than for a camel to
10.37 your throne in your glorious **Kingdom,** we want you to let us
11.10 God bless the coming **kingdom** of King David, our father!
12.34 he told him, "You are not far from the **Kingdom of God."**
14.25 the day I drink the new wine in the **Kingdom of God."**
15.42 Council, who was waiting for the coming of the **Kingdom of God.**
Lk 1.33 his **kingdom** will never end!"
4.43 Good News about the **Kingdom of God** in other towns also,
6.20 the **Kingdom of God** is yours!
7.28 who is least in the **Kingdom of God** is greater than John."
8. 1 and villages, preaching the Good News about the **Kingdom of God.**
8.10 the secrets of the **Kingdom of God** has been given to you,
9. 2 out to preach the **Kingdom of God** and to heal the sick,
9.11 to them about the **Kingdom of God,** and healed those who
9.27 who will not die until they have seen the **Kingdom of God."**
9.60 You go and proclaim the **Kingdom of God."**
9.62 keeps looking back is of no use to the **Kingdom of God."**
10. 9 to the people there, 'The **Kingdom of God** has come near you.'
10.11 But remember that the **Kingdom of God** has come near you!'
11. 2 may your **Kingdom** come.
11.20 proves that the **Kingdom of God** has already come to you.
12.31 Instead, be concerned with his **Kingdom,** and he will provide
12.32 flock, for your Father is pleased to give you the **Kingdom.**
13.18 Jesus asked, "What is the **Kingdom of God** like?
13.20 Jesus asked, "What shall I compare the **Kingdom of God** with?
13.28 prophets in the **Kingdom of God,** while you are thrown out!

Lk	13.29	south, and sit down at the feast in the **Kingdom of God.**
	14.15	who will sit down at the feast in the **Kingdom of God!"**
	16.16	Good News about the **Kingdom of God** is being told, and
	17.20	Some Pharisees asked Jesus when the **Kingdom of God** would come.
	17.20	His answer was, "The **Kingdom of God** does not come in such
	17.21	because the **Kingdom of God** is within you."
	18.16	because the **Kingdom of God** belongs to such as these.
	18.17	does not receive the **Kingdom of God** like a child will never
	18.24	hard it is for rich people to enter the **Kingdom of God!**
	18.25	person to enter the **Kingdom of God** than for a camel to
	18.29	the sake of the **Kingdom of God** [30] will receive much more in
	19.11	supposed that the **Kingdom of God** was just about to appear.
	21.31	you will know that the **Kingdom of God** is about to come.
	22.16	until it is given its full meaning in the **Kingdom of God."**
	22.18	I will not drink this wine until the **Kingdom of God** comes."
	22.30	at my table in my **Kingdom,** and you will sit on thrones
	23.50	man, who was waiting for the coming of the **Kingdom of God.**
Jn	3. 3	one can see the **Kingdom of God** unless he is born again."
	3. 5	one can enter the **Kingdom of God** unless he is born of
	18.36	Jesus said, "My **kingdom** does not belong to this world;
	18.36	if my **kingdom** belonged to this world, my followers would
	18.36	No, my **kingdom** does not belong here!"
Acts	1. 3	saw him, and he talked with them about the **Kingdom of God.**
	1. 6	"Lord, will you at this time give the **Kingdom** back to Israel?"
	8.12	good news of the **Kingdom of God** and about Jesus Christ,
	14.22	through many troubles to enter the **Kingdom of God,"** they taught.
	19. 8	them and trying to convince them about the **Kingdom of God.**
	20.25	gone about among all of you, preaching the **Kingdom of God.**
	28.23	his message about the **Kingdom of God,** and he tried to
	28.31	He preached about the **Kingdom of God** and taught about
Rom	14.17	For **God's Kingdom** is not a matter of eating and drinking,
1 Cor	4.20	For the **Kingdom of God** is not a matter of words but
	6. 9	Surely you know that the wicked will not possess **God's Kingdom.**
	6.10	or are thieves—none of these will possess **God's Kingdom.**
	15.24	powers, and will hand over the **Kingdom** to God the Father.
	15.50	blood cannot share in **God's Kingdom,** and what is mortal cannot
Gal	5.21	who do these things will not possess the **Kingdom of God.**
Eph	5. 5	ever receive a share in the **Kingdom** of Christ and of God.
Col	1.11	God has reserved for his people in the **kingdom** of light.
	1.13	brought us safe into the **kingdom** of his dear Son, [14] by
	4.11	with me for the **Kingdom of God,** and they have been a
1 Thes	2.12	God, who calls you to share in his own **Kingdom** and glory.
2 Thes	1. 5	will become worthy of his **Kingdom,** for which you are suffering.
2 Tim	4.18	from all evil and take me safely into his **heavenly Kingdom.**
Heb	1. 8	"Your **kingdom,** O God, will last for ever and ever!
	12.28	because we receive a **kingdom** that cannot be shaken.
Jas	2. 5	and to possess the **kingdom** which he promised to those who
	2. 8	the law of the **Kingdom,** which is found in the scripture,
2 Pet	1.11	right to enter the eternal **Kingdom** of our Lord and Saviour
Rev	1. 6	and made us a **kingdom** of priests to serve his God
	1. 9	the suffering that comes to those who belong to his **Kingdom.**
	5.10	You have made them a **kingdom** of priests to serve our God,

KINGDOM (2)

Gen	10.10	At first his **kingdom** included Babylon, Erech, and Accad,
	20. 9	you to make you bring this disaster on me and my **kingdom?**
Josh	11.10	(At that time Hazor was the most powerful of all those **kingdoms.)**
	12. 2	His **kingdom** included half of Gilead:
	12. 5	His **kingdom** included Mount Hermon, Salecah, and all of Bashan
	13.12	It included the **kingdom** of Og,
	13.21	the whole **kingdom** of the Amorite king Sihon,
	13.27	the rest of the **kingdom** of King Sihon of Heshbon.
	13.30	the whole **kingdom** of Og, the king of Bashan,
	13.31	Ashtaroth and Edrei, the capital cities of Og's **kingdom**
1 Sam	15.28	"The Lord has torn the **kingdom** of Israel away from you
	24.20	the **kingdom** will continue under your rule.
	28.17	he has taken the **kingdom** away from you
2 Sam	3. 9	he would take the **kingdom** away from Saul and his descendants
	5.12	and was making his **kingdom** prosperous
	7.12	make one of your sons king and will keep his **kingdom** strong.
	7.16	and I will make your **kingdom** last for ever.
	12. 8	I gave you his **kingdom** and his wives;
	16. 3	restore to him the **kingdom** of his grandfather Saul."
	16. 8	You took Saul's **kingdom,** and now the Lord is punishing you
	16. 8	The Lord has given the **kingdom** to your son Absalom,
1 Kgs	2.24	his promise and given the **kingdom** to me and my descendants.
	2.45	he will make David's **kingdom** secure for ever."
	4.21	Solomon's **kingdom** included all the nations from the
	9.19	to build in Jerusalem, in Lebanon, and elsewhere in his **kingdom.**
	10.19	No throne like this had ever existed in any other **kingdom.**
	11.11	that I will take the **kingdom** away from you
	11.13	And I will not take the whole **kingdom** away from him;
	11.31	am going to take the **kingdom** away from Solomon,
	11.34	will not take the whole **kingdom** away from Solomon,
	11.35	I will take the **kingdom** away from Solomon's son
	12.19	the northern **kingdom** of Israel have been in rebellion
	14. 8	I took the **kingdom** away from David's descendants
2 Kgs	8.20	Edom revolted against Judah and became an independent **kingdom.**
	17.18	leaving only the **kingdom** of Judah.
	19.15	you alone are God, ruling all the **kingdoms** of the world.
	20.13	or anywhere in his **kingdom** that he did not show them.
1 Chr	2.23	But the **kingdoms** of Geshur and Aram conquered sixty towns
	10.14	gave control of the **kingdom** to David son of Jesse.
	11.10	as the Lord had promised, and they kept his **kingdom** strong.
	14. 2	and was making his **kingdom** prosperous
	16.20	wandered from country to country, from one **kingdom** to another.
	17.11	make one of your sons king and will keep his **kingdom** strong.
	17.14	put him in charge of my people and my **kingdom** for ever.
1 Chr	27. 1	officials who administered the work of the **kingdom.**
	28. 1	administered the work of the **kingdom,**
	28. 5	he chose Solomon to rule over Israel, the Lord's **kingdom.**
	28. 7	I will make his **kingdom** last for ever
	29.30	that happened to him, to Israel, and to the surrounding **kingdoms.**
2 Chr	1. 1	took firm control of the **kingdom** of Israel,
	9.19	No throne like this had ever existed in any other **kingdom.**
	10.19	the northern **kingdom** of Israel have been in rebellion
	11.17	This strengthened the **kingdom** of Judah,
	14. 5	the **kingdom** was at peace under his rule.
	15. 9	and were living in his **kingdom,** because they had seen
	17. 5	Jehoshaphat firm control over the **kingdom** of Judah,
	17.10	Lord made all the surrounding **kingdoms** afraid to go to war
	21. 4	firm control of the **kingdom,** he had all his brothers killed,
	21. 8	Edom revolted against Judah and became an independent **kingdom.**
	22. 9	No member of Ahaziah's family was left who could rule the **kingdom.**
	25. 7	The Lord is not with these men from the Northern **Kingdom.**
	28.12	leading men of the Northern **Kingdom,**
	34. 7	the territory of the Northern **Kingdom** he smashed the altars
	34. 9	rest of the Northern **Kingdom,** and from the people of Judah,
Neh	9.22	"You let them conquer nations and **kingdoms,**
Esth	1.14	Persia and Media who held the highest offices in the **kingdom.**
Ps	45. 6	The **kingdom** that God has given you will last for ever
	46. 6	Nations are terrified, **kingdoms** are shaken;
	68.32	Sing to God, **kingdoms** of the world, sing praise to the Lord,
	72. 8	His **kingdom** will reach from sea to sea,
	89.25	extend his **kingdom** from the Mediterranean to the River Euphrates.
	89.36	I will watch over his **kingdom** as long as the sun shines.
	102.22	when nations and **kingdoms** come together and worship the Lord.
	105.13	They wandered from country to country, from one **kingdom** to another.
	132.18	with shame, but his **kingdom** will prosper and flourish."
Is	7.17	since the **kingdom** of Israel separated from Judah—
	8.14	catch the people of the **kingdoms** of Judah and Israel
	9. 8	has pronounced judgement on the **kingdom** of Israel,
	10.10	my hand to punish those **kingdoms** that worship idols,
	11.13	The **kingdom** of Israel will not be jealous of Judah
	13. 4	the sound of nations and **kingdoms** gathering.
	13.19	Babylonia is the most beautiful **kingdom** of all;
	14.16	'Is this the man who shook the earth and made **kingdoms** tremble?
	23.11	stretched out his hand over the sea and overthrown **kingdoms.**
	23.17	she will hire herself out to all the **kingdoms** of the world.
	28. 1	The **kingdom** of Israel is doomed!
	37.16	you alone are God, ruling all the **kingdoms** of the world.
	39. 2	anywhere in his **kingdom** that he did not show them.
Jer	1.10	authority over nations and **kingdoms** to uproot
	18. 7	or destroy any nation or **kingdom,**
	18. 9	build up any nation or **kingdom,**
	27. 8	"But if any nation or **kingdom** will not submit to his rule,
	28. 8	and disease would come to many nations and powerful **kingdoms.**
	29.16	the king who rules the **kingdom** that David ruled
	36.30	no descendant of yours will ever rule over David's **kingdom.**
	51.20	to crush nations and **kingdoms,** [21] to shatter horses
	51.27	Tell the **kingdoms** of Ararat, Minni, and Ashkenaz to attack.
Lam	2. 2	He brought disgrace on the **kingdom** and its rulers.
Ezek	29.14	they will be a weak **kingdom,** [15] the weakest kingdom of all,
	37.16	stick and write on it the words, 'The **kingdom** of Judah.'
	37.16	stick and write on it the words, 'The **kingdom** of Israel.'
	37.22	be divided into two nations or split into two **kingdoms.**
	47.16	between the territory of the **kingdom** of Damascus
	47.16	and that of the **kingdom** of Hamath), and to the city
	48. 1	to the boundary between the **kingdoms** of Damascus and Hamath.
Dan	1.20	than any fortune-teller or magician in his whole **kingdom.**
	4.17	God has power over human **kingdoms**
	4.25	Supreme God controls all human **kingdoms,**
	4.32	God has power over human **kingdoms**
	4.36	and the glory of my **kingdom** were given back to me.
	5. 7	round his neck, and be the third in power in the **kingdom."**
	5.11	is a man in your **kingdom** who has the spirit of the
	5.16	your neck, and be the third in power in the **kingdom."**
	5.21	Supreme God controls all human **kingdoms**
	5.26	numbered the days of your **kingdom** and brought it to an end;
	5.28	divisions, your **kingdom** is divided up
	5.29	And he made him the third in power in the **kingdom.**
	7.27	and greatness of all the **kingdoms** on earth will be given
	8.20	two horns represents the **kingdoms** of Media and Persia.
	8.21	The goat represents the **kingdom** of Greece,
	8.22	represent the four **kingdoms** into which that nation will be
	8.22	and which will not be as strong as the first **kingdom.**
	8.23	"When the end of those **kingdoms** is near
	9. 1	the son of Xerxes, ruled over the **kingdom** of Babylonia.
	10.13	The angel prince of the **kingdom** of Persia opposed me
	11. 2	he will challenge the **kingdom** of Greece.
	11. 5	however, will be even stronger and rule a greater **kingdom.**
	11.17	to destroy his enemy's **kingdom,** he will make an alliance
	11.20	taxes in order to increase the wealth of his **kingdom.**
Amos	6. 2	Were they any better than the **kingdoms** of Judah and Israel?
	9. 8	watching this sinful **kingdom** of Israel, and I will destroy
	9.11	when I will restore the **kingdom** of David,
Mic	4. 8	once again be the capital of the **kingdom** that was yours.
Zeph	3. 8	to gather nations and **kingdoms,** in order to let them feel
Hag	2.22	to shake heaven and earth [22] and overthrow **kingdoms**
Mt	4. 8	and showed him all the **kingdoms** of the world in all their
	12.26	is fighting another in Satan's **kingdom,** this means that it is
	24. 7	will fight each other, **kingdoms** will attack one another.
Mk	3.26	So if Satan's **kingdom** divides into groups, it cannot last,
	6.23	you anything you ask for, even as much as half my **kingdom!"**
	13. 8	**kingdoms** will attack one another.

Lk 4. 5 and showed him in a second all the **kingdoms** of the world.
11.18 So if Satan's **kingdom** has groups fighting each other,
21.10 **kingdoms** will attack one another.
Acts 15.16 I will return, says the Lord, and restore the **kingdom** of David.
Rev 16.10 Darkness fell over the beast's **kingdom,** and people bit their

KINSMAN

Gen 31.25 up his camp with his **kinsmen** in the hill-country of Gilead.
Num 20.14 "This message is from your **kinsmen,** the tribes of Israel.

KISH (1)
Saul's father.

1 Sam 9. 1 influential man named **Kish,** from the tribe of Benjamin;
9. 3 Some donkeys belonging to **Kish** had wandered off,
10.11 asked one another, "What has happened to the son of **Kish?**
10.21 of Matri came forward, and Saul son of **Kish** was picked out.
14.51 Saul's father **Kish** and Abner's father Ner were sons of Abiel.
2 Sam 21.14 the grave of Saul's father **Kish,**
1 Chr 8.33 Ner was the father of **Kish,**
8.33 and **Kish** was the father of King Saul.
9.39 Ner was the father of **Kish,**
9.39 and **Kish** was the father of Saul.
Acts 13.21 gave them Saul son of **Kish** from the tribe of Benjamin,

KISLEV
The ninth month of the Hebrew calendar.

Neh 1. 1 In the month of **Kislev** in the twentieth year that
Zech 7. 1 month (the month of **Kislev),** the Lord gave me a message.

KISS

Gen 27.26 his father said to him, "Come closer and **kiss** me, my son."
27.27 As he came up to **kiss** him, Isaac smelt his clothes—so
29.11 Then he **kissed** her and began to cry for joy.
29.13 meet him, hugged him and **kissed** him, and brought him
31.28 even let me **kiss** my grandchildren and my daughters good-bye.
31.55 Laban **kissed** his grandchildren and his daughters good-bye,
33. 4 ran to meet him, threw his arms round him, and **kissed** him.
45.15 he embraced each of his brothers and **kissed** them.
48.10 brought the boys to him, and he hugged them and **kissed** them.
50. 1 Joseph threw himself on his father, crying and **kissing** his face.
Ex 4.27 and when he met him, he **kissed** him.
18. 7 Moses went out to meet him, bowed before him, and **kissed** him.
Ruth 1. 9 So Naomi **kissed** them good-bye.
1.14 Then Orpah **kissed** her mother-in-law good-bye
1 Sam 10. 1 poured it on Saul's head, **kissed** him, and said, "The Lord
20.41 Both he and Jonathan were crying as they **kissed** each other;
2 Sam 14.33 The king welcomed him with a **kiss.**
15. 5 him, Absalom would reach out, take hold of him, and **kiss**
19.39 He **kissed** Barzillai and gave him his blessing,
20. 9 of his beard with his right hand in order to **kiss** him.
1 Kgs 19.18 to me and have not bowed to Baal or **kissed** his idol."
19.20 and said, "Let me **kiss** my father and mother good-bye,
Job 31.27 to honour them by **kissing** my hand in reverence to them.
Prov 5. 3 sweet as honey and her **kisses** as smooth as olive-oil,
7.13 arms round the young man, **kissed** him,
Ecc 3. 5 the time for **kissing** and the time for not kissing.
Song 1. 2 Your lips cover me with **kisses;**
5.16 His mouth is sweet to **kiss;**
8. 1 in the street, I could **kiss** you and no one would mind.
Hos 13. 2 How can men **kiss** those idols—idols in the shape of bulls!
Mt 26.48 "The man I **kiss** is the one you want.
26.49 and said, "Peace be with you, Teacher," and **kissed** him.
Mk 14.44 "The man I **kiss** is the one you want.
14.45 and **kissed** him.
Lk 7.38 his feet with her hair, **kissed** them, and poured the perfume
7.45 not welcome me with a **kiss,**
7.45 but she has not stopped **kissing** my feet since I came.
15.20 and he ran, threw his arms round his son, and **kissed** him.
22.47 He came up to Jesus to **kiss** him.
22.48 "Judas, is it with a **kiss** that you betray the Son of
Acts 20.37 were all crying as they hugged him and **kissed** him good-bye.
Rom 16.16 Greet one another with a brotherly **kiss.**
1 Cor 16.20 Greet one another with a brotherly **kiss.**
2 Cor 13.12 Greet one another with a brotherly **kiss.**
1 Thes 5.26 Greet all the believers with a brotherly **kiss.**
1 Pet 5.14 Greet one another with the **kiss** of Christian love.

KITCHEN

Ezek 46.24 "These are the **kitchens** where the temple servants are to

KNEE

Judg 5.27 He sank to his **knees,** fell down and lay still
5.27 At her feet he sank to his **knees** and fell;
7. 5 from everyone who gets down on his **knees** to drink."
7. 6 all the others got down on their **knees** to drink.
7.15 what it meant, he fell to his **knees** and worshipped the Lord.
1 Sam 14.13 pass on his hands and **knees,** and the young man followed him.
20.41 fell on his **knees** and bowed
1 Kgs 18.42 bowed down to the ground, with his head between his **knees.**
2 Kgs 1.13 fell on his **knees** in front of Elijah, and pleaded,
Job 3.12 Why did my mother hold me on her **knees?**
Ps 109.24 My **knees** are weak from lack of food;
Is 35. 3 that are tired and to **knees** that tremble with weakness.
Ezek 7.17 Everyone's hands will be weak, and their **knees** will shake.
21. 7 their courage will fail, and their **knees** will tremble.
Ezek 47. 4 five hundred metres, and the water came up to my **knees.**
Dan 5. 6 pale and was so frightened that his **knees** began to shake.
10.10 took hold of me and raised me to my hands and **knees;**
Nah 2.10 **knees** tremble, strength is gone;
Mt 18.26 The servant fell on his **knees** before the king.
Mk 5. 6 he ran, fell on his **knees** before him, [7]and screamed in a
15.19 spat on him, fell on their **knees,** and bowed down to him.
Lk 5. 8 happened, he fell on his **knees** before Jesus and said, "Go
Eph 3.14 reason I fall on my **knees** before the Father, [15]from whom
Phil 2.10 below will fall on their **knees,** [11]and all will openly proclaim
Heb 12.12 up your tired hands, then, and strengthen your trembling **knees!**

KNEEL
[KNELT]

Gen 24.11 he made the camels **kneel** down at the well
24.26 Then the man **knelt** down and worshipped the Lord.
24.48 I **knelt** down and worshipped the Lord.
43.28 And they **knelt** and bowed down before him.
Ex 12.27 The Israelites **knelt** down and worshipped.
1 Kgs 8.54 the altar, where he had been **kneeling** with uplifted hands.
2 Chr 6.13 mounted this platform, **knelt** down where everyone could see him,
29.29 Then King Hezekiah and all the people **knelt** down
29.30 So everyone sang with great joy as they **knelt** and worshipped
Ezra 9. 5 I **knelt** in prayer
Neh 8. 6 They **knelt** in worship, with their faces to the ground.
Esth 3. 2 show their respect for Haman by **kneeling** and bowing to him.
3. 5 Mordecai was not going to **kneel** and bow to him,
Ps 95. 6 let us **kneel** before the Lord, our Maker!
Is 45.23 Everyone will come and **kneel** before me and vow to be loyal
Dan 6.10 he **knelt** down at the open windows
Mt 2.11 child with his mother Mary, they **knelt** down and worshipped him.
4. 9 you," the Devil said, "if you **kneel** down and worship me."
8. 2 dreaded skin-disease came to him, **knelt** down before him, and said,
9.18 Jewish official came to him, **knelt** down before him, and said,
17.14 a man came to Jesus, **knelt** before him, [15]and said, "Sir,
27.29 then they **knelt** before him and mocked him.
Mk 1.40 dreaded skin-disease came to Jesus, **knelt** down, and begged him
5.33 she came, trembling with fear, **knelt** at his feet, and told
10.17 again, a man ran up, **knelt** before him, and asked him, "Good
Lk 22.41 the distance of a stone's throw and **knelt** down and prayed.
Jn 9.38 the man said, and **knelt** down before Jesus.
Acts 7.60 He **knelt** down and cried out in a loud voice, "Lord!
9.40 put them all out of the room, and **knelt** down and prayed;
20.36 When Paul finished, he **knelt** down with them and prayed.
21. 5 of the city to the beach, where we all **knelt** and prayed.
Rom 14.11 says the Lord, everyone will **kneel** before me, and everyone will

KNIFE
[PRUNING-KNIVES]

Gen 22. 6 and he himself carried a **knife** and live coals
22.10 Then he picked up the **knife** to kill him.
Josh 5. 2 Lord told Joshua, "Make some **knives** out of flint and circumcise
Judg 19.29 When he arrived, he went into the house and got a **knife.**
1 Kgs 18.28 cut themselves with **knives** and daggers, according to their ritual,
Is 2. 4 their swords into ploughs and their spears into **pruning-knives.**
18. 5 the Sudanese as easily as a **knife** cuts branches from a vine.
Jer 36.23 off with a small **knife** and threw them into the fire.
Joel 3.10 ploughs into swords and your **pruning-knives** into spears.
Mic 4. 3 their swords into ploughs and their spears into **pruning-knives.**

Am **KNOCK**
see also **HURL**

KNOCK

Ex 21.27 If he **knocks** out a tooth, he is to free the slave
Lev 24.20 if he **knocks** out a tooth,
24.20 one of his teeth shall be **knocked** out.
1 Sam 14.13 Jonathan attacked the Philistines and **knocked** them down,
Neh 4. 3 Even a fox could **knock** it down!"
Song 5. 2 I dreamt my lover **knocked** at the door.
Ezek 39. 3 Then I will **knock** his bow out of his left hand
Mt 7. 7 **knock,** and the door will be opened to you.
7. 8 and the door will be opened to him who **knocks.**
Lk 9.42 boy was coming, the demon **knocked** him to the ground and
11. 9 **knock,** and the door will be opened to you.
11.10 and the door will be opened to anyone who **knocks.**
12.36 When he comes and **knocks,** they will open the door for him
13.25 stand outside and begin to **knock** on the door and say, 'Open
Acts 12.13 Peter **knocked** at the outside door, and a servant-girl
12.16 Meanwhile Peter kept on **knocking.**
Rev 3.20 I stand at the door and **knock;**

KNOT

Judg 15. 4 he tied their tails together and put torches in the **knots.**

KNOW
[KNEW]

Gen 3. 5 God said that, because he **knows** that when you eat it
3. 5 will be like God and **know** what is good
4. 9 He answered, "I don't **know.**
8.11 So Noah **knew** that the water had gone down.
8.21 I **know** that from the time he is young his thoughts are
15. 8 "Sovereign Lord, how can I **know** that it will be mine?"
19.33 But he was so drunk that he didn't **know** it.

Gen 19.35 Again he was so drunk that he didn't **know** it.
20. 6 in the dream, "Yes, I **know** that you did it
20.16 everyone will **know** that you have done no wrong."
21.26 Abimelech said, "I don't **know** who did this.
22.12 "Now I **know** that you honour and obey God,
24.14 If this happens, I will **know** that you have kept your promise
26.28 They answered, "Now we **know** that the Lord is with you,
27.11 said to his mother, "You **know** that Esau is a hairy man,
28.16 He is in this place, and I didn't **know** it!"
29. 5 He asked, "Do you **know** Laban son of Nahor?"
30.26 You **know** how well I have served you."
30.29 Jacob answered, "You **know** how I have worked for you
30.33 that isn't black, you will **know** that it has been stolen."
31. 6 You both **know** that I have worked for your father
31.20 Jacob deceived Laban by not letting him **know** that he was leaving.
31.30 I **know** that you left because you were so anxious
31.32 Jacob did not **know** that Rachel had stolen Laban's gods.
31.50 even though I don't **know** about it, remember that God is
32.29 But he answered, "Why do you want to **know** my name?"
33.13 Jacob answered, "You **know** that the children are weak,
38. 9 But Onan **knew** that the children would not belong to him,
38.14 As she well **knew**, Judah's youngest son Shelah had now grown up,
38.16 (He did not **know** that she was his daughter-in-law.)
41.21 but no one would have **known** it, because they looked
42. 7 recognized them, but he acted as if he did not **know** them.
42.23 but they did not **know** it, because they had been speaking
42.34 Then I will **know** that you are not spies, but honest men;
43. 7 How could we **know** that he would tell us to bring our
43.22 We do not **know** who put our money back in our sacks."
44. 8 You **know** that we brought back to you from the land of
44.15 Didn't you **know** that a man in my position could find you
44.27 father said to us, 'You **know** that my wife Rachel bore me
46.30 that I have seen you and **know** that you are still alive."
48.19 His father refused, saying, "I **know**, my son, I know.
Ex 1. 8 Then, a new king, who **knew** nothing about Joseph,
3. 7 I **know** all about their sufferings, [8]and so I have come down
3.19 I **know** that the king of Egypt will not let you go
4.14 I **know** that he can speak well.
5. 2 I do not **know** the Lord;
6. 3 I did not make myself **known** to them by my holy name,
6. 7 You will **know** that I am the Lord your God
6.30 Moses answered, "You **know** that I am such a poor speaker;
7. 5 The Egyptians will then **know** that I am the Lord,
8.10 and then you will **know** that there is no other god
8.22 this so that you will **know** that I, the Lord,
9.14 well, so that you may **know** that there is no one like
9.29 hail, so that you may **know** that the earth belongs to the
9.30 But I **know** that you and your officials do not yet fear
10. 2 All of you will **know** that I am the Lord."
10.26 there, we will not **know** what animals to sacrifice to him."
11. 7 Then you will **know** that I, the Lord, make a distinction
14. 4 Then the Egyptians will **know** that I am the Lord."
14.18 I defeat them, the Egyptians will **know** that I am the Lord."
16. 6 Israelites, "This evening you will **know** that it was the Lord
16.12 Then they will **know** that I, the Lord, am their God."
16.15 Israelites saw it, they didn't **know** what it was
18.11 Now I **know** that the Lord is greater than all the gods,
21.36 But if it was **known** that the bull had been in the
23. 9 you **know** how it feels to be a foreigner, because you were
29.46 They will **know** that I am the Lord their God who brought
32. 1 to him, "We do not **know** what has happened to this man
32. 9 I **know** how stubborn these people are.
32.22 you **know** how determined these people are to do evil.
32.23 said to me, 'We don't **know** what has happened to this man
33.12 You have said that you **know** me well and are pleased with
33.16 How will anyone **know** that you are pleased with your people
33.17 you have asked, because I **know** you very well and I am
34.29 but he did not **know** it.
36. 1 skill and understanding, who **know** how to make everything needed
Lev 4.14 soon as the sin becomes **known**, the community shall bring
18.29 You **know** that whoever does any of these disgusting things
23.43 your descendants may **know** that the Lord made the people
Num 10.31 "You **know** where we can camp in the wilderness,
14.34 You will **know** what it means to have me against you!
16.28 "This is how you will **know** that the Lord has sent me
16.30 of the dead, you will **know** that these men have rejected
20.14 You **know** the hardships we have suffered,
22. 5 "I want you to **know** that a whole nation has come from
22. 6 I **know** that when you pronounce a blessing, people are blessed,
22.34 I did not **know** that you were standing in the road
23. 9 They **know** they are blessed more than other nations.
24. 1 By now Balaam **knew** that the Lord wanted him to bless
Deut 1.39 are still too young to **know** right from wrong,
3.19 I **know** you have a lot of livestock
3.24 prayed, [24]'Sovereign Lord, I **know** that you have shown me
8. 2 you, so that he might **know** what you intended to do
9.13 Lord also said to me, 'I **know** how stubborn these people are.
9.24 Ever since I have **known** you, you have rebelled
9.25 because I **knew** that he was determined to destroy
11. 5 You **know** what the Lord did for you in the desert before
21. 1 going to give you, and you do not **know** who killed him.
21. 7 not murder the man, and we do not **know** who did it.
22. 2 or if you don't **know** who owns it, then take it
28.49 a nation whose language you do not **know**.
30.14 You **know** it and can quote it, so now obey it.
31.21 I **know** what they are thinking."
31.27 I **know** how stubborn and rebellious they are.
31.29 I **know** that after my death the people will become wicked
32.17 gods their ancestors had never **known**,
Deut 32.31 Their enemies **know** that their own gods are weak,
34. 6 to this day no one **knows** the exact place of his burial.
Josh 2. 4 she answered, "but I don't **know** where they were from.
2. 9 and said to them, "I **know** that the Lord has given you
3.10 You will **know** that the living God is among you
4.24 everyone on earth will **know** how great the Lord's power is,
8.14 same place as before, not **knowing** that he was about to be
14. 6 said to him, "You **know** what the Lord said in Kadesh
22.22 He **knows** why we did this,
22.22 and we want you to **know** too!
22.31 said to them, "Now we **know** that the Lord is with us.
23.14 Every one of you **knows** in his heart and soul
24. 7 You **know** what I did to Egypt.
Judg 6.37 the ground, then I will **know** that you are going to use
13.15 Manoah did not **know** that it was the Lord's angel,
13.18 The angel asked, "Why do you want to **know** my name?
14. 4 His parents did not **know** that it was the Lord
14.18 been ploughing with my cow, You wouldn't **know** the answer now."
15.11 "Don't you **know** that the Philistines are our rulers?
16. 9 So they still did not **know** the secret of his strength.
16.20 He did not **know** that the Lord had left him.
17.13 Levite as my priest, I **know** that the Lord will make things
18.14 to their companions, "Did you **know** that here in one of
Ruth 1.13 No, my daughters, you **know** that's impossible.
2.11 I **know** how you left your father and mother and your own
2.11 you came to live among a people you had never **known** before.
3. 3 threshing, but don't let him **know** you are there until he has
3.11 as everyone in town **knows**, you are a fine woman.
3.14 Boaz did not want anyone to **know** that she had been there.
4. 4 relative Elimelech, [4]and I think you ought to **know** about it.
1 Sam 2. 3 Lord is a God who **knows**, and he judges all that people
3. 6 The boy did not **know** that it was the Lord, because the
3.13 Eli **knew** they were doing this, but he did not stop them.
3.20 **knew** that Samuel was indeed a prophet
6. 9 it doesn't, then we will **know** that he did not send the
10.11 People who had **known** him before saw him doing this
14. 3 The men did not **know** that Jonathan had left.
16.15 servants said to him, "We **know** that an evil spirit sent by
16.16 will look for a man who **knows** how to play the harp.
17.46 Then the whole world will **know** that Israel has a God,
19. 3 If I find out anything, I will let you **know**."
20. 3 But David answered, "Your father **knows** very well
20. 3 decided not to let you **know** what he plans to do, because
20. 7 he becomes angry, you will **know** that he is determined to
20. 9 "If I **knew** for certain that my father was determined to
20.10 "Who will let me **know** if your father answers you angrily?"
20.13 if I don't let you **know** about it and get you safely
20.30 Now I **know** you are taking sides with David and are
20.39 returned to his master, [39]not **knowing** what it all meant;
20.39 only Jonathan and David **knew**.
21. 2 me not to let anyone **know** what he sent me to do.
22.15 I don't **know** anything about this matter!"
22.17 that he had run away, even though they **knew** it all along."
22.22 Doeg there that day, I **knew** that he would be sure
23.17 He **knows** very well that you are the one who will be
23.20 We **know**, Your Majesty, how much you want to capture him;
24. 4 cut off a piece of Saul's robe without Saul's **knowing** it.
24.13 You **know** the old saying, 'Evil is done only by evil men.'
25. 7 and he wants you to **know** that your shepherds have been with
25.11 and give them to men who come from I don't **know** where!"
26.10 David continued, "I **know** that the Lord himself will kill
26.12 No one saw it or **knew** what had happened
28. 9 "Surely you **know** what King Saul has done,
28.14 Then Saul **knew** that it was Samuel, and he bowed
2 Sam 1. 5 "How do you **know** that Saul and Jonathan are dead?"
1.10 killed him, because I **knew** that he would die anyway
3.25 Surely you **know** that!"
3.26 but David **knew** nothing about it.
3.28 news, he said, "The Lord **knows** that my subjects and I are
7.20 You **know** me, your servant.
7.22 we have always **known** that you alone are God.
11.16 sent Uriah to a place where he **knew** the enemy was strong.
14. 1 Joab **knew** that King David missed Absalom very much,
14.20 as the angel of God and **knows** everything that happens."
14.22 Now I **know** that you are pleased with me,
15.11 they **knew** nothing of the plot and went in all good faith.
15.20 I don't even **know** where I'm going.
16.21 Then everyone in Israel will **know** that your father regards
17. 8 You **know** that your father David and his men are hard
17.10 because everyone in Israel **knows** that your father is a great
17.12 and attack him before he **knows** what's happening.
17.28 They **knew** that David and his men would be hungry,
19.20 I **know**, sir, that I have sinned,
19.26 He answered, "As you **know**, Your Majesty, I am
22.24 He **knows** that I am faultless,
22.25 I do what is right, because he **knows** that I am innocent.
22.44 people I did not **know** have now become my subjects.
24. 2 I want to **know** how many there are."
1 Kgs 1.11 And King David doesn't **know** anything about it!
1.18 Adonijah has already become king, and you don't **know** anything about it.
2. 6 You **know** what to do;
2. 9 You **know** what to do, and you must see to it
2.15 He answered, "You **know** that I should have become king
2.17 "Please ask King Solomon—I **know** he won't refuse you—
2.44 You **know** very well all the wrong that you did to my
3. 7 even though I am very young and don't **know** how to rule.
3. 9 justice and to **know** the difference between good and evil.
3.28 respect for him, because they **knew** then that God had given
5. 3 "You **know** that because of the constant wars my father David
5. 6 well know, my men don't **know** how to cut down trees

1 Kgs 8.39 You alone **know** the thoughts of the human heart.
8.43 peoples of the world may **know** you and obey you,
8.43 Then they will **know** that this Temple I have built
8.60 nations of the world will **know** that the Lord alone is God
13. 3 Then you will **know** that the Lord has spoken through me."
14. 6 I **know** you are Jeroboam's wife.
17.24 She answered, "Now I **know** that you are a man of God
18.37 so that this people will **know** that you, the Lord, are God,
20.13 over it today, and you will **know** that I am the Lord.' "
20.28 and you and your people will **know** that I am the Lord.' "
2 Kgs 2. 3 and asked him, "Do you **know** that the Lord is going to
2. 3 "Yes, I **know,"** Elisha answered.
2. 5 and asked him, "Do you **know** that the Lord is going to
2. 5 "Yes, I **know,"** Elisha answered.
2.19 Elisha and said, "As you **know,** sir, this is a fine city,
4. 1 As you **know,** he was a God-fearing man, but now a man
4.39 sliced them up into the stew, not **knowing** what they were.
5.15 men and said, "Now I **know** that there is no god but
7.12 They **know** about the famine here, so they have left their
8. 4 the king wanted to **know** about Elisha's miracles.
8.12 "Because I **know** the horrible things you will do
9.11 "You **know** what he wanted," Jehu answered.
9.18 him, "The king wants to **know** if you come as a friend."
17.26 cities of Samaria did not **know** the law of the god of
18.19 emperor wanted to **know** what made King Hezekiah so confident.
19.17 We all **know,** Lord, that the emperors of Assyria have
19.19 nations of the world will **know** that only you, O Lord, are
19.27 "But I **know** everything about you,
19.27 I **know** how you rage against me.
1 Chr 12.17 the God of our ancestors will **know** it and punish you."
12.23 (these leaders **knew** what Israel should do
17.18 You **know** me well, and yet you honour me, your servant.
17.20 we have always **known** that you alone are God.
21. 2 I want to **know** how many there are."
28. 9 He **knows** all our thoughts and desires.
29.15 You **know,** O Lord, that we pass through life like exiles
29.17 I **know** that you test everyone's heart
2 Chr 2. 8 I **know** how skilful your woodmen are, so send me cedar,
2.14 He **knows** how to make things out of gold, silver, bronze,
6.30 You alone **know** the thoughts of the human heart.
6.33 peoples of the world may **know** you and obey you, as your
6.33 Then they will **know** that this Temple I have built is where
13. 5 "Don't you **know** that the Lord, the God of Israel,
20. 8 to honour you, **knowing** [9]that if any disaster struck them
20.12 We do not **know** what to do, but we look to you
25.16 "Now I **know** that God has decided to destroy
28.10 Don't you **know** that you also have committed sins against the
29. 8 You **know** this very well.
32.13 Don't you **know** what my ancestors and I have done
Ezra 4.12 "We want Your Majesty to **know** that the Jews who came
5. 8 "Your Majesty should **know** that we went to the province of
7.25 You must teach that Law to anyone who does not **know** it.
9.13 we **know** that you, our God, have punished
Neh 2.16 None of the local officials **knew** where I had been
4.11 would not see them or **know** what was happening
5.18 But I **knew** what heavy burdens the people had to bear,
6.16 had lost face, since everyone **knew** that the work had been
9.10 because you **knew** how they oppressed your people.
13.13 I **knew** I could trust these men to be honest
13.24 and didn't **know** how to speak our language.
13.30 and the Levites so that each one would **know** his duty;
Esth 1.13 called for his advisers, who would **know** what should be done.
2.20 she had still not let it be **known** that she was Jewish.
4.11 from the king's advisers to the people in the provinces, **knows**
4.14 Yet who **knows**—maybe it was for a time like this
Job 3. 8 those who **know** how to control Leviathan.
6.10 If I **knew** he would, I would leap for joy,
6.10 I **know** that God is holy;
7. 9 he is forgotten by all who **knew** him.
8. 9 Our life is short, we **know** nothing at all;
8.18 pull them up— no one will ever **know** they were there.
9.27 I **know** that God does hold me guilty.
9.35 I am going to talk because I **know** my own heart.
10. 7 You **know** that I am not guilty,
10.13 But now I **know** that all that time you were secretly
11. 8 God **knows** the world of the dead,
11. 8 but you do not **know** it.
11.11 God **knows** which men are worthless;
12. 3 everyone **knows** all that you have said.
12. 9 All of them **know** that the Lord's hand made them.
13. 1 I **know** as much as you do.
13.18 to state my case, because I **know** I am in the right.
14.21 win honour, but he never **knows** it, nor is he told
15. 9 There is nothing you **know** that we don't know.
15.17 Now listen, Job, to what I **know.**
15.23 He **knows** his future is dark;
17.12 say that light is near, but I **know** I remain in darkness.
19.13 I am a stranger to those who **knew** me;
19.25 But I **know** there is someone in heaven who will come
19.29 on sin, so that you will **know** there is one who judges.
20. 3 said is an insult, but I **know** how to reply to you.
20. 4 Surely you **know** that from ancient times,
20. 7 Those who used to **know** him will wonder where he has gone.
21.14 they don't want to **know** his will for their lives.
21.27 I **know** what spiteful thoughts you have.
21.29 Don't you **know** the reports they bring back?
22.13 And yet you ask, "What does God **know?**
23. 3 How I wish I **knew** where to find him,
23. 3 and **knew** how to go where he is.
23. 5 I want to **know** what he would say and how he would
23.10 Yet God **knows** every step I take;
Job 26.14 Who can **know** how truly great God is?
28.13 No one **knows** its true value.
28.23 God alone **knows** the way, Knows the place where wisdom is found,
30.23 I **know** you are taking me off to my death, to the
31. 4 God **knows** everything I do;
31.21 have ever cheated an orphan, **knowing** I could win in court,
31.31 who work for me **know** that I have always welcomed strangers.
32. 9 that makes men wise or helps them to **know** what is right.
32.22 I don't **know** how to flatter,
34. 3 You **know** good food when you taste it, but not wise words
34.25 Because he **knows** what they do he overthrows them
35.16 it is clear you don't **know** what you are saying.
36. 3 I will use what I **know** to show that God, my Creator,
36.26 We cannot fully **know** his greatness
36.29 No one **knows** how the clouds move or how the thunder
36.33 the approaching storm, and the cattle **know** it is coming.
37.15 Do you **know** how God gives the command and makes lightning
37.16 Do you **know** how clouds float in the sky,
38. 4 If you **know** so much, tell me about it.
38. 5 Do you **know** all the answers?
38.18 Answer me if you **know.**
38.19 Do you **know** where the light comes from
38.33 Do you **know** the laws that govern the skies,
39. 1 Do you **know** when mountain-goats are born?
39. 2 Do you **know** how long they carry their young?
39. 2 Do you **know** the time for their birth?
39. 3 Do you **know** when they will crouch down and bring their
39.22 They do not **know** the meaning of fear,
42. 2 I **know,** Lord, that you are all-powerful;
42. 3 about marvels too great for me to **know.**
42. 5 In the past I **knew** only what others had told me,
Ps 6.10 My enemies will **know** the bitter shame of defeat;
7. 8 you **know** that I am innocent.
9.10 Those who **know** you, Lord, will trust you;
9.20 make them **know** that they are only mortal beings.
11. 4 He watches people everywhere and **knows** what they are doing.
14. 4 "Don't they **know?"**
17. 2 You will judge in my favour, because you **know** what is right.
17. 3 You **know** my heart.
18.23 He **knows** that I am faultless, that I have kept myself
18.24 I do what is right, because he **knows** that I am innocent.
18.43 people I did not **know** have now become my subjects.
20. 6 Now I **know** that the Lord gives victory to his chosen king;
23. 6 I **know** that your goodness and love will be with me all
25. 4 make them **known** to me.
27.13 I **know** that I will live to see the Lord's goodness in
31. 7 you **know** my trouble.
31.11 those who **know** me are afraid of me;
31.19 Everyone **knows** how good you are,
33.15 He forms all their thoughts and **knows** everything they do.
35. 8 But destruction will catch them before they **know** it;
35.11 accuse me of crimes I **know** nothing about.
36.10 Continue to love those who **know** you and to do good to
37.13 wicked men, because he **knows** they will soon be destroyed.
37.35 I once **knew** a wicked man who was a tyrant;
38. 9 O Lord, you **know** what I long for;
39. 6 he gathers wealth, but doesn't **know** who will get it.
40. 9 You **know** that I will never stop telling it.
40.11 Lord, I **know** you will never stop being merciful to me.
41.11 over me, and I will **know** that you are pleased with me.
44.21 surely have discovered it, because you **know** our secret thoughts.
46.10 "Stop fighting," he says, "and **know** that I am God,
53. 4 "Don't they **know?"**
56. 8 You **know** how troubled I am;
56. 9 I **know** this:
58. 9 Before they **know** it, they are cut down like weeds;
59.13 Then everyone will **know** that God rules in Israel,
67. 2 kindness, [2]so that the whole world may **know** your will;
67. 2 so that all nations may **know** your salvation.
69. 5 you **know** how foolish I have been.
69.19 You **know** how I am insulted, how I am disgraced
73.11 They say, "God will not **know;**
74. 9 no prophets left, and no one **knows** how long this will last.
76. 1 God is **known** in Judah;
76. 8 You made your judgement **known** from heaven;
78. 3 things we have heard and **known,** things that our fathers told us.
83.18 May they **know** that you alone are the Lord,
89. 2 I **know** that your love will last for all time,
90.11 Who **knows** what fear your fury can bring?
92. 6 This is something a fool cannot **know;**
92. 9 We **know** that your enemies will die,
94.11 The Lord **knows** what they think;
94.11 he **knows** how senseless their reasoning is.
98. 2 he made his saving power **known** to the nations.
103.14 He **knows** what we are made of;
104.19 the sun **knows** the time to set.
109.27 Make my enemies **know** that you are the one who saves me.
119.20 I want to **know** your judgements at all times.
119.75 I **know** that your judgements are righteous, Lord,
119.79 honour you come to me— all those who **know** your commands.
119.125 give me understanding, so that I may **know** your teachings.
135. 5 I **know** that our Lord is great, greater than all the gods.
139. 1 Lord, you have examined me and you **know** me.
139. 2 You **know** everything I do;
139. 3 you **know** all my actions.
139. 4 Even before I speak, you already **know** what I will say.
139.14 I **know** it with all my heart.
139.15 growing there in secret, you **knew** that I was there—
139.23 Examine me, O God, and **know** my mind;
140.12 Lord, I **know** that you defend the cause of the poor

Ps 142. 3 I am ready to give up, he **knows** what I should do.
145.12 so that everyone will **know** your mighty deeds
147.20 they do not **know** his laws.
Prov 2. 5 If you do, you will **know** what it means to fear
2. 9 listen to me, you will **know** what is right, just, and fair.
2. 9 You will **know** what you should do.
3. 5 Never rely on what you think you **know.**
5. 2 Then you will **know** how to behave properly,
6.34 his revenge **knows** no limits.
7.23 he did not **know** that his life was in danger.
9.10 If you **know** the Holy One, you have understanding.
9.18 Her victims do not **know** that the people die who go to
10.32 Righteous people **know** the kind thing to say,
12.16 When a fool is annoyed, he quickly lets it be **known.**
12.23 keep quiet about what they **know,** but stupid people advertise
14. 8 Because he **knows** what to do.
14. 8 Because he only thinks he **knows.**
14.24 but fools are **known** by their foolishness.
14.33 fools **know** nothing about wisdom.
15.11 of the dead can keep the Lord from **knowing** what is there;
16.21 A wise, mature person is **known** for his understanding.
18. 1 they will disagree with what everyone else **knows** is right.
19.25 so that people who don't **know** any better can learn a lesson.
19.27 stop learning, you will soon neglect what you already **know.**
20. 8 The king sits in judgement and **knows** evil when he sees it.
20.15 If you **know** what you are talking about,
21.12 God, the righteous one, **knows** what goes on in the homes
24.12 of your business, but God **knows** and judges your motives.
24.12 he **knows.**
24.18 The Lord will **know** if you are gloating,
25. 3 You never **know** what a king is thinking;
25. 5 king and his government will be **known** for its justice.
27. 1 You don't **know** what will happen between now and then.
28. 5 Evil people do not **know** what justice is,
28.11 a poor person who has insight into character **knows** better.
28.22 rich that they do not **know** when poverty is about to strike.
29. 7 A good person **knows** the rights of the poor,
30. 3 learned any wisdom, and I **know** nothing at all about God.
30. 4 Who is he, if you **know?**
31.18 She **knows** the value of everything she makes,
Ecc 1.16 I **know** what wisdom and knowledge really are."
1.18 the more you **know,** the more it hurts.
2.13 Oh, I **know,** "Wisdom is better than foolishness,
2.14 But I also **know** that the same fate is waiting for us
2.18 because I **knew** that I would have to leave
2.19 and he might be wise, or he might be foolish—who **knows?**
3.10 I **know** the heavy burdens that God has laid on us.
3.11 given us a desire to **know** the future,
3.14 I **know** that everything God does will last for ever.
3.22 no way for us to **know** what will happen after we die.
5. 1 people who don't **know** right from wrong.
6. 5 the light of day or **knows** what life is like,
6. 8 does it do a poor man to **know** how to face life?
6.10 long ago, and we all **know** that a man cannot argue with
6.12 How can anyone **know** what is best for a man
6.12 How can anyone **know** what will happen in the world
7.14 you never **know** what is going to happen next.
7.22 and you **know** yourself that you have insulted
8. 1 Only a wise man **knows** what things really mean.
8. 5 safe, and a wise man **knows** how and when to do it.
8. 6 a right way to do everything, but we **know** so little!
8. 7 None of us **knows** what is going to happen,
8.12 Oh yes, I **know** what they say:
8.17 Wise men may claim to **know,** but they don't.
9. 1 No one **knows** anything about what lies ahead of him.
9. 5 Yes, the living **know** they are going to die,
9. 5 but the dead **know** nothing.
9.12 You never **know** when your time is coming.
10. 3 he lets everyone **know** that he is a fool.
10.11 **Knowing** how to charm a snake is of no use
10.14 No one **knows** what is going to happen next,
11. 2 because you never **know** what kind of bad luck
11. 6 You never **know** whether it will all grow well
12. 9 Philosopher was wise, he kept on teaching the people what he **knew.**
Song 1. 8 Don't you **know** the place, loveliest of women?
8.10 My lover **knows** that with him I find contentment and peace.
Is 1. 3 Cattle **know** who owns them,
1. 3 and donkeys **know** where their master feeds them.
1. 3 But that is more than my people Israel **know.**
3.12 misleading you, so that you do not **know** which way to turn.
6. 9 how much you look, you will not **know** what is happening."
9. 9 in the city of Samaria, will **know** that he has done this.
11. 2 He will **know** the Lord's will and have reverence for him,
16. 6 We **know** that they are arrogant and conceited,
26.11 Your enemies do not **know** that you will punish them.
28.26 He **knows** how to do his work, because God has taught him.
28.28 threshing it endlessly, and he **knows** how to thresh it
29.11 take it to someone who **knows** how to read and ask him
29.12 read it to you, he will answer that he doesn't **know** how.
29.15 think no one will see them or **know** what they are doing.
29.16 can it say to him, "You don't **know** what you are doing"?
31. 2 He **knows** what he is doing!
36. 4 emperor wanted to **know** what made King Hezekiah so confident.
37.18 We all **know,** Lord, that the emperors of Assyria
37.20 nations of the world will **know** that you alone are God."
37.28 "But I **know** everything about you, what you do
37.28 I **know** how you rage against me.
40.14 consult in order to **know** and understand and to learn
40.21 Do you not **know?**
40.26 out like an army, he **knows** how many there are and calls
Is 40.27 complain that the Lord doesn't **know** your troubles
40.28 Don't you **know?**
41.11 "Those who are angry with you will **know** the shame of defeat.
41.20 People will see this and **know** that I, the Lord, have
41.22 so that we will **know** it when it takes place.
41.23 the future holds— then we will **know** that you are gods!
42.25 but we never **knew** what was happening;
43.10 servant, so that you would **know** me and believe in me and
44. 8 You **know** that from ancient times until now I have predicted
44.18 Such people are too stupid to **know** what they are doing.
45. 3 then you will **know** that I am the Lord, and that the
45. 4 I have given you great honour, although you do not **know** me.
45. 5 you the strength you need, although you do not **know** me.
45. 6 world to the other may **know** that I am the Lord and
45.19 I make **known** what is right."
45.20 that cannot save them— those people **know** nothing at all!
48. 4 I **knew** that you would prove to be stubborn,
48. 7 If it had, you would claim that you **knew** all about it.
48. 8 I **knew** that you couldn't be trusted,
48. 8 that you have always been **known** as a rebel.
48.20 make it **known** everywhere:
49.23 Then you will **know** that I am the Lord;
49.26 Then all mankind will **know** that I am the Lord, the one
49.26 They will **know** that I am Israel's powerful God."
50. 7 I **know** that I will not be disgraced, [8] for God is near,
51. 7 "Listen to me, you that **know** what is right, who have my
52.15 They will see and understand something they had never **known."**
53.11 he will **know** that he did not suffer in vain.
55. 5 one time they did not **know** you, but now they will come
56.10 They **know** nothing.
58. 2 that they are eager to **know** my ways and obey my laws.
59. 9 The people say, "Now we **know** why God does not save us
60.16 You will **know** that I, the Lord, have saved you, That the
61. 9 Everyone who sees them will **know** That they are a people whom
62.10 so that the nations can **know** [11] That the Lord is announcing
66.14 Then you will **know** that I, the Lord, help those who obey
66.18 I **know** their thoughts and their deeds.
66.19 power can do [19] and will **know** that I am the one who
Jer 1. 6 I answered, "Sovereign Lord, I don't **know** how to speak;
2. 8 My own priests did not **know** me.
2.33 You certainly **know** how to chase after lovers.
4.22 they don't **know** me.
5. 4 they don't **know** what their God requires, what the Lord
5. 5 Surely they **know** what their God requires, what the Lord
5.15 and ancient nation, a nation whose language you do not **know.**
6.15 they don't even **know** how to blush.
7. 9 and worship gods that you had not **known** before.
8. 7 Even storks **know** when it is time to return;
8. 7 swallows, and thrushes **know** when it is time to migrate.
8. 7 my people, you do not **know** the laws by which I rule
8. 8 you say that you are wise, and that you **know** my laws?
8.12 you don't even **know** how to blush!
9.24 he should boast that he **knows** and understands me,
10.23 Lord, I **know** that no one is the master of his own
11.19 killed, and I did not **know** that it was against me that
12. 3 But, Lord, you **know** me;
13.12 They will answer that they **know** every wine-jar should be
14.13 I said, "Sovereign Lord, you **know** that the prophets are
14.18 on their work, but they don't **know** what they are doing."
15.14 enemies in a land they **know** nothing about,
16.13 a land that neither you nor your ancestors have ever **known.**
16.21 all I will make the nations **know** my power and my might;
16.21 they will **know** that I am the Lord."
17. 4 enemies in a land you **know** nothing about,
17.16 Lord, you **know** this;
17.16 you **know** what I have said.
18.23 But, Lord, you **know** all their plots to kill me.
19. 4 ancestors nor the kings of Judah have **known** anything about.
20.12 you **know** what is in their hearts and minds.
22.16 That is what it means to **know** the Lord.
22.28 been taken into exile to a land they **know** nothing about?"
23.18 "None of these prophets has ever **known** the Lord's secret thoughts.
23.22 If they had **known** my secret thoughts,
23.24 Do you not **know** that I am everywhere in heaven and on
23.25 I **know** what those prophets have said who speak lies
24. 7 will give them the desire to **know** that I am the Lord.
29.11 I alone **know** the plans I have for you, plans to bring
29.23 he **knows** what they have done, and he is a witness
31.34 to teach his fellow-countryman to **know** the Lord,
31.34 because all will **know** me,
32. 8 So I **knew** that the Lord had really spoken to me.
32.20 so that you are now **known** everywhere.
33. 3 marvellous things that you **know** nothing about.
36.19 Don't let anyone **know** where you are."
38.24 "Don't let anyone **know** about this conversation,
40.14 said to him, "Don't you **know** that King Baalis of Ammon
40.15 go and kill Ishmael, and no one will **know** who did it.
41. 4 The next day, before anyone **knew** about Gedaliah's murder,
44.15 all the men who **knew** that their wives offered sacrifices
44.21 that the Lord did not **know** about them or that he forgot
44.28 Then the survivors will **know** whose words have come true,
48.17 you that live near by, all of you that **know** its fame.
48.30 I, the Lord, **know** of their arrogance.
50.24 trap I set for you, even though you did not **know** it.
50.29 Send out everyone who **knows** how to use the bow and arrow.
Lam 3. 1 I am one who **knows** what it is to be punished by
3.34 The Lord **knows** when our spirits are crushed in prison;
3.35 He **knows** when we are denied the rights he gave us;
3.36 When justice is perverted in court, he **knows.**
3.59 you **know** the wrongs done against me.

Lam 3.60 You **know** how my enemies hate me and how they plot
3.61 you **know** all their plots.
Ezek 2. 5 you or not, they will **know** that a prophet has been among
6. 9 they will remember me and **know** that I have punished them
6.10 They will **know** that I am the Lord and that my warnings
6.13 Then everyone will **know** that I am the Lord.
6.14 Then everyone will **know** that I am the Lord."
7. 4 have done, so that you will **know** that I am the Lord."
7. 9 done, so that you will **know** that I am the Lord, and
11. 5 "People of Israel, I **know** what you are saying and what you
11.10 Then everyone will **know** that I am the Lord.
11.12 You will **know** that I am the Lord and that while you
12.15 and in foreign countries, they will **know** that I am the Lord.
12.20 Then they will **know** that I am the Lord."
13. 9 Then you will **know** that I am the Sovereign Lord.
13.14 Then everyone will **know** that I am the Lord.
13.21 Then you will **know** that I am the Lord.
13.23 your power, so that you will **know** that I am the Lord."
14. 8 my people, so that you will **know** that I am the Lord.
14.23 you will **know** that there was good reason for everything
15. 7 When I punish them, you will **know** that I am the Lord.
16.50 things that I hate, so I destroyed them, as you well **know.**
16.62 covenant with you, and you will **know** that I am the Lord.
17. 3 a parable [3] to let them **know** what I, the Sovereign Lord, am
17.12 "Ask these rebels if they **know** what the parable means.
17.21 Then you will **know** that I, the Lord, have spoken."
17.24 the trees in the land will **know** that I am the Lord.
20.38 Then you will **know** that I am the Lord."
20.42 to your ancestors, then you will **know** that I am the Lord.
20.44 my honour, you Israelites will **know** that I am the Lord,
21. 5 Everyone will **know** that I, the Lord, have drawn my sword
21.24 Everyone **knows** how guilty you are.
22.16 will dishonour you, but you will **know** that I am the Lord."
22.22 and then they will **know** that they are feeling the anger
23.18 She exposed herself publicly and let everyone **know** she was a whore.
23.49 Then you will **know** that I am the Sovereign Lord."
24.24 happens, you will **know** that he is the Sovereign Lord."
24.27 to the people, and they will **know** that I am the Lord."
25. 5 keep sheep, so that you will **know** that I am the Lord.
25. 7 Then you will **know** that I am the Lord."
25.11 will punish Moab, and they will **know** that I am the Lord."
25.14 Edom will **know** what it means to be the object of my
25.17 Then they will **know** that I am the Lord."
26. 6 Then Tyre will **know** that I am the Lord."
28.19 nations that had come to **know** you are terrified,
28.22 They will **know** that I am the Lord, when I show how
28.23 Then you will **know** that I am the Lord."
28.24 And they will **know** that I am the Sovereign Lord."
28.25 them, and all the nations will **know** that I am holy.
28.26 Then they will **know** that I am the Lord their God."
29. 6 all the people of Egypt will **know** that I am the Lord."
29. 9 Then you will **know** that I am the Lord.
29.16 Then Israel will **know** that I am the Sovereign Lord."
29.21 hear you, so that they will **know** that I am the Lord."
30. 8 are killed, then they will **know** that I am the Lord.
30.19 Egypt in this way, they will **know** that I am the Lord."
30.25 everyone will **know** that I am the Lord.
30.26 Then they will **know** that I am the Lord."
32.15 all who live there, they will **know** that I am the Lord.
33.29 country a waste, then they will **know** that I am the Lord."
33.33 come true—then they will **know** that a prophet has been among
34.27 made them slaves, then they will **know** that I am the Lord.
34.30 Everyone will **know** that I protect Israel
35. 4 Then you will **know** that I am the Lord.
35. 9 Then you will **know** that I am the Lord.
35.11 They will **know** that I am punishing you for what you did
35.12 Then you will **know** that I, the Lord, heard you say
35.15 Then everyone will **know** that I am the Lord."
36.11 Then you will **know** that I am the Lord.
36.23 disgraced among them—then they will **know** that I am the Lord.
36.32 Israel, I want you to **know** that I am not doing all
36.36 nations that have survived will **know** that I, the Lord, rebuild
36.38 Then they will **know** that I am the Lord."
37. 6 Then you will **know** that I am the Lord."
37.13 and bring them out, they will **know** that I am the Lord.
37.14 Then they will **know** that I am the Lord.
37.28 then the nations will **know** that I, the Lord, have chosen
38.23 They will **know** then that I am the Lord."
39. 6 undisturbed, and everyone will **know** that I am the Lord.
39. 7 sure that my people Israel **know** my holy name,
39. 7 Then the nations will **know** that I, the Lord, am the Holy
39.22 The Israelites will **know** from then on that I am the Lord
39.23 the nations will **know** that the Israelites went into exile
39.28 Then my people will **know** that I am the Lord their God.
39.28 They will **know** this, because I sent them into captivity
Dan 1.20 these four **knew** ten times more than any fortune-teller
2. 3 I want to **know** what it means."
2. 9 was, and then I will **know** that you can also tell me
2.10 who can tell Your Majesty what you want to **know.**
2.22 he **knows** what is hidden in darkness,
2.47 I **know** this because you have been able to explain this mystery."
4. 9 chief of the fortune-tellers, I **know** that the spirit of
4.17 let all people everywhere **know** that the Supreme God has power
5.22 not humbled yourself, even though you **knew** all this.
5.23 gods that cannot see or hear and that do not **know** anything.
6.15 "Your Majesty **knows** that according to the laws
6.22 He did this because he **knew** that I was innocent
7.19 Then I wanted to **know** more about the fourth beast,
7.20 And I wanted to **know** about the ten horns on its head
9.17 restore it so that everyone will **know** that you are God.
Dan 9.19 In order that everyone will **know** that you are God,
10.20 He said, "Do you **know** why I came to you?
Hos 4.12 A stick tells them what they want to **know!**
5. 3 I **know** what Israel is like—she cannot hide from me.
6. 3 Let us try to **know** the Lord.
6. 6 rather have my people **know** me than burn offerings to me.
7. 9 Their days are numbered, but they don't even **know** it.
8. 2 my people and that they **know** me, [3] they have rejected what
9. 7 When that happens, Israel will **know** it!
Joel 2.27 Then, Israel, you will **know** that I am among you,
3.17 "Then, Israel, you will **know** that I am the Lord your God.
Amos 3. 2 you are the only one I have **known** and cared for.
3.10 They don't even **know** how to be honest.
4.13 He makes his thoughts **known** to man;
5.12 I **know** how terrible your sins are
Jon 1.12 I **know** it is my fault that you are caught in this
4. 2 I **knew** that you are a loving and merciful God, always patient,
Mic 1.11 you will **know** that there is no refuge there.
4.12 But these nations do not **know** what is in the Lord's mind.
Nah 3.17 out, they fly away, and no one **knows** where they have gone!
Hab 2. 7 But before you **know** it, you that have conquered others
Zech 2. 9 everyone will **know** that the Lord Almighty sent me.
2.11 and you will **know** that he has sent me
4. 5 "Don't you **know?"**
4. 9 this happens, my people will **know** that it is I who sent
4.13 He asked me, "Don't you **know?"**
6.15 it is rebuilt, you will **know** that the Lord Almighty sent me
8. 3 It will be **known** as the faithful city,
11.11 were watching me, and they **knew** that the Lord was speaking
14. 7 When this will happen is **known** only to the Lord.
14. 9 will worship him as God and **know** him by the same name.
Mal 2. 4 Then you will **know** that I have given you this command,
2.14 It is because he **knows** you have broken your promise
Mt 2. 8 you find him, let me **know,** so that I too may go
5. 3 "Happy are those who **know** they are spiritually poor;
6. 3 a way that even your closest friend will not **know** about it.
6. 8 Your Father already **knows** what you need before you ask him.
6.18 so that others cannot **know** that you are fasting—
6.18 only your Father, who is unseen, will **know.**
6.32 Your Father in heaven **knows** that you need all these things.
7.11 Bad as you are, you **know** how to give good things to
7.16 You will **know** them by what they do.
7.20 So then, you will **know** the false prophets by what they do.
7.23 Then I will say to them, 'I never **knew** you.
10.26 up will be uncovered, and every secret will be made **known.**
11.27 No one **knows** the Son except the Father,
11.27 and no one **knows** the Father except the Son and
12. 7 If you really **knew** what this means, you would not condemn
12.25 Jesus **knew** what they were thinking, so he said to them,
12.33 A tree is **known** by the kind of fruit it bears.
15.12 and said, "Do you **know** that the Pharisees had their feelings
16. 8 Jesus **knew** what they were saying, so he asked them, "Why
20.22 "You don't **know** what you are asking for," Jesus answered
20.25 all together and said, "You **know** that the rulers of the
21.27 So they answered Jesus, "We don't **know."**
21.45 heard Jesus' parables and **knew** that he was talking about them,
22.16 "Teacher," they said, "we **know** that you tell the truth.
22.29 It is because you don't **know** the Scriptures or God's power.
24.32 it starts putting out leaves, you **know** that summer is near.
24.33 all these things, you will **know** that the time is near,
24.36 "No one **knows,** however, when that day and hour will come—
24.36 the Father alone **knows.**
24.42 because you do not **know** what day your Lord will come.
24.43 the owner of a house **knew** the time when the thief would
24.50 does not expect him and at a time he does not **know.**
25.12 I don't **know** you,' the bridegroom answered."
25.13 guard, then, because you do not **know** the day or the hour.
25.24 came in and said, 'Sir, I **know** you are a hard man;
25.26 'You **knew,** did you, that I reap harvests where I did not
26. 2 "In two days, as you **know,** it will be the Passover Festival,
26.10 Jesus **knew** what they were saying, so he said to them,
26.34 tonight, you will say three times that you do not **know** me."
26.53 Don't you **know** that I could call on my Father for help,
26.70 "I don't **know** what you are talking about," he answered,
26.72 it and answered, "I swear that I don't **know** that man!"
26.74 I do not **know** that man!"
26.75 you will say three times that you do not **know** me."
27.18 **knew** very well that the Jewish authorities had handed Jesus over
28. 5 "I **know** you are looking for Jesus, who was crucified.
Mk 1.24 I **know** who you are—you are God's holy messenger!"
1.34 let the demons say anything, because they **knew** who he was.
2. 8 At once Jesus **knew** what they were thinking, so he said to
4.27 Yet he does not **know** how it happens.
5.30 At once Jesus **knew** that power had gone out of him,
6.20 afraid of John because he **knew** that John was a good and
6.33 however, saw them leave and **knew** at once who they were;
7.24 did not want anyone to **know** he was there, but he could
8.17 Jesus **knew** what they were saying, so he asked them,
8.17 Don't you **know** or understand yet?
9. 6 others were so frightened that he did not **know** what to say.
9.30 did not want anyone to **know** where he was, [31] because he was
10.19 You **know** the commandments:
10.38 Jesus said to them, "You don't **know** what you are asking for.
10.42 to him and said, "You **know** that the men who are considered
11.33 So their answer to Jesus was, "We don't **know."**
12.12 to arrest Jesus, because they **knew** that he had told this
12.14 and said, "Teacher, we **know** that you tell the truth, without
12.24 And do you **know** why?
12.24 It is because you don't **know** the Scriptures or God's power.
13.19 any the world has ever **known** from the very beginning when
13.28 it starts putting out leaves, you **know** that summer is near.

Mk	13.29	these things happening, you will **know** that the time is near,
	13.32	"No one **knows,** however, when that day or hour will
	13.32	only the Father **knows.**
	13.33	be alert, for you do not **know** when the time will come.
	13.35	because you do not **know** when the master of the house
	14.30	tonight, you will say three times that you do not **know** me."
	14.40	And they did not **know** what to say to him.
	14.68	"I don't **know.**
	14.71	I do not **know** the man you are talking about!"
	14.72	you will say three times that you do not **know** me."
	15.10	He **knew** very well that the chief priests had handed
	16. 6	"I **know** you are looking for Jesus of Nazareth, who was crucified.
Lk	1. 4	so that you will **know** the full truth about everything which
	1.18	said to the angel, "How shall I **know** if this is so?
	1.22	to them, and so they **knew** that he had seen a vision
	2.43	His parents did not **know** this;
	2.49	Didn't you **know** that I had to be in my Father's house?"
	4.34	I **know** who you are:
	4.41	let them speak, because they **knew** that he was the Messiah.
	5.22	Jesus **knew** their thoughts and said to them, "Why do you
	6. 8	But Jesus **knew** their thoughts and said to the man, "Stand
	6.44	Every tree is **known** by the fruit it bears;
	7.39	were a prophet, he would **know** who this woman is
	7.39	he would **know** what kind of sinful life she lives!"
	8.46	"Someone touched me, for I **knew** it when power went out of
	8.53	They all laughed at him, because they **knew** that she was dead.
	9.33	(He did not really **know** what he was saying.)
	9.45	But the disciples did not **know** what this meant.
	9.47	Jesus **knew** what they were thinking, so he took a child,
	10.22	No one **knows** who the Son is except the Father,
	10.22	and no one **knows** who the Father is except the
	11.13	Bad as you are, you **know** how to give good things to
	11.17	But Jesus **knew** what they were thinking, so he said to them,
	11.44	are like unmarked graves which people walk on without **knowing** it."
	12. 2	up will be uncovered, and every secret will be made **known.**
	12.30	Your Father **knows** that you need these things.
	12.39	the owner of a house **knew** the time when the thief would
	12.46	does not expect him and at a time he does not **know.**
	12.47	"The servant who **knows** what his master wants him to do,
	12.48	the servant who does not **know** what his master wants, and yet
	12.56	why, then, don't you **know** the meaning of this present time?
	13.25	he will answer you, 'I don't **know** where you come from!'
	13.27	But he will say again, 'I don't **know** where you come from.
	16. 4	Now I **know** what I will do!
	16.15	right in other people's sight, but God **knows** your hearts.
	18.20	You **know** the commandments:
	18.34	and they did not **know** what Jesus was talking about.
	19.22	You **know** that I am a hard man, taking what is not
	19.42	saying, "If you only **knew** today what is needed for peace!
	20. 7	So they answered, "We don't **know** where it came from."
	20.19	on the spot, because they **knew** that he had told this parable
	20.21	said to Jesus, "Teacher, we **know** that what you say and
	20.21	We **know** that you pay no attention to a man's status,
	21.20	armies, then you will **know** that she will soon be destroyed.
	21.30	their leaves beginning to appear, you **know** that summer is near.
	21.31	these things happening, you will **know** that the Kingdom of
	22. 6	Jesus over to them without the people **knowing** about it.
	22.34	until you have said three times that you do not **know** me."
	22.57	But Peter denied it, "Woman, I don't even **know** him!"
	22.60	Peter answered, "Man, I don't **know** what you are talking about!"
	22.61	tonight, you will say three times that you do not **know** me."
	23.34	They don't **know** what they are doing."
	23.49	All those who **knew** Jesus personally, including the women who
	24.18	in Jerusalem who doesn't **know** the things that have been happening
	24.39	Feel me, and you will **know,** for a ghost doesn't have flesh
Jn	1.18	God and is at the Father's side, he has made him **known.**
	1.26	with water, but among you stands the one you do not **know.**
	1.31	I did not **know** who he would be, but I came baptizing
	1.31	water in order to make him **known** to the people of Israel."
	1.33	I still did not **know** that he was the one, but God,
	1.48	Nathanael asked him, "How do you **know** me?"
	2. 9	He did not **know** where this wine had come from
	2. 9	(but, of course, the servants who had drawn out the water **knew);**
	2.24	Jesus did not trust himself to them, because he **knew** them all.
	2.25	about them, because he himself **knew** what was in their hearts.
	3. 2	said to him, "Rabbi, we **know** that you are a teacher sent
	3. 8	makes, but you do not **know** where it comes from or where
	3.10	"You are a great teacher in Israel, and you don't **know** this?
	3.11	we speak of what we **know** and report what we have seen,
	4.10	Jesus answered, "If only you **knew** what God gives and
	4.22	You Samaritans do not really **know** whom you worship;
	4.22	but we Jews **know** whom we worship, because it is from the
	4.25	woman said to him, "I **know** that the Messiah will come,
	4.32	"I have food to eat that you **know** nothing about."
	4.42	have heard him, and we **know** that he really is the Saviour
	5. 6	him lying there, and he **knew** that the man had been ill
	5.13	had been healed did not **know** who Jesus was, for there was
	5.32	on my behalf, and I **know** that what he says about me
	5.42	But I **know** what kind of people you are,
	5.42	and I **know** that you have no love for
	6. 6	actually he already **knew** what he would do.)
	6.15	Jesus **knew** that they were about to come and seize him in
	6.22	They **knew** that Jesus had not gone in it with his disciples,
	6.42	We **know** his father and mother.
	6.61	Without being told, Jesus **knew** that they were grumbling about
	6.64	(Jesus **knew** from the very beginning who were the ones that
	6.69	And now we believe and **know** that you are the Holy One
	7. 4	hides what he is doing if he wants to be well **known.**
	7. 4	doing these things, let the whole world **know** about you!"
Jn	7.15	said, "How does this man **know** so much when he has never
	7.17	do what God wants will **know** whether what I teach comes from
	7.26	Can it be that they really **know** that he is the Messiah?
	7.27	when the Messiah comes, no one will **know** where he is from.
	7.27	And we all **know** where this man comes from."
	7.28	"Do you really know me and **know** where I am from?
	7.28	You do not **know** him,
	7.29	but I **know** him, because I come from him
	7.48	"Have you ever **known** one of the authorities or one
	7.49	This crowd does not **know** the Law of Moses, so they are
	8.14	say is true, because I **know** where I came from and where
	8.14	You do not **know** where I came from or where I am
	8.19	"You **know** neither me nor my Father," Jesus answered.
	8.19	"If you **knew** me, you would know my Father also."
	8.28	Son of Man, you will **know** that 'I Am Who I Am';
	8.28	then you will **know** that I do nothing on my own authority,
	8.32	you will **know** the truth, and the truth will set you free."
	8.37	I **know** you are Abraham's descendants.
	8.55	You have never known him, but I **know** him.
	8.55	say that I do not **know** him, I would be a liar
	8.55	But I do **know** him, and I obey his word.
	9.12	"I don't **know,"** he answered.
	9.20	His parents answered, "We **know** that he is our son,
	9.20	and we **know** that he was born blind.
	9.21	But we do not **know** how it is that he is now
	9.21	to see, nor do we **know** who cured him of his blindness.
	9.24	We **know** that this man who cured you is a sinner."
	9.25	"I do not **know** if he is a sinner or not,"
	9.25	"One thing I do **know:**
	9.29	We **know** that God spoke to Moses;
	9.29	fellow, however, we do not even **know** where he comes from!"
	9.30	You do not **know** where he comes from, but he cured me
	9.31	We **know** that God does not listen to sinners;
	10. 4	and the sheep follow him, because they **know** his voice.
	10. 5	from such a person, because they do not **know** his voice."
	10.14	As the Father **knows** me and I know the Father,
	10.14	in the same way I **know** my sheep and they know me.
	10.27	I **know** them, and they follow me.
	10.35	We **know** that what the scripture says is true for ever;
	10.38	in order that you may **know** once and for all that the
	11.22	But I **know** that even now God will give you whatever you
	11.24	"I **know,"** she replied, "that he will rise to life on
	11.42	I **know** that you always listen to me, but I say this
	11.57	given orders that if anyone **knew** where Jesus was, he must
	12.35	who walks in the dark does not **know** where he is going.
	12.50	And I **know** that his command brings eternal life.
	13. 1	Jesus **knew** that the hour had come for him to leave this
	13. 3	Jesus **knew** that the Father had given him complete power;
	13. 3	he **knew** that he had come from God and was going to
	13.11	(Jesus already **knew** who was going to betray him;
	13.17	Now that you **know** this truth, how happy you will be if
	13.18	I **know** those I have chosen.
	13.35	one another, then everyone will **know** that you are my disciples."
	13.38	you will say three times that you do not **know** me.
	14. 4	You **know** the way that leads to the place where I am
	14. 5	said to him, "Lord, we do not **know** where you are going;
	14. 5	so how can we **know** the way to get there?"
	14. 7	Now that you have **known** me," he said to them,
	14. 7	"you will **know** my Father also,
	14. 7	from now on you do **know** him and you have seen him."
	14. 9	yet you do not **know** me, Philip?
	14.17	cannot receive him, because it cannot see him or **know** him.
	14.17	But you **know** him, because he remains with you and is in
	14.20	that day comes, you will **know** that I am in my Father
	14.31	but the world must **know** that I love the Father;
	15.15	because a servant does not **know** what his master is doing.
	15.21	for they do not **know** the one who sent me.
	16. 3	to you because they have not **known** either the Father or me.
	16.18	We don't **know** what he is talking about!"
	16.19	Jesus **knew** that they wanted to question him, so he said
	16.30	We **know** now that you know everything;
	17. 3	And eternal life means **knowing** you, the only true God,
	17. 3	and **knowing** Jesus Christ, whom you sent.
	17. 6	"I have made you **known** to those you gave me out of
	17. 7	your word, [7] and now they **know** that everything you gave me
	17. 8	they **know** that it is true that I came from you,
	17.23	order that the world may **know** that you sent me and that
	17.25	The world does not **know** you,
	17.25	but I know you, and these **know** that you sent me.
	17.26	I made you **known** to them, and I will continue to do
	18. 2	Judas, the traitor, **knew** where it was, because many times Jesus
	18. 4	Jesus **knew** everything that was going to happen to him, so
	18.15	That other disciple was well **known** to the High Priest, so he
	18.21	Ask them what I told them—they **know** what I said."
	19.28	Jesus **knew** that by now everything had been completed;
	19.35	he said is true, and he **knows** that he speaks the truth.)
	20. 2	from the tomb, and we don't **know** where they have put him!"
	20.13	Lord away, and I do not **know** where they have put him!"
	20.14	but she did not **know** that it was Jesus.
	21. 4	edge, but the disciples did not **know** that it was Jesus.
	21.12	because they **knew** it was the Lord.
	21.15	"Yes, Lord," he answered, "you **know** that I love you."
	21.16	"Yes, Lord," he answered, "you **know** that I love you."
	21.17	so he said to him, "Lord, you **know** everything;
	21.17	you **know** that I love you!"
	21.24	and we **know** that what he said is true.
Acts	1. 7	and it is not for you to **know** when they will be.
	1.23	Joseph, who was called Barsabbas (also **known** as Justus),
	1.24	they prayed, "Lord, you **know** the thoughts of everyone, so show
	2.22	You yourselves **know** this, for it happened here among you.
	2.30	He was a prophet, and he **knew** what God had promised him:

Acts 2.36 of Israel, then, are to **know** for sure that this Jesus, whom
3.16 What you see and **know** was done by faith in his name;
3.17 "And now, my brothers, I **know** that what you and your
4.10 then you should all **know,** and all the people
4.10 people of Israel should **know,** that this man stands here before
4.16 "Everyone in Jerusalem **knows** that this extraordinary miracle
5. 7 three hours later his wife, not **knowing** what had happened, came
6. 3 men among you who are **known** to be full of the Holy
7.13 second visit Joseph made himself **known** to his brothers,
7.13 and the king of Egypt came to **know** about Joseph's family.
7.18 a king who did not **know** about Joseph began to rule in
7.40 We do not **know** what has happened to that man Moses, who
8.10 is that power of God **known** as 'The Great Power'," they
9.15 to make my name **known** to Gentiles and kings and to
10.28 said to them, "You yourselves **know** very well that a Jew is
10.36 You **know** the message he sent to the people of Israel,
10.37 You **know** of the great event that took place throughout the
10.38 You **know** about Jesus of Nazareth and how God poured out
12. 9 out of the prison, not **knowing,** however, if what the angel
12.11 to him, and said, "Now I **know** that it is really true!
13. 9 Then Saul—also **known** as Paul—was filled with the Holy Spirit;
13.27 and their leaders did not **know** that he is the Saviour,
13.38 want you to **know,** my fellow-Israelites, that it is through Jesus
15. 7 and said, "My brothers, you **know** that a long time ago God
15. 8 And God, who **knows** the thoughts of everyone, showed his approval
15.18 So says the Lord, who made this **known** long ago.'
16. 3 who lived in those places **knew** that Timothy's father was Greek.
17.19 said, "We would like to **know** what this new teaching is that
17.20 strange to us, and we would like to **know** what they mean."
17.23 even though you do not **know** it, is what I now proclaim
17.30 times when people did not **know** him, but now he commands all
18.25 However, he **knew** only the baptism of John.
19.15 spirit said to them, "I **know** Jesus, and I know about Paul;
19.25 said to them, "Men, you **know** that our prosperity comes from
19.32 most of them did not even **know** why they had come together.
19.35 "Everyone **knows** that the city of Ephesus is the keeper of
20.18 he said to them, "You **know** how I spent the whole time
20.20 You **know** that I did not hold back anything that would be
20.22 to Jerusalem, not **knowing** what will happen to me there.
20.23 I only **know** that in every city the Holy Spirit has
20.25 And now I **know** that none of you will ever see me
20.29 I **know** that after I leave, fierce wolves will come among you,
20.34 You yourselves **know** that I have worked with these hands
21.24 In this way everyone will **know** that there is no truth in
22.14 has chosen you to **know** his will, to see his righteous
22.19 'Lord,' I answered, 'they **know** very well that I went to
23. 5 "My fellow-Israelites, I did not **know** that he was the High Priest.
23.28 I wanted to **know** what they were accusing him of,
24.10 and Paul said, "I **know** that you have been a judge
25.10 have done no wrong to the Jews, as you yourself well **know.**
26. 3 particularly since you **know** so well all the Jewish customs
26. 4 "All the Jews **know** how I have lived ever since I was
26. 4 They **know** how I have spent my whole life, at first in
26. 5 They have always **known,** if they are willing to testify, that
26.26 to you with all boldness, because you **know** about these things.
26.27 I **know** that you do!"
28.22 your ideas, because we **know** that everywhere people speak against
28.28 "You are to **know,** then, that God's message of salvation has

Rom 1. 9 God **knows** that I remember you [10] every time I pray.
1.18 people whose evil ways prevent the truth from being **known.**
1.19 because what can be **known** about God is plain to them,
1.21 They **know** God, but they do not give him the honour that
1.32 They **know** that God's law says that people who live in
2. 2 We **know** that God is right when he judges the people who
2. 4 Surely you **know** that God is kind, because he is trying to
2.18 you **know** what God wants you to do, and you have learnt
3.17 have not **known** the path of peace, [18] nor have they learnt
3.19 Now we **know** that everything in the Law applies to those
3.20 the Law does is to make man **know** that he has sinned.
5. 3 of our troubles, because we **know** that trouble produces endurance,
6. 3 For surely you **know** that when we were baptized into union
6. 6 And we **know** that our old being has been put to death
6. 9 For we **know** that Christ has been raised from death and
6.16 Surely you **know** that when you surrender yourselves as slaves
7. 1 to say, my brothers, because all of you **know** about law.
7. 7 But it was the Law that made me **know** what sin is.
7. 7 to someone else," I would not have **known** such a desire.
7.14 We **know** that the Law is spiritual;
7.18 I **know** that good does not live in me—that is, in
8.22 For we **know** that up to the present time all of creation
8.26 For we do not **know** how we ought to pray;
8.27 who sees into our hearts, **knows** what the thought of the
8.28 We **know** that in all things God works for good with those
9.22 He wanted to show his anger and to make his power **known.**
10. 3 They have not **known** the way in which God puts people right
11. 2 You **know** what the scripture says in the passage where Elijah
11.25 which I want you to **know,** for it will keep you from
11.34 As the scripture says, "Who **knows** the mind of the Lord?
12. 2 you will be able to **know** the will of God—what is
13.11 must do this, because you **know** that the time has come for
15.29 I come to you, I **know** that I shall come with
16. 7 well **known** among the apostles, and they became Christians before
16.26 eternal God it is made **known** to all nations, so that all

1 Cor 1.21 it impossible for people to **know** him by means of their own
2. 8 None of the rulers of this world **knew** this wisdom.
2. 8 If they had **known** it, they would not have crucified the Lord
2.10 to us that God made **known** his secret by means of his
2.11 a person's own spirit within him that **knows** all about him;
2.11 in the same way, only God's Spirit **knows** all about God.
2.12 God, so that we may **know** all that God has given us.
2.16 As the scripture says, "Who **knows** the mind of the Lord?
3.16 Surely you **know** that you are God's temple and that God's
3.20 scripture says, "The Lord **knows** that the thoughts of the wise
5. 6 You **know** the saying, "A little bit of yeast makes the whole
5. 7 dough without any yeast, as indeed I **know** you actually are.
6. 2 Don't you **know** that God's people will judge the world?
6. 3 Do you not **know** that we shall judge the angels?
6. 9 Surely you **know** that the wicked will not possess God's Kingdom.
6.15 You **know** that your bodies are parts of the body of Christ.
6.16 Or perhaps you don't **know** that the man who joins his
6.19 Don't you **know** that your body is the temple of the Holy
8. 2 Whoever thinks he **knows** something
8. 2 really doesn't know as he ought to **know.**
8. 3 But the person who loves God is **known** by him.
8. 4 we **know** that an idol stands for something that does not
8. 4 we **know** that there is only the one God.
8. 7 But not everyone **knows** this truth.
9.13 Surely you **know** that the men who work in the Temple get
9.24 Surely you **know** that many runners take part in a race,
12. 1 I want you to **know** the truth about them, my brothers.
12. 2 You **know** that while you were still heathen, you were led
12. 3 I want you to **know** that no one who is led by
13.12 What I **know** now is only partial;
14. 7 the harp—how will anyone **know** the tune that is being played
14.11 But if I do not **know** the language being spoken, the
14.16 He has no way of **knowing** what you are saying.
15.34 declare to your shame that some of you do not **know** God.
15.58 for the Lord, since you **know** that nothing you do in the
16.15 You **know** about Stephanas and his family;

2 Cor 1. 7 we **know** that just as you share in our sufferings, you also
1.23 I call God as my witness—he **knows** my heart!
1.24 we **know** that you stand firm in the faith.
2. 8 beg you to let him **know** that you really do love him.
2.11 for we **know** what his plans are.
3. 2 have, written on our hearts for everyone to **know** and read.
4.14 We **know** that God, who raised the Lord Jesus to life,
5. 1 For we **know** that when this tent we live in—our body
5. 6 We **know** that as long as we are at home in the
5.11 We **know** what it means to fear the Lord,
5.11 God **knows** us completely,
5.11 and I hope that in your hearts you **know** me as well.
6. 9 as unknown, yet we are **known** by all;
8. 1 brothers, we want you to **know** what God's grace has accomplished
8. 9 You **know** the grace of our Lord Jesus Christ;
8.24 be sure of it and **know** that we are right in boasting
9. 2 I **know** that you are willing to help, and I have boasted
11.11 God **knows** I love you!
11.31 **knows** that I am not lying.
12. 2 I **know** a certain Christian man who fourteen years ago was
12. 2 (I do not **know** whether this actually happened
12. 2 or whether he had a vision—only God **knows).**
12. 3 I repeat, I **know** that this man was snatched to Paradise
12. 3 (again, I do not **know** whether this actually happened or whether
12. 3 was a vision—only God **knows),** and there he heard things
13. 5 Surely you **know** that Christ Jesus is in you?
13. 6 I trust you will **know** that we are not failures.

Gal 1.20 God **knows** that I am not lying!
1.22 of the churches in Judaea did not **know** me personally.
1.23 They **knew** only what others were saying:
2.16 Yet we **know** that a person is put right with God only
4. 8 the past you did not **know** God, and so you were slaves
4. 9 But now that you **know** God—or, I should say,
4. 9 now that God **knows** you—

Eph 1. 9 he had purposed, and made **known** to us the secret plan he
1.17 wise and reveal God to you, so that you will **know** him.
1.18 light, so that you will **know** what is the hope to which
3. 3 God revealed his secret plan and made it **known** to me.
3.19 Yes, may you come to **know** his love—
3.19 it can never be fully **known**—and so be completely filled with
6.19 that I may speak boldly and make **known** the gospel's secret.
6.21 about me, so that you may **know** how I am getting on.

Phil 1.12 I want you to **know,** my brothers, that the things that
1.13 and all the others here **know** that I am in prison because
1.16 so from love, because they **know** that God has given me the
1.19 to be happy, [19] because I **know** that by means of your
1.25 am sure of this, and so I **know** that I will stay.
2.22 And you yourselves **know** how he has proved his worth, how
2.23 as soon as I **know** how things are going to turn
3.10 All I want is to **know** Christ and to experience the power
4.12 I **know** what it is to be in need and what it
4.15 You Philippians **know** very well that when I left Macedonia

Col 1. 6 grace of God and came to **know** it as it really is.
1.27 God's plan is to make **known** his secret to his people,
2. 1 Laodicea and for all others who do not **know** me personally.
2. 2 In this way they will **know** God's secret, which is Christ himself.
4. 6 and interesting, and you should **know** how to give the right

1 Thes 1. 4 Our brothers, we **know** that God loves you and has chosen
1. 5 You **know** how we lived when we were with you;
2. 1 Our brothers, you yourselves **know** that our visit to you
2. 2 You **know** how we had already been ill-treated and insulted in
2. 5 You **know** very well that we did not come to you with
2.11 You **know** that we treated each one of you just as a
3. 3 You yourselves **know** that such persecutions are part of God's will
3. 4 and as you well **know,** that is exactly what happened.
4. 2 For you **know** the instructions we gave you by the authority
4. 4 Each of you men should **know** how to live with his wife
4. 5 with a lustful desire, like the heathen who do not **know** God.

1 Thes 4.13 brothers, we want you to **know** the truth about those who have
5. 2 For you yourselves **know** very well that the Day of the Lord
2 Thes 2. 6 that keeps this from happening now, and you **know** what it is.
3. 7 You yourselves **know** very well that you should do just what
1 Tim 1. 4 they do not serve God's plan, which is **known** by faith.
1. 8 We **know** that the Law is good if it is used as
1.13 yet have faith and so did not **know** what I was doing.
2. 4 wants everyone to be saved and to come to **know** the truth.
3. 5 if a man does not **know** how to manage his own family,
3.15 this letter will let you **know** how we should conduct
4. 3 by those who are believers and have come to **know** the truth.
6. 4 of our religion [4] is swollen with pride and **knows** nothing.
2 Tim 1.12 full of confidence, because I **know** whom I have trusted, and
1.15 You **know** that everyone in the province of Asia, including
1.18 And you **know** very well how much he did for me in
2.19 "The Lord **knows** those who are his" and "Whoever says that
2.23 you **know** that they end up in quarrels.
2.25 them the opportunity to repent and come to **know** the truth.
3. 7 trying to learn but who can never come to **know** the truth.
3.11 You **know** all that happened to me in Antioch, Iconium, and
3.14 You **know** who your teachers were, [15] and you remember that
3.15 were a child, you have **known** the Holy Scriptures, which are
Tit 1.16 They claim that they **know** God, but their actions deny it.
3.11 You **know** that such a person is corrupt, and his sins
Phlm 21 I ask—in fact I **know** that you will do even more.
Heb 6. 5 they **knew** from experience that God's word is good, and
6. 9 We **know** that you have the better blessings that belong to
7.14 It is well **known** that he was born a member of the
8.11 or say to his fellow-countryman, '**Know** the Lord.'
8.11 For they will all **know** me, from the least to the greatest.
9. 7 sins which the people have committed without **knowing** they were
10.26 go on sinning after the truth has been made **known** to us.
10.30 For we **know** who said, "I will take revenge, I will repay";
10.34 your loss gladly, because you **knew** that you still possessed
11. 8 He left his own country without **knowing** where he was going.
12.17 Afterwards, you **know,** he wanted to receive his father's blessing;
13. 2 were some who did that and welcomed angels without **knowing** it.
13.23 I want you to **know** that our brother Timothy has been let
Jas 1. 3 come your way, [3] for you **know** that when your faith succeeds
3. 1 As you **know,** we teachers will be judged with greater strictness
4. 4 Don't you **know** that to be the world's friend means to be
4.14 You don't even **know** what your life tomorrow will be!
4.17 not do the good he **knows** he should do is guilty of
5.11 of Job's patience, and you **know** how the Lord provided for
1 Pet 1.18 For you **know** what was paid to set you free from the
2.10 one time you did not **know** God's mercy, but now you have
5. 9 and resist him, because you **know** that your fellow-believers in
2 Pet 1.12 even though you already **know** them and are firmly grounded in
1.14 I **know** that I shall soon put off this mortal body,
1.16 on made-up stories in making **known** to you the mighty coming
2. 9 And so the Lord **knows** how to rescue godly people from
2.21 for them never to have **known** the way of righteousness
2.21 than to **know** it and then turn away
3.17 But you, my friends, already **know** this.
1 Jn 1. 2 life which was with the Father and was made **known** to us.
2. 3 we obey God's commands, then we are sure that we **know** him.
2. 4 If someone says that he **knows** him, but does not obey his
2.11 in it and does not **know** where he is going, because the
2.13 to you, fathers, because you **know** him who has existed from
2.14 I am writing to you, my children, because you **know** the Father.
2.14 to you, fathers, because you **know** him who has existed from
2.18 have already appeared, and so we **know** that the end is near.
2.20 on you by Christ, and so all of you **know** the truth.
2.21 writing to you, then, not because you do not **know** the truth;
2.21 it is because you do **know** it,
2.21 and you also **know** that no lie ever comes from
2.29 You **know** that Christ is righteous;
2.29 you should **know,** then, that everyone who does what is right
3. 1 This is why the world does not **know** us:
3. 1 it has not **known** God.
3. 2 But we **know** that when Christ appears, we shall be like him,
3. 5 You **know** that Christ appeared in order to take away sins,
3. 6 whoever continues to sin has never seen him or **known** him.
3.14 We **know** that we have left death and come over into life;
3.14 we **know** it because we love our brothers.
3.15 is a murderer, and you **know** that a murderer has not got
3.16 This is how we **know** what love is:
3.19 then, is how we will **know** that we belong to the truth;
3.20 our conscience condemns us, we **know** that God is greater
3.20 greater than our conscience and that he **knows** everything.
3.24 God has given us we **know** that God lives in union with
4. 2 how you will be able to **know** whether it is God's Spirit:
4. 6 Whoever **knows** God listens to us;
4. 7 Whoever loves is a child of God and **knows** God.
4. 8 Whoever does not love does not **know** God, for God is love.
4.16 And we ourselves **know** and believe the love which God has
5. 2 This is how we **know** that we love God's children:
5.13 so that you may **know** that you have eternal life—you
5.15 know this is true, we **know** also that he gives us what
5.18 We **know** that no child of God keeps on sinning, for the
5.19 We **know** that we belong to God even though the whole
5.20 We **know** that the Son of God has come
5.20 has given us understanding, so that we **know** the true God.
2 Jn 1 only one, but all who **know** the truth love you, [2] because the
3 Jn 2 be in good health—as I **know** you are well in spirit.
12 add our testimony, and you **know** that what we say is true.
Jude 5 For even though you **know** all this, I want to remind you
10 and those things that they **know** by instinct, like wild animals,
Rev 1. 1 Christ made these things **known** to his servant John by
2. 2 I **know** what you have done;
2. 2 I **know** how hard you have worked and how patient you have
Rev 2. 2 I **know** that you cannot tolerate evil men and that you have
2. 9 I **know** your troubles;
2. 9 I **know** that you are poor—but really you are rich!
2. 9 I **know** the evil things said against you by those who claim
2.13 I **know** where you live, there where Satan has his throne.
2.17 new name that no one **knows** except the one who receives it.
2.19 I **know** what you do.
2.19 I **know** your love, your faithfulness, your service, and your
2.19 I **know** that you are doing more now than you did at
2.23 then all the churches will **know** that
2.23 I am the one who **knows** everyone's thoughts and wishes.
3. 1 I **know** what you are doing;
3. 1 I **know** that you have the reputation of being alive, even
3. 3 and you will not even **know** the time when I will come.
3. 8 I **know** what you do;
3. 8 I **know** that you have a little power;
3. 9 They will all **know** that I love you.
3.15 I **know** what you have done;
3.15 I **know** that you are neither cold nor hot.
3.17 But you do not **know** how miserable and pitiful you are!
7.14 "I don't **know,** sir.
12.12 filled with rage, because he **knows** that he has only a little
14. 5 They have never been **known** to tell lies;
18. 7 I am no widow, I will never **know** grief!'
19.12 written on him, but no one except himself **knows** what it is.

KNOWLEDGE

Gen 2. 9 and the tree that gives **knowledge** of what is good
2.17 except the tree that gives **knowledge** of what is good
3.22 one of us and has **knowledge** of what is good
Num 24.16 And receive the **knowledge** that comes from the Most High.
1 Kgs 2.32 murders, which he committed without my father David's **knowledge.**
4.29 wisdom and insight, and **knowledge** too great to be measured.
2 Chr 1.10 give me the wisdom and **knowledge** I need to rule over them.
1.11 have asked for wisdom and **knowledge** so that you can rule
1.12 I will give you wisdom and **knowledge.**
Ezra 7. 6 scholar with a thorough **knowledge** of the Law which the Lord,
7.11 scholar, who had a thorough **knowledge** of the laws
Job 11. 6 there are things too deep for human **knowledge.**
26. 3 and share your **knowledge** with a fool like me!
36. 3 My **knowledge** is wide;
Ps 19.11 They give **knowledge** to me, your servant;
94.10 He is the teacher of all men—hasn't he any **knowledge?**
119.66 Give me wisdom and **knowledge,** because I trust in your commands.
139. 6 Your **knowledge** of me is too deep;
Prov 1. 5 can even add to the **knowledge** of wise men and give guidance
1. 7 To have **knowledge,** you must first have reverence for the Lord.
1.22 How long will you enjoy pouring scorn on **knowledge?**
1.23 I will give you good advice and share my **knowledge** with you.
1.29 never had any use for **knowledge**
2. 3 Yes, beg for **knowledge;**
2. 6 from him come **knowledge** and understanding.
2.10 and your **knowledge** will give you pleasure.
3.19 by his **knowledge** he set the sky in place.
5. 2 and your words will show that you have **knowledge.**
8.10 choose **knowledge** rather than the finest gold.
8.12 I have **knowledge** and sound judgement.
9. 6 Follow the way of **knowledge."**
9. 9 Whatever you tell a righteous man will add to his **knowledge.**
10.14 The wise get all the **knowledge** they can,
12. 1 Anyone who loves **knowledge** wants to be told when he is wrong.
14.18 but the clever are rewarded with **knowledge.**
15. 2 wise people speak, they make **knowledge** attractive,
15. 7 **Knowledge** is spread by people who are wise, not by fools.
16.16 better—to have wisdom and **knowledge** than gold and silver.
19. 2 Enthusiasm without **knowledge** is not good;
22.20 They contain **knowledge** and good advice,
24. 4 Where there is **knowledge,** the rooms are furnished with valuable,
24. 5 yes, **knowledge** is more important than strength.
30. 4 Who has ever mastered heavenly **knowledge?**
Ecc 1.16 I know what wisdom and **knowledge** really are."
1.17 to learn the difference between **knowledge** and foolishness,
2.21 with all your wisdom, **knowledge,** and skill,
2.26 God gives wisdom, **knowledge,** and happiness to those who please him,
5.11 All you gain is the **knowledge** that you are rich.
7.12 Wisdom keeps you safe—this is the advantage of **knowledge.**
7.25 But I devoted myself to **knowledge** and study;
9.10 no action, no thought, no **knowledge,** no wisdom in the world
Is 11. 2 him wisdom, and the **knowledge** and skill to rule his people.
11. 9 will be as full of **knowledge** of the Lord as the seas
33. 6 He always protects his people and gives them wisdom and **knowledge.**
47.10 Your wisdom and **knowledge** led you astray,
Dan 1.17 gave the four young men **knowledge** and skill in literature
5.11 this man showed good sense, **knowledge,** and wisdom
5.14 and that you are skilful and have **knowledge** and wisdom.
Hab 2.14 be as full of the **knowledge** of the Lord's glory as the
Mal 2. 7 is the duty of priests to teach the true **knowledge** of God.
Mt 13.11 "The **knowledge** about the secrets of the Kingdom of heaven
Lk 8.10 and he answered, "The **knowledge** of the secrets of the Kingdom
11.52 kept the key that opens the door to the house of **knowledge;**
Acts 18.24 eloquent speaker and had a thorough **knowledge** of the Scriptures.
Rom 1.28 keep in mind the true **knowledge** about God, he has given them
2.20 the Law you have the full content of **knowledge** and of truth.
10. 2 but their devotion is not based on true **knowledge.**
11.33 How deep are his wisdom and **knowledge!**
15.14 goodness, that you have all **knowledge,** and that you are able

1 Cor 1. 5 become rich in all things, including all speech and all **knowledge.**
8. 1 true, of course, that "all of us have **knowledge,"** as they
8. 1 Such **knowledge,** however, puffs a person up with pride;
8.10 you, who have so-called **"knowledge,"** eating in the temple of
8.11 for whom Christ died, will perish because of your **"knowledge"**!
12. 8 person the same Spirit gives a message full of **knowledge.**
13. 2 I may have all **knowledge** and understand all secrets;
13. 8 there is **knowledge,** but it will pass.
13. 9 our gifts of **knowledge** and of inspired messages are only partial;
13.12 it will be complete—as complete as God's **knowledge** of me.
14. 6 revelation from God or some **knowledge** or some inspired message,
2 Cor 2.14 uses us to make the **knowledge** about Christ spread everywhere
4. 6 hearts, to bring us the **knowledge** of God's glory shining in
6. 6 By our purity, **knowledge,** patience, and kindness we have shown
8. 7 in faith, speech, and **knowledge,** in your eagerness to help
10. 5 every proud obstacle that is raised against the **knowledge** of God;
11. 6 I am an amateur in speaking, but certainly not in **knowledge;**
Eph 4.13 in our faith and in our **knowledge** of the Son of God;
Phil 1. 9 and more, together with true **knowledge** and perfect judgement,
3. 8 much more valuable, the **knowledge** of Christ Jesus my Lord.
Col 1. 9 to fill you with the **knowledge** of his will, with all the
1.10 of good deeds, and you will grow in your **knowledge** of God.
2. 3 that opens all the hidden treasures of God's wisdom and **knowledge.**
3.10 image, in order to bring you to a full **knowledge** of himself.
1 Tim 6.20 foolish arguments of what some people wrongly call **"Knowledge."**
2 Pet 1. 2 in full measure through your **knowledge** of God and of Jesus
1. 3 religious life through our **knowledge** of the one who called us
1. 5 to your goodness add **knowledge;**
1. 6 to your **knowledge** add self-control;
1. 8 active and effective in your **knowledge** of our Lord Jesus Christ.
2.20 the world through their **knowledge** of our Lord and Saviour Jesus
3.18 grow in the grace and **knowledge** of our Lord and Saviour

KOHATH
Levi's son and Moses' grandfather.

Gen 46.11 Gershon, **Kohath,** and Merari.
Ex 6.16 Gershon, **Kohath,** and Merari;
6.18 **Kohath** had four sons:
6.18 **Kohath** lived 133 years.
Num 3.17 Gershon, **Kohath,** and Merari, who were the ancestors of the clans
3.17 **Kohath** had four sons:
3.27 The clan of **Kohath** was composed of the families of Amram,
4. 2 of the Levite clan of **Kohath** by sub-clans and families,
4.15 break camp, the clan of **Kohath** shall come to carry the
4.15 The clan of **Kohath** must not touch the sacred objects,
4.15 responsibilities of the clan of **Kohath** whenever the Tent
4.18 not let the clan of **Kohath** [19] be killed by coming near
4.20 But if the **Kohathites** enter the Tent and see the priests
4.34 took a census of the three Levite clans, **Kohath,** Gershon,
4.34 **Kohath** 2,750
7. 9 wagons or oxen to the **Kohathites,** because the sacred objects
10.21 Then the Levite clan of **Kohath** would start out,
16. 1 the Levite clan of **Kohath,** rebelled against the leadership
26.57 tribe of Levi consisted of the clans of Gershon, **Kohath,**
26.58 **Kohath** was the father of Amram,
Josh 21. 4 of the Levite clan of **Kohath** were the first to be assigned
21. 5 rest of the clan of **Kohath** was assigned ten cities
21.10 were of the clan of **Kohath,** which was descended from Levi.
21.20 of the Levite clan of **Kohath** were assigned some cities
21.26 families of the clan of **Kohath** received ten cities in all,
1 Chr 6. 1 Gershon, **Kohath,** and Merari.
6. 2 **Kohath** had four sons:
6.16 Gershon, **Kohath,** and Merari.
6.18 **Kohath** was the father of Amram, Izhar, Hebron, and
6.22 These are the descendants of **Kohath**
6.33 The clan of **Kohath:**
6.38 Izhar, **Kohath,** Levi, Jacob.
6.54 assigned to the descendants of Aaron of the clan of **Kohath.**
6.61 lot to the rest of the clan of **Kohath,** family by family.
6.66 families of the clan of **Kohath** were assigned towns
9.32 the clan of **Kohath** were responsible for preparing
15. 5 From the Levite clan of **Kohath** came Uriel,
23. 6 Gershon, **Kohath,** and Merari.
23.12 **Kohath** had four sons:
23.18 **Kohath's** second son, Izhar, had a son, Shelomith,
23.19 **Kohath's** third son, Hebron, had four sons:
23.20 **Kohath's** fourth son, Uzziel, had two sons,
2 Chr 20.19 of the Levite clans of **Kohath** and Korah stood up
29.12 From the clan of **Kohath,** Mahath son of Amasai and Joel son
34.12 Zechariah and Meshullam of the clan of **Kohath.**

KOR
Measure equal to ten ephahs, about 17.5 litres.

Ezek 45.13 10 baths = 1 homer = 1 **kor.)**

KORAH (1)
Grandson of Kohath, and the clan descended from him.

Ex 6.21 **Korah,** Nepheg, and Zichri.
6.24 **Korah** had three sons:
6.24 were the ancestors of the divisions of the clan of **Korah.**
Num 16. 1 **Korah** son of Izhar, from the Levite clan of Kohath,
16. 5 Then he said to **Korah** and his followers, "Tomorrow morning
16. 8 Moses continued to speak to **Korah.**
16.16 Moses said to **Korah,** "Tomorrow you and your 250 followers
16.19 Then **Korah** gathered the whole community,
16.24 to move away from the tents of **Korah,** Dathan, and Abiram."
16.27 they moved away from the tents of **Korah,** Dathan, and Abiram.
16.32 together with all of **Korah's** followers and their possessions.
16.40 Otherwise he would be destroyed like **Korah** and his men.
16.49 14,700, not counting those who died in **Korah's** rebellion.
26. 9 the followers of **Korah** when they rebelled against the Lord.
26.10 they died with **Korah** and his followers when fire destroyed
26.11 But the sons of **Korah** were not killed.)
26.58 included the subclans of Libni, Hebron, Mahli, Mushi, and **Korah.**
27. 3 the followers of **Korah,** who rebelled against the Lord;
1 Chr 6.37 Tahath, Assir, Ebiasaph, **Korah,**
9.19 the clan of **Korah,** was responsible for guarding the entrance
9.31 Shallum, of the clan of **Korah,** was responsible for preparing
12. 3 Jashobeam, of the clan of **Korah** Joelah and Zebadiah,
26. 1 From the clan of **Korah** there was Meshelemiah son of Kore,
26.19 guard duty to the clan of **Korah** and the clan of Merari.
2 Chr 20.19 Levite clans of Kohath and **Korah** stood up and with a loud
Jude 11 have rebelled as **Korah** rebelled, and like him they are destroyed.

LABAN (1)
Rebecca's brother and Jacob's uncle.

Gen 24.1-67 **A wife for Isaac**
27.30-45 **Esau begs for Isaac's blessing**
27.46-28.5 **Isaac sends Jacob to Laban**
29.1-14 **Jacob arrives at Laban's home**
15-30 **Jacob serves Laban for Rachel and Leah**
30.25-43 **Jacob's bargain with Laban**
31.1-21 **Jacob flees from Laban**
22-42 **Laban pursues Jacob**
43-55 **The agreement between Jacob and Laban**

Gen 25.20 (an Aramean from Mesopotamia) and sister of **Laban.**
32. 4 I have been staying with **Laban**
46.18 Zilpah, the slave-girl whom **Laban** gave to his daughter Leah.
46.25 Bilhah, the slave-girl whom **Laban** gave to his daughter Rachel.

LABOUR (1)

Ex 1.11 slave-drivers over them to crush their spirits with hard **labour.**
2.11 and he saw how they were forced to do hard **labour.**
Deut 20.11 are all to become your slaves and do forced **labour** for you.
2 Sam 20.24 Adoniram was in charge of the forced **labour;**
1 Kgs 4. 6 In charge of the forced **labour:** Adoniram
5.13 drafted 30,000 men as forced **labour** from all over Israel,
9.15 King Solomon used forced **labour** to build the Temple
9.17 Using his forced **labour,** Solomon also rebuilt Lower Beth Horon,
9.20 For his forced **labour** Solomon used the descendants
9.23 **labour** working on Solomon's various building projects.
11.28 charge of all the forced **labour** in the territory of the
12.18 in charge of the forced **labour,** to go to the Israelites,
1 Chr 27.25 Farm **labour:** Ezri son of Chelub
2 Chr 8. 7 Solomon employed in forced **labour** all the descendants
8. 9 were not used in forced **labour,** but served as soldiers,
8.10 in charge of the forced **labour** working on the various building
10.18 in charge of the forced **labour,** to go to the Israelites,
Neh 3. 5 refused to do the manual **labour** assigned to them
Esth 10. 1 King Xerxes imposed forced **labour** on the people
Job 7. 1 a life of hard manual **labour,** [2] like a slave
Prov 16.26 A **labourer's** appetite makes him work harder,
Ecc 1. 3 You spend your life working, **labouring,** and what do you have
5.16 We **labour,** trying to catch the wind, and what do we get?
8.15 least do this as he **labours** during the life that God has
Hab 2.13 wore themselves out in useless **labour,**

LABOUR (2)

Gen 35.16 Rachel to have her baby, and she was having difficult **labour.**
35.17 When her **labour** pains were at their worst,
38.28 While she was in **labour,** one of them put out an arm;
1 Sam 4.19 she suddenly went into **labour** and gave birth.
Is 13. 8 and overcome with pain, like the pain of a woman in **labour.**
21. 3 with terror and pain, pain like that of a woman in **labour.**
26.17 us cry out, as a woman in **labour** cries out in pain.
42.14 I cry out like a woman in **labour.**
66. 7 suddenly gives birth to a child, without ever going into **labour.**
Jer 4.31 cry, like a woman in **labour,** a scream like a woman bearing
6.24 we are seized by anguish and pain like a woman in **labour.**
22.23 pains strike you, pains like those of a woman in **labour.**
30. 6 man with his hands on his stomach like a woman in **labour?**
48.41 Moab's soldiers will be as frightened as a woman in **labour.**
49.22 Edom's soldiers will be as frightened as a woman in **labour."**
49.24 They are in pain and misery like a woman in **labour.**
50.43 He is seized by anguish, by pain like a woman in **labour.**
Mic 4. 9 Why are you suffering like a woman in **labour?**
1 Thes 5. 3 come upon a woman in **labour,** and people will not escape.

LACHISH
Important city in Judah.

Josh 10. 3 Jarmuth, King Japhia of **Lachish,** and to King Debir of Eglon:
10. 5 kings of Jerusalem, Hebron, Jarmuth, **Lachish,** and Eglon,
10.23 kings of Jerusalem, Hebron, Jarmuth, **Lachish,** and Eglon
10.31 from Libnah to **Lachish,** surrounded it and attacked it.
10.32 gave the Israelites victory over **Lachish**
10.33 came to the aid of **Lachish,** but Joshua defeated him
10.34 army went on from **Lachish** to Eglon, surrounded it and attacked
10.35 everyone there to death, just as they had done at **Lachish.**
12.11 Jarmuth, **Lachish,**
15.39 **Lachish,** Bozkath, Eglon,
2 Kgs 14.19 fled to the city of **Lachish,** but his enemies followed him
18.14 Hezekiah sent a message to Sennacherib, who was in **Lachish:**
18.17 emperor sent a large army from **Lachish** to attack Hezekiah

2 Kgs	19. 8	that the emperor had left **Lachish** and was fighting
2 Chr	11. 9	Adoraim, **Lachish,** Azekah,
	25.27	fled to the city of **Lachish,** but his enemies followed him
	32. 9	his army were still at **Lachish,** he sent the following message
Neh	11.30	They lived in **Lachish** and on the farms near by, and in
Is	36. 2	chief official to go from **Lachish** to Jerusalem
	37. 8	that the emperor had left **Lachish** and was fighting
Jer	34. 7	The army was also attacking **Lachish** and Azekah,
Mic	1.13	You that live in **Lachish,** hitch the horses to the chariots.

LACK

1 Kgs	17. 7	a while the brook dried up because of the **lack** of rain.
1 Chr	29. 1	God has chosen, but he is still young and **lacks** experience.
Job	4.21	he dies, still **lacking** wisdom."
Ps	19. 7	the Lord are trustworthy, giving wisdom to those who **lack** it.
	34.10	Even lions go hungry for **lack** of food,
	34.10	but those who obey the Lord **lack** nothing good.
	109.24	My knees are weak from **lack** of food;
Prov	1.32	Stupid people are destroyed by their own **lack** of concern.
Song	4.13	There is no **lack** of henna and nard, [14] of saffron, calamus,
Is	50. 2	desert, so that the fish in them die for **lack** of water.
Lk	22.35	that time without purse, bag, or shoes, did you **lack** anything?"
1 Cor	7. 5	in to Satan's temptation because of your **lack** of self-control.
Gal	5. 6	neither circumcision nor the **lack** of it makes any difference
Heb	4.11	us will fail as they did because of their **lack** of faith.
Jas	1. 4	so that you may be perfect and complete, **lacking** nothing.
	1. 5	But if any of you **lacks** wisdom, he should pray to God,

LADY

Judg	5.29	Her wisest **ladies** answered her,
Ps	45. 9	Among the **ladies** of your court are daughters of kings,
Prov	11.16	A gracious **lady** is respected, but a woman without virtue
2 Jn	1	Elder— To the dear **Lady** and to her children,
	5	And so I ask you, dear **Lady:**

LAKE

Num	34.11	on the eastern shore of **Lake Galilee,**
Deut	3.17	to the River Jordan, from **Lake Galilee** in the north
	33.23	Their land reaches to the south from **Lake Galilee."**
Josh	11. 2	the Jordan Valley south of **Lake Galilee,** in the foothills,
	12. 3	included the Jordan Valley from **Lake Galilee** south
	13.27	border was the River Jordan as far north as **Lake Galilee.**
1 Kgs	15.20	Beth Maacah, the area near **Lake Galilee,**
Job	14.11	rivers that stop running, and **lakes** that go dry,
Is	35. 7	burning sand will become a **lake,** and dry land will be filled
Mt	4.13	Capernaum, a town by **Lake Galilee,** in the territory of Zebulun
	4.18	walked along the shore of **Lake Galilee,** he saw two brothers
	4.18	his brother Andrew, catching fish in the **lake** with a net.
	8.18	ordered his disciples to go to the other side of the **lake.**
	8.24	a fierce storm hit the **lake,** and the boat was in danger
	8.28	the other side of the **lake,** he was met by two men
	8.32	down the side of the cliff into the **lake** and was drowned.
	9. 1	and went back across the **lake** to his own town, [2] where some
	13. 1	house and went to the **lake-side,** where he sat down to teach.
	13.47	their net out in the **lake** and catch all kinds of fish.
	14.22	the other side of the **lake,** while he sent the people away.
	14.24	was far out in the **lake,** tossed about by the waves, because
	14.34	They crossed the **lake** and came to land at Gennesaret,
	15.29	Jesus left there and went along by **Lake Galilee.**
	16. 5	the other side of the **lake,** they forgot to take any bread.
	17.27	So go to the **lake** and drop in a line.
Mk	1.16	walked along the shore of **Lake Galilee,** he saw two fishermen,
	2.13	Jesus went back again to the shore of **Lake Galilee.**
	3. 7	disciples went away to **Lake Galilee,** and a large crowd followed
	4. 1	Again Jesus began to teach beside **Lake Galilee.**
	4.35	"Let us go across to the other side of the **lake."**
	5. 1	the other side of **Lake Galilee,** in the territory of Gerasa.
	5.13	down the side of the cliff into the **lake** and was drowned.
	5.21	Jesus went back across to the other side of the **lake.**
	5.21	There at the **lakeside** a large crowd gathered round him.
	6.45	the other side of the **lake,** while he sent the crowd away.
	6.47	in the middle of the **lake,** while Jesus was alone on land.
	6.53	They crossed the **lake** and came to land at Gennesaret,
	7.31	went on through Sidon to **Lake Galilee,** going by way of the
	8.13	the boat, and started across to the other side of the **lake.**
Lk	5. 1	standing on the shore of **Lake Gennesaret** while the people
	8.22	"Let us go across to the other side of the **lake."**
	8.23	wind blew down on the **lake,** and the boat began to fill
	8.26	the territory of Gerasa, which is across the **lake** from Galilee.
	8.33	down the side of the cliff into the **lake** and was drowned.
	8.40	the other side of the **lake,** the people welcomed him, because
Jn	6. 1	After this, Jesus went across **Lake Galilee** (or, Lake Tiberias,
	6.16	disciples went down to the **lake,** [17] got into a boat, and
	6.17	into a boat, and went back across the **lake** towards Capernaum.
	6.22	the other side of the **lake** realized that there had been only
	6.25	the other side of the **lake,** they said to him, "Teacher,
	21. 1	Jesus appeared once more to his disciples at **Lake Tiberias.**
Rev	19.20	thrown alive into the **lake** of fire that burns with sulphur.
	20.10	them, was thrown into the **lake** of fire and sulphur, where
	20.14	the world of the dead were thrown into the **lake** of fire.
	20.14	(This **lake** of fire is the second death.)
	20.15	of the living was thrown into the **lake** of fire.
	21. 8	place for them is the **lake** burning with fire and sulphur,

LAMB

Gen	4. 4	Then Abel brought the first **lamb** born to one of his sheep,
	21.28	Abraham separated seven **lambs** from his flock,
Gen	21.30	Abraham answered, "Accept these seven **lambs.**
	22. 7	and the wood, but where is the **lamb** for the sacrifice?"
	30.32	today and take every black **lamb** and every spotted or speckled
Ex	12. 3	man must choose either a **lamb** or a young goat
	12.21	you is to choose a **lamb** or a young goat and kill
	13.13	every first-born male donkey by offering a **lamb** in its place.
	29.38	sacrifice on the altar two one-year-old **lambs.**
	29.39	Sacrifice one of the **lambs** in the morning
	29.40	With the first **lamb** offer one kilogramme of fine wheat
	29.41	Sacrifice the second **lamb** in the evening,
	34.20	buy back every first-born donkey by offering a **lamb**
Lev	9. 3	a one-year-old **lamb** without any defects for a burnt-offering,
	12. 6	the Lord's presence a one-year-old **lamb** for a burnt-offering
	12. 8	the woman cannot afford a **lamb,** she shall bring two doves
	14.10	he shall bring two male **lambs** and one female lamb a year
	14.12	take one of the male **lambs** and together with the one-third
	14.13	He shall kill the **lamb** in the place where the animals
	14.14	of the blood of the **lamb** and put it on the lobe
	14.17	of the blood of the **lamb** and put them on the lobe
	14.21	his purification only one male **lamb** as his repayment-offering, a
	14.24	The priest shall take the **lamb** and the olive-oil
	14.25	He shall kill the **lamb** and take some of the blood
	22.26	When a calf or a **lamb** or a kid is born,
	22.28	or a sheep and its **lamb** or a goat and its kid
	23.12	a burnt-offering a one-year-old male **lamb** that has no defects.
	23.18	is to present seven one-year-old **lambs,** one bull, and two rams,
	23.19	and two one-year-old male **lambs** as a fellowship-offering.
	23.20	the bread with the two **lambs** as a special gift
	27.26	A calf, a **lamb,** or a kid belongs to the Lord,
Num	6.12	As a repayment offering he shall bring a one-year-old **lamb.**
	6.14	a one-year-old male **lamb** for a burnt-offering,
	6.14	a one-year-old ewe **lamb** for a sin-offering,
	7.12	one ram, and a one-year-old **lamb,** for the burnt-offering;
	7.12	and five one-year-old **lambs** for the fellowship-offering.
	7.84	and twelve one-year-old **lambs,** together with the grain-offerings
	7.84	sixty goats, sixty one-year-old **lambs,** for the fellowship-offerings
	28. 3	two one-year-old male **lambs** without any defects.
	28. 4	Offer the first **lamb** in the morning,
	28. 7	the wine-offering with the first **lamb,** pour out at the altar
	28. 8	the evening offer the second **lamb** in the same way
	28. 9	offer two one-year-old male **lambs** without any defects,
	28.11	seven one-year-old male **lambs,** all without any defects.
	28.13	and with each **lamb,** one kilogramme.
	28.14	a half litres with the ram, and one litre with each **lamb.**
	28.19	seven one-year-old male **lambs,** all without any defects.
	28.21	and one kilogramme with each **lamb.**
	28.27	seven one-year-old male **lambs,** all without any defects.
	28.29	and one kilogramme with each **lamb.**
	29. 2	seven one-year-old male **lambs,** all without any defects.
	29. 4	and one kilogramme with each **lamb.**
	29. 8	seven one-year-old male **lambs,** all without any defects.
	29.10	and one kilogramme with each **lamb.**
	29.13	fourteen one-year-old male **lambs,** all without any defects.
	29.15	and one kilogramme with each **lamb,**
	29.17	fourteen one-year-old male **lambs,** all without any defects.
	29.20	fourteen one-year-old male **lambs,** all without any defects.
	29.23	fourteen one-year-old male **lambs,** all without any defects.
	29.26	fourteen one-year-old male **lambs,** all without any defects.
	29.29	fourteen one-year-old male **lambs,** all without any defects.
	29.32	fourteen one-year-old male **lambs,** all without any defects.
	29.36	seven one-year-old male **lambs,** all without any defects.
Deut	14.26	whatever you want—beef, **lamb,** wine, beer—and there,
1 Sam	7. 9	Samuel killed a young **lamb** and burnt it whole as a
	15. 9	the best calves and **lambs,** or anything else that was good;
	17.34	a bear carries off a **lamb,** [35] I go after it, attack it,
	17.35	a lamb, [35] I go after it, attack it, and rescue the **lamb.**
2 Sam	12. 3	while the poor man had only one **lamb,** which he had bought.
	12. 3	The **lamb** was like a daughter to him.
	12. 4	he took the poor man's **lamb** and cooked a meal
2 Kgs	3. 4	100,000 **lambs,** and the wool from 100,000 sheep.
1 Chr	29.21	thousand rams, and a thousand **lambs,** which they burnt whole
2 Chr	29.21	they took seven bulls, seven sheep, seven **lambs,** and seven goats.
	29.22	sheep, and then the **lambs,** and sprinkled the blood of each
	29.32	and two hundred **lambs** as burnt-offerings for the Lord;
	30.15	they killed the **lambs** for the Passover sacrifice.
	30.17	could not kill the Passover **lambs,**
	30.17	Levites did it for them, and dedicated the **lambs** to the Lord.
	35. 6	You are to kill the Passover **lambs** and goats.
	35. 7	thirty thousand sheep, **lambs,** and young goats,
	35. 8	priests two thousand six hundred **lambs** and young goats
	35. 9	and Jozabad—contributed five thousand **lambs** and young goats
	35.11	After the **lambs** and goats had been killed, the Levites skinned them,
Ezra	6. 9	young bulls, sheep, or **lambs** to be burnt as offerings
	6.17	hundred sheep, and four hundred **lambs** as sacrifices,
	7.17	buy bulls, rams, **lambs,** corn, and wine and offer them
	8.35	They offered 12 bulls for all Israel, 96 rams, and 77 **lambs;**
Neh	10.36	our cows, and the first **lamb** or kid born to each
Job	21.11	children run and play like **lambs** [12] and dance to the music
Ps	114. 4	the hills jumped about like **lambs.**
	114. 6	You hills, why did you jump about like **lambs?**
Is	5.17	the ruins of the cities **lambs** will eat grass
	16. 1	people of Moab send a **lamb** as a present to the one
	34. 6	the blood and fat of **lambs** and goats that are sacrificed.
	40.11	he will gather the **lambs** together and carry them in his arms;
	53. 7	Like a **lamb** about to be slaughtered, like a sheep about to
	65.25	Wolves and **lambs** will eat together;
	66. 3	whether they sacrifice a **lamb** or break a dog's neck;
Jer	11.19	I was like a trusting **lamb** taken out to be killed,
	51.40	I will take them to be slaughtered, like **lambs,**
Ezek	27.21	land of Kedar paid for your merchandise with **lambs,** sheep,

Ezek	39.18	will be killed like rams or **lambs** or goats or fat bulls.
	46. 4	to be burnt whole, six **lambs** and one ram,
	46. 5	of corn, and with each **lamb** he is to bring whatever he
	46. 6	offer a young bull, six **lambs,** and a ram,
	46. 7	of corn, and with each **lamb** the offering is to be whatever
	46.11	and whatever the worshipper wants to give with each **lamb.**
	46.13	says, "Every morning a one-year-old **lamb** without any defects
	46.15	The **lamb,** the flour, and the olive-oil are to be offered
Hos	4.16	How can I feed them like **lambs** in a meadow?
Amos	6. 4	on your luxurious couches, feasting on veal and **lamb!**
Mk	14.12	the day the **lambs** for the Passover meal were killed,
Lk	10. 3	I am sending you like **lambs** among wolves.
	22. 7	of Unleavened Bread when the **lambs** for the Passover meal
Jn	1.29	said, "There is the **Lamb of God,** who takes away the sin
	1.36	"There is the **Lamb of God!"**
	21.15	Jesus said to him, "Take care of my **lambs."**
Acts	8.32	to be slaughtered, like a **lamb** that makes no sound when its
1 Cor	5. 7	now that Christ, our Passover **lamb,** has been sacrificed.
1 Pet	1.19	of Christ, who was like a **lamb** without defect or flaw.
Rev	5. 6	Then I saw a **Lamb** standing in the centre of the throne,
	5. 6	The **Lamb** appeared to have been killed.
	5. 7	The **Lamb** went and took the scroll from the right hand of
	5. 8	creatures and the twenty-four elders fell down before the **Lamb.**
	5.12	"The **Lamb** who was killed is worthy to receive power, wealth,
	5.13	the throne and to the **Lamb,** be praise and honour, glory and
	6. 1	Then I saw the **Lamb** break open the first of the seven
	6. 3	Then the **Lamb** broke open the second seal;
	6. 5	Then the **Lamb** broke open the third seal;
	6. 7	Then the **Lamb** broke open the fourth seal;
	6. 9	Then the **Lamb** broke open the fifth seal.
	6.12	And I saw the **Lamb** break open the sixth seal.
	6.16	who sits on the throne and from the anger of the **Lamb!**
	7. 9	the throne and of the **Lamb,** dressed in white robes and
	7.10	from our God, who sits on the throne, and from the **Lamb!"**
	7.14	their robes and made them white with the blood of the **Lamb.**
	7.17	will burn them, [17] because the **Lamb,** who is in the centre
	8. 1	When the **Lamb** broke open the seventh seal, there was silence
	12.11	by the blood of the **Lamb** and by the truth which they
	13. 8	of the living which belongs to the **Lamb** that was killed.
	13.11	had two horns like a **lamb's** horns, and it spoke like a
	14. 1	Then I looked, and there was the **Lamb** standing on Mount Zion;
	14. 4	They follow the **Lamb** wherever he goes.
	14. 4	the first ones to be offered to God and to the **Lamb.**
	14.10	in fire and sulphur before the holy angels and the **Lamb.**
	15. 3	of Moses, the servant of God, and the song of the **Lamb:**
	17.14	They will fight against the **Lamb;**
	17.14	**Lamb,** together with his called, chosen, and faithful followers,
	19. 7	for the wedding of the **Lamb,** and his bride has prepared
	19. 9	who have been invited to the wedding-feast of the **Lamb."**
	21. 9	and I will show you the Bride, the wife of the **Lamb."**
	21.14	were written the names of the twelve apostles of the **Lamb.**
	21.22	because its temple is the Lord God Almighty and the **Lamb.**
	21.23	glory of God shines on it, and the **Lamb** is its lamp.
	21.27	names are written in the **Lamb's** book of the living will
	22. 1	of God and of the **Lamb** [2] and flowing down the middle of
	22. 3	of God and of the **Lamb** will be in the city,

LAME

Lev	21.18	no one who is blind, **lame,** disfigured, or deformed;
Job	29.15	I was eyes for the blind, and feet for the **lame.**
Is	33.22	will be so much that even **lame** men can have a share.
	35. 6	The **lame** will leap and dance,
Jer	31. 8	The blind and the **lame** will come with them,
Zeph	3.19	I will rescue all the **lame** and bring the exiles home.
Mal	1. 8	a blind or sick or **lame** animal to sacrifice to me, do
	1.13	you bring a stolen animal or one that is **lame** or sick.
Mt	11. 5	the blind can see, the **lame** can walk, those who suffer
	15.30	bringing with them the **lame,** the blind, the crippled, the dumb,
	15.31	the crippled made whole, the **lame** walking, and the blind seeing;
Lk	7.22	the blind can see, the **lame** can walk, those who suffer from
	14.13	a feast, invite the poor, the crippled, the **lame,** and the
	14.21	bring back the poor, the crippled, the blind, and the **lame.'**
Jn	5. 3	lying in the porches—the blind, the **lame,** and the paralysed.
Acts	3. 2	was called, was a man who had been **lame** all his life.
	3.16	the power of his name that gave strength to this **lame** man.
	4. 9	good deed done to the **lame** man and how he was healed,
	8. 7	a loud cry, and many paralysed and **lame** people were healed.
	14. 8	a man who had been **lame** from birth and had never been
Heb	12.13	straight paths, so that the **lame** foot may not be disabled,

LAMENT

2 Sam	1.17	David sang this **lament** for Saul and his son Jonathan,
	3.33	David sang this **lament** for Abner:
2 Chr	35.25	The prophet Jeremiah composed a **lament** for King Josiah.
	35.25	The song is found in the collection of **laments.**
Mic	1. 8	Then Micah said, "Because of this I will mourn and **lament.**

LAMP

Ex	25. 6	oil for the **lamps;**
	25.37	Make seven **lamps** for the lamp-stand and set them up
	27.20	the best olive-oil for the **lamp,** so that it can be lit
	27.21	are to set up the **lamp** in the Tent of my presence
	30. 7	Aaron comes to get the **lamps** ready,
	30. 8	must do the same when he lights the **lamps** in the evening.
	35. 8	oil for the **lamps;**
	35.14	the **lamps** with their oil;
	35.28	spices and oil for the **lamps,** for the anointing oil,
	37.23	He made seven **lamps** for the lamp-stand,
Ex	39.37	its lamps, all its equipment, and the oil for the **lamps;**
	40. 4	Also bring in the lamp-stand and set up the **lamps** on it.
	40.25	he lit the **lamps,** just as the Lord had commanded.
Lev	24. 2	the finest quality for the **lamps** in the Tent,
	24. 4	shall take care of the **lamps** on the lampstand of pure gold
Num	4. 9	cover the lampstand, with its **lamps,** tongs, trays,
	4.16	for the oil for the **lamps,** the incense, the grain-offerings,
	8. 2	when he puts the seven **lamps** on the lamp-stand,
	8. 3	placed the **lamps** facing the front of the lamp-stand.
1 Sam	3. 3	Before dawn, while the **lamp** was still burning, [4] the Lord
1 Kgs	7.49	the flowers, **lamps,** and tongs;
	7.50	the cups, **lamp** snuffers, bowls, dishes for incense,
2 Kgs	4.10	table, a chair, and a **lamp** in it, and he can stay
	12.13	tools for tending the **lamps,** or any other article of silver
	25.14	tools used in tending the **lamps,** the bowls used for catching
1 Chr	28.15	making the utensils, [15] for each **lamp** and lampstand,
2 Chr	4.20	the lampstands and the **lamps** of fine gold
	4.21	the flower decorations, the **lamps,** and the tongs;
	4.22	the **lamp** snuffers, the bowls, the dishes for incense,
	13.11	and every evening they light the **lamps** on the gold lampstand.
	29. 7	let the **lamps** go out,
Job	18. 6	The **lamp** in his tent will be darkened.
Ps	119.105	Your word is a **lamp** to guide me and a light for
Prov	13. 9	the wicked are like a **lamp** flickering out.
	20.20	life will end like a **lamp** that goes out in the dark.
Ecc	12. 6	chain will snap, and the golden **lamp** will fall and break;
Is	42. 3	not break off a bent reed or put out a flickering **lamp.**
	43.17	fell, never to rise, snuffed out like the flame of a **lamp!**
Jer	25.10	have no oil for their **lamps,** and there will be no more
	52.18	tools used in tending the **lamps,** the bowls used for catching
Dan	5. 5	where the light from the **lamps** was shining most brightly.
Zeph	1.12	"At that time I will take a **lamp** and search Jerusalem.
Zech	4. 2	On the lamp-stand are seven **lamps,**
	4.10b	said to me, "The seven **lamps** are the seven eyes
Mt	5.15	No one lights a **lamp** and puts it under a bowl;
	6.22	"The eyes are like a **lamp** for the body.
	12.20	not break off a bent reed, or put out a flickering **lamp.**
	25. 1	girls who took their oil **lamps** and went out to meet the
	25. 3	The foolish ones took their **lamps** but did not take any
	25. 4	while the wise ones took containers full of oil for their **lamps.**
	25. 7	The ten girls woke up and trimmed their **lamps.**
	25. 8	us have some of your oil, because our **lamps** are going out.'
Mk	4.21	anyone ever bring in a **lamp** and put it under a bowl
Lk	8.16	"No one lights a **lamp** and covers it with a bowl or
	11.33	"No one lights a **lamp** and then hides it or puts it
	11.34	Your eyes are like a **lamp** for the body.
	11.36	over, as when a **lamp** shines on you with its brightness."
	12.35	and with your **lamps** lit, [36] like servants who are waiting
	15. 8	She lights a **lamp,** sweeps her house, and looks carefully
Jn	5.35	John was like a **lamp,** burning and shining, and you were
Acts	20. 8	Many **lamps** were burning in the upstairs room where we were
2 Pet	1.19	because it is like a **lamp** shining in a dark place until
Rev	11. 4	two olive-trees and the two **lamps** that stand before the Lord
	18.23	Never again will the light of a **lamp** be seen in you;
	21.23	glory of God shines on it, and the Lamb is its **lamp.**
	22. 5	and they will not need **lamps** or sunlight, because the Lord

LAMP-STAND

Ex	25.31	"Make a **lamp-stand** of pure gold.
	25.34	shaft of the **lamp-stand** is to have four decorative flowers
	25.36	the branches, and the **lamp-stand** are to be a single piece
	25.37	Make seven lamps for the **lamp-stand** and set them up
	25.39	pure gold to make the **lamp-stand** and all this equipment.
	26.35	and the **lamp-stand** against the south side.
	30.27	and all its equipment, the **lamp-stand** and its equipment,
	31. 8	table and its equipment, the **lamp-stand** of pure gold
	35.14	the **lamp-stand** for the light and its equipment;
	37.17	He made the **lamp-stand** of pure gold.
	37.20	The shaft of the **lamp-stand** had four decorative flowers
	37.22	the branches, and the **lamp-stand** were a single piece
	37.23	made seven lamps for the **lamp-stand,**
	37.24	pure gold to make the **lamp-stand** and all its equipment.
	39.37	the **lamp-stand** of pure gold, its lamps, all its equipment,
	40. 4	Also bring in the **lamp-stand** and set up the lamps on it.
	40.24	He put the **lamp-stand** in the Tent, on the south side,
Lev	24. 4	of the lamps on the **lampstand** of pure gold and must see
Num	3.31	Covenant Box, the table, the **lamp-stand,** the altars,
	4. 9	and cover the **lampstand,** with its lamps, tongs, trays,
	8. 2	the seven lamps on the **lamp-stand,** he should place them
	8. 3	placed the lamps facing the front of the **lamp-stand.**
	8. 4	From top to bottom the **lamp-stand** was made of hammered gold,
1 Kgs	7.49	offered to God, [49] the ten **lamp-stands** that stood in front
1 Chr	28.15	for each lamp and **lampstand,**
2 Chr	4. 7	They made ten gold **lampstands**
	4. 7	five **lampstands** and five tables on each side.
	4.20	the **lampstands** and the lamps of fine gold
	13.11	and every evening they light the lamps on the gold **lampstand.**
Jer	52.19	the ash containers, the **lampstands,** the bowls used for incense,
Zech	4. 2	"A **lamp-stand** made of gold," I answered.
	4. 2	On the **lamp-stand** are seven lamps,
	4. 3	are two olive-trees beside the **lamp-stand,** one on each side
	4.11	"What do the two olive-trees on either side of the **lamp-stand** mean?
Mt	5.15	he puts it on the **lampstand,** where it gives light for
Mk	4.21	Doesn't he put it on the **lampstand?**
Lk	8.16	he puts it on the **lampstand,** so that people will see the
	11.33	he puts it on the **lampstand,** so that people may see the
Heb	9. 2	In it were the **lampstand** and the table with the bread
Rev	1.12	and I saw seven gold **lamp-stands,** [13] and among them there was
	1.20	you see in my right hand, and of the seven gold **lamp-stands:**

Rev 1.20 and the seven **lamp-stands** are the seven churches.
2. 1 right hand and who walks among the seven gold **lamp-stands.**
2. 5 I will come to you and take your **lamp-stand** from its place.

LANCE

Job 41.26 no spear or arrow or **lance** that can harm him.

LAND
[PROMISED LAND]
see also **CANAAN, EGYPT, ISRAEL, JUDAH, LANDOWNER, LANDSLIDE**

Gen 1. 9 one place, so that the **land** will appear"—and it was done.
1.10 He named the **land** "Earth,"
2. 5 sent any rain, and there was no one to cultivate the **land;**
4.14 You are driving me off the **land** and away from your presence.
4.16 and lived in a **land** called "Wandering,"
8. 9 water still covered all the **land,** the dove did not find a
10.11 From that **land** he went to Assyria and built the cities
10.30 The **land** in which they lived extended from Mesha to Sephar
12. 1 and go to a **land** that I am going to show
12. 6 Abram travelled through the **land** until he came to the sacred
12. 6 (At that time the Canaanites were still living in the **land.)**
13. 6 there was not enough pasture **land** for the two of them to
13. 7 Canaanites and the Perizzites were still living in the **land.)**
13. 9 Choose any part of the **land** you want.
13.15 and your descendants all the **land** that you see,
13.17 and look over the whole **land,** because I am going to give
14. 7 They conquered all the **land** of the Amalekites
15. 7 of Ur in Babylonia, to give you this **land** as your own."
15.13 "Your descendants will be strangers in a foreign **land;**
15.14 when they leave that foreign **land,** they will take great wealth
15.18 give your descendants all this **land** from the border of Egypt
15.19 including the **lands** of the Kenites, the Kenizzites, the
17. 8 and to your descendants this **land** in which you are now a
19.25 all the people there and everything that grew on the **land.**
19.28 smoke rising from the **land,** like smoke from a huge furnace.
20.13 my father's house into foreign **lands,** I said to her, 'You
20.15 He said to Abraham, "Here is my whole **land;**
23. 4 sell me some **land,** so that I can bury my wife."
23.15 "Sir, **land** worth only four hundred pieces of silver—
24. 5 girl will not leave home to come with me to this **land?**
24. 5 Shall I send your son back to the **land** you came from?"
24. 7 my father and from the **land** of my relatives,
24. 7 promised me that he would give this **land** to my descendants.
25. 6 sent these sons to the **land** of the East, away from his
26. 1 another famine in the **land** besides the earlier one
26. 2 stay in this **land,** where I tell you to stay.
26.12 Isaac sowed seed in that **land,** and that year he harvested
26.22 to live in the **land,** and we will be prosperous here."
28. 4 you take possession of this **land,** in which you have lived
28.13 and to your descendants this **land** on which you are lying.
28.15 wherever you go, and I will bring you back to this **land.**
29. 1 continued on his way and went towards the **land** of the East.
31. 3 him, "Go back to the **land** of your fathers
31.13 get ready to go back to the **land** where you were born.' "
32. 9 to go back to my **land** and to my relatives, and you
34.21 let them live in the **land** with us and travel freely.
34.21 The **land** is large enough for them also.
34.30 Perizzites, and everybody else in the **land** will hate me.
35.12 I will give you the **land** which I gave to Abraham and
35.22 Jacob was living in that **land,** Reuben had sexual intercourse
36. 6 and went away from his brother Jacob to another **land.**
36. 7 He left because the **land** where he and Jacob were living
40.15 I was kidnapped from the **land** of the Hebrews, and even here
41.45 He left the king's court and travelled all over the **land.**
41.47 seven years of plenty the **land** produced abundant crops,
41.52 "God has given me children in the **land** of my trouble";
43.11 the best products of the **land** in your packs as a present
45. 6 This is only the second year of famine in the **land;**
46. 4 Egypt, and I will bring your descendants back to this **land.**
47. 6 settle in the region of Goshen, the best part of the **land.**
47.11 in the best of the **land** near the city of Rameses, as
47.18 is nothing left to give you except our bodies and our **lands.**
47.19 Buy us and our **land** in exchange for food.
47.19 We will be the king's slaves, and he will own our **land.**
47.20 Joseph bought all the **land** in Egypt for the king.
47.20 forced to sell his **land,** because the famine was so severe;
47.20 and all the **land** became the king's property.
47.22 The only **land** he did not buy
47.22 was the **land** that belonged to the priests.
47.22 not have to sell their **lands,** because the king gave them an
47.23 see, I have now bought you and your **lands** for the king.
47.26 Only the **lands** of the priests did not become the king's property.
48. 4 I will give this **land** to your descendants as their possession
48.21 and will take you back to the **land** of your ancestors.
49.15 the resting-place is good And that the **land** is delightful.
49.20 "Asher's **land** will produce rich food.
50.24 this land to the **land he solemnly promised** to Abraham,
50.25 God leads you to that **land,** you will take my body with
Ex 1.12 increased in number and the further they spread through the **land.**
2.22 am a foreigner in this **land,** and so I name him Gershom."
3. 8 of Egypt to a spacious **land,** one which is rich and fertile
3.17 to a rich and fertile **land**—the land of the Canaanites,
6. 1 fact, I will force him to drive them out of his **land."**
6. 4 the land of Canaan, the **land** in which they had lived
6. 8 you to the **land that I solemnly promised** to give to Abraham,
6.11 of Egypt that he must let the Israelites leave his **land."**
7. 3 Egypt and lead the tribes of my people out of the **land.**
7.19 and all over the **land** there will be blood,
Ex 8. 6 and the frogs came out and covered the **land.**
8. 7 used magic, and they too made frogs come up on the **land.**
8.14 them up in great heaps, until the **land** stank with them.
8.22 will know that I, the Lord, am at work in this **land.**
10.13 to blow on the **land** all that day
12.25 When you enter the **land** that the Lord has promised
13. 5 to give you the **land** of the Canaanites, the Hittites,
13. 5 into that rich and fertile **land,** you must celebrate this
13. 7 must be no yeast or leavened bread anywhere in your **land.**
13.11 will bring you into the **land** of the Canaanites,
14.21 It blew all night and turned the sea into dry **land.**
15.13 by your strength you guided them to your sacred **land.**
18. 3 (Moses had said, "I have been a foreigner in a strange **land";**
20.12 live a long time in the **land** that I am giving you.
23.23 and take you into the **land** of the Amorites, the Hittites,
23.26 In your **land** no woman will have a miscarriage
23.29 if I did, the **land** would become deserted,
23.30 there are enough of you to take possession of the **land.**
23.31 make the borders of your **land** extend from the Gulf of Aqaba
23.31 over the inhabitants of the **land,** and you will drive them
32.13 their descendants all that **land you promised** would be their
33. 1 and go to the **land that I promised** to give to Abraham,
33. 3 You are going to a rich and fertile **land.**
33.12 lead these people to that **land,** but you did not tell me
Lev 11. 2 You may eat any **land** animal [3]that has divided hoofs
16.22 carry all their sins away with him into some uninhabited **land.**
18.24 pagans who lived in the **land** before you and whom the Lord
18.25 Their actions made the **land** unclean,
18.25 the Lord is punishing the **land** and making it reject
18.26 disgusting things and made the **land** unclean,
18.28 and commands, [28]and then the **land** will not reject you,
18.30 people who lived in the **land** before you,
19.29 turn to other gods and the **land** will be full of immorality.
19.33 "Do not ill-treat foreigners who are living in your **land.**
20.23 am driving out those pagans so that you can enter the **land.**
20.24 you this rich and fertile **land** as your possession,
22.24 This is not permitted in your **land.**
23. 9 When you come into the **land** that the Lord is giving
25. 2 When you enter the **land** that the Lord is giving you,
25. 2 honour the Lord by not cultivating the **land** every seventh year.
25. 4 of complete rest for the **land,** a year dedicated to the Lord.
25. 5 it is a year of complete rest for the **land.**
25. 6 Although the **land** has not been cultivated during that year,
25. 9 send a man to blow a trumpet throughout the whole **land.**
25.10 proclaim freedom to all the inhabitants of the **land.**
25.14 So when you sell **land** to your fellow-Israelite
25.14 or buy **land** from him, do not deal unfairly.
25.15 the number of years the **land** can produce crops
25.16 is being sold is the number of crops the **land** can produce.
25.18 and commands, so that you may live in safety in the **land.**
25.19 The **land** will produce its crops, and you will have all
25.21 The Lord will bless the **land** in the sixth year
25.23 Your **land** must not be sold on a permanent basis,
25.24 When **land** is sold, the right of the original owner to
25.25 is forced to sell his **land,** his closest relative is to buy
25.27 Year of Restoration, when he would in any event recover his **land.**
25.28 money to buy the **land** back, it remains under the control
25.34 pasture **land** round the Levite cities shall never be sold;
25.45 Such children born in your **land** may become your property,
26. 4 right time, so that the **land** will produce crops
26. 5 and you will live in safety in your **land.**
26. 6 give you peace in your **land,** and you will sleep without
26. 6 the dangerous animals in the **land,** and there will be no more
26.19 be no rain, and your **land** will be dry
26.20 because your **land** will not produce crops
26.32 I will destroy your **land** so completely that the enemies
26.33 I will bring war on you and scatter you in foreign **lands.**
26.33 Your **land** will be deserted, and your cities left in ruins.
26.34 Then the **land** will enjoy the years of complete rest
26.34 while you are in exile in the **land** of your enemies.
26.38 will die in exile, swallowed up by the **land** of your enemies.
26.39 you who survive in the **land** of your enemies will waste away
26.41 and send them into exile in the **land** of their enemies.
26.42 and I will renew my promise to give my people the **land.**
26.43 First, however, the **land** must be rid of its people,
26.44 they are still in the **land** of their enemies,
27.16 man dedicates part of his **land** to the Lord, the price shall
27.17 If he dedicates the **land** immediately after a Year of
27.28 whether it is a human being, an animal, or **land.**
27.30 all the produce of the **land,** whether grain or fruit,
Num 10. 9 are at war in your **land,** defending yourselves
10.30 Hobab answered, "No, I am going back to my native **land."**
11.12 all the way to the **land you promised** to their ancestors?
13.16 These are the spies Moses sent to explore the **land.**
13.19 Find out whether the **land** is good or bad
13.20 whether the soil is fertile and whether the **land** is wooded.
13.21 went north and explored the **land** from the wilderness of Zin
13.22 the southern part of the **land** and came to Hebron,
13.25 After exploring the **land** for forty days, the spies returned
13.27 "We explored the **land** and found it to be rich
13.29 Amalekites live in the southern part of the **land;**
13.30 and said, "We should attack now and take the **land;**
13.32 a false report among the Israelites about the **land**
13.32 "That **land** doesn't even produce enough to feed the people
14. 3 Why is the Lord taking us into that **land?**
14. 7 "The **land** we explored is an excellent land.
14. 8 will take us there and give us that rich and fertile **land.**
14.14 they will tell it to the people who live in this **land.**
14.16 able to bring them into the **land you promised** to give them.
14.22 none of these people will live to enter that **land.**
14.23 They will never enter the **land** which I promised

Num 14.24 will bring him into the **land** which he explored,
14.24 his descendants will possess the **land**
14.29 none of you over twenty years of age will enter that **land.**
14.31 will bring them into the **land** that you rejected,
14.34 for each of the forty days you spent exploring the **land.**
14.36 had sent to explore the **land** brought back a false report
15. 2 to observe in the **land** that he was going to give
15.18 to observe in the **land** that he was going to give
16.13 us out of the fertile **land** of Egypt to kill us here
16.14 brought us into a fertile **land** or given us fields
20.12 not lead them into the **land that I promised** to give them."
20.17 Please permit us to pass through your **land.**
20.24 not going to enter the **land** which I promised to give
21.22 "Let us pass through your **land.**
21.24 and occupied their **land** from the River Arnon north
21.26 and had captured all his **land** as far as the River Arnon.
21.34 give you victory over him, all his people, and his **land.**
21.35 leaving no survivors, and then they occupied his **land.**
22. 5 spreading out everywhere and threatening to take over our **land.**
22. 6 be able to defeat them and drive them out of the **land.**
22.11 who came from Egypt has spread out over the whole **land.**
24.18 in Edom And make their **land** his property,
26.53 said to Moses, [53]"Divide the **land** among the tribes,
26.54 Divide the **land** by drawing lots,
27.12 and look out over the **land** that I am giving
32. 1 they saw how suitable the **land** of Jazer and Gilead was
32. 3 Nebo, and Beon—is good **land** for livestock,
32. 5 Please give us this **land** as our property,
32. 7 crossing the Jordan into the **land** which the Lord has given
32. 8 did when I sent them from Kadesh Barnea to explore the **land.**
32. 9 and saw the **land,** but when they returned, they discouraged
32. 9 the people from entering the **land** which the Lord had given
32.11 Egypt will enter the **land that I promised** to Abraham, Isaac,
32.17 until we have settled them in the **land** that will be theirs.
32.17 in the fortified towns, safe from the people of this **land.**
32.18 the other Israelites have taken possession of the **land**
32.22 until the Lord defeats them [22]and takes possession of the **land.**
32.22 will acknowledge that this **land** east of the Jordan is yours.
32.29 are able to conquer the **land,** then give them the land of
33.52 you must drive out all the inhabitants of the **land.**
33.53 Occupy the **land** and settle in it, because I am giving it
33.54 Divide the **land** among the various tribes and clans
33.55 out the inhabitants of the **land,** those that are left will be
34. 2 "When you enter Canaan, the **land** which I am giving you,
34.12 "These will be the four borders of your **land."**
34.13 the Israelites, "This is the **land** that you will receive
34.13 by drawing lots, the **land** that the Lord has assigned
34.17 and Joshua son of Nun will divide the **land** for the people.
35. 2 Levites some cities to live in and pasture **land** round the cities.
35. 3 The pasture **land** will be for their cattle
35. 4 The pasture **land** is to extend outwards from the city walls
35. 7 forty-two other cities [7]with their pasture **land,**
35.33 did this, you would defile the **land** where you are living.
35.33 Murder defiles the **land,** and except by the death of the
35.33 of purification for the **land** where a man has been murdered.
35.34 Do not defile the **land** where you are living,
36. 2 commanded you to distribute the **land** to the people of Israel
Deut 1. 8 All of this is the **land** which I, the Lord, promised
1.22 us to spy out the **land,** so that they can tell us
1.25 and reported that the **land** which the Lord our God was
1.26 and you would not enter the **land.**
1.35 the fertile **land that I promised** to give your ancestors.
1.36 give him and his descendants the **land** that he has explored.'
1.37 'Not even you, Moses, will enter the **land.**
1.38 He will lead Israel to occupy the **land.'**
1.39 will enter the **land**—the children you said would be
1.39 I will give the **land** to them, and they will occupy it.
2. 5 to give you so much as a square metre of their **land.**
2. 9 and I am not going to give you any of their **land.'"**
2.12 their enemies out of the **land** that the Lord gave them.)
2.19 will then be near the **land** of the Ammonites,
2.19 to give you any of the **land** that I have given them.'"
2.20 is also known as the **land** of the Rephaim, the name of
2.21 so that the Ammonites took over their **land** and settled there.
2.22 the Edomites took over their **land** and settled there,
2.23 The **land** along the Mediterranean coast had been settled
2.23 had taken over all their **land** as far south as the city
2.24 Sihon, the Amorite king of Heshbon, along with his **land.**
2.24 Attack him, and begin occupying his **land.**
2.29 the River Jordan into the **land** that the Lord our God is
2.31 'Look, I have made King Sihon and his **land** helpless
2.31 take his **land** and occupy it.'
3. 8 those two Amorite kings the **land** east of the River Jordan,
3.12 we took possession of the **land,** I assigned to the tribes
3.13 (Bashan was known as the **land** of the Rephaim.
3.18 God has given you this **land** east of the Jordan to occupy.
3.18 other tribes of Israel, to help them to occupy their **land.**
3.20 until they occupy the **land** that the Lord is giving them
3.20 you may return to this **land** which I have assigned to you.'
3.21 he will do the same to everyone else whose **land** you invade.
3.25 and see the fertile **land** on the other side,
3.28 lead the people across to occupy the **land** that you see.'
4. 1 will live and occupy the **land** which the Lord, the God of
4. 5 Obey them in the **land** that you are about to invade
4.14 are to obey in the **land** that you are about to invade
4.21 River Jordan to enter the fertile **land** which he is giving you.
4.22 I will die in this **land** and never cross the river,
4.22 but you are about to go across and occupy that fertile **land.**
4.25 you have been in the **land** a long time and have children
4.26 if you disobey me, you will soon disappear from the **land.**
4.26 live very long in the **land** across the Jordan

Deut 4.38 give you their land, the **land** which still belongs to you.
4.40 continue to live in the **land** which the Lord your God
4.47 They occupied his **land** and the land of King Og of Bashan,
4.48 This **land** extended from the town of Aroer,
5.16 live a long time in the **land** that I am giving you.
5.21 not desire his house, his **land,** his slaves, his cattle,
5.31 they will obey them in the **land** that I am giving them.'
5.33 continue to live in the **land** that you are going to occupy.
6. 1 Obey them in the **land** that you are about to enter
6. 2 so that you may live in that **land** a long time.
6. 3 in that rich and fertile **land,** just as the Lord, the God
6.10 he will give you a **land** with large and prosperous cities
6.11 Lord brings you into this **land** and you have all you want
6.18 of the fertile **land that the Lord promised** your ancestors,
6.23 and give us this **land,** as he had promised our ancestors
7. 1 will bring you into the **land** which you are going to occupy,
7.13 these blessings in the **land that he promised** your ancestors
8. 1 occupy the **land which the Lord promised** to your ancestors.
8. 7 into a fertile land—a **land** that has rivers and springs,
8. 8 a **land** that produces wheat and barley, grapes, figs,
8.10 Lord your God for the fertile **land** that he has given you.
8.15 In that dry and waterless **land** he made water flow out
9. 1 River Jordan and occupy the **land** belonging to nations greater
9. 4 brought you in to possess this **land** because you deserved it.
9. 5 what is right that the Lord is letting you take their **land.**
9. 6 is not giving you this fertile **land** because you deserve it.
9.23 and take possession of the **land** that he was giving you,
9.28 take your people into the **land that you had promised** them.
10. 9 the tribe of Levi received no **land** as the other tribes did;
10.11 possession of the **land that he had promised** to give to your
11. 8 the river and occupy the **land** that you are about to enter.
11. 9 rich and fertile **land that the Lord promised** to give your
11.10 The **land** that you are about to occupy is not like
11.11 but the **land** that you are about to enter
11.11 is a land of mountains and valleys, a **land** watered by rain.
11.12 God takes care of this **land** and watches over it
11.14 will send rain on your **land** when it is needed,
11.17 even though it is a good **land** that he is giving you.
11.21 a long time in the **land** that the Lord your God promised
11.23 you will occupy the **land** belonging to nations greater
11.25 Wherever you go in that **land,** the Lord your God will
11.29 Lord brings you into the **land** that you are going to occupy,
11.31 River Jordan and occupy the **land** that the Lord your God
12. 1 as you live in the **land** that the Lord, the God of
12. 2 In the **land** that you are taking, destroy all the places
12. 9 have not yet entered the **land** that the Lord your God is
12.10 the Lord will let you occupy the **land** and live there.
12.12 remember that the Levites will have no **land** of their own.
12.19 to neglect the Levites, as long as you live in your **land.**
12.29 nations as you invade their **land,** and you will occupy it
15. 4 God will bless you in the **land** that he is giving you.
15. 7 of the towns in the **land** that the Lord your God is
16. 4 no one in your **land** is to have any yeast
16. 5 and nowhere else in the **land** that the Lord your God
16.20 that you will occupy the **land** that the Lord your God
17.14 have taken possession of the **land** that the Lord your God
18. 1 of Levi is not to receive any share of **land** in Israel;
18. 2 They are to own no **land,** as the other tribes do;
18. 9 "When you come into the **land** that the Lord your God
18.12 he is driving those nations out of the **land** as you advance.
18.14 Then Moses said, "In the **land** you are about to occupy,
19. 1 has destroyed the people whose **land** he is giving you
19. 8 gives you all the **land he has promised,** [9]then you are to
19. 9 (He will give you this **land** if you do everything that I
19.10 them to death in the **land** that the Lord is giving you.
19.14 established long ago in the **land** that the Lord your God
20.15 cities that are far away from the **land** you will settle in.
20.16 you capture cities in the **land** that the Lord your God
21. 1 in a field in the **land** that the Lord your God
21.23 dead body hanging on a post brings God's curse on the **land.**
21.23 you will not defile the **land** that the Lord your God
23. 7 you once lived in their **land.**
23.20 everything you do in the **land** that you are going to occupy.
24. 4 a terrible sin in the **land** that the Lord your God
25.15 a long time in the **land** that the Lord your God
25.19 God has given you the **land** and made you safe
26. 1 "After you have occupied the **land** that the Lord your God
26. 3 I have entered the **land that he promised** our ancestors to
26. 9 He brought us here and gave us this rich and fertile **land.**
26.15 also the rich and fertile **land** that you have given us,
27. 2 River Jordan and enter the **land** that the Lord your God
27. 3 entered the rich and fertile **land** that the Lord,
28. 8 He will bless you in the **land** that he is giving you.
28.11 abundant crops in the **land that he promised** your ancestors
28.21 left in the **land** that you are about to occupy.
28.36 king away to a foreign **land,** where neither you nor your
28.40 will grow everywhere in your **land,** but you will not have any
28.43 "Foreigners who live in your **land** will gain more
28.52 attack every town in the **land** that the Lord your God
28.63 be uprooted from the **land** that you are about to occupy.
29. 8 we defeated them, [8]took their **land,** and divided it
29.22 descendants and foreigners from distant **lands** will see the
29.22 disasters and sufferings that the Lord has brought on your **land.**
29.23 Your **land** will be like the cities of Sodom and Gomorrah,
29.24 world will ask, 'Why did the Lord do this to their **land?**
29.27 and brought on their **land** all the disasters written in this
29.28 he uprooted them from their **land**
29.28 threw them into a foreign **land,** and there they are today.'
30. 5 may again take possession of the **land** where your ancestors
30. 6 all your heart, and you will continue to live in that **land.**
30.16 will bless you in the **land** that you are about to occupy.

Deut 30.18 not live long in that **land** across the Jordan
30.20 long in the **land that he promised** to give your ancestors,
31. 3 the nations living there, so that you can occupy their **land;**
31. 7 occupy the **land that the Lord promised** to their ancestors.
31.13 as they live in the **land** that you are about to occupy
31.16 the pagan gods of the **land** they are about to enter.
31.20 this rich and fertile **land,** as I promised their ancestors.
31.21 take them into the **land that I promised** to give them, I
31.23 of Israel into the **land that I promised** them, and I will
32. 8 The Most High assigned nations their **lands;**
32.47 will live long in that **land** across the Jordan
32.52 You will look at the **land** from a distance,
32.52 you will not enter the **land** that I am giving the people
33.13 "May the Lord bless their **land** with rain
33.14 May their **land** be blessed with sun-ripened fruit,
33.16 May their **land** be filled with all that is good,
33.21 They took the best of the **land** for themselves;
33.23 Their **land** reaches to the south from Lake Galilee."
33.24 And may his **land** be rich with olive-trees.
33.28 in peace, secure in a **land** full of corn and wine,
34. 1 of Jericho, and there the Lord showed him the whole **land:**
34. 4 Moses, "This is the **land that I promised** Abraham, Isaac,
Josh 1. 2 cross the River Jordan into the **land** that I am giving them.
1. 3 my people the entire **land** that you will be marching over.
1. 6 as they occupy this **land** which I promised their ancestors.
1.11 River Jordan to occupy the **land** that the Lord your God
1.13 God would give you this **land** on the east side
1.15 until they have occupied the **land** west of the Jordan
1.15 settle here in your own **land** east of the Jordan, which
2. 9 to them, "I know that the Lord has given you this **land.**
2.14 when the Lord gives us this **land,** we will treat you well."
2.18 When we invade your **land,** tie this red cord to the window
5. 4 rich and fertile **land that he had promised** their ancestors.
7. 2 near Bethaven, with orders to go and explore the **land.**
8. 1 his people, city, and **land** will be yours.
9. 6 and the men of Israel, "We have come from a distant **land.**
9. 9 come from a very distant **land,** sir, because we have heard of
9.11 people that live in our **land** told us to get some food
9.24 to give you the whole **land** and to kill the people living
10.21 No one in the **land** dared even to speak against the Israelites.
10.40 Joshua conquered the whole **land.**
11.16 Joshua captured all the **land**—
11.23 Joshua captured the whole **land,** as the Lord had commanded
12. 1 already conquered and occupied the **land** east of the Jordan,
12. 6 the Lord's servant, gave their **land** to the tribes of Reuben
12. 7 Joshua divided this **land** among the tribes and gave it to
12. 8 This **land** had been the home of the Hittites, the Amorites,
13. 1 but there is still much **land** to be taken:
13. 3 (The **land** from the stream of Shihor, at the Egyptian border,
13. 5 the **land** of the Gebalites;
13. 6 You must divide the **land** among the Israelites,
13. 7 Now then, divide this **land** among the other nine tribes
13. 8 Manasseh had already received the **land** that Moses,
13.14 Moses had given no **land** to the tribe of Levi.
13.15 given a part of the **land** to the families of the tribe
13.21 All of them had ruled the **land** for King Sihon.
13.24 given a part of the **land** to the families of the tribe
13.26 their **land** extended from Heshbon to Ramath Mizpeh
13.29 given a part of the **land** to the families of half the
13.32 is how Moses divided the **land** east of Jericho and the Jordan
13.33 But Moses did not assign any **land** to the tribe of Levi.
14. 3 Moses had already assigned the **land** east of the Jordan
14. 5 people of Israel divided the **land** as the Lord had commanded
14. 7 Moses sent me from Kadesh Barnea to spy out this **land.**
14. 9 would certainly receive as our possession the **land**
14.15 There was now peace in the **land.**
15. 1 tribe of Judah received a part of the **land**
15. 1 The **land** reached south to the southernmost point of the
15.19 The **land** you have given me is in the dry country."
15.20 This is the **land** that the families of the tribe of Judah
16. 1 southern boundary of the **land** assigned to the descendants
16. 4 tribes of Ephraim and West Manasseh, received this **land**
16. 8 This was the **land** given to the families of the tribe
17. 1 A part of the **land** west of the Jordan was assigned to
17. 2 **Land** west of the Jordan was assigned to the rest
17. 4 well as our male relatives, a part of the **land** to possess."
17. 4 they were given **land** along with their male relatives.
17. 6 female descendants as well as his male descendants were assigned **land.**
17. 8 The **land** round Tappuah belonged to Manasseh,
17.14 us only one part of the **land** to possess as our own?
17.15 ground for yourselves in the **land** of the Perizzites
18. 1 After they had conquered the **land,** the entire community
18. 2 Israel who had not yet been assigned their share of the **land.**
18. 3 go in and take the **land** that the Lord,
18. 5 The **land** will be divided among them in seven parts;
18. 7 receive a share of the **land** with the rest of you,
18. 7 Manasseh have already received their **land** east of the Jordan,
18. 8 way to map out the **land** after Joshua had given them these
18. 8 "Go all over the **land** and map it out, and come back
18. 9 men went all over the **land** and set down in writing how
18.10 the remaining tribes of Israel a certain part of the **land.**
18.11 Their **land** lay between the tribes of Judah and Joseph.
18.20 were the borders of the **land** which the families of the tribe
18.28 This is the **land** which the families of the tribe of Benjamin
19. 1 extended into the **land** assigned to the tribe of Judah.
19. 8 This was the **land** which the families of the tribe of Simeon
19.10 The **land** which they received reached as far as Sarid.
19.16 their towns were in the **land** which the families of the tribe
19.23 their towns were in the **land** which the families of the tribe
19.31 their towns were in the **land** which the families of the tribe

Josh 19.39 their towns were in the **land** which the families of the tribe
19.47 people of Dan lost their **land,** they went to Laish
19.48 their towns were in the **land** which the families of the tribe
19.49 Israel finished dividing up the **land,** they gave Joshua
19.49 son of Nun a part of the **land** as his own.
19.51 assigned these parts of the **land** by drawing lots
19.51 In this way they finished dividing the **land.**
21. 2 as well as pasture **land** round them for our livestock."
21. 3 certain cities and pasture **lands** out of their own territories.
21. 8 these cities and their pasture **lands** to the Levites, as the
21.11 in the hill-country of Judah, along with the pasture **land**
21.16 Ain, Juttah, and Beth Shemesh, with their pasture **lands:**
21.18 Geba, [18]Anathoth, and Almon, with their pasture **lands.**
21.19 in all, with their pasture **lands,** were given to the priests,
21.21 Shechem and its pasture **lands** in the hill-country of Ephraim
21.22 Kibzaim, and Beth Horon, with their pasture **lands.**
21.24 Aijalon, and Gathrimmon, with their pasture **lands.**
21.25 Taanach and Gathrimmon, with their pasture **lands.**
21.26 Kohath received ten cities in all, with their pasture **lands.**
21.27 and Beeshterah, with their pasture **lands.**
21.29 Jarmuth, and Engannim, with their pasture **lands.**
21.31 Abdon, [31]Helkath, and Rehob, with their pasture **lands.**
21.32 with its pasture **lands** (one of the cities of refuge),
21.32 Hammoth Dor, and Kartan, with their pasture **lands.**
21.33 Gershon received a total of thirteen cities with their pasture **lands.**
21.35 Kartah, [35]Dimnah, and Nahalal, with their pasture **lands.**
21.37 Jahaz, [37]Kedemoth, and Mephaath, with their pasture **lands.**
21.38 with its pasture **lands** (one of the cities of refuge),
21.39 Mahanaim, [39]Heshbon, and Jazer, with their pasture **lands.**
21.41 From the **land** that the people of Israel possessed,
21.41 forty-eight cities, with the pasture **lands** round them, was
21.43 gave to Israel all the **land** that he had solemnly promised
21.44 gave them peace throughout the **land,** just as he had promised
22. 4 go back home to the **land** which you claimed for your own,
22. 4 the **land** on the east side
22. 6 Moses had given **land** east of the Jordan to one half of
22. 6 other half Joshua had given **land** west of the Jordan,
22. 9 started out for their own **land,** the land of Gilead,
22.19 Now then, if your **land** is not fit to worship in,
22.19 come over into the Lord's **land,** where his Tent is.
22.19 Claim some **land** among us.
22.33 to war to devastate the **land** where the people of Reuben
23. 4 possession of your tribes the **land** of the nations that are
23. 5 You shall have their **land,** as the Lord your God has promised
23.13 are left in this good **land** which the Lord your God has
23.16 will be left in this good **land** that he has given you."
24. 3 Abraham, your ancestor, from the **land** beyond the Euphrates
24. 8 I brought you to the **land** of the Amorites,
24. 8 You took their **land,** and I destroyed them as you advanced.
24.13 I gave you a **land** that you had never cultivated and
24.15 the gods of the Amorites, in whose **land** you are now living.
24.18 As we advanced into this **land,** the Lord drove out all
24.28 away, and everyone returned to his own part of the **land.**
24.30 buried him on his own **land** at Timnath Serah in the
24.32 Shechem, in the piece of **land** that Jacob had bought from the
24.32 This **land** was inherited by Joseph's descendants.
Judg 1. 2 I am giving them control of the **land."**
1.15 The **land** you have given me is in the dry country."
2. 1 brought you to the **land that I promised** to your ancestors.
2. 2 not make any covenant with the people who live in this **land.**
2. 6 man went to take possession of his own share of the **land.**
2. 9 his own part of the **land** at Timnath Serah in the
2.21 of the nations that were still in the **land** when Joshua died.
2.23 So the Lord allowed those nations to remain in the **land;**
3. 1 left some nations in the **land** to test the Israelites who had
3. 3 Those left in the **land** were the five Philistine cities,
3.11 There was peace in the **land** for forty years, and then
3.30 Moab, and there was peace in the **land** for eighty years.
5. 6 went through the **land,** and travellers used the side roads.
5. 8 was war in the **land** when the Israelites chose new gods.
5.31 And there was peace in the **land** for forty years.
6. 4 They would camp on the **land** and destroy the crops as far
6. 5 They came and devastated the **land,** [6]and Israel was helpless
6. 9 from the people who fought against you here in this **land.**
6. 9 drove them out as you advanced, and I gave you their **land.**
6.10 the gods of the Amorites, whose **land** you are now living in.
8.28 The **land** was at peace for forty years, until Gideon died.
11.13 Egypt, they took away my **land** from the River Arnon to the
11.15 Israel took away the land of Moab or the **land** of Ammon.
11.17 the king of Edom to ask permission to go through his **land.**
11.17 of Moab, but neither would he let them go through his **land.**
11.19 for permission to go through his country to their own **land.**
15.20 Samson led Israel for twenty years while the Philistines ruled the **land.**
16.24 enemy, who devastated our **land** and killed so many of us!"
18. 1 had not yet received any **land** of their own among the tribes
18. 2 of Zorah and Eshtaol with instructions to explore the **land.**
18. 9 We saw the **land,** and it's very good.
Ruth 1. 1 before Israel had a king, there was a famine in the **land.**
1 Sam 6. 5 Perhaps he will stop punishing you, your gods, and your **land.**
12. 8 who brought them out of Egypt and settled them in this **land.**
25. 2 town of Maon, and who owned **land** near the town of Carmel.
26.19 me out from the Lord's **land** to a country where I can
27. 8 He would raid their **land** as far as Shur, all the way
2 Sam 3.12 was at Hebron, to say, "Who is going to rule this **land?**
3.21 what you have wanted and will rule over the whole **land."**
5. 9 starting at the place where **land** was filled in on the east
7.10 Ever since they entered this **land,** they have been attacked
8. 1 Philistines again, defeated them, and ended their control over the **land.**
9. 7 back all the **land** that belonged to your grandfather Saul,

2 Sam	9.10	your servants will farm the **land** for your master Saul's
	14.16	me and so remove us from the **land** God gave his people.
	24.13	years of famine in your **land** or three months of running away
	24.13	from your enemies or three days of an epidemic in your **land?**
1 Kgs	4.19	there was one governor over the whole **land.**
	4.24	Solomon ruled over all the **land** west of the River Euphrates,
	8.34	them back to the **land** which you gave to their ancestors.
	8.36	Lord, send rain on this **land** of yours, which you gave to
	8.37	there is famine in the **land** or an epidemic, or the crops
	8.40	time they live in the **land** which you gave to our ancestors.
	8.41	who lives in a distant **land** hears of your fame and of
	8.46	as prisoners to some other **land,** even if that land is far
	8.46	other land, even if that **land** is far away, [47] listen to
	8.47	If there in that **land** they repent and pray to you,
	8.48	If in that **land** they truly and sincerely repent, and
	8.48	they face towards this **land** which you gave to our ancestors,
	9. 7	my people Israel from the **land** that I have given them.
	9. 8	'Why did the Lord do this to this **land** and this Temple?'
	9.15	the palace, to fill in **land** on the east side of the
	9.20	Israelites had not killed when they took possession of their **land.**
	9.24	Solomon filled in the **land** on the east side of the city,
	11.18	king, who gave Hadad some **land** and a house and provided him
	11.27	Solomon was filling in the **land** on the east side of
	14.15	Israel from this good **land** which he gave to their ancestors,
	14.24	had driven out of the **land** as the Israelites advanced into
	18. 5	and every river-bed in the **land** to see if we can find
	18. 6	on which part of the **land** each one would explore, and set
	21. 2	palace, and I want to use the **land** for a vegetable garden.
	21.26	driven out of the **land** as the people of Israel advanced.)
2 Kgs	4.38	was a famine throughout the **land,** Elisha returned to Gilgal.
	8. 1	a famine on the **land,** which would last for seven years,
	8. 3	ask for her house and her **land** to be restored to her.
	12.20	the house built on the **land** that was filled in on the
	16. 3	Lord had driven out of the **land** as the Israelites advanced.
	17.11	of the people whom the Lord had driven out of the **land.**
	17.26	of the god of that **land,** and so the god had sent
	17.27	to teach the people the law of the god of that **land."**
	18.32	it is a **land** of olives, olive-oil, and honey.
	19.17	destroyed many nations, made their **lands** desolate, [18] and
	19.24	and drank water in foreign **lands** and that the feet of your
	21. 2	had driven out of the **land** as his people advanced, Manasseh
	21. 8	be driven out of the **land** that I gave to their ancestors."
	21. 9	the Lord had driven out of the **land** as his people advanced.
	21.14	their enemies, who will conquer them and plunder their **land.**
	25.21	of Judah were carried away from their **land** into exile.
	25.24	Settle in this **land,** serve the king of Babylonia, and all
1 Chr	4.10	the God of Israel, "Bless me, God, and give me much **land.**
	4.40	found plenty of fertile pasture **lands** there in a stretch of
	5. 9	and so they occupied the **land** as far east as the desert
	5.10	and occupied their **land** in the eastern part of Gilead.
	5.16	in the towns there and all over the pasture **lands** of Sharon.
	5.25	gods of the nations whom God had driven out of the **land.**
	6.54	They received the first share of the **land** assigned to the Levites.
	6.55	Hebron in the territory of Judah and the pasture **lands** round it.
	6.57	Debir, Ashan, and Beth Shemesh, with their pasture **lands.**
	6.60	they were assigned the following towns with their pasture **lands:**
	6.64	together with the pasture **lands** round the towns.
	6.66	assigned towns and pasture **lands** in the territory of Ephraim:
	6.70	of Aner and Bileam with the surrounding pasture **lands.**
	6.71	assigned the following towns, with the surrounding pasture **lands:**
	6.77	assigned the following towns with the surrounding pasture **lands:**
	11. 4	original inhabitants of the **land,** were still living there.
	11. 8	starting at the place where **land** was filled in on the east
	17. 9	Ever since they entered this **land** they have been attacked by
	19. 3	as spies to explore the **land,** so that he can conquer it!"
	21.12	sends an epidemic on your **land,** using his angel to bring
	22.18	used to live in this **land,** and they are now subject to
	28. 8	continue to possess this good **land** and so that you may hand
2 Chr	6.25	bring them back to the **land** which you gave to them and
	6.27	Lord, send rain on this **land** of yours, which you gave to
	6.28	there is famine in the **land** or an epidemic or the crops
	6.31	time they live in the **land** which you gave to our ancestors.
	6.32	who lives in a distant **land** hears how great and powerful you
	6.36	as prisoners to some other **land,** even if that land is far
	6.36	other land, even if that **land** is far away, [37] listen to
	6.37	If there in that **land** they repent and pray to you,
	6.38	If in that **land** they truly and sincerely repent and pray
	6.38	they face towards this **land** which you gave to our ancestors,
	7.14	forgive their sins, and make their **land** prosperous again.
	7.20	will remove you from the **land** that I gave you, and I
	7.21	'Why did the Lord do this to this **land** and this Temple?'
	8. 7	Israelites had not killed when they took possession of the **land.**
	11.14	pastures and other **land** and moved to Judah and Jerusalem,
	14. 1	as king, and under Asa the **land** enjoyed peace for ten years.
	14. 7	We have control of the **land** because we have done the will
	15. 5	because there was trouble and disorder in every **land.**
	15.17	places of worship in the **land,** he remained faithful to the
	20. 7	people Israel moved into this **land,** you drove out the people
	20. 7	living here and gave the **land** to the descendants of Abraham,
	20.10	allow them to enter those **lands,** so our ancestors went round
	20.11	come to drive us out of the **land** that you gave us.
	26.10	vineyards in the hill-country and to farm the fertile **land.**
	28. 3	Lord had driven out of the **land** as the Israelites advanced.
	30. 6	You have survived the Assyrian conquest of the **land.**
	31.19	or in the pasture **lands** belonging to these cities,
	32. 5	the defences built on the **land** that was filled in on the
	32.31	that had happened in the **land,** God let Hezekiah go his own
	33. 2	had driven out of the **land** as his people advanced, Manasseh
	33. 8	be driven out of the **land** that I gave to their ancestors."
	33. 9	the Lord had driven out of the **land** as his people advanced.
	34. 8	after he had purified the **land** and the Temple by ending
2 Chr	36.21	"The **land** will lie desolate for seventy years, to make up
Ezra	3. 3	who were living in the **land,** they rebuilt the altar where it
	4. 4	had been living in the **land** tried to discourage and frighten
	6.21	who were living in the **land** and who had come to worship
	9.11	They told us that the **land** we were going to occupy
	9.11	was an impure **land** because the people who lived in
	9.12	we wanted to enjoy the **land** and pass it on to our
	10.11	the foreigners living in our **land** and get rid of your
Neh	4. 4	have, and let them be taken as prisoners to a foreign **land.**
	9. 6	You made **land** and sea and everything in them;
	9. 8	Hittites and the Amorites, the **land** of the Perizzites, the
	9. 8	Girgashites, to be a **land** where his descendants would live.
	9.10	and the people of his **land,** because you knew how they
	9.15	to take control of the **land** which you had promised to give
	9.22	conquer nations and kingdoms, **lands** that bordered their own.
	9.23	conquer and live in the **land** that you had promised their
	9.25	fortified cities, fertile **land,** houses full of wealth,
	9.35	when they lived in the broad, fertile **land** you gave them;
	9.36	land that you gave us, this fertile **land** which gives us food.
	9.37	What the **land** produces goes to the kings that you put
	10.28	the foreigners living in our **land,** we, together with our
	10.30	We will not intermarry with the foreigners living in our **land.**
	10.31	we will not farm the **land,** and we will cancel all debts.
	10.37	villages, the tithes from the crops that grow on our **land.**
Job	5.10	He sends rain on the **land** and he waters the fields.
	10.21	going to a **land** that is dark and
	10.22	is dark and gloomy, [22] a **land** of darkness, shadows, and
	15.19	Their **land** was free from foreigners;
	18.18	be driven out of the **land** of the living, driven from light
	22. 8	your power and your position to take over the whole **land.**
	24. 2	Men move boundary stones to get more **land;**
	24.18	away by floods, and the **land** he owns is under God's curse;
	24.19	drought, so a sinner vanishes from the **land** of the living.
	30. 8	They were driven out of the **land.**
	31.38	If I have stolen the **land** I farm and taken it from
	37.17	suffer in the heat when the south wind oppresses the **land.**
	38.27	Who waters the dry and thirsty **land,** so that grass springs up?
Ps	10.16	Those who worship other gods will vanish from his **land.**
	25.13	They will always be prosperous, and their children will possess the **land.**
	37. 3	live in the **land** and be safe.
	37. 9	the Lord will possess the **land,** but the wicked will be
	37.11	the humble will possess the **land** and enjoy prosperity and peace.
	37.18	those who obey him, and the **land** will be theirs for ever.
	37.22	the Lord will possess the **land,** but those who are cursed by
	37.27	do good, and your descendants will always live in the **land;**
	37.29	The righteous will possess the **land** and live in it for ever.
	37.34	you by giving you the **land,** and you will see the wicked
	41. 2	he will make them happy in the **land;**
	44. 2	out the heathen and established your people in their **land;**
	44. 3	Your people did not conquer the **land** with their swords;
	47. 4	He chose for us the **land** where we live, the proud
	49.11	stay for all time, though they once had **lands** of their own.
	58. 2	evil you can do, and commit crimes of violence in the **land.**
	60. 2	You have made the **land** tremble, and you have cut it open;
	63. 1	worn-out, and waterless **land,** my soul is thirsty for you.
	65. 9	You show your care for the **land** by sending rain;
	66. 6	He changed the sea into dry **land;**
	67. 6	The **land** has produced its harvest;
	68. 6	freedom, but rebels will have to live in a desolate **land.**
	68. 9	You caused abundant rain to fall and restored your worn-out **land;**
	69.35	His people will live there and possess the **land;**
	72. 3	May the **land** enjoy prosperity;
	72. 6	like rain on the fields, like showers falling on the **land.**
	72.16	May there be plenty of corn in the **land;**
	74. 8	they burnt down every holy place in the **land.**
	74.20	There is violence in every dark corner of the **land.**
	78.45	that tormented them, and frogs that ruined their **land.**
	78.54	brought them to his holy **land,** to the mountains which he
	78.55	he divided their **land** among the tribes of Israel and gave
	79. 1	O God, the heathen have invaded your **land.**
	80. 6	You let the surrounding nations fight over our **land;**
	80. 8	you drove out other nations and planted it in their **land.**
	80. 9	its roots went deep, and it spread out over the whole **land.**
	83.12	"We will take for our own the **land** that belongs to God."
	85. 1	Lord, you have been merciful to your **land;**
	85. 9	him, and his saving presence will remain in our **land.**
	85.12	and our **land** will produce rich harvests.
	88.12	of darkness or your goodness in the **land** of the forgotten?
	94. 6	and orphans, and murder the strangers who live in our **land.**
	94.17	me, I would have gone quickly to the **land** of silence.
	95. 5	the **land** also, which he himself formed.
	95.11	'You will never enter the **land** where I would have given
	101. 8	Day after day I will destroy the wicked in our **land;**
	105.21	him ruler over all the **land,** [22] with power over the king's
	105.32	He sent hail and lightning on their **land** instead of rain;
	105.35	they ate all the plants in the **land;**
	105.44	He gave them the **lands** of other peoples and let them
	106. 9	he led his people across on dry **land.**
	106.24	Then they rejected the pleasant **land,** because they did
	106.38	children, and the **land** was defiled by those murders.
	107.35	into pools of water and dry **land** into flowing springs.
	111. 6	power to his people by giving them the **lands** of foreigners.
	112. 2	The good man's children will be powerful in the **land;**
	114. 1	Jacob's descendants left that foreign **land,**
	115.17	the dead, by any who go down to the **land** of silence.
	125. 3	The wicked will not always rule over the **land** of the righteous;
	135.12	He gave their **lands** to his people;
	136.21	He gave their **lands** to his people;
	137. 4	can we sing a song to the Lord in a foreign **land?**
	146. 9	He protects the strangers who live in our **land;**

Prov 2.21 Righteous men—men of integrity—will live in this **land** of ours.
2.22 snatch wicked men from the **land** and pull sinners out of it
3. 9 an offering from the best of all that your **land** produces.
10.30 have security, but the wicked will not survive in the **land.**
23.10 Never move an old boundary-mark or take over **land** owned by orphans.
25.25 good news from a distant **land** is like a drink of cold
27.26 of your sheep and buy **land** with the money you get from
31.16 She looks at **land** and buys it, and with money she has
Ecc 2. 8 and gold from the royal treasuries of the **lands** I ruled.
Is 1. 7 foreigners take over your **land** and bring everything to ruin.
1.19 obey me, you will eat the good things the **land** produces.
2. 6 The **land** is full of magic practices from the east and from
2. 7 Their **land** is full of silver and gold, and there is no
2. 7 Their **land** is full of horses, and there is no end to
2. 8 Their **land** is full of idols, and they worship objects that
4. 2 every plant and tree in the **land** grow large and beautiful.
4. 2 take delight and pride in the crops that the **land** produces.
5. 8 anyone else to live, and you alone will live in the **land.**
5.10 growing on ten hectares of **land** will yield only eight litres
6.11 are uninhabited—until the **land** itself is a desolate waste.
6.12 send the people far away and make the whole **land** desolate.
6.13 out of ten remains in the **land,** he too will be destroyed;
7.16 before that time comes, the **lands** of those two kings who
7.18 and for the Assyrians to come from their **land** like bees.
7.22 few survivors left in the **land** will have milk and honey to
8. 8 His outspread wings protect the **land.**
8.21 The people will wander through the **land,** discouraged and hungry.
9. 1 The **land** of the tribes of Zebulun and Naphtali was once disgraced,
9. 1 the Mediterranean eastwards to the **land** on the other side of
9. 2 They lived in a **land** of shadows, but now light is shining
9.19 like a fire throughout the **land** and destroys the people, and
11. 9 The **land** will be as full of knowledge of the Lord as
11.11 Assyria and Egypt, in the **lands** of Pathros, Sudan, Elam,
14. 1 them live in their own **land** again, and foreigners will come
14. 2 Israel to return to the **land** which the Lord gave them, and
16. 4 Let us stay in your **land.**
17.14 That is the fate of everyone who plunders our **land.**
18. 1 of Sudan there is a **land** where the sound of wings is
18. 2 From that **land** ambassadors come down the Nile in boats
18. 2 a message back to your **land** divided by rivers, to your
18. 7 will receive offerings from this **land** divided by rivers,
21. 1 the desert, disaster will come from a terrifying **land.**
23.10 Go and farm the **land,** you people in the colonies in Spain!
24.11 it has been banished from the **land.**
25. 5 attack like a winter storm, [5]like drought in a dry **land.**
26.10 Even here in a **land** of righteous people they still do wrong;
26.18 We have won no victory for our **land;**
28. 2 a rushing, overpowering flood, and will overwhelm the **land.**
32. 2 desert, like the shadow of a giant rock in a barren **land.**
32.13 and thorn-bushes and briars are growing on my people's **land.**
32.15 The waste **land** will become fertile,
32.16 Everywhere in the **land** righteousness and justice will be done.
33. 9 The **land** lies idle and deserted.
33.17 in splendour over a **land** that stretches in all directions.
33.24 one who lives in our **land** will ever again complain of being
34.10 The **land** will lie waste age after age, and no one will
34.11 Owls and ravens will take over the **land.**
34.17 Lord who will divide the **land** among them and give each of
34.17 They will live in the **land** age after age, and it will
35. 7 become a lake, and dry **land** will be filled with springs.
37.18 destroyed many nations, made their **lands** desolate, [19]and
37.25 and drank water in foreign **lands,** and that the feet of your
41. 1 "Be silent and listen to me, you distant **lands!**
41. 5 "The people of distant **lands** have seen what I have done;
41.18 into pools of water and the dry **land** into flowing springs.
41.19 Forests will grow in barren **land,** forests of pine and
42. 4 Distant **lands** eagerly wait for his teaching."
42.10 Sing, distant **lands** and all who live there!
42.12 those who live in distant **lands** give praise and glory to the
43. 6 return from distant **lands,** from every part of the world.
44. 3 give water to the thirsty **land** and make streams flow on the
49. 8 you settle once again in your **land** that is now laid waste.
49.20 day say to you, 'This **land** is too small— we need
51. 3 Though her **land** is a desert, I will make it a garden,
51. 5 Distant **lands** wait for me to come;
51.19 your **land** has been devastated by war,
54. 3 will get back the **land** that the other nations now occupy.
57.13 me will live in the **land** and will worship me in my
58.14 and you will enjoy the **land** I gave to your ancestor, Jacob.
59.18 what they have done, even those who live in distant **lands.**
60. 9 ships coming from distant **lands,** Bringing God's people home.
60.21 all do what is right, And will possess the **land** for ever.
61. 5 of your flocks And farm your **land** and tend your vineyards.
61. 7 live in your own **land,** And your wealth will be doubled;
62. 4 "Forsaken," Or your **land** be called "The Deserted Wife."
62. 4 Your **land** will be called "Happily Married," Because the Lord
62. 4 pleased with you And will be like a husband to your **land.**
65. 9 and their descendants will possess my **land** of mountains.
65.16 Anyone in the **land** who asks for a blessing will ask to
66.19 the nations and the distant **lands** that have not heard of my
Jer 1.14 all who live in this **land,** [15]because I am calling all the
1.18 Everyone in this **land**—the kings of Judah, the officials, the
2. 2 through the desert, through a **land** that had not been sown.
2. 6 a **land** of deserts and sand-dunes, a dry and dangerous land
2. 7 brought them into a fertile **land,** to enjoy its harvests and
2. 7 But instead they ruined my **land;**
2.15 they have made his **land** a desert, and his towns lie in
2.31 been like a desert to you, like a dark and dangerous **land?**
3. 1 This would completely defile the **land.**
3. 2 You have defiled the **land** with your prostitution.
Jer 3. 9 She defiled the **land,** and she committed adultery by
3.16 have become numerous in that **land,** people will no longer
3.18 and will return to the **land** that I gave your ancestors as
3.19 and give you a delightful **land,** the most beautiful land in
4. 5 Blow the trumpet throughout the **land!**
4.26 The fertile **land** had become a desert;
5.19 foreign gods in their own **land,** so they will serve strangers
5.19 in a **land** that is not theirs."
5.30 A terrible and shocking thing has happened in the **land:**
6.12 I am going to punish the people of this **land.**
6.20 they bring me from Sheba, or the spices from a distant **land?**
7. 6 Stop killing innocent people in this **land.**
7. 7 on living here in the **land** which I gave your ancestors as
7.34 The **land** will become a desert.
8.13 I have allowed outsiders to take over the **land."**
8.16 The whole **land** trembles when their horses neigh.
8.16 have come to destroy our **land** and everything in it, our city
8.19 Throughout the **land** I hear my people crying out, "Is the
9. 3 dishonesty instead of truth rules the **land.**
9.12 "Lord, why is the **land** devastated and dry as a desert,
9.19 We must leave our **land;**
10.18 The Lord is going to throw you out of this **land;**
11. 4 them out of Egypt, the **land** that was like a blazing furnace
11. 5 give them the rich and fertile **land** which they now have."
12. 4 How long will our **land** be dry, and the grass in every
12.10 they have turned my lovely **land** into a desert.
12.11 The whole **land** has become a desert, and no one cares.
12.12 I have sent war to destroy the entire **land;**
12.14 who have ruined the **land** I gave to my people Israel.
12.15 each nation back to its own **land** and to its own country.
13.13 fill the people in this **land** with wine until they are drunk:
14. 8 like a stranger in our **land,** like a traveller who stays for
14.13 they say, that there will be only peace in our **land."**
14.15 starvation will not strike this **land**—I will kill them in war
15. 7 In every town in the **land** I threw you to the wind
15. 8 are more widows in your **land** than grains of sand by the
15.10 I have to quarrel and argue with everyone in the **land.**
15.13 them for the sins they have committed throughout the **land.**
15.14 serve their enemies in a **land** they know nothing about,
16. 6 poor will die in this **land,** but no one will bury them
16.13 throw you out of this **land** into a land that neither you
16.15 Israel out of a northern **land** and out of all the other
16.15 their own country, to the **land** that I gave their ancestors.
16.18 because they have defiled my **land** with idols that are as
17. 3 of all the sins you have committed throughout your **land.**
17. 4 have to give up the **land** I gave you, and I will
17. 4 serve your enemies in a **land** you know nothing about, because
18.16 They have made this **land** a thing of horror, to be
22.10 to return, never again to see the **land** where he was born.
22.12 have taken him, and he will never again see this **land."**
22.28 been taken into exile to a **land** they know nothing about?"
22.29 O **land,** land, land!
23. 5 wisely and do what is right and just throughout the **land.**
23. 8 Israel out of a northern **land** and out of all the other
23. 8 Then they will live in their own **land."**
23.10 The **land** is full of people unfaithful to the Lord;
23.10 the Lord's curse the **land** mourns and the pastures are dry.
23.15 because they have spread ungodliness throughout the **land."**
24. 6 I will watch over them and bring them back to this **land.**
24. 8 who have stayed in this **land** or moved to Egypt—I, the
24.10 of them left in the **land** that I gave to them and
25. 5 go on living in the **land** that the Lord gave you and
25.11 This whole **land** will be left in ruins and will be a
25.19 all the kings of the Mediterranean **lands;**
27.11 stay on in its own **land,** to farm it and live there.
29.14 you will find me, and I will restore you to your **land.**
29.14 bring you back to the **land** from which I had sent you
30. 3 bring them back to the **land** that I gave their ancestors, and
30.10 that distant land, from the **land** where you are prisoners.
30.18 my people to their **land** and have mercy on every family;
31.16 they will return from the enemy's **land.**
31.23 restore the people to their **land,** they will once again say
32.15 fields, and vineyards will again be bought in this **land."**
32.22 rich and fertile **land,** as you had promised their ancestors.
32.23 when they came into this **land** and took possession of it,
32.41 them, and I will establish them permanently in this **land.**
32.43 people are saying that this **land** will be like a desert where
32.43 But fields will once again be bought in this **land.**
32.44 I will restore the people to their **land.**
33.11 I will make this **land** as prosperous as it was before.
33.12 Lord Almighty said, "In this **land** that is like a desert and
33.15 That king will do what is right and just throughout the **land.**
35. 7 build houses or farm the **land,** and not to plant vineyards or
35. 7 we might remain in this **land** where we live like strangers.
35.15 go on living in the **land** that I gave you and your
36.29 would come and destroy this **land** and kill its people and its
40. 2 Lord your God threatened this **land** with destruction, [3]and
40. 6 Mizpah and lived among the people who were left in the **land.**
40. 7 made Gedaliah governor of the **land** and had placed him in
40. 7 been taken away to Babylonia—the poorest people in the **land.**
40. 9 Settle down in this **land,** serve the king of Babylonia, and
41.17 whom the king of Babylonia had made governor of the **land.**
42.10 go on living in this **land,** then I will build you up
42.13 disobey the Lord your God and refuse to live in this **land.**
42.22 starvation or disease in the **land** where you want to go and
44.21 and the people of the **land** offered in the towns of Judah
44.22 This very day your **land** lies in ruins and no one lives
46.27 that distant land, from the **land** where you are prisoners.
47. 2 They will cover the **land** and everything on it, cities and
48.33 and joy have been taken away from the fertile **land** of Moab.
49. 1 Is there no one to defend their **land?**

Jer	49. 2	Then Israel will take its **land** back from those who took it
	49.19	up to the green pasture **land,** I will come and make the
	50.19	I will restore the people of Israel to their **land.**
	50.22	battle is heard in the **land,** and there is great destruction.
	50.38	Bring a drought on its **land** and dry up its rivers.
	50.38	Babylonia is a **land** of terrifying idols, that have made
	50.44	up to the green pasture **land,** I, the Lord, will come and
	51. 2	they will attack from every side and leave the **land** bare.
	51.46	of violence in the **land** and of one king fighting another.
	51.54	in Babylon, of mourning for the destruction in the **land.**
	52.27	of Judah were carried away from their **land** into exile.
Lam	1. 3	They live in other **lands,** with no place to call their own
	2. 2	in Judah And tore down the forts that defended the **land.**
Ezek	7. 2	This is the end for the whole **land!**
	7. 7	The end is coming for you people who live in the **land.**
	7.23	"Everything is in confusion—the **land** is full of murders
	9. 9	all over the **land** and have filled Jerusalem with crime.
	11.15	He has given us possession of the **land.'**
	11.16	be present with them in the **lands** where they have gone.
	12.19	the people of Jerusalem who are still living in their **land:**
	12.19	Their **land** will be stripped bare, because everyone who lives
	13. 9	you will never return to your **land.**
	14.15	kill the people, making the **land** so dangerous that no one
	14.16	their own lives, and the **land** would become a wilderness.
	17. 4	which he carried to a **land** of commerce, and placed in a
	17.24	All the trees in the **land** will know that I am the
	19. 7	The people of the **land** were terrified every time he roared.
	19.13	it is planted in the desert, in a dry and waterless **land.**
	20. 6	and lead them to a **land** I had chosen for them,
	20. 6	a rich and fertile **land,** the finest land of all.
	20.15	not take them to the **land** I had given them,
	20.15	a rich and fertile **land,** the finest land of all.
	20.28	I brought them to the **land I had promised** to give them.
	20.38	take them out of the **lands** where they are living now, but
	20.40	There in the **land,** on my holy mountain, the high
	20.42	back to Israel, the **land that I promised** I would give to
	21.30	where you were created, in the **land** where you were born.
	22.24	"tell the Israelites that their **land** is unholy, and so I am
	22.30	have crumbled and defend the **land** when my anger is about to
	23.48	Throughout the **land** I will put a stop to immorality, as
	26.20	be inhabited and take your place in the **land** of the living.
	27.15	people of many coastal **lands** gave you ivory and ebony in
	27.26	you out to sea, An east wind wrecked you far from **land.**
	28.25	in their own land, the **land** that I gave to my servant
	29. 2	him how he and all the **land** of Egypt will be punished.
	29.19	I am giving the **land** of Egypt to King Nebuchadnezzar.
	30. 7	The **land** will be the most desolate in the world, and its
	30.11	He and his ruthless army will come to devastate the **land.**
	30.11	Egypt with swords, and the **land** will be full of corpses.
	32.23	Yet once they terrified the **land** of the living.
	33. 2	"tell your people what happens when I bring war to a **land.**
	33.24	'Abraham was only one man, and he was given the whole **land.**
	33.24	There are many of us, so now the **land** is ours.'
	33.25	What makes you think that the **land** belongs to you?
	33.26	What makes you think that the **land** is yours?
	34.13	gather them together, and bring them back to their own **land.**
	34.25	the dangerous animals in the **land,** so that my sheep can live
	34.27	crops, and everyone will live in safety on his own **land.**
	34.29	them fertile fields and put an end to hunger in the **land.**
	35. 4	I will leave your cities in ruins And your **land** desolate;
	35.10	and Israel, together with their **lands,** belonged to you and
	36. 5	they captured my **land** and took possession of its pastures.
	36. 9	will make sure that your **land** is ploughed again and that
	36.12	bring you, my people Israel, back to live again in the **land.**
	36.12	It will be your own **land,** and it will never again let
	36.13	true that people call the **land** a man-eater, and they say
	36.15	The **land** will no longer have to listen to the nations
	36.15	The **land** will no longer rob the nation of its children.
	36.17	Israelites were living in their **land,** they defiled it by the
	36.18	they had committed in the **land** and because of the idols by
	36.20	the people of the Lord, but they had to leave his **land.'**
	36.24	nation and country and bring you back to your own **land.**
	36.28	Then you will live in the **land** I gave your ancestors.
	36.35	Everyone will say how this **land,** which was once a wilderness,
	37.14	them back to life, and let them live in their own **land.**
	37.21	gather them together, and bring them back to their own **land.**
	37.22	into one nation in the **land,** on the mountains of Israel.
	37.25	They will live on the **land** I gave to my servant Jacob,
	37.25	the **land** where their ancestors lived.
	37.26	put my Temple in their **land,** where it will stay for ever.
	38. 6	the fighting men of the **lands** of Gomer and Beth Togarmah in
	38. 9	will attack like a storm and cover the **land** like a cloud."
	38.16	attack my people Israel like a storm moving across the **land.**
	38.16	send you to invade my **land** in order to show the nations
	39. 6	start a fire in the **land** of Magog and along all the
	39.12	to bury all the corpses and make the **land** clean again.
	39.13	Everyone in the **land** will help to bury them, and they
	39.14	chosen to travel through the **land** in order to find and bury
	39.14	on the ground, so that they can make the **land** clean.
	39.16	And so the **land** will be made clean again."
	39.26	in safety in their own **land,** with no one to threaten them,
	39.28	them back into their own **land,** not leaving even one of them
	45. 1	When the **land** is divided to give each tribe a share, one
	45. 2	be a square plot of **land** for the Temple, 250 metres along
	45. 4	contain their houses and the section of **land** for the Temple.
	45. 7	**Land** is also to be set aside for the ruling prince.
	45. 9	You must never again drive my people off their **land.**
	45.16	"All the people of the **land** must take these offerings
	46.16	prince gives any of the **land** he owns to one of his
	46.17	prince gives any of his **land** to anyone who is in his
	46.18	Any **land** he gives to his sons must be from the land
Ezek	46.18	will not oppress any of my people by taking their **land."**
	47. 8	"This water flows through the **land** to the east and down
	47.13	are the boundaries of the **land** that is to be divided among
	47.14	ancestors that I would give them possession of this **land;**
	47.21	"Divide this **land** among your tribes;
	47.22	also to receive their share of the **land** when you divide it.
	47.22	lots for shares of the **land** along with the tribes of Israel.
	48. 1	The northern boundary of the **land** runs eastwards from
	48. 1	to receive one section of **land** extending from the eastern
	48. 8	The next section of the **land** is to be set apart for
	48.14	best part of all the **land,** and none of it may be
	48.15	They may live there and use the **land.**
	48.18	The **land** that is left after the city has been built in
	48.18	to be used as farm **land** by the people who live in
	48.19	no matter which tribe he comes from, may farm that **land.**
	48.21	contains the Temple, the priests' **land,** the Levites' land,
	48.21	the remaining **land** belongs to the ruling prince.
	48.23	to receive one section of **land** running from the eastern
	48.29	"That is the way the **land** is to be divided into sections
Dan	8. 9	the south and the east and towards the **Promised Land.**
	11.16	He will stand in the **Promised Land** and have it completely in
	11.19	the fortresses of his own **land,** but he will be defeated, and
	11.28	will do as he pleases and then return to his own **land.**
	11.39	put them into high offices, and give them **land** as a reward.
	11.41	He will even invade the **Promised Land** and kill tens of thousands,
Hos	1.11	and once again they will grow and prosper in their **land.**
	2. 3	like a dry and barren **land,** and she will die of thirst.
	2.18	weapons of war from the **land,** all swords and bows, and will
	2.23	I will establish my people in the **land** and make them prosper.
	4. 1	to bring against the people who live in this **land.**
	4. 1	faithfulness or love in the **land,** and the people do not
	4. 3	And so the **land** will dry up, and everything that lives on
	5. 7	So now they and their **lands** will soon be destroyed.
	5.10	of Judah have invaded Israel and stolen **land** from her.
	5.11	she has lost **land** that was rightfully hers, because she
	6. 7	soon as they entered the **land** at Adam, they broke the
	8. 1	Enemies are swooping down on my **land** like eagles!
	9. 1	All over the **land** you have sold yourselves like prostitutes
	9. 3	not remain in the Lord's **land,** but will have to go back
	9. 4	In those foreign **lands** they will not be able to make
	9.15	evil they have done, I will drive them out of my **land.**
	10. 1	The more productive their **land** was, the more beautiful they
	13. 5	I took care of you in a dry, desert **land.**
	13. 6	you entered the good **land,** you became full and satisfied,
	14. 5	be to the people of Israel like rain in a dry **land.**
Joel	1. 6	An army of locusts has attacked our **land;**
	2. 3	In front of them the **land** is like the Garden of Eden,
	2.18	Then the Lord showed concern for his **land;**
	3. 2	Israelites in foreign countries and divided up Israel, my **land.**
Amos	2. 3	kill the ruler of Moab and all the leaders of the **land."**
	2.10	years, and gave you the **land** of the Amorites to be your
	3.11	an enemy will surround their **land,** destroy their defences,
	5.27	you into exile in a **land** beyond Damascus," says the Lord,
	7. 2	green thing in the **land,** and then I said, "Sovereign Lord,
	7. 4	ocean under the earth, and started to burn up the **land.**
	7.11	Israel will be taken away from their **land** into exile.' "
	7.17	Your **land** will be divided up and given to others, and you
	7.17	Israel will certainly be taken away from their own **land** into exile.' "
	8. 8	will quake, and everyone in the **land** will be in distress.
	8.11	"The time is coming when I will send famine on the **land.**
	9.14	I will bring my people back to their **land.**
	9.15	plant my people on the **land** I gave them, and they will
Obad	17	of Jacob will possess the **land** that is theirs by right.
Jon	1. 9	the Lord, the God of heaven, who made **land** and sea."
	2. 6	mountains, into the **land** whose gates lock shut for ever.
Mic	2. 4	The Lord has taken our **land** away And given it to those
	2. 5	the time comes for the **land** to be given back to the
	2.12	pasture full of sheep, your **land** will once again be filled
	5.11	the cities in your **land** and tear down all your defences.
	5.14	of the goddess Asherah in your **land** and destroy your cities.
	7. 2	an honest person left in the **land,** no one loyal to God.
	7.14	apart in the wilderness, there is fertile **land** around them.
Nah	1.15	The wicked will never invade your **land** again.
Hab	1. 6	They are marching out across the world to conquer other **lands.**
	1. 8	Their horsemen come riding from distant **lands;**
Zeph	2. 3	all you humble people of the **land,** who obey his commands.
	2. 6	Your **land** by the sea will become open fields with shepherds'
	2. 7	The people of Judah who survive will occupy your **land.**
	2. 8	my people, and boasting that they would seize their **land.**
	2. 9	people who survive will plunder them and take their **land."**
	2.11	then every nation will worship him, each in its own **land.**
Hag	1.11	have brought drought on the **land**—on its hills, cornfields,
	2. 6	"Before long I will shake heaven and earth, **land** and sea.
Zech	2.12	the Lord in his sacred **land,** and Jerusalem will be the city
	3. 9	a single day I will take away the sin of this **land.**
	5. 3	written the curse that is to go out over the whole **land.**
	5. 3	it says that every thief will be removed from the **land;**
	5. 6	a basket, and it stands for the sin of the whole **land."**
	7. 5	"Tell the people of the **land** and the priests that when they
	7.14	This good **land** was left a desolate place, with no one living
	8. 7	rescue my people from the **lands** where they have been taken,
	9. 8	I will guard my **land** and keep armies from passing through it.
	9.16	They will shine in his **land** like the jewels of a crown.
	9.17	How good and beautiful the **land** will be!
	10.10	the whole **land** will be filled with people.
	12.12	Each family in the **land** will mourn by itself:
	13. 2	of the idols from the **land,** and no one will remember them
	13. 5	I am a farmer—I have farmed the **land** all my life.'
	13. 8	and throughout the **land** two-thirds of the people will die.
	14.10	Jerusalem will tower above the **land** round it;

Zech 14.17 Lord Almighty as king, then rain will not fall on their **land.**
Mal 1. 3 I have devastated Esau's hill-country and abandoned the **land**
3.12 call you happy, because your **land** will be a good place to
Mt 2. 6 'Bethlehem in the **land** of Judah, you are by no means the
2.20 and go back to the **land** of Israel, because those who tried
4.15 "Land of Zebulun and **land** of Naphtali, on the road to
4.15 other side of the Jordan, Galilee, **land** of the Gentiles!
4.16 who live in the dark **land** of death the light will shine."
4.25 from Jerusalem, Judaea, and the **land** on the other side of
14.13 about it, so they left their towns and followed him by **land.**
14.34 and came to **land** at Gennesaret, [35] where the people recognized
Mk 6.33 towns and ran ahead by **land** and arrived at the place ahead
6.47 in the middle of the lake, while Jesus was alone on **land.**
6.53 the lake and came to **land** at Gennesaret, where they tied up
Lk 4.25 years and a severe famine spread throughout the whole **land.**
12.16 was once a rich man who had **land** which bore good crops.
21.23 distress will come upon this **land,** and God's punishment will fall
Jn 6.21 immediately the boat reached **land** at the place they were heading
21. 8 They were not very far from **land,** about a hundred metres away.
Acts 7. 3 and country and go to the **land** that I will show you.'
7. 4 God made him move to this **land** where you now live.
7.29 fled from Egypt and went to live in the **land** of Midian.
7.45 Joshua and took over the **land** from the nations that God
10.37 took place throughout the **land** of Israel, beginning in Galilee
10.39 that he did in the **land** of Israel and in Jerusalem.
13.19 destroyed seven nations in the **land** of Canaan
13.19 and made his people the owners of the **land.**
20.13 told us to do this, because he was going there by **land.**
27.27 midnight the sailors suspected that we were getting close to **land.**
Eph 6. 3 with you, and you may live a long time in the **land."**
Heb 3.11 'They will never enter the **land** where I would have given
3.18 "They will never enter the **land** where I would have given
3.19 not able to enter the **land,** because they did not believe.
4. 3 'They will never enter the **land** where I would have given
4. 5 "They will never enter that **land** where I would have given
11.29 Israelites able to cross the Red Sea as if on dry **land;**
Jas 5. 7 is as he waits for his **land** to produce precious crops.
5.17 no rain fell on the **land** for three and a half years.
Rev 10. 2 his left foot on the **land,** [3] and called out in a loud
10. 5 the sea and on the **land** raised his right hand to heaven
10. 8 hand of the angel standing on the sea and on the **land."**

LANDOWNER

Mt 21.33 "There was once a **landowner** who planted a vineyard,

LANDSLIDE

Prov 26.27 People who start **landslides** get crushed.

LANE

Lk 14.23 to the country roads and **lanes** and make people come in,

LANGUAGE

Gen 10. 5 tribes and countries, each group speaking its own **language.**
10.20 tribes and countries, each group speaking its own **language.**
10.31 tribes and countries, each group speaking its own **language.**
11. 1 whole world had only one **language** and used the same words.
11. 6 "Now then, these are all one people and they speak one **language;**
11. 7 down and mix up their **language** so that they will not
11. 9 the Lord mixed up the **language** of all the people, and from
Deut 28.49 ends of the earth, a nation whose **language** you do not know.
Neh 13.24 Half their children spoke the **language** of Ashdod
13.24 other language and didn't know how to speak our **language.**
Esth 1.22 sent a message in the **language** and the system of writing of
3.12 to be translated into every **language** and system of writing
8. 9 each province in its own **language** and system of writing
8. 9 and to the Jews in their **language** and system of writing.
Is 19.18 that time comes, the Hebrew **language** will be spoken in five
28.11 some strange-sounding **language** to teach you a lesson.
33.19 foreigners who speak a **language** that you can't understand.
Jer 5.15 and ancient nation, a nation whose **language** you do not know.
Ezek 3. 5 speaks a difficult foreign **language,** but to the Israelites.
3. 6 that spoke difficult **languages** you didn't understand,
Dan 1. 4 Ashpenaz was to teach them to read and write the Babylonian **language.**
3. 4 a loud voice, "People of all nations, races, and **languages!**
3. 7 all the nations, races, and **languages** bowed down and
3.29 of any nation, race, or **language** speaks disrespectfully of
4. 1 people of all nations, races, and **languages** in the world:
5.19 races, and **languages** were afraid of him and trembled.
6.25 the people of all nations, races, and **languages** on earth:
7.14 people of all nations, races, and **languages** would serve him.
Acts 1.19 and so in their own **language** they call that field Akeldama,
2. 4 began to talk in other **languages,** as the Spirit enabled them
2. 6 of them heard the believers speaking in his own **language.**
2. 8 all of us hear them speaking in our own native **languages?**
2.11 speaking in our own **languages** about the great things that God
14.11 in their own Lycaonian **language,** "The gods have become like men
Rom 6.19 (I use everyday **language** because of the weakness of your
1 Cor 1.17 tell it without using the **language** of human wisdom, in order
13. 1 be able to speak the **languages** of men and even of angels,
14.10 are many different **languages** in the world, yet none of them
14.11 I do not know the **language** being spoken, the person who uses
14.21 of men speaking strange **languages** I will speak to my people,
Eph 5. 4 fitting for you to use **language** which is obscene, profane,
1 Pet 2. 1 more lying or hypocrisy or jealousy or insulting **language.**
Rev 5. 9 you bought for God people from every tribe, **language,** nation,
7. 9 every race, tribe, nation, and **language,** and they stood in front
10.11 must proclaim God's message about many nations, races, **languages,**
11. 9 People from all nations, tribes, **languages,** and races will look
13. 7 was given authority over every tribe, nation, **language,** and race.
14. 6 peoples of the earth, to every race, tribe, **language,** and nation.
17.15 prostitute is sitting, are nations, peoples, races, and **languages.**

LANTERN

Jn 18. 3 they were armed and carried **lanterns** and torches.

LAP (1)

Gen 48.12 Joseph took them from Jacob's **lap** and bowed down before him
Judg 16.19 Samson to sleep in her **lap** and then called a man, who
2 Sam 12. 3 let it drink from his cup, and hold it in his **lap.**
2 Kgs 4.20 who held him in her **lap** until noon, at which time he

LAP (2)

Judg 7. 5 to him, "Separate everyone who **laps** up the water with his
7. 6 men who scooped up water in their hands and **lapped** it;
7. 7 Midianites with the three hundred men who **lapped** the water.
Ps 68.23 blood, and your dogs may **lap** up as much as they want."

LARGE

Gen 1.16 So God made the two **larger** lights, the sun to rule over
1.24 domestic and wild, **large** and small"—and it was done.
1.26 and all animals, domestic and wild, **large** and small."
7.14 of animal, domestic and wild, **large** and small, and every
24.22 in her nose and put two **large** gold bracelets on her arms.
29. 2 from this well, which had a **large** stone over the opening.
34.21 The land is **large** enough for them also.
Ex 10.14 It was the **largest** swarm of locusts that had ever been seen
12.38 A **large** number of other people and many sheep, goats,
16.13 In the evening a **large** flock of quails flew in, enough
Num 13.28 and their cities are very **large** and well fortified.
14.12 a nation that is **larger** and more powerful than they are!"
22.15 Then Balak sent a **larger** number of leaders, who were
26.54 a large share to a **large** tribe and a small one to
33.54 by drawing lots, giving a **large** piece of property to a large
Deut 6.10 give you a land with **large** and prosperous cities which you
7. 1 drive out seven nations **larger** and more powerful than you:
9. 1 Their cities are **large,** with walls that reach the sky.
9.14 father of a nation **larger** and more powerful than they are.'
17.16 is not to have a **large** number of horses for his army,
26. 5 went there, but they became a **large** and powerful nation.
27. 2 are to set up some **large** stones, cover them with plaster,
33.20 "Praise God, who made their territory **large.**
Josh 7. 3 it is not a **large** city."
10. 2 this because Gibeon was as **large** as any of the cities that
10. 2 it was **larger** than Ai, and its men were good fighters.
10.11 Israelite army, the Lord made **large** hailstones fall down on
10.27 **Large** stones were placed at the entrance to the cave, and
14.12 giants called the Anakim were there in **large** walled cities.
19. 9 Since Judah's assignment was **larger** than was needed, part
22.10 they built a **large,** impressive altar there by the river.
24.26 Then he took a **large** stone and set it up under the
1 Sam 6.14 in Beth Shemesh, and it stopped there near a **large** rock.
6.15 the gold models in it, and placed them on the **large** rock.
6.18 The **large** rock in the field of Joshua of Beth Shemesh, on
9.22 and his servant into the **large** room and gave them a place
14. 4 Philistine camp, there were two **large** jagged rocks, one on
19.22 When he came to the **large** well in Secu, he asked where
2 Sam 3.22 from a raid, bringing a **large** amount of loot with them.
12.30 He also took a **large** amount of loot from the city [31] and
13.34 on sentry duty saw a **large** crowd coming down the hill on
18. 9 as it went under a **large** oak-tree, Absalom's head got caught
20. 8 When they reached the **large** rock at Gibeon, Amasa met them.
1 Kgs 4.13 of Argob in Bashan, sixty **large** towns in all, fortified with
5.17 Solomon's command they quarried fine **large** stones for the
7.10 The foundations were made of **large** stones prepared at the quarry,
8. 5 Covenant Box and sacrificed a **large** number of sheep and
8.27 Not even all heaven is **large** enough to hold you,
8.27 so how can this Temple that I have built be **large** enough?
10. 2 She brought with her a **large** group of attendants, as well
10. 2 loaded with spices, jewels, and a **large** amount of gold.
10.10 of gold and a very **large** amount of spices and jewels.
10.11 from there a **large** amount of juniper wood and jewels.
10.16 Solomon made two hundred **large** shields, and had each
10.18 He also had a **large** throne made.
18.32 dug a trench round it, **large** enough to hold almost fourteen
20.25 call up an army as **large** as the one that deserted you,
2 Kgs 6.14 he sent a **large** force there with horses and chariots.
7. 6 like the advance of a **large** army, with horses and chariots,
12.10 Whenever there was a **large** amount of money in the box,
16.15 "Use this **large** altar of mine for the morning
17. 9 their towns, from the smallest village to the **largest** city.
18. 8 the smallest village to the **largest** city, including Gaza and
18.17 The Assyrian emperor sent a **large** army from Lachish to
25.13 the Temple, together with the **large** bronze tank, and they
25.16 the carts, and the **large** tank—were too heavy to weigh.
1 Chr 5. 9 They had **large** herds in the land of Gilead, and so they
20. 2 He also took a **large** amount of loot from the city.
22. 3 He supplied a **large** amount of iron for making nails and
22. 4 Tyre and Sidon to bring him a **large** number of cedar logs.
22. 5 So David got **large** amounts of the materials ready before he died.
22.15 carpenters, as well as a **large** number of craftsmen of every

2 Chr	2. 9	to assist yours [9]in preparing **large** quantities of timber,
	2. 9	this temple I intend to build will be **large** and magnificent.
	4. 6	The water in the **large** tank was for the priests to use
	5. 6	Covenant Box and sacrificed a **large** number of sheep and
	6.18	Not even all heaven is **large** enough to hold you,
	6.18	so how can this Temple that I have built be **large** enough?
	9. 1	She brought with her a **large** group of attendants, as well as
	9. 1	loaded with spices, jewels, and a **large** amount of gold.
	9. 9	of gold and a very **large** amount of spices and jewels.
	9.15	Solomon made two hundred **large** shields, each of which
	9.17	The king also had a **large** throne made.
	14.13	Lord and his army, and the army took **large** amounts of loot.
	14.14	plundered all those cities and captured **large** amounts of loot.
	14.15	some shepherds, capturing **large** numbers of sheep and camels.
	16. 8	the Libyans have **large** armies with many chariots and horsemen?
	17.11	brought Jehoshaphat a **large** amount of silver and other gifts,
	18. 2	with him, Ahab had a **large** number of sheep and cattle
	20. 2	"A **large** army from Edom has come from the other side of
	20.12	in the face of this **large** army that is attacking us.
	20.15	not be discouraged or be afraid to face this **large** army.
	21. 3	Their father gave them **large** amounts of gold, silver, and
	24.11	And so they collected a **large** sum of money.
	24.23	leaders, and took **large** amounts of loot back to Damascus.
	24.24	let them defeat a much **larger** Judaean army because the
	26.10	many cisterns, because he had **large** herds of livestock in
	26.11	He had a **large** army ready for battle.
	26.15	shooting arrows and for throwing **large** stones from the
	28. 5	defeat him and take a **large** number of Judaeans back to
	28. 8	them back to Samaria, along with **large** amounts of loot.
	30. 5	Passover according to the Law, in **larger** numbers than ever before.
	30.24	A **large** number of priests went through the ritual of purification.
	31. 6	sheep, and they also brought **large** quantities of gifts,
	31.10	there has been enough to eat and a **large** surplus besides.
	32. 3	The officials led a **large** number of people out and stopped
	32. 5	He also had a **large** number of spears and shields made.
Ezra	5. 8	God is being rebuilt with **large** stone blocks and with wooden
	10. 1	and confessing these sins, a **large** group of Israelites—men,
Neh	3.27	from a point opposite the **large** tower guarding the Temple as
	5. 2	Some said, "We have **large** families, we need corn to keep
	7. 4	Jerusalem was a **large** city, but not many people were
	12.31	them in charge of two **large** groups to march round the city,
	13. 5	allowed Tobiah to use a **large** room that was intended only
Job	1. 3	He also had a **large** number of servants and was the richest
	38. 5	Who decided how **large** it would be?
Ps	74.15	you dried up **large** rivers.
	80. 5	given us sorrow to eat, a **large** cup of tears to drink.
	104.25	large and wide, where countless creatures live, **large** and small alike.
Prov	16. 8	honestly earned, than to have a **large** income gained dishonestly.
Is	2.16	He will sink even the **largest** and most beautiful ships.
	4. 2	every plant and tree in the land grow **large** and beautiful.
	8. 1	large piece of writing material and write on it in **large** letters:
	22.18	up like a ball and throw you into a much **larger** country.
	36. 2	Lachish to Jerusalem with a **large** military force to demand
	54. 2	Make the tent you live in **larger;**
	57. 8	clothes and climb into your **large** beds with your lovers,
Jer	40.12	and there they gathered in **large** amounts of wine and fruit.
	41. 9	he had killed was the **large** one that King Asa had dug
	41.12	their men and overtook him near the **large** pool at Gibeon.
	43. 9	said to me, [9]"Get some **large** stones and bury them in the
	44.15	lived in southern Egypt—a **large** crowd in all—said to me,
	52.17	the Temple, together with the **large** bronze tank, and they
	52.20	two columns, the carts, the **large** tank, and the twelve bulls
Ezek	6.13	every green tree and every **large** oak, in every place where
	17.15	and sent agents to Egypt to get horses and a **large** army.
	23.24	bringing a **large** army with chariots and supply wagons.
	23.32	it is **large** and deep.
	27.25	Your merchandise was carried in fleets of the **largest** cargo ships.
	38.15	the far north, leading a **large,** powerful army of soldiers
	38.20	fish and bird, every animal **large** and small, and every human
Dan	11.10	king of Syria will prepare for war and gather a **large** army.
	11.13	will go back and gather a **larger** army than he had before.
	11.13	time comes, he will return with a **large,** well-equipped army.
	11.25	"He will boldly raise a **large** army to attack the king
Hos	10.13	your chariots and in the **large** number of your soldiers,
Amos	3.15	every **large** house will be destroyed."
	6. 2	Was their territory **larger** than yours?
	6.11	Lord gives the command, houses **large** and small will be
Jon	1.17	At the Lord's command a **large** fish swallowed Jonah, and
	3. 3	to Nineveh, a city so **large** that it took three days to
Hag	1. 9	"You hoped for **large** harvests, but they turned out to be small.
Zech	14. 4	be split in two from east to west by a **large** valley.
Mt	4.25	**Large** crowds followed him from Galilee and the Ten Towns,
	8. 1	When Jesus came down from the hill, **large** crowds followed him.
	8.30	Not far away there was a **large** herd of pigs feeding.
	9.37	his disciples, "The harvest is **large,** but there are few workers
	12.15	and **large** crowds followed him.
	13. 2	gathered round him was so **large** that he got into a boat
	14.14	and when he saw the **large** crowd, his heart was filled with
	15.30	**Large** crowds came to him, bringing with them the lame,
	18. 6	that person to have a **large** millstone tied round his neck
	19. 2	**Large** crowds followed him, and he healed them there.
	20.29	his disciples were leaving Jericho, a **large** crowd was following.
	21. 8	A **large** crowd of people spread their cloaks on the road
	23. 5	on their foreheads and arms, and notice how **large** they are!
	25.21	small amounts, so I will put you in charge of **large** amounts.
	25.23	small amounts, so I will put you in charge of **large** amounts.
	26. 9	have been sold for a **large** amount and the money given to
	26.47	With him was a **large** crowd armed with swords and clubs
	27.60	Then he rolled a **large** stone across the entrance to the tomb
Mt	28.12	they gave a **large** sum of money to the soldiers [13]and said,
Mk	2.15	**large** number of tax collectors and other outcasts were following
	3. 7	went away to Lake Galilee, and a **large** crowd followed him.
	3. 9	The crowd was so **large** that Jesus told his disciples to
	3.20	Again such a **large** crowd gathered that Jesus and his disciples
	4. 1	gathered round him was so **large** that he got into a boat
	4.32	It puts out such **large** branches that the birds come and make
	5.11	There was a **large** herd of pigs near by, feeding on
	5.21	There at the lakeside a **large** crowd gathered round him.
	6.34	the boat, he saw this **large** crowd, and his heart was filled
	8. 1	Not long afterwards another **large** crowd came together.
	9.14	disciples, they saw a **large** crowd round them and some teachers
	9.42	that person to have a **large** millstone tied round his neck
	10.46	his disciples and a **large** crowd, a blind beggar named Bartimaeus
	12.37	A **large** crowd was listening to Jesus gladly.
	14.15	he will show you a **large** upstairs room, prepared and furnished,
	15.46	Then he rolled a **large** stone across the entrance to the tomb.
	16. 3	(It was a very **large** stone.)
Lk	5. 6	and caught such a **large** number of fish that the nets
	5. 9	were all amazed at the **large** number of fish they had caught.
	5.29	among the guests was a **large** number of tax collectors and
	6.17	stood on a level place with a **large** number of his disciples.
	6.17	A **large** crowd of people was there from all over Judaea
	7.11	town called Nain, accompanied by his disciples and a **large** crowd.
	7.12	was a widow, and a **large** crowd from the town was with
	8.32	There was a **large** herd of pigs near by, feeding on
	9.37	went down from the hill, and a **large** crowd met Jesus.
	10. 2	to them, "There is a **large** harvest, but few workers to
	14.25	Once when **large** crowds of people were going along with Jesus,
	16.10	is faithful in small matters will be faithful in **large** ones;
	16.10	is dishonest in small matters will be dishonest in **large** ones.
	17. 2	better for him if a **large** millstone were tied round his neck
	19.37	the Mount of Olives, the **large** crowd of his disciples began
	22.12	He will show you a **large** furnished room upstairs, where you
	23.27	A **large** crowd of people followed him;
Jn	2. 6	jars were there, each one **large** enough to hold about a
	5. 3	A **large** crowd of sick people were lying in the porches—
	6. 2	A **large** crowd followed him, because they had seen his miracles
	6. 5	round and saw that a **large** crowd was coming to him,
	12. 9	A **large** number of people heard that Jesus was in Bethany,
	12.12	The next day the **large** crowd that had come to the
Acts	2. 6	When they heard this noise, a **large** crowd gathered.
	6. 7	disciples in Jerusalem grew **larger and larger,** and a great number
	7.17	Abraham, the number of our people in Egypt had grown much **larger.**
	10.11	down that looked like a **large** sheet being lowered by its
	11. 5	down that looked like a **large** sheet being lowered by its
	11.26	met with the people of the church and taught a **large** group.
	17. 4	women and a **large** group of Greeks who worshipped God.
	22.28	said, "I became one by paying a **large** amount of money."
	28.23	date with Paul, and a **large** number of them came that day
2 Cor	9. 6	the one who sows many seeds will have a **large** crop.
Eph	1. 8	grace of God, [8]which he gave to us in such **large** measure!
2 Tim	2.20	In a **large** house there are dishes and bowls of all kinds:
Heb	12. 1	As for us, we have this **large** crowd of witnesses round us.
Jas	3. 5	Just think how **large** a forest can be set on fire by
Rev	6. 4	He was given a **large** sword.
	8.10	A **large** star, burning like a torch, dropped from the sky
	9. 2	smoke poured out of it, like the smoke from a **large** furnace;
	12.14	the two wings of a **large** eagle in order to fly to
	18.21	stone the size of a **large** millstone and threw it into the
	19. 1	like the roar of a **large** crowd of people in heaven, saying,
	19. 6	heard what sounded like a **large** crowd, like the sound of

LASH

Deut	25. 2	The number of **lashes** will depend on the crime he has committed.
	25. 3	He may be given as many as forty **lashes,** but no more;
Dan	7. 2	from all directions and **lashing** the surface of the ocean.
2 Cor	11.24	Five times I was given the thirty-nine **lashes** by the Jews;

LAST (1)

Gen	47. 9	"My life of wandering has **lasted** a hundred and thirty years.
Lev	26.10	so plentiful that they will **last** for a year, and even then
Num	28.17	a religious festival begins which **lasts** seven days, during
Deut	20.19	its fruit-trees, even though the siege **lasts** a long time.
Josh	23.13	And this will **last** until none of you are left in this
2 Sam	7.16	descendants, and I will make your kingdom **last** for ever.
	21. 1	there was a severe famine which **lasted** for three full years.
	24.15	an epidemic on Israel, which **lasted** from that morning until
2 Kgs	8. 1	on the land, which would **last** for seven years, and that she
1 Chr	16.15	covenant, which he made to **last** for ever, [16]the covenant
	16.17	Lord made a covenant with Jacob, one that will **last** for ever.
	28. 7	I will make his kingdom **last** for ever if he continues to
Esth	1. 5	It **lasted** a whole week and was held in the gardens of
	2.12	beauty treatment for the women **lasted** a year—massages with
Job	15.29	nothing he owns will **last.**
	19.24	in stone and write them so that they would **last** for ever.
Ps	21. 4	asked for life, and you gave it, a long and **lasting** life.
	30. 5	His anger **lasts** only a moment, his goodness for a lifetime.
	33.11	his purposes **last** eternally.
	45. 6	kingdom that God has given you will **last** for ever and ever.
	49.19	his ancestors in death, where the darkness **lasts** for ever.
	72. 7	his lifetime, and may prosperity **last** as long as the moon
	72.17	may his fame **last** as long as the sun.
	74. 9	no prophets left, and no one knows how long this will **last.**
	78.66	He drove his enemies back in **lasting** and shameful defeat.
	81.15	their punishment would **last** for ever.
	89. 2	know that your love will **last** for all time, that your

Ps 89.28 to him, and my covenant with him will **last** for ever.
90. 5 we **last** no longer than a dream.
90.13 How much longer will your anger **last?**
100. 5 his love is eternal and his faithfulness **lasts** for ever.
103.17 honour the Lord, his love **lasts** for ever, and his goodness
104.31 May the glory of the Lord **last** for ever!
105.10 Lord made a covenant with Jacob, one that will **last** for ever.
111. 8 They **last** for all time;
119.89 Your word, O Lord, will **last** for ever;
119.142 Your righteousness will **last** for ever, and your law is always true.
119.152 you made them to **last** for ever.
Prov 18.24 Some friendships do not **last,** but some friends are more
27.24 Not even nations **last** for ever.
Ecc 3.14 I know that everything God does will **last** for ever.
12.11 collected proverbs are as **lasting** as firmly driven nails.
Is 24. 5 laws and by violating the covenant he made to **last** for ever.
40. 6 they **last** no longer than wild flowers.
42. 3 He will bring **lasting** justice to all.
45.17 Israel is saved by the Lord, and her victory **lasts** for ever;
45.18 formed and made the earth— he made it firm and **lasting.**
51. 6 But the deliverance I bring will **last** for ever;
51. 8 But the deliverance I bring will **last** for ever;
55. 3 I will make a **lasting** covenant with you and give you the
55.13 be a sign that will **last** for ever, a reminder of what
60.20 be your eternal light, More **lasting** than the sun and moon.
61. 7 Your joy will **last** for ever.
66.12 The Lord says, "I will bring you **lasting** prosperity;
Jer 31.36 long as the natural order **lasts,** so long will Israel be a
48.30 amount to nothing, and the things they do will not **last.**
Ezek 4. 4 you to one day for each year their punishment will **last.**
4.10 a day, and it will have to **last** until the next day.
16.60 I will make a covenant with you that will **last** for ever.
25.12 Judah, and that revenge has brought **lasting** guilt on Edom.
39. 9 and clubs, and will have enough to **last** for seven years.
Dan 2.44 destroy all those empires, and then **last** for ever.
4.34 will rule for ever, and his kingdom will **last** for all time.
7.14 His authority would **last** for ever, and his kingdom would never end.
11. 6 But the alliance will not **last,** and she, her husband, her
Mt 5.18 long as heaven and earth **last,** not the least point nor the
12.25 into groups which fight each other will not **last** very long.
13.21 it does not sink deep into them, and they don't **last** long.
27.45 country was covered with darkness, which **lasted** for three hours.
Mk 3.26 divides into groups, it cannot **last,** but will fall apart and
4.17 it does not sink deep into them, and they don't **last** long.
15.33 country was covered with darkness, which **lasted** for three hours.
Lk 11.17 into groups which fight each other will not **last** very long;
11.18 Satan's kingdom has groups fighting each other, how can it **last?**
Jn 6.27 instead, work for the food that **lasts** for eternal life.
Rom 11.25 is not permanent, but will **last** only until the complete
1 Cor 7.31 For this world, as it is now, will not **last** much longer.
9.25 in order to be crowned with a wreath that will not **last;**
9.25 but we do it for one that will **last** for ever.
2 Cor 3.11 was glory in that which **lasted** for a while,
3.11 how much more glory is there in that which **lasts** for ever!
4.18 What can be seen **lasts** only for a time,
4.18 but what cannot be seen **lasts** for ever.
5. 1 a home he himself has made, which will **last** for ever.
9. 9 his kindness **lasts** for ever."
Gal 3.19 it was meant to **last** until the coming of Abraham's descendant,
Heb 1. 8 "Your kingdom, O God, will **last** for ever and ever!
10.34 still possessed something much better, which would **last** for ever.
Rev 2.10 thrown into prison, and your troubles will **last** ten days.

LAST (2)

Gen 33. 7 and her children came, and **last** of all Joseph and Rachel
35.18 and as she breathed her **last,** she named her son Benoni, but
Ex 26. 5 loops matching them on the **last** piece of the second set.
26.10 on the edge of the **last** piece of one set, and fifty
36.12 loops matching them on the **last** piece of the second set.
36.17 on the edge of the **last** piece of one set and fifty
Num 2.17 first two divisions and the **last** two the Levites are to
2.25 The division of Dan shall march **last.**
14.33 for your unfaithfulness, until the **last** one of you dies.
24.19 Israel will trample them down And wipe out the **last** survivors."
Deut 3.11 (King Og was the **last** of the Rephaim.
Josh 12. 4 Og of Bashan, who was one of the **last** of the Rephaim;
13.12 the kingdom of Og, the **last** of the Rephaim, who had ruled
1 Sam 25.22 I don't kill every **last** one of those men before morning!"
2 Sam 14. 7 They will destroy my **last** hope and leave my husband without
15.17 men were leaving the city, they stopped at the **last** house.
19.11 "Why should you be the **last** to help bring the king back
19.12 why should you be the **last** to bring me back?"
23. 1 These are David's **last** words:
1 Kgs 2. 1 called his son Solomon and gave him his **last** instructions:
17.12 That will be our **last** meal, and then we will starve to
19.19 teams ahead of him, and he was ploughing with the **last** one.
2 Kgs 4. 6 "That was the **last** one," one of her sons answered.
1 Chr 26. 6 the **last** two were especially talented.
2 Chr 7. 9 On the **last** day they had a closing celebration, [10] and on
Neh 3.32 and the merchants built the **last** section, from the room at
8.18 of the festival to the **last** they read a part of God's
Esth 8.11 slaughter them to the **last** man and take their possessions.
Job 16. 3 Do you always have to have the **last** word?
27.19 One **last** time they will lie down rich, and when they
42.12 The Lord blessed the **last** part of Job's life even more
Ps 75. 8 they drink it down to the **last** drop.
Prov 16. 1 We may make our plans, but God has the **last** word.
18.14 are sick, but if you lose it, your **last** hope is gone.
Is 24.13 off every tree and the **last** grapes picked from the vines.
44. 6 "I am the first, the **last,** the only God;
48.12 I am God, the first, the **last,** the only God!
Jer 25.19 **Last** of all, the king of Babylonia will drink from it.
Ezek 5.12 and I will scatter the **last** third to the winds and pursue
40.15 to the far side of the **last** room was twenty-five metres.
Zeph 1. 4 I will destroy the **last** trace of the worship of Baal there,
Zech 4. 7 and as you put the **last** stone in place, the people will
Mt 5.26 I tell you, until you pay the **last** penny of your fine.
19.30 now are first will be **last,**
19.30 and many who now are **last** will be first.
20. 8 with those who were hired **last** and ending with those who
20.12 'These men who were hired **last** worked only one hour,'
20.14 this man who was hired **last** as much as I have given
20.16 concluded, "So those who are **last** will be first,
20.16 and those who are first will be **last."**
21.37 **Last** of all he sent his son to them.
22.27 **Last** of all, the woman died.
27.19 because in a dream **last** night I suffered much on account
27.50 Jesus again gave a loud cry and breathed his **last.**
27.64 This **last** lie would be even worse than the first one."
Mk 9.35 be first must place himself **last** of all and be the servant
10.31 now are first will be **last,**
10.31 and many who now are **last** will be first."
12. 6 **Last** of all, then, he sent his son to the tenants.
12.22 **Last** of all, the woman died.
16.14 **Last** of all, Jesus appeared to the eleven disciples as
Lk 1.25 "Now at **last** the Lord has helped me," she said.
12.59 I tell you, until you pay the **last** penny of your fine."
13.30 Then those who are now **last** will be first,
13.30 and those who are now first will be **last."**
15.17 At **last** he came to his senses and said, 'All my father's
18. 4 refused to act, but at **last** he said to himself, 'Even though
20.32 **Last** of all, the woman died.
24.18 the things that have been happening there these **last** few days?"
Jn 6.39 that I should raise them all to life on the **last day.**
6.40 And I will raise them to life on the **last day."**
6.44 and I will raise him to life on the **last day.**
6.54 and I will raise him to life on the **last day.**
7.37 On the **last** and most important day of the festival Jesus
11.24 she replied, "that he will rise to life on the **last day."**
12.48 words I have spoken will be his judge on the **last day!**
Acts 2.17 'This is what I will do in the **last days,** God says:
7.18 At **last** a king who did not know about Joseph began to
12.10 the second, and came at **last** to the iron gate leading into
12.16 At **last** they opened the door, and when they saw him,
19.35 At **last** the town clerk was able to calm the crowd.
27.23 For **last** night an angel of the God to whom I belong
Rom 1.10 his good will may at **last** make it possible for me to
1 Cor 4. 9 God has given the very **last** place to us apostles, like men
15. 8 **Last** of all he appeared also to me—even though I am
15.26 The **last** enemy to be defeated will be death.
15.45 but the **last Adam** is the life-giving Spirit.
15.51 all die, but when the **last** trumpet sounds, we shall all be
2 Cor 8.10 is better for you to finish now what you began **last** year.
9. 2 Achaia," I said, "have been ready to help since **last** year."
1 Thes 2.16 And now God's anger has at **last** come down on them!
2 Tim 3. 1 Remember that there will be difficult times in the **last days.**
Heb 1. 2 the prophets, [2] but in these **last days** he has spoken to us
Jas 5. 3 You have piled up riches in these **last days.**
1 Pet 1.20 the world and was revealed in these **last days** for your sake.
2 Pet 3. 3 understand that in these **last days** some people will appear whose
Jude 18 said to you, "When the **last days** come, people will appear
Rev 1. 8 am the first and the **last,"** says the Lord God Almighty, who
1.17 I am the first and the **last.**
2. 8 who is the first and the **last,** who died and lived again.
15. 1 plagues, which are the **last** ones, because they are the final
21. 6 I am the first and the **last,** the beginning and the end.
21. 9 bowls full of the seven **last** plagues came to me and said,
22.13 I am the first and the **last,** the beginning and the end."

LATE (1)

Gen 24.11 It was **late** afternoon, the time when women came out to get
Judg 5.28 "Why is his chariot so **late** in coming?"
19.10 It was **late** in the day when they came near Jebus (that
2 Sam 11. 2 One day, **late** in the afternoon, David got up from his nap
21. 9 It was **late** in the spring, at the beginning of the barley
Ps 127. 2 hard for a living, getting up early and going to bed **late.**
Prov 31.18 of everything she makes, and works **late** into the night.
Jer 6. 4 they will say, "It's too **late,** the day is almost over, and
51. 9 said, 'We tried to help Babylonia, but it was too **late.**
Mt 14.15 said, "It is already very **late,** and this is a lonely place.
25. 5 The bridegroom was **late** in coming, so the girls began to
Mk 6.35 When it was getting **late,** his disciples came to him and said,
6.35 "It is already very **late,** and this is a lonely place.
11.11 But since it was already **late** in the day, he went out
Jn 20.19 **late** that Sunday evening, and the disciples were gathered together
Acts 4. 3 them in jail until the next day, since it was already **late.**

LATE (2)

2 Kgs 10.13 met some relatives of the **late** King Ahaziah of Judah and
2 Chr 23. 3 Jehoiada said to them, "Here is the son of the **late** king!

LATER

Mt 16.21 to death, but three days **later** I will be raised to life."
17. 1 Six days **later** Jesus took with him Peter and the brothers
17.23 but three days **later** he will be raised to life."
20.19 but three days **later** he will be raised to life."
21.29 to,' he answered, but **later** he changed his mind and went.

Mt 21.32 this, you did not **later** change your minds and believe him.
25.11 "**Later** the other girls arrived.
26.61 down God's Temple and three days **later** build it up again."'
27.63 alive he said, 'I will be raised to life three days **later.**'
Mk 2. 1 A few days **later** Jesus went back to Capernaum, and the
2.15 **Later** on Jesus was having a meal in Levi's house.
8.31 put to death, but three days **later** he will rise to life."
9. 2 Six days **later** Jesus took with him Peter, James, and John,
9.31 Three days **later,** however, he will rise to life."
10.34 but three days **later** he will rise to life."
14.70 A little while **later** the bystanders accused Peter again,
Lk 1.24 Some time **later** his wife Elizabeth became pregnant
2.21 A week **later,** when the time came for the baby to be
8. 1 Some time **later** Jesus travelled through towns and villages,
9.22 to death, but three days **later** he will be raised to life."
12.38 ready, even if he should come at midnight or even **later!**
18.33 and kill him, but three days **later** he will rise to life."
22.59 And about an hour **later** another man insisted strongly,
24. 7 men, be crucified, and three days **later** rise to life."'
24.46 rise from death three days **later,** [47]and in his name the
Jn 2. 1 Two days **later** there was a wedding in the town of Cana
6.58 like the bread that your ancestors ate, but then **later** died.
13. 7 now what I am doing, but you will understand **later."**
13.36 "but **later** you will follow me."
16.16 any more, and then a little while **later** you will see me."
16.17 and then a little while **later** we will see him;
16.19 and then a little while **later** you will see me.'
20.26 week **later** the disciples were together again indoors, and Thomas
Acts 1.15 A few days **later** there was a meeting of the believers,
5. 7 About three hours **later** his wife, not knowing what had happened,
6. 1 Some time **later,** as the number of disciples kept growing,
7.45 **Later** on, our ancestors who received the tent from their fathers
10.40 him from death three days **later** and caused him to appear,
15.36 Some time **later** Paul said to Barnabas, "Let us go back
20. 6 Unleavened Bread, and five days **later** we joined them in Troas,
20.15 A day **later** we came to Samos, and the following day we
24. 1 Five days **later** the High Priest Ananias went to Caesarea
25.13 Some time **later** King Agrippa and Bernice came to Caesarea
27.28 a little **later** they did the same and found that it was
Rom 4.11 He was circumcised **later,** and his circumcision was a sign
1 Cor 15. 4 raised to life three days **later,** as written in the Scriptures;
15.37 other grain, not the full-bodied plant that will **later** grow up.
Gal 1.18 It was three years **later** that I went to Jerusalem to
2. 1 Fourteen years **later** I went back to Jerusalem with Barnabas,
3.17 four hundred and thirty years **later,** cannot break that covenant
1 Tim 1.16 for all those who would **later** believe in him and receive
4. 1 clearly that some people will abandon the faith in **later** times;
5.24 but the sins of others are seen only **later.**
Heb 4. 7 Many years **later** he spoke of it through David in the
4. 8 had promised, God would not have spoken **later** about another day.
7.28 the vow, which came **later** than the Law, appoints the Son,
12.11 **Later,** however, those who have been disciplined by such punishment

LATEST

Acts 17.21 spend all their time telling and hearing the **latest** new thing.)

LATIN

Jn 19.20 The notice was written in Hebrew, **Latin,** and Greek.

LATRINE

2 Kgs 10.27 turned the temple into a **latrine**—which it still is today.

LATTICE

Judg 5.28 she gazed from behind the **lattice.**
Song 2. 9 He looks in through the window and glances through the **lattice.**

LAUGH

Gen 17.17 ground, but he began to **laugh** when he thought, "Can a man
18.12 So Sarah **laughed** to herself and said, "Now that I am
18.13 asked Abraham, "Why did Sarah **laugh** and say, 'Can I really
18.15 "I didn't **laugh,"** she said.
18.15 "You **laughed."**
21. 6 Sarah said, "God has brought me joy and **laughter.**
21. 6 Everyone who hears about it will **laugh** with me."
38.23 We don't want people to **laugh** at us.
1 Sam 2. 1 I **laugh** at my enemies;
2 Kgs 19.21 "The city of Jerusalem **laughs** at you, Sennacherib,
2 Chr 30.10 of Zebulun, but people **laughed** at them and ridiculed them.
36.16 messengers, ignoring his words and **laughing** at his prophets,
Neh 2.19 were planning to do, they **laughed** at us and said, "What do
Job 5.22 You will **laugh** at violence and hunger and not be afraid
8.21 He will let you **laugh** and shout again, [22]but he will
9.23 When an innocent man suddenly dies, God **laughs.**
12. 4 Even my friends **laugh** at me now;
12. 4 they **laugh,** although I am righteous and blameless;
19.18 Children despise me and **laugh** when they see me.
22.19 and innocent men **laugh** when they see the wicked punished.
30. 9 Now they come and **laugh** at me;
39.18 she begins to run, she can **laugh** at any horse and rider.
41.29 is a piece of straw, and he **laughs** when men throw spears.
Ps 2. 4 in heaven the Lord **laughs** and mocks their feeble plans.
37.13 But the Lord **laughs** at wicked men, because he knows they
39. 8 me from all my sins, and don't let fools **laugh** at me.
44.13 you did to us, and they mock us and **laugh** at us.
52. 6 then they will **laugh** at you and say, [7]"Look, here is a
Ps 59. 8 But you **laugh** at them, Lord;
69.11 I dress myself in clothes of mourning, and they **laugh** at me.
73. 8 They **laugh** at other people and speak of evil things;
74.10 How long, O God, will our enemies **laugh** at you?
74.18 O Lord, that your enemies **laugh** at you, that they are
74.22 Remember that godless people **laugh** at you all day long.
79. 4 they **laugh** at us and mock us.
89.41 all his neighbours **laugh** at him.
109.25 When people see me, they **laugh** at me;
126. 2 How we **laughed,** how we sang for joy!
Prov 1.26 So when you get into trouble, I will **laugh** at you.
14.13 **Laughter** may hide sadness.
17. 5 If you **laugh** at poor people, you insult the God who made
29. 9 a fool, the fool only **laughs** and becomes loud and abusive.
Ecc 2. 2 I discovered that **laughter** is foolish,
7. 3 Sorrow is better than **laughter;**
7. 6 When a fool **laughs,** it is like thorns crackling in a fire.
Is 22.13 Instead, you **laughed** and celebrated.
28.22 Don't **laugh** at the warning I am giving you!
37.22 "The city of Jerusalem **laughs** at you, Sennacherib,
Jer 6.10 they **laugh** at what you tell me to say.
15.17 my time with other people, **laughing** and having a good time.
48.26 Moab will roll in its own vomit, and people will **laugh.**
Lam 1. 7 Her conquerors **laughed** at her downfall.
2.15 They shake their heads and **laugh** at the ruins of Jerusalem.
3.14 People **laugh** at me all day long;
4.21 **Laugh** on, people of Edom and Uz;
Hos 7.16 will die a violent death, and the Egyptians will **laugh."**
Obad 12 You should not have **laughed** at them in their distress.
Hab 1.10 They treat kings with contempt and **laugh** at high officials.
Mt 9.24 Then they all **laughed** at him.
Mk 5.40 They **laughed** at him, so he put them all out, took the
Lk 6.21 you will **laugh!**
6.25 "How terrible for you who **laugh** now;
8.53 They all **laughed** at him, because they knew that she was dead.
14.29 and all who see what happened will **laugh** at him.
1 Cor 7.30 those who **laugh,** as though they were not happy;
Jas 4. 9 change your **laughter** into crying, your joy into gloom!

LAUNCH

1 Sam 13. 6 Then they **launched** a strong attack against the Israelites,
2 Sam 11.25 Tell him to **launch** a stronger attack on the city and capture
1 Kgs 20. 1 up, laid siege to Samaria, and **launched** attacks against it.
Ezek 29.18 "King Nebuchadnezzar of Babylonia **launched** an attack on Tyre.

LAUREL-TREE

Is 44.14 Or he might plant a **laurel-tree** and wait for the rain to

AV LAVER see BASIN

LAW
[MOSES' LAW]
see also **LAW-BREAKER, LAWFUL, LAWGIVER, LAWLESS, LAWSUIT, LAWYER**

Gen 26. 5 Abraham obeyed me and kept all my **laws** and commands."
31.36 "What **law** have I broken that gives you the right to hunt
47.26 So Joseph made it a **law** for the land of Egypt that
47.26 This **law** still remains in force today.
Ex 13. 9 to recite and study the **Law** of the Lord, because the Lord
15.25 There the Lord gave them **laws** to live by, and there he
18.16 them is right, and I tell them God's commands and **laws."**
20. 6 of generations of those who love me and obey my **laws.**
21. 1 "Give the Israelites the following **laws:**
24.12 tablets which contain all the **laws** that I have written for
25.22 I will give you all my **laws** for the people of Israel.
34.11 Obey the **laws** that I am giving you today.
34.32 Moses gave them all the **laws** that the Lord had given him
Lev 7.27 Anyone who breaks this **law** will no longer be considered
10. 9 This is a **law** to be kept by all your descendants.
10.11 people of Israel all the **laws** which I have given to you
11.46 This, then, is the **law** about animals and birds, about
13.59 This, then, is the **law** about mildew on clothing, whether
14.32 This is the **law** for the man who has a dreaded
14.54 These are the **laws** about dreaded skin-diseases;
14.57 These **laws** determine when something is unclean and when it is clean.
17. 3 of the Tent of the Lord's presence has broken the **Law.**
18. 4 Obey my **laws** and do what I command.
18. 5 Follow the practices and the **laws** that I give you;
18.26 you, must keep the Lord's **laws** and commands, [28]and then
19.37 Obey all my **laws** and commands.
20. 8 Obey my **laws,** because I am the Lord and I make you
20.22 Lord said, "Keep all my **laws** and commands, so that you will
24.22 This **law** applies to all of you, to Israelites and to
25.18 Obey all the Lord's **laws** and commands, so that you may
26. 3 you live according to my **laws** and obey my commands, [4]I will
26.15 you refuse to obey my **laws** and commands and break the
26.43 full penalty for having rejected my **laws** and my commands.
26.46 All these are the **laws** and commands that the Lord gave
Num 5.29 This is the **law** in cases where a man is jealous
6.20 the leg of the ram which by **law** belong to the priest.
9.14 The same **law** applies to everyone, whether native or foreigner."
15.16 the same **laws** and regulations apply to you and to them.
Deut 1. 5 Moab that Moses began to explain God's **laws** and teachings.
4. 1 the people, "Obey all the **laws** that I am teaching you, and
4. 5 have taught you all the **laws,** as the Lord my God told
4. 6 they hear of all these **laws,** they will say, 'What wisdom and

Deut 4. 8 no matter how great, has **laws** so just as those that I
4.14 to teach you all the **laws** that you are to obey in
4.40 Obey all his **laws** that I have given you today, and all
4.44 Moses gave God's **laws** and teachings to the people of Israel.
4.45 opposite the town of Bethpeor, that he gave them these **laws.**
5. 1 Israel, listen to all the **laws** that I am giving you today.
5.10 of generations of those who love me and obey my **laws.**
5.31 with me, and I will give you all my **laws** and commands.
5.32 Do not disobey any of his **laws.**
6. 1 "These are all the **laws** that the Lord your God commanded
6. 2 God and obey all his **laws** that I am giving you, so
6.17 sure that you obey all the **laws** that he has given you.
6.20 did the Lord our God command us to obey all these **laws?'**
6.24 God commanded us to obey all these **laws** and to honour him.
7.11 obey all the **laws** that I have given you today.
8. 1 "Obey faithfully all the **laws** that I have given you today,
8. 6 live according to his **laws** and obey him.
8.11 to obey any of his **laws** that I am giving you today.
10.13 serve him with all your heart, [13] and obey all his **laws.**
11. 1 "Love the Lord your God and always obey all his **laws.**
11. 8 "Obey all the **laws** that I have given you today.
11.22 "Obey faithfully all the **laws** that I have given you:
11.32 sure to obey all the **laws** that I am giving you today.
12. 1 "Here are the **laws** that you are to obey as long as
17.18 of the book of God's **laws** and teachings made from the
26.16 "Today the Lord your God commands you to obey all his **laws;**
26.17 him, to keep all his **laws,** and to do all that he
26.18 and he commands you to obey all his **laws.**
27. 3 plaster, [3] and write on them all these **laws** and teachings.
27. 8 with plaster write clearly every word of God's **laws."**
27.10 him and keep all his **laws** that I am giving you today."
27.26 anyone who does not obey all of God's **laws** and teachings.'
28.15 keep all his commands and **laws** that I am giving you today,
28.45 Lord your God and keep all the **laws** that he gave you.
28.61 in this book of God's **laws** and teachings, and you will be
29.29 but he has revealed his **Law,** and we and our descendants are
30.10 him and keep all his **laws** that are written in this book
30.16 him, and keep all his **laws,** then you will prosper and become
31. 9 So Moses wrote down God's **Law** and gave it to the
31.13 who have never heard the **Law** of the Lord your God will
31.24 Moses wrote God's **Law** in a book, taking care not to
31.26 "Take this book of God's **Law** and place it beside the
33. 4 We obey the **Law** that Moses gave us, our nation's most
33.10 They will teach your people to obey your **Law;**
33.21 obeyed the Lord's commands and **laws** When the leaders of
Josh 1. 7 that you obey the whole **Law** that my servant Moses gave you.
1. 8 that the book of the **Law** is always read in your worship.
8.31 had given the Israelites, as it says in the **Law of Moses:**
8.32 on the stones a copy of the **Law** which Moses had written.
8.34 aloud the whole **Law,** including the blessings and the curses,
8.34 just as they are written in the book of the **Law.**
22. 5 Make sure you obey the **law** that Moses commanded you:
23. 6 everything that is written in the book of the **Law of Moses.**
24.25 and there at Shechem he gave them **laws** and rules to follow.
24.26 Joshua wrote these commands in the book of the **Law** of God.
2 Sam 15. 3 Absalom would say, "Look, the **law** is on your side, but
22.22 I have obeyed the **law** of the Lord;
22.23 I have observed all his **laws;**
1 Kgs 2. 3 Obey all his **laws** and commands,
2. 3 as written in the **Law of Moses,** so that wherever you go
3.14 obey me and keep my **laws** and commands, as your father David
6.12 "If you obey all my **laws** and commands, I will do for
8.58 and keep all the **laws** and commands he gave our ancestors.
8.61 God, obeying all his **laws** and commands, as you do today."
9. 4 and if you obey my **laws** and do everything I have commanded
9. 6 me, if you disobey the **laws** and commands I have given you,
10. 9 you their king so that you can maintain **law** and justice."
11.33 and has not kept my **laws** and commands as his father David
11.34 David, whom I chose and who obeyed my **laws** and commands.
11.38 me completely, live by my **laws,** and win my approval by doing
2 Kgs 10.31 with all his heart the **law** of the Lord, the God of
11.12 head, and gave him a copy of the **laws** governing kingship.
14. 6 followed what the Lord had commanded in the **Law of Moses:**
17.13 which are contained in the **Law** I gave to your ancestors and
17.16 They broke all the **laws** of the Lord their God and made
17.19 of Judah did not obey the **laws** of the Lord their God;
17.26 Samaria did not know the **law** of the god of that land,
17.27 to teach the people the **law** of the god of that land."
17.34 nor do they obey the **laws** and commands which he gave to
17.37 You shall always obey the **laws** and commands that I wrote
18.12 them and disobeyed all the **laws** given by Moses, the servant
21. 8 and keep the whole **Law** that my servant Moses gave them,
22. 2 ancestor King David, strictly obeying all the **laws** of God.
22. 8 that he had found the book of the **Law** in the Temple.
23. 3 obey him, to keep his **laws** and commands with all his heart
23.24 In order to enforce the **laws** written in the book that
23.25 his heart, mind, and strength, obeying all the **Law of Moses;**
1 Chr 16.40 what was written in the **Law** which the Lord gave to Israel.
22.12 wisdom so that you may govern Israel according to his **Law.**
22.13 If you obey all the **laws** which the Lord gave to Moses
28. 7 to obey carefully all my **laws** and commands as he does now.'
2 Chr 6.16 provided that they carefully obeyed your **Law** just as he did.
7.17 father David did, obeying my **laws** and doing everything I
7.19 people ever disobey the **laws** and commands I have given you,
8.13 to the requirements of the **Law of Moses** for each holy day:
9. 8 you their king so that you can maintain **law** and justice."
12. 1 king, he and all his people abandoned the **Law** of the Lord.
15. 3 true God, without priests to teach them, and without a **law.**
17. 9 took the book of the **Law** of the Lord and went through
19. 8 involving a violation of the **Law** of the Lord or legal
19.10 any other violation of a **law** or commandment, you must

2 Chr 23.11 head, and gave him a copy of the **laws** governing kingship.
23.18 offered to the Lord in accordance with the **Law of Moses.**
25. 4 followed what the Lord had commanded in the **Law of Moses:**
29.15 Temple ritually clean, according to the **Law** of the Lord.
30. 5 Passover according to the **Law,** in larger numbers than ever before.
30.16 to the instructions in the **Law of Moses,** the man of God.
31. 3 other festivals which are required by the **Law** of the Lord.
31. 4 all their time to the requirements of the **Law** of the Lord.
31.21 or in observance of the **Law,** he did in a spirit of
33. 8 and keep the whole **Law** that my servant Moses gave them,
34. 2 ancestor King David, strictly obeying all the **laws** of God.
34.14 Law of the Lord, the **Law** that God had given to Moses.
34.15 "I have found the book of the **Law** here in the Temple."
34.31 obey him, to keep his **laws** and commands with all his heart
35.12 them according to the instructions in the **Law of Moses.**
35.26 Lord, his obedience to the **Law,** [27] and his history from
Ezra 3. 2 instructions written in the **Law of Moses,** the man of God.
7. 6 a thorough knowledge of the **Law** which the Lord, the God of
7.10 his life to studying the **Law** of the Lord, to practising it,
7.10 and to teaching all its **laws** and regulations to the people
7.11 a thorough knowledge of the **laws** and commands which the Lord
7.12 Ezra the priest, scholar in the **Law** of the God of Heaven.
7.14 to see how well the **Law** of your God, which has been
7.21 priest and scholar in the **Law** of the God of Heaven,
7.25 people in West Euphrates who live by the **Law** of your God.
7.25 You must teach that **Law** to anyone who does not know it.
7.26 If anyone disobeys the **laws** of your God or the laws of
10. 3 We will do what God's **Law** demands.
Neh 1. 7 We have not kept the **laws** which you gave us through Moses,
8. 1 priest and scholar of the **Law** which the Lord
8. 1 had given Israel through Moses, to get the book of the **Law.**
8. 3 the gate he read the **Law** to them from dawn until noon,
8. 7 places, and the following Levites explained the **Law** to them:
8. 8 an oral translation of God's **Law** and explained it so that
8. 9 the people heard what the **Law** required, they were so moved
8. 9 priest and scholar of the **Law,** and the Levites
8. 9 who were explaining the **Law** told all the people,
8.13 the Levites, went to Ezra to study the teachings of the **Law.**
8.14 They discovered that the **Law,** which the Lord gave through Moses,
8.15 according to the instructions written in the **Law."**
8.18 to the last they read a part of God's **Law** every day.
8.18 day there was a closing ceremony, as required in the **Law.**
9. 3 For about three hours the **Law** of the Lord their God was
9.13 to your people and gave them good **laws** and sound teachings.
9.14 and through your servant Moses you gave them your **laws.**
9.26 they turned their backs on your **Law.**
9.29 in pride they rejected your **laws,** although keeping your Law
9.29 your laws, although keeping your **Law** is the way to life.
9.34 our kings, leaders, and priests have not kept your **Law.**
10.28 who in obedience to God's **Law** have separated themselves from
10.29 will live according to God's **Law,** which God gave through his
10.29 and that we will keep all his **laws** and requirements.
10.34 the Lord our God, according to the requirements of the **Law.**
10.36 Temple and there, as required by the **Law,** dedicate him to God.
12.26 time of Ezra, the priest who was a scholar of the **Law.**
12.44 for the priests and the Levites which the **Law** required.
13. 1 When the **Law of Moses** was being read aloud to the people,
13. 3 people of Israel heard this **law** read, they excluded all
13.13 Zadok, a scholar of the **Law;**
Esth 1.13 expert opinion on questions of **law** and order, so he called
1.15 What does the **law** say that we should do with her?"
1.19 to be written into the **laws** of Persia and Media, so that
3. 8 they do not obey the **laws** of the empire, so it is
4.11 That is the **law;**
4.11 There is only one way to get round this **law:**
4.16 will go to the king, even though it is against the **law.**
8.13 was to be proclaimed as **law** and made known to everyone in
Job 38.33 Do you know the **laws** that govern the skies, and can you
Ps 1. 2 find joy in obeying the **Law** of the Lord, and they study
18.21 I have obeyed the **law** of the Lord;
18.22 I have observed all his **laws;**
19. 7 The **law** of the Lord is perfect;
19. 8 The **laws** of the Lord are right, and those who obey them
37.31 He keeps the **law** of his God in his heart and never
40. 7 your instructions for me are in the book of the **Law.**
78. 5 He gave **laws** to the people of Israel and commandments to
78. 5 our ancestors to teach his **laws** to their children, [6] so that
78.10 they refused to obey his **law.**
81. 4 This is the **law** in Israel, an order from the God of
89.30 if his descendants disobey my **law** and do not live according
93. 5 Your **laws** are eternal, Lord, and your Temple is holy indeed,
94.12 person you instruct, the one to whom you teach your **law!**
99. 7 they obeyed the **laws** and commands that he gave them.
105.45 his people would obey his **laws** and keep all his commands.
119. 1 are faultless, who live according to the **law** of the Lord.
119. 4 you have given us your **laws** and told us to obey them
119. 8 I will obey your **laws;**
119.11 I keep your **law** in my heart, so that I will not
119.13 I will repeat aloud all the **laws** you have given.
119.16 I take pleasure in your **laws;**
119.18 eyes, so that I may see the wonderful truths in your **law.**
119.22 their insults and scorn, because I have kept your **laws.**
119.27 Help me to understand your **laws,** and I will meditate on
119.29 the wrong way, and in your goodness teach me your **law.**
119.33 Lord, the meaning of your **laws,** and I will obey them at
119.34 Explain your **law** to me, and I will obey it;
119.36 me the desire to obey your **laws** rather than to get rich.
119.44 I will always obey your **law,** for ever and ever.
119.51 scornful of me, but I have not departed from your **law.**

Ps 119.53 I see the wicked breaking your **law,** I am filled with anger.
119.55 the night I remember you, Lord, and I think about your **law.**
119.57 I promise to obey your **laws.**
119.61 laid a trap for me, but I do not forget your **law.**
119.63 friend of all who serve you, of all who obey your **laws.**
119.70 These men have no understanding, but I find pleasure in your **law.**
119.72 The **law** that you gave means more to me than all the
119.73 give me understanding, so that I may learn your **laws.**
119.77 me, and I will live because I take pleasure in your **law.**
119.85 who do not obey your **law,** have dug pits to trap me.
119.88 love be good to me, so that I may obey your **laws.**
119.92 If your **law** had not been the source of my joy, I
119.95 are waiting to kill me, but I will meditate on your **laws.**
119.97 How I love your **law!**
119.104 I gain wisdom from your **laws,** and so I hate all bad
119.109 I have not forgotten your **law.**
119.112 I have decided to obey your **laws** until the day I die.
119.113 who are not completely loyal to you, but I love your **law.**
119.118 You reject everyone who disobeys your **laws;**
119.126 for you to act, because people are disobeying your **law.**
119.135 Bless me with your presence and teach me your **laws.**
119.136 down like a river, because people do not obey your **law.**
119.137 You are righteous, Lord, and your **laws** are just.
119.142 Your righteousness will last for ever, and your **law** is always true.
119.146 save me, and I will keep your **laws.**
119.150 My cruel persecutors are coming closer, people who never keep your **law.**
119.153 and save me, because I have not neglected your **law.**
119.155 wicked will not be saved, for they do not obey your **laws.**
119.157 and oppressors, but I do not fail to obey your **laws.**
119.160 The heart of your **law** is truth, and all your righteous
119.161 Powerful men attack me unjustly, but I respect your **law.**
119.163 I hate and detest all lies, but I love your **law.**
119.165 Those who love your **law** have perfect security, and
119.171 I will always praise you, because you teach me your **laws.**
119.172 I will sing about your **law,** because your commands are just.
119.174 I find happiness in your **law.**
119.176 me, your servant, because I have not neglected your **laws.**
147.19 message to his people, his instructions and **laws** to Israel.
147.20 they do not know his **laws.**
Prov 8.15 I help kings to govern and rulers to make good **laws.**
19.16 Keep God's **laws** and you will live longer;
28. 4 have no regard for the **law,** you are on the side of
28. 7 A young man who obeys the **law** is intelligent.
28. 9 you do not obey the **law,** God will find your prayers too
29.18 Happy is the man who keeps God's **law!**
31. 5 they drink, they forget the **laws** and ignore the rights of
Is 10. 1 You make unjust **laws** that oppress my people.
24. 5 the earth by breaking God's **laws** and by violating the
42.21 save, so he exalted his **laws** and teachings, and he wanted
51. 4 my **laws** will bring them light.
58. 2 that they are eager to know my ways and obey my **laws.**
58. 2 me to give them just **laws** and that they take pleasure in
Jer 8. 7 people, you do not know the **laws** by which I rule you.
8. 8 you say that you are wise, and that you know my **laws?**
8. 8 Look, the **laws** have been changed by dishonest scribes.
31.33 I will put my **law** within them and write it on their
33.25 night, and I have made the **laws** that control earth and sky.
44.10 lived according to all the **laws** that I gave you and your
Lam 2. 9 The **Law** is no longer taught, and the prophets have no
Ezek 4.13 to eat food which the **Law** forbids, when I scatter them to
5. 6 Jerusalem rejected my commands and refused to keep my **laws.**
5. 7 By not obeying my **laws** or keeping my commands, you have
11.12 while you were keeping the **laws** of the neighbouring nations,
11.12 you were breaking my **laws** and disobeying my commands."
11.20 Then they will keep my **laws** and faithfully obey all my commands.
18. 9 Such a man obeys my commands and carefully keeps my **laws.**
18.17 He keeps my **laws** and obeys my commands.
18.19 He kept my **laws** and followed them carefully, and so he will
18.21 stops sinning and keeps my **laws,** if he does what is right
20.11 commands and taught them my **laws,** which bring life to anyone
20.13 They broke my **laws** and rejected my commands, which bring
20.16 rejected my commands, broken my **laws,** and profaned the
20.18 Do not keep the **laws** your ancestors made;
20.19 Obey my **laws** and my commands.
20.21 They broke my **laws** and did not keep my commands, which bring
20.24 rejected my commands, broken my **laws,** profaned the Sabbath,
20.25 "Then I gave them **laws** that are not good and commands
22.26 The priests break my **law** and have no respect for what is
23.24 over to them, and they will judge you by their own **laws.**
33.15 stops sinning and follows the **laws** that give life, he will
36.27 it that you follow my **laws** and keep all the commands I
37.24 be united under one ruler and will obey my **laws** faithfully.
43.12 This is the **law** of the Temple:
44.24 the priests are to decide the case according to my **laws.**
Dan 6. 8 will be in force, a **law** of the Medes and Persians, which
6.12 "Yes, a strict order, a **law** of the Medes and Persians,
6.15 knows that according to the **laws** of the Medes and Persians
7.25 try to change their religious **laws** and festivals, and God's
9.10 to live according to the **laws** which you gave us through your
9.11 All Israel broke your **laws** and refused to listen to what
9.11 the curses that are written in the **Law of Moses,** your
9.13 giving us all the punishment described in the **Law of Moses.**
Mic 3.11 bribes, the priests interpret the **Law** for pay, the prophets
Hab 1. 4 The **law** is weak and useless, and justice is never done.
1. 7 terror, and in their pride they are a **law** to themselves.
Zeph 3. 4 is sacred, and twist the **law** of God to their own advantage.
Zech 3. 7 "If you obey my **laws** and perform the duties I have assigned
Mal 3. 7 you, have turned away from my **laws** and have not kept them.
4. 4 of my servant Moses, the **laws** and commands which I gave him
Mt 5.17 do away with the **Law of Moses** and the teachings of the

Mt 5.18 the smallest detail of the **Law** will be done away with—
5.19 other hand, whoever obeys the **Law** and teaches others to do
7.12 the meaning of the **Law of Moses** and of the teachings of
11.13 the prophets and the **Law of Moses** spoke about the Kingdom;
12. 2 "Look, it is against our **Law** for your disciples to do this
12. 4 though it was against the **Law** for them to eat it—
12. 5 not read in the **Law of Moses** that every Sabbath the priests
12. 5 Temple actually break the Sabbath **law,** yet they are not guilty?
12.10 asked him, "Is it against our **Law** to heal on the Sabbath?"
12.12 So then, our **Law** does allow us to help someone on the
15. 9 because they teach man-made rules as though they were my **laws!'"**
19. 3 him by asking, "Does our **Law** allow a man to divorce his
19. 7 then, did Moses give the **law** for a man to hand his
22.17 Is it against our **Law** to pay taxes to the Roman Emperor,
22.36 he asked, "which is the greatest commandment in the **Law?"**
22.40 whole **Law of Moses** and the teachings of the prophets depend
23. 2 and the Pharisees are the authorized interpreters of **Moses' Law.**
27. 6 and it is against our **Law** to put it in the temple
Mk 2.24 "Look, it is against our **Law** for your disciples to do that
2.26 According to our **Law** only the priests may eat this bread—
3. 4 the people, "What does our **Law** allow us to do on the
7. 7 because they teach man-made rules as though they were God's **laws!'**
7. 9 clever way of rejecting God's **law** in order to uphold your
10. 2 they asked, "does our **Law** allow a man to divorce his
10. 3 Jesus answered with a question, "What **law** did Moses give you?"
10. 5 "Moses wrote this **law** for you because you are so
12.14 is it against our **Law** to pay taxes to the Roman
12.19 to Jesus and said, [19]"Teacher, Moses wrote this **law** for us:
Lk 1. 6 God's sight and obeyed fully all the Lord's **laws** and commands.
2.22 the ceremony of purification, as the **Law of Moses** commanded.
2.23 as it is written in the **law** of the Lord:
2.24 or two young pigeons, as required by the **law** of the Lord.
2.27 do for him what the **Law** required, [28]Simeon took the child
2.39 that was required by the **law** of the Lord, they returned to
6. 2 are you doing what our **Law** says you cannot do on the
6. 4 Yet it is against our **Law** for anyone except the priests to
6. 9 What does our **Law** allow us to do on the Sabbath?
14. 3 and the Pharisees, "Does our **Law** allow healing on the
16.16 "The **Law of Moses** and the writings of the prophets were
16.17 for the smallest detail of the **Law** to be done away with.
20.22 is it against our **Law** for us to pay taxes to
20.28 to Jesus and said, [28]"Teacher, Moses wrote this **law** for us:
23.56 On the Sabbath they rested, as the **Law** commanded.
24.44 about me in the **Law of Moses,** the writings of the prophets,
Jn 1.17 God gave the **Law** through Moses, but grace and truth came
1.45 in the book of the **Law** and whom the prophets also wrote
5.10 and it is against our **Law** for you to carry your mat."
5.18 had he broken the Sabbath **law,** but he had said that God
7.19 Moses gave you the **Law,** didn't he?
7.19 But not one of you obeys the **Law.**
7.23 on the Sabbath so that **Moses' Law** is not broken, why are
7.49 does not know the **Law of Moses,** so they are under God's
7.51 "According to our **Law** we cannot condemn a man before
8. 3 The teachers of the **Law** and the Pharisees brought in a
8. 5 In our **Law** Moses commanded that such a woman must be
8.17 It is written in your **Law** that when two witnesses agree,
9.16 cannot be from God, for he does not obey the Sabbath **law."**
10.34 is written in your own **Law** that God said, 'You are gods.'
12.34 crowd answered, "Our **Law** tells us that the Messiah will live
15.25 happen so that what is written in their **Law** may come true:
18.31 yourselves take him and try him according to your own **law."**
19. 7 answered back, "We have a **law** that says he ought to die,
Acts 6.13 "is always talking against our sacred Temple and the **Law of Moses.**
7.53 the ones who received God's **law,** that was handed down by
13.15 the reading from the **Law of Moses** and from the writings of
13.38 sins from which the **Law of Moses** could not set you free.
15. 1 saved unless you are circumcised as the **Law of Moses** requires."
15. 5 Gentiles must be circumcised and told to obey the **Law of Moses."**
15.21 For the **Law of Moses** has been read for a very long
16.21 They are teaching customs that are against our **law;**
17. 7 They are all breaking the **laws** of the Emperor, saying that
18.13 people to worship God in a way that is against the **law!"**
18.15 and names and your own **law,** you yourselves must settle it.
21.20 become believers, and how devoted they all are to the **Law.**
21.21 to abandon the **Law of Moses,** telling them not to circumcise
21.24 that you yourself live in accordance with the **Law of Moses.**
21.28 the people of Israel, the **Law of Moses,** and this Temple.
22. 3 received strict instruction in the **Law** of our ancestors and was
22.12 religious man who obeyed our **Law** and was highly respected by
23. 3 judge me according to the **Law,**
23. 3 yet you break the **Law** by ordering them to strike me!"
23.29 against him had to do with questions about their own **law.**
24.14 everything written in the **Law of Moses** and the books of the
25. 8 done nothing wrong against the **Law** of the Jews or against
25.11 If I have broken the **law** and done something for which I
28.23 by quoting from the **Law of Moses** and the writings of the
Rom 1.32 They know that God's **law** says that people who live in
2.12 The Gentiles do not have the **Law of Moses;**
2.12 they sin and are lost apart from the **Law.**
2.12 The Jews have the **Law;**
2.12 they sin and are judged by the **Law.**
2.13 is not by hearing the **Law** that people
2.13 are put right with God, but by doing what the **Law** commands.
2.14 The Gentiles do not have the **Law;**
2.14 by instinct what the **Law** commands, they are their own law,
2.14 even though they do not have the **Law.**
2.15 shows that what the **Law** commands is written in their hearts.
2.17 you depend on the **Law** and boast about God;

Rom 2.18 and you have learnt from the **Law** to choose what is right;
2.20 are certain that in the **Law** you have the full content of
2.23 You boast about having God's **law**—
2.23 but do you bring shame on God by breaking his **law?**
2.25 If you obey the **Law,** your circumcision is of value;
2.25 but if you disobey the **Law,** you might as well never have
2.26 obeys the commands of the **Law,** will God not regard him as
2.27 because you break the **Law,** even though you have it written
2.27 obey the **Law,** even though they are not physically circumcised.
2.29 this is the work of God's Spirit, not of the written **Law.**
3.19 know that everything in the **Law** applies to those
3.19 who live under the **Law,** in order to stop all human
3.20 is put right in God's sight by doing what the **Law** requires;
3.20 what the **Law** does is to make man know that he has
3.21 has nothing to do with **law,**
3.21 even though the **Law of Moses** and the prophets gave their
3.27 Is it that we obey the **Law?**
3.28 God only through faith, and not by doing what the **Law** commands.
3.31 this mean that by this faith we do away with the **Law?**
3.31 instead, we uphold the **Law.**
4.13 not because Abraham obeyed the **Law,** but because he believed
4.14 to those who obey the **Law,** then man's faith means nothing
4.15 The **Law** brings down God's anger;
4.15 where there is no law, there is no disobeying of the **law.**
4.16 to those who obey the **Law,** but also to those who believe
5.13 There was sin in the world before the **Law** was given;
5.13 but where there is no **law,** no account is kept of sins.
5.20 **Law** was introduced in order to increase wrongdoing;
6.14 for you do not live under **law** but under God's grace.
6.15 we sin, because we are not under **law** but under God's grace?
7. 1 to say, my brothers, because all of you know about **law.**
7. 1 The **law** rules over people only as long as they live.
7. 2 example, is bound by the **law** to her husband as long as
7. 2 then she is free from the **law** that bound her to him.
7. 4 As far as the **Law** is concerned, you also have died because
7. 5 desires stirred up by the **Law** were at work in our bodies,
7. 6 we are free from the **Law,** because we died to that which
7. 6 old way of a written **law,** but in the new way of
7. 7 Shall we say, then, that the **Law** itself is sinful?
7. 7 But it was the **Law** that made me know what sin is.
7. 7 If the **Law** had not said, "Do not desire what belongs to
7. 8 Apart from **law,** sin is a dead thing.
7. 9 I myself was once alive apart from **law;**
7.12 So then, the **Law** itself is holy, and the commandment is holy,
7.14 We know that the **Law** is spiritual;
7.16 this shows that I agree that the **Law** is right.
7.21 So I find that this **law** is at work:
7.22 My inner being delights in the **law** of God.
7.23 But I see a different **law** at work in my body—
7.23 a law that fights against the **law** which my mind approves of.
7.23 me a prisoner to the **law** of sin which is at work
7.25 own I can serve God's **law** only with my mind,
7.25 while my human nature serves the **law** of sin.
8. 2 For the **law** of the Spirit, which brings us life in union
8. 2 Jesus, has set me free from the **law** of sin and death.
8. 3 What the **Law** could not do, because human nature was weak,
8. 4 the righteous demands of the **Law** might be fully satisfied in
8. 7 he does not obey God's **law,** and in fact he cannot obey
9. 4 he made his covenants with them and gave them the **Law;**
9.31 people, who were seeking a **law** that would put them right
10. 4 For Christ has brought the **Law** to an end, so that everyone
10. 5 this about being put right with God by obeying the **Law:**
10. 5 "Whoever obeys the commands of the **Law** will live."
13. 8 Whoever does this has obeyed the **Law.**
13.10 to love, then, is to obey the whole **Law.**
1 Cor 9. 8 to these everyday examples, because the **Law** says the same thing.
9. 9 We read in the **Law of Moses,** "Do not muzzle an ox
9.20 not subject to the **Law of Moses,** I live as though I
9.21 a Gentile, outside the Jewish **Law,** in order to win Gentiles.
9.21 This does not mean that I don't obey God's **law;**
9.21 I am really under Christ's **law.**
14.34 as the Jewish **Law** says, they must not be in charge.
15.56 to hurt from sin, and sin gets its power from the **Law.**
2 Cor 3. 6 which consists not of a written **law** but of the Spirit.
3. 6 The written **law** brings death, but the Spirit gives life.
3. 7 The **Law** was carved in letters on stone tablets, and God's
3. 7 If the **Law,** which brings death when it is in force, came
3.15 whenever they read the **Law of Moses,** the veil still covers
Gal 2.16 faith in Jesus Christ, never by doing what the **Law** requires.
2.16 our faith in Christ, and not by doing what the **Law** requires.
2.16 one is put right with God by doing what the **Law** requires.
2.18 to rebuild the system of **Law** that I tore down,
2.18 then I show myself to be someone who breaks the **Law.**
2.19 So far as the **Law** is concerned, however, I am dead—
2.19 killed by the **Law** itself—in order that I might
2.21 right with God through the **Law,** it means that Christ died
3. 2 Spirit by doing what the **Law** requires or by hearing the
3. 5 because you do what the **Law** requires or because you hear the
3.10 Those who depend on obeying the **Law** live under a curse.
3.10 is written in the book of the **Law** is under God's curse!"
3.11 God by means of the **Law,** because the scripture says, "Only
3.12 But the **Law** has nothing to do with faith.
3.12 says, "Whoever does everything the **Law** requires will live."
3.13 Christ has redeemed us from the curse that the **Law** brings;
3.17 The **Law,** which was given four hundred and thirty years later,
3.18 God's gift depends on the **Law,** then it no longer depends on
3.19 What, then, was the purpose of the **Law?**
3.19 The **Law** was handed down by angels, with a man acting as
3.21 Does this mean that the **Law** is against God's promises?
3.21 if mankind had received a **law** that could bring life, then
3.23 time for faith came, the **Law** kept us all locked up as
Gal 3.24 And so the **Law** was in charge of us until Christ came,
3.25 for faith is here, the **Law** is no longer in charge of
4. 4 and lived under the Jewish **Law,** [5] to redeem those
4. 5 those who were under the **Law,** so that we might become God's
4.21 ask those of you who want to be subject to the **Law:**
4.21 do you not hear what the **Law** says?
5. 3 to be circumcised that he is obliged to obey the whole **Law.**
5. 4 God by obeying the **Law** have cut yourselves off from Christ.
5.14 For the whole **Law** is summed up in one commandment:
5.18 the Spirit leads you, then you are not subject to the **Law.**
5.23 There is no **law** against such things as these.
6. 2 burdens, and in this way you will obey the **law** of Christ.
6.13 Even those who practise circumcision do not obey the **Law;**
Eph 2.15 He abolished the Jewish **Law** with its commandments and rules,
Phil 3. 5 as keeping the Jewish **Law** is concerned, I was a Pharisee,
3. 6 by obeying the commands of the **Law,** I was without fault.
3. 9 of my own, the kind that is gained by obeying the **Law.**
Col 2.13 of your sins and because you were Gentiles without the **Law.**
1 Tim 1. 8 We know that the **Law** is good if it is used as
1. 9 of course, that **laws** are made, not for good people,
2.14 it was the woman who was deceived and broke God's **law.**
Tit 3. 9 long lists of ancestors, quarrels, and fights about the **Law.**
Heb 7. 5 priests are commanded by the **Law** to collect a tenth from the
7.11 the levitical priesthood that the **Law** was given to the people
7.12 is changed, there also has to be a change in the **law.**
7.19 For the **Law of Moses** could not make anything perfect.
7.28 The **Law of Moses** appoints men who are imperfect to be
7.28 which came later than the **Law,** appoints the Son, who has
8. 4 are priests who offer the gifts required by the Jewish **Law.**
8.10 I will put my **laws** in their minds and write them on
9.19 to the people all the commandments as set forth in the **Law.**
9.19 on the book of the **Law** and all the people, using a
9.22 according to the **Law** almost everything is purified by blood,
10. 1 The Jewish **Law** is not a full and faithful model of the
10. 1 How can the **Law,** then, by means of these sacrifices make
10. 7 as it is written of me in the book of the **Law.'** "
10. 8 even though all these sacrifices are offered according to the **Law.**
10.16 I will put my **laws** in their hearts and write them on
10.28 Anyone who disobeys the **Law of Moses** is put to death
Jas 1.25 looks closely into the perfect **law** that sets people free,
2. 8 if you obey the **law** of the Kingdom, which is found
2. 9 guilty of sin, and the **Law** condemns you as a law-breaker.
2.12 people who will be judged by the **law** that sets us free.
4.11 Christian brother or judges him, criticizes the **Law** and judges it.
4.11 If you judge the **Law,** then you are no longer
4.11 one who obeys the **Law,** but one who judges it.
1 Jn 3. 4 is guilty of breaking God's **law,**
3. 4 because sin is a breaking of the **law.**

LAW-BREAKER

Ezek 7.21 them," says the Lord, "and **law-breakers** will take all
1 Tim 1. 9 but for **lawbreakers** and criminals, for the godless and
Jas 2. 9 guilty of sin, and the Law condemns you as a **law-breaker.**
2.11 you have become a **law-breaker** if you commit murder.

LAWFUL

see also **LEGAL**

Acts 22.25 officer standing there, "Is it **lawful** for you to whip a

LAWGIVER

Jas 4.12 God is the only **lawgiver** and judge.

LAWLESS

Ps 11. 5 the **lawless** he hates with all his heart.
Ezek 12.19 stripped bare, because everyone who lives there is **lawless.**
22. 5 countries far away sneer at you because of your **lawlessness.**
2 Pet 2. 7 who was distressed by the immoral conduct of **lawless** people.
3.17 away by the errors of **lawless** people and fall from your safe

LAWSUIT

Prov 29. 9 an intelligent man brings a **lawsuit** against a fool, the fool
Mt 5.25 someone brings a **lawsuit** against you and takes you to court,
Lk 12.58 someone brings a **lawsuit** against you and takes you to court,

LAWYER

Acts 24. 1 went to Caesarea with some elders and a **lawyer** named Tertullus.
Tit 3.13 best to help Zenas the **lawyer** and Apollos to get started on

Am **LAY (nets)** see **SPREAD**

LAY

see also **LIE (1)**

LAY (1)

Josh 6.26 Whoever **lays** the foundation will lose his eldest son;
7.23 and all the Israelites, and **laid** them down in the presence
1 Sam 19.13 she took the household idol, **laid** it on the bed, put a
2 Sam 22.16 floor of the ocean was **laid** bare, and the foundations of the
1 Kgs 6.37 foundation of the Temple was **laid** in the second month,
13.31 bury me in this grave and **lay** my body next to his.
16.34 eldest son Abiram when he **laid** the foundation of Jericho,
17.19 the room where he was staying, and **laid** him on the bed.

1 Kgs 18.33 altar, cut the bull in pieces, and **laid** it on the wood.
20. 1 he marched up, **laid** siege to Samaria, and launched attacks
2 Kgs 6.24 army against Israel and **laid** siege to the city of Samaria.
2 Chr 8.14 Following the rules **laid** down by his father David,
8.16 From the **laying** of the foundation of the Lord's Temple to
29.23 and to the other worshippers, who **laid their hands on** them.
Ezra 3.10 When the men started to **lay** the foundation of the Temple,
3.12 watched the foundation of this Temple being **laid,**
5.16 So Sheshbazzar came and **laid** its foundation;
Job 19.12 they dig trenches and **lay** siege to my tent.
38. 6 Who **laid** the corner-stone of the world?
Ps 18.15 floor of the ocean was **laid** bare, and the foundations
24. 2 waters beneath the earth and **laid** its foundations
35. 7 Without any reason they **laid** a trap for me
38.12 who want to kill me **lay** traps for me, and those who
119.61 The wicked have **laid** a trap for me,
119.110 Wicked men **lay** a trap for me, but I have not disobeyed
140. 5 they have **laid** their snares and along the path they have
Prov 8.29 I was there when he **laid** the earth's foundations.
9. 2 for a feast, mixed spices in the wine, and **laid** the table.
Ecc 1.13 God has **laid** a miserable fate upon us.
3.10 I know the heavy burdens that God has **laid** on us.
Is 21. 2 Army of Media, **lay** siege to the cities!
44.28 Jerusalem to be rebuilt and the Temple foundations to be **laid.'** "
49. 8 you settle once again in your land that is now **laid** waste.
51.13 who stretched out the heavens and **laid** the earth's foundations?
51.16 I stretched out the heavens and **laid** the earth's foundations;
Ezek 32.30 those killed in battle and are **laid** to rest, uncircumcised.
32.32 killed and **laid** to rest with all the uncircumcised
Dan 11.15 the king of Syria will **lay** siege to a fortified city and
Obad 7 Those friends who ate with you have **laid** a trap for you;
Mic 1. 6 into the valley, and will **lay** bare the city's foundations.
Zech 4. 9 He said, "Zerubbabel has **laid** the foundation of the Temple,
8. 9 the foundation was being **laid** for rebuilding my Temple.
Lk 2. 7 in strips of cloth and **laid** him in a manger—there was
6.48 his house, dug deep and **laid** the foundation on rock.
6.49 like a man who built his house without **laying** a foundation;
11.54 about many things, [54]trying to **lay** traps for him and catch
14.29 not be able to finish the tower after **laying** the foundation;
Jn 7.30 seize him, but no one **laid** a hand on him, because his
7.44 wanted to seize him, but no one **laid** a hand on him.
Acts 9.37 Her body was washed and **laid** in a room upstairs.
15.10 God to the test by **laying** a load on the backs of
Rom 15.20 so as not to build on a foundation **laid** by someone else.
1 Cor 3.10 of an expert builder and **laid** the foundation, and another
3.11 and only foundation, and no other foundation can be **laid.**
2 Cor 1. 8 The burdens **laid** upon us were so great and so heavy that
8. 8 I am not **laying** down any rules.
Eph 2.20 are built upon the foundation **laid** by the apostles and prophets,
1 Tim 4.14 the prophets spoke and the elders **laid their hands on** you.
5.22 Be in no hurry to **lay hands on** someone to dedicate him
2 Tim 1. 6 gift that God gave you when I **laid my hands on** you.
2.19 But the solid foundation that God has **laid** cannot be shaken;
Heb 6. 1 We should not **lay** again the foundation of turning away from
6. 2 of the teaching about baptisms and the **laying on of hands;**

LAY (2)

Is 34.15 Owls will build their nests, **lay eggs,** hatch their young,
Jer 17.11 dishonestly is like a bird that hatches eggs it didn't **lay.**

LAYER

1 Kgs 6.36 with walls which had one **layer** of cedar beams
6.36 for every three **layers** of stone.
7.12 Temple had walls with one **layer** of cedar beams
7.12 for every three **layers** of cut stones.
Ezra 6. 4 to be built with one **layer** of wood
6. 4 on top of every three **layers** of stone.

LAYMEN

1 Chr 9. 2 Israelite **laymen,** priests, Levites, and temple workmen.

LAZARUS (1)
Poor man in parable.

Lk 16.20 also a poor man named **Lazarus,** covered with sores,
16.23 up and saw Abraham, far away, with **Lazarus** at his side.
16.24 pity on me, and send **Lazarus** to dip his finger in some
16.25 all the good things, while **Lazarus** got all the bad things.
16.27 beg you, father Abraham, send **Lazarus** to my father's house,

LAZARUS (2)
Martha and Mary's brother.

Jn 11. 1 A man named **Lazarus,** who lived in Bethany, was ill.
11. 2 it was her brother **Lazarus** who was ill.)
11. 4 result of this illness will not be the death of **Lazarus;**
11. 5 Jesus loved Martha and her sister and **Lazarus.**
11. 6 he received the news that **Lazarus** was ill, he stayed where
11.11 then added, "Our friend **Lazarus** has fallen asleep, but I will
11.13 Jesus meant that **Lazarus** had died, but they thought he meant
11.14 Jesus told them plainly, **"Lazarus** is dead, [15]but for your sake
11.17 Jesus arrived, he found that **Lazarus** had been buried four days
11.37 Could he not have kept **Lazarus** from dying?"
11.43 said this, he called out in a loud voice, **"Lazarus,** come
12. 1 to Bethany, the home of **Lazarus,** the man he had raised from
12. 2 **Lazarus** was one of those who were sitting at the table with
12. 9 Jesus but also to see **Lazarus,** whom Jesus had raised from death.
Jn 12.10 priests made plans to kill **Lazarus** too, [11]because on his account
12.17 with Jesus when he called **Lazarus** out of the grave and

LAZY

Ex 5.17 The king answered, "You are **lazy** and don't want to work,
Prov 6. 6 **Lazy** people should learn a lesson from the way ants live.
6. 9 How long is the **lazy** man going to lie in bed?
10. 4 Being **lazy** will make you poor, but hard work will make you
10.26 Never get a **lazy** man to do something for you;
11.16 A **lazy** man will never have money, but an aggressive man
12.24 being **lazy** will make you a slave.
12.27 If you are **lazy,** you will never get what you are after,
13. 4 No matter how much a **lazy** person may want something, he
15.19 If you are **lazy,** you will meet difficulty everywhere,
18. 9 A **lazy** person is as bad as someone who is destructive.
19.15 Be **lazy** if you want to;
19.24 Some people are too **lazy** to put food in their own mouths.
20. 4 A farmer who is too **lazy** to plough his fields at the
21.25 A **lazy** man who refuses to work is only killing himself;
22.13 The **lazy** man stays at home;
24.30 I walked through the fields and vineyards of a **lazy,**
26.13 Why doesn't the **lazy** man ever get out of the house?
26.14 The **lazy** man turns over in bed.
26.15 Some people are too **lazy** to put food in their own mouths.
26.16 A **lazy** man will think he is more intelligent than seven
Ecc 10.18 When a man is too **lazy** to repair his roof, it will
Mt 25.26 'You bad and **lazy** servant!'
Rom 12.11 Work hard and do not be **lazy.**
2 Thes 3. 6 brothers who are living a **lazy** life and who do not follow
3. 7 We were not **lazy** when we were with you.
3.11 people among you who live **lazy** lives and who do nothing
Tit 1.12 "Cretans are always liars, wicked beasts, and **lazy** gluttons."
Heb 6.12 not want you to become **lazy,** but to be like those who

LEAD (1)
[LED]

Gen 15. 7 "I am the Lord, who **led** you out of Ur in Babylonia,
19.16 two daughters by the hand and **led** them out of the city.
24.27 The Lord has **led** me straight to my master's relatives."
24.48 Abraham, who had **led** me straight to my master's relative,
48.15 May God, who has **led** me to this very day, bless them!
50.24 take care of you and **lead** you out of this land to
50.25 he said, "that when God **leads** you to that land, you will
Ex 3. 1 the priest of Midian, he **led** the flock across the desert and
3.10 Egypt so that you can **lead** my people out of his country."
6.13 I have ordered you to **lead** the Israelites out of Egypt."
6.26 to whom the Lord said, **"Lead** the tribes of Israel out of
7. 3 severe punishment on Egypt and **lead** the tribes of my people
13.18 Instead, he **led** them in a roundabout way through the
15.13 Faithful to your promise, you **led** the people you had rescued;
15.22 Then Moses **led** the people of Israel away from the Red
18. 1 and the people of Israel when he **led** them out of Egypt.
19.17 Moses **led** them out of the camp to meet God, and they
20.26 not build an altar for me with steps **leading** up to it;
32. 1 has happened to this man Moses, who **led** us out of Egypt;
32. 1 so make us a god to **lead** us."
32. 4 said, "Israel, this is our god, who **led** us out of Egypt!"
32. 7 because your people, whom you **led** out of Egypt, have sinned
32. 8 saying that this is their god, who **led** them out of Egypt.
32.12 able to say that you **led** your people out of Egypt, planning
32.23 so make us a god to **lead** us.'
32.34 Now go, **lead** the people to the place I told you about.
33.12 you have told me to **lead** these people to that land, but
34.16 those foreign women, who would **lead** them to be unfaithful to
Lev 23.43 Israel live in simple shelters when he **led** them out of Egypt.
Num 10.14 the banner of the division **led** by the tribe of Judah started
10.18 the banner of the division **led** by the tribe of Reuben would
10.22 the banner of the division **led** by the tribe of Ephraim would
10.25 the banner of the division **led** by the tribe of Dan, serving
11.21 the Lord, "Here I am **leading** 600,000 people, and you say
20.12 of Israel, you will not **lead** them into the land that I
20.16 our cry and sent an angel, who **led** us out of Egypt.
21. 4 Hor by the road that **leads** to the Gulf of Aqaba, in
27.16 pray, a man who can **lead** the people [17]and can command them
31.16 Balaam's instructions and at Peor **led** the people to be
32.17 our fellow-Israelites into battle and **lead** the attack until
Deut 1. 9 you, 'The responsibility for **leading** you is too much for me.
1.30 The Lord your God will **lead** you, and he will fight for
1.38 He will **lead** Israel to occupy the land.'
3.28 his determination, because he will **lead** the people across to
7. 4 them, [4]because then they would **lead** your children away from
8. 2 how the Lord your God **led** you on this long journey through
8.15 He **led** you through that vast and terrifying desert where
9.12 because your people, whom you **led** out of Egypt, have become
10.11 told me to go and **lead** you, so that you could take
11.16 Do not let yourselves be **led** away from the Lord to
13. 2 a wonder, [2]in order to **lead** you to worship and serve gods
13. 5 evil and is trying to **lead** you away from the life that
13.10 He tried to **lead** you away from the Lord your God, who
27.18 " 'God's curse on anyone who **leads** a blind man in the
29. 5 For forty years the Lord **led** you through the desert, and
30.17 refuse to listen, and are **led** away to worship other gods,
31. 7 are the one who will **lead** these people to occupy the land
31. 8 The Lord himself will **lead** you and be with you.
31.23 You will **lead** the people of Israel into the land that I
32.12 The Lord alone **led** his people without the help of a
Josh 8. 6 will pursue us until we have **led** them away from the city.
8.10 Then he and the leaders of Israel **led** them to Ai.
24. 3 land beyond the Euphrates and **led** him through the whole land

Josh	24. 5	But I **led** you out;
Judg	3.27	then he **led** them down from the hills.
	4. 6	tribes of Naphtali and Zebulun and **lead** them to Mount Tabor.
	4.14	The Lord is **leading** you!
	5.12	**Lead** on, Deborah, lead on!
	5.12	**Lead** on! Sing a song! Lead on!
	5.12	Forward, Barak son of Abinoam, **lead** your captives away!
	9.29	I wish I were **leading** this people!
	9.39	Gaal **led** the men of Shechem out and fought Abimelech.
	10. 3	He **led** Israel for twenty-two years.
	10.18	another, "Who will **lead** the fight against the Ammonites?
	11. 6	They said, "Come and **lead** us, so that we can fight the
	11. 8	fight the Ammonites and **lead** all the people of Gilead."
	12. 7	Jephthah **led** Israel for six years.
	12. 8	After Jephthah, Ibzan from Bethlehem **led** Israel.
	12. 9	Ibzan **led** Israel for seven years, [10]then he died and was
	12.11	After Ibzan, Elon from Zebulun **led** Israel for ten years.
	12.13	After Elon, Abdon son of Hillel from Pirathon **led** Israel.
	12.14	Abdon **led** Israel for eight years, [15]then he died and was
	13.12	What kind of a life must he **lead?"**
	14. 4	was the Lord who was **leading** Samson to do this, for the
	15.20	Samson **led** Israel for twenty years while the Philistines ruled the land.
	16.26	to the boy who was **leading** him by the hand, "Let me
	20.31	Benjaminites came out to fight and were **led** away from the city.
	20.32	had planned to retreat and **lead** them away from the city on
1 Sam	8.20	to rule us and to **lead** us out to war and to
	9.22	Then Samuel **led** Saul and his servant into the large
	10. 3	One of them will be **leading** three young goats, another one
	10. 7	When these things happen, do whatever God **leads** you to do.
	11. 1	later King Nahash of Ammon **led** his army against the town of
	12. 2	king to rule you, [2]and now you have him to **lead** you.
	17.52	all along the road that **leads** to Shaaraim, as far as Gath
	18.13	David **led** his men in battle [14]and was successful in all he
	30.15	"Will you **lead** me to those raiders?"
	30.16	And he **led** David to them.
2 Sam	5. 2	was still our king, you **led** the people of Israel in battle,
	5. 2	you that you would **lead** his people and be their ruler."
	6. 2	of thirty thousand men, [2]and **led** them to Baalah in Judah,
	17.11	the sea-shore, and that you **lead** them personally in battle.
1 Kgs	6. 8	of the Temple, with stairs **leading** up to the second and
	10.19	The throne had six steps **leading** up to it, with
	11. 4	he was old they had **led** him into the worship of foreign
	14.16	Jeroboam sinned and **led** the people of Israel into sin."
	15.26	him, he sinned against the Lord and **led** Israel into sin.
	15.34	him, he sinned against the Lord and **led** Israel into sin.
	16. 2	have sinned like Jeroboam and have **led** my people into sin.
	16.13	their idolatry and because they **led** Israel into sin, Baasha
	16.19	the Lord by his own sins and by **leading** Israel into sin.
	16.26	by his sins and by **leading** the people into sin and idolatry.
	18.40	seized them all, and Elijah **led** them down to the River
	20.14	"Who will **lead** the attack?"
	20.19	The young soldiers **led** the attack, followed by the Israelite army,
	21.22	you have stirred up my anger by **leading** Israel into sin.'
	22.52	Jezebel, and King Jeroboam, who had **led** Israel into sin.
2 Kgs	3. 3	of Nebat before him, he **led** Israel into sin, and would not
	6.19	Follow me, and I will **lead** you to the man you are
	6.19	And he **led** them to Samaria.
	6.24	later King Benhadad of Syria **led** his entire army against
	10.29	sin of King Jeroboam, who **led** Israel into the sin of
	10.31	followed the example of Jeroboam, who **led** Israel into sin.
	11.12	Then Jehoiada **led** Joash out, placed the crown on his head,
	12.18	to King Hazael, who then **led** his army away from Jerusalem.
	13. 2	him he sinned against the Lord and **led** Israel into sin;
	13. 6	King Jeroboam had **led** Israel, but kept on committing them;
	13.11	evil example of King Jeroboam, who had **led** Israel into sin.
	14.24	King Jeroboam son of Nebat, who **led** Israel into sin.
	15. 9	of King Jeroboam son of Nebat, who **led** Israel into sin.
	15.18	Jeroboam son of Nebat, who **led** Israel into sin till the day
	15.24	of King Jeroboam son of Nebat, who **led** Israel into sin.
	15.28	of King Jeroboam son of Nebat, who **led** Israel into sin.
	17. 7	from the king of Egypt and had **led** them out of Egypt.
	17.21	Jeroboam made them abandon the Lord and **led** them into terrible sins.
	19. 9	the Egyptian army, **led** by King Tirhakah of Sudan,
	21. 9	obey the Lord, and Manasseh **led** them to commit even greater
	21.11	with his idols he has **led** the people of Judah into sin.
	21.16	in addition to **leading** the people of Judah into idolatry,
	23.15	by King Jeroboam son of Nebat, who **led** Israel into sin.
	23.29	king, King Neco of Egypt **led** an army to the River Euphrates
1 Chr	4.42	They were **led** by the sons of Ishi:
	8. 6	Gera, the father of Uzza and Ahihud, **led** them in this move.
	11. 2	was still our king, you **led** the people of Israel in battle,
	11. 2	you that you would **lead** his people and be their ruler."
	11. 6	mother was Zeruiah, **led** the attack and became commander.
	16. 4	some of the Levites to **lead** the worship of the Lord, the
	20. 1	usually go to war, Joab **led** out the army and invaded the
	25. 1	chose the following Levite clans to **lead** the services of worship:
	25. 1	list of persons chosen to **lead** the worship,
2 Chr	6. 5	and I did not choose anyone to **lead** my people Israel.
	9.18	Six steps **led** up to the throne, and there was a
	13.15	The Judaeans gave a loud shout, and **led** by Abijah, they
	20.16	of the valley that **leads** to the wild country near Jeruel.
	20.27	Jehoshaphat **led** his troops back to Jerusalem in triumph,
	21.11	in the Judaean highlands and **led** the people of Judah and
	21.13	kings of Israel and have **led** the people of Judah and
	21.13	as Ahab and his successors **led** Israel into unfaithfulness.
	22. 1	Some Arabs had **led** a raid and killed all King Jehoram's
	22. 2	King Omri of Israel—gave him advice that **led** him into evil.
	22. 4	Ahab's family became his advisers, and they **led** to his downfall.
2 Chr	23.11	Then Jehoiada **led** Joash out, placed the crown on his head,
	23.13	with their instruments were **leading** the celebration.
	25.11	summoned up his courage and **led** his army to the Valley of
	26.16	he grew arrogant, and that **led** to his downfall.
	29.11	incense to him and to **lead** the people in worshipping him."
	32. 3	The officials **led** a large number of people out and stopped
	32. 7	afraid of the Assyrian emperor or of the army he is **leading.**
	33. 9	Manasseh **led** the people of Judah to commit even greater
	35.20	Temple, King Neco of Egypt **led** an army to fight at
Ezra	8.21	and to ask him to **lead** us on our journey and protect
Neh	3.15	garden, as far as the steps **leading** down from David's City.
	9. 7	Lord God, chose Abram and **led** him out of Ur in Babylonia;
	9.11	a path for your people and **led** them through on dry ground.
	9.12	With a cloud you **led** them in day-time, and at night you
	9.18	bull-calf and said it was the god who **led** them from Egypt!
	11.17	He **led** the temple choir in singing the prayer of thanksgiving.
	11.23	should take turns in **leading** the temple music each day.
	12.36	Ezra the scholar **led** this group in the procession.
	12.37	up the steps that **led** to David's City, past David's palace,
	12.42	The singers, **led** by Jezrahiah, sang at the top of their voices.
	12.46	long ago, the musicians have **led** songs of praise and
Esth	6. 9	man in these robes and **lead** him, mounted on the horse,
	6.11	on the horse, and Haman **led** him through the city square,
Job	14. 1	All **lead** the same short, troubled life.
	15.19	there was no one to **lead** them away from God.
	24.13	they don't understand it or go where it **leads.**
	29.25	led them as a king **leads** his troops, and gave them comfort
	31.27	I have not been **led** astray to honour them by kissing my
	36.18	not to let bribes deceive you, or riches **lead** you astray.
Ps	5. 8	**Lead** me to do your will;
	16.11	You will show me the path that **leads** to life;
	23. 2	fields of green grass and **leads** me to quiet pools of fresh
	25. 9	He **leads** the humble in the right way and teaches them his
	25.10	With faithfulness and love he **leads** all who keep his
	26. 3	your faithfulness always **leads** me.
	27.11	want me to do, and **lead** me along a safe path, because
	31. 3	guide me and **lead** me as you have promised.
	37. 8	it only **leads** to trouble.
	42. 4	the house of God and **led** them as they walked along,
	43. 3	may they **lead** me and bring me back to Zion, your sacred
	45.14	her colourful gown she is **led** to the king, followed by her
	48.14	he will **lead** us for all time to come."
	60. 9	Who will **lead** me to Edom?
	68. 6	home to live in and **leads** prisoners out into happy freedom,
	68. 7	O God, when you **led** your people, when you marched across
	77.20	You **led** your people like a shepherd, with Moses and
	78.14	By day he **led** them with a cloud and all night long
	78.52	Then he **led** his people out like a shepherd and guided
	78.53	He **led** them safely, and they were not afraid;
	78.72	of them with unselfish devotion and **led** them with skill.
	105.37	Then he **led** the Israelites out;
	105.43	So he **led** his chosen people out, and they sang and
	106. 9	he **led** his people across on dry land.
	107. 7	He **led** them by a straight road to a city where they
	108.10	Who will **lead** me to Edom?
	136.11	He **led** the people of Israel out of Egypt;
	136.14	he **led** his people through it;
	136.16	He **led** his people through the desert;
	139.10	you would be there to **lead** me, you would be there to
Prov	3.17	Wisdom can make your life pleasant and **lead** you safely through
	6.22	Their teaching will **lead** you when you travel, protect you at night,
	10.16	for doing good is life, but sin **leads** only to more sin.
	10.28	The hopes of good men **lead** to joy, but wicked people can
	12.17	the truth, justice is done, but lies **lead** to injustice.
	12.26	his friend, but the path of the wicked **leads** them astray.
	14.12	What you think is the right road may **lead** to death.
	15.24	leads upwards to life, not the road that **leads** downwards to death.
	16.18	Pride **leads** to destruction, and arrogance to downfall.
	16.25	What you think is the right road may **lead** to death.
	16.29	Violent people deceive their friends and **lead** them to disaster.
	21. 6	but not before they **lead** you into the jaws of death.
	28.20	Honest people will **lead** a full, happy life.
Ecc	1. 8	Everything **leads** to weariness—a weariness too great for words.
	5. 6	Don't let your own words **lead** you into sin, so that you
Song	1. 7	Tell me, my love, Where will you **lead** your flock to graze?
Is	9.16	Those who **lead** these people have misled them
	19.13	They were supposed to **lead** the nation, but they have misled it.
	20. 4	The emperor of Assyria will **lead** away naked the prisoners
	37. 9	the Egyptian army, **led** by King Tirhakah of Sudan, was
	40.11	he will gently **lead** their mothers.
	40.26	The one who **leads** them out like an army, he knows how
	42.16	"I will **lead** my blind people by roads they have never travelled.
	43.17	He **led** a mighty army to destruction, an army of chariots
	47.10	Your wisdom and knowledge **led** you astray, and you said to yourself,
	48.15	I **led** him out and gave him success.
	48.21	When the Lord **led** his people through a hot, dry desert,
	49.10	hurt them, for they will be **led** by one who loves them.
	49.10	He will **lead** them to springs of water.
	51.18	There is no one to **lead** you, no one among your people
	52.12	The Lord your God will **lead** you and protect you on every
	53. 8	was arrested and sentenced and **led** off to die, and no one
	55.12	you will be **led** out of the city in peace.
	57.18	I will **lead** them and help them, and I will comfort those
	63.12	of the sea and **leading** his people through the deep water,
	63.12	**Led** by the Lord, they were as sure-footed as wild horses,
	63.14	As cattle are **led** into a fertile valley, so the Lord
	63.14	He **led** his people and brought honour to his name.
	65.10	will worship me and will **lead** their sheep and cattle to
Jer	2. 6	I rescued them from Egypt and **led** them through the wilderness:

Jer 2.17 the Lord your God, while I was **leading** you along the way.
21. 8 way that leads to life and the way that **leads** to death.
23.13 spoken in the name of Baal and have **led** my people astray.
23.32 They tell these dreams and **lead** my people astray with their
31. 9 My people will return weeping, praying as I **lead** them back.
31.32 I took them by the hand and **led** them out of Egypt.
38.22 in Judah's royal palace being **led** out to the king of
51.27 Appoint an officer to **lead** the attack.
Ezek 7.19 Gold and silver **led** them into sin.
14. 3 hearts to idols and are letting idols **lead** them into sin.
14. 4 to idols and lets them **lead** him into sin and who then
20. 6 them out of Egypt and **lead** them to a land I had
20. 9 to Israel that I was going to **lead** them out of Egypt.
20.10 "And so I **led** them out of Egypt into the desert.
20.14 the nations which had seen me **lead** Israel out of Egypt.
23. 7 Assyrian officers, and her lust **led** her to defile herself by
28.16 buying and selling, and this **led** you to violence and sin.
34.13 I will **lead** them back to the mountains and the streams of
37. 2 He **led** me all round the valley, and I could see that
38.15 place in the far north, **leading** a large, powerful army of
39. 2 in a new direction and **lead** him out of the far north
40. 7 passage three metres long that **led** to an entrance room which
40.14 The room at the far end **led** out to a courtyard.
40.19 a gateway at a higher level that **led** to the inner courtyard.
40.20 gateway on the north side that **led** into the outer courtyard.
40.22 Here seven steps **led** up to the gate, and the entrance room
40.23 gateway was another gateway **leading** to the inner courtyard,
40.26 Seven steps **led** up to it, and its entrance room was also
40.27 Here, too, there was a gateway **leading** to the inner courtyard.
40.31 Eight steps **led** up to this gate.
40.34 Eight steps **led** up to this gate.
40.37 Eight steps **led** up to this gate.
40.49 Steps **led** up to the entrance room, which was ten metres
41. 1 He measured the passage **leading** into it:
41. 3 He measured the passage **leading** into it:
41.23 the end of the passage **leading** to the Holy Place and one
41.23 at the end of the passage **leading** to the Most Holy Place.
42. 1 into the outer courtyard and **led** me to a building on the
44. 1 The man **led** me to the outer gate at the east side
44.12 Israel and in this way **led** the people into sin, I, the
46.21 Then he **led** me to the outer courtyard and showed
47. 1 The man **led** me back to the entrance of the Temple.
47. 2 of the north gate and **led** me round to the gate that
Hos 12. 9 the Lord your God who **led** you out of Egypt, I will
13. 4 "I am the Lord your God, who **led** you out of Egypt.
Amos 2. 4 They have been **led** astray by the same false gods that their
2.10 brought you out of Egypt, **led** you through the desert for
5.25 during those forty years that I **led** you through the desert.
Mic 2.13 will open the way for them and **lead** them out of exile.
2.13 Their king, the Lord himself, will **lead** them out.
6. 4 I sent Moses, Aaron, and Miriam to **lead** you.
Zech 12. 8 The descendants of David will **lead** them like the angel of
Mal 2. 8 Your teaching has **led** many to do wrong.
Mt 4. 1 Then the Spirit **led** Jesus into the desert to be tempted by
7.13 wide and the road that **leads** to it is easy, and there
7.14 narrow and the way that **leads** to it is hard, and there
15.14 when one blind man **leads** another, both fall into a ditch."
15.19 come the evil ideas which **lead** him to kill, commit adultery,
17. 1 brothers James and John and **led** them up a high mountain
27. 2 They put him in chains, **led** him off, and handed him over
27.31 Then they **led** him out to crucify him.
Mk 7.21 come the evil ideas which **lead** him to do immoral things,
8.23 blind man by the hand and **led** him out of the village.
9. 2 Peter, James, and John, and **led** them up a high mountain,
15. 1 They put Jesus in chains, **led** him away, and handed him over
15.20 Then they **led** him out to crucify him.
Lk 2.27 **Led** by the Spirit, Simeon went into the Temple.
4. 1 the Holy Spirit and was **led** by the Spirit into the desert,
6.39 "One blind man cannot **lead** another one;
22.47 speaking when a crowd arrived, **led** by Judas, one of the
23.26 The soldiers **led** Jesus away, and as they were going,
23.32 of them criminals, were also **led** out to be put to death
24.50 Then he **led** them out of the city as far as Bethany,
Jn 10. 3 he calls his own sheep by name, and he **leads** them out.
14. 4 You know the way that **leads** to the place where I am
16.13 the truth about God, he will **lead** you into all the truth.
Acts 2.28 shown me the paths that **lead** to life, and your presence will
3.15 You killed the one who **leads** to life, but God raised him
5.19 Lord opened the prison gates, **led** the apostles out, and said
7.36 He **led** the people out of Egypt, performing miracles and
7.40 they said to Aaron, 'Make us some gods who will **lead** us.
9. 8 So they took him by the hand and **led** him into Damascus.
12.10 and came at last to the iron gate **leading** into the city.
13.11 walked about trying to find someone to **lead** him by the hand.
13.50 the Jews stirred up the **leading** men of the city and the
16.30 Then he **led** them out and asked, "Sirs, what must I do
16.39 then they **led** them out of the prison and asked them to
17. 4 so did many of the **leading** women and a large group of
20.30 group will tell lies to **lead** the believers away after them.
21.38 started a revolution and **led** four thousand armed terrorists out
22.11 my companions took me by the hand and **led** me into Damascus.
23.18 The officer took him, **led** him to the commander, and said,
23.19 took him by the hand, **led** him off by himself, and asked
25.23 with the military chiefs and the **leading** men of the city.
Rom 1. 5 of Christ, in order to **lead** people of all nations to believe
2. 4 God is kind, because he is trying to **lead** you to repent.
5.21 means of righteousness, **leading** us to eternal life through Jesus
8.14 Those who are **led** by God's Spirit are God's sons.
15.18 Christ has done through me to **lead** the Gentiles to obey God.
1 Cor 3. 5 We are simply God's servants, by whom you were **led** to believe.
12. 2 were still heathen, you were **led** astray in many ways to the
1 Cor 12. 3 that no one who is **led** by God's Spirit can say
2 Cor 2.14 with Christ we are always **led** by God as prisoners in
7.10 a change of heart that **leads** to salvation—and there is no
11.29 when someone is **led** into sin, I am filled with distress.
Gal 5.18 If the Spirit **leads** you, then you are not subject to the
Eph 4.14 teaching of deceitful men, who **lead** others into error
4.26 do not let your anger **lead** you into sin,
6.18 Pray on every occasion, as the Spirit **leads.**
Col 2.15 public spectacle of them by **leading** them as captives in his
2 Thes 3. 5 May the Lord **lead** you into a greater understanding of
3.12 people and warn them to **lead** orderly lives and work to earn
2 Tim 3.15 the wisdom that **leads** to salvation through faith in Christ
Tit 1. 1 God's chosen people and to **lead** them to the truth taught by
Heb 2.10 For Jesus is the one who **leads** them to salvation.
3.16 All those who were **led** out of Egypt by Moses.
8. 9 I took them by the hand and **led** them out of Egypt.
13. 9 all kinds of strange teachings **lead** you from the right way.
1 Pet 3.18 man on behalf of sinners, in order to **lead** you to God.
2 Pet 2.14 They **lead** weak people into a trap.
3.17 that you will not be **led** away by the errors of lawless
1 Jn 5.16 a sin that does not **lead** to death, you should pray to
5.16 This applies to those whose sins do not **lead** to death.
5.16 But there is sin which **leads** to death, and I do not
5.17 is sin, but there is sin which does not **lead** to death.
Rev 2.14 who taught Balak how to **lead** the people of Israel into sin

LEAD (2)

Ex 15.10 they sank like **lead** in the terrible water.
Num 31.22 silver, bronze, iron, tin, or **lead,** is to be purified by
Ezek 22.18 metal—copper, tin, iron, and **lead**—left over after silver has
22.20 ore of silver, copper, iron, **lead,** and tin is put in a
27.12 iron, tin, and **lead** in payment for your abundant goods.
Zech 5. 7 The basket had a lid made of **lead.**

LEADER

Gen 23. 6 We look upon you as a mighty **leader;**
Ex 3.16 Go and gather the **leaders** of Israel together and tell
3.18 you must go with the **leaders** of Israel to the king of
4.29 Aaron went to Egypt and gathered all the Israelite **leaders**
12.21 Moses called for all the **leaders** of Israel and said to them,
15.15 The **leaders** of Edom are terrified;
16.22 All the **leaders** of the community came and told Moses about it,
17. 5 Moses, "Take some of the **leaders** of Israel with you, and go
17. 6 Moses did so in the presence of the **leaders** of Israel.
18.12 and Aaron and all the **leaders** of Israel went with him to
18.21 some capable men and appoint them as **leaders** of the people:
18.21 **leaders** of thousands, hundreds, fifties, and tens.
18.25 He appointed them as **leaders** of thousands, hundreds,
19. 7 went down and called the **leaders** of the people together and
22.28 evil of God, and do not curse a **leader** of your people.
24. 1 Aaron, Nadab, Abihu, and seventy of the **leaders** of Israel;
24. 9 Abihu, and seventy of the **leaders** of Israel went up the
24.14 Moses said to the **leaders,** "Wait here in the camp for
34.31 and Aaron and all the **leaders** of the community went to him,
35.27 The **leaders** brought carnelians and other jewels to be
Lev 4.15 the **leaders** of the community shall put their hands on its head,
9. 1 Moses called Aaron and his sons and the **leaders** of Israel.
Num 1. 5 These are the men, **leaders** within their tribes, who
2. 3 of Judah shall camp in their groups, under their **leaders,** as
2.10 of Reuben shall camp in their groups, under their **leaders,**
2.18 of Ephraim shall camp in their groups, under their **leaders,**
2.25 of Dan shall camp in their groups, under their **leaders,** as
4.34 command, Moses, Aaron, and the **leaders** of the community took
7. 2 the clan chiefs who were **leaders** in the tribes of Israel,
7. 3 a wagon for every two **leaders**
7. 3 and an ox for each **leader.**
7.10 The **leaders** also brought offerings to celebrate the dedication
7.11 twelve days one of the **leaders** is to present his gifts for
7.84 offerings brought by the twelve **leaders** for the dedication
10. 4 is sounded, then only the **leaders** of the clans are to gather
11.16 men who are recognized as **leaders** of the people, bring them
11.24 He assembled seventy of the **leaders** and placed them round the Tent.
11.25 he had given to Moses and gave it to the seventy **leaders.**
11.26 Two of the seventy **leaders,** Eldad and Medad, had stayed
11.30 Then Moses and the seventy **leaders** of Israel went back to camp.
13. 2 Moses, [2]"Choose one of the **leaders** from each of the twelve
13. 3 and from the wilderness of Paran he sent out **leaders,** as
14. 4 another, "Let's choose a **leader** and go back to Egypt!"
16. 1 Levite clan of Kohath, rebelled against the **leadership** of Moses.
16. 1 Peleth—and by 250 other Israelites, well-known **leaders** chosen by the community.
16.25 Then Moses, accompanied by the **leaders** of Israel, went
17. 2 give you twelve sticks, one from the **leader** of each tribe.
17. 3 There will be one stick for each tribal **leader.**
17. 6 Israelites, and each of their **leaders** gave him a stick, one
17. 9 what had happened, and each **leader** took his own stick back.
21.18 dug by princes And by **leaders** of the people, Dug with a
22. 4 The Moabites said to the **leaders** of the Midianites, "This
22. 7 So the Moabite and Midianite **leaders** took with them the
22. 8 So the Moabite **leaders** stayed with Balaam.
22.15 sent a larger number of **leaders,** who were more important
22.21 Balaam saddled his donkey and went with the Moabite **leaders.**
22.40 of the meat to Balaam and the **leaders** who were with him.
23. 6 standing by his burnt-offering, with all the **leaders** of Moab.
23.17 still standing by his burnt-offering, with the **leaders** of Moab.
24.17 He will strike the **leaders** of Moab And beat down all the
25. 4 to Moses, "Take all the **leaders** of Israel and, in obedience
27. 2 Moses, Eleazar the priest, the **leaders,** and the whole

Num	30. 1	instructions to the **leaders** of the tribes of Israel.
	31.13	Eleazar, and all the other **leaders** of the community went out
	31.26	Eleazar, together with the other **leaders** of the community,
	32. 2	Eleazar, and the other **leaders** of the community and said,
	32.28	to Eleazar, Joshua, and the other **leaders** of Israel:
	33. 1	Egypt in their tribes under the **leadership** of Moses and Aaron.
	34.18	Take also one **leader** from each tribe to help them divide it."
	36. 1	Manasseh son of Joseph, went to Moses and the other **leaders.**
Deut	1.15	the wise and experienced **leaders** you chose from your tribes,
	5.23	voice from the darkness, your **leaders** and the chiefs of your
	19.12	In that case, the **leaders** of his own town are to send
	20. 9	finished speaking to the army, **leaders** are to be chosen for
	21. 2	Your **leaders** and judges are to go out and measure the
	21. 3	Then the **leaders** of the town nearest to where the body was
	21. 6	Then all the **leaders** from the town nearest the place where
	21.19	to take him before the **leaders** of the town where he lives
	22.15	and they are to show it in court to the town **leaders.**
	22.18	Then the town **leaders** are to take the husband and beat him.
	25. 7	to go before the town **leaders** and say, 'My husband's brother
	25. 8	Then the town **leaders** are to summon him and speak to him.
	25. 9	presence of the town **leaders,** take off one of his sandals,
	27. 1	Then Moses, together with the **leaders** of Israel, said to the people,
	28.13	God will make you the **leader** among the nations and not a
	29.10	God, all of you—your **leaders** and officials, your men,
	31. 2	twenty years old and am no longer able to be your **leader.**
	31. 3	and Joshua will be your **leader,** as the Lord has said.
	31. 9	of the Lord's Covenant Box, and to the **leaders** of Israel.
	31.28	Assemble all your tribal **leaders** and officials before me,
	33. 5	Israel when their tribes and **leaders** were gathered together.
	33.16	of Joseph, Because he was the **leader** among his brothers.
	33.21	A **leader's** share was assigned to them.
	33.21	When the **leaders** of Israel were gathered together."
Josh	1. 6	for you will be the **leader** of these people as they occupy
	1.10	Then Joshua ordered the **leaders** to [11] go through the
	3. 2	Three days later the **leaders** went through the camp [3] and
	7. 6	Joshua and the **leaders** of Israel tore their clothes in grief,
	8.10	Then he and the **leaders** of Israel led them to Ai.
	8.33	The Israelites, with their **leaders,** officers, and
	9.11	Our **leaders** and all the people that live in our land
	9.15	The **leaders** of the community of Israel gave their solemn
	9.18	not kill them, because their **leaders** had made a solemn
	9.18	complained to the **leaders** about this, [19] but they answered,
	9.21	This was what the **leaders** suggested.
	14. 1	son of Nun, and the **leaders** of the families of the Israelite
	17. 4	of Nun and to the **leaders,** and said, "The Lord commanded
	19.51	son of Nun, and the **leaders** of the families of the tribes
	20. 4	to the city, and explain to the **leaders** what happened.
	21. 1	The **leaders** of the Levite families went to Eleazar the priest,
	22.32	Then Phinehas and the **leaders** left the people of Reuben
	23. 2	the elders, **leaders,** judges, and officers of the people,
	24. 1	He called the elders, the **leaders,** the judges, and the
	24.31	so as long as those **leaders** were alive who had seen for
Judg	2. 7	so as long as the **leaders** were alive who had seen for
	2.16	Lord gave the Israelites **leaders** who saved them from the raiders.
	2.17	But the Israelites paid no attention to their **leaders.**
	2.18	the Lord gave Israel a **leader,** the Lord would help him and
	2.18	the people from their enemies as long as that **leader** lived.
	2.19	But when the **leader** died, the people used to return to
	3.10	of the Lord came upon him, and he became Israel's **leader.**
	3.31	The next **leader** was Shamgar son of Anath.
	5.13	Then the faithful ones came down to their **leaders;**
	5.15	The **leaders** of Issachar came with Deborah;
	8. 6	But the **leaders** of Sukkoth said, "Why should we give your
	8.16	the desert and used them to punish the **leaders** of Sukkoth.
	9.51	man and woman in the city, including the **leaders,** ran to it.
	10. 2	He was Israel's **leader** for twenty-three years.
	10.18	There the people and the **leaders** of the Israelite tribes
	10.18	Whoever does will be the **leader** of everyone in Gilead."
	11. 5	When this happened, the **leaders** of Gilead went to bring
	11.11	So Jephthah went with the **leaders** of Gilead,
	11.11	and the people made him their ruler and **leader.**
	16.31	He had been Israel's **leader** for twenty years.
	20. 2	The **leaders** of all the tribes of Israel were present at
	21.16	So the **leaders** of the gathering said, "There are no
Ruth	4. 2	Boaz got ten of the **leaders** of the town and asked them
	4. 9	Then Boaz said to the **leaders** and all the others there,
	4.11	The **leaders** and the others said, "Yes, we are witnesses.
1 Sam	4. 3	came back to camp, the **leaders** of Israel said, "Why did the
	4.18	He had been a **leader** in Israel for forty years.
	8. 4	Then all the **leaders** of Israel met together, went to
	11. 3	The **leaders** of Jabesh said, "Give us seven days to send
	12. 2	I have been your **leader** from my youth until now.
	14.38	Then Saul said to the **leaders** of the people, "Come here
	15.17	no importance, you are the **leader** of the tribes of Israel.
	15.30	respect in front of the **leaders** of my people and all Israel.
	16. 4	to Bethlehem, where the city **leaders** came trembling to meet
	18.16	Israel and Judah loved David because he was such a successful **leader.**
	19.20	prophets dancing and shouting, with Samuel as their **leader.**
	22. 2	about four hundred men in all, and he became their **leader.**
	30.26	loot to his friends, the **leaders** of Judah, with the message,
2 Sam	1.19	"On the hills of Israel our **leaders** are dead!
	3.17	Abner went to the **leaders** of Israel and said to them,
	3.38	you realize that this day a great **leader** in Israel has died?
	4. 2	who were **leaders** of raiding parties, Baanah and Rechab,
	5. 3	So all the **leaders** of Israel came to King David at Hebron.
	6.21	and his family to make me the **leader** of his people Israel.
	7. 7	never asked any of the **leaders** that I appointed why they had
	7. 9	make you as famous as the greatest **leaders** in the world.
	10. 3	arrived in Ammon, [3] the Ammonite **leaders** said to the king,
	15.19	said to Ittai, their **leader,** "Why are you going with us?
2 Sam	17. 4	This seemed like good advice to Absalom and all the Israelite **leaders.**
	17.15	the Israelite **leaders** and what Ahithophel had given.
	19.11	and Abiathar to ask the **leaders** of Judah, "Why should you
	23. 8	Josheb Basshebeth from Tachemon, who was the **leader** of "The Three";
	23.18	the **leader** of "The Famous Thirty."
	23.19	"The Thirty" and became their **leader,** but he was not as
1 Kgs	8. 1	King Solomon summoned all the **leaders** of the tribes and
	8. 3	When all the **leaders** had gathered, the priests lifted the
	11.24	Zobah, [24] and had become the **leader** of a gang of outlaws.
	16. 2	a nobody, but I made you the **leader** of my people Israel.
	20. 7	Ahab called in all the **leaders** of the country and said,
	20. 8	The **leaders** and the people answered, "Don't pay any attention
	22.17	And the Lord said, 'These men have no **leader;**
2 Kgs	9.20	And he added, "The **leader** of the group is driving his
	10. 7	Jehu's letter was received, the **leaders** of Samaria killed
	13. 5	The Lord sent Israel a **leader,** who freed them from the Syrians,
	23. 1	King Josiah summoned all the **leaders** of Judah and Jerusalem,
1 Chr	5. 4	Tiglath Pileser, captured Beerah, a **leader** of the tribe,
	5. 7	list the following clan **leaders** in the tribe of Reuben:
	5.24	They were all outstanding soldiers, well-known **leaders** of their clans.
	6.33	Heman, the **leader** of the first choir, was the son of Joel.
	6.39	Asaph was **leader** of the second choir.
	6.44	of the clan of Merari was the **leader** of the third choir.
	7.40	They were heads of families, famous fighting men, outstanding **leaders.**
	9. 4	son Perez had as their **leader** Uthai, the son of Ammihud and
	9. 4	son Shelah had as their **leader** Asaiah, who was the head of
	9. 4	The descendants of Judah's son Zerah had Jeuel as their **leader.**
	9.17	Shallum was their **leader.**
	9.34	They were the **leaders** who lived in Jerusalem.
	11. 3	So all the **leaders** of Israel came to King David at Hebron.
	11.11	Jashobeam of the clan of Hachmon, the **leader** of "The Three."
	11.20	Joab's brother Abishai was the **leader** of "The Famous Thirty."
	11.21	"The Thirty" and became their **leader,** but he was not as
	12. 3	soldier and one of the **leaders** of "The Thirty"
	12.23	200 **leaders,** together with the men under their command
	12.23	(these **leaders** knew what Israel should do
	12.23	1,000 **leaders,** together with 37,000 men armed with shields
	15.12	to the Levites, "You are the **leaders** of the Levite clans.
	15.16	David commanded the **leaders** of the Levites to assign
	15.25	So King David, the **leaders** of Israel, and the military
	15.27	were the musicians, Chenaniah their **leader,** and the Levites
	16. 5	Asaph was appointed **leader,** with Zechariah as his assistant.
	17. 6	never asked any of the **leaders** that I appointed why they had
	17. 8	make you as famous as the greatest **leaders** in the world.
	19. 3	on King Hanun, [3] the Ammonite **leaders** said to the king, "Do
	21.16	Then David and the **leaders** of the people—all of whom were
	22.17	David commanded all the **leaders** of Israel to help Solomon.
	23. 2	all the Israelite **leaders** and all the priests and Levites.
	23.16	The **leader** among Gershom's sons was Shebuel.
	24. 5	were temple officials and spiritual **leaders** among the
	25. 1	King David and the **leaders** of the Levites chose the
	25. 9	groups of twelve, with a **leader** in charge of each group.
	26.10	(his father made him the **leader,** even though he was not the
	26.26	of families, **leaders** of clan groups, and army officers.
	26.31	Jeriah was the **leader** of the descendants of Hebron.
	27. 1	heads of families and clan **leaders** and their officials who
	27. 2	he was the **leader** of "The Thirty" (his son Amizzabad
	28. 1	work of the kingdom, the **leaders** of the clans, the
	28. 4	tribe of Judah to provide **leadership,** and out of Judah he
	28.21	and all the people and their **leaders** are at your command."
2 Chr	5. 2	King Solomon summoned all the **leaders** of the tribes and
	5. 4	When all the **leaders** had gathered, then the Levites lifted
	12. 5	King Rehoboam and the Judaean **leaders** who had gathered in
	12. 6	The king and the **leaders** admitted that they had sinned,
	13.12	God himself is our **leader** and his priests are here with trumpets,
	18.16	And the Lord said, 'These men have no **leader;**
	22. 8	group made up of Judaean **leaders** and of Ahaziah's nephews
	24. 6	he called in Jehoiada, their **leader,** and demanded, "Why
	24.10	pleased the people and their **leaders,** and they brought their
	24.17	once Jehoiada was dead, the **leaders** of Judah persuaded King
	24.23	and Jerusalem, killed all the **leaders,** and took large
	28.14	to the people and their **leaders,** [15] and the four men were
	28.21	and the homes of the **leaders** of the people, and gave it
	29.30	The king and the **leaders** of the nation told the Levites
	34.29	King Josiah summoned all the **leaders** of Judah and Jerusalem,
	35. 9	The **leaders** of the Levites—Conaniah, Shemaiah and his
	36.14	In addition, the **leaders** of Judah, the priests, and the
Ezra	2. 2	Their **leaders** were Zerubbabel, Joshua, Nehemiah, Seraiah,
	2.68	in Jerusalem, some of the **leaders** of the clans gave freewill
	5. 5	was watching over the Jewish **leaders,** and the Persian
	5. 9	"We then asked the **leaders** of the people to tell us who
	5.10	that we could inform you who the **leaders** of this work are.
	6. 7	of Judah and the Jewish **leaders** rebuild the Temple of God
	6.14	The Jewish **leaders** made good progress with the building
	8.16	I sent for nine of the **leaders:**
	8.29	hand them over to the **leaders** of the priests and of the
	8.29	the Levites, and to the **leaders** of the people of Israel in
	9. 1	been done, some of the **leaders** of the people of Israel came
	9. 2	The **leaders** and officials were the chief offenders.
	10. 5	Ezra began by making the **leaders** of the priests, of the Levites,
	10. 8	meet in Jerusalem [8] by order of the **leaders** of the people.
	10.14	time, together with the **leaders** and the judges of his city.
Neh	2.16	my fellow-Jews—the priests, the **leaders,** the officials, or
	4.14	to them and to their **leaders** and officials, "Don't be
	4.16	And our **leaders** gave their full support to the people
	4.19	people and their officials and **leaders,** "The work is spread
	5. 7	I denounced the **leaders** and officials of the people and told them,

Neh	5. 8	The **leaders** were silent and could find nothing to say.
	5.12	The **leaders** replied, "We'll do as you say.
	5.12	the priests and made the **leaders** swear in front of them to
	5.13	And the **leaders** kept their promise.
	5.17	the Jewish people and their **leaders,** besides all the people
	6.17	the Jewish **leaders** had been in correspondence with Tobiah.
	7. 5	assemble the people and their **leaders** and officials and to
	7. 7	Their **leaders** were Zerubbabel, Joshua, Nehemiah, Azariah,
	9.17	their pride they chose a **leader** to take them back to slavery
	9.27	you sent them **leaders** who rescued them from their foes.
	9.32	Our kings, our **leaders,** our priests and prophets, our
	9.34	our kings, **leaders,** and priests have not kept your Law.
	9.38	solemn written agreement, and our **leaders,** our Levites, and
	10.14	**Leaders** of the people:
	10.29	do hereby join with our **leaders** in an oath, under
	11. 1	The **leaders** settled in Jerusalem, and the rest of the
	11. 9	son of Zichri was their **leader,** and Judah son of Hassenuah
	11.14	Their **leader** was Zabdiel, a member of a leading family.
	12. 2	These men were **leaders** among all their fellow-priests in
	12.31	I assembled the **leaders** of Judah on top of the wall and
	12.32	behind the singers, followed by half the **leaders** of Judah.
	12.40	In addition to the **leaders** who were with me, [41] my group
	13.17	I reprimanded the Jewish **leaders** and said, "Look at the
Job	12.17	away the wisdom of rulers and makes **leaders** act like fools.
	12.24	He makes their **leaders** foolish
	29. 9	The **leaders** of the people would stop talking;
	34.24	to remove **leaders** and replace them with others.
Ps	68.27	smallest tribe, then the **leaders** of Judah with their group,
	68.27	followed by the **leaders** of Zebulun and Naphtali.
	80. 1	hear us, **leader** of your flock.
	83.11	Do to their **leaders** what you did to Oreb and Zeeb;
	107.32	people and praise him before the council of the **leaders.**
	118. 9	to trust in the Lord than to depend on human **leaders.**
	146. 3	Don't put your trust in human **leaders;**
	149. 8	to bind their kings in chains, their **leaders** in chains of iron;
Prov	6. 7	They have no **leader,** chief, or ruler, [8] but they store up
	28. 2	and endure when it has intelligent, sensible **leaders.**
Ecc	10.16	its king is a youth and its **leaders** feast all night long.
	10.17	his own decisions and **leaders** who eat at the proper time,
Is	1.23	Your **leaders** are rebels and friends of thieves;
	3. 3	statesmen, [3] their military and civilian **leaders,** their
	3. 6	to wear, so be our **leader** in this time of trouble."
	3. 7	Don't make me your **leader!"**
	3.12	My people, your **leaders** are misleading you, so that you do
	3.14	Lord is bringing the elders and **leaders** of his people to judgement.
	5.13	Your **leaders** will starve to death, and the common people
	9.14	day the Lord will punish Israel's **leaders** and its people;
	19.11	The **leaders** of the city of Zoan are fools!
	19.13	The **leaders** of Zoan and Memphis are fools.
	22. 3	All your **leaders** ran away and were captured before they
	24.23	on Mount Zion, and the **leaders** of the people will see his
	28. 1	the crowns of flowers on the heads of its drunken **leaders.**
	28. 3	The pride of those drunken **leaders** will be trampled underfoot.
	28. 4	fading glory of those proud **leaders** will disappear like the
	32. 1	integrity, and national **leaders** who govern with justice.
	34.12	king to rule the country, and the **leaders** will all be gone.
	43.27	your **leaders** sinned against me,
	55. 4	I made him a **leader** and commander of nations, and through
	56.10	He says, "All the **leaders,** who are supposed to warn my people,
	56.11	These **leaders** have no understanding.
	63.11	the Lord, who saved the **leaders** of his people from the sea?
Jer	10.21	I answered, "Our **leaders** are stupid;
	22.22	Your **leaders** will be blown away by the wind, your allies
	24. 1	to Babylonia, together with the **leaders** of Judah, the
	25.18	with its kings and **leaders,** were made to drink from it,
	25.19	the king of Egypt, his officials and **leaders;**
	25.34	Cry, you **leaders,** you shepherds of my people, cry out
	26.10	When the **leaders** of Judah heard what had happened, they
	26.11	the prophets said to the **leaders** and to the people, "This
	26.16	Then the **leaders** and the people said to the priests and
	29. 1	the priests, the prophets, the **leaders** of the people, and to
	29. 2	the palace officials, the **leaders** of Judah and of Jerusalem,
	32.32	with their kings and **leaders,** their priests and prophets.
	34.10	All the people and their **leaders** agreed to free their
	34.18	the priests, and all the **leaders,** made a covenant with me by
	40.13	After this, Johanan and the **leaders** of the soldiers who
	41.11	Johanan and all the army **leaders** with him heard of the
	41.13	saw Johanan and the **leaders** of the forces with him,
	41.16	Then Johanan and the **leaders** of the forces with him took
	42. 1	Then all the army **leaders,** including Johanan son of Kareah
	42. 8	together Johanan, all the army **leaders** who were with him,
	44.17	ancestors, our king and our **leaders,** used to do in the towns
	44.21	ancestors, your kings and your **leaders,** and the people of
	49.19	Then the **leader** I choose will rule the nation.
	49.38	destroy their kings and **leaders,** and set up my throne there.
	50.44	Then the **leader** I choose will rule the nation.
	51.28	the kings of Media, their **leaders** and officials, and the
	51.57	will make its rulers drunk— men of wisdom, **leaders,** and
Lam	1. 6	Her **leaders** are like deer that are weak from hunger, Whose
	1.19	The priests and the **leaders** died in the city streets,
	4.14	Her **leaders** wandered through the streets like blind men,
	4.16	He showed no regard for our priests and **leaders.**
	5.12	Our **leaders** have been taken and hanged;
Ezek	8. 1	year of our exile, the **leaders** of the exiles from Judah were
	8.11	Seventy Israelite **leaders** were there,
	8.12	do you see what the Israelite **leaders** are doing in secret?
	9. 6	So they began with the **leaders** who were standing there at
	11. 1	Azzur and Pelatiah son of Benaiah, two **leaders** of the nation.
	14. 1	Some of the **leaders** of the Israelites came to consult me
	20. 1	Some of the **leaders** of the Israelite community came to
	21.12	is meant for my people and for all the **leaders** of Israel.
Ezek	22. 6	All Israel's **leaders** trust in their own strength and commit murder.
	22.25	The **leaders** are like lions roaring
Dan	9.25	rebuild Jerusalem, until God's chosen **leader** comes, seven
	9.26	of that time God's chosen **leader** will be killed unjustly.
	11.18	But a foreign **leader** will defeat him and put an end to
	11.33	Wise **leaders** of the people will share their wisdom
	11.35	Some of those wise **leaders** will be killed, but as a
	12. 3	The wise **leaders** will shine with all the brightness of the sky.
Hos	1.11	choose for themselves a single **leader,** and once again they
	3. 4	or **leaders,** without sacrifices or sacred stone pillars,
	5.10	"I am angry because the **leaders** of Judah have invaded
	7.16	Because their **leaders** talk arrogantly, they will die
	8. 4	They appointed **leaders,** but without my approval.
	9.15	all their **leaders** have rebelled against me.
	13.10	for a king and for **leaders,** but how can they save the
Joel	1.14	Gather the **leaders** and all the people of Judah into the
Amos	2. 3	kill the ruler of Moab and all the **leaders** of the land."
Mic	1.15	The **leaders** of Israel will go and hide in the cave at
	5. 1	They are attacking the **leader** of Israel!
	5. 5	defences, we will send our strongest **leaders** to fight them.
Hab	3.13	You struck down the **leader** of the wicked and completely
Zech	10. 2	They are in trouble because they have no **leader.**
	10. 4	come rulers, **leaders,** and commanders to govern my people.
Mt	2. 6	you will come a **leader** who will guide my people Israel.' "
	15.14	They are blind **leaders** of the blind;
	20.25	have power over them, and the **leaders** have complete authority.
	23.10	Nor should you be called **'Leader',**
	23.10	because your one and only **leader** is the Messiah.
Mk	10.42	have power over them, and the **leaders** have complete authority.
	12.12	The Jewish **leaders** tried to arrest Jesus, because they knew
Lk	18.18	A Jewish **leader** asked Jesus, "Good Teacher, what must I do
	19.47	of the Law, and the **leaders** of the people wanted to kill
	22.26	like the youngest, and the **leader** must be like the servant.
	23.13	together the chief priests, the **leaders,** and the people,
	23.35	stood there watching while the Jewish **leaders** jeered at him:
Jn	3. 1	There was a Jewish **leader** named Nicodemus, who belonged to the
Acts	3.17	that what you and your **leaders** did to Jesus was due to
	4. 5	The next day the Jewish **leaders,** the elders, and the teachers
	4. 8	of the Holy Spirit, answered them, **"Leaders** of the people
	5.31	to his right-hand side as **Leader** and Saviour, to give the
	13.27	live in Jerusalem and their **leaders** did not know that he is
	14. 5	and Jews, together with their **leaders,** decided to ill-treat
	18. 8	Crispus, who was the **leader** of the synagogue, believed in the
	18.17	They all seized Sosthenes, the **leader** of the synagogue,
	24. 2	Your wise **leadership** has brought us a long period of peace,
	24. 5	the world and is a **leader** of the party of the Nazarenes.
	25. 2	priests and the Jewish **leaders** brought their charges against Paul.
	25. 5	Let your **leaders** go to Caesarea with me and accuse the man
	28.17	Paul called the local Jewish **leaders** to a meeting.
1 Cor	16.16	my brothers, [16] to follow the **leadership** of such people as these,
Gal	2. 2	a private meeting with the **leaders** I explained the gospel message
	2. 6	who seemed to be the **leaders**—I say this because it makes
	2. 6	outward appearances—those **leaders,** I say, made no new suggestions
	2. 9	who seemed to be the **leaders,** recognized that God had given
Phil	1. 1	union with Christ Jesus, including the church **leaders** and helpers:
1 Tim	3. 1	eager to be a church **leader,** he desires an excellent work.
	3. 2	A church **leader** must be without fault;
	5.17	do good work as **leaders** should be considered worthy of receiving
Tit	1. 7	For since a church **leader** is in charge of God's work,
Heb	13. 7	Remember your former **leaders,** who spoke God's message to you.
	13.17	Obey your **leaders** and follow their orders.
	13.24	Give our greetings to all your **leaders** and to all God's people.
3 Jn	9	who likes to be their **leader,** will not pay any attention to

LEADING

Gen	50. 7	court, and all the **leading** men of Egypt went with Joseph.
Ex	24.11	God did not harm these **leading** men of Israel;
Josh	22.14	Ten **leading** men went with Phinehas, one from each of the
	22.30	the priest and the ten **leading** men of the community who were
Judg	8.14	Gideon the names of the seventy-seven **leading** men of Sukkoth.
	9.46	When all the **leading** men in the fort at Shechem heard
1 Kgs	21. 8	sent them to the officials and **leading** citizens of Jezreel.
	21.11	The officials and **leading** citizens of Jezreel
2 Kgs	10. 1	of the city, to the **leading** citizens, and to the guardians
	10. 5	city, together with the **leading** citizens and the guardians,
	10. 6	under the care of the **leading** citizens of Samaria, who were
	24.14	royal princes, and all the **leading** men, ten thousand in all.
	24.15	his wives, his officials, and the **leading** men of Judah.
1 Chr	5.12	was the founder of the **leading** clan, and Shapham of the
	11.15	day three of the thirty **leading** soldiers went to a rock
	11.26	Adina son of Shiza (a **leading** member of the tribe of Reuben,
	12.23	22 **leading** men;
	28. 1	indeed all the palace officials, **leading** soldiers, and
2 Chr	19. 8	priests, and some of the **leading** citizens as judges in cases
	23.20	The army officers, the **leading** citizens, the officials,
	28.12	Four of the **leading** men of the Northern Kingdom,
	29.20	delay King Hezekiah assembled the **leading** men of the city,
Ezra	8.24	From among the **leading** priests I chose Sherebiah,
Neh	3. 5	the next section, but the **leading** men of the town refused to
	11. 3	is the list of the **leading** citizens of the province of Judah
	11.14	Their leader was Zabdiel, a member of a **leading** family.
Prov	31.23	Her husband is well known, one of the **leading** citizens.
Jer	27.19	of Jehoiakim, and the **leading** men of Judah and Jerusalem,
Nah	3.10	Their **leading** men were carried off in chains and divided
Mt	2. 6	are by no means the least of the **leading** cities of Judah;
Mk	6.21	the military commanders, and the **leading** citizens of Galilee.
Lk	14. 1	eat a meal at the home of one of the **leading** Pharisees;

LEAF

Gen 1.30 I have provided grass and **leafy** plants for food"—and it was
3. 7 so they sewed fig **leaves** together and covered themselves.
8.11 him in the evening with a fresh olive **leaf** in its beak.
40.10 As soon as the **leaves** came out, the blossoms appeared, and
Lev 23.40 branches and the branches of **leafy** trees, and begin a
26.36 that the sound of a **leaf** blowing in the wind will make
Job 13.25 I'm nothing but a **leaf;**
Ps 1. 3 fruit at the right time, and whose **leaves** do not dry up.
29. 9 the oaks and strips the **leaves** from the trees while everyone
Prov 11.28 wealth will fall like the **leaves** of autumn,
11.28 but the righteous will prosper like the **leaves** of summer.
Song 6.11 valley, to see the new **leaves** on the vines and the blossoms
Is 33. 9 on Mount Carmel the **leaves** are falling from the trees.
34. 4 the stars will fall like **leaves** dropping from a vine or a
64. 6 our sins we are like **leaves** that wither and are blown away
Jer 8.13 even the **leaves** have withered.
11.16 I once called them a **leafy** olive-tree, full of beautiful fruit;
11.16 I will set its **leaves** on fire and break its branches.
17. 8 when hot weather comes, because its **leaves** stay green;
Ezek 17. 6 The vine was covered with branches and **leaves.**
17. 7 towards him and turned its **leaves** towards him, in the hope
17. 8 so that it could grow **leaves** and bear grapes and be a
19.10 of water, the vine was covered with **leaves** and fruit.
19.11 everyone saw how **leafy** and tall it was.
36. 8 the trees will again grow **leaves** and bear fruit for you, my
47.12 Their **leaves** will never wither,
47.12 food, and their **leaves** will be used for healing people."
Dan 4.12 Its **leaves** were beautiful, and it was loaded down with
4.14 strip off its **leaves** and scatter its fruit.
4.21 Its **leaves** were beautiful, and it had enough fruit on it
Mt 21.19 road and went to it, but found nothing on it except **leaves.**
24.32 it starts putting out **leaves,** you know that summer is near.
Mk 11.13 distance a fig-tree covered with **leaves,** so he went to see
11.13 to it, he found only **leaves,** because it was not the right
13.28 it starts putting out **leaves,** you know that summer is near.
Lk 21.30 you see their **leaves** beginning to appear, you know that summer
Heb 9. 4 Aaron's stick that had sprouted **leaves,** and the two stone tablets
Rev 22. 2 and its **leaves** are for the healing of the nations.

LEAH

Jacob's wife.

Gen 29.16 the elder was named **Leah,** and the younger Rachel.
29.17 **Leah** had lovely eyes, but Rachel was shapely and beautiful.
29.23 instead of Rachel, he took **Leah** to Jacob, and Jacob had
29.24 (Laban gave his slave-girl Zilpah to his daughter **Leah**
29.25 Not until the next morning did Jacob discover that it was **Leah.**
29.30 with Rachel also, and he loved her more than **Leah.**
29.31 When the Lord saw that **Leah** was loved less than Rachel,
29.32 **Leah** became pregnant and gave birth to a son.
30. 9 When **Leah** realized that she had stopped having children,
30.11 **Leah** said, "I have been lucky";
30.13 Zilpah bore Jacob another son, [13]and **Leah** said, "How happy I am!
30.14 and found mandrakes, which he brought to his mother **Leah.**
30.14 Rachel said to **Leah,** "Please give me some of your son's mandrakes."
30.15 **Leah** answered, "Isn't it enough that you have taken away my husband?
30.16 the fields in the evening, **Leah** went out to meet him
30.17 God answered **Leah's** prayer, and she became pregnant
30.18 **Leah** said, "God has given me my reward,
30.19 **Leah** became pregnant again and bore Jacob a sixth son.
31. 4 sent word to Rachel and **Leah** to meet him in the field
31.14 Rachel and **Leah** answered Jacob, "There is nothing left
31.33 then he went into **Leah's** tent, and the tent of the two
33. 1 the children among **Leah,** Rachel, and the two concubines.
33. 2 and their children first, then **Leah** and her children, and
33. 7 then **Leah** and her children came, and last of all Joseph
34. 1 the daughter of Jacob and **Leah,** went to visit some of the
35.23 The sons of **Leah** were Reuben (Jacob's eldest son),
35.26 The sons of **Leah's** slave Zilpah were Gad and Asher.
46.15 These are the sons that **Leah** had borne to Jacob in Mesopotamia,
46.15 In all, his descendants by **Leah** numbered thirty-three.
46.18 Zilpah, the slave-girl whom Laban gave to his daughter **Leah.**
49.31 and that is where I buried **Leah.**
Ruth 4.11 like Rachel and **Leah,** who bore many children to Jacob.

LEAK

Ecc 10.18 repair his roof, it will **leak,** and the house will fall in.

LEAN

Judg 16.26 I want to **lean** on them."
2 Sam 1. 6 I saw that Saul was **leaning** on his spear and that the
Job 8.15 If they **lean** on a web, will it hold them up?
Ezek 29. 7 When they **leaned** on you, you broke, pierced their armpits,
Jn 21.20 the one who had **leaned** close to Jesus at the meal
Heb 11.21 He **leaned** on the top of his walking-stick and worshipped God.

LEAP

Deut 33.22 He **leaps** out from Bashan."
1 Chr 15.29 saw King David dancing and **leaping** for joy, and she was
Job 6.10 knew he would, I would **leap** for joy, no matter how great
39.20 Did you make them **leap** like locusts and frighten men
41.21 flames **leap** out of his mouth.
Ps 29. 6 like calves and makes Mount Hermon **leap** like a young bull.
Is 35. 6 The lame will **leap** and dance, and those who cannot speak
Dan 3.24 Suddenly Nebuchadnezzar **leapt** to his feet in amazement.
Joel 2. 5 As they **leap** on the tops of the mountains, they rattle

LEARN

[UNLEARNED]

Gen 9.24 Noah was sober again and **learnt** what his youngest son had
22.20 Some time later Abraham **learnt** that Milcah had borne
28. 6 Esau **learnt** that Isaac had blessed Jacob and sent him away
28. 6 He also **learnt** that when Isaac blessed him, he commanded him
30.27 I have **learnt** by divination that the Lord has blessed me
34. 5 Jacob **learnt** that his daughter had been disgraced, but
42. 1 When Jacob **learnt** that there was corn in Egypt, he said to
Ex 18.15 do this because the people come to me to **learn** God's will.
Lev 10.16 the sin-offering and **learnt** that it had already been burnt.
Num 20.29 The whole community **learnt** that Aaron had died, and they
22.19 did, so that I may **learn** whether or not the Lord has
27.21 Eleazar the priest, who will **learn** my will by using the Urim
Deut 4.10 say, so that they will **learn** to obey me as long as
5. 1 **Learn** them and be sure that you obey them.
11. 2 Remember today what you have **learned** about the Lord
14.23 this so that you may **learn** to honour the Lord your God
17.19 life, so that he will **learn** to honour the Lord and to
31.12 everyone may hear it and **learn** to honour the Lord your God
31.13 And so they will **learn** to obey him as long as they
Josh 9.16 had been made, the Israelites **learnt** that these people did
9.24 did it, sir, because we **learnt** that it was really true that
Judg 4.12 When Sisera **learnt** that Barak had gone up to Mount Tabor,
15. 6 who had done this, they **learnt** that Samson had done it
1 Sam 26. 3 the wilderness, and when he **learnt** that Saul had come to
2 Sam 11. 3 out who she was, and **learnt** that she was Bathsheba, the
2 Kgs 11. 1 King Ahaziah's mother Athaliah **learnt** of her son's murder,
17. 4 When Shalmaneser **learnt** of this, he had Hoshea arrested and
19. 8 The Assyrian official **learnt** that the emperor had left
2 Chr 12. 8 conquer them, and they will **learn** the difference between
22.10 King Ahaziah's mother Athaliah **learnt** of her son's murder,
Neh 13.10 I also **learnt** that the temple musicians and other
Esth 2.22 Mordecai **learnt** about it and told Queen Esther, who then
3. 6 to him, [6]and when he **learnt** that Mordecai was a Jew, he
4. 1 When Mordecai **learnt** of all that had been done, he tore
Job 5.27 Job, we have **learnt** this by long study.
8. 8 consider the truths our fathers **learnt.**
15.10 We **learnt** our wisdom from grey-haired men— men born
15.18 taught me truths which they **learnt** from their fathers, and
28.12 Where can we **learn** to understand?
28.20 Where can we **learn** to understand?
39.26 Does a hawk **learn** from you how to fly when it spreads
Ps 2.10 **learn** this lesson, you rulers of the world:
25.12 reverence for the Lord will **learn** from him the path they
78. 6 that the next generation might **learn** them and in turn should
94. 8 When will you ever **learn?**
119. 7 As I **learn** your righteous judgements, I will praise you
119.71 was good for me, because it made me **learn** your commands.
119.73 give me understanding, so that I may **learn** your laws.
119.96 I have **learnt** that everything has limits;
119.152 Long ago I **learnt** about your instructions;
Prov 1. 7 Stupid people have no respect for wisdom and refuse to **learn.**
1.22 Will you never **learn?**
2. 1 **Learn** what I teach you, my son, and never forget what I
2. 5 to fear the Lord and you will succeed in **learning** about God.
4.13 Always remember what you have **learnt.**
5.12 eaten away, [12]and you will say, "Why would I never **learn?**
6. 6 Lazy people should **learn** a lesson from the way ants live.
8. 5 **Learn** to be mature.
8. 5 **Learn** to have sense.
13.18 Someone who will not **learn** will be poor and disgraced.
14. 6 but intelligent people **learn** easily.
15.14 Intelligent people want to **learn,**
15.32 If you refuse to **learn,** you are hurting yourself.
16.33 Men cast lots to **learn** God's will, but God himself
17.10 An intelligent person **learns** more from one rebuke
17.10 than a fool **learns** from being beaten a hundred times.
18.15 Intelligent people are always eager and ready to **learn.**
19. 8 Do yourself a favour and **learn** all you can;
19. 8 then remember what you **learn** and you will prosper.
19.18 Discipline your children while they are young enough to **learn.**
19.20 advice and are willing to **learn,** one day you will be wise.
19.25 so that people who don't know any better can **learn** a lesson.
19.25 If you are wise, you will **learn** when you are corrected.
19.27 Son, when you stop **learning,** you will soon neglect what
21.11 his punishment, even an unthinking person **learns** a lesson.
21.11 One who is wise will **learn** from what he is taught.
22.25 You might **learn** their habits and not be able to change.
23.12 Pay attention to your teacher and **learn** all you can.
23.23 wisdom, **learning,** and good sense—these are worth paying for, but
24.32 at this, thought about it, and **learned** a lesson from it:
25.10 Otherwise everyone will **learn** that you can't keep a secret,
27.17 People **learn** from one another, just as iron sharpens iron.
30. 3 I have never **learned** any wisdom, and I know nothing at all
Ecc 1.17 determined to **learn** the difference between knowledge and foolishness,
4. 4 I have also **learnt** why people work so hard to succeed:
5. 1 better to go there to **learn** than to offer sacrifices as
7.25 and to **learn** how wicked and foolish stupidity is.
7.29 This is all that I have **learnt:**
8.16 tried to become wise and **learn** what goes on in the world,
Is 1.17 Yes, stop doing evil [17]and **learn** to do right.
23. 1 As your ships return from Cyprus, you **learn** the news.
23. 5 and dismayed when they **learn** that Tyre has been destroyed.
26. 9 earth and its people, they will all **learn** what justice is.
26.10 kind to wicked men, they never **learn** to do what is right.

Is 29.24 Foolish people will **learn** to understand, and those who
37. 8 The Assyrian official **learnt** that the emperor had left
40.14 know and understand and to **learn** how things should be done?
42.25 we **learnt** from it nothing at all.
Jer 2.19 You will **learn** how bitter and wrong it is to abandon me,
2.33 Even the worst of women can **learn** from you.
5. 3 he crushed you, but you refused to **learn.**
6.18 said, "Listen, you nations, and **learn** what is going to
7.28 obey me, the Lord their God, or **learn** from their punishment.
10. 8 What can they **learn** from wooden idols?
13.23 that do nothing but evil could **learn** to do what is right.
17.23 they would not obey me or **learn** from me.
32.33 I kept on teaching them, they would not listen and **learn.**
Lam 3.27 And it is best to **learn** this patience in our youth.
Ezek 19. 6 He too **learnt** to hunt and became a man-eater.
Dan 1. 4 quick to **learn,** and free from physical defects,
2.30 so that Your Majesty may **learn** the meaning of your dream and
6.10 When Daniel **learnt** that the order had been signed, he
Mal 2. 7 should go to them to **learn** my will, because they are the
Mt 2.16 accordance with what he had **learned** from the visitors about
11.25 you have shown to the **unlearned**
11.25 what you have hidden from the wise and **learned.**
11.29 put it on you, and **learn** from me, because I am gentle
13.18 "Listen, then, and **learn** what the parable of the sower means.
27. 3 When Judas, the traitor, **learnt** that Jesus had been condemned,
Lk 10.21 you have shown to the **unlearned**
10.21 what you have hidden from the wise and **learned.**
23. 7 When he **learnt** that Jesus was from the region ruled by Herod,
Jn 6.45 Anyone who hears the Father and **learns** from him comes to me.
7.52 the Scriptures and you will **learn** that no prophet ever comes
Acts 2.42 spent their time in **learning** from the apostles, taking part in
4.13 and John were and to **learn** that they were ordinary men
10.17 men sent by Cornelius had **learnt** where Simon's house was,
14. 6 When the apostles **learnt** about it, they fled to the cities
23.27 I **learnt** that he was a Roman citizen, so I went with
24. 8 yourself will be able to **learn** from him all the things that
26.24 Your great **learning** is driving you mad!"
28. 1 safely ashore, we **learnt** that the island was called Malta.
Rom 2.18 and you have **learnt** from the Law to choose what
3.18 the path of peace, [18] nor have they **learnt** reverence for God."
1 Cor 2. 1 God's secret truth, I did not use big words and great **learning.**
4. 6 so that you may **learn** what the saying means, "Observe the
14.31 one by one, so that everyone will **learn** and be encouraged.
Eph 3. 4 I have written, you can **learn** about my understanding of the
3.10 in the heavenly world might **learn** of his wisdom in all its
4.20 That was not what you **learnt** about Christ!
5.10 Try to **learn** what pleases the Lord.
Phil 4. 9 Put into practice what you **learnt** and received from me,
4.11 feel neglected, for I have **learnt** to be satisfied with what
4.12 I have **learnt** this secret, so that anywhere, at any time,
Col 1. 7 You **learnt** of God's grace from Epaphras, our dear fellow-servant,
1 Thes 4. 1 Finally, our brothers, you **learnt** from us how you should live
1 Tim 2.11 Women should **learn** in silence and all humility.
5. 4 they should **learn** first to carry out their religious
5.13 They also **learn** to waste their time in going round from
5.13 but even worse, they **learn** to be gossips and busybodies,
2 Tim 3. 7 who are always trying to **learn** but who can never come to
Tit 3.14 Our people must **learn** to spend their time doing good,
Heb 5. 8 God's Son, he **learnt** through his sufferings to be obedient.
Rev 2.24 you have not **learnt** what the others call 'the deep secrets
14. 3 they were singing a new song, which only they could **learn.**

LEAST

Judg 6.15 and I am the **least** important member of my family."
1 Sam 9.21 and my family is the **least** important one in the tribe.
Jer 31.34 because all will know me, from the **least** to the greatest.
50.12 Babylonia will be the **least** important nation of all;
Dan 4.17 to anyone he chooses—even to the **least** important of men.'
Jon 3. 5 from the greatest to the **least,** put on sackcloth to show
Mt 2. 6 are by no means the **least** of the leading cities of Judah;
5.18 and earth last, not the **least** point nor the smallest detail
5.19 whoever disobeys even the **least** important of the commandments
5.19 to do the same, will be **least** in the Kingdom of heaven.
10.42 water to one of the **least** of these my followers because he
11.11 But he who is **least** in the Kingdom of heaven is greater
25.40 for one of the **least** important of these brothers of mine,
25.45 to help one of these **least** important ones, you refused to
Lk 7.28 But he who is **least** in the Kingdom of God is greater
9.48 For he who is **least** among you all is the greatest."
1 Cor 15. 9 For I am the **least** of all the apostles—I do not
2 Cor 11. 5 think that I am the **least** bit inferior to those very special
Eph 3. 8 I am less than the **least** of all God's people;
Heb 8.11 For they will all know me, from the **least** to the greatest.

LEATHER

Gen 21.14 Abraham gave Hagar some food and a **leather** bag full of water.
21.19 She went and filled the **leather** bag with water and gave some
Ex 25. 5 fine **leather;**
26.14 and the other of fine **leather,** to serve as the outer cover.
35. 7 fine **leather;**
35.23 or fine **leather,** brought it.
36.19 and the other of fine **leather,** to serve as an outer cover.
39.34 the covering of fine **leather;**
Lev 11.32 any article of wood, cloth, **leather,** or sacking, no matter
13.48 wool cloth or on **leather**
13.48 or anything made of **leather,**
13.56 has faded, he shall tear it out of the clothing or **leather.**
13.59 or on linen or wool cloth or on anything made of **leather;**
Lev 15.17 Anything made of cloth or **leather** on which the semen
Num 4. 6 They shall put a fine **leather** cover over it, spread a blue
4. 8 all this, put a fine **leather** cover over it, and then insert
4.10 its equipment in a fine **leather** cover and place it on a
4.11 gold altar, put a fine **leather** cover over it, and then
4.12 blue cloth, put a fine **leather** cover over them, and place
4.14 they shall put a fine **leather** cover over it and insert the
4.25 its outer cover, the fine **leather** cover on top of it, the
31.20 piece of clothing and everything made of **leather,** goats'
Judg 4.19 She opened a **leather** bag of milk, gave him a drink, and
1 Sam 1.24 ten kilogrammes of flour, and a **leather** bag full of wine.
10. 3 and the third one will have a **leather** bag full of wine.
16.20 a donkey loaded with bread, and a **leather** bag full of wine.
25.18 hundred loaves of bread, two **leather** bags full of wine, five
2 Sam 16. 1 bunches of fresh fruit, and a **leather** bag full of wine.
2 Kgs 1. 8 of animal skins, tied with a **leather** belt," they answered.
Jer 27. 2 myself a yoke out of **leather** straps and wooden crossbars and
Ezek 16.10 you shoes of the best **leather,** a linen headband, and a silk
Mt 3. 4 he wore a **leather** belt round his waist, and his food was
Mk 1. 6 of camel's hair, with a **leather** belt round his waist, and
Acts 9.43 Joppa for many days with a tanner of **leather** named Simon.
10. 6 home of a tanner of **leather** named Simon, who lives by the
10.32 home of Simon the tanner of **leather,** who lives by the sea.'

LEAVE

[LEFT, LEFT OVER, LEFTOVER PIECES, LEFTOVERS]
see also **LEFT OVER**

Gen 2.24 That is why a man **leaves** his father and mother and is
6.16 roof for the boat and **leave** a space of 44 centimetres
7.23 The only ones **left** were Noah and those who were with him
11.31 wife, and with them he **left** the city of Ur in Babylonia
12. 1 The Lord said to Abram, **"Leave** your country, your relatives,
13. 3 Then he **left** there and moved from place to place, going
13.14 After Lot had **left,** the Lord said to Abram, "From where
15.14 enslaves them, and when they **leave** that foreign land, they
17.22 When God finished speaking to Abraham, he **left** him.
18.16 Then the men **left** and went to a place where they could
18.22 Then the two men **left** and went on towards Sodom, but the
21.14 She **left** and wandered about in the wilderness of Beersheba.
21.15 water was all gone, she **left** the child under a bush [16] and
23. 3 He **left** the place where his wife's body was lying, went to
24. 5 if the girl will not **leave** home to come with me to
25. 5 Abraham **left** everything he owned to Isaac;
25.34 He ate and drank and then got up and **left.**
26.16 Then Abimelech said to Isaac, **"Leave** our country.
26.17 So Isaac **left** and set up his camp in the Valley of
26.23 Isaac **left** and went to Beersheba.
26.27 unfriendly to me before and made me **leave** your country?"
26.29 We were kind to you and let you **leave** peacefully.
27.30 and as soon as Jacob **left,** his brother Esau came in from
28.10 Jacob **left** Beersheba and started towards Haran.
28.15 I will not **leave** you until I have done all that I
30.26 that I have earned by working for you, and I will **leave.**
31.14 answered Jacob, "There is nothing **left** for us to inherit
31.20 Jacob deceived Laban by not letting him know that he was **leaving.**
31.21 He took everything he owned and **left** in a hurry.
31.30 I know that you **left** because you were so anxious to get
31.55 and his daughters good-bye, and **left** to go back home.
32.16 "Go ahead of me, and **leave** a space between each herd and
32.31 sun rose as Jacob was **leaving** Peniel, and he was limping
33.12 Esau said, "Let's prepare to **leave.**
33.15 Esau said, "Then let me **leave** some of my men with you."
34.17 our terms and be circumcised, we will take her and **leave."**
34.26 Then they took Dinah from Shechem's house and **left.**
35. 3 We are going to **leave** here and go to Bethel, where I
35. 5 and his sons started to **leave,** great fear fell on the people
35.13 Then God **left** him.
35.16 Jacob and his family **left** Bethel, and when they were
36. 7 He **left** because the land where he and Jacob were living
37.17 The man said, "They have already **left.**
38. 1 About that time Judah **left** his brothers and went to stay
39.12 But he escaped and ran outside, **leaving** his robe in her hand.
39.13 she saw that he had **left** his robe and had run out
39.15 me scream, he ran outside, **leaving** his robe beside me."
39.18 But when I screamed, he ran outside, **leaving** his robe beside me."
41.45 He **left** the king's court and travelled all over the land.
42.15 will never **leave** unless your youngest brother comes here.
42.24 Joseph **left** them and began to cry.
42.26 donkeys with the corn they had bought, and then they **left.**
42.33 rest will take corn for your starving families and **leave.**
42.38 his brother is dead, and he is the only one **left.**
43. 8 father, "Send the boy with me, and we will **leave** at once.
43.30 Then Joseph **left** suddenly, because his heart was full of
44.22 and we answered that the boy could not **leave** his father;
44.28 One of them has already **left** me.
44.28 by wild animals, because I have not seen him since he **left.**
45. 1 of his servants, so he ordered them all to **leave** the room.
45.20 They are not to worry about **leaving** their possessions behind;
45.24 brothers off and as they **left,** he said to them, "Don't
45.25 They **left** Egypt and went back home to their father Jacob
47.10 Jacob gave the king a farewell blessing and **left.**
47.18 There is nothing **left** to give you except our bodies and our
Ex 2.20 "Why did you **leave** the man out there?
3.21 so that when my people **leave,** they will not go empty-handed.
5.20 As they were **leaving,** they met Moses and Aaron, who were
6.11 of Egypt that he must let the Israelites **leave** his land."
7. 2 will tell the king to let the Israelites **leave** his country.
8. 3 of frogs that they will **leave** it and go into your palace,
8. 9 frogs, and there will be none **left** except in the Nile."

Ex 8.11 the frogs, and there will be none **left** except in the Nile."
8.12 Then Moses and Aaron **left** the king, and Moses prayed to
8.29 answered, "As soon as I **leave,** I will pray to the Lord
8.29 the flies will **leave** you, your officials, and your people.
8.30 Moses **left** the king and prayed to the Lord, [31]and the
8.31 The flies **left** the king, his officials, and his people;
9.19 on the people and animals **left** outside unprotected, and they
9.21 to the Lord's warning and **left** their slaves and animals out
9.33 Moses **left** the king, went out of the city, and lifted up
10. 5 that the hail did not destroy, even the trees that are **left.**
10. 6 Then Moses turned and **left.**
10.15 everything that the hail had **left,** including all the fruit
10.15 Not a green thing was **left** on any tree or plant in
10.18 Moses **left** the king and prayed to the Lord.
10.19 Not one locust was **left** in all Egypt.
10.23 see each other, and no one **left** his house during that time.
10.26 not one will be **left** behind.
11. 1 After that he will let you **leave.**
11. 8 After that, I will **leave."**
11. 8 Then in great anger Moses **left** the king.
11.10 and he would not let the Israelites **leave** his country.
12.10 You must not **leave** any of it until morning;
12.10 if any is **left over,** it must be burnt.
12.22 Not one of you is to **leave** the house until morning.
12.31 **Leave** my country;
12.32 Take your sheep, goats, and cattle, and **leave.**
12.33 The Egyptians urged the people to hurry and **leave** the country;
12.33 they said, "We will all be dead if you don't **leave."**
12.41 all the tribes of the Lord's people **left** Egypt.
13. 3 the day on which you **left** Egypt, the place where you were
13. 4 You are **leaving** Egypt on this day in the first month, the
13. 8 because of what the Lord did for you when you **left** Egypt.
13.20 The Israelites **left** Sukkoth and camped at Etham on the
14. 8 he pursued the Israelites, who were **leaving** triumphantly.
14.12 Didn't we tell you before we **left** that this would happen?
14.12 We told you to **leave** us alone and let us go on
14.28 not one of them was **left.**
16. 1 second month after they had **left** Egypt, they came to the
16.21 when the sun grew hot, what was **left** on the ground melted.
16.23 Whatever is **left** should be put aside and kept for tomorrow."
16.24 they kept what was **left** until the next day;
16.29 where he is on the seventh day and not **leave** his home."
17. 1 The whole Israelite community **left** the desert of Sin,
18. 2 who had been **left** behind, [3]and Gershom and Eliezer,
19. 1 The people of Israel **left** Rephidim, and on the first
19. 1 third month after they had **left** Egypt they came to the
21. 3 he is not to take a wife with him when he **leaves;**
21. 4 belong to the master, and the man shall **leave** by himself.
23.11 grows there, and the wild animals can have what is **left.**
23.15 the month in which you **left** Egypt, celebrate the Festival of
23.18 festivals is not to be **left** until the following morning.
25.15 The poles are to be **left** in the rings and must not
27. 8 altar out of boards and **leave** it hollow, according to the
28.35 Holy Place or when he **leaves** it, the sound of the bells
29.32 are to eat it along with the bread **left** in the basket.
32. 8 They have already **left** the way that I commanded them to follow;
33. 1 The Lord said to Moses, **"Leave** this place, you and the
33. 6 So after they **left** Mount Sinai, the people of Israel no
33.15 you do not go with us, don't make us **leave** this place.
34.18 of Abib, because it was in that month that you **left** Egypt.
35.20 All the people of Israel **left,** [21]and everyone who
40.17 the second year after they **left** Egypt, the Tent of the
Lev 6. 2 return what a fellow-Israelite has **left** as a deposit or by
6. 9 A burnt-offering is to be **left** on the altar all night long,
6.10 shall remove the greasy ashes **left** on the altar and put them
7.15 none of it may be **left** until the next morning.
7.16 offered, but any that is **left over** may be eaten on the
8.32 Burn up any meat or bread that is **left over.**
8.33 You shall not **leave** the entrance of the Tent for seven days,
10. 6 Eleazar and Ithamar, "Do not **leave** your hair uncombed or
10. 7 Do not **leave** the entrance of the Tent or you will die,
10.12 "Take the grain-offering that is **left over** from the food
13.23 it is only the scar **left** from the boil, and the priest
13.45 must wear torn clothes, **leave** his hair uncombed,
14.38 into the wall, [38]he shall **leave** the house and lock it up
16.23 before entering the Most Holy Place, and **leave** them there.
19. 6 Any meat **left** on the third day must be burnt, [7]because it
19. 9 not go back to cut the ears of corn that were **left.**
19.10 **leave** them for poor people and foreigners.
21.10 garments, so he must not **leave** his hair uncombed or tear his
21.11 defile my sacred Tent by **leaving** it and entering a house
22.30 it the same day and **leave** none of it until the next
23.22 not go back to cut the ears of corn that were **left;**
23.22 **leave** them for poor people and foreigners.
25.41 he and his children shall **leave** you and return to his family
25.46 your property, [46]and you may **leave** them as an inheritance
25.51 to the number of years **left,** [53]as if he had been hired
26.10 to throw away what is **left** of the old harvest to make
26.22 children, destroy your livestock, and **leave** so few of you
26.33 Your land will be deserted, and your cities **left** in ruins.
27.18 the number of years **left** until the next Year of Restoration,
Num 1. 1 after the people of Israel **left** Egypt, the Lord spoke to
9. 1 the second year after the people of Israel had **left** Egypt.
9.12 Do not **leave** any of the food until the following morning
10.11 second year after the people **left** Egypt, the cloud over the
10.31 "Please don't **leave** us," Moses said.
10.33 When the people **left** Sinai, the holy mountain, they
11.20 to him that you should never have **left** Egypt.' "
12.10 he departed [10]and the cloud **left** the Tent, Miriam's skin
12.16 Then they **left** Hazeroth and set up camp in the
14.19 as you have forgiven them ever since they **left** Egypt."
Num 14.44 neither the Lord's Covenant Box nor Moses **left** the camp.
16.48 the plague, and he was **left** standing between the living and
18.30 the farmer keeps what is **left** after he makes his offering.
20.17 and our cattle will not **leave** the road or go into your
20.22 The whole community of Israel **left** Kadesh
21. 4 The Israelites **left** Mount Hor by the road that leads to
21.11 After **leaving** that place, they camped at the ruins of
21.22 and our cattle will not **leave** the road and go into your
21.35 sons, and all his people, **leaving** no survivors, and then
22.23 there holding a sword, it **left** the road and turned into the
25. 7 Aaron the priest, saw this, he got up and **left** the assembly.
26.64 was not even one man **left** among those whom Moses and Aaron
27. 3 "Our father died in the wilderness without **leaving** any sons.
27. 8 whenever a man dies without **leaving** a son, his daughter is
33. 1 set up camp after they **left** Egypt in their tribes under the
33. 3 The people of Israel **left** Egypt on the fifteenth day of
33. 3 Under the Lord's protection they **left** the city of Rameses in
33. 5 The people of Israel **left** Rameses and set up camp at Sukkoth.
33. 8 They **left** Pi Hahiroth and passed through the Red Sea into
33.10 They **left** Elim and camped near the Gulf of Suez.
33.38 of the fortieth year after the Israelites had **left** Egypt.
33.55 the land, those that are **left** will be as troublesome as
35.26 the man guilty of manslaughter **leaves** the city of refuge to
Deut 1. 3 fortieth year after they had **left** Egypt, Moses told the
1.19 We **left** Mount Sinai and went through that vast and fearful
2. 8 "So we moved on and **left** the road that goes from the
2.14 This was thirty-eight years after we had **left** Kadesh Barnea.
2.27 We will go straight through and not **leave** the road.
2.34 We **left** no survivors.
9. 7 From the day that you **left** Egypt until the day you arrived
13.16 It must be **left** in ruins for ever and never again be
15.16 "But your slave may not want to **leave;**
16. 3 you did when you had to **leave** Egypt in such a hurry.
16. 5 Do it at sunset, the time of day when you **left** Egypt.
24.19 it is to be **left** for the foreigners, orphans, and widows, so
24.20 olives once, do not go back and get those that are **left;**
24.21 the grapes that are **left** are for the foreigners, orphans,
25. 5 and one of them dies, **leaving** no son, then his widow is
26.13 the Lord, 'None of the sacred tithe is **left** in my house;
28.21 is not one of you **left** in the land that you are
28.51 They will not **leave** you any corn, wine, olive-oil,
28.54 wife he loves or to any of his children who are **left.**
31.24 God's Law in a book, taking care not to **leave** out anything.
Josh 2. 4 They **left** at sunset before the city gate was closed.
2. 7 The king's men **left** the city, and then the gate was shut.
2.10 the Red Sea in front of you when you were **leaving** Egypt.
3. 1 of Israel got up early, **left** the camp at Acacia, and went
3.14 When the people **left** the camp to cross the Jordan, the
5. 4 When the people of Israel **left** Egypt, all the males
5. 4 of fighting age when they **left** Egypt had died because they
6. 1 No one could enter or **leave** the city.
8.17 Israelites, and the city was **left** wide open, with no one to
8.28 Joshua burnt Ai and **left** it in ruins.
8.29 of Ai from a tree and **left** his body there until evening.
9.12 When we **left** home with it and started out to meet you,
10.28 no one was **left** alive.
10.33 Joshua defeated him and his army and **left** none of them alive.
10.37 No one in it was **left** alive.
11. 8 The fight continued until none of the enemy was **left** alive.
11.11 no one was **left** alive, and the city was burnt.
11.14 no one was **left** alive.
11.22 None of the Anakim were **left** in the land of Israel;
11.22 a few, however, were **left** in Gaza, Gath, and Ashdod.
22. 6 Then they **left** for home.
22. 9 They **left** the rest of the people of Israel at Shiloh in
22.32 Then Phinehas and the leaders **left** the people of Reuben
23. 4 the nations that are still **left,** as well as of all the
23. 7 not associate with these peoples **left** among you or speak the
23.12 that are still **left** among you and intermarry with them,
23.13 until none of you are **left** in this good land which the
23.16 none of you will be **left** in this good land that he
24.16 "We would never **leave** the Lord to serve other gods!
24.20 no rivals, [20]and if you **leave** him to serve foreign gods,
Judg 1.24 city, [24]who saw a man **leaving** and said to him, "Show us
3. 1 So then, the Lord **left** some nations in the land to test
3. 3 Those **left** in the land were the five Philistine cities,
3.19 So the king ordered his servants, **"Leave** us alone!"
3.24 closed the doors behind him, locked them, [24]and **left.**
4.16 Not a man was **left.**
5. 4 Lord, when you **left** the mountains of Seir, when you came
6. 4 sheep, cattle, and donkeys, and **leave** nothing for the
6.13 Lord has abandoned us and **left** us to the mercy of the
6.18 Please do not **leave** until I bring you an offering of food."
8.10 Of the whole army of desert tribesmen, only about 15,000 were **left;**
10.10 sinned against you, for we **left** you, our God, and worshipped
10.13 But you still **left** me and worshipped other gods, so I am
11. 2 and when they grew up, they forced Jephthah to **leave** home.
11. 7 me so much that you forced me to **leave** my father's house.
11.16 when the Israelites **left** Egypt, they went through the desert
11.37 **Leave** me alone for two months, so that I can go with
14. 8 On the way he **left** the road to look at the lion
16.20 He did not know that the Lord had **left** him.
17. 8 He **left** Bethlehem to find somewhere else to live.
18. 7 So the five men **left** and went to the town of Laish.
18.11 the tribe of Dan **left** Zorah and Eshtaol, ready for battle.
18.24 What have I got **left?"**
19. 8 fifth day he started to **leave,** but the girl's father said,
19. 9 servant once more started to **leave,** the father said, "Look,
19.30 Nothing like this has ever happened since the Israelites **left** Egypt!
21. 7 do to provide wives for the men of Benjamin who are **left?**
21.16 shall we do to provide wives for the men who are **left?**

Judg	21.24	the rest of the Israelites **left**, and every man went back to
Ruth	1. 3	Elimelech died, and Naomi was **left** alone with her two sons,
	1. 5	and Naomi was **left** all alone, without husband or sons.
	1. 6	so she got ready to **leave** Moab with her daughters-in-law.
	1.16	But Ruth answered, "Don't ask me to **leave** you!
	1.21	When I **left** here, I had plenty, but the Lord has brought
	2. 2	fields to gather the corn that the harvest workers **leave**.
	2. 3	behind the workers, picking up the corn which they **left**.
	2.11	I know how you **left** your father and mother and your own
	2.14	she was satisfied, and she still had some food **left over**.
	2.15	After she had **left** to go on picking up corn, Boaz
	2.15	corn from the bundles and **leave** it for her to pick up."
	2.18	She also gave her the food **left over** from the meal.
1 Sam	2. 5	seven children, but the mother of many is **left** with none.
	4.21	Ichabod, explaining, "God's glory has **left** Israel"—
	4.22	"God's glory has **left** Israel," she said, "because
	5. 4	only the body was **left**.
	6. 6	God made fools of them until they let the Israelites **leave** Egypt.
	9. 7	"There is no food **left** in our packs, and we haven't
	9.27	The servant **left**, and Samuel continued, "Stay here a minute,
	10. 2	When you **leave** me today, you will meet two men near
	10. 9	When Saul turned to **leave** Samuel, God gave Saul a new nature.
	13.15	Samuel **left** Gilgal and went on his way.
	14. 3	The men did not know that Jonathan had **left**.
	15. 3	Don't **leave** a thing;
	15. 6	"Go away and **leave** the Amalekites, so that I won't kill you
	15. 6	So the Kenites **left**.
	15.27	Then Samuel turned to **leave**, but Saul caught hold of his cloak,
	16.14	The Lord's spirit **left** Saul, and an evil spirit sent by
	16.23	The evil spirit would **leave**, and Saul would feel better and
	17.20	up early the next morning, **left** someone else in charge of
	17.22	David **left** the food with the officer in charge of the supplies,
	20.22	other side of you,' then **leave**, because the Lord is sending
	20.41	After the boy had **left**, David got up from behind the
	20.42	Then David **left**, and Jonathan went back to the town.
	21. 8	The king's orders made me **leave** in such a hurry that I
	21.10	So David **left**, fleeing from Saul, and went to King
	22. 4	So David **left** his parents with the king of Moab, and they
	22. 5	So David **left** and went to the forest of Hereth.
	23.13	about six hundred in all—**left** Keilah at once and kept on
	23.24	So they **left** and returned to Ziph ahead of Saul.
	23.29	David **left** and went to the region of Engedi, where he
	24. 7	Saul got up, **left** the cave, and started on his way.
	25.13	buckled on his sword and **left** with about four hundred
	25.13	of his men, **leaving** two hundred behind with the supplies.
	26.12	jar from just beside Saul's head, and he and Abishai **left**.
	28. 3	Saul had forced all the fortune-tellers and mediums to **leave** Israel.
	28. 9	he forced the fortune-tellers and mediums to **leave** Israel.
	28.25	And they **left** that same night.
	29.10	morning all of you who **left** Saul and came over to me
	29.10	have to get up early and **leave** as soon as it's light."
	30. 2	anyone, but had taken everyone with them when they **left**.
	30.13	"My master **left** me behind three days ago because I was ill.
2 Sam	3.26	After **leaving** David, Joab sent messengers to get Abner,
	5.21	When the Philistines fled, they **left** their idols behind,
	9. 1	One day David asked, "Is there anyone **left** of Saul's family?
	9. 3	asked him, "Is there anyone **left** of Saul's family to whom I
	11. 8	Uriah **left**, and David sent a present to his home.
	13. 9	He said, "Send everyone away"—and they all **left**.
	13.25	the king would not give in, and he asked Absalom to **leave**.
	13.30	"Absalom has killed all your sons—not one of them is **left**!"
	14. 7	If they do this, I will be **left** without a son.
	14. 7	destroy my last hope and **leave** my husband without a son to
	14.32	'Why did I **leave** Geshur and come here?
	15.16	So the king **left**, accompanied by all his family and officials,
	15.16	for ten concubines, whom he **left** behind to take care of the
	15.17	and all his men were **leaving** the city, they stopped at the
	15.23	The people cried loudly as David's followers **left**.
	15.24	pick it up again until all the people had **left** the city.
	16.11	so **leave** him alone and let him do it.
	16.21	your father's concubines whom he **left** behind to take care of
	17.13	a single stone will be **left** there on top of the hill."
	17.21	After they **left**, Ahimaaz and Jonathan came up out of the
	18. 9	The mule ran on and Absalom was **left** hanging in mid air.
	19. 9	but now he has fled from Absalom and **left** the country.
	19.19	please forget the wrong I did that day you **left** Jerusalem.
	19.24	time the king **left** Jerusalem until he returned victorious.
	20. 3	the ten concubines he had **left** to take care of the palace,
	20. 7	and all the other soldiers **left** Jerusalem with Abishai to go
	20.22	signal for his men to **leave** the city, and they went back
	21. 5	wanted to destroy us and **leave** none of us alive anywhere in
	24. 4	they **left** his presence and went out to count the people of
1 Kgs	1.49	and they all got up and **left**, each going his own way.
	2.36	Live in it and don't **leave** the city.
	2.37	If you ever **leave** and go beyond the brook of Kidron, you
	2.42	"I made you promise in the Lord's name not to **leave** Jerusalem.
	6. 1	after the people of Israel **left** Egypt, during the fourth
	8.10	As the priests were **leaving** the Temple, it was suddenly
	8.57	may he never **leave** us, or abandon us;
	10. 5	It **left** her breathless and amazed.
	11.13	instead, I will **leave** him one tribe for the sake of my
	11.18	They **left** Midian and went to Paran, where some other men
	12. 5	So they **left**.
	12.17	the people of Israel rebelled, [17]**leaving** Rehoboam as king
	12.25	Then he **left** and fortified the town of Penuel.
	13.12	"Which way did he go when he **left**?"
	15.18	silver and gold that was **left** in the Temple and the palace,
	16.17	Omri and his troops **left** Gibbethon and went and besieged Tirzah.
	17. 3	the Lord said to Elijah, [3]"**Leave** this place and go east
	18.12	carries you off to some unknown place as soon as I **leave**?
	18.22	prophet of the Lord still **left**, but there are 450 prophets
1 Kgs	19. 3	**Leaving** the servant there, [4]Elijah walked a whole day
	19.10	I am the only one **left**—and they are trying to kill
	19.14	I am the only one **left**—and they are trying to kill
	19.18	Yet I will **leave** seven thousand people alive in
	19.19	Elijah **left** and found Elisha ploughing with a team of oxen;
	19.20	Elisha then **left** his oxen, ran after Elijah, and said,
	20. 9	The messengers **left** and then returned with another message
	20.36	command, a lion will kill you as soon as you **leave** me."
	20.36	And as soon as he **left**, a lion came along and killed
	22.24	"Since when did the Lord's spirit **leave** me and speak to you?"
	22.46	pagan altars who were still **left** from the days of his father
2 Kgs	2. 2	the living Lord and to you that I will not **leave** you."
	2. 4	the living Lord and to you that I will not **leave** you."
	2. 6	the living Lord and to you that I will not **leave** you."
	2.16	has carried him away and **left** him on some mountain or in
	2.23	Elisha **left** Jericho to go to Bethel, and on the way
	3. 6	At once King Joram **left** Samaria and gathered all his troops.
	3. 9	and there was none **left** for the men or the pack-animals.
	3.25	city of Kir Heres was **left**, and the slingers surrounded it
	4. 7	there will be enough money **left over** for you and your sons
	4.21	put him on the bed and **left**, closing the door behind her.
	4.27	about to push her away, but Elisha said, "**Leave** her alone.
	4.30	the living Lord and to you that I will not **leave** you!"
	4.37	then she took her son and **left**.
	4.43	Lord says that they will eat and still have some **left over**."
	4.44	had said, they all ate and there was still some **left over**.
	5.11	But Naaman **left** in a rage, saying, "I thought that he
	5.19	And Naaman **left**.
	5.27	When Gehazi **left**, he had the disease—his skin was as white
	7. 7	horses, and donkeys, and **leaving** the camp just as it was.
	7.10	So they **left** the Syrian camp, went back to Samaria and
	7.10	untied, and the tents are just as the Syrians **left** them."
	7.12	famine here, so they have **left** their camp to go and hide
	7.12	They think that we will **leave** the city to find food, and
	7.13	of the horses that are **left**, so that we can find out
	8. 1	years, and that she should **leave** with her family and go and
	9. 3	Then **leave** there as fast as you can."
	9.10	After saying this, the young prophet **left** the room and fled.
	10. 8	city gate and to be **left** there until the following morning.
	10.11	not one of them was **left** alive.
	10.12	Jehu **left** Jezreel to go to Samaria.
	10.14	people in all, and not one of them was **left** alive.
	13. 7	Jehoahaz had no armed forces **left** except fifty horsemen,
	17.18	them from his sight, **leaving** only the kingdom of Judah.
	19. 8	learnt that the emperor had **left** Lachish and was fighting
	20. 4	Isaiah **left** the king, but before he had passed through the
	20.17	Nothing will be **left**.
	23.18	"**Leave** it as it is," Josiah ordered.
	24.14	skilled workmen, including the blacksmiths, **leaving** only the
	25. 3	that the people had nothing **left** to eat, [4]the city walls
	25. 4	They **left** by way of the royal garden, went through the
	25.11	Babylonia the people who were **left** in the city, the
	25.12	But he **left** in Judah some of the poorest people, who
	25.26	together with the army officers, **left** and went to Egypt,
1 Chr	13.13	Instead, he **left** it at the house of a man named Obed
	14.12	When the Philistines fled, they **left** their idols behind,
	21.21	King David approaching, he **left** the threshing-place and bowed low,
	24. 2	before their father did, and **left** no descendants, so their
2 Chr	1.13	So Solomon **left** the place of worship at Gibeon, where
	5.11	As the priests were **leaving** the Temple, it was suddenly
	9. 4	It **left** her breathless and amazed.
	10. 5	So the people **left**.
	10.17	the people of Israel rebelled, [17]**leaving** Rehoboam as king
	18.23	"Since when did the Lord's spirit **leave** me and speak to you?"
	22. 9	No member of Ahaziah's family was **left** who could rule the kingdom.
	26.18	**Leave** this holy place.
	26.20	forehead in horror, and then forced him to **leave** the Temple.
	35.15	gates did not need to **leave** their posts, because the other
Ezra	2. 1	Many of the exiles **left** the province of Babylon and
	7. 8	They **left** Babylonia on the first day of the first month,
	7.18	silver and gold that is **left over** for whatever you and your
	8.31	the first month that we **left** the Ahava Canal to go to
	9. 9	We were slaves, but you did not **leave** us in slavery.
Neh	2.13	was still night as I **left** the city through the Valley Gate
	5.13	and everything you own, and will **leave** you with nothing."
	6. 1	that there were no gaps **left** in it, although we still had
	6.10	grandson of Mehetabel, who was unable to **leave** his house.
	7. 6	Many of the exiles **left** the province of Babylon and
	13.10	musicians and other Levites had **left** Jerusalem and gone back
	13.28	the town of Beth Horon, so I made Joiada **leave** Jerusalem.
Esth	4.17	Mordecai then **left** and did everything that Esther had
	5. 9	When Haman **left** the banquet he was happy and in a good
	7. 7	got up in a fury, **left** the room, and went outside to
	8.15	Mordecai **left** the palace, wearing royal robes of blue and white,
Job	1.12	So Satan **left**.
	2. 7	Then Satan **left** the Lord's presence and made sores break
	6.13	I have no strength **left** to save myself;
	7.16	**Leave** me alone.
	10.20	**Leave** me alone!
	10.20	Let me enjoy the time I have **left**.
	11. 3	That your mocking words will **leave** us speechless?
	14. 6	Look away from him and **leave** him alone;
	17. 1	there is nothing **left** for me but the grave.
	19.10	He uproots my hope and **leaves** me to wither and die.
	20.21	he eats, there is nothing **left over**, but now his prosperity
	21.14	The wicked tell God to **leave** them alone;
	22. 6	you took away his clothes and **left** him nothing to wear.
	22.20	own is destroyed, and fire burns up anything that is **left**.
	39.14	The ostrich **leaves** her eggs on the ground for the heat

Job 41.32 He **leaves** a shining path behind him and turns the sea to
Ps 3. 7 You punish all my enemies and **leave** them powerless to harm me.
7. 5 me down and kill me and **leave** me lifeless on the ground!
12. 1 There is not a good man **left;**
17.14 children and some **left over** for their children's children!
22.15 You have **left** me for dead in the dust.
27. 9 don't **leave** me, don't abandon me, O God, my saviour.
39.13 **Leave** me alone so that I may have some happiness before
41. 8 he will never **leave** his bed again."
44.19 Yet you **left** us helpless among wild animals;
49.10 They all **leave** their riches to their descendants.
55.22 **Leave** your troubles with the Lord, and he will defend you;
69.25 May their camps be **left** deserted;
69.25 may no one be **left** alive in their tents.
74. 9 there are no prophets **left,** and no one knows how long this
79. 1 They have desecrated your holy Temple and **left** Jerusalem in ruins.
79. 2 They **left** the bodies of your people for the vultures, the
79. 3 through Jerusalem, and no one was **left** to bury the dead.
89.40 down the walls of his city and **left** his forts in ruins.
105.38 The Egyptians were afraid of them and were glad when they **left.**
106.11 not one of them was **left.**
109.12 be kind to him or care for the orphans he **leaves** behind.
114. 1 When the people of Israel **left** Egypt,
114. 1 when Jacob's descendants **left** that foreign land,
139.19 How I wish violent men would **leave** me alone!
Prov 5. 4 is all over, she **leaves** you nothing but bitterness and pain.
9. 6 **Leave** the company of ignorant people, and live.
12. 7 men meet their downfall and **leave** no descendants, but the
13.22 man will have wealth to **leave** to his grandchildren, but the
Ecc 2.18 that I would have to **leave** it to my successor, [19] and he
2.21 and then you have to **leave** it all to someone who hasn't
5.14 and end up with nothing **left** to pass on to their children.
5.15 We **leave** this world just as we entered it—with nothing.
Song 3. 4 As soon as I **left** them, I found him.
Is 1. 8 Jerusalem alone is **left,** a city under siege—as defenceless
3.17 punish them—I will shave their heads and **leave** them bald."
4. 3 Everyone who is **left** in Jerusalem, whom God has chosen for survival,
5.25 of those who die will be **left** in the streets like rubbish.
7.22 Yes, the few survivors **left** in the land will have milk and
10.19 will be so few trees **left** that even a child will be
10.28 They **left** their supplies at Michmash!
11.11 of his people who are **left** in Assyria and Egypt, in the
11.15 to dry up the Euphrates, **leaving** only seven tiny streams, so
11.16 just as there was for their ancestors when they **left** Egypt.
14.22 I will **leave** nothing—no children, no survivors at all.
14.30 on you Philistines, and it will not **leave** any of you alive.
15. 6 the grass beside it has withered, and nothing green is **left.**
15. 9 there will be a bloody slaughter of everyone **left** in Moab.
17. 6 very top, or a few that are **left** on the lower branches.
17. 9 cities will be deserted and **left** in ruins like the cities
18. 6 of their soldiers will be **left** exposed to the birds and the
21.17 the bravest men of Kedar, but few of them will be **left.**
22. 4 Now **leave** me alone to weep bitterly over all those of my
23.13 the fortifications of Tyre, and **left** the city in ruins.
24. 1 The Lord is going to devastate the earth and **leave** it desolate.
27. 9 incense-altars or symbols of the goddess Asherah are **left.**
28. 8 are all covered with vomit, and not a clean spot is **left.**
30.17 Nothing will be **left** of your army except a lonely flagstaff
37. 8 learnt that the emperor had **left** Lachish and was fighting
39. 6 Nothing will be **left.**
46. 3 to me, descendants of Jacob, all who are **left** of my people.
47.15 They all will **leave** you and go their own way,
47.15 and none will be **left** to save you."
49.17 are coming soon, and those who destroyed you will **leave.**
49.19 And those who **left** you in ruins will be far removed from
49.21 I was **left** all alone— where did these children come from?' "
52.11 Make sure you **leave** Babylonia,
52.11 keep yourselves holy and **leave.**
52.12 This time you will not have to **leave** in a hurry;
54. 1 more children than a woman whose husband never **left** her!
54. 7 "For one brief moment I **left** you;
55. 7 Let the wicked **leave** their way of life and change their
55.12 "You will **leave** Babylon with joy;
59. 7 You **leave** ruin and destruction wherever you go, [8] and no one
66.24 "As they **leave,** they will see the dead bodies of those
Jer 3. 1 his wife, and she **leaves** him and becomes another man's wife,
4. 7 cities of Judah will be **left** in ruins, and no one will
4.20 the whole country is **left** in ruins.
4.29 Every town will be **left** empty, and no one will live in
5.23 you have turned aside and **left** me.
9.19 We must **leave** our land;
9.22 fields, like corn cut and **left** behind by the reapers, corn
10.18 is going to crush you until not one of you is **left.**
10.20 there is no one **left** to put up our tents again;
10.25 they have destroyed us completely and **left** our country in ruins.
15. 3 eat them, and wild animals will devour what is **left over.**
17.19 through which the kings of Judah enter and **leave** the city;
19.14 Then I **left** Topheth, where the Lord had sent me to
24.10 is not one of them **left** in the land that I gave
25. 9 nation and its neighbours and **leave** them in ruins for ever,
25.11 This whole land will be **left** in ruins and will be a
25.12 I will destroy that country and **leave** it in ruins for ever.
25.36 your nation and **left** your peaceful country in ruins.
25.38 Lord has abandoned his people like a lion that **leaves** its cave.
26. 2 Do not **leave** out anything.
27.19 Judah and Jerusalem, he **left** the columns, the bronze tank,
27.21 about the treasures that are **left** in the Temple and in the
28.11 Then I **left.**
31. 7 he has rescued all who are **left.'**
Jer 31.21 find again the way by which you **left.**
31.21 Come back, people of Israel, come home to the towns you **left.**
34. 7 Lachish and Azekah, the only other fortified cities **left** in Judah.
37.10 that only wounded men are **left,** lying in their tents, those
37.12 So I started to **leave** Jerusalem and go to the territory
38. 4 is doing the same thing to everyone else **left** in the city.
38.22 I saw all the women **left** in Judah's royal palace being led
38.22 feet have sunk in the mud, his friends have **left** him.' "
39. 4 They **left** by way of the royal garden, went through the
39. 9 Babylonia the people who were **left** in the city, together
39.10 He **left** in the land of Judah some of the poorest people,
40. 6 Mizpah and lived among the people who were **left** in the land.
40.12 So they **left** the places where they had been scattered,
40.15 bring disaster on all the people who are **left** in Judah."
42. 2 now only a few of us are **left,** as you can see.
42.13 "But you people who are **left** in Judah must not
42.19 told you people who are **left** in Judah not to go to
43. 5 army officers took everybody **left** in Judah away to Egypt,
43. 6 the commanding officer had **left** under the care of Gedaliah,
43.12 pick the land of Egypt clean and then **leave** victorious.
44. 6 They were **left** in ruins and became a horrifying sight, as
44. 7 and babies, so that none of your people will be **left?**
44.12 people of Judah who are **left** and are determined to go and
44.14 people of Judah who are **left** and have come to Egypt to
44.27 in war or of disease, until not one of you is **left.**
48. 9 Its towns will be **left** in ruins, and no one will live
48.11 Moab is like wine **left** to settle undisturbed and never
48.18 Moab's destroyer is here and has **left** its forts in ruins.
48.28 "You people who live in Moab, **leave** your towns!
49. 2 battle, and it will be **left** in ruins and its villages burnt
49. 9 When men pick grapes, they **leave** a few on the vines, and
49.10 Not one of them is **left.**
49.11 **Leave** your orphans with me, and I will take care of them.
50. 8 **Leave** the country!
50. 8 Be the first to **leave!**
50.13 it will be **left** in ruins, and all who pass by will
50.26 **Leave** nothing at all!
51. 2 they will attack from every side and **leave** the land bare.
51. 9 Let's **leave** her now and go back home.
51.25 of you, level you to the ground, and **leave** you in ashes.
52. 6 that the people had nothing **left** to eat, [7] the city walls
52. 7 They **left** by way of the royal garden, went through the
52.15 Babylonia the people who were **left** in the city, the
52.16 But he **left** in Judah some of the poorest people, who
Lam 1. 2 Of all her former friends, not one is **left** to comfort her.
1.13 Then he abandoned me and **left** me in constant pain.
1.16 my people have nothing **left.**
2. 5 He has **left** her forts and palaces in ruins.
3. 4 He has **left** my flesh open and raw, and has broken my
3.11 chased me off the road, tore me to pieces, and **left** me.
5.16 Nothing is **left** of all we were proud of.
Ezek 5.10 you and scatter in every direction any who are **left** alive.
9. 8 Jerusalem that you are going to kill everyone **left** in Israel?"
10. 7 The man took the coals and **left.**
10.18 light of the Lord's presence **left** the entrance of the Temple
11.13 Are you going to kill everyone **left** in Israel?"
11.23 Then the dazzling light **left** the city and moved to the
12. 3 Let everyone see you **leaving** and going to another place.
12. 4 then let them watch you **leave** in the evening as if you
12. 7 While everyone watched, I put the pack on my shoulder and **left.**
13.14 to shatter it, and to **leave** the foundation stones bare.
14. 6 Turn back and **leave** your disgusting idols.
16.39 your clothes and jewels and **leave** you completely naked.
22.14 you will have any courage **left** or have strength enough to
22.18 copper, tin, iron, and lead—**left over** after silver has been
22.25 they can get, and by their murders **leave** many widows.
23.29 you have worked for and **leave** you stripped naked, exposed
24. 6 after piece of meat is taken out, and not one is **left.**
24. 8 I have **left** the blood there, where it cannot be hidden,
24.21 of your families who are **left** in Jerusalem will be killed in
25.16 I will destroy everyone **left** living there on the Philistine Plain.
26. 4 will sweep away all the dust and **leave** only a bare rock.
26.14 I will **leave** only a bare rock where fishermen can dry
28.16 So I forced you to **leave** my holy mountain, and the angel
28.17 you to the ground and **left** you as a warning to other
29. 5 Your body will fall on the ground and be **left** unburied.
30. 4 The country will be plundered And **left** in ruins.
30. 7 in the world, and its cities will be **left** totally in ruins.
31.12 Ruthless foreigners will cut it down and **leave** it.
35. 4 I will **leave** your cities in ruins And your land desolate;
36. 4 to you places that were **left** in ruins, and to you deserted
36.10 in the cities and rebuild everything that was **left** in ruins.
36.20 the people of the Lord, but they had to **leave** his land.'
36.35 were torn down, looted, and **left** in ruins, are now inhabited
39.28 into their own land, not **leaving** even one of them behind.
42.14 the outer courtyard, they must **leave** in these rooms the holy
44. 3 He is to enter and **leave** the gateway through the entrance
44.19 on duty in the Temple and **leave** them in the holy rooms.
46. 8 The prince must **leave** the entrance room of the gateway and
46. 9 the north gate are to **leave** by the south gate after they
46. 9 enter by the south gate are to **leave** by the north gate.
46. 9 same way as he entered, but must **leave** by the opposite gate.
46.10 to come in when the people come, and **leave** when they leave.
48.15 the special area that is **left,** twelve and a half kilometres
48.18 The land that is **left** after the city has been built in
Dan 2.35 The wind carried it all away, **leaving** not a trace.
4.15 But **leave** the stump in the ground with a band of iron
4.15 **Leave** it there in the field with the grass.
4.23 tree down and destroy it, but **leave** the stump in the ground.
4.23 and bronze round it, and **leave** it there in the field with
4.26 The angel ordered the stump to be **left** in the ground.

Dan 10. 8 I was **left** there alone, watching this amazing vision.
10. 8 I had no strength **left,** and my face was so changed that
10.13 to help me, because I had been **left** there alone in Persia.
10.17 I have no strength or breath **left** in me."
11.41 of Edom, Moab, and what is **left** of Ammon will escape.
Hos 1. 2 In the same way, my people have **left** me and become unfaithful."
4.12 They have **left** me.
5. 6 They cannot find him, for he has **left** them.
5.14 I myself will tear them to pieces and then **leave** them.
7.13 They have **left** me and rebelled against me.
9.12 up children, I would take them away and not **leave** one alive.
Joel 1. 4 what one swarm **left,** the next swarm devoured.
2.16 Even newly married couples must **leave** their room and come.
Amos 1. 8 of Ekron, and all the Philistines who are **left** will die."
5.15 to the people of this nation who are still **left** alive.
6. 9 If there are ten men **left** in a family, they will die.
6.10 call to whoever is still **left** in the house, "Is anyone else
7. 9 The holy places of Israel will be **left** in ruins.
9.12 Israel will conquer what is **left** of the land of Edom and
Obad 5 When people gather grapes, they always **leave** a few.
Jon 4. 2 didn't I say before I **left** home that this is just what
Mic 2.12 gather you together, all you people of Israel that are **left.**
4. 7 beginning with those who are **left,** and they will become a
4.10 now you will have to **leave** the city and live in the
5. 8 Those who are **left** among the nations will be like a lion
5.12 charms you use and **leave** you without any fortune-tellers.
7. 1 man who finds no fruit **left** on the trees and no grapes
7. 2 is not an honest person **left** in the land, no one loyal
Zeph 1. 3 I will destroy all mankind, and no survivors will be **left.**
2. 4 No one will be **left** in the city of Gaza.
2. 5 He will destroy you, and not one of you will be **left.**
3. 3 hungry wolves, too greedy to **leave** a bone until morning.
3. 6 their cities and **left** their walls and towers in ruins.
3. 6 the streets are empty—no one is **left.**
3.12 I will **leave** there a humble and lowly people, who will
Hag 2.19 Although there is no corn **left,** and the grapevines,
Zech 5. 4 It will remain in their houses and **leave** them in ruins."
7.14 This good land was **left** a desolate place, with no one living
8. 6 the nation who are now **left,** but it's not impossible for me.
9. 5 Gaza will lose her king, and Ashkelon will be **left** deserted.
11. 9 Those who are **left** will destroy one another."
Mal 4. 1 they will burn up, and there will be nothing **left** of them.
Mt 2. 9 And so they **left,** and on their way they saw the same
2.13 After they had **left,** an angel of the Lord appeared in
2.13 escape to Egypt, and stay there until I tell you to **leave."**
2.14 child and his mother, and **left** during the night for Egypt,
4.11 Then the Devil **left** Jesus;
4.20 At once they **left** their nets and went with him.
4.22 and at once they **left** the boat and their father, and
5.24 brother has something against you, [24]**leave** your gift there in
8.15 the fever **left** her, and she got up and began to wait
8.32 so they **left** and went off into the pigs.
8.34 they saw him, they begged him to **leave** their territory.
9. 9 Jesus **left** that place, and as he walked along, he saw
9.27 Jesus **left** that place, and as he walked along, two blind
9.31 But they **left** and spread the news about Jesus all over
9.32 As the men were **leaving,** some people brought to Jesus a
10.11 welcome you, and stay with him until you **leave** that place.
10.14 or listen to you, then **leave** that place and shake the dust
11. 1 to his twelve disciples, he **left** that place and went off to
11. 7 While John's disciples were **leaving,** Jesus spoke about him to
12. 9 Jesus **left** that place and went to a synagogue,
12.14 Then the Pharisees **left** and made plans to kill Jesus.
13. 1 That same day Jesus **left** the house and went to the lake-side,
13.36 When Jesus had **left** the crowd and gone indoors, his disciples
13.53 finished telling these parables, he **left** that place [54]and went
14.13 the news about John, he **left** there in a boat and went
14.13 heard about it, so they **left** their towns and followed him by
14.16 "They don't have to **leave,"** answered Jesus.
14.20 disciples took up twelve baskets full of what was **left over.**
15.21 Jesus **left** that place and went off to the territory near
15.27 the dogs eat the **leftovers** that fall from their masters' table."
15.29 Jesus **left** there and went along by Lake Galilee.
15.37 Then the disciples took up seven baskets full of pieces **left over.**
16. 4 So he **left** them and went away.
18.12 He will **leave** the other ninety-nine grazing on the hillside
19. 1 finished saying these things, he **left** Galilee and went to the
19. 5 this reason a man will **leave** his father and mother and unite
19.27 "Look," he said, "we have **left** everything and followed you.
19.29 And everyone who has **left** houses or brothers or sisters
20.29 Jesus and his disciples were **leaving** Jericho, a large crowd was
21.17 Jesus **left** them and went out of the city to Bethany,
22.22 they **left** him and went away.
22.25 having children, so he **left** his widow to his brother.
24. 1 Jesus **left** and was going away from the Temple when his
24. 2 not a single stone here will be **left** in its place;
24.40 one will be taken away, the other will be **left** behind.
24.41 one will be taken away, the other will be **left** behind.
25.15 Then he **left** on his journey.
26.31 you will run away and **leave** me, for the scripture says,
26.33 to Jesus, "I will never **leave** you, even though all the rest
26.44 Again Jesus **left** them, went away, and prayed the third time,
26.56 Then all the disciples **left** him and ran away.
27. 5 Judas threw the coins down in the Temple and **left;**
27.53 They **left** the graves, and after Jesus rose from death,
27.66 So they **left** and made the tomb secure
27.66 putting a seal on the stone and **leaving** the guard on watch.
28. 8 So they **left** the tomb in a hurry, afraid and yet filled
Mk 1.18 At once they **left** their nets and went with him.
1.20 they **left** their father Zebedee in the boat with the hired
1.29 disciples, including James and John, **left** the synagogue and went
Mk 1.31 The fever **left** her, and she began to wait on them.
1.35 long before daylight, Jesus got up and **left** the house.
1.42 At once the disease **left** the man, and he was clean.
2. 2 that there was no room **left,** not even out in front of
3. 6 So the Pharisees **left** the synagogue and met at once with
4.36 So they **left** the crowd;
5.17 So they asked Jesus to **leave** their territory.
5.20 So the man **left** and went all through the Ten Towns,
6. 1 Jesus **left** that place and went back to his home town,
6.10 welcomed, stay in the same house until you **leave** that place.
6.11 will not listen to you, **leave** it and shake the dust off
6.27 The guard **left,** went to the prison, and cut John's head off;
6.33 Many people, however, saw them **leave** and knew at once
6.43 baskets full of what was **left** of the bread and the fish.
6.54 As they **left** the boat, people recognized Jesus at once.
7.17 When he **left** the crowd and went into the house, his
7.24 Then Jesus **left** and went away to the territory near the
7.28 "even the dogs under the table eat the children's **leftovers!"**
7.31 Jesus then **left** the neighbourhood of Tyre and went on through
8. 1 the people had nothing **left** to eat, Jesus called the disciples
8. 8 Then the disciples took up seven baskets full of pieces **left over.**
8.13 He **left** them, got back into the boat, and started across
8.19 How many baskets full of **leftover pieces** did you take up?"
8.20 "how many baskets full of **leftover pieces** did you take up?"
9.30 Jesus and his disciples **left** that place and went on through
10. 1 Then Jesus **left** that place, went to the province of Judaea,
10. 7 this reason a man will **leave** his father and mother and unite
10.28 Peter spoke up, "Look, we have **left** everything and followed you."
10.29 tell you that anyone who **leaves** home or brothers or sisters
10.46 Jericho, and as Jesus was **leaving** with his disciples and a
11.19 When evening came, Jesus and his disciples **left** the city.
12. 1 let out the vineyard to tenants and **left** home on a journey.
12. 6 The only one **left** to send was the man's own dear son.
12.12 were afraid of the crowd, so they **left** him and went away.
12.19 'If a man dies and **leaves** a wife but no children,
13. 1 As Jesus was **leaving** the Temple, one of his disciples said,
13. 2 Not a single stone here will be **left** in its place;
13.34 home on a journey and **leaves** his servants in charge, after
14. 6 But Jesus said, **"Leave** her alone!
14.16 The disciples **left,** went to the city, and found everything
14.27 you will run away and **leave** me, for the scripture says,
14.29 Peter answered, "I will never **leave** you, even though all the
14.50 Then all the disciples **left** him and ran away.
14.52 arrest him, [52]but he ran away naked, **leaving** the cloth behind.
Lk 1.24 Elizabeth became pregnant and did not **leave** the house for five
1.38 And the angel **left** her.
2.36 She never **left** the Temple;
4.13 tempting Jesus in every way, he **left** him for a while.
4.38 Jesus **left** the synagogue and went to Simon's house.
4.39 and stood at her bedside and ordered the fever to **leave** her.
4.39 The fever **left** her, and she got up at once and began
4.42 At daybreak Jesus **left** the town and went off to a lonely
4.42 when they found him, they tried to keep him from **leaving.**
5. 2 the fishermen had **left** them and were washing the nets.
5.11 the boats up on the beach, **left** everything, and followed Jesus.
5.13 At once the disease **left** the man.
5.28 Levi got up, **left** everything, and followed him.
7.24 John's messengers had **left,** Jesus began to speak about him to
8.37 So Jesus got into the boat and **left.**
9. 4 welcomed, stay in the same house until you **leave** that town;
9. 5 people don't welcome you, **leave** that town and shake the dust
9. 6 The disciples **left** and travelled through all the villages,
9.17 the disciples took up twelve baskets of what was **left over.**
9.33 As the men were **leaving** Jesus, Peter said to him, "Master,
10.30 stripped him, and beat him up, **leaving** him half dead.
10.40 care that my sister has **left** me to do all the work
11.53 When Jesus **left** that place, the teachers of the Law and
12.13 brother to divide with me the property our father **left** us."
13. 8 the gardener answered, **'Leave** it alone, sir, just one more year;
15. 4 He **leaves** the other ninety-nine sheep in the pasture and goes
15.13 sold his part of the property and **left** home with the money.
15.14 spread over that country, and he was **left** without a thing.
17.29 On the day Lot **left** Sodom, fire and sulphur rained down
17.34 one will be taken away, the other will be **left** behind.
17.35 one will be taken away, the other will be **left** behind."
18.28 We have **left** our homes to follow you."
18.29 assure you that anyone who **leaves** home or wife or brothers
19.13 Before he **left,** he called his ten servants and gave them
19.44 a single stone will they **leave** in its place, because you did
20. 9 it out to tenants, and then **left** home for a long time.
20.28 'If a man dies and **leaves** a wife but no children,
21. 6 when not a single stone here will be **left** in its place;
21.21 are in the city must **leave,** and those who are out in
22.39 Jesus **left** the city and went, as he usually did, to the
Jn 2. 3 out, Jesus' mother said to him, "They have no wine **left."**
4. 3 was being said, he **left** Judaea and went back to Galilee;
4.28 Then the woman **left** her water jar, went back to the town,
4.30 So they **left** the town and went to Jesus.
4.43 After spending two days there, Jesus **left** and went to Galilee.
4.52 "It was one o'clock yesterday afternoon when the fever **left** him."
5.15 Then the man **left** and told the Jewish authorities that
6.12 he said to his disciples, "Gather the pieces **left over;**
6.13 baskets with the pieces **left over** from the five barley loaves
6.22 it with his disciples, but that they had **left** without him.
6.67 twelve disciples, "And you—would you also like to **leave?"**
7. 3 Jesus' brothers said to him, **"Leave** this place and go to Judaea,
8. 9 they heard this, they all **left,** one by one, the older ones
8. 9 Jesus was **left** alone, with the woman still standing there.
8.10 Is there no one **left** to condemn you?"
8.29 he has not **left** me alone, because I always do what pleases
8.59 to throw at him, but Jesus hid himself and **left** the Temple.

Jn 10.12 sees a wolf coming, he **leaves** the sheep and runs away;
11.54 travel openly in Judaea, but **left** and went to a place near
12. 7 But Jesus said, "**Leave** her alone!
13. 1 had come for him to **leave** this world and go to the
13.31 After Judas had **left,** Jesus said, "Now the Son of Man's
14.18 "When I go, you will not be **left** all alone;
14.27 "Peace is what I **leave** with you;
14.28 say to you, 'I am **leaving,** but I will come back to
16.28 and now I am **leaving** the world and going to the Father."
16.32 one to his own home, and I will be **left** all alone.
18. 1 had said this prayer, he **left** with his disciples and went
Acts 1. 4 "Do not **leave** Jerusalem, but wait for the gift I told you
1.25 the place of Judas, who **left** to go to the place where
4.15 So they told them to **leave** the Council room, and then
5.38 **Leave** them alone!
5.41 As the apostles **left** the Council, they were happy, because God
7. 3 and said to him, '**Leave** your family and country and go
7. 4 And so he **left** his country and went to live in Haran.
7.58 The witnesses **left** their cloaks in the care of a young man
12.10 They walked down a street, and suddenly the angel **left** Peter.
12.17 then he **left** and went somewhere else.
12.19 After this, Herod **left** Judaea and spent some time in Caesarea.
13.13 Pamphylia, where John Mark **left** them and went back to Jerusalem.
13.42 Paul and Barnabas were **leaving** the synagogue, the people invited
13.43 the people had **left** the meeting, Paul and Barnabas were followed
13.46 of eternal life, we will **leave** you and go to the Gentiles.
15.38 mission, but had turned back and **left** them in Pamphylia.
15.40 while Paul chose Silas and **left,** commended by the believers
16.10 vision, we got ready to **leave** for Macedonia, because we decided
16.11 **left** by ship from Troas and sailed straight across to Samothrace,
16.36 You may **leave,** then, and go in peace."
16.39 them out of the prison and asked them to **leave** the city.
16.40 Paul and Silas **left** the prison and went to Lydia's house.
16.40 met the believers, spoke words of encouragement to them, and **left.**
17.33 And so Paul **left** the meeting.
18. 1 After this, Paul **left** Athens and went on to Corinth.
18. 2 the Emperor Claudius had ordered all the Jews to **leave** Rome.
18. 7 So he **left** them and went to live in the house of
18.18 for many days, then **left** them and sailed off with Priscilla
18.19 They arrived in Ephesus, where Paul **left** Priscilla and Aquila.
18.21 he told them as he **left,** "If it is the will of
18.23 spending some time there, he **left** and went through the
19. 9 So Paul **left** them and took the believers with him, and every
20. 1 Then he **left** and went on to Macedonia.
20. 7 until midnight, since he was going to **leave** the next day.
20.11 with them for a long time, even until sunrise, Paul **left.**
20.29 I know that after I **leave,** fierce wolves will come among you,
21. 1 We said good-bye to them and **left.**
21. 5 time with them was over, we **left** and went on our way.
21. 8 On the following day we **left** and arrived in Caesarea.
21.15 time there, we got our things ready and **left** for Jerusalem.
22.18 'Hurry and **leave** Jerusalem quickly, because the people here
23.23 hundred spearmen, and be ready to **leave** by nine o'clock tonight.
23.32 returned to the fort and **left** the horsemen to go on with
24.25 Day of Judgement, Felix was afraid and said, "You may **leave** now.
24.27 to gain favour with the Jews so he **left** Paul in prison.
25.14 "There is a man here who was **left** a prisoner by Felix;
26.31 others got up, [31] and after **leaving** they said to each other,
27. 2 which was ready to **leave** for the seaports of the province
28.25 So they **left,** disagreeing among themselves, after Paul had
Rom 3.16 they **leave** ruin and destruction wherever they go.
4.20 His faith did not **leave** him, and he did not doubt God's
9.29 Lord Almighty had not **left** us some descendants, we would have
11. 3 I am the only one **left,** and they are trying to kill
11. 5 there is a small number **left** of those whom God has chosen
15.28 raised for them, I shall **leave** for Spain and visit you on
1 Cor 1.20 So then, where does that **leave** the wise?
7.10 a wife must not **leave** her husband;
7.15 not a believer wishes to **leave** the Christian partner, let it
7.29 there is not much time **left,** and from now on married men
2 Cor 2. 2 to make you sad, who would be **left** to cheer me up?
5. 8 and would much prefer to **leave** our home in the body and
6.17 the Lord says, "You must **leave** them and separate yourselves from
Gal 4.27 have more children than the woman whose husband never **left** her."
Eph 5.31 this reason a man will **leave** his father and mother and unite
Phil 1.23 I want very much to **leave** this life and be with Christ,
4.15 very well that when I **left** Macedonia in the early days of
2 Tim 2.18 They have **left** the way of truth and are upsetting the
4. 6 the time is here for me to **leave** this life.
4.13 you come, bring my coat that I **left** in Troas with Carpus;
4.20 stayed in Corinth, and I **left** Trophimus in Miletus, because he
Tit 1. 5 I **left** you in Crete, so that you could put in order
Heb 6. 1 then, to mature teaching and **leave** behind us the first
10.27 Instead, all that is **left** is to wait in fear for the
11. 8 He **left** his own country without knowing where he was going.
11.15 They did not keep thinking about the country they had **left;**
11.22 from Egypt, and **leave** instructions about what should be done
11.27 was faith that made Moses **leave** Egypt without being afraid of
13. 5 For God has said, "I will never **leave** you;
1 Pet 2.21 himself suffered for you and **left** you an example, so that
5. 7 **Leave** all your worries with him, because he cares for you.
2 Pet 2.15 They have **left** the straight path and have lost their way;
1 Jn 2.19 not belong to our fellowship, and that is why they **left** us;
2.19 But they **left** so that it might be clear that none of
3.14 We know that we have **left** death and come over into life;
Rev 3.12 in the temple of my God, and he will never **leave** it.
Rev 12.12 because he knows that he has only a little time **left.**"
17.16 they will take away everything she has and **leave** her naked;

LEAVEN

see also **UNLEAVENED, YEAST**

Ex 12.39 time to get their food ready or to prepare **leavened** dough.
13. 3 No **leavened** bread is to be eaten.
13. 7 must be no yeast or **leavened** bread anywhere in your land.

LEBANON

Mountain range in n. Palestine.

Deut 1. 7 Canaan and on beyond the **Lebanon** Mountains as far as the
3.25 the beautiful hill-country and the **Lebanon** Mountains.'
11.24 in the south to the **Lebanon** Mountains in the north, and from
Josh 1. 4 desert in the south to the **Lebanon** Mountains in the north;
9. 1 plain of the Mediterranean Sea as far north as **Lebanon;**
11.17 the north, in the valley of **Lebanon** south of Mount Hermon.
12. 7 Baalgad in the valley of **Lebanon** to Mount Halak in the south
13. 5 all of **Lebanon** to the east, from Baalgad, which is south of
13. 6 between the **Lebanon** Mountains and Misrephoth Maim.
Judg 3. 3 Hivites who lived in the **Lebanon** Mountains from Mount Baal
9.15 of my thorny branches and burn up the cedars of **Lebanon.**'
1 Kgs 4.33 trees and plants, from the **Lebanon** cedars to the hyssop that
5. 6 So send your men to **Lebanon** to cut down cedars for me.
5. 9 bring the logs down from **Lebanon** to the sea, and will tie
5.14 group spent one month in **Lebanon** and two months back home.
7. 2 Hall of the Forest of **Lebanon** was 44 metres long, 22 metres
9.19 in Jerusalem, in **Lebanon,** and elsewhere in his kingdom.
10.17 these shields placed in the Hall of the Forest of **Lebanon.**
10.21 in the Hall of the Forest of **Lebanon** were of pure gold.
2 Kgs 14. 9 a thorn bush on the **Lebanon** Mountains sent a message to a
19.23 chariots you had conquered the highest mountains of **Lebanon.**
2 Chr 2. 8 so send me cedar, cypress, and juniper logs from **Lebanon.**
2.16 In the mountains of **Lebanon** we will cut down all the
8. 6 for building in Jerusalem, in **Lebanon,** and throughout the
9.16 had them all placed in the Hall of the Forest of **Lebanon.**
9.20 in the Hall of the Forest of **Lebanon** were of pure gold.
25.18 a thorn bush in the **Lebanon** Mountains sent a message to a
Ezra 3. 7 in exchange for cedar-trees from **Lebanon,** which were to be
Ps 29. 5 of the Lord breaks the cedars, even the cedars of **Lebanon.**
29. 6 He makes the mountains of **Lebanon** jump like calves and
37.35 he towered over everyone like a cedar of **Lebanon;**
72.16 be covered with crops, as fruitful as those of **Lebanon.**
92.12 they will grow like the cedars of **Lebanon.**
104.16 The cedars of **Lebanon** get plenty of rain— the Lord's own
Song 4. 8 Come with me from the **Lebanon** Mountains, my bride;
4. 8 come with me from **Lebanon.**
4.11 Your clothing has all the fragrance of **Lebanon.**
4.15 water, brooks gushing down from the **Lebanon** Mountains.
5.15 He is majestic, like the **Lebanon** Mountains
7. 4 as the tower of **Lebanon** that stands guard at Damascus.
Is 2.13 destroy the tall cedars of **Lebanon** and all the oaks in the
10.34 down with an axe, as even the finest trees of **Lebanon** fall!
14. 8 and the cedars of **Lebanon** rejoice over the fallen king,
33. 9 The forests of **Lebanon** have withered, the fertile valley of
35. 2 be as beautiful as the **Lebanon** Mountains and as fertile as
37.24 chariots you had conquered the highest mountains of **Lebanon.**
40.16 animals in the forests of **Lebanon** are not enough for a
60.13 from the forests of **Lebanon,** Will be brought to rebuild you,
Jer 18.14 Are **Lebanon's** rocky heights ever without snow?
22. 6 as the land of Gilead and as the **Lebanon** Mountains;
22.20 People of Jerusalem, go to **Lebanon** and shout, go to the
22.23 You rest secure among the cedars brought from **Lebanon;**
Ezek 17. 3 He flew to the **Lebanon** Mountains and broke off the top of
27. 5 And a cedar from **Lebanon** for your mast.
31. 3 are like a cedar in **Lebanon,** With beautiful, shady branches,
31.15 will bring darkness over the **Lebanon** Mountains and make all
31.16 the choice, well-watered trees of **Lebanon** who have gone to
Hos 14. 5 they will be firmly rooted like the trees of **Lebanon.**
14. 6 They will be fragrant like the cedars of **Lebanon.**
14. 7 They will be as famous as the wine of **Lebanon.**
Nah 1. 4 Mount Carmel turns brown, and the flowers of **Lebanon** fade.
Hab 2.17 You have cut down the forests of **Lebanon;**
Zech 10.10 I will settle them in Gilead and **Lebanon** also;
11. 1 Open your doors, **Lebanon,**

LECTURE HALL

Acts 19. 9 every day he held discussions in the **lecture hall** of Tyrannus.

LEDGE

Ezek 40.43 **Ledges** seventy-five millimetres wide ran round the edge

LEECH

Prov 30.15 A **leech** has two daughters, and both are named "Give me!"

LEEKS

Num 11. 5 the cucumbers, the water-melons, the **leeks,** the onions, and

LEFT

see also **LEAVE**

Gen 48.13 Joseph put Ephraim at Jacob's **left** and Manasseh at his right.
48.14 was the younger, and his **left hand** on the head of Manasseh,
Lev 14.15 the palm of his own **left hand,** [16] dip a finger of his
14.26 the palm of his own **left hand** [27] and with a finger of

Judg 3.15 This was Ehud, a **left-handed** man, who was the son of Gera,
3.21 With his **left hand** Ehud took the sword from his right
7.20 torches in their **left hands,** the trumpets in their right,
20.15 Gibeah gathered seven hundred specially chosen men who were **left-handed.**
2 Kgs 23. 8 governor, which was to the **left** of the main gate as one
1 Chr 12. 2 shoot arrows and sling stones either right-handed or **left-handed.**
Neh 8. 4 and the following stood at his **left:**
12.38 gave thanks went to the **left** along the top of the wall,
Song 2. 6 His **left hand** is under my head, and his right hand
8. 3 Your **left hand** is under my head, and your right hand
Is 30.21 to the right or the **left,** you will hear his voice behind
Ezek 1.10 a bull's face at the **left,** and an eagle's face at the
4. 4 "Then lie down on your **left** side, and I will place on
4. 9 eat during the 390 days you are lying on your **left** side.
21.16 Cut to the right and the **left,** you sharp sword!
39. 3 his bow out of his **left hand** and his arrows out of
Mt 5.39 you on the right cheek, let him slap your **left** cheek too.
20.21 will sit at your right and your **left** when you are King."
20.23 right to choose who will sit at my right and my **left.**
25.33 righteous people on his right and the others on his **left.**
25.41 say to those on his **left,** 'Away from me, you that are
27.38 with Jesus, one on his right and the other on his **left.**
Mk 10.37 sit with you, one at your right and one at your **left."**
10.40 right to choose who will sit at my right and my **left.**
15.27 with Jesus, one on his right and the other on his **left.**
Lk 23.33 two criminals, one on his right and the other on his **left.**
Rev 10. 2 on the sea and his **left** foot on the land, [3] and called

LEFT OVER
see also **LEAVE**

Ex 12.10 if any is **left over,** it must be burnt.
Lev 7.16 offered, but any that is **left over** may be eaten on the
8.32 Burn up any meat or bread that is **left over.**
10.12 "Take the grain-offering that is **left over** from the food
Ruth 2.14 she was satisfied, and she still had some food **left over.**
2.18 She also gave her the food **left over** from the meal.
2 Kgs 4. 7 there will be enough money **left over** for you and your sons
4.43 Lord says that they will eat and still have some **left over."**
4.44 had said, they all ate and there was still some **left over.**
Ezra 7.18 silver and gold that is **left over** for whatever you and your
Job 20.21 he eats, there is nothing **left over,** but now his prosperity
Ps 17.14 children and some **left over** for their children's children!
Jer 15. 3 eat them, and wild animals will devour what is **left over.**
Ezek 22.18 copper, tin, iron, and lead—**left over** after silver has been
Mt 14.20 disciples took up twelve baskets full of what was **left over.**
15.27 the dogs eat the **leftovers** that fall from their masters' table."
15.37 Then the disciples took up seven baskets full of pieces **left over.**
Mk 7.28 "even the dogs under the table eat the children's **leftovers!"**
8. 8 Then the disciples took up seven baskets full of pieces **left over.**
8.19 How many baskets full of **leftover pieces** did you take up?"
8.20 "how many baskets full of **leftover pieces** did you take up?"
Lk 9.17 the disciples took up twelve baskets of what was **left over.**
Jn 6.12 he said to his disciples, "Gather the pieces **left over;**
6.13 baskets with the pieces **left over** from the five barley loaves

LEG

Ex 12. 9 including the head, the **legs,** and the internal organs.
25.12 attach them to its four **legs,** with two rings on each side.
25.26 it and put them at the four corners, where the **legs** are.
29.17 internal organs and its hind **legs,** and put them on top of
37.13 it and put them at the four corners, where the **legs** were.
Lev 1. 9 internal organs and the hind **legs,** and the officiating
1.13 internal organs and the hind **legs,** and the priest will
4.11 its flesh, its head, its **legs,** and its internal organs
7.32 The right hind **leg** of the animal shall be given as a
7.34 gift, and the right hind **leg** is a special contribution that
8.20 organs and the hind **legs** with water, and burnt the head,
8.25 the kidneys with the fat on them, and the right hind **leg.**
8.26 put them on top of the fat and the right hind **leg.**
9.14 internal organs and the hind **legs** and burnt them on the
9.21 breasts and the right hind **legs** as the special gift to the
10.14 the breast and the hind **leg** that are presented as the
10.15 They shall bring the hind **leg** and the breast at the time
11.42 whether they crawl, or walk on four **legs,** or have many legs.
Num 6.20 to the breast and the **leg** of the ram which by law
18.18 the breast and the right hind **leg** of the special offering.
Deut 28.35 The Lord will cover your **legs** with incurable, painful
Judg 3.22 king's belly, and it stuck out behind, between his **legs.**
1 Sam 9.24 the choice piece of the **leg** and placed it before Saul.
17. 6 His **legs** were also protected by bronze armour, and he
Job 17. 7 my arms and **legs** are as thin as shadows.
18.13 spreads over his body and causes his arms and **legs** to rot.
40.17 up like a cedar, and the muscles in his **legs** are strong.
40.18 are as strong as bronze, and his **legs** are like iron bars.
41.12 me tell you about Leviathan's **legs** and describe how great
Prov 26. 7 proverb about as well as a crippled man can use his **legs.**
Ecc 12. 3 will tremble, and your **legs,** now strong, will grow weak.
Ezek 1. 7 Their **legs** were straight, and they had hoofs like those of
24. 4 the shoulders and the **legs**— fill it with choice bony
Dan 2.33 its **legs** of iron, and its feet partly of iron and partly
7. 5 The second beast looked like a bear standing on its hind **legs.**
10. 6 His arms and **legs** shone like polished bronze, and his voice
Amos 3.12 a shepherd recovers only two **legs** or an ear of a sheep
Lk 14. 2 A man whose **legs** and arms were swollen came to Jesus,
Jn 19.31 allow them to break the **legs** of the men who had been
19.32 soldiers went and broke the **legs** of the first man and then
19.33 that he was already dead, so they did not break his **legs.**
Rev 10. 1 was like the sun, and his **legs** were like pillars of fire.

LEGAL
see also **LAWFUL**

Lev 19.15 "Be honest and just when you make decisions in **legal** cases;
Num 27.11 to observe this as a **legal** requirement, just as I, the Lord,
Deut 21. 5 they are to decide every **legal** case involving violence.
21.17 first son and give him the share he is **legally** entitled to.
2 Chr 19. 8 **legal** disputes between inhabitants of the city.
Ps 94.20 corrupt judges, who make injustice **legal,** [21] who plot
Ezek 44.24 When a **legal** dispute arises, the priests are to decide
Lk 3.13 "Don't collect more than is **legal,"** he told them.
Acts 19.39 it will have to be settled in a **legal** meeting of citizens.
Rom 7. 3 her husband dies, she is **legally** a free woman and does not
1 Cor 6. 7 very fact that you have **legal** disputes among yourselves shows

LEGEND

1 Tim 1. 4 to give up those **legends** and those long lists of ancestors,
4. 7 But keep away from those godless **legends,** which are not worth
2 Tim 4. 4 from listening to the truth and give their attention to **legends.**
Tit 1.14 longer hold on to Jewish **legends** and to human commandments which

LEND

Ex 22.25 "If you **lend** money to any of my people who are poor,
Lev 25.37 interest on the money you **lend** him, and do not make a
Deut 15. 2 Everyone who has **lent** money to a fellow-Israelite is to
15. 6 You will **lend** money to many nations, but you will not have
15. 8 Instead, be generous and **lend** him as much as he needs.
15. 9 Do not refuse to **lend** him something, just because the year
23.19 "When you **lend** money or food or anything else to a fellow-Israelite,
23.20 charge interest on what you **lend** to a foreigner,
23.20 but not on what you **lend** to a fellow-Israelite.
24. 6 "When you **lend** a man something, you are not to take as
24.10 "When you **lend** a man something, do not go into his
28.12 work, so that you will **lend** to many nations, but you will
28.44 They will have money to **lend** you,
28.44 but you will have none to **lend** them.
Ps 37.26 times he gives freely and **lends** to others, and his children
Prov 19.17 the poor, it is like **lending** to the Lord, and the Lord
22. 7 Borrow money and you are the **lender's** slave.
Is 24. 2 and masters, buyers and sellers, **lenders** and borrowers,
Jer 15.10 I have not **lent** any money or borrowed any;
Ezek 18. 8 He doesn't **lend** money for profit.
18.13 worships disgusting idols, [13] and **lends** money for profit.
18.17 He refuses to do evil and doesn't **lend** money for profit.
Mt 5.42 when someone wants to borrow something, **lend** it to him.
Lk 6.34 And if you **lend** only to those from whom you hope to
6.34 Even sinners **lend** to sinners, to get back the same amount!
6.35 **lend** and expect nothing back.

LENGTH, LENGTHEN see LONG (1)

LEOPARD

Song 4. 8 Mount Senir and Mount Hermon, where the lions and **leopards** live.
Is 11. 6 in peace, and **leopards** will lie down with young goats.
Jer 5. 6 to pieces, and **leopards** will prowl through their towns.
13.23 the colour of his skin, or a **leopard** remove its spots?
Dan 7. 6 It looked like a **leopard,** but on its back there were four
Hos 13. 7 Like a **leopard** I will lie in wait along your path.
Hab 1. 8 "Their horses are faster than **leopards,** fiercer than hungry wolves.
Rev 13. 2 The beast looked like a **leopard,** with feet like a bear's

AV LEPER (LEPROSY) see SKIN-DISEASE

LESS

Gen 29.31 saw that Leah was loved **less** than Rachel, he made it
Ex 5. 8 the same number of bricks as before, not one brick **less.**
16.17 The Israelites did this, some gathering more, others **less.**
16.18 much, and those who gathered **less** did not have too little.
30.15 more, nor the poor man **less,** when they pay this amount for
Num 11.31 from the sea, flying **less** than a metre above the ground.
11.32 no one gathered **less** than a thousand kilogrammes.
Ezra 9.13 our God, have punished us **less** than we deserve and have
Job 11. 6 God is punishing you **less** than you deserve.
Prov 20.21 easily you get your wealth, the **less** good it will do you.
Jon 1. 5 order to **lessen** the danger, they threw the cargo overboard.
Jn 3.30 He must become more important while I become **less** important."
11.18 Bethany was **less** than three kilometres from Jerusalem,
2 Cor 12.15 Will you love me **less** because I love you so much?
Eph 3. 8 I am **less** than the least of all God's people;
1 Thes 2.19 After all, it is you—you, no **less** than others!
Heb 12.25 How much **less** shall we escape, then, if we turn away from

LESSON

Ps 2.10 learn this **lesson,** you rulers of the world:
Prov 6. 6 Lazy people should learn a **lesson** from the way ants live.
19.25 so that people who don't know any better can learn a **lesson.**
21.11 his punishment, even an unthinking person learns a **lesson.**
24.32 at this, thought about it, and learned a **lesson** from it:
Is 28.10 us letter by letter, line by line, **lesson by lesson."**
28.11 some strange-sounding language to teach you a **lesson.**

Is	28.13	teach you letter by letter, line by line, **lesson by lesson.**
Zeph	3. 7	that they would never forget the **lesson** I taught them.
Mt	24.32	"Let the fig-tree teach you a **lesson.**
Mk	13.28	"Let the fig-tree teach you a **lesson.**
Heb	5.12	need someone to teach you the first **lessons** of God's message.
	6. 1	and leave behind us the first **lessons** of the Christian message.

LET

Mt	21.33	Then he **let** out the vineyard to tenants and went on a
	21.41	they answered, "and **let** the vineyard out to other tenants,
Mk	12. 1	Then he **let** out the vineyard to tenants and left home on
Lk	20. 9	man who planted a vineyard, **let** it out to tenants, and then

LET GO

Gen	30.25	Jacob said to Laban, **"Let me go,** so that I can return
	32.26	The man said, **"Let me go;**
Ex	3.19	of Egypt will not **let you go** unless he is forced to
	3.20	After that he will **let you go.**
	4.21	make the king stubborn, and he will not **let the people go.**
	4.23	I told you to **let my son go,** so that he might
	5. 1	God of Israel, says, **'Let my people go,** so that they can
	6. 1	I will force him to **let my people go.**
	7.14	"The king is very stubborn and refuses to **let the people go.**
	7.16	to tell you to **let his people go,** so that they can
	8. 1	that the Lord says, **'Let my people go,** so that they can
	8. 8	frogs, and I will **let your people go,** so that they can
	8.20	that the Lord says, **'Let my people go,** so that they can
	8.32	became stubborn, and again he would not **let the people go.**
	9. 1	of the Hebrews, says, **'Let my people go,** so that they may
	9. 2	you again refuse to **let them go,** [3] I will punish you by
	9. 7	But he was stubborn and would not **let the people go.**
	9.13	of the Hebrews, says, **'Let my people go,** so that they may
	9.17	Yet you are still arrogant and refuse to **let my people go.**
	9.28	I promise to **let you go;**
	9.35	through Moses, the king would not **let the Israelites go.**
	10. 3	**Let my people go,** so that they may worship me.
	10. 7	**Let the Israelite men go,** so that they can worship the Lord
	10.20	the king stubborn, and he did not **let the Israelites go.**
	10.27	Lord made the king stubborn, and he would not **let them go.**
	13.15	stubborn and refused to **let us go,** the Lord killed every
	13.17	the king of Egypt **let the people go,** God did not take
2 Sam	23.10	was so stiff that he could not **let go** of his sword.
1 Kgs	11.21	"Just **let me go,"** Hadad answered the king.
	20.34	He made a treaty with him and **let him go.**
2 Kgs	2.17	But they insisted until he gave in and **let them go.**
2 Chr	28.11	**Let them go,** or the Lord will punish you in his anger."
Job	41. 3	Will he beg you to **let him go?**
Prov	3. 3	Never **let go** of loyalty and faithfulness.
	17.15	Condemning the innocent or **letting the wicked go**—both
Song	3. 4	held him and wouldn't **let him go** until I took him to
Is	43. 6	tell the north to **let them go** and the south not to
Jer	50.33	them are guarding them closely and will not **let them go.**

LETTER (1)

Is	8. 1	piece of writing material and write on it in large **letters:**
	28.10	teach us **letter by letter,** line by line, lesson by lesson."
	28.13	teach you **letter by letter,** line by line, lesson by lesson.
2 Cor	3. 7	The Law was carved in **letters** on stone tablets, and God's
Gal	6.11	See what big **letters** I make as I write to you now

LETTER (2)

2 Sam	11.14	next morning David wrote a **letter** to Joab and sent it by
1 Kgs	21. 8	Then she wrote some **letters,** signed them with Ahab's name,
	21. 9	The **letters** said:
2 Kgs	5. 5	"Go to the king of Israel and take this **letter** to him."
	5. 6	The **letter** that he took read:
	5. 6	"This **letter** will introduce my officer Naaman.
	5. 7	king of Israel read the **letter,** he tore his clothes in
	10. 1	Jehu wrote a **letter** and sent copies to the rulers of the
	10. 1	The **letter** read:
	10. 2	soon as you receive this **letter,** [3] you are to choose the
	10. 6	Jehu wrote them another **letter:**
	10. 7	When Jehu's **letter** was received, the leaders of Samaria
	19. 9	heard this, he sent a **letter** to King Hezekiah of Judah
	19.14	King Hezekiah took the **letter** from the messengers and read it.
	19.14	to the Temple, placed the **letter** there in the presence of
	20.12	had been ill, so he sent him a **letter** and a present.
2 Chr	2.11	King Hiram sent Solomon a **letter** in reply.
	21.12	The prophet Elijah sent Jehoram a **letter,** which read as follows:
	30. 1	took special care to send **letters** to the tribes of Ephraim
	32.17	The **letter** that the emperor wrote defied the Lord, the
Ezra	4. 7	Tabeel, and their associates wrote a **letter** to the emperor.
	4. 7	The **letter** was written in Aramaic and was to be translated
	4. 8	wrote the following **letter** to Artaxerxes about Jerusalem:
	4.11	This is the text of the **letter:**
	4.18	"The **letter** which you sent has been translated and read to me.
	4.23	As soon as this **letter** from Artaxerxes was read to Rehum,
Neh	2. 7	the favour of giving me **letters** to the governors of West
	2. 8	I asked also for a **letter** to Asaph, keeper of the royal
	2. 9	There I gave the emperor's **letters** to the governors.
	6. 5	fifth message, this one in the form of an unsealed **letter.**
	6.19	And he kept sending me **letters** to try to frighten me.
Esth	8. 9	the king's secretaries and dictated **letters** to the Jews and
	8. 9	The **letters** were written to each province in its own
	8.10	Mordecai had the **letters** written in the name of King Xerxes,
	8.11	These **letters** explained that the king would allow the
	9.20	events written down and sent **letters** to all the Jews, near
Esth	9.26	Because of Mordecai's **letter** and because of all that had
	9.29	with Mordecai, also wrote a **letter,**
	9.29	her full authority behind the **letter** about Purim,
	9.30	The **letter** was addressed to all the Jews, and copies
Is	37. 9	heard this, he sent a **letter** to King Hezekiah [10] of Judah
	37.14	King Hezekiah took the **letter** from the messengers and read it.
	37.14	to the Temple, placed the **letter** there in the presence of
	39. 1	had been ill, so he sent him a **letter** and a present.
Jer	29. 1	I wrote a **letter** to the priests, the prophets, the leaders
	29. 3	I gave the **letter** to Elasah son of Shaphan and to Gemariah
	29.24	Nehelam, who had sent a **letter** in his own name to all
	29.24	In this **letter,** Shemaiah wrote to Zephaniah:
	29.29	Zephaniah read the **letter** to me, [30] and then the Lord
Acts	9. 2	and asked for **letters** of introduction to the synagogues in
	15.20	Instead, we should write a **letter** telling them not to
	15.23	and Silas, [23] and they sent the following **letter** by them:
	15.30	gathered the whole group of believers and gave them the **letter.**
	21.25	we have sent them a **letter** telling them we decided that they
	22. 5	I received from them **letters** written to fellow-Jews in Damascus,
	23.25	Then the commander wrote a **letter** that went like this:
	23.33	Caesarea, delivered the **letter** to the governor, and handed Paul
	23.34	The governor read the **letter** and asked Paul what province he
	28.21	"We have not received any **letters** from Judaea about you,
Rom	15.15	in this **letter** I have been quite bold about certain subjects
	16.22	Tertius, the writer of this **letter,** send you Christian greetings.
1 Cor	5. 9	In the **letter** that I wrote you I told you not to
	16. 3	I come, I shall give **letters** of introduction to the men you
2 Cor	2. 3	is why I wrote that **letter** to you—I did not want
	2. 9	I wrote you that **letter** because I wanted to find out how
	3. 1	other people, we need **letters** of recommendation to you or from
	3. 2	You yourselves are the **letter** we have, written on our hearts
	3. 3	that Christ himself wrote this **letter** and sent it by us.
	7. 8	For even if that **letter** of mine made you sad, I am
	7.12	even though I wrote that **letter,** it was not because of the
	10. 9	to appear that I am trying to frighten you with my **letters.**
	10.10	Someone will say, "Paul's **letters** are severe and strong,
	10.11	what we write in our **letters** when we are away and what
Col	4.16	After you read this **letter,** make sure that it is read
	4.16	you are to read the **letter** that the brothers in Laodicea
1 Thes	5.27	of the Lord to read this **letter** to all the believers.
2 Thes	2. 2	prophesying or preaching, or that we wrote it in a **letter.**
	2.15	we taught you, both in our preaching and in our **letter.**
	3.14	there will not obey the message we send you in this **letter.**
	3.17	This is the way I sign every **letter;**
1 Tim	3.14	As I write this **letter** to you, I hope to come and
	3.15	if I am delayed, this **letter** will let you know how we
Heb	13.22	for this **letter** I have written to you is not very long.
1 Pet	5.12	I write you this brief **letter** with the help of Silas,
2 Pet	3. 1	this is now the second **letter** I have written to you.
	3. 1	In both **letters** I have tried to arouse pure thoughts in your
	3.16	he says in all his **letters** when he writes on the subject.
	3.16	things in his **letters** which ignorant and unstable people explain
3 Jn	9	I wrote a short **letter** to the church;

LEVEL

Ex	14.27	sea, and at daybreak the water returned to its normal **level.**
Is	2.14	He will **level** the high mountains and hills, [15] every high tower,
	26. 7	the road they travel is **level.**
	40. 4	**level** every mountain.
	45. 2	"I myself will prepare your way, **levelling** mountains and hills.
Jer	51.25	will take hold of you, **level** you to the ground, and leave
Ezek	40.18	This outer courtyard was at a lower **level** than the inner courtyard.
	40.19	a gateway at a higher **level** that led to the inner courtyard.
	41. 8	the ground and it was **level** with the foundation of the rooms
	42. 3	It was built on three **levels,** each one set further back than
	42. 5	The rooms at the upper **level** of the building were narrower
	42. 5	middle and lower **levels** because they were set further back.
	42. 6	The rooms at all three **levels** were on terraces and were
	42. 7	At the lower **level** the outer wall of the building was
	42. 7	At the top **level** there were rooms in the entire length of
Zech	14.10	in the north to Rimmon in the south, will be made **level.**
Lk	3. 5	valley must be filled up, every hill and mountain **levelled** off.
	6.17	apostles, he stood on a **level** place with a large number of

LEVI (1)

Jacob and Leah's son and the priestly tribe descended from him.
see also **LEVITES**

Gen	29.34	so she named him **Levi.**
	34.25	of Jacob's sons, Simeon and **Levi,** the brothers of Dinah,
	34.30	Jacob said to Simeon and **Levi,** "You have brought trouble on me;
	35.23	Leah were Reuben (Jacob's eldest son), Simeon, **Levi,** Judah,
	46.11	**Levi** and his sons:
	49. 5	"Simeon and **Levi** are brothers.
Ex	1. 2	his family, were [2] Reuben, Simeon, **Levi,** Judah, [3] Issachar,
	2. 1	man from the tribe of **Levi** married a woman of his own
	6.16	**Levi** had three sons:
	6.16	**Levi** lived 137 years.
	6.19	These are the clans of **Levi** with their descendants.
	6.25	heads of the families and the clans of the tribe of **Levi.**
Num	1.49	fit for military service, do not include the tribe of **Levi.**
	3. 6	"Bring forward the tribe of **Levi** and appoint them as
	3.17	**Levi** had three sons:
	17. 3	and then write Aaron's name on the stick representing **Levi.**
	17. 8	he saw that Aaron's stick, representing the tribe of **Levi,**
	18. 2	your relatives, the tribe of **Levi,** to work with you and help
	26.57	The tribe of **Levi** consisted of the clans of Gershon,
	26.59	Amram, [59] who was married to **Levi's** daughter Jochebed, who
Deut	10. 8	men of the tribe of **Levi** to be in charge of the
	10. 9	is why the tribe of **Levi** received no land as the other

Deut 18. 1 “The priestly tribe of **Levi** is not to receive any share
18. 5 your tribes the tribe of **Levi** to serve him as priests for
27.12 Simeon, **Levi**, Judah, Issachar, Joseph, and Benjamin.
33. 8 About the tribe of **Levi** he said:
Josh 13.14 Moses had given no land to the tribe of **Levi.**
13.33 But Moses did not assign any land to the tribe of **Levi.**
21.10 were of the clan of Kohath, which was descended from **Levi.**
1 Kgs 12.31 priests from families who were not of the tribe of **Levi.**
1 Chr 2. 1 Reuben, Simeon, **Levi,** Judah, Issachar, Zebulun, [2]Dan,
6. 1 **Levi** had three sons:
6.16 **Levi** had three sons:
6.39 His family line went back to **Levi** as follows:
6.44 His family line went back to **Levi** as follows:
21. 6 did not take any census of the tribes of **Levi** and Benjamin.
23.24 These were the descendants of **Levi,** by clans and families,
24.20 These are other heads of families descended from **Levi:**
27.16 **Levi** Hashabiah son of
Jer 33.18 priests from the tribe of **Levi** to serve me and to offer
33.21 from the tribe of **Levi** that they would always serve me;
33.22 priests from the tribe of **Levi,** so that it will be as
Ezek 40.46 members of the tribe of **Levi** who are permitted to go into
43.19 belonging to the tribe of **Levi** who are descended from Zadok
44.15 belonging to the tribe of **Levi** who are descended from Zadok,
48.11 doing wrong, as the other members of the tribe of **Levi** did.
48.30 in the north wall are named after Reuben, Judah, and **Levi;**
Zech 12.12 descended from **Levi,** the family descended from Shimei,
Mal 2. 4 the priests, the descendants of **Levi,** will not be broken.
Heb 7. 5 And those descendants of **Levi** who are priests are commanded by
7. 6 Melchizedek was not descended from **Levi,** but he collected
7. 9 Abraham paid the tenth, **Levi** (whose descendants collect the tenth)
7.10 For **Levi** had not yet been born, but was, so to speak,
Rev 7. 5 Manasseh, Simeon, **Levi,** Issachar, Zebulun, Joseph, and Benjamin.
also 1 Chr 6.38 1 Chr 6.43 1 Chr 6.47 1 Chr 12.23

LEVI (2)
An ancestor of Jesus.

Lk 3.24 Matthat, the son of **Levi,** the son of Melchi,

LEVI (3)
An ancestor of Jesus.

Lk 3.29 Matthat, the son of **Levi,** [30]the son of Simeon,

LEVI (4)
Tax-collector who followed Jesus. see also MATTHEW

Mk 2.14 he saw a tax collector, **Levi** son of Alphaeus,
2.14 **Levi** got up and followed him.
2.15 Later on Jesus was having a meal in **Levi's** house.
Lk 5.27 and saw a tax collector named **Levi,** sitting in his office.
5.28 **Levi** got up, left everything, and followed him.
5.29 Then **Levi** had a big feast in his house for Jesus,

LEVIATHAN
Legendary sea-monster.

Job 3. 8 to curse that day, those who know how to control **Leviathan.**
41. 1 Can you catch **Leviathan** with a fish-hook or tie his tongue
41. 9 Anyone who sees **Leviathan** loses courage and falls to the ground.
41.12 Let me tell you about **Leviathan's** legs and describe how
Ps 74.14 the heads of the monster **Leviathan** and fed his body to
104.26 and in it plays **Leviathan,** that sea-monster which you made.
Is 27. 1 sword to punish **Leviathan,** that wriggling, twisting dragon,

LEVITES
[FELLOW-LEVITES]
Israelites with certain priestly functions, and later subordinate members of the Temple staff.

Ex 4.14 Moses and said, “What about your brother Aaron, the **Levite?**
32.26 So all the **Levites** gathered round him, [27]and he said to them,
32.28 The **Levites** obeyed, and killed about three thousand men that day.
32.29 Moses said to the **Levites,** “Today you have consecrated
38.21 Moses and made by the **Levites** who worked under the direction
Lev 25.32 However, **Levites** have the right to buy back at any time
25.33 cities is sold by a **Levite** and is not bought back, it
25.33 because the houses which the **Levites** own in their cities are
25.34 But the pasture land round the **Levite** cities shall never be sold;
Num 1.47 The **Levites** were not registered with the other tribes,
1.50 Instead, put the **Levites** in charge of the Tent of my
1.51 you move your camp, the **Levites** shall take the Tent down and
1.53 But the **Levites** shall camp round the Tent to guard it,
2.17 and the last two the **Levites** are to march carrying the Tent.
2.33 Lord had commanded Moses, the **Levites** were not registered
3. 9 The only responsibility the **Levites** have is to serve Aaron
3.12 “The **Levites** are now to be mine.
3.12 the first-born sons of Israel as my own, I have the **Levites;**
3.15 Moses [15]to register the **Levites** by clans and families,
3.32 The chief of the **Levites** was Eleazar son of Aaron the priest.
3.39 total number of all the **Levite** males one month old or older
3.40 But in place of them I claim all the **Levites** as mine!
3.40 claim the livestock of the **Levites** in place of all the
3.45 to Moses, [45]“Now dedicate the **Levites** as mine in place of
3.45 dedicate the livestock of the **Levites** in place of the
3.46 first-born Israelite sons outnumber the **Levites** by 273, you
4. 2 take a census of the **Levite** clan of Kohath by sub-clans and
4.22 take a census of the **Levite** clan of Gershon by sub-clans and
4.29 take a census of the **Levite** clan of Merari by sub-clans and
4.34 took a census of the three **Levite** clans, Kohath, Gershon,
Num 7. 5 give them to the **Levites** according to the work they have to
7. 6 So Moses gave the wagons and the oxen to the **Levites.**
8. 6 said to Moses, [6]“Separate the **Levites** from the rest of the
8. 9 of Israel and make the **Levites** stand in front of the Tent
8.10 on the heads of the **Levites,** [11]and then Aaron shall
8.11 then Aaron shall dedicate the **Levites** to me as a special
8.12 The **Levites** shall then put their hands on the heads of
8.12 to perform the ritual of purification for the **Levites.**
8.13 “Dedicate the **Levites** as a special gift to me, and put
8.14 Separate the **Levites** in this way from the rest of the Israelites,
8.15 have purified and dedicated the **Levites,** they will be
8.18 I am now taking the **Levites** instead of all the
8.19 and I assign the **Levites** to Aaron and his sons,
8.20 Israel dedicated the **Levites,** as the Lord commanded Moses.
8.21 The **Levites** purified themselves and washed their clothes,
8.22 everything the Lord had commanded Moses concerning the **Levites.**
8.22 And so the **Levites** were qualified to work in the Tent under
8.24 the age of twenty-five each **Levite** shall perform his duties
8.26 that, he may help his **fellow-Levites** in performing their
8.26 This is how you are to regulate the duties of the **Levites.”**
10.21 Then the **Levite** clan of Kohath would start out, carrying
16. 1 son of Izhar, from the **Levite** clan of Kohath, rebelled
16. 6 You **Levites** are the ones who have gone too far!”
16. 8 “Listen, you **Levites!**
16.10 you and all the other **Levites** have this honour—and now you
18. 1 “You, your sons, and the **Levites** must suffer the
18. 6 has chosen your relatives the **Levites** from among the
18.21 “I have given to the **Levites** every tithe that the people of
18.23 From now on only the **Levites** will take care of the Tent
18.23 The **Levites** shall have no permanent property in Israel,
18.26 The Lord commanded Moses [26]to say to the **Levites:**
26.62 The male **Levites** who were one month old or older numbered 23,000.
31.30 Give them to the **Levites** who are in charge of the Lord's
31.47 commanded, gave them to the **Levites** who were in charge of
35. 2 receive they must give the **Levites** some cities to live in
35. 3 These cities will belong to the **Levites,** and they will live there.
35. 6 You are to give the **Levites** six cities of refuge to which
35. 8 The number of **Levite** cities in each tribe is to be
Deut 12.12 your servants, and the **Levites** who live in your towns;
12.12 remember that the **Levites** will have no land of their own.
12.18 with your servants and the **Levites** who live in your towns,
12.19 also, not to neglect the **Levites,** as long as you live in
14.27 “Do not neglect the **Levites** who live in your towns;
14.29 This food is for the **Levites,** since they own no property,
16.11 children, your servants, and the **Levites,** foreigners,
16.14 children, your servants, and the **Levites,** foreigners,
17. 9 present your case to the **levitical** priests and to the judge
17.18 made from the original copy kept by the **levitical** priests.
18. 6 “Any **Levite** who wants to may come from any town in
18. 7 Lord his God, like the other **Levites** who are serving there.
21. 5 The **levitical** priests are to go there also, because they
24. 8 be sure to do exactly what the **levitical** priests tell you;
26.11 and let the **Levites** and the foreigners who live among you
26.12 of your crops—to the **Levites,** the foreigners, the orphans,
26.13 have given it to the **Levites,** the foreigners, the orphans,
27. 9 Then Moses, together with the **levitical** priests, said to
27.14 The **Levites** will speak these words in a loud voice:
31. 9 and gave it to the **levitical** priests, who were in charge of
31.25 finished, he said to the **levitical** priests, who were in
33. 8 Urim and Thummim Through your faithful servants, the **Levites;**
Josh 8.33 Lord's Covenant Box, facing the **levitical** priests who carried it.
14. 3 However, Moses gave the **Levites** no portion of the territory.
18. 7 The **Levites,** however, will not receive a share of the land
21. 1 The leaders of the **Levite** families went to Eleazar the priest,
21. 3 people of Israel gave the **Levites** certain cities and pasture
21. 4 The families of the **Levite** clan of Kohath were the first
21. 8 their pasture lands to the **Levites,** as the Lord had
21.20 The other families of the **Levite** clan of Kohath were
21.27 Another group of **Levites,** the clan of Gershon, received
21.34 The rest of the **Levites,** the clan of Merari, received
21.41 the pasture lands round them, was given to the **Levites.**
Judg 17. 7 time there was a young **Levite** who had been living in the
17. 9 He answered, “I am a **Levite** from Bethlehem in Judah.
17.11 The young **Levite** agreed to stay with Micah and became
17.13 “Now that I have a **Levite** as my priest, I know that
18. 3 the accent of the young **Levite,** so they went up to him
18.15 Levite lived, and asked the **Levite** how he was getting on.
19. 1 a king, there was a **Levite** living far back in the
19. 3 The girl showed the **Levite** into the house, and when her
19. 5 father said to the **Levite,** “Have something to eat first.
19. 7 The **Levite** got up to go, but the father urged him to
19.18 The **Levite** answered, “We have been to Bethlehem in Judah,
19.25 So the **Levite** took his concubine and put her outside with them.
20. 4 The **Levite** whose concubine had been murdered answered,
1 Sam 6.15 The **Levites** lifted off the Covenant Box of the Lord and
2 Sam 15.24 with him were the **Levites,** carrying the sacred Covenant Box.
1 Kgs 8. 4 The **Levites** and the priests also moved the Tent of the
1 Chr 6.48 Their **fellow-Levites** were assigned all the other duties
6.54 They received the first share of the land assigned to the **Levites.**
6.64 Israel assigned towns for the **Levites** to live in, together
9. 2 Israelite laymen, priests, **Levites,** and temple workmen.
9.14 The following **Levites** lived in Jerusalem:
9.18 had stood guard at the gates to the camps of the **Levites.**
9.26 chief guards were **Levites** and had the final responsibility.
9.28 Other **Levites** were responsible for the utensils used in worship.
9.31 A **Levite** named Mattithiah, eldest son of Shallum, of
9.33 Some **Levite** families were responsible for the temple music.
9.34 of **Levite** families, according to their ancestral lines.
13. 2 and to the priests and **Levites** in their towns, and tell them

1 Chr 15. 2 Then he said, "Only **Levites** should carry the Covenant Box,
15. 4 Next he sent for the descendants of Aaron and for the **Levites.**
15. 5 From the **Levite** clan of Kohath came Uriel, in charge of
15.11 and Abiathar and the six **Levites,** Uriel, Asaiah, Joel,
15.12 He said to the **Levites,**
15.12 "You are the leaders of the **Levite** clans.
15.12 Purify yourselves and your **fellow-Levites,**
15.14 Then the priests and the **Levites** purified themselves in
15.15 The **Levites** carried it on poles on their shoulders, as
15.16 the leaders of the **Levites** to assign various Levites
15.17 chose the following **Levites** to play the high-pitched harps:
15.17 To play the low-pitched harps they chose the following **Levites:**
15.22 Chenaniah was chosen to be in charge of the **levitical** musicians.
15.26 God would help the **Levites** who were carrying the Covenant Box.
15.27 Chenaniah their leader, and the **Levites** who carried the Box.
16. 4 David appointed some of the **Levites** to lead the worship
16. 7 first gave Asaph and his **fellow-Levites** the responsibility
16.37 David put Asaph and his **fellow-Levites** in permanent charge
23. 2 all the Israelite leaders and all the priests and **Levites.**
23. 3 took a census of all the male **Levites** aged thirty or older.
23. 6 David divided the **Levites** into three groups,
23.14 of Moses, the man of God, were included among the **Levites.)**
23.26 longer any need for the **Levites** to carry the Tent of the
23.27 of David's final instructions all **Levites** were registered
23.31 made specifying the number of **Levites** assigned to do this
23.31 The **Levites** were assigned the duty of worshipping the Lord
24. 6 Shemaiah son of Nethanel, a **Levite** secretary.
24. 6 families and of the **Levite** families, were all witnesses.
24.30 These are the families of the **Levites.**
24.31 families of the priests and of the **Levites** were witnesses.
25. 1 and the leaders of the **Levites**
25. 1 chose the following **Levite** clans to lead the services
25. 7 and their **fellow-Levites** were trained musicians.
26. 1 of work for the **Levites** who served as temple guards.
26.12 duties in the Temple, just as the other **Levites** were.
26.20 Others of their **fellow-Levites** were in charge of the
28.13 organizing the priests and **Levites** to perform their duties,
28.21 The priests and the **Levites** have been assigned duties to
29. 8 was administered by Jehiel of the **Levite** clan of Gershon.
2 Chr 5. 4 leaders had gathered, then the **Levites** lifted the Covenant
5. 5 The priests and the **Levites** also moved the Tent of the
5.11 And all the **Levite** musicians—Asaph, Heman, and Jeduthun, and
5.11 The **Levites** stood near the east side of the altar with
7. 6 and facing them stood the **Levites,** praising the Lord with
8.14 the priests and of the **Levites** who assisted the priests in
8.15 given the priests and the **Levites** concerning the storehouses
11.13 territory of Israel priests and **Levites** came south to Judah.
11.14 The **Levites** abandoned their pastures and other land and
11.16 God of Israel, followed the **Levites** to Jerusalem, so that
13. 9 the descendants of Aaron, and you drove out the **Levites.**
13.10 perform their duties, and **Levites** assist them.
17. 8 They were accompanied by nine **Levites** and two priests.
17. 8 The **Levites** were Shemaiah, Nethaniah, Zebadiah, Asahel,
19. 8 In Jerusalem Jehoshaphat appointed **Levites,** priests, and
19.11 The **Levites** have the responsibility of seeing that the
20.14 the Lord came upon a **Levite** who was present in the crowd.
20.19 The members of the **Levite** clans of Kohath and Korah
23. 2 with them to Jerusalem the **Levites** and all the heads of the
23. 4 When the priests and **Levites** come on duty on the Sabbath,
23. 6 except the priests and the **Levites** who are on duty.
23. 7 The **Levites** are to stand guard round the king, with their
23. 8 The **Levites** and the people of Judah carried out Jehoiada's
23.18 Jehoiada put the priests and **Levites** in charge of the
24. 5 ordered the priests and the **Levites** to go to the cities of
24. 5 but the **Levites** delayed, [6]so he called in Jehoiada,
24. 6 seen to it that the **Levites** collect from Judah and Jerusalem
24. 8 The king ordered the **Levites** to make a box for
24.11 Every day the **Levites** would take the box to the royal
29. 4 a group of priests and **Levites** in the east courtyard of the
29. 5 He said, "You **Levites** are to consecrate yourselves and
29.12 The following **Levites** were there:
29.15 These men assembled their **fellow-Levites,**
29.16 From there the **Levites** took it all outside the city to the
29.18 The **Levites** made the following report to King Hezekiah:
29.25 he stationed **Levites** in the Temple, with harps and cymbals,
29.30 of the nation told the **Levites** to sing to the Lord the
29.34 kill all these animals, the **Levites** helped them until the
29.34 (The **Levites** were more faithful in keeping ritually clean
30.15 The priests and **Levites** who were not ritually clean were so
30.16 The **Levites** gave the blood of the sacrifices to the priests,
30.17 the Passover lambs, so the **Levites** did it for them, and
30.21 and day after day the **Levites** and the priests praised the
30.22 Hezekiah praised the **Levites** for their skill in
30.25 of Judah, the priests, the **Levites,** the people who had come
30.27 The priests and the **Levites** asked the Lord's blessing
31. 2 organization of the priests and **Levites,** under which they
31. 4 which the priests and the **Levites** were entitled, so that
31. 9 to the priests and the **Levites** about these gifts, [10]and
31.12 They placed a **Levite** named Conaniah in charge and made his
31.13 Ten **Levites** were assigned to work under them:
31.14 Kore son of Imnah, a **Levite** who was chief guard at the
31.15 lived, he was faithfully assisted in this by other **Levites:**
31.15 to their **fellow-Levites** according to what their duties were,
31.17 duties by clans, and the **Levites** twenty years of age or
31.19 and to everyone who was on the rolls of the **Levite** clans.
34. 9 The money that the **Levite** guards had collected in the
34.12 They were supervised by four **Levites:**
34.12 (The **Levites** were all skilful musicians.)
34.13 Other **Levites** were in charge of transporting materials
34.30 by the priests and the **Levites** and all the rest of the
35. 3 these instructions to the **Levites,** the teachers of Israel,
2 Chr 35. 8 for the people, the priests, and the **Levites** to use.
35. 9 The leaders of the **Levites**—Conaniah, Shemaiah and his brother
35. 9 five hundred bulls for the **Levites** to offer as sacrifices.
35.10 Passover, the priests and the **Levites** took their places, as
35.11 goats had been killed, the **Levites** skinned them, and the
35.13 The **Levites** roasted the Passover sacrifices over the fire,
35.14 After this was done, the **Levites** provided meat for
35.15 The following musicians of the **Levite** clan of Asaph were
35.15 because the other **Levites** prepared the Passover for them.
35.18 King Josiah, the priests, the **Levites,** and the people of Judah,
Ezra 1. 5 and Benjamin, the priests and **Levites,** and everyone else
2.40 Clans of **Levites** who returned from exile:
2.70 The priests, the **Levites,** and some of the people settled
3. 8 fellow-countrymen, the priests, and the **Levites,** in fact all
3. 8 All the **Levites** twenty years of age or older were put in
3. 9 The **Levite** Jeshua and his sons and relatives, and Kadmiel
3. 9 (They were helped by the **Levites** of the clan of Henadad.)
3.10 in their hands, and the **Levites** of the clan of Asaph stood
3.12 Many of the older priests, **Levites,** and heads of clans
6.16 of Israel—the priests, the **Levites,** and all the others who
6.18 and the **Levites** for the temple services in Jerusalem,
6.20 All the priests and the **Levites** had purified themselves
6.20 The **Levites** killed the animals for the Passover sacrifices
7. 6 Israelites which included priests, **Levites,** temple musicians,
7.13 the Israelite people, priests, and **Levites** that so desire be
7.24 any taxes from the priests, **Levites,** musicians, guards,
8.15 I found that there were priests in the group, but no **Levites.**
8.18 Sherebiah, an able man, a **Levite** from the clan of Mahli, and
8.20 by King David and his officials to assist the **Levites.**
8.29 the priests and of the **Levites,** and to the leaders of the
8.30 So the priests and the **Levites** took charge of the silver,
8.33 son of Phinehas and two **Levites,** Jozabad son of Jeshua and
9. 1 people, the priests, and the **Levites** had not kept themselves
10. 5 of the priests, of the **Levites,** and of the rest of the
10.15 had the support of Meshullam and of Shabbethai, a **Levite.**
10.23 **Levites:**
Neh 3.17 **Levites** rebuilt the next several sections of the wall:
7. 1 choir, and the other **Levites** had been assigned their work.
7.43 Clans of **Levites** who returned from exile:
7.73 The priests, the **Levites,** the temple guards, the
8. 7 places, and the following **Levites** explained the Law to them:
8. 9 of the Law, and the **Levites** who were explaining the Law told
8.11 The **Levites** went about calming the people and telling
8.13 with the priests and the **Levites,** went to Ezra to study the
9. 4 was a platform for the **Levites,** and on it stood Jeshua,
9. 5 The following **Levites** gave a call to worship:
9.38 agreement, and our leaders, our **Levites,** and our priests put
10. 9 **Levites:**
10.28 the **Levites,** the temple guards, the temple musicians,
10.34 We, the people, priests, and **Levites,** will draw lots
10.37 We will take to the **Levites,** who collect tithes in our
10.38 are to be with the **Levites** when tithes are collected, and
10.38 use in the Temple the **Levites** are to take to the temple
10.39 people of Israel and the **Levites** are to take the
11. 3 of Israel, the priests, the **Levites,** the temple workmen, and
11.15 **Levites:**
11.16 Shabbethai and Jozabad, prominent **Levites** in charge of
11.18 In all, 284 **Levites** lived in the holy city of Jerusalem.
11.20 and the remaining priests and **Levites** lived on their own
11.22 The supervisor of the **Levites** who lived in Jerusalem was Uzzi,
11.36 Some groups of **Levites** that had lived in the territory
12. 1 list of the priests and **Levites** who returned from exile with
12. 8 **Levites:**
12. 9 Bakbukiah, Unno, and their **fellow-Levites.**
12.22 of the heads of the **Levite** families and of the priestly
12.23 The heads of the **Levite** families, however, were recorded
12.24 Binnui, and Kadmiel, the **Levites** were organized into groups.
12.27 of Jerusalem was dedicated, the **Levites** were brought in from
12.28 The **Levite** families of singers gathered from the area
12.30 The priests and the **Levites** performed ritual purification
12.44 for the priests and the **Levites** which the Law required.
12.44 the **Levites,** [45]because they performed the ceremonies
12.47 a sacred offering to the **Levites,** and the Levites gave the
13. 5 and olive-oil given to the **Levites,** to the temple musicians,
13.10 the temple musicians and other **Levites** had left Jerusalem
13.11 And I brought the **Levites** and musicians back to the Temple
13.13 and Pedaiah, a **Levite.**
13.22 I ordered the **Levites** to purify themselves and to go and
13.29 and the covenant you made with the priests and the **Levites.**
13.30 for the priests and the **Levites** so that each one would know
Ps 135.20 Praise the Lord, you **Levites;**
Is 66.21 I will make some of them priests and **Levites.**
Ezek 44.10 me, "I am punishing those **Levites** who, together with the
45. 5 as the possession of the **Levites,** who do the work in the
48.12 the area belonging to the **Levites,** and it will be the
48.13 The **Levites** also are to have a special area, south of
48.21 Temple, the priests' land, the **Levites'** land, and the city,
Lk 10.32 In the same way a **Levite** also came along, went over and
Jn 1.19 Jerusalem sent some priests and **Levites** to John, to ask him,
Acts 4.36 it was that Joseph, a **Levite** born in Cyprus, whom the
Heb 7.11 on the basis of the **levitical** priesthood that the Law was
7.11 if the work of the **levitical** priests had been perfect,

LIAR see **LIE (2)**

LIBERTY

Lk 4.18 has sent me to proclaim **liberty** to the captives and recovery

AV LIBERTY

Ezek 46.17 property again when the **Year of Restoration** comes round.
Acts 27. 3 was kind to Paul and **allowed** him to go and see his
Heb 13.23 to know that our brother Timothy has been let out of **prison.**

LIBNAH (1)

Important city in Judah.

Josh 10.29 his army went on from Makkedah to **Libnah** and attacked it.
10.31 his army went on from **Libnah** to Lachish, surrounded it and
10.32 as they had done at **Libnah,** they spared no one, but killed
10.39 what he had done to Hebron and to **Libnah** and its king.
12.15 Gezer, [13]Debir, Geder, [14]Hormah, Arad, [15]**Libnah,**
15.42 There were also **Libnah,** Ether, Ashan, [43]Iphtah,
21.13 **Libnah,** [14]Jattir, Eshtemoa, [15]Holon, Debir, [16]Ain, Juttah, and Beth Shemesh,
2 Kgs 8.22 During this same period the city of **Libnah** also revolted.
19. 8 Lachish and was fighting against the nearby city of **Libnah;**
23.31 Hamutal, the daughter of Jeremiah from the city of **Libnah.**
24.18 Hamutal, the daughter of Jeremiah from the city of **Libnah.**
1 Chr 6.57 Jattir, and the towns of **Libnah,** Eshtemoa, Hilen, Debir,
2 Chr 21.10 same period, the city of **Libnah** also revolted, because
Is 37. 8 Lachish and was fighting against the nearby city of **Libnah;**
Jer 52. 1 daughter of the Jeremiah who lived in the city of **Libnah.**

LICE

Jer 43.12 picks his clothes clean of **lice,** so the king of Babylonia

LICK

1 Kgs 21.19 licked up Naboth's blood they will **lick** up your blood!' "
22.38 pool of Samaria, where dogs **licked** up his blood and
Lk 16.21 Even the dogs would come and **lick** his sores.

LID

Ex 25.17 "Make a **lid** of pure gold, 110 centimetres long and 66
25.19 creatures of hammered gold, [19]one for each end of the **lid.**
25.19 Make them so that they form one piece with the **lid.**
25.20 face each other across the **lid,** and their outspread wings
25.21 tablets inside the box and put the **lid** on top of it.
25.22 there, and from above the **lid** between the two winged
26.34 Put the **lid** on the Covenant Box.
31. 7 Covenant Box and its **lid,** all the furnishings of the Tent,
35.12 Covenant Box, its poles, its **lid,** and the curtain to screen
37. 6 He made a **lid** of pure gold, 110 centimetres long and 66
37. 8 creatures of hammered gold, [8]one for each end of the **lid.**
37. 8 He made them so that they formed one piece with the **lid.**
37. 9 other across the **lid,** and their outspread wings covered it.
39.35 Covenant Box containing the stone tablets, its poles, and its **lid;**
40.20 in the rings of the box and put the **lid** on it.
Lev 16. 2 I appear in a cloud above the **lid** on the Covenant Box.
16.13 the incense will hide the **lid** of the Covenant Box so that
16.14 on the front of the **lid** and then sprinkle some of it
16.15 and sprinkle it on the **lid** and then in front of the
Num 7.89 to him from above the **lid** on the Covenant Box, between the
19.15 in the tent that has no **lid** on it also becomes unclean.
2 Kgs 12. 9 made a hole in the **lid,** and placed the box by the
Zech 5. 7 The basket had a **lid** made of lead.
5. 7 As I watched, the **lid** was raised, and there in the basket
5. 8 pushed her down into the basket and put the **lid** back down.

LIE (1)

[LAY]

Gen 9.21 drunk, took off his clothes, and **lay** naked in his tent.
23. 3 where his wife's body was **lying,** went to the Hittites, and
28.11 He **lay** down to sleep, resting his head on a stone.
28.13 and to your descendants this land on which you are **lying.**
29. 2 out in the fields with three flocks of sheep **lying** round it.
49. 9 and returning to his den, Stretching out and **lying** down.
49.14 a donkey That **lies** stretched out between its saddlebags.
49.33 instructions to his sons, he **lay** down again and died.
Ex 14.30 and the Israelites saw them **lying** dead on the seashore.
Lev 14.47 Anyone who **lies** down or eats in the house must wash his
15. 4 Any bed on which he sits or **lies** is unclean.
15.20 which she sits or **lies** during her monthly period is unclean.
15.24 for seven days, and any bed on which he **lies** is unclean.
15.26 Any bed on which she **lies** and anything on which she sits
26.34 it will **lie** abandoned and get its rest while you are in
Num 22.27 This time, when the donkey saw the angel, it **lay** down.
Deut 9.18 Then once again I **lay** face downwards in the Lord's
9.25 "So I **lay** face downwards in the Lord's presence those
25. 2 is to make him **lie** face downwards and have him whipped.
Josh 7. 6 the Lord's Covenant Box, and **lay** there till evening, with
7.10 Why are you **lying** on the ground like this?
18.11 Their land **lay** between the tribes of Judah and Joseph.
Judg 3.25 And there was their master, **lying** dead on the floor.
5.27 sank to his knees, fell down and **lay** still at her feet.
7.13 The tent collapsed and **lay** flat on the ground."
19.27 way, he found his concubine **lying** in front of the house with
Ruth 2.15 even where the bundles are **lying,** and don't say anything to
3. 4 to notice where he **lies** down, and after he falls asleep,
3. 4 go and lift the covers and **lie** down at his feet.
3. 7 He went to the pile of barley and **lay** down to sleep.
3. 7 lifted the covers and **lay** down at his feet.
3. 8 and was surprised to find a woman **lying** at his feet.
3.13 Now **lie** down and stay here till morning."
3.14 So she **lay** there at his feet, but she got up before
1 Sam 5. 4 both its arms were broken off and were **lying** in the doorway;
19.24 shouted in Samuel's presence, and **lay** naked all that day and
28.20 once Saul fell down and **lay** stretched out on the ground,
31. 8 the bodies of Saul and his three sons **lying** on Mount Gilboa.
2 Sam 1.21 For the shields of the brave **lie** there in disgrace;
1.25 Jonathan **lies** dead in the hills.
2.23 to the place where he was **lying** stopped and stood there.
8. 2 He made the prisoners **lie** down on the ground and put two
12.16 went into his room and spent the night **lying** on the floor.
20.12 covered with blood, was **lying** in the middle of the road.
22.39 they **lie** defeated before me.
1 Kgs 1. 2 She will **lie** close to you and keep you warm."
13.24 His body **lay** on the road, and the donkey and the lion
13.28 and found the prophet's body **lying** on the road, with the
19. 5 He **lay** down under the tree and fell asleep.
19. 6 He ate and drank, and **lay** down again.
21. 4 He **lay** down on his bed, facing the wall, and would not
2 Kgs 4.32 into the room and saw the boy **lying** dead on the bed.
4.34 Then he **lay** down on the boy, placing his mouth, eyes,
4.34 As he **lay** stretched out over the boy, the boy's body started
13.14 fatal disease, and as he **lay** dying King Jehoash of Israel
19.35 At dawn the next day, there they **lay,** all dead!
1 Chr 10. 8 found the bodies of Saul and his sons **lying** on Mount Gilboa.
2 Chr 20.24 enemy and saw that they were all **lying** on the ground, dead.
36.21 "The land will **lie** desolate for seventy years, to make up
Esth 4. 3 wailed, and most of them put on sackcloth and **lay** in ashes.
Job 6.17 heat they disappear, and the stream beds **lie** bare and dry.
7. 4 When I **lie** down to sleep, the hours drag;
7.13 I **lie** down and try to rest;
11. 8 sky is no limit for God, but it **lies** beyond your reach.
17.13 the dead, where I will **lie** down to sleep in the dark.
21.33 procession, and even the earth **lies** gently on his body.
26. 6 The world of the dead **lies** open to God;
27.19 One last time they will **lie** down rich, and when they
38.40 they hide in their caves, or **lie** in wait in their dens?
40.21 He **lies** down under the thorn-bushes, and hides among the
Ps 3. 5 I **lie** down and sleep, and all night long the Lord protects
4. 4 think deeply about this, when you **lie** in silence on your beds.
4. 8 When I **lie** down, I go to sleep in peace;
10. 9 He **lies** in wait for the poor;
10.10 The helpless victims **lie** crushed;
18.38 they **lie** defeated before me.
36. 4 He makes evil plans as he **lies** in bed;
36.12 There they **lie,** unable to rise.
44.25 we **lie** defeated in the dust.
63. 6 As I **lie** in bed, I remember you;
88. 5 I am like the slain **lying** in their graves, those you have
88. 7 Your anger **lies** heavy on me, and I am crushed beneath its
102. 7 I **lie** awake;
104.22 the sun rises, they go back and **lie** down in their dens.
119.25 I **lie** defeated in the dust;
119.148 All night long I **lie** awake, to meditate on your instructions.
131. 2 As a child **lies** quietly in its mother's arms, so my heart
139. 8 if I **lay** down in the world of the dead, you would
Prov 4.16 They **lie** awake unless they have hurt someone.
5.11 You will **lie** groaning on your deathbed, your flesh and
6. 9 How long is the lazy man going to **lie** in bed?
Ecc 9. 1 No one knows anything about what **lies** ahead of him.
11. 3 in which direction a tree falls, it will **lie** where it fell.
Song 1.12 My king was **lying** on his couch, and my perfume filled
1.13 lover has the scent of myrrh as he **lies** upon my breasts.
Is 11. 6 in peace, and leopards will **lie** down with young goats.
11. 7 together, and their calves and cubs will **lie** down in peace.
14.11 You **lie** on a bed of maggots and are covered with a
14.18 the kings of the earth **lie** in their magnificent tombs,
21. 9 All the idols they worshipped **lie** shattered on the ground."
24. 3 The earth will **lie** shattered and ruined.
27.10 The fortified city **lies** in ruins.
28. 1 Their proud heads are well perfumed, but there they **lie,**
33. 9 The land **lies** idle and deserted.
34. 3 will not be buried, but will **lie** there rotting and stinking;
34.10 The land will **lie** waste age after age, and no one will
37.36 At dawn the next day there they **lay,** all dead!
51.23 to those who made you **lie** down in the streets and trampled
56.10 watchdogs that don't bark—they only **lie** about and dream.
58. 5 of grass, and spread out sackcloth and ashes to **lie** on.
Jer 2.15 a desert, and his towns **lie** in ruins, completely abandoned.
3.25 We should **lie** down in shame and let our disgrace cover us.
5.26 they **lie** in wait like men who spread nets to catch birds,
8. 2 buried, their bones will be like manure **lying** on the ground.
12.11 it **lies** desolate before me.
14. 2 cities are dying, its people **lie** on the ground in sorrow,
16. 4 Their bodies will **lie** like piles of manure on the ground.
25.33 the Lord has killed will **lie** scattered from one end of the
25.33 They will **lie** on the ground like piles of manure.
37.10 only wounded men are left, **lying** in their tents, those men
44.22 This very day your land **lies** in ruins and no one lives
Lam 1. 1 How lonely **lies** Jerusalem, once so full of people!
2. 8 The towers and walls now **lie** in ruins together.
2. 9 The gates **lie** buried in rubble, their bars smashed to pieces.
2.21 Young and old alike **lie** dead in the streets, Young men
4. 1 the stones of the Temple **lie** scattered in the streets.
4. 8 they **lie** unknown in the streets, their faces blackened in death;
5.18 our tears, [18]because Mount Zion **lies** lonely and deserted,
Ezek 4. 4 "Then **lie** down on your left side, and I will place on
4. 9 eat during the 390 days you are **lying** on your left side.
29. 3 I am your enemy, you monster crocodile, **lying** in the river.
29.12 the cities of Egypt will **lie** in ruins, ruins worse than
32.19 to the world of the dead and **lie** there among the ungodly.
32.21 killed in battle have come down here, and here they **lie!'**
32.24 In life they spread terror, but now they **lie** dead and disgraced.

Ezek 32.25 Elam **lies** down among those killed in battle, and the
32.25 spread terror, but now they **lie** dead and disgraced, sharing
32.28 is how the Egyptians will **lie** crushed among the
32.29 powerful soldiers, but now they **lie** in the world of the dead
Dan 10. 9 I fell to the ground unconscious and **lay** there face downwards.
Hos 13. 7 Like a leopard I will **lie** in wait along your path.
Amos 5. 2 She **lies** abandoned on the ground, And no one helps her up.
Jon 1. 5 had gone below and was **lying** in the ship's hold, sound
Mic 2. 1 terrible it will be for those who **lie** awake and plan evil!
Nah 3. 7 They will say, 'Nineveh **lies** in ruins!
Zeph 1.17 and their dead bodies will **lie** rotting on the ground."
2.14 flocks, herds, and animals of every kind will **lie** down.
Hag 1. 4 living in well-built houses while my Temple **lies** in ruins?
1. 9 Because my Temple **lies** in ruins while every one of you is
Zech 1.11 found that the whole world **lies** helpless and subdued."
Mt 8.20 but the Son of Man has nowhere to **lie** down and rest."
9. 2 some people brought to him a paralysed man, **lying** on a bed.
28. 6 Come here and see the place where he was **lying.**
Mk 2. 4 made an opening, they let the man down, **lying** on his mat.
5.40 and went into the room where the child was **lying.**
6.55 they brought to him sick people **lying** on their mats.
7.30 She went home and found her child **lying** on the bed;
Lk 2.12 a baby wrapped in strips of cloth and **lying** in a manger."
2.16 found Mary and Joseph and saw the baby **lying** in the manger.
5.25 the bed he had been **lying** on, and went home, praising God.
9.58 but the Son of Man has nowhere to **lie** down and rest."
16.26 there is a deep pit **lying** between us, so that those who
Jn 5. 3 crowd of sick people were **lying** in the porches—the blind,
5. 6 Jesus saw him **lying** there, and he knew that the man had
20. 6 He saw the linen wrappings **lying** there [7] and the cloth which
20. 7 It was not **lying** with the linen wrappings but was rolled up
Heb 4.13 in all creation is exposed and **lies** open before his eyes.
12. 1 let us run with determination the race that **lies** before us.
Rev 11. 8 and their bodies will **lie** in the street of the great

LIE (2)
[LIAR]

Ex 5. 9 that they won't have time to listen to a pack of **lies."**
Lev 6. 3 by cheating him [3] or by **lying** about something that has been
19.11 "Do not steal or cheat or **lie.**
19.16 Do not spread **lies** about anyone, and when someone is on
Num 23.19 God is not like men, who **lie;**
Josh 7.11 They stole them, **lied** about it, and put them with their own
1 Sam 15.29 Israel's majestic God does not **lie** or change his mind.
2 Sam 19.27 He **lied** about me to Your Majesty, but you are like God's
1 Kgs 13.18 But the old prophet was **lying.**
22.22 replied, 'I will go and make all Ahab's prophets tell **lies.'**
22.23 The Lord has made these prophets of yours **lie** to you.
2 Kgs 4.16 "Please, sir, don't **lie** to me.
2 Chr 18.21 replied, 'I will go and make all Ahab's prophets tell **lies.'**
18.22 The Lord has made these prophets of yours **lie** to you.
Job 6.28 I won't **lie.**
6.30 But you think I am **lying**— you think I can't tell
13. 4 You cover up your ignorance with **lies;**
13. 7 Why are you **lying?**
13. 7 Do you think your **lies** will benefit God?
21.34 Every answer you give is a **lie!**
27. 4 never say anything evil, my tongue will never tell a **lie.**
34. 6 He asks, "How could I **lie** and say I am wrong?
Ps 5. 6 You destroy all **liars** and despise violent, deceitful men.
10. 7 His speech is filled with curses, **lies,** and threats;
12. 2 All of them **lie** to one another;
27.12 me to my enemies, who attack me with **lies** and threats.
31.18 Silence those **liars**— all the proud and arrogant who
34.13 Then hold back from speaking evil and from telling **lies.**
35.19 Don't let my enemies, those **liars,** gloat over my defeat.
35.20 instead they invent all kinds of **lies** about peace-loving people.
36. 3 His speech is wicked and full of **lies;**
43. 1 deliver me from **lying** and evil men!
50.19 you never hesitate to tell **lies.**
52. 2 You are always inventing **lies.**
52. 4 You love to hurt people with your words, you **liar!**
55.23 will bring those murderers and **liars** to their graves before
58. 3 they tell **lies** from the day they are born.
59.12 Because they curse and **lie,** [13] destroy them in your anger;
62. 4 you take pleasure in **lies.**
63.11 name will praise him, but the mouths of **liars** will be shut.
64. 4 They are quick to spread their shameless **lies;**
69. 4 My enemies tell **lies** against me;
78.36 But their words were all **lies;**
89.35 I will never **lie** to David.
101. 7 No **liar** will live in my palace;
109. 2 Wicked men and **liars** have attacked me.
109. 2 They tell **lies** about me [3] and they say evil things about me,
119.69 Proud men have told **lies** about me, but with all my heart
119.86 men persecute me with **lies**—help me!
119.163 I hate and detest all **lies,** but I love your law.
120. 2 Save me, Lord, from **liars** and deceivers.
120. 3 You **liars,** what will God do to you?
144. 8 who never tell the truth and **lie** even under oath.
144.11 who never tell the truth and **lie** even under oath.
Prov 4.24 Have nothing to do with **lies** and misleading words.
6.12 Worthless, wicked people go around telling **lies.**
6.16 a **lying** tongue,
6.16 a witness who tells one **lie** after
8. 7 **lies** are hateful to me.
10.18 A man who hides his hatred is a **liar.**
12.17 the truth, justice is done, but **lies** lead to injustice.
12.19 A **lie** has a short life, but truth lives on for ever.
12.22 The Lord hates **liars,** but is pleased with those who keep
Prov 13. 5 Honest people hate **lies,** but the words of wicked people
14. 5 the truth, but an unreliable one tells nothing but **lies.**
14.25 when he tells **lies,** he betrays people.
17. 4 Evil people listen to evil ideas, and liars listen to **lies.**
17. 7 Respected people do not tell **lies,** and fools have nothing
19. 1 better to be poor but honest than to be a **lying** fool.
19. 5 If you tell **lies** in court, you will be punished—there will
19. 9 No one who tells **lies** in court can escape punishment;
19.22 poor people are better off than **liars.**
21.28 The testimony of a **liar** is not believed, but the word of
22.12 that truth is kept safe by disproving the words of **liars.**
26.28 You have to hate someone to want to hurt him with **lies.**
29.12 to false information, all his officials will be **liars.**
30. 6 said, he will reprimand you and show that you are a **liar."**
30. 8 keep me from **lying,** and let me be neither rich nor poor.
Is 9.15 head—and the tail is the prophets whose teachings are **lies!**
28.15 because you depend on **lies** and deceit to keep you safe.
28.17 will sweep away all the **lies** you depend on, and floods will
29.21 criminals, and those who tell **lies** to keep honest men from
30. 9 always rebelling against God, always **lying,** always refusing
32. 7 to ruin the poor with **lies** and to prevent them getting their
53. 9 though he had never committed a crime or ever told a **lie."**
57. 4 Who are you **liars** jeering at?
57.11 afraid, so that you tell me **lies** and forget me completely?
59. 3 You are guilty of **lying,** violence, and murder.
59. 4 You depend on **lies** to win your case.
59.13 our words are **lies.**
Jer 5.31 prophets speak nothing but **lies;**
7. 9 adultery, tell **lies** under oath, offer sacrifices to Baal,
9. 3 They are always ready to tell **lies;**
9. 5 have taught their tongues to **lie** and will not give up their
9. 8 they always tell **lies.**
14.14 But the Lord replied, "The prophets are telling **lies** in my name;
20. 6 all your friends to whom you have told so many **lies.'"**
23.14 they commit adultery and tell **lies;**
23.25 prophets have said who speak **lies** in my name and claim that
23.26 prophets mislead my people with the **lies** they have invented?
23.32 the prophets who tell their dreams that are full of **lies.**
23.32 lead my people astray with their **lies** and their boasting.
27.15 send them and that they are **lying** to you in his name.
27.15 you and the prophets who are telling you these **lies."**
27.16 They are **lying** to you.
28.15 not send you, and you are making these people believe a **lie.**
29. 9 They are telling you **lies** in my name.
29.21 Zedekiah son of Maaseiah, who are telling you **lies** in his name.
29.23 committed adultery and have told **lies** in the Lord's name.
29.31 as if he were a prophet, and he made you believe **lies.**
43. 2 and all the other arrogant men said to me, "You are **lying.**
50.36 Death to its **lying** prophets— what fools they are!
Lam 2.14 Your prophets had nothing to tell you but **lies;**
Ezek 13. 6 Their visions are false, and their predictions are **lies.**
13. 7 you see are false, and the predictions you make are **lies.**
13. 8 to them, "Your words are false, and your visions are **lies.**
13.19 So you tell **lies** to my people, and they believe you."
13.22 "By your **lies** you discourage good people, whom I do not
21.29 you see are false, and the predictions you make are **lies.**
22. 9 Some of your people tell **lies** about others in order to
Dan 2. 9 to go on telling me **lies** because you hope that in time
11.27 their motives will be evil, and they will **lie** to each other.
Hos 4. 2 they **lie,** murder, steal, and commit adultery.
10.13 You have eaten the fruit produced by your **lies.**
11.12 Israel have surrounded me with **lies** and deceit, and the
Mic 2.11 who goes about full of **lies** and deceit and says, 'I prophesy
6.12 Your rich men exploit the poor, and all of you are **liars.**
Nah 3. 1 Doomed is the **lying,** murderous city, full of wealth to be
Hab 2.18 that a man has made, and it tells you nothing but **lies.**
Zeph 3.13 do no wrong to anyone, tell no **lies,** nor try to deceive.
Zech 5. 3 says that everyone who tells **lies** under oath will also be
5. 4 thief and the house of everyone who tells **lies** under oath.
8.17 I hate **lying,** injustice, and violence."
10. 2 but the answers they get are **lies** and nonsense.
13. 3 he claimed to speak the Lord's word, but spoke **lies** instead.
Mt 5.11 tell all kinds of evil **lies** against you because you are my
15.19 to rob, **lie,** and slander others.
26.60 even though many people came forward and told **lies** about him.
27.63 we remember that while that **liar** was still alive he said,
27.64 This last **lie** would be even worse than the first one."
Mk 14.56 Many witnesses told **lies** against Jesus,
Jn 8.44 because he is a **liar** and the father of all lies.
8.55 I do not know him, I would be a **liar** like you.
Acts 5. 3 of you and make you **lie** to the Holy Spirit by keeping
5. 4 You have not **lied** to men—you have lied to God!"
6.13 Then they brought in some men to tell **lies** about him.
13.10 you always keep trying to turn the Lord's truths into **lies!**
20.30 your own group will tell **lies** to lead the believers away
Rom 1.25 They exchange the truth about God for a **lie;**
3. 4 God must be true, even though every man is a **liar.**
3.13 wicked **lies** roll off their tongues, and dangerous threats,
9. 1 I belong to Christ and I do not **lie.**
9. 1 me that I am not **lying** [2] when I say how great is
1 Cor 15.15 we are shown to be **lying** about God, because we said that
2 Cor 6. 8 We are treated as **liars,** yet we speak the truth;
11. 3 same way that Eve was deceived by the snake's clever **lies.**
11.13 false apostles, who **lie** about their work and disguise themselves
11.31 knows that I am not **lying.**
12.16 will say that I was crafty, and trapped you with **lies.**
Gal 1.20 God knows that I am not **lying!**
Eph 4.25 No more **lying,** then!
Col 3. 9 Do not **lie** to one another, for you have taken off the
1 Tim 1.10 for kidnappers, for those who **lie** and give false testimony or
2. 7 I am not **lying;**

1 Tim 4. 1 will obey **lying** spirits and follow the teachings of demons.
4. 2 are spread by deceitful **liars,** whose consciences are dead,
Tit 1. 2 God, who does not **lie,** promised us this life before the
1.12 "Cretans are always **liars,** wicked beasts, and lazy gluttons."
Heb 6.18 things, then, that cannot change and about which God cannot **lie.**
1 Pet 2. 1 more **lying** or hypocrisy or jealousy or insulting language.
2.22 and no one ever heard a **lie** come from his lips.
3.10 times, must keep from speaking evil and stop telling **lies.**
1 Jn 1. 6 in the darkness, we are **lying** both in our words and in
1.10 God out to be a **liar,** and his word is not in
2. 4 such a person is a **liar** and there is no truth in
2.21 and you also know that no **lie** ever comes from the truth.
2.22 Who, then, is the **liar?**
4.20 says he loves God, but hates his brother, he is a **liar.**
5.10 him out to be a **liar,** because he has not believed what
3 Jn 10 the terrible things he says about us and the **lies** he tells!
Rev 2. 2 but are not, and have found out that they are **liars.**
3. 9 that belongs to Satan, those **liars** who claim that they are
14. 5 They have never been known to tell **lies;**
21. 8 who worship idols, and all **liars**—the place for them is the
21.27 the city, nor anyone who does shameful things or tells **lies.**
22.15 idols and those who are **liars** both in words and deeds.

LIEUTENANT-GOVERNORS

Dan 3. 2 come together—the princes, governors, **lieutenant-governors,**
3.27 All the princes, governors, **lieutenant-governors,** and
6. 7 the supervisors, the governors, the **lieutenant-governors,**

LIFE (1)

[ETERNAL LIFE, LIVES]
see also **LIFE (2) (TO LIFE), LIFELESS, LIFETIME**

Gen 1.24 "Let the earth produce all kinds of animal **life:**
2. 7 he breathed **life-giving** breath into his nostrils and the man
2. 9 stood the tree that gives **life** and the tree that gives
3.17 to work hard all your **life** to make it produce enough food
3.22 from the tree that gives **life,** eat it, and live for ever."
3.24 to keep anyone from coming near the tree that gives **life.**
4.15 If anyone kills you, seven **lives** will be taken in revenge."
4.24 If seven **lives** are taken to pay for killing Cain,
5.24 He spent his **life** in fellowship with God, and then he disappeared,
6.12 it was evil, for the people were all living evil **lives.**
9. 4 I forbid this because the **life** is in the blood.
9. 5 If anyone takes human **life,** he will be punished.
9. 5 I will punish with death any animal that takes a human **life.**
19.15 you will not lose your **lives** when the city is destroyed."
19.17 Then one of the angels said, "Run for your **lives!**
19.19 You have done me a great favour and saved my **life.**
25.27 man who loved the outdoor **life,** but Jacob was a quiet man
26.35 They made **life** miserable for Isaac and Rebecca.
42.18 God-fearing man, and I will spare your **lives** on one condition.
43. 9 I will pledge my own **life,** and you can hold me responsible
44.30 His **life** is wrapped up with the life of the boy, and
44.32 is more, I pledged my **life** to my father for the boy.
44.32 boy back to him, I would bear the blame all my **life.**
45. 5 really God who sent me ahead of you to save people's **lives.**
46.34 of livestock all your **lives,** just as your ancestors did.
47. 9 Jacob answered, "My **life** of wandering has lasted a
47.25 They answered, "You have saved our **lives;**
50.20 in order to preserve the **lives** of many people who are alive
Ex 1.13 the Israelites [13-14] and made their **lives** miserable by
4.25 And so the Lord spared Moses' **life.**
21. 6 Then he will be his slave for **life.**
21.23 shall be life for **life,** [24] eye for eye, tooth for tooth,
21.30 a fine to save his **life,** he must pay the full amount
23.26 I will give you long **lives.**
30.12 me a price for his **life,** so that no disaster will come
30.15 poor man less, when they pay this amount for their **lives.**
30.16 be the payment for their **lives,** and I will remember to
Lev 17.11 The **life** of every living thing is in the blood, and that
17.11 Blood, which is **life,** takes away sins.
17.14 The **life** of every living thing is in the blood, and that
18. 5 you will save your **life** by doing so.
19.16 is on trial for his **life,** speak out if your testimony can
24.18 The principle is a **life** for a life.
26.16 that will make you blind and cause your **life** to waste away.
Num 16.22 ground and said, "O, God, you are the source of all **life.**
22.30 not the same donkey on which you have ridden all your **life?**
27.16 "Lord God, source of all **life,** appoint, I pray, a man
31.50 as a payment for our **lives,** so that he will protect us."
Deut 12.23 for the **life** is in the blood,
12.23 and you must not eat the **life** with the meat.
13. 5 lead you away from the **life** that the Lord has commanded you
15.17 he will then be your slave for **life.**
17.19 read from it all his **life,** so that he will learn to
19.21 punishment is to be a **life** for a life, an eye for
22. 7 bird go, so that you will live a long and prosperous **life.**
28.66 Your **life** will always be in danger.
29.16 "You remember what **life** was like in Egypt and what it
30.15 you a choice between good and evil, between **life** and death.
30.19 giving you the choice between **life** and death,
30.19 Choose **life.**
32.18 God, their mighty saviour, the one who had given them **life.**
32.39 I kill and I give **life,** I wound and I heal,
32.47 they are your very **life.**
Josh 2.14 her, "May God take our **lives** if we don't do as we
4.14 They honoured him all his **life,** just as they had honoured Moses.
6.25 But Joshua spared the **lives** of the prostitute Rahab and
9.24 we were in fear of our **lives.**
Judg 5.18 Zebulun and Naphtali risked their **lives** on the battlefield.
Judg 9.17 He risked his **life** to save you from the Midianites.
12. 3 going to, I risked my **life** and crossed the border to fight
13.12 What kind of a **life** must he lead?"
16.30 people at his death than he had killed during his **life.**
Ruth 1.20 "call me Marah, because Almighty God has made my **life** bitter.
4.15 grandson, who will bring new **life** to you and give you
1 Sam 1.11 to you for his whole **life** and that he will never have
1.22 the house of the Lord, where he will stay all his **life."**
2. 9 "He protects the **lives** of his faithful people, but the
9. 2 a son named Saul, a handsome man in the prime of **life.**
15. 9 and his men spared Agag's **life** and did not kill the best
17.33 just a boy, and he has been a soldier all his **life!"**
19. 5 He risked his **life** when he killed Goliath, and the Lord
26.21 harm you again, because you have spared my **life** tonight.
26.24 as I have spared your **life** today, may the Lord do the
27.12 Israelites that he will have to serve me all his **life."**
28.21 "Please, sir, I risked my **life** by doing what you asked.
2 Sam 1.23 together in **life,** together in death;
19. 5 the men who saved your **life**
19. 5 and the **lives** of your sons and daughters
19. 7 be the worst disaster you have suffered in all your **life."**
20. 3 confined for the rest of their **lives,** living like widows.
23.17 drinking the blood of these men who risked their **lives!"**
1 Kgs 1.12 save your life and the **life** of your son Solomon, I would
2.23 if I don't make Adonijah pay with his **life** for asking this!
3.11 rule justly, instead of long **life** for yourself or riches or
3.13 all your **life** you will have wealth and honour, more than
3.14 as your father David did, I will give you a long **life."**
4.21 They paid him taxes and were subject to him all his **life.**
12. 4 these burdens lighter and make **life** easier for us, we will
15.14 of worship, he remained faithful to the Lord all his **life.**
19. 3 Elijah was afraid, and fled for his **life;**
19. 4 "Take away my **life;**
20.31 ropes round our necks, and maybe he will spare your **life."**
20.32 Ahab and said, "Your servant Benhadad pleads with you for his **life."**
20.39 pay for it with your **life** or else pay a fine of
20.42 pay for it with your **life,** and your army will be destroyed
2 Kgs 1.13 Spare our **lives!**
4.31 child, but there was no sound or any other sign of **life.**
5. 7 think that I am God, with the power of **life** and death?
7. 4 can do is kill us, but maybe they will spare our **lives."**
7. 7 Syrians had fled for their **lives,** abandoning their tents,
10.24 lets one of them escape will pay for it with his **life!"**
12. 2 Throughout his **life** he did what pleased the Lord, because
15. 5 skin-disease that stayed with him the rest of his **life.**
25.29 to dine at the king's table for the rest of his **life.**
1 Chr 11.19 drinking the blood of these men who risked their **lives!"**
29.15 Lord, that we pass through **life** like exiles and strangers,
2 Chr 1.11 enemies or even for long **life** for yourself, you have asked
10. 4 these burdens lighter and make **life** easier for us, we will
15.17 in the land, he remained faithful to the Lord all his **life.**
17. 3 example of his father's early **life** and did not worship Baal.
26.21 For the rest of his **life** King Uzziah was ritually
Ezra 7.10 Ezra had devoted his **life** to studying the Law of the Lord,
9. 8 You have freed us from slavery and given us new **life.**
Neh 6.11 I would try to save my **life** by hiding in the Temple?
9. 6 you gave **life** to all.
9.29 your laws, although keeping your Law is the way to **life.**
Esth 4.11 gold sceptre to someone, then that person's **life** is spared.
7. 7 this, so he stayed behind to beg Queen Esther for his **life.**
7. 9 that he could hang Mordecai, who saved Your Majesty's **life.**
Job 4. 6 You worshipped God, and your **life** was blameless;
7. 1 Human **life** is like forced army service, like a life of
7. 7 Remember, O God, my **life** is only a breath;
7.16 My **life** makes no sense.
8. 9 Our **life** is short, we know nothing at all;
9.18 he has filled my **life** with bitterness.
9.26 My **life** passes like the swiftest boat, as fast as an
10. 5 Is your **life** as short as ours?
10.12 You have given me **life** and constant love, and your care
10.20 Isn't my **life** almost over?
11.17 Your **life** will be brighter than sunshine at noon,
11.17 and **life's** darkest hours will shine
12.10 It is God who directs the **lives** of his creatures;
12.10 every man's **life** is in his power.
13.14 I am ready to risk my **life.**
14. 1 All lead the same short, troubled **life.**
14. 5 The length of his **life** is decided beforehand— the number
14. 6 let him enjoy his hard **life**—if he can.
14.19 so you destroy man's hope for **life.**
17. 1 The end of my **life** is near.
19.20 I have barely escaped with my **life.**
21.13 They live out their **lives** in peace and quietly die
21.14 they don't want to know his will for their **lives.**
21.21 When a man's **life** is over, does he really care whether
27. 1 me justice and makes my **life** bitter— [3] as long as God
27. 8 for godless men in the hour when God demands their **life?**
29. 2 If only my **life** could once again be as it was when
29.18 expected to live a long **life** and to die at home in
31.18 All my **life** I have taken care of them.
33. 4 God's spirit made me and gave me **life.**
33.30 he saves a person's **life,** and gives him the joy of living.
34.14 took back the breath of **life,** [15] then everyone living would
36.11 him, they live out their **lives** in peace and prosperity.
36.14 while they are still young, worn out by a **life** of disgrace.
38.12 have you ever in all your **life** commanded a day to dawn?
42.12 the last part of Job's **life** even more than he had blessed
Ps 16.11 You will show me the path that leads to **life;**
17.14 save me from those who in this **life** have all they want,
21. 4 asked for life, and you gave it, a long and lasting **life.**

Ps	22.20	save my **life** from these dogs.
	23. 6	that your goodness and love will be with me all my **life;**
	27. 4	Lord's house all my **life,** to marvel there at his goodness,
	27.13	I will live to see the Lord's goodness in this present **life.**
	30. 3	on my way to the depths below, but you restored my **life.**
	31.10	I am exhausted by sorrow, and weeping has shortened my **life.**
	34.12	Would you like to enjoy **life?**
	34.12	Do you want long **life** and happiness?
	35.17	save my **life** from these lions!
	36. 9	are the source of all **life,** and because of your light we
	39. 4	Tell me how soon my **life** will end."
	39. 5	How short you have made my **life!**
	41. 2	The Lord will protect them and preserve their **lives;**
	42. 8	a song at night, a prayer to the God of my **life.**
	49. 8	life, [8] because the payment for a human **life** is too great.
	49.18	man is satisfied with this **life** and is praised because he is
	51.14	Spare my **life,** O God, and save me, and I will gladly
	55.23	and liars to their graves before half their **life** is over.
	58. 3	Evil men go wrong all their **lives;**
	61. 4	Let me live in your sanctuary all my **life;**
	61. 6	Add many years to the king's **life;**
	63. 3	constant love is better than **life** itself, and so I will
	64. 1	I am afraid of my enemies—save my **life!**
	71. 6	I have relied on you all my **life;**
	71. 7	My **life** has been an example to many, because you have been
	72.13	he saves the **lives** of those in need.
	72.14	their **lives** are precious to him.
	78.33	days like a breath and their **lives** with sudden disaster.
	78.50	anger or spare their **lives,** but killed them with a plague.
	82. 7	your **life** will end like that of any prince."
	89.47	Remember how short my **life** is;
	90. 9	Our **life** is cut short by your anger;
	90.10	**life** is soon over, and we are gone.
	90.12	Teach us how short our **life** is, so that we may become
	90.14	love, so that we may sing and be glad all our **life.**
	91.16	I will reward them with long **life;**
	97.10	he protects the **lives** of his people;
	101. 2	I will live a pure **life** in my house, [3] and will never
	102. 3	My **life** is disappearing like smoke;
	102.11	My **life** is like the evening shadows;
	102.23	he has shortened my **life.**
	102.27	But you are always the same, and your **life** never ends.
	103. 5	He fills my **life** with good things, so that I stay young
	103.15	As for us, our **life** is like grass.
	104.30	you give new **life** to the earth.
	104.33	I will sing to the Lord all my **life;**
	109. 8	May his **life** soon be ended;
	119. 1	Happy are those whose **lives** are faultless, who live
	119. 9	How can a young man keep his **life** pure?
	119.40	give me new **life,** for you are righteous.
	119.50	I was comforted because your promise gave me **life.**
	119.54	During my brief earthly **life** I compose songs about your commands.
	119.109	I am always ready to risk my **life;**
	119.149	show your mercy, and preserve my **life!**
	119.175	Give me **life,** so that I may praise you;
	128. 5	May you see Jerusalem prosper all the days of your **life!**
	133. 3	the Lord has promised his blessing— **life** that never ends.
	142. 5	you are all I want in this **life.**
	146. 2	I will sing to my God all my **life.**
Prov	1.19	Robbery always claims the **life** of the robber—this is
	2.13	who have abandoned a righteous **life** to live in the darkness
	2.19	He never returns to the road to **life.**
	2.20	follow the example of good men and live a righteous **life.**
	3. 2	My teaching will give you a long and prosperous **life.**
	3.16	Wisdom offers you long **life,** as well as wealth and honour.
	3.17	Wisdom can make your **life** pleasant and lead you safely through it.
	3.18	wisdom will give them **life.**
	3.22	They will provide you with **life**—a pleasant and happy life.
	4.10	what I am telling you, and you will live a long **life.**
	4.13	Your education is your **life**—guard it well.
	4.22	They will give **life** and health to anyone who understands them.
	4.23	your **life** is shaped by your thoughts.
	5. 6	She does not stay on the road to **life;**
	7.23	a net—he did not know that his **life** was in danger.
	8.35	man who finds me finds **life,** and the Lord will be pleased
	9.11	Wisdom will add years to your **life.**
	10. 2	will do you no good, but honesty can save your **life.**
	10.11	words are a fountain of **life,** but a wicked man's words hide
	10.16	reward for doing good is **life,** but sin leads only to more
	11. 4	on the day you face death, but honesty can save your **life.**
	11. 5	Honesty makes a good man's **life** easier, but a wicked man
	11.30	Righteousness gives **life,** but violence takes it away.
	12.19	A lie has a short **life,** but truth lives on for ever.
	12.28	Righteousness is the road to **life;**
	13. 3	Be careful what you say and protect your **life.**
	13. 8	his money to save his **life,** but no one threatens a poor
	13.14	The teachings of the wise are a fountain of **life;**
	13.14	they will help you escape when your **life** is in danger.
	14.25	A witness saves **lives** when he tells the truth;
	14.27	Reverence for the Lord is a fountain of **life.**
	15. 4	Kind words bring **life,** but cruel words crush your spirit.
	15.15	The **life** of the poor is a constant struggle,
	15.15	but happy people always enjoy **life.**
	15.24	road that leads upwards to **life,** not the road that leads
	16.15	the clouds that bring rain in the springtime—**life** is there.
	16.17	so watch where you are going—it may save your **life.**
	16.22	Wisdom is a fountain of **life** to the wise, but trying to
	16.31	Long **life** is the reward of the righteous;
	18.21	What you say can preserve **life** or destroy it;
Prov	19.23	and you will live a long **life,** content and safe from harm.
	20.20	you curse your parents, your **life** will end like a lamp that
	20.24	can anyone understand the direction his own **life** is taking?
	21.21	Be kind and honest and you will live a long **life;**
	22. 4	humble, and you will get riches, honour, and a long **life.**
	22. 5	If you love your **life,** stay away from the traps that catch
	22. 6	how he should live, and he will remember it all his **life.**
	22.23	them and threaten the **life** of anyone who threatens theirs.
	23.14	As a matter of fact, it may save his **life.**
	23.17	let reverence for the Lord be the concern of your **life.**
	23.26	Pay close attention, son, and let my **life** be your example.
	28.13	You will never succeed in **life** if you try to hide your
	28.20	Honest people will lead a full, happy **life.**
	29.10	righteous people will protect the **life** of such a person.
Ecc	1. 2	**Life** is useless, all useless.
	1. 3	You spend your **life** working, labouring, and what do you
	2. 3	the best way people can spend their short **lives** on earth.
	2.17	So **life** came to mean nothing to me, because everything
	2.22	and worry your way through **life,** and what do you have to
	3.19	off than an animal, because **life** has no meaning for either.
	4. 7	I have noticed something else in **life** that is useless.
	5.17	We have to live our **lives** in darkness and grief,
	5.18	has worked for during the short **life** that God has given him;
	5.20	happy, he will not worry too much about how short **life** is.
	6. 5	of day or knows what **life** is like, but at least it
	6. 6	the man who never enjoys **life,** though he may live two
	6. 8	does it do a poor man to know how to face **life?**
	6.12	short, useless life of his—a **life** that passes like a shadow?
	7.15	My **life** has been useless, but in it I have seen everything.
	7.24	How can anyone discover what **life** means?
	8.13	Their **life** is like a shadow and they will die young, because
	8.15	pleasure he has in this **life** is eating and drinking and
	8.15	as he labours during the **life** that God has given him in
	9. 9	Enjoy **life** with the woman you love,
	9. 9	as you live the useless **life** that God has given you
	11. 5	than you understand how new **life** begins in the womb of a
	12. 1	and years come when you will say, "I don't enjoy **life."**
	12. 7	earth, and the breath of **life** will go back to God, who
Is	10.31	The people of Madmenah and Gebim are running for their **lives.**
	32. 9	women who live an easy **life,** free from worries, listen to
	32.11	You have been living an easy **life,** free from worries;
	32.13	people were happy and for the city that was full of **life.**
	38.10	that in the prime of **life** I was going
	38.10	to the world of the dead, Never to live out my **life.**
	38.12	My **life** was cut off and ended, Like a tent that is
	38.12	I thought that God was ending my **life.**
	38.13	I thought that God was ending my **life.**
	38.17	You save my **life** from all danger;
	42. 5	he gave **life** and breath to all its people.
	43. 4	whole nations to save your **life,** because you are precious to
	47.15	do you— those astrologers you've consulted all your **life.**
	51.14	they will live a long **life** and have all the food they
	53.10	he will live a long **life,** and through him my purpose will
	53.11	After a **life** of suffering, he will again have joy;
	53.12	He willingly gave his **life** and shared the fate of evil men.
	55. 3	come to me, and you will have **life!**
	55. 7	leave their way of **life** and change their way of thinking.
	57. 2	Those who live good **lives** find peace and rest in death.
	57.16	I gave my people **life,** and I will not continue to accuse
	65.20	in infancy, and all people will live out their **life** span.
	65.21	Like trees, my people will live long **lives.**
Jer	1. 5	you before I gave you **life,** and before you were born I
	3.21	because they have lived sinful **lives** and have forgotten the
	10.23	no person has control over his own **life.**
	17.11	In the prime of **life** he will lose his riches, and in
	17.21	that if they love their **lives,** they must not carry any load
	18.11	them to stop living sinful **lives**—to change their ways and
	20.18	to have trouble and sorrow, to end my **life** in disgrace?
	21. 8	the way that leads to **life** and the way that leads to
	21. 9	he will at least escape with his **life.**
	22.15	Your father enjoyed a full **life.**
	22.21	That is what you've done all your **life;**
	23.10	they live wicked **lives** and misuse their power.
	23.22	them give up the evil **lives** they live and the wicked things
	25. 5	from your wicked way of **life** and from the evil things you
	32.39	I will give them a single purpose in **life:**
	38. 2	he will at least escape with his **life."**
	38.16	the God who gave us **life,** that I will not put you
	38.17	king of Babylonia's officers, your **life** will be spared, and
	38.20	all will go well with you, and your **life** will be spared.
	38.24	this conversation, and your **life** will not be in danger.
	39.18	You will escape with your **life** because you have put your
	45. 5	you will at least escape with your **life,** wherever you go.
	48. 6	'Quick, run for your **lives!'**
	49. 5	one will run for his **life,** and there will be no one
	50.20	I will forgive those people whose **lives** I have spared.
	51. 6	Run for your **lives!**
	51.13	but its time is up, and its thread of **life** is cut.
	51.14	has sworn by his own **life** that he will bring many men
	51.45	Run for your **life** from my fierce anger.
	52.33	to dine at the king's table for the rest of his **life.**
Lam	3.58	"You came to my rescue, Lord, and saved my **life.**
	4.20	the source of our **life,** the king the Lord had chosen,
	5. 9	we risk our **lives** when we look for food.
	5.15	Happiness has gone out of our **lives;**
Ezek	3.18	that he can save his **life,** he will die, still a sinner,
	3.19	he will die, still a sinner, but your **life** will be spared.
	3.21	he will stay alive, and your **life** will also be spared."
	13.18	so that they can have power over other people's **lives.**
	13.18	to possess the power of **life** and death over my people and
	13.20	that you use in your attempt to control **life** and death.

Ezek 13.22 You prevent evil people from giving up evil and saving their **lives.**
14.14 living there, their goodness would save only their own **lives."**
14.16 would save only their own **lives,** and the land would become a
14.18 able to save even their children, but only their own **lives.**
14.19 in my anger take many **lives,** killing people and animals,
14.20 Their goodness would save only their own **lives."**
16.22 During your disgusting **life** as a prostitute you never
18. 4 The **life** of every person belongs to me,
18. 4 the **life** of the parent as well as
18.27 sinning and does what is right and good, he saves his **life.**
20.11 them my laws, which bring **life** to anyone who obeys them.
20.13 my commands, which bring **life** to anyone who obeys them.
20.21 keep my commands, which bring **life** to anyone who obeys them.
20.25 laws that are not good and commands that do not bring **life.**
32.10 all of them will tremble in fear for their own **lives."**
32.24 In **life** they spread terror, but now they lie dead and disgraced.
32.25 In **life** they spread terror, but now they lie dead and disgraced,
33. 8 that he can save his **life,** then he will die, still a
33. 9 will die, still a sinner, but your **life** will be spared."
33.12 if a good man starts sinning, his **life** will not be spared.
33.13 I may promise **life** to a good man, but if he starts
33.15 follows the laws that give **life,** he will not die, but live.
33.19 and does what is right and good, he has saved his **life.**
47. 9 Dead Sea fresh, and wherever it flows, it will bring **life.**
Dan 3.28 my orders and risked their **lives** rather than bow down and
12. 2 enjoy **eternal life,** and some will suffer eternal disgrace.
Amos 2.14 and soldiers will not be able to save their own **lives.**
2.15 away, and men on horses will not escape with their **lives.**
6. 1 that have such an easy **life** in Zion and for you that
Jon 1. 6 Maybe he will feel sorry for us and spare our **lives."**
1.14 pray, don't punish us with death for taking this man's **life!**
2. 7 When I felt my **life** slipping away, then, O Lord, I prayed
Hab 2.19 covered with silver and gold, but there is no **life** in it.
Zeph 3.17 in you, and in his love he will give you new **life.**
Zech 1. 4 telling them not to live evil, sinful **lives** any longer.
12. 1 out the skies, created the earth, and gave **life** to man.
13. 5 I am a farmer—I have farmed the land all my **life.'**
Mal 2. 5 my covenant I promised them **life** and well-being, and this is
Mt 6.25 After all, isn't **life** worth more than food?
7.14 But the gate to **life** is narrow and the way that leads
10.39 Whoever tries to gain his own **life** will lose it;
10.39 but whoever loses his **life** for my sake will gain it.
13.22 but the worries about this **life** and the love for riches
14. 2 Baptist, who has come back to **life,"** he told his officials.
16.25 For whoever wants to save his own **life** will lose it;
16.25 but whoever loses his **life** for my sake will find it.
16.26 gain anything if he wins the whole world but loses his **life?**
16.26 There is nothing he can give to regain his **life.**
18. 8 better for you to enter **life** without a hand or a foot
18. 9 better for you to enter **life** with only one eye than to
19.16 "what good thing must I do to receive **eternal life?"**
19.17 Keep the commandments if you want to enter **life."**
19.29 receive a hundred times more and will be given **eternal life.**
20.28 but to serve and to give his **life** to redeem many people."
23.29 and decorate the monuments of those who lived good **lives;**
25.46 to eternal punishment, but the righteous will go to **eternal life."**
Mk 3. 4 To save a man's **life** or to destroy it?"
4.19 the worries about this **life,** the love for riches, and all
6.14 Some people were saying, "John the Baptist has come back to **life!**
6.16 had his head cut off, but he has come back to **life!"**
8.35 For whoever wants to save his own **life** will lose it;
8.35 but whoever loses his **life** for me and for the gospel will
8.36 gain anything if he wins the whole world but loses his **life?**
8.37 There is nothing he can give to regain his **life.**
9.43 better for you to enter **life** without a hand than to keep
9.45 better for you to enter **life** without a foot than to keep
10.17 "Good Teacher, what must I do to receive **eternal life?"**
10.30 and in the age to come he will receive **eternal life.**
10.45 came to serve and to give his **life** to redeem many people."
Lk 1. 6 They both lived good **lives** in God's sight and obeyed fully
1.75 be holy and righteous before him all the days of our **life.**
6. 9 To save a man's **life** or destroy it?"
6.24 you have had your easy **life!**
7.37 In that town was a woman who lived a sinful **life.**
7.39 he would know what kind of sinful **life** she lives!"
8.14 riches and pleasures of this **life** crowd in and choke them,
8.55 Her **life** returned, and she got up at once, and Jesus
9. 7 were saying that John the Baptist had come back to **life.**
9. 8 one of the prophets of long ago had come back to **life.**
9.19 one of the prophets of long ago has come back to **life."**
9.24 wants to save his own **life** will lose it,
9.24 but whoever loses his **life** for my sake will save it.
10.25 "Teacher," he asked, "what must I do to receive **eternal life?"**
12.15 because a person's true **life** is not made up of the things
12.19 Take **life** easy, eat, drink, and enjoy yourself!'
12.20 This very night you will have to give up your **life;**
12.23 **Life** is much more important than food, and the body much
17.33 Whoever tries to save his own **life** will lose it;
17.33 whoever loses his **life** will save it.
18.18 "Good Teacher, what must I do to receive **eternal life?"**
18.30 in this present age and **eternal life** in the age to come."
21.34 with the worries of this **life,** or that Day may suddenly
Jn 1. 4 Word was the source of **life,**
1. 4 and this **life** brought light to mankind.
3.15 so that everyone who believes in him may have **eternal life.**
3.16 who believes in him may not die but have **eternal life.**
3.36 Whoever believes in the Son has **eternal life;**
3.36 Son will not have **life,** but will remain under God's punishment.
4.10 you would ask him, and he would give you **life-giving** water."
4.11 Where would you get that **life-giving** water?
4.14 provide him with **life-giving** water

Jn 4.14 and give him **eternal life."**
4.36 is being paid and gathers the crops for **eternal life;**
5.21 the dead and gives them **life,** in the same way
5.21 the Son gives **life** to those he wants to.
5.24 my words and believes in him who sent me has **eternal life.**
5.24 not be judged, but has already passed from death to **life.**
5.25 Son of God, and those who hear it will come to **life.**
5.26 is himself the source of **life,** in the same way
5.26 he has made his Son to be the source of **life.**
5.39 because you think that in them you will find **eternal life.**
5.40 are not willing to come to me in order to have **life.**
6.27 instead, work for the food that lasts for **eternal life.**
6.33 he who comes down from heaven and gives **life** to the world."
6.35 "I am the bread of **life,"** Jesus told them.
6.40 who see the Son and believe in him should have **eternal life.**
6.47 he who believes has **eternal life.**
6.48 I am the bread of **life.**
6.53 Man and drink his blood, you will not have **life** in yourselves.
6.54 drinks my blood has **eternal life,**
6.54 and I will raise him to **life** on the last day.
6.63 What gives **life** is God's Spirit;
6.63 The words I have spoken to you bring God's **life-giving** Spirit.
6.68 You have the words that give **eternal life.**
7.38 believes in me, streams of **life-giving** water will pour out
8.12 have the light of **life** and will never walk in darkness."
10.10 in order that you might have **life**—life in all its fullness.
10.17 willing to give up my **life,** in order that I may receive
10.18 No one takes my **life** away from me.
10.28 I give them **eternal life,** and they shall never die.
11.25 Jesus said to her, "I am the resurrection and the **life.**
12.25 Whoever loves his own **life** will lose it;
12.25 whoever hates his own **life** in this world
12.25 will keep it for **life eternal.**
12.50 And I know that his command brings **eternal life.**
14. 6 Jesus answered him, "I am the way, the truth, and the **life;**
15.13 can have for his friends is to give his **life** for them.
17. 2 so that he might give **eternal life** to all those you gave
17. 3 And **eternal life** means knowing you, the only true God,
20.31 God, and that through your faith in him you may have **life.**
Acts 2.28 the paths that lead to **life,** and your presence will fill me
3. 2 was called, was a man who had been lame all his **life.**
3.15 the one who leads to **life,** but God raised him from death
5.20 the Temple, and tell the people all about this new **life."**
8.33 about his descendants, because his **life** on earth has come to
13.46 not consider yourselves worthy of **eternal life,** we will leave
13.48 those who had been chosen for **eternal life** became believers.
15.26 Paul, [26] who have risked their **lives** in the service of our
17.25 is he himself who gives **life** and breath and everything else
20.24 But I reckon my own **life** to be worth nothing to me;
26. 4 I have spent my whole **life,** at first in my own country
27.10 the cargo and to the ship, and loss of **life** as well."
27.22 Not one of you will lose his **life;**
27.24 to you has spared the **lives** of all those who are sailing
Rom 2. 7 keep on doing good, and seek glory, honour, and immortal **life;**
2. 7 to them God will give **eternal life.**
4.12 circumcised, also live the same **life** of faith that our
5.10 God's friends, how much more will we be saved by Christ's **life!**
5.17 freely put right with him will rule in **life** through Christ.
5.18 one righteous act sets all mankind free and gives them **life.**
5.21 righteousness, leading us to **eternal life** through Jesus Christ
6. 4 power of the Father, so also we might live a new **life.**
6.10 and now he lives his **life** in fellowship with God.
6.22 Your gain is a **life** fully dedicated to him,
6.22 and the result is **eternal life.**
6.23 but God's free gift is **eternal life** in union with Christ
7. 9 when the commandment came, sin sprang to **life,** [10] and I died.
7.10 which was meant to bring **life,** in my case brought death.
8. 2 the Spirit, which brings us **life** in union with Christ Jesus,
8. 6 to be controlled by the Spirit results in **life** and peace.
8.10 in you, the Spirit is **life** for you because you have been
8.11 from death will also give **life** to your mortal bodies by the
8.38 neither death nor **life,** neither angels nor other heavenly rulers
11.15 It will be **life** for the dead!
11.17 and now you share the strong spiritual **life** of the Jews.
15. 8 I tell you that Christ's **life** of service was on behalf of
16. 4 they risked their **lives** for me.
1 Cor 3.22 this world, **life** and death, the present and the future—all
4.15 guardians in your Christian **life,** you have only one father.
4.15 For in your **life** in union with Christ Jesus I have become
4.17 who is my own dear and faithful son in the Christian **life.**
4.17 I follow in the new **life** in union with Christ Jesus
6. 3 How much more, then, the things of this **life!**
9. 2 Because of your **life** in union with the Lord you yourselves
11.11 In our **life** in the Lord, however, woman is not
15.19 Christ is good for this **life** only and no more, then we
15.31 have in you, in our **life** in union with Christ Jesus our
15.36 in the ground, it does not sprout to **life** unless it dies.
15.45 but the last Adam is the **life-giving** Spirit.
2 Cor 1.12 conscience assures us that our **lives** in this world, and
1.21 together with you, sure of our **life** in union with Christ;
2.16 who are being saved, it is a fragrance that brings **life.**
3. 6 The written law brings death, but the Spirit gives **life.**
4.10 of Jesus, so that his **life** also may be seen in our
4.11 Throughout our **lives** we are always in danger of death for Jesus'
4.11 sake, in order that his **life** may be seen in this mortal
4.12 is at work in us, but **life** is at work in you.
5. 4 over us, so that what is mortal will be transformed by **life.**
5. 7 For our **life** is a matter of faith, not of sight.
5.10 to everything he has done, good or bad, in his bodily **life.**
13. 4 relations with you we shall share God's power in his **life.**
Gal 2.20 This **life** that I live now, I live by faith in the

Gal 2.20 Son of God, who loved me and gave his **life** for me.
3.21 a law that could bring **life,** then everyone could be put
3.27 are clothed, so to speak, with the **life** of Christ himself.
5.10 Our **life** in union with the Lord makes me confident that you
5.16 let the Spirit direct your **lives,** and you will not satisfy
5.25 The Spirit has given us **life;**
5.25 he must also control our **lives.**
6. 8 from the Spirit he will gather the harvest of **eternal life.**
6.16 follow this rule in their **lives,** may peace and mercy be with
Eph 1. 1 who are faithful in their **life** in union with Christ Jesus:
2.10 has created us for a **life** of good deeds, which he has
4. 1 live a **life** that measures up to the standard God set when
4.18 have no part in the **life** that God gives, for they are
4.24 reveals itself in the true **life** that is upright and holy.
5. 2 Your **life** must be controlled by love, just as Christ
5. 2 loved us and gave his **life** for us as a sweet-smelling
5.25 just as Christ loved the church and gave his **life** for it.
Phil 1.11 Your **lives** will be filled with the truly good qualities
1.21 For what is **life?**
1.23 very much to leave this **life** and be with Christ, which is
1.26 be proud of me in your **life** in union with Christ Jesus.
1.27 is that your way of **life** should be as the gospel of
2. 1 Your **life** in Christ makes you strong, and his love comforts you.
2.16 up the sky, [16]as you offer them the message of **life.**
2.17 Perhaps my **life's** blood is to be poured out like an
2.30 because he risked his **life** and nearly died for the sake
3. 3 Spirit and rejoice in our **life** in union with Christ Jesus.
3.14 which is God's call through Christ Jesus to the **life** above.
3.18 there are many whose **lives** make them enemies of Christ's
4. 1 is how you should stand firm in your **life** in the Lord.
4.10 In my **life** in union with the Lord it is a great
Col 1.10 Your **lives** will produce all kinds of good deeds, and you
1.18 he is the source of the body's **life.**
2. 7 deep in him, build your **lives** on him, and become stronger in
2.10 and you have been given full **life** in union with him.
3. 3 you have died, and your **life** is hidden with Christ in God.
3. 4 Your real **life** is Christ and when he appears, then you too
3. 7 according to such desires, when your **life** was dominated by them.
1 Thes 2. 8 not only the Good News from God but even our own **lives.**
2.12 to live the kind of **life** that pleases God, who calls you
3. 8 if you stand firm in your **life** in union with the Lord.
4.11 aim to live a quiet **life,** to mind your own business,
5.12 among you, who guide and instruct you in the Christian **life.**
5.18 God wants from you in your **life** in union with Christ Jesus.
2 Thes 1.11 make you worthy of the **life** he has called you to live.
3. 6 who are living a lazy **life** and who do not follow the
3.11 among you who live lazy **lives** and who do nothing except
3.12 warn them to lead orderly **lives** and work to earn their own
1 Tim 1.16 those who would later believe in him and receive **eternal life.**
2. 2 live a quiet and peaceful **life** with all reverence towards God
4. 7 Keep yourself in training for a godly **life.**
4. 8 every way, because it promises **life** both for the present and
6.12 in the race of faith, and win **eternal life** for yourself;
6.12 for it was to this **life** that God called you when you
6.13 Before God, who gives **life** to all things, and before Christ
6.17 in the things of this **life** not to be proud, but to
6.19 they will be able to win the **life** which is true life.
2 Tim 1. 1 sent to proclaim the promised **life** which we have in union
1.10 power of death and through the gospel has revealed immortal **life.**
2. 4 so does not get mixed up in the affairs of civilian **life.**
3.10 followed my teaching, my conduct, and my purpose in **life;**
3.12 wants to live a godly **life** in union with Christ Jesus will
4. 6 the time is here for me to leave this **life.**
Tit 1. 2 our religion, [2]which is based on the hope for **eternal life.**
1. 2 not lie, promised us this **life** before the beginning of time,
2. 3 older women to behave as women should who live a holy **life.**
2.12 live self-controlled, upright, and godly **lives** in this world,
3. 3 We spent our **lives** in malice and envy;
3. 5 Spirit, who gives us new birth and new **life** by washing us.
3. 7 God and come into possession of the **eternal life** we hope for.
3.14 they should not live useless **lives.**
Phlm 6 blessing which we have in our **life** in union with Christ.
Heb 1.12 But you are always the same, and your **life** never ends."
2.15 were slaves all their **lives** because of their fear of death.
5. 7 In his **life** on earth Jesus made his prayers and requests
6.19 We have this hope as an anchor for our **lives.**
7.16 but through the power of a **life** which has no end.
11.35 died under torture in order to be raised to a better **life.**
12.11 by such punishment reap the peaceful reward of a righteous **life.**
12.14 try to live a holy **life,** because no one will see the
13. 5 Keep your **lives** free from the love of money, and be
Jas 1.12 receive as his reward the **life** which God has promised to
2.16 if you don't give them the necessities of **life?**
3.13 prove it by his good **life,** by his good deeds performed with
4.14 You don't even know what your **life** tomorrow will be!
5. 5 Your **life** here on earth has been full of luxury and pleasure.
1 Pet 1. 3 he gave us new **life** by raising Jesus Christ from death.
1.14 and do not allow your **lives** to be shaped by those desires
1.17 spend the rest of your **lives** here on earth in reverence for
1.18 from the worthless manner of **life** handed down by your ancestors.
3. 7 they also will receive, together with you, God's gift of **life.**
3.10 "Whoever wants to enjoy **life** and wishes to see good times,
4. 2 the rest of your earthly **lives** controlled by God's will and
4. 3 Your **lives** were spent in indecency, lust, drunkenness, orgies, drinking parties,
2 Pet 1. 3 to live a truly religious **life** through our knowledge of the
3. 3 will appear whose **lives** are controlled by their own lusts.
3.11 Your **lives** should be holy and dedicated to God, [12]as you
1 Jn 1. 1 you about the Word of **life,** which has existed from the very
1. 2 When this **life** became visible, we saw it;
1. 2 and tell you about the **eternal life** which was with the
2.25 this is what Christ himself promised to give us—**eternal life.**
3.14 We know that we have left death and come over into **life;**
3.15 you know that a murderer has not got **eternal life** in him.
3.16 Christ gave his **life** for us.
3.16 We too, then, ought to give our **lives** for our brothers!
4. 9 Son into the world, so that we might have **life** through him.
4.17 will have it because our **life** in this world is the same
5.11 God has given us **eternal life,**
5.11 and this **life** has its source in his Son.
5.12 Whoever has the Son has this **life;**
5.12 whoever does not have the Son of God does not have **life.**
5.13 may know that you have **eternal life**—you that believe in the
5.16 to death, you should pray to God, who will give him **life.**
5.20 This is the true God, and this is **eternal life.**
Jude 21 Lord Jesus Christ in his mercy to give you **eternal life.**
Rev 2. 7 fruit of the tree of **life** that grows in the Garden of
2.10 death, and I will give you **life** as your prize of victory.
4.11 and by your will they were given existence and **life."**
7.17 he will guide them to springs of **life-giving** water.
11.11 and a half days a **life-giving** breath came from God and
12.11 and they were willing to give up their **lives** and die.
13.15 beast was allowed to breathe **life** into the image of the
18.13 sheep, horses and carriages, slaves, and even human **lives.**
21. 6 from the spring of the water of **life** without paying for it.
22. 1 river of the water of **life,** sparkling like crystal,
22. 2 river was the tree of **life,** which bears fruit twelve times a
22.14 fruit from the tree of **life** and to go through the gates
22.17 accept the water of **life** as a gift, whoever wants it.
22.19 fruit of the tree of **life** and of the Holy City, which

LIFE (2) (TO LIFE)

1 Sam 2. 6 The Lord kills and restores **to life;**
2 Sam 12.23 Could I bring the child back **to life?**
14.14 not bring the dead back **to life,** but the king can at
1 Kgs 17.21 and prayed, "O Lord my God, restore this child **to life!"**
2 Kgs 8. 1 son he had brought back **to life,** that the Lord was sending
8. 5 brought a dead person back **to life,** the woman made her
8. 5 and here is her son whom Elisha brought back **to life!"**
13.21 Elisha's bones, the man came back **to life** and stood up.
Neh 9.29 your laws, although keeping your Law is the way **to life.**
Job 14. 7 it can come back **to life** and sprout.
14.14 If a man dies, can he come back **to life?**
Ps 16.11 You will show me the path that leads **to life;**
Prov 2.19 He never returns to the road **to life.**
5. 6 She does not stay on the road **to life;**
12.28 Righteousness is the road **to life;**
15.24 the road that leads upwards **to life,** not the road that leads
Is 26.19 Their bodies will come back **to life.**
Jer 21. 8 between the way that leads **to life** and the way that leads
Ezek 37. 3 to me, "Mortal man, can these bones come back **to life?"**
37. 5 going to put breath into you and bring you back **to life.**
37. 6 I will put breath into you and bring you back **to life.**
37. 9 into these dead bodies, and to bring them back **to life."**
37.10 Breath entered the bodies, and they came **to life** and stood up.
37.14 in them, bring them back **to life,** and let them live in
Mt 10. 8 bring the dead back **to life,** heal those who suffer from
11. 5 the dead are brought back **to life,** and the Good News is
16.21 to death, but three days later I will be raised **to life."**
17.23 but three days later he will be raised **to life."**
20.19 but three days later he will be raised **to life."**
22.28 day when the dead rise **to life,** whose wife will she be?
22.30 For when the dead rise **to life,** they will be like the
22.31 Now, as for the dead rising **to life:**
26.32 But after I am raised **to life,** I will go to Galilee
27.52 and many of God's people who had died were raised **to life.**
27.63 alive he said, 'I will be raised **to life** three days later.'
Mk 8.31 put to death, but three days later he will rise **to life."**
9.31 Three days later, however, he will rise **to life."**
10.34 but three days later he will rise **to life."**
12.23 when all the dead rise **to life** on the day of resurrection,
12.25 For when the dead rise **to life,** they will be like the
14.28 But after I am raised **to life,** I will go to Galilee
Lk 7.22 the dead are raised **to life,** and the Good News is
9.22 to death, but three days later he will be raised **to life."**
18.33 and kill him, but three days later he will rise **to life."**
20.33 day when the dead rise **to life,** whose wife will she be?
20.37 And Moses clearly proves that the dead are raised **to life.**
24. 7 to sinful men, be crucified, and three days later rise **to life.' "**
Jn 5.24 not be judged, but has already passed from death **to life.**
6.39 that I should raise them all **to life** on the last day.
6.40 And I will raise them **to life** on the last day."
6.44 and I will raise him **to life** on the last day.
6.54 and I will raise him **to life** on the last day.
11.23 "Your brother will rise **to life,"** Jesus told her.
11.24 she replied, "that he will rise **to life** on the last day."
Acts 4. 2 from death, which proved that the dead will rise **to life.**
13.32 for us, who are their descendants, by raising Jesus **to life.**
23. 6 of the hope I have that the dead will rise **to life!"**
24.21 you today for believing that the dead will rise **to life.' "**
Rom 4.17 God who brings the dead **to life** and whose command brings
4.25 and he was raised **to life** in order to put us
6. 5 be one with him by being raised **to life** as he was.
6.13 been brought from death **to life,** and surrender your whole being
8.34 or rather, who was raised **to life** and is at the right-hand
14. 9 For Christ died and rose **to life** in order to be the
1 Cor 15. 4 and that he was raised **to life** three days later, as written
15.12 of you say that the dead will not be raised **to life?**
15.15 the dead are not raised **to life,** then he did not raise
15.22 way all will be raised **to life** because of their union with
15.29 the dead are not raised **to life,** why are those people being

1 Cor 15.32 the dead are not raised **to life,** then, as the saying goes,
15.35 Someone will ask, "How can the dead be raised **to life?**
15.42 is how it will be when the dead are raised **to life.**
2 Cor 4.14 who raised the Lord Jesus **to life,** will also raise us up
5.15 for him who died and was raised **to life** for their sake.
Eph 2. 5 dead in our disobedience he brought us **to life** with Christ.
Phil 3.11 the hope that I myself will be raised from death **to life.**
Col 2.13 But God has now brought you **to life** with Christ.
3. 1 You have been raised **to life** with Christ, so set your
1 Thes 4.16 Those who have died believing in Christ will rise **to life** first;
Heb 11.35 women received their dead relatives raised back **to life.**
Rev 20. 4 They came **to life** and ruled as kings with Christ for a
20. 5 the dead did not come **to life** until the thousand years were

LIFE-BLOOD see BLOOD

LIFELESS

Ps 7. 5 me down and kill me and leave me **lifeless** on the ground!
106.28 of Baal, and ate sacrifices offered to **lifeless** gods.
Jer 10.14 because the gods they make are false and **lifeless.**
16.18 with idols that are as **lifeless** as corpses, and have filled
51.17 because the gods they make are false and **lifeless.**
1 Cor 12. 2 led astray in many ways to the worship of **lifeless** idols.
14. 7 Take such **lifeless** musical instruments as the flute

LIFETIME

Num 3. 4 Eleazar and Ithamar served as priests during Aaron's **lifetime.**
Deut 31.27 against the Lord during my **lifetime,** and they will rebel
2 Sam 18.18 During his **lifetime** Absalom had built a monument for
1 Kgs 11.12 not do this in your **lifetime,** but during the reign of your
11.25 He was an enemy of Israel during the **lifetime** of Solomon.
15. 6 Rehoboam and Jeroboam continued throughout Abijah's **lifetime.**
21.29 this, I will not bring disaster on him during his **lifetime;**
21.29 will be during his son's **lifetime** that I will bring disaster
2 Kgs 20.19 peace and security during his **lifetime,** so he replied, "The
Neh 12.22 families during the **lifetimes** of the following High Priests:
Ps 30. 5 His anger lasts only a moment, his goodness for a **lifetime.**
39. 5 In your sight my **lifetime** seems nothing.
72. 7 May righteousness flourish in his **lifetime,** and may
Is 23.15 Tyre will be forgotten for seventy years, the **lifetime** of a king.
39. 8 peace and security during his **lifetime,** so he replied, "The
Ezek 12.25 In your own **lifetime,** you rebels, I will do what I have
Lk 16.25 my son, that in your **lifetime** you were given all the good

LIFT
[UPLIFTED]

Gen 41.44 Egypt shall so much as **lift** a hand or a foot without
Ex 9.29 of the city, I will **lift** up my hands in prayer
9.33 out of the city, and **lifted** up his hands in prayer
14.16 **Lift** up your stick and hold it out over the sea.
40.36 to another place only when the cloud **lifted** from the Tent.
Num 9.17 Whenever the cloud **lifted,** the people of Israel broke camp,
9.21 morning, and they moved on as soon as the cloud **lifted.**
9.21 Whenever the cloud **lifted,** they moved on.
9.22 but when it **lifted,** they moved.
10.11 Tent of the Lord's presence **lifted,** [12] and the Israelites
Josh 8.19 and as soon as he **lifted** his hand, the men who had
Ruth 3. 4 he falls asleep, go and **lift** the covers and lie down at
3. 7 Ruth slipped over quietly, **lifted** the covers and lay down at
3.15 of barley and helped her to **lift** it on her shoulder.
1 Sam 2. 8 He **lifts** the poor from the dust and raises the needy from
5. 3 So they **lifted** it up and put it back in its place.
6.15 The Levites **lifted** off the Covenant Box of the Lord and
22.17 But the guards refused to **lift** a hand to kill the Lord's
2 Sam 18.12 of silver, I wouldn't **lift** a finger against the king's son.
1 Kgs 8. 3 leaders had gathered, the priests **lifted** the Covenant Box
8.54 the altar, where he had been kneeling with **uplifted** hands.
2 Chr 5. 4 had gathered, then the Levites **lifted** the Covenant Box [5] and
35.24 They **lifted** him out of his chariot, placed him in a
Ps 28. 2 for help, when I **lift** my hands towards your holy Temple.
35. 3 **Lift** up your spear and your axe against those who pursue me.
69.29 **lift** me up, O God, and save me!
77. 2 all night long I **lift** my hands in prayer, but I cannot
88. 9 I call to you and **lift** my hands to you in prayer.
107.26 The ships were **lifted** high in the air and plunged down
113. 7 he **lifts** the needy from their misery [8] and makes them
141. 2 my prayer as incense, my **uplifted** hands as an evening sacrifice.
143. 6 I **lift** up my hands to you in prayer;
145.14 he **lifts** those who have fallen.
146. 8 He **lifts** those who have fallen;
Is 1.15 "When you **lift** your hands in prayer, I will not look at
10.15 A club doesn't **lift** up a man;
10.15 a man **lifts** up a club."
46. 7 They **lift** it to their shoulders and carry it;
47. 2 **Lift** up your skirts to cross the streams!
Ezek 3.12 Then God's spirit **lifted** me up, and I heard behind me
8. 3 in this vision God's spirit **lifted** me high in the air and
11. 1 God's spirit **lifted** me up and took me to the east gate
11.24 vision the spirit of God **lifted** me up and brought me back
22.14 or have strength enough to **lift** your hand when I am finished
43. 5 The Lord's spirit **lifted** me up and took me into the inner
Dan 7. 4 The beast was **lifted** up and made to stand like a man.
Hos 11. 7 that is on them, but no one will **lift** it from them.
Zech 12. 3 heavy stone—any nation that tries to **lift** it will be hurt.
Mt 11.23 Did you want to **lift** yourself up to heaven?
12.11 Will he not take hold of it and **lift** it out?
23. 4 they aren't willing even to **lift** a finger to help them carry
Lk 1.52 mighty kings from their thrones, and **lifted** up the lowly.
10.15 Did you want to **lift** yourself up to heaven?
Jn 3.14 As Moses **lifted** up the bronze snake on a pole in the
3.14 Son of Man must be **lifted** up, [15] so that everyone who
8.28 said to them, "When you **lift** up the Son of Man, you
12.32 When I am **lifted** up from the earth, I will draw everyone
12.34 can you say that the Son of Man must be **lifted** up?
19.29 put on a stalk of hyssop, and **lifted** up to his lips.
1 Tim 2. 8 dedicated to God and can **lift** up their hands in prayer
Heb 12.12 **Lift** up your tired hands, then, and strengthen your trembling knees!
Jas 1. 9 must be glad when God **lifts** him up, [10] and the rich
4.10 Humble yourselves before the Lord, and he will **lift** you up.
1 Pet 5. 6 hand, so that he will **lift** you up in his own good

LIGAMENTS

Col 2.19 together by its joints and **ligaments,** and it grows as God

LIGHT (1)

Gen 1. 3 Then God commanded, "Let there be **light"**—and light appeared.
1. 4 Then he separated the **light** from the darkness, [5] and he
1. 5 and he named the **light** "Day" and the darkness "Night".
1.14 Then God commanded, "Let **lights** appear in the sky to
1.15 in the sky to give **light** to the earth"—and it was
1.16 God made the two larger **lights,** the sun to rule over the
1.17 He placed the **lights** in the sky to shine on the earth,
1.18 the day and the night, and to separate **light** from darkness.
Ex 10.23 But the Israelites had **light** where they were living.
13.21 of fire to give them **light,** so that they could travel night
14.20 for the Egyptians, but gave **light** to the people of Israel,
16. 7 you will see the dazzling **light** of the Lord's presence.
16.10 desert, and suddenly the dazzling **light** of the Lord appeared
24.16 The dazzling **light** of the Lord's presence came down
24.16 To the Israelites the **light** looked like a fire burning on
29.43 of Israel, and the dazzling **light** of my presence will make
33.18 "Please, let me see the dazzling **light** of your presence."
33.22 When the dazzling **light** of my presence passes by, I will
35. 3 Do not even **light** a fire in your homes on the Sabbath."
35.14 the lamp-stand for the **light** and its equipment;
40.34 Tent and the dazzling **light** of the Lord's presence filled it.
Lev 9. 6 this, so that the dazzling **light** of his presence can appear
9.23 the people, and the dazzling **light** of the Lord's presence
13.21 the surrounding skin, but is **light** in colour, the priest
13.26 the surrounding skin, but is **light** in colour, the priest
13.28 does not spread and is **light** in colour, it is not a
24. 2 in the Tent, so that a **light** may be kept burning regularly.
Num 5.15 a suspicious husband, made to bring the truth to **light.**
8. 2 place them so that the **light** shines towards the front."
14.10 the people saw the dazzling **light** of the Lord's presence
14.22 They have seen the dazzling **light** of my presence and the
16.19 Suddenly the dazzling **light** of the Lord's presence appeared
16.42 that the dazzling **light** of the Lord's presence had appeared.
20. 6 the ground, and the dazzling **light** of the Lord's presence
Ruth 3.14 got up before it was **light** enough for her to be seen,
1 Sam 29.10 have to get up early and leave as soon as it's **light."**
2 Sam 22.29 You, Lord, are my **light;**
1 Kgs 8.11 shining with the dazzling **light** of the Lord's presence,
2 Chr 5.11 shining with the dazzling **light** of the Lord's presence,
7. 1 been offered, and the dazzling **light** of the Lord's presence
7. 2 full of the dazzling **light,** the priests could not enter it.
7. 3 fall from heaven and the **light** fill the Temple, they fell
Neh 9.12 in day-time, and at night you **lighted** their way with fire.
Job 3. 4 never again let **light** shine on it.
3.20 Why give **light** to men in grief?
10.22 shadows, and confusion, where the **light** itself is darkness.
12.22 He sends **light** to places dark as death.
17.12 they say that **light** is near, but I know I remain in
18. 5 The wicked man's **light** will still be put out;
18.18 of the land of the living, driven from **light** into darkness.
21.17 Was a wicked man's **light** ever put out?
22.28 succeed in all you do, and **light** will shine on your path.
24.13 There are men who reject the **light;**
24.16 into houses, but by day they hide and avoid the **light.**
24.17 They fear the **light** of day, but darkness holds no terror
25. 3 Is there any place where God's **light** does not shine?
26.10 He divided **light** from darkness by a circle drawn on the
28.11 to the sources of rivers And bring to **light** what is hidden.
29. 3 me then and gave me **light** as I walked through the darkness.
30.26 I hoped for happiness and **light,** but trouble and darkness came
37.21 And now the **light** in the sky is dazzling, too bright for
38.15 The **light** of day is too bright for the wicked and
38.19 Do you know where the **light** comes from or what the
41.18 **Light** flashes when he sneezes, and his eyes glow like
Ps 18.28 O Lord, you give me **light;**
27. 1 The Lord is my **light** and my salvation;
36. 9 of all life, and because of your **light** we see the light.
43. 3 Send your **light** and your truth;
56.13 presence of God, in the **light** that shines on the living.
58. 8 they be like a baby born dead that never sees the **light.**
72. 5 shines, as long as the moon gives **light,** for ages to come.
72. 7 and may prosperity last as long as the moon gives **light.**
77.18 rolled out, and flashes of lightning **lit** up the world;
78.14 a cloud and all night long with the **light** of a fire.
89.15 you with songs, who live in the **light** of your kindness!
97. 4 His lightning **lights** up the world;
97.11 **Light** shines on the righteous, and gladness on the good.
104. 2 you cover yourself with **light.**
105.39 over his people and a fire at night to give them **light.**
112. 4 **Light** shines in the darkness for good men, for those who

Ps 119.105 is a lamp to guide me and a **light** for my path.
119.130 teachings gives **light** and brings wisdom to the ignorant.
139.11 to hide me or the **light** round me to turn into night,
139.12 Darkness and **light** are the same to you.
Prov 6.23 Their instructions are a shining **light;**
13. 9 The righteous are like a **light** shining brightly;
Ecc 2.13 better than foolishness, just as **light** is better than darkness.
6. 5 It never sees the **light** of day or knows what life is
11. 7 is good to be able to enjoy the pleasant **light** of day.
12. 2 That is when the **light** of the sun, the moon, and the
Is 2. 5 Jacob, let us walk in the **light** which the Lord gives us!
5.20 You turn darkness into **light** and light into darkness.
5.30 The **light** is swallowed by darkness.
9. 2 The people who walked in darkness have seen a great **light.**
9. 2 in a land of shadows, but now **light** is shining on them.
10.17 God, the **light** of Israel, will become a fire.
13.10 be dark when it rises, and the moon will give no **light.**
30.26 brighter than usual, like the **light** of seven days in one.
42. 6 through you I will bring **light** to the nations.
42.16 will turn their darkness into **light** and make rough country
45. 7 I create both **light** and darkness;
49. 6 will also make you a **light** to the nations— so that
49. 9 and to those who are in darkness, 'Come out to the **light!'**
51. 4 my laws will bring them **light.**
59. 9 We hope for **light** to walk by, but there is only darkness,
60. 2 by darkness, But on you the **light** of the Lord will shine;
60. 3 will be drawn to your **light,** And kings to the dawning of
60.19 will the sun be your **light** by day
60.19 Or the moon be your **light** by night;
60.19 I, the Lord, will be your eternal **light;**
60.19 The **light** of my glory will shine on you.
60.20 Lord, will be your eternal **light,** More lasting than the sun
Jer 4.23 at the sky—there was no **light.**
13.16 before he turns into deep darkness the **light** you hoped for.
31.35 Lord provides the sun for **light** by day, the moon and the
Ezek 1.27 all over with a bright **light** [28] that had in it all the
1.28 This was the dazzling **light** that shows the presence of the Lord.
8. 4 There I saw the dazzling **light** that shows the presence of
9. 3 Then the dazzling **light** of the presence of the God of
10. 4 The dazzling **light** of the Lord's presence rose up from the
10. 4 the Temple, and the courtyard was blazing with the **light.**
10.18 Then the dazzling **light** of the Lord's presence left the
10.19 gate of the Temple, and the dazzling **light** was over them.
11.22 The dazzling **light** of the presence of the God of Israel was
11.23 Then the dazzling **light** left the city and moved to the
32. 7 hide behind the clouds, and the moon will give no **light.**
32. 8 will put out all the **lights** of heaven and plunge your world
43. 2 from the east the dazzling **light** of the presence of the God
43. 2 of the sea, and the earth shone with the dazzling **light.**
43. 4 The dazzling **light** passed through the east gate and went
44. 4 the Lord was filled with the dazzling **light** of his presence.
Dan 2.22 hidden in darkness, and he himself is surrounded by **light.**
5. 5 of the palace, where the **light** from the lamps was shining
Amos 5.18 you it will be a day of darkness and not of **light.**
5.20 The day of the Lord will bring darkness and not **light;**
Mic 7. 8 We are in darkness now, but the Lord will give us **light.**
7. 9 He will bring us out to the **light;**
Hab 3. 4 **light** flashes from his hand, there where his power is hidden.
Mt 4.16 The people who live in darkness will see a great **light.**
4.16 who live in the dark land of death the **light** will shine."
5.14 "You are like **light** for the whole world.
5.15 lampstand, where it gives **light** for everyone in the house.
5.16 In the same way your **light** must shine before people, so
6.22 your eyes are sound, your whole body will be full of **light;**
6.23 So if the **light** in you is darkness, how terribly dark it
Lk 2.32 A **light** to reveal your will to the Gentiles and bring
8.16 so that people will see the **light** as they come in.
8.17 whatever is covered up will be found and brought to **light.**
11.33 lampstand, so that people may see the **light** as they come in.
11.34 When your eyes are sound, your whole body is full of **light;**
11.35 Make certain, then, that the **light** in you is not darkness.
11.36 whole body is full of **light,** with no part of it in
16. 8 their affairs than the people who belong to the **light."**
17.24 flashes across the sky and **lights** it up from one side to
Jn 1. 4 the source of life, and this life brought **light** to mankind.
1. 5 The **light** shines in the darkness, and the darkness has
1. 7 to tell people about the **light,** so that all should hear the
1. 8 He himself was not the **light;**
1. 8 he came to tell about the **light.**
1. 9 This was the real **light**—the light that comes into the
3.19 the **light** has come into the world, but people love the
3.19 darkness rather than the **light,** because their deeds are evil.
3.20 does evil things hates the **light** and
3.20 will not come to the **light,** because he does not want his
3.21 is true comes to the **light**
3.21 in order that the **light** may show that what he did
5.35 and you were willing for a while to enjoy his **light.**
8.12 "I am the **light** of the world," he said.
8.12 follows me will have the **light** of life and will never walk
9. 5 I am in the world, I am the **light** for the world."
11. 9 does not stumble, for he sees the **light** of this world.
11.10 during the night he stumbles, because he has no **light."**
12.35 Jesus answered, "The **light** will be among you a little longer.
12.35 way while you have the **light,** so that the darkness will not
12.36 Believe in the **light,** then, while you have it,
12.36 so that you will be the people of the **light."**
12.46 come into the world as **light,** so that everyone who believes
Acts 9. 3 suddenly a **light** from the sky flashed round him.
12. 7 of the Lord stood there, and a **light** shone in the cell.
13.11 blind and will not see the **light** of day for a time."
13.47 'I have made you a **light** for the Gentiles, so that all
Acts 16.29 The jailer called for a **light,** rushed in, and fell
22. 6 about midday a bright **light** from the sky flashed suddenly round
22. 9 men with me saw the **light,** but did not hear the voice
22.11 blind because of the bright **light,** and so my companions took
26.13 Majesty, that I saw a **light** much brighter than the sun,
26.18 from the darkness to the **light** and from the power of Satan
26.23 from death, to announce the **light** of salvation to the Jews
Rom 2.19 guide for the blind, a **light** for those who are in darkness,
13.12 dark, and let us take up weapons for fighting in the **light.**
13.13 who live in the **light** of day—no orgies or drunkenness,
1 Cor 4. 5 he will bring to **light** the dark secrets and expose the
2 Cor 4. 2 In the full **light** of truth we live in God's sight and
4. 4 keeps them from seeing the **light** shining on them,
4. 4 the **light** that comes from the Good News
4. 6 The God who said, "Out of darkness the **light** shall shine!"
4. 6 same God who made his **light** shine in our hearts,
6.14 How can **light** and darkness live together?
11.14 Even Satan can disguise himself to look like an angel of **light!**
Eph 1.18 be opened to see his **light,** so that you will know what
5. 8 you have become the Lord's people, you are in the **light.**
5. 8 people who belong to the **light,**
5. 9 for it is the **light** that brings a rich harvest
5.11 Instead, bring them out to the **light.**
5.13 are brought out to the **light,** then their true nature is
5.14 for anything that is clearly revealed becomes **light.**
Phil 2.15 shine among them like stars **lighting** up the sky, [16] as you
Col 1.11 God has reserved for his people in the kingdom of **light.**
1 Thes 5. 5 are people who belong to the **light,** who belong to the day.
1 Tim 6.16 he lives in the **light** that no one can approach.
Heb 6. 4 They were once in God's **light;**
10.32 In those days, after God's **light** had shone on you, you
Jas 1.17 the Creator of the heavenly **lights,** who does not change or
1 Pet 2. 9 God, who called you out of darkness into his own marvellous **light.**
2 Pet 1.19 the Day dawns and the **light** of the morning star shines in
1 Jn 1. 5 God is **light,** and there is no darkness at all in him.
1. 7 if we live in the **light**—
1. 7 as he is in the **light**—then we have fellowship with one
2. 8 darkness is passing away, and the real **light** is already shining.
2. 9 that he is in the **light,** yet hates his brother, is in
2.10 his brother lives in the **light,** and so there is nothing in
Rev 8.12 stars, so that their **light** lost a third of its brightness;
8.12 there was no **light** during a third of the day and a
18.23 Never again will the **light** of a lamp be seen in you;
21.24 world will walk by its **light,** and the kings of the earth
22. 5 Lord God will be their **light,** and they will rule as kings

LIGHT (2)

Ex 27.20 olive-oil for the lamp, so that it can be **lit** each evening.
30. 8 must do the same when he **lights** the lamps in the evening.
40.25 in the Lord's presence he **lit** the lamps, just as the Lord
Lev 1. 7 and the priests shall arrange fire-wood on the altar and **light** it.
24. 3 Each evening Aaron shall **light** them and keep them burning
1 Kgs 18.23 pieces, and put it on the wood—but don't **light** the fire.
2 Chr 13.11 every evening they **light** the lamps on the gold lampstand.
21.19 His subjects did not **light** a bonfire in mourning for him as
Job 20.26 a fire not **lit** by human hands burns him and all his
Lam 4.11 he **lit** a fire in Zion that burnt it to the ground.
Mal 1.10 as to prevent you from **lighting** useless fires on my altar.
Mt 5.15 No one **lights** a lamp and puts it under a bowl;
Lk 8.16 "No one **lights** a lamp and covers it with a bowl or
11.33 "No one **lights** a lamp and then hides it or puts it
12.35 action and with your lamps **lit,** [36] like servants who are waiting
15. 8 She **lights** a lamp, sweeps her house, and looks carefully
22.55 A fire had been **lit** in the centre of the courtyard,
Acts 28. 2 and was cold, so they **lit** a fire and made us all
Rev 4. 5 front of the throne seven **lighted** torches were burning,

LIGHT (3)

1 Kgs 12. 4 If you make these burdens **lighter** and make life easier for us,
12. 9 people who are asking me to make their burdens **lighter?"**
2 Chr 10. 4 If you make these burdens **lighter** and make life easier for us,
10. 9 people who are asking me to make their burdens **lighter?"**
Job 4.15 A **light** breeze touched my face, and my hair bristled with fright.
Ps 62. 9 they are **lighter** than a mere breath.
Is 28.27 instead he uses **light** sticks of the proper size.
40.15 the distant islands are as **light** as dust.
Dan 5.27 have been weighed on the scales and found to be too **light;**
Mt 11.30 is easy, and the load I will put on you is **light."**
Lk 12.48 he deserves a whipping, will be punished with a **light** whipping.
Acts 27.38 everyone had eaten enough, they **lightened** the ship by throwing

LIGHTNING

Ex 9.23 Lord sent thunder and hail, and **lightning** struck the ground.
9.24 The Lord sent [24] a heavy hailstorm, with **lightning** flashing
19.16 day there was thunder and **lightning,** a thick cloud appeared
20.18 blast and saw the **lightning** and the smoking mountain,
2 Sam 22.13 burning coals flamed up from the **lightning** before him.
22.15 with flashes of **lightning** he sent them running.
Job 1.16 another servant came and said, **"Lightning** struck the sheep
36.30 He sends **lightning** through all the sky, but the depths
36.32 He seizes the **lightning** with his hands and commands it
37. 3 He sends the **lightning** across the sky, from one end of the
37. 4 sound of thunder, and all the while the **lightning** flashes.
37.11 **Lightning** flashes from the clouds, [12] as they move at God's will.
37.15 God gives the command and makes **lightning** flash from the clouds?
38.35 And if you command the **lightning** to flash, will it come
Ps 18.12 of fire came from the **lightning** before him and broke through

Ps 18.14 with flashes of **lightning** he sent them running.
29. 7 The voice of the Lord makes the **lightning** flash.
77.17 thunder crashed from the sky, and **lightning** flashed
77.18 rolled out, and flashes of **lightning** lit up the world;
78.48 He killed their cattle with hail and their flocks with **lightning.**
97. 4 His **lightning** lights up the world;
104. 4 your messengers and flashes of **lightning** as your servants.
105.32 He sent hail and **lightning** on their land instead of rain;
135. 7 he makes **lightning** for the storms, and he brings out the
144. 6 Send flashes of **lightning** and scatter your enemies;
148. 8 **lightning** and hail, snow and clouds, strong winds that obey his command.
Jer 10.13 He makes **lightning** flash in the rain and sends the wind from
51.16 He makes **lightning** flash in the rain and sends the wind from
Ezek 1. 4 **Lightning** was flashing from a huge cloud, and the sky round
1. 4 Where the **lightning** was flashing, something shone like bronze.
1.13 The fire would blaze up and shoot out flashes of **lightning.**
1.14 creatures themselves darted to and fro with the speed of **lightning.**
21.10 It is sharpened to kill, polished to flash like **lightning.**
21.15 a sword that flashes like **lightning** and is ready to kill.
21.28 It is polished to kill, to flash like **lightning.**
Dan 10. 6 as a flash of **lightning,** and his eyes blazed like fire.
Nah 2. 4 They flash like torches and dart about like **lightning.**
Hab 3. 4 He comes with the brightness of **lightning;**
3. 9 Your **lightning** split open the earth.
Zech 9.14 he will shoot his arrows like **lightning.**
Mt 24.27 Man will come like the **lightning** which flashes across the
28. 3 His appearance was like **lightning,** and his clothes were white as snow.
Lk 10.18 "I saw Satan fall like **lightning** from heaven.
17.24 As the **lightning** flashes across the sky and lights it up
Rev 4. 5 From the throne came flashes of **lightning,** rumblings,
8. 5 peals of thunder, flashes of **lightning,** and an earthquake.
11.19 Then there were flashes of **lightning,** rumblings
16.18 There were flashes of **lightning,** rumblings

LIKE
[WELL-LIKED]

Gen 6. 2 girls were beautiful, so they took the ones they **liked.**
20.15 live anywhere you **like."**
27. 4 of that tasty food that I **like,** and bring it to me.
27. 9 them and make some of that food your father **likes** so much.
27.14 her, and she cooked the kind of food that his father **liked.**
Ex 21. 8 his wife, but he doesn't **like** her, then she is to be
Deut 21.11 them a beautiful woman that you **like** and want to marry.
24. 1 because he finds something about her that he doesn't **like.**
Josh 18. 4 territory that they would **like** to have as their possession.
Judg 10.15 Do whatever you **like,** but please, save us today."
14. 3 I **like** her."
14. 7 Then he went and talked to the girl, and he **liked** her.
1 Sam 16.21 Saul **liked** him very much and chose him as the man to
16.22 "I **like** David.
18. 8 Saul did not **like** this, and he became very angry.
20. 3 very well how much you **like** me, and he has decided not
2 Sam 9. 1 If there is, I would **like** to show him kindness for
1 Kgs 3. 5 and asked him, "What would you **like** me to give you?"
5. 9 On your part, I would **like** you to supply the food for
9.12 Hiram went to see them, and he did not **like** them.
2 Kgs 4.13 Maybe she would **like** me to go to the king or the
5.22 Ephraim arrived, and he would **like** you to give them three
2 Chr 1. 7 Solomon and asked, "What would you **like** me to give you?"
Esth 1.21 The king and his officials **liked** this idea, and the king
2. 4 Then take the girl you **like** best and make her queen in
2. 9 Hegai **liked** Esther, and she won his favour.
2.14 the king again unless he **liked** her enough to ask for her
2.17 The king **liked** her more than any of the other girls, and
3.11 do as you **like** with them."
5. 4 please Your Majesty, I would **like** you and Haman to be my
5. 8 grant my request, I would **like** you and Haman to be my
10. 3 He was honoured and **well-liked** by his fellow-Jews.
Job 21. 3 to speak and then, when I am through, sneer if you **like.**
34. 8 He **likes** the company of evil men and goes about with sinners.
Ps 22. 8 If the Lord **likes** you, why doesn't he help you?"
34.12 Would you **like** to enjoy life?
Prov 14.20 one, not even his neighbour, **likes** a poor man, but the rich
15.12 Conceited people do not **like** to be corrected;
17.19 To **like** sin is to like making trouble.
21.26 all he does is think about what he would **like** to have.
24.18 will know if you are gloating, and he will not **like** it;
Ecc 8. 3 The king can do anything he **likes,** so depart from his presence;
Is 8.10 Talk as much as you **like!**
Ezek 16.37 lovers together—the ones you **liked** and the ones you hated.
24.21 You **like** to look at it and to visit it, but the
24.25 pride and joy, which they **liked** to look at and to visit.
Hos 3. 1 turn to other gods and **like** to take offerings of raisins to
Amos 6. 5 You **like** to compose songs, as David did, and play them on
Mal 2.17 in fact he **likes** them."
Mk 6.20 He **liked** to listen to him, even though he became greatly
6.22 the king said to the girl, "What would you **like** to have?
Lk 1.62 father, asking him what name he would **like** the boy to have.
Jn 5.44 You **like** to receive praise from one another, but you do
6.67 the twelve disciples, "And you—would you also **like** to leave?"
9.27 Maybe you, too, would **like** to be his disciples?"
Acts 13.22 the kind of man I **like,** a man who will do all
17.19 and said, "We would **like** to know what this new teaching
17.20 strange to us, and we would **like** to know what they mean."
17.21 foreigners who lived there **liked** to spend all their time telling
25.22 Agrippa said to Festus, "I would **like** to hear this man myself."
28.22 But we would **like** to hear your ideas, because we know
Rom 7.15 don't do what I would **like** to do, but instead I do
Rom 13. 3 Would you **like** to be unafraid of the man in authority?
15.24 I would **like** to see you on my way to Spain, and
1 Cor 7.32 I would **like** you to be free from worry.
14. 5 I would **like** all of you to speak in strange tongues;
2 Cor 11.17 saying now is not what the Lord would **like** me to say;
12.20 different from what I would **like** you to be and you will
12.20 will find me different from what you would **like** me to be.
Phlm 13 I would **like** to keep him here with me, while I am
14 rather, I would **like** you to do it of your own free
1 Pet 1.12 These are things which even the angels would **like** to understand.
3 Jn 9 but Diotrephes, who **likes** to be their leader, will not pay

LIKENESS

1 Cor 15.49 Just as we wear the **likeness** of the man made of earth,
15.49 so we will wear the **likeness** of the Man from heaven.
2 Cor 3.18 Spirit, transforms us into his **likeness** in an ever greater degree
4. 4 about the glory of Christ, who is the exact **likeness** of God.
Eph 4.24 which is created in God's **likeness** and reveals itself in the
Phil 2. 7 He became like man and appeared in human **likeness.**
Col 1.15 Christ is the visible **likeness** of the invisible God.
Heb 1. 3 glory and is the exact **likeness** of God's own being, sustaining
Jas 3. 9 curse our fellow-man, who is created in the **likeness** of God.

AV LIKENESS

Gen 1.26 they will be like us and **resemble** us.
Deut 4.25 sin by making for yourselves an idol in any **form** at all.
Ps 17.15 and when I awake, your **presence** will fill me with joy.
Ezek 1. 5 four living creatures in human **form,** [6]but each of them had

LILY

1 Kgs 7.19 The capitals were shaped like **lilies,** 1.8 metres tall,
7.22 The **lily-shaped** bronze capitals were on top of the columns.
7.26 rim of a cup, curving outwards like the petals of a **lily.**
Song 2. 1 only a wild flower in Sharon, a **lily** in a mountain valley.
2. 2 Like a **lily** among thorns is my darling among women.
2.16 feeds his flock among the **lilies** [17]until the morning
4. 5 Your breasts are like gazelles, twin deer feeding among **lilies.**
5.13 His lips are like **lilies,** wet with liquid myrrh.
6. 2 He is feeding his flock in the garden and gathering **lilies.**
6. 3 he feeds his flock among the **lilies.**
7. 2 A sheaf of wheat is there, surrounded by **lilies.**

Am LIMB see BOUGH

LIMB

Job 16. 9 In anger God tears me **limb from limb;**
Dan 2. 5 I'll have you torn **limb from limb** and make your houses a
3.29 is to be torn **limb from limb,** and his house is to
Mt 5.30 to lose one of your **limbs** than for your whole body to

LIME

Is 33.12 like rocks burnt to make **lime,** like thorns burnt to ashes.

LIMIT

Num 11.23 "Is there a **limit** to my power?"
Ezra 7.22 you for, [22]up to a **limit** of 3,400 kilogrammes of silver,
Esth 1. 8 There were no **limits** on the drinks;
Job 11. 7 Can you discover the **limits** and bounds of the greatness
11. 8 The sky is no **limit** for God, but it lies beyond your
Ps 74.17 you set the **limits** of the earth;
119.96 I have learnt that everything has **limits;**
Prov 6.34 his revenge knows no **limits.**
Ecc 4.16 There may be no **limit** to the number of people a king
Jer 5.28 There is no **limit** to their evil deeds.
Lam 5.22 Is there no **limit** to your anger?
Ezek 4.11 You will also have a **limited** amount of water to drink,
Dan 7.12 but they were permitted to go on living for a **limited** time.
Amos 1.11 Their anger had no **limits,** and they never let it die.
Nah 3. 9 She ruled Sudan and Egypt, there was no **limit** to her power;
Acts 17.26 the exact times and the **limits** of the places where they
1 Cor 9. 8 I don't have to **limit** myself to these everyday examples,
10.29 "why should my freedom to act be **limited** by another person's conscience?
2 Cor 10.13 however, our boasting will not go beyond certain **limits;**
10.13 it will stay within the **limits** of the work which God has
10.14 since you are within those **limits,** we were not going beyond
10.15 work that others have done beyond the **limits** God set for us.
10.15 work among you, always within the **limits** that God has set.
Jude 6 did not stay within the **limits** of their proper authority,

LIMP (1)

Is 13. 7 Everyone's hands will hang **limp,** and everyone's courage will fail.
Jer 6.24 say the people of Jerusalem, "and our hands hang **limp;**
47. 3 their hands will hang **limp** at their sides.
50.43 The king of Babylonia hears the news, and his hands hang **limp.**
Ezek 21. 7 fear, their hands will hang **limp,** their courage will fail,
Hab 3.16 My body goes **limp,** and my feet stumble beneath me.
Zeph 3.16 Do not let your hands hang **limp!**

LIMP (2)

Gen 32.31 Jacob was leaving Peniel, and he was **limping** because of his hip.

LINE (1)

Num	34. 7	northern border will follow a **line** from the Mediterranean to
	34.10	"The eastern border will follow a **line** from Hazar Enan to Shepham.
1 Sam	17. 3	The Philistines **lined** up on one hill and the Israelites on another,
	17. 8	Israelites, "What are you doing there, **lined** up for battle?
	17.20	Israelites were going out to their battle **line,**
	17.22	supplies, ran to the battle **line,** went to his brothers, and
	17.48	David ran quickly towards the Philistine battle **line** to fight him.
2 Sam	11.15	"Put Uriah in the front **line,** where the fighting is heaviest,
2 Kgs	3.26	his way through the enemy **lines** and escape to the king of
Job	6. 4	God has **lined** up his terrors against me.
Is	28.10	us letter by letter, **line by line,** lesson by lesson."
	28.13	teach you letter by letter, **line by line,** lesson by lesson.
Jer	31.39	And the boundary **line** will continue from there on the
	46. 4	Fall in **line** and put on your helmets!
	50. 9	They will **line** up in battle against the country and conquer it.
	50.14	"Bowmen, **line** up for battle against Babylon and surround it.
Ezek	4. 1	front of you, and scratch **lines** on it to represent the city
Joel	2. 5	They are **lined** up like a great army ready for battle.
Amos	7. 8	that my people are like a wall that is out of **line.**
Gal	2.14	a straight path in **line** with the truth of the gospel,

LINE (2)

Gen	10.32	by nation, according to their different **lines** of descent.
Deut	25. 6	dead man, so that his family **line** will continue in Israel.
Ruth	4.10	man's family, and his family **line** will continue among his
	4.18	This is the family **line** from Perez to David:
1 Chr	1.24	The family **line** from Shem to Abram is as follows:
	2.10	The family **line** from Ram to Jesse is as follows:
	2.36	The family **line** from Attai to Elishama is as follows:
	3.10	This is the **line** of King Solomon's descendants from father to son:
	4.26	Then from Mishma the **line** descended through Hammuel,
	6.33	The family **lines** of those who held this office are as follows:
	6.33	His family **line** went back to Jacob as follows:
	6.39	His family **line** went back to Levi as follows:
	6.44	His family **line** went back to Levi as follows:
	6.50	This is the **line** of Aaron's descendants:
	9.34	of Levite families, according to their ancestral **lines.**
	26.31	was made of the family **line** of Hebron's descendants, and
Is	11. 1	The royal **line** of David is like a tree that has been
	11.10	new king from the royal **line** of David will be a symbol
Mic	5. 2	for Israel, whose family **line** goes back to ancient times."

LINE (3)

[MEASURING-LINE, PLUMB-LINE]

Job	38. 5	Who stretched the **measuring-line** over it?
Is	28.17	Justice will be the **measuring-line** for the foundation,
	28.17	and honesty will be its **plumb-line."**
Amos	7. 7	with the help of a **plumb-line,**
	7. 7	and there was a **plumb-line** in his hand.
	7. 8	"A **plumb-line,"** I answered.
Zech	2. 1	vision I saw a man with a **measuring-line** in his hand.
	2. 4	that young man with the **measuring-line** that there are going
Mt	17.27	So go to the lake and drop in a **line.**
Acts	27.28	So they dropped a **line** with a weight tied to it

LINEN

Gen	41.42	He put a fine **linen** robe on him, and placed a gold
Ex	25. 4	fine **linen;**
	26. 1	of ten pieces of fine **linen** woven with blue, purple, and red
	26.31	"Make a curtain of fine **linen** woven with blue, purple,
	26.36	make a curtain of fine **linen** woven with blue, purple, and
	27. 9	Tent of my presence make an enclosure out of fine **linen** curtains.
	27.16	metres long made of fine **linen** woven with blue, purple, and
	27.18	are to be made of fine **linen** and the bases of bronze.
	28. 5	blue, purple, and red wool, gold thread, and fine **linen.**
	28. 6	gold thread, and fine **linen,** decorated with embroidery.
	28.39	"Weave Aaron's shirt of fine **linen**
	28.39	make a turban of fine **linen** and also a sash
	28.42	Make **linen** shorts for them, reaching from the waist to the thighs,
	35. 6	fine **linen;**
	35.23	Everyone who had fine **linen;**
	35.25	skilled women brought fine **linen** thread and thread of blue,
	35.35	done by engravers, designers, and weavers of fine **linen;**
	36. 8	of ten pieces of fine **linen** woven with blue, purple, and red
	36.35	made a curtain of fine **linen,** woven with blue, purple, and
	36.37	made a curtain of fine **linen** woven with blue, purple, and
	38. 9	Lord's presence he made the enclosure out of fine **linen** curtains.
	38.16	All the curtains round the enclosure were made of fine **linen.**
	38.18	enclosure was made of fine **linen** woven with blue, purple,
	38.23	and a weaver of fine **linen** and of blue, purple, and red
	39. 2	They made the ephod of fine **linen;**
	39. 3	be worked into the fine **linen** and into the blue, purple, and
	39.24	they put pomegranates of fine **linen** and of blue, purple, and
	39.28	the turban, the caps, the **linen** shorts, [29] and the sash of
	39.29	and the sash of fine **linen** and of blue, purple, and red
Lev	6.10	Then the priest, wearing his **linen** robe and linen shorts,
	13.47	on clothing, whether wool or **linen,**
	13.48	or on any piece of **linen** or wool cloth
	13.59	whether it is wool or **linen,** or on linen or wool cloth
	16. 4	the **linen** robe and shorts, the belt, and the turban.
Deut	22.11	"Do not wear cloth made by weaving wool and **linen** together.
Judg	14.12	you a piece of fine **linen** and a change of fine clothes
1 Sam	2.18	Samuel continued to serve the Lord, wearing a sacred **linen** apron.
2 Sam	6.14	David, wearing only a **linen** cloth round his waist,
1 Chr	4.21	clan of **linen-weavers,** who lived in the town of Beth Ashbea;
1 Chr	15.27	robe made of the finest **linen,** and so were the musicians,
	15.27	David also wore a **linen** ephod.
2 Chr	2.14	He can work with blue, purple, and red cloth, and with **linen.**
	3.14	Holy Place was made of **linen** and of other material, which
	5.11	and the members of their clans—were wearing **linen** clothing.
Esth	1. 6	of fine purple **linen** to silver rings on marble columns.
	8.15	a cloak of fine purple **linen,** and a magnificent gold crown.
Prov	7.16	I've covered my bed with sheets of coloured **linen** from Egypt.
	31.13	She keeps herself busy making wool and **linen** cloth.
	31.22	She makes bedspreads and wears clothes of fine purple **linen.**
Is	3.23	their revealing garments, their **linen** handkerchiefs, and
	19. 9	Those who make **linen** cloth will be in despair;
Jer	13. 1	go and buy myself some **linen** shorts and to put them on;
Ezek	9. 2	dressed in **linen** clothes, carrying something to write with.
	9. 3	to the man dressed in **linen,** [4] "Go through the whole city
	9.11	Then the man wearing **linen** clothes returned
	10. 2	said to the man wearing **linen** clothes, "Go between the
	10. 6	Lord commanded the man wearing **linen** clothes to take some
	10. 7	coals, and put them in the hands of the man in **linen.**
	16.10	of the best leather, a **linen** headband, and a silk cloak.
	16.13	and you always wore clothes of embroidered **linen** and silk.
	27. 7	Your sails were made of **linen,** Embroidered linen from Egypt,
	27.16	emeralds, purple cloth, embroidery, fine **linen,** coral, and
	40. 3	He was holding a **linen** tape-measure and a measuring-rod
	44.17	courtyard of the Temple, they are to put on **linen** clothing.
	44.18	they are to wear linen turbans and **linen** trousers, but no
Dan	10. 5	saw someone who was wearing **linen** clothes and a belt of fine
	12. 1	The angel wearing **linen** clothes said, "At that time the
Hos	2. 4	me food and water, wool and **linen,** olive-oil and wine."
	2. 9	take away the wool and the **linen** I gave her for clothing.
Mt	27.59	wrapped it in a new **linen** sheet, [60] and placed it in his
Mk	14.51	young man, dressed only in a **linen** cloth, was following Jesus.
	15.46	Joseph bought a **linen** sheet, took the body down, wrapped
Lk	23.53	down, wrapped it in a **linen** sheet, and placed it in a
	24.12	he bent down and saw the **linen** wrappings but nothing else.
Jn	19.40	body and wrapped it in **linen** with the spices according to
	20. 5	bent over and saw the **linen** wrappings, but he did not go
	20. 6	He saw the **linen** wrappings lying there [7] and the cloth which
	20. 7	was not lying with the **linen** wrappings but was rolled up
Rev	15. 6	dressed in clean shining **linen** and with gold belts tied around
	18.12	their goods of **linen,** purple cloth, silk, and scarlet cloth;
	18.16	used to dress herself in **linen,** purple, and scarlet,
	19. 8	She has been given clean shining **linen** to wear."
	19. 8	(The **linen** is the good deeds of God's people.)
	19.14	riding on white horses and dressed in clean white **linen.**

LION

Gen	49. 9	Judah is like a **lion,** Killing his victim and returning to
Num	23.24	The nation of Israel is like a mighty **lion:**
	24. 9	The nation is like a mighty **lion;**
Deut	33.20	Gad waits like a **lion** To tear off an arm or a
	33.22	"Dan is a young **lion;**
Judg	14. 5	through the vineyards there, he heard a young **lion** roaring.
	14. 6	strong, and he tore the **lion** apart with his bare hands, as
	14. 8	road to look at the **lion** he had killed, and he was
	14. 9	he had taken the honey from the dead body of a **lion.**
	14.18	What could be stronger than a **lion?"**
1 Sam	17.34	Whenever a **lion** or a bear carries off a lamb, [35] I go
	17.35	And if the **lion** or bear turns on me, I grab it
	17.36	I have killed **lions** and bears, and I will do the same
	17.37	The Lord has saved me from **lions** and bears;
2 Sam	1.23	swifter than eagles, stronger than **lions.**
	17.10	bravest men, as fearless as **lions,** will be afraid because
	23.20	down into a pit on a snowy day and killed a **lion.**
1 Kgs	7.29	frames, [29] with the figures of **lions,** bulls, and winged
	7.29	frames, above and underneath the **lions** and bulls, there were
	7.36	with figures of winged creatures, **lions,** and palm-trees,
	10.19	with the figure of a **lion** at each end of every step,
	10.19	a total of twelve **lions.**
	10.19	beside each of the two arms was the figure of a **lion.**
	13.24	On the way, a **lion** met him and killed him.
	13.24	on the road, and the donkey and the **lion** stood beside it.
	13.25	saw the body on the road, with the **lion** standing near by.
	13.26	so the Lord sent the **lion** to attack and kill him, just
	13.28	the road, with the donkey and the **lion** still standing by it.
	13.28	The **lion** had not eaten the body or attacked the donkey.
	20.36	disobeyed the Lord's command, a **lion** will kill you as soon
	20.36	as soon as he left, a **lion** came along and killed him.
2 Kgs	17.25	the Lord, and so he sent **lions,** which killed some of them.
	17.26	and so the god had sent **lions,** which were killing them.
1 Chr	11.22	down into a pit on a snowy day and killed a **lion.**
	12. 8	as fierce-looking as **lions** and as quick as mountain deer.
2 Chr	9.18	the throne, and the figure of a **lion** stood at each side.
	9.19	Twelve figures of **lions** were on the steps, one at either
Job	4.10	wicked roar and growl like **lions,** but God silences them and
	4.11	Like **lions** with nothing to kill and eat, they die, and
	10.16	have any success at all, you hunt me down like a **lion;**
	28. 8	No **lion** or other fierce beast Ever travels those lonely roads.
	38.39	Do you find food for **lions** to eat,
	38.39	and satisfy hungry young **lions** [40] when they hide in their caves,
Ps	7. 2	me, [2] or else like a **lion** they will carry me off where
	10. 9	he waits in his hiding place like a **lion.**
	17.12	They are like **lions,** waiting for me, wanting to tear me
	22.13	They open their mouths like **lions,** roaring and tearing at me.
	22.21	Rescue me from these **lions;**
	34.10	Even **lions** go hungry for lack of food, but those who
	35.17	save my life from these **lions!**
	57. 4	I am surrounded by enemies, who are like man-eating **lions.**
	58. 6	Break the teeth of these fierce **lions,** O God.

Ps 91.13 You will trample down **lions** and snakes, fierce lions and poisonous snakes.
104.21 The young **lions** roar while they hunt, looking for the
Prov 19.12 like the roar of a **lion,** but his favour is like welcome
20. 2 Fear an angry king as you would a growling **lion;**
22.13 he says a **lion** might get him if he goes outside.
26.13 What is he afraid of? **Lions?**
28. 1 chasing them, but an honest person is as brave as a **lion.**
28.15 he is as dangerous as a growling **lion** or a prowling bear.
30.30 **lions,** strongest of all animals and afraid of none;
Ecc 9. 4 a live dog is better off than a dead **lion.**
Song 4. 8 Mount Senir and Mount Hermon, where the **lions** and leopards live.
Is 5.29 The soldiers roar like **lions** that have killed an animal
11. 6 Calves and **lion** cubs will feed together, and little children
11. 7 **Lions** will eat straw as cattle do.
30. 6 travel through dangerous country, where **lions** live and where
31. 4 they can't scare away a **lion** from an animal that it has
35. 9 No **lions** will be there;
38.13 cried out with pain, As if a **lion** were breaking my bones.
65.25 **lions** will eat straw, as cattle do, and snakes will no
Jer 2.15 They have roared at him like **lions;**
2.30 Like a raging **lion,** you have murdered your prophets.
4. 7 Like a **lion** coming from its hiding place, a destroyer of
5. 6 That is why **lions** from the forest will kill them;
12. 8 like a **lion** in the forest they have roared at me, and
25.38 Lord has abandoned his people like a **lion** that leaves its cave.
49.19 Like a **lion** coming out of the thick woods along the
50.17 "The people of Israel are like sheep, chased and scattered by **lions.**
50.44 "Like a **lion** coming out of the thick woods along the
51.38 The Babylonians all roar like **lions**
51.38 and growl like **lion** cubs.
Lam 3.10 he pounced on me like a **lion.**
Ezek 1.10 human face in front, a **lion's** face at the right, a bull's
10.14 third the face of a **lion,** and the fourth the face of
19. 2 She reared her cubs among the fierce male **lions.**
19. 5 reared another of her cubs, and he grew into a fierce **lion.**
19. 6 When he was full-grown, he prowled with the other **lions.**
22.25 leaders are like **lions** roaring over the animals they have killed.
32. 2 You act like a **lion** among the nations, but you are more
41.19 on one side, and a **lion's** face that was turned towards the
Dan 6. 7 this order is to be thrown into a pit filled with **lions.**
6.12 except you, would be thrown into a pit filled with **lions."**
6.16 arrested and he was thrown into the pit filled with **lions.**
6.20 God you serve so loyally able to save you from the **lions?"**
6.22 shut the mouths of the **lions** so that they would not hurt
6.24 wives and their children, into the pit filled with **lions.**
6.24 bottom of the pit, the **lions** pounced on them and broke all
6.27 He saved Daniel from being killed by the **lions."**
7. 4 first one looked like a **lion,** but had wings like an eagle.
Hos 5.14 I will attack the people of Israel and Judah like a **lion.**
11.10 will follow me when I roar like a **lion** at their enemies.
13. 7 So I will attack you like a **lion.**
13. 8 Like a **lion** I will devour you on the spot, and will
Joel 1. 6 their teeth are as sharp as those of a **lion.**
Amos 3. 4 Does a **lion** roar in the forest unless he has found a
3. 4 Does a young **lion** growl in his den unless he has caught
3. 8 When a **lion** roars, who can avoid being afraid?
3.12 of a sheep that a **lion** has eaten, so only a few
5.19 like a man who runs from a **lion** and meets a bear!
Mic 5. 8 nations will be like a **lion** hunting for food in a forest
Nah 2.11 was like a den of **lions,** the place where young lions were
2.11 lions were fed, where the **lion** and the lioness would go and
2.12 The **lion** killed his prey and tore it to pieces for his
Zeph 3. 3 Its officials are like roaring **lions;**
Zech 11. 3 Listen to the roaring of the **lions;**
Heb 11.33 They shut the mouths of **lions,** [34]put out fierce fires,
1 Pet 5. 8 roams round like a roaring **lion,** looking for someone to devour.
Rev 4. 7 The first one looked like a **lion;**
5. 5 The **Lion** from Judah's tribe, the great descendant of David,
9. 8 hair was like women's hair, their teeth were like **lions'** teeth.
9.17 The horses' heads were like **lions'** heads, and from their mouths
10. 3 out in a loud voice that sounded like the roar of **lions.**
13. 2 feet like a bear's feet and a mouth like a **lion's** mouth.

LIONESS

Ezek 19. 2 What a **lioness** your mother was!
Nah 2.11 where the lion and the **lioness** would go and their cubs would

LIPS

1 Sam 1.12 to the Lord for a long time, and Eli watched her **lips.**
1.13 her **lips** were moving, but she made no sound.
2 Sam 23. 2 his message is on my **lips.**
Job 27. 4 God gives me breath, [4]my **lips** will never say anything evil,
Ps 59.12 Sin is on their **lips;**
141. 3 guard at my mouth, a sentry at the door of my **lips.**
Prov 5. 3 The **lips** of another man's wife may be as sweet as honey
Song 1. 2 Your **lips** cover me with kisses;
4. 3 Your **lips** are like a scarlet ribbon;
4.11 The taste of honey is on your **lips,** my darling;
5.13 His **lips** are like lilies, wet with liquid myrrh.
7. 9 flow straight to my lover, flowing over his **lips** and teeth.
Is 6. 5 every word that passes my **lips** is sinful, and I live among
6. 7 He touched my **lips** with the burning coal and said,
6. 7 "This has touched your **lips,** and now your guilt is gone,
Jer 1. 9 out his hand, touched my **lips,** and said to me, "Listen, I
Lam 2.16 They curl their **lips** and sneer, "We have destroyed it!
Ezek 33.31 Loving words are on their **lips,** but they continue their greedy ways.
Dan 10.16 like a man, stretched out his hand and touched my **lips.**
Hab 3.16 my **lips** quiver with fear.
Mk 15.36 Then he held it up to Jesus' **lips** and said, "Wait!
Jn 19.29 put on a stalk of hyssop, and lifted up to his **lips.**
Rom 3.13 and dangerous threats, like snake's poison, from their **lips;**
10. 8 is near you, on your **lips** and in your heart"—that is,
1 Cor 14.21 I will speak through **lips** of foreigners, but even then my
2 Cor 12. 3 be put into words, things that human **lips** may not speak.
Col 3. 8 No insults or obscene talk must ever come from your **lips.**
Heb 13.15 is the offering presented by **lips** that confess him as Lord.
1 Pet 2.22 sin, and no one ever heard a lie come from his **lips.**

LIQUID

Ex 30.23 six kilogrammes of **liquid** myrrh, three
Song 5. 5 with myrrh, my fingers with **liquid** myrrh, as I grasped the
5.13 His lips are like lilies, wet with **liquid** myrrh.
Ezek 45.11 dry measure is to be equal to the bath for **liquid** measure.

LIQUOR

Is 28. 7 so much wine and **liquor** that they stumble in confusion.
Amos 4. 1 and demand that your husbands keep you supplied with **liquor!**
Mic 2.11 says, 'I prophesy that wine and **liquor** will flow for you.'

LIST

Gen 5. 1 This is the **list** of the descendants of Adam.
25.13 had the following sons, **listed** in the order of their birth:
Ex 38.21 Here is a **list** of the amounts of the metals used in
38.21 The **list** was ordered by Moses and made by the Levites who
Num 1. 2 **List** the names of all the men [3]twenty years old or older
26.62 They were **listed** separately from the rest of the Israelites,
26.63 All these clans were **listed** by Moses and Eleazar when
26.64 whom Moses and Aaron had **listed** in the first census in the
31.32 The following is a **list** of what was captured by the soldiers,
Deut 29.21 accordance with all the curses **listed** in the covenant that
Josh 18. 9 divided it into seven parts, making a **list** of the towns.
1 Chr 5. 7 The family records **list** the following clan leaders in the
7. 5 Issachar **listed** 87,000 men eligible for military service.
7. 9 families **listed** 20,200 men eligible for military service.
9. 1 people of Israel were **listed** according to their families,
11.10 This is the **list** of David's famous soldiers.
25. 1 This is the **list** of persons chosen to lead the worship, with
26. 2 He had seven sons, **listed** in order of age:
26. 4 God blessed by giving him eight sons, **listed** in order of age:
27. 1 This is the **list** of the Israelite heads of families and
27.16 This is the **list** of the administrators of the tribes of Israel:
27.25 This is the **list** of those who administered the royal property:
Ezra 2. 2 This is the **list** of the clans of Israel, with the number
2.36 This is the **list** of the priestly clans that returned from exile:
8. 1 This is the **list** of the heads of the clans who had
8.20 They were all **listed** by name.
10.18 This is the **list** of the men who had foreign wives:
10.18 Priests, **listed** by clans:
Neh 7. 8 This is the **list** of the clans of Israel, with the
7.39 This is the **list** of the priestly clans that returned from exile:
11. 3 The following is the **list** of the leading citizens of the
12. 1 The following is a **list** of the priests and Levites who
Ps 56. 8 Aren't they **listed** in your book?
69.28 may they not be included in the **list** of your people.
87. 4 Egypt and Babylonia when I **list** the nations that obey me;
87. 6 The Lord will write a **list** of the peoples and include them
Jer 25.19 Here is the **list** of all the others who had to
Ezek 13. 9 will not be included in the **list** of the citizens of Israel;
Mt 1. 1 This is the **list** of the ancestors of Jesus Christ,
1. 2 From Abraham to King David, the following ancestors are **listed:**
1. 6 taken into exile in Babylon, the following ancestors are **listed:**
1.12 Babylon to the birth of Jesus, the following ancestors are **listed:**
1 Tim 1. 4 and those long **lists of ancestors,** which only produce arguments;
5. 9 add any widow to the **list** of widows unless she is over
5.11 But do not include younger widows in the **list;**
Tit 3. 9 avoid stupid arguments, long **lists of ancestors,** quarrels,

LISTEN

Gen 3.17 said to the man, "You **listened** to your wife and ate the
4.23 "Adah and Zillah, **listen** to me:
18.10 Sarah was behind him, at the door of the tent, **listening.**
23. 6 They answered, [6]**"Listen** to us, sir.
23.11 he answered in the hearing of everyone there, [11]**"Listen,**
23.13 everyone could hear, "May I ask you, please, to **listen.**
27. 5 While Isaac was talking to Esau, Rebecca was **listening.**
27. 8 Now, my son," Rebecca continued, **"listen** to me and do
27.42 sent for Jacob and said, **"Listen,** your brother Esau is
37. 6 He said, **"Listen** to the dream I had.
42.21 was in when he begged for help, but we would not **listen.**
42.22 "I told you not to harm the boy, but you wouldn't **listen.**
49. 2 "Come together and **listen,** sons of Jacob.
49. 2 **Listen** to your father Israel.
Ex 3.18 "My people will **listen** to what you say to them.
4. 1 do not believe me and will not **listen** to what I say.
4. 9 and if they refuse to **listen** to what you say, take some
5. 2 "Why should I **listen** to him and let Israel go?
5. 9 that they won't have time to **listen** to a pack of lies."
6. 9 Israelites, but they would not **listen** to him, because their
6.12 "Even the Israelites will not **listen** to me, so why should
6.30 why should the king **listen** to me?"
7. 3 stubborn, and he will not **listen** to you, no matter how many
7.13 Lord had said, the king would not **listen** to Moses and Aaron.
7.16 But until now you have not **listened.**

Ex 7.22 Lord had said, the king refused to **listen** to Moses and Aaron.
8.15 Lord had said, the king would not **listen** to Moses and Aaron.
8.19 Lord had said, the king would not **listen** to Moses and Aaron.
9.12 Lord had said, the king would not **listen** to Moses and Aaron.
11. 9 will continue to refuse to **listen** to you, in order that I
16.20 some of them did not **listen** to Moses and saved part of
20.19 They said to Moses, "If you speak to us, we will **listen;**
23.13 **"Listen** to everything that I, the Lord, have said to you.
Lev 26.23 punishment you still do not **listen** to me, but continue to
Num 16. 8 **"Listen,** you Levites!
20.10 community in front of the rock, and Moses said, **"Listen,**
23.18 Balak son of Zippor, And **listen** to what I have to say.
Deut 1.16 that time I instructed them, **'Listen** to the disputes that
1.45 help, but he would not **listen** to you or pay any attention
3.26 you people the Lord was angry with me and would not **listen.**
5. 1 to them, "People of Israel, **listen** to all the laws that I
5.27 Go back, Moses, and **listen** to everything that the Lord
5.27 We will **listen** and obey.'
6. 3 **Listen** to them, people of Israel, and obey them!
7.12 "If you **listen** to these commands and obey them faithfully,
9. 1 **"Listen,** people of Israel!
9.19 but once again the Lord **listened** to me.
10.10 The Lord **listened** to me once more and agreed not to destroy
10.12 "Now, people of Israel, **listen** to what the Lord your
12. 1 **Listen** to them!
13. 8 do not even **listen** to him.
20. 3 come forward and say to the army, [3]'Men of Israel, **listen!**
23. 5 But the Lord your God would not **listen** to Balaam;
27. 9 "Give me your attention, people of Israel, and **listen** to me.
30.17 you disobey and refuse to **listen,** and are led away to
31.30 Moses recited the entire song while all the people of Israel **listened.**
32. 1 "Earth and sky, hear my words, **listen** closely to what I say.
33. 7 "Lord, **listen** to their cry for help;
Josh 3. 9 the people, "Come here and **listen** to what the Lord your God
22.11 The rest of the people of Israel were told, **"Listen!**
24.10 But I would not **listen** to Balaam, so he blessed you, and
Judg 5. 3 **Listen,** you kings!
5.16 to **listen** to shepherds calling the flocks?
6.10 But you did not **listen** to me."
9. 7 and shouted out to them, **"Listen** to me, you men of Shechem,
9. 7 and God may **listen** to you!
19.25 But the men would not **listen** to him.
1 Sam 2.25 But they would not **listen** to their father, for the Lord had
2.31 **Listen,** the time is coming when I will kill all the
3. 9 you again, say, 'Speak, Lord, your servant is **listening.'"**
3.10 your servant is **listening."**
3.21 And when Samuel spoke, all Israel **listened.**
4. 6 heard the shouting and said, **"Listen** to all that shouting
8. 7 Lord, [7]and the Lord said, **"Listen** to everything the people
8. 9 So then, **listen** to them, but give them strict warnings and
8.18 chose, but the Lord will not **listen** to your complaints."
8.21 Samuel **listened** to everything they said and then went
12.14 Lord your God, serve him, **listen** to him, and obey his commands,
12.15 But if you do not **listen** to the Lord but disobey his
15. 1 Now **listen** to what the Lord Almighty says.
17.25 **"Listen** to his challenge!
22. 7 and he said to his officers, **"Listen,** men of Benjamin!
22.12 Saul said to Ahimelech, **"Listen,** Ahimelech!"
24. 9 and said, "Why do you **listen** to people who say that I
25.17 He is so pigheaded that he won't **listen** to anybody!"
25.24 at David's feet, and said to him, "Please, sir, **listen**
26.19 Your Majesty, **listen** to what I have to say.
2 Sam 13.14 But he would not **listen** to her;
13.16 But Amnon would not **listen** to her;
14.16 I thought you would **listen** to me and save me from the
20.16 wise woman in the city who shouted from the wall, **"Listen!**
20.17 **"Listen** to me, sir," she said.
20.17 "I'm **listening,"** he answered.
22. 7 he **listened** to my cry for help.
1 Kgs 4.34 world heard of his wisdom and sent people to **listen** to him.
8.28 **Listen** to my prayer, and grant the requests I make to you
8.32 O Lord, **listen** in heaven and judge your servants.
8.34 to you for forgiveness, [34]**listen** to them in heaven.
8.36 Temple, humbly praying to you, [36]**listen** to them in heaven.
8.38 disease or sickness among them, [38]**listen** to their prayers.
8.39 **Listen** to them in your home in heaven, forgive them, and
8.43 you and to pray at this Temple, [43]**listen** to his prayer.
8.45 Temple which I have built for you, [45]**listen** to their prayers.
8.47 that land is far away, [47]**listen** to your people's prayers.
8.49 Temple which I have built for you, [49]then **listen** to their prayers.
10.24 world wanted to come and **listen** to the wisdom that God had
12.16 that the king would not **listen** to them, they shouted, "Down
22.19 "Now **listen** to what the Lord says!
22.28 And he added, **"Listen,** everyone, to what I have said!"
2 Kgs 7. 1 Elisha answered, **"Listen** to what the Lord says!
14.11 But Amaziah refused to **listen,** so King Jehoash marched
17.40 But those people would not **listen,** and they continued to
18.12 They would not **listen** and they would not obey.
18.26 all the people on the wall are **listening."**
18.28 up and shouted in Hebrew, **"Listen** to what the emperor of
18.31 Don't **listen** to Hezekiah.
19.16 **Listen** to all the things that Sennacherib is saying to insult you,
22.18 You **listened** to what is written in the book, [19]and you
1 Chr 28. 2 "My countrymen, **listen** to me.
2 Chr 6.19 **Listen** to my prayer and grant the requests I make to you.
6.23 O Lord, **listen** in heaven and judge your servants.
6.25 to you for forgiveness, [25]**listen** to them in heaven.
6.27 praying to you, [27]O Lord, **listen** to them in heaven and
6.29 disease or sickness among them, [29]**listen** to their prayers.
6.30 **Listen** to them in your home in heaven and forgive them.

2 Chr 6.33 he comes to pray at this Temple, [33]**listen** to his prayer.
6.35 Temple which I have built for you, [35]**listen** to their prayers.
6.37 that land is far away, [37]**listen** to your people's prayers.
6.39 I have built for you, [39]then **listen** to their prayers.
6.40 God, look on us and **listen** to the prayers offered in this
10.16 that the king would not **listen** to them, they shouted, "Down
13. 4 **"Listen** to me!"
15. 2 He called out, **"Listen** to me, King Asa, and all you people
18.18 "Now **listen** to what the Lord says!
18.27 And he added, **"Listen,** everyone, to what I have said!"
24.17 of Judah persuaded King Joash to **listen** to them instead.
24.19 them to return to him, but the people refused to **listen.**
25.20 But Amaziah refused to **listen.**
28.11 **Listen** to me!
33.10 the Lord warned Manasseh and his people, they refused to **listen.**
34.26 You **listened** to what is written in the book, [27]and you
35.22 He refused to **listen** to what God was saying through King Neco,
36.12 the Lord and did not **listen** humbly to the prophet Jeremiah,
Neh 1.11 **Listen** now to my prayer and to the prayers of all your
4. 4 I prayed, **"Listen** to them mocking us, O God!
8. 3 Law to them from dawn until noon, and they all **listened**
9.34 They did not **listen** to your commands and warnings.
Esth 3. 4 urged him to give in, but he would not **listen** to them.
Job 6.24 I will be quiet and **listen** to you.
8.10 **listen** to what they had to say:
9.16 he lets me speak, I can't believe he would **listen** to me.
10. 1 **Listen** to my bitter complaint.
13. 6 **Listen** while I state my case.
13.17 Now **listen** to my words of explanation.
15.17 Now **listen,** Job, to what I know.
18. 1 If you stopped to **listen,** we could talk to you.
19. 7 I protest against his violence, but no one is **listening;**
21. 1 **Listen** to what I am saying;
23. 6 No, he would **listen** as I spoke.
29.21 people were silent and **listened** carefully to what I said;
31.13 complained against me, I would **listen** and treat him fairly.
31.35 Will no one **listen** to what I am saying?
32.10 So now I want you to **listen** to me;
32.11 I **listened** patiently while you were speaking and waited
33. 1 And now, Job, **listen** carefully to all that I have to say.
33.16 He makes them **listen** to what he says, and they are
33.31 Now, Job, **listen** to what I am saying;
33.33 if not, be quiet and **listen** to me, and I will teach
34. 1 **listen** now to what I am saying.
34.10 **Listen** to me, you men who understand!
34.16 Now **listen** to me, if you are wise.
36. 1 Be patient and **listen** a little longer to what I am
36.10 He makes them **listen** to his warning to turn away from evil.
37. 2 **Listen,** all of you, to the voice of God, to the thunder
37.14 Pause a moment, Job, and **listen;**
42. 4 You told me to **listen** while you spoke and to try to
Ps 2.10 Now **listen** to this warning, you kings;
5. 1 **Listen** to my words, O Lord, and hear my sighs.
5. 2 **Listen** to my cry for help, my God and king!
6. 9 he **listens** to my cry for help and will answer my prayer.
10.17 You will **listen,** O Lord, to the prayers of the lowly;
17. 1 **Listen,** O Lord, to my plea for justice;
17. 1 **Listen** to my honest prayer.
17. 6 so turn to me and **listen** to my words.
18. 6 he **listened** to my cry for help.
28. 1 **Listen** to my cry!
34. 2 may all who are oppressed **listen** and be glad!
34.11 Come, my young friends, and **listen** to me, and I will
34.15 The Lord watches over the righteous and **listens** to their cries;
34.17 The righteous call to the Lord, and he **listens;**
39.12 Hear my prayer, Lord, and **listen** to my cry;
40. 1 then he **listened** to me and heard my cry.
45.10 Bride of the king, **listen** to what I say— forget your
49. 1 **Listen,** all people everywhere, [2]great and small alike,
50. 7 **"Listen,** my people, and I will speak;
50.22 **"Listen** to this, you that ignore me, or I will destroy you,
54. 2 **listen** to my words!
55. 2 **Listen** to me and answer me;
59. 7 **Listen** to their insults and threats.
61. 1 **listen** to my prayer!
64. 1 I am in trouble, God—**listen** to my prayer!
66.16 Come and **listen,** all who honour God, and I will tell you
66.18 ignored my sins, the Lord would not have **listened** to me.
66.19 he has **listened** to my prayer.
68.33 **Listen** to him shout with a mighty roar.
69.33 The Lord **listens** to those in need and does not forget
71. 2 **Listen** to me and save me!
78. 1 **Listen,** my people, to my teaching, and pay attention to
79.11 **Listen** to the groans of the prisoners, and by your great
80. 1 **Listen** to us, O Shepherd of Israel;
81. 8 **Listen,** my people, to my warning;
81. 8 Israel, how I wish you would **listen** to me!
81.11 "But my people would not **listen** to me;
81.13 How I wish my people would **listen** to me;
84. 8 **Listen,** O God of Jacob!
85. 8 I am **listening** to what the Lord God is saying;
86. 1 **Listen** to me, Lord, and answer me, for I am helpless and
86. 6 **Listen,** Lord, to my prayer;
87. 3 **Listen,** city of God, to the wonderful things he says about you:
88. 2 **listen** to my cry for help!
95. 7 **Listen** today to what he says:
102. 1 **Listen** to my prayer, O Lord, and hear my cry for help!
102. 2 **Listen** to me, and answer me quickly when I call!
102.17 He will hear his forsaken people and **listen** to their prayer.
103.20 angels, who obey his commands, who **listen** to what he says.
106.25 their tents and grumbled and would not **listen** to the Lord.

Ps 116. 1 he **listens** to my prayers.
116. 2 He **listens** to me every time I call to him.
118.15 **Listen** to the glad shouts of victory in the tents of
119.170 **Listen** to my prayer, and save me according to your promise!
130. 2 **listen** to my call for help!
141. 1 **Listen** to me when I call to you.
142. 6 **Listen** to my cry for help, for I am sunk in despair.
143. 1 In your righteousness **listen** to my plea;
Prov 1.23 **Listen** when I reprimand you;
1.24 calling you, inviting you to come, but you would not **listen.**
1.33 But whoever **listens** to me will have security.
2. 2 **Listen** to what is wise and try to understand it.
2. 9 If you **listen** to me, you will know what is right, just,
4. 1 **Listen** to what your father teaches you, my sons.
4.10 **Listen** to me, my son.
4.20 **Listen** to my words.
5. 1 Pay attention, my son, and **listen** to my wisdom and insight.
5. 7 Now **listen** to me, my sons, and never forget what I am
5.13 I wouldn't **listen** to my teachers.
7.24 Now then, my sons, **listen** to me.
8. 6 **Listen** to my excellent words;
8.32 "Now, young men, **listen** to me.
8.33 **Listen** to what you are taught.
8.34 The man who **listens** to me will be happy— the man
10.17 People who **listen** when they are corrected will live, but
12.15 Wise people **listen** to advice.
13.18 Anyone who **listens** to correction is respected.
15.29 good people pray, the Lord **listens,** but he ignores those who
17. 4 Evil people **listen** to evil ideas, and liars listen to lies.
18.13 **Listen** before you answer.
19.20 If you **listen** to advice and are willing to learn, one
20.12 has given us eyes to see with and ears to **listen** with.
21.13 If you refuse to **listen** to the cry of the poor, your
22.17 **Listen,** and I will teach you what wise men have said.
23.19 **Listen,** my son, be wise and give serious thought to the
23.22 **Listen** to your father;
25.12 person to someone willing to **listen** is more valuable than
31. 4 **Listen,** Lemuel.
Ecc 9.17 It is better to **listen** to the quiet words of a wise
Is 1. 2 The Lord said, "Earth and sky, **listen** to what I am saying!
1.10 **Listen** to what the Lord is saying to you.
1.15 you pray, I will not **listen,** for your hands are covered with
1.23 orphans in court or **listen** when widows present their case.
1.24 So now, **listen** to what the Lord Almighty, Israel's powerful God,
5. 1 **Listen** while I sing you this song, a song of my friend
6. 9 "No matter how much you **listen,** you will not understand.
7.13 To that Isaiah replied, **"Listen,** now, descendants of King David.
8. 9 **Listen,** you distant parts of the earth.
8.20 You are to answer them, **"Listen** to what the Lord is
8.20 Don't **listen** to mediums—what they tell you will do you no
10.30 **Listen,** people of Laishah!
13. 4 **Listen** to the noise on the mountains—the sound of a great
18. 3 **Listen,** everyone who lives on earth!
18. 3 **Listen** for the blowing of the bugle!
24.17 **Listen** to me, everyone!
28.11 If you won't **listen** to me, then God will use foreigners
28.12 comfort to all of you, but you refused to **listen** to him.
28.14 Jerusalem over this people, **listen** to what the Lord is saying.
28.23 **Listen** to what I am saying;
30. 9 lying, always refusing to **listen** to the Lord's teachings.
32. 9 an easy life, free from worries, **listen** to what I am saying.
34. 1 Gather round and **listen.**
34. 1 whole earth and everyone living on it come here and **listen.**
36.11 all the people on the wall are **listening."**
36.13 up and shouted in Hebrew, **"Listen** to what the emperor of
36.16 Don't **listen** to Hezekiah!
37.17 **Listen** to all the things that Sennacherib is saying to insult you,
41. 1 "Be silent and **listen** to me, you distant lands!
42.18 **"Listen,** you deaf people!
42.23 Will any of you **listen** to this?
42.23 From now on will you **listen** with care?
44. 1 **"Listen** now, Israel, my servant, my chosen people,
46. 3 **"Listen** to me, descendants of Jacob, all who are left of
46.12 **"Listen** to me, you stubborn people who think that
47. 8 **"Listen** to this, you lover of pleasure, you that think
48. 1 **Listen** to this, people of Israel,
48.12 **"Listen** to me, Israel, the people I have called!
48.14 "Assemble and **listen,** all of you!
48.18 "If only you had **listened** to my commands!
49. 1 **Listen** to me, distant nations, you people who live far away!
51. 1 **"Listen** to me, you that want to be saved, you that come
51. 4 **"Listen** to me, my people, listen to what I say:
51. 7 **"Listen** to me, you that know what is right, who have my
55. 2 **Listen** to me and do what I say, and you will enjoy
55. 3 **"Listen** now, my people, and come to me;
58. 4 this kind of fasting will make me **listen** to your prayers?
65.12 did not answer when I called you or **listen** when I spoke.
66. 4 no one answered when I called or **listened** when I spoke.
66. 5 **Listen** to what the Lord says, you that fear him and obey
Jer 1. 9 lips, and said to me, **"Listen,** I am giving you the words
1.18 **Listen,** Jeremiah!
2. 4 **Listen** to the Lord's message, you descendants of Jacob,
2.31 People of Israel, **listen** to what I am saying.
6.10 I answered, "Who would **listen** to me if I spoke to them
6.10 They are stubborn and refuse to **listen** to your message;
6.17 the Lord appointed watchmen to **listen** for the trumpet's warning.
6.17 But they said, "We will not **listen."**
6.18 So the Lord said, **"Listen,** you nations, and learn what
6.19 **Listen,** earth!
7.13 I spoke to you over and over again, you refused to **listen.**
7.16 do not plead with me, for I will not **listen** to you.
Jer 7.26 Yet no one **listened** or paid any attention.
7.27 these words to my people, but they will not **listen** to you;
8. 6 I **listened** carefully, but you did not speak the truth.
9.15 So then, **listen** to what I, the Lord Almighty, the God of
9.19 **Listen** to the sound of crying in Zion,
9.20 **"Listen** to the Lord, you women, and pay attention to his words.
10. 1 People of Israel, **listen** to the message that the Lord has
11. 2 The Lord said to me, [2]**"Listen** to the terms of the covenant.
11. 6 and tell the people to **listen** to the terms of the covenant
11. 8 But they did not **listen** or obey.
11.11 cry out to me for help, I will not **listen** to them.
11.14 and call to me for help, I will not **listen** to them."
13.15 Be humble and **listen** to him.
13.17 If you will not **listen,** I will cry in secret because of
14.12 if they fast, I will not **listen** to their cry for help;
15.16 You spoke to me, and I **listened** to every word.
16. 9 **Listen** to what I, the Lord Almighty, the God of Israel,
17.20 Jerusalem and enters these gates, to **listen** to what I say.
17.23 Their ancestors did not **listen** to me or pay any attention.
18.18 Let's bring charges against him, and stop **listening** to what he says."
18.19 what I am saying and **listen** to what my enemies are saying
19. 3 people of Jerusalem, **listen** to what I, the Lord Almighty,
19.15 you are stubborn and will not **listen** to what I say."
21. 8 Then the Lord told me to say to the people, **"Listen!**
21.11 **"Listen** to what I, the Lord, am saying.
22. 1 the people of Jerusalem to **listen** to what the Lord had said:
22.21 to you when you were prosperous, but you refused to **listen.**
22.29 **Listen** to what the Lord has said:
23.16 of Jerusalem, "Do not **listen** to what the prophets say;
23.17 the people who refuse to **listen** to what I have said, they
23.18 understood his message, or ever **listened** or paid attention
23.32 **Listen** to what I, the Lord, say!
25. 4 You would not **listen** or pay attention, even though the
25. 7 But the Lord himself says that you refused to **listen** to him.
25. 8 because you would not **listen** to him, the Lord Almighty says,
26. 3 Perhaps the people will **listen** and give up their evil ways.
27. 9 Do not **listen** to your prophets or to anyone who claims he
27.14 Do not **listen** to the prophets who tell you not to
27.16 "Do not **listen** to the prophets who say that the temple
27.17 Don't **listen** to them!
27.21 **"Listen** to what I, the Lord Almighty, the God of Israel,
28. 7 But **listen** to what I say to you and to the people.
28.15 Then I told Hananiah this, and added, **"Listen,**
29.16 **Listen** to what the Lord says about the king who rules
29.19 They refused to **listen.**
29.20 sent into exile in Babylonia, **listen** to what I, the Lord,
31.10 "Nations, **listen** to me, and proclaim my words
32.33 I kept on teaching them, they would not **listen** and learn.
32.36 Now **listen** to what else I have to say.
34. 4 Zedekiah, **listen** to what I say about you.
34.14 not pay any attention to me or **listen** to what I said.
35.12 you why you refuse to **listen** to me and to obey my
35.15 But you would not **listen** to me or pay attention to me.
35.17 this because you would not **listen** when I spoke to you, and
36.10 while all the people were **listening,** Baruch read from the
37.14 But Irijah would not **listen** to me.
37.20 Majesty, I beg you to **listen** to me and do what I
38.22 **Listen** to what they were saying as they went:
44. 5 But you would not **listen** or pay any attention.
44.16 to me, [16]"We refuse to **listen** to what you have told us
44.26 But now **listen** to the vow that I, the Lord, have made
48. 4 **listen** to the children crying.
49.20 So **listen** to the plan that I have made against the
50.45 So **listen** to the plan that I have made against the city
51.54 **"Listen** to the sound of crying in Babylon, of mourning for
Lam 1.18 **Listen** to me, people everywhere;
1.21 **"Listen** to my groans;
3. 8 I cry aloud for help, but God refuses to **listen;**
3.56 And when I begged you to **listen** to my cry, you heard.
Ezek 2. 5 Whether those rebels **listen** to you or not, they will know
2. 7 them whatever I tell you to say, whether they **listen** or not.
2. 8 "Mortal man, **listen** to what I tell you.
3. 6 languages you didn't understand, they would **listen** to you.
3. 7 But none of the people of Israel will be willing to **listen;**
3. 7 they will not even **listen** to me.
3.21 not to sin and he **listens** to you and doesn't sin, he
3.27 Some of them will **listen,** but some will ignore you, for they
5. 7 Now **listen,** Jerusalem, to what I, the Sovereign Lord, am
8.18 as loud as they can, but I will not **listen** to them."
13. 2 Tell them to **listen** to the word of the Lord."
18.25 **Listen** to me, you Israelites.
20. 8 But they defied me and refused to **listen.**
25. 3 Tell them to **listen** to what I, the Sovereign Lord, am
33.32 They **listen** to all your words and don't obey a single one
34. 7 "Now, you shepherds, **listen** to what I, the Lord, am telling you.
34. 8 as I am the living God, you had better **listen** to me.
34. 9 So **listen** to me, you shepherds.
36. 1 Israel and tell them to **listen** to the message which I, [2]the
36. 4 So now **listen** to what I, the Sovereign Lord, say to you
36.15 will no longer have to **listen** to the nations mocking it or
37. 4 Tell these dry bones to **listen** to the word of the Lord.
40. 4 **Listen** carefully and pay close attention to everything I show you,
43.18 Lord said to me, "Mortal man, **listen** to what I tell you.
Dan 4. 2 **Listen** to my account of the wonders and miracles which the
4.31 from heaven, "King Nebuchadnezzar, **listen** to what I say!
9. 6 We have not **listened** to your servants the prophets, who
9.10 We did not **listen** to you, O Lord our God, when you
9.11 Israel broke your laws and refused to **listen** to what you said.
9.14 always do what is right, and we did not **listen** to you.
9.18 **Listen** to us, O God;

Dan 9.19 Lord, **listen** to us, and act!
10.11 Stand up and **listen** carefully to what I am going to say.
Hos 4. 1 **Listen,** Israel, to what he says:
5. 1 **"Listen** to this, you priests!
5. 1 **Listen,** you that belong to the royal family!
9.17 reject his people, because they have not **listened** to him.
Joel 1. 2 everyone in Judah, **listen.**
Amos 3. 1 People of Israel, **listen** to this message which the Lord
3.13 **Listen** now, and warn the descendants of Jacob," says
4. 1 **Listen** to this, you women of Samaria, who grow fat like
5. 1 **Listen,** people of Israel, to this funeral song which I
5.23 I do not want to **listen** to your harps.
7.16 So now **listen** to what the Lord says.
8. 4 **Listen** to this, you that trample on the needy and try to
Mic 1. 2 **listen** to this, all who live on earth!
3. 1 **Listen,** you rulers of Israel!
3. 4 He will not **listen** to your prayers, for you have done evil.
3. 9 **Listen** to me, you rulers of Israel, you that hate justice
6. 1 **Listen** to the Lord's case against Israel.
6. 2 foundations of the earth, **listen** to the Lord's case!
6. 9 He calls to the city, **"Listen,** you people who assemble in
Hab 1. 2 help before you **listen,** before you save us from violence?
Zeph 3. 2 It has not **listened** to the Lord or accepted his discipline.
Zech 1. 4 But they would not **listen** to me or obey me.
3. 8 **Listen** then, Joshua, you who are the High Priest;
3. 8 and **listen,** you fellow-priests of his, you that are the sign
7.11 "But my people stubbornly refused to **listen.**
7.12 Because they would not **listen** to the teaching which I sent
7.13 Because they did not **listen** when I spoke, I did not
11. 3 **Listen** to the roaring of the lions;
Mal 2. 2 If you will not **listen** to what I say, then I will
3.16 one another, and the Lord **listened** and heard what they said.
Mt 8. 4 Then Jesus said to him, **"Listen!**
10.14 will not welcome you or **listen** to you, then leave that place
11.15 **Listen,** then, if you have ears!
12.42 way from her country to **listen** to King Solomon's wise teaching;
13. 9 And Jesus concluded, **"Listen,** then, if you have ears!"
13.13 do not see, and they **listen,** but do not hear or understand.
13.14 'This people will **listen** and listen, but not understand;
13.18 **"Listen,** then, and learn what the parable of the sower means.
13.43 **Listen,** then, if you have ears!
15.10 the crowd to him and said to them, **"Listen** and understand!
17. 5 my own dear Son, with whom I am pleased—**listen** to him!"
18.15 If he **listens** to you, you have won your brother back.
18.16 But if he will not **listen** to you, take one or two
18.17 And if he will not **listen** to them, then tell the whole
18.17 Finally, if he will not **listen** to the church, treat him as
20.13 **'Listen, friend,'** the owner answered one of them, 'I have not
20.18 **"Listen,"** he told them, "we are going up to Jerusalem,
21.33 **"Listen** to another parable," Jesus said.
Mk 1.44 after saying to him, **"Listen,** don't tell anyone about this.
4. 9 And Jesus concluded, **"Listen,** then, if you have ears!"
4.12 they may **listen** and listen, yet not understand.
4.23 **Listen,** then, if you have ears!"
6.11 welcome you or will not **listen** to you, leave it and shake
6.20 He liked to **listen** to him, even though he became greatly
7.14 more and said to them, **"Listen** to me, all of you,
9. 7 from the cloud, "This is my own dear Son—**listen** to him!"
10.33 **"Listen,"** he told them, "we are going up to Jerusalem
12.29 **'Listen,** Israel!
12.37 A large crowd was **listening** to Jesus gladly.
15. 4 **Listen** to all their accusations!"
15.35 heard him and said, **"Listen,** he is calling for Elijah!"
Lk 2.46 sitting with the Jewish teachers, **listening** to them and asking
4.25 **"Listen** to me:
5. 1 their way up to him to **listen** to the word of God.
6.47 who comes to me and **listens** to my words and obeys them
8. 8 And Jesus concluded, **"Listen,** then, if you have ears!"
8.10 they may look but not see, and **listen** but not understand.
8.18 "Be careful, then, how you **listen;**
9.35 "This is my Son, whom I have chosen—**listen** to him!"
10.16 Jesus said to his disciples, "Whoever **listens** to you listens to me;
10.39 down at the feet of the Lord and **listened** to his teaching.
11.31 from her country to **listen** to King Solomon's wise teaching;
14.35 **Listen,** then, if you have ears!"
15. 1 and other outcasts came to **listen** to Jesus, [2]the Pharisees
16.29 your brothers should **listen** to what they say.'
16.31 said, 'If they will not **listen** to Moses and the prophets,
18. 6 And the Lord continued, **"Listen** to what that corrupt judge said.
18.31 Jesus took the twelve disciples aside and said to them, **"Listen!**
19. 8 Zacchaeus stood up and said to the Lord, **"Listen,** sir!
19.11 While the people were **listening** to this, Jesus continued
19.48 all the people kept **listening** to him, not wanting to miss
20.45 As all the people **listened** to him, Jesus said to his disciples,
21.38 morning all the people went to the Temple to **listen** to him.
Jn 3.29 friend, who stands by and **listens,** is glad when he hears the
5.14 him in the Temple and said, **"Listen,** you are well now;
6.60 Who can **listen** to it?"
8.43 It is because you cannot bear to **listen** to my message.
8.47 He who comes from God **listens** to God's words.
8.47 are not from God, and that is why you will not **listen."**
9.27 already told you," he answered, "and you would not **listen.**
9.31 We know that God does not **listen** to sinners;
9.31 he does **listen** to people who respect him and do what he
10. 8 thieves and robbers, but the sheep did not **listen** to them.
10.16 they will **listen** to my voice, and they will become one flock
10.20 Why do you **listen** to him?"
10.27 My sheep **listen** to my voice;
11.41 up and said, "I thank you, Father, that you **listen** to me.
11.42 I know that you always **listen** to me, but I say this
18.37 Whoever belongs to the truth **listens** to me."
Acts 2.14 you who live in Jerusalem, **listen** to me and let me tell
2.22 **"Listen** to these words, fellow-Israelites!
5.25 Then a man came in and said to them, **"Listen!**
7. 2 Stephen answered, "Brothers and fathers, **listen** to me!
7.26 **'Listen,** men,' he said, 'you are fellow-Israelites;
7.54 members of the Council **listened** to Stephen, they became furious
8. 6 what Philip said, as they **listened** to him and saw the
10.19 understand what the vision meant, when the Spirit said, **"Listen!**
10.44 Spirit came down on all those who were **listening** to his message.
14. 9 He sat there and **listened** to Paul's words.
15.13 **"Listen** to me, my brothers!
16.25 hymns to God, and the other prisoners were **listening** to them.
17.11 They **listened** to the message with great eagerness, and every day
22. 1 "My fellow-Israelites, **listen** to me as I make my defence
22.22 The people **listened** to Paul until he said this;
23.21 don't **listen** to them, because there are more than forty men
24. 4 I beg you to be kind and **listen** to our brief account.
24.24 He sent for Paul and **listened** to him as he talked about
26. 3 I ask you, then, to **listen** to me with patience.
26.29 rest of you who are **listening** to me today might become what
27.21 said, "Men, you should have **listened** to me and not have
28.26 You will **listen** and listen, but not understand;
28.28 They will **listen!"**
1 Cor 14.21 foreigners, but even then my people will not **listen** to me."
15.51 **Listen** to this secret truth:
2 Cor 13.11 **listen** to my appeals;
1 Tim 1.19 Some men have not **listened** to their conscience and have made
5.19 Do not **listen** to an accusation against an elder unless
2 Tim 2.14 It does no good, but only ruins the people who **listen.**
4. 3 when people will not **listen** to sound doctrine, but will follow
4. 4 They will turn away from **listening** to the truth and give
Heb 13.22 my brothers, to **listen** patiently to this message of encouragement;
Jas 1.19 Everyone must be quick to **listen,** but slow to speak and slow
1.22 Do not deceive yourselves by just **listening** to his word;
1.23 Whoever **listens** to the word but does not put it into
1.25 it and does not simply **listen** and then forget it, but puts
2. 5 **Listen,** my dear brothers!
4.13 Now **listen** to me, you that say, "Today or tomorrow we
5. 1 And now, you rich people, **listen** to me!
5. 4 **Listen** to their complaints!
1 Pet 3.12 the Lord watches over the righteous and **listens** to their prayers;
1 Jn 4. 5 the world, and the world **listens** to them because they belong
4. 6 Whoever knows God **listens** to us;
4. 6 whoever does not belong to God does not **listen** to us.
Rev 1. 3 and happy are those who **listen** to the words of this
2. 7 "If you have ears, then, **listen** to what the Spirit says
2.11 "If you have ears, then, **listen** to what the Spirit says
2.17 "If you have ears, then, **listen** to what the Spirit says
2.29 "If you have ears, then, **listen** to what the Spirit says
3. 6 "If you have ears, then, **listen** to what the Spirit says
3.13 "If you have ears, then, **listen** to what the Spirit says
3.22 "If you have ears, then, **listen** to what the Spirit says
13. 9 **"Listen,** then, if you have ears!
also Judg 5.11 Ruth 3.2 2 Sam 20.16 Prov 1.20 Prov 8.1 Is 66.6 Jer 8.19 Jer 10.22 Mic 1.2 Nah 3.2 Mt 10.16 Mt 24.25 Mk 4.3 Lk 10.19 Lk 22.31 Acts 13.25 2 Cor 6.2 Gal 5.2 Rev 2.10 Rev 3.9 Rev 3.20 Rev 16.15 Rev 22.7 Rev 22.12

LITERATURE

Dan 1.17 young men knowledge and skill in **literature** and philosophy.

LITRE

Ex 16.16 Ex 16.22 Ex 16.33 Ex 16.36 Ex 29.40 Ex 29.40 Ex 30.24 Lev 14.10 Lev 14.12 Lev 14.21 Lev 23.13 Num 15.4 Num 15.4 Num 15.6 Num 15.7 Num 15.9 Num 15.10 Num 28.5 Num 28.7 Num 28.14 Num 28.14 Num 28.14 1 Kgs 4.22 1 Kgs 5.11 1 Kgs 7.26 1 Kgs 7.38 1 Kgs 18.32 2 Chr 2.10 2 Chr 2.10 2 Chr 4.5 Ezra 7.22 Is 5.10 Is 5.10 Ezek 45.24 Ezek 46.5 Ezek 46.5 Ezek 46.7 Ezek 46.7 Ezek 46.11 Ezek 46.11 Ezek 46.14 Hag 2.16 Mt 13.33 Lk 13.21 Jn 2.6 Jn 12.3 Rev 6.6 Rev 6.6

LITTLE

Gen 19.20 Do you see that **little** town?
30.30 The **little** you had before I came has grown enormously,
43. 2 to his sons, "Go back and buy a **little** food for us."
43.11 a **little** resin, a little honey, spices, pistachio nuts, and
44.25 Then he told us to return and buy a **little** food.
Ex 16.18 much, and those who gathered less did not have too **little.**
23.30 I will drive them out **little** by little, until there are
Deut 7.22 **Little** by little he will drive out these nations as you advance.
Judg 8. 2 Even the **little** that you men of Ephraim did is worth more
19.12 pass on and go a **little** farther and spend the night at
1 Sam 2.19 his mother would make a **little** robe and take it to him
14.43 Jonathan answered, "I ate a **little** honey with the stick I
2 Sam 16. 1 When David had gone a **little** beyond the top of the hill,
19.36 I will go just a **little** way with you beyond the Jordan.
1 Kgs 12.10 'My **little** finger is thicker than my father's waist!'
17.12 back home and prepare what **little** I have for my son and
18.44 and said, "I saw a **little** cloud no bigger than a man's
18.45 In a **little** while the sky was covered with dark clouds,
2 Kgs 5. 2 Syrians had carried off a **little** Israelite girl, who became
10.18 served the god Baal a **little,** but I will serve him much
2 Chr 10.10 'My **little** finger is thicker than my father's waist.'
Esth 2.20 had obeyed him when she was a **little** girl under his care.
Job 35.15 God does not punish, that he pays **little** attention to sin.
36. 1 Be patient and listen a **little** longer to what I am
38.32 season by season and direct the Great and the **Little** Bear?
Ps 37.16 The **little** that a good man owns is worth more than the

Ps 39.12 all my ancestors I am only your guest for a **little** while.
44.12 people for a small price as though they had **little** value.
119.19 I am here on earth for just a **little** while;
Prov 4. 3 When I was only a **little** boy, my parents' only son, [4]my
16. 8 is better to have a **little,** honestly earned, than to have a
Ecc 4. 6 better to have only a **little,** with peace of mind, than to
7.27 Philosopher, I found this out **little** by little while I was
8. 6 and a right way to do everything, but we know so **little!**
9.14 There was a **little** town without many people in it.
10. 1 of perfume stink, and a **little** stupidity can cancel out the
Song 2.15 Catch the foxes, the **little** foxes, before they ruin our
Is 3.16 They take dainty **little** steps,
10.25 In only a **little** while I will finish punishing you, and
11. 6 feed together, and **little** children will take care of them.
26.20 Hide yourselves for a **little** while until God's anger is over.
59.15 There is so **little** honesty that anyone who stops doing
63.18 people, were driven out by our enemies for a **little** while:
Ezek 16.47 No, in only a **little** while you were behaving worse than they
Dan 7. 8 the horns, I saw a **little** horn coming up among the others.
7.11 I could still hear the **little** horn bragging and boasting.
8. 9 these four horns grew a **little** horn, whose power extended
11.34 God's people will receive a **little** help, even though many
Hag 1. 6 You have sown much corn, but have harvested very **little.**
Zech 4.10 They are disappointed because so **little** progress is being made.
Mt 6.30 How **little** faith you have!
8.26 "How **little** faith you have!"
9.24 The **little** girl is not dead—she is only sleeping!"
13. 5 Some of it fell on rocky ground, where there was **little** soil.
13.12 will have taken away from him even the **little** he has.
14.31 grabbed hold of him and said, "How **little** faith you have!
16. 8 How **little** faith you have!
18. 6 should cause one of these **little** ones to lose his faith in
18.10 "See that you don't despise any of these **little** ones.
18.14 heaven does not want any of these **little** ones to be lost.
24.19 for women who are pregnant and for mothers with **little** babies!
25.29 who has nothing, even the **little** that he has will be taken
26.39 He went a **little** farther on, threw himself face downwards
26.73 After a **little** while the men standing there came to Peter.
Mk 1.19 He went a **little** farther on and saw two other brothers,
4. 5 Some of it fell on rocky ground, where there was **little** soil.
4.25 will have taken away from him even the **little** he has."
5.23 begged him earnestly, "My **little** daughter is very ill.
5.41 "Talitha, koum," which means, **"Little** girl, I tell you to get
9.42 should cause one of these **little** ones to lose his faith in
12.42 and dropped in two **little** copper coins, worth about a penny.
13.17 for women who are pregnant and for mothers with **little** babies!
14.35 He went a **little** farther on, threw himself on the ground,
14.70 A **little** while later the bystanders accused Peter again,
Lk 5. 3 Simon—and asked him to push off a **little** from the shore.
7.47 But whoever has been forgiven **little** shows only a little love."
8.18 have taken away from him even the **little** he thinks he has."
12.28 How **little** faith you have!
12.32 "Do not be afraid, **little** flock, for your Father is pleased
17. 2 than for him to cause one of these **little** ones to sin.
19. 3 was, but he was a **little** man and could not see Jesus
19.26 who has nothing, even the **little** that he has will be taken
21. 2 saw a very poor widow dropping in two **little** copper coins.
21.23 women who are pregnant and for mothers with **little** babies!
22.58 After a **little** while a man noticed Peter and said, "You
Jn 6. 7 everyone to have even a **little,** it would take more than two
7.33 shall be with you a **little** while longer, and then I shall
12.35 Jesus answered, "The light will be among you a **little** longer.
14.19 In a **little** while the world will see me no more,
16.16 "In a **little** while you will not see me any more,
16.16 and then a **little** while later you will see me."
16.17 tells us that in a **little** while we will not see him,
16.17 and then a **little** while later we will see him;
16.18 What does this 'a **little** while' mean?
16.19 them, "I said, 'In a **little** while you will not see me,
16.19 and then a **little** while later you will see me.'
Acts 27.16 when we passed to the south of the **little** island of Cauda.
27.28 a **little** later they did the same and found that it was
1 Cor 5. 6 You know the saying, "A **little** bit of yeast makes the whole
2 Cor 8.15 and the one who gathered **little** did not have too little."
11.16 a fool, so that I will have a **little** to boast of.
Gal 5. 9 "It takes only a **little** yeast to make the whole batch of
Phil 4.12 am full or hungry, whether I have too much or too **little.**
1 Thes 2.17 separated from you for a **little** while—not in our thoughts,
1 Tim 5.23 water only, but take a **little** wine to help your digestion,
Heb 2. 7 You made him for a **little** while lower than the angels;
2. 9 see Jesus, who for a **little** while was made lower than the
10.37 the scripture says, "Just a **little** while longer, and he who
11.25 God's people rather than to enjoy sin for a **little** while.
1 Pet 5.10 you have suffered for a **little** while, the God of all grace,
Rev 3. 8 I know that you have a **little** power;
6.11 were told to rest a **little** while longer, until the complete
10. 9 to the angel and asked him to give me the **little** scroll.
10.10 I took the **little** scroll from his hand and ate it,
12.12 because he knows that he has only a **little** time left."
17.10 when he comes, he must rule only a **little** while.
20. 3 After that he must be let loose for a **little** while.

LITTLE WHILE see WHILE

LIVE (1)

[EVER-LIVING, LIVING BEING, LIVING CREATURE, LIVING FOR EVER, LIVING GOD, LIVING LORD, LIVING THING, LIVING-QUARTERS]

Gen 1.20 filled with many kinds of **living beings,** and let the air be
1.21 all kinds of creatures that **live** in the water, and all kinds
Gen 1.22 and told the creatures that **live** in the water to reproduce,
1.28 so that your descendants will **live** all over the earth and
2. 7 breath into his nostrils and the man began to **live.**
2.18 God said, "It is not good for the man to **live** alone.
3.14 and you will have to eat dust as long as you **live.**
3.22 from the tree that gives life, eat it, and **live** for ever."
3.24 of the garden he put **living creatures** and a flaming sword
4.16 Lord's presence and **lived** in a land called "Wandering,"
4.20 the ancestor of those who raise livestock and **live** in tents.
5. 4 After that, Adam **lived** another 800 years.
5. 7 105, he had a son, Enosh, [7]and then **lived** another 807 years.
5.10 90, he had a son, Kenan, [10]and then **lived** another 815 years.
5.13 he had a son, Mahalalel, [13]and then **lived** another 840 years.
5.16 65, he had a son, Jared, [16]and then **lived** another 830 years.
5.19 162, he had a son, Enoch, [19]and then **lived** another 800 years.
5.22 After that, Enoch **lived** in fellowship with God for 300
5.23 He **lived** to be 365 years old.
5.26 187, he had a son, Lamech, [26]and then **lived** another 782 years.
5.30 Lamech **lived** another 595 years.
6. 3 the Lord said, "I will not allow people to **live** for ever;
6. 3 From now on they will **live** no longer than a hundred and
6. 9 He **lived** in fellowship with God, [11]but everyone else was
6.12 it was evil, for the people were all **living** evil lives.
6.17 to send a flood on the earth to destroy every **living being.**
7. 4 order to destroy all the **living beings** that I have made."
7.15 female of each kind of **living being** went into the boat with
7.21 Every **living being** on the earth died—every bird, every
7.23 The Lord destroyed all **living beings** on the earth—human beings,
8.21 again will I destroy all **living beings,** as I have done this
9. 1 so that your descendants will **live** all over the earth.
9. 2 All the animals, birds, and fish will **live** in fear of you.
9. 7 so that your descendants will **live** all over the earth."
9.10 your descendants, [10]and with all **living beings—**all birds
9.11 never again will all **living beings** be destroyed by a flood;
9.12 with you and with all **living beings,** [13]I am putting my bow
9.15 that a flood will never again destroy all **living beings.**
9.16 covenant between me and all **living beings** on earth.
9.17 of the promise which I am making to all **living beings."**
9.27 May his descendants **live** with the people of Shem!
9.28 After the flood Noah **lived** for 350 years [29]and died at
10. 5 ancestors of the people who **live** along the coast and on the
10. 5 of Japheth, **living** in their different tribes and countries,
10.20 of Ham, **living** in their different tribes and countries,
10.30 The land in which they **lived** extended from Mesha to
10.31 of Shem, **living** in their different tribes and countries,
11.11 After that, he **lived** another 500 years and had other children.
11.13 after that, he **lived** another 403 years and had other children.
11.15 after that, he **lived** another 403 years and had other children.
11.17 after that, he **lived** another 430 years and had other children.
11.19 after that, he **lived** another 209 years and had other children.
11.21 after that, he **lived** another 207 years and had other children.
11.23 after that, he **lived** another 200 years and had other children.
11.25 after that, he **lived** another 119 years and had other children.
11.28 city, Ur in Babylonia, while his father was still **living.**
12. 6 (At that time the Canaanites were still **living** in the land.)
12.10 Abram went farther south to Egypt, to **live** there for a while.
12.12 my wife, and so they will kill me and let you **live.**
12.13 because of you they will let me **live** and treat me well."
13. 7 Canaanites and the Perizzites were still **living** in the land.)
14. 7 Amalekites and defeated the Amorites who **lived** in Hazazon Tamar.
14.12 Lot, Abram's nephew, was **living** in Sodom, so they took
14.13 Abram, the Hebrew, who was **living** near the sacred trees
15.15 You yourself will **live** to a ripe old age, die in peace,
16. 3 (This happened after Abram had **lived** in Canaan for ten years.)
16.12 But your son will **live** like a wild donkey;
16.12 He will **live** apart from all his relatives."
16.13 "Have I really seen God and **lived** to tell about it?"
16.14 Kadesh and Bered "The Well of the **Living** One Who Sees Me."
19.12 sons-in-law, or any other relatives **living** in the city—get
19.29 the valley where Lot was **living,** he kept Abraham in mind and
19.30 two daughters moved up into the hills and **lived** in a cave.
20. 1 southern part of Canaan and **lived** between Kadesh and Shur.
20. 1 Later, while he was **living** in Gerar, [2]he said that his wife
20.15 **live** anywhere you like."
21.20 **lived** in the wilderness of Paran and became a skilful hunter.
21.23 loyal to me and to this country in which you are **living."**
21.34 Abraham **lived** in Philistia for a long time.
23. 1 Sarah **lived** to be a hundred and twenty-seven years old.
23. 4 and said, [4]"I am a foreigner **living** here among you;
24.10 to the city where Nahor had **lived** in northern Mesopotamia.
24.62 of "The Well of the **Living** One Who Sees Me" and was
24.67 that his mother Sarah had **lived** in, and she became his wife.
25.11 who lived near "The Well of the **Living** One Who Sees Me."
25.18 The descendants of Ishmael **lived** in the territory between
25.18 They **lived** apart from the other descendants of Abraham.
26. 3 **Live** here, and I will be with you and bless you.
26. 6 So Isaac **lived** at Gerar.
26.22 has given us freedom to **live** in the land, and we will
27.40 You will **live** by your sword, But be your brother's slave.
28. 4 in which you have **lived** and which God gave to Abraham!"
34.10 **live** anywhere you wish, trade freely, and own property."
34.21 let them **live** in the land with us and travel freely.
34.22 these men will agree to **live** among us and be one people
34.23 So let us agree that they can **live** among us."
35. 1 God said to Jacob, "Go to Bethel at once, and **live** there.
35.22 While Jacob was **living** in that land, Reuben had sexual
35.27 Isaac at Mamre, near Hebron, where Abraham and Isaac had **lived.**
35.28 Isaac **lived** to be a hundred and eighty years old [29]and
36. 7 where he and Jacob were **living** was not able to support them;

Gen 36. 8 So Esau **lived** in the hill-country of Edom.
36.40 where each of these tribes **lived** was known by the name of
37. 1 Jacob continued to **live** in the land of Canaan, where his
37. 1 Canaan, where his father had **lived**, [2]and this is the story
39. 2 He **lived** in the house of his Egyptian master, [3]who saw that
42.16 Otherwise, as sure as the king **lives**, you are spies."
43. 7 about us and our family, 'Is your father still **living?**
45.10 You can **live** in the region of Goshen, where you can be
45.18 in Egypt, and they will have more than enough to **live** on.
46.31 father's family, who were **living** in Canaan, have come to me.
46.34 this way he will let you **live** in the region of Goshen."
47. 4 "We have come to **live** in this country, because in the
47. 4 Please give us permission to **live** in the region of Goshen."
47.22 lands, because the king gave them an allowance to **live** on.
47.27 The Israelites **lived** in Egypt in the region of Goshen,
47.28 Jacob **lived** in Egypt for seventeen years, until he was a
48.16 of my fathers Abraham and Isaac **live** on through these boys!
49.13 "Zebulun will **live** beside the sea.
50.22 Joseph continued to **live** in Egypt with his father's family;
50.23 He **lived** to see Ephraim's children and grandchildren.
50.23 He also **lived** to receive the children of Machir son of
Ex 1.16 but if it is a girl, let it **live.**"
1.17 instead, they let the boys **live.**
1.18 Why are you letting the boys **live?**"
1.22 and throw him into the Nile, but let all the girls **live.**"
2.15 but Moses fled and went to **live** in the land of Midian.
2.21 So Moses agreed to **live** there, and Jethro gave him his
3. 8 the Perizzites, the Hivites, and the Jebusites now **live.**
3.22 and to any Egyptian woman **living** in her house and will ask
6. 4 of Canaan, the land in which they had **lived** as foreigners.
6.16 Levi **lived** 137 years.
6.18 Kohath **lived** 133 years.
6.20 Amram **lived** 137 years.
8.22 of Goshen, where my people **live**, so that there will be no
9.16 power I have let you **live** so that my fame might spread
9.26 of Goshen, where the Israelites **lived**, was the only place
10.23 But the Israelites had light where they were **living.**
12.13 will be a sign to mark the houses in which you **live.**
12.40 The Israelites had **lived** in Egypt for 430 years.
15.25 Lord gave them laws to **live** by, and there he also tested
18.20 to them how they should **live** and what they should do.
20.10 your animals, nor the foreigners who **live** in your country.
20.12 mother, so that you may **live** a long time in the land
23.33 Do not let those people **live** in your country;
25. 8 a sacred tent for me, so that I may **live** among them.
29.45 I will **live** among the people of Israel, and I will be
29.46 brought them out of Egypt so that I could **live** among them.
Lev 3.17 to be kept for ever by all Israelites wherever they **live.**
7.26 No matter where the Israelites **live**, they must never use
11.10 fins and scales, [10]but anything **living** in the water that
11.12 must not eat anything that **lives** in the water and does not
11.46 and birds, about everything that **lives** in the water, and
13.46 and he must **live** outside the camp, away from others.
14. 8 the camp, but he must **live** outside his tent for seven days.
16.29 the Israelites and the foreigners **living** among them must
17. 8 Any Israelite or any foreigner **living** in the community who
17.10 any Israelite or any foreigner **living** in the community eats
17.11 The life of every **living thing** is in the blood, and that
17.12 neither they nor any foreigner **living** among them shall eat
17.13 any Israelite or any foreigner **living** in the community hunts
17.14 The life of every **living thing** is in the blood, and that
18. 3 of Egypt, where you once **lived**, or of the people in the
18.18 as one of your wives, as long as your wife is **living.**
18.24 themselves unclean, those pagans who **lived** in the land
18.25 the land and making it reject the people who **lived** there.
18.26 you, whether Israelites or foreigners **living** with you, must
18.28 you, as it rejected the pagans who **lived** there before you.
18.30 practices of the people who **lived** in the land before you,
19.33 "Do not ill-treat foreigners who are **living** in your land.
20. 2 of you or any foreigner **living** among you who gives any of
20.23 Do not adopt the customs of people who **live** there;
21. 3 brother, [3]or unmarried sister **living** in his house.
22.13 and who has returned to **live** in her father's house as a
22.18 or any foreigner **living** in Israel presents a burnt-offering, whether
23. 3 The Sabbath belongs to the Lord, no matter where you **live.**
23.21 regulation for all time to come, no matter where they **live.**
23.31 applies to all your descendants, no matter where they **live.**
23.42 the people of Israel shall **live** in shelters for seven days,
23.43 made the people of Israel **live** in simple shelters when he
24.16 Any Israelite or any foreigner **living** in Israel who curses
24.22 to Israelites and to foreigners **living** among you, because I
25. 6 the foreigners **living** with you, [7]your domestic animals,
25.18 and commands, so that you may **live** in safety in the land.
25.19 will have all you want to eat and will **live** in safety.
25.35 If a fellow-Israelite **living** near you becomes poor and cannot support himself,
25.35 a hired man, so that he can continue to **live** near you.
25.36 but obey God and let your fellow-Israelite **live** near you.
25.39 If a fellow-Israelite **living** near you becomes so poor
25.45 buy the children of the foreigners who are **living** among you.
25.46 to your sons, whom they must serve as long as they **live.**
25.47 Suppose a foreigner **living** with you becomes rich, while
26. 3 "If you **live** according to my laws and obey my commands,
26. 5 want to eat, and you will **live** in safety in your land.
26.11 I will **live** among you in my sacred tent, and I will
Num 5. 3 will not defile the camp, where I **live** among my people."
9.14 "If a foreigner **living** among you wants to keep the Passover,
13.18 it is, how many people **live** there, and how strong they are.
13.19 bad and whether the people **live** in open towns or in
13.22 descendants of a race of giants called the Anakim, **lived.**
13.28 But the people who **live** there are powerful, and their
Num 13.29 Amalekites **live** in the southern part of the land;
13.29 Hittites, Jebusites, and Amorites **live** in the hill-country;
13.29 Canaanites **live** by the Mediterranean Sea
13.32 even produce enough to feed the people who **live** there.
14. 9 the Lord and don't be afraid of the people who **live** there.
14.14 they will tell it to the people who **live** in this land.
14.21 that as surely as I **live** and as surely as my presence
14.22 none of these people will **live** to enter that land.
14.25 in whose valleys the Amalekites and the Canaanites now **live.**
14.28 that as surely as I **live**, I will do to you just
14.30 I promised to let you **live** there, but not one of you
14.45 Amalekites and the Canaanites who **lived** there attacked and
15.14 at any time a foreigner **living** among you, whether on a
15.15 are binding on you and on the foreigners who **live** among you.
15.26 Israel and the foreigners **living** among them will be forgiven,
16.48 and he was left standing between the **living** and the dead.
19.10 the Israelites and for the foreigners **living** among them.
20.15 how our ancestors went to Egypt, where we **lived** many years.
21.32 surrounding towns and drove out the Amorites **living** there.
23. 9 They are a nation that **lives** alone;
24.21 "The place where you **live** is secure, Safe as a nest set
30. 3 When a young woman still **living** in her father's house
30.16 made by an unmarried woman **living** in her father's house or
32.17 our dependants can **live** here in the fortified towns,
32.40 Moses gave Gilead to the clan of Machir, and they **lived** there.
35. 2 the Levites some cities to **live** in and pasture land round
35. 3 These cities will belong to the Levites, and they will **live** there.
35.25 He must **live** there until the death of the man who is
35.29 These rules apply to you and your descendants wherever you may **live.**
35.33 did this, you would defile the land where you are **living.**
35.34 the land where you are **living**, because I am the Lord
35.34 and I **live** among the people of Israel."
Deut 1.16 your own people or involves foreigners who **live** among you.
1.28 we are, and that they **live** in cities with walls that reach
1.44 Then the Amorites who **lived** in those hills came out
2.10 mighty race of giants called the Emim used to **live** in Ar.
2.12 The Horites used to **live** in Edom, but the descendants of
2.20 the Rephaim, the name of the people who used to **live** there;
2.22 descendants of Esau, who **live** in the hill-country of Edom.
2.22 took over their land and settled there, where they still **live.**
2.29 The descendants of Esau, who **live** in Edom,
2.29 and the Moabites, who **live** in Ar, allowed us to pass
3.20 until the Lord lets them **live** there in peace, as he has
4. 1 teaching you, and you will **live** and occupy the land which
4. 9 forget, as long as you **live**, what you have seen with your
4.10 me as long as they **live** and so that they will teach
4.26 You will not **live** very long in the land across the Jordan
4.33 Have any people ever **lived** after hearing a god speak to
4.40 You will continue to **live** in the land which the Lord your
4.47 Bashan, the other Amorite king who **lived** east of the Jordan.
5. 3 with our fathers, but with all of us who are **living** today.
5.14 your animals, nor the foreigners who **live** in your country.
5.16 and so that you may **live** a long time in the land
5.24 a man to continue to **live**, even though God has spoken to
5.26 Has any human being ever **lived**
5.26 after hearing the **living God** speak from a fire?
5.33 that you will continue to **live** in the land that you are
6. 2 As long as you **live**, you and your descendants are to
6. 2 you, so that you may **live** in that land a long time.
6. 3 a mighty nation and **live** in that rich and fertile land,
8. 1 today, so that you may **live**, increase in number, and occupy
8. 6 **live** according to his laws and obey him.
8.12 have built good houses to **live** in [13]and when your cattle
10.18 he loves the foreigners who **live** with our people, and gives
11. 9 And you will **live** a long time in the rich and fertile
11.10 is not like the land of Egypt, where you **lived** before.
11.21 you and your children will **live** a long time in the land
11.21 You will **live** there as long as there is a sky above
11.30 territory of the Canaanites who **live** in the Jordan Valley.
12. 1 obey as long as you **live** in the land that the Lord,
12. 9 Lord your God is giving you, where you can **live** in peace.
12.10 the Lord will let you occupy the land and **live** there.
12.10 you safe from all your enemies, and you will **live** in peace.
12.12 your servants, and the Levites who **live** in your towns;
12.15 you are free to kill and eat your animals wherever you **live.**
12.17 the Lord is to be eaten in the places where you **live:**
12.18 servants and the Levites who **live** in your towns, are to eat
12.19 to neglect the Levites, as long as you **live** in your land.
13. 5 away from the life that the Lord has commanded you to **live.**
13. 7 gods of the people who **live** near you
13. 7 or the gods of those who **live** far away.
13.12 "When you are **living** in the towns that the Lord your
13.16 possessions of the people who **live** there and pile them up in
14. 2 own people from among all the peoples who **live** on earth.
14.10 fins and scales, [10]but anything **living** in the water that
14.21 may let the foreigners who **live** among you eat it, or you
14.27 "Do not neglect the Levites who **live** in your towns;
14.29 the foreigners, orphans, and widows who **live** in your towns.
16. 3 that as long as you **live** you will remember the day you
16.11 foreigners, orphans, and widows who **live** in your towns.
16.14 foreigners, orphans, and widows who **live** in your towns.
16.20 Lord your God is giving you and will continue to **live** there.
18. 1 instead, they are to **live** on the offerings and other
19. 9 love the Lord your God and **live** according to his teachings.)
21.19 leaders of the town where he **lives** and make him stand trial.
22. 2 But if its owner **lives** a long way off or if you
22. 7 bird go, so that you will **live** a long and prosperous life.
22.19 wife, and he can never divorce her as long as he **lives.**
22.21 married, while she was still **living** in her father's house.
22.29 He can never divorce her as long as he **lives.**

Deut 23. 7 you once **lived** in their land.
23.16 He may **live** in any of your towns that he chooses, and
24.14 fellow-Israelite or a foreigner **living** in one of your towns.
25. 5 "If two brothers **live** on the same property and one of
25.15 measures, so that you may **live** a long time in the land
25.19 from all your enemies who **live** around you, be sure to kill
26. 5 a wandering Aramean, who took his family to Egypt to **live.**
26.11 the foreigners who **live** among you join in the celebration.
28.30 You will build a house—but never **live** in it.
28.36 where neither you nor your ancestors ever **lived** before;
28.43 "Foreigners who **live** in your land will gain more and more power,
28.66 with terror, and you will **live** in constant fear of death.
29.11 children, and the foreigners who **live** among you and cut wood
30. 1 to you, and you are **living** among the nations where the Lord
30. 5 take possession of the land where your ancestors once **lived.**
30. 6 all your heart, and you will continue to **live** in that land.
30.18 You will not **live** long in that land across the Jordan that
30.20 you and your descendants will **live** long in the land that he
31. 3 you and destroy the nations **living** there, so that you can
31.12 children, and the foreigners who **live** in your towns, so that
31.13 him as long as they **live** in the land that you are
31.14 Then the Lord said to Moses, "You haven't much longer to **live.**
31.20 have all the food they want, and they will **live** comfortably.
32. 8 he determined where peoples should **live.**
32.40 surely as I am the **living God,** I raise my hand and
32.47 Obey them and you will **live** long in that land across the
33.25 protected with iron gates, And may he always **live** secure."
33.28 So Jacob's descendants **live** in peace, secure in a land
Josh 1. 5 one will be able to defeat you as long as you **live.**
2.15 Rahab **lived** in a house built into the city wall, so she
3.10 You will know that the **living God** is among you [11] when the
6.25 (Her descendants have **lived** in Israel to this day.)
8.22 got away, and no one **lived** through it [23] except the king of
8.35 and children, as well as the foreigners **living** among them.
9. 7 Maybe you **live** nearby."
9.10 Sihon of Heshbon and King Og of Bashan, who **lived** in Ashtaroth.
9.11 and all the people that **live** in our land told us to
9.15 with the people of Gibeon and allowed them to **live.**
9.16 Israelites learnt that these people did indeed **live** nearby.
9.17 days later arrived at the cities where these people **lived:**
9.20 We must let them **live** because of our promise;
9.21 Let them **live,** but they will have to cut wood and carry
9.22 us that you were from far away, when you **live** right here?
9.24 land and to kill the people **living** in it as you advanced.
10. 1 had made peace with the Israelites and were **living** among them.
11. 3 as to the Hivites who **lived** at the foot of Mount Hermon
11.19 of Israel was Gibeon, where some of the Hivites **lived.**
11.21 called the Anakim who **lived** in the hill-country—in Hebron,
13. 3 the kings of the Philistines **lived** at Gaza, Ashdod,
13. 6 territory of the Sidonians, who **live** in the hill-country
13.13 they still **live** in Israel.
14. 3 Instead, they received cities to **live** in, with fields for
15.12 Within these borders **lived** the people of the families of Judah.
15.15 From there he went to attack the people **living** in Debir.
15.63 not able to drive out the Jebusites, who **lived** in Jerusalem.
15.63 The Jebusites still **live** there with the people of Judah.
16. 2 Luz, passing on to Ataroth Addar, where the Archites **lived.**
16.10 drive out the Canaanites who **lived** in Gezer,
16.10 the Canaanites have **lived** among the Ephraimites to this day,
17.12 to drive out the people **living** in those cities,
17.12 so the Canaanites continued to **live** there.
17.16 both those who **live** in Beth Shan and its surrounding
17.16 towns and those who **live** in the Valley of Jezreel."
20. 4 give him a place to **live** in, so that he can stay
20. 9 people of Israel and for any foreigner **living** among them.
21. 2 to be given cities to **live** in, as well as pasture land
22.22 keep faith with the Lord, do not let us **live** any longer!
24. 2 'Long ago your ancestors **lived** on the other side of the
24. 7 'You **lived** in the desert a long time.
24. 8 land of the Amorites, who **lived** on the east side of the
24.13 Now you are **living** there and eating grapes from vines that
24.15 the gods of the Amorites, in whose land you are now **living.**
24.18 land, the Lord drove out all the Amorites who **lived** here.
24.31 As long as Joshua **lived,** the people of Israel served the Lord,
Judg 1. 9 Canaanites who **lived** in the hill-country, in the foothills,
1.10 They marched against the Canaanites **living** in the city of Hebron,
1.17 defeated the Canaanites who **lived** in the city of Zephath.
1.18 These people **living** along the coast had iron chariots, and
1.21 not drive out the Jebusites **living** in Jerusalem,
1.21 the Jebusites have continued to **live** there with the people
1.27 not drive out the people **living** in the cities of Beth Shan,
1.27 the Canaanites continued to **live** there.
1.29 not drive out the Canaanites **living** in the city of Gezer,
1.29 and so the Canaanites continued to **live** there with them.
1.30 not drive out the people **living** in the cities of Kitron and
1.30 so the Canaanites continued to **live** there with them and were
1.31 not drive out the people **living** in the cities of Acco,
1.32 The people of Asher **lived** with the local Canaanites,
1.33 not drive out the people **living** in the cities of Beth Shemesh
1.33 The people of Naphtali **lived** with the local Canaanites, but
1.35 The Amorites continued to **live** at Aijalon,
2. 2 not make any covenant with the people who **live** in this land.
2. 7 As long as Joshua **lived,** the people of Israel served the Lord,
2.18 the people from their enemies as long as that leader **lived.**
3. 3 Sidonians, and the Hivites who **lived** in the Lebanon
4. 2 Sisera, who **lived** at Harosheth-of-the-Gentiles.
5.23 of the Lord, "a curse, a curse on those who **live** there.
5.24 the Kenite— the most fortunate of women who **live** in tents.
6. 4 donkeys, and leave nothing for the Israelites to **live** on.
6.10 the gods of the Amorites, whose land you are now **living** in.
8.29 Gideon went back to his own home and **lived** there.
Judg 9. 1 where all his mother's relatives **lived,** and told them [2] to
9.21 Abimelech, Jotham ran away and went to **live** at Beer.
9.41 Abimelech **lived** in Arumah, and Zebul drove Gaal and his
9.41 out of Shechem, so that they could no longer **live** there.
10. 1 the tribe of Issachar and **lived** at Shamir in the
10. 8 persecuted all the Israelites who **lived** in Amorite country
11. 3 Jephthah fled from his brothers and **lived** in the land of Tob.
11.21 all the territory of the Amorites who **lived** in that country.
13. 7 be dedicated to God as a Nazirite as long as he **lives."**
16. 4 a woman named Delilah, who **lived** in the Valley of Sorek.
17. 1 a man named Micah, who **lived** in the hill-country of Ephraim.
17. 7 young Levite who had been **living** in the town of Bethlehem in
17. 8 He left Bethlehem to find somewhere else to **live.**
17. 9 I am looking for somewhere to **live."**
17.12 Micah appointed him as his priest, and he **lived** in Micah's home.
18. 7 saw how safely the people there were **living,** like the Sidonians.
18. 7 They **lived** far away from the Sidonians and had no dealings
18.15 house, where the young Levite **lived,** and asked the Levite
19. 1 king, there was a Levite **living** far back in the hill-country
19.16 hill-country of Ephraim, but he was now **living** in Gibeah.
20. 8 "None of us, whether he **lives** in a tent or in a
21.23 their own territory, rebuilt their towns, and **lived** there.
Ruth 1. 1 clan of Ephrath and who **lived** in Bethlehem in Judah, went
1. 1 sons Mahlon and Chilion to **live** for a while in the country
1. 1 While they were **living** there, [3] Elimelech died, and Naomi
1.16 wherever you **live,** I will live.
2.11 and how you came to **live** among a people you had never
2.20 "The Lord always keeps his promises to the **living** and the dead."
2.23 And she continued to **live** with her mother-in-law.
3.13 then I swear by the **living Lord** that I will take the
1 Sam 1. 1 the tribe of Ephraim, who **lived** in the town of Ramah in
1.28 As long as he **lives,** he will belong to the Lord."
2.31 so that no man in your family will **live** to be old.
2.32 no one in your family will ever again **live** to old age.
6.14 a man named Joshua, who **lived** in Beth Shemesh, and it
7. 1 the house of a man named Abinadab, who **lived** on a hill.
7.13 from invading Israel's territory as long as Samuel **lived.**
7.15 Samuel ruled Israel as long as he **lived.**
9. 9 So they went to the town where the holy man **lived.**
9.18 the gate, and asked, "Tell me, where does the seer **live?"**
10.12 A man who **lived** there asked, "How about these other
10.24 All the people shouted, "Long **live** the king!"
11. 4 at Gibeah, where Saul **lived,** and when they told the news,
12.11 us rescued you from your enemies, and you **lived** in safety.
14.39 I promise by the **living Lord,** who gives Israel victory,
14.45 We promise by the **living Lord** that he will not lose even
14.52 As long as he **lived,** Saul had to fight fiercely against
15.35 As long as Samuel **lived,** he never again saw the king;
17.26 heathen Philistine to defy the army of the **living God?"**
17.36 Philistine, who has defied the army of the **living God.**
18.29 afraid of David and was his enemy as long as he **lived.**
20. 3 swear to you by the **living Lord** that I am only a
20.21 I swear by the **living Lord** that you will be in no
25.26 swear to you by the **living Lord** that your enemies and all
25.28 and you will not do anything evil as long as you **live.**
25.34 But I swear by the **living God** of Israel that if you
26.10 By the **living Lord,"** David continued, "I know that the
26.16 I swear by the **living Lord** that all of you deserve to
27. 5 are my friend, let me have a small town to **live** in.
27. 5 need, sir, for me to **live** with you in the capital city."
27. 7 David **lived** in Philistia for sixteen months.
27. 8 and Amalek, who had been **living** in the region a very long
27.10 of Jerahmeel or to the territory where the Kenites **lived.**
27.11 This is what David did the whole time he **lived** in Philistia.
28.10 "By the **living Lord** I promise that you will not be punished
29. 6 him, "I swear by the **living God** of Israel that you have
2 Sam 1.13 He answered, "I'm an Amalekite, but I **live** in your country."
2.27 "I swear by the **living God,"** Joab answered, "that if
4. 3 had fled to Gittaim, where they have **lived** ever since.)
4. 9 make a vow by the **living Lord,** who has saved me from
5. 6 The Jebusites, who **lived** there, thought that David would not
5. 9 After capturing the fortress, David **lived** in it and named
7. 2 Nathan, "Here I am **living** in a house built of cedar,
7. 5 not the one to build a temple for me to **live** in.
7. 6 Israel from Egypt until now, I have never **lived** in a temple;
7. 6 I have travelled round **living** in a tent.
7.10 where they will **live** without being oppressed any more.
9.13 was crippled in both feet, **lived** in Jerusalem, eating all
12. 1 and said, "There were two men who **lived** in the same town;
12. 5 said, "I swear by the **living Lord** that the man who did
12.18 said, "While the child was **living,** David wouldn't answer us
13.20 So Tamar **lived** in Absalom's house, sad and lonely.
14. 2 much, [2] so he sent for a clever woman who **lived** in Tekoa.
14.11 "I promise by the **living Lord,"** David replied, "that
14.24 gave orders that Absalom should not **live** in the palace.
14.24 So Absalom **lived** in his own house and did not appear before
14.28 Absalom **lived** two years in Jerusalem without seeing the king.
15. 8 While I was **living** in Geshur in Syria, I promised the Lord
15.20 You have **lived** here only a short time, so why should I
16.16 trusted friend, met Absalom, he shouted, "Long **live** the king!
16.16 Long **live** the king!"
19.34 But Barzillai answered, "I haven't long to **live;**
20. 3 confined for the rest of their lives, **living** like widows.
22.47 The Lord **lives!**
24. 3 they are now, and may you **live** to see him do it.
1 Kgs 1.25 feasting with him and shouting, 'Long **live** King Adonijah!'
1.29 "I promise you by the **living Lord,** who has rescued me from
1.31 bowed low and said, "May my lord the king **live** for ever!"
1.34 Then blow the trumpet and shout, 'Long **live** King Solomon!'
1.39 and all the people shouted, "Long **live** King Solomon!"
1.48 succeed me as king, and has let me **live** to see it!' "

1 Kgs 2.24 I swear by the **living Lord** that Adonijah will die this very
2.36 **Live** in it and don't leave the city.
2.38 So he **lived** in Jerusalem a long time.
3. 1 He brought her to **live** in David's City until he had finished
3.17 Majesty, this woman and I **live** in the same house, and I
3.22 The **living** child is mine, and the dead one is yours!"
3.22 The dead child is yours, and the **living** one is mine!"
3.23 of you claims that the **living** child is hers and that the
3.25 brought, [25] he said, "Cut the **living** child in two and give
4.25 As long as he **lived,**
4.25 people throughout Judah and Israel **lived** in safety, each
6.13 I will **live** among my people Israel in this Temple that
7.13 man named Huram, a craftsman **living** in the city of Tyre, who
7.14 father, who was no longer **living,** was from Tyre, and had
8.12 sky, yet you have chosen to **live** in clouds and darkness.
8.13 temple for you, a place for you to **live** in for ever."
8.23 your love when they **live** in whole-hearted obedience to you.
8.27 "But can you, O God, really **live** on earth?
8.40 you all the time they **live** in the land which you gave
8.41 "When a foreigner who **lives** in a distant land
8.43 In heaven, where you **live,** hear him and do what he asks
8.58 so that we will always **live** as he wants us to live,
10. 5 served at his table, the **living quarters** for his officials,
11.20 queen in the palace, where he **lived** with the king's sons.
11.24 and his men went and **lived** in Damascus, where his men made
11.34 and I will keep him in power as long as he **lives.**
11.38 If you obey me completely, **live** by my laws, and win my
12.17 only of the people who **lived** in the territory of Judah.
12.25 in the hill-country of Ephraim and **lived** there for a while.
13.11 At that time there was an old prophet **living** in Bethel.
14. 2 Shiloh, where the prophet Ahijah **lives,** the one who said I
17. 1 name of the Lord, the **living God** of Israel, whom I serve,
17. 9 I have commanded a widow who **lives** there to feed you."
17.12 She answered, "By the **living Lord** your God I swear
18.10 By the **living Lord,** your God, I swear that the king has
18.15 Elijah answered, "By the **living Lord,** whom I serve, I
22.14 But Micaiah answered, "By the **living Lord** I promise
2 Kgs 2. 2 by my loyalty to the **living Lord** and to you that I
2. 3 A group of prophets who **lived** there went to Elisha and
2. 4 by my loyalty to the **living Lord** and to you that I
2. 5 A group of prophets who **lived** there went to Elisha and
2. 6 by my loyalty to the **living Lord** and to you that I
3.14 Elisha answered, "By the **living Lord,** whom I serve, I
4. 7 enough money left over for you and your sons to **live** on."
4. 8 One day Elisha went to Shunem, where a rich woman **lived.**
4.30 by my loyalty to the **living Lord** and to you that I
5. 3 that my master could go to the prophet who **lives** in Samaria!
5.16 Elisha answered, "By the **living Lord,** whom I serve, I
5.20 By the **living Lord,** I will run after him and get something
5.24 reached the hill where Elisha **lived,** Gehazi took the two
6. 1 complained to him, "The place where we **live** is too small!
6. 2 down some trees, so that we can build a place to **live."**
6.10 Israel warned the men who **lived** in that place, and they were
8. 1 had told the woman who **lived** in Shunem, whose son he had
8. 1 should leave with her family and go and **live** somewhere else.
8. 2 with her family to **live** in Philistia for the seven years.
10. 1 descendants of King Ahab **living** in the city of Samaria.
10.11 relatives of Ahab **living** in Jezreel, and all his officers,
10.33 where the tribes of Gad, Reuben, and East Manasseh **lived.**
11.12 The people clapped their hands and shouted, "Long **live** the king!"
13. 5 from the Syrians, and so the Israelites **lived** in peace, as
14.17 King Amaziah of Judah **lived** fifteen years after the
15. 5 He **lived** in a house on his own, relieved of all duties,
16. 6 city of Elath, and drove out the Judaeans who **lived** there.
16. 6 The Edomites settled in Elath, and still **live** there.)
17.23 Israel were taken into exile to Assyria, where they still **live.**
17.24 They took possession of these cities and **lived** there.
17.27 make him go back and **live** there, in order to teach the
17.28 deported from Samaria went and **lived** in Bethel, where he
17.29 different group made idols in the cities they were **living** in:
18.32 If you do what he commands, you will not die, but **live.**
19. 4 emperor has sent his chief official to insult the **living God.**
19.12 the people of Betheden who **lived** in Telassar, and none of
19.16 that Sennacherib is saying to insult you, the **living God.**
19.26 The people who **lived** there were powerless;
20. 6 I will let you **live** fifteen years longer.
22.14 Huldah, a prophet who **lived** in the newer part of Jerusalem.
23. 7 He destroyed the **living-quarters** in the Temple
23.11 from the **living-quarters** of Nathan Melech, a high official.)
25.30 for as long as he **lived,** he was given a regular allowance
1 Chr 2.23 All the people who **lived** there were descendants of Machir,
2.53 and of the following clans that **lived** in Kiriath Jearim:
2.55 in writing and copying documents **lived** in the town of Jabez:
4. 2 Ahumai and Lahad, the ancestors of the people who **lived** in Zorah.
4.12 The descendants of these men **lived** in Recah.
4.19 the clan of Garm, which **lived** in the town of Keilah, and
4.19 the clan of Maacath, which **lived** in the town of Eshtemoa.
4.21 clan of linen-weavers, who **lived** in the town of Beth Ashbea;
4.22 Jokim and the people who **lived** in the town of Cozeba;
4.23 service of the king and **lived** in the towns of Netaim and
4.28 the descendants of Simeon **lived** in the following towns:
4.32 They also **lived** in five other places:
4.33 kept of their families and of the places where they **lived.**
4.40 The people who had **lived** there before were Hamites.
4.41 destroyed the tents and huts of the people who **lived** there.
4.43 surviving Amalekites, and they have **lived** there ever since.
5. 8 This clan **lived** in Aroer and in the territory from there
5.11 The tribe of Gad **lived** to the north of Reuben in the
5.16 They **lived** in the territory of Bashan and Gilead, in the
5.22 And they went on **living** in that territory until the exile.
6.60 a total of thirteen towns for all their families to **live** in.
1 Chr 6.64 towns for the Levites to **live** in, together with the pasture
7.29 places where the descendants of Joseph son of Jacob **lived.**
8. 6 were heads of families that **lived** in Geba,
8. 6 but which were forced out and went to **live** in Manahath.
8. 8 Later, when he **lived** in the country of Moab, he married
8.13 and drove out the people who **lived** in the city of Gath.
8.28 and their principal descendants who **lived** in Jerusalem.
8.32 descendants **lived** in Jerusalem near other families of their clan.
9. 3 Benjamin, Ephraim, and Manasseh went to **live** in Jerusalem.
9. 4 690 families of the tribe of Judah who **lived** in Jerusalem.
9. 7 following members of the tribe of Benjamin **lived** in Jerusalem:
9. 9 There were 956 families of this tribe **living** there.
9.10 The following priests **lived** in Jerusalem:
9.14 The following Levites **lived** in Jerusalem:
9.14 and grandson of Elkanah, who **lived** in the territory that
9.17 The following temple guards **lived** in Jerusalem:
9.22 They were registered according to the villages where they **lived.**
9.25 assisted by their relatives, who **lived** in the villages and
9.27 They **lived** near the Temple, because it was their duty to
9.33 The heads of these families **lived** in some of the temple
9.34 They were the leaders who **lived** in Jerusalem.
9.38 descendants **lived** in Jerusalem near other families of their clan.
10. 7 When the Israelites who **lived** in the Valley of Jezreel
11. 4 original inhabitants of the land, were still **living** there.
11. 7 Because David went to **live** in the fortress, it came to be
12. 1 David was **living** in Ziklag, where he had gone to escape
12.15 river, scattering the people who **lived** in the valleys both
17. 1 King David was now **living** in his palace.
17. 1 to him, "Here I am **living** in a house built of cedar,
17. 4 not the one to build a temple for me to **live** in.
17. 5 Israel from Egypt until now, I have never **lived** in a temple;
17. 5 I have always **lived** in tents and moved from place to place.
17. 9 where they will **live** without being oppressed any more.
22. 2 orders for all the foreigners **living** in the land of Israel
22.18 the people who used to **live** in this land, and they are
23.25 his people, and he himself will **live** in Jerusalem for ever.
26.31 to this family were found **living** at Jazer in the territory
2 Chr 2.17 census of all the foreigners **living** in the land of Israel,
6. 1 "Lord, you have chosen to **live** in clouds and darkness.
6. 2 temple for you, a place for you to **live** in for ever."
6.14 your love when they **live** in wholehearted obedience to you.
6.18 can you, O God, really **live** on earth among men and women?
6.31 you all the time they **live** in the land which you gave
6.32 "When a foreigner who **lives** in a distant land hears
6.33 In heaven, where you **live,** hear him and do what he asks
8.11 He said, "She must not **live** in the palace of King David
9. 4 served at his table, the **living-quarters** for his officials,
10.17 only of the people who **lived** in the territory of Judah.
11.17 Rehoboam son of Solomon and **lived** as they had under the rule
15. 3 For a long time Israel **lived** without the true God, without
15. 9 Manasseh, and Simeon, and were **living** in his kingdom,
18.13 But Micaiah answered, "By the **living Lord,** I will say
19. 4 Even though King Jehoshaphat **lived** in Jerusalem, he
20. 7 out the people who were **living** here and gave the land to
20. 8 They have **lived** here and have built a temple to honour you,
21.16 Some Philistines and Arabs **lived** near where some
23.11 Joash, and everyone shouted, "Long **live** the king!"
26. 5 adviser, was **living,** he served the Lord faithfully,
26. 7 Philistines, the Arabs **living** at Gurbaal, and the Meunites.
26.21 enter the Temple again, he **lived** in his own house, relieved
28. 9 Oded, a prophet of the Lord, **lived** in the city of Samaria.
31. 6 All the people who **lived** in the cities of Judah brought
31.15 the other cities where priests **lived,** he was faithfully
31.19 priests who **lived** in the cities assigned to Aaron's descendants,
32.22 He let the people **live** in peace with all the neighbouring countries.
34.22 Huldah, a prophet who **lived** in the newer part of Jerusalem.
34.33 and as long as he **lived,** he required the people to serve
Ezra 2. 1 Their families had been **living** in exile in Babylonia ever
2.21 whose ancestors had **lived** in the following towns also returned:
2.70 Israelites settled in the towns where their ancestors had **lived.**
3. 3 of the people who were **living** in the land, they rebuilt the
4. 2 Esarhaddon, emperor of Assyria, sent us here to **live."**
4. 4 the people who had been **living** in the land tried to
4. 6 the enemies of the people **living** in Judah and Jerusalem
4.17 and to their associates who **live** in Samaria and in the rest
5. 1 God of Israel to the Jews who **lived** in Judah and Jerusalem.
6.21 the other people who were **living** in the land and who had
7.25 people in West Euphrates who **live** by the Law of your God.
9. 8 escape from slavery and **live** in safety in this holy place.
9. 9 permit us to go on **living** and to rebuild your Temple, which
9.11 land because the people who **lived** in it filled it from one
10. 6 Temple into the **living-quarters** of Jehohanan son of Eliashib,
10. 9 ninth month, all the men **living** in the territory of Judah
10.11 Separate yourselves from the foreigners **living** in our land
Neh 1. 3 that the foreigners who **lived** near by looked down on them.
2. 3 I was startled [3] and answered, "May Your Majesty **live** for ever!
2. 8 the city walls, and for the house I was to **live** in.
3.25 of the city called Ophel, where the temple workmen **lived.)**
4.12 after time Jews who were **living** among our enemies came to
7. 3 from among the people who **lived** in Jerusalem and to assign
7. 4 but not many people were **living** in it, and not many houses
7. 6 Their families had been **living** in exile in Babylonia ever
7.26 whose ancestors had **lived** in the following towns also returned:
8.14 the people of Israel to **live** in temporary shelters during
8.17 come back from captivity built shelters and **lived** in them.
9. 8 Girgashites, to be a land where his descendants would **live.**
9.23 and let them conquer and **live** in the land that you had
9.24 you overcame the people **living** there.
9.35 ruled your people when they **lived** in the broad, fertile land
10.28 separated themselves from the foreigners **living** in our land,
10.29 break it, that we will **live** according to God's Law, which

Neh 10.30 We will not intermarry with the foreigners **living** in our land.
11. 1 every ten to go and **live** in the holy city of Jerusalem,
11. 1 while the rest were to **live** in the other cities and towns.
11. 2 people praised anyone else who volunteered to **live** in Jerusalem.
11. 3 the descendants of Solomon's servants **lived** on their own
11. 3 citizens of the province of Judah who **lived** in Jerusalem:
11. 6 descendants of Perez, 468 outstanding men **lived** in Jerusalem.
11. 8 In all, 928 Benjaminites **lived** in Jerusalem.
11.18 In all, 284 Levites **lived** in the holy city of Jerusalem.
11.20 the remaining priests and Levites **lived** on their own
11.21 The temple workmen **lived** in the part of Jerusalem called
11.22 supervisor of the Levites who **lived** in Jerusalem was Uzzi,
11.25 Many of the people **lived** in towns near their farms.
11.25 of the tribe of Judah **lived** in Kiriath Arba, Dibon, and
11.26 They also **lived** in the cities of Jeshua, Moladah, Bethpelet,
11.28 They **lived** in the city of Ziklag, in Meconah and its villages,
11.30 They **lived** in Lachish and on the farms near by, and in
11.30 say, the people of Judah **lived** in the territory between
11.31 of the tribe of Benjamin **lived** in Geba, Michmash, Ai, Bethel
11.36 groups of Levites that had **lived** in the territory of Judah
11.36 were assigned to **live** with the people of Benjamin.
12.26 These people **lived** during the time of Joiakim, the son
12.27 in from wherever they were **living**, so that they could join
13.10 the people had not been giving them enough to **live** on.
13.16 the city of Tyre were **living** in Jerusalem, and they brought
Esth 2. 5 There in Susa **lived** a Jew named Mordecai son of Jair;
7. 3 wish is that I may **live** and that my people may live.
9.19 This is why Jews who **live** in small towns observe the
Job 1. 1 was a man named Job, **living** in the land of Uz, who
3.20 Why let men go on **living** in misery?
5.24 Then you will **live** at peace in your tent;
5.26 ripens till harvest time, you will **live** to a ripe old age.
6.11 What strength have I got to keep on **living?**
6.11 Why go on **living** when I have no hope?
7. 3 Month after month I have nothing to **live** for;
7.15 I would rather be strangled than **live** in this miserable body.
7.16 I am tired of **living.**
9.21 I am sick of **living.**
10. 1 I am tired of **living.**
11.18 You will **live** secure and full of hope;
12. 6 But thieves and godless men **live** in peace, though their
14. 5 is decided beforehand— the number of months he will **live.**
15.20 oppresses others will be in torment as long as he **lives.**
16.12 I was **living** in peace, but God took me by the throat
18.14 from the tent where he **lived** secure, and is dragged off to
18.15 Now anyone may **live** in his tent— after sulphur is
18.18 of the land of the **living,** driven from light into darkness.
20. 9 He will disappear from the place where he used to **live;**
20.17 He will not **live** to see rivers of olive-oil or streams
21. 7 does God let evil men **live,** let them grow old and prosper?
21. 8 and grandchildren, and **live** to watch them all grow up.
21. 9 they never have to **live** in terror.
21.13 They **live** out their lives in peace and quietly die
21.25 they **live** and die with bitter hearts.
22.12 Doesn't God **live** in the highest heavens and look down on
24.19 drought, so a sinner vanishes from the land of the **living.**
24.23 God may let him **live** secure, but keeps an eye on him
27. 1 I swear by the **living** Almighty God, who refuses me
28. 4 Far from where anyone **lives** Or human feet ever travel, Men
28.21 No **living creature** can see it, Not even a bird in flight.
29.18 I always expected to **live** a long life and to die at
30. 6 They had to **live** in caves, in holes dug in the sides
31.16 never have I let widows **live** in despair [17] or let orphans
33.30 he saves a person's life, and gives him the joy of **living.**
34.15 breath of life, [15] then everyone **living** would die and turn
36. 6 He does not let sinners **live** on, and he always treats the
36.11 God and serve him, they **live** out their lives in peace and
38.26 Who makes rain fall where no one **lives?**
39. 6 to be their home, and let them **live** on the salt plains.
42.16 Job **lived** a hundred and forty years after this, long
Ps 11. 7 those who do them will **live** in his presence.
14. 4 They **live** by robbing my people, and they never pray to me."
18.46 The Lord **lives!**
23. 6 and your house will be my home as long as I **live.**
24. 1 the earth and all who **live** on it are his.
25. 5 Teach me to **live** according to your truth, for you are my
26. 8 love the house where you **live,** O Lord, the place where your
27. 4 to **live** in the Lord's house all my life, to marvel there
27.13 I know that I will **live** to see the Lord's goodness in
33.14 where he rules, he looks down on all who **live** on earth.
37. 3 **live** in the land and be safe.
37.25 I have **lived** a long time, but I have never seen a
37.27 do good, and your descendants will always **live** in the land;
37.29 The righteous will possess the land and **live** in it for ever.
39. 4 "Lord, how long will I **live?**
39. 5 Indeed every **living** man is no more than a puff of wind,
42. 2 I thirst for you, the **living God;**
43. 3 Zion, your sacred hill, and to your Temple, where you **live.**
47. 4 the land where we **live,** the proud possession of his people,
49. 9 to keep him from the grave, to let him **live** for ever.
50.11 wild birds are mine and all **living things** in the fields.
52. 5 he will remove you from the world of the **living.**
53. 4 They **live** by robbing my people, and they never pray to me."
55. 7 I would fly far away and **live** in the wilderness.
56.13 presence of God, in the light that shines on the **living.**
58. 9 anger God will blow them away while they are still **living.**
61. 4 Let me **live** in your sanctuary all my life;
61. 6 let him **live** on and on!
63. 4 I will give you thanks as long as I **live;**
65. 4 whom you choose, whom you bring to **live** in your sanctuary.
68. 5 God, who **lives** in his sacred Temple, cares for orphans and

Ps 68. 6 the lonely a home to **live** in and leads prisoners out into
68. 6 freedom, but rebels will have to **live** in a desolate land.
68.16 look with scorn on the mountain on which God chose to **live?**
68.16 The Lord will **live** there for ever!
68.18 The Lord God will **live** there.
69.28 May their names be erased from the book of the **living;**
69.35 His people will **live** there and possess the land;
69.36 will inherit it, and those who love him will **live** there.
72.15 Long **live** the king!
74. 2 Remember Mount Zion, where once you **lived.**
75. 3 every **living creature** tremble and the earth itself be shaken, I
76. 2 he **lives** on Mount Zion.
78.60 his tent in Shiloh, the home where he had **lived** among us.
84. 2 With my whole being I sing for joy to the **living God.**
84. 4 How happy are those who **live** in your Temple, always
84.10 house of my God than **live** in the homes of the wicked.
89.15 you with songs, who **live** in the light of your kindness!
89.30 my law and do not **live** according to my commands, [31] if they
89.48 Who can **live** and never die?
94. 6 and orphans, and murder the strangers who **live** in our land.
98. 7 sing, earth, and all who **live** on you!
101. 2 I will **live** a pure life in my house, [3] and will never
101. 6 are faithful to God and will let them **live** in my palace.
101. 7 No liar will **live** in my palace;
102.24 O Lord, you **live** for ever;
102.28 Our children will **live** in safety, and under your
104.18 The wild goats **live** in the high mountains, and the
104.25 where countless creatures **live,** large and small alike.
104.33 as long as I **live** I will sing praises to my God.
107. 4 and could not find their way to a city to **live** in.
107. 7 them by a straight road to a city where they could **live.**
107.10 Some were **living** in gloom and darkness,
107.34 because of the wickedness of those who **lived** there.
107.36 people settle there, and they built a city to **live** in.
109.10 may they be driven from the ruins they **live** in!
113. 5 He **lives** in the heights above, [6] but he bends down to see
115.18 But we, the **living,** will give thanks to him now and for
116. 9 in the presence of the Lord in the world of the **living.**
118.17 instead, I will **live** and proclaim what the Lord has done.
119. 1 whose lives are faultless, who **live** according to the law of
119.17 your servant, so that I may **live** and obey your teachings.
119.45 I will **live** in perfect freedom, because I try to obey
119.77 on me, and I will **live** because I take pleasure in your
119.116 Give me strength, as you promised, and I shall **live;**
119.144 give me understanding, and I shall **live.**
120. 5 **Living** among you is as bad as living in Meshech
120. 6 I have **lived** too long with people who hate peace!
128. 1 Happy are those who obey the Lord, who **live** by his commands.
128. 6 May you **live** to see your grandchildren!
132.14 "This is where I will **live** for ever;
133. 1 how pleasant, for God's people to **live** together in harmony!
136.25 He gives food to every **living creature;**
139. 9 away beyond the east or **lived** in the farthest place in the
140.13 they will **live** in your presence.
145.15 All **living things** look hopefully to you, and you give
146. 2 I will praise him as long as I **live;**
146. 9 He protects the strangers who **live** in our land;
148. 1 Praise the Lord from heaven, you that **live** in the heights above.
150. 6 Praise the Lord, all **living creatures!**
Prov 1. 3 teach you how to **live** intelligently and how to be honest,
1.19 is what happens to anyone who **lives** by violence.
2.13 abandoned a righteous life to **live** in the darkness of sin,
2.20 follow the example of good men and **live** a righteous life.
2.21 Righteous men—men of integrity—will **live** in this land of ours.
3.29 he **lives** beside you, trusting you.
4. 4 Do as I tell you, and you will **live.**
4.10 what I am telling you, and you will **live** a long life.
4.11 I have taught you wisdom and the right way to **live.**
6. 6 Lazy people should learn a lesson from the way ants **live.**
6.23 their correction can teach you how to **live.**
7. 2 Do what I say, and you will **live.**
7. 8 the street near the corner where a certain woman **lived.**
9. 6 Leave the company of ignorant people, and **live.**
10.17 when they are corrected will **live,** but those who will not
10.27 Obey the Lord, and you will **live** longer.
11.19 determined to do right will **live,** but anyone who insists on
12. 7 no descendants, but the families of righteous men **live** on.
12.19 A lie has a short life, but truth **lives** on for ever.
15.27 Don't take bribes and you will **live** longer.
18.14 Your will to **live** can sustain you when you are sick, but
18.20 You will have to **live** with the consequences of everything you say.
19.10 Fools should not **live** in luxury, and slaves should not
19.16 Keep God's laws and you will **live** longer;
19.23 the Lord and you will **live** a long life, content and safe
21. 9 Better to **live** on the roof than share the house with a
21.19 Better to **live** out in the desert than with a nagging,
21.20 Wise people **live** in wealth and luxury, but stupid people
21.21 Be kind and honest and you will **live** a long life;
22. 6 a child how he should **live,** and he will remember it all
23.19 son, be wise and give serious thought to the way you **live.**
25.10 keep a secret, and you will never **live** down the shame.
25.24 Better to **live** on the roof than share the house with a
29.16 But the righteous will **live** to see the downfall of such men.
31.12 As long as she **lives,** she does him good and never harm.
Ecc 2. 7 livestock than anyone else who had ever **lived** in Jerusalem.
2. 9 anyone else who had ever **lived** in Jerusalem, and my wisdom
2.23 As long as you **live,** everything you do brings nothing
4. 8 Here is a man who **lives** alone.
4. 8 This is useless, too—and a miserable way to **live.**
4.15 about all the people who **live** in this world, and I realized
5.17 We have to **live** our lives in darkness and grief,

Ecc 6. 3 have a hundred children and **live** a long time,
6. 3 no matter how long he **lives,** if he does not get his
6. 6 never enjoys life, though he may **live** two thousand years.
7. 2 is a party, because the **living** should always remind
7.11 Everyone who **lives** ought to be wise;
7.15 may die while another man **lives** on, even though he is evil.
8.12 A sinner may commit a hundred crimes and still **live.**
9. 3 As long as people **live,** their minds are full of evil and
9. 4 who is alive in the world of the **living** has some hope;
9. 5 Yes, the **living** know they are going to die, but the dead
9. 9 love, as long as you **live** the useless life that God has
9.15 A man **lived** there who was poor, but so clever that he
11. 8 Be grateful for every year you **live.**
11. 8 No matter how long you **live,** remember that you will be dead
Song 4. 8 Mount Senir and Mount Hermon, where the lions and leopards **live.**
Is 5. 3 friend says, "You people who **live** in Jerusalem and Judah,
5. 8 nowhere for anyone else to **live,**
5. 8 and you alone will **live** in the land.
6. 5 lips is sinful, and I **live** among a people whose every word
8.18 has sent us as **living** messages to the people of Israel.
8.19 the spirits and consult the dead on behalf of the **living."**
9. 1 and even to Galilee itself, where the foreigners **live.**
9. 2 They **lived** in a land of shadows, but now light is shining
9. 9 people of Israel, everyone who **lives** in the city of Samaria,
10.13 Like a bull I have trampled on the people who **live** there.
10.24 says to his people who **live** in Zion, "Do not be afraid
11. 6 Wolves and sheep will **live** together in peace, and leopards
11.14 on the west and plunder the people who **live** to the east.
12. 6 Let everyone who **lives** in Zion shout and sing!
12. 6 Israel's holy God is great, and he **lives** among his people."
13.14 "The foreigners **living** in Babylon will run away
13.20 No one will ever **live** there again.
13.21 where desert animals **live** and where owls build their nests.
13.21 Ostriches will **live** there,
14. 1 He will let them **live** in their own land again,
14. 1 and foreigners will come and **live** there with them.
14.23 I will turn Babylon into a marsh, and owls will **live** there.
14.30 the poor of his people and will let them **live** in safety.
18. 3 Listen, everyone who **lives** on earth!
20. 6 time comes, the people who **live** along the coast of Philistia
22.14 "This evil will never be forgiven them as long as they **live.**
24.15 The people who **live** along the sea will praise the Lord, the
26. 5 destroyed the strong city they **lived** in, and sent its walls
26.14 Now they are dead and will not **live** again;
26.19 Those of our people who have died will **live** again!
27. 1 dragon, and to kill the monster that **lives** in the sea.
29.18 the blind, who have been **living** in darkness, will open their
30. 6 through dangerous country, where lions **live** and where there
30.19 You people who **live** in Jerusalem will not weep any more.
32. 9 You women who **live** an easy life, free from worries, listen
32.11 You have been **living** an easy life, free from worries;
33.20 What a safe place it will be to **live** in!
33.21 We will **live** beside broad rivers and streams, but hostile
33.24 No one who **lives** in our land will ever again complain of
34. 1 whole earth and everyone **living** on it come here and listen.
34.13 and walled towns, and jackals and owls will **live** in them.
34.16 the Lord's book of **living creatures** and read what it says.
34.17 They will **live** in the land age after age, and it will
35. 7 Where jackals used to **live,** marsh grass and reeds will grow.
37. 4 emperor has sent his chief official to insult the **living God.**
37.12 the people of Betheden who **lived** in Telassar, and none of
37.17 that Sennacherib is saying to insult you, the **living God.**
37.27 The people who **lived** there were powerless;
38. 5 I will let you **live** fifteen years longer.
38.10 to the world of the dead, Never to **live** out my life.
38.11 in this world of the **living**
38.11 I would never again see the Lord Or any **living** person.
38.16 Lord, I will **live** for you, for you alone;
38.16 Heal me and let me **live.**
38.19 It is the **living** who praise you, As I praise you now.
38.20 your praise, Sing praise in your Temple as long as we **live.**
40.22 the sky like a curtain, like a tent in which to **live.**
41.25 "I have chosen a man who **lives** in the east;
42. 5 he fashioned the earth and all that **lives** there;
42.10 Sing, distant lands and all who **live** there!
42.11 Let those who **live** in the city of Sela shout for joy
42.12 Let those who **live** in distant lands give praise and
42.24 We would not **live** as he wanted us to live or obey
44.26 tell Jerusalem that people will **live** there again, and the
45.12 one who made the earth and created mankind to **live** there.
45.18 it a desolate waste, but a place for people to **live** in.
49. 1 Listen to me, distant nations, you people who **live** far away!
49.18 surely as I am the **living God,** you will be proud of
49.19 will be too small for those who are coming to **live** there.
49.20 land is too small— we need more room to **live** in!'
51. 3 show compassion to Jerusalem, to all who **live** in her ruins.
51.13 Why should you **live** in constant fear of the fury of those
51.14 they will **live** a long life and have all the food they
52. 4 When you went to **live** in Egypt as foreigners, you did so
53.10 he will **live** a long life, and through him my purpose will
54. 2 Make the tent you **live** in larger;
57. 2 Those who **live** good lives find peace and rest in death.
57.13 who trust in me will **live** in the land and will worship
57.15 "I am the high and holy God, who **lives** for ever.
57.15 I **live** in a high and holy place,
57.15 but I also **live** with people who are humble
59.18 what they have done, even those who **live** in distant lands.
61. 7 You will **live** in your own land, And your wealth will be
63.15 us from heaven, where you **live** in your holiness and glory.
64. 5 what is right, those who remember how you want them to **live.**
65. 9 My chosen people, who serve me, will **live** there.
Is 65.20 in infancy, and all people will **live** out their life span.
65.20 Those who **live** to be a hundred will be considered young.
65.21 People will build houses and **live** in them
65.21 Like trees, my people will **live** long lives.
66. 1 build for me, what kind of place for me to **live** in?
Jer 1.14 the north on all who **live** in this land, [15]because I am
2. 6 land where no one **lives** and no one will even travel.
3.21 and pleading, because they have **lived** sinful lives and have
4. 7 will be left in ruins, and no one will **live** in them.
4.18 by the way you have **lived** and by the things you have
4.29 will be left empty, and no one will **live** in them again.
5.26 "Evil men **live** among my people;
6. 8 turn your city into a desert, a place where no one **lives."**
6.16 Walk on it, and you will **live** in peace."
7. 1 "Change the way you are **living** and the things you are doing,
7. 1 and I will let you go on **living** here.
7. 5 "Change the way you are **living** and stop doing the things
7. 7 will let you go on **living** here in the land which I
7.23 And I told them to **live** as I had commanded them, so
8. 1 of the other people who **lived** in Jerusalem, will be taken
8. 3 evil nation who survive, who **live** in the places where I have
8. 3 them, will prefer to die rather than to go on **living.**
9.11 make Jerusalem a pile of ruins, a place where jackals **live;**
9.11 Judah will become a desert, a place where no one **lives."**
10.10 the true God, you are the **living God** and the eternal king.
10.22 of Judah into a desert, a place where jackals **live."**
12.12 no one can **live** in peace.
12.16 will swear, 'As the Lord **lives'**—as they once taught my
16. 9 The people here will **live** to see this happen.
16.14 swear by me as the **living God** who brought the people of
16.15 swear by me as the **living God** who brought the people of
17.10 according to the way he **lives,** according to what he does."
17.20 and everyone who **lives** in Jerusalem and enters these gates,
18.11 Tell them to stop **living** sinful lives—to change their ways
21. 6 I will kill everyone **living** in this city;
22. 6 but I will make it a desolate place where no one **lives.**
22.24 surely as I am the **living God,** even if you were the
23. 6 will be safe, and the people of Israel will **live** in peace.
23. 7 swear by me as the **living God** who brought the people of
23. 8 swear by me as the **living God** who brought the people of
23. 8 Then they will **live** in their own land."
23.10 they **live** wicked lives and misuse their power.
23.22 up the evil lives they **live** and the wicked things they do.
23.36 the words of their God, the **living God,** the Lord Almighty.
25. 5 that you could go on **living** in the land that the Lord
26. 9 this city will be destroyed and no one will **live** in it?"
26.13 change the way you are **living** and the things you are doing,
27. 5 world, mankind, and all the animals that **live** on the earth;
27.11 stay on in its own land, to farm it and **live** there.
27.12 Serve him and his people, and you will **live.**
27.17 Submit to the king of Babylonia and you will **live!**
29. 8 deceived by the prophets who **live** among you or by any others
29.31 He will not **live** to see the good things that I am
30.10 You will come back home and **live** in peace;
30.19 The people who **live** there will sing praise;
31.23 sacred hill of Jerusalem, the holy place where he **lives.'**
31.24 People will **live** in Judah and in all its towns, and
32.23 not obey your commands or **live** according to your teaching;
32.37 them back to this place and let them **live** here in safety.
32.43 where neither people nor animals **live,** and that it will be
33.10 a desert, that it has no people or animals **living** in it.
33.10 no people or animals **live** there.
33.12 where no people or animals **live,** there will once again be
33.16 Judah and of Jerusalem will be rescued and will **live** in safety.
34.22 make the towns of Judah like a desert where no one **lives.**
35. 7 He commanded us always to **live** in tents,
35. 7 we might remain in this land where we **live** like strangers.
35. 9 build houses for homes—we **live** in tents—and we own no
35.11 That is why we are **living** in Jerusalem."
35.15 that you could go on **living** in the land that I gave
36. 9 was kept by all who **lived** in Jerusalem and by all who
38.16 secret, "I swear by the **living God,** the God who gave us
40. 5 may stay with him and **live** among the people, or you may
40. 6 with Gedaliah in Mizpah and **lived** among the people who were
40.10 fruit, and olive-oil, and **live** in the villages you occupy."
42.10 are willing to go on **living** in this land, then I will
42.13 disobey the Lord your God and refuse to **live** in this land.
42.13 'No, we will go and **live** in Egypt, where we won't face
42.13 are determined to go and **live** in Egypt, [16]then the war
42.17 are determined to go and **live** in Egypt will die either in
42.22 or disease in the land where you want to go and **live."**
43. 2 send you to tell us not to go and **live** in Egypt.
44. 1 me concerning all the Israelites **living** in Egypt, in the
44. 2 in ruins, and no one **lives** in them [3]because their people
44. 8 to other gods here in Egypt, where you have come to **live?**
44.10 have not honoured me or **lived** according to all the laws that
44.12 are determined to go and **live** in Egypt, I will see to
44.13 I will punish those who **live** in Egypt, just as I
44.14 left and have come to Egypt to **live** will escape or survive.
44.14 will return to Judah, where they long to **live** once again.
44.15 there, including the Israelites who **lived** in southern
44.22 day your land lies in ruins and no one **lives** in it.
44.24 Israel, was saying to the people of Judah **living** in Egypt:
44.26 a vow by saying, 'I swear by the **living** Sovereign Lord!'
46. 8 I will destroy cities and the people who **live** there.
46.18 I am the **living God.**
46.19 Memphis will be made a desert, a ruin where no one **lives.**
46.26 But later on, people will **live** in Egypt again, as they did
46.27 You will come back home and **live** in peace;
47. 2 and everything on it, cities and the people who **live** there.
47. 7 to attack Ashkelon and the people who **live** on the coast."

Jer 48. 9 will be left in ruins, and no one will **live** there again."
48.11 Lord said, "Moab has always **lived** secure and has never been
48.17 for that nation, you that **live** near by, all of you that
48.18 You that **live** in Dibon, come down from your place of
48.19 You that **live** in Aroer, stand by the road and wait;
48.28 "You people who **live** in Moab, leave your towns!
48.28 Go and **live** on the cliffs!
49.16 You **live** on the rocky cliffs, high on top of the mountain;
49.16 but even though you **live** as high up as an eagle, the
49.18 No one will ever **live** there again.
49.33 be made a desert for ever, a place where only jackals **live.**
49.33 No one will ever **live** there again.
50. 3 Men and animals will run away, and no one will **live** there."
50.13 Because of my anger no one will **live** in Babylon;
50.16 Every foreigner **living** there will be afraid of the attacking
50.39 Never again will people **live** there, not for all time to come.
50.40 No one will ever **live** there again.
51. 9 Foreigners **living** there said, 'We tried to help Babylonia,
51.29 out his plan to make Babylonia a desert, where no one **lives.**
51.37 That country will become a pile of ruins where wild animals **live.**
51.37 no one will **live** there, and all who see it will be
51.43 like a waterless desert, where no one **lives** or even travels.
51.62 that there would be no **living creature** in it, neither man
52. 1 daughter of the Jeremiah who **lived** in the city of Libnah.
52.34 for as long as he **lived,** he was given a regular allowance
Lam 1. 3 They **live** in other lands, with no place to call their own
3. 6 He has forced me to **live** in the stagnant darkness of death.
3.18 I have not much longer to **live;**
3.47 we **live** in danger and fear.
5. 2 foreigners are **living** in our homes.
Ezek 1. 1 priest, son of Buzi, was **living** with the Jewish exiles by
1. 5 saw what looked like four **living creatures** in human form,
1.10 Each **living creature** had four different faces:
2. 6 it will be like **living** among scorpions.
3.15 Chebar, where the exiles were **living,** and for seven days I
5.11 "Therefore, as I am the **living God**—this is the word of
6. 9 among the nations, [9] where they will **live** in exile.
6.14 not sparing any place where the Israelites **live.**
7. 7 The end is coming for you people who **live** in the land.
7.13 No merchant will **live** long enough to get back what he
10. 1 over the heads of the **living creatures** and above them was
11.15 he said, "the people who **live** in Jerusalem are talking
11.16 one who sent them to **live** in far-off nations and scattered
11.22 The **living creatures** began to fly, and the wheels went with them.
12. 2 "Mortal man," he said, "you are **living** among rebellious people.
12.10 ruling in Jerusalem and for all the people who **live** there.
12.19 the people of Jerusalem who are still **living** in their land:
12.19 stripped bare, because everyone who **lives** there is lawless.
13. 4 are as useless as foxes **living** among the ruins of a city.
13.19 to die, and you keep people alive who don't deserve to **live.**
14. 7 one of the foreigners who **live** in the Israelite community
14.14 Noah, Danel, and Job, were **living** there, their goodness
14.16 even if those three men **lived** there—as surely as I,
14.16 the Sovereign Lord, am the **living God**—they would not be able
14.18 even if those three men **lived** there—as surely as I,
14.18 the Sovereign Lord, am the **living God**—they would not be able
14.20 if Noah, Danel, and Job **lived** there—as surely as I,
14.20 the Sovereign Lord, am the **living God**—they would not be able
15. 6 the people who **live** in Jerusalem [7] and will punish them.
16.48 sure as I am the **living God,"** the Sovereign Lord says,
16.49 had plenty to eat and **lived** in peace and quiet, but they
17. 9 Will this vine **live** and grow?
17.10 Yes, it is planted, but will it **live** and grow?
17.16 surely as I am the **living God,"** says the Sovereign Lord,
17.19 surely as I am the **living God,** I will punish him for
17.23 Birds of every kind will **live** there and find shelter in its
18. 3 surely as I am the **living God,"** says the Sovereign Lord,
18. 9 He is righteous, and he will **live,"** says the Sovereign Lord.
18.13 Will he **live?**
18.17 because of his father's sins, but he will certainly **live.**
18.19 and followed them carefully, and so he will certainly **live.**
18.21 he will certainly **live.**
18.22 be forgiven, and he will **live,** because he did what is right.
18.23 "No, I would rather see him repent and **live.**
18.24 disgusting things that evil men do, will he go on **living?**
18.28 sinning, so he will certainly not die, but go on **living.**
18.32 "Turn away from your sins and **live."**
20. 3 surely as I am the **living God,** I will not let you
20. 9 people among whom they were **living** I had announced to Israel
20.31 the Sovereign Lord, am the **living God,** I will not let you
20.32 nations, like the people who **live** in other countries and
20.33 the Sovereign Lord, am the **living God,** I warn you that in
20.38 the lands where they are **living** now, but I will not let
23. 3 When they were young, **living** in Egypt, they lost their
25.16 I will destroy everyone left **living** there on the Philistine Plain.
26. 6 they will kill those who **live** in her towns on the mainland.
26. 8 Those who **live** in the towns on the mainland will be killed
26.15 being conquered, the people who **live** along the coast will be
26.17 ruled the seas And terrified all who **lived** on the coast.
26.19 make you as desolate as ruined cities where no one **lives.**
26.20 of the dead to join the people who **lived** in ancient times.
26.20 be inhabited and take your place in the land of the **living.**
27. 3 and does business with the people **living** on every seacoast.
27.35 "Everyone who **lives** along the coast is shocked at your fate.
28.13 You **lived** in Eden, the garden of God, and wore gems of
28.14 You **lived** on my holy mountain and walked among sparkling gems.
28.22 show how holy I am by punishing those who **live** in you.
28.25 The people of Israel will **live** in their own land, the land
28.26 They will **live** there in safety.
29.11 For forty years nothing will **live** there.
Ezek 29.12 They will flee to every country and **live** among other peoples."
29.14 and I will let them **live** in southern Egypt, their original home.
31.12 the nations that have been **living** in its shade will go away.
31.17 And all who **live** under its shadow will be scattered among
32.15 waste and destroy all who **live** there, they will know that I
32.23 Yet once they terrified the land of the **living.**
32.26 Yet once they terrified the **living.**
32.27 These heroes were once powerful enough to terrify the **living.**
32.32 king of Egypt terrorize the **living,** but he and all his army
33.10 How can we **live?'**
33.11 the Sovereign Lord, am the **living God,** I do not enjoy seeing
33.11 I would rather see him stop sinning and **live.**
33.15 follows the laws that give life, he will not die, but **live.**
33.16 has committed, and he will **live** because he has done what is
33.24 said, "the people who are **living** in the ruined cities of
33.27 surely as I am the **living God,**
33.27 the people who **live** in the ruined cities will be
33.27 Those **living** in the country will be eaten by wild animals.
34. 8 surely as I am the **living God,** you had better listen to
34.25 so that my sheep can **live** safely in the fields and sleep
34.26 "I will bless them and let them **live** round my sacred hill.
34.27 crops, and everyone will **live** in safety on his own land.
34.28 They will **live** in safety, and no one will terrify them.
35. 6 the Sovereign Lord, am the **living God**—death is your fate,
35. 9 for ever, and no one will **live** in your cities again.
35.11 the Sovereign Lord, am the **living God,** I will pay you back
36.10 You will **live** in the cities and rebuild everything that was
36.11 I will let you **live** there as you used to live, and
36.12 bring you, my people Israel, back to **live** again in the land.
36.17 said, "when the Israelites were **living** in their land,
36.17 they defiled it by the way they **lived** and acted.
36.19 them for the way they **lived** and acted, and I scattered them
36.28 Then you will **live** in the land I gave your ancestors.
36.33 sins, I will let you **live** in your cities again and let
37.14 them back to life, and let them **live** in their own land.
37.25 They will **live** on the land I gave to my servant Jacob,
37.25 I gave to my servant Jacob, the land where their ancestors **lived.**
37.25 They will **live** there for ever, and so will their children
37.27 I will **live** there with them;
38. 8 from many nations and have **lived** without fear of war.
38. 8 so long, but where all the people now **live** in safety.
38.11 helpless country where the people **live** in peace and security
38.12 and loot the people who **live** in cities that were once in
38.12 livestock and property and **live** at the crossroads of the world.
38.14 "Now while my people Israel **live** in security, you will set
39. 6 all the coasts where people **live** undisturbed, and everyone
39. 9 The people who **live** in the cities of Israel will go out
39.26 When they are once more **living** in safety in their own land,
39.27 people back from all the countries where their enemies **live.**
43. 7 I will **live** here among the people of Israel and rule over
43. 9 If they do, I will **live** among them for ever."
44. 9 even a foreigner who **lives** among the people of Israel."
45. 5 There will be towns there for them to **live** in.
45. 6 for a city where any of the people of Israel may **live.**
47.22 The foreigners who are **living** among you and who have had
47.23 share with the people of the tribe among whom he is **living.**
48.15 They may **live** there and use the land.
48.18 used as farm land by the people who **live** in the city.
48.19 Anyone who **lives** in the city, no matter which tribe he
Dan 2. 4 "May Your Majesty **live** for ever!
2.11 except the gods, and they do not **live** among human beings."
3. 9 "May Your Majesty **live** for ever!
4. 4 "I was **living** comfortably in my palace,
4.12 its branches, and every kind of **living being** ate its fruit.
4.15 this man, and let him **live** with the animals and the plants.
4.23 this man, and let him **live** there with the animals for seven
4.25 away from human society and will **live** with wild animals.
4.32 driven away from human society, **live** with wild animals, and
4.34 and gave honour and glory to the one who **lives** for ever.
5.10 She said, "May Your Majesty **live** for ever!
5.21 He **lived** with wild donkeys, ate grass like an ox, and slept
5.23 God who determines whether you **live** or die and who controls
6. 6 and said, "King Darius, may Your Majesty **live** for ever!
6.20 called out anxiously, "Daniel, servant of the **living God!**
6.21 Daniel answered, "May Your Majesty **live** for ever!
6.26 "He is a **living God,** and he will rule for ever.
7. 9 One who had been **living for ever** sat down on one of
7.12 but they were permitted to go on **living** for a limited time.
7.13 one who had been **living for ever** and was presented to him.
7.22 one who had been **living for ever** came and pronounced
9. 7 of all of us who **live** in Judaea and in Jerusalem and
9.10 when you told us to **live** according to the laws which you
12. 2 Many of those who have already died will **live** again:
Hos 1.10 say to them, "You are the children of the **living God!"**
2.18 and bows, and will let my people **live** in peace and safety.
3. 4 of Israel will have to **live** for a long time without kings
4. 1 to bring against the people who **live** in this land.
4. 3 land will dry up, and everything that **lives** on it will die.
4.15 or make promises there in the name of the **living Lord.**
6. 2 days he will revive us, and we will **live** in his presence.
10. 5 The people who **live** in the city of Samaria will be afraid
12. 9 Egypt, I will make you **live** in tents again, as you did
13.13 Israel has a chance to **live,** but is too foolish to take
14. 7 Once again they will **live** under my protection.
14. 9 are right, and righteous people **live** by following them, but
Joel 3.17 I **live** on Zion, my sacred hill.
3.20 for ever, and I the Lord, will **live** on Mount Zion."
Amos 3. 9 Announce to those who **live** in the palaces of Egypt and Ashdod:
5. 4 to the people of Israel, "Come to me, and you will **live.**
5. 6 Go to the Lord, and you will **live.**
5.11 And so you will not **live** in the fine stone houses you

Amos 5.14 what is right, not what is evil, so that you may **live.**
9. 5 all who **live** there mourn.
9.14 They will rebuild their ruined cities and **live** there;
Mic 1. 2 listen to this, all who **live** on earth!
1. 9 the gates of Jerusalem itself, where my people **live."**
1.11 Those who **live** in Zaanan dare not come out of their city.
1.13 You that **live** in Lachish, hitch the horses to the chariots.
4. 4 Everyone will **live** in peace among his own vineyards and fig-trees, and
4.10 will have to leave the city and **live** in the open country.
5. 4 His people will **live** in safety because people all over the
6. 8 love, and to **live** in humble fellowship with our God.
7. 9 we will **live** to see him save us.
7.13 a desert because of the wickedness of those who **live** on it.
7.14 Although they **live** apart in the wilderness, there is fertile
Nah 1.14 a grave for the Assyrians—they don't deserve to **live!"**
Hab 2. 4 righteous will **live** because they are faithful to God.' "
Zeph 1.11 you hear this, you that **live** in the lower part of the
1.13 They will never **live** in the houses they are building or
1.18 put an end—a sudden end—to everyone who **lives** on earth.
2. 5 You Philistines are doomed, you people who **live** along the coast.
2. 9 surely as I am the **living Lord,** the God of Israel, I
2.14 Owls will **live** among its ruins and hoot from the windows.
Hag 1. 4 people, why should you be **living** in well-built houses while
1. 6 And the working man cannot earn enough to **live** on.
Zech 1. 4 telling them not to **live** evil, sinful lives any longer.
2. 5 protect it and that he will **live** there in all his glory."
2.10 I am coming to **live** among you!"
2.11 He will **live** among you, and you will know that he has
6.15 Men who **live** far away will come and help to rebuild the
7. 7 when there were many people **living** not only in the towns
7.10 oppress widows, orphans, foreigners who **live** among you, or
7.12 the prophets who **lived** long ago, I became very angry.
7.14 Like a storm I swept them away to **live** in foreign countries.
7.14 land was left a desolate place, with no one **living** in it."
8. 3 I will return to Jerusalem, my holy city, and **live** there.
8. 8 bring them back from east and west to **live** in Jerusalem.
9. 6 People of mixed race will **live** in Ashdod.
12. 5 Almighty gives strength to his people who **live** in Jerusalem.'
12. 8 Lord will protect those who **live** in Jerusalem, and even the
14.11 The people will **live** there in safety, no longer threatened
Mal 2. 6 They **lived** in harmony with me;
3.12 happy, because your land will be a good place to **live** in.
Mt 4. 4 "The scripture says, 'Man cannot **live** on bread alone,
4.13 in Nazareth, but went to **live** in Capernaum, a town by Lake
4.16 The people who **live** in darkness will see a great light.
4.16 On those who **live** in the dark land of death the light
5.12 This is how the prophets who **lived** before you were persecuted.
6.27 Can any of you **live** a bit longer by worrying about it?
9.18 but come and place your hands on her, and she will **live."**
11. 8 People who dress like that **live** in palaces!
11.11 John the Baptist is greater than any man who has ever **lived.**
12.45 spirits even worse than itself, and they come and **live** there.
13.56 Aren't all his sisters **living** here?
15.22 A Canaanite woman who **lived** in that region came to him.
16.16 Peter answered, "You are the Messiah, the Son of the **living God."**
22.25 Now, there were seven brothers who used to **live** here.
22.32 He is the God of the **living,** not of the dead."
23.21 Temple, he is swearing by it and by God, who **lives** there;
23.29 and decorate the monuments of those who **lived** good lives;
23.30 that if you had **lived** during the time of your ancestors,
24.34 things will happen before the people now **living** have all died.
26.63 "In the name of the **living God** I now put you on
27.29 "Long **live** the King of the Jews!"
Mk 5. 3 man had an evil spirit in him [3] and **lived** among the tombs.
5.23 your hands on her, so that she will get well and **live!"**
6. 3 Aren't his sisters **living** here?"
9.50 friendship among yourselves, and **live** in peace with one another."
12.27 He is the God of the **living,** not of the dead.
12.44 in all she had—she gave all she had to **live** on."
13.30 things will happen before the people now **living** have all died.
15.18 "Long **live** the King of the Jews!"
16.10 the sacred and **ever-living** message of eternal salvation.
Lk 1. 6 They both **lived** good lives in God's sight and obeyed fully
1.79 heaven on all those who **live** in the dark shadow of death,
1.80 He **lived** in the desert until the day when he appeared
2.25 At that time there was a man named Simeon **living** in Jerusalem.
4. 4 "The scripture says, 'Man cannot **live** on bread alone.' "
4.26 but only to a widow **living** in Zarephath in the territory of
4.27 from a dreaded skin-disease who **lived** in Israel during the
7.25 who dress like that and **live** in luxury are found in palaces!
7.28 Jesus added, "John is greater than any man who has ever **lived.**
7.37 In that town was a woman who **lived** a sinful life.
7.39 he would know what kind of sinful life she **lives!"**
10. 6 If a peace-loving man **lives** there, let your greeting of
10.28 "do this and you will **live."**
11.26 spirits even worse than itself, and they come and **live** there.
12.25 Can any of you **live** a bit longer by worrying about it?
13. 4 they were worse than all the other people **living** in Jerusalem?
15.13 far away, where he wasted his money in reckless **living.**
16.19 most expensive clothes and **lived** in great luxury every day.
20.35 to rise from death and **live** in the age to come will
20.38 is the God of the **living,** not of the dead, for to
21. 4 she, poor as she is, gave all she had to **live** on."
21.32 will take place before the people now **living** have all died.
Jn 1.14 a human being and, full of grace and truth, **lived** among us.
1.38 They answered, "Where do you **live,** Rabbi?"
1.39 him and saw where he **lived,** and spent the rest of that
1.44 (Philip was from Bethsaida, the town where Andrew and Peter **lived.)**
4.18 men, and the man you **live** with now is not really your

Jn 4.50 Jesus said to him, "Go, your son will **live!"**
4.51 met him with the news, "Your boy is going to **live!"**
4.53 very hour when Jesus had told him, "Your son will **live."**
5.29 done good will rise and **live,** and those who have done evil
6.51 I am the **living** bread that came down from heaven.
6.51 If anyone eats this bread, he will **live** for ever.
6.51 is my flesh, which I give so that the world may **live."**
6.56 and drinks my blood lives in me, and I **live** in him.
6.57 The living Father sent me, and because of him I **live** also.
6.57 In the same way whoever eats me will **live** because of me.
6.58 The one who eats this bread will **live** for ever."
7.35 Greek cities where our people **live,** and teach the Greeks?
7.42 David and will be born in Bethlehem, the town where David **lived."**
11. 1 A man named Lazarus, who **lived** in Bethany, was ill.
11. 1 Bethany was the town where Mary and her sister Martha **lived.**
11.25 Whoever believes in me will **live,** even though he dies;
11.26 and whoever **lives** and believes in me will never die.
12.34 "Our Law tells us that the Messiah will **live** for ever.
14.19 and because I **live,** you also will live.
14.23 my Father and I will come to him and **live** with him.
19. 3 came to him and said, "Long **live** the King of the Jews!"
19.27 From that time the disciple took her to **live** in his home.
21.22 "If I want him to **live** until I come, what is that
21.23 "If I want him to **live** until I come, what is that
Acts 1.19 All the people **living** in Jerusalem heard about it, and
1.20 may no one **live** in it.'
2. 5 There were Jews **living** in Jerusalem, religious men who had come
2.14 and all of you who **live** in Jerusalem, listen to me
3.21 God announced through his holy prophets who **lived** long ago.
7. 2 ancestor Abraham had gone to **live** in Haran, the God of glory
7. 4 And so he left his country and went to **live** in Haran.
7. 4 died, God made him move to this land where you now **live.**
7. 6 'Your descendants will **live** in a foreign country,
7.29 fled from Egypt and went to **live** in the land of Midian.
7.38 Sinai, and he received God's **living** messages to pass on to us.
7.48 the Most High God does not **live** in houses built by men;
7.49 Where is the place for me to **live** in?
8. 9 A man named Simon **lived** there, who for some time had
9.22 that the Jews who **lived** in Damascus could not answer him.
9.31 and grew in numbers, as it **lived** in reverence for the Lord.
9.32 occasion he went to visit God's people who **lived** in Lydda.
9.35 All the people **living** in Lydda and Sharon saw him, and
10. 6 of a tanner of leather named Simon, who **lives** by the sea."
10.32 home of Simon the tanner of leather, who **lives** by the sea.'
10.42 one whom God has appointed judge of the **living** and the dead.
11.18 given to the Gentiles also the opportunity to repent and **live!"**
11.29 he could to help their fellow-believers who **lived** in Judaea.
13.17 nation during the time they **lived** as foreigners in Egypt.
13.27 For the people who **live** in Jerusalem and their leaders
13.43 and encouraged them to keep on **living** in the grace of God.
14.15 these worthless things to the **living God,** who made heaven,
15.23 brothers of Gentile birth who **live** in Antioch, Syria, and Cilicia.
16. 1 to Derbe and Lystra, where a Christian named Timothy **lived.**
16. 3 because all the Jews who **lived** in those places knew that
17.21 Athens and the foreigners who **lived** there liked to spend all
17.24 Lord of heaven and earth and does not **live** in man-made temples.
17.26 races of mankind and made them **live** throughout the whole earth.
17.26 times and the limits of the places where they would **live.**
17.28 as someone has said, 'In him we **live** and move and exist.'
18. 7 left them and went to **live** in the house of a Gentile
19.10 that all the people who **lived** in the province of Asia, both
19.17 All the Jews and Gentiles who **lived** in Ephesus heard about this;
21.21 teaching all the Jews who **live** in Gentile countries to
21.24 you, but that you yourself **live** in accordance with the Law
22.12 Law and was highly respected by all the Jews **living** there.
22.22 He's not fit to **live!"**
23. 1 way in which I have **lived** before God to this very day."
25.24 They scream that he should not **live** any longer.
26. 4 the Jews know how I have **lived** ever since I was young.
26. 5 the very first I have **lived** as a member of the strictest
28. 4 Fate will not let him **live,** even though he escaped from the
28.16 Rome, Paul was allowed to **live** by himself with a soldier
28.30 For two years Paul **lived** in a place he rented for himself,
Rom 1.15 to preach the Good News to you also who **live** in Rome.
1.17 "The person who is put right with God through faith shall **live."**
1.32 God's law says that people who **live** in this way deserve death.
3.19 Law applies to those who **live** under the Law, in order to
4.12 addition to being circumcised, also **live** the same life of faith
4.12 that our father Abraham **lived** before he was circumcised.
5. 2 into this experience of God's grace, in which we now **live.**
6. 1 Should we continue to **live** in sin so that God's grace will
6. 2 died to sin—how then can we go on **living** in it?
6. 4 power of the Father, so also we might **live** a new life.
6. 8 with Christ, we believe that we will also **live** with him.
6.10 and now he **lives** his life in fellowship with God.
6.11 sin is concerned, but **living** in fellowship with God
6.14 for you do not **live** under law but under God's grace.
7. 1 The law rules over people only as long as they **live.**
7. 2 bound by the law to her husband as long as he **lives;**
7. 3 So then, if she **lives** with another man while her husband
7. 5 For when we **lived** according to our human nature, the
7.17 rather it is the sin that **lives** in me.
7.18 know that good does not **live** in me—that is, in my
7.20 instead, it is the sin that **lives** in me.
8. 1 now for those who **live** in union with Christ Jesus.
8. 4 fully satisfied in us who **live** according to the Spirit,
8. 5 Those who **live** as their human nature tells them to, have
8. 5 Those who **live** as the Spirit tells them to, have their minds
8. 9 But you do not **live** as your human nature tells you to;

Rom 8. 9 instead, you **live** as the Spirit tells you to—if, in fact,
8. 9 Spirit tells you to—if, in fact, God's Spirit **lives** in you.
8.10 But if Christ **lives** in you, the Spirit is life for you
8.11 who raised Jesus from death, **lives** in you, then he who
8.12 but it is not to **live** as our human nature wants us
8.13 For if you **live** according to your human nature, you are
8.13 Spirit you put to death your sinful actions, you will **live.**
9.26 there they will be called the sons of the **living God."**
10. 5 "Whoever obeys the commands of the Law will **live."**
12. 1 Offer yourselves as a **living** sacrifice to God,
12.18 Do everything possible on your part to **live** in peace with everybody.
13.13 ourselves properly, as people who **live** in the light of day—
14. 7 None of us **lives** for himself only, none of us dies for
14. 8 If we **live,** it is for the Lord that we live,
14. 8 So whether we **live** or die, we belong to the Lord.
14. 9 order to be the Lord of the **living** and of the dead.
14.11 surely as I am the **living God,** says the Lord, everyone will
1 Cor 3. 3 because you still live as the people of this world **live.**
3. 3 prove that you belong to this world, **living** by its standards?
3.16 you are God's temple and that God's Spirit **lives** in you!
6.19 of the Holy Spirit, who **lives** in you and who was given
7. 8 be better for you to continue to **live** alone as I do.
7.12 she agrees to go on **living** with him, he must not divorce
7.13 he agrees to go on **living** with her, she must not divorce
7.15 God has called you to **live** in peace.
7.17 Each one should go on **living** according to the Lord's
7.29 on married men should **live** as though they were not married;
7.39 A married woman is not free as long as her husband **lives;**
8. 6 who is the Creator of all things and for whom we **live;**
8. 6 through whom all things were created and through whom we **live.**
9.20 working with the Jews, I **live** like a Jew in order to
9.20 the Law of Moses, I **live** as though I were when working
9.21 working with Gentiles, I **live** like a Gentile, outside the Jewish
10.11 For we **live** at a time when the end is about to
10.32 **Live** in such a way as to cause no trouble either to
15.39 And the flesh of **living beings** is not all the same kind
15.45 "The first man, Adam, was created a **living being";**
2 Cor 3. 3 with the Spirit of the **living God,** and not on stone tablets
4. 2 full light of truth we **live** in God's sight and try to
5. 1 that when this tent we **live** in—our body here on earth
5. 1 in heaven for us to **live** in, a home he himself has
5. 4 While we **live** in this earthly tent, we groan with a
5.15 so that those who **live** should no longer live for themselves,
6. 9 as though we were dead, but, as you see, we **live** on.
6.14 How can light and darkness **live** together?
6.16 For we are the temple of the **living God!**
6.16 "I will make my home with my people and **live** among them;
7. 1 and let us be completely holy by **living** in awe of God.
7. 3 to us that we are always together, whether we **live** or die.
10. 3 It is true that we **live** in the world, but we do
13. 4 death on the cross, it is by God's power that he **lives.**
13. 5 judge yourselves, to find out whether you are **living** in faith.
13.11 **live** in peace.
Gal 1.13 told how I used to **live** when I was devoted to the
2.14 Jew, yet you have been **living** like a Gentile, not like a
2.14 How, then, can you try to force Gentiles to **live** like Jews?"
2.19 by the Law itself—in order that I might **live** for God.
2.20 is no longer I who **live,**
2.20 but it is Christ who **lives** in me.
2.20 This life that I **live** now,
2.20 I **live** by faith in the Son
3.10 Those who depend on obeying the Law **live** under a curse.
3.11 person who is put right with God through faith shall **live."**
3.12 scripture says, "Whoever does everything the Law requires will **live."**
4. 4 of a human mother and **lived** under the Jewish Law, [5] to
Eph 2. 3 were like them and **lived** according to our natural desires,
2.12 to his people, and you **lived** in this world without hope and
2.22 the others into a place where God **lives** through his Spirit.
4. 1 **live** a life that measures up to the standard God set when
4.17 do not continue to **live** like the heathen, whose thoughts
4.22 old self, which made you **live** as you used to—the old
5. 8 So you must **live** like people who belong to the light, [9] for
5.15 So be careful how you **live.**
5.15 Don't **live** like ignorant people, but like wise people.
6. 3 with you, and you may **live** a long time in the land."
Phil 1.20 being I shall bring honour to Christ, whether I **live** or die.
1.22 But if by continuing to **live** I can do more worthwhile work,
2.15 as God's perfect children, who **live** in a world of corrupt
4. 3 whose names are in God's book of the **living.**
Col 1.10 you will be able to **live** as the Lord wants and will
2. 6 have accepted Christ Jesus as Lord, **live** in union with him.
2. 9 content of divine nature **lives** in Christ, in his humanity,
2.20 Why, then, do you **live** as though you belonged to this world?
3. 7 time you yourselves used to **live** according to such desires,
3.16 Christ's message in all its richness must **live** in your hearts.
1 Thes 1. 5 You know how we **lived** when we were with you;
1. 9 to serve the true and **living God** [10] and to wait for his
2.12 we kept urging you to **live** the kind of life that pleases
3. 8 us, [8] because now we really **live** if you stand firm in your
4. 1 learnt from us how you should **live** in order to please God.
4. 1 This is, of course, how you have been **living.**
4. 4 men should know how to **live** with his wife in a holy
4. 7 God did not call us to **live** in immorality, but in holiness.
4.11 Make it your aim to **live** a quiet life, to mind your
4.17 then we who are **living** at that time will be gathered up
5.10 in order that we might **live** together with him, whether we
2 Thes 1.11 make you worthy of the life he has called you to **live.**
3. 6 from all brothers who are **living** a lazy life and who do
3.11 some people among you who **live** lazy lives and who do nothing
1 Tim 2. 2 in authority, that we may **live** a quiet and peaceful life
3.15 is the church of the **living God,** the pillar and support of
4.10 placed our hope in the **living God,** who is the Saviour of
5. 6 herself to pleasure has already died, even though she **lives.**
6.16 he **lives** in the light that no one can approach.
2 Tim 1.14 of the Holy Spirit, who **lives** in us, keep the good things
2.11 "If we have died with him, we shall also **live** with him.
3.12 Everyone who wants to **live** a godly life in union with
3.16 giving instruction for right **living,** [17] so that the person
4. 1 Jesus, who will judge the **living** and the dead, and because
Tit 2. 3 older women to behave as women should who **live** a holy life.
2.12 us to give up ungodly **living** and worldly passions,
2.12 and to **live** self-controlled, upright, and godly lives
3.14 they should not **live** useless lives.
Heb 3.12 and unbelieving that he will turn away from the **living God.**
7. 8 tenth was collected by one who **lives,** as the scripture says.
7.24 But Jesus **lives** on for ever, and his work as priest does
7.25 God through him, because he **lives for ever** to plead with God
9.14 from useless rituals, so that we may serve the **living God.**
10.20 us a new way, a **living** way, through the curtain—that is,
10.31 terrifying thing to fall into the hands of the **living God!**
10.38 My righteous people, however, will believe and **live;**
11. 9 By faith he **lived** as a foreigner in the country that God
11. 9 He **lived** in tents, as did Isaac and Jacob, who received the
11.38 in the deserts and hills, **living** in caves and holes in the
12. 9 then, should we submit to our spiritual Father and **live!**
12.14 with everyone, and try to **live** a holy life, because no one
12.22 to the city of the **living God,** the heavenly Jerusalem,
13. 7 Think back on how they **lived** and died, and imitate their faith.
Jas 4.15 the Lord is willing, we will **live** and do this or that."
1 Pet 1. 1 To God's chosen people who **live** as refugees scattered
1. 3 This fills us with a **living** hope, [4] and so we look forward
1.23 For through the **living** and eternal word of God you have
2. 4 Come to the Lord, the **living** stone rejected by man
2. 5 Come as **living** stones, and let yourselves be used in building
2.16 **Live** as free people;
2.16 your freedom to cover up any evil, but **live** as God's slaves.
2.24 so that we might die to sin and **live** for righteousness.
3. 7 same way you husbands must **live** with your wives with the
4. 2 now on, then, you must **live** the rest of your earthly lives
4. 4 the same wild and reckless **living,** and so they insult you.
4. 5 to God, who is ready to judge the **living** and the dead.
4. 6 in their spiritual existence they may **live** as God lives.
2 Pet 1. 3 us everything we need to **live** a truly religious life through
2. 8 That good man **lived** among them, and day after day he
2.18 beginning to escape from among people who **live** in error.
1 Jn 1. 6 yet at the same time **live** in the darkness, we are lying
1. 7 But if we **live** in the light—just as he is in
2. 6 in union with God should **live** just as Jesus Christ did.
2.10 Whoever loves his brother **lives** in the light, and so
2.14 the word of God **lives** in you, and you have defeated the
2.17 but he who does the will of God **lives for ever.**
2.24 message, then you will always **live** in union with the Son and
3. 6 So everyone who **lives** in union with Christ does not continue
3.24 Whoever obeys God's commands **lives** in union with God
3.24 and God **lives** in union with him.
3.24 has given us we know that God **lives** in union with us.
4.12 we love one another, God **lives** in union with us, and his
4.13 We are sure that we **live** in union with God
4.13 and that he **lives** in union with us,
4.15 the Son of God, he **lives** in union with God
4.15 and God **lives** in union with him.
4.16 God is love, and whoever **lives** in love
4.16 lives in union with God and God **lives** in union with him.
5.20 We **live** in union with the true God—in union with his
2 Jn 4 that some of your children **live** in the truth, just as the
6 of means that we must **live** in obedience to God's commands.
6 from the beginning, is that you must all **live** in love.
3 Jn 3 are to the truth—just as you always **live** in the truth.
4 me happier than to hear that my children **live** in the truth.
Jude 1 been called by God, who **live** in the love of God the
Rev 1.18 I am the **living** one!
2. 8 who is the first and the last, who died and **lived** again.
2.13 I know where you **live,** there where Satan has his throne.
2.13 Antipas, my faithful witness, was killed there where Satan **lives.**
3. 5 I will not remove their names from the book of the **living.**
4. 6 of its sides, were four **living creatures** covered with eyes
4. 8 Each one of the four **living creatures** had six wings, and
4. 9 The four **living creatures** sing songs of glory and honour
4. 9 one who sits on the throne, who **lives for ever and ever.**
4.10 on the throne, and worship him who **lives for ever and ever.**
5. 6 surrounded by the four **living creatures** and the elders.
5. 8 he did so, the four **living creatures** and the twenty-four elders
5.11 round the throne, the four **living creatures,** and the elders,
5.13 and in the sea—all **living beings** in the universe—and they
5.14 The four **living creatures** answered, "Amen!"
6. 1 heard one of the four **living creatures** say in a voice that
6. 3 and I heard the second **living creature** say, "Come!"
6. 5 and I heard the third **living creature** say, "Come!"
6. 6 coming from among the four **living creatures,** which said,
6. 7 and I heard the fourth **living creature** say, "Come!"
7. 2 coming up from the east with the seal of the **living God.**
7.11 stood round the throne, the elders, and the four **living creatures.**
8. 9 blood, [9] a third of the **living creatures** in the sea died,
8.13 will be for all who **live** on earth when the sound comes
10. 6 the name of God, who **lives for ever and ever,** who created
12.12 And so be glad, you heavens, and all you that **live** there!
13. 6 the place where he **lives,**
13. 6 and all those who **live** in heaven.
13. 8 All people **living** on earth will worship it, except those
13. 8 in the book of the **living** which belongs to the Lamb that

Rev 13.12 the earth and all who **live** on it to worship the first
13.14 it deceived all the people **living** on earth by means of the
13.14 the beast that had been wounded by the sword and yet **lived.**
14. 3 people stood before the throne, the four **living creatures,**
15. 7 Then one of the four **living creatures** gave the seven
15. 7 full of the anger of God, who **lives for ever and ever.**
16. 3 a dead person, and every **living creature** in the sea died.
17. 8 That beast was once alive, but **lives** no longer;
17. 8 The people **living** on earth whose names have not been written
17. 8 in the book of the **living,** will all be amazed as they
17. 8 now it no longer **lives,** but it will reappear.
17.11 that was once alive, but **lives** no longer, is itself an
18. 2 all kinds of filthy and hateful birds **live** in her.
19. 4 the four **living creatures** fell down and worshipped God,
20.12 and then another book was opened, the book of the **living.**
20.15 in the book of the **living** was thrown into the lake of
21. 3 He will **live** with them, and they shall be his people.
21.27 in the Lamb's book of the **living** will enter the city.

LIVE (2)

Gen 22. 6 carried a knife and **live** coals for starting the fire.
Ex 21.35 the two men shall sell the **live** bull and divide the money;
21.36 giving the other man a **live** bull, but he may keep the
Lev 10. 1 each took his fire-pan, put **live** coals in it, added incense,
14. 7 He shall let the **live** bird fly away over the open fields.
14.51 the red cord, and the **live** bird and shall dip them in
14.52 blood, the fresh water, the **live** bird, the cedar-wood, the
14.53 Then he shall let the **live** bird fly away outside the
16.20 shall present to the Lord the **live** goat chosen for Azazel.
Num 16. 6 followers take firepans, put **live** coals and incense on them,
16.18 man took his firepan, put **live** coals and incense on it, and
16.46 "Take your firepan, put **live** coals from the altar in it,
1 Kgs 7.50 for incense, and the pans used for carrying **live** coals;
2 Kgs 25.15 the small bowls and the pans used for carrying **live** coals.
2 Chr 4.22 for incense, and the pans used for carrying **live** coals.
Ecc 9. 4 a **live** dog is better off than a dead lion.
Jer 52.19 the pans used for carrying **live** coals, the bowls for holding

LIVER

Ex 29.13 the best part of the **liver,** and the two kidneys with the
29.22 the best part of the **liver,** the two kidneys with the fat
Lev 3. 4 and the fat on them, and the best part of the **liver.**
3.10 and the fat on them, and the best part of the **liver.**
3.15 and the fat on them, and the best part of the **liver.**
4. 9 and the fat on them, and the best part of the **liver.**
7. 4 and the fat on them, and the best part of the **liver.**
8.16 the best part of the **liver,** and the kidneys with the fat
8.25 the best part of the **liver,** the kidneys with the fat on
9.10 the best part of the **liver,** just as the Lord had commanded
Ezek 21.21 he examines the **liver** of a sacrificed animal.

Am **LIVESTOCK** see **CATTLE**

LIVESTOCK

Gen 4.20 the ancestor of those who raise **livestock** and live in tents.
32.13 there, Jacob chose from his **livestock** as a present for his
33.13 I must think of the sheep and **livestock** with their young.
33.14 as I can with the **livestock** and the children until I catch
33.17 he built a house for himself and shelters for his **livestock.**
34. 5 in the fields with his **livestock,** he did nothing until they
34.23 Won't all their **livestock** and everything else they own be ours?
36. 6 house, together with all his **livestock** and all the
36. 7 had too much **livestock** and could no longer stay together.
45.11 I do not want you, your family, and your **livestock** to starve.' "
46. 6 They took their **livestock** and the possessions they had
46.32 shepherds and take care of **livestock** and that you have
46.34 you have taken care of **livestock** all your lives, just as
47. 6 men among them, put them in charge of my own **livestock."**
47.16 Joseph answered, "Bring your **livestock;**
47.17 So they brought their **livestock** to Joseph, and he gave
47.17 them with food in exchange for all their **livestock.**
47.18 that our money is all gone and our **livestock** belongs to you.
Ex 9.19 Now give orders for your **livestock** and everything else
17. 3 To kill us and our children and our **livestock** with thirst?"
Lev 26.22 kill your children, destroy your **livestock,** and leave so few
Num 3.40 I also claim the **livestock** of the Levites
3.40 in place of all the first-born of the **livestock."**
3.45 Israelite sons, and dedicate the **livestock** of the Levites
3.45 in place of the first-born of the Israelites' **livestock.**
32. 1 The tribes of Reuben and Gad had a lot of **livestock.**
32. 3 Beon—is good land for **livestock,** and we have so much livestock.
Deut 2.35 We took the **livestock** and plundered the towns.
3. 7 We took the **livestock** and plundered the towns.
3.19 Only your wives, children, and **livestock—**
3.19 you have a lot of **livestock—**will remain behind in the towns
7.13 will bless you by giving you a lot of **livestock** and sheep.
7.14 None of you nor any of your **livestock** will be sterile.
11.15 and olive-oil for you, [15]and grass for your **livestock.**
13.15 all the people in that town and all their **livestock** too.
20.14 children, the **livestock,** and everything else in the city.
28.51 They will eat your **livestock** and your crops, and you
28.51 They will not leave you any corn, wine, olive-oil, **livestock,**
30. 9 children and a lot of **livestock,** and your fields will
Josh 1.14 and your **livestock** will stay here, but your soldiers,
8. 2 time you may keep its goods and **livestock** for yourselves.
8.27 kept for themselves the **livestock** and goods captured in the city,
11.14 took all the valuables and **livestock** from these cities and
Josh 21. 2 live in, as well as pasture land round them for our **livestock."**
22. 6 rich, with a lot of **livestock,** silver, gold, bronze, iron,
Judg 6. 5 would come with their **livestock** and tents, as thick as locusts.
18.21 children, their **livestock,** and their belongings going ahead.
1 Sam 23. 5 they killed many of them and took their **livestock.**
30.20 his men drove all the **livestock** in front of them and said,
2 Kgs 3.17 with water, and you, your **livestock,** and your pack-animals
1 Chr 7.21 they tried to steal the **livestock** belonging to the native
28. 1 supervisors of the property and **livestock** that belonged to
2 Chr 26.10 herds of **livestock** in the western foothills and plains.
Neh 9.37 with us and our **livestock,** and we are in deep distress!"
Ecc 2. 7 I owned more **livestock** than anyone else who had ever lived
Is 30.23 harvest, and your **livestock** will have plenty of pasture.
Jer 9.10 The sound of **livestock** is no longer heard;
49.32 "Take their camels and all their **livestock!**
Ezek 38.12 nations, and now they have **livestock** and property and live
38.13 to get silver and gold, **livestock** and property, and to march
Zech 2. 4 many people and so much **livestock** in Jerusalem that it will

LIVING

see also **LIVE (1)**

Ps 107.23 over the ocean in ships, earning their **living** on the seas.
127. 2 work so hard for a **living,** getting up early and going to
Prov 12. 9 ordinary man working for a **living** than to play the part of
14.23 Work and you will earn a **living;**
24.27 are ready, and you are sure that you can earn a **living.**
30.14 that is the way they make their **living.**
Ecc 9.11 do not always earn a **living,** intelligent men do not always
Is 19. 8 Everyone who earns his **living** by fishing in the Nile will
Acts 18. 3 them, because he earned his **living** by making tents, just as
1 Cor 9. 6 and I the only ones who have to work for our **living?**
9.14 who preach the gospel should get their **living** from it.
Eph 4.28 order to earn an honest **living** for himself and to be able
1 Thes 4.11 and to earn your own **living,** just as we told you before.
2 Thes 3.12 to lead orderly lives and work to earn their own **living.**
Rev 18.17 all others who earn their **living** on the sea, stood a long

LIVING BEING see **LIVE (1)**

LIVING CREATURE see **LIVE (1)**

LIVING FOR EVER see **LIVE (1)**

LIVING GOD see **GOD (1), LIVE (1)**

LIVING LORD see **LIVE (1)**

LIVING THING see **LIVE (1)**

LIVING-QUARTERS see **LIVE (1), QUARTER (2)**

LIZARD

Lev 11.29 Moles, rats, mice, and **lizards** must be considered unclean.
Prov 30.28 **Lizards:**

LOAD

[MULE-LOADS]

Gen 22. 3 some wood for the sacrifice, **loaded** his donkey, and took
37.25 Their camels were **loaded** with spices and resins.
42.26 The brothers **loaded** their donkeys with the corn they had bought,
44.13 tore their clothes in sorrow, **loaded** their donkeys, and
45.17 Joseph, "Tell your brothers to **load** their animals and to
45.23 sent his father ten donkeys **loaded** with the best Egyptian goods
45.23 and ten donkeys **loaded** with corn, bread,
49.15 his back to carry the **load** And is forced to work as
Ex 23. 5 donkey has fallen under its **load,** help him get the donkey to
Josh 9. 4 and got some food and **loaded** their donkeys with worn-out
1 Sam 16.20 a young goat, a donkey **loaded** with bread, and a leather bag
25.18 two hundred cakes of dried figs, and **loaded** them on donkeys.
2 Sam 16. 1 a couple of donkeys **loaded** with two hundred loaves of bread,
1 Kgs 10. 2 attendants, as well as camels **loaded** with spices, jewels,
2 Kgs 5.17 then let me have two **mule-loads** of earth to take home with
8. 9 So Hazael **loaded** forty camels with all kinds of the finest
1 Chr 12.40 donkeys, camels, mules, and oxen **loaded** with food—flour,
2 Chr 9. 1 attendants, as well as camels **loaded** with spices, jewels,
Neh 13.15 Others were **loading** corn, wine, grapes, figs, and other
Ps 81. 6 I let you put down your **loads** of bricks.
Is 30. 6 They **load** their donkeys and camels with expensive gifts for
46. 1 worshipped, but now they are **loaded** on donkeys, a burden for
Jer 17.21 their lives, they must not carry any **load** on the Sabbath;
17.24 They must not carry any **load** in through the gates of this
17.27 They must not carry any **load** through the gates of Jerusalem
Lam 5.13 boys go staggering under heavy **loads** of wood.
Ezek 27.25 You were like a ship at sea **Loaded** with heavy cargo.
29.18 his soldiers carry such heavy **loads** that their heads were
Dan 4.12 were beautiful, and it was **loaded** down with fruit—enough for
Amos 2.13 the ground, and you will groan like a cart **loaded** with corn.
Mal 3.11 your crops, and your grapevines will be **loaded** with grapes.
Mt 11.28 tired from carrying heavy **loads,** and I will give you rest.
11.30 you is easy, and the **load** I will put on you is
23. 4 tie on to people's backs **loads** that are heavy and hard to

Mt 23. 4 even to lift a finger to help them carry those **loads.**
Lk 11.46 You put **loads** on people's backs which are hard to carry, but
11.46 not stretch out a finger to help them carry those **loads.**
Acts 15.10 the test by laying a **load** on the backs of the believers
Gal 6. 5 For everyone has to carry his own **load.**

LOAF

Ex 29.23 which has been offered to me, take one **loaf** of each kind:
29.23 one **loaf** made with olive-oil and one made without it and one
Lev 2. 4 It may be thick **loaves** made of flour mixed with olive-oil or
7.12 either thick **loaves** made of flour mixed with olive-oil or
7.13 In addition, he shall offer **loaves** of bread baked without yeast.
8.26 Then he took one **loaf** of bread from the basket of
8.26 to the Lord, one **loaf** made with oil, and one biscuit,
23.17 family is to bring two **loaves** of bread and present them to
23.17 Each **loaf** shall be made of two kilogrammes of flour baked
24. 5 Take twelve kilogrammes of flour and bake twelve **loaves** of bread.
24. 6 Put the **loaves** in two rows, six in each row, on the
Num 6.15 thick **loaves** made of flour mixed with olive-oil and biscuits
6.19 it, together with one thick **loaf** of bread and one biscuit
15.20 you bake bread, the first **loaf** of the first bread made from
Judg 7.13 saying, "I dreamt that a **loaf** of barley bread rolled into
8. 5 men of the town, "Please give my men some **loaves** of bread.
1 Sam 10. 3 one will be carrying three **loaves** of bread, and the third
10. 4 and offer you two of the **loaves,** which you are to accept.
17.17 roasted grain and these ten **loaves** of bread, and hurry with
21. 3 Give me five **loaves** of bread or anything else you have."
21. 6 bread he had was the **loaves** offered to God, which had been
25.18 Abigail quickly collected two hundred **loaves** of bread,
2 Sam 6.19 and woman in Israel a **loaf** of bread, a piece of roasted
16. 1 donkeys loaded with two hundred **loaves** of bread, a hundred
1 Kgs 14. 3 Take him ten **loaves** of bread, some cakes, and a jar of
17.13 But first make a small **loaf** from what you have and bring
19. 6 looked round, and saw a **loaf** of bread and a jar of
2 Kgs 4.42 Baal Shalishah, bringing Elisha twenty **loaves** of bread made
1 Chr 16. 3 and woman in Israel a **loaf** of bread, a piece of roasted
28.16 on which were placed the **loaves** of bread offered to God.
Prov 6.26 for the price of a **loaf** of bread, but adultery will cost
Jer 37.21 day I was given a **loaf** of bread from the bakeries until
Ezek 44.30 give the priests the first **loaf** as an offering, and my
Hos 7. 8 "The people of Israel are like a half-baked **loaf** of bread.
Mt 14.17 "All we have here are five **loaves** and two fish,"
14.19 then he took the five **loaves** and the two fish, looked up
14.19 He broke the **loaves** and gave them to the disciples, and the
15.34 "Seven **loaves,**" they answered, "and a few small fish."
15.36 Then he took the seven **loaves** and the fish, gave thanks
16. 9 when I broke the five **loaves** for the five thousand men?
16.10 And what about the seven **loaves** for the four thousand men?
Mk 6.38 found out, they told him, "Five **loaves** and also two fish."
6.41 Then Jesus took the five **loaves** and the two fish, looked
6.41 He broke the **loaves** and gave them to his disciples to
8. 5 "Seven **loaves,**" they answered.
8. 6 Then he took the seven **loaves,** gave thanks to God, broke
8.14 enough bread and had only one **loaf** with them in the boat.
8.19 when I broke the five **loaves** for the five thousand people?
8.20 when I broke the seven **loaves** for the four thousand people,"
Lk 9.13 They answered, "All we have are five **loaves** and two fish.
9.16 Jesus took the five **loaves** and two fish, looked up to
11. 5 say to him, 'Friend, let me borrow three **loaves** of bread.
Jn 6. 9 boy here who has five **loaves** of barley bread and two fish.
6.13 from the five barley **loaves** which the people had eaten.
Rom 11.16 bread is given to God, then the whole **loaf** is his also;
1 Cor 10.17 Because there is the one **loaf** of bread, all of us,
10.17 though many, are one body, for we all share the same **loaf.**

LOAFERS

Acts 17. 5 gathered some of the worthless **loafers** from the streets and formed

LOAN

Deut 15. 9 you refuse to make the **loan,** he will cry out to the
24.17 and do not take a widow's garment as security for a **loan.**
Ps 15. 5 He makes **loans** without charging interest and cannot be
112. 5 is generous with his **loans,** who runs his business honestly.
Ezek 22.12 Some charge interest on the **loans** they make to their
33.15 security he took for a **loan** or gives back what he stole

LOBE

Ex 29.20 and put it on the **lobes** of the right ears of Aaron
Lev 8.23 and put it on the **lobe** of Aaron's right ear, on the
8.24 of the blood on the **lobes** of their right ears, on the
14.14 and put it on the **lobe** of the right ear, on the
14.17 and put them on the **lobe** of the right ear, on the
14.25 and put it on the **lobe** of the man's right ear, on
14.28 on the **lobe** of the man's right ear, on the thumb of

LOCAL

Deut 17. 8 be too difficult for the **local** judges to decide, such as
Judg 1.32 of Asher lived with the **local** Canaanites, since they did not
1.33 of Naphtali lived with the **local** Canaanites, but forced them
1 Chr 27.25 **Local** storerooms:
Neh 2.16 None of the **local** officials knew where I had been or
Mk 5.22 Jairus, an official of the **local** synagogue, arrived,
Lk 8.41 he was an official in the **local** synagogue.
Acts 5.17 his companions, members of the **local** party of the Sadducees,
28.17 After three days Paul called the **local** Jewish leaders

LOCATED

Josh 15. 8 the hill where the Jebusite city of Jerusalem was **located.**
1 Sam 26. 5 He went at once and **located** the exact place where Saul and
1 Chr 4.39 eastern side of the valley in which that city is **located.**
2 Chr 1. 3 Lord's presence was **located,** which Moses, the Lord's servant,
Neh 7. 5 I **located** the records of those who had first returned
Ezek 47.16 Berothah and Sibraim (they are **located** between the territory
47.16 to the city of Ticon (**located** by the border of the district

LOCK (1)

Lev 14.38 he shall leave the house and **lock** it up for seven days.
14.46 house while it is **locked** up will be unclean until evening.
Deut 3. 5 walls, gates, and bars to **lock** the gates, and there were
Judg 3.23 Ehud went outside, closed the doors behind him, **locked** them,
3.24 saw that the doors were **locked,** but they only thought that
9.51 They **locked** themselves in and went up to the roof.
16. 3 the city gate and pulled it up—doors, posts, **lock,** and all.
2 Sam 13.17 Throw her out and **lock** the door!"
13.18 The servant put her out and **locked** the door.
Neh 3. 3 place, and put in the bolts and bars for **locking** the gate.
3. 6 place, and put in the bolts and bars for **locking** the gate.
3.13 bolts and the bars for **locking** the gate, and repaired the
3.14 and put in the bolts and the bars for **locking** the gate.
6.10 Place of the Temple and **lock** the doors, because they are
Prov 6.21 Keep their words with you always, **locked** in your heart.
Is 24.10 and people **lock** themselves in their houses for safety.
42.22 they are **locked** up in dungeons and hidden away in prisons.
Jer 32. 2 attacking Jerusalem, and I was **locked** up in the courtyard of
37.15 me to be beaten and **locked** up in the house of Jonathan,
37.21 King Zedekiah ordered me to be **locked** up in the palace courtyard.
49.31 Their city has no gates or **locks** and is completely unprotected.'
Jon 2. 6 mountains, into the land whose gates **lock** shut for ever.
Mt 23.13 You **lock** the door to the Kingdom of heaven in people's faces,
Lk 11. 7 The door is already **locked,** and my children and I are in
Jn 20.19 disciples were gathered together behind **locked** doors,
20.26 The doors were **locked,** but Jesus came and stood among them
Acts 5.23 the jail, we found it **locked** up tight and all the guards
16.23 into jail, and the jailer was ordered to **lock** them up tight.
Gal 3.23 the Law kept us all **locked** up as prisoners until this coming
Rev 20. 3 threw him into the abyss, **locked** it, and sealed it, so that

LOCK (2)

Judg 16.13 "If you weave my seven **locks** of hair into a loom, and
16.14 to sleep, took his seven **locks** of hair, and wove them into
16.19 then called a man, who cut off Samson's seven **locks** of hair.

LOCUST

Ex 10. 4 then I will bring **locusts** into your country tomorrow.
10.12 "Raise your hand over the land of Egypt to bring the **locusts.**
10.13 By morning it had brought the **locusts.**
10.14 was the largest swarm of **locusts** that had ever been seen or
10.19 wind, which picked up the **locusts** and blew them into the
10.19 Not one **locust** was left in all Egypt.
Lev 11.22 You may eat **locusts,** crickets, or grasshoppers.
Deut 28.38 a small harvest, because the **locusts** will eat your crops.
Judg 6. 5 They would come with their livestock and tents, as thick as **locusts.**
7.12 valley like a swarm of **locusts,** and they had as many camels
1 Kgs 8.37 scorching winds or swarms of **locusts,** or when your people
2 Chr 6.28 scorching winds or swarms of **locusts,** or when your people
7.13 back the rain or send **locusts** to eat up the crops or
Job 39.20 leap like **locusts** and frighten men with their snorting?
Ps 78.46 He sent **locusts** to eat their crops and to destroy their fields.
105.34 He commanded, and the **locusts** came, countless millions of them;
Prov 30.27 **Locusts:**
Jer 46.23 their soldiers outnumber the **locusts.**
51.14 like a swarm of **locusts,** and they will shout with victory.
51.27 Bring up the horses like a swarm of **locusts.**
Joel 1. 4 Swarm after swarm of **locusts** settled on the crops;
1. 6 An army of **locusts** has attacked our land;
2. 2 The great army of **locusts** advances like darkness spreading
2.20 I will remove the **locust** army that came from the north
2.25 lost in the years when swarms of **locusts** ate your crops.
Amos 4. 9 The **locusts** ate up all your gardens and vineyards, your
7. 1 him create a swarm of **locusts** just after the king's share of
7. 2 my vision I saw the **locusts** eat up every green thing in
Nah 3.15 You will be wiped out like crops eaten up by **locusts.**
3.15 You multiplied like **locusts!**
3.16 now they are gone, like **locusts** that spread their wings and
3.17 are like a swarm of **locusts** that stay in the walls on
Mt 3. 4 round his waist, and his food was **locusts** and wild honey.
Mk 1. 6 round his waist, and his food was **locusts** and wild honey.
Rev 9. 3 **Locusts** came down out of the smoke upon the earth, and
9. 5 The **locusts** were not allowed to kill these people, but
9. 7 The **locusts** looked like horses ready for battle;

LODGING

Lk 9.12 and find food and **lodging,** because this is a lonely place."

LOG

2 Sam 5.11 he provided him with cedar **logs** and with carpenters and
1 Kgs 5. 9 My men will bring the **logs** down from Lebanon to the sea,
5.10 all the cedar and pine **logs** that he wanted, [11] and Solomon
1 Chr 14. 1 he provided him with cedar **logs** and with stone-masons and
22. 4 Tyre and Sidon to bring him a large number of cedar **logs.**
2 Chr 2. 3 King David, when you sold him cedar **logs** for building his palace.
2. 8 so send me cedar, cypress, and juniper **logs** from Lebanon.
Mt 7. 3 eye, and pay no attention to the **log** in your own eye?
7. 4 of your eye,' when you have a **log** in your own eye?
7. 5 First take the **log** out of your own eye, and then you
Lk 6.41 eye, but pay no attention to the **log** in your own eye?
6.42 your eye,' yet cannot even see the **log** in your own eye?
6.42 First take the **log** out of your own eye, and then you

LONELY

2 Sam 13.20 So Tamar lived in Absalom's house, sad and **lonely.**
Job 28. 4 There they work in **loneliness,** Clinging to ropes in the pits.
28. 8 No lion or other fierce beast Ever travels those **lonely** roads.
30.29 voice is as sad and **lonely** as the cries of a jackal
Ps 25.16 Lord, and be merciful to me, because I am **lonely** and weak.
68. 6 He gives the **lonely** a home to live in and leads prisoners
102. 7 I am like a **lonely** bird on a house-top.
Is 30.17 of your army except a **lonely** flagstaff on the top of a
54. 4 as a young wife, and your desperate **loneliness** as a widow.
Lam 1. 1 How **lonely** lies Jerusalem, once so full of people!
1. 7 A **lonely** ruin now, Jerusalem recalls her ancient splendour.
5.18 tears, [18] because Mount Zion lies **lonely** and deserted,
Mt 14.13 there in a boat and went to a **lonely** place by himself.
14.15 said, "It is already very late, and this is a **lonely** place.
Mk 1.35 went out of the town to a **lonely** place, where he prayed.
1.45 Instead, he stayed out in **lonely** places, and people came to
6.32 started out in a boat by themselves for a **lonely** place.
6.35 said, "It is already very late, and this is a **lonely** place.
Lk 4.42 daybreak Jesus left the town and went off to a **lonely** place.
5.16 But he would go away to **lonely** places, where he prayed.
9.12 and find food and lodging, because this is a **lonely** place."

LONG (1)
[LENGTH, LENGTHEN]

Gen 6. 4 They were the great heroes and famous men of **long ago.**
6.15 Make it 133 metres **long,** 22 metres wide, and 13 metres high.
21.34 Abraham lived in Philistia for a **long** time.
37. 3 He made a **long** robe with full sleeves for him.
37.23 brothers, they ripped off his **long** robe with full sleeves.
37.34 He mourned for his son a **long** time.
40. 4 They spent a **long** time in prison, and the captain assigned
43.10 we had not waited so **long,** we could have been there and
46.29 his arms round his father's neck and cried for a **long** time.
47. 9 few and difficult, unlike the **long** years of my ancestors in
50.10 they mourned loudly for a **long** time, and Joseph performed
Ex 20.12 that you may live a **long** time in the land that I
20.18 mountain, they trembled with fear and stood a **long** way off.
20.21 people continued to stand a **long** way off, and only Moses
23.26 I will give you **long** lives.
25.10 of acacia-wood, 110 centimetres **long,** 66 centimetres wide,
25.17 of pure gold, 110 centimetres **long** and 66 centimetres wide.
25.23 of acacia-wood, 88 centimetres **long,** 44 centimetres wide,
26. 2 piece the same size, twelve metres **long** and two metres wide.
26. 8 all the same size, thirteen metres **long** and two metres wide.
26.13 on each side of the **length** is to hang over the sides
26.16 is to be four metres **long** and 66 centimetres wide, [17] with
27. 1 to be square, 2.2 metres **long** and 2.2 metres wide, and it
27. 9 are to be 44 metres **long,** [10] supported by twenty bronze
27.12 to be curtains 22 metres **long,** with ten posts and ten bases.
27.16 be a curtain 9 metres **long** made of fine linen woven with
27.18 is to be 44 metres **long,** 22 metres wide, and 2.2 metres
28.16 folded double, 22 centimetres **long** and 22 centimetres wide.
30. 2 to be square, 45 centimetres **long** and 45 centimetres wide,
32. 1 but was staying there a **long** time, they gathered round Aaron
36. 9 was the same size, twelve metres **long** and two metres wide.
36.15 all the same size, thirteen metres **long** and two metres wide.
37. 1 of acacia-wood, 110 centimetres **long,** 66 centimetres wide,
37. 6 of pure gold, 110 centimetres **long** and 66 centimetres wide.
37.10 of acacia-wood, 88 centimetres **long,** 44 centimetres wide,
37.25 It was square, 45 centimetres **long** and 45 centimetres wide,
38. 1 It was square, 2.2 metres **long** and 2.2 metres wide, and it
38. 9 the curtains were 44 metres **long,** [10] supported by twenty
38.12 there were curtains 22 metres **long,** with ten posts and ten
38.18 It was 9 metres **long** and 2 metres high, like the curtains
39. 9 folded double, 22 centimetres **long** and 22 centimetres wide.
Lev 19.35 not cheat anyone by using false measures of **length,** weight,
Num 9.19 over the Tent for a **long** time, they obeyed the Lord and
9.22 a month, a year, or **longer,** as long as the cloud remained
10. 3 When **long** blasts are sounded on both trumpets, the whole
10. 7 call the community together, **long** blasts are to be sounded.
11.25 them, they began to shout like prophets, but not for **long.**
24. 6 of Israel are beautiful, [6] Like **long** rows of palms Or
Deut 1. 6 God said to us, 'You have stayed **long** enough at this mountain.
1.46 stayed at Kadesh for a **long** time, [1] we finally turned and
2. 1 commanded, and we spent a **long** time wandering about in the
3.11 of stone, was four metres **long** and almost two metres wide
4.25 in the land a **long** time and have children and grandchildren,
4.26 You will not live very **long** in the land across the Jordan
5.16 that you may live a **long** time in the land that I
6. 2 you, so that you may live in that land a **long** time.
8. 2 God led you on this **long** journey through the desert these
11. 9 And you will live a **long** time in the rich and fertile
Deut 11.21 your children will live a **long** time in the land that the
19.14 your neighbour's boundary mark, established **long ago** in the
20.19 its fruit-trees, even though the siege lasts a **long** time.
22. 2 if its owner lives a **long** way off or if you don't
22. 7 bird go, so that you will live a **long** and prosperous life.
25.15 that you may live a **long** time in the land that the
30.18 You will not live **long** in that land across the Jordan that
30.20 and your descendants will live **long** in the land that he
32. 7 "Think of the past, of the time **long ago;**
32.47 them and you will live **long** in that land across the Jordan
Josh 6. 5 Then they are to sound one **long** note.
9.13 Our clothes and sandals are worn out from the **long** journey."
11.17 of this territory for a **long** time, but he captured them all
24. 2 **'Long ago** your ancestors lived on the other side of the
24. 7 'You lived in the desert a **long** time.
Judg 3.16 made himself a double-edged sword nearly fifty centimetres **long.**
18.27 them, because Laish was a **long** way from Sidon, and they had
Ruth 1. 1 **Long ago,** in the days before Israel had a king, there
1 Sam 1.12 to the Lord for a **long** time, and Eli watched her lips.
7. 2 Lord stayed in Kiriath Jearim a **long** time, some twenty years.
10.24 All the people shouted, **"Long** live the king!"
27. 8 Amalek, who had been living in the region a very **long** time.
29. 3 He has been with me for quite a **long** time now.
2 Sam 3. 1 Saul's family and those supporting David went on for a **long** time.
3.17 said to them, "For a **long** time you have wanted David to
11.10 he asked him, "You have just returned after a **long** absence;
13.18 Tamar was wearing a **long** robe with full sleeves, the usual
13.37 David mourned a **long** time for his son Amnon;
14. 2 like a woman who has been in mourning for a **long** time.
14.26 cut it once a year, when it grew too **long** and heavy.
16.16 met Absalom, he shouted, **"Long** live the king!
16.16 **Long** live the king!"
19.34 But Barzillai answered, "I haven't **long** to live;
20.18 She said, **"Long ago** they used to say, 'Go and get your
1 Kgs 1.25 feasting with him and shouting, **'Long** live King Adonijah!'
1.34 Then blow the trumpet and shout, **'Long** live King Solomon!'
1.39 and all the people shouted, **"Long** live King Solomon!"
2.38 So he lived in Jerusalem a **long** time.
3.11 to rule justly, instead of **long** life for yourself or riches
3.14 as your father David did, I will give you a **long** life."
6. 2 Inside it was 27 metres **long,** 9 metres wide, and 13.5
6.16 It was nine metres **long** and was partitioned off by cedar
6.17 in front of the Most Holy Place was eighteen metres **long.**
6.20 inner room was nine metres **long,** nine metres wide, and nine
6.24 wings, each wing 2.2 metres **long,** so that the distance from
7. 2 of Lebanon was 44 metres **long,** 22 metres wide, and 13.5
7. 6 The Hall of Columns was 22 metres **long** and 13.5 metres wide.
7.10 three and a half metres **long** and others four metres long.
7.27 was 1.8 metres **long,** 1.8 metres wide, and 1.3 metres high.
2 Kgs 3. 8 "We will go the **long** way, through the wilderness of Edom,"
6.33 Why should I wait any **longer** for him to do something?"
11.12 people clapped their hands and shouted, **"Long** live the king!"
19.25 "Have you never heard that I planned all this **long ago?**
20. 6 I will let you live fifteen years **longer.**
2 Chr 1.11 your enemies or even for **long** life for yourself, you have
3. 3 King Solomon built was twenty-seven metres **long** and
3. 8 Holy Place, was nine metres **long** and nine metres wide, which
3.11 wings, each wing 2.2 metres **long,** which were spread out so
15. 3 For a **long** time Israel lived without the true God, without
23.11 Joash, and everyone shouted, **"Long** live the king!"
Neh 12.46 David and the musician Asaph **long ago,** the musicians have
13. 4 temple storerooms, had for a **long** time been on good terms
Job 2.12 While they were still a **long** way off they saw Job, but
5.27 Job, we have learnt this by **long** study.
7.19 Won't you look away **long** enough for me to swallow my spittle?
14. 5 The **length** of his life is decided beforehand— the number
15.29 He will not remain rich for **long;**
20. 5 placed on earth, [5] no wicked man has been happy for **long.**
29.18 always expected to live a **long** life and to die at home
36. 1 patient and listen a little **longer** to what I am saying on
39. 2 Do you know how **long** they carry their young?
42.16 and forty years after this, **long** enough to see his
Ps 12. 5 I will give them the security they **long** for."
21. 4 asked for life, and you gave it, a **long** and lasting life.
25. 6 and constant love which you have shown from **long ago.**
34.12 Do you want **long** life and happiness?
37.25 I have lived a **long** time, but I have never seen a
44. 1 things you did in their time, in the days of **long ago:**
72.15 **Long** live the king!
74. 2 whom you chose for yourself **long ago,** whom you brought out
77. 5 I think of days gone by and remember years of **long ago.**
89.19 In a vision **long ago** you said to your faithful servants,
90. 5 we last no **longer** than a dream.
91.16 I will reward them with **long** life;
102.25 **long ago** you created the earth, and with your own
119.52 I remember your judgements of **long ago,**
119.152 **Long ago** I learnt about your instructions;
120. 6 I have lived too **long** with people who hate peace!
123. 4 We have been mocked too **long** by the rich and scorned by
143. 3 a dark prison, and I am like those who died **long ago.**
Prov 3. 2 My teaching will give you a **long** and prosperous life.
3.16 Wisdom offers you **long** life, as well as wealth and honour.
4.10 what I am telling you, and you will live a **long** life.
7.19 He's gone away on a **long** journey.
8.22 created me first of all, the first of his works, **long ago.**
10.27 Obey the Lord, and you will live **longer.**
15.27 Don't take bribes and you will live **longer.**
16.31 **Long** life is the reward of the righteous;
19.16 Keep God's laws and you will live **longer;**
19.23 and you will live a **long** life, content and safe from harm.
21.21 Be kind and honest and you will live a **long** life;

Prov	22. 4	humble, and you will get riches, honour, and a **long** life.
	28.16	One who hates dishonesty will rule a **long** time.
	29.14	the rights of the poor, he will rule for a **long** time.
Ecc	6. 3	hundred children and live a **long** time,
	6. 3	but no matter how **long** he lives, if he does not
	6.10	that happens was already determined **long ago,** and we all
	6.11	The **longer** you argue, the more useless it is, and you
	9. 1	I thought **long** and hard about all this and saw that God
	11. 8	No matter how **long** you live,
	11. 8	remember that you will be dead much **longer.**
	11.10	You aren't going to be young very **long.**
Is	1.26	give you rulers and advisers like those you had **long ago.**
	3.23	and the scarves and **long** veils they wear on their heads.
	5.11	start drinking, and you spend **long** evenings getting drunk.
	9. 4	people, just as you defeated the army of Midian **long ago.**
	22.11	God, who planned all this **long ago** and who caused it to
	23. 7	Can this be the joyful city of Tyre, founded so **long ago?**
	25. 1	you have faithfully carried out the plans you made **long ago.**
	26.19	so the Lord will revive those who have **long** been dead.
	29.17	saying goes, before **long** the dense forest will become farmland,
	30.33	**Long ago** a place was prepared where a huge fire will
	37.26	"Have you never heard that I planned all this **long ago?**
	38. 5	I will let you live fifteen years **longer.**
	40. 2	Tell them they have suffered **long** enough and their sins are
	40.21	Were you not told **long ago?**
	42.14	"For a **long** time I kept silent;
	43.16	**Long ago** the Lord made a road through the sea, a path
	43.18	to events of the past or dwell on what happened **long ago.**
	45.21	Who predicted **long ago** what would happen?
	46. 9	Remember what happened **long ago;**
	46.10	**long ago** I foretold what would happen.
	48. 3	**"Long ago** I predicted what would take place;
	48. 5	so I predicted your future **long ago,** announcing events
	51.14	they will live a **long** life and have all the food they
	53.10	he will live a **long** life, and through him my purpose will
	54. 2	**lengthen** its ropes and strengthen the pegs!
	56. 5	Temple and among my people **longer** than if you had sons and
	57.11	stopped honouring me because I have kept silent for so **long?**
	58.12	people will rebuild what has **long** been in ruins, building
	61. 4	They will rebuild cities that have **long** been in ruins.
	65.21	Like trees, my people will live **long** lives.
	66. 8	Zion will not have to suffer **long,** before the nation is born.
Jer	2.20	"Israel, **long ago** you rejected my authority;
	6. 4	is almost over, and the evening shadows are growing **long.**
	15. 5	Who will stop **long** enough to ask how you are?
	28. 8	The prophets who spoke **long ago,** before my time and yours,
	29.28	be prisoners there a **long** time and should build houses,
	32.20	**Long ago,** you performed miracles and wonders in Egypt,
	37.16	was put in an underground cell and kept there a **long** time.
Lam	2.17	He has destroyed us without mercy, as he warned us **long ago.**
	3.18	I have not much **longer** to live;
	5.20	Why have you abandoned us so **long?**
Ezek	7.13	No merchant will live **long** enough to get back what he
	31. 5	Its branches grew thick and **long.**
	31. 7	How beautiful the tree was— So tall, with such **long** branches.
	38. 8	were desolate and deserted so **long,** but where all the people
	38.17	one I was talking about **long ago,** when I announced through
	40. 5	which was three metres **long,** and measured the wall.
	40. 7	was a passage three metres **long** that led to an entrance room
	40.15	The total **length** of the gateway from the outside wall of
	40.21	The total **length** of the gateway was twenty-five metres and
	40.25	The total **length** of the gateway was twenty-five metres, and
	40.29	The total **length** was twenty-five metres and the width twelve
	40.33	The total **length** was twenty-five metres and the width twelve
	40.36	Its total **length** was twenty-five metres and its width twelve
	41. 2	it was twenty metres **long,** and ten metres wide.
	41.12	a building forty-five metres **long** and thirty-five metres wide;
	41.13	the outside of the Temple, and it was fifty metres **long.**
	41.15	He measured the **length** of the building to the west,
	42. 2	This building was fifty metres **long** and twenty-five metres wide.
	42. 4	wide and fifty metres **long,** with entrances on that side.
	42. 7	building was solid for twenty-five metres, half its **length;**
	42. 7	level there were rooms in the entire **length** of the building.
	42.17	each side had the same **length,** 250 metres, [20] so that the
	44.20	must neither shave their heads nor let their hair grow **long.**
	44.20	They are to keep it a proper **length.**
	45. 1	be twelve and a half kilometres **long** by ten kilometres wide.
	45. 6	twelve and a half kilometres **long** and two and a half
	45. 7	so that its **length** will be the same
	45. 7	as the **length** of one of the areas allotted
	45. 9	Lord said, "You have sinned too **long,** you rulers of Israel!
	46.21	courtyard, twenty metres **long** and fifteen metres wide.
	48. 8	and the same **length** from east to west
	48.35	The total **length** of the wall on all four sides
Dan	4.33	and his hair grew as **long** as eagles' feathers
	4.33	and his nails as **long** as birds' claws.
	8. 3	long horns, one of which was **longer** and newer than the other.
	8.26	because it will be a **long** time before it does come true."
	9.24	times seventy years is the **length** of time God has set for
Hos	1. 4	because it will not be **long** before I punish the king of
	3. 3	told her that for a **long** time she would have to wait
	3. 4	have to live for a **long** time without kings or leaders,
Amos	9.11	I will rebuild it and make it as it was **long ago.**
Mic	7.14	rich pastures of Bashan and Gilead, as they did **long ago.**
	7.20	Abraham and of Jacob, as you promised our ancestors **long ago.**
Hag	2. 6	"Before **long** I will shake heaven and earth, land and sea.
Zech	1. 4	**Long ago** the prophets gave them my message, telling them not
	2. 2	he answered, "to see how **long** and how wide it is."
	5. 2	it is nine metres **long** and four and a half metres wide."
	7. 9	**"Long ago** I gave these commands to my people:
	7.12	the prophets who lived **long ago,** I became very angry.
Mt	5.18	Remember that as **long** as heaven and earth last, not the
	6. 7	their gods will hear them because their prayers are **long.**
	6.27	Can any of you live a bit **longer** by worrying about it?
	9.15	party to be sad as **long** as the bridegroom is with them?
	11.21	Sidon, the people there would **long ago** have put on sackcloth
	12. 1	Not **long** afterwards Jesus was walking through some cornfields
	12.25	into groups which fight each other will not last very **long.**
	13.21	it does not sink deep into them, and they don't last **long.**
	17.17	How **long** must I stay with you?
	17.17	How **long** do I have to put up with you?
	23. 5	Notice also how **long** are the tassels on their cloaks!
	24.48	not come back for a **long** time, [49] and he will begin to
	25.19	"After a **long** time the master of those servants came back
	27.29	**"Long** live the King of the Jews!"
Mk	1. 9	Not **long** afterwards Jesus came from Nazareth in the province
	1.35	Very early the next morning, **long** before daylight, Jesus got up
	2.19	As **long** as the bridegroom is with them, they will not do
	4.17	it does not sink deep into them, and they don't last **long.**
	5.35	Why bother the Teacher any **longer?"**
	6.15	"He is a prophet, like one of the prophets of **long ago."**
	8. 1	Not **long** afterwards another large crowd came together.
	8. 3	because some of them have come a **long** way."
	9.19	How **long** must I stay with you?
	9.19	How **long** do I have to put up with you?
	9.21	"How **long** has he been like this?"
	12.38	to walk around in their **long** robes and be greeted with
	12.40	and then make a show of saying **long** prayers.
	15.18	**"Long** live the King of the Jews!"
Lk	1.70	promised through his holy prophets **long ago** [71] that he would
	5. 5	"we worked hard all night **long** and caught nothing.
	5.34	go without food as **long** as the bridegroom is with them?
	8.49	"don't bother the Teacher any **longer."**
	9. 8	one of the prophets of **long ago** had come back to life.
	9.19	one of the prophets of **long ago** has come back to life."
	9.41	How **long** must I stay with you?
	9.41	How **long** do I have to put up with you?"
	10.13	Sidon, the people there would **long ago** have sat down, put on
	11.17	groups which fight each other will not last very **long;**
	12.25	Can any of you live a bit **longer** by worrying about it?
	14.32	for terms of peace while he is still a **long** way off.
	15.20	"He was still a **long** way from home when his father saw
	16. 2	because you cannot be my manager any **longer.'**
	20.46	to walk about in their **long** robes and love to be greeted
	20.47	and then make a show of saying **long** prayers!
Jn	7.33	with you a little while **longer,** and then I shall go away
	9. 4	As **long** as it is day, we must keep on doing the
	10.24	asked, "How **long** are you going to keep us
	12.35	Jesus answered, "The light will be among you a little **longer.**
	13.33	My children, I shall not be with you very much **longer.**
	14.30	cannot talk with you much **longer,** because the ruler of this
	15.15	not call you servants any **longer,** because a servant does not
	19. 3	came to him and said, **"Long** live the King of the Jews!"
Acts	3.18	God announced **long ago** through all the prophets
	3.21	as God announced through his holy prophets who lived **long ago.**
	7.52	They killed God's messengers, who **long ago** announced the coming
	15. 7	After a **long** debate Peter stood up and said, "My brothers,
	15.18	So says the Lord, who made this known **long ago.'**
	18.20	The people asked him to stay **longer,** but he would not consent.
	22.16	And now, why wait any **longer?**
	24. 2	leadership has brought us a **long** period of peace, and many
	25.24	They scream that he should not live any **longer.**
Rom	1. 2	The Good News was promised **long ago** by God
	7. 1	The law rules over people only as **long** as they live.
	7. 2	bound by the law to her husband as **long** as he lives;
	10.21	Israel he says, "All day **long** I held out my hands to
	11.13	As **long** as I am an apostle to the Gentiles, I will
	16.25	the secret truth which was hidden for **long** ages in the past.
1 Cor	7.31	For this world, as it is now, will not last much **longer.**
	7.39	A married woman is not free as **long** as her husband lives;
	11.14	nature itself teaches you that **long** hair on a man is a
	11.15	Her **long** hair has been given her to serve as a covering.
2 Cor	5. 6	We know that as **long** as we are at home in the
Eph	2.19	you Gentiles are not foreigners or strangers any **longer;**
	3.18	to understand how broad and **long,** how high and deep, is
Phil	1.18	am happy about it—so **long** as Christ is preached in every
	4.10	to me that after so **long** a time you once more had
1 Thes	3. 1	Finally, we could not bear it any **longer.**
	3. 5	could not bear it any **longer,** so I sent him to find
1 Tim	1. 4	those legends and those **long** lists of ancestors, which only
Tit	3. 9	But avoid stupid arguments, **long** lists of ancestors, quarrels,
Heb	3.13	one another every day, as **long** as the word "Today" in the
	9. 8	not yet been opened as **long** as the outer Tent still stands.
	10.17	"I will not remember their sins and evil deeds any **longer."**
	10.37	says, "Just a little while **longer,** and he who is coming
	11.13	had promised, but from a **long** way off they saw them
	13.22	for this letter I have written to you is not very **long.**
2 Pet	1.13	your memory of these matters as **long** as I am still alive.
	3. 2	the words that were spoken **long ago** by the holy prophets,
	3. 5	purposely ignore the fact that **long ago** God gave a command,
1 Jn	2.27	As **long** as his Spirit remains in you, you do not need
Jude	4	**Long ago** the Scriptures predicted the condemnation
	14	sixth direct descendant from Adam, who **long ago** prophesied this
Rev	6.10	How **long** will it be until you judge the people on earth
	6.11	to rest a little while **longer,** until the complete number of
	12. 8	his angels were not allowed to stay in heaven any **longer.**
	14.20	a flood three hundred kilometres **long** and nearly two metres deep.
	18.10	They stand a **long** way off, because they are afraid of
	18.11	mourn for her, because no one buys their goods any **longer;**
	18.15	that city, will stand a **long** way off, because they are
	18.17	on the sea, stood a **long** way off, [18] and cried out

Rev	21.16	The city was perfectly square, as wide as it was **long.**
	21.16	it was 2,400 kilometres **long**
	21.16	and was as wide and as high as it was **long.**

LONG (2)

2 Sam	13.39	Amnon's death, he was filled with **longing** for his son Absalom.
Job	7. 2	hard manual labour, [2]like a slave **longing** for cool shade;
	7. 4	I toss all night and **long** for dawn.
Ps	38. 9	O Lord, you know what I **long** for;
	42. 1	As a deer **longs** for a stream of cool water,
	42. 1	so I **long** for you, O God.
	63. 1	O God, you are my God, and I **long** for you.
	84. 2	I **long** to be in the Lord's Temple.
	119.20	My heart aches with **longing;**
	119.174	How I **long** for your saving help, O Lord!
Ecc	5.10	if you **long** to be rich, you will never get all you
Is	21. 4	I had been **longing** for evening to come, but it has brought
	26. 9	At night I **long** for you with all my heart;
	59.11	We **long** for God to save us from oppression and wrong, but
Jer	22.27	You will **long** to see this country again, but you will
	31. 2	When the people of Israel **longed** for rest, [3]I appeared to
	44.14	will return to Judah, where they **long** to live once again.
Amos	5.18	will be for you who **long** for the day of the Lord!
Zech	8. 2	"I have **longed** to help Jerusalem because of my deep love
Mal	3. 1	messenger you **long** to see will come and proclaim my covenant."
Rom	8.19	waits with eager **longing** for God to reveal his sons.
Heb	11.16	it was a better country they **longed** for, the heavenly country.
Rev	18.14	"All the good things you **longed** to own have disappeared,

LOOK

see also **LOOK AFTER, LOOK DOWN ON, LOOK FOR, LOOK LIKE, LOOK OUT**

Gen	1.31	God **looked** at everything he had made, and he was very pleased.
	6.12	God **looked** at the world and saw that it was evil, for
	8.13	the covering of the boat, **looked** round, and saw that the
	13.10	Lot **looked** round and saw that the whole Jordan Valley,
	13.14	"From where you are, **look** carefully in all directions.
	13.17	Now, go and **look** over the whole land, because I am going
	15. 5	took him outside and said, **"Look** at the sky and try to
	18. 2	part of the day, [2]he **looked** up and saw three men standing
	18.16	a place where they could **look** down at Sodom, and Abraham
	19. 8	**Look,** I have two daughters who are still virgins.
	19.17	Don't **look** back and don't stop in the valley.
	19.26	But Lot's wife **looked** back and was turned into a pillar
	19.28	He **looked** down at Sodom and Gomorrah and the whole
	22.13	Abraham **looked** round and saw a ram caught in a bush by
	23. 6	We **look** upon you as a mighty leader;
	26. 8	for some time, King Abimelech **looked** down from his window
	29. 6	**"Look,** here comes his daughter Rachel with his flock."
	31.12	**'Look,'** he continued, 'all the male goats that are mating
	33. 5	When Esau **looked** round and saw the women and the children,
	38.25	**Look** at them and see whose they are—this seal with its
	39. 8	refused and said to her, **"Look,** my master does not have to
	39.14	she called to her house servants and said, **"Look** at this!
	40. 7	He asked them, "Why do you **look** so worried today?"
	41.21	have known it, because they **looked** just as bad as before.
	43.33	had been seated, they **looked** at one another in amazement.
Ex	2.12	Moses **looked** all round, and when he saw that no one was
	3. 6	Moses covered his face, because he was afraid to **look** at God.
	7.17	**Look,** I am going to strike the surface of the river with
	14.11	**Look** what you have done by bringing us out of Egypt!
	14.24	Just before dawn the Lord **looked** down from the pillar of
	19.21	people not to cross the boundary to come and **look** at me;
	34.30	Aaron and all the people **looked** at Moses and saw that
Lev	13. 5	in his opinion the sore **looks** the same and has not spread,
	14.44	scraped and plastered, [44]the priest shall go and **look.**
	14.48	when the priest comes to **look,** the mildew has not reappeared
Num	6.26	May the Lord **look** on you with favour and give you peace.
	12.10	When Aaron **looked** at her and saw that she was covered with
	13.33	and that is how we must have **looked** to them."
	21. 8	that anyone who was bitten could **look** at it and be healed.
	21. 9	who had been bitten would **look** at the bronze snake and be
	21.20	below the top of Mount Pisgah, **looking** out over the desert.
	23.23	Now people will say about Israel, **'Look** what God has done!'
	24.17	I **look** into the future, And I see the nation of Israel.
	27.12	up the Abarim Mountains and **look** out over the land that I
	35.23	Or suppose that, without **looking,** a man throws a stone
Deut	1.20	**Look,** there it is.
	2.31	the Lord said to me, **'Look,** I have made King Sihon and
	3.27	peak of Mount Pisgah and **look** to the north and to the
	3.27	**Look** carefully at what you see, because you will never go
	22.17	**look** at the bloodstains on the wedding sheet!'
	26.15	**Look** down from your holy place in heaven and bless your
	28.31	be dragged away while you **look** on, and they will not be
	28.32	will be given as slaves to foreigners while you **look** on.
	28.32	you will strain your eyes, **looking** in vain for your children
	32.49	climb Mount Nebo and **look** at the land of Canaan that I
	32.52	You will **look** at the land from a distance, but you will
Josh	2.22	The king's men **looked** for them all over the countryside for
	8.20	When the men of Ai **looked** back, they saw the smoke
	8.32	There, with the Israelites **looking** on, Joshua made on
	9.12	**Look** at our bread.
	9.13	When we filled these wineskins, they were new, but **look!**
	14.10	But now, **look.**
	14.10	**Look** at me!
	22.28	this should ever happen, our descendants could say, **'Look!**
Judg	5.28	Sisera's mother **looked** out of the window;
	9.36	Gaal saw them and said to Zebul, **"Look!**
	9.37	Gaal said again, **"Look!**
Judg	13. 6	come to me, and he **looked** as frightening as the angel of
	13.10	with her, [10]so she ran at once and said to him, **"Look!**
	14. 8	he left the road to **look** at the lion he had killed,
	14.16	He said, **"Look,** I haven't even told my father and mother.
	16.10	Delilah said to Samson, **"Look,** you've been making a
	17. 2	**Look,** I have the money.
	19. 9	to leave, the father said, **"Look,** it's almost evening now;
	20.40	The Benjaminites **looked** behind them and were amazed to see
1 Sam	1.11	"Almighty Lord, **look** at me, your servant!
	2.29	Why, then, do you **look** with greed at the sacrifices and
	2.32	You will be troubled and **look** with envy on all the
	6.13	when suddenly they **looked** up and saw the Covenant Box.
	6.19	of Beth Shemesh because they **looked** inside the Covenant Box.
	8. 5	Ramah, [5]and said to him, **"Look,** you are getting old and
	9.24	Samuel said, **"Look,** here is the piece that was kept for you.
	14.11	let the Philistines see them, and the Philistines said, **"Look!**
	14.33	Saul was told, **"Look,** the people are sinning against
	16. 7	Man **looks** at the outward appearance, but I look at the heart."
	17.25	**"Look** at him!"
	17.42	when he got a good **look** at David, he was filled with
	20.21	And if I tell him, **'Look,** the arrows are on this side
	21.14	So Achish said to his officials, **"Look!**
	24.11	**Look,** my father, look at the piece of your robe I am
	24.14	**Look** at what the king of Israel is trying to kill!
	24.14	**Look** at what he is chasing!
	24.15	May he **look** into the matter, defend me, and save me from
2 Sam	2.20	Abner **looked** back and said, "Is that you, Asahel?"
	6.16	the city, Michal, Saul's daughter, **looked** out of the window
	13. 4	the king's son, yet day after day I see you **looking** sad.
	13.32	You could tell by **looking** at Absalom that he had made up
	14.25	no one in Israel as famous for his good **looks** as Absalom;
	14.30	said to his servants, **"Look,** Joab's field is next to mine,
	15. 3	from, [3]Absalom would say, **"Look,** the law is on your side,
	15.27	on to say to Zadok, **"Look,** take your son Ahimaaz and
	18.24	he **looked** out and saw a man running alone.
	18.26	running alone, and he called down to the gatekeeper, **"Look!**
	24.20	Araunah **looked** down and saw the king and his officials
1 Kgs	1.20	the people of Israel are **looking** to you to tell them who
	3.21	I **looked** at it more closely and saw that it was not
	8.52	"Sovereign Lord, may you always **look** with favour on
	17.23	to his mother and said to her, **"Look,** your son is alive!"
	18. 5	Obadiah, "Let us go and **look** at every spring and every
	18.43	He said to his servant, "Go and **look** towards the sea."
	18.43	Seven times in all Elijah told him to go and **look.**
	19. 6	He **looked** round, and saw a loaf of bread and a jar
2 Kgs	2.17	fifty of them went and **looked** high and low for Elijah for
	3.22	was shining on the water, making it **look** as red as blood.
	4.25	servant Gehazi, **"Look**—there comes the woman from Shunem!
	6.17	his prayer, and Elisha's servant **looked** up and saw the
	8.11	at him with a horrified **look** on his face until Hazael became
	9.30	arranged her hair, and stood **looking** down at the street from
	9.32	Jehu **looked** up and shouted, "Who is on my side?"
	9.32	Two or three palace officials **looked** down at him from a window,
	19.16	Now, Lord, **look** at what is happening to us.
	23.16	Then Josiah **looked** round and saw some tombs there on the hill;
	23.16	King Josiah **looked** round and saw the tomb of the prophet who
	25. 7	While Zedekiah was **looking** on, his sons were put to death;
1 Chr	15.29	the city, Michal, Saul's daughter, **looked** out of the window
2 Chr	6.40	"Now, O my God, **look** on us and listen to the prayers
	13.14	The Judaeans **looked** round and saw that they were surrounded.
	20.12	not know what to do, but we **look** to you for help."
	20.24	was in the desert, they **looked** towards the enemy and saw
Neh	1. 6	**Look** at me, Lord, and hear my prayer, as I pray day
	2. 1	He had never seen me **look** sad before, [2]so he asked, "Why
	2. 2	look sad before, [2]so he asked, "Why are you **looking** so sad?
	2. 3	How can I help **looking** sad when the city where my ancestors
	2.15	valley of the Kidron and rode along, **looking** at the wall.
	13.17	Jewish leaders and said, **"Look** at the evil you're doing!
Esth	8. 7	Esther and Mordecai, the Jew, **"Look,** I have hanged Haman
Job	5. 3	I have seen fools who **looked** secure, but I called down a
	5.24	when you **look** at your sheep, you will find them safe.
	6.28	**Look** me in the face.
	7.19	Won't you **look** away long enough for me to swallow my spittle?
	8. 8	**Look** for a moment at ancient wisdom;
	11.20	But the wicked will **look** round in despair and find that
	13. 9	If God **looks** at you closely, will he find anything good?
	14. 3	Will you even **look** at me, God, or put me on trial
	14. 6	**Look** away from him and leave him alone;
	19.19	My closest friends **look** at me with disgust;
	21. 5	**Look** at me.
	22.12	in the highest heavens and **look** down on the stars, even
	31. 1	made a solemn promise never to **look** with lust at a girl.
	33.20	his appetite, and even the finest food **looks** revolting.
	35. 5	**Look** at the sky!
	37.21	the sky is dazzling, too bright for us to **look** at it;
	40.11	**Look** at those who are proud;
	40.12	Yes, **look** at them and bring them down;
	40.15	**Look** at the monster Behemoth;
Ps	4. 6	**Look** on us with kindness!"
	8. 3	When I **look** at the sky, which you have made, at the
	13. 3	**Look** at me, O Lord my God, and answer me.
	14. 2	The Lord **looks** down from heaven at mankind to see if there
	22.17	My enemies **look** at me and stare.
	25.15	I **look** to the Lord for help at all times, and he
	31.16	**Look** on your servant with kindness;
	33.13	The Lord **looks** down from heaven and sees all mankind.
	33.14	From where he rules, he **looks** down on all who live on
	34. 5	The oppressed **look** to him and are glad;
	35.17	How much longer, Lord, will you just **look** on?
	52. 7	laugh at you and say, [7]**"Look,** here is a man who did
	53. 2	God **looks** down from heaven at mankind to see if there are

Ps 67. 1 **look** on us with kindness, [2]so that the whole world may
68.16 your mighty peaks do you **look** with scorn on the mountain on
80.14 **Look** down from heaven at us;
80.16 **look** at them in anger and destroy them!
85.11 earth, and God's righteousness will **look** down from heaven.
91. 8 You will **look** and see how the wicked are punished.
102.19 The Lord **looked** down from his holy place on high,
102.19 he **looked** down from heaven to earth.
104.32 He **looks** at the earth, and it trembles;
114. 3 The Red Sea **looked** and ran away;
119.153 **Look** at my suffering, and save me, because I have not
119.158 When I **look** at those traitors, I am filled with disgust,
121. 1 I **look** to the mountains;
123. 1 Lord, I **look** up to you, up to heaven, where you rule.
123. 2 mistress, so we will keep **looking** to you, O Lord our God,
142. 4 When I **look** beside me, I see that there is no one
145.15 All living things **look** hopefully to you, and you give
Prov 4.25 **Look** straight ahead with honest confidence;
6.16 A proud **look,**
7. 6 Once I was **looking** out of the window of my house, [7]and
7.13 the young man, kissed him, **looked** him straight in the eye,
10.28 lead to joy, but wicked people can **look** forward to nothing.
15.13 they smile, but when they are sad, they **look** depressed.
24.20 A wicked person has no future—nothing to **look** forward to.
24.32 I **looked** at this, thought about it, and learned a lesson
31.16 She **looks** at land and buys it, and with money she has
Ecc 1.10 **"Look,"** they say, "here is something new!"
4. 1 Then I **looked** again at all the injustice that goes on in
8.14 **Look** at what happens in the world:
9. 8 Always **look** happy and cheerful.
11. 8 There is nothing at all to **look** forward to.
Song 2. 9 He **looks** in through the window and glances through the lattice.
3. 2 I **looked,** but couldn't find him.
4. 9 The **look** in your eyes, my sweetheart and bride, and the
6. 9 All women **look** at her and praise her;
7.12 will get up early and **look** at the vines to see whether
Is 1. 7 While you **look** on, foreigners take over your land and bring
1.15 you lift your hands in prayer, I will not **look** at you.
3.16 The Lord said, **"Look** how proud the women of Jerusalem are!
5.30 **Look** at this country!
6. 9 No matter how much you **look,** you will not know what is
8.21 They may **look** up to the sky [22]or stare at the ground,
13. 8 They will **look** at each other in fear, and their faces will
13.16 While they **look** on helplessly, their babies will be battered
18. 4 said to me, "I will **look** down from heaven as quietly as
20. 6 coast of Philistia will say, **'Look** at what has happened to
33.20 **Look** at Zion, the city where we celebrate our religious festivals.
33.20 **Look** at Jerusalem!
37.17 Now, Lord, hear us and **look** at what is happening to us.
38.14 My eyes grew tired from **looking** to heaven.
40.22 the people below **look** as tiny as ants.
40.26 **Look** up at the sky!
41.28 When I **looked** among the gods, none of them had a thing
42.18 **Look** closely, you that are blind!
49.18 **Look** around and see what is happening!
51. 6 **Look** up at the heavens;
51. 6 **look** at the earth!
52.14 he was so disfigured that he hardly **looked** human.
53. 3 No one would even **look** at him— we ignored him as
60. 4 **Look** around you and see what is happening:
63. 5 I was amazed when I **looked** and saw that there was no
63.15 Lord, **look** upon us from heaven, where you live in your
Jer 2.21 But **look** what you have become!
2.23 **Look** how you sinned in the valley;
3. 2 **Look** up at the hill-tops.
4.13 **Look,** the enemy is coming like clouds.
4.23 I **looked** at the earth—it was a barren waste;
4.24 I **looked** at the mountains—they were shaking, and the
5. 1 **Look** around!
6.16 The Lord said to his people, "Stand at the crossroads and **look.**
7. 8 **"Look,** you put your trust in deceitful words.
8. 8 **Look,** the laws have been changed by dishonest scribes.
13.20 Jerusalem, **look!**
33.24 And so they **look** with contempt on my people and no longer
39. 6 to death while Zedekiah was **looking** on, and he also executed
46. 5 they run as fast as they can and do not **look** back.
52.10 to death while Zedekiah was **looking** on and he also had the
Lam 1.11 **"Look** at me, Lord," the city cries;
1.12 **"Look** at me!"
1.18 **look** at me in my pain.
1.20 **"Look,** O Lord, at my agony, at the anguish of my soul!
2.15 People passing by the city **look** at you in scorn.
2.20 **Look,** O Lord!
2.20 **Look** at those you are torturing!
3.50 Until the Lord **looks** down from heaven and sees us.
4.17 We looked until we could **look** no longer for help
5. 1 **Look** at us, and see our disgrace.
Ezek 1. 4 I **looked** up and saw a storm coming from the north.
1.15 As I was **looking** at the four creatures, I saw four
5. 5 The Sovereign Lord said, **"Look** at Jerusalem.
5.15 They will **look** at you with disgust and will mock you.
6. 2 "Mortal man," he said, **"look** towards the mountains of
8. 2 I **looked** up and saw a vision of a fiery human form.
8. 5 God said to me, "Mortal man, **look** towards the north."
8. 5 I **looked,** and there near the altar by the entrance of the
8. 6 **Look** at the disgusting things the people of Israel are doing here,
8. 9 to me, "Go in and **look** at the evil, disgusting things they
8.10 So I went in and **looked.**
8.17 **Look** how they insult me in the most offensive way possible!
10. 1 I **looked** at the dome over the heads of the living
10.22 Their faces **looked** exactly like the faces I had seen by

Ezek 13.17 Lord said, "Now, mortal man, **look** at the women among your
14.22 survive and save his children, **look** at them when they come
16.51 Your corruption makes your sisters **look** innocent by comparison.
16.52 those of your sisters that they **look** innocent beside you.
16.52 bear your shame, because you make your sisters **look** pure."
20.46 "Mortal man," he said, **"look** towards the south.
23.27 You won't **look** at any more idols or think about Egypt any
24.21 You like to **look** at it and to visit it, but the
24.25 pride and joy, which they liked to **look** at and to visit.
28.18 All who **look** at you now see you reduced to ashes.
44. 4 As I **looked,** I saw that the Temple of the Lord was
Dan 1.10 drink, and if you don't **look** as fit as the other young
1.13 the royal court, and base your decision on how we **look."**
1.15 the time was up, they **looked** healthier and stronger than all
2.31 giant statue, bright and shining, and terrifying to **look** at.
2.34 While you were **looking** at it, a great stone broke loose
3.27 of the king gathered to **look** at the three men, who had
4.30 palace in Babylon, [30]he said, **"Look** how great Babylon is!
4.34 passed," said the king, "I **looked** up at the sky, and my
4.35 He **looks** on the people of the earth as nothing;
5.10 Please do not be so disturbed and **look** so pale.
7. 6 It had a **look** of authority about it.
7. 9 While I was **looking,** thrones were put in place.
7.11 While I was **looking,** I could still hear the little horn
7.21 While I was **looking,** that horn made war on God's people
9.18 **look** at us, and see the trouble we are in and the
10. 5 I **looked** up and saw someone who was wearing linen clothes
Hos 13. 1 they **looked up** to Ephraim.
Joel 1.16 We **look** on helpless as our crops are destroyed.
Amos 6. 2 Go and **look** at the city of Calneh.
8.12 They will **look** everywhere for a message from the Lord, but
Nah 1.15 **Look,** a messenger is coming over the mountains with good news!
Hab 1. 3 How can you endure to **look** on such wrongdoing?
1.13 eyes are too holy to **look** at evil, and you cannot stand
Hag 2. 3 How does it **look** to you now?
Zech 5. 1 I **looked** again, and this time I saw a scroll flying
5. 5 The angel appeared again and said, **"Look!**
5. 9 I **looked** up and saw two women flying towards me with
9. 9 **Look,** your king is coming to you!
12.10 They will **look** at the one whom they stabbed to death, and
Mt 5.28 anyone who **looks** at a woman and wants to possess her is
6.26 **Look** at the birds:
6.28 **Look** how the wild flowers grow:
7. 3 Why, then, do you **look** at the speck in your brother's eye,
11.19 he ate and drank, and everyone said, **'Look** at this man!
12. 2 this, they said to Jesus, **"Look,** it is against our Law for
12.47 people there said to him, **"Look,** your mother and brothers
12.49 Then he pointed to his disciples and said, **"Look!**
13.13 to them is that they **look,** but do not see, and they
13.14 they will **look** and look, but not see, [15]because their minds
14.19 loaves and the two fish, **looked** up to heaven, and gave
16. 3 can predict the weather by **looking** at the sky, but you
17. 2 As they **looked** on, a change came over Jesus:
17. 8 So they **looked** up and saw no one there but Jesus.
19.26 Jesus **looked** straight at them and answered, "This is
19.27 **"Look,"** he said, "we have left everything and followed you.
21. 5 "Tell the city of Zion, **Look,** your king is coming to you!
22.11 "The king went in to **look** at the guests and saw a
23. 5 **Look** at the straps with scripture verses on them which they
23.27 are like whitewashed tombs, which **look** fine on the outside but
24. 2 "Yes," he said, "you may well **look** at all these.
24.23 "Then, if anyone says to you, **'Look,** here is the Messiah!'
24.26 if people should tell you, **'Look,** he is out in the desert!"
24.26 or if they say, **'Look,** he is hiding here!"
26.46 **Look,** here is the man who is betraying me!"
27.55 There were many women there, **looking** on from a distance,
28. 1 Mary Magdalene and the other Mary went to **look** at the tomb.
Mk 2.24 the Pharisees said to Jesus, **"Look,** it is against our Law
3. 5 Jesus was angry as he **looked** round at them, but at the
3.32 and they said to him, **"Look,** your mother and your brothers
3.34 He looked at the people sitting round him and said, **"Look!**
4.12 of parables, [12]so that, 'They may **look** and look, yet not
5.32 But Jesus kept **looking** round to see who had done it.
6.41 loaves and the two fish, **looked** up to heaven, and gave
7.34 Then Jesus **looked** up to heaven, gave a deep groan, and
8.24 The man **looked** up and said, "Yes, I can see people,
8.25 This time the man **looked** intently, his eyesight returned,
8.33 Jesus turned round, **looked** at his disciples, and rebuked Peter.
9. 2 As they **looked** on, a change came over Jesus, [3]and his
9. 8 They took a quick **look** round but did not see anyone else;
10.21 Jesus **looked** straight at him with love and said, "You need
10.23 Jesus **looked** round at his disciples and said to them,
10.27 Jesus **looked** straight at them and answered, "This is
10.28 Peter spoke up, **"Look,** we have left everything and followed you."
11.11 Jerusalem, went into the Temple, and **looked** round at everything.
11.21 said to Jesus, **"Look,** Teacher, the fig-tree you cursed
13. 1 leaving the Temple, one of his disciples said, **"Look,** Teacher!
13.21 "Then, if anyone says to you, **'Look,** here is the Messiah!'
13.21 or, **'Look,** there he is!'
14.41 **Look,** the Son of Man is now being handed over
14.42 **Look,** here is the man who is betraying me!"
14.67 saw Peter warming himself, she **looked** straight at him and said,
15.40 Some women were there, **looking** on from a distance.
16. 3 Then they **looked** up and saw that the stone had already been
16. 6 **Look,** here is the place where they put him.
Lk 6.10 He **looked** around at them all;
6.20 Jesus **looked** at his disciples and said, "Happy are you poor;
6.41 "Why do you **look** at the speck in your brother's eye,
7.34 and he ate and drank, and you said, **'Look** at this man!
8.10 so that they may **look** but not see, and listen but
9.16 five loaves and two fish, **looked** up to heaven, thanked God

Lk 9.38 I beg you, **look** at my son—my only son!
9.62 to plough and then keeps **looking** back is of no use to
10.32 came along, went over and **looked** at the man, and then walked
12.24 **Look** at the crows:
12.27 **Look** how the wild flowers grow:
12.56 You can **look** at the earth and the sky and predict the
13. 7 he said to his gardener, **'Look,** for three years I have been
14.18 'I have bought a field and must go and **look** at it;
15. 8 sweeps her house, and **looks** carefully everywhere until she finds
15.29 he answered his father, **'Look,** all these years I have worked
16.15 the ones who make yourselves **look** right in other people's sight,
16.23 was in great pain, he **looked** up and saw Abraham, far away,
17. 7 has a servant who is ploughing or **looking** after the sheep.
17.21 No one will say, **'Look,** here it is!'
17.23 There will be those who will say to you, **'Look,** over there!'
17.23 or, **'Look,** over here!'
18.28 Then Peter said, **"Look!**
19. 5 came to that place, he **looked** up and said to Zacchaeus,
20.17 Jesus **looked** at them and asked, "What, then, does this
21. 1 Jesus **looked** round and saw rich men dropping their gifts in
21. 5 the Temple, how beautiful it **looked** with its fine stones
22.38 The disciples said, **"Look!**
22.56 there at the fire, she **looked** straight at him and said,
22.61 The Lord turned round and **looked** straight at Peter,
24. 5 to them, "Why are you **looking** among the dead for one who
24.39 **Look** at my hands and my feet, and see
Jn 1.42 Jesus **looked** at him and said, "Your name is Simon son of
4.35 But I tell you, take a good **look** at the fields;
6. 5 Jesus **looked** round and saw that a large crowd was coming
11.41 Jesus **looked** up and said, "I thank you, Father, that you
11.47 **Look** at all the miracles this man is performing!
12.19 **Look,** the whole world is following him!"
13.22 The disciples **looked** at one another, completely puzzled
17. 1 Jesus finished saying this, he **looked** up to heaven and said,
19. 4 and said to the crowd, **"Look,** I will bring him out here
19. 5 Pilate said to them, **"Look!**
19.37 scripture that says, "People will **look** at him whom they pierced."
20.11 crying, she bent over and **looked** in the tomb [12]and saw two
20.27 to Thomas, "Put your finger here, and **look** at my hands;
Acts 1.11 "Galileans, why are you standing there **looking** up at the sky?
3. 4 They looked straight at him, and Peter said, **"Look** at us!"
3. 5 So he **looked** at them, expecting to get something from them.
7.31 went near the bush to get a better **look.**
7.32 Moses trembled with fear and dared not **look.**
7.55 full of the Holy Spirit, **looked** up to heaven and saw God's
11. 6 I **looked** closely inside and saw domesticated and wild animals,
13. 9 he **looked** straight at the magician [10]and said, "You son
13.41 **'Look,** you scoffers!
14. 9 could be healed, so he **looked** straight at him [10]and said
17.23 through your city and **looked** at the places where you worship,
22.13 At that very moment I saw again and **looked** at him.
23. 1 Paul **looked** straight at the Council and said,
28.26 you will **look** and look, but not see,
Rom 9.33 **"Look,** I place in Zion a stone that will make people stumble,
1 Cor 10.24 No one should be **looking** to his own interests, but to
12.23 of the body which don't **look** very nice are treated with
2 Cor 10. 7 You are **looking** at the outward appearance of things.
Phil 2. 4 And **look** out for one another's interests, not just for your own.
Jas 1.23 is like a man who **looks** in a mirror and sees himself
1.24 He takes a good **look** at himself and then goes away
1.25 whoever **looks** closely into the perfect law that sets people free,
1 Pet 1. 4 and so we **look** forward to possessing the rich blessings
2 Pet 2.14 They want to **look** at nothing but immoral women;
3.15 **Look** on our Lord's patience as the opportunity he is
Rev 1. 7 **Look,** he is coming on the clouds!
5. 3 world below who could open the scroll and **look** inside it.
5. 4 found who was worthy to open the scroll or **look** inside it.
5.11 Again I **looked,** and I heard angels, thousands and millions
6. 2 I **looked,** and there was a white horse.
6. 5 I **looked,** and there was a black horse.
6. 8 I **looked,** and there was a pale-coloured horse.
7. 9 After this I **looked,** and there was an enormous crowd—no
8.13 Then I **looked,** and I heard an eagle that was flying high
11. 9 tribes, languages, and races will **look** at their bodies for three
14. 1 Then I **looked,** and there was the Lamb standing on Mount Zion;
14.14 Then I **looked,** and there was a white cloud, and sitting
17. 8 the living, will all be amazed as they **look** at the beast.
also Josh 9.12 Judg 19.24 1 Sam 26.16 Ps 59.3 Ps 83.2 Jer 47.2 Ezek 20.47 Mt 25.20 Mt 25.22 Mt 25.25 Mt 26.45 Lk 22.21 Jn 7.26 Acts 7.56 Rev 5.5

LOOK AFTER

Gen 39.23 jailer did not have to **look after** anything for which Joseph
1 Sam 25.16 the whole time we were with them **looking after** our flocks.
2 Sam 7. 8 him, 'I took you from **looking after** sheep in the fields and
1 Chr 17. 7 him, 'I took you from **looking after** sheep in the fields and
Ps 78.71 from the pastures, [71]where he **looked after** his flocks, and
Prov 27.23 **Look after** your sheep and cattle as carefully as you can,
31.27 She is always busy and **looks after** her family's needs.
Dan 6. 2 the governors and to **look after** the king's interests.

LOOK DOWN ON

2 Sam 19.43 Why do you **look down on** us?
Neh 1. 3 that the foreigners who lived near by **looked down on** them.
Esth 1.17 the empire will begin to **look down on** her husband as soon
Job 41.34 He **looks down on** even the proudest animals;
Prov 12. 8 if you are stupid, people will **look down on** you.
Song 1. 6 Don't **look down on** me because of my colour, because the
Dan 9.16 people in the neighbouring countries **look down on** Jerusalem
1 Cor 1.28 He chose what the world **looks down on** and despises,
16.11 No one should **look down on** him, but you must help him
2 Cor 11.20 you or traps you or **looks down on** you or slaps you
1 Tim 4.12 Do not let anyone **look down on** you because you are young,
Tit 2.15 Let none of them **look down on** you.

LOOK FOR

Gen 31.32 with our men as witnesses, **look for** anything that belongs to
37.15 a man saw him and asked him, "What are you **looking for?"**
37.16 "I am **looking for** my brothers, who are taking care of
Ex 5.12 So the people went all over Egypt **looking for** straw.
Lev 13.36 If the sore has spread, he need not **look for** yellowish hairs;
Num 24. 1 he did not go to **look for** omens, as he had done
Deut 4.29 There you will **look for** the Lord your God, and if you
18.10 your people practise divination or **look for** omens or use
18.14 those who practise divination and **look for** omens, but the
22. 2 When its owner comes **looking for** it, give it to him.
Josh 2. 7 They went **looking for** the Israelite spies as far as the
2.22 The king's men **looked for** them all over the countryside for
20. 3 can go there and escape the man who is **looking for** revenge.
20. 5 If the man **looking for** revenge follows him there, the
20. 9 find protection there from the man **looking for** revenge;
Judg 4.22 When Barak came **looking for** Sisera, Jael went out to
4.22 I'll show you the man you're **looking for."**
14. 4 this, for the Lord was **looking for** a chance to fight the
17. 9 I am **looking for** somewhere to live."
18. 1 the tribe of Dan was **looking for** territory to claim and
Ruth 3.10 You might have gone **looking for** a young man, either rich or
1 Sam 9. 3 of the servants with you and go and **look for** the donkeys."
10. 2 that the donkeys you were **looking for** have been found, so
10.14 **"Looking for** the donkeys," Saul answered.
10.21 They **looked for** him, but when they could not find him,
16.16 order, sir, and we will **look for** a man who knows how
22. 8 men, is at this moment **looking for** a chance to kill me,
23.25 his men set out to **look for** David, but he heard about
24. 2 soldiers in Israel and went **looking for** David and his men
26. 2 the wilderness of Ziph to **look for** David, [3]and camped by
26. 3 that Saul had come to **look for** him, [4]he sent spies and
27. 1 Then Saul will give up **looking for** me in Israel, and I
2 Sam 17.20 The men **looked for** them but could not find them, and so
22.42 They **look for** help, but no one saves them;
2 Kgs 2.16 Let us go and **look for** your master.
6.19 this is not the town you are **looking for.**
9. 2 and when you get there **look for** Jehu, the son of
2 Chr 15. 2 If you **look for** him, he will let you find him, but
Job 6.18 Caravans get lost **looking for** water;
7. 8 If you **look for** me, I'll be gone.
7.13 I **look for** relief from my pain.
7.21 in my grave, and I'll be gone when you **look for** me.
19.28 You **looked for** some excuse to attack me.
Ps 37.10 you may **look for** them, but you won't find them;
37.36 I **looked for** him, but couldn't find him.
52. 7 his great wealth and **looked for** security in being wicked."
69. 3 I have strained my eyes, **looking for** your help.
104.21 while they hunt, **looking for** the food that God provides.
119.176 so come and **look for** me, your servant, because I have not
Prov 1.28 You may **look for** me everywhere, but you will not find me.
2. 4 **Look for** it as hard as you would for silver or some
7.15 So I came out **looking for** you.
8.17 whoever **looks for** me can find me.
11.27 respected, but if you are **looking for** trouble, that is what
16.27 Evil people **look for** ways to harm others;
Ecc 7.27 this out little by little while I was **looking for** answers.
7.28 I have **looked for** other answers but have found none.
Song 1. 7 Why should I need to **look for** you among the flocks of
3. 1 I was **looking for** him, but couldn't find him.
3. 2 I **looked for** the one I love.
5. 6 I **looked for** him, but couldn't find him;
Is 18. 3 **Look for** a signal flag to be raised on the tops of
34.14 The night monster will come there **looking for** a place to rest.
41.17 my people in their need **look for** water, when their throats
45.19 the people of Israel to **look for** me in a desolate waste.
57.10 You wear yourselves out **looking for** other gods, but you
Jer 5. 3 Surely the Lord **looks for** faithfulness.
14.19 We **looked for** peace, but nothing good happened;
45. 5 Are you **looking for** special treatment for yourself?
46.11 People of Egypt, go to Gilead and **look for** medicine!
50. 4 both Israel and Judah will come weeping, **looking for** me,
Lam 1.11 Her people groan as they **look for** something to eat;
1.19 city streets, **Looking for** food to keep themselves alive.
5. 9 we risk our lives when we **look for** food.
Ezek 7.25 You will **look for** peace and never find it.
22.30 I **looked for** someone who could build a wall, who could
26.21 People may **look for** you, but you will never be found."
34. 4 those that wandered off, or **looked for** those that were lost.
34. 6 the earth, and no one **looked for** them or tried to find
34.11 you that I myself will **look for** my sheep and take care
34.16 "I will **look for** those that are lost, bring back those
Hos 2. 7 She will **look for** them but will not find them.
5.15 have suffered enough for their sins and come **looking for** me.
Zech 11.16 nor does he **look for** the lost, or heal those that are
Mal 3. 1 Then the Lord you are **looking for** will suddenly come to his
Mt 2.13 and said, "Herod will be **looking for** the child in order to
10.11 or village, go in and **look for** someone who is willing to
12.43 it travels over dry country **looking for** a place to rest.
13.45 A man is **looking for** fine pearls, [46]and when he finds one
18.12 grazing on the hillside and go and **look for** the lost sheep.
26.16 From then on Judas was **looking for** a good chance to hand
28. 5 "I know you are **looking for** Jesus, who was crucified.
Mk 1.37 when they found him, they said, "Everyone is **looking for** you."

Mk 11.18 of this, so they began **looking for** some way to kill Jesus.
14. 1 teachers of the Law were **looking for** a way to arrest Jesus
14.11 So Judas started **looking for** a good chance to hand Jesus
16. 6 "I know you are **looking for** Jesus of Nazareth, who was crucified.
Lk 2.44 whole day and then started **looking for** him among their relatives
2.45 find him, so they went back to Jerusalem **looking for** him.
2.49 He answered them, "Why did you have to **look for** me?
4.42 The people started **looking for** him, and when they found him,
11.24 it travels over dry country **looking for** a place to rest.
13. 6 He went **looking for** figs on it but found none.
13. 7 I have been coming here **looking for** figs on this fig-tree,
15. 4 in the pasture and goes **looking for** the one that got lost
17.23 But don't go out **looking for** it.
20.20 So they **looked for** an opportunity.
22. 6 agreed to it and started **looking for** a good chance to hand
Jn 1.38 saw them following him, and asked, "What are you **looking for?"**
5.41 "I am not **looking for** human praise.
6.24 got into those boats and went to Capernaum, **looking for** him.
6.26 you are **looking for** me because you ate the bread and had
7.11 The Jewish authorities were **looking for** him at the festival.
7.34 You will **look for** me, but you will not find me,
7.36 He says that we will **look for** him but will not find
8.21 you will **look for** me, but you will die in your sins.
11.56 were **looking for** Jesus, and as they gathered in the Temple,
13.33 You will **look for** me;
18. 4 forward and asked them, "Who is it you are **looking for?"**
18. 7 Again Jesus asked them, "Who is it you are **looking for?"**
18. 8 "If, then, you are **looking for** me, let these others go."
20.15 "Who is it that you are **looking for?"**
Acts 10.19 Three men are here **looking for** you.
10.21 said to the men, "I am the man you are **looking for.**
11.25 Then Barnabas went to Tarsus to **look for** Saul.
17.27 so that they would **look for** him, and perhaps find him
Rom 10.20 says, "I was found by those who were not **looking for** me;
11. 7 The people of Israel did not find what they were **looking for.**
1 Cor 1.22 Jews want miracles for proof, and Greeks **look for** wisdom.
7.27 Then don't **look for** a wife.
2 Tim 1.17 in Rome, he started **looking for** me until he found me.
Heb 11.14 it clear that they are **looking for** a country of their own.
12.17 what he had done, even though in tears he **looked for** it.
13.14 we are **looking for** the city which is to come.
1 Pet 5. 8 roams round like a roaring lion, **looking for** someone to devour.

LOOK LIKE

Ex 24.10 Beneath his feet was what **looked like** a pavement of sapphire,
24.16 To the Israelites the light **looked like** a fire burning on
Num 9.15 At night the cloud **looked like** fire.
Judg 8.18 They answered, "They **looked like** you—every one of them
1 Sam 28.14 "What does it **look like?"**
1 Kgs 20.27 The Israelites **looked like** two small flocks of goats
2 Kgs 1. 7 "What did the man **look like?"**
Ps 74. 5 They **looked like** woodmen cutting down trees with their axes.
Jer 3. 3 You even **look like** a prostitute;
Ezek 1. 5 the storm, I saw what **looked like** four living creatures in
1.13 that **looked like** a blazing torch, constantly moving.
1.22 creatures there was something that **looked like** a dome made
1.26 was something that **looked like** a throne made of sapphire,
1.26 sitting on the throne was a figure that **looked like** a man.
8. 2 the waist down his body **looked like** fire, and from the waist
10. 8 that each creature had what **looked like** a human hand under
10.21 faces, four wings, and what **looked like** a human hand under
37.17 to end in your hand so that they **look like** one stick.
40. 2 front of me a group of buildings that **looked like** a city.
41.21 there was something that **looked like** [22]a wooden altar.
Dan 3.25 of being hurt—and the fourth one **looks like** an angel."
7. 4 The first one **looked like** a lion, but had wings like an
7. 5 The second beast **looked like** a bear standing on its hind legs.
7. 6 It **looked like** a leopard, but on its back there were four
7.13 vision in the night, I saw what **looked like** a human being.
10.16 Then the angel, who **looked like** a man, stretched out his
Joel 2. 4 They **look like** horses;
Mt 7.15 they come to you **looking like** sheep on the outside,
Mk 8.24 "Yes, I can see people, but they **look like** trees walking about."
9.26 The boy **looked like** a corpse, and everyone said, "He is dead!"
Jn 9. 9 he just **looks like** him."
Acts 2. 3 Then they saw what **looked like** tongues of fire which
6.15 and saw that his face **looked like** the face of an angel.
10.11 something coming down that **looked like** a large sheet being
11. 5 something coming down that **looked like** a large sheet being
Rom 1.23 they worship images made to **look like** mortal man or birds or
2 Cor 11.13 disguise themselves to **look like** real apostles of Christ.
11.14 Even Satan can disguise himself to **look like** an angel of light!
11.15 disguise themselves to **look like** servants of righteousness.
Jas 1.24 then goes away and at once forgets what he **looks like.**
Rev 1.13 among them there was what **looked like** a human being, wearing
4. 6 the throne there was what **looked like** a sea of glass, clear
4. 7 The first one **looked like** a lion;
4. 7 the second **looked like** a bull;
4. 7 and the fourth **looked like** an eagle in flight.
8. 8 Something that **looked like** a huge mountain on fire was thrown
9. 7 The locusts **looked like** horses ready for battle;
9. 9 chests were covered with what **looked like** iron breastplates,
11. 1 given a stick that **looked like** a measuring-rod, and was told,
13. 2 The beast **looked like** a leopard, with feet like a bear's
14.14 on the cloud was what **looked like** a human being,
15. 2 Then I saw what **looked like** a sea of glass mixed with
16.13 Then I saw three unclean spirits that **looked like** frogs.

LOOK OUT

Gen 30.30 it is time for me to **look out** for my own interests."
1 Kgs 12.16 Let Rehoboam **look out** for himself!"
2 Chr 10.16 Let Rehoboam **look out** for himself!"

LOOM

Judg 16.13 locks of hair into a **loom,** and make it tight with a
16.14 took his seven locks of hair, and wove them into the **loom.**
16.14 But he woke up and pulled his hair loose from the **loom.**
1 Sam 17. 7 the bar on a weaver's **loom,** and its iron head weighed about
2 Sam 21.19 had a shaft as thick as the bar on a weaver's **loom.**
1 Chr 20. 5 had a shaft as thick as the bar on a weaver's **loom.**
Is 38.12 that is taken down, Like cloth that is cut from a **loom.**

LOOPS

Ex 26. 4 Make **loops** of blue cloth on the edge of the outside piece
26. 5 Put fifty **loops** on the first piece of the first set
26. 5 and fifty **loops** matching them on the last piece
26.10 Put fifty **loops** on the edge of the last piece
26.10 of one set, and fifty **loops** on the edge of the other
26.11 and put them in the **loops** to join the two sets so
36.11 They made **loops** of blue cloth on the edge of the outside
36.12 They put fifty **loops** on the first piece of the first set
36.12 and fifty **loops** matching them on the last piece
36.17 They put fifty **loops** on the edge of the last piece
36.17 of one set and fifty **loops** on the edge of the other

LOOSE

Ex 23. 4 enemy's cow or donkey running **loose,** take it back to him.
28.28 breast-piece rests above the belt and does not come **loose.**
39.21 breast-piece rested above the belt and did not come **loose.**
Num 5.18 Then he shall **loosen** the woman's hair and put the
Deut 22. 1 cow or sheep running **loose,** do not ignore it;
Judg 15. 5 and turned the foxes **loose** in the Philistine cornfields.
16.14 But he woke up and pulled his hair **loose** from the loom.
16.20 woke up and thought, "I'll get **loose** and go free, as
Job 12.15 floods come when he turns water **loose.**
19.20 My skin hangs **loose** on my bones;
38.31 the Pleiades together or **loosen** the bonds that hold Orion?
39. 5 Who turned them **loose** and let them roam?
Prov 25.19 trying to chew with a **loose** tooth or walk with a crippled
Is 5.27 Not a belt is **loose;**
22.25 the peg that was firmly fastened will work **loose** and fall.
Jer 2.23 on heat, running about **loose,** [24]rushing
Lam 4.11 The Lord turned **loose** the full force of his fury;
Ezek 13.10 put up a wall of **loose** stones, and then the prophets have
21.31 anger when I turn it **loose** on you like a blazing fire.
22.31 I will turn my anger **loose** on them, and like a fire
Dan 2.34 it, a great stone broke **loose** from a cliff without anyone
2.45 saw how a stone broke **loose** from a cliff without anyone
Acts 3.14 Pilate to do you the favour of turning **loose** a murderer.
Rev 20. 3 After that he must be let **loose** for a little while.
20. 7 Satan will be let **loose** from his prison, [8]and he will

LOOT

Gen 14.16 of Damascus, [16]and recovered the **loot** that had been taken.
14.20 Abram gave Melchizedek a tenth of all the **loot** he had recovered.
14.21 said to Abram, "Keep the **loot,** but give me back all my
34.27 the slaughter Jacob's other sons **looted** the town to take
Num 31.11 They took all the **loot** that they had captured, including
31.53 Those who were not officers kept the **loot** they had taken.
1 Sam 15.19 you rush to seize the **loot,** and so do what displeases the
17.53 back from pursuing the Philistines, they **looted** their camp.
30.16 of the enormous amount of **loot** they had captured from
30.19 and daughters, and all the **loot** the Amalekites had taken.
30.22 with us, and so we won't give them any of the **loot.**
30.26 he sent part of the **loot** to his friends, the leaders of
30.26 for you from the **loot** we took from the Lord's enemies."
2 Sam 3.22 from a raid, bringing a large amount of **loot** with them.
8.12 as well as part of the **loot** he had taken from Hadadezer.
12.30 took a large amount of **loot** from the city [31]and put its
2 Kgs 3.23 Let's go and **loot** their camp!"
7.16 The people of Samaria rushed out and **looted** the Syrian camp.
1 Chr 2. 7 of Israel by keeping **loot** that had been devoted to God.
20. 2 He also took a large amount of **loot** from the city.
26.27 They took some of the **loot** they captured in battle and
2 Chr 14.13 Lord and his army, and the army took large amounts of **loot.**
14.14 army plundered all those cities and captured large amounts of **loot.**
15.11 sacrifices to the Lord from the **loot** they had brought back:
20.25 moved in to take the **loot,** and they found many cattle,
20.25 spent three days gathering the **loot,** but there was so much
21.17 They invaded Judah, **looted** the royal palace, and carried
24.23 leaders, and took large amounts of **loot** back to Damascus.
25.13 killed three thousand men, and captured quantities of **loot.**
25.24 took back to Samaria as **loot** all the gold and silver in
28. 8 them back to Samaria, along with large amounts of **loot.**
28.14 handed the prisoners and the **loot** over to the people and
28.15 provide the prisoners with clothing from the captured **loot.**
36.18 The king of Babylonia **looted** the Temple, the temple treasury,
Esth 9. 7 However, there was no **looting.**
9.15 But again, they did no **looting.**
9.16 But they did no **looting.**
Prov 1.13 We'll find all kinds of riches and fill our houses with **loot!**
16.19 be one of the arrogant and get a share of their **loot.**
Is 8. 1 'Quick **Loot,** Fast Plunder.'

Is 8. 4 of Damascus and all the **loot** of Samaria will be carried off
10. 6 I sent them to **loot** and steal and trample on the people
13.16 houses will be **looted,** and their wives will be raped."
33. 4 Their belongings are pounced upon and taken as **loot.**
42.24 Who gave Israel up to the **looters?**
49.24 Can you take away a soldier's **loot?**
49.25 will be taken away, and the tyrant's **loot** will be seized.
Jer 5.27 cage with birds, they have filled their houses with **loot.**
50.10 Babylonia will be **looted,**
50.10 and those who **loot** it will take everything they want.
50.26 Pile up the **loot** like piles of grain!
50.37 plunder and **loot.**
Ezek 29.19 He will **loot** and plunder it and carry off all the wealth
36.35 cities which were torn down, **looted,** and left in ruins, are
38.12 You will plunder and **loot** the people who live in cities
38.13 your army and attacked in order to **loot** and plunder?
39.10 They will **loot** and plunder those who looted and plundered them."
Dan 11.28 return home with all the **loot** he has captured, determined to
Obad 6 Descendants of Esau, your treasures have been **looted.**
Nah 3. 1 murderous city, full of wealth to be **looted** and plundered!
Zeph 1. 9 and kill in order to fill their master's house with **loot.**
1.13 Their wealth will be **looted** and their houses destroyed.
Zech 14. 1 Then Jerusalem will be **looted,**
14. 1 and the **loot** will be divided up
14. 2 The city will be taken, the houses **looted,** and the women raped.
14.14 They will take as **loot** the wealth of all the nations—

LORD

[OUR LORD, POWER OF THE LORD, THE LORD GOD, THE LORD YOUR SAVIOUR]

In this translation "LORD" *stands for the Hebrew name "Yahweh" (some translations use "Jehovah"). Sometimes it refers to the name itself, sometimes to a pronoun standing for the name. It is listed below as* **" Lord ".**

Gen 2. 4 When the **Lord God** made the universe, [5]there were no plants
2. 7 Then the **Lord God** took some soil from the ground and
2. 8 Then the **Lord God** planted a garden in Eden, in the East,
2.15 Then the **Lord God** placed the man in the Garden of Eden
2.18 Then the **Lord God** said, "It is not good for the man
2.21 Then the **Lord God** made the man fall into a deep sleep,
3. 1 was the most cunning animal that the **Lord God** had made.
3. 8 That evening they heard the **Lord God** walking in the garden,
3. 9 But the **Lord God** called out to the man, "Where are you?"
3.13 The **Lord God** asked the woman, "Why did you do this?"
3.14 Then the **Lord God** said to the snake, "You will be
3.21 And the **Lord God** made clothes out of animal skins for
3.22 Then the **Lord God** said, "Now the man has become like
3.23 So the **Lord God** sent him out of the Garden of Eden
4. 1 son and said, "By the **Lord's** help I have acquired a son."
4. 3 of his harvest and gave it as an offering to the **Lord.**
4. 4 The **Lord** was pleased with Abel and his offering, [5]but he
4. 6 Then the **Lord** said to Cain, "Why are you angry?
4. 9 The **Lord** asked Cain, "Where is your brother Abel?"
4.10 Then the **Lord** said, "Why have you done this terrible thing?
4.13 And Cain said to the **Lord,** "This punishment is too hard
4.15 But the **Lord** answered, "No.
4.15 So the **Lord** put a mark on Cain to warn anyone who
4.16 Cain went away from the **Lord's** presence and lived in a land
4.26 that people began using the **Lord's** holy name in worship.
5.29 very ground on which the **Lord** put a curse, this child will
6. 3 Then the **Lord** said, "I will not allow people to live for
6. 5 When the **Lord** saw how wicked everyone on earth was and how
6. 8 But the **Lord** was pleased with Noah.
7. 1 The **Lord** said to Noah, "Go into the boat with your whole
7. 5 And Noah did everything that the **Lord** commanded.
7.16 Then the **Lord** shut the door behind Noah.
7.23 The **Lord** destroyed all living beings on the earth—human beings,
8.20 Noah built an altar to the **Lord;**
8.21 of the sacrifice pleased the **Lord,** and he said to himself,
9.26 Give praise to the **Lord,** the God of Shem!
10. 9 By the **Lord's** help he was a great hunter, and that is
10. 9 why people say, "May the **Lord** make you as great a hunter
11. 5 Then the **Lord** came down to see the city and the tower
11. 8 So the **Lord** scattered them all over the earth, and they
11. 9 called Babylon, because there the **Lord** mixed up the language
12. 1 The **Lord** said to Abram, "Leave your country, your relatives,
12. 4 started out from Haran, as the **Lord** had told him to do;
12. 7 The **Lord** appeared to Abram and said to him, "This is the
12. 7 built an altar there to the **Lord,** who had appeared to him.
12. 8 There also he built an altar and worshipped the **Lord.**
12.17 king had taken Sarai, the **Lord** sent terrible diseases on him
13. 4 There he worshipped the **Lord.**
13.10 like the Garden of the **Lord** or like the land of Egypt.
13.10 (This was before the **Lord** had destroyed the cities of Sodom
13.13 whose people were wicked and sinned against the **Lord.**
13.14 After Lot had left, the **Lord** said to Abram, "From where
13.18 Mamre at Hebron, and there he built an altar to the **Lord.**
14.22 "I solemnly swear before the **Lord,** the Most High God, Maker
15. 1 a vision and heard the **Lord** say to him, "Do not be
15. 2 But Abram answered, "Sovereign **Lord,** what good will your reward do me,
15. 4 Then he heard the **Lord** speaking to him again:
15. 5 The **Lord** took him outside and said, "Look at the sky and
15. 6 put his trust in the **Lord,** and because of this the Lord
15. 7 Then the **Lord** said to him, "I am the Lord, who led
15. 8 But Abram asked, "Sovereign **Lord,** how can I know that it
15.13 The **Lord** said to him, "Your descendants will be
15.18 Then and there the **Lord** made a covenant with Abram.
16. 2 said to Abram, "The **Lord** has kept me from having children.
16. 5 May the **Lord** judge which of us is right, you or me!"

Gen 16. 7 The angel of the **Lord** met Hagar at a spring in the
16.11 Ishmael, because the **Lord** has heard your cry of distress.
16.13 So she called the **Lord** who had spoken to her "A God
17. 1 ninety-nine years old, the **Lord** appeared to him and said,
18. 1 The **Lord** appeared to Abraham at the sacred trees of Mamre.
18.13 Then the **Lord** asked Abraham, "Why did Sarah laugh and say,
18.14 Is anything too hard for the **Lord?**
18.17 And the **Lord** said to himself, "I will not hide from
18.20 Then the **Lord** said to Abraham, "There are terrible
18.22 went on towards Sodom, but the **Lord** remained with Abraham.
18.23 Abraham approached the **Lord** and asked, "Are you really
18.26 The **Lord** answered, "If I find fifty innocent people in Sodom,
18.27 "Please forgive my boldness in continuing to speak to you, **Lord.**
18.28 The **Lord** answered, "I will not destroy the city if I find
18.30 Abraham said, "Please don't be angry, **Lord,** but I must speak again.
18.31 "Please forgive my boldness in continuing to speak to you, **Lord.**
18.32 said, "Please don't be angry, **Lord,** and I will speak just
18.33 Abraham, the **Lord** went away, and Abraham returned home.
19.13 The **Lord** has heard the terrible accusations against these
19.14 the **Lord** is going to destroy this place."
19.16 The **Lord,** however, had pity on him;
19.24 Suddenly the **Lord** rained burning sulphur on the cities
19.27 the place where he had stood in the presence of the **Lord.**
20. 4 had not come near her, and he said, **"Lord,** I am innocent!
20.17 to Sarah, Abraham's wife, the **Lord** had made it impossible
21. 1 The **Lord** blessed Sarah, as he had promised, [2]and she
21.33 in Beersheba and worshipped the **Lord,** the Everlasting God.
22.11 But the angel of the **Lord** called to him from heaven,
22.14 Abraham named that place "The **Lord** Provides."
22.14 And even today people say, "On the **Lord's** mountain he provides."
22.15 The angel of the **Lord** called to Abraham from heaven a
22.16 by my own name—the **Lord** is speaking—that I will richly
24. 1 now very old, and the **Lord** had blessed him in everything he
24. 3 in the name of the **Lord,** the God of heaven and earth,
24. 7 The **Lord,** the God of heaven, brought me from the home of
24.12 He prayed, **"Lord,** God of my master Abraham, give me
24.21 her in silence, to see if the **Lord** had given him success.
24.26 Then the man knelt down and worshipped the **Lord.**
24.27 He said, "Praise the **Lord,** the God of my master Abraham,
24.27 The **Lord** has led me straight to my master's relatives."
24.31 You are a man whom the **Lord** has blessed.
24.35 "The **Lord** has greatly blessed my master and made him a
24.40 He answered, 'The **Lord,** whom I have always obeyed, will
24.42 the well today, I prayed, **'Lord,** God of my master Abraham,
24.48 I knelt down and worshipped the **Lord.**
24.48 I praised the **Lord,** the God of my master Abraham, who had
24.50 this matter comes from the **Lord,** it is not for us to
24.51 wife of your master's son, as the **Lord** himself has said."
24.52 Abraham heard this, he bowed down and worshipped the **Lord.**
24.56 The **Lord** has made my journey a success;
25.21 Because Rebecca had no children, Isaac prayed to the **Lord** for her.
25.21 The **Lord** answered his prayer, and Rebecca became pregnant.
25.22 So she went to ask the **Lord** for an answer.
25.23 The **Lord** said to her,
26. 2 The **Lord** had appeared to Isaac and had said, "Do not go
26.12 times as much as he had sown, because the **Lord** blessed him.
26.22 He said, "Now the **Lord** has given us freedom to live in
26.24 That night the **Lord** appeared to him and said, "I am the
26.25 Isaac built an altar there and worshipped the **Lord.**
26.28 "Now we know that the **Lord** is with you, and we think
26.29 Now it is clear that the **Lord** has blessed you."
27. 7 you my blessing in the presence of the **Lord** before I die.'
27.20 Jacob answered, **"The Lord your God** helped me to find it."
27.27 is like the smell of a field which the **Lord** has blessed.
28.13 And there was the **Lord** standing beside him.
28.13 "I am the **Lord,** the God of Abraham and Isaac," he said.
28.16 Jacob woke up and said, "The **Lord** is here!
28.20 Then Jacob made a vow to the **Lord:**
29.31 When the **Lord** saw that Leah was loved less than Rachel,
29.32 She said, "The **Lord** has seen my trouble, and now my husband
29.33 She said, "The **Lord** has given me this son also, because he
29.35 She said, "This time I will praise the **Lord";**
30.24 May the **Lord** give me another son";
30.27 by divination that the **Lord** has blessed me because of you.
30.30 enormously, and the **Lord** has blessed you wherever I went.
31. 3 Then the **Lord** said to him, "Go back to the land of
31.49 Laban also said, "May the **Lord** keep an eye on us while
32. 9 You told me, **Lord,** to go back to my land and to
38. 7 evil, and it displeased the **Lord,** so the Lord killed him.
38.10 What he did displeased the **Lord,** and the Lord killed him also.
39. 2 The **Lord** was with Joseph and made him successful.
39. 3 master, [3]who saw that the **Lord** was with Joseph and had made
39. 5 on, because of Joseph the **Lord** blessed the household of the
39.21 But the **Lord** was with Joseph and blessed him, so that
39.23 Joseph was responsible, because the **Lord** was with Joseph and
49.18 "I wait for your deliverance, **Lord.**
Ex 3. 2 There the angel of the **Lord** appeared to him as a flame
3. 4 When the **Lord** saw that Moses was coming closer, he called
3. 7 Then the **Lord** said, "I have seen how cruelly my people
3.15 the Israelites that I, the **Lord,** the God of their ancestors,
3.16 tell them that I, the **Lord,** the God of their ancestors, the
3.18 and say to him, 'The **Lord,** the God of the Hebrews, has
3.18 into the desert to offer sacrifices to **the Lord, our God.'**
4. 1 Then Moses answered the **Lord,** "But suppose the Israelites
4. 2 So the **Lord** asked him, "What are you holding?"
4. 3 The **Lord** said, "Throw it on the ground."
4. 4 Then the **Lord** said to Moses, "Bend down and pick it up
4. 5 The **Lord** said, "Do this to prove to the Israelites that
4. 5 to the Israelites that the **Lord,** the God of their ancestors,

Ex
4. 6 The **Lord** spoke to Moses again, "Put your hand inside your robe."
4. 7 Then the **Lord** said, "Put your hand inside your robe again."
4. 8 The **Lord** said, "If they will not believe you or be
4.10 But Moses said, "No, **Lord,** don't send me.
4.11 The **Lord** said to him, "Who gives man his mouth?
4.11 It is I, the **Lord.**
4.13 But Moses answered, "No, **Lord,** please send someone else."
4.14 At this the **Lord** became angry with Moses and said,
4.19 was still in Midian, the **Lord** said to him, "Go back to
4.21 Again the **Lord** said to Moses, "Now that you are going
4.22 him that I, the **Lord,** say, 'Israel is my first-born son.
4.24 the way to Egypt, the **Lord** met Moses and tried to kill
4.25 And so the **Lord** spared Moses' life.
4.27 Meanwhile the **Lord** had said to Aaron, "Go into the
4.28 told Aaron everything that the **Lord** had said when he told
4.28 the miracles which the **Lord** had ordered him to perform.
4.30 told them everything that the **Lord** had said to Moses, and
4.31 when they heard that the **Lord** had come to them and had
5. 1 of Egypt and said, "The **Lord,** the God of Israel, says, 'Let
5. 2 "Who is the **Lord?"**
5. 2 I do not know the **Lord;**
5. 3 into the desert to offer sacrifices to **the Lord our God.**
5.17 ask me to let you go and offer sacrifices to the **Lord.**
5.21 to Moses and Aaron, "The **Lord** has seen what you have done
5.22 Then Moses turned to the **Lord** again and said, "Lord,
5.22 Lord again and said, **"Lord,** why do you ill-treat your people?
6. 1 Then the **Lord** said to Moses, "Now you are going to see
6. 2 God spoke to Moses and said, "I am the **Lord.**
6. 3 not make myself known to them by my holy name, the **Lord.**
6. 6 tell the Israelites that I say to them, 'I am the **Lord;**
6. 7 know that I am **the Lord your God** when I set you
6. 8 I am the **Lord.'"**
6.10 Then the **Lord** said to Moses, [11] "Go and tell the king
6.13 The **Lord** commanded Moses and Aaron:
6.26 the ones to whom the **Lord** said, "Lead the tribes of Israel
6.28 When the **Lord** spoke to Moses in the land of Egypt,
6.29 Moses in the land of Egypt, [29] he said, "I am the **Lord.**
7. 1 The **Lord** said, "I am going to make you like God to
7. 5 know that I am the **Lord,** when I raise my hand against
7. 6 Moses and Aaron did what the **Lord** commanded.
7. 8 The **Lord** said to Moses and Aaron, [9] "If the king demands
7.10 Aaron went to the king and did as the **Lord** had commanded.
7.13 stubborn and, just as the **Lord** had said, the king would not
7.14 Then the **Lord** said to Moses, "The king is very stubborn
7.16 say to the king, 'The **Lord,** the God of the Hebrews, sent
7.17 Now, Your Majesty, the **Lord** says that you will find out
7.19 The **Lord** said to Moses, "Tell Aaron to take his stick
7.20 Then Moses and Aaron did as the **Lord** commanded.
7.22 Just as the **Lord** had said, the king refused to listen to
7.25 Seven days passed after the **Lord** struck the river.
8. 1 Then the **Lord** said to Moses, "Go to the king
8. 1 and tell him that the **Lord** says, 'Let my people go,
8. 5 The **Lord** said to Moses, "Tell Aaron to hold out his stick
8. 8 and said, "Pray to the **Lord** to take away these frogs, and
8. 8 people go, so that they can offer sacrifices to the **Lord."**
8.10 know that there is no other god like **the Lord, our God.**
8.12 and Moses prayed to the **Lord** to take away the frogs which
8.13 The **Lord** did as Moses asked, and the frogs in the houses,
8.15 again and, just as the **Lord** had said, the king would not
8.16 The **Lord** said to Moses, "Tell Aaron to strike the
8.19 stubborn and, just as the **Lord** had said, the king would not
8.20 The **Lord** said to Moses, "Early tomorrow morning go and
8.20 and tell him that the **Lord** says, 'Let my people go, so
8.22 will know that I, the **Lord,** am at work in this land.
8.24 The **Lord** sent great swarms of flies into the king's
8.26 sacrificing the animals that we offer to **the Lord our God.**
8.27 to offer sacrifices to **the Lord our God,** just as he
8.28 go to sacrifice to **the Lord, your God,** in the desert, if
8.29 I will pray to the **Lord** that tomorrow the flies will leave
8.29 prevent the people from going to sacrifice to the **Lord."**
8.30 king and prayed to the **Lord,** [31] and the Lord did as Moses
8.31 and prayed to the Lord, [31] and the **Lord** did as Moses asked.
9. 1 The **Lord** said to Moses, "Go to the king
9. 1 and tell him that the **Lord,** the God of the Hebrews, says,
9. 5 I, the **Lord,** have set tomorrow as the time when I will
9. 6 The next day the **Lord** did as he had said, and all
9. 8 Then the **Lord** said to Moses and Aaron, "Take a few
9.12 But the **Lord** made the king stubborn and, just as the Lord
9.13 The **Lord** then said to Moses, "Early tomorrow morning
9.13 and tell him that the **Lord,** the God of the Hebrews, says,
9.20 afraid because of what the **Lord** had said, and they brought
9.21 paid no attention to the **Lord's** warning and left their
9.22 Then the **Lord** said to Moses, "Raise your hand towards the sky,
9.23 towards the sky, and the **Lord** sent thunder and hail, and
9.23 The **Lord** sent [24] a heavy hailstorm, with lightning flashing to and fro.
9.27 the **Lord** is in the right, and my people and I are
9.28 Pray to the **Lord!**
9.29 city, I will lift up my hands in prayer to the **Lord.**
9.29 so that you may know that the earth belongs to the **Lord.**
9.30 that you and your officials do not yet fear the **Lord God."**
9.33 the city, and lifted up his hands in prayer to the **Lord.**
9.35 ever [35] and, just as the **Lord** had foretold through Moses,
10. 1 Then the **Lord** said to Moses, "Go and see the king.
10. 2 All of you will know that I am the **Lord."**
10. 3 and said to him, "The **Lord,** the God of the Hebrews, says
10. 7 Israelite men go, so that they can worship **the Lord their God.**
10. 8 said to them, "You may go and worship **the Lord your God.**
10. 9 because we must hold a festival to honour the **Lord."**
10.10 said, "I swear by the **Lord** that I will never let you
10.11 may go and worship the **Lord** if that is what you want."

Ex
10.12 Then the **Lord** said to Moses, "Raise your hand over the
10.13 raised his stick, and the **Lord** caused a wind from the east
10.16 "I have sinned against **the Lord your God** and against you.
10.17 once and pray to **the Lord your God** to take away this
10.18 Moses left the king and prayed to the **Lord.**
10.19 And the **Lord** changed the east wind into a very strong
10.20 But the **Lord** made the king stubborn, and he did not let
10.21 The **Lord** then said to Moses, "Raise your hand towards the sky,
10.24 called Moses and said, "You may go and worship the **Lord;**
10.25 sacrifices and burnt-offerings to offer to **the Lord our God.**
10.26 select the animals with which to worship **the Lord our God.**
10.27 The **Lord** made the king stubborn, and he would not let
11. 1 Then the **Lord** said to Moses, "I will send only one more
11. 3 The **Lord** made the Egyptians respect the Israelites.
11. 4 said to the king, "The **Lord** says, 'At about midnight I will
11. 7 will know that I, the **Lord,** make a distinction between the
11. 9 The **Lord** had said to Moses, "The king will continue to
11.10 before the king, but the **Lord** made him stubborn, and he
12. 1 The **Lord** spoke to Moses and Aaron in Egypt:
12.11 It is the Passover Festival to honour me, the **Lord.**
12.12 I am the **Lord.**
12.14 religious festival to remind you of what I, the **Lord,** have
12.15 The **Lord** said, "For seven days you must not eat any
12.23 When the **Lord** goes through Egypt to kill the Egyptians,
12.25 enter the land that the **Lord** has promised to give you, you
12.27 of Passover to honour the **Lord,** because he passed over the
12.28 went and did what the **Lord** had commanded Moses and Aaron.
12.29 At midnight the **Lord** killed all the first-born sons in Egypt,
12.31 go and worship the **Lord,** as you asked.
12.36 The **Lord** made the Egyptians respect the people and give
12.41 430 years ended, all the tribes of the **Lord's** people left Egypt.
12.42 was a night when the **Lord** kept watch to bring them out
12.42 night is dedicated to the **Lord** for all time to come as
12.43 The **Lord** said to Moses and Aaron, "These are the Passover regulations:
12.48 celebrate Passover to honour the **Lord,** you must first
12.50 Israelites obeyed and did what the **Lord** had commanded Moses and Aaron.
12.51 On that day the **Lord** brought the Israelite tribes out of Egypt.
13. 1 The **Lord** said to Moses, [2] "Dedicate all the first-born males to me,
13. 3 This is the day the **Lord** brought you out by his great
13. 5 The **Lord** solemnly promised your ancestors to give you the
13. 6 seventh day there is to be a festival to honour the **Lord.**
13. 8 this because of what the **Lord** did for you when you left
13. 9 study the Law of the **Lord,** because the Lord brought you out
13.11 "The **Lord** will bring you into the land of the Canaanites,
13.12 you, [12] you must offer every first-born male to the **Lord.**
13.12 your animals belongs to the **Lord,** [13] but you must buy back
13.14 'By using great power the **Lord** brought us out of Egypt, the
13.15 to let us go, the **Lord** killed every first-born male in the
13.15 male animal to the **Lord,** but buy back our first-born sons.
13.16 will remind us that the **Lord** brought us out of Egypt by
13.21 During the day the **Lord** went in front of them in a
14. 1 Then the **Lord** said to Moses, [2] "Tell the Israelites to
14. 4 Then the Egyptians will know that I am the **Lord."**
14. 8 The **Lord** made the king stubborn, and he pursued the Israelites,
14.10 they were terrified and cried out to the **Lord** for help.
14.13 you will see what the **Lord** will do to save you today;
14.14 The **Lord** will fight for you, and there is no need for
14.15 The **Lord** said to Moses, "Why are you crying out for help?
14.18 I defeat them, the Egyptians will know that I am the **Lord."**
14.21 over the sea, and the **Lord** drove the sea back with a
14.24 Just before dawn the **Lord** looked down from the pillar of
14.25 The Egyptians said, "The **Lord** is fighting for the Israelites against us.
14.26 The **Lord** said to Moses, "Hold out your hand over the sea,
14.27 escape from the water, but the **Lord** threw them into the sea.
14.30 On that day the **Lord** saved the people of Israel from the
14.31 Lord had defeated the Egyptians, they stood in awe of the **Lord;**
14.31 and they had faith in the **Lord** and in his servant Moses.
15. 1 Then Moses and the Israelites sang this song to the **Lord:**
15. 1 "I will sing to the **Lord,** because he has won a glorious
15. 2 The **Lord** is my strong defender;
15. 3 The **Lord** is a warrior;
15. 3 the **Lord** is his name.
15. 6 "Your right hand, **Lord,** is awesome in power;
15.10 But one breath from you, **Lord,** and the Egyptians were drowned;
15.11 **"Lord,** who among the gods is like you?
15.16 They see your strength, O **Lord,** and stand helpless with fear
15.17 the place that you, **Lord,** have chosen for your home,
15.18 You, **Lord,** will be king for ever and ever."
15.19 went into the sea, the **Lord** brought the water back, and it
15.21 "Sing to the **Lord,** because he has won a glorious victory;
15.25 Moses prayed earnestly to the **Lord,** and the Lord showed
15.25 There the **Lord** gave them laws to live by, and there he
15.26 I am the **Lord,** the one who heals you."
16. 3 to them, "We wish that the **Lord** had killed us in Egypt.
16. 4 The **Lord** said to Moses, "Now I am going to make food
16. 6 know that it was the **Lord** who brought you out of Egypt.
16. 7 you will see the dazzling light of the **Lord's** presence.
16. 8 Moses said, "It is the **Lord** who will give you meat to
16. 8 When you complain against us, you are really complaining against the **Lord."**
16. 9 before the **Lord,** because he has heard their complaints."
16.10 suddenly the dazzling light of the **Lord** appeared in a cloud.
16.11 The **Lord** said to Moses, [12] "I have heard the
16.12 Then they will know that I, the **Lord,** am their God."
16.15 "This is the food that the **Lord** has given you to eat.
16.16 The **Lord** has commanded that each of you is to gather as
16.23 he said to them, "The **Lord** has commanded that tomorrow is a
16.25 of rest dedicated to the **Lord,** and you will not find any

Ex 16.28 Then the **Lord** said to Moses, "How much longer will you
16.29 Remember that I, the **Lord,** have given you a day of rest,
16.32 Moses said, "The **Lord** has commanded us to save some manna,
16.33 and place it in the **Lord's** presence to be kept for our
16.34 As the **Lord** had commanded Moses, Aaron put it in front
17. 1 moving from one place to another at the command of the **Lord.**
17. 2 Why are you putting the **Lord** to the test?"
17. 4 Moses prayed earnestly to the **Lord** and said, "What can I
17. 5 The **Lord** said to Moses, "Take some of the leaders of
17. 7 Israelites complained and put the **Lord** to the test
17. 7 when they asked, "Is the **Lord** with us or not?"
17.14 Then the **Lord** said to Moses, "Write an account of this victory,
17.15 Moses built an altar and named it "The **Lord is my Banner."**
17.16 He said, "Hold high the banner of the **Lord!**
17.16 The **Lord** will continue to fight against the Amalekites for ever!"
18. 8 told Jethro everything that the **Lord** had done to the king
18. 8 had faced on the way and how the **Lord** had saved them.
18.10 happy [10]and said, "Praise the **Lord,** who saved you from
18.10 Praise the **Lord,** who saved his people from slavery!
18.11 Now I know that the **Lord** is greater than all the gods,
19. 3 The **Lord** called to him from the mountain and told him to
19. 4 "You saw what I, the **Lord,** did to the Egyptians and how
19. 7 and told them everything that the **Lord** had commanded him.
19. 8 the Lord has said," and Moses reported this to the **Lord.**
19. 9 The **Lord** said to Moses, "I will come to you in a
19. 9 Moses told the **Lord** what the people had answered, [10]and the Lord
19.10 people had answered, [10]and the **Lord** said to him, "Go to
19.18 covered with smoke, because the **Lord** had come down on it in
19.20 The **Lord** came down on the top of Mount Sinai and called
19.21 Moses went up [21]and the **Lord** said to him, "Go down and
19.23 Moses said to the **Lord,** "The people cannot come up,
19.24 The **Lord** replied, "Go down and bring Aaron back with you.
19.25 down to the people and told them what the **Lord** had said.
20. 2 "I am **the Lord your God** who brought you out of Egypt,
20. 5 it, because I am **the Lord your God** and I tolerate no
20. 7 evil purposes, for I, **the Lord your God,** will punish anyone
20.11 In six days I, the **Lord,** made the earth, the sky, the
20.11 That is why I, the **Lord,** blessed the Sabbath and made it
20.22 The **Lord** commanded Moses to say to the Israelites:
20.22 have seen how I, the **Lord,** have spoken to you from heaven.
22.20 who offers sacrifices to any god except to me, the **Lord.**
22.23 If you do, I, the **Lord,** will answer them when they cry
23.13 "Listen to everything that I, the **Lord,** have said to you.
23.17 all your men must come to worship me, **the Lord your God.**
23.19 to the house of **the Lord your God** the first corn that
23.25 If you worship me, **the Lord your God,** I will bless you
24. 1 The **Lord** said to Moses, "Come up the mountain to me, you
24. 3 the people all the **Lord's** commands and all the ordinances,
24. 3 together, "We will do everything that the **Lord** has said."
24. 4 Moses wrote down all the **Lord's** commands.
24. 5 the **Lord** and sacrificed some cattle as fellowship-offerings.
24. 7 the covenant, in which the **Lord's** commands were written, and
24. 7 said, "We will obey the **Lord** and do everything that he has
24. 8 seals the covenant which the **Lord** made with you when he gave
24.12 The **Lord** said to Moses, "Come up the mountain to me,
24.16 The dazzling light of the **Lord's** presence came down on the mountain.
24.16 on the seventh day the **Lord** called to Moses from the cloud.
25. 1 The **Lord** said to Moses, [2]"Tell the Israelites to make an
28.12 so that I, the **Lord,** will always remember my people.
28.29 Israel, so that I, the **Lord,** will always remember my people.
28.36 of pure gold and engrave on it 'Dedicated to the **Lord.'**
28.38 forehead, so that I, the **Lord,** will accept all the offerings
29. 6 sacred sign of dedication engraved 'Dedicated to the **Lord.'**
29.28 This is the people's gift to me, the **Lord.**
29.41 a food offering to me, the **Lord,** and its odour pleases me.
29.46 know that I am **the Lord their God** who brought them out
29.46 I am **the Lord their God.**
30.10 This altar is to be completely holy, dedicated to me, the **Lord."**
30.11 The **Lord** said to Moses, [12]"When you take a census of
30.17 The **Lord** said to Moses, [18]"Make a bronze basin with a
30.22 The **Lord** said to Moses, [23]"Take the finest spices—six
30.34 The **Lord** said to Moses, "Take an equal part of each of
31. 1 The **Lord** said to Moses, [2]"I have chosen Bezalel, the son
31.12 The **Lord** commanded Moses [13]to say to the people of Israel,
31.13 to show that I, the **Lord,** have made you my own people.
31.17 and me, because I, the **Lord,** made heaven and earth in six
32. 5 "Tomorrow there will be a festival to honour the **Lord."**
32. 7 The **Lord** said to Moses, "Go back down at once, because
32.11 But Moses pleaded with **the Lord his God** and said,
32.14 So the **Lord** changed his mind and did not bring on his
32.26 "Everyone who is on the **Lord's** side come over here!"
32.27 he said to them, "The **Lord God** of Israel commands every one
32.29 the service of the **Lord** by killing your sons and brothers,
32.29 so the **Lord** has given you his blessing."
32.30 But now I will again go up the mountain to the **Lord;**
32.31 Moses then returned to the **Lord** and said, "These people
32.33 The **Lord** answered, "It is those who have sinned against
32.35 So the **Lord** sent a disease on the people, because they
33. 1 The **Lord** said to Moses, "Leave this place, you and the
33. 5 For the **Lord** had commanded Moses to say to them, "You are
33. 7 called the Tent of the **Lord's** presence,
33. 7 anyone who wanted to consult the **Lord** would go out to it.
33. 9 of the Tent, and the **Lord** would speak to Moses from the
33.11 The **Lord** would speak with Moses face to face, just as a
33.12 Moses said to the **Lord,** "It is true that you have told
33.14 The **Lord** said, "I will go with you, and I will give
33.17 The **Lord** said to Moses, "I will do just as you have
33.19 The **Lord** answered, "I will make all my splendour pass
33.19 I am the **Lord,** and I show compassion and pity on those
34. 1 The **Lord** said to Moses, "Cut two stone tablets like the

Ex 34. 4 them up Mount Sinai, just as the **Lord** had commanded.
34. 5 The **Lord** came down in a cloud, stood with him there,
34. 5 and pronounced his holy name, the **Lord.**
34. 6 The **Lord** then passed in front of him and called out, "I,
34. 6 and called out, "I, the **Lord,** am a God who is full
34. 9 He said, **"Lord,** if you really are pleased with me, I ask
34.10 The **Lord** said to Moses, "I now make a covenant with the
34.10 what great things I, the **Lord,** can do, because I am going
34.14 any other god, because I, the **Lord,** tolerate no rivals.
34.23 men must come to worship me, the **Lord,** the God of Israel.
34.26 to the house of the **Lord** the first corn that you harvest.
34.27 The **Lord** said to Moses, "Write these words down,
34.28 Moses stayed there with the **Lord** forty days and nights,
34.29 face was shining because he had been speaking with the **Lord;**
34.32 all the laws that the **Lord** had given him on Mount Sinai.
34.34 into the Tent of the **Lord's** presence
34.34 to speak to the **Lord,** he took the veil off.
34.35 on until the next time he went to speak to the **Lord.**
35. 1 to them, "This is what the **Lord** has commanded you to do:
35. 2 be sacred, a solemn day of rest dedicated to me, the **Lord.**
35. 4 the people of Israel, "This is what the **Lord** has commanded:
35. 5 Make an offering to the **Lord.**
35.10 you are to come and make everything that the **Lord** commanded:
35.21 brought an offering to the **Lord**
35.21 for making the Tent of the **Lord's** presence.
35.22 all kinds of gold jewellery and dedicated them to the **Lord.**
35.24 brought their offering for the **Lord,** and all who had
35.29 brought their offering to the **Lord** for the work which he had
35.30 said to the Israelites, "The **Lord** has chosen Bezalel, the
35.34 The **Lord** has given to him and to Oholiab son of Ahisamach,
36. 1 to whom the **Lord** has given skill and understanding,
36. 1 are to make everything just as the **Lord** has commanded."
36. 2 skilled men to whom the **Lord** had given ability and who were
36. 5 needed for the work which the **Lord** commanded to be done."
36. 8 those doing the work made the Tent of the **Lord's** presence.
38. 8 served at the entrance of the Tent of the **Lord's** presence.
38. 9 For the Tent of the **Lord's** presence he made the enclosure
38.21 in the Tent of the **Lord's** presence, where the two stone
38.22 tribe of Judah, made everything that the **Lord** had commanded.
38.24 had been dedicated to the **Lord** for the sacred Tent weighed a
38.29 The bronze which was dedicated to the **Lord** amounted to 2,425 kilogrammes.
38.30 of the Tent of the **Lord's** presence, the bronze altar with
39. 1 garments for Aaron, as the **Lord** had commanded Moses.
39. 5 to form one piece with it, as the **Lord** had commanded Moses.
39. 7 tribes of Israel, just as the **Lord** had commanded Moses.
39.21 Just as the **Lord** had commanded Moses, they tied the
39.24 bells of pure gold, just as the **Lord** had commanded Moses.
39.29 decorated with embroidery, as the **Lord** had commanded Moses.
39.30 gold, and they engraved on it "Dedicated to the **Lord."**
39.31 with a blue cord, just as the **Lord** had commanded Moses.
39.32 on the Tent of the **Lord's** presence was finally completed.
39.32 The Israelites made everything just as the **Lord** had commanded Moses.
39.42 had done all the work just as the **Lord** had commanded Moses.
39.43 that they had made it all just as the **Lord** had commanded.
40. 1 The **Lord** said to Moses, [2]"On the first day of the first
40. 2 of the first month set up the Tent of the **Lord's** presence.
40.16 Moses did everything just as the **Lord** had commanded.
40.17 they left Egypt, the Tent of the **Lord's** presence was set up.
40.19 the outer covering over it, just as the **Lord** had commanded.
40.21 off the Covenant Box, just as the **Lord** had commanded.
40.23 bread offered to the **Lord,** just as the Lord had commanded.
40.25 and there in the **Lord's** presence he lit the lamps,
40.25 just as the **Lord** had commanded.
40.27 and burnt the sweet-smelling incense, just as the **Lord** had commanded.
40.29 and the grain-offering, just as the **Lord** had commanded.
40.32 the Tent or to the altar, just as the **Lord** had commanded.
40.34 Tent and the dazzling light of the **Lord's** presence filled it.
40.38 see the cloud of the **Lord's** presence over the Tent during
Lev 1. 1 The **Lord** called to Moses
1. 1 from the Tent of the **Lord's** presence and gave him the
1. 3 Tent of the Lord's presence so that the **Lord** will accept him.
1. 5 present the blood to the **Lord** and then throw it against all
1. 9 The smell of this food-offering is pleasing to the **Lord.**
1.13 present the sacrifice to the **Lord** and burn all of it on
1.13 The smell of this food-offering is pleasing to the **Lord.**
1.17 The smell of this food-offering is pleasing to the **Lord.**
2. 1 offering of grain to the **Lord,** he must first grind it into
2. 2 as a token that it has all been offered to the **Lord.**
2. 2 The smell of this food-offering is pleasing to the **Lord.**
2. 3 holy, since it is taken from the food offered to the **Lord.**
2. 8 as an offering to the **Lord** and present it to the priest,
2. 9 all been offered to the **Lord,** and he will burn it on
2. 9 The smell of this food-offering is pleasing to the **Lord.**
2.10 holy, since it is taken from the food offered to the **Lord.**
2.11 which you present to the **Lord** may be made with yeast;
2.11 must never use yeast or honey in food offered to the **Lord.**
2.12 shall be brought to the **Lord,** but it is not to be
2.14 When you bring to the **Lord** an offering of the first corn
2.16 and also all the incense, as a food-offering to the **Lord.**
3. 2 kill it at the entrance of the Tent of the **Lord's** presence.
3. 3 parts of the animal as a food-offering to the **Lord:**
3. 5 The smell of this food-offering is pleasing to the **Lord.**
3. 9 parts of the animal as a food-offering to the **Lord:**
3.11 burn all this on the altar as a food-offering to the **Lord.**
3.14 and present the following parts as a food-offering to the **Lord:**
3.16 this on the altar as a food-offering pleasing to the **Lord.**
3.16 All the fat belongs to the **Lord.**
4. 1 The **Lord** commanded Moses [2]to tell the people of Israel

Lev 4. 2 and broke any of the **Lord's** commands without intending to,
4. 3 any defects and sacrifice it to the **Lord** for his sin.
4. 4 hand on its head, and kill it there in the **Lord's** presence.
4.13 of breaking one of the **Lord's** commands without intending to,
4.14 They shall bring it to the Tent of the **Lord's** presence;
4.22 of breaking one of the **Lord's** commands without intending to,
4.27 of breaking one of the **Lord's** commands without intending to,
4.31 burn it on the altar so that the smell pleases the **Lord.**
4.35 the altar along with the food-offerings given to the **Lord.**
5. 6 he must bring to the **Lord** a female sheep or goat as
5. 7 he shall bring to the **Lord** as the payment for his sin
5.12 all been offered to the **Lord,** and he will burn it on
5.14 The **Lord** gave the following regulations to Moses.
5.15 that are sacred to the **Lord,** he shall bring as his
5.15 as his repayment-offering to the **Lord** a male sheep or goat
5.17 by breaking any of the **Lord's** commands, he is guilty and
5.19 It is a repayment-offering for the sin he committed against the **Lord.**
6. 1 The **Lord** gave the following regulations to Moses.
6. 2 any one sins against the **Lord** by refusing to return what a
6. 6 as his repayment-offering to the **Lord** a male sheep or goat
6. 8 The **Lord** commanded Moses [9] to give Aaron and his sons the
6.14 the grain-offering to the **Lord** in front of the altar.
6.15 a token that all of it has been offered to the **Lord.**
6.15 The smell of this offering is pleasing to the **Lord.**
6.16 place, the courtyard of the Tent of the **Lord's** presence.
6.16 The **Lord** has given it to the priests as their part of
6.18 as their continuing share of the food offered to the **Lord.**
6.19 The **Lord** gave Moses the following regulations [20] for
6.20 as an offering to the **Lord** one kilogramme of flour (the same
6.21 presented as a grain-offering, a smell pleasing to the **Lord.**
6.22 It shall be completely burnt as a sacrifice to the **Lord.**
6.24 The **Lord** commanded Moses [25] to give Aaron and his sons
6.26 place, the courtyard of the Tent of the **Lord's** presence.
7. 5 all the fat on the altar as a food-offering to the **Lord.**
7.11 The following are the regulations for the fellowship-offerings presented to the **Lord.**
7.14 of each kind of bread as a special contribution to the **Lord;**
7.22 The **Lord** gave Moses the following regulations [23] for the people of Israel.
7.25 as a food-offering to the **Lord** will no longer be considered
7.28 The **Lord** gave Moses the following regulations [29] for the people of Israel.
7.29 a special gift to the **Lord,** [30] bringing it with his own
7.30 its breast and present it as a special gift to the **Lord.**
7.34 a special contribution that the **Lord** has taken from the
7.35 the food offered to the **Lord** that was given to Aaron and
7.36 On that day the **Lord** commanded the people of Israel to
7.38 Sinai in the desert, the **Lord** gave these commands to Moses
8. 1 The **Lord** said to Moses, [2] "Take Aaron and his sons to the
8. 4 Moses did as the **Lord** had commanded, and when the
8. 5 I am now about to do is what the **Lord** has commanded."
8. 9 sign of dedication, just as the **Lord** had commanded him.
8.10 on the Tent of the **Lord's** presence and everything that was
8.10 it, and in this way he dedicated it all to the **Lord.**
8.11 basin and its base, in order to dedicate them to the **Lord.**
8.13 tied caps on their heads, just as the **Lord** had commanded.
8.17 burnt it outside the camp, just as the **Lord** had commanded.
8.20 of the ram on the altar, just as the **Lord** had commanded.
8.20 a food-offering, and the smell was pleasing to the **Lord.**
8.26 bread dedicated to the **Lord,** one loaf made with oil,
8.27 sons, and they presented it as a special gift to the **Lord.**
8.28 This was a food-offering, and the smell was pleasing to the **Lord.**
8.29 the breast and presented it as a special gift to the **Lord.**
8.29 Moses did everything just as the **Lord** had commanded.
8.30 In this way he consecrated them and their clothes to the **Lord.**
8.31 of the Tent of the **Lord's** presence, boil it, and eat it
8.31 basket of ordination offerings, just as the **Lord** commanded.
8.34 The **Lord** commanded us to do what we have done today, in
8.35 and night for seven days, doing what the **Lord** has commanded.
8.35 This is what the **Lord** has commanded me."
8.36 did everything that the **Lord** had commanded through Moses.
9. 2 and offer them to the **Lord,** the bull for a sin-offering and
9. 4 them to the **Lord** with the grain-offering mixed with oil.
9. 4 They must do this because the **Lord** will appear to them today."
9. 5 and the whole community assembled there to worship the **Lord.**
9. 6 Moses said, "The **Lord** has commanded you to do all this,
9. 7 away the sins of the people, just as the **Lord** commanded."
9.10 part of the liver, just as the **Lord** had commanded Moses.
9.21 the special gift to the **Lord** for the priests, as Moses had
9.23 the Tent of the **Lord's** presence, and when they came out,
9.23 light of the **Lord's** presence appeared to all the people.
9.24 Suddenly the **Lord** sent a fire, and it consumed the
10. 1 coals in it, added incense, and presented it to the **Lord.**
10. 1 was not holy, because the **Lord** had not commanded them to
10. 2 Suddenly the **Lord** sent fire, and it burnt them to death
10. 2 there in the presence of the **Lord.**
10. 3 "This is what the **Lord** was speaking about when he said,
10. 6 you will die, and the **Lord** will be angry with the whole
10. 6 to mourn this death caused by the fire which the **Lord** sent.
10. 7 have been consecrated by the anointing oil of the **Lord."**
10. 8 The **Lord** said to Aaron, [9] "You and your sons are not to
10.12 the food offered to the **Lord,** make unleavened bread with it
10.13 to you and your sons from the food offered to the **Lord.**
10.13 That is what the **Lord** commanded me.
10.14 and the special contribution to the **Lord** for the priests.
10.15 time the fat is presented as a food-offering to the **Lord.**
10.15 and your children for ever, just as the **Lord** commanded."
10.17 is very holy, and the **Lord** has given it to you in
10.19 "If I had eaten the sin-offering today, would the **Lord** have approved?

Lev 10.19 to the **Lord** today, and they brought their burnt-offering,
11. 1 The **Lord** gave Moses and Aaron the following regulations
11.44 I am **the Lord your God,** and you must keep yourselves holy,
11.45 I am the **Lord** who brought you out of Egypt so that
12. 1 The **Lord** gave Moses the following regulations [2] for the people of Israel.
12. 6 of the Tent of the **Lord's** presence a one-year-old lamb for a
12. 7 present her offering to the **Lord** and perform the ritual to
13. 1 The **Lord** gave Moses and Aaron these regulations.
14. 1 The **Lord** gave Moses [2] the following regulations about the
14.11 to the entrance of the Tent of the **Lord's** presence.
14.12 present them as a special gift to the **Lord** for the priest.
14.16 some of it seven times there in the **Lord's** presence.
14.21 a special gift to the **Lord** for the priest.
14.24 present them as a special gift to the **Lord** for the priest.
14.27 some of it seven times there in the **Lord's** presence.
14.33 The **Lord** gave Moses and Aaron [34-35] the following
14.34 land of Canaan, which the **Lord** was going to give them as
14.34 If someone finds that the **Lord** has sent mildew on his house,
15. 1 The **Lord** gave Moses and Aaron the following regulations
15.14 of the Tent of the **Lord's** presence and give them to the
15.29 priest at the entrance of the Tent of the **Lord's** presence.
15.31 The **Lord** told Moses to warn the people of Israel about
16. 1 The **Lord** spoke to Moses after the death of the two sons
16. 1 Aaron who were killed when they offered unholy fire to the **Lord.**
16. 4 Then the **Lord** gave the following instructions.
16. 7 goats to the entrance of the Tent of the **Lord's** presence.
16. 8 one marked "for the **Lord"** and the other "for Azazel."
16. 9 chosen by lot for the **Lord** and offer it as a sin-offering.
16.10 be presented alive to the **Lord** and sent off into the desert
16.13 There in the **Lord's** presence he shall put the incense on
16.20 of the Tent of the **Lord's** presence, and the altar, he shall
16.20 shall present to the **Lord** the live goat chosen for Azazel.
16.33 of the Tent of the **Lord's** presence, the altar, the priests,
16.34 So Moses did as the **Lord** had commanded.
17. 1 The **Lord** commanded Moses [2] to give Aaron and his sons and
17. 3 as an offering to the **Lord** anywhere except at the entrance
17. 3 of the Tent of the **Lord's** presence has broken the Law.
17. 5 shall now bring to the **Lord** the animals which they used to
17. 6 the fat to produce a smell that is pleasing to the **Lord.**
17. 7 longer be unfaithful to the **Lord** by killing their animals in
17. 9 as an offering to the **Lord** anywhere except at the entrance
17.10 blood still in it, the **Lord** will turn against him and no
17.11 and that is why the **Lord** has commanded that all blood be
17.12 That is why the **Lord** has told the people of Israel that
17.14 and that is why the **Lord** has told the people of Israel
18. 1 The **Lord** told Moses [2] to say to the people of Israel, "I
18. 2 say to the people of Israel, "I am **the Lord your God.**
18. 4 I am **the Lord your God.**
18. 5 I am the **Lord."**
18. 6 The **Lord** gave the following regulations.
18.21 that would bring disgrace on the name of God, the **Lord.**
18.24 before you and whom the **Lord** is driving out so that you
18.25 land unclean, and so the **Lord** is punishing the land and
18.26 with you, must keep the **Lord's** laws and commands, [28] and
18.30 And the **Lord** said, "Obey the commands I give and do not
18.30 I am **the Lord your God."**
19. 1 The **Lord** told Moses [2] to say to the community of Israel,
19. 2 of Israel, "Be holy, because I, **the Lord your God,** am holy.
19. 3 I am **the Lord your God.**
19. 4 I am **the Lord your God.**
19.10 I am **the Lord your God.**
19.12 I am **the Lord your God.**
19.14 I am **the Lord your God.**
19.16 I am the **Lord.**
19.18 I am the **Lord.**
19.24 as an offering to show your gratitude to me, the **Lord.**
19.25 I am **the Lord your God.**
19.28 I am the **Lord.**
19.30 I am the **Lord.**
19.31 I am **the Lord your God.**
19.32 I am the **Lord.**
19.34 I am **the Lord your God.**
19.36 I am **the Lord your God,** and I brought you out of
19.37 I am the **Lord."**
20. 1 The **Lord** told Moses [2] to say to the people of Israel,
20. 7 Keep yourselves holy, because I am **the Lord your God.**
20. 8 my laws, because I am the **Lord** and I make you holy."
20. 9 The **Lord** gave the following regulations.
20.22 The **Lord** said, "Keep all my laws and commands, so that
20.24 I am **the Lord your God,** and I have set you apart
20.26 only to me, because I am the **Lord** and I am holy.
21. 1 The **Lord** commanded Moses to say to the Aaronite priests,
21. 8 I am the **Lord;**
21.15 I am the **Lord** and I have set him apart as the
21.16 The **Lord** commanded Moses [17] to say to Aaron, "None of
21.23 holy things, because I am the **Lord** and I make them holy."
22. 1 The **Lord** commanded Moses [2] to say to Aaron and his sons,
22. 2 I am the **Lord.**
22. 3 I am the **Lord.**
22. 8 I am the **Lord.**
22. 9 I am the **Lord** and I make them holy.
22.16 I am the **Lord** and I make the offerings holy."
22.17 The **Lord** commanded Moses [18] to give Aaron and his sons
22.20 any animal that has any defect, the **Lord** will not accept it.
22.21 presents a fellowship-offering to the **Lord,** whether in
22.22 Do not offer to the **Lord** any animal that is blind or
22.24 Do not offer to the **Lord** any animal whose testicles have
22.29 sacrifice of thanksgiving to the **Lord,** follow the rules so
22.31 The **Lord** said, "Obey my commands;
22.31 I am the **Lord.**

Lev 22.32 I am the **Lord** and I make you holy;
22.33 I am the **Lord."**
23. 1 The **Lord** gave Moses [2]the following regulations for the religious festivals,
23. 3 The Sabbath belongs to the **Lord,** no matter where you live.
23. 5 Passover, celebrated to honour the **Lord,** begins at sunset on
23. 8 Offer your food-offerings to the **Lord** for seven days.
23. 9 into the land that the **Lord** is giving you and you harvest
23.11 a special offering to the **Lord,** so that you may be accepted.
23.13 The smell of this offering is pleasing to the **Lord.**
23.15 which you bring your sheaf of corn to present to the **Lord.**
23.16 Sabbath, present to the **Lord** another new offering of corn.
23.17 of bread and present them to the **Lord** as a special gift.
23.17 shall be presented to the **Lord** as an offering of the first
23.18 as a burnt-offering to the **Lord,**
23.18 The smell of this offering is pleasing to the **Lord.**
23.20 two lambs as a special gift to the **Lord** for the priests.
23.22 The **Lord is your God.**
23.25 Present a food-offering to the **Lord** and do none of your
23.26 for worship, and present a food-offering to the **Lord.**
23.30 work on that day, the **Lord** himself will put him to death.
23.37 on which you honour the **Lord** by gathering together for
23.38 and your freewill offerings that you give to the **Lord.)**
23.40 and begin a religious festival to honour **the Lord your God.**
23.43 descendants may know that the **Lord** made the people of Israel
23.43 He is **the Lord your God.**
23.44 Israel the regulations for observing the religious festivals to honour the **Lord.**
24. 1 The **Lord** told Moses [2]to give the following orders to the
24. 3 until morning, there in the **Lord's** presence outside the
24. 4 must see that they burn regularly in the **Lord's** presence.
24. 6 covered with pure gold, which is in the **Lord's** presence.
24. 7 a token food-offering to the **Lord** to take the place of the
24. 8 come, the bread must be placed in the presence of the **Lord.**
24. 9 holy part of the food offered to the **Lord** for the priests.
24.12 guard, and waited for the **Lord** to tell them what to do
24.13 The **Lord** said to Moses, [14]"Take that man out of the camp.
24.16 in Israel who curses the **Lord** shall be stoned to death by
24.22 living among you, because I am **the Lord your God."**
24.23 the people of Israel did what the **Lord** had commanded Moses.
25. 1 The **Lord** spoke to Moses on Mount Sinai and commanded him
25. 2 enter the land that the **Lord** is giving you,
25. 2 you shall honour the **Lord** by not cultivating the land
25. 4 of complete rest for the land, a year dedicated to the **Lord.**
25.17 Do not cheat a fellow-Israelite, but obey **the Lord your God.**
25.18 Obey all the **Lord's** laws and commands, so that you may
25.21 The **Lord** will bless the land in the sixth year so that
25.38 is the command of **the Lord your God,** who brought you out
25.42 people of Israel are the **Lord's** slaves, and he brought them
25.55 slave, because the people of Israel are the **Lord's** slaves.
25.55 he is **the Lord their God.**
26. 1 The **Lord** said, "Do not make idols or set up statues,
26. 1 I am **the Lord your God.**
26. 2 I am the **Lord.**
26.13 I, **the Lord your God,** brought you out of Egypt so that
26.14 The **Lord** said, "If you will not obey my commands, you
26.44 to my covenant with them, and I am **the Lord their God.**
26.45 of Egypt, in order that I, the **Lord,** might be their God."
26.46 laws and commands that the **Lord** gave to Moses on Mount Sinai
27. 1 The **Lord** gave Moses [2]the following regulations for the people of Israel.
27. 2 has been given to the **Lord** in fulfilment of a special vow,
27. 9 as an offering to the **Lord,** then every gift made to the
27. 9 every gift made to the **Lord** is sacred, [10]and the man who
27.10 If he does, both animals belong to the **Lord.**
27.11 as an offering to the **Lord,** the man shall take the animal
27.14 dedicates his house to the **Lord,** the priest shall fix the
27.16 of his land to the **Lord,** the price shall be fixed according
27.20 buying it back from the **Lord,** he loses the right to buy
27.21 Year of Restoration the field will become the **Lord's** permanent property;
27.22 a man dedicates to the **Lord** a field that he has bought,
27.23 the money belongs to the **Lord.**
27.26 animal already belongs to the **Lord,** so no one may dedicate
27.26 a kid belongs to the **Lord,** [27]but the first-born of an
27.28 dedicated to the **Lord,** whether it is a human being,
27.28 It belongs permanently to the **Lord.**
27.30 of the land, whether grain or fruit, belongs to the **Lord.**
27.32 One out of every ten domestic animals belongs to the **Lord.**
27.32 When the animals are counted, every tenth one belongs to the **Lord.**
27.33 animals will belong to the **Lord** and may not be bought back.
27.34 are the commands that the **Lord** gave Moses on Mount Sinai for

Num 1. 1 of Israel left Egypt, the **Lord** spoke to Moses there in the
1.19 were recorded and counted, [19]as the **Lord** had commanded.
1.48 the other tribes, [48]because the **Lord** had said to Moses,
1.54 of Israel did everything that the **Lord** had commanded Moses.
2. 1 The **Lord** gave Moses and Aaron the following instructions.
2.33 As the **Lord** had commanded Moses, the Levites were not
2.34 So the people of Israel did everything the **Lord** had commanded Moses.
3. 1 Moses at the time the **Lord** spoke to Moses on Mount Sinai.
3. 4 they offered unholy fire to the **Lord** in the Sinai Desert.
3. 5 The **Lord** said to Moses, [6]"Bring forward the tribe of
3.11 The **Lord** said to Moses, [12-13]"The Levites are now to be mine.
3.12 I am the **Lord."**
3.14 In the Sinai Desert the **Lord** commanded Moses [15]to
3.39 Moses enrolled by clans at the command of the **Lord,** was
3.40 The **Lord** said to Moses, "All of Israel's
3.40 I am the **Lord!**
3.44 The **Lord** said to Moses, [45]"Now dedicate the Levites

Num 4. 1 The **Lord** told Moses [2]to take a census of the Levite clan
4. 3 were qualified to work in the Tent of the **Lord's** presence.
4. 5 The **Lord** gave Moses the following instructions.
4. 7 the bread offered to the **Lord** and put on it the dishes,
4.16 else in the Tent that has been consecrated to the **Lord.**
4.17 The **Lord** said to Moses and Aaron, [18]"Do not let the
4.21 The **Lord** told Moses [22]to take a census of the Levite
4.23 were qualified to work in the Tent of the **Lord's** presence.
4.29 The **Lord** told Moses to take a census of the Levite clan
4.30 were qualified to work in the Tent of the **Lord's** presence.
4.34 Following the **Lord's** command, Moses, Aaron, and
4.34 qualified to work in the Tent of the **Lord's** presence, as
4.49 Each man was registered as the **Lord** had commanded Moses;
4.49 at the command of the **Lord** given through Moses, each man was
5. 1 The **Lord** said to Moses, [2]"Command the people of Israel
5. 5 The **Lord** gave Moses [6]the following instructions for the people of Israel.
5. 6 unfaithful to the **Lord** and commits a wrong against someone,
5. 8 be made, it shall be given to the **Lord** for the priest.
5. 9 the Israelites offer to the **Lord** belongs to the priest to
5.11 The **Lord** commanded Moses [12-14]to give the Israelites the following instructions.
5.17 of the Tent of the **Lord's** presence and put it in the
5.21 have committed adultery, [21]may the **Lord** make your name a
5.22 may the **Lord** do so."
5.25 out in dedication to the **Lord,** and present it on the altar.
6. 1 The **Lord** commanded Moses [2]to give the following
6. 2 himself to the **Lord** [3]shall abstain from wine and beer.
6. 5 he is dedicated to the **Lord,** and he shall let his hair
6. 8 long as he is a Nazirite, he is consecrated to the **Lord.**
6.10 priest at the entrance of the Tent of the **Lord's** presence.
6.12 hair [12]and rededicate to the **Lord** his time as a Nazirite.
6.14 Tent [14]and present to the **Lord** three animals without any defects:
6.16 present all these to the **Lord** and offer the sin-offering and
6.17 sacrifice the ram to the **Lord** as a fellowship-offering, and
6.20 the priest shall present them as a special gift to the **Lord;**
6.22 The **Lord** commanded Moses [23]to tell Aaron and his sons
6.24 May the **Lord** bless you and take care of you;
6.25 May the **Lord** be kind and gracious to you;
6.26 May the **Lord** look on you with favour and give you peace.
6.27 And the **Lord** said, "If they pronounce my name as a
7. 1 up the Tent of the **Lord's** presence, he anointed and
7. 3 charge of the census, [3]brought their offerings to the **Lord:**
7. 4 they had presented them, [4]the **Lord** said to Moses,
7.11 gifts at the altar, [11]the **Lord** said to Moses, "Tell them
7.89 Tent to talk with the **Lord,** he heard the Lord speaking to
8. 1 The **Lord** said to Moses, [2]"Tell Aaron that when he puts
8. 4 according to the pattern that the **Lord** had shown Moses.
8. 5 The **Lord** said to Moses, [6]"Separate the Levites from the
8.20 Israel dedicated the Levites, as the **Lord** commanded Moses.
8.21 and Aaron dedicated them as a special gift to the **Lord.**
8.22 The people did everything the **Lord** had commanded Moses concerning the Levites.
8.23 The **Lord** said to Moses, [24]"From the age of
9. 1 The **Lord** spoke to Moses in the Sinai Desert in the first
9. 5 The people did everything just as the **Lord** had commanded Moses.
9. 7 be excluded from presenting the **Lord's** offering with the
9. 8 Moses answered, "Wait until I receive instructions from the **Lord."**
9. 9 The **Lord** told Moses [10]to say to the people of Israel,
9.15 day the Tent of the **Lord's** presence was set up, a cloud
9.18 at the command of the **Lord,** and at his command they set
9.19 a long time, they obeyed the **Lord** and did not move on.
9.20 in camp or moved, according to the command of the **Lord.**
9.23 to the commands which the **Lord** gave through Moses.
10. 1 The **Lord** said to Moses, [2]"Make two trumpets of hammered
10. 9 I, **the Lord your God,** will help you and save you from
10.10 I am **the Lord your God."**
10.11 over the Tent of the **Lord's** presence lifted, [12]and the
10.13 at the command of the **Lord** through Moses, [14]and each time
10.29 out for the place which the **Lord** said he would give us.
10.32 share with you all the blessings that the **Lord** gives us."
10.33 The **Lord's** Covenant Box always went ahead of them to find a
10.34 each camp, the cloud of the **Lord** was over them by day.
10.35 Whenever the Covenant Box started out, Moses would say, "Arise, **Lord;**
10.36 stopped, he would say, "Return, **Lord,** to the thousands of
11. 1 The people began to complain to the **Lord** about their troubles.
11. 1 When the **Lord** heard them, he was angry and sent fire on
11. 2 he prayed to the **Lord,** and the fire died down.
11. 3 because there the fire of the **Lord** burnt among them.
11.10 He was distressed because the **Lord** was angry with them,
11.11 and he said to the **Lord,** "Why have you treated me so
11.16 The **Lord** said to Moses, "Assemble seventy respected men
11.18 The **Lord** has heard you whining and saying that you wished
11.18 Now the **Lord** will give you meat, and you will have to
11.20 because you have rejected the **Lord** who is here among you and
11.21 Moses said to the **Lord,** "Here I am leading 600,000 people,
11.23 the **Lord** answered.
11.24 Moses went out and told the people what the **Lord** had said.
11.25 Then the **Lord** came down in the cloud and spoke to him.
11.29 I wish that the **Lord** would give his spirit to all his
11.31 Suddenly the **Lord** sent a wind that brought quails from the sea,
11.33 for them to eat, the **Lord** became angry with the people and
12. 2 They said, "Has the **Lord** spoken only through Moses?
12. 2 The **Lord** heard what they said.
12. 4 Suddenly the **Lord** said to Moses, Aaron, and Miriam, "I
12. 5 They went, [5]and the **Lord** came down in a pillar of cloud,
12. 6 them stepped forward, [6]and the **Lord** said, "Now hear what I
12. 9 The **Lord** was angry with them;
12.13 So Moses cried out to the **Lord,** "O God, heal her!"
12.14 The **Lord** answered, "If her father had spat in her face,

Num 13. 1 The **Lord** said to Moses, [2]"Choose one of the leaders from
14. 3 Why is the **Lord** taking us into that land?
14. 8 If the **Lord** is pleased with us, he will take us there
14. 9 Do not rebel against the **Lord** and don't be afraid of the
14. 9 The **Lord** is with us and has defeated the gods who protected
14.10 dazzling light of the **Lord's** presence appear over the tent.
14.11 The **Lord** said to Moses, "How much longer will these
14.13 But Moses said to the **Lord**, "You brought these people
14.14 have already heard that you, **Lord**, are with us, that you are
14.17 So now **Lord**, I pray, show us your power and do what
14.18 when you said, [18]'I, the **Lord**, am not easily angered, and
14.19 And now, **Lord**, according to the greatness of your unchanging love,
14.20 The **Lord** answered, "I will forgive them, as you have asked.
14.26 The **Lord** said to Moses and Aaron, [27]"How much longer
14.28 I, the **Lord**.
14.35 I, the **Lord**, have spoken.' "
14.36 report which caused the people to complain against the **Lord**.
14.36 And so the **Lord** struck them with a disease, and they died.
14.39 Moses told the Israelites what the **Lord** had said, they mourned bitterly.
14.40 ready to go to the place which the **Lord** told us about.
14.41 But Moses said, "Then why are you disobeying the **Lord** now?
14.42 The **Lord** is not with you, and your enemies will defeat you.
14.43 the **Lord** will not be with you, because you have refused to
14.44 hill-country, even though neither the **Lord's** Covenant Box
15. 1 The **Lord** gave Moses [2]the following regulations for the
15. 3 may be presented to the **Lord** as a burnt-offering or as a
15. 3 the smell of these food-offerings is pleasing to the **Lord**.
15. 4 as a burnt-offering to the **Lord** is to bring with each animal
15. 7 The smell of these sacrifices is pleasing to the **Lord**.
15. 8 bull is offered to the **Lord** as a burnt-offering or as a
15.10 The smell of this sacrifice is pleasing to the **Lord**.
15.13 he presents a food-offering, a smell pleasing to the **Lord**.
15.14 a smell that pleases the **Lord**, he is to observe the same
15.15 You and they are alike in the **Lord's** sight;
15.17 The **Lord** gave Moses [18]the following regulations for
15.19 is to be set aside as a special contribution to the **Lord**.
15.20 is to be presented as a special contribution to the **Lord**.
15.21 is to be given to the **Lord** from the bread you bake.
15.22 some of these regulations which the **Lord** has given Moses.
15.23 to do everything that the **Lord** commanded through Moses.
15.24 the **Lord**, with the proper grain-offering and wine-offering.
15.25 brought their sin-offering as a food-offering to the **Lord**.
15.30 is guilty of treating the **Lord** with contempt, and he shall
15.31 he has rejected what the **Lord** said and has deliberately
15.35 Then the **Lord** said to Moses, "The man must be put to
15.36 camp and stoned him to death, as the **Lord** had commanded.
15.37 The **Lord** commanded Moses [38]to say to the people of Israel:
15.41 I am **the Lord your God;**
15.41 I am the **Lord."**
16. 3 belong to the Lord, and the **Lord** is with all of us.
16. 3 Moses, do you set yourself above the **Lord's** community?"
16. 5 his followers, "Tomorrow morning the **Lord** will show us who
16. 6 Then we will see which of us the **Lord** has chosen.
16. 9 perform your service in the **Lord's** Tent, and minister to the
16.11 it is really against the **Lord** that you and your followers
16.13 Do you also have to **lord** it over us?
16.15 angry and said to the **Lord**, "Do not accept any offerings
16.16 250 followers must come to the Tent of the **Lord's** presence;
16.19 of the **Lord's** presence appeared to the whole community,
16.20 whole community, [20]and the **Lord** said to Moses and Aaron,
16.23 The **Lord** said to Moses, [24]"Tell the people to move
16.28 you will know that the **Lord** has sent me to do all
16.29 some punishment from God, then the **Lord** did not send me.
16.30 But if the **Lord** does something unheard of, and the earth
16.30 you will know that these men have rejected the **Lord."**
16.35 Then the **Lord** sent a fire that blazed out and burnt up
16.36 Then the **Lord** said to Moses, [37]"Tell Eleazar son of
16.38 They became holy when they were presented at the **Lord's** altar.
16.40 Aaron should come to the altar to burn incense for the **Lord**.
16.40 All this was done as the **Lord** had commanded Eleazar through Moses.
16.41 Aaron and said, "You have killed some of the **Lord's** people."
16.42 that the dazzling light of the **Lord's** presence had appeared.
16.44 of the Tent, [44]and the **Lord** said to Moses, [45]"Stand
16.46 The **Lord's** anger has already broken out and an epidemic has
17. 1 The **Lord** said to Moses, [2]"Tell the people of Israel to
17. 7 the sticks in the Tent in front of the **Lord's** Covenant Box.
17.10 The **Lord** said to Moses, "Put Aaron's stick back in
17.11 Moses did as the **Lord** commanded.
18. 1 The **Lord** said to Aaron, "You, your sons, and the Levites
18. 8 The **Lord** said to Aaron, "Remember that I am giving you
18.20 The **Lord** said to Aaron, "You will not receive any
18.20 I, the **Lord**, am all you need."
18.21 The **Lord** said, "I have given to the Levites every tithe
18.25 The **Lord** commanded Moses [26]to say to the Levites:
18.26 Israelites the tithe that the **Lord** gives you as your possession,
18.26 present a tenth of it as a special contribution to the **Lord**.
18.28 contribution that belongs to the **Lord** from all the tithes
18.28 this special contribution for the **Lord** to Aaron the priest.
18.32 long as you have presented the best of it to the **Lord**.
19. 1 The **Lord** commanded Moses and Aaron [2]to give the
19.13 He defiles the **Lord's** Tent, and he will no longer be
19.20 He defiles the **Lord's** Tent and will no longer be considered
20. 3 front of the **Lord's** Tent along with our fellow-Israelites.
20. 6 the dazzling light of the **Lord's** presence appeared to them.
20. 7 The **Lord** said to Moses, [8]"Take the stick that is in
20. 9 Moses went and got the stick, as the **Lord** had commanded.
20.12 But the **Lord** reprimanded Moses and Aaron.
20.13 people of Israel complained against the **Lord** and where he

Num 20.16 our ancestors and us, [16]and we cried to the **Lord** for help.
20.23 There the **Lord** said to Moses and Aaron, [24]"Aaron is not
20.27 Moses did what the **Lord** had commanded.
21. 2 Then the Israelites made a vow to the **Lord:**
21. 3 The **Lord** heard them and helped them to conquer the Canaanites.
21. 6 Then the **Lord** sent poisonous snakes among the people, and
21. 7 "We sinned when we spoke against the **Lord** and against you.
21. 7 Now pray to the **Lord** to take these snakes away."
21. 8 Then the **Lord** told Moses to make a metal snake and put
21.14 That is why The Book of the **Lord's** Battles speaks of
21.16 place called Wells, where the **Lord** said to Moses, "Bring
21.34 The **Lord** said to Moses, "Do not be afraid of him.
22. 8 tomorrow I will report to you whatever the **Lord** tells me."
22.13 the **Lord** has refused to let me go with you."
22.18 disobey the command of **the Lord my God** in even the smallest
22.19 whether or not the **Lord** has something else to tell me."
22.22 servants, the angel of the **Lord** stood in the road to bar
22.28 Then the **Lord** gave the donkey the power of speech, and
22.31 Then the **Lord** let Balaam see the angel standing there
23. 3 I go to see whether or not the **Lord** will meet me.
23. 5 The **Lord** told Balaam what to say and sent him back to
23. 8 has not cursed, Or speak of doom when the **Lord** has not?
23.12 answered, "I can say only what the **Lord** tells me to say."
23.16 The **Lord** met Balaam, told him what to say, and sent him
23.17 Balak asked what the **Lord** had said, [18]and Balaam uttered this prophecy:
23.21 **The Lord their God** is with them;
23.26 you that I had to do everything that the **Lord** told me?"
24. 1 now Balaam knew that the **Lord** wanted him to bless the people
24. 6 Like aloes planted by the **Lord** Or cedars beside the water.
24.11 to reward you, but the **Lord** has kept you from getting the
24.13 disobey the command of the **Lord** by doing anything of myself.
24.13 I will say only what the **Lord** tells me to say."
25. 3 So the **Lord** was angry with them [4]and said to Moses, "Take
25. 6 mourning at the entrance of the Tent of the **Lord's** presence.
25.10 The **Lord** said to Moses, [11]"Because of what Phinehas has done,
25.16 The **Lord** commanded Moses, [17]"Attack the Midianites and destroy them,
26. 1 After the epidemic the **Lord** said to Moses and Eleazar son
26. 9 the followers of Korah when they rebelled against the **Lord**.
26.52 The **Lord** said to Moses, [53]"Divide the land among the tribes,
26.61 Nadab and Abihu died when they offered unholy fire to the **Lord**.
26.65 The **Lord** had said that all of them would die in the
27. 2 of the Tent of the **Lord's** presence and said, [3]"Our father
27. 3 among the followers of Korah, who rebelled against the **Lord;**
27. 5 their case to the **Lord**, [6]and the Lord said to him,
27. 6 to the Lord, [6]and the **Lord** said to him, [7]"What the
27.11 requirement, just as I, the **Lord**, have commanded you."
27.12 The **Lord** said to Moses, "Go up the Abarim Mountains and
27.16 Moses prayed, [16]**"Lord God,** source of all life,
27.18 The **Lord** said to Moses, "Take Joshua son of Nun, a
27.22 Moses did as the **Lord** had commanded him.
27.23 As the **Lord** had commanded, Moses put his hands on
28. 1 The **Lord** commanded Moses [2]to instruct the Israelites to
28. 3 These are the food-offerings that are to be presented to the **Lord:**
28. 6 Mount Sinai as a food-offering, a smell pleasing to the **Lord**.
28. 8 It also is a food-offering, a smell pleasing to the **Lord**.
28.11 Present a burnt-offering to the **Lord** at the beginning of each month:
28.13 These burnt-offerings are food-offerings, a smell pleasing to the **Lord**.
28.16 Festival in honour of the **Lord** is to be held on the
28.19 Offer a burnt-offering as a food-offering to the **Lord:**
28.24 seven days offer to the **Lord** a food-offering, a smell
28.26 of new corn to the **Lord**, you are to gather for worship,
28.27 Offer a burnt-offering as a smell pleasing to the **Lord:**
29. 2 Present a burnt-offering to the **Lord**, a smell pleasing to him:
29. 6 These food-offerings are a smell pleasing to the **Lord**.
29. 8 Offer a burnt-offering to the **Lord**, a smell pleasing to him:
29.12 festival in honour of the **Lord** for seven days and do no
29.13 offer a food-offering to the **Lord**, a smell pleasing to him:
29.36 as a food-offering to the **Lord**, a smell pleasing to him:
29.39 you are to make to the **Lord** at your appointed festivals.
29.40 of Israel everything that the **Lord** had commanded him.
30. 2 to give something to the **Lord** or takes an oath to abstain
30. 3 something to the **Lord** or promises to abstain from something,
30. 5 The **Lord** will forgive her, because her father refused to let
30. 8 The **Lord** will forgive her.
30.12 The **Lord** will forgive her, because her husband prevented her
30.16 are the rules that the **Lord** gave Moses concerning vows made
31. 1 The **Lord** said to Moses, [2]"Punish the Midianites for what
31. 3 attack Midian and punish them for what they did to the **Lord**.
31. 7 They attacked Midian, as the **Lord** had commanded Moses, and
31.16 and at Peor led the people to be unfaithful to the **Lord**.
31.16 That was what brought the epidemic on the **Lord's** people.
31.21 "These are the regulations that the **Lord** has given to Moses.
31.25 The **Lord** said to Moses, [26]"You and Eleazar, together
31.28 as a tax for the **Lord** one out of every five hundred
31.29 to Eleazar the priest as a special contribution to the **Lord**.
31.30 them to the Levites who are in charge of the **Lord's** Tent."
31.31 Moses and Eleazar did what the **Lord** commanded.
31.36 sheep and goats, of which 675 were the tax for the **Lord;**
31.36 for the soldiers, of which 72 were the tax for the **Lord;**
31.36 for the soldiers, of which 61 were the tax for the **Lord;**
31.36 for the soldiers, of which 32 were the tax for the **Lord**.
31.41 contribution to the **Lord**, as the Lord had commanded.
31.47 and animals, and as the **Lord** had commanded, gave them to the
31.47 them to the Levites who were in charge of the **Lord's** Tent.
31.50 We offer them to the **Lord** as a payment for our lives,
31.54 Tent, so that the **Lord** would protect the people of Israel.
32. 3 said, [3-4]"This region which the **Lord** has helped the

Num
32. 7 the Jordan into the land which the **Lord** has given them?
32. 9 people from entering the land which the **Lord** had given them.
32.10 The **Lord** was angry that day and made a promise:
32.12 they remained loyal to the **Lord.**
32.13 The **Lord** was angry with the people and made them wander
32.14 to bring down the fierce anger of the **Lord** on Israel again.
32.20 in the presence of the **Lord** get ready to go into battle.
32.21 under the command of the **Lord** they are to attack our enemies
32.21 attack our enemies until the **Lord** defeats them [22] and takes
32.22 your obligation to the **Lord** and to your fellow-Israelites.
32.22 Then the **Lord** will acknowledge that this land east of the
32.23 I warn you that you will be sinning against the **Lord.**
32.27 of us are ready to go into battle under the **Lord's** command.
32.29 ready for battle at the **Lord's** command and if with their
32.31 Reuben answered, "Sir, we will do as the **Lord** has commanded.
33. 2 At the command of the **Lord,** Moses wrote down the name of
33. 3 Under the **Lord's** protection they left the city of Rameses in
33. 4 who were burying the first-born sons that the **Lord** had killed.
33. 4 By doing this, the **Lord** showed that he was more powerful
33.38 At the command of the **Lord,** Aaron the priest climbed Mount Hor.
33.50 the Jordan from Jericho the **Lord** gave Moses [51] the
34. 1 The **Lord** gave Moses [2] the following instructions for the people of Israel:
34.13 lots, the land that the **Lord** has assigned to the nine and
34.16 The **Lord** said to Moses, [17] "Eleazar the priest and
34.19 These are the men the **Lord** chose:
34.29 are the men that the **Lord** assigned to divide the property
35. 1 the Jordan from Jericho the **Lord** said to Moses, [2] "Tell the
35. 9 The **Lord** told Moses [10] to say to the people of Israel:
35.34 living, because I am the **Lord** and I live among the people
36. 2 They said, "The **Lord** commanded you to distribute the land
36. 5 Moses gave the people of Israel the following command from the **Lord.**
36. 6 is right, [6] and so the **Lord** says that the daughters of
36.10 of Zelophehad, did as the **Lord** had commanded Moses, and they
36.13 rules and regulations that the **Lord** gave the Israelites

Deut
1. 3 people everything the **Lord** had commanded him to tell them.
1. 4 This was after the **Lord** had defeated King Sihon of the Amorites,
1. 6 were at Mount Sinai, **the Lord our God** said to us, 'You
1. 8 land which I, the **Lord,** promised to give to your ancestors,
1.10 **The Lord your God** has made you as numerous as the stars
1.11 May the **Lord,** the God of your ancestors, make you
1.19 "We did what **the Lord our God** commanded us.
1.20 of the Amorites, which **the Lord our God,** the God of our
1.25 that the land which **the Lord our God** was giving us was
1.26 against the command of **the Lord your God,** and you would not
1.27 'The **Lord** hates us.
1.30 **The Lord your God** will lead you, and he will fight for
1.32 still would not trust the **Lord,** [33] even though he always
1.34 "The **Lord** heard your complaints and became angry, and
1.37 Because of you the **Lord** also became angry with me and said,
1.39 "Then the **Lord** said to all of us, 'Your children, who
1.41 "You replied, 'Moses, we have sinned against the **Lord.**
1.41 now we will attack, just as **the Lord our God** commanded us.'
1.42 "But the **Lord** said to me, 'Warn them not to attack,
1.43 I told you what the **Lord** had said, but you paid no
1.45 you cried out to the **Lord** for help, but he would not
2. 1 Gulf of Aqaba, as the **Lord** had commanded, and we spent a
2. 2 "Then the **Lord** told me [3] that we had spent enough time
2. 7 "Remember how **the Lord your God** has blessed you in
2. 9 The **Lord** said to me, 'Don't trouble the people of Moab,
2.12 their enemies out of the land that the **Lord** gave them.)
2.13 we crossed the River Zered as the **Lord** told us to do.
2.14 that generation had died, as the **Lord** had said they would.
2.15 The **Lord** kept on opposing them until he had destroyed them all.
2.17 they had all died, [17] the **Lord** said to us, [18] 'Today you
2.21 But the **Lord** destroyed them, so that the Ammonites took over
2.22 The **Lord** had done the same thing for the Edomites, the
2.24 had passed through Moab, the **Lord** said to us, 'Now, start
2.29 Jordan into the land that **the Lord our God** is giving us.
2.30 **The Lord your God** had made him stubborn and rebellious, so
2.31 "Then the **Lord** said to me, 'Look, I have made King
2.33 town of Jahaz, [33] but **the Lord our God** put him in our
2.36 **The Lord our God** let us capture all the towns from Aroer,
2.37 any other place where **the Lord our God** had commanded us not
3. 2 But the **Lord** said to me, 'Don't be afraid of him.
3. 3 "So the **Lord** also placed King Og and his people in our
3.18 **'The Lord our God** has given you this land east of the
3.20 occupy the land that the **Lord** is giving them west of the
3.20 the Jordan and until the **Lord** lets them live there in peace,
3.21 have seen all that **the Lord your God** did to those two
3.22 afraid of them, for **the Lord your God** will fight for you.'
3.24 time I earnestly prayed, [24] 'Sovereign **Lord,** I know that
3.25 me cross the River Jordan, **Lord,** and see the fertile land on
3.26 because of you people the **Lord** was angry with me and would
4. 1 occupy the land which the **Lord,** the God of your ancestors,
4. 2 Obey the commands of **the Lord your God** that I have given
4. 3 You yourselves saw what the **Lord** did at Mount Peor.
4. 4 were faithful to **the Lord your God** are still alive today.
4. 5 all the laws, as **the Lord my God** told me to do.
4. 7 when they need him as **the Lord our God** is to us.
4.10 in the presence of **the Lord your God** at Mount Sinai, when
4.12 Tell them how the **Lord** spoke to you from the fire, how
4.14 The **Lord** told me to teach you all the laws that you
4.15 "When the **Lord** spoke to you from the fire on Mount Sinai,
4.19 **The Lord your God** has given these to all other peoples for
4.21 Because of you **the Lord your God** was angry with me and
4.23 forget the covenant that **the Lord your God** made with you.
4.24 kind of idol, [24] because **the Lord your God** is like a
4.25 This is evil in the **Lord's** sight, and it will make him
4.27 The **Lord** will scatter you among other nations, where

Deut
4.29 you will look for **the Lord your God,** and if you search
4.30 you, then you will finally turn to the **Lord** and obey him.
4.34 them his own, as **the Lord your God** did for you in
4.35 The **Lord** has shown you this, to prove to you that he
4.39 the **Lord is God** in heaven and on earth.
4.40 in the land which **the Lord your God** is giving you to
5. 2 At Mount Sinai **the Lord our God** made a covenant, [3] not
5. 4 There on the mountain the **Lord** spoke to you face-to-face
5. 5 stood between you and the **Lord** at that time to tell you
5. 6 Lord said, [6] 'I am **the Lord your God,** who rescued you from
5. 9 it, for I am **the Lord your God** and I tolerate no
5.11 evil purposes, for I, **the Lord your God,** will punish anyone
5.12 keep it holy, as I, **the Lord your God,** have commanded you.
5.15 Egypt, and that I, **the Lord your God,** rescued you by my
5.16 your mother, as I, **the Lord your God,** command you, so that
5.22 "These are the commandments the **Lord** gave to all of
5.24 to me [24] and said, **'The Lord our God** showed us his
5.25 sure to die if we hear **the Lord our God** speak again.
5.27 Moses, and listen to everything that **the Lord our God** says.
5.28 "When the **Lord** heard this, he said to me, 'I have
5.32 you do everything that **the Lord your God** has commanded you.
6. 1 all the laws that **the Lord your God** commanded me to teach
6. 2 descendants are to honour **the Lord your God** and obey all his
6. 3 fertile land, just as the **Lord,** the God of our ancestors,
6. 4 The **Lord**—and the Lord alone—is our God.
6. 5 Love **the Lord your God** with all your heart, with all your
6.10 "Just as **the Lord your God** promised your ancestors,
6.11 When the **Lord** brings you into this land and you have all
6.12 you do not forget the **Lord** who rescued you from Egypt, where
6.13 Honour **the Lord your God,** worship only him, and make
6.15 do worship other gods, the **Lord's** anger will come against
6.15 destroy you completely, because **the Lord your God,** who is
6.16 "Do not put **the Lord your God** to the test, as you
6.18 Do what the **Lord** says is right and good, and all will
6.18 the fertile land that the **Lord** promised your ancestors,
6.20 ask you, 'Why did **the Lord our God** command us to obey
6.21 king of Egypt, and the **Lord** rescued us by his great power.
6.24 Then **the Lord our God** commanded us to obey all these
7. 1 **"The Lord your God** will bring you into the land which you
7. 2 When **the Lord your God** places these people in your power
7. 4 lead your children away from the **Lord** to worship other gods.
7. 4 If that happens, the **Lord** will be angry with you and destroy
7. 6 Do this because you belong to **the Lord your God.**
7. 7 "The **Lord** did not love you and choose you because you
7. 8 But the **Lord** loved you and wanted to keep the promise that
7. 9 Remember that **the Lord your God** is the only God and that
7.12 obey them faithfully, then **the Lord your God** will continue
7.15 The **Lord** will protect you from all sickness, and he will
7.16 Destroy every nation that **the Lord your God** places in your power,
7.18 remember what **the Lord your God** did to the king of Egypt
7.19 power and strength by which **the Lord your God** set you free.
7.21 **The Lord your God** is with you;
7.23 The **Lord** will put your enemies in your power and make
7.25 If you do, that will be fatal, because the **Lord** hates idolatry.
7.26 these idols, because they are under the **Lord's** curse.
8. 1 occupy the land which the **Lord** promised to your ancestors.
8. 2 Remember how **the Lord your God** led you on this long
8. 3 alone to sustain him, but on everything that the **Lord** says.
8. 5 Remember that **the Lord your God** corrects and punishes you
8. 6 So then, do as the **Lord** has commanded you:
8. 7 **The Lord your God** is bringing you into a fertile land—a
8.10 will give thanks to **the Lord your God** for the fertile land
8.11 "Make certain that you do not forget **the Lord your God;**
8.14 become proud and forget **the Lord your God** who rescued you
8.18 Remember that it is **the Lord your God** who gives you the
8.19 Never forget **the Lord your God** or turn to other gods to
8.20 you do not obey the **Lord,** then you will be destroyed just
9. 3 see for yourselves that **the Lord your God** will go ahead of
9. 4 "After **the Lord your God** has driven them out for you, do
9. 4 No, the **Lord** is going to drive these people out for you
9. 5 what is right that the **Lord** is letting you take their land.
9. 6 can be sure that the **Lord** is not giving you this fertile
9. 7 forget how you made **the Lord your God** angry in the desert.
9. 8 Mount Sinai you made the **Lord** angry—angry enough to destroy you.
9. 9 was written the covenant that the **Lord** had made with you.
9.10 Then the **Lord** gave me the two stone tablets on which he
9.11 forty days and nights the **Lord** gave me the two stone tablets
9.12 "Then the **Lord** said to me, 'Go down the mountain at once,
9.13 "The **Lord** also said to me, 'I know how stubborn these
9.16 disobeyed the command that **the Lord your God** had given you,
9.18 lay face downwards in the **Lord's** presence for forty days and
9.18 you had sinned against the **Lord** and had made him angry.
9.19 I was afraid of the **Lord's** fierce anger, because he was
9.19 but once again the **Lord** listened to me.
9.20 The **Lord** was also angry enough with Aaron to kill him,
9.22 "You also made **the Lord your God** angry when you were
9.24 Ever since I have known you, you have rebelled against the **Lord.**
9.25 in the **Lord's** presence those forty days and nights,
9.26 And I prayed, 'Sovereign **Lord,** don't destroy your own people,
10. 1 "Then the **Lord** said to me, 'Cut two stone tablets like
10. 4 Then the **Lord** wrote on those tablets the same words that
10. 4 The **Lord** gave me the tablets, [5] and I turned and went down
10. 5 Then, just as the **Lord** had commanded, I put them in the
10. 8 At the mountain the **Lord** appointed the men of the tribe of
10. 9 the privilege of being the **Lord's** priests,
10. 9 as **the Lord your God** promised.)
10.10 The **Lord** listened to me once more and agreed not to destroy
10.12 of Israel, listen to what **the Lord your God** demands of you:
10.12 Worship the **Lord** and do all that he commands.
10.14 To the **Lord** belong even the highest heavens;

Deut 10.15 But the **Lord's** love for your ancestors was so strong
10.16 from now on be obedient to the **Lord** and stop being stubborn.
10.17 **The Lord your God** is supreme over all gods and over all
10.20 Obey **the Lord your God** and worship only him.
10.22 But now **the Lord your God** has made you as numerous as
11. 1 "Love **the Lord your God** and always obey all his laws.
11. 2 learned about the **Lord** through your experiences with him.
11. 2 You saw the **Lord's** greatness, his power, his might, [3]and his miracles.
11. 4 You saw how the **Lord** completely wiped out the Egyptian army,
11. 5 You know what the **Lord** did for you in the desert before
11. 7 have seen all these great things that the **Lord** has done.
11. 9 and fertile land that the **Lord** promised to give your
11.12 **The Lord your God** takes care of this land and watches
11.13 love **the Lord your God** and serve him with all your heart.
11.16 be led away from the **Lord** to worship and serve other gods.
11.17 If you do, the **Lord** will become angry with you.
11.21 in the land that **the Lord your God** promised to give to
11.22 Love **the Lord your God,** do everything he commands, and be
11.25 go in that land, **the Lord your God** will make the people
11.27 obey the commands of **the Lord your God** that I am giving
11.29 When the **Lord** brings you into the land that you are
11.31 and occupy the land that **the Lord your God** is giving you.
12. 1 in the land that the **Lord,** the God of your ancestors, is
12. 4 "Do not worship **the Lord your God** in the way that these
12. 5 of all your tribes the **Lord** will choose the one place where
12. 6 that you promise to the **Lord,** your freewill offerings, and
12. 7 in the presence of **the Lord your God,** who has blessed you,
12. 9 entered the land that **the Lord your God** is giving you, where
12.10 cross the River Jordan, the **Lord** will let you occupy the
12.11 The **Lord** will choose a single place where he is to be
12.11 and those special gifts that you have promised to the **Lord.**
12.14 the one place that the **Lord** will choose in the territory of
12.15 You may eat as many as the **Lord** gives you.
12.17 that you offer to the **Lord** is to be eaten in the
12.17 that you promise to the **Lord,** your freewill offerings, or
12.18 in the presence of **the Lord your God,**
12.18 in the one place of worship chosen by **the Lord your God.**
12.20 "When **the Lord your God** enlarges your territory, as he has promised,
12.21 cattle or sheep that the **Lord** has given you, and you may
12.25 you obey this command, the **Lord** will be pleased, and all
12.26 offerings and the gifts that you have promised the **Lord.**
12.27 which are to be completely burnt on the **Lord's** altar.
12.28 be doing what is right and what pleases **the Lord your God.**
12.29 **"The Lord your God** will destroy the nations as you invade their
12.30 After the **Lord** destroys those nations, make sure that
12.31 Do not worship **the Lord your God** in the way they worship
12.31 they do all the disgusting things that the **Lord** hates.
13. 3 **The Lord your God** is using him to test you,
13. 3 to see if you love the **Lord** with all your heart.
13. 4 Follow the **Lord** and honour him;
13. 5 you to rebel against the **Lord,** who rescued you from Egypt,
13. 5 away from the life that the **Lord** has commanded you to live.
13.10 lead you away from **the Lord your God,** who rescued you from
13.12 in the towns that **the Lord your God** gives you, you may
13.16 and everything in it as an offering to **the Lord your God.**
13.17 to destruction, and then the **Lord** will turn from his fierce
14. 1 "You are the people of **the Lord your God.**
14. 2 You belong to **the Lord your God;**
14. 3 "Do not eat anything that the **Lord** has declared unclean.
14.21 But you belong to **the Lord your God;**
14.23 the one place where **the Lord your God** has chosen to be
14.23 so that you may learn to honour **the Lord your God** always.
14.24 of the produce that the **Lord** has blessed you with, then do
14.26 in the presence of **the Lord your God,** you and your families
14.29 Do this, and **the Lord your God** will bless you in everything
15. 2 the **Lord** himself has declared the debt cancelled.
15. 4 **"The Lord your God** will bless you in the land that he
15. 6 The **Lord** will bless you, as he has promised.
15. 7 in the land that **the Lord your God** is giving you there
15. 9 will cry out to the **Lord** against you, and you will be
15.10 freely and unselfishly, and the **Lord** will bless you in
15.14 generously from what the **Lord** has blessed you with—sheep,
15.15 were slaves in Egypt and **the Lord your God** set you free;
15.18 Do this, and **the Lord your God** will bless you in all
15.19 "Set aside for **the Lord your God** all the first-born
15.20 to eat them in the **Lord's** presence at the one place of
15.21 defect, you must not sacrifice them to **the Lord your God.**
16. 1 "Honour **the Lord your God** by celebrating Passover in the
16. 2 or cattle for the Passover meal to honour **the Lord your God.**
16. 5 else in the land that **the Lord your God** will give you.
16. 8 day assemble to worship **the Lord your God,** and do no work
16.10 Harvest Festival, to honour **the Lord your God,** by bringing
16.11 Be joyful in the **Lord's** presence, together with your children,
16.15 Honour **the Lord your God** by celebrating this festival
16.15 Be joyful, because the **Lord** has blessed your harvest and your work.
16.16 to come to worship the **Lord** three times a year at the
16.17 to the blessings that **the Lord your God** has given him.
16.18 officials in every town that **the Lord your God** gives you.
16.20 occupy the land that **the Lord your God** is giving you and
16.21 make an altar for **the Lord your God,** do not put beside
16.22 the **Lord** hates them.
17. 1 "Do not sacrifice to **the Lord your God** cattle or sheep
17. 1 the **Lord** hates this.
17. 2 woman has sinned against the **Lord** and broken his covenant
17. 3 or the moon or the stars, contrary to the **Lord's** command.
17. 8 of worship chosen by **the Lord your God,** [9]and present your
17.14 of the land that **the Lord your God** is going to give
17.15 choose to be king is the one whom the **Lord** has chosen.

Deut 17.16 to buy horses, because the **Lord** has said that his people are
17.17 wives, because this would make him turn away from the **Lord;**
17.19 will learn to honour the **Lord** and to obey faithfully
17.20 and from disobeying the **Lord's** commands in any way.
18. 1 on the offerings and other sacrifices given to the **Lord.**
18. 2 of being the **Lord's** priests, as the Lord has promised.
18. 5 The **Lord** chose from all your tribes the tribe of Levi to
18. 7 as a priest of **the Lord his God,** like the other Levites
18. 9 into the land that **the Lord your God** is giving you, don't
18.12 **The Lord your God** hates people who do these disgusting things,
18.13 Be completely faithful to the **Lord."**
18.14 look for omens, but **the Lord your God** does not allow you
18.16 begged not to hear the **Lord** speak again or to see his
18.17 So the **Lord** said to me, 'They have made a wise request.
18.21 tell when a prophet's message does not come from the **Lord.**
18.22 in the name of the **Lord** and what he says
18.22 does not come true, then it is not the **Lord's** message.
19. 1 "After **the Lord your God** has destroyed the people whose
19. 8 "When **the Lord your God** enlarges your territory, as he
19. 9 and if you love **the Lord your God** and live according to
19.10 them to death in the land that the **Lord** is giving you.
19.14 ago in the land that **the Lord your God** is giving you.
20. 1 **The Lord your God,** who rescued you from Egypt, will be with
20. 4 **The Lord your God** is going with you, and he will give
20.13 Then, when **the Lord your God** lets you capture the city,
20.14 The **Lord** has given it to you.
20.16 in the land that **the Lord your God** is giving you, kill
20.17 Hivites, and the Jebusites, as the **Lord** ordered you to do.
20.18 make you sin against the **Lord** by teaching you to do all
21. 1 in the land that **the Lord your God** is going to give
21. 5 **The Lord your God** has chosen them to serve him and to
21. 8 **Lord,** forgive your people Israel, whom you rescued from Egypt.
21. 9 so, by doing what the **Lord** requires, you will not be held
21.10 "When **the Lord your God** gives you victory in battle
21.23 not defile the land that **the Lord your God** is giving you.
22. 5 **the Lord your God** hates people who do such things.
23. 1 has been cut off may be included among the **Lord's** people.
23. 2 tenth generation, may be included among the **Lord's** people.
23. 3 tenth generation—may be included among the **Lord's** people.
23. 5 But **the Lord your God** would not listen to Balaam;
23. 8 their descendants may be included among the **Lord's** people.
23.14 camp ritually clean, because **the Lord your God** is with you
23.14 indecent that would cause the **Lord** to turn his back on you.
23.18 into the house of **the Lord your God** in fulfilment of a
23.18 The **Lord** hates temple prostitutes.
23.20 Obey this rule, and **the Lord your God** will bless everything
23.21 make a vow to **the Lord your God,** do not put off
23.21 the **Lord** will hold you to your vow, and it is a
23.22 make a vow to the **Lord,** [23]but if you make one voluntarily,
24. 4 If he married her again, it would be offensive to the **Lord.**
24. 4 sin in the land that **the Lord your God** is giving you.
24. 9 Remember what **the Lord your God** did to Miriam as you were
24.13 will be grateful, and **the Lord your God** will be pleased with
24.15 out against you to the **Lord,** and you will be guilty of
24.18 slaves in Egypt and that **the Lord your God** set you free;
24.19 and widows, so that **the Lord your God** will bless you in
25.15 time in the land that **the Lord your God** is giving you.
25.16 The **Lord** hates people who cheat.
25.19 So then, when **the Lord your God** has given you the land
26. 1 occupied the land that **the Lord your God** is giving you and
26. 3 'I now acknowledge to **the Lord my God** that I have entered
26. 4 you and place it before the altar of **the Lord your God.**
26. 5 Then, in the **Lord's** presence you will recite these words:
26. 7 cried out for help to the **Lord,** the God of our ancestors.
26.10 now I bring to the **Lord** the first part of the harvest
26.10 "Then set the basket down in the **Lord's** presence and worship there.
26.11 the good things that **the Lord your God** has given you and
26.13 done this, [13]say to the **Lord,** 'None of the sacred tithe is
26.14 I have obeyed you, O **Lord;**
26.16 "Today **the Lord your God** commands you to obey all his laws;
26.17 Today you have acknowledged the **Lord** as your God;
26.18 Today the **Lord** has accepted you as his own people, as he
27. 2 enter the land that **the Lord your God** is giving you, you
27. 3 and fertile land that the **Lord,** the God of your ancestors,
27. 6 altar you build for **the Lord your God** must be made of
27. 7 and be grateful in the presence of **the Lord your God.**
27. 9 Today you have become the people of **the Lord your God;**
27.15 the **Lord** hates idolatry.'
28. 1 "If you obey **the Lord your God** and faithfully keep all
28. 2 Obey **the Lord your God** and all these blessings will be yours:
28. 3 "The **Lord** will bless your towns and your fields.
28. 4 "The **Lord** will bless you with many children, with abundant crops,
28. 5 "The **Lord** will bless your corn crops and the food you
28. 6 "The **Lord** will bless everything you do.
28. 7 "The **Lord** will defeat your enemies when they attack you.
28. 8 **"The Lord your God** will bless your work and fill your
28. 9 "If you obey **the Lord your God** and do everything he commands,
28.10 earth will see that the **Lord** has chosen you to be his
28.11 The **Lord** will give you many children, many cattle, and
28.13 **The Lord your God** will make you the leader among the
28.15 "But if you disobey **the Lord your God** and do not
28.16 "The **Lord** will curse your towns and your fields.
28.17 "The **Lord** will curse your corn crops and the food you
28.18 "The **Lord** will curse you by giving you only a few children,
28.19 "The **Lord** will curse everything you do.
28.20 do evil and reject the **Lord,** he will bring on you disaster,
28.22 The **Lord** will strike you with infectious diseases, with swelling and fever;
28.24 Instead of rain, the **Lord** will send down duststorms and
28.25 "The **Lord** will give your enemies victory over you.

Deut 28.27 The **Lord** will send boils on you, as he did on the
28.28 The **Lord** will make you lose your mind;
28.35 The **Lord** will cover your legs with incurable, painful
28.36 "The **Lord** will take you and your king away to a
28.37 the countries to which the **Lord** will scatter you, the people
28.45 you did not obey **the Lord your God** and keep all the
28.47 The **Lord** blessed you in every way, but you would not
28.48 the enemies that the **Lord** is going to send against you.
28.48 The **Lord** will oppress you harshly until you are destroyed.
28.49 The **Lord** will bring against you a nation from the ends
28.52 in the land that **the Lord your God** is giving you, and
28.53 even eat the children that **the Lord your God** has given you.
28.58 and awesome name of **the Lord your God,** [59]he will send on
28.62 will survive, because you did not obey **the Lord your God.**
28.63 Just as the **Lord** took delight in making you prosper and
28.64 "The **Lord** will scatter you among all the nations, from
28.65 the **Lord** will overwhelm you with anxiety, hopelessness, and
28.68 The **Lord** will send you back to Egypt in ships, even
29. 1 of the covenant that the **Lord** commanded Moses to make with
29. 1 to the covenant which the **Lord** had made with them at Mount
29. 2 saw for yourselves what the **Lord** did to the king of Egypt,
29. 3 the miracles, and the great wonders that the **Lord** performed.
29. 5 For forty years the **Lord** led you through the desert, and
29. 6 beer to drink, but the **Lord** provided for your needs in order
29.10 in the presence of **the Lord your God,** all of you—your
29.12 into this covenant that **the Lord your God** is making with you
29.13 its obligations, [13]so that the **Lord** may now confirm you as
29.14 only ones with whom the **Lord** is making this covenant with
29.18 here today turns from **the Lord our God** to worship the gods
29.20 The **Lord** will not forgive such a man.
29.20 Instead, the **Lord's** burning anger will flame up against him,
29.20 fall on him until the **Lord** has destroyed him completely.
29.21 The **Lord** will make an example of him before all the
29.21 that is written in this book of the **Lord's** teachings.
29.22 and sufferings that the **Lord** has brought on your land.
29.23 Admah and Zeboiim, which the **Lord** destroyed when he was furiously angry.
29.24 world will ask, 'Why did the **Lord** do this to their land?
29.25 be, 'It is because the **Lord's** people broke the covenant they
29.26 before, gods that the **Lord** had forbidden them to worship.
29.27 And so the **Lord** became angry with his people and brought
29.28 The **Lord** became furiously angry, and in his great anger
29.29 "There are some things that **the Lord our God** has kept secret;
30. 1 among the nations where **the Lord your God** has scattered you,
30. 2 will turn back to the **Lord** and with all your heart obey
30. 3 giving you today, [3]then **the Lord your God** will have mercy
30. 4 corners of the earth, **the Lord your God** will gather you
30. 6 **The Lord your God** will give you and your descendants obedient hearts,
30. 9 The **Lord** will make you prosperous in all that you do;
30.16 obey the commands of **the Lord your God,** which I give you
30.16 **The Lord your God** will bless you in the land that you
30.20 Love **the Lord your God,** obey him and be faithful to him,
31. 2 And besides this, the **Lord** has told me that I will not
31. 3 **The Lord your God** himself will go before you and destroy the
31. 3 and Joshua will be your leader, as the **Lord** has said.
31. 4 The **Lord** will destroy those people, just as he defeated
31. 5 The **Lord** will give you victory over them, and you are to
31. 6 Your God, the **Lord** himself, will be with you.
31. 7 occupy the land that the **Lord** promised to their ancestors.
31. 8 The **Lord** himself will lead you and be with you.
31. 9 were in charge of the **Lord's** Covenant Box, and to the
31.11 they come to worship **the Lord your God** at the one place
31.12 and learn to honour **the Lord your God** and to obey his
31.13 never heard the Law of **the Lord your God** will hear it.
31.14 Then the **Lord** said to Moses, "You haven't much longer to live.
31.15 to the Tent, [15]and the **Lord** appeared to them there in a
31.16 The **Lord** said to Moses, "You will soon die, and after
31.23 Then the **Lord** spoke to Joshua son of Nun and said to
31.25 were in charge of the **Lord's** Covenant Box, [26]"Take this
31.26 the Covenant Box of **the Lord your God,** so that it will
31.27 They have rebelled against the **Lord** during my lifetime, and
31.29 they will have made the **Lord** angry by doing what he has
32. 3 praise the name of the **Lord,** and his people will tell of
32. 4 "The **Lord** is your mighty defender, perfect and just in
32. 6 you should treat the **Lord,** you foolish, senseless people?
32.11 on its spreading wings, the **Lord** kept Israel from falling.
32.12 The **Lord** alone led his people without the help of a
32.15 "The **Lord's** people grew rich, but rebellious;
32.16 Their idolatry made the **Lord** jealous;
32.19 "When the **Lord** saw this, he was angry and rejected his
32.30 **The Lord, their God,** had abandoned them;
32.34 "The **Lord** remembers what their enemies have done;
32.35 The **Lord** will take revenge and punish them;
32.36 The **Lord** will rescue his people when he sees that their
32.37 Then the **Lord** will ask his people, 'Where are those
32.43 "Nations, you must praise the **Lord's** people— he
32.48 That same day the **Lord** said to Moses, [49]"Go to the
33. 2 The **Lord** came from Mount Sinai;
33. 3 The **Lord** loves his people and protects those who belong to him.
33. 5 The **Lord** became king of his people Israel when their
33. 7 **"Lord,** listen to their cry for help;
33. 7 Fight for them, **Lord,** And help them against their enemies."
33. 8 "You, **Lord,** reveal your will by the Urim and Thummim
33.11 **Lord,** help their tribe to grow strong;
33.12 "This is the tribe the **Lord** loves and protects;
33.13 "May the **Lord** bless their land with rain And with water
33.16 the goodness of the **Lord,** Who spoke from the burning bush.
33.21 They obeyed the **Lord's** commands and laws When the leaders of
33.23 "Naphtali is richly blessed by the **Lord's** good favour;
33.29 There is no one like you, a nation saved by the **Lord.**

Deut 33.29 The **Lord** himself is your shield and your sword, to defend
34. 1 of Jericho, and there the **Lord** showed him the whole land:
34. 4 Then the **Lord** said to Moses, "This is the land that I
34. 5 So Moses, the **Lord's** servant, died there in the land of Moab,
34. 5 in the land of Moab, as the **Lord** had said he would.
34. 6 The **Lord** buried him in a valley in Moab, opposite the town
34. 9 the commands that the **Lord** had given them through Moses.
34.10 the **Lord** spoke with him face to face.
34.11 wonders like those that the **Lord** sent Moses to perform

Josh 1. 1 After the death of the **Lord's** servant Moses,
1. 1 the **Lord** spoke to Moses' helper,
1. 9 or discouraged, for I, **the Lord your God,** am with you
1.11 to occupy the land that **the Lord your God** is giving you."
1.13 "Remember how Moses, the **Lord's** servant, told you that the Lord
1.13 servant, told you that **the Lord your God** would give you this
1.15 west of the Jordan that **the Lord your God** has given them.
1.15 the Jordan, which Moses, the **Lord's** servant, gave to you."
1.17 obeyed Moses, and may **the Lord your God** be with you as
2. 9 to them, "I know that the **Lord** has given you this land.
2.10 We have heard how the **Lord** dried up the Red Sea in
2.11 **The Lord your God** is God in heaven above and here on
2.14 promise you that when the **Lord** gives us this land, we will
2.24 "We are sure that the **Lord** has given us the whole country.
3. 3 the Covenant Box of **the Lord your God,** break camp and follow
3. 5 "Purify yourselves, because tomorrow the **Lord** will perform miracles among you."
3. 7 The **Lord** said to Joshua, "What I do today will make all
3. 9 here and listen to what **the Lord your God** has to say.
3.11 the Covenant Box of the **Lord** of all the earth crosses the
3.13 the Covenant Box of the **Lord** of all the earth put their
3.17 ground, the priests carrying the **Lord's** Covenant Box stood
4. 1 the Jordan, the **Lord** said to Joshua, [2]"Choose twelve men,
4. 5 the Jordan ahead of the Covenant Box of **the Lord your God.**
4. 6 These stones will remind the people of what the **Lord** has done.
4. 7 Jordan stopped flowing when the **Lord's** Covenant Box crossed the river.
4. 8 As the **Lord** had commanded Joshua, they took twelve stones
4.10 had been done that the **Lord** ordered Joshua to tell the
4.11 side, the priests with the **Lord's** Covenant Box went on ahead
4.13 In the presence of the **Lord** about forty thousand men
4.14 What the **Lord** did that day made the people of Israel
4.15 Then the **Lord** told Joshua [16]to command the priests
4.23 Tell them that **the Lord your God** dried up the water of
4.24 will know how great the **Lord's** power is,
4.24 and you will honour **the Lord your God** for ever."
5. 1 Mediterranean Sea heard that the **Lord** had dried up the
5. 2 Then the **Lord** told Joshua, "Make some knives out of flint
5. 3 So Joshua did as the **Lord** had commanded, and he
5. 4 left Egypt had died because they had disobeyed the **Lord.**
5. 9 The **Lord** said to Joshua, "Today I have removed from you
5.14 "I am here as the commander of the **Lord's** army."
5.15 And the commander of the **Lord's** army told him, "Take
6. 2 The **Lord** said to Joshua, "I am putting into your hands Jericho,
6. 7 an advance guard going on ahead of the **Lord's** Covenant Box.
6.11 of men to take the **Lord's** Covenant Box round the city once.
6.12 then, the priests carrying the **Lord's** Covenant Box;
6.16 to shout, and he said, "The **Lord** has given you the city!
6.17 in it must be totally destroyed as an offering to the **Lord.**
6.19 of silver, gold, bronze, or iron is set apart for the **Lord.**
6.19 It is to be put in the **Lord's** treasury."
6.24 and iron, which they took and put in the **Lord's** treasury.
6.26 rebuild the city of Jericho will be under the **Lord's** curse.
6.27 So the **Lord** was with Joshua, and his fame spread through
7. 1 The **Lord's** command to Israel not to take from Jericho
7. 1 that order, and so the **Lord** was furious with the Israelites.
7. 6 to the ground before the **Lord's** Covenant Box, and lay there
7. 7 And Joshua said, "Sovereign **Lord!**
7. 8 What can I say, O **Lord,** now that Israel has retreated from
7.10 The **Lord** said to Joshua, "Get up!
7.13 ready tomorrow, because I, the **Lord God** of Israel, have this
7.19 the truth here before the **Lord,** the God of Israel, and
7.20 have sinned against the **Lord, Israel's God,** and this is what
7.23 Israelites, and laid them down in the presence of the **Lord.**
7.25 The **Lord** will now bring trouble on you!"
7.26 Then the **Lord** was no longer furious.
8. 1 The **Lord** said to Joshua, "Take all the soldiers with you
8. 7 **The Lord your God** will give it to you.
8. 8 the city, set it on fire, just as the **Lord** has commanded.
8.18 Then the **Lord** said to Joshua, "Point your spear at Ai;
8.27 and goods captured in the city, as the **Lord** had told Joshua.
8.30 on Mount Ebal an altar to the **Lord,** the God of Israel.
8.31 that Moses, the **Lord's** servant, had given the Israelites,
8.31 **Lord,** and they also presented their fellowship-offerings.
8.33 on two sides of the **Lord's** Covenant Box, facing the
8.33 The **Lord's** servant Moses had commanded them to do this when
9. 9 land, sir, because we have heard of **the Lord your God.**
9.14 some food from them, but did not consult the **Lord** about it.
9.18 promise to them in the name of the **Lord, Israel's God.**
9.19 promise to them in the name of the **Lord God** of Israel.
9.24 was really true that **the Lord your God** had commanded his
9.27 water for the people of Israel and for the **Lord's** altar.
9.27 in the place where the **Lord** has chosen to be worshipped.
10. 8 The **Lord** said to Joshua, "Do not be afraid of them.
10.10 The **Lord** made the Amorites panic at the sight of Israel's army.
10.11 from the Israelite army, the **Lord** made large hailstones fall
10.12 On the day that the **Lord** gave the men of Israel
10.12 victory over the Amorites, Joshua spoke to the **Lord.**
10.14 been a day like it, when the **Lord** obeyed a human being.
10.14 The **Lord** fought on Israel's side!
10.19 **The Lord your God** has given you victory over them."
10.25 because this is what the **Lord** is going to do to all

Josh 10.30 The **Lord** also gave the Israelites victory over this city
10.32 The **Lord** gave the Israelites victory over Lachish on the
10.40 This was what the **Lord God** of Israel had commanded.
10.42 because the **Lord, Israel's God,** was fighting for Israel.
11. 6 The **Lord** said to Joshua, "Do not be afraid of them.
11. 8 The **Lord** gave the Israelites victory over them;
11. 9 Joshua did to them what the **Lord** had commanded:
11.12 everyone to death, just as Moses, the **Lord's** servant,
11.15 The **Lord** had given his commands to his servant Moses,
11.15 He did everything that the **Lord** had commanded Moses.
11.20 The **Lord** had made them determined to fight the Israelites,
11.20 This was what the **Lord** had commanded Moses.
11.23 Joshua captured the whole land, as the **Lord** had commanded Moses.
12. 6 Moses, the **Lord's** servant, gave their land to the tribes of
13. 1 The **Lord** said to him, "You are very old, but there is
13. 8 the land that Moses, the **Lord's** servant, had given them;
13.14 As the **Lord** had told Moses, they were to receive as their
13.14 sacrifices burnt on the altar to the **Lord God** of Israel.
13.33 be a share of the offerings to the **Lord God** of Israel.
14. 2 As the **Lord** had commanded Moses, the territories of the
14. 5 of Israel divided the land as the **Lord** had commanded Moses.
14. 6 him, "You know what the **Lord** said in Kadesh Barnea about
14. 7 forty years old when the **Lord's** servant Moses sent me from
14. 8 But I faithfully obeyed **the Lord my God.**
14.10 It has been forty-five years since the **Lord** said that to Moses.
14.10 through the desert, and the **Lord,** as he promised, has kept
14.12 me the hill-country that the **Lord** promised me on that day
14.12 Maybe the **Lord** will be with me,
14.12 and I will drive them out, just as the **Lord** said."
14.14 because he faithfully obeyed the **Lord,** the God of Israel.
15.13 As the **Lord** commanded Joshua, part of the territory of
17. 4 leaders, and said, "The **Lord** commanded Moses to give us,
17. 4 So, as the **Lord** had commanded, they were given land along
17.14 There are very many of us because the **Lord** has blessed us."
18. 1 at Shiloh and set up the Tent of the **Lord's** presence.
18. 3 take the land that the **Lord,** the God of your ancestors, has
18. 6 I will draw lots to consult **the Lord our God** for you.
18. 7 you, because their share is to serve as the **Lord's** priests.
18. 7 Jordan, which Moses, the **Lord's** servant, gave to them."
18. 8 in Shiloh I will consult the **Lord** for you by drawing lots."
18.10 drew lots to consult the **Lord** for them, and assigned each of
19.50 As the **Lord** had commanded, they gave him the city he
19.51 drawing lots to consult the **Lord** at Shiloh,
19.51 at the entrance of the Tent of the **Lord's** presence.
20. 1 Then the **Lord** told Joshua [2]to say to the people of Israel,
21. 2 they said to them, "The **Lord** commanded through Moses that
21. 3 So in accordance with the **Lord's** command the people of
21. 8 to the Levites, as the **Lord** had commanded through Moses.
21.43 So the **Lord** gave to Israel all the land that he had
21.44 The **Lord** gave them peace throughout the land, just as he
21.44 stand against them, because the **Lord** gave the Israelites the
21.45 The **Lord** kept every one of the promises that he had made
22. 2 everything that Moses the **Lord's** servant ordered you to do,
22. 3 have been careful to obey the commands of **the Lord your God.**
22. 4 Now, as he promised, **the Lord your God** has given your
22. 4 east side of the Jordan, that Moses, the **Lord's** servant,
22. 5 love **the Lord your God,** do his will, obey his commandments,
22. 9 had taken as the **Lord** had commanded them through Moses.
22.16 the whole community of the **Lord,** they said to them, "Why
22.16 You have rebelled against the **Lord** by building this altar for yourselves!
22.17 sin at Peor, when the **Lord** punished his own people with an
22.18 If you rebel against the **Lord** today, he will be angry with
22.19 in, come over into the **Lord's** land, where his Tent is.
22.19 But don't rebel against the **Lord** or make rebels out of us
22.19 an altar in addition to the altar of **the Lord our God.**
22.22 He is the **Lord!**
22.22 He is the **Lord!**
22.22 not keep faith with the **Lord,** do not let us live any
22.23 If we disobeyed the **Lord** and built our own altar to burn
22.23 or fellowship-offerings, let the **Lord** himself punish us.
22.24 do you have to do with the **Lord,** the God of Israel?
22.25 You have nothing to do with the **Lord.'**
22.25 Then your descendants might make our descendants stop worshipping the **Lord.**
22.27 we do indeed worship the **Lord** before his sacred Tent with
22.27 from saying that ours have nothing to do with the **Lord.**
22.28 Our ancestors made an altar just like the **Lord's** altar.
22.29 certainly not rebel against the **Lord** or stop following him
22.29 than the altar of **the Lord our God** that stands in front
22.31 said to them, "Now we know that the **Lord** is with us.
22.31 saved the people of Israel from the **Lord's** punishment."
22.34 is a witness to all of us that the **Lord is God."**
23. 1 Much later the **Lord** gave Israel security from their enemies around them.
23. 3 have seen everything that **the Lord your God** has done to all
23. 3 **The Lord your God** has been fighting for you.
23. 5 **The Lord your God** will make them retreat from you, and he
23. 5 have their land, as **the Lord your God** has promised you.
23. 8 Instead, be faithful to the **Lord,** as you have been till now.
23. 9 The **Lord** has driven great and powerful nations out as you
23.10 men run away, because **the Lord your God** is fighting for you,
23.11 Be careful, then, to love **the Lord your God.**
23.13 may be sure that **the Lord your God** will no longer drive
23.13 in this good land which **the Lord your God** has given you.
23.14 heart and soul that **the Lord your God** has given you all
23.16 keep the covenant which **the Lord your God** commanded you to
24. 2 people, "This is what the **Lord,** the God of Israel, has to
24.14 Joshua continued, "honour the **Lord** and serve him sincerely and faithfully.

Josh 24.14 in Mesopotamia and in Egypt, and serve only the **Lord.**
24.15 As for my family and me, we will serve the **Lord."**
24.16 "We would never leave the **Lord** to serve other gods!
24.17 **The Lord our God** brought our fathers and us out of
24.18 advanced into this land, the **Lord** drove out all the Amorites
24.18 So we also will serve the **Lord;**
24.19 the people, "But you may not be able to serve the **Lord.**
24.21 We will serve the **Lord."**
24.22 to the fact that you have chosen to serve the **Lord."**
24.23 "and pledge your loyalty to the **Lord,** the God of Israel."
24.24 then said to Joshua, "We will serve **the Lord our God.**
24.26 and set it up under the oak-tree in the **Lord's** sanctuary.
24.27 has heard all the words that the **Lord** has spoken to us.
24.29 After that, the **Lord's** servant Joshua son of Nun died at
24.31 people of Israel served the **Lord,** and after his death they
24.31 themselves everything that the **Lord** had done for Israel.
Judg 1. 1 people of Israel asked the **Lord,** "Which of our tribes
1. 2 The **Lord** answered, "The tribe of Judah will go first.
1. 4 The **Lord** gave them victory over the Canaanites and the Perizzites,
1.18 The **Lord** helped the people of Judah, and they took
1.22 The **Lord** helped them.
2. 1 The angel of the **Lord** went from Gilgal to Bochim and said
2. 5 There they offered sacrifices to the **Lord.**
2. 7 people of Israel served the **Lord,** and after his death they
2. 7 all the great things that the **Lord** had done for Israel.
2. 8 The **Lord's** servant Joshua son of Nun died at the age of
2.10 the next generation forgot the **Lord** and what he had done for
2.11 Israel sinned against the **Lord** and began to serve the Baals.
2.12 They stopped worshipping the **Lord,** the God of their ancestors,
2.12 They bowed down to them and made the **Lord** angry.
2.13 They stopped worshipping the **Lord** and served the Baals and the Astartes.
2.14 And so the **Lord** became furious with Israel and let
2.15 they went into battle, the **Lord** was against them, just as he
2.16 Then the **Lord** gave the Israelites leaders who saved
2.17 Israel was unfaithful to the **Lord** and worshipped other gods.
2.17 Their fathers had obeyed the **Lord's** commands, but this new
2.18 Whenever the **Lord** gave Israel a leader, the Lord would
2.18 The **Lord** would have mercy on them because they groaned under
2.20 Then the **Lord** would become furious with Israel and say,
2.23 So the **Lord** allowed those nations to remain in the land;
3. 1 So then, the **Lord** left some nations in the land to test
3. 4 that the **Lord** had given their ancestors through Moses.
3. 7 The people of Israel forgot **the Lord their God;**
3. 8 So the **Lord** became angry with Israel and let King Cushan
3. 9 Israelites cried out to the **Lord,** and he sent a man who
3.10 The spirit of the **Lord** came upon him, and he became
3.10 went to war, and the **Lord** gave him victory over the king
3.12 The people of Israel sinned against the **Lord** again.
3.12 Because of this the **Lord** made King Eglon of Moab stronger
3.15 Israelites cried out to the **Lord,** and he sent a man to
3.28 The **Lord** has given you victory over your enemies, the Moabites."
4. 1 After Ehud died, the people of Israel sinned against the **Lord** again.
4. 2 So the **Lord** let them be conquered by Jabin, a Canaanite
4. 3 Then the people of Israel cried out to the **Lord** for help.
4. 6 and said to him, "The **Lord,** the God of Israel, has given
4. 9 for the victory, because the **Lord** will hand Sisera over to a
4.14 The **Lord** is leading you!
4.15 attacked with his army, the **Lord** threw Sisera into confusion
5. 2 Praise the **Lord!**
5. 3 I will sing, I will play music to Israel's God, the **Lord.**
5. 4 **Lord,** when you left the mountains of Seir, when you came
5. 5 The mountains quaked before the **Lord** of Sinai, before the Lord,
5. 9 Praise the **Lord!**
5.11 of the **Lord's** victories, the victories of Israel's people!
5.11 Then the **Lord's** people marched down from their cities.
5.13 the **Lord's** people came to him ready to fight.
5.23 says the angel of the **Lord,** "a curse, a curse on those
5.23 not come to help the **Lord,** come as soldiers to fight for
5.31 enemies die like that, O **Lord,** but may your friends shine
6. 1 of Israel sinned against the **Lord,** so he let the people of
6. 7 Israel cried out to the **Lord** for help against the Midianites,
6. 8 brought them this message from the **Lord,** the God of Israel:
6.10 you that I am **the Lord your God** and that you should
6.11 Then the **Lord's** angel came to the village of Ophrah and
6.12 The **Lord's** angel appeared to him there and said, "The Lord
6.12 him there and said, "The **Lord** is with you, brave and mighty
6.13 has all this happened to us if the **Lord** is with us?
6.13 our fathers told us the **Lord** used to do—how he brought
6.13 The **Lord** has abandoned us and left us to the mercy of
6.14 Then the **Lord** ordered him, "Go with all your great
6.15 Gideon replied, "But **Lord,** how can I rescue Israel?
6.16 The **Lord** answered, "You can do it because I will help you.
6.17 with me, give me some proof that you are really the **Lord.**
6.19 pot, brought them to the **Lord's** angel under the oak-tree,
6.21 Then the **Lord's** angel reached out and touched the meat
6.22 realized that it was the **Lord's** angel he had seen,
6.22 and he said in terror, "Sovereign **Lord!**
6.23 But the **Lord** said to him, "Peace.
6.24 altar to the Lord there and named it "The **Lord is Peace."**
6.25 That night the **Lord** told Gideon, "Take your father's
6.26 a well-constructed altar to **the Lord your God** on top of this
6.27 ten of his servants and did what the **Lord** had told him.
6.34 The spirit of the **Lord** took control of Gideon, and he
7. 2 The **Lord** said to Gideon, "The men you have are too many
7. 4 Then the **Lord** said to Gideon, "You still have too many men.
7. 5 to the water, and the **Lord** said to him, "Separate everyone
7. 7 The **Lord** said to Gideon, "I will rescue you and give you

Judg 7. 9 That night the **Lord** commanded Gideon, "Get up and attack the camp;
7.15 what it meant, he fell to his knees and worshipped the **Lord.**
7.15 The **Lord** is giving you victory over the Midianite army!"
7.18 round the camp and shout, 'For the **Lord** and for Gideon!' "
7.20 right, and shouted, "A sword for the **Lord** and for Gideon!"
7.22 were blowing their trumpets, the **Lord** made the enemy troops
8. 7 When the **Lord** has handed Zebah and Zalmunna over to me, I
8.23 The **Lord** will be your ruler."
8.34 and no longer served **the Lord their God,** who had saved them
10. 6 the Israelites sinned against the **Lord** by worshipping the
10. 6 They abandoned the **Lord** and stopped worshipping him.
10. 7 So the **Lord** became angry with the Israelites, and let the
10.10 Israelites cried out to the **Lord** and said, "We have sinned
10.11 The **Lord** gave them this answer:
10.15 But the people of Israel said to the **Lord,** "We have sinned.
10.16 So they got rid of their foreign gods and worshipped the **Lord;**
11. 9 fight the Ammonites and the **Lord** gives me victory, I will be
11.10 The **Lord** is our witness."
11.11 Jephthah stated his terms at Mizpah in the presence of the **Lord.**
11.21 But the **Lord,** the God of Israel, gave the Israelites
11.23 So it was the **Lord,** the God of Israel, who drove out
11.24 going to keep everything that **the Lord, our God,** has given
11.27 The **Lord** is the judge.
11.29 Then the spirit of the **Lord** came upon Jephthah.
11.30 Jephthah promised the **Lord:**
11.32 river to fight the Ammonites, and the **Lord** gave him victory.
11.35 a solemn promise to the **Lord,** and I cannot take it back!"
11.36 made a promise to the **Lord,** do what you said you would
11.36 do to me, since the **Lord** has given you revenge on your
11.39 what he had promised the **Lord,** and she died still a virgin.
12. 3 to fight them, and the **Lord** gave me victory over them.
13. 1 The Israelites sinned against the **Lord** again, and he let
13. 3 The **Lord's** angel appeared to her and said, "You have
13. 8 Then Manoah prayed to the **Lord,** "Please, Lord, let the
13.13 The **Lord's** angel answered, "Your wife must be sure to
13.15 know that it was the **Lord's** angel, so he said to him,
13.15 want to prepare it, burn it as an offering to the **Lord."**
13.19 them on the rock altar to the **Lord** who works wonders.
13.20 and his wife saw the **Lord's** angel go up towards heaven in
13.20 the man had been the **Lord's** angel, and he and his wife
13.23 his wife answered, "If the **Lord** had wanted to kill us, he
13.24 The child grew and the **Lord** blessed him.
13.25 And the **Lord's** power began to strengthen him while he
14. 4 know that it was the **Lord** who was leading Samson to do
14. 4 to do this, for the **Lord** was looking for a chance to
14. 6 Suddenly the **power of the Lord** made Samson strong, and he
14.19 Suddenly the **power of the Lord** made him strong, and he
15.14 Suddenly the **power of the Lord** made him strong, and he broke
15.18 so he called to the **Lord** and said, "You gave me this
16.20 He did not know that the **Lord** had left him.
16.28 Then Samson prayed, "Sovereign **Lord,** please remember me;
17. 2 His mother said, "May the **Lord** bless you, my son!"
17. 3 son, I myself am solemnly dedicating the silver to the **Lord.**
17.13 priest, I know that the **Lord** will make things go well for
18. 6 The **Lord** is taking care of you on this journey."
20. 1 They gathered in one body in the **Lord's** presence at Mizpah.
20.18 The **Lord** answered, "The tribe of Judah."
20.22 and mourned in the presence of the **Lord** until evening.
20.22 The **Lord** answered, "Yes."
20.26 They sat there in the **Lord's** presence and did not eat until
20.26 burnt some sacrifices whole—all in the presence of the **Lord.**
20.27 The people asked the **Lord,** "Should we go out to fight our
20.27 The **Lord** answered, "Fight.
20.35 The **Lord** gave Israel victory over the army of Benjamin.
21. 1 at Mizpah, they had made a solemn promise to the **Lord:**
21. 3 **"Lord God** of Israel, why has this happened?
21. 5 not go to the gathering in the **Lord's** presence at Mizpah?"
21. 7 a solemn promise to the **Lord** that we will not give them
21.15 for the Benjaminites because the **Lord** had broken the unity
21.19 "The yearly festival of the **Lord** at Shiloh is coming soon."

Ruth 1. 6 later Naomi heard that the **Lord** had blessed his people by
1. 8 May the **Lord** be as good to you as you have been
1. 9 And may the **Lord** make it possible for each of you to
1.13 The **Lord** has turned against me, and I feel very sorry for
1.17 May the **Lord's** worst punishment come upon me if I let
1.21 I had plenty, but the **Lord** has brought me back without a
1.21 call me Naomi when the **Lord Almighty** has condemned me and
2. 4 "The **Lord** be with you!"
2. 4 "The **Lord** bless you!"
2.12 May the **Lord** reward you for what you have done.
2.12 a full reward from the **Lord God** of Israel,
2.20 "May the **Lord** bless Boaz!"
2.20 "The **Lord** always keeps his promises to the living and the dead."
3.10 "The **Lord** bless you," he said.
3.13 I swear by the living **Lord** that I will take the responsibility.
4.11 May the **Lord** make your wife become like Rachel and Leah, who
4.12 May the children that the **Lord** will give you by this
4.13 The **Lord** blessed her, and she became pregnant and had a son.
4.14 The women said to Naomi, "Praise the **Lord!**

1 Sam 1. 3 and offer sacrifices to the **Lord Almighty** at Shiloh, where
1. 3 the two sons of Eli, were priests of the **Lord.**
1. 5 share, because the **Lord** had kept her from having children.
1. 6 and humiliate her, because the **Lord** had kept her childless.
1. 7 to the house of the **Lord,** Peninnah would upset Hannah so
1. 9 meal in the house of the **Lord** at Shiloh, Hannah got up.
1. 9 and she cried bitterly as she prayed to the **Lord.**
1.11 "Almighty **Lord,** look at me, your servant!
1.12 continued to pray to the **Lord** for a long time, and Eli
1.15 I have been praying, pouring out my troubles to the **Lord.**
1.19 after worshipping the **Lord,** they went back home to Ramah.
1.19 with his wife Hannah, and the **Lord** answered her prayer.
1.20 She named him Samuel, and explained, "I asked the **Lord** for him."
1.21 Shiloh and offer to the **Lord** the yearly sacrifice and the
1.22 to the house of the **Lord,** where he will stay all his
1.23 And may the **Lord** make your promise come true."
1.24 young as he was, to the house of the **Lord** at Shiloh.
1.26 I am the woman you saw standing here, praying to the **Lord.**
1.28 So I am dedicating him to the **Lord.**
1.28 As long as he lives, he will belong to the **Lord."**
1.28 Then they worshipped the **Lord** there.
2. 1 "The **Lord** has filled my heart with joy;
2. 2 "No one is holy like the **Lord;**
2. 3 For the **Lord** is a God who knows, and he judges all
2. 6 The **Lord** kills and restores to life;
2. 8 The foundations of the earth belong to the **Lord;**
2.10 The **Lord's** enemies will be destroyed;
2.10 The **Lord** will judge the whole world;
2.11 Samuel stayed in Shiloh and served the **Lord** under the priest Eli.
2.12 paid no attention to the **Lord** [13] or to the regulations
2.17 was extremely serious in the **Lord's** sight,
2.17 treated the offerings to the **Lord** with such disrespect.
2.18 Samuel continued to serve the **Lord,** wearing a sacred linen apron.
2.20 say to Elkanah, "May the **Lord** give you other children by
2.21 The **Lord** did bless Hannah, and she had three more sons
2.21 The boy Samuel grew up in the service of the **Lord.**
2.22 worked at the entrance to the Tent of the **Lord's** presence.
2.24 is an awful thing the people of the **Lord** are talking about!
2.25 but who can defend a man who sins against the **Lord?"**
2.25 to their father, for the **Lord** had decided to kill them.
2.26 grow and to gain favour both with the **Lord** and with men.
2.27 A prophet came to Eli with this message from the **Lord:**
2.30 I, the **Lord God** of Israel, promised in the past that
3. 1 boy Samuel was serving the **Lord** under the direction of Eli,
3. 1 very few messages from the **Lord,** and visions from him were
3. 4 Before dawn, while the lamp was still burning, [4] the **Lord** called Samuel.
3. 6 The **Lord** called Samuel again.
3. 6 know that it was the **Lord,** because the Lord had never spoken
3. 8 The **Lord** called Samuel a third time;
3. 8 realized that it was the **Lord** who was calling the boy, [9] so
3. 9 you again, say, 'Speak, **Lord,** your servant is listening.' "
3.10 The **Lord** came and stood there, and called as he had before,
3.11 The **Lord** said to him, "Some day I am going to do
3.15 got up and opened the doors of the house of the **Lord.**
3.17 "What did the **Lord** tell you?"
3.18 Eli said, "He is the **Lord;**
3.19 As Samuel grew up, the **Lord** was with him and made
3.20 other, knew that Samuel was indeed a prophet of the **Lord.**
3.21 The **Lord** continued to reveal himself at Shiloh, where he
4. 3 Israel said, "Why did the **Lord** let the Philistines defeat us today?
4. 3 Let's go and bring the **Lord's** Covenant Box from Shiloh, so
4. 4 to Shiloh and fetched the Covenant Box of the **Lord Almighty;**
4. 6 they found out that the **Lord's** Covenant Box had arrived in
5. 3 downwards on the ground in front of the **Lord's** Covenant Box.
5. 6 The **Lord** punished the people of Ashdod severely and terrified them.
5. 9 after it arrived there, the **Lord** punished that city too and
6. 1 After the **Lord's** Covenant Box had been in Philistia for seven months,
6. 2 asked, "What shall we do with the Covenant Box of the **Lord?**
6. 8 Take the **Lord's** Covenant Box, put it on the wagon, and
6.14 the cows and offered them as a burnt-sacrifice to the **Lord.**
6.15 the Covenant Box of the **Lord** and the box with the gold
6.15 Beth Shemesh offered burnt-sacrifices and other sacrifices to the **Lord.**
6.17 five gold tumours to the **Lord** as a gift to pay for
6.18 on which they placed the **Lord's** Covenant Box, is still there
6.19 The **Lord** killed seventy of the men of Beth Shemesh
6.19 the people mourned because the **Lord** had caused such a great
6.20 Beth Shemesh said, "Who can stand before the **Lord,** this
6.21 Kiriath Jearim to say, "The Philistines have returned the **Lord's** Covenant Box.
7. 1 of Kiriath Jearim fetched the **Lord's** Covenant Box and took
7. 2 The Covenant Box of the **Lord** stayed in Kiriath Jearim a
7. 2 During this time all the Israelites cried to the **Lord** for help.
7. 3 going to turn to the **Lord** with all your hearts, you must
7. 3 Dedicate yourselves completely to the **Lord** and worship only him,
7. 4 idols of Baal and Astarte, and worshipped only the **Lord.**
7. 5 Mizpah, saying, "I will pray to the **Lord** for you there."
7. 6 out as an offering to the **Lord** and fasted that whole day.
7. 6 They said, "We have sinned against the **Lord."**
7. 8 Samuel, "Keep praying to **the Lord our God** to save us from
7. 9 young lamb and burnt it whole as a sacrifice to the **Lord.**
7. 9 the Lord to help Israel, and the **Lord** answered his prayer.
7.10 but just then the **Lord** thundered from heaven against them.
7.12 and Shen, and said, "The **Lord** has helped us all the way"
7.13 Philistines were defeated, and the **Lord** prevented them from
7.17 In Ramah he built an altar to the **Lord.**
8. 6 so he prayed to the **Lord,** [7] and the Lord said, "Listen to
8. 7 to the Lord, [7] and the **Lord** said, "Listen to everything the
8.10 him for a king everything that the **Lord** had said to him.
8.18 chose, but the **Lord** will not listen to your complaints."
8.21 to everything they said and then went and told the **Lord.**
8.22 The **Lord** answered, "Do what they want and give them a king."
9.15 on the previous day the **Lord** had said to Samuel,
9.17 caught sight of Saul, the **Lord** said to him, "This is the
10. 1 kissed him, and said, "The **Lord** anoints you as ruler of his
10. 1 proof to you that the **Lord** has chosen you to be the
10. 6 Suddenly the spirit of the **Lord** will take control of you,
10.18 and said to them, "The **Lord,** the God of Israel, says,
10.19 yourselves before the **Lord** by tribes and by clans.' "

1 Sam 10.20 come forward, and the **Lord** picked the tribe of Benjamin.
10.22 they asked the **Lord,** "Is there still someone else?"
10.22 The **Lord** answered, "Saul is over there, hiding behind the supplies."
10.24 said to the people, "Here is the man the **Lord** has chosen!
11. 7 were afraid of what the **Lord** might do, and all of them,
11.13 death today, for this is the day the **Lord** rescued Israel."
12. 3 in the presence of the **Lord** and the king he has chosen.
12. 5 Samuel replied, "The **Lord** and the king he has chosen are
12. 5 "Yes, the **Lord** is our witness," they answered.
12. 6 Samuel continued, "The **Lord** is the one who chose Moses
12. 7 will accuse you before the **Lord** by reminding you of
12. 7 all the mighty actions the **Lord** did to save you
12. 8 your ancestors cried to the **Lord** for help, and he sent Moses
12. 9 But the people forgot **the Lord their God,**
12.10 Then they cried to the **Lord** for help
12.10 we turned away from you, **Lord,** and worshipped the idols
12.11 And the **Lord** sent Gideon, Barak, Jephthah, and finally me.
12.12 attack you, you rejected the **Lord** as your king and said to
12.13 asked for him, and now the **Lord** has given him to you.
12.14 you if you honour **the Lord your God,** serve him, listen to
12.15 do not listen to the **Lord** but disobey his commands, he will
12.16 will see the great thing which the **Lord** is going to do.
12.17 But I will pray, and the **Lord** will send thunder and rain.
12.17 a great sin against the **Lord** when you asked him for a
12.18 prayed, and on that same day the **Lord** sent thunder and rain.
12.18 people became afraid of the **Lord** and of Samuel, [19]and they
12.19 "Please, sir, pray to **the Lord your God** for us, so that
12.20 not turn away from the **Lord,** but serve him with all your
12.22 The **Lord** has made a solemn promise, and he will not
12.23 As for me, the **Lord** forbid that I should sin against him
12.24 Obey the **Lord** and serve him faithfully with all your heart.
13.12 in Gilgal, and I have not tried to win the **Lord's** favour.'
13.13 "You have not obeyed the command **the Lord your God** gave you.
13.14 you have disobeyed him, the **Lord** will find the kind of man
14. 3 Phinehas and grandson of Eli, the priest of the **Lord** in Shiloh.)
14. 6 Maybe the **Lord** will help us;
14.10 be the sign that the **Lord** has given us victory over them."
14.12 The **Lord** has given Israel victory over them."
14.19 Saul said to him, "There's no time to consult the **Lord!"**
14.23 The **Lord** saved Israel that day.
14.33 people are sinning against the **Lord** by eating meat with the
14.34 must not sin against the **Lord** by eating meat with blood in
14.35 built an altar to the **Lord,** the first one that he built.
14.39 I promise by the living **Lord,** who gives Israel victory,
14.41 Saul said to the **Lord,** the God of Israel, "Lord, why
14.41 **Lord,** God of Israel, answer me by the sacred stones.
14.45 We promise by the living **Lord** that he will not lose even
15. 1 am the one whom the **Lord** sent to anoint you king of
15. 1 Now listen to what the **Lord Almighty** says.
15.10 The **Lord** said to Samuel, [11]"I am sorry that I made
15.11 Samuel was angry, and all night long he pleaded with the **Lord.**
15.13 up to Saul, who greeted him, saying, "The **Lord** bless you,
15.13 I have obeyed the **Lord's** command."
15.15 as a sacrifice to **the Lord your God,** and the rest we
15.16 I will tell you what the **Lord** said to me last night."
15.17 The **Lord** anointed you king of Israel, [18]and he sent you
15.19 to seize the loot, and so do what displeases the **Lord?"**
15.20 "I did obey the **Lord,"** Saul replied.
15.21 to Gilgal to offer as a sacrifice to **the Lord your God."**
15.22 Samuel said, "Which does the **Lord** prefer:
15.23 Because you rejected the **Lord's** command, he has rejected you as king."
15.24 "I disobeyed the **Lord's** command and your instructions.
15.25 and go back with me, so that I can worship the **Lord."**
15.26 "You rejected the **Lord's** command, and he has rejected you
15.28 Samuel said to him, "The **Lord** has torn the kingdom of
15.30 back with me so that I can worship **the Lord your God."**
15.31 So Samuel went back with him, and Saul worshipped the **Lord.**
15.35 The **Lord** was sorry that he had made Saul king of Israel.
16. 1 The **Lord** said to Samuel, "How long will you go on
16. 2 The **Lord** answered, "Take a calf with you
16. 2 say that you are there to offer a sacrifice to the **Lord.**
16. 4 Samuel did what the **Lord** told him to do and went to
16. 5 "I have come to offer a sacrifice to the **Lord.**
16. 6 man standing here in the **Lord's** presence is surely the one
16. 7 But the **Lord** said to him, "Pay no attention to how tall
16. 8 But Samuel said, "No, the **Lord** hasn't chosen him either."
16. 9 "No, the **Lord** hasn't chosen him either," Samuel said.
16.10 Samuel said to him, "No, the **Lord** hasn't chosen any of these."
16.12 The **Lord** said to Samuel, "This is the one—anoint him!"
16.13 Immediately the spirit of the **Lord** took control of David and
16.14 The **Lord's** spirit left Saul,
16.14 and an evil spirit sent by the **Lord** tormented him.
16.18 The **Lord** is with him."
17.37 The **Lord** has saved me from lions and bears;
17.37 "Go, and the **Lord** be with you."
17.45 in the name of the **Lord Almighty,** the God of the Israelite
17.46 This very day the **Lord** will put you in my power;
17.47 here will see that the **Lord** does not need swords or spears
18.12 afraid of David because the **Lord** was with David but had
18.14 was successful in all he did, because the **Lord** was with him.
18.17 a brave and loyal soldier, and fight the **Lord's** battles."
18.28 Saul realized clearly that the **Lord** was with David and
19. 5 killed Goliath, and the **Lord** won a great victory for Israel.
19. 6 made a vow in the **Lord's** name that he would not kill
19. 9 One day an evil spirit from the **Lord** took control of Saul.
20. 3 to you by the living **Lord** that I am only a step
20.12 said to David, "May the **Lord God** of Israel be our witness!
20.13 to harm you, may the **Lord** strike me dead if I don't
20.13 May the **Lord** be with you as he was with my father!

1 Sam 20.15 And when the **Lord** has completely destroyed all your enemies,
20.16 If it is broken, the **Lord** will punish you."
20.21 I swear by the living **Lord** that you will be in no
20.22 of you,' then leave, because the **Lord** is sending you away.
20.23 made to each other, the **Lord** will make sure that we will
20.42 The **Lord** will make sure that you and I, and your descendants
22.10 Ahimelech asked the **Lord** what David should do,
22.17 to the guards standing near him, "Kill the **Lord's** priests!
22.17 guards refused to lift a hand to kill the **Lord's** priests.
22.21 He told him how Saul had slaughtered the priests of the **Lord.**
23. 2 So he asked the **Lord,** "Shall I go and attack the Philistines?"
23. 2 "Yes," the **Lord** answered.
23. 4 So David consulted the **Lord** again, and the Lord said to him,
23.10 Then David said, **"Lord,** God of Israel, I have heard
23.11 **Lord,** God of Israel, I beg you to answer me!"
23.11 The **Lord** answered, "Saul will come."
23.12 "They will," the **Lord** answered.
23.21 Saul answered, "May the **Lord** bless you for being so
24. 4 The **Lord** has told you that he would put your enemy in
24. 6 to his men, "May the **Lord** keep me from doing any harm
24. 6 any harm to my master, whom the **Lord** chose as king!
24. 6 in the least, because he is the king chosen by the **Lord!"**
24.10 just now in the cave the **Lord** put you in my power.
24.10 because you are the one whom the **Lord** chose to be king.
24.12 May the **Lord** judge which one of us is wrong!
24.15 The **Lord** will judge, and he will decide which one of us
24.18 not kill me, even though the **Lord** put me in your power.
24.19 The **Lord** bless you for what you have done to me today!
24.21 But promise me in the **Lord's** name that you will spare my
25.26 It is the **Lord** who has kept you from taking revenge and
25.26 to you by the living **Lord** that your enemies and all who
25.28 The **Lord** will make you king, and your descendants also,
25.29 try to kill you, **the Lord your God** will keep you safe,
25.30 And when the **Lord** has done all the good things he has
25.31 And when the **Lord** has blessed you, sir, please do not forget
25.32 said to her, "Praise the **Lord,** the God of Israel, who sent
25.34 The **Lord** has kept me from harming you.
25.38 Some ten days later the **Lord** struck Nabal and he died.
25.39 When David heard that Nabal had died, he said, "Praise the **Lord!**
25.39 The **Lord** has punished Nabal for his evil."
26. 9 The **Lord** will certainly punish whoever harms his chosen king.
26.10 By the living **Lord,"** David continued, "I know that the Lord
26.11 The **Lord** forbid that I should try to harm
26.11 to harm the one whom the **Lord** has made king!
26.12 all sound asleep, because the **Lord** had sent a heavy sleep on
26.16 I swear by the living **Lord** that all of you deserve to
26.16 you have not protected your master, whom the **Lord** made king.
26.19 If it is the **Lord** who has turned you against me,
26.19 if men have done it, may the **Lord's** curse fall on them.
26.19 driven me out from the **Lord's** land to a country where I
26.20 Don't let me be killed on foreign soil, away from the **Lord.**
26.23 The **Lord** rewards those who are faithful and righteous.
26.23 power, but I did not harm you, whom the **Lord** made king.
26.24 your life today, may the **Lord** do the same to me and
28. 6 he was terrified, [6]and so he asked the **Lord** what to do.
28. 6 But the **Lord** did not answer him at all, either by dreams
28.10 "By the living **Lord** I promise that you will not be punished
28.16 you call me when the **Lord** has abandoned you and become your
28.17 The **Lord** has done to you what he told you through me:
28.18 You disobeyed the **Lord's** command and did not completely
28.18 That is why the **Lord** is doing this to you now.
28.19 will join me, and the **Lord** will also hand the army of
30. 6 but **the Lord his God** gave him courage.
30. 8 David asked the **Lord,** "Shall I go after those raiders?
30.23 brothers, you can't do this with what the **Lord** has given us!
30.26 for you from the loot we took from the **Lord's** enemies."

2 Sam 1.12 Israel, the people of the **Lord,** because so many had been
1.14 "How is it that you dared to kill the **Lord's** chosen king?"
1.16 that you killed the one whom the **Lord** chose to be king."
2. 1 After this, David asked the **Lord,** "Shall I go and take
2. 1 "Yes," the **Lord** answered.
2. 1 "Hebron," the **Lord** said.
2. 5 "May the **Lord** bless you for showing your loyalty to your
2. 6 And now may the **Lord** be kind and faithful to you.
3. 9 The **Lord** promised David that he would take the
3.18 Remember that the **Lord** has said, 'I will use my servant
3.28 the news, he said, "The **Lord** knows that my subjects and I
3.39 May the **Lord** punish these criminals as they deserve!"
4. 8 Today the **Lord** has allowed Your Majesty to take revenge on
4. 9 a vow by the living **Lord,** who has saved me from all
5. 2 Israel in battle, and the **Lord** promised you that you would
5. 8 "The blind and the crippled cannot enter the **Lord's** house.")
5.10 all the time, because the **Lord God** Almighty was with him.
5.12 so David realized that the **Lord** had established him as king
5.19 David asked the **Lord,** "Shall I attack the Philistines?
5.19 the **Lord** answered.
5.20 He said, "The **Lord** has broken through my enemies like a flood."
5.23 Once more David consulted the **Lord,** who answered,
5.25 David did what the **Lord** had commanded, and was able to
6. 2 bearing the name of the **Lord Almighty,** who is enthroned
6. 5 dancing and singing with all their might to honour the **Lord.**
6. 7 At once the **Lord God** became angry with Uzzah and killed
6. 8 David was furious because the **Lord** had punished Uzzah in anger.
6. 9 David was afraid of the **Lord** and said, "How can I take
6.11 months, and the **Lord** blessed Obed Edom and his family.
6.12 of the Covenant Box the **Lord** had blessed Obed Edom's family
6.13 stop while he offered the **Lord** a sacrifice of a bull and
6.14 his waist, danced with all his might to honour the **Lord.**
6.17 Then he offered sacrifices and fellowship-offerings to the **Lord.**
6.18 in the name of the **Lord Almighty** [19]and distributed food to
6.21 was dancing to honour the **Lord,** who chose me instead of your

2 Sam 6.21 to honour the **Lord,** [22] and will disgrace myself even more.
7. 1 in his palace, and the **Lord** kept him safe from all his
7. 3 "Do whatever you have in mind, because the **Lord** is with you."
7. 4 But that night the **Lord** said to Nathan, [5] "Go and tell my
7. 8 servant David that I, the **Lord Almighty,** say to him, 'I took
7.18 into the Tent of the **Lord's** presence, sat down and prayed,
7.18 have already done for me, Sovereign **Lord,** nor is my family.
7.19 Yet now you are doing even more, Sovereign **Lord;**
7.19 And you let a man see this, Sovereign **Lord!**
7.22 How great you are, Sovereign **Lord!**
7.24 own people for ever, and you, **Lord,** have become their God.
7.25 "And now, **Lord God,** fulfil for all time the promise
7.26 will for ever say, 'The **Lord Almighty** is God over Israel.'
7.27 Almighty **Lord,** God of Israel!
7.28 "And now, Sovereign **Lord,** you are God;
7.29 You, Sovereign **Lord,** have promised this, and your blessing
8. 6 The **Lord** made David victorious everywhere.
8.14 The **Lord** made David victorious everywhere.
10.12 And may the **Lord's** will be done!"
11.27 But the **Lord** was not pleased with what David had done.
12. 1 The **Lord** sent the prophet Nathan to David.
12. 5 "I swear by the living **Lord** that the man who did this
12. 7 "And this is what the **Lord God** of Israel says:
12.13 "I have sinned against the **Lord,"** David said.
12.13 Nathan replied, "The **Lord** forgives you;
12.14 shown such contempt for the **Lord** in doing this, your child
12.15 The **Lord** caused the child that Uriah's wife had borne to
12.20 Then he went and worshipped in the house of the **Lord.**
12.22 I thought that the **Lord** might be merciful to me and not
12.24 The **Lord** loved the boy [25] and commanded the prophet Nathan
12.25 Nathan to name the boy Jedidiah, because the **Lord** loved him.
14.11 Majesty, please pray to **the Lord your God,** so that my
14.11 "I promise by the living **Lord,"** David replied, "that
14.17 May **the Lord your God** be with you!"
15. 7 go to Hebron and keep a promise I made to the **Lord.**
15. 8 in Syria, I promised the **Lord** that if he would take me
15.20 with you—and may the **Lord** be kind and faithful to you."
15.21 swear to you in the **Lord's** name that I will always go
15.25 If the **Lord** is pleased with me, some day he will let
15.31 Absalom's rebellion, he prayed, "Please, **Lord,** turn Ahithophel's advice into nonsense!"
16. 8 Saul's kingdom, and now the **Lord** is punishing you for
16. 8 The **Lord** has given the kingdom to your son Absalom, and you
16.10 he curses me because the **Lord** told him to, who has the
16.11 The **Lord** told him to curse;
16.12 Perhaps the **Lord** will notice my misery and give me some
16.18 the one chosen by the **Lord,** by these people, and by all
17.14 The **Lord** had decided that Ahithophel's good advice would not be followed,
18.19 good news that the **Lord** has saved him from his enemies."
18.28 him, and said, "Praise **the Lord your God,** who has given you
18.31 Today the **Lord** has given you victory over all who rebelled
19. 7 I swear by the **Lord's** name that if you don't, not one
19.21 because he cursed the one whom the **Lord** chose as king."
20.19 Do you want to ruin what belongs to the **Lord?"**
21. 1 So David consulted the **Lord** about it, and the Lord said,
21. 3 done to you, so that you will bless the **Lord's** people."
21. 6 will hang them before the **Lord** at Gibeah,
21. 6 the town of Saul, the **Lord's** chosen king."
21. 9 on the mountain before the **Lord**—and all seven of them died
22. 1 When the **Lord** saved David from Saul and his other enemies,
22. 1 David sang this song to the **Lord:**
22. 2 The **Lord** is my protector;
22. 4 I call to the **Lord,** and he saves me from my enemies.
22. 4 Praise the **Lord!**
22. 7 In my trouble I called to the **Lord;**
22.14 Then the **Lord** thundered from the sky, and the voice of
22.16 earth were uncovered when the **Lord** rebuked his enemies and
22.17 The **Lord** reached down from above and took hold of me;
22.19 I was in trouble, they attacked me, but the **Lord** protected me.
22.21 The **Lord** rewards me because I do what is right;
22.22 I have obeyed the law of the **Lord;**
22.26 O **Lord,** you are faithful to those who are faithful to you,
22.29 You, **Lord,** are my light;
22.32 The **Lord** alone is God;
22.36 O **Lord,** you protect me and save me;
22.42 they call to the **Lord,** but he does not answer.
22.47 The **Lord** lives!
22.49 O **Lord,** you give me victory over my enemies and protect me
23. 2 The spirit of the **Lord** speaks through me;
23.10 The **Lord** won a great victory that day.
23.12 The **Lord** won a great victory that day.
23.16 as an offering to the **Lord** [17] and said, "Lord, I could
23.17 to the Lord [17] and said, **"Lord,** I could never drink this!
24. 1 The **Lord** was angry with Israel once more, and he made
24. 1 The **Lord** said to him, "Go and count the people of Israel
24. 3 king, "Your Majesty, may **the Lord your God** make the people
24.10 and he said to the **Lord,** "I have committed a terrible sin
24.11 The **Lord** said to Gad, David's prophet, "Go and
24.13 him, told him what the **Lord** had said, and asked, "Which is
24.13 over, and tell me what answer to take back to the **Lord."**
24.14 Let the **Lord** himself be the one to punish us, for he
24.15 So the **Lord** sent an epidemic on Israel, which lasted
24.16 When the **Lord's** angel was about to destroy Jerusalem,
24.16 the **Lord** changed his mind
24.17 the people, and said to the **Lord,** "I am the guilty one.
24.18 "Go up to Araunah's threshing-place and build an altar to the **Lord."**
24.19 David obeyed the **Lord's** command and went as Gad had told him.
24.21 an altar for the **Lord,** in order to stop the epidemic."

2 Sam 24.22 Your Majesty," Araunah said, "and offer to the **Lord** whatever you wish."
24.23 to him, "May **the Lord your God** accept your offering."
24.24 will not offer to **the Lord my God** sacrifices that have cost
24.25 **Lord** and offered burnt-offerings and fellowship-offerings.
24.25 The **Lord** answered his prayer, and the epidemic in Israel was stopped.

1 Kgs 1.17 in the name of **the Lord your God** that my son Solomon
1.29 promise you by the living **Lord,** who has rescued me from all
1.30 in the name of the **Lord,** the God of Israel, that your
1.31 bowed low and said, "May my **lord** the king live for ever!"
1.36 answered Benaiah, "and may **the Lord your God** confirm it.
1.37 As the **Lord** has been with Your Majesty, may he also be
1.39 from the Tent of the **Lord's** presence, and anointed Solomon.
1.48 prayed, 'Let us praise the **Lord,** the God of Israel, who has
1.50 to the Tent of the **Lord's** presence and took hold of the
2. 3 and do what **the Lord your God** orders you to do.
2. 4 If you obey him, the **Lord** will keep the promise he made
2. 8 in the name of the **Lord** that I would not have him
2.15 and my brother became king, because it was the **Lord's** will.
2.23 a solemn promise in the **Lord's** name, "May God strike me
2.24 The **Lord** has firmly established me on the throne of my
2.24 I swear by the living **Lord** that Adonijah will die this very
2.26 were in charge of the **Lord's** Covenant Box while you were
2.27 as a priest of the **Lord,**
2.27 so he made what the **Lord** had said in Shiloh
2.28 to the Tent of the **Lord's** presence and took hold of the
2.29 he had fled to the **Lord** because he was afraid of Solomon.
2.30 to the Tent of the **Lord's** presence and said to Joab, "The
2.32 The **Lord** will punish Joab for those murders, which he
2.33 But the **Lord** will always give success to David's descendants
2.34 to the Tent of the **Lord's** presence and killed Joab, and he
2.42 "I made you promise in the **Lord's** name not to leave Jerusalem.
2.44 The **Lord** will punish you for it.
3. 2 yet been built for the **Lord,** and so the people were still
3. 3 Solomon loved the **Lord** and followed the instructions of his father David,
3. 5 That night the **Lord** appeared to him in a dream and asked
3. 7 O **Lord God,** you have let me succeed my father as king,
3.10 The **Lord** was pleased that Solomon had asked for this,
3.15 stood in front of the **Lord's** Covenant Box
3.15 and offered burnt-offerings and fellowship-offerings to the **Lord.**
5. 3 for the worship of **the Lord his God**
5. 3 until the **Lord** had given him victory
5. 4 But now **the Lord my God** has given me peace on all
5. 5 The **Lord** promised my father David, 'Your son, whom I will
5. 5 to build that temple for the worship of **the Lord my God.**
5. 7 and he said, "Praise the **Lord** today for giving David such a
5.12 The **Lord** kept his promise and gave Solomon wisdom.
6.11 The **Lord** said to Solomon, [12] "If you obey all my laws
6.19 was built, where the **Lord's** Covenant Box was to be placed.
7.40 He completed all his work for King Solomon for the **Lord's** Temple.
7.51 David had dedicated to the **Lord**—the silver, gold, and other articles.
8. 1 in order to take the **Lord's** Covenant Box from Zion, David's
8. 4 moved the Tent of the **Lord's** presence and all its equipment
8. 9 at Mount Sinai, when the **Lord** made a covenant with the
8.11 the dazzling light of the **Lord's** presence, and they could
8.12 "You, **Lord,** have placed the sun in the sky, yet you have
8.15 He said, "Praise the **Lord God** of Israel!
8.17 for the worship of the **Lord God** of Israel, [18] but the Lord
8.18 God of Israel, [18] but the **Lord** said to him, 'You were right
8.20 "And now the **Lord** has kept his promise.
8.20 built the Temple for the worship of the **Lord God** of Israel.
8.21 of the covenant which the **Lord** made with our ancestors when
8.23 raised his arms [23] and prayed, **"Lord God** of Israel, there
8.25 And now, **Lord God** of Israel, I pray that you will also
8.28 **Lord** my God, I am your servant.
8.32 that he is innocent, [32] O **Lord,** listen in heaven and judge
8.36 Then, O **Lord,** send rain on this land of yours, which you
8.47 sinful and wicked they have been, hear their prayers O **Lord.**
8.52 "Sovereign **Lord,** may you always look with favour on
8.54 had finished praying to the **Lord,** he stood up in front of
8.56 He said, [56] "Praise the **Lord** who has given his people peace,
8.57 May **the Lord our God** be with us, as he was with
8.59 May **the Lord our God** remember at all times this prayer
8.60 world will know that the **Lord** alone is God—there is no
8.61 always be faithful to **the Lord our God,** obeying all his laws
8.62 King Solomon and all the people there offered sacrifices to the **Lord.**
8.66 all the blessings that the **Lord** had given his servant David
9. 2 he wanted to build, [2] the **Lord** appeared to him again, as he
9. 3 The **Lord** said to him, "I have heard your prayer.
9. 8 'Why did the **Lord** do this to this land and this Temple?'
9. 9 because they abandoned **the Lord their God,** who brought their
9. 9 That is why the **Lord** has brought this disaster on them.' "
9.25 fellowship-offerings on the altar he had built to the **Lord.**
9.25 He also burnt incense to the **Lord.**
10. 9 Praise **the Lord your God!**
11. 2 married them even though the **Lord** had commanded the
11. 4 was not faithful to **the Lord his God,** as his father David
11. 6 He sinned against the **Lord** and was not true to him as
11. 9 Even though the **Lord,** the God of Israel, had
11. 9 Solomon did not obey the **Lord,** but turned away from him.
11. 9 So the **Lord** was angry with Solomon [11] and said to him,
11.14 So the **Lord** caused Hadad, of the royal family of Edom,
11.31 pieces for yourself, because the **Lord,** the God of Israel,
12.15 was the will of the **Lord** to bring about what he had
12.24 They all obeyed the **Lord's** command and went back home.
12.26 and offer sacrifices to the **Lord** in the Temple there, they

1 Kgs	13. 1	At the **Lord's** command a prophet from Judah went to Bethel
	13. 2	Following the **Lord's** command, the prophet denounced the altar:
	13. 2	"O altar, altar, this is what the **Lord** says:
	13. 3	Then you will know that the **Lord** has spoken through me."
	13. 5	as the prophet had predicted in the name of the **Lord.**
	13. 6	pray for me to **the Lord your God,** and ask him to
	13. 6	The prophet prayed to the **Lord,** and the king's arm was healed.
	13. 9	The **Lord** has commanded me not to eat or drink a thing,
	13.17	with you here, [17] because the **Lord** has commanded me not to
	13.18	like you, and at the **Lord's** command an angel told me to
	13.20	table, the word of the **Lord** came to the old prophet, [21] and
	13.21	the prophet from Judah, "The **Lord** says that you disobeyed
	13.26	"That is the prophet who disobeyed the **Lord's** command!
	13.26	And so the **Lord** sent the lion to attack and kill him,
	13.26	just as the **Lord** said he would."
	13.32	that he spoke at the **Lord's** command against the altar in
	14. 5	The **Lord** had told him that Jeroboam's wife was coming to
	14. 5	And the **Lord** told Ahijah what to say.
	14. 7	that this is what the **Lord,** the God of Israel, says to
	14.11	I, the **Lord,** have spoken.'"
	14.13	only one with whom the **Lord,** the God of Israel, is pleased.
	14.14	The **Lord** is going to place a king over Israel who will
	14.15	The **Lord** will punish Israel, and she will shake like a
	14.16	The **Lord** will abandon Israel because Jeroboam sinned and
	14.18	and buried him, as the **Lord** had said through his servant,
	14.21	Jerusalem, the city which the **Lord** had chosen from all the
	14.22	of Judah sinned against the **Lord** and did more to arouse his
	14.24	by the people whom the **Lord** had driven out of the land
	15. 3	not completely loyal to **the Lord his God,** as his
	15. 4	But for David's sake, **the Lord his God** gave Abijah a son
	15. 5	The **Lord** did this because David had done what pleased him
	15.11	Asa did what pleased the **Lord,** as his ancestor David had done.
	15.14	of worship, he remained faithful to the **Lord** all his life.
	15.26	him, he sinned against the **Lord** and led Israel into sin.
	15.29	In accordance with what the **Lord** had said through his servant,
	15.30	aroused the anger of the **Lord,** the God of Israel, by the
	15.34	him, he sinned against the **Lord** and led Israel into sin.
	16. 1	The **Lord** spoke to the prophet Jehu son of Hanani and gave
	16. 7	That message from the **Lord** against Baasha and his family
	16. 7	Jehu because of the sins that Baasha committed against the **Lord.**
	16. 7	He aroused the **Lord's** anger not only because of the evil he
	16.12	in accordance with what the **Lord** had said against Baasha
	16.13	Elah had aroused the anger of the **Lord,** the God of Israel.
	16.19	This happened because of his sins against the **Lord.**
	16.19	predecessor Jeroboam he displeased the **Lord** by his own sins
	16.25	Omri sinned against the **Lord** more than any of his predecessors.
	16.26	aroused the anger of the **Lord,** the God of Israel, by his
	16.30	He sinned against the **Lord** more than any of his predecessors.
	16.33	arouse the anger of the **Lord,** the God of Israel, than all
	16.34	As the **Lord** had foretold through Joshua son of Nun, Hiel
	17. 1	"In the name of the **Lord,** the living God of Israel, whom
	17. 2	Then the **Lord** said to Elijah, [3] "Leave this place and go
	17. 5	Elijah obeyed the **Lord's** command, and went and stayed by
	17. 8	Then the **Lord** said to Elijah, [9] "Now go to the town of
	17.12	She answered, "By the living **Lord** your God I swear
	17.14	For this is what the **Lord,** the God of Israel, says:
	17.14	out of oil before the day that I, the **Lord,** send rain.'"
	17.16	As the **Lord** had promised through Elijah, the bowl did
	17.20	Then he prayed aloud, "O **Lord** my God, why have you done
	17.21	three times and prayed, "O **Lord** my God, restore this child
	17.22	The **Lord** answered Elijah's prayer;
	17.24	a man of God and that the **Lord** really speaks through you!"
	18. 1	year of the drought, the **Lord** said to Elijah, "Go and
	18. 3	a devout worshipper of the **Lord,** [4] and when Jezebel was
	18. 4	when Jezebel was killing the **Lord's** prophets, Obadiah took a
	18.10	By the living **Lord,** your God, I swear that the king has
	18.12	if the spirit of the **Lord** carries you off to some unknown
	18.12	a devout worshipper of the **Lord** ever since I was a boy.
	18.13	killing the prophets of the **Lord** I hid a hundred of them
	18.15	Elijah answered, "By the living **Lord,** whom I serve, I
	18.18	You are disobeying the **Lord's** commands and worshipping the idols of Baal.
	18.21	If the **Lord** is God, worship him;
	18.22	the only prophet of the **Lord** still left, but there are 450
	18.24	I will pray to the **Lord,** and the one who answers by
	18.30	repairing the altar of the **Lord** which had been torn down.
	18.31	Jacob, the man to whom the **Lord** had given the name Israel.
	18.32	stones he rebuilt the altar for the worship of the **Lord.**
	18.36	the altar and prayed, "O **Lord,** the God of Abraham, Isaac,
	18.37	Answer me, **Lord,** answer me, so that this people
	18.37	will know that you, the **Lord,** are God,
	18.38	The **Lord** sent fire down, and it burnt up the sacrifice,
	18.39	themselves on the ground and exclaimed, "The **Lord is God;**
	18.39	the **Lord** alone is God!"
	18.46	The **power of the Lord** came on Elijah;
	19. 4	"It's too much, **Lord,"** he prayed.
	19. 7	The **Lord's** angel returned and woke him up a second time,
	19. 9	Suddenly the **Lord** spoke to him, "Elijah, what are you doing here?"
	19.10	He answered, **"Lord God** Almighty, I have always served you—
	19.11	before me on top of the mountain," the **Lord** said to him.
	19.11	Then the **Lord** passed by and sent a furious wind that split
	19.11	and shattered the rocks—but the **Lord** was not in the wind.
	19.11	was an earthquake—but the **Lord** was not in the earthquake.
	19.12	there was a fire—but the **Lord** was not in the fire.
	19.14	He answered, **"Lord God** Almighty, I have always served you—
	19.15	The **Lord** said, "Return to the wilderness near Damascus,
	20. 4	"Tell my **lord,** King Benhadad, that I agree;
	20. 9	to Benhadad's messengers, "Tell my **lord** the king that I
	20.13	King Ahab and said, "The **Lord** says, 'Don't be afraid of
	20.13	over it today, and you will know that I am the **Lord.'"**
1 Kgs	20.14	The prophet answered, "The **Lord** says that the young
	20.28	went to King Ahab and said, "This is what the **Lord** says:
	20.28	and you and your people will know that I am the **Lord.'"**
	20.35	At the **Lord's** command a member of a group of prophets
	20.36	"Because you have disobeyed the **Lord's** command, a lion will
	20.42	then said to the king, "This is the word of the **Lord:**
	21. 3	"The **Lord** forbid that I should let you have it!"
	21.17	Then the **Lord** said to Elijah, the prophet from Tishbe,
	21.19	Tell him that I, the **Lord,** say to him, 'After murdering
	21.20	completely to doing what is wrong in the **Lord's** sight.
	21.21	So the **Lord** says to you, 'I will bring disaster on you.
	21.23	And concerning Jezebel, the **Lord** says that dogs will eat
	21.25	to doing wrong in the **Lord's** sight as Ahab—all at the
	21.26	Amorites had done, whom the **Lord** had driven out of the land
	21.28	The **Lord** said to the prophet Elijah, [29] "Have you
	22. 5	But first let's consult the **Lord."**
	22. 6	"The **Lord** will give you victory."
	22. 7	"Isn't there another prophet through whom we can consult the **Lord?"**
	22.11	iron horns and said to Ahab, "This is what the **Lord** says:
	22.12	"The **Lord** will give you victory."
	22.14	Micaiah answered, "By the living **Lord** I promise that I will
	22.15	The **Lord** will give you victory."
	22.16	speak to me in the name of the **Lord,** tell the truth!
	22.17	And the **Lord** said, 'These men have no leader;
	22.19	"Now listen to what the **Lord** says!
	22.19	I saw the **Lord** sitting on his throne in heaven, with all
	22.20	The **Lord** asked, 'Who will deceive Ahab so that he will
	22.21	approached the **Lord,** and said, 'I will deceive him.'
	22.22	'How?' the **Lord** asked.
	22.22	The **Lord** said, 'Go and deceive him.
	22.23	The **Lord** has made these prophets of yours lie to you.
	22.24	asked, "Since when did the **Lord's** spirit leave me and speak
	22.28	Micaiah exclaimed, "then the **Lord** has not spoken through me!"
	22.38	washed themselves, as the **Lord** had said would happen.
	22.43	him, he did what was right in the sight of the **Lord;**
	22.52	He sinned against the **Lord,** following the wicked example
	22.53	him, he aroused the anger of the **Lord,** the God of Israel.
2 Kgs	1. 3	But an angel of the **Lord** commanded Elijah, the prophet from Tishbe,
	1. 4	Tell the king that the **Lord** says, 'You will not recover
	1. 4	Elijah did as the **Lord** commanded, [5] and the messengers
	1. 6	and tell you that the **Lord** says to you, 'Why are you
	1.15	The angel of the **Lord** said to Elijah, "Go down with him,
	1.16	the king [16] and said to him, "This is what the **Lord** says:
	1.17	Ahaziah died, as the **Lord** had said through Elijah.
	2. 1	The time came for the **Lord** to take Elijah up to heaven
	2. 2	the **Lord** has ordered me to go to Bethel."
	2. 2	my loyalty to the living **Lord** and to you that I will
	2. 3	"Do you know that the **Lord** is going to take your master
	2. 4	the **Lord** has ordered me to go to Jericho."
	2. 4	my loyalty to the living **Lord** and to you that I will
	2. 5	"Do you know that the **Lord** is going to take your master
	2. 6	the **Lord** has ordered me to go to the River Jordan."
	2. 6	my loyalty to the living **Lord** and to you that I will
	2.14	Elijah's cloak, and said, "Where is the **Lord,** the God of Elijah?"
	2.16	Maybe the spirit of the **Lord** has carried him away and left
	2.21	salt in the water, and said, "This is what the **Lord** says:
	2.24	glared at them, and cursed them in the name of the **Lord.**
	3. 2	He sinned against the **Lord,** but he was not as bad as
	3.10	"The **Lord** has put the three of us at the mercy of
	3.11	"Is there a prophet here through whom we can consult the **Lord?"**
	3.13	"It is the **Lord** who has put us three kings at the
	3.14	Elisha answered, "By the living **Lord,** whom I serve, I
	3.15	played his harp, the **power of the Lord** came on Elisha,
	3.16	on Elisha, [16] and he said, "This is what the **Lord** says:
	3.18	continued, "But this is an easy thing for the **Lord** to do;
	4.27	And the **Lord** has not told me a thing about it."
	4.30	my loyalty to the living **Lord** and to you that I will
	4.33	He closed the door and prayed to the **Lord.**
	4.43	them to eat, because the **Lord** says that they will eat and
	4.44	before them, and, as the **Lord** had said, they all ate and
	5. 1	Syria, because through Naaman the **Lord** had given victory to
	5.11	to me, pray to **the Lord his God,** wave his hand over
	5.16	Elisha answered, "By the living **Lord,** whom I serve, I
	5.17	sacrifices or burnt-offerings to any god except the **Lord.**
	5.18	So I hope that the **Lord** will forgive me when I accompany
	5.18	Surely the **Lord** will forgive me!"
	5.20	By the living **Lord,** I will run after him and get something
	6.17	Then he prayed, "O **Lord,** open his eyes and let him see!"
	6.17	The **Lord** answered his prayer, and Elisha's servant looked up
	6.18	When the Syrians attacked, Elisha prayed, "O **Lord,** strike these men blind!"
	6.18	The **Lord** answered his prayer and struck them blind.
	6.20	Elisha prayed, "Open their eyes, **Lord,** and let them see."
	6.20	The **Lord** answered his prayer;
	6.27	He replied, "If the **Lord** won't help you, what help can
	6.33	arrived and said, "It's the **Lord** who has brought this
	7. 1	Elisha answered, "Listen to what the **Lord** says!
	7. 2	happen—not even if the **Lord** himself were to send grain at
	7. 6	The **Lord** had made the Syrians hear what sounded like the
	7.16	And, as the **Lord** had said, three kilogrammes of the best
	7.19	happen—not even if the **Lord** himself were to send grain at
	8. 1	back to life, that the **Lord** was sending a famine on the
	8. 8	ask him to consult the **Lord** to find out whether or not
	8.10	Elisha answered, "The **Lord** has revealed to me that he will die;
	8.13	"The **Lord** has shown me that you will be king of Syria,"
	8.18	He sinned against the **Lord,** [19] but the Lord was not willing
	8.19	the Lord, [19] but the **Lord** was not willing to destroy Judah,
	8.27	he sinned against the **Lord,** just as Ahab's family did.
	9. 3	his head, and say, 'The **Lord** proclaims that he anoints you

2 Kgs 9. 6 head and said to him, "The **Lord,** the God of Israel,
9.12 "He told me that the **Lord** proclaims:
9.25 King Joram's father Ahab, the **Lord** spoke these words against Ahab:
9.26 belonged to Naboth, so as to fulfil the **Lord's** promise."
9.36 said, "This is what the **Lord** said would happen, when he
10.10 proves that everything that the **Lord** said about the
10.10 The **Lord** has done what he promised through his prophet Elijah."
10.16 me and see for yourself how devoted I am to the **Lord."**
10.17 This is what the **Lord** had told Elijah would happen.
10.23 present and that no worshipper of the **Lord** has come in."
10.30 The **Lord** said to Jehu, "You have done to Ahab's
10.31 all his heart the law of the **Lord,** the God of Israel;
10.32 At that time the **Lord** began to reduce the size of
11.17 covenant with the Lord that they would be the **Lord's** people;
12. 2 the **Lord,** because Jehoiada the priest instructed him.
12.18 Ahaziah had dedicated to the **Lord,** added to them his own
13. 2 him he sinned against the **Lord** and led Israel into sin;
13. 3 So the **Lord** was angry with Israel, and he allowed King
13. 4 Then Jehoahaz prayed to the **Lord,** and the Lord, seeing how
13. 5 The **Lord** sent Israel a leader, who freed them from the Syrians,
13.11 He too sinned against the **Lord** and followed the evil
13.17 prophet exclaimed, "You are the **Lord's** arrow, with which he
13.23 Jehoahaz' reign, [23] but the **Lord** was kind and merciful to them.
14. 3 what was pleasing to the **Lord,** but he was not like his
14. 6 children but followed what the **Lord** had commanded in the Law
14.24 He sinned against the **Lord,** following the wicked example
14.25 This was what the **Lord,** the God of Israel, had promised
14.26 The **Lord** saw the terrible suffering of the Israelites;
14.27 But it was not the **Lord's** purpose to destroy Israel
15. 3 example of his father, he did what was pleasing to the **Lord.**
15. 5 The **Lord** struck Uzziah with a dreaded skin-disease that
15. 9 He, like his predecessors, sinned against the **Lord.**
15.12 promise was fulfilled which the **Lord** had made to King Jehu:
15.18 He sinned against the **Lord,** for until the day of his
15.24 He sinned against the **Lord,** following the wicked example
15.28 He sinned against the **Lord,** following the wicked example
15.34 his father Uzziah, Jotham did what was pleasing to the **Lord.**
15.37 he was king that the **Lord** first sent King Rezin of Syria
16. 2 was not pleasing to **the Lord his God** [3] and followed the
16. 3 of the people whom the **Lord** had driven out of the land
16.14 bronze altar dedicated to the **Lord** was between the new altar
17. 2 He sinned against the **Lord,** but not as much as the kings
17. 7 the Israelites sinned against **the Lord their God,** who had rescued them
17. 8 of the people whom the **Lord** had driven out as his people
17. 9 The Israelites did things that **the Lord their God** disapproved of.
17.11 of the people whom the **Lord** had driven out of the land.
17.11 They aroused the **Lord's** anger with all their wicked deeds
17.12 and disobeyed the **Lord's** command not to worship idols.
17.13 The **Lord** had sent his messengers and prophets to warn
17.14 their ancestors, who had not trusted in **the Lord their God.**
17.15 nations, disobeying the **Lord's** command not to imitate them.
17.16 all the laws of **the Lord their God** and made two metal
17.17 what is wrong in the **Lord's** sight, and so aroused his anger.
17.18 The **Lord** was angry with the Israelites and banished them
17.19 of Judah did not obey the laws of **the Lord their God;**
17.20 The **Lord** rejected all the Israelites, punishing them and
17.21 After the **Lord** had separated Israel from Judah, the
17.21 Jeroboam made them abandon the **Lord** and led them into terrible sins.
17.23 until at last the **Lord** banished them from his sight,
17.25 they did not worship the **Lord,** and so he sent lions, which
17.28 Bethel, where he taught the people how to worship the **Lord.**
17.32 These people also worshipped the **Lord** and chose from
17.33 So they worshipped the **Lord,** but they also worshipped
17.34 They do not worship the **Lord** nor do they obey the laws
17.35 The **Lord** had made a covenant with them and had ordered them:
17.36 You shall obey me, the **Lord,** who brought you out of
17.39 You shall obey me, **the Lord your God,** and I will rescue
17.41 So those people worshipped the **Lord,** but they also worshipped their idols;
18. 3 ancestor King David, he did what was pleasing to the **Lord.**
18. 5 Hezekiah trusted in the **Lord,** the God of Israel;
18. 6 He was faithful to the **Lord** and never disobeyed him, but
18. 6 kept all the commands that the **Lord** had given Moses.
18. 7 So the **Lord** was with him, and he was successful in
18.12 Israelites did not obey **the Lord their God,** but broke the
18.12 all the laws given by Moses, the servant of the **Lord.**
18.22 you tell me that you are relying on **the Lord your God?**
18.22 It was the **Lord's** shrines and altars that Hezekiah destroyed,
18.25 I have attacked your country and destroyed it without the **Lord's** help?
18.25 The **Lord** himself told me to attack it and destroy it."
18.30 And don't let him persuade you to rely on the **Lord.**
18.30 Don't think that the **Lord** will save you, and that he will
18.32 Hezekiah fool you into thinking that the **Lord** will rescue you.
18.35 Then what makes you think the **Lord** can save Jerusalem?"
19. 1 grief, put on sackcloth, and went to the Temple of the **Lord.**
19. 4 May **the Lord your God** hear these insults and punish those
19. 6 "The **Lord** tells you not to let the Assyrians frighten you
19. 7 The **Lord** will cause the emperor to hear a rumour that will
19. 7 his own country, and the **Lord** will have him killed there."
19.14 in the presence of the **Lord,** [15] and prayed, "O Lord, the
19.15 the Lord, [15] and prayed, "O **Lord,** the God of Israel,
19.16 Now, **Lord,** look at what is happening to us.
19.17 We all know, **Lord,** that the emperors of Assyria have
19.19 Now, **Lord** our God, rescue us from the Assyrians, so that
19.19 of the world will know that only you, O **Lord,** are God."
19.21 to the king's prayer [21] the **Lord** had said, "The city of
19.31 because the **Lord** is determined to make this happen.

2 Kgs 19.32 "This is what the **Lord** has said about the Assyrian emperor:
19.33 I, the **Lord,** have spoken.
19.35 night an angel of the **Lord** went to the Assyrian camp and
20. 1 and said to him, "The **Lord** tells you that you are to
20. 3 "Remember, **Lord,** that I have served you faithfully and loyally,
20. 4 courtyard of the palace the **Lord** told him [5] to go back to
20. 5 to Hezekiah, ruler of the **Lord's** people, and say to him,
20. 5 "I, the **Lord,** the God of your ancestor David,
20. 8 sign to prove that the **Lord** will heal me and that three
20. 9 Isaiah replied, "The **Lord** will give you a sign to prove
20.11 Isaiah prayed to the **Lord,** and the Lord made the shadow
20.16 said to the king, "The **Lord Almighty** says that [17] a time
20.19 "The message you have given me from the **Lord** is good."
21. 2 of the nations whom the **Lord** had driven out of the land
21. 2 as his people advanced, Manasseh sinned against the **Lord.**
21. 4 Temple, the place that the **Lord** had said was where he should
21. 6 He sinned greatly against the **Lord** and stirred up his anger.
21. 7 the place about which the **Lord** had said to David and his
21. 9 Judah did not obey the **Lord,** and Manasseh led them to commit
21. 9 by the nations whom the **Lord** had driven out of the land
21.10 his servants the prophets the **Lord** said, [11] "King Manasseh
21.12 So I, the **Lord God** of Israel, will bring such a disaster
21.16 Judah into idolatry, causing them to sin against the **Lord.**
21.20 Like his father Manasseh, he sinned against the **Lord;**
21.22 He rejected the **Lord,** the God of his ancestors,
21.22 and disobeyed the **Lord's** commands.
22. 2 Josiah did what was pleasing to the **Lord;**
22.13 "Go and consult the **Lord** for me and for all the people
22.13 The **Lord** is angry with us because our ancestors have not
22.16 king and give him [16] the following message from the **Lord:**
22.18 king himself, this is what I, the **Lord God** of Israel, say:
23. 3 made a covenant with the **Lord** to obey him, to keep his
23.19 the kings of Israel, who thereby aroused the **Lord's** anger.
23.21 Passover in honour of **the Lord their God,** as written in the
23.25 him before, who served the **Lord** with all his heart, mind,
23.26 But the **Lord's** fierce anger had been aroused against
23.27 The **Lord** said, "I will do to Judah what I have done
23.32 Following the example of his ancestors, he sinned against the **Lord.**
23.37 Following the example of his ancestors, Jehoiakim sinned against the **Lord.**
24. 2 The **Lord** sent armed bands of Babylonians, Syrians,
24. 2 to destroy Judah, as the **Lord** had said through his servants
24. 3 This happened at the **Lord's** command, in order to banish
24. 4 The **Lord** could not forgive Manasseh for that.
24. 9 Following the example of his father, Jehoiachin sinned against the **Lord.**
24.13 As the **Lord** had foretold, Nebuchadnezzar broke up all the
24.19 King Zedekiah sinned against the **Lord,** just as King Jehoiakim had done.
24.20 The **Lord** became so angry with the people of Jerusalem

1 Chr 2. 3 His eldest son, Er, was so evil that the **Lord** killed him.
6.15 of Judah and Jerusalem whom the **Lord** sent into exile.
6.32 at the Tent of the **Lord's** presence during the time before
9.19 to the Tent of the **Lord's** presence, just as their ancestors
9.19 had been when they were in charge of the **Lord's** camp.
9.20 Phineas son of Eleazar—may the **Lord** be with him!—
9.21 a guard at the entrance to the Tent of the **Lord's** presence.
10.13 Saul died because he was unfaithful to the **Lord.**
10.13 He disobeyed the **Lord's** commands;
10.14 the spirits of the dead [14] instead of consulting the **Lord.**
10.14 So the **Lord** killed him and gave control of the kingdom to
11. 2 Israel in battle, and **the Lord your God** promised you that
11. 3 of Israel, just as the **Lord** had promised through Samuel.
11. 9 stronger and stronger, because the **Lord Almighty** was with him.
11.10 to become king, as the **Lord** had promised, and they kept his
11.14 The **Lord** gave him a great victory.
11.18 as an offering to the **Lord** [19] and said, "I could never
12.23 make him king in place of Saul, as the **Lord** had promised.
13. 2 is the will of **the Lord our God,** let us send messengers
13. 6 the name of the **Lord** enthroned above the winged creatures.
13.10 At once the **Lord** became angry with Uzzah and killed him
13.11 David was furious because the **Lord** had punished Uzzah in anger.
13.14 there three months, and the **Lord** blessed Obed Edom's family
14. 2 so David realized that the **Lord** had established him as king
14.10 The **Lord** answered, "Yes, attack!
14.17 everywhere, and the **Lord** made every nation afraid of him.
15. 2 they are the ones the **Lord** chose to carry it and to
15.12 the Covenant Box of the **Lord God** of Israel to the place
15.13 it the first time, **the Lord our God** punished us for not
15.14 order to move the Covenant Box of the **Lord God** of Israel.
15.15 their shoulders, as the **Lord** had commanded through Moses.
16. 2 in the name of the **Lord** [3] and distributed food to them all.
16. 4 lead the worship of the **Lord,** the God of Israel, in front
16. 7 Asaph and his fellow-Levites the responsibility for singing praises to the **Lord.**
16. 8 Give thanks to the **Lord,** proclaim his greatness;
16. 9 Sing praise to the **Lord;**
16.11 Go to the **Lord** for help, and worship him continually.
16.14 The **Lord is our God;**
16.17 The **Lord** made a covenant with Jacob, one that will last
16.23 Sing to the **Lord,** all the world!
16.25 The **Lord** is great and is to be highly praised;
16.26 nations are only idols, but the **Lord** created the heavens.
16.28 Praise the **Lord,** all people on earth, praise his glory and might.
16.29 Praise the **Lord's** glorious name;
16.31 Tell the nations that the **Lord is king.**
16.33 will shout for joy when the **Lord** comes to rule the earth.
16.34 Give thanks to the **Lord,** because he is good;
16.36 Praise the **Lord,** the God of Israel!
16.36 Then all the people said, "Amen," and praised the **Lord.**

1 Chr 16.39 of the worship of the **Lord** at the place of worship in
16.40 what was written in the Law which the **Lord** gave to Israel.
16.41 chosen to sing praises to the **Lord** for his eternal love.
17. 1 built of cedar, but the **Lord's** Covenant Box is kept in a
17. 7 servant David that I, the **Lord Almighty,** say to him, 'I took
17.16 into the Tent of the **Lord's** presence, sat down, and prayed,
17.16 you have already done for me, **Lord God,** nor is my family.
17.17 years to come, and you, **Lord God,** are already treating me
17.20 **Lord,** there is none like you;
17.22 own people for ever, and you, **Lord,** have become their God.
17.23 "And now, O **Lord,** fulfil for all time the promise you
17.24 will for ever say, 'The **Lord Almighty** is God over Israel.'
17.26 You, **Lord,** are God, and you have made this wonderful
17.27 You, **Lord,** have blessed them, and your blessing will rest on
18. 6 The **Lord** made David victorious everywhere.
18.13 The **Lord** made David victorious everywhere.
19.13 And may the **Lord's** will be done."
21. 3 Joab answered, "May the **Lord** make the people of Israel a
21. 9 Then the **Lord** said to Gad, David's prophet, [10]"Go and
21.11 David, told him what the **Lord** had said, and asked, "Which
21.12 three days during which the **Lord** attacks you with his sword
21.12 What answer shall I give the **Lord?"**
21.13 Let the **Lord** himself be the one to punish me, because he
21.14 So the **Lord** sent an epidemic on the people of Israel,
21.17 **Lord,** my God, punish me and my family, and spare your people."
21.18 The angel of the **Lord** told Gad to command David to go
21.18 and build an altar to the **Lord** at Araunah's threshing-place.
21.19 David obeyed the **Lord's** command and went, as Gad had
21.22 I can build an altar to the **Lord,** to stop the epidemic.
21.24 as an offering to the **Lord** something that belongs to you,
21.26 **Lord** there and offered burnt-offerings and fellowship-offerings.
21.26 He prayed, and the **Lord** answered him by sending fire from
21.27 The **Lord** told the angel to put his sword away, and the
21.28 saw by this that the **Lord** had answered his prayer, so he
21.29 The Tent of the **Lord's** presence which Moses had made in
21.30 because he was afraid of the sword of the **Lord's** angel.
22. 1 said, "This is where the Temple of the **Lord God** will be.
22. 6 him to build a temple for the **Lord,** the God of Israel.
22. 7 I wanted to build a temple to honour **the Lord my God.**
22. 8 But the **Lord** told me that I had killed too many people
22.11 "Now, my son, may **the Lord your God** be with you, and
22.12 And may **the Lord your God** give you insight and wisdom so
22.13 all the laws which the **Lord** gave to Moses for Israel, you
22.16 Now begin the work, and may the **Lord** be with you."
22.18 He said, **"The Lord your God** has been with you and given
22.18 land, and they are now subject to you and to the **Lord.**
22.19 Now serve **the Lord your God** with all your heart and soul.
22.19 the Covenant Box of the **Lord** and all the other sacred
23. 5 four thousand to praise the **Lord,** using the musical
23.13 in the worship of the **Lord,** to serve him, and to bless
23.24 or older, had a share in the work of the **Lord's** Temple.
23.25 David said, "The **Lord God** of Israel has given peace to
23.26 carry the Tent of the **Lord's** presence and all the equipment
23.30 to praise and glorify the **Lord** every morning and every
23.31 and whenever offerings to the **Lord** are burnt on the Sabbath,
23.31 Levites were assigned the duty of worshipping the **Lord** for all time.
23.32 of the Tent of the **Lord's** presence and the Temple, and of
24.19 Aaron in obedience to the commands of the **Lord God** of Israel.
25. 3 the music of harps, and sang praise and thanks to the **Lord.**
27.23 of twenty, because of the **Lord's** promise to make the people
28. 2 for the Covenant Box, the footstool of **the Lord our God.**
28. 4 The **Lord,** the God of Israel, chose me and my descendants
28. 5 he chose Solomon to rule over Israel, the **Lord's** kingdom.
28. 6 "The **Lord** said to me, 'Your son Solomon is the one who
28. 8 assembly of all Israel, the **Lord's** people, I charge you to
28. 8 carefully everything that **the Lord our God** has commanded us,
28.10 You must realize that the **Lord** has chosen you to build
28.12 the temple equipment and the gifts dedicated to the **Lord.**
28.18 that spread their wings over the **Lord's** Covenant Box.
28.19 instructions which the **Lord** himself gave me to carry out."
28.20 The **Lord God,** whom I serve, will be with you.
29. 1 not a palace for men but a temple for the **Lord God.**
29. 5 else is willing to give a generous offering to the **Lord?"**
29. 9 had given willingly to the **Lord,** and they were happy that so
29.10 There in front of the whole assembly King David praised the **Lord.**
29.10 He said, **"Lord God** of our ancestor Jacob, may you be
29.15 You know, O **Lord,** that we pass through life like exiles
29.16 O **Lord,** our God, we have brought together all this
29.18 **Lord God** of our ancestors Abraham, Isaac, and Jacob,
29.20 Then David commanded the people, "Praise **the Lord your God!"**
29.20 whole assembly praised the **Lord,** the God of their ancestors,
29.20 low and gave honour to the **Lord** and also to the king.
29.21 sacrifices, dedicating them to the **Lord,** and then gave them
29.22 happy as they ate and drank in the presence of the **Lord.**
29.22 In the name of the **Lord** they anointed him as their ruler
29.23 father David on the throne which the **Lord** had established.
29.25 The **Lord** made the whole nation stand in awe of Solomon,

2 Chr 1. 1 kingdom of Israel, and **the Lord his God** blessed him and made
1. 3 where the Tent of the **Lord's** presence was located,
1. 3 which Moses, the **Lord's** servant, had made in the wilderness.
1. 5 also in Gibeon in front of the Tent of the **Lord's** presence.
1. 5 King Solomon and all the people worshipped the **Lord** there.
1. 6 Tent the king worshipped the **Lord** by offering sacrifices on
1. 9 O **Lord God,** fulfil the promise you made to my father.
1.13 Tent of the **Lord's** presence was, and returned to Jerusalem.
2. 1 build a temple where the **Lord** would be worshipped, and also
2. 4 I am building a temple to honour **the Lord my God.**
2. 4 New Moon Festivals, and other holy days honouring **the Lord our God.**
2.11 He wrote, "Because the **Lord** loves his people, he has made

2 Chr 2.12 Praise the **Lord God** of Israel, Creator of heaven and earth!
2.12 to build a temple for the **Lord** and a palace for himself.
3. 1 on Mount Moriah, where the **Lord** appeared to David, the place
4.11 King Solomon had commanded, for use in the Temple of the **Lord.**
5. 1 David had dedicated to the **Lord**—the silver, gold, and other articles.
5. 2 in order to take the **Lord's** Covenant Box from Zion, David's
5. 5 moved the Tent of the **Lord's** presence and all its equipment
5. 7 the Covenant Box of the **Lord** into the Temple and put it
5.10 at Mount Sinai, when the **Lord** made a covenant with the
5.11 cymbals, and other instruments, as they praised the **Lord,**
5.11 "Praise the **Lord,** because he is good, And his love is eternal."
5.11 the dazzling light of the **Lord's** presence, and they could
6. 1 **"Lord,** you have chosen to live in clouds and darkness.
6. 4 He said, "Praise the **Lord God** of Israel!
6. 7 for the worship of the **Lord God** of Israel, [8]but the Lord
6. 8 God of Israel, [8]but the **Lord** said to him, 'You were right
6.10 "Now the **Lord** has kept his promise:
6.10 built a temple for the worship of the **Lord God** of Israel.
6.11 covenant which the **Lord** made with the people of Israel."
6.14 He prayed, **"Lord God** of Israel, in all heaven and earth
6.16 Now, **Lord God** of Israel, keep the other promise you made
6.17 So now, **Lord God** of Israel, let everything come true
6.19 **Lord** my God, I am your servant.
6.23 that he is innocent, [23]O **Lord,** listen in heaven and judge
6.27 humbly praying to you, [27]O **Lord,** listen to them in heaven
6.27 Then, O **Lord,** send rain on this land of yours, which you
6.37 and wicked they have been, hear their prayers, O **Lord.**
6.41 Rise up now, **Lord God,** and with the Covenant Box, the
6.42 **Lord God,** do not reject the king you have chosen.
7. 1 the dazzling light of the **Lord's** presence filled the Temple.
7. 4 Then Solomon and all the people offered sacrifices to the **Lord.**
7. 6 stood the Levites, praising the **Lord** with the musical
7.10 the blessings that the **Lord** had given to his people Israel,
7.12 his plans for them, [12]the **Lord** appeared to him at night.
7.21 will ask, 'Why did the **Lord** do this to this land and
7.22 because they abandoned **the Lord their God,** who brought their
7.22 That is why the **Lord** has brought this disaster on them.' "
8.12 Solomon offered sacrifices to the **Lord** on the altar
8.16 of the foundation of the **Lord's** Temple to its completion,
9. 8 Praise **the Lord your God!**
10.15 was the will of the **Lord God** to bring about what he
11. 2 But the **Lord** told the prophet Shemaiah [3]to give this
11. 4 They obeyed the **Lord's** command and did not go to fight Jeroboam.
11.14 successors would not let them serve as priests of the **Lord.**
11.16 sincerely wanted to worship the **Lord,** the God of Israel,
11.16 offer sacrifices to the **Lord,** the God of their ancestors.
12. 1 king, he and all his people abandoned the Law of the **Lord.**
12. 2 Rehoboam's reign their disloyalty to the **Lord** was punished.
12. 5 He said to them, "This is the **Lord's** message to you:
12. 6 sinned, and they said, "What the **Lord** is doing is just."
12. 7 When the **Lord** saw this, he spoke again to Shemaiah and
12.12 Because he submitted to the **Lord,**
12.12 the **Lord's** anger did not completely destroy him,
12.13 Jerusalem, the city which the **Lord** had chosen from all the
12.14 was evil, because he did not try to find the **Lord's** will.
13. 5 "Don't you know that the **Lord,** the God of Israel, made an
13. 8 royal authority that the **Lord** gave to David's descendants.
13. 9 You drove out the **Lord's** priests, the descendants of Aaron,
13.10 "But we still serve **the Lord our God** and have not
13.11 We do what the **Lord** has commanded, but you have abandoned him.
13.12 don't fight against the **Lord,** the God of your ancestors!
13.14 They cried to the **Lord** for help, and the priests blew the
13.18 they relied on the **Lord,** the God of their ancestors.
13.20 Finally the **Lord** struck him down, and he died.
14. 2 Asa pleased **the Lord, his God,** by doing what was right and
14. 4 do the will of the **Lord,** the God of their ancestors, and
14. 6 years there was no war, because the **Lord** gave him peace.
14. 7 land because we have done the will of **the Lord our God.**
14.11 Asa prayed to **the Lord his God,** "O Lord, you can help
14.11 Help us now, O **Lord** our God, because we are relying on
14.11 **Lord,** you are our God;
14.12 The **Lord** defeated the Sudanese army when Asa and the
14.13 They were overpowered by the **Lord** and his army, and the army
14.14 Gerar, because the people there were terrified of the **Lord.**
15. 2 The **Lord** is with you as long as you are with him.
15. 4 trouble came, they turned to the **Lord,** the God of Israel.
15. 8 the altar of the **Lord** that stood in the temple courtyard.
15. 9 kingdom, because they had seen that the **Lord** was with him.
15.11 they offered sacrifices to the **Lord** from the loot they had
15.12 they agreed to worship the **Lord,** the God of their ancestors,
15.14 took an oath in the **Lord's** name that they would keep the
15.15 took delight in worshipping the **Lord,** and he accepted them
15.17 in the land, he remained faithful to the **Lord** all his life.
16. 7 instead of relying on **the Lord your God,** the army of the
16. 8 you relied on the **Lord,** he gave you victory over them.
16. 9 The **Lord** keeps close watch over the whole world, to give
16.12 he did not turn to the **Lord** for help, but to doctors.
17. 3 The **Lord** blessed Jehoshaphat because he followed the
17. 5 The **Lord** gave Jehoshaphat firm control over the kingdom of Judah,
17. 6 took pride in serving the **Lord** and destroyed all the pagan
17. 9 of the Law of the **Lord** and went through all the towns
17.10 The **Lord** made all the surrounding kingdoms afraid to go
17.16 (Amasiah had volunteered to serve the **Lord.)**
18. 4 Then he added, "But first let's consult the **Lord."**
18. 6 "Isn't there another prophet through whom we can consult the **Lord?"**
18.10 Ahab, "This is what the **Lord** says, 'With these you will

2 Chr	18.11	"The **Lord** will give you victory."
	18.13	Micaiah answered, "By the living **Lord,** I will say what my
	18.14	The **Lord** will give you victory."
	18.15	speak to me in the name of the **Lord,** tell the truth!
	18.16	And the **Lord** said, 'These men have no leader;
	18.18	"Now listen to what the **Lord** says!
	18.18	I saw the **Lord** sitting on his throne in heaven, with all
	18.19	The **Lord** asked, 'Who will deceive Ahab so that he will
	18.20	approached the **Lord,** and said, 'I will deceive him.'
	18.20	the **Lord** asked.
	18.21	The **Lord** said, 'Go and deceive him.
	18.22	The **Lord** has made these prophets of yours lie to you.
	18.23	asked, "Since when did the **Lord's** spirit leave me and speak
	18.27	Micaiah exclaimed, "then the **Lord** has not spoken through me!"
	18.31	gave a shout, and the **Lord God** rescued him and turned the
	19. 2	wicked and to take the side of those who hate the **Lord?**
	19. 2	What you have done has brought the **Lord's** anger on you.
	19. 4	the people back to the **Lord,** the God of their ancestors.
	19. 6	on the authority of the **Lord,** and he is with you when
	19. 7	Honour the **Lord** and act carefully,
	19. 7	because **the Lord our God** does not tolerate fraud
	19. 8	of the Law of the **Lord** or legal disputes between inhabitants
	19. 9	duties in reverence for the **Lord,** faithfully obeying him in
	19.10	that they do not become guilty of sinning against the **Lord.**
	19.10	fellow-citizens will feel the force of the **Lord's** anger.
	19.11	these instructions, and may the **Lord** be on the side of the
	20. 3	Jehoshaphat was frightened and prayed to the **Lord** for guidance.
	20. 4	to Jerusalem to ask the **Lord** for guidance, [5]and they and
	20. 6	them [6]and prayed aloud, "O **Lord God** of our ancestors, you
	20.14	The spirit of the **Lord** came upon a Levite who was
	20.15	of Judah and Jerusalem, the **Lord** says that you must not be
	20.17	you will see the **Lord** give you victory.
	20.17	Go out to battle, and the **Lord** will be with you!"
	20.18	and all the people bowed with him and worshipped the **Lord.**
	20.19	and with a loud shout praised the **Lord,** the God of Israel.
	20.20	Put your trust in **the Lord your God,** and you will stand
	20.21	"Praise the **Lord!**
	20.22	they began to sing, the **Lord** threw the invading armies into
	20.26	Valley of Beracah and praised the **Lord** for all he had done.
	20.27	Jerusalem in triumph, because the **Lord** had defeated their enemies.
	20.29	how the **Lord** had defeated Israel's enemies was terrified,
	20.32	him, he did what was right in the sight of the **Lord;**
	20.37	with Ahaziah, the **Lord** will destroy what you have built."
	21. 6	He sinned against the **Lord,** [7]but the Lord was not willing
	21. 7	against the Lord, [7]but the **Lord** was not willing to destroy
	21.10	Jehoram had abandoned the **Lord,** the God of his ancestors.
	21.11	the people of Judah and Jerusalem to sin against the **Lord.**
	21.12	"The **Lord,** the God of your ancestor David, condemns you,
	21.14	As a result, the **Lord** will severely punish your people,
	21.16	The **Lord** incited them to go to war against Jehoram.
	21.18	Then after all this, the **Lord** brought on the king a
	22. 4	He sinned against the **Lord,** because after his father's
	22. 7	son of Nimshi, whom the **Lord** had chosen to destroy the
	22. 9	King Jehoshaphat, who had done all he could to serve the **Lord.**
	23. 3	to be king, as the **Lord** promised that King David's
	23. 6	people must obey the **Lord's** instructions and stay outside.
	23.16	in making a covenant that they would be the **Lord's** people.
	23.18	the sacrifices offered to the **Lord** in accordance with the
	24. 2	what was pleasing to the **Lord** as long as Jehoiada the priest
	24. 6	Moses, the servant of the **Lord,** required the people to pay
	24. 6	to pay for support of the Tent of the **Lord's** presence?"
	24. 9	everyone to bring to the **Lord** the tax which Moses, God's
	24.18	in the Temple of the **Lord,** the God of their ancestors, and
	24.18	these sins brought the **Lord's** anger on Judah and Jerusalem.
	24.19	The **Lord** sent prophets to warn them to return to him,
	24.20	him and called out, "The **Lord God** asks why you have
	24.22	he called out, "May the **Lord** see what you are doing and
	24.24	army was small, but the **Lord** let them defeat a much larger
	24.24	people had abandoned him, the **Lord God** of their ancestors.
	25. 2	He did what was pleasing to the **Lord,** but did it reluctantly.
	25. 4	children, but followed what the **Lord** had commanded in the
	25. 7	The **Lord** is not with these men from the Northern Kingdom.
	25. 9	The prophet replied, "The **Lord** can give you back more than that!"
	25.15	This made the **Lord** angry, so he sent a prophet to Amaziah.
	25.27	when he rebelled against the **Lord,** there had been a plot
	26. 4	example of his father, he did what was pleasing to the **Lord.**
	26. 5	living, he served the **Lord** faithfully, and God blessed him.
	26.16	He defied **the Lord his God** by going into the Temple to
	26.18	You have no right to burn incense to the **Lord.**
	26.18	You have offended the **Lord God,** and you no longer have his
	26.20	He hurried to get out, because the **Lord** had punished him.
	27. 2	what was pleasing to the **Lord,** just as his father had done;
	27. 6	Jotham grew powerful because he faithfully obeyed **the Lord his God.**
	28. 1	was not pleasing to the **Lord** [2]and followed the example of
	28. 3	of the people whom the **Lord** had driven out of the land
	28. 5	Because King Ahaz sinned, **the Lord his God** let the
	28. 5	The **Lord** also let the king of Israel, Pekah son of Remaliah,
	28. 5	The **Lord,** the God of their ancestors, permitted this to happen,
	28. 9	Oded, a prophet of the **Lord,** lived in the city of Samaria.
	28. 9	city, and he said, "The **Lord God** of your ancestors was
	28.10	that you also have committed sins against **the Lord your God?**
	28.11	Let them go, or the **Lord** will punish you in his anger."
	28.13	have already sinned against the **Lord** and made him angry
	28.19	and had defied the **Lord,** the Lord brought troubles on Judah.
	28.22	worst, that man Ahaz sinned against the **Lord** more than ever.
	28.25	on himself the anger of the **Lord,** the God of his ancestors.
	29. 2	ancestor King David, he did what was pleasing to the **Lord.**
	29. 5	purify the Temple of the **Lord,** the God of your ancestors.
2 Chr	29. 6	ancestors were unfaithful to **the Lord our God** and did what
	29. 8	Because of this the **Lord** has been angry with Judah and Jerusalem,
	29.10	make a covenant with the **Lord,** the God of Israel, so that
	29.11	are the ones that the **Lord** has chosen to burn incense to
	29.15	Temple ritually clean, according to the Law of the **Lord.**
	29.19	It is all in front of the **Lord's** altar."
	29.25	followed the instructions that the **Lord** had given to King
	29.27	people sang praise to the **Lord,** and the musicians began to
	29.30	Levites to sing to the **Lord** the songs of praise that were
	29.31	bring sacrifices as offerings of thanksgiving to the **Lord."**
	29.32	and two hundred lambs as burnt-offerings for the **Lord;**
	30. 1	the Passover in honour of the **Lord,** the God of Israel.
	30. 6	Now return to the **Lord,** the God of Abraham, Isaac, and
	30. 7	fellow-Israelites who were unfaithful to **the Lord their God.**
	30. 8	Do not be stubborn as they were, but obey the **Lord.**
	30. 8	Temple in Jerusalem, which **the Lord your God** has made holy
	30. 9	If you return to the **Lord,** then those who have taken your
	30. 9	**The Lord your God** is kind and merciful, and if you return
	30.15	they dedicated themselves to the **Lord,** and now they could
	30.17	Levites did it for them, and dedicated the lambs to the **Lord.**
	30.19	"O **Lord,** the God of our ancestors, in your goodness
	30.20	The **Lord** answered Hezekiah's prayer;
	30.21	Levites and the priests praised the **Lord** with all their strength.
	30.22	Levites for their skill in conducting the worship of the **Lord.**
	30.22	in praise of the **Lord,** the God of their ancestors,
	30.27	The priests and the Levites asked the **Lord's** blessing on the people.
	31. 3	other festivals which are required by the Law of the **Lord.**
	31. 4	all their time to the requirements of the Law of the **Lord.**
	31. 6	of gifts, which they dedicated to **the Lord their God.**
	31. 8	given, they praised the **Lord** and praised his people Israel.
	31.10	We have all this because the **Lord** has blessed his people."
	31.14	the gifts offered to the **Lord** and of distributing them.
	31.20	what was right and what was pleasing to **the Lord his God.**
	32. 1	King Hezekiah served the **Lord** faithfully, Sennacherib, the emperor of Assyria,
	32. 8	power, but we have **the Lord our God** to help us and
	32.11	Hezekiah tells you that **the Lord your God** will save you
	32.12	the one who destroyed the **Lord's** shrines and altars and then
	32.16	things about the **Lord God** and Hezekiah, the Lord's servant.
	32.17	that the emperor wrote defied the **Lord,** the God of Israel.
	32.21	**The Lord** sent an angel that killed the soldiers and
	32.22	In this way the **Lord** rescued King Hezekiah and the
	32.23	bringing offerings to the **Lord** and gifts to Hezekiah,
	32.24	He prayed, and the **Lord** gave him a sign that he would
	32.25	show gratitude for what the **Lord** had done for him, and Judah
	32.26	humbled themselves, and so the **Lord** did not punish the
	32.32	and his devotion to the **Lord** are recorded in The Vision of
	33. 2	of the nations whom the **Lord** had driven out of the land
	33. 2	as his people advanced, Manasseh sinned against the **Lord.**
	33. 4	Temple, the place that the **Lord** had said was where he should
	33. 6	He sinned greatly against the **Lord** and stirred up his anger.
	33. 9	by the nations whom the **Lord** had driven out of the land
	33.10	Although the **Lord** warned Manasseh and his people, they refused to listen.
	33.11	So the **Lord** let the commanders of the Assyrian army invade Judah.
	33.12	became humble, turned to **the Lord his God,** and begged him
	33.13	This convinced Manasseh that the **Lord** was God.
	33.16	repaired the altar where the **Lord** was worshipped, and he
	33.16	the people of Judah to worship the **Lord,** the God of Israel.
	33.17	places of worship, they offered them only to the **Lord.**
	33.18	in the name of the **Lord,** the God of Israel, are all
	33.22	Manasseh, he sinned against the **Lord,** and he worshipped the
	33.23	his father, he did not become humble and turn to the **Lord;**
	34. 2	He did what was pleasing to the **Lord;**
	34. 8	Josiah sent three men to repair the Temple of the **Lord God:**
	34.14	of the Law of the **Lord,** the Law that God had given
	34.21	"Go and consult the **Lord** for me and for the people who
	34.21	The **Lord** is angry with us because our ancestors have not
	34.21	obeyed the word of the **Lord** and have not done what this
	34.24	king and give him [24]the following message from the **Lord:**
	34.26	king himself, this is what I, the **Lord God** of Israel, say:
	34.31	made a covenant with the **Lord** to obey him, to keep his
	34.33	the people to serve the **Lord,** the God of their ancestors.
	35. 1	King Josiah celebrated the Passover at Jerusalem in honour of the **Lord;**
	35. 3	the teachers of Israel, who were dedicated to the **Lord:**
	35. 3	you are to serve **the Lord your God** and his people Israel.
	35. 6	the instructions which the **Lord** gave through Moses."
	35.16	worship of the **Lord,** the keeping of the Passover Festival,
	35.26	did—his devotion to the **Lord,** his obedience to the Law,
	36. 5	He sinned against **the Lord his God.**
	36. 9	He too sinned against the **Lord.**
	36.12	He sinned against the **Lord** and did not listen humbly
	36.12	to the prophet Jeremiah, who spoke the word of the **Lord.**
	36.13	refused to repent and return to the **Lord,** the God of Israel.
	36.14	defiled the Temple, which the **Lord** himself had made holy.
	36.15	The **Lord,** the God of their ancestors, had continued to
	36.16	prophets, until at last the **Lord's** anger against his people
	36.17	So the **Lord** brought the king of Babylonia to attack them.
	36.21	And so what the **Lord** had foretold through the prophet
	36.22	of Persia was emperor, the **Lord** made what he had said
	36.23	The **Lord,** the God of Heaven, has made me ruler over the
	36.23	people, go there, and may **the Lord your God** be with you."
Ezra	1. 1	of Persia was emperor, the **Lord** made what he had said
	1. 2	The **Lord,** the God of Heaven, has made me ruler over the
	1. 3	rebuild the Temple of the **Lord,** the God of Israel, the God
	1. 5	got ready to go and rebuild the **Lord's** Temple in Jerusalem.
	2.68	the exiles arrived at the **Lord's** Temple in Jerusalem, some

Ezra	3. 5	regular assemblies at which the **Lord** is worshipped,
	3. 5	all the offerings that were given to the **Lord** voluntarily.
	3. 6	day of the seventh month to burn sacrifices to the **Lord.**
	3.10	They praised the **Lord** according to the instructions handed
	3.11	They sang the **Lord's** praises, repeating the refrain:
	3.11	"The **Lord** is good, and his love for Israel is eternal."
	3.11	all his might, praising the **Lord,** because the work on the
	4. 1	were rebuilding the Temple of the **Lord,** the God of Israel.
	4. 3	need your help to build a temple for **the Lord our God.**
	6.21	land and who had come to worship the **Lord God** of Israel.
	6.22	full of joy because the **Lord** had made the emperor of Assyria
	7. 6	of the Law which the **Lord,** the God of Israel, had given
	7. 6	had the blessing of **the Lord his God,** the emperor gave him
	7.10	studying the Law of the **Lord,** to practising it, and to
	7.11	the laws and commands which the **Lord** had given to Israel:
	7.27	Ezra said, "Praise the **Lord,** the God of our ancestors!
	7.27	to honour in this way the Temple of the **Lord** in Jerusalem.
	7.28	**the Lord my God** has given me courage, and I have been
	8.28	"You are sacred to the **Lord,** the God of your ancestors, and
	8.35	All these animals were burnt as sacrifices to the **Lord.**
	9. 5	in prayer and stretched out my hands to **the Lord my God.**
	9. 8	for a short time, O **Lord** our God, you have been gracious
	9.15	**Lord God** of Israel, you are just, but you have let us
	10.11	confess your sins to the **Lord,** the God of your ancestors,
Neh	1. 5	I prayed to God, [5] **"Lord God** of Heaven!
	1. 6	Look at me, **Lord,** and hear my prayer, as I pray day
	1.10	**"Lord,** these are your servants, your own people.
	4.14	the **Lord** is, and fight for your fellow-countrymen,
	5.13	and praised the **Lord.**
	8. 1	of the Law which the **Lord** had given Israel through Moses, to
	8. 6	Ezra said, "Praise the **Lord,** the great God!"
	8. 9	day is holy to **the Lord your God,** so you are not
	8.10	Today is holy to **our Lord,** so don't be sad.
	8.10	The joy that the **Lord** gives you will make you strong."
	8.14	that the Law, which the **Lord** gave through Moses, ordered the
	9. 3	hours the Law of **the Lord their God** was read to them,
	9. 3	they confessed their sins and worshipped **the Lord their God.**
	9. 4	They prayed aloud to **the Lord their God.**
	9. 5	"Stand up and praise **the Lord your God;**
	9. 6	"You, **Lord,** you alone are Lord;
	9. 7	You, **Lord God,** chose Abram and led him out of Ur in
	9.18	How much they insulted you, **Lord!**
	10.29	that we will obey all that the Lord, **our Lord,** commands us;
	10.34	the sacrifices offered to **the Lord our God,** according to the
Job	1. 6	to appear before the **Lord,** Satan was there among them.
	1. 7	The **Lord** asked him, "What have you been doing?"
	1. 8	the **Lord** asked.
	1.12	"All right," the **Lord** said to Satan, "everything he
	1.21	The **Lord** gave, and now he has taken away.
	2. 1	to appear before the **Lord** again, Satan was there among them.
	2. 2	The **Lord** asked him, "Where have you been?"
	2. 3	the **Lord** asked.
	2. 6	So the **Lord** said to Satan, "All right, he is in your
	2. 7	Then Satan left the **Lord's** presence and made sores break
	12. 9	All of them know that the **Lord's** hand made them.
	28.28	to men, "To be wise, you must have reverence for the **Lord.**
	38. 1	Then out of the storm the **Lord** spoke to Job.
	38. 1	The **Lord**
	40. 3	I spoke foolishly, **Lord.**
	40. 6	Then out of the storm the **Lord** spoke to Job once again.
	40. 6	The **Lord**
	42. 1	Then Job answered the **Lord.**
	42. 2	I know, **Lord,** that you are all-powerful;
	42. 7	After the **Lord** had finished speaking to Job, he said to Eliphaz,
	42. 9	Lord had told them to do, and the **Lord** answered Job's prayer.
	42.10	for his three friends, the **Lord** made him prosperous again
	42.11	him for all the troubles the **Lord** had brought on him.
	42.12	The **Lord** blessed the last part of Job's life even more
Ps	1. 2	obeying the Law of the **Lord,** and they study it day and
	1. 6	guided and protected by the **Lord,** but the evil are on the
	2. 2	together against the **Lord** and against the king he chose.
	2. 4	in heaven the **Lord** laughs and mocks their feeble plans.
	2. 7	"I will announce," says the king, "what the **Lord** has declared.
	2.11	Serve the **Lord** with fear;
	3. 1	I have so many enemies, **Lord,** so many who turn against me!
	3. 3	But you, O **Lord,** are always my shield from danger;
	3. 4	I call to the **Lord** for help, and from his sacred hill
	3. 5	down and sleep, and all night long the **Lord** protects me.
	3. 7	Come, **Lord!**
	3. 8	Victory comes from the **Lord**— may he bless his people.
	4. 3	Remember that the **Lord** has chosen the righteous for his own,
	4. 5	right sacrifices to the **Lord,** and put your trust in him.
	4. 6	"Give us more blessings, O **Lord.**
	4. 8	you alone, O **Lord,** keep me perfectly safe.
	5. 1	Listen to my words, O **Lord,** and hear my sighs.
	5. 2	I pray to you, O **Lord;**
	5. 8	**Lord,** I have so many enemies!
	5.12	You bless those who obey you, **Lord;**
	6. 1	**Lord,** don't be angry and rebuke me!
	6. 2	I am worn out, O **Lord;**
	6. 3	How long, O **Lord,** will you wait to help me?
	6. 4	Come and save me, **Lord;**
	6. 8	The **Lord** hears my weeping;
	7. 1	O **Lord,** my God, I come to you for protection;
	7. 3	O **Lord,** my God, if I have wronged anyone, if I have
	7. 6	Rise in your anger, O **Lord!**
	7. 8	Judge in my favour, O **Lord;**
	7.17	I thank the **Lord** for his justice,
	7.17	I sing praises to the **Lord,** the Most High.
	8. 1	O Lord, **our Lord,** your greatness is seen in all the world!
	8. 9	O Lord, **our Lord,** your greatness is seen in all the world!
Ps	9. 1	I will praise you, **Lord,** with all my heart;
	9. 7	But the **Lord is king** for ever;
	9. 9	The **Lord** is a refuge for the oppressed, a place of safety
	9.10	Those who know you, **Lord,** will trust you;
	9.11	Sing praise to the **Lord,** who rules in Zion!
	9.13	Be merciful to me, O **Lord!**
	9.13	Rescue me from death, O **Lord,** [14] that I may stand before
	9.16	The **Lord** has revealed himself by his righteous judgements,
	9.19	Come, **Lord!**
	9.20	Make them afraid, O **Lord;**
	10. 1	Why are you so far away, O **Lord?**
	10. 3	the greedy man curses and rejects the **Lord.**
	10. 4	A wicked man does not care about the **Lord;**
	10.12	O **Lord,** punish those wicked men!
	10.16	The **Lord is king** for ever and ever.
	10.17	You will listen, O **Lord,** to the prayers of the lowly;
	11. 1	I trust in the **Lord** for safety.
	11. 4	The **Lord** is in his holy temple;
	11. 7	The **Lord** is righteous and loves good deeds;
	12. 1	Help us, **Lord!**
	12. 3	Silence those flattering tongues, O **Lord!**
	12. 5	I will come," says the **Lord,** "because the needy are
	12. 6	The promises of the **Lord** can be trusted;
	12. 7	Keep us always safe, O **Lord,** and preserve us from such people.
	13. 1	How much longer will you forget me, **Lord?**
	13. 3	Look at me, O **Lord** my God, and answer me.
	13. 6	will sing to you, O **Lord,** because you have been good to
	14. 2	The **Lord** looks down from heaven at mankind to see if there
	14. 4	asks the **Lord.**
	14. 6	plans of the humble man, but the **Lord** is his protection.
	14. 7	Israel will be when the **Lord** makes them prosperous again!
	15. 1	**Lord,** who may enter your Temple?
	15. 4	whom God rejects, but honours those who obey the **Lord.**
	16. 2	I say to the **Lord,** "You are my Lord;
	16. 3	How excellent are the **Lord's** faithful people!
	16. 5	You, **Lord,** are all I have, and you give me all I
	16. 7	I praise the **Lord,** because he guides me, and in the night
	16. 8	I am always aware of the **Lord's** presence;
	17. 1	Listen, O **Lord,** to my plea for justice;
	17.13	Come, **Lord!**
	18. 1	How I love you, **Lord!**
	18. 2	The **Lord** is my protector;
	18. 3	I call to the **Lord,** and he saves me from my enemies.
	18. 3	Praise the **Lord!**
	18. 6	In my trouble I called to the **Lord;**
	18.13	Then the **Lord** thundered from the sky;
	18.15	rebuked your enemies, **Lord,** and roared at them in anger.
	18.16	The **Lord** reached down from above and took hold of me;
	18.18	I was in trouble, they attacked me, but the **Lord** protected me.
	18.20	The **Lord** rewards me because I do what is right;
	18.21	I have obeyed the law of the **Lord;**
	18.25	O **Lord,** you are faithful to those who are faithful to you;
	18.28	O **Lord,** you give me light;
	18.31	The **Lord** alone is God;
	18.35	O **Lord,** you protect me and save me;
	18.41	they call to the **Lord,** but he does not answer.
	18.46	The **Lord** lives!
	18.48	O **Lord,** you give me victory over my enemies and protect me
	19. 7	The law of the **Lord** is perfect;
	19. 7	The commands of the **Lord** are trustworthy, giving wisdom to
	19. 8	The laws of the **Lord** are right, and those who obey them
	19. 8	The commands of the **Lord** are just and give understanding to
	19. 9	Reverence for the **Lord** is good;
	19. 9	The judgements of the **Lord** are just;
	19.12	deliver me, **Lord,** from hidden faults!
	19.14	be acceptable to you, O **Lord,** my refuge and my redeemer!
	20. 1	May the **Lord** answer you when you are in trouble!
	20. 5	May the **Lord** answer all your requests.
	20. 6	Now I know that the **Lord** gives victory to his chosen king;
	20. 7	but we trust in the power of **the Lord our God.**
	20. 9	Give victory to the king, O **Lord;**
	21. 1	The king is glad, O **Lord,** because you gave him strength;
	21. 7	The king trusts in the **Lord Almighty;**
	21. 7	and because of the **Lord's** constant love he will always be secure.
	21. 9	The **Lord** will devour them in his anger, and fire will
	21.13	We praise you, **Lord,** for your great strength!
	22. 8	"You relied on the **Lord,"** they say.
	22. 8	If the **Lord** likes you, why doesn't he help you?"
	22.19	O **Lord,** don't stay away from me!
	22.23	"Praise him, you servants of the **Lord!**
	22.26	those who come to the **Lord** will praise him.
	22.27	All nations will remember the **Lord.**
	22.28	The **Lord is king,** and he rules the nations.
	22.30	men will speak of the **Lord** to the coming generation.
	22.31	"The **Lord** saved his people."
	23. 1	The **Lord** is my shepherd;
	23. 4	darkness, I will not be afraid, **Lord,** for you are with me.
	24. 1	The world and all that is in it belong to the **Lord;**
	24. 3	Who has the right to go up the **Lord's** hill?
	24. 5	The **Lord** will bless them and save them;
	24. 8	He is the **Lord,** strong and mighty,
	24. 8	the **Lord,** victorious in battle.
	24.10	The triumphant **Lord**—he is the great king!
	25. 1	To you, O **Lord,** I offer my prayer;
	25. 4	Teach me your ways, O **Lord;**
	25. 6	Remember, O **Lord,** your kindness and constant love which
	25. 7	In your constant love and goodness, remember me, **Lord!**
	25. 8	Because the **Lord** is righteous and good, he teaches sinners
	25.11	Keep your promise, **Lord,** and forgive my sins, for they are many.
	25.12	who have reverence for the **Lord** will learn from him the path
	25.14	The **Lord** is the friend of those who obey him and he

Ps
25.15 I look to the **Lord** for help at all times, and he
25.16 Turn to me, **Lord,** and be merciful to me, because I am
26. 1 Declare me innocent, O **Lord,** because I do what is right
26. 2 Examine me and test me, **Lord;**
26. 6 **Lord,** I wash my hands to show that I am innocent and
26. 8 where you live, O **Lord,** the place where your glory dwells.
26.12 in the assembly of his people I praise the **Lord.**
27. 1 The **Lord** is my light and my salvation;
27. 1 The **Lord** protects me from all danger;
27. 4 I have asked the **Lord** for one thing;
27. 4 to live in the **Lord's** house all my life, to marvel there
27. 6 I will sing, I will praise the **Lord.**
27. 7 Hear me, **Lord,** when I call to you!
27. 8 "Come and worship me," I answered, "I will come, **Lord;**
27.10 mother may abandon me, but the **Lord** will take care of me.
27.11 Teach me, **Lord,** what you want me to do, and lead me
27.13 I will live to see the **Lord's** goodness in this present life.
27.14 Trust in the **Lord.**
27.14 Trust in the **Lord.**
28. 1 O **Lord,** my defender, I call to you.
28. 5 no notice of what the **Lord** has done or of what he
28. 6 Give praise to the **Lord;**
28. 7 The **Lord** protects and defends me;
28. 8 The **Lord** protects his people;
28. 9 Save your people, **Lord,** and bless those who are yours.
29. 1 Praise the **Lord,** you heavenly beings;
29. 2 Praise the **Lord's** glorious name;
29. 3 The voice of the **Lord** is heard on the seas;
29. 4 The voice of the **Lord** is heard in all its might and
29. 5 The voice of the **Lord** breaks the cedars, even the cedars
29. 7 The voice of the **Lord** makes the lightning flash.
29. 9 The **Lord's** voice shakes the oaks and strips the leaves
29.10 The **Lord** rules over the deep waters;
29.11 The **Lord** gives strength to his people and blesses them with peace.
30. 1 I praise you, **Lord,** because you have saved me and kept my
30. 2 to you for help, O **Lord** my God, and you healed me;
30. 4 Sing praise to the **Lord,** all his faithful people!
30. 7 You were good to me, **Lord;**
30. 8 I called to you, **Lord;**
30.10 Hear me, **Lord,** and be merciful!
30.10 Help me, **Lord!"**
30.12 **Lord,** you are my God, I will give you thanks for ever.
31. 1 I come to you, **Lord,** for protection;
31. 5 You will save me, **Lord;**
31. 9 Be merciful to me, **Lord,** for I am in trouble;
31.14 But my trust is in you, O **Lord;**
31.17 I call to you, **Lord;**
31.21 Praise the **Lord!**
31.23 Love the **Lord,** all his faithful people.
31.23 The **Lord** protects the faithful, but punishes the proud as they deserve.
31.24 Be strong, be courageous, all you that hope in the **Lord.**
32. 2 is the man whom the **Lord** does not accuse of doing wrong
32. 4 Day and night you punished me, **Lord;**
32. 8 The **Lord** says, "I will teach you the way you should go;
32.10 who trust in the **Lord** are protected by his constant love.
32.11 be glad and rejoice because of what the **Lord** has done.
33. 1 are righteous, shout for joy for what the **Lord** has done;
33. 2 Give thanks to the **Lord** with harps, sing to him with
33. 4 The words of the **Lord** are true and all his works are
33. 5 The **Lord** loves what is righteous and just;
33. 6 The **Lord** created the heavens by his command, the sun,
33. 8 Worship the **Lord,** all the earth!
33.10 The **Lord** frustrates the purposes of the nations;
33.12 Happy is the nation whose God is the **Lord;**
33.13 The **Lord** looks down from heaven and sees all mankind.
33.18 The **Lord** watches over those who obey him, those who
33.20 We put our hope in the **Lord;**
33.22 constant love be with us, **Lord,** as we put our hope in
34. 1 I will always thank the **Lord;**
34. 3 Proclaim with me the **Lord's** greatness;
34. 4 I prayed to the **Lord,** and he answered me;
34. 7 those who honour the **Lord** and rescues them from danger.
34. 8 Find out for yourself how good the **Lord** is.
34. 9 Honour the **Lord,** all his people;
34.10 of food, but those who obey the **Lord** lack nothing good.
34.11 listen to me, and I will teach you to honour the **Lord.**
34.15 The **Lord** watches over the righteous and listens to their cries;
34.17 The righteous call to the **Lord,** and he listens;
34.18 The **Lord** is near to those who are discouraged;
34.19 many troubles, but the **Lord** saves him from them all;
34.20 the **Lord** preserves him completely;
34.22 The **Lord** will save his people;
35. 1 Oppose those who oppose me, **Lord,** and fight those who
35. 5 blown by the wind as the angel of the **Lord** pursues them!
35. 6 and slippery while the angel of the **Lord** strikes them down!
35. 9 Then I will be glad because of the **Lord;**
35.10 I will say to the **Lord,** "There is no one like you.
35.17 How much longer, **Lord,** will you just look on?
35.22 But you, O **Lord,** have seen this.
35.22 So don't be silent, **Lord;**
35.23 Rouse yourself, O **Lord,** and defend me;
35.24 You are righteous, O **Lord,** so declare me innocent;
35.27 for joy and sing again and again, "How great is the **Lord!**
36. 5 **Lord,** your constant love reaches the heavens;
37. 3 Trust in the **Lord** and do good;
37. 4 Seek your happiness in the **Lord,** and he will give you your
37. 5 Give yourself to the **Lord;**
37. 7 Be patient and wait for the **Lord** to act;
37. 9 Those who trust in the **Lord** will possess the land, but the
37.13 But the **Lord** laughs at wicked men, because he knows they

Ps
37.17 all the wicked, [17]because the **Lord** will take away the
37.18 The **Lord** takes care of those who obey him, and the land
37.20 the enemies of the **Lord** will vanish like wild flowers;
37.22 who are blessed by the **Lord** will possess the land, but those
37.23 The **Lord** guides a man in the way he should go and
37.24 will not stay down, because the **Lord** will help them up.
37.25 man abandoned by the **Lord** or his children begging for food.
37.28 for the **Lord** loves what is right and does not abandon
37.33 but the **Lord** will not abandon him to his enemy's power
37.34 Put your hope in the **Lord** and obey his commands;
37.39 The **Lord** saves righteous men and protects them in times of trouble.
38. 1 O **Lord,** don't punish me in your anger!
38. 9 O **Lord,** you know what I long for;
38.15 But I trust in you, O **Lord;**
38.15 and you, O **Lord** my God, will answer me.
38.21 Do not abandon me, O **Lord;**
38.22 Help me now, O **Lord** my saviour!
39. 4 **"Lord,** how long will I live?
39. 7 What, then, can I hope for, **Lord?**
39.12 Hear my prayer, **Lord,** and listen to my cry;
40. 1 I waited patiently for the **Lord's** help;
40. 3 will take warning and will put their trust in the **Lord.**
40. 4 are those who trust the **Lord,** who do not turn to idols
40. 5 You have done many things for us, O **Lord** our God;
40. 9 assembly of all your people, **Lord,** I told the good news that
40.11 **Lord,** I know you will never stop being merciful to me.
40.13 Save me, **Lord!**
40.16 for your salvation always say, "How great is the **Lord!"**
40.17 am weak and poor, O **Lord,** but you have not forgotten me.
41. 1 the **Lord** will help them when they are in trouble.
41. 2 The **Lord** will protect them and preserve their lives;
41. 3 The **Lord** will help them when they are sick and will
41. 4 I said, "I have sinned against you, **Lord;**
41.10 Be merciful to me, **Lord,** and restore my health, and I
41.13 Praise the **Lord,** the God of Israel!
42. 8 May the **Lord** show his constant love during the day, so
44.23 Wake up, **Lord!**
46. 7 The **Lord Almighty** is with us;
46. 8 Come and see what the **Lord** has done.
46.11 The **Lord Almighty** is with us;
47. 2 The **Lord,** the Most High, is to be feared;
47. 5 of joy and the blast of trumpets, as the **Lord** goes up.
48. 1 The **Lord** is great and is to be highly praised in the
48. 8 have seen it in the city of our God, the **Lord Almighty;**
50. 1 The Almighty God, the **Lord,** speaks;
51.15 Help me to speak, **Lord,** and I will praise you.
54. 4 The **Lord** is my defender.
54. 6 I will gladly offer you a sacrifice, O **Lord;**
55. 9 Confuse the speech of my enemies, O **Lord!**
55.16 But I call to the **Lord God** for help, and he will
55.22 Leave your troubles with the **Lord,** and he will defend you;
56. 3 When I am afraid, O **Lord Almighty,** I put my trust in
56.10 God is on my side— [10]the **Lord,** whose promises I praise.
57. 9 I will thank you, O **Lord,** among the nations.
59. 4 any fault of mine, O **Lord,** that they hurry to their places.
59. 5 Rise, **Lord God** Almighty, and come to my aid;
59. 8 But you laugh at them, **Lord;**
59.11 Scatter them by your strength and defeat them, O **Lord,** our protector.
62.12 You yourself, O **Lord,** reward everyone according to his deeds.
64.10 All righteous people will rejoice because of what the **Lord** has done.
66.18 ignored my sins, the **Lord** would not have listened to me.
68. 4 His name is the **Lord**—be glad in his presence!
68.11 The **Lord** gave the command, and many women carried the news:
68.16 The **Lord** will live there for ever!
68.17 thousands of mighty chariots the **Lord** comes from Sinai into
68.18 The **Lord God** will live there.
68.19 Praise the **Lord,** who carries our burdens day after day;
68.20 he is the Lord, **our Lord,** who rescues us from death.
68.22 The **Lord** has said, "I will bring your enemies back from Bashan;
68.26 praise the **Lord,** all you descendants of Jacob!"
68.32 world, sing praise to the **Lord,** [33]to him who rides in the
69. 6 shame on those who trust in you, Sovereign **Lord Almighty!**
69.13 But as for me, I will pray to you, **Lord;**
69.16 Answer me, **Lord,** in the goodness of your constant love;
69.31 This will please the **Lord** more than offering him cattle,
69.33 The **Lord** listens to those in need and does not forget
70. 1 **Lord,** help me now!
70. 5 You are my saviour, O **Lord**— hurry to my aid!
71. 1 **Lord,** I have come to you for protection;
71. 5 Sovereign **Lord,** I put my hope in you;
71.16 I will praise your power, Sovereign **Lord;**
72.18 Praise the **Lord,** the God of Israel!
73.20 when you rouse yourself, O **Lord,** they disappear.
73.28 find protection with the Sovereign **Lord** and to proclaim all
74.18 But remember, O **Lord,** that your enemies laugh at you,
75. 8 The **Lord** holds a cup in his hand, filled with the strong
76. 7 But you, **Lord,** are feared by all.
76.11 Give **the Lord your God** what you promised him;
77. 2 In times of trouble I pray to the **Lord;**
77. 7 "Will the **Lord** always reject us?
77.11 I will remember your great deeds, **Lord;**
78. 4 the next generation about the **Lord's** power and his great
78.21 And so the **Lord** was angry when he heard them;
78.65 At last the **Lord** woke up as though from sleep;
79. 5 **Lord,** will you be angry with us for ever?
79.12 **Lord,** pay the other nations back seven times for all the
80. 4 How much longer, **Lord God** Almighty, will you be angry with
80.19 Bring us back, **Lord God** Almighty.

Ps 81.10 I am **the Lord your God,** who brought you out of Egypt.
83.16 with shame, O **Lord,** and make them acknowledge your power.
83.18 you alone are the **Lord,** supreme ruler over all the earth.
84. 1 How I love your Temple, **Lord Almighty!**
84. 2 I long to be in the **Lord's** Temple.
84. 3 young near your altars, **Lord Almighty,** my king and my God.
84. 8 Hear my prayer, **Lord God** Almighty.
84.11 The **Lord** is our protector and glorious king, blessing us
84.12 **Lord Almighty,** how happy are those who trust in you!
85. 1 **Lord,** you have been merciful to your land;
85. 7 your constant love, O **Lord,** and give us your saving help.
85. 8 I am listening to what the **Lord God** is saying;
85.12 The **Lord** will make us prosperous, and our land will
85.13 Righteousness will go before the **Lord** and prepare the path for him.
86. 1 Listen to me, **Lord,** and answer me, for I am helpless and
86. 4 Make your servant glad, O **Lord,** because my prayers go up
86. 6 Listen, **Lord,** to my prayer;
86. 8 no god like you, O **Lord,** not one has done what you
86.11 Teach me, **Lord,** what you want me to do, and I will
86.12 I will praise you with all my heart, O **Lord** my God;
86.15 But you, O **Lord,** are a merciful and loving God, always patient,
86.17 Show me proof of your goodness, **Lord;**
87. 1 The **Lord** built his city on the sacred hill;
87. 6 The **Lord** will write a list of the peoples and include them
88. 1 **Lord God,** my saviour, I cry out all day, and at night
88. 9 **Lord,** every day I call to you and lift my hands to
88.13 **Lord,** I call to you for help;
88.14 Why do you reject me, **Lord?**
89. 1 O **Lord,** I will always sing of your constant love;
89. 5 the holy ones sing of your faithfulness, **Lord.**
89. 6 No one in heaven is like you, **Lord;**
89. 8 **Lord God** Almighty, none is as mighty as you;
89. 8 in all things you are faithful, O **Lord.**
89.18 You, O **Lord,** chose our protector;
89.46 **Lord,** will you hide yourself for ever?
89.49 **Lord,** where are the former proofs of your love?
89.51 Your enemies insult your chosen king, O **Lord!**
89.52 Praise the **Lord** for ever!
90. 1 O **Lord,** you have always been our home.
90.13 Have pity, O **Lord,** on your servants!
90.17 **Lord** our God, may your blessings be with us.
91. 1 Whoever goes to the **Lord** for safety, whoever remains under
91. 9 You have made the **Lord** your defender, the Most High your protector,
91.14 love me and will protect those who acknowledge me as **Lord.**
92. 1 give thanks to you, O **Lord,** to sing in your honour, O
92. 4 Your mighty deeds, O **Lord,** make me glad;
92. 5 How great are your actions, **Lord!**
92. 8 destroyed, [8]because you, **Lord,** are supreme for ever.
92.13 in the house of the **Lord,** that flourish in the Temple of
92.15 This shows that the **Lord** is just, that there is no wrong
93. 1 The **Lord is king.**
93. 2 Your throne, O **Lord,** has been firm from the beginning, and
93. 3 The ocean depths raise their voice, O **Lord;**
93. 4 The **Lord** rules supreme in heaven, greater than the roar of
93. 5 Your laws are eternal, **Lord,** and your Temple is holy indeed,
94. 1 **Lord,** you are a God who punishes;
94. 3 How much longer, **Lord?**
94. 5 They crush your people, **Lord;**
94. 7 They say, "The **Lord** does not see us;
94.11 The **Lord** knows what they think;
94.12 **Lord,** how happy is the person you instruct, the one to
94.14 The **Lord** will not abandon his people;
94.17 If the **Lord** had not helped me, I would have gone quickly
94.18 but your constant love, O **Lord,** held me up.
94.22 But the **Lord** defends me;
94.23 **the Lord our God** will destroy them.
95. 1 Come, let us praise the **Lord!**
95. 3 For the **Lord** is a mighty God, a mighty king over all
95. 6 let us kneel before the **Lord,** our Maker!
96. 1 Sing a new song to the **Lord!**
96. 1 Sing to the **Lord,** all the world!
96. 2 Sing to the **Lord,** and praise him!
96. 4 The **Lord** is great and is to be highly praised;
96. 5 nations are only idols, but the **Lord** created the heavens.
96. 7 Praise the **Lord,** all people on earth;
96. 8 Praise the **Lord's** glorious name;
96.10 Say to all the nations, "The **Lord is king!**
96.13 shout for joy [13]when the **Lord** comes to rule the earth.
97. 1 The **Lord is king!**
97. 5 like wax before the Lord, before the **Lord** of all the earth.
97. 7 all the gods bow down before the **Lord.**
97. 8 cities of Judah rejoice because of your judgements, O **Lord.**
97. 9 **Lord Almighty,** you are ruler of all the earth;
97.10 The **Lord** loves those who hate evil;
97.12 are righteous be glad because of what the **Lord** has done!
98. 1 Sing a new song to the **Lord;**
98. 2 The **Lord** announced his victory;
98. 4 Sing for joy to the **Lord,** all the earth;
98. 5 Sing praises to the **Lord!**
98. 6 trumpets and horns, and shout for joy to the **Lord,** our
98. 8 together with joy before the **Lord,** [9]because he comes to
99. 1 The **Lord is king;**
99. 2 The **Lord** is mighty in Zion;
99. 5 Praise **the Lord our God;**
99. 6 they called to the **Lord,** and he answered them.
99. 8 O **Lord,** our God, you answered your people;
99. 9 Praise **the Lord our God,** and worship at his sacred hill!
99. 9 **The Lord our God** is holy.
100. 1 Sing to the **Lord,** all the world!

Ps 100. 2 Worship the **Lord** with joy;
100. 3 Acknowledge that the **Lord is God.**
100. 5 The **Lord** is good;
101. 1 about loyalty and justice, and I sing it to you, O **Lord.**
101. 8 I will expel all evil men from the city of the **Lord.**
102. 1 Listen to my prayer, O **Lord,** and hear my cry for help!
102.12 But you, O **Lord,** are king for ever;
102.15 The nations will fear the **Lord;**
102.16 When the **Lord** rebuilds Zion, he will reveal his greatness.
102.18 the coming generation what the **Lord** has done, so that people
102.19 The **Lord** looked down from his holy place on high, he
102.22 Jerusalem [22]when nations and kingdoms come together and worship the **Lord.**
102.23 The **Lord** has made me weak while I am still young;
102.24 O **Lord,** you live for ever;
103. 1 Praise the **Lord,** my soul!
103. 2 Praise the **Lord,** my soul, and do not forget how kind he
103. 6 The **Lord** judges in favour of the oppressed and gives them
103. 8 The **Lord** is merciful and loving, slow to become angry and
103.13 to his children, so the **Lord** is kind to those who honour
103.17 for those who honour the **Lord,** his love lasts for ever, and
103.19 The **Lord** placed his throne in heaven;
103.20 Praise the **Lord,** you strong and mighty angels, who obey his commands,
103.21 Praise the **Lord,** all you heavenly powers, you servants of his,
103.22 Praise the **Lord,** all his creatures in all the places he rules.
103.22 Praise the **Lord,** my soul!
104. 1 Praise the **Lord,** my soul!
104. 1 O **Lord,** my God, how great you are!
104.16 get plenty of rain— the **Lord's** own trees, which he planted.
104.24 **Lord,** you have made so many things!
104.31 May the glory of the **Lord** last for ever!
104.31 May the **Lord** be happy with what he has made!
104.33 I will sing to the **Lord** all my life;
104.35 Praise the **Lord,** my soul!
104.35 Praise the **Lord!**
105. 1 Give thanks to the **Lord,** proclaim his greatness;
105. 2 Sing praise to the **Lord;**
105. 4 Go to the **Lord** for help;
105. 7 The **Lord is our God;**
105.10 The **Lord** made a covenant with Jacob, one that will last
105.16 The **Lord** sent famine to their country and took away all
105.19 The word of the **Lord** proved him right.
105.24 The **Lord** gave many children to his people and made them
105.45 Praise the **Lord!**
106. 1 Praise the **Lord!**
106. 1 Give thanks to the **Lord,** because he is good;
106. 4 Remember me, **Lord,** when you help your people;
106.16 jealous of Moses and of Aaron, the **Lord's** holy servant.
106.25 their tents and grumbled and would not listen to the **Lord.**
106.29 They stirred up the **Lord's** anger by their actions, and a
106.32 Meribah the people made the **Lord** angry, and Moses was in
106.34 kill the heathen, as the **Lord** had commanded them to do,
106.40 So the **Lord** was angry with his people;
106.43 Many times the **Lord** rescued his people, but they chose
106.44 Yet the **Lord** heard them when they cried out, and he took
106.47 Save us, O **Lord** our God, and bring us back from among
106.48 Praise the **Lord,** the God of Israel;
106.48 Praise the **Lord!**
107. 1 "Give thanks to the **Lord,** because he is good;
107. 2 words in praise to the **Lord,** all you whom he has saved.
107. 6 trouble they called to the **Lord,** and he saved them from
107. 8 They must thank the **Lord** for his constant love, for the
107.13 trouble they called to the **Lord,** and he saved them from
107.15 They must thank the **Lord** for his constant love, for the
107.19 trouble they called to the **Lord,** and he saved them from
107.21 They must thank the **Lord** for his constant love, for the
107.24 They saw what the **Lord** can do, his wonderful acts on the
107.28 trouble they called to the **Lord,** and he saved them from
107.31 They must thank the **Lord** for his constant love, for the
107.33 The **Lord** made rivers dry up completely and stopped springs from flowing.
107.43 may they consider the **Lord's** constant love.
108. 3 I will thank you, O **Lord,** among the nations.
109.14 May the **Lord** remember the evil of his ancestors and
109.15 May the **Lord** always remember their sins, but may they
109.20 **Lord,** punish my enemies in that way— those who say such
109.21 But my Sovereign **Lord,** help me as you have promised, and
109.26 Help me, O **Lord** my God;
109.30 I will give loud thanks to the **Lord;**
110. 1 The **Lord** said to my lord, the king, "Sit here at my
110. 2 From Zion the **Lord** will extend your royal power.
110. 4 The **Lord** made a solemn promise and will not take it back:
110. 5 The **Lord** is at your right side;
111. 1 Praise the **Lord!**
111. 1 heart I will thank the **Lord** in the assembly of his people.
111. 2 How wonderful are the things the **Lord** does!
111. 4 The **Lord** does not let us forget his wonderful actions;
111.10 The way to become wise is to honour the **Lord;**
112. 1 Praise the **Lord!**
112. 1 the person who honours the **Lord,** who takes pleasure in
112. 7 his faith is strong, and he trusts in the **Lord.**
113. 1 Praise the **Lord!**
113. 1 You servants of the **Lord,** praise his name!
113. 3 From the east to the west praise the name of the **Lord!**
113. 4 The **Lord** rules over all nations;
113. 5 There is no one like **the Lord our God.**
113. 9 Praise the **Lord!**
114. 2 foreign land, [2]Judah became the **Lord's** holy people, Israel
114. 7 Tremble, earth, at the **Lord's** coming, at the presence of
115. 1 To you alone, O **Lord,** to you alone, and not to us,

Ps 115. 9 Trust in the **Lord,** you people of Israel.
115.10 Trust in the **Lord,** you priests of God.
115.11 Trust in the **Lord,** all you that worship him.
115.12 The **Lord** remembers us and will bless us;
115.14 May the **Lord** give you children— you and your descendants!
115.15 May you be blessed by the **Lord,** who made heaven and earth!
115.16 Heaven belongs to the **Lord** alone, but he gave the earth
115.17 The **Lord** is not praised by the dead, by any who go
115.18 Praise the **Lord!**
116. 1 I love the **Lord,** because he hears me;
116. 4 Then I called to the Lord, "I beg you, **Lord,** save me!"
116. 5 The **Lord** is merciful and good;
116. 6 The **Lord** protects the helpless;
116. 7 Be confident, my heart, because the **Lord** has been good to me.
116. 8 The **Lord** saved me from death;
116. 9 in the presence of the **Lord** in the world of the living.
116.12 What can I offer the **Lord** for all his goodness to me?
116.13 a wine-offering to the **Lord,** to thank him for saving me.
116.15 painful it is to the **Lord** when one of his people dies!
116.16 I am your servant, **Lord;**
116.18 Praise the **Lord!**
117. 1 Praise the **Lord,** all nations!
117. 2 Praise the **Lord!**
118. 1 Give thanks to the **Lord,** because he is good, and his love
118. 5 In my distress I called to the **Lord;**
118. 6 The **Lord** is with me, I will not be afraid;
118. 7 It is the **Lord** who helps me, and I will see my
118. 8 is better to trust in the **Lord** than to depend on man.
118. 9 to trust in the **Lord** than to depend on human leaders.
118.10 but I destroyed them by the **power of the Lord!**
118.11 but I destroyed them by the **power of the Lord!**
118.12 by the **power of the Lord** I destroyed them.
118.13 attacked and was being defeated, but the **Lord** helped me.
118.14 The **Lord** makes me powerful and strong;
118.15 "The **Lord's** mighty power has done it!
118.17 instead, I will live and proclaim what the **Lord** has done.
118.19 I will go in and give thanks to the **Lord!**
118.20 This is the gate of the **Lord;**
118.21 I praise you, **Lord,** because you heard me, because you
118.23 This was done by the **Lord;**
118.24 This is the day of the **Lord's** victory;
118.25 Save us, **Lord,** save us!
118.25 Give us success, O **Lord!**
118.26 God bless the one who comes in the name of the **Lord!**
118.26 From the Temple of the **Lord** we bless you.
118.27 The **Lord is God;**
118.29 Give thanks to the **Lord,** because he is good, and his
119. 1 are faultless, who live according to the law of the **Lord.**
119. 3 they walk in the **Lord's** ways.
119. 4 **Lord,** you have given us your laws and told us to obey
119.12 I praise you, O **Lord;**
119.31 I have followed your instructions, **Lord;**
119.33 Teach me, **Lord,** the meaning of your laws, and I will
119.41 how much you love me, **Lord,** and save me according to your
119.52 judgements of long ago, and they bring me comfort, O **Lord.**
119.55 the night I remember you, **Lord,** and I think about your law.
119.57 You are all I want, O **Lord;**
119.64 **Lord,** the earth is full of your constant love;
119.65 You have kept your promise, **Lord,** and you are good to me,
119.75 that your judgements are righteous, **Lord,** and that you
119.81 I am worn out, **Lord,** waiting for you to save me;
119.89 Your word, O **Lord,** will last for ever;
119.107 My sufferings, **Lord,** are terrible indeed;
119.108 Accept my prayer of thanks, O **Lord,** and teach me your commands.
119.126 **Lord,** it is time for you to act, because people are
119.137 You are righteous, **Lord,** and your laws are just.
119.145 answer me, **Lord,** and I will obey your commands!
119.149 Because your love is constant, hear me, O **Lord;**
119.151 are near to me, **Lord,** and all your commands are permanent.
119.156 But your compassion, **Lord,** is great;
119.159 See how I love your instructions, **Lord.**
119.166 for you to save me, **Lord,** and I do what you command.
119.169 Let my cry for help reach you, **Lord!**
119.174 How I long for your saving help, O **Lord!**
120. 1 was in trouble, I called to the **Lord,** and he answered me.
120. 2 Save me, **Lord,** from liars and deceivers.
121. 2 My help will come from the **Lord,** who made heaven and earth.
121. 5 The **Lord** will guard you;
121. 7 The **Lord** will protect you from all danger;
122. 1 when they said to me, "Let us go to the **Lord's** house."
122. 4 to give thanks to the **Lord** according to his command.
122. 9 of the house of **the Lord our God** I pray for your
123. 1 **Lord,** I look up to you, up to heaven, where you rule.
123. 2 keep looking to you, O **Lord** our God, until you have mercy
123. 3 Be merciful to us, **Lord,** be merciful;
124. 1 What if the **Lord** had not been on our side?
124. 2 "If the **Lord** had not been on our side when our enemies
124. 6 Let us thank the **Lord,** who has not let our enemies destroy
124. 8 Our help comes from the **Lord,** who made heaven and earth.
125. 1 Those who trust in the **Lord** are like Mount Zion, which can
125. 2 mountains surround Jerusalem, so the **Lord** surrounds his
125. 4 **Lord,** do good to those who are good, to those who obey
126. 1 When the **Lord** brought us back to Jerusalem, it was like a
126. 2 said about us, "The **Lord** did great things for them."
126. 4 **Lord,** make us prosperous again, just as the rain brings
127. 1 If the **Lord** does not build the house, the work of the
127. 1 if the **Lord** does not protect the city, it is useless for
127. 2 For the **Lord** provides for those he loves, while they are asleep.
127. 3 Children are a gift from the **Lord;**
128. 1 Happy are those who obey the **Lord,** who live by his commands.

Ps 128. 4 A man who obeys the **Lord** will surely be blessed like this.
128. 5 May the **Lord** bless you from Zion!
129. 4 But the **Lord,** the righteous one, has freed me from slavery."
129. 8 No one who passes by will say, "May the **Lord** bless you!
129. 8 We bless you in the name of the **Lord."**
130. 1 From the depths of my despair I call to you, **Lord.**
130. 2 Hear my cry, O **Lord;**
130. 5 I wait eagerly for the **Lord's** help, and in his word I
130. 6 I wait for the **Lord** more eagerly than watchmen wait for
130. 7 Israel, trust in the **Lord,** because his love is constant
131. 1 **Lord,** I have given up my pride and turned away from my
131. 3 Israel, trust in the **Lord** now and for ever!
132. 1 **Lord,** do not forget David and all the hardships he endured.
132. 2 Remember, **Lord,** what he promised, the vow he made to you,
132. 5 provide a place for the **Lord,** a home for the Mighty God
132. 7 We said, "Let us go to the **Lord's** house;
132. 8 Come to the Temple, **Lord,** with the Covenant Box, the
132.10 do not reject your chosen king, **Lord.**
132.13 The **Lord** has chosen Zion;
133. 3 That is where the **Lord** has promised his blessing— life that
134. 1 Come, praise the **Lord,** all his servants, all who serve in
134. 2 Raise your hands in prayer in the Temple, and praise the **Lord!**
134. 3 May the **Lord,** who made heaven and earth, bless you from Zion!
135. 1 Praise the **Lord!**
135. 1 you servants of the **Lord,** [2]who stand in the Lord's house,
135. 2 Lord, [2]who stand in the **Lord's** house, in the Temple of our
135. 3 Praise the **Lord,** because he is good;
135. 5 I know that **our Lord** is great, greater than all the gods.
135.13 **Lord,** you will always be proclaimed as God;
135.14 The **Lord** will defend his people;
135.19 Praise the **Lord,** people of Israel;
135.20 Praise the **Lord,** you Levites;
135.21 Praise the **Lord** in Zion, in Jerusalem, his home.
135.21 Praise the **Lord!**
136. 1 Give thanks to the **Lord,** because he is good;
137. 4 can we sing a song to the **Lord** in a foreign land?
137. 7 Remember, **Lord,** what the Edomites did the day Jerusalem was captured.
138. 1 I thank you, **Lord,** with all my heart;
138. 4 praise you, **Lord,** because they have heard your promises.
138. 8 **Lord,** your love is eternal.
139. 1 **Lord,** you have examined me and you know me.
139.21 O **Lord,** how I hate those who hate you!
140. 1 Save me, **Lord,** from evil men;
140. 4 Protect me, **Lord,** from the power of the wicked;
140. 6 I say to the **Lord,** "You are my God."
140. 6 Hear my cry for help, **Lord!**
140. 7 My Sovereign **Lord,** my strong defender, you have protected me in battle.
140. 8 **Lord,** don't give the wicked what they want;
140.12 **Lord,** I know that you defend the cause of the poor and
141. 1 I call to you, **Lord;**
141. 3 **Lord,** place a guard at my mouth, a sentry at the door
141. 8 But I keep trusting in you, my Sovereign **Lord.**
142. 1 I call to the **Lord** for help;
142. 5 **Lord,** I cry to you for help;
142. 5 you, **Lord,** are my protector;
143. 1 **Lord,** hear my prayer!
143. 7 Answer me now, **Lord!**
143. 9 I go to you for protection, **Lord;**
143.11 Rescue me, **Lord,** as you have promised;
144. 1 Praise the **Lord,** my protector!
144. 3 **Lord,** what is man, that you notice him;
144. 5 O **Lord,** tear the sky apart and come down;
144.15 happy are the people whose God is the **Lord!**
145. 3 The **Lord** is great and is to be highly praised;
145. 8 The **Lord** is loving and merciful, slow to become angry and
145.10 All your creatures, **Lord,** will praise you, and all your
145.13 The **Lord** is faithful to his promises, and he is merciful in
145.17 The **Lord** is righteous in all he does, merciful in all
145.21 I will always praise the **Lord;**
146. 1 Praise the **Lord!**
146. 1 Praise the **Lord,** my soul!
146. 5 who depends on **the Lord his God,** [6]the Creator of heaven,
146. 7 The **Lord** sets prisoners free [8]and gives sight to the blind.
146.10 The **Lord is king** for ever.
146.10 Praise the **Lord!**
147. 1 Praise the **Lord!**
147. 2 The **Lord** is restoring Jerusalem;
147. 5 Great and mighty is **our Lord;**
147. 7 Sing hymns of praise to the **Lord;**
147.12 Praise the **Lord,** O Jerusalem!
147.20 Praise the **Lord!**
148. 1 Praise the **Lord!**
148. 1 Praise the **Lord** from heaven, you that live in the heights above.
148. 5 Let them all praise the name of the **Lord!**
148. 7 Praise the **Lord** from the earth, sea-monsters and all ocean depths;
148.13 Let them all praise the name of the **Lord!**
148.14 Praise the **Lord!**
149. 1 Praise the **Lord!**
149. 1 Sing a new song to the **Lord;**
149. 4 The **Lord** takes pleasure in his people;
149. 9 Praise the **Lord!**
150. 1 Praise the **Lord!**
150. 6 Praise the **Lord,** all living creatures!
150. 6 Praise the **Lord!**

Prov 1. 7 To have knowledge, you must first have reverence for the **Lord.**
1.29 use for knowledge and have always refused to obey the **Lord.**
2. 5 it means to fear the **Lord** and you will succeed in learning
2. 6 It is the **Lord** who gives wisdom;
3. 5 Trust in the **Lord** with all your heart.

Prov 3. 6 Remember the **Lord** in everything you do, and he will show
3. 7 simply obey the **Lord** and refuse to do wrong.
3. 9 Honour the **Lord** by making him an offering from the best of
3.11 When the **Lord** corrects you, my son, pay close attention
3.12 The **Lord** corrects those he loves, as a father corrects a
3.19 The **Lord** created the earth by his wisdom;
3.26 The **Lord** will keep you safe.
3.32 as they do, [32] because the **Lord** hates people who do evil,
3.33 The **Lord** puts a curse on the homes of wicked men, but
5.21 The **Lord** sees everything you do.
6.16 There are seven things that the **Lord** hates and cannot tolerate:
8.13 To honour the **Lord** is to hate evil;
8.22 "The **Lord** created me first of all, the first of his works,
8.35 finds me finds life, and the **Lord** will be pleased with him.
9.10 To be wise you must first have reverence for the **Lord.**
10. 3 The **Lord** will not let good people go hungry, but he will
10.22 It is the **Lord's** blessing that makes you wealthy.
10.27 Obey the **Lord,** and you will live longer.
10.29 The **Lord** protects honest people, but destroys those who do wrong.
11. 1 The **Lord** hates people who use dishonest scales.
11.20 The **Lord** hates evil-minded people, but loves those who do right.
12. 2 The **Lord** is pleased with good people, but condemns those
12.22 The **Lord** hates liars, but is pleased with those who keep
14. 2 Be honest and you show that you have reverence for the **Lord;**
14.26 Reverence for the **Lord** gives confidence and security to
14.27 Reverence for the **Lord** is a fountain of life.
15. 3 The **Lord** sees what happens everywhere;
15. 8 The **Lord** is pleased when good men pray, but hates the
15. 9 The **Lord** hates the ways of evil people, but loves those
15.11 of the dead can keep the **Lord** from knowing what is there;
15.16 be poor and fear the **Lord** than to be rich and in
15.25 The **Lord** will destroy the homes of arrogant men, but he
15.26 The **Lord** hates evil thoughts, but he is pleased with friendly words.
15.29 When good people pray, the **Lord** listens, but he ignores
15.33 Reverence for the **Lord** is an education in itself.
16. 2 you do is right, but the **Lord** judges your motives.
16. 3 Ask the **Lord** to bless your plans, and you will be
16. 4 Everything the **Lord** has made has its destiny;
16. 5 The **Lord** hates everyone who is arrogant;
16. 6 Obey the **Lord** and nothing evil will happen to you.
16. 7 When you please the **Lord,** you can make your enemies into friends.
16.11 The **Lord** wants weights and measures to be honest and
16.20 trust in the **Lord** and you will be happy.
17. 3 tested by fire, and a person's heart is tested by the **Lord.**
17.15 or letting the wicked go—both are hateful to the **Lord.**
18.10 The **Lord** is like a strong tower, where the righteous can
18.22 it shows that the **Lord** is good to you.
19. 3 by their own stupid actions and then blame the **Lord.**
19.14 parents, but only the **Lord** can give him a sensible wife.
19.17 like lending to the Lord, and the **Lord** will pay you back.
19.21 kinds of things, but the **Lord's** will is going to be done.
19.23 Obey the **Lord** and you will live a long life, content and
20.10 The **Lord** hates people who use dishonest weights and measures.
20.12 The **Lord** has given us eyes to see with and ears to
20.22 Trust the **Lord** and he will make it right.
20.23 The **Lord** hates people who use dishonest scales and weights.
20.24 The **Lord** has determined our path;
20.27 The **Lord** gave us mind and conscience;
21. 1 The **Lord** controls the mind of a king as easily as he
21. 2 is right, but remember that the **Lord** judges your motives.
21. 3 that pleases the **Lord** more than bringing him sacrifices.
21.27 The **Lord** hates it when wicked men offer him sacrifices,
21.30 insight—they are of no help if the **Lord** is against you.
21.31 ready for battle, but it is the **Lord** who gives victory.
22. 2 the **Lord** made them both.
22. 4 Obey the **Lord,** be humble, and you will get riches, honour,
22.12 The **Lord** sees to it that truth is kept safe by
22.14 is a trap—it catches those with whom the **Lord** is angry.
22.19 I want you to put your trust in the **Lord;**
22.23 The **Lord** will argue their case for them and threaten the
23.11 The **Lord** is their powerful defender, and he will argue
23.17 let reverence for the **Lord** be the concern of your life.
24.18 The **Lord** will know if you are gloating, and he will not
24.21 Have reverence for the **Lord,** my son, and honour the king.
25.22 make him burn with shame, and the **Lord** will reward you.
28. 5 is, but those who worship the **Lord** understand it well.
28.14 Always obey the **Lord** and you will be happy.
28.25 You are much better off to trust the **Lord.**
29.13 have this in common—the **Lord** gave eyes to both of them.
29.25 think of you, but if you trust the **Lord,** you are safe.
29.26 of the ruler, but only from the **Lord** can you get justice.
31.30 but a woman who honours the **Lord** should be praised.

Is 1. 2 The **Lord** said, "Earth and sky, listen to what I am saying!
1. 4 You have rejected the **Lord,** the holy God of Israel, and have
1. 9 If the **Lord Almighty** had not let some of the people survive,
1.10 Listen to what the **Lord** is saying to you.
1.18 The **Lord** says, "Now, let's settle the matter.
1.20 I, the **Lord,** have spoken."
1.24 listen to what the **Lord Almighty,** Israel's powerful God,
1.27 Because the **Lord** is righteous, he will save Jerusalem
2. 3 up the hill of the **Lord,** to the Temple of Israel's God.
2. 3 For the **Lord's** teaching comes from Jerusalem;
2. 5 Jacob, let us walk in the light which the **Lord** gives us!
2. 9 Do not forgive them, **Lord!**
2.10 try to escape from the **Lord's** anger and to hide from his
2.11 Then the **Lord** alone will be exalted.
2.12 On that day the **Lord Almighty** will humble everyone who is powerful,
2.17 will completely disappear, and the **Lord** alone will be
2.19 try to escape from the **Lord's** anger and to hide from his

Is 2.21 When the **Lord** comes to shake the earth, people will hide
3. 1 Now the **Lord,** the Almighty Lord, is about to take away
3. 4 The **Lord** will let the people be governed by immature boys.
3. 8 Everything they say and do is against the **Lord;**
3.13 The **Lord** is ready to state his case;
3.14 The **Lord** is bringing the elders and leaders of his
3.15 I, the Sovereign **Lord Almighty,** have spoken."
3.16 The **Lord** said, "Look how proud the women of Jerusalem are!
3.18 day is coming when the **Lord** will take away from the women
4. 2 time is coming when the **Lord** will make every plant and tree
4. 4 By his power the **Lord** will judge and purify the nation and
4. 5 who are gathered there, the **Lord** will send a cloud in the
5. 7 Israel is the vineyard of the **Lord Almighty;**
5. 9 I have heard the **Lord Almighty** say, "All these big, fine
5.12 you don't understand what the **Lord** is doing, [13] and so you
5.16 But the **Lord Almighty** shows his greatness by doing what is right,
5.19 You say, "Let the **Lord** hurry up and do what he says
5.24 you have rejected what the **Lord Almighty,** Israel's holy God,
5.25 The **Lord** is angry with his people and has stretched out
5.25 Yet even then the **Lord's** anger will not be ended, but his
5.26 The **Lord** gives a signal to call for a distant nation.
6. 1 In the year that King Uzziah died, I saw the **Lord.**
6. 3 The **Lord Almighty** is holy!
6. 5 my own eyes, I have seen the King, the **Lord Almighty!"**
6. 8 Then I heard the **Lord** say, "Whom shall I send?
6.11 I asked, "How long will it be like this, **Lord?"**
7. 3 The **Lord** said to Isaiah, "Take your son Shear Jashub, and
7. 7 "But I, the **Lord,** declare that this will never happen.
7.10 The **Lord** sent another message to Ahaz:
7.11 "Ask **the Lord your God** to give you a sign.
7.12 I refuse to put the **Lord** to the test."
7.14 Well then, the **Lord** himself will give you a sign:
7.17 "The **Lord** is going to bring on you, on your people, and
7.18 "When that time comes, the **Lord** will whistle as a
7.20 "When that time comes, the **Lord** will hire a barber from
8. 1 The **Lord** said to me, "Take a large piece of writing
8. 3 the **Lord** said to me, "Name him 'Quick-Loot-Fast-Plunder.'
8. 5 The **Lord** spoke to me again.
8. 7 and King Pekah, [7] I, the **Lord,** will bring the emperor of
8.11 With his great power the **Lord** warned me not to follow
8.13 Remember that I, the **Lord Almighty,** am holy;
8.17 The **Lord** has hidden himself from his people, but I trust
8.18 Here I am with the children the **Lord** has given me.
8.18 The **Lord Almighty,** whose throne is on Mount Zion, has sent
8.20 to answer them, "Listen to what the **Lord** is teaching you!
9. 3 You have given them great joy, **Lord;**
9. 7 The **Lord Almighty** is determined to do all this.
9. 8 The **Lord** has pronounced judgement on the kingdom of Israel,
9.11 The **Lord** has stirred up their enemies to attack them.
9.12 Yet even so the **Lord's** anger is not ended;
9.13 even though the **Lord Almighty** has punished them, they have
9.14 In a single day the **Lord** will punish Israel's leaders
9.17 And so the **Lord** will not let any of the young men
9.17 Yet even so the **Lord's** anger will not be ended, but his
9.19 Because the **Lord Almighty** is angry, his punishment burns
9.21 Yet even so the **Lord's** anger is not ended;
10. 4 Yet even so the **Lord's** anger will not be ended;
10. 5 The **Lord** said, "Assyria!
10.12 But the **Lord** says, "When I finish what I am doing on
10.15 But the **Lord** says, "Can an axe claim to be greater than
10.16 The **Lord Almighty** is going to send disease to punish
10.20 They will truly put their trust in the **Lord,** Israel's holy God.
10.23 country the Sovereign **Lord Almighty** will bring destruction,
10.24 The Sovereign **Lord Almighty** says to his people who live in Zion,
10.26 I, the **Lord Almighty,** will beat them with my whip as I
10.33 The **Lord Almighty** will bring them crashing down like
10.34 The **Lord** will cut them down as trees in the heart of
11. 2 The spirit of the **Lord** will give him wisdom, and the
11. 2 He will know the **Lord's** will and have reverence for him,
11. 9 full of knowledge of the **Lord** as the seas are full of
11.11 When that day comes, the **Lord** will once again use his
11.12 The **Lord** will raise a signal flag to show the nations
11.15 The **Lord** will dry up the Gulf of Suez, and he will
12. 1 "I praise you, **Lord!**
12. 2 The **Lord** gives me power and strength;
12. 4 "Give thanks to the **Lord!**
12. 5 Sing to the **Lord** because of the great things he has done.
13. 3 The **Lord** has called out his proud and confident soldiers
13. 4 The **Lord** of Armies is preparing his troops for battle.
13. 5 In his anger the **Lord** is coming to devastate the whole country.
13. 6 The day of the **Lord** is near, the day when the Almighty
13. 9 The day of the **Lord** is coming—that cruel day of his
13.11 The **Lord** says, "I will bring disaster on the earth and
13.13 place on that day when I, the **Lord Almighty,** show my anger.
13.17 The **Lord** says, "I am stirring up the Medes to attack Babylon.
13.19 But I, the **Lord,** will overthrow Babylon as I did Sodom and
14. 1 The **Lord** will once again be merciful to his people Israel
14. 2 to the land which the **Lord** gave them, and there the nations
14. 3 The **Lord** will give the people of Israel relief from their
14. 5 The **Lord** has ended the power of the evil rulers [6] who
14.22 The **Lord Almighty** says, "I will attack Babylon and
14.22 I, the **Lord,** have spoken.
14.23 I, the **Lord Almighty,** have spoken."
14.24 The **Lord Almighty** has sworn an oath:
14.27 The **Lord Almighty** is determined to do this;
14.30 The **Lord** will be a shepherd to the poor of his people
14.32 will tell them that the **Lord** has established Zion and that
16.13 That is the message the **Lord** gave earlier about Moab.
16.14 And now the **Lord** says, "In exactly three years Moab's
17. 1 The **Lord** said, "Damascus will not be a city any longer;
17. 3 I, the **Lord Almighty,** have spoken."

Is 17. 4 The **Lord** said, "A day is coming when Israel's greatness
17. 6 I, the **Lord God** of Israel, have spoken."
18. 4 The **Lord** said to me, "I will look down from heaven as
18. 7 time is coming when the **Lord Almighty** will receive offerings
18. 7 come to Mount Zion, where the **Lord Almighty** is worshipped.
19. 1 The **Lord** is coming to Egypt, riding swiftly on a cloud.
19. 2 The **Lord** says, "I will stir up civil war in Egypt and
19. 4 I, the **Lord Almighty,** have spoken."
19.12 can tell you what plans the **Lord Almighty** has for Egypt.
19.14 The **Lord** has made them give confusing advice.
19.16 when they see that the **Lord Almighty** has stretched out his
19.17 of the fate that the **Lord Almighty** has prepared for them.
19.18 will take their oaths in the name of the **Lord Almighty.**
19.19 be an altar to the **Lord** in the land of Egypt and
19.20 They will be symbols of the **Lord Almighty's** presence in Egypt.
19.20 and call out to the **Lord** for help, he will send someone
19.21 The **Lord** will reveal himself to the Egyptian people, and
19.22 The **Lord** will punish the Egyptians, but then he will heal them.
19.25 The **Lord Almighty** will bless them and say, "I will bless you,
20. 2 Three years earlier the **Lord** had told Isaiah son of Amoz
20. 3 When Ashdod was captured, the **Lord** said, "My servant
21. 6 Then the **Lord** said to me, "Go and post a sentry, and
21.10 I have heard from the **Lord Almighty,** the God of Israel.
21.16 Then the **Lord** said to me, "In exactly one year the
21.17 I, the **Lord God** of Israel, have spoken."
22. 5 Vision, and the Sovereign **Lord Almighty** has sent it on us.
22.12 The Sovereign **Lord Almighty** was calling you then to weep
22.14 The Sovereign **Lord Almighty** himself spoke to me and said,
22.14 I, the Sovereign **Lord Almighty,** have spoken."
22.15 The Sovereign **Lord Almighty** told me to go to Shebna, the
22.17 may be important, but the **Lord** will pick you up and throw
22.19 The **Lord** will remove you from office and bring you down
22.20 The **Lord** said to Shebna, "When that happens, I will
22.25 The **Lord** has spoken.
23. 9 The **Lord Almighty** planned it.
23.11 The **Lord** has stretched out his hand over the sea and
23.17 seventy years are over, the **Lord** will let Tyre go back to
23.18 The money she earns by commerce will be dedicated to the **Lord.**
23.18 but those who worship the **Lord** will use her money to buy
24. 1 The **Lord** is going to devastate the earth and leave it desolate.
24. 3 The **Lord** has spoken and it will be done.
24.14 will tell how great the **Lord** is, [15]and those in the east
24.15 live along the sea will praise the **Lord,** the God of Israel.
24.21 time is coming when the **Lord** will punish the powers above
24.23 will no longer shine, for the **Lord Almighty** will be king.
25. 1 **Lord,** you are my God;
25. 5 But you, **Lord,** have silenced our enemies;
25. 6 Here on Mount Zion the **Lord Almighty** will prepare a
25. 8 The Sovereign **Lord** will destroy death for ever!
25. 8 The **Lord** himself has spoken!
25. 9 He is the **Lord!**
25.10 The **Lord** will protect Mount Zion, but the people of Moab
26. 3 You, **Lord,** give perfect peace to those who keep their
26. 4 Trust in the **Lord** for ever;
26. 7 **Lord,** you make the path smooth for good men;
26.11 **Lord,** put them to shame and let them suffer;
26.12 You will give us prosperity, **Lord;**
26.13 **Lord** our God, we have been ruled by others,
26.13 but you alone are **our Lord.**
26.15 **Lord,** you have made our nation grow, enlarging its
26.16 You punished your people, **Lord,** and in anguish they prayed to you.
26.17 You, **Lord,** have made us cry out, as a woman in labour
26.19 refreshes the earth, so the **Lord** will revive those who have
26.21 The **Lord** is coming from his heavenly dwelling-place to
27. 1 On that day the **Lord** will use his powerful and deadly
27. 2 On that day the **Lord** will say of his pleasant vineyard,
27. 7 not been punished by the **Lord** as severely as its enemies,
27. 8 The **Lord** punished his people by sending them into exile.
27.12 to the Egyptian border, the **Lord** will gather his people one
27.13 come and worship the **Lord** in Jerusalem, on his sacred hill.
28. 2 The **Lord** has someone strong and powerful ready to attack them,
28. 5 day is coming when the **Lord Almighty** will be like a glorious
28.13 That is why the **Lord** is going to teach you letter by
28.14 Jerusalem over this people, listen to what the **Lord** is saying.
28.16 This, now, is what the Sovereign **Lord** says:
28.21 The **Lord** will fight as he did at Mount Perazim and in
28.22 the **Lord Almighty's** decision to destroy the whole country.
28.29 All this wisdom comes from the **Lord Almighty.**
29. 6 Suddenly and unexpectedly [6]the **Lord Almighty** will rescue
29.10 The **Lord** has made you drowsy, ready to fall into a deep
29.13 The **Lord** said, "These people claim to worship me, but
29.15 Those who try to hide their plans from the **Lord** are doomed!
29.19 find the happiness which the **Lord,** the holy God of Israel,
29.22 So now the **Lord,** the God of Israel, who rescued Abraham
30. 1 The **Lord** has spoken:
30. 9 lying, always refusing to listen to the **Lord's** teachings.
30.15 The Sovereign **Lord,** the holy God of Israel, says to the people,
30.18 And yet the **Lord** is waiting to be merciful to you.
30.18 Happy are those who put their trust in the **Lord.**
30.19 The **Lord** is compassionate, and when you cry to him for help,
30.20 The **Lord** will make you go through hard times, but he
30.23 you sow your seeds, the **Lord** will send rain to make them
30.26 will all happen when the **Lord** bandages and heals the wounds
30.27 The **Lord's** power and glory can be seen in the distance.
30.29 way to the Temple of the **Lord,** the defender of Israel.
30.30 The **Lord** will let everyone hear his majestic voice and
30.31 terrified when they hear the **Lord's** voice and feel the force
30.32 As the **Lord** strikes them again and again, his people
30.33 The **Lord** will breathe out a stream of flame to set it
31. 1 do not rely on the **Lord,** the holy God of Israel, or

Is 31. 3 When the **Lord** acts, the strong nation will crumble, and the
31. 4 The **Lord** said to me, "No matter how shepherds yell and shout,
31. 4 can keep me, the **Lord Almighty,** from protecting Mount Zion.
31. 5 its young, so I, the **Lord Almighty,** will protect Jerusalem
31. 6 The **Lord** said, "People of Israel, you have sinned against
31. 9 The **Lord** has spoken—the Lord who is worshipped in Jerusalem
32. 6 are an insult to the **Lord,** and he never feeds the hungry
33. 2 **Lord,** have mercy on us.
33. 5 How great the **Lord** is!
33. 6 Their greatest treasure is their reverence for the **Lord.**
33.10 The **Lord** says to the nations, "Now I will act.
33.21 The **Lord** will show us his glory.
33.22 The **Lord** himself will be our king;
34. 2 The **Lord** is angry with all the nations and all their armies.
34. 5 The **Lord** has prepared his sword in heaven, and now it will
34. 6 The **Lord** will offer this sacrifice in the city of Bozrah;
34. 8 is the time when the **Lord** will rescue Zion and take
34.11 The **Lord** will make it a barren waste again, as it was
34.16 Search in the **Lord's** book of living creatures and read
34.16 The **Lord** has commanded it to be so;
34.17 It is the **Lord** who will divide the land among them and
35. 2 Everyone will see the **Lord's** splendour, see his greatness and power.
35. 9 Those whom the **Lord** has rescued will travel home by that road.
36. 7 you tell me that you are relying on **the Lord your God?**
36. 7 It was the **Lord's** shrines and altars that Hezekiah destroyed
36.10 I have attacked your country and destroyed it without the **Lord's** help?
36.10 The **Lord** himself told me to attack it and destroy it."
36.15 And don't let him persuade you to rely on the **Lord.**
36.15 Don't think that the **Lord** will save you and that he will
36.18 Hezekiah fool you into thinking that the **Lord** will rescue you.
36.20 Then what makes you think the **Lord** can save Jerusalem?"
37. 1 grief, put on sackcloth, and went to the Temple of the **Lord.**
37. 4 May **the Lord your God** hear these insults and punish those
37. 6 "The **Lord** tells you not to let the Assyrians frighten you
37. 7 The **Lord** will cause the emperor to hear a rumour that will
37. 7 his own country, and the **Lord** will have him killed there."
37.14 presence of the **Lord,** [15]and prayed, [16]"Almighty Lord,
37.17 Now, **Lord,** hear us and look at what is happening to us.
37.18 We all know, **Lord,** that the emperors of Assyria have
37.20 Now, **Lord** our God, rescue us from the Assyrians, so that
37.22 to the king's prayer [22]the **Lord** had said, "The city of
37.32 who will survive, because the **Lord Almighty** is determined to
37.33 "This is what the **Lord** has said about the Assyrian emperor:
37.34 I, the **Lord,** have spoken.
37.36 An angel of the **Lord** went to the Assyrian camp and
38. 1 and said to him, "The **Lord** tells you that you are to
38. 3 "Remember, **Lord,** that I have served you faithfully and loyally,
38. 4 Then the **Lord** commanded Isaiah [5]to go back to Hezekiah
38. 5 say to him, "I, the **Lord,** the God of your ancestor David,
38. 7 Isaiah replied, "The **Lord** will give you a sign to prove
38. 8 built by King Ahaz, the **Lord** will make the shadow go back
38.11 I would never again see the **Lord** Or any living person.
38.14 **Lord,** rescue me from all this trouble.
38.15 The **Lord** has done this.
38.16 **Lord,** I will live for you, for you alone;
38.20 **Lord,** you have healed me.
39. 5 then told the king, "The **Lord Almighty** says that [6]a time
39. 8 "The message you have given me from the **Lord** is good."
40. 3 cries out, "Prepare in the wilderness a road for the **Lord!**
40. 5 Then the glory of the **Lord** will be revealed, and all
40. 5 The **Lord** himself has promised this."
40. 7 fade, when the **Lord** sends the wind blowing over them.
40.10 The Sovereign **Lord** is coming to rule with power,
40.13 Can anyone tell the **Lord** what to do?
40.15 To the **Lord** the nations are nothing, no more than a drop
40.24 When the **Lord** sends a wind, they dry up and blow away
40.27 do you complain that the **Lord** doesn't know your troubles or
40.28 The **Lord** is the everlasting God;
40.31 those who trust in the **Lord** for help will find their
41. 4 I, the **Lord,** was there at the beginning, and I, the Lord,
41.13 I am **the Lord your God;**
41.14 The **Lord** says,
41.17 with thirst, then I, the **Lord,** will answer their prayer;
41.20 will see this and know that I, the **Lord,** have done it.
41.21 The **Lord,** the king of Israel, has this to say:
41.27 I, the **Lord,** was the first to tell Zion the news;
42. 1 The **Lord** says,
42. 5 And now the **Lord God** says to his servant, [6]"I, the Lord,
42. 8 "I alone am **the Lord your God.**
42.10 Sing a new song to the **Lord;**
42.12 live in distant lands give praise and glory to the **Lord!**
42.13 The **Lord** goes out to fight like a warrior;
42.18 The **Lord** says,
42.21 The **Lord** is a God who is eager to save, so he
42.24 It was the **Lord** himself, against whom we sinned!
43. 1 Israel, the **Lord** who created you says,
43. 3 For I am **the Lord your God,** the holy God of Israel,
43.11 "I alone am the **Lord,** the only one who can save you.
43.14 Israel's holy God, the **Lord** who saves you, says,
43.15 I am the **Lord,** your holy God.
43.16 Long ago the **Lord** made a road through the sea, a path
43.18 But the **Lord** says,
43.22 The **Lord** says,
44. 1 The **Lord** says,
44. 2 I am the **Lord** who created you;
44. 5 "One by one, people will say, 'I am the **Lord's.'**
44. 5 mark the name of the **Lord** on his arm and call himself
44. 6 The **Lord,** who rules and protects Israel,
44. 6 the **Lord Almighty,** has this to say:

Is 44.21 The **Lord** says,
44.23 The **Lord** has shown his greatness by saving his people Israel.
44.24 "I am **the Lord, your saviour;**
44.24 I am the **Lord,** the Creator of all things.
45. 1 The **Lord** has chosen Cyrus to be king!
45. 1 the **Lord** will open the gates of cities for him.
45. 1 To Cyrus the **Lord** says, [2]"I myself will prepare your way,
45. 3 know that I am the **Lord,** and that the God of Israel
45. 5 "I am the **Lord;**
45. 6 know that I am the **Lord** and that there is no other
45. 7 I, the **Lord,** do all these things.
45. 8 I, the **Lord,** will make this happen."
45.11 The **Lord,** the holy God of Israel, the one who shapes the
45.13 The **Lord Almighty** has spoken.
45.14 The **Lord** says to Israel,
45.17 Israel is saved by the **Lord,** and her victory lasts for ever;
45.18 The **Lord** created the heavens— he is the one who is
45.18 who says, "I am the **Lord,** and there is no other god.
45.19 I am the **Lord,** and I speak the truth;
45.20 The **Lord** says,
45.21 Was it not I, the **Lord,** the God who saves his people?
45.25 I, the **Lord,** will rescue all the descendants of Jacob,
46. 5 says the **Lord.**
47. 1 The **Lord** says,
47. 4 of Israel sets us free— his name is the **Lord Almighty.**
47. 5 The **Lord** says to Babylon,
48. 1 by the name of the **Lord** and claim to worship the God
48. 2 depend on Israel's God, whose name is the **Lord Almighty.**
48. 3 The **Lord** says to Israel,
48.12 The **Lord** says,
48.16 (Now the Sovereign **Lord** has given me his power and sent me.)
48.17 The holy God of Israel, the **Lord** who saves you, says:
48.17 "I am **the Lord your God,** the one who wants to teach
48.20 "The **Lord** has saved his servant Israel!"
48.21 When the **Lord** led his people through a hot, dry desert,
48.22 "There is no safety for sinners," says the **Lord.**
49. 1 Before I was born, the **Lord** chose me and appointed me to
49. 4 Yet I can trust the **Lord** to defend my cause;
49. 5 Before I was born, the **Lord** appointed me;
49. 5 The **Lord** gives me honour;
49. 6 The **Lord** said to me,
49. 7 This will happen because the **Lord** has chosen his servant;
49. 8 The **Lord** says to his people,
49.13 The **Lord** will comfort his people;
49.14 "The **Lord** has abandoned us!
49.15 So the **Lord** answers,
49.22 The Sovereign **Lord** says to his people:
49.23 Then you will know that I am the **Lord;**
49.25 The **Lord** replies,
49.26 know that I am the **Lord,** the one who saves you and
50. 1 The **Lord** says,
50. 4 The Sovereign **Lord** has taught me what to say, so that I
50. 5 The **Lord** has given me understanding, and I have not
50. 7 cannot hurt me because the Sovereign **Lord** gives me help.
50. 9 The Sovereign **Lord** himself defends me— who, then, can
50.10 of you that honour the **Lord** and obey the words of his
50.10 be dark indeed, but trust in the **Lord,** rely on your God.
50.11 The **Lord** himself will make this happen;
51. 1 The **Lord** says,
51. 9 Wake up, **Lord,** and help us!
51.12 The **Lord** says,
51.13 Have you forgotten the **Lord** who made you, who stretched
51.15 "I am **the Lord your God;**
51.15 My name is the **Lord Almighty!**
51.17 cup of punishment that the **Lord** in his anger gave you to
51.22 you were drunk, [22]**the Lord your God** defends you and says,
52. 3 The Sovereign **Lord** says to his people, "When you became slaves,
52. 8 see with their own eyes the return of the **Lord** to Zion!
52. 9 The **Lord** will rescue his city and comfort his people.
52.10 The **Lord** will use his holy power;
52.12 **The Lord your God** will lead you and protect you on every
52.13 The **Lord** says,
53. 1 Who could have seen the **Lord's** hand in this?
53. 2 was the will of the **Lord** that his servant should grow like
53. 6 But the **Lord** made the punishment fall on him, the punishment
53.10 The **Lord** says,
54. 5 like a husband to you— the **Lord Almighty** is his name.
54. 6 But the **Lord** calls you back to him and says:
54. 8 So says the **Lord** who saves you.
54.10 So says the **Lord** who loves you.
54.11 The **Lord** says,
54.17 The **Lord** has spoken.
55. 1 The **Lord** says,
55. 5 I, **the Lord your God,** the holy God of Israel, will make
55. 6 Turn to the **Lord** and pray to him, now that he is
55. 7 Let them turn to **the Lord, our God;**
55. 8 "My thoughts," says the **Lord,** "are not like yours, and
55.13 last for ever, a reminder of what I, the **Lord,** have done."
56. 1 The **Lord** says to his people, "Do what is just and right,
56. 3 who has joined the **Lord's** people should not say,
56. 3 "The **Lord** will not let me worship
56. 4 The **Lord** says to such a man, "If you honour me by
56. 6 And the **Lord** says to those foreigners who become part of
56. 8 The Sovereign **Lord,** who has brought his people Israel home from exile,
56. 9 The **Lord** has told the foreign nations to come like wild
57.11 The **Lord** says, "Who are these gods that make you afraid,
57.14 The **Lord** says, "Let my people return to me.
57.21 There is no safety for sinners," says the **Lord.**
58. 1 The **Lord** says, "Shout as loud as you can!
58. 3 The people ask, "Why should we fast if the **Lord** never notices?

Is 58. 3 The **Lord** says to them, "The truth is that at the same
58.13 The **Lord** says, "If you treat the Sabbath as sacred and
58.14 I, the **Lord,** have spoken."
59. 1 Don't think that the **Lord** is too weak to save you or
59.12 **"Lord,** our crimes against you are many.
59.15 The **Lord** has seen this, and he is displeased that there is
59.20 The **Lord** says to his people, "I will come to Jerusalem
60. 1 The glory of the **Lord** is shining on you!
60. 2 by darkness, But on you the light of the **Lord** will shine;
60. 6 People will tell the good news of what the **Lord** has done!
60. 7 as sacrifices And offered on the altar to please the **Lord.**
60. 7 The **Lord** will make his Temple more glorious than ever.
60. 9 honour the name of the **Lord,** The holy God of Israel, Who
60.10 The **Lord** says to Jerusalem, "Foreigners will rebuild your walls,
60.14 you 'The City of the **Lord,'** 'Zion, the City of Israel's Holy
60.16 will know that I, the **Lord,** have saved you, That the mighty
60.19 I, the **Lord,** will be your eternal light;
60.20 I, the **Lord,** will be your eternal light, More lasting than
60.22 I am the **Lord!"**
61. 1 The Sovereign **Lord** has filled me with his spirit.
61. 2 time has come When the **Lord** will save his people And defeat
61. 3 They will be like trees That the **Lord** himself has planted.
61. 6 known as the priests of the **Lord,** The servants of our God.
61. 8 The **Lord** says,
61.10 Jerusalem rejoices because of what the **Lord** has done.
61.11 sprout and grow, The Sovereign **Lord** will save his people,
62. 2 called by a new name, A name given by the **Lord** himself.
62. 3 You will be like a beautiful crown for the **Lord.**
62. 4 called "Happily Married," Because the **Lord** is pleased with
62. 6 They must remind the **Lord** of his promises And never let him
62. 8 The **Lord** has made a solemn promise, And by his power he
62. 9 harvested the corn Will eat the bread and praise the **Lord.**
62.11 can know [11]That the **Lord** is announcing to all the earth:
62.11 people of Jerusalem That the **Lord** is coming to save you,
62.12 "God's Holy People," "The People the **Lord** Has Saved."
63. 1 "It is the **Lord,** powerful to save, coming to announce his victory."
63. 3 The **Lord** answers, "I have trampled the nations like grapes,
63. 7 I will tell of the **Lord's** unfailing love;
63. 8 The **Lord** said, "They are my people;
63. 9 It was not an angel, but the **Lord** himself who saved them.
63.10 So the **Lord** became their enemy and fought against them.
63.11 Moses, the servant of the **Lord,** and they asked,
63.11 "Where now is the **Lord,** who saved the leaders
63.11 Where is the **Lord,** who gave his spirit to Moses?
63.12 Where is the **Lord,** who by his power did great
63.12 Led by the **Lord,** they were as sure-footed as wild horses,
63.14 led into a fertile valley, so the **Lord** gave his people rest.
63.15 **Lord,** look upon us from heaven, where you live in your
63.16 not acknowledge us, but you, **Lord,** are our father, the one
64. 8 But you are our father, **Lord.**
64.12 **Lord,** are you unmoved by all this?
65. 1 The **Lord** said, "I was ready to answer my people's prayers,
65. 8 The **Lord** says, "No one destroys good grapes;
65.15 I, the Sovereign **Lord,** will put you to death.
65.17 The **Lord** says, "I am making a new earth and new heavens.
66. 1 The **Lord** says, "Heaven is my throne, and the earth is my
66. 5 Listen to what the **Lord** says, you that fear him and obey
66. 5 you and say, 'Let the **Lord** show his greatness and save you,
66. 6 the Temple, is the sound of the **Lord** punishing his enemies!
66. 9 The **Lord** has spoken.
66.12 The **Lord** says, "I will bring you lasting prosperity;
66.14 will know that I, the **Lord,** help those who obey me, and
66.15 The **Lord** will come with fire.
66.17 The **Lord** says, "The end is near for those who purify
66.23 will come to worship me here in Jerusalem," says the **Lord.**

Jer 1. 2 The **Lord** spoke to Jeremiah in the thirteenth year that
1. 3 After that, the **Lord** spoke to him many times, until the
1. 4 The **Lord** said to me, [5]"I chose you before I gave you
1. 6 I answered, "Sovereign **Lord,** I don't know how to speak;
1. 7 But the **Lord** said to me, "Do not say that you are
1. 8 I, the **Lord,** have spoken!"
1. 9 Then the **Lord** stretched out his hand, touched my lips, and
1.11 The **Lord** asked me, "Jeremiah, what do you see?"
1.12 "You are right," the **Lord** said, "and I am watching to
1.13 Then the **Lord** spoke to me again.
1.18 I, the **Lord,** have spoken."
2. 1 The **Lord** told me [2]to proclaim this message to everyone in Jerusalem.
2. 3 I, the **Lord,** have spoken."
2. 4 Listen to the **Lord's** message, you descendants of Jacob,
2. 5 The **Lord** says:
2. 8 The priests did not ask, 'Where is the **Lord?'**
2. 9 "And so I, the **Lord,** will state my case against my people
2.17 You deserted me, **the Lord your God,** while I was leading
2.19 is to abandon me, **the Lord your God,** and no longer to
2.19 I, the Sovereign **Lord Almighty,** have spoken."
2.20 The Sovereign **Lord** says,
2.26 The **Lord** says, "Just as a thief is disgraced when caught,
2.35 surely the **Lord** is no longer angry with me.'
2.35 But I, the **Lord,** will punish you because you deny that you
2.37 I, the **Lord,** have rejected those you trust;
3. 1 The **Lord** says, "If a man divorces his wife, and she
3. 6 When Josiah was king, the **Lord** said to me, "Have you seen
3.10 I, the **Lord,** have spoken."
3.11 Then the **Lord** told me that, even though Israel had
3.13 and that you have rebelled against **the Lord, your God.**
3.13 I, the **Lord,** have spoken.
3.17 called 'The Throne of the **Lord,'** and all nations will gather
3.19 The **Lord** says,
3.20 I, the **Lord,** have spoken."
3.21 they have lived sinful lives and have forgotten **the Lord their God.**

Jer 3.22 Return, all of you who have turned away from the **Lord;**
3.22 "Yes, we are coming to the **Lord,** because he is our God.
3.23 Help for Israel comes only from **the Lord our God.**
3.25 We and our ancestors have always sinned against **the Lord our God;**
4. 1 The **Lord** says, "People of Israel, if you want to turn,
4. 3 The **Lord** says to the people of Judah and Jerusalem,
4. 4 covenant with me, your **Lord,** and dedicate yourselves to me,
4. 6 The **Lord** is bringing disaster and great destruction from the north.
4. 8 fierce anger of the **Lord** has not turned away from Judah.
4. 9 The **Lord** said, "On that day kings and officials will lose
4.10 Then I said, "Sovereign **Lord,** you have completely
4.12 wind that comes at the **Lord's** command will be much stronger
4.12 It is the **Lord** himself who is pronouncing judgement on his people.
4.17 a field, because her people have rebelled against the **Lord.**
4.17 The **Lord** has spoken.
4.22 The **Lord** says, "My people are stupid;
4.26 its cities were in ruins because of the **Lord's** fierce anger.
4.27 (The **Lord** has said that the whole earth will become a wilderness,
4.28 The **Lord** has spoken and will not change his mind.
5. 1 If you can, the **Lord** will forgive Jerusalem.
5. 2 you claim to worship the **Lord,** you do not mean what you
5. 3 Surely the **Lord** looks for faithfulness.
5. 4 what their God requires, what the **Lord** wants them to do.
5. 5 what their God requires, what the **Lord** wants them to do."
5. 5 have rejected the **Lord's** authority and refuse to obey him.
5. 7 The **Lord** asked, "Why should I forgive the sins of my people?
5.11 I, the **Lord,** have spoken."
5.12 The **Lord's** people have denied him and have said, "He
5.13 but windbags and that they have no message from the **Lord.**
5.13 The **Lord God** Almighty said to me, "Jeremiah, because these
5.15 People of Israel, the **Lord** is bringing a nation from
5.18 The **Lord** says, "Yet even in those days I will not
5.20 The **Lord** says, "Tell the descendants of Jacob, tell the
5.22 I am the **Lord;**
5.29 "But I, the **Lord,** will punish them for these things;
6. 6 The **Lord Almighty** has ordered these kings to cut down
6. 9 The **Lord Almighty** said to me, "Israel will be stripped
6.11 them burns in me too, **Lord,** and I can't hold it in
6.11 Then the **Lord** said to me, "Pour out my anger on the
6.15 I, the **Lord,** have spoken."
6.16 The **Lord** said to his people, "Stand at the crossroads and look.
6.17 Then the **Lord** appointed watchmen to listen for the trumpet's warning.
6.18 So the **Lord** said, "Listen, you nations, and learn what
6.22 The **Lord** says, "People are coming from a country in the north;
6.26 The **Lord** says to his people, "Put on sackcloth and roll
6.30 worthless dross, because I, the **Lord,** have rejected them."
7. 1 The **Lord** sent me to the gate of the Temple where the
7. 1 and announce what the **Lord Almighty,** the God of Israel,
7. 4 This is the **Lord's** Temple, this is the Lord's Temple,
7. 4 this is the **Lord's** Temple!'
7.15 I, the **Lord,** have spoken."
7.16 The **Lord** said, "Jeremiah, do not pray for these people.
7.20 And so I, the Sovereign **Lord,** will pour out my fierce
7.21 But what I, the **Lord,** say is that you might as well
7.28 does not obey me, **the Lord their God,** or learn from their
7.29 the hill-tops, because I, the **Lord,** am angry, and have
8. 3 I, the **Lord Almighty,** have spoken."
8. 4 The **Lord** told me to say to his people, "When someone
8.12 I, the **Lord,** have spoken.
8.14 **The Lord our God** has condemned us to die;
8.17 the **Lord** says, "I am sending snakes among you, poisonous
8.19 hear my people crying out, "Is the **Lord** no longer in Zion?
8.19 The **Lord,** their king, replies, "Why have you made me angry
9. 3 The **Lord** says,
9. 5 The **Lord** says that his people reject him.
9. 7 Because of this the **Lord Almighty** says, "I will refine my
9. 9 I, the **Lord,** have spoken."
9.11 The **Lord** says, "I will make Jerusalem a pile of ruins,
9.12 I asked, **"Lord,** why is the land devastated and dry as a
9.13 The **Lord** answered, "This has happened because my people
9.15 listen to what I, the **Lord Almighty,** the God of Israel, will
9.17 The **Lord Almighty** said,
9.20 "Listen to the **Lord,** you women, and pay attention to his words.
9.22 This is what the **Lord** has told me to say."
9.23 The **Lord** says,
9.24 I, the **Lord,** have spoken."
9.25 The **Lord** says, "The time is coming when I will
10. 1 of Israel, listen to the message that the **Lord** has for you.
10. 6 **Lord,** there is no one like you;
10.10 But you, **Lord,** are the true God, you are the living God
10.12 The **Lord** made the earth by his power;
10.15 they will be destroyed when the **Lord** comes to deal with them.
10.16 The **Lord Almighty** is his name.
10.18 The **Lord** is going to throw you out of this land;
10.18 The **Lord** has spoken.
10.21 they do not ask the **Lord** for guidance.
10.23 **Lord,** I know that no one is the master of his own
10.24 Correct your people, **Lord;**
11. 1 The **Lord** said to me, [2]"Listen to the terms of the covenant.
11. 3 of Jerusalem [3]that I, the **Lord God** of Israel, have placed a
11. 5 I said, "Yes, **Lord."**
11. 6 Then the **Lord** said to me, "Go to the cities of Judah
11. 9 Then the **Lord** said to me, "The people of Judah and of
11.11 So now, I, the **Lord,** warn them that I am going to
11.15 The **Lord** says, "The people I love are doing evil things.
11.17 "I, the **Lord Almighty,** planted Israel and Judah;
11.18 The **Lord** informed me of the plots that my enemies were
11.20 Then I prayed, "Almighty **Lord,** you are a just judge;
11.21 would kill me if I kept on proclaiming the **Lord's** message.

Jer 11.22 So the **Lord Almighty** said, "I will punish them!
12. 1 **Lord,** if I argued my case with you, you would prove to
12. 3 But, **Lord,** you know me;
12. 5 The **Lord** said,
12. 7 The **Lord** says,
12.14 The **Lord** says, "I have something to say about Israel's
12.16 and will swear, 'As the **Lord** lives'—as they once taught my
12.17 I, the **Lord,** have spoken."
13. 1 The **Lord** told me to go and buy myself some linen shorts
13. 3 Then the **Lord** spoke to me again, and said, [4]"Go to the
13. 6 Some time later the **Lord** told me to go back to the
13. 8 Then the **Lord** spoke to me again.
13.12 The **Lord God** said to me, "Jeremiah, tell the people of
13.13 tell them that I, the **Lord,** am going to fill the people
13.15 People of Israel, the **Lord** has spoken!
13.16 Honour **the Lord, your God,** before he brings darkness,
13.17 tears will flow because the **Lord's** people have been taken
13.18 The **Lord** said to me, "Tell the king and his mother to
13.24 The **Lord** will scatter you like straw that is blown away
13.26 The **Lord** himself will strip off your clothes and expose
14. 1 The **Lord** said to me concerning the drought,
14. 7 our sins accuse us, help us, **Lord,** as you have promised.
14. 9 Surely, **Lord,** you are with us!
14.10 The **Lord** says about these people, "They love to run
14.11 The **Lord** said to me, "Do not ask me to help these
14.13 Then I said, "Sovereign **Lord,** you know that the
14.14 But the **Lord** replied, "The prophets are telling lies in my name;
14.15 I, the **Lord,** tell you what I am going to do to
14.17 The **Lord** commanded me to tell the people about my sorrow
14.19 **Lord,** have you completely rejected Judah?
14.20 We have sinned against you, **Lord;**
14.22 our hope in you, O **Lord** our God, because you are the
15. 1 Then the **Lord** said to me, "Even if Moses and Samuel were
15. 3 I, the **Lord,** have decided that four terrible things will
15. 5 The **Lord** says,
15. 9 I, the **Lord,** have spoken."
15.11 **Lord,** may all their curses come true if I have not
15.13 The **Lord** said to me, "I will send enemies to carry away
15.15 Then I said, **"Lord,** you understand.
15.16 I belong to you, **Lord God** Almighty, and so your words filled
15.19 To this the **Lord** replied, "If you return, I will take
15.21 I, the **Lord,** have spoken."
16. 1 Again the **Lord** spoke to me and said, [2]"Do not marry or
16. 9 Listen to what I, the **Lord Almighty,** the God of Israel,
16.10 and what sin they have committed against **the Lord their God.**
16.11 Then tell them that the **Lord** has said, 'Your ancestors
16.14 The **Lord** says, "The time is coming when people will no
16.15 I, the **Lord,** have spoken."
16.16 The **Lord** says, "I am sending for many fishermen to come
16.19 **Lord,** you are the one who protects me and gives me strength;
16.21 "So then," says the **Lord,** "once and for all I will
16.21 they will know that I am the **Lord."**
17. 1 The **Lord** says, "People of Judah, your sin is written with
17. 5 The **Lord** says,
17.10 I, the **Lord,** search the minds and test the hearts of men.
17.13 **Lord,** you are Israel's hope;
17.13 have abandoned you, the **Lord,** the spring of fresh water.
17.14 **Lord,** heal me and I will be completely well;
17.15 to me, "Where are those threats the **Lord** made against us?
17.16 But, **Lord,** I never urged you to bring disaster on them;
17.16 **Lord,** you know this;
17.18 Bring disgrace on those who persecute me, but spare me, **Lord.**
17.19 The **Lord** said to me, "Jeremiah, go and announce my
18. 1 The **Lord** said to me, [2]"Go down to the potter's house,
18. 5 Then the **Lord** said to me, [6]"Haven't I the right to do
18.13 The **Lord** says,
18.19 So I prayed, **"Lord,** hear what I am saying and listen to
18.21 But now, **Lord,** let their children starve to death;
18.23 But, **Lord,** you know all their plots to kill me.
19. 1 The **Lord** told me to go and buy a clay jar.
19. 3 The **Lord** told me to say, "Kings of Judah and people of
19. 3 listen to what I, the **Lord Almighty,** the God of Israel, have
19.10 Then the **Lord** told me to break the jar in front of
19.11 to tell them that the **Lord Almighty** had said, "I will break
19.14 I left Topheth, where the **Lord** had sent me to proclaim his
19.15 the people [15]that the **Lord Almighty,** the God of Israel,
20. 3 chains, I said to him, "The **Lord** did not name you Pashhur.
20. 4 The **Lord** himself has said, 'I am going to make you a
20. 7 **Lord,** you have deceived me, and I was deceived.
20. 8 **Lord,** I am ridiculed and scorned all the time because I
20. 9 say, "I will forget the **Lord** and no longer speak in his
20.11 But you, **Lord,** are on my side, strong and mighty, and
20.12 But, Almighty **Lord,** you test men justly;
20.13 Sing to the **Lord!**
20.13 Praise the **Lord!**
20.16 May he be like those cities that the **Lord** destroyed without mercy.
21. 2 "Please speak to the **Lord** for us, because King
21. 2 Maybe the **Lord** will perform one of his miracles for us and
21. 3 Then the **Lord** spoke to me, and I told the men who
21. 4 to tell Zedekiah that the **Lord,** the God of Israel, had
21. 7 I, the **Lord,** have spoken."
21. 8 Then the **Lord** told me to say to the people, "Listen!
21. 8 I, the **Lord,** am giving you a choice between the way that
21.10 I, the **Lord,** have spoken."
21.11 The **Lord** told me to give this message to the royal
21.11 "Listen to what I, the **Lord,** am saying.
21.14 I, the **Lord,** have spoken."
22. 1 The **Lord** told me to go to the palace of the king
22. 1 the people of Jerusalem to listen to what the **Lord** had said:
22. 3 "I, the **Lord,** command you to do what is just and right.
22. 5 I, the **Lord,** have spoken.

Jer 22. 8 one another why I, the **Lord,** have done such a thing to
22.11 The **Lord** says concerning Josiah's son Joahaz, who
22.16 That is what it means to know the **Lord.**
22.17 The **Lord** has spoken.
22.18 So then, the **Lord** says about Josiah's son Jehoiakim, king of Judah,
22.21 The **Lord** spoke to you when you were prosperous, but you
22.21 you never would obey the **Lord.**
22.24 The **Lord** said to King Jehoiachin, son of King Jehoiakim of Judah,
22.29 Listen to what the **Lord** has said:
22.30 I, the **Lord,** have spoken."
23. 1 How terrible will be the **Lord's** judgement on those rulers
23. 2 This is what the **Lord,** the God of Israel, says about the
23. 4 I, the **Lord,** have spoken."
23. 5 The **Lord** says, "The time is coming when I will choose as
23. 6 He will be called 'The **Lord** Our Salvation.'
23. 7 time is coming," says the **Lord,** "when people will no
23. 9 Because of the **Lord,** because of his holy words, I am like
23.10 The land is full of people unfaithful to the **Lord;**
23.10 Because of the **Lord's** curse the land mourns and the pastures
23.11 The **Lord** says,
23.12 I, the **Lord,** have spoken.
23.15 this is what I, the **Lord Almighty,** say about the prophets of
23.16 The **Lord Almighty** said to the people of Jerusalem, "Do
23.18 "None of these prophets has ever known the **Lord's** secret thoughts.
23.21 The **Lord** said, "I did not send these prophets, but even
23.32 Listen to what I, the **Lord,** say!
23.32 I, the **Lord,** have spoken."
23.33 The **Lord** said to me, "Jeremiah, when one of my people
23.33 prophet or a priest asks you, 'What is the **Lord's** message?'
23.33 are a burden to the **Lord,** and he is going to get
23.34 even uses the words 'the **Lord's** burden,' I will punish him
23.35 friends and his relatives, 'What answer has the **Lord** given?
23.35 What has the **Lord** said?'
23.36 use the words 'the **Lord's** burden,' because if anyone does,
23.36 the words of their God, the living God, the **Lord Almighty.**
23.37 Jeremiah, ask the prophets, 'What answer did the **Lord** give you?
23.37 What did the **Lord** say?'
23.38 and use the words 'the **Lord's** burden,' then tell them that
24. 1 The **Lord** showed me two baskets of figs placed in front of
24. 3 Then the **Lord** said to me, "Jeremiah, what do you see?"
24. 4 So the **Lord** said to me, [5] "I, the Lord, the God of
24. 5 said to me, [5] "I, the **Lord,** the God of Israel, consider
24. 7 will give them the desire to know that I am the **Lord.**
24. 8 moved to Egypt—I, the **Lord,** will treat them all like these
25. 1 a message from the **Lord** concerning all the people of Judah.
25. 3 until this very day, the **Lord** has spoken to me, and I
25. 4 pay attention, even though the **Lord** has continued to send
25. 5 in the land that the **Lord** gave you and your ancestors as
25. 6 and not to make the **Lord** angry by worshipping the idols you
25. 6 If you had obeyed the **Lord,** then he would not have punished
25. 7 But the **Lord** himself says that you refused to listen to him.
25. 8 not listen to him, the **Lord Almighty** says, [9] 'I am going to
25. 9 I, the **Lord,** have spoken.
25.15 The **Lord,** the God of Israel, said to me, "Here is a
25.17 took the cup from the **Lord's** hand, gave it to all the
25.17 the nations to whom the **Lord** had sent me, and made them
25.27 Then the **Lord** said to me, "Tell the people
25.27 that I, the **Lord Almighty,** the God of Israel,
25.28 then tell them that the **Lord Almighty** has said that they
25.29 I, the **Lord Almighty,** have spoken.
25.30 'The **Lord** will roar from heaven and thunder from the heights
25.31 The **Lord** has a case against the nations.
25.31 The **Lord** has spoken.' "
25.32 The **Lord Almighty** says that disaster is coming on one
25.33 bodies of those whom the **Lord** has killed will lie scattered
25.36 out in distress because the **Lord** in his anger has destroyed
25.38 The **Lord** has abandoned his people like a lion that
25.38 horrors of war and the **Lord's** fierce anger have turned the
26. 2 became king of Judah, [2] the **Lord** said to me, "Stand in the
26. 4 The **Lord** told me to say to the people, "I, the Lord,
26. 8 had finished all that the **Lord** had commanded me to speak,
26. 9 have you said in the **Lord's** name that this Temple will
26.12 Then I said, "The **Lord** sent me to proclaim everything
26.13 the things you are doing, and must obey **the Lord your God.**
26.15 man, because it is the **Lord** who sent me to give you
26.16 man spoke to us in the name of **the Lord our God;**
26.18 Moresheth told all the people that the **Lord Almighty** had said,
26.19 Hezekiah honoured the **Lord** and tried to win his favour.
26.19 And the **Lord** changed his mind about the disaster that he
26.20 in the name of the **Lord** against this city and nation just
27. 1 became king of Judah, the **Lord** told me [2] to make myself a
27. 3 Then the **Lord** told me to send a message to the kings
27. 4 The **Lord Almighty,** the God of Israel, told me to command
27. 4 to command them to tell their kings that the **Lord** had said:
27.11 I, the **Lord,** have spoken."
27.13 That is what the **Lord** has said will happen to any nation
27.15 The **Lord** himself has said that he did not send them and
27.16 I told the priests and the people that the **Lord** had said:
27.18 let them ask me, the **Lord Almighty,** not to allow the
27.21 "Listen to what I, the **Lord Almighty,** the God of Israel,
27.22 I, the **Lord,** have spoken."
28. 2 he told me [2] that the **Lord Almighty,** the God of Israel, had
28. 4 I, the **Lord,** have spoken."
28. 6 I hope the **Lord** will do this!
28. 9 as a prophet whom the **Lord** has truly sent when that
28.11 "The **Lord** has said that this is how he will break the
28.12 Some time after this the **Lord** told me [13] to go and say
28.13 "The **Lord** has said that you may be able to break a
28.14 The **Lord Almighty,** the God of Israel, has said that he
28.14 The **Lord** has said that he will make even the wild animals

Jer 28.15 The **Lord** did not send you, and you are making these people
28.16 And so the **Lord** himself says that he is going to get
28.16 you have told the people to rebel against the **Lord."**
29. 4 "The **Lord Almighty,** the God of Israel, says to all those
29. 8 I, the **Lord,** the God of Israel, warn you not to let
29. 9 I, the **Lord Almighty,** have spoken.'
29.10 "The **Lord** says, 'When Babylonia's seventy years are over,
29.14 I, the **Lord,** have spoken.'
29.15 "You say that the **Lord** has given you prophets in Babylonia.
29.16 Listen to what the **Lord** says about the king who rules
29.17 The **Lord Almighty** says, 'I am bringing war, starvation,
29.20 sent into exile in Babylonia, listen to what I, the **Lord,**
29.21 "The **Lord Almighty,** the God of Israel, has spoken about
29.22 will say, 'May the **Lord** treat you like Zedekiah and Ahab,
29.23 committed adultery and have told lies in the **Lord's** name.
29.23 This was against the **Lord's** will;
29.23 The **Lord** has spoken."
29.24 The **Lord Almighty,** the God of Israel, gave me a
29.26 "The **Lord** made you a priest in place of Jehoiada, and
29.30 to me, [30] and then the **Lord** told me [31-32] to send to
29.31 "I, the **Lord,** will punish Shemaiah and all his descendants.
29.31 I, the **Lord,** have spoken."
30. 1 The **Lord,** the God of Israel, [2] said to me:
30. 3 I, the **Lord,** have spoken."
30. 4 The **Lord** says to the people of Israel and Judah:
30. 8 The **Lord Almighty** says:
30. 9 they will serve me, **the Lord their God,** and a descendant of
30.11 I, the **Lord,** have spoken."
30.12 The **Lord** says to his people,
30.17 I, the **Lord,** have spoken."
30.18 The **Lord** says,
30.21 I, the **Lord,** have spoken."
30.23 The **Lord's** anger is a storm, a furious wind that
31. 1 The **Lord** says, "The time is coming when I will be the
31. 6 of Ephraim, 'Let's go up to Zion, to **the Lord our God.' "**
31. 7 The **Lord** says,
31. 7 Sing your song of praise, 'The **Lord** has saved his people;
31.10 The **Lord** says,
31.14 I, the **Lord,** have spoken."
31.15 The **Lord** says,
31.17 I, the **Lord,** have spoken.
31.18 Israel say in grief, **'Lord,** we were like an untamed animal,
31.18 we are ready to return to you, **the Lord our God.**
31.23 The **Lord Almighty,** the God of Israel, says, "When I
31.23 'May the **Lord** bless the sacred hill of Jerusalem, the holy
31.27 "I, the **Lord,** say that the time is coming when I will
31.31 The **Lord** says, "The time is coming when I will make a
31.34 to know the **Lord,** because all will know me,
31.34 I, the **Lord,** have spoken."
31.35 The **Lord** provides the sun for light by day, the moon and
31.35 his name is the **Lord Almighty.**
31.37 The **Lord** has spoken.
31.38 time is coming," says the **Lord,** "when all Jerusalem will
32. 1 The **Lord** spoke to me in the tenth year that Zedekiah was
32. 3 me of announcing that the **Lord** had said, "I am going to
32. 5 I, the **Lord,** have spoken."
32. 6 The **Lord** told me [7] that Hanamel, my uncle Shallum's son,
32. 8 Then, just as the **Lord** had said, Hanamel came to me there
32. 8 So I knew that the **Lord** had really spoken to me.
32.14 I said to Baruch, [14] "The **Lord Almighty,** the God of Israel,
32.15 The **Lord Almighty,** the God of Israel, has said that houses,
32.17 to Baruch, I prayed, [17] "Sovereign **Lord,** you made the
32.18 you are the **Lord Almighty.**
32.25 Yet, Sovereign **Lord,** you are the one who ordered me to
32.26 Then the **Lord** said to me, [27] "I am the Lord, the God
32.27 said to me, [27] "I am the **Lord,** the God of all mankind.
32.36 The **Lord,** the God of Israel, said to me, "Jeremiah, the
32.44 I, the **Lord,** have spoken."
33. 1 in the courtyard, the **Lord's** message came to me again.
33. 2 The **Lord,** who made the earth, who formed it and set it
33. 2 He whose name is the **Lord** said, [3] "Call to me, and I
33. 4 I, the **Lord,** the God of Israel, say that the houses of
33.10 The **Lord** said, "People are saying that this place is
33.11 'Give thanks to the **Lord Almighty,** because he is good and
33.11 I, the **Lord,** have spoken."
33.12 The **Lord Almighty** said, "In this land that is like a
33.13 I, the **Lord,** have spoken."
33.14 The **Lord** said, "The time is coming when I will fulfil
33.16 The city will be called 'The **Lord** Our Salvation.'
33.17 I, the **Lord,** promise that there will always be a
33.19 The **Lord** said to me, [20] "I have made a covenant with
33.23 The **Lord** said to me, [24] "Have you noticed how people
33.25 But I, the **Lord,** have a covenant with day and night, and
34. 1 The **Lord** spoke to me when King Nebuchadnezzar of Babylonia
34. 2 The **Lord,** the God of Israel, told me to go and say
34. 2 Zedekiah of Judah, "I, the **Lord,** will hand this city over
34. 5 I, the **Lord,** have spoken."
34.12 Then the **Lord,** [13] the God of Israel, told me to say to
34.17 So now, I, the **Lord,** say that you have disobeyed me:
34.22 I, the **Lord,** have spoken."
35. 1 was king of Judah, the **Lord** said to me, [2] "Go to the
35.12 Then the **Lord Almighty,** the God of Israel, told me
35.12 Judah and Jerusalem, "I, the **Lord,** ask you why you refuse
35.17 So now, I, the **Lord Almighty,** the God of Israel, will
35.18 Rechabite clan that the **Lord Almighty,** the God of Israel,
35.19 So I, the **Lord Almighty,** the God of Israel, promise that
36. 1 was king of Judah, the **Lord** said to me, [2] "Get a scroll
36. 4 and dictated to him everything that the **Lord** had said to me.
36. 6 will hear everything that the **Lord** has said to me and that
36. 7 they will pray to the **Lord** and turn from their evil ways,
36. 7 because the **Lord** has threatened this people

Jer 36. 8 So Baruch read the **Lord's** words in the Temple exactly as I
36. 9 king of Judah, the people fasted to gain the **Lord's** favour.
36.11 heard Baruch read from the scroll what the **Lord** had said.
36.26 But the **Lord** had hidden us.
36.27 had dictated to Baruch, the **Lord** told me [28] to take another
36.29 The **Lord** told me to say to the king, "You have burnt
36.30 So now, I, the **Lord,** say to you, King Jehoiakim, that no
37. 2 the people obeyed the message which the **Lord** had given me.
37. 3 me to pray to **the Lord our God** on behalf of our
37. 6 Then the **Lord,** the God of Israel, told me [7] to say to
37. 9 I, the **Lord,** warn you not to deceive yourselves into
37.17 asked me privately, "Is there any message from the **Lord?"**
38. 2 telling the people that [2] the **Lord** had said, "Whoever stays
38. 3 also telling them that the **Lord** had said, "I am going to
38.17 I told Zedekiah that the **Lord Almighty,** the God of Israel,
38.20 I beg you to obey the **Lord's** message;
38.21 But the **Lord** has shown me in a vision what will happen
39.15 in the palace courtyard, the **Lord** told me [16] to tell
39.16 Ebedmelech the Sudanese that the **Lord Almighty,** the God of Israel,
39.17 But I, the **Lord,** will protect you, and you will not be
39.18 I, the **Lord,** have spoken."
40. 1 The **Lord** spoke to me after Nebuzaradan, the commanding officer,
40. 2 me aside and said, **"The Lord your God** threatened this land
40. 3 your people sinned against the **Lord** and disobeyed him.
42. 2 Pray to **the Lord our God** for us.
42. 3 Pray that **the Lord our God** will show us the way we
42. 4 I will pray to **the Lord our God,** just as you have
42. 5 said to me, "May the **Lord** be a true and faithful witness
42. 5 all the commands that **the Lord our God** gives you for us.
42. 6 not, we will obey **the Lord our God,** to whom we are
42. 7 Ten days later the **Lord** spoke to me;
42. 9 I said to them, "The **Lord,** the God of Israel, to whom
42.12 I, the **Lord,** have spoken.'
42.13 Judah must not disobey **the Lord your God** and refuse to live
42.13 you say this, then the **Lord Almighty,** the God of Israel,
42.18 "The **Lord,** the God of Israel, says, 'Just as my anger
42.19 Then I continued, "The **Lord** has told you people who are
42.20 me to pray to **the Lord our God** for you, and you
42.21 are disobeying everything that **the Lord our God** sent me to
43. 1 the people everything that **the Lord their God** had sent me to
43. 2 **The Lord our God** did not send you to tell us not
43. 4 the people would obey the **Lord's** command to remain in the
43. 7 They disobeyed the **Lord's** command and went into Egypt as
43. 8 There the **Lord** said to me, [9] "Get some large stones and
43.10 tell them that I, the **Lord Almighty,** the God of Israel, am
44. 1 The **Lord** spoke to me concerning all the Israelites living in Egypt,
44. 2 The **Lord Almighty,** the God of Israel, said, "You
44. 7 "And so I, the **Lord Almighty,** the God of Israel, now ask
44.11 "So then, I, the **Lord Almighty,** the God of Israel, will
44.16 to what you have told us in the name of the **Lord.**
44.21 do you think that the **Lord** did not know about them or
44.22 as a curse because the **Lord** could no longer endure your
44.23 sinned against the **Lord** by not obeying all his commands."
44.24 the women, what the **Lord Almighty,** the God of Israel,
44.26 the vow that I, the **Lord,** have made in my mighty name
44.26 a vow by saying, 'I swear by the living Sovereign **Lord!'**
44.29 I, the **Lord,** will give you proof that I will punish you
45. 2 I told him [2] that the **Lord,** the God of Israel, had said,
45. 3 The **Lord** has added sorrow to my troubles.
45. 4 "But I, the **Lord,** am tearing down what I have built and
45. 5 I, the **Lord,** have spoken."
46. 1 The **Lord** spoke to me about the nations, [2] beginning with Egypt.
46. 5 asks the **Lord.**
46.10 This is the day of the Sovereign **Lord Almighty:**
46.13 Nebuchadnezzar of Babylonia came to attack Egypt, the **Lord** spoke to me.
46.15 The **Lord** has struck him down!'
46.18 I, the **Lord Almighty,** am king.
46.24 I, the **Lord,** have spoken."
46.25 The **Lord Almighty,** the God of Israel, says, "I am going
46.26 I, the **Lord,** have spoken."
46.28 I, the **Lord,** have spoken."
47. 1 Egypt attacked Gaza, the **Lord** spoke to me about Philistia.
47. 4 I, the **Lord,** will destroy the Philistines, all who came from
47. 6 You cry out, 'Sword of the **Lord!**
48. 1 This is what the **Lord Almighty** said about Moab:
48. 8 I, the **Lord,** have spoken.
48.10 man who does not do the **Lord's** work with all his heart!
48.11 The **Lord** said, "Moab has always lived secure and has
48.15 I am the king, the **Lord Almighty,** and I have spoken.
48.25 I, the **Lord,** have spoken."
48.26 The **Lord** said, "Make Moab drunk, because it has rebelled against me.
48.30 I, the **Lord,** know of their arrogance.
48.35 I, the **Lord,** have spoken.
48.39 I, the **Lord,** have spoken."
48.40 The **Lord** has promised that a nation will swoop down on
48.43 The **Lord** has spoken.
48.44 in the traps, because the **Lord** has set the time for Moab's
48.47 But in days to come the **Lord** will make Moab prosperous again.
48.47 of this is what the **Lord** has said will happen to Moab.
49. 1 This is what the **Lord** said about Ammon:
49. 6 I, the **Lord,** have spoken."
49. 7 This is what the **Lord Almighty** said about Edom:
49.13 I, the **Lord,** have spoken."
49.14 I said, "Edom, I have received a message from the **Lord.**
49.15 The **Lord** is going to make you weak, and no one will
49.16 as high up as an eagle, the **Lord** will bring you down.
49.16 The **Lord** has spoken."

Jer 49.17 The **Lord** said, "The destruction that will come on Edom
49.18 I, the **Lord,** have spoken.
49.23 This is what the **Lord** said about Damascus:
49.27 I, the **Lord Almighty,** have spoken."
49.28 This is what the **Lord** said about the tribe of Kedar and
49.30 "People of Hazor, I, the **Lord,** warn you to run far away
49.33 I, the **Lord,** have spoken."
49.34 became king of Judah, the **Lord Almighty** spoke to me about
49.39 I, the **Lord,** have spoken."
50. 1 is the message that the **Lord** gave me about the city of
50. 4 The **Lord** says, "When that time comes, the people of both
50. 7 say, 'They sinned against the **Lord,** and so what we have done
50. 7 Their ancestors trusted in the **Lord,** and they themselves
50.10 I, the **Lord,** have spoken."
50.11 The **Lord** says, "People of Babylonia, you plundered my nation.
50.14 at Babylon, because it has sinned against me, the **Lord.**
50.17 The **Lord** says, "The people of Israel are like sheep,
50.18 Because of this, I, the **Lord Almighty,** the God of Israel,
50.20 I, the **Lord,** have spoken."
50.21 The **Lord** says, "Attack the people of Merathaim and of Pekod.
50.21 I, the **Lord,** have spoken.
50.25 out, because I, the Sovereign **Lord Almighty,** have work to do
50.28 and they tell how **the Lord our God** took revenge for what
50.30 I, the **Lord,** have spoken.
50.31 pride, so I, the Sovereign **Lord Almighty,** am against you!
50.33 The **Lord Almighty** says, "The people of Israel and of
50.34 will rescue them is strong—his name is the **Lord Almighty.**
50.35 The **Lord** says,
50.40 I, the **Lord,** have spoken.
50.44 green pasture land, I, the **Lord,** will come and make the
51. 1 The **Lord** says, "I am bringing a destructive wind against
51. 5 I, the **Lord God** Almighty, have not abandoned Israel and Judah,
51.10 The **Lord** says, "My people shout, 'The Lord has shown
51.10 says, "My people shout, 'The **Lord** has shown that we are in
51.10 the people in Jerusalem what **the Lord our God** has done.' "
51.11 The **Lord** has stirred up the kings of Media, because he
51.12 The **Lord** has done what he said he would do to the
51.14 The **Lord Almighty** has sworn by his own life that he will
51.15 The **Lord** made the earth by his power;
51.18 they will be destroyed when the **Lord** comes to deal with them.
51.19 The **Lord Almighty** is his name.
51.20 The **Lord** says,
51.24 The **Lord** says, "You will see me repay Babylonia and its
51.25 that destroys the whole world, but I, the **Lord,** am your
51.26 I, the **Lord,** have spoken.
51.29 trembles and shakes because the **Lord** is carrying out his
51.33 I, the **Lord Almighty,** the God of Israel, have spoken."
51.36 And so the **Lord** said to the people of Jerusalem, "I
51.40 I, the **Lord,** have spoken."
51.41 The **Lord** says about Babylon:
51.49 I, the **Lord,** have spoken."
51.50 The **Lord** says to his people in Babylonia:
51.50 home, think about me, your **Lord,** and remember Jerusalem.
51.53 I, the **Lord,** have spoken."
51.54 The **Lord** says,
51.57 I, the king, have spoken, I am the **Lord Almighty.**
51.58 I, the **Lord Almighty,** have spoken."
51.62 Then pray, **'Lord,** you have said that you would destroy this place,
51.64 the destruction that the **Lord** is going to bring on it.' "
52. 2 King Zedekiah sinned against the **Lord,** just as King Jehoiakim had done.
52. 3 The **Lord** became so angry with the people of Jerusalem and

Lam 1. 5 The **Lord** has made her suffer for all her many sins;
1. 9 Her enemies have won, and she cries to the **Lord** for mercy.
1.10 Temple itself, Where the **Lord** had forbidden Gentiles to go.
1.11 "Look at me, **Lord,"** the city cries;
1.12 like mine, Pain that the **Lord** brought on me in the time
1.14 The **Lord** gave me to my foes, and I was helpless against
1.15 "The **Lord** jeered at all my strongest soldiers;
1.17 The **Lord** has called enemies against me from every side;
1.18 "But the **Lord** is just, for I have disobeyed him.
1.20 "Look, O **Lord,** at my agony, at the anguish of my soul!
2. 1 The **Lord** in his anger has covered Zion with darkness.
2. 2 The **Lord** destroyed without mercy every village in Judah
2. 5 Like an enemy, the **Lord** has destroyed Israel;
2. 7 The **Lord** rejected his altar and deserted his holy Temple;
2. 8 The **Lord** was determined that the walls of Zion should fall;
2. 9 taught, and the prophets have no visions from the **Lord.**
2.17 The **Lord** has finally done what he threatened to do:
2.18 O Jerusalem, let your very walls cry out to the **Lord!**
2.19 night get up again and again to cry out to the **Lord;**
2.20 Look, O **Lord!**
3.18 my hope in the **Lord** is gone.
3.22 The **Lord's** unfailing love and mercy still continue, [23] Fresh as the morning,
3.24 The **Lord** is all I have, and so I put my hope
3.25 The **Lord** is good to everyone who trusts in him, [26] So
3.31 The **Lord** is merciful and will not reject us for ever.
3.34 The **Lord** knows when our spirits are crushed in prison;
3.37 The will of the **Lord** alone is always carried out.
3.40 Let us examine our ways and turn back to the **Lord.**
3.42 sinned and rebelled, and you, O **Lord,** have not forgiven us.
3.50 a ceaseless stream [50] Until the **Lord** looks down from heaven
3.55 bottom of the pit, O **Lord,** I cried out to you, [56] And
3.58 "You came to my rescue, **Lord,** and saved my life.
3.61 "You have heard them insult me, O **Lord;**
3.64 "Punish them for what they have done, O **Lord;**
4.11 The **Lord** turned loose the full force of his fury;
4.16 The **Lord** had no more concern for them;
4.20 our life, the king the **Lord** had chosen, the one we had
4.22 the **Lord** will not keep us in exile any longer.

Lam 4.22 But Edom, the **Lord** will punish you;
5. 1 Remember, O **Lord**, what has happened to us.
5.19 But you, O **Lord**, are king for ever, and will rule to
5.21 Bring us back to you, **Lord!**
Ezek 1. 3 River Chebar, I heard the **Lord** speak to me and I felt
1.28 This was the dazzling light that shows the presence of the **Lord.**
2. 4 to tell them what I, the Sovereign **Lord**, am saying to them.
3.11 them what I, the Sovereign **Lord**, am saying to them, whether
3.12 that said, "Praise the glory of the **Lord** in heaven above!"
3.14 The **power of the Lord** came on me with great force, and
3.16 After the seven days had passed, the **Lord** spoke to me.
3.22 the powerful presence of the **Lord** and heard him say to me,
3.23 saw the glory of the **Lord**, just as I had seen it
3.24 The **Lord** said to me, "Go home and shut yourself up in
3.27 speech, you will tell them what I, the Sovereign **Lord**, am
4.13 The **Lord** said, "This represents the way the Israelites
4.14 But I replied, "No, Sovereign **Lord!**
5. 1 The **Lord** said, "Mortal man, take a sharp sword and use it
5. 5 The Sovereign **Lord** said, "Look at Jerusalem.
5. 7 Now listen, Jerusalem, to what I, the Sovereign **Lord**, am
5. 8 And so I, the Sovereign **Lord**, am telling you that I am
5.11 the word of the Sovereign **Lord**—because you defiled my Temple
5.13 be convinced that I, the **Lord**, have spoken to you because I
5.17 I, the **Lord**, have spoken."
6. 1 The **Lord** spoke to me.
6. 3 hear the word of the **Lord**—
6. 3 hear what I, the Sovereign **Lord**, am telling the mountains,
6. 7 and those who survive will acknowledge that I am the **Lord.**
6.10 know that I am the **Lord** and that my warnings were not
6.11 The Sovereign **Lord** said, "Wring your hands!
6.13 Then everyone will know that I am the **Lord.**
6.14 Then everyone will know that I am the **Lord."**
7. 1 The **Lord** spoke to me.
7. 2 is what I, the Sovereign **Lord**, am saying to the land of
7. 4 have done, so that you will know that I am the **Lord."**
7. 5 This is what the Sovereign **Lord** is saying, "One disaster
7. 9 know that I am the **Lord**, and that I am the one
7.19 nor gold can save them when the **Lord** pours out his fury.
7.20 That is why the **Lord** has made their wealth repulsive to them.
7.21 foreigners rob them," says the **Lord**, "and law-breakers
7.27 This will show you that I am the **Lord."**
8. 1 Suddenly the **power of the Sovereign Lord** came on me.
8.12 'The **Lord** doesn't see us!
8.13 Then the **Lord** said to me, "You are going to see them
8.17 The **Lord** said to me, "Mortal man, do you see that?
9. 3 The **Lord** called to the man dressed in linen, [4]"Go through
9. 8 the ground and shouted, "Sovereign **Lord**, are you so angry
9. 9 They say that I, the **Lord**, have abandoned their country and
9.11 reported to the **Lord**, "I have carried out your orders."
10. 4 The dazzling light of the **Lord's** presence rose up from the
10. 6 When the **Lord** commanded the man wearing linen clothes to
10.18 the dazzling light of the **Lord's** presence left the entrance
11. 5 The spirit of the **Lord** took control of me, and the Lord
11. 7 "So this is what I, the Sovereign **Lord**, am saying to you.
11.10 Then everyone will know that I am the **Lord.**
11.12 know that I am the **Lord** and that while you were keeping
11.13 downwards on the ground and shouted, "No, Sovereign **Lord!**
11.14 The **Lord** spoke to me.
11.15 They say, 'The exiles are too far away to worship the **Lord.**
11.17 "So tell them what I, the Sovereign **Lord**, am saying.
11.21 The Sovereign **Lord** has spoken.
11.25 and I told the exiles everything that the **Lord** had shown me.
12. 1 The **Lord** spoke to me.
12. 7 I did what the **Lord** told me to do.
12. 8 The next morning the **Lord** spoke to me.
12.10 tell them what I, the Sovereign **Lord**, am saying to them.
12.15 and in foreign countries, they will know that I am the **Lord.**
12.16 have been and will acknowledge that I am the **Lord."**
12.17 The **Lord** spoke to me.
12.19 the message of the Sovereign **Lord** to the people of Jerusalem
12.20 Then they will know that I am the **Lord."**
12.21 The **Lord** spoke to me.
12.23 them what I, the Sovereign **Lord**, have to say about that.
12.25 I, the **Lord**, will speak to them, and what I say will
12.25 I have spoken," says the Sovereign **Lord.**
12.26 The **Lord** said to me, [27]"Mortal man, the Israelites
12.28 So tell them that I, the Sovereign **Lord**, am saying:
12.28 I, the Sovereign **Lord**, have spoken!"
13. 1 The **Lord** spoke to me.
13. 2 Tell them to listen to the word of the **Lord."**
13. 3 This is what the Sovereign **Lord** says:
13. 5 cannot be defended when war comes on the day of the **Lord.**
13. 8 So the Sovereign **Lord** says to them, "Your words are false,
13. 9 Then you will know that I am the Sovereign **Lord.**
13.13 Now this is what the Sovereign **Lord** says:
13.14 Then everyone will know that I am the **Lord.**
13.16 The Sovereign **Lord** has spoken.
13.17 The **Lord** said, "Now, mortal man, look at the women
13.18 and tell them what the Sovereign **Lord** is saying to them:
13.20 Now this is what the Sovereign **Lord** says:
13.21 Then you will know that I am the **Lord.**
13.23 your power, so that you will know that I am the **Lord."**
14. 1 of the Israelites came to consult me about the **Lord's** will.
14. 2 Then the **Lord** spoke to me.
14. 4 and tell them what I, the Sovereign **Lord**, am saying to them:
14. 6 "Now then, tell the Israelites what I, the Sovereign **Lord**,
14. 7 to consult a prophet, I, the **Lord**, will give him his answer!
14. 8 my people, so that you will know that I am the **Lord.**
14. 9 false answer, it is because I, the **Lord**, have deceived him.
14.11 The Sovereign **Lord** has spoken.
14.12 The **Lord** spoke to me.

Ezek 14.14 The Sovereign **Lord** has spoken.
14.16 surely as I, the Sovereign **Lord**, am the living God—they
14.18 surely as I, the Sovereign **Lord**, am the living God—they
14.20 surely as I, the Sovereign **Lord**, am the living God—they
14.21 This is what the Sovereign **Lord** is saying:
14.23 The Sovereign **Lord** has spoken.
15. 1 The **Lord** spoke to me.
15. 6 this is what the Sovereign **Lord** is saying, "Just as a vine
15. 7 When I punish them, you will know that I am the **Lord.**
15. 8 The Sovereign **Lord** has spoken.
16. 1 The **Lord** spoke to me again.
16. 3 Tell Jerusalem what the Sovereign **Lord** is saying to her:
16. 8 This is what the Sovereign **Lord** says.
16.14 This is what the Sovereign **Lord** says.
16.19 This is what the Sovereign **Lord** says.
16.23 The Sovereign **Lord** said, "You are doomed!
16.30 This is what the Sovereign **Lord** is saying:
16.35 Hear what the **Lord** is saying.
16.36 This is what the Sovereign **Lord** says:
16.43 The Sovereign **Lord** has spoken.
16.44 The **Lord** said, "People will use this proverb about you,
16.48 the living God," the Sovereign **Lord** says, "your sister
16.53 The **Lord** said to Jerusalem, "I will make them
16.58 The **Lord** has spoken.
16.59 The Sovereign **Lord** says, "I will treat you as you deserve,
16.62 covenant with you, and you will know that I am the **Lord.**
16.63 The Sovereign **Lord** has spoken.
17. 1 The **Lord** spoke to me.
17. 3 let them know what I, the Sovereign **Lord**, am saying to them:
17. 9 "So I, the Sovereign **Lord**, ask:
17.11 The **Lord** said to me, [12]"Ask these rebels if they know
17.16 living God," says the Sovereign **Lord**, "this king will die
17.19 The Sovereign **Lord** says, "As surely as I am the living God,
17.21 Then you will know that I, the **Lord**, have spoken."
17.22 This is what the Sovereign **Lord** says:
17.24 the trees in the land will know that I am the **Lord.**
17.24 I, the **Lord**, have spoken.
18. 1 The **Lord** spoke to me [2]and said, "What is this proverb
18. 3 living God," says the Sovereign **Lord**, "you will not repeat
18. 9 He is righteous, and he will live," says the Sovereign **Lord.**
18.23 asks the Sovereign **Lord.**
18.25 "But you say, 'What the **Lord** does isn't right.'
18.29 And you Israelites say, 'What the **Lord** does isn't right.'
18.30 "Now I, the Sovereign **Lord**, am telling you Israelites
18.32 I do not want anyone to die," says the Sovereign **Lord.**
19. 1 The **Lord** told me to sing this song of sorrow for two
20. 1 to consult me about the **Lord's** will, and they sat down in
20. 2 Then the **Lord** spoke to me.
20. 3 these men and tell them that the Sovereign **Lord** is saying:
20. 3 I, the Sovereign **Lord**, have spoken.
20. 5 I am **the Lord your God.**
20. 7 the false gods of Egypt, because I am **the Lord their God.**
20.12 between us, to remind them that I, the **Lord**, make them holy.
20.19 I am **the Lord your God.**
20.20 made, and will remind you that I am **the Lord your God.**
20.26 was to punish them and show them that I am the **Lord.**
20.27 Israelites what I, the Sovereign **Lord**, am saying to them.
20.30 Now tell the Israelites what I, the Sovereign **Lord**, am
20.31 surely as I, the Sovereign **Lord**, am the living God, I will
20.33 surely as I, the Sovereign **Lord**, am the living God, I warn
20.36 I condemned your fathers in the Sinai Desert," says the Sovereign **Lord.**
20.38 Then you will know that I am the **Lord."**
20.39 The Sovereign **Lord** said, "And now, all you Israelites, please yourselves!
20.42 to your ancestors, then you will know that I am the **Lord.**
20.44 know that I am the **Lord**, because I do not deal with
20.44 The Sovereign **Lord** has spoken.
20.45 The **Lord** spoke to me.
20.47 Tell the southern forest to hear what the Sovereign **Lord** is saying:
20.48 all see that I, the **Lord**, set it on fire and that
20.49 But I protested, "Sovereign **Lord**, don't make me do it!
21. 1 The **Lord** spoke to me.
21. 3 Warn the land of Israel [3]that I, the **Lord**, am saying:
21. 5 will know that I, the **Lord**, have drawn my sword and that
21. 7 The Sovereign **Lord** has spoken.
21. 8 The **Lord** said to me, [9]"Mortal man, prophesy.
21. 9 Tell the people what I, the **Lord**, am saying:
21.17 I, the **Lord**, have spoken."
21.18 The **Lord** spoke to me.
21.24 This then is what I, the Sovereign **Lord**, am saying:
21.26 I, the Sovereign **Lord**, have spoken.
21.28 Announce what I, the Sovereign **Lord**, am saying to the Ammonites,
21.32 The **Lord** has spoken.
22. 1 The **Lord** spoke to me.
22. 3 Tell the city what I, the Sovereign **Lord**, am saying:
22.12 The Sovereign **Lord** has spoken.
22.14 I, the **Lord**, have spoken, and I keep my word.
22.16 will dishonour you, but you will know that I am the **Lord."**
22.17 The **Lord** said to me, [18]"Mortal man, the Israelites
22.19 So now I, the Sovereign **Lord**, am telling them that they
22.22 will know that they are feeling the anger of the **Lord."**
22.23 The **Lord** spoke to me again.
22.28 Sovereign Lord, but I, the **Lord**, have not spoken to them.
22.31 The Sovereign **Lord** has spoken.
23. 1 The **Lord** spoke to me.
23.22 this is what I, the Sovereign **Lord**, am saying to you.
23.28 This is what the Sovereign **Lord** says:
23.32 The Sovereign **Lord** says,
23.34 I, the Sovereign **Lord**, have spoken."

Ezek 23.35 Now this is what the Sovereign **Lord** is saying:
23.36 The **Lord** said to me, "Mortal man, are you ready to
23.46 This is what the Sovereign **Lord** says:
23.49 Then you will know that I am the Sovereign **Lord."**
24. 1 of the ninth year of our exile, the **Lord** spoke to me.
24. 3 this parable that I, the Sovereign **Lord,** have for them:
24. 6 This is what the Sovereign **Lord** is saying:
24. 9 This is what the Sovereign **Lord** is saying:
24.14 I, the Sovereign **Lord,** have spoken.
24.14 The Sovereign **Lord** has spoken.
24.15 The **Lord** spoke to me.
24.20 I said to them, "The **Lord** spoke to me and told me
24.21 and to visit it, but the **Lord** is going to profane it.
24.24 The **Lord** says that when this happens,
24.24 you will know that he is the Sovereign **Lord."**
24.25 The **Lord** said, "Now, mortal man, I will take away from
24.27 to the people, and they will know that I am the **Lord."**
25. 1 The **Lord** spoke to me.
25. 3 Tell them to listen to what I, the Sovereign **Lord,** am
25. 5 keep sheep, so that you will know that I am the **Lord.**
25. 6 "This is what the Sovereign **Lord** is saying:
25. 7 Then you will know that I am the **Lord."**
25. 8 The Sovereign **Lord** said, "Because Moab has said that
25.11 will punish Moab, and they will know that I am the **Lord."**
25.12 The Sovereign **Lord** said, "The people of Edom took cruel
25.14 The Sovereign **Lord** has spoken.
25.15 The Sovereign **Lord** said, "The Philistines have taken
25.17 Then they will know that I am the **Lord."**
26. 1 of the eleventh year of our exile, the **Lord** spoke to me.
26. 3 "Now then, this is what I, the Sovereign **Lord,** am saying:
26. 5 I, the Sovereign **Lord,** have spoken.
26. 6 Then Tyre will know that I am the **Lord."**
26. 7 The Sovereign **Lord** says, "I am going to bring the
26.14 I, the Sovereign **Lord,** have spoken."
26.15 The Sovereign **Lord** has this to say to the city of Tyre:
26.19 The Sovereign **Lord** says:
26.21 The Sovereign **Lord** has spoken.
27. 1 The **Lord** said to me, [2]"Mortal man, sing a funeral song
27. 3 Tell her what the Sovereign **Lord** is saying:
28. 1 The **Lord** spoke to me.
28. 2 ruler of Tyre what I, the Sovereign **Lord,** am saying to him:
28. 6 "Now then, this is what I, the Sovereign **Lord,** am saying:
28.10 I, the Sovereign **Lord,** have given the command."
28.11 The **Lord** spoke to me again.
28.12 Tell him what I, the Sovereign **Lord,** am saying:
28.20 The **Lord** said to me, [21]"Mortal man, denounce the city of Sidon.
28.22 Tell the people there what I, the Sovereign **Lord,** say about them:
28.22 know that I am the **Lord,** when I show how holy I
28.23 Then you will know that I am the **Lord."**
28.24 The **Lord** said, "None of the surrounding nations that
28.24 And they will know that I am the Sovereign **Lord."**
28.25 The Sovereign **Lord** said, "I will bring back the people
28.26 Then they will know that I am **the Lord their God."**
29. 1 of the tenth year of our exile, the **Lord** spoke to me.
29. 3 is what the Sovereign **Lord** is telling the king of Egypt:
29. 6 all the people of Egypt will know that I am the **Lord."**
29. 6 The **Lord** says, "The Israelites relied on you Egyptians for support,
29. 8 Now then, I, the Sovereign **Lord,** am telling you that I
29. 9 Then you will know that I am the **Lord.**
29.13 The Sovereign **Lord** says, "After forty years I will
29.16 Then Israel will know that I am the Sovereign **Lord."**
29.17 the twenty-seventh year of our exile, the **Lord** spoke to me.
29.19 So now this is what I, the Sovereign **Lord,** am saying:
29.20 I, the Sovereign **Lord,** have spoken.
29.21 hear you, so that they will know that I am the **Lord."**
30. 1 The **Lord** spoke again.
30. 2 he said, "prophesy and announce what I, the Sovereign **Lord,**
30. 3 near, the day when the **Lord** will act, A day of clouds
30. 6 The **Lord** says, "From Migdol in the north to Aswan in the
30. 6 I, the Sovereign **Lord,** have spoken.
30. 8 are killed, then they will know that I am the **Lord.**
30.10 The Sovereign **Lord** says, "I will use King
30.12 I, the **Lord,** have spoken."
30.13 The Sovereign **Lord** says, "I will destroy the idols and
30.19 Egypt in this way, they will know that I am the **Lord."**
30.20 of the eleventh year of our exile, the **Lord** spoke to me.
30.22 Now then, this is what I, the Sovereign **Lord,** say:
30.25 it towards Egypt, everyone will know that I am the **Lord.**
30.26 Then they will know that I am the **Lord."**
31. 1 of the eleventh year of our exile, the **Lord** spoke to me.
31.10 "Now then, I, the Sovereign **Lord,** will tell you what is
31.15 This is what the Sovereign **Lord** says:
31.18 I have spoken," says the Sovereign **Lord.**
32. 1 of the twelfth year of our exile, the **Lord** spoke to me.
32. 8 I, the Sovereign **Lord,** have spoken.
32.11 The Sovereign **Lord** says to the king of Egypt, "You will
32.14 I, the Sovereign **Lord,** have spoken.
32.15 all who live there, they will know that I am the **Lord.**
32.16 I, the Sovereign **Lord,** have spoken."
32.17 of the twelfth year of our exile, the **Lord** spoke to me.
32.31 the king of Egypt and his army," says the Sovereign **Lord.**
32.32 The Sovereign **Lord** has spoken.
33. 1 The **Lord** spoke to me.
33.10 The **Lord** spoke to me.
33.11 surely as I, the Sovereign **Lord,** am the living God, I do
33.22 he came, I had felt the powerful presence of the **Lord.**
33.22 arrived the next morning, the **Lord** gave me back the power of
33.23 The **Lord** spoke to me.
33.25 "Tell them what I, the Sovereign **Lord,** am saying:
33.27 them that I, the Sovereign **Lord,** warn them that as surely as

Ezek 33.29 country a waste, then they will know that I am the **Lord."**
33.30 The **Lord** said, "Mortal man, your people are talking
33.30 'Let's go and hear what word has come from the **Lord** now.'
34. 1 The **Lord** spoke to me.
34. 2 them, and tell them what I, the Sovereign **Lord,** say to them:
34. 7 "Now, you shepherds, listen to what I, the **Lord,** am telling you.
34.10 I, the Sovereign **Lord,** declare that I am your enemy.
34.11 "I, the Sovereign **Lord,** tell you that I myself will
34.15 I, the Sovereign **Lord,** have spoken.
34.17 my flock, I, the Sovereign **Lord,** tell you that I will judge
34.20 "So now, I, the Sovereign **Lord,** tell you that I will
34.24 I, the **Lord,** will be their God, and a king like my
34.27 made them slaves, then they will know that I am the **Lord.**
34.30 I, the Sovereign **Lord,** have spoken.
34.31 my people, and I am your God," says the Sovereign **Lord.**
35. 1 The **Lord** spoke to me.
35. 3 Tell the people what I, the Sovereign **Lord,** am saying:
35. 4 Then you will know that I am the **Lord.**
35. 6 surely as I, the Sovereign **Lord,** am the living God—death is
35. 9 Then you will know that I am the **Lord.**
35.10 you would possess them, even though I, the **Lord,** was their
35.11 surely as I, the Sovereign **Lord,** am the living God, I will
35.12 will know that I, the **Lord,** heard you say with contempt that
35.14 The Sovereign **Lord** says, "I will make you so desolate
35.15 Then everyone will know that I am the **Lord."**
36. 1 The **Lord** said, "Mortal man, speak to the mountains of
36. 2 listen to the message which I, [2]the Sovereign **Lord,** have
36. 3 "Prophesy, then, and announce what I, the Sovereign **Lord,**
36. 4 what I, the Sovereign **Lord,** say to you mountains and hills,
36. 5 "I, the Sovereign **Lord,** have spoken out in the heat of my
36. 6 valleys what I, the Sovereign **Lord,** am saying in jealous
36. 7 I, the Sovereign **Lord,** solemnly promise that the
36.11 Then you will know that I am the **Lord.**
36.13 "I, the Sovereign **Lord,** say:
36.14 I, the Sovereign **Lord,** have spoken.
36.15 I, the Sovereign **Lord,** have spoken."
36.16 The **Lord** spoke to me.
36.20 are the people of the **Lord,** but they had to leave his
36.22 the Israelites the message that I, the Sovereign **Lord,** have
36.23 disgraced among them—then they will know that I am the **Lord.**
36.23 I, the Sovereign **Lord,** have spoken.
36.32 I, the Sovereign **Lord,** have spoken."
36.33 The Sovereign **Lord** says, "When I make you clean from
36.36 will know that I, the **Lord,** rebuild ruined cities and
36.36 I, the **Lord,** have promised that I would do this—and I
36.37 The Sovereign **Lord** says, "I will once again let the
36.38 Then they will know that I am the **Lord."**
37. 1 the powerful presence of the **Lord,** and his spirit took me
37. 3 I replied, "Sovereign **Lord,** only you can answer that!"
37. 4 Tell these dry bones to listen to the word of the **Lord.**
37. 5 Tell them that I, the Sovereign **Lord,** am saying to them:
37. 6 Then you will know that I am the **Lord."**
37. 9 the wind that the Sovereign **Lord** commands it to come from
37.12 that I, the Sovereign **Lord,** am going to open their graves.
37.13 and bring them out, they will know that I am the **Lord.**
37.14 Then they will know that I am the **Lord.**
37.14 I, the **Lord,** have spoken."
37.15 The **Lord** spoke to me again.
37.19 them that I, the Sovereign **Lord,** am going to take the stick
37.21 them that I, the Sovereign **Lord,** am going to take all my
37.28 will know that I, the **Lord,** have chosen Israel to be my
38. 1 The **Lord** spoke to me.
38. 3 him, [3]and tell him that I, the Sovereign **Lord,** am his
38.10 This is what the Sovereign **Lord** says to Gog:
38.14 So the Sovereign **Lord** sent me to tell Gog what he was
38.17 The Sovereign **Lord** has spoken.
38.18 The Sovereign **Lord** says, "On the day when Gog invades Israel,
38.21 I, the Sovereign **Lord,** have spoken.
38.23 They will know then that I am the **Lord."**
39. 1 The Sovereign **Lord** said, "Mortal man, denounce Gog, the
39. 5 I, the Sovereign **Lord,** have spoken.
39. 6 live undisturbed, and everyone will know that I am the **Lord.**
39. 7 will know that I, the **Lord,** am the Holy God of Israel."
39. 8 The Sovereign **Lord** said, "The day I spoke about is
39.10 The Sovereign **Lord** has spoken.
39.11 The **Lord** said, "When all this happens, I will give Gog
39.13 I, the Sovereign **Lord,** have spoken.
39.17 The Sovereign **Lord** said to me, "Mortal man, call all
39.20 I, the Sovereign **Lord,** have spoken."
39.21 The **Lord** said, "I will let the nations see my glory and
39.22 will know from then on that I am **the Lord their God.**
39.25 The Sovereign **Lord** said, "But now I will be merciful to
39.28 Then my people will know that I am **the Lord their God.**
39.29 I, the Sovereign **Lord,** have spoken."
40. 1 the powerful presence of the **Lord,** and he carried me away.
40.46 are permitted to go into the **Lord's** presence to serve him.
41.22 "This is the table which stands in the presence of the **Lord."**
42.13 who enter the **Lord's** presence eat the holiest offerings.
42.14 rooms the holy clothing they wore while serving the **Lord.**
43. 5 The **Lord's** spirit lifted me up and took me into the inner
43. 5 saw that the Temple was filled with the glory of the **Lord.**
43. 6 there, and I heard the **Lord** speak to me out of the
43.10 And the **Lord** continued, "Mortal man, tell the people of
43.18 The Sovereign **Lord** said to me, "Mortal man, listen to
43.19 I, the Sovereign **Lord,** command this.
43.27 I, the Sovereign **Lord,** have spoken."
44. 2 gate was closed, [2]and the **Lord** said to me, "This gate will
44. 2 use it, because I, the **Lord God** of Israel, have entered
44. 4 that the Temple of the **Lord** was filled with the dazzling
44. 5 on the ground, [5]and the **Lord** said to me, "Mortal man, pay
44. 6 Israel that I, the Sovereign **Lord,** will no longer tolerate

Ezek 44. 9 "I, the Sovereign **Lord,** declare that no uncircumcised foreigner,
44.10 The **Lord** said to me, "I am punishing those Levites who,
44.12 into sin, I, the Sovereign **Lord,** solemnly swear that they
44.15 The Sovereign **Lord** said, "Those priests belonging to
44.27 I, the Sovereign **Lord,** have spoken.
45. 1 tribe a share, one part is to be dedicated to the **Lord.**
45. 4 set aside for the priests who serve the **Lord** in his Temple.
45. 9 The Sovereign **Lord** said, "You have sinned too long, you
45. 9 I, the Sovereign **Lord,** am telling you this.
45.13 I, the Sovereign **Lord,** command it.
45.18 The Sovereign **Lord** said, "On the first day of the first
45.23 is to sacrifice to the **Lord** seven bulls and seven rams
46. 1 The Sovereign **Lord** says, "The east gateway to the inner
46. 3 to bow down and worship the **Lord** in front of the gate.
46. 4 is to bring to the **Lord,** as sacrifices to be burnt whole,
46. 9 people come to worship the **Lord** at any festival, those who
46.12 a voluntary offering to the **Lord,** either an offering to be
46.13 The **Lord** says, "Every morning a one-year-old lamb
46.13 defects is to be burnt whole as an offering to the **Lord.**
46.14 for this offering to the **Lord** are to be in force for
46.15 are to be offered to the **Lord** every morning for ever."
46.16 The Sovereign **Lord** commands:
47.13 The Sovereign **Lord** said, "These are the boundaries of
47.23 I, the Sovereign **Lord,** have spoken."
48. 9 kilometres by ten kilometres is to be dedicated to the **Lord.**
48.10 The Temple of the **Lord** is to be in the middle of
48.14 The area dedicated to the **Lord** is the best part of all
48.14 It is holy and belongs to the **Lord.**
48.29 The Sovereign **Lord** said, "That is the way the land is
Dan 1. 2 The **Lord** let him capture King Jehoiakim and seize some of
2.47 greatest of all gods, the **Lord** over kings, and the one who
5.23 You acted against the **Lord** of heaven and brought in the
9. 2 according to what the **Lord** had told the prophet Jeremiah.
9. 3 I prayed earnestly to the **Lord God,** pleading with him,
9. 4 I prayed to **the Lord my God** and confessed the sins of
9. 4 I said, **"Lord God,** you are great, and we honour you.
9. 7 You, **Lord,** always do what is right, but we have always
9. 8 have acted shamefully and sinned against you, **Lord.**
9.10 not listen to you, O **Lord** our God, when you told us
9.13 But even now, O **Lord** our God, we have not tried to
9.14 You, O **Lord** our God, were prepared to punish us, and you
9.15 "O **Lord** our God, you showed your power by bringing
9.19 **Lord,** hear us.
9.19 **Lord,** forgive us.
9.19 **Lord,** listen to us, and act!
9.20 Israel, and pleading with **the Lord my God** to restore his
Hos 1. 1 is the message which the **Lord** gave Hosea son of Beeri during
1. 2 When the **Lord** first spoke to Israel through Hosea, he
1. 4 a son, the **Lord** said to Hosea, "Name him 'Jezreel,'
1. 6 The **Lord** said to Hosea, "Name her 'Unloved,' because I will
1. 7 I, **the Lord their God,** will save them, but I will not
1. 9 The **Lord** said to Hosea, "Name him 'Not-My-People,'
2.13 The **Lord** has spoken.
2.20 and make you mine, and you will acknowledge me as **Lord.**
3. 1 The **Lord** said to me, "Go again and show your love for
3. 5 once again turn to **the Lord their God,** and to a descendant
3. 5 Then they will fear the **Lord** and will receive his good gifts.
4. 1 The **Lord** has an accusation to bring against the people who
4. 4 The **Lord** says, "Let no one accuse the people or
4.11 The **Lord** says, "Wine, both old and new, is robbing my
4.15 or make promises there in the name of the living **Lord.**
5. 4 powerful hold on them, and they do not acknowledge the **Lord.**
5. 6 offer as sacrifices to the **Lord,** but it does them no good.
5. 7 They have been unfaithful to the **Lord;**
5.10 The **Lord** says, "I am angry because the leaders of
6. 1 The people say, "Let's return to the **Lord!**
6. 3 Let us try to know the **Lord.**
6. 4 But the **Lord** says, "Israel and Judah, what am I going to
7. 3 The **Lord** says, "People deceive the king and his officers
7. 8 The **Lord** says, "The people of Israel are like a
7.10 happened, they have not returned to me, **the Lord their God.**
8. 1 The **Lord** says, "Sound the alarm!
8.13 But I, the **Lord,** am not pleased with them, and now I
9. 3 will not remain in the **Lord's** land, but will have to go
9. 4 of wine to the **Lord,** or bring their sacrifices to him.
9. 4 of it will be taken as an offering to the **Lord's** Temple.
9. 5 festivals in honour of the **Lord,** what will they do then?
9.10 The **Lord** says, "When I first found Israel, it was like
9.13 **Lord,** I can see their children being hunted down and killed.
9.15 The **Lord** says, "All their evil-doing began in Gilgal.
10. 3 saying, "We have no king because we did not fear the **Lord.**
10. 9 The **Lord** says, "The people of Israel have not stopped
10.12 to turn to me, your **Lord,** and I will come and pour
11. 1 The **Lord** says,
11.11 I, the **Lord,** have spoken."
11.12 The **Lord** says, "The people of Israel have surrounded
12. 2 The **Lord** has an accusation to bring against the people of Judah;
12. 5 This was the **Lord God** Almighty—the Lord is the name by
12. 7 The **Lord** says, "The people of Israel are as dishonest as
12. 9 But I, **the Lord your God** who led you out of Egypt,
12.13 The **Lord** sent a prophet to rescue the people of Israel
12.14 The people of Israel have made the **Lord** bitterly angry;
12.14 The **Lord** will punish them for the disgrace they have brought
13. 4 Lord says, "I am **the Lord your God,** who led you out
14. 1 Return to **the Lord your God,** people of Israel.
14. 2 Return to the **Lord,** and let this prayer be your offering
14. 3 O **Lord,** you show mercy to those who have no one else
14. 4 The **Lord** says,
14. 9 The **Lord's** ways are right, and righteous people live by following them,
Joel 1. 1 This is the **Lord's** message to Joel son of Pethuel.
Joel 1. 9 the priests mourn because they have no offerings for the **Lord.**
1.14 into the Temple of **the Lord your God** and cry out to
1.15 The day of the **Lord** is near;
1.19 I cry out to you, **Lord,** because the pastures and trees
2. 1 The day of the **Lord** is coming soon.
2.11 The **Lord** thunders commands to his army.
2.11 How terrible is the day of the **Lord!**
2.12 "But even now," says the **Lord,** "repent sincerely and
2.13 Come back to **the Lord your God.**
2.14 Perhaps **the Lord your God** will change his mind and bless
2.17 The priests, serving the **Lord** between the altar and the
2.17 "Have pity on your people, **Lord.**
2.18 Then the **Lord** showed concern for his land;
2.21 joyful and glad because of all the **Lord** has done for you.
2.23 Zion, rejoice at what **the Lord your God** has done for you.
2.26 You will praise **the Lord your God,** who has done wonderful
2.27 you, and that I, the **Lord,** am your God and there is
2.31 blood before the great and terrible day of the **Lord** comes.
2.32 But all who ask the **Lord** for help will be saved.
2.32 As the **Lord** has said, 'Some in Jerusalem will escape;
3. 1 The **Lord** says,
3. 8 I, the **Lord,** have spoken.
3.11 Send down, O **Lord,** your army to attack them.
3.12 There I, the **Lord,** will sit to judge all the surrounding nations.
3.14 It is there that the day of the **Lord** will soon come.
3.16 The **Lord** roars from Mount Zion;
3.17 "Then, Israel, you will know that I am **the Lord your God.**
3.18 from the Temple of the **Lord,** and it will water the Valley
3.20 for ever, and I the **Lord,** will live on Mount Zion."
Amos 1. 2 "The **Lord** roars from Mount Zion;
1. 3 The **Lord** says, "The people of Damascus have sinned again and again,
1. 6 The **Lord** says, "The people of Gaza have sinned again and again,
1. 9 The **Lord** says, "The people of Tyre have sinned again and again,
1.11 The **Lord** says, "The people of Edom have sinned again and again,
1.13 The **Lord** says, "The people of Ammon have sinned again and again,
2. 1 The **Lord** says, "The people of Moab have sinned again and again,
2. 4 The **Lord** says, "The people of Judah have sinned again and again,
2. 6 The **Lord** says, "The people of Israel have sinned again and again,
2.11 I, the **Lord,** have spoken.
2.16 The **Lord** has spoken.
3. 1 to this message which the **Lord** has spoken about you, the
3. 6 Does disaster strike a city unless the **Lord** sends it?
3. 7 The Sovereign **Lord** never does anything without revealing
3. 8 When the Sovereign **Lord** speaks, who can avoid proclaiming his message?
3.10 The **Lord** says, "These people fill their mansions with
3.12 The **Lord** says, "As a shepherd recovers only two legs
3.13 descendants of Jacob," says the Sovereign **Lord Almighty.**
4. 2 As the Sovereign **Lord** is holy, he has promised, "The days
4. 4 The Sovereign **Lord** says, "People of Israel, go to the
4.11 Still you did not come back to me," says the **Lord.**
4.13 the **Lord God** Almighty!
5. 3 The Sovereign **Lord** says, "A city in Israel sends out a
5. 4 The **Lord** says to the people of Israel, "Come to me, and
5. 6 Go to the **Lord,** and you will live.
5. 8 The **Lord** made the stars, the Pleiades and Orion.
5. 8 His name is the **Lord.**
5.14 Then the **Lord God** Almighty really will be with you, as you
5.15 Perhaps the **Lord** will be merciful to the people of this
5.16 And so the Sovereign **Lord Almighty** says, "There will
5.17 The **Lord** has spoken.
5.18 will be for you who long for the day of the **Lord!**
5.20 The day of the **Lord** will bring darkness and not light;
5.21 The **Lord** says, "I hate your religious festivals;
5.27 Damascus," says the **Lord,** whose name is Almighty God.
6. 8 The Sovereign **Lord Almighty** has given this solemn warning:
6.10 We must be careful not even to mention the **Lord's** name."
6.11 When the **Lord** gives the command, houses large and small
6.14 The **Lord God** Almighty himself says, "People of Israel,
7. 1 I had a vision from the Sovereign **Lord.**
7. 2 and then I said, "Sovereign **Lord,** forgive your people!
7. 3 The **Lord** changed his mind and said, "What you saw will
7. 4 I had another vision from the Sovereign **Lord.**
7. 5 Then I said, "Stop, Sovereign **Lord!**
7. 6 The **Lord** changed his mind again and said, "This will not
7. 7 I had another vision from the **Lord.**
7.15 But the **Lord** took me from my work as a shepherd and
7.16 So now listen to what the **Lord** says.
7.17 And so, Amaziah, the **Lord** says to you, 'Your wife will
8. 1 I had another vision from the Sovereign **Lord.**
8. 1 The **Lord** asked, "Amos, what do you see?"
8. 1 The **Lord** said to me, "The end has come for my people
8. 7 The **Lord,** the God of Israel, has sworn, "I will never
8. 9 I, the Sovereign **Lord,** have spoken.
8.11 They will hunger and thirst for a message from the **Lord.**
8.11 I, the Sovereign **Lord,** have spoken.
8.12 for a message from the **Lord,** but they will not find it.
9. 1 I saw the **Lord** standing by the altar.
9. 5 The Sovereign **Lord Almighty** touches the earth, and it quakes;
9. 6 The **Lord** builds his home in the heavens, and over the
9. 6 His name is the **Lord!**
9. 7 The **Lord** says, "People of Israel, I think as much of the
9. 8 I, the Sovereign **Lord,** am watching this sinful kingdom of Israel,
9.11 The **Lord** says, "A day is coming when I will restore
9.12 once mine," says the **Lord,** who will cause this to happen.
9.13 days are coming," says the **Lord,** "when corn will grow
9.15 **The Lord your God** has spoken.
Obad 1 Obadiah—what the Sovereign **Lord** said about the nation of Edom.
2 The **Lord** says to Edom, "I will make you weak;

Obad 15 The **Lord** has sent his messenger to the nations, and we have
15 "The day is near when I, the **Lord,** will judge all nations.
18 I, the **Lord,** have spoken.
21 And the **Lord** himself will be King."

Jon 1. 1 One day, the **Lord** spoke to Jonah son of Amittai.
1. 3 the opposite direction in order to get away from the **Lord.**
1. 3 to sail to Spain, where he would be away from the **Lord.**
1. 4 But the **Lord** sent a strong wind on the sea, and the
1. 9 "I worship the **Lord,** the God of heaven, who made land and
1.10 on to tell them that he was running away from the **Lord.**
1.14 they cried out to the **Lord,** "O Lord, we pray, don't punish
1.14 You, O **Lord,** are responsible for all this;
1.16 sailors so afraid of the **Lord** that they offered a sacrifice
1.17 At the **Lord's** command a large fish swallowed Jonah, and
2. 1 From deep inside the fish Jonah prayed to **the Lord his God:**
2. 2 "In my distress, O **Lord,** I called to you, and you
2. 6 But you, O **Lord** my God, brought me back from the depths
2. 7 life slipping away, then, O **Lord,** I prayed to you, and in
2. 9 Salvation comes from the **Lord!"**
2.10 Then the **Lord** ordered the fish to spew Jonah up on the
3. 1 Once again the **Lord** spoke to Jonah.
3. 3 So Jonah obeyed the **Lord** and went to Nineveh, a city so
4. 2 So he prayed, **"Lord,** didn't I say before I left home that
4. 3 Now, **Lord,** let me die.
4. 4 The **Lord** answered, "What right have you to be angry?"
4. 6 Then the **Lord God** made a plant grow up over Jonah to
4.10 The **Lord** said to him, "This plant grew up in one night

Mic 1. 1 were kings of Judah, the **Lord** gave this message to Micah,
1. 1 The **Lord** revealed to Micah all these things about Samaria and Jerusalem.
1. 2 The Sovereign **Lord** will testify against you.
1. 3 The **Lord** is coming from his holy place;
1. 6 So the **Lord** says, "I will make Samaria a pile of ruins
1.12 because the **Lord** has brought disaster close to Jerusalem.
1.15 People of Mareshah, the **Lord** will hand you over to an enemy,
2. 3 And so the **Lord** says, "I am planning to bring disaster on
2. 4 The **Lord** has taken our land away And given it to those
2. 5 be given back to the **Lord's** people, there will be no share
2. 7 Has the **Lord** lost his patience?
2. 8 The **Lord** replies, "You attack my people like enemies.
2.13 Their king, the **Lord** himself, will lead them out.
3. 4 will cry out to the **Lord,** but he will not answer you.
3. 5 To these prophets the **Lord** says, [6] "Prophets, your day is almost over;
3. 8 But as for me, the **Lord** fills me with his spirit and
3.11 for money—and they all claim that the **Lord** is with them.
3.11 "The **Lord** is with us."
4. 2 up the hill of the **Lord,** to the Temple of Israel's God.
4. 2 For the **Lord's** teaching comes from Jerusalem;
4. 4 The **Lord Almighty** has promised this.
4. 5 will worship and obey **the Lord our God** for ever and ever.
4. 6 time is coming," says the **Lord,** "when I will gather
4.10 Babylon, but there the **Lord** will save you from your enemies.
4.12 But these nations do not know what is in the **Lord's** mind.
4.13 The **Lord** says, "People of Jerusalem, go and punish your enemies!
4.13 you will present to me, the **Lord** of the whole world."
5. 2 The **Lord** says, "Bethlehem Ephrathah, you are one of the
5. 3 So the **Lord** will abandon his people to their enemies until
5. 4 from the Lord and with the majesty of the **Lord God** himself.
5. 7 refreshing dew sent by the **Lord** for many nations, like
5.10 The **Lord** says, "At that time I will take away your
6. 1 Listen to the **Lord's** case against Israel.
6. 1 Arise, O **Lord,** and present your case;
6. 2 foundations of the earth, listen to the **Lord's** case!
6. 2 The **Lord** has a case against his people.
6. 3 The **Lord** says, "My people, what have I done to you?
6. 6 shall I bring to the **Lord,** the God of heaven, when I
6. 7 Will the **Lord** be pleased if I bring him thousands of sheep
6. 8 No, the **Lord** has told us what is good.
6. 9 It is wise to fear the **Lord.**
7. 7 But I will watch for the **Lord;**
7. 8 We are in darkness now, but the **Lord** will give us light.
7. 9 We have sinned against the **Lord,** so now we must endure his
7.10 who taunted us by asking, "Where is **the Lord your God?"**
7.14 Be a shepherd to your people, **Lord,** the people you have chosen.
7.15 Work miracles for us, **Lord,** as you did in the days when
7.17 They will turn in fear to **the Lord our God.**
7.18 There is no other god like you, O **Lord;**

Nah 1. 2 The **Lord God** tolerates no rivals;
1. 3 The **Lord** does not easily become angry, but he is powerful
1. 3 Where the **Lord** walks, storms arise;
1. 5 Mountains quake in the presence of the **Lord;**
1. 5 The earth shakes when the **Lord** appears;
1. 7 The **Lord** is good;
1. 9 What are you plotting against the **Lord?**
1.11 a man full of wicked schemes, who plotted against the **Lord.**
1.12 This is what the **Lord** says to his people Israel:
1.14 This is what the **Lord** has decreed about the Assyrians:
2. 2 (The **Lord** is about to restore the glory of Israel, as it
2.13 says the **Lord Almighty.**
3. 5 The **Lord Almighty** says,

Hab 1. 1 This is the message that the **Lord** revealed to the prophet Habakkuk.
1. 2 O **Lord,** how long must I call for help before you listen,
1. 5 Then the **Lord** said to his people, "Keep watching the
1.12 **Lord,** from the very beginning you are God.
1.12 **Lord,** my God and protector, you have chosen the Babylonians
2. 1 wait to see what the **Lord** will tell me to say and
2. 2 The **Lord** gave me this answer:
2.13 The **Lord Almighty** has done this.
2.14 of the knowledge of the **Lord's** glory as the seas are full

Hab 2.16 The **Lord** will make you drink your own cup of punishment, and
2.20 The **Lord** is in his holy Temple;
3. 2 O **Lord,** I have heard of what you have done, and I
3. 8 Was it the rivers that made you angry, **Lord?**
3.18 be joyful and glad, because the **Lord God** is my saviour.
3.19 The Sovereign **Lord** gives me strength.

Zeph 1. 1 is the message that the **Lord** gave to Zephaniah during the
1. 2 The **Lord** said, "I am going to destroy everything on earth,
1. 3 I, the **Lord,** have spoken.
1. 7 The day is near when the **Lord** will sit in judgement;
1. 7 The **Lord** is preparing to sacrifice his people and has
1. 8 slaughter," says the **Lord,** "I will punish the officials,
1.10 "On that day," says the **Lord,** "you will hear the
1.12 who say to themselves, 'The **Lord** never does anything, one
1.14 The great day of the **Lord** is near—very near and coming
1.17 The **Lord** says, "I will bring such disasters on mankind
1.18 On the day when the **Lord** shows his fury, not even all
2. 2 the burning anger of the **Lord** comes upon you, before the day
2. 3 Turn to the **Lord,** all you humble people of the land, who
2. 3 Do what is right, and humble yourselves before the **Lord.**
2. 3 escape punishment on the day when the **Lord** shows his anger.
2. 5 The **Lord** has passed sentence on you.
2. 7 **The Lord their God** will be with them and make them prosper
2. 8 The **Lord Almighty** says, "I have heard the people of Moab
2. 9 as I am the living **Lord,** the God of Israel, I swear
2.10 arrogance and for insulting the people of the **Lord Almighty.**
2.11 The **Lord** will terrify them.
2.12 The **Lord** will also put the people of Sudan to death.
2.13 The **Lord** will use his power to destroy Assyria.
3. 2 It has not listened to the **Lord** or accepted his discipline.
3. 2 not put its trust in the **Lord** or asked for his help.
3. 5 But the **Lord** is still in the city;
3. 6 The **Lord** says, "I have wiped out whole nations;
3. 8 "Just wait," the **Lord** says.
3.15 The **Lord** has ended your punishment;
3.15 The **Lord,** the king of Israel, is with you;
3.17 **The Lord your God** is with you;
3.17 The **Lord** will take delight in you, and in his love he
3.18 The **Lord** says,
3.20 The **Lord** has spoken.

Hag 1. 1 the sixth month, the **Lord** spoke through the prophet Haggai.
1. 2 The **Lord Almighty** said to Haggai, "These people say that
1. 3 The **Lord** then gave this message to the people through the
1.12 in Babylonia, did what **the Lord their God** told them to do.
1.12 They were afraid and obeyed the prophet Haggai, the **Lord's** messenger.
1.13 Then Haggai gave the **Lord's** message to the people:
1.14 The **Lord** inspired everyone to work on the Temple:
1.14 on the Temple of the **Lord Almighty,** their God, [15] on the
2. 1 same year, the **Lord** spoke again through the prophet Haggai.
2. 9 The **Lord Almighty** has spoken.
2.10 that Darius was emperor, the **Lord Almighty** spoke again to
2.14 Then Haggai said, "The **Lord** says that the same thing
2.15 The **Lord** says, "Can't you see what has happened to you?
2.20 twenty-fourth of the month, the **Lord** gave Haggai a second
2.23 The **Lord Almighty** has spoken.

Zech 1. 1 was emperor of Persia, the **Lord** gave this message to the
1. 2 The **Lord Almighty** told Zechariah to say to the people,
1. 2 "I, the **Lord,** was very angry with your ancestors,
1. 6 and acknowledged that I, the **Lord Almighty,** had punished
1. 7 (the month of Shebat), the **Lord** gave me a message in a
1. 8 I saw an angel of the **Lord** riding a red horse.
1.10 The **Lord** sent them to go and inspect the earth."
1.12 Then the angel said, "Almighty **Lord,** you have been
1.13 The **Lord** answered the angel with comforting words,
1.14 angel told me to proclaim what the **Lord Almighty** had said:
1.17 "The **Lord Almighty** says that his cities will be prosperous
1.20 Then the **Lord** showed me four workmen with hammers.
2. 5 The **Lord** has promised that he himself will be a wall of
2. 6 The **Lord** said to his people, "I scattered you in all directions.
2. 8 So the **Lord Almighty** sent me with this message for the
2. 9 "The **Lord** himself will fight against you, and you will be
2. 9 everyone will know that the **Lord Almighty** sent me.
2.10 The **Lord** said, "Sing for joy, people of Jerusalem!
2.11 many nations will come to the **Lord** and become his people.
2.12 the special possession of the **Lord** in his sacred land, and
2.13 in the presence of the **Lord,** for he is coming from his
3. 1 In another vision the **Lord** showed me the High Priest
3. 1 High Priest Joshua standing before the angel of the **Lord.**
3. 2 of the **Lord** said to Satan, "May the **Lord** condemn you,
3. 2 May the **Lord,** who loves Jerusalem, condemn you.
3. 5 new clothes on him while the angel of the **Lord** stood there.
3. 7 Then the angel told Joshua that [7] the **Lord Almighty** had said:
4. 6 The angel told me to give Zerubbabel this message from the **Lord:**
4. 8 Another message came to me from the **Lord.**
4.10b the seven eyes of the **Lord,** which see all over the earth."
4.14 and anointed to serve him, the **Lord** of the whole earth."
5. 4 The **Lord Almighty** says that he will send this curse out,
6. 5 just come from the presence of the **Lord** of all the earth."
6. 8 north to Babylonia have calmed down the **Lord's** anger."
6. 9 The **Lord** gave me this message.
6.12 Tell him that the **Lord Almighty** says, 'The man who is
6.12 The Branch will flourish where he is and rebuild the **Lord's** Temple.
6.14 be a memorial in the **Lord's** Temple in honour of Heldai,
6.15 away will come and help to rebuild the Temple of the **Lord.**
6.15 you will know that the **Lord Almighty** sent me to you.
6.15 happen if you fully obey the commands of **the Lord your God.**
7. 1 month (the month of Kislev), the **Lord** gave me a message.
7. 2 to the Temple of the **Lord Almighty** to pray for the Lord's
7. 2 Almighty to pray for the **Lord's** blessing [3] and to ask the

Zech 7. 4 This is the message of the **Lord** that came to me.
7. 7 This is what the **Lord** said through the earlier prophets at
7. 8 The **Lord** gave this message to Zechariah:
8. 1 The **Lord Almighty** gave this message to Zechariah:
8. 3 and the hill of the **Lord Almighty** will be called the sacred
8.14 The **Lord Almighty** says, "When your ancestors made me angry,
8.18 The **Lord Almighty** gave this message to Zechariah:
8.20 The **Lord Almighty** says, "The time is coming when people
8.21 to worship the **Lord Almighty** and pray for his blessing.
8.22 to Jerusalem to worship the **Lord Almighty,** and to pray for
9. 1 This is the **Lord's** message:
9. 1 of Israel, but also the capital of Syria belong to the **Lord.**
9. 4 But the **Lord** will take away everything she has.
9. 6 The **Lord** says, "I will humble all these proud Philistines.
9.10 The **Lord** says,
9.11 The **Lord** says,
9.14 The **Lord** will appear above his people;
9.14 The Sovereign **Lord** will sound the trumpet;
9.15 The **Lord Almighty** will protect his people, and they will
9.16 When that day comes, the **Lord** will save his people, as a
10. 1 Ask the **Lord** for rain in the spring of the year.
10. 1 It is the **Lord** who sends rain clouds and showers, making the
10. 3 The **Lord** says, "I am angry with those foreigners who rule
10. 3 are mine, and I, the **Lord Almighty,** will take care of them.
10. 5 They will fight because the **Lord** is with them, and they will
10. 6 I am **the Lord their God;**
10. 7 this victory and be glad because of what the **Lord** has done.
10.11 sea of trouble, I, the **Lord,** will strike the waves, and the
10.12 The **Lord** has spoken.
11. 4 **The Lord my God** said to me, "Act the part of the
11. 5 They sell the meat and say, 'Praise the **Lord!**
11. 6 (The **Lord** said, "I will no longer pity anyone on earth.
11.10 the covenant which the **Lord** had made with all the nations.
11.11 and they knew that the **Lord** was speaking through what I did.
11.13 The **Lord** said to me, "Put them in the temple treasury."
11.15 Then the **Lord** said to me, "Once again act the part of
12. 1 Israel from the Lord, the **Lord** who spread out the skies,
12. 5 will say to themselves, 'The **Lord God** Almighty gives
12. 7 "I, the **Lord,** will give victory to the armies of Judah first,
12. 8 At that time the **Lord** will protect those who live in Jerusalem,
12. 8 will lead them like the angel of the **Lord,** like God himself.
13. 1 that time comes," says the **Lord Almighty,** "a fountain will
13. 3 he claimed to speak the **Lord's** word, but spoke lies instead.
13. 7 The **Lord Almighty** says, "Wake up, sword, and attack the
14. 1 The day when the **Lord** will sit in judgement is near.
14. 2 The **Lord** will bring all the nations together to make war
14. 3 Then the **Lord** will go out and fight against those nations,
14. 5 **The Lord my God** will come, bringing all the angels with him.
14. 7 When this will happen is known only to the **Lord.**
14. 9 Then the **Lord** will be king over all the earth;
14.12 The **Lord** will bring a terrible disease on all the
14.13 At that time the **Lord** will make them so confused and
14.16 each year to worship the **Lord Almighty** as king, and to
14.17 to go and worship the **Lord Almighty** as king, then rain will
14.18 the same disease that the **Lord** will send on every nation
14.20 will be inscribed with the words "Dedicated to the **Lord."**
14.21 be set apart for use in the worship of the **Lord Almighty.**
14.21 longer be any merchant in the Temple of the **Lord Almighty.**
Mal 1. 1 is the message that the **Lord** gave Malachi to tell the people
1. 2 The **Lord** says to his people, "I have always loved you."
1. 2 The **Lord** answers, "Esau and Jacob were brothers, but I
1. 4 will rebuild them," then the **Lord** will reply, "Let them
1. 4 and 'The nation with whom the **Lord** is angry for ever.' "
1. 5 and they will say, "The **Lord** is mighty even outside the
1. 6 The **Lord Almighty** says to the priests, "A son honours his father,
1.10 The **Lord Almighty** says, "I wish one of you would close
2. 1 The **Lord Almighty** says to the priests, "This command is for you:
2. 7 will, because they are the messengers of the **Lord Almighty.**
2.11 They have defiled the Temple which the **Lord** loves.
2.12 May the **Lord** remove from the community of Israel those
2.12 in the offerings our nation brings to the **Lord Almighty.**
2.13 You drown the **Lord's** altar with tears, weeping and wailing
2.16 "I hate divorce," says the **Lord God** of Israel.
2.17 You have tired the **Lord** out with your talk.
2.17 By saying, "The **Lord Almighty** thinks all evildoers are good;
3. 1 The **Lord Almighty** answers, "I will send my messenger to
3. 1 Then the **Lord** you are looking for will suddenly come to his
3. 3 and gold, so the **Lord's** messenger will purify the priests,
3. 3 they will bring to the **Lord** the right kind of offerings.
3. 4 and Jerusalem bring to the **Lord** will be pleasing to him, as
3. 5 The **Lord Almighty** says, "I will appear among you to judge,
3. 6 "I am the **Lord,** and I do not change.
3.13 "You have said terrible things about me," says the **Lord.**
3.14 of trying to show the **Lord Almighty** that we are sorry for
3.16 the people who feared the **Lord** spoke to one another, and the
3.16 one another, and the **Lord** listened and heard what they said.
3.16 a record of those who feared the **Lord** and respected him.
3.17 "They will be my people," says the **Lord Almighty.**
4. 1 The **Lord Almighty** says, "The day is coming when all proud
4. 5 and terrible day of the **Lord** comes, I will send you the
Mt 1.22 order to make what the **Lord** had said through the prophet
2.15 done to make what the **Lord** had said through the prophet come
3. 3 "Someone is shouting in the desert, 'Prepare a road for the **Lord;**
4. 7 also says, 'Do not put the **Lord** your God to the test.' "
4.10 scripture says, 'Worship the **Lord** your God and serve only him!' "
5.33 promise, but do what you have vowed to the **Lord** to do.'
7.21 "Not everyone who calls me **'Lord, Lord'** will enter the
7.22 When Judgement Day comes, many will say to me, **'Lord, Lord!**
8.25 "Save us, **Lord!"**
11.25 At that time Jesus said, "Father, **Lord** of heaven and earth!
12. 8 for the Son of Man is **Lord** of the Sabbath."
Mt 14.28 **"Lord,** if it is really you, order me to come out on
14.30 "Save me, **Lord!"**
16.22 "God forbid it, **Lord!"**
17. 4 up and said to Jesus, **"Lord,** how good it is that we
18.21 came to Jesus and asked, **"Lord,** if my brother keeps on
21. 9 God bless him who comes in the name of the **Lord!**
21.42 This was done by the **Lord;**
22.37 answered, " 'Love **the Lord your God** with all your heart,
22.43 Jesus asked, "did the Spirit inspire David to call him **'Lord'?**
22.44 David said, [44] 'The **Lord** said to my Lord:
22.45 If, then, David called him **'Lord,'** how can the Messiah be
23.39 'God bless him who comes in the name of the **Lord.'"**
24.42 because you do not know what day your **Lord** will come.
25.37 will then answer him, 'When, **Lord,** did we ever see you
25.44 they will answer him, 'When, **Lord,** did we ever see you
26.22 one after the other, "Surely, **Lord,** you don't mean me?"
27.10 to buy the potter's field, as the **Lord** had commanded me."
Mk 1. 3 shouting in the desert, 'Get the road ready for the **Lord;**
2.28 So the Son of Man is **Lord** even of the Sabbath."
5.19 tell them how much the **Lord** has done for you and how
11. 9 God bless him who comes in the name of the **Lord!**
12.11 This was done by the **Lord;**
12.29 **The Lord our God** is the only Lord.
12.30 Love **the Lord your God** with all your heart, with all
12.32 you say, that only the **Lord** is God and that there is
12.36 'The **Lord** said to my Lord:
12.37 David himself called him **'Lord';**
13.20 But the **Lord** has reduced the number of those days;
16.19 After the **Lord Jesus** had talked with them, he was taken
16.20 preached everywhere, and the **Lord** worked with them
Lk 1. 6 God's sight and obeyed fully all the **Lord's** laws and commands.
1. 9 into the Temple of the **Lord,** [10] while the crowd of people
1.15 He will be a great man in the **Lord's** sight.
1.16 back many of the people of Israel to **the Lord their God.**
1.17 will go ahead of the **Lord,** strong and mighty like the
1.17 he will get the **Lord's** people ready for him."
1.25 "Now at last the **Lord** has helped me," she said.
1.28 The **Lord** is with you and has greatly blessed you!"
1.32 The **Lord God** will make him a king, as his ancestor David
1.38 "I am the **Lord's** servant," said Mary;
1.43 thing happen to me, that my **Lord's** mother comes to visit me?
1.45 to believe that the **Lord's** message to you will come true!"
1.46 Mary said, "My heart praises the **Lord;**
1.58 heard how wonderfully good the **Lord** had been to her,
1.66 For it was plain that the **Lord's** power was upon him.
1.68 "Let us praise the **Lord,** the God of Israel!
1.76 will go ahead of the **Lord** to prepare his road for him,
2. 9 appeared to them, and the glory of the **Lord** shone over them.
2.11 day in David's town your Saviour was born—Christ the **Lord!**
2.15 this thing that has happened, which the **Lord** has told us."
2.22 to present him to the **Lord,**
2.23 as it is written in the law of the **Lord:**
2.23 "Every first-born male is to be dedicated to the **Lord."**
2.24 or two young pigeons, as required by the law of the **Lord.**
2.26 not die before he had seen the **Lord's** promised Messiah.
2.29 "Now, **Lord,** you have kept your promise, and you may let
2.39 by the law of the **Lord,** they returned to their home town
3. 4 'Get the road ready for the **Lord;**
4. 8 scripture says, 'Worship **the Lord your God** and serve only him!' "
4.12 says, 'Do not put **the Lord your God** to the test.' "
4.18 written, [18] "The Spirit of the **Lord** is upon me, because he
4.19 that the time has come when the **Lord** will save his people."
5. 8 on his knees before Jesus and said, "Go away from me, **Lord!**
5.17 The power of the **Lord** was present for Jesus to heal
6. 5 And Jesus concluded, "The Son of Man is **Lord** of the Sabbath."
6.46 "Why do you call me, **'Lord, Lord,'** and yet don't do
7.13 When the **Lord** saw her, his heart was filled with pity
7.19 and sent them to the **Lord** to ask him, "Are you the
9.54 John saw this, they said, **"Lord,** do you want us to call
10. 1 After this the **Lord** chose another seventy-two men and sent them
10.17 **"Lord,"** they said, "even the demons obeyed us when we
10.21 Holy Spirit and said, "Father, **Lord** of heaven and earth!
10.27 The man answered, " 'Love **the Lord your God** with all
10.39 down at the feet of the **Lord** and listened to his teaching.
10.40 so she came and said, **"Lord,** don't you care that my sister
10.41 The **Lord** answered her, "Martha, Martha!
11. 1 his disciples said to him, **"Lord,** teach us to pray,
11.39 So the **Lord** said to him, "Now then, you Pharisees clean
12.41 Peter said, **"Lord,** does this parable apply to us, or do
12.42 **Lord** answered, "Who, then, is the faithful and wise servant?
13.15 The **Lord** answered him, "You hypocrites!
13.35 say, 'God bless him who comes in the name of the **Lord.'"**
17. 5 The apostles said to the **Lord,** "Make our faith greater."
17. 6 The **Lord** answered, "If you had faith as big as a mustard
17.37 The disciples asked him, "Where, **Lord?"**
18. 6 the **Lord** continued, "Listen to what that corrupt judge said.
19. 8 Zacchaeus stood up and said to the **Lord,** "Listen, sir!
19.38 "God bless the king who comes in the name of the **Lord!**
20.37 bush he speaks of the **Lord** as 'the God of Abraham,
20.42 says in the book of Psalms, 'The **Lord** said to my Lord:
20.44 David called him **'Lord';**
22.33 Peter answered, **"Lord,** I am ready to go to prison with
22.38 Here are two swords, **Lord!"**
22.49 to happen, they asked, "Shall we use our swords, **Lord?"**
22.61 The **Lord** turned round and looked straight at Peter,
22.61 and Peter remembered that the **Lord** had said to him,
24. 3 but they did not find the body of the **Lord Jesus.**
24.34 with the others [34] and saying, "The **Lord** is risen indeed!
24.35 how they had recognized the **Lord** when he broke the bread.
24.36 telling them this, suddenly the **Lord** himself stood among
Jn 1.23 Make a straight path for the **Lord** to travel!' "

Jn 6.23 crowd had eaten the bread after the **Lord** had given thanks.
6.68 Simon Peter answered him, **"Lord,** to whom would we go?
9.38 "I believe, **Lord!"**
11. 2 poured the perfume on the **Lord's** feet and wiped them with
11. 3 **"Lord,** your dear friend is ill."
11.12 disciples answered, "If he is asleep, **Lord,** he will get well."
11.21 "If you had been here, **Lord,** my brother would not have died!
11.27 "Yes, **Lord!"**
11.32 **"Lord,"** she said, "if you had been here, my brother would
11.34 "Come and see, **Lord,"** they answered.
11.39 man's sister, answered, "There will be a bad smell, **Lord.**
12.13 God bless him who comes in the name of the **Lord!**
12.38 **"Lord,** who believed the message we told?
12.38 To whom did the **Lord** reveal his power?"
13. 6 who said to him, "Are you going to wash my feet, **Lord?"**
13. 9 Simon Peter answered, **"Lord,** do not wash only my feet,
13.13 "You call me Teacher and **Lord,** and it is right that you
13.14 I, your **Lord** and Teacher, have just washed your feet.
13.25 moved closer to Jesus' side and asked, "Who is it, **Lord?"**
13.36 "Where are you going, **Lord?"**
13.37 **"Lord,** why can't I follow you now?"
14. 5 Thomas said to him, **"Lord,** we do not know where you are
14. 8 Philip said to him, **"Lord,** show us the Father;
14.22 Judas (not Judas Iscariot) said, **"Lord,** how can it be that
20. 2 "They have taken the **Lord** from the tomb, and we don't
20.13 answered, "They have taken my **Lord** away, and I do not know
20.18 that she had seen the **Lord** and related to them what he
20.20 The disciples were filled with joy at seeing the **Lord.**
20.25 So the other disciples told him, "We have seen the **Lord!"**
20.28 Thomas answered him, "My **Lord** and my God!"
21. 7 The disciple whom Jesus loved said to Peter, "It is the **Lord!"**
21. 7 heard that it was the **Lord,** he wrapped his outer garment
21.12 because they knew it was the **Lord.**
21.15 "Yes, **Lord,"** he answered, "you know that I love you."
21.16 "Yes, **Lord,"** he answered, "you know that I love you."
21.17 so he said to him, **"Lord,** you know everything;
21.20 meal and had asked, **"Lord,** who is going to betray you?"
21.21 Peter saw him, he asked Jesus, **"Lord,** what about this man?"
Acts 1. 6 with Jesus, they asked him, **"Lord,** will you at this time
1.21 join us as a witness to the resurrection of the **Lord Jesus.**
1.21 the whole time that the **Lord Jesus** travelled about with us,
1.24 Then they prayed, **"Lord,** you know the thoughts of everyone,
2.20 blood, before the great and glorious Day of the **Lord** comes.
2.21 then, whoever calls out to the **Lord** for help will be saved.'
2.25 said about him, 'I saw the **Lord** before me at all times;
2.34 rather he said, 'The **Lord** said to my Lord:
2.36 crucified, is the one that God has made **Lord** and Messiah!"
2.39 are far away—all whom **the Lord our God** calls to himself."
2.47 And every day the **Lord** added to their group those who were
3.20 strength will come from the **Lord,** and he will send Jesus,
3.22 For Moses said, **'The Lord your God** will send you a prophet,
4.26 and the rulers met together against the **Lord** and his Messiah.'
4.29 And now, **Lord,** take notice of the threats they have made,
4.33 the resurrection of the **Lord Jesus,** and God poured rich blessings
5. 9 your husband decide to put the **Lord's** Spirit to the test?
5.14 group—a crowd of men and women who believed in the **Lord.**
7.31 But he heard the **Lord's** voice:
7.33 The **Lord** said to him, 'Take your sandals off, for the
7.49 is my throne, says the **Lord,** and the earth is my footstool.
7.59 called out to the **Lord, "Lord Jesus,** receive my spirit!"
7.60 He knelt down and cried out in a loud voice, **"Lord!**
8.16 they had only been baptized in the name of the **Lord Jesus.**
8.22 yours, and pray to the **Lord** that he will forgive you for
8.24 John, "Please pray to the **Lord** for me, so that none of
8.25 and proclaimed the **Lord's** message, Peter and John went back
8.39 out of the water, the Spirit of the **Lord** took Philip away.
9. 1 violent threats of murder against the followers of the **Lord.**
9. 2 of the Way of the **Lord,** he would be able to arrest
9. 5 "Who are you, **Lord?"**
9.10 He had a vision, in which the **Lord** said to him, "Ananias!"
9.10 "Here I am, **Lord,"** he answered.
9.11 The **Lord** said to him, "Get ready and go to Straight Street,
9.13 Ananias answered, **"Lord,** many people have told me about this
9.15 The **Lord** said to him, "Go, because I have chosen him to
9.17 "Brother Saul," he said, "the **Lord** has sent me—Jesus himself,
9.27 how Saul had seen the **Lord** on the road
9.27 and that the **Lord** had spoken to him.
9.28 over Jerusalem, preaching boldly in the name of the **Lord.**
9.31 and grew in numbers, as it lived in reverence for the **Lord.**
9.35 in Lydda and Sharon saw him, and they turned to the **Lord.**
9.42 spread all over Joppa, and many people believed in the **Lord.**
10.14 But Peter said, "Certainly not, **Lord!**
10.33 to hear anything that the **Lord** has instructed you to say."
10.36 Good News of peace through Jesus Christ, who is **Lord** of all.
11. 8 But I said, 'Certainly not, **Lord!**
11.16 Then I remembered what the **Lord** had said:
11.17 that he gave us when we believed in the **Lord Jesus Christ;**
11.20 Gentiles also, telling them the Good News about the **Lord Jesus.**
11.21 The **Lord's** power was with them,
11.21 a great number of people believed and turned to the **Lord.**
11.23 to be faithful and true to the **Lord** with all their hearts.
11.24 Holy Spirit and faith, and many people were brought to the **Lord.**
12.11 The **Lord** sent his angel to rescue me from Herod's power
12.17 to them how the **Lord** had brought him out of prison.
13. 2 While they were serving the **Lord** and fasting, the Holy Spirit
13.10 you always keep trying to turn the **Lord's** truths into lies!
13.11 The **Lord's** hand will come down on you now;
13.12 for he was greatly amazed at the teaching about the **Lord.**
13.44 everyone in the town came to hear the word of the **Lord.**
13.47 For this is the commandment that the **Lord** has given us:
13.48 heard this, they were glad and praised the **Lord's** message;
Acts 13.49 The word of the **Lord** spread everywhere in that region.
14. 3 speaking boldly about the **Lord,** who proved that their message
14.23 they commended them to the **Lord,** in whom they had put their
15.11 saved by the grace of the **Lord Jesus,** just as they are."
15.16 I will return, says the **Lord,** and restore the kingdom of David.
15.18 So says the **Lord,** who made this known long ago.'
15.26 risked their lives in the service of our **Lord Jesus Christ.**
15.35 many others they taught and preached the word of the **Lord.**
15.36 preached the word of the **Lord,** and let us find out how
15.40 commended by the believers to the care of the **Lord's** grace.
16.14 worshipped God, and the **Lord** opened her mind to pay attention
16.15 you have decided that I am a true believer in the **Lord."**
16.31 answered, "Believe in the **Lord Jesus,** and you will be saved
16.32 preached the word of the **Lord** to him and to all the
17.24 and everything in it, is **Lord** of heaven and earth and does
18. 8 believed in the **Lord,** together with all his family;
18. 9 a vision in which the **Lord** said to him, "Do not be
18.25 in the Way of the **Lord,** and with great enthusiasm he
19. 5 this, they were baptized in the name of the **Lord Jesus.**
19. 9 whole group they said evil things about the Way of the **Lord.**
19.10 both Jews and Gentiles, heard the word of the **Lord.**
19.13 tried to use the name of the **Lord Jesus** to do this.
19.17 and the name of the **Lord Jesus** was given greater honour.
19.20 way the word of the **Lord** kept spreading and growing stronger.
19.23 serious trouble in Ephesus because of the Way of the **Lord.**
20.19 did my work as the **Lord's** servant during the hard times that
20.21 turn from their sins to God and believe in our **Lord Jesus.**
20.24 finish the work that the **Lord Jesus** gave me to do,
20.35 remembering the words that the **Lord Jesus** himself said,
21.13 but even to die there for the sake of the **Lord Jesus."**
21.14 so we gave up and said, "May the **Lord's** will be done."
22. 8 'Who are you, **Lord?'**
22.10 I asked, 'What shall I do, **Lord?'**
22.10 and the **Lord** said to me, 'Get up and go into Damascus,
22.18 in which I saw the **Lord,** as he said to me, 'Hurry
22.19 **'Lord,'** I answered, 'they know very well that I went to
22.21 'Go,' the **Lord** said to me, 'for I will send you far
23.11 That night the **Lord** stood by Paul and said, "Don't be afraid!
26.15 'Who are you, **Lord?'**
26.15 And the **Lord** answered, 'I am Jesus, whom you persecute.
28.31 taught about the **Lord Jesus Christ,** speaking with all boldness
Rom 1. 3 It is about his Son, our **Lord Jesus Christ:**
1. 7 God our Father and the **Lord Jesus** Christ give you grace
4. 8 the person whose sins the **Lord** will not keep account of!"
4.24 who believe in him who raised Jesus **our Lord** from death.
5. 1 we have peace with God through our **Lord Jesus Christ.**
5.11 God has done through our **Lord Jesus Christ,** who has now made
5.21 leading us to eternal life through Jesus Christ **our Lord.**
6.23 gift is eternal life in union with Christ Jesus **our Lord.**
7.25 Thanks be to God, who does this through our **Lord Jesus Christ!**
8.39 love of God which is ours through Christ Jesus **our Lord.**
9.28 the **Lord** will quickly settle his full account with the world."
9.29 had said before, "If the **Lord** Almighty had not left us some
10. 9 you confess that Jesus is **Lord** and believe that God raised
10.12 God is the same **Lord** of all and richly blesses all
10.13 "Everyone who calls out to the **Lord** for help will be saved."
10.16 Isaiah himself said, **"Lord,** who believed our message?"
11. 3 **"Lord,** they have killed your prophets and torn down your altars;
11.34 As the scripture says, "Who knows the mind of the **Lord?**
12.11 Serve the **Lord** with a heart full of devotion.
12.19 "I will take revenge, I will pay back, says the **Lord."**
13.14 the weapons of the **Lord Jesus Christ,** and stop paying attention
14. 4 will succeed, because the **Lord** is able to make him succeed.
14. 6 highly of a certain day does so in honour of the **Lord;**
14. 6 so in honour of the **Lord,** because he gives thanks to God
14. 6 so in honour of the **Lord,** and he gives thanks to God.
14. 8 live, it is for the **Lord** that we live,
14. 8 and if we die, it is for the **Lord** that we die.
14. 8 So whether we live or die, we belong to the **Lord.**
14. 9 in order to be the **Lord** of the living and of the
14.11 the living God, says the **Lord,** everyone will kneel before me,
14.14 My union with the **Lord Jesus** makes me certain that no
15. 6 with one voice the God and Father of our **Lord Jesus Christ.**
15.11 And again, "Praise the **Lord,** all Gentiles;
15.30 urge you, brothers, by our **Lord Jesus Christ** and by the love
16. 2 Receive her in the **Lord's** name, as God's people should,
16. 8 to Ampliatus, my dear friend in the fellowship of the **Lord.**
16.12 Tryphosa, who work in the **Lord's** service, and to my dear
16.12 dear friend Persis, who has done so much work for the **Lord.**
16.13 that outstanding worker in the **Lord's** service, and to his mother,
16.18 are not serving Christ **our Lord,** but their own appetites.
16.20 The grace of our **Lord Jesus** be with you.
1 Cor 1. 2 people everywhere who worship our **Lord Jesus Christ,**
1. 2 their **Lord** and ours:
1. 3 God our Father and the **Lord Jesus Christ** give you grace
1. 7 as you wait for our **Lord Jesus Christ** to be revealed.
1. 8 you will be faultless on the Day of our **Lord Jesus Christ.**
1. 9 you to have fellowship with his Son Jesus Christ, **our Lord.**
1.10 By the authority of our **Lord Jesus Christ** I appeal to
1.31 "Whoever wants to boast must boast of what the **Lord** has done."
2. 8 known it, they would not have crucified the **Lord** of glory.
2.16 As the scripture says, "Who knows the mind of the **Lord?**
3. 5 of us does the work which the **Lord** gave him to do:
3.20 another scripture says, "The **Lord** knows that the thoughts of
4. 4 The **Lord** is the one who passes judgement on me.
4. 5 Final judgement must wait until the **Lord** comes;
4.19 If the **Lord** is willing, however, I will come to you soon,
5. 3 in the name of our **Lord Jesus** already passed judgement on
5. 3 by the power of our **Lord Jesus** present with us, [5] you are
5. 5 that his spirit may be saved in the Day of the **Lord.**
6.11 right with God by the **Lord Jesus Christ** and by the Spirit

1 Cor 6.13 not to be used for sexual immorality, but to serve the **Lord;**
6.13 and the **Lord** provides for the body.
6.14 God raised the **Lord** from death, and he will also raise
6.17 joins himself to the **Lord** becomes spiritually one with him.
7.10 I have a command which is not my own but the **Lord's:**
7.12 To the others I say (I, myself, not the **Lord**):
7.17 on living according to the **Lord's** gift to him, and as he
7.22 who has been called by the **Lord**
7.22 is the **Lord's** free man;
7.25 have a command from the **Lord,** but I give my opinion
7.25 as one who by the **Lord's** mercy is worthy of trust.
7.32 man concerns himself with the **Lord's** work,
7.32 because he is trying to please the **Lord.**
7.34 concerns herself with the **Lord's** work, because she wants to be
7.35 to give yourselves completely to the **Lord's** service without any
8. 6 there is only one **Lord,** Jesus Christ, through whom all things
9. 1 Haven't I seen Jesus **our Lord?**
9. 1 And aren't you the result of my work for the **Lord?**
9. 2 life in union with the **Lord** you yourselves are proof of the
9. 5 the other apostles and the **Lord's** brothers and Peter, by
9.14 In the same way, the **Lord** has ordered that those who
10. 9 We must not put the **Lord** to the test, as some of
10.21 You cannot drink from the **Lord's** cup and also from the
10.21 you cannot eat at the **Lord's** table and also at the table
10.22 Or do we want to make the **Lord** jealous?
10.26 "The earth and everything in it belong to the **Lord.**"
11.11 In our life in the **Lord,** however, woman is not
11.23 For I received from the **Lord** the teaching that I passed
11.23 that the **Lord Jesus,** on the night he was betrayed, took a
11.26 from this cup you proclaim the **Lord's** death until he comes.
11.27 that if anyone eats the **Lord's** bread or drinks from his cup
11.27 him, he is guilty of sin against the **Lord's** body and blood.
11.29 recognize the meaning of the **Lord's** body when he eats the
11.32 judged and punished by the **Lord,** so that we shall not be
12. 3 one can confess "Jesus is **Lord,**" unless he is guided by
12. 5 are different ways of serving, but the same **Lord** is served.
14.21 strange languages I will speak to my people, says the **Lord.**
14.37 realize that what I am writing to you is the **Lord's** command.
15.31 in union with Christ Jesus **our Lord,** makes me declare this.
15.57 God who gives us the victory through our **Lord Jesus Christ!**
15.58 in your work for the **Lord,** since you know
15.58 that nothing you do in the **Lord's** service is ever useless.
16. 7 to spend quite a long time with you, if the **Lord** allows.
16.10 because he is working for the **Lord,** just as I am.
16.22 Whoever does not love the **Lord**—a curse on him!
16.22 Marana tha—**Our Lord,** come!
16.23 The grace of the **Lord Jesus** be with you.
2 Cor 1. 2 God our Father and the **Lord Jesus Christ** give you grace
1. 3 God and Father of our **Lord Jesus Christ,** the merciful Father,
1.13 in the Day of our **Lord Jesus** you can be as proud
2.12 Christ, I found that the **Lord** had opened the way for the
3.16 "His veil was removed when he turned to the **Lord.**"
3.17 Now, "the **Lord**" in this passage is the Spirit;
3.17 where the Spirit of the **Lord** is present, there is freedom.
3.18 then, reflect the glory of the **Lord** with uncovered faces;
3.18 same glory, coming from the **Lord,** who is the Spirit, transforms
4. 5 we preach Jesus Christ as **Lord,** and ourselves as your servants
4.14 that God, who raised the **Lord Jesus** to life, will also raise
5. 6 at home in the body we are away from the **Lord's** home.
5. 8 our home in the body and be at home with the **Lord.**
5.11 it means to fear the **Lord,** and so we try to persuade
6.17 so the **Lord** says, "You must leave them and separate yourselves
6.18 shall be my sons and daughters, says the **Lord** Almighty."
8. 5 First they gave themselves to the **Lord;**
8. 9 You know the grace of **our Lord** Jesus Christ;
8.19 for the sake of the **Lord's** glory, and in order to show
8.21 in the sight of the **Lord,** but also in the sight of
10. 8 the authority that the **Lord** has given us—authority to build
10.17 "Whoever wants to boast must boast about what the **Lord** has done."
10.18 For it is when the **Lord** thinks well of a person that
11.17 saying now is not what the **Lord** would like me to say;
11.31 God and Father of the **Lord Jesus**—blessed be his name
12. 1 now talk about visions and revelations given me by the **Lord.**
12. 8 I prayed to the **Lord** about this and asked him
13.10 using the authority that the **Lord** has given me—
13.13 The grace of the **Lord Jesus Christ,** the love of God,
Gal 1. 3 God our Father and the **Lord Jesus Christ** give you grace
1.19 did not see any other apostle except James, the **Lord's** brother.
5.10 life in union with the **Lord** makes me confident that you will
6.14 I will boast only about the cross of our **Lord Jesus Christ;**
6.18 May the grace of our **Lord Jesus Christ** be with you all,
Eph 1. 2 God our Father and the **Lord Jesus** Christ give you grace
1. 3 give thanks to the God and Father of our **Lord Jesus Christ!**
1.15 of your faith in the **Lord Jesus** and your love for all
1.17 ask the God of our **Lord Jesus Christ,** the glorious Father,
1.22 and gave him to the church as supreme **Lord** over all things.
2.21 makes it grow into a sacred temple dedicated to the **Lord.**
3.11 eternal purpose, which he achieved through Christ Jesus **our Lord.**
4. 1 then—I who am a prisoner because I serve the **Lord:**
4. 5 There is one **Lord,** one faith, one baptism;
4. 6 of all mankind, who is **Lord** of all, works through all,
4.17 In the **Lord's** name, then, I warn you:
5. 8 you have become the **Lord's** people, you are in the light.
5.10 Try to learn what pleases the **Lord.**
5.17 but try to find out what the **Lord** wants you to do.
5.19 hymns and psalms to the **Lord** with praise in your hearts.
5.20 In the name of our **Lord Jesus Christ,** always give thanks
5.22 Wives, submit to your husbands as to the **Lord.**
6. 7 cheerfully, as though you served the **Lord,** and not merely men.
6. 8 that the **Lord** will reward everyone, whether slave or free,
Eph 6.10 strength in union with the **Lord** and by means of his mighty
6.21 and faithful servant in the **Lord's** work, will give you all
6.23 God the Father and the **Lord Jesus Christ** give to all
6.24 all those who love our **Lord Jesus Christ** with undying love.
Phil 1. 2 God our Father and the **Lord Jesus Christ** give you grace
1.14 brothers more confidence in the **Lord,** so that they grow bolder
2.11 proclaim that Jesus Christ is **Lord,** to the glory of God
2.19 If it is the **Lord's** will, I hope that I will be
2.24 And I trust in the **Lord** that I myself will be able
2.29 Receive him, then, with joy, as a brother in the **Lord.**
3. 1 In conclusion, my brothers, be joyful in your union with the **Lord.**
3. 8 much more valuable, the knowledge of Christ Jesus my **Lord.**
3.20 for our Saviour, the **Lord Jesus Christ,** to come from heaven.
4. 1 is how you should stand firm in your life in the **Lord.**
4. 2 please, I beg you, try to agree as sisters in the **Lord.**
4. 4 May you always be joyful in your union with the **Lord.**
4. 5 The **Lord** is coming soon.
4.10 life in union with the **Lord** it is a great joy to
4.23 May the grace of the **Lord Jesus Christ** be with you all.
Col 1. 3 God, the Father of our **Lord Jesus Christ,** when we pray for
1.10 able to live as the **Lord** wants and will always do what
2. 6 have accepted Christ Jesus as **Lord,** live in union with him.
3.13 You must forgive one another just as the **Lord** has forgiven you.
3.17 in the name of the **Lord Jesus,** as you give thanks
3.22 with a sincere heart because of your reverence for the **Lord.**
3.23 as though you were working for the **Lord** and not for men.
3.24 Remember that the **Lord** will give you as a reward what he
4. 7 worker and fellow-servant in the **Lord's** work, will give you all
4.17 to finish the task you were given in the **Lord's** service."
1 Thes 1. 1 belong to God the Father and the **Lord Jesus Christ:**
1. 3 hard, and how your hope in our **Lord Jesus Christ** is firm.
1. 6 You imitated us and the **Lord;**
1. 8 the message about the **Lord** go out from you throughout Macedonia
2.15 the Jews, [15] who killed the **Lord Jesus** and the prophets,
2.19 our victory in the presence of our **Lord Jesus** when he comes.
3. 8 if you stand firm in your life in union with the **Lord.**
3.11 and Father himself and our **Lord Jesus** prepare the way for us
3.12 May the **Lord** make your love for one another and for all
3.13 God and Father when our **Lord Jesus** comes with all who belong
4. 1 you in the name of the **Lord Jesus** to do even more.
4. 2 instructions we gave you by the authority of the **Lord Jesus.**
4. 6 warned you that the **Lord** will punish those who do that.
4.15 What we are teaching you now is the **Lord's** teaching:
4.15 alive on the day the **Lord** comes will not go ahead of
4.16 God's trumpet, and the **Lord** himself will come down from heaven.
4.17 with them in the clouds to meet the **Lord** in the air.
4.17 And so we will always be with the **Lord.**
5. 2 that the Day of the **Lord** will come as a thief comes
5. 9 possess salvation through our **Lord Jesus Christ,** [10] who died for
5.23 from every fault at the coming of our **Lord Jesus Christ.**
5.27 by the authority of the **Lord** to read this letter to all
5.28 The grace of our **Lord Jesus Christ** be with you.
2 Thes 1. 1 who belong to God our Father and the **Lord Jesus Christ:**
1. 2 God our Father and the **Lord Jesus Christ** give you grace
1. 7 will do this when the **Lord Jesus** appears from heaven with
1. 8 and who do not obey the Good News about our **Lord Jesus.**
1. 9 from the presence of the **Lord** and from his glorious might,
1.12 way the name of our **Lord Jesus** will receive glory from you,
1.12 by the grace of our God and of the **Lord Jesus Christ.**
2. 1 Concerning the coming of our **Lord Jesus Christ** and our being
2. 2 upset by the claim that the Day of the **Lord** has come.
2. 8 be revealed, but when the **Lord Jesus** comes, he will kill him
2.13 God at all times for you, brothers, you whom the **Lord** loves.
2.14 to possess your share of the glory of our **Lord Jesus Christ.**
2.16 our **Lord Jesus Christ** himself and God our Father, who loved
3. 1 pray for us, that the **Lord's** message may continue to spread
3. 3 But the **Lord** is faithful, and he will strengthen you and
3. 4 And the **Lord** gives us confidence in you, and we are sure
3. 5 the **Lord** lead you into a greater understanding of God's love
3. 6 in the name of our **Lord Jesus Christ** to keep away from
3.12 In the name of the **Lord Jesus Christ** we command these
3.16 May the **Lord** Himself, who is our source of peace, give
3.16 The **Lord** be with you all.
3.18 May the grace of our **Lord Jesus Christ** be with you all.
1 Tim 1. 2 the Father and Christ Jesus **our Lord** give you grace, mercy,
1.12 give thanks to Christ Jesus **our Lord,** who has given me
1.14 And **our Lord** poured out his abundant grace on me
5.22 lay hands on someone to dedicate him to the **Lord's** service.
6. 3 the true words of our **Lord Jesus Christ** and with the
6.14 faithfully until the Day when our **Lord Jesus Christ** will appear.
6.15 and only Ruler, the King of kings and the **Lord of lords.**
2 Tim 1. 2 the Father and Christ Jesus **our Lord** give you grace, mercy,
1. 8 Do not be ashamed, then, of witnessing for **our Lord;**
1.16 May the **Lord** show mercy to the family of Onesiphorus,
1.18 May the **Lord** grant him his mercy on that Day!
2. 7 I am saying, because the **Lord** will enable you to understand
2.19 "The **Lord** knows those who are his" and "Whoever says
2.19 he belongs to the **Lord** must turn away from wrongdoing."
2.22 who with a pure heart call out to the **Lord** for help.
2.24 The **Lord's** servant must not quarrel.
3.11 But the **Lord** rescued me from them all.
4. 8 right with God, which the **Lord,** the righteous Judge, will give
4.14 the **Lord** will reward him according to what he has done.
4.17 But the **Lord** stayed with me and gave me strength, so
4.18 And the **Lord** will rescue me from all evil and take me
4.22 The **Lord** be with your spirit.
Phlm 3 God our Father and the **Lord Jesus Christ** give you grace
5 all God's people and the faith you have in the **Lord Jesus.**
16 both as a slave and as a brother in the **Lord!**
20 So, my brother, please do me this favour for the **Lord's** sake;

Phlm 25 May the grace of the **Lord Jesus Christ** be with you all.
Heb 1.10 He also said, "You, **Lord,** in the beginning created the earth,
2. 3 The **Lord** himself first announced this salvation, and those who
7.13 And **our Lord,** of whom these things are said, belonged to
7.21 God said to him, "The **Lord** has made a solemn promise
8. 2 real tent which was put up by the **Lord,** not by man.
8. 8 days are coming, says the **Lord,** when I will draw up
8.10 the people of Israel in the days to come, says the **Lord:**
8.11 fellow-citizen or say to his fellow-countryman, 'Know the **Lord.'**
10.16 will make with them in the days to come, says the **Lord:**
10.25 since you see that the Day of the **Lord** is coming nearer.
10.30 and who also said, "The **Lord** will judge his people."
12. 5 son, pay attention when the **Lord** corrects you, and do not be
12. 6 the **Lord** corrects everyone he loves, and punishes everyone he
12.14 a holy life, because no one will see the **Lord** without it.
13. 6 bold, then, and say, "The **Lord** is my helper, I will not
13.15 is the offering presented by lips that confess him as **Lord.**
13.20 has raised from death our **Lord Jesus,** who is the Great
Jas 1. 1 From James, a servant of God and of the **Lord Jesus Christ:**
1. 7 must not think that he will receive anything from the **Lord.**
2. 1 as believers in our **Lord Jesus Christ,** the Lord of glory,
3. 9 it to give thanks to **our Lord** and Father and also to
4.10 Humble yourselves before the **Lord,** and he will lift you up.
4.15 "If the **Lord** is willing, we will live and do this or
5. 4 your crops have reached the ears of God, the **Lord** Almighty.
5. 7 Be patient, then, my brothers, until the **Lord** comes.
5. 8 your hopes high, for the day of the **Lord's** coming is near.
5.10 remember the prophets who spoke in the name of the **Lord.**
5.11 and you know how the **Lord** provided for him in the end.
5.11 For the **Lord** is full of mercy and compassion.
5.14 and rub olive-oil on him in the name of the **Lord.**
5.15 the **Lord** will restore him to health, and the sins he has
1 Pet 1. 3 give thanks to the God and Father of our **Lord Jesus Christ!**
1.25 fall, [25] but the word of the **Lord** remains for ever."
2. 3 "You have found out for yourselves how kind the **Lord** is."
2. 4 Come to the **Lord,** the living stone rejected by man as
2.13 For the sake of the **Lord** submit to every human authority:
3.12 the **Lord** watches over the righteous and listens to their prayers;
3.15 reverence for Christ in your hearts, and honour him as **Lord.**
2 Pet 1. 2 through your knowledge of God and of Jesus **our Lord.**
1. 8 active and effective in your knowledge of our **Lord Jesus Christ.**
1.11 the eternal Kingdom of **our Lord** and Saviour Jesus Christ.
1.14 this mortal body, as our **Lord Jesus Christ** plainly told me.
1.16 known to you the mighty coming of our **Lord Jesus Christ.**
2. 9 And so the **Lord** knows how to rescue godly people from
2.11 do not accuse them with insults in the presence of the **Lord.**
2.20 through their knowledge of **our Lord** and Saviour Jesus Christ,
3. 2 and the command from the **Lord** and Saviour which was given
3. 8 is no difference in the **Lord's** sight between one day and a
3. 9 The **Lord** is not slow to do what he has promised,
3.10 But the Day of the **Lord** will come like a thief.
3.15 Look on **our Lord's** patience as the opportunity he is
3.18 grace and knowledge of **our Lord** and Saviour Jesus Christ.
Jude 4 and who reject Jesus Christ, our only Master and **Lord.**
5 remind you of how the **Lord** once rescued the people of Israel
9 the Devil with insulting words, but said, "The **Lord** rebuke you!"
14 "The **Lord** will come with many thousands of his holy angels
17 told in the past by the apostles of our **Lord Jesus Christ.**
21 as you wait for our **Lord Jesus Christ** in his mercy to
25 through Jesus Christ **our Lord,** be glory, majesty, might,
Rev 1. 8 and the last," says the **Lord God** Almighty, who is, who was,
1.10 On the **Lord's** day the Spirit took control of me, and I
4. 8 "Holy, holy, holy, is the **Lord God** Almighty, who was, who
4.11 down in front of the throne and say, [11] **"Our Lord** and God!
6.10 They shouted in a loud voice, "Almighty **Lord,** holy and
11. 4 and the two lamps that stand before the **Lord** of the earth.
11. 8 street of the great city, where their **Lord** was crucified.
11.15 the world belongs now to **our Lord** and his Messiah,
11.17 **"Lord God** Almighty, the one who is and who was!
14.13 those who from now on die in the service of the **Lord!"**
15. 3 **"Lord God** Almighty, how great and wonderful are your deeds!
15. 4 Who will not stand in awe of you, **Lord?**
16. 7 I heard a voice from the altar saying, **"Lord God** Almighty!
17.14 them, because he is **Lord of lords** and King of kings."
18. 8 burnt with fire, because the **Lord God,** who judges her, is
19. 6 For the **Lord,** our Almighty God, is King!
19.16 "King of kings and **Lord of lords."**
21.22 because its temple is the **Lord God** Almighty and the Lamb.
22. 5 lamps or sunlight, because the **Lord God** will be their light,
22. 6 And the **Lord God,** who gives his Spirit to the prophets,
22.20 Come, **Lord Jesus!**
22.21 May the grace of the **Lord Jesus** be with everyone.

LORD GOD see **GOD (1), LORD**

LORD OUR SALVATION

Jer 23. 6 He will be called **'The Lord Our Salvation.'**
33.16 The city will be called **'The Lord Our Salvation.'**

LORD-IS-HERE

Ezek 48.35 The name of the city from now on will be, **"The-Lord-Is-Here!"**

LORD'S ANGEL see **ANGEL**

LORD'S ANGER see **ANGER**

LORD'S KINGDOM see **KINGDOM (1)**

LORD'S NAME see **NAME (2)**

LORD'S PEOPLE see **GOD'S PEOPLE**

LORD'S POWER see **POWER**

LORD'S SPIRIT see **SPIRIT (1)**

LORD'S SUPPER

1 Cor 10.16 cup we use in the **Lord's Supper** and for which we give
11.20 as a group, it is not the **Lord's Supper** that you eat.
11.33 gather together to eat the **Lord's Supper,** wait for one another.

LORD'S WILL see **WILL (1)**

LORD'S WORD see **WORD (1)**

AV **LORD (not addressed to God)** see **SIR**

LORD(S)

Ps 110. 1 The Lord said to my **lord,** the king, "Sit here at my
136. 3 Give thanks to the mightiest of all **lords;**
Jer 22.18 No one will weep for him or cry, 'My **lord!**
1 Cor 8. 5 many of these "gods" and **"lords,"** [6] yet there is for us
Eph 1.21 there above all heavenly rulers, authorities, powers, and **lords;**
Col 1.16 seen and the unseen things, including spiritual powers, **lords,**

LOSE
[LOST]

Gen 19.15 so that you will not **lose** your lives when the city is
27.45 Why should I **lose** both my sons on the same day?"
31.36 Then Jacob **lost** his temper.
34.19 Shechem, [19] and the young man **lost** no time in doing what
42.36 to them, "Do you want to make me **lose** all my children?
43.14 for me, if I must **lose** my children, I must lose them."
Ex 14. 5 Israelites escape, and we have **lost** them as our slaves!"
15.15 the people of Canaan **lose** their courage.
21.18 is to pay for his **lost** time and take care of him
21.22 pregnant woman so that she **loses** her child, but she is not
21.26 the eye so that he **loses** the use of it, he is
22. 9 sheep, clothing, or any other **lost** object, the two men
Lev 6. 3 about something that has been **lost** and swearing that he did
13.40 If a man **loses** his hair at the back or the front
25.30 back within the year, he **loses** the right of repurchase, and
27.20 back from the Lord, he **loses** the right to buy it back.
Num 21. 4 on the way the people **lost** their patience [5] and spoke
22.27 Balaam **lost** his temper and began to beat the donkey with his
36. 4 into which they marry and will be **lost** to our tribe."
Deut 20. 3 Do not be afraid of your enemies, or **lose** courage, or panic.
20. 8 there any man here who has **lost** his nerve and is afraid?
22. 3 or anything else that your fellow-Israelite may have **lost.**
28.28 The Lord will make you **lose** your mind;
28.34 Your sufferings will make you **lose** your mind.
28.41 and daughters, but you will **lose** them, because they will be
28.43 gain more and more power, while you gradually **lose** yours.
31. 8 you or abandon you, so do not **lose** courage or be afraid."
Josh 2.11 we have all **lost** our courage because of you.
5. 1 They became afraid and **lost** their courage
6.26 Whoever lays the foundation will **lose** his eldest son;
6.26 Whoever builds the gates will **lose** his youngest."
7. 5 Then the Israelites **lost** their courage and were afraid.
19.47 When the people of Dan **lost** their land, they went to
Judg 16.17 hair were cut, I would **lose** my strength and be as weak
16.19 Then she began to torment him, for he had **lost** his strength.
21. 6 Israel has **lost** one of its tribes.
21.17 Israel must not **lose** one of its twelve tribes.
1 Sam 2.33 he will become blind and **lose** all hope,
4. 7 We're **lost!**
9.20 for the donkeys that were **lost** three days ago, don't worry
14.45 Lord that he will not **lose** even a hair from his head.
30. 6 were all very bitter about **losing** their children, and they
2 Sam 21.17 hope of Israel, and we don't want to **lose** you," they said.
22.46 They **lose** their courage and come trembling from their fortresses.
1 Kgs 16.34 Joshua son of Nun, Hiel **lost** his eldest son Abiram when he
2 Kgs 3.26 Moab realized that he was **losing** the battle, he took seven
1 Chr 5. 1 of his father's concubines, he **lost** the rights belonging to
2 Chr 29.11 My sons, do not **lose** any time.
Ezra 10. 8 be confiscated, and he would **lose** his right to be a member
Neh 6.16 they realized that they had **lost** face, since everyone knew
Esth 2. 9 He **lost** no time in beginning her beauty treatment of massage
6.13 said to him, "You are beginning to **lose** power to Mordecai.
Job 6.18 Caravans get **lost** looking for water;
8. 7 All the wealth you **lost** will be nothing compared with what
12.24 lets them wander confused and **lost;**
13.15 I've **lost** all hope, so what if God kills me?
15.33 He will be like a vine that **loses** its unripe grapes;
29.24 I smiled on them when they had **lost** confidence;
33.20 The sick man **loses** his appetite, and even the finest

Job 41. 9 Anyone who sees Leviathan **loses** courage and falls to the ground.
Ps 18.45 They **lose** their courage and come trembling from their fortresses.
34.18 he saves those who have **lost** all hope.
38.10 strength is gone, and my eyes have **lost** their brightness.
40.12 than the hairs of my head, and I have **lost** my courage.
73. 2 But I had nearly **lost** confidence;
79. 8 we have **lost** all hope.
102. 4 I have **lost** my desire for food.
107.26 In such danger the men **lost** their courage;
119.176 I wander about like a **lost** sheep;
143. 7 I have **lost** all hope.
Prov 13.11 easily you get your wealth, the sooner you will **lose** it.
15. 6 wealth, but wicked men **lose** theirs when hard times come.
18. 3 **Lose** your honour, and you will get scorn in its place.
18.14 are sick, but if you **lose** it, your last hope is gone.
Ecc 3. 6 finding and the time for **losing,** the time for saving and the
5.14 may need it, [14] and then **lose** it all in some unlucky deal
Song 1. 4 We will be happy together, drink deep, and **lose** ourselves in love.
Is 17. 3 Damascus will **lose** its independence.
19. 1 before him, and the people of Egypt **lose** their courage.
27. 7 as severely as its enemies, nor has she **lost** as many men.
42. 4 He will not **lose** hope or courage;
47. 9 the magic you use, you will **lose** your husband and children.
49.21 I **lost** my children and could have no more.
53. 6 were like sheep that were **lost,** each of us going his own
Jer 3.24 of shame, has made us **lose** flocks and herds, sons and
4. 9 "On that day kings and officials will **lose** their courage;
4.13 We are **lost!**
15. 9 The mother who **lost** her seven children has fainted,
16. 7 not even for someone who has **lost** his father or mother.
17.11 prime of life he will **lose** his riches, and in the end
18.21 Let the women **lose** their husbands and children;
22.30 "This man is condemned to **lose** his children, to be a
38. 4 the soldiers in the city **lose** their courage, and he is doing
49. 7 "Have the people of Edom **lost** their good judgement?
50. 6 whose shepherds have let them get **lost** in the mountains.
51.30 They have **lost** their courage and have become like women.
51.46 Do not **lose** courage or be afraid because of the rumours
Ezek 7.13 back what he has **lost,** because God's anger is on everyone.
7.24 Your strongest men will **lose** their confidence when I let the
21.15 It makes my people **lose** courage and stumble.
23. 3 in Egypt, they **lost** their virginity and became prostitutes.
23. 8 as a prostitute in Egypt, where she **lost** her virginity.
23.21 men played with your breasts and you **lost** your virginity.)
24.27 of speech which you had **lost,** and you will talk with him.
27.27 ship— All, all were **lost** at sea When your ship was
34. 4 those that wandered off, or looked for those that were **lost.**
34.16 for those that are **lost,** bring back those that wander off,
Dan 3.19 Then Nebuchadnezzar **lost** his temper, and his face
5.20 removed from his royal throne and **lost** his place of honour.
Hos 5.11 she has **lost** land that was rightfully hers, because she
13. 8 like a bear that has **lost** her cubs, and I will tear
Joel 2.25 give you back what you **lost** in the years when swarms of
Amos 2.14 strong men will **lose** their strength, and soldiers will not
Mic 2. 7 Has the Lord **lost** his patience?
Zech 9. 5 Gaza will **lose** her king, and Ashkelon will be left deserted.
10. 2 So the people wander about like **lost** sheep.
10.11 mighty Egypt will **lose** her power.
11. 8 I **lost** patience with three other shepherds, who hated me,
11.16 does he look for the **lost,** or heal those that are hurt,
12.10 mourn bitterly, like those who have **lost** their first-born son.
Mal 3. 6 And so you, the descendants of Jacob, are not yet completely **lost.**
Mt 5.13 But if salt **loses** its saltiness, there is no way to make
5.29 much better for you to **lose** a part of your body than
5.30 much better for you to **lose** one of your limbs than for
10. 6 are to go to the **lost** sheep of the people of Israel.
10.39 Whoever tries to gain his own life will **lose** it;
10.39 but whoever **loses** his life for my sake will gain it.
15.24 been sent only to the **lost** sheep of the people of Israel."
16.25 For whoever wants to save his own life will **lose** it;
16.25 but whoever **loses** his life for my sake will find it.
16.26 gain anything if he wins the whole world but **loses** his life?
18. 6 of these little ones to **lose** his faith in me, it would
18. 7 that there are things that make people **lose** their faith!
18. 8 or your foot makes you **lose** your faith, cut it off
18. 9 if your eye makes you **lose** your faith, take it out
18.12 does who has a hundred sheep and one of them gets **lost?**
18.12 grazing on the hillside and go and look for the **lost** sheep.
18.13 one sheep than over the ninety-nine that did not get **lost.**
18.14 heaven does not want any of these little ones to be **lost.**
Mk 8.35 For whoever wants to save his own life will **lose** it;
8.35 but whoever **loses** his life for me and for the gospel will
8.36 gain anything if he wins the whole world but **loses** his life?
9.42 of these little ones to **lose** his faith in me, it would
9.43 So if your hand makes you **lose** your faith, cut it off!
9.45 And if your foot makes you **lose** your faith, cut it off!
9.47 And if your eye makes you **lose** your faith, take it out!
9.50 but if it **loses** its saltiness, how can you make it salty
13.15 of his house must not **lose** time by going down into the
Lk 9.24 save his own life will **lose** it,
9.24 but whoever **loses** his life for my sake
9.25 if he wins the whole world but is himself **lost** or defeated?
14.34 is good, but if it **loses** its saltiness, there is no way
15. 4 has a hundred sheep and **loses** one of them—what does he
15. 4 goes looking for the one that got **lost** until he finds it.
15. 6 says to them, 'I am so happy I found my **lost** sheep.
15. 8 who has ten silver coins **loses** one of them—what does she
15. 9 to them, 'I am so happy I found the coin I **lost.**
15.24 he was **lost,** but now he has been found.'
15.32 he was **lost,** but now he has been found.' "
17.33 Whoever tries to save his own life will **lose** it;
Lk 17.33 whoever **loses** his life will save it.
19.10 The Son of Man came to seek and to save the **lost."**
21.18 But not a single hair from your heads will be **lost.**
Jn 6.39 me that I should not **lose** any of all those he has
12.25 Whoever loves his own life will **lose** it;
17.12 not one of them was **lost,** except the man who
17.12 was bound to be **lost**—so that the scripture might come
18. 9 "Father, I have not **lost** even one of those you gave me.")
Acts 18. 6 to them, "If you are **lost,** you yourselves must take the
20.16 Ephesus, so as not to **lose** any time in the province of
20.26 if any of you should be **lost,** I am not responsible.
25.17 they came here, then, I **lost** no time, but on the very
27.22 Not one of you will **lose** his life;
27.22 only the ship will be **lost.**
27.34 Not even a hair of your heads will be **lost."**
Rom 2.12 they sin and are **lost** apart from the Law.
8.20 creation was condemned to **lose** its purpose, not of its own
1 Cor 1.18 death on the cross is nonsense to those who are being **lost;**
2. 6 powers that rule this world—powers that are **losing** their power.
3.15 But if anyone's work is burnt up, then he will **lose** it;
8. 8 we shall not **lose** anything if we do not eat, nor shall
15.17 faith is a delusion and you are still **lost** in your sins.
15.18 mean that the believers in Christ who have died are **lost.**
2 Cor 2.15 those who are being saved and those who are being **lost.**
2.16 For those who are being **lost,** it is a deadly stench that
4. 3 it is hidden only from those who are being **lost.**
Eph 4.19 They have **lost** all feeling of shame;
Phil 1.28 to them that they will **lose** and that you will win, because
1 Tim 1. 6 away from these and have **lost** their way in foolish discussions.
6.21 and as a result they have **lost** the way of faith.
Heb 10.35 Do not **lose** your courage, then, because it brings with it
10.39 We are not people who turn back and are **lost.**
1 Pet 2.25 were like sheep that had **lost** their way, but now you have
5. 4 receive the glorious crown which will never **lose** its brightness.
2 Pet 2.15 They have left the straight path and have **lost** their way;
2 Jn 8 so that you will not **lose** what we have worked for,
Rev 8.12 stars, so that their light **lost** a third of its brightness;
18.17 And in one hour she has **lost** all this wealth!"
18.19 And in one hour she has **lost** everything!"

LOSS

Gen 24.67 and so he was comforted for the **loss** of his mother.
31.39 was killed by wild animals, I always bore the **loss** myself.
Ex 21.21 The **loss** of his property is punishment enough.
21.36 he must make good the **loss** by giving the other man a
22. 5 he must make good the **loss** with the crops from his own
22.11 the owner shall accept the **loss,** and the other man need not
22.15 a hired animal, the **loss** is covered by the hiring charge.
Lev 12. 4 days before she is ritually clean from her **loss** of blood;
12. 5 days before she is ritually clean from her **loss** of blood.
Ps 144.14 May our cattle reproduce plentifully without miscarriage or **loss.**
Is 47. 8 would never be a widow or suffer the **loss** of your children.
Hos 10. 5 afraid and will mourn the **loss** of the gold bull at Bethel.
Acts 27.10 the cargo and to the ship, and **loss** of life as well."
27.21 then we would have avoided all this damage and **loss.**
Phil 3. 7 count as profit I now reckon as **loss** for Christ's sake.
3. 8 I reckon everything as complete **loss** for the sake of what is
4.15 you were the only ones who shared my profits and **losses.**
Heb 10.34 were seized, you endured your **loss** gladly, because you knew

LOST see LOSE

LOT (1)

Lev 16. 8 There he shall draw **lots,** using two stones, one marked
16. 9 sacrifice the goat chosen by **lot** for the Lord and offer it
Num 26.54 Divide the land by drawing **lots,** and give a large
33.54 tribes and clans by drawing **lots,** giving a large piece of
34.13 you will receive by drawing **lots,** the land that the Lord has
36. 2 distribute the land to the people of Israel by drawing **lots.**
Josh 14. 2 tribes west of the Jordan were determined by drawing **lots.**
18. 6 Then I will draw **lots** to consult the Lord our God for
18. 8 in Shiloh I will consult the Lord for you by drawing **lots."**
18.10 Joshua drew **lots** to consult the Lord for them, and
19.51 of the land by drawing **lots** to consult the Lord at Shiloh,
21. 8 By drawing **lots,** the people of Israel assigned these
Judg 20. 9 we will draw **lots** and choose some men to attack Gibeah.
1 Chr 6.61 West Manasseh were assigned by **lot** to the rest of the clan
6.65 mentioned above, were also assigned by drawing **lots.)**
24. 5 Eleazar and Ithamar, assignments were made by drawing **lots.**
24. 6 The descendants of Eleazar and of Ithamar took turns in drawing **lots.**
24.31 of his younger brothers drew **lots** for their assignments,
25. 8 duties they all drew **lots,** whether they were young or old,
26.13 family, regardless of size, drew **lots** to see which gate it
Neh 10.34 priests, and Levites, will draw **lots** each year to determine
11. 1 rest of the people drew **lots** to choose one family out of
Esth 3. 7 of Nisan, Haman ordered the **lots** to be cast ("purim," they
9.24 Jewish people—had cast **lots** (or "purim," as they were called)
Prov 16.33 Men cast **lots** to learn God's will, but God himself
18.18 each other in court, casting **lots** can settle the issue.
Ezek 47.22 citizens and are to draw **lots** for shares of the land along
Jon 1. 7 to one another, "Let's draw **lots** and find out who is to
Lk 1. 9 priests, he was chosen by **lot** to burn incense on the altar.
Acts 1.26 Then they drew **lots** to choose between the two men,

LOT (2)
Abraham's nephew (rescued when Sodom and Gomorrah were destroyed).

Gen 11.27 Haran was the father of **Lot,**
11.31 his son Abram, his grandson **Lot,** who was the son of Haran,
12. 4 and **Lot** went with him.
12. 5 his wife Sarai, his nephew **Lot,** and all the wealth
13. 1 his wife and everything he owned, and **Lot** went with him.
13. 5 **Lot** also had sheep, goats, and cattle,
13. 7 of Abram's animals and those who took care of **Lot's** animals.
13. 8 Then Abram said to **Lot,** "We are relatives, and your men
13.10 **Lot** looked round and saw that the whole Jordan Valley,
13.11 So **Lot** chose the whole Jordan Valley for himself
13.12 the land of Canaan, and **Lot** settled among the cities in the
13.14 After **Lot** had left, the Lord said to Abram, "From where
14.12 **Lot,** Abram's nephew, was living in Sodom,
14.16 also brought back his nephew **Lot** and his possessions,
19. 1 to Sodom that evening, **Lot** was sitting at the city gate.
19. 3 **Lot** ordered his servants to bake some bread and prepare a
19. 5 They called out to **Lot** and asked, "Where are the men who
19. 6 **Lot** went outside and closed the door behind him.
19. 9 They pushed **Lot** back and moved up to break down the door.
19.10 men inside reached out, pulled **Lot** back into the house,
19.12 The two men said to **Lot,** "If you have anyone else here
19.14 Then **Lot** went to the men that his daughters were going
19.15 At dawn the angels tried to make **Lot** hurry.
19.16 **Lot** hesitated.
19.18 But **Lot** answered, "No, please don't make us do that,
19.22 Because **Lot** called it small, the town was named Zoar.
19.23 The sun was rising when **Lot** reached Zoar.
19.26 But **Lot's** wife looked back and was turned into a pillar
19.29 cities of the valley where **Lot** was living,
19.29 kept Abraham in mind and allowed **Lot** to escape to safety.
19.30 Because **Lot** was afraid to stay in Zoar,
19.36 In this way both of **Lot's** daughters became pregnant
Deut 2. 9 Moab, the descendants of **Lot,** or start a war against them.
2.19 be near the land of the Ammonites, the descendants of **Lot.**
Ps 83. 8 ally of the Ammonites and Moabites, the descendants of **Lot.**
Lk 17.28 It will be as it was in the time of **Lot.**
17.29 On the day **Lot** left Sodom, fire and sulphur rained down
17.32 Remember **Lot's** wife!
2 Pet 2. 7 He rescued **Lot,** a good man, who was distressed

Am **LOTS**
see also **PURIM**

LOUD

Gen 27.34 heard this, he cried out **loudly** and bitterly and said,
39.14 tried to rape me, but I screamed as **loud** as I could.
45. 2 He cried with such **loud** sobs that the Egyptians heard it,
50.10 of the Jordan, they mourned **loudly** for a long time, and
Ex 11. 6 There will be **loud** crying all over Egypt, such as there
12.30 There was **loud** crying throughout Egypt, because there was
19.16 on the mountain, and a very **loud** trumpet blast was heard.
19.19 The sound of the trumpet became **louder and louder.**
Deut 27.14 The Levites will speak these words in a **loud** voice:
Josh 6. 5 men are to give a **loud** shout, and the city walls will
6.20 heard it, they gave a **loud** shout, and the walls collapsed.
Judg 21. 2 **Loudly** and bitterly they mourned:
1 Sam 2. 3 Stop your **loud** boasting;
4. 5 the Israelites gave such a **loud** shout of joy that the earth
2 Sam 15.23 The people cried **loudly** as David's followers left.
19. 4 The king covered his face and cried **loudly,** "O my son!
1 Kgs 8.55 In a **loud** voice he asked God's blessings on all the
18.27 "Pray **louder!**
18.28 So the prophets prayed **louder** and cut themselves
2 Chr 13.15 The Judaeans gave a **loud** shout, and led by Abijah, they
15.14 In a **loud** voice they took an oath in the Lord's name
20.19 stood up and with a **loud** shout praised the Lord, the God
Ezra 3.13 noise they made was so **loud** that it could be heard far
Esth 4. 1 walked through the city, wailing **loudly** and bitterly,
4. 3 was made known, there was **loud** mourning among the Jews.
Job 40. 9 Can your voice thunder as **loud** as mine?
Ps 47. 1 Praise God with **loud** songs!
109.30 I will give **loud** thanks to the Lord;
150. 5 Praise him with **loud** cymbals.
Prov 1.21 the streets and market-places, [21] calling **loudly** at the
9.13 Stupidity is like a **loud,** ignorant, shameless woman.
20. 1 Drinking too much makes you **loud** and foolish.
27.14 as wake him up early in the morning with a **loud** greeting.
29. 9 a fool, the fool only laughs and becomes **loud** and abusive.
Is 5.30 day comes, they will roar over Israel as **loudly** as the sea.
15. 5 some escape to Horonaim, grieving **loudly.**
40. 9 Call out with a **loud** voice, Zion;
42. 2 or raise his voice or make **loud** speeches in the streets.
58. 1 The Lord says, "Shout as **loud** as you can!
66. 6 That **loud** noise in the city, that sound in the Temple, is
Jer 4. 5 Shout **loud** and clear!
25.34 Cry, you leaders, you shepherds of my people, cry out **loud!**
Ezek 3.12 I heard behind me the **loud** roar of a voice that said,
3.13 air, and the noise of the wheels, as **loud** as an earthquake.
8.18 shout prayers to me as **loud** as they can, but I will
Dan 3. 4 a herald announced in a **loud** voice, "People of all nations,
4.14 He proclaimed in a **loud** voice, 'Cut the tree down and
Mic 4. 9 Why do you cry out so **loudly?**
Mt 12.19 not argue or shout, or make **loud** speeches in the streets.
20.31 But they shouted even more **loudly,** "Son of David!
27.46 Jesus cried out with a **loud** shout, "Eli, Eli, lema sabachthani?"
Mt 27.50 Jesus again gave a **loud** cry and breathed his last.
Mk 1.26 the man hard, gave a **loud** scream, and came out of him.
5. 7 and screamed in a **loud** voice, "Jesus, Son of the Most
5.38 Jesus saw the confusion and heard all the **loud** crying and wailing.
10.48 But he shouted even more **loudly,** "Son of David, take pity
15.14 They shouted all the **louder,** "Crucify him!"
15.34 cried out with a **loud** shout, "Eloi, Eloi, lema sabachthani?"
15.37 With a **loud** cry Jesus died.
Lk 1.42 Spirit [42] and said in a **loud** voice, "You are the most
4.33 he screamed out in a **loud** voice, [34] "Ah!
8.28 saw Jesus, he gave a **loud** cry, threw himself down at his
17.15 he was healed, he came back, praising God in a **loud** voice.
18.39 But he shouted even more **loudly,** "Son of David!
19.37 God and praise him in **loud** voices for all the great things
23.46 Jesus cried out in a **loud** voice, "Father!
Jn 7.28 Temple, he said in a **loud** voice, "Do you really know me
7.37 and said in a **loud** voice, "Whoever is thirsty should come
11.43 said this, he called out in a **loud** voice, "Lazarus, come
12.44 Jesus said in a **loud** voice, "Whoever believes in me believes
Acts 2.14 eleven apostles and in a **loud** voice began to speak to the
7.57 With a **loud** cry the members of the Council covered their
7.60 He knelt down and cried out in a **loud** voice, "Lord!
8. 2 devout men buried Stephen, mourning for him with **loud** cries.
8. 7 from many people with a **loud** cry, and many paralysed and
14.10 and said in a **loud** voice, "Stand up straight on your
23. 9 The shouting became **louder,** and some of the teachers of
Heb 5. 7 his prayers and requests with **loud** cries and tears to God,
Rev 1.10 and I heard a **loud** voice, that sounded like a trumpet,
5. 2 angel, who announced in a **loud** voice, "Who is worthy to
5.12 living creatures, and the elders, [12] and sang in a **loud** voice:
6.10 They shouted in a **loud** voice, "Almighty Lord, holy and
7. 2 He called out in a **loud** voice to the four angels to
7.10 They called out in a **loud** voice:
8.13 flying high in the air say in a **loud** voice, "O horror!
10. 3 and called out in a **loud** voice that sounded like the roar
11.12 the two prophets heard a **loud** voice say to them from heaven,
11.15 and there were **loud** voices in heaven, saying, "The power
12.10 I heard a **loud** voice in heaven saying, "Now God's salvation
14. 2 sounded like a roaring waterfall, like a **loud** peal of thunder.
14. 7 He said in a **loud** voice, "Honour God and praise his greatness!
14. 9 first two, saying in a **loud** voice, "Whoever worships the beast
14.15 and cried out in a **loud** voice to the one who was
14.18 He shouted in a **loud** voice to the angel who had the
16. 1 Then I heard a **loud** voice speaking from the temple to the
16.17 A **loud** voice came from the throne in the temple, saying,
18. 2 He cried out in a **loud** voice:
19. 6 the sound of a roaring waterfall, like **loud** peals of thunder.
19.17 He shouted in a **loud** voice to all the birds flying in
21. 3 I heard a **loud** voice speaking from the throne:

LOVE
[BELOVED, CONSTANT LOVE, LOVING, LOVINGLY]
see also **LOVER**

Gen 22. 2 only son, Isaac, whom you **love** so much, and go to the
24.67 Isaac **loved** Rebecca, and so he was comforted for the loss of
25.27 skilled hunter, a man who **loved** the outdoor life, but Jacob
26. 8 down from his window and saw Isaac and Rebecca making **love.**
29.18 Jacob was in **love** with Rachel, so he said, "I will work
29.20 seemed like only a few days to him, because he **loved** her.
29.30 with Rachel also, and he **loved** her more than Leah.
29.31 Lord saw that Leah was **loved** less than Rachel, he made it
29.32 Lord has seen my trouble, and now my husband will **love** me";
29.33 me this son also, because he heard that I was not **loved";**
34. 3 attractive that he fell in **love** with her and tried to win
34. 8 him, "My son Shechem has fallen in **love** with your daughter;
34.19 was suggested, because he was in **love** with Jacob's daughter.
37. 3 Jacob **loved** Joseph more than all his other sons, because
37. 4 saw that their father **loved** Joseph more than he loved them,
44.20 his father **loves** him very much.'
Ex 20. 6 But I show my **love** to thousands of generations
20. 6 of those who **love** me and obey my laws.
21. 5 the slave declares that he **loves** his master, his wife, and
34. 6 easily angered and who shows great **love** and faithfulness.
Lev 19.18 to hate him, but **love** your neighbour as you love yourself.
19.34 a fellow-Israelite, and **love** them as you love yourselves.
Num 14.18 angered, and I show great **love** and faithfulness and forgive
14.19 the greatness of your unchanging **love,** forgive, I pray, the
Deut 4.37 Because he **loved** your ancestors, he chose you, and by
5.10 But I show my **love** to thousands of generations
5.10 of those who **love** me and obey my laws.
6. 5 **Love** the Lord your God with all your heart, with all your
7. 7 "The Lord did not **love** you and choose you because you
7. 8 But the Lord **loved** you and wanted to keep the promise that
7. 9 his covenant and show his **constant love** to a thousand
7. 9 of those who **love** him and obey his commands,
7.12 show you his **constant love,** as he promised your ancestors.
7.13 He will **love** you and bless you, so that you will
10.12 **Love** him, serve him with all your heart, [13] and obey all
10.15 But the Lord's **love** for your ancestors was so strong
10.18 he **loves** the foreigners who live with our people, and gives
10.19 So then, show **love** for those foreigners, because you
11. 1 **"Love** the Lord your God and always obey all his laws.
11.13 **love** the Lord your God and serve him with all your heart.
11.22 **Love** the Lord your God, do everything he commands, and be
13. 3 you, to see if you **love** the Lord with all your heart.
13. 6 daughter or the wife you **love** or your closest friend may
15.16 he may **love** you and your family and be content to stay.
19. 9 you today and if you **love** the Lord your God and live
23. 5 he turned the curse into a blessing, because he **loved** you.
28.54 or to the wife he **loves** or to any of his children

Deut	28.56	with the husband she **loves** or with any of her children.
	30. 6	hearts, so that you will **love** him with all your heart, and
	30.16	give you today, if you **love** him, obey him, and keep all
	30.20	**Love** the Lord your God, obey him and be faithful to him,
	33. 3	The Lord **loves** his people and protects those who belong to him.
	33.12	"This is the tribe the Lord **loves** and protects;
Josh	22. 5	**love** the Lord your God, do his will, obey his commandments,
	23.11	Be careful, then, to **love** the Lord your God.
Judg	14.16	wife went to him in tears and said, "You don't **love** me!
	16. 4	After this, Samson fell in **love** with a woman named Delilah,
	16.15	"How can you say you **love** me, when you don't mean it?
Ruth	4.15	Your daughter-in-law **loves** you, and has done more for
1 Sam	1. 5	And even though he **loved** Hannah very much he would give
	18. 1	David and came to love him as much as he **loved** himself.
	18.16	everyone in Israel and Judah **loved** David because he was such
	18.20	daughter Michal, however, fell in **love** with David, and when
	18.28	Lord was with David and also that his daughter Michal **loved** him.
	20.17	Jonathan made David promise to **love** him,
	20.17	for Jonathan loved David as much as he **loved** himself.
2 Sam	1.26	How wonderful was your **love** for me,
	1.26	better even than the **love** of women.
	11. 4	they brought her to him and he made **love** to her.
	12.24	The Lord **loved** the boy [25]and commanded the prophet Nathan
	12.25	to name the boy Jedidiah, because the Lord **loved** him.
	13. 1	Amnon, another of David's sons, fell in **love** with her.
	13. 2	He was so much in **love** with her that he became ill,
	13. 4	"I'm in **love** with Tamar, the sister of my half-brother Absalom,"
	13.15	he hated her now even more than he had **loved** her before.
	19. 6	You oppose those who **love** you and support those who hate you!
	21.20	battle at Gath, where there was a giant who **loved** to fight.
	22.51	he shows **constant love** to the one he has chosen, to David
1 Kgs	3. 3	Solomon **loved** the Lord and followed the instructions
	3. 6	"You always showed great **love** for my father David,
	3. 6	show him your great and **constant love** by giving him a son
	3.26	mother, her heart full of **love** for her son, said to the
	8.23	people and show them your **love** when they live in
	10. 9	Because his **love** for Israel is eternal, he has made you
	11. 1	Solomon **loved** many foreign women.
1 Chr	16.34	his **love** is eternal.
	16.41	chosen to sing praises to the Lord for his eternal **love.**
	29. 3	my personal property because of my **love** for God's Temple.
2 Chr	1. 8	"You always showed great **love** for my father David,
	2.11	He wrote, "Because the Lord **loves** his people, he has made
	5.11	"Praise the Lord, because he is good, And his **love** is eternal."
	6.14	people and show them your **love** when they live in
	6.42	Remember the **love** you had for your servant David."
	7. 3	God and praising him for his goodness and his eternal **love.**
	7. 6	singing the hymn, "His **Love** Is Eternal!"
	9. 8	Because he **loves** his people Israel and wants to preserve
	11.21	his wives and concubines he **loved** Maacah best, [22]and he
	20.21	His **love** is eternal!"
	26.10	Because he **loved** farming, he encouraged the people to plant
Ezra	3.11	"The Lord is good, and his **love** for Israel is eternal."
Neh	1. 5	covenant with those who **love** you and do what you command.
	9.17	you are gracious and **loving,** slow to be angry.
	13.22	for this also, and spare me because of your great **love.**
	13.26	God **loved** him and made him king over all Israel, and yet
Job	10.12	have given me life and **constant love,** and your care has kept
	19.19	those I **loved** most have turned against me.
Ps	4. 2	How long will you **love** what is worthless and go after what
	5. 7	But because of your great **love** I can come into your house;
	5.11	Protect those who **love** you;
	5.12	your **love** protects them like a shield.
	11. 7	The Lord is righteous and **loves** good deeds;
	13. 5	I rely on your **constant love;**
	17. 7	Reveal your wonderful **love** and save me;
	18. 1	How I **love** you, Lord!
	18.50	he shows **constant love** to the one he has chosen, to David
	21. 7	and because of the Lord's **constant love** he will always be secure.
	23. 6	know that your goodness and **love** will be with me all my
	25. 6	O Lord, your kindness and **constant love** which you have shown
	25. 7	In your **constant love** and goodness, remember me, Lord!
	25.10	With faithfulness and **love** he leads all who keep his
	26. 3	Your **constant love** is my guide;
	26. 8	I **love** the house where you live, O Lord, the place where
	31. 7	I will be glad and rejoice because of your **constant love.**
	31.16	save me in your **constant love.**
	31.21	How wonderfully he showed his **love** for me when I was
	31.23	**Love** the Lord, all his faithful people.
	32.10	who trust in the Lord are protected by his **constant love.**
	33. 5	The Lord **loves** what is righteous and just;
	33. 5	his **constant love** fills the earth.
	33.18	those who obey him, those who trust in his **constant love.**
	33.22	May your **constant love** be with us, Lord, as we put our
	36. 5	Lord, your **constant love** reaches the heavens;
	36. 7	How precious, O God, is your **constant love!**
	36.10	Continue to **love** those who know you and to do good to
	37.28	for the Lord **loves** what is right and does not abandon
	39.11	by your rebukes, and like a moth you destroy what he **loves.**
	40. 8	How I **love** to do your will, my God!
	40.10	I have not been silent about your loyalty and **constant love.**
	40.11	Your **love** and loyalty will always keep me safe.
	42. 8	May the Lord show his **constant love** during the day, so
	44. 3	of your presence, which showed that you **loved** them.
	44.26	Because of your **constant love** save us!
	45. 7	you **love** what is right and hate what is evil.
	47. 4	we live, the proud possession of his people, whom he **loves.**
	48. 9	Inside your Temple, O God, we think of your **constant love.**
	51. 1	Be merciful to me, O God, because of your **constant love.**
	52. 3	You **love** evil more than good and falsehood more than truth.
	52. 4	You **love** to hurt people with your words, you liar!
Ps	52. 8	I trust in his **constant love** for ever and ever.
	57. 3	God will show me his **constant love** and faithfulness.
	57.10	Your **constant love** reaches the heavens;
	59.10	My God **loves** me and will come to me;
	59.16	every morning I will sing aloud of your **constant love.**
	59.17	My refuge is God, the God who **loves** me.
	60. 5	our prayer, so that the people you **love** may be rescued.
	61. 7	protect him with your **constant love** and faithfulness.
	62.12	power belongs to him [12]and that his **love is constant.**
	63. 3	Your **constant love** is better than life itself, and so I
	66.20	reject my prayer or keep back his **constant love** from me.
	68.30	Scatter those people who **love** to make war!
	69.13	me because of your great **love,** because you keep your promise
	69.16	Answer me, Lord, in the goodness of your **constant love;**
	69.36	will inherit it, and those who **love** him will live there.
	77. 8	Has he stopped **loving** us?
	78.68	the tribe of Judah and Mount Zion, which he dearly **loves.**
	84. 1	How I **love** your Temple, Lord Almighty!
	85. 7	Show us your **constant love,** O Lord, and give us your
	85.10	**Love** and faithfulness will meet;
	86. 5	us and forgiving, full of **constant love** for all who pray to
	86.13	How great is your **constant love** for me!
	86.15	Lord, are a merciful and **loving** God, always patient, always
	87. 2	any other place in Israel he **loves** the city of Jerusalem.
	88.11	Is your **constant love** spoken of in the grave or your
	89. 1	O Lord, I will always sing of your **constant love;**
	89. 2	I know that your **love** will last for all time, that your
	89.14	**love** and faithfulness are shown in all you do.
	89.17	in your **love** you make us triumphant.
	89.24	I will **love** him and be loyal to him;
	89.33	But I will not stop **loving** David or fail to keep my
	89.49	Lord, where are the former proofs of your **love?**
	90.14	us each morning with your **constant love,** so that we may sing
	91.14	"I will save those who **love** me and will protect those who
	92. 2	High God, [2]to proclaim your **constant love** every morning and
	94.18	but your **constant love,** O Lord, held me up.
	97.10	The Lord **loves** those who hate evil;
	98. 3	people of Israel with loyalty and **constant love** for them.
	99. 4	Mighty king, you **love** what is right;
	100. 5	his **love** is eternal and his faithfulness lasts for ever.
	102.14	Your servants **love** her, even though she is destroyed;
	103. 4	keeps me from the grave and blesses me with **love** and mercy.
	103. 8	The Lord is merciful and **loving,**
	103. 8	slow to become angry and full of **constant love.**
	103.11	the earth, so great is his **love** for those who honour him.
	103.17	who honour the Lord, his **love** lasts for ever, and his
	106. 1	his **love** is eternal.
	106. 7	times he showed them his **love,** and they rebelled against the
	106.45	his covenant, and because of his great **love** he relented.
	107. 1	his **love** is eternal!"
	107. 8	thank the Lord for his **constant love,**
	107.15	thank the Lord for his **constant love,**
	107.21	thank the Lord for his **constant love,**
	107.31	thank the Lord for his **constant love,**
	107.43	may they consider the Lord's **constant love.**
	108. 4	Your **constant love** reaches above the heavens;
	108. 6	my prayer, so that the people you **love** may be rescued.
	109. 4	me, even though I **love** them and have prayed for them.
	109. 5	They pay me back evil for good and hatred for **love.**
	109.17	He **loved** to curse—may he be cursed!
	109.21	and rescue me because of the goodness of your **love.**
	109.26	because of your **constant love,** save me!
	115. 1	be given because of your **constant love** and faithfulness.
	116. 1	I **love** the Lord, because he hears me;
	117. 2	His **love** for us is strong and his faithfulness is eternal.
	118. 1	to the Lord, because he is good, and his **love** is eternal.
	118. 2	Let the people of Israel say, "His **love** is eternal."
	118. 3	Let the priests of God say, "His **love** is eternal."
	118. 4	Let all who worship him say, "His **love** is eternal."
	118.29	to the Lord, because he is good, and his **love** is eternal.
	119.41	Show me how much you **love** me, Lord, and save me
	119.47	I find pleasure in obeying your commands, because I **love** them.
	119.48	I respect and **love** your commandments;
	119.64	Lord, the earth is full of your **constant love;**
	119.76	Let your **constant love** comfort me, as you have promised me,
	119.88	Because of your **constant love** be good to me, so that I
	119.97	How I **love** your law!
	119.113	who are not completely loyal to you, but I **love** your law.
	119.119	the wicked like rubbish, and so I **love** your instructions.
	119.124	Treat me according to your **constant love,** and teach me your commands.
	119.127	I **love** your commands more than gold, more than the finest gold.
	119.132	mercy on me as you do on all those who **love** you.
	119.140	How I **love** it!
	119.149	Because your **love is constant,** hear me, O Lord;
	119.159	See how I **love** your instructions, Lord.
	119.159	Your **love** never changes, so save me!
	119.163	I hate and detest all lies, but I **love** your law.
	119.165	Those who **love** your law have perfect security, and
	119.167	I **love** them with all my heart.
	122. 6	"May those who **love** you prosper.
	127. 2	For the Lord provides for those he **loves,** while they are asleep.
	130. 7	the Lord, because his **love is constant** and he is always
	136	his **love** is eternal.
	138. 2	your name because of your **constant love** and faithfulness,
	138. 8	Lord, your **love** is eternal.
	143. 8	me each morning of your **constant love,** for I put my trust
	143.12	Because of your **love** for me, kill my enemies and destroy
	145. 8	The Lord is **loving** and merciful,
	145. 8	slow to become angry and full of **constant love.**
	145.20	He protects everyone who **loves** him,

Ps 146. 8 he **loves** his righteous people.
147.11 who honour him, in those who trust in his **constant love.**
Prov 3.12 The Lord corrects those he **loves,** as a father corrects a
4. 6 **love** her, and she will keep you safe.
4. 8 **Love** wisdom, and she will make you great.
5.15 faithful to your own wife and give your **love** to her alone.
5.19 let her surround you with her **love.**
5.20 Why should you give your **love** to another woman, my son?
7.18 Let's make **love** all night long.
8.17 I **love** those who love me;
8.21 giving wealth to those who **love** me,
8.36 anyone who hates me **loves** death."
10.12 Hate stirs up trouble, but **love** overlooks all offences.
11.20 The Lord hates evil-minded people, but **loves** those who do right.
12. 1 Anyone who **loves** knowledge wants to be told when he is wrong.
13.24 If you don't punish your son, you don't **love** him.
13.24 If you do **love** him, you will correct him.
15. 9 ways of evil people, but **loves** those who do what is right.
15.17 eat vegetables with people you **love** than to eat the finest
17.17 Friends always show their **love.**
18. 8 Gossip is so tasty—how we **love** to swallow it!
19.28 Wicked people **love** the taste of evil.
22. 5 If you **love** your life, stay away from the traps that catch
22.11 If you **love** purity of heart and graciousness of speech,
26.22 How we **love** to swallow it!
30.19 a man and a woman falling in **love.**
Ecc 3. 5 the time for making **love**
3. 5 the time for not making **love,**
3. 8 He sets the time for **love** and the time for hate,
5.10 If you **love** money, you will never be satisfied;
7.26 The **love** she offers you will catch you like a trap or
9. 1 of wise and righteous men, even their **love** and their hate.
9. 6 Their **loves,** their hates, their passions, all died with them.
9. 9 life with the woman you **love,** as long as you live the
Song 1. 2 your **love** is better than wine.
1. 3 No woman could help **loving** you.
1. 4 We will be happy together, drink deep, and lose ourselves in **love.**
1. 4 No wonder all women **love** you!
1. 7 Tell me, my **love,** Where will you lead your flock to graze?
1. 9 You, my **love,** excite men as a mare excites the stallions
1.15 How beautiful you are, my **love;**
1.15 how your eyes shine with **love!**
2. 3 I **love** to sit in its shadow, and its fruit is sweet
2. 4 his banqueting hall and raised the banner of **love** over me.
2. 7 deer and the gazelles that you will not interrupt our **love.**
2.10 Come then, my **love;**
2.13 Come then, my **love;**
3. 1 my bed, night after night I dreamt of the one I **love;**
3. 2 I looked for the one I **love.**
3. 5 deer and the gazelles that you will not interrupt our **love.**
3.10 purple cloth, **lovingly** woven by the women of Jerusalem.
4. 1 How beautiful you are, my **love!**
4. 1 How your eyes shine with **love** behind your veil.
4. 7 How beautiful you are, my **love;**
4.10 Your **love** delights me, my sweetheart and bride.
4.10 Your **love** is better than wine;
5. 1 Eat, lovers, and drink until you are drunk with **love!**
6. 4 My **love,** you are as beautiful as Jerusalem, as lovely as
6. 9 But I **love** only one, and she is as lovely as a
6.12 made me as eager for **love** as a chariot driver is for
7. 6 how complete the delights of your **love.**
7.12 There I will give you my **love.**
8. 2 you to my mother's house, where you could teach me **love.**
8. 4 Promise me, women of Jerusalem, that you will not interrupt our **love.**
8. 6 Close your heart to every **love** but mine;
8. 6 **Love** is as powerful as death;
8. 7 if anyone tried to buy **love** with his wealth, contempt is all
8.13 Let me hear your voice from the garden, my **love;**
Is 16. 5 and he will rule the people with faithfulness and **love.**
26.11 Show them how much you **love** your people.
43. 4 precious to me and because I **love** you and give you honour.
44. 2 you are my servant, my chosen people whom I **love.**
49.10 hurt them, for they will be led by one who **loves** them.
49.15 woman forget her own baby and not **love** the child she bore?
54. 7 with deep **love** I will take you back.
54. 8 only a moment, but I will show you my **love** for ever."
54.10 and hills may crumble, but my **love** for you will never end;
54.10 So says the Lord who **loves** you.
56. 6 part of his people, who **love** him and serve him, who observe
56.10 How they **love** to sleep!
61. 8 "I **love** justice and I hate oppression and crime.
62.12 called "The City That God **Loves,**" "The City That God Did
63. 7 I will tell of the Lord's unfailing **love;**
63. 7 people of Israel because of his mercy and **constant love.**
63. 9 In his **love** and compassion he rescued them.
63.15 Where are your **love** and compassion?
64.11 All the places we **loved** are in ruins.
66.10 be glad for her, all you that **love** this city!
66.12 by its mother, carried in her arms, and treated with **love.**
Jer 2. 2 were young, how you **loved** me when we were first married;
2.25 I have **loved** foreign gods and will go after them.' "
3. 4 my father, and you have **loved** me ever since I was a
3.13 tree you have given your **love** to foreign gods and that you
8. 2 stars, which these people have **loved** and served, and which
9.24 understands me, because my **love is constant,** and I do what
11.15 The Lord says, "The people I **love** are doing evil things.
12. 3 you see what I do, and how I **love** you.
12. 7 given the people I **love** into the power of their enemies.
14.10 says about these people, "They **love** to run away from me,
16. 5 bless my people with peace or show them **love** and mercy.

Jer 16. 7 or drink with anyone to comfort him when a **loved** one dies.
17.21 Tell them that if they **love** their lives, they must not
31. 3 I have always **loved** you,
31. 3 so I continue to show you my **constant love.**
31.20 "Israel, you are my dearest son, the child I **love** best.
31.20 Whenever I mention your name, I think of you with **love.**
32.18 You have shown **constant love** to thousands, but you also
33.11 Lord Almighty, because he is good and his **love** is eternal.'
Lam 2.13 O Jerusalem, **beloved** Jerusalem, what can I say?
2.20 Women are eating the bodies of the children they **loved!**
2.22 They murdered my children, whom I had reared and **loved.**
3.22 The Lord's unfailing **love** and mercy still continue, [23] Fresh as the morning,
3.32 bring us sorrow, but his **love** for us is sure and strong.
4.10 **loving** mothers boiled their own children for food.
Ezek 11.21 punish the people who **love** to worship filthy, disgusting idols.
16. 5 When you were born, no one **loved** you.
16. 8 saw that the time had come for you to fall in **love.**
16. 8 your naked body with my coat and promised to **love** you.
16.32 adultery with strangers instead of **loving** her husband.
20. 7 away the disgusting idols they **loved** and not to make
24.16 blow I am going to take away the person you **love** most.
33.31 **Loving** words are on their lips, but they continue their greedy ways.
33.32 thân an entertainer singing **love** songs or playing a harp.
Dan 9. 4 to your covenant and show **constant love** to those who love
9.23 He **loves** you, and so I have come to tell you the
10.11 The angel said to me, "Daniel, God **loves** you.
10.19 He said, "God **loves** you, so don't let anything worry
11.37 god his ancestors served, and also the god that women **love.**
Hos 1. 6 I will no longer show **love** to the people of Israel or
1. 7 But to the people of Judah I will show **love.**
2.14 there I will win her back with words of **love.**
2.19 I will show you **constant love** and mercy and make you mine
2.23 I will show **love** to those who were called "Unloved," and
3. 1 "Go again and show your **love** for a woman who is committing
3. 1 You must **love** her just as I still love the people of
4. 1 "There is no faithfulness or **love** in the land, and the
6. 4 Your **love** for me disappears as quickly as morning mist;
6. 6 I want your **constant love,** not your animal sacrifices.
9. 1 the god Baal and have **loved** the corn you thought he paid
9.10 Baal, and soon became as disgusting as the gods they **loved.**
9.15 I will not **love** them any more;
11. 1 Israel was a child, I **loved** him and called him out of
11. 4 I drew them to me with affection and **love.**
11. 8 My **love** for you is too strong.
12. 7 they **love** to cheat their customers with false scales.
14. 4 I will **love** them with all my heart;
Amos 4. 5 This is the kind of thing you **love** to do.
5.15 Hate what is evil, **love** what is right, and see that
Jon 4. 2 knew that you are a **loving** and merciful God, always patient,
Mic 1.16 cut off your hair in mourning for the children you **love.**
2. 9 out of the homes they **love,** and you have robbed their
3. 2 yet you hate what is good and you **love** what is evil.
6. 8 what is just, to show **constant love,** and to live in humble
7.18 but you take pleasure in showing us your **constant love.**
7.20 show your faithfulness and **constant love** to your people,
Zeph 3.17 in you, and in his **love** he will give you new life.
Zech 1.14 "I have a deep **love** and concern for Jerusalem, my holy
2.12 land, and Jerusalem will be the city he **loves** most of all.
3. 2 May the Lord, who **loves** Jerusalem, condemn you.
8. 2 Jerusalem because of my deep **love** for her people,
8. 2 a **love** which has made me angry
8.19 You must **love** truth and peace."
Mal 1. 2 The Lord says to his people, "I have always **loved** you."
1. 2 But they reply, "How have you shown your **love** for us?"
1. 2 were brothers, but I have **loved** Jacob and his descendants,
2.11 They have defiled the Temple which the Lord **loves.**
Mt 5.43 heard that it was said, '**Love** your friends, hate your enemies.'
5.44 **love** your enemies and pray for those who persecute you,
5.46 God reward you if you **love** only the people who love you?
6. 5 They **love** to stand up and pray in the houses of worship
6.24 he will hate one and **love** the other;
10.37 "Whoever **loves** his father or mother more than me is not
10.37 whoever **loves** his son or daughter more than me is not fit
12.18 have chosen, the one I **love,** and with whom I am pleased.
13.22 about this life and the **love** for riches choke the message,
19.19 and love your neighbour as you **love** yourself."
22.37 Jesus answered, "'**Love** the Lord your God with all your heart,
22.39 '**Love** your neighbour as you love yourself.'
23. 6 They **love** the best places at feasts and the reserved seats
23. 7 they **love** to be greeted with respect in the market-places
24.12 the spread of evil that many people's **love** will grow cold.
Mk 4.19 worries about this life, the **love** for riches, and all other
10.21 looked straight at him with **love** and said, "You need only
12.30 **Love** the Lord your God with all your heart, with all
12.31 '**Love** your neighbour as you love yourself.'
12.33 And man must **love** God with all his heart and with all
12.33 and he must **love** his neighbour as he loves himself.
Lk 6.27 **Love** your enemies, do good to those who hate you, [28] bless
6.32 "If you **love** only the people who love you, why should
6.32 Even sinners love those who **love** them!
6.35 **Love** your enemies and do good to them;
7. 5 He **loves** our people and he himself built a synagogue for us."
7.42 Which one, then, will **love** him more?"
7.47 tell you, then, the great **love** she has shown proves that her
7.47 But whoever has been forgiven little shows only a little **love.**"
10.27 The man answered, "'**Love** the Lord your God with all
10.27 and '**Love** your neighbour as you love yourself.' "
11.42 the other herbs, but you neglect justice and **love** for God.
11.43 You **love** the reserved seats in the synagogues and to be

Lk 14.26 be my disciple unless he **loves** me more
14.26 than he **loves** his father and his mother,
16.13 he will hate one and **love** the other;
16.14 heard all this, they sneered at Jesus, because they **loved** money.
20.46 in their long robes and **love** to be greeted with respect in
Jn 3.16 For God **loved** the world so much that he gave his only
3.19 world, but people **love** the darkness rather than the light,
3.35 The Father **loves** his Son and has put everything in his power.
5.20 For the Father **loves** the Son and shows him all that he
5.42 I know that you have no **love** for God in your hearts.
8.42 were your Father, you would **love** me, because I came from God
10.17 "The Father **loves** me because I am willing to give up my
11. 5 Jesus **loved** Martha and her sister and Lazarus.
11.36 "See how much he **loved** him!"
12.25 Whoever **loves** his own life will lose it;
12.43 They **loved** the approval of men rather than the approval of God.
13. 1 He had always **loved** those in the world who were his own,
13. 1 and he **loved** them to the very end.
13.23 disciples, the one whom Jesus **loved,** was sitting next to Jesus.
13.34 **love** one another.
13.34 As I have loved you, so you must **love** one another.
13.35 If you have **love** for one another, then everyone will know
14.15 "If you **love** me, you will obey my commandments.
14.21 my commandments and obeys them is the one who **loves** me.
14.21 My Father will **love** whoever loves me;
14.21 I too will **love** him and reveal myself to him."
14.23 Jesus answered him, "Whoever **loves** me will obey my teaching.
14.23 My Father will **love** him, and my Father and I will come
14.24 Whoever does not **love** me does not obey my teaching.
14.28 If you **loved** me, you would be glad that I am going
14.31 but the world must know that I **love** the Father;
15. 9 I **love** you just as the Father loves me;
15. 9 remain in my **love.**
15.10 you will remain in my **love,** just as I
15.10 have obeyed my Father's commands and remain in his **love.**
15.12 **love** one another, just as I love you.
15.13 The greatest **love** a person can have for his friends is
15.17 **love** one another.
15.19 to the world, then the world would **love** you as its own.
16.27 ask him on your behalf, [27] for the Father himself **loves** you.
16.27 He loves you because you **love** me and have believed that I
17.23 you sent me and that you **love** them as you love me.
17.24 for you **loved** me before the world was made.
17.26 so, in order that the **love** you have for me may be
19.26 Jesus saw his mother and the disciple he **loved** standing there;
20. 2 disciple, whom Jesus **loved,** and told them, "They have taken
21. 7 The disciple whom Jesus **loved** said to Peter, "It is the Lord!"
21.15 son of John, do you **love** me more than these others do?"
21.15 "Yes, Lord," he answered, "you know that I **love** you."
21.16 Jesus said to him, "Simon son of John, do you **love** me?"
21.16 "Yes, Lord," he answered, "you know that I **love** you."
21.17 time Jesus said, "Simon son of John, do you **love** me?"
21.17 because Jesus asked him the third time, "Do you **love** me?"
21.17 you know that I **love** you!"
21.20 other disciple, whom Jesus **loved**—the one who had leaned close
Rom 1. 7 you in Rome whom God **loves** and has called to be his
5. 5 God has poured out his **love** into our hearts by means of
5. 8 shown us how much he **loves** us—it was while we were
8.28 for good with those who **love** him, those whom he has called
8.35 Who, then, can separate us from the **love** of Christ?
8.37 these things we have complete victory through him who **loved** us!
8.38 For I am certain that nothing can separate us from his **love:**
8.39 to separate us from the **love** of God which is ours through
9.13 As the scripture says, "I **loved** Jacob, but I hated Esau."
9.25 The nation that I did not **love**
9.25 I will call 'My **Beloved.**'
12. 9 **Love** must be completely sincere.
12.10 **Love** one another warmly as Christian brothers, and be eager to
13. 8 no one—the only obligation you have is to **love** one another.
13. 9 in the one command, **"Love** your neighbour as you love yourself."
13.10 If you **love** someone, you will never do him wrong;
13.10 to **love,** then, is to obey the whole Law.
14.15 something you eat, then you are no longer acting from **love.**
15.30 our Lord Jesus Christ and by the **love** that the Spirit gives:
1 Cor 2. 9 is the very thing God prepared for those who **love** him."
4.21 you with a whip, or in a spirit of **love** and gentleness?
8. 1 but **love** builds up.
8. 3 But the person who **loves** God is known by him.
13. 1 but if I have no **love,** my speech is no more than
13. 2 to move mountains—but if I have no **love,** I am nothing.
13. 3 —but if I have no **love,** this does me no good.
13. 4 **Love** is patient and kind;
13. 5 **love** is not ill-mannered or selfish or irritable;
13. 5 **love** does not keep a record of wrongs;
13. 6 **love** is not happy with evil, but is happy with the truth.
13. 7 **Love** never gives up;
13. 8 **Love** is eternal.
13.13 faith, hope, and **love;**
13.13 and the greatest of these is **love.**
14. 1 It is **love,** then, that you should strive for.
16.14 Do all your work in **love.**
16.22 Whoever does not **love** the Lord—a curse on him!
16.24 My **love** be with you all in Christ Jesus.
2 Cor 2. 4 sad, but to make you realize how much I **love** you all.
2. 8 beg you to let him know that you really do **love** him.
5.14 We are ruled by the **love** of Christ, now that we
6. 6 Holy Spirit, by our true **love,** [7] by our message of truth,
7.15 And so his **love** for you grows stronger, as he remembers
8. 6 continue it and help you complete this special service of **love.**
8. 7 in your eagerness to help and in your **love** for us.
8. 7 we want you to be generous also in this service of **love.**
2 Cor 8. 8 I am trying to find out how real your own **love** is.
8.19 carry out this service of **love** for the sake of the Lord's
8.24 Show your **love** to them, so that all the churches will be
9. 7 for God **loves** the one who gives gladly.
11.11 Do I say this because I don't **love** you?
11.11 God knows I **love** you!
12.15 Will you **love** me less because I love you so much?
13.11 And the God of **love** and peace will be with you.
13.13 the Lord Jesus Christ, the **love** of God, and the fellowship
Gal 2.20 the Son of God, who **loved** me and gave his life for
5. 6 what matters is faith that works through **love.**
5.13 Instead, let **love** make you serve one another.
5.14 **"Love** your neighbour as you love yourself."
5.22 But the Spirit produces **love,** joy, peace, patience, kindness,
Eph 1. 4 Because of his **love** [5] God had already decided that through
1.15 the Lord Jesus and your **love** for all God's people, [16] I
2. 4 is so abundant, and his **love** for us is so great, [5] that
2. 7 of his grace in the **love** he showed us in Christ Jesus.
3.17 roots and foundation in **love,** [18] so that you, together with
3.18 how broad and long, how high and deep, is Christ's **love.**
3.19 you come to know his **love**—although it can never be fully
4. 2 Show your **love** by being tolerant with one another.
4.15 truth in a spirit of **love,** we must grow up in every
4.16 the whole body grows and builds itself up through **love.**
5. 2 life must be controlled by **love,** just as Christ loved us
5.25 Husbands, **love** your wives just as Christ loved the church and
5.28 to love their wives just as they **love** their own bodies.
5.28 A man who **loves** his wife loves himself.
5.33 every husband must **love** his wife as himself, and every wife
6.23 Christ give to all Christian brothers peace and **love** with faith.
6.24 all those who love our Lord Jesus Christ with undying **love.**
Phil 1. 9 I pray that your **love** will keep on growing more and more,
1.16 These do so from **love,** because they know that God has
2. 1 life in Christ makes you strong, and his **love** comforts you.
2. 2 same thoughts, sharing the same **love,** and being one in soul
Col 1. 4 faith in Christ Jesus and of your **love** for all God's people.
1. 5 So your faith and **love** are based on what you hope for,
1. 8 has told us of the **love** that the Spirit has given you.
2. 2 may be drawn together in **love,** and so have the full wealth
3.12 he **loved** you and chose you for his own.
3.14 all these qualities add **love,** which binds all things together
3.19 Husbands, **love** your wives and do not be harsh with them.
1 Thes 1. 3 faith into practice, how your **love** made you work so hard,
1. 4 brothers, we know that God **loves** you and has chosen you to
2. 8 Because of our **love** for you we were ready to share with
3. 6 has brought us the welcome news about your faith and **love.**
3.12 May the Lord make your **love** for one another and for all
3.12 more and more and become as great as our **love** for you.
4. 9 need to write to you about **love** for your fellow-believers.
4. 9 have been taught by God how you should **love** one another.
5. 8 We must wear faith and **love** as a breastplate, and our hope
5.13 the greatest respect and **love** because of the work they do.
2 Thes 1. 3 growing so much and the **love** each of you has for the
2.10 they did not welcome and **love** the truth so as to be
2.13 God at all times for you, brothers, you whom the Lord **loves.**
2.16 and God our Father, who **loved** us and in his grace gave
3. 5 a greater understanding of God's **love** and the endurance that is
1 Tim 1. 5 order is to arouse the **love** that comes from a pure heart,
1.14 gave me the faith and **love** which are ours in union with
2.15 if she perseveres in faith and **love** and holiness, with modesty.
3. 3 he must not **love** money;
4.12 in your speech, your conduct, your **love,** faith, and purity.
6. 2 those who benefit from their work are believers whom they **love.**
6.10 For the **love** of money is a source of all kinds of
6.11 Strive for righteousness, godliness, faith, **love,** endurance,
2 Tim 1. 7 his Spirit fills us with power, **love,** and self-control.
1.13 remain in the faith and **love** that are ours in union with
2.22 strive for righteousness, faith, **love,** and peace, together with
3. 4 they will **love** pleasure rather than God;
3.10 faith, my patience, my **love,** my endurance, [11] my persecutions,
4. 8 but to all those who wait with **love** for him to appear.
4.10 Demas fell in **love** with this present world and has deserted me,
Tit 1. 8 He must be hospitable and **love** what is good.
2. 2 to be sound in their faith, **love,** and endurance.
2. 4 train the younger women to **love** their husbands and children,
3. 4 But when the kindness and **love** of God our Saviour was revealed,
Phlm 5 For I hear of your **love** for all God's people and the
7 Your **love,** dear brother, has brought me great joy and much
9 But because I **love** you, I make a request instead.
Heb 1. 9 You **love** what is right and hate what is wrong.
6.10 work you did or the **love** you showed for him in the
10.24 another, to help one another to show **love** and to do good.
12. 6 the Lord corrects everyone he **loves,** and punishes everyone he
13. 1 Keep on **loving** one another as Christian brothers.
13. 5 your lives free from the **love** of money, and be satisfied
Jas 1.12 the life which God has promised to those who **love** him.
2. 5 possess the kingdom which he promised to those who **love** him.
2. 8 in the scripture, **"Love** your neighbour as you love yourself."
1 Pet 1. 8 You **love** him, although you have not seen him, and you
1.22 come to have a sincere **love** for your fellow-believers,
1.22 **love** one another earnestly
2.17 Respect everyone, **love** your fellow-believers, honour God,
3. 8 **love** one another as brothers, and be kind and humble with
4. 8 **love** one another earnestly, because love covers over many sins.
5.14 Greet one another with the kiss of Christian **love.**
2 Pet 1. 7 and to your brotherly affection add **love.**
2.15 Balaam son of Beor, who **loved** the money he would get for
1 Jn 2. 5 word is the one whose **love** for God has really been made
2.10 Whoever **loves** his brother lives in the light,
2.15 Do not **love** the world or anything that belongs to the world.
2.15 If you **love** the world, you do not love the Father.

1 Jn 3. 1 See how much the Father has **loved** us!
3. 1 His **love** is so great that we are called God's children—
3.10 is right or does not **love** his brother is not God's child.
3.11 we must **love** one another.
3.14 we know it because we **love** our brothers.
3.14 Whoever does not **love** is still under the power of death.
3.16 This is how we know what **love** is:
3.17 against his brother, how can he claim that he **loves** God?
3.18 My children, our **love** should not be just words and talk;
3.18 it must be true **love**, which shows itself in action.
3.23 Son Jesus Christ and **love** one another, just as Christ commanded
4. 7 friends, let us **love** one another, because love comes from God.
4. 7 Whoever **loves** is a child of God and knows God.
4. 8 Whoever does not love does not know God, for God is **love.**
4. 9 And God showed his **love** for us by sending his only Son
4.10 This is what **love** is:
4.10 is not that we have **loved** God,
4.10 but that he **loved** us and sent his Son
4.11 if this is how God **loved** us,
4.11 then we should **love** one another.
4.12 seen God, but if we **love** one another, God lives in
4.12 union with us, and his **love** is made perfect in us.
4.16 ourselves know and believe the **love** which God has for us.
4.16 God is **love,**
4.16 and whoever lives in **love** lives in union with God
4.17 **Love** is made perfect in us in order that we may have
4.18 There is no fear in **love;**
4.18 perfect **love** drives out all fear.
4.18 So then, **love** has not been made perfect in anyone who is
4.19 We **love** because God first loved us.
4.20 If someone says he **loves** God, but hates his brother, he
4.20 For he cannot **love** God, whom he has not seen,
4.20 if he does not **love** his brother, whom he has seen.
4.21 whoever loves God must **love** his brother also.
5. 1 and whoever loves a father **loves** his child also.
5. 2 This is how we know that we **love** God's children:
5. 2 it is by **loving** God and obeying his commands.
5. 3 For our **love** for God means that we obey his commands.
2 Jn 1 To the dear Lady and to her children, whom I truly **love.**
1 all who know the truth **love** you, [2]because the truth remains
3 may they be ours in truth and **love.**
5 let us all **love** one another.
6 This **love** I speak of means that we must live in obedience
6 from the beginning, is that you must all live in **love.**
3 Jn 1 From the Elder— To my dear Gaius, whom I truly **love.**
6 They have spoken to the church here about your **love.**
Jude 1 who live in the **love** of God the Father and the
2 May mercy, peace, and **love** be yours in full measure.
21 and keep yourselves in the **love** of God, as you wait for
Rev 1. 5 He **loves** us, and by his sacrificial death he has freed us
2. 4 you do not **love** me now as you did at first.
2.19 I know your **love,** your faithfulness, your service,
3. 9 They will all know that I **love** you.
3.19 I rebuke and punish all whom I **love.**
20. 9 the camp of God's people and the city that he **loves.**

LOVED-BY-THE-LORD

Hos 2. 1 call your fellow-Israelites "God's People" and **"Loved-by-the-Lord."**

LOVELY

Gen 29.17 Leah had **lovely** eyes, but Rachel was shapely and beautiful.
49.21 "Naphtali is a deer that runs free, Who bears **lovely** fawns.
Song 1. 8 Don't you know the place, **loveliest** of women?
2.14 Let me see your **lovely** face and hear your enchanting voice.
4. 3 how **lovely** they are when you speak.
5.13 His cheeks are as **lovely** as a garden
6. 4 as beautiful as Jerusalem, as **lovely** as the city of Tirzah,
6. 9 I love only one, and she is as **lovely** as a dove.
7. 4 Your nose is as **lovely** as the tower of Lebanon that stands
Jer 12.10 they have turned my **lovely** land into a desert.
Lam 2.15 "Is this that **lovely** city?
Ezek 16.14 beauty, because I was the one who made you so **lovely."**
Phil 4. 8 that are true, noble, right, pure, **lovely,** and honourable.

LOVER

Song 1.13 My **lover** has the scent of myrrh
1.14 My **lover** is like the wild flowers that bloom
2. 8 I hear my **lover's** voice.
2. 9 My **lover** is like a gazelle, like a young stag.
2.10 My **lover** speaks to me.
2.16 My **lover** is mine, and I am his.
3. 3 I asked them, "Have you found my **lover?"**
4.16 Let my **lover** come to his garden and eat
5. 1 Eat, **lovers,** and drink until you are drunk with love!
5. 2 I dreamt my **lover** knocked at the door.
5. 4 My **lover** put his hand to the door, and I was thrilled
5. 6 I opened the door for my **lover,** but he had already gone.
5. 8 that if you find my **lover,** you will tell him I am
5. 9 is your **lover** different from everyone else?
5.10 My **lover** is handsome and strong;
5.16 This is what my **lover** is like, women of Jerusalem.
6. 1 Most beautiful of women, where has your **lover** gone?
6. 1 Tell us which way your **lover** went, so that we can help
6. 2 My **lover** has gone to his garden, where the balsam-trees grow.
6. 3 My **lover** is mine, and I am his;
7. 9 flow straight to my **lover,** flowing over his lips and teeth.
7.10 I belong to my **lover,** and he desires me.
Song 8. 5 is this coming from the desert, arm in arm with her **lover?**
8.10 My **lover** knows that with him I find contentment and peace.
8.14 Come to me, my **lover,** like a gazelle, like a young stag
Is 47. 8 "Listen to this, you **lover** of pleasure,
57. 8 your large beds with your **lovers,** whom you pay to sleep with
Jer 2.33 You certainly know how to chase after **lovers.**
3. 1 Israel, you have had many **lovers,** and now you want to return
3. 2 You waited for **lovers** along the roadside, as an Arab waits
4.30 Your **lovers** have rejected you and want to kill you.
30.14 All your **lovers** have forgotten you;
Ezek 16.33 gave presents to all your **lovers** and bribed them to come
16.36 yourself to your **lovers** and to all your disgusting idols,
16.37 will bring all your former **lovers** together—
16.41 a prostitute and make you stop giving gifts to your **lovers.**
23. 5 prostitute and was full of lust for her **lovers** from Assyria.
23. 9 her over to her Assyrian **lovers** whom she wanted so much.
23.22 You are tired of those **lovers,** but I will make them angry
Hos 2. 4 "I will go to my **lovers**—they give me food and water,
2. 7 She will run after her **lovers** but will not catch them.
2.10 naked in front of her **lovers,** and no one will be able
2.12 which she said her **lovers** gave her for serving them.
2.13 Baal and put on her jewellery to go chasing after her **lovers.**
3. 1 love for a woman who is committing adultery with a **lover.**

LOVING see LOVE

AV LOVINGKINDNESS see LOVE

LOW

Ex 28.26 and attach them to the **lower** corners of the breast-piece on
28.27 and attach them to the **lower** part of the front of the
28.33 All round its **lower** hem put pomegranates of blue,
39.19 and attached them to the **lower** corners of the breast-piece,
39.20 and attached them to the **lower** part of the front of the
39.24 All round its **lower** hem they put pomegranates of
Lev 13.45 his hair uncombed, cover the **lower** part of his face, and
25.16 years, the price shall be **lower,** because what is being sold
27. 8 the priest will set a **lower** price, according to the ability
Josh 15.19 So Caleb gave her the upper and **lower** springs.
16. 3 of the Japhletites, as far as the area of **Lower** Beth Horon.
18.13 to Ataroth Addar, on the mountain south of **Lower** Beth Horon.
Judg 1.15 So Caleb gave her the upper and **lower** springs.
1 Kgs 1.16 Bathsheba bowed **low** before the king, and he asked,
1.23 was there, and Nathan went in and bowed **low** before the king.
1.31 Bathsheba bowed **low** and said, "May my lord the king
1.53 to the king and bowed **low** before him, and the king said
6. 6 Each room in the **lowest** storey was 2.2 metres wide, in the
6. 8 The entrance to the **lowest** storey of the annexe was on
9.17 forced labour, Solomon also rebuilt **Lower** Beth Horon,
18. 7 He recognized him, bowed **low** before him, and asked, "Is it
2 Kgs 2.17 went and looked high and **low** for Elijah for three days, but
18.24 no match for even the **lowest** ranking Assyrian official, and
1 Chr 7.24 the towns of Upper and **Lower** Beth Horon, and Uzzen Sheerah.
15.17 To play the **low-pitched** harps they chose the following Levites:
21.16 sackcloth—bowed **low,** with their faces touching the ground.
21.21 and bowed **low,** with his face touching the ground.
29.20 their ancestors, and they bowed **low** and gave honour to the
2 Chr 8. 5 Upper Beth Horon and **Lower** Beth Horon (fortified cities with
20.18 Then King Jehoshaphat bowed **low,**
Ps 35.13 prayed with my head bowed **low,** [14]as I would pray for a
Is 17. 6 very top, or a few that are left on the **lower** branches.
19. 5 The water will be **low** in the Nile, and the river will
36. 9 no match for even the **lowest** ranking Assyrian official, and
49. 7 also will see it, and they will bow **low** to honour you."
49.23 They will bow **low** before you and honour you;
58. 5 you bow your heads **low** like a blade of grass, and spread
60.14 oppressed you will come And bow **low** to show their respect.
Ezek 8.16 the sanctuary and were bowing **low** towards the east,
17. 6 The plant sprouted and became a **low,** wide-spreading grapevine.
40.12 the guardrooms there was a **low** wall fifty centimetres high
40.18 This outer courtyard was at a **lower** level
41. 7 possible to go from the **lower** storey to the middle and the
42. 5 those at the middle and **lower** levels because they were set
42. 7 At the **lower** level the outer wall of the building was
43.14 The **lowest** section of the altar, from the top of the base,
Zeph 1.11 you that live in the **lower** part of the city, because all
Lk 14. 9 would be embarrassed and have to sit in the **lowest** place.
14.10 go and sit in the **lowest** place, so that your host will
Eph 4. 9 that first he came down to the **lowest** depths of the earth.
Heb 2. 7 You made him for a little while **lower** than the angels;
2. 9 a little while was made **lower** than the angels, so that

LOWER

Gen 24.14 to one of them, 'Please, **lower** your jar and let me have
24.18 said, "Drink, sir," and quickly **lowered** her jar from her
24.46 She quickly **lowered** her jar from her shoulder and said,
44.11 So they quickly **lowered** their sacks to the ground, and
Acts 9.25 through an opening in the wall, **lowering** him in a basket.
10.11 like a large sheet being **lowered** by its four corners to the
11. 5 a large sheet being **lowered** by its four corners from heaven,
27.17 coast of Libya, so they **lowered** the sail and let the ship
27.29 on the rocks, so they **lowered** four anchors from the back
27.30 they **lowered** the boat into the water and pretended that they

LOWLANDS

Deut 1. 7 the hill-country and the **lowlands,** to the southern region,

LOWLY

Ps 10.17 You will listen, O Lord, to the prayers of the **lowly;**
138. 6 above, you care for the **lowly,** and the proud cannot hide
Zeph 3.12 leave there a humble and **lowly** people, who will come to me
Lk 1.48 God my Saviour, [48] for he has remembered me, his **lowly** servant!
1.52 down mighty kings from their thrones, and lifted up the **lowly.**

LOYAL

Gen 20.13 her, 'You can show how **loyal** you are to me by telling
21.23 I have been **loyal** to you,
21.23 that you will also be **loyal** to me and to this country
Num 14.24 different attitude and has remained **loyal** to me, I will
32.11 because they did not remain **loyal** to me, none of the men
32.12 they remained **loyal** to the Lord.
Deut 33. 9 They showed greater **loyalty** to you Than to parents,
Josh 24.23 he demanded, "and pledge your **loyalty** to the Lord, the God
Judg 9.28 Be **loyal** to your ancestor Hamor, who founded your clan!
Ruth 3.10 are showing even greater family **loyalty** in what you are
1 Sam 18.17 a brave and **loyal** soldier, and fight the Lord's battles."
20.14 alive, please keep your sacred promise and be **loyal** to me;
20.15 show the same kind of **loyalty** to my family for ever.
29. 6 the living God of Israel that you have been **loyal** to me;
29. 9 "I consider you as **loyal** as an angel of God.
2 Sam 2. 5 you for showing your **loyalty** to your king by burying him.
2.10 the tribe of Judah was **loyal** to David, [11] and he ruled in
3. 6 David's forces and the forces **loyal** to Saul's family, Abner
3. 8 very first I have been **loyal** to the cause of your father
9. 3 to whom I can show **loyalty** and kindness, as I promised God
10. 2 David said, "I must show **loyal** friendship to Hanun, as his
15. 6 came to the king for justice, and so he won their **loyalty.**
15.13 "The Israelites are pledging their **loyalty** to Absalom."
16.17 "What has happened to your **loyalty** to your friend David?"
19.14 David's words won the complete **loyalty** of all the men of Judah,
20. 2 the men of Judah remained **loyal** and followed David from the
20.19 a great city, one of the most peaceful and **loyal** in Israel.
1 Kgs 1.52 Solomon replied, "If he is **loyal,** not even a hair on
3. 6 servant, and he was good, **loyal,** and honest in his relations
11. 2 cause the Israelites to give their **loyalty** to other gods.
12. 4 make life easier for us, we will be your **loyal** subjects."
12. 7 to their request, and they will always serve you **loyally."**
12.20 Only the tribe of Judah remained **loyal** to David's descendants.
14. 8 David, who was completely **loyal** to me, obeyed my commands,
15. 3 father and was not completely **loyal** to the Lord his God, as
19.18 Israel—all those who are **loyal** to me and have not bowed
2 Kgs 2. 2 answered, "I swear by my **loyalty** to the living Lord and to
2. 4 answered, "I swear by my **loyalty** to the living Lord and to
2. 6 answered, "I swear by my **loyalty** to the living Lord and to
4.30 Elisha, "I swear by my **loyalty** to the living Lord and to
20. 3 have served you faithfully and **loyally,** and that I have
1 Chr 12.23 (most of the people of Benjamin had remained **loyal** to Saul);
12.23 50,000 **loyal** and reliable men ready to fight, trained to use
19. 2 David said, "I must show **loyal** friendship to Hanun, as his
29.24 David's other sons promised to be **loyal** to Solomon as king.
2 Chr 10. 4 make life easier for us, we will be your **loyal** subjects."
10. 7 a considerate answer, they will always serve you **loyally."**
16. 9 to give strength to those whose hearts are **loyal** to him.
24.22 The king forgot about the **loyal** service that Zechariah's
31.21 in a spirit of complete **loyalty** and devotion to his God.
36.13 forced him to swear in God's name that he would be **loyal.**
Job 6.14 trouble like this I need **loyal** friends— whether I've
Ps 32. 6 So all your **loyal** people should pray to you in times of
40.10 I have not been silent about your **loyalty** and constant love.
40.11 Your love and **loyalty** will always keep me safe.
51.10 me, O God, and put a new and **loyal** spirit in me.
78.37 They were not **loyal** to him;
85.11 Man's **loyalty** will reach up from the earth, and God's
86. 2 Save me from death, because I am **loyal** to you;
89.24 I will love him and be **loyal** to him;
98. 3 people of Israel with **loyalty** and constant love for them.
101. 1 My song is about **loyalty** and justice, and I sing it to
119.113 those who are not completely **loyal** to you, but I love your
Prov 3. 3 Never let go of **loyalty** and faithfulness.
16. 6 Be **loyal** and faithful, and God will forgive your sin.
18.24 do not last, but some friends are more **loyal** than brothers.
20. 6 Everyone talks about how **loyal** and faithful he is, but
Is 38. 3 have served you faithfully and **loyally,** and that I have
45.23 come and kneel before me and vow to be **loyal** to me.
Jer 2.19 the Lord your God, and no longer to remain **loyal** to me.
Ezek 14. 5 me, but by my answer I hope to win back their **loyalty.**
17.13 made a treaty with him, and made him swear to be **loyal.**
Dan 6.16 to Daniel, "May your God, whom you serve so **loyally,** rescue
6.20 the God you serve so **loyally** able to save you from the
Hos 12. 6 Be **loyal** and just, and wait patiently for your God to act.
Jon 2. 8 Those who worship worthless idols have abandoned their **loyalty**
Mic 7. 2 an honest person left in the land, no one **loyal** to God.
Zeph 1. 5 who worship me and swear **loyalty** to me, but then take oaths
Mt 6.24 he will be **loyal** to one and despise the other.
Lk 16.13 he will be **loyal** to one and despise the other.
Rom 16.10 Greetings to Apelles, whose **loyalty** to Christ has been proved.
16.19 Everyone has heard of your **loyalty** to the gospel,
2 Cor 9.13 glory to God for your **loyalty** to the gospel of Christ,
10. 6 have proved your complete **loyalty,** we will be ready to punish
2 Tim 2. 3 Take your part in suffering, as a **loyal** soldier of Christ Jesus.
Rev 17. 6 those who were killed because they had been **loyal** to Jesus.

LUCK
[UNLUCKY]

Gen 30.11 Leah said, "I have been **lucky";**
Ecc 5.14 lose it all in some **unlucky** deal and end up with nothing
9.11 Bad **luck** happens to everyone.
11. 2 know what kind of bad **luck** you are going to have in
Is 65.11 hill, and worship Gad and Meni, the gods of **luck** and fate.
Lk 12.19 Then I will say to myself, **Lucky** man!
23.29 when people will say, 'How **lucky** are the women who never had

LUKEWARM

Rev 3.16 But because you are **lukewarm,** neither hot nor cold, I am

LULLED

Judg 16.14 Delilah then **lulled** him to sleep, took his seven locks of hair,
16.19 Delilah **lulled** Samson to sleep in her lap and then

Am LUMBER see TIMBER

LUMP

Job 38.38 out the rain, [38] rain that hardens the dust into **lumps?**
Rom 9.21 two pots from the same **lump** of clay, one for special

LUNCH

Lk 14.12 host, "When you give a **lunch** or a dinner, do not invite

LUST

Job 31. 1 made a solemn promise never to look with **lust** at a girl.
Is 57. 8 And there you satisfy your **lust.**
Jer 5. 8 wild with desire, each **lusting** for his neighbour's wife.
13.27 like a man **lusting** after his neighbour's wife
Ezek 16.26 You let your **lustful** neighbours, the Egyptians, go to bed with you,
22. 9 Some are always satisfying their **lusts.**
23. 5 prostitute and was full of **lust** for her lovers from Assyria.
23. 7 the Assyrian officers, and her **lust** led her to defile
23.12 She too was full of **lust** for the Assyrian noblemen and
23.16 them, she was filled with **lust** and sent messengers to them
23.20 She was filled with **lust** for oversexed men
23.20 who had all the **lustfulness** of donkeys and stallions."
23.27 put a stop to your **lust** and to the obscenities you have
23.29 Your **lust** and your prostitution [30] have brought this on you.
23.35 me, you will suffer for your **lust** and your prostitution."
2 Cor 12.21 immoral things they have done—their **lust** and their sexual sins.
Col 3. 5 such as sexual immorality, indecency, **lust,** evil passions,
1 Thes 4. 5 honourable way, [5] not with a **lustful** desire, like the heathen
1 Pet 4. 3 lives were spent in indecency, **lust,** drunkenness, orgies,
2 Pet 1. 4 may escape from the destructive **lust** that is in the world,
2.10 who follow their filthy bodily **lusts** and despise God's authority.
2.18 and use immoral bodily **lusts** to trap those who are just
3. 3 people will appear whose lives are controlled by their own **lusts.**
Jude 23 but hate their very clothes, stained by their sinful **lusts.**
Rev 14. 8 drink her wine—the strong wine of her immoral **lust!"**
18. 3 have drunk her wine—the strong wine of her immoral **lust.**
18. 3 the businessmen of the world grew rich from her unrestrained **lust."**
18. 9 part in her immorality and **lust** will cry and weep over the

LUXURY

Prov 19.10 Fools should not live in **luxury,** and slaves should not
21.17 **luxuries,** wine, and rich food will never make you wealthy.
21.20 people live in wealth and **luxury,** but stupid people spend
Lam 4. 5 those raised in **luxury** are pawing through refuse for food.
Ezek 26.12 They will pull down your walls and shatter your **luxurious** houses.
27.24 They sold you **luxurious** clothing,
Amos 3.12 of Samaria's people, who now recline on **luxurious** couches.
6. 4 out on your **luxurious** couches, feasting on veal and lamb!
6. 8 I despise their **luxurious** mansions.
Lk 7.25 who dress like that and live in **luxury** are found in palaces!
16.19 the most expensive clothes and lived in great **luxury** every day.
Jas 5. 5 Your life here on earth has been full of **luxury** and pleasure.
Rev 18. 7 and grief as the glory and **luxury** she gave herself.

LYING see LIE (1), LIE (2)

LYRE
A kind of harp.

1 Sam 10. 5 altar on the hill, playing harps, drums, flutes, and **lyres.**
18. 6 dancing, and playing tambourines and **lyres.**
2 Sam 6. 5 They were playing harps, **lyres,** drums, rattles, and
1 Kgs 10.12 palace, and also to make harps and **lyres** for the musicians.
2 Chr 9.11 his palace, and to make harps and **lyres** for the musicians.
Ps 57. 8 Wake up, my harp and **lyre!**
81. 2 play pleasant music on the harps and the **lyres.**
108. 2 Wake up, my harp and **lyre!**
150. 3 Praise him with harps and **lyres.**
Dan 3. 5 the trumpets, followed by the playing of oboes, **lyres,**
3.15 sound of the trumpets, oboes, **lyres,** zithers, harps, and all

MACEDONIA

Acts	16. 9	in which he saw a **Macedonian** standing and begging him,
	16. 9	"Come over to **Macedonia** and help us!"
	16.10	got ready to leave for **Macedonia,** because we decided that God
	16.12	inland to Philippi, a city of the first district of **Macedonia;**
	18. 5	and Timothy arrived from **Macedonia,** Paul gave his whole time
	19.21	his mind to travel through **Macedonia** and Achaia and go on to
	19.22	two of his helpers, to **Macedonia,** while he spent more time
	19.29	Gaius and Aristarchus, two **Macedonians** who were travelling
	20. 1	Then he left and went on to **Macedonia.**
	20. 3	so he decided to go back through **Macedonia.**
	27. 2	Aristarchus, a **Macedonian** from Thessalonica, was with us.
Rom	15.26	the churches in **Macedonia** and Achaia have freely decided to give
1 Cor	16. 5	after I have gone through **Macedonia**—
	16. 5	for I have to go through **Macedonia.**
2 Cor	1.16	you on my way to **Macedonia** and again on my way back,
	2.13	I said good-bye to the people there and went on to **Macedonia.**
	7. 5	Even after we arrived in **Macedonia,** we had no rest.
	8. 1	what God's grace has accomplished in the churches in **Macedonia.**
	9. 2	help, and I have boasted of you to the people in **Macedonia.**
	9. 4	if the people from **Macedonia** should come with me and find
	11. 9	brothers who came from **Macedonia** brought me everything I needed.
Phil	4.15	well that when I left **Macedonia** in the early days of
1 Thes	1. 7	you became an example to all believers in **Macedonia** and Achaia.
	1. 8	go out from you throughout **Macedonia** and Achaia, but the news
	4.10	behaved like this towards all the brothers in all **Macedonia.**
1 Tim	1. 3	as I urged you when I was on my way to **Macedonia.**

MACHIR (1)

Manasseh's eldest son and the clan descended from him.

Gen	50.23	the children of **Machir** son of Manasseh into the family.
Num	26.29	**Machir** son of Manasseh was the father of Gilead, and the
	27. 1	son of Gilead, son of **Machir,** son of Manasseh,
	32.39	The clan of **Machir** son of Manasseh invaded the land of Gilead,
	32.40	Moses gave Gilead to the clan of **Machir,** and they lived there.
	36. 1	of Gilead, the son of **Machir** and grandson of Manasseh son of
Deut	3.15	Gilead to the clan of **Machir** of the tribe of Manasseh.
Josh	13.31	to half the families descended from **Machir** son of Manasseh.
	17. 1	**Machir,** the father of Gilead, was Manasseh's eldest son
	17. 3	son of Gilead, son of **Machir,** son of Manasseh,
Judg	5.14	The commanders came down from **Machir,** the officers down from Zebulun.
1 Chr	2.21	old, he married **Machir's** daughter, the sister of Gilead.
	2.23	there were descendants of **Machir,** the father of Gilead.
	7.14	By his Aramean concubine, Manasseh had two sons, Asriel and **Machir.**
	7.14	**Machir** was the father of Gilead.
	7.15	**Machir** found a wife for Huppim and one for Shuppim.
	7.15	**Machir's** second son was Zelophehad, and he had only daughters.
	7.16	Maacah, **Machir's** wife, gave birth to two sons, whom
	7.17	of Gilead, the son of **Machir** and grandson of Manasseh.

MAD

1 Sam	18.10	control of Saul, and he raved in his house like a **madman.**
	21.13	and acted like a **madman** when they tried to restrain him;
	21.14	The man is **mad!**
	21.15	Haven't I got enough **madmen** already?
2 Kgs	9.20	is driving his chariot like a **madman,** just like Jehu!"
Job	16.14	he attacks like a soldier gone **mad** with hate.
Prov	26.18	only joking is like a **madman** playing with a deadly weapon.
Ecc	1.17	between knowledge and foolishness, wisdom and **madness.**
	9. 3	minds are full of evil and **madness,** and suddenly they die.
	10.13	He starts out with silly talk and ends up with pure **madness.**
Jer	29.26	duty to see that every **madman** who pretends to be a prophet
Zech	12. 4	terrify all their horses and make all their riders go **mad.**
Mk	3.21	take charge of him, because people were saying, "He's gone **mad!"**
Jn	10.20	He is **mad!**
Acts	12.15	"You are **mad!"**
	26.24	himself in this way, Festus shouted at him, "You are **mad,**
	26.24	Your great learning is driving you **mad!"**
	26.25	Paul answered, "I am not **mad,** Your Excellency!
2 Cor	11.23	I sound like a **madman**—but I am a better servant than

MADE-UP

2 Pet	1.16	We have not depended on **made-up** stories in making known
	2. 3	teachers will make a profit out of telling you **made-up** stories.

MAGGOT

Is	14.11	lie on a bed of **maggots** and are covered with a blanket

MAGIC

Gen	41. 8	so he sent for all the **magicians** and wise men of Egypt.
	41.24	told the dreams to the **magicians,** but none of them could
Ex	7.11	for his wise men and **magicians,**
	7.11	and by their **magic** they did the same thing.
	7.22	Then the king's **magicians** did the same thing
	7.22	by means of their **magic,** and the king was as stubborn
	8. 7	But the magicians used **magic,** and they too made frogs come
	8.18	The **magicians** tried to use their magic to make gnats appear,
	8.19	gnats everywhere, [19] and the **magicians** said to the king,
	9.11	The **magicians** were not able to appear before Moses,
	22.18	"Put to death any woman who practises **magic.**
Lev	19.26	Do not practise any kind of **magic.**
Num	23.23	There is no **magic** charm, no witchcraft, That can be used
1 Sam	6. 2	called the priests and the **magicians** and asked, "What shall
2 Kgs	21. 6	He practised divination and **magic** and consulted fortune-tellers
2 Chr	33. 6	He practised divination and **magic** and consulted fortune-tellers
Ps	58. 5	of the snake-charmer, or the chant of the clever **magician.**
Prov	17. 8	Some people think a bribe works like **magic;**
Is	2. 6	The land is full of **magic** practices from the east and from
	3. 3	politicians and everyone who uses **magic** to control events.
	3.20	**magic** charms they wear on their arms and at their waists;
	47. 9	In spite of all the **magic** you use, you will lose your
	47.11	will come upon you, and none of your **magic** can stop it.
	47.12	Keep all your **magic** spells and charms;
Jer	27. 9	or by calling up the spirits of the dead or by **magic.**
Ezek	13.18	You sew **magic** wristbands for everyone and make magic scarves for
Dan	1.20	than any fortune-teller or **magician** in his whole kingdom.
	2. 2	he sent for his fortune-tellers, **magicians,** sorcerers, and
	2.10	ever made such a demand of his fortune-tellers, **magicians,**
	2.27	Majesty, there is no wizard, **magician,** fortune-teller, or
	4. 7	**magicians,** wizards, and astrologers were brought in, and
	5. 7	He shouted for someone to bring in the **magicians,**
	5.11	father, made him chief of the fortune-tellers, **magicians,**
	5.15	The advisers and **magicians** were brought in to read this
Mic	5.12	I will destroy the **magic** charms you use and leave you
Mal	3. 5	once against those who practise **magic,** against adulterers,
Acts	8. 9	who for some time had astounded the Samaritans with his **magic.**
	8.11	for such a long time he had astonished them with his **magic.**
	13. 6	they met a certain **magician** named Bar-Jesus, a Jew who claimed
	13. 8	they were opposed by the **magician** Elymas (that is his name
	13. 9	he looked straight at the **magician** [10] and said, "You son
	19.19	of those who had practised **magic** brought their books together
Rev	9.21	repent of their murders, their **magic,** their sexual immorality,
	18.23	and with your false **magic** you deceived all the peoples of
	21. 8	the immoral, those who practise **magic,** those who worship idols,
	22.15	and those who practise **magic,** the immoral and the murderers,

MAGISTRATE

Dan	3. 2	commissioners, treasurers, judges, **magistrates,**

MAGNIFICENT

Ex	31.10	the **magnificent** priestly garments for Aaron and
	35.19	and the **magnificent** garments the priests are to wear
	39. 1	red wool they made the **magnificent** garments which the
	39.41	and the **magnificent** garments the priests were to wear in
2 Chr	2. 9	this temple I intend to build will be large and **magnificent.**
Esth	8.15	a cloak of fine purple linen, and a **magnificent** gold crown.
Is	14.18	lie in their **magnificent** tombs, [19] but you have no tomb,
Ezek	17. 8	grow leaves and bear grapes and be a **magnificent** vine.
	17.23	grow branches and bear seed and become a **magnificent** cedar.
Zech	11.13	thirty pieces of silver—the **magnificent** sum they thought I

MAID

Gen	29.24	(Laban gave his slave-girl Zilpah to his daughter Leah as her **maid.)**
	29.29	(Laban gave his slave-girl Bilhah to his daughter Rachel as her **maid.)**
1 Sam	25.42	Accompanied by her five **maids,** she went with David's
Ps	123. 2	as a **maid** depends on her mistress,

MAIN

Num	20.17	We will stay on the **main** road until we are out of
	20.19	"We will stay on the **main** road, and if we or our
	21.22	we will stay on the **main** road until we are out of
Josh	8.11	with him went towards the **main** entrance to the city and set
	8.13	arranged for battle with the **main** camp north of the city and
Judg	20.33	So when the **main** army of the Israelites pulled back and
	20.36	The **main** body of the Israelite army had retreated from the
	20.38	The **main** Israelite army and the men in hiding had
	20.42	They were caught between the **main** army and the men who were
1 Kgs	6.29	The walls of the **main** room and of the inner room were
	6.33	For the entrance to the **main** room a rectangular
	20.14	"Who will command the **main** force?"
2 Kgs	23. 8	to the left of the **main** gate as one enters the city.
2 Chr	3. 5	The **main** room was panelled with cedar
	4. 7	and placed them in the **main** room of the Temple, five
	23.20	They entered by the **main** gate, and the king took his place
Mt	22. 9	Now go to the **main** streets and invite to the feast as

MAINLAND

Ezek	26. 6	they will kill those who live in her towns on the **mainland.**
	26. 8	in the towns on the **mainland** will be killed in the fighting.

MAINTAIN

2 Sam	22.44	rebellious people and **maintained** my rule over the nations;
1 Kgs	10. 9	you their king so that you can **maintain** law and justice."
2 Chr	9. 8	you their king so that you can **maintain** law and justice."
Jer	33.26	so I will **maintain** my covenant with Jacob's descendants and

MAJESTY

Gen	41.16	Joseph answered, "I cannot, Your **Majesty,** but God will
Ex	5.15	and complained, "Why do you do this to us, Your **Majesty?**
	7.17	Now, Your **Majesty,** the Lord says that you will find out
	15. 7	In **majestic** triumph you overthrow your foes;
Judg	3.19	to Eglon, and said, "Your **Majesty,** I have a secret message
1 Sam	15.29	Israel's **majestic** God does not lie or change his mind.

1 Sam 17.32 David said to Saul, "Your **Majesty,** no one should be
17.34 "Your **Majesty,**" David said, "I take care of my father's sheep.
17.55 "I have no idea, Your **Majesty,**" Abner answered.
22.15 for plotting against you, Your **Majesty** must not accuse me or
23.20 We know, Your **Majesty,** how much you want to capture him;
24. 8 Then David went out after him and called to him, "Your **Majesty!**"
26.17 "Yes, Your **Majesty,**" David answered.
26.19 Your **Majesty,** listen to what I have to say.
26.22 David replied, "Here is your spear, Your **Majesty.**
2 Sam 3.21 "I will go now and win all Israel over to Your **Majesty.**
4. 8 the Lord has allowed Your **Majesty** to take revenge on Saul
9.11 Ziba answered, "I will do everything Your **Majesty** commands."
11.24 the wall, and some of Your **Majesty's** officers were killed;
13.24 David and said, "Your **Majesty,** I am having my sheep sheared.
13.32 said, "Your **Majesty,** they haven't killed all your sons.
14. 4 the ground in respect, and said, "Help me, Your **Majesty!**"
14. 9 "Your **Majesty,**" she said, "whatever you do, my family
14.11 She said, "Your **Majesty,** please pray to the Lord your God,
14.12 "Please, Your **Majesty,** let me say just one more thing,"
14.15 Now, Your **Majesty,** the reason I have come to speak to
14.18 "Ask me anything, Your **Majesty,**" she answered.
14.19 all that is sacred, Your **Majesty,** that there is no way to
14.20 Your **Majesty** is as wise as the angel of God and knows
14.22 David in respect, and said, "God bless you, Your **Majesty!**
15.15 "Yes, Your **Majesty,**" they answered.
15.21 But Ittai answered, "Your **Majesty,** I swear to you in
16. 2 "The donkeys are for Your **Majesty's** family to ride, the
16. 4 "May I always please Your **Majesty!**"
16. 9 said to the king, "Your **Majesty,** why do you let this dog
18.28 victory over the men who rebelled against Your **Majesty!**"
18.31 and said to the king, "I have good news for Your **Majesty!**
19.19 of him [19]and said, "Your **Majesty,** please forget the wrong
19.20 the northern tribes to come and meet Your **Majesty** today."
19.26 He answered, "As you know, Your **Majesty,** I am
19.27 lied about me to Your **Majesty,** but you are like God's angel,
19.28 put to death by Your **Majesty,** but you gave me the right
19.28 no right to ask for any more favours from Your **Majesty.**"
19.30 "It's enough for me that Your **Majesty** has come home safely."
19.34 why should I go with Your **Majesty** to Jerusalem?
19.35 I would only be a burden to Your **Majesty.**
19.37 take him with you, Your **Majesty,** and do for him as you
19.41 and said to him, "Your **Majesty,** why did our brothers, the
24. 3 Joab answered the king, "Your **Majesty,** may the Lord your
24. 3 But why does Your **Majesty** want to do this?"
24.21 of David [21]and asked, "Your **Majesty,** why are you here?"
24.22 "Take it, Your **Majesty,**" Araunah said, "and offer to
1 Kgs 1. 2 officials said to him, "Your **Majesty,** let us find a young
1.13 David and ask him, 'Your **Majesty,** didn't you solemnly
1.17 She answered, "Your **Majesty,** you made me a solemn
1.20 Your **Majesty,** all the people of Israel are looking to
1.24 Then he said, "Your **Majesty,** have you announced that
1.27 Did Your **Majesty** approve all this and not even tell your
1.37 Lord has been with Your **Majesty,** may he also be with Solomon,
1.43 "His **Majesty** King David has made Solomon king.
1.47 pay their respects to His **Majesty** King David, and said, 'May
2.38 "Very well, Your **Majesty,**" Shimei answered.
3.17 One of them said, "Your **Majesty,** this woman and I live
3.26 to the king, "Please, Your **Majesty,** don't kill the child!
8.13 Now I have built a **majestic** temple for you, a place for
20.39 to him and said, "Your **Majesty,** I was fighting in the
2 Kgs 6.12 One of them answered, "No one is, Your **Majesty.**
6.26 wall when a woman cried out, "Help me, Your **Majesty!**"
8. 5 Gehazi said to him, "Your **Majesty,** here is the woman and
1 Chr 16.27 Glory and **majesty** surround him, power and joy fill his Temple.
21. 3 Your **Majesty,** they are all your servants.
21.23 "Take it, Your **Majesty,**" Araunah said, "and do whatever
29.11 You are great and powerful, glorious, splendid, and **majestic.**
2 Chr 6. 2 Now I have built a **majestic** temple for you, a place for
20.15 Jahaziel said, "Your **Majesty** and all you people of Judah
Ezra 4.12 "We want Your **Majesty** to know that the Jews who came
4.13 Your **Majesty,** if this city is rebuilt and its walls
4.14 are under obligation to Your **Majesty,** we do not want to see
4.16 its walls are completed, Your **Majesty** will no longer be able
5. 8 "Your **Majesty** should know that we went to the province of
5.17 "Now, if it please Your **Majesty,** let a search be made
Neh 2. 3 I was startled [3]and answered, "May Your **Majesty** live for ever!
2. 5 to the emperor, "If Your **Majesty** is pleased with me and is
6. 7 His **Majesty** is certain to hear about this, so I suggest that
Esth 1. 4 of the imperial court with all its splendour and **majesty.**
1.19 If it please Your **Majesty,** issue a royal proclamation
3. 9 If it please Your **Majesty,** issue a decree that they are to
5. 4 replied, "If it please Your **Majesty,** I would like you and
5. 8 Esther replied, [8]"If Your **Majesty** is kind enough to grant
7. 3 "If it please Your **Majesty** to grant my humble request,
7. 9 that he could hang Mordecai, who saved Your **Majesty's** life.
8. 5 said, [5]"If it please Your **Majesty,** and if you care about
9.13 answered, "If it please Your **Majesty,** let the Jews in Susa
Job 37. 4 his voice is heard, the **majestic** sound of thunder, and all
40.10 clothe yourself with **majesty** and glory.
Ps 21. 5 you have given him fame and **majesty.**
29. 4 voice of the Lord is heard in all its might and **majesty.**
45. 3 you are glorious and **majestic.**
45. 4 Ride on in **majesty** to victory for the defence of truth and
68.34 his **majesty** is over Israel, his might is in the skies.
76. 4 How **majestic,** as you return from the mountains where you
93. 1 He is clothed with **majesty** and strength.
96. 6 Glory and **majesty** surround him;
99. 3 Everyone will praise his great and **majestic** name.
104. 1 You are clothed with **majesty** and glory;
111. 3 All he does is full of honour and **majesty;**
145. 5 speak of your glory and **majesty,** and I will meditate on your
Ps 145.12 your mighty deeds and the glorious **majesty** of your kingdom.
Song 5.15 He is **majestic,** like the Lebanon Mountains
Is 30.30 will let everyone hear his **majestic** voice and feel the force
Jer 37.20 And now, Your **Majesty,** I beg you to listen to me and
38. 9 said to the king, [9]"Your **Majesty,** what these men have done
Dan 2. 4 answered the king in Aramaic, "May Your **Majesty** live for ever!
2. 7 the king again, "If Your **Majesty** will only tell us what the
2.10 the earth who can tell Your **Majesty** what you want to know.
2.11 What Your **Majesty** is asking for is so difficult that no
2.25 who can tell Your **Majesty** the meaning of your dream."
2.27 Daniel replied, "Your **Majesty,** there is no wizard, magician,
2.28 He has informed Your **Majesty** what will happen in the future.
2.29 "While Your **Majesty** was sleeping, you dreamt about the future;
2.30 else, but so that Your **Majesty** may learn the meaning of your
2.31 "Your **Majesty,** in your vision you saw standing before
2.36 Now I will tell Your **Majesty** what it means.
2.37 Your **Majesty,** you are the greatest of all kings.
2.45 God is telling Your **Majesty** what will happen in the future.
3. 9 said to King Nebuchadnezzar, "May Your **Majesty** live for ever!
3.10 Your **Majesty** has issued an order that as soon as the
3.12 Shadrach, Meshach, and Abednego—who are disobeying Your **Majesty's** orders.
3.16 Meshach, and Abednego answered, "Your **Majesty,** we will not
3.18 even if he doesn't, Your **Majesty** may be sure that we will
3.24 They answered, "Yes, we did, Your **Majesty.**"
4.19 Belteshazzar replied, "Your **Majesty,** I wish that the dream
4.22 "Your **Majesty,** you are the tree, tall and strong.
4.23 While Your **Majesty** was watching, an angel came down from
4.24 is what it means, Your **Majesty,** and this is what the Supreme
4.27 So then, Your **Majesty,** follow my advice.
4.30 city to display my power and might, my glory and **majesty.**"
4.36 sanity returned, my honour, my **majesty,** and the glory of my
5.10 She said, "May Your **Majesty** live for ever!
5.17 I will read for Your **Majesty** what has been written and tell
5.18 Nebuchadnezzar a great king and gave him dignity and **majesty.**
6. 6 and said, "King Darius, may Your **Majesty** live for ever!
6. 7 officials—have agreed that Your **Majesty** should issue an
6. 7 from any god or from any man except from Your **Majesty.**
6. 8 So let Your **Majesty** issue this order and sign it, and it
6.12 They said, "Your **Majesty,** you signed an order that for the
6.13 does not respect Your **Majesty** or obey the order you issued.
6.15 and said to him, "Your **Majesty** knows that according to the
6.21 Daniel answered, "May Your **Majesty** live for ever!
6.22 I was innocent and because I have not wronged you, Your **Majesty.**"
Mic 5. 4 from the Lord and with the **majesty** of the Lord God himself.
Acts 26. 7 because of this hope, Your **Majesty,** that I am being accused
26.13 the road at midday, Your **Majesty,** that I saw a light much
Heb 8. 1 at the right of the throne of the Divine **Majesty** in heaven.
Jude 25 Christ our Lord, be glory, **majesty,** might, and authority,

MAJORITY

Ex 23. 2 Do not follow the **majority** when they do wrong

MAKE

[MADE BY CHRIST, MADE FROM, MADE OF, MADE OUT OF, MAN-MADE, WELL-MADE]

Gen 14.22 Lord, the Most High God, **Maker** of heaven and earth, [23]that
Neh 3. 8 Hananiah, a **maker** of perfumes, built the next section, as
Ps 95. 6 let us kneel before the Lord, our **Maker!**
Is 7. 3 the road where the cloth **makers** work, at the end of the
44.19 The **maker** of idols hasn't the wit or the sense to say,
45. 9 dare to argue with its **maker,** a pot that is like all
45. 9 Does the pot complain that its **maker** has no skill?
Ezek 27.24 brightly coloured carpets, and **well-made** cords and ropes.
Hos 8.14 Israel have built palaces, but they have forgotten their own **Maker.**
Hab 2.18 does it do for its **maker** to trust it—a god that
Mt 3. 4 John's clothes were **made of** camel's hair;
15. 9 because they teach **man-made** rules as though they were my
Mk 1. 6 John wore clothes **made of** camel's hair, with a leather belt
2.27 Jesus concluded, "The Sabbath was **made** for the good of man;
2.27 man was not **made** for the Sabbath.
7. 7 because they teach **man-made** rules as though they were God's
14. 3 jar full of a very expensive perfume **made of** pure nard.
14.58 this Temple which men have **made,** and after three days I will
Jn 1. 3 Through him God **made** all things;
1. 3 not one thing in all creation was **made** without him.
1.10 the world, and though God **made** the world through him,
12. 3 of a very expensive perfume **made of** pure nard, poured it on
17. 5 the same glory I had with you before the world was **made.**
17.24 for you loved me before the world was **made.**
19.23 took the robe, which was **made of** one piece of woven cloth
Acts 7.41 and had a feast in honour of what they themselves had **made.**
17.24 Lord of heaven and earth and does not live in **man-made** temples.
19.26 He says that **man-made** gods are not gods at all,
Rom 1.20 they are perceived in the things that God has **made.**
1 Cor 2. 7 already chosen for our glory even before the world was **made.**
11.12 For as woman was **made from** man, in the same way man
12.12 one body, even though it is **made** up of different parts.
12.14 the body itself is not **made** up of only one part,
15.47 The first Adam, **made of** earth, came from the earth;
15.48 to the earth are like the one who was **made of** earth;
15.49 the likeness of the man **made of** earth, so we will wear
15.50 brothers, is that what is **made of** flesh and blood cannot
2 Cor 5. 1 a home he himself has **made,** which will last for ever.
Eph 1. 4 Even before the world was **made,** God had already chosen us
Col 2.11 the circumcision **made by Christ,** which consists of being freed
2.22 they are only **man-made** rules and teachings.
2 Tim 2.20 some are **made of** silver and gold, others of wood and clay;

2 Tim	4.13	the books too, and especially the ones **made of** parchment.
Heb	9. 1	rules for worship and a **man-made** place for worship as well.
	9.11	it is not a **man-made** tent, that is, it is not a
	9.24	did not go into a **man-made** Holy Place, which was a copy
	11. 3	what can be seen was **made out of** what cannot be seen.
Rev	9.20	did not turn away from what they themselves had **made.**
	14. 7	Worship him who **made** heaven, earth, sea, and the springs of
	18.12	all kinds of objects **made of** ivory and of expensive wood,
	21.18	The wall was **made of** jasper,
	21.18	and the city itself was **made of** pure gold,
	21.21	each gate was **made from** a single pearl.

MALE

Gen	1.27	He created them **male** and female, [28]blessed them, and said,
	5. 2	He created them **male** and female, blessed them,
	6.19	the boat with you a **male** and a female of every kind
	7. 8	A **male** and a female of every kind of animal and bird,
	7.15	A **male** and a female of each kind of living being went
	17.10	must all agree to circumcise every **male** among you.
	17.14	Any **male** who has not been circumcised will no longer be
	17.23	Ishmael and all the other **males** in his household, including
	24.35	and goats, cattle, silver, gold, **male** and female slaves,
	30.35	that day Laban removed the **male** goats that had stripes or
	31.10	and I saw that the **male** goats that were mating were striped,
	31.12	he continued, 'all the **male** goats that are mating are striped,
	32.13	hundred female goats and twenty **males,**
	32.13	sheep and twenty **males,** thirty
	32.13	cows and ten bulls, twenty female donkeys and ten **males.**
	34.15	that you become like us by circumcising all your **males.**
	34.22	that we circumcise all our **males,** as they are circumcised.
	34.24	Hamor and Shechem proposed, and all the **males** were circumcised.
Ex	12. 5	but it must be a one-year-old **male** without any defects.
	12.12	Egypt, killing every first-born **male,** both human and animal,
	12.48	you must first circumcise all the **males** of his household.
	13. 2	"Dedicate all the first-born **males** to me,
	13. 2	for every first-born **male** Israelite
	13. 2	and every first-born **male** animal belongs to me."
	13.12	you, [12]you must offer every first-born **male** to the Lord.
	13.12	Every first-born **male** of your animals belongs to the Lord,
	13.13	back from him every first-born **male** donkey by offering a
	13.13	You must buy back every first-born **male** child of yours.
	13.15	the Lord killed every first-born **male** in the land of Egypt,
	13.15	why we sacrifice every first-born **male** animal to the Lord,
	21. 7	slave, she is not to be set free, as **male** slaves are.
	21.20	and beats his slave, whether **male** or female, and the slave
	21.26	"If a man hits his **male** or female slave in the eye
	21.32	If the bull kills a **male** or female slave, its owner
	22.30	Let the first-born **male** stay with its mother for seven days,
	34.19	first-born son and first-born **male** domestic animal belongs to me, [20]but
Lev	1.10	his sheep or goats, it must be a **male** without any defects.
	3. 6	a fellowship-offering, it may be **male** or female, but it must
	4.23	shall bring as his offering a **male** goat without any defects.
	5.15	to the Lord a **male** sheep or goat without any defects.
	5.18	repayment-offering a **male** sheep or goat without any defects.
	6. 6	to the Lord a **male** sheep or goat without any defects.
	6.18	to come any of the **male** descendants of Aaron may eat it
	6.29	Any **male** of the priestly families may eat this offering;
	7. 6	Any **male** of the priestly families may eat it, but it must
	9. 3	of Israel to take a **male** goat for a sin-offering, a
	14.10	day he shall bring two **male** lambs and one female lamb a
	14.12	shall take one of the **male** lambs and together with the
	14.21	purification only one **male** lamb as his repayment-offering,
	16. 5	Israel shall give Aaron two **male** goats for a sin-offering
	22.19	To be accepted, it must be a **male** without any defects.
	23.12	burnt-offering a one-year-old **male** lamb that has no defects.
	23.19	Also offer one **male** goat as a sin-offering
	23.19	and two one-year-old **male** lambs as a fellowship-offering.
	27. 3	adult **male,** twenty to sixty years old:
	27. 3	—young **male,** five to twenty years old:
	27. 3	—infant **male** under five:
	27. 3	—**male** above sixty years of age:
Num	3.15	and families, enrolling every **male** a month old or older,
	3.22	The total number of **males** one month old or older that
	3.28	The total number of **males** one month old or older that
	3.34	The total number of **males** one month old or older that
	3.39	number of all the Levite **males** one month old or older that
	3.40	every first-born **male** Israelite, one month old or older.
	3.42	all the first-born **males** [43]one month old or older;
	6.14	a one-year-old **male** lamb for a burnt-offering, a
	15.24	In addition, they are to offer a **male** goat as a sin-offering.
	18.10	these things in a holy place, and only **males** may eat them;
	26.62	The **male** Levites who were one month old or older numbered 23,000.
	28. 3	two one-year-old **male** lambs without any defects.
	28. 9	offer two one-year-old **male** lambs without any defects, two
	28.11	ram, seven one-year-old **male** lambs, all without any defects.
	28.15	its wine-offering, offer one **male** goat as a sin-offering.
	28.19	and seven one-year-old **male** lambs, all without any defects.
	28.22	Also offer one **male** goat as a sin-offering, and in this
	28.27	and seven one-year-old **male** lambs, all without any defects.
	28.30	Also offer one **male** goat as a sin-offering, and in this
	29. 2	and seven one-year-old **male** lambs, all without any defects.
	29. 5	Also offer one **male** goat as a sin-offering, and in this
	29. 8	and seven one-year-old **male** lambs, all without any defects.
	29.11	Also offer one **male** goat as a sin-offering, in addition
	29.13	fourteen one-year-old **male** lambs, all without any defects.
	29.16	Also offer one **male** goat as a sin-offering.
	29.17	fourteen one-year-old **male** lambs, all without any defects.
Num	29.20	fourteen one-year-old **male** lambs, all without any defects.
	29.23	fourteen one-year-old **male** lambs, all without any defects.
	29.26	fourteen one-year-old **male** lambs, all without any defects.
	29.29	fourteen one-year-old **male** lambs, all without any defects.
	29.32	fourteen one-year-old **male** lambs, all without any defects.
	29.36	and seven one-year-old **male** lambs, all without any defects.
Deut	15.19	Lord your God all the first-born **males** of your cattle and sheep;
Josh	5. 4	Israel left Egypt, all the **males** were already circumcised.
	17. 2	These were **male** descendants of Manasseh son of Joseph, and
	17. 4	us, as well as our **male** relatives, a part of the land
	17. 4	they were given land along with their **male** relatives.
	17. 6	as well as his **male** descendants were assigned land.
Judg	21.11	Kill all the **males,** and also every woman who is not a
2 Sam	21. 6	hand over seven of his **male** descendants, and we will hang
1 Kgs	11.15	that time they killed every **male** in Edom [17]except Hadad
	14.10	will kill all your **male** descendants, young and old alike.
	15.12	from the country all the **male** and female prostitutes serving
	16.11	Every **male** relative and friend was put to death.
	21.21	and get rid of every **male** in your family, young and old
	22.46	got rid of all the **male** and female prostitutes serving at
2 Kgs	9. 8	will get rid of every **male** in his family, young and old
1 Chr	23. 3	took a census of all the **male** Levites aged thirty or older.
	24. 4	done because there were more **male** heads of families among
2 Chr	15.13	Anyone, young or old, **male** or female, who did not
	31.16	gave a share to all **males** thirty years of age or older
	31.19	the food to all the **males** in the priestly families and to
Ezra	2.64	Their **male** and female servants - 7,337
	2.64	**Male** and female musicians - 200
Neh	7.66	Their **male** and female servants - 7,337
	7.66	**Male** and female musicians - 245
Jer	2.24	No **male** that wants her has to trouble himself;
	34. 9	free [9]their Hebrew slaves, both **male** and female, so that no
	35.19	of Rechab will always have a **male** descendant to serve me."
Ezek	16.17	it to make **male** images, and committed adultery with them.
	19. 2	She reared her cubs among the fierce **male** lions.
	43.22	you are to take a **male** goat without any defects and offer
	45.23	is also to sacrifice a **male** goat each day as a sin-offering.
Mt	19. 4	that in the beginning the Creator made people **male** and female?
Mk	10. 6	'God made them **male** and female,' as the scripture says.
Lk	2.23	"Every first-born **male** is to be dedicated to the Lord."

MALICE

Rom	1.29	are full of jealousy, murder, fighting, deceit, and **malice.**
Tit	3. 3	We spent our lives in **malice** and envy;

MAN

[FELLOW-MAN, MEN AND WOMEN]

see also **MAN OF GOD, MAN-EATER, MAN-MADE, MANKIND, MORTAL (Man), SON OF MAN**

Gen	2. 7	some soil from the ground and formed a **man** out of it;
	2. 7	breath into his nostrils and the **man** began to live.
	2. 8	in the East, and there he put the **man** he had formed.
	2.15	the Lord God placed the **man** in the Garden of Eden to
	2.18	God said, "It is not good for the **man** to live alone.
	2.19	he brought them to the **man** to see what he would name
	2.20	So the **man** named all the birds and all the animals;
	2.21	the Lord God made the **man** fall into a deep sleep, and
	2.21	took out one of the **man's** ribs and closed up the flesh.
	2.23	Then the **man** said,
	2.23	'Woman' is her name because she was taken out of **man."**
	2.24	That is why a **man** leaves his father and mother and is
	2.25	The **man** and the woman were both naked, but they were not
	3. 9	But the Lord God called out to the **man,** "Where are you?"
	3.12	The **man** answered, "The woman you put here with me gave
	3.17	And he said to the **man,** "You listened to your wife and
	3.22	Lord God said, "Now the **man** has become like one of us
	4.23	I have killed a young **man** because he struck me.
	6. 9	had no faults and was the only good **man** of his time.
	8.21	I put the earth under a curse because of what **man** does;
	9. 6	**Man** was made like God,
	9. 6	so whoever murders a **man**
	9. 6	will himself be killed by his **fellow-man.**
	14.13	But a **man** escaped and reported all this to Abram, the
	17.17	when he thought, "Can a **man** have a child when he is
	18. 2	of the day, [2]he looked up and saw three **men** standing there.
	18.22	Then the two **men** left and went on towards Sodom, but the
	18.27	I am only a **man** and have no right to say anything.
	19. 4	All the **men** of the city, both young and old, were there.
	19. 5	and asked, "Where are the **men** who came to stay with you
	19. 8	But don't do anything to these **men;**
	19.12	The two **men** said to Lot, "If you have anyone else here
	19.31	old, and there are no **men** in the whole world to marry
	24.31	You are a **man** whom the Lord has blessed.
	24.58	Rebecca and asked, "Do you want to go with this **man?"**
	24.65	"Who is that **man** walking towards us in the field?"
	26.11	"Anyone who ill-treats this **man** or his wife will be put to
	27.11	know that Esau is a hairy **man,** but I have smooth skin.
	32.24	Then a **man** came and wrestled with him until just before daybreak.
	32.25	When the **man** saw that he was not winning the struggle,
	32.26	The **man** said, "Let me go;
	32.28	The **man** said, "Your name will no longer be Jacob.
	32.28	You have struggled with God and with **men,** and you have won;
	34.30	I haven't many **men;**
	38.25	"I am pregnant by the **man** who owns these things.
	41.33	"Now you should choose some **man** with wisdom and insight
	41.38	will never find a better **man** than Joseph,
	41.38	a **man** who has God's spirit in him."
	42.13	all, sir, sons of the same **man** in the land of Canaan.

Gen	42.18	them, "I am a God-fearing **man,** and I will spare your lives
	42.33	The **man** answered, 'This is how I will find out if you
	42.38	I am an old **man,** and the sorrow you would cause me
	43. 3	Judah said to him, "The **man** sternly warned us that we
	43. 6	trouble by telling the **man** that you had another brother?"
	43. 7	They answered, "The **man** kept asking about us and our family,
	43.14	May Almighty God cause the **man** to have pity on you, so
	43.21	opened our sacks, and each **man** found his money in the top
	44.11	their sacks to the ground, and each **man** opened his sack.
	44.15	Didn't you know that a **man** in my position could find you
	44.26	not be admitted to the **man's** presence unless our youngest
	49. 3	the first child of my **manhood,** The proudest and strongest of
	49. 6	For they killed **men** in anger
	50. 7	and all the leading **men** of Egypt went with Joseph.
	50. 9	**Men** in chariots and men on horseback also went with him;
Ex	4.11	The Lord said to him, "Who gives **man** his mouth?
	10. 7	Let the Israelite **men** go, so that they can worship the Lord
	10.11	Only the **men** may go and worship the Lord if that is
	11. 3	and all the people considered Moses to be a very great **man.**
	12.37	about six hundred thousand **men,** not counting women and children.
	15.15	Moab's mighty **men** are trembling;
	17. 9	"Pick out some **men** to go and fight the Amalekites
	18.21	choose some capable **men** and appoint them as leaders
	18.21	They must be God-fearing **men** who can be trusted
	18.25	and chose capable **men** from among all the Israelites.
	19.13	This applies to both **men** and animals;
	20.17	"Do not desire another **man's** house;
	21.12	"Whoever hits a **man** and kills him is to be put to
	21.13	not mean to kill the **man,** he can escape to a place
	21.14	But when a **man** gets angry and deliberately kills another man,
	21.16	"Whoever kidnaps a **man,** either to sell him or to keep
	21.22	"If some **men** are fighting and hurt a pregnant woman so
	24. 5	Then he sent young **men,** and they burnt sacrifices to the
	24.11	God did not harm these leading **men** of Israel;
	30.32	not be poured on ordinary **men,** and you must not use the
	33.11	Moses face to face, just as a **man** speaks with a friend.
	33.11	But the young **man** who was his helper, Joshua son of Nun,
	35.22	All who wanted to, both **men** and women, brought decorative pins,
	38.26	There were 603,550 **men** twenty years old or older enrolled in
Lev	7.21	ritually unclean, whether from a **man** or an animal, he shall
	18.22	No **man** is to have sexual relations with another man;
	18.23	No **man** or woman is to have sexual relations with an animal;
	20.13	If a **man** has sexual relations with another man, they
	24.10	There was a **man** whose father was an Egyptian and
	24.10	There in the camp this **man** quarrelled with an Israelite.
	24.14	The Lord said to Moses, [14]"Take that **man** out of the camp.
	24.21	replace it, but whoever kills a **man** shall be put to death.
	24.23	of Israel, they took the **man** outside the camp and stoned him
Num	1. 2	the names of all the **men** [3]twenty years old or older who
	1. 5	These are the **men,** leaders within their tribes, who
	1.17	the help of these twelve **men** Moses and Aaron [18]called
	1.18	The names of all the **men** twenty years old or older were
	1.20	The **men** twenty years old or older who were fit for
	1.49	take a census of the **men** fit for military service, do not
	1.52	camp, company by company, each **man** with his own group and
	2. 2	Israelites set up camp, each **man** will camp under the banner
	4. 3	and to register all the **men** between the ages of thirty and
	4.19	go in and assign each **man** his task and tell him what
	4.23	and to register all the **men** between the ages of thirty
	4.30	and to register all the **men** between the ages of thirty
	4.32	Each **man** will be responsible for carrying specific items.
	4.34	families and registered all the **men** between the ages of
	4.49	Each **man** was registered as the Lord had commanded Moses;
	4.49	Lord given through Moses, each **man** was assigned
	5.12	has defiled herself by having intercourse with another **man.**
	7. 2	tribes of Israel, the same **men** who were in charge of the
	9. 6	But there were some **men** who were ritually unclean because
	11.16	"Assemble seventy respected **men** who are recognized as leaders of
	11.27	A young **man** ran out to tell Moses what Eldad and Medad
	11.28	since he was a young **man,** spoke up and said to Moses,
	13.21	So the **men** went north and explored the land
	13.23	heavy that it took two **men** to carry it on a pole
	15.32	still in the wilderness, a **man** was found gathering firewood
	15.35	the Lord said to Moses, "The **man** must be put to death;
	16.18	So every **man** took his firepan, put live coals and
	16.22	When one **man** sins, do you get angry with the whole community?"
	17. 2	Write each **man's** name on his stick [3]and then write Aaron's
	17. 5	Then the stick of the **man** I have chosen will sprout.
	21.29	Your god let the **men** become refugees,
	23.19	God is not like **men,** who lie;
	24. 3	Beor, The words of the **man** who can see clearly, [4]Who can
	24.15	Beor, The words of the **man** who can see clearly, [16]Who can
	25. 8	a spear, [8]followed the **man** and the woman into the tent,
	26. 2	community of Israel, of all **men** twenty years old or older
	26. 3	Eleazar obeyed, and called together all the **men** of that age group.
	26.64	There was not even one **man** left among those whom Moses
	27. 8	of Israel that whenever a **man** dies without leaving a son,
	27.16	life, appoint, I pray, a **man** who can lead the people [17]and
	27.18	son of Nun, a capable **man,** and place your hands on his
	31. 4	From each tribe of Israel send a thousand **men** to war."
	31. 5	So a thousand **men** were chosen from each tribe,
	31. 5	a total of twelve thousand **men** ready for battle.
	31. 7	killed all the **men,** [8]including the five kings of Midian:
	32.11	to me, none of the **men** twenty years old or older who
	32.21	All your fighting **men** are to cross the Jordan and under
	36. 3	But remember, if they marry **men** of another tribe, their
Deut	2.34	destroyed every town, and put everyone to death, **men,** women,
	3. 6	put to death all the **men,** women, and children, just as we
	4.16	any form at all—whether **man** or woman, [17]animal or bird,
Deut	4.32	way back to the time when God created **man** on the earth.
	5.24	it is possible for a **man** to continue to live, even though
	8. 3	this to teach you that **man** must not depend on bread alone
	13. 5	Such a **man** is evil and is trying to lead you away
	15.12	"If a fellow-Israelite, **man** or woman, sells himself to
	17. 2	one of your towns some **man** or woman has sinned against the
	17.15	Make sure that the **man** you choose to be king is the
	19. 6	might catch him and in his anger kill an innocent **man.**
	19. 6	by accident that he killed a **man** who was not his enemy.
	19.15	"One witness is not enough to convict a **man** of a crime;
	19.18	**man** has made a false accusation against his fellow-Israelite,
	20. 5	and say, 'Is there any **man** here who has just built a
	20. 6	Is there any **man** here who has just planted a vineyard, but
	20. 8	the men, 'Is there any **man** here who has lost his nerve
	20.13	your God lets you capture the city, kill every **man** in it.
	21. 8	not hold us responsible for the murder of an innocent **man.'**
	22. 5	"Women are not to wear **men's** clothing,
	22. 5	and **men** are not to wear women's clothing;
	22.16	gave my daughter to this **man** in marriage, and now he doesn't
	22.25	Then only the **man** is to be put to death;
	22.26	same as when one **man** attacks another man and murders him.
	23. 1	"No **man** who has been castrated or whose penis has been
	23.17	"No Israelite, **man** or woman, is to become a temple prostitute.
	24. 2	Then suppose she marries another **man,** [3]and he also
	25.11	hold of the other **man's** genitals, [12]show her no mercy;
	28.54	Even the most refined **man** of noble birth will
	29.10	your leaders and officials, your **men,** [11]women, and
	29.18	Make sure that no **man,** woman, family, or tribe standing
	29.20	The Lord will not forgive such a **man.**
	31.12	Call together all the **men,** women, and children, and the
	32.25	Young **men** and young women will die;
	32.25	neither babies nor old **men** will be spared.
Josh	2. 4	"Some **men** did come to my house," she answered, "but
	3. 7	honour you as a great **man,** and they will realize that I
	3.12	Now choose twelve **men,** one from each of the tribes of Israel.
	4. 2	said to Joshua, [2]"Choose twelve **men,** one from each tribe,
	4. 4	Then Joshua called the twelve **men** he had chosen, [5]and
	4.13	the Lord about forty thousand **men** ready for war crossed over
	4.14	day made the people of Israel consider Joshua a great **man.**
	5. 4	of that time all the **men** who were of fighting age when
	5.13	Jericho, he suddenly saw a **man** standing in front of him,
	5.14	"Neither," the **man** answered.
	6. 5	you hear it, all the **men** are to give a loud shout,
	6.21	they killed everyone in the city, **men** and women, young and
	7. 3	Send only about two or three thousand **men.**
	7.14	The family that I pick out will come forward, **man** by man.
	7.18	then brought Zabdi's family forward, **man** by man, and Achan,
	8.12	He took about five thousand **men** and put them in hiding
	8.16	All the **men** in the city had been called together to go
	8.25	of Ai was killed that day—twelve thousand **men** and women.
	10. 2	it was larger than Ai, and its **men** were good fighters.
	11. 4	an army with as many **men** as there are grains of sand
	18. 4	Let me have three **men** from each tribe.
	22.14	Ten leading **men** went with Phinehas, one from each of the
	22.30	priest and the ten leading **men** of the community who were
	23.10	you can make a thousand **men** run away,
Judg	1.24	the city, [24]who saw a **man** leaving and said to him, "Show
	1.25	killed everyone in the city, except this **man** and his family.
	2. 6	on their way, and each **man** went to take possession of his
	3. 9	out to the Lord, and he sent a **man** who freed them.
	3.15	out to the Lord, and he sent a **man** to free them.
	3.15	This was Ehud, a left-handed **man,** who was the son of Gera,
	3.17	he took the gifts to Eglon, who was a very fat **man.**
	3.28	they did not allow a single **man** to cross.
	4.16	Not a **man** was left.
	4.22	I'll show you the **man** you're looking for."
	6.12	and said, "The Lord is with you, brave and mighty **man!"**
	6.16	the Midianites as easily as if they were only one **man."**
	7. 2	Lord said to Gideon, "The **men** you have are too many for
	7. 4	Then the Lord said to Gideon, "You still have too many **men.**
	7. 4	If I tell you a **man** should go with you, he will
	7. 4	If I tell you a **man** should not go with you, he
	7. 6	There were three hundred **men** who scooped up water in their
	7. 7	Midianites with the three hundred **men** who lapped the water.
	7.13	Gideon arrived, he heard a **man** telling a friend about a dream.
	7.16	three groups and gave each **man** a trumpet and a jar with
	7.19	Gideon and his hundred **men** came to the edge of the camp
	7.21	Every **man** stood in his place round the camp, and the
	8. 4	Gideon and his three hundred **men** had come to the River
	8.14	he captured a young **man** from Sukkoth and questioned him.
	8.14	The young **man** wrote down for Gideon the names of the
	8.21	It takes a **man** to do a man's job."
	9. 2	governed by all seventy of Gideon's sons or by just one **man?**
	9. 9	producing my oil, which is used to honour gods and **men.'**
	9.13	to stop producing my wine, that makes gods and **men** happy.'
	9.18	You killed his sons—seventy **men** on a single stone—and just
	9.28	Gaal said, "What kind of **men** are we in Shechem?
	9.36	There are **men** coming down from the mountain-tops!"
	9.36	"Those are not **men,"** Zebul answered.
	9.37	There are **men** coming down the crest of the mountain and one
	9.38	These are the **men** you were treating so scornfully.
	9.49	So every **man** cut off a branch of a tree;
	9.49	the people of the fort died—about a thousand **men** and women.
	9.51	strong tower there, and every **man** and woman in the city,
	9.54	he quickly called the young **man** who was carrying his weapons
	9.54	So the young **man** ran him through, and he died.
	13.10	The **man** who came to me the other day has appeared to
	13.11	He went to the **man** and asked,
	13.11	"Are you the **man** who was talking to my wife?"
	13.20	Manoah realized then that the **man** had been the Lord's angel,
	14.10	This was a custom among the young **men.**

Judg 14.20 wife was given to the **man**
14.20 that had been his best **man** at the wedding.
15.16 "With the jaw-bone of a donkey I killed a thousand **men;**
16. 9 She had some **men** waiting in another room, so she shouted,
16.12 The **men** were waiting in another room.
16.19 lap and then called a **man,** who cut off Samson's seven locks
16.27 The building was crowded with **men** and women.
16.27 there were about three thousand **men** and women on the roof,
18. 7 So the five **men** left and went to the town of Laish.
18.11 So six hundred **men** from the tribe of Dan left Zorah and
18.19 a whole Israelite tribe than for the family of one **man?"**
19. 3 Then the **man** decided to go after her and try to persuade
19. 6 So the two **men** sat down and ate and drank together.
19. 8 So the two **men** ate together.
19. 9 When the **man,** his concubine, and the servant once more
19.10 But the **man** did not want to spend another night there,
19.16 they were there, an old **man** came by at the end of
19.17 The old **man** noticed the traveller in the city square and
19.20 The old **man** said, "You are welcome in my home!
19.22 They said to the old **man,**
19.22 "Bring out that **man** that came home with you!
19.23 But the old **man** went outside and said to them, "No,
19.23 This **man** is my guest.
19.24 But don't do such an awful thing to this **man!"**
19.25 But the **men** would not listen to him.
19.26 at the door of the old **man's** house, where her husband was.
20.10 One tenth of the **men** in Israel will provide food for the
20.34 Ten thousand **men,** specially chosen out of all Israel, attacked Gibeah,
20.42 the main army and the **men** who were now coming out of
20.47 But six hundred **men** were able to escape to the open
20.48 Benjaminites and killed them all—**men,** women, and children,
21.10 twelve thousand of their bravest **men** with the orders, "Go
21.16 shall we do to provide wives for the **men** who are left?
21.24 the Israelites left, and every **man** went back to his own

Ruth 2. 1 Boaz, a rich and influential **man** who belonged to the family
2. 5 Boaz asked the **man** in charge, "Who is that young woman?"
2. 6 The **man** answered, "She is the foreign girl who came back
2.19 May God bless the **man** who took an interest in you!"
2.20 And she went on, "That **man** is a close relative of ours,
3.10 gone looking for a young **man,** either rich or poor, but you
3.12 you, but there is a **man** who is a closer relative than
4. 1 Then Elimelech's nearest relative, the **man** whom Boaz had mentioned,
4. 4 The **man** said, "I will buy it."
4. 6 The **man** answered, "In that case I will give up my right
4. 8 So when the **man** said to Boaz, "You buy it," he took

1 Sam 2. 7 He makes some **men** poor and others rich;
2. 9 a **man** does not triumph by his own strength.
2.13 Instead, when a **man** was offering his sacrifice, the priest's
2.15 come and say to the **man** offering the sacrifice, "Give me
2.16 If the **man** answered, "Let us do what is right and burn
2.25 If a **man** sins against another man, God can defend him;
2.25 but who can defend a **man** who sins against the Lord?"
2.26 grow and to gain favour both with the Lord and with **men.**
2.31 will kill all the young **men** in your family and your clan,
2.31 so that no **man** in your family will live
4. 9 Fight like **men,** or we will become slaves to the Hebrews,
4. 9 So fight like **men!"**
4.12 A **man** from the tribe of Benjamin ran all the way from
4.13 The **man** spread the news throughout the town, and everyone
4.14 The **man** hurried to Eli to tell him the news.
4.16 The **man** said, "I have escaped from the battle and have
4.18 When the **man** mentioned the Covenant Box, Eli fell
9. 2 a son named Saul, a handsome **man** in the prime of life.
9. 6 town there is a holy **man** who is highly respected because
9. 9 So they went to the town where the holy **man** lived.
9.16 time I will send you a **man** from the tribe of Benjamin;
9.17 Lord said to him, "This is the **man** I told you about.
10. 2 today, you will meet two **men** near Rachel's tomb at Zelzah in
10. 3 where you will meet three **men** on their way to offer a
10.12 A **man** who lived there asked, "How about these other
10.24 said to the people, "Here is the **man** the Lord has chosen!
11.11 The survivors scattered, each **man** running off by himself.
13. 2 The rest of the **men** Saul sent home.
13.14 will find the kind of **man** he wants and make him ruler
14. 1 Jonathan said to the young **man** who carried his weapons,
14. 2 he had about six hundred **men** with him.
14. 6 Jonathan said to the young **man,** "Let's cross over to the
14. 7 The young **man** answered, "Whatever you want to do, I'm with you."
14.12 called out to Jonathan and the young **man,** "Come on up here!
14.12 Jonathan said to the young **man,** "Follow me.
14.13 pass on his hands and knees, and the young **man** followed him.
14.13 Philistines and knocked them down, and the young **man** killed them.
14.14 slaughter Jonathan and the young **man** killed about twenty men
14.17 Jonathan and the young **man** who carried his weapons were missing.
14.52 So whenever he found a **man** who was strong or brave, he
15. 3 kill all the **men,** women, children, and babies;
15.28 and given it to someone who is a better **man** than you.
15.29 He is not a **man**—he does not change his mind."
16. 3 You will anoint as king the **man** I tell you to."
16. 6 and said to himself, "This **man** standing here in the Lord's
16. 7 I have rejected him, because I do not judge as **man** judges.
16. 7 **Man** looks at the outward appearance, but I look at the heart."
16.12 He was a handsome, healthy young **man,** and his eyes sparkled.
16.16 we will look for a **man** who knows how to play the
16.16 spirit comes on you, the **man** can play his harp, and you
16.17 ordered them, "Find me a **man** who plays well and bring him
16.18 also a brave and handsome **man,** a good soldier, and an able
16.21 very much and chose him as the **man** to carry his weapons.
17. 8 Choose one of your **men** to fight me.
17.12 the time Saul was king, he was already a very old **man.**
17.25 promised to give a big reward to the **man** who kills him;
17.26 near him, "What will the **man** get who kills this Philistine
17.27 told him what would be done for the **man** who killed Goliath.
17.30 He turned to another **man** and asked him the same question,
17.58 Saul asked him, "Young **man,** whose son are you?"
19. 5 do wrong to an innocent **man** and kill David for no reason
21. 2 As for my **men,** I have told them to meet me at
21. 4 it if your **men** haven't had sexual relations recently."
21.11 This is the **man** about whom the women sang, as they danced,
21.14 The **man** is mad!
22.19 **men** and women, children and babies, cattle, donkeys, and
24.13 You know the old saying, 'Evil is done only by evil **men.'**
24.19 How often does a **man** catch his enemy and then let him
25. 2 He was a very rich **man,** the owner of three thousand sheep
25. 2 but he was a mean, bad-tempered **man.**
25.22 I don't kill every last one of those **men** before morning!"
25.29 God will keep you safe, as a **man** guards a precious treasure.
25.29 throw them away, as a **man** hurls stones with his catapult.
26.15 David answered, "Abner, aren't you the greatest **man** in Israel?
26.19 but if **men** have done it, may the Lord's curse fall on
26.22 Let one of your **men** come over and get it.
27. 9 Egypt, [9]killing all the **men** and women and taking the sheep,
27.11 David would kill everyone, **men** and women, so that no one
28. 8 "Call up the spirit of the **man** I name."
28.14 "It's an old **man** coming up," she answered.
31. 4 He said to the young **man** carrying his weapons, "Draw your
31. 4 But the young **man** was too terrified to do it.
31. 5 The young **man** saw that Saul was dead, so he too threw
31. 6 that is how Saul, his three sons, and the young **man** died;

2 Sam 1. 2 The next day a young **man** arrived from Saul's camp.
1.13 David asked the young **man** who had brought him the news,
1.15 The **man** struck the Amalekite and mortally wounded him,
2.16 Each **man** caught his opponent by the head and plunged his
3.29 generation may there be some **man** in his family who has
4.11 evil men who murder an innocent **man** asleep in his own house!
6.19 He gave each **man** and woman in Israel a loaf of bread,
7.19 And you let a **man** see this, Sovereign Lord!
12. 1 and said, "There were two **men** who lived in the same town;
12. 2 The rich **man** had many cattle and sheep,
12. 3 while the poor **man** had only one lamb,
12. 4 One day a visitor arrived at the rich **man's** home.
12. 4 The rich **man** didn't want to kill one of his own animals
12. 4 instead, he took the poor **man's** lamb and cooked a meal for
12. 5 very angry with the rich **man** and said, "I swear by
12. 5 the living Lord that the **man** who did this ought to die!
12. 7 "You are that **man,"** Nathan said to David.
12.11 I take your wives from you and give them to another **man;**
13. 2 as a virgin, she was kept from meeting **men.**
14.14 at least find a way to bring a **man** back from exile.
14.21 Go and get the young **man** Absalom and bring him back here."
15. 2 And after the **man** had told him what tribe he was from,
15. 5 When the **man** approached Absalom to bow down before him,
17. 3 You want to kill only one **man;**
17.10 Then even the bravest **men,** as fearless as lions, will be
17.18 off to hide in the house of a certain **man** in Bahurim.
18. 5 "For my sake don't harm the young **man** Absalom."
18.12 But the **man** answered, "Even if you gave me a thousand
18.12 'For my sake don't harm the young **man** Absalom.'
18.17 All the Israelites fled, each **man** to his own home.
18.24 he looked out and saw a **man** running alone.
18.26 Then the watchman saw another **man** running alone,
18.26 There's another **man** running!"
18.27 said, "I can see that the first **man** runs like Ahimaaz."
18.27 "He's a good **man,"** the king said, "and he is bringing
18.29 "Is the young **man** Absalom safe?"
18.32 "Is the young **man** Absalom safe?"
19. 8 Meanwhile all the Israelites had fled, each **man** to his own home.
19.32 Barzillai was a very old **man,** eighty years old.
20.12 Joab's **man** saw that everybody was stopping, so he dragged
20.21 Hand over this one **man,** and I will withdraw from the city."
23. 1 son of Jesse was the **man** whom God made great, whom the
23. 6 But godless **men** are like thorns that are thrown away;
23.21 killed an Egyptian, a huge **man** who was armed with a spear.
24.14 But I don't want to be punished by **men.**

1 Kgs 1. 1 was now a very old **man,** and although his servants covered
1. 5 He was a very handsome **man.**
1.42 "You're a good **man**—you must be bringing good news."
4. 7 king and his household, each **man** being responsible for one
7.13 King Solomon sent for a **man** named Huram, a craftsman
11.26 Another **man** who turned against King Solomon
11.28 Jeroboam was an able young **man,** and when Solomon noticed
13. 4 he pointed at him and ordered, "Seize that **man!"**
13.14 "I am," the **man** answered.
18.31 the sons of Jacob, the **man** to whom the Lord had given
18.44 no bigger than a **man's** hand, coming up from the sea."
20. 7 country and said, "You see that this **man** wants to ruin us.
20.20 Israelite army, [20]and each one killed the **man** he fought.
20.37 Then this same prophet went to another **man** and said,
20.37 This **man** did so;
20.39 brought a captured enemy to me and said, 'Guard this **man;**
20.40 But I got busy with other things, and the **man** escaped."
20.42 'Because you allowed the **man** to escape whom I had ordered to
21.19 to him, 'After murdering the **man,** are you taking over his
22.17 And the Lord said, 'These **men** have no leader;
22.36 "Every **man** go back to his own country and city!"

2 Kgs 1. 6 "We were met by a **man** who told us to come back
1. 7 "What did the **man** look like?"

2 Kgs 4. 1 know, he was a God-fearing **man,**
4. 1 but now a **man** he owed money to has come
4. 9 "I am sure that this **man**
4. 9 who comes here so often is a holy **man.**
4.14 "Well, she has no son, and her husband is an old **man."**
4.16 You are a **man** of God!"
4.42 Another time, a **man** came from Baal Shalishah, bringing
5. 7 "How can the king of Syria expect me to cure this **man?**
5. 8 Send the **man** to me, and I'll show him that there is
5.21 When Naaman saw a **man** running after him, he got down from
5.26 there in spirit when the **man** got out of his chariot to
6. 6 The **man** showed him the place, and Elisha cut off a stick,
6. 7 out," he ordered, and the **man** bent down and picked it up.
6.19 me, and I will lead you to the **man** you are after."
9.17 "I see some **men** riding up!"
13. 7 ten chariots, and ten thousand **men** on foot, because the king
13.21 contact with Elisha's bones, the **man** came back to life and
18.23 thousand horses if you can find that many **men** to ride them!
20.14 and asked, "Where did these **men** come from and what did they
24.14 royal princes, and all the leading **men,** ten thousand in all.
24.15 his wives, his officials, and the leading **men** of Judah.
24.16 Nebuchadnezzar deported all the important **men** to Babylonia,
24.16 all of them able-bodied **men** fit for military duty.
1 Chr 7.40 They were heads of families, famous fighting **men,** outstanding leaders.
10. 4 He said to the young **man** carrying his weapons, "Draw your
10. 4 But the young **man** was too terrified to do it.
10. 5 The young **man** saw that Saul was dead, so he too threw
11. 6 David said, "The first **man** to kill a Jebusite will be
11.19 drinking the blood of these **men** who risked their lives!"
11.23 killed an Egyptian, a huge **man** over two metres tall, who was
16. 3 He gave each **man** and woman in Israel a loaf of bread,
17.17 you, Lord God, are already treating me like a great **man.**
21.13 But I don't want to be punished by **men.**
26. 6 They were important **men** in their clan
26. 8 a total of sixty-two highly qualified **men** for this work.
26.30 of his relatives, all outstanding **men,** were put in charge of
28. 1 leading soldiers, and important **men**—gathered in Jerusalem.
29. 1 is not a palace for **men** but a temple for the Lord
2 Chr 2. 7 Now send me a **man** with skill in engraving, in working gold,
6.18 can you, O God, really live on earth among **men** and women?
8.18 of his own officers and **manned** by experienced sailors.
18.16 And the Lord said, 'These **men** have no leader;
21.13 You even murdered your brothers, who were better **men** than you are.
35.25 Israel for the singers, both **men** and women, to use this song
36.17 on anyone, young or old, **man** or woman, sick or healthy.
Ezra 9. 2 Jewish **men** were marrying foreign women, and so God's holy
10. 1 of Israelites—**men,** women, and children—gathered round him,
10.17 they investigated all the cases of **men** with foreign wives.
10.18 This is the list of the **men** who had foreign wives:
10.44 All these **men** had foreign wives.
Neh 4.18 The **man** who was to sound the alarm on the bugle stayed
5. 1 many of the people, both **men** and women, began to complain
6.11 I answered, "I'm not the kind of **man** that runs and hides.
7. 2 Hananiah was a reliable and God-fearing **man** without an equal.
8. 2 where the people had gathered—**men,** women, and the children
13.23 that many of the Jewish **men** had married women from Ashdod,
13.26 He was a **man** who was greater than any of the kings
Esth 1.16 but also his officials—in fact, every **man** in the empire!
4.11 "If anyone, **man** or woman, goes to the inner courtyard
6. 6 What should I do for this **man?"**
6. 7 to be brought for this **man**—robes that you yourself wear.
6. 9 noblemen to dress the **man** in these robes and lead him,
6. 9 'See how the king rewards a **man** he wishes to honour!' "
6.11 "See how the king rewards a **man** he wishes to honour!"
7. 5 Where is this **man?"**
7. 8 king cried out, "Is this **man** going to rape the queen
8.11 attacked the Jewish **men,** their children or their women,
8.11 slaughter them to the last **man** and take their possessions.
9. 4 Mordecai was now a powerful **man** in the palace and was
Job 1. 1 He was a good **man,** careful not to do anything evil.
1. 3 number of servants and was the richest **man** in the East.
2. 4 Satan replied, "A **man** will give up everything in order to
3.20 Why let **men** go on living in misery?
3.20 Why give light to **men** in grief?
4. 7 Name a single case where a righteous **man** met with disaster.
4.20 A **man** may be alive in the morning, but die unnoticed
5. 7 **Man** brings trouble on himself, as surely as sparks fly up
5.12 upsets the plans of cunning **men,**
5.12 and traps wise **men** in their own schemes,
7. 9 cloud that fades and is gone, a **man** dies and never returns;
7.17 Why is **man** so important to you?
8.10 But let the ancient wise **men** teach you;
8.13 Godless **men** are like those reeds;
8.16 Evil **men** sprout like weeds in the sun,
8.19 Yes, that's all the joy evil **men** have;
8.20 never abandon the faithful or ever give help to evil **men.**
9. 1 But how can a **man** win his case against God?
9. 4 no **man** can stand up against him.
9.23 When an innocent **man** suddenly dies, God laughs.
10. 3 And then to smile on the schemes of wicked **men?**
11. 1 Does talking so much put a **man** in the right?
11.11 God knows which **men** are worthless;
11.12 Stupid **men** will start being wise when wild donkeys are born tame.
12. 5 you hit a **man** who is about to fall.
12. 6 But thieves and godless **men** live in peace,
12.10 every **man's** life is in his power.
12.12 Old **men** have wisdom, but God has wisdom and power.
12.12 Old **men** have insight;
12.14 who can rebuild, and who can free the **man** God imprisons?
Job 12.19 he humbles priests and **men** of power.
12.20 He silences **men** who are trusted,
12.20 and takes the wisdom of old **men** away.
13. 9 Do you think you can fool God as you fool **men?**
13.16 will save me, since no wicked **man** would dare to face God.
14. 4 Nothing clean can ever come from anything as unclean as **man.**
14.10 But a **man** dies, and that is the end of him;
14.14 If a **man** dies, can he come back to life?
14.19 so you destroy **man's** hope for life.
14.20 You overpower a **man** and send him away for ever;
15. 3 No wise **man** would talk as you do or defend himself with
15. 7 Do you think you were the first **man** born?
15.10 wisdom from grey-haired **men**— men born before your father.
15.14 Can any **man** be really pure?
15.16 And **man** drinks evil as if it were water;
15.16 yes, **man** is corrupt;
15.16 **man** is worthless.
15.18 Wise **men** have taught me truths which they learnt
15.20 A wicked **man** who oppresses others will be in torment as
15.25 is the fate of the **man** who shakes his fist at God
15.26 That **man** is proud and rebellious;
15.28 That is the **man** who captured cities and seized houses
15.34 be no descendants for godless **men,** and fire will destroy the
15.35 These are the **men** who plan trouble and do evil;
16.11 God has handed me over to evil **men.**
16.21 plead with God for me, as a **man** pleads for his friend.
17. 5 In the old proverb a **man** betrays his friends for money,
18. 5 The wicked **man's** light will still be put out;
18.21 is the fate of evil **men,** the fate of those who care
20. 4 that from ancient times, when **man** was first placed on earth,
20. 5 no wicked **man** has been happy for long.
20.15 The wicked **man** vomits up the wealth he stole;
20.16 What the evil **man** swallows is like poison;
20.27 Heaven reveals this **man's** sin,
20.29 is the fate of wicked **men,** the fate that God assigns to
21. 4 My quarrel is not with mortal **men;**
21. 7 Why does God let evil **men** live, let them grow old and
21.17 Was a wicked **man's** light ever put out?
21.21 When a **man's** life is over, does he really care whether
21.22 Can a **man** teach God, who judges even those in high places?
21.23 Some **men** stay healthy till the day they die;
21.28 house of the great **man** now, the man who practised evil?"
21.30 and punishes, it is the wicked **man** who is always spared.
21.31 one to accuse a wicked **man** or pay him back for all
22. 1 Is there any **man,** even the wisest, who could ever be
22.15 to walk in the paths that evil **men** have always followed?
22.17 These are the **men** who rejected God
22.19 Good **men** are glad and innocent men laugh when they see
24. 2 **Men** move boundary stones to get more land;
24. 6 don't own, and gather grapes in wicked **men's** vineyards.
24. 9 Evil **men** make slaves of fatherless infants and take the
24. 9 and take the poor **man's** children in payment for debts.
24.13 There are **men** who reject the light;
24.18 The wicked **man** is swept away by floods, and the land he
24.22 God acts—and the wicked **man** dies.
24.24 For a while the wicked **man** prospers, but then he withers
25. 6 Then what about **man,** that worm, that insect?
25. 6 What is **man** worth in God's eyes?
26. 1 help you are to me— poor, weak **man** that I am!
27. 5 I will never say that you **men** are right;
27. 7 fight against me be punished like wicked, unrighteous **men.**
27. 8 hope is there for godless **men** in the hour when God demands
27.13 This is how Almighty God punishes wicked, violent **men.**
27.17 but some good **man** will wear the clothes,
27.17 and some honest **man** will get the silver.
28. 2 **Men** dig iron out of the ground And melt copper out of
28. 3 **Men** explore the deepest darkness.
28. 4 Or human feet ever travel, **Men** dig the shafts of mines.
28. 9 **Men** dig the hardest rocks, Dig mountains away at their base.
28.13 Wisdom is not to be found among **men;**
28.28 God said to **men,** "To be wise, you must have reverence
29. 8 my place among them, [8] young **men** stepped aside as soon as
29. 8 they saw me, and old **men** stood up to show me respect.
29.10 even the most important **men** kept silent.
29.13 **Men** who were in deepest misery praised me, and I helped
29.17 I destroyed the power of cruel **men** and rescued their victims.
30. 1 But **men** younger than I am make fun of me now!
30. 2 were a bunch of worn-out **men,** too weak to do any work
30.24 do you attack a ruined **man,** one who can do nothing but
31.10 let my wife cook another **man's** food
31.10 and sleep in another **man's** bed.
31.31 All the **men** who work for me know that I have always
31.33 Other **men** try to hide their sins, but I have never
32. 1 own innocence, the three **men** gave up trying to answer him.
32. 5 he saw that the three **men** could not answer Job, he was
32. 7 to speak, that you older **men** should share your wisdom.
32. 8 of Almighty God that comes to **men** and gives them wisdom.
32. 9 not growing old that makes **men** wise or helps them to know
33.12 God is greater than any **man.**
33.13 Why do you accuse God of never answering a **man's** complaints?
33.15 At night when **men** are asleep, God speaks in dreams and visions.
33.19 God corrects a **man** by sending sickness and filling his
33.20 The sick **man** loses his appetite, and even the finest
33.23 of God's thousands of angels, who remind **men** of their duty.
34. 1 You **men** are so wise, so clever;
34. 7 Have you ever seen anyone like this **man** Job?
34. 8 He likes the company of evil **men** and goes about with sinners.
34.10 Listen to me, you **men** who understand!
34.20 A **man** may suddenly die at night.
34.20 God strikes **men** down and they perish;
34.21 He watches every step **men** take.

Job 34.23 to set a time for **men** to go and be judged by
34.29 If he hid his face, **men** would be helpless.
34.34 any wise **man** who hears me will say [35] that Job is
34.36 you will see that he talks like an evil **man.**
35. 8 It is your **fellow-man** who suffers from your sins, and the
35. 9 When **men** are oppressed, they groan;
35.12 but God doesn't answer, for they are proud and evil **men.**
36. 4 you see before you a truly wise **man.**
36.15 But God teaches **men** through suffering and uses distress
37. 7 He brings the work of **men** to a stop;
37.13 may send it to punish **men,** or to show them his favour.
37.23 he is righteous and just in his dealings with **men.**
38. 3 Stand up now like a **man** and answer the questions I ask
39.20 leap like locusts and frighten **men** with their snorting?
40. 7 Stand up now like a **man,** and answer my questions.
41.29 is a piece of straw, and he laughs when **men** throw spears.
Ps 1. 1 reject the advice of evil **men,** who do not follow the example
1. 4 But evil **men** are not like this at all;
5. 5 You cannot stand the sight of proud **men;**
5. 6 You destroy all liars and despise violent, deceitful **men.**
6. 8 Keep away from me, you evil **men!**
7. 9 Stop the wickedness of evil **men** and reward those who are good.
8. 4 what is **man,** that you think of him;
8. 4 mere **man,** that you care for him?
9.19 Do not let **men** defy you!
10. 3 The wicked **man** is proud of his evil desires;
10. 3 the greedy **man** curses and rejects the Lord.
10. 4 A wicked **man** does not care about the Lord;
10. 5 A wicked **man** succeeds in everything.
10.11 The wicked **man** says to himself, "God doesn't care!
10.12 O Lord, punish those wicked **men!**
10.13 How can a wicked **man** despise God and say to himself,
10.14 The helpless **man** commits himself to you;
10.15 Break the power of wicked and evil **men;**
10.18 their favour, so that mortal **men** may cause terror no more.
11. 2 aimed their arrows to shoot from the shadows at good **men.**
11. 3 There is nothing a good **man** can do when everything falls apart."
12. 1 There is not a good **man** left;
12. 1 honest **men** can no longer be found.
12. 7 Wicked **men** are everywhere, and everyone praises what is evil.
14. 6 plans of the humble **man,** but the Lord is his protection.
18.48 me victory over my enemies and protect me from violent **men.**
22. 6 But I am no longer a **man;**
22.16 A gang of evil **men** is round me;
22.29 All proud **men** will bow down to him;
22.29 all mortal **men** will bow down before him.
22.30 **men** will speak of the Lord to the coming generation.
26. 5 I hate the company of evil **men** and avoid the wicked.
26.10 the fate of murderers— [10] **men** who do evil all the time
27. 2 When evil **men** attack me and try to kill me, they stumble
28. 3 those who do evil— **men** whose words are friendly, but who
31.18 and arrogant who speak with contempt about righteous **men.**
31.20 them in the safety of your presence from the plots of **men;**
32. 2 Happy is the **man** whom the Lord does not accuse of doing
34.19 The good **man** suffers many troubles, but the Lord saves
35.11 Evil **men** testify against me and accuse me of crimes I
35.16 Like **men** who would mock a cripple, they glared at me
36. 1 Sin speaks to the wicked **man** deep in his heart;
36. 6 **Men** and animals are in your care.
36.11 let proud men attack me or wicked **men** make me run away.
36.12 See where evil **men** have fallen.
37.12 The wicked **man** plots against the good man and glares at
37.13 the Lord laughs at wicked **men,** because he knows they will
37.16 The little that a good **man** owns is worth more than the
37.21 The wicked **man** borrows and never pays back,
37.21 but the good **man** is generous with his gifts.
37.23 The Lord guides a **man** in the way he should go and
37.25 I am an old **man** now;
37.25 have never seen a good **man** abandoned by the Lord or his
37.30 A good **man's** words are wise, and he is always fair.
37.32 A wicked **man** watches a good man and tries to kill him;
37.35 I once knew a wicked **man** who was a tyrant;
37.37 Notice the good **man,** observe the righteous man;
37.37 a peaceful **man** has descendants,
37.39 The Lord saves righteous **men** and protects them in times of trouble.
38.13 I am like a deaf **man** and cannot hear,
38.13 like a dumb **man** and cannot speak.
38.14 I am like a **man** who does not answer, because he cannot
39. 1 I will not say anything while evil **men** are near."
39. 5 Indeed every living **man** is no more than a puff of wind,
39.11 You punish a **man's** sins by your rebukes, and like a moth
39.11 Indeed a **man** is no more than a puff of wind!
43. 1 deliver me from lying and evil **men!**
45. 2 You are the most handsome of **men;**
49. 6 surrounded by enemies, [6] by evil **men** who trust in their
49.10 that even wise men die, as well as foolish and stupid **men.**
49.12 A **man's** greatness cannot save him from death;
49.16 Don't be upset when a **man** becomes rich, when his wealth
49.18 Even if a **man** is satisfied with this life and is praised
49.20 A **man's** greatness cannot save him from death;
52. 1 Why do you boast, great **man,** of your evil?
52. 7 say, [7] "Look, here is a **man** who did not depend on God
54. 3 Proud **men** are coming to attack me;
54. 3 cruel **men** are trying to kill me—
54. 3 **men** who do not care about God.
55.22 he never lets honest **men** be defeated.
58. 1 Do you judge all **men** fairly?
58. 3 Evil **men** go wrong all their lives;
59. 2 Save me from those evil **men;**
59. 3 cruel **men** are gathering against me.
Ps 62. 3 all of you attack a **man** who is no stronger than a
62. 9 **Men** are all like a puff of breath;
64. 2 me from the plots of the wicked, from mobs of evil **men.**
64. 4 they destroy good **men** with cowardly slander.
64. 6 The heart and mind of **man** are a mystery.
66. 5 Come and see what God has done, his wonderful acts among **men.**
68.18 he receives gifts from rebellious **men.**
71. 4 God, rescue me from wicked **men,**
71. 4 from the power of cruel and evil **men.**
73. 9 and give arrogant orders to **men** on earth, [10] so that even
76.10 **Men's** anger only results in more praise for you;
76.11 God makes **men** fear him;
78.31 killed their strongest **men,** the best young men of Israel.
78.63 Young **men** were killed in war, and young women had no one
78.65 he was like a strong **man** excited by wine.
82. 4 Rescue them from the power of evil **men.**
82. 7 But you will die like **men;**
85.11 **Man's** loyalty will reach up from the earth, and God's
86.14 Proud **men** are coming against me, O God;
86.14 a gang of cruel **men** is trying to kill me— people
89. 3 You said, "I have made a covenant with the **man** I chose;
89.48 How can **man** keep himself from the grave?
90. 3 You tell **man** to return to what he was;
92. 6 a stupid **man** cannot understand:
94. 2 You are the judge of all **men;**
94.10 He is the teacher of all **men**—hasn't he any knowledge?
94.21 who plot against good **men** and sentence the innocent to death.
101. 5 I will not tolerate a **man** who is proud and arrogant.
101. 8 I will expel all evil **men** from the city of the Lord.
104.14 the cattle and plants for **man** to use, so that he can
105. 5 you descendants of Jacob, the **man** he chose:
105.17 But he sent a **man** ahead of them, Joseph, who had been
107.26 In such danger the **men** lost their courage;
107.27 staggered like drunken **men**— all their skill was useless.
109. 2 Wicked **men** and liars have attacked me.
109. 8 may another **man** take his job!
109.16 That **man** never thought of being kind;
109.31 because he defends the poor **man** and saves him from those
110. 3 of early morning your young **men** will come to you on the
112. 2 The good **man's** children will be powerful in the land;
112. 4 in the darkness for good **men,** for those who are merciful,
115.16 belongs to the Lord alone, but he gave the earth to **man.**
118. 8 is better to trust in the Lord than to depend on **man.**
119. 9 How can a young **man** keep his life pure?
119.69 Proud **men** have told lies about me, but with all my heart
119.70 These **men** have no understanding, but I find pleasure in your law.
119.85 Proud **men,** who do not obey your law, have dug pits to
119.86 **men** persecute me with lies—help me!
119.95 Wicked **men** are waiting to kill me, but I will meditate
119.100 I have greater wisdom than old **men,** because I obey your commands.
119.110 Wicked **men** lay a trap for me, but I have not disobeyed
119.122 don't let arrogant **men** oppress me!
119.161 Powerful **men** attack me unjustly, but I respect your law.
127. 4 The sons a **man** has when he is young are like arrows
127. 5 Happy is the **man** who has many such arrows.
128. 4 A **man** who obeys the Lord will surely be blessed like this.
135. 8 In Egypt he killed all the first-born of **men** and animals alike.
137. 8 Happy is the **man** who pays you back for what you have
139.19 How I wish violent **men** would leave me alone!
140. 1 Save me, Lord, from evil **men;**
140. 1 keep me safe from violent **men.**
140. 4 keep me safe from violent **men** who plot my downfall.
140. 5 Proud **men** have set a trap for me;
140.11 may evil overtake violent **men** and destroy them.
141. 4 to do wrong and from joining evil **men** in their wickedness.
141. 5 A good **man** may punish me and rebuke me in kindness, but
141. 5 never accept honour from evil **men,** because I am always
144. 3 Lord, what is **man,** that you notice him;
144. 3 mere **man,** that you pay attention to him?
146. 5 Happy is the **man** who has the God of Jacob to help
148.12 girls and young **men,** old people and children too.
Prov 1. 4 person clever and teach young **men** how to be resourceful.
1. 5 the knowledge of wise **men** and give guidance to the educated,
1. 6 meanings of proverbs and the problems that wise **men** raise.
1.18 to catch is watching, [18] but **men** like that are setting a
2. 7 He provides help and protection for righteous, honest **men.**
2.13 trouble by what they say— [13] **men** who have abandoned a
2.14 in the darkness of sin, [14] **men** who find pleasure in doing
2.15 senseless evil, [15] unreliable **men** who cannot be trusted.
2.20 follow the example of good **men** and live a righteous life.
2.21 Righteous **men**—men of integrity—will live in this land of ours.
2.22 But God will snatch wicked **men** from the land and pull
3. 4 you do this, both God and **man** will be pleased with you.
3.13 Happy is the **man** who becomes wise—who gains understanding.
3.32 who do evil, but he takes righteous **men** into his confidence.
3.33 on the homes of wicked **men,** but blesses the homes of the
3.35 Wise **men** will gain an honourable reputation,
3.35 but stupid **men** will only add to their own disgrace.
4.14 Do not go where evil **men** go.
5. 9 had, and you will die young at the hands of merciless **men.**
5.22 The sins of a wicked **man** are a trap.
6. 9 How long is the lazy **man** going to lie in bed?
6.16 and a **man** who stirs up
6.26 A **man** can hire a prostitute for the price of a loaf
6.32 But a **man** who commits adultery hasn't any sense.
7. 7 I saw many inexperienced young **men,** but noticed one foolish
7.13 her arms round the young **man,** kissed him, looked him
7.26 been the ruin of many **men** and caused the death of too
8. 9 To the **man** with insight, it is all clear;
8.32 "Now, young **men,** listen to me.

Prov 8.34 The **man** who listens to me will be happy—
8.34 the **man** who stays at my door
8.35 The **man** who finds me finds life, and the Lord will be
8.36 The **man** who does not find me hurts himself;
9. 4 And to the foolish **man** she says, [5]"Come, eat my food and
9. 7 If you correct a conceited **man,** you will only be insulted.
9. 7 If you reprimand an evil **man,** you will only get hurt.
9. 8 Never correct a conceited **man;**
9. 8 But if you correct a wise **man,** he will respect you.
9. 9 Anything you say to a wise **man** will make him wiser.
9. 9 Whatever you tell a righteous **man** will add to his knowledge.
9.16 To the foolish **man** she says, [17]"Stolen water is sweeter.
10. 5 A sensible **man** gathers the crops when they are ready;
10. 6 A good **man** will receive blessings.
10. 6 A wicked **man's** words hide a violent nature.
10.11 A good **man's** words are a fountain of life,
10.11 but a wicked **man's** words hide a violent nature.
10.18 A **man** who hides his hatred is a liar.
10.20 A good **man's** words are like pure silver;
10.20 a wicked **man's** ideas are worthless.
10.21 A good **man's** words will benefit many people, but you can
10.26 Never get a lazy **man** to do something for you;
10.28 The hopes of good **men** lead to joy, but wicked people can
11. 5 Honesty makes a good **man's** life easier,
11. 5 but a wicked **man** will cause his own downfall.
11. 6 Righteousness rescues the honest **man,** but someone who
11. 7 When a wicked **man** dies, his hope dies with him.
11.10 fortune, and there are joyful shouts when wicked **men** die.
11.11 A city becomes great when righteous **men** give it their blessing;
11.16 A lazy **man** will never have money,
11.16 but an aggressive **man** will get rich.
11.21 evil men will be punished, but righteous **men** will escape.
11.26 People curse a **man** who hoards grain, waiting for a higher price,
11.29 The **man** who brings trouble on his family will have
11.29 Foolish **men** will always be servants to the wise.
12. 6 The words of wicked **men** are murderous, but the words of
12. 7 Wicked **men** meet their downfall and leave no descendants,
12. 7 but the families of righteous **men** live on.
12. 9 better to be an ordinary **man** working for a living
12. 9 than to play the part of a great **man** but go hungry.
12.10 A good **man** takes care of his animals,
12.10 but wicked **men** are cruel to theirs.
12.13 A wicked **man** is trapped by his own words,
12.13 but an honest **man** gets himself out of trouble.
12.26 The righteous **man** is a guide to his friend, but the path
13. 8 A rich **man** has to use his money to save his life,
13. 8 but no one threatens a poor **man.**
13.22 A good **man** will have wealth to leave to his grandchildren,
13.22 but the wealth of sinners will go to righteous **men.**
13.23 for the poor, but unjust **men** keep them from being farmed.
14. 3 a wise **man's** words protect him.
14.11 A good **man's** house will still be standing
14.11 after an evil **man's** house has been destroyed.
14.20 likes a poor **man,** but the rich have many friends.
14.26 Lord gives confidence and security to a **man** and his family.
14.33 Wisdom is in every thought of an intelligent **man;**
15. 6 Righteous **men** keep their wealth,
15. 6 but wicked **men** lose theirs when hard times come.
15. 8 Lord is pleased when good **men** pray,
15. 8 but hates the sacrifices that wicked **men** bring him.
15.11 how then can a **man** hide his thoughts from God?
15.25 destroy the homes of arrogant **men,** but he will protect a
16.14 A wise **man** will try to keep the king happy;
16.33 **Men** cast lots to learn God's will, but God himself
17. 6 Old **men** are proud of their grandchildren, just as boys are
17.18 Only a **man** with no sense would promise to be responsible
18.17 The first **man** to speak in court always seems right until
18.18 If two powerful **men** are opposing each other in court,
18.23 When the poor **man** speaks, he has to beg politely,
18.23 but when the rich **man** answers, he is rude.
19. 7 Even the brothers of a poor **man** have no use for him;
19.14 A **man** can inherit a house and money from his parents,
21.22 a city defended by strong **men,** and destroy the walls they
21.25 A lazy **man** who refuses to work is only killing himself;
21.26 A righteous **man,** however, can give, and give generously.
21.27 Lord hates it when wicked **men** offer him sacrifices,
22. 7 Poor people are the rich **man's** slaves.
22.13 The lazy **man** stays at home;
22.17 Listen, and I will teach you what wise **men** have said.
22.29 Show me a **man** who does a good job,
22.29 I will show you a **man** who is better than most
23. 1 to eat with an important **man,** keep in mind who he is.
23. 6 the table of a stingy **man** or be greedy for the fine
23.24 A righteous **man's** father has good reason to be happy.
23.28 for you like robbers and cause many **men** to be unfaithful.
24.15 scheme to rob an honest **man** or to take away his home.
24.16 how often an honest **man** falls, he always gets up again;
24.22 such **men** could be ruined in a moment.
24.23 Wise **men** have also said these things:
24.30 I walked through the fields and vineyards of a lazy, stupid **man.**
25. 1 of Solomon's proverbs, copied by **men** at the court of King
26. 7 proverb about as well as a crippled **man** can use his legs.
26. 9 reminds you of a drunk **man** trying to pick a thorn out
26.13 Why doesn't the lazy **man** ever get out of the house?
26.14 The lazy **man** turns over in bed.
26.16 A lazy **man** will think he is more intelligent
26.16 than seven **men** who can give good reasons
26.18 A **man** who misleads someone and then claims that he
27. 8 A **man** away from home is like a bird away from its
28. 3 A **man** in authority who oppresses poor people is like a
28. 7 A young **man** who obeys the law is intelligent.

Prov 28.12 When good **men** come to power, everybody celebrates,
28.12 but when bad **men** rule, people stay in hiding.
28.17 A **man** guilty of murder is digging his own grave as fast
28.28 People stay in hiding when bad **men** come to power.
28.28 But when they fall from power, righteous **men** will rule again.
29. 9 When an intelligent **man** brings a lawsuit against a fool,
29.13 A poor **man** and his oppressor have this in common—the
29.16 When evil **men** are in power, crime increases.
29.16 But the righteous will live to see the downfall of such **men.**
29.18 Happy is the **man** who keeps God's law!
30. 2 I am more like an animal than a **man;**
30. 2 I do not have the sense a **man** should have.
30.19 and a **man** and a woman falling in love.

Ecc 1.16 "I have become a great **man,** far wiser than anyone who ruled
2. 8 **Men** and women sang to entertain me,
2. 8 and I had all the women a **man** could want.
2.14 Wise **men** can see where they are going, and fools cannot."
2.16 No one remembers wise **men,** and no one remembers fools.
2.24 The best thing a **man** can do is to eat and drink
3.19 After all, the same fate awaits **man** and animal alike.
3.21 anyone be sure that a **man's** spirit goes upwards while an
4. 5 They say that a **man** would be a fool to fold his
4. 8 Here is a **man** who lives alone.
4.12 Two **men** can resist an attack
4.12 that would defeat one **man** alone.
4.13 A **man** may rise from poverty to become king of his country,
4.13 as well off as a young **man** who is poor but intelligent.
4.15 them there is a young **man** who will take the king's place.
5.12 A working **man** may or may not have enough to eat,
5.12 A rich **man,** however, has so much that he stays awake worrying.
5.18 this is **man's** fate.
5.19 If God gives a **man** wealth and property and lets him
6. 3 A **man** may have a hundred children and live a long time,
6. 6 rest—[6] more so than the **man** who never enjoys life, though he
6. 7 A **man** does all his work just to get something to eat,
6. 8 How is a wise **man** better off than a fool?
6. 8 does it do a poor **man** to know how to face life?
6.10 we all know that a **man** cannot argue with someone who is
6.12 what is best for a **man** in this short, useless life of
7. 7 When a wise **man** cheats someone, he is acting like a fool.
7.15 A good **man** may die while another man lives on, even though
7.26 A **man** who pleases God can get away, but she will catch
7.28 I found one **man** in a thousand that I could respect, but
8. 1 Only a wise **man** knows what things really mean.
8. 5 are safe, and a wise **man** knows how and when to do
8. 9 world, a world where some **men** have power and others have to
8.10 Yes, I have seen wicked **men** buried and in their graves,
8.14 sometimes righteous **men** get the punishment of the wicked,
8.14 and wicked **men** get the reward of the righteous.
8.15 I am convinced that a **man** should enjoy himself, because the
8.17 Wise **men** may claim to know, but they don't.
9. 1 of wise and righteous **men,** even their love and their hate.
9. 2 A good **man** is no better off than a sinner;
9. 2 a **man** who takes an oath is no better off than one
9.11 Wise **men** do not always earn a living,
9.11 intelligent **men** do not always get rich,
9.11 and capable **men** do not always rise
9.15 A **man** lived there who was poor, but so clever that he
9.16 one thinks of a poor **man** as wise or pays any attention
9.17 quiet words of a wise **man** than to the shouts of a
10. 2 is natural for a wise **man** to do the right thing and
10. 6 given positions of authority while rich **men** are ignored.
10.12 What a wise **man** says brings him honour, but a fool is
10.18 When a **man** is too lazy to repair his roof, it will
12.11 The sayings of wise **men** are like the sharp sticks that
12.13 his commands, because this is all that **man** was created for.

Song 1. 9 You, my love, excite **men** as a mare excites the stallions
2. 3 of the forest, so is my dearest compared with other **men.**
8. 8 What will we do for her when a young **man** comes courting?

Is 1.31 by a spark, so powerful **men** will be destroyed
2.22 Put no more confidence in mortal **men.**
3.10 Righteous **men** will be happy, and things will go well for them.
3.11 But evil **men** are doomed;
4. 1 will grab hold of one **man** and say, "We can feed and
7.13 wear out the patience of **men**—must you wear out God's
9.15 The old and honourable **men** are the head—
9.19 and destroys the people, and it is every **man** for himself.
10.15 an axe claim to be greater than the **man** who uses it?
10.15 Is a saw more important than the **man** who saws with it?
10.15 A club doesn't lift up a **man;**
10.15 a **man** lifts up a club."
10.18 in the same way that a fatal sickness destroys a **man.**
14.16 will ask, 'Is this the **man** who shook the earth and made
14.17 Is this the **man** who destroyed cities and turned the
14.17 Is this the **man** who never freed his prisoners or let them
19.11 Egypt's wisest **men** give stupid advice!
19.14 and staggers like a drunken **man** slipping on his own vomit.
21. 7 If he sees **men** coming on horseback, two by two,
21. 7 and **men** riding on donkeys and camels,
21. 9 **Men** on horseback, two by two.
21.17 The bowmen are the bravest **men** of Kedar, but few of them
22. 2 Your **men** who died in this war did not die fighting.
23. 2 You sent **men** [3]across the sea to buy and sell the corn
23. 8 whose merchant princes were the most honoured **men** on earth?
23. 9 in what they had done and to humiliate their honoured **men.**
23.16 Play and sing your songs again to bring **men** back once more.
24.20 will stagger like a drunken **man** and sway like a hut in
25. 4 Cruel **men** attack like a winter storm, [5]like drought in a
25. 5 silence the shouts of cruel **men,** as a cloud cools a hot
26. 7 Lord, you make the path smooth for good **men;**
26.10 you are kind to wicked **men,** they never learn to do what

Is 27. 7 as severely as its enemies, nor has she lost as many **men.**
28. 9 They say, "Who does that **man** think he's teaching?
28.14 Now you arrogant **men** who rule here in Jerusalem over this people,
28.20 You will be like the **man** in the proverb, who tries to
29. 8 will be like a starving **man** who dreams he is eating
29. 8 or like a **man** dying of thirst who dreams he
29.16 Can something a **man** has made say to him, "You didn't make
29.21 who tell lies to keep honest **men** from getting justice.
31. 2 his threats to punish evil **men** and those who protect them.
31. 8 run from battle, and their young **men** will be made slaves.
33. 7 Brave **men** are calling for help.
33.22 will be so much that even lame **men** can have a share.
36. 8 thousand horses if you can find that many **men** to ride them.
39. 3 and asked, "Where did these **men** come from
40.20 The **man** who cannot afford silver or gold chooses wood
40.30 young **men** can fall exhausted.
41. 7 The **man** who beats the idol smooth encourages the one who
41.25 "I have chosen a **man** who lives in the east;
44.13 in the form of a **man,** a handsome human figure, to be
44.15 A **man** uses part of a tree for fuel and part of
46.11 I am calling a **man** to come from the east;
48.14 predict that the **man** I have chosen would attack Babylon;
50. 1 I sent my people away like a **man** who divorces his wife?
50. 1 into captivity like a **man** who sells his children as slaves?
51.12 Why should you fear mortal **man,** who is no more enduring
53. 9 in a grave with evil **men,** he was buried with the rich,
53.12 a place of honour, a place among great and powerful **men.**
53.12 He willingly gave his life and shared the fate of evil **men.**
56. 3 A **man** who has been castrated should never think that
56. 4 Lord says to such a **man,** "If you honour me by observing
57.20 But evil **men** are like the restless sea, whose waves
62. 5 Like a young **man** taking a virgin as his bride, He who
63. 2 red, like that of a **man** who tramples grapes to make wine?"

Jer 3. 1 The Lord says, "If a **man** divorces his wife, and she
3. 1 leaves him and becomes another **man's** wife, he cannot take
5.26 "Evil **men** live among my people;
5.26 they lie in wait like **men** who spread nets to catch birds,
5.26 but they have set their traps to catch **men.**
6.11 in the streets and on the gatherings of the young **men.**
7.18 The children gather firewood, the **men** build fires, and
8. 9 Your wise **men** are put to shame;
8.10 their fields to new owners and their wives to other **men.**
8.13 "I wanted to gather my people, as a **man** gathers his harvest;
9.21 in the streets and the young **men** in the market-places.
9.23 "Wise **men** should not boast of their wisdom,
9.23 strong men of their strength, nor rich **men** of their wealth.
10. 7 you among all the wise **men** of the nations or among any
10.14 At the sight of this, **men** feel stupid and senseless;
11.22 Their young **men** will be killed in war;
12. 1 Why are wicked **men** so prosperous?
12. 1 Why do dishonest **men** succeed?
12. 3 Drag these evil **men** away like sheep to be butchered;
12. 5 tired racing against **men,** how can you race against horses?
12.12 Across all the desert highlands **men** have come to plunder.
13.23 Can a black **man** change the colour of his skin, or a
13.27 in the fields, like a **man** lusting after his neighbour's wife
14. 9 Why are you like a **man** taken by surprise, like a soldier
14.18 into the fields, I see the bodies of **men** killed in war;
15. 8 I killed your young **men** in their prime and made their
15.10 What an unhappy **man** I am!
15.21 I will rescue you from the power of wicked and violent **men.**
16.20 Can a **man** make his own gods?
17. 5 and puts his trust in **man,** in the strength of mortal man.
17.10 I, the Lord, search the minds and test the hearts of **men.**
18.18 priests to instruct us, wise **men** to give us counsel, and
18.21 let the **men** die of disease and the young men be killed
19.10 jar in front of the **men** who had gone with me [11] and
20.12 But, Almighty Lord, you test **men** justly;
20.13 He rescues the oppressed from the power of evil **men.**
20.15 Curse the **man** who made my father glad when he brought
21. 3 me, and I told the **men** who had been sent to me
22. 7 I am sending **men** to destroy it.
22.13 Doomed is the **man** who builds his house by injustice and
22.14 Doomed is the **man** who says, "I will build myself a mansion
22.30 "This **man** is condemned to lose his children,
22.30 to be a **man** who will never succeed.
23. 9 I am like a **man** who is drunk,
23. 9 a **man** who has had too much wine.
25.30 he will shout like a **man** treading grapes.
26.11 and to the people, "This **man** deserves to be sentenced to
26.15 guilty of killing an innocent **man,** because it is the Lord
26.16 priests and the prophets, "This **man** spoke to us in the name
30. 6 Can a **man** give birth to a child?
30. 6 then do I see every **man** with his hands on his stomach
31.13 and **men,** young and old, will rejoice.
31.22 and different, as different as a woman protecting a **man."**
32.12 and of the **men** who were sitting in the courtyard.
37.10 so that only wounded **men** are left, lying in their tents,
37.10 those **men** would still get up
38. 4 to the king and said, "This **man** must be put to death.
38. 9 king, [9] "Your Majesty, what these **men** have done is wrong.
38.10 to take with him three **men** and to pull me out of
38.16 or hand you over to the **men** who want to kill you."
39.17 will not be handed over to the **men** you are afraid of.
43. 6 the **men,** the women, the children, and the king's daughters.
44. 7 to bring destruction on **men** and women, children and babies,
46. 9 **men** from Sudan and Libya, carrying shields,
46.23 Their **men** are too many to count;
48.10 (Curse the **man** who does not do the Lord's work with all
48.10 Curse the **man** who does not slash and kill!)
48.15 its finest young **men** have been slaughtered.
49. 1 "Where are the **men** of Israel?
49. 9 When **men** pick grapes, they leave a few on the vines, and
49.26 On that day her young **men** will be killed in the city
50. 3 **Men** and animals will run away, and no one will live there."
50.30 So its young **men** will be killed in the city streets, and
50.35 Death to its people, to its rulers, to its **men** of wisdom.
51. 3 Do not spare the young **men!**
51.12 Place **men** in ambush!"
51.17 At the sight of this, **men** feel stupid and senseless;
51.22 and their drivers, [22] to kill **men** and women, to slay old
51.57 will make its rulers drunk— **men** of wisdom, leaders, and
51.62 living creature in it, neither **man** nor animal, and it would

Lam 1.15 He sent an army to destroy my young **men.**
1.18 My young **men** and women have been taken away captive.
2.10 Jerusalem's old **men** sit on the ground in silence, With
2.21 the streets, Young **men** and women, killed by enemy swords.
4. 2 Zion's young **men** were as precious to us as gold, but now
4.14 through the streets like blind **men,** so stained with blood
5. 8 We are ruled by **men** who are no better than slaves, and
5.12 our old **men** are shown no respect.
5.13 Our young **men** are forced to grind corn like slaves;

Ezek 1.26 sitting on the throne was a figure that looked like a **man.**
3.18 I announce that an evil **man** is going to die but you
3.19 you do warn an evil **man** and he doesn't stop sinning, he
3.20 "If a truly good **man** starts doing evil and I put him
3.21 you do warn a good **man** not to sin and he listens
7.24 Your strongest **men** will lose their confidence when I let the
9. 2 With them was a **man** dressed in linen clothes, carrying
9. 3 The Lord called to the **man** dressed in linen, [4] "Go through
9. 6 Kill the old **men,** young men, young women, mothers, and
9.11 Then the **man** wearing linen clothes returned
10. 2 God said to the **man** wearing linen clothes, "Go between
10. 6 When the Lord commanded the **man** wearing linen clothes to
10. 6 were under the creatures, the **man** went in and stood by one
10. 7 coals, and put them in the hands of the **man** in linen.
10. 7 The **man** took the coals and left.
11. 8 I will bring **men** with swords to attack you.
14.14 Even if those three **men,** Noah, Danel, and Job, were living there,
14.16 and even if those three **men** lived there—as surely as I,
14.18 and even if those three **men** lived there—as surely as I,
18. 5 "Suppose there is a truly good **man,** righteous and honest.
18. 6 He doesn't seduce another **man's** wife
18. 9 Such a **man** obeys my commands and carefully keeps my laws.
18.10 "Then suppose this **man** has a son who robs and kills,
18.14 "Now suppose this second **man** has a son.
18.15 He doesn't seduce another **man's** wife [16] or oppress anyone
18.20 A good **man** will be rewarded for doing good,
18.20 and an evil **man** will suffer for the evil
18.21 "If an evil **man** stops sinning and keeps my laws,
18.23 Do you think I enjoy seeing an evil **man** die?"
18.24 "But if a righteous **man** stops doing good and starts
18.24 disgusting things that evil **men** do, will he go on living?
18.26 When a righteous **man** stops doing good and starts doing
18.27 When an evil **man** stops sinning and does what is right
20. 3 "Mortal **man,"** he said, "speak to these men and tell
21.31 And I will hand you over to brutal **men,** experts at destruction.
23. 8 time she was a girl, **men** slept with her and treated her
23.20 filled with lust for oversexed **men** who had all the
23.21 a girl in Egypt, where **men** played with your breasts and you
25.13 that I will punish Edom and kill every **man** and animal there.
27. 8 Your own skilful **men** were the sailors.
27. 9 The ship's carpenters Were well-trained **men** from Byblos.
27.10 They are the **men** who won glory for you.
27.11 They are the **men** who made you beautiful.
30.12 up the Nile and put Egypt under the power of evil **men.**
31.14 doomed to die like mortal **men,** doomed to join those who go
33. 8 I announce that an evil **man** is going to die but you
33. 9 you do warn an evil **man** and he doesn't stop sinning, he
33.12 Israelites that when a good **man** sins, the good he has done
33.12 If an evil **man** stops doing evil, he won't be punished,
33.12 and if a good **man** starts sinning, his life will not
33.13 promise life to a good **man,** but if he starts thinking that
33.14 I may warn an evil **man** that he is going to die,
33.18 When a righteous **man** stops doing good and starts doing evil,
33.19 When an evil **man** gives up sinning and does what is right
33.21 year of our exile, a **man** who had escaped from Jerusalem came
33.22 When the **man** arrived the next morning, the Lord gave me back
33.24 'Abraham was only one **man,** and he was given the whole land.
40. 3 took me closer, and I saw a **man** who shone like bronze.
40. 5 The **man** took his measuring-rod, which was three metres long,
40.11 Next, the **man** measured the width of the passage in the gateway.
40.17 The **man** took me through the gateway into the courtyard.
40.19 The **man** measured the distance between the two gateways, and
40.20 Then the **man** measured the gateway on the north side that
40.23 The **man** measured the distance between these two gateways,
40.24 Next, the **man** took me to the south side, and there we
40.27 The **man** measured the distance to this second gateway, and it
40.28 The **man** took me through the south gateway into the inner courtyard.
40.32 The **man** took me through the east gateway into the inner courtyard.
40.35 Then the **man** took me to the north gateway.
40.45 The **man** told me that the room which faced south was for
40.47 The **man** measured the inner courtyard,
41. 1 Next, the **man** took me into the central room, the Holy Place.
41. 5 The **man** measured the thickness of the inner wall of the
41.13 The **man** measured the outside of the Temple, and it was
41.22 The **man** said to me, "This is the table which stands in
42. 1 Then the **man** took me into the outer courtyard and led me
42.13 The **man** said to me, "Both these buildings are holy.

Ezek 42.15 When the **man** had finished measuring inside the temple area,
43. 1 The **man** took me to the gate that faces east,
43. 6 The **man** stood beside me there, and I heard the Lord speak
43. 7 "Mortal **man,** here is my throne.
44. 1 The **man** led me to the outer gate at the east side
44. 4 Then the **man** took me through the north gate to the front
46.19 Then the **man** took me to the entrance of the rooms facing
46.24 The **man** told me, "These are the kitchens where the
47. 1 The **man** led me back to the entrance of the Temple.
47. 2 The **man** then took me out of the temple area by way
47. 3 With his measuring-rod the **man** measured five hundred
47. 6 Then the **man** took me back to the bank of the river,
Dan 1.13 compare us with the young **men** who are eating the food of
1.17 God gave the four young **men** knowledge and skill in
1.18 the king, Ashpenaz took all the young **men** to Nebuchadnezzar.
3.13 a rage and ordered the three **men** to be brought before him.
3.20 army to tie the three **men** up and throw them into the
3.22 flames burnt up the guards who took the **men** to the furnace.
3.24 "Didn't we tie up three **men** and throw them into the blazing
3.25 "Then why do I see four **men** walking about in the fire?"
3.27 to look at the three **men,** who had not been harmed by
3.28 his angel and rescued these **men** who serve and trust him.
4.15 the dew fall on this **man,** and let him live with the
4.17 to anyone he chooses—even to the least important of **men.'**
4.23 the dew fall on this **man,** and let him live there with
5.11 There is a **man** in your kingdom who has the spirit of
5.11 your father was king, this **man** showed good sense, knowledge,
5.12 send for this **man** Daniel, whom the king named Belteshazzar,
6. 7 from any god or from any **man** except from Your Majesty.
6.12 any god or from any **man** except you, would be thrown into
6.15 Then the **men** came back to the king and said to him,
7. 4 The beast was lifted up and made to stand like a **man.**
8.24 He will bring destruction on powerful **men** and on God's own people.
10.16 angel, who looked like a **man,** stretched out his hand and
11.14 And some violent **men** from your nation, Daniel, will rebel
11.21 Syria will be an evil **man** who has no right to be
12. 5 Then I saw two **men** standing by a river, one on each
Hos 6. 9 like a gang of robbers who wait in ambush for a **man.**
9. 7 This inspired **man** is insane."
11. 9 For I am God and not **man.**
12.12 wife, he worked for another **man** and took care of his sheep.
13. 2 How can **men** kiss those idols—idols in the shape of bulls!
Joel 1. 8 who mourns the death of the **man** she was going to marry.
2.28 men will have dreams, and your young **men** will see visions.
2.29 pour out my spirit even on servants, both **men** and women.
Amos 2. 6 They sell into slavery honest **men** who cannot pay their debts,
2. 6 poor **men** who cannot repay even the price
2. 7 A **man** and his father have intercourse with the same slave-girl,
2.14 strong **men** will lose their strength, and soldiers will not
3. 3 Do two **men** start travelling together without arranging to meet?
4.13 He makes his thoughts known to **man;**
5.12 You persecute good **men,** take bribes, and prevent the poor
5.19 It will be like a **man** who runs from a lion and
5.19 Or like a **man** who comes home and puts his hand on
6. 9 If there are ten **men** left in a family, they will die.
6.12 Do **men** plough the sea with oxen?
8. 6 We'll find a poor **man** who can't pay his debts, not even
8.13 even healthy young **men** and women will collapse from thirst.
Obad 8 I will destroy their clever **men** and wipe out all their wisdom.
Jon 1.14 pray, don't punish us with death for taking this **man's** life!
Mic 2. 2 No **man's** family or property is safe.
2. 8 **Men** return from battle, thinking they are safe at home, but
5. 7 They will depend on God, not **man.**
6.10 In the houses of evil **men** are treasures which they got dishonestly.
6.11 How can I forgive **men** who use false scales and weights?
6.12 Your rich **men** exploit the poor, and all of you are liars.
7. 1 I am like a hungry **man** who finds no fruit left on
7. 3 The influential **man** tells them what he wants, and so they
7. 6 a **man's** enemies are the members of his own family.
Nah 1.11 you, Nineveh, there came a **man** full of wicked schemes, who
2. 1 **Man** the defences!
3. 3 high, dead bodies without number— **men** stumble over them!
3.10 Their leading **men** were carried off in chains and divided
Hab 1. 4 Evil **men** get the better of the righteous,
1.11 wind and are gone, these **men** whose power is their god."
1.13 But how can you stand these treacherous, evil **men?**
2. 5 Greedy **men** are proud and restless—like death itself they are
2.18 is only something that a **man** has made, and it tells you
Zeph 1.17 on mankind that everyone will grope about like a blind **man.**
Hag 1. 6 And the working **man** cannot earn enough to live on.
1.11 crop the ground produces, on **men** and animals, on everything
2.13 Then Haggai asked, "Suppose a **man** is defiled because he
Zech 1.21 I asked, "What have these **men** come to do?"
2. 1 vision I saw a **man** with a measuring-line in his hand.
2. 4 "Run and tell that young **man** with the measuring-line that
3. 2 This **man** is like a stick snatched from the fire."
3. 4 "Take away the filthy clothes this **man** is wearing."
4.14 "These are the two **men** whom God has chosen and anointed
6.10 All these **men** have returned from exile in Babylonia.
6.12 the Lord Almighty says, 'The **man** who is called The Branch
6.15 **Men** who live far away will come and help to rebuild the
8. 4 Once again old **men** and women, so old that they use a
8.10 could afford to hire either **men** or animals, and no one was
9.15 shout in battle like drunken **men** and will shed the blood of
10. 7 like soldiers, happy like **men** who have been drinking wine.
12. 1 out the skies, created the earth, and gave life to **man.**
12. 2 nations round her will drink and stagger like drunken **men.**
12.12 and the **men** of each family will mourn separately
14.13 that everyone will seize the **man** next to him and attack him.
Mal 2.11 **Men** have married women who worship foreign gods.
Mal 3.15 Evil **men** not only prosper, but they test God's patience with
Mt 1.19 Joseph was a **man** who always did what was right,
2. 1 afterwards, some **men** who studied the stars came from the east
3. 3 John was the **man** the prophet Isaiah was talking about when
4. 4 answered, "The scripture says, **'Man** cannot live on bread alone,
4.19 "Come with me, and I will teach you to catch **men."**
5.32 if a **man** divorces his wife, for any cause other than her
5.32 and the **man** who marries her commits adultery also.
8. 2 Then a **man** suffering from a dreaded skin-disease came to him,
8. 3 At once the **man** was healed of his disease.
8. 9 I, too, am a **man** under the authority of superior officers,
8.21 Another **man,** who was a disciple, said, "Sir, first let
8.27 "What kind of **man** is this?"
8.28 he was met by two **men** who came out of the burial
8.28 These **men** had demons in them and were so fierce that no
8.33 The **men** who had been taking care of the pigs ran away
8.33 story and what had happened to the **men** with the demons.
9. 3 of the Law said to themselves, "This **man** is speaking blasphemy!"
9. 7 The **man** got up and went home.
9. 8 afraid, and praised God for giving such authority to **men.**
9.32 As the **men** were leaving, some people
9.32 brought to Jesus a **man** who could not talk
9.33 demon was driven out, the **man** started talking, and everyone was
10. 5 These twelve **men** were sent out by Jesus with the following
10.17 for there will be **men** who will arrest you and take
10.21 **"Men** will hand over their own brothers to be put to death,
10.36 a **man's** worst enemies will be the members of his own family.
11. 8 A **man** dressed up in fancy clothes?
11.11 John the Baptist is greater than any **man** who has ever lived.
11.19 he ate and drank, and everyone said, 'Look at this **man!**
12. 3 what David did that time when he and his **men** were hungry?
12. 4 and he and his **men** ate the bread offered to God,
12.10 where there was a **man** who had a paralysed hand.
12.12 And a **man** is worth much more than a sheep!
12.13 Then he said to the **man** with the paralysed hand,
12.22 people brought to Jesus a **man** who was blind and could not
12.22 Jesus healed the **man,** so that he was able to talk
12.29 can break into a strong **man's** house and take away his
13. 3 "Once there was a **man** who went out to sow corn.
13.24 A **man** sowed good seed in his field.
13.27 The **man's** servants came to him and said, 'Sir, it was
13.31 A **man** takes a mustard seed and sows it in his field.
13.37 Jesus answered, "The **man** who sowed the good seed is the
13.44 A **man** happens to find a treasure hidden in a field.
13.45 A **man** is looking for fine pearls, [46] and when he finds one
14.21 number of **men** who ate was about five thousand, not counting
15.38 The number of **men** who ate was four thousand, not
16. 9 when I broke the five loaves for the five thousand **men?**
16.10 And what about the seven loaves for the four thousand **men?**
16.23 these thoughts of yours don't come from God, but from **man."**
17.14 to the crowd, a **man** came to Jesus, knelt before him,
17.22 is about to be handed over to **men** [23] who will kill him;
18.12 "What do you think a **man** does who has a hundred sheep
18.28 "Then the **man** went out and met one of his fellow-servants
19. 3 "Does our Law allow a **man** to divorce his wife for whatever
19. 5 said, 'For this reason a **man** will leave his father and
19. 6 **Man** must not separate, then, what God has joined together."
19. 7 give the law for a **man** to hand his wife a divorce
19. 9 tell you, then, that any **man** who divorces his wife, for any
19.10 how it is between a **man** and his wife, it is better
19.12 For there are different reasons why **men** cannot marry:
19.12 others, because **men** made them that way;
19.16 Once a **man** came to Jesus.
19.26 "This is impossible for **man,** but for God everything is possible."
20. 1 Once there was a **man** who went out early in the morning
20. 1 to hire some **men** to work in his vineyard.
20. 3 nine o'clock and saw some **men** standing there doing nothing,
20. 6 to the market-place and saw some other **men** still standing there.
20. 9 The **men** who had begun to work at five o'clock were paid
20.10 So when the **men** who were the first to be hired came
20.12 'These **men** who were hired last worked only one hour,'
20.14 I want to give this **man** who was hired last as much
21.25 was it from God or from **man?"**
21.26 But if we say, 'From **man,'** we are afraid of what the
21.28 There was once a **man** who had two sons.
21.36 Again the **man** sent other slaves, more than the first time,
22.11 guests and saw a **man** who was not wearing wedding clothes.
22.12 But the **man** said nothing.
22.16 truth about God's will for **man,** without worrying about what
22.16 people think, because you pay no attention to a **man's** status.
22.24 "Moses said that if a **man** who has no children dies,
24. 5 Many **men,** claiming to speak for me, will come and say,
24.17 A **man** who is on the roof of his house must not
24.18 A **man** who is in the field must not go back to
24.38 people ate and drank, **men and women** married, up to the very
24.40 At that time two **men** will be working in a field:
25.14 Once there was a **man** who was about to go on a
26. 6 the house of Simon, a **man** who had suffered from a dreaded
26.18 "Go to a certain **man** in the city," he said to them,
26.24 but how terrible for that **man** who betrays the Son of Man!
26.24 have been better for that **man** if he had never been born!"
26.46 Look, here is the **man** who is betraying me!"
26.48 "The **man** I kiss is the one you want.
26.60 Finally two **men** stepped up [61] and said, "This man said, 'I
26.61 stepped up [61] and said, "This **man** said, 'I am able to tear
26.71 and said to the **men** there, "He was with Jesus of
26.72 it and answered, "I swear that I don't know that **man!"**
26.73 After a little while the **men** standing there came to Peter.
26.74 I do not know that **man!"**
27.24 and said, "I am not responsible for the death of this **man!**
27.32 going out, they met a **man** from Cyrene named Simon,

Mk 1. 7 announced to the people, "The **man** who will come after me is
1.17 "Come with me, and I will teach you to catch **men.**"
1.23 Just then a **man** with an evil spirit in him came into
1.25 Jesus ordered the spirit, "Be quiet, and come out of the **man!**"
1.26 The evil spirit shook the **man** hard, gave a loud scream,
1.27 This **man** has authority to give orders to the evil spirits,
1.40 A **man** suffering from a dreaded skin-disease came to Jesus,
1.42 At once the disease left the **man,** and he was clean.
1.45 But the **man** went away and began to spread the news everywhere.
2. 3 message to them [3]when four **men** arrived, carrying a paralysed man
2. 4 of the crowd, however, they could not get the **man** to him.
2. 4 made an opening, they let the **man** down, lying on his mat.
2.12 While they all watched, the **man** got up, picked up his mat,
2.25 He and his **men** were hungry, [26]so he went into the house
2.26 bread—but David ate it and even gave it to his **men.**"
2.27 Jesus concluded, "The Sabbath was made for the good of **man;**
2.27 **man** was not made for the Sabbath.
3. 1 synagogue, where there was a **man** who had a paralysed hand.
3. 2 closely to see whether he would heal the **man** on the Sabbath.
3. 3 Jesus said to the **man,** "Come up here to the front."
3. 4 To save a **man's** life or to destroy it?"
3. 5 Then he said to the **man,** "Stretch out your hand."
3.13 went up a hill and called to himself the **men** he wanted.
4. 3 Once there was a **man** who went out to sow corn.
4.26 A **man** scatters seed in his field.
4.29 the corn is ripe, the **man** starts cutting it with his sickle,
4.31 A **man** takes a mustard seed, the smallest seed in the world,
4.41 terribly afraid and said to one another, "Who is this **man?**
5. 2 he was met by a **man** who came out of the burial
5. 2 This **man** had an evil spirit in him [3]and lived among the
5. 8 because Jesus was saying, "Evil spirit, come out of this **man!**")
5. 9 The **man** answered, "My name is 'Mob'—there are so many of
5.13 the evil spirits went out of the **man** and entered the pigs.
5.14 The **men** who had been taking care of the pigs ran away
5.15 to Jesus, they saw the **man** who used to have the mob
5.16 what had happened to the **man** with the demons, and about the
5.18 getting into the boat, the **man** who had had the demons begged
5.20 So the **man** left and went all through the Ten Towns,
6.44 The number of **men** who were fed was five thousand.
7. 8 "You put aside God's command and obey the teachings of **men.**"
7.32 Some people brought him a **man** who was deaf and could
7.33 fingers in the man's ears, spat, and touched the **man's** tongue.
7.34 and said to the **man,** "Ephphatha," which means, "Open up!"
7.35 At once the **man** was able to hear, his speech impediment
8.23 After spitting on the **man's** eyes, Jesus placed his hands on
8.24 The **man** looked up and said, "Yes, I can see people,
8.25 Jesus again placed his hands on the **man's** eyes.
8.25 This time the **man** looked intently, his eyesight returned,
8.33 "Your thoughts don't come from God but from **man!**"
9.17 A **man** in the crowd answered, "Teacher, I brought my son
9.31 of Man will be handed over to **men** who will kill him.
9.38 "Teacher, we saw a **man** who was driving out demons in
10. 2 asked, "does our Law allow a **man** to divorce his wife?"
10. 4 "Moses gave permission for a **man** to write a divorce notice
10. 7 'And for this reason a **man** will leave his father and
10. 9 **Man** must not separate, then, what God has joined together."
10.11 He said to them, "A **man** who divorces his wife and
10.12 divorces her husband and marries another **man** commits adultery."
10.17 on his way again, a **man** ran up, knelt before him,
10.20 "Teacher," the **man** said, "ever since I was young, I have
10.22 When the **man** heard this, gloom spread over his face,
10.27 and answered, "This is impossible for **man,** but not for God;
10.42 said, "You know that the **men** who are considered rulers of
11. 6 just as Jesus had told them, and the **men** let them go.
11.30 was it from God or from **man?**"
11.32 But if we say, 'From **man**
12. 1 "Once there was a **man** who planted a vineyard, put a fence
12. 6 The only one left to send was the **man's** own dear son.
12. 9 will come and kill those **men** and hand the vineyard over to
12.14 pay no attention to a **man's** status,
12.14 but teach the truth about God's will for **man.**
12.19 'If a **man** dies and leaves a wife but no children,
12.19 that **man's** brother must marry the widow
12.33 And **man** must love God with all his heart and with all
13. 6 Many **men,** claiming to speak for me, will come and say, 'I
13.12 **Men** will hand over their own brothers to be put to death,
13.15 A **man** who is on the roof of his house must not
13.16 A **man** who is in the field must not go back to
13.34 It will be like a **man** who goes away from home on
14. 3 the house of Simon, a **man** who had suffered from a dreaded
14.13 into the city, and a **man** carrying a jar of water will
14.21 but how terrible for that **man** who betrays the Son of Man!
14.21 have been better for that **man** if he had never been born!"
14.42 Look, here is the **man** who is betraying me!"
14.44 "The **man** I kiss is the one you want.
14.57 Then some **men** stood up and told this lie against Jesus:
14.58 tear down this Temple which **men** have made, and after three
14.58 I will build one that is not made by **men.'** "
14.71 I do not know the **man** you are talking about!"
15. 7 At that time a **man** named Barabbas was in prison with the
15.21 the way they met a **man** named Simon, who was coming into
15.39 "This **man** was really the Son of God!"

Lk 1.27 promised in marriage to a **man** named Joseph, who was a
2.25 At that time there was a **man** named Simeon living in Jerusalem.
2.52 in body and in wisdom, gaining favour with God and **men.**
3.11 must give one to the **man** who has none, and whoever has
4. 4 answered, "The scripture says, **'Man** cannot live on bread alone.' "
4.33 In the synagogue was a **man** who had the spirit of an

Lk 4.35 Jesus ordered the spirit, "Be quiet and come out of the **man!**"
4.35 The demon threw the **man** down in front of them and went
4.36 authority and power this **man** gives orders to the evil spirits,
5.10 from now on you will be catching **men.**"
5.12 town where there was a **man** who was suffering from a dreaded
5.13 At once the disease left the **man.**
5.18 Some **men** came carrying a paralysed man on a bed, and
5.20 he said to the **man,** "Your sins are forgiven, my friend."
5.21 say to themselves, "Who is this **man** who speaks such blasphemy!
5.25 At once the **man** got up in front of them all, took
6. 3 you read what David did when he and his **men** were hungry?
6. 4 offered to God, ate it, and gave it also to his **men.**
6. 6 A **man** was there whose right hand was paralysed.
6. 8 thoughts and said to the **man,** "Stand up and come here to
6. 8 The **man** got up and stood there.
6. 9 To save a **man's** life or destroy it?"
6.10 then he said to the **man,** "Stretch out your hand."
6.48 He is like a **man** who, in building his house, dug deep
6.49 obey them is like a **man** who built his house without laying
7. 2 the **man** was sick and about to die.
7. 4 and begged him earnestly, "This **man** really deserves your help.
7. 8 I, too, am a **man** placed under the authority of superior officers,
7.14 and touched the coffin, and the **men** carrying it stopped.
7.25 A **man** dressed up in fancy clothes?
7.28 Jesus added, "John is greater than any **man** who has ever lived.
7.34 and he ate and drank, and you said, 'Look at this **man!**
7.39 said to himself, "If this **man** really were a prophet, he
7.41 "There were two **men** who owed money to a money-lender,"
8. 5 "Once there was a **man** who went out to sow corn.
8.25 and afraid, and said to one another, "Who is this **man?**
8.27 he was met by a **man** from the town who had demons
8.27 For a long time this **man** had gone without clothes and would
8.33 They went out of the **man** and into the pigs.
8.34 The **men** who had been taking care of the pigs saw what
8.35 to Jesus, they found the **man** from whom the demons had gone
8.36 had seen it told the people how the **man** had been cured.
8.38 The **man** from whom the demons had gone out begged Jesus,
8.39 The **man** went through the town, telling what Jesus had done
8.41 Then a **man** named Jairus arrived;
9. 9 but who is this **man** I hear these things about?"
9.14 (There were about five thousand **men** there.)
9.30 Suddenly two **men** were there talking with him.
9.32 saw Jesus' glory and the two **men** who were standing with him.
9.33 As the **men** were leaving Jesus, Peter said to him, "Master,
9.38 A **man** shouted from the crowd, "Teacher!
9.41 Then he said to the **man,** "Bring your son here."
9.44 Man is going to be handed over to the power of **men.**"
9.49 "Master, we saw a **man** driving out demons in your name,
9.57 went on their way, a **man** said to Jesus, "I will follow
9.59 He said to another **man,** "Follow me."
9.59 But that **man** said, "Sir, first let me go back and bury
9.61 Another **man** said, "I will follow you, sir;
10. 1 the Lord chose another seventy-two **men** and sent them out two
10.17 The seventy-two **men** came back in great joy.
10.27 The **man** answered, " 'Love the Lord your God with all
10.30 "There was once a **man** who was going down from Jerusalem
10.31 but when he saw the **man,** he walked on by, on the
10.32 over and looked at the **man,** and then walked on by,
10.33 that way came upon the **man,** and when he saw him, his
10.34 then he put the **man** on his own animal and took him
10.36 acted like a neighbour towards the **man** attacked by the robbers?"
11.14 and when the demon went out, the **man** began to talk.
12.13 A **man** in the crowd said to Jesus, "Teacher, tell my
12.45 the other servants, both the **men** and the women, and eats
13. 6 "There was once a **man** who had a fig-tree growing in his
13.19 A **man** takes a mustard seed and sows it in his field.
14. 2 A **man** whose legs and arms were swollen came to Jesus,
14. 4 Jesus took the **man,** healed him, and sent him away.
14.15 When one of the **men** sitting at table heard this, he said
14.16 "There was once a **man** who was giving a great feast
14.24 all that none of those **men** who were invited will taste my
14.30 'This **man** began to build but can't finish the job!'
14.31 goes out with ten thousand **men** to fight another king who
14.31 against him with twenty thousand **men,** he will sit down first
15. 2 grumbling, "This **man** welcomes outcasts and even eats with
15.11 on to say, "There was once a **man** who had two sons.
15.12 So the **man** divided his property between his two sons.
16.15 of great value by **man** are worth nothing in God's sight.
16.18 "Any **man** who divorces his wife and marries another woman
16.18 and the **man** who marries a divorced woman commits adultery.
17.12 he was met by ten **men** suffering from a dreaded skin-disease.
17.16 The **man** was a Samaritan.
17.17 Jesus said, "There were ten **men** who were healed;
17.27 eating and drinking, and **men and women** married, up to the
17.31 "On that day the **man** who is on the roof of his
17.31 in the same way the **man** who is out in the field
18. 2 there was a judge who neither feared God nor respected **man.**
18. 4 don't fear God or respect **man,** [5]yet because of all the
18.10 "Once there were two **men** who went up to the Temple to
18.21 The **man** replied, "Ever since I was young, I have obeyed
18.23 But when the **man** heard this, he became very sad, because
18.27 answered, "What is impossible for **man** is possible for God."
19. 7 saw it started grumbling, "This **man** has gone as a guest to
19. 9 house today, for this **man,** also, is a descendant of Abraham.
19.12 said, "There was once a **man** of high rank who was going
19.14 him to say, 'We don't want this **man** to be our king.'
19.15 "The **man** was made king and came back.
20. 4 did John's right to baptize come from God or from **man?**"
20. 6 But if we say 'From **man,'** this whole crowd here will stone
20. 9 "There was once a **man** who planted a vineyard, let it out
20.16 will come and kill those **men,** and hand the vineyard over to

Lk 20.20 They bribed some **men** to pretend they were sincere, and they
20.21 pay no attention to a **man's** status,
20.21 but teach the truth about God's will for **man.**
20.28 'If a **man** dies and leaves a wife but no children,
20.28 wife but no children, that **man's** brother must marry the widow
20.34 Jesus answered them, "The **men and women** of this age marry,
20.35 but the **men and women** who are worthy to rise
21. 8 Many **men,** claiming to speak for me, will come and say,
22.10 go into the city, a **man** carrying a jar of water will
22.22 God has decided, but how terrible for that **man** who betrays him!"
22.51 He touched the **man's** ear and healed him.
22.56 straight at him and said, "This **man** too was with Jesus!"
22.58 After a little while a **man** noticed Peter and said, "You
22.58 But Peter answered, **"Man,** I am not!"
22.59 about an hour later another **man** insisted strongly, "There
22.59 isn't any doubt that this **man** was with Jesus,
22.60 Peter answered, **"Man,** I don't know what you are talking about!"
22.63 The **men** who were guarding Jesus mocked him and beat him.
23. 2 caught this **man** misleading our people, telling them not to pay
23. 4 and the crowds, "I find no reason to condemn this **man."**
23. 6 When Pilate heard this, he asked, "Is this **man** a Galilean?"
23.14 to them, "You brought this **man** to me and said that he
23.15 There is nothing this **man** has done to deserve death.
23.25 He set free the **man** they wanted, the one who had been
23.26 were going, they met a **man** from Cyrene named Simon who was
23.32 Two other **men,** both of them criminals, were also led out
23.50 was a **man** named Joseph from Arimathea, a town in Judaea.
24. 4 when suddenly two **men** in bright shining clothes stood by
24. 5 to the ground, as the **men** said to them, "Why are you
24.19 "This **man** was a prophet and was considered by God and by
Jn 1. 6 God sent his messenger, a **man** named John, [7] who came to
1.30 about when I said, 'A **man** is coming after me, but he
1.33 'You will see the Spirit come down and stay on a **man;**
2. 8 out and take it to the **man** in charge of the feast."
2.14 in the Temple he found **men** selling cattle, sheep, and pigeons,
2.16 and he ordered the **men** who sold the pigeons, "Take them
3.26 said, "Teacher, you remember the **man** who was with you on
4.18 have been married to five **men,** and the man you live with
4.29 "Come and see the **man** who told me everything I have
4.36 The **man** who reaps the harvest is being paid and gathers
4.36 man who sows and the **man** who reaps will be glad together.
4.37 The saying is true, 'One **man** sows, another man reaps.'
4.50 The **man** believed Jesus' words and went.
5. 5 A **man** was there who had been ill for thirty-eight years.
5. 6 and he knew that the **man** had been ill for such a
5. 9 Immediately the **man** got well;
5.10 Jewish authorities told the **man** who had been healed, "This is
5.11 He answered, "The **man** who made me well told me to pick
5.12 asked him, "Who is the **man** who told you to do this?"
5.13 But the **man** who had been healed did not know who Jesus
5.15 Then the **man** left and told the Jewish authorities that
5.34 It is not that I must have a **man's** witness;
6.10 there were about five thousand **men.**
6.42 So they said, "This **man** is Jesus son of Joseph, isn't
6.52 "How can this **man** give us his flesh to eat?"
6.63 **man's** power is of no use at all.
7.15 and said, "How does this **man** know so much when he has
7.23 with me because I made a **man** completely well on the Sabbath?
7.25 said, "Isn't this the **man** the authorities are trying to kill?
7.27 And we all know where this **man** comes from."
7.31 Messiah comes, will he perform more miracles than this **man** has?"
7.40 him say this and said, "This **man** is really the Prophet!"
7.46 The guards answered, "Nobody has ever talked like this **man!"**
7.50 Pharisees there was Nicodemus, the **man** who had gone to see
7.51 Law we cannot condemn a **man** before hearing him and finding
9. 1 was walking along, he saw a **man** who had been born blind.
9. 6 rubbed the mud on the **man's** eyes [7] and said, "Go and wash
9. 7 So the **man** went, washed his face, and came back seeing.
9. 8 asked, "Isn't this the **man** who used to sit and beg?"
9. 9 So the **man** himself said, "I am the man."
9.11 He answered, "The **man** called Jesus made some mud, rubbed it
9.13 Then they took to the Pharisees the **man** who had been blind.
9.15 The Pharisees, then, asked the **man** again how he had received
9.16 of the Pharisees said, "The **man** who did this cannot be from
9.16 however, said, "How could a **man** who is a sinner perform
9.17 So the Pharisees asked the **man** once more, "You say he
9.17 "He is a prophet," the **man** answered.
9.24 time they called back the **man** who had been born blind,
9.24 We know that this **man** who cured you is a sinner."
9.25 not know if he is a sinner or not," the **man** replied.
9.30 The **man** answered, "What a strange thing that is!
9.33 Unless this **man** came from God, he would not be able to
9.35 had happened, he found the **man** and asked him, "Do you
9.36 The **man** answered, "Tell me who he is, sir, so that I
9.38 the **man** said, and knelt down before Jesus.
10. 1 the **man** who does not enter the sheepfold by the gate,
10. 2 The **man** who goes in through the gate is the shepherd of
10.21 But others were saying, "A **man** with a demon could not
10.33 You are only a **man,** but you are trying to make yourself
10.41 they said, "but everything he said about this **man** was true."
11. 1 A **man** named Lazarus, who lived in Bethany, was ill.
11.47 Look at all the miracles this **man** is performing!
11.50 for you to let one **man** die for the people, instead of
12. 1 Bethany, the home of Lazarus, the **man** he had raised from death.
12.43 loved the approval of **men** rather than the approval of God.
13.18 come true that says, 'The **man** who shared my food turned
13.26 he is the **man."**
17.12 them was lost, except the **man** who was bound to be lost
18.14 it was better that one **man** should die for all the people.
18.17 Peter, "Aren't you also one of the disciples of that **man?"**
Jn 18.25 "Aren't you also one of the disciples of that **man?"**
18.26 slaves, a relative of the **man** whose ear Peter had cut off,
18.29 to them and asked, "What do you accuse this **man** of?"
19. 5 Here is the **man!"**
19.11 So the **man** who handed me over to you is guilty of
19.18 they also crucified two other **men,** one on each side, with
19.21 the Jews,' but rather, 'This **man** said, I am the King of
19.31 break the legs of the **men** who had been crucified, and to
19.32 and then of the other **man** who had been crucified with Jesus.
19.40 The two **men** took Jesus' body and wrapped it in linen
21.21 Peter saw him, he asked Jesus, "Lord, what about this **man?"**
Acts 1. 2 the Holy Spirit to the **men** he had chosen as his apostles.
1.10 he went away, when two **men** dressed in white suddenly stood
1.21 must be one of the **men** who were in our group during
1.23 So they proposed two **men:**
1.26 choose between the two **men,** and the one chosen was Matthias,
2.18 on my servants, both **men and women,** I will pour out my
2.22 Jesus of Nazareth was a **man** whose divine authority was clearly
3. 2 it was called, was a **man** who had been lame all his
3. 7 At once the **man's** feet and ankles became strong;
3.11 As the **man** held on to Peter and John in Solomon's Porch,
3.12 of our own power or godliness that we made this **man** walk?
4. 4 and the number of **men** grew to about five thousand.
4.10 know, that this **man** stands here before you completely well
4.14 because they saw the **man** who had been healed standing there
4.16 "What shall we do with these **men?"**
4.17 let us warn these **men** never again to speak to anyone
4.22 The **man** on whom this miracle of healing had been performed
5. 1 But there was a **man** named Ananias, who with his wife
5. 4 You have not lied to **men**—you have lied to God!"
5. 9 The **men** who buried your husband are now at the door,
5.14 group—a crowd of **men and women** who believed in the Lord.
5.25 Then a **man** came in and said to them, "Listen!
5.25 The **men** you put in prison are in the Temple teaching the
5.26 officer went off with his **men** and brought the apostles back.
5.28 orders not to teach in the name of this **man,"** he said;
5.29 and the other apostles replied, "We must obey God, not **men.**
5.35 the Council, "Fellow-Israelites, be careful what you do to these **men.**
5.36 to be somebody great, and about four hundred **men** joined him.
5.38 I tell you, do not take any action against these **men.**
6. 3 So then, brothers, choose seven **men** among you who are
6. 5 so they chose Stephen, a **man** full of faith and the Holy
6. 8 Stephen, a **man** richly blessed by God and full of power,
6. 9 he was opposed by some **men** who were members of the synagogue
6.11 they bribed some **men** to say, "We heard him speaking against
6.13 Then they brought in some **men** to tell lies about him.
6.13 "This **man,"** they said, "is always talking against our sacred
7.26 'Listen, **men,'** he said, 'you are fellow-Israelites;
7.40 what has happened to that **man** Moses, who brought us out of
7.48 the Most High God does not live in houses built by **men;**
8. 3 believers, both **men and women,** and threw them into jail.
8. 9 A **man** named Simon lived there, who for some time had
8.12 God and about Jesus Christ, they were baptized, both **men and women.**
9. 2 to arrest them, both **men and women,** and bring them back to
9. 7 The **men** who were travelling with Saul had stopped, not
9.11 the house of Judas ask for a **man** from Tarsus named Saul.
9.12 vision he has seen a **man** named Ananias come in and place
9.13 have told me about this **man** and about all the terrible
9.21 who in Jerusalem was killing those who worship that **man** Jesus?
9.33 There he met a **man** named Aeneas, who was paralysed and
9.38 in Lydda, they sent two **men** to him with the message,
10. 1 There was a **man** in Caesarea named Cornelius, who was a
10. 5 And now send some **men** to Joppa
10. 5 for a certain **man** whose full name is Simon Peter.
10.17 meaning of this vision, the **men** sent by Cornelius had learnt
10.19 Three **men** are here looking for you.
10.21 said to the men, "I am the **man** you are looking for.
10.23 Peter invited the **men** in and persuaded them to spend the
10.26 "I myself am only a **man."**
10.30 Suddenly a **man** dressed in shining clothes stood in front of
10.32 someone to Joppa for a **man** whose full name is Simon Peter.
11.11 At that very moment three **men** who had been sent to me
11.13 someone to Joppa for a **man** whose full name is Simon Peter.
11.20 other believers, **men** from Cyprus and Cyrene, went to Antioch
12.20 First they convinced Blastus, the **man** in charge of the palace,
12.22 "It isn't a **man** speaking, but a god!"
13.22 of man I like, a **man** who will do all I want
13.50 Jews stirred up the leading **men** of the city and the Gentile
14. 8 In Lystra there was a **man** who had been lame from birth
14.10 The **man** jumped up and started walking around.
14.11 "The gods have become like **men** and have come down to us!"
15. 1 Some **men** came from Judaea to Antioch and started teaching the
15.22 decided to choose some **men** from the group and send them
15.22 They chose two **men** who were highly respected by the believers,
15.24 We have heard that some **men** who went from our group have
16.17 Paul and us, shouting, "These **men** are servants of the Most
16.20 officials and said, "These **men** are Jews, and they are causing
16.35 sent police officers with the order, "Let those **men** go."
17. 5 attacked the home of a **man** called Jason, in an attempt to
17. 6 city authorities and shouted, "These **men** have caused trouble
17.15 The **men** who were taking Paul went with him as far as
17.26 From one **man** he created all races of mankind and made
17.29 or silver or stone, shaped by the art and skill of **man.**
17.31 whole world with justice by means of a **man** he has chosen.
17.31 proof of this to everyone by raising that **man** from death!"
17.34 Some **men** joined him and believed, among whom was Dionysius,
18.13 "This **man,"** they said, "is trying to persuade people to
19. 7 They were about twelve **men** in all.

Acts	19.16	The **man** who had the evil spirit in him attacked them
	19.25	and said to them, **"Men,** you know that our prosperity comes
	19.37	You have brought these **men** here even though they have not
	20.30	time will come when some **men** from your own group will tell
	21. 8	evangelist, one of the seven **men** who had been chosen as
	21.16	to the house of the **man** we were going to stay with
	21.23	There are four **men** here who have taken a vow.
	21.26	So Paul took the **men** and the next day performed the
	21.28	**"Men** of Israel!"
	21.28	This is the **man** who goes everywhere teaching everyone against
	21.33	Then he asked, "Who is this **man,** and what has he done?"
	21.34	happened, so he ordered his **men** to take Paul up into the
	22. 4	I arrested **men and women** and threw them into prison.
	22. 9	The **men** with me saw the light, but did not hear the
	22.12	"In that city was a **man** named Ananias, a religious man
	22.24	Roman commander ordered his **men** to take Paul into the fort,
	22.26	That **man** is a Roman citizen!"
	22.29	At once the **men** who were going to question Paul drew
	23. 4	The **men** close to Paul said to him, "You are insulting
	23. 9	"We cannot find anything wrong with this **man!**
	23.21	there are more than forty **men** who will be hiding and waiting
	23.27	The Jews seized this **man** and were about to kill him.
	24. 5	We found this **man** to be a dangerous nuisance;
	24. 8	If you question this **man,** you yourself will be able to
	24.16	best always to have a clear conscience before God and **man.**
	24.20	Or let these **men** here tell what crime they found me
	25. 5	with me and accuse the **man** if he has done anything wrong."
	25.14	"There is a **man** here who was left a prisoner by Felix;
	25.16	habit of handing over any **man** accused of a crime before he
	25.17	sat in the court and ordered the **man** to be brought in.
	25.19	their own religion and about a **man** named Jesus, who has
	25.22	Agrippa said to Festus, "I would like to hear this **man**
	25.24	You see this **man** against whom all the Jewish people, both
	26.13	the sky and shining round me and the **men** travelling with me.
	26.31	said to each other, "This **man** has not done anything for
	26.32	Agrippa said to Festus, "This **man** could have been released if
	27.10	**"Men,** I see that our voyage from here on will be dangerous;
	27.12	so most of the **men** were in favour of putting out to
	27.13	began to blow, and the **men** thought that they could carry out
	27.21	After the **men** had gone a long time without food, Paul
	27.21	stood before them and said, **"Men,** you should have listened
	27.25	So take heart, **men!**
	27.43	Instead, he ordered all the **men** who could swim to jump
	28. 4	said to one another, "This **man** must be a murderer, but Fate
Rom	1.23	to look like mortal **man** or birds or animals or reptiles.
	1.27	In the same way the **men** give up natural sexual relations
	1.27	**Men** do shameful things with each other, and as a result they
	2.28	It is not the **man** who is a Jew on the outside,
	2.29	Such a person receives his praise from God, not from **man.**
	3. 4	God must be true, even though every **man** is a liar.
	3.20	the Law does is to make **man** know that he has sinned.
	4.14	obey the Law, then **man's** faith means nothing and God's promise
	5.12	into the world through one **man,** and his sin brought death
	5.15	that many people died because of the sin of that one **man.**
	5.15	so many people through the grace of the one **man,** Jesus
	5.16	is a difference between God's gift and the sin of one **man.**
	5.17	through the sin of one **man** death began to rule
	5.17	because of that one **man.**
	5.17	the result of what was done by the one **man,** Jesus Christ!
	5.19	of the disobedience of one **man,** in the same way they will
	5.19	with God as the result of the obedience of the one **man.**
	7. 3	if she lives with another **man** while her husband is alive,
	7. 3	and does not commit adultery if she marries another **man.**
	7.14	but I am a mortal **man,** sold as a slave to sin.
	8. 3	came with a nature like **man's** sinful nature, to do away with
	9.16	everything depends, not on what **man** wants or does, but only
	9.20	pot does not ask the **man** who made it, "Why did you
	9.21	After all, the **man** who makes the pots has the right to
	11. 4	kept for myself seven thousand **men** who have not worshipped the
	13. 3	Would you like to be unafraid of the **man** in authority?
	16. 5	Epaenetus, who was the first **man** in the province of Asia to
1 Cor	3. 8	difference between the man who sows and the **man** who waters;
	3.10	and laid the foundation, and another **man** is building on it.
	3.21	No one, then, should boast about what **men** can do.
	4. 9	place to us apostles, like **men** condemned to die in public as
	5. 1	I am told that a **man** is sleeping with his stepmother!
	5. 2	filled with sadness, and the **man** who has done such a thing
	5. 3	passed judgement on the **man** who has done this terrible thing.
	5. 5	you are to hand this **man** over to Satan for his body
	6.16	you don't know that the **man** who joins his body to a
	6.18	Any other sin a **man** commits does not affect his body;
	6.18	but the **man** who is guilty of sexual immorality sins against
	7. 1	A **man** does well not to marry.
	7. 2	is so much immorality, every **man** should have his own wife,
	7. 3	A **man** should fulfil his duty as a husband, and a woman
	7.13	woman is married to a **man** who is an unbeliever and he
	7.19	For whether or not a **man** is circumcised means nothing;
	7.23	so do not become slaves of **men.**
	7.26	think it is better for a **man** to stay as he is.
	7.36	if the **man** feels that he is not acting properly towards the
	7.37	But if a **man,** without being forced to do so, has firmly
	7.38	So the **man** who marries does well, but the one who
	7.39	to be married to any **man** she wishes, but only if he
	9.10	man who ploughs and the **man** who reaps should do their work
	9.13	Surely you know that the **men** who work in the Temple get
	9.22	become all things to all **men,** that I may save some of
	11. 3	Christ is supreme over every **man,** the husband is supreme over
	11. 4	So a **man** who prays or proclaims God's message in public
	11. 7	A **man** has no need to cover his head, because he reflects
	11. 7	But woman reflects the glory of **man;**
	11. 8	for **man** was not created from woman, but woman from man.
1 Cor	11. 9	Nor was **man** created for woman's sake,
	11. 9	but woman was created for **man's** sake.
	11.11	is not independent of **man,** nor is man independent of woman.
	11.12	as woman was made from **man,**
	11.12	in the same way **man** is born of woman;
	11.14	that long hair on a **man** is a disgrace, [15] but on a
	13. 1	to speak the languages of **men** and even of angels, but if
	13.11	now that I am a **man,** I have no more use for
	14. 8	And if the **man** who plays the bugle does not sound a
	14.21	"By means of **men** speaking strange languages I will speak
	15.21	came by means of a **man,** in the same way
	15.21	the rising from death comes by means of a **man.**
	15.45	says, "The first **man,** Adam, was created a living being";
	15.49	wear the likeness of the **man** made of earth,
	15.49	so we will wear the likeness of the **Man** from heaven.
	16. 3	letters of introduction to the **men** you have approved, and send
	16.18	Such **men** as these deserve notice.
2 Cor	5.12	who boast about a **man's** appearance and not about his character.
	5.14	we recognize that one **man** died for everyone, which means that
	8.21	the sight of the Lord, but also in the sight of **man.**
	10.16	to boast about work already done in another **man's** field.
	11. 2	I have promised in marriage to one **man** only, Christ himself.
	11.13	Those **men** are not true apostles—they are false apostles,
	12. 3	I know that this **man** was snatched to Paradise
	12. 5	I will boast about this **man**—but I will not boast about
Gal	1. 1	apostle did not come from **man** or by means of man,
	1.10	Does this sound as if I am trying to win **man's** approval?
	1.10	Am I trying to be popular with **men?**
	1.12	not receive it from any **man,** nor did anyone teach it to
	1.23	"The **man** who used to persecute us is now preaching the
	2. 4	to be fellow-believers, these **men** slipped into our group as spies,
	2.12	Before some **men** who had been sent by James arrived there,
	2.12	But after these **men** arrived, he drew back and would not eat
	3.19	handed down by angels, with a **man** acting as a go-between.
	3.28	and Gentiles, between slaves and free men, between **men and women;**
	4. 2	he is young, there are **men** who take care of him
	5. 3	Once more I warn any **man** who allows himself to be
	5.10	different view and that the **man** who is upsetting you,
	6. 6	The **man** who is being taught the Christian message should share
Eph	2.11	circumcised" (which refers to what **men** do to their bodies)—
	4.28	The **man** who used to rob must stop robbing and start working,
	5.28	**Men** ought to love their wives
	5.28	A **man** who loves his wife loves himself.
	5.31	says, "For this reason a **man** will leave his father and
	6. 7	as though you served the Lord, and not merely **men.**
Phil	2. 7	He became like **man** and appeared in human likeness.
	3. 2	those dogs, those **men** who insist on cutting the body.
Col	2. 8	the teachings handed down by **men** and from the ruling spirits
	2.11	circumcision that is made by **men,** but with the circumcision made
	3.23	as though you were working for the Lord and not for **men.**
1 Thes	2. 4	do not try to please **men,** but to please God, who tests
	2.13	and accepted it, not as **man's** message but as God's message,
	4. 4	Each of you **men** should know how to live with his wife
	4. 6	then, no **man** should do wrong to his fellow-Christian
	4. 8	this teaching is not rejecting **man,** but God,
1 Tim	1.19	Some **men** have not listened to their conscience
	2. 5	and mankind together, the **man** Christ Jesus, [6] who gave himself
	2. 8	church service I want the **men** to pray,
	2. 8	**men** who are dedicated to God
	2.12	do not allow them to teach or to have authority over **men;**
	3. 1	If a **man** is eager to be a church leader, he desires
	3. 5	For if a **man** does not know how to manage his own
	3. 7	He should be a **man** who is respected by the people outside
	6.11	But you, **man** of God, avoid all these things.
2 Tim	2.17	Two **men** who have taught such things are Hymenaeus and Philetus.
Heb	2. 6	"What is **man,** O God, that you should think of him;
	2. 6	mere **man,** that you should care for him?
	2. 8	It says that God made **man** "ruler over all things";
	2. 8	We do not, however, see **man** ruling over all things now.
	3. 3	A **man** who builds a house receives more honour
	4.12	It judges the desires and thoughts of **man's** heart.
	5. 1	priest is chosen from his **fellow-men** and appointed to serve
	5. 4	by God's call that a **man** is made a high priest—
	7. 6	Abraham and blessed him, the **man** who received God's promises.
	7. 8	case of the priests the tenth is collected by **men** who die;
	7.28	The Law of Moses appoints **men** who are imperfect
	8. 2	real tent which was put up by the Lord, not by **man.**
	11.12	practically dead, from this one **man** came as many descendants as
Jas	1.20	**Man's** anger does not achieve God's righteous purpose.
	1.23	into practice is like a **man** who looks in a mirror
	3. 7	**Man** is able to tame and has tamed all other creatures—
	3. 9	and also to curse our **fellow-man,** who is created in the
	4.12	Who do you think you are, to judge your **fellow-man?**
	5. 4	not paid any wages to the **men** who work in your fields.
1 Pet	2. 4	the living stone rejected by **man** as worthless but chosen by
2 Pet	1.21	the will of man, but **men** were under the control of the
	2.12	But these **men** act by instinct, like wild animals born to
	2.17	These **men** are like dried-up springs, like clouds blown along
1 Jn	5. 9	We believe **man's** testimony;
Rev	4. 7	the third had a face like a **man's** face;
	6. 4	bring war on the earth, so that **men** should kill each other.
	6.15	the powerful, and all other **men,** slave and free, hid themselves
	9. 7	to be crowns of gold, and their faces were like **men's** faces.
	13.18	of the beast, because the number stands for a **man's** name.
	14. 4	They are the **men** who have kept themselves pure
	16.18	There has never been such an earthquake since the creation of **man;**

MAN OF GOD

Deut 33. 1 blessings that Moses, the **man of God,** pronounced
Josh 14. 6 Kadesh Barnea about you and me to Moses, the **man of God.**
Judg 13. 6 to her husband, "A **man of God** has come to me,
13. 8 "Please, Lord, let the **man of God** that you sent come back
1 Kgs 17.18 She said to Elijah, **"Man of God,** why did you do this
17.24 that you are a **man of God** and that the Lord really
2 Kgs 1. 9 and said to him, **"Man of God,** the king orders you to
1.10 "If I am a **man of God,"** Elijah answered, "may fire
1.11 and said to Elijah, **"Man of God,** the king orders you to
1.12 "If I am a **man of God,"** Elijah answered, "may fire
1.13 of Elijah, and pleaded, **"Man of God,** be merciful to me
4.16 You are a **man of God!"**
1 Chr 23.14 of Moses, the **man of God,** were included among the Levites.)
2 Chr 8.14 in accordance with the commands of David, the **man of God.**
30.16 to the instructions in the Law of Moses, the **man of God.**
Ezra 3. 2 instructions written in the Law of Moses, the **man of God.**
Neh 12.24 with the instructions given by King David, the **man of God.**
12.36 of the kind played by King David, the **man of God.**

MAN-EATER

Ps 57. 4 I am surrounded by enemies, who are like **man-eating** lions.
Ezek 19. 3 he became a **man-eater.**
19. 6 He too learnt to hunt and became a **man-eater.**
36.13 people call the land a **man-eater,** and they say that it robs
36.14 will no longer be a **man-eater** who robs you of your children.

MAN-MADE

see also **MAKE**

Mt 15. 9 because they teach **man-made** rules
Mk 7. 7 because they teach **man-made** rules as though they were God's
Acts 17.24 Lord of heaven and earth and does not live in **man-made** temples.
19.26 He says that **man-made** gods are not gods at all,
Col 2.22 they are only **man-made** rules and teachings.
Heb 9. 1 rules for worship and a **man-made** place for worship as well.
9.11 it is not a **man-made** tent,
9.24 did not go into a **man-made** Holy Place, which was a copy

MANAGE

Is 22.15 to go to Shebna, the **manager** of the royal household, and say
Mt 25.21 'You have been faithful in **managing** small amounts,
25.23 'You have been faithful in **managing** small amounts,
Lk 12.26 If you can't **manage** even such a small thing, why worry
16. 1 once a rich man who had a servant who **managed** his property.
16. 1 man was told that the **manager** was wasting his master's money,
16. 2 of my property, because you cannot be my **manager** any longer.'
16. 6 'Here is your account,' the **manager** told him;
16. 7 'Here is your account,' the **manager** told him;
16. 8 master of this dishonest **manager** praised him for doing such a
Acts 27.16 with some difficulty, we **managed** to make the ship's boat secure.
Gal 4. 2 take care of him and **manage** his affairs until the time set
1 Tim 3. 4 he must be able to **manage** his own family well
3. 5 does not know how to **manage** his own family, how can he
3.12 wife, and be able to **manage** his children and family well.
1 Pet 4.10 Each one, as a good **manager** of God's different gifts, must

MANASSEH (1)

[EAST MANASSEH, WEST MANASSEH]
Joseph's son, the tribe descended from him and its territory.

Gen 41.51 so he named his first son **Manasseh.**
46.20 Egypt Joseph had two sons, **Manasseh** and Ephraim, by Asenath,
48. 1 he took his two sons, **Manasseh** and Ephraim, and went to see
48. 5 Ephraim and **Manasseh** are just as much my sons as Reuben and
48. 6 inheritance they get will come through Ephraim and **Manasseh.**
48.13 Joseph put Ephraim at Jacob's left and **Manasseh** at his right.
48.14 his left hand on the head of **Manasseh,** who was the elder.
48.17 hand to move it from Ephraim's head to the head of **Manasseh.**
48.19 **Manasseh's** descendants will also become a great people.
48.20 They will say, 'May God make you like Ephraim and **Manasseh.'** "
48.20 In this way Jacob put Ephraim before **Manasseh.**
50.23 the children of Machir son of **Manasseh** into the family.
Num 10.23 command of the tribe of **Manasseh,** [24]and Abidan son of
26.28 who was the father of two sons, **Manasseh** and Ephraim.
26.29 The tribe of **Manasseh:**
26.29 Machir son of **Manasseh** was the father of Gilead, and the
27. 1 son of Gilead, son of Machir, son of **Manasseh,** son of
32.33 to half the tribe of **Manasseh** all the territory of King
32.39 clan of Machir son of **Manasseh** invaded the land of Gilead,
32.41 Jair, of the tribe of **Manasseh,** attacked and captured
34.14 the eastern half of **Manasseh** have received their property,
36. 1 of Machir and grandson of **Manasseh** son of Joseph, went to
36. 5 said, "What the tribe of **Manasseh** says is right, [6]and so
36.12 clans of the tribe of **Manasseh** son of Joseph, and their
Deut 3.13 To half the tribe of **Manasseh** I assigned the rest of
3.14 Jair, from the tribe of **Manasseh,** took the entire region of Argob,
3.15 Gilead to the clan of Machir of the tribe of **Manasseh.**
4.43 and for the tribe of **Manasseh** there was Golan, in the
29. 8 tribes of Reuben and Gad, and half the tribe of **Manasseh.**
33.17 His horns are **Manasseh's** thousands And Ephraim's ten thousands.
34. 2 the territories of Ephraim and **Manasseh;**
Josh 1.12 of **Manasseh,** [13]"Remember how Moses, the Lord's servant,
4.12 of half the tribe of **Manasseh,** ready for battle, crossed
12. 6 Gad and to half the tribe of **Manasseh,** to be their possession.
13. 7 half of the tribe of **Manasseh,** for them to possess as their
13. 8 half of the tribe of **Manasseh** had already received the land
13.29 families of half the tribe of **Manasseh** as their possession.
Josh 13.31 to half the families descended from Machir son of **Manasseh.**
16. 4 Ephraim and **West Manasseh,** received this land as their possession.
16. 9 the borders of **Manasseh,** but given to the Ephraimites.
17. 1 of the families descended from Joseph's elder son **Manasseh.**
17. 1 of Gilead, was **Manasseh's** eldest son and a military hero,
17. 2 Jordan was assigned to the rest of the families of **Manasseh:**
17. 2 These were male descendants of **Manasseh** son of Joseph, and
17. 3 son of Machir, son of **Manasseh,** did not have any sons, but
17. 5 That is why **Manasseh** received ten shares in addition to
17. 6 Gilead was assigned to the rest of the descendants of **Manasseh.**
17. 7 The territory of **Manasseh** reached from Asher to Michmethath,
17. 8 round Tappuah belonged to **Manasseh,** but the town of Tappuah,
17. 9 Ephraim, even though they were in the territory of **Manasseh.**
17. 9 The border of **Manasseh** proceeded along the north side of the
17.10 was to the south, and **Manasseh** was to the north, with the
17.11 Issachar and Asher, **Manasseh** possessed Beth Shan and Ibleam,
17.12 The people of **Manasseh,** however, were not able to drive
17.17 Ephraim and **West Manasseh,** "There are indeed many of you,
18. 7 of Gad, Reuben, and **East Manasseh** have already received
20. 8 and Golan in Bashan, in the territory of **Manasseh.**
21. 5 from the territories of Ephraim, Dan, and **West Manasseh.**
21. 6 of Issachar, Asher, Naphtali, and **East Manasseh.**
21.25 From the territory of **West Manasseh** they were given two cities:
21.27 received from the territory of **East Manasseh** two cities:
22. 1 the people of the tribes of Reuben, Gad, and **East Manasseh.**
22. 6 half of the tribe of **Manasseh,** but to the other half Joshua
22. 9 the tribes of Reuben, Gad, and **East Manasseh** went back home.
22.10 of Reuben, Gad, and **East Manasseh** arrived at Geliloth, still
22.11 Gad, and **East Manasseh** have built an altar at Geliloth,
22.13 of Reuben, Gad, and **East Manasseh** in the land of Gilead.
22.15 of Reuben, Gad, and **East Manasseh,** [16]and speaking for the
22.21 of Reuben, Gad, and **East Manasseh** answered the heads of the
22.30 of Reuben, Gad, and **East Manasseh** had to say, and they were
Judg 1.22 The tribes of Ephraim and **Manasseh** went to attack
1.25 people of Ephraim and **Manasseh** killed everyone in the city,
1.27 The tribe of **Manasseh** did not drive out the people
1.35 the tribes of Ephraim and **Manasseh** kept them under their
6.15 weakest in the tribe of **Manasseh,** and I am the least
6.35 of both parts of **Manasseh** to call them to follow him.
7.23 Asher, and both parts of **Manasseh** were called out, and they
11.29 He went through Gilead and **Manasseh** and returned to Mizpah
12. 4 "You Gileadites in Ephraim and **Manasseh,** you are deserters from
1 Kgs 4.13 of Jair, a descendant of **Manasseh,** and the region of Argob
11.28 in the territory of the tribes of **Manasseh** and Ephraim.
2 Kgs 10.33 where the tribes of Gad, Reuben, and **East Manasseh** lived.
1 Chr 5.18 Reuben, Gad, and **East Manasseh** there were 44,760 soldiers,
5.23 The people of **East Manasseh** settled in the territory of
5.26 and **East Manasseh** and settled them permanently in Halah,
6.61 in the territory of **West Manasseh** were assigned by lot to
6.62 of Issachar, Asher, Naphtali, and **East Manasseh** in Bashan.
6.70 In the territory of **West Manasseh** they were assigned the
6.71 In the territory of **East Manasseh:**
7.14 By his Aramean concubine, **Manasseh** had two sons,
7.17 of Gilead, the son of Machir and grandson of **Manasseh.**
7.29 The descendants of **Manasseh** controlled the cities of Beth Shan,
9. 3 Benjamin, Ephraim, and **Manasseh** went to live in Jerusalem.
12.19 soldiers from the tribe of **Manasseh** went over to David's
12.20 These are the soldiers from **Manasseh** who went over to
12.20 In **Manasseh** they had all commanded units of a thousand men.
12.23 Tribes east of the Jordan—Reuben, Gad, and **East Manasseh:**
26.32 River Jordan—the territories of Reuben, Gad, and **East Manasseh.**
2 Chr 15. 9 to Asa's side from Ephraim, **Manasseh,** and Simeon, and were
30. 1 the tribes of Ephraim and **Manasseh,** inviting them to come to
30.10 the tribes of Ephraim and **Manasseh,** and as far north as the
30.11 from the tribes of Asher, **Manasseh,** and Zebulun who were
30.18 from the tribes of Ephraim, **Manasseh,** Issachar, and Zebulun
31. 1 and the territories of Benjamin, Ephraim, and **Manasseh;**
34. 6 and the devastated areas of **Manasseh,** Ephraim, and Simeon,
34. 9 the people of Ephraim and **Manasseh** and the rest
Ps 60. 7 Gilead is mine, and **Manasseh** too;
80. 2 reveal yourself to the tribes of Ephraim, Benjamin, and **Manasseh.**
108. 8 Gilead is mine, and **Manasseh** too;
Is 9.21 people of **Manasseh** and the people of Ephraim attack each other,
Ezek 48. 1 Dan Asher Naphtali **Manasseh** Ephraim Reuben Judah
Rev 7. 5 Reuben, Gad, Asher, Naphtali, **Manasseh,** Simeon, Levi, Issachar,
also Num 1.5 Num 1.20 Num 2.18 Num 7.12 Num 13.3 Num 34.19 Josh 14.3 1 Chr 12.23 1 Chr 27.16 1 Chr 27.16

MANASSEH (2)

King of Judah.

2 Kgs 20.21 Hezekiah died, and his son **Manasseh** succeeded him as king.
21. 1 **Manasseh** was twelve years old when he became king of Judah,
21. 2 as his people advanced, **Manasseh** sinned against the Lord.
21. 3 **Manasseh** also worshipped the stars.
21. 9 not obey the Lord, and **Manasseh** led them to commit even
21.11 Lord said, [11]"King **Manasseh** has done these disgusting things,
21.16 **Manasseh** killed so many innocent people that the
21.17 Everything else that **Manasseh** did, including the sins he committed,
21.18 **Manasseh** died and was buried in the palace garden,
21.20 Like his father **Manasseh,** he sinned against the Lord;
23.12 altars put up by King **Manasseh** in the two courtyards
23.26 against Judah by what King **Manasseh** had done, and even now
24. 3 all the sins that King **Manasseh** had committed,
24. 4 The Lord could not forgive **Manasseh** for that.
1 Chr 3.13 Amaziah, Uzziah, Jotham, [13]Ahaz, Hezekiah, **Manasseh,** [14]Amon, and Josiah.
2 Chr 32.33 His son **Manasseh** succeeded him as king.

2 Chr 33. 1 **Manasseh** was twelve years old when he became king of Judah,
33. 2 as his people advanced, **Manasseh** sinned against the Lord.
33. 9 **Manasseh** led the people of Judah to commit even greater
33.10 Although the Lord warned **Manasseh** and his people,
33.11 They captured **Manasseh,** stuck hooks in him, put him in chains,
33.13 God accepted **Manasseh's** prayer and answered it
33.13 This convinced **Manasseh** that the Lord was God.
33.14 After this, **Manasseh** increased the height of the outer
33.18 Everything else that **Manasseh** did, the prayer he made to his God,
33.20 **Manasseh** died and was buried at the palace,
33.22 Like his father **Manasseh,** he sinned against the Lord,
Jer 15. 4 because of what Hezekiah's son **Manasseh** did in Jerusalem
Mt 1. 6 Jotham, Ahaz, Hezekiah, **Manasseh,** Amon, Josiah, and Jehoiachin

MANDRAKE

A small plant; it was believed that eating its root or fruit would help a woman to have children.

Gen 30.14 into the fields and found **mandrakes,** which he brought
30.14 Rachel said to Leah, "Please give me some of your son's **mandrakes."**
30.15 Now you are even trying to take away my son's **mandrakes."**
30.15 your son's **mandrakes,** you can sleep with Jacob tonight."
30.16 because I have paid for you with my son's **mandrakes."**
Song 7.13 can smell the scent of **mandrakes,** and all the pleasant

MANE

Job 39.19 made horses so strong and gave them their flowing **manes?**

MANGER

Lk 2. 7 and laid him in a **manger**—there was no room for them
2.12 a baby wrapped in strips of cloth and lying in a **manger."**
2.16 found Mary and Joseph and saw the baby lying in the **manger.**

MANKIND

Gen 5. 2 male and female, blessed them, and named them **"Mankind.")**
6. 1 When **mankind** had spread all over the world, and girls were
6.13 to Noah, "I have decided to put an end to all **mankind.**
Job 36.28 the rain pour from the clouds in showers for all **mankind.**
Ps 7. 8 You are the judge of all **mankind.**
14. 2 looks down from heaven at **mankind** to see if there are any
33.13 The Lord looks down from heaven and sees all **mankind.**
53. 2 looks down from heaven at **mankind** to see if there are any
Prov 8. 4 "I appeal to you, **mankind;**
Is 40. 5 of the Lord will be revealed, and all **mankind** will see it.
40. 6 "Proclaim that all **mankind** are like grass;
45.12 one who made the earth and created **mankind** to live there.
49.26 Then all **mankind** will know that I am the Lord, the one
66.24 The sight of them will be disgusting to all **mankind."**
Jer 27. 5 strength I created the world, **mankind,** and all the animals
32.27 said to me, [27] "I am the Lord, the God of all **mankind.**
45. 5 am bringing disaster on all **mankind,** but you will at least
Zeph 1. 3 I will destroy all **mankind,** and no survivors will be left.
1.17 will bring such disasters on **mankind** that everyone will
Mt 5.13 "You are like salt for all **mankind.**
24. 9 All **mankind** will hate you because of me.
24.14 preached through all the world for a witness to all **mankind;**
Mk 16.15 "Go throughout the whole world and preach the gospel to all **mankind.**
Lk 3. 6 All **mankind** will see God's salvation!' "
Jn 1. 4 the source of life, and this life brought light to **mankind.**
1. 9 light that comes into the world and shines on all **mankind.**
17. 2 authority over all **mankind,** so that he might give eternal
Acts 15.17 so all the rest of **mankind** will come to me, all the
17.26 he created all races of **mankind** and made them live throughout
Rom 5.14 death ruled over all **mankind,** even over those who did not
5.18 the one sin condemned all **mankind,** in the same way
5.18 one righteous act sets all **mankind** free and gives them life.
11.15 when they were rejected, **mankind** was changed from God's enemies
1 Cor 2. 7 wisdom, which is hidden from **mankind,** but which he had already
4. 9 as a spectacle for the whole world of angels and of **mankind.**
2 Cor 5.19 is that God was making all **mankind** his friends through Christ.
Gal 3. 8 "Through you God will bless all **mankind."**
3.21 For if **mankind** had received a law that could bring life,
Eph 3. 5 In past times **mankind** was not told this secret, but God
4. 6 God and Father of all **mankind,** who is Lord of all, works
4. 8 he gave gifts to **mankind."**
4.11 It was he who "gave gifts to **mankind"**;
Col 1.26 all past ages from all **mankind** but has now revealed to his
1 Tim 2. 5 one who brings God and **mankind** together, the man Christ Jesus,
2. 6 who gave himself to redeem all **mankind.**
Tit 2.11 For God has revealed his grace for the salvation of all **mankind.**
Heb 1. 3 forgiveness for the sins of **mankind,** he sat down in heaven
12.23 is the judge of all **mankind,** and to the spirits of good
1 Pet 1.24 As the scripture says, "All **mankind** are like grass, and all
Rev 9.15 they had been kept ready to kill a third of all **mankind.**
9.18 A third of **mankind** was killed by those three plagues:
9.20 The rest of **mankind,** all those who had not been killed
11.10 because those two prophets brought much suffering upon **mankind.**
14. 3 Of all **mankind** they are the only ones who have been redeemed.
14. 4 redeemed from the rest of **mankind** and are the first ones to
14. 7 For the time has come for him to judge **mankind.**
21. 3 "Now God's home is with **mankind!**

MANNA

A food eaten by the Israelites during their travels in the wilderness. It was white and flaky, and looked like small seeds.

Ex 16.31 The people of Israel called the food **manna.**
16.32 us to save some **manna,** to be kept for our descendants,
16.33 jar, put two litres of **manna** in it, and place it in
16.35 The Israelites ate **manna** for the next forty years, until
Num 11. 6 at all to eat—nothing but this **manna** day after day!"
11. 7 (**Manna** was like small seeds, whitish yellow in colour.
Deut 8. 3 and then he gave you **manna** to eat, food that you and
8.16 the desert he gave you **manna** to eat, food that your
Josh 5.12 The **manna** stopped falling then,
Neh 9.20 you fed them with **manna** and gave them water to drink.
Ps 78.24 grain from heaven, by sending down **manna** for them to eat.
Jn 6.31 Our ancestors ate **manna** in the desert, just as the scripture
6.49 Your ancestors ate **manna** in the desert, but they died.
Heb 9. 4 the gold jar with the **manna** in it, Aaron's stick that had
Rev 2.17 who win the victory I will give some of the hidden **manna.**

MANNER

Mk 16.12 Jesus appeared in a different **manner** to two of them while
Acts 7.10 God gave him a pleasing **manner** and wisdom, and the king made
Heb 9.28 In the same **manner** Christ also was offered in sacrifice once
1 Pet 1.18 you free from the worthless **manner** of life handed down by

MANOAH

Samson's father.

Judg 13. 2 time there was a man named **Manoah** from the town of Zorah.
13. 8 Then **Manoah** prayed to the Lord, "Please, Lord, let the man
13. 9 God did what **Manoah** asked, and his angel came back to the
13. 9 Her husband **Manoah** was not with her, [10] so she ran at once
13.11 **Manoah** got up and followed his wife.
13.12 Then **Manoah** asked, "When your words come true, what
13.15 **Manoah** did not know that it was the Lord's angel,
13.17 **Manoah** replied, "Tell us your name, so that we can
13.19 So **Manoah** took a young goat and some grain, and offered
13.20 going up from the altar, **Manoah** and his wife saw the Lord's
13.20 **Manoah** realized then that the man had been the Lord's angel,
13.22 **Manoah** said to his wife, "We are sure to die, because
16.31 between Zorah and Eshtaol in the tomb of his father **Manoah.**

MANSION

Jer 22.14 "I will build myself a **mansion** with spacious rooms upstairs."
Amos 3.10 says, "These people fill their **mansions** with things taken
3.11 land, destroy their defences, and plunder their **mansions."**
6. 8 I despise their luxurious **mansions.**

MANSLAUGHTER

Num 35.12 A man accused of **manslaughter** is not to be put to death
35.25 the man guilty of **manslaughter** from the dead man's relative,
35.26 If the man guilty of **manslaughter** leaves the city of
35.28 The man guilty of **manslaughter** must remain in the city
Deut 17. 8 that involve a distinction between murder and **manslaughter.**

MANUAL

Neh 3. 5 town refused to do the **manual** labour assigned to them by the
Job 7. 1 like a life of hard **manual** labour, [2] like a slave longing

MANURE

Is 25.10 Moab will be trampled down, just as straw is trampled in **manure.**
Jer 8. 2 buried, their bones will be like **manure** lying on the ground.
9.22 scattered everywhere, like piles of **manure** on the fields,
16. 4 Their bodies will lie like piles of **manure** on the ground.
25.33 They will lie on the ground like piles of **manure.**
Lk 13. 8 I will dig round it and put in some **manure.**
14.35 It is no good for the soil or for the **manure** heap;

MANY

Mt 7.13 leads to it is easy, and there are **many** who travel it.
7.22 When Judgement Day comes, **many** will say to me, 'Lord,
8.11 I assure you that **many** will come from the east and the
8.16 people brought to Jesus **many** who had demons in them.
19.30 But **many** who now are first will be last,
19.30 and **many** who now are last will be first.
20.28 but to serve and to give his life to redeem **many people."**
22. 9 streets and invite to the feast as **many people** as you find.'
22.14 And Jesus concluded, **"Many** are invited, but few are chosen."
24. 5 **Many** men, claiming to speak for me, will come and say,
24. 5 and they will deceive **many people.**
24.10 **Many** will give up their faith at that time;
24.11 Then many false prophets will appear and deceive **many people.**
24.12 the spread of evil that **many people's** love will grow cold.
26.28 my blood poured out for **many** for the forgiveness of sins.
26.60 not find any, even though **many people** came forward and told
27.53 they went into the Holy City, where **many people** saw them.
Mk 1. 5 **Many people** from the province of Judaea and the city of
1.34 Jesus healed **many** who were sick with all kinds of diseases
2. 2 So **many people** came together that there was no room left,
3.10 He had healed **many people,** and all those who were ill
5. 9 man answered, "My name is 'Mob'—there are so **many** of us!"
5.24 So **many people** were going along with Jesus that they were
6. 2 **Many people** were there;
6.31 There were so **many people** coming and going that Jesus

Mk 6.33 **Many people,** however, saw them leave and knew at once
10.31 But **many** who now are first will be last,
10.31 and **many** who now are last will be first.
10.45 came to serve and to give his life to redeem **many people."**
11. 8 **Many people** spread their cloaks on the road, while others cut
13. 6 **Many** men, claiming to speak for me, will come and say,
13. 6 and they will deceive **many people.**
14.24 is poured out for **many,** my blood which seals God's covenant.
Lk 1. 1 **Many people** have done their best to write a report of the
2.34 God for the destruction and the salvation of **many** in Israel.
2.34 a sign from God which **many people** will speak against [35] and
4.27 there were **many people** suffering from a dreaded skin-disease
4.41 Demons also went out from **many people,** screaming, "You are
7.21 that very time Jesus cured **many people** of their sicknesses,
13.24 because **many people** will surely try to go in but will not
14.16 was giving a great feast to which he invited **many people.**
Jn 2.23 during the Passover Festival, **many** believed in him as they saw
4.41 **Many** more believed because of his message, [42] and they said
10.41 **Many people** came to him.
10.42 And **many people** there believed in him.
11.55 Festival was near, and **many people** went up from the country
19.20 **Many people** read it, because the place where Jesus was
21.11 even though there were so **many,** still the net did not tear.
Acts 4. 4 But **many** who heard the message believed;
8. 7 Evil spirits came out from **many people** with a loud cry,
9.13 Ananias answered, "Lord, **many people** have told me about this
9.42 spread all over Joppa, and **many people** believed in the Lord.
10.27 he went into the house, where he found **many people** gathered.
11.24 Holy Spirit and faith, and **many people** were brought to the Lord.
12.12 of John Mark, where **many people** had gathered and were praying.
18.10 able to harm you, for **many** in this city are my people."
19.26 he has succeeded in convincing **many people,** both here in Ephesus
Rom 4.17 the scripture says, "I have made you father of **many** nations."
4.18 for hoping, and so became "the father of **many** nations."
5.15 It is true that **many people** died because of the sin of
5.15 his free gift to so **many people** through the grace of the
12. 4 We have **many** parts in the one body, and all these parts
12. 5 same way, though we are **many,** we are one body in union
16. 2 has been a good friend to **many people** and also to me.
1 Cor 9.19 everybody's slave in order to win as **many people** as possible.
10.17 bread, all of us, though **many,** are one body, for we all
12.12 Christ is like a single body, which has **many** parts;
12.14 is not made up of only one part, but of **many** parts.
12.20 As it is, there are **many** parts but one body.
2 Cor 1.11 **many** will raise their voices to him in thanksgiving for us.
6.10 we seem poor, but we make **many people** rich;
9.11 at all times, so that **many** will thank God for your gifts
9.13 this service of yours brings, **many** will give glory to God
11.18 since there are so **many** who boast for merely human reasons,
12.21 and I shall weep over **many** who sinned in the past and
Gal 3.16 the plural "descendants," meaning **many people,** but the singular
Phil 3.18 there are **many** whose lives make them enemies of Christ's
Tit 1.10 there are **many,** especially converts from Judaism, who rebel and
Heb 6.14 you that I will bless you and give you **many** descendants."
9.28 was offered in sacrifice once to take away the sins of **many.**
Jas 3. 1 My brothers, not **many** of you should become teachers.
Rev 8.11 water turned bitter, and **many people** died from drinking the water,

MAP

Josh 18. 4 over the whole country to **map** out the territory that they
18. 8 went on their way to **map** out the land after Joshua had
18. 8 all over the land and **map** it out, and come back to
Is 47.13 who study the stars, who **map** out the zones of the heavens

MARANA THA

1 Cor 16.22 **Marana tha**—Our Lord, come!

MARBLE

1 Chr 29. 2 and gems, stones for mosaics, and quantities of **marble.**
Esth 1. 6 of fine purple linen to silver rings on **marble** columns.
1. 6 with white **marble,** red feldspar, shining mother-of-pearl,
Rev 18.12 of ivory and of expensive wood, of bronze, iron, and **marble;**

MARCH

Ex 14.10 the king and his army **marching** against them, they were
15.16 fear until your people have **marched** past— the people you set
Num 2. 3 The division of Judah shall **march** first.
2.10 The division of Reuben shall **march** second.
2.17 and the last two the Levites are to **march** carrying the Tent.
2.17 Each division shall **march** in the same order as they camp,
2.18 The division of Ephraim shall **march** third.
2.25 The division of Dan shall **march** last.
2.34 his own banner, and they **marched,** each with his own clan.
10.13 They began to **march** at the command of the Lord through Moses,
10.28 then, was the order of **march,** company by company, whenever
20.18 If you try, we will **march** out and attack you."
20.20 and they **marched** out with a powerful army to attack the
21.33 and King Og of Bashan **marched** out with his army to attack
33. 8 after a three days' **march** they camped at Marah.
Deut 1.43 him, and in your pride you **marched** into the hill-country.
11.24 All the ground that you **march** over will be yours.
Josh 1. 3 my people the entire land that you will be **marching** over.
6. 3 and your soldiers are to **march** round the city once a day
6. 4 and your soldiers are to **march** round the city seven times
6. 7 ordered his men to start **marching** round the city, with an
Josh 6.12 time the priests and soldiers **marched** round the city in the
6.14 this second day they again **marched** round the city once and
6.15 got up at daybreak and **marched** seven times round the city in
6.15 was the only day that they **marched** round it seven times.
10. 9 night Joshua and his army **marched** from Gilgal to Gibeon, and
Judg 1.10 They **marched** against the Canaanites living in the city of Hebron,
1.11 there the men of Judah **marched** against the city of Debir, at
5.11 Then the Lord's people **marched** down from their cities.
5.21 I shall **march,** march on, with strength!
20.24 They **marched** against the army of Benjamin a second time.
20.30 the third successive day they **marched** against the army of
1 Sam 7.11 The Israelites **marched** out from Mizpah and pursued the
14.20 Then he and his men **marched** into battle against the Philistines,
23. 8 his troops to war, to **march** against Keilah and besiege David
29. 2 The five Philistine kings **marched** out with their units of
29. 2 David and his men **marched** in the rear with King Achish.
31.12 the bravest men started out and **marched** all night to Beth Shan.
2 Sam 2.29 Abner and his men **marched** through the Jordan Valley
2.29 the River Jordan, and after **marching** all the next morning,
2.32 Then they **marched** all night and at dawn arrived back at Hebron.
5.24 you hear the sound of **marching** in the tree-tops,
5.24 attack because I will be **marching** ahead of you
10. 8 The Ammonites **marched** out and took up their position at
10.17 crossed the River Jordan, and **marched** to Helam, where the
15.22 **"March** on!"
18. 4 the gate as his men **marched** out in units of a thousand
1 Kgs 20. 1 horses and chariots, he **marched** up, laid siege to Samaria,
20.26 called up his men and **marched** with them to the city of
20.27 **marched** out and camped in two groups facing the Syrians.
22.12 **"March** against Ramoth and you will win," they said.
2 Kgs 3. 9 After **marching** for seven days, they ran out of water, and
14.11 to listen, so King Jehoash **marched** out with his men and
16. 9 to Ahaz' plea, **marched** out with his army against Damascus,
24. 7 Egypt and his army never **marched** out of Egypt again, because
24.10 King Nebuchadnezzar's officers, **marched** against Jerusalem
1 Chr 12.19 David's side when he was **marching** out with the Philistines
14. 8 So David **marched** out to meet them.
14.15 you hear the sound of **marching** in the tree-tops, then
14.15 attack, because I will be **marching** ahead of you to defeat
19. 9 The Ammonites **marched** out and took up their position at
2 Chr 18.11 **"March** against Ramoth and you will win," they said.
20.21 wore on sacred occasions and to **march** ahead of the army,
20.28 they reached the city, they **marched** to the Temple, to the
Neh 12.31 of two large groups to **march** round the city, giving thanks
12.32 Hoshaiah **marched** behind the singers,
12.33 The following priests, blowing trumpets, **marched**
12.38 We **marched** past the Tower of the Ovens to the Broad Wall,
12.39 We ended our **march** near the gate to the Temple.
Ps 26. 6 that I am innocent and **march** in worship round your altar.
44. 9 you no longer **march** out with our armies.
60.10 Aren't you going to **march** out with our armies?
68. 7 when you **marched** across the desert, [8] the earth shook,
68.24 O God, your **march** of triumph is seen by all, the
108.11 Aren't you going to **march** out with our armies?
118.27 your hands, start the festival and **march** round the altar.
Is 41. 3 He follows in pursuit and **marches** safely on, so fast that
63. 1 dressed in red, **marching** along in power and strength?"
Jer 46. 3 'Get your shields ready and **march** into battle!
48. 2 armies will **march** against it.
Ezek 38.13 and property, and to **march** off with all those spoils?' "
Joel 2. 7 They all keep **marching** straight ahead and do not change
3. 9 gather all your soldiers and **march!**
Hab 1. 6 They are **marching** out across the world to conquer other lands.
3.12 You **marched** across the earth in anger;
Zech 9.14 he will **march** in the storms from the south.
Heb 11.30 fall down after the Israelites had **marched** round them for seven

MARE

Song 1. 9 men as a **mare** excites the stallions of Pharaoh's chariots.
Jer 13.27 after his neighbour's wife or like a stallion after a **mare.**

MARITAL RELATIONS

1 Cor 7. 5 but then resume normal **marital relations.**

MARK (1)

[UNMARKED]

Gen 4.15 So the Lord put a **mark** on Cain to warn anyone who
35.20 stone there, and it still **marks** Rachel's grave to this day.
Ex 12.13 will be a sign to **mark** the houses in which you live.
19.12 **Mark** a boundary round the mountain that the people must not cross,
19.23 the mountain sacred and to **mark** a boundary round it."
Lev 16. 8 lots, using two stones, one **marked** "for the Lord" and the
Deut 19.14 not move your neighbour's boundary **mark,** established long
27.17 " 'God's curse on anyone who moves a neighbour's boundary **mark.'**
Job 36.32 lightning with his hands and commands it to hit the **mark.**
38.10 I **marked** a boundary for the sea and kept it behind
Ps 104.19 You created the moon to **mark** the months;
Is 44. 5 Each one will **mark** the name of the Lord on his arm
Jer 18.15 they walk on **unmarked** paths.
31.21 Set up signs and **mark** the road;
50. 9 They are skilful hunters, shooting arrows that never miss the **mark.**
Ezek 9. 4 of Jerusalem and put a **mark** on the forehead of everyone who
9. 6 But don't touch anyone who has the **mark** on his forehead.
21.19 "Mortal man," he said, **"mark** out two roads by which
21.22 His right hand holds the arrow **marked** 'Jerusalem'!
39.15 bone, they will put a **marker** beside it so that the

Lk 11.44 You are like **unmarked** graves which people walk on without knowing
Jn 6.27 God, the Father, has put his **mark** of approval on him."
1 Cor 7.18 God's call, he should not try to remove the **marks** of circumcision;
2 Cor 1.22 who has placed his **mark** of ownership upon us, and who
Eph 4.30 for the Spirit is God's **mark** of ownership on you, a
Rev 7. 3 or the trees, until we **mark** the servants of our God with
7. 4 of those who were **marked** with God's seal on their foreheads
9. 4 who did not have the **mark** of God's seal on their foreheads.
13.16 and free, to have a **mark** placed on their right hands or
13.17 sell unless he had this **mark**, that is, the beast's name or
14. 9 its image and receives the **mark** on his forehead or on his
14.11 and its image, for anyone who has the **mark** of its name."
16. 2 on those who had the **mark** of the beast and on those
19.20 deceived those who had the **mark** of the beast and those who
20. 4 nor had they received the **mark** of the beast on their

MARK (2)
John Mark, Paul's companion and fellow worker.

Acts 12.12 Mary, the mother of **John Mark,** where many people had gathered
12.25 mission and returned from Jerusalem, taking **John Mark** with them.
13. 5 They had **John Mark** with them to help in the work.
13.13 city in Pamphylia, where **John Mark** left them and went back
15.37 Barnabas wanted to take **John Mark** with them, 38 but Paul
15.39 Barnabas took **Mark** and sailed off for Cyprus, 40 while Paul
Col 4.10 sends you greetings, and so does **Mark,** the cousin of Barnabas.
4.10 received instructions to welcome **Mark** if he comes your way.)
2 Tim 4.11 Get **Mark** and bring him with you, because he can help me
Phlm 24 so do my fellow-workers **Mark,** Aristarchus, Demas, and Luke.
1 Pet 5.13 chosen by God, sends you greetings, and so does my son **Mark.**

MARKET
[MEAT-MARKET]

Prov 1.20 out in the streets and **market-places,** 21 calling loudly at
7.12 sometimes in the streets, sometimes in the **market-place.**
Jer 5. 1 Search the **market-places!**
9.21 in the streets and the young men in the **market-places.**
Mt 11.16 They are like children sitting in the **market-place.**
20. 3 went out again to the **market-place** at nine o'clock and saw
20. 6 when he went to the **market-place** and saw some other men
23. 7 be greeted with respect in the **market-places** and to be called
Mk 6.56 who were ill to the **market-places** and beg him to let them
7. 4 that comes from the **market** unless they wash it first.
12.38 greeted with respect in the **market-place,** 39 who choose the
Lk 7.32 They are like children sitting in the **market-place.**
11.43 the synagogues and to be greeted with respect in the **market-places.**
20.46 and love to be greeted with respect in the **market-place;**
Jn 2.16 Stop making my Father's house a **market-place!"**
1 Cor 10.25 eat anything sold in the **meat-market,** without asking any

MARKET OF APPIUS

Acts 28.15 as the towns of **Market of Appius** and Three Inns to meet

MARROW

Heb 4.12 soul and spirit meet, to where joints and **marrow** come together.

MARRY
[INTERMARRIAGE, INTERMARRY]
see also **MARITAL RELATIONS**

Gen 11.29 Abram **married** Sarai, and Nahor married Milcah,
19.14 his daughters were going to **marry,** and said, "Hurry up and
19.31 in the whole world to **marry** us so that we can have
20. 3 she is already **married."**
20.12 of my father, but not of my mother, and I **married** her.
25. 1 Abraham **married** another wife, whose name was Keturah.
25.20 forty years old when he **married** Rebecca, the daughter of
26.34 was forty years old, he **married** two Hittite girls, Judith
27.46 If Jacob also **marries** one of these Hittite girls, I might as
28. 1 him, and said to him, "Don't **marry** a Canaanite girl.
28. 2 your grandfather Bethuel, and **marry** one of the girls there,
28. 3 May Almighty God bless your **marriage** and give you many children,
28. 6 he commanded him not to **marry** a Canaanite woman.
28. 9 Ishmael son of Abraham and **married** his daughter Mahalath,
29.18 seven years for you, if you will let me **marry** Rachel."
29.21 let me **marry** your daughter."
29.26 to give the younger daughter in **marriage** before the elder.
29.27 Wait until the week's **marriage** celebrations are over,
29.28 and when the week of **marriage** celebrations was over, Laban
31.50 my daughters or if you **marry** other women, even though I
34. 8 please let him **marry** her.
34. 9 that there will be **intermarriage** between our people and yours.
34.12 you whatever you ask, if you will only let me **marry** her."
34.14 "We cannot let our sister **marry** a man who is not circumcised;
34.16 Then we will agree to **intermarriage.**
34.21 Let us **marry** their daughters and give them ours in marriage.
36. 2 Esau **married** Canaanite women:
38. 2 He **married** her, 3 and she bore him a son, whom he named
38.14 up, and yet she had not been given to him in **marriage.**
38.26 her—I should have given her to my son Shelah in **marriage."**
Ex 2. 1 from the tribe of Levi **married** a woman of his own tribe,
2.21 his daughter Zipporah in **marriage,** 22 who bore him a son.
6.20 Amram **married** his father's sister Jochebed,

Ex 6.23 Aaron **married** Elisheba, the daughter of Amminadab
6.25 Eleazar, Aaron's son, **married** one of Putiel's daughters,
21. 3 but if he was **married** when he became your slave, he may
22.16 engaged, he must pay the bride-price for her and **marry** her.
22.17 father refuses to let him **marry** her, he must pay the father
34.16 Your sons might **marry** those foreign women, who would
Lev 20.14 If a man **marries** a woman and her mother, all three shall
20.17 If a man **marries** his sister or half-sister, they shall
20.21 If a man **marries** his brother's wife, they will die childless.
21. 4 unclean at the death of those related to him by **marriage.**
21. 7 A priest shall not **marry** a woman who has been a prostitute
21.13 He shall **marry** a virgin, 14 not a widow or a divorced
21.14 He shall **marry** only a virgin from his own clan.
22.12 A priest's daughter who **marries** someone who is not a
Num 12. 1 Moses had **married** a Cushite woman, and Miriam and Aaron
26.59 of Amram, 59 who was **married** to Levi's daughter Jochebed,
30. 6 abstain from something, and then **marries,** 7 she must do
30.10 If a **married** woman makes a vow or promises to abstain
30.16 woman living in her father's house or by a **married** woman.
36. 3 But remember, if they **marry** men of another tribe, their
36. 4 the tribe into which they **marry** and will be lost to our
36. 6 of Zelophehad are free to **marry** anyone they wish but only
36. 8 an Israelite tribe must **marry** a man belonging to that tribe.
36.10 Lord had commanded Moses, and they **married** their cousins.
36.12 They **married** within the clans of the tribe of Manasseh
Deut 7. 3 Do not **marry** any of them,
7. 3 do not let your children **marry** any of them, 4 because then
20. 7 Is there anyone here who is engaged to be **married?**
20. 7 someone else will **marry** the woman he is engaged to.'
21.11 them a beautiful woman that you like and want to **marry.**
21.13 after that, you may **marry** her.
22.13 "Suppose a man **marries** a girl and later he decides he
22.14 accusing her of not being a virgin when they got **married.**
22.16 to this man in **marriage,** and now he doesn't want her.
22.17 her, saying that she was not a virgin when he **married** her.
22.21 having intercourse before she was **married,** while she was
24. 1 "Suppose a man **marries** a woman and later decides that he
24. 2 Then suppose she **marries** another man, 3 and he also
24. 4 In either case, her first husband is not to **marry** her again;
24. 4 If he **married** her again, it would be offensive to the Lord.
24. 5 "When a man is newly **married,** he is not to be drafted
25. 5 widow is not to be **married** to someone outside the family;
25. 5 it is the duty of the dead man's brother to **marry** her.
25. 7 brother does not want to **marry** her, she is to go before
25. 8 If he still refuses to **marry** her, 9 his brother's widow is
28.30 will be engaged to a girl—but someone else will **marry** her.
Josh 15.16 give my daughter Achsah in **marriage** to the man who succeeds
15.17 the city, so Caleb gave him his daughter Achsah in **marriage.**
23.12 still left among you and **intermarry** with them, 13 you may be
Judg 1.12 give my daughter Achsah in **marriage** to the man who succeeds
1.13 the city, so Caleb gave him his daughter Achsah in **marriage.**
3. 6 They **intermarried** with them and worshipped their gods.
12. 9 He gave his daughters in **marriage** outside the clan and
12. 9 thirty girls from outside the clan for his sons to **marry.**
14. 2 I want to **marry** her."
14. 8 A few days later Samson went back to **marry** her.
21. 1 us will allow a Benjaminite to **marry** a daughter of ours."
21.18 we cannot allow them to **marry** our daughters, because we have
21.18 who allows a Benjaminite to **marry** one of our daughters."
Ruth 1. 4 her two sons, 4 who **married** Moabite girls, Orpah and Ruth.
1. 9 possible for each of you to **marry** again and have a home."
1.11 Do you think I could have sons again for you to **marry?**
1.12 Go back home, for I am too old to get **married** again.
1.12 still hope, and so got **married** tonight and had sons,
1.13 Would this keep you from **marrying** someone else?
3. 9 So please **marry** me."
1 Sam 17.25 give him his daughter to **marry** and will not require his
18.22 now is a good time for you to **marry** his daughter."
18.27 So Saul had to give his daughter Michal in **marriage** to David.
25.39 Then David sent a proposal of **marriage** to Abigail.
25.43 David had **married** Ahinoam from Jezreel, and now Abigail
2 Sam 3.14 I paid a hundred Philistine foreskins in order to **marry** her."
1 Kgs 3. 1 an alliance with the king of Egypt by **marrying** his daughter.
4.11 Benabinadab, who was **married** to Solomon's daughter Taphath:
4.15 Ahimaaz, who was **married** to Basemath, another of Solomon's
9.16 when she **married** Solomon, 17 and
11. 1 king of Egypt he **married** Hittite women and women from Moab,
11. 2 He **married** them even though the Lord had commanded the
11. 2 commanded the Israelites not to **intermarry** with these people,
11. 3 Solomon **married** seven hundred princesses
11.19 the sister of Queen Tahpenes, to Hadad in **marriage.**
16.31 he went further and **married** Jezebel, the daughter of King
2 Kgs 8.27 to King Ahab by **marriage,** he sinned against the Lord,
14. 9 'Give your daughter in **marriage** to my son.'
1 Chr 2.17 other daughter Abigail **married** Jether, a descendant of Ishmael,
2.18 Caleb **married** Azubah and had a daughter named Jerioth.
2.19 the death of Azubah, Caleb **married** Ephrath, and they had a
2.21 old, he **married** Machir's daughter, the sister of Gilead.
2.24 Hezron died, his son Caleb **married** Ephrath, his father's widow.
2.29 Abishur **married** a woman named Abihail, and they had two sons,
2.35 Jarha, 35 to whom he gave one of his daughters in **marriage.**
2.55 They were Kenites who had **intermarried** with the Rechabites.)
4.17 Mered **married** Bithiah, a daughter of the king of Egypt, and
4.17 Mered also **married** a woman from the tribe of Judah, and they
4.19 Hodiah **married** the sister of Naham.
4.22 and Joash and Saraph, who **married** Moabite women and then
8. 8 the country of Moab, he **married** Hodesh and had seven sons:
14. 3 There in Jerusalem, David **married** more wives and had more
23.22 His daughters **married** their cousins, the sons of Kish.
2 Chr 11.18 Rehoboam **married** Mahalath, whose father was Jerimoth
11.20 Later he **married** Maacah, the daughter of Absalom, and

2 Chr 18. 1 and famous, he arranged a **marriage** between a member of his
21. 6 of Israel, because he had **married** one of Ahab's daughters.
22.11 Jehosheba, who was **married** to a priest named Jehoiada.
25.18 'Give your daughter in **marriage** to my son.'
Ezra 2.61 priestly clan of Barzillai had **married** a woman from the clan
9. 2 Jewish men were **marrying** foreign women, and so God's holy
9.12 that we were never to **intermarry** with those people and never
9.14 can we ignore your commandments again and **intermarry** with
10. 2 broken faith with God by **marrying** foreign women, but even so
10.10 and have brought guilt on Israel by **marrying** foreign women.
Neh 6.18 addition, his son Jehohanan had **married** the daughter of
7.63 priestly clan of Barzillai had **married** a woman from the clan
10.30 will not **intermarry** with the foreigners living in our land.
13.23 of the Jewish men had **married** women from Ashdod, Ammon,
13.25 again would they or their children **intermarry** with foreigners.
13.27 example and disobey our God by **marrying** foreign women?"
13.28 but one of Joiada's sons **married** the daughter of Sanballat,
Ps 78.63 were killed in war, and young women had no one to **marry.**
106.35 but they **intermarried** with them and adopted their pagan
Prov 5.18 with the girl you **married—**[19] pretty and graceful as a deer.
30.23 a hateful woman who gets **married,**
Is 62. 4 land will be called "Happily **Married,**" Because the Lord is
62. 5 a virgin as his bride, He who formed you will **marry** you.
Jer 2. 2 were young, how you loved me when we were first **married;**
16. 2 me and said, [2]"Do not **marry** or have children in a place
29. 6 **Marry** and have children.
29. 6 Then let your children get **married,** so that they also may
Ezek 16. 8 I made a **marriage** covenant with you, and you became mine."
23. 4 I **married** both of them, and they bore me children.
44.22 No priest may **marry** a divorced woman;
44.22 he is to **marry** only an Israelite virgin or the widow of
Dan 2.43 to unite their families by **intermarriage,** but they will not
11. 6 the king of Syria and give him his daughter in **marriage.**
11.17 an alliance with him and offer him his daughter in **marriage;**
Hos 1. 2 Israel through Hosea, he said to Hosea, "Go and get **married;**
1. 3 So Hosea **married** a woman named Gomer, the daughter of Diblaim.
Joel 1. 8 who mourns the death of the man she was going to **marry.**
2.16 Even newly **married** couples must leave their room and come.
Mal 2.11 Men have **married** women who worship foreign gods.
2.14 your promise to the wife you **married** when you were young.
Mt 1.12 Matthan, Jacob, and Joseph, who **married** Mary, the mother of Jesus,
1.18 Joseph, but before they were **married,** she found out that she
1.24 when Joseph woke up, he **married** Mary, as the angel of the
5.32 guilty of making her commit adultery if she **marries** again;
5.32 and the man who **marries** her commits adultery also.
14. 4 Herod, "It isn't right for you to be **married** to Herodias!"
19. 9 commits adultery if he **marries** some other woman."
19.10 between a man and his wife, it is better not to **marry."**
19.12 For there are different reasons why men cannot **marry:**
19.12 and others do not **marry** for the sake of the Kingdom
22.24 dies, his brother must **marry** the widow so that they can
22.25 The eldest got **married** and died without having children,
22.28 All of them had **married** her."
22.30 they will be like the angels in heaven and will not **marry.**
24.38 and drank, men and women **married,** up to the very day Noah
Mk 6.17 of Herodias, whom he had **married,** even though she was the
6.18 "It isn't right for you to be **married** to your brother's wife!"
10.11 who divorces his wife and **marries** another woman commits adultery
10.12 divorces her husband and **marries** another man commits adultery."
12.19 that man's brother must **marry** the widow so that they can
12.20 the eldest got **married** and died without having children.
12.21 Then the second one **married** the woman, and he also died
12.22 all seven brothers **married** the woman and died without having
12.23 All seven of them had **married** her."
12.25 they will be like the angels in heaven and will not **marry.**
Lk 1.27 for a girl promised in **marriage** to a man named Joseph,
2. 5 to register with Mary, who was promised in **marriage** to him.
2.36 She had been **married** for only seven years and was now
3.19 because he had **married** Herodias, his brother's wife, and had
14.20 said, 'I have just got **married,** and for that reason I cannot
16.18 "Any man who divorces his wife and **marries** another woman
16.18 and the man who **marries** a divorced woman commits adultery.
17.27 drinking, and men and women **married,** up to the very day Noah
20.28 that man's brother must **marry** the widow so that they can
20.29 the eldest got **married** and died without having children.
20.30 Then the second one **married** the woman, [31] and then the third.
20.33 All seven of them had **married** her."
20.34 and women of this age **marry,** [35] but the men and women who
20.35 death and live in the age to come will not then **marry.**
Jn 4.18 You have been **married** to five men, and the man you live
Rom 7. 2 A **married** woman, for example, is bound by the law to her
7. 3 free woman and does not commit adultery if she **marries** another
1 Cor 7. 1 A man does well not to **marry.**
7. 9 your desires, go ahead and **marry—**
7. 9 it is better to **marry** than to burn with passion.
7.10 For **married** people I have a command which is not my own
7.13 if a Christian woman is **married** to a man who is an
7.28 But if you do **marry,** you haven't committed a sin;
7.28 if an unmarried woman **marries,** she hasn't committed a sin.
7.28 spare you the everyday troubles that **married** people will have.
7.29 married men should live as though they were not **married;**
7.33 But a **married** man concerns himself with worldly matters,
7.34 but a **married** woman concerns herself with worldly matters,
7.36 the case of an engaged couple who have decided not to **marry:**
7.36 feels that they ought to **marry,** then they should get married,
7.37 up his mind not to **marry,** and if he has his will
1 Cor 7.37 what to do—then he does well not to **marry** the girl.
7.38 So the man who **marries** does well,
7.38 but the one who doesn't **marry** does even better.
7.39 A **married** woman is not free as long as her husband lives;
7.39 she is free to be **married** to any man she wishes,
2 Cor 11. 2 I have promised in **marriage** to one man only, Christ himself.
1 Tim 4. 3 teach that it is wrong to **marry** and to eat certain foods.
5. 9 she must have been **married** only once [10] and have a reputation
5.11 desires make them want to **marry,** they turn away from Christ,
5.14 the younger widows get **married,** have children, and take care of
Heb 13. 4 **Marriage** is to be honoured by all, and husbands and wives

MARSH

Is 14.23 I will turn Babylon into a **marsh,** and owls will live there.
35. 7 Where jackals used to live, **marsh** grass and reeds will grow.
Ezek 47.11 But the water in the **marshes** and ponds along the shore

MARTHA

Lazarus and Mary's sister.

Lk 10.38 village where a woman named **Martha** welcomed him in her home.
10.40 **Martha** was upset over all the work she had to do,
10.41 The Lord answered her, **"Martha, Martha!**
Jn 11. 1 Bethany was the town where Mary and her sister **Martha** lived.
11. 5 Jesus loved **Martha** and her sister and Lazarus.
11.19 Judaeans had come to see **Martha** and Mary to comfort them
11.20 When **Martha** heard that Jesus was coming, she went out to
11.21 **Martha** said to Jesus, "If you had been here, Lord, my
11.28 **Martha** said this, she went back and called her sister Mary
11.30 but was still in the place where **Martha** had met him.)
11.39 **Martha,** the dead man's sister, answered, "There will be a bad
12. 2 prepared a dinner for him there, which **Martha** helped to serve;

MARVEL

Job 42. 3 I did not understand, about **marvels** too great for me to know.
Ps 27. 4 house all my life, to **marvel** there at his goodness, and to
Is 52.15 But now many nations will **marvel** at him, and kings will
Jer 33. 3 wonderful and **marvellous** things that you know nothing about.
Lk 4.22 impressed with him and **marvelled** at the eloquent words that he
5.26 praised God, saying, "What **marvellous** things we have seen today!"
9.43 The people were still **marvelling** at everything Jesus was doing,
1 Pet 2. 9 who called you out of darkness into his own **marvellous** light.

MARY (1)

Jesus' mother.

Mt 1.12 Joseph, who married **Mary,** the mother of Jesus,
1.18 His mother **Mary** was engaged to Joseph,
1.19 but he did not want to disgrace **Mary** publicly;
1.20 do not be afraid to take **Mary** to be your wife.
1.24 Joseph woke up, he married **Mary,** as the angel of the Lord
2.11 child with his mother **Mary,** they knelt down and worshipped him.
13.55 Isn't **Mary** his mother, and aren't James, Joseph, Simon, and
Mk 6. 3 the carpenter, the son of **Mary,** and the brother of James,
Lk 1.27 The girl's name was **Mary.**
1.29 **Mary** was deeply troubled by the angel's message,
1.30 The angel said to her, "Don't be afraid, **Mary;**
1.34 **Mary** said to the angel, "I am a virgin.
1.38 "I am the Lord's servant," said **Mary;**
1.39 Soon afterwards **Mary** got ready and hurried off to a town
1.41 Elizabeth heard **Mary's** greeting, the baby moved within her.
1.46 **Mary** said, "My heart praises the Lord;
1.56 **Mary** stayed about three months with Elizabeth and then went
2. 5 He went to register with **Mary,** who was promised in marriage
2.16 they hurried off and found **Mary** and Joseph and saw the baby
2.19 **Mary** remembered all these things and thought deeply about them.
2.22 came for Joseph and **Mary** to perform the ceremony of purification,
2.34 blessed them and said to **Mary,** his mother, "This child is
2.39 When Joseph and **Mary** had finished doing all that was required
Acts 1.14 with the women and with **Mary** the mother of Jesus

MARY (2)

Mary Magdalene.

Mt 27.56 Among them were **Mary Magdalene,** Mary the mother of James
27.61 **Mary Magdalene** and the other Mary were sitting there, facing
28. 1 as Sunday morning was dawning, **Mary Magdalene** and the other Mary
Mk 15.40 Among them were **Mary Magdalene,** Mary the mother of the younger
15.47 **Mary Magdalene** and Mary the mother of Joseph were watching
16. 1 the Sabbath was over, **Mary Magdalene,** Mary the mother of James,
16. 9 he appeared first to **Mary Magdalene,** from whom he had driven
Lk 8. 2 **Mary** (who was called Magdalene), from whom seven demons had been
24.10 The women were **Mary Magdalene,** Joanna, and Mary the mother
Jn 19.25 his mother's sister, Mary the wife of Clopas, and **Mary Magdalene.**
20. 1 while it was still dark, **Mary Magdalene** went to the tomb
20.11 **Mary** stood crying outside the tomb.
20.16 Jesus said to her, **"Mary!"**
20.18 **Mary Magdalene** went and told the disciples that she had seen

MARY (3)
James and Joseph's mother.

Mt	27.56	them were Mary Magdalene, **Mary** the mother of James and Joseph,
	27.61	Magdalene and the other **Mary** were sitting there, facing the tomb.
	28. 1	Mary Magdalene and the other **Mary** went to look at the tomb.
Mk	15.40	them were Mary Magdalene, **Mary** the mother of the younger James
	15.47	Mary Magdalene and **Mary** the mother of Joseph were watching
	16. 1	Sabbath was over, Mary Magdalene, **Mary** the mother of James, and
Lk	24.10	women were Mary Magdalene, Joanna, and **Mary** the mother of James;

MARY (4)
Wife of Clopas, perhaps the same as (3).

Jn	19.25	his mother, his mother's sister, **Mary** the wife of Clopas,

MARY (5)
Lazarus and Martha's sister.

Lk	10.39	She had a sister named **Mary**, who sat down at the feet
	10.42	**Mary** has chosen the right thing, and it will not be taken
Jn	11. 1	Bethany was the town where **Mary** and her sister Martha lived.
	11. 2	(This **Mary** was the one who poured the perfume on the
	11.19	come to see Martha and **Mary** to comfort them over their
	11.20	she went out to meet him, but **Mary** stayed in the house.
	11.28	Martha said this, she went back and called her sister **Mary**
	11.29	When **Mary** heard this, she got up and hurried out
	11.31	were in the house with **Mary**, comforting her, followed her
	11.32	**Mary** arrived where Jesus was, and as soon as she saw him,
	11.45	who had come to visit **Mary** saw what Jesus did, and they
	12. 3	Then **Mary** took half a litre of a very expensive perfume

MARY (6)
John Mark's mother.

Acts	12.12	went to the home of **Mary**, the mother of John Mark,

MARY (7)
Church worker in Rome.

Rom	16. 6	Greetings to **Mary**, who has worked so hard for you.

MASON
[STONE-MASONS]

2 Sam	5.11	logs and with carpenters and **stone-masons** to build a palace.
2 Kgs	12.12	the builders, [12]the **masons**, and the stone-cutters,
	22. 6	carpenters, the builders, and the **masons**, and buy the timber
1 Chr	14. 1	logs and with **stone-masons** and carpenters to build a palace.
	22.15	stone quarries, and there are **masons** and carpenters, as well
2 Chr	24.12	the Temple, and they hired **stonemasons**, carpenters, and
Ezra	3. 7	to pay the **stonemasons** and the carpenters and gave food,

MASSAGE

Esth	2. 9	beginning her beauty treatment of **massage** and special diet.
	2.12	the women lasted a year—**massages** with oil of myrrh for six

MAST

Ezek	27. 5	Mount Hermon for timber And a cedar from Lebanon for your **mast**.

MASTER

Gen	24. 9	the thighs of Abraham, his **master**, and made a vow to do
	24.10	property, took ten of his **master's** camels and went to the
	24.12	prayed, "Lord, God of my **master** Abraham,
	24.12	give me success today and keep your promise to my **master**.
	24.14	I will know that you have kept your promise to my **master**."
	24.27	Lord, the God of my **master** Abraham,
	24.27	who has faithfully kept his promise to my **master**.
	24.27	The Lord has led me straight to my **master's** relatives."
	24.35	Lord has greatly blessed my **master** and made him a rich man.
	24.36	Sarah, my **master's** wife, bore him a son when she was old,
	24.36	and my **master** has given everything he owns
	24.37	My **master** made me promise with a vow to obey his command.
	24.39	And I asked my **master**, 'What if the girl will not come
	24.42	prayed, 'Lord, God of my **master** Abraham, please give me
	24.44	one that you have chosen as the wife for my **master's** son.'
	24.48	Lord, the God of my **master** Abraham, who had led me straight
	24.48	led me straight to my **master's** relative,
	24.48	where I found his daughter for my **master's** son.
	24.49	your responsibility towards my **master** and treat him fairly,
	24.51	become the wife of your **master's** son, as the Lord himself
	24.54	in the morning, he said, "Let me go back to my **master**."
	24.56	let me go back to my **master**."
	24.65	"He is my **master**," the servant answered.
	27.37	"I have already made him **master** over you, and I have made
	32. 4	obedient servant, report to my **master** Esau that I have been
	32.17	"When my brother Esau meets you and asks, 'Who is your **master**?
	32.18	He sends them as a present to his **master** Esau.
	39. 2	the house of his Egyptian **master**, [3]who saw that the Lord
	39. 7	and after a while his **master's** wife began to desire Joseph
	39. 8	said to her, "Look, my **master** does not have to concern
	39.16	She kept his robe with her until Joseph's **master** came home.
	39.19	Joseph's **master** was furious [20]and had Joseph arrested
Gen	44. 5	Why did you steal my **master's** silver cup?
	44. 8	Why then should we steal silver or gold from your **master's** house?
Ex	21. 4	If his **master** gave him a wife and she bore him sons
	21. 4	her children belong to the **master**, and the man shall leave
	21. 5	declares that he loves his **master**, his wife, and his
	21. 6	be set free, [6]then his **master** shall take him to the place
	21. 8	her **master** cannot sell her to foreigners, because he has
	21.21	for a day or two, the **master** is not to be punished.
Lev	25.53	His **master** must not treat him harshly.
Judg	3.25	And there was their **master**, lying dead on the floor.
	19.10	the servant said to his **master**, "Why don't we stop and
	19.12	But his **master** said, "We're not going to stop in
1 Sam	20.38	returned to his **master**, [39]not knowing what it all meant;
	24. 6	doing any harm to my **master**, whom the Lord chose as king!
	25.14	with greetings for our **master**, but he insulted them.
	25.17	This could be disastrous for our **master** and all his family.
	26.15	So why aren't you protecting your **master**, the king?
	26.15	Just now someone entered the camp to kill your **master**.
	26.16	you have not protected your **master**, whom the Lord made king.
	29. 4	him to win back his **master's** favour than by the death of
	29. 8	I go with you, my **master** and king, and fight your enemies?"
	30.13	David asked him, "Who is your **master**, and where are you from?"
	30.13	"My **master** left me behind three days ago because I was ill.
	30.15	you will not kill me or hand me over to my **master**."
2 Sam	9. 9	"I am giving Mephibosheth, your **master's** grandson,
	9.10	farm the land for your **master** Saul's family and bring in the
	16. 3	"Where is Mephibosheth, the grandson of your **master** Saul?"
	16.19	After all, whom should I serve, if not my **master's** son?
1 Kgs	11.23	Rezon had fled from his **master**, King Hadadezer of Zobah,
	18. 8	"Go and tell your **master** the king that I am here."
2 Kgs	2. 3	Lord is going to take your **master** away from you today?"
	2. 5	Lord is going to take your **master** away from you today?"
	2.16	Let us go and look for your **master**.
	5. 3	mistress, "I wish that my **master** could go to the prophet
	5.20	Gehazi said to himself, "My **master** has let Naaman get away
	5.22	"But my **master** sent me to tell you that just now two
	9. 7	You are to kill your **master** the king, that son of Ahab,
1 Chr	12.19	betray them to his former **master** Saul, so they sent him back
2 Chr	2.13	sending you a wise and skilful **master** craftsman named Huram.
	4.11	Huram the **master** craftsman made all these objects
Esth	1.22	every husband should be the **master** of his home and speak
Ps	45.11	he is your **master**, so you must obey him.
	123. 2	a servant depends on his **master**, as a maid depends on her
Prov	17. 2	will gain authority over a **master's** worthless son and
	27.18	A servant who takes care of his **master** will be honoured.
	30. 4	Who has ever **mastered** heavenly knowledge?
	30.10	Never criticize a servant to his **master**.
Is	1. 3	owns them, and donkeys know where their **master** feeds them.
	22.18	You are a disgrace to your **master's** household.
	24. 2	and **masters**, buyers and sellers, lenders and borrowers,
Jer	10.23	I know that no one is the **master** of his own destiny;
Dan	10.17	I am like a slave standing before his **master**.
Zeph	1. 9	and kill in order to fill their **master's** house with loot.
Mal	1. 6	"A son honours his father, and a servant honours his **master**.
	1. 6	I am your **master**—why don't you respect me?
Mt	6.24	"No one can be a slave of two **masters**;
	10.24	no slave is greater than his **master**.
	10.25	to become like his teacher, and a slave like his **master**.
	15.27	the dogs eat the leftovers that fall from their **masters'** table."
	21. 3	And if anyone says anything, tell him, 'The **Master** needs them';
	24.45	is the one that his **master** has placed in charge of the
	24.46	that servant is if his **master** finds him doing this when he
	24.47	I tell you, the **master** will put that servant in charge
	24.48	will tell himself that his **master** will not come back for a
	24.50	that servant's **master** will come back one day when the servant
	24.51	The **master** will cut him in pieces and make him share the
	25.18	dug a hole in the ground, and hid his **master's** money.
	25.19	"After a long time the **master** of those servants came back
	25.21	you good and faithful servant!' said his **master**.
	25.23	you good and faithful servant!' said his **master**.
	25.26	" 'You bad and lazy servant!' his **master** said.
Mk	11. 3	tell him that the **Master** needs it and will send it
	13.35	do not know when the **master** of the house is coming—
Lk	5. 5	**"Master,"** Simon answered, "we worked hard all night long and
	8.24	went to Jesus and woke him up, saying, **"Master, Master!**
	8.45	denied it, and Peter said, **"Master,** the people are all round
	9.33	Jesus, Peter said to him, **"Master,** how good it is that we
	9.49	John spoke up, **"Master,** we saw a man driving out demons
	12.36	who are waiting for their **master** to come back from a wedding
	12.37	happy are those servants whose **master** finds them awake and ready
	12.42	is the one that his **master** will put in charge, to run
	12.43	that servant is if his **master** finds him doing this when he
	12.44	I tell you, the **master** will put that servant in charge
	12.45	says to himself that his **master** is taking a long time to
	12.46	and gets drunk, [46]then the **master** will come back one day
	12.46	The **master** will cut him in pieces and make him share the
	12.47	servant who knows what his **master** wants him to do, but does
	12.48	does not know what his **master** wants, and yet does something
	13.25	The **master** of the house will get up and close the door;
	14.21	"The servant went back and told all this to his **master**.
	14.21	The **master** was furious and said to his servant, 'Hurry out
	14.23	So the **master** said to the servant, 'Go out to the
	16. 1	the manager was wasting his **master's** money, [2]so he called
	16. 3	servant said to himself, 'My **master** is going to dismiss me
	16. 5	called in all the people who were in debt to his **master**.
	16. 5	He asked the first one, 'How much do you owe my **master?'**
	16. 8	"As a result the **master** of this dishonest manager praised him
	16.13	"No servant can be the slave of two **masters;**
	17.13	**Master!** Take pity on us!"
	19.31	why you are untying it, tell him that the **Master** needs it."

Lk 19.34 “The **Master** needs it,” they answered, [35]and they took
Jn 13.16 slave is greater than his **master,** and no messenger is greater
15.15 because a servant does not know what his **master** is doing.
15.20 ‘No slave is greater than his **master.’**
Acts 4.24 **“Master** and Creator of heaven, earth, and sea, and all that
Rom 6.14 Sin must not be your **master;**
6.16 fact the slaves of the **master** you obey—either of sin, which
14. 4 It is his own **Master** who will decide whether he succeeds or
1 Cor 4. 2 of such a servant is that he be faithful to his **master.**
7. 4 A wife is not the **master** of her own body, but her
7. 4 a husband is not the **master** of his own body, but his
Eph 6. 5 Slaves, obey your human **masters** with fear and trembling;
6. 9 **Masters,** behave in the same way towards your slaves and stop
6. 9 slaves belong to the same **Master** in heaven, who judges everyone
Col 3.22 Slaves, obey your human **masters** in all things, not only when
3.24 For Christ is the real **Master** you serve.
4. 1 **Masters,** be fair and just in the way you treat your slaves.
4. 1 Remember that you too have a **Master** in heaven.
1 Tim 6. 1 are slaves must consider their **masters** worthy of all respect,
6. 2 Slaves belonging to Christian **masters** must not despise them,
2 Tim 2.21 dedicated and useful to his **Master,** ready to be used for
Tit 2. 9 to submit to their **masters** and please them in all things.
1 Pet 2.18 must submit to your **masters** and show them complete respect,
3. 6 she obeyed Abraham and called him her **master.**
2 Pet 2. 1 and will deny the **Master** who redeemed them, and so they
Jude 4 and who reject Jesus Christ, our only **Master** and Lord.

MAT

Mk 2. 4 made an opening, they let the man down, lying on his **mat.**
2. 9 forgiven’, or to say, ‘Get up, pick up your **mat,** and walk’?
2.11 “I tell you, get up, pick up your **mat,** and go home!”
2.12 the man got up, picked up his **mat,** and hurried away.
6.55 they brought to him sick people lying on their **mats.**
Jn 5. 8 Jesus said to him, “Get up, pick up your **mat,** and walk.”
5. 9 he picked up his **mat** and started walking.
5.10 and it is against our Law for you to carry your **mat.”**
5.11 made me well told me to pick up my **mat** and walk.”
Acts 5.15 and placed on beds and **mats** so that at least Peter’s shadow

MATCH

Ex 26. 5 first set and fifty loops **matching** them on the last piece of
26.17 66 centimetres wide, [17]with two **matching** projections, so
36.12 first set and fifty loops **matching** them on the last piece of
36.22 centimetres wide, [22]with two **matching** projections,
2 Kgs 18.24 You are no **match** for even the lowest ranking Assyrian official,
Song 4. 2 they are all perfectly **matched.**
6. 6 they are all perfectly **matched.**
Is 36. 9 You are no **match** for even the lowest ranking Assyrian official,
Lk 5.36 coat, and the piece of new cloth will not **match** the old.

MATE

Gen 30.38 there, because the animals **mated** when they came to drink.
30.41 When the healthy animals were **mating,** Jacob put the
31.10 that the male goats that were **mating** were striped, spotted,
31.12 ‘all the male goats that are **mating** are striped, spotted,
Is 34.16 will be missing, and not one will be without its **mate.**
Jer 2.24 she is always available at **mating** time.
Nah 2.12 prey and tore it to pieces for his **mate** and her cubs;

MATERIAL (1)

Ex 28. 8 belt made of the same **materials** is to be attached to the
28.15 be made of the same **materials** as the ephod and with similar
39. 5 belt, made of the same **materials,** was attached to the ephod
39. 8 the breast-piece of the same **materials** as the ephod and with
Lev 19.19 Do not wear clothes made of two kinds of **material.**
1 Kgs 15.22 With this **material** Asa fortified Mizpah and Geba, a city in
2 Kgs 12.14 the workmen and to buy the **materials** used in the repairs.
1 Chr 22. 5 So David got large amounts of the **materials** ready before he died.
29. 2 made every effort to prepare **materials** for the Temple—gold,
2 Chr 2. 2 thousand men to work transporting **materials,** and eighty
2.18 70,000 of them to transport **materials** and 80,000 to cut
3.14 of linen and of other **material,** which was dyed blue, purple,
34.13 were in charge of transporting **materials** and supervising the
Neh 4.17 Even those who carried building **materials** worked with one
Is 8. 1 a large piece of writing **material** and write on it in large

MATERIAL (2)

Rom 15.27 Gentiles ought to use their **material** blessings to help the Jews.
1 Cor 7.31 those who deal in **material** goods, as though they were not
9.11 Is it too much if we reap **material** benefits from you?

MATTER

Judg 18.23 The men from Dan turned round and asked Micah, “What’s the **matter?**
18.24 Micah answered, “What do you mean, ‘What’s the **matter?’**
2 Sam 13. 4 What’s the **matter?”**
Job 9.21 Nothing **matters;**
Ps 10. 4 in his pride he thinks that God doesn’t **matter.**
1 Cor 3. 7 one who sows and the one who waters really do not **matter.**
3. 7 It is God who **matters,** because he makes the plant grow.
7.19 what **matters** is to obey God’s commandments.
Gal 5. 6 what **matters** is faith that works through love.
6.15 It does not **matter** at all whether or not one is circumcised;
6.15 what does **matter** is being a new creature.
Phil 1.18 It does not **matter!**

MATURE

Prov 8. 5 Learn to be **mature.**
16.21 A wise, **mature** person is known for his understanding.
1 Cor 2. 6 proclaim a message of wisdom to those who are spiritually **mature.**
Gal 4. 3 spirits of the universe before we reached spiritual **maturity.**
Eph 4.13 we shall become **mature** people, reaching to the very height of
Phil 3.15 of us who are spiritually **mature** should have this same attitude.
Col 1.28 into God’s presence as a **mature** individual in union with Christ.
4.12 make you stand firm, as **mature** and fully convinced Christians,
1 Tim 3. 6 He must be **mature** in the faith, so that he will not
Heb 6. 1 us go forward, then, to **mature** teaching and leave behind us

MEADOW

Ezek 34.14 in safety in the mountain **meadows** and the valleys and in all
45.13 1 sheep out of every 200 from the **meadows** of Israel
Hos 4.16 How can I feed them like lambs in a **meadow?**

MEAL (1)

Gen 19. 3 to bake some bread and prepare a fine **meal** for the guests.
31.46 Then they ate a **meal** beside the pile of rocks.
31.54 on the mountain, and he invited his men to the **meal.**
43.31 and controlling himself, he ordered the **meal** to be served.
Ex 12.43 foreigner shall eat the Passover **meal,** [44]but any slave
12.46 The whole **meal** must be eaten in the house in which it
18.12 with him to eat the sacred **meal** as an act of worship.
Deut 16. 2 or cattle for the Passover **meal** to honour the Lord your God.
16. 3 When you eat this **meal,** do not eat bread prepared with yeast.
Judg 19. 4 The couple had their **meals** and spent the nights there.
19.21 His guests washed their feet and had a **meal.**
Ruth 2.14 At **meal-time** Boaz said to Ruth, “Come and have a piece
2.18 She also gave her the food left over from the **meal.**
1 Sam 1. 9 after they had finished their **meal** in the house of the Lord
20.18 your absence will be noticed if you aren’t at the **meal.**
20.24 King Saul came to the **meal** [25]and sat in his usual place
20.27 “Why didn’t David come to the **meal** either yesterday or today?”
2 Sam 9.13 in Jerusalem, eating all his **meals** at the king’s table.
12. 4 kill one of his own animals to prepare a **meal** for him;
12. 4 took the poor man’s lamb and cooked a **meal** for his guest.”
1 Kgs 13.15 “Come home and have a **meal** with me,” he said.
13.19 went home with the old prophet and had a **meal** with him.
13.22 you returned and ate a **meal** in a place he had ordered
17.12 That will be our last **meal,** and then we will starve to
17.13 “Go ahead and prepare your **meal.**
2 Kgs 4. 8 She invited him to a **meal,** and from then on every time
4. 8 he went to Shunem he would have his **meals** at her house.
9.34 over her body, [34]entered the palace, and had a **meal.**
Jer 41. 1 they were all eating a **meal** together, [2]Ishmael and the ten
Ezek 44. 3 however, may go there to eat a holy **meal** in my presence.
Mt 9.10 Jesus was having a **meal** in Matthew’s house, many tax collectors
26.17 do you want us to get the Passover **meal** ready for you?”
26.19 did as Jesus had told them and prepared the Passover **meal.**
26.21 During the **meal** Jesus said, “I tell you, one of you
Mk 2.15 Later on Jesus was having a **meal** in Levi’s house.
14.12 lambs for the Passover **meal** were killed, Jesus’ disciples asked
14.12 want us to go and get the Passover **meal** ready for you?”
14.14 room where my disciples and I will eat the Passover **meal?’**
14.16 and they prepared the Passover **meal.**
Lk 14. 1 Jesus went to eat a **meal** at the home of one of
17. 7 the field, do you tell him to hurry and eat his **meal?**
17. 8 after that you may have your **meal.’**
22. 7 when the lambs for the Passover **meal** were to be killed.
22. 8 “Go and get the Passover **meal** ready for us to eat.”
22.11 room where my disciples and I will eat the Passover **meal?’**
22.13 Jesus had told them, and they prepared the Passover **meal.**
22.15 so much to eat this Passover **meal** with you before I suffer!
Jn 18.28 clean, in order to be able to eat the Passover **meal.**
21.20 close to Jesus at the **meal** and had asked, “Lord, who is
Acts 2.42 fellowship, and sharing in the fellowship **meals** and the prayers.
2.46 and they had their **meals** together in their homes, eating with
20. 7 On Saturday evening we gathered together for the fellowship **meal.**
1 Cor 10.27 unbeliever invites you to a **meal** and you decide to go, eat
11.21 goes ahead with his own **meal,** so that some are hungry while
Heb 12.16 Esau, who for a single **meal** sold his rights as the elder
2 Pet 2.13 join you in your **meals,** all the while enjoying their deceitful
Jude 12 carousing they are like dirty spots in your fellowship **meals.**

MEAL (2)

Lev 2.14 first corn harvested, offer roasted grain or ground **meal.**
2.16 burn that part of the **meal** and oil that is to serve
2 Sam 17.28 wheat, barley, **meal,** roasted grain, beans, peas, honey,
1 Kgs 4.22 litres of fine flour and ten thousand litres of **meal;**
2 Kgs 4.41 Elisha asked for some **meal,** threw it into the pot, and
Mt 24.41 Two women will be at a mill grinding **meal:**

MEAN (1)

Gen 33. 8 What did that **mean?”**
40. 5 each had a dream, and the dreams had different **meanings.**
40. 8 and there is no one here to explain what the dreams **mean.”**
40.12 Joseph said, “This is what it **means:**
40.18 Joseph answered, “This is what it **means:**
41.11 of us had a dream, and the dreams had different **meanings.**
41.25 Joseph said to the king, “The two dreams **mean** the same thing;
41.26 they have the same **meaning.**
41.32 The repetition of your dream **means** that the matter is

Gen 44. 7 answered him, "What do you **mean,** sir, by talking like this?
Ex 5. 4 and Aaron, "What do you **mean** by making the people neglect
12.26 When your children ask you, 'What does this ritual **mean?'**
13.14 son asks what this observance **means,** you will answer him,
21.13 accident and he did not **mean** to kill the man, he can
Lev 13.15 An open sore **means** a dreaded skin-disease,
17. 5 The **meaning** of this command is that the people of Israel
Num 11.34 named Kibroth Hattaavah (which **means** "Graves of Craving"),
14.34 You will know what it **means** to have me against you!
32.20 Moses answered, "If you really **mean** what you say, then
Josh 4. 6 children ask what these stones **mean** to you, [7] you will tell
4.21 ask you what these stones **mean,** [22] you will tell them about
Judg 7.14 It can't **mean** anything else!
7.15 man's dream and what it **meant,** he fell to his knees and
14.12 you can't tell me its **meaning** before the seven days of the
14.15 "Trick your husband into telling us what the riddle **means.**
14.16 my friends a riddle and didn't tell me what it **means!"**
14.17 told her what the riddle **meant,** for she nagged him about it
16.15 "How can you say you love me, when you don't **mean** it?
18.24 Micah answered, "What do you **mean,** 'What's the matter?'
Ruth 4. 6 the field, because it would **mean** that my own children would
1 Sam 1. 8 Don't I **mean** more to you than ten sons?"
4. 6 What does it **mean?"**
6. 9 town of Beth Shemesh, this **means** that it is the God of
20.21 get them,' that **means** that you are safe and can come out.
20.39 returned to his master, [39] not knowing what it all **meant;**
25.25 He is exactly what his name **means**—a fool!
2 Sam 15.21 go with you wherever you go, even if it **means** death."
19. 6 it clear that your officers and men **mean** nothing to you.
1 Kgs 1.41 trumpet, he asked, "What's the **meaning** of all that noise in
2 Kgs 10.19 of Jehu by which he **meant** to kill all the worshippers of
20.19 King Hezekiah understood this to **mean** that there would
Esth 5.13 But none of this **means** a thing to me as long as
Job 15. 3 as you do or defend himself with such **meaningless** words.
39.22 They do not know the **meaning** of fear, and no sword can
Ps 49. 4 to proverbs and explain their **meaning** as I play the harp.
119.33 Teach me, Lord, the **meaning** of your laws, and I will
119.72 The law that you gave **means** more to me than all the
Prov 1. 2 and good advice, and understand sayings with deep **meaning.**
1. 6 they can understand the hidden **meanings** of proverbs and the
2. 5 you will know what it **means** to fear the Lord and you
11.14 Many advisers **mean** security.
23. 7 on and have some more," he says, but he doesn't **mean** it.
27. 6 A friend **means** well, even when he hurts you.
Ecc 2.11 worked doing it, and I realized that it didn't **mean** a thing.
2.12 started thinking about what it **meant** to be wise or reckless
2.17 So life came to **mean** nothing to me, because everything
2.18 had worked for and earned **meant** a thing to me, because I
3.19 off than an animal, because life has no **meaning** for either.
5. 6 that you have to tell God's priest that you didn't **mean** it.
7. 6 It doesn't **mean** a thing.
7.24 How can anyone discover what life **means?**
8. 1 Only a wise man knows what things really **mean.**
Is 29.11 The **meaning** of every prophetic vision will be hidden from you;
29.13 words are **meaningless,** and their hearts are somewhere else.
32. 4 will act with understanding and will say what they **mean.**
39. 8 King Hezekiah understood this to **mean** that there would be
41.22 court the events of the past, and tell us what they **mean.**
42.20 you have seen so much, but what has it **meant** to you?
48. 1 God of Israel— but you don't **mean** a word you say.
Jer 5. 2 claim to worship the Lord, you do not **mean** what you say.
22.16 That is what it **means** to know the Lord.
Ezek 7.12 selling will have no more **meaning,** because God's punishment
17.12 me, [12] "Ask these rebels if they know what the parable **means.**
21.12 this sword is **meant** for my people and for all the leaders
25.14 Edom will know what it **means** to be the object of my
37.18 to tell them what this **means,** [19] tell them that I, the
Dan 2. 3 I want to know what it **means."**
2. 5 must tell me the dream and then tell me what it **means.**
2. 6 both the dream and its **meaning,** I will reward you with gifts
2. 6 Now then, tell me what the dream was and what it **means."**
2. 9 I will know that you can also tell me what it **means."**
2.16 time, so that he could tell the king what the dream **meant.**
2.24 to the king, and I will tell him what his dream **means."**
2.25 who can tell Your Majesty the **meaning** of your dream."
2.26 Belteshazzar), "Can you tell me what I dreamt and what it **means?"**
2.30 Your Majesty may learn the **meaning** of your dream and
2.36 Now I will tell Your Majesty what it **means.**
2.41 This **means** that it will be a divided empire.
2.42 partly iron and partly clay—**mean** that part of the empire
2.43 This **means** that the rulers of that empire will try to unite
2.45 what you dreamt, and have given you its true **meaning."**
4. 6 to me so that they could tell me what the dream **meant.**
4. 9 Tell me what it **means.**
4.18 "Now, Belteshazzar, tell me what it **means.**
4.24 "This, then, is what it **means,** Your Majesty, and this
4.26 This **means** that you will become king again when you
5. 7 and tell me what it **means** will be dressed in robes of
5. 8 them could read the writing or tell the king what it **meant.**
5.12 Belteshazzar, and he will tell you what all this **means."**
5.15 and tell me what it **means,**
5.15 but they could not discover the **meaning.**
5.16 heard that you can find hidden **meanings** and explain mysteries.
5.16 and tell me what it **means,** you will be dressed in robes
5.17 Your Majesty what has been written and tell you what it **means.**
5.26 And this is what it **means:**
7.16 So he told me the **meaning.**
8. 5 I was wondering what this **meant,** a goat came rushing out of
8.15 to understand what the vision **meant,** when suddenly someone
8.16 "Gabriel, explain to him the **meaning** of what he saw."
Dan 8.17 He said to me, "Mortal man, understand the **meaning.**
Zech 1. 9 I asked him, "Sir, what do these horses **mean?"**
1. 9 He answered, "I will show you what they **mean.**
1.19 that had been speaking to me, "What do these horns **mean?"**
4.11 "What do the two olive-trees on either side of the lamp-stand **mean?**
4.12 And what is the **meaning** of the two olive branches beside
6. 4 Then I asked the angel, "Sir, what do these chariots **mean?"**
Mt 1.23 he will be called Immanuel" (which **means,** "God is with us").
6. 7 not use a lot of **meaningless** words, as the pagans do,
7.12 this is the **meaning** of the Law of Moses and of the
9.13 Go and find out what is **meant** by the scripture that says:
12. 7 you really knew what this **means,** you would not condemn people
12.26 another in Satan's kingdom, this **means** that it is already divided
13.18 "Listen, then, and learn what the parable of the sower **means.**
13.36 "Tell us what the parable about the weeds in the field **means."**
13.52 replied, "This **means,** then, that every teacher of the Law
17.26 replied Jesus, "that **means** that the citizens don't have to
24. 6 must happen, but they do not **mean** that the end has come.
24.15 be sure to understand what this **means!)**
26.22 one after the other, "Surely, Lord, you don't **mean** me?"
26.25 "Surely, Teacher, you don't **mean** me?"
27.33 a place called Golgotha, which **means,** "The Place of the Skull."
27.46 which **means,** "My God, my God, why did you abandon me?"
Mk 3.17 gave them the name Boanerges, which **means** "Men of Thunder");
5.41 to her, "Talitha, koum," which **means,** "Little girl, I tell you
6.52 had not understood the real **meaning** of the feeding of the
7.11 says, 'This is Corban' (which **means,** it belongs to God),
7.34 and said to the man, "Ephphatha," which **means,** "Open up!"
9.10 discussing the matter, "What does this 'rising from death' **mean?"**
9.32 understand what this teaching **meant,** and they were afraid to ask
13. 7 must happen, but they do not **mean** that the end has come.
13.14 be sure to understand what this **means!)**
14.19 him, one after the other, "Surely you don't **mean** me, do
15.22 a place called Golgotha, which **means** "The Place of the Skull."
15.34 which **means,** "My God, my God, why did you abandon me?"
Lk 1.29 by the angel's message, and she wondered what his words **meant.**
4.29 They **meant** to throw him over the cliff, [30] but he walked
8. 9 asked Jesus what this parable **meant,** [10] and he answered,
8.11 "This is what the parable **means:**
9.45 But the disciples did not know what this **meant.**
12. 1 guard against the yeast of the Pharisees—I **mean** their hypocrisy.
12.41 this parable apply to us, or do you **mean** it for everyone?"
12.56 why, then, don't you know the **meaning** of this present time?
18.34 the **meaning** of the words was hidden from them, and they did
20.17 looked at them and asked, "What, then, does this scripture **mean?**
21. 9 happen first, but they do not **mean** that the end is near."
22.16 until it is given its full **meaning** in the Kingdom of God."
Jn 1.38 (This word **means** "Teacher.")
1.41 (This word **means** "Christ.")
1.42 (This is the same as Peter and **means** "a rock.")
6.46 This does not **mean** that anyone has seen the Father;
7.36 What does he **mean?"**
8.22 Does this **mean** that he will kill himself?"
8.33 What do you **mean,** then, by saying, 'You will be free'?"
9. 7 (This name **means** "Sent.")
9.40 and asked him, "Surely you don't **mean** that we are blind,
9.41 that you can see, this **means** that you are still guilty."
10. 6 this parable, but they did not understand what he **meant.**
11.13 Jesus **meant** that Lazarus had died,
11.13 but they thought he **meant** natural sleep.
13.22 looked at one another, completely puzzled about whom he **meant.**
16.17 of his disciples asked among themselves, "What does this **mean?**
16.18 What does this 'a little while' **mean?**
17. 3 And eternal life **means** knowing you, the only true God,
19.12 you set him free, that **means** that you are not the Emperor's
20.16 (This **means** "Teacher.")
Acts 1.19 they call that field Akeldama, which **means** "Field of Blood.")
2.12 and confused, they kept asking each other, "What does this **mean?"**
2.14 listen to me and let me tell you what this **means.**
4.36 the apostles called Barnabas (which **means** "One who Encourages"),
9.36 (Her name in Greek is Dorcas, **meaning** "a deer.")
10.17 Peter was wondering about the **meaning** of this vision,
10.19 trying to understand what the vision **meant,** when the Spirit said,
17.20 strange to us, and we would like to know what they **mean."**
19.27 goddess Artemis will come to **mean** nothing and that her greatness
Rom 1.12 What I **mean** is that both you and I will be helped
3. 3 Does this **mean** that God will not be faithful?
3.31 Does this **mean** that by this faith we do away with the
4. 6 This is what David **meant** when he spoke of the happiness of
4.14 then man's faith **means** nothing and God's promise is worthless.
7.10 And the commandment which was **meant** to bring life, in my
7.13 But does this **mean** that what is good caused my death?
7.20 don't want to do, this **means** that I am no longer the
9. 8 This **means** that the children born in the usual way are not
1 Cor 1.29 This **means** that no one can boast in God's presence.
4. 6 you may learn what the saying **means,** "Observe the proper rules."
5.10 Now I did not **mean** pagans who are immoral or greedy or
5.11 What I **meant** was that you should not associate with a
7.19 For whether or not a man is circumcised **means** nothing;
7.29 What I **mean,** my brothers, is this:
9.10 Didn't he really **mean** us when he said that?
9.21 This does not **mean** that I don't obey God's law;
11.26 This **means** that every time you eat this bread and drink
11.29 he does not recognize the **meaning** of the Lord's body when he
14.10 languages in the world, yet none of them is without **meaning.**
14.26 This is what I **mean,** my brothers.
15.13 If that is true, it **means** that Christ was not raised;

1 Cor 15.18 It would also **mean** that the believers in Christ who have
15.50 What I **mean,** brothers, is that what is made of flesh
2 Cor 4.12 This **means** that death is at work in us, but life is
5.11 We know what it **means** to fear the Lord, and so we
5.14 died for everyone, which **means** that all share in his death.
Gal 2.17 the Gentiles are—does this **mean** that Christ is serving the
2.21 God through the Law, it **means** that Christ died for nothing!
3. 4 Did all your experience **mean** nothing at all?
3. 4 Surely it **meant** something!
3.16 not use the plural "descendants," **meaning** many people, but the
3.16 singular "descendant," **meaning** one person only, namely, Christ.
3.17 What I **mean** is that God made a covenant with Abraham
3.19 wrongdoing is, and it was **meant** to last until the coming of
3.21 Does this **mean** that the Law is against God's promises?
5. 2 yourselves to be circumcised, it **means** that Christ is of no
5.17 two are enemies, and this **means** that you cannot do what you
Eph 4. 9 Now, what does "he went up" **mean?**
4. 9 It **means** that first he came down to the lowest depths of
Phil 4.10 I don't **mean** that you had stopped caring for me—you just
Col 1.27 Christ is in you, which **means** that you will share in the
Phlm 16 How much he **means** to me!
16 how much more he will **mean** to you, both as a slave
Heb 2.17 This **means** that he had to become like his brothers in
7. 2 first **meaning** of Melchizedek's name is "King of Righteousness";
7. 2 was king of Salem, his name also **means** "King of Peace.")
9. 9 It **means** that the offerings and animal sacrifices presented to
9.17 has died, [17] for a will **means** nothing while the person who
12. 8 all his sons are, it **means** you are not real sons,
Jas 4. 4 know that to be the world's friend **means** to be God's enemy?
5.12 Say only "Yes" when you **mean** yes,
5.12 and "No" when you **mean** no,
1 Pet 4.14 this **means** that the glorious Spirit, the Spirit of God, is
1 Jn 5. 3 For our love for God **means** that we obey his commands.
2 Jn 6 This love I speak of **means** that we must live in obedience
Rev 1.20 This is the secret **meaning** of the seven stars that you
2.10 to me, even if it **means** death, and I will give you
9.11 in Greek the name is Apollyon **(meaning** "The Destroyer").
13.10 Whoever is **meant** to be captured will surely be captured;
13.10 whoever is **meant** to be killed by the sword will surely be
13.18 can work out the **meaning** of the number of the beast,
17. 5 On her forehead was written a name that has a secret **meaning:**
17. 7 will tell you the secret **meaning** of the woman and of the

MEAN (2)

1 Sam 25. 2 but he was a **mean,** bad-tempered man.
30.22 But some **mean** and worthless men who had gone with David said,

MEANS
[BY MEANS OF, BY NATURAL MEANS]

Ex 7.22 did the same thing **by means of** their magic, and the king
Lev 6. 4 ways, he must repay whatever he got by dishonest **means.**
Deut 24. 6 away the family's **means** of preparing food to keep alive.
Jer 32.21 **By means of** miracles and wonders that terrified our enemies,
Mk 4.11 hear all things **by means of** parables, [12] so that, 'They may
Lk 8.10 the rest it comes **by means of** parables, so that they may
11.20 No, it is rather **by means of** God's power that I drive
Jn 1.13 not become God's children **by natural means,** that is, by being
11. 4 and it will be the **means** by which the Son of God
17.17 Dedicate them to yourself **by means of** the truth;
Acts 3.12 think that it was **by means of** our own power or godliness
4.25 **By means of** the Holy Spirit you spoke through our ancestor
17.31 whole world with justice **by means of** a man he has chosen.
Rom 3.25 he should become the **means** by which people's sins are forgiven
5. 5 love into our hearts **by means of** the Holy Spirit, who is
5.21 just as sin ruled **by means of** death, so also
5.21 God's grace rules **by means of** righteousness, leading us to
7. 8 But **by means of** that commandment sin found its chance to
7.11 found its chance, and **by means of** the commandment it
7.13 And so, **by means of** the commandment sin is shown to be
10.19 and **by means of** a nation of fools I will make my
15.13 all joy and peace **by means of** your faith in him,
15.18 He has done this **by means of** words and deeds,
1 Cor 1.21 for people to know him **by means of** their own wisdom.
1.21 Instead, **by means of** the so-called "foolish" message we preach,
2.10 that God made known his secret **by means of** his Spirit.
9.22 I may save some of them by whatever **means** are possible.
14.21 it is written, **"By means of** men speaking strange languages
15.21 just as death came **by means of** a man, in the
15.21 same way the rising from death comes **by means of** a man.
2 Cor 1.11 as you help us **by means of** your prayers for us.
8. 9 in order to make you rich **by means of** his poverty.
Gal 1. 1 come from man or **by means of** man, but from Jesus Christ
3.11 put right with God **by means of** the Law, because the
3.14 given to the Gentiles **by means of** Christ Jesus, so that
6.14 for **by means of** his cross the world is dead to me,
Eph 1. 9 plan he had already decided to complete **by means of** Christ.
2.16 **by means of** the cross he united both races into one body
3. 6 The secret is that **by means of** the gospel the Gentiles
3.10 at the present time, **by means of** the church, the angelic
3.20 To him who **by means of** his power working in us is
4. 3 which the Spirit gives **by means of** the peace that binds you
6.10 in union with the Lord and **by means of** his mighty power.
Phil 1.19 because I know that **by means of** your prayers and the
3. 3 for we worship God **by means of** his Spirit and rejoice in
Col 1.22 But now, **by means of** the physical death of his Son, God
1.24 sufferings for you, for **by means of** my physical sufferings I
2. 8 no one enslaves you **by means of** the worthless deceit of
2 Tim 1. 9 gave us this grace **by means of** Christ Jesus before the
Heb 7.21 Jesus became a priest **by means of** a vow when God said
10. 1 can the Law, then, **by means of** these sacrifices make perfect
10.19 into the Most Holy Place **by means of** the death of Jesus.
11. 4 **By means of** his faith Abel still speaks, even though he is
2 Pet 1. 4 he promised, so that **by means of** these gifts you may escape
1 Jn 2. 2 And Christ himself is the **means** by which our sins are forgiven,
4.10 his Son to be the **means** by which our sins are forgiven.
5. 4 we win the victory over the world **by means of** our faith.
Rev 6. 8 the earth, to kill **by means of** war, famine, disease, and
13.14 people living on earth **by means of** the miracles which it was

MEASURE
[TAPE-MEASURE]

Gen 41.49 much corn that Joseph stopped **measuring** it—it was like the
Ex 16.18 When they **measured** it, those who gathered much did not
16.36 (The standard dry **measure** then in use equalled twenty litres.)
Lev 19.35 not cheat anyone by using false **measures** of length, weight,
19.36 Use honest scales, honest weights, and honest **measures.**
Num 35. 5 there is a square area **measuring** 900 metres on each side,
Deut 3.11 almost two metres wide according to standard **measurements.**
21. 2 are to go out and **measure** the distance from the place where
25.13 "Do not cheat when you use weights and **measures.**
25.15 true and honest weights and **measures,** so that you may live a
1 Kgs 4.29 wisdom and insight, and knowledge too great to be **measured.**
7. 9 the quarry and cut to **measure,** with their inner and outer
7.11 of them were other stones, cut to **measure,** and cedar beams.
1 Chr 23.29 to weigh and **measure** the temple offerings;
Job 38. 5 Who stretched the **measuring-line** over it?
Ps 147. 5 his wisdom cannot be **measured.**
Prov 16.11 The Lord wants weights and **measures** to be honest and
20.10 The Lord hates people who use dishonest weights and **measures.**
Is 28.17 Justice will be the **measuring-line** for the foundation,
40.12 Can anyone **measure** the ocean by handfuls
40.12 or **measure** the sky with his hands?
44.13 The carpenter **measures** the wood.
Jer 31.37 day the sky could be **measured** and the foundations of the
Lam 2. 8 He **measured** them off to make sure of total destruction.
Ezek 4.16 distressed and anxious as they **measure** out the food they eat
40. 3 He was holding a linen **tape-measure**
40. 3 and a **measuring-rod** and was standing by a gateway.
40. 5 The man took his **measuring-rod,** which was three metres long,
40. 5 and **measured** the wall.
40. 6 went up the steps, and at the top he **measured** the entrance;
40. 8 He **measured** this room, and found it was four metres deep.
40.11 Next, the man **measured** the width of the passage in the gateway.
40.13 Then he **measured** the distance from the back wall of one
40.14 He **measured** that room and found it was ten metres wide.
40.19 The man **measured** the distance between the two gateways, and
40.20 Then the man **measured** the gateway on the north side that
40.21 all had the same **measurements** as those in the east gateway.
40.23 The man **measured** the distance between these two gateways,
40.24 He **measured** its inner walls and its entrance room, and they
40.27 The man **measured** the distance to this second gateway, and it
40.28 He **measured** the gateway, and it was the same size as the
40.32 He **measured** the gateway, and it was the same size as the
40.33 room, and its inner walls **measured** the same as those in the
40.35 He **measured** it, and it was the same size as the others.
40.47 The man **measured** the inner courtyard, and it was fifty metres
40.48 He **measured** the entrance:
41. 1 He **measured** the passage leading into it:
41. 2 He **measured** the room itself:
41. 3 He **measured** the passage leading into it:
41. 4 He **measured** the room itself, and it was ten metres square.
41. 5 The man **measured** the thickness of the inner wall of the
41.13 The man **measured** the outside of the Temple, and it was
41.15 He **measured** the length of the building to the west,
42.11 It had the same **measurements,** the same design, and the same
42.15 When the man had finished **measuring** inside the temple area,
42.15 the east gate and then **measured** the outside of the area.
42.16 He took the **measuring-rod** and measured the east side,
42.17 Then he **measured** the north side, the south side,
43.13 These are the **measurements** of the altar, using the same
43.13 the same unit of measurement as in **measuring** the Temple.
45. 3 a half kilometres by five kilometres, is to be **measured** off;
45.10 "Everyone must use honest weights and **measures:**
45.11 "The ephah for dry **measure** is to be
45.11 equal to the bath for liquid **measure.**
45.11 The resulting **measures** are as follows:
45.13 **(Measure** it by the bath:
47. 3 With his **measuring-rod** the man measured five hundred
47. 4 Then he **measured** another five hundred metres, and the
47. 5 He **measured** five hundred metres more, and there the stream
48.10 their portion is to **measure** twelve and a half kilometres,
48.16 and it will be a square, **measuring** 2,250 metres on each side.
48.20 apart will be a square **measuring** twelve and a half
48.30 Each of the four walls **measures** 2,250 metres and has three
Hos 1.10 the sand of the sea, more than can be counted or **measured.**
Amos 8. 5 we can overcharge, use false **measures,** and tamper with the
Mic 6.10 They use false **measures,** a thing that I hate.
Zech 2. 1 vision I saw a man with a **measuring-line** in his hand.
2. 2 "To **measure** Jerusalem," he answered, "to see how long
2. 4 that young man with the **measuring-line** that there are going
Lk 6.38 you will receive a full **measure,** a generous helping, poured into
6.38 The **measure** you use for others is the one that God will
Rom 15.29 I shall come with a full **measure** of the blessing of Christ.
2 Cor 10.12 up their own standards to **measure** themselves by, and they judge
Eph 1. 8 grace of God, [8] which he gave to us in such large **measure!**
4. 1 live a life that **measures** up to the standard God set when
1 Pet 1. 2 May grace and peace be yours in full **measure.**
2 Pet 1. 2 peace be yours in full **measure** through your knowledge of God
Jude 2 May mercy, peace, and love be yours in full **measure.**

Rev 11. 1 stick that looked like a **measuring-rod,**
11. 1 and was told, "Go and **measure** the temple of God
11. 2 do not **measure** the outer courts, because they have been given
21.15 had a gold measuring-rod to **measure** the city, its gates,
21.16 The angel measured the city with his **measuring-rod:**
21.17 angel also **measured** the wall, and it was sixty metres high,
21.17 according to the standard unit of **measure** which he was using.

MEAT

Gen 9. 4 thing you must not eat is **meat** with blood still in it;
18. 8 cream, some milk, and the **meat,** and set the food before the
27.19 and eat some of the **meat** that I have brought you, so
27.25 Isaac said, "Bring me some of the **meat.**
27.31 and eat some of the **meat** that I have brought you, so
Ex 12. 8 That night the **meat** is to be roasted, and eaten with
16. 3 least sit down and eat **meat** and as much other food as
16. 8 Lord who will give you **meat** to eat in the evening and
16.12 at twilight they will have **meat** to eat, and in the morning
21.35 they shall also divide up the **meat** from the dead animal.
22.31 you must not eat the **meat** of any animal that has been
29.31 "Take the **meat** of the ram used for the ordination of
29.34 If some of the **meat** or some of the bread is not
Lev 6.28 clay pot in which the **meat** is boiled must be broken, and
7. 7 the **meat** belongs to the priest who offers the sacrifice.
7.17 Any **meat** that still remains on the third day must be burnt.
7.19 If the **meat** comes into contact with anything ritually unclean,
7.19 ritually clean may eat the **meat,** [20] but if anyone who is
7.21 Also, if anyone eats the **meat** of this offering after he
8.31 and his sons, "Take the **meat** to the entrance of the Tent
8.32 Burn up any **meat** or bread that is left over.
9.11 But he burnt the **meat** and the skin outside the camp.
16.27 Skin, **meat,** and intestines shall all be burnt.
17.10 living in the community eats **meat** with blood still in it,
17.12 among them shall eat any **meat** with blood still in it.
17.14 they shall not eat any **meat** with blood still in it and
17.15 Israelite or foreigner, who eats **meat** from an animal that
19. 6 The **meat** must be eaten on the day the animal is killed
19. 6 Any **meat** left on the third day must be burnt, [7] because it
19.26 "Do not eat any **meat** with blood still in it.
22. 8 He shall not eat the **meat** of any animal that has died
Num 11. 4 had a strong craving for **meat,** and even the Israelites
11. 4 "If only we could have some **meat!**
11.13 Where could I get enough **meat** for all these people?
11.13 They keep whining and asking for **meat.**
11.18 you will have **meat** to eat.
11.18 you wished you had some **meat** and that you were better off
11.18 the Lord will give you **meat,** and you will have to eat
11.21 you say that you will give them enough **meat** for a month?
11.33 there was still plenty of **meat** for them to eat, the Lord
11.34 because there they buried the people who had craved **meat.**
18.18 The **meat** from them belongs to you, like the breast and
19. 5 The whole animal, including skin, **meat,** blood, and intestines,
22.40 and gave some of the **meat** to Balaam and the leaders who
Deut 12.15 them, just as you would eat the **meat** of deer or antelope.
12.20 as he has promised, you may eat **meat** whenever you wish.
12.21 and you may eat the **meat** at home, as I have told
12.22 or unclean, may eat that **meat,**
12.22 just as he would eat the **meat** of deer or antelope.
12.23 Only do not eat **meat** with blood still in it, for the
12.23 the blood, and you must not eat the life with the **meat.**
12.27 in which you eat the **meat** and pour the blood out on
16. 4 and the **meat** of the animal killed on the evening of the
16. 7 Boil the **meat** and eat it at the one place of worship;
28.31 your very eyes, but you will not eat any of the **meat.**
Judg 6.19 He put the **meat** in a basket and the broth in a
6.20 ordered him, "Put the **meat** and the bread on this rock,
6.21 reached out and touched the **meat** and the bread with the end
6.21 out of the rock and burnt up the **meat** and the bread.
1 Sam 1. 4 give one share of the **meat** to Peninnah and one share to
2.13 While the **meat** was still cooking, [14] he would stick the
2.15 the sacrifice, "Give me some **meat** for the priest to roast;
2.15 he won't accept boiled **meat** from you, only raw meat."
9.23 cook, "Bring the piece of **meat** I gave you, which I told
14.32 the spot, and ate the **meat** with the blood still in it.
14.33 against the Lord by eating **meat** with the blood in it."
14.34 not sin against the Lord by eating **meat** with blood in it."
2 Sam 6.19 a loaf of bread, a piece of roasted **meat,** and some raisins.
1 Kgs 17. 6 brought him bread and **meat** every morning and every evening.
19.21 killed them, and cooked the **meat,** using the yoke as fuel for
19.21 He gave the **meat** to the people, and they ate it.
1 Chr 16. 3 a loaf of bread, a piece of roasted **meat,** and some raisins.
2 Chr 35.13 and pans, and quickly distributed the **meat** to the people.
35.14 was done, the Levites provided **meat** for themselves and for
Ps 78.20 he also provide us with bread and give his people **meat?"**
Prov 7.14 made my offerings today and have the **meat** from the sacrifices.
15.17 you love than to eat the finest **meat** where there is hate.
Is 44.16 he roasts **meat,** eats it, and is satisfied.
44.19 some bread on the embers and I roasted **meat** and ate it.
65. 4 and drink broth made from **meat** offered in pagan sacrifices.
Ezek 4.14 on I have never eaten **meat** from any animal that died a
11. 3 and we are like the **meat** in it, but at least it
11. 7 This city is indeed a cooking-pot, but what is the **meat?**
11.11 will not protect you as a pot protects the **meat** in it.
24. 4 in the best pieces of **meat**— the shoulders and the legs
24. 5 Use the **meat** of the finest sheep;
24. 5 boil the bones and the **meat."**
24. 6 Piece after piece of **meat** is taken out, and not one is
24.10 Cook the **meat!**
33.25 You eat **meat** with the blood still in it.
39.17 of Israel, where they can eat **meat** and drink blood.
Ezek 40.43 All the **meat** to be offered in sacrifice was placed on the
46.20 priests are to boil the **meat** offered as sacrifices for sin
Dan 7. 5 said to it, "Go on, eat as much **meat** as you can!"
10. 3 any rich food or any **meat,** drink any wine, or comb my
Hos 8.13 They offer sacrifices to me and eat the **meat** of the sacrifices.
Mic 3. 3 break their bones, and chop them up like **meat** for the pot.
Hag 2.12 takes a piece of consecrated **meat** from a sacrifice and
Zech 9. 7 They will no longer eat **meat** with blood in it, or other
11. 5 They sell the **meat** and say, 'Praise the Lord!
11.16 Instead, he eats the **meat** of the fattest sheep and tears off
14.21 will use them for boiling the **meat** of the sacrifices.
Rom 14.21 to keep from eating **meat,** drinking wine, or doing anything else
1 Cor 8.13 sin, I will never eat **meat** again, so as not to make
10.25 eat anything sold in the **meat-market,** without asking any

MEDDLE

2 Thes 3.11 and who do nothing except **meddle** in other people's business.
1 Pet 4.15 thief or a criminal or a **meddler** in other people's affairs.

MEDIA

[MEDE, MEDES]

Powerful nation known as the Medes in what is now Iran.

2 Kgs 17. 6 in the district of Gozan, and some in the cities of **Media.**
18.11 in the district of Gozan, and some in the cities of **Media.**
Ezra 6. 2 Ecbatana in the province of **Media** that a scroll was found,
Esth 1. 3 The armies of Persia and **Media** were present, as well as the
1.14 seven officials of Persia and **Media** who held the highest
1.18 royal officials of Persia and **Media** hear about the queen's
1.19 the laws of Persia and **Media,** so that it can never be
10. 2 in the official records of the kings of Persia and **Media.**
Is 13.17 The Lord says, "I am stirring up the **Medes** to attack Babylon.
21. 2 Army of **Media,** lay siege to the cities!
Jer 25.19 all the kings of Zimri, Elam, and **Media;**
51.11 the kings of **Media,** because he intends to destroy Babylonia.
51.28 Send for the kings of **Media,** their leaders and officials,
Dan 5.28 is divided up and given to the **Medes** and Persians."
5.31 and Darius the **Mede,** who was then sixty-two years old,
6. 8 a law of the **Medes** and Persians, which cannot be changed."
6.12 a law of the **Medes** and Persians, which cannot be changed."
6.15 to the laws of the **Medes** and Persians no order which the
8.20 had two horns represents the kingdoms of **Media** and Persia.
9. 1 Darius the **Mede,** who was the son of Xerxes, ruled over the
Acts 2. 9 We are from Parthia, **Media,** and Elam;

Am MEDICINE

see also **OINTMENT**

MEDICINE

Prov 3. 8 it will be like good **medicine,** healing your wounds and
Jer 8.22 Is there no **medicine** in Gilead?
46.11 People of Egypt, go to Gilead and look for **medicine!**
46.11 All your **medicine** has proved useless;
51. 8 Get **medicine** for its wounds, and perhaps it can be healed.

MEDITATE

Ps 77. 3 when I **meditate,** I feel discouraged.
77. 6 I **meditate,** and this is what I ask myself:
77.12 I will **meditate** on all your mighty acts.
119.27 your laws, and I will **meditate** on your wonderful teachings.
119.48 I will **meditate** on your instructions.
119.78 as for me, I will **meditate** on your instructions.
119.95 are waiting to kill me, but I will **meditate** on your laws.
119.99 all my teachers, because I **meditate** on your instructions.
119.148 All night long I lie awake, to **meditate** on your instructions.
145. 5 and majesty, and I will **meditate** on your wonderful deeds.

MEDITERRANEAN

Modern name for the sea extending from Palestine to Spain.

Ex 23.31 Gulf of Aqaba to the **Mediterranean** Sea and from the desert
Num 13.29 Canaanites live by the **Mediterranean** Sea and along the River
34. 5 valley at the border of Egypt and end at the **Mediterranean.**
34. 6 "The western border will be the **Mediterranean** Sea.
34. 7 follow a line from the **Mediterranean** to Mount Hor [8] and from
Deut 1. 7 to the southern region, and to the **Mediterranean** coast.
2.23 The land along the **Mediterranean** coast had been settled
11.24 Euphrates in the east to the **Mediterranean** Sea in the west.
34. 2 the territory of Judah as far west as the **Mediterranean** Sea;
Josh 1. 4 the Hittite country, to the **Mediterranean** Sea in the west.
5. 1 the Canaanite kings along the **Mediterranean** Sea heard that
9. 1 plain of the **Mediterranean** Sea as far north as Lebanon;
15. 4 of Egypt to the **Mediterranean** Sea, where the border ended.
15.11 the **Mediterranean** Sea, [12] which formed the western border.
15.46 and towns near Ashdod, from Ekron to the **Mediterranean** Sea.
15.47 the border of Egypt and the coast of the **Mediterranean** Sea.
16. 3 on from there to Gezer and ended at the **Mediterranean** Sea.
16. 6 Upper Beth Horon, [6] and from there to the **Mediterranean** Sea.
16. 8 to the stream of Kanah and ended at the **Mediterranean** Sea.
17. 9 north side of the stream and ended at the **Mediterranean** Sea.
17.10 north, with the **Mediterranean** Sea as their western border.
19.29 then it turned to Hosah and ended at the **Mediterranean** Sea.
23. 4 River Jordan in the east to the **Mediterranean** Sea in the west.
Ps 80.11 extended its branches to the **Mediterranean** Sea and as far as
89.25 I will extend his kingdom from the **Mediterranean** to
Is 9. 1 to this region, from the **Mediterranean** eastwards to the land
Jer 25.19 all the kings of the **Mediterranean** lands;

Ezek	45. 7	the holy area it will extend west to the **Mediterranean** Sea;
	47.10	kinds of fish there as there are in the **Mediterranean** Sea.
	47.15	eastwards from the **Mediterranean** Sea to the city of Hethlon,
	47.17	runs from the **Mediterranean** eastwards to the city of Enon,
	47.19	along the Egyptian border to the **Mediterranean** Sea.
	47.20	boundary is formed by the **Mediterranean** and runs north to a
	48. 1	eastwards from the **Mediterranean** Sea to the city of Hethlon,
	48. 1	eastern boundary westwards to the **Mediterranean** Sea, in the
	48.21	boundary and westwards to the **Mediterranean** Sea, and is
	48.23	eastern boundary westwards to the **Mediterranean** Sea, in the
	48.28	along the Egyptian border to the **Mediterranean** Sea.
Joel	2.20	into the Dead Sea, their rear ranks into the **Mediterranean.**
Amos	8.12	the Dead Sea to the **Mediterranean** and then on from the north
Zech	14. 8	it to the Dead Sea and the other half to the **Mediterranean.**
Acts	27.27	were being driven about in the **Mediterranean** by the storm.

MEDIUM

A person who believes that he or she can communicate with the dead.

1 Sam	28. 3	had forced all the fortune-tellers and **mediums** to leave Israel.
	28. 7	a woman who is a **medium,** and I will go and consult
	28. 9	he forced the fortune-tellers and **mediums** to leave Israel.
2 Kgs	17.17	they consulted **mediums** and fortune-tellers,
	21. 6	divination and magic and consulted fortune-tellers and **mediums.**
	23.24	rest of Judah all the **mediums** and fortune-tellers,
2 Chr	33. 6	divination and magic and consulted fortune-tellers and **mediums.**
Is	8.19	from fortune-tellers and **mediums,** who chirp and mutter.
	8.20	Don't listen to **mediums**—what they tell you will do you no
	19. 3	they will go and consult **mediums** and ask the spirits of the

MEEK

2 Cor	10. 1	who am said to be **meek** and mild when I am with

AV **MEEK** see **GENTLE, HUMBLE**

MEET

Gen	4.15	on Cain to warn anyone who **met** him not to kill him.
	14.17	of Sodom went out to **meet** him in the Valley of Shaveh
	16. 7	The angel of the Lord **met** Hagar at a spring in the
	18. 2	As soon as he saw them, he ran out to **meet** them.
	19. 1	as he saw them, he got up and went to **meet** them.
	23.10	the other Hittites at the **meeting-place** at the city gate;
	24.17	The servant ran to **meet** her and said, "Please give me a
	29.13	nephew Jacob, he ran to **meet** him, hugged him and kissed him,
	30.16	evening, Leah went out to **meet** him and said, "You are going
	31. 4	to Rachel and Leah to **meet** him in the field where his
	32. 1	As Jacob went on his way, some angels **met** him.
	32. 6	brother Esau, and he is already on his way to **meet** you.
	32.17	servant, "When my brother Esau **meets** you and asks, 'Who is
	32.19	"This is what you must say to Esau when you **meet** him.
	32.20	gifts, and when I **meet** him, perhaps he will forgive me."
	33. 4	But Esau ran to **meet** him, threw his arms round him, and
	33. 8	Esau asked, "What about that other group I **met?**
	34.20	son Shechem went to the **meeting-place** at the city gate and
	38. 2	There Judah **met** a Canaanite girl whose father was named Shua.
	46.28	Jacob sent Judah ahead to ask Joseph to **meet** them in Goshen.
	46.29	got in his chariot and went to Goshen to **meet** his father.
	46.29	When they **met,** Joseph threw his arms round his father's neck
Ex	4.14	he is now coming to **meet** you and will be glad to
	4.24	way to Egypt, the Lord **met** Moses and tried to kill him.
	4.27	Lord had said to Aaron, "Go into the desert to **meet** Moses."
	4.27	So he went to **meet** him at the holy mountain;
	4.27	and when he **met** him, he kissed him.
	5.20	As they were leaving, they **met** Moses and Aaron, who were
	7.15	So go and **meet** him in the morning when he goes down
	8.20	"Early tomorrow morning go and **meet** the king as he goes to
	9.13	to Moses, "Early tomorrow morning **meet** with the king and
	12.16	and again on the seventh day you are to **meet** for worship.
	18. 7	so Moses went out to **meet** him, bowed before him, and
	19. 3	Mount Sinai, [3] and Moses went up the mountain to **meet** with God.
	19.17	out of the camp to **meet** God, and they stood at the
	25.22	I will **meet** you there, and from above the lid between
	29.42	That is where I will **meet** my people and speak to you.
	29.43	There I will **meet** the people of Israel, and the dazzling
	30. 6	That is the place where I will **meet** you.
	34. 2	and come up Mount Sinai to **meet** me there at the top.
Num	17. 4	put them in front of the Covenant Box, where I **meet** you.
	22.36	was coming, he went to **meet** him at Ar, a city on
	23. 3	I go to see whether or not the Lord will **meet** me.
	23. 4	went alone to the top of a hill, [4] and God **met** him.
	23.15	here by your burnt-offering, and I will **meet** God over there."
	23.16	The Lord **met** Balaam, told him what to say, and sent him
	28.25	**Meet** for worship on the seventh day and do no work.
	31.13	of the community went out of the camp to **meet** the army.
Deut	31.29	time to come they will **meet** with disaster, because they will
Josh	9.11	some food ready for a journey and to go and **meet** you.
	9.12	with it and started out to **meet** you, it was still warm.
Judg	4.18	Jael went out to **meet** Sisera and said to him, "Come in,
	4.22	Sisera, Jael went out to **meet** him and said to him, "Come
	11.31	out of my house to **meet** me, when I come back from
	11.34	coming out to **meet** him, dancing and playing the tambourine.
	16. 1	city of Gaza, where he **met** a prostitute and went to bed
	16.23	The Philistine kings **met** together to celebrate and
Ruth	4. 1	Boaz went to the **meeting place** at the town gate and sat
1 Sam	7. 5	for all the Israelites to **meet** at Mizpah, saying, "I will
	8. 4	the leaders of Israel **met** together, went to Samuel in Ramah,
	9. 9	hill to the town, they **met** some girls who were coming out
1 Sam	10. 2	leave me today, you will **meet** two men near Rachel's tomb at
	10. 3	at Tabor, where you will **meet** three men on their way to
	10. 5	to the town you will **meet** a group of prophets coming down
	10. 8	I will **meet** you and offer burnt-sacrifices and
	10.10	his servant arrived at Gibeah, a group of prophets **met** him.
	13.10	Saul went out to **meet** him and welcome him, [11] but Samuel said,
	16. 4	city leaders came trembling to **meet** him and asked, "Is this
	17.40	With his catapult ready, he went out to **meet** Goliath.
	18. 6	women from every town in Israel came out to **meet** King Saul.
	20.35	Jonathan went to the fields to **meet** David, as they had agreed.
	21. 1	Ahimelech came out trembling to **meet** him and asked, "Why
	21. 2	men, I have told them to **meet** me at a certain place.
	25.20	a hillside when suddenly she **met** David and his men coming
	25.32	Lord, the God of Israel, who sent you today to **meet** me!
	25.34	you had not hurried to **meet** me, all of Nabal's men would
	30.21	They came forward to **meet** David and his men, and David went
2 Sam	2.13	Zeruiah, and David's other officials **met** them at the pool,
	6.20	went home to greet his family, Michal came out to **meet** him.
	13. 2	as a virgin, she was kept from **meeting** men.
	15.32	trusted friend Hushai the Archite **met** him with his clothes
	16. 1	he was suddenly **met** by Ziba, the servant of Mephibosheth,
	16. 5	of Gera, came out to **meet** him, cursing him as he came.
	16.16	When Hushai, David's trusted friend, **met** Absalom, he
	17.27	arrived at Mahanaim, he was **met** by Shobi son of Nahash, from
	18. 9	Suddenly Absalom **met** some of David's men.
	19.15	way back the king was **met** at the River Jordan by the
	19.16	Gera from Bahurim hurried to the Jordan to **meet** King David.
	19.20	the northern tribes to come and **meet** Your Majesty today."
	19.24	Then Mephibosheth, Saul's grandson, came down to **meet** the king.
	19.25	Mephibosheth arrived from Jerusalem to **meet** the king, the
	20. 8	When they reached the large rock at Gibeon, Amasa **met** them.
1 Kgs	2. 8	to Mahanaim, but when he **met** me at the River Jordan, I
	10. 2	When she and Solomon **met,** she asked him all the questions
	11.29	the prophet Ahijah, from Shiloh, **met** him alone on the road
	13.24	On the way, a lion **met** him and killed him.
	18. 7	As Obadiah was on his way, he suddenly **met** Elijah.
	18.16	King Ahab and told him, and Ahab set off to **meet** Elijah.
	18.19	order all the people of Israel to **meet** me at Mount Carmel.
	18.20	Israelites and the prophets of Baal to **meet** at Mount Carmel.
	22.23	But he himself has decreed that you will **meet** with disaster!"
2 Kgs	1. 3	from Tishbe, to go and **meet** the messengers of King Ahaziah
	1. 6	They answered, "We were **met** by a man who told us to
	2.15	They went to **meet** him, bowed down before him, [16] and said,
	4.29	stop to greet anyone you **meet,** and if anyone greets you,
	4.31	So he went back to **meet** Elisha and said, "The boy didn't
	5.21	his chariot to **meet** him, and asked, "Is something wrong?"
	5.26	spirit when the man got out of his chariot to **meet** you?
	8. 9	When Hazael **met** him, he said, "Your servant King Benhadad
	9.21	King Ahaziah rode out, each in his own chariot, to **meet**
	9.21	They **met** him at the field which had belonged to Naboth.
	10.13	place called "Shepherds' Camp," [13] he **met** some relatives
	10.15	and on his way he was **met** by Jonadab son of Rechab.
	16.10	Ahaz went to Damascus to **meet** Emperor Tiglath Pileser, he
	18.18	King Hezekiah, and three of his officials went out to **meet** them:
1 Chr	12.17	David went to **meet** them and said, "If you are coming as
	14. 8	So David marched out to **meet** them.
2 Chr	9. 1	When she and Solomon **met,** she asked him all the questions
	13. 4	The armies **met** in the hill-country of Ephraim.
	15. 2	upon Azariah son of Oded, [2] and he went to **meet** King Asa.
	18.22	But he himself has decreed that you will **meet** with disaster!"
	19. 2	son of Hanani, went to **meet** the king and said to him,
	20.16	You will **meet** them at the end of the valley that leads
	25.21	They **met** at Beth Shemesh in Judah, [22] the Judaean army was
	28. 9	He **met** the returning Israelite army with its Judaean
Ezra	10. 7	returned from exile were to **meet** in Jerusalem [8] by order of
Neh	6. 2	a message, suggesting that I **meet** with them in one of the
	6. 7	I suggest that you and I **meet** to talk the situation over."
Job	4. 7	Name a single case where a righteous man **met** with disaster.
	21.17	Did one of them ever **meet** with disaster?
	29. 7	Whenever the city elders **met** and I took my place among them,
	31.29	enemies suffered, or pleased when they **met** with disaster;
	41.22	His neck is so powerful that all who **meet** him are terrified.
Ps	85.10	Love and faithfulness will **meet;**
	119.23	The rulers **meet** and plot against me, but I will study
	127. 5	never be defeated when he **meets** his enemies in the place of
Prov	7.10	And then she **met** him;
	12. 7	Wicked men **meet** their downfall and leave no descendants,
	15.19	you are lazy, you will **meet** difficulty everywhere, but if
	17.12	It is better to **meet** a mother bear robbed of her cubs
	17.12	than to **meet** some fool busy with a stupid
	18.16	Do you want to **meet** an important person?
	24.17	be glad when your enemy **meets** disaster, and don't rejoice
Ecc	10. 3	will be evident even to strangers he **meets** along the way;
Song	8. 1	Then, if I **met** you in the street, I could kiss you
Is	7. 3	"Take your son Shear Jashub, and go to **meet** King Ahaz.
	24. 2	Everyone will **meet** the same fate—the priests and the people,
	36. 3	Three Judaeans came out to **meet** him:
	65.23	successful, and their children will not **meet** with disaster.
Jer	41. 6	Ishmael went out from Mizpah to **meet** them, weeping as he went.
Lam	4. 6	the inhabitants of Sodom, which **met** with a sudden downfall
Ezek	33.30	talking about you when they **meet** by the city walls or in
Dan	9.27	one who put it there **meets** the end which God has prepared
Amos	3. 3	Do two men start travelling together without arranging to **meet?**
	5.19	like a man who runs from a lion and **meets** a bear!
Zech	2. 3	to me step forward, and another angel came to **meet** him.
Mt	8. 5	entered Capernaum, a Roman officer **met** him and begged for help:
	8.28	of the lake, he was **met** by two men who came out
	8.34	So everyone from the town went out to **meet** Jesus;
	18.28	the man went out and **met** one of his fellow-servants who owed
	25. 1	took their oil lamps and went out to **meet** the bridegroom.

Mt 25. 6 Come and **meet** him!'
26. 3 priests and the elders **met** together in the palace of Caiaphas,
27.32 they were going out, they **met** a man from Cyrene named Simon,
27.62 chief priests and the Pharisees **met** with Pilate [63] and said,
28. 9 Suddenly Jesus **met** them and said, "Peace be with you."
28.12 The chief priests **met** with the elders and made their plan;
Mk 3. 6 Pharisees left the synagogue and **met** at once with some members
5. 2 of the boat, he was **met** by a man who came out
6.30 The apostles returned and **met** with Jesus, and told him all
14.13 city, and a man carrying a jar of water will **meet** you.
15. 1 the chief priests **met** hurriedly with the elders, the teachers
15.21 On the way they **met** a man named Simon, who was coming
Lk 8.27 Jesus stepped ashore, he was **met** by a man from the town
9.37 went down from the hill, and a large crowd **met** Jesus.
14.32 he will send messengers to **meet** the other king, to ask for
17.12 a village when he was **met** by ten men suffering from a
22.10 the city, a man carrying a jar of water will **meet** you.
22.66 teachers of the Law **met** together, and Jesus was brought before
23.26 as they were going, they **met** a man from Cyrene named Simon
Jn 4.51 his way home his servants **met** him with the news, "Your boy
11.20 coming, she went out to **meet** him, but Mary stayed in the
11.29 Mary heard this, she got up and hurried out to **meet** him.
11.30 but was still in the place where Martha had **met** him.)
11.47 Pharisees and the chief priests **met** with the Council and said,
12.13 branches of palm-trees and went out to **meet** him, shouting,
12.18 That was why the crowd **met** him—because they heard that
18. 2 because many times Jesus had **met** there with his disciples.
Acts 1. 6 When the apostles **met** together with Jesus, they asked him,
2.46 Day after day they **met** as a group in the Temple,
4. 6 They **met** with the High Priest Annas and with Caiaphas, John,
4.26 and the rulers **met** together against the Lord and his
4.27 Herod and Pontius Pilate **met** together in this city with the
4.31 finished praying, the place where they were **meeting** was shaken.
5.12 All the believers **met** together in Solomon's Porch.
9.23 had gone by, the Jews **met** together and made plans to kill
9.33 There he **met** a man named Aeneas, who was paralysed and
10.25 about to go in, Cornelius **met** him, fell at his feet,
11.26 a whole year the two **met** with the people of the church
13. 6 to Paphos, where they **met** a certain magician named Bar-Jesus,
15. 6 apostles and the elders **met** together to consider this question.
15.25 And so we have **met** together and have all agreed to
16.16 place of prayer, we were **met** by a slave-girl who had
16.40 they **met** the believers, spoke words of encouragement to them,
18. 2 There he **met** a Jew named Aquila, born in Pontus, who had
20. 8 lamps were burning in the upstairs room where we were **meeting.**
20.14 When he **met** us in Assos, we took him aboard and went
20.17 to Ephesus, asking the elders of the church to **meet** him.
22.30 and ordered the chief priests and the whole Council to **meet.**
23.12 The next morning some Jews **met** together and made a plan.
25.16 a crime before he has **met** his accusers face to face
28.15 the towns of Market of Appius and Three Inns to **meet** us.
Rom 16. 5 Greetings also to the church that **meets** in their house.
16.23 Gaius, in whose house the church **meets,** sends you his greetings;
1 Cor 5. 3 As you **meet** together, and I meet with you in my spirit,
11.20 When you **meet** together as a group, it is not the Lord's
11.34 you will not come under God's judgement as you **meet** together.
14.23 the whole church **meets** together and everyone starts speaking in
14.26 When you **meet** for worship, one person has a hymn, another a
16.19 and the church that **meets** in their house send warm Christian
2 Cor 9.12 service you perform not only **meets** the needs of God's people,
Col 4.15 Laodicea and to Nympha and the church that **meets** in her house.
1 Thes 4.17 with them in the clouds to **meet** the Lord in the air.
Phlm 2 and the church that **meets** in your house, and our sister
Heb 4.12 to where soul and spirit **meet,** to where joints and marrow
7. 1 defeated the four kings, Melchizedek **met** him and blessed him,
7.10 in the body of his ancestor Abraham when Melchizedek **met** him.
7.26 Jesus, then, is the High Priest that **meets** our needs.
10.25 give up the habit of **meeting** together, as some are doing.
Rev 21. 2 prepared and ready, like a bride dressed to **meet** her husband.

MEETING

Gen 23.18 by all the Hittites who were there at the **meeting.**
49. 6 I take part in their **meetings,** For they killed men in anger
1 Kgs 12.20 they invited him to a **meeting** of the people and made him
Ezra 10. 9 and the importance of the **meeting** everyone was trembling.
Ps 68.26 "Praise God in the **meeting** of his people;
Hos 2.11 and her Sabbath celebrations—all her religious **meetings.**
Joel 2.16 prepare them for a sacred **meeting;**
Mt 2. 7 the east to a secret **meeting** and found out from them the
Acts 1.15 days later there was a **meeting** of the believers, about a
5.21 all the Jewish elders for a full **meeting** of the Council;
13.43 the people had left the **meeting,** Paul and Barnabas were followed
17.33 And so Paul left the **meeting.**
19.32 Meanwhile the whole **meeting** was in an uproar:
19.39 it will have to be settled in a legal **meeting** of citizens.
19.41 After saying this, he dismissed the **meeting.**
28.17 three days Paul called the local Jewish leaders to a **meeting.**
1 Cor 11.17 because your **meetings** for worship actually do more harm
11.18 I have been told that there are opposing groups in your **meetings;**
14.16 person taking part in the **meeting** say "Amen" to your
14.30 if someone sitting in the **meeting** receives a message from God,
14.34 of God's people, [34] the women should keep quiet in the **meetings.**
Gal 2. 2 In a private **meeting** with the leaders I explained the gospel
Heb 2.12 I will praise you in their **meeting."**
Jas 2. 2 fine clothes comes to your **meeting,** and a poor man in ragged

MEGIDDO

Important city in West Manasseh.

Josh 12.21 Shimron Meron, Achshaph, [21] Taanach, **Megiddo,**
17.11 Endor, Taanach, **Megiddo,** and their surrounding towns.
Judg 1.27 Beth Shan, Taanach, Dor, Ibleam, **Megiddo,** and the nearby towns;
5.19 At Taanach, by the stream of **Megiddo,** the kings came and fought;
1 Kgs 4.12 of Taanach, **Megiddo,** and all the region near Beth Shan,
9.15 also used it to rebuild the cities of Hazor, **Megiddo,**
2 Kgs 9.27 keep going until he reached the city of **Megiddo,**
23.29 stop the Egyptian army at **Megiddo** and was killed in battle.
1 Chr 7.29 cities of Beth Shan, Taanach, **Megiddo,** and Dor,
2 Chr 35.22 himself and went into battle on the plain of **Megiddo.**
Zech 12.11 as the mourning for Hadad-rimmon in the plain of **Megiddo.**

MELCHIZEDEK

King contemporary with Abraham.

Gen 14.18 And **Melchizedek,** who was king of Salem and also a priest
14.20 And Abram gave **Melchizedek** a tenth of all the loot
Ps 110. 4 a priest for ever in the priestly order of **Melchizedek."**
Heb 5. 6 a priest for ever, in the priestly order of **Melchizedek."**
5.10 to be high priest, in the priestly order of **Melchizedek.**
6.20 a high priest for ever, in the priestly order of **Melchizedek.**
7. 1 This **Melchizedek** was king of Salem and a priest
7. 1 he defeated the four kings, **Melchizedek** met him and blessed him,
7. 2 first meaning of **Melchizedek's** name is "King of Righteousness";
7. 3 There is no record of **Melchizedek's** father or mother
7. 6 **Melchizedek** was not descended from Levi, but he collected a tenth
7. 8 as for **Melchizedek** the tenth was collected by one who lives,
7.10 in the body of his ancestor Abraham when **Melchizedek** met him.
7.11 one who is in the priestly order of **Melchizedek,**
7.15 a different priest has appeared, who is like **Melchizedek.**
7.17 a priest for ever, in the priestly order of **Melchizedek."**

MELODY

Ps 92. 3 the music of stringed instruments and with **melody** on the harp.

MELON

[WATER-MELONS]

Num 11. 5 Remember the cucumbers, the **water-melons,** the leeks, the
Jer 10. 5 Such idols are like scarecrows in a field of **melons;**

MELT

Ex 16.21 when the sun grew hot, what was left on the ground **melted.**
32. 4 He took the earrings, **melted** them, poured the gold into a mould,
32. 8 made a bull-calf out of **melted** gold and have worshipped it
32.20 which they had made, **melted** it, ground it into fine powder,
2 Kgs 12.10 the High Priest would come, **melt** down the silver, and weigh
Job 28. 2 iron out of the ground And **melt** copper out of the stones.
Ps 22.14 my heart is like **melted** wax.
68. 2 as wax **melts** in front of the fire, so do the wicked
97. 5 The hills **melt** like wax before the Lord, before the Lord
147.18 Then he gives a command, and the ice **melts;**
Jer 6.29 fiercely, but the waste metals do not **melt** and run off.
Ezek 22.20 My anger and rage will **melt** them
22.20 just as fire **melts** ore.
22.21 build a fire under them, and **melt** them with my anger.
22.22 They will be **melted** in Jerusalem
22.22 just as silver is **melted** in a furnace,
Mic 1. 4 Then the mountains will **melt** under him like wax in a fire;
Nah 1. 5 hills **melt** before him.
2.10 Hearts **melt** with fear;
2 Pet 3.12 and the heavenly bodies will be **melted** by the heat.

MEMBER

[FELLOW-MEMBERS]

Gen 34.19 He was the most important **member** of his family.
46. 8 The **members** of Jacob's family who went to Egypt with him
Ex 16.16 as he needs, two litres for each **member** of his household."
Lev 22.10 "Only a **member** of a priestly family may eat any of the
22.13 Only a **member** of a priestly family may eat any of it.
22.14 person who is not a **member** of a priestly family eats any
25.47 a slave to that foreigner or to a **member** of his family.
Num 16. 1 He was joined by three **members** of the tribe of Reuben—Dathan
16. 3 All the **members** of the community belong to the Lord, and the
18.11 Every **member** of your family who is ritually clean may eat them.
18.13 Every **member** of your family who is ritually clean may eat it.
Judg 6.15 and I am the least important **member** of my family."
13. 2 He was a **member** of the tribe of Dan.
2 Sam 9.12 All the **members** of Ziba's family became servants of Mephibosheth.
20.14 Beth Maacah, and all the **members** of the clan of Bikri
23.24 Other **members** of "The Thirty" included:
1 Kgs 14.11 Any **members** of your family who die in the city will be
14.13 He will be the only **member** of Jeroboam's family who will be
15.29 At once he began killing all the **members** of Jeroboam's family.
16. 4 Any **members** of your family who die in the city will be
16.11 he killed off all the **members** of Baasha's family.
20.35 At the Lord's command a **member** of a group of prophets
2 Kgs 4. 1 The widow of a **member** of a group of prophets went to
5.22 you that just now two **members** of the group of prophets in
11. 1 gave orders for all the **members** of the royal family to be
25.25 and grandson of Elishama, a **member** of the royal family, went
1 Chr 2.53 cities of Zorah and Eshtaol were **members** of these clans.)
4. 9 Jabez, who was the most respected **member** of his family.

1 Chr 4.42 Five hundred other **members** of the tribe of Simeon went
5.13 The other **members** of the tribe belonged to the following
8.40 All those named above were **members** of the tribe of Benjamin.
9. 7 following **members** of the tribe of Benjamin lived in Jerusalem:
9.18 Down to that time **members** of their clans had been
9.19 together with his **fellow-members** of the clan of Korah,
9.32 **Members** of the clan of Kohath were responsible for
11.26 son of Shiza (a leading **member** of the tribe of Reuben, with
12. 2 reliable soldiers, [2]**members** of the tribe of Benjamin,
15. 5 of Kohath came Uriel, in charge of 120 **members** of his clan;
16.42 **members** of Jeduthun's clan were in charge of guarding the gates.
26.11 In all there were thirteen **members** of Hosah's family who
26.26 Shelomith and the **members** of his family were in charge
27. 2 of Zabdiel (he was a **member** of the clan of Perez, a
27. 2 from Hushah (he was a **member** of the clan of Zerah, a
27. 2 from Netophah (he was a **member** of the clan of Zerah)
2 Chr 2.14 His mother was a **member** of the tribe of Dan and his
5.11 Heman, and Jeduthun, and the **members** of their clans—were
18. 1 arranged a marriage between a **member** of his family and the
20.14 he was a **member** of the clan of Asaph and was descended
20.19 The **members** of the Levite clans of Kohath and Korah
22. 4 after his father's death other **members** of King Ahab's family
22. 9 No **member** of Ahaziah's family was left who could rule
22.10 gave orders for all the **members** of the royal family of Judah
26.11 under the supervision of Hananiah, a **member** of the king's staff.
Ezra 10. 8 he would lose his right to be a **member** of the community.
Neh 7. 1 and the temple guards, the **members** of the sacred choir, and
10.39 the temple guards, and the **members** of the temple choir have
11. 4 **Members** of the tribe of Judah:
11. 7 **Members** of the tribe of Benjamin:
11.12 In all, 822 **members** of this clan served in the Temple.
11.13 In all, 242 **members** of this clan were heads of families.
11.14 were 128 **members** of this clan who were outstanding soldiers.
11.14 Their leader was Zabdiel, a **member** of a leading family.
12.36 He was followed by other **members** of his clan—Shemaiah,
Is 3. 6 time will come when the **members** of a clan will choose one
Jer 12. 6 your brothers, **members** of your own family, have betrayed you;
35. 2 to me, [2]"Go to the **members** of the Rechabite clan and talk
41. 1 and grandson of Elishama, a **member** of the royal family and
Ezek 12.14 in every direction all the **members** of his court and his
24.21 And the younger **members** of your families who are left in
40.46 they are the only **members** of the tribe of Levi who are
48.11 doing wrong, as the other **members** of the tribe of Levi did.
Dan 1. 5 the same food and wine as the **members** of the royal court.
1.19 So they became **members** of the king's court.
Mic 7. 6 a man's enemies are the **members** of his own family.
Mt 10.25 is called Beelzebul, the **members** of the family will be called
10.36 a man's worst enemies will be the **members** of his own family.
22.16 some of their disciples and some **members** of Herod's party.
Mk 3. 6 met at once with some **members** of Herod's party, and they
12.13 Pharisees and some **members** of Herod's party were sent to Jesus
15.42 He was a respected **member** of the Council, who was waiting
Lk 23.50 Although he was a **member** of the Council, he had not agreed
Acts 1.17 Judas was a **member** of our group, for he had been chosen
4.13 The **members** of the Council were amazed to see how bold
5.17 Priest and all his companions, **members** of the local party of
5.33 the **members** of the Council heard this, they were so furious
6. 9 by some men who were **members** of the synagogue of the
7.54 As the **members** of the Council listened to Stephen,
7.57 With a loud cry the **members** of the Council covered their
12. 1 King Herod began to persecute some **members** of the church.
17.34 and believed, among whom was Dionysius, a **member** of the council;
26. 5 I have lived as a **member** of the strictest party of our
Rom 11. 1 a descendant of Abraham, a **member** of the tribe of Benjamin.
1 Cor 5.12 But should you not judge the **members** of your own fellowship?
Gal 1.22 At that time the **members** of the churches in Judaea did
Eph 2.19 fellow-citizens with God's people and **members** of the family of
3. 6 they are **members** of the same body and share in the promise
4.25 because we are all **members** together in the body of Christ.
5.30 for we are **members** of his body.)
Col 4.12 Greetings from Epaphras, another **member** of your group and a
1 Tim 5. 8 of his relatives, especially the **members** of his own family,
Heb 7.13 a different tribe, and no **member** of his tribe ever served as
7.14 known that he was born a **member** of the tribe of Judah;

AV **MEMBER** see **BODY, PART**

MEMORIAL

Gen 28.18 that was under his head, and set it up as a **memorial.**
28.22 This **memorial** stone which I have set up will be the
31.13 dedicated a stone as a **memorial** by pouring olive-oil on it
31.45 So Jacob took a stone and set it up as a **memorial.**
31.51 I have piled up between us, and here is the **memorial** stone.
31.52 Both this pile and this **memorial** stone are reminders.
31.52 go beyond it or beyond this **memorial** stone to attack me.
35.14 him, Jacob set up a **memorial** stone and consecrated it by
35.20 Jacob set up a **memorial** stone there, and it still marks
Zech 6.14 The crown will be a **memorial** in the Lord's Temple in

MEMORY

Judg 9.16 Did you respect Gideon's **memory** and treat his family properly,
Job 11.16 troubles will fade from your **memory,** like floods that are
Is 29.13 rules and traditions, which they have simply **memorized.**
33.18 of foreign tax-collectors and spies will be only a **memory.**
Mt 26.13 world, what she has done will be told in **memory** of her."
Mk 14. 9 world, what she has done will be told in **memory** of her."
Lk 22.19 Do this in **memory** of me."
1 Cor 11.24 Do this in **memory** of me."
11.25 Whenever you drink it, do so in **memory** of me."
2 Pet 1.13 me to stir up your **memory** of these matters as long as

MEN OF THUNDER

Mk 3.17 (Jesus gave them the name Boanerges, which means **"Men of Thunder");**

MEND

Josh 9. 5 put on ragged clothes and worn-out sandals that had been **mended.**
Ecc 3. 7 tearing and the time for **mending,** the time for silence

MENIAL

Ezek 44.14 am assigning to them the **menial** work that is to be done

MENTION

Gen 23.16 the amount that Ephron had **mentioned** in the hearing of the
40.14 please be kind enough to **mention** me to the king and help
Ex 23.13 do not even **mention** their names.
Deut 2.25 Everyone will tremble with fear at the **mention** of your name.'
3.26 Don't **mention** this again!
28.61 and epidemics that are not **mentioned** in this book of God's
Ruth 4. 1 the man whom Boaz had **mentioned,** came by, and Boaz called to
1 Sam 4.18 When the man **mentioned** the Covenant Box, Eli fell
1 Chr 6.65 of Judah, Simeon, and Benjamin, **mentioned** above, were also
Jer 31.20 Whenever I **mention** your name, I think of you with love.
Amos 6.10 We must be careful not even to **mention** the Lord's name."
2 Cor 11.28 And not to **mention** other things, every day I am under
Eph 5. 3 or indecency or greed should even be **mentioned** among you.
1 Thes 1. 2 thank God for you all and always **mention** you in our prayers.
Phlm 4 every time I pray, I **mention** you and give thanks to my
Heb 7.14 Moses did not **mention** this tribe when he spoke of priests.

MEPHIBOSHETH (1)

Saul's grandson.
see also MERIBBAAL

2 Sam 4. 4 of Saul was Jonathan's son **Mephibosheth,** who was five years
9. 6 When **Mephibosheth,** the son of Jonathan and grandson of Saul,
9. 6 David said, **"Mephibosheth,"** and he answered, "At your service,
9. 8 **Mephibosheth** bowed again and said, "I am no better than
9. 9 said, "I am giving **Mephibosheth,** your master's grandson,
9.10 But **Mephibosheth** himself will always be a guest at my table."
9.11 So **Mephibosheth** ate at the king's table,
9.12 **Mephibosheth** had a young son named Mica.
9.12 All the members of Ziba's family became servants of **Mephibosheth.**
9.13 **Mephibosheth,** who was crippled in both feet, lived in Jerusalem,
16. 1 by Ziba, the servant of **Mephibosheth,** who had with him
16. 3 "Where is **Mephibosheth,** the grandson of your master Saul?"
16. 4 "Everything that belonged to **Mephibosheth** is yours."
19.24 Then **Mephibosheth,** Saul's grandson, came down to meet the king.
19.25 When **Mephibosheth** arrived from Jerusalem to meet the king,
19.25 the king said to him, **"Mephibosheth,** you didn't go with me.
19.30 "Let Ziba have it all," **Mephibosheth** answered.
21. 7 David spared Jonathan's son **Mephibosheth,** the grandson of Saul.

MERARI

Levi's son, whose name was given to a group of Levites.

Gen 46.11 Gershon, Kohath, and **Merari.**
Ex 6.16 Gershon, Kohath, and **Merari;**
6.19 **Merari** had two sons:
Num 3.17 Gershon, Kohath, and **Merari,** who were the ancestors of the
3.17 and **Merari** had two sons:
3.33 The clan of **Merari** was composed of the families of Mahli
4.29 of the Levite clan of **Merari** by sub-clans and families,
4.33 are the responsibilities of the **Merari** clan in their service
4.34 of the three Levite clans, Kohath, Gershon, and **Merari.**
4.34 **Merari** 3,200
7. 8 and four wagons and eight oxen to the **Merarites.**
10.17 of Gershon and **Merari,** who carried it, would start out.
26.57 Levi consisted of the clans of Gershon, Kohath, and **Merari.**
Josh 21. 7 families of the clan of **Merari** were assigned twelve cities
21.34 the Levites, the clan of **Merari,** received from the territory
21.40 So the clan of **Merari** was assigned a total of twelve cities.
1 Chr 6. 1 Gershon, Kohath, and **Merari.**
6.16 Gershon, Kohath, and **Merari.**
6.19 and **Merari** was the father of Mahli and Mushi.
6.29 the descendants of **Merari** from generation to generation:
6.44 Ethan of the clan of **Merari** was the leader of the third
6.47 Amzi, Bani, Shemer, [47]Mahli, Mushi, **Merari,** Levi.
6.63 Zebulun were assigned to the clan of **Merari,** family by family.
6.77 families of the clan of **Merari** were assigned the following
9.14 Hashabiah, of the clan of **Merari** Bakbakkar, Heresh, and
15. 6 from the clan of **Merari** came Asaiah, in charge of 220;
15.17 Berechiah, and Ethan son of Kushaiah, of the clan of **Merari.**
23. 6 Gershon, Kohath, and **Merari.**
23.21 **Merari** had two sons, Mahli and Mushi.
23.23 **Merari's** second son, Mushi, had three sons:
24.26 Mahli, Mushi, and Jaaziah, descendants of **Merari.**
26.10 From the clan of **Merari** there was Hosah, who had four sons:
26.19 guard duty to the clan of Korah and the clan of **Merari.**
2 Chr 29.12 Azariah From the clan of **Merari,** Kish son of Abdi and
34.12 Obadiah of the clan of **Merari,** and Zechariah and Meshullam
Ezra 8.19 Jeshaiah of the clan of **Merari,** with twenty of their relatives.

MERCHANT

Gen 23.16 according to the standard weights used by the **merchants.**
1 Kgs 10.15 to the taxes paid by **merchants,** the profits from trade, and
2 Chr 9.14 in addition to the taxes paid by the traders and **merchants.**
Neh 3.31 workmen and the **merchants,** which was by the Miphkad Gate,
3.32 The goldsmiths and the **merchants** built the last section,
13.20 Once or twice **merchants** who sold all kinds of goods
Job 41. 6 Will **merchants** cut him up to sell?
Prov 31.14 food from out-of-the-way places, as **merchant** ships do.
31.24 She makes clothes and belts, and sells them to **merchants.**
Is 23. 2 Wail, you **merchants** of Sidon!
23. 8 Tyre, that imperial city, whose **merchant** princes were the
Ezek 7.13 No **merchant** will live long enough to get back what he
17. 4 to a land of commerce, and placed in a city of **merchants.**
26.12 Your enemies will help themselves to your wealth and **merchandise.**
27.16 people of Syria bought your **merchandise** and your many products.
27.18 of Damascus bought your **merchandise** and your products,
27.21 land of Kedar paid for your **merchandise** with lambs, sheep,
27.22 For your goods the **merchants** of Sheba and Raamah exchanged
27.23 Haran, Canneh, and Eden, the **merchants** of Sheba, the cities
27.25 **merchandise** was carried in fleets of the largest cargo ships.
27.27 All your wealth of **merchandise,** All the sailors in your crew,
27.27 Your ship's carpenters and your **merchants,** Every soldier on
27.33 When your **merchandise** went overseas, You filled the needs
27.36 for ever, and **merchants** all over the world are terrified,
38.13 Sheba and Dedan and the **merchants** from the towns of Spain
Nah 3.16 You produced more **merchants** than there are stars in the sky!
Zeph 1.11 part of the city, because all the **merchants** will be dead!
Zech 14.21 will no longer be any **merchant** in the Temple of the Lord
Lk 19.45 to drive out the **merchants,** [46] saying to them, "It is written
2 Cor 2.17 others, who handle God's message as if it were cheap **merchandise;**

MERCY

Ex 1.13 and in their fields, and they had no **mercy** on them.
22.27 to me for help, I will answer him because I am **merciful.**
Deut 4.31 He is a **merciful** God.
7. 2 Do not make an alliance with them or show them any **mercy.**
7.16 God places in your power, and do not show them any **mercy.**
13. 8 Show him no **mercy** or pity, and do not protect him.
13.17 the Lord will turn from his fierce anger and show you **mercy.**
13.17 He will be **merciful** to you and make you a numerous people,
19.13 Show him no **mercy.**
19.21 In such cases show no **mercy;**
25.12 hold of the other man's genitals, [12] show her no **mercy;**
28.50 will be ruthless and show no **mercy** to anyone, young or old.
30. 3 you today, [3] then the Lord your God will have **mercy** on you.
32.36 He will have **mercy** on those who serve him, when he sees
33.29 come begging for **mercy,** and you will trample them down.
Josh 11.20 to total destruction and all be killed without **mercy.**
Judg 2.18 The Lord would have **mercy** on them because they groaned under
6.13 abandoned us and left us to the **mercy** of the Midianites."
2 Sam 1.22 the sword of Saul was **merciless,** striking down the mighty,
12.22 that the Lord might be **merciful** to me and not let the
24.14 Lord himself be the one to punish us, for he is **merciful."**
1 Kgs 8.49 In your home in heaven hear them and be **merciful** to them.
8.59 May he always be **merciful** to the people of Israel and to
20.31 said, "We have heard that the Israelite kings are **merciful.**
2 Kgs 1.13 and pleaded, "Man of God, be **merciful** to me and my men.
1.14 but please be **merciful** to me!"
3.10 the three of us at the **mercy** of the king of Moab!"
3.13 put us three kings at the **mercy** of the king of Moab."
13.23 Jehoahaz' reign, [23] but the Lord was kind and **merciful** to them.
1 Chr 21.13 Lord himself be the one to punish me, because he is **merciful."**
2 Chr 6.39 heaven hear them and be **merciful** to them and forgive all the
30. 9 your God is kind and **merciful,** and if you return to him,
36.17 He had no **mercy** on anyone, young or old, man or woman,
Neh 1.11 Give me success today and make the emperor **merciful** to me."
9.17 Your **mercy** is great;
9.19 abandon them there in the desert, for your **mercy** is great.
9.27 In your great **mercy** you sent them leaders who rescued them
9.28 and time after time you rescued them in your great **mercy.**
9.31 And yet, because your **mercy** is great, you did not
9.31 You are a gracious and **merciful** God!
Esth 3.13 were to be slaughtered without **mercy** and their belongings
4. 8 with the king and beg him to have **mercy** on her people.
7. 8 Esther's couch to beg for **mercy,** when the king came back
Job 9.15 all I can do is beg for **mercy** from God my judge.
33.24 In **mercy** the angel will say, "Release him!
41. 3 Will he plead with you for **mercy?**
Ps 6. 4 in your **mercy** rescue me from death.
9.13 Be **merciful** to me, O Lord!
25.16 to me, Lord, and be **merciful** to me, because I am lonely
26.11 be **merciful** to me and save me!
27. 7 Be **merciful** and answer me!
30.10 Hear me, Lord, and be **merciful!**
31. 9 Be **merciful** to me, Lord, for I am in trouble;
40.11 Lord, I know you will never stop being **merciful** to me.
41. 4 be **merciful** to me and heal me."
41.10 Be **merciful** to me, Lord, and restore my health, and I
51. 1 Be **merciful** to me, O God, because of your constant love.
51. 1 Because of your great **mercy** wipe away my sins!
56. 1 Be **merciful** to me, O God, because I am under attack;
57. 1 Be **merciful** to me, O God, be merciful, because I come to
59. 5 show no **mercy** to evil traitors!
67. 1 God, be **merciful** to us and bless us;
77. 9 Has God forgotten to be **merciful?**
78.38 But God was **merciful** to his people.
Ps 79. 8 Have **mercy** on us now;
80. 3 Show us your **mercy,** and we will be saved!
80. 7 Show us your **mercy,** and we will be saved!
80.19 Show us your **mercy,** and we will be saved.
85. 1 Lord, you have been **merciful** to your land;
86. 3 You are my God, so be **merciful** to me;
86.15 you, O Lord, are a **merciful** and loving God, always patient,
86.16 Turn to me and have **mercy** on me;
102.13 the time has come to have **mercy** on her;
103. 4 keeps me from the grave and blesses me with love and **mercy.**
103. 8 The Lord is **merciful** and loving, slow to become angry and
111. 4 he is kind and **merciful.**
112. 4 darkness for good men, for those who are **merciful,** kind, and
116. 5 The Lord is **merciful** and good;
119.58 all my heart to have **mercy** on me, as you have promised!
119.77 Have **mercy** on me, and I will live because I take
119.132 Turn to me and have **mercy** on me as you do on
119.149 show your **mercy,** and preserve my life!
119.156 show your **mercy** and save me!
123. 2 to you, O Lord our God, until you have **mercy** on us.
123. 3 Be **merciful** to us, Lord, be merciful;
145. 8 The Lord is loving and **merciful,** slow to become angry and
145.13 to his promises, and he is **merciful** in all his acts.
145.17 Lord is righteous in all he does, **merciful** in all his acts.
Prov 5. 9 had, and you will die young at the hands of **merciless** men.
21.10 they have no **mercy** on anyone.
28.13 then God will show **mercy** to you.
Is 13.18 They will show no **mercy** to babies and take no pity on
14. 1 Lord will once again be **merciful** to his people Israel and
27.11 God their Creator will not pity them or show them any **mercy.**
30.18 And yet the Lord is waiting to be **merciful** to you.
33. 2 Lord, have **mercy** on us.
47. 6 I put them in your power, and you showed them no **mercy;**
55. 7 he is **merciful** and quick to forgive.
60.10 punished you, But now I will show you my favour and **mercy.**
63. 7 people of Israel because of his **mercy** and constant love.
64. 9 be **merciful** to us.
Jer 3.12 I am **merciful** and will not be angry;
5.16 Their bowmen are mighty soldiers who kill without **mercy.**
6.23 they are cruel and **merciless.**
12.15 after I have taken them away, I will have **mercy** on them;
13.14 No pity, compassion, or **mercy** will stop me from killing them."
15. 1 pleading with me, I would not show these people any **mercy.**
16. 5 bless my people with peace or show them love and **mercy.**
16.13 other gods day and night, and I will show you no **mercy.' "**
20.16 May he be like those cities that the Lord destroyed without **mercy.**
21. 7 any of you or show **mercy** or pity to any of you.
30.18 my people to their land and have **mercy** on every family;
31. 2 In the desert I showed **mercy** to those people who had
31.20 I will be **merciful.**
33.26 I will be **merciful** to my people and make them prosperous again."
42.12 Because I am **merciful,**
42.12 I will make him have **mercy** on you and let you go
50.42 they are cruel and **merciless.**
Lam 1. 9 Her enemies have won, and she cries to the Lord for **mercy.**
2. 2 The Lord destroyed without **mercy** every village in Judah
2.17 He has destroyed us without **mercy,** as he warned us long ago.
2.19 heart and beg him for **mercy** on your children— Children
2.21 You slaughtered them without **mercy** on the day of your anger.
3. 3 And beat me again and again with **merciless** blows.
3.22 The Lord's unfailing love and **mercy** still continue,
3.31 The Lord is **merciful** and will not reject us for ever.
3.43 your **mercy** was hidden by your anger, [44] By a cloud of fury
Ezek 5.11 things you did, I will cut you down without **mercy.**
7. 4 I will not spare you or show you any **mercy.**
7. 9 I will not spare you or show you any **mercy.**
8.18 I will not spare them or show them any **mercy.**
9. 5 have **mercy** on no one.
24.14 I will not ignore your sins or show pity or be **merciful.**
39.25 "But now I will be **merciful** to Jacob's descendants, the
Dan 2.18 the God of heaven for **mercy** and to ask him to explain
4.27 Stop sinning, do what is right, and be **merciful** to the poor.
9. 9 You are **merciful** and forgiving, although we have rebelled
9.18 because you are **merciful,** not because we have done right.
Hos 2. 4 I will not show **mercy** to her children;
2.19 you constant love and **mercy** and make you mine for ever.
14. 3 O Lord, you show **mercy** to those who have no one else
Joel 2.13 He is kind and full of **mercy;**
2.18 he had **mercy** on his people.
Amos 1.11 their brothers, the Israelites, and showed them no **mercy.**
5.15 Perhaps the Lord will be **merciful** to the people of this
Jon 4. 2 you are a loving and **merciful** God, always patient, always
Mic 7.19 You will be **merciful** to us once again.
Hab 1.17 for ever and keep on destroying nations without **mercy?**
3. 2 Be **merciful,** even when you are angry.
Zech 1.12 How much longer will it be before you show them **mercy?"**
1.16 I have come back to Jerusalem to show **mercy** to the city.
7. 9 is done, and must show kindness and **mercy** to one another.
12.10 Jerusalem with the spirit of **mercy** and the spirit of prayer.
Mal 3.17 I will be **merciful** to them,
3.17 as a father is **merciful** to the son who serves him.
Mt 5. 7 "Happy are those who are **merciful** to others;
5. 7 God will be **merciful** to them!
10.15 Day God will show more **mercy** to the people of Sodom
11.22 Day God will show more **mercy** to the people of Tyre
11.24 Judgement Day God will show more **mercy** to Sodom than to you!"
15.22 "Have **mercy** on me, sir!
17.15 knelt before him, [15] and said, "Sir, have **mercy** on my son!
18.33 You should have had **mercy** on your fellow-servant,
18.33 just as I had **mercy** on you.'
23.23 teachings of the Law, such as justice and **mercy** and honesty.

Lk 1.50 to another he shows **mercy** to those who honour him.
1.55 He has remembered to show **mercy** to Abraham and to all
1.72 He said he would show **mercy** to our ancestors and
1.78 Our God is **merciful** and tender.
6.36 Be **merciful** just as your Father is merciful.
10.12 Day God will show more **mercy** to Sodom than to that town!
10.14 God will show more **mercy** on Judgement Day to Tyre and
Rom 9.15 he said to Moses, "I will have **mercy** on anyone I wish;
9.16 not on what man wants or does, but only on God's **mercy.**
9.18 So then, God has **mercy** on anyone he wishes, and he makes
9.23 are the objects of his **mercy,** those of us whom he has
11.30 you have received God's **mercy** because the Jews were disobedient.
11.31 same way, because of the **mercy** that you have received, the
11.31 God, in order that they also may now receive God's **mercy.**
11.32 prisoners of disobedience, so that he might show **mercy** to them
12. 1 because of God's great **mercy** to us I appeal to you:
15. 9 to enable even the Gentiles to praise God for his **mercy.**
1 Cor 7.25 opinion as one who by the Lord's **mercy** is worthy of trust.
2 Cor 1. 3 our Lord Jesus Christ, the **merciful** Father, the God from
4. 1 God in his **mercy** has given us this work to do,
Gal 1.13 how I persecuted without **mercy** the church of God and did
6.16 their lives, may peace and **mercy** be with them—with them and
Eph 2. 4 But God's **mercy** is so abundant, and his love for us is
1 Tim 1. 2 and Christ Jesus our Lord give you grace, **mercy,** and peace.
1.13 But God was **merciful** to me because I did not yet have
1.16 of them, [16] but God was **merciful** to me in order that Christ
2 Tim 1. 2 and Christ Jesus our Lord give you grace, **mercy,** and peace.
1.16 May the Lord show **mercy** to the family of Onesiphorus,
1.18 May the Lord grant him his **mercy** on that Day!
3. 3 they will be unkind, **merciless,** slanderers, violent, and
Tit 3. 5 but because of his own **mercy** that he saved us, through the
Heb 2.17 to be their faithful and **merciful** High Priest in his service
4.16 There we will receive **mercy** and find grace to help us just
10.28 put to death without any **mercy** when judged guilty on the
Jas 2.13 For God will not show **mercy** when he judges
2.13 the person who has not been **merciful;**
2.13 but **mercy** triumphs over judgement.
5.11 For the Lord is full of **mercy** and compassion.
1 Pet 1. 3 Because of his great **mercy** he gave us new life by raising
2.10 not know God's mercy, but now you have received his **mercy.**
2 Jn 3 Jesus Christ, the Father's Son, give us grace, **mercy,** and peace;
Jude 2 May **mercy,** peace, and love be yours in full measure.
21 Lord Jesus Christ in his **mercy** to give you eternal life.
22 Show **mercy** towards those who have doubts;
23 and to others show **mercy** mixed with fear, but hate their

AV **MERCY SEAT see LID**

MERE

Ps 8. 4 **mere** man, that you care for him?
56. 4 What can a **mere** human being do to me?
56.11 What can a **mere** human being do to me?
62. 9 they are lighter than a **mere** breath.
144. 3 **mere** man, that you pay attention to him?
Ezek 8.17 Judah are not satisfied with **merely** doing all the disgusting

MERIBAH

Place where God provided the Israelites with water from a rock.
see also KADESH MERIBAH, MASSAH

Ex 17. 7 place was named Massah and **Meribah,** because the Israelites
Num 20.13 This happened at **Meribah,** where the people of Israel
20.24 the two of you rebelled against my command at **Meribah.**
27.14 community complained against me at **Meribah,** you refused to
27.14 **(Meribah** is the spring at Kadesh in the wilderness of Zin.)
Deut 32.51 were at the waters of **Meribah,** near the town of Kadesh
33. 8 at Massah And proved them true at the waters of **Meribah.**
Ps 81. 7 I put you to the test at the springs of **Meribah.**
95. 8 as your ancestors were at **Meribah,** as they were that day
106.32 At the springs of **Meribah** the people made the Lord angry,

MERRY

Esth 1.10 king was drinking and feeling **merry,** so he called in the

MESHACH

One of Daniel's three friends, also known as "Mishael".

Dan 1. 7 Belteshazzar, Shadrach, **Meshach,** and Abednego.
2.49 request the king put Shadrach, **Meshach,** and Abednego in
3.12 the province of Babylon—Shadrach, **Meshach,** and Abednego—
3.14 He said to them, "Shadrach, **Meshach,** and Abednego,
3.16 Shadrach, **Meshach,** and Abednego answered, "Your Majesty,
3.19 and his face turned red with anger at Shadrach, **Meshach,**
3.23 Then Shadrach, **Meshach,** and Abednego, still tied up,
3.26 "Shadrach! **Meshach!** Abednego!
3.28 The king said, "Praise the God of Shadrach, **Meshach,**
3.29 of the God of Shadrach, **Meshach,** and Abednego, he is to be
3.30 And the king promoted Shadrach, **Meshach,** and Abednego

MESOPOTAMIA

Area between R. Tigris and R. Euphrates, now known as Iraq.

Gen 24.10 to the city where Nahor had lived in northern **Mesopotamia.**
25.20 Bethuel (an Aramean from **Mesopotamia)** and sister of Laban.
28. 2 Go instead to **Mesopotamia,** to the home of your grandfather
28. 5 Isaac sent Jacob away to **Mesopotamia,** to Laban, who was
28. 6 Jacob and sent him away to **Mesopotamia** to find a wife.
Gen 28. 7 Jacob had obeyed his father and mother and had gone to **Mesopotamia.**
31.17 of him, with everything that he had acquired in **Mesopotamia.**
33.18 On his return from **Mesopotamia** Jacob arrived safely
35. 9 When Jacob returned from **Mesopotamia,** God appeared to him
35.26 These sons were born in **Mesopotamia.**
46.15 Leah had borne to Jacob in **Mesopotamia,**
48. 7 not far from Ephrath, as I was returning from **Mesopotamia.**
Deut 23. 4 of Beor, from the city of Pethor in **Mesopotamia,** to curse
Josh 24.14 ancestors used to worship in **Mesopotamia** and in Egypt, and
24.15 worshipped in **Mesopotamia** or the gods of the Amorites,
Judg 3. 8 let King Cushan Rishathaim of **Mesopotamia** conquer them, and
3.10 and the Lord gave him victory over the king of **Mesopotamia.**
1 Chr 19. 6 chariots and charioteers from Upper **Mesopotamia** and from the
Hos 12.12 Jacob had to flee to **Mesopotamia,** where, in order to get a
Acts 2. 9 from **Mesopotamia,** Judaea, and Cappadocia;
7. 2 glory appeared to him in **Mesopotamia** [3] and said to him,

MESSAGE

Gen 50. 4 king's officials, "Please take this **message** to the king:
50.16 So they sent a **message** to Joseph:
50.17 Joseph cried when he received this **message.**
Num 20.14 "This **message** is from your kinsmen, the tribes of Israel.
22. 5 They brought him this **message** from Balak:
22. 7 for the curse, went to Balaam, and gave him Balak's **message.**
22.16 They went to Balaam and gave him this **message** from Balak:
23. 5 say and sent him back to Balak to give him his **message.**
23.16 say, and sent him back to Balak to give him his **message.**
24. 3 "The **message** of Balaam son of Beor, The words of the man
24.15 "The **message** of Balaam son of Beor, The words of the man
Deut 18.20 prophet dares to speak a **message** in my name when I did
18.21 tell when a prophet's **message** does not come from the Lord.
18.22 says does not come true, then it is not the Lord's **message.**
Josh 10. 3 So Adonizedek sent the following **message** to King Hoham of Hebron,
Judg 3.19 said, "Your Majesty, I have a secret **message** for you."
3.20 to him and said, "I have a **message** from God for you."
6. 8 prophet who brought them this **message** from the Lord, the God
11.28 of Ammon paid no attention to this **message** from Jephthah.
16.18 truth, she sent a **message** to the Philistine kings and said,
1 Sam 2.27 A prophet came to Eli with this **message** from the Lord:
3. 1 Eli, there were very few **messages** from the Lord, and visions
11. 9 people of Jabesh received the **message,** they were overjoyed
16.22 Then Saul sent a **message** to Jesse:
25. 9 David's men delivered this **message** to Nabal in David's name.
30.26 leaders of Judah, with the **message,** "Here is a present for
2 Sam 2. 5 Gilead had buried Saul, [5] he sent some men there with the **message:**
11. 5 she was pregnant and sent a **message** to David to tell him.
11. 6 David then sent a **message** to Joab:
17.16 Send a **message** to David not to spend the night at the
23. 2 his **message** is on my lips.
1 Kgs 5. 2 Solomon sent back this **message** to Hiram:
5. 7 pleased when he received Solomon's **message,** and he said,
5. 8 Then Hiram sent Solomon the following **message:**
5. 8 "I have received your **message** and I am ready to do what
12.23 prophet Shemaiah [23] to give this **message** to Rehoboam and to
15.18 son of Tabrimmon and grandson of Hezion, with this **message:**
16. 1 Jehu son of Hanani and gave him this **message** for Baasha:
16. 7 That **message** from the Lord against Baasha and his family
19. 2 She sent a **message** to Elijah:
20. 7 He sent me a **message** demanding my wives and children, my
20. 9 and then returned with another **message** [10] from Benhadad:
21.14 The **message** was sent to Jezebel:
21.15 soon as Jezebel received the **message,** she said to Ahab,
2 Kgs 9. 5 He said, "Sir, I have a **message** for you."
10. 5 citizens and the guardians, sent this **message** to Jehu:
14. 9 bush on the Lebanon Mountains sent a **message** to a cedar:
16. 7 Tiglath Pileser, the emperor of Assyria, with this **message:**
18.14 Hezekiah sent a **message** to Sennacherib, who was in Lachish:
19. 3 This is the **message** which he told them to give Isaiah:
19. 5 When Isaiah received King Hezekiah's **message,** [6] he sent back
19.20 Then Isaiah sent a **message** telling King Hezekiah that
20.19 lifetime, so he replied, "The **message** you have given me
22.16 king and give him [16] the following **message** from the Lord:
22.20 The men returned to King Josiah with this **message.**
1 Chr 25. 1 They were to proclaim God's **messages,** accompanied by the
25. 2 who proclaimed God's **messages** whenever the king commanded.
25. 3 proclaimed God's **message,** accompanied by the music of harps,
2 Chr 2. 3 Solomon sent a **message** to King Hiram of Tyre:
11. 3 prophet Shemaiah [3] to give this **message** to King Rehoboam and
12. 5 He said to them, "This is the Lord's **message** to you:
16. 2 to Damascus, to King Benhadad of Syria, with this **message:**
25.17 He then sent a **message** to King Jehoash of Israel, who was
25.18 bush in the Lebanon Mountains sent a **message** to a cedar:
32. 9 Lachish, he sent the following **message** to Hezekiah and the
33.18 to his God, and the **messages** of the prophets who spoke to
34.24 king and give him [24] the following **message** from the Lord:
34.28 The men returned to King Josiah with this **message.**
35.21 Josiah tried to stop him, [21] but Neco sent Josiah this **message:**
Ezra 5. 2 son of Jehozadak heard their **messages,** they began to rebuild
10. 7 A **message** was sent throughout Jerusalem and Judah that all
Neh 6. 2 and Geshem sent me a **message,** suggesting that I meet with
6. 4 They sent me the same **message** four times, and each time I
6. 5 to me with a fifth **message,** this one in the form of
Esth 1.22 royal provinces he sent a **message** in the language and the
4.10 and Esther gave him this **message** to take back to Mordecai:
4.12 When Mordecai received Esther's **message,** [13] he sent her
Job 4.12 Once a **message** came quietly, so quietly I could hardly hear it.
Ps 19. 4 yet their **message** goes out to all the world and is heard

Ps 147.19 He gives his **message** to his people, his instructions and
Prov 26. 6 let a fool deliver a **message,** you might as well cut off
Ecc 10.20 A bird might carry the **message** and tell them what you said.
Is 1. 1 This book contains the **messages** about Judah and Jerusalem
2. 1 This is the **message** which God gave to Isaiah son of Amoz
6. 9 So he told me to go and give the people this **message:**
7.10 The Lord sent another **message** to Ahaz:
8.16 to guard and preserve the **messages** that God has given me.
8.18 has sent us as living **messages** to the people of Israel.
8.19 you to ask for **messages** from fortune-tellers and mediums,
8.19 all, people should ask for **messages** from the spirits and
13. 1 This is a **message** about Babylon, which Isaiah son of Amoz
14.28 This is a **message** that was proclaimed in the year that
15. 1 This is a **message** about Moab.
16.13 That is the **message** the Lord gave earlier about Moab.
18. 2 Take a **message** back to your land divided by rivers, to your
19. 1 This is a **message** about Egypt.
21. 1 This is a **message** about Babylonia.
21.11 This is a **message** about Edom.
21.13 This is a **message** about Arabia.
22. 1 This is a **message** about the Valley of Vision.
23. 1 This is a **message** about Tyre.
28. 9 Who needs his **message?**
28.19 Each new **message** from God will bring new terror!
30. 6 This is God's **message** about the animals of the southern desert:
37. 3 This is the **message** which he told them to give to Isaiah:
37. 5 When Isaiah received King Hezekiah's **message,** [6]he sent back
37.21 Then Isaiah sent a **message** telling King Hezekiah that in
39. 8 lifetime, so he replied, "The **message** you have given me
40. 6 A voice cries out, "Proclaim a **message!"**
40. 6 "What **message** shall I proclaim?"
Jer 2. 2 Lord told me [2]to proclaim this **message** to everyone in Jerusalem.
2. 4 Listen to the Lord's **message,** you descendants of Jacob,
5.13 but windbags and that they have no **message** from the Lord.
6.10 They are stubborn and refuse to listen to your **message;**
10. 1 of Israel, listen to the **message** that the Lord has for you.
11. 6 Proclaim my **message** there and tell the people to listen to
11.21 would kill me if I kept on proclaiming the Lord's **message.**
15.19 proclaim a worthwhile **message,** you will be my prophet again.
17.19 "Jeremiah, go and announce my **message** at the People's Gate,
18. 2 to the potter's house, where I will give you my **message."**
18.18 to give us counsel, and prophets to proclaim God's **message.**
19. 2 There I was to proclaim the **message** that he would give me.
19.14 Topheth, where the Lord had sent me to proclaim his **message.**
20. 8 and scorned all the time because I proclaim your **message.**
20. 9 in his name," then your **message** is like a fire burning deep
21.11 told me to give this **message** to the royal house of Judah,
23.18 ever heard or understood his **message,** or ever listened or
23.21 did not give them any **message,** but still they spoke in my
23.22 they could have proclaimed my **message** to my people and could
23.25 claim that I have given them my **messages** in their dreams.
23.28 heard my **message** should proclaim that message faithfully.
23.29 My **message** is like a fire, and like a hammer that breaks
23.30 who take each other's words and proclaim them as my **message.**
23.33 prophet or a priest asks you, 'What is the Lord's **message?'**
23.36 anyone does, I will make my **message** a real burden to him.
25. 1 of Judah, I received a **message** from the Lord concerning all
27. 3 told me to send a **message** to the kings of Edom, Moab,
27.18 and if they have my **message,** let them ask me, the Lord
29.19 they did not obey the **message** that I kept on sending to
29.24 of Israel, gave me a **message** for Shemaiah of Nehelam, who
29.31 to all the prisoners in Babylon this **message** about Shemaiah:
33. 1 in the courtyard, the Lord's **message** came to me again.
34. 6 Then I gave this **message** to King Zedekiah in Jerusalem
36.32 first scroll and similar **messages** that I dictated to him.
37. 2 the people obeyed the **message** which the Lord had given me.
37.17 asked me privately, "Is there any **message** from the Lord?"
38.20 I beg you to obey the Lord's **message;**
49.14 I said, "Edom, I have received a **message** from the Lord.
50. 1 This is the **message** that the Lord gave me about the city
Ezek 6. 2 "look towards the mountains of Israel and give them my **message.**
11. 5 me, and the Lord told me to give the people this **message:**
12.10 This **message** is for the prince ruling in Jerusalem and for
12.19 nation that this is the **message** of the Sovereign Lord to the
13. 6 that they are speaking my **message,** but I have not sent them.
24.21 to me and told me [21]to give you Israelites this **message:**
32. 2 Give him this **message** from me:
36. 1 them to listen to the **message** which I, [2]the Sovereign Lord,
36.22 give the Israelites the **message** that I, the Sovereign Lord,
Dan 4. 1 King Nebuchadnezzar sent the following **message** to the people
4.19 "Belteshazzar, don't let the dream and its **message** alarm you."
10. 1 was emperor of Persia, a **message** was revealed to Daniel, who
10. 1 The **message** was true but extremely hard to understand.
Hos 1. 1 This is the **message** which the Lord gave Hosea son of Beeri
6. 5 to you with my **message** of judgement and destruction.
Joel 1. 1 This is the Lord's **message** to Joel son of Pethuel.
2.28 your sons and daughters will proclaim my **message;**
Amos 2.12 and ordered the prophets not to speak my **message.**
3. 1 of Israel, listen to this **message** which the Lord has spoken
3. 8 the Sovereign Lord speaks, who can avoid proclaiming his **message?**
8.11 They will hunger and thirst for a **message** from the Lord.
8.12 will look everywhere for a **message** from the Lord, but they
Obad 1 messenger to the nations, and we have heard his **message:**
Jon 3. 2 and proclaim to the people the **message** I have given you."
3. 5 The people of Nineveh believed God's **message.**
Mic 1. 1 Judah, the Lord gave this **message** to Micah, who was from the
Nah 1. 1 This is a **message** about Nineveh, the account of a vision
Hab 1. 1 is the **message** that the Lord revealed to the prophet Habakkuk.
2. 4 And this is the **message:**
Zeph 1. 1 This is the **message** that the Lord gave to Zephaniah during
Hag 1. 1 The **message** was for the governor of Judah, Zerubbabel
1. 3 The Lord then gave this **message** to the people through the
1.13 Then Haggai gave the Lord's **message** to the people:
2.20 Lord gave Haggai a second **message** [21] for Zerubbabel,
Zech 1. 1 Persia, the Lord gave this **message** to the prophet Zechariah,
1. 4 gave them my **message,** telling them not to live evil,
1. 7 Shebat), the Lord gave me a **message** in a vision at night.
2. 8 Almighty sent me with this **message** for the nations that had
4. 6 The angel told me to give Zerubbabel this **message** from the Lord:
4. 8 Another **message** came to me from the Lord.
6. 9 The Lord gave me this **message.**
7. 1 month (the month of Kislev), the Lord gave me a **message.**
7. 4 This is the **message** of the Lord that came to me.
7. 8 The Lord gave this **message** to Zechariah:
8. 1 The Lord Almighty gave this **message** to Zechariah:
8.18 The Lord Almighty gave this **message** to Zechariah:
9. 1 This is the Lord's **message:**
12. 1 This is a **message** about Israel from the Lord, the Lord who
Mal 1. 1 This is the **message** that the Lord gave Malachi to tell the
Mt 4.17 From that time Jesus began to preach his **message:**
7.22 your name we spoke God's **message,** by your name we drove out
11.12 the time John preached his **message** until this very day
11.14 willing to believe their **message,** John is Elijah, whose coming
13.19 who hear the **message** about the Kingdom but do not understand
13.20 for those who receive the **message** gladly as soon as they
13.21 persecution comes because of the **message,** they give up at once.
13.22 among thorn bushes stand for those who hear the **message;**
13.22 for riches choke the **message,** and they don't bear fruit.
13.23 soil stand for those who hear the **message** and understand it:
22. 4 So he sent other servants with this **message** for the guests:
27.19 sitting in the judgement hall, his wife sent him a **message:**
Mk 2. 2 Jesus was preaching the **message** to them [3]when four men arrived,
3.31 outside the house and sent in a **message,** asking for him.
4.14 The sower sows God's **message.**
4.15 as they hear the **message,** Satan comes and takes it away.
4.16 As soon as they hear the **message,** they receive it gladly.
4.17 persecution comes because of the **message,** they give up at once.
4.18 ones who hear the **message,** [19]but the worries about this life,
4.19 crowd in and choke the **message,** and they don't bear fruit.
4.20 They hear the **message,** accept it, and bear fruit:
4.33 Jesus preached his **message** to the people, using many other
16. 7 Now go and give this **message** to his disciples, including Peter:
16.10 the sacred and ever-living **message** of eternal salvation.
Lk 1. 2 saw these things from the beginning and who proclaimed the **message.**
1.20 you have not believed my **message,** which will come true at
1.27 He had a **message** for a girl promised in marriage to a
1.29 deeply troubled by the angel's **message,** and she wondered what
1.45 to believe that the Lord's **message** to you will come true!"
1.67 was filled with the Holy Spirit, and he spoke God's **message:**
8.12 Devil comes and takes the **message** away from their hearts in
8.13 stand for those who hear the **message** and receive it gladly.
8.15 for those who hear the **message** and retain it in a good
24.47 in his name the **message** about repentance and the forgiveness of
Jn 1. 7 the light, so that all should hear the **message** and believe.
3.11 have seen, yet none of you is willing to accept our **message.**
3.32 what he has seen and heard, yet no one accepts his **message.**
3.33 whoever accepts his **message** confirms by this that God is truthful.
4.41 believed because of his **message,** [42]and they said to the woman,
5.38 you do not keep his **message** in your hearts, for you do
8.43 It is because you cannot bear to listen to my **message.**
10.35 those people gods, the people to whom his **message** was given.
11. 3 The sisters sent Jesus a **message:**
12.38 "Lord, who believed the **message** we told?
12.47 If anyone hears my **message** and does not obey it, I will
12.48 and does not accept my **message** has one who will judge him.
17. 8 I gave them the **message** that you gave me, and they
17.14 I gave them your **message,** and the world hated them,
17.20 also for those who believe in me because of their **message.**
Acts 1.21 the time John preached his **message** of baptism until the day
2.17 Your sons and daughters will proclaim my **message;**
2.18 my Spirit in those days, and they will proclaim my **message.**
2.41 Many of them believed his **message** and were baptized,
3.24 prophets who had a **message,** including Samuel and those who came
4. 4 But many who heard the **message** believed;
4.29 allow us, your servants, to speak your **message** with all boldness.
4.31 the Holy Spirit and began to proclaim God's **message** with boldness.
7.14 So Joseph sent a **message** to his father Jacob, telling him
7.38 Sinai, and he received God's living **messages** to pass on to us.
7.51 "How heathen your hearts, how deaf you are to God's **message!**
8. 4 believers who were scattered went everywhere, preaching the **message.**
8.12 But when they believed Philip's **message** about the good news
8.25 testimony and proclaimed the Lord's **message,** Peter and John went
9.38 to him with the **message,** "Please hurry and come to us."
10.36 You know the **message** he sent to the people of Israel,
10.37 beginning in Galilee after John preached his **message** of baptism.
10.44 Spirit came down on all those who were listening to his **message.**
11.19 Phoenicia, Cyprus, and Antioch, telling the **message** to Jews only.
11.20 to Antioch and proclaimed the **message** to Gentiles also, telling
13.15 the prophets, the officials of the synagogue sent them a **message:**
13.15 people if you have a **message** of encouragement for them."
13.26 it is to us that this **message** of salvation has been sent!
13.38 is through Jesus that the **message** about forgiveness of sins is
13.48 Gentiles heard this, they were glad and praised the Lord's **message;**
14. 3 Lord, who proved that their **message** about his grace was true

Acts 14.25 they preached the **message** in Perga and then went to Attalia,
15.31 they were filled with joy by the **message** of encouragement.
16. 6 did not let them preach the **message** in the province of Asia.
17.11 They listened to the **message** with great eagerness, and every day
18. 5 whole time to preaching the **message,** testifying to the Jews that
18. 8 people in Corinth heard the **message,** believed, and were baptized.
19. 6 spoke in strange tongues and also proclaimed God's **message.**
19.31 friends, also sent him a **message** begging him not to show
20. 2 through those regions and encouraged the people with many **messages.**
20.17 Miletus Paul sent a **message** to Ephesus, asking the elders of
20.32 of God and to the **message** of his grace, which is able
21. 9 He had four unmarried daughters who proclaimed God's **message.**
28.23 he explained to them his **message** about the Kingdom of God,
28.28 to know, then, that God's **message** of salvation has been sent
Rom 3. 2 In the first place, God trusted his **message** to the Jews.
10. 8 "God's **message** is near you, on your lips and in your heart"
10. 8 that is, the **message** of faith that we preach.
10.14 And how can they believe if they have not heard the **message?**
10.14 And how can they hear if the **message** is not proclaimed?
10.15 And how can the **message** be proclaimed if the messengers are
10.16 Isaiah himself said, "Lord, who believed our **message?"**
10.17 faith comes from hearing the **message,**
10.17 and the **message** comes through preaching Christ.
10.18 Is it true that they did not hear the **message?**
12. 6 gift is to speak God's **message,** we should do it according to
1 Cor 1. 6 The **message** about Christ has become so firmly established in
1.18 the **message** about Christ's death on the cross is nonsense to
1.21 the so-called "foolish" **message** we preach, God decided to save
1.23 proclaim the crucified Christ, a **message** that is offensive to
1.24 both Jews and Gentiles, this **message** is Christ, who is the
2. 4 my teaching and **message** were not delivered with skilful words
2. 6 Yet I do proclaim a **message** of wisdom to those who are
11. 4 prays or proclaims God's **message** in public worship with his head
11. 5 prays or proclaims God's **message** in public worship with nothing
12. 8 Spirit gives one person a **message** full of wisdom, while to
12. 8 another person the same Spirit gives a **message** full of knowledge.
12.10 to another, the gift of speaking God's **message;**
13. 8 There are inspired **messages,** but they are temporary;
13. 9 our gifts of knowledge and of inspired **messages** are only partial;
14. 1 spiritual gifts, especially the gift of proclaiming God's **message.**
14. 3 the one who proclaims God's **message** speaks to people and gives
14. 4 but the one who proclaims God's **message** helps the whole church.
14. 5 I would rather that you had the gift of proclaiming God's **message.**
14. 5 the person who proclaims God's **message** is of greater value than
14. 6 or some knowledge or some inspired **message,** or some teaching.
14. 9 are talking about if your **message** given in strange tongues
14.22 gift of proclaiming God's **message** is proof for believers, not for
14.24 if everyone is proclaiming God's **message** when some unbeliever
14.26 revelation from God, another a **message** in strange tongues,
14.29 three who are given God's **message** should speak, while the others
14.30 in the meeting receives a **message** from God, the one who is
14.31 of you may proclaim God's **message,** one by one, so that
14.32 proclaiming God's **message** should be under the speaker's control,
14.39 your heart on proclaiming God's **message,** but do not forbid the
15. 2 That is the gospel, the **message** that I preached to you.
15.12 since our **message** is that Christ has been raised from death,
2 Cor 2.17 others, who handle God's **message** as if it were cheap merchandise;
5.19 Our **message** is that God was making all mankind his friends
5.19 he has given us the **message** which tells how he makes them
6. 7 our true love, [7] by our **message** of truth, and by the power
Gal 2. 2 I explained the gospel **message** that I preach to the Gentiles.
6. 6 is being taught the Christian **message** should share all the good
Eph 1.13 when you heard the true **message,** the Good News that brought
6.19 God will give me a **message** when I am ready to speak,
Phil 1.14 they grow bolder all the time to preach the **message** fearlessly.
2.16 up the sky, [16] as you offer them the **message** of life.
Col 1. 5 When the true **message,** the Good News, first came to you,
1.25 task of fully proclaiming his **message,** [26] which is the secret
3.16 Christ's **message** in all its richness must live in your hearts.
4. 3 opportunity to preach his **message** about the secret of Christ.
1 Thes 1. 6 suffered much, you received the **message** with the joy that comes
1. 8 For not only did the **message** about the Lord go out from
2.13 When we brought you God's **message,** you heard it and accepted it,
2.13 as man's message but as God's **message,** which indeed it is.
2.16 from preaching to the Gentiles the **message** that would bring them
5.20 do not despise inspired **messages.**
2 Thes 1.10 because you have believed the **message** that we told you.
3. 1 for us, that the Lord's **message** may continue to spread rapidly
3. 2 for not everyone believes the **message.**
3.14 there will not obey the **message** we send you in this letter.
1 Tim 2. 7 teacher of the Gentiles, to proclaim the **message** of faith and
2 Tim 2.15 his work, one who correctly teaches the **message** of God's truth.
4. 2 urge you [2] to preach the **message,** to insist upon proclaiming it
4.15 him yourself, because he was violently opposed to our **message.**
4.17 to proclaim the full **message** for all the Gentiles to hear;
Tit 1. 3 and at the right time he revealed it in his **message.**
1. 9 must hold firmly to the **message** which can be trusted and
2. 5 no one will speak evil of the **message** that comes from God.
Heb 2. 2 The **message** given to our ancestors by the angels was shown
4. 2 They heard the **message,** but it did them no good, because
5.12 someone to teach you the first lessons of God's **message.**
6. 1 and leave behind us the first lessons of the Christian **message.**
12.25 the one who gave the divine **message** on earth did not escape.
13. 7 Remember your former leaders, who spoke God's **message** to you.
13.22 brothers, to listen patiently to this **message** of encouragement;
1 Pet 4.11 Whoever preaches must preach God's **messages;**
2 Pet 1.19 even more confident of the **message** proclaimed by the prophets.
1.21 For no prophetic **message** ever came just from the will of man,
2 Pet 1.21 Holy Spirit as they spoke the **message** that came from God.
1 Jn 1. 5 Now the **message** that we have heard from his Son and
2. 7 The old command is the **message** you have already heard.
2.24 in your hearts the **message** you heard from the beginning.
2.24 If you keep that **message,** then you will always live in union
3.11 The **message** you heard from the very beginning is this:
Jude 4 persons who distort the **message** about the grace of our God
Rev 1. 2 his report concerning the **message** from God and the truth revealed
1. 3 the words of this prophetic **message** and obey what is written
2. 1 "This is the **message** from the one who holds the seven
2. 8 "This is the **message** from the one who is the first
2.12 "This is the **message** from the one who has the sharp
2.18 "This is the **message** from the Son of God, whose eyes blaze
3. 1 "This is the **message** from the one who has the seven
3. 7 "This is the **message** from the one who is holy and true.
3.14 "This is the **message** from the Amen, the faithful and true
10.11 again you must proclaim God's **message** about many nations, races,
11. 3 and they will proclaim God's **message** during those 1,260 days."
11. 6 will be no rain during the time they proclaim God's **message.**
11. 7 When they finish proclaiming their **message,** the beast that
14. 6 the air, with an eternal **message** of Good News to announce to

MESSENGER

Gen 32. 3 Jacob sent **messengers** ahead of him to his brother Esau in
32. 6 When the **messengers** came back to Jacob, they said, "We
Num 20.14 Moses sent **messengers** from Kadesh to the king of Edom.
21.21 the people of Israel sent **messengers** to the Amorite king
22. 5 So King Balak [5] sent **messengers** to summon Balaam son of Beor,
22.13 Balaam went to Balak's **messengers** and said, "Go back home;
24.12 Balaam answered, "I told the **messengers** you sent to me
Deut 2.26 "Then I sent **messengers** from the desert of Kedemoth to
Judg 6.35 He sent **messengers** throughout the territory of both
6.35 He sent **messengers** to the tribes of Asher, Zebulun, and
7.24 Gideon sent **messengers** through all the hill-country of Ephraim
9.31 He sent **messengers** to Abimelech at Arumah to say, "Gaal
11.12 Then Jephthah sent **messengers** to the king of Ammon to say,
11.13 king of Ammon answered Jephthah's **messengers,** "When the
11.14 Jephthah sent **messengers** back to the king of Ammon
11.17 Then they sent **messengers** to the king of Edom to ask
11.19 the Israelites sent **messengers** to Sihon, the Amorite king
20.12 The Israelite tribes sent **messengers** all through the
1 Sam 4. 4 So they sent **messengers** to Shiloh and fetched the Covenant
4.17 The **messenger** answered, "Israel ran away from the Philistines;
5. 8 So they sent **messengers** and called together all five of
6.21 They sent **messengers** to the people of Kiriath Jearim to say,
11. 3 "Give us seven days to send **messengers** throughout the land
11. 4 The **messengers** arrived at Gibeah, where Saul lived, and
11. 5 They told him what the **messengers** from Jabesh had reported.
11. 7 them in pieces, and sent **messengers** to carry the pieces
11. 9 They said to the **messengers** from Jabesh, "Tell your
13. 3 Then Saul sent **messengers** to call the Hebrews to war by
16.19 So Saul sent **messengers** to Jesse to say, "Send me your
19.21 of this, he sent more **messengers,** and they also began to
19.21 He sent **messengers** the third time, and the same thing
23.27 Just then a **messenger** arrived and said to Saul, "Come
25.14 David sent some **messengers** from the wilderness with greetings
31. 9 off his armour, and sent **messengers** with them throughout
2 Sam 3.12 Abner sent **messengers** to David, who at that time was at Hebron,
3.14 And David also sent **messengers** to Ishbosheth to say,
3.26 After leaving David, Joab sent **messengers** to get Abner,
4.10 The **messenger** who came to me at Ziklag and told me of
10. 2 So David sent **messengers** to express his sympathy.
10. 4 Hanun seized David's **messengers,** shaved off one side of their
11. 3 So he sent a **messenger** to find out who she was, and
11. 4 David sent **messengers** to fetch her;
11.19 battle, [19] and he instructed the **messenger,** "After you
11.22 So the **messenger** went to David and told him what Joab
11.25 David said to the **messenger,** "Encourage Joab and tell
12.27 He sent **messengers** to David to report:
15.10 But he sent **messengers** to all the tribes of Israel to say,
15.13 A **messenger** reported to David, "The Israelites are
1 Kgs 2.29 the altar, Solomon sent a **messenger** to Joab to ask him why
20. 2 He sent **messengers** into the city to King Ahab of Israel to
20. 5 **messengers** came back to Ahab with another demand from Benhadad:
20. 9 So Ahab replied to Benhadad's **messengers,** "Tell my lord
20. 9 The **messengers** left and then returned with another message
2 Kgs 1. 2 So he sent some **messengers** to consult Baalzebub, the god of
1. 3 to go and meet the **messengers** of King Ahaziah and ask them,
1. 5 Lord commanded, [5] and the **messengers** returned to the king.
1. 6 you, 'Why are you sending **messengers** to consult Baalzebub,
1.16 'Because you sent **messengers** to consult Baalzebub, the god
6.32 And he sent a **messenger** to get Elisha.
6.32 Before the king's **messenger** arrived, Elisha said to the elders,
9.18 The **messenger** rode out to Jehu and said to him, "The
9.18 the watch-tower reported that the **messenger** had reached the
9.19 Another **messenger** was sent out, who asked Jehu the same
9.20 the guard reported that the **messenger** had reached the group
14. 8 Then Amaziah sent **messengers** to King Jehoash of Israel,
17. 4 But one year Hoshea sent **messengers** to So, king of Egypt,
17.13 The Lord had sent his **messengers** and prophets to warn
19.14 King Hezekiah took the letter from the **messengers** and read it.
19.23 You sent your **messengers** to boast to me that with all
20.13 Hezekiah welcomed the **messengers** and showed them his
1 Chr 10. 9 off his armour, and sent **messengers** with them throughout
13. 2 our God, let us send **messengers** to the rest of our
19. 2 So David sent **messengers** to express his sympathy.
19. 4 Hanun seized David's **messengers,** shaved off their beards,

2 Chr 20. 2 Some **messengers** came and announced to King Jehoshaphat:
30. 6 **Messengers** went out at the command of the king and his
30.10 The **messengers** went to every city in the territory of
36.16 But they ridiculed God's **messengers,** ignoring his words
Neh 6. 3 I sent **messengers** to say to them, "I am doing important
Job 1.14 their eldest brother, [14]a **messenger** came running to Job.
Ps 78.49 anger and fierce rage, which came as **messengers** of death.
104. 4 use the winds as your **messengers** and flashes of lightning as
Prov 13.17 Unreliable **messengers** cause trouble,
17.11 will come like a cruel **messenger** to wicked people who are
25.13 A reliable **messenger** is refreshing to the one who sends him,
Is 6. 8 Who will be our **messenger?"**
14.32 How shall we answer the **messengers** that come to us from Philistia?
18. 2 Go back home, swift **messengers!**
37.14 King Hezekiah took the letter from the **messengers** and read it.
39. 2 Hezekiah welcomed the **messengers** and showed them his
41.27 I sent a **messenger** to Jerusalem to say, 'Your people are coming!
42.19 blind than my servant, more deaf than the **messenger** I send?
44.26 prediction, when I send a **messenger** to reveal my plans, I
52. 7 it is to see a **messenger** coming across the mountains,
57. 9 gods to worship, you send **messengers** far and wide, even to
Jer 4.15 **Messengers** from the city of Dan and from the hills of
49.14 He has sent a **messenger** to tell the nations to assemble
51.31 **Messenger** after messenger runs to tell the king of
Ezek 23.16 filled with lust and sent **messengers** to them in Babylonia.
23.40 "Again and again they sent **messengers** to invite men to
30. 9 is destroyed, I will send **messengers** in ships to arouse the
Obad 1 The Lord has sent his **messenger** to the nations, and we have
Nah 1.15 Look, a **messenger** is coming over the mountains with good news!
Hag 1.12 were afraid and obeyed the prophet Haggai, the Lord's **messenger.**
Mal 2. 7 will, because they are the **messengers** of the Lord Almighty.
3. 1 "I will send my **messenger** to prepare the way for me.
3. 1 The **messenger** you long to see will come and proclaim
3. 3 and gold, so the Lord's **messenger** will purify the priests,
Mt 10.41 Whoever welcomes God's **messenger** because
10.41 he is God's **messenger,** will share in his reward.
11.10 said, I will send my **messenger** ahead of you to open the
23.37 You kill the prophets and stone the **messengers** God has sent you!
Mk 1. 2 said, 'I will send my **messenger** ahead of you to clear the
1.24 I know who you are—you are God's holy **messenger!"**
5.35 Jesus was saying this, some **messengers** came from Jairus' house
Lk 4.34 you are God's holy **messenger!"**
7.10 The **messengers** went back to the officer's house and found
7.22 answered John's **messengers,** "Go back and tell John what you have
7.24 John's **messengers** had left, Jesus began to speak about him to
7.27 said, I will send my **messenger** ahead of you to open the
8.49 Jesus was saying this, a **messenger** came from the official's
9.52 He sent **messengers** ahead of him, who went into a village
11.49 Wisdom of God said, 'I will send them prophets and **messengers;**
13.34 You kill the prophets, you stone the **messengers** God has sent you!
14.32 he isn't, he will send **messengers** to meet the other king,
19.14 and so they sent **messengers** after him to say, 'We don't
Jn 1. 6 God sent his **messenger,** a man named John, [7]who came to
1.24 **messengers,** who had been sent by the Pharisees, [25]then asked John,
5.33 to whom you sent your **messengers,** and he spoke on behalf of
13.16 than his master, and no **messenger** is greater than the one
Acts 7.52 They killed God's **messengers,** who long ago announced the coming
15.25 all agreed to choose some **messengers** and send them to you.
15.30 The **messengers** were sent off and went to Antioch, where they
Rom 10.15 message be proclaimed if the **messengers** are not sent out?
10.15 "How wonderful is the coming of **messengers** who bring good news!"
1 Cor 14.37 anyone supposes he is God's **messenger** or has a spiritual gift,
2 Cor 12. 7 ailment, which acts as Satan's **messenger** to beat me and keep
12.17 I take advantage of you through any of the **messengers** I sent?
Phil 2.25 my side and who has served as your **messenger** in helping me.
1 Pet 1.12 have now heard from the **messengers** who announced the Good News
Rev 2.20 that woman Jezebel, who calls herself a **messenger** of God.

MESSIAH

Hebrew title (meaning "the anointed one") given to the saviour whose coming was promised by the Hebrew prophets.
see also **CHRIST, (God's) CHOSEN (leader)**

Mt 1.12 Mary, the mother of Jesus, who was called the **Messiah.**
1.17 Babylon, and fourteen from then to the birth of the **Messiah.**
2. 4 the Law and asked them, "Where will the **Messiah** be born?"
16.16 Peter answered, "You are the **Messiah,** the Son of the living God."
16.20 his disciples not to tell anyone that he was the **Messiah.**
22.42 Jesus asked them, [42]"What do you think about the **Messiah?**
22.45 called him 'Lord,' how can the **Messiah** be David's descendant?"
23.10 called 'Leader', because your one and only leader is the **Messiah.**
24. 5 to speak for me, will come and say, 'I am the **Messiah!'**
24.23 "Then, if anyone says to you, 'Look, here is the **Messiah!'**
24.24 For false **Messiahs** and false prophets will appear;
26.63 tell us if you are the **Messiah,** the Son of God."
26.68 those who slapped him [68]said, "Prophesy for us, **Messiah!**
27.17 Jesus Barabbas or Jesus called the **Messiah?"**
27.22 "What, then, shall I do with Jesus called the **Messiah?"**
Mk 8.29 Peter answered, "You are the **Messiah."**
12.35 Law say that the **Messiah** will be the descendant of David?
12.37 so how can the **Messiah** be David's descendant?"
13.21 "Then, if anyone says to you, 'Look, here is the **Messiah!'**
13.22 For false **Messiahs** and false prophets will appear.
14.61 "Are you the **Messiah,** the Son of the Blessed God?"
Mk 15.32 Let us see the **Messiah,** the king of Israel, come down
Lk 2.26 not die before he had seen the Lord's promised **Messiah.**
3.15 began to wonder whether John perhaps might be the **Messiah.**
4.41 let them speak, because they knew that he was the **Messiah.**
9.20 Peter answered, "You are God's **Messiah."**
20.41 it be said that the **Messiah** will be the descendant of David?
20.44 how, then, can the **Messiah** be David's descendant?"
22.67 "Tell us," they said, "are you the **Messiah?"**
23. 2 and claiming that he himself is the **Messiah,** a king."
23.35 him save himself if he is the **Messiah** whom God has chosen!"
23.39 "Aren't you the **Messiah?**
24.26 it not necessary for the **Messiah** to suffer these things and
24.46 **Messiah** must suffer and must rise from death three days later,
Jn 1.20 "I am not the **Messiah."**
1.25 "If you are not the **Messiah** nor Elijah nor the Prophet, why
1.41 brother Simon and told him, "We have found the **Messiah."**
3.28 said, 'I am not the **Messiah,** but I have been sent ahead
4.25 "I know that the **Messiah** will come, and when he comes,
4.29 Could he be the **Messiah?"**
7.26 Can it be that they really know that he is the **Messiah?**
7.27 But when the **Messiah** comes, no one will know where he is
7.31 said, "When the **Messiah** comes, will he perform more miracles
7.41 Others said, "He is the **Messiah!"**
7.41 But others said, "The **Messiah** will not come from Galilee!
7.42 scripture says that the **Messiah** will be a descendant of King
9.22 believed that Jesus was the **Messiah** would be expelled from the
10.24 are you the **Messiah?"**
11.27 believe that you are the **Messiah,** the Son of God, who was
12.34 "Our Law tells us that the **Messiah** will live for ever.
20.31 believe that Jesus is the **Messiah,** the Son of God, and that
Acts 2.31 about the resurrection of the **Messiah** when he said, 'He was
2.36 crucified, is the one that God has made Lord and **Messiah!"**
3.18 ago through all the prophets that his **Messiah** had to suffer;
3.20 Jesus, who is the **Messiah** he has already chosen for you.
4.26 and the rulers met together against the Lord and his **Messiah.'**
4.27 of Israel against Jesus, your holy Servant, whom you made **Messiah.**
5.42 to teach and preach the Good News about Jesus the **Messiah.**
8. 5 principal city in Samaria and preached the **Messiah** to the people
9.22 proofs that Jesus was the **Messiah** were so convincing that the
17. 3 proving from them that the **Messiah** had to suffer and rise
17. 3 "This Jesus whom I announce to you," Paul said, "is the **Messiah."**
18. 5 the message, testifying to the Jews that Jesus is the **Messiah.**
18.28 debates by proving from the Scriptures that Jesus is the **Messiah.**
26.23 that the **Messiah** must suffer and be the first one to
Heb 11.26 to suffer scorn for the **Messiah** was worth far more than all
1 Jn 2.22 It is anyone who says that Jesus is not the **Messiah.**
5. 1 Whoever believes that Jesus is the **Messiah** is a child of God;
Rev 11.15 to our Lord and his **Messiah,** and he will rule for ever
12.10 Now his **Messiah** has shown his authority!

AV **MESSIAS** see **MESSIAH**

METAL

Ex 34.17 "Do not make and worship gods of **metal.**
38.21 of the amounts of the **metals** used in the Tent of the
Lev 6.28 be broken, and if a **metal** pot is used, it must be
19. 4 do not make gods of **metal** and worship them.
Num 21. 8 told Moses to make a **metal** snake and put it on a
33.52 Destroy all their stone and **metal** idols and all their places
Deut 9.16 him by making yourselves a **metal** idol in the form of a
9.21 that you had made—that **metal** bull-calf—and threw it into the
27.15 an idol of stone, wood, or **metal** and secretly worships it;
Judg 17. 4 and gave them to a **metal-worker,** who made an idol, carving
1 Kgs 14. 9 my anger by making idols and **metal** images to worship.
2 Kgs 17.16 Lord their God and made two **metal** bull-calves to worship;
2 Chr 3.10 two winged creatures out of **metal,** cover them with gold, and
24.12 carpenters, and **metalworkers** to make the repairs.
28. 2 He had **metal** images of Baal made, [3]burnt incense in the
Job 37.18 stretch out the sky and make it as hard as polished **metal?**
Is 1.25 will purify you just as **metal** is refined, and will remove
40.19 idol that workmen make, that **metalworkers** cover with gold
44.10 It's no good making a **metal** image to worship as a god!
44.12 The **metalworker** takes a piece of metal and works with it
44.12 His strong arm swings a hammer to pound the **metal** into shape.
Jer 6.27 people, as you would test **metal,** and find out what they are
6.29 fiercely, but the waste **metals** do not melt and run off.
9. 7 will refine my people like **metal** and put them to the test.
52.21 They were hollow, and the **metal** was 75 millimetres thick.
Ezek 22.18 They are like the waste **metal**—copper, tin, iron, and
Hos 13. 2 sinning by making **metal** images to worship—idols of silver,
Mal 3. 2 He will be like strong soap, like a fire that refines **metal.**
3. 3 As a **metal-worker** refines silver and gold, so the Lord's
2 Tim 4.14 Alexander the **metal-worker** did me much harm;

Are you looking for

a word? Continue in this section.
a theme? Turn to the **Thematic Index.**
a name? Turn to the **Concordance of Biblical Names.**
For more detailed instructions, turn to 'How to use the Concordance' on page ix.

METRE
see also **SQUARE (Metre)**

Gen 6.15 Gen 7.20 Gen 21.16 Ex 26.2 Ex 26.8 Ex 26.16 Ex 27.1 Ex 27.1 Ex 27.9 Ex 27.12 Ex 27.13 Ex 27.14 Ex 27.16 Ex 27.18 Ex 27.18 Ex 36.9 Ex 36.15 Ex 36.21 Ex 38.1 Ex 38.1 Ex 38.9 Ex 38.12 Ex 38.13 Ex 38.14 Ex 38.18 Num 11.31 Num 35.4 Num 35.5 Deut 2.5 Deut 3.11 Deut 3.11 1 Sam 17.4 1 Kgs 6.2 1 Kgs 6.3 1 Kgs 6.5 1 Kgs 6.6 1 Kgs 6.6 1 Kgs 6.6 1 Kgs 6.10 1 Kgs 6.16 1 Kgs 6.17 1 Kgs 6.20 1 Kgs 6.20 1 Kgs 6.23 1 Kgs 6.24 1 Kgs 6.24 1 Kgs 7.2 1 Kgs 7.2 1 Kgs 7.6 1 Kgs 7.10 1 Kgs 7.15 1 Kgs 7.16 1 Kgs 7.19 1 Kgs 7.23 1 Kgs 7.23 1 Kgs 7.27 1 Kgs 7.38 2 Kgs 14.13 2 Kgs 25.17 2 Kgs 25.17 1 Chr 11.23 2 Chr 3.3 2 Chr 3.4 2 Chr 3.8 2 Chr 3.11 2 Chr 3.11 2 Chr 3.15 2 Chr 3.15 2 Chr 4.1 2 Chr 4.1 2 Chr 4.2 2 Chr 4.2 2 Chr 6.13 2 Chr 25.23 Ezra 6.3 Neh 3.13 Esth 5.14 Esth 7.9 Jer 52.21 Jer 52.21 Ezek 40.5 Ezek 40.5 Ezek 40.6 Ezek 40.7 Ezek 40.7 Ezek 40.7 Ezek 40.8 Ezek 40.8 Ezek 40.11 Ezek 40.11 Ezek 40.12 Ezek 40.13 Ezek 40.14 Ezek 40.15 Ezek 40.19 Ezek 40.21 Ezek 40.21 Ezek 40.23 Ezek 40.25 Ezek 40.25 Ezek 40.27 Ezek 40.29 Ezek 40.29 Ezek 40.33 Ezek 40.33 Ezek 40.36 Ezek 40.36 Ezek 40.47 Ezek 40.48 Ezek 40.48 Ezek 40.49 Ezek 41.1 Ezek 41.2 Ezek 41.2 Ezek 41.3 Ezek 41.3 Ezek 41.4 Ezek 41.5 Ezek 41.5 Ezek 41.8 Ezek 41.8 Ezek 41.8 Ezek 41.8 Ezek 41.12 Ezek 41.12 Ezek 41.13 Ezek 41.13 Ezek 41.14 Ezek 41.15 Ezek 41.22 Ezek 42.2 Ezek 42.3 Ezek 42.4 Ezek 42.7 Ezek 42.7 Ezek 42.16 Ezek 42.17 Ezek 42.20 Ezek 43.14 Ezek 43.14 Ezek 43.15 Ezek 43.16 Ezek 43.17 Ezek 45.2 Ezek 45.2 Ezek 46.21 Ezek 47.3 Ezek 47.4 Ezek 47.4 Ezek 47.5 Ezek 48.16 Ezek 48.17 Ezek 48.30 Ezek 48.35 Dan 3.1 Zech 5.2 Jn 21.8 Acts 27.28 Acts 27.28 Rev 14.20 Rev 21.17

METRIC see TON

MICAH (1)
Man who employed a young Levite, Jonathan, as his priest.

Judg 17. 1 was once a man named **Micah**, who lived in the hill-country
17. 4 It was placed in **Micah's** house.
17. 5 This man **Micah** had his own place of worship.
17. 8 he came to **Micah's** house in the hill-country of Ephraim.
17. 9 **Micah** asked him, "Where do you come from?"
17.10 **Micah** said, "Stay with me.
17.11 Levite agreed to stay with **Micah** and became like a son
17.12 **Micah** appointed him as his priest, and he lived in Micah's home.
17.13 **Micah** said, "Now that I have a Levite as my priest, I
18. 2 the hill-country of Ephraim, they stayed at **Micah's** house.
18. 4 "I have an arrangement with **Micah**, who pays me to serve as
18.13 and came to **Micah's** house in the hill-country of Ephraim.
18.15 So they went into **Micah's** house, where the young Levite lived,
18.18 the men went into **Micah's** house and took the sacred objects,
18.22 the house when **Micah** called his neighbours out for battle.
18.23 men from Dan turned round and asked **Micah**, "What's the matter?
18.24 **Micah** answered, "What do you mean, 'What's the matter?'
18.26 **Micah** saw that they were too strong for him, so he turned
18.27 priest and the things that **Micah** had made, they went and
18.31 **Micah's** idol remained there all the time that the Tent

MICAIAH (1)
Prophet who predicted King Ahab's defeat.

1 Kgs 22. 8 Ahab answered, "There is one more, **Micaiah** son of Imlah.
22. 9 official and told him to go and fetch **Micaiah** at once.
22.13 who had gone to get **Micaiah** said to him, "All the other
22.14 But **Micaiah** answered, "By the living Lord I promise
22.15 Ahab, the king asked him, **"Micaiah**, should King Jehoshaphat
22.15 "Attack!" **Micaiah** answered.
22.17 **Micaiah** answered, "I can see the army of Israel
22.19 **Micaiah** went on:
22.23 And **Micaiah** concluded:
22.24 prophet Zedekiah went up to **Micaiah**, slapped his face, and
22.25 when you go into some back room to hide," **Micaiah** replied.
22.26 one of his officers, "Arrest **Micaiah** and take him to Amon,
22.28 "If you return safely," **Micaiah** exclaimed, "then the
2 Chr 18. 7 Ahab answered, "There is one more, **Micaiah** son of Imlah.
18. 8 official and told him to go and fetch **Micaiah** at once.
18.12 who had gone to fetch **Micaiah** said to him, "All the other
18.13 But **Micaiah** answered, "By the living Lord, I will say
18.14 Ahab, the king asked him, **"Micaiah**, should King Jehoshaphat
18.14 "Attack!" **Micaiah** answered.
18.16 **Micaiah** answered, "I can see the army of Israel
18.18 **Micaiah** went on:
18.22 And **Micaiah** concluded:
18.23 prophet Zedekiah went up to **Micaiah**, slapped his face, and
18.24 when you go into some back room to hide," **Micaiah** replied.
18.25 one of his officers, "Arrest **Micaiah** and take him to Amon,
18.27 "If you return safely," **Micaiah** exclaimed, "then the

MICE

Lev 11.29 Moles, rats, **mice**, and lizards must be considered unclean.
1 Sam 6. 4 of tumours and five gold **mice**, one of each for each
6. 5 the tumours and of the **mice** that are ravaging your country,
6.11 containing the gold models of the **mice** and of the tumours.
6.18 They also sent gold **mice**, one for each of the cities
Is 66.17 and who eat pork and **mice** and other disgusting foods.

MICHAEL (1)
Israel's guardian angel.

Dan 10.13 Then **Michael**, one of the chief angels, came to help me,
10.20 no one to help me except **Michael**, Israel's guardian angel.
12. 1 that time the great angel **Michael**, who guards your people,
Jude 9 Not even the chief angel **Michael** did this.
9 have the body of Moses, **Michael** did not dare to condemn the
Rev 12. 7 **Michael** and his angels fought against the dragon, who fought

MICHAL
Saul's daughter who married David, and was later taken from him by her father.

1 Sam 14.49 His elder daughter was named Merab, and the younger one **Michal**.
18.20 Saul's daughter **Michal**, however, fell in love with David,
18.21 He said to himself, "I'll give **Michal** to David;
18.27 So Saul had to give his daughter **Michal** in marriage to David.
18.28 Lord was with David and also that his daughter **Michal** loved him.
19.11 **Michal**, David's wife, warned him, "If you don't get away tonight,
19.14 men came to get David, **Michal** told them that he was ill.
19.17 Saul asked **Michal**, "Why have you tricked me like this
25.44 Saul had given his daughter **Michal**, who had been David's wife,
2 Sam 3.13 you must bring Saul's daughter **Michal** to me when you come
3.14 to Ishbosheth to say, "Give me back my wife **Michal**.
6.16 being brought into the city, **Michal**, Saul's daughter, looked
6.20 went home to greet his family, **Michal** came out to meet him.
6.23 **Michal**, Saul's daughter, never had any children.
1 Chr 15.29 being brought into the city, **Michal**, Saul's daughter, looked

MICHMASH
Site of encounter between Jonathan and the Philistines.

1 Sam 13. 2 with him in **Michmash** and in the hill-country of Bethel
13. 5 They went to **Michmash**, east of Bethaven, and camped there.
13.11 besides that, the Philistines are gathering at **Michmash**.
13.16 the Philistine camp was at **Michmash**.
13.23 sent a group of soldiers to defend the pass of **Michmash**.
14. 4 In the pass of **Michmash**, which Jonathan had to go through
14. 5 side of the pass, facing **Michmash**, and the other was on the
14.31 fighting all the way from **Michmash** to Aijalon.
Ezra 2.21 **Michmash** – 122
Neh 7.26 **Michmash** – 122
11.31 Benjamin lived in Geba, **Michmash**, Ai, Bethel
Is 10.28 They left their supplies at **Michmash**!

MID AIR see AIR

MIDDAY

2 Sam 4. 5 there about noon, while he was taking his **midday** rest.
Acts 22. 6 coming near Damascus, about **midday** a bright light from the sky
26.13 was on the road at **midday**, Your Majesty, that I saw a
Rev 1.16 His face was as bright as the **midday** sun.

MIDDLE

Gen 2. 9 In the **middle** of the garden stood the tree that gives life
3. 3 the woman answered, [3] "except the tree in the **middle** of it.
Ex 3. 2 to him as a flame coming from the **middle** of a bush.
3. 4 called to him from the **middle** of the bush and said, "Moses!
26.28 The **middle** cross-bar, set half-way up the frames, is to
36.33 The **middle** cross-bar, set half-way up the frames,
Lev 15.31 Tent of his presence, which was in the **middle** of the camp.
16.16 because it stands in the **middle** of the camp, which is
Num 16.47 his firepan and ran into the **middle** of the assembled people.
35. 5 900 metres on each side, with the city in the **middle**.
Deut 2.36 and the city in the **middle** of that valley, all the way
3.16 The **middle** of the river was their southern boundary, and
Josh 3.17 on dry ground in the **middle** of the Jordan until all the
4. 3 twelve stones out of the **middle** of the Jordan, from the very
4. 8 took twelve stones from the **middle** of the Jordan, one for
4. 9 up twelve stones in the **middle** of the Jordan, where the
4.10 The priests stood in the **middle** of the Jordan until
10.13 sun stood still in the **middle** of the sky and did not
12. 2 and the city in the **middle** of that valley, as far as
13. 9 and the city in the **middle** of that valley and included all
13.16 and the city in the **middle** of that valley and included all
Judg 16.29 Samson took hold of the two **middle** pillars holding up
2 Sam 20.12 covered with blood, was lying in the **middle** of the road.
24. 5 Aroer, the city in the **middle** of the valley, in the
1 Kgs 6. 6 2.2 metres wide, in the **middle** storey 2.7 metres wide, and
6.27 touched each other in the **middle** of the room, and the other
18.29 kept on ranting and raving until the **middle** of the afternoon;
1 Chr 11.14 made a stand in the **middle** of the field and fought the
2 Chr 6.13 a bronze platform and put it in the **middle** of the courtyard.
Neh 2.12 Then in the **middle** of the night I got up and went
Ps 78.28 they fell in the **middle** of the camp all round the tents.
119.62 In the **middle** of the night I wake up to praise you
Ezek 1.27 seemed to be shining like bronze in the **middle** of a fire.
15. 4 are burnt up and the **middle** is charred, can you make
41. 7 from the lower storey to the **middle** and the upper storeys.
41.24 They were double doors that swung open in the **middle**.
42. 5 narrower than those at the **middle** and lower levels because
43.17 The **middle** section was also a square, seven metres on each
43.20 on the corners of the **middle** section of the altar, and all
48.10 of the Lord is to be in the **middle** of this area.
Dan 4.10 a vision of a huge tree in the **middle** of the earth.

Mk 6.47 the boat was in the **middle** of the lake, while Jesus was
Lk 4.30 but he walked through the **middle** of the crowd and went
5.19 on his bed into the **middle** of the group in front of
Acts 14.14 and ran into the **middle** of the crowd, shouting, [15]"Why are
Rev 22. 2 the Lamb [2]and flowing down the **middle** of the city's street.

MIDDLE GATE

Jer 39. 3 their places at the **Middle Gate,** including Nergal Sarezer,

MIDIAN

Abraham's son and the tribe, distantly related to Israel, descended from him.

Gen 25. 2 She bore him Zimran, Jokshan, Medan, **Midian,** Ishbak, and
25. 4 The sons of **Midian** were Ephah, Epher, Hanoch, Abida, and
36.31 from Avith (he defeated the **Midianites** in a battle in the
37.28 agreed, [28]and when some **Midianite** traders came by,
37.36 in Egypt, the **Midianites** had sold Joseph to Potiphar,
Ex 2.15 but Moses fled and went to live in the land of **Midian.**
2.15 of Jethro, the priest of **Midian,** came to draw water and fill
3. 1 father-in-law Jethro, the priest of **Midian,** he led the flock
4.19 While Moses was still in **Midian,** the Lord said to him,
18. 1 father-in-law Jethro, the priest of **Midian,** heard about
Num 10.29 Hobab son of Jethro the **Midianite,** "We are about to start
22. 4 to the leaders of the **Midianites,** "This horde will soon
22. 7 So the Moabite and **Midianite** leaders took with them the
25. 6 of the Israelites took a **Midianite** woman into his tent in
25.14 was killed with the **Midianite** woman was Zimri son of Salu,
25.15 Zur, her father, was chief of a group of **Midianite** clans.
25.17 commanded Moses, [17]"Attack the **Midianites** and destroy them,
31. 2 said to Moses, [2]"Punish the **Midianites** for what they did
31. 3 so that you can attack **Midian** and punish them for what they
31. 7 They attacked **Midian,** as the Lord had commanded Moses, and
31. 8 killed all the men, [8]including the five kings of **Midian:**
31. 9 people of Israel captured the **Midianite** women and children,
Josh 13.21 Moses defeated him, as well as the rulers of **Midian:**
Judg 6. 1 so he let the people of **Midian** rule them for seven years.
6. 2 The **Midianites** were stronger than Israel, and the people
6. 3 Israelites sowed any seed, the **Midianites** would come with
6. 7 Lord for help against the **Midianites,** [8]and he sent them a
6.11 in a winepress, so that the **Midianites** would not see him.
6.13 abandoned us and left us to the mercy of the **Midianites."**
6.14 all your great strength and rescue Israel from the **Midianites.**
6.16 You will crush the **Midianites** as easily as if they were only
6.33 the **Midianites,** the Amalekites, and the desert tribes assembled,
7. 1 The **Midianite** camp was in the valley to the north of them
7. 2 too many for me to give them victory over the **Midianites.**
7. 7 give you victory over the **Midianites** with the three hundred
7. 8 The **Midianite** camp was below them in the valley.
7.12 The **Midianites,** the Amalekites, and the desert tribesmen
7.14 God has given him victory over **Midian** and our whole army!"
7.15 The Lord is giving you victory over the **Midianite** army!"
7.23 Manasseh were called out, and they pursued the **Midianites.**
7.24 of Ephraim to say, "Come down and fight the **Midianites.**
7.24 as Bethbarah, to keep the **Midianites** from crossing them."
7.25 They captured the two **Midianite** chiefs, Oreb and Zeeb;
7.25 They continued to pursue the **Midianites** and brought the
8. 1 "Why didn't you call us when you went to fight the **Midianites?**
8. 3 power of God you killed the two **Midianite** chiefs, Oreb and
8. 5 I am pursuing Zebah and Zalmunna, the **Midianite** kings."
8.12 The two **Midianite** kings, Zebah and Zalmunna, ran away,
8.22 You have saved us from the **Midianites."**
8.24 (The **Midianites,** like other desert people, wore gold earrings.)
8.26 clothes that the kings of **Midian** wore, nor the collars that
8.28 So **Midian** was defeated by the Israelites and was no
9.17 He risked his life to save you from the **Midianites.**
1 Kgs 11.18 They left **Midian** and went to Paran, where some other men
1 Chr 1.32 Zimran, Jokshan, Medan, **Midian,** Ishbak, and Shuah.
1.33 **Midian** had five sons:
1.43 from Avith (he defeated the **Midianites** in a battle in the
Ps 83. 9 what you did to the **Midianites,** and to Sisera and Jabin at
Is 9. 4 people, just as you defeated the army of **Midian** long ago.
10.26 as I beat the people of **Midian** at the Rock of Oreb.
60. 6 Great caravans of camels will come, from **Midian** and Ephah.
Hab 3. 7 people of Cushan afraid and the people of **Midian** tremble.
Acts 7.29 fled from Egypt and went to live in the land of **Midian.**

MIDNIGHT

Ex 11. 4 "The Lord says, 'At about **midnight** I will go through Egypt,
12.29 At **midnight** the Lord killed all the first-born sons in Egypt,
Judg 7.19 camp a short while before **midnight,** just after the guard had
16. 3 But Samson stayed in bed only until **midnight.**
Mt 25. 6 "It was already **midnight** when the cry rang out, 'Here is
Mk 13.35 in the evening or at **midnight** or before dawn or at sunrise.
Lk 11. 5 to a friend's house at **midnight** and say to him, 'Friend, let
12.38 ready, even if he should come at **midnight** or even later!
Acts 16.25 About **midnight** Paul and Silas were praying and singing hymns
20. 7 and kept on speaking until **midnight,** since he was going to
27.27 About **midnight** the sailors suspected that we were getting close

MIDST

Deut 33.12 them all the day long, And he dwells in their **midst."**

MIDWIFE

Gen 35.17 at their worst, the **midwife** said to her, "Don't be afraid,
38.28 the **midwife** caught it, tied a red thread round it, and said,
38.29 Then the **midwife** said, "So this is how you break your way
Ex 1.15 Shiphrah and Puah, the two **midwives** who helped the Hebrew women.
1.17 But the **midwives** feared God and so did not obey the king;
1.18 the king sent for the **midwives** and asked them, "Why are you
1.20 Because the **midwives** feared God, he was good to

MIGHT

Gen 18.18 will become a great and **mighty** nation, and through him I
23. 6 We look upon you as a **mighty** leader;
49.24 By the power of the **Mighty** God of Jacob, By the Shepherd,
Ex 6. 6 I will raise my **mighty** arm to bring terrible punishment
15.11 Who can work miracles and **mighty** acts like yours?
15.15 Moab's **mighty** men are trembling;
32.11 whom you rescued from Egypt with great **might** and power?
Num 23.24 The nation of Israel is like a **mighty** lion:
24. 9 The nation is like a **mighty** lion;
Deut 2.10 (A **mighty** race of giants called the Emim used to live
2.21 There were many of them, and they were a **mighty** race.
3.24 on earth who can do the **mighty** things that you have done!
5.22 When he spoke with a **mighty** voice from the fire and from
6. 3 and you will become a **mighty** nation and live in that rich
7. 8 saved you by his great **might** and set you free from slavery
9.29 you brought out of Egypt by your great power and **might.'**
10.17 He is great and **mighty,** and he is to be feared.
11. 2 You saw the Lord's greatness, his power, his **might,**
32. 4 "The Lord is your **mighty** defender, perfect and just in
32.15 They abandoned God their Creator and rejected their **mighty** saviour.
32.18 They forgot their God, their **mighty** saviour, the one who
32.30 their **mighty** God had given them up.
32.31 that their own gods are weak, not **mighty** like Israel's God.
32.37 will ask his people, 'Where are those **mighty** gods you trusted?
Josh 22.22 "The **Mighty** One is God!
22.22 The **Mighty** One is God!
Judg 6.12 and said, "The Lord is with you, brave and **mighty** man!"
16.30 He pushed with all his **might,** and the building fell down on
1 Sam 12. 7 reminding you of all the **mighty** actions the Lord did to save
2 Sam 1.22 Saul was merciless, striking down the **mighty,**
6. 5 dancing and singing with all their **might** to honour the Lord.
6.14 his waist, danced with all his **might** to honour the Lord.
2 Kgs 2.12 **Mighty** defender of Israel!
13.14 "You have been the **mighty** defender of Israel!"
18.20 that words can take the place of military skill and **might?**
1 Chr 13. 8 all the people danced with all their **might** to honour God.
16.24 Proclaim his glory to the nations, his **mighty** deeds
16.28 Praise the Lord, all people on earth, praise his glory and **might.**
2 Chr 20. 6 You are powerful and **mighty,** and no one can oppose you.
Ezra 3.11 Everyone shouted with all his **might,** praising the Lord,
Job 24.22 God, in his strength, destroys the **mighty;**
34.20 he kills the **mighty** with no effort at all.
Ps 24. 8 the Lord, strong and **mighty,** the Lord, victorious in battle.
29. 4 voice of the Lord is heard in all its **might** and majesty.
45. 3 Buckle on your sword, **mighty** king;
54. 1 set me free by your **might!**
60. 5 Save us by your **might;**
63. 2 let me see how **mighty** and glorious you are.
65. 6 in place by your strength, showing your **mighty** power.
66. 7 rules for ever by his **might** and keeps his eyes on the
68.15 What a **mighty** mountain is Bashan, a mountain of many peaks!
68.16 Why from your **mighty** peaks do you look with scorn on the
68.17 With his many thousands of **mighty** chariots the Lord
68.33 Listen to him shout with a **mighty** roar.
68.34 his majesty is over Israel, his **might** is in the skies.
71.18 I proclaim your power and **might** to all generations to come.
74.13 With your **mighty** strength you divided the sea and
77.12 I will meditate on all your **mighty** acts.
77.14 you showed your **might** among the nations.
78.43 their enemies [43]and performed his **mighty** acts and miracles
86.10 You are **mighty** and do wonderful things;
89. 8 Lord God Almighty, none is as **mighty** as you;
89.10 with your **mighty** strength you defeated your enemies.
90.16 Let us, your servants, see your **mighty** deeds;
90.16 let our descendants see your glorious **might.**
92. 4 Your **mighty** deeds, O Lord, make me glad;
95. 3 Lord is a mighty God, a **mighty** king over all the gods.
96. 3 Proclaim his glory to the nations, his **mighty** deeds
96. 7 praise his glory and **might.**
99. 2 The Lord is **mighty** in Zion;
99. 4 **Mighty** king, you love what is right;
103. 7 to Moses and let the people of Israel see his **mighty** deeds.
103.20 Lord, you strong and **mighty** angels, who obey his commands,
105.27 They did God's **mighty** acts and performed miracles in Egypt.
106.21 the God who had saved them by his **mighty** acts in Egypt.
107.25 He commanded, and a **mighty** wind began to blow and
108. 6 Save us by your **might;**
111. 9 Holy and **mighty** is he!
118.15 "The Lord's **mighty** power has done it!
118.16 His power has brought us victory— his **mighty** power in battle!"
132. 2 promised, the vow he made to you, the **Mighty** God of Jacob:
132. 5 place for the Lord, a home for the **Mighty** God of Jacob."
136. 3 Give thanks to the **mightiest** of all lords;
145. 4 they will proclaim your **mighty** acts.
145. 6 People will speak of your **mighty** deeds, and I will
145.11 power and tell of your **might,** [12]so that everyone will know
145.12 that everyone will know your **mighty** deeds and the glorious
147. 5 Great and **mighty** is our Lord;
150. 2 Praise him for the **mighty** things he has done.
Is 9. 6 "Wonderful Counsellor," **"Mighty** God,"
10.21 of the people of Israel will come back to their **mighty** God.
17.10 God who rescues you and who protects you like a **mighty** rock.

Is 36. 5 that words can take the place of military skill and **might?**
43.17 He led a **mighty** army to destruction, an army of chariots
60.16 saved you, That the **mighty** God of Israel sets you free.
Jer 5.16 Their bowmen are **mighty** soldiers who kill without mercy.
6.22 a **mighty** nation far away is preparing for war.
10. 6 you are **mighty,** and your name is great and powerful.
16.21 all I will make the nations know my power and my **might;**
20.11 on my side, strong and **mighty,** and those who persecute me
21. 5 against you with all my **might,** my anger, my wrath, and my
31.11 Israel's people free and have saved them from a **mighty** nation.
32.17 made the earth and the sky by your great power and **might;**
32.19 You make wise plans and do **mighty** things;
32.21 you used your power and **might** to bring your people Israel
44.26 Lord, have made in my **mighty** name to all you Israelites in
46.15 Why has your **mighty** god Apis fallen?
48. 1 Kiriathaim is captured, its **mighty** fortress torn down, and
48.17 its glory and **might** are no more.'
48.25 Moab's **might** has been crushed;
50.41 from a country in the north, a **mighty** nation far away;
51. 9 Babylonia with all his **might** and has destroyed it completely.' "
51.58 The walls of **mighty** Babylon will be thrown to the ground,
Ezek 17. 9 not take much strength or a **mighty** nation to pull it up.
26.11 Your **mighty** pillars will be thrown to the ground.
Dan 2.37 heaven has made you emperor and given you power, **might,** and
4.30 city to display my power and **might,** my glory and majesty."
10. 4 year, I was standing on the bank of the **mighty** River Tigris.
Joel 2.11 The troops that obey him are many and **mighty.**
Amos 4. 4 Go to Gilgal and sin with all your **might!**
5. 9 He brings destruction on the **mighty** and their strongholds.
Jon 1.13 tried to get the ship to shore, rowing with all their **might.**
2. 3 all round me, and all your **mighty** waves rolled over me.
Hab 3.15 trampled the sea with your horses, and the **mighty** waters foamed.
Zech 4. 6 will succeed, not by military **might** or by your own strength,
10.11 Assyria will be humbled, and **mighty** Egypt will lose her power.
Mal 1. 5 "The Lord is **mighty** even outside the land of Israel!"
Lk 1.17 of the Lord, strong and **mighty** like the prophet Elijah.
1.49 because of the great things the **Mighty** God has done for me.
1.51 He has stretched out his **mighty** arm and scattered the proud
1.52 He has brought down **mighty** kings from their thrones,
1.69 has provided for us a **mighty** Saviour, a descendant of his
9.43 All the people were amazed at the **mighty** power of God.
Eph 1.19 is the same as the **mighty** strength [20] which he used when he
6.10 in union with the Lord and by means of his **mighty** power.
Col 1.29 and struggle, using the **mighty** strength which Christ supplies
2 Thes 1. 7 appears from heaven with his **mighty** angels, [8] with a flaming fire,
1. 9 Lord and from his glorious **might,** [10] when he comes on that
Heb 11.34 were **mighty** in battle and defeated the armies of foreigners.
1 Pet 5. 6 Humble yourselves, then, under God's **mighty** hand, so that he
2 Pet 1.16 known to you the **mighty** coming of our Lord Jesus Christ.
2.11 are so much stronger and **mightier** than these false teachers,
Jude 25 our Lord, be glory, majesty, **might,** and authority, from all ages
Rev 5. 2 And I saw a **mighty** angel, who announced in a loud voice,
5.13 Lamb, be praise and honour, glory and **might,** for ever and ever!"
7.12 thanksgiving, honour, power, and **might** belong to our God for ever
10. 1 Then I saw another **mighty** angel coming down out of heaven.
18. 8 fire, because the Lord God, who judges her, is **mighty."**
18.10 This great and **mighty** city Babylon!
18.21 Then a **mighty** angel picked up a stone the size of a

MIGRATE

Jer 8. 7 swallows, and thrushes know when it is time to **migrate.**

MILD

2 Cor 10. 1 said to be meek and **mild** when I am with you,

MILDEW

Lev 13.47 When there is **mildew** on clothing, whether wool or linen,
13.49 or reddish, it is a spreading **mildew** and must be shown to
13.51 day, and if the **mildew** has spread, the object is unclean.
13.52 it is a spreading **mildew** which must be destroyed by fire.
13.53 priest finds that the **mildew** has not spread on the object,
13.55 examine it, and if the **mildew** has not changed colour, even
13.56 priest examines it again, the **mildew** has faded, he shall
13.57 Then, if the **mildew** reappears, it is spreading again,
13.59 then, is the law about **mildew** on clothing, whether it is
14.34 following regulations about houses affected by spreading **mildew.**
14.34 that the Lord has sent **mildew** on his house, then he must
14.36 moved out of the house before he goes to examine the **mildew;**
14.37 Then he shall go to the house [37] and examine the **mildew.**
14.39 If the **mildew** has spread, [40] he shall order
14.40 the stones on which the **mildew** is found to be removed and
14.43 If the **mildew** breaks out again in the house after the
14.48 priest comes to look, the **mildew** has not reappeared after
14.48 clean, because the **mildew** has been completely removed.
14.55 and about **mildew** in clothes or houses.

AV MILE see KILOMETRE

Am for MILES see FAR (and wide)

MILITARY

Num 1. 3 twenty years old or older who are fit for **military service.**
1.20 older who were fit for **military service** were registered by
1.49 of the men fit for **military service,** do not include the
26. 2 years old or older who are fit for **military service."**
Deut 24. 5 be drafted into **military service** or any other public duty;
Josh 17. 1 Manasseh's eldest son and a **military** hero, so Gilead and Bashan,
2 Sam 8. 6 Then he set up **military** camps in their territory, and they
8.14 He set up **military** camps throughout Edom, and the people
24. 9 king the total number of men capable of **military service:**
2 Kgs 18.20 that words can take the place of **military** skill and might?
20.13 his spices and perfumes, and all his **military** equipment.
24.16 all of them able-bodied men fit for **military** duty.
25.19 charge of **military** records, and sixty other important men.
1 Chr 7. 4 were able to provide 36,000 men for **military service.**
7. 5 Issachar listed 87,000 men eligible for **military service.**
7. 7 descendants included 22,034 men eligible for **military service.**
7. 9 families listed 20,200 men eligible for **military service.**
7.11 descendants included 17,200 men eligible for **military service.**
7.40 descendants included 26,000 men eligible for **military service.**
15.25 leaders of Israel, and the **military** commanders went to the
18. 6 Then he set up **military** camps in their territory, and they
18.13 He set up **military** camps throughout Edom, and the people
21. 5 King David the total number of men capable of **military service:**
Is 3. 3 and their statesmen, [3] their **military** and civilian leaders,
31. 1 They are relying on Egypt's vast **military** strength—horses,
36. 2 to Jerusalem with a large **military** force to demand that King
36. 5 that words can take the place of **military** skill and might?
39. 2 his spices and perfumes, and all his **military** equipment.
Jer 52.25 charge of **military** records, and sixty other important men.
Hos 1. 5 I will at that time destroy Israel's **military** power."
Zech 4. 6 "You will succeed, not by **military** might or by your own strength,
Mk 6.21 government officials, the **military** commanders, and the leading
Acts 25.23 the audience hall with the **military** chiefs and the leading
Rev 6.15 the rulers and the **military** chiefs, the rich and the powerful,

MILK

Gen 18. 8 He took some cream, some **milk,** and the meat, and set the
32.13 sheep and twenty males, thirty **milk** camels with their young,
49.12 from drinking wine, His teeth white from drinking **milk.**
Ex 23.19 "Do not cook a young sheep or goat in its mother's **milk.**
34.26 "Do not cook a young sheep or goat in its mother's **milk."**
Deut 14.21 "Do not cook a young sheep or goat in its mother's **milk.**
32.14 Their cows and goats gave plenty of **milk;**
Judg 4.19 opened a leather bag of **milk,** gave him a drink, and hid
5.25 Sisera asked for water, but she gave him **milk;**
Job 20.17 of olive-oil or streams that flow with **milk** and honey.
29. 6 and goats gave plenty of **milk,** and my olive-trees grew in
Prov 27.27 of the goats will provide **milk** for you and your family, and
30.33 If you churn **milk,** you get butter.
Song 4.11 your tongue is **milk** and honey for me.
5. 1 I am drinking my wine and **milk.**
5.12 brook, doves washed in **milk** and standing by the stream.
Is 7.15 decisions, people will be drinking **milk** and eating honey.
7.22 they will give so much **milk** that he will have all he
7.22 survivors left in the land will have **milk** and honey to eat.
55. 1 Buy wine and **milk**— it will cost you nothing!
Ezek 25. 4 the fruit and drink the **milk** that should have been yours.
34. 3 You drink the **milk,** wear clothes made from the wool, and
1 Cor 3. 2 had to feed you with **milk,** not solid food, because you were
9. 7 What shepherd does not use the **milk** from his own sheep?
Heb 5.12 Instead of eating solid food, you still have to drink **milk.**
5.13 Anyone who has to drink **milk** is still a child, without
1 Pet 2. 2 thirsty for the pure spiritual **milk,** so that by drinking it

MILL
see also **MILLSTONE**

Judg 16.21 and put him to work grinding at the **mill** in the prison.
Ecc 12. 4 be able to hear the **mill** as it grinds or music
Mt 24.41 Two women will be at a **mill** grinding meal:

MILLET
A cultivated grain that is grown as a food crop.

Ezek 4. 9 "Now take some wheat, barley, beans, peas, **millet,**

MILLIMETRE

Ex 25.25 Ex 37.12 1 Kgs 7.26 2 Chr 4.5 Jer 52.21 Ezek 40.43

MILLION

Gen 24.60 "May you, sister, become the mother of **millions!**
2 Chr 13.17 defeat—half a **million** of Israel's best soldiers were killed.
14. 9 with an army of a **million** men and three hundred chariots and
Ps 105.34 He commanded, and the locusts came, countless **millions** of them;
Dan 7.10 there to serve him, and **millions** of people stood before him.
Mt 18.24 one of them was brought in who owed him **millions** of pounds.
Rev 5.11 I looked, and I heard angels, thousands and **millions** of them!

MILLSTONE

Deut 24. 6 take as security his **millstones** used for grinding his corn.
Judg 9.53 But a woman threw a **millstone** down on his head and
2 Sam 11.21 where a woman threw a **millstone** down from the wall and
Job 41.24 is without fear, as unyielding and hard as a **millstone.**
Is 47. 2 Turn the **millstone!**
Mt 18. 6 person to have a large **millstone** tied round his neck and be
Mk 9.42 person to have a large **millstone** tied round his neck and be
Lk 17. 2 for him if a large **millstone** were tied round his neck
Rev 18.21 the size of a large **millstone** and threw it into the sea,
18.22 and the sound of the **millstone** will be heard no more!

MINA

Weight equal to 60 shekels.

Ezek 45.12 20 gerahs = 1 shekel 60 shekels = 1 **mina**

MIND (1)

Gen 19.29 living, he kept Abraham in **mind** and allowed Lot to escape to
Ex 13.17 the people to change their **minds** and return to Egypt when
14. 5 officials changed their **minds** and said, "What have we done?
32.12 your **mind** and do not bring this disaster on your people.
32.14 So the Lord changed his **mind** and did not bring on his
Num 23.19 He is not a human who changes his **mind.**
Deut 15. 9 Do not let such an evil thought enter your **mind.**
28.28 The Lord will make you lose your **mind;**
28.34 Your sufferings will make you lose your **mind.**
1 Sam 15.29 Israel's majestic God does not lie or change his **mind.**
15.29 He is not a man—he does not change his **mind."**
26.19 me, an offering to him will make him change his **mind;**
2 Sam 7. 3 "Do whatever you have in **mind,** because the Lord is with you."
13.32 he had made up his **mind** to do this from the time
24.16 Jerusalem, the Lord changed his **mind** about punishing the
1 Kgs 18.21 "How much longer will it take you to make up your **minds?**
2 Kgs 23.25 Lord with all his heart, **mind,** and strength, obeying all the
1 Chr 17. 2 "Do whatever you have in **mind,** because God is with you."
21.15 Jerusalem, but he changed his **mind** and said to the angel,
28. 9 and to serve him with an undivided heart and a willing **mind.**
28.12 for all he had in **mind** for the courtyards and the rooms
Job 14.22 pain of his own body and the grief of his own **mind.**
17. 4 You have closed their **minds** to reason;
33. 2 I am ready to say what's on my **mind.**
37.19 our **minds** are blank;
Ps 19. 8 of the Lord are just and give understanding to the **mind.**
45. 1 Beautiful words fill my **mind,** as I compose this song for
51. 6 fill my **mind** with your wisdom.
64. 6 The heart and **mind** of man are a mystery.
73. 7 out evil, and their **minds** are busy with wicked schemes.
73.26 My **mind** and my body may grow weak, but God is my
139.23 Examine me, O God, and know my **mind;**
143. 5 all that you have done, I bring to **mind** all your deeds.
Prov 6.14 in their perverted **minds,** stirring up trouble everywhere.
6.16 a **mind** that thinks up wicked plans,
14.30 Peace of **mind** makes the body healthy, but jealousy is
17. 1 of bread with peace of **mind** than to have a banquet in
20.27 The Lord gave us **mind** and conscience;
21. 1 The Lord controls the **mind** of a king as easily as he
23. 1 to eat with an important man, keep in **mind** who he is.
27. 9 you feel happier, but trouble shatters your peace of **mind.**
Ecc 2.23 Even at night your **mind** can't rest.
4. 6 a little, with peace of **mind,** than to be busy all the
9. 3 as people live, their **minds** are full of evil and madness,
Is 1. 5 covered with wounds, and your heart and **mind** are sick.
5.19 let's see what he has in **mind."**
6.10 said to me, "Make the **minds** of these people dull, their
10. 7 But the Assyrian emperor has his own violent plans in **mind.**
44.18 They close their eyes and their **minds** to the truth.
Jer 4.28 The Lord has spoken and will not change his **mind.**
7.31 command them to do this—it did not even enter my **mind.**
17.10 I, the Lord, search the **minds** and test the hearts of men.
19. 5 it never even entered my **mind.**
20.12 you know what is in their hearts and **minds.**
21.10 I have made up my **mind** not to spare this city, but
25.16 and go out of their **minds** because of the war I am
26. 3 then I will change my **mind** about the destruction I plan to
26.13 do, he will change his **mind** about the destruction that he
26.19 And the Lord changed his **mind** about the disaster that he
32.35 did not even enter my **mind** that they would do such a
34.11 but later they changed their **minds,** took them back, and
34.15 few days ago you changed your **minds** and did what pleased me.
34.16 But then you changed your **minds** again and dishonoured me.
51. 7 The nations drank its wine and went out of their **minds.**
Ezek 11.19 I will give them a new heart and a new **mind.**
18.31 have been doing, and get yourselves new **minds** and hearts.
20.32 You have made up your **minds** that you want to be like
36.26 I will give you a new heart and a new **mind.**
Dan 1. 8 Daniel made up his **mind** not to let himself become
2. 5 "I have made up my **mind** that you must tell me the
2. 8 I have made up my **mind** [9] to give all of you the
4.16 will not have a human **mind,** but the mind of an animal.
5.21 human society, and his **mind** became like that of an animal.
7. 4 And then a human **mind** was given to it.
Hos 13. 2 of silver, designed by human **minds,** made by human hands.
Joel 2.14 God will change his **mind** and bless you with abundant crops.
Amos 7. 3 The Lord changed his **mind** and said, "What you saw will
7. 6 The Lord changed his **mind** again and said, "This will not
7. 8 I will not change my **mind** again about punishing them.
8. 1 I will not change my **mind** again about punishing them.
Jon 3. 9 Perhaps God will change his **mind;**
3.10 So he changed his **mind** and did not punish them as he
4. 2 kind, and always ready to change your **mind** and not punish.
Mic 4.12 But these nations do not know what is in the Lord's **mind.**
Zeph 3. 8 I have made up my **mind** to gather nations and kingdoms, in
Zech 7.11 closed their **minds** [12] and made their hearts as hard as rock.
8.14 them and did not change my **mind,** but carried out my plans.
Mt 3.14 But John tried to make him change his **mind.**
13.15 because their **minds** are dull, and they have stopped
13.15 their **minds** would understand, and they would turn
21.29 to,' he answered, but later he changed his **mind** and went.
21.32 this, you did not later change your **minds** and believe him.
22.37 all your heart, with all your soul, and with all your **mind.'**
Mk 5.15 He was sitting there, clothed and in his right **mind;**
Mk 6.52 their **minds** could not grasp it.
8.17 Are your **minds** so dull?
12.30 your soul, with all your **mind,** and with all your strength.'
12.33 his heart and with all his **mind** and with all his strength;
Lk 8.35 sitting at the feet of Jesus, clothed and in his right **mind;**
9.51 heaven, he made up his **mind** and set out on his way
10.27 your soul, with all your strength, and with all your **mind';**
21.14 Make up your **minds** beforehand not to worry about how you
24.38 Why are these doubts coming up in your **minds?**
24.45 Then he opened their **minds** to understand the Scriptures,
Jn 12.40 their eyes and closed their **minds,** so that their eyes would
12.40 not see, and their **minds** would not understand,
Acts 4.32 The group of believers was one in **mind** and heart.
16.14 and the Lord opened her **mind** to pay attention to what Paul
19.21 Paul made up his **mind** to travel through Macedonia and Achaia
28. 6 they changed their **minds** and said, "He is a god!"
28.27 because this people's **minds** are dull, and they have stopped
28.27 their ears would hear, their **minds** would understand, and they
Rom 1.21 nonsense, and their empty **minds** are filled with darkness.
1.28 people refuse to keep in **mind** the true knowledge about God,
1.28 given them over to corrupted **minds,** so that they do the
7.23 a law that fights against the law which my **mind** approves of.
7.25 God's law only with my **mind,** while my human nature serves
8. 5 have their **minds** controlled by what human nature wants.
8. 5 have their **minds** controlled by what the Spirit wants.
11. 8 As the scripture says, "God made their **minds** and hearts dull;
11.29 God does not change his **mind** about whom he chooses and blesses.
11.34 As the scripture says, "Who knows the **mind** of the Lord?
12. 2 God transform you inwardly by a complete change of your **mind.**
14. 5 Each one should firmly make up his own **mind.**
1 Cor 2. 2 I made up my **mind** to forget everything except Jesus Christ
2.16 As the scripture says, "Who knows the **mind** of the Lord?
2.16 We, however, have the **mind** of Christ.
4. 5 the dark secrets and expose the hidden purposes of people's **minds.**
7.37 has firmly made up his **mind** not to marry, and if he
7.37 already decided in his own **mind** what to do—then he does
14.14 my spirit prays indeed, but my **mind** has no part in it.
14.15 pray with my spirit, but I will pray also with my **mind;**
14.15 sing with my spirit, but I will sing also with my **mind.**
2 Cor 2. 1 So I made up my **mind** not to come to you again
3.14 Their **minds,** indeed, were closed;
3.14 to this very day their **minds** are covered with the same veil
3.15 read the Law of Moses, the veil still covers their **minds.**
4. 4 do not believe, because their **minds** have been kept in the
11. 3 I am afraid that your **minds** will be corrupted and that you
Eph 1.18 I ask that your **minds** may be opened to see his light,
2. 3 doing whatever suited the wishes of our own bodies and **minds.**
4.18 whose thoughts are worthless [18] and whose **minds** are in the dark.
4.23 Your hearts and **minds** must be made completely new,
Phil 2. 2 sharing the same love, and being one in soul and **mind.**
4. 7 keep your hearts and **minds** safe in union with Christ Jesus.
4. 8 my brothers, fill your **minds** with those things that are good
Col 3. 2 Keep your **minds** fixed on things there, not on things here
1 Tim 6. 5 constant arguments from people whose **minds** do not function
2 Tim 3. 8 to the truth—people whose **minds** do not function and who are
Tit 1.15 unbelieving, for their **minds** and consciences have been defiled.
Heb 8.10 put my laws in their **minds** and write them on their hearts.
10.16 put my laws in their hearts and write them on their **minds."**
Jas 1. 7 unable to make up his **mind** and undecided in all he does,
1 Pet 1.13 So then, have your **minds** ready for action.
2 Pet 3. 1 arouse pure thoughts in your **minds** by reminding you of these

MIND (2)

2 Kgs 4.23 "Never **mind,"** she answered.
Prov 9.15 to people passing by, who are **minding** their own business:
Song 8. 1 in the street, I could kiss you and no one would **mind.**
1 Cor 7.21 Well, never **mind;**
Phil 3. 1 I don't **mind** repeating what I have written before, and you
1 Thes 4.11 live a quiet life, to **mind** your own business, and to earn

MINE

Deut 8. 9 have iron in them, and from its hills you can **mine** copper.
Job 28. 1 There are **mines** where silver is dug;
28. 4 Or human feet ever travel, Men dig the shafts of **mines.**
28. 7 sees the roads to the **mines,** And no vulture ever flies over

MINISTER

Num 16. 9 Lord's Tent, and **minister** to the community and serve them?
Esth 3. 1 promoted a man named Haman to the position of prime **minister.**

AV MINISTER

see also **HELP, SERVANT, SERVE, WORK**

Ex 24.13 Moses and his **helper** Joshua got ready, and Moses began to
Num 4.14 on it all the equipment used in the **service** at the altar:
Deut 17.12 judge or the priest on **duty** is to be put to death;
Josh 1. 1 the Lord spoke to Moses' **helper,** Joshua son of Nun.
1 Kgs 1. 4 on the king and took **care** of him, but he did not
1.15 and Abishag, the girl from Shunem, was taking **care** of him.
8.11 and they could not go back in to **perform** their duties.
10. 5 organization of his palace **staff** and the uniforms they wore,
2 Kgs 25.14 all the other bronze articles used in the temple **service.**
1 Chr 6.32 They took regular turns of **duty** at the Tent of the
16. 4 the Levites to lead the **worship** of the Lord, the God of
16.37 in permanent charge of the **worship** that was held at the
26.12 and they were assigned **duties** in the Temple,
28. 1 the officials who **administered** the work of the kingdom,

2 Chr 5.11 and they could not continue the **service** of worship.
9. 4 organization of his palace **staff** and the uniforms they wore,
13.10 Priests descended from Aaron perform their **duties,**
22. 8 Ahaziah's nephews that had **accompanied** Ahaziah on his visit.
23. 6 except the priests and the Levites who are on **duty.**
29.11 incense to him and to lead the people in **worshipping** him."
31. 2 taking part in the temple **worship,** and giving praise and
Neh 10.39 the priests who are on **duty,** the temple guards, and the
Jer 52.18 all the other bronze articles used in the temple **service.**
Ezek 20.40 of Israel, all you people of Israel will **worship** me.
44.12 because they conducted the **worship of idols** for the people
44.16 Temple, serve at my altar, and conduct the temple **worship.**
44.17 wool when they are on **duty** in the inner courtyard or in
44.19 the clothes they wore on **duty** in the Temple and leave them
45. 5 possession of the Levites, who do the **work** in the Temple.
Mt 8.15 left her, and she got up and began to **wait on** him.
Mk 1.31 The fever left her, and she began to **wait on** them.
Lk 4.39 and she got up at once and began to **wait on** them.
Acts 24.23 freedom and allow his friends to **provide** for his needs.
Rom 15. 8 you that Christ's life of **service** was on behalf of the Jews,
15.25 I am going to Jerusalem in the **service** of God's people there.
2 Cor 9.10 And God, who **supplies** seed to sow and bread to eat,
9.10 will also **supply** you with all the seed
1 Tim 1. 4 and those long lists of ancestors, which only **produce** arguments;
Heb 10.11 Every Jewish priest performs his **services** every day and

AV MINISTRATION

Lk 1.23 When his period of **service** in the Temple was over,
Acts 6. 1 widows were being neglected in the daily **distribution** of funds.
2 Cor 3. 8 is the glory that belongs to the **activity** of the Spirit!
3. 9 The **system** which brings condemnation was glorious;
3. 9 much more glorious is the **activity** which brings salvation!
9.13 of the proof which this **service** of yours brings, many will

AV MINISTRY

Acts 1.17 for he had been chosen to have a part in our **work."**
1.25 two you have chosen [25] to **serve** as an apostle in the place
6. 4 give our full time to prayer and the **work** of preaching."
12.25 Barnabas and Saul finished their **mission** and returned from
20.24 my mission and finish the **work** that the Lord Jesus gave me
21.19 that God had done among the Gentiles through his **work.**
Rom 12. 7 if it is to **serve,** we should serve;
1 Cor 16.15 Achaia and have given themselves to the **service** of God's people.
2 Cor 4. 1 mercy has given us this **work** to do, and so we are
5.18 and gave us the **task** of making others his friends also.
6. 3 to find fault with our **work,** so we try not to put
Eph 4.12 for the work of Christian **service,** in order to build up the
Col 4.17 "Be sure to finish the **task** you were given in the Lord's
1 Tim 1.12 worthy and appointing me to **serve** him, [13] even though in
2 Tim 4. 5 Good News, and perform your whole duty as a **servant** of God.
4.11 bring him with you, because he can help me in the **work.**
Heb 8. 6 Jesus has been given priestly **work** which is superior to theirs,
9.21 the Covenant Tent and over all the things used in **worship.**

MINT

Mt 23.23 seasoning herbs, such as **mint,** dill, and cumin, but you neglect
Lk 11.42 the seasoning herbs, such as **mint** and rue and all the other

MINUTE

1 Sam 9.27 Samuel continued, "Stay here a **minute,** and I will tell you
Job 7.18 You inspect him every morning and test him every **minute.**
Gal 2. 5 for you, we did not give in to them for a **minute.**

MIPHKAD GATE

Neh 3.31 merchants, which was by the **Miphkad Gate,** near the room on

MIRACLE

Ex 4. 8 by the first **miracle,** then this one will convince them.
4. 9 spite of these two **miracles** they still will not believe you,
4.17 for with it you will perform **miracles."**
4.21 before the king all the **miracles** which I have given you the
4.28 also told him about the **miracles** which the Lord had ordered
4.30 Moses performed all the **miracles** in front of the people.
7. 9 prove yourselves by performing a **miracle,** tell Aaron to take
8.23 This **miracle** will take place tomorrow.'"
10. 1 that I may perform these **miracles** among them [2] and in order
10. 2 I made fools of the Egyptians when I performed the **miracles.**
11. 9 in order that I may do more of my **miracles** in Egypt."
11.10 and Aaron performed all these **miracles** before the king, but
15.11 Who can work **miracles** and mighty acts like yours?
Num 14.11 even though I have performed so many **miracles** among them?
14.22 of my presence and the **miracles** that I performed in Egypt
Deut 4.34 brought plagues and war, worked **miracles** and wonders, and
6.22 eyes we saw him work **miracles** and do terrifying things to
7.19 with your own eyes, the **miracles** and wonders, and the great
11. 3 saw the Lord's greatness, his power, his might, [3] and his **miracles.**
13. 1 of dreams may promise a **miracle** or a wonder, [2] in order to
26. 8 He worked **miracles** and wonders, and caused terrifying things
29. 3 saw the terrible plagues, the **miracles,** and the great
34.11 other prophet has ever done **miracles** and wonders like those
Josh 3. 5 because tomorrow the Lord will perform **miracles** among you."
24.17 slavery in Egypt, and we saw the **miracles** that he performed.
2 Kgs 8. 4 the king wanted to know about Elisha's **miracles.**
1 Chr 16.12 whom God chose, remember the **miracles** that God performed
Neh 9.10 You worked amazing **miracles** against the king, against
9.17 they forgot the **miracles** you had performed.
Job 5. 9 great things he does, and to his **miracles** there is no end.
9.10 great things he does, and to his **miracles** there is no end.
10.16 to hurt me you even work **miracles.**
Ps 77.14 You are the God who works **miracles;**
78.11 what he had done, the **miracles** they had seen him perform.
78.12 their ancestors watched, God performed **miracles** in the plain
78.32 in spite of his **miracles** they did not trust him.
78.43 performed his mighty acts and **miracles** in the plain of Zoan
88.10 Do you perform **miracles** for the dead?
88.12 Are your **miracles** seen in that place of darkness or your
105. 5 **miracles** that God performed and the judgements that he gave.
105.27 They did God's mighty acts and performed **miracles** in Egypt.
135. 9 There he performed **miracles** and wonders to punish the king
136. 4 He alone performs great **miracles;**
Jer 21. 2 will perform one of his **miracles** for us and force
32.20 Long ago, you performed **miracles** and wonders in Egypt,
32.21 By means of **miracles** and wonders that terrified our enemies,
Dan 4. 2 account of the wonders and **miracles** which the Supreme God
4. 3 How powerful are the **miracles** he performs!
6.27 he performs wonders and **miracles** in heaven and on earth.
Mic 7.15 Work **miracles** for us, Lord, as you did in the days when
Mt 7.22 name we drove out many demons and performed many **miracles!'**
11.20 performed most of his **miracles** did not turn from their sins,
11.21 If the **miracles** which were performed in you had been
11.23 If the **miracles** which were performed in you had been
12.38 "Teacher," they said, "we want to see you perform a **miracle."**
12.39 "You ask me for a **miracle?**
12.39 The only **miracle** you will be given
12.39 is the **miracle** of the prophet Jonah.
13.54 "And what about his **miracles?**
13.58 did not have faith, he did not perform many **miracles** there.
14. 2 "That is why he has this power to perform **miracles."**
16. 1 asked him to perform a **miracle** for them, to show that God
16. 4 You ask me for a **miracle?**
16. 4 The only miracle you will be given is the **miracle** of Jonah."
24.24 they will perform great **miracles** and wonders in order to deceive
Mk 6. 2 How does he perform **miracles?**
6. 5 not able to perform any **miracles** there, except that he placed
6.14 That is why he has this power to perform **miracles."**
8.11 asked him to perform a **miracle** to show that God approved of
8.12 said, "Why do the people of this day ask for a **miracle?**
9.39 no one who performs a **miracle** in my name will be able
13.22 They will perform **miracles** and wonders in order to deceive even
16.17 Believers will be given the power to perform **miracles:**
16.20 proved that their preaching was true by the **miracles** that were
Lk 10.13 If the **miracles** which were performed in you had been
11.16 asked him to perform a **miracle** to show that God approved of
11.29 They ask for a **miracle,**
11.29 but none will be given them except the **miracle** of Jonah.
23. 8 He was hoping to see Jesus perform some **miracle.**
Jn 2.11 Jesus performed this first **miracle** in Cana in Galilee;
2.18 replied with a question, "What **miracle** can you perform to show
2.23 many believed in him as they saw the **miracles** he performed.
3. 2 No one could perform the **miracles** you are doing unless God
4.48 "None of you will ever believe unless you see **miracles** and
4.54 This was the second **miracle** that Jesus performed after coming
6. 2 they had seen his **miracles** of healing those who were ill.
6.14 Seeing this **miracle** that Jesus had performed, the people
6.26 and had all you wanted, not because you understood my **miracles.**
6.30 replied, "What **miracle** will you perform so that we may see
7.21 answered, "I performed one **miracle,** and you were all surprised.
7.31 Messiah comes, will he perform more **miracles** than this man has?"
9.16 a man who is a sinner perform such **miracles** as these?"
10.41 "John performed no **miracles,"** they said, "but everything he
11.47 Look at all the **miracles** this man is performing!
12.18 met him—because they heard that he had performed this **miracle.**
12.37 had performed all these **miracles** in their presence, they did not
20.30 Jesus performed many other **miracles** which are not written down in
Acts 2.19 I will perform **miracles** in the sky above and wonders on
2.22 by all the **miracles** and wonders which God performed through
2.43 **miracles** and wonders were being done through the apostles,
4.16 knows that this extraordinary **miracle** has been performed by them,
4.22 The man on whom this **miracle** of healing had been performed
4.30 grant that wonders and **miracles** may be performed through the name
5.12 **miracles** and wonders were being performed among the people
6. 8 and full of power, performed great **miracles** and wonders among
7.36 people out of Egypt, performing **miracles** and wonders in Egypt
8. 6 they listened to him and saw the **miracles** that he performed.
8.13 he saw the great wonders and **miracles** that were being performed.
14. 3 by giving them the power to perform **miracles** and wonders.
15.12 Paul report all the **miracles** and wonders that God had performed
19.11 God was performing unusual **miracles** through Paul.
Rom 15.19 by the power of **miracles** and wonders, and by the power
1 Cor 1.22 Jews want **miracles** for proof, and Greeks look for wisdom.
12.10 The Spirit gives one person the power to work **miracles;**
12.28 then those who perform **miracles,** followed by those who are given
12.29 has the power to work **miracles** [30] or to heal diseases or to
2 Cor 12.12 The many **miracles** and wonders that prove that I am an
Gal 3. 5 you the Spirit and work **miracles** among you because you do
2 Thes 2. 9 all kinds of false **miracles** and wonders, [10] and use every kind
Heb 2. 4 performing all kinds of **miracles** and wonders and by distributing
Rev 13.13 This second beast performed great **miracles;**
13.14 earth by means of the **miracles** which it was allowed to

Rev 16.14 They are the spirits of demons that perform **miracles.**
19.20 together with the false prophet who had performed **miracles**
19.20 (It was by those **miracles** that he had deceived those who had

MIRIAM (1)
Moses and Aaron's sister.

Ex 15.20 The prophet **Miriam,** Aaron's sister, took her tambourine,
15.21 **Miriam** sang for them:
Num 12. 1 a Cushite woman, and **Miriam** and Aaron criticized him for it.
12. 4 said to Moses, Aaron, and **Miriam,** "I want the three of you
12. 5 **Miriam!"**
12.10 the cloud left the Tent, **Miriam's** skin was suddenly covered
12.15 **Miriam** was shut out of the camp for seven days, and the
20. 1 There **Miriam** died and was buried.
26.59 She bore Amram two sons, Aaron and Moses, and a daughter, **Miriam.**
Deut 24. 9 Lord your God did to **Miriam** as you were coming from Egypt.
1 Chr 6. 3 Amram had two sons, Aaron and Moses, and one daughter, **Miriam.**
Mic 6. 4 I sent Moses, Aaron, and **Miriam** to lead you.

MIRROR

Ex 38. 8 bronze base out of the **mirrors** belonging to the women who
1 Cor 13.12 What we see now is like a dim image in a **mirror;**
Jas 1.23 man who looks in a **mirror** and sees himself as he is.

MISCARRIAGE

Ex 23.26 no woman will have a **miscarriage** or be without children.
2 Kgs 2.19 fine city, but the water is bad and causes **miscarriages."**
2.21 and it will not cause any more deaths or **miscarriages.' "**
Ps 144.14 May our cattle reproduce plentifully without **miscarriage**

MISERY

Gen 26.35 They made life **miserable** for Isaac and Rebecca.
Ex 1.13 made their lives **miserable** by forcing them into cruel slavery.
Num 20. 5 of Egypt into this **miserable** place where nothing will grow?
21. 5 We can't stand any more of this **miserable** food!"
Deut 26. 7 He heard us and saw our suffering, hardship, and **misery.**
1 Sam 1.16 I have been praying like this because I'm so **miserable."**
2. 8 poor from the dust and raises the needy from their **misery.**
2 Sam 16.12 the Lord will notice my **misery** and give me some blessings to
Neh 4. 2 he said, "What do these **miserable** Jews think they're doing?
Job 3.20 Why let men go on living in **misery?**
7.15 I would rather be strangled than live in this **miserable** body.
10.15 I am **miserable** and covered with shame.
20.22 of his success all the weight of **misery** will crush him.
29.13 Men who were in deepest **misery** praised me, and I helped
Ps 90.15 as the sadness you gave us during all our years of **misery.**
107.41 rescued the needy from their **misery** and made their families
113. 7 from their **misery** [8]and makes them companions of princes,
Prov 1.27 fierce winds of trouble, and you are in pain and **misery.**
23.29 I will show you someone **miserable** and sorry for himself,
29. 2 me a wicked ruler and I will show you a **miserable** people.
31. 6 is for people who are dying, for those who are in **misery.**
Ecc 1.13 God has laid a **miserable** fate upon us.
4. 8 This is useless, too—and a **miserable** way to live.
Is 50.11 you will suffer a **miserable** fate.
Jer 49.24 They are in pain and **misery** like a woman in labour.
Lam 1.11 "see me in my **misery."**
1.22 I groan in **misery,** and I am sick at heart."
3. 5 He has shut me in a prison of **misery** and anguish.
Ezek 23.33 It will make you **miserable** and drunk, that cup of fear
Jas 5. 1 Weep and wail over the **miseries** that are coming upon you!
Rev 3.17 But you do not know how **miserable** and pitiful you are!

MISFORTUNE

Num 23.21 I foresee that Israel's future Will bring her no **misfortune**
Prov 17. 5 You will be punished if you take pleasure in someone's **misfortune.**
Obad 12 have gloated over the **misfortune** of your brothers in Judah.

MISLEAD

Deut 13.13 men of your nation have **misled** the people of their town to
2 Chr 32.15 Now don't let Hezekiah deceive you or **mislead** you like that.
Prov 4.24 Have nothing to do with lies and **misleading** words.
8. 8 nothing is false or **misleading.**
24.28 without good reason, or say **misleading** things about him.
26.18 A man who **misleads** someone and then claims that he
Is 3.12 My people, your leaders are **misleading** you, so that you do
9.16 Those who lead these people have **misled** them and totally confused them.
19.13 They were supposed to lead the nation, but they have **misled** it.
35. 8 no fools will **mislead** those who follow it.
44.20 His foolish ideas have so **misled** him that he is beyond help.
Jer 9. 5 They all **mislead** their friends, and no one tells the truth;
23.26 much longer will those prophets **mislead** my people with the
38.22 'The king's best friends **misled** him, they overruled him.
Ezek 12.24 there will be no more false visions or **misleading** prophecies.
13. 9 who have false visions and make **misleading** predictions.
13.10 "The prophets **mislead** my people by saying that all is well.
13.23 So now your false visions and **misleading** predictions are over.
Mic 3. 6 Because you **mislead** my people, you will have no more prophetic visions,
Zech 10. 2 Some interpret dreams, but only **mislead** you;
Lk 23. 2 caught this man **misleading** our people, telling them not to pay
23.14 this man to me and said that he was **misleading** the people.
Jn 7.12 "No," others said, "he is **misleading** the people."
Rev 2.20 she **misleads** my servants into practising sexual immorality

MISS

Lev 19.10 gather the grapes that were **missed** or to pick up the grapes
Judg 20.15 could sling a stone at a strand of hair and never **miss.**
2 Sam 14. 1 Joab knew that King David **missed** Absalom very much, [2]so
Jer 8. 4 If someone **misses** the road, doesn't he turn back?
46.17 Egypt a new name— 'Noisy Braggart Who **Missed** His Chance.'
50. 9 skilful hunters, shooting arrows that never **miss** the mark.
Lk 19.48 kept listening to him, not wanting to **miss** a single word.
Phil 4. 1 brothers, how dear you are to me and how I **miss** you!
1 Thes 2.17 only in body—how we **missed** you and how hard we tried

MISSING

Num 31.49 soldiers under our command and not one of them is **missing.**
1 Sam 14.17 his men, "Count the soldiers and find out who is **missing."**
14.17 Jonathan and the young man who carried his weapons were **missing.**
30.19 nothing at all was **missing.**
2 Sam 2.30 that nineteen of them were **missing,** in addition to Asahel.
Song 4. 2 Not one of them is **missing;**
6. 6 Not one of them is **missing;**
Is 34.16 of these creatures will be **missing,** and not one will be
40.26 power is so great— not one of them is ever **missing!**

MISSION

1 Sam 18. 5 was successful in all the **missions** on which Saul sent him,
21. 5 ritually pure even when we go out on an ordinary **mission;**
21. 5 how much more this time when we are on a special **mission!"**
2 Sam 5.11 King Hiram of Tyre sent a trade **mission** to David;
1 Chr 14. 1 King Hiram of Tyre sent a trade **mission** to David;
Acts 12.25 Barnabas and Saul finished their **mission** and returned from
13.25 was about to finish his **mission,** he said to the people, 'Who
15.38 to the end of their **mission,** but had turned back and left
20.24 only want to complete my **mission** and finish the work that

MIST

Song 5. 2 is wet with dew, and my hair is damp from the **mist.**
Hos 6. 4 Your love for me disappears as quickly as morning **mist;**
13. 3 people will disappear like morning **mist,** like the dew that
Acts 13.11 once Elymas felt a dark **mist** cover his eyes, and he walked

MISTAKE

Gen 43.12 Maybe it was a **mistake.**
Num 15.24 the **mistake** was made because of the ignorance of the community,
15.25 will be forgiven, because the **mistake** was unintentional and
15.26 be forgiven, because everyone was involved in the **mistake.**
32.23 Make no **mistake** about it;
Prov 14.22 if you work for evil, you are making a **mistake.**
Ecc 7.20 does what is right all the time and never makes a **mistake.**
Jer 42.20 so I warn you now [20]that you are making a fatal **mistake.**
Heb 5. 2 to be gentle with those who are ignorant and make **mistakes.**
Jas 3. 2 All of us often make **mistakes.**
3. 2 a person never makes a **mistake** in what he says, he is

Am **MISTREAT** see **ILL-TREAT**

MISTRESS

Gen 16. 8 She answered, "I am running away from my **mistress."**
2 Kgs 5. 3 day she said to her **mistress,** "I wish that my master could
Ps 123. 2 a maid depends on her **mistress,** so we will keep looking to
Prov 30.23 place of her **mistress.**

MISUSE

Ex 20. 7 the Lord your God, will punish anyone who **misuses** my name.
Deut 5.11 the Lord your God, will punish anyone who **misuses** my name.
Is 56. 2 those who always observe the Sabbath and do not **misuse** it.
Jer 23.10 they live wicked lives and **misuse** their power.

MIX

Gen 11. 7 Let us go down and **mix** up their language so that they
11. 9 Babylon, because there the Lord **mixed** up the language of all
Ex 29.40 of fine wheat flour **mixed** with one litre of pure olive-oil.
30.25 and make a sacred anointing oil, **mixed** like perfume.
30.32 must not use the same formula to make any **mixture** like it.
30.35 Use them to make incense, **mixed** like perfume.
32.20 it, ground it into fine powder, and **mixed** it with water.
37.29 and the pure sweet-smelling incense, **mixed** like perfume.
Lev 2. 4 thick loaves made of flour **mixed** with olive-oil or biscuits
2. 5 to be made of flour **mixed** with olive-oil but without yeast.
6.21 It is to be **mixed** with oil and cooked on a griddle
7.10 But all uncooked grain-offerings, whether **mixed** with oil or dry,
7.12 thick loaves made of flour **mixed** with olive-oil or biscuits
7.12 with olive-oil or cakes made of flour **mixed** with olive-oil.
9. 4 them to the Lord with the grain-offering **mixed** with oil.
14.10 defects, three kilogrammes of flour **mixed** with olive-oil,
14.21 only one kilogramme of flour **mixed** with olive-oil for a
23.13 of flour **mixed** with olive-oil as a food-offering.
Num 6.15 thick loaves made of flour **mixed** with olive-oil and biscuits
7.12 of them full of flour **mixed** with oil for the grain-offering;
8. 8 the required grain-offering of flour **mixed** with olive-oil;

Num 15. 4 animal a kilogramme of flour **mixed** with a litre of olive-oil
15. 6 offered, two kilogrammes of flour **mixed** with one and a half
15. 9 of three kilogrammes of flour **mixed** with two litres of
28. 5 of one kilogramme of flour, **mixed** with one litre of the best
28. 9 of flour **mixed** with olive-oil as a grain-offering,
28.12 As a grain-offering, offer flour **mixed** with olive-oil:
28.20 Offer the proper grain-offering of flour **mixed** with olive-oil:
28.28 Offer the proper grain-offering of flour **mixed** with olive-oil:
29. 3 Offer the proper grain-offering of flour **mixed** with olive-oil:
29. 9 Offer the proper grain-offering of flour **mixed** with olive-oil:
29.14 Offer the proper grain-offering of flour **mixed** with olive-oil:
1 Chr 9.30 responsibility for **mixing** the spices belonged to the priests.
23.29 the baked offerings, and the flour **mixed** with olive-oil;
Ps 102. 9 ashes are my food, and my tears are **mixed** with my drink.
Prov 9. 2 animal killed for a feast, **mixed** spices in the wine, and
9. 5 "Come, eat my food and drink the wine that I have **mixed.**
Is 5.22 Brave and fearless when it comes to **mixing** drinks!
Jer 7.18 build fires, and the women **mix** dough to bake cakes for the
15.12 the iron from the north that is **mixed** with bronze.)
Ezek 4. 9 **Mix** them all together and make bread.
46.14 with one litre of olive-oil for **mixing** with the flour.
Dan 2.41 of iron, because there was iron **mixed** with the clay.
2.43 You also saw that the iron was **mixed** with the clay.
2.43 not be able to, any more than iron can **mix** with clay.
Zech 9. 6 People of **mixed** race will live in Ashdod.
Mt 13.33 woman takes some yeast and **mixes** it with forty litres of
27.34 There they offered Jesus wine **mixed** with a bitter substance;
Mk 15.23 tried to give him wine **mixed** with a drug called myrrh,
Lk 13.21 woman takes some yeast and **mixes** it with forty litres of
Jn 19.39 about thirty kilogrammes of spices, a **mixture** of myrrh and aloes.
2 Tim 2. 4 and so does not get **mixed** up in the affairs of civilian
Heb 9.19 blood of bulls and goats, **mixed** it with water, and sprinkled
Jude 23 and to others show mercy **mixed** with fear, but hate their
Rev 8. 7 Hail and fire, **mixed** with blood, came pouring down on the earth.
15. 2 I saw what looked like a sea of glass **mixed** with fire.

MIZPAH (1)

Town in Benjamin.

Josh 18.26 were also Gibeon, Ramah, Beeroth, [26]**Mizpah,** Chephirah,
Judg 20. 1 They gathered in one body in the Lord's presence at **Mizpah.**
20. 3 Benjamin heard that all the other Israelites had gathered at **Mizpah.**
21. 1 the Israelites had gathered at **Mizpah,** they had made a
21. 5 not go to the gathering in the Lord's presence at **Mizpah?"**
21. 5 anyone who had not gone to **Mizpah** would be put to death.)
21. 8 gone to the gathering at **Mizpah,** they found out that no one
1 Sam 7. 5 the Israelites to meet at **Mizpah,** saying, "I will pray to
7. 6 So they all gathered at **Mizpah.**
7. 6 at **Mizpah** that Samuel settled disputes among the Israelites.)
7. 7 the Israelites had gathered at **Mizpah,** the five Philistine
7.11 The Israelites marched out from **Mizpah** and pursued the
7.12 stone, set it up between **Mizpah** and Shen, and said, "The
7.16 round to Bethel, Gilgal, and **Mizpah,** and in these places he
10.17 for a religious gathering at **Mizpah** [18]and said to them,
1 Kgs 15.22 With this material Asa fortified **Mizpah** and Geba, a city in
2 Kgs 25.23 heard about this, they joined Gedaliah at **Mizpah.**
25.25 the royal family, went to **Mizpah** with ten men, attacked
2 Chr 16. 6 they used them to fortify the cities of Geba and **Mizpah.**
Neh 3. 7 the men of Gibeon and **Mizpah** built the next section, as far
3.15 ruler of the **Mizpah** District, rebuilt the Fountain Gate.
3.19 son of Jeshua, ruler of **Mizpah,** built the next section in
Jer 40. 6 to stay with Gedaliah in **Mizpah** and lived among the people
40. 8 Jezaniah from Maacah went with their men to Gedaliah at **Mizpah.**
40.10 I myself will stay in **Mizpah** and be your representative
40.12 They came to Gedaliah at **Mizpah,** and there they gathered in
40.13 surrendered came to Gedaliah at **Mizpah** [14]and said to him,
41. 1 chief officers, went to **Mizpah** with ten men to see Gedaliah.
41. 3 who were with Gedaliah at **Mizpah** and the Babylonian soldiers
41. 6 So Ishmael went out from **Mizpah** to meet them, weeping as
41.10 rest of the people in **Mizpah,** whom Nebuzaradan the
41.16 as prisoners from **Mizpah** after murdering Gedaliah—soldiers,

MOAB

Lot's son, the people descended from him, and their country e. of the Dead Sea.

see also PAHATH MOAB

Gen 19.37 The elder daughter had a son, whom she named **Moab.**
19.37 He was the ancestor of the present-day **Moabites.**
36.31 battle in the country of **Moab)**
Ex 15.15 **Moab's** mighty men are trembling;
Num 21.11 ruins of Abarim in the wilderness east of **Moabite** territory.
21.13 (The Arnon was the border between the **Moabites** and the Amorites.)
21.15 extend to the town of Ar and towards the border of **Moab."**
21.20 territory of the **Moabites,** below the top of Mount Pisgah,
21.26 against the former king of **Moab** and had captured all his
21.28 the city of Ar in **Moab** And devoured the hills of the
21.29 How terrible for you, people of **Moab!**
22. 1 camp in the plains of **Moab** east of the Jordan and opposite
22. 2 When the king of **Moab,** Balak son of Zippor, heard what the
22. 4 The **Moabites** said to the leaders of the Midianites, "This
22. 7 So the **Moabite** and Midianite leaders took with them the
22. 8 So the **Moabite** leaders stayed with Balaam.
22.10 He answered, "King Balak of **Moab** has sent them to tell
22.21 Balaam saddled his donkey and went with the **Moabite** leaders.
22.36 Ar, a city on the River Arnon at the border of **Moab.**
23. 6 standing by his burnt-offering, with all the leaders of **Moab.**
23. 7 "Balak king of **Moab** has brought me From Syria, from the
Num 23.17 still standing by his burnt-offering, with the leaders of **Moab.**
24.17 will strike the leaders of **Moab** And beat down all the people
25. 1 sexual intercourse with the **Moabite** women who were there.
25. 2 to sacrificial feasts, where the god of **Moab** was worshipped.
26. 3 in the plains of **Moab** across the River Jordan from Jericho.
26.63 in the plains of **Moab** across the River Jordan from Jericho.
31.12 camp on the plains of **Moab** across the Jordan from Jericho.
33.41 Hor to the plains of **Moab** the Israelites set up camp at
33.41 Abarim in the territory of **Moab,** Dibon Gad, Almon Diblathaim,
33.41 in the plains of **Moab** across the River Jordan from Jericho,
33.50 There in the plains of **Moab** across the Jordan from
35. 1 In the plains of **Moab** across the Jordan from Jericho the
36.13 in the plains of **Moab** across the River Jordan from Jericho.
Deut 1. 5 Jordan in the territory of **Moab** that Moses began to explain
2. 8 Eziongeber to the Dead Sea, and we turned north-east towards **Moab.**
2. 9 'Don't trouble the people of **Moab,** the descendants of Lot,
2.11 but the **Moabites** called them Emim.
2.18 are to pass through the territory of **Moab** by way of Ar.
2.24 "After we had passed through **Moab,** the Lord said to us,
2.29 live in Edom, and the **Moabites,** who live in Ar, allowed us
23. 3 "No Ammonite or **Moabite**—or any of their descendants, even
29. 1 to make with the people of Israel in the land of **Moab;**
32.49 Mountains in the land of **Moab** opposite the city of Jericho;
34. 1 up from the plains of **Moab** to Mount Nebo, to the top
34. 5 there in the land of **Moab,** as the Lord had said he
34. 6 him in a valley in **Moab,** opposite the town of Bethpeor, but
34. 8 Israel mourned for him for thirty days in the plains of **Moab.**
Josh 13.32 Jericho and the Jordan when he was in the plains of **Moab.**
24. 9 Then the king of **Moab,** Balak son of Zippor, fought against you.
Judg 3.12 this the Lord made King Eglon of **Moab** stronger than Israel.
3.15 Israel sent Ehud to King Eglon of **Moab** with gifts for him.
3.28 The Lord has given you victory over your enemies, the **Moabites."**
3.28 the place where the **Moabites** were to cross the Jordan;
3.29 they killed about ten thousand of the best **Moabite** soldiers;
3.30 That day the Israelites defeated **Moab,** and there was
10. 6 of Syria, of Sidon, of **Moab,** of Ammon, and of Philistia.
11.15 Israel took away the land of **Moab** or the land of Ammon.
11.17 also asked the king of **Moab,** but neither would he let them
11.18 Edom and the land of **Moab** until they came to
11.18 to the east side of **Moab,** on the other side of the
11.18 did not cross the Arnon because it was the boundary of **Moab.**
11.25 you are any better than Balak son of Zippor, king of **Moab?**
Ruth 1. 1 and Chilion to live for a while in the country of **Moab.**
1. 4 her two sons, [4]who married **Moabite** girls, Orpah and Ruth.
1. 6 so she got ready to leave **Moab** with her daughters-in-law.
1.22 Naomi came back from **Moab** with Ruth, her Moabite daughter-in-law.
2. 6 "She is the foreign girl who came back from **Moab** with Naomi.
4. 3 Naomi has come back from **Moab,** she wants to sell the field
4. 5 are also buying Ruth, the **Moabite** widow, so that the field
4.10 In addition, Ruth the **Moabite,** Mahlon's widow, becomes my wife.
1 Sam 12. 9 Philistines and the king of **Moab** and Sisera, commander of
14.47 the people of **Moab,** of Ammon, and of Edom, the kings of
22. 3 from there to Mizpah in **Moab**
22. 3 said to the king of **Moab,** "Please let my father and mother
22. 4 parents with the king of **Moab,** and they stayed there as long
2 Sam 8. 2 Then he defeated the **Moabites.**
8. 2 So the **Moabites** became his subjects and paid taxes to him.
8.12 nations he had conquered—[12]Edom, **Moab,** Ammon, Philistia,
23.20 brave deeds, including killing two great **Moabite** warriors.
1 Kgs 11. 1 he married Hittite women and women from **Moab,** Ammon, Edom,
11. 7 the disgusting god of **Moab,** and a place to worship Molech,
11.33 Chemosh, the god of **Moab;**
2 Kgs 1. 1 the country of **Moab** rebelled against Israel.
3. 4 King Mesha of **Moab** bred sheep, and every year he gave as
3. 7 "The king of **Moab** has rebelled against me;
3.10 the three of us at the mercy of the king of **Moab!"**
3.13 put us three kings at the mercy of the king of **Moab."**
3.18 he will also give you victory over the **Moabites.**
3.21 When the **Moabites** heard that the three kings had come
3.24 Israelites kept up the pursuit, slaughtering the **Moabites**
3.26 When the king of **Moab** realized that he was losing the battle,
3.27 on the city wall as a sacrifice to the god of **Moab.**
13.20 Every year bands of **Moabites** used to invade the land of Israel.
23.13 Sidon, Chemosh the god of **Moab,** and Molech the god of Ammon.
24. 2 armed bands of Babylonians, Syrians, **Moabites,** and Ammonites
1 Chr 1.43 battle in the country of **Moab)**
4.22 Joash and Saraph, who married **Moabite** women and then settled
8. 8 lived in the country of **Moab,** he married Hodesh and had
11.22 brave deeds, including killing two great **Moabite** warriors.
11.26 Elnaam Ithmah from **Moab** Eliel, Obed, and Jaasiel from Zobah
18. 2 He also defeated the **Moabites,** who became his subjects and
18.11 took from the nations he conquered—Edom, **Moab,** Ammon,
2 Chr 20. 1 the armies of **Moab** and Ammon, together with their allies,
20.10 "Now the people of Ammon, **Moab,** and Edom have attacked us.
20.23 The Ammonites and the **Moabites** attacked the Edomite army
24.26 and Jehozabad, the son of a **Moabite** woman named Shimrith.)
Ezra 9. 1 countries of Ammon, **Moab,** and Egypt or from the Canaanites,
Neh 13. 1 said that no Ammonite or **Moabite** was ever to be permitted to
13. 2 the people of Ammon and **Moab** did not give food and water
13.23 Jewish men had married women from Ashdod, Ammon, and **Moab.**
Ps 60. 8 But I will use **Moab** as my wash-basin and I will throw
83. 6 the people of **Moab** and the Hagrites;
83. 8 ally of the Ammonites and **Moabites,** the descendants of Lot.
108. 9 But I will use **Moab** as my wash-basin and I will throw
Is 11.14 the people of Edom and **Moab,** and the people of Ammon will
15. 1 This is a message about **Moab.**
15. 1 in a single night, and silence covers the land of **Moab.**
15. 2 The people of **Moab** wail in grief over the cities of Nebo

Is 15. 5 My heart cries out for **Moab!**
15. 8 Everywhere at **Moab's** borders the sound of crying is heard.
15. 9 there will be a bloody slaughter of everyone left in **Moab.**
16. 1 the desert the people of **Moab** send a lamb as a present
16. 6 Judah say, "We have heard how proud the people of **Moab** are.
16. 7 people of **Moab** will weep because of the troubles they suffer.
16.11 I groan with sadness for **Moab,** with grief for Kir Heres.
16.12 The people of **Moab** wear themselves out going to their
16.13 That is the message the Lord gave earlier about **Moab.**
16.14 "In exactly three years **Moab's** great wealth will disappear.
25.10 Zion, but the people of **Moab** will be trampled down, just as
25.12 will destroy the fortresses of **Moab** with their high walls
Jer 9.25 of Egypt, Judah, Edom, Ammon, **Moab,** and the desert people,
22.20 out from the mountains of **Moab,** because all your allies have
25.19 all the people of Edom, **Moab,** and Ammon;
27. 3 to the kings of Edom, **Moab,** Ammon, Tyre, and Sidon through
40.11 Israelites who were in **Moab,** Ammon, Edom, and other countries,
48. 1 This is what the Lord Almighty said about **Moab:**
48. 1 the splendour of **Moab** is gone.
48. 2 captured Heshbon and plot to destroy the nation of **Moab.**
48. 4 **"Moab** has been destroyed;
48. 7 **"Moab,** you trusted in your strength and your wealth, but
48. 9 Set up a tombstone for **Moab;**
48.11 The Lord said, **"Moab** has always lived secure and has
48.11 **Moab** is like wine left to settle undisturbed and never
48.12 coming when I will send people to pour **Moab** out like wine.
48.13 the **Moabites** will be disillusioned with their god Chemosh,
48.14 "Men of **Moab,** why do you claim to be heroes, brave
48.15 **Moab** and its cities are destroyed;
48.16 **Moab's** doom approaches;
48.18 **Moab's** destroyer is here and has left its forts in ruins.
48.20 **'Moab** has fallen,' they will answer, 'weep for it;
48.20 Announce along the River Arnon that **Moab is destroyed!'**
48.24 Judgement has come on all the cities of **Moab,** far and near.
48.25 **Moab's** might has been crushed;
48.26 The Lord said, "Make **Moab** drunk, because it has rebelled
48.26 **Moab** will roll in its own vomit, and people will laugh.
48.27 **Moab,** remember how you jeered at the people of Israel?
48.28 "You people who live in **Moab,** leave your towns!
48.29 **Moab** is very proud!
48.31 will weep for everyone in **Moab** and for the people of Kir
48.33 and joy have been taken away from the fertile land of **Moab.**
48.35 will stop the people of **Moab** from making burnt-offerings at
48.36 "So my heart mourns for **Moab** and for the people of Kir
48.38 On all the house-tops of **Moab** and in all its public
48.38 mourning, because I have broken **Moab** like a jar that no one
48.39 **Moab** has been shattered!
48.39 **Moab** has been disgraced.
48.40 nation will swoop down on **Moab** like an eagle with its
48.41 On that day **Moab's** soldiers will be as frightened as a woman
48.42 **Moab** will be destroyed and will no longer be a nation,
48.43 Terror, pits, and traps are waiting for the people of **Moab.**
48.44 because the Lord has set the time for **Moab's** destruction.
48.45 and the mountain heights of the war-loving people of **Moab.**
48.46 Pity the people of **Moab!**
48.47 But in days to come the Lord will make **Moab** prosperous again.
48.47 of this is what the Lord has said will happen to **Moab.**
Ezek 25. 8 The Sovereign Lord said, "Because **Moab** has said that
25. 9 that defend the border of **Moab** be attacked, including even
25.10 of the eastern desert conquer **Moab,** together with Ammon,
25.10 so that **Moab** will no longer be a nation.
25.11 I will punish **Moab,** and they will know that I am the
Dan 11.41 but the countries of Edom, **Moab,** and what is left of Ammon
Amos 2. 1 Lord says, "The people of **Moab** have sinned again and again,
2. 1 fire upon the land of **Moab** and burn down the fortresses of
2. 2 The people of **Moab** will die in the noise of battle while
2. 3 will kill the ruler of **Moab** and all the leaders of the
Mic 6. 5 remember what King Balak of **Moab** planned to do to you and
Zeph 2. 8 have heard the people of **Moab** and Ammon insulting and
2. 9 of Israel, I swear that **Moab** and Ammon are going to be
2.10 is how the people of **Moab** and Ammon will be punished for

MOAN

Is 38.14 My voice was thin and weak, And I **moaned** like a dove.
Jer 25.36 You **moan** and cry out in distress because the Lord
Ezek 7.16 All of them wil! **moan** over their sins.
Nah 2. 7 her servants **moan** like doves and beat their breasts in sorrow.

MOB (1)

Mk 5. 9 man answered, "My name is **'Mob'**—there are so many of us!"
5.15 the man who used to have the **mob** of demons in him.
Lk 8.30 "My name is **'Mob,' "** he answered—because many demons had gone

MOB (2)

Judg 18.23 Why all this **mob?"**
Job 30.12 This **mob** attacks me head-on;
Ps 64. 2 me from the plots of the wicked, from **mobs** of evil men.
Jer 9. 2 They are all unfaithful, a **mob** of traitors.
18.22 Send a **mob** to plunder their homes without warning;
Ezek 23.46 "Bring a **mob** to terrorize them and rob them.
23.47 Let the **mob** stone them and attack them with swords, kill
Acts 17. 5 of the worthless loafers from the streets and formed a **mob.**
17.13 they came there and started exciting and stirring up the **mob.**.
19.29 The **mob** seized Gaius and Aristarchus, two Macedonians who were
21.31 The **mob** was trying to kill Paul, when a report was sent
21.35 the soldiers had to carry him because the **mob** was so wild.
2 Cor 6. 5 We have been beaten, imprisoned, and **mobbed;**

MOCK

Neh 4. 4 I prayed, "Listen to them **mocking** us, O God!
Job 11. 3 That your **mocking** words will leave us speechless?
17. 2 I watch how bitterly everyone **mocks** me.
34.37 in front of us all he **mocks** God.
Ps 2. 4 in heaven the Lord laughs and **mocks** their feeble plans.
35.15 trouble, they were all glad and gathered round to **mock** me;
35.16 Like men who would **mock** a cripple, they glared at me
44.13 you did to us, and they **mock** us and laugh at us.
55.12 If it were an enemy that **mocked** me, I could endure it;
59. 8 you **mock** all the heathen.
79. 4 they laugh at us and **mock** us.
102. 8 those who **mock** me use my name in cursing.
123. 4 We have been **mocked** too long by the rich and scorned by
Prov 1.26 I will **mock** you when terror strikes—[27] when it comes on you
Is 14. 4 does this, they are to **mock** the king of Babylonia and say:
66. 5 They **mock** you and say, 'Let the Lord show his greatness and
Jer 20. 7 they **mock** me all day long.
24. 9 People will **mock** them, make jokes about them, ridicule them,
29.18 People will **mock** them and use their name as a curse.
Lam 2.16 All your enemies **mock** you and glare at you with hate.
3.46 "We are insulted and **mocked** by all our enemies.
Ezek 5.15 They will look at you with disgust and will **mock** you.
22. 4 I have let the nations **mock** you and all the countries sneer
23.32 Everyone will scorn and **mock** you;
36. 4 were plundered and **mocked** by all the surrounding nations.
36.15 to listen to the nations **mocking** it or see the peoples sneer
Joel 2.17 other nations despise us and **mock** us by saying, 'Where is
Mt 20.19 the Gentiles, who will **mock** him, whip him, and crucify him;
27.29 then they knelt before him and **mocked** him.
27.31 When they had finished **mocking** him, they took the robe off
Mk 10.34 to the Gentiles, [34] who will **mock** him, spit on him, whip
15.20 they had finished **mocking** him, they took off the purple robe
Lk 18.32 to the Gentiles, who will **mock** him, insult him, and spit on
22.63 The men who were guarding Jesus **mocked** him and beat him.
23.11 Herod and his soldiers **mocked** Jesus and treated him with
23.36 The soldiers also **mocked** him:
Heb 11.36 Some were **mocked** and whipped, and others were put in chains
2 Pet 3. 3 They will **mock** you [4] and will ask, "He promised to come,
Jude 18 people will appear who will **mock** you, people who follow

MODEL

1 Sam 6. 4 They answered, "Five gold **models** of tumours and five gold mice,
6. 5 You must make these **models** of the tumours and of the mice
6. 8 box beside it the gold **models** that you are sending to him
6.11 the box containing the gold **models** of the mice
6.15 the box with the gold **models** in it, and placed them on
2 Kgs 16.10 Uriah the priest an exact **model** of it, down to the smallest
Acts 19.24 named Demetrius made silver **models** of the temple of the goddess
Heb 10. 1 Law is not a full and faithful **model** of the real things;

MODEST

Prov 11. 2 It is wiser to be **modest.**
Rom 12. 3 be **modest** in your thinking, and judge yourself according to the
1 Cor 12.23 treated with special **modesty,** [24] which the more beautiful parts
1 Tim 2. 9 want the women to be **modest** and sensible about their clothes
2.15 if she perseveres in faith and love and holiness, with **modesty.**

MOISTURE

Ps 32. 4 strength was completely drained, as **moisture** is dried up by
Lk 8. 6 plants sprouted, they dried up because the soil had no **moisture.**

MOLE

Lev 11.29 **Moles,** rats, mice, and lizards must be considered unclean.
Is 2.20 they have made, and abandon them to the **moles** and the bats.

MOLECH

Understood to be the name of a god, often written in Hebrew as "Milcom".

Lev 18.21 the worship of the god **Molech,** because that would bring
20. 2 the worship of the god **Molech** shall be stoned to death by
20. 3 one of his children to **Molech** and makes my sacred Tent
20. 5 join him in being unfaithful to me and worshipping **Molech.**
2 Sam 12.30 idol of the Ammonite god **Molech** David took a gold crown
1 Kgs 11. 5 the goddess of Sidon, and **Molech** the disgusting god of Ammon.
11. 7 and a place to worship **Molech,** the disgusting god of Ammon.
11.33 and **Molech,** the god of Ammon.
2 Kgs 23.10 his son or daughter as a burnt-offering to the god **Molech.**
23.13 Sidon, Chemosh the god of Moab, and **Molech** the god of Ammon.
1 Chr 20. 2 The Ammonite idol **Molech** had a gold crown which weighed
Is 57. 9 perfumes and ointments and go to worship the god **Molech.**
Jer 32.35 to sacrifice their sons and daughters to the god **Molech.**
49. 1 let the people who worship **Molech** take the territory of the
49. 3 Your god **Molech** will be taken into exile, together with his
Zeph 1. 5 me, but then take oaths in the name of the god **Molech.**
Acts 7.43 the tent of the god **Molech** that you carried, and the image

MOLEST

Ruth 2. 9 I have ordered my men not to **molest** you.
2.22 You might be **molested** if you went to someone else's field."
2 Sam 13.20 brother Absalom saw her, he asked, "Has Amnon **molested** you?

MOMENT

Ex	33. 5	with you even for a **moment,** I would completely destroy you.
Lev	13.14	But from the **moment** an open sore appears, he is unclean.
1 Sam	22. 8	own men, is at this **moment** looking for a chance to kill
Job	3.11	died in my mother's womb or died the **moment** I was born.
	8. 8	Look for a **moment** at ancient wisdom;
	37.14	Pause a **moment,** Job, and listen;
Ps	30. 5	His anger lasts only a **moment,** his goodness for a lifetime.
Prov	24.22	such men could be ruined in a **moment.**
Ecc	9.12	we are trapped at some evil **moment** when we least expect it.
Is	47. 9	But in a **moment,** in a single day, both of these things
	54. 7	"For one brief **moment** I left you;
	54. 8	away angry for only a **moment,** but I will show you my
Rom	13.11	For the **moment** when we will be saved is closer now than
Jas	4.14	of smoke, which appears for a **moment** and then disappears.

MONEY

Gen	31.15	now he has spent all the **money** he was paid for us.
	42.25	corn, to put each man's **money** back in his sack, and to
	42.27	his donkey and found his **money** at the top of the sack.
	42.28	"My **money** has been returned to me," he called to his brothers.
	42.35	out their sacks, every one of them found his bag of **money;**
	42.35	and when they saw the **money,** they and their father Jacob
	43.12	you also twice as much **money,** because you must
	43.12	take back the **money** that was returned
	43.15	gifts and twice as much **money,** and set out for Egypt with
	43.18	brought here because of the **money** that was returned in our
	43.21	and each man found his **money** in the top of his sack
	43.22	have also brought some more **money** with us to buy more food.
	43.22	We do not know who put our **money** back in our sacks."
	43.23	your father, must have put the **money** in your sacks for you.
	44. 1	carry, and put each man's **money** in the top of his sack.
	44. 2	brother's sack, together with the **money** for his corn."
	44. 8	the land of Canaan the **money** we found in the top of
	47.14	Joseph collected all the **money** and took it to the palace.
	47.15	When all the **money** in Egypt and Canaan was spent, the
	47.15	Our **money** is all gone."
	47.16	you food in exchange for it if your **money** is all gone."
	47.18	from you, sir, that our **money** is all gone and our livestock
Ex	21.34	He is to pay the **money** to the owner and may keep
	21.35	the two men shall sell the live bull and divide the **money;**
	22. 7	agrees to keep another man's **money** or other valuables for
	22.17	the father a sum of **money** equal to the bride-price for a
	22.25	"If you lend **money** to any of my people who are poor,
	30.13	amount of **money,** weighed according to the official standard.
	30.16	Collect this **money** from the people of Israel and spend
Lev	22.11	slaves, bought with his own **money** or born in his home, may
	25.28	he does not have enough **money** to buy the land back, it
	25.37	him pay interest on the **money** you lend him, and do not
	27. 2	sums of **money,** [3-7]according to the official standard:
	27.23	the **money** belongs to the Lord.
Num	3.48	standard, [48]and give this **money** to Aaron and his sons."
	35.31	He cannot escape this penalty by the payment of **money.**
Deut	14.25	your produce and take the **money** with you to the one place
	15. 1	you are to cancel the debts of those who owe you **money.**
	15. 2	Everyone who has lent **money** to a fellow-Israelite is to
	15. 2	he must not try to collect the **money;**
	15. 6	You will lend **money** to many nations, but you will not have
	21.20	he wastes **money** and is a drunkard.'
	22.19	of silver and give the **money** to the girl's father, because
	23.18	Also, no **money** earned in this way may be brought into
	23.19	"When you lend **money** or food or anything else
	24.15	he needs the **money** and has counted on getting it.
	27.25	curse on anyone who accepts **money** to murder an innocent person.'
	28.44	They will have **money** to lend you, but you will have none
Judg	9. 4	of Baal-of-the-Covenant, and with this **money** he hired a
	16.18	Then they came and brought the **money** with them.
	17. 2	Look, I have the **money.**
	17. 3	He gave the **money** back to his mother, and she said, "To
1 Sam	2.36	priest and ask him for **money** and food, and beg to be
	8. 3	were interested only in making **money,** so they accepted
2 Kgs	4. 1	now a man he owed **money** to has come to take away
	4. 7	and there will be enough **money** left over for you and your
	5.26	to accept **money** and clothes, olive-groves and vineyards,
	12. 4	them to save up the **money** paid in connection with the
	12. 4	regular sacrifices and the **money** given as free-will gifts.
	12. 5	to be responsible for the **money** brought by those he served,
	12. 5	and the **money** was to be used to repair
	12. 7	From now on you are not to keep the **money** you receive;
	12. 9	put in the box all the **money** given by the worshippers.
	12.10	was a large amount of **money** in the box, the royal secretary
	12.13	None of the **money,** however, was used to pay for making
	12.16	The **money** given for the repayment offerings and for the
	15.20	Menahem got the **money** from the rich men of Israel by
	22. 4	report on the amount of **money** that the priests on duty at
	22. 5	Tell him to give the **money** to the men who are in
	22. 9	"Your servants have taken the **money** that was in the Temple
2 Chr	24. 5	from all the people enough **money** to make the annual repairs
	24.10	and they brought their tax **money** and filled the box with it.
	24.11	Priest's representative would take the **money** out and return
	24.11	And so they collected a large sum of **money.**
	24.12	and Jehoiada would give the **money** to those who were in
	34. 9	The **money** that the Levite guards had collected in the
	34.10	This **money** was then handed over to the three men in
	34.14	While the **money** was being taken out of the storeroom,
	34.17	We have taken the **money** that was kept in the Temple and
Ezra	3. 7	The people gave **money** to pay the stonemasons and the
	7.17	"You are to spend this **money** carefully and buy bulls,
Neh	5. 4	said, "We had to borrow **money** to pay the royal tax on
	5.10	have let the people borrow **money** and corn from me, and so
	5.11	the debts they owe you—**money** or corn or wine or olive-oil.
	13. 2	Instead, they paid **money** to Balaam to curse Israel, but our
Esth	3.11	The king told him, "The people and their **money** are yours;
	4. 7	him and just how much **money** Haman had promised to put into
Job	17. 5	his friends for **money,** and his children suffer for it.
	22. 6	your brother repay you the **money** he owed, you took away his
	42.11	Each of them gave him some **money** and a gold ring.
Ps	119.72	gave means more to me than all the **money** in the world.
Prov	7.20	He took plenty of **money** with him and won't be back for
	11.16	lazy man will never have **money,** but an aggressive man will
	11.24	Some people spend their **money** freely and still grow richer.
	13. 8	man has to use his **money** to save his life, but no
	17.16	fool no good to spend **money** on an education, because he has
	19.14	can inherit a house and **money** from his parents, but only the
	21.20	but stupid people spend their **money** as fast as they get it.
	22. 7	Borrow **money** and you are the lender's slave.
	23. 5	Your **money** can be gone in a flash, as if it had
	27.26	and buy land with the **money** you get from selling some of
	29. 3	It is a foolish waste to spend **money** on prostitutes.
	29. 4	he is only concerned with **money,** he will ruin his country.
	31. 3	spend all your energy on sex and all your **money** on women;
	31.16	and buys it, and with **money** she has earned she plants a
Ecc	5.10	If you love **money,** you will never be satisfied;
	5.13	people save up their **money** for a time when they may need
	7.12	and will give you as much security as **money** can.
	10.19	cheers you up, but you can't have either without **money.**
	11. 1	Invest your **money** in foreign trade, and one of these days
Is	23.18	The **money** she earns by commerce will be dedicated to the Lord.
	23.18	the Lord will use her **money** to buy the food and the
	52. 3	people, "When you became slaves, no **money** was paid for you;
	55. 1	Come, you that have no **money**— buy corn and eat!
	55. 2	Why spend **money** on what does not satisfy?
Jer	6.13	Everyone, great and small, tries to make **money** dishonestly;
	8.10	Everyone, great and small, tries to make **money** dishonestly.
	15.10	I have not lent any **money** or borrowed any;
	17.11	The person who gets **money** dishonestly is like a bird
	32. 9	the field from Hanamel and weighed out the **money** to him;
	32.10	deed, had it witnessed, and weighed out the **money** on scales.
Ezek	16.31	But you are not out for **money** like a common prostitute.
	18. 8	He doesn't lend **money** for profit.
	18.13	worships disgusting idols, [13]and lends **money** for profit.
	18.17	He refuses to do evil and doesn't lend **money** for profit.
	22.25	the people, take all the **money** and property they can get,
Amos	2. 8	wine which they have taken from those who owe them **money.**
Mic	3.11	prophets give their revelations for **money**—and they all claim
Mt	6.24	You cannot serve both God and **money.**
	10. 9	Do not carry any gold, silver, or copper **money** in your pockets;
	19.21	you have and give the **money** to the poor, and you will
	20.11	took their **money** and started grumbling against the employer.
	20.15	have the right to do as I wish with my own **money?**
	25.16	at once and invested his **money** and earned another five thousand.
	25.18	dug a hole in the ground, and hid his master's **money.**
	25.25	afraid, so I went off and hid your **money** in the ground.
	25.27	you should have deposited my **money** in the bank, and I would
	25.28	Now, take the **money** away from him and give it to the
	26. 9	sold for a large amount and the **money** given to the poor!"
	27. 6	and said, "This is blood **money,** and it is against our Law
	27. 7	about it, they used the **money** to buy Potter's Field, as a
	27.10	for him, [10]and used the **money** to buy the potter's field,
	28.12	gave a large sum of **money** to the soldiers [13]and said,
	28.15	The guards took the **money** and did what they were told to
Mk	5.26	She had spent all her **money,** but instead of getting better
	6. 8	a stick—no bread, no beggar's bag, no **money** in your pockets.
	10.21	you have and give the **money** to the poor, and you will
	12.41	he watched the people as they dropped in their **money.**
	12.41	Many rich men dropped in a lot of **money;**
	14. 5	three hundred silver coins and the **money** given to the poor!"
	14.11	hear what he had to say, and promised to give him **money.**
Lk	3.14	said to them, "Don't take **money** from anyone by force or
	7.41	"There were two men who owed **money** to a money-lender,"
	9. 3	no beggar's bag, no food, no **money,** not even an extra shirt.
	12.33	Sell all your belongings and give the **money** to the poor.
	14.28	cost, to see if he has enough **money** to finish the job.
	15.13	sold his part of the property and left home with the **money.**
	15.13	far away, where he wasted his **money** in reckless living.
	16. 1	manager was wasting his master's **money,** [2]so he called him in
	16.13	You cannot serve both God and **money."**
	16.14	heard all this, they sneered at Jesus, because they loved **money.**
	18.22	you have and give the **money** to the poor, and you will
	19.23	Well, then, why didn't you put my **money** in the bank?
	22. 5	They were pleased and offered to pay him **money.**
Jn	12. 5	hundred silver coins and the **money** given to the poor?"
	12. 6	He carried the **money bag** and would help himself from it.
	13.29	was in charge of the **money bag,** some of the disciples
Acts	1.18	(With the **money** that Judas got for his evil act he
	2.45	and distribute the **money** among all, according to what each
	3. 2	the gate to beg for **money** from the people who were going
	3. 6	to him, "I have no **money** at all, but I give you
	4.34	would sell them, bring the **money** received from the sale,
	4.35	**money** was distributed to each one according to his need.
	4.37	field he owned, brought the **money,** and handed it over to the
	5. 2	he kept part of the **money** for himself and handed the rest
	5. 3	by keeping part of the **money** you received for the property?
	5. 4	and after you sold it, the **money** was yours.
	7.16	had bought from the clan of Hamor for a sum of **money.**
	8.18	So he offered **money** to Peter and John, [19]and said, "Give
	8.20	"May you and your **money** go to hell,
	8.20	for thinking that you can buy God's gift with **money!**
	11.30	this, then, and sent the **money** to the church elders by

Acts 16.16 She earned a lot of **money** for her owners by telling fortunes.
16.19 that their chance of making **money** was gone, they seized Paul
17. 9 pay the required amount of **money** to be released, and then
22.28 said, "I became one by paying a large amount of **money."**
24.17 went there to take some **money** to my own people and to
24.26 same time he was hoping that Paul would give him some **money;**
Rom 15.28 over to them all the **money** that has been raised for them,
1 Cor 16. 1 what you wrote about the **money** to be raised to help God's
16. 2 you must put aside some **money,** in proportion to what he has
16. 2 that there will be no need to collect **money** when I come.
2 Cor 11. 9 you I did not bother you for help when I needed **money;**
12.14 It is you I want, not your **money.**
1 Tim 3. 3 he must not love **money;**
3. 8 they must not drink too much wine or be greedy for **money;**
6.10 For the love of **money** is a source of all kinds of
Tit 1. 7 or quick-tempered, or a drunkard or violent or greedy for **money.**
1.11 not, and all for the shameful purpose of making **money.**
Heb 13. 5 free from the love of **money,** and be satisfied with what you
Jas 4.13 a year and go into business and make a lot of **money."**
2 Pet 2.15 of Beor, who loved the **money** he would get for doing wrong
Jude 11 For the sake of **money** they have given themselves over to the

MONEY-CHANGERS

Mt 21.12 overturned the tables of the **money-changers** and the stools of
Mk 11.15 overturned the tables of the **money-changers** and the stools of
Jn 2.14 and pigeons, and also the **money-changers** sitting at their tables.
2.15 he overturned the tables of the **money-changers** and scattered

MONEY-LENDER

Ex 22.25 not act like a **money-lender** and require him to pay interest.
Is 3.12 **Money-lenders** oppress my people, and their creditors cheat them.
Lk 7.41 were two men who owed money to a **money-lender,"** Jesus began.

MONKEY

1 Kgs 10.22 return, bringing gold, silver, ivory, apes, and **monkeys.**
2 Chr 9.21 return, bringing gold, silver, ivory, apes, and **monkeys.**

MONSTER
[SEA-MONSTER]

Gen 1.21 So God created the great **sea-monsters,** all kinds of
Job 7.12 Do you think I am a **sea-monster?**
9. 8 God spread out the heavens or trample the **sea-monster's** back.
9.13 He crushed his enemies who helped Rahab, the **sea-monster,**
26.12 by his skill he destroyed the **monster** Rahab.
26.13 sky clear, and his hand that killed the escaping **monster.**
40.15 Look at the **monster** Behemoth;
Ps 74.13 divided the sea and smashed the heads of the **sea-monsters;**
74.14 crushed the heads of the **monster** Leviathan and fed his body
89.10 You crushed the **monster** Rahab and killed it;
104.26 and in it plays Leviathan, that **sea-monster** which you made.
148. 7 Praise the Lord from the earth, **sea-monsters** and all ocean depths;
Is 27. 1 dragon, and to kill the **monster** that lives in the sea.
34.14 The night **monster** will come there looking for a place to rest.
51. 9 It was you that cut the **sea-monster** Rahab to pieces.
Jer 51.34 like a **monster** he swallowed it.
Ezek 29. 3 I am your enemy, you **monster** crocodile, lying in the river.
Amos 9. 3 of the sea, I will command the **sea-monster** to bite them.

MONTH

Gen 7.11 seventeenth day of the second **month** all the outlets of the
8. 4 seventeenth day of the seventh **month** the boat came to rest
8. 5 day of the tenth **month** the tops of the mountains appeared.
8.13 on the first day of the first **month,** the water was gone.
8.14 day of the second **month** the earth was completely dry.
18.10 One of them said, "Nine **months** from now I will come back,
18.11 were very old, and Sarah had stopped having her **monthly periods.**
18.14 As I said, nine **months** from now I will return, and Sarah
29.14 Jacob stayed there a whole **month.**
31.35 I am having my **monthly period."**
38.24 About three **months** later someone said to Judah, "Your
Ex 2. 2 what a fine baby he was, she hid him for three **months.**
12. 2 "This **month** is to be the first month of the year for
12. 3 the tenth day of this **month** each man must choose either a
12. 6 the fourteenth day of the **month,** the whole community of
12.18 fourteenth day of the first **month** to the evening of the
13. 4 Egypt on this day in the first **month,** the month of Abib.
13. 5 celebrate this festival in the first **month** of every year.
16. 1 fifteenth day of the second **month** after they had left Egypt,
19. 1 first day of the third **month** after they had left Egypt they
23.15 In the **month** of Abib, the month in which you left Egypt,
34.18 for seven days in the **month** of Abib,
34.18 because it was in that **month** that you left Egypt.
40. 2 first day of the first **month** set up the Tent of the
40.17 first day of the first **month** of the second year after they
Lev 12. 2 is ritually unclean, as she is during her **monthly period.**
12. 5 is ritually unclean, as she is during her **monthly period.**
15.19 When a woman has her **monthly period,** she remains unclean
15.20 which she sits or lies during her **monthly period** is unclean.
15.25 for several days outside her **monthly period** or if her flow
15.25 flow continues, just as she is during her **monthly period.**
15.33 semen, [33]a woman during her **monthly period,** or a man who
16.29 tenth day of the seventh **month** the Israelites and the
18.19 during her **monthly period,** because she is ritually unclean.
20.18 with a woman during her **monthly period,** both of them are to
23. 5 begins at sunset on the fourteenth day of the first **month.**
Lev 23.23 day of the seventh **month** observe a special day of rest,
23.26 tenth day of the seventh **month** is the day when the annual
23.32 the ninth day of the **month** to sunset on the tenth observe
23.33 day of the seventh **month** and continues for seven days.
23.39 days, beginning on the fifteenth day of the seventh **month.**
25. 9 tenth day of the seventh **month,** the Day of Atonement, send a
Num 1. 1 first day of the second **month** in the second year after the
1.18 first day of the second **month** and registered all the people
3.15 families, enrolling every male a **month** old or older, [16]and
3.22 total number of males one **month** old or older that were
3.28 total number of males one **month** old or older that were
3.34 total number of males one **month** old or older that were
3.39 all the Levite males one **month** old or older that Moses
3.40 every first-born male Israelite, one **month** old or older.
3.43 all the first-born males [43]one **month** old or older;
9. 1 Sinai Desert in the first **month** of the second year after the
9. 2 the fourteenth day of this **month,** beginning at sunset, the
9. 5 fourteenth day of the first **month** they did so in the Sinai
9.11 permitted to observe it one **month** later instead,
9.11 on the evening of the fourteenth day of the second **month.**
9.22 it was two days, a **month,** a year, or longer, as long
10.11 twentieth day of the second **month** in the second year after
11.20 days, [20]but for a whole **month,** until it comes out of your
11.21 you say that you will give them enough meat for a **month?**
18.16 at the age of one **month** for the fixed price of five
20. 1 In the first **month** the whole community of Israel came to
26.62 male Levites who were one **month** old or older numbered 23,000.
28.11 a burnt-offering to the Lord at the beginning of each **month:**
28.14 for the first day of each **month** throughout the year.
28.16 is to be held on the fourteenth day of the first **month.**
29. 1 day of the seventh **month** you are to gather for worship,
29. 6 the first day of the **month** with its grain-offering, and the
29. 7 Gather for worship on the tenth day of the seventh **month;**
29.12 Gather for worship on the fifteenth day of the seventh **month.**
33. 3 fifteenth day of the first **month** of the year, the day after
33.38 first day of the fifth **month** of the fortieth year after the
Deut 1. 3 first day of the eleventh **month** of the fortieth year after
16. 1 Lord your God by celebrating Passover in the **month** of Abib;
16. 1 on a night in that **month** that he rescued you from Egypt.
21.13 stay in your home and mourn for her parents for a **month;**
Josh 4.19 tenth day of the first **month** and made camp at Gilgal, east
5.10 Passover on the evening of the fourteenth day of the **month.**
Judg 11.37 Leave me alone for two **months,** so that I can go with
11.38 He told her to go and sent her away for two **months.**
11.39 After two **months** she came back to her father.
19. 2 father's house in Bethlehem, and stayed there four **months.**
20.47 to the Rock of Rimmon, and they stayed there four **months.**
1 Sam 6. 1 been in Philistia for seven **months,** [2]the people called the
11. 1 About a **month** later King Nahash of Ammon led his army
27. 7 David lived in Philistia for sixteen **months.**
2 Sam 6.11 It stayed there three **months,** and the Lord blessed Obed
11. 4 (She had just finished her **monthly** ritual of purification.)
24. 8 So after nine **months** and twenty days they returned to Jerusalem,
24.13 in your land or three **months** of running away from your
1 Kgs 4. 7 each man being responsible for one **month** out of the year.
4.27 governors, each one in the **month** assigned to him, supplied
5.14 and each group spent one **month** in Lebanon
5.14 and two **months** back home.
6. 1 in the second month, the **month** of Ziv, Solomon began work on
6.37 was laid in the second **month,** the month of Ziv, in the
6.38 In the eighth **month,** the month of Bul, in the eleventh
8. 2 Festival of Shelters in the seventh **month,** in the month of Ethanim.
11.15 men remained in Edom six **months,** and during that time they
12.32 day of the eighth **month,** like the festival in Judah.
12.33 fifteenth day of the eighth **month,** the day that he himself
2 Kgs 15. 8 king of Israel, and he ruled in Samaria for six **months.**
15.13 king of Israel, and he ruled in Samaria for one **month.**
23.31 king of Judah, and he ruled in Jerusalem for three **months.**
24. 8 king of Judah, and he ruled in Jerusalem for three **months.**
25. 1 tenth day of the tenth **month** of the ninth year of Zedekiah's
25. 3 ninth day of the fourth **month** of that same year, when the
25. 8 seventh day of the fifth **month** of the nineteenth year of
25.25 But in the seventh **month** of that year, Ishmael, the son
25.27 twenty-seventh day of the twelfth **month** of the
1 Chr 12.15 In the first **month** of one year, the time when the River
13.14 It stayed there three **months,** and the Lord blessed Obed
21.12 Or three **months** of running away from the armies of your enemies?
27. 1 Each **month** of the year a different group of twenty-four
27. 1 men was on duty under the commander for that **month.**
27. 2 The following were the commanders for each **month:**
27. 2 First **month:**
27. 2 Second **month:**
27. 2 Third **month:**
27. 2 Fourth **month:**
27. 2 Fifth **month:**
27. 2 Sixth **month:**
27. 2 Seventh **month:**
27. 2 Eighth **month:**
27. 2 Ninth **month:**
27. 2 Tenth **month:**
27. 2 Eleventh **month:**
27. 2 Twelfth **month:**
2 Chr 3. 2 the construction [2]in the second **month** of the fourth year
7.10 day of the seventh **month,** Solomon sent the people home.
15.10 in Jerusalem in the third **month** of the fifteenth year that
29. 3 In the first **month** of the year after Hezekiah became king,
29.17 first day of the first **month,** and by the eighth day they
29.17 sixteenth of the **month,** preparing the Temple for worship.
30. 1 proper time, in the first **month,** because not enough priests

2 Chr 30. 1 celebrate it in the second **month,** and the king sent word to
30.13 in Jerusalem in the second **month** to celebrate the Festival
30.15 the fourteenth day of the **month** they killed the lambs for
31. 7 started arriving in the third **month** and continued to pile up
31. 7 month and continued to pile up for the next four **months.**
35. 1 fourteenth day of the first **month** they killed the animals
36. 2 king of Judah, and he ruled in Jerusalem for three **months.**
36. 9 and he ruled in Jerusalem for three **months** and ten days.
Ezra 3. 1 By the seventh **month** the people of Israel were all settled
3. 6 day of the seventh **month** to burn sacrifices to the Lord.
3. 8 So in the second **month** of the year after they came back
6.15 the third day of the **month** Adar in the sixth year of
6.19 the fourteenth day of the first **month** of the following year.
7. 8 first day of the first **month,** and with God's help they
7. 8 arrived in Jerusalem on the first day of the fifth **month.**
8.31 twelfth day of the first **month** that we left the Ahava Canal
10. 9 twentieth day of the ninth **month,** all the men living in the
10.16 first day of the tenth **month** they began their investigation,
10.17 and within the next three **months** they investigated all
Neh 1. 1 In the **month** of Kislev in the twentieth year that
2. 1 One day four **months** later, when Emperor Artaxerxes was dining,
6.15 was finished on the twenty-fifth day of the **month** of Elul.
8. 1 By the seventh **month** the people of Israel were all settled
8. 1 the first day of that **month** they all assembled in Jerusalem,
9. 1 twenty-fourth day of the same **month** the people of Israel
Esth 1. 4 For six whole **months** he made a show of the riches of
2.12 oil of myrrh for six **months** and with oil of balsam for
2.16 in the tenth month, the **month** of Tebeth, Esther was brought
3. 7 in the first month, the **month** of Nisan, Haman ordered the
3. 7 find out the right day and **month** to carry out his plot.
3. 7 of the twelfth month, the **month** of Adar, was decided on.
3.12 thirteenth day of the first **month** Haman called the king's
4.11 But it has been a **month** since the king sent for me."
8. 9 the twenty-third day of the third **month,** the month of Sivan.
8.12 of the Jews, the thirteenth of Adar, the twelfth **month.**
9.19 the fourteenth day of the **month** of Adar as a joyous holiday,
9.22 this was a **month** that had been turned from a time of
Job 7. 3 **Month** after month I have nothing to live for;
14. 5 is decided beforehand— the number of **months** he will live.
Ps 104.19 You created the moon to mark the **months;**
Is 47.13 tell you from month to **month** what is going to happen to
Jer 1. 3 In the fifth **month** of that year the people of Jerusalem were
28. 1 same year, in the fifth **month** of the fourth year that
28.17 And Hananiah died in the seventh **month** of that same year.
36. 9 In the ninth **month** of the fifth year that Jehoiakim was
39. 1 In the tenth **month** of the ninth year that Zedekiah was
39. 2 day of the fourth **month** of Zedekiah's eleventh year as king,
41. 1 In the seventh **month** of that year, Ishmael, the son of
52. 4 tenth day of the tenth **month** of the ninth year of Zedekiah's
52. 6 ninth day of the fourth **month** of that same year, when the
52.12 tenth day of the fifth **month** of the nineteenth year of King
52.31 twenty-fifth day of the twelfth **month** of the thirty-seventh
Ezek 1. 1 fifth day of the fourth **month** of the thirtieth year, I,
8. 1 fifth day of the sixth **month** of the sixth year of our
20. 1 tenth day of the fifth **month** of the seventh year of our
24. 1 tenth day of the tenth **month** of the ninth year of our
26. 1 **month** of the eleventh year of our exile, the Lord spoke to
29. 1 twelfth day of the tenth **month** of the tenth year of our
29.17 first day of the first **month** of the twenty-seventh year of
30.20 seventh day of the first **month** of the eleventh year of our
31. 1 first day of the third **month** of the eleventh year of our
32. 1 first day of the twelfth **month** of the twelfth year of our
32.17 fifteenth day of the first **month** of the twelfth year of our
33.21 fifth day of the tenth **month** of the twelfth year of our
36.17 ritually unclean as a woman is during her **monthly period.**
39.12 will take the Israelites seven **months** to bury all the
39.14 After the seven **months** are over, men will be chosen to
45.18 first day of the first **month** you are to sacrifice a bull
45.20 the seventh day of the **month** you are to do the same
45.21 fourteenth day of the first **month** you will begin the
45.25 fifteenth day of the seventh **month,** the prince will offer on
47.12 will have fresh fruit every **month,** because they are watered
Dan 4.29 Only twelve **months** later, while he was walking about on
10. 4 twenty-fourth day of the first **month** of the year, I was
Hos 2.11 her festivities—her annual and **monthly** festivals and her
Hag 1. 1 first day of the sixth **month,** the Lord spoke through the
1.15 twenty-fourth day of the sixth **month** of the second year that
2. 1 twenty-first day of the seventh **month** of that same year, the
2.10 twenty-fourth day of the ninth **month** of the second year that
2.18 twenty-fourth day of the ninth **month,** the day that the
2.20 day, the twenty-fourth of the **month,** the Lord gave Haggai a
Zech 1. 1 In the eighth **month** of the second year that Darius was
1. 7 of the eleventh month (the **month** of Shebat), the Lord gave
7. 1 of the ninth month (the **month** of Kislev), the Lord gave me
7. 3 by fasting in the fifth **month** as we have done for so
7. 5 in the fifth and seventh **months** during these seventy years,
8.19 fourth, fifth, seventh, and tenth **months** will become
11. 8 me, and I got rid of them all in a single **month.**
Lk 1.24 became pregnant and did not leave the house for five **months.**
1.26 the sixth **month** of Elizabeth's pregnancy God sent the angel
1.36 she herself is now six **months** pregnant, even though she is
1.56 Mary stayed about three **months** with Elizabeth and then went
Jn 4.35 You have a saying, 'Four more **months** and then the harvest.'
Acts 7.20 for at home for three **months,** [21] and when he was put out
19. 8 synagogue and during three **months** spoke boldly with the people,
20. 3 Then he came to Achaia, [3] where he stayed three **months.**
28.11 After three **months** we sailed away on a ship from Alexandria,
Gal 4.10 You pay special attention to certain days, **months,** seasons,
Heb 11.23 of Moses hide him for three **months** after he was born.
Rev 9. 5 kill these people, but only to torture them for five **months.**
9. 6 During those five **months** they will seek death, but will not
Rev 9.10 that they have the power to hurt people for five **months.**
9.15 very day of this very **month** and year they had been kept
11. 2 who will trample on the Holy City for forty-two **months.**
13. 5 and it was permitted to have authority for forty-two **months.**
22. 2 which bears fruit twelve times a year, once each **month;**

MONUMENT

1 Sam 15.12 where he had built a **monument** to himself, and then had gone
2 Sam 18.18 Absalom had built a **monument** for himself in King's Valley,
18.18 himself, and to this day it is known as Absalom's **Monument.**
Jer 43.13 will destroy the sacred stone **monuments** at Heliopolis in
Mt 23.29 and decorate the **monuments** of those who lived good lives;

MOO

1 Sam 6.12 They were **mooing** as they went.
15.14 "Why, then, do I hear cattle **mooing** and sheep bleating?"

MOOD

Ruth 3. 7 Boaz had finished eating and drinking, he was in a good **mood.**
1 Sam 25.36 drunk and in a good **mood,** so she did not tell him
Esth 5. 9 Haman left the banquet he was happy and in a good **mood.**

MOON

[NEW MOON FESTIVAL]

Gen 1.16 rule over the day and the **moon** to rule over the night;
37. 9 I saw the sun, the **moon,** and eleven stars bowing down to
Num 10.10 joyful occasions—at your **New Moon Festivals** and your other
Deut 4.19 you see in the sky—the sun, the **moon,** and the stars.
17. 3 or the sun or the **moon** or the stars, contrary to the
Josh 10.12 **Moon,** stop over Aijalon Valley."
10.13 sun stood still and the **moon** did not move until the nation
1 Sam 20. 5 "Tomorrow is the **New Moon Festival,"** David replied,
20.18 "Since tomorrow is the **New Moon Festival,** your absence will
20.24 At the **New Moon Festival,** King Saul came to the meal [25]and
20.27 after the **New Moon Festival,** David's place was still empty,
20.34 nothing that day—the second day of the **New Moon Festival.**
2 Kgs 4.23 "It's neither a Sabbath nor a **New Moon Festival."**
23. 5 to Baal, to the sun, the **moon,** the planets, and the stars.
1 Chr 23.31 on the Sabbath, the **New Moon Festival,** and other festivals.
2 Chr 2. 4 well as on Sabbaths, **New Moon Festivals,** and other holy days
8.13 Sabbaths, **New Moon Festivals,** and the three annual
31. 3 the Sabbath, at the **New Moon Festival,** and at the other
Ezra 3. 5 be offered at the **New Moon Festival** and at all the other
Neh 10.33 for Sabbaths, **New Moon Festivals,** and other festivals,
Job 25. 5 In his eyes even the **moon** is not bright, nor the stars
26. 9 He hides the full **moon** behind a cloud.
31.26 the sun in its brightness or the **moon** in all its beauty.
Ps 8. 3 you have made, at the **moon** and the stars, which you set
33. 6 his command, the sun, **moon,** and stars by his spoken word.
72. 5 shines, as long as the **moon** gives light, for ages to come.
72. 7 and may prosperity last as long as the **moon** gives light.
74.16 you set the sun and the **moon** in their places;
81. 3 festival, when the moon is new and when the **moon** is full.
89.37 permanent as the **moon,** that faithful witness in the sky."
104.19 You created the **moon** to mark the months;
121. 6 not hurt you during the day, nor the **moon** during the night.
136. 7 He made the sun and the **moon;**
136. 9 the **moon** and the stars to rule over the night;
148. 3 Praise him, sun and **moon;**
Ecc 12. 2 light of the sun, the **moon,** and the stars will grow dim
Song 6.10 beautiful and bright, as dazzling as the sun or the **moon.**
Is 1.13 I cannot stand your **New Moon Festivals,** your Sabbaths, and
1.14 I hate your **New Moon Festivals** and holy days;
13.10 be dark when it rises, and the **moon** will give no light.
24.23 The **moon** will grow dark, and the sun will no longer shine,
30.26 The **moon** will be as bright as the sun, and the sun
34. 4 The sun, **moon,** and stars will crumble to dust.
45.12 I control the sun, the **moon,** and the stars.
60.19 your light by day Or the **moon** be your light by night;
60.20 be your eternal light, More lasting than the sun and **moon.**
66.23 On every **New Moon Festival** and every Sabbath, people of
Jer 8. 2 out before the sun, the **moon,** and the stars, which these
31.35 for light by day, the **moon** and the stars to shine at
Ezek 32. 7 hide behind the clouds, and the **moon** will give no light.
45.17 of Israel at the **New Moon Festivals,** the Sabbaths, and the
46. 1 to be opened on the Sabbath and at the **New Moon Festival.**
46. 3 Each Sabbath and each **New Moon Festival** all the people are
46. 6 At the **New Moon Festival** he will offer a young bull, six
Joel 2.10 The sun and the **moon** grow dark, and the stars no longer
2.31 will be darkened, and the **moon** will turn red as blood before
3.15 The sun and the **moon** grow dark, and the stars no longer
Hab 3.11 of your shining spear, the sun and the **moon** stood still.
Zeph 1. 5 on the roof and worships the sun, the **moon,** and the stars.
Mt 24.29 sun will grow dark, the **moon** will no longer shine, the stars
Mk 13.24 sun will grow dark, the **moon** will no longer shine, [25] the
Lk 21.25 be strange things happening to the sun, the **moon,** and the
Acts 2.20 will be darkened, and the **moon** will turn red as blood,
1 Cor 15.41 has its own beauty, the **moon** another beauty, and the stars a
Rev 6.12 black cloth, and the **moon** turned completely red like blood.
8.12 and a third of the **moon,** and a third of the stars,
12. 1 sun and who had the **moon** under her feet and a crown
21.23 of the sun or the **moon** to shine on it, because the

MORALE

Deut 20. 8 Otherwise, he will destroy the **morale** of the others.'
Is 19. 3 the plans of the Egyptians and destroy their **morale.**

MORDECAI (1)

Esther's cousin.

Esth 2.1-18 **Esther becomes queen**
19-23 **Mordecai saves the king's life**
3.1-15 **Haman plots to destroy the Jews**
4.1-17 **Mordecai asks for Esther's help**
5.9-14 **Haman plots to kill Mordecai**
6.1-13 **The king honours Mordecai**
6.14–7.10 **Haman is put to death**
8.1-17 **The Jews are told to fight back**
9.1-19 **The Jews destroy their enemies**
20-32 **The Festival of Purim**
10.1-3 **The greatness of Xerxes and Mordecai**

MORE

Mt 6.25 After all, isn't life worth **more** than food?
6.25 And isn't the body worth **more** than clothes?
6.26 Aren't you worth much **more** than birds?
10.31 you are worth much **more** than many sparrows!
10.37 loves his father or mother **more** than me is not fit to
10.37 loves his son or daughter **more** than me is not fit to
11. 9 Yes indeed, but you saw much **more** than a prophet.
12.12 And a man is worth much **more** than a sheep!
13.12 will be given more, so that he will have **more** than enough;
20.10 be hired came to be paid, they thought they would get **more;**
21.36 the man sent other slaves, **more** than the first time, and the
25.29 even more will be given, and he will have **more** than enough;
26.53 at once he would send me **more** than twelve armies of angels?
Mk 4.25 has something will be given **more,** and the person who has
7.36 but the more he ordered them not to, the **more** they spoke.
9.24 Help me to have **more!"**
10.30 for the gospel, [30] will receive much **more** in this present age.
14. 5 could have been sold for **more** than three hundred silver coins
Lk 3.13 "Don't collect **more** than is legal," he told them.
7.26 Yes indeed, but you saw much **more** than a prophet.
7.42 Which one, then, will love him **more?"**
7.43 Simon, "that it would be the one who was forgiven **more."**
8.18 has something will be given **more,** but whoever has nothing will
12. 7 you are worth much **more** than many sparrows!
12.24 You are worth so much **more** than birds!
12.48 more is required from the person to whom much **more** is given.
14.22 has been carried out, sir, but there is room for **more.'**
14.26 disciple unless he loves me **more** than he loves his father
15.17 my father's hired workers have **more** than they can eat, and
19.26 'that to every person who has something, even **more** will be given;
21. 3 you that this poor widow put in **more** than all the others.
Jn 6. 7 a little, it would take **more** than two hundred silver coins
12.24 grain of wheat remains no **more** than a single grain unless it
21.15 son of John, do you love me **more** than these others do?"
Acts 5.14 But **more and more** people were added to the group—
23.13 There were **more** than forty who planned this together.
23.21 to them, because there are **more** than forty men who will be
24.11 for yourself, it was no **more** than twelve days ago that I
1 Cor 4.13 We are no **more** than this world's refuse;
13. 1 love, my speech is no **more** than a noisy gong or a
14.18 that I speak in strange tongues much **more** than any of you.
15. 6 Then he appeared to **more** than five hundred of his followers
15.15 **More** than that, we are shown to be lying about God,
16. 7 I want to see you **more** than just briefly in passing;
2 Cor 4.15 and as God's grace reaches **more and more** people, they will
5. 9 **More** than anything else, however, we want to please him,
8. 3 gave as much as they could, and even **more** than they could.
8. 5 It was **more** than we could have hoped for!
9. 8 is able to give you **more** than you need, so that you
9. 8 need for yourselves and **more** than enough for every good cause.
Eph 3.20 able to do so much **more** than we can ever ask for,
Phil 1. 9 love will keep on growing **more and more,** together with true
1.21 Death, then, will bring **more.**
4.12 be in need and what it is to have **more** than enough.
4.16 **More** than once when I needed help in Thessalonica, you
4.18 you have given me—and it has been **more** than enough!
1 Thes 2.18 myself tried to go back **more** than once, but Satan would not
3.12 and for all people grow **more and more** and become as great
4. 1 you in the name of the Lord Jesus to do even **more.**
4.10 So we beg you, our brothers, to do even **more.**
2 Tim 4. 3 collect for themselves **more and more** teachers who will tell them
Phlm 16 he is not just a slave, but much **more** than a slave:
21 I ask—in fact I know that you will do even **more.**
Heb 11.26 Messiah was worth far **more** than all the treasures of Egypt,

MORNING

Gen 1. 5 Evening passed and **morning** came—that was the first day.
1. 8 Evening passed and **morning** came—that was the second day.
1.13 Evening passed and **morning** came—that was the third day.
1.19 Evening passed and **morning** came—that was the fourth day.
1.23 Evening passed and **morning** came—that was the fifth day.
1.31 Evening passed and **morning** came—that was the sixth day.
19. 2 In the **morning** you can get up early and go on your
19.27 Early the next **morning** Abraham hurried to the place
20. 8 Early the next **morning** Abimelech called all his officials
21.14 Early the next **morning** Abraham gave Hagar some food and
22. 3 Early the next **morning** Abraham cut some wood for the sacrifice,
24.54 they got up in the **morning,** he said, "Let me go back
26.31 Early next **morning** each man made his promise and sealed
28.18 Jacob got up early next **morning,** took the stone that was
29.25 Not until the next **morning** did Jacob discover that it was Leah.
31.55 Early the next **morning** Laban kissed his grandchildren
40. 6 came to them in the **morning,** he saw that they were upset.
Gen 41. 8 In the **morning** he was worried, so he sent for all the
44. 3 Early in the **morning** the brothers were sent on their way
49.27 **Morning** and evening he kills and devours."
Ex 7.15 and meet him in the **morning** when he goes down to the
8.20 said to Moses, "Early tomorrow **morning** go and meet the king
9.13 said to Moses, "Early tomorrow **morning** meet with the king
10.13 By **morning** it had brought the locusts.
12.10 You must not leave any of it until **morning;**
12.22 Not one of you is to leave the house until **morning.**
16. 7 In the **morning** you will see the dazzling light of the
16. 8 as you want in the **morning,** because he has heard how much
16.12 to eat, and in the **morning** they will have all the bread
16.13 the camp, and in the **morning** there was dew all round the
16.20 The next **morning** it was full of worms and smelt rotten, and
16.21 Every **morning** each one gathered as much as he needed;
18.13 the people, and he was kept busy from **morning** till night.
18.14 standing here from **morning** till night to consult you?"
19.16 On the **morning** of the third day there was thunder and lightning,
23.18 festivals is not to be left until the following **morning.**
24. 4 Early the next **morning** he built an altar at the foot of
27.21 There in my presence it is to burn from evening until **morning.**
29.34 the bread is not eaten by **morning,** it is to be burnt;
29.39 of the lambs in the **morning** and the other in the evening.
29.41 amounts of flour, olive-oil, and wine as in the **morning.**
30. 7 Every **morning** when Aaron comes to get the lamps ready, he
32. 6 Early the next **morning** they brought some animals to burn
34. 2 Be ready tomorrow **morning,** and come up Mount Sinai to meet
34. 4 and early the next **morning** he carried them up Mount Sinai,
34.25 not keep until the following **morning** any part of the animal
36. 3 Israel continued to bring Moses their offerings every **morning.**
Lev 6.12 Every **morning** the priest shall put firewood on it, arrange
6.20 half in the **morning** and half in the evening.
7.15 none of it may be left until the next **morning.**
22.30 the same day and leave none of it until the next **morning.**
24. 3 and keep them burning until **morning,** there in the Lord's
Num 9.12 the food until the following **morning** and do not break any of
9.21 remained only from evening until **morning,** and they moved on
11. 8 The next **morning** the people would go round and gather it,
14.40 Early the next **morning** they started out to invade
16. 5 Korah and his followers, "Tomorrow **morning** the Lord will
16. 6 Tomorrow **morning** you and your followers take firepans,
22.13 The next **morning** Balaam went to Balak's messengers and said,
22.21 So the next **morning** Balaam saddled his donkey and went
22.41 Next **morning** Balak took Balaam up to Bamoth Baal, from
28. 4 first lamb in the **morning,** and the second in the evening,
28. 8 as the **morning** offering, together with its wine-offering.
28.23 Offer these in addition to the regular **morning** burnt-offering.
Deut 16. 7 and the next **morning** return home.
28.67 Every **morning** you will wish for evening;
28.67 every evening you will wish for **morning.**
Josh 3. 1 The next **morning** Joshua and all the people of Israel got
6.12 got up early the next **morning,** and for the second time the
7.14 tell them that in the **morning** they will be brought forward,
7.16 Early the next **morning** Joshua brought Israel forward,
8.10 Early in the **morning** Joshua got up and called the soldiers
Judg 6.28 got up early the next **morning,** they found that the altar to
6.31 Anyone who stands up for him will be killed before **morning.**
6.37 If in the **morning** there is dew only on the wool but
6.38 got up early the next **morning,** he squeezed the wool and
6.40 The next **morning** the wool was dry, but the ground was wet
9.33 Get up tomorrow **morning** at sunrise and make a sudden
19. 5 On the **morning** of the fourth day they woke up early and
19. 8 Early in the **morning** of the fifth day he started to leave,
19.25 abused her all night long and didn't stop until **morning.**
19.27 Her husband got up that **morning,** and when he opened the
20.19 Israelites started out the next **morning** and made camp near
21. 4 Early the next **morning** the people built an altar there,
Ruth 2. 7 has been working since early **morning** and has just now
3.13 the night, and in the **morning** we will find out whether or
3.13 Now lie down and stay here till **morning."**
1 Sam 1.19 The next **morning** Elkanah and his family got up early,
3.15 Samuel stayed in bed until **morning;**
5. 3 Early next **morning** the people of Ashdod saw that the
5. 4 Early the following **morning** they saw that the statue had
9.19 Tomorrow **morning** I will answer all your questions and send
15.12 Early the following **morning** he went off to find Saul.
17.16 Goliath challenged the Israelites every **morning** and evening
17.20 got up early the next **morning,** left someone else in charge
19. 2 Please be careful tomorrow **morning;**
19.11 men to watch David's house and kill him the next **morning.**
20.35 following **morning** Jonathan went to the fields to meet David,
25.22 I don't kill every last one of those men before **morning!"**
25.34 me, all of Nabal's men would have been dead by **morning!"**
25.36 so she did not tell him anything until the next **morning.**
29.10 So then, David, tomorrow **morning** all of you who left
29.11 out early the following **morning** to go back to Philistia,
2 Sam 2.27 men would have kept on chasing you until tomorrow **morning."**
2.29 all the next **morning,** they arrived back at Mahanaim.
11.14 The next **morning** David wrote a letter to Joab and sent
19. 7 don't, not one of them will be with you by tomorrow **morning.**
24.11 The next **morning,** after David got up, [13] Gad went to him,
24.15 Israel, which lasted from that **morning** until the time that
1 Kgs 3.21 The next **morning,** when I woke up and was going to feed
17. 6 brought him bread and meat every **morning** and every evening.
2 Kgs 3.20 next **morning,** at the time of the regular morning sacrifice,
3.22 they got up the following **morning,** the sun was shining on
4.18 the boy went out one **morning** to join his father, who was
6.15 Early the next **morning** Elisha's servant got up, went out
7. 9 If we wait until **morning** to tell it, we are sure to
10. 8 city gate and to be left there until the following **morning.**
10. 9 In the **morning,** he went out to the gate and said to

2 Kgs 16.15 the **morning** burnt-offerings and the evening grain-offerings,
1 Chr 9.27 their duty to guard it and to open the gates every **morning.**
16.40 Every **morning** and evening they were to burn sacrifices
23.30 and glorify the Lord every **morning** and every evening [31] and
2 Chr 2. 4 we will offer burnt-offerings every **morning** and evening, as
13.11 Every **morning** and every evening they offer him incense
20.20 Early the next **morning** the people went out to the wild
31. 3 animals for the burnt-offerings each **morning** and evening,
Ezra 3. 3 to burn on it the regular **morning** and evening sacrifices.
Neh 7. 3 of Jerusalem opened in the **morning** until well after sunrise
13.21 them, "It's no use waiting out there for **morning** to come.
Esth 2.14 the evening, and the next **morning** she would be taken to
5.14 Tomorrow **morning** you can ask the king to have Mordecai
Job 1. 5 The **morning** after each feast, Job would get up early and
3. 9 Keep the **morning** star from shining;
4.20 in the **morning,** but die unnoticed before evening comes.
7.18 You inspect him every **morning** and test him every minute.
Ps 5. 3 you hear my voice in the **morning;**
19. 5 it comes out in the **morning** like a happy bridegroom,
30. 5 Tears may flow in the night, but joy comes in the **morning.**
55.17 **Morning,** noon, and night my complaints and groans go up to him,
59.16 every **morning** I will sing aloud of your constant love.
73.14 every **morning** you have punished me.
73.20 They are like a dream that goes away in the **morning;**
88.13 every **morning** I pray to you.
90. 5 sprout in the **morning,** [6] that grow and burst into bloom,
90.14 Fill us each **morning** with your constant love, so that we
92. 2 love every **morning** and your faithfulness every night,
110. 3 Like the dew of early **morning** your young men will come to
143. 8 Remind me each **morning** of your constant love, for I put my
Prov 23.32 The next **morning** you will feel as if you had been bitten
27.14 as wake him up early in the **morning** with a loud greeting.
Ecc 11. 6 Do your sowing in the **morning** and in the evening, too.
Song 2.17 until the **morning** breezes blow and the darkness disappears.
4. 6 until the **morning** breezes blow and the darkness disappears.
Is 5.11 get up early in the **morning** to start drinking, and you spend
14.12 "King of Babylonia, bright **morning** star,
17.11 sprouted and blossomed the very **morning** you planted them,
17.14 In the evening they cause terror, but by **morning** they are gone.
21.12 I answer, "**Morning** is coming, but night will come again.
28.19 It will strike you again and again, **morning** after morning.
50. 4 Every **morning** he makes me eager to hear what he is going
58. 8 shine on you like the **morning** sun, and your wounds will be
Jer 20. 3 The next **morning,** after Pashhur had released me from the chains,
20.16 cries of pain in the **morning** and the battle alarm at noon,
Lam 3.23 continue, [23] Fresh as the **morning,** as sure as the sunrise.
3.63 From **morning** till night they jeer at me.
Ezek 12. 8 The next **morning** the Lord spoke to me.
33.22 the man arrived the next **morning,** the Lord gave me back the
46.13 The Lord says, "Every **morning** a one-year-old lamb
46.14 is to be made every **morning,** together with one litre of
46.15 are to be offered to the Lord every **morning** for ever."
Dan 8.14 during which evening and **morning** sacrifices will not be offered.
8.26 vision about the evening and **morning** sacrifices which has
Hos 6. 4 Your love for me disappears as quickly as **morning** mist;
7. 6 anger smouldered, and in the **morning** it burst into flames.
12. 1 Israel do from **morning** to night is useless and destructive.
13. 3 these people will disappear like **morning** mist, like the dew
Amos 4. 4 bring animals to be sacrificed **morning** after morning, and
Mic 2. 1 When **morning** comes, as soon as they have the chance, they do
Zeph 3. 3 hungry wolves, too greedy to leave a bone until **morning.**
3. 5 Every **morning** without fail, he brings justice to his people.
Mt 14.25 and six o'clock in the **morning** Jesus came to the disciples,
16. 3 And early in the **morning** you say, 'It is going to rain,
20. 1 went out early in the **morning** to hire some men to work
21.18 way back to the city early next **morning,** Jesus was hungry.
27. 1 Early in the **morning** all the chief priests and the elders
28. 1 After the Sabbath, as Sunday **morning** was dawning, Mary
Mk 1.35 early the next **morning,** long before daylight, Jesus got up
6.48 and six o'clock in the **morning** he came to them, walking on
11.20 Early next **morning,** as they walked along the road, they saw
15. 1 Early in the **morning** the chief priests met hurriedly with the
15.25 It was nine o'clock in the **morning** when they crucified him.
16. 2 Very early on Sunday **morning,** at sunrise, they went to the tomb.
Lk 21.38 Early each **morning** all the people went to the Temple to
24. 1 Very early on Sunday **morning** the women went to the tomb,
Jn 8. 2 Early the next **morning** he went back to the Temple.
18.28 Early in the **morning** Jesus was taken from Caiaphas' house
20. 1 Early on Sunday **morning,** while it was still dark, Mary
Acts 2.15 it is only nine o'clock in the **morning.**
12.18 **morning** came, there was a tremendous confusion among the guards—
16.35 The next **morning** the Roman authorities sent police officers
23.12 The next **morning** some Jews met together and made a plan.
28.23 From **morning** till night he explained to them his message about
2 Pet 1.19 and the light of the **morning** star shines in your hearts.
Rev 2.26 I will also give them the **morning** star.
22.16 I am the bright **morning** star."

MORTAL

Gen 6. 3 they are **mortal.**
2 Sam 1.15 man struck the Amalekite and **mortally** wounded him, [16] and
Job 21. 4 My quarrel is not with **mortal** men;
Ps 9.20 make them know that they are only **mortal** beings.
10.18 their favour, so that **mortal** men may cause terror no more.
22.29 all **mortal** men will bow down before him.
78.39 remembered that they were only **mortal** beings, like a wind
89.47 remember that you created all of us **mortal!**
Is 2.22 Put no more confidence in **mortal** men.
Is 51.12 Why should you fear **mortal** man, who is no more enduring
Jer 17. 5 and puts his trust in man, in the strength of **mortal** man.
Ezek 2. 1 Then I heard a voice [1] saying, "**Mortal man,** stand up.
2. 3 I heard the voice continue, [3] "**Mortal man,** I am sending you
2. 6 "But you, **mortal man,** must not be afraid of them or of
2. 8 "**Mortal man,** listen to what I tell you.
3. 1 God said, "**Mortal man,** eat this scroll;
3. 3 He said, "**Mortal man,** eat this scroll that I give you;
3. 4 Then God said, "**Mortal man,** go to the people of Israel
3.10 God continued, "**Mortal man,** pay close attention and
3.17 "**Mortal man,**" he said, "I am making you a watchman
3.25 will be tied with ropes, **mortal man,** and you will not be
4. 1 God said, "**Mortal man,** get a brick, put it in front of
4.16 And he added, "**Mortal man,** I am going to cut off the
5. 1 The Lord said, "**Mortal man,** take a sharp sword and use it
6. 2 "**Mortal man,**" he said, "look towards the mountains of
7. 2 "**Mortal man,**" he said, "this is what I, the Sovereign Lord,
8. 5 God said to me, "**Mortal man,** look towards the north."
8. 6 God said to me, "**Mortal man,** do you see what is happening?
8. 8 He said, "**Mortal man,** break through the wall here."
8.12 God asked me, "**Mortal man,** do you see what the
8.15 He asked, "**Mortal man,** do you see that?
8.17 The Lord said to me, "**Mortal man,** do you see that?
11. 2 God said to me, "**Mortal man,** these men make evil plans
11. 4 Now then, denounce them, **mortal man.**"
11.15 "**Mortal man,**" he said, "the people who live in
12. 2 "**Mortal man,**" he said, "you are living among rebellious people.
12. 3 "Now, **mortal man,** pack a bundle just as a refugee would,
12. 9 "**Mortal man,**" he said, "now that those Israelite rebels
12.18 "**Mortal man,**" he said, "tremble when you eat, and
12.22 "**Mortal man,**" he said, "why do the people of Israel
12.27 The Lord said to me, [27] "**Mortal man,** the Israelites
13. 2 "**Mortal man,**" he said, "denounce the prophets of Israel
13.17 The Lord said, "Now, **mortal man,** look at the women
14. 3 "**Mortal man,**" he said, "these men have given their
14.13 "**Mortal man,**" he said, "if a country sins and is
15. 2 "**Mortal man,**" he said, "how does a vine compare with a tree?
16. 2 "**Mortal man,**" he said, "point out to Jerusalem what
17. 2 "**Mortal man,**" he said, "tell the Israelites a parable
20. 3 "**Mortal man,**" he said, "speak to these men and tell
20. 4 "Are you ready to pass sentence on them, **mortal man?**
20.27 **mortal man,** tell the Israelites what I, the Sovereign Lord,
20.46 "**Mortal man,**" he said, "look towards the south.
21. 2 "**Mortal man,**" he said, "denounce Jerusalem.
21. 6 "**Mortal man,** groan as if your heart is breaking with despair.
21. 9 The Lord said to me, [9] "**Mortal man,** prophesy.
21.12 Howl in grief, **mortal man;**
21.14 "Now, **mortal man,** prophesy.
21.19 "**Mortal man,**" he said, "mark out two roads by which
21.28 "**Mortal man,** prophesy.
22. 2 "**Mortal man,**" he said, "are you ready to judge the city
22.18 The Lord said to me, [18] "**Mortal man,** the Israelites
22.24 "**Mortal man,**" he said, "tell the Israelites that their land
23. 2 "**Mortal man,**" he said, "there were once two sisters.
23.36 The Lord said to me, "**Mortal man,** are you ready to
24. 2 "**Mortal man,**" he said, "write down today's date,
24.16 "**Mortal man,**" he said, "with one blow I am going to
24.25 The Lord said, "Now, **mortal man,** I will take away from
25. 2 "**Mortal man,**" he said, "denounce the country of Ammon.
26. 2 "**Mortal man,**" he said, "this is what the people in the
27. 2 The Lord said to me, [2] "**Mortal man,** sing a funeral song
28. 2 "**Mortal man,**" he said, "tell the ruler of Tyre what I,
28.12 "**Mortal man,**" he said, "grieve for the fate that is
28.21 Lord said to me, [21] "**Mortal man,** denounce the city of Sidon.
29. 2 "**Mortal man,**" he said, "denounce the king of Egypt.
29.18 "**Mortal man,**" he said, "King Nebuchadnezzar of
30. 2 "**Mortal man,**" he said, "prophesy and announce what I,
30.21 "**Mortal man,**" he said, "I have broken the arm of the
31. 2 "**Mortal man,**" he said, "say to the king of Egypt and
32. 2 "**Mortal man,**" he said, "give a solemn warning to the
32.18 "**Mortal man,**" he said, "mourn for all the many people
33. 2 "**Mortal man,**" he said, "tell your people what happens
33. 7 "Now, **mortal man,** I am making you a watchman for the
33.10 "**Mortal man,**" he said, "repeat to the Israelites what they
33.12 "Now, **mortal man,** tell the Israelites that when a good man sins,
33.24 "**Mortal man,**" he said, "the people who are living in
33.30 The Lord said, "**Mortal man,** your people are talking
34. 2 "**Mortal man,**" he said, "denounce the rulers of Israel.
35. 2 "**Mortal man,**" he said, "denounce the country of Edom.
36. 1 The Lord said, "**Mortal man,** speak to the mountains of
36.17 "**Mortal man,**" he said, "when the Israelites were living
37. 3 He said to me, "**Mortal man,** can these bones come back to
37. 9 God said to me, "**Mortal man,** prophesy to the wind.
37.11 God said to me, "**Mortal man,** the people of Israel are
37.16 "**Mortal man,**" he said, "take a wooden stick and write
38. 2 "**Mortal man,**" he said, "denounce Gog, chief ruler of
39. 1 The Sovereign Lord said, "**Mortal man,** denounce Gog, the
39.17 Sovereign Lord said to me, "**Mortal man,** call all the birds
40. 4 He said to me, "Watch, **mortal man.**
43. 7 "**Mortal man,** here is my throne.
43.10 And the Lord continued, "**Mortal man,** tell the people of
43.18 Sovereign Lord said to me, "**Mortal man,** listen to what I
44. 5 the Lord said to me, "**Mortal man,** pay attention to
47. 6 He said to me, "**Mortal man,** note all this carefully."
Dan 8.17 He said to me, "**Mortal man,** understand the meaning.
Acts 2.26 And I, **mortal** though I am, will rest assured in hope,
Rom 1.23 images made to look like **mortal** man or birds or animals or
6.12 no longer rule in your **mortal** bodies, so that you obey the
7.14 but I am a **mortal** man, sold as a slave to sin.
8.11 also give life to your **mortal** bodies by the presence of his
1 Cor 15.42 When the body is buried, it is **mortal;**

1 Cor 15.50 in God's Kingdom, and what is **mortal** cannot possess immortality.
15.53 For what is **mortal** must be changed into what is immortal;
15.54 takes place, and the **mortal** has been changed into the immortal,
2 Cor 4.10 times we carry in our **mortal** bodies the death of Jesus,
4.11 that his life may be seen in this **mortal** body of ours.
5. 4 over us, so that what is **mortal** will be transformed by life.
Phil 3.21 He will change our weak **mortal** bodies and make them like
1 Pet 1.23 as the children of a parent who is immortal, not **mortal.**
2 Pet 1.14 shall soon put off this **mortal** body, as our Lord Jesus

MORTAR

Jer 43. 9 and bury them in the **mortar** of the pavement in front of

MORTGAGE

Neh 5. 3 said, "We have had to **mortgage** our fields and vineyards and

MOSAIC

1 Chr 29. 2 and gems, stones for **mosaics,** and quantities of marble.

MOSES

[LAW OF MOSES]
Law-giver and leader of the Israelites in their escape from Egypt.

Ex 2.1-10 **The birth of Moses**
11-25 **Moses escapes to Midian**
3.1-22 **God calls Moses**
4.1-17 **God gives Moses miraculous power**
18-31 **Moses returns to Egypt**
5.1-21 **Moses and Aaron before the king of Egypt**
5.22–6.1 **Moses complains to the LORD**
6.2-13 **God calls Moses**
14-27 **The family record of Moses and Aaron**
6.28–7.7 **The LORD's command to Moses and Aaron**
7.8-13 **Aaron's stick**
7.14–10.29 **Disasters strike Egypt**
11.1-10 **Moses announces the death of the first-born**
12.1-14 **The Passover**
21-28 **The first Passover**
29-36 **The death of the first-born**
43-51 **Regulations about Passover**
13.1-2 **Dedication of the first-born**
3-10 **The Festival of Unleavened Bread**
17-22 **The pillar of cloud and the pillar of fire**
14.1-31 **Crossing the Red Sea**
15.1-18 **The Song of Moses**
22-27 **Bitter water**
16.1-36 **The manna and the quails**
17.1-7 **Water from the rock**
8-16 **War with the Amalekites**
18.1-12 **Jethro visits Moses**
13-27 **The appointment of judges**
19.1-25 **The Israelites at Mount Sinai**
20.18-21 **The people's fear**
22-26 **Laws about altars**
24.1-11 **The covenant is sealed**
12-18 **Moses on Mount Sinai**
(25.1–31.18 **The Covenant Tent and instructions for worship)**
32.1-35 **The gold bull-calf**
33.1-6 **The LORD orders Israel to leave Mount Sinai**
7-11 **The Tent of the LORD's presence**
12-23 **The LORD promises to be with his people**
34.1-9 **The second set of stone tablets**
10-28 **The covenant is renewed**
29-35 **Moses goes down from Mount Sinai**
35.1-3 **Regulations for the Sabbath**
(35.4–40.38 **The Covenant Tent)**
Lev (1.1–7.38 **Laws about offerings and sacrifices)**
8.1-36 **The ordination of Aaron and his sons**
9.1-24 **Aaron offers sacrifices**
10.1-7 **The sin of Nadab and Abihu**
8-20 **Rules for priests**
(11.1–15.33 **Laws about ritual cleanness and uncleanness)**
16.1-34 **The Day of Atonement**
(17.1–27.34 **Laws about holiness in life and worship)**
Num (1.1–4.49 **The first census)**
(5.1–8.26 **Various laws and rules)**
9.1-14 **The second Passover**
15-23 **The fiery cloud**
10.1-10 **The silver trumpets**
11-32 **The Israelites break camp**
33-36 **The people set out**
11.1-3 **The place named Taberah**
4-30 **Moses chooses seventy leaders**
12.1-16 **Miriam is punished**
13.1-33 **The spies**
14.1-10 **The people complain**
11-25 **Moses prays for the people**
26-38 **The LORD punishes the people for complaining**
39-45 **The first attempt to invade the land**
15.1-31 **Laws about sacrifice**
32-36 **The man who broke the Sabbath**
37-41 **Rules about tassels**
16.1-35 **The rebellion of Korah, Dathan, and Abiram**
36-40 **The firepans**
41-50 **Aaron saves the people**
17.1-13 **Aaron's stick**
18.25-32 **The Levites' tithe**
19.1-10 **Ashes of the red cow**
Num 20.1-13 **Events at Kadesh**
14-21 **The King of Edom refuses to let Israel pass**
22-29 **The death of Aaron**
21.4-9 **The snake made of bronze**
10-20 **From Mount Hor to the valley of the Moabites**
21-35 **Victory over King Sihon and King Og**
25.1-18 **The people of Israel at Peor**
26.1-65 **The second census**
27.1-11 **The daughters of Zelophehad**
12-23 **Joshua is chosen as successor to Moses**
(28.1–30.16 **Rules about offerings and vows)**
31.1-12 **The holy war against Midian**
13-24 **The army returns**
25-54 **Division of the loot**
32.1-42 **The tribes east of the Jordan**
33.1-49 **The journey from Egypt to Moab**
(33.50–36.13 **Instructions before crossing the Jordan)**
Deut 1.1-8 **Introduction**
9-18 **Moses appoints judges**
34-45 **The LORD punishes Israel**
3.23-29 **Moses is not permitted to enter Canaan**
4.1-14 **Moses urges Israel to be obedient**
41-43 **The cities of refuge east of the Jordan**
44-49 **Introduction to the giving of God's Law**
5.1-22 **The Ten Commandments**
23-33 **The people's fear**
10.1-11 **Moses receives the commandments again**
18.14-22 **The promise to send a prophet**
27.1-10 **God's laws written on stones**
11-26 **The curses on disobedience**
29.1-29 **The LORD's covenant with Israel in the land of Moab**
31.1-8 **Joshua becomes Moses' successor**
9-13 **The Law is to be read every seven years**
14-29 **The LORD's last instruction to Moses**
31.30–32.44 **The Song of Moses**
32.45-52 **Moses' final instructions**
33.1-29 **Moses blesses the tribes of Israel**
34.1-12 **The death of Moses**
Josh 1. 1 death of the Lord's servant **Moses,**
1. 1 the Lord spoke to **Moses'** helper, Joshua son of Nun.
1. 2 He said, "My servant **Moses** is dead.
1. 3 As I told **Moses,** I have given you and all my people
1. 5 I will be with you as I was with **Moses.**
1. 7 that you obey the whole Law that my servant **Moses** gave you.
1.13 of Manasseh, [13]"Remember how **Moses,** the Lord's servant,
1.15 the Jordan, which **Moses,** the Lord's servant, gave to you."
1.17 just as we always obeyed **Moses,**
1.17 the Lord your God be with you as he was with **Moses!**
3. 7 will realize that I am with you as I was with **Moses.**
4.10 This is what **Moses** had commanded.
4.12 the rest of the people, as **Moses** had told them to do.
4.14 They honoured him all his life, just as they had honoured **Moses.**
8.31 to the instructions that **Moses,** the Lord's servant,
8.31 had given the Israelites, as it says in the **Law of Moses:**
8.32 on the stones a copy of the Law which **Moses** had written.
8.33 The Lord's servant **Moses** had commanded them to do this when
8.35 one of the commandments of **Moses** was read by Joshua to the
9.24 God had commanded his servant **Moses** to give you the whole
11.12 everyone to death, just as **Moses,** the Lord's servant,
11.15 to his servant **Moses,**
11.15 **Moses** had given them to Joshua,
11.15 He did everything that the Lord had commanded **Moses.**
11.20 This was what the Lord had commanded **Moses.**
11.23 Joshua captured the whole land, as the Lord had commanded **Moses.**
12. 6 These two kings were defeated by **Moses** and the people of Israel.
12. 6 **Moses,** the Lord's servant, gave their land to the tribes of
13. 8 the land that **Moses,** the Lord's servant, had given them;
13.12 **Moses** had defeated these people and driven them out.
13.14 **Moses** had given no land to the tribe of Levi.
13.14 As the Lord had told **Moses,** they were to receive as their
13.15 **Moses** had given a part of the land to the families of
13.21 **Moses** defeated him, as well as the rulers of Midian:
13.24 **Moses** had also given a part of the land to the families
13.29 **Moses** had given a part of the land to the families of
13.32 That is how **Moses** divided the land east of Jericho and
13.33 But **Moses** did not assign any land to the tribe of Levi.
14. 2 As the Lord had commanded **Moses,** the territories of the
14. 3 **Moses** had already assigned the land east of the Jordan
14. 3 However, **Moses** gave the Levites no portion of the territory.
14. 5 of Israel divided the land as the Lord had commanded **Moses.**
14. 6 Kadesh Barnea about you and me to **Moses,** the man of God.
14. 7 old when the Lord's servant **Moses** sent me from Kadesh Barnea
14. 9 Because I did, **Moses** promised me that my children and I
14.10 It has been forty-five years since the Lord said that to **Moses.**
14.11 just as strong today as I was when **Moses** sent me out.
17. 4 and said, "The Lord commanded **Moses** to give us, as well as
18. 7 Jordan, which **Moses,** the Lord's servant, gave to them."
20. 2 cities of refuge that I commanded **Moses** to tell you about.
21. 2 them, "The Lord commanded through **Moses** that we were to be
21. 8 to the Levites, as the Lord had commanded through **Moses.**
22. 2 "You have done everything that **Moses** the Lord's servant
22. 4 east side of the Jordan, that **Moses,** the Lord's servant,
22. 5 Make sure you obey the law that **Moses** commanded you:
22. 6 **Moses** had given land east of the Jordan to one half of
22. 9 had taken as the Lord had commanded them through **Moses.**
23. 6 everything that is written in the book of the **Law of Moses.**
24. 5 Later I sent **Moses** and Aaron, and I brought great trouble
Judg 1.16 The descendants of **Moses'** father-in-law, the Kenite,
1.20 As **Moses** had commanded, Hebron was given to Caleb, who

Judg 3. 4 that the Lord had given their ancestors through **Moses.**
4.11 the descendants of Hobab, the brother-in-law of **Moses.**
18.30 of Gershom and grandson of **Moses,** served as a priest for the
1 Sam 12. 6 is the one who chose **Moses** and Aaron and who brought your
12. 8 for help, and he sent **Moses** and Aaron, who brought them out
1 Kgs 2. 3 as written in the **Law of Moses,** so that wherever you go
8. 9 stone tablets which **Moses** had placed there at Mount Sinai,
8.53 told them through your servant **Moses** when you brought our
8.56 all the generous promises he made through his servant **Moses.**
2 Kgs 14. 6 followed what the Lord had commanded in the **Law of Moses:**
18. 4 snake that **Moses** had made, which was called Nehushtan.
18. 6 kept all the commands that the Lord had given **Moses.**
18.12 all the laws given by **Moses,** the servant of the Lord.
21. 8 whole Law that my servant **Moses** gave them, then I will not
23.25 his heart, mind, and strength, obeying all the **Law of Moses;**
1 Chr 6. 3 Amram had two sons, Aaron and **Moses,** and one daughter,
6.49 all this in accordance with the instructions given by **Moses,**
15.15 their shoulders, as the Lord had commanded through **Moses.**
21.29 the Lord's presence which **Moses** had made in the wilderness,
22.13 the Lord gave to **Moses** for Israel, you will be successful.
23.13 His eldest son, Amram, was the father of Aaron and **Moses.**
23.14 But the sons of **Moses,** the man of God, were included
23.15 **Moses** had two sons, Gershom and Eliezer.
26.24 Shebuel, of the clan of **Moses'** son Gershom, was the
2 Chr 1. 3 Lord's presence was located, which **Moses,** the Lord's servant,
5.10 stone tablets which **Moses** had placed there at Mount Sinai,
8.13 to the requirements of the **Law of Moses** for each holy day:
23.18 offered to the Lord in accordance with the **Law of Moses.**
24. 6 and Jerusalem the tax which **Moses,** the servant of the Lord,
24. 9 the Lord the tax which **Moses,** God's servant, had first
25. 4 followed what the Lord had commanded in the **Law of Moses:**
30.16 to the instructions in the **Law of Moses,** the man of God.
33. 8 whole Law that my servant **Moses** gave them, then I will not
34.14 Law of the Lord, the Law that God had given to **Moses.**
35. 6 the instructions which the Lord gave through **Moses."**
35.12 them according to the instructions in the **Law of Moses.**
Ezra 3. 2 instructions written in the **Law of Moses,** the man of God.
6.18 to the instructions contained in the book of **Moses.**
7. 6 Law which the Lord, the God of Israel, had given to **Moses.**
Neh 1. 7 not kept the laws which you gave us through **Moses,** your
1. 8 Remember now what you told **Moses:**
8. 1 Lord had given Israel through **Moses,** to get the book of the
8.14 which the Lord gave through **Moses,** ordered the people of
9.14 and through your servant **Moses** you gave them your laws.
10.29 to God's Law, which God gave through his servant **Moses;**
13. 1 When the **Law of Moses** was being read aloud to the people,
Ps 77.20 people like a shepherd, with **Moses** and Aaron in charge.
99. 6 **Moses** and Aaron were his priests, and Samuel was one who
103. 7 He revealed his plans to **Moses** and let the people of
105.26 Then he sent his servant **Moses,** and Aaron, whom he had chosen.
106.16 desert they were jealous of **Moses** and of Aaron, the Lord's
106.23 his people, his chosen servant, **Moses,** stood up against God
106.32 the Lord angry, and **Moses** was in trouble on their account.
Is 63.11 the past, the days of **Moses,** the servant of the Lord, and
63.11 Where is the Lord, who gave his spirit to **Moses?**
63.12 power did great things through **Moses,** dividing the waters of
Jer 15. 1 said to me, "Even if **Moses** and Samuel were standing here
Dan 9.11 the curses that are written in the **Law of Moses,** your
9.13 giving us all the punishment described in the **Law of Moses.**
Mic 6. 4 I sent **Moses,** Aaron, and Miriam to lead you.
Mal 4. 4 the teachings of my servant **Moses,** the laws and commands
Mt 5.17 do away with the **Law of Moses** and the teachings of the
7.12 the meaning of the **Law of Moses** and of the teachings of
8. 4 that you are cured, offer the sacrifice that **Moses** ordered."
11.13 the prophets and the **Law of Moses** spoke about the Kingdom;
12. 5 not read in the **Law of Moses** that every Sabbath the priests
17. 3 the three disciples saw **Moses** and Elijah talking with Jesus.
17. 4 here, one for you, one for **Moses,** and one for Elijah."
19. 7 asked him, "Why, then, did **Moses** give the law for a man
19. 8 **"Moses** gave you permission to divorce your wives because you
22.24 "Teacher," they said, **"Moses** said that if a man who
22.40 whole **Law of Moses** and the teachings of the prophets depend
23. 2 and the Pharisees are the authorized interpreters of **Moses' Law.**
Mk 1.44 that you are cured, offer the sacrifice that **Moses** ordered."
7.10 For **Moses** commanded, 'Respect your father and your mother,'
9. 4 the three disciples saw Elijah and **Moses** talking with Jesus.
9. 5 tents, one for you, one for **Moses,** and one for Elijah."
10. 3 Jesus answered with a question, "What law did **Moses** give you?"
10. 4 Their answer was, **"Moses** gave permission for a man to
10. 5 Jesus said to them, **"Moses** wrote this law for you because
12.19 to Jesus and said, [19]"Teacher, **Moses** wrote this law for us:
12.26 in the Book of **Moses** the passage about the burning bush?
12.26 written that God said to **Moses,** 'I am the God of Abraham,
Lk 2.22 the ceremony of purification, as the **Law of Moses** commanded.
5.14 that you are cured, offer the sacrifice as **Moses** ordered."
9.30 They were **Moses** and Elijah, [31]who appeared in heavenly glory
9.33 tents, one for you, one for **Moses,** and one for Elijah."
16.16 "The **Law of Moses** and the writings of the prophets were
16.29 said, 'Your brothers have **Moses** and the prophets to warn them;
16.31 they will not listen to **Moses** and the prophets, they will
20.28 to Jesus and said, [28]"Teacher, **Moses** wrote this law for us:
20.37 And **Moses** clearly proves that the dead are raised to life.
24.27 beginning with the books of **Moses** and the writings of all
24.44 about me in the **Law of Moses,** the writings of the prophets,
Jn 1.17 God gave the Law through **Moses,** but grace and truth came
1.45 have found the one whom **Moses** wrote about in the book of
3.14 As **Moses** lifted up the bronze snake on a pole in the
5.45 **Moses,** in whom you have put your hope, is the very one
5.46 If you had really believed **Moses,** you would have believed me,
6.32 "What **Moses** gave you was not the bread from heaven;
7.19 **Moses** gave you the Law, didn't he?
Jn 7.22 **Moses** ordered you to circumcise your sons
7.22 (although it was not **Moses** but your ancestors who started it),
7.23 on the Sabbath so that **Moses' Law** is not broken, why are
7.49 does not know the **Law of Moses,** so they are under God's
8. 5 In our Law **Moses** commanded that such a woman must be
9.28 but we are **Moses'** disciples.
9.29 We know that God spoke to **Moses;**
Acts 3.22 For **Moses** said, 'The Lord your God will send you a prophet,
6.11 to say, "We heard him speaking against **Moses** and against God!"
6.13 "is always talking against our sacred Temple and the **Law of Moses.**
6.14 all the customs which have come down to us from **Moses!"**
7.20 at this time that **Moses** was born, a very beautiful child.
7.23 "When **Moses** was forty years old, he decided to find out
7.27 But the one who was ill-treating the other pushed **Moses** aside.
7.29 When **Moses** heard this, he fled from Egypt and went to
7.30 an angel appeared to **Moses** in the flames of a burning
7.31 **Moses** was amazed by what he saw, and went near the bush
7.32 **Moses** trembled with fear and dared not look.
7.35 **"Moses** is the one who was rejected by the people of Israel.
7.37 **Moses** is the one who said to the people of Israel, 'God
7.40 happened to that man **Moses,** who brought us out of Egypt.'
7.44 made as God had told **Moses** to make it,
7.44 according to the pattern that **Moses** had been shown.
13.15 the reading from the **Law of Moses** and from the writings of
13.38 sins from which the **Law of Moses** could not set you free.
15. 1 saved unless you are circumcised as the **Law of Moses** requires."
15. 5 Gentiles must be circumcised and told to obey the **Law of Moses."**
15.21 For the **Law of Moses** has been read for a very long
21.21 to abandon the **Law of Moses,** telling them not to circumcise
21.24 that you yourself live in accordance with the **Law of Moses.**
21.28 the people of Israel, the **Law of Moses,** and this Temple.
24.14 everything written in the **Law of Moses** and the books of the
26.22 thing which the prophets and **Moses** said was going to happen:
28.23 by quoting from the **Law of Moses** and the writings of the
Rom 2.12 The Gentiles do not have the **Law of Moses;**
3.21 even though the **Law of Moses** and the prophets gave their
5.14 Adam to the time of **Moses** death ruled over all mankind, even
9.15 For he said to **Moses,** "I will have mercy on anyone I
10. 5 **Moses** wrote this about being put right with God by obeying
10.19 **Moses** himself is the first one to answer:
1 Cor 9. 9 We read in the **Law of Moses,** "Do not muzzle an ox
9.20 not subject to the **Law of Moses,** I live as though I
10. 1 my brothers, what happened to our ancestors who followed **Moses.**
10. 2 and in the sea they were all baptized as followers of **Moses.**
2 Cor 3. 7 Even though the brightness on **Moses'** face was fading, it was
3.13 We are not like **Moses,** who had to put a veil over
3.15 whenever they read the **Law of Moses,** the veil still covers
3.16 But it can be removed, as the scripture says about **Moses:**
2 Tim 3. 8 and Jambres were opposed to **Moses,** so also these people are
Heb 3. 2 do this work, just as **Moses** was faithful in his work in
3. 3 same way Jesus is worthy of much greater honour than **Moses.**
3. 5 **Moses** was faithful in God's house as a servant, and he
3.16 All those who were led out of Egypt by **Moses.**
7.14 **Moses** did not mention this tribe when he spoke of priests.
7.19 For the **Law of Moses** could not make anything perfect.
7.28 The **Law of Moses** appoints men who are imperfect to be
8. 5 It is the same as it was with **Moses.**
9.19 First, **Moses** proclaimed to the people all the commandments
9.21 In the same way **Moses** also sprinkled the blood on the
10.28 Anyone who disobeys the **Law of Moses** is put to death
11.23 that made the parents of **Moses** hide him for three months
11.24 It was faith that made **Moses,** when he had grown up,
11.27 It was faith that made **Moses** leave Egypt without being afraid
12.21 was so terrifying that **Moses** said, "I am trembling and afraid!"
Jude 9 would have the body of **Moses,** Michael did not dare to
Rev 15. 3 and singing the song of **Moses,** the servant of God, and the

MOST HIGH

Gen 14.18 also a priest of the **Most High God,** brought bread and wine
14.19 him, and said, "May the **Most High God,** who made heaven and
14.20 May the **Most High God,** who gave you victory over your enemies,
14.22 swear before the Lord, the **Most High God,** Maker of heaven
Num 24.16 And receive the knowledge that comes from the **Most High.**
Deut 32. 8 The **Most High** assigned nations their lands;
Ps 7.17 for his justice, I sing praises to the Lord, the **Most High.**
18.13 and the voice of the **Most High** was heard.
46. 4 the city of God, to the sacred house of the **Most High.**
47. 2 The Lord, the **Most High,** is to be feared;
57. 2 I call to God, the **Most High,** to God, who supplies my
73.11 the **Most High** will not find out."
78.17 God, and in the desert they rebelled against the **Most High.**
82. 6 'all of you are sons of the **Most High.'**
91. 9 the Lord your defender, the **Most High** your protector,
92. 1 sing in your honour, O **Most High God,** [2]to proclaim your
Mk 5. 7 screamed in a loud voice, "Jesus, Son of the **Most High God!**
Lk 1.32 great and will be called the Son of the **Most High God.**
1.76 my child, will be called a prophet of the **Most High God.**
6.35 great reward, and you will be sons of the **Most High God.**
8.28 at his feet, and shouted, "Jesus, Son of the **Most High God!**
Acts 7.48 "But the **Most High God** does not live in houses built by
16.17 us, shouting, "These men are servants of the **Most High God!**
Heb 7. 1 was king of Salem and a priest of the **Most High God.**

MOST HOLY PLACE see HOLY PLACE

MOTH

Job 4.19 clay, a thing of dust that can be crushed like a **moth?**
13.28 I crumble like rotten wood, like a **moth-eaten** coat.
Ps 39.11 by your rebukes, and like a **moth** you destroy what he loves.
Is 50. 9 they will vanish like **moth-eaten** cloth.
51. 8 they will vanish like **moth-eaten** clothing!
Mt 6.19 here on earth, where **moths** and rust destroy, and robbers break
6.20 in heaven, where **moths** and rust cannot destroy, and robbers
Lk 12.33 no thief can get to them, and no **moth** can destroy them.
Jas 5. 2 have rotted away, and your clothes have been eaten by **moths.**

MOTHER

[FATHER AND MOTHER]

Gen 2.24 a man leaves his **father and mother** and is united with his
3.20 wife Eve, because she was the **mother** of all human beings.
17.16 and she will become the **mother** of nations, and there will be
20.12 of my father, but not of my **mother,** and I married her.
21.21 His **mother** found an Egyptian wife for him.
24.28 The girl ran to her **mother's** house and told the whole story.
24.53 He also gave expensive gifts to her brother and to her **mother.**
24.55 But Rebecca's brother and her **mother** said, "Let the
24.60 "May you, sister, become the **mother** of millions!
24.67 into the tent that his **mother** Sarah had lived in, and she
24.67 and so he was comforted for the loss of his **mother.**
27.11 But Jacob said to his **mother,** "You know that Esau is a
27.13 His **mother** answered, "Let any curse against you fall on me,
27.29 and may your **mother's** descendants bow down before you.
28. 5 and the brother of Rebecca, the **mother** of Jacob and Esau.
28. 7 Jacob had obeyed his **father and mother** and had gone to Mesopotamia.
30. 3 In this way I can become a **mother** through her."
30.14 and found mandrakes, which he brought to his **mother** Leah.
37.10 Do you think that your **mother,** your brothers, and I are
44.20 and he is the only one of his **mother's** children still alive;
48. 7 I am doing this because of your **mother** Rachel.
Ex 2. 8 So the girl went and brought the baby's own **mother.**
20.12 "Respect your **father and your mother,** so that you may
21.15 "Whoever hits his **father or his mother** is to be put to
21.17 "Whoever curses his **father or his mother** is to be put
22.30 first-born male stay with its **mother** for seven days, and on
23.19 "Do not cook a young sheep or goat in its **mother's** milk.
34.26 "Do not cook a young sheep or goat in its **mother's** milk."
Lev 18. 7 Do not disgrace your father by having intercourse with your **mother.**
18. 7 You must not disgrace your own **mother.**
18.12 whether she is your father's sister or your **mother's** sister.
19. 3 of you must respect his **mother** and his father, and must keep
20. 9 Anyone who curses his **father or his mother** shall be put to
20.14 marries a woman and her **mother,** all three shall be burnt to
21. 2 dies, [2]unless it is his **mother,** father, son, daughter,
21.11 a dead person, even if it is his own **father or mother.**
22.26 not be taken from its **mother** for seven days, but after that
24.10 Egyptian and whose **mother** was an Israelite named Shelomith,
Num 6. 6 a corpse, not even that of his father, **mother,** brother, or
Deut 5.16 " 'Respect your **father and your mother,** as I, the Lord your God,
14.21 "Do not cook a young sheep or goat in its **mother's** milk
22. 6 on the ground with the **mother** bird sitting either on the
22. 6 or with her young, you are not to take the **mother** bird
22. 7 but you must let the **mother** bird go, so that you will
27.16 " 'God's curse on anyone who dishonours his **father or mother.'**
Josh 2.13 you will save my **father and mother,** my brothers and sisters,
2.18 Get your **father and mother,** your brothers,
6.23 out, along with her **father and mother,** her brothers, and the
Judg 5. 7 they stood empty until you came, came like a **mother** for Israel.
5.28 Sisera's **mother** looked out of the window;
8.19 Gideon said, "They were my brothers, my own **mother's** sons.
9. 1 of Shechem, where all his **mother's** relatives lived, and told
9. 3 His **mother's** relatives talked to the men of Shechem about
14. 2 and said to his **father and mother,** "There is a Philistine
14. 3 But his **father and mother** asked him, "Why do you have to
14. 5 So Samson went down to Timnah with his **father and mother.**
14. 9 Then he went to his **father and mother** and gave them some.
14.16 He said, "Look, I haven't even told my **father and mother.**
17. 2 He said to his **mother,** "When someone stole those eleven
17. 2 His **mother** said, "May the Lord bless you, my son!"
17. 3 the money back to his **mother,** and she said, "To stop the
17. 4 Then he gave them back to his **mother.**
Ruth 1. 8 she said to them, "Go back home and stay with your **mothers.**
2.11 how you left your **father and mother** and your own country and
1 Sam 2. 5 seven children, but the **mother** of many is left with none.
2.19 Each year his **mother** would make a little robe and take
15.33 has made many **mothers** childless,
15.33 so now will your **mother** become childless."
20.30 said to him, "How rebellious and faithless your **mother** was!
20.30 David and are disgracing yourself and that **mother** of yours!
22. 3 Moab, "Please let my **father and mother** come and stay with
26. 6 the brother of Joab (their **mother** was Zeruiah), "Which of
2 Sam 2.13 Joab, whose **mother** was Zeruiah, and David's other
3. 2 Amnon, whose **mother** was Ahinoam, from Jezreel;
3. 3 Chileab, whose **mother** was Abigail, Nabal's widow, from
3. 3 **mother** was Maacah, the daughter of King Talmai
3. 4 Adonijah, whose **mother** was Haggith;
3. 4 Shephatiah, whose **mother** was Abital;
3. 5 Ithream, whose **mother** was Eglah.
8.16 Joab, whose **mother** was Zeruiah, was the commander of the army;
16. 9 Abishai, whose **mother** was Zeruiah, said to the king,
17. 8 they are as fierce as a **mother** bear robbed of her cubs.
17.25 his **mother** was Abigail, the daughter of Nahash
2 Sam 17.25 and the sister of Joab's **mother** Zeruiah.)
23.18 Joab's brother Abishai (their **mother** was Zeruiah) was
1 Kgs 1. 7 He talked with Joab (whose **mother** was Zeruiah) and with
1.11 Nathan went to Bathsheba, Solomon's **mother,** and asked her,
2.13 Then Adonijah, whose **mother** was Haggith, went to
2.13 went to Bathsheba, who was Solomon's **mother.**
2.19 The king stood up to greet his **mother** and bowed to her.
2.20 "What is it, **mother?"**
3.26 The real **mother,** her heart full of love for her son,
3.27 Give it to the first woman—she is its real **mother."**
7.14 his **mother** was from the tribe of Naphtali.
11.26 His **mother** was a widow named Zeruah.
14.21 Rehoboam's **mother** was Naamah from Ammon.
15. 2 His **mother** was Maacah, the daughter of Absalom.
15.13 from her position as queen **mother,** because she had made an
17.23 boy back downstairs to his **mother** and said to her, "Look,
19.20 "Let me kiss my **father and mother** good-bye, and then I will
22.42 His **mother** was Azubah, the daughter of Shilhi.
22.52 of his father Ahab, his **mother** Jezebel, and King Jeroboam,
2 Kgs 3. 2 he was not as bad as his father or his **mother** Jezebel;
3.13 "Go and consult those prophets that your **father and mother** consulted."
4.19 "Carry the boy to his **mother,"** the father said to a servant.
4.20 the boy back to his **mother,** who held him in her lap
4.36 Elisha called Gehazi and told him to call the boy's **mother.**
8.26 His **mother** was Athaliah, the daughter of King Ahab and
9.22 witchcraft and idolatry that your **mother** Jezebel started?"
11. 1 as King Ahaziah's **mother** Athaliah learnt of her son's murder,
12. 1 His **mother** was Zibiah from the city of Beersheba.
14. 2 His **mother** was Jehoaddin, from Jerusalem.
15. 2 His **mother** was Jecoliah from Jerusalem.
15.33 His **mother** was Jerusha, the daughter of Zadok.
18. 2 His **mother** was Abijah, the daughter of Zechariah.
21. 1 His **mother** was Hephzibah.
21.19 His **mother** was Meshullemeth, the daughter of Haruz, from the
22. 1 His **mother** was Jedidah, the daughter of Adaiah, from the
23.31 His **mother** was Hamutal, the daughter of Jeremiah from the
23.36 His **mother** was Zebidah, the daughter of Pedaiah from the
24. 8 His **mother** was Nehushta, the daughter of Elnathan from Jerusalem.
24.12 King Jehoiachin, along with his **mother,** his sons, his
24.15 a prisoner, together with Jehoiachin's **mother,** his wives,
24.18 His **mother** was Hamutal, the daughter of Jeremiah from the
1 Chr 3. 1 Amnon, whose **mother** was Ahinoam from Jezreel
3. 1 Daniel, whose **mother** was Abigail from Carmel
3. 1 Absalom, whose **mother** was Maacah, daughter of King Talmai
3. 1 Adonijah, whose **mother** was Haggith
3. 1 Shephatiah, whose **mother** was Abital
3. 1 Ithream, whose **mother** was Eglah
4. 9 His **mother** had given him the name Jabez, because his birth
11. 6 **mother** was Zeruiah, led the attack and became commander.
18.12 Abishai, whose **mother** was Zeruiah, defeated the
27.24 Joab, whose **mother** was Zeruiah, began to take a census,
2 Chr 2.14 His **mother** was a member of the tribe of Dan and his
11.18 son of David, and whose **mother** was Abihail, the daughter of
12.13 Rehoboam's **mother** was Naamah, from the land of Ammon.
13. 2 His **mother** was Micaiah daughter of Uriel, from the city
15.16 from her position as queen **mother,** because she had made an
20.31 His **mother** was Azubah, the daughter of Shilhi.
22. 2 King Ahab's family, since his **mother** Athaliah—the daughter
22.10 as King Ahaziah's **mother** Athaliah learnt of her son's murder,
24. 1 His **mother** was Zibiah from the city of Beersheba.
25. 1 His **mother** was Jehoaddin from Jerusalem.
26. 3 His **mother** was Jecoliah from Jerusalem.
27. 1 His **mother** was Jerushah, the daughter of Zadok.
29. 1 His **mother** was Abijah, the daughter of Zechariah.
Job 3.11 I had died in my **mother's** womb or died the moment I
3.12 Why did my **mother** hold me on her knees?
10.10 you made me grow in my **mother's** womb.
17.14 worms that eat me I will call my **mother** and my sisters.
24.20 Not even his **mother** remembers him now;
38.29 Who is the **mother** of the ice and the frost, [30]which
Ps 27.10 My **father and mother** may abandon me, but the Lord will
35.14 bent over in mourning, as one who mourns for his **mother.**
86.16 and save me, because I serve you, just as my **mother** did.
109.14 evil of his ancestors and never forgive his **mother's** sins.
116.16 I serve you, just as my **mother** did.
131. 2 child lies quietly in its **mother's** arms, so my heart is
139.13 you put me together in my **mother's** womb.
139.15 carefully put together in my **mother's** womb, when I was
Prov 1. 8 Pay attention to what your **father and mother** tell you, my
6.20 you, my son, and never forget what your **mother** taught you.
10. 1 a foolish one brings his **mother** grief.
15.20 Only a fool despises his **mother.**
17.12 is better to meet a **mother** bear robbed of her cubs than
17.25 grief to his father and bitter regrets to his **mother.**
19.26 ill-treat his father or turn his **mother** away from his home.
23.22 When your **mother** is old, show her your appreciation.
23.25 Make your **father and mother** proud of you;
23.25 give your **mother** that happiness.
29.15 has his own way, he will make his **mother** ashamed of him.
30.11 and do not show their appreciation for their **mothers.**
30.17 his father or despises his **mother** in her old age ought to
31. 1 the solemn words which King Lemuel's **mother** said to him:
Song 3. 4 I took him to my **mother's** house, to the room where I
3.11 wearing the crown that his **mother** placed on his head on his
6. 9 She is her **mother's** only daughter, her mother's favourite child.
8. 1 my brother, that my **mother** had nursed you at her breast.
8. 2 would take you to my **mother's** house, where you could teach
Is 40.11 he will gently lead their **mothers.**
49.15 Even if a **mother** should forget her child, I will never

Is	49.23	queens will be like **mothers.**
	60.16	and kings will care for you As a **mother** nurses her child.
	66.11	enjoy her prosperity, like a child at its **mother's** breast.
	66.12	that is nursed by its **mother,** carried in her arms, and
	66.13	I will comfort you in Jerusalem, as a **mother** comforts her child.
Jer	2.27	a tree is your father and that a rock is your **mother.**
	13.18	"Tell the king and his **mother** to come down from their thrones,
	14. 5	In the field the **mother** deer abandons her new-born fawn
	15. 8	young men in their prime and made their **mothers** suffer.
	15. 9	The **mother** who lost her seven children has fainted,
	15.10	Why did my **mother** bring me into the world?
	16. 7	not even for someone who has lost his **father or mother.**
	20.14	Forget the day my **mother** gave me birth!
	20.17	Then my **mother's** womb would have been my grave.
	22.26	I am going to force you and your **mother** into exile.
	29. 2	it after King Jehoiachin, his **mother,** the palace officials,
	52. 1	His **mother's** name was Hamutal, the daughter of the Jeremiah
Lam	2.12	Hungry and thirsty, they cry to their **mothers;**
	2.12	they were wounded, And slowly die in their **mothers'** arms.
	4. 3	Even a **mother** wolf will nurse her cubs, but my people are
	4.10	loving **mothers** boiled their own children for food.
	5. 3	been killed by the enemy, and now our **mothers** are widows.
Ezek	9. 6	Kill the old men, young men, young women, **mothers,** and
	16. 3	Your father was an Amorite, and your **mother** was a Hittite.
	16.44	'Like **mother,** like daughter.'
	16.45	You really are your **mother's** daughter.
	16.45	sister cities had a Hittite **mother** and an Amorite father.
	19. 2	What a lioness your **mother** was!
	19.10	Your **mother** was like a grapevine planted near a stream.
Dan	5.10	The queen **mother** heard the noise made by the king and
Hos	2. 2	My children, plead with your **mother**—though she is no
	4. 5	I am going to destroy Israel, your **mother.**
	10.14	of Betharbel in battle, and **mothers** and their children were
	12. 3	Esau while the two of them were still in their **mother's** womb;
Mic	7. 6	like fools, daughters oppose their **mothers,** and young women
Zech	13. 3	on prophesying, his own **father and mother** will tell him that
	13. 3	his own **father and mother** will stab him to death.
Mt	1. 2	then Perez and Zerah (their **mother** was Tamar),
	1. 2	Boaz (his **mother** was Rahab),
	1. 2	Obed (his **mother** was Ruth),
	1. 6	Solomon (his **mother** was the woman who had been Uriah's wife),
	1.12	Joseph, who married Mary, the **mother** of Jesus,
	1.18	His **mother** Mary was engaged to Joseph, but before they were
	2.11	the child with his **mother** Mary, they knelt down and worshipped
	2.13	take the child and his **mother** and escape to Egypt,
	2.14	took the child and his **mother,** and left during the night
	2.20	take the child and his **mother,** and go back to the land
	2.21	took the child and his **mother,** and went back to Israel.
	10.35	sons against their fathers, daughters against their **mothers,**
	10.37	"Whoever loves his **father or mother** more than me is not
	12.46	still talking to the people when his **mother** and brothers arrived.
	12.47	to him, "Look, your **mother** and brothers are standing outside,
	12.48	Jesus answered, "Who is my **mother?**
	12.49	Here are my **mother** and my brothers!
	12.50	wants him to do is my brother, my sister, and my **mother."**
	13.55	Isn't Mary his **mother,** and aren't James, Joseph, Simon, and
	14. 8	At her **mother's** suggestion she asked him, "Give me here and
	14.11	dish and given to the girl, who took it to her **mother.**
	15. 4	God said, 'Respect your **father and your mother,'**
	15. 4	curses his father or his **mother** is to be put to death.'
	15. 5	use to help his **father or mother,** but says, 'This belongs to
	19. 5	will leave his **father and mother** and unite with his wife,
	19.19	respect your **father and your mother;**
	19.29	brothers or sisters or **father or mother** or children or fields
	24.19	for women who are pregnant and for **mothers** with little babies!
	27.56	were Mary Magdalene, Mary the **mother** of James and Joseph, and
Mk	3.31	Then Jesus' **mother** and brothers arrived.
	3.32	said to him, "Look, your **mother** and your brothers and sisters
	3.33	Jesus answered, "Who is my **mother?**
	3.34	Here are my **mother** and my brothers!
	3.35	God wants him to do is my brother, my sister, my **mother."**
	5.40	out, took the child's **father and mother** and his three disciples,
	6.24	went out and asked her **mother,** "What shall I ask for?"
	6.28	and gave it to the girl, who gave it to her **mother.**
	7.10	Moses commanded, 'Respect your **father and your mother,'**
	7.10	curses his father or his **mother** is to be put to death.'
	7.11	use to help his **father or mother,** but says, 'This is Corban'
	7.12	he is excused from helping his **father or mother.**
	10. 7	will leave his **father and mother** and unite with his wife,
	10.19	respect your **father and your mother.'** "
	10.29	or brothers or sisters or **mother** or father or children or
	10.30	more houses, brothers, sisters, **mothers,** children and fields—
	13.17	for women who are pregnant and for **mothers** with little babies!
	15.40	were Mary Magdalene, Mary the **mother** of the younger James
	15.47	Mary Magdalene and Mary the **mother** of Joseph were watching
	16. 1	Mary Magdalene, Mary the **mother** of James, and Salome bought
Lk	1.43	thing happen to me, that my Lord's **mother** comes to visit me?
	1.60	But his **mother** said, "No!
	2.33	child's **father and mother** were amazed at the things Simeon said
	2.34	and said to Mary, his **mother,** "This child is chosen by God
	2.48	they saw him, and his **mother** said to him, "My son, why
	2.51	His **mother** treasured all these things in her heart.
	7.15	and began to talk, and Jesus gave him back to his **mother.**
	8.19	Jesus' **mother** and brothers came to him, but were unable to
	8.20	said to Jesus, "Your **mother** and brothers are standing outside
	8.21	said to them all, "My **mother** and brothers are those who
	8.51	except Peter, John, and James, and the child's **father and mother.**
	12.53	**mothers** will be against their daughters,
	12.53	and daughters against their **mothers;**
	14.26	loves his father and his **mother,** his wife and his children,
Lk	18.20	respect your **father and your mother.'** "
	21.23	for women who are pregnant and for **mothers** with little babies!
	24.10	women were Mary Magdalene, Joanna, and Mary the **mother** of James;
Jn	2. 1	Jesus' **mother** was there, [2] and Jesus and his disciples had also
	2. 3	wine had given out, Jesus' **mother** said to him, "They have
	2. 5	Jesus' **mother** then told the servants, "Do whatever he tells
	2.12	Jesus and his **mother,** brothers, and disciples went to Capernaum
	3. 4	"He certainly cannot enter his **mother's** womb and be born a
	6.42	We know his **father and mother.**
	19.25	Jesus' cross were his **mother,** his mother's sister, Mary the wife
	19.26	Jesus saw his **mother** and the disciple he loved standing there;
	19.26	so he said to his **mother,** "He is your son."
	19.27	Then he said to the disciple, "She is your **mother."**
Acts	1.14	and with Mary the **mother** of Jesus and with his brothers.
	12.12	the home of Mary, the **mother** of John Mark, where many people
	16. 1	His **mother,** who was also a Christian, was Jewish, but his
Rom	16.13	Lord's service, and to his **mother,** who has always treated me
Gal	4. 4	the son of a human mother and lived under the Jewish Law,
	4.19	Once again, just like a **mother** in childbirth, I feel the
	4.26	But the heavenly Jerusalem is free, and she is our **mother.**
Eph	5.31	will leave his **father and mother** and unite with his wife,
	6. 2	"Respect your **father and mother"** is the first commandment that
1 Thes	2. 7	we were with you, like a **mother** taking care of her children.
1 Tim	1. 9	who kill their fathers or **mothers,** for murderers,
	5. 2	the older women as **mothers,** and the younger women as sisters,
2 Tim	1. 5	faith that your grandmother Lois and your **mother** Eunice also had.
Heb	7. 3	no record of Melchizedek's **father or mother** or of any of his
Rev	17. 5	"Great Babylon, the **mother** of all the prostitutes and perverts

MOTHER-IN-LAW

Deut	27.23	"'God's curse on anyone who has intercourse with his **mother-in-law.'**
Ruth	1.14	Then Orpah kissed her **mother-in-law** good-bye and went back home,
	2.11	have done for your **mother-in-law** since your husband died.
	2.18	town and showed her **mother-in-law** how much she had gathered.
	2.23	And she continued to live with her **mother-in-law.**
	3. 6	and did just what her **mother-in-law** had told her.
	3.10	are doing now than in what you did for your **mother-in-law.**
	3.16	When she arrived home, her **mother-in-law** asked her,
Mic	7. 6	mothers, and young women quarrel with their **mothers-in-law;**
Mt	8.14	There he saw Peter's **mother-in-law** sick in bed with a fever.
	10.35	daughters-in-law against their **mothers-in-law;**
Mk	1.30	Simon's **mother-in-law** was sick in bed with a fever,
Lk	4.38	Simon's **mother-in-law** was sick with a high fever, and they spoke
	12.53	**mothers-in-law** will be against their daughters-in-law,
	12.53	and daughters-in-law against their **mothers-in-law."**

MOTHER-OF-PEARL

Esth	1. 6	red feldspar, shining **mother-of-pearl,** and blue turquoise.

MOTION

Lk	5. 7	So they **motioned** to their partners in the other boat to
Jn	13.24	Simon Peter **motioned** to him and said, "Ask him whom he
Acts	12.17	He **motioned** with his hand for them to be quiet, and he
	13.16	Paul stood up, **motioned** with his hand, and began to speak:
	19.33	Then Alexander **motioned** with his hand for the people to be silent,
	21.40	stood on the steps and **motioned** with his hand for the people
	24.10	The governor then **motioned** to Paul to speak, and Paul said,

MOTIVE

Prov	16. 2	you do is right, but the Lord judges your **motives.**
	21. 2	is right, but remember that the Lord judges your **motives.**
	21.27	him sacrifices, especially if they do it from evil **motives.**
	24.12	of your business, but God knows and judges your **motives.**
Dan	11.27	the same table, but their **motives** will be evil, and they
1 Cor	15.32	here in Ephesus simply from human **motives,** what have I gained?
2 Cor	1.17	I make them from selfish **motives,** ready to say "Yes, yes"
	10. 2	harshly with those who say that we act from worldly **motives.**
	10. 3	live in the world, but we do not fight from worldly **motives.**
	12.18	act from the very same **motives** and behave in the same way?
Phil	1.18	preached in every way possible, whether from wrong or right **motives.**
1 Thes	2. 3	based on error or impure **motives,** nor do we try to trick
	2. 4	try to please men, but to please God, who tests our **motives.**
Jas	2. 4	among yourselves and of making judgements based on evil **motives.**
	4. 3	ask, you do not receive it, because your **motives** are bad;

MOULD

Ex	32. 4	poured the gold into a **mould,** and made a gold bull-calf.
Nah	3.14	Trample the clay to make bricks, and get the brick **moulds** ready!

MOULDY

Josh	9. 5	The bread they took with them was dry and **mouldy.**
	9.12	Now it is dry and **mouldy.**

MOUND

[SIEGE-MOUNDS]

Deut	20.20	use them in the **siege mounds** until the city is captured.
Josh	11.13	cities built on **mounds,** except Hazor, which Joshua did burn.
Judg	6.26	altar to the Lord your God on top of this **mound.**

2 Kgs	19.32	near the city, and no **siege-mounds** will be built round it.
Is	37.33	near the city, and no **siege-mounds** will be built round it.
Jer	6. 6	down trees and build **mounds** in order to besiege Jerusalem.
	32.24	"The Babylonians have built **siege mounds** round the city

MOUNT (1)

Ex	17. 6	I will stand before you on a rock at **Mount Sinai.**
	19. 1	camp at the foot of **Mount Sinai,** [3]and Moses went up the
	19.11	I will come down on **Mount Sinai,** where all the people can
	19.18	The whole of **Mount Sinai** was covered with smoke, because
	19.20	down on the top of **Mount Sinai** and called Moses to the
	24.15	Moses went up **Mount Sinai,** and a cloud covered it.
	31.18	finished speaking to Moses on **Mount Sinai,** he gave him the
	33. 6	So after they left **Mount Sinai,** the people of Israel no
	34. 2	tomorrow morning, and come up **Mount Sinai** to meet me there
	34. 4	morning he carried them up **Mount Sinai,** just as the Lord had
	34.29	Moses went down from **Mount Sinai** carrying the Ten Commandments,
	34.32	all the laws that the Lord had given him on **Mount Sinai.**
Lev	7.38	There on **Mount Sinai** in the desert, the Lord gave these
	25. 1	Lord spoke to Moses on **Mount Sinai** and commanded him [2]to
	26.46	Lord gave to Moses on **Mount Sinai** for the people of Israel.
	27.34	Lord gave Moses on **Mount Sinai** for the people of Israel.
Num	3. 1	Moses at the time the Lord spoke to Moses on **Mount Sinai.**
	20.22	Kadesh and arrived at **Mount Hor,** [23]on the border of Edom.
	20.25	and his son Eleazar up **Mount Hor,** [26]and there remove
	20.27	They went up **Mount Hor** in the sight of the whole community,
	21. 4	The Israelites left **Mount Hor** by the road that leads to
	21.20	below the top of **Mount Pisgah,** looking out over the desert.
	23.14	him to the field of Zophim on the top of **Mount Pisgah.**
	23.28	took Balaam to the top of **Mount Peor** overlooking the desert.
	28. 6	which was first offered at **Mount Sinai** as a food-offering, a
	33.15	From Rephidim to **Mount Hor** they set up camp at the
	33.15	Rimmon Perez, Libnah, Rissah, Kehelathah, **Mount Shepher,**
	33.15	Zin (that is, Kadesh), and **Mount Hor,** at the edge of the
	33.38	At the command of the Lord, Aaron the priest climbed **Mount Hor.**
	33.41	From **Mount Hor** to the plains of Moab the
	33.41	Diblathaim, the Abarim Mountains near **Mount Nebo,** and in the
	34. 7	line from the Mediterranean to **Mount Hor** [8]and from there to
Deut	1. 2	eleven days to travel from **Mount Sinai** to Kadesh Barnea by
	1. 6	said, [6]"When we were at **Mount Sinai,** the Lord our God said
	1. 9	"While we were still at **Mount Sinai,** I told you, 'The
	1.19	We left **Mount Sinai** and went through that vast and fearful
	3. 8	of the River Jordan, from the River Arnon to **Mount Hermon.**
	3. 9	**(Mount Hermon** is called Sirion by the Sidonians, and Senir
	3.17	the south and to the foot of **Mount Pisgah** on the east.
	3.27	Go to the peak of **Mount Pisgah** and look to the north
	4. 3	You yourselves saw what the Lord did at **Mount Peor.**
	4.10	the Lord your God at **Mount Sinai,** when he said to me,
	4.15	you from the fire on **Mount Sinai,** you did not see any
	4.48	all the way north to **Mount Sirion,** that is, Mount Hermon.
	4.49	as the Dead Sea and east to the foot of **Mount Pisgah.**
	5. 2	At **Mount Sinai** the Lord our God made a covenant, [3]not
	9. 8	Even at **Mount Sinai** you made the Lord angry—angry enough
	11.29	to proclaim the blessing from **Mount Gerizim**
	11.29	and the curse from **Mount Ebal.**
	18.16	that you were gathered at **Mount Sinai,** you begged not to
	27. 4	set up these stones on **Mount Ebal,** as I am instructing you
	27.12	tribes are to stand on **Mount Gerizim** when the blessings are
	27.13	will stand on **Mount Ebal** when the curses are pronounced:
	29. 1	covenant which the Lord had made with them at **Mount Sinai.**
	32.49	climb **Mount Nebo** and look at the land of Canaan that I
	32.50	your brother Aaron died on **Mount Hor,** [51]because both of
	33. 2	The Lord came from **Mount Sinai;**
	33. 2	the sun over Edom and shone on his people from **Mount Paran.**
	34. 1	the plains of Moab to **Mount Nebo,**
	34. 1	to the top of **Mount Pisgah** east of Jericho, and there
Josh	8.30	Then Joshua built on **Mount Ebal** an altar to the Lord,
	8.33	stood with their backs to **Mount Gerizim**
	8.33	and the other half with their backs to **Mount Ebal.**
	11. 3	lived at the foot of **Mount Hermon** in the land of Mizpah.
	11.17	The territory extended from **Mount Halak** in the south near Edom,
	11.17	the north, in the valley of Lebanon south of **Mount Hermon.**
	12. 1	Valley up the Jordan Valley and as far north as **Mount Hermon.**
	12. 3	of the Dead Sea) and on towards the foot of **Mount Pisgah.**
	12. 5	His kingdom included **Mount Hermon,** Salecah, and all of
	12. 7	the valley of Lebanon to **Mount Halak** in the south near Edom.
	13. 5	Baalgad, which is south of **Mount Hermon,** to Hamath Pass.
	13.11	of Geshur and Maacah, all **Mount Hermon,** and all of Bashan as
	13.20	Bethpeor, the slopes of **Mount Pisgah,** and Beth Jeshimoth.
	15. 9	Springs of Nephtoah and out to the cities near **Mount Ephron.**
	15.10	on the north side of **Mount Jearim** (or Chesalon), down to
	15.11	towards Shikkeron, past **Mount Baalah,** and on to Jamnia.
	24.30	in the hill-country of Ephraim north of **Mount Gaash.**
Judg	1.35	live at Aijalon, Shaalbim, and **Mount Heres,** but the tribes
	2. 9	in the hill-country of Ephraim north of **Mount Gaash.**
	3. 3	in the Lebanon Mountains from **Mount Baal Hermon** as far as
	4. 6	tribes of Naphtali and Zebulun and lead them to **Mount Tabor.**
	4.12	Barak had gone up to **Mount Tabor,** [13]he called out his nine
	4.14	So Barak went down from **Mount Tabor** with his ten thousand men.
	7. 3	go back home, and we will stay here at **Mount Gilead.'"**
	9. 7	and stood on top of **Mount Gerizim** and shouted out to them,
	9.48	there, [48]so he went up to **Mount Zalmon** with his men.
1 Sam	23.19	our territory at Horesh on **Mount Hachilah,** in the southern
	26. 1	that David was hiding on **Mount Hachilah** at the edge of the
	26. 3	look for David, [3]and camped by the road on **Mount Hachilah.**
	28. 4	Saul gathered the Israelites and camped at **Mount Gilboa.**
	31. 1	fought a battle against the Israelites on **Mount Gilboa.**
1 Sam	31. 8	the bodies of Saul and his three sons lying on **Mount Gilboa.**
2 Sam	1. 6	"I happened to be on **Mount Gilboa,** and I saw that Saul
	15.30	David went on up the **Mount of Olives** weeping;
	21.12	the bodies on the day they killed Saul on **Mount Gilboa.)**
1 Kgs	8. 9	Moses had placed there at **Mount Sinai,** when the Lord made a
	18.19	order all the people of Israel to meet me at **Mount Carmel.**
	18.20	Israelites and the prophets of Baal to meet at **Mount Carmel.**
	18.42	climbed to the top of **Mount Carmel,** where he bowed down to
2 Kgs	2.25	Elisha went on to **Mount Carmel,** and later returned to Samaria.
	4.25	So she set out, and went to **Mount Carmel,** where Elisha was.
	19.31	people in Jerusalem and on **Mount Zion** who will survive,
	23.13	of Jerusalem, south of the **Mount of Olives,** for the worship
1 Chr	5.23	Senir, and **Mount Hermon,** and their population increased greatly.
	10. 1	fought a battle against the Israelites on **Mount Gilboa.**
	10. 8	found the bodies of Saul and his sons lying on **Mount Gilboa.**
2 Chr	3. 1	It was in Jerusalem, on **Mount Moriah,** where the Lord
	5.10	Moses had placed there at **Mount Sinai,** when the Lord made a
	13. 4	King Abijah went up **Mount Zemaraim** and called out to
Neh	9.13	At **Mount Sinai** you came down from heaven;
Ps	20. 2	you help from his Temple and give you aid from **Mount Zion.**
	29. 6	like calves and makes **Mount Hermon** leap like a young bull.
	42. 6	down to the Jordan from **Mount Hermon and Mount Mizar.**
	48. 4	The kings gathered together and came to attack **Mount Zion.**
	68.14	God scattered the kings on **Mount Zalmon,** he caused snow to
	74. 2	Remember **Mount Zion,** where once you lived.
	76. 2	he lives on **Mount Zion.**
	78.68	the tribe of Judah and **Mount Zion,** which he dearly loves.
	84. 5	you, who are eager to make the pilgrimage to **Mount Zion.**
	89.12	**Mount Tabor and Mount Hermon** sing to you for joy.
	125. 1	in the Lord are like **Mount Zion,** which can never be shaken,
	133. 3	is like the dew on **Mount Hermon,** falling on the hills of
Song	4. 8	down from the top of **Mount Amana, from Mount Senir**
	4. 8	and **Mount Hermon,** where the lions and leopards
	7. 5	Your head is held high like **Mount Carmel.**
Is	4. 5	Then over **Mount Zion** and over all who are gathered there,
	8.18	Almighty, whose throne is on **Mount Zion,** has sent us as
	10.12	what I am doing on **Mount Zion** and in Jerusalem, I will
	10.32	their fists at **Mount Zion,** at the city of Jerusalem.
	18. 7	will come to **Mount Zion,** where the Lord Almighty is worshipped.
	24.23	will rule in Jerusalem on **Mount Zion,** and the leaders of the
	25. 6	Here on **Mount Zion** the Lord Almighty will prepare a
	25.10	The Lord will protect **Mount Zion,** but the people of Moab
	28.21	fight as he did at **Mount Perazim** and in the valley of
	31. 4	can keep me, the Lord Almighty, from protecting **Mount Zion.**
	33. 9	and in Bashan and on **Mount Carmel** the leaves are falling
	37.32	people in Jerusalem and on **Mount Zion** who will survive,
Jer	3.14	from each clan, and I will bring you back to **Mount Zion.**
	31.12	and sing for joy on **Mount Zion** and be delighted with my
	46.18	As **Mount Tabor** towers above the mountains
	46.18	and **Mount Carmel** stands high above the sea,
	50.19	the food that grows on **Mount Carmel** and in the region of
Lam	5.11	Our wives have been raped on **Mount Zion** itself;
	5.18	our tears, [18]because **Mount Zion** lies lonely and deserted,
Ezek	27. 5	They used fir-trees from **Mount Hermon** for timber And a
Hos	5. 1	Mizpah, a net spread on **Mount Tabor,** [2]a deep pit at Acacia
	9.10	But when they came to **Mount Peor,** they began to worship Baal,
Joel	2.15	Blow the trumpet on **Mount Zion;**
	3.16	The Lord roars from **Mount Zion;**
	3.20	for ever, and I the Lord, will live on **Mount Zion."**
Amos	1. 2	"The Lord roars from **Mount Zion;**
	1. 2	The pastures dry up, and the grass on **Mount Carmel** turns brown."
	9. 3	hide on the top of **Mount Carmel,** I will search for them
Obad	17	"But on **Mount Zion** some will escape, and it will be a
Mic	4. 7	will rule over them on **Mount Zion** from that time on and
Nah	1. 4	The fields of Bashan wither, **Mount Carmel** turns brown, and
Zech	14. 4	he will stand on the **Mount of Olives,** to the east of
	14. 4	Then the **Mount of Olives** will be split in two from east
Mal	4. 4	which I gave him at **Mount Sinai** for all the people of
Mt	21. 1	approached Jerusalem, they came to Bethphage at the **Mount of Olives.**
	24. 3	Jesus sat on the **Mount of Olives,** the disciples came to him
	26.30	they sang a hymn and went out to the **Mount of Olives.**
Mk	11. 1	of Bethphage and Bethany, they came to the **Mount of Olives.**
	13. 3	was sitting on the **Mount of Olives,** across from the Temple,
	14.26	they sang a hymn and went out to the **Mount of Olives.**
Lk	19.29	and Bethany at the **Mount of Olives,** he sent two disciples
	19.37	road went down the **Mount of Olives,** the large crowd of his
	21.37	would go out and spend the night on the **Mount of Olives.**
	22.39	city and went, as he usually did, to the **Mount of Olives;**
Jn	8. 1	Then everyone went home, but Jesus went to the **Mount of Olives.**
Acts	1.12	to Jerusalem from the **Mount of Olives,** which is about a
	7.30	the flames of a burning bush in the desert near **Mount Sinai.**
	7.38	who spoke to him on **Mount Sinai,** and he received God's
Gal	4.24	is Hagar, and she represents the covenant made at **Mount Sinai.**
	4.25	Hagar, who stands for **Mount Sinai** in Arabia, is a figure
Heb	12.18	what you can feel, to **Mount Sinai** with its blazing fire, the
	12.22	Instead, you have come to **Mount Zion** and to the city of
Rev	14. 1	Then I looked, and there was the Lamb standing on **Mount Zion;**

MOUNT (2)

Gen	24.61	young women got ready and **mounted** the camels to go with
1 Sam	25.42	She rose quickly and **mounted** her donkey.
	30.17	four hundred young men who **mounted** camels and got away, none
2 Sam	13.29	All the rest of David's sons **mounted** their mules and fled.
2 Chr	6.13	He **mounted** this platform, knelt down where everyone could see
Esth	6. 9	these robes and lead him, **mounted** on the horse, through the
	8.10	They were delivered by riders **mounted** on fast horses from
	8.14	the king's command the riders **mounted** royal horses and rode
Jer	46. 4	Harness your horses and **mount** them!

Dan 7. 9 His throne, **mounted** on fiery wheels, was blazing with fire,
Rev 9.16 I was told the number of the **mounted** troops:

MOUNT (3)

Ex 28.11 of the sons of Jacob, and **mount** the stones in gold settings.
28.17 **Mount** four rows of precious stones on it;
28.17 in the first row **mount** a ruby, a topaz, and a garnet;
28.20 These are to be **mounted** in gold settings.
39. 6 They prepared the carnelians and **mounted** them in gold settings;
39.10 They **mounted** four rows of precious stones on it:
39.10 in the first row they **mounted** a ruby, a topaz, and a
39.13 These were **mounted** in gold settings.

MOUNTAIN

Gen 7.19 It became so deep that it covered the highest **mountains;**
7.20 it was about seven metres above the tops of the **mountains.**
8. 4 the boat came to rest on a **mountain** in the Ararat range.
8. 5 day of the tenth month the tops of the **mountains** appeared.
14. 6 and the Horites in the **mountains** of Edom, pursuing them as
14.10 but the other three kings escaped to the **mountains.**
22. 2 There on a **mountain** that I will show you, offer him as
22.14 even today people say, "On the Lord's **mountain** he provides."
31.25 up his camp on a **mountain,** and Laban set up his camp
31.54 as a sacrifice on the **mountain,** and he invited his men to
31.54 After they had eaten, they spent the night on the **mountain.**
49.26 Blessings of ancient **mountains,** Delightful things
Ex 3. 1 across the desert and came to Sinai, the holy **mountain.**
3.12 people out of Egypt, you will worship me on this **mountain.**
4.27 So he went to meet him at the holy **mountain;**
15.17 and plant them on your **mountain,** the place that you, Lord,
18. 5 into the desert where Moses was camped at the holy **mountain.**
19. 3 Mount Sinai, [3]and Moses went up the **mountain** to meet with God.
19. 3 called to him from the **mountain** and told him to say to
19.12 a boundary round the **mountain** that the people must not cross,
19.12 them not to go up the **mountain** or even get near it.
19.13 is blown, then the people are to go up to the **mountain."**
19.14 Then Moses came down the **mountain** and told the people to
19.16 thick cloud appeared on the **mountain,** and a very loud
19.17 to meet God, and they stood at the foot of the **mountain.**
19.20 of Mount Sinai and called Moses to the top of the **mountain.**
19.23 commanded us to consider the **mountain** sacred and to mark a
20.18 the lightning and the smoking **mountain,** they trembled with
24. 1 to Moses, "Come up the **mountain** to me, you and Aaron,
24. 2 The people are not even to come up the **mountain."**
24. 4 at the foot of the **mountain** and set up twelve stones, one
24. 9 of Israel went up the **mountain** [10]and they saw the God of
24.12 to Moses, "Come up the **mountain** to me, and while you are
24.13 Joshua got ready, and Moses began to go up the holy **mountain.**
24.16 dazzling light of the Lord's presence came down on the **mountain.**
24.16 the light looked like a fire burning on top of the **mountain.**
24.16 The cloud covered the **mountain** for six days, and on the
24.18 Moses went on up the **mountain** into the cloud.
25.40 according to the plan that I showed you on the **mountain.**
26.30 Tent according to the plan that I showed you on the **mountain.**
27. 8 according to the plan that I showed you on the **mountain.**
32. 1 not come down from the **mountain** but was staying there a long
32.12 to kill them in the **mountains** and destroy them completely?
32.15 Moses went back down the **mountain,** carrying the two
32.19 at the foot of the **mountain,** he threw down the tablets he
32.30 But now I will again go up the **mountain** to the Lord;
34. 3 no one is to be seen on any part of the **mountain;**
34. 3 sheep or cattle are to graze at the foot of the **mountain."**
Num 10.33 Sinai, the holy **mountain,** they travelled for three days.
20.28 on the top of the **mountain** Aaron died, and Moses and Eleazar
23. 7 Moab has brought me From Syria, from the eastern **mountains.**
27.12 Moses, "Go up the Abarim **Mountains** and look out over the
33.41 Gad, Almon Diblathaim, the Abarim **Mountains** near Mount Nebo,
Deut 1. 6 God said to us, 'You have stayed long enough at this **mountain.**
1. 7 and on beyond the Lebanon **Mountains** as far as the great
3.25 the beautiful hill-country and the Lebanon **Mountains.'**
4.11 at the foot of the **mountain** which was covered with thick
5. 4 There on the **mountain** the Lord spoke to you face-to-face
5. 5 were afraid of the fire and would not go up the **mountain.**
5.22 gave to all of you when you were gathered at the **mountain.**
5.23 "When the whole **mountain** was on fire and you heard the
9. 9 I went up the **mountain** to receive the stone tablets on
9.10 on the day that you were gathered there at the **mountain.**
9.12 to me, 'Go down the **mountain** at once, because your people,
9.15 turned and went down the **mountain,** carrying the two stone
9.15 Flames of fire were coming from the **mountain.**
9.21 the dust into the stream that flowed down the **mountain.**
10. 1 up to me on the **mountain,** [2]and I will write on those
10. 3 tablets like the first ones and took them up the **mountain.**
10. 4 from the fire on the day you were gathered at the **mountain.**
10. 5 me the tablets, [5]and I turned and went down the **mountain.**
10. 8 At the **mountain** the Lord appointed the men of the tribe of
10.10 "I stayed on the **mountain** forty days and nights, as I
11.11 enter is a land of **mountains** and valleys, a land watered by
11.24 the south to the Lebanon **Mountains** in the north, and from
11.30 (These two **mountains** are west of the River Jordan in the
12. 2 gods on high **mountains,** on hills, and under green trees.
32.22 to the world below and consume the roots of the **mountains.**
32.49 Moses, [49]"Go to the Abarim **Mountains** in the land of Moab
32.50 You will die on that **mountain** as your brother Aaron died
33.19 They invite foreigners to their **mountain** And offer the right
Josh 1. 4 desert in the south to the Lebanon **Mountains** in the north;
10.10 and pursued them down the **mountain** pass at Beth Horon,
13. 6 between the Lebanon **Mountains** and Misrephoth Maim.
18.13 to Ataroth Addar, on the **mountain** south of Lower Beth Horon.
Josh 18.14 the western side of this **mountain** and going to Kiriath Baal
18.16 foot of the **mountain** that overlooks the Valley of Hinnom,
Judg 3. 3 who lived in the Lebanon **Mountains** from Mount Baal Hermon as
5. 4 Lord, when you left the **mountains** of Seir, when you came
5. 5 The **mountains** quaked before the Lord of Sinai, before the Lord,
9.25 ambush against Abimelech on the **mountain-tops,** and they
9.36 There are men coming down from the **mountain-tops!"**
9.36 "They are just shadows on the **mountains."**
9.37 down the crest of the **mountain** and one group is coming along
11.37 friends to wander in the **mountains** and grieve that I must
11.38 friends went up into the **mountains** and grieved because she
2 Sam 21. 9 who hanged them on the **mountain** before the Lord—and all
22.34 he keeps me safe on the **mountains.**
1 Kgs 11. 7 On the **mountain** east of Jerusalem he built a place to
19. 8 strength to walk forty days to Sinai, the holy **mountain.**
19.11 before me on top of the **mountain,"** the Lord said to him.
20.23 "The gods of Israel are **mountain** gods, and that is why the
2 Kgs 2.16 him away and left him on some **mountain** or in some valley."
14. 9 bush on the Lebanon **Mountains** sent a message to a cedar:
19.23 chariots you had conquered the highest **mountains** of Lebanon.
1 Chr 12. 8 as fierce-looking as lions and as quick as **mountain** deer.
2 Chr 2.16 In the **mountains** of Lebanon we will cut down all the
2.18 to cut stones in the **mountains,** and appointed 3,600
25.18 bush in the Lebanon **Mountains** sent a message to a cedar:
27. 4 In the **mountains** of Judah he built cities, and in the
Job 9. 5 Without warning he moves **mountains** and in anger he destroys
14.18 There comes a time when **mountains** fall and solid cliffs
15. 7 Were you there when God made the **mountains?**
18. 4 Will God move **mountains** to satisfy you?
24. 8 rain that falls on the **mountains,** and they huddle beside the
28. 9 Men dig the hardest rocks, Dig **mountains** away at their base.
39. 1 Do you know when **mountain-goats** are born?
39. 8 The **mountains** are the pastures where they feed, where they
39.27 for your command to build its nest high in the **mountains?**
Ps 11. 1 like a bird to the **mountains,** [2]because the wicked have
18. 7 the foundations of the **mountains** rocked and quivered,
18.33 he keeps me safe on the **mountains.**
29. 6 He makes the **mountains** of Lebanon jump like calves
30. 7 you protected me like a **mountain** fortress.
36. 6 Your righteousness is towering like the **mountains;**
46. 2 earth is shaken and **mountains** fall into the ocean depths;
48. 2 Zion, the **mountain** of God, is high and beautiful;
65. 6 You set the **mountains** in place by your strength, showing
68.15 What a mighty **mountain** is Bashan, a mountain of many peaks!
68.16 look with scorn on the **mountain** on which God chose to live?
76. 4 you return from the **mountains** where you defeated your foes.
78.54 his holy land, to the **mountains** which he himself conquered.
104. 6 over it like a robe, and the water covered the **mountains.**
104. 8 They flowed over the **mountains** and into the valleys, to
104.18 goats live in the high **mountains,** and the rock-badgers hide
104.32 he touches the **mountains,** and they pour out smoke.
114. 4 The **mountains** skipped like goats;
114. 6 You **mountains,** why did you skip like goats?
121. 1 I look to the **mountains;**
125. 2 As the **mountains** surround Jerusalem, so the Lord surrounds
144. 5 touch the **mountains,** and they will pour out smoke.
148. 9 Praise him, hills and **mountains,** fruit-trees and forests;
Prov 8.25 I was born before the **mountains,** before the hills were
Song 2. 1 only a wild flower in Sharon, a lily in a **mountain** valley.
2. 8 He comes running over the **mountains,** racing across the hills
2.17 like a gazelle, like a stag on the **mountains** of Bether.
4. 8 Come with me from the Lebanon **Mountains,** my bride;
4.15 water, brooks gushing down from the Lebanon **Mountains.**
5.15 He is majestic, like the Lebanon **Mountains**
8.14 like a young stag on the **mountains** where spices grow.
Is 2. 2 In days to come the **mountain** where the Temple stands will
2.14 He will level the high **mountains** and hills,
5.25 The **mountains** will shake, and the bodies of those who die
13. 4 to the noise on the **mountains**—the sound of a great crowd
14.13 like a king on that **mountain** in the north where the gods
14.25 in my land of Israel and trample upon them on my **mountains.**
16.12 themselves out going to their **mountain** shrines and to their
18. 3 a signal flag to be raised on the tops of the **mountains!**
30.25 of water will flow from every **mountain** and every hill.
34. 3 and the **mountains** will be red with blood.
35. 2 as beautiful as the Lebanon **Mountains** and as fertile as the
37.24 chariots you had conquered the highest **mountains** of Lebanon.
40. 4 level every **mountain.**
40. 9 Jerusalem, go up on a high **mountain** and proclaim the good news!
40.12 earth in a cup or weigh the **mountains** and hills on scales?
41.15 You will thresh **mountains** and destroy them;
42.11 city of Sela shout for joy from the tops of the **mountains!**
42.15 will destroy the hills and **mountains** and dry up the grass
44.23 Shout for joy, **mountains,** and every tree of the forest!
45. 2 "I myself will prepare your way, levelling **mountains** and hills.
49.11 make a highway across the **mountains** and prepare a road for
49.13 Let the **mountains** burst into song!
52. 7 a messenger coming across the **mountains,** bringing good news,
54.10 The **mountains** and hills may crumble, but my love for you
55.12 The **mountains** and hills will burst into singing, and the
57. 7 You go to the high **mountains** to offer sacrifices and have sex.
64. 1 The **mountains** would see you and shake with fear.
64. 3 the **mountains** saw you and shook with fear.
65. 9 and their descendants will possess my land of **mountains.**
Jer 4.24 I looked at the **mountains**—they were shaking, and the
9.10 "I will mourn for the **mountains** and weep for the pastures,
13.16 he brings darkness, and you stumble on the **mountains;**
16.16 hunt them down on every **mountain** and hill and in the caves
17. 3 on the hill-tops [3]and on the **mountains** in the open country.
17.12 throne, standing on a high **mountain** from the beginning.
17.26 the foothills, from the **mountains,** and from southern Judah.

Jer 18.14 Do its cool **mountain** streams ever run dry?
22. 6 as the land of Gilead and as the Lebanon **Mountains;**
22.20 call out from the **mountains** of Moab, because all your allies
46.18 Mount Tabor towers above the **mountains** and Mount Carmel
48.45 up the frontiers and the **mountain** heights of the war-loving
49.16 You live on the rocky cliffs, high on top of the **mountain;**
50. 6 whose shepherds have let them get lost in the **mountains.**
50. 6 wandered like sheep from one **mountain** to another, and they
51.25 Babylonia, you are like a **mountain** that destroys the whole world,
Ezek 6. 2 he said, "look towards the **mountains** of Israel and give
6. 3 Tell the **mountains** of Israel to hear the word of the Lord
6. 3 Sovereign Lord, am telling the **mountains,** the hills, the
6.13 on the top of every **mountain,** under every green tree and
7. 7 more celebrations at the **mountain** shrines, only confusion.
7.16 Some will escape to the **mountains** like doves frightened
11.23 light left the city and moved to the **mountain** east of it.
17. 3 He flew to the Lebanon **Mountains** and broke off the top of
17.22 I will plant it on a high **mountain,**
17.23 on Israel's highest **mountain.**
20.40 the land, on my holy **mountain,** the high mountain of Israel,
28.14 You lived on my holy **mountain** and walked among sparkling gems.
28.16 you to leave my holy **mountain,** and the angel who guarded you
31.12 will fall on every **mountain** and valley in the country.
31.15 bring darkness over the Lebanon **Mountains** and make all the
32. 5 I will cover **mountains** and valleys with your rotting corpse.
32. 6 until it spreads over the **mountains** and fills the streams.
33.27 Those hiding in the **mountains** and in caves will die of disease.
33.28 The **mountains** of Israel will be so wild that no one will
34. 6 So my sheep wandered over the high hills and the **mountains.**
34.13 lead them back to the **mountains** and the streams of Israel
34.14 graze in safety in the **mountain** meadows and the valleys and
35. 3 I am your enemy, **mountains** of Edom!
35. 8 I will cover the **mountains** with corpses, and the bodies of
35.12 say with contempt that the **mountains** of Israel were desolate
35.15 The **mountains** of Seir, yes, all the land of Edom, will be
36. 1 "Mortal man, speak to the **mountains** of Israel and tell them
36. 3 nations captured and plundered the **mountains** of Israel, all
36. 4 Sovereign Lord, say to you **mountains** and hills, to you
36. 6 **mountains,** hills, brooks, and valleys what I,
36. 8 But on the **mountains** of Israel the trees will again grow
37.22 into one nation in the land, on the **mountains** of Israel.
38. 8 He will invade the **mountains** of Israel, which were desolate
38.20 **Mountains** will fall, cliffs will crumble, and every wall
39. 2 of the far north until he comes to the **mountains** of Israel.
39. 4 will fall dead on the **mountains** of Israel, and I will let
39.17 a huge feast on the **mountains** of Israel, where they can eat
40. 2 to the land of Israel and put me on a high **mountain.**
43.12 it on the top of the **mountain** is sacred and holy."
Dan 2.35 stone grew to be a **mountain** that covered the whole earth.
11.45 between the sea and the **mountain** on which the Temple stands.
Hos 4.13 At sacred places on the **mountain-tops** they offer sacrifices,
10. 8 The people will call out to the **mountains,** "Hide us!"
Joel 2. 2 army of locusts advances like darkness spreading over the **mountains.**
2. 5 on the tops of the **mountains,** they rattle like chariots;
3.18 At that time the **mountains** will be covered with vineyards,
Amos 4.13 God is the one who made the **mountains** and created the winds.
9.13 The **mountains** will drip with sweet wine, and the hills will
Obad 3 home is high in the **mountains,** and so you say to yourself,
Jon 2. 6 the very roots of the **mountains,** into the land whose gates
Mic 1. 3 he will come down and walk on the tops of the **mountains.**
1. 4 Then the **mountains** will melt under him like wax in a fire;
4. 1 In days to come the **mountain** where the Temple stands will
6. 1 let the **mountains** and the hills hear what you say.
6. 2 You **mountains,** you everlasting foundations of the earth,
7.12 of the Euphrates, from distant seas and far-off **mountains.**
Nah 1. 5 **Mountains** quake in the presence of the Lord;
1.15 Look, a messenger is coming over the **mountains** with good news!
3.18 people are scattered on the **mountains,** and there is no one
Hab 3. 6 The eternal **mountains** are shattered;
3.10 When the **mountains** saw you, they trembled;
3.19 sure-footed as a deer, and keeps me safe on the **mountains.**
Zech 4. 7 Obstacles as great as **mountains** will disappear before you.
6. 1 I saw four chariots coming out from between two bronze **mountains.**
14. 4 Half the **mountain** will move northwards and half of it southwards.
14. 5 escape through this valley that divides the **mountain** in two.
Mt 4. 8 Jesus to a very high **mountain** and showed him all the
17. 1 John and led them up a high **mountain** where they were alone.
17. 9 they came down the **mountain,** Jesus ordered them, "Don't tell
Mk 9. 2 John, and led them up a high **mountain,** where they were alone.
9. 9 they came down the **mountain,** Jesus ordered them, "Don't tell
Lk 3. 5 valley must be filled up, every hill and **mountain** levelled off.
23.30 the time when people will say to the **mountains,** 'Fall on
Jn 4.20 ancestors worshipped God on this **mountain,** but you Jews say that
4.21 not worship the Father either on this **mountain** or in Jerusalem.
1 Cor 13. 2 the faith needed to move **mountains**—but if I have no love,
Heb 8. 5 according to the pattern you were shown on the **mountain."**
12.20 animal touches the **mountain,** it must be stoned to death."
2 Pet 1.18 from heaven, when we were with him on the holy **mountain.**
Rev 6.14 being rolled up, and every **mountain** and island was moved
6.15 hid themselves in caves and under rocks on the **mountains.**
6.16 They called out to the **mountains** and to the rocks,
8. 8 that looked like a huge **mountain** on fire was thrown into the
16.20 All the islands disappeared, all the **mountains** vanished.
21.10 the angel carried me to the top of a very high **mountain.**

MOUNTAIN-GOATS see **GOAT**

Am **MOUNTAINSIDE** see **HILLSIDE**

MOURN

Gen 23. 2 Hebron in the land of Canaan, and Abraham **mourned** her death.
27.41 He thought, "The time to **mourn** my father's death is near;
37.34 He **mourned** for his son a long time.
37.35 down to the world of the dead still **mourning** for my son."
37.35 So he continued to **mourn** for his son Joseph.
38.12 had finished the time of **mourning,** he and his friend Hirah
50. 3 The Egyptians **mourned** for him seventy days.
50. 4 When the time of **mourning** was over, Joseph said to the
50.10 east of the Jordan, they **mourned** loudly for a long time, and
50.10 and Joseph performed **mourning** ceremonies for seven days.
50.11 of Canaan saw those people **mourning** at Atad, they said,
50.11 "What a solemn ceremony of **mourning** the Egyptians are holding!"
Ex 33. 4 heard this, they began to **mourn** and did not wear jewellery
Lev 10. 6 or tear your clothes to show that you are in **mourning.**
10. 6 your fellow-Israelites are allowed to **mourn** this death
19.28 yourselves or cut gashes in your body to **mourn** for the dead.
21. 5 cut gashes on his body to show that he is in **mourning.**
21.10 uncombed or tear his clothes to show that he is in **mourning.**
Num 14.39 the Israelites what the Lord had said, they **mourned** bitterly.
20.29 Aaron had died, and they all **mourned** for him for thirty days.
25. 6 whole community, while they were **mourning** at the entrance of
Deut 14. 1 So when you **mourn** for the dead, don't gash yourselves or
21.13 stay in your home and **mourn** for her parents for a month;
26.14 I have not eaten any of it when I was **mourning;**
34. 8 The people of Israel **mourned** for him for thirty days in
Judg 20.22 the place of worship and **mourned** in the presence of the Lord
20.26 Then all the people of Israel went up to Bethel and **mourned.**
21. 2 Loudly and bitterly they **mourned:**
1 Sam 6.19 And the people **mourned** because the Lord had caused such a
25. 1 Samuel died, and all the Israelites came together and **mourned**
28. 3 and all the Israelites had **mourned** for him and had buried
2 Sam 1.12 They grieved and **mourned** and fasted until evening for
1.24 "Women of Israel, **mourn** for Saul!
3.31 to tear their clothes, wear sackcloth, and **mourn** for Abner.
11.26 Bathsheba heard that her husband had been killed, she **mourned**
11.27 When the time of **mourning** was over, David sent for her
13.37 David **mourned** a long time for his son Amnon;
14. 2 arrived, he said to her, "Pretend that you are in **mourning;**
14. 2 put on your **mourning** clothes, and don't comb your hair.
14. 2 like a woman who has been in **mourning** for a long time.
19. 1 was told that King David was weeping and **mourning** for Absalom.
19. 2 because they heard that the king was **mourning** for his son.
1 Kgs 13.29 brought it back to Bethel to **mourn** over it and bury it.
13.30 he and his sons **mourned** over it, saying, "Oh my brother,
14.13 All the people of Israel will **mourn** for him and bury him.
14.18 The people of Israel **mourned** for him and buried him, as
1 Chr 7.22 Their father Ephraim **mourned** for them for many days, and
2 Chr 16.14 burial, and they built a huge bonfire to **mourn** his death.
21.19 not light a bonfire in **mourning** for him as had been done
35.24 All the people of Judah and Jerusalem **mourned** his death.
35.25 men and women, to use this song when they **mourn** for him.
Neh 1. 4 For several days I **mourned** and did not eat.
8. 9 the Lord your God, so you are not to **mourn** or cry.
Esth 4. 3 was made known, there was loud **mourning** among the Jews.
9.31 rules for the observance of fasts and times of **mourning.**
Job 3.24 Instead of eating, I **mourn,** and I can never stop groaning.
5.11 God who raises the humble and gives joy to all who **mourn.**
16.15 I **mourn** and wear clothes made of sackcloth, and I sit
27.15 disease, and even their widows will not **mourn** their death.
30.31 I heard joyful music, now I hear only **mourning** and weeping.
Ps 35.13 But when they were sick, I dressed in **mourning;**
35.14 went about bent over in **mourning,**
35.14 as one who **mourns** for his mother.
38. 6 I **mourn** all day long.
69.11 I dress myself in clothes of **mourning,** and they laugh at me.
78.64 died by violence, and their widows were not allowed to **mourn.**
Ecc 3. 4 for joy, the time for **mourning** and the time for dancing,
7. 2 a home where there is **mourning** than to one where there is
12. 5 place, and then there will be **mourning** in the streets.
Is 3.26 The city gates will **mourn** and cry, and the city itself
15. 3 the city squares and on the house-tops people **mourn** and cry.
22.12 you then to weep and **mourn,** to shave your heads and wear
50. 3 sky turn dark, as if it were in **mourning** for the dead."
57.18 lead them and help them, and I will comfort those who **mourn.**
61. 2 me to comfort all who **mourn,**
61. 3 To give to those who **mourn** in Zion Joy and gladness
66.10 Rejoice with her now, all you that have **mourned** for her!
Jer 4.28 The earth will **mourn;**
6.26 **Mourn** with bitter tears as you would for an only son,
7.29 **"Mourn,** people of Jerusalem;
8.21 I **mourn;**
9.10 I said, "I will **mourn** for the mountains and weep for
9.17 Call for the **mourners** to come, for the women who sing
9.20 Teach your daughters how to **mourn,** and your friends how to
14. 2 "Judah is in **mourning;**
16. 4 diseases, and no one will **mourn** for them or bury them.
16. 5 "You must not enter a house where there is **mourning.**
16. 6 this land, but no one will bury them or **mourn** for them.
22.10 do not **mourn** his death.
22.18 "No one will **mourn** his death or say, 'How terrible, my
23.10 the Lord's curse the land **mourns** and the pastures are dry.
25.33 No one will **mourn** for them, and they will not be taken
25.34 **Mourn** and roll in the dust.
31.13 turn their **mourning** into joy, their sorrow into gladness.
34. 5 They will **mourn** over you and say, 'Our king is dead!'

Jer 47. 5 How long will the rest of Philistia **mourn?**
48.17 **"Mourn** for that nation, you that live near by, all of
48.36 "So my heart **mourns** for Moab and for the people of Kir
48.38 squares there is nothing but **mourning,** because I have broken
49. 3 Women of Rabbah, go into **mourning!**
49. 3 Put on sackcloth and **mourn.**
51. 8 **Mourn** over it!
51.54 in Babylon, of **mourning** for the destruction in the land.
Ezek 7.27 The king will **mourn,** the prince will give up hope, and
24.17 Do not go bareheaded or barefoot as a sign of **mourning.**
24.17 Don't cover your face or eat the food that **mourners** eat."
24.22 will not cover your faces or eat the food that **mourners** eat.
24.23 You will not go bareheaded or barefoot or **mourn** or cry.
27.30 They all **mourn** bitterly for you, Throwing dust on their
31.15 make the underground waters cover it as a sign of **mourning.**
32.16 nations will sing it to **mourn** for Egypt and all its people.
32.18 he said, **"mourn** for all the many people of Egypt.
Dan 10. 2 At that time, I was **mourning** for three weeks.
Hos 10. 5 will be afraid and will **mourn** the loss of the gold bull
Joel 1. 8 people, like a girl who **mourns** the death of the man she
1. 9 the priests **mourn** because they have no offerings for the Lord.
1.10 the ground **mourns** because the corn is destroyed, the grapes
1.13 Go into the Temple and **mourn** all night!
2.12 and return to me with fasting and weeping and **mourning.**
Amos 5.16 to mourn the dead along with those who are paid to **mourn.**
6. 6 perfumes, but you do not **mourn** over the ruin of Israel.
8. 3 day the songs in the palace will become cries of **mourning.**
8.10 and you will be like parents **mourning** for their only son.
9. 5 all who live there **mourn.**
Mic 1. 8 Then Micah said, "Because of this I will **mourn** and lament.
1.11 hear the people of Bethezel **mourn,** you will know that there
1.16 cut off your hair in **mourning** for the children you love.
Zech 7. 3 "Should we continue to **mourn** because of the destruction
7. 5 that when they fasted and **mourned** in the fifth and seventh
12.10 will mourn for him like those who **mourn** for an only child.
12.10 **mourn** bitterly, like those who have lost their first-born son.
12.11 At that time the **mourning** in Jerusalem will be
12.11 as great as the **mourning** for Hadad-rimmon in the plain of
12.12 Each family in the land will **mourn** by itself:
12.12 Each family will **mourn** by itself,
12.12 men of each family will **mourn** separately from the women.
Mt 5. 4 "Happy are those who **mourn;**
Mk 16.10 They were **mourning** and crying;
Lk 6.25 you will **mourn** and weep!
8.52 Everyone there was crying and **mourning** for the child.
Acts 8. 2 devout men buried Stephen, **mourning** for him with loud cries.
Rev 1. 7 All peoples on earth will **mourn** over him.
18.11 the earth also cry and **mourn** for her, because no one buys
18.15 They will cry and **mourn,** [16]and say, "How terrible!
18.19 threw dust on their heads, they cried and **mourned,** saying,

MOUTH

Gen 4.11 if it had opened its **mouth** to receive it when you killed
Ex 4.11 The Lord said to him, "Who gives man his **mouth?**
2 Sam 22. 9 a consuming flame and burning coals from his **mouth.**
2 Kgs 4.34 on the boy, placing his **mouth,** eyes, and hands on
4.34 on the boy's **mouth,** eyes, and hands.
19.28 and a bit in your **mouth,** and take you back by the
Job 20.12 him that he keeps some in his **mouth** to enjoy its flavour.
37. 2 the voice of God, to the thunder that comes from his **mouth.**
41.19 Flames blaze from his **mouth,** and streams of sparks fly out.
41.21 flames leap out of his **mouth.**
Ps 12. 3 Close those boastful **mouths** that say, [4]"With our words
18. 8 a consuming flame and burning coals from his **mouth.**
22.13 They open their **mouths** like lions, roaring and tearing at me.
22.15 as dust, and my tongue sticks to the roof of my **mouth.**
59. 7 are like swords in their **mouths,** yet they think that no one
63.11 name will praise him, but the **mouths** of liars will be shut.
81.10 Open your **mouth,** and I will feed you.
115. 5 They have **mouths,** but cannot speak, and eyes, but cannot see.
119.131 In my desire for your commands I pant with open **mouth.**
135.16 They have **mouths,** but cannot speak, and eyes, but cannot see.
141. 3 place a guard at my **mouth,** a sentry at the door of
Prov 17.28 and intelligent if he stays quiet and keeps his **mouth** shut.
19.24 Some people are too lazy to put food in their own **mouths.**
20.17 but sooner or later it will be like a **mouthful** of sand.
24. 2 time they open their **mouth** someone is going to be hurt.
26.15 Some people are too lazy to put food in their own **mouths.**
Ecc 5.11 The richer you are, the more **mouths** you must feed.
Song 5.16 His **mouth** is sweet to kiss;
7. 9 fragrance of apples, [9]and your **mouth** like the finest wine.
Is 5.14 the dead is hungry for them, and it opens its **mouth** wide.
9.12 Philistia on the west have opened their **mouths** to devour Israel.
37.29 and a bit in your **mouth** and will take you back by
Jer 5.13 things, I will make my words like a fire in your **mouth.**
Ezek 2. 8 Open your **mouth** and eat what I am going to give you."
3. 2 So I opened my **mouth,** and he gave me the scroll to
16.63 will remember them and be too ashamed to open your **mouth."**
Dan 4.31 words were out of his **mouth,** a voice spoke from heaven,
6.17 stone was put over the **mouth** of the pit, and the king
6.22 his angel to shut the **mouths** of the lions so that they
7. 8 This horn had human eyes and a **mouth** that was boasting proudly.
7.20 It had eyes and a **mouth** and was boasting proudly.
Mic 7.16 In dismay they will close their **mouths** and cover their ears.
Nah 3.12 shake the trees, and the fruit falls right into your **mouth!**
Mt 12.34 For the **mouth** speaks what the heart is full of.
15.11 not what goes into a person's **mouth** that makes him ritually
15.17 that goes into a person's **mouth** goes into his stomach and
15.18 that come out of the **mouth** come from the heart, and these
17.27 you hook, and in its **mouth** you will find a coin worth
Mk 9.18 and he foams at the **mouth,** grits his teeth, and becomes
9.20 fell on the ground and rolled round, foaming at the **mouth.**
Lk 6.45 For the **mouth** speaks what the heart is full of.
9.39 throws him into a fit, so that he foams at the **mouth;**
Acts 11. 8 No ritually unclean or defiled food has ever entered my **mouth.'**
23. 2 who were standing close to Paul to strike him on the **mouth.**
2 Thes 2. 8 with the breath from his **mouth** and destroy him with his
Heb 11.33 They shut the **mouths** of lions, [34]put out fierce fires,
Jas 3. 3 put a bit into the **mouth** of a horse to make it
3.10 Words of thanksgiving and cursing pour out from the same **mouth.**
Rev 1.16 and a sharp two-edged sword came out of his **mouth.**
2.16 those people with the sword that comes out of my **mouth.**
3.16 nor cold, I am going to spit you out of my **mouth!**
9.17 and from their **mouths** came out fire, smoke, and sulphur.
9.18 the smoke, and the sulphur coming out of the horses' **mouths.**
9.19 of the horses is in their **mouths** and also in their tails.
10. 9 your stomach, but in your **mouth** it will be sweet as honey."
10.10 and ate it, and it tasted sweet as honey in my **mouth.**
11. 5 fire comes out of their **mouths** and destroys their enemies;
12.15 And then from his **mouth** the dragon poured out a flood of
12.16 it opened its **mouth** and swallowed the water
12.16 that had come from the dragon's **mouth.**
13. 2 feet like a bear's feet and a **mouth** like a lion's mouth.
16.13 were coming out of the **mouth** of the dragon,
16.13 the mouth of the beast, and the **mouth** of the false prophet.
19.15 Out of his **mouth** came a sharp sword, with which he will
19.21 that comes out of the **mouth** of the one who was riding

MOVE

Gen 1. 2 darkness, and the power of God was **moving** over the water.
12. 8 After that, he **moved** on south to the hill-country east of
12. 9 Then he **moved** on from place to place, going towards the
13. 3 Then he left there and **moved** from place to place, going
13.11 Jordan Valley for himself and **moved** away towards the east.
13.18 So Abram **moved** his camp and settled near the sacred
19. 9 They pushed Lot back and **moved** up to break down the door.
19.30 he and his two daughters **moved** up into the hills and lived
20. 1 Abraham **moved** from Mamre to the southern part of Canaan
26.22 He **moved** away from there and dug another well.
27.22 Jacob **moved** closer to his father, who felt him and said,
35.21 Jacob **moved** on and set up his camp on the other side
48.17 took his father's hand to **move** it from Ephraim's head to the
Ex 14.15 Tell the people to **move** forward.
14.19 front of the army of Israel, **moved** and went to the rear.
14.19 The pillar of cloud also **moved** until it was [20]between the
14.25 get stuck, so that they **moved** with great difficulty.
17. 1 left the desert of Sin, **moving** from one place to another at
40.36 The Israelites **moved** their camp to another place only
40.37 as the cloud stayed there, they did not **move** their camp.
Lev 11.41 animals that **move** on the ground, [42]whether they crawl,
11.46 lives in the water, and everything that **moves** on the ground.
14.36 shall order everything to be **moved** out of the house before
Num 1.51 Whenever you **move** your camp, the Levites shall take the
4.15 of the clan of Kohath whenever the Tent is **moved.**
4.20 preparing the sacred objects for **moving,** they will die."
9.19 a long time, they obeyed the Lord and did not **move** on.
9.20 they remained in camp or **moved,** according to the command of
9.21 evening until morning, and they **moved** on as soon as the
9.21 Whenever the cloud lifted, they **moved** on.
9.22 as the cloud remained over the Tent, they did not **move** on;
9.22 but when it lifted, they **moved.**
10. 5 are sounded, the tribes camped on the east will **move** out.
10. 6 a second time, the tribes on the south will **move** out.
10.14 and each time they **moved,** they were in the same order.
10.34 As they **moved** on from each camp, the cloud of the Lord
11.35 From there the people **moved** to Hazeroth, where they made camp.
12.15 and the people did not **move** on until she was brought back
16.24 "Tell the people to **move** away from the tents of Korah,
16.27 So they **moved** away from the tents of Korah, Dathan, and
20. 6 Moses and Aaron **moved** away from the people and stood at
21.10 The Israelites **moved** on and camped at Oboth.
21.13 From there they **moved** again and camped on the north side
21.18 They **moved** from the wilderness to Mattanah, [19]and from
22. 1 The Israelites **moved** on and set up camp in the plains of
22.25 donkey saw the angel, it **moved** over against the wall and
22.26 Once more the angel **moved** ahead;
Deut 1. 7 Break camp and **move** on.
2. 8 "So we **moved** on and left the road that goes from the
3. 1 "Next, we **moved** north towards the region of Bashan, and
19.14 "Do not **move** your neighbour's boundary mark,
23.13 when you have a bowel **movement** you can dig a hole and
27.17 " 'God's curse on anyone who **moves** a neighbour's boundary mark.'
Josh 10.13 and the moon did not **move** until the nation had conquered its
Judg 4.11 had **moved** away from the other Kenites, the descendants of Hobab,
5.20 as they **moved** across the sky, they fought against Sisera.
9.32 you and your men should **move** by night and hide in the
9.34 all his men made their **move** at night and hid outside Shechem
1 Sam 1.13 her lips were **moving,** but she made no sound.
7.10 Samuel was offering the sacrifice, the Philistines **moved** forward
23.13 hundred in all—left Keilah at once and kept on the **move.**
2 Sam 5.13 After **moving** from Hebron to Jerusalem, David took more
1 Kgs 8. 4 Levites and the priests also **moved** the Tent of the Lord's
9.24 the king of Egypt, had **moved** from David's City to the palace
20.12 get ready to attack the city, so they **moved** into position.
2 Kgs 16.14 and the Temple, so Ahaz **moved** it to the north side of
23.18 "His bones are not to be **moved."**
23.18 So his bones were not **moved,** neither were those of the

1 Chr 6.31 worship in Jerusalem after the Covenant Box was **moved** there.
8. 6 Gera, the father of Uzza and Ahihud, led them in this **move.**
15.14 purified themselves in order to **move** the Covenant Box of the
16.30 The earth is set firmly in place and cannot be **moved.**
17. 5 I have always lived in tents and **moved** from place to place.
2 Chr 5. 5 priests and the Levites also **moved** the Tent of the Lord's
8.11 Solomon **moved** his wife, the daughter of the king of Egypt,
11.14 pastures and other land and **moved** to Judah and Jerusalem,
20. 7 When your people Israel **moved** into this land, you drove out
20.25 Jehoshaphat and his troops **moved** in to take the loot,
Ezra 1. 5 else whose heart God had **moved** got ready to go and rebuild
4.10 the great and powerful Ashurbanipal **moved** from their homes
5. 8 is being done with great care and is **moving** ahead steadily.
Neh 8. 9 the Law required, they were so **moved** that they began to cry.
Job 9. 5 Without warning he **moves** mountains and in anger he destroys
14.18 a time when mountains fall and solid cliffs are **moved** away.
18. 4 Will God **move** mountains to satisfy you?
24. 2 Men **move** boundary stones to get more land;
33.11 he watches every **move** I make."
36.29 one knows how the clouds **move** or how the thunder roars
37.12 flashes from the clouds, [12]as they **move** at God's will.
Ps 93. 1 The earth is set firmly in place and cannot be **moved.**
96.10 The earth is set firmly in place and cannot be **moved;**
104. 5 firmly on its foundations, and it will never be **moved.**
125. 1 like Mount Zion, which can never be shaken, never be **moved.**
Prov 22.28 Never **move** an old boundary-mark that your ancestors established.
23.10 Never **move** an old boundary-mark or take over land owned
30.19 a snake **moving** on a rock,
30.27 they have no king, but they **move** in formation.
Is 16. 2 of the River Arnon and **move** aimlessly to and fro, like birds
33.20 a tent that is never **moved,** whose pegs are never pulled up
38. 8 And the shadow **moved** back ten steps.
46. 7 and there it stands, unable to **move** from where it is.
Jer 24. 8 stayed in this land or **moved** to Egypt—I, the Lord, will
37. 4 prison and was still **moving** about freely among the people.
Ezek 1. 9 When they **moved,** they moved as a group without turning
1.13 that looked like a blazing torch, constantly **moving.**
1.17 so that the wheels could **move** in any of the four directions.
1.19 Whenever the creatures **moved,** the wheels moved with them,
1.21 So every time the creatures **moved** or stopped or rose in
5. 2 it up with your sword as you **move** about outside the city.
9. 3 where it had been, and **moved** to the entrance of the Temple.
10. 4 from the creatures and **moved** to the entrance of the Temple.
10.11 When the creatures **moved,** they could go in any direction
10.11 They all **moved** together in the direction they wanted to go,
10.16 rose in the air [16]and **moved,** the wheels went with them.
10.18 of the Temple and **moved** to a place above the creatures.
10.22 Each creature **moved** straight ahead.
11.23 light left the city and **moved** to the mountain east of it.
38.16 attack my people Israel like a storm **moving** across the land.
Dan 8. 5 rushing out of the west, **moving** so fast that his feet didn't
Zech 14. 4 Half the mountain will **move** northwards and half of it southwards.
Mt 8. 6 in bed at home, unable to **move** and suffering terribly."
Lk 1.41 Elizabeth heard Mary's greeting, the baby **moved** within her.
10. 7 Don't **move** round from one house to another.
Jn 11.33 his heart was touched, and he was deeply **moved.**
11.38 Deeply **moved** once more, Jesus went to the tomb, which
13.25 So that disciple **moved** closer to Jesus' side and asked,
18. 6 "I am he," they **moved** back and fell to the ground.
Acts 7. 4 father died, God made him **move** to this land where you now
17.28 as someone has said, 'In him we live and **move** and exist.'
27.41 got stuck and could not **move,** while the back part was being
1 Cor 13. 2 all the faith needed to **move** mountains—but if I have no
Rev 6.14 and every mountain and island was **moved** from its place.

MOVEMENT

Acts 5.36 all his followers were scattered, and his **movement** died out.

MUCH

Lk 12.48 Much is required from the person to whom **much** is given;
Jn 8.26 I have **much** to say about you, much to condemn you for.
Rom 3. 2 **Much,** indeed, in every way!
2 Cor 8.15 says, "The one who gathered **much** did not have too much,
Phil 4.12 am full or hungry, whether I have too **much** or too little.
Heb 5.11 There is **much** we have to say about this matter, but it
2 Jn 12 I have so **much** to tell you, but I would rather not
3 Jn 13 I have so **much** to tell you, but I do not want

MUCK

Is 57.20 whose waves never stop rolling in, bringing filth and **muck.**

MUD

2 Sam 22.43 I trample on them like **mud** in the streets.
Job 30.19 He throws me down in the **mud;**
41.30 they tear up the **muddy** ground like a threshing-sledge.
Ps 18.42 I trample on them like **mud** in the streets.
69. 2 I am sinking in deep **mud,** and there is no solid ground;
69.14 Save me from sinking in the **mud;**
89.39 covenant with your servant and thrown his crown in the **mud.**
Is 41.25 rulers as if they were **mud,** like a potter trampling clay.
Jer 38. 6 water in the well, only **mud,** and I sank down in it.
38.22 feet have sunk in the **mud,** his friends have left him.' "
Ezek 16.25 You dragged your beauty through the **mud.**
32. 2 You **muddy** the water with your feet and pollute the rivers.
32.13 will be no people or cattle to **muddy** the water any more.
34.18 You drink the clear water and **muddy** what you don't drink!
Ezek 34.19 the grass you trample down and drink the water you **muddy.**
Mic 7.10 will see them defeated, trampled down like **mud** in the streets.
Zech 10. 5 who trample their enemies into the **mud** of the streets.
Jn 9. 6 Jesus spat on the ground and made some **mud** with the spittle;
9. 6 he rubbed the **mud** on the man's eyes [7]and said, "Go
9.11 man called Jesus made some **mud,** rubbed it on my eyes,
9.14 day that Jesus made the **mud** and cured him of his blindness
9.15 He told them, "He put some **mud** on my eyes;
2 Pet 2.22 pig that has been washed goes back to roll in the **mud."**

MUFFLED

Is 29. 4 under the ground, a **muffled** voice coming from the dust.

MULBERRY TREE

Lk 17. 6 you could say to this **mulberry tree,** 'Pull yourself up by

MULE

2 Sam 13.29 All the rest of David's sons mounted their **mules** and fled.
18. 9 Absalom was riding a **mule,** and as it went under a large
18. 9 The **mule** ran on and Absalom was left hanging in mid air.
1 Kgs 1.33 son Solomon ride my own **mule,** and escort him down to the
1.38 put Solomon on King David's **mule,** and escorted him to the
1.44 him ride on the king's **mule,** [45]and Zadok and Nathan
10.25 silver and gold, robes, weapons, spices, horses, and **mules.**
18. 5 we can find enough grass to keep the horses and **mules** alive.
2 Kgs 5.17 then let me have two **mule-loads** of earth to take home with
1 Chr 12.40 donkeys, camels, **mules,** and oxen loaded with food—flour,
2 Chr 9.24 silver and gold, robes, weapons, spices, horses, and **mules.**
Ezra 2.64 **Mules** - 245
Neh 7.66 **Mules** - 245
Ps 32. 9 like a horse or a **mule,** which must be controlled with a
Is 66.20 hill in Jerusalem on horses, **mules,** and camels, and in
Ezek 27.14 You sold your goods for draught-horses, war-horses, and **mules**
Hos 4.16 The people of Israel are as stubborn as **mules.**
Zech 14.15 fall on the horses, the **mules,** the camels, and the

MULTIPLY

Nah 3.15 You **multiplied** like locusts!

AV **MULTITUDE** see **CROWD**

MUMMY

Is 8. 4 is old enough to say **'Mummy'** and 'Daddy,' all the wealth of

MURDER

Gen 9. 6 made like God, so whoever **murders** a man will himself be
37.26 we gain by killing our brother and covering up the **murder?**
Ex 20.13 "Do not commit **murder.**
22. 2 is killed, the one who killed him is not guilty of **murder.**
22. 2 But if it happens during the day, he is guilty of **murder.**
Lev 24.17 "Anyone who commits **murder** shall be put to death,
Num 35.16 someone, he is guilty of **murder** and is to be put to
35.19 has the responsibility for putting the **murderer** to death.
35.21 fist, he is guilty of **murder** and is to be put to
35.21 has the responsibility for putting the **murderer** to death.
35.27 finds him and kills him, this act of revenge is not **murder.**
35.30 "A man accused of **murder** may be found guilty and put to
35.30 is not sufficient to support an accusation of **murder.**
35.31 A **murderer** must be put to death.
35.33 **Murder** defiles the land, and except by the death of the murderer
35.33 of purification for the land where a man has been **murdered.**
Deut 5.17 " 'Do not commit **murder.**
17. 8 that involve a distinction between **murder** and manslaughter.
19.11 "But suppose a man deliberately **murders** his enemy in
19.12 for taking revenge for the **murder,** so that he may be put
19.13 Rid Israel of this **murderer,** so that all will go well with
21. 1 "Suppose a man is found **murdered** in a field in the land
21. 6 nearest the place where the **murdered** man was found are to
21. 7 and say, 'We did not **murder** the man, and we do not
21. 8 not hold us responsible for the **murder** of an innocent man.'
21. 9 Lord requires, you will not be held responsible for the **murder.**
22.26 same as when one man attacks another man and **murders** him.
27.24 " 'God's curse on anyone who secretly commits **murder.'**
27.25 " 'God's curse on anyone who accepts money to **murder** an innocent
Judg 9.24 Shechem, who encouraged him to **murder** Gideon's seventy sons,
20. 4 Levite whose concubine had been **murdered** answered, "My
1 Sam 25.33 me from the crime of **murder** and from taking my own revenge.
2 Sam 3.27 Abner was **murdered** because he had killed Joab's brother Asahel.
3.28 and I are completely innocent of the **murder** of Abner.
3.37 understood that the king had no part in the **murder** of Abner.
4.11 be for evil men who **murder** an innocent man asleep in his
4.11 take revenge on you for **murdering** him and will wipe you off
14. 7 them, so that they can kill him for **murdering** his brother.
16. 7 **Murderer!**
16. 8 Lord is punishing you for **murdering** so many of Saul's family.
16. 8 to your son Absalom, and you are ruined, you **murderer!"**
21. 1 the Lord said, "Saul and his family are guilty of **murder;**
1 Kgs 2. 5 You remember how he **murdered** them in time of peace in
2.32 will punish Joab for those **murders,** which he committed
2.33 The punishment for their **murders** will fall on Joab and
21.19 Lord, say to him, 'After **murdering** the man, are you taking
2 Kgs 6.32 the elders, "That **murderer** is sending someone to kill me!

2 Kgs 9. 7 may punish Jezebel for **murdering** my prophets and my other servants.
9.26 'I saw the **murder** of Naboth and his sons yesterday.
11. 1 Athaliah learnt of her son's **murder,** she gave orders for all
2 Chr 21.13 You even **murdered** your brothers, who were better men than you
22.10 Athaliah learnt of her son's **murder,** she gave orders for all
22.11 who were about to be **murdered** and hid him and a nurse
24.25 his bed to avenge the **murder** of the son of Jehoiada the
25. 3 he executed the officials who had **murdered** his father.
Job 24.14 At dawn the **murderer** gets up and goes out to kill the
Ps 10. 8 hides himself in the villages, waiting to **murder** innocent people.
26. 9 me from the fate of **murderers**— [10]men who do evil all
55.23 O God, will bring those **murderers** and liars to their graves
59. 2 rescue me from those **murderers!**
94. 6 kill widows and orphans, and **murder** the strangers who live
106.38 children, and the land was defiled by those **murders.**
Prov 12. 6 words of wicked men are **murderous,** but the words of the
28.17 A man guilty of **murder** is digging his own grave as fast
Is 1.21 filled with righteous men, but now only **murderers** remain.
5. 7 to do what was good, but instead they committed **murder.**
26.21 The **murders** that were secretly committed on the earth will be
33.15 those who plan to commit **murder** or to do other evil things.
49.26 they will be drunk with **murder** and rage.
59. 3 You are guilty of lying, violence, and **murder.**
59. 7 You never hesitate to **murder** innocent people.
Jer 2.30 Like a raging lion, you have **murdered** your prophets.
7. 9 You steal, **murder,** commit adultery, tell lies under oath,
40.14 that King Baalis of Ammon has sent Ishmael to **murder** you?"
40.15 Why should he be allowed to **murder** you?
41. 4 about Gedaliah's **murder,** [5]eighty men
41.16 as prisoners from Mizpah after **murdering** Gedaliah—soldiers,
41.17 the Babylonians because Ishmael had **murdered** Gedaliah, whom
Lam 1.20 There is **murder** in the streets;
2.22 They **murdered** my children, whom I had reared and loved.
5. 9 **Murderers** roam through the countryside;
Ezek 7.23 the land is full of **murders** and the cities are full of
9. 9 They have committed **murder** all over the land and have filled
11. 6 You have **murdered** so many people here in the city that the
16.38 condemn you for adultery and **murder,** and in my anger and
22. 2 "are you ready to judge the city that is full of **murderers?**
22. 3 Because you have **murdered** so many of your own people and
22. 4 You are guilty of those **murders** and are defiled by the
22. 6 All Israel's leaders trust in their own strength and commit **murder.**
22.12 Some of your people **murder** for pay.
22.13 "I will bring my fist down on your robberies and **murders.**
22.25 they can get, and by their **murders** leave many widows.
22.27 They commit **murder** in order to get rich.
23.37 They have committed adultery and **murder**—
23.37 adultery with idols and **murder** of the sons they bore me.
23.45 the charge of adultery and **murder,** because they practise
24. 6 "The city of **murderers** is doomed!
24. 7 There was **murder** in the city, but the blood was not spilt
24. 9 "The city of **murderers** is doomed!
28. 9 When you face your **murderers,** you will be mortal and not at
33.25 You commit **murder.**
35. 6 You are guilty of **murder,** and murder will follow you.
36.18 my anger because of the **murders** they had committed in the
Hos 1. 4 king of Israel for the **murders** that his ancestor Jehu
4. 2 they lie, **murder,** steal, and commit adultery.
4. 2 Crimes increase, and there is one **murder** after another.
6. 8 Gilead is a city full of evil men and **murderers.**
6. 9 on the road to the holy place at Shechem they commit **murder.**
7. 7 "In the heat of their anger they **murdered** their rulers.
Mic 3.10 God's city, Jerusalem, on a foundation of **murder** and injustice.
7. 2 Everyone is waiting for a chance to commit **murder.**
Nah 3. 1 Doomed is the lying, **murderous** city, full of wealth to be
Hab 2. 8 plunder you because of the **murders** you have committed and
2.12 You founded a city on crime and built it up by **murder.**
2.17 will happen because of the **murders** you have committed and
Mt 5.21 that people were told in the past, 'Do not commit **murder;**
19.18 Jesus answered, "Do not commit **murder;**
22. 7 soldiers, who killed those **murderers** and burnt down their city.
23.31 that you are the descendants of those who **murdered** the prophets!
23.35 result, the punishment for the **murder** of all innocent men will
23.35 fall on you, from the **murder** of innocent Abel
23.35 to the **murder** of Zachariah son of Berachiah,
23.35 whom you **murdered** between the Temple and the altar.
23.36 the punishment for all these **murders** will fall on the people
Mk 10.19 'Do not commit **murder;**
15. 7 prison with the rebels who had committed **murder** in the riot.
Lk 11.47 tombs for the prophets—the very prophets your ancestors **murdered.**
11.48 they **murdered** the prophets, and you build their tombs.
11.50 will be punished for the **murder** of all the prophets killed
11.51 of the world, [51]from the **murder** of Abel
11.51 to the **murder** of Zechariah, who was killed between
18.20 do not commit **murder;**
23.19 a riot that had taken place in the city, and for **murder.)**
23.25 in prison for riot and **murder,** and he handed Jesus over for
Jn 8.44 very beginning he was a **murderer** and has never been on the
Acts 3.14 Pilate to do you the favour of turning loose a **murderer.**
7.52 And now you have betrayed and **murdered** him.
8. 1 And Saul approved of his **murder.**
9. 1 his violent threats of **murder** against the followers of the Lord.
22.20 was there, approving of his **murder**
22.20 and taking care of the cloaks of his **murderers.'**
28. 4 "This man must be a **murderer,** but Fate will not let him
Rom 1.29 they are full of jealousy, **murder,** fighting, deceit, and
13. 9 do not commit **murder;**
1 Tim 1. 9 their fathers or mothers, for **murderers,** [10]for the immoral,
Jas 2.11 "Do not commit adultery," also said, "Do not commit **murder."**
Jas 2.11 adultery, you have become a law-breaker if you commit **murder.**
5. 6 You have condemned and **murdered** innocent people,
1 Pet 4.15 be because he is a **murderer** or a thief or a criminal
1 Jn 3.12 belonged to the Evil One and **murdered** his own brother Abel.
3.12 Why did Cain **murder** him?
3.15 hates his brother is a **murderer,**
3.15 and you know that a **murderer** has not got eternal life in
Rev 9.21 did they repent of their **murders,** their magic, their sexual
21. 8 But cowards, traitors, perverts, **murderers,** the immoral,
22.15 the immoral and the **murderers,** those who worship idols and those

MUSCLE

Gen 32.32 Israel do not eat the **muscle** which is on the hip-joint,
32.32 because it was on this **muscle** that Jacob was struck.
Job 10.11 and sinews and covered the bones with **muscles** and skin.
40.16 is in his body, and what power there is in his **muscles!**
40.17 up like a cedar, and the **muscles** in his legs are strong.
Prov 5.11 your deathbed, your flesh and **muscles** being eaten away,
Ezek 37. 6 I will give you sinews and **muscles,** and cover you with skin.
37. 8 were covered with sinews and **muscles,** and then with skin.

MUSIC

Gen 31.27 rejoicing and singing to the **music** of tambourines and harps.
Judg 5. 3 I will sing, I will play **music** to Israel's God, the Lord.
1 Chr 6.31 put in charge of the **music** at the place of worship in
9.33 Some Levite families were responsible for the temple **music.**
13. 8 They sang and played **musical** instruments—harps, drums,
15.16 Levites to sing and to play joyful **music** on harps and cymbals.
15.22 Because of his skill in **music** Chenaniah was chosen to
15.28 of trumpets, horns, and cymbals, and the **music** of harps.
23. 5 praise the Lord, using the **musical** instruments provided by
25. 1 God's messages, accompanied by the **music** of harps and cymbals.
25. 3 God's message, accompanied by the **music** of harps, and sang
2 Chr 7. 6 praising the Lord with the **musical** instruments that King
20.28 marched to the Temple, to the **music** of harps and trumpets.
23.18 They were also in charge of the **music** and the celebrations.
29.28 and the rest of the **music** continued until all the sacrifices
Neh 11.22 that was responsible for the **music** in the temple services.
11.23 should take turns in leading the temple **music** each day.
12.27 of thanksgiving and with the **music** of cymbals and harps.
12.36 Hanani—all of whom carried **musical** instruments of the kind
Job 21.12 like lambs [12]and dance to the **music** of harps and flutes.
30.31 Where once I heard joyful **music,** now I hear only
Ps 81. 2 Start the **music** and beat the tambourines;
81. 2 play pleasant **music** on the harps and the lyres.
92. 3 faithfulness every night, [3]with the **music** of stringed
98. 5 Play **music** on the harps!
147. 7 play **music** on the harp to our God.
Ecc 12. 4 mill as it grinds or **music** as it plays, but even the
Is 14.11 to be honoured with the **music** of harps, but now here you
24. 8 now sad, [8]and the joyful **music** of their harps and drums has
30.29 those who walk to the **music** of flutes on their way to
30.32 his people will keep time with the **music** of drums and harps.
Lam 5.14 the city gate, and the young people no longer make **music.**
Ezek 26.13 all your songs, and I will silence the **music** of your harps.
Dan 3. 5 As soon as the **music** starts, you are to bow down and
3.10 that as soon as the **music** starts, everyone is to bow down
Mt 11.17 'We played wedding **music** for you, but you wouldn't dance!
Lk 7.32 'We played wedding **music** for you, but you wouldn't dance!
15.25 he came close to the house, he heard the **music** and dancing.
1 Cor 14. 7 Take such lifeless **musical** instruments as the flute or the harp—
Rev 14. 2 It sounded like the **music** made by musicians playing their harps.
18.22 The **music** of harps and of human voices, of players of

MUSICIAN

Gen 4.21 Jubal, the ancestor of all **musicians** who play the harp and
1 Sam 16.18 the town of Bethlehem, has a son who is a good **musician.**
1 Kgs 10.12 palace, and also to make harps and lyres for the **musicians.**
2 Kgs 3.15 Now get me a **musician."**
3.15 As the **musician** played his harp, the power of the Lord came
1 Chr 15.22 Chenaniah was chosen to be in charge of the levitical **musicians.**
15.27 linen, and so were the **musicians,** Chenaniah their leader,
25. 7 and their fellow-Levites were trained **musicians.**
2 Chr 5.11 And all the Levite **musicians**—Asaph, Heman, and Jeduthun, and
9.11 his palace, and to make harps and lyres for the **musicians.**
20.21 people, the king ordered some **musicians** to put on the robes
23.13 blowing trumpets, and the temple **musicians** with their
29.27 to the Lord, and the **musicians** began to play the trumpets
34.12 (The Levites were all skilful **musicians.)**
35.15 The following **musicians** of the Levite clan of Asaph were
Ezra 2.40 Temple **musicians** (descendants of Asaph) - 128
2.64 Male and female **musicians** - 200
2.70 the **musicians,** the temple guards, and the temple workmen
7. 6 Israelites which included priests, Levites, temple **musicians,**
7.24 taxes from the priests, Levites, **musicians,** guards, workmen,
10.24 **Musicians:**
Neh 7.43 Temple **musicians**
7.66 Male and female **musicians** - 245
7.73 temple guards, the **musicians,** many of the ordinary people,
10.28 the temple guards, the temple **musicians,** the temple workmen,
12.45 The temple **musicians** and the temple guards also performed
12.46 of King David and the **musician** Asaph long ago,
12.46 the **musicians** have led songs of praise
12.47 the support of the temple **musicians** and the temple guards.
13. 5 Levites, to the temple **musicians,** and to the temple guards.
13.10 also learnt that the temple **musicians** and other Levites had
13.11 I brought the Levites and **musicians** back to the Temple and

Ps	45. 8	**musicians** entertain you in palaces decorated with ivory.
	68.25	singers are in front, the **musicians** are behind, in between
Mt	9.23	When he saw the **musicians** for the funeral and the people all
Rev	14. 2	It sounded like the music made by **musicians** playing their harps.

MUSTARD SEED
A very small seed which grows into a large plant. The seeds are ground into powder and used as spice on food.

Mt	13.31	A man takes a **mustard seed** and sows it in his field.
	17.20	faith as big as a **mustard seed,** you can say to this
Mk	4.31	A man takes a **mustard seed,** the smallest seed in the world,
Lk	13.19	A man takes a **mustard seed** and sows it in his field.
	17. 6	faith as big as a **mustard seed,** you could say to this

MUTILATED

Lev	22.22	is blind or crippled or **mutilated,** or that has a running

MUTTER

Is	8.19	from fortune-tellers and mediums, who chirp and **mutter.**

MUZZLE

Deut	25. 4	"Do not **muzzle** an ox when you are using it to thresh
1 Cor	9. 9	Law of Moses, "Do not **muzzle** an ox when you are using
1 Tim	5.18	the scripture says, "Do not **muzzle** an ox when you are using

MYRRH
A sweet-smelling resin that was very valuable. It served as a medicine and was used by the Jews in preparing bodies for burial.

Ex	30.23	liquid **myrrh,** three kilogrammes of sweet-smelling cinnamon,
Esth	2.12	year—massages with oil of **myrrh** for six months and with oil
Ps	45. 8	The perfume of **myrrh** and aloes is on your clothes;
Prov	7.17	I've perfumed it with **myrrh,** aloes, and cinnamon.
Song	1.13	lover has the scent of **myrrh** as he lies upon my breasts.
	3. 6	with incense and **myrrh,** the incense sold by the traders?
	4. 6	stay on the hill of **myrrh,** the hill of incense, until the
	4.14	**Myrrh** and aloes grow there with all the most fragrant perfumes.
	5. 1	I am gathering my spices and **myrrh;**
	5. 5	My hands were covered with **myrrh,** my fingers with liquid myrrh,
	5.13	His lips are like lilies, wet with liquid **myrrh.**
Mt	2.11	gifts of gold, frankincense, and **myrrh,** and presented them to him.
Mk	15.23	with a drug called **myrrh,** but Jesus would not drink it.
Jn	19.39	about thirty kilogrammes of spices, a mixture of **myrrh** and aloes.
Rev	18.13	and cinnamon, spice, incense, **myrrh,** and frankincense;

MYRTLE
A kind of evergreen shrub or tree.

Neh	8.15	get branches from pines, olives, **myrtles,** palms, and other
Is	41.19	in the desert, and acacias and **myrtles** and olive-trees.
	55.13	**myrtle-trees** will come up in place of thorns.
Zech	1. 8	He had stopped among some **myrtle-trees** in a valley, and

MYSTERY

Ps	64. 6	The heart and mind of man are a **mystery.**
	78. 2	use wise sayings and explain **mysteries** from the past,
Prov	30.18	four things that are too **mysterious** for me to understand:
Is	28.21	He will complete his work, his **mysterious** work.
Dan	2.18	ask him to explain the **mystery** to them so that they would
	2.19	Then that same night the **mystery** was revealed to Daniel
	2.28	But there is a God in heaven, who reveals **mysteries.**
	2.29	who reveals **mysteries,** showed you what is going to happen.
	2.30	Now, this **mystery** was revealed to me, not because I am
	2.47	the Lord over kings, and the one who reveals **mysteries.**
	2.47	I know this because you have been able to explain this **mystery."**
	4. 9	holy gods is in you, and that you understand all **mysteries.**
	5.12	dreams, solving riddles, and explaining **mysteries;**
	5.16	heard that you can find hidden meanings and explain **mysteries.**
2 Thes	2. 7	The **Mysterious Wickedness** is already at work, but what is going
Rev	12. 1	Then a great and **mysterious** sight appeared in the sky.
	12. 3	Another **mysterious** sight appeared in the sky.
	15. 1	I saw in the sky another **mysterious** sight, great and amazing.

NAAMAN (1)
Syrian general healed of skin-disease in R. Jordan.

2 Kgs	5. 1	**Naaman,** the commander of the Syrian army, was highly
	5. 1	king of Syria, because through **Naaman** the Lord had given
	5. 2	Israelite girl, who became a servant of **Naaman's** wife.
	5. 4	When **Naaman** heard of this, he went to the king and told
	5. 5	So **Naaman** set out, taking thirty thousand pieces of silver,
	5. 6	"This letter will introduce my officer **Naaman.**
	5. 9	So **Naaman** went with his horses and chariot, and stopped
	5.11	But **Naaman** left in a rage, saying, "I thought that he
	5.14	So **Naaman** went down to the Jordan, dipped himself in it
	5.16	**Naaman** insisted that he accept it, but he would not.
	5.17	So **Naaman** said, "If you won't accept my gift, then let
	5.19	And **Naaman** left.
	5.20	"My master has let **Naaman** get away without paying a thing!
	5.21	So he set off after **Naaman.**
	5.21	When **Naaman** saw a man running after him, he got down from
	5.23	"Please take six thousand pieces of silver," **Naaman** replied.
	5.24	Then he sent **Naaman's** servants back.
	5.27	And now **Naaman's** disease will come upon you, and you and
Lk	4.27	not one of them was healed, but only **Naaman** the Syrian."

NABAL
David's wife Abigail's first husband.

1 Sam	25. 2	the clan of Caleb named **Nabal,** who was from the town of
	25. 2	**Nabal** was shearing his sheep in Carmel, [4]and David, who
	25. 5	to go to Carmel, find **Nabal,** and give him his greetings.
	25. 6	He instructed them to say to **Nabal:**
	25. 9	David's men delivered this message to **Nabal** in David's name.
	25.10	Then they waited there, [10]and **Nabal** finally answered,
	25.12	men went back to him and told him what **Nabal** had said.
	25.14	One of **Nabal's** servants said to Nabal's wife Abigail,
	25.25	don't pay any attention to **Nabal,** that good-for-nothing!
	25.26	and all who want to harm you will be punished like **Nabal.**
	25.34	to meet me, all of **Nabal's** men would have been dead by
	25.36	Abigail went back to **Nabal,** who was at home having a
	25.38	Some ten days later the Lord struck **Nabal** and he died.
	25.39	David heard that **Nabal** had died, he said, "Praise the Lord!
	25.39	He has taken revenge on **Nabal** for insulting me and has kept
	25.39	The Lord has punished **Nabal** for his evil."
	27. 3	Ahinoam from Jezreel, and Abigail, **Nabal's** widow, from Carmel.
2 Sam	2. 2	Jezreel, and Abigail, **Nabal's** widow, who was from Carmel.
	3. 3	Chileab, whose mother was Abigail, **Nabal's** widow, from

NABOTH
Owner of a vineyard, killed on Jezebel's orders.

1 Kgs	21. 1	in Jezreel there was a vineyard owned by a man named **Naboth.**
	21. 2	One day Ahab said to **Naboth,** "Let me have your vineyard;
	21. 3	"I inherited this vineyard from my ancestors," **Naboth** replied.
	21. 4	home, depressed and angry over what **Naboth** had said to him.
	21. 6	He answered, "Because of what **Naboth** said to me.
	21. 7	I will get you **Naboth's** vineyard!"
	21. 9	the people together, and give **Naboth** the place of honour.
	21.12	the people together, and gave **Naboth** the place of honour.
	21.14	**"Naboth** has been put to death."
	21.15	received the message, she said to Ahab, **"Naboth** is dead.
	21.18	You will find him in **Naboth's** vineyard, about to take
	21.19	that the dogs licked up **Naboth's** blood they will lick up
2 Kgs	9.21	They met him at the field which had belonged to **Naboth.**
	9.25	his body and throw it in the field that belonged to **Naboth.**
	9.26	'I saw the murder of **Naboth** and his sons yesterday.
	9.26	the field that belonged to **Naboth,** so as to fulfil the

NADAB (1)
Aaron's son, killed for the wrong use of fire.

Ex	6.23	she bore him **Nadab,** Abihu, Eleazar, and Ithamar.
	24. 1	to me, you and Aaron, **Nadab,** Abihu, and seventy of the
	24. 9	Moses, Aaron, **Nadab,** Abihu, and seventy of the leaders of
	28. 1	"Summon your brother Aaron and his sons, **Nadab,** Abihu,
Lev	10. 1	Aaron's sons **Nadab** and Abihu, each took his fire-pan, put
Num	3. 2	**Nadab,** the eldest, Abihu, Eleazar, and Ithamar.
	3. 4	and ordained as priests, [4]but **Nadab** and Abihu were killed
	26.60	Aaron had four sons, **Nadab,** Abihu, Eleazar, and Ithamar.
	26.61	**Nadab** and Abihu died when they offered unholy fire to the Lord.
1 Chr	6. 3	**Nadab,** Abihu, Eleazar, and Ithamar.
	24. 1	**Nadab,** Abihu, Eleazar, and Ithamar.
	24. 2	**Nadab** and Abihu died before their father did,

NAG

Judg	14.17	what the riddle meant, for she **nagged** him about it so much.
	16.16	sick and tired of her **nagging** him about it [17]that he
Prov	19.13	A **nagging** wife is like water going drip-drip-drip.
	21. 9	live on the roof than share the house with a **nagging** wife.
	21.19	out in the desert than with a **nagging,** complaining wife.
	25.24	live on the roof than share the house with a **nagging** wife.
	27.15	A **nagging** wife is like water going drip-drip-drip on a rainy day.

NAHASH (1)
King of Ammon.

1 Sam	11. 1	About a month later King **Nahash** of Ammon led his army
	11. 1	men of Jabesh said to **Nahash,** "Make a treaty with us, and
	11. 2	**Nahash** answered, "I will make a treaty with you on one condition:
	11.10	and said to **Nahash,** "Tomorrow we will surrender to you,
	12.12	when you saw that King **Nahash** of Ammon was about to attack
2 Sam	10. 1	Some time later King **Nahash** of Ammon died, and his son
	10. 2	loyal friendship to Hanun, as his father **Nahash** did to me."
	17.27	met by Shobi son of **Nahash,** from the city of Rabbah in
1 Chr	19. 1	Some time later King **Nahash** of Ammon died, and his son
	19. 2	loyal friendship to Hanun, as his father **Nahash** did to me."

NAHOR (1)
Terah's son and Abraham's brother.

Gen	11.26	70 years old, he became the father of Abram, **Nahor,** and
	11.27	descendants of Terah, who was the father of Abram, **Nahor,**
	11.29	and **Nahor** married Milcah, the daughter of Haran,
	22.20	learnt that Milcah had borne eight children to his brother **Nahor:**
	22.23	Milcah bore these eight sons to **Nahor,** Abraham's brother.
	22.24	Reumah, **Nahor's** concubine, bore Tebah, Gaham, Tahash,
	24.10	to the city where **Nahor** had lived in northern Mesopotamia.
	24.15	was the son of Abraham's brother **Nahor** and his wife Milcah.
	24.24	"My father is Bethuel son of **Nahor** and Milcah," she
	24.47	she answered, 'My father is Bethuel son of **Nahor** and Milcah.'
	29. 5	He asked, "Do you know Laban son of **Nahor?"**
	31.53	God of Abraham and the God of **Nahor** will judge between us."
Josh	24. 2	One of those ancestors was Terah, the father of Abraham and **Nahor.**

NAIL (1)

1 Sam 31.10 the goddess Astarte, and they **nailed** his body to the wall of
1 Chr 22. 3 of iron for making **nails** and clamps for the wooden gates,
2 Chr 3. 9 gold were used for making **nails,** and the walls of the upper
Ecc 12.11 collected proverbs are as lasting as firmly driven **nails.**
Is 41. 7 the idol smooth encourages the one who **nails** it together.
41. 7 is good'— and they fasten the idol in place with **nails.**
Jer 10. 4 It is fastened down with **nails** to keep it from falling over.
Jn 20.25 see the scars of the **nails** in his hands and put my
Acts 5.30 death, after you had killed him by **nailing** him to a cross.
10.39 Then they put him to death by **nailing** him to a cross.
Col 2.14 and did away with it completely by **nailing** it to the cross.

NAIL (2)

[FINGERNAILS]

Deut 21.12 her head, cut her **fingernails,** [13]and change her clothes.
Dan 4.33 long as eagles' feathers and his **nails** as long as birds'

NAKED

Gen 2.25 the woman were both **naked,** but they were not embarrassed.
3. 7 were given understanding and realized that they were **naked;**
3.10 I was afraid and hid from you, because I was **naked."**
3.11 "Who told you that you were **naked?"**
9.21 drunk, took off his clothes, and lay **naked** in his tent.
9.22 saw that his father was **naked,** he went out and told his
9.23 keeping their faces turned away so as not to see him **naked.**
Deut 28.48 You will be hungry, thirsty, and **naked**—in need of everything.
1 Sam 19.24 in Samuel's presence, and lay **naked** all that day and all
Is 3.26 will be like a woman sitting on the ground, stripped **naked.**
20. 2 He obeyed and went about **naked** and barefoot.
20. 3 Isaiah has been going about **naked** and barefoot for three years.
20. 4 of Assyria will lead away **naked** the prisoners he captures
20. 4 will walk barefoot and **naked,** with their buttocks exposed,
47. 3 People will see you **naked;**
Lam 1. 8 she is **naked** and held in contempt.
4.21 you too will stagger **naked** in shame.
Ezek 16. 7 well-formed, and your hair had grown, but you were **naked.**
16. 8 I covered your **naked** body with my coat and promised to love
16.22 you were **naked,** squirming in your own blood."
16.37 I will strip off your clothes and let them see you **naked.**
16.39 your clothes and jewels and leave you completely **naked.**
18. 7 he feeds the hungry and gives clothing to the **naked.**
18.16 He feeds the hungry and gives clothing to the **naked.**
23.10 They stripped her **naked,** seized her sons and daughters,
23.29 for and leave you stripped **naked,** exposed like a prostitute.
Hos 2. 3 I will strip her as **naked** as she was on the day
2.10 I will strip her **naked** in front of her lovers, and no
Mic 1. 8 To show my sorrow, I will walk about barefoot and **naked.**
1.11 You people of Shaphir, go into exile, **naked** and ashamed.
Nah 3. 5 I will strip you **naked** and let the nations see you, see
Mt 25.36 you received me in your homes, [36]**naked** and you clothed me;
25.38 and welcome you in our homes, or **naked** and clothe you?
25.43 welcome me in your homes, **naked** but you would not clothe me;
25.44 thirsty or a stranger or **naked** or sick or in prison,
Mk 14.52 arrest him, [52]but he ran away **naked,** leaving the cloth behind.
Rev 3.17 You are poor, **naked,** and blind.
3.18 clothing to dress yourself and cover up your shameful **nakedness.**
16.15 he will not walk around **naked** and be ashamed in public!"
17.16 they will take away everything she has and leave her **naked;**

NAME (1)

[NICKNAMED, RENAMED]

see also **NAME (2) (NAME OF GOD, OF JESUS, OF THE LORD)**

Gen 1. 5 from the darkness, [5]and he **named** the light "Day" and the
1. 8 He **named** the dome "Sky."
1.10 He **named** the land "Earth,"
1.10 and the water which had come together he **named** "Sea."
2.19 brought them to the man to see what he would **name** them;
2.19 and that is how they all got their **names.**
2.20 So the man **named** all the birds and all the animals;
2.23 'Woman' is her **name** because she was taken out of man."
3.20 Adam **named** his wife Eve, because she was the mother of
4. 1 So she **named** him Cain.
4.17 Cain and his wife had a son and **named** him Enoch.
4.17 Then Cain built a city and **named** it after his son.
4.18 Enoch had a son **named** Irad, who was the father of Mehujael,
4.18 and Mehujael had a son **named** Methushael, who was the father
4.25 So she **named** him Seth.
4.26 Seth had a son whom he **named** Enosh.
5. 2 male and female, blessed them, and **named** them "Mankind.")
5. 3 had a son who was like him, and he **named** him Seth.
5.29 so he **named** him Noah.
10. 2 Tiras—were the ancestors of the peoples who bear their **names.**
10. 6 Canaan—were the ancestors of the peoples who bear their **names.**
10. 8 Cush had a son **named** Nimrod, who became the world's first
10.15 Heth—were the ancestors of the peoples who bear their **names.**
10.22 Aram—were the ancestors of the peoples who bear their **names.**
10.25 one was **named** Peleg, because during his time the people of
10.25 and the other was **named** Joktan.
11. 4 that we can make a **name** for ourselves and not be scattered
12. 2 bless you and make your **name** famous, so that you will be
16. 1 she had an Egyptian slave-girl **named** Hagar, [2]and so she
16.11 a son, and you will **name** him Ishmael, because the Lord has
16.15 Hagar bore Abram a son, and he **named** him Ishmael.
17. 5 Your **name** will no longer be Abram, but Abraham, because I
17.15 from now on her **name** is Sarah.
17.19 Sarah will bear you a son and you will **name** him Isaac.
Gen 19.22 Because Lot called it small, the town was **named** Zoar.
19.37 The elder daughter had a son, whom she **named** Moab.
19.38 The younger daughter also had a son, whom she **named** Benammi.
21. 3 Abraham **named** him Isaac, [4]and when Isaac was eight days old,
22.14 Abraham **named** that place "The Lord Provides."
24.29 Now Rebecca had a brother **named** Laban, and he ran
25. 1 Abraham married another wife, whose **name** was Keturah.
25.16 of twelve tribes, and their **names** were given to their
25.25 his skin was like a hairy robe, so he was **named** Esau.
25.26 on tightly to the heel of Esau, so he was **named** Jacob.
26.18 the wells the same **names** that his father had given them.
26.20 So Isaac **named** the well "Quarrel."
26.21 a quarrel about that one also, so he **named** it "Enmity."
26.22 There was no dispute about this one, so he **named** it "Freedom."
26.33 He **named** the well "Vow."
26.33 That is how the city of Beersheba got its **name.**
27.36 No wonder his **name** is Jacob.
28.19 He **named** the place Bethel.
29.16 the elder was **named** Leah, and the younger Rachel.
29.32 so she **named** him Reuben.
29.33 so she **named** him Simeon.
29.34 so she **named** him Levi.
29.35 so she **named** him Judah.
30. 6 so she **named** him Dan.
30. 8 so she **named** him Naphtali.
30.11 so she **named** him Gad.
30.13 so she **named** him Asher.
30.18 so she **named** her son Issachar.
30.20 so she **named** him Zebulun.
30.21 Later she bore a daughter, whom she **named** Dinah.
30.24 so she **named** him Joseph.
30.28 **Name** your wages, and I will pay them."
31.47 Laban **named** it Jegar Sahadutha, while Jacob named it Galeed.
31.48 That is why that place was **named** Galeed.
31.49 So the place was also **named** Mizpah.
32.27 "What is your **name?"**
32.28 The man said, "Your **name** will no longer be Jacob.
32.28 so your **name** will be Israel."
32.29 Jacob said, "Now tell me your **name."**
32.29 But he answered, "Why do you want to know my **name?"**
32.30 so he **named** the place Peniel.
33.17 That is why the place was **named** Sukkoth.
33.20 up an altar there and **named** it after El, the God of
35. 7 built an altar there and **named** the place after the God of
35. 8 So it was **named** "Oak of Weeping."
35.10 God said to him, "Your **name** is Jacob, but from now on
35.10 So God **named** him Israel.
35.15 He **named** the place Bethel.
35.18 named her son Benoni, but his father **named** him Benjamin.
36.22 (Lotan had a sister **named** Timna.)
36.25 Anah also had a daughter **named** Oholibamah.
36.40 of these tribes lived was known by the **name** of the tribe.
38. 1 to stay with a man **named** Hirah, who was from the town
38. 2 There Judah met a Canaanite girl whose father was **named** Shua.
38. 3 married her, [3]and she bore him a son, whom he **named** Er.
38. 4 became pregnant again and bore another son and **named** him Onan.
38. 5 Again she had a son and **named** him Shelah.
38. 6 his first son Er, Judah got a wife whose **name** was Tamar.
38.29 So he was **named** Perez.
38.30 with the red thread on his arm, and he was **named** Zerah.
41.45 He gave Joseph the Egyptian **name** Zaphenath Paneah,
41.51 so he **named** his first son Manasseh.
41.52 so he **named** his second son Ephraim.
42.15 I swear by the **name** of the king that you will never
48.16 May my **name** and the name of my fathers Abraham and Isaac
48.20 Israelites will use your **names** when they pronounce blessings.
50.11 That is why the place was **named** Abel Mizraim.
Ex 2.10 pulled him out of the water, and so I **name** him Moses."
2.22 am a foreigner in this land, and so I **name** him Gershom."
6.14 they were the ancestors of the clans that bear their **names.**
6.15 they were the ancestors of the clans that bear their **names.**
6.16 they were the ancestors of the clans that bear their **names.**
15.23 That is why it was **named** Marah.
17. 7 The place was **named** Massah and Meribah, because the
17.15 Moses built an altar and **named** it "The Lord is my Banner."
18. 3 so he had **named** one son Gershom.
18. 4 so he had **named** the other son Eliezer.
23.13 do not even mention their **names.**
28. 9 and engrave on them the **names** of the twelve sons of Jacob,
28.11 on the two stones the **names** of the sons of Jacob, and
28.12 way Aaron will carry their **names** on his shoulders, so that
28.21 have engraved on it the **name** of one of the sons of
28.29 engraved with the **names** of the tribes of Israel,
32.32 then remove my **name** from the book
32.32 in which you have written the **names** of your people."
32.33 sinned against me whose **names** I will remove from my book.
39. 6 engraved with the **names** of the twelve sons of Jacob.
39.14 had engraved on it the **name** of one of the sons of
Lev 24.10 whose mother was an Israelite **named** Shelomith, the daughter
Num 1. 2 List the **names** of all the men [3]twenty years old or older
1.18 The **names** of all the men twenty years old or older were
1.20 were registered by **name** according to clan and family,
3.17 who were the ancestors of the clans that bear their **names.**
3.17 They were the ancestors of the families that bear their **names.**
3.40 So register by **name** every first-born male Israelite, one
5.21 may the Lord make your **name** a curse among your people.
5.27 Her **name** will become a curse among her people.
11. 3 So the place was **named** Taberah, because there the fire of
11.34 was **named** Kibroth Hattaavah (which means "Graves of Craving"),

Num 13.16 He changed the **name** of Hoshea son of Nun to Joshua.
13.24 (That place was **named** the Valley of Eshcol because of
17. 2 Write each man's **name** on his stick
17. 3 and then write Aaron's **name** on the stick representing Levi.
21. 3 destroyed them and their cities, and **named** the place Hormah.
25.14 The **name** of the Israelite who was killed with the
25.15 The woman's **name** was Cozbi.
26.33 their **names** were Mahlah, Noah, Hoglah, Milcah, and Tirzah.
26.46 Asher had a daughter **named** Serah.
27. 4 no sons, why should our father's **name** disappear from Israel?
32.38 Kiriathaim, [38] Nebo, Baal Meon (this **name** was changed),
32.38 They gave new **names** to the towns they rebuilt.
32.41 captured some villages and **named** them "Villages of Jair."
32.42 Kenath and its villages, and he **renamed** it Nobah, after himself.
33. 1 The following account gives the **names** of the places where
33. 2 Lord, Moses wrote down the **name** of the place each time they
Deut 2.20 land of the Rephaim, the **name** of the people who used to
2.25 Everyone will tremble with fear at the mention of your **name.'**
3.14 He **named** the villages after himself, and they are still
18.20 so must any prophet who speaks in the **name** of other gods.'
Josh 2. 1 to spend the night in the house of a prostitute **named** Rahab.
5. 9 is why the place was **named** Gilgal,
5. 9 the **name** it still has.
7. 1 A man **named** Achan disobeyed that order, and so the Lord was
17. 3 Their **names** were Mahlah, Noah, Hoglah, Milcah, and Tirzah.
19.47 settled there and changed the **name** of the city
19.47 from Laish to Dan, **naming** it after their ancestor Dan.
21. 9 These are the **names** of the cities from the territories of
22.34 And so they **named** it "Witness."
23. 7 among you or speak the **names** of their gods
23. 7 or use those **names** in taking vows or worship those
Judg 1.17 put a curse on the city, destroyed it, and **named** it Hormah.
1.26 built a city there, and **named** it Luz,
1.26 which is still its **name.**
6.24 altar to the Lord there and **named** it "The Lord is Peace."
8.14 wrote down for Gideon the **names** of the seventy-seven leading
8.31 she bore him a son, and he **named** him Abimelech.
13. 2 time there was a man **named** Manoah from the town of Zorah.
13. 6 him where he came from, and he didn't tell me his **name.**
13.17 Manoah replied, "Tell us your **name,** so that we can
13.18 The angel asked, "Why do you want to know my **name?**
13.18 It is a **name** of wonder."
13.24 The woman gave birth to a son and **named** him Samson.
15.17 The place where this happened was **named** Ramath Lehi.
15.19 So the spring was **named** Hakkore;
16. 4 in love with a woman **named** Delilah, who lived in the Valley
17. 1 There was once a man **named** Micah, who lived in the
18.29 They changed its **name** from Laish to Dan, after their ancestor
Ruth 1. 1 So a man **named** Elimelech, who belonged to the clan of
2. 1 Naomi had a relative **named** Boaz, a rich and influential
2.19 had been working in a field belonging to a man **named** Boaz.
4.17 The women of the neighbourhood **named** the boy Obed.
1 Sam 1. 1 There was a man **named** Elkanah, from the tribe of Ephraim,
1.20 **named** him Samuel, and explained, "I asked the Lord for him."
4.21 She **named** the boy Ichabod, explaining, "God's glory has left Israel"—
6.14 belonging to a man **named** Joshua, who lived in Beth Shemesh,
7. 1 the house of a man **named** Abinadab, who lived on a hill.
7.12 helped us all the way"—and he **named** it "Stone of Help."
8. 2 The elder son was **named** Joel and the younger one Abijah;
9. 1 and influential man **named** Kish, from the tribe of Benjamin;
9. 2 He had a son **named** Saul, a handsome man in the prime
14.49 His elder daughter was **named** Merab, and the younger one Michal.
16. 1 to Bethlehem, to a man **named** Jesse, because I have chosen
17. 4 A man **named** Goliath, from the city of Gath, came out from
18.19 she was given instead to a man **named** Adriel from Meholah.
24.21 my name and my family's **name** will not be completely forgotten."
25. 2 of the clan of Caleb **named** Nabal, who was from the town
25. 9 David's men delivered this message to Nabal in David's **name.**
25.25 He is exactly what his **name** means—a fool!
28. 8 "Call up the spirit of the man I **name."**
2 Sam 5. 9 fortress, David lived in it and **named** it "David's City."
6.20 "The king of Israel made a big **name** for himself today!"
9. 2 a servant of Saul's family **named** Ziba, and he was told to
9.12 Mephibosheth had a young son **named** Mica.
12.24 with her, and she bore a son, whom David **named** Solomon.
12.25 commanded the prophet Nathan to **name** the boy Jedidiah,
13. 1 David's son Absalom had a beautiful unmarried sister **named** Tamar.
13. 3 friend, a very shrewd man **named** Jonadab, the son of David's
14. 7 leave my husband without a son to keep his **name** alive."
14.27 sons and one daughter **named** Tamar, a very beautiful woman.
18.18 King's Valley, because he had no son to keep his **name** alive.
18.18 So he **named** it after himself, and to this day it is
20. 1 in Gilgal a worthless character **named** Sheba son of Bikri, of
20.21 A man **named** Sheba son of Bikri, who is from the hill-country
21.16 A giant **named** Ishbibenob, who was carrying a bronze
21.18 which Sibbecai from Hushah killed a giant **named** Saph.
23. 8 These are the **names** of David's famous soldiers:
1 Kgs 1. 3 they found such a girl **named** Abishag, and brought her to the
4. 8 The following are the **names** of these twelve officers and
7.13 Solomon sent for a man **named** Huram, a craftsman living in
7.21 on the south side was **named** Jachin,
7.21 and the one on the north was **named** Boaz.
11.26 His mother was a widow **named** Zeruah.
13. 2 A child, whose **name** will be Josiah, will be born to the
16.24 for six thousand pieces of silver from a man **named** Shemer.
16.24 built a town there, and **named** it Samaria, after Shemer, the
17. 1 prophet **named** Elijah, from Tishbe in Gilead, said to King Ahab,
18.31 each of the twelve tribes **named** after the sons of Jacob,
1 Kgs 18.31 the man to whom the Lord had given the **name** Israel.
21. 1 in Jezreel there was a vineyard owned by a man **named** Naboth.
21. 8 signed them with Ahab's **name,** sealed them with his seal,
2 Kgs 14. 7 Sela in battle and called it Joktheel, the **name** it still has.
17.34 he gave to the descendants of Jacob, whom he **named** Israel.
18.23 will make a bargain with you in the **name** of the emperor.
22.14 went to consult a woman **named** Huldah, a prophet who lived in
22.19 sight, a place whose **name** people will use as a curse.
23.34 Judah as successor to Josiah, and changed his **name** to Jehoiakim.
24.17 Mattaniah king of Judah and changed his **name** to Zedekiah.
1 Chr 1. 5 Tiras—were the ancestors of the peoples who bear their **names.**
1. 8 Canaan—were the ancestors of the peoples who bear their **names.**
1.10 (Cush had a son **named** Nimrod, who became the world's
1.13 Heth—were the ancestors of the peoples who bear their **names.**
1.17 Meshek—were the ancestors of the peoples who bear their **names.**
1.19 one was **named** Peleg, because during his time the people
1.19 of the world were divided, and the other was **named** Joktan.
1.29 Nebaioth (from the **name** of Ishmael's eldest son), Kedar,
1.32 Abraham had a concubine **named** Keturah, who bore him six sons:
1.38 (Lotan had a sister **named** Timna.)
2.17 a descendant of Ishmael, and they had a son **named** Amasa.
2.18 Caleb married Azubah and had a daughter **named** Jerioth.
2.19 Azubah, Caleb married Ephrath, and they had a son **named** Hur.
2.21 They had a son **named** Segub,
2.22 and Segub had a son **named** Jair.
2.24 They had a son **named** Ashhur, who founded the town of Tekoa.
2.26 had another wife, a woman **named** Atarah, and they had a son,
2.29 Abishur married a woman **named** Abihail, and they had two sons,
2.34 He had an Egyptian servant **named** Jarha, [35] to whom he gave
2.35 They had a son **named** Attai.
2.42 The eldest son of Caleb, Jerahmeel's brother, was **named** Mesha.
2.46 Caleb had a concubine **named** Ephah, and by her he had
2.46 Haran also had a son **named** Gazez.
2.47 (A man **named** Jahdai had six sons:
2.49 In addition, Caleb had a daughter **named** Achsah.
4. 9 There was a man **named** Jabez, who was the most respected
4. 9 mother had given him the **name** Jabez, because his birth had
4.41 Hezekiah of Judah, the men **named** above went to Gerar and
7.15 His sister's **name** was Maacah.
7.16 gave birth to two sons, whom they **named** Peresh and Sheresh.
7.17 sons, Ulam and Rakem, [17] and Ulam had a son **named** Bedan.
7.23 They **named** him Beriah, because of the trouble that had come
7.24 Ephraim had a daughter **named** Sheerah.
7.25 Ephraim also had a son **named** Rephah, whose descendants were
8.29 His wife was **named** Maacah, [30] and his eldest son, Abdon.
8.40 All those **named** above were members of the tribe of Benjamin.
9. 9 All the men **named** above were heads of families.
9.31 A Levite **named** Mattithiah, eldest son of Shallum, of
9.34 The men **named** above were heads of Levite families,
9.35 His wife was **named** Maacah.
12. 8 These are the **names** of the famous, experienced soldiers
13.13 the house of a man **named** Obed Edom, a native of the
20. 4 killed a giant **named** Sippai, and the Philistines were defeated.
22. 9 His **name** will be Solomon, because during his reign I will
23.24 by clans and families, every one of them registered by **name.**
2 Chr 2.13 sending you a wise and skilful master craftsman **named** Huram.
3.17 on the south side was **named** Jachin,
3.17 and the one on the north side was **named** Boaz.
14. 9 A Sudanese **named** Zerah invaded Judah with an army of a
20. 2 (This is another **name** for Engedi.)
20.14 His **name** was Jahaziel son of Zechariah;
22. 7 were confronted by a man **named** Jehu son of Nimshi, whom the
22.11 Jehosheba, who was married to a priest **named** Jehoiada.
24.26 son of an Ammonite woman **named** Shimeath,
24.26 and Jehozabad, the son of a Moabite woman **named** Shimrith).
28. 7 An Israelite soldier **named** Zichri killed King Ahaz' son
28. 9 A man **named** Oded, a prophet of the Lord, lived in the
31.12 They placed a Levite **named** Conaniah in charge and made his
34.22 went to consult a woman **named** Huldah, a prophet who lived in
36. 4 Eliakim king of Judah and changed his **name** to Jehoiakim.
Ezra 2.61 of Gilead and had taken the **name** of his father-in-law's clan.)
5. 4 They also asked for the **names** of all the men who were
5.10 We also asked them their **names** so that we could inform
5.14 utensils over to a man **named** Sheshbazzar, whom he appointed
7. 1 Artaxerxes was emperor of Persia, there was a man **named** Ezra.
8.20 They were all listed by **name.**
10.16 from among the heads of the clans and recorded their **names.**
Neh 2.19 Sanballat, Tobiah, and an Arab **named** Geshem heard what we
7.63 of Gilead and taken the **name** of his father-in-law's clan.)
9. 7 you changed his **name** to Abraham.
Esth 2. 5 There in Susa lived a Jew **named** Mordecai son of Jair;
2. 7 He had a cousin, Esther, whose Hebrew **name** was Hadassah;
2.14 again unless he liked her enough to ask for her by **name.**
3. 1 King Xerxes promoted a man **named** Haman to the position of
3.12 It was issued in the **name** of King Xerxes and stamped with
7. 9 one of them, who was **named** Harbonah, said, "Haman even went
8. 8 proclamation issued in the king's **name** and stamped with the
8. 8 may write it in my **name** and stamp it with the royal
8.10 the letters written in the **name** of King Xerxes, and he
Job 1. 1 There was a man **named** Job, living in the land of Uz,
4. 7 **Name** a single case where a righteous man met with disaster.
30. 8 A worthless bunch of **nameless** nobodies!
32. 2 a bystander **named** Elihu could not control his anger any longer,
Ps 69.28 May their **names** be erased from the book of the living;
72.17 May the king's **name** never be forgotten;
102. 8 those who mock me use my **name** in cursing.
109.13 die, and may his **name** be forgotten in the next generation.
147. 4 decided the number of the stars and calls each one by **name.**
Prov 22.10 be no more arguments, quarrelling, or calling of **names.**
30.15 A leech has two daughters, and both are **named** "Give me!"
Song 1. 3 the sound of your **name** recalls it.

Is 7.14 is pregnant will have a son and will **name** him 'Immanuel.'
8. 3 the Lord said to me, "**Name** him 'Quick-Loot-Fast-Plunder.'
30. 7 So I have **nicknamed** Egypt, 'The Harmless Dragon.' "
36. 8 will make a bargain with you in the **name** of the emperor.
40.26 he knows how many there are and calls each one by **name!**
43. 1 I have called you by **name**—you are mine.
45. 3 Lord, and that the God of Israel has called you by **name.**
49.16 I have written your **name** on the palms of my hands.
56. 5 keep my covenant, [5]then your **name** will be remembered in my
62. 2 called by a new name, A **name** given by the Lord himself.
62. 4 Your new **name** will be "God Is Pleased with Her."
65.15 My chosen people will use your **name** as a curse.
65.15 But I will give a new **name** to those who obey me.
66.22 by my power, so your descendants and your **name** will endure.
Jer 2. 8 prophets spoke in the **name** of Baal and worshipped useless idols.
17.13 They will disappear like **names** written in the dust, because
20. 3 chains, I said to him, "The Lord did not **name** you Pashhur.
20. 3 The **name** he has given you is 'Terror Everywhere.'
23.13 they have spoken in the **name** of Baal and have led my
24. 9 ridicule them, and use their **name** as a curse everywhere I
25.18 that people would use their **name** as a curse—as they still
26. 6 the world will use the **name** of this city as a curse."
29.18 People will mock them and use their **name** as a curse.
29.24 a letter in his own **name** to all the people of Jerusalem
31.20 Whenever I mention your **name,** I think of you with love.
37.13 there, a man by the **name** of Irijah, the son of Shelemiah
42.18 will treat you with scorn and use your **name** as a curse.
44. 8 will treat you with scorn and use your **name** as a curse?
44.12 will treat them with scorn and use their **name** as a curse.
44.22 sight, and people use its **name** as a curse because the Lord
46.17 king of Egypt a new **name**— 'Noisy Braggart Who Missed His
49.13 people will jeer at it and use its **name** as a curse.
52. 1 His mother's **name** was Hamutal, the daughter of the Jeremiah
Ezek 13. 9 your **names** will not be included in the list of the citizens
23. 4 The older one was **named** Oholah (she represents Samaria),
23. 4 the younger one was **named** Oholibah (she represents Jerusalem).
39.16 (There will be a town near by **named** after the army.)
48.30 has three gates in it, each **named** after one of the tribes.
48.30 gates in the north wall are **named** after Reuben, Judah, and Levi;
48.30 those in the west wall are **named** after Gad, Asher, and Naphtali.
48.35 The **name** of the city from now on will be, "The-Lord-Is-Here!"
Dan 1. 7 The chief official gave them new **names:**
4. 8 (He is also called Belteshazzar, after the **name** of my god.)
5.12 man Daniel, whom the king **named** Belteshazzar, and he will
12. 1 people of your nation whose **names** are written in God's book
Hos 1. 3 So Hosea married a woman **named** Gomer, the daughter of Diblaim.
1. 4 the Lord said to Hosea, "**Name** him 'Jezreel,' because it
1. 6 The Lord said to Hosea, "**Name** her 'Unloved,' because I will
1. 9 The Lord said to Hosea, "**Name** him 'Not-My-People,'
2.17 I will never let her speak the **name** of Baal again.
Jon 1. 7 They did so, and Jonah's **name** was drawn.
Nah 1.14 "They will have no descendants to carry on their **name.**
Zeph 1. 5 me, but then take oaths in the **name** of the god Molech.
Zech 13. 2 time I will remove the **names** of the idols from the land,
Mt 1.25 And Joseph **named** him Jesus.
2.23 of Galilee [23]and made his home in a town **named** Nazareth.
9. 9 he saw a tax collector, **named** Matthew, sitting in his office.
10. 2 These are the **names** of the twelve apostles:
10.25 the members of the family will be called even worse **names!**
22.20 and he asked them, "Whose face and **name** are these?"
26.14 twelve disciples—the one **named** Judas Iscariot—went to the chief
27.16 that time there was a well-known prisoner **named** Jesus Barabbas.
27.32 met a man from Cyrene **named** Simon, and the soldiers forced
27.57 his **name** was Joseph, and he also was a disciple of Jesus.
Mk 3.14 came to him, [14]and he chose twelve, whom he **named** apostles.
3.16 Simon (Jesus gave him the **name** Peter);
3.17 (Jesus gave them the **name** Boanerges, which means "Men of Thunder");
5. 9 So Jesus asked him, "What is your **name?"**
5. 9 The man answered, "My **name** is 'Mob'—there are so many of
10.46 a blind beggar **named** Bartimaeus son of Timaeus was sitting
12.16 him one, and he asked, "Whose face and **name** are these?"
15. 7 At that time a man **named** Barabbas was in prison with the
15.21 way they met a man **named** Simon, who was coming into the
Lk 1. 5 there was a priest **named** Zechariah, who belonged to the priestly
1. 5 His wife's **name** was Elizabeth;
1.13 You are to **name** him John.
1.26 God sent the angel Gabriel to a town in Galilee **named** Nazareth.
1.27 in marriage to a man **named** Joseph, who was a descendant of
1.27 The girl's **name** was Mary.
1.59 and they were going to **name** him Zechariah, after his father.
1.60 His **name** is to be John."
1.61 They said to her, "But you have no relatives with that **name!"**
1.62 his father, asking him what **name** he would like the boy to
1.63 asked for a writing tablet and wrote, "His **name** is John."
2.21 to be circumcised, he was **named** Jesus, the name which the
2.25 At that time there was a man **named** Simeon living in Jerusalem.
2.36 very old prophetess, a widow **named** Anna, daughter of Phanuel
5.27 and saw a tax collector **named** Levi, sitting in his office.
6.13 to him and chose twelve of them, whom he **named** apostles:
6.14 Simon (whom he **named** Peter) and his brother Andrew;
8.30 Jesus asked him, "What is your **name?"**
8.30 "My **name** is 'Mob,' " he answered—because many demons had gone
8.41 Then a man **named** Jairus arrived;
10.20 rather be glad because your **names** are written in heaven."
10.38 village where a woman **named** Martha welcomed him in her home.
10.39 She had a sister **named** Mary, who sat down at the feet
16.20 was also a poor man **named** Lazarus, covered with sores, who
Lk 19. 2 was a chief tax collector there **named** Zacchaeus, who was rich.
20.24 Whose face and **name** are these on it?"
23.26 met a man from Cyrene **named** Simon who was coming into the
23.50 was a man **named** Joseph from Arimathea, a town in Judaea.
24.13 to a village **named** Emmaus, about eleven kilometres from Jerusalem,
24.18 One of them, **named** Cleopas, asked him, "Are you the only
Jn 1. 6 sent his messenger, a man **named** John, [7]who came to tell
1.42 at him and said, "Your **name** is Simon son of John,
3. 1 was a Jewish leader **named** Nicodemus, who belonged to the party
4. 5 he came to a town **named** Sychar, which was not far from
9. 7 (This **name** means "Sent.")
10. 3 he calls his own sheep by **name,** and he leads them out.
11. 1 A man **named** Lazarus, who lived in Bethany, was ill.
11.49 One of them, **named** Caiaphas, who was High Priest that year,
11.54 the desert, to a town **named** Ephraim, where he stayed with
18.10 The **name** of the slave was Malchus.
19.13 (In Hebrew the **name** is "Gabbatha.")
Acts 4. 7 What power have you got or whose **name** did you use?"
5. 1 But there was a man **named** Ananias, who with his wife
5.34 one of them, a Pharisee **named** Gamaliel, who was a teacher of
7.58 left their cloaks in the care of a young man **named** Saul.
8. 9 A man **named** Simon lived there, who for some time had
9.10 There was a Christian in Damascus **named** Ananias.
9.11 the house of Judas ask for a man from Tarsus **named** Saul.
9.12 he has seen a man **named** Ananias come in and place his
9.33 There he met a man **named** Aeneas, who was paralysed and
9.36 In Joppa there was a woman **named** Tabitha, who was a believer.
9.36 (Her **name** in Greek is Dorcas, meaning "a deer.")
9.43 Joppa for many days with a tanner of leather **named** Simon.
10. 1 was a man in Caesarea **named** Cornelius, who was a captain in
10. 5 to Joppa for a certain man whose full **name** is Simon Peter.
10. 6 of a tanner of leather **named** Simon, who lives by the sea."
10.18 asked, "Is there a guest here by the **name** of Simon Peter?"
10.32 someone to Joppa for a man whose full **name** is Simon Peter.
11.13 someone to Joppa for a man whose full **name** is Simon Peter.
11.28 One of them, **named** Agabus, stood up and by the power of
12.13 outside door, and a servant-girl **named** Rhoda came to answer it.
13. 6 they met a certain magician **named** Bar-Jesus, a Jew who claimed
13. 8 magician Elymas (that is his **name** in Greek), who tried to
14.12 They gave Barnabas the **name** Zeus, and Paul the name Hermes,
16. 1 on to Derbe and Lystra, where a Christian **named** Timothy lived.
17.34 was also a woman **named** Damaris, and some other people.
18. 2 There he met a Jew **named** Aquila, born in Pontus, who had
18. 7 house of a Gentile **named** Titius Justus, who worshipped God;
18.15 argument about words and **names** and your own law, you yourselves
18.24 At that time a Jew **named** Apollos, who had been born in
19.14 sons of a Jewish High Priest **named** Sceva, were doing this.
19.24 A certain silversmith **named** Demetrius made silver models of
19.27 then, that this business of ours will get a bad **name.**
20. 9 A young man **named** Eutychus was sitting in the window,
21.10 for several days when a prophet **named** Agabus arrived from Judaea.
22.12 that city was a man **named** Ananias, a religious man who
24. 1 went to Caesarea with some elders and a lawyer **named** Tertullus.
25.19 their own religion and about a man **named** Jesus, who has
Rom 14.16 Do not let what you regard as good get a bad **name.**
Eph 3.15 every family in heaven and on earth receives its true **name.**
Phil 4. 3 all my other fellow-workers, whose **names** are in God's book of
Heb 6.13 than himself, he used his own **name** when he made his vow.
6.16 a vow, he uses the **name** of someone greater than himself,
7. 2 first meaning of Melchizedek's **name** is "King of Righteousness";
7. 2 was king of Salem, his **name** also means "King of Peace.")
12.23 of God's first-born sons, whose **names** are written in heaven.
Jas 2. 7 speak evil of that good **name** which has been given to you.
Rev 2.17 which is written a new **name** that no one knows except the
3. 5 I will not remove their **names** from the book of the living.
3.12 of my God and the **name** of the city of my God,
6. 8 Its rider was **named** Death, and Hades followed close behind.
8.11 (The **name** of the star is "Bitterness.")
9.11 His **name** in Hebrew is Abaddon;
9.11 in Greek the **name** is Apollyon (meaning "The Destroyer").
11. 8 The symbolic **name** of that city is Sodom, or Egypt.
13. 1 of its heads there was a **name** that was insulting to God.
13. 8 except those whose **names** were written before the creation of
13.17 the beast's name or the number that stands for the **name.**
13.18 of the beast, because the number stands for a man's **name.**
14.11 and its image, for anyone who has the mark of its **name."**
15. 2 and over the one whose **name** is represented by a number.
16. 9 and they cursed the **name** of God, who has authority over
17. 3 a red beast that had **names** insulting to God written all over
17. 5 On her forehead was written a **name** that has a secret meaning:
17. 8 people living on earth whose **names** have not been written before
19.12 He had a **name** written on him, but no one except himself
19.13 His **name** is "The Word of God."
19.16 On his robe and on his thigh was written the **name:**
20.15 Whoever did not have his **name** written in the book of the
21.12 the gates were written the **names** of the twelve tribes of the
21.14 on which were written the **names** of the twelve apostles of
21.27 Only those whose **names** are written in the Lamb's book of the
22. 4 his face, and his **name** will be written on their foreheads.

NAME (2) (NAME OF GOD, OF JESUS)

[IN THE NAME OF, LORD'S NAME]

Gen 4.26 that people began using the Lord's holy **name** in worship.
22.16 a vow by my own **name**—the Lord is speaking—that I
24. 3 a vow in the **name of the Lord,** the God of heaven
31.53 in the **name** of the God whom his father Isaac worshipped,
Ex 3.13 sent me to you,' they will ask me, 'What is his **name?'**

Ex 3.15 This is my **name** for ever;
6. 3 not make myself known to them by my holy **name,** the Lord.
15. 3 the Lord is his **name.**
20. 7 "Do not use my **name** for evil purposes, for I,
20. 7 the Lord your God, will punish anyone who misuses my **name.**
33.19 you and in your presence I will pronounce my sacred **name.**
34. 5 cloud, stood with him there, and pronounced his holy **name,**
Lev 18.21 because that would bring disgrace on the **name** of God, the
19.12 not make a promise **in my name** if you do not intend
19.12 that brings disgrace on my **name.**
20. 3 unclean and disgraces my holy **name,** I will turn against him
21. 6 He must be holy and must not disgrace my **name.**
22. 2 bring disgrace on my holy **name,** so treat with respect the
22.32 Do not bring disgrace on my holy **name;**
Num 6.27 said, "If they pronounce my **name** as a blessing upon the
Deut 5.11 "'Do not use my **name** for evil purposes, for I,
5.11 the Lord your God, will punish anyone who misuses my **name.**
6.13 worship only him, and make your promises **in his name** alone.
10. 8 him as priests, and to pronounce blessings **in his name.**
10.20 Be faithful to him and make your promises **in his name** alone.
18.19 He will speak **in my name,** and I will punish anyone who
18.20 to speak a message **in my name** when I did not command
18.22 prophet speaks in the **name of the Lord** and what he says
21. 5 them to serve him and to pronounce blessings **in his name.**
26.19 created, and you will bring praise and honour to his **name.**
28.58 the wonderful and awesome **name of the Lord** your God, [59]he
32. 3 I will praise the **name of the Lord,** and his people will
Josh 9.18 solemn promise to them in the **name of the Lord,** Israel's
9.19 promise to them in the **name of the Lord** God of Israel.
1 Sam 17.45 against you in the **name of the Lord** Almighty, the God of
19. 6 made a vow in the **Lord's name** that he would not kill
24.21 But promise me in the **Lord's name** that you will spare my
30.15 you promise me in God's **name** that you will not kill me
2 Sam 6. 2 Covenant Box, bearing the **name of the Lord** Almighty, who is
6.18 the people in the **name of the Lord** Almighty [19]and
15.21 swear to you in the **Lord's name** that I will always go
19. 7 I swear by the **Lord's name** that if you don't, not one
1 Kgs 1.17 solemn promise in the **name of the Lord** your God that my
1.30 to you in the **name of the Lord,** the God of Israel,
2. 8 solemn promise in the **name of the Lord** that I would not
2.23 a solemn promise in the **Lord's name,** "May God strike me
2.42 "I made you promise in the **Lord's name** not to leave Jerusalem.
13. 5 as the prophet had predicted in the **name of the Lord.**
17. 1 King Ahab, "In the **name of the Lord,** the living God of
22.16 speak to me in the **name of the Lord,** tell the truth!
2 Kgs 2.24 glared at them, and cursed them in the **name of the Lord.**
1 Chr 13. 6 God, which bears the **name of the Lord** enthroned above the
16. 2 the people in the **name of the Lord** [3]and distributed food to
16.29 Praise the Lord's glorious **name;**
16.35 so that we may be thankful and praise your holy **name."**
23.13 Lord, to serve him, and to bless the people **in his name.**
29.13 God, we give you thanks, and we praise your glorious **name.**
29.16 temple to honour your holy **name,** but it all came from you
29.22 In the **name of the Lord** they anointed him as their ruler
2 Chr 9. 8 is with you by making you king, to rule **in his name.**
14.11 on you, and in your **name** we have come out to fight
15.14 took an oath in the **Lord's name** that they would keep the
18.15 speak to me in the **name of the Lord,** tell the truth!
33.18 to him in the **name of the Lord,** the God of Israel,
36.13 forced him to swear in God's **name** that he would be loyal.
Ezra 5. 1 began to speak in the **name** of the God of Israel to
Neh 9. 5 Let everyone praise his glorious **name,** although no human
13.25 take an oath in God's **name** that never again would they or
Job 1.21 May his **name** be praised!"
Ps 29. 2 Praise the Lord's glorious **name;**
33.21 we trust in his holy **name.**
34. 3 let us praise his **name** together!
63.11 who make promises in God's **name** will praise him, but the
66. 2 Sing to the glory of his **name;**
66. 4 they sing praises to you, they sing praises to your **name."**
68. 4 Sing to God, sing praises to his **name;**
68. 4 His **name** is the Lord—be glad in his presence!
72.19 Praise his glorious **name** for ever!
74.10 Will they insult your **name** for ever?
76. 1 his **name** is honoured in Israel.
89.35 "Once and for all I have promised by my holy **name:**
96. 8 Praise the Lord's glorious **name;**
99. 3 Everyone will praise his great and majestic **name.**
102.21 And so his **name** will be proclaimed in Zion, and he will
103. 1 All my being, praise his holy **name!**
106.47 so that we may be thankful and praise your holy **name.**
113. 1 You servants of the Lord, praise his **name!**
113. 2 May his **name** be praised, now and for ever.
113. 3 From the east to the west praise the **name of the Lord!**
118.26 God bless the one who comes in the **name of the Lord!**
129. 8 We bless you in the **name of the Lord."**
135. 1 Praise his **name,** you servants of the Lord, [2]who stand in
135. 3 sing praises to his **name,** because he is kind.
138. 2 bow down, and praise your **name** because of your constant love
138. 2 have shown that your **name** and your commands are supreme.
139.20 they speak evil things against your **name.**
145.21 let all his creatures praise his holy **name** for ever.
148. 5 Let them all praise the **name of the Lord!**
148.13 Let them all praise the **name of the Lord!**
148.13 His **name** is greater than all others;
149. 3 Praise his **name** with dancing;
Is 19.18 will take their oaths in the **name of the Lord** Almighty.
25. 1 I will honour you and praise your **name.**
44. 5 one will mark the **name of the Lord** on his arm and
47. 4 of Israel sets us free— his **name** is the Lord Almighty.
48. 1 You swear by the **name of the Lord** and claim to worship

Is 48. 2 depend on Israel's God, whose **name** is the Lord Almighty.
48. 9 that people will praise my **name,** I am holding my anger in
48.11 I will not let my **name** be dishonoured or let anyone else
51.15 My **name** is the Lord Almighty!
54. 5 like a husband to you— the Lord Almighty is his **name.**
60. 9 gold To honour the **name of the Lord,** The holy God of
63.14 He led his people and brought honour to his **name.**
65.16 takes an oath will swear by the **name** of the Faithful God.
Jer 4. 2 hate, [2]it will be right for you to swear by my **name.**
10. 6 you are mighty, and your **name** is great and powerful.
10.16 The Lord Almighty is his **name.**
13.11 be my people and would bring praise and honour to my **name;**
14.14 But the Lord replied, "The prophets are telling lies **in my name;**
14.15 send but who speak **in my name** and say war and starvation
20. 9 and no longer speak **in his name,"** then your message is like
23.21 not give them any message, but still they spoke **in my name.**
23.25 said who speak lies **in my name** and claim that I have
26. 9 have you said in the **Lord's name** that this Temple will
26.16 man spoke to us in the **name of the Lord** our God;
26.20 who spoke in the **name of the Lord** against this city and
27.15 send them and that they are lying to you **in his name.**
29. 9 They are telling you lies **in my name.**
29.21 Zedekiah son of Maaseiah, who are telling you lies **in his name.**
29.23 committed adultery and have told lies in the **Lord's name.**
31.35 his **name** is the Lord Almighty.
33. 2 He whose **name** is the Lord said, [3]"Call to me, and I
44.16 to what you have told us in the **name of the Lord.**
44.26 have made in my mighty **name** to all you Israelites in Egypt:
44.26 any of you use my **name** to make a vow by saying,
50.34 will rescue them is strong—his **name** is the Lord Almighty.
51.19 The Lord Almighty is his **name.**
Ezek 17.19 for breaking the treaty which he swore **in my name** to keep.
20. 9 have brought dishonour to my **name,** for in the presence of
20.14 have brought dishonour to my **name** among the nations which
20.22 have brought dishonour to my **name** among the nations which
20.39 dishonouring my holy **name** by offering gifts to your idols.
36.20 brought disgrace on my holy **name,** because people would say,
36.21 me concerned for my holy **name,** since the Israelites brought
36.22 the sake of my holy **name,** which you have disgraced in every
36.23 the holiness of my great **name**—the name you disgraced among
39. 7 people Israel know my holy **name,**
39. 7 and I will not let my **name** be disgraced any more.
39.25 I will protect my holy **name.**
43. 7 ever again disgrace my holy **name** by worshipping other gods
43. 8 disgraced my holy **name** by all the disgusting things they did,
Dan 9. 6 prophets, who spoke in your **name** to our kings, our rulers,
9.18 are in and the suffering of the city that bears your **name.**
12. 7 and made a solemn promise in the **name** of the Eternal God.
Hos 4.15 or make promises there in the **name** of the living Lord.
12. 5 Almighty—the Lord is the **name** by which he is to be
Amos 2. 7 with the same slave-girl, and so profane my holy **name.**
4.13 This is his **name:**
5. 8 His **name** is the Lord.
5.27 Damascus," says the Lord, whose **name** is Almighty God.
6.10 We must be careful not even to mention the **Lord's name."**
9. 6 His **name** is the Lord!
Hag 2.23 my servant, and I will appoint you to rule **in my name.**
Zech 14. 9 will worship him as God and know him by the same **name.**
Mt 1.21 a son, and you will **name** him Jesus—because he will save
6. 9 May your holy **name** be honoured;
7.22 **In your name** we spoke God's message,
7.22 by your **name** we drove out many demons
18. 5 And whoever welcomes **in my name** one such child as this,
18.20 or three come together **in my name,** I am there with them."
21. 9 God bless him who comes **in the name of** the Lord!
23.39 say, 'God bless him who comes **in the name of** the Lord.' "
26.63 Priest spoke to him, **"In the name of** the living God I
28.19 baptize them **in the name of** the Father, the Son, and the
Mk 9.37 "Whoever welcomes **in my name** one of these children, welcomes
9.38 was driving out demons **in your name,** and we told him to
9.39 who performs a miracle **in my name** will be able soon
11. 9 God bless him who comes **in the name of** the Lord!
16.17 they will drive out demons **in my name;**
Lk 1.31 and give birth to a son, and you will **name** him Jesus.
1.49 His **name** is holy;
2.21 he was named Jesus, the **name** which the angel had given him
9.48 to them, "Whoever welcomes this child **in my name,** welcomes
me;
9.49 man driving out demons **in your name,** and we told him to
10.17 demons obeyed us when we gave them a command **in your name!"**
11. 2 May your holy **name** be honoured;
13.35 say, 'God bless him who comes **in the name of** the Lord.' "
19.38 "God bless the king who comes **in the name of** the Lord!
24.47 three days later, [47]and **in his name** the message about repentance
Jn 12.13 God bless him who comes **in the name of** the Lord!
12.28 Father, bring glory to your **name!"**
14.13 whatever you ask for **in my name,** so that the Father's glory
14.14 you ask me for anything **in my name,** I will do it.
14.26 the Father will send **in my name,** will teach you everything
15.16 Father will give you whatever you ask of him **in my name.**
16.23 Father will give you whatever you ask him for **in my name.**
16.24 Until now you have not asked for anything **in my name;**
16.26 When that day comes, you will ask him **in my name;**
17.11 by the power of your **name,** the name you gave me,
17.12 safe by the power of your name, the **name** you gave me.
Acts 2.38 and be baptized **in the name of** Jesus Christ, so that
3. 6 **in the name of** Jesus Christ of Nazareth I order you to
3.16 was the power of his **name** that gave strength to this lame
3.16 What you see and know was done by faith **in his name;**
4.10 the power of the **name of Jesus** Christ of Nazareth—whom you
4.17 men never again to speak to anyone **in the name of** Jesus."

Acts 4.18 were they to speak or to teach **in the name of** Jesus.
4.30 may be performed through the **name** of your holy Servant Jesus."
5.28 orders not to teach **in the name of** this man," he said;
5.40 and ordered them never again to speak **in the name of** Jesus;
8.16 they had only been baptized **in the name of** the Lord Jesus.
9.15 serve me, to make my **name** known to Gentiles and kings
9.27 boldly Saul had preached **in the name of** Jesus in Damascus.
9.28 all over Jerusalem, preaching boldly **in the name of** the Lord.
10.43 will have his sins forgiven through the power of his **name."**
10.48 he ordered them to be baptized **in the name of** Jesus Christ.
16.18 said to the spirit, **"In the name of** Jesus Christ I order
17. 7 saying that there is another king, whose **name** is Jesus."
19. 5 this, they were baptized **in the name of** the Lord Jesus.
19.13 tried to use the **name of the Lord** Jesus to do this.
19.13 "I command you **in the name of** Jesus, whom Paul preaches."
19.17 with fear, and the **name of the Lord** Jesus was given greater
Rom 16. 2 Receive her in the **Lord's name,** as God's people should,
1 Cor 5. 3 with you, I have **in the name of** our Lord Jesus already
2 Cor 11.31 and Father of the Lord Jesus—blessed be his **name** for ever!
Eph 4.17 In the **Lord's name,** then, I warn you:
5.20 **In the name of** our Lord Jesus Christ, always give thanks
Phil 2. 9 gave him the name that is greater than any other **name.**
2.10 in honour of the **name of Jesus** all beings in heaven,
Col 3.17 then, should be done **in the name of** the Lord Jesus,
1 Thes 4. 1 beg and urge you **in the name of** the Lord Jesus to
2 Thes 1.12 In this way the **name of our Lord** Jesus will receive
3. 6 brothers, we command you **in the name of** our Lord Jesus
3.12 **In the name of** the Lord Jesus Christ we command these
1 Tim 6. 1 will speak evil of the **name of God** and of our teaching.
Heb 1. 4 the angels, just as the **name** that God gave him is greater
Jas 5.10 remember the prophets who spoke **in the name of** the Lord.
5.14 and rub olive-oil on him **in the name of** the Lord.
1 Pet 4.16 ashamed of it, but thank God that you bear Christ's **name.**
Rev 3.12 write on him the **name of my God** and the name of
3.12 I will also write on him my new **name.**
10. 6 and took a vow **in the name of** God, who lives for
13. 6 began to curse God, his **name,** the place where he lives,
14. 1 have his name and his Father's **name** written on their foreheads.
16. 9 and they cursed the **name of God,** who has authority over
22. 4 his face, and his **name** will be written on their foreheads.

Am **NAME-CALLING** see **NAME (1)**

NAMELY

Acts 24.15 that these themselves have, **namely,** that all people,
Gal 3.16 singular "descendant," meaning one person only, **namely,** Christ.

NAOMI
Ruth's mother-in-law.
see also MARAH (2)

Ruth 1. 1 Judah, went with his wife **Naomi** and their two sons Mahlon
1. 3 living there, [3]Elimelech died, and **Naomi** was left alone
1. 5 and Chilion also died, and **Naomi** was left all alone, without
1. 6 Some time later **Naomi** heard that the Lord had blessed his
1. 9 So **Naomi** kissed them good-bye.
1.11 "You must go back, my daughters," **Naomi** answered.
1.15 So **Naomi** said to her, "Ruth, your sister-in-law has
1.18 When **Naomi** saw that Ruth was determined to go with her,
1.19 and the women there exclaimed, "Is this really **Naomi?"**
1.20 "Don't call me **Naomi,"** she answered;
1.21 Why call me **Naomi** when the Lord Almighty has condemned me
1.22 This, then, was how **Naomi** came back from Moab with Ruth,
2. 1 **Naomi** had a relative named Boaz, a rich and influential
2. 2 One day Ruth said to **Naomi,** "Let me go to the fields
2. 2 **Naomi** answered, "Go ahead, my daughter."
2. 6 "She is the foreign girl who came back from Moab with **Naomi.**
2.19 **Naomi** asked her, "Where did you gather all this?
2.19 So Ruth told **Naomi** that she had been working in a field
2.20 **Naomi** exclaimed.
2.22 **Naomi** said to Ruth, "Yes, my daughter,
3. 1 Some time later **Naomi** said to Ruth, "I must find a
3.18 **Naomi** said to her, "Now be patient, Ruth, until you
4. 3 to his relative, "Now that **Naomi** has come back from Moab,
4. 5 you buy the field from **Naomi,** then you are also buying Ruth,
4. 9 that I have bought from **Naomi** everything that belonged to
4.14 The women said to **Naomi,** "Praise the Lord!
4.16 **Naomi** took the child, held him close, and took care of him.
4.17 They told everyone, "A son has been born to **Naomi!"**

NAP

2 Sam 11. 2 David got up from his **nap** and went to the palace roof.
Prov 6.10 "I'll just take a short **nap,"** he says;
24.33 Have a **nap** and sleep if you want to.

NAPHTALI
Jacob and Bilhah's son, the tribe descended from him and its territory.

Gen 30. 8 so she named him **Naphtali.**
35.25 The sons of Rachel's slave Bilhah were Dan and **Naphtali.**
46.24 **Naphtali** and his sons:
49.21 **"Naphtali** is a deer that runs free, Who bears lovely fawns.
Ex 1. 4 Issachar, Zebulun, Benjamin, [4]Dan, **Naphtali,** Gad, and Asher.
Num 1. 5 **Naphtali** Ahira son of Enan
10.27 Ahira son of Enan was in command of the tribe of **Naphtali.**
13. 3 **Naphtali** Nahbi son of Vophsi
26.48 The tribe of **Naphtali:**
Num 34.19 **Naphtali** Pedahel son of Ammihud
Deut 27.13 Reuben, Gad, Asher, Zebulun, Dan, and **Naphtali.**
33.23 About the tribe of **Naphtali** he said:
33.23 **"Naphtali** is richly blessed by the Lord's good favour;
34. 2 the entire territory of **Naphtali;**
Josh 19.32 made was for the families of the tribe of **Naphtali.**
19.39 of the tribe of **Naphtali** received as their possession.
20. 7 they set aside Kedesh in Galilee, in the hill-country of **Naphtali;**
21. 6 of Issachar, Asher, **Naphtali,** and East Manasseh.
21.32 From the territory of **Naphtali** they received three cities:
Judg 1.33 The tribe of **Naphtali** did not drive out the people
1.33 The people of **Naphtali** lived with the local Canaanites, but
4. 6 the city of Kedesh in **Naphtali** and said to him, "The Lord,
4. 6 men from the tribes of **Naphtali** and Zebulun and lead them to
4.10 the tribes of Zebulun and **Naphtali** to Kedesh, and ten
5.18 Zebulun and **Naphtali** risked their lives on the battlefield.
6.35 tribes of Asher, Zebulun, and **Naphtali,** and they also came
7.23 men from the tribes of **Naphtali,** Asher, and both parts of
1 Kgs 4.15 the territory of **Naphtali**
7.14 his mother was from the tribe of **Naphtali.**
15.20 area near Lake Galilee, and the whole territory of **Naphtali.**
2 Kgs 15.29 territories of Gilead, Galilee, and **Naphtali,** and took the
1 Chr 2. 2 Judah, Issachar, Zebulun, [2]Dan, Joseph, Benjamin, **Naphtali,**
6.62 of Issachar, Asher, **Naphtali,** and East Manasseh in Bashan.
6.76 In the territory of **Naphtali:**
7.13 **Naphtali** had four sons:
12.40 Zebulun, and **Naphtali,** people came bringing donkeys,
27.16 **Naphtali** Jeremoth son of Azriel
2 Chr 16. 4 and all the cities of **Naphtali** where supplies were stored.
34. 6 Manasseh, Ephraim, and Simeon, and as far north as **Naphtali.**
Ps 68.27 with their group, followed by the leaders of Zebulun and **Naphtali.**
Is 9. 1 the tribes of Zebulun and **Naphtali** was once disgraced, but
Ezek 48. 1 Dan Asher **Naphtali** Manasseh Ephraim Reuben Judah
48.30 in the west wall are named after Gad, Asher, and **Naphtali.**
Mt 4.13 by Lake Galilee, in the territory of Zebulun and **Naphtali.**
4.15 of Zebulun and land of **Naphtali,** on the road to the sea,
Rev 7. 5 Judah, Reuben, Gad, Asher, **Naphtali,** Manasseh, Simeon,
also Num 1.20 Num 2.25 Num 7.12 1 Chr 12.23

NARD
An expensive perfume made from a plant.

Song 4.13 no lack of henna and **nard,** [14]of saffron, calamus, and
Mk 14. 3 jar full of a very expensive perfume made of pure **nard.**
Jn 12. 3 expensive perfume made of pure **nard,** poured it on Jesus' feet,

NARROW

Num 22.24 angel stood where the road **narrowed** between two vineyards
22.26 he stood in a **narrow** place where there was no room at
1 Kgs 6. 4 Temple had openings in them, **narrower** on the outside than on
Is 28.20 out on, with a blanket too **narrow** to wrap himself in.
Ezek 42. 5 level of the building were **narrower** than those at the middle
Mt 7.13 "Go in through the **narrow** gate, because the gate to
7.14 the gate to life is **narrow** and the way that leads to
Lk 13.24 "Do your best to go in through the **narrow** door;

NATHAN (1)
Prophet in David's time.

2 Sam 7. 2 king said to the prophet **Nathan,** "Here I am living in a
7. 3 **Nathan** answered, "Do whatever you have in mind, because
7. 4 night the Lord said to **Nathan,** [5]"Go and tell my servant
7.17 **Nathan** told David everything that God had revealed to him.
12. 1 The Lord sent the prophet **Nathan** to David.
12. 1 **Nathan** went to him and said, "There were two men who lived
12. 7 "You are that man," **Nathan** said to David.
12.13 **Nathan** replied, "The Lord forgives you;
12.15 Then **Nathan** went home.
12.25 and commanded the prophet **Nathan** to name the boy Jedidiah,
1 Kgs 1. 8 priest, Benaiah son of Jehoiada, **Nathan** the prophet, Shimei,
1.10 his half brother Solomon or **Nathan** the prophet, or Benaiah,
1.11 Then **Nathan** went to Bathsheba, Solomon's mother, and
1.14 **Nathan** added, "Then, while you are still talking with King David,
1.22 She was still speaking, when **Nathan** arrived at the palace.
1.23 the prophet was there, and **Nathan** went in and bowed low
1.32 Then King David sent for Zadok, **Nathan,** and Benaiah.
1.34 of Gihon, [34]where Zadok and **Nathan** are to anoint him as
1.38 So Zadok, **Nathan,** Benaiah, and the royal bodyguard put
1.44 He sent Zadok, **Nathan,** Benaiah, and the royal bodyguard
1.45 king's mule, [45]and Zadok and **Nathan** anointed him as king
1 Chr 17. 1 he sent for the prophet **Nathan** and said to him, "Here I
17. 2 **Nathan** answered, "Do whatever you have in mind, because
17. 3 that night God said to **Nathan,** [4]"Go and tell my servant
17.15 **Nathan** told David everything that God had revealed to him.
29.29 in the records of the three prophets, Samuel, **Nathan,**
2 Chr 9.29 recorded in The History of **Nathan** the Prophet, in The
29.25 through Gad, the king's prophet, and through the prophet **Nathan;**

NATION

Gen 10.32 are the descendants of Noah, **nation** by nation, according to
10.32 After the flood all the **nations** of the earth were descended
12. 2 you many descendants, and they will become a great **nation.**
12. 3 And through you I will bless all the **nations."**
15.14 But I will punish the **nation** that enslaves them, and
17. 4 I promise that you will be the ancestor of many **nations.**
17. 5 because I am making you the ancestor of many **nations.**
17. 6 You will have so many descendants that they will become **nations.**
17.16 will become the mother of **nations,** and there will be kings
17.20 princes, and I will make a great **nation** of his descendants.

Gen 18.18 become a great and mighty **nation,**
18.18 and through him I will bless all the **nations.**
21.13 son of the slave-girl, so that they will become a **nation.**
21.18 I will make a great **nation** out of his descendants."
22.18 All the **nations** will ask me to bless them as I have
25.23 "Two **nations** are within you;
26. 4 All the **nations** will ask me to bless them as I have
27.29 **nations** be your servants, and may peoples bow down before you.
28. 3 so that you will become the father of many **nations!**
28.14 you and your descendants I will bless all the **nations.**
35.11 **Nations** will be descended from you, and you will be the
46. 3 I will make your descendants a great **nation** there.
48. 4 children, so that your descendants will become many **nations;**
48.19 than he, and his descendants will become great **nations."**
49.10 **Nations** will bring him tribute And bow in obedience before him.
Ex 15.14 The **nations** have heard, and they tremble with fear;
32.10 Then I will make you and your descendants into a great **nation."**
33.13 Remember also that you have chosen this **nation** to be your own."
34.10 never been done anywhere on earth among any of the **nations.**
34.24 driven out the **nations** before you and extended your territory,
Lev 20.24 your God, and I have set you apart from the other **nations.**
20.26 you apart from the other **nations** so that you would belong to
25.44 need slaves, you may buy them from the **nations** round you.
26.45 when I showed all the **nations** my power by bringing my people
Num 14.12 you the father of a **nation** that is larger and more powerful
14.15 kill all your people, the **nations** who have heard of your
22. 5 want you to know that a whole **nation** has come from Egypt;
23. 9 They are a **nation** that lives alone;
23. 9 They know they are blessed more than other **nations.**
23.23 witchcraft, That can be used against the **nation** of Israel.
23.24 The **nation** of Israel is like a mighty lion:
24. 9 The **nation** is like a mighty lion;
24.17 I look into the future, And I see the **nation** of Israel.
24.17 A king, like a bright star, will arise in that **nation.**
24.19 The **nation** of Israel will trample them down And wipe out
24.20 "Amalek was the most powerful **nation** of all, But at the end
Deut 2.12 out, destroyed their **nation,** and settled there themselves,
4. 6 this will show the people of other **nations** how wise you are.
4. 6 say, 'What wisdom and understanding this great **nation** has!'
4. 7 "No other **nation,** no matter how great, has a god who is
4. 8 No other **nation,** no matter how great, has laws so just as
4.27 will scatter you among other **nations,** where only a few of
4.34 take a people from another **nation** and make them his own, as
4.38 he drove out **nations** greater and more powerful than you,
6. 3 you will become a mighty **nation** and live in that rich and
6.24 he will always watch over our **nation** and keep it prosperous.
7. 1 going to occupy, and he will drive many **nations** out of it.
7. 1 drive out seven **nations** larger and more powerful than you:
7. 7 you were the smallest **nation** on earth.
7.16 Destroy every **nation** that the Lord your God places in your power,
7.22 Little by little he will drive out these **nations** as you advance.
8.20 be destroyed just like those **nations** that he is going to
9. 1 belonging to **nations** greater and more powerful than you.
9.14 you the father of a **nation** larger and more powerful than
11.23 will drive out all those **nations** as you advance, and you
11.23 belonging to **nations** greater and more powerful than you.
12.29 your God will destroy the **nations** as you invade their land,
12.30 After the Lord destroys those **nations,** make sure that
13.13 some worthless men of your **nation** have misled the people of
15. 6 will lend money to many **nations,** but you will not have to
15. 6 will have control over many **nations,**
15. 6 but no **nation** will have control over you.
16.16 "All the men of your **nation** are to come to worship the
17.14 will decide you need a king like all the **nations** round you.
18. 9 the disgusting practices of the **nations** that are there.
18.12 why he is driving those **nations** out of the land as you
23. 6 long as you are a **nation,** never do anything to help
23. 6 to help these **nations** or to make them prosperous.
26. 5 went there, but they became a large and powerful **nation.**
26.19 you greater than any other **nation** that he has created, and
28. 1 he will make you greater than any other **nation** on earth.
28.12 you will lend to many **nations,** but you will not have to
28.13 make you the leader among the **nations** and not a follower;
28.33 A foreign **nation** will take all the crops that you have
28.49 will bring against you a **nation** from the ends of the earth,
28.49 a **nation** whose language you do not know.
28.64 scatter you among all the **nations,** from one end of the earth
29.16 was like to travel through the territory of other **nations.**
29.18 from the Lord our God to worship the gods of other **nations.**
30. 1 you are living among the **nations** where the Lord your God has
30. 3 bring you back from the **nations** where he has scattered you,
30.16 then you will prosper and become a **nation** of many people.
31. 3 before you and destroy the **nations** living there, so that you
32. 5 unworthy to be his people, a sinful and deceitful **nation.**
32. 6 He is your father, your Creator, he made you into a **nation.**
32. 8 The Most High assigned **nations** their lands;
32. 8 He assigned to each **nation** a god, [9]but Jacob's descendants
32.21 So I will use a so-called **nation** to make them angry;
32.21 I will make them jealous with a **nation** of fools.
32.28 "Israel is a **nation** without sense;
32.43 **"Nations,** you must praise the Lord's people— he
33. 4 Law that Moses gave us, our **nation's** most treasured possession.
33.17 With them he gores the **nations** And pushes them to the ends
33.29 There is no one like you, a **nation** saved by the Lord.
Josh 4. 1 When the whole **nation** had crossed the Jordan, the Lord
5. 8 circumcision was completed, the whole **nation** stayed in the
10.13 did not move until the **nation** had conquered its enemies.
23. 3 Lord your God has done to all these **nations** because of you.
23. 4 tribes the land of the **nations** that are still left,
23. 4 well as of all the **nations** that I have already conquered,
23. 9 has driven great and powerful **nations** out as you advanced

Josh 23.12 disloyal and join with the **nations** that are still left among
23.13 God will no longer drive these **nations** out as you advance.
24.17 we went among all the **nations** through which we passed.
Judg 2.20 with Israel and say, "This **nation** has broken the covenant
2.21 drive out any of the **nations** that were still in the land
2.23 So the Lord allowed those **nations** to remain in the land;
3. 1 then, the Lord left some **nations** in the land to test the
1 Sam 8.20 we will be like other **nations,** with our own king to rule
2 Sam 7.23 There is no other **nation** on earth like Israel, whom you
7.23 drove out other **nations** and their gods as your people advanced,
8.11 gold he took from the **nations** he had conquered—[12]Edom,
22.44 rebellious people and maintained my rule over the **nations;**
22.48 he subdues the **nations** under me [49]and saves me from my foes.
22.50 And so I praise you among the **nations;**
1 Kgs 4.21 Solomon's kingdom included all the **nations** from the
5. 7 a wise son to succeed him as king of that great **nation!"**
8.60 And so all the **nations** of the world will know that the
2 Kgs 17.15 the customs of the surrounding **nations,** disobeying the
18.33 the gods of any other **nations** save their countries from the
19.17 Assyria have destroyed many **nations,** made their lands desolate,
19.19 Assyrians, so that all the **nations** of the world will know
21. 2 the disgusting practices of the **nations** whom the Lord had
21. 9 than those committed by the **nations** whom the Lord had driven
23.22 Israel or of Judah, since the time when judges ruled the **nation.**
1 Chr 5.25 worship the gods of the **nations** whom God had driven out of
14.17 everywhere, and the Lord made every **nation** afraid of him.
16. 8 tell the **nations** what he has done.
16.24 Proclaim his glory to the **nations,** his mighty deeds
16.26 The gods of all other **nations** are only idols, but the
16.31 Tell the **nations** that the Lord is king.
16.35 rescue us from the **nations,** so that we may be thankful and
17.21 There is no other **nation** on earth like Israel, whom you
17.21 Egypt and drove out other **nations** as your people advanced.
18.11 gold he took from the **nations** he conquered—Edom, Moab,
21. 3 do you want to do this and make the whole **nation** guilty?"
29.23 successful king, and the whole **nation** of Israel obeyed him.
29.25 The Lord made the whole **nation** stand in awe of Solomon,
2 Chr 13. 9 you appointed priests in the same way that other **nations** do.
15. 6 One **nation** oppressed another nation, and one city oppressed
20. 6 you rule in heaven over all the **nations** of the world.
20.29 Every **nation** that heard how the Lord had defeated
28.23 This brought disaster on him and on his **nation.**
29.30 and the leaders of the **nation** told the Levites to sing to
32.13 my ancestors and I have done to the people of other **nations?**
32.13 the gods of any other **nation** save their people from the
32.15 No god of any **nation** has ever been able to save his
32.17 said, "The gods of the **nations** have not saved their people
32.23 that from then on all the **nations** held Hezekiah in honour.
33. 2 the disgusting practices of the **nations** whom the Lord had
33. 9 than those committed by the **nations** whom the Lord had driven
36.14 example of the **nations** round them in worshipping idols,
Ezra 6.12 worshipped overthrow any king or **nation** that defies this
Neh 1. 8 to me, I will scatter you among the other **nations.**
5.17 all the people who came to me from the surrounding **nations.**
6.16 our enemies in the surrounding **nations** heard this, they
9.22 "You let them conquer **nations** and kingdoms,
9.30 were deaf, so you let them be conquered by other **nations.**
13.26 man who was greater than any of the kings of other **nations.**
Esth 8.11 If armed men of any **nationality** in any province attacked the
Job 12.23 He makes **nations** strong and great, but then he defeats
34.30 There would be nothing that **nations** could do to keep
36.20 Don't wish for night to come, the time when **nations** will perish.
Ps 2. 1 Why do the **nations** plan rebellion?
2. 8 Ask, and I will give you all the **nations;**
9. 8 he judges the **nations** with justice.
9.11 Tell every **nation** what he has done!
18.43 a rebellious people and made me ruler over the **nations;**
18.47 he subdues the **nations** under me [48]and saves me from my foes.
18.49 And so I praise you among the **nations;**
22.27 All **nations** will remember the Lord.
22.28 The Lord is king, and he rules the **nations.**
33.10 The Lord frustrates the purposes of the **nations;**
33.12 Happy is the **nation** whose God is the Lord;
44. 2 punished the other **nations** and caused your own to prosper.
44.14 You have made us an object of contempt among the **nations;**
45. 5 **nations** fall down at your feet.
46. 6 **Nations** are terrified, kingdoms are shaken;
46.10 I am God, supreme among the **nations,** supreme over the world."
47. 3 he made us rule over the **nations.**
47. 8 he rules over the **nations.**
47. 9 The rulers of the **nations** assemble with the people of the
57. 9 I will thank you, O Lord, among the **nations.**
66. 7 for ever by his might and keeps his eyes on the **nations.**
66. 8 Praise our God, all **nations;**
67. 2 so that all **nations** may know your salvation.
67. 4 May the **nations** be glad and sing for joy, because you
67. 4 the peoples with justice and guide every **nation** on earth.
68.30 rebuke the **nations,** that herd of bulls with their calves,
72.11 all **nations** will serve him.
72.17 May all **nations** ask God to bless them as he has blessed
76.11 bring gifts to him, all you nearby **nations.**
77.14 you showed your might among the **nations.**
79. 4 The surrounding **nations** insult us;
79. 6 Turn your anger on the **nations** that do not worship you, on
79.10 Why should the **nations** ask us, "Where is your God?"
79.10 us see you punish the **nations** for shedding the blood of your
79.12 Lord, pay the other **nations** back seven times for all the
80. 6 You let the surrounding **nations** fight over our land;
80. 8 you drove out other **nations** and planted it in their land.
80.17 the people you have chosen, the **nation** you made so strong.
82. 8 all the **nations** are yours.

Ps 83. 4 say, "let us destroy their **nation,** so that Israel will be
86. 9 All the **nations** that you have created will come and bow
87. 4 Egypt and Babylonia when I list the **nations** that obey me;
87. 5 will be said that all **nations** belong there and that the
94.10 He scolds the **nations**—won't he punish them?
96. 3 Proclaim his glory to the **nations,** his mighty deeds
96. 5 The gods of all other **nations** are only idols, but the Lord
96.10 Say to all the **nations,** "The Lord is king!
97. 6 proclaim his righteousness, and all the **nations** see his glory.
98. 2 he made his saving power known to the **nations.**
99. 2 he is supreme over all the **nations.**
102.15 The **nations** will fear the Lord;
102.22 be praised in Jerusalem [22] when **nations** and kingdoms come
105. 1 tell the **nations** what he has done.
105.20 the ruler of **nations** set him free.
106. 5 in the happiness of your **nation,** in the glad pride of those
106.47 us back from among the **nations,** so that we may be thankful
108. 3 I will thank you, O Lord, among the **nations.**
110. 6 on the **nations** and fill the battlefield with corpses;
113. 4 The Lord rules over all **nations;**
115. 2 Why should the **nations** ask us, "Where is your God?"
117. 1 Praise the Lord, all **nations!**
126. 2 Then the other **nations** said about us, "The Lord did great
135.10 He destroyed many **nations** and killed powerful kings:
135.15 The gods of the **nations** are made of silver and gold;
144. 2 He subdues the **nations** under me.
144.15 Happy is the **nation** of whom this is true;
147.20 He has not done this for other **nations;**
148.14 He made his **nation** strong, so that all his people praise
149. 7 hands [7] to defeat the **nations** and to punish the peoples;
149. 9 to punish the **nations** as God has commanded.
Prov 11.14 A **nation** will fall if it has no guidance.
14.34 Righteousness makes a **nation** great;
14.34 sin is a disgrace to any **nation.**
27.24 Not even **nations** last for ever.
28. 2 When a **nation** sins, it will have one ruler after another.
28. 2 But a **nation** will be strong and endure when it has intelligent,
29. 4 is concerned with justice, the **nation** will be strong, but
29.18 A **nation** without God's guidance is a nation without order.
Is 1. 4 You are doomed, you sinful **nation,** you corrupt and evil people!
2. 2 Many **nations** will come streaming to it, [3] and their people
2. 4 He will settle disputes among great **nations.**
2. 4 **Nations** will never again go to war, never prepare for battle again.
4. 4 will judge and purify the **nation** and wash away the guilt of
5.26 The Lord gives a signal to call for a distant **nation.**
7. 8 years it will be too shattered to survive as a **nation.**
8. 9 Gather together in fear, you **nations!**
9. 4 defeated the **nation** that oppressed and exploited your people,
10. 6 to attack a godless **nation,** people who have made me angry.
10. 7 He is determined to destroy many **nations.**
10.13 wiped out the boundaries between **nations** and took the
10.14 The **nations** of the world were like a bird's nest, and I
10.20 no longer rely on the **nation** that almost destroyed them.
11.10 the royal line of David will be a symbol to the **nations.**
11.12 signal flag to show the **nations** that he is gathering
12. 4 Tell all the **nations** what he has done!
13. 4 of people, the sound of **nations** and kingdoms gathering.
14. 2 Many **nations** will help the people of Israel to return to
14. 2 and there the **nations** will serve Israel as slaves.
14. 6 never stopped persecuting the **nations** they had conquered.
14.12 In the past you conquered **nations,** but now you have been
14.26 world, and my arm is stretched out to punish the **nations."**
16. 8 whose wine used to make the rulers of the **nations** drunk.
17.12 Powerful **nations** are in commotion with a sound like the
17.13 The **nations** advance like rushing waves, but God
18. 2 and powerful **nation,** to your tall and smooth-skinned people,
18. 7 and powerful **nation,** this tall and smooth-skinned people,
19.13 They were supposed to lead the **nation,** but they have misled it.
19.23 fro between them, and the two **nations** will worship together.
19.24 and Assyria, and these three **nations** will be a blessing to
23. 3 that grew in Egypt and to do business with all the **nations.**
24.13 This is what will happen in every **nation** all over the world.
24.16 will hear songs in praise of Israel, the righteous **nation.**
25. 3 The people of powerful **nations** will praise you;
25. 3 you will be feared in the cities of cruel **nations.**
25. 6 a banquet for all the **nations** of the world—a banquet of
25. 7 cloud of sorrow that has been hanging over all the **nations.**
26. 2 gates and let the faithful **nation** enter,
26. 2 the **nation** whose people do what is right.
26.15 Lord, you have made our **nation** grow, enlarging its
29. 7 the armies of the **nations** attacking the city of God's altar,
29. 8 All the **nations** that assemble to attack Jerusalem will be
30. 5 they ever trusted that unreliable **nation,**
30. 5 a **nation** that fails them when they expect
30. 6 expensive gifts for a **nation** that cannot give them any help.
30.28 It sweeps **nations** to destruction and puts an end to their
31. 3 the Lord acts, the strong **nation** will crumble,
31. 3 and the weak **nation** it helped will fall.
32. 1 integrity, and **national** leaders who govern with justice.
33. 3 When you fight for us, **nations** run away from the noise of
33. 6 with justice and integrity [6] and give stability to the **nation.**
33.10 The Lord says to the **nations,** "Now I will act.
34. 1 Come, people of all **nations!**
34. 2 The Lord is angry with all the **nations** and all their armies.
36.18 the gods of any other **nations** save their countries from the
37.18 Assyria have destroyed many **nations,** made their lands desolate,
37.20 Assyrians, so that all the **nations** of the world will know
40.15 To the Lord the **nations** are nothing, no more than a drop
40.17 The **nations** are nothing at all to him.
41. 2 Who gives him victory over kings and **nations?**
41.21 "You gods of the **nations,** present your case.
Is 42. 1 with my spirit, and he will bring justice to every **nation.**
42. 6 through you I will bring light to the **nations.**
43. 4 I will give up whole **nations** to save your life, because
43. 9 Summon the **nations** to come to the trial.
45. 1 He has appointed him to conquer **nations;**
45.20 "Come together, people of the **nations,** all who survive the
47. 5 no more will they call you the queen of **nations!**
49. 1 Listen to me, distant **nations,** you people who live far away!
49. 6 you a light to the **nations**— so that all the world
49. 7 who is hated by the **nations** and is the servant of rulers:
49.22 "I will signal to the **nations,** and they will bring your
51. 4 I give my teaching to the **nations;**
51. 5 I myself will rule over the **nations.**
52.15 But now many **nations** will marvel at him, and kings will
54. 3 will get back the land that the other **nations** now occupy.
55. 4 a leader and commander of **nations,** and through him I showed
55. 5 Now you will summon foreign **nations;**
56. 7 called a house of prayer for the people of all **nations."**
56. 9 Lord has told the foreign **nations** to come like wild animals
60. 2 Other **nations** will be covered by darkness, But on you the
60. 3 **Nations** will be drawn to your light, And kings to the
60. 5 The wealth of the **nations** will be brought to you;
60. 9 God of Israel, Who has made all **nations** honour his people.
60.11 So that the kings of the **nations** May bring you their wealth.
60.12 But **nations** that do not serve you Will be completely destroyed.
60.16 **Nations** and kings will care for you As a mother nurses
60.22 humblest family Will become as great as a powerful **nation.**
61. 6 enjoy the wealth of the **nations** And be proud that it is
61. 9 They will be famous among the **nations;**
61.11 Lord will save his people, And all the **nations** will praise him.
62. 2 Jerusalem, the **nations** will see you victorious!
62.10 a signal so that the **nations** can know [11] That the Lord is
63. 3 answers, "I have trampled the **nations** like grapes, and no
63. 6 In my anger I trampled whole **nations** and shattered them.
64. 2 your enemies, and make the **nations** tremble at your presence!
65. 1 The **nation** did not pray to me, even though I was always
66. 8 Has a **nation** ever been born in a day?
66. 8 Zion will not have to suffer long, before the **nation** is born.
66.12 the wealth of the **nations** will flow to you like a river
66.18 I am coming to gather the people of all the **nations.**
66.19 and send them to the **nations** and the distant lands that have
66.19 Among these **nations** they will proclaim my greatness.
66.20 all your fellow-countrymen from the **nations** as a gift to me.
66.23 every Sabbath, people of every **nation** will come to worship
Jer 1. 5 were born I selected you to be a prophet to the **nations."**
1.10 I give you authority over **nations** and kingdoms to uproot and
1.15 because I am calling all the **nations** in the north to come.
2.11 No other **nation** has ever changed its gods, even though
2.36 have cheapened yourself by turning to the gods of other **nations.**
3.17 the Lord,' and all **nations** will gather there to worship me.
4. 2 Then all the **nations** will ask me to bless them, and they
4. 7 from its hiding place, a destroyer of **nations** has set out.
4.16 have come to warn the **nations** and to tell Jerusalem that
5. 9 for these things and take revenge on a **nation** such as this?
5.15 the Lord is bringing a **nation** from afar to attack you.
5.15 is a strong and ancient **nation,**
5.15 a **nation** whose language you do not know.
5.29 I will take revenge on this **nation.**
6.18 the Lord said, "Listen, you **nations,** and learn what is
6.22 a mighty **nation** far away is preparing for war.
7.28 will tell them that their **nation** does not obey me, the Lord
8. 3 the people of this evil **nation** who survive, who live in the
9. 9 Will I not take revenge on a **nation** like this?
9.16 I will scatter them among **nations** that neither they nor
10. 2 "Do not follow the ways of other **nations;**
10. 2 sights in the sky, even though other **nations** are terrified.
10. 7 Who would not honour you, the king of all **nations?**
10. 7 the wise men of the **nations** or among any of their kings.
10.10 the **nations** cannot endure your anger.
10.22 There is a great commotion in a **nation** to the north;
10.25 Turn your anger on the **nations** that do not worship you
12. 7 I have rejected my chosen **nation.**
12.15 I will bring each **nation** back to its own land and to
12.17 But if any **nation** will not obey, then I will completely
14.22 None of the idols of the **nations** can send rain;
16.19 **Nations** will come to you from the ends of the earth and
16.21 all I will make the **nations** know my power and my might;
18. 7 break down, or destroy any **nation** or kingdom,
18. 8 but then that **nation** turns from its evil, I will
18. 9 plant or build up any **nation** or kingdom,
18.10 but then that **nation** disobeys me and does evil,
18.13 "Ask every **nation** if such a thing has ever happened before.
24. 9 on them that all the **nations** of the world will be terrified.
25. 9 Judah and its inhabitants and against all the neighbouring **nations.**
25. 9 am going to destroy this **nation** and its neighbours and leave
25.11 shocking sight, and the neighbouring **nations** will serve the
25.13 threatened to bring on the **nations** when I spoke through
25.14 they have done, and many **nations** and great kings will make
25.15 Take it to all the **nations** to whom I send you, and
25.17 gave it to all the **nations** to whom the Lord had sent
25.19 Every **nation** on the face of the earth had to drink from
25.31 The Lord has a case against the **nations.**
25.32 disaster is coming on one **nation** after another, and a great
25.36 his anger has destroyed your **nation** and left your peaceful
26. 6 to Shiloh, and all the **nations** of the world will use the
26.20 the Lord against this city and **nation** just as Jeremiah did.
27. 6 has placed all these **nations** under the power of my servant,
27. 7 All **nations** will serve him, and they will serve his son
27. 7 grandson until the time comes for his own **nation** to fall.
27. 7 Then his **nation** will serve powerful nations and great kings.
27. 8 "But if any **nation** or kingdom will not submit to his rule,

Jer 27. 8 then I will punish that **nation** by war, starvation, and
27.11 But if any **nation** submits to the king of Babylonia and
27.13 said will happen to any **nation** that does not submit to the
28. 8 disease would come to many **nations** and powerful kingdoms.
28.11 King Nebuchadnezzar has put on the neck of all the **nations;**
28.14 iron yoke on all these **nations** and that they will serve King
29.18 and disease, and all the **nations** of the world will be
30.11 I will destroy all the **nations** where I have scattered you,
30.20 I will restore the **nation's** ancient power and establish it
30.21 from their own **nation,** their prince from their own people.
31. 7 "Sing with joy for Israel, the greatest of the **nations.**
31. 8 They will come back a great **nation.**
31.10 **"Nations,** listen to me, and proclaim my words on the far-off shores.
31.11 Israel's people free and have saved them from a mighty **nation.**
31.36 the natural order lasts, so long will Israel be a **nation.**
32.20 and among all the other **nations,** so that you are now known
33. 9 and every **nation** in the world will fear and tremble when
33.24 contempt on my people and no longer consider them a **nation.**
34. 1 by troops from all the **nations** and races that were subject
34.17 I will make every **nation** in the world horrified at what I
36. 2 I have told you about Israel and Judah and all the **nations.**
37. 3 to pray to the Lord our God on behalf of our **nation.**
43. 5 had returned from the **nations** where they had been scattered:
44. 8 destroy yourselves, so that every **nation** on earth will treat
46. 1 The Lord spoke to me about the **nations,** [2]beginning with Egypt.
46.12 **Nations** have heard of your shame;
46.28 I will destroy all the **nations** where I have scattered you,
48. 2 captured Heshbon and plot to destroy the **nation** of Moab.
48.17 "Mourn for that **nation,** you that live near by, all of
48.39 It is in ruins, and all the surrounding **nations** jeer at it.
48.40 Lord has promised that a **nation** will swoop down on Moab like
48.42 will no longer be a **nation,** because it rebelled against me.
49.14 a messenger to tell the **nations** to assemble their armies and
49.19 Then the leader I choose will rule the **nation.**
50. 2 "Tell the news to the **nations!**
50. 3 "A **nation** from the north has come to attack Babylonia and
50. 9 up a group of strong **nations** in the north and make them
50.11 The Lord says, "People of Babylonia, you plundered my **nation.**
50.12 Babylonia will be the least important **nation** of all;
50.23 All the **nations** are shocked at what has happened to that country.
50.32 Your proud **nation** will stumble and fall, and no one will
50.41 from a country in the north, a mighty **nation** far away;
50.44 Then the leader I choose will rule the **nation.**
50.46 the cries of alarm will be heard by the other **nations."**
51. 7 The **nations** drank its wine and went out of their minds.
51.20 I used you to crush **nations** and kingdoms, [21]to shatter
51.27 Blow the trumpet so that the **nations** can hear!
51.27 Prepare the **nations** for war against Babylonia!
51.28 Prepare the **nations** for war against Babylonia.
51.41 What a horrifying sight Babylon has become to the **nations!**
51.44 the **nations** will not worship him any more.
51.58 The work of the **nations** is all for nothing;
Lam 4.12 not even rulers of foreign **nations,** believed that any
4.15 So they wandered from **nation** to nation, welcomed by no one.
4.17 kept waiting for help from a **nation** that had none to give.
Ezek 3. 5 you to a **nation** that speaks a difficult foreign language,
3. 6 I sent you to great **nations** that spoke difficult languages
3.17 said, "I am making you a watchman for the **nation** of Israel.
3.27 some will ignore you, for they are a **nation** of rebels."
4. 3 This will be a sign to the **nation** of Israel.
4. 4 I will place on you the guilt of the **nation** of Israel.
5. 4 From them fire will spread to the whole **nation** of Israel."
5. 6 more wicked than the other **nations,** more disobedient than
5. 7 you have caused more trouble than the **nations** around you.
5. 7 You have followed the customs of other **nations.**
5. 8 will pass judgement on you where all the **nations** can see it.
5.14 Everyone from the **nations** around you who passes by will
5.15 punish you, all the **nations** around you will be terrified.
6. 8 among the **nations,** [9]where they will live in exile.
7.24 will bring the most evil **nations** here and let them have your
7.24 when I let the **nations** profane the places where you worship.
11. 1 Azzur and Pelatiah son of Benaiah, two leaders of the **nation.**
11.12 the laws of the neighbouring **nations,** you were breaking my
11.16 in far-off **nations** and scattered them in other countries.
12.15 them among the other **nations** and in foreign countries,
12.16 so that there among the **nations** they will realize how
12.19 Tell the whole **nation** that this is the message of the
16.14 You became famous in every **nation** for your perfect beauty,
16.29 prostitute for the Babylonians, that **nation** of businessmen,
17. 9 not take much strength or a mighty **nation** to pull it up.
17.14 as hostages [14]to keep the **nation** from rising again and to
19. 4 The **nations** heard about him and trapped him in a pit.
19. 8 The **nations** gathered to fight him;
20.14 to my name among the **nations** which had seen me lead Israel
20.22 to my name among the **nations** which had seen me bring Israel
20.32 to be like the other **nations,** like the people who live in
20.35 into the 'Desert of the **Nations,'** and there I will condemn
20.41 that you burn, and the **nations** will see that I am holy.
22. 4 why I have let the **nations** mock you and all the countries
22.15 people to every country and **nation** and will put an end to
22.16 And so the other **nations** will dishonour you, but you
23.30 for the **nations** and defiled yourself with their idols.
25. 7 hand you over to other **nations** who will rob you and plunder
25. 7 you will not be a **nation** any more or have a country
25. 8 is like all the other **nations,** [9]I will let the cities that
25.10 with Ammon, so that Moab will no longer be a **nation.**
26. 3 I will bring many **nations** to attack you, and they will come
26. 5 The **nations** will plunder Tyre, [6]and with their swords they
26.16 of the seafaring **nations** will come down from their thrones.
27.33 merchandise went overseas, You filled the needs of every **nation.**
Ezek 28.19 for ever, and all the **nations** that had come to know you
28.24 said, "None of the surrounding **nations** that treated Israel
28.25 people of Israel from the **nations** where I scattered them,
28.25 and all the **nations** will know that I am holy.
29.13 Egyptians back from the **nations** where I have scattered them,
29.15 of all, and they will never again rule over other **nations.**
29.15 will not be able to bend any other **nation** to their will.
30. 3 Lord will act, A day of clouds and trouble for the **nations.**
31. 6 The **nations** of the world rested in its shade.
31.12 All the **nations** that have been living in its shade will go
31.16 the dead, the noise of its downfall will shake the **nations.**
31.17 live under its shadow will be scattered among the **nations.**
32. 2 like a lion among the **nations,** but you are more like a
32. 3 When many **nations** gather, I will catch you in my net and
32. 9 "Many **nations** will be troubled when I spread the news of
32.10 What I do to you will shock many **nations.**
32.12 will let soldiers from cruel **nations** draw their swords and
32.16 The women of the **nations** will sing it to mourn for Egypt
32.18 with the other powerful **nations** to the world of the dead.
33. 7 man, I am making you a watchman for the **nation** of Israel.
34.28 The heathen **nations** will not plunder them any more, and
34.29 The other **nations** will not sneer at them any more.
35.10 "You said that the two **nations,** Judah and Israel,
36. 3 When the neighbouring **nations** captured and plundered
36. 4 were plundered and mocked by all the surrounding **nations.**
36. 5 the surrounding **nations,** and especially against Edom.
36. 6 of the way the **nations** have insulted and humiliated them.
36. 7 promise that the surrounding **nations** will be humiliated.
36.13 and they say that it robs the **nation** of its children.
36.15 have to listen to the **nations** mocking it or see the peoples
36.15 The land will no longer rob the **nation** of its children.
36.23 When I demonstrate to the **nations** the holiness of my
36.23 I will use you to show the **nations** that I am holy.
36.24 will take you from every **nation** and country and bring you
36.30 will be no more famines to disgrace you among the **nations.**
36.36 Then the neighbouring **nations** that have survived will know
37.21 my people out of the **nations** where they have gone, gather
37.22 will unite them into one **nation** in the land, on the
37.22 be divided into two **nations** or split into two kingdoms.
37.28 them for ever, then the **nations** will know that I, the Lord,
38. 2 Gog, chief ruler of the **nations** of Meshech and Tubal in the
38. 6 north are with him, and so are men from many other **nations.**
38. 8 brought back together from many **nations** and have lived
38. 9 his army and the many **nations** with him will attack like a
38.12 have been gathered from the **nations,** and now they have
38.15 of soldiers from many **nations,** all of them on horseback.
38.16 in order to show the **nations** who I am, to show my
38.22 his army and on the many **nations** that are on his side.
38.23 I will show all the **nations** that I am great and that
39. 1 the chief ruler of the **nations** of Meshech and Tubal, and
39. 7 Then the **nations** will know that I, the Lord, am the Holy
39.21 said, "I will let the **nations** see my glory and show them
39.23 And the **nations** will know that the Israelites went into
39.27 order to show the many **nations** that I am holy, I will
45.17 the wine-offerings for the whole **nation** of Israel at the New
Dan 3. 4 announced in a loud voice, "People of all **nations,** races,
3. 7 the people of all the **nations,** races, and languages bowed
3.29 that if anyone of any **nation,** race, or language speaks
4. 1 people of all **nations,** races, and languages in the world:
5.19 great that people of all **nations,** races, and languages were
6.25 the people of all **nations,** races, and languages on earth:
7.14 people of all **nations,** races, and languages would serve him.
8.22 four kingdoms into which that **nation** will be divided and
9. 6 our kings, our rulers, our ancestors, and our whole **nation.**
11.14 some violent men from your **nation,** Daniel, will rebel
11.18 that he will attack the **nations** by the sea and conquer many
11.23 treaties, he will deceive other **nations,** and he will grow
11.23 and stronger, even though he rules only a small **nation.**
12. 1 troubles, the worst since **nations** first came into existence.
12. 1 all the people of your **nation** whose names are written in
Hos 7. 8 They rely on the **nations** around them [9]and do not realize
8. 8 has become like any other **nation** and is as useless as a
8. 9 from Assyria, and have paid other **nations** to protect them.
9.17 They will become wanderers among the **nations.**
10.10 **Nations** will join together against them, and they will be
13.10 a king and for leaders, but how can they save the **nation?**
Joel 2.17 Do not let other **nations** despise us and mock us by saying,
2.19 Other **nations** will no longer despise you.
3. 2 I will gather all the **nations** and bring them to the Valley
3. 9 "Make this announcement among the **nations:**
3.11 Hurry and come, all you surrounding **nations,** and gather
3.12 "The **nations** must get ready and come to the Valley of Judgement.
3.12 There I, the Lord, will sit to judge all the surrounding **nations.**
Amos 1. 6 They carried off a whole **nation** and sold them as slaves to
1. 9 They carried off a whole **nation** into exile in the land of
3. 1 about you, the entire **nation** that he brought out of Egypt;
3. 2 "Of all the **nations** on earth, you are the only one I
5.15 to the people of this **nation** who are still left alive.
6. 1 great men of this great **nation** Israel, you to whom the
7.13 This is the king's place of worship, the **national** temple."
9. 9 them among the **nations** to remove all who are worthless.
9.12 of Edom and all the **nations** that were once mine," says the
Obad 1 Obadiah—what the Sovereign Lord said about the **nation** of Edom.
1 messenger to the **nations,** and we have heard his message:
15 "The day is near when I, the Lord, will judge all **nations.**
16 But all the surrounding **nations** will drink a still more
Jon 1. 8 What is your **nationality?"**
Mic 1. 2 Hear this, all you **nations;**
4. 1 Many **nations** will come streaming to it, [2]and their people
4. 3 will settle disputes among the **nations,** among the great

Mic 4. 3 **Nations** will never again go to war, never prepare for battle again.
4. 5 Each **nation** worships and obeys its own god, but we will
4. 7 those who are left, and they will become a great **nation.**
4.11 Many **nations** have gathered to attack you.
4.12 But these **nations** do not know what is in the Lord's mind.
4.13 You will crush many **nations,** and the wealth they got by
5. 7 the Lord for many **nations,** like showers on growing plants.
5. 8 who are left among the **nations** will be like a lion hunting
5.15 I will take revenge on all **nations** that have not obeyed me."
7.16 The **nations** will see this and be frustrated in spite of
Nah 3. 4 full of deadly charms, she enchanted **nations** and enslaved them.
3. 5 you naked and let the **nations** see you, see you in all
Hab 1. 5 his people, "Keep watching the **nations** round you, and you
1.17 for ever and keep on destroying **nations** without mercy?
2. 5 That is why they conquer **nation** after nation for themselves.
2. 8 plundered the people of many **nations,** but now those who have
2.10 many **nations** you have only brought ruin on yourself.
2.13 **nations** you conquered wore themselves out in useless labour,
3. 6 at his glance the **nations** tremble.
3.12 in fury you trampled the **nations.**
Zeph 2. 1 Shameless **nation,** come to your senses [2]before you are
2.11 to nothing, and then every **nation** will worship him, each in
3. 6 The Lord says, "I have wiped out whole **nations;**
3. 8 "Wait for the day when I rise to accuse the **nations.**
3. 8 up my mind to gather **nations** and kingdoms, in order to let
3. 9 change the people of the **nations,** and they will pray to me
Hag 2. 7 I will overthrow all the **nations,** and their treasures will
2.14 to the people of this **nation** and to everything they produce;
Zech 1.15 I am very angry with the **nations** that enjoy quiet and peace.
1.15 anger against my people, those **nations** made the sufferings
1.21 to terrify and overthrow the **nations** that completely crushed
2. 8 this message for the **nations** that had plundered his people:
2.11 At that time many **nations** will come to the Lord and
8. 6 impossible to those of the **nation** who are now left, but it's
8.11 But now I am treating the survivors of this **nation** differently.
8.12 all these blessings to the people of my **nation** who survive.
8.22 Many peoples and powerful **nations** will come to Jerusalem
9.10 Your king will make peace among the **nations;**
10. 9 have scattered them among the **nations,** yet in far-off places
11.10 the covenant which the Lord had made with all the **nations.**
12. 2 **nations** round her will drink and stagger like drunken men.
12. 3 like a heavy stone—any **nation** that tries to lift it will
12. 3 All the **nations** of the world will join forces to attack her.
12. 6 of ripe corn—they will destroy all the surrounding **nations.**
12. 9 I will destroy every **nation** that tries to attack Jerusalem.
14. 2 Lord will bring all the **nations** together to make war
14. 3 out and fight against those **nations,** as he has fought in
14.12 disease on all the **nations** that make war on Jerusalem.
14.14 the wealth of all the **nations**—gold, silver, and clothing in
14.16 all the survivors from the **nations** that have attacked
14.17 If any **nation** refuses to go and worship the Lord
14.18 that the Lord will send on every **nation** that refuses to go.
14.19 and on all the other **nations** if they do not celebrate the
Mal 1. 4 'The evil country' and 'The **nation** with whom the Lord is
1.14 I am a great king, and people of all **nations** fear me."
2.12 in the offerings our **nation** brings to the Lord Almighty.
3. 9 is on all of you because the whole **nation** is cheating me.
3.12 Then the people of all **nations** will call you happy,
Mt 12.18 Spirit upon him, and he will announce my judgement to the **nations.**
25.32 and the people of all the **nations** will be gathered before him.
Mk 11.17 be called a house of prayer for the people of all **nations.'**
Lk 24.47 forgiveness of sins must be preached to all **nations,** beginning
Jn 11.48 authorities will take action and destroy our Temple and our **nation!"**
11.50 for the people, instead of having the whole **nation** destroyed?"
Acts 7.45 over the land from the **nations** that God drove out as they
13.17 made the people a great **nation** during the time they lived
13.19 He destroyed seven **nations** in the land of Canaan and
24.10 been a judge over this **nation** for many years, and so I
Rom 1. 5 in order to lead people of all **nations** to believe and obey.
4.17 the scripture says, "I have made you father of many **nations.**"
4.18 for hoping, and so became "the father of many **nations.**"
9.25 The **nation** that I did not love I will call 'My Beloved.'
10.19 "I will use a so-called **nation** to make my people jealous;
10.19 and by means of a **nation** of fools I will make my
16.26 is made known to all **nations,** so that all may believe
1 Tim 3.16 He was preached among the **nations,** was believed in throughout
1 Pet 2. 9 the holy **nation,** God's own people, chosen to proclaim
Rev 2.26 give them authority over the **nations,** to rule them with an
5. 9 for God people from every tribe, language, **nation,** and race.
7. 9 from every race, tribe, **nation,** and language, and they stood in
10.11 must proclaim God's message about many **nations,** races, languages,
11. 9 People from all **nations,** tribes, languages, and races will look
12. 5 a son, who will rule over all **nations** with an iron rod.
13. 7 was given authority over every tribe, **nation,** language, and race.
14. 6 peoples of the earth, to every race, tribe, language, and **nation.**
15. 3 King of the **nations,** how right and true are your ways!
15. 4 All the **nations** will come and worship you, because your just
17.15 on which the prostitute is sitting, are **nations,** peoples, races,
18. 3 For all the **nations** have drunk her wine—the strong wine of
19.15 came a sharp sword, with which he will defeat the **nations.**
20. 3 could not deceive the **nations** any more until the thousand years
20. 8 go out to deceive the **nations** scattered over the whole world,
21.26 and the wealth of the **nations** will be brought into the city.
22. 2 and its leaves are for the healing of the **nations.**

NATIVE

Gen 11.28 and Haran died in his **native** city, Ur in Babylonia,
Ex 12.19 your houses, for if anyone, **native-born** or foreign, eats
12.48 to be treated like a **native-born** Israelite and may join in
12.49 The same regulations apply to **native-born** Israelites and
Num 9.14 The same law applies to everyone, whether **native** or foreigner."
10.30 Hobab answered, "No, I am going back to my **native** land."
15.13 Every **native** Israelite is to do this when he presents
15.29 whether he is a **native** Israelite or a resident foreigner.
15.30 deliberately, whether he is a **native** or a foreigner, is
2 Sam 6.10 the house of Obed Edom, a **native** of the city of Gath.
1 Chr 7.21 the livestock belonging to the **native** inhabitants of Gath.
13.13 a man named Obed Edom, a **native** of the city of Gath.
2 Chr 2.14 the tribe of Dan and his father was a **native** of Tyre.
Acts 2. 8 all of us hear them speaking in our own **native** languages?
6. 1 a quarrel between the Greek-speaking Jews and the **native** Jews.
28. 2 The **natives** there were very friendly to us.
28. 4 The **natives** saw the snake hanging on Paul's hand and said

NATURAL

Lev 7.24 animal that has died a **natural** death or has been killed by
17.15 animal that has died a **natural** death or has been killed by
22. 8 animal that has died a **natural** death or has been killed by
Num 16.29 If these men die a **natural** death without some punishment
19.16 killed or has died a **natural** death out of doors or if
Deut 14.21 "Do not eat any animal that dies a **natural** death.
1 Sam 26.10 time comes to die a **natural** death or when he dies in
1 Kgs 2. 6 you must not let him die a **natural** death.
Ps 109.18 He cursed as **naturally** as he dressed himself;
Prov 22.15 Children just **naturally** do silly, careless things, but a
Ecc 10. 2 It is **natural** for a wise man to do the right thing
Jer 31.36 that as long as the **natural** order lasts, so long will Israel
Ezek 4.14 any animal that died a **natural** death or was killed by wild
44.31 or animal that dies a **natural** death or is killed by another
Jn 1.13 not become God's children by **natural** means, that is, by being
8.44 is only doing what is **natural** to him, because he is a
11.13 that Lazarus had died, but they thought he meant **natural** sleep.
Rom 1.26 Even the women pervert the **natural** use of their sex by
1.27 way the men give up **natural** sexual relations with women and
3. 5 (This would be the **natural** question to ask.)
6.12 bodies, so that you obey the desires of your **natural** self.
6.19 everyday language because of the weakness of your **natural** selves.)
11.21 God did not spare the Jews, who are like **natural** branches;
Gal 6. 8 in the field of his **natural** desires, from it he will gather
Eph 2. 3 lived according to our **natural** desires, doing whatever suited
2. 3 In our **natural** condition we, like everyone else, were destined
Jude 19 who are controlled by their **natural** desires, who do not have

NATURE

1 Sam 10. 9 When Saul turned to leave Samuel, God gave Saul a new **nature.**
Prov 10. 6 A wicked man's words hide a violent **nature.**
10.11 of life, but a wicked man's words hide a violent **nature.**
Acts 17.29 should not suppose that his **nature** is anything like an image
Rom 1.20 his eternal power and his divine **nature,** have been clearly seen;
7. 5 lived according to our human **nature,** the sinful desires stirred
7.13 in order that its true **nature** as sin might be revealed.
7.18 good does not live in me—that is, in my human **nature.**
7.25 with my mind, while my human **nature** serves the law of sin.
8. 3 the Law could not do, because human **nature** was weak, God
8. 3 He condemned sin in human **nature** by sending his own Son,
8. 3 with a nature like man's sinful **nature,** to do away with sin.
8. 4 live according to the Spirit, and not according to human **nature.**
8. 5 who live as their human **nature** tells them to,
8. 5 have their minds controlled by what human **nature** wants.
8. 6 To be controlled by human **nature** results in death;
8. 7 an enemy of God when he is controlled by his human **nature;**
8. 8 Those who obey their human **nature** cannot please God.
8. 9 But you do not live as your human **nature** tells you to;
8.12 it is not to live as our human **nature** wants us to.
8.13 live according to your human **nature,** you are going to die;
11.24 then, contrary to **nature,** is joined to a cultivated olive-tree.
13.14 stop paying attention to your sinful **nature** and satisfying its
1 Cor 11.14 Why, **nature** itself teaches you that long hair on a man
Gal 4.19 kind of pain for you until Christ's **nature** is formed in you.
5.16 and you will not satisfy the desires of the human **nature.**
5.17 For what our human **nature** wants is opposed to what the
5.17 the Spirit wants is opposed to what our human **nature** wants.
5.19 What human **nature** does is quite plain.
5.24 death their human **nature** with all its passions and desires.
Eph 3.19 and so be completely filled with the very **nature** of God.
5.13 out to the light, then their true **nature** is clearly revealed;
Phil 2. 6 He always had the **nature** of God, but he did not think
2. 7 gave up all he had, and took the **nature** of a servant.
Col 1.19 decision that the Son has in himself the full **nature** of God.
2. 9 full content of divine **nature** lives in Christ, in his humanity,
Heb 2.14 Jesus himself became like them and shared their human **nature.**
2 Pet 1. 4 is in the world, and may come to share the divine **nature.**
1 Jn 3. 9 does not continue to sin, for God's very **nature** is in him;

NAZARENE

Someone from the town of Nazareth. The name was used as a title for Jesus and also as a name for the early Christians.

Mt 2.23 "He will be called a **Nazarene.**"
Acts 24. 5 the world and is a leader of the party of the **Nazarenes.**

NAZARETH

Place in n. Palestine where Jesus was brought up.

Mt 2.23 of Galilee [23]and made his home in a town named **Nazareth.**
4.13 He did not stay in **Nazareth,** but went to live in Capernaum,
21.11 "This is the prophet Jesus, from **Nazareth** in Galilee,"
26.71 said to the men there, "He was with Jesus of **Nazareth."**
Mk 1. 9 afterwards Jesus came from **Nazareth** in the province of Galilee,
1.24 and screamed, [24]"What do you want with us, Jesus of **Nazareth?**
10.47 heard that it was Jesus of **Nazareth,** he began to shout,
14.67 at him and said, "You, too, were with Jesus of **Nazareth."**
16. 6 "I know you are looking for Jesus of **Nazareth,** who was crucified.
Lk 1.26 God sent the angel Gabriel to a town in Galilee named **Nazareth.**
2. 4 went from the town of **Nazareth** in Galilee to the town of
2.39 they returned to their home town of **Nazareth** in Galilee.
2.51 back with them to **Nazareth,** where he was obedient to them.
4.16 Then Jesus went to **Nazareth,** where he had been brought up,
4.34 What do you want with us, Jesus of **Nazareth?**
18.37 "Jesus of **Nazareth** is passing by," they told him.
24.19 "The things that happened to Jesus of **Nazareth,"** they
Jn 1.45 He is Jesus son of Joseph, from **Nazareth."**
1.46 "Can anything good come from **Nazareth?"**
18. 5 "Jesus of **Nazareth,"** they answered.
18. 7 "Jesus of **Nazareth,"** they said.
19.19 "Jesus of **Nazareth,** the King of the Jews," is what he wrote.
Acts 2.22 Jesus of **Nazareth** was a man whose divine authority was clearly
3. 6 name of Jesus Christ of **Nazareth** I order you to get up
4.10 name of Jesus Christ of **Nazareth**—whom you crucified and whom
6.14 say that this Jesus of **Nazareth** will tear down the Temple
10.38 You know about Jesus of **Nazareth** and how God poured out
22. 8 'I am Jesus of **Nazareth,** whom you persecute,' he said to me.
26. 9 do everything I could against the cause of Jesus of **Nazareth.**

NAZIRITE

Person under a vow of dedication to God.

Num 6. 2 special vow to become a **Nazirite** and dedicates himself
6. 4 long as he is a **Nazirite,** he shall not eat anything that
6. 5 as he is under the **Nazirite** vow, he must not cut his
6. 8 long as he is a **Nazirite,** he is consecrated to the Lord.
6. 9 the consecrated hair of a **Nazirite** is defiled because he is
6.12 hair [12]and rededicate to the Lord his time as a **Nazirite.**
6.13 When a **Nazirite** completes his vow, he shall perform the ritual.
6.18 entrance of the Tent the **Nazirite** shall shave off his hair
6.19 one biscuit from the basket, into the hands of the **Nazirite.**
6.20 After that, the **Nazirite** may drink wine.
6.21 These are the regulations for **Nazirites;**
6.21 but if a **Nazirite** promises an offering beyond what his vow
Judg 13. 5 of his birth he will be dedicated to God as a **Nazirite.**
13. 7 be dedicated to God as a **Nazirite** as long as he lives."
16.17 dedicated to God as a **Nazirite** from the time I was born.
Amos 2.11 to be prophets, and some of your young men to be **Nazirites.**
2.12 But you made the **Nazirites** drink wine,

NEAR

Gen 3.24 to keep anyone from coming **near** the tree that gives life.
10.19 Sidon southwards to Gerar **near** Gaza,
10.19 eastwards to Sodom, Gomorrah, Admah, and Zeboiim **near** Lasha.
13.12 in the valley and camped **near** Sodom, [13]whose people were
13.18 moved his camp and settled **near** the sacred trees of Mamre at
14.13 the Hebrew, who was living **near** the sacred trees belonging
19.20 It is **near** enough.
20. 4 But Abimelech had not come **near** her, and he said, "Lord,
23. 9 sell me Machpelah Cave, which is **near** the edge of his field.
25.11 his son Isaac, who lived **near** "The Well of the Living One
27.41 He thought, "The time to mourn my father's death is **near;**
33.18 Canaan and set up his camp in a field **near** the city.
35. 4 He buried them beneath the oak-tree **near** Shechem.
35. 5 on the people of the **nearby** towns, and they did not pursue
35.27 his father Isaac at Mamre, **near** Hebron, where Abraham and
41.32 God and that he will make it happen in the **near** future.
45.10 you can be **near** me—you, your children, your grandchildren,
47.11 the best of the land **near** the city of Rameses, as the
47.29 When the time drew **near** for him to die, he called for
Ex 14. 2 Pi Hahiroth, between Migdol and the Red Sea, **near** Baal Zephon.
14. 9 camped by the Red Sea **near** Pi Hahiroth and Baal Zephon.
14.20 and so the armies could not come **near** each other all night.
19.12 them not to go up the mountain or even get **near** it.
19.22 Even the priests who come **near** me must purify themselves,
20.21 off, and only Moses went **near** the dark cloud where God was.
24. 2 You alone, and none of the others, are to come **near** me.
25.27 poles for carrying the table are to be placed **near** the rim.
28.27 two shoulder-straps of the ephod **near** the seam and above the
34.30 his face was shining, and they were afraid to go **near** him.
37.14 the poles for carrying the table were placed **near** the rim.
39.20 shoulder straps of the ephod, **near** the seam and above the
Lev 3. 9 entire fat tail cut off **near** the backbone, all the fat
21.23 defect, he shall not come **near** the sacred curtain or
22. 3 he is ritually unclean, comes **near** the sacred offerings
25.35 If a fellow-Israelite living **near** you becomes poor
25.35 a hired man, so that he can continue to live **near** you.
25.36 but obey God and let your fellow-Israelite live **near** you.
25.39 If a fellow-Israelite living **near** you becomes so poor
26.36 battle, and you will fall when there is no enemy **near** you.
Num 1.51 Anyone else who comes **near** the Tent shall be put to death.
1.53 that no one may come **near** and cause my anger to strike
4.19 Kohath [19]be killed by coming **near** these most sacred objects.
6. 6 not defile himself by going **near** a corpse, not even that of
8.19 would strike them if they came too **near** the Holy Place."
13.21 south all the way to Rehob, **near** Hamath Pass in the north.
Num 17.13 If anyone who even comes **near** the Tent must die, then we
18. 7 Any unqualified person who comes **near** the sacred objects
21.30 Heshbon to Dibon, From Nashim to Nophah, **near** Medeba."
22. 5 Beor, who was at Pethor **near** the River Euphrates in the land
33. 7 to Pi Hahiroth, east of Baal Zephon, and camped **near** Migdol.
33.10 They left Elim and camped **near** the Gulf of Suez.
33.41 Almon Diblathaim, the Abarim Mountains **near** Mount Nebo, and
Deut 1. 1 were in the Jordan Valley **near** Suph, between the town of
2.19 You will then be **near** the land of the Ammonites, the
2.32 his men to fight us **near** the town of Jahaz, [33]but the
2.37 But we did not go **near** the territory of the Ammonites or
3. 1 with all his men to fight us **near** the town of Edrei.
3.12 of the town of Aroer **near** the River Arnon and part of
4. 7 a god who is so **near** when they need him as the
11.30 far from the sacred trees of Moreh **near** the town of Gilgal.)
13. 7 of the people who live **near** you or the gods of those
15. 9 just because the year when debts are cancelled is **near.**
17.19 is to keep this book **near** him and read from it all
21. 2 place where the body was found to each of the **nearby** towns.
21. 3 the leaders of the town **nearest** to where the body was found
21. 4 it down to a spot **near** a stream that never runs dry
21. 6 the leaders from the town **nearest** the place where the
32.35 the day of their doom is **near.**
32.51 at the waters of Meribah, **near** the town of Kadesh in the
Josh 3. 4 But do not get **near** the Covenant Box;
3. 8 the river, they must wade in and stand **near** the bank."
3.16 off, and the people were able to cross over **near** Jericho.
4.13 men ready for war crossed over to the plain **near** Jericho.
5.10 at Gilgal on the plain **near** Jericho, they observed Passover
5.13 While Joshua was **near** Jericho, he suddenly saw a man
6.23 all, family and slaves, to safety **near** the Israelite camp.
7. 2 a city east of Bethel, **near** Bethaven, with orders to go and
9. 7 Maybe you live **nearby."**
9.16 Israelites learnt that these people did indeed live **nearby.**
10.37 everyone else in the city as well as in the **nearby** towns.
10.39 He captured it, with its king and all the **nearby** towns.
10.41 in the south to Gaza **near** the coast, including all the area
11. 2 Lake Galilee, in the foothills, and on the coast **near** Dor,
11.17 Mount Halak in the south **near** Edom, as far as Baalgad in
12. 7 the valley of Lebanon to Mount Halak in the south **near** Edom.
12. 9 Jericho, Ai **(near** Bethel), [10]Jerusalem, Hebron,
15. 9 Springs of Nephtoah and out to the cities **near** Mount Ephron.
15.21 to them, those that were **near** the border of Edom, were
15.46 all the cities and towns **near** Ashdod, from Ekron to the
16. 1 Joseph started from the Jordan **near** Jericho, at a point east
Judg 1.27 Beth Shan, Taanach, Dor, Ibleam, Megiddo, and the **nearby** towns;
3.19 back at the carved stones **near** Gilgal, went back to Eglon,
4.11 up his tent close to Kedesh **near** the oak-tree at Zanannim.
7.22 Beth Shittah, as far as the town of Abel Meholah **near** Tabbath.
19.10 the day when they came **near** Jebus (that is, Jerusalem), so
20.19 out the next morning and made camp **near** the city of Gibeah.
1 Sam 6.14 in Beth Shemesh, and it stopped there **near** a large rock.
9.18 over to Samuel, who was **near** the gate, and asked, "Tell me,
10. 2 you will meet two men **near** Rachel's tomb at Zelzah in the
17.26 asked the men who were **near** him, "What will the man get
22. 1 of Gath and went to a cave **near** the town of Adullam.
22.17 to the guards standing **near** him, "Kill the Lord's priests!
23.14 in hiding in the hill-country, in the wilderness **near** Ziph.
23.15 David was at Horesh, in the wilderness **near** Ziph.
24. 1 he was told that David was in the wilderness **near** Engedi.
25. 2 town of Maon, and who owned land **near** the town of Carmel.
26. 7 the camp with his spear stuck in the ground **near** his head.
28. 4 Philistine troops assembled and camped **near** the town of Shunem;
2 Sam 4.12 hands and feet, which they hung up **near** the pool in Hebron.
5.23 to attack them from the other side, **near** the balsam-trees.
11.20 you, 'Why did you go so **near** the city to fight them?
11.21 Why, then, did you go so **near** the wall?'
13.23 sheep sheared at Baal Hazor, **near** the town of Ephraim, and
17.18 He had a well **near** his house, and they got down into
18.25 The runner came **nearer and nearer.**
19. 8 the king got up, and went and sat **near** the city gate.
19.37 Then let me go back home and die **near** my parents' grave.
23.13 **Near** the beginning of harvest time three of "The Thirty"
23.24 Pirathon Hiddai from the valleys **near** Gaash Abialbon from
1 Kgs 1. 9 fattened calves at Snake Rock, **near** the spring of Enrogel.
4.12 the region near Beth Shan, **near** the town of Zarethan, south
9.26 ships at Eziongeber, which is **near** Elath, on the shore of
13.25 saw the body on the road, with the lion standing **near by.**
15.20 Abel Beth Maacah, the area **near** Lake Galilee, and the whole
17. 3 go east and hide yourself **near** the brook of Cherith, east of
17. 9 "Now go to the town of Zarephath, **near** Sidon, and stay there.
19. 6 a loaf of bread and a jar of water **near** his head.
19.15 said, "Return to the wilderness **near** Damascus, then enter
21. 1 **Near** King Ahab's palace in Jezreel there was a vineyard
22.36 **Near** sunset the order went out through the Israelite ranks:
2 Kgs 6. 9 warning him not to go **near** that place, because the Syrians
9.27 chariot on the road up to Gur, **near** the town of Ibleam.
10.14 seized them, and he put them to death **near** a pit there.
11. 8 Anyone who comes **near** you is to be killed."
17. 6 the city of Halah, some **near** the River Habor in the district
18.11 the city of Halah, some **near** the River Habor in the district
19. 8 Lachish and was fighting against the **nearby** city of Libnah;
19.32 soldiers with shields will come **near** the city, and no
23. 4 objects outside the city **near** the valley of the Kidron,
23. 5 of Judah and in places **near** Jerusalem—all the priests who
23. 8 dedicated to the goat-demons **near** the gate built by Joshua,
23.11 kept in the temple courtyard, **near** the gate and not far from
25. 5 captured him in the plains **near** Jericho, and all his
1 Chr 2.23 the villages of Jair and Kenath, and the towns **near by.**
8.32 lived in Jerusalem **near** other families of their clan.
9.27 They lived **near** the Temple, because it was their duty to

1 Chr 9.38 lived in Jerusalem **near** other families of their clan.
11.15 rock where David was staying **near** the cave of Adullam, while
11.26 Pirathon Hurai from the valleys **near** Gaash Abiel from Arbah
14.14 to attack them from the other side, **near** the balsam-trees.
18. 3 the Syrian state of Zobah, **near** the territory of Hamath,
19. 7 the army of the king of Maacah came and camped **near** Medeba.
26.18 **Near** the western pavilion there were four guards by the
2 Chr 4.10 The tank was placed **near** the south-east corner of the Temple.
5.11 The Levites stood **near** the east side of the altar with
13.19 and Ephron, and the villages **near** each of these cities.
14.10 up their positions in the Valley of Zephathah **near** Mareshah.
20.16 of the valley that leads to the wild country **near** Jeruel.
20.20 morning the people went out to the wild country **near** Tekoa.
21.16 Some Philistines and Arabs lived **near** where some
26. 6 Ashdod, and built fortified cities **near** Ashdod and in the
32. 3 Assyrians from having any water when they got **near** Jerusalem.
33.14 a point in the valley **near** the spring of Gihon north to
34. 4 Baal was worshipped and tore down the incense-altars **near** them.
Ezra 2.70 and some of the people settled in or **near** Jerusalem;
2.70 guards, and the temple workmen settled in **nearby** towns;
Neh 1. 3 that the foreigners who lived **near by** looked down on them.
3.10 Harumaph built the next section, which was **near** his own house.
3.25 the tower of the upper palace **near** the court of the guard;
3.25 a point on the east **near** the Water Gate and the tower
3.25 (This was **near** that part of the city called Ophel, where the
3.27 tower guarding the Temple as far as the wall **near** Ophel.
3.31 was by the Miphkad Gate, **near** the room on top of the
11.25 Many of the people lived in towns **near** their farms.
11.25 Dibon, and Jekabzeel, and in the villages **near** these cities.
11.30 in Zanoah, in Adullam, and in the villages **near** these towns.
11.30 Lachish and on the farms **near by,** and in Azekah and its
11.31 Michmash, Ai, Bethel and the **nearby** villages, [32] Anathoth,
12.39 We ended our march **near** the gate to the Temple.
12.44 for collecting from the farms **near** the various cities the
Esth 9.20 all the Jews, **near** and far, throughout the Persian Empire,
Job 1.14 oxen," he said, "and the donkeys were in a **nearby** pasture.
17. 1 The end of my life is **near.**
17.12 they say that light is **near,** but I know I remain in
19.17 smell of my breath, and my own brothers won't come **near** me.
37.23 God's power is so great that we cannot come **near** him;
39.25 a battle before they get **near,** and they hear the officers
39.29 From there it watches **near** and far for something to kill
Ps 16. 8 he is **near,** and nothing can shake me.
22.11 Trouble is **near,** and there is no one to help.
34.18 The Lord is **near** to those who are discouraged;
38. 7 I am burning with fever and I am **near** to death.
38.11 and neighbours will not come **near** me, because of my sores;
39. 1 I will not say anything while evil men are **near."**
73.28 me, how wonderful to be **near** God, to find protection with
76.11 bring gifts to him, all you **nearby** nations.
84. 3 they keep their young **near** your altars, Lord Almighty, my
88.15 Ever since I was young, I have suffered and been **near** death;
91.10 will strike you, no violence will come **near** your home.
104.12 In the trees **near by,** the birds make their nests and sing.
119.151 But you are **near** to me, Lord, and all your commands
137. 2 On the willows **near by** we hung up our harps.
145.18 He is **near** to those who call to him, who call to
Prov 5. 8 Don't even go **near** her door!
7. 8 was walking along the street **near** the corner where a certain
7. 8 He was passing **near** her house [9] in the evening after it was
8. 2 On the hilltops **near** the road and at the cross-roads she stands.
27.10 a neighbour **near by** can help you more than a brother who
Song 1. 8 find pasture for your goats **near** the tents of the shepherds.
5. 4 hand to the door, and I was thrilled that he was **near.**
7. 4 in the city of Heshbon, **near** the gate of that great city.
7.13 mandrakes, and all the pleasant fruits are **near** our door.
Is 11. 8 baby will not be harmed if it plays **near** a poisonous snake.
13. 6 day of the Lord is **near,** the day when the Almighty brings
16. 8 The farms **near** Heshbon and the vineyards of Sibmah are
33.13 Let everyone **near** and far hear what I have done and
37. 8 Lachish and was fighting against the **nearby** city of Libnah;
37.33 soldiers with shields will come **near** the city, and no
46.13 bringing the day of victory **near**— it is not far away
50. 8 for God is **near,** and he will prove me innocent.
51. 5 the time of my victory is **near.**
55. 6 to the Lord and pray to him, now that he is **near.**
57. 5 as sacrifices in the rocky caves **near** the bed of a stream.
57.19 I offer peace to all, both **near** and far!
59.14 Justice is driven away, and right cannot come **near.**
66.17 Lord says, "The end is **near** for those who purify themselves
Jer 13. 5 So I went and hid them **near** the Euphrates.
17. 8 is like a tree growing **near** a stream and sending out roots
19.15 this city and on every **nearby** town all the punishment that I
20. 2 beaten and placed in chains **near** the upper Benjamin Gate in
25.19 the kings of the north, far and **near,** one after another.
34. 1 to him, were attacking Jerusalem and its **nearby** towns.
35. 4 in the Temple, and **near** the rooms of the other officials.
36.10 was in the upper court **near** the entrance of the New Gate
39. 5 pursued them and captured Zedekiah in the plains **near** Jericho.
41.12 their men and overtook him **near** the large pool at Gibeon.
41.17 On the way, they stopped at Chimham, **near** Bethlehem.
46. 2 of Babylonia defeated at Carchemish **near** the River Euphrates
48.17 that nation, you that live **near by,** all of you that know
48.24 Judgement has come on all the cities of Moab, far and **near.**
49.13 All the **near-by** villages will be in ruins for ever.
49.18 and Gomorrah, when they and the **near-by** towns were destroyed.
50.40 and Gomorrah, when I destroyed them and the **near-by** towns.
52. 8 captured him in the plains **near** Jericho, and all his
Lam 3.54 Water began to close over me, and I thought death was **near.**
Ezek 6.12 those **near by** will be killed in war;
7. 7 The time is **near** when there will be no more celebrations at
Ezek 7.12 The day is **near** when buying and selling will have no more
8. 5 I looked, and there **near** the altar by the entrance of the
8.16 There **near** the entrance of the sanctuary, between the altar
11. 1 There **near** the gate I saw twenty-five men, including
19.10 Your mother was like a grapevine planted **near** a stream.
22. 5 Countries **near by** and countries far away sneer at you
30. 3 The day is **near,** the day when the Lord will act, A
39.16 (There will be a town **near by** named after the army.)
40. 8 of the gateway which was **nearest** the Temple, and at its far
44.13 as priests or to go **near** anything that is holy to me
46.19 of the rooms facing north **near** the gate on the south side
Dan 8.23 end of those kingdoms is **near** and they have become so wicked
9. 7 whom you scattered in countries **near** and far because they
Joel 1.15 The day of the Lord is **near;**
Amos 4. 3 will be dragged to the **nearest** break in the wall and thrown
9.10 those who say, 'God will not let any harm come **near** us.'
Obad 15 "The day is **near** when I, the Lord, will judge all nations.
Mic 4. 3 among the nations, among the great powers **near** and far.
Zeph 1. 7 The day is **near** when the Lord will sit in judgement;
1.14 great day of the Lord is near—very **near** and coming fast!
Zech 14. 1 The day when the Lord will sit in judgement is **near.**
Mt 3. 2 sins," he said, "because the Kingdom of heaven is **near!"**
4.17 "Turn away from your sins, because the Kingdom of heaven is **near!"**
10. 7 Go and preach, 'The Kingdom of heaven is **near!'**
24.32 it starts putting out leaves, you know that summer is **near.**
24.33 you will know that the time is **near,** ready to begin.
28.18 Jesus drew **near** and said to them, "I have been given
Mk 1.15 time has come," he said, "and the Kingdom of God is **near!**
5.11 was a large herd of pigs **near** by, feeding on a hillside.
6.36 let them go to the **nearby** farms and villages in order to
13.28 it starts putting out leaves, you know that summer is **near.**
13.29 you will know that the time is **near,** ready to begin.
Lk 8.32 was a large herd of pigs **near** by, feeding on a hillside.
9.51 As the time drew **near** when Jesus would be taken up to
10. 9 to the people there, 'The Kingdom of God has come **near** you.'
10.11 But remember that the Kingdom of God has come **near** you!'
18.40 When he came **near,** Jesus asked him, [41] "What do you want
19.29 As he came **near** Bethphage and Bethany at the Mount of Olives,
19.37 When he came **near** Jerusalem, at the place where the road
21. 9 happen first, but they do not mean that the end is **near."**
21.28 stand up and raise your heads, because your salvation is **near."**
21.30 leaves beginning to appear, you know that summer is **near.**
22. 1 The time was **near** for the Festival of Unleavened Bread,
24.15 and discussed, Jesus himself drew **near** and walked along with them;
24.28 As they came **near** the village to which they were going,
Jn 5. 2 **Near** the Sheep Gate in Jerusalem there is a pool with five
6. 4 The time for the Passover Festival was **near.**
7. 2 Festival of Shelters was **near,** [3] so Jesus' brothers said to him,
11.55 for the Passover Festival was **near,** and many people went up
Acts 2.25 he is **near** me, and I will not be troubled.
7.17 "When the time drew **near** for God to keep the promise he
Rom 10. 8 "God's message is **near** you, on your lips and in your heart"
Eph 2.13 far away have been brought **near** by the sacrificial death of Christ.
2.17 away from God, and to the Jews, who were **near** to him.
Heb 7.19 hope has been provided through which we come **near** to God.
9.26 all ages of time are **nearing** the end, he has appeared once
10.22 So let us come **near** to God with a sincere heart
10.25 since you see that the Day of the Lord is coming **nearer.**
Jas 4. 8 Come **near** to God, and he will come near to you.
5. 8 your hopes high, for the day of the Lord's coming is **near.**
5. 9 The Judge is **near,** ready to appear.
1 Pet 4. 7 The end of all things is **near.**
1 Jn 2.18 My children, the end is **near!**
2.18 have already appeared, and so we know that the end is **near.**
Jude 7 Sodom and Gomorrah, and the **nearby** towns, whose people acted as
Rev 1. 3 For the time is **near** when all these things will happen.
22.10 secret, because the time is **near** when all this will happen.

NEBUCHADNEZZAR

King of Babylonia who conquered Jerusalem.

2 Kgs 24. 1 King **Nebuchadnezzar** of Babylonia invaded Judah,
24.10 Babylonian army, commanded by King **Nebuchadnezzar's** officers,
24.11 During the siege **Nebuchadnezzar** himself came to Jerusalem,
24.12 In the eighth year of **Nebuchadnezzar's** reign he took
24.13 As the Lord had foretold, **Nebuchadnezzar** broke up all the
24.14 **Nebuchadnezzar** carried away as prisoners the people of Jerusalem,
24.15 **Nebuchadnezzar** took Jehoiachin to Babylon as a prisoner,
24.16 **Nebuchadnezzar** deported all the important men to Babylonia,
24.17 **Nebuchadnezzar** made Jehoiachin's uncle Mattaniah king
25. 1 Zedekiah rebelled against King **Nebuchadnezzar** of Babylonia,
25. 1 so **Nebuchadnezzar** came with all his army and
25. 6 Zedekiah was taken to King **Nebuchadnezzar,** who was in the
25. 6 of Riblah, and there **Nebuchadnezzar** passed sentence on him.
25. 7 **Nebuchadnezzar** had Zedekiah's eyes put out, placed him in chains,
25. 8 year of King **Nebuchadnezzar** of Babylonia, Nebuzaradan,
25.22 King **Nebuchadnezzar** of Babylonia made Gedaliah, the son
1 Chr 6.15 King **Nebuchadnezzar** deported Jehozadak along with the
2 Chr 36. 6 **Nebuchadnezzar** of Babylonia invaded Judah, captured Jehoiakim,
36. 7 **Nebuchadnezzar** carried off some of the treasures of the
36.10 King **Nebuchadnezzar** took Jehoiachin to Babylonia as a prisoner,
36.10 **Nebuchadnezzar** made Jehoiachin's uncle Zedekiah king of Judah
36.13 Zedekiah rebelled against King **Nebuchadnezzar,** who had
Ezra 1. 7 bowls and cups that King **Nebuchadnezzar** had taken from the

Ezra 2. 1 Babylonia ever since King **Nebuchadnezzar** had taken them there
5.12 them be conquered by King **Nebuchadnezzar** of Babylonia, a
5.14 and silver temple utensils which **Nebuchadnezzar** had taken
6. 5 and silver utensils which King **Nebuchadnezzar** brought to
Neh 7. 6 Babylonia ever since King **Nebuchadnezzar** had taken them there
Esth 2. 6 When King **Nebuchadnezzar** of Babylon took King Jehoiachin
Jer 21. 2 Lord for us, because King **Nebuchadnezzar** of Babylonia and
21. 2 his miracles for us and force **Nebuchadnezzar** to retreat."
21. 7 you be captured by King **Nebuchadnezzar** and by your enemies,
21. 7 **Nebuchadnezzar** will put you to death.
22.25 I will give you to King **Nebuchadnezzar** of Babylonia
24. 1 **Nebuchadnezzar** of Babylonia had taken away Jehoiakim's son,
25. 1 was the first year that **Nebuchadnezzar** was king of Babylonia.)
25. 9 north and for my servant, King **Nebuchadnezzar** of Babylonia.
27. 6 power of my servant, King **Nebuchadnezzar** of Babylonia, and I
27. 8 until I have let **Nebuchadnezzar** destroy it completely.
27.19 King **Nebuchadnezzar** took away to Babylonia the king of Judah,
28. 3 temple treasures that King **Nebuchadnezzar** took to Babylonia.
28.11 break the yoke that King **Nebuchadnezzar** has put on the neck
28.14 and that they will serve King **Nebuchadnezzar** of Babylonia.
28.14 he will make even the wild animals serve **Nebuchadnezzar."**
29. 1 to all the others whom **Nebuchadnezzar** had taken away
29. 3 King Zedekiah of Judah was sending to King **Nebuchadnezzar**
29. 4 those people whom he allowed **Nebuchadnezzar** to take away as
29.21 to the power of King **Nebuchadnezzar** of Babylonia,
32. 1 the eighteenth year of King **Nebuchadnezzar** of Babylonia.
32.28 city over to King **Nebuchadnezzar** of Babylonia and his army;
34. 1 to me when King **Nebuchadnezzar** of Babylonia and his army,
35.11 But when King **Nebuchadnezzar** invaded the country, we
37. 1 King **Nebuchadnezzar** of Babylonia made Zedekiah son of
39. 1 was king of Judah, King **Nebuchadnezzar** of Babylonia came
39. 5 they took him to King **Nebuchadnezzar,** who was in the city of
39. 5 of Hamath, and there **Nebuchadnezzar** passed sentence on him.
39.11 **Nebuchadnezzar** commanded Nebuzaradan, the commanding officer,
43.10 my servant King **Nebuchadnezzar** of Babylonia to this place,
43.11 **Nebuchadnezzar** will come and defeat Egypt.
44.30 Zedekiah of Judah to King **Nebuchadnezzar** of Babylonia, who
46. 2 Neco of Egypt, which King **Nebuchadnezzar** of Babylonia
46.13 When King **Nebuchadnezzar** of Babylonia came to attack Egypt,
46.26 kill them, to King **Nebuchadnezzar** of Babylonia and his army.
49.28 which were conquered by King **Nebuchadnezzar** of Babylonia:
49.30 King **Nebuchadnezzar** of Babylonia has plotted against you,
50.17 then King **Nebuchadnezzar** of Babylonia gnawed their bones.
50.18 of Israel, will punish King **Nebuchadnezzar** and his country,
52. 3 Zedekiah rebelled against King **Nebuchadnezzar** of Babylonia,
52. 4 and so **Nebuchadnezzar** came with all his army and
52. 9 Zedekiah was taken to King **Nebuchadnezzar,** who was in the
52. 9 of Hamath, and there **Nebuchadnezzar** passed sentence on him.
52.12 year of King **Nebuchadnezzar** of Babylonia, Nebuzaradan,
52.28 of the people that **Nebuchadnezzar** took away as prisoners:
Ezek 26. 7 king of all—King **Nebuchadnezzar** of Babylonia—to attack Tyre.
29.18 "Mortal man," he said, "King **Nebuchadnezzar** of
29.19 I am giving the land of Egypt to King **Nebuchadnezzar.**
30.10 says, "I will use King **Nebuchadnezzar** of Babylonia to put
Dan 1. 1 was king of Judah, King **Nebuchadnezzar** of Babylonia attacked
1.18 the king, Ashpenaz took all the young men to **Nebuchadnezzar.**
2. 1 In the second year that **Nebuchadnezzar** was king, he had a dream.
2.25 Arioch took Daniel into King **Nebuchadnezzar's** presence
2.46 Then King **Nebuchadnezzar** bowed to the ground and gave
3. 1 King **Nebuchadnezzar** had a gold statue made, twenty-seven
3. 2 of the statue which King **Nebuchadnezzar** had set up.
3. 5 worship the gold statue that King **Nebuchadnezzar** has set up.
3. 7 the gold statue which King **Nebuchadnezzar** had set up.
3. 9 said to King **Nebuchadnezzar,** "May Your Majesty live for ever!
3.19 Then **Nebuchadnezzar** lost his temper, and his face
3.24 Suddenly **Nebuchadnezzar** leapt to his feet in amazement.
3.26 So **Nebuchadnezzar** went up to the door of the blazing
4. 1 King **Nebuchadnezzar** sent the following message to the people
4.18 "This is the dream I had," said King **Nebuchadnezzar.**
4.28 All this did happen to King **Nebuchadnezzar.**
4.31 from heaven, "King **Nebuchadnezzar,** listen to what I say!
4.33 **Nebuchadnezzar** was driven out of human society and ate grass
4.37 I, **Nebuchadnezzar,** praise, honour, and glorify the King of Heaven.
5. 2 and bowls which his father **Nebuchadnezzar** had carried off
5.11 **Nebuchadnezzar,** your father, made him chief of the fortune-tellers,
5.18 Supreme God made your father **Nebuchadnezzar** a great king and

NEBUZARADAN
Commander of the Babylonian army which conquered Jerusalem.

2 Kgs 25. 8 of King Nebuchadnezzar of Babylonia, **Nebuzaradan,** adviser to
25.11 Then **Nebuzaradan** took away to Babylonia the people
25.18 In addition, **Nebuzaradan,** the commanding officer, took
25.20 **Nebuzaradan** took them to the king of Babylonia,
Jer 39. 9 Finally **Nebuzaradan,** the commanding officer, took away
39.11 Nebuchadnezzar commanded **Nebuzaradan,** the commanding officer,
39.13 So **Nebuzaradan,** together with the high officials Nebushazban
40. 1 Lord spoke to me after **Nebuzaradan,** the commanding officer,
40. 5 When I did not answer, **Nebuzaradan** said, "Go back to Gedaliah,
41.10 the people in Mizpah, whom **Nebuzaradan** the commanding
43. 6 They took everyone whom **Nebuzaradan** the commanding officer
52.12 of King Nebuchadnezzar of Babylonia, **Nebuzaradan,** adviser to
52.15 Then **Nebuzaradan** took away to Babylonia the people who
52.24 In addition, **Nebuzaradan,** the commanding officer, took
52.26 **Nebuzaradan** took them to the king of Babylonia, who was
52.30 and in his twenty-third year, 745—taken away by **Nebuzaradan.**

NECESSARY

Lk 24.26 Was it not **necessary** for the Messiah to suffer these things
Acts 13.46 "It was **necessary** that the word of God should be spoken
15.28 put any other burden on you besides these **necessary** rules:
24. 2 period of peace, and many **necessary** reforms are being made for
2 Cor 9. 5 So I thought it was **necessary** to urge these brothers to go
Gal 5.11 to preach that circumcision is **necessary,** why am I still being
Phil 2.25 have thought it **necessary** to send you our brother Epaphroditus,
Tit 1.11 is **necessary** to stop their talk, because they are upsetting
Heb 9.16 of a will it is **necessary** to prove that the person who
Jas 2.16 if you don't give them the **necessities** of life?
1 Pet 1. 6 though it may now be **necessary** for you to be sad for
3. 1 It will not be **necessary** for you to say a word,

NECK

Gen 27.16 goats on his arms and on the hairless part of his **neck.**
41.42 linen robe on him, and placed a gold chain round his **neck.**
46.29 his arms round his father's **neck** and cried for a long time.
49. 8 You hold your enemies by the **neck.**
Ex 13.13 you do not want to buy back the donkey, break its **neck.**
34.20 If you do not buy it back, break its **neck.**
Lev 1.15 at the altar, wring its **neck,** and burn its head on the
5. 8 He will break its **neck** without pulling off its head [9]and
Deut 21. 4 ploughed or planted, and there they are to break its **neck.**
Josh 10.24 to come and put their feet on the **necks** of the kings.
Judg 5.30 for Sisera, embroidered pieces for the **neck** of the queen."
8.21 took the ornaments that were on the **necks** of their camels.
8.26 nor the collars that were round the **necks** of their camels.
1 Sam 4.18 old and fat that the fall broke his **neck,** and he died.
1 Kgs 20.31 waists and ropes round our **necks,** and maybe he will spare
20.32 waists and ropes round their **necks,** went to Ahab and said,
Job 41.22 His **neck** is so powerful that all who meet him are terrified.
Ps 69. 1 The water is up to my **neck;**
105.18 iron collar was round his **neck,** [19]until what he had
Prov 3. 3 Tie them round your **neck;**
Song 1.10 upon your cheeks and falls along your **neck** like jewels.
4. 4 Your **neck** is like the tower of David, round and smooth,
7. 4 Your **neck** is like a tower of ivory.
Is 3.18 on their heads, on their **necks,** [19]and on their wrists.
66. 3 whether they sacrifice a lamb or break a dog's **neck;**
Jer 27. 2 straps and wooden crossbars and to put it on my **neck.**
28.10 took the yoke off my **neck,** broke it in pieces, [11]and said
28.11 King Nebuchadnezzar has put on the **neck** of all the nations;
29.26 is placed in chains with an iron collar round his **neck.**
30. 8 yoke that is round their **necks** and remove their chains, and
Lam 1.14 He hung them round my **neck,** and I grew weak beneath the
Ezek 21.29 The sword is going to fall on your **necks.**
Dan 5. 7 chain of honour round his **neck,** and be the third in power
5.16 chain of honour round your **neck,** and be the third in power
5.29 purple and to hang a gold chain of honour round his **neck.**
Hos 10.11 a yoke on her beautiful **neck** and to harness her for harder
Mt 18. 6 large millstone tied round his **neck** and be drowned in the
Mk 9.42 millstone tied round his **neck** and be thrown into the sea.
Lk 17. 2 millstone were tied round his **neck** and he were thrown into

NECKLACE

Ex 35.22 brought decorative pins, earrings, rings, **necklaces,** and all
Num 31.50 rings, earrings, and **necklaces** that each of us has taken.
Judg 8.26 did not include the ornaments, **necklaces,** and purple clothes
Ps 73. 6 they wear pride like a **necklace** and violence like a robe;
Prov 1. 9 a handsome turban or a **necklace** improves your appearance.
Song 4. 4 round and smooth, with a **necklace** like a thousand shields
4. 9 sweetheart and bride, and the **necklace** you are wearing have
Ezek 16.11 I put jewels on you—bracelets and **necklaces.**

NECO
King of Egypt who defeated and killed King Josiah.

2 Kgs 23.29 While Josiah was king, King **Neco** of Egypt led an army
23.33 His reign ended when King **Neco** of Egypt took him
23.34 King **Neco** made Josiah's son Eliakim king of Judah
23.34 Joahaz was taken to Egypt by King **Neco,** and there he died.
2 Chr 35.20 this for the Temple, King **Neco** of Egypt led an army
35.21 Josiah tried to stop him, [21]but **Neco** sent Josiah this message:
35.22 God was saying through King **Neco,** so he disguised himself
36. 3 King **Neco** of Egypt took him prisoner and made Judah pay
36. 4 **Neco** made Joahaz' brother Eliakim king of Judah and
36. 4 Joahaz was taken to Egypt by **Neco.**
Jer 46. 2 about the army of King **Neco** of Egypt,

NEED

Gen 33.11 God has been kind to me and given me everything I **need."**
33.15 Jacob answered, "There is no **need** for that for I only want
Ex 14.14 for you, and there is no **need** for you to do anything."
16.16 much of it as he **needs,** two litres for each member of
16.18 Each had gathered just what he **needed.**
16.21 Every morning each one gathered as much as he **needed;**
22.11 shall accept the loss, and the other man **need** not repay him;
22.13 he **need** not pay for what has been killed by wild animals.
22.15 happens when the owner is present, the man **need** not repay.
35.21 They brought everything **needed** for use in worship and for
36. 1 know how to make everything **needed** to build the sacred Tent,
36. 5 are bringing more than is **needed** for the work which the Lord
Lev 13.11 is no **need** to isolate him, because he is obviously unclean.
13.36 If the sore has spread, he **need** not look for yellowish hairs;
25.44 If you **need** slaves, you may buy them from the nations
26.26 so that ten women will **need** only one oven to bake all

Num 18.20 I, the Lord, am all you **need."**
Deut 2. 7 these forty years, and you have had everything you **needed.**
4. 7 is so near when they **need** him as the Lord our God
8. 9 There you will never go hungry or ever be in **need.**
11.14 your land when it is **needed,** in the autumn and in the
14.29 They are to come and get all they **need.**
15. 7 there is a fellow-Israelite in **need,** then do not be selfish
15. 8 Instead, be generous and lend him as much as he **needs.**
15.11 who are poor and in **need,** and so I command you to
17.14 then you will decide you **need** a king like all the nations
23.12 camp where you can go when you **need** to relieve yourselves.
24.14 not cheat a poor and **needy** hired servant, whether he is a
24.15 he **needs** the money and has counted on getting it.
26.12 that in every community they will have all they **need** to eat.
28.48 You will be hungry, thirsty, and naked—in **need** of everything.
29. 6 the Lord provided for your **needs** in order to teach you that
Josh 7. 3 "There is no **need** for everyone to attack Ai.
19. 9 assignment was larger than was **needed,** part of its territory
Judg 18. 7 they had all they **needed.**
19.19 We have everything we **need."**
1 Sam 2. 8 poor from the dust and raises the **needy** from their misery.
17.47 that the Lord does not **need** swords or spears to save his
27. 5 There is no **need,** sir, for me to live with you in
2 Sam 20. 3 He provided for their **needs,** but did not have intercourse with them.
1 Kgs 3. 9 give me the wisdom I **need** to rule your people with justice
4.22 The supplies Solomon **needed** each day were five thousand
4.27 supplied the food King Solomon **needed** for himself and for
4.27 they always supplied everything **needed.**
4.28 and straw, where it was **needed,** for the chariot-horses and
8.59 of Israel and to their king, according to their daily **needs.**
2 Kgs 4.13 for all the trouble she has had in providing for our **needs.**
4.13 "I have all I **need** here among my own people," she
4.22 I **need** to go to the prophet Elisha.
12. 5 the money was to be used to repair the Temple, as **needed.**
12.15 honest, so there was no **need** to require them to account for
22. 7 honest, so there is no **need** to require them to account for
23.35 order to raise the amount **needed** to pay the tribute demanded
25.24 word that there is no **need** for you to be afraid of
25.30 he lived, he was given a regular allowance for his **needs.**
1 Chr 23.26 there is no longer any **need** for the Levites to carry the
2 Chr 1.10 give me the wisdom and knowledge I **need** to rule over them.
2.16 down all the cedars you **need,** bind them together in rafts,
35.15 the temple gates did not **need** to leave their posts, because
Ezra 1. 4 of his people in exile **need** help to return, their neighbours
4. 3 said to them, "We don't **need** your help to build a temple
6. 9 the priests in Jerusalem whatever they tell you they **need:**
7.20 And anything else which you **need** for the Temple, you may
Neh 5. 2 "We have large families, we **need** corn to keep us alive."
9.21 Through forty years in the desert you provided all that they **needed;**
10.33 sins of Israel, and anything else **needed** for the Temple.
Job 5.15 he saves the **needy** from oppression.
6.14 In trouble like this I **need** loyal friends— whether I've
15. 6 There is no **need** for me to condemn you;
21.15 They think there is no **need** to serve God nor any
24. 4 getting their rights and force the **needy** to run and hide.
27.16 much silver to count and more clothes than anyone **needs;**
30.25 with people in trouble and feel sorry for those in **need?**
31.19 When I found someone in **need,** too poor to buy clothes,
34.23 God does not **need** to set a time for men to go
34.24 He does not **need** an investigation to remove leaders and
35. 7 There is nothing God **needs** from you.
Ps 9.18 The **needy** will not always be neglected;
10.14 you have always helped the **needy.**
12. 5 says the Lord, "because the **needy** are oppressed and the
16. 5 Lord, are all I have, and you give me all I **need;**
23. 1 I have everything I **need.**
32. 6 all your loyal people should pray to you in times of **need;**
34. 9 those who obey him have all they **need.**
37.14 to kill the poor and **needy,** to slaughter those who do what
50. 9 And yet I do not **need** bulls from your farms or goats
57. 2 to God, the Most High, to God, who supplies my every **need.**
69.33 Lord listens to those in **need** and does not forget his people
72. 4 may he help the **needy** and defeat their oppressors.
72.12 who call to him, and those who are **needy** and neglected.
72.13 he saves the lives of those in **need.**
73.26 he is all I ever **need.**
74.21 let those poor and **needy** people praise you.
82. 3 be fair to the **needy** and the helpless.
91. 5 You **need** not fear any dangers at night or sudden attacks
104.27 them depend on you to give them food when they **need** it.
107.41 But he rescued the **needy** from their misery and made
109.16 he persecuted and killed the poor, the **needy,** and the helpless.
109.22 I am poor and **needy;**
112. 9 He gives generously to the **needy,** and his kindness never fails;
113. 7 he lifts the **needy** from their misery [8] and makes them
128. 2 Your work will provide for your **needs;**
132.15 I will richly provide Zion with all she **needs;**
140.12 defend the cause of the poor and the rights of the **needy.**
145.15 hopefully to you, and you give them food when they **need** it.
145.16 You give them enough and satisfy the **needs** of all.
145.19 He supplies the **needs** of those who honour him;
Prov 3.27 Whenever you possibly can, do good to those who **need** it.
10.13 but stupid people **need** to be punished.
23.35 I **need** another drink."
25.16 Never eat more honey than you **need;**
28.27 Give to the poor and you will never be in **need.**
30. 8 So give me only as much food as I **need.**
30. 9 I have more, I might say that I do not **need** you.
30.14 There are people who take cruel advantage of the poor and **needy;**
Prov 30.16 dry ground that **needs** rain,
31. 5 forget the laws and ignore the rights of people in **need.**
31. 9 Protect the rights of the poor and **needy."**
31.20 She is generous to the poor and **needy.**
31.27 She is always busy and looks after her family's **needs.**
Ecc 5.13 a time when they may **need** it, [14] and then lose it all
Song 1. 7 Why should I **need** to look for you among the flocks of
Is 7.22 will give so much milk that he will have all he **needs.**
22. 9 You found the places where the walls of Jerusalem **needed** repair.
23.18 use her money to buy the food and the clothing they **need.**
28. 9 Who **needs** his message?
32. 3 eyes and ears will be open to the **needs** of the people.
41.17 "When my people in their **need** look for water, when
45. 5 you the strength you **need,** although you do not know me.
49.20 land is too small— we **need** more room to live in!'
51.14 will live a long life and have all the food they **need.**
58.10 satisfy those who are in **need,** then the darkness around you
Jer 3.16 they will not even **need** it, nor will they make another one.
15.19 back to you, and you will not **need** to go to them.
31.12 they will have everything they **need.**
31.14 the richest food and satisfy all the **needs** of my people.
40. 9 word that there is no **need** for you to be afraid to
52.34 he lived, he was given a regular allowance for his **needs.**
Lam 2.14 They made you think you did not **need** to repent.
5. 4 we must buy the wood we **need** for fuel.
Ezek 27.33 You filled the **needs** of every nation.
34.26 I will bless them with showers of rain when they **need** it.
44.28 I am all they **need.**
Amos 4. 7 I held back the rain when your crops **needed** it most.
8. 4 you that trample on the **needy** and try to destroy the poor
Zeph 3.11 my people, will no longer **need** to be ashamed that you
Zech 7.10 foreigners who live among you, or anyone else in **need.**
Mt 4. 4 on bread alone, but **needs** every word that God speaks.' "
6. 2 you give something to a **needy** person, do not make a big
6. 3 But when you help a **needy** person, do it in such a
6. 8 Your Father already knows what you **need** before you ask him.
6.11 Give us today the food we **need.**
6.25 the food and drink you **need** in order to stay alive,
6.32 Your Father in heaven knows that you **need** all these things.
6.34 There is no **need** to add to the troubles each day brings.
9.12 who are well do not **need** a doctor, but only those who
10.10 A worker should be given what he **needs.**
15. 6 'This belongs to God,' [6] he does not **need** to honour his father.
19.20 "What else do I **need** to do?"
21. 3 And if anyone says anything, tell him, 'The Master **needs** them';
26.65 We don't **need** any more witnesses!
Mk 2.17 who are well do not **need** a doctor, but only those who
2.25 what David did that time when he **needed** something to eat?
10.21 at him with love and said, "You **need** only one thing.
11. 3 tell him that the Master **needs** it and will send it back
14.63 tore his robes and said, "We don't **need** any more witnesses!
Lk 5.31 who are well do not **need** a doctor, but only those who
9.11 about the Kingdom of God, and healed those who **needed** it.
10.42 and troubled over so many things, [42] but just one is **needed.**
11. 3 Give us day by day the food we **need.**
11. 8 and give you everything you **need** because you are not ashamed
12.19 You have all the good things you **need** for many years.
12.22 worry about the food you **need** to stay alive
12.22 or about the clothes you **need** for your body.
12.30 Your Father knows that you **need** these things.
15. 7 over ninety-nine respectable people who do not **need** to repent.
18.22 "There is still one more thing you **need** to do.
19.31 why you are untying it, tell him that the Master **needs** it."
19.34 "The Master **needs** it," they answered, [35] and they took
19.42 saying, "If you only knew today what is **needed** for peace!
22.71 And they said, "We don't **need** any witnesses!
Jn 2.25 There was no **need** for anyone to tell him about them,
13.29 go and buy what they **needed** for the festival, or to give
14. 8 that is all we **need."**
16.30 you do not **need** someone to ask you questions.
Acts 2.45 distribute the money among all, according to what each one **needed.**
4.34 There was no one in the group who was in **need.**
4.35 money was distributed to each one according to his **need.**
17.25 Nor does he **need** anything that we can supply by working
20.34 to provide everything that my companions and I have **needed.**
24.23 freedom and allow his friends to provide for his **needs.**
27. 3 to go and see his friends, to be given what he **needed.**
27.34 you **need** it in order to survive.
28.10 we sailed, they put on board what we **needed** for the voyage.
Rom 12.13 Share your belongings with your **needy** fellow-Christians,
16. 2 and give her any help she may **need** from you;
1 Cor 4. 8 Do you already have everything you **need?**
7. 3 duty as a wife, and each should satisfy the other's **needs.**
11. 7 A man has no **need** to cover his head, because he reflects
11.22 of God and put to shame the people who are in **need?**
12.21 the eye cannot say to the hand, "I don't **need** you!"
12.21 can the head say to the feet, "Well, I don't **need** you!"
12.24 special modesty, [24] which the more beautiful parts do not **need.**
12.24 way as to give greater honour to those parts that **need** it.
13. 2 may have all the faith **needed** to move mountains—but if I
16. 2 that there will be no **need** to collect money when I come.
2 Cor 2.10 I forgive—if, indeed, I **need** to forgive anything—I do it
3. 1 like some other people, we **need** letters of recommendation to you
8.13 is only fair that you should help those who are in **need.**
8.13 Then, when you are in **need** and they have plenty, they will
9. 1 There is really no **need** for me to write to you about
9. 8 give you more than you **need,** so that you will
9. 8 always have all you **need** for yourselves and more than enough
9. 9 As the scripture says, "He gives generously to the **needy;**
9.10 with all the seed you **need** and will make it grow

2 Cor	9.12	not only meets the **needs** of God's people, but also produces
	11. 9	I did not bother you for help when I **needed** money;
	11. 9	brothers who came from Macedonia brought me everything I **needed.**
	12. 9	"My grace is all you **need,** for my power is greatest when
Gal	2.10	that we should remember the **needy** in their group, which is
	3.20	a go-between is not **needed** when only one person is involved;
Eph	4.29	and provide what is **needed,** so that what you say will
Phil	4. 6	ask God for what you **need,** always asking him with a thankful
	4.12	it is to be in **need** and what it is to have
	4.16	More than once when I **needed** help in Thessalonica, you sent
	4.18	I have all I **need** now that Epaphroditus has brought me all
	4.19	wealth through Christ Jesus, my God will supply all your **needs.**
1 Thes	1. 8	There is nothing, then, that we **need** to say.
	3.10	see you personally and supply what is **needed** in your faith.
	4. 9	There is no **need** to write to you about love for your
	4.12	you will not have to depend on anyone for what you **need.**
	5. 1	There is no **need** to write to you, brothers, about the
Tit	1. 5	the things that still **needed** doing and appoint church elders
	3.13	travels, and see to it that they have everything they **need.**
	3.14	their time doing good, in order to provide for real **needs;**
Heb	4.16	mercy and find grace to help us just when we **need** it.
	5.12	be teachers—yet you still **need** someone to teach you the
	7.11	there would have been no **need** for a different kind of priest
	7.26	Jesus, then, is the High Priest that meets our **needs.**
	7.27	he does not **need** to offer sacrifices every day for his own
	8. 7	covenant, there would have been no **need** for a second one.
	10.18	an offering to take away sins is no longer **needed.**
	10.36	You **need** to be patient, in order to do the will of
	13.20	with every good thing you **need** in order to do his will,
Jas	2.15	are brothers or sisters who **need** clothes and don't have
2 Pet	1. 3	has given us everything we **need** to live a truly religious
	1. 8	These are the qualities you **need,** and if you have them in
1 Jn	2.27	Spirit remains in you, you do not **need** anyone to teach you.
	2.28	be full of courage and **need** not hide in shame from him
	3.17	person sees his brother in **need,** yet closes his heart against
Jude	3	when I felt the **need** of writing at once to encourage
Rev	3.17	I have all I **need.'**
	21.23	The city has no **need** of the sun or the moon to
	22. 5	night, and they will not **need** lamps or sunlight, because the

NEEDLE

Mt	19.24	than for a camel to go through the eye of a **needle."**
Mk	10.25	than for a camel to go through the eye of a **needle."**
Lk	18.25	than for a camel to go through the eye of a **needle."**

NEGLECT

Ex	5. 4	"What do you mean by making the people **neglect** their work?
Deut	12.19	Be sure, also, not to **neglect** the Levites, as long as
	14.27	"Do not **neglect** the Levites who live in your towns;
Josh	1. 7	Do not **neglect** any part of it and you will succeed wherever
	23. 6	Do not **neglect** any part of it, [7]and then you will not
Neh	10.39	We will not **neglect** the house of our God.
	13.11	I reprimanded the officials for letting the Temple be **neglected.**
Job	20.19	wealth, [19]because he oppressed and **neglected** the poor and
Ps	9.18	The needy will not always be **neglected;**
	22.24	He does not **neglect** the poor or ignore their suffering;
	72.12	who call to him, and those who are needy and **neglected.**
	119.87	in killing me, but I have not **neglected** your commands.
	119.93	I will never **neglect** your instructions, because by them
	119.102	I have not **neglected** your instructions,
	119.141	am unimportant and despised, but I do not **neglect** your teachings.
	119.153	and save me, because I have not **neglected** your law.
	119.176	me, your servant, because I have not **neglected** your laws.
Prov	8.33	do not **neglect** it.
	19.27	stop learning, you will soon **neglect** what you already know.
Mt	6.16	They **neglect** their appearance so that everyone will see that
	23.23	but you **neglect** to obey the really important teachings
	23.23	These you should practise, without **neglecting** the others.
Lk	11.42	the other herbs, but you **neglect** justice and love for God.
	11.42	These you should practise, without **neglecting** the others.
Acts	6. 1	widows were being **neglected** in the daily distribution of funds.
	6. 2	not right for us to **neglect** the preaching of God's word in
Phil	4.11	saying this because I feel **neglected,** for I have learnt to
1 Tim	4.14	Do not **neglect** the spiritual gift that is in you, which

NEIGH

Jer	8.16	The whole land trembles when their horses **neigh.**
	50.11	threshing corn or like a **neighing** horse, [12]but your own

NEIGHBOUR

Ex	3.22	will go to her Egyptian **neighbours** and to any Egyptian woman
	11. 2	to ask their **neighbours** for gold and silver jewellery."
	12. 4	animal, he and his next-door **neighbour** may share an animal,
	32.27	and kill his brothers, his friends, and his **neighbours."**
Lev	19.18	to hate him, but love your **neighbour** as you love yourself.
Deut	19.14	"Do not move your **neighbour's** boundary mark,
	27.17	"'God's curse on anyone who moves a **neighbour's** boundary mark.'
Judg	18.22	the house when Micah called his **neighbours** out for battle.
1 Kgs	4.24	and he was at peace with all the **neighbouring** countries.
	4.31	his fame spread throughout all the **neighbouring** countries.
2 Kgs	4. 3	"Go to your **neighbours** and borrow as many empty jars as
2 Chr	32.22	the people live in peace with all the **neighbouring** countries.
Ezra	1. 4	help to return, their **neighbours** are to give them this help.
	1. 6	All their **neighbours** helped them by giving them many things:
	9. 1	from the people in the **neighbouring** countries of Ammon,
Neh	6. 6	is going round among the **neighbouring** peoples that you and
Job	31. 9	have been attracted to my **neighbour's** wife, and waited,
Ps	15. 3	to his friends nor spreads rumours about his **neighbours.**
	31.11	and especially my **neighbours,** treat me with contempt;
	38.11	My friends and **neighbours** will not come near me, because
	44.13	Our **neighbours** see what you did to us, and they mock us
	89.41	all his **neighbours** laugh at him.
Prov	3.28	Never tell your **neighbour** to wait until tomorrow if you
	3.29	Don't plan anything that will hurt your **neighbour;**
	14.20	No one, not even his **neighbour,** likes a poor man, but
	25. 9	If you and your **neighbour** have a difference of opinion,
	25.17	Don't visit your **neighbour** too often;
	27.10	a **neighbour** near by can help you more than a brother who
Ecc	4. 4	it is because they envy their **neighbours.**
Is	19. 2	turn brother against brother and **neighbour** against neighbour.
Jer	5. 8	wild with desire, each lusting for his **neighbour's** wife.
	6.21	Fathers and sons will die, and so will friends and **neighbours."**
	9. 8	speaks friendly words to his **neighbour,** but is really
	12.14	something to say about Israel's **neighbours** who have ruined
	13.27	a man lusting after his **neighbour's** wife or like a stallion
	25. 9	Judah and its inhabitants and against all the **neighbouring** nations.
	25. 9	destroy this nation and its **neighbours** and leave them in
	25.11	a shocking sight, and the **neighbouring** nations will serve
Ezek	11.12	keeping the laws of the **neighbouring** nations, you were
	16.26	You let your lustful **neighbours,** the Egyptians, go to bed with you,
	16.57	the Philistines, and your other **neighbours** who hate you.
	28.26	I will punish all their **neighbours** who treated them with scorn,
	36. 3	When the **neighbouring** nations captured and plundered
	36.36	Then the **neighbouring** nations that have survived will know that I,
Dan	9.16	All the people in the **neighbouring** countries look down on
Mic	7. 5	Don't believe your **neighbour** or trust your friend.
Hab	2.15	In your fury you humiliated and disgraced your **neighbours;**
Zech	3.10	of you will invite his **neighbour** to come and enjoy peace and
Mt	19.19	and love your **neighbour** as you love yourself."
	22.39	'Love your **neighbour** as you love yourself.'
Mk	12.31	'Love your **neighbour** as you love yourself.'
	12.33	and he must love his **neighbour** as he loves himself.
Lk	1.58	Her **neighbours** and relatives heard how wonderfully good the
	1.65	The **neighbours** were all filled with fear, and the news about
	10.27	and 'Love your **neighbour** as you love yourself.'"
	10.29	to justify himself, so he asked Jesus, "Who is my **neighbour?"**
	10.36	these three acted like a **neighbour** towards the man attacked by
	14.12	relatives or your rich **neighbours**—for they will invite you back,
	15. 6	he calls his friends and **neighbours** together and says to them,
	15. 9	she calls her friends and **neighbours** together, and says to them,
Jn	9. 8	His **neighbours,** then, and the people who had seen him begging
Rom	13. 9	in the one command, "Love your **neighbour** as you love yourself."
Gal	5.14	"Love your **neighbour** as you love yourself."
Jas	2. 8	in the scripture, "Love your **neighbour** as you love yourself."

NEIGHBOURHOOD

Ruth	4.17	The women of the **neighbourhood** named the boy Obed.
Mt	2.16	boys in Bethlehem and its **neighbourhood** who were two years old
Mk	7.31	Jesus then left the **neighbourhood** of Tyre and went on through

NEPHEW

Gen	12. 5	took his wife Sarai, his **nephew** Lot, and all the wealth and
	14.12	Lot, Abram's **nephew,** was living in Sodom, so they took
	14.14	When Abram heard that his **nephew** had been captured, he
	14.16	He also brought back his **nephew** Lot and his possessions,
	29.13	heard the news about his **nephew** Jacob, he ran to meet him,
2 Chr	22. 8	Judaean leaders and of Ahaziah's **nephews** that had

NERVE

Deut	20. 8	there any man here who has lost his **nerve** and is afraid?

NEST

Num	24.21	is secure, Safe as a **nest** set high on a cliff, [22]But
Deut	22. 6	happen to find a bird's **nest** in a tree or on the
Job	39.27	for your command to build its **nest** high in the mountains?
Ps	84. 3	the sparrows have built a **nest,** and the swallows have their
	104.12	In the trees near by, the birds make their **nests** and sing.
	104.17	There the birds build their **nests;**
	104.17	the storks **nest** in the fir-trees.
Prov	27. 8	man away from home is like a bird away from its **nest.**
Is	10.14	world were like a bird's **nest,** and I gathered their wealth
	13.21	where desert animals live and where owls build their **nests.**
	16. 2	aimlessly to and fro, like birds driven from their **nest.**
	31. 5	a bird hovers over its **nest** to protect its young, so I,
	34.15	Owls will build their **nests,** lay eggs, hatch their young,
Jer	48.28	the dove that makes its **nest** in the sides of a ravine.
Ezek	31. 6	Every kind of bird built **nests** in its branches;
Dan	4.12	in its shade, birds built **nests** in its branches, and every
	4.21	under it, and birds made their **nests** in its branches.
Obad	4	as high as an eagle's **nest,** so that it seems to be
Mt	8.20	have holes, and birds have **nests,** but the Son of Man has
	13.32	so that birds come and make their **nests** in its branches."
Mk	4.32	that the birds come and make their **nests** in its shade."
Lk	9.58	have holes, and birds have **nests,** but the Son of Man has
	13.19	a tree, and the birds make their **nests** in its branches."

NET

Job	18. 8	He walks into a **net,** and his feet are caught;
Ps	57. 6	My enemies have spread a **net** to catch me;
Prov	1.17	no good to spread a **net** when the bird you want to

Prov 5.22 He gets caught in the **net** of his own sin.
7.23 a bird going into a **net**—he did not know that his
Ecc 7.26 offers you will catch you like a trap or like a **net;**
9.12 like fish caught in a **net,** we are trapped at some evil
Is 19. 8 their hooks and their **nets** will be useless.
51.20 they are like deer caught in a hunter's **net.**
Jer 5.26 wait like men who spread **nets** to catch birds, but they have
Ezek 12.13 But I will spread out my **net** and trap him in it.
17.20 I will spread out a hunter's **net** and catch him in it.
19. 8 They spread their hunting **nets** and caught him in their trap.
26. 5 Fishermen will dry their **nets** on it, there where it stands
26.14 leave only a bare rock where fishermen can dry their **nets.**
32. 3 catch you in my net and let them drag the **net** ashore.
47.10 the sea, and they will spread out their **nets** there to dry.
Hos 5. 1 a trap at Mizpah, a **net** spread on Mount Tabor, [2]a deep
7.12 I will spread out a **net** and catch them like birds as
Hab 1.15 They drag them off in **nets** and shout for joy over their
1.16 They even worship their **nets** and offer sacrifices to them,
1.16 because their **nets** provide them with the best
Mt 4.18 his brother Andrew, catching fish in the lake with a **net.**
4.20 At once they left their **nets** and went with him.
4.21 their boat with their father Zebedee, getting their **nets** ready.
13.47 Some fishermen throw their **net** out in the lake and catch all
13.48 When the **net** is full, they pull it to shore and sit
Mk 1.16 fishermen, Simon and his brother Andrew, catching fish with a **net.**
1.18 At once they left their **nets** and went with him.
1.19 They were in their boat getting their **nets** ready.
Lk 5. 2 the fishermen had left them and were washing the **nets.**
5. 4 and you and your partners let down your **nets** for a catch."
5. 5 But if you say so, I will let down the **nets."**
5. 6 a large number of fish that the **nets** were about to break.
Jn 21. 6 said to them, "Throw your **net** out on the right side of
21. 6 So they threw the **net** out and could not pull it back
21. 8 came to shore in the boat, pulling the **net** full of fish.
21.11 went aboard and dragged the **net** ashore full of big fish,
21.11 even though there were so many, still the **net** did not tear.

NEVER AGAIN

Gen 8.21 and he said to himself, **"Never again** will I put the earth
8.21 **Never again** will I destroy all living beings, as I have done
9.11 I promise that **never again** will all living beings be
9.11 **never again** will a flood destroy the earth.
9.15 that a flood will **never again** destroy all living beings.
Lev 22. 3 have dedicated to me, he can **never again** serve at the altar.
Deut 12. 3 that they will **never again** be worshipped at those places.
13.16 must be left in ruins for ever and **never again** be rebuilt.
1 Sam 15.35 As long as Samuel lived, he **never again** saw the king;
2 Sam 21.17 David promise that he would **never again** go out with them to
1 Chr 19.19 The Syrians were **never again** willing to help the Ammonites.
Neh 13.25 oath in God's name that **never again** would they or their
Esth 1.19 that Vashti may **never again** appear before the king.
Job 3. 4 **Never again** remember that day;
3. 4 **never again** let light shine on it.
7. 8 You see me now, but **never again.**
Ps 77. 7 Will he **never again** be pleased with us?
Ecc 9. 6 They will **never again** take part in anything that happens in
Is 2. 4 Nations will **never again** go to war, never prepare for battle again.
38.11 of the living I would **never again** see the Lord Or any
54. 9 the time of Noah I promised **never again** to flood the earth.
Jer 3.19 you to call me father, and **never again** turn away from me.
22.10 him away, never to return, **never again** to see the land where
22.12 have taken him, and he will **never again** see this land."
31.40 The city will **never again** be torn down or destroyed."
44.26 **Never again** will I let any of you use my name to
50.39 **Never again** will people live there, not for all time to come.
Ezek 19.14 The branches will **never again** be strong, will never be royal sceptres.
26.20 As a result you will **never again** be inhabited and take your
29.15 of all, and they will **never again** rule over other nations.
29.16 Israel will **never again** depend on them for help.
34.10 away from you and **never again** let you be their shepherds;
34.10 **never again** will I let you take care only of yourselves.
36.12 own land, and it will **never again** let your children starve.
39.29 on the people of Israel and **never again** turn away from them.
45. 9 You must **never again** drive my people off their land.
Hos 14. 3 We will **never again** say to our idols that they are our
Mic 4. 3 Nations will **never again** go to war, never prepare for battle again.
Zeph 3.11 and arrogant, and you will **never again** rebel against me on
Mal 2.12 those who did this, and **never again** let them participate in

NEW

see also **NEW GATE, NEW MOON FESTIVAL, NEW-BORN**

Ex 1. 8 Then, a **new** king, who knew nothing about Joseph, came to
Lev 14.42 stones that were removed, and **new** plaster will be used to
23.14 not eat any of the **new** corn, whether raw, roasted, or baked
23.16 Sabbath, present to the Lord another **new** offering of corn.
26.10 is left of the old harvest to make room for the **new.**
Num 1.51 Tent down and set it up again at each **new** camping place.
15.20 first bread made from the **new** corn is to be presented as
18.27 offering which the farmer makes of **new** corn and new wine.
28.26 you present the offering of **new** corn to the Lord, you are
32.14 taken your fathers' place, a **new** generation of sinful men
32.38 They gave **new** names to the towns they rebuilt.
Deut 22. 8 "When you build a **new** house, be sure to put a railing
24. 5 "When a man is **newly** married, he is not to be drafted
32.17 that are not real, **new** gods their ancestors had never known,
Josh 5. 7 and it was this **new** generation that Joshua circumcised.
9.13 When we filled these wineskins, they were **new,** but look!
Judg 2.17 Lord's commands, but this **new** generation soon stopped doing so.
Judg 5. 8 was war in the land when the Israelites chose **new** gods.
15.13 tied him up with two **new** ropes and brought him back from
16. 7 tie me up with seven **new** bowstrings that are not dried out,
16. 8 seven **new** bowstrings that were not dried out,
16.11 "If they tie me with **new** ropes that have never been used,
16.12 So Delilah got some **new** ropes and tied him up.
Ruth 4.15 a grandson, who will bring **new** life to you and give you
1 Sam 6. 7 So prepare a **new** wagon and two cows that have never been
10. 9 When Saul turned to leave Samuel, God gave Saul a **new** nature.
23. 1 town of Keilah and were stealing the **newly-harvested** corn.
2 Sam 6. 3 Abinadab's home on the hill and placed it on a **new** cart.
15.19 Go back and stay with the **new** king.
21.16 who was wearing a **new** sword, thought he could kill David.
1 Kgs 11.30 Ahijah took off the **new** robe he was wearing, tore it
2 Kgs 2.20 "Put some salt in a **new** bowl, and bring it to me,"
11.14 There she saw the **new** king standing by the column at the
16.14 the Lord was between the **new** altar and the Temple,
16.14 so Ahaz moved it to the north side of his **new** altar.
22.14 Huldah, a prophet who lived in the **newer** part of Jerusalem.
1 Chr 12.22 Almost every day **new** men joined David's forces, so that
13. 7 brought out the Covenant Box and put it on a **new** cart.
2 Chr 20. 5 of Jerusalem gathered in the **new** courtyard of the Temple.
23.13 There she saw the **new** king at the temple entrance,
34.22 Huldah, a prophet who lived in the **newer** part of Jerusalem.
Ezra 9. 8 You have freed us from slavery and given us **new** life.
Esth 2. 8 the king had issued his **new** proclamation and many girls were
Job 10.17 you always plan some **new** attack.
32.19 to speak, I will burst like a wineskin full of **new** wine.
Ps 19. 7 it gives **new** strength.
23. 3 He gives me **new** strength.
33. 3 Sing a **new** song to him, play the harp with skill, and
40. 3 taught me to sing a **new** song, a song of praise to
51.10 me, O God, and put a **new** and loyal spirit in me.
81. 3 festival, when the moon is **new** and when the moon is full.
96. 1 Sing a **new** song to the Lord!
98. 1 Sing a **new** song to the Lord;
104.30 you give **new** life to the earth.
119.40 give me **new** life, for you are righteous.
144. 9 I will sing you a **new** song, O God;
149. 1 Sing a **new** song to the Lord;
Prov 19. 4 Rich people are always finding **new** friends, but the poor
23.29 has to try out some **new** drink, and I will show you
Ecc 1. 9 There is nothing **new** in the whole world.
1.10 "Look," they say, "here is something **new!"**
11. 5 does than you understand how **new** life begins in the womb of
Song 6.11 the valley, to see the **new** leaves on the vines and the
7.13 Darling, I have kept for you the old delights and the **new.**
Is 6.13 (The stump represents a **new** beginning for God's people.)
11. 1 but just as **new** branches sprout from a stump,
11. 1 so a **new** king will arise from among David's
11.10 day is coming when the **new** king from the royal line of
28.19 Each **new** message from God will bring new terror!
41.15 like a threshing-board, with spikes that are **new** and sharp.
42. 9 I will tell you of **new** things even before they begin to
42.10 Sing a **new** song to the Lord;
43.19 Watch for the **new** thing I am going to do.
48. 6 I will tell you of **new** things to come, events that I
60. 3 to your light, And kings to the dawning of your **new** day.
62. 2 will be called by a **new** name, A name given by the
62. 4 Your **new** name will be "God Is Pleased with Her."
65.15 But I will give a **new** name to those who obey me.
65.17 The Lord says, "I am making a **new** earth and new heavens.
65.18 The **new** Jerusalem I make will be full of joy, and her
66.22 the new earth and the **new** heavens will endure by my power,
Jer 8.10 will give their fields to **new** owners and their wives to
31.22 I have created something **new** and different, as different as
31.31 when I will make a **new covenant** with the people of Israel
31.33 The **new covenant** that I will make with the people of
46.17 the king of Egypt a **new** name— 'Noisy Braggart Who Missed
Ezek 11.19 I will give them a **new** heart and a new mind.
18.31 have been doing, and get yourselves **new** minds and hearts.
36.26 I will give you a **new** heart and a new mind.
39. 2 will turn him in a **new** direction and lead him out of
40. 1 the tenth day of the **new** year, which was the twenty-fifth
Dan 1. 7 The chief official gave them **new** names:
8. 3 horns, one of which was longer and **newer** than the other.
Hos 4.11 says, "Wine, both old and **new,** is robbing my people of
10.12 I said, 'Plough **new** ground for yourselves, plant righteousness,
14. 6 They will be alive with **new** growth, and beautiful like olive-trees.
Joel 1. 5 the grapes for making **new** wine have been destroyed.
2.16 Even **newly** married couples must leave their room and come.
Mic 4. 7 but I will make a **new** beginning with those who are left,
Zeph 1.10 will hear wailing in the **newer** part of the city and a
3.17 in you, and in his love he will give you **new life.**
Hag 2. 9 The **new** Temple will be more splendid than the old one, and
Zech 3. 4 away your sin and will give you **new** clothes to wear."
3. 5 and then they put the **new** clothes on him while the angel
Mt 9.16 coat with a piece of **new** cloth,
9.16 for the **new** patch will shrink and make an
9.17 Nor does anyone pour **new** wine into used wineskins,
9.17 Instead, **new** wine is poured into fresh wineskins, and both will
13.52 of a house who takes **new** and old things out of his
19.28 his glorious throne in the **New Age,** then you twelve
26.29 the day I drink the **new** wine with you in my Father's
27.59 wrapped it in a **new** linen sheet, [60]and placed it in
Mk 1.27 Is it some kind of **new** teaching?
2.21 one uses a piece of **new** cloth to patch up
2.21 an old coat, because the **new** patch will shrink and tear off
2.22 Nor does anyone pour **new** wine into used wineskins,
2.22 Instead, **new** wine must be poured into fresh wineskins."
14.25 the day I drink the **new** wine in the Kingdom of God."

Lk 5.36 tears a piece off a **new** coat to patch up an old
5.36 he will have torn the **new** coat,
5.36 and the piece of **new** cloth will not match the old.
5.37 Nor does anyone pour **new** wine into used wineskins,
5.37 because the **new** wine will burst the skins,
5.38 Instead, **new** wine must be poured into fresh wineskins!
5.39 And no one wants **new** wine after drinking old wine.
22.20 saying, "This cup is God's **new covenant** sealed with my blood,
Jn 13.34 And now I give you a **new** commandment:
19.41 in it there was a **new** tomb where no one had ever
Acts 3.21 all things to be made **new**, as God announced through his holy
5.20 the Temple, and tell the people all about this **new life."**
17.19 like to know what this **new** teaching is that you are talking
17.21 spend all their time telling and hearing the latest **new** thing.)
Rom 6. 4 power of the Father, so also we might live a **new life.**
7. 6 of a written law, but in the **new** way of the Spirit.
1 Cor 4.17 which I follow in the **new life** in union with Christ Jesus
5. 7 you will be like a **new** batch of dough without any yeast,
11.25 "This cup is God's **new covenant**, sealed with my blood.
2 Cor 3. 6 us capable of serving the **new covenant**, which consists not
5.17 When anyone is joined to Christ, he is a **new** being;
5.17 the old is gone, the **new** has come.
Gal 2. 6 appearances—those leaders, I say, made no **new** suggestions to me.
6.15 what does matter is being a **new** creature.
Eph 2.15 of the two races one **new** people in union with himself,
4.23 minds must be made completely **new**, [24]and you must put on
4.24 you must put on the **new** self, which is created in God's
Col 3.10 old self with its habits [10]and have put on the **new** self.
3.10 This is the **new** being which God, its Creator, is constantly
Tit 3. 5 Spirit, who gives us new birth and **new life** by washing us.
Heb 2. 5 angels as rulers over the **new** world to come—the world of
8. 8 I will draw up a **new covenant** with the people of Israel
8.13 By speaking of a **new covenant**, God has made the first
9.10 only until the time when God will establish the **new** order.
9.15 the one who arranges a **new covenant**, so that those who have
10.20 He opened for us a **new** way, a living way, through the
12.24 Jesus, who arranged the **new covenant**, and to the sprinkled blood
1 Pet 1. 3 great mercy he gave us **new life** by raising Jesus Christ from
2 Pet 3.13 **new** heavens and a new earth, where righteousness will be at home.
1 Jn 2. 7 dear friends, this command I am writing to you is not **new;**
2. 8 now writing to you is **new**, because its truth is seen in
2 Jn 5 This is no **new** command I am writing to you;
Rev 2.17 on which is written a **new** name that no one knows except
3.12 city of my God, the **new** Jerusalem, which will come down out
3.12 I will also write on him my **new** name.
5. 9 They sang a **new** song:
14. 3 they were singing a **new** song, which only they could learn.
21. 1 Then I saw a **new** heaven and a new earth.
21. 2 saw the Holy City, the **new** Jerusalem, coming down out of
21. 5 sits on the throne said, "And now I make all things **new!"**

NEW GATE

Jer 26.10 palace to the Temple and took their places at the **New Gate.**
36.10 court near the entrance of the **New Gate** of the Temple.

NEW MOON FESTIVAL
see also **MOON**

Num 10.10 joyful occasions—at your **New Moon Festivals** and your other
1 Sam 20. 5 "Tomorrow is the **New Moon Festival,"** David replied,
20.18 "Since tomorrow is the **New Moon Festival**, your absence will
20.24 At the **New Moon Festival**, King Saul came to the meal [25]and
20.27 after the **New Moon Festival**, David's place was still empty,
20.34 nothing that day—the second day of the **New Moon Festival.**
2 Kgs 4.23 "It's neither a Sabbath nor a **New Moon Festival."**
1 Chr 23.31 on the Sabbath, the **New Moon Festival**, and other festivals.
2 Chr 2. 4 well as on Sabbaths, **New Moon Festivals**, and other holy days
8.13 Sabbaths, **New Moon Festivals**, and the three annual
31. 3 the Sabbath, at the **New Moon Festival**, and at the other
Ezra 3. 5 be offered at the **New Moon Festival** and at all the other
Neh 10.33 for Sabbaths, **New Moon Festivals**, and other festivals,
Is 1.13 I cannot stand your **New Moon Festivals**, your Sabbaths, and
1.14 I hate your **New Moon Festivals** and holy days;
66.23 On every **New Moon Festival** and every Sabbath, people of
Ezek 45.17 of Israel at the **New Moon Festivals**, the Sabbaths, and the
46. 1 to be opened on the Sabbath and at the **New Moon Festival.**
46. 3 Each Sabbath and each **New Moon Festival** all the people are
46. 6 At the **New Moon Festival** he will offer a young bull, six
Col 2.16 or about holy days or the **New Moon Festival** or the Sabbath.

NEW-BORN

Ex 1.22 "Take every **new-born** Hebrew boy and throw him into the Nile,
Deut 28.56 secretly eat her **newborn** child and the afterbirth as well.
Jer 14. 5 deer abandons her **new-born** fawn because there is no grass.
1 Pet 2. 2 like **new-born babies**, always thirsty for the pure spiritual milk,

NEWS
see also **GOOD NEWS**

Gen 29.13 and when he heard the **news** about his nephew Jacob, he
45. 2 Egyptians heard it, and the **news** was taken to the king's palace.
45.16 When the **news** reached the palace that Joseph's brothers had come,
Josh 11. 1 When the **news** of Israel's victories reached King Jabin of Hazor,
1 Sam 4.13 The man spread the **news** throughout the town, and everyone
4.14 The man hurried to Eli to tell him the **news.**
11. 4 they told the **news**, the people started crying in despair.
1 Sam 31. 9 Philistia to tell the good **news** to their idols and to their
2 Sam 1.13 man who had brought him the **news**, "Where are you from?"
3.28 When David heard the **news**, he said, "The Lord knows
4. 4 When the **news** about their death came from the city of Jezreel,
4.10 told me of Saul's death thought he was bringing good **news.**
4.10 That was the reward I gave him for his good **news!**
12.18 and David's officials were afraid to tell him the **news.**
13.33 So don't believe the **news** that all your sons are dead;
15.28 crossings in the wilderness until I receive **news** from you."
18.19 the king with the good **news** that the Lord has saved him
18.20 "No," Joab said, "today you will not take any good **news.**
18.22 please let me take the **news** also."
18.25 the king said, "If he is alone, he is bringing good **news."**
18.26 The king answered, "This one also is bringing good **news."**
18.27 man," the king said, "and he is bringing good **news."**
18.31 and said to the king, "I have good **news** for Your Majesty!
19.11 The **news** of what the Israelites were saying reached King David.
1 Kgs 1.42 "You're a good man—you must be bringing good **news."**
2.29 When the **news** reached King Solomon that Joab had fled to
11.21 When the **news** reached Hadad in Egypt that David had
12. 2 from King Solomon, heard this **news**, he returned from Egypt.
14. 6 I have bad **news** for you.
2 Kgs 7. 9 We have good **news** and we shouldn't keep it to ourselves.
7.11 The guards announced the **news**, and it was reported in the palace.
1 Chr 10. 9 Philistia to tell the good **news** to their idols and to their
16.23 Proclaim every day the good **news** that he has saved us.
2 Chr 10. 2 to escape from King Solomon, heard this **news**, he returned home.
Esth 3.15 city of Susa, and runners carried the **news** to the provinces.
Ps 40. 9 your people, Lord, I told the good **news** that you save us.
40.10 I have not kept the **news** of salvation to myself;
41. 6 they gather bad **news** about me and then go out and tell
68.11 The Lord gave the command, and many women carried the **news:**
96. 2 Proclaim every day the good **news** that he has saved us.
112. 7 He is not afraid of receiving bad **news;**
Prov 15.30 Smiling faces make you happy, and good **news** makes you feel better.
25.25 Finally, hearing good **news** from a distant land is like a
Is 12. 5 Let the whole world hear the **news.**
21. 9 The sentry gives the **news**, "Babylon has fallen!
21.10 announced to you the good **news** that I have heard from the
23. 1 As your ships return from Cyprus, you learn the **news.**
40. 9 Jerusalem, go up on a high mountain and proclaim the good **news!**
40. 9 announce the good **news!**
41.27 I, the Lord, was the first to tell Zion the **news;**
48.20 Shout the **news** gladly;
52. 7 the mountains, bringing good **news**, the news of peace!
60. 6 People will tell the good **news** of what the Lord has done!
61. 1 sent me To bring good **news** to the poor, To heal the
Jer 4.15 of Dan and from the hills of Ephraim announce the bad **news.**
6.24 "We have heard the **news,"** say the people of Jerusalem,
10.22 **News** has come!
20.15 my father glad when he brought him the **news**, "It's a boy!
49.23 Arpad are worried and troubled because they have heard bad **news.**
50. 2 "Tell the **news** to the nations!
50. 2 Give the signal and announce the **news!**
50.43 The king of Babylonia hears the **news**, and his hands hang limp.
Ezek 7.26 another, and a steady stream of bad **news** will pour in.
21. 7 tell them it is because of the **news** that is coming.
32. 9 troubled when I spread the **news** of your destruction through
Dan 11.44 Then **news** that comes from the east and the north will
Nah 1.15 Look, a messenger is coming over the mountains with good **news!**
3.19 All those who hear the **news** of your destruction clap their
Mt 4.24 The **news** about him spread through the whole country of Syria,
9.26 The **news** about this spread all over that part of the country.
9.31 they left and spread the **news** about Jesus all over that part
14.13 When Jesus heard the **news** about John, he left there in a
24. 6 noise of battles close by and the **news** of battles far away;
Mk 1.28 And so the **news** about Jesus spread quickly everywhere in the
1.45 the man went away and began to spread the **news** everywhere.
2. 1 back to Capernaum, and the **news** spread that he was at home.
5.14 ran away and spread the **news** in the town and among the
13. 7 the noise of battles close by and **news** of battles far away.
Lk 1.19 sent me to speak to you and tell you this good **news.**
1.65 filled with fear, and the **news** about these things spread through
2.10 I am here with good **news** for you, which will bring great
4.14 The **news** about him spread throughout all that territory.
4.18 because he has chosen me to bring good **news** to the poor.
5.15 But the **news** about Jesus spread all the more widely,
7.17 This **news** about Jesus went out through all the country and
8.34 ran off and spread the **news** in the town and among the
Jn 4.51 met him with the **news**, "Your boy is going to live!"
11. 6 Yet when he received the **news** that Lazarus was ill, he
Acts 8.12 Philip's message about the good **news** of the Kingdom of God
9.42 The **news** about this spread all over Joppa, and many people
11.22 **news** about this reached the church in Jerusalem, so they sent
15. 3 this **news** brought great joy to all the believers.
28.21 come from there with any **news** or anything bad to say about
Rom 10.15 "How wonderful is the coming of messengers who bring good **news!"**
Eph 6.21 will give you all the **news** about me, so that you may
Phil 2.19 you soon, so that I may be encouraged by **news** about you.
Col 4. 7 in the Lord's work, will give you all the **news** about me.
1 Thes 1. 8 Macedonia and Achaia, but the **news** about your faith in God
3. 6 has brought us the welcome **news** about your faith and love.

NEXT

Mk 1.21 of Capernaum, and on the **next** Sabbath Jesus went to the
Lk 13. 9 Then if the tree bears figs **next** year, so much the better;
Jn 13.23 the one whom Jesus loved, was sitting **next** to Jesus.

Acts 11. 5 by its four corners from heaven, and it stopped **next** to me.
13.42 them to come back the **next** Sabbath and tell them more about
13.44 The **next** Sabbath nearly everyone in the town came to
18. 7 his house was **next** to the synagogue.
1 Cor 16. 6 me to continue my journey, wherever it is I shall go **next.**
2 Cor 12.21 I am afraid that the **next** time I come my God will
13. 2 the **next** time I come nobody will escape punishment.
Eph 1.21 to all titles of authority in this world and in the **next.**

NEXT-DOOR

Ex 12. 4 animal, he and his **next-door** neighbour may share an animal,

NICE

1 Sam 17.42 scorn for him because he was just a **nice,** good-looking boy.
Is 44.16 He warms himself and says, "How **nice** and warm!
1 Cor 12.23 body which don't look very **nice** are treated with special modesty,

NICKNAMED see NAME (1)

NIGHT

[DAY AND NIGHT, OVERNIGHT]

Gen 1. 5 and he named the light "Day" and the darkness **"Night".**
1.14 sky to separate day from **night** and to show the time when
1.16 rule over the day and the moon to rule over the **night;**
1.18 the day and the **night,** and to separate light from darkness.
7. 4 fall for forty days and **nights,** in order to destroy all the
7.12 and rain fell on the earth for forty days and **nights.**
8.22 be cold and heat, summer and winter, day and **night."**
14.15 into groups, attacked the enemy by **night,** and defeated them.
19. 2 You can wash your feet and stay the **night.**
19. 2 "No, we will spend the **night** here in the city square."
19.33 That **night** they gave him wine to drink, and the elder
19.34 daughter said to her sister, "I slept with him last **night;**
19.35 So that **night** they made him drunk, and the younger
20. 3 One **night** God appeared to him in a dream and said:
24.23 in his house for my men and me to spend the **night?"**
24.54 the men with him ate and drank, and spent the **night** there.
26.24 That **night** the Lord appeared to him and said, "I am the
29.23 But that **night,** instead of Rachel, he took Leah to Jacob,
30.16 So he had intercourse with her that **night.**
31.24 In a dream that **night** God came to Laban and said to
31.29 do you harm, but last **night** the God of your father warned
31.39 anything that was stolen during the day or during the **night.**
31.40 from the heat during the day and from the cold at **night.**
31.42 work I have done, and last **night** he gave his judgement."
31.54 After they had eaten, they spent the **night** on the mountain.
32.13 After spending the **night** there, Jacob chose from
32.21 the gifts on ahead of him and spent that **night** in camp.
32.22 That same **night** Jacob got up, took his two wives, his
37. 5 One **night** Joseph had a dream, and when he told his
40. 5 One **night** there in prison the wine steward and the chief
41.11 One **night** each of us had a dream, and the dreams had
42.27 place where they spent the **night,** one of them opened his
46. 2 spoke to him in a vision at **night** and called, "Jacob,
Ex 10.13 to blow on the land all that day and all that **night.**
12. 8 That **night** the meat is to be roasted, and eaten with
12.12 "On that **night** I will go through the land of Egypt,
12.30 That **night,** the king, his officials, and all the other
12.31 That same **night** the king sent for Moses and Aaron and said,
12.42 It was a **night** when the Lord kept watch to bring them
12.42 this same **night** is dedicated to the Lord for all time
12.42 as a **night** when the Israelites must keep watch.
13.21 the way, and during the **night** he went in front of them
13.21 to give them light, so that they could travel **night** and day.
13.22 the people during the day, and the pillar of fire at **night.**
14.20 and so the armies could not come near each other all **night.**
14.21 It blew all **night** and turned the sea into dry land.
18.13 the people, and he was kept busy from morning till **night.**
18.14 standing here from morning till **night** to consult you?"
22. 2 breaking into a house at **night** and is killed, the one who
24.18 There he stayed for forty days and **nights.**
34.28 the Lord forty days and **nights,** eating and drinking nothing.
40.38 the day and a fire burning above it during the **night.**
Lev 6. 9 left on the altar all **night** long, and the fire is to
8.35 of the Tent day and **night** for seven days, doing what the
19.13 the wages of someone you have hired, not even for one **night.**
Num 9.15 At **night** the cloud looked like fire.
11. 8 It fell on the camp at **night** along with the dew.
11.32 So all that day, all **night,** and all the next day, the
14. 1 All **night** long the people cried out in distress.
14.14 pillar of cloud by day and a pillar of fire by **night.**
22. 8 said to them, "Spend the **night** here, and tomorrow I will
22.19 But please stay the **night,** as the others did, so that I
22.20 That **night** God came to Balaam and said, "If these men
Deut 1.33 a pillar of fire by **night** and in a pillar of cloud
9. 9 stayed there forty days and **nights** and did not eat or drink
9.11 after those forty days and **nights** the Lord gave me the two
9.18 presence for forty days and **nights** and did not eat or drink
9.25 presence those forty days and **nights,** because I knew that he
10.10 the mountain forty days and **nights,** as I did the first time.
16. 1 it was on a **night** in that month that he rescued you
16. 4 the evening of the first day must be eaten that same **night.**
21.23 is hung on a post, [23] it is not to remain there **overnight.**
23.10 a wet dream during the **night,** he is to go outside the
24.12 If he is a poor man, do not keep it **overnight;**
28.66 Day and **night** you will be filled with terror, and you will
Josh 1. 8 Study it day and **night,** and make sure that you obey
Josh 2. 1 they went to spend the **night** in the house of a prostitute
2. 2 some Israelites had come that **night** to spy out the country,
2. 8 spies settled down for the **night,** Rahab went up on the roof
6.11 Then they came back to camp and spent the **night** there.
8. 3 best troops and sent them out at **night** [4] with these orders:
8. 9 Joshua spent the **night** in camp.
8.13 Joshua spent the **night** in the valley.
10. 9 All **night** Joshua and his army marched from Gilgal to Gibeon,
Judg 6.25 That **night** the Lord told Gideon, "Take your father's
6.27 town to do it by day, so he did it at **night.**
6.40 That **night** God did that very thing.
7. 9 That **night** the Lord commanded Gideon, "Get up and attack
9.32 and your men should move by **night** and hide in the fields.
9.34 men made their move at **night** and hid outside Shechem in four
16. 2 place and waited for him all **night** long at the city gate.
16. 2 They were quiet all **night,** thinking to themselves, "We'll wait
19. 4 The couple had their meals and spent the **nights** there.
19. 6 to him, "Please spend the **night** here and enjoy yourself."
19. 7 father urged him to stay, so he spent another **night** there.
19. 9 you might as well stay all **night.**
19.10 not want to spend another **night** there, so he and his
19.10 we stop and spend the **night** here in this Jebusite city?"
19.12 a little farther and spend the **night** at Gibeah or Ramah."
19.15 They turned off the road to go and spend the **night** there.
19.15 square, but no one offered to take them home for the **night.**
19.18 put us up for the **night,** [19] even though we have fodder and
19.20 you don't have to spend the **night** in the square."
19.25 abused her all **night** long and didn't stop until morning.
20. 4 to Gibeah in the territory of Benjamin to spend the **night.**
20. 5 Gibeah came to attack me and surrounded the house at **night.**
Ruth 3. 8 During the **night** he woke up suddenly, turned over, and was
3.13 here the rest of the **night,** and in the morning we will
1 Sam 3. 2 One **night** Eli, who was now almost blind, was sleeping in
11.11 That **night** Saul divided his men into three groups, and
14.34 So that **night** they all brought their cattle and slaughtered them
14.36 the Philistines in the **night,** plunder them until dawn,
15.11 Samuel was angry, and all **night** long he pleaded with the Lord.
15.16 I will tell you what the Lord said to me last **night."**
19.11 That same **night** Saul sent some men to watch David's
19.24 Samuel's presence, and lay naked all that day and all that **night.**
25.16 They protected us day and **night** the whole time we were
26. 7 So that **night** David and Abishai entered Saul's camp and
28.20 because he had not eaten anything all day and all **night.**
28.25 And they left that same **night.**
31.12 the bravest men started out and marched all **night** to Beth Shan.
2 Sam 2.29 Abner and his men marched through the Jordan Valley all that **night;**
2.32 Then they marched all **night** and at dawn arrived back at Hebron.
4. 7 with them, and walked all **night** through the Jordan Valley.
7. 4 But that **night** the Lord said to Nathan, [5] "Go and tell my
11.13 But again that **night** Uriah did not go home;
12.16 and every **night** he went into his room
12.16 and spent the **night** lying on the floor.
17. 8 experienced soldier and does not stay with his men at **night.**
17.16 David not to spend the **night** at the river crossings in the
21.10 from the corpses, and at **night** she would protect them from
1 Kgs 3. 5 That **night** the Lord appeared to him in a dream and asked
3.19 Then one **night** she accidentally rolled over on her baby
3.20 She got up during the **night,** took my son from my side
8.29 over this Temple day and **night,** this place where you have
19. 9 There he went into a cave to spend the **night.**
2 Kgs 6.14 They reached the town at **night** and surrounded it.
7.12 It was still **night,** but the king got out of bed and
8.21 During the **night** he and his chariot commanders managed to
19.35 That **night** an angel of the Lord went to the Assyrian
25. 4 all the soldiers escaped during the **night.**
1 Chr 9.33 from other duties, because they were on call day and **night.**
17. 3 But that **night** God said to Nathan, [4] "Go and tell my
2 Chr 1. 7 That **night** God appeared to Solomon and asked, "What
6.20 Watch over this Temple day and **night.**
7.12 his plans for them, [12] the Lord appeared to him at **night.**
21. 9 surrounded them, but during the **night** they managed to break
35.14 priests were kept busy until **night,** burning the animals that
Ezra 10. 6 of Eliashib, and spent the **night** there grieving over the
Neh 1. 6 as I pray day and **night** for your servants, the people of
2.12 in the middle of the **night** I got up and went out,
2.13 It was still **night** as I left the city through the Valley
4. 9 our God and kept men on guard against them day and **night.**
4.21 the stars came out at **night,** half of us worked on the
4.22 to stay in Jerusalem at **night,**
4.22 could guard the city at **night** as well as work
4.23 my clothes even at **night,** neither did any of my companions
6.10 Any **night** now they will come to kill you."
9.12 in day-time, and at **night** you lighted their way with fire.
9.19 or the fire that showed them the path by day and **night.**
13.20 kinds of goods spent Friday **night** outside the city walls.
Esth 4.16 Don't eat or drink anything for three days and **nights.**
6. 1 That same **night** the king could not get to sleep, so he
Job 2.13 him for seven days and **nights** without saying a word, because
3. 2 put a curse on the **night** when I was conceived!
3. 6 Blot that **night** out of the year, and never let it be
3. 7 make it a barren, joyless **night.**
3. 9 give that **night** no hope of dawn.
3.10 Curse that **night** for letting me be born, for exposing me
7. 3 **night** after night brings me grief.
7. 4 I toss all **night** and long for dawn.
9. 7 the sun from rising, and the stars from shining at **night.**
17.12 But my friends say **night** is daylight;
20. 8 a dream, like a vision at **night,** and never be seen again.
24. 7 At **night** they sleep with nothing to cover them, nothing to
24.14 and goes out to kill the poor, and at **night** he steals.

Job 24.16 At **night** thieves break into houses, but by day they hide
27.20 a wind in the **night** will blow them away;
30. 3 would gnaw dry roots— at **night,** in wild, desolate places.
30.17 At **night** my bones all ache;
33.15 At **night** when men are asleep, God speaks in dreams and visions.
34.20 A man may suddenly die at **night.**
34.25 what they do he overthrows them and crushes them by **night.**
36.20 Don't wish for **night** to come, the time when nations will perish.
39. 9 Is he willing to spend the **night** in your stable?
Ps 1. 2 the Law of the Lord, and they study it day and **night.**
3. 5 down and sleep, and all **night** long the Lord protects me.
6. 6 every **night** my bed is damp from my weeping;
13. 2 How long will sorrow fill my heart day and **night?**
16. 7 he guides me, and in the **night** my conscience warns me.
17. 3 You have come to me at **night;**
19. 2 each **night** repeats it to the next.
22. 2 I call at **night,** but get no rest.
30. 5 Tears may flow in the **night,** but joy comes in the morning.
32. 4 Day and **night** you punished me, Lord;
42. 3 Day and **night** I cry, and tears are my only food;
42. 8 may have a song at **night,** a prayer to the God of
55.10 surrounding it day and **night,** filling it with crime and trouble.
55.17 Morning, noon, and **night** my complaints and groans go up to him,
63. 6 all **night** long I think of you, [7]because you have always
74.16 You created the day and the **night;**
77. 2 all **night** long I lift my hands in prayer, but I cannot
77. 4 He keeps me awake all **night;**
77. 6 I spend the **night** in deep thought;
78.14 with a cloud and all **night** long with the light of a
88. 1 I cry out all day, and at **night** I come before you.
90. 4 yesterday, already gone, like a short hour in the **night.**
91. 5 not fear any dangers at **night** or sudden attacks during the
92. 2 morning and your faithfulness every **night,** [3]with the music
104.20 You made the **night,** and in the darkness all the wild
105.39 over his people and a fire at **night** to give them light.
119.55 In the **night** I remember you, Lord, and I think about
119.62 In the middle of the **night** I wake up to praise you
119.148 All **night** long I lie awake, to meditate on your instructions.
121. 6 not hurt you during the day, nor the moon during the **night.**
134. 1 all his servants, all who serve in his Temple at **night.**
136. 9 the moon and the stars to rule over the **night;**
139.11 round me to turn into **night,** [12]but even darkness is not
139.12 dark for you, and the **night** is as bright as the day.
149. 5 God's people rejoice in their triumph and sing joyfully all **night** long.
Prov 3.24 you go to bed, and you will sleep soundly through the **night.**
4.19 The road of the wicked, however, is dark as **night.**
6.22 travel, protect you at **night,** and advise you during the day.
7.18 Let's make love all **night** long.
31.18 of everything she makes, and works late into the **night.**
Ecc 2.23 Even at **night** your mind can't rest.
5.12 to eat, but at least he can get a good **night's** sleep.
8.16 that you could stay awake **night** and day [17]and never be
10.16 its king is a youth and its leaders feast all **night** long.
Song 3. 1 Asleep on my bed, **night** after night I dreamt of the one
3. 8 is armed with a sword, on guard against a **night** attack.
7.11 out to the countryside and spend the **night** in the villages.
Is 4. 5 cloud in the daytime and smoke and a bright flame at **night.**
10.29 They have crossed the pass and are spending the **night** at Geba!
15. 1 are destroyed in a single **night,** and silence covers the land
18. 4 dew forms in the warm **nights** of harvest time, as serenely as
21. 8 "Sir, I have been standing guard at my post day and **night."**
21.11 to me from Edom, "Sentry, how soon will the **night** be over?
21.12 I answer, "Morning is coming, but **night** will come again.
26. 9 At **night** I long for you with all my heart;
27. 3 I guard it **night** and day so that no one will harm
28.19 You will have to bear it day and **night.**
29. 7 vanish like a dream, like something imagined in the **night.**
30.29 and sing as you do on the **night** of a sacred festival.
34.10 It will burn day and **night,** and smoke will rise from it
34.14 The **night** monster will come there looking for a place to rest.
38.13 All **night** I cried out with pain, As if a lion were
59.10 noon, as if it were **night,** as if we were in the
60.11 Day and **night** your gates will be open, So that the kings
60.19 your light by day Or the moon be your light by **night;**
62. 1 is saved, And her victory shines like a torch in the **night.**
62. 6 They must never be silent day or **night.**
65. 4 At **night** they go to caves and tombs to consult the spirits
Jer 6. 5 We'll attack by **night;**
9. 1 I could cry day and **night** for my people who have been
14. 8 in our land, like a traveller who stays for only one **night?**
14.17 flow with tears day and **night,** may I never stop weeping, for
16.13 serve other gods day and **night,** and I will show you no
31.35 light by day, the moon and the stars to shine at **night.**
33.20 the day and with the **night,** so that they always come at
33.25 a covenant with day and **night,** and I have made the laws
36.30 to the sun during the day and to the frost at **night.**
39. 4 they tried to escape from the city during the **night.**
49. 9 when robbers come at **night,** they take only what they want.
52. 7 all the soldiers escaped during the **night.**
Lam 1. 2 All **night** long she cries;
2.18 Let your tears flow like rivers **night** and day;
2.19 All through the **night** get up again and again to cry out
3.63 From morning till **night** they jeer at me.
Ezek 12. 3 just as a refugee would, and start out before **nightfall.**
Dan 2.19 Then that same **night** the mystery was revealed to Daniel
5. 1 One **night** King Belshazzar invited a thousand noblemen
5.30 That same **night** Belshazzar, the king of Babylonia, was
6.18 palace and spent a sleepless **night,** without food or any form
7. 1 Babylonia, I had a dream and saw a vision in the **night.**
7. 2 down, and this is the record [2]of what I saw that **night:**
Dan 7.13 During this vision in the **night,** I saw what looked like
Hos 4. 5 **Night** and day you blunder on, and the prophets do no
7. 6 All **night** their anger smouldered, and in the morning it
12. 1 Israel do from morning to **night** is useless and destructive.
Joel 1.13 Go into the Temple and mourn all **night!**
Amos 4.13 he changes day into **night.**
5. 8 He turns darkness into daylight, and day into **night.**
Obad 5 "When thieves come at **night,** they take only what they want.
Jon 1.17 and he was inside the fish for three days and **nights.**
4.10 "This plant grew up in one **night** and disappeared the next;
Zech 1. 7 Shebat), the Lord gave me a message in a vision at **night.**
14. 7 There will always be daylight, even at **night-time.**
Mt 2.14 and left during the **night** for Egypt, [15]where he stayed until
4. 2 After spending forty days and **nights** without food, Jesus was hungry.
12.40 that Jonah spent three days and **nights** in the big fish, so
12.40 of Man spend three days and **nights** in the depths of the
13.25 One **night,** when everyone was asleep, an enemy came and sowed
21.17 went out of the city to Bethany, where he spent the **night.**
26.31 said to them, "This very **night** all of you will run away
27.19 because in a dream last **night** I suffered much on account of
28.13 his disciples came during the **night** and stole his body while
Mk 4.27 He sleeps at **night,** is up and about during the day,
5. 5 **Day and night** he wandered among the tombs and through the hills,
Lk 2. 8 country who were spending the **night** in the fields, taking
2.36 **day and night** she worshipped God, fasting and praying.
5. 5 answered, "we worked hard all **night** long and caught nothing.
6.12 hill to pray and spent the whole **night** there praying to God.
12.20 This very **night** you will have to give up your life;
17.34 On that **night,** I tell you, there will be two people
18. 7 his own people who cry to him **day and night** for help?
21.37 would go out and spend the **night** on the Mount of Olives.
Jn 3. 2 One **night** he went to Jesus and said to him, "Rabbi, we
6.17 **Night** came on, and Jesus still had not come to them.
9. 4 **night** is coming when no one can work.
11.10 if he walks during the **night** he stumbles, because he has no
13.30 It was **night.**
19.39 gone to see Jesus at **night,** went with Joseph, taking with
21. 3 a boat, but all that **night** they did not catch a thing.
Acts 5.19 But that **night** an angel of the Lord opened the prison gates,
9.24 **Day and night** they watched the city gates in order to kill
9.25 But one **night** Saul's followers took him and let him down
10.23 the men in and persuaded them to spend the **night** there.
12. 6 The **night** before Herod was going to bring him out to the
16. 9 That **night** Paul had a vision in which he saw a Macedonian
16.33 that very hour of the **night** the jailer took them and washed
17.10 As soon as **night** came, the believers sent Paul and Silas
18. 9 One **night** Paul had a vision in which the Lord said to
20.31 that with many tears, **day and night,** I taught every one of
23.11 That **night** the Lord stood by Paul and said, "Don't be afraid!
23.31 They got Paul and took him that **night** as far as Antipatris.
26. 7 people hope to receive, as they worship God **day and night.**
27.23 For last **night** an angel of the God to whom I belong
27.27 It was the fourteenth **night,** and we were being driven about
28.23 From morning till **night** he explained to them his message about
Rom 13.12 The **night** is nearly over, day is almost here.
1 Cor 11.23 the Lord Jesus, on the **night** he was betrayed, took a piece
1 Thes 2. 9 We worked **day and night** so that we would not be any
3.10 **Day and night** we ask him with all our heart to let
5. 2 Day of the Lord will come as a thief comes at **night.**
5. 5 We do not belong to the **night** or to the darkness.
5. 7 It is at **night** that people sleep;
5. 7 it is at **night** that they get drunk.
2 Thes 3. 8 we kept working **day and night** so as not to be an
1 Tim 5. 5 continues to pray and ask him for his help **night and day.**
2 Tim 1. 3 him as I remember you always in my prayers **night and day.**
Rev 4. 8 **Day and night** they never stop singing:
7.15 God's throne and serve him **day and night** in his temple.
8.12 during a third of the day and a third of the **night.**
12.10 and accused our brothers **day and night** has been thrown out
20.10 and they will be tormented **day and night** for ever and ever.
21.25 will never be closed, because there will be no **night** there.
22. 5 There shall be no more **night,** and they will not need lamps

NIGHTMARE

Job 4.13 Like a **nightmare** it disturbed my sleep.
7.14 you send me visions and **nightmares** [15]until I would

NILE

River that flows through Egypt into the Mediterranean Sea.

Gen 41. 1 was standing by the River **Nile,** [2]when seven cows, fat and
41.17 on the bank of the **Nile,** [18]when seven cows, fat and sleek,
Ex 1.22 and throw him into the **Nile,** but let all the girls live."
4. 9 take some water from the **Nile** and pour it on the ground.
7.15 meet him in the morning when he goes down to the **Nile.**
8. 3 The **Nile** will be so full of frogs that they will leave
8. 9 frogs, and there will be none left except in the **Nile."**
8.11 the frogs, and there will be none left except in the **Nile."**
17. 5 Take along the stick with which you struck the **Nile.**
2 Kgs 19.24 that the feet of your soldiers tramped the River **Nile** dry.
Job 38.36 tells the ibis when the **Nile** will flood, or who tells the
Is 7.18 the farthest branches of the **Nile,** and for the Assyrians to
18. 2 land ambassadors come down the **Nile** in boats made of reeds.
19. 5 will be low in the **Nile,** and the river will gradually dry
19. 7 along the banks of the **Nile** will dry up and be blown
19. 8 earns his living by fishing in the **Nile** will groan and cry;
37.25 that the feet of your soldiers tramped the River **Nile** dry.
Jer 2.18 will gain by going to Egypt to drink water from the **Nile?**

Jer 46. 7 that rises like the **Nile,** like a river flooding its banks?
46. 8 rising like the **Nile,** like a river flooding its banks.
Ezek 29. 3 You say that the **Nile** is yours and that you made it.
29. 4 you up out of the **Nile,** with all the fish sticking to
29. 9 "Because you said that the **Nile** is yours and you made it,
29.10 made it, [10]I am your enemy and the enemy of your **Nile.**
30.12 I will dry up the **Nile** and put Egypt under the power
Amos 8. 8 it will rise and fall like the River **Nile.**
9. 5 The whole world rises and falls like the River **Nile.**
Nah 3. 8 river to protect her like a wall—the **Nile** was her defence.
Zech 10.11 strike the waves, and the depths of the **Nile** will go dry.

NINE
[NINTH]

Gen 18.10 One of them said, "**Nine** months from now I will come back,
18.14 As I said, **nine** months from now I will return, and Sarah
Ex 27.16 is to be a curtain **9** metres long made of fine linen
38.18 It was **9** metres long and 2 metres high, like the curtains
Lev 23.32 From sunset on the **ninth** day of the month to sunset on
Num 29.26 On the fifth day offer **nine** young bulls, two rams, and
34.13 that the Lord has assigned to the **nine** and a half tribes.
Josh 13. 7 this land among the other **nine** tribes and half of the tribe
14. 2 Moses, the territories of the **nine** and a half tribes west of
15.44 **nine** cities, along with the towns round them.
15.54 **nine** cities, along with the towns round them.
21.16 **nine** cities from the tribes of Judah and Simeon.
2 Sam 24. 8 So after **nine** months and twenty days they returned to Jerusalem,
1 Kgs 6. 2 it was 27 metres long, **9** metres wide, and 13.5 metres high.
6. 3 was 4.5 metres deep and **9** metres wide, as wide as the
6.16 It was **nine** metres long and was partitioned off by cedar
6.20 This inner room was **nine** metres long,
6.20 **nine** metres wide, and nine metres high,
2 Kgs 17. 1 king of Israel, and he ruled in Samaria for **nine** years.
17. 6 siege, [6]which was the **ninth** year of the reign of Hoshea,
18.10 of Hezekiah's reign, and the **ninth** year of Hoshea's reign.
25. 1 of the tenth month of the **ninth** year of Zedekiah's reign.
25. 3 On the **ninth** day of the fourth month of that same year,
1 Chr 3. 6 He had **nine** other sons:
7. 8 Becher had **nine** sons:
27. 2 clan of Zerah, a part of the tribe of Judah) **Ninth** month:
2 Chr 3. 3 King Solomon built was twenty-seven metres long and **nine** metres wide.
3. 4 of the Temple, **nine** metres, and was fifty-four metres high.
3. 8 Most Holy Place, was **nine** metres long and nine metres wide,
3.11 room, stretching across the full width of about **nine** metres.
4. 1 bronze altar made, which was **nine** metres square and four and
17. 8 They were accompanied by **nine** Levites and two priests.
Ezra 8.16 I sent for **nine** of the leaders:
10. 9 the twentieth day of the **ninth** month, all the men living in
Jer 36. 9 In the **ninth** month of the fifth year that Jehoiakim was
39. 1 the tenth month of the **ninth** year that Zedekiah was king of
39. 2 On the **ninth** day of the fourth month of Zedekiah's
52. 4 of the tenth month of the **ninth** year of Zedekiah's reign.
52. 6 On the **ninth** day of the fourth month of that same year,
Ezek 24. 1 the tenth month of the **ninth** year of our exile, the Lord
Hag 2.10 the twenty-fourth day of the **ninth** month of the second year
2.18 the twenty-fourth day of the **ninth** month, the day that the
Zech 5. 2 it is **nine** metres long and four and a half metres wide."
7. 1 the fourth day of the **ninth** month (the month of Kislev), the
Mt 20. 3 again to the market-place at **nine** o'clock and saw some men
Mk 15.25 It was **nine** o'clock in the morning when they crucified him.
Lk 17.17 where are the other **nine?**
Acts 2.15 it is only **nine** o'clock in the morning.
23.23 hundred spearmen, and be ready to leave by **nine** o'clock tonight.
Rev 21.20 the eighth beryl, the **ninth** topaz, the tenth chalcedony,
also Num 7.12 1 Chr 24.7 1 Chr 25.9

NINEVEH
Chief city of the Assyrian empire.

Gen 10.11 and built the cities of **Nineveh,** Rehoboth Ir, Calah,
10.12 and Resen, which is between **Nineveh** and the great city of Calah.
2 Kgs 19.36 the Assyrian emperor Sennacherib withdrew and returned to **Nineveh.**
Is 37.37 the Assyrian emperor Sennacherib withdrew and returned to **Nineveh.**
Jon 1. 2 He said, "Go to **Nineveh,** that great city, and speak out
3. 2 He said, "Go to **Nineveh,** that great city, and proclaim to
3. 3 the Lord and went to **Nineveh,** a city so large that it
3. 4 he proclaimed, "In forty days **Nineveh** will be destroyed!"
3. 5 The people of **Nineveh** believed God's message.
3. 6 When the king of **Nineveh** heard about it, he got up from
3. 7 He sent out a proclamation to the people of **Nineveh:**
4. 5 in its shade, waiting to see what would happen to **Nineveh.**
4.11 more, then, should I have pity on **Nineveh,** that great city.
Nah 1. 1 This is a message about **Nineveh,** the account of a vision
1.11 From you, **Nineveh,** there came a man full of wicked schemes,
2. 1 **Nineveh,** you are under attack!
2. 8 Like water from a broken dam the people rush from **Nineveh!**
2.10 **Nineveh** is destroyed, deserted, desolate!
3. 4 **Nineveh** the whore is being punished.
3. 5 "I will punish you, **Nineveh!**
3. 7 They will say, '**Nineveh** lies in ruins!
3. 8 **Nineveh,** are you any better than Thebes, the capital of Egypt?
3.11 **Nineveh,** you too will fall into a drunken stupor!
Zeph 2.13 the city of **Nineveh** a deserted ruin, a waterless desert.
Mt 12.41 Judgement Day the people of **Nineveh** will stand up and accuse you,
Lk 11.30 sign for the people of **Nineveh,** so the Son of Man will
Lk 11.32 Judgement Day the people of **Nineveh** will stand up and accuse you,

NINTH see NINE

NISAN
First month of the Hebrew calendar, also called Abib.

Esth 3. 7 first month, the month of **Nisan,** Haman ordered the lots to

NO

Gen 4.15 But the Lord answered, **"No.**
17.19 But God said, **"No.**
19. 2 But they answered, **"No,** we will spend the night here in
19.18 But Lot answered, **"No,** please don't make us do that,
33.10 Jacob said, **"No,** please, if I have gained your favour,
42.10 **"No,** sir," they answered.
42.12 Joseph said to them, **"No!**
44.17 Joseph said, "Oh, **no!**
Ex 4.10 But Moses said, **"No,** Lord, don't send me.
4.13 But Moses answered, **"No,** Lord, please send someone else."
10.11 **No!**
Num 10.30 Hobab answered, **"No,** I am going back to my native land."
13.31 had gone with Caleb said, **"No,** we are not strong enough to
Deut 9. 4 **No,** the Lord is going to drive these people out for you
9. 6 **No,** you are a stubborn people.
30.14 **No,** it is here with you.
Josh 24.21 The people said to Joshua, **"No!**
Judg 4.20 if anyone comes and asks you if someone is here, say **no."**
11.27 **No,** I have not done you any wrong.
12. 5 If he said, **"No,"** [6]they would tell him to say "Shibboleth."
19.23 the old man went outside and said to them, **"No,** my friends!
Ruth 1.10 But they started crying [10]and said to her, **"No!**
1.13 **No,** my daughters, you know that's impossible.
1 Sam 1.15 **"No,** I'm not drunk, sir," she answered.
2.16 take what you want," the priest's servant would say, **"No!**
8.19 The people paid no attention to Samuel, but said **"No!**
12. 4 The people answered, **"No,** you have not cheated us or oppressed us;
16. 8 But Samuel said, **"No,** the Lord hasn't chosen him either."
16. 9 **"No,** the Lord hasn't chosen him either," Samuel said.
16.10 And Samuel said to him, **"No,** the Lord hasn't chosen any of
17.33 **"No,"** answered Saul.
2 Sam 13.25 **"No,** my son," the king answered.
18.20 **"No,"** Joab said, "today you will not take any good news.
24.24 But the king answered, **"No,** I will pay you for it.
1 Kgs 2.30 **"No,"** Joab answered.
3.22 But the other woman said, **"No!**
3.22 The first woman answered, **"No!**
2 Kgs 2.16 **"No,** you must not go," Elisha answered.
5.22 **"No,"** Gehazi answered.
18.27 **No,** I am also talking to the people who are sitting on
1 Chr 21.24 But the king answered, **"No,** I will pay you the full price.
Job 22. 5 **No,** it's because you have sinned so much;
23. 6 **No,** he would listen as I spoke.
27.12 But **no,** after all, you have seen for yourselves;
37.17 **No,** you can only suffer in the heat when the south wind
Ecc 1.10 But **no,** it has all happened before, long before we were born.
Is 36.12 **No,** I am also talking to the people who are sitting on
50. 1 **No,** you went away captive because of your sins;
Jer 2.25 But you say, **'No!**
6.15 **No,** they were not at all ashamed;
6.16 But they said, **"No,** we will not!"
7.19 **No,** they are hurting themselves and bringing shame on themselves.
8.12 **No,** you were not ashamed at all;
16.20 **No,** if he did, they would not really be gods."
18.12 They will answer, **'No,** why should we?
25.29 **No,** they will be punished, for I am going to send war
42.13 You must not say, **'No,** we will go and live in Egypt,
49.12 **No,** you must drink from the cup!
Ezek 4.14 But I replied, **"No,** Sovereign Lord!
8.17 **No,** they must come and do them here in the Temple itself
11.13 downwards on the ground and shouted, **"No,** Sovereign Lord!
16.47 **No,** in only a little while you were behaving worse than they
18.23 **"No,** I would rather see him repent and live.
28. 2 pretend to be a god, but, **no,** you are mortal, not divine.
33.17 **No,** it's their way that isn't right.
Amos 6.10 A voice will answer, **"No!"**
Mic 6. 8 **No,** the Lord has told us what is good.
Hag 2.12 When the question was asked, the priests answered, **"No."**
Zech 4. 5 **"No,** I don't, sir," I replied.
4.13 **"No,** I don't, sir," I answered.
Mt 5.37 Just say 'Yes' or **'No'**—anything else you say comes from
8. 8 "Oh **no,** sir," answered the officer.
10.34 **No,** I did not come to bring peace, but a sword.
12.28 **No,** it is not Beelzebul, but God's Spirit, who gives me
13.29 **'No,'** he answered, 'because as you gather the weeds you might
18.22 **"No,** not seven times," answered Jesus, "but seventy times
25. 9 **'No,** indeed,' the wise ones answered, 'there is not enough for
Mk 8.12 **No,** I tell you!
Lk 1.60 But his mother said, **"No!**
11.20 **No,** it is rather by means of God's power that I drive
12.51 **No,** not peace, but division.
Jn 1.21 **"No,** I am not," John answered.
7.12 **"No,"** others said, "he is misleading the people."
8.14 **"No,"** Jesus answered, "even though I do testify on my own
9. 9 Some said, "He is the one," but others said, **"No** he
18.17 **"No,** I am not," answered Peter.

Jn 18.25 **"No,** I am not," he said.
18.27 Again Peter said **"No"**—and at once a cock crowed.
18.36 **No,** my kingdom does not belong here!"
18.40 They answered him with a shout, **"No,** not him!
Rom 3.27 **No,** but that we believe.
2 Cor 1.17 ready to say "Yes, yes" and **"No,** no" at the same time?
1.18 my promise to you was not a "Yes" and a **"No."**
1.19 Silas, Timothy, and myself, is not one who is "Yes" and **"No."**
Jas 5.12 when you mean yes, and **"No"** when you mean no, and then
also Ex 10.26 Num 22.30 Josh 22.24 1 Sam 14.45 2 Sam 13.12 2 Sam 13.16 2 Kgs 3.13 2 Kgs 6.22 2 Kgs 9.12 Job 5.7 Job 7.11 Job 21.19 Ps 58.2 Ezek 18.13 Ezek 18.24 Lk 13.3 Lk 13.5 Jn 1.21 Rom 3.31 Rom 4.9 Gal 1.10 Gal 3.21

NO ONE

see also **NOBODY**

Gen 2. 5 sent any rain, and there was **no one** to cultivate the land;
13.16 you so many descendants that **no one** will be able to count
16.10 you so many descendants that **no one** will be able to count
20. 9 **No one** should ever do what you have done to me.
20.11 thought that there would be **no one** here who has reverence
40. 8 a dream, and there is **no one** here to explain what the
41. 8 told them his dreams, but **no one** could explain them to him.
41.15 him, "I have had a dream, and **no one** can explain it.
41.21 up the fat ones, [21] but **no one** would have known it, because
41.44 "I am the king—and **no one** in all Egypt shall so
45. 1 **No one** else was with him when Joseph told his brothers who
49. 9 **No one** dares disturb him.
Ex 2.12 and when he saw that **no one** was watching, he killed the
9.14 may know that there is **no one** like me in all the
10.23 not see each other, and **no one** left his house during that
16.19 Moses said to them, **"No one** is to keep any of it
20.10 On that day **no one** is to work—neither you, your children,
33.20 you see my face, because **no one** can see me and stay
34. 3 **No one** is to come up with you;
34. 3 **no one** is to be seen on any part of the mountain;
34.20 **"No one** is to appear before me without an offering.
34.24 you and extended your territory, **no one** will try to conquer
36. 6 command throughout the camp that **no one** was to make any
Lev 16.17 until he comes out, there must be **no one** in the Tent.
21.18 **no one** who is blind, lame, disfigured, or deformed;
21.19 **no one** with a crippled hand or foot;
21.20 **no one** who is a hunchback or a dwarf;
21.20 **no one** with any eye or skin disease;
22.10 **no one** else may eat them—not even someone staying with a
26.17 so terrified that you will run when **no one** is chasing you.
26.37 stumble over one another when **no one** is chasing you, and you
27.26 belongs to the Lord, so **no one** may dedicate it to him
27.28 **No one** may sell or buy back what he has unconditionally
Num 1.53 to guard it, so that **no one** may come near and cause
11.32 **no one** gathered less than a thousand kilogrammes.
16.40 warning to the Israelites that **no one** who was not a
24. 9 When it is sleeping, **no one** dares wake it.
Deut 5.14 On that day **no one** is to work—neither you, your children,
7.24 **No one** will be able to stop you;
9. 2 you have heard it said that **no one** can stand against them.
9.14 destroy them so that **no one** will remember them any longer.
11.25 as he has promised, and **no one** will be able to stop
13.11 they will be afraid, and **no one** will ever again do such
16. 4 For seven days **no one** in your land is to have any
17.13 it and be afraid, and **no one** else will dare to act
19.20 they will be afraid, and **no one** will ever again do such
22.27 although she cried for help, there was **no one** to help her.
23. 2 **"No one** born out of wedlock or any descendant of such a
25.19 Amalekites, so that **no one** will remember them any longer.
28.26 your bodies, and there will be **no one** to scare them off.
28.29 oppressed and robbed, and there will be **no one** to help you.
28.31 to your enemies, and there will be **no one** to help you.
28.68 your enemies as slaves, but **no one** will want to buy you."
29.19 Make sure that there is **no one** here today who hears
32.26 them completely, so that **no one** would remember them.
32.39 wound and I heal, and **no one** can oppose what I do.
32.42 I will spare **no one** who fights against me;
33.29 There is **no one** like you, a nation saved by the Lord.
34. 6 Bethpeor, but to this day **no one** knows the exact place of
Josh 1. 5 Joshua, **no one** will be able to defeat you as long as
6. 1 **No one** could enter or leave the city.
8.17 the city was left wide open, with **no one** to defend it.
8.22 **No one** got away, and no one lived through it
10.21 **No one** in the land dared even to speak against the Israelites.
10.28 **no one** was left alive.
10.30 They spared **no one,** but killed every person in it.
10.32 done at Libnah, they spared **no one,** but killed every person
10.37 **No one** in it was left alive.
10.40 He spared **no one;**
11.11 **no one** was left alive, and the city was burnt.
11.14 **no one** was left alive.
23. 9 out as you advanced and **no one** has ever been able to
Judg 18.27 There was **no one** to save them, because Laish was a long
19.15 down in the square, but **no one** offered to take them home
19.18 **No one** will put us up for the night, [19] even though we
21. 8 Mizpah, they found out that **no one** from Jabesh in Gilead had
21. 9 the roll call of the army **no one** from Jabesh had responded.
1 Sam 2. 2 **"No one** is holy like the Lord;
2.32 other people of Israel, but **no one** in your family will ever
10.24 There is **no one** else among us like him."
11. 3 If **no one** will help us, then we will surrender to you."
11.13 But Saul said, **"No one** will be put to death today, for
14.26 were full of honey, but **no one** ate any of it because
14.39 But **no one** said anything.
1 Sam 17.32 said to Saul, "Your Majesty, **no one** should be afraid of
22. 8 **No one** is concerned about me or tells me that David, one
26.12 **No one** saw it or knew what had happened or even woke
27.11 men and women, so that **no one** could go back to Gath
30.24 **No one** can agree with what you say!
2 Sam 14. 6 the fields, where there was **no one** to separate them, and one
14.25 There was **no one** in Israel as famous for his good looks
17.19 grain over it, so that **no one** would notice anything.
22.42 They look for help, but **no one** saves them;
23. 6 **no one** can touch them with bare hands.
1 Kgs 3.18 of us were there in the house—**no one** else was present.
8.46 against you—and there is **no one** who does not sin—and
14. 2 wife, "Disguise yourself so that **no one** will recognize you,
21.25 (There was **no one** else who had devoted himself so
22.31 thirty-two chariot commanders to attack **no one** else except
2 Kgs 6.12 One of them answered, **"No one** is, Your Majesty.
7. 5 the Syrian camp, but when they reached it, **no one** was there.
9.14 with me, make sure that **no one** slips out of Ramoth to
9.37 there like dung, so that **no one** will be able to identify
10.19 **No one** is excused;
14.26 there was **no one** at all to help them.
23.10 Valley of Hinnom, so that **no one** could sacrifice his son or
1 Chr 16.21 But God let **no one** oppress them;
22. 3 wooden gates, and so much bronze that **no one** could weigh it.
2 Chr 2. 6 Yet **no one** can really build a temple for God, because even
4.18 many objects were made that **no one** determined the total
6.36 against you—and there is **no one** who does not sin—and
14.11 **no one** can hope to defeat you."
15. 5 In those days **no one** could come and go in safety, because
18.30 his chariot commanders to attack **no one** else except the king
20. 6 You are powerful and mighty, and **no one** can oppose you.
23. 6 **No one** is to enter the temple buildings except the priests
Ezra 3.13 **No one** could distinguish between the joyful shouts and the crying,
9.14 that you will destroy us completely and let **no one** survive.
10.15 **No one** was opposed to the plan except Jonathan son of
Esth 4. 2 go in because **no one** wearing sackcloth was allowed inside.
5.12 Esther gave a banquet for **no one** but the king and me,
9. 2 were afraid of them, and **no one** could stand against them.
Job 1. 8 "There is **no one** on earth as faithful and good as he
2. 3 "There is **no one** on earth as faithful and good as he
5. 4 **no one** stands up to defend them in court.
8.18 then pull them up— **no one** will ever know they were
9. 3 He can ask a thousand questions that **no one** could ever answer.
9. 8 **No one** helped God spread out the heavens or trample the
9.12 He takes what he wants, and **no one** can stop him;
9.12 **no one** dares ask him, "What are you doing?"
9.33 But there is **no one** to step between us—
9.33 **no one** to judge both God and
10. 7 I am not guilty, that **no one** can save me from you.
11. 1 Will **no one** answer all this nonsense?
15. 4 If you had your way, **no one** would fear God;
15. 4 **no one** would pray to him.
15.19 there was **no one** to lead them away from God.
17. 3 There is **no one** else to support what I say.
18.17 **no one** remembers him any more.
19. 7 I protest against his violence, but **no one** is listening;
19. 7 **no one** hears my cry for justice.
21.31 There is **no one** to accuse a wicked man or pay him
23.13 **No one** can oppose him or stop him from doing what he
24.15 he covers his face so that **no one** can see him.
28.13 **No one** knows its true value.
30.13 and there is **no one** to stop them.
31.35 Will **no one** listen to what I am saying?
33.14 God speaks again and again, **no one** pays attention to what he
34.29 God decided to do nothing at all, **no one** could criticize him.
36. 5 He despises **no one;**
36.23 **No one** can tell God what to do or accuse him of
36.29 **No one** knows how the clouds move or how the thunder
38.26 Who makes rain fall where **no one** lives?
39. 7 from the noisy cities, and **no one** can tame them and make
41.10 **no one** would dare to stand before him.
41.11 **No one** in all the world can do it.
41.13 **No one** can tear off his outer coat or pierce the armour
Ps 6. 5 **no one** can praise you there.
7. 2 will carry me off where **no one** can save me, and there
12. 4 We will say what we wish, and **no one** can stop us."
14. 1 there is **no one** who does what is right.
18.41 They cry for help, but **no one** saves them;
19.12 **No one** can see his own errors;
22.11 Trouble is near, and there is **no one** to help.
27. 1 I will fear **no one.**
35.10 I will say to the Lord, "There is **no one** like you.
40. 5 there is **no one** like you!
50.22 will destroy you, and there will be **no one** to save you.
53. 1 there is **no one** who does what is right.
59. 7 in their mouths, yet they think that **no one** hears them.
64. 5 **"No one** can see them," they say.
69.25 may **no one** be left alive in their tents.
71.11 there is **no one** to rescue him."
71.19 there is **no one** like you.
74. 9 are no prophets left, and **no one** knows how long this will
76. 7 **No one** can stand in your presence when you are angry.
78.63 were killed in war, and young women had **no one** to marry.
79. 3 water all through Jerusalem, and **no one** was left to bury the
89. 6 **No one** in heaven is like you, Lord;
103.16 on it, and it is gone— **no one** sees it again.
105.14 But God let **no one** oppress them;
107.12 they would fall down, and **no one** would help.
109.12 May **no one** ever be kind to him or care for the
109.17 He hated to give blessings—may **no one** bless him!
113. 5 There is **no one** like the Lord our God.

Ps	116.11	even when I was afraid and said, **"No one** can be trusted."
	129. 7	**no one** gathers it up or carries it away in bundles.
	129. 8	**No one** who passes by will say, "May the Lord bless you!
	142. 4	there is no one to help me, **no one** to protect me.
	142. 4	**No one** cares for me.
	143. 2	**no one** is innocent in your sight.
	147.17	**no one** can endure the cold he sends!
Prov	2.19	**No one** who visits her ever comes back.
	11.13	**No one** who gossips can be trusted with a secret, but you
	13. 8	money to save his life, but **no one** threatens a poor man.
	14.10	**No one** can share them with you.
	14.20	**No one,** not even his neighbour, likes a poor man, but
	18.12	**No one** is respected unless he is humble;
	19. 9	**No one** who tells lies in court can escape punishment;
	28. 1	The wicked run when **no one** is chasing them, but an honest
Ecc	1.11	**No one** remembers what has happened in the past,
	1.11	and **no one** in days to come
	2.16	**No one** remembers wise men, and no one remembers fools.
	2.16	No one remembers wise men, and **no one** remembers fools.
	4. 1	The oppressed were weeping, and **no one** would help them.
	4. 1	**No one** would help them, because their oppressors had power
	4.10	it's just too bad, because there is **no one** to help him.
	4.16	when he is gone, **no one** will be grateful for what he
	7.20	There is **no one** on earth who does what is right all
	8. 4	acts with authority, and **no one** can challenge what he does.
	8. 7	is going to happen, and there is **no one** to tell us.
	8. 8	**No one** can keep himself from dying or put off the day
	9. 1	**No one** knows anything about what lies ahead of him.
	9.15	But **no one** thought about him.
	9.16	is better than strength, but **no one** thinks of a poor man
	10.14	**No one** knows what is going to happen next,
	10.14	and **no one** can tell us what will
Song	8. 1	in the street, I could kiss you and **no one** would mind.
	8. 6	hold **no one** in your arms but me.
Is	1.30	wither like a dying oak, like a garden that **no one** waters.
	1.31	their own evil deeds, and **no one** will be able to stop
	5.29	are carrying it off where **no one** can take it away from
	7.25	will be so overgrown with thorns that **no one** will go there.
	13.20	**No one** will ever live there again.
	14. 8	fallen king, because there is **no one** to cut them down, now
	14.27	stretched out his arm to punish, and **no one** can stop him.
	16. 3	hide us where **no one** can find us.
	16.10	**No one** is happy now in the fertile fields.
	16.10	**No one** shouts or sings in the vineyards.
	16.10	**No one** tramples grapes to make wine;
	17. 2	for sheep and cattle, and **no one** will drive them away.
	19.15	**No one** in Egypt, rich or poor, important or unknown, can
	22.22	what he opens, **no one** will shut,
	22.22	and what he shuts, **no one** will open.
	23.10	There is **no one** to protect you any more.
	24. 9	**no one** enjoys its taste any more.
	26.14	**No one** remembers them any more.
	27. 3	guard it night and day so that **no one** will harm it.
	29.15	schemes in secret and think **no one** will see them or know
	32. 5	**No one** will think that a fool is honourable or say that
	33. 1	have robbed and betrayed, although **no one** has robbed them or
	33. 8	The highways are so dangerous that **no one** travels on them.
	33. 8	**No one** is respected any more.
	33.24	**No one** who lives in our land will ever again complain of
	34.10	waste age after age, and **no one** will ever travel through it
	38.18	**No one** in the world of the dead can praise you;
	40.28	**No one** understands his thoughts.
	41.26	**no one** heard you say a thing!
	42.22	robbed and plundered, with **no one** to come to their rescue.
	43.13	**No one** can escape from my power;
	43.13	**no one** can change what I do."
	44.24	when I made the earth, **no one** helped me.
	45.13	**No one** has hired him or bribed him to do this."
	46. 9	alone am God and that there is **no one** else like me.
	47. 3	I will take vengeance, and **no one** will stop me."
	47. 8	great as God— that there is **no one** else like you.
	47.10	you thought that **no one** could see you.
	47.10	yourself, 'I am God— there is **no one** else like me.'
	49.23	**no one** who waits for my help will be disappointed."
	51.18	There is **no one** to lead you, no one among your people
	51.19	There is **no one** to show you sympathy.
	53. 3	**No one** would even look at him— we ignored him as
	53. 8	and led off to die, and **no one** cared about his fate.
	54.11	you suffering, helpless city, with **no one** to comfort you, I
	57. 1	Good people die, and **no one** understands or even cares.
	59. 8	destruction wherever you go, [8]and **no one** is safe when you
	59. 8	follow a crooked path, and **no one** who walks that path will
	59.16	to see that there is **no one** to help the oppressed.
	63. 3	the nations like grapes, and **no one** came to help me.
	63. 5	I looked and saw that there was **no one** to help me.
	64. 4	**No one** has ever seen or heard of a God like you,
	64. 7	**No one** turns to you in prayer;
	64. 7	**no one** goes to you for help.
	65. 8	The Lord says, **"No one** destroys good grapes;
	66. 4	they are afraid of—because **no one** answered when I called or
Jer	2. 6	land where no one lives and **no one** will even travel.
	4. 4	will burn, and there will be **no one** to put it out."
	4. 7	will be left in ruins, and **no one** will live in them.
	4.29	will be left empty, and **no one** will live in them again.
	6. 8	turn your city into a desert, a place where **no one** lives."
	7.20	anger will be like a fire that **no one** can put out.
	7.26	Yet **no one** listened or paid any attention.
	7.33	wild animals, and there will be **no one** to scare them off.
	9. 4	guard against his friend, and **no one** can trust his brother;
	9. 5	They all mislead their friends, and **no one** tells the truth;
	9.10	they have dried up, and **no one** travels through them.
Jer	9.11	Judah will become a desert, a place where **no one** lives."
	9.12	and dry as a desert, so that **no one** travels through it?
	9.22	and left behind by the reapers, corn that **no one** gathers.
	10. 6	Lord, there is **no one** like you;
	10. 7	There is **no one** like you among all the wise men of
	10.20	there is **no one** left to put up our tents again;
	10.20	there is **no one** to hang their curtains."
	10.23	Lord, I know that **no one** is the master of his own
	11.19	let's kill him so that **no one** will remember him any more."
	12.11	The whole land has become a desert, and **no one** cares.
	12.12	**no one** can live in peace.
	13.19	**no one** can get through to them.
	14.16	streets of Jerusalem, and there will be **no one** to bury them.
	15.12	**(No one** can break iron, especially the iron from the
	16. 4	die of terrible diseases, and **no one** will mourn for them or
	16. 6	die in this land, but **no one** will bury them or mourn
	16. 6	**No one** will gash himself or shave his head to show his
	16. 7	**No one** will eat or drink with anyone to comfort him when
	16. 7	**No one** will show sympathy, not even for someone who has lost
	17.27	the palaces of Jerusalem, and **no one** will be able to put
	21.13	You say that **no one** can attack you or break through your
	22. 6	but I will make it a desolate place where **no one** lives.
	22.18	**"No one** will mourn his death or say, 'How terrible, my
	22.18	**No one** will weep for him or cry, 'My lord!
	22.28	a broken jar that is thrown away and that **no one** wants?
	23.14	to do wrong, so that **no one** stops doing what is evil.
	23.24	**No one** can hide where I cannot see him.
	25.33	**No one** will mourn for them, and they will not be taken
	26. 9	this city will be destroyed and **no one** will live in it?"
	30.10	you will be secure, and **no one** will make you afraid.
	30.13	There is **no one** to take care of you, no remedy for
	30.17	**no one** cares about her.'
	34. 9	male and female, so that **no one** would have a
	34.22	make the towns of Judah like a desert where **no one** lives.
	38.27	could do, because **no one** had overheard the conversation.
	40.15	go and kill Ishmael, and **no one** will know who did it.
	44. 2	are still in ruins, and **no one** lives in them [3]because their
	44.14	**No one** will return except a few refugees."
	44.22	day your land lies in ruins and **no one** lives in it.
	46.19	Memphis will be made a desert, a ruin where **no one** lives.
	46.27	you will be secure, and **no one** will make you afraid.
	48. 9	will be left in ruins, and **no one** will live there again."
	48.33	there is **no one** to make the wine and shout for joy.
	48.38	because I have broken Moab like a jar that **no one** wants.
	49. 1	Is there **no one** to defend their land?
	49. 4	in your power and say that **no one** would dare attack you?
	49. 5	life, and there will be **no one** to bring your troops together
	49.15	is going to make you weak, and **no one** will respect you.
	49.16	**No one** fears you as much as you think they do.
	49.18	**No one** will ever live there again.
	49.33	**No one** will ever live there again.
	50. 3	Men and animals will run away, and **no one** will live there."
	50.13	Because of my anger **no one** will live in Babylon;
	50.32	nation will stumble and fall, and **no one** will help you up.
	50.40	**No one** will ever live there again.
	51.29	out his plan to make Babylonia a desert, where **no one** lives.
	51.37	**no one** will live there, and all who see it will be
	51.43	like a waterless desert, where **no one** lives or even travels.
Lam	1. 4	**No one** comes to the Temple now to worship on the holy
	1. 7	she fell to the enemy, there was **no one** to help her;
	1. 9	**no one** can comfort her.
	1.12	**"No one** has ever had pain like mine, Pain that the Lord
	1.16	**No one** can comfort me;
	1.16	**no one** can give me courage.
	1.17	"I stretch out my hands, but **no one** will help me.
	1.21	there is **no one** to comfort me.
	2.13	**No one** has ever suffered like this.
	2.22	terror all round me, And **no one** could escape on that day
	4. 4	children are begging for food that **no one** will give them.
	4.12	**No one** anywhere, not even rulers of foreign nations,
	4.14	men, so stained with blood that **no one** would touch them.
	4.15	So they wandered from nation to nation, welcomed by **no one.**
	5. 8	no better than slaves, and **no one** can save us from their
Ezek	7.14	But **no one** goes off to war, for God's anger will fall
	9. 5	Spare **no one;**
	9. 5	have mercy on **no one.**
	14.15	the land so dangerous that **no one** could travel through it,
	16. 4	When you were born, **no one** cut your umbilical cord or
	16. 5	**No one** took enough pity on you to do any of these
	16. 5	When you were born, **no one** loved you.
	16.34	**No one** forced you to become one.
	20.48	set it on fire and that **no one** can put it out."
	21.32	your own country, and **no one** will remember you any more.' "
	22. 7	**No one** in the city honours his parents.
	22.30	anger is about to destroy it, but I could find **no one.**
	26.19	make you as desolate as ruined cities where **no one** lives.
	30.13	There will be **no one** to rule over Egypt, and I will
	30.21	**No one** has bandaged it or put it in a sling so
	33.28	will be so wild that **no one** will be able to travel
	34. 6	face of the earth, and **no one** looked for them or tried
	34.28	They will live in safety, and **no one** will terrify them.
	35. 9	you desolate for ever, and **no one** will live in your cities
	39.26	in their own land, with **no one** to threaten them, they will
	44. 9	that no uncircumcised foreigner, **no one** who disobeys me,
	46. 9	**No one** may go out by the same way as he entered,
Dan	2.10	The advisers replied, "There is **no one** on the face of
	2.11	for is so difficult that **no one** can do it for you
	4.35	**No one** can oppose his will or question what he does.
	6. 7	orders that for thirty days **no one** be permitted to request
	6.17	noblemen on the stone, so that **no one** could rescue Daniel.
	8. 7	and trampled on, and there was **no one** who could save him.

Dan 10. 8 my face was so changed that **no one** could have recognized me.
10.20 There is **no one** to help me except Michael, Israel's guardian angel.
11.45 But he will die, with **no one** there to help him."
Hos 2.10 front of her lovers, and **no one** will be able to save
4. 4 The Lord says, "Let **no one** accuse the people or
5.14 When I drag them off, **no one** will be able to save
7. 7 one after another, but **no one** prays to me for help."
11. 7 that is on them, but **no one** will lift it from them.
12. 8 And **no one** can accuse us of getting rich dishonestly.'
14. 3 show mercy to those who have **no one** else to turn to."
Amos 5. 2 She lies abandoned on the ground, And **no one** helps her up.
5. 6 the people of Bethel, and **no one** will be able to put
9. 1 **No one** will get away;
Jon 3. 7 **No one** is to eat anything;
Mic 4. 4 vineyards and fig-trees, and **no one** will make him afraid.
7. 2 an honest person left in the land, **no one** loyal to God.
Nah 1. 9 **No one** opposes him more than once.
2. 8 the cry rings out— but **no one** turns back.
3.17 out, they fly away, and **no one** knows where they have gone!
3.18 the mountains, and there is **no one** to bring them home again.
Zeph 1. 4 worship of Baal there, and **no one** will even remember the
2. 4 **No one** will be left in the city of Gaza.
3. 6 the streets are empty—**no one** is left.
3.13 They will be prosperous and secure, afraid of **no one."**
Zech 7.14 land was left a desolate place, with **no one** living in it."
8.10 Before that time **no one** could afford to hire either men
8.10 or animals, and **no one** was safe from his enemies.
13. 2 idols from the land, and **no one** will remember them any more.
Mt 5.15 **No one** lights a lamp and puts it under a bowl;
6.24 **"No one** can be a slave of two masters;
8.28 and were so fierce that **no one** dared travel on that road.
9.16 **"No one** patches up an old coat with a piece of new
11.27 **No one** knows the Son except the Father,
11.27 and **no one** knows the Father except the
12.29 **"No one** can break into a strong man's house and take
17. 8 So they looked up and saw **no one** there but Jesus.
20. 7 **'No one** hired us,' they answered.
22.46 **No one** was able to give Jesus any answer,
22.46 and from that day on **no one** dared to ask him any
24.36 **"No one** knows, however, when that day and hour will come—
Mk 2.21 **"No one** uses a piece of new cloth to patch up an
3.27 **"No one** can break into a strong man's house and take
9.39 Jesus told them, "because **no one** who performs a miracle in
10.18 **"No one** is good except God alone.
11.14 Jesus said to the fig-tree, **"No one** shall ever eat figs
13.32 **"No one** knows, however, when that day or hour will come—
Lk 5.36 **"No one** tears a piece off a new coat to patch up
5.39 And **no one** wants new wine after drinking old wine.
8.16 **"No one** lights a lamp and covers it with a bowl or
8.43 she had on doctors, but **no one** had been able to cure
9.36 about all this, and told **no one** at that time anything they
10.22 **No one** knows who the Son is except the Father,
10.22 and **no one** knows who the Father is
11.33 **"No one** lights a lamp and then hides it or puts it
15.16 pods the pigs ate, but **no one** gave him anything to eat.
17.21 **No one** will say, 'Look, here it is!'
18.19 **"No one** is good except God alone.
Jn 1.18 **No one** has ever seen God.
3. 2 **No one** could perform the miracles you are doing unless God
3. 3 **no one** can see the Kingdom of God unless he is born
3. 5 **"No one** can enter the Kingdom of God unless he is born
3.13 And **no one** has ever gone up to heaven except the Son
3.27 John answered, **"No one** can have anything unless God gives it
3.32 what he has seen and heard, yet **no one** accepts his message.
5. 7 man answered, "Sir, I have **no one** here to put me in
6.44 **No one** can come to me unless the Father who sent me
6.65 reason I told you that **no one** can come to me unless
7. 4 **No one** hides what he is doing if he wants to be
7.13 But **no one** talked about him openly, because they were afraid
7.27 But when the Messiah comes, **no one** will know where he is
7.30 tried to seize him, but **no one** laid a hand on him,
7.44 wanted to seize him, but **no one** laid a hand on him.
8.10 Is there **no one** left to condemn you?"
8.11 **"No one,** sir," she answered.
8.15 I pass judgement on **no one.**
8.20 And **no one** arrested him, because his hour had not come.
9. 4 night is coming when **no one** can work.
10.18 **No one** takes my life away from me.
10.28 **No one** can snatch them away from me.
10.29 is greater than everything, and **no one** can snatch them away
14. 6 **no one** goes to the Father except by me.
15.24 not done among them the things that **no one** else ever did;
16.22 the kind of gladness that **no one** can take away from you.
19.41 there was a new tomb where **no one** had ever been buried.
Acts 1.20 may **no one** live in it.'
4.12 all the world there is **no one** else whom God has given
4.32 **No one** said that any of his belongings was his own,
4.34 There was **no one** in the group who was in need.
5.23 but when we opened the gates, we found **no one** inside!"
8.33 **No one** will be able to tell about his descendants, because
18.10 **No one** will be able to harm you, for many in this
25.11 charges they bring against me, **no one** can hand me over to
Rom 3.10 "There is **no one** who is righteous, [11] no one who is wise
3.12 **no one** does what is right, not even one.
3.20 For **no one** is put right in God's sight by doing what
13. 8 Be under obligation to **no one**—the only obligation you have
1 Cor 1.15 **No one** can say, then, that you were baptized as my disciples.
1.29 This means that **no one** can boast in God's presence.
2. 9 as the scripture says, "What **no one** ever saw or heard,
2. 9 what **no one** ever thought could happen,
1 Cor 2.15 the value of everything, but **no one** is able to judge him.
3.18 **No one** should fool himself.
3.21 **No one,** then, should boast about what men can do.
10.24 **No one** should be looking to his own interests, but to
12. 3 want you to know that **no one** who is led by God's
12. 3 and **no one** can confess "Jesus is Lord," unless he is
14. 2 speak to others but to God, because **no one** understands him.
14.28 But if **no one** is there who can explain, then the one
16.11 **No one** should look down on him, but you must help him
2 Cor 7. 2 We have wronged **no one;**
7. 2 have ruined **no one,** nor tried to take advantage of anyone.
11.16 **no one** should think that I am a fool.
Gal 2.16 For **no one** is put right with God by doing what the
3.11 Now, it is clear that **no one** is put right with God
3.15 matter and sign an agreement, **no one** can break it or add
6. 7 **no one** makes a fool of God.
6.17 let **no one** give me any more trouble, because the scars I
Eph 2. 8 but God's gift, so that **no one** can boast about it.
5. 5 You may be sure that **no one** who is immoral, indecent, or
5.29 **(No one** ever hates his own body.
Col 2. 8 See to it, then, that **no one** enslaves you by means of
2.16 So let **no one** make rules about what you eat or drink
1 Thes 5.15 See that **no one** pays back wrong for wrong, but at all
1 Tim 3.16 **No one** can deny how great is the secret of our religion:
5. 5 who is all alone, with **no one** to take care of her,
5. 7 these instructions, so that **no one** will find fault with them.
6. 1 of all respect, so that **no one** will speak evil of the
6.16 he lives in the light that **no one** can approach.
6.16 **No one** has ever seen him;
6.16 **no one** can ever see him.
2 Tim 4.16 **No one** stood by me the first time I defended myself;
Tit 2. 5 to their husbands, so that **no one** will speak evil of the
Heb 3.12 My fellow-believers, be careful that **no one** among you has a
4.11 receive that rest, so that **no one** of us will fail
5. 4 **No one** chooses for himself the honour of being a high priest.
6.13 Since there was **no one** greater than himself, he used his own
11. 6 **No one** can please God without faith, for whoever comes to
12.14 live a holy life, because **no one** will see the Lord without
12.15 Let **no one** become like a bitter plant that grows up
12.16 Let **no one** become immoral or unspiritual like Esau,
Jas 1.13 God cannot be tempted by evil, and he himself tempts **no one.**
3. 8 But **no one** has ever been able to tame the tongue.
1 Pet 2.22 He committed no sin, and **no one** ever heard a lie come
2 Pet 1.20 all else, however, remember that **no one** can explain by himself
1 Jn 3. 7 Let **no one** deceive you, my children!
4.12 **No one** has ever seen God, but if we love one another,
Rev 2.17 written a new name that **no one** knows except the one who
3. 7 when he opens a door, **no one** can close it,
3. 7 and when he closes it, **no one** can open it.
3. 8 opened a door in front of you, which **no one** can close.
3.11 what you have, so that **no one** will rob you of your
5. 3 But there was **no one** in heaven or on earth or in
5. 4 I cried bitterly because **no one** could be found who was
7. 9 was an enormous crowd—**no one** could count all the people!
13.17 **No one** could buy or sell unless he had this mark,
15. 8 and power of God, and **no one** could go into the temple
18.11 mourn for her, because **no one** buys their goods any longer;
18.12 **no one** buys their gold, silver, precious stones, and
19.12 name written on him, but **no one** except himself knows what it

NOAH (1)

Head of the family which survived the Flood.

Gen 5.29 so he named him **Noah.**
5.32 After **Noah** was 500 years old, he had three sons, Shem,
6. 8 But the Lord was pleased with **Noah.**
6. 9 This is the story of **Noah.**
6. 9 **Noah** had no faults and was the only good man of his
6.13 God said to **Noah,** "I have decided to put an end to
6.22 **Noah** did everything that God commanded.
7. 1 The Lord said to **Noah,** "Go into the boat with your whole
7. 5 And **Noah** did everything that the Lord commanded.
7. 6 **Noah** was six hundred years old when the flood came on the
7. 9 went into the boat with **Noah,** as God had commanded.
7.11 When **Noah** was six hundred years old, on the seventeenth
7.13 On that same day **Noah** and his wife went into the boat
7.15 went into the boat with **Noah,** [16] as God had commanded.
7.16 Then the Lord shut the door behind **Noah.**
7.23 The only ones left were **Noah** and those who were with him
8. 1 God had not forgotten **Noah** and all the animals with him in
8. 6 After forty days **Noah** opened a window [7] and sent out a raven.
8. 8 Meanwhile, **Noah** sent out a dove to see if the water had
8. 9 back to the boat, and **Noah** reached out and took it in.
8.11 So **Noah** knew that the water had gone down.
8.13 When **Noah** was 601 years old, on the first day of the
8.13 **Noah** removed the covering of the boat, looked round, and saw
8.15 God said to **Noah,** [16] "Go out of the boat with your wife,
8.18 So **Noah** went out of the boat with his wife, his sons,
8.20 **Noah** built an altar to the Lord;
9. 1 God blessed **Noah** and his sons and said, "Have many children,
9. 8 God said to **Noah** and his sons, [9] "I am now making my
9.18 The sons of **Noah** who went out of the boat were Shem,
9.19 These three sons of **Noah** were the ancestors of all the
9.20 **Noah,** who was a farmer, was the first man to plant a
9.24 When **Noah** was sober again and learnt what his youngest
9.28 After the flood **Noah** lived for 350 years [29] and died at
10. 1 These are the descendants of **Noah's** sons, Shem, Ham,
10.32 peoples are the descendants of **Noah,** nation by nation,
10.32 nations of the earth were descended from the sons of **Noah.**
1 Chr 1. 4 Methuselah was the father of Lamech, [4] who was the father of **Noah.**

1 Chr 1. 4 **Noah** had three sons:
Is 54. 9 "In the time of **Noah** I promised never again to flood the
Ezek 14.14 Even if those three men, **Noah**, Daniel, and Job, were living there,
14.20 people and animals, [20] even if **Noah**, Daniel, and Job lived
Mt 24.37 of Man will be like what happened in the time of **Noah.**
24.38 women married, up to the very day **Noah** went into the boat;
Lk 3.36 of Shem, the son of **Noah**, the son of Lamech,
17.26 was in the time of **Noah** so shall it be in the
17.27 up to the very day **Noah** went into the boat and the
Heb 11. 7 It was faith that made **Noah** hear God's warnings
11. 7 world was condemned, and **Noah** received from God the righteousness
1 Pet 3.20 waited patiently during the days that **Noah** was building his boat.
2 Pet 2. 5 only ones he saved were **Noah**, who preached righteousness, and

NOBLE

Deut 28.54 the most refined man of **noble** birth will become so desperate
28.56 the most refined woman of **noble** birth, so rich that she has
Esth 1. 3 as well as the governors and **noblemen** of the provinces.
6. 9 get one of your highest **noblemen** to dress the man in these
6. 9 Let the **nobleman** announce as they go:
Prov 8.16 governs with my help, statesmen and **noblemen** alike.
19.10 live in luxury, and slaves should not rule over **noblemen.**
Ecc 10. 7 slaves on horseback while **noblemen** go on foot like slaves.
Is 5.14 It gulps down the **nobles** of Jerusalem along with the noisy
Lam 1. 1 The **noblest** of cities has fallen into slavery.
2. 9 The king and the **noblemen** now are in exile.
Ezek 23. 6 in uniforms of purple, **noblemen** and high-ranking officers;
23.12 of lust for the Assyrian **noblemen** and officers—soldiers in
23.23 gather all those handsome young **noblemen** and officers, all
Dan 1. 3 young men of the royal family and of the **noble** families.
4.36 My officials and my **noblemen** welcomed me, and I was given
5. 1 King Belshazzar invited a thousand **noblemen** to a great banquet,
5. 2 them so that he, his **noblemen**, his wives, and his concubines
5. 9 grew even paler, and his **noblemen** had no idea what to do.
5.10 the king and his **noblemen** and entered the banqueting-hall.
5.23 You, your **noblemen**, your wives, and your concubines drank
6.17 and the seal of his **noblemen** on the stone, so that no
Nah 3.18 governors are dead, and your **noblemen** are asleep for ever!
Phil 4. 8 that are true, **noble**, right, pure, lovely, and honourable.

NOBODY

see also **NO ONE**

Ex 3.11 But Moses said to God, "I am **nobody.**
1 Sam 14.24 So **nobody** had eaten anything all day.
1 Kgs 16. 2 "You were a **nobody**, but I made you the leader of my
2 Kgs 8.13 "I'm a **nobody!"**
2 Chr 21.20 **Nobody** was sorry when he died.
Job 30. 8 A worthless bunch of nameless **nobodies!**
Mt 24.22 had he not done so, **nobody** would survive.
Mk 5. 3 **Nobody** could keep him chained up any more;
12.34 After this **nobody** dared to ask Jesus any more questions.
13.20 if he had not, **nobody** would survive.
Jn 7.46 The guards answered, **"Nobody** has ever talked like this man!"
9.32 beginning of the world **nobody** has ever heard of anyone giving
Acts 5.13 **Nobody** outside the group dared to join them, even though the
19.36 **Nobody** can deny these things.
1 Cor 9.15 **Nobody** is going to turn my rightful boast into empty words!
9.19 I am a free man, **nobody's** slave;
2 Cor 13. 2 the next time I come **nobody** will escape punishment.
Gal 6. 3 somebody when really he is **nobody**, he is only deceiving himself.
Heb 11. 5 taken up to God, and **nobody** could find him, because God had

NOD

Mt 25. 5 late in coming, so the girls began to **nod** and fall asleep.

NOISE

Judg 5.11 **noisy** crowds round the wells are telling of the Lord's victories,
1 Sam 4.14 Eli heard the **noise** and asked, "What is all this noise about?"
1 Kgs 1.40 playing flutes, making enough **noise** to shake the ground.
1.41 his guests were finishing the feast, they heard the **noise.**
1.41 asked, "What's the meaning of all that **noise** in the city?"
1.45 That's the **noise** you just heard.
6. 7 so that there was no **noise** made by hammers, axes, or any
2 Kgs 11.13 Queen Athaliah heard the **noise** being made by the guards
Ezra 3.13 and the crying, because the **noise** they made was so loud that
Neh 12.43 in the celebration, and the **noise** they all made could be
Job 39. 7 keep far away from the **noisy** cities, and no one can tame
Ps 65. 7 calm the roar of the seas and the **noise** of the waves;
74.23 of your enemies, the continuous **noise** made by your foes.
Ecc 12. 4 Your ears will be deaf to the **noise** of the street.
Is 5.14 of Jerusalem along with the **noisy** crowd of common people.
13. 4 Listen to the **noise** on the mountains—the sound of a great
22. 2 The whole city is in an uproar, filled with **noise** and excitement.
33. 3 you fight for us, nations run away from the **noise** of battle.
66. 6 That loud **noise** in the city, that sound in the Temple, is
Jer 3.21 A **noise** is heard on the hill-tops:
4.29 At the **noise** of the horsemen and bowmen everyone will run away.
46.17 Egypt a new name— **'Noisy** Braggart Who Missed His Chance.'
49. 2 city of Rabbah hear the **noise** of battle, and it will be
49.21 there will be such a **noise** that the entire earth will shake,
50.22 The **noise** of battle is heard in the land, and there is
50.46 there will be such a **noise** that the entire earth will shake,
51.55 The armies rush in like roaring waves and attack with **noisy** shouts.
Ezek 1.24 I heard the **noise** their wings made in flight;
1.24 of the sea, like the **noise** of a huge army, like the
3.13 in the air, and the **noise** of the wheels, as loud as
10. 5 The **noise** made by the creatures' wings was heard even in
26.10 The **noise** of their horses pulling wagons and chariots will
31.16 world of the dead, the **noise** of its downfall will shake the
37. 7 speaking, I heard a rattling **noise**, and the bones began to
Dan 5.10 The queen mother heard the **noise** made by the king and
Amos 2. 2 Moab will die in the **noise** of battle while soldiers are
5.23 Stop your **noisy** songs;
Mt 15.23 She is following us and making all this **noise!"**
24. 6 are going to hear the **noise** of battles close by and the
Mk 13. 7 troubled when you hear the **noise** of battles close by and
Acts 2. 2 Suddenly there was a **noise** from the sky which sounded like
2. 6 When they heard this **noise**, a large crowd gathered.
1 Cor 13. 1 speech is no more than a **noisy** gong or a clanging bell.
2 Pet 3.10 disappear with a shrill **noise**, the heavenly bodies will burn up
Rev 9. 9 their wings was like the **noise** of many horse-drawn chariots

NONE

Lk 3.11 to the man who has **none**, and whoever has food must share
11.29 ask for a miracle, but **none** will be given them except the
13. 6 He went looking for figs on it but found **none.**
14.24 I tell you all that **none** of those men who were invited
14.33 the same way," concluded Jesus, **"none** of you can be my
21.15 such words and wisdom that **none** of your enemies will be able
Jn 3.11 what we have seen, yet **none** of you is willing to accept
4.27 But **none** of them said to her, "What do you want?"
4.48 Jesus said to him, **"None** of you will ever believe
13.28 **None** of the others at the table understood why Jesus
16. 5 him who sent me, yet **none** of you asks me where I
21.12 **None** of the disciples dared ask him, "Who are you?"
Acts 8.24 Lord for me, so that **none** of these things you spoke of
20.25 And now I know that **none** of you will ever see me
Rom 14. 7 **None** of us lives for himself only,
14. 7 **none** of us dies for himself only.
1 Cor 2. 8 **None** of the rulers of this world knew this wisdom.
4. 6 **None** of you should be proud of one person and despise another.
5.12 After all, it is **none** of my business to judge outsiders.
6.10 or are thieves—**none** of these will possess God's Kingdom.
14.10 languages in the world, yet **none** of them is without meaning.
1 Thes 3. 3 help your faith, [3] so that **none** of you should turn back
Tit 2.15 Let **none** of them look down on you.
Heb 3.13 Instead, in order that **none** of you be deceived by sin
4. 1 us take care, then, that **none** of you will be found to
8.11 **None** of them will have to teach his fellow-citizen or
1 Jn 2.16 people are so proud of—**none** of this comes from the Father;
2.19 it might be clear that **none** of them really belonged to us.

NONSENSE

2 Sam 15.31 Absalom's rebellion, he prayed, "Please, Lord, turn Ahithophel's advice into **nonsense!"**
Job 2.10 Job answered, "You are talking **nonsense!**
6.25 Honest words are convincing, but you are talking **nonsense.**
11. 1 Will no one answer all this **nonsense?**
21.34 You try to comfort me with **nonsense!**
27.12 so why do you talk such **nonsense?**
Prov 15. 2 knowledge attractive, but stupid people spout **nonsense.**
Ecc 8.14 But this is **nonsense.**
Jer 15.19 If instead of talking **nonsense** you proclaim a worthwhile message,
Zech 10. 2 but the answers they get are lies and **nonsense.**
Lk 24.11 the women said was **nonsense**, and they did not believe them.
Rom 1.21 thoughts have become complete **nonsense**, and their empty minds
1 Cor 1.18 death on the cross is **nonsense** to those who are being lost;
1.23 that is offensive to the Jews and **nonsense** to the Gentiles;
1.27 what the world considers **nonsense** in order to shame the wise,
2.14 they are **nonsense** to him, because their value can be judged
3.19 this world considers to be wisdom is **nonsense** in God's sight.
Tit 1.10 from Judaism, who rebel and deceive others with their **nonsense.**

NOON

Gen 43.16 to eat with me at **noon**, so kill an animal and prepare
43.25 Joseph when he arrived at **noon**, because they had been told
1 Sam 11. 9 "Tell your people that before **noon** tomorrow they will be rescued."
11.11 By **noon** they had slaughtered them.
2 Sam 4. 5 house and arrived there about **noon**, while he was taking his
1 Kgs 18.26 brought to them, prepared it, and prayed to Baal until **noon.**
18.27 At **noon** Elijah started making fun of them:
20.16 The attack began at **noon**, as Benhadad and his
2 Kgs 4.20 held him in her lap until **noon**, at which time he died.
Neh 8. 3 from dawn until **noon**, and they all listened attentively.
Job 5.14 even at **noon** they grope in darkness.
11.17 be brighter than sunshine at **noon**, and life's darkest hours
Ps 37. 6 he will make your righteousness shine like the **noonday** sun.
55.17 Morning, **noon**, and night my complaints and groans go up to him,
Song 1. 7 Where will they rest from the **noonday** sun?
Is 16. 3 shadow in the heat of **noon**, and let us rest in your
58.10 the darkness around you will turn to the brightness of **noon.**
59.10 We stumble at **noon**, as if it were night, as if we
Jer 6. 4 We'll attack at **noon!"**
20.16 and the battle alarm at **noon**, [17] because he didn't kill me
Amos 8. 9 the sun go down at **noon** and the earth grow dark in
Mt 27.45 At **noon** the whole country was covered with darkness,
Mk 15.33 At **noon** the whole country was covered with darkness,
Jn 4. 6 It was about **noon.**
19.14 It was then almost **noon** of the day before the Passover.
Acts 10. 9 on the roof of the house about **noon** in order to pray.

NORMAL
see also **ABNORMAL**

Gen 50. 3 It took forty days, the **normal** time for embalming.
Ex 14.27 sea, and at daybreak the water returned to its **normal** level.
Lev 11.34 Any food which could **normally** be eaten, but on which
14.32 afford the **normal** offerings required for his purification.
1 Cor 7. 5 but then resume **normal** marital relations.
10.13 you have experienced is the kind that **normally** comes to people.

NORTH

Gen 13. 1 Abram went **north** out of Egypt to the southern part of
14.15 them as far as Hobah, **north** of Damascus, [16]and recovered
24.10 to the city where Nahor had lived in **northern** Mesopotamia.
Ex 26.20 Make twenty frames for the **north** side of the Tent
26.35 put the table against the **north** side of the Tent and the
27.11 same is to be done on the **north** side of the enclosure.
36.25 made twenty frames for the **north** side of the Tent [26]and
38.11 The enclosure was the same on the **north** side.
40.22 in the Tent, on the **north** side outside the curtain, [23]and
Lev 1.11 shall kill it on the **north** side of the altar, and the
4.24 and kill it on the **north** side of the altar, where the
4.29 and kill it on the **north** side of the altar, where the
4.33 and kill it on the **north** side of the altar, where the
6.25 shall be killed on the **north** side of the altar, where the
7. 2 to be killed on the **north** side of the altar, where the
Num 2.25 On the **north,** those under the banner of the
3.35 was to camp on the **north** side of the Tent, with Zuriel
13.17 he said to them, "Go **north** from here into the southern part
13.21 So the men went **north** and explored the land from the
13.21 south all the way to Rehob, near Hamath Pass in the **north.**
21.13 again and camped on the **north** side of the River Arnon,
21.24 land from the River Arnon **north** to the Jabbok, that is,
24.23 "Who are these people gathering in the **north?**
34. 7 "The **northern** border will follow a line from the
Deut 2. 3 wandering about in those hills and that we should go **north.**
3. 1 "Next, we moved **north** towards the region of Bashan, and
3.12 Reuben and Gad the territory **north** of the town of Aroer near
3.16 boundary, and their **northern** boundary was the River Jabbok,
3.17 from Lake Galilee in the **north** down to the Dead Sea in
3.27 Pisgah and look to the **north** and to the south,
4.48 River Arnon, all the way **north** to Mount Sirion,
11.24 the Lebanon Mountains in the **north,** and from the River
34. 1 the territory of Gilead as far **north** as the town of Dan;
Josh 1. 4 desert in the south to the Lebanon Mountains in the **north;**
8.11 set up camp on the **north** side, with a valley between
8.13 battle with the main camp **north** of the city and the rest
9. 1 plain of the Mediterranean Sea as far **north** as Lebanon;
10.41 all the area of Goshen, and as far **north** as Gibeon.
11. 2 in the hill-country in the **north,** in the Jordan Valley south
11. 8 and pursued them as far **north** as Misrephoth Maim and Sidon,
11.16 the hill-country and foothills, both **north** and south, all
11.17 far as Baalgad in the **north,** in the valley of Lebanon south
12. 1 Valley up the Jordan Valley and as far **north** as Mount Hermon.
13. 3 the Egyptian border, as far **north** as the border of Ekron was
13.27 border was the River Jordan as far **north** as Lake Galilee.
15. 5 The **northern** border began there, [6]extended up to Beth Hoglah,
15. 6 to Beth Hoglah, and went **north** of the ridge overlooking the
15. 7 to Debir, and then turned **north** towards Gilgal, which faces
15. 8 Valley of Hinnom, at the **northern** end of the Valley of Rephaim.
15.10 Edom, went on the **north** side of Mount Jearim (or Chesalon),
15.11 out to the hill **north** of Ekron, turned towards Shikkeron,
16. 6 Michmethath was on their **north.**
17. 9 of Manasseh proceeded along the **north** side of the stream and
17.10 and Manasseh was to the **north,** with the Mediterranean Sea as
18. 5 in the south, and Joseph in its territory in the **north.**
18.12 On the **north** their border began at the Jordan and then
18.12 then went up the slope **north** of Jericho and westwards
18.16 Valley of Hinnom, at the **north** end of the Valley of Rephaim.
18.17 It then turned **north** to Enshemesh and then on to Geliloth,
18.18 son of Reuben) [18]and passed **north** of the ridge overlooking
18.19 the valley, [19]passing **north** of the ridge of Beth Hoglah,
18.19 Hoglah, and ended at the **northern** inlet on the Dead Sea,
19.14 On the **north** the border turned towards Hannathon, ending
19.27 Valley of Iphtahel on the way **north** to Bethemek and Neiel.
19.27 It continued **north** to Cabul, [28]Ebron, Rehob, Hammon, and
24.30 Timnath Serah in the hill-country of Ephraim **north** of Mount Gaash.
Judg 1.36 **North** of Sela, the Edomite border ran through Akrabbim Pass.
2. 9 Timnath Serah in the hill-country of Ephraim **north** of Mount Gaash.
7. 1 was in the valley to the **north** of them by Moreh Hill.
11.22 to the Jabbok in the **north** and from the desert on the
20. 1 Israel from Dan in the **north** to Beersheba in the south, as
21.19 (Shiloh is **north** of Bethel, south of Lebonah, and east of
1 Sam 14. 5 One was on the **north** side of the pass, facing Michmash,
2 Sam 19.20 the first one from the **northern** tribes to come and meet Your
24. 5 From there they went **north** to Jazer, [6]and on to Gilead and
1 Kgs 7.21 was named Jachin, and the one on the **north** was named Boaz.
7.39 side of the Temple, and the other five on the **north** side;
7.49 Holy Place, five on the south side and five on the **north;**
8.65 as Hamath Pass in the **north** and the Egyptian border in the
12. 1 where all the people of **northern** Israel had gathered to make
12. 3 The people of the **northern** tribes sent for him, and then
12.19 time the people of the **northern** kingdom of Israel have been
12.21 and restore his control over the **northern** tribes of Israel.
2 Kgs 14.25 from Hamath Pass in the **north** to the Dead Sea in the
16.14 so Ahaz moved it to the **north** side of his new altar.
24. 7 from the River Euphrates to the **northern** border of Egypt.
1 Chr 5. 8 and in the territory from there **north** to Nebo and Baal Meon.
5.11 of Gad lived to the **north** of Reuben in the land of
5.23 territory of Bashan as far **north** as Baal Hermon, Senir, and
9.24 gate facing in each direction, **north,** south, east, and west,
12.40 as far away as the **northern** tribes of Issachar, Zebulun, and
13. 5 to Hamath Pass in the **north,** in order to bring the Covenant
26.14 a man who always gave good advice, drew the **north** gate.
26.17 duty each day, on the **north,** four, and on the south, four.
2 Chr 3.17 named Jachin, and the one on the **north** side was named Boaz.
4. 6 the south side of the Temple and five on the **north** side.
7. 8 as Hamath Pass in the **north** and the Egyptian border in the
10. 1 where all the people of **northern** Israel had gathered to make
10. 3 The people of the **northern** tribes sent for him, and they
10.19 time the people of the **northern** kingdom of Israel have been
11. 1 and restore his control over the **northern** tribes of Israel.
19. 4 hill-country of Ephraim in the **north,** in order to call the
25. 7 The Lord is not with these men from the **Northern** Kingdom.
28.12 men of the **Northern** Kingdom, Azariah son of Jehohanan,
30. 5 Israelites, from Dan in the **north** to Beersheba in the south,
30.10 and Manasseh, and as far **north** as the tribe of Zebulun, but
30.25 who had come from the **north,** and the foreigners who had
33.14 near the spring of Gihon **north** to the Fish Gate and the
34. 6 Manasseh, Ephraim, and Simeon, and as far **north** as Naphtali.
34. 7 Throughout the territory of the **Northern** Kingdom he
34. 9 and the rest of the **Northern** Kingdom, and from the people of
Neh 2.14 of the city I went **north** to the Fountain Gate and the
3.28 built the next section, going **north** from the Horse Gate,
11.30 Beersheba in the south and the Valley of Hinnom in the **north.**
Job 23. 9 been at work in the **north** and the south, but still I
26. 7 God stretched out the **northern** sky and hung the earth in
37. 9 come from the south, and the biting cold from the **north.**
37.22 glow is seen in the **north,** and the glory of God fills
Ps 75. 6 east or from the west, from the **north** or from the south;
89.12 You created the **north** and the south;
107. 3 countries, from east and west, from **north** and south.
Prov 25.23 Gossip brings anger just as surely as the **north** wind brings rain.
Ecc 1. 6 south, the wind blows **north**—round and round and back again.
Song 4.16 Wake up, **North** Wind.
Is 14.13 king on that mountain in the **north** where the gods assemble.
14.31 dust is coming from the **north**—it is an army with no
41.25 I will bring him to attack from the **north.**
43. 6 I will tell the **north** to let them go and the south
49.12 from far away, from the **north** and the west, and from Aswan
Jer 1.13 a pot boiling in the **north,** and it is about to tip
1.14 will boil over from the **north** on all who live in this
1.15 because I am calling all the nations in the **north** to come.
3.18 in the country in the **north** and will return to the land
4. 6 The Lord is bringing disaster and great destruction from the **north.**
6. 1 Disaster and destruction are about to come from the **north.**
6.22 The Lord says, "People are coming from a country in the **north;**
10.22 There is a great commotion in a nation to the **north;**
13.20 Your enemies are coming down from the **north!**
15.12 the iron from the **north** that is mixed with bronze.)
16.15 of Israel out of a **northern** land and out of all the
23. 8 of Israel out of a **northern** land and out of all the
25. 9 all the peoples from the **north** and for my servant, King
25.19 the kings of the **north,** far and near, one after another.
31. 8 will bring them from the **north** and gather them from the ends
46. 6 In the **north,** by the Euphrates, they stumble and fall.
46.10 Today the Almighty sacrifices his victims in the **north,**
46.20 a splendid cow, attacked by a stinging fly from the **north.**
46.24 they are conquered by the people of the **north.**
47. 2 Waters are rising in the **north** and will rush like a river
50. 3 "A nation from the **north** has come to attack Babylonia and
50. 9 strong nations in the **north** and make them attack Babylonia.
50.41 from a country in the **north,** a mighty nation far away;
51.48 falls to the people who come from the **north** to destroy it.
Ezek 1. 4 I looked up and saw a storm coming from the **north.**
6.14 city of Riblah in the **north,** not sparing any place where the
8. 3 the inner entrance of the **north** gate of the Temple, where
8. 5 God said to me, "Mortal man, look towards the **north."**
8.14 he took me to the **north** gate of the Temple and showed
9. 2 men came from the outer **north** gate of the Temple, each one
16.46 "Your elder sister is Samaria, in the **north,** with her villages.
20.47 will spread from south to **north,** and everyone will feel the
21. 4 I will use my sword against everyone from **north** to south.
23.24 will attack you from the **north,** bringing a large army with
26. 7 He will come from the **north** with a huge army, with horses
29.10 city of Migdol in the **north** to the city of Aswan in
30. 6 says, "From Migdol in the **north** to Aswan in the south, all
30.14 desolate and set fire to the city of Zoan in the **north.**
32.30 "All the princes of the **north** are there, and so are the
38. 6 and Beth Togarmah in the **north** are with him, and so are
38.15 your place in the far **north,** leading a large, powerful army
39. 2 him out of the far **north** until he comes to the mountains
40.20 measured the gateway on the **north** side that led into the
40.23 Across the courtyard from this **north** gateway was another
40.35 Then the man took me to the **north** gateway.
40.38 an annexe attached to the inner gateway on the **north** side.
40.40 two on either side of the entrance of the **north** gate.
40.44 one facing south beside the **north** gateway
40.44 and the other facing **north** beside the south gateway.
40.46 and the room which faced **north** was for the priests who
41. 8 into the rooms on the **north** side of the Temple, and one
42. 1 to a building on the **north** side of the Temple, not far
42. 4 Along the **north** side of this building was a passage five
42.11 there was a passage just like the one on the **north** side.
42.17 Then he measured the **north** side, the south side,
44. 4 man took me through the **north** gate to the front of the
46. 9 those who enter by the **north** gate are to leave by the
46. 9 enter by the south gate are to leave by the **north** gate.
46.19 entrance of the rooms facing **north** near the gate on the

Ezek 47. 2 area by way of the **north** gate and led me round to
47.15 "The **northern** boundary runs eastwards from the
47.17 So the **northern** boundary runs from the Mediterranean
47.17 border regions of Damascus and Hamath to the **north** of it.
47.20 by the Mediterranean and runs **north** to a point west of
48. 1 The **northern** boundary of the land runs eastwards from
48. 1 Mediterranean Sea, in the following order from **north** to south:
48. 8 a half kilometres wide from **north** to south, and the same
48.10 a half kilometres, and from **north** to south, five kilometres.
48.13 from east to west, by five kilometres from **north** to south.
48.21 and is bounded on the **north** by the section belonging to
48.23 Mediterranean Sea, in the following order from **north** to south:
48.30 The gates in the **north** wall are named after Reuben, Judah,
Dan 8. 4 butting with his horns to the west, the **north,** and the
11.44 from the east and the **north** will frighten him, and he will
Joel 2.20 army that came from the **north** and will drive some of them
Amos 6.14 from Hamath Pass in the **north** to the brook of the Arabah
8.12 to the Mediterranean and then on from the **north** to the east.
Obad 20 The army of exiles from **northern** Israel will return
20 and conquer Phoenicia as far **north** as Zarephath.
Zech 6. 6 the black horses was going **north** to Babylonia, the white
6. 8 me, "The horses that went **north** to Babylonia have calmed
14. 4 Half the mountain will move **northwards** and half of it southwards.
14.10 region, from Geba in the **north** to Rimmon in the south, will
Lk 13.29 and the west, from the **north** and the south, and sit down
Rev 21.13 on the south, three on the **north,** and three on the west.

NORTH GATE

2 Kgs 15.35 It was Jotham who built the **North Gate** of the Temple.
2 Chr 27. 3 was Jotham who built the **North Gate** of the Temple and did

NORTH-EAST

Deut 2. 8 Eziongeber to the Dead Sea, and we turned **north-east** towards Moab.
Josh 17.10 Asher was to the north-west, and Issachar to the **north-east.**
Neh 3.31 near the room on top of the **north-east** corner of the wall.

NORTH-EASTER

Acts 27.14 very strong wind—the one called **"North-easter"**—blew down from

NORTH-WEST

Num 34. 4 Then it will turn **north-west** to Hazar Addar and on to Azmon,
Josh 17.10 Asher was to the **north-west,** and Issachar to the north-east.
Ezek 47.19 of Kadesh Meribah, and then **north-west** along the Egyptian
48.28 oasis of Kadesh, and then **north-west** along the Egyptian
Acts 27.12 Phoenix is a harbour in Crete that faces south-west and **north-west.**

NOSE

Gen 24.22 and put it in her **nose** and put two large gold bracelets
24.30 Laban had seen the **nose-ring** and the bracelets on his
24.47 put the ring in her **nose** and the bracelets on her arms.
2 Kgs 19.28 put a hook through your **nose** and a bit in your mouth,
Job 41.20 comes pouring out of his **nose,** like smoke from weeds burning
Ps 115. 6 They have ears, but cannot hear, and **noses,** but cannot smell.
Prov 30.33 If you hit someone's **nose,** it bleeds.
Song 7. 4 Your **nose** is as lovely as the tower of Lebanon that stands
Is 3.16 They walk along with their **noses** in the air.
3.21 the rings they wear on their fingers and in their **noses;**
37.29 put a hook through your **nose** and a bit in your mouth
Ezek 16.12 I gave you a **nose-ring** and earrings and a beautiful
23.25 They will cut off your **nose** and your ears and kill your
Mal 1.13 and you turn up your **nose** at me.

NOSTRILS

Gen 2. 7 breath into his **nostrils** and the man began to live.
2 Sam 22. 9 Smoke poured out of his **nostrils,** a consuming flame and
Ps 18. 8 Smoke poured out of his **nostrils,** a consuming flame and
Amos 4.10 I filled your **nostrils** with the stink of dead bodies in your

NOT WORTH see WORTHLESS

NOT YET

Jn 2. 4 "My time has **not yet** come."
7. 6 said to them, "The right time for me has **not yet** come.
7.30 laid a hand on him, because his hour had **not yet** come.
7.39 that time the Spirit had **not yet** been given, because Jesus
11.30 (Jesus had **not yet** arrived in the village, but was still
20.17 told her, "because I have **not yet** gone back up to the
Acts 8.16 For the Holy Spirit had **not yet** come down on any of
1 Tim 1.13 to me because I did **not yet** have faith and so did
Heb 7.10 For Levi had **not yet** been born, but was, so to speak,
9. 8 the Most Holy Place has **not yet** been opened as long as
12. 4 struggle against sin you have **not yet** had to resist to the
1 Jn 3. 2 God's children, but it is **not yet** clear what we shall become.
Rev 3. 2 what you have done is **not yet** perfect in the sight of
17.10 one still rules, and the other one has **not yet** come;
17.12 are ten kings who have **not yet** begun to rule, but who

NOT-MY-PEOPLE

Hos 1. 9 said to Hosea, "Name him **'Not-My-People,'** because the
2.23 to those who were called **"Not-My-People"** I will say, "You

NOTE (1)

2 Sam 3.36 They took **note** of this and were pleased.
Lam 1.14 "He took **note** of all my sins and tied them all together;
Ezek 44. 5 **Note** carefully which persons are allowed to go in and out of
47. 6 He said to me, "Mortal man, **note** all this carefully."
Dan 9.25 **Note** this and understand it:
2 Thes 3.14 If so, take **note** of him and have nothing to do with

NOTE (2)

Josh 6. 5 Then they are to sound one long **note.**
1 Cor 14. 7 tune that is being played unless the **notes** are sounded distinctly?

NOTHING

Gen 14.24 I will take **nothing** for myself.
27.37 Now there is **nothing** that I can do for you, my son!"
29.15 work for me for **nothing** just because you are my relative.
31.14 Leah answered Jacob, "There is **nothing** left for us to
31.43 But since I can do **nothing** to keep my daughters and their
32.10 I crossed the Jordan with **nothing** but a walking-stick, and
34. 5 with his livestock, he did **nothing** until they came back.
46.34 Egyptians will have **nothing** to do with shepherds.
47.18 There is **nothing** left to give you except our bodies and our
50.21 You have **nothing** to fear.
Ex 1. 8 a new king, who knew **nothing** about Joseph, came to power in
5.23 And you have done **nothing** to help them!"
22. 2 If he owns **nothing,** he shall be sold as a slave to
34.28 the Lord forty days and nights, eating and drinking **nothing.**
Lev 23.32 a special day of rest, during which **nothing** may be eaten.
Num 11. 5 to eat all the fish we wanted, and it cost us **nothing.**
11. 6 nothing at all to eat—**nothing** but this manna day after day!"
20. 5 of Egypt into this miserable place where **nothing** will grow?
Deut 12.17 **Nothing** that you offer to the Lord is to be eaten in
22.26 **nothing** is to be done to the girl, because she has not
28.33 receive **nothing** but constant oppression and harsh treatment.
29.23 **nothing** will be planted, and not even weeds will grow there.
Josh 22.25 You have **nothing** to do with the Lord.'
22.27 from saying that ours have **nothing** to do with the Lord.
24.12 Your swords and bows had **nothing** to do with it.
Judg 6. 4 donkeys, and leave **nothing** for the Israelites to live on.
8. 2 was able to do is **nothing** compared with what you have done.
18. 6 The priest answered, "You have **nothing** to worry about.
18. 9 Don't stay here doing **nothing;**
19.30 **Nothing** like this has ever happened since the Israelites left Egypt!
Ruth 1.18 Ruth was determined to go with her, she said **nothing** more.
1 Sam 4. 7 **Nothing** like this has ever happened to us before!
14. 6 if he does, **nothing** can keep him from giving us the victory,
20.26 but Saul said **nothing** that day, because he thought,
20.34 in a rage and ate **nothing** that day—the second day of
25. 7 **Nothing** that belonged to them was stolen all the time they
25.15 them in the fields, **nothing** that belonged to us was stolen.
25.19 But she said **nothing** to her husband.
29. 3 He has done **nothing** I can find fault with since the day
30.19 **nothing** at all was missing.
2 Sam 2.26 see that in the end there will be **nothing** but bitterness?
3.26 but David knew **nothing** about it.
6.22 You may think I am **nothing,** but those girls will think
15.11 they knew **nothing** of the plot and went in all good faith.
19. 6 it clear that your officers and men mean **nothing** to you.
19.35 eighty years old, and **nothing** gives me pleasure any more.
24.24 to the Lord my God sacrifices that have cost me **nothing."**
1 Kgs 8. 9 There was **nothing** inside the Covenant Box except the two
10. 3 there was **nothing** too difficult for him to explain.
2 Kgs 3.14 swear that I would have **nothing** to do with you if I
4. 2 **"Nothing** at all, except a small jar of olive-oil," she
4.41 And then there was **nothing** wrong with it.
9.35 out to bury her found **nothing** except her skull, and the
20.13 There was **nothing** in his storerooms or anywhere in his
20.15 There is **nothing** in the storerooms that I didn't show them."
20.17 **Nothing** will be left.
25. 3 bad that the people had **nothing** left to eat, ʻthe city
1 Chr 21.24 Lord something that belongs to you, something that costs me **nothing."**
2 Chr 5.10 There was **nothing** inside the Covenant Box except the two
9. 2 there was **nothing** too difficult for him to explain.
9.11 **Nothing** like that had ever been seen before in the land of
30.26 was filled with joy, because **nothing** like this had happened
Neh 5. 8 The leaders were silent and could find **nothing** to say.
5.13 and everything you own, and will leave you with **nothing."**
6. 8 **"Nothing** of what you are saying is true.
13.19 gates to make sure that **nothing** was brought into the city on
Esth 6. 3 His servants answered, **"Nothing** has been done for him."
7. 4 If it were **nothing** more serious than being sold into slavery,
Job 1. 9 "Would Job worship you if he got **nothing** out of it?
1.21 "I was born with **nothing,** and I will die with nothing.
2.10 In spite of everything he suffered, Job said **nothing** against God.
4.11 Like lions with **nothing** to kill and eat, they die, and
5.12 men in their own schemes, so that **nothing** they do succeeds;
6.26 You think I am talking **nothing** but wind;
7. 3 Month after month I have **nothing** to live for;
8. 7 wealth you lost will be **nothing** compared with what God will
8. 9 Our life is short, we know **nothing** at all;
9.21 **Nothing** matters;
13. 5 Say **nothing,** and someone may think you are wise!

Job 13.25 I'm **nothing** but a leaf;
14. 4 **Nothing** clean can ever come from anything as unclean as man.
15. 9 There is **nothing** you know that we don't know.
15.29 **nothing** he owns will last.
16. 6 But **nothing** I say helps, and being silent does not calm my
17. 1 there is **nothing** left for me but the grave.
18.21 of evil men, the fate of those who care **nothing** for God.
20.21 When he eats, there is **nothing** left over, but now his
22. 6 you took away his clothes and left him **nothing** to wear.
22.17 rejected God and believed that he could do **nothing** to them.
24. 7 nothing to cover them, **nothing** to keep them from the cold.
29.22 they had **nothing** to add when I had finished.
30. 9 I am **nothing** but a joke to them.
30.24 a ruined man, one who can do **nothing** but beg for pity?
32.16 They stand there with **nothing** more to say.
33. 9 I have done **nothing** wrong.
33.21 His body wastes away to **nothing;**
34.29 If God decided to do **nothing** at all, no one could
34.30 There would be **nothing** that nations could do to keep
34.35 speaking from ignorance and that **nothing** he says makes sense.
35. 7 There is **nothing** God needs from you.
36. 4 **Nothing** I say to you is false;
36. 5 there is **nothing** he doesn't understand.
37.19 we have **nothing** to say.
41.17 so firmly together that **nothing** can ever pull them apart.
41.33 There is **nothing** on earth to compare with him;
Ps 11. 3 There is **nothing** a good man can do when everything falls apart."
16. 8 he is near, and **nothing** can shake me.
19. 6 **Nothing** can hide from its heat.
26. 4 I have **nothing** to do with hypocrites.
34.10 of food, but those who obey the Lord lack **nothing** good.
35.11 against me and accuse me of crimes I know **nothing** about.
36. 4 **nothing** he does is good, and he never rejects anything evil.
39. 5 In your sight my lifetime seems **nothing.**
39. 6 All he does is for **nothing;**
50.21 this, and I have said **nothing,** so you thought that I was
62. 9 Put them on the scales, and they weigh **nothing;**
73.13 Is it for **nothing,** then, that I have kept myself pure
78.36 **nothing** they said was sincere.
94.20 You have **nothing** to do with corrupt judges,
101. 3 I will have **nothing** to do with them.
102. 5 I am **nothing** but skin and bones.
109.24 I am **nothing** but skin and bones.
119.165 security, and there is **nothing** that can make them fall.
Prov 3.15 **nothing** you could want can compare with it.
4.12 **Nothing** will stand in your way if you walk wisely, and
4.24 Have **nothing** to do with lies and misleading words.
5. 4 is all over, she leaves you **nothing** but bitterness and pain.
8. 8 **nothing** is false or misleading.
8.11 **nothing** you want can compare with me.
10.28 lead to joy, but wicked people can look forward to **nothing.**
11. 7 Confidence placed in riches comes to **nothing.**
11.29 brings trouble on his family will have **nothing** at the end.
12.21 **Nothing** bad happens to righteous people,
12.21 but the wicked have **nothing** but trouble.
13. 7 Some people pretend to be rich, but have **nothing.**
13.10 Arrogance causes **nothing** but trouble.
14. 5 the truth, but an unreliable one tells **nothing** but lies.
14. 7 they have **nothing** to teach you.
14.28 without them he is **nothing.**
14.33 fools know **nothing** about wisdom.
16. 6 Obey the Lord and **nothing** evil will happen to you.
17. 7 do not tell lies, and fools have **nothing** worthwhile to say.
17.20 speaks evil can expect to find **nothing** good—only disaster.
17.21 There is **nothing** but sadness and sorrow for a father
20. 4 his fields at the right time will have **nothing** to harvest.
24. 7 He has **nothing** to say when important matters are being discussed.
24. 9 People hate a person who has **nothing** but scorn for others.
24.20 A wicked person has no future—**nothing** to look forward to.
24.21 Have **nothing** to do with people who rebel against them;
26.28 Insincere talk brings **nothing** but ruin.
27. 3 of stone and sand is **nothing** compared to the trouble that
27. 4 cruel and destructive, but it is **nothing** compared to jealousy.
30. 3 learned any wisdom, and I know **nothing** at all about God.
Ecc 1. 9 There is **nothing** new in the whole world.
2.15 **"Nothing,"** I answered, "not a thing."
2.17 So life came to mean **nothing** to me,
2.17 because everything in it had brought me **nothing** but trouble.
2.18 **Nothing** that I had worked for and earned meant a thing
2.23 everything you do brings **nothing** but worry and heartache.
3.22 There is **nothing** else we can do.
5.14 deal and end up with **nothing** left to pass on to their
5.15 We leave this world just as we entered it—with **nothing.**
5.15 of all our work there is **nothing** we can take with us.
9. 5 know they are going to die, but the dead know **nothing.**
11. 8 There is **nothing** at all to look forward to.
Is 8.22 ground, but they will see **nothing** but trouble and darkness,
11. 9 On Zion, God's sacred hill, there will be **nothing** harmful or evil.
13.17 They care **nothing** for silver and are not tempted by gold.
14.22 I will leave **nothing**—no children, no survivors at all.
15. 6 the grass beside it has withered, and **nothing** green is left.
21. 4 evening to come, but it has brought me **nothing** but terror.
26.18 We were in pain and agony, but we gave birth to **nothing.**
26.18 we have accomplished **nothing.**
27.11 Because the people have understood **nothing,** God their Creator
29.13 Their religion is **nothing** but human rules and traditions,
30.17 **Nothing** will be left of your army except a lonely flagstaff
31. 4 the same way, there is **nothing** that can keep me, the Lord
39. 2 There was **nothing** in his storerooms or anywhere in his
39. 4 There is **nothing** in the storerooms that I didn't show them."
Is 39. 6 **Nothing** will be left.
40.15 the Lord the nations are **nothing,** no more than a drop of
40.17 The nations are **nothing** at all to him.
40.23 He brings down powerful rulers and reduces them to **nothing.**
41.10 I am your God—let **nothing** terrify you!
41.24 You and all you do are **nothing;**
41.29 they can do **nothing** at all— these idols are weak and
42.25 we learnt from it **nothing** at all.
44.11 The people who make idols are human beings and **nothing** more.
45.20 that cannot save them— those people know **nothing** at all!
48. 7 **nothing** like this took place in the past.
49. 4 I have used up my strength, but have accomplished **nothing."**
52. 3 in the same way **nothing** will be paid to set you free.
52. 4 however, took you away by force and paid **nothing** for you.
52. 5 you are captives, and **nothing** was paid for you.
53. 2 nothing attractive about him, **nothing** that would draw us to him.
53. 3 look at him— we ignored him as if he were **nothing.**
55. 1 Buy wine and milk— it will cost you **nothing!**
56. 2 I will bless those who do **nothing** evil."
56.10 They know **nothing.**
58. 7 clothes to those who have **nothing** to wear, and do not refuse
59.11 God to save us from oppression and wrong, but **nothing** happens.
64.12 Are you going to do **nothing** and make us suffer more than
65.25 On Zion, my sacred hill, there will be **nothing** harmful or evil."
66. 5 own people hate you and will have **nothing** to do with you.
Jer 2.10 You will see that **nothing** like this has ever happened before.
2.11 brought them honour, for gods that can do **nothing** for them.
4.30 You are making yourself beautiful for **nothing!**
5.13 said that the prophets are **nothing** but windbags and that
5.31 prophets speak **nothing** but lies;
12.13 they have worked hard, but got **nothing** for it.
13.23 could, then you that do **nothing** but evil could learn to do
14.19 We looked for peace, but **nothing** good happened;
15.14 in a land they know **nothing** about, because my anger is like
16.17 **Nothing** is hidden from me;
16.19 "Our ancestors had nothing but false gods, **nothing** but useless idols.
17. 4 in a land you know **nothing** about, because my anger is like
17. 6 dry wilderness, on salty ground where **nothing** else grows.
17. 6 **Nothing** good ever happens to him.
17. 9 There is **nothing** else so deceitful;
17.11 his riches, and in the end he is **nothing** but a fool.
22.13 countrymen work for **nothing** and does not pay their wages.
22.28 been taken into exile to a land they know **nothing** about?"
32.17 **nothing** is too difficult for you.
32.23 they did **nothing** that you had ordered them to do.
32.27 **Nothing** is too difficult for me.
33. 3 wonderful and marvellous things that you know **nothing** about.
38.27 There was **nothing** else they could do, because no one had
44.18 to her, we have had **nothing,** and our people have died in
46.11 **nothing** can heal you.
48.30 Their boasts amount to **nothing,** and the things they do
48.38 its public squares there is **nothing** but mourning, because I
50.26 Leave **nothing** at all!
51.58 The work of the nations is all for **nothing;**
52. 6 bad that the people had **nothing** left to eat, [7] the city
Lam 1.16 my people have **nothing** left.
2.14 Your prophets had **nothing** to tell you but lies;
5.16 **Nothing** is left of all we were proud of.
Ezek 7.11 **Nothing** of theirs will remain, nothing of their wealth,
7.26 The priests will have **nothing** to teach the people, and the
12. 2 They have eyes, but they see **nothing;**
12. 2 ears, but they hear **nothing,** because they are rebellious.
12.22 'Time goes by, and predictions come to **nothing'?**
20.47 **Nothing** will be able to put it out.
21.26 **Nothing** will be the same again.
29.11 For forty years **nothing** will live there.
33.32 To them you are **nothing** more than an entertainer singing
46.20 offerings of flour, so that **nothing** holy is carried to the
Dan 4.35 He looks on the people of the earth as **nothing;**
5.21 in the open air with **nothing** to protect him from the dew.
Hos 14. 8 The people of Israel will have **nothing** more to do with idols;
Joel 2. 3 **Nothing** escapes them.
2. 8 They swarm through defences, and **nothing** can stop them.
Amos 5. 5 not try to find me at Bethel—Bethel will come to **nothing.**
Hab 2.18 that a man has made, and it tells you **nothing** but lies.
Zeph 2.11 gods of the earth to **nothing,** and then every nation will
Hag 1.10 That is why there is no rain and **nothing** can grow.
2. 3 It must seem like **nothing** at all.
Mal 1. 8 to me, do you think there's **nothing** wrong with that?
4. 1 they will burn up, and there will be **nothing** left of them.
Mt 13.12 but the person who has **nothing** will have taken away from him
15.32 been with me for three days and now have **nothing** to eat.
16.26 There is **nothing** he can give to regain his life.
20. 3 some men standing there doing **nothing,** [4] so he told them,
20. 6 'Why are you wasting the whole day here doing **nothing?'**
21.19 road and went to it, but found **nothing** on it except leaves.
22.12 But the man said **nothing.**
25.29 but the person who has **nothing,** even the little that he has
27.12 But he said **nothing** in response to the accusations of the
27.19 "Have **nothing** to do with that innocent man, because in a
28.14 you are innocent, and you will have **nothing** to worry about."
Mk 4.25 and the person who has **nothing** will have taken away from him
7.15 There is **nothing** that goes into a person from the outside
7.18 **Nothing** that goes into a person from the outside can really
8. 1 the people had **nothing** left to eat, Jesus called the disciples
8. 2 been with me for three days and now have **nothing** to eat.
8.37 There is **nothing** he can give to regain his life.
9.29 **"nothing** else can."
16. 8 They said **nothing** to anyone, because they were afraid.
Lk 1.37 For there is **nothing** that God cannot do."

Lk	4. 2	all that time he ate **nothing,** so that he was hungry when
	5. 5	answered, "we worked hard all night long and caught **nothing.**
	6.35	lend and expect **nothing** back.
	8.18	given more, but whoever has **nothing** will have taken away
	9. 3	after saying to them, "Take **nothing** with you for the journey:
	10.19	all the power of the Enemy, and **nothing** will hurt you.
	16.15	of great value by man are worth **nothing** in God's sight.
	19.26	but the person who has **nothing,** even the little that he has
	23.15	There is **nothing** this man has done to deserve death.
	24.12	he bent down and saw the linen wrappings but **nothing** else.
Jn	1.47	there is **nothing** false in him!"
	4.32	"I have food to eat that you know **nothing** about."
	5.19	the Son can do **nothing** on his own;
	5.30	"I can do **nothing** on my own authority;
	7.18	who sent him is honest, and there is **nothing** false in him.
	7.26	He is talking in public, and they say **nothing** against him!
	8.13	what you say proves **nothing."**
	8.28	will know that I do **nothing** on my own authority, but I
	8.40	Abraham did **nothing** like this!
	8.54	"If I were to honour myself, that honour would be worth **nothing.**
	9. 3	Jesus answered, "His blindness has **nothing** to do with his sins
	15. 5	for you can do **nothing** without me.
Acts	4.14	But there was **nothing** that they could say, because they saw
	19.27	Artemis will come to mean **nothing** and that her greatness
	20.24	But I reckon my own life to be worth **nothing** to me;
	25. 8	"I have done **nothing** wrong against the Law of the Jews
	25.26	But I have **nothing** definite about him to write to the Emperor.
	28.17	even though I did **nothing** against our people or the customs
	28.18	found that I had done **nothing** for which I deserved to die.
Rom	3.21	It has **nothing** to do with law, even though the Law of
	3.27	**Nothing!**
	4.14	then man's faith means **nothing** and God's promise is worthless.
	8.38	For I am certain that **nothing** can separate us from his love:
	8.39	the world below—there is **nothing** in all creation that will
1 Cor	1.28	despises, and thinks is **nothing,** in order to destroy what the
	7.19	For whether or not a man is circumcised means **nothing;**
	11. 5	message in public worship with **nothing** on her head disgraces her
	11.13	to pray to God in public worship with **nothing** on her head.
	13. 2	to move mountains—but if I have no love, I am **nothing.**
	15. 2	firmly to it—unless it was for **nothing** that you believed.
	15.14	we have nothing to preach and you have **nothing** to believe.
	15.58	Lord, since you know that **nothing** you do in the Lord's
2 Cor	3. 5	There is **nothing** in us that allows us to claim that we
	6.10	we seem to have **nothing,** yet we really possess everything.
	6.17	Have **nothing** to do with what is unclean, and I will accept
	10.10	with us in person, he is weak, and his words are **nothing!"**
	12.11	For even if I am **nothing,** I am in no way inferior
Gal	2.21	God through the Law, it means that Christ died for **nothing!**
	3. 4	Did all your experience mean **nothing** at all?
	3.12	But the Law has **nothing** to do with faith.
	4.11	it be that all my work for you has been for **nothing?**
Eph	5. 7	So have **nothing** at all to do with such people.
	5.11	Have **nothing** to do with the worthless things that people do,
1 Thes	1. 8	There is **nothing,** then, that we need to say.
	3. 5	Devil had tempted you and all our work had been for **nothing!**
2 Thes	3.11	and who do **nothing** except meddle in other people's business.
	3.14	note of him and have **nothing** to do with him, so that
1 Tim	4. 4	**nothing** is to be rejected, but everything is to be received
	6. 4	teaching of our religion [4] is swollen with pride and knows **nothing.**
	6. 7	**Nothing!**
	6. 7	**Nothing!**
Tit	1.15	but **nothing** is pure to those who are defiled and unbelieving,
	3.10	causes divisions, and then have **nothing** more to do with him.
Heb	4.13	There is **nothing** that can be hidden from God;
	6. 8	But if it grows thorns and weeds, it is worth **nothing;**
	8. 7	If there had been **nothing** wrong with the first covenant,
	9.17	for a will means **nothing** while the person who made it
	12. 2	waiting for him, he thought **nothing** of the disgrace of dying
Jas	1. 4	so that you may be perfect and complete, lacking **nothing.**
1 Pet	3. 7	Do this so that **nothing** will interfere with your prayers.
2 Pet	2.14	They want to look at **nothing** but immoral women;
1 Jn	2.10	and so there is **nothing** in him that will cause someone
3 Jn	4	**Nothing** makes me happier than to hear that my children
Rev	21.27	But **nothing** that is impure will enter the city, nor anyone
	22. 3	**Nothing** that is under God's curse will be found in the city.

NOTICE (1)

Gen	31. 5	said to them, "I have **noticed** that your father is not as
Ex	2. 5	Suddenly she **noticed** the basket in the tall grass and sent a
Judg	14. 1	went down to Timnah, where he **noticed** a certain Philistine girl.
	19.17	The old man **noticed** the traveller in the city square and
Ruth	3. 4	Be sure to **notice** where he lies down, and after he falls
1 Sam	18.15	Saul **noticed** David's success and became even more afraid of him.
	20. 6	If your father **notices** that I am not at table, tell him
	20.18	your absence will be **noticed** if you aren't at the meal.
	20.19	The day after tomorrow your absence will be **noticed** even more;
2 Sam	12.19	When David **noticed** them whispering to each other, he
	13.28	**"Notice** when Amnon has had too much to drink, and then when
	16.12	Perhaps the Lord will **notice** my misery and give me some
	17.19	grain over it, so that no one would **notice** anything.
1 Kgs	11.28	young man, and when Solomon **noticed** how hard he worked, he
	21.29	the prophet Elijah, [29] "Have you **noticed** how Ahab has
Job	1. 8	"Did you **notice** my servant Job?"
	2. 3	"Did you **notice** my servant Job?"
Ps	10.14	you take **notice** of trouble and suffering and are always
	28. 5	They take no **notice** of what the Lord has done or of
	37.37	**Notice** the good man, observe the righteous man;
	48.13	take **notice** of the walls and examine the fortresses,
	94. 7	the God of Israel does not **notice."**
	106.44	when they cried out, and he took **notice** of their distress.
Ps	144. 3	Lord, what is man, that you **notice** him;
Prov	7. 7	young men, but **noticed** one foolish fellow in particular.
Ecc	3.16	In addition, I have also **noticed** that in this world you
	4. 7	I have **noticed** something else in life that is useless.
	6. 1	I have **noticed** that in this world a serious injustice is done.
Is	53. 2	had no dignity or beauty to make us take **notice** of him.
	58. 3	The people ask, "Why should we fast if the Lord never **notices?**
Jer	33.24	said to me, [24] "Have you **noticed** how people are saying
Ezek	12. 3	Maybe those rebels will **notice** you.
Mt	8.18	Jesus **noticed** the crowd round him, he ordered his disciples to
	14.30	when he **noticed** the strong wind, he was afraid and started
	23. 5	on their foreheads and arms, and **notice** how large they are!
	23. 5	**Notice** also how long are the tassels on their cloaks!
Mk	7. 2	**noticed** that some of his disciples were eating their food with
	9.25	Jesus **noticed** that the crowd was closing in on them, so
	10.14	Jesus **noticed** this, he was angry and said to his disciples,
	12.34	Jesus **noticed** how wise his answer was, and so he told him,
Lk	11.38	Pharisee was surprised when he **noticed** that Jesus had not washed
	14. 7	Jesus **noticed** how some of the guests were choosing the best
	22.58	a little while a man **noticed** Peter and said, "You are one
Acts	4.29	And now, Lord, take **notice** of the threats they have made,
	10.31	your prayer and has taken **notice** of your works of charity.
	17.16	was greatly upset when he **noticed** how full of idols the city
	26.26	sure that you have taken **notice** of every one of them,
	27.39	recognize the coast, but they **noticed** a bay with a beach
1 Cor	16.18	Such men as these deserve **notice.**

NOTICE (2)

[DIVORCE NOTICE]

Mt	5.31	his wife must give her a written **notice of divorce.'**
	19. 7	man to hand his wife a **divorce notice** and send her away?"
	27.37	head they put the written **notice** of the accusation against him:
Mk	10. 4	a man to write a **divorce notice** and send his wife away."
	15.26	The **notice** of the accusation against him said:
Jn	19.19	Pilate wrote a **notice** and had it put on the cross.
	19.20	The **notice** was written in Hebrew, Latin, and Greek.
Acts	21.26	into the Temple and gave **notice** of how many days it would

NOURISH

[WELL-NOURISHED]

Job	21.23	they die happy and at ease, their bodies **well-nourished.**
Col	2.19	the whole body is **nourished** and held together by its joints

NOW

Mt	3.15	But Jesus answered him, "Let it be so for **now.**
	10.26	Whatever is **now** covered up will be uncovered, and every secret
	12.32	against the Holy Spirit will not be forgiven—**now** or ever.
	14. 8	"Give me here and **now** the head of John the Baptist
	19.30	But many who **now** are first will be last,
	19.30	and many who **now** are last will be first.
	22. 4	'My feast is ready **now;**
	23.39	From **now** on, I tell you, you will never see me again
	24.34	things will happen before the people **now** living have all died.
	27.42	he comes down off the cross **now,** we will believe in him!
	27.43	Well, then, let us see if God wants to save him **now!"**
Mk	6.25	to give me here and **now** the head of John the Baptist
	10.31	But many who **now** are first will be last,
	10.31	and many who **now** are last will be first."
	13.30	things will happen before the people **now** living have all died.
	14.41	the Son of Man is **now** being handed over to the power
	15.32	come down from the cross **now,** and we will believe in him!"
Lk	1.25	**"Now** at last the Lord has helped me," she said.
	1.48	From **now** on all people will call me happy, [49] because of
	5.10	from **now** on you will be catching men."
	6.21	"Happy are you who are hungry **now;**
	6.21	"Happy are you who weep **now;**
	6.24	"But how terrible for you who are rich **now;**
	6.25	"How terrible for you who are full **now;**
	6.25	"How terrible for you who laugh **now;**
	12.52	From **now** on a family of five will be divided, three
	13.30	Then those who are **now** last will be first,
	13.30	and those who are **now** first will be last."
	15.12	said to him, 'Father, give me my share of the property **now.'**
	15.24	For this son of mine was dead, but **now** he is alive;
	15.24	he was lost, but **now** he has been found.'
	15.32	happy, because your brother was dead, but **now** he is alive;
	15.32	he was lost, but **now** he has been found.' "
	21.32	will take place before the people **now** living have all died.
	22.18	I tell you that from **now** on I will not drink this
	22.36	"But **now,"** Jesus said, "whoever has a purse or a bag
	22.69	But from **now** on the Son of Man will be seated on
	23. 5	He began in Galilee and **now** has come here."
Jn	2.10	But you have kept the best wine until **now!"**
	3.26	Well, he is baptizing **now,** and everyone is going to him!"
	4.35	the crops are **now** ripe and ready to be harvested!
	4.42	the woman, "We believe **now,** not because of what you said,
	8.42	love me, because I came from God and **now** I am here.
	8.52	They said to him, **"Now** we are certain that you have a
	9.10	"How is it that you can **now** see?"
	9.15	I washed my face, and **now** I can see."
	9.18	had been blind and could **now** see, until they called his
	9.19	how is it, then, that he can **now** see?"
	9.21	it is that he is **now** able to see, nor do we
	9.25	I was blind, and **now** I see."
	12.23	answered them, "The hour has **now** come for the Son of Man
	12.27	**"Now** my heart is troubled—and what shall I say?
	12.31	**Now** is the time for this world to be judged;

Jn 12.31 **now** the ruler of this world will be overthrown.
13. 7 "You do not understand **now** what I am doing, but you
13.19 I tell you this **now** before it happens, so that when it
13.31 Judas had left, Jesus said, **"Now** the Son of Man's glory is
13.31 **now** God's glory is revealed through him.
13.34 And **now** I give you a new commandment:
13.36 "You cannot follow me **now** where I am going," answered Jesus;
13.37 "Lord, why can't I follow you **now?"**
14. 7 my Father also, and from **now** on you do know him
14.29 I have told you this **now** before it all happens, so that
16. 5 But **now** I am going to him who sent me, yet none
16. 6 And **now** that I have told you, your hearts are full of
16.12 more to tell you, but **now** it would be too much for
16.22 **now** you are sad, but I will see you again, and your
16.24 Until **now** you have not asked for anything in my name;
16.28 and **now** I am leaving the world and going to the Father."
16.29 his disciples said to him, **"Now** you are speaking plainly,
16.30 We know **now** that you know everything;
16.31 Jesus answered them, "Do you believe **now?**
17. 5 me glory in your presence **now,** the same glory I had with
19.28 Jesus knew that by **now** everything had been completed;
Acts 2.33 What you **now** see and hear is his gift that he has
17.30 did not know him, but **now** he commands all of them everywhere
18. 6 From **now** on I will go to the Gentiles."
Rom 3.21 But **now** God's way of putting people right with himself has
5. 1 **Now** that we have been put right with God through faith,
5. 2 into this experience of God's grace, in which we **now** live.
5. 9 By his sacrificial death we are **now** put right with God;
5.11 our Lord Jesus Christ, who has **now** made us God's friends.
6.10 and **now** he lives his life in fellowship with God.
6.22 But **now** you have been set free from sin and are the
7. 4 and **now** you belong to him who was raised from death in
7. 6 **Now,** however, we are free from the Law, because we died to
13.11 will be saved is closer **now** than it was when we first
1 Cor 3. 2 And even **now** you are not ready for it, [3]because you still
7.29 much time left, and from **now** on married men should live as
7.31 For this world, as it is **now,** will not last much longer.
13.11 **now** that I am a man, I have no more use for
13.12 What we see **now** is like a dim image in a mirror;
13.12 What I know **now** is only partial;
2 Cor 1.13 But even though you **now** understand us only in part, I hope
8.10 is better for you to finish **now** what you began last year.
8.11 were to plan it, and do it with what you **now** have.
Gal 1. 9 We have said it before, and **now** I say it again:
1.23 used to persecute us is **now** preaching the faith that he once
2.20 This life that I live **now,** I live by faith in the
5.21 I warn you **now** as I have before:
Eph 6.13 So put on God's armour **now!**
Phil 1. 5 the work of the gospel from the very first day until **now.**
1.20 times, and especially just **now,** I shall be full of courage,
3.16 according to the same rules we have followed until **now.**
2 Thes 2. 6 that keeps this from happening **now,** and you know what it is.
Heb 2. 8 We do not, however, see man ruling over all things **now.**
2. 9 We see him **now** crowned with glory and honour because of the
2.18 And **now** he can help those who are tempted, because he
7.19 And **now** a better hope has been provided through which we
7.25 And so he is able, **now** and always, to save those who
8. 6 But **now,** Jesus has been given priestly work which is superior
9. 5 But **now** is not the time to explain everything in detail.
9.26 Instead, **now** when all ages of time are nearing the end, he
10.13 There he **now** waits until God puts his enemies as a
12. 2 the cross, and he is **now** seated at the right-hand side of
1 Pet 1. 8 and you believe in him, although you do not **now** see him.
2.10 time you were not God's people, but **now** you are his people;
2.10 not know God's mercy, but **now** you have received his mercy.
2.25 had lost their way, but **now** you have been brought back to
3. 6 You are **now** her daughters if you do good and are not
3.21 which was a symbol pointing to baptism, which **now** saves you.
4. 2 From **now** on, then, you must live the rest of your earthly
2 Pet 3. 7 heavens and the earth that **now** exist are being preserved by
3.18 To him be the glory, **now** and for ever!
1 Jn 3. 2 My dear friends, we are **now** God's children, but it is not
4. 3 that it would come, and **now** it is here in the world
Jude 25 from all ages past, and **now,** and for ever and ever!
Rev 1.18 I was dead, but **now** I am alive for ever and ever.
1.19 both the things that are **now** and the things that will happen
2. 4 you do not love me **now** as you did at first.
2.19 know that you are doing more **now** than you did at first.
14.13 Happy are those who from **now** on die in the service of

NOWADAYS

1 Sam 25.10 The country is full of runaway slaves **nowadays!**
Acts 8.26 (This road is not used **nowadays.)**

NUISANCE

Acts 24. 5 We found this man to be a dangerous **nuisance;**

NUMBER

Gen 1.22 fill the sea, and he told the birds to increase in **number.**
46.15 In all, his descendants by Leah **numbered** thirty-three.
46.26 The total **number** of the direct descendants of Jacob who
46.27 seventy the total **number** of Jacob's family who went there.
Ex 1. 5 **number** of these people directly descended from Jacob was seventy.
1.12 the more they increased in **number** and the further they
5. 8 them to make the same **number** of bricks as before, not one
5.11 it, but you must still make the same **number** of bricks."
5.13 them to make the same **number** of bricks every day as they
Ex 5.14 making the same **number** of bricks as you made before?"
5.18 straw, but you must still make the same **number** of bricks."
5.19 had to make the same **number** of bricks every day as they
12. 4 animal, in proportion to the **number** of people and the amount
12.38 A large **number** of other people and many sheep, goats,
Lev 25.15 be fixed according to the **number** of years the land can
25.16 is being sold is the **number** of crops the land can produce.
25.51 purchase price according to the **number** of years left,
27.18 cash value according to the **number** of years left until the
27.23 its value according to the **number** of years until the next
Num 2.32 The total **number** of the people of Israel enrolled in the divisions,
3.22 The total **number** of males one month old or older that
3.28 The total **number** of males one month old or older that
3.34 The total **number** of males one month old or older that
3.39 The total **number** of all the Levite males one month old
16.49 The **number** of people who died was 14,700, not counting
22.15 Then Balak sent a larger **number** of leaders, who were
26. 7 These clans **numbered** 43,730 men.
26.14 These clans **numbered** 22,200 men.
26.18 These clans **numbered** 40,500 men.
26.22 These clans **numbered** 76,500 men.
26.25 These clans **numbered** 64,300 men.
26.27 These clans **numbered** 60,500 men.
26.34 These clans **numbered** 52,700 men.
26.37 These clans **numbered** 32,500 men.
26.41 These clans **numbered** 45,600 men.
26.43 the clan of Shuham, [43]which **numbered** 64,400 men.
26.47 These clans **numbered** 53,400 men.
26.50 These clans **numbered** 45,400 men.
26.51 The total **number** of the Israelite men was 601,730.
26.62 The male Levites who were one month old or older **numbered** 23,000.
35. 8 The **number** of Levite cities in each tribe is to be
Deut 7.13 so that you will increase in **number** and have many children;
7.22 for, if you did, the **number** of wild animals would increase
8. 1 you may live, increase in **number,** and occupy the land which
17.16 not to have a large **number** of horses for his army, and
25. 2 The **number** of lashes will depend on the crime he has committed.
26. 5 They were few in **number** when they went there, but they
28.63 in making you increase in **number,** so he will take delight in
2 Sam 15.12 gained strength, and Absalom's followers grew in **number.**
24. 9 king the total **number** of men capable of military service:
1 Kgs 8. 5 Box and sacrificed a large **number** of sheep and cattle—too
20.25 deserted you, with the same **number** of horses and chariots.
2 Kgs 17.32 chose from among their own **number** all sorts of people to
1 Chr 7. 2 At the time of King David their descendants **numbered** 22,600.
12.23 Their **numbers** were as follows:
16.19 God's people were few in **number,** strangers in the land of Canaan.
21. 5 King David the total **number** of men capable of military service:
22. 4 Tyre and Sidon to bring him a large **number** of cedar logs.
22.15 as well as a large **number** of craftsmen of every sort who
23.31 Rules were made specifying the **number** of Levites assigned to
2 Chr 5. 6 Box and sacrificed a large **number** of sheep and cattle—too
14.15 some shepherds, capturing large **numbers** of sheep and camels.
18. 2 A **number** of years later Jehoshaphat went to the city of
18. 2 Ahab had a large **number** of sheep and cattle slaughtered
28. 5 him and take a large **number** of Judaeans back to Damascus as
30. 5 Passover according to the Law, in larger **numbers** than ever before.
30.13 A great **number** of people gathered in Jerusalem in the
30.24 A large **number** of priests went through the ritual of purification.
32. 3 The officials led a large **number** of people out and stopped
32. 5 He also had a large **number** of spears and shields made.
Ezra 2. 2 clans of Israel, with the **number** of those from each clan who
2.58 The total **number** of descendants of the temple workmen
2.64 Total **number** of exiles who returned - 42,360
Neh 7. 8 clans of Israel, with the **number** of those from each clan who
7.60 The total **number** of descendants of the temple workmen
7.66 Total **number** of exiles who
Esth 9.11 That same day the **number** of people killed in Susa was
Job 1. 3 He also had a large **number** of servants and was the richest
14. 5 is decided beforehand— the **number** of months he will live.
36.26 fully know his greatness or count the **number** of his years.
Ps 40. 5 could never speak of them all— their **number** is so great!
87. 4 I will **number** among the inhabitants of Jerusalem
105.12 God's people were few in **number,** strangers in the land of Canaan.
147. 4 He has decided the **number** of the stars and calls each one
Ecc 4.16 may be no limit to the **number** of people a king rules;
Song 6. 8 sixty queens, eighty concubines, young women without **number!**
Is 3. 6 will choose one of their **number** and say to him, "You at
Jer 23. 3 They will have many children and increase in **number.**
29. 6 You must increase in **numbers** and not decrease.
30.19 By my blessing they will increase in **numbers;**
33.22 I will increase the **number** of descendants of my servant David
33.22 and the **number** of priests from the tribe of
Ezek 33. 2 of that country choose one of their **number** to be a watchman.
36.11 I will make people and cattle increase in **number.**
36.37 I will let them increase in **numbers** like a flock of sheep.
Dan 5.25 **'Number,** number, weight, divisions.'
5.26 number, God has **numbered** the days of your kingdom and
11. 6 After a **number** of years the king of Egypt will make an
Hos 7. 9 Their days are **numbered,** but they don't even know it.
10.13 chariots and in the large **number** of your soldiers, [14]war
Nah 3. 3 high, dead bodies without **number**— men stumble over them!
Mt 14.21 The **number** of men who ate was about five thousand,
15.38 The **number** of men who ate was four thousand,
24.22 But God has already reduced the **number** of days;
Mk 2.15 large **number** of tax collectors and other outcasts were following
6.44 The **number** of men who were fed was five thousand.
13.20 But the Lord has reduced the **number** of those days;
Lk 5. 6 and caught such a large **number** of fish that the nets were

Lk 5. 9 were all amazed at the large **number** of fish they had caught.
5.29 was a large **number** of tax collectors and other people.
6.17 stood on a level place with a large **number** of his disciples.
Jn 12. 9 A large **number** of people heard that Jesus was in Bethany,
Acts 4. 4 and the **number** of men grew to about five thousand.
6. 1 Some time later, as the **number** of disciples kept growing,
6. 7 The **number** of disciples in Jerusalem grew larger and larger,
6. 7 and a great **number** of priests accepted the faith.
7.17 had made to Abraham, the **number** of our people in Egypt had
9.31 was strengthened and grew in **numbers,** as it lived in reverence
11.21 with them, and a great **number** of people believed and turned
14. 1 that a great **number** of Jews and Gentiles became believers.
16. 5 made stronger in the faith and grew in **numbers** every day.
28.23 with Paul, and a large **number** of them came that day to
Rom 11. 5 there is a small **number** left of those whom God has chosen
11.12 blessings will be when the complete **number** of Jews is included!
11.25 last only until the complete **number** of Gentiles comes to God.
Heb 11.12 as many as the **numberless** grains of sand on the sea-shore.
Rev 6.11 while longer, until the complete **number** of their fellow-servants
7. 4 I was told that the **number** of those who were marked with
9.16 I was told the **number** of the mounted troops:
13.17 the beast's name or the **number** that stands for the name.
13.18 out the meaning of the **number** of the beast,
13.18 because the **number** stands for a man's name.
13.18 Its **number** is 666.
15. 2 and over the one whose name is represented by a **number.**

NUMEROUS

Gen 28.14 They will be as **numerous** as the specks of dust on the
Ex 1. 7 many children and became so **numerous** and strong that Egypt
1. 9 people, "These Israelites are so **numerous** and strong that
1.10 some way to keep them from becoming even more **numerous."**
5. 5 You people have become more **numerous** than the Egyptians.
Deut 1.10 God has made you as **numerous** as the stars in the sky.
10.22 God has made you as **numerous** as the stars in the sky.
13.17 make you a **numerous** people, as he promised your ancestors,
28.62 Although you become as **numerous** as the stars in the sky,
30. 5 prosperous and more **numerous** than your ancestors ever were.
2 Sam 24. 3 Israel a hundred times more **numerous** than they are now, and
1 Kgs 4.20 Judah and Israel were as **numerous** as the grains of sand on
1 Chr 21. 3 of Israel a hundred times more **numerous** than they are now!
27.23 the people of Israel as **numerous** as the stars in the sky.
Ps 69. 4 for no reason are more **numerous** than the hairs of my head.
Is 10.10 idols more **numerous** than those of Jerusalem and Samaria.
48.19 Your descendants would be as **numerous** as grains of sand,
51. 2 I made his descendants **numerous.**
Jer 3.16 Then when you have become **numerous** in that land, people
5. 6 apart because their sins are **numerous** and time after time
Nah 1.12 Assyrians are strong and **numerous,** they will be destroyed
Hab 1. 9 Their captives are as **numerous** as grains of sand.
Zech 10. 8 rescue them and make them as **numerous** as they used to be.

NUN

Father of Joshua (1).

Ex 33.11 who was his helper, Joshua son of **Nun,** stayed in the Tent.
Num 11.28 Then Joshua son of **Nun,** who had been Moses' helper since
13. 3 Ephraim Hoshea son of **Nun**
13.16 He changed the name of Hoshea son of **Nun** to Joshua.
14. 6 And Joshua son of **Nun** and Caleb son of Jephunneh, two of
26.65 Caleb son of Jephunneh and Joshua son of **Nun** they all did.
27.18 Moses, "Take Joshua son of **Nun,** a capable man, and place
32.12 Caleb son of Jephunneh the Kenizzite and Joshua son of **Nun;**
34.17 priest and Joshua son of **Nun** will divide the land for the
Deut 1.38 But strengthen the determination of your helper, Joshua son of **Nun.**
31.23 spoke to Joshua son of **Nun** and said to him, "Be confident
32.44 Moses and Joshua son of **Nun** recited this song, so that
34. 9 Joshua son of **Nun** was filled with wisdom, because Moses
Josh 1. 1 Moses, the Lord spoke to Moses' helper, Joshua son of **Nun.**
14. 1 the priest, Joshua son of **Nun,** and the leaders of the
17. 4 and to Joshua son of **Nun** and to the leaders, and said,
19.49 they gave Joshua son of **Nun** a part of the land as
19.51 the priest, Joshua son of **Nun,** and the leaders of the
21. 1 the priest, Joshua son of **Nun,** and to the heads of the
24.29 Lord's servant Joshua son of **Nun** died at the age of a
Judg 2. 8 Lord's servant Joshua son of **Nun** died at the age of a
1 Kgs 16.34 foretold through Joshua son of **Nun,** Hiel lost his eldest son
1 Chr 7.27 Telah, Tahan, [26] Ladan, Ammihud, Elishama, [27] **Nun,**
Neh 8.17 of Joshua son of **Nun,** and everybody was excited and happy.

Am **NURSE**
see also **WEAN**

NURSE

[WET-NURSE]

Gen 21. 7 "Who would have said to Abraham that Sarah would **nurse** children?
35. 8 Rebecca's **nurse** Deborah died and was buried beneath the
Ex 2. 7 I go and call a Hebrew woman to act as a **wet-nurse?"**
2. 9 woman, "Take this baby and **nurse** him for me, and I will
2. 9 So she took the baby and **nursed** him.
Num 11.12 me to act like a **nurse** and carry them in my arms
1 Sam 1.23 So Hannah stayed at home and **nursed** her child.
2 Sam 4. 4 from the city of Jezreel, his **nurse** picked him up and fled;
2 Kgs 11. 2 She took him and his **nurse** into a bedroom in the Temple
2 Chr 22.11 and hid him and a **nurse** in a bedroom at the Temple.
Song 8. 1 my brother, that my mother had **nursed** you at her breast.
Is 60.16 and kings will care for you As a mother **nurses** her child.
66.12 like a child that is **nursed** by its mother, carried in her
Lam 4. 3 Even a mother wolf will **nurse** her cubs, but my people are
Hos 9.14 Make them unable to **nurse** their babies!
Lk 11.27 "How happy is the woman who bore you and **nursed** you!"
23.29 never had children, who never bore babies, who never **nursed** them!'

NUT

Gen 43.11 a little resin, a little honey, spices, pistachio **nuts,** and

O'CLOCK

Mt 14.25 Between three and **six o'clock** in the morning Jesus came to
20. 3 to the market-place at **nine o'clock** and saw some men standing
20. 5 twelve o'clock and again at **three o'clock** he did the same thing.
20. 6 It was nearly **five o'clock** when he went to the market-place
20. 9 begun to work at **five o'clock** were paid a silver coin each.
27.46 At about **three o'clock** Jesus cried out with a loud shout,
Mk 6.48 time between three and **six o'clock** in the morning he came to
15.25 It was **nine o'clock** in the morning when they crucified him.
15.34 At **three o'clock** Jesus cried out with a loud shout,
Lk 23.44 It was about **twelve o'clock** when the sun stopped shining
23.44 and darkness covered the whole country until **three o'clock;**
Jn 1.39 (It was then about **four o'clock** in the afternoon.)
4.52 "It was **one o'clock** yesterday afternoon when the fever left
Acts 2.15 it is only **nine o'clock** in the morning.
3. 1 to the Temple at **three o'clock** in the afternoon, the hour
10. 3 It was about **three o'clock** one afternoon when he had a vision,
10.30 I was praying in my house at **three o'clock** in the afternoon.
23.23 hundred spearmen, and be ready to leave by **nine o'clock** tonight.

OAK

Gen 35. 4 He buried them beneath the **oak-tree** near Shechem.
35. 8 Deborah died and was buried beneath the **oak** south of Bethel.
Josh 19.33 went from Heleph to the **oak** in Zaanannim, on to Adaminekeb
24.26 and set it up under the **oak-tree** in the Lord's sanctuary.
Judg 4.11 up his tent close to Kedesh near the **oak-tree** at Zanannim.
6.11 Ophrah and sat under the **oak-tree** that belonged to Joash, a
6.19 the Lord's angel under the **oak-tree,** and gave them to him.
9. 6 and went to the sacred **oak-tree** at Shechem, where they made
9.37 along the road from the **oak-tree** of the fortune-tellers!"
2 Sam 18. 9 it went under a large **oak-tree,** Absalom's head got caught in
18.10 to Joab, "Sir, I saw Absalom hanging in an **oak-tree!"**
18.14 Absalom's chest while he was still alive, hanging in the **oak-tree.**
1 Kgs 13.14 the prophet from Judah and found him sitting under an **oak.**
1 Chr 10.12 They buried them there under an **oak** and fasted for seven days.
Ps 29. 9 The Lord's voice shakes the **oaks** and strips the leaves
Is 1.30 will wither like a dying **oak,** like a garden that no one
2.13 cedars of Lebanon and all the **oaks** in the land of Bashan.
6.13 be like the stump of an **oak-tree** that has been cut down."
44.14 to use, or choose **oak** or cypress wood from the forest.
Ezek 6.13 green tree and every large **oak,** in every place where they
27. 6 They took **oak-trees** from Bashan to make oars;
Amos 2. 9 men who were as tall as cedar-trees and as strong as **oaks.**
Zech 11. 2 Weep and wail, **oaks** of Bashan— the dense forest has been

OAK OF WEEPING

Gen 35. 8 So it was named **"Oak of Weeping."**

OARS

Ezek 27. 6 They took oak-trees from Bashan to make **oars;**
27. 8 Your **oarsmen** were from the cities of Sidon and Arvad.
27.26 When your **oarsmen** brought you out to sea, An east wind
Mk 6.48 disciples were straining at the **oars,** because they were rowing
Acts 27.40 same time they untied the ropes that held the steering **oars.**

OASIS

Ezek 47.19 south-west from Tamar to the **oasis** of Kadesh Meribah, and
48.28 south-west from Tamar to the **oasis** of Kadesh, and then

OATH

Ex 22. 8 there he must take an **oath** that he has not stolen the
22.11 of worship and take an **oath** that he has not stolen the
Num 5.19 make the woman agree to this **oath** spoken by the priest:
30. 2 the Lord or takes an **oath** to abstain from something, he must
Judg 21. 5 (They had taken a solemn **oath** that anyone who had not gone
1 Sam 14.24 day, because Saul, with a solemn **oath,** had given the order:
1 Kgs 8.31 this Temple to take an **oath** that he is innocent, [32] O Lord,
2 Kgs 11. 4 he made them agree under **oath** to what he planned to do.
2 Chr 6.22 this Temple to take an **oath** that he is innocent, [23] O Lord,
15.14 loud voice they took an **oath** in the Lord's name that they
Ezra 10. 5 of the people take an **oath** that they would do what Shecaniah
Neh 10.29 with our leaders in an **oath,** under penalty of a curse if
13.25 I made them take an **oath** in God's name that never again
Ps 144. 8 who never tell the truth and lie even under **oath.**
144.11 who never tell the truth and lie even under **oath.**
Ecc 9. 2 a man who takes an **oath** is no better off than one
Is 14.24 The Lord Almighty has sworn an **oath:**
19.18 people there will take their **oaths** in the name of the Lord
65.16 Whoever takes an **oath** will swear by the name of the Faithful
Jer 7. 9 adultery, tell lies under **oath,** offer sacrifices to Baal,
Ezek 17.16 Babylonia because he broke his **oath** and the treaty he had
17.18 He broke his **oath** and the treaty he had made.
Zeph 1. 5 to me, but then take **oaths** in the name of the god

Zech 5. 3 everyone who tells lies under **oath** will also be taken away.
5. 4 thief and the house of everyone who tells lies under **oath.**
8.17 Do not give false testimony under **oath.**
Mt 26.63 the name of the living God I now put you on **oath:**
Lk 1.73 With a solemn **oath** to our ancestor Abraham he promised
Jas 5.12 my brothers, do not use an **oath** when you make a promise.

OBED EDOM (1)

Man who looked after the Covenant Box before it was taken to Jerusalem.

2 Sam 6.10 it to the house of **Obed Edom,** a native of the city
6.11 months, and the Lord blessed **Obed Edom** and his family.
6.12 Box the Lord had blessed **Obed Edom's** family and all that he
6.12 fetched the Covenant Box from **Obed's** house to take it to
1 Chr 13.13 house of a man named **Obed Edom,** a native of the city
13.14 and the Lord blessed **Obed Edom's** family
15.25 went to the house of **Obed Edom** to fetch the Covenant Box,

OBED EDOM (2)

Levite singer and Temple Guard.

1 Chr 15.17 Azaziah, and the temple guards, **Obed Edom** and Jeiel.
15.23 Berechiah and Elkanah, along with **Obed Edom** and Jehiah,
16. 5 Shemiramoth, Jehiel, Mattithiah, Eliab, Benaiah, **Obed Edom,**
16.38 **Obed Edom** son of Jeduthun and sixty-eight men of his
16.38 Hosah and **Obed Edom** were in charge of guarding the gates.
26. 4 There was also **Obed Edom,** whom God blessed by giving him
26. 6 **Obed Edom's** eldest son, Shemaiah, had six sons:
26. 8 **Obed Edom's** family furnished a total of sixty-two highly
26.15 **Obed Edom** was allotted the south gate, and his sons were
2 Chr 25.24 by the descendants of **Obed Edom,** and the palace treasures.

OBEY

[OBEDIENCE, OBEDIENT]

Gen 17. 1 **Obey** me and always do what is right.
17.23 On that same day Abraham **obeyed** God and circumcised his
18.19 sons and his descendants to **obey** me and to do what is
22.12 know that you honour and **obey** God, because you have not kept
22.18 I have blessed your descendants—all because you **obeyed** my command."
24.37 My master made me promise with a vow to **obey** his command.
24.40 Lord, whom I have always **obeyed,** will send his angel with
26. 5 will bless you, because Abraham **obeyed** me and kept all my
28. 7 found out that Jacob had **obeyed** his father and mother and
32. 4 "I, Jacob, your **obedient** servant, report to my master Esau
41.40 of my country, and all my people will **obey** your orders.
49.10 Nations will bring him tribute And bow in **obedience** before him.
Ex 1.17 But the midwives feared God and so did not **obey** the king;
4. 6 Moses **obeyed;**
12.24 You and your children must **obey** these rules for ever.
12.50 All the Israelites **obeyed** and did what the Lord had
15.26 He said, "If you will **obey** me completely by doing what
16.28 "How much longer will you people refuse to **obey** my commands?
19. 5 Now, if you will **obey** me and keep my covenant, you will
20. 6 of generations of those who love me and **obey** my laws.
20.20 and make you keep on **obeying** him, so that you will not
23.21 Pay attention to him and **obey** him.
23.22 But if you **obey** him and do everything I command, I will
24. 7 They said, "We will **obey** the Lord and do everything that he
32.28 The Levites **obeyed,** and killed about three thousand men that day.
34.11 **Obey** the laws that I am giving you today.
Lev 7.36 that the people of Israel must **obey** for all time to come.
18. 4 **Obey** my laws and do what I command.
18.30 And the Lord said, **"Obey** the commands I give and do not
19.14 **Obey me;**
19.19 **"Obey** my commands.
19.32 Reverently **obey** me;
19.37 **Obey** all my laws and commands.
20. 8 **Obey** my laws, because I am the Lord and I make you
22.31 The Lord said, **"Obey** my commands;
25.17 Do not cheat a fellow-Israelite, but **obey** the Lord your God.
25.18 **Obey** all the Lord's laws and commands, so that you may
25.36 charge him any interest, but **obey** God and let your
25.43 Do not treat them harshly, but **obey** your God.
26. 3 according to my laws and **obey** my commands, [4] I will send you
26.14 "If you will not **obey** my commands, you will be punished.
26.15 If you refuse to **obey** my laws and commands and break the
26.18 this you still do not **obey** me, I will increase your
26.21 resist me and refuse to **obey** me, I will again increase your
26.27 defy me and refuse to **obey** me, [28] then in my anger I
Num 3.42 Moses **obeyed,** and registered all the first-born males
3.49 Moses **obeyed** and took [50] the 1,365 pieces of silver
5. 4 The Israelites **obeyed** and expelled them all from the camp.
8. 3 Aaron **obeyed** and placed the lamps facing the front
9.19 for a long time, they **obeyed** the Lord and did not move
9.23 camp and broke camp in **obedience** to the commands which the
13. 3 Moses **obeyed** and from the wilderness of Paran he sent out leaders,
14.22 my patience over and over again and have refused to **obey** me.
15.39 see them you will remember all my commands and **obey** them;
16.47 Aaron **obeyed,** took his firepan and ran into the middle
25. 4 leaders of Israel and, in **obedience** to me, execute them in
26. 3 Moses and Eleazar **obeyed,** and called together all the
27.20 so that the whole community of Israel will **obey** him.
Deut 4. 1 Moses said to the people, **"Obey** all the laws that I am
4. 2 **Obey** the commands of the Lord your God that I have given
4. 5 **Obey** them in the land that you are about to invade and
4. 6 **Obey** them faithfully, and this will show the people of
4.10 that they will learn to **obey** me as long as they live

Deut 4.13 made with you—you must **obey** the Ten Commandments, which he
4.14 laws that you are to **obey** in the land that you are
4.23 **Obey** his command not to make yourselves any kind of idol,
4.30 you, then you will finally turn to the Lord and **obey** him.
4.40 **Obey** all his laws that I have given you today, and all
5. 1 Learn them and be sure that you **obey** them.
5.10 of generations of those who love me and **obey** my laws.
5.27 We will listen and **obey.'**
5.29 would always honour me and **obey** all my commands, so that
5.31 people, so that they will **obey** them in the land that I
5.33 **Obey** them all, so that everything will go well with you
6. 1 **Obey** them in the land that you are about to enter and
6. 2 the Lord your God and **obey** all his laws that I am
6. 3 Listen to them, people of Israel, and **obey** them!
6.17 Be sure that you **obey** all the laws that he has given
6.20 did the Lord our God command us to **obey** all these laws?'
6.24 our God commanded us to **obey** all these laws and to honour
6.25 If we faithfully **obey** everything that God has commanded us,
7. 9 those who love him and **obey** his commands, [10] but he will
7.11 So now, **obey** what you have been taught;
7.11 **obey** all the laws that I have given you today.
7.12 listen to these commands and **obey** them faithfully, then the
8. 1 **"Obey** faithfully all the laws that I have given you today,
8. 2 you intended to do and whether you would **obey** his commands.
8. 6 live according to his laws and **obey** him.
8.11 do not fail to **obey** any of his laws that I am
8.20 If you do not **obey** the Lord, then you will be destroyed
9.23 you did not trust him or **obey** him.
10.13 serve him with all your heart, [13] and **obey** all his laws.
10.16 then, from now on be **obedient** to the Lord and stop being
10.20 **Obey** the Lord your God and worship only him.
11. 1 "Love the Lord your God and always **obey** all his laws.
11. 8 **"Obey** all the laws that I have given you today.
11.13 "So then, **obey** the commands that I have given you today;
11.22 **"Obey** faithfully all the laws that I have given you:
11.27 curse—[27] a blessing, if you **obey** the commands of the Lord
11.32 settle there, [32] be sure to **obey** all the laws that I am
12. 1 laws that you are to **obey** as long as you live in
12.25 If you **obey** this command, the Lord will be pleased, and
12.28 **Obey** faithfully everything that I have commanded you,
13. 4 **obey** him and keep his commands;
13.18 promised your ancestors, [18] if you **obey** all his commands
15. 5 will be poor [5] if you **obey** him and carefully observe
16.12 Be sure that you **obey** these commands;
17.19 honour the Lord and to **obey** faithfully everything that is
18.15 me from among your own people, and you are to **obey** him.
18.19 my name, and I will punish anyone who refuses to **obey** him.
21.18 a son who will not **obey** his parents, even though they punish
21.20 'Our son is stubborn and rebellious and refuses to **obey** us;
23.20 **Obey** this rule, and the Lord your God will bless everything
26.14 I have **obeyed** you, O Lord;
26.16 "Today the Lord your God commands you to **obey** all his laws;
26.16 so **obey** them faithfully with all your heart.
26.17 you have promised to **obey** him, to keep all his laws, and
26.18 and he commands you to **obey** all his laws.
27. 1 Israel, said to the people, **"Obey** all the instructions that
27.10 so **obey** him and keep all his laws that I am giving
27.26 anyone who does not **obey** all of God's laws and teachings.'
28. 1 "If you **obey** the Lord your God and faithfully keep all
28. 2 **Obey** the Lord your God and all these blessings will be yours:
28. 9 "If you **obey** the Lord your God and do everything he commands,
28.13 and never fail if you **obey** faithfully all his commands that
28.45 destroyed, because you did not **obey** the Lord your God and
28.58 "If you do not **obey** faithfully all God's teachings
28.62 will survive, because you did not **obey** the Lord your God.
29. 9 **Obey** faithfully all the terms of this covenant, so that
29.29 Law, and we and our descendants are to **obey** it for ever.
30. 2 and with all your heart **obey** his commands that I am giving
30. 6 give you and your descendants **obedient** hearts, so that you
30. 8 you, [8] and you will again **obey** him and keep all his commands
30.10 but you will have to **obey** him and keep all his laws
30.12 down for us, so that we can hear it and **obey** it?'
30.13 it to us, so that we may hear it and **obey** it?'
30.14 You know it and can quote it, so now **obey** it.
30.16 If you **obey** the commands of the Lord your God, which I
30.16 today, if you love him, **obey** him, and keep all his laws,
30.20 Love the Lord your God, **obey** him and be faithful to him,
31.12 the Lord your God and to **obey** his teachings faithfully.
31.13 so they will learn to **obey** him as long as they live
32.17 that Israel had never **obeyed,** [18] They forgot their God,
32.46 he said, "Make sure you **obey** all these commands that I
32.46 so that they may faithfully **obey** all God's teachings.
32.47 **Obey** them and you will live long in that land across the
33. 3 So we bow at his feet and **obey** his commands.
33. 4 We **obey** the Law that Moses gave us, our nation's most
33. 9 They **obeyed** your commands And were faithful to your covenant.
33.10 They will teach your people to **obey** your Law;
33.21 They **obeyed** the Lord's commands and laws When the leaders of
34. 9 The people of Israel **obeyed** Joshua and kept the commands
Josh 1. 7 and make sure that you **obey** the whole Law that my servant
1. 8 night, and make sure that you **obey** everything written in it.
1.17 We will **obey** you, just as we always obeyed Moses, and
7. 1 Jericho anything that was to be destroyed was not **obeyed.**
10.14 been a day like it, when the Lord **obeyed** a human being.
11.15 Moses had given them to Joshua, and Joshua **obeyed** them.
14. 8 But I faithfully **obeyed** the Lord my God.
14.14 because he faithfully **obeyed** the Lord, the God of Israel.
22. 2 ordered you to do, and you have **obeyed** all my commands.
22. 3 You have been careful to **obey** the commands of the Lord your
22. 5 Make sure you **obey** the law that Moses commanded you:

Josh 22. 5 God, do his will, **obey** his commandments, be faithful to him,
22.20 son of Zerah refused to **obey** the command about the things
23. 6 So be careful to **obey** and do everything that is written in
24.24 We will **obey** his commands."
Judg 2.17 Their fathers had **obeyed** the Lord's commands, but this new
2.20 Because they have not **obeyed** me, [21] I will no longer drive
3. 4 or not the Israelites would **obey** the commands that the Lord
1 Sam 12.14 him, listen to him, and **obey** his commands, and if you and
12.24 **Obey** the Lord and serve him faithfully with all your heart.
13.13 "You have not **obeyed** the command the Lord your God gave you.
13.13 If you had **obeyed,** he would have let you and your
15.13 I have **obeyed** the Lord's command."
15.19 Why, then, did you not **obey** him?
15.20 "I did **obey** the Lord," Saul replied.
15.22 **obedience** or offerings and sacrifices?
15.22 It is better to **obey** him than to sacrifice the best sheep
2 Sam 22.22 I have **obeyed** the law of the Lord;
22.45 when they hear me, they **obey.**
23. 3 with justice, who rules in **obedience** to God, [4] is like the
24. 4 But the king made Joab and his officers **obey** his order;
24.19 David **obeyed** the Lord's command and went as Gad had told him.
1 Kgs 2. 3 **Obey** all his laws and commands, as written in the Law of
2. 4 If you **obey** him, the Lord will keep the promise he made
2. 4 as they were careful to **obey** his commands faithfully with
2.42 you not agree to it and say that you would **obey** me?
3.14 And if you **obey** me and keep my laws and commands, as
6.12 said to Solomon, [12] "If you **obey** all my laws and commands,
8.23 your love when they live in whole-hearted **obedience** to you.
8.25 of Israel, provided they **obeyed** you as carefully as he did.
8.40 so that your people may **obey** you all the time they live
8.43 world may know you and **obey** you, as your people Israel do.
8.58 may he make us **obedient** to him, so that we will always
8.61 to the Lord our God, **obeying** all his laws and commands, as
9. 4 David did, and if you **obey** my laws and do everything I
11. 9 foreign gods, Solomon did not **obey** the Lord, but turned away
11.34 David, whom I chose and who **obeyed** my laws and commands.
11.38 If you **obey** me completely, live by my laws, and win my
12.24 They all **obeyed** the Lord's command and went back home.
14. 8 was completely loyal to me, **obeyed** my commands, and did only
17. 5 Elijah **obeyed** the Lord's command, and went and stayed by
2 Kgs 10.31 But Jehu did not **obey** with all his heart the law of
11. 9 The officers **obeyed** Jehoiada's instructions and brought
17.13 "Abandon your evil ways and **obey** my commands, which are
17.14 But they would not **obey;**
17.15 They refused to **obey** his instructions, they did not keep
17.19 people of Judah did not **obey** the laws of the Lord their
17.34 the Lord nor do they **obey** the laws and commands which he
17.36 You shall **obey** me, the Lord, who brought you out of
17.37 You shall always **obey** the laws and commands that I wrote
17.37 You shall not **obey** other gods, [38] and you shall not forget
17.39 You shall **obey** me, the Lord your God, and I will rescue
18.12 because the Israelites did not **obey** the Lord their God, but
18.12 They would not listen and they would not **obey.**
21. 8 the people of Israel will **obey** all my commands and keep the
21. 9 people of Judah did not **obey** the Lord, and Manasseh led them
22. 2 ancestor King David, strictly **obeying** all the laws of God.
23. 3 covenant with the Lord to **obey** him, to keep his laws and
23.25 his heart, mind, and strength, **obeying** all the Law of Moses;
1 Chr 21. 4 But the king made Joab **obey** the order.
21.19 David **obeyed** the Lord's command and went, as Gad had
21.27 told the angel to put his sword away, and the angel **obeyed.**
22.13 If you **obey** all the laws which the Lord gave to Moses
24.19 by their ancestor Aaron in **obedience** to the commands of the
28. 7 ever if he continues to **obey** carefully all my laws and
28. 8 people, I charge you to **obey** carefully everything that the
29.19 Solomon a wholehearted desire to **obey** everything that you
29.23 successful king, and the whole nation of Israel **obeyed** him.
2 Chr 6.14 your love when they live in wholehearted **obedience** to you.
6.16 provided that they carefully **obeyed** your Law just as he did.
6.31 people may honour you and **obey** you all the time they live
6.33 world may know you and **obey** you, as your people Israel do.
7.17 as your father David did, **obeying** my laws and doing
11. 4 They **obeyed** the Lord's command and did not go to fight Jeroboam.
14. 4 God of their ancestors, and to **obey** his teachings and commands.
17. 4 He served his father's God, **obeyed** God's commands, and did
19. 9 for the Lord, faithfully **obeying** him in everything you do.
23. 6 people must **obey** the Lord's instructions and stay outside.
27. 6 Jotham grew powerful because he faithfully **obeyed** the Lord
29.31 They **obeyed,** and some of them also voluntarily brought
30. 8 Do not be stubborn as they were, but **obey** the Lord.
30.12 people in their determination to **obey** his will by following
33. 8 the people of Israel will **obey** all my commands and keep the
34. 2 ancestor King David, strictly **obeying** all the laws of God.
34.21 because our ancestors have not **obeyed** the word of the Lord
34.31 covenant with the Lord to **obey** him, to keep his laws and
34.32 so the people of Jerusalem **obeyed** the requirements of the
35.26 devotion to the Lord, his **obedience** to the Law, [27] and his
Ezra 6.12 It is to be fully **obeyed."**
7.14 your God, which has been entrusted to you, is being **obeyed.**
Neh 5. 9 You ought to **obey** God and do what's right.
9.16 grew proud and stubborn and refused to **obey** your commands.
9.17 They refused to **obey;**
9.29 You warned them to **obey** your teachings, but in pride
9.29 Obstinate and stubborn, they refused to **obey.**
10.28 and all others who in **obedience** to God's Law have separated
10.29 that we will **obey** all that the Lord, our Lord, commands us;
Esth 1.15 to Queen Vashti with a command, and she refused to **obey** it!
2.20 to tell anyone, and she **obeyed** him in this,
2.20 just as she had **obeyed** him when she was a little
3. 8 Moreover, they do not **obey** the laws of the empire, so it

Job 36.11 If they **obey** God and serve him, they live out their
Ps 1. 2 Instead, they find joy in **obeying** the Law of the Lord, and
5.12 You bless those who **obey** you, Lord;
7.10 he saves those who **obey** him.
14. 5 they will be terrified, for God is with those who **obey** him.
15. 2 A person who **obeys** God in everything and always does what
15. 4 whom God rejects, but honours those who **obey** the Lord.
17. 4 I have **obeyed** your command and have not followed paths of violence.
18.21 I have **obeyed** the law of the Lord;
18.44 when they hear me, they **obey.**
19. 8 of the Lord are right, and those who **obey** them are happy.
19.11 I am rewarded for **obeying** them.
25.10 he leads all who keep his covenant and **obey** his commands.
25.14 the friend of those who **obey** him and he affirms his covenant
32.11 You that **obey** him, shout for joy!
33. 1 praise him, all you that **obey** him.
33.18 Lord watches over those who **obey** him, those who trust in his
34. 9 those who **obey** him have all they need.
34.10 of food, but those who **obey** the Lord lack nothing good.
37.18 takes care of those who **obey** him, and the land will be
37.34 Put your hope in the Lord and **obey** his commands;
45.11 he is your master, so you must **obey** him.
50.23 that honours me, and I will surely save all who **obey** me."
51.12 comes from your salvation, and make me willing to **obey** you.
78. 7 forget what he has done, but always **obey** his commandments.
78.10 they refused to **obey** his law.
78.56 They did not **obey** his commandments, [57] but were rebellious
81.11 Israel would not **obey** me.
81.13 how I wish they would **obey** me!
86.11 what you want me to do, and I will **obey** you faithfully;
87. 4 Egypt and Babylonia when I list the nations that **obey** me;
95.10 They refuse to **obey** my commands.'
99. 7 they **obeyed** the laws and commands that he gave them.
103.18 true to his covenant and who faithfully **obey** his commands.
103.20 strong and mighty angels, who **obey** his commands, who listen
105.28 on the country, but the Egyptians did not **obey** his command.
105.45 so that his people would **obey** his laws and keep all his
106. 3 Happy are those who **obey** his commands, who always do what
111.10 he gives sound judgement to all who **obey** his commands.
112. 1 the Lord, who takes pleasure in **obeying** his commands.
119. 2 who follow his commands, who **obey** him with all their heart.
119. 4 given us your laws and told us to **obey** them faithfully.
119. 8 I will **obey** your laws;
119. 9 By **obeying** your commands.
119.17 your servant, so that I may live and **obey** your teachings.
119.30 I have chosen to be **obedient;**
119.32 I will eagerly **obey** your commands, because you will give
119.33 meaning of your laws, and I will **obey** them at all times.
119.34 Explain your law to me, and I will **obey** it;
119.35 Keep me **obedient** to your commandments,
119.36 Give me the desire to **obey** your laws rather than to get
119.38 your servant— the promise you make to those who **obey** you.
119.40 I want to **obey** your commands;
119.44 I will always **obey** your law, for ever and ever.
119.45 in perfect freedom, because I try to **obey** your teachings.
119.47 I find pleasure in **obeying** your commands, because I love them.
119.56 I find my happiness in **obeying** your commands.
119.57 I promise to **obey** your laws.
119.60 Without delay I hurry to **obey** your commands.
119.63 friend of all who serve you, of all who **obey** your laws.
119.67 me, I used to go wrong, but now I **obey** your word.
119.69 about me, but with all my heart I **obey** your instructions.
119.80 May I perfectly **obey** your commandments and be spared the
119.85 Proud men, who do not **obey** your law, have dug pits to
119.88 love be good to me, so that I may **obey** your laws.
119.94 I have tried to **obey** your commands.
119.100 I have greater wisdom than old men, because I **obey** your commands.
119.101 avoided all evil conduct, because I want to **obey** your word.
119.106 I will keep my solemn promise to **obey** your just instructions.
119.112 I have decided to **obey** your laws until the day I die.
119.115 I will **obey** the commands of my God.
119.129 I **obey** them with all my heart.
119.134 those who oppress me, so that I may **obey** your commands.
119.136 down like a river, because people do not **obey** your law.
119.145 answer me, Lord, and I will **obey** your commands!
119.155 wicked will not be saved, for they do not **obey** your laws.
119.157 and oppressors, but I do not fail to **obey** your laws.
119.167 I **obey** your teachings;
119.168 I **obey** your commands and your instructions;
125. 4 to those who are good, to those who **obey** your commands.
128. 1 Happy are those who **obey** the Lord, who live by his commands.
128. 4 A man who **obeys** the Lord will surely be blessed like this.
148. 8 snow and clouds, strong winds that **obey** his command.
Prov 1.29 use for knowledge and have always refused to **obey** the Lord.
3. 7 simply **obey** the Lord and refuse to do wrong.
10.27 **Obey** the Lord, and you will live longer.
16. 6 **Obey** the Lord and nothing evil will happen to you.
19.23 **Obey** the Lord and you will live a long life, content and
22. 4 **Obey** the Lord, be humble, and you will get riches, honour,
28. 4 but if you **obey** it, you are against them.
28. 7 A young man who **obeys** the law is intelligent.
28. 9 If you do not **obey** the law, God will find your prayers
28.14 Always **obey** the Lord and you will be happy.
Ecc 8. 5 As long as you **obey** his commands, you are safe, and a
8.12 "If you **obey** God, everything will be all right, [13] but it
8.13 and they will die young, because they do not **obey** God."
12.13 Have reverence for God, and **obey** his commands, because this
Is 1.19 If you will only **obey** me, you will eat the good things
11. 3 have reverence for him, [3] and find pleasure in **obeying** him.

Is 11.14 of Edom and Moab, and the people of Ammon will **obey** them.
20. 2 He **obeyed** and went about naked and barefoot.
42.24 he wanted us to live or **obey** the teachings he gave us.
50.10 that honour the Lord and **obey** the words of his servant, the
58. 2 that they are eager to know my ways and **obey** my laws.
59.21 now on you are to **obey** me and teach your children
59.21 and your descendants to **obey** me for all time to come."
65.13 that those who worship and **obey** me will have plenty to eat
65.15 But I will give a new name to those who **obey** me.
66. 2 who are humble and repentant, who fear me and **obey** me.
66. 5 to what the Lord says, you that fear him and **obey** him:
66.14 the Lord, help those who **obey** me, and I show my anger
Jer 2.20 you refused to **obey** me and worship me.
3.13 to foreign gods and that you have not **obeyed** my commands.
3.15 will give you rulers who **obey** me, and they will rule you
3.25 we have never **obeyed** his commands."
5. 5 have rejected the Lord's authority and refuse to **obey** him.
6.19 they have rejected my teaching and have not **obeyed** my words.
7.23 I did command them to **obey** me, so that I would be
7.24 But they did not **obey** or pay any attention.
7.28 that their nation does not **obey** me, the Lord their God, or
9.13 They have not **obeyed** me or done what I told them.
11. 3 on everyone who does not **obey** the terms of this covenant.
11. 4 I told them to **obey** me and to do everything that I
11. 4 told them that if they **obeyed,** they would be my people and
11. 6 to listen to the terms of the covenant and to **obey** them.
11. 7 I solemnly warned them to **obey** me, and I have kept on
11. 8 But they did not listen or **obey.**
12.17 if any nation will not **obey,** then I will completely uproot
13.10 These evil people have refused to **obey** me.
13.11 but they would not **obey** me."
15.17 In **obedience** to your orders I stayed by myself and was
16.11 They abandoned me and did not **obey** my teachings.
16.12 of you are stubborn and evil, and you do not **obey** me.
17.23 they would not **obey** me or learn from me.
17.24 "Tell these people that they must **obey** all my commands.
17.27 But they must **obey** me and observe the Sabbath as a
22. 5 But if you do not **obey** my commands, then I swear to
22.21 you never would **obey** the Lord.
25. 6 If you had **obeyed** the Lord, then he would not have punished
26. 4 have said that you must **obey** me by following the teaching
26. 5 You have never **obeyed** what they said.
26.13 the things you are doing, and must **obey** the Lord your God.
29.19 them because they did not **obey** the message that I kept on
31.18 we were like an untamed animal, but you taught us to **obey.**
32.23 of it, they did not **obey** your commands or live according to
35. 8 We have **obeyed** all the instructions that Jonadab gave us.
35. 9 fully **obeyed** everything that our ancestor Jonadab commanded us.
35.12 why you refuse to listen to me and to **obey** my instructions.
35.14 Jonadab's descendants have **obeyed** his command not to drink wine,
35.14 have kept on speaking to you, and you have not **obeyed** me.
35.16 Jonadab's descendants have **obeyed** the command
35.16 their ancestor gave them, but you people have not **obeyed** me.
35.18 Israel, had said, "You have **obeyed** the command that your
37. 2 his officials nor the people **obeyed** the message which the
38.20 I beg you to **obey** the Lord's message;
42. 5 us if we do not **obey** all the commands that the Lord
42. 6 us or not, we will **obey** the Lord our God, to whom
42. 6 All will go well with us if we **obey** him."
43. 4 any of the people would **obey** the Lord's command to remain in
44.23 sinned against the Lord by not **obeying** all his commands."
Ezek 5. 7 By not **obeying** my laws or keeping my commands, you have
11.19 heart of stone and will give them an **obedient** heart.
11.20 Then they will keep my laws and faithfully **obey** all my commands.
18. 9 Such a man **obeys** my commands and carefully keeps my laws.
18.17 He keeps my laws and **obeys** my commands.
20.11 them my laws, which bring life to anyone who **obeys** them.
20.13 my commands, which bring life to anyone who **obeys** them.
20.19 **Obey** my laws and my commands.
20.21 keep my commands, which bring life to anyone who **obeys** them.
20.37 will take firm control of you and make you **obey** my covenant.
20.39 this you will have to **obey** me and stop dishonouring my holy
33.32 to all your words and don't **obey** a single one of them.
36.26 your stubborn heart of stone and give you an **obedient** heart.
37.24 be united under one ruler and will **obey** my laws faithfully.
44. 7 foreigners, people who do not **obey** me, enter the Temple when
Dan 6.13 does not respect Your Majesty or **obey** the order you issued.
7.27 end and all rulers on earth will serve and **obey** them."
Joel 2.11 The troops that **obey** him are many and mighty.
Jon 3. 3 So Jonah **obeyed** the Lord and went to Nineveh, a city so
Mic 4. 5 Each nation worships and **obeys** its own god, but we will
4. 5 but we will worship and **obey** the Lord our God for ever
5.15 I will take revenge on all nations that have not **obeyed** me."
Zeph 2. 3 all you humble people of the land, who **obey** his commands.
3. 9 They will all **obey** me.
Hag 1.12 They were afraid and **obeyed** the prophet Haggai,
Zech 1. 4 But they would not listen to me or **obey** me.
3. 7 "If you **obey** my laws and perform the duties I have assigned
6.15 all happen if you fully **obey** the commands of the Lord your
10.12 they will worship and **obey** me."
Mal 2. 9 you because you do not **obey** my will, and when you teach
4. 2 But for you who **obey** me, my saving power will rise on
4. 4 him at Mount Sinai for all the people of Israel to **obey.**
Mt 5.19 On the other hand, whoever **obeys** the Law and teaches others
7.24 these words of mine and **obeys** them is like a wise man
7.26 of mine and does not **obey** them is like a foolish man
8.27 "Even the winds and the waves **obey** him!"
19.20 have **obeyed** all these commandments," the young man replied.
23. 3 So you must **obey** and follow everything they tell you to do;
23.23 but you neglect to **obey** the really important teachings of the
Mt 28.20 and teach them to **obey** everything I have commanded you.
Mk 1.27 to give orders to the evil spirits, and they **obey** him!"
4.41 Even the wind and the waves **obey** him!"
7. 8 "You put aside God's command and **obey** the teachings of men."
9.10 **obeyed** his order, but among themselves they started discussing
10.20 "ever since I was young, I have **obeyed** all these commandments."
12.33 It is more important to **obey** these two commandments than to
Lk 1. 6 lives in God's sight and **obeyed** fully all the Lord's laws
2.51 back with them to Nazareth, where he was **obedient** to them.
6.47 listens to my words and **obeys** them—I will show you what
6.49 my words and does not **obey** them is like a man who
7.29 were the ones who had **obeyed** God's righteous demands and had
8.15 in a good and **obedient** heart, and they persist until they
8.21 brothers are those who hear the word of God and **obey** it."
8.25 He gives orders to the winds and waves, and they **obey** him!"
10.17 they said, "even the demons **obeyed** us when we gave them a
10.20 But don't be glad because the evil spirits **obey** you;
11.28 happy are those who hear the word of God and **obey** it!"
17. 6 and it would **obey** you.
17. 9 The servant does not deserve thanks for **obeying** orders,
18.21 "Ever since I was young, I have **obeyed** all these commandments."
Jn 3.21 light may show that what he did was in **obedience** to God.
4.34 said to them, "is to **obey** the will of the one who
7.19 But not one of you **obeys** the Law.
8.31 believed in him, "If you **obey** my teaching, you are really
8.51 whoever **obeys** my teaching will never die."
8.52 yet you say that whoever **obeys** your teaching will never die.
8.55 But I do know him, and I **obey** his word.
9.16 cannot be from God, for he does not **obey** the Sabbath law."
12.47 my message and does not **obey** it, I will not judge him.
14.15 "If you love me, you will **obey** my commandments.
14.21 "Whoever accepts my commandments and **obeys** them is the one
14.23 Jesus answered him, "Whoever loves me will **obey** my teaching.
14.24 Whoever does not love me does not **obey** my teaching.
15.10 If you **obey** my commands, you will remain in my love,
15.10 just as I have **obeyed** my Father's commands and remain in
15.20 if they obeyed my teaching, they will **obey** yours too.
17. 6 They have **obeyed** your word, [7] and now they know that everything
Acts 3.22 You are to **obey** everything that he tells you to do.
3.23 who does not **obey** that prophet shall be separated from God's
4.19 is right in God's sight—to **obey** you or to obey God.
5.21 The apostles **obeyed,** and at dawn they entered the Temple
5.29 and the other apostles replied, "We must **obey** God, not men.
5.32 the Holy Spirit, who is God's gift to those who **obey** him."
7.39 "But our ancestors refused to **obey** him;
7.53 that was handed down by angels—yet you have not **obeyed** it!"
15. 5 Gentiles must be circumcised and told to **obey** the Law of Moses."
16. 4 and elders in Jerusalem, and told them to **obey** those rules.
20.22 And now, in **obedience** to the Holy Spirit I am going to
22.12 Ananias, a religious man who **obeyed** our Law
Rom 1. 5 in order to lead people of all nations to believe and **obey.**
2.25 If you **obey** the Law, your circumcision is of value;
2.26 Gentile, who is not circumcised, **obeys** the commands of the Law,
2.27 **obey** the Law, even though they are not physically circumcised.
3.27 Is it that we **obey** the Law?
4.13 not because Abraham **obeyed** the Law, but because he believed
4.14 be given to those who **obey** the Law, then man's faith means
4.16 not just to those who **obey** the Law, but also to those
5.19 with God as the result of the **obedience** of the one man.
6.12 bodies, so that you **obey** the desires of your natural self.
6.16 surrender yourselves as slaves to **obey** someone, you are in fact
6.16 slaves of the master you **obey**—either of sin, which results
6.16 or of **obedience,** which results in being put right
6.17 slaves to sin, you have **obeyed** with all your heart the
8. 7 does not obey God's law, and in fact he cannot **obey** it.
8. 8 Those who **obey** their human nature cannot please God.
10. 5 this about being put right with God by **obeying** the Law:
10. 5 "Whoever **obeys** the commands of the Law will live."
13. 1 Everyone must **obey** the state authorities, because no authority
13. 5 For this reason you must **obey** the authorities—not just because
13. 8 Whoever does this has **obeyed** the Law.
13.10 to love, then, is to **obey** the whole Law.
15.18 Christ has done through me to lead the Gentiles to **obey** God.
16.26 known to all nations, so that all may believe and **obey.**
1 Cor 7.19 what matters is to **obey** God's commandments.
9.21 This does not mean that I don't **obey** God's law;
2 Cor 2. 9 and whether you are always ready to **obey** my instructions.
7.15 of you were ready to **obey** his instructions, how you welcomed
10. 5 we take every thought captive and make it **obey** Christ.
Gal 1. 4 himself for our sins, in **obedience** to the will of our God
3.10 Those who depend on **obeying** the Law live under a curse.
3.10 "Whoever does not always **obey** everything that is written in the
3.21 then everyone could be put right with God by **obeying** it.
5. 3 to be circumcised that he is obliged to **obey** the whole Law.
5. 4 put right with God by **obeying** the Law have cut yourselves
5. 7 Who made you stop **obeying** the truth?
6. 2 burdens, and in this way you will **obey** the law of Christ.
6.13 Even those who practise circumcision do not **obey** the Law;
Eph 2. 2 you **obeyed** the ruler of the spiritual powers in space,
5. 6 that God's anger will come upon those who do not **obey** him.
6. 1 is your Christian duty to **obey** your parents, for this is the
6. 5 Slaves, **obey** your human masters with fear and trembling;
Phil 2. 8 and walked the path of **obedience** all the way to death—
2.12 dear friends, as you always **obeyed** me when I was with you,
2.12 even more important that you **obey** me now while I am away
2.13 to make you willing and able to **obey** his own purpose.
3. 6 person can be righteous by **obeying** the commands of the Law,
3. 9 of my own, the kind that is gained by **obeying** the Law.
Col 2.20 Why do you **obey** such rules as [21] "Don't handle this,"
3. 6 God's anger will come upon those who do not **obey** him.

Col 3.20 is your Christian duty to **obey** your parents always, for that
3.22 Slaves, **obey** your human masters in all things, not only when
4.12 fully convinced Christians, in complete **obedience** to God's will.
2 Thes 1. 8 God and who do not **obey** the Good News about our Lord
3.14 that someone there will not **obey** the message we send you in
1 Tim 3. 4 family well and make his children **obey** him with all respect.
4. 1 will **obey** lying spirits and follow the teachings of demons.
5.21 solemnly call upon you to **obey** these instructions
6.14 I command you [14]to **obey** your orders and keep them faithfully
2 Tim 2. 5 in a race cannot win the prize unless he **obeys** the rules.
2.26 the Devil, who had caught them and made them **obey** his will.
Tit 3. 1 to rulers and authorities, to **obey** them, and to be ready to
Heb 2. 2 follow it or **obey** it received the punishment he deserved.
3.10 'They are always disloyal and refuse to **obey** my commands.'
5. 8 God's Son, he learnt through his sufferings to be **obedient.**
5. 9 salvation for all those who **obey** him, [10]and God declared him
9.20 seals the covenant that God has commanded you to **obey."**
11. 7 He **obeyed** God and built a boat in which he and his
11. 8 was faith that made Abraham **obey** when God called him to go
13. 9 strength from God's grace, and not by **obeying** rules about foods;
13. 9 those who **obey** these rules have not been helped by them.
13.17 **Obey** your leaders and follow their orders.
13.17 If you **obey** them, they will do their work gladly;
Jas 2. 8 the right thing if you **obey** the law of the Kingdom,
3. 3 a horse to make it **obey** us, and we are able to
4.11 are no longer one who **obeys** the Law, but one who judges
1 Pet 1. 2 people by his Spirit, to **obey** Jesus Christ and be purified
1.14 Be **obedient** to God, and do not allow your lives to be
1.22 Now that by your **obedience** to the truth you have purified
3. 6 she **obeyed** Abraham and called him her master.
3.20 of those who had not **obeyed** God when he waited patiently
1 Jn 2. 3 If we **obey** God's commands, then we are sure that we know
2. 4 knows him, but does not **obey** his commands, such a person is
2. 5 But whoever **obeys** his word is the one whose love for God
2.27 **Obey** the Spirit's teaching, then, and remain in union with Christ.
3.22 whatever we ask, because we **obey** his commands and do what
3.24 Whoever **obeys** God's commands lives in union with God
5. 2 it is by loving God and **obeying** his commands.
5. 3 For our love for God means that we **obey** his commands.
2 Jn 6 means that we must live in **obedience** to God's commands.
Rev 1. 3 prophetic message and **obey** what is written in this book!
3. 3 **obey** it and turn from your sins.
12.17 all those who **obey** God's commandments and are faithful to
14.12 God's people, those who **obey** God's commandments and are faithful
22. 7 Happy are those who **obey** the prophetic words in this book!"
22. 9 prophets and of all those who **obey** the words in this book.

OBJECT (1)

Ex 22. 9 clothing, or any other lost **object,** the two men claiming the
Lev 13.50 shall examine it and put the **object** away for seven days.
13.51 day, and if the mildew has spread, the **object** is unclean.
13.53 has not spread on the **object,** [54]he shall order it to be
13.55 you must burn the **object,** whether the rot is on the front
13.57 it is spreading again, and the owner shall burn the **object.**
13.58 If he washes the **object** and the spot disappears, he
Num 4.15 come to carry the sacred **objects** only after Aaron and his
4.15 Kohath must not touch the sacred **objects,** or they will die.
4.19 Kohath [19]be killed by coming near these most sacred **objects.**
4.20 preparing the sacred **objects** for moving, they will die."
4.24 They shall be responsible for carrying the following **objects:**
4.26 and all the fittings used in setting up these **objects.**
7. 9 the Kohathites, because the sacred **objects** they took care of
10.21 Levite clan of Kohath would start out, carrying the sacred **objects.**
18. 3 have any contact with sacred **objects** in the Holy Place or
18. 7 who comes near the sacred **objects** shall be put to death."
31. 6 of the sacred **objects** and the trumpets for giving signals.
Judg 18.18 house and took the sacred **objects,** the priest asked them,
18.20 so he took the sacred **objects** and went along with them.
1 Kgs 7.47 did not have these bronze **objects** weighed, because there
15.15 the Temple all the **objects** his father had dedicated to God,
15.15 as the gold and silver **objects** that he himself dedicated.
2 Kgs 23. 4 of the Temple all the **objects** used in the worship of Baal,
23. 4 The king burnt all these **objects** outside the city near the
23.24 gods, idols, and all other pagan **objects** of worship.
25.16 The bronze **objects** that King Solomon had made for the
1 Chr 22.19 all the other sacred **objects** used in worshipping him."
23.13 in charge of the sacred **objects** for ever, to burn incense in
29. 5 all the **objects** which the craftsmen are to make.
2 Chr 4.11 He completed all the **objects** that he had promised King
4.11 craftsman made all these **objects** out of polished bronze,
4.18 So many **objects** were made that no one determined the
4.22 All these **objects** were made of pure gold.
15.18 in the Temple all the **objects** his father Abijah had
15.18 as the gold and silver **objects** that he himself dedicated.
20.25 many cattle, supplies, clothing, and other valuable **objects.**
24. 7 used many of the sacred **objects** in the worship of Baal.)
32.27 stones, spices, shields, and other valuable **objects.**
Ps 44.14 You have made us an **object** of contempt among the nations;
Is 2. 8 of idols, and they worship **objects** that they have made with
Jer 52.20 The bronze **objects** that King Solomon had made for the
Ezek 25.14 will know what it means to be the **object** of my revenge."
Rom 9.22 enduring those who were the **objects** of his anger, who were
9.23 on us who are the **objects** of his mercy, those of us
2 Thes 2. 4 oppose every so-called god or **object** of worship and will put
Rev 18.12 woods and all kinds of **objects** made of ivory and of

OBJECT (2)

Num 30. 4 her father raises an **objection** when he hears about it.
30. 7 her husband raises an **objection** when he hears about it.
30.11 her husband raises an **objection** when he hears about it.
30.14 vow, he has raised no **objection,** she must do everything that
30.14 affirmed the vow by not **objecting** on the day he heard of
Job 34.33 Since you **object** to what God does, can you expect him to
Jer 5.31 as the prophets command, and my people offer no **objections.**
Acts 10.29 And so when you sent for me, I came without any **objection.**

OBLIGATION

Gen 38. 8 Fulfil your **obligation** to her as her husband's brother, so
38.26 I have failed in my **obligation** to her—I should have given
Num 32.22 you will have fulfilled your **obligation** to the Lord and to
Deut 29.12 you and to accept its **obligations,** [13]so that the Lord may
29.14 whom the Lord is making this covenant with its **obligations.**
1 Sam 21. 7 that day, because he had to fulfil a religious **obligation.)**
Ezra 4.14 Now, because we are under **obligation** to Your Majesty, we
Rom 1.14 For I have an **obligation** to all peoples, to the civilized
8.12 my brothers, we have an **obligation,** but it is not to live
13. 8 Be under **obligation** to no one—
13. 8 the only **obligation** you have is to love
15.27 as a matter of fact, they have an **obligation** to help them.
Gal 5. 3 to be circumcised that he is **obliged** to obey the whole Law.

OBOE

Dan 3. 5 the trumpets, followed by the playing of **oboes,** lyres,
3.15 the sound of the trumpets, **oboes,** lyres, zithers, harps, and

OBSCENE

1 Kgs 15.13 had made an **obscene** idol of the fertility goddess Asherah.
2 Chr 15.16 had made an **obscene** idol of the fertility goddess Asherah.
Is 57. 8 You set up your **obscene** idols just inside your front doors.
57.10 You think your **obscene** idols give you strength, and so you
Ezek 16.58 You must suffer for the **obscene,** disgusting things you have done."
23.27 your lust and to the **obscenities** you have committed ever
Eph 5. 4 for you to use language which is **obscene,** profane, or vulgar.
Col 3. 8 No insults or **obscene** talk must ever come from your lips.
Rev 17. 4 a gold cup full of **obscene** and filthy things, the result of

OBSERVE

Ex 13. 9 This **observance** will be a reminder, like something tied on
13.14 son asks what this **observance** means, you will answer him,
13.16 This **observance** will be a reminder, like something tied
20. 8 **"Observe** the Sabbath and keep it holy.
30.21 which they and their descendants are to **observe** for ever."
Lev 1. 2 for the Israelites to **observe** when they offer their sacrifices.
4. 2 would have to **observe** the following rules.
16.29 The following regulations are to be **observed** for all time to come.
16.31 These regulations are to be **observed** for all time to come.
16.34 These regulations are to be **observed** for all time to come.
22. 9 "All priests shall **observe** the regulations that I have given.
23.14 This regulation is to be **observed** by all your descendants
23.21 Your descendants are to **observe** this regulation for all time
23.23 day of the seventh month **observe** a special day of rest, and
23.32 to sunset on the tenth **observe** this day as a special day
23.44 of Israel the regulations for **observing** the religious
24. 3 This regulation is to be **observed** for all time to come.
Num 9. 2 people of Israel are to **observe** the Passover according to
9. 4 Moses told the people to **observe** the Passover, [5]and on the
9.11 you are permitted to **observe** it one month later instead,
9.12 **Observe** the Passover according to all the regulations.
9.13 journey and who does not **observe** the Passover, shall no
9.14 keep the Passover, he must **observe** it according to all the
10. 8 "The following rule is to be **observed** for all time to come.
15. 2 the people of Israel to **observe** in the land that he was
15.14 pleases the Lord, he is to **observe** the same regulations.
15.18 the people of Israel to **observe** in the land that he was
19.21 You are to **observe** this rule for all time to come.
27.11 people of Israel are to **observe** this as a legal requirement,
Deut 5.12 **" 'Observe** the Sabbath and keep it holy, as I, the Lord
5.15 That is why I command you to **observe** the Sabbath.
15. 5 and carefully **observe** everything that I command you today.
Josh 5.10 the plain near Jericho, they **observed** Passover on the
2 Sam 22.23 I have **observed** all his laws;
2 Chr 20. 3 orders for a fast to be **observed** throughout the country.
30.18 and so they were **observing** Passover improperly.
31.21 for the Temple or in **observance** of the Law, he did in
36.21 make up for the Sabbath rest that has not been **observed."**
Esth 3. 8 They **observe** customs that are not like those of any other people.
9.19 who live in small towns **observe** the fourteenth day of the
9.21 Persian Empire, [21]telling them to **observe** the fourteenth
9.22 They were told to **observe** these days with feasts and parties,
9.27 be regularly **observed** according to Mordecai's instructions.
9.28 every city should remember and **observe** the days of Purim for
9.31 them and their descendants to **observe** the days of Purim at
9.31 rules for the **observance** of fasts and times of mourning.
Ps 18.22 I have **observed** all his laws;
37.37 Notice the good man, **observe** the righteous man;
Is 21. 7 on donkeys and camels, he is to **observe** them carefully."
56. 2 will bless those who always **observe** the Sabbath and do not
56. 4 "If you honour me by **observing** the Sabbath and if you do
56. 6 him and serve him, who **observe** the Sabbath and faithfully
Jer 17.22 they must **observe** it as a sacred day, as I commanded their
17.24 They must **observe** the Sabbath as a sacred day and must not
17.27 they must obey me and **observe** the Sabbath as a sacred day.

Dan 6.11 When Daniel's enemies **observed** him praying to God,
1 Cor 4. 6 you may learn what the saying means, **"Observe** the proper rules."
2 Tim 3.10 you have **observed** my faith, my patience, my love, my endurance,

OBSTACLE

Is 57.14 Remove every **obstacle** from their path!
Zech 4. 7 **Obstacles** as great as mountains will disappear before you.
Mt 16.23 You are an **obstacle** in my way, because these thoughts of
1 Cor 9.12 order not to put any **obstacle** in the way of the Good
2 Cor 6. 3 our work, so we try not to put **obstacles** in anyone's way.
10. 5 we pull down every proud **obstacle** that is raised against the

OBSTINATE

Neh 9.29 **Obstinate** and stubborn, they refused to obey.

OBTAIN

Ex 32.30 perhaps I can **obtain** forgiveness for your sin."
Lev 22.25 not offer as a food-offering any animal **obtained** from a foreigner.
Dan 2.16 Daniel went at once and **obtained** royal permission for more time,
Mt 23.25 is full of what you have **obtained** by violence and selfishness.
Gal 1.18 I went to Jerusalem to **obtain** information from Peter,
2 Tim 2.10 that they too may **obtain** the salvation that comes through Christ
Heb 9.12 he took his own blood and **obtained** eternal salvation for us.

OCCASION

Mk 2.18 On one **occasion** the followers of John the Baptist and the
Acts 1. 7 to them, "The times and **occasions** are set by my Father's
9.32 everywhere, and on one **occasion** he went to visit God's people
Rom 9.21 one for special **occasions** and the other for ordinary use.
Eph 6.18 Pray on every **occasion,** as the Spirit leads.
1 Thes 5. 1 about the times and **occasions** when these things will happen.
2 Tim 2.20 some are for special **occasions,** others for ordinary use.

OCCUPY (1)

Lev 26.32 completely that the enemies who **occupy** it will be shocked at
Num 21.24 the enemy in battle and **occupied** their land from the River
21.35 leaving no survivors, and then they **occupied** his land.
32. 3 has helped the Israelites to **occupy**—the towns of Ataroth,
32.39 invaded the land of Gilead, **occupied** it, and drove out the
33.53 **Occupy** the land and settle in it, because I am giving it
Deut 1. 8 Go and **occupy** it.' "
1.20 Go and **occupy** it as he commanded.
1.38 He will lead Israel to **occupy** the land.'
1.39 I will give the land to them, and they will **occupy** it.
2.24 Attack him, and begin **occupying** his land.
2.30 defeat him and take his territory, which we still **occupy.**
2.31 take his land and **occupy** it.'
3.18 God has given you this land east of the Jordan to **occupy.**
3.18 other tribes of Israel, to help them to **occupy** their land.
3.20 Help your fellow-Israelites until they **occupy** the land
3.28 lead the people across to **occupy** the land that you see.'
4. 1 and you will live and **occupy** the land which the Lord, the
4. 5 them in the land that you are about to invade and **occupy.**
4.14 obey in the land that you are about to invade and **occupy.**
4.22 but you are about to go across and **occupy** that fertile land.
4.26 in the land across the Jordan that you are about to **occupy.**
4.47 They **occupied** his land and the land of King Og of Bashan,
5.33 continue to live in the land that you are going to **occupy.**
6. 1 them in the land that you are about to enter and **occupy.**
7. 1 which you are going to **occupy,** and he will drive many
8. 1 live, increase in number, and **occupy** the land which the Lord
9. 1 cross the River Jordan and **occupy** the land belonging to
11. 8 to cross the river and **occupy** the land that you are about
11.10 that you are about to **occupy** is not like the land of
11.23 you advance, and you will **occupy** the land belonging to
11.29 that you are going to **occupy,** you are to proclaim the
11.31 cross the River Jordan and **occupy** the land that the Lord
12.10 the Lord will let you **occupy** the land and live there.
12.29 invade their land, and you will **occupy** it and settle there.
16.20 just, so that you will **occupy** the land that the Lord your
18.14 land you are about to **occupy,** people follow the advice of
23.20 everything you do in the land that you are going to **occupy.**
26. 1 "After you have **occupied** the land that the Lord your God
28.21 of you left in the land that you are about to **occupy.**
28.63 be uprooted from the land that you are about to **occupy.**
30.16 will bless you in the land that you are about to **occupy.**
30.18 in that land across the Jordan that you are about to **occupy.**
31. 3 the nations living there, so that you can **occupy** their land;
31. 7 will lead these people to **occupy** the land that the Lord
31.13 the land that you are about to **occupy** across the Jordan."
32.47 that land across the Jordan that you are about to **occupy."**
Josh 1. 6 of these people as they **occupy** this land which I promised
1.11 cross the River Jordan to **occupy** the land that the Lord your
1.15 help them [15] until they have **occupied** the land west of the
12. 1 already conquered and **occupied** the land east of the Jordan,
Judg 11.22 They **occupied** all the Amorite territory from the Arnon
11.26 three hundred years Israel has **occupied** Heshbon and Aroer,
18. 1 for territory to claim and **occupy** because they had not yet
1 Sam 31. 7 Then the Philistines came and **occupied** them.
2 Sam 5.18 The Philistines arrived at the Valley of Rephaim and **occupied** it.
5.22 went back to the Valley of Rephaim and **occupied** it again.
20. 6 him, or else he may **occupy** some fortified towns and escape
23.14 hill, and a group of Philistines had **occupied** Bethlehem.
2 Kgs 18.17 they **occupied** the road where the clothmakers work,
23. 7 living-quarters in the Temple **occupied** by the temple prostitutes.
1 Chr 5. 9 of Gilead, and so they **occupied** the land as far east as
5.10 killed them in battle, and **occupied** their land in the
10. 7 Then the Philistines came and **occupied** them.
11.16 hill, and a group of Philistines had **occupied** Bethlehem.
2 Chr 13.19 Abijah pursued Jeroboam's army and **occupied** some of his cities:
Ezra 9.11 land we were going to **occupy** was an impure land because the
Is 36. 2 The official **occupied** the road where the clothmakers work,
54. 3 will get back the land that the other nations now **occupy.**
Jer 40.10 fruit, and olive-oil, and live in the villages you **occupy."**
Ezek 48.20 side, and it will include the area **occupied** by the city.
Amos 6.14 I am going to send a foreign army to **occupy** your country.
Obad 19 "People from southern Judah will **occupy** Edom;
Zeph 2. 7 The people of Judah who survive will **occupy** your land.
Mt 5.41 And if one of the **occupation troops** forces you to carry
Jas 3. 6 is a world of wrong, **occupying** its place in our bodies

OCCUPY (2)

Gen 46.33 you and asks what your **occupation** is, [34] be sure to tell
47. 3 The king asked them, "What is your **occupation?"**
Lk 21.34 Don't let yourselves become **occupied** with too much feasting and
1 Cor 7.31 material goods, as though they were not fully **occupied** with them.

OCEAN

Gen 1. 2 The raging **ocean** that covered everything was engulfed in total darkness,
Deut 30.13 Nor is it on the other side of the **ocean.**
30.13 'Who will go across the **ocean** and bring it to us, so
2 Sam 22.16 The floor of the **ocean** was laid bare, and the
1 Kgs 10.22 He had a fleet of **ocean-going** ships sailing with Hiram's fleet.
22.48 King Jehoshaphat built **ocean-going** ships to sail to the
2 Chr 9.21 He had a fleet of **ocean-going** ships
20.36 At the port of Eziongeber they built **ocean-going** ships.
Job 28.14 The depths of the **oceans** and seas Say that wisdom is not
38.16 Have you walked on the floor of the **ocean?**
Ps 18.15 The floor of the **ocean** was laid bare, and the
24. 2 the earth and laid its foundations in the **ocean** depths.
29. 3 the glorious God thunders, and his voice echoes over the **ocean.**
33. 7 he shut up the **ocean** depths in storerooms.
46. 2 earth is shaken and mountains fall into the **ocean** depths;
68.22 from the depths of the **ocean,** [23] so that you may wade in
93. 3 The **ocean** depths raise their voice, O Lord;
93. 4 than the roar of the **ocean,** more powerful than the waves of
104. 6 You placed the **ocean** over it like a robe, and the water
104.25 There is the **ocean,** large and wide,
107.23 Some sailed over the **ocean** in ships, earning their
148. 7 Praise the Lord from the earth, sea-monsters and all **ocean** depths;
Prov 8.24 I was born before the **oceans,** when there were no springs
8.27 stretched the horizon across the **ocean,** [28] when he placed
8.28 opened the springs of the **ocean** [29] and ordered the waters
18. 4 of wisdom, deep as the **ocean,** fresh as a flowing stream.
23.34 you were out on the **ocean,** sea-sick, swinging high up in the
25. 3 like the heights of the sky or the depths of the **ocean.**
Is 23. 1 Howl with grief, you sailors out on the **ocean!**
23. 4 The sea and the great **ocean** depths disown you and say, "I
23.14 Howl with grief, you sailors out on the **ocean!**
40.12 Can anyone measure the **ocean** by handfuls or measure the
44.27 With a word of command I dry up the **ocean.**
Lam 2.13 Your disaster is boundless as the **ocean;**
Ezek 26.19 I will cover you with the water of the **ocean** depths.
27.34 You have sunk to the **ocean** depths.
Dan 7. 2 from all directions and lashing the surface of the **ocean.**
7. 3 up out of the **ocean,** each one different from the others.
Amos 7. 4 fire burnt up the great **ocean** under the earth, and started

ODOUR

Gen 8.21 The **odour** of the sacrifice pleased the Lord, and he said
Ex 29.18 The **odour** of this offering pleases me.
29.25 The **odour** of this offering pleases me.
29.41 a food offering to me, the Lord, and its **odour** pleases me.

OFFEND

Gen 40. 1 Egypt's wine steward and his chief baker **offended** the king.
Ex 8.26 "because the Egyptians would be **offended** by our sacrificing
8.26 we use these animals and **offend** the Egyptians by sacrificing
Deut 24. 4 If he married her again, it would be **offensive** to the Lord.
2 Chr 26.18 You have **offended** the Lord God, and you no longer have his
Ezra 9. 2 The leaders and officials were the chief **offenders.**
Prov 10.12 Hate stirs up trouble, but love overlooks all **offences.**
Ezek 8.17 Look how they insult me in the most **offensive** way possible!
Mt 17.27 But we don't want to **offend** these people.
1 Cor 1.23 Christ, a message that is **offensive** to the Jews and nonsense

OFFER

see also **ANIMAL-OFFERING, BURNT-OFFERING, FELLOWSHIP-OFFERING, FOOD-OFFERING, GRAIN-OFFERING, ORDINATION OFFERING, REPAYMENT-OFFERING, SIN-OFFERING, THANK-OFFERING, THANKSGIVING-OFFERING, WINE-OFFERING**

Gen 4. 3 of his harvest and gave it as an **offering** to the Lord.
4. 4 killed it, and gave the best parts of it as an **offering.**
4. 4 pleased with Abel and his **offering,**
4. 5 but he rejected Cain and his **offering.**
22. 2 that I will show you, **offer him as a sacrifice** to me."
22.13 went and got it and **offered** it as a burnt-offering
24.44 If she agrees and also **offers** to bring water for my camels,

Gen 31.54 an animal, which he **offered as a sacrifice** on the mountain,
46. 1 went to Beersheba, where he **offered sacrifices** to the God of
Ex 3.18 days into the desert to **offer sacrifices** to the Lord, our
5. 3 into the desert to **offer sacrifices** to the Lord our God.
5. 8 asking me to let them go and **offer sacrifices** to their God!
5.17 ask me to let you go and **offer sacrifices** to the Lord.
8. 8 people go, so that they can **offer sacrifices** to the Lord."
8.25 Aaron and said, "Go and **offer sacrifices** to your God here
8.27 into the desert to **offer sacrifices** to the Lord our God,
10.25 sacrifices and burnt-offerings to **offer** to the Lord our God.
13.12 you, [12]you must **offer** every first-born male to the Lord.
13.13 first-born male donkey by **offering** a lamb in its place.
18.12 Then Jethro brought an **offering** to be burnt whole and
18.12 and other sacrifices to be **offered** to God;
20.24 sheep and your cattle as **offerings** to be completely burnt
22.20 "Condemn to death anyone who **offers sacrifices** to any
22.29 "Give me the **offerings** from your corn, your wine, and
22.30 for seven days, and on the eighth day **offer** it to me.
23.15 Never come to worship me without bringing an **offering.**
23.18 "Do not **offer** bread made with yeast when you sacrifice
25. 2 to Moses, [2]"Tell the Israelites to make an **offering** to me.
25. 2 Receive whatever **offerings** any man wishes to give.
25. 3 These **offerings** are to be:
25.30 table there is always to be the sacred bread **offered** to me.
28.38 accept all the **offerings** that the Israelites dedicate to me,
28.38 even if the people commit some error in **offering** them.
29. 3 them in a basket and **offer** them to me when you sacrifice
29.13 them and burn them on the altar as an **offering** to me.
29.14 This is an **offering** to take away the sins of the priests.
29.18 Burn the whole ram on the altar as a food **offering.**
29.18 The odour of this **offering** pleases me.
29.23 of bread which has been **offered** to me, take one loaf of
29.25 The odour of this **offering** pleases me.
29.36 Each day you must **offer** a bull as a sacrifice, so that
29.40 With the first lamb **offer** one kilogramme of fine wheat
29.40 Pour out one litre of wine as an **offering.**
29.41 lamb in the evening, and **offer** with it the same amounts of
29.41 This is a food **offering** to me, the Lord, and its odour
29.42 this burnt-offering is to be **offered** in my presence at the
30. 8 This **offering** of incense is to continue without interruption
30. 9 Do not **offer** on this altar any forbidden
30.13 Everyone must pay this as an **offering** to me.
30.20 the Tent or approach the altar to **offer** the food offering.
30.28 the altar for burning **offerings,** together with all its equipment,
32. 8 gold and have worshipped it and **offered sacrifices** to it.
34.15 will be tempted to eat the food they **offer** to their gods.
34.20 every first-born donkey by **offering** a lamb in its place.
34.20 "No one is to appear before me without an **offering.**
34.25 "Do not **offer** bread made with yeast when you sacrifice
35. 5 Make an **offering** to the Lord.
35. 5 do so is to bring an **offering** of gold, silver, or bronze;
35.13 the bread **offered** to God;
35.16 which to burn **offerings,** with its bronze grating attached,
35.21 to do so brought an **offering** to the Lord for making the
35.24 silver or bronze brought their **offering** for the Lord, and
35.29 who wanted to brought their **offering** to the Lord for the
36. 3 received from him all the **offerings** which the Israelites had
36. 3 Israel continued to bring Moses their **offerings** every morning.
38. 1 For burning **offerings,** he made an altar out of acacia-wood.
39.36 the table and all its equipment, and the bread **offered** to God;
40. 6 Put in front of the Tent the altar for burning **offerings.**
40.23 placed on it the bread **offered** to the Lord, just as the
40.29 of the curtain he placed the altar for burning **offerings.**
Lev 1. 2 for the Israelites to observe when they **offer their sacrifices.**
1. 2 When anyone **offers** an animal sacrifice, it may be one of
1. 3 If he is **offering** one of his cattle as a burnt-offering,
1.10 If the man is **offering** one of his sheep or goats, it
1.14 If the man is **offering** a bird as a burnt-offering, it
2. 1 When anyone presents an **offering** of grain to the Lord, he
2. 2 as a token that it has all been **offered** to the Lord.
2. 3 holy, since it is taken from the food **offered** to the Lord.
2. 4 If the **offering** is bread baked in an oven, it must be
2. 5 If the **offering** is bread cooked on a griddle, it is to
2. 6 pour the oil on it when you present it as an **offering.**
2. 7 If the **offering** is bread cooked in a pan, it is to
2. 8 Bring it as an **offering** to the Lord and present it to
2. 9 that it has all been **offered** to the Lord, and he will
2.10 The rest of the **offering** belongs to the priests;
2.10 holy, since it is taken from the food **offered** to the Lord.
2.11 must never use yeast or honey in food **offered** to the Lord.
2.12 An **offering** of the first corn that you harvest each year
2.13 (You must put salt on all your **offerings.)**
2.14 to the Lord an **offering** of the first corn harvested,
2.14 **offer** roasted grain or ground meal.
3. 1 When anyone **offers** one of his cattle as a fellowship-offering,
3. 7 If a man **offers** a sheep, [8]he shall put his hand on
3.12 If a man **offers** a goat, [13]he shall put his hand on
4.21 it, just as he burns the bull **offered** for his own sin.
4.21 This is an **offering** to take away the sin of the community.
4.23 shall bring as his **offering** a male goat without any defects.
4.24 This is an **offering** to take away sin.
4.26 way the priest shall **offer the sacrifice** for the sin of the
4.28 bring as his **offering** a female goat without any defects.
4.31 way the priest shall **offer the sacrifice** for the man's sin,
4.35 way the priest shall **offer the sacrifice** for the man's sin,
5. 6 bring to the Lord a female sheep or goat as an **offering.**
5. 6 The priest shall **offer the sacrifice** for the man's sin.
5. 8 priest, who will first **offer** the bird for the sin-offering.
5. 9 This is an **offering** to take away sin.
5.10 Then he shall **offer** the second bird as a burnt-offering,
5.10 way the priest shall **offer the sacrifice** for the man's sin,
Lev 5.12 that it has all been **offered** to the Lord, and he will
5.12 It is an **offering** to take away sin.
5.13 way the priest shall **offer the sacrifice** for the man's sin,
5.16 priest, and the priest shall **offer** the animal as a sacrifice
5.18 The priest shall **offer the sacrifice** for the sin which the
6. 2 An **offering** is to be made if any one sins against the
6. 7 The priest shall **offer the sacrifice** for the man's sin,
6.15 a token that all of it has been **offered** to the Lord.
6.15 The smell of this **offering** is pleasing to the Lord.
6.18 as their continuing share of the food **offered** to the Lord.
6.20 he shall present as an **offering** to the Lord one kilogramme
6.22 all time to come this **offering** is to be made by every
6.25 altar, where the animals for the burnt **offerings** are killed.
6.25 This is a very holy **offering.**
6.29 Any male of the priestly families may eat this **offering;**
7. 2 The animal for this **offering** is to be killed on the north
7. 3 All its fat shall be removed and **offered** on the altar:
7. 7 the meat belongs to the priest who **offers the sacrifice.**
7. 8 The skin of an animal **offered** as a burnt-offering belongs
7. 8 belongs to the priest who **offers the sacrifice.**
7. 9 a griddle belongs to the priest who has **offered** it to God.
7.12 If a man makes this **offering** as a thank-offering to God,
7.12 to be sacrificed, an **offering** of bread made without yeast:
7.13 In addition, he shall **offer** loaves of bread baked without yeast.
7.16 or as his own freewill **offering,** not all of it has to
7.16 on the day it is **offered,** but any that is left over
7.18 on the third day, God will not accept the man's **offering.**
7.18 The **offering** will not be counted to his credit but will be
7.21 eats the meat of this **offering** after he has touched anything
7.25 an animal that may be **offered** as a food-offering to the Lord
7.29 Whoever **offers** a fellowship-offering must bring part of it
7.33 contribution [33]to the priest who **offers** the blood and the
7.35 the part of the food **offered** to the Lord that was given
7.36 the people of Israel to give them this part of the **offering.**
7.38 day he told the people of Israel to make their **offerings.**
8.28 on top of the burnt-offering, as an ordination **offering.**
8.31 basket of ordination **offerings,** just as the Lord commanded.
9. 2 ram without any defects and **offer** them to the Lord, the bull
9. 7 "Go to the altar and **offer** the sin-offering and the
9. 7 Present this **offering** to take away the sins of the people,
9.15 After that, he presented the people's **offerings.**
9.15 goat that was to be **offered** for the people's sins,
9.15 killed it, and **offered** it, as he had done with
9.16 burnt-offering and **offered** it according to the regulations.
10.12 left over from the food **offered** to the Lord, make unleavened
10.12 eat it beside the altar, because this **offering** is very holy.
10.13 to you and your sons from the food **offered** to the Lord.
10.14 These **offerings** have been given to you and your children as
12. 7 The priest shall present her **offering** to the Lord and
14.11 take the man and these **offerings** to the entrance of the Tent
14.12 of a litre of oil he shall **offer** it as a repayment-offering.
14.19 Then the priest shall **offer** the sin-offering and perform
14.20 animal for the burnt-offering [20]and **offer** it with the
14.30 Then he shall **offer** one of the doves or pigeons [31]as
14.32 afford the normal **offerings** required for his purification.
15.15 The priest shall **offer** one of them as a sin-offering and
15.30 The priest shall **offer** one of them as a sin-offering and
16. 1 Aaron who were killed when they **offered** unholy fire to the Lord.
16. 6 He shall **offer** a bull as a sacrifice to take away his
16. 9 chosen by lot for the Lord and **offer** it as a sin-offering.
16.24 he shall go out and **offer** the burnt-offering to remove his
17. 3 or a goat as an **offering** to the Lord anywhere except at
17. 8 living in the community who **offers** a burnt-offering or any
17. 9 any other sacrifice [9]as an **offering** to the Lord anywhere
19. 5 that I have given you, and I will accept the **offering.**
19. 7 and if anyone eats it, I will not accept the **offering.**
19.24 be dedicated as an **offering** to show your gratitude to me,
21. 6 He **offers** food-offerings to me, and he must be holy.
21.18 No man with any physical defect may make the **offering:**
21.22 man may eat the food **offered** to me, both the holy
22. 2 treat with respect the sacred **offerings** that the people of
22. 3 unclean, comes near the sacred **offerings** which the people of
22. 4 eat any of the sacred **offerings** until he is ritually clean.
22. 6 eat any of the sacred **offerings** until he has had a bath.
22. 7 then he may eat the sacred **offerings,** which are his food.
22.10 of a priestly family may eat any of the sacred **offerings;**
22.12 is not a priest may not eat any of the sacred **offerings.**
22.14 eats any of the sacred **offerings** without intending to, he
22.15 shall not profane the sacred **offerings** [16]by letting any
22.16 I am the Lord and I make the **offerings** holy."
22.18 vow or as a freewill **offering,** the animal must not have any
22.20 If you **offer** any animal that has any defect, the Lord
22.21 vow or as a freewill **offering,** the animal must be without
22.22 Do not **offer** to the Lord any animal that is blind or
22.22 Do not **offer** any such animals on the altar as a food-offering.
22.23 a freewill offering you may **offer** an animal that is stunted
22.24 Do not **offer** to the Lord any animal whose testicles have
22.25 Do not **offer** as a food-offering any animal obtained from a foreigner.
22.29 When you **offer a sacrifice** of thanksgiving to the Lord,
23. 8 **Offer** your food-offerings to the Lord for seven days.
23.11 present it as a special **offering** to the Lord, so that you
23.12 the day you present the **offering** of corn, also sacrifice as
23.13 The smell of this **offering** is pleasing to the Lord.
23.13 shall also present with it an **offering** of one litre of wine.
23.14 into bread, until you have brought this **offering** to God.
23.16 Sabbath, present to the Lord another new **offering** of corn.
23.17 to the Lord as an **offering** of the first corn to be
23.18 They shall be **offered** as a burnt-offering to the Lord,
23.18 The smell of this **offering** is pleasing to the Lord.
23.19 Also **offer** one male goat as a sin-offering and two

Lev 23.20 These **offerings** are holy.
23.38 the regular Sabbaths, and these **offerings** are in addition
23.38 to your regular gifts, your **offerings** in fulfilment of vows,
23.38 and your freewill **offerings** that you give to the Lord.)
24. 9 holy part of the food **offered** to the Lord for the priests.
27. 9 that is acceptable as an **offering** to the Lord, then every
27.11 is not acceptable as an **offering** to the Lord, the man shall
27.26 so no one may dedicate it to him as a freewill **offering.**
Num 3. 4 Abihu were killed when they **offered** unholy fire to the Lord
4. 7 the table for the bread **offered** to the Lord and put on
4. 7 dishes, the incense bowls, the **offering** bowls, and the jars
5. 9 special contribution which the Israelites **offer** to the Lord
5.10 Each priest shall keep the **offerings** presented to him.
5.15 the required **offering** of one kilogramme of barley flour,
5.15 it, because it is an **offering** from a suspicious husband,
5.18 the woman's hair and put the **offering** of flour in her hands.
5.25 the priest shall take the **offering** of flour out of the
5.26 of it as a token **offering** and burn it on the altar.
6.11 The priest shall **offer** one as a sin-offering and the
6.12 As a repayment **offering** he shall bring a one-year-old lamb.
6.15 He shall also **offer** a basket of bread made without yeast:
6.15 and in addition the required **offerings** of corn and wine.
6.16 the Lord and **offer** the sin-offering and the burnt-offering.
6.17 fellowship-offering, and **offer** it with the basket of bread;
6.17 he shall also present the **offerings** of corn and wine.
6.20 they are a sacred **offering** for the priest, in addition to
6.21 if a Nazirite promises an **offering** beyond what his vow
7. 3 charge of the census, [3]brought their **offerings** to the Lord:
7.10 The leaders also brought **offerings** to celebrate the dedication
7.12 They presented their **offerings** in the following order:
7.12 The **offerings** each one brought were identical:
7.84 The totals of the **offerings** brought by the twelve
8.12 one is to be **offered** as a sin-offering and the other as
9. 7 the Lord's **offering** with the rest of the Israelites?"
9.13 he did not present the **offering** to me at the appointed time.
15. 3 vow or as a freewill **offering**
15. 3 or as an **offering** at your regular religious festivals;
15. 6 When a ram is **offered,** two kilogrammes of flour mixed with
15. 8 When a bull is **offered** to the Lord as a burnt-offering or
15.11 That is what shall be **offered** with each bull, ram,
15.12 more than one animal is **offered,**
15.12 the accompanying **offering** is to be increased proportionately.
15.24 the community, they are to **offer** a bull as a burnt-offering,
15.24 In addition, they are to **offer** a male goat as a sin-offering.
15.27 sins unintentionally, he is to **offer** a one-year-old female
16.15 to the Lord, "Do not accept any **offerings** these men bring.
18. 9 Of the most sacred **offerings** not burnt on the altar, the
18. 9 the sin-offerings, and the repayment **offerings.**
18. 9 to me as a sacred **offering** belongs to you and your sons.
18.18 the breast and the right hind leg of the special **offering.**
18.27 as the equivalent of the **offering** which the farmer makes of
18.30 the farmer keeps what is left after he makes his **offering.**
18.32 by eating any of the gifts before the best part is **offered;**
23. 2 told, and he and Balaam **offered** a bull and a ram on
23. 4 built the seven altars and **offered** a bull and a ram on
23.14 he built seven altars and **offered** a bull and a ram on
23.30 as he was told, and **offered** a bull and a ram on
26.61 Nadab and Abihu died when they **offered** unholy fire to the Lord.
28. 4 **Offer** the first lamb in the morning, and the second in the
28. 6 This is the daily **offering** that is completely burnt,
28. 6 which was first **offered** at Mount Sinai as a food-offering,
28. 8 In the evening **offer** the second lamb in the same way
28. 8 as the morning **offering,** together with its wine-offering.
28. 9 On the Sabbath day **offer** two one-year-old male lambs
28.10 This burnt-offering is to be **offered** every Sabbath
28.10 in addition to the daily **offering** with its wine-offering.
28.12 As a grain-offering, **offer** flour mixed with olive-oil:
28.15 its wine-offering, **offer** one male goat as a sin-offering.
28.19 **Offer** a burnt-offering as a food-offering to the Lord:
28.20 **Offer** the proper grain-offering of flour mixed with olive-oil:
28.22 Also **offer** one male goat as a sin-offering, and in this
28.23 **Offer** these in addition to the regular morning burnt-offering.
28.24 same way, for seven days **offer** to the Lord a food-offering,
28.24 **Offer** this in addition to the daily burnt-offering and wine-offering.
28.26 when you present the **offering** of new corn to the Lord,
28.27 **Offer** a burnt-offering as a smell pleasing to the Lord:
28.28 **Offer** the proper grain-offering of flour mixed with olive-oil:
28.30 Also **offer** one male goat as a sin-offering, and in this
28.31 **Offer** these and the wine-offering in addition to the
29. 3 **Offer** the proper grain-offering of flour mixed with olive-oil:
29. 5 Also **offer** one male goat as a sin-offering, and in this
29. 6 **Offer** these in addition to the regular burnt-offering for
29. 8 **Offer** a burnt-offering to the Lord, a smell pleasing to him:
29. 9 **Offer** the proper grain-offering of flour mixed with olive-oil:
29.11 Also **offer** one male goat as a sin-offering,
29.11 in addition to the goat **offered** in the ritual of
29.13 On this first day **offer** a food-offering to the Lord, a
29.14 **Offer** the proper grain-offering of flour mixed with olive-oil:
29.16 Also **offer** one male goat as a sin-offering.
29.16 **Offer** these in addition to the daily burnt-offering with its
29.17 On the second day **offer** twelve young bulls, two rams,
29.18 **Offer** with them all the other offerings required for the first day.
29.20 On the third day **offer** eleven young bulls, two rams, and
29.21 **Offer** with them all the other offerings required for the first day.
29.23 On the fourth day **offer** ten young bulls, two rams, and
29.24 **Offer** with them all the other offerings required for the first day.
29.26 On the fifth day **offer** nine young bulls, two rams, and
29.27 **Offer** with them all the other offerings required for the first day.
29.29 On the sixth day **offer** eight young bulls, two rams, and
29.30 **Offer** with them all the other offerings required for the first day.
29.32 On the seventh day **offer** seven young bulls, two rams,
Num 29.33 **Offer** with them all the other offerings required for the first day.
29.36 **Offer** a burnt-offering as a food-offering to the Lord, a
29.37 **Offer** with them all the other offerings required for the first day.
29.39 are in addition to the **offerings**
29.39 you give in fulfilment of a vow or as freewill **offerings.**
31.50 We **offer** them to the Lord as a payment for our lives,
Deut 2.26 to King Sihon of Heshbon with the following **offer** of peace:
12. 6 There you are to **offer your sacrifices** that are to be
12. 6 sacrifices, your tithes and your **offerings,** the gifts that
12. 6 to the Lord, your freewill **offerings,** and the first-born of
12.11 sacrifices, your tithes and your **offerings,** and those
12.13 You are not to **offer your sacrifices** wherever you choose;
12.14 you must **offer** them only in the one place that the Lord
12.14 there are you to **offer your sacrifices** that are to be burnt
12.17 Nothing that you **offer** to the Lord is to be eaten in
12.17 the Lord, your freewill **offerings,** or any other offerings.
12.18 towns, are to eat these **offerings** only in the presence of
12.26 one place of worship your **offerings** and the gifts that you
12.27 **Offer there the sacrifices** which are to be completely
12.27 Also **offer those sacrifices** in which you eat the meat and
13.16 and everything in it as an **offering** to the Lord your God.
16.10 by bringing him a freewill **offering** in proportion to the
18. 1 are to live on the **offerings** and other sacrifices given to
26.14 have not given any of it as an **offering** for the dead.
27. 6 There you are to **offer the sacrifices** that are to be burnt,
32.38 the fat of your sacrifices and **offered** them wine to drink.
33.10 They will **offer sacrifices** on your altar.
33.19 And **offer the right sacrifices** there.
Josh 6.17 in it must be totally destroyed as an **offering** to the Lord.
8.31 On it they **offered burnt sacrifices** to the Lord, and they
13.33 be a share of the **offerings** to the Lord God of Israel.
22.26 to burn sacrifices or make **offerings,** [27]but instead, as a
22.27 his sacred Tent with our **offerings** to be burnt and with
22.28 It was not for burning **offerings** or for sacrifice, but as a
22.29 to burn **offerings** on or for grain-offerings or sacrifices.
Judg 2. 5 There they **offered sacrifices** to the Lord.
6.18 Please do not leave until I bring you an **offering** of food."
6.26 burn it whole as an **offering,** using for firewood the symbol
11.31 I will burn as an **offering** the first person that comes
11.31 I will **offer** that person to you as a sacrifice."
13.15 want to prepare it, burn it as an **offering** to the Lord."
13.19 goat and some grain, and **offered** them on the rock altar to
13.23 wanted to kill us, he would not have accepted our **offerings;**
16.23 to celebrate and **offer a great sacrifice** to their god Dagon.
19.15 the square, but no one **offered** to take them home for the
20.26 They **offered fellowship sacrifices** and burnt some sacrifices
21. 4 **offered fellowship sacrifices** and burnt some sacrifices whole.
21.13 were at the Rock of Rimmon and **offered** to end the war.
1 Sam 1. 3 from Ramah to worship and **offer sacrifices** to the Lord
1. 4 Each time Elkanah **offered his sacrifice,** he would give one
1.21 to go to Shiloh and **offer** to the Lord the yearly sacrifice
2.13 when a man was **offering his sacrifice,** the priest's servant
2.14 Israelites who came to Shiloh to **offer sacrifices**
2.15 say to the man **offering the sacrifice,** "Give me some meat
2.17 treated the **offerings** to the Lord with such disrespect.
2.19 she accompanied her husband to **offer the yearly sacrifice.**
2.29 the sacrifices and **offerings** which I require from my people?
2.29 the best parts of all the sacrifices my people **offer** to me?
3.14 Eli that no sacrifice or **offering** will ever be able to
6.14 the cows and **offered them as a burnt-sacrifice** to the Lord.
6.15 the people of Beth Shemesh **offered burnt-sacrifices** and
7. 6 poured it out as an **offering** to the Lord and fasted that
7.10 While Samuel was **offering the sacrifice,** the Philistines moved
9.12 people are going to **offer a sacrifice** on the altar on the
10. 3 men on their way to **offer a sacrifice** to God at Bethel.
10. 4 They will greet you and **offer** you two of the loaves, which
10. 8 I will meet you and **offer burnt-sacrifices**
11.15 They **offered fellowship-sacrifices,** and Saul and all the
13. 9 He **offered a burnt-sacrifice,** [10]and just as he was finishing,
13.12 So I felt I had to **offer a sacrifice."**
15.15 sheep and cattle to **offer as a sacrifice** to the Lord your
15.21 here to Gilgal to **offer as a sacrifice** to the Lord your
15.22 obedience or **offerings** and sacrifices?
16. 2 say that you are there to **offer a sacrifice** to the Lord.
16. 5 "I have come to **offer a sacrifice** to the Lord.
16.11 "We won't **offer the sacrifice** until he comes."
21. 6 he had was the loaves **offered** to God, which had been removed
26.19 turned you against me, an **offering** to him will make him
2 Sam 6.13 stop while he **offered the Lord a sacrifice** of a bull and
6.17 Then he **offered sacrifices** and fellowship-offerings to the Lord.
6.18 When he had finished **offering the sacrifices,** he blessed
13.11 As she **offered** them to him, he grabbed her and said,
15.12 And while he was **offering sacrifices,** Absalom also sent
23.16 poured it out as an **offering** to the Lord [17]and said,
24.22 "and **offer** to the Lord whatever you wish.
24.22 Here are these oxen to burn as an **offering** on the altar;
24.23 to him, "May the Lord your God accept your **offering."**
24.24 I will not **offer** to the Lord my God sacrifices that have
24.25 Lord and **offered** burnt-offerings and fellowship-offerings.
1 Kgs 1. 9 One day Adonijah **offered a sacrifice** of sheep, bulls, and
1.19 He has **offered a sacrifice** of many bulls, sheep,
1.25 he has gone and **offered a sacrifice** of many bulls, sheep,
3. 2 were still **offering sacrifices** at many different altars.
3. 3 animals and **offered them as sacrifices** on various altars.
3. 4 he went to Gibeon to **offer sacrifices** because that was where
3. 4 He had **offered** hundreds of burnt-offerings there in the past.
3.15 **offered** burnt-offerings and fellowship-offerings to the Lord.
7.48 the table for the bread **offered** to God, [49]the ten
8.62 all the people there **offered sacrifices** to the Lord.
8.64 **offered there the sacrifices** burnt whole, the grain-offerings,
8.64 the bronze altar was too small for all these **offerings.**

1 Kgs 9.25 Three times a year Solomon **offered** burnt-offerings and
10. 5 him at feasts, and the sacrifices he **offered** in the Temple.
11. 8 could burn incense and **offer sacrifices** to their own gods.
12.26 people go to Jerusalem and **offer sacrifices** to the Lord in
12.32 the altar in Bethel he **offered sacrifices** to the gold
12.33 went to Bethel and **offered a sacrifice** on the altar in
13. 1 there as Jeroboam stood at the altar to **offer the sacrifice.**
13. 2 at the pagan altars who **offer sacrifices** on you, and he will
13.18 me to take you home with me and **offer** you my hospitality."
18.33 jars with water and pour it on the **offering** and the wood."
21. 6 I **offered** to buy his vineyard, or, if he preferred, to give
22.43 people continued to **offer sacrifices** and burn incense there.
22.49 Then King Ahaziah of Israel **offered** to let his men sail
22.49 with Jehoshaphat's men, but Jehoshaphat refused the **offer.**
2 Kgs 3.27 succeed him as king, and **offered** him on the city wall as
5.17 now on I will not **offer sacrifices** or burnt-offerings to any
5.20 He should have accepted what that Syrian **offered** him.
10.19 I am going to **offer a great sacrifice** to Baal, and whoever
10.24 Jonadab went in to **offer sacrifices** and burnt-offerings to Baal.
10.25 as Jehu had presented the **offerings,** he said to the guards
12. 3 continued to **offer sacrifices** and burn incense there.
12.16 money given for the repayment **offerings**
12.16 and for the **offerings** for sin was not deposited in
12.18 took all the **offerings** that his predecessors Jehoshaphat,
12.18 added to them his own **offerings** and all the gold in the
14. 4 continued to **offer sacrifices** and burn incense there.
15. 4 people continued to **offer sacrifices** and burn incense there.
15.35 people continued to **offer sacrifices** and burn incense there.
16. 4 shady tree, Ahaz **offered sacrifices** and burnt incense.
17.32 places of worship and to **offer sacrifices** for them there.
17.35 bow down to them or serve them or **offer sacrifices** to them.
17.36 you are to bow down to me and **offer sacrifices** to me.
22.17 have rejected me and have **offered sacrifices** to other gods,
23. 5 of Judah had ordained to **offer sacrifices** on the pagan
23. 5 Jerusalem—all the priests who **offered sacrifices** to Baal, to
23. 8 he desecrated the altars where they had **offered sacrifices.**
1 Chr 6.49 offerings of incense and **offered the sacrifices** that were
9.31 Korah, was responsible for preparing the baked **offerings.**
11.18 poured it out as an **offering** to the Lord [19] and said, "I
16. 1 Then they **offered sacrifices** and fellowship-offerings to God.
16. 2 After David had finished **offering the sacrifices,** he
16.29 bring an **offering** and come into his Temple.
21.23 oxen to burn as an **offering** on the altar, and here are
21.23 to use as fuel, and wheat to give as an **offering.**
21.24 will not give as an **offering** to the Lord something that
21.26 and **offered** burnt-offerings and fellowship-offerings.
21.28 answered his prayer, so he **offered sacrifices** on the altar
22. 1 where the people of Israel are to **offer** burnt-offerings."
23.29 be responsible for the bread **offered** to God,
23.29 the flour used in **offerings,** the wafers made without yeast,
23.29 the baked **offerings,** and the flour mixed with olive-oil;
23.29 to weigh and measure the temple **offerings;**
23.31 and every evening [31] and whenever **offerings** to the Lord are
28.16 on which were placed the loaves of bread **offered** to God.
29. 5 else is willing to give a generous **offering** to the Lord?"
29.17 are gathered here have been happy to bring **offerings** to you.
29.21 They also brought the **offerings** of wine.
2 Chr 1. 6 the Lord by **offering sacrifices** on the bronze altar;
2. 4 will present **offerings** of sacred bread to him continuously,
2. 4 we will **offer** burnt-offerings every morning and evening,
4.19 the altar and the tables for the bread **offered** to God;
6.40 look on us and listen to the prayers **offered** in this place.
7. 1 the sacrifices that had been **offered,** and the dazzling light
7. 4 Then Solomon and all the people **offered sacrifices** to the Lord.
7. 7 **offered there the sacrifices** burnt whole, the grain-offerings,
7. 7 which he had made was too small for all these **offerings.**
7.12 Temple as the place where sacrifices are to be **offered** to me.
7.15 all the prayers that are **offered** here, [16] because I have
8.12 Solomon **offered sacrifices** to the Lord on the altar
8.13 He **offered** burnt-offerings according to the requirements
9. 4 him at feasts, and the sacrifices he **offered** in the Temple.
11.16 Jerusalem, so that they could **offer sacrifices** to the Lord,
13.11 morning and every evening they **offer** him incense and animal
13.11 They present the **offerings** of bread on a table that is
15.11 On that day they **offered sacrifices** to the Lord from the
23.18 and to burn the sacrifices **offered** to the Lord in accordance
24.14 sacrifices were **offered** regularly at the Temple.
28. 4 every shady tree Ahaz **offered sacrifices** and burnt incense.
28.23 He **offered sacrifices** to the gods of the Syrians, who
29. 7 failed to burn incense or **offer** burnt-offerings in the
29.21 As an **offering** to take away the sins of the royal family
29.21 of Aaron, to **offer the animals as sacrifices** on the altar.
29.27 as the **offering** began, the people sang praise to the Lord,
29.31 bring sacrifices as **offerings** of thanksgiving to the Lord."
29.35 In addition to **offering the sacrifices** that were burnt whole,
29.35 that was **offered from the sacrifices** which the people ate,
30.14 been used in Jerusalem for **offering sacrifices** and burning
30.18 King Hezekiah **offered** this prayer for them:
30.22 during which they **offered sacrifices** in praise of the Lord,
31. 2 **offering** the burnt-offerings and the fellowship-offerings,
31. 3 and evening, and for those **offered** on the Sabbath, at the
31. 4 of Jerusalem to bring the **offerings** to which the priests and
31.14 charge of receiving the gifts **offered** to the Lord and of
32.23 people came to Jerusalem, bringing **offerings** to the Lord and
33.17 people continued to **offer sacrifices** at other places of worship,
33.17 they **offered** them only to the Lord.
34.25 have rejected me and have **offered sacrifices** to other gods,
35. 9 five hundred bulls for the Levites to **offer as sacrifices.**
35.12 burnt-offerings, so that they could **offer** them according to
35.13 regulations, and boiled the sacred **offerings** in pots,
35.16 and the **offering** of burnt-offerings on the altar.
Ezra 1. 4 pack animals, as well as **offerings** to present in the Temple
1. 6 animals, other valuables, and **offerings** for the Temple.
1. 9 gold bowls for **offerings** 30
1. 9 silver bowls for **offerings** 1,000
2.63 could not eat the food **offered** to God until there was a
2.68 of the clans gave freewill **offerings** to help rebuild the
3. 4 each day they **offered the sacrifices** required for that day;
3. 5 and in addition they **offered the regular sacrifices** to be
3. 5 whole and those to be **offered** at the New Moon Festival and
3. 5 as well as all the **offerings** that were given to the Lord
4. 2 have been **offering sacrifices** to him ever since Esarhaddon,
6. 3 a place where sacrifices are made and **offerings** are burnt.
6. 9 lambs to be burnt as **offerings** to the God of Heaven, or
6.10 done so that they can **offer sacrifices** that are acceptable
6.17 For the dedication they **offered** a hundred bulls,
6.17 sacrifices, and twelve goats as **offerings** for sin, one for
7.15 you the gold and silver **offerings** which I and my counsellors
7.16 province of Babylon and the **offerings** which the Israelite
7.17 lambs, corn, and wine and **offer** them on the altar of the
8.28 and gold utensils brought to him as freewill **offerings.**
8.35 returned from exile then brought **offerings** to be burnt as
8.35 They **offered** 12 bulls for all Israel, 96 rams, and 77 lambs;
8.35 they also **offered** 12 goats to purify themselves from sin.
9. 4 the evening sacrifice to be **offered,** and people began to
10.19 divorce their wives, and they **offered** a ram as a sacrifice
Neh 4. 2 Do they think that by **offering sacrifices** they can finish
7.65 could not eat the food **offered** to God until there was a
10.33 the sacred **offerings** for Sabbaths, New Moon Festivals,
10.33 other festivals, the other sacred **offerings,**
10.33 the **offerings** to take away the sins
10.34 wood to burn the sacrifices **offered** to the Lord our God,
10.35 the Temple each year an **offering** of the first corn we
10.37 each year and our other **offerings** of wine, olive-oil, and
12.43 That day many sacrifices were **offered,** and the people
12.47 The people gave a sacred **offering** to the Levites, and the
13. 5 was intended only for storing **offerings** of corn and incense,
13. 5 used in the Temple, the **offerings** for the priests, and the
13.31 wood used for burning the **offerings** to be brought at the
13.31 the people to bring their **offerings** of the first corn and
Job 1. 5 would get up early and **offer sacrifices** for each of his
15.11 God **offers** you comfort;
42. 8 rams to Job and **offer them as a sacrifice** for yourselves.
Ps 4. 5 **Offer the right sacrifices** to the Lord, and put your trust
5. 3 at sunrise I **offer** my prayer and wait for your answer.
20. 3 May he accept all your **offerings** and be pleased with all
22.25 who worship you I will **offer the sacrifices** I promised.
25. 1 To you, O Lord, I **offer** my prayer;
27. 6 With shouts of joy I will **offer sacrifices** in his Temple;
40. 6 You do not want sacrifices and **offerings;**
50. 5 who made a covenant with me by **offering a sacrifice."**
51.16 You do not want sacrifices, or I would **offer** them;
54. 6 I will gladly **offer** you a sacrifice, O Lord;
56.12 O God, I will **offer** you what I have promised;
56.12 I will give you my **offering** of thanksgiving, [13] because
61. 8 praises to you, as I **offer** you daily what I have promised.
66. 2 **offer** him glorious praise!
66.13 I will **offer** you what I promised.
66.15 I will **offer** sheep to be burnt on the altar;
68.30 calves, until they all bow down and **offer** you their silver.
69.21 when I was thirsty, they **offered** me vinegar.
69.31 please the Lord more than **offering** him cattle, more than
72.10 The kings of Spain and of the islands will **offer** him gifts;
72.10 the kings of Sheba and Seba will bring him **offerings.**
96. 8 bring an **offering** and come into his Temple.
106.28 of Baal, and ate sacrifices **offered** to lifeless gods.
106.37 They **offered** their own sons and daughters as sacrifices
116.12 What can I **offer** the Lord for all his goodness to me?
116.17 you a sacrifice of thanksgiving and **offer** my prayer to you.
Prov 3. 9 Lord by making him an **offering** from the best of all that
3.16 Wisdom **offers** you long life, as well as wealth and honour.
7.14 and said, [14] "I made my **offerings** today and have the meat
20.25 Think carefully before you promise an **offering** to God.
21.27 it when wicked men **offer him sacrifices,** especially if they
Ecc 5. 1 to learn than to **offer sacrifices** as foolish people do,
7.26 The love she **offers** you will catch you like a trap or
9. 2 to those who **offer sacrifices** and those who do not.
Is 1.11 think I want all these sacrifices you keep **offering** to me?
1.13 It's useless to bring your **offerings.**
18. 7 Lord Almighty will receive **offerings** from this land
19.15 Egypt, rich or poor, important or unknown, can **offer** help.
19.21 and worship him, and bring him sacrifices and **offerings.**
28.12 He **offered** rest and comfort to all of you, but you
34. 6 The Lord will **offer this sacrifice** in the city of Bozrah;
43.23 not burden you by demanding **offerings** or wear you out by
56. 7 of prayer, and accept the sacrifices you **offer** on my altar.
57. 5 You **offer your children as sacrifices** in the rocky caves
57. 6 You pour out wine as **offerings** to them and bring them
grain-offerings.
57. 7 You go to the high mountains to **offer sacrifices** and have sex.
57.19 I **offer** peace to all, both near and far!
60. 7 to you as sacrifices And **offered** on the altar to please the
65. 3 They **offer pagan sacrifices** in sacred gardens and burn
65. 4 and drink broth made from meat **offered in pagan sacrifices.**
66. 3 whether they present a grain-offering or **offer** pigs' blood;
66. 3 whether they **offer** incense or pray to an idol.
Jer 1.16 have abandoned me, have **offered sacrifices** to other gods,
6.20 I will not accept their **offerings**
7. 9 adultery, tell lies under oath, **offer sacrifices** to Baal,
11.12 the gods to whom they **offer sacrifices** and will cry out to
11.15 by making promises and by **offering animal sacrifices?**
11.17 they have made me angry by **offering sacrifices** to Baal."

Jer 14.12 even if they **offer** me burnt-offerings and grain-offerings,
19. 4 and defiled this place by **offering sacrifices** here to other
19.13 been poured out as an **offering** to other gods—they will all
33.18 Levi to serve me and to **offer** burnt-offerings, grain-offerings, and sacrifices."
35. 2 one of the rooms in the Temple and **offer** them some wine."
41. 5 They were taking corn and incense to **offer** in the Temple.
44. 3 They **offered sacrifices** to other gods and served gods that
44.15 who knew that their wives **offered sacrifices** to other gods,
44.17 We will **offer sacrifices** to our goddess, the Queen of Heaven,
44.19 like the Queen of Heaven, **offered sacrifices** to her, and
44.21 the people of the land **offered** in the towns of Judah and
44.23 come on you because you **offered sacrifices** to other gods and
44.24 You promised that you would **offer sacrifices** to her and pour
48.35 of worship and from **offering sacrifices** to their gods.
52.19 and the bowls used for pouring out **offerings** of wine.
Ezek 16.18 on the images, and you **offered** to the images the olive-oil
16.19 olive-oil, and honey—but you **offered** it as a sacrifice to
16.20 you had borne me and **offered them as sacrifices** to idols.
16.25 You **offered** yourself to everyone who came by, and you were
18. 6 or eat the sacrifices **offered** at forbidden shrines.
18.11 He eats sacrifices **offered** at forbidden shrines
18.15 or eat the sacrifices **offered** at forbidden shrines.
20.26 defile themselves with their own **offerings,** and I let them
20.28 and green trees, they **offered sacrifices** at all of them.
20.28 they burnt and by the wine they brought as **offerings.**
20.31 Even today you **offer** the same gifts and defile
20.39 dishonouring my holy name by **offering gifts to your idols.**
20.40 your sacrifices, your best **offerings,** and your holy gifts.
22. 9 Some of them eat sacrifices **offered** to idols.
36.38 of the sheep which were **offered as sacrifices** at a festival.
40.39 the animals to be **offered as sacrifices,** either to be burnt
40.42 annexe, used to prepare the **offerings** to be burnt whole,
40.43 meat to be **offered in sacrifice** was placed on the tables.
42.13 who enter the Lord's presence eat the holiest **offerings.**
42.13 holy, the priests will place the holiest **offerings** there:
42.13 the sacrifices **offered** for sin or as repayment-offerings.
43.19 give them a young bull to **offer as a sacrifice** for sin.
43.21 the bull that is **offered as a sacrifice** for sin and burn
43.22 without any defects and **offer it as a sacrifice** for sin.
43.24 sprinkle salt on them and burn them as an **offering** to me.
43.25 seven days you are to **offer** a goat, a bull, and a
43.27 the priests are to begin **offering** on the altar the
44. 7 fat and the blood of the sacrifices are being **offered** to me.
44.11 the people **offer** for burnt-offerings and for sacrifices,
44.15 come into my presence to **offer** me the fat and the blood
44.27 of the Temple and **offer a sacrifice** for his purification, so
44.30 first harvest and of everything else that is **offered** to me.
44.30 the first loaf as an **offering,** and my blessing will rest on
45.13 "This is the basis on which you are to make your **offerings:**
45.16 must take these **offerings** to the ruling prince of Israel.
45.17 the grain-offerings, the **offerings** to be burnt whole,
45.22 festival the ruling prince must **offer** a bull as a sacrifice
45.24 there is to be an **offering** of seventeen and a half litres
45.25 seventh month, the prince will **offer** on each of the seven
45.25 sacrifice for sin, the same **offerings** to be burnt whole,
45.25 and the same **offerings** of corn and olive-oil."
46. 2 his sacrifices whole and **offer** his fellowship-offerings.
46. 5 he is to bring an **offering** of seventeen and a half litres
46. 6 New Moon Festival he will **offer** a young bull, six lambs, and
46. 7 bull and each ram the **offering** is to be seventeen and a
46. 7 and with each lamb the **offering** is to be whatever the prince
46. 7 are to be **offered** with each such grain-offering of corn.
46.11 olive-oil are to be **offered** with each such grain-offering.
46.12 wants to make a voluntary **offering** to the Lord,
46.12 either an **offering** to be burnt whole or a
46.12 He is to make the **offering** in the same way as he
46.13 defects is to be burnt whole as an **offering** to the Lord.
46.13 This **offering** must be made every day.
46.14 Also an **offering** of two kilogrammes of flour is to be
46.14 The rules for this **offering** to the Lord are to be in
46.15 the olive-oil are to be **offered** to the Lord every morning
46.20 **offered as sacrifices** for sin or as repayment-offerings,
46.20 to bake the **offerings** of flour,
46.24 servants are to boil the sacrifices the people **offer."**
Dan 2.46 orders for sacrifices and **offerings** to be made to Daniel.
8.11 stopped the daily sacrifices **offered** to him,
8.12 there instead of **offering the proper daily sacrifices,** and
8.14 evening and morning sacrifices will not be **offered.**
9.21 It was the time for the evening sacrifice to be **offered.**
9.27 is past, he will put an end to sacrifices and **offerings.**
11.17 an alliance with him and **offer** him his daughter in marriage;
11.38 He will **offer** gold, silver, jewels, and other rich gifts to
Hos 3. 1 gods and like to take **offerings** of raisins to idols."
4.13 places on the mountain-tops they **offer sacrifices,** and on
4.14 prostitutes, and together with them you **offer pagan sacrifices.**
5. 6 sheep and cattle to **offer as sacrifices** to the Lord, but it
6. 6 rather have my people know me than burn **offerings** to me.
8.13 They **offer sacrifices** to me and eat the meat of the sacrifices.
9. 4 not be able to make **offerings** of wine to the Lord, or
9. 4 of it will be taken as an **offering** to the Lord's Temple.
13. 2 And then they say, **"Offer sacrifices** to them!"
14. 2 to the Lord, and let this prayer be your **offering** to him:
Joel 1. 9 There is no corn or wine to **offer** in the Temple;
1. 9 the priests mourn because they have no **offerings** for the Lord.
1.13 There is no corn or wine to **offer** your God.
2.14 Then you can **offer** him corn and wine.
Amos 4. 5 Go ahead and **offer** your bread in thanksgiving to God,
4. 5 and boast about the extra **offerings** you bring!
5.22 the animals you have fattened to bring me as **offerings.**
5.25 did not demand sacrifices and **offerings** during those forty
Jon 1.16 Lord that they **offered a sacrifice** and promised to serve him.
2. 9 I will **offer** you a sacrifice and do what I have promised.
Mic 6. 6 Shall I bring the best calves to burn as **offerings** to him?
6. 7 Shall I **offer** him my first-born child to pay for my sins?
Hab 1.16 even worship their nets and **offer sacrifices** to them,
Zeph 3.10 from distant Sudan my scattered people will bring **offerings** to me.
Hag 2.14 and so everything they **offer** on the altar is defiled."
Zech 14.21 The people who **offer sacrifices** will use them for boiling
Mal 1. 7 This is how—by **offering** worthless food on my altar.
1.10 I will not accept the **offerings** you bring me.
1.11 Everywhere they burn incense to me and **offer acceptable sacrifices.**
1.12 is worthless and when you **offer** on it food that you despise.
1.13 As your **offering** to me you bring a stolen animal or one
2.12 let them participate in the **offerings** our nation brings to
2.13 because he no longer accepts the **offerings** you bring him.
3. 3 they will bring to the Lord the right kind of **offerings.**
3. 4 Then the **offerings** which the people of Judah and Jerusalem
3. 8 In the matter of tithes and **offerings.**
Mt 5.23 if you are about to **offer** your gift to God at the
5.24 brother, and then come back and **offer** your gift to God.
8. 4 that you are cured, **offer the sacrifice** that Moses ordered."
12. 4 his men ate the bread **offered** to God, even though it was
21.16 'You have trained children and babies to **offer** perfect praise.'"
27.34 There they **offered** Jesus wine mixed with a bitter substance;
Mk 1.44 that you are cured, **offer the sacrifice** that Moses ordered."
2.26 into the house of God and ate the bread **offered** to God.
12.33 these two commandments than to **offer** animals and other sacrifices
Lk 2.24 They also went to **offer a sacrifice** of a pair of doves
5.14 that you are cured, **offer the sacrifice** as Moses ordered."
5.33 of John fast frequently and **offer** prayers, and the disciples of
6. 4 took the bread **offered** to God, ate it, and gave
10. 7 eating and drinking whatever they **offer** you, for a worker should
13. 1 whom Pilate had killed while they were **offering sacrifices** to God.
21. 4 For the others **offered** their gifts from what they had to
21. 5 it looked with its fine stones and the gifts **offered** to God.
22. 5 They were pleased and **offered** to pay him money.
23.36 came up to him and **offered** him cheap wine, [37]and said,
Jn 4.23 Father as he really is, **offering** him the true worship that
Acts 7.41 the shape of a bull, **offered sacrifice** to it, and had a
8.18 So he **offered** money to Peter and John, [19]and said, "Give
14.13 and the crowds wanted to **offer sacrifice** to the apostles.
14.18 could hardly keep the crowd from **offering a sacrifice** to them.
15.20 that is ritually unclean because it has been **offered** to idols;
15.29 eat no food that has been **offered** to idols;
21.25 any food that has been **offered** to idols, or any blood,
21.26 purification, when a sacrifice would be **offered** for each one
24.17 to take some money to my own people and to **offer sacrifices.**
Rom 3.25 God **offered** him, so that by his sacrificial death
8.32 even keep back his own Son, but **offered** him for us all!
11.16 roots of a tree are **offered** to God, the branches are his
12. 1 **Offer** yourselves as a living sacrifice to God, dedicated to his
12. 1 This is the true worship that you should **offer.**
15.16 Gentiles may be an **offering** acceptable to God, dedicated to him
15.26 freely decided to give an **offering** to help the poor among
1 Cor 8. 1 Now, concerning what you wrote about food **offered** to idols.
8. 4 So then, about eating the food **offered** to idols:
8.10 will not this encourage him to eat food **offered** to idols?
9.13 Temple and that those who **offer the sacrifices** on the altar
10.18 those who eat what is **offered in sacrifice** share in the
10.19 idol or the food **offered** to it really amounts to anything?
10.20 is sacrificed on pagan altars is **offered** to demons, not to
10.28 to you, "This food was **offered** to idols," then do not eat
2 Cor 2.15 are like a sweet-smelling incense **offered** by Christ to God,
4.15 and more people, they will **offer** to the glory of God more
Eph 5. 2 as a sweet-smelling **offering** and sacrifice that pleases God.
Phil 2.16 as you **offer** them the message of life.
2.17 be poured out like an **offering** on the sacrifice
2.17 that your faith **offers** to God.
4.18 They are like a sweet-smelling **offering** to God, a sacrifice which
Col 1. 5 News, first came to you, you heard about the hope it **offers.**
1 Tim 2. 1 requests, and thanksgivings be **offered** to God for all people;
Heb 4. 1 Now, God has **offered** us the promise that we may receive
5. 1 on their behalf, to offer sacrifices and **offerings** for sins.
5. 3 is himself weak, he must **offer sacrifices** not only for the
7.27 he does not need to **offer sacrifices** every day for his own
7.27 **offered one sacrifice,** once and for all, when he offered himself.
8. 3 is appointed to present **offerings** and animal sacrifices to God,
8. 3 and so our High Priest must also have something to **offer.**
8. 4 there are priests who **offer** the gifts required by the Jewish
9. 2 the lampstand and the table with the bread **offered** to God.
9. 7 with him blood which he **offers** to God on behalf of himself
9. 9 that the **offerings** and animal sacrifices presented to God cannot
9.12 take the blood of goats and bulls to **offer as a sacrifice;**
9.14 Through the eternal Spirit he **offered** himself as a perfect sacrifice
9.25 did not go in to **offer** himself many times, [26]for then he
9.28 Christ also was **offered in sacrifice** once to take away
10. 1 The same sacrifices are **offered** for ever, year after year.
10. 5 not want sacrifices and **offerings,** but you have prepared a body
10. 8 pleased with sacrifices and **offerings** or with animals burnt on
10. 8 even though all these sacrifices are **offered** according to the Law.
10.10 purified from sin by the **offering** that he made of his own
10.11 his services every day and **offers** the same sacrifices many times;
10.12 Christ, however, **offered one sacrifice** for sins,
10.12 an **offering** that is effective for ever,
10.18 these have been forgiven, an **offering** to take away sins is
11. 4 was faith that made Abel **offer** to God a better sacrifice
11.17 was faith that made Abraham **offer** his son Isaac as a
11.17 yet he was ready to **offer** his only son as a sacrifice.

Heb 13.11 the Most Holy Place to **offer it as a sacrifice** for sins;
13.15 Let us, then, always **offer** praise to God as our sacrifice
13.15 which is the **offering** presented by lips that confess him
Jas 2.21 his actions, when he **offered** his son Isaac on the altar.
1 Pet 2. 5 as holy priests to **offer** spiritual and acceptable sacrifices
Rev 2.14 eat food that had been **offered** to idols and to practise
2.20 sexual immorality and eating food that has been **offered** to idols.
8. 3 all God's people and to **offer** it on the gold altar that
14. 4 the first ones to be **offered** to God and to the Lamb.

OFFERING BOX

Mk 12.43 poor widow put more in the **offering box** than all the others.
Jn 8.20 Temple, in the room where the **offering boxes** were placed.

OFFICE

Deut 17. 9 the judge who is in **office** at that time, and let them
19.17 be judged by the priests and judges who are then in **office.**
2 Kgs 23. 5 He removed from **office** the priests that the kings of Judah
1 Chr 6.33 The family lines of those who held this **office** are as follows:
Neh 5.15 governor who had been in **office** before me had been a burden
13.29 those people defiled both the **office** of priest and the
Esth 1.14 Persia and Media who held the highest **offices** in the kingdom.
2.21 Mordecai held **office** in the palace, Bigthana and Teresh,
5.11 had promoted him to high **office,** and how much more important
10. 2 Mordecai to high **office,** are recorded in the official
Is 22.19 Lord will remove you from **office** and bring you down from
22.22 He will have the keys of **office;**
Dan 6. 1 and twenty governors to hold **office** throughout his empire.
11.39 ruler, put them into high **offices,** and give them land as a
Mt 9. 9 he saw a tax collector, named Matthew, sitting in his **office.**
Mk 2.14 tax collector, Levi son of Alphaeus, sitting in his **office.**
Lk 5.27 and saw a tax collector named Levi, sitting in his **office.**

OFFICER

[FELLOW-OFFICERS]

Gen 37.36 Potiphar, one of the king's **officers,** who was the captain of
39. 1 Potiphar, one of the king's **officers,** who was the captain of
Ex 5.21 punish you for making the king and his **officers** hate us.
7.10 of the king and his **officers,** and it turned into a snake.
7.20 of the king and his **officers,** Aaron raised his stick and
8. 9 when I am to pray for you, your **officers,** and your people.
14. 7 the six hundred finest, commanded by their **officers.**
15. 4 the best of its **officers** were drowned in the Red Sea.
Num 31.14 Moses was angry with the **officers,**
31.48 Then the **officers** who had commanded the army went to
31.52 The total contribution of the **officers**
31.53 Those who were not **officers** kept the loot they had taken.
Deut 20. 5 "Then the **officers** will address the men and say, 'Is
20. 8 "The **officers** will also say to the men, 'Is there any
20. 9 When the **officers** have finished speaking to the army,
Josh 8.33 The Israelites, with their leaders, **officers,** and
10.24 to him and ordered the **officers** who had gone with him to
10.25 Then Joshua said to his **officers,** "Don't be afraid
23. 2 the elders, leaders, judges, and **officers** of the people, and
24. 1 leaders, the judges, and the **officers** of Israel, and they
Judg 5.14 commanders came down from Machir, the **officers** down from Zebulun.
1 Sam 8.12 will make some of them **officers** in charge of a thousand men,
8.15 of your grapes for his court **officers** and other officials.
17.18 And take these ten cheeses to the commanding **officer.**
17.22 left the food with the **officer** in charge of the supplies,
18. 5 sent him, and so Saul made him an **officer** in his army.
18. 5 This pleased all of Saul's **officers** and men.
18.30 David was more successful than any of Saul's other **officers.**
22. 6 in his hand, and all his **officers** were standing round him.
22. 7 and he said to his **officers,** "Listen, men of Benjamin!
22. 7 vineyards to all of you, and make you **officers** in his army?
22. 9 was standing there with Saul's **officers,** and he said, "I
22.14 Ahimelech answered, "David is the most faithful **officer** you have!
28.23 But his **officers** also urged him to eat.
28.25 set the food before Saul and his **officers,** and they ate it.
2 Sam 4. 2 Ishbosheth had two **officers** who were leaders of raiding parties,
11. 1 David sent out Joab with his **officers** and the Israelite army;
11.11 commander Joab and his **officers** are camping out in the open.
11.17 some of David's **officers** were killed, and so was Uriah.
11.21 this, tell him, 'Your **officer** Uriah was also killed.' "
11.24 the wall, and some of Your Majesty's **officers** were killed;
11.24 your **officer** Uriah was also killed."
14.19 It was indeed your **officer** Joab who told me what to do
18. 1 and of a hundred, and placed **officers** in command of them.
18. 5 And all the troops heard David give this command to his **officers.**
18.29 Ahimaaz answered, "Sir, when your **officer** Joab sent me, I
19. 6 it clear that your **officers** and men mean nothing to you.
24. 2 "Go with your **officers** through all the tribes of Israel
24. 4 But the king made Joab and his **officers** obey his order;
1 Kgs 4. 8 the names of these twelve **officers** and the districts they
9.22 as his soldiers, **officers,** commanders, chariot captains,
14.27 to the **officers** responsible for guarding the palace gates.
15.20 proposal and sent his commanding **officers** and their armies
16. 9 Zimri, one of his **officers** who was in charge of half the
20. 6 however, I will send my **officers** to search your palace and
22.26 Ahab ordered one of his **officers,** "Arrest Micaiah and take
2 Kgs 1. 9 Then he sent an **officer** with fifty men to get Elijah.
1. 9 The **officer** found him sitting on a hill and said to him,
1.10 At once fire came down and killed the **officer** and his men.
1.11 The king sent another **officer** with fifty men, who went
1.12 fire of God came down and killed the **officer** and his men.
1.13 Once more the king sent an **officer** with fifty men.

2 Kgs 1.14 The two other **officers** and their men were killed by fire
1.15 So Elijah went with the **officer** to the king [16] and said to
3.11 An **officer** of King Joram's forces answered, "Elisha son of
5. 6 "This letter will introduce my **officer** Naaman.
6. 8 He consulted his **officers** and chose a place to set up his
6.11 he called in his **officers** and asked them, "Which one of you
7. 9 Let's go at once and tell the king's **officers!"**
7.17 the command of the **officer** who was his personal attendant.
7.17 The **officer** was trampled to death there by the people and died,
7.19 of silver, [19] to which the **officer** had answered, "That
9. 5 Ramoth, [5] where he found the army **officers** in a conference.
9.11 Jehu went back to his **fellow-officers,** who asked him,
9.13 At once Jehu's **fellow-officers** spread their cloaks at
9.14 So Jehu said to his **fellow-officers,** "If you are with me,
10. 5 So the **officer** in charge of the palace and the official in
10.11 Ahab living in Jezreel, and all his **officers,** close friends,
10.25 said to the guards and **officers,** "Go in and kill them all;
11. 4 the priest sent for the **officers** in charge of the royal
11. 9 The **officers** obeyed Jehoiada's instructions and brought
11.10 He gave the **officers** the spears and shields that had
11.14 He was surrounded by the **officers** and the trumpeters, and
11.15 Athaliah killed in the temple area, so he ordered the army **officers:**
11.19 Temple, [19] and then he, the **officers,** the royal bodyguard,
15.25 An **officer** of Pekahiah's forces, Pekah son of Remaliah,
24.10 King Nebuchadnezzar's **officers,** marched against Jerusalem
24.12 mother, his sons, his **officers,** and the palace officials,
25.18 In addition, Nebuzaradan, the commanding **officer,** took
25.19 the city he took the **officer** who had been in command of
25.23 When the Judaean **officers** and soldiers who had not surrendered
25.23 These **officers** were Ishmael son of Nethaniah, Johanan son of Kareah,
25.26 together with the army **officers,** left and went to Egypt,
1 Chr 12.14 of Gad were senior **officers** in command of a thousand men,
12.14 and others were junior **officers** in command of a hundred.
12.18 David welcomed them and made them **officers** in his army.
12.21 They served David as **officers** over his troops,
12.21 Later they were **officers** in the Israelite army.
13. 1 David consulted with all the **officers** in command of units of
21. 2 to Joab and the other **officers,** "Go through Israel, from
26.26 of families, leaders of clan groups, and army **officers.**
2 Chr 1. 2 an order to all the **officers** in charge of units of a
8. 9 but served as soldiers, **officers,** chariot commanders,
8.18 of his own **officers** and manned by experienced sailors.
8.18 They sailed with Solomon's **officers** to the land of Ophir and
12.10 to the **officers** responsible for guarding the palace gates.
16. 4 proposal and sent his commanding **officers** and their armies
17.13 In Jerusalem he stationed outstanding **officers,**
18.25 Ahab ordered one of his **officers,** "Arrest Micaiah and take
21. 9 So Jehoram and his **officers** set out with chariots and invaded Edom.
23. 1 He made a pact with five army **officers:**
23. 9 Jehoiada gave the **officers** the spears and shields that had
23.13 and surrounded by the army **officers** and the trumpeters.
23.14 he called out the army **officers** and said, "Take her out
23.20 The army **officers,** the leading citizens, the officials,
25. 5 they belonged to, and placed **officers** in command of units of
26.12 The army was commanded by 2,600 **officers.**
32. 6 under the command of army **officers** and ordered them to
32.21 that killed the soldiers and **officers** of the Assyrian army.
33.14 He also stationed an army **officer** in command of a unit of
Neh 2. 9 The emperor sent some army **officers** and a troop of
7. 2 Hanani and Hananiah, commanding **officer** of the fortress.
Job 39.25 get near, and they hear the **officers** shouting commands.
Is 21. 5 **"Officers!**
31. 9 away in terror, and the **officers** will be so frightened that
Jer 20. 1 Immer, who was the chief **officer** of the Temple, heard me
29.26 Jehoiada, and you are now the chief **officer** in the Temple.
37.13 reached the Benjamin Gate, the **officer** in charge of the
38.17 the king of Babylonia's **officers,** your life will be spared,
38.22 being led out to the king of Babylonia's **officers.**
39. 9 Finally Nebuzaradan, the commanding **officer,** took away as
39.11 King Nebuchadnezzar commanded Nebuzaradan, the commanding **officer,**
39.13 Sarezer and all the other **officers** of the king of Babylonia,
40. 1 the commanding **officer,** had set me free at Ramah.
40. 2 The commanding **officer** took me aside and said, "The Lord
40. 7 Some of the Judaean **officers** and soldiers had not surrendered.
41. 1 one of the king's chief **officers,** went to Mizpah with ten
41.10 Mizpah, whom Nebuzaradan the commanding **officer** had placed
43. 4 nor any of the army **officers** nor any of the people would
43. 5 Johanan and all the army **officers** took everybody left in
43. 6 everyone whom Nebuzaradan the commanding **officer** had left
46. 3 "The Egyptian **officers** shout, 'Get your shields ready
51.11 The attacking **officers** command, "Sharpen your arrows!
51.27 Appoint an **officer** to lead the attack.
52.24 In addition, Nebuzaradan, the commanding **officer,** took
52.25 the city he took the **officer** who had been in command of
Ezek 23. 6 soldiers in uniforms of purple, noblemen and high-ranking **officers;**
23. 6 all of them were handsome young cavalry **officers.**
23. 7 whore for all the Assyrian **officers,** and her lust led her to
23.12 for the Assyrian noblemen and **officers**—soldiers in bright
23.12 for the cavalry **officers,** all those handsome young men.
23.23 those handsome young noblemen and **officers,**
23.23 all those important officials and high-ranking cavalry **officers.**
Dan 11.20 king, who will send an **officer** to oppress the people with
Hos 7. 3 "People deceive the king and his **officers** by their evil plots.
Amos 1.15 Their king and his **officers** will go into exile."
Nah 2. 5 The **officers** are summoned;
Mt 8. 5 Jesus entered Capernaum, a Roman **officer** met him and begged for

Mt 8. 8 "Oh no, sir," answered the **officer.**
8. 9 the authority of superior **officers,** and I have soldiers under me.
8.13 Jesus said to the **officer,** "Go home, and what you believe
8.13 And the **officer's** servant was healed that very moment.
27.54 the army **officer** and the soldiers with him who were watching
Mk 15.39 The army **officer** who was standing there in front of the
15.44 He called the army **officer** and asked him if Jesus had been
15.45 After hearing the **officer's** report, Pilate told Joseph
Lk 7. 2 A Roman **officer** there had a servant who was very dear to
7. 3 When the **officer** heard about Jesus, he sent some Jewish elders
7. 6 from the house when the **officer** sent friends to tell him,
7. 8 the authority of superior **officers,** and I have soldiers under me.
7.10 went back to the **officer's** house and found his servant well.
8. 3 Joanna, whose husband Chuza was an **officer** in Herod's court;
22. 4 the chief priests and the **officers** of the temple guard about
22.52 the chief priests and the **officers** of the temple guard and
23.47 The army **officer** saw what had happened, and he praised God,
Jn 18.12 Roman soldiers with their commanding **officer** and the Jewish guards arrested Jesus,
Acts 4. 1 when some priests, the **officer** in charge of the temple guards,
5.24 the chief priests and the **officer** in charge of the temple
5.26 So the **officer** went off with his men and brought the
16.35 the Roman authorities sent police **officers** with the order,
16.37 Paul said to the police **officers,** "We were not found guilty of
16.38 police **officers** reported these words to the Roman officials;
21.32 the commander took some **officers** and soldiers and rushed down
22.25 Paul said to the **officer** standing there, "Is it lawful for
22.26 the **officer** heard this, he went to the commander and asked
23.17 Paul called one of the **officers** and said to him, "Take this
23.18 The **officer** took him, led him to the commander, and said,
23.23 called two of his **officers** and said, "Get two hundred soldiers
24.23 He ordered the **officer** in charge of Paul to keep him
27. 1 prisoners over to Julius, an **officer** in the Roman regiment called
27. 6 There the **officer** found a ship from Alexandria that was going
27.11 But the army **officer** was convinced by what the captain
27.31 Paul said to the army **officer** and soldiers, "If the sailors
27.43 But the army **officer** wanted to save Paul, so he stopped
2 Tim 2. 4 wants to please his commanding **officer** and so does not get

OFFICIAL

[FELLOW-OFFICIALS]

Gen 12.15 Some of the court **officials** saw her and told the king
20. 8 Abimelech called all his **officials** and told them what had happened,
40. 2 was angry with these two **officials** [3] and put them in prison
40.20 days later the king gave a banquet for all his **officials;**
40.20 and his chief baker and brought them before his **officials.**
41.34 You must also appoint other **officials** and take a fifth
41.37 The king and his **officials** approved this plan, [38] and
45. 8 He has made me the king's highest **official.**
45.16 the king and his **officials** were pleased.
50. 4 Joseph said to the king's **officials,** "Please take this
50. 7 All the king's **officials,** the senior men of his court, and
Ex 8. 3 bed, the houses of your **officials** and your people, and even
8. 4 They will jump up on you, your people, and all your **officials.'"**
8.11 You, your **officials,** and your people will be rid of the frogs,
8.21 by sending flies on you, your **officials,** and your people.
8.24 of flies into the king's palace and the houses of his **officials.**
8.29 the flies will leave you, your **officials,** and your people.
8.31 The flies left the king, his **officials,** and his people;
9.14 will punish not only your **officials** and your people, but I
9.20 Some of the king's **officials** were afraid because of what
9.30 know that you and your **officials** do not yet fear the Lord
9.34 He and his **officials** remained as stubborn as ever [35] and,
10. 1 have made him and his **officials** stubborn, in order that I
10. 6 and the houses of all your **officials** and all your people.
10. 7 The king's **officials** said to him, "How long is this man
11. 3 Indeed, the **officials** and all the people considered Moses to
11. 8 concluded by saying, "All your **officials** will come to me
12.30 That night, the king, his **officials,** and all the other
14. 5 escaped, he and his **officials** changed their minds and said,
Lev 5. 1 If someone is **officially** summoned to give evidence in court
Num 25. 5 Moses said to the **officials,** "Each of you is to kill
Deut 1.15 I also appointed other **officials** throughout the tribes.
6.22 to the Egyptians and to their king and to all his **officials.**
16.18 "Appoint judges and other **officials** in every town that
29. 2 king of Egypt, to his **officials,** and to his entire country.
29.10 of you—your leaders and **officials,** your men, [11] women, and
31.28 all your tribal leaders and **officials** before me, so that I
34.11 the king of Egypt, his **officials,** and the entire country.
1 Sam 8.14 vineyards, and olive-groves, and give them to his **officials.**
8.15 of your grapes for his court officers and other **officials.**
18.22 He ordered his **officials** to speak privately to David
18.22 "The king is pleased with you and all his **officials** like you;
18.24 The **officials** told Saul what David had said, [25] and
18.26 Saul's **officials** reported to David what Saul had said,
19. 1 Jonathan and all his **officials** that he planned to kill David.
21.11 The king's **officials** said to Achish, "Isn't this David,
21.14 So Achish said to his **officials,** "Look!
28. 7 Then Saul ordered his **officials,** "Find me a woman who is
29. 3 "This is David, an **official** of King Saul of Israel.
2 Sam 2.12 Abner and the **officials** of Ishbosheth went from
2.13 Zeruiah, and David's other **officials** met them at the pool,
3.22 on Joab and David's other **officials** returned from a raid,
3.38 The king said to his **officials,** "Don't you realize that
6.20 fool in the sight of the servant-girls of his **officials!"**
8. 7 carried by Hadadezer's **officials** and took them to Jerusalem.
12.17 His court **officials** went to him and tried to make him
12.18 the child died, and David's **officials** were afraid to tell
2 Sam 12.21 "We don't understand this," his **officials** said to him.
13.24 Will you and your **officials** come and take part in the festivities?"
13.36 crying, and David and his **officials** also wept bitterly.
15.14 David said to all his **officials** who were with him in Jerusalem,
15.16 by all his family and **officials,** except for ten concubines,
15.18 All his **officials** stood next to him as the royal
16. 6 stones at David and his **officials,** even though David was
16.11 Abishai and to all his **officials,** "My own son is trying to
17.20 Absalom's **officials** came to the house and asked the woman,
19.14 and they sent him word to return with all his **officials.**
24.20 down and saw the king and his **officials** coming up to him.
1 Kgs 1. 2 So his **officials** said to him, "Your Majesty, let us find
1. 9 King David and the king's **officials** who were from Judah to
1.27 and not even tell your **officials** who is to succeed you as
1.33 in, [33] he said to them, "Take my court **officials** with you;
1.47 What is more, the court **officials** went in to pay their
3.15 After that he gave a feast for all his **officials.**
4. 2 Solomon was king of all Israel, [2] and these were his high **officials:**
9.23 There were 550 **officials** in charge of the forced labour
10. 5 the living quarters for his **officials,** the organization of
11.11 kingdom away from you and give it to one of your **officials.**
11.26 Solomon was one of his **officials,** Jeroboam son of Nebat,
15.18 it by some of his **officials** to Damascus, to King Benhadad of
20. 6 and the homes of your **officials,** and to take everything they
20.23 King Benhadad's **officials** said to him, "The gods of
20.31 His **officials** went to him and said, "We have heard that
20.33 Benhadad's **officials** were watching for a good sign, and
21. 8 sent them to the **officials** and leading citizens of Jezreel.
21.11 **officials** and leading citizens of Jezreel did what Jezebel
22. 3 Ahab asked his **officials,** "Why is it that we have not
22. 9 Ahab called in a court **official** and told him to go and
22.13 Meanwhile, the **official** who had gone to get Micaiah said to him,
2 Kgs 7.12 bed and said to his **officials,** "I'll tell you what the
7.13 One of his **officials** said, "The people here in the
8. 6 so the king called an **official** and told him to give back
8. 8 Hazael, one of his **officials,** "Take a gift to the prophet,
9.28 His **officials** took his body back to Jerusalem in a
9.32 Two or three palace **officials** looked down at him from a window,
10. 5 of the palace and the **official** in charge of the city,
12.20 King Joash's **officials** plotted against him, and two of them,
14. 5 power, he executed the **officials** who had killed his father,
18.17 it was commanded by his three highest **officials.**
18.18 King Hezekiah, and three of his **officials** went out to meet them:
18.19 One of the Assyrian **officials** told them that the emperor
18.22 The Assyrian **official** went on, "Or will you tell me
18.24 even the lowest ranking Assyrian **official,** and yet you
18.26 Shebna, and Joah told the **official,** "Speak Aramaic to us,
18.28 Then the **official** stood up and shouted in Hebrew,
18.37 reported to the king what the Assyrian **official** had said.
19. 2 He sent Eliakim, the **official** in charge of the palace,
19. 4 emperor has sent his chief **official** to insult the living God.
19. 8 The Assyrian **official** learnt that the emperor had left
21.23 Amon's **officials** plotted against him and assassinated him
23.11 from the living-quarters of Nathan Melech, a high **official.)**
23.30 His **officials** placed his body in a chariot and took it
24.12 and the palace **officials,** surrendered to the Babylonians.
24.15 Jehoiachin's mother, his wives, his **officials,**
25.18 in rank, and the three other important temple **officials.**
25.24 is no need for you to be afraid of the Babylonian **officials.**
1 Chr 7. 5 The **official** records of all the families of the tribe of
7. 9 The **official** record of their descendants by families
9.10 son of Hilkiah (the chief **official** in the Temple), whose
18. 7 carried by Hadadezer's **officials** and took them to Jerusalem.
24. 5 Since there were temple **officials** and spiritual leaders
24. 6 The king, his **officials,** the priest Zadok,
26.24 the chief **official** responsible for the temple treasury.
27. 1 and clan leaders and their **officials** who administered the
27.24 were never recorded in King David's **official** records.
28. 1 King David commanded all the **officials** of Israel to assemble
28. 1 So all the **officials** of the tribes,
28. 1 the **officials** who administered the work of the
28. 1 sons—indeed all the palace **officials,** leading soldiers, and
29. 6 heads of the clans, the **officials** of the tribes, the
29.24 All the **officials** and soldiers, and even all of David's
2 Chr 1. 2 all the government **officials,** all the heads of families,
8.10 There were 250 **officials** in charge of the forced labour
9. 4 table, the living-quarters for his **officials,** the
17. 7 he sent out the following **officials** to teach in the cities
18. 8 Ahab called in a court **official** and told him to go and
18.12 the **official** who had gone to fetch Micaiah said to him,
21. 4 all his brothers killed, and also some Israelite **officials.**
23.20 officers, the leading citizens, the **officials,** and all the
24.11 the box to the royal **official** who was in charge of it.
24.25 enemy withdrew, two of his **officials** plotted against him and
25. 3 he executed the **officials** who had murdered his father.
30. 1 So King Hezekiah, his **officials,** and the people of Jerusalem
30. 6 of the king and his **officials** through all Judah and Israel
30.12 by following the commands of the king and his **officials.**
30.24 kill and eat, and the **officials** gave them another thousand
31. 8 When King Hezekiah and his **officials** saw how much had been given,
32. 3 he and his **officials** decided to cut off the supply
32. 3 The **officials** led a large number of people out
32.16 The Assyrian **officials** said even worse things about the
32.18 The **officials** shouted this in Hebrew in order to
33.24 Amon's **officials** plotted against him and assassinated him
34. 8 of Jerusalem, and Joah son of Joahaz, a high **official.**
35. 8 His **officials** also made contributions for the people, the
35. 8 And the **officials** in charge of the Temple—
36.18 king and his **officials,** and took everything back to Babylon.

Ezra 4. 5 They also bribed Persian government **officials** to work against them.
4. 9 all the other **officials,** who are men originally from Erech,
5. 3 their **fellow-officials** came to Jerusalem and demanded:
5. 5 Jewish leaders, and the Persian **officials** decided to take no
6. 6 your **fellow-officials** in West Euphrates.
6.13 their **fellow-officials** did exactly as the emperor had
7.21 "I command all the treasury **officials** in the province
7.28 of his counsellors, and of all his powerful **officials;**
8.20 by King David and his **officials** to assist the Levites.
8.25 the emperor, his advisers and **officials,** and the people of
8.36 governors and **officials** of the province of West Euphrates,
9. 2 The leaders and **officials** were the chief offenders.
10.14 Let our **officials** stay in Jerusalem and take charge of the matter.
Neh 2.10 and Tobiah, an **official** in the province of Ammon,
2.16 None of the local **officials** knew where I had been or
2.16 the priests, the leaders, the **officials,** or anyone else who
4.14 leaders and **officials,** "Don't be afraid of our enemies.
4.19 told the people and their **officials** and leaders, "The work
5. 7 I denounced the leaders and **officials** of the people and told them,
7. 5 leaders and **officials** and to check their family records.
9.10 the king, against his **officials** and the people of his land,
11. 9 Judah son of Hassenuah was the second senior **official** in the city.
12.23 however, were recorded in the **official** records only until
13.11 I reprimanded the **officials** for letting the Temple be neglected.
Esth 1. 3 he gave a banquet for all his **officials** and administrators.
1.11 to show off her beauty to the **officials** and all his guests.
1.14 Meres, Marsena, and Memucan—seven **officials** of Persia and
1.16 Then Memucan declared to the king and his **officials:**
1.16 the king but also his **officials**—in fact, every man in the
1.18 the wives of the royal **officials** of Persia and Media hear
1.21 The king and his **officials** liked this idea, and the king
2. 3 You can appoint **officials** in every province of the empire
2.18 Esther's honour and invited all his **officials** and administrators.
2.23 to be written down in the **official** records of the empire.
3. 2 The king ordered all the **officials** in his service to show
3. 3 The other **officials** in the royal service asked him why he
3.10 stamp proclamations and make them **official,** and gave it to
3.12 and to be sent to all the rulers, governors, and **officials.**
5.11 important he was than any of the king's other **officials.**
6. 1 sleep, so he ordered the **official** records of the empire to
6. 4 "Are any of my **officials** in the palace?"
8. 9 to the governors, administrators, and **officials** of all the
9. 3 In fact, all the provincial **officials**—governors, administrators,
10. 2 office, are recorded in the **official** records of the kings of
Ps 105.22 with power over the king's **officials** and authority to instruct
135. 9 and wonders to punish the king and all his **officials.**
Prov 14.35 Kings are pleased with competent **officials,** but they
29.12 to false information, all his **officials** will be liars.
Ecc 5. 8 Every **official** is protected by the one over him,
5. 8 and both are protected by still higher **officials.**
Is 22.21 I will put your **official** robe and belt on him and give
36. 2 Then he ordered his chief **official** to go from Lachish to
36. 2 The **official** occupied the road where the clothmakers work,
36. 3 **official** in charge of the palace, Eliakim son of Hilkiah;
36. 3 the **official** in charge of the records, Joah son of Asaph.
36. 4 The Assyrian **official** told them that the emperor wanted to
36. 7 The Assyrian **official** went on, "Or will you tell me that
36. 9 even the lowest ranking Assyrian **official,** and yet you
36.11 and Joah said to the **official,** "Speak Aramaic to us.
36.13 Then the **official** stood up and shouted in Hebrew,
36.22 reported to the king what the Assyrian **official** had said.
37. 2 He sent Eliakim, the **official** in charge of the palace,
37. 4 emperor has sent his chief **official** to insult the living God.
37. 8 The Assyrian **official** learnt that the emperor had left
Jer 1.18 the kings of Judah, the **officials,** the priests, and the
2.26 Israel will be disgraced—your kings and **officials,**
4. 9 "On that day kings and **officials** will lose their courage;
8. 1 the kings and of the **officials** of Judah, as well as the
21. 7 But as for you, your **officials,** and the people who survive
22. 1 there tell the king, his **officials,** and the people of
22. 4 And they, together with their **officials** and their people,
25.19 the king of Egypt, his **officials** and leaders;
26.21 his soldiers and **officials** heard what Uriah had said,
29. 2 Jehoiachin, his mother, the palace **officials,** the leaders of
34.18 The **officials** of Judah and of Jerusalem,
34.18 with the palace **officials,** the priests, and all the leaders,
34.21 Zedekiah of Judah and his **officials** to those who want to
35. 4 son of Shallum, an important **official** in the Temple,
35. 4 and near the rooms of the other **officials.**
36.12 court secretary, where all the **officials** were in session.
36.12 Zedekiah son of Hananiah, and all the other **officials** were there.
36.14 Then the **officials** sent Jehudi (the son of Nethaniah,
36.20 The **officials** put the scroll in the room of Elishama,
36.21 the king and all the **officials** who were standing round him.
36.24 king nor any of his **officials** who heard all this was afraid
36.31 you, your descendants, and your **officials** because of the
37. 2 But neither Zedekiah nor his **officials** nor the people
37.14 Instead, he arrested me and took me to the **officials.**
37.18 committed against you or your **officials** or this people, to
38. 4 Then the **officials** went to the king and said, "This man
38.25 If the **officials** hear that I have talked with you, they
38.27 Then all the **officials** came and questioned me, and I
39. 3 was captured, all the high **officials** of the king of
39. 6 and he also executed the **officials** of Judah.
39.13 Nebuzaradan, together with the high **officials** Nebushazban
51.23 and their horses, to crush rulers and high **officials."**
51.28 of Media, their leaders and **officials,** and the armies of all
52.10 looking on and he also had the **officials** of Judah executed.
52.24 in rank, and the three other important temple **officials.**
Ezek 17.12 took the king and his **officials** back with him to Babylonia.
Ezek 22.27 The government **officials** are like wolves tearing apart
23.14 the images of high Babylonian **officials** carved into the wall
23.23 those important **officials** and high-ranking cavalry officers.
Dan 1. 3 king ordered Ashpenaz, his chief **official,** to select from
1. 7 The chief **official** gave them new names:
3. 2 orders for all his **officials** to come together—the princes,
3. 2 magistrates, and all the other **officials** of the provinces.
3. 3 When all these **officials** gathered for the dedication and
3.24 He asked his **officials,** "Didn't we tie up three men and
3.27 governors, lieutenant-governors, and other **officials**
4.36 My **officials** and my noblemen welcomed me, and I was given
6. 7 the lieutenant-governors, and the other **officials**—have
Hos 7. 5 made the king and his **officials** drunk and foolish with wine.
Jon 3. 7 "This is an order from the king and his **officials:**
Mic 7. 3 **Officials** and judges ask for bribes.
Nah 3.17 Your **officials** are like a swarm of locusts that stay in
Hab 1.10 They treat kings with contempt and laugh at high **officials.**
Zeph 1. 8 Lord, "I will punish the **officials,** the king's sons, and
3. 3 Its **officials** are like roaring lions;
Mt 9.18 was saying this, a Jewish **official** came to him, knelt down
9.23 Then Jesus went into the **official's** house.
14. 2 Baptist, who has come back to life," he told his **officials.**
Mk 5.22 Jairus, an **official** of the local synagogue, arrived,
6.21 for all the chief government **officials,** the military commanders,
Lk 8.41 he was an **official** in the local synagogue.
8.49 Jesus was saying this, a messenger came from the **official's** house.
13.14 **official** of the synagogue was angry that Jesus had healed on
Jn 4.46 A government **official** was there whose son was ill in Capernaum.
4.49 replied the **official,** "come with me before my child dies."
Acts 5.22 when the **officials** arrived, they did not find the apostles in
8.27 eunuch, who was an important **official** in charge of the treasury
8.31 **official** replied, "How can I understand unless someone explains it
8.34 **official** asked Philip, "Tell me, of whom is the prophet saying
8.36 was some water, and the **official** said, "Here is some water.
8.38 The **official** ordered the carriage to stop,
8.38 and both Philip and the **official** went down into the water,
8.39 The **official** did not see him again, but continued on his way,
13.15 writings of the prophets, the **officials** of the synagogue sent
16.20 them before the Roman **officials** and said, "These men are Jews,
16.22 Then the **officials** tore the clothes off Paul and Silas
16.36 the jailer told Paul, "The **officials** have sent an order for
16.37 The Roman **officials** themselves must come here and let us out."
16.38 The police officers reported these words to the Roman **officials;**
28. 7 fields that belonged to Publius, the chief **official** of the island.

OFFICIAL STANDARD see STANDARD

OFFICIATE

Lev 1. 9 the hind legs, and the **officiating** priest will burn the
1.12 man cuts it up, the **officiating** priest shall put on the fire
2. 2 The **officiating** priest shall take a handful of the flour and
3.11 The **officiating** priest shall burn all this on the altar

OFFSPRING

Gen 3.15 her **offspring** and yours will always be enemies.
3.15 Her **offspring** will crush your head, and you will bite their heel."

OG

King of Bashan, e. of the Jordan, at the time of Israel's conquest of Canaan.

Num 21.33 road to Bashan, and King **Og** of Bashan marched out
21.35 So the Israelites killed **Og,** his sons, and all his people,
32.33 of the Amorites and King **Og** of Bashan, including the towns
Deut 1. 4 town of Heshbon, and King **Og** of Bashan, who ruled in the
3. 1 region of Bashan, and King **Og** came out with all his men
3. 3 the Lord also placed King **Og** and his people in our power,
3. 4 whole region of Argob, where King **Og** of Bashan ruled.
3.10 We took all the territory of King **Og** of Bashan:
3.11 (King **Og** was the last of the Rephaim.
3.13 also all of Bashan, where **Og** had ruled,
3.21 the Lord your God did to those two kings, Sihon and **Og;**
4.47 and the land of King **Og** of Bashan, the other Amorite king
29. 7 Sihon of Heshbon and King **Og** of Bashan came out to fight
31. 4 as he defeated Sihon and **Og,** kings of the Amorites,
Josh 2.10 how you killed Sihon and **Og,** the two Amorite kings
9.10 Sihon of Heshbon and King **Og** of Bashan, who lived in Ashtaroth.
12. 4 They also defeated King **Og** of Bashan,
13.12 It included the kingdom of **Og,** the last of the Rephaim,
13.30 the whole kingdom of **Og,** the king of Bashan,
13.31 Ashtaroth and Edrei, the capital cities of **Og's** kingdom in Bashan.
1 Kgs 4.19 of the Amorites and King **Og** of Bashan
Neh 9.22 Sihon ruled, and the land of Bashan, where **Og** was king.
Ps 135.11 Sihon, king of the Amorites, **Og,** king of Bashan,
136.20 and **Og,** king of Bashan;

OIL

see also **OLIVE-OIL**

Ex 25. 6 **oil** for the lamps;
25. 6 for the anointing **oil** and for the sweet-smelling incense;
29. 2 it, and some in the form of biscuits brushed with **oil.**
29. 7 Then take the anointing **oil,** pour it on his head, and
29.21 and some of the anointing **oil,** and sprinkle it on Aaron and
30.25 and make a sacred anointing **oil,** mixed like perfume.
30.31 of Israel, 'This holy anointing **oil** is to be used in my
31.11 serve as priests, [11] the anointing **oil,** and the
35. 8 **oil** for the lamps;

Ex 35. 8 for the anointing **oil** and for the sweet-smelling incense;
35.14 the lamps with their **oil;**
35.15 the anointing **oil;**
35.28 and spices and **oil** for the lamps,
35.28 for the anointing **oil,** and for the sweet-smelling incense.
37.29 sacred anointing **oil** and the pure sweet-smelling incense,
39.37 its lamps, all its equipment, and the **oil** for the lamps;
39.38 the anointing **oil;**
40. 9 by anointing it with the sacred **oil,** and it will be holy.
Lev 2. 2 handful of the flour and **oil** and all of the incense and
2. 6 it up and pour the **oil** on it when you present it
2.16 part of the meal and **oil** that is to serve as a
6.15 handful of the flour and **oil,** and the incense on it, and
6.21 is to be mixed with **oil** and cooked on a griddle and
7.10 uncooked grain-offerings, whether mixed with **oil** or dry,
8. 2 the anointing **oil,** the young bull for the sin-offering,
8.10 Then Moses took the anointing **oil** and put it on the Tent
8.11 He took some of the **oil** and sprinkled it seven times on
8.12 Aaron by pouring some of the anointing **oil** on his head.
8.26 Lord, one loaf made with **oil,** and one biscuit, and he put
8.30 took some of the anointing **oil** and some of the blood that
9. 4 them to the Lord with the grain-offering mixed with **oil.**
10. 7 have been consecrated by the anointing **oil** of the Lord."
14.12 one-third of a litre of **oil** he shall offer it as a
14.17 shall take some of the **oil** that is in the palm of
14.18 put the rest of the **oil** that is in the palm of
14.26 shall pour some of the **oil** into the palm of his own
14.28 shall put some of the **oil** on the same places as he
14.29 The rest of the **oil** that is in his palm he shall
21.10 Priest has had the anointing **oil** poured on his head and has
Num 4.16 whole Tent and for the **oil** for the lamps, the incense,
4.16 the grain-offerings, the anointing **oil,**
7.12 of them full of flour mixed with **oil** for the grain-offering;
Judg 9. 9 have to stop producing my **oil,** which is used to honour gods
2 Sam 1.21 the shield of Saul is no longer polished with **oil.**
1 Kgs 17.14 the jar run out of **oil** before the day that I, the
17.16 run out of flour nor did the jar run out of **oil.**
2 Kgs 4. 4 house, close the door, and start pouring **oil** into the jars.
4. 5 jar of olive-oil, and poured **oil** into the jars as her sons
2 Chr 16.14 They used spices and perfumed **oils** to prepare his body for burial,
Esth 2.12 massages with **oil** of myrrh for six months
2.12 and with **oil** of balsam for six more.
Job 24.11 They press olives for **oil,** and grapes for wine, but they
41.31 like boiling water and makes it bubble like a pot of **oil.**
Ps 55.21 were as soothing as **oil,** but they cut like sharp swords.
89.20 made my servant David king by anointing him with holy **oil.**
109.18 soak into his body like water and into his bones like **oil!**
133. 2 is like the precious anointing **oil** running down from Aaron's
Prov 27. 9 Perfume and fragrant **oils** make you feel happier,
27.16 stop the wind or ever tried to hold a handful of **oil?**
Jer 25.10 They will have no **oil** for their lamps, and there will be
Mic 6.15 You will press **oil** from olives, but never be able to use
Zech 4. 2 "At the top is a bowl for the **oil.**
Mt 25. 1 ten girls who took their **oil** lamps and went out to meet
25. 3 did not take any extra **oil** with them, [4] while the wise ones
25. 4 while the wise ones took containers full of **oil** for their lamps.
25. 8 us have some of your **oil,** because our lamps are going out.'
25.10 So the foolish girls went off to buy some **oil;**
Lk 10.34 went over to him, poured **oil** and wine on his wounds
Rev 18.13 wine and **oil,** flour and wheat, cattle and sheep,

OINTMENT

Is 1. 6 No **ointment** has been put on them.
57. 9 put on your perfumes and **ointments** and go to worship the god
Rev 3.18 Buy also some **ointment** to put on your eyes, so that you

OLD

[YEARS OLD]

Gen 5. 3 When Adam was 130 **years old,** he had a son who was
5.23 He lived to be 365 **years old.**
5.32 After Noah was 500 **years old,** he had three sons, Shem,
7. 6 Noah was six hundred **years old** when the flood came on the
7.11 When Noah was six hundred **years old,** on the seventeenth
8.13 When Noah was 601 **years old,** on the first day of the
11.10 flood, when Shem was 100 **years old,** he had a son,
11.12 When Arpachshad was 35 **years old,** he had a son, Shelah;
11.14 When Shelah was 30 **years old,** he had a son, Eber;
11.16 When Eber was 34 **years old,** he had a son, Peleg;
11.18 When Peleg was 30 **years old,** he had a son, Reu;
11.20 When Reu was 32 **years old,** he had a son, Serug;
11.22 When Serug was 30 **years old,** he had a son, Nahor;
11.24 When Nahor was 29 **years old,** he had a son, Terah;
11.26 After Terah was 70 **years old,** he became the father of Abram,
12. 4 When Abram was seventy-five **years old,** he started out from Haran,
15. 9 ram, each of them three **years old,** and a dove and a
15.15 will live to a ripe **old age,** die in peace, and be
16.16 Abram was eighty-six **years old** at the time.
17. 1 When Abram was ninety-nine **years old,** the Lord appeared to
17.11 when he is eight days **old,** including slaves born in your
17.17 a man have a child when he is a hundred **years old?**
17.24 Abraham was ninety-nine **years old** when he was circumcised,
18.11 Abraham and Sarah were very **old,** and Sarah had stopped
18.12 said, "Now that I am **old** and worn out, can I still
18.12 And besides, my husband is **old** too."
18.13 say, 'Can I really have a child when I am so **old?'**
19. 4 All the men of the city, both young and **old,** were there.
19.31 sister, "Our father is getting **old,** and there are no men in
21. 2 became pregnant and bore a son to Abraham when he was **old.**
Gen 21. 4 when Isaac was eight days **old,** Abraham circumcised him, as
21. 5 Abraham was a hundred **years old** when Isaac was born.
21. 7 Yet I have borne him a son in his **old age."**
23. 1 Sarah lived to be a hundred and twenty-seven **years old.**
24. 1 Abraham was now very **old,** and the Lord had blessed him in
24. 2 He said to his **oldest** servant, who was in charge of all
24.36 a son when she was **old,** and my master has given everything
24.59 they let Rebecca and her **old** family servant go with
25. 7 Abraham died at the ripe **old age** of a hundred and seventy-five.
25.17 Ishmael was a hundred and thirty-seven **years old** when he died.
25.20 Isaac was forty **years old** when he married Rebecca, the
25.23 The **older** will serve the younger."
25.26 Isaac was sixty **years old** when they were born.
26.34 When Esau was forty **years old,** he married two Hittite girls,
27. 1 Isaac was now **old** and had become blind.
27. 2 Isaac said, "You see that I am **old** and may die soon.
35.28 be a hundred and eighty **years old** [29] and died at a ripe
35.29 hundred and eighty years old [29] and died at a ripe **old age;**
37. 3 sons, because he had been born to him when he was **old.**
41.45 Joseph was thirty **years old** when he began to serve the king
42.38 I am an **old** man, and the sorrow you would cause me
43.27 then said, "You told me about your **old** father—how is he?
44.20 have a father who is **old** and a younger brother,
44.20 born to him in his **old age.**
44.29 sorrow you would cause me would kill me, **old** as I am.'
44.30 boy, and he is so **old** that the sorrow we would cause
47. 8 blessing, [8] and the king asked him, "How **old** are you?"
47.28 years, until he was a hundred and forty-seven **years old.**
50.22 he was a hundred and ten **years old** when he died.
Ex 2.10 Later, when the child was **old** enough, she took him to
7. 7 Moses was eighty **years old,** and Aaron was eighty-three.
10. 9 "We will all go, including our children and our **old** people.
30.14 that is, every man twenty **years old** or older, is to pay
38.26 There were 603,550 men twenty **years old** or older enrolled in
Lev 14.10 one female lamb a year **old** that are without any defects,
19.32 "Show respect for **old** people and honour them.
26.10 what is left of the **old** harvest to make room for the
27. 3 adult male, twenty to sixty **years old:**
27. 3 —young male, five to twenty **years old:**
Num 1. 3 of all the men [3] twenty **years old** or older who are fit
1.18 of all the men twenty **years old** or older were recorded and
1.20 The men twenty **years old** or older who were fit for
3.15 every male a month old or **older,** [16] and Moses did so.
3.22 males one month old or **older** that were enrolled was 7,500.
3.28 males one month old or **older** that were enrolled was 8,600.
3.34 males one month old or **older** that were enrolled was 6,200.
3.39 males one month old or **older** that Moses enrolled by clans at
3.40 every first-born male Israelite, one month old or **older.**
3.43 all the first-born males [43] one month old or **older;**
26. 2 Israel, of all men twenty **years old** or older who are fit
26.62 The male Levites who were one month old or **older** numbered 23,000.
32.11 none of the men twenty **years old** or older who came out
Deut 28.50 will be ruthless and show no mercy to anyone, young or **old.**
31. 2 now a hundred and twenty **years old** and am no longer able
32. 7 you what happened, ask the **old** men to tell of the past.
32.25 neither babies nor **old** men will be spared.
34. 7 Moses was a hundred and twenty **years old** when he died;
Josh 6.21 killed everyone in the city, men and women, young and **old.**
13. 1 Joshua was now very **old.**
13. 1 to him, "You are very **old,** but there is still much land
14. 7 I was forty **years old** when the Lord's servant Moses sent
14.10 I am eighty-five **years old** [11] and I'm just as strong today
23. 1 that time Joshua was very **old,** [2] so he called all Israel,
23. 2 and officers of the people, and said, "I am very **old** now.
Judg 2.19 used to return to the **old** ways and behave worse than the
6.25 bull and another bull seven **years old,** tear down your
8.32 Joash died at a ripe **old age** and was buried in the
19.16 While they were there, an **old** man came by at the end
19.17 The **old** man noticed the traveller in the city square and
19.20 The **old** man said, "You are welcome in my home!
19.22 They said to the **old** man, "Bring out that man that came
19.23 But the **old** man went outside and said to them, "No, my
19.26 at the door of the **old** man's house, where her husband was.
Ruth 1.12 Go back home, for I am too **old** to get married again.
4.15 new life to you and give you security in your **old age."**
1 Sam 2.22 Eli was now very **old.**
2.31 so that no man in your family will live to be **old.**
2.32 no one in your family will ever again live to **old age.**
4.15 (Eli was now ninety-eight **years old** and almost completely blind.)
4.18 He was so **old** and fat that the fall broke his neck,
5. 9 in all the people of the city, young and **old** alike.
8. 1 When Samuel grew **old,** he made his sons judges in Israel.
8. 5 him, "Look, you are getting **old** and your sons don't follow
12. 2 As for me, I am **old** and grey, and my sons are
17.12 the time Saul was king, he was already a very **old** man.
24.13 You know the **old** saying, 'Evil is done only by evil men.'
28.14 "It's an **old** man coming up," she answered.
2 Sam 2.10 He was forty **years old** when he was made king of Israel,
4. 4 son Mephibosheth, who was five **years old** when Saul and
5. 4 David was thirty **years old** when he became king, and he
19.32 Barzillai was a very **old** man, eighty years old.
19.35 I am already eighty **years old,** and nothing gives me
1 Kgs 1. 1 David was now a very **old** man, and although his servants
1.15 He was very **old,** and Abishag, the girl from Shunem, was
11. 4 by the time he was **old** they had led him into the
12. 6 King Rehoboam consulted the **older** men who had served as
12. 8 ignored the advice of the **older** men and went instead to the
12.13 ignored the advice of the **older** men and spoke harshly to the
13.11 At that time there was an **old** prophet living in Bethel.
13.12 the **old** prophet asked them.

1 Kgs 13.18 Then the **old** prophet from Bethel said to him, "I, too,
13.18 But the **old** prophet was lying.
13.19 Judah went home with the **old** prophet and had a meal with
13.20 the Lord came to the **old** prophet, [21]and he cried out to
13.23 they had finished eating, the **old** prophet saddled the donkey
13.26 When the **old** prophet heard about it, he said, "That is
13.29 The **old** prophet picked up the body, put it on the donkey,
14. 4 **Old age** had made Ahijah blind.
14.10 will kill all your male descendants, young and **old** alike.
14.21 Solomon's son Rehoboam was forty-one **years old** when he
15.23 But in his **old age** he was crippled by a foot disease.
21.21 get rid of every male in your family, young and **old** alike.
2 Kgs 3.21 could bear arms, from the **oldest** to the youngest, were
4.14 "Well, she has no son, and her husband is an **old** man."
9. 8 get rid of every male in his family, young and **old** alike.
17.34 They still carry on their **old** customs to this day.
17.40 not listen, and they continued to follow their **old** customs.
21. 1 Manasseh was twelve **years old** when he became king of Judah,
21.19 Amon was twenty-two **years old** when he became king of Judah,
22. 1 Josiah was eight **years old** when he became king of Judah,
23.31 Joahaz was twenty-three **years old** when he became king of Judah,
23.36 Jehoiakim was twenty-five **years old** when he became king of Judah,
24. 8 Jehoiachin was eighteen **years old** when he became king of Judah,
24.18 Zedekiah was twenty-one **years old** when he became king of Judah,
1 Chr 2.21 When Hezron was sixty **years old,** he married Machir's daughter,
4.22 (These traditions are very **old.)**
23. 1 When David was very **old,** he made his son Solomon king of
23. 3 took a census of all the male Levites aged thirty or **older.**
23.24 twenty years of age or **older,** had a share in the work
25. 8 lots, whether they were young or **old,** experts or beginners.
29.28 He died at a ripe **old age,** wealthy and respected, and
2 Chr 10. 6 King Rehoboam consulted the **older** men who had served as
10. 8 ignored the advice of the **older** men and went instead to the
10.13 ignored the advice of the **older** men and spoke harshly to the
12.13 He was forty-one **years old** when he became king, and he ruled
15.13 Anyone, young or **old,** male or female, who did not
24.15 After reaching the very **old age** of a hundred and thirty,
25. 5 all men twenty years of age or **older,** 300,000 in all.
27. 8 Jotham was twenty-five **years old** when he became king, and
31.16 thirty years of age or **older** who had daily responsibilities
31.17 years of age or **older** were assigned theirs by work groups.
32. 5 filled in on the east side of the **old** part of Jerusalem.
33. 1 Manasseh was twelve **years old** when he became king of Judah,
33.21 Amon was twenty-two **years old** when he became king of Judah,
34. 1 Josiah was eight **years old** when he became king of Judah,
36. 2 Joahaz was twenty-three **years old** when he became king of Judah,
36. 5 Jehoiakim was twenty-five **years old** when he became king of Judah,
36. 9 Jehoiachin was eighteen **years old** when he became king of Judah,
36.11 Zedekiah was twenty-one **years old** when he became king of Judah,
36.17 on anyone, young or **old,** man or woman, sick or healthy.
Ezra 2.68 offerings to help rebuild the Temple on its **old** site.
3. 8 twenty years of age or **older** were put in charge of the
3.12 Many of the **older** priests, Levites, and heads of clans
Neh 8. 2 women, and the children who were **old** enough to understand.
10.28 wives and all our children **old** enough to understand, [29]do
Esth 3.13 Adar, all Jews—young and **old,** women and children—were to be
Job 5.26 ripens till harvest time, you will live to a ripe **old age.**
12.12 **Old** men have wisdom, but God has wisdom and power.
12.12 **Old** men have insight;
12.20 men who are trusted, and takes the wisdom of **old** men away.
14. 8 Even though its roots grow **old,** and its stump dies in the
17. 5 In the **old** proverb a man betrays his friends for money,
21. 7 does God let evil men live, let them grow **old** and prosper?
29. 8 as they saw me, and **old** men stood up to show me
32. 6 am young, and you are **old,** so I was afraid to tell
32. 7 to speak, that you **older** men should share your wisdom.
32. 9 It is not growing **old** that makes men wise or helps them
38.21 you can, because you're so **old** and were there when the world
Ps 37.25 I am an **old** man now;
71. 9 Do not reject me now that I am **old;**
71.18 Now that I am **old** and my hair is grey, do not
89.45 You have made him **old** before his time and covered him
92.14 that still bear fruit in **old age** and are always green
102.24 O God, do not take me away now before I grow **old.**
119.100 I have greater wisdom than **old** men, because I obey your commands.
148.12 girls and young men, **old** people and children too.
Prov 17. 6 **Old** men are proud of their grandchildren, just as boys are
22.28 Never move an **old** boundary-mark that your ancestors established.
23.10 Never move an **old** boundary-mark or take over land owned by orphans.
23.22 When your mother is **old,** show her your appreciation.
30.17 despises his mother in her **old age** ought to be eaten by
Ecc 4.13 throne, but if in his **old age** he is too foolish to
7.10 ask, "Oh, why were things so much better in the **old** days?"
Song 7.13 Darling, I have kept for you the **old** delights and the new.
Is 7.15 By the time he is **old** enough to make his own decisions,
8. 4 Before the boy is **old** enough to say 'Mummy' and 'Daddy,'
9.15 The **old** and honourable men are the head—and the tail is
20. 4 Young and **old,** they will walk barefoot and naked, with their
22.11 the city to hold the water flowing down from the **old** pool.
23.17 Tyre go back to her **old** trade, and she will hire herself
Is 33.18 Your **old** fears of foreign tax-collectors and spies will
46. 4 care of you until you are **old** and your hair is grey.
51. 6 earth will wear out like **old** clothing, and all its people
58.12 long been in ruins, building again on the **old** foundations.
Jer 6.11 be taken away, and even the very **old** will not be spared.
13.14 them like jars against one another, **old** and young alike.
18.15 the way they should go, they no longer follow the **old** ways;
19. 1 people and some of the **older** priests, [2]and to go through
31.13 will dance and be happy, and men, young and **old,** will
31.32 will not be like the **old covenant** that I made with their
51.22 men and women, to slay **old** and young, to kill boys and
52. 1 Zedekiah was twenty-one **years old** when he became king of Judah,
Lam 2.10 Jerusalem's **old** men sit on the ground in silence, With
2.21 Young and **old** alike lie dead in the streets, Young men
5.12 our **old** men are shown no respect.
5.14 The **old** people no longer sit at the city gate, and the
Ezek 9. 6 Kill the **old** men, young men, young women, mothers, and
23. 4 The **older** one was named Oholah (she represents Samaria),
Dan 5.31 who was then sixty-two **years old,** seized the royal power.
Hos 4.11 The Lord says, "Wine, both **old** and new, is robbing my
Joel 1. 2 Pay attention, you **older** people;
2.16 bring the **old** people;
2.28 your **old** men will have dreams, and your young men will see
Hag 2. 9 be more splendid than the **old** one, and there I will give
Zech 8. 4 old men and women, so **old** that they use a stick when
Mt 2.16 its neighbourhood who were two **years old** and younger—this
9.16 "No one patches up an **old** coat with a piece of new
13.52 a house who takes new and **old** things out of his storeroom."
Mk 2.21 cloth to patch up an **old** coat, because the new patch will
2.21 tear off some of the **old** cloth, making an even bigger hole.
5.42 (She was twelve **years old.)**
Lk 1. 7 not have any, and she and Zechariah were both very **old.**
1.18 I am an **old** man, and my wife is old also."
1.36 is now six months pregnant, even though she is very **old.**
1.59 the baby was a week **old,** they came to circumcise him,
2.36 There was a very **old** prophetess, a widow named Anna,
2.36 for only seven years and was now eighty-four **years old.**
2.42 When Jesus was twelve **years old,** they went to the
3.23 When Jesus began his work, he was about thirty **years old.**
5.36 a piece off a new coat to patch up an **old** coat.
5.36 coat, and the piece of new cloth will not match the **old.**
5.39 And no one wants new wine after drinking **old** wine.
5.39 'The **old** is better,' he says."
8.42 because his only daughter, who was twelve **years old,**
Jn 8. 9 heard this, they all left, one by one, the **older** ones first.
8.57 "You are not even fifty **years old**—and you have seen Abraham?"
9.21 he is **old** enough, and he can answer for himself!"
9.23 That is why his parents said, "He is **old** enough;
21.18 but when you are **old,** you will stretch out your hands
Acts 2.17 men will see visions, and your **old** men will have dreams.
4.22 of healing had been performed was over forty **years old.**
7.23 "When Moses was forty **years old,** he decided to find out
Rom 4.19 He was then almost one hundred **years old;**
6. 6 And we know that our **old** being has been put to death
7. 6 do we serve in the **old** way of a written law,
1 Cor 5. 7 You must remove the **old** yeast of sin so that you will
5. 8 not with bread having the **old** yeast of sin and wickedness,
2 Cor 3.14 the same veil as they read the books of the **old** covenant.
5.17 the **old** is gone, the new has come.
Eph 4.22 So get rid of your **old** self, which made you live
4.22 as you used to—the **old** self that was being destroyed by
Phil 3. 5 I was circumcised when I was a week **old.**
Col 3. 9 you have taken off the **old** self with its habits [10]and have
1 Tim 5. 1 Do not rebuke an **older** man, but appeal to him as if
5. 2 as your brothers, [2]the **older** women as mothers, and the younger
Tit 2. 2 Instruct the **older** men to be sober, sensible, and
2. 3 the same way instruct the **older** women to behave as women
Heb 7.18 The **old** rule, then, is set aside, because it was weak
8.13 speaking of a new covenant, God has made the first one **old;**
8.13 anything that becomes **old** and worn out will soon disappear.
10. 9 does away with all the **old** sacrifices and puts the sacrifice
11.11 even though he was too **old** and Sarah herself could not have
1 Pet 5. 5 the same way you younger men must submit to the **older** men.
2 Pet 3. 6 the water of the flood, that the **old** world was destroyed.
1 Jn 2. 7 it is the **old** command, the one you have had from the
2. 7 The **old** command is the message you have already heard.
Rev 21. 4 The **old** things have disappeared."

OLIVE

[MOUNT OF OLIVES]

Gen 8.11 him in the evening with a fresh **olive** leaf in its beak.
Ex 23.11 Do the same with your vineyards and your **olive-trees.**
Deut 6.11 and vineyards and **olive** orchards that you did not plant.
8. 8 wheat and barley, grapes, figs, pomegranates, **olives,**
24.20 When you have picked your **olives** once, do not go back
28.40 **Olive-trees** will grow everywhere in your land, but you
28.40 not have any olive-oil, because the **olives** will drop off.
32.13 their **olive-trees** flourished in stony ground.
33.24 of his brothers, And may his land be rich with **olive-trees.**
Josh 24.13 you did not plant, and **olives** from trees that you did not
Judg 9. 8 They said to the **olive-tree,** 'Be our king.'
9. 9 The **olive-tree** answered, 'In order to govern you, I would
15. 5 was still in the fields, and the **olive** orchards as well.
1 Sam 8.14 vineyards, and **olive-groves,** and give them to his officials.
2 Sam 15.30 David went on up the **Mount of Olives** weeping;
1 Kgs 6.23 winged creatures were made of **olive** wood and placed in the
6.31 A double door made of **olive** wood was set in place at
6.33 main room a rectangular door-frame of **olive** wood was made.
2 Kgs 5.26 and clothes, **olive-groves** and vineyards, sheep and cattle,

2 Kgs 18.32 it is a land of **olives,** olive-oil, and honey.
23.13 south of the **Mount of Olives,** for the worship of disgusting
1 Chr 27.25 **Olives** and sycomore-trees (in the western foothills):
Neh 5.11 And give them back their fields, vineyards, **olive-groves,**
8.15 and get branches from pines, **olives,** myrtles, palms, and
9.25 already dug, **olive-trees,** fruit-trees, and vineyards.
Job 15.33 like an **olive-tree** that drops its blossoms.
24.11 They press **olives** for oil, and grapes for wine, but they
29. 6 of milk, and my **olive-trees** grew in the rockiest soil.
Ps 52. 8 But I am like an **olive-tree** growing in the house of God;
128. 3 your sons will be like young **olive-trees** round your table.
Is 17. 6 Israel will be like an **olive-tree**
17. 6 from which all the **olives** have been picked
24.13 end of harvest, when the **olives** have been beaten off every
41.19 in the desert, and acacias and myrtles and **olive-trees.**
Jer 11.16 I once called them a leafy **olive-tree,** full of beautiful fruit;
Hos 2.21 and the earth will produce corn and grapes and **olives.**
14. 6 They will be alive with new growth, and beautiful like **olive-trees.**
Joel 1.10 the grapes are dried up, and the **olive-trees** are withered.
Amos 4. 9 your gardens and vineyards, your fig-trees and **olive-trees.**
Mic 6.15 You will press oil from **olives,** but never be able to use
Hab 3.17 the vines, even though the **olive-crop** fails and the fields
Hag 1.11 its hills, cornfields, vineyards, and **olive** orchards—on
2.19 pomegranates, and **olive-trees** have not yet produced,
Zech 4. 3 There are two **olive-trees** beside the lamp-stand, one on
4.11 him, "What do the two **olive-trees** on either side of the
4.12 the meaning of the two **olive** branches beside the two gold
14. 4 will stand on the **Mount of Olives,** to the east of Jerusalem.
14. 4 Then the **Mount of Olives** will be split in two from east
Mt 21. 1 approached Jerusalem, they came to Bethphage at the **Mount of Olives.**
24. 3 Jesus sat on the **Mount of Olives,** the disciples came to him
26.30 they sang a hymn and went out to the **Mount of Olives.**
Mk 11. 1 of Bethphage and Bethany, they came to the **Mount of Olives.**
13. 3 was sitting on the **Mount of Olives,** across from the Temple,
14.26 they sang a hymn and went out to the **Mount of Olives.**
Lk 19.29 and Bethany at the **Mount of Olives,** he sent two disciples
19.37 road went down the **Mount of Olives,** the large crowd of his
21.37 would go out and spend the night on the **Mount of Olives.**
22.39 city and went, as he usually did, to the **Mount of Olives;**
Jn 8. 1 Then everyone went home, but Jesus went to the **Mount of Olives.**
Acts 1.12 to Jerusalem from the **Mount of Olives,** which is about a
Rom 11.17 the branches of the cultivated **olive-tree** have been broken off,
11.17 and a branch of a wild **olive-tree** has been joined to it.
11.17 Gentiles are like that wild **olive-tree,** and now you share the
11.24 the branch of a wild **olive-tree** that is broken off and then,
11.24 contrary to nature, is joined to a cultivated **olive-tree.**
Jas 3.12 A fig-tree, my brothers, cannot bear **olives;**
Rev 6. 6 But do not damage the **olive-trees** and the vineyards!"
11. 4 two witnesses are the two **olive-trees** and the two lamps that

OLIVE-OIL

Gen 28.18 Then he poured **olive-oil** on it to dedicate it to God.
31.13 as a memorial by pouring **olive-oil** on it and where you made
35.14 and consecrated it by pouring wine and **olive-oil** on it.
Ex 22.29 your corn, your wine, and your **olive-oil** when they are due.
27.20 to bring you the best **olive-oil** for the lamp, so that it
28.41 them by anointing them with **olive-oil,** so that they may
29. 2 and make some bread with **olive-oil,** some without it, and
29.23 one loaf made with **olive-oil** and one made without it and one
29.36 Then anoint it with **olive-oil** to make it holy.
29.40 of fine wheat flour mixed with one litre of pure **olive-oil.**
29.41 amounts of flour, **olive-oil,** and wine as in the morning.
30.24 Add four litres of **olive-oil,** [25]and make a sacred anointing oil,
Lev 2. 1 He must put **olive-oil** and incense on it [2]and bring it to
2. 4 loaves made of flour mixed with **olive-oil**
2. 4 or biscuits brushed with **olive-oil.**
2. 5 to be made of flour mixed with **olive-oil** but without yeast.
2. 7 in a pan, it is to be made of flour and **olive-oil.**
2.15 Add **olive-oil** and put incense on it.
5.11 He shall not put any **olive-oil** or any incense on it, because
7.12 made of flour mixed with **olive-oil**
7.12 or biscuits brushed with **olive-oil**
7.12 or cakes made of flour mixed with **olive-oil.**
14.10 kilogrammes of flour mixed with **olive-oil,**
14.10 and a third of a litre of **olive-oil.**
14.15 shall take some of the **olive-oil** and pour it in the palm
14.21 kilogramme of flour mixed with **olive-oil** for a grain-offering
14.21 and a third of a litre of **olive-oil.**
14.24 take the lamb and the **olive-oil** and present them as a
23.13 of flour mixed with **olive-oil** as a food-offering.
24. 2 Bring pure **olive-oil** of the finest quality for the lamps in
Num 4. 9 its lamps, tongs, trays, and all the **olive-oil** containers.
5.15 he shall not pour any **olive-oil** on it or put any incense
6.15 made of flour mixed with **olive-oil**
6.15 and biscuits brushed with **olive-oil,**
8. 8 the required grain-offering of flour mixed with **olive-oil;**
11. 8 It tasted like bread baked with **olive-oil.)**
15. 4 mixed with a litre of **olive-oil** as a grain-offering,
15. 6 and a half litres of **olive-oil** are to be presented as a
15. 9 mixed with two litres of **olive-oil** is to be presented,
18.12 **olive-oil,** wine, and corn.
28. 5 of flour, mixed with one litre of the best **olive-oil.**
28. 9 with **olive-oil** as a grain-offering, and the wine-offering.
28.12 As a grain-offering, offer flour mixed with **olive-oil:**
28.20 Offer the proper grain-offering of flour mixed with **olive-oil:**
28.28 Offer the proper grain-offering of flour mixed with **olive-oil:**
29. 3 Offer the proper grain-offering of flour mixed with **olive-oil:**
29. 9 Offer the proper grain-offering of flour mixed with **olive-oil:**
29.14 Offer the proper grain-offering of flour mixed with **olive-oil:**
Deut 7.13 fields, so that you will have corn, wine, and **olive-oil;**
11.14 will be corn, wine, and **olive-oil** for you, [15]and grass for
12.17 corn, your wine, or your **olive-oil,** nor the first-born of
14.23 of your corn, wine, and **olive-oil,** and the first-born of
18. 4 to receive the first share of the corn, wine, **olive-oil,** and
28.40 not have any **olive-oil,** because the olives will drop off.
28.51 They will not leave you any corn, wine, **olive-oil,**
1 Sam 10. 1 Samuel took a jar of **olive-oil** and poured it on Saul's head,
16. 1 But now get some **olive-oil** and go to Bethlehem, to a man
16.13 Samuel took the **olive-oil** and anointed David
1 Kgs 1.39 Zadok took the container of **olive-oil** which he had
5.11 litres of pure **olive-oil** every year to feed his men.
17.12 flour in a bowl and a drop of **olive-oil** in a jar.
2 Kgs 4. 2 "Nothing at all, except a small jar of **olive-oil,"** she
4. 5 took the small jar of **olive-oil,** and poured oil into the
4. 6 And the **olive-oil** stopped flowing.
4. 7 said to her, "Sell the **olive-oil** and pay all your debts,
9. 1 Take this jar of **olive-oil** with you, [2]and when you get
9. 3 from his companions, [3]pour this **olive-oil** on his head, and
9. 6 the young prophet poured the **olive-oil** on Jehu's head and
18.32 it is a land of olives, **olive-oil,** and honey.
1 Chr 9.29 other sacred equipment, and of the flour, wine, **olive-oil,**
12.40 loaded with food—flour, figs, raisins, wine, and **olive-oil.**
23.29 the baked offerings, and the flour mixed with **olive-oil;**
27.25 **Olive-oil** storage:
2 Chr 2.10 of wine, and four hundred thousand litres of **olive-oil."**
2.15 us the wheat, barley, wine, and **olive-oil** that you promised.
11.11 he placed supplies of food, **olive-oil,** and wine, [12]and
28.15 enough to eat and drink, and put **olive-oil** on their wounds.
31. 5 finest corn, wine, **olive-oil,** honey, and other farm produce,
32.28 he had storehouses built for his corn, wine, and **olive-oil;**
Ezra 3. 7 and gave food, drink, and **olive-oil** to be sent to the cities
6. 9 to the God of Heaven, or wheat, salt, wine, or **olive-oil.**
7.22 2,000 litres of **olive-oil,** and as much salt as necessary.
Neh 5.11 the debts they owe you—money or corn or wine or **olive-oil.**
10.37 other offerings of wine, **olive-oil,** and all kinds of fruit.
10.39 contributions of corn, wine, and **olive-oil** to the storerooms
13. 5 tithes of corn, wine, and **olive-oil** given to the Levites, to
13.12 temple storerooms their tithes of corn, wine, and **olive-oil.**
Job 20.17 live to see rivers of **olive-oil** or streams that flow with
Ps 104.15 wine to make him happy, **olive-oil** to make him cheerful, and
Prov 5. 3 kisses as smooth as **olive-oil,** [4]but when it is all over,
Jer 31.12 of corn and wine and **olive-oil,** gifts of sheep and cattle.
40.10 store up wine, fruit, and **olive-oil,** and live in the
41. 8 We have wheat, barley, **olive-oil,** and honey hidden in the fields."
Ezek 16. 9 I rubbed **olive-oil** on your skin.
16.13 from the best flour, and had honey and **olive-oil** to eat.
16.18 to the images the **olive-oil** and incense I had given you.
16.19 you food—the best flour, **olive-oil,** and honey—but you
23.41 the incense and the **olive-oil** that I had given them.
27.17 and Israel paid for your goods with wheat, honey, **olive-oil,**
45.13 **Olive-oil:**
45.24 and a half litres of corn and three litres of **olive-oil.**
45.25 whole, and the same offerings of corn and **olive-oil."**
46. 5 For each such grain-offering he is to bring three litres of **olive-oil.**
46. 7 Three litres of **olive-oil** are to be offered with each such
46.11 Three litres of **olive-oil** are to be offered
46.14 with one litre of **olive-oil** for mixing with the flour.
46.15 lamb, the flour, and the **olive-oil** are to be offered to the
Hos 2. 4 me food and water, wool and linen, **olive-oil** and wine."
2. 8 the corn, the wine, the **olive-oil,** and all the silver and
9. 2 have enough corn and **olive-oil,** and there will be no wine.
Joel 2.19 you corn and wine and **olive-oil,** and you will be satisfied.
2.24 the pits beside the presses will overflow with wine and **olive-oil.**
Mic 6. 7 I bring him thousands of sheep or endless streams of **olive-oil?**
Hag 2.12 any bread, cooked food, wine, **olive-oil,** or any kind of food
Zech 4.12 the two gold pipes from which the **olive-oil** pours?"
Mk 6.13 and rubbed **olive-oil** on many sick people and healed
Lk 7.46 You provided no **olive-oil** for my head, but she has
16. 6 'One hundred barrels of **olive-oil,'** he answered.
Jas 5.14 pray for him and rub **olive-oil** on him in the name of

OMEN

Num 24. 1 did not go to look for **omens,** as he had done before.
Deut 18.10 divination or look for **omens** or use spells [11]or charms,
18.14 practise divination and look for **omens,** but the Lord your

OMRI (1)

King of the n. kingdom (Israel), father of King Ahab.

1 Kgs 16.16 they all proclaimed their commander **Omri** king of Israel.
16.17 **Omri** and his troops left Gibbethon and went and besieged Tirzah.
16.21 son of Ginath king, and the others were in favour of **Omri.**
16.22 In the end, those in favour of **Omri** won;
16.22 Tibni died and **Omri** became king.
16.23 of King Asa of Judah, **Omri** became king of Israel, and he
16.24 **Omri** fortified the hill, built a town there, and named it Samaria,
16.25 **Omri** sinned against the Lord more than any of his predecessors.
16.27 Everything else that **Omri** did and all his
16.28 **Omri** died and was buried in Samaria, and his son Ahab
16.29 of Judah, Ahab son of **Omri** became king of Israel, and he
2 Kgs 8.26 of King Ahab and granddaughter of King **Omri** of Israel.
2 Chr 22. 2 Ahab and granddaughter of King **Omri** of Israel—gave him
Mic 6.16 the evil practices of King **Omri** and of his son, King Ahab.

ONCE

see also **AT ONCE**

Gen 18.32 "Please don't be angry, Lord, and I will speak just **once** more.
Ex 10.17 Now forgive my sin this **once** and pray to the Lord your

Ex 30.10 **Once** a year Aaron is to perform the ritual for purifying
Lev 16.34 This ritual must be performed **once** a year to purify the
Deut 24.20 you have picked your olives **once,** do not go back and get
24.21 you have gathered your grapes **once,** do not go back over the
Josh 6. 3 are to march round the city **once** a day for six days.
6.11 of men to take the Lord's Covenant Box round the city **once.**
6.14 again marched round the city **once** and then returned to camp.
Judg 6.39 let me speak just **once** more.
16.18 the Philistine kings and said, "Come back just **once** more.
16.28 give me my strength just **once** more, so that with this one
2 Sam 14.26 he had to cut it **once** a year, when it grew too
1 Kgs 18.34 "Do it **once** more," he said—and they did.
Job 23. 7 he would declare me innocent **once and for all.**
41. 8 Touch him **once** and you'll never try it again;
Ps 89.35 **"Once and for all** I have promised by my holy name:
Prov 19.19 get him out of trouble **once,** you will have to do it
Jer 16.21 "So then," says the Lord, **"once** and for all I will
Ezek 13.21 and let my people escape from your power **once** and for all.
16.22 as a prostitute you never **once** remembered your
Nah 1. 9 No one opposes him more than **once.**
Jn 10.38 that you may know **once and for all** that the Father is
Rom 7. 6 Law, because we died to that which **once** held us prisoners.
7. 9 I myself was **once** alive apart from law;
2 Cor 11.25 and **once** I was stoned.
11.25 been in three shipwrecks, and **once** I spent twenty-four hours in
Gal 1.23 is now preaching the faith that he **once** tried to destroy!"
Phil 4.16 More than **once** when I needed help in Thessalonica, you
Col 2.22 these refer to things which become useless **once** they are used;
1 Thes 2.18 to go back more than **once,** but Satan would not let us.
1 Tim 5. 9 must have been married only **once** [10]and have a reputation
Tit 3. 3 For we ourselves were **once** foolish, disobedient, and
Heb 6. 4 They were **once** in God's light;
7.27 He offered one sacrifice, **once and for all,** when he offered himself.
9. 7 into the inner Tent, and he does so only **once** a year.
9.12 the tent and entered **once and for all** into the Most Holy
9.26 he has appeared **once and for all,** to remove sin through
9.27 Everyone must die **once,** and after that be judged by God.
9.28 also was offered in sacrifice **once** to take away the sins of
10.10 offering that he made of his own body **once and for all.**
1 Pet 3.18 Christ died for sins **once and for all,** a good man
Jude 3 for the faith which **once and for all** God has given to
5 of how the Lord **once** rescued the people of Israel from
Rev 17. 8 That beast was **once** alive, but lives no longer;
17. 8 It was **once** alive;
17.11 And the beast that was **once** alive, but lives no longer,
22. 2 which bears fruit twelve times a year, **once** each month;

ONE

Gen 1. 9 the sky come together in **one** place, so that the land will
2.20 but not **one** of them was a suitable companion to help him.
2.21 was sleeping, he took out **one** of the man's ribs and closed
2.23 "At last, here is **one** of my own kind— Bone taken
2.24 mother and is united with his wife, and they become **one.**
7. 2 ritually clean animal, but only **one** pair of each kind of
8.20 he took **one** of each kind of ritually clean animal and bird,
9. 4 The **one** thing you must not eat is meat with blood still
11. 1 whole world had only **one** language and used the same words.
11. 6 "Now then, these are all **one** people and they speak one language;
13. 9 You go **one** way, and I'll go the other."
24.41 There is only **one** way for you to be free from your
25.23 **One** will be stronger than the other;
27.38 "Have you only **one** blessing, father?
33.13 are driven hard for even **one** day, the whole herd will die.
34.16 We will settle among you and become **one** people with you.
34.22 live among us and be **one** people with us only on condition
36.10 Esau's wife Adah bore him **one** son, Eliphaz, and
36.10 And by another wife, Timna, he had **one** more son, Amalek.
36.10 Esau's wife Basemath bore him **one** son, Reuel, and Reuel had
41. 5 Seven ears of corn, full and ripe, were growing on **one** stalk.
41.22 ears of corn which were full and ripe, growing on **one** stalk.
42.13 **One** brother is dead, and the youngest is now with our father."
42.32 **One** brother is dead, and the youngest is still in Canaan
42.38 his brother is dead, and he is the only **one** left.
43.32 Joseph was served at **one** table and his brothers at another.
44.28 **One** of them has already left me.
47.21 slaves of the people from **one** end of Egypt to the other.
Ex 5. 8 the same number of bricks as before, not **one** brick less.
8.31 not **one** fly remained.
9. 6 the Egyptians died, but not **one** of the animals of the
10.19 Not **one** locust was left in all Egypt.
10.26 not **one** will be left behind.
11. 1 Moses, "I will send only **one** more punishment on the king of
12. 5 but it must be a **one-year-old** male without any defects.
12.22 Not **one** of you is to leave the house until morning.
12.30 Egypt, because there was not **one** home in which there was not
14.28 not **one** of them was left.
15.10 But **one** breath from you, Lord, and the Egyptians were drowned;
22. 1 pay five cows for one cow and four sheep for **one** sheep.
22. 2 is found alive in his possession, he shall pay two for **one.**
23.29 I will not drive them out within **one** year;
24. 4 and set up twelve stones, **one** for each of the twelve tribes
25.19 creatures of hammered gold, [19]**one** for each end of the lid.
25.19 Make them so that they form **one** piece with the lid.
25.31 including buds and petals, are to form **one** piece with it.
25.35 There is to be **one** bud below each of the three pairs
26. 3 five of them together in **one** set, and do the same with
26. 6 gold hooks with which to join the two sets into **one** piece.
26. 9 five of them together in **one** set, and the other six in
26.10 of the last piece of **one** set, and fifty loops on the
26.11 loops to join the two sets so as to form **one** cover.
Ex 27. 2 They are to form **one** piece with the altar, and the whole
28. 8 attached to the ephod so as to form **one** piece with it.
29. 1 Take **one** young bull and two rams without any defects.
29.15 "Take **one** of the rams and tell Aaron and his sons to
29.23 which has been offered to me, take **one** loaf of each kind:
29.23 **one** loaf made with olive-oil
29.23 and **one** made without it and one biscuit.
29.38 time to come, sacrifice on the altar two **one-year-old** lambs.
30. 2 at the four corners are to form **one** piece with it.
36.10 five of them together in **one** set and did the same with
36.13 gold hooks, with which to join the two sets into **one** piece.
36.16 five of them together in **one** set and the other six in
36.17 of the last piece of **one** set and fifty loops on the
36.18 hooks to join the two sets, so as to form **one** cover.
37. 8 creatures of hammered gold, [8]**one** for each end of the lid.
37. 8 He made them so that they formed **one** piece with the lid.
37.17 including buds and petals, formed **one** piece with it.
37.21 There was **one** bud below each of the three pairs of branches.
37.25 Its projections at the four corners formed **one** piece with it.
38. 2 four corners, so that they formed **one** piece with the altar.
39. 5 ephod so as to form **one** piece with it, as the Lord
Lev 7. 7 There is **one** regulation that applies to both the
8.26 Then he took **one** loaf of bread from the basket of
8.26 bread dedicated to the Lord, **one** loaf made with oil,
8.26 and **one** biscuit, and he put them on
9. 3 a one-year-old calf, and a **one-year-old** lamb without any
12. 6 of the Lord's presence a **one-year-old** lamb for a
14.10 bring two male lambs and **one** female lamb a year old that
14.21 purification only **one** male lamb as his repayment-offering,
19.13 the wages of someone you have hired, not even for **one** night.
23.12 burnt-offering a **one-year-old** male lamb that has no defects.
23.18 community is to present seven **one-year-old** lambs,
23.18 **one** bull, and two rams,
23.19 Also offer **one** male goat as a sin-offering
23.19 and two **one-year-old** male lambs as a fellowship-offering.
24.20 blinds him in one eye, **one** of his eyes shall be blinded;
24.20 he knocks out a tooth, **one** of his teeth shall be knocked
26.26 ten women will need only **one** oven to bake all the bread
27.32 **One** out of every ten domestic animals belongs to the Lord.
Num 1. 4 Ask **one** clan chief from each tribe to help you."
3.22 The total number of males **one** month old or older that
3.28 The total number of males **one** month old or older that
3.34 The total number of males **one** month old or older that
3.39 of all the Levite males **one** month old or older that Moses
3.40 every first-born male Israelite, **one** month old or older.
3.43 all the first-born males [43]**one** month old or older;
6.12 As a repayment offering he shall bring a **one-year-old** lamb.
6.14 **one-year-old** male lamb for a burnt-offering,
6.14 a **one-year-old** ewe lamb for a sin-offering,
6.19 and put it, together with **one** thick loaf of bread
6.19 and **one** biscuit from the basket, into the
7.12 **one** silver bowl weighing 1.5 kilogrammes and one silver basin
7.12 **one** gold dish weighing 110 grammes, full of incense;
7.12 **one** young bull, one ram, and a one-year-old lamb, for the burnt-offering;
7.12 **one** goat for the sin-offering;
7.12 and five **one-year-old** lambs for the fellowship-offering.
7.84 bulls, twelve rams, and twelve **one-year-old** lambs, together
7.84 sixty **one-year-old** lambs, for the fellowship-offerings
10. 4 But when only **one** trumpet is sounded, then only the
11.19 eat it not just for **one** or two days, or five, or
13.23 off a branch which had **one** bunch of grapes on it so
14.34 your sin for forty years, **one** year for each of the forty
15.27 he is to offer a **one-year-old** female goat as a sin-offering.
16.22 When **one** man sins, do you get angry with the whole community?"
17. 2 give you twelve sticks, **one** from the leader of each tribe.
17. 3 There will be **one** stick for each tribal leader.
17. 6 leaders gave him a stick, **one** for each tribe, twelve in all,
18.16 back at the age of **one** month for the fixed price of
26.62 The male Levites who were **one** month old or older numbered 23,000.
26.64 There was not even **one** man left among those whom Moses
28. 3 two **one-year-old** male lambs without any defects.
28. 9 two **one-year-old** male lambs without any defects,
28.11 two young bulls, **one** ram,
28.11 seven **one-year-old** male lambs, all without any defects.
28.15 its wine-offering, offer **one** male goat as a sin-offering.
28.19 two young bulls, **one** ram,
28.19 seven **one-year-old** male lambs, all without any defects.
28.22 Also offer **one** male goat as a sin-offering, and in this
28.27 two young bulls, **one** ram,
28.27 and seven **one-year-old** male lambs, all without any defects.
28.30 Also offer **one** male goat as a sin-offering, and in this
29. 2 **one** young bull, one ram,
29. 2 seven **one-year-old** male lambs, all without any defects.
29. 5 Also offer **one** male goat as a sin-offering, and in this
29. 8 **one** young bull, one ram,
29. 8 seven **one-year-old** male lambs, all without any defects.
29.11 Also offer **one** male goat as a sin-offering, in addition
29.13 fourteen **one-year-old** male lambs, all without any defects.
29.16 Also offer **one** male goat as a sin-offering.
29.17 fourteen **one-year-old** male lambs, all without any defects.
29.20 fourteen **one-year-old** male lambs, all without any defects.
29.23 fourteen **one-year-old** male lambs, all without any defects.
29.26 fourteen **one-year-old** male lambs, all without any defects.
29.29 fourteen **one-year-old** male lambs, all without any defects.
29.32 fourteen **one-year-old** male lambs, all without any defects.
29.36 **one** young bull, one ram,
29.36 seven **one-year-old** male lambs, all without any defects.
31.28 a tax for the Lord **one** out of every five hundred prisoners
31.30 rest of the people, take **one** out of every fifty prisoners

Num 31.47 From this share Moses took **one** out of every fifty
31.49 soldiers under our command and not **one** of them is missing.
34.18 Take also **one** leader from each tribe to help them divide it."
35.30 the evidence of **one** witness is not sufficient to support an
Deut 1.23 thing to do, so I selected twelve men, **one** from each tribe.
1.35 so he solemnly declared, [35] 'Not **one** of you from this evil
3. 4 all his towns—there was not **one** that we did not take.
12. 5 the Lord will choose the **one** place where the people are to
12.14 offer them only in the **one** place that the Lord will choose
12.18 Lord your God, in the **one** place of worship chosen by the
12.21 If the **one** place of worship is too far away, then,
12.26 Take to the **one** place of worship your offerings and the
14.23 Then go to the **one** place where the Lord your God has
14.25 and take the money with you to the **one** place of worship.
15. 4 Not **one** of your people will be poor [5] if you obey him
15.20 eat them in the Lord's presence at the **one** place of worship.
16. 2 Go to the **one** place of worship and slaughter there one of
16. 5 the Passover animals at the **one** place of worship—and nowhere
16. 7 Boil the meat and eat it at the **one** place of worship;
16.11 Do this at the **one** place of worship.
16.15 this festival for seven days at the **one** place of worship.
16.16 the Lord three times a year at the **one** place of worship:
17. 6 not to be put to death if there is only **one** witness.
17. 8 this happens, go to the **one** place of worship chosen by the
18. 6 town in Israel to the **one** place of worship [7] and may serve
19. 6 If there were only **one** city, the distance to it might be
19.15 "**One** witness is not enough to convict a man of a crime;
19.17 are to go to the **one** place of worship and be judged
24. 5 be excused from duty for **one** year, so that he can stay
26. 2 you must take it with you to the **one** place of worship.
28. 7 They will attack from **one** direction, but they will run from
28.21 you until there is not **one** of you left in the land
28.25 You will attack them from **one** direction, but you will run
31.11 to worship the Lord your God at the **one** place of worship.
32.30 a thousand defeated by **one,** and ten thousand by only two?
Josh 3.13 the water coming downstream will pile up in **one** place."
6. 5 Then they are to sound **one** long note.
8.35 Every **one** of the commandments of Moses was read by
10. 8 Not **one** of them will be able to stand against you."
10.42 kings and their territory in **one** campaign because the Lord,
17.14 have you given us only **one** part of the land to possess
17.17 You shall have more than **one** share.
21.45 The Lord kept every **one** of the promises that he had made
23.10 Any **one** of you can make a thousand men run away, because
23.14 not **one** has failed.
Judg 6.16 the Midianites as easily as if they were only **one** man."
6.39 Please let me make **one** more test with the wool.
8.24 he went on to say, "Let me ask **one** thing of you.
9. 2 governed by all seventy of Gideon's sons or by just **one** man?
11.37 But she asked her father, "Do this **one** thing for me.
16. 5 Each **one** of us will give you eleven hundred pieces of silver."
16.28 more, so that with this **one** blow I can get even with
18.19 a whole Israelite tribe than for the family of **one** man?"
19.29 into twelve pieces, and sent **one** piece to each of the twelve
20. 1 They gathered in **one** body in the Lord's presence at Mizpah.
20. 6 it in pieces, and sent **one** piece to each of the twelve
20.11 in Israel assembled with **one** purpose—to attack the town.
1 Sam 1. 5 he would give her only **one** share, because the Lord had kept
2.33 Yet I will keep **one** of your descendants alive, and he
6. 4 and five gold mice, **one** of each for each Philistine king.
6.17 to pay for their sins, **one** each for the cities of Ashdod,
6.18 They also sent gold mice, **one** for each of the cities
13.21 the charge was **one** small coin for sharpening axes and
25.22 I don't kill every last **one** of those men before morning!"
26. 8 to the ground with just **one** blow—I won't have to strike
2 Sam 10. 4 David's messengers, shaved off **one** side of their beards,
12. 3 while the poor man had only **one** lamb, which he had bought.
13.30 "Absalom has killed all your sons—not **one** of them is left!"
14.12 Your Majesty, let me say just **one** more thing," the woman said.
14.27 Absalom had three sons and **one** daughter named Tamar, a
17. 3 You want to kill only **one** man;
19. 7 that if you don't, not **one** of them will be with you
20.21 Hand over this **one** man, and I will withdraw from the city."
23. 8 eight hundred men and killed them all in **one** battle.
1 Kgs 2.16 And now I have **one** request to make;
4. 7 each man being responsible for **one** month out of the year.
4.19 Besides these twelve, there was **one** governor over the whole land.
5.14 men, and each group spent **one** month in Lebanon and two
6.36 enclosed with walls which had **one** layer of cedar beams for
7.12 the Temple had walls with **one** layer of cedar beams for every
7.24 had been cast all in **one** piece with the rest of the
7.32 the panels, and the axles were of **one** piece with the carts.
7.34 corners of each cart, which were of **one** piece with the cart.
7.35 its supports and the panels were of **one** piece with the cart.
7.38 Huram also made ten basins, **one** for each cart.
11.13 instead, I will leave him **one** tribe for the sake of my
11.32 Solomon will keep **one** tribe, for the sake of my servant
11.36 will let Solomon's son keep **one** tribe, so that I will always
15.29 not **one** survived.
18.31 He took twelve stones, **one** for each of the twelve tribes
22. 8 Ahab answered, "There is **one** more, Micaiah son of Imlah.
2 Kgs 4. 6 "That was the last **one,**" one of her sons answered.
7. 1 or six kilogrammes of barley for **one** piece of silver."
7.16 kilogrammes of barley were sold for **one** piece of silver.
7.18 be sold in Samaria for **one** piece of silver, [19] to which the
8.26 age of twenty-two, and he ruled in Jerusalem for **one** year.
10.11 not **one** of them was left alive.
10.14 people in all, and not **one** of them was left alive.
10.17 Jehu killed all of Ahab's relatives, not sparing even **one.**
10.21 not **one** of them failed to come.
15.13 king of Israel, and he ruled in Samaria for **one** month.

2 Kgs 15.20 Israel by forcing each **one** to contribute fifty pieces of silver.
1 Chr 2. 8 Ethan had **one** son, Azariah.
3.19 of two sons, Meshullam and Hananiah, and **one** daughter,
3.22 Shecaniah had **one** son, Shemaiah, and five grandsons:
4. 3 Jezreel, Ishma, and Idbash, and **one** daughter, Hazzelelponi.
6. 3 Amram had two sons, Aaron and Moses, and **one** daughter,
7. 3 Uzzi had **one** son, Izrahiah.
7.10 Jediael had **one** son, Bilhan, and Bilhan had seven sons:
7.12 Dan had **one** son, Hushim.
7.30 and **one** daughter, Serah.
7.32 and **one** daughter, Shua.
11.11 against three hundred men and killed them all in **one** battle.
23.10 have many descendants, so they were counted as **one** clan.
23.17 Eliezer had only **one** son, Rehabiah,
23.24 by clans and families, every **one** of them registered by name.
24.28 Eleazar had no sons, but Kish had **one** son, Jerahmeel.
2 Chr 4. 3 had been cast all in **one** piece with the rest of the
18. 7 Ahab answered, "There is **one** more, Micaiah son of Imlah.
20.24 Not **one** had escaped.
22. 2 age of twenty-two, and he ruled in Jerusalem for **one** year.
28. 5 Ahaz and kill 120,000 of the bravest Judaean soldiers in **one** day.
32.12 Judah and Jerusalem to worship and burn incense at **one** altar only.
Ezra 6. 4 are to be built with **one** layer of wood on top of
Neh 4. 2 by offering sacrifices they can finish the work in **one** day?
5.18 Every day I served **one** ox, six of the best sheep, and
11. 1 people drew lots to choose **one** family out of every ten to
Esth 4.11 There is only **one** way to get round this law:
Job 1.15 They killed every **one** of your servants except me.
9.25 My days race by, not **one** of them good.
11.20 Their **one** hope is that death will come.
17.10 stood before me, I would not find even **one** of them wise.
19.29 on sin, so that you will know there is **one** who judges.
23.14 that plan is just **one** of the many he has;
27.19 **One** last time they will lie down rich, and when they
Ps 14. 3 Not **one** of them does what is right, not a single one.
27. 4 I have asked the Lord for **one** thing;
27. 4 **one** thing only do I want:
33. 7 He gathered all the seas into **one** place;
34.20 not **one** of his bones is broken.
53. 3 Not **one** of them does what is right, not a single one.
84.10 **One** day spent in your Temple is better than a thousand
86. 8 like you, O Lord, not **one** has done what you have done.
89.34 covenant with him or take back even **one** promise I made him.
90. 4 A thousand years to you are like **one** day;
106.11 not **one** of them was left.
147. 4 decided the number of the stars and calls each **one** by name.
Prov 4.27 Don't go **one** step off the right way.
7. 7 young men, but noticed **one** foolish fellow in particular.
17.10 intelligent person learns more from **one** rebuke than a fool
Ecc 3.14 And **one** thing God does is to make us stand in awe
4. 9 Two are better off than **one,** because together they can
4.10 If **one** of them falls down, the other can help him up.
4.12 Two men can resist an attack that would defeat **one** man alone.
7.28 I found **one** man in a thousand that I could
7.28 but not **one** woman.
9. 3 **One** fate comes to all alike, and this is as wrong as
9.18 more good than weapons, but **one** sinner can undo a lot of
11. 6 all grow well or whether **one** sowing will do better than the
12.11 They have been given by God, the **one** Shepherd of us all.
12.13 After all this, there is only **one** thing to say:
Song 4. 2 Not **one** of them is missing;
5.10 he is **one** in ten thousand.
6. 6 Not **one** of them is missing;
6. 9 But I love only **one,** and she is as lovely as a
8.11 each **one** pays a thousand silver coins.
Is 4. 1 women will grab hold of **one** man and say, "We can feed
6.13 Even if **one** person out of ten remains in the land, he
7.21 been able to save only **one** young cow and two goats, [22] they
10. 8 He boasts, "Every **one** of my commanders is a king!
14.10 You are **one** of us!
14.29 When **one** snake dies, a worse one comes in its place.
21.16 said to me, "In exactly **one** year the greatness of the
27.12 Lord will gather his people **one by one,** like someone
29.14 So I will startle them with **one** unexpected blow after another.
30. 1 sign treaties against my will, piling **one** sin on another.
30.17 run away when you see **one** enemy soldier, and five soldiers
30.26 brighter than usual, like the light of seven days in **one.**
34.15 Vultures will gather there, **one** after another.
34.16 Not **one** of these creatures will be missing,
34.16 and not **one** will be without its mate.
36. 7 people of Judah and Jerusalem to worship at **one** altar only.
40.26 he knows how many there are and calls each **one** by name!
40.26 power is so great— not **one** of them is ever missing!
41.28 not **one** could answer the questions I asked.
44. 5 "**One by one,** people will say, 'I am the Lord's.'
44. 5 Each **one** will mark the name of the Lord on his arm
44.15 With **one** part he builds a fire to warm himself and bake
54. 7 "For **one** brief moment I left you;
55. 5 at **one** time they did not know you, but now they will
Jer 3.14 I will take **one** of you from each town and two from
4.20 **One** disaster follows another;
5. 1 Can you find **one** person who does what is right and tries
6. 3 round the city, and each **one** will camp wherever he wants.
8. 6 Not **one** of you has been sorry for his wickedness;
8. 6 not **one** of you has asked, 'What have I done wrong?'
9. 3 "My people do **one** evil thing after another, and do not
9. 5 They do **one** violent thing after another,
9. 5 and **one** deceitful act follows another.
10.18 is going to crush you until not **one** of you is left.
14. 8 in our land, like a traveller who stays for only **one** night?

Jer	14.14	did I give them any orders or speak **one** word to them.
	21. 2	Maybe the Lord will perform **one** of his miracles for us and
	23.23	am a God who is everywhere and not in **one** place only.
	24.10	them until there is not **one** of them left in the land
	42.17	Not **one** of them will survive,
	42.17	not **one** will escape the disaster
	44.14	Not **one** of them will return to Judah, where they long to
	44.27	in war or of disease, until not **one** of you is left.
	49.10	Not **one** of them is left.
Lam	1. 2	Of all her former friends, not **one** is left to comfort her.
	3.21	Yet hope returns when I remember this **one** thing:
Ezek	1. 8	wings, they each had four human hands, **one** under each wing.
	1.15	I saw four wheels touching the ground, **one** beside each of them.
	4. 4	I have sentenced you to **one** day for each year their
	4. 6	of Judah for forty days—**one** day for each year of their
	10. 9	there were four wheels, all alike, **one** beside each creature.
	15. 7	They have escaped **one** fire, but now fire will burn them up.
	24. 6	after piece of meat is taken out, and not **one** is left.
	24.16	"Mortal man," he said, "with **one** blow I am going to
	33.24	'Abraham was only **one** man, and he was given the whole land.
	33.32	to all your words and don't obey a single **one** of them.
	34.23	servant David to be their **one** shepherd, and he will take
	37.17	to end in your hand so that they look like **one** stick.
	37.19	the two I will make **one** stick and hold it in my
	37.22	I will unite them into **one** nation in the land, on the
	37.22	They will have **one** king to rule over them, and they will
	37.24	will all be united under **one** ruler and will obey my laws
	39.28	into their own land, not leaving even **one** of them behind.
	45.11	**1** homer = 10 ephahs = 10 baths
	45.12	20 gerahs = **1** shekel 60 shekels = 1 mina
	45.13	10 baths = **1** homer = 1 kor.)
	45.13	**1** sheep out of every 200 from the meadows of Israel
	46. 4	burnt whole, six lambs and **one** ram, all without any defects.
	46.13	"Every morning a **one-year-old** lamb without any defects
Dan	8. 3	that had two long horns, **one** of which was longer and newer
	8. 5	He had **one** prominent horn between his eyes.
	12. 5	I saw two men standing by a river, **one** on each bank.
Hos	9.12	up children, I would take them away and not leave **one** alive.
Joel	1. 4	what **one** swarm left, the next swarm devoured.
Amos	4. 7	I sent rain on **one** city, but not on another.
	4. 7	Rain fell on **one** field, but another field dried up.
	9. 1	not **one** will escape.
Jon	4.10	"This plant grew up in **one** night and disappeared the next;
Zeph	1.12	'The Lord never does anything, **one** way or the other.'
	2. 5	He will destroy you, and not **one** of you will be left.
Hag	1. 9	lies in ruins while every **one** of you is busy working on
Zech	8.21	Those from **one** city will say to those from another, 'We
	8.23	ten foreigners will come to **one** Jew and say, 'We want to
Mal	2.15	Didn't God make you **one** body and spirit with her?
Mt	5.30	better for you to lose **one** of your limbs than for your
	5.41	to carry his pack **one** kilometre, carry it two kilometres.
	6.24	he will hate **one** and love the other;
	6.24	he will be loyal to **one** and despise the other.
	6.29	his wealth had clothes as beautiful as **one** of these flowers.
	10.23	When they persecute you in **one** town, run away to another one.
	10.29	buy two sparrows, yet not **one** sparrow falls to the ground
	10.42	drink of cold water to **one** of the least of these my
	11.16	**One** group shouts to the other, [17]'We played wedding music for you,
	12.26	So if **one** group is fighting another in Satan's kingdom,
	15.14	when **one** blind man leads another, both fall into a ditch."
	17. 4	here, one for you, **one** for Moses, and one for Elijah."
	18. 5	whoever welcomes in my name **one** such child as this, welcomes
	18. 6	"If anyone should cause **one** of these little ones to lose
	18. 9	to enter life with only **one** eye than to keep both eyes
	18.12	who has a hundred sheep and **one** of them gets lost?
	18.13	feels far happier over this **one** sheep than over the ninety-nine
	18.16	not listen to you, take **one** or two other persons with you,
	18.35	in heaven will treat every **one** of you unless you forgive
	19. 5	and unite with his wife, and the two will become **one.'**
	19. 6	So they are no longer two, but **one.**
	19.17	"There is only **One** who is good.
	20.12	were hired last worked only **one** hour,' they said, 'while we
	20.13	you agreed to do a day's work for **one** silver coin.
	21.24	"I will ask you just **one** question, and if you give me
	21.35	The tenants seized his slaves, beat **one,** killed another,
	22. 5	**one** went to his farm, another to his shop, [6]while others
	23. 7	are all brothers of one another and have only **one** Teacher.
	23. 9	on earth 'Father', because you have only the **one** Father in heaven.
	23.10	because your **one** and only leader is the Messiah.
	23.15	You sail the seas and cross whole countries to win **one** convert;
	24. 2	every **one** of them will be thrown down."
	24.31	gather his chosen people from **one** end of the world to the
	24.40	**one** will be taken away, the other will be left behind.
	24.41	**one** will be taken away, the other will be left behind.
	25.15	to **one** he gave five thousand gold coins, to another he gave
	25.40	whenever you did this for **one** of the least important of
	25.45	whenever you refused to help **one** of these least important ones,
	26.40	were not able to keep watch with me even for **one** hour?
	27.15	habit of setting free any **one** prisoner the crowd asked for.
	27.38	crucified two bandits with Jesus, **one** on his right and the
Mk	8.14	enough bread and had only **one** loaf with them in the boat.
	9. 5	tents, one for you, **one** for Moses, and one for Elijah."
	9.37	"Whoever welcomes in my name **one** of these children, welcomes me;
	9.42	"If anyone should cause **one** of these little ones to
	9.47	Kingdom of God with only **one** eye than to keep both eyes
	10. 8	and unite with his wife, [8]and the two will become **one.'**
	10. 8	So they are no longer two, but **one.**
	10.21	at him with love and said, "You need only **one** thing.
	10.37	sit with you, one at your right and **one** at your left."
Mk	11.29	"I will ask you just **one** question, and if you give me
	13. 2	every **one** of them will be thrown down."
	13.27	gather God's chosen people from **one** end of the world to the
	14.18	one of you will betray me—**one** who is eating with me."
	14.37	Weren't you able to stay awake even for **one** hour?"
	15. 6	habit of setting free any **one** prisoner the people asked for.
	15.27	crucified two bandits with Jesus, **one** on his right and the
Lk	3.11	has two shirts must give **one** to the man who has none,
	4.27	not **one** of them was healed, but only Naaman the Syrian."
	4.40	placed his hands on every **one** of them and healed them all.
	6.29	If anyone hits you on **one** cheek,
	6.39	**"One** blind man cannot lead another one;
	7.32	**One** group shouts to the other, 'We played wedding music for you,
	7.41	**"One** owed him five hundred silver coins, and the other owed
	9.33	tents, one for you, **one** for Moses, and **one** for Elijah."
	10.36	"In your opinion, which **one** of these three acted like a
	10.42	and troubled over so many things, [42]but just **one** is needed.
	12. 6	Yet not **one** sparrow is forgotten by God.
	12.27	his wealth had clothes as beautiful as **one** of these flowers.
	13. 8	the gardener answered, 'Leave it alone, sir, just **one** more year;
	15. 4	a hundred sheep and loses **one** of them—what does he do?
	15. 4	and goes looking for the **one** that got lost until he finds
	15. 7	more joy in heaven over **one** sinner who repents than over
	15. 8	has ten silver coins loses **one** of them—what does she do?
	15.10	the angels of God rejoice over **one** sinner who repents."
	16.13	he will hate **one** and love the other;
	16.13	he will be loyal to **one** and despise the other.
	17. 2	than for him to cause **one** of these little ones to sin.
	17. 4	against you seven times in **one** day, and each time he comes
	17.24	and lights it up from **one** side to the other, so will
	17.34	**one** will be taken away, the other will be left behind.
	17.35	**one** will be taken away, the other will be left behind."
	18.10	**one** was a Pharisee, the other a tax collector.
	18.22	"There is still **one** more thing you need to do.
	19.16	I have earned ten gold coins with the **one** you gave me.'
	19.18	I have earned five gold coins with the **one** you gave me.'
	21. 6	every **one** will be thrown down."
	23.33	and the two criminals, **one** on his right and the other
	23.39	**One** of the criminals hanging there hurled insults at him:
Jn	1. 3	not **one** thing in all creation was made without him.
	4.37	The saying is true, **'One** man sows, another man reaps.'
	4.52	"It was **one** o'clock yesterday afternoon when the fever
	6.22	the lake realized that there had been only **one** boat there.
	6.70	Yet **one** of you is a devil!"
	7.19	But not **one** of you obeys the Law.
	7.21	"I performed **one** miracle, and you were all surprised.
	8. 9	heard this, they all left, **one** by one, the older ones first.
	9.25	**"One** thing I do know:
	10.16	and they will become **one** flock with one shepherd.
	10.30	The Father and I are **one."**
	11.50	better for you to let **one** man die for the people,
	11.52	also to bring together into **one** body all the scattered
	13.10	All of you are clean—all except **one."**
	13.11	that is why he said, "All of you, except **one,** are clean.")
	17.11	that they may be one just as you and I are **one.**
	17.12	I protected them, and not **one** of them was lost, except the
	17.21	I pray that they may all be **one.**
	17.21	May they be **one,** so that the world will believe that you
	17.22	that they may be one, just as you and I are **one:**
	17.23	that they may be completely **one,** in order that the world may
	18. 9	"Father, I have not lost even **one** of those you gave me.")
	18.14	that it was better that **one** man should die for all the
	18.37	the world for this **one** purpose, to speak about the truth.
	19.18	also crucified two other men, **one** on each side, with Jesus
	19.23	clothes and divided them into four parts, **one** part for each
	19.23	robe, which was made of **one** piece of woven cloth without any
	19.36	"Not **one** of his bones will be broken."
	20.12	body of Jesus had been, **one** at the head and the other
	21.25	all written down one by **one,** I suppose that the whole world
Acts	2. 1	all the believers were gathered together in **one** place.
	4.32	The group of believers was **one** in mind and heart.
	17.26	From **one** man he created all races of mankind and made
	24.21	the Council—[21]except for the **one** thing I called out when I
	27.22	Not **one** of you will lose his life;
	28.25	disagreeing among themselves, after Paul had said this **one** thing:
Rom	3.12	no one does what is right, not even **one.**
	3.30	God is **one,** and he will put the Jews right with himself
	5.12	came into the world through **one** man, and his sin brought
	5.15	that many people died because of the sin of that **one** man.
	5.15	so many people through the grace of the **one** man, Jesus
	5.16	is a difference between God's gift and the sin of **one** man.
	5.16	After the **one** sin, came the judgement of "Guilty";
	5.17	that through the sin of **one** man
	5.17	death began to rule because of that **one** man.
	5.17	the result of what was done by the **one** man, Jesus Christ!
	5.18	So then, as the **one** sin condemned all mankind,
	5.18	in the same way the **one** righteous act sets all mankind free
	5.19	result of the disobedience of **one** man, in the same way they
	5.19	with God as the result of the obedience of the **one** man.
	6. 5	For since we have become **one** with him in dying
	6. 5	same way we shall be **one** with him by being raised to
	9.11	order that the choice of **one** son might be completely the
	9.21	the same lump of clay, **one** for special occasions and the
	12. 4	have many parts in the **one** body, and all these parts have
	12. 5	we are **one** body in union with Christ,
	12. 5	are all joined to each other as different parts of **one** body.
	13. 9	are summed up in the **one** command, "Love your neighbour as
	15. 6	you together may praise with **one** voice the God and Father of
1 Cor	1.10	Be completely united, with only **one** thought and one purpose.
	3.11	placed Jesus Christ as the **one** and only foundation, and no
	4. 2	The **one** thing required of such a servant is that he be

1 Cor 4.15 guardians in your Christian life, you have only **one** father.
6. 5 Surely there is at least **one** wise person in your fellowship
6.16 joins his body to a prostitute becomes physically **one** with her?
6.16 The scripture says quite plainly, "The two will become **one** body."
6.17 joins himself to the Lord becomes spiritually **one** with him.
8. 4 we know that there is only the **one** God.
8. 6 there is for us only **one** God, the Father, who is the
8. 6 and there is only **one** Lord, Jesus Christ, through whom all
9.24 part in a race, but only **one** of them wins the prize.
10. 8 and in **one** day twenty-three thousand of them fell
10.17 Because there is the **one** loaf of bread, all of us,
10.17 though many, are **one** body, for we all share the
12. 9 **One** and the same Spirit gives faith to one person,
12.11 But it is **one** and the same Spirit who does all this;
12.12 it is still **one** body, even though it is made up of
12.13 have been baptized into the **one** body by the same Spirit,
12.13 and we have all been given the **one** Spirit to drink.
12.14 is not made up of only **one** part, but of many parts.
12.19 would not be a body if it were all only **one** part!
12.20 As it is, there are many parts but **one** body.
12.26 If **one** part of the body suffers, all the other parts
12.26 **one** part is praised, all the other parts share its happiness.
14.31 proclaim God's message, one by **one**, so that everyone will learn
2 Cor 5.14 now that we recognize that **one** man died for everyone,
11. 2 I have promised in marriage to **one** man only, Christ himself.
Gal 3. 2 Tell me this **one** thing:
3.16 singular "descendant," meaning **one** person only, namely, Christ.
3.20 a go-between is not needed when only **one** person is involved;
3.20 and God is **one.**
3.28 you are all **one** in union with Christ Jesus.
4.22 that Abraham had two sons, **one** by a slave-woman, the other
5.14 For the whole Law is summed up in **one** commandment:
Eph 2.14 has brought us peace by making Jews and Gentiles **one** people.
2.15 out of the two races **one** new people in union with himself,
2.16 he united both races into **one** body and brought them back
2.18 able to come in the **one** Spirit into the presence of the
4. 4 There is **one** body and one Spirit,
4. 4 just as there is **one** hope to which God has called
4. 5 There is **one** Lord, one faith, one baptism;
4. 6 there is **one** God and Father of all mankind, who is Lord
4.13 all come together to that **oneness** in our faith and in our
5.31 and unite with his wife, and the two will become **one."**
Phil 1.27 you are standing firm with **one** common purpose
1.27 and that with only **one** desire you are fighting together
2. 2 sharing the same love, and being **one** in soul and mind.
3.13 the **one** thing I do, however, is to forget what is behind
Col 3.15 God has called you together in the **one** body.
1 Tim 2. 5 For there is **one** God,
2. 5 and there is **one** who brings God and mankind together,
3. 2 he must have only **one** wife, be sober, self-controlled, and
3.12 church helper must have only **one** wife,
Tit 1. 6 he must have only **one** wife, and his children must be
Heb 7.27 He offered **one** sacrifice, once and for all, when he offered himself.
10.12 Christ, however, offered **one** sacrifice for sins,
10.14 With **one** sacrifice, then, he has made perfect for ever those
11.12 practically dead, from this **one** man came as many descendants as
Jas 2.10 Whoever breaks **one** commandment is guilty of breaking them all.
2.19 Do you believe that there is only **one** God?
2 Pet 3. 8 But do not forget **one** thing, my dear friends!
3. 8 in the Lord's sight between **one** day and a thousand years;
Rev 17.12 authority to rule as kings for **one** hour with the beast.
18. 8 Because of this, in **one** day she will be struck with
18.10 In just **one** hour you have been punished!"
18.17 And in **one** hour she has lost all this wealth!"
18.19 And in **one** hour she has lost everything!"
also 1 Chr 24.7 1 Chr 25.9

ONE ANOTHER
see also **EACH OTHER**

Mt 23. 8 are all brothers of **one another** and have only one Teacher.
24. 7 Countries will fight each other, kingdoms will attack **one another.**
24.10 they will betray **one another** and hate one another.
Mk 1.27 that they started saying to **one another,** "What is this?
4.41 terribly afraid and said to **one another,** "Who is this man?
9.50 friendship among yourselves, and live in peace with **one another."**
10.26 amazed and asked **one another,** "Who, then, can be saved?"
12. 7 But those tenants said to **one another,** 'This is the owner's son.
13. 8 kingdoms will attack **one another.**
14. 4 became angry and said to **one another,** "What was the use of
16. 3 the way they said to **one another,** "Who will roll away the
Lk 2.15 the shepherds said to **one another,** "Let's go to Bethlehem
4.36 all amazed and said to **one another,** "What kind of words are
8.25 and afraid, and said to **one another,** "Who is this man?
20.14 they said to **one another,** 'This is the owner's son.
21.10 kingdoms will attack **one another.**
Jn 5.44 like to receive praise from **one another,** but you do not try
11.56 in the Temple, they asked **one another,** "What do you think?
12.19 The Pharisees then said to **one another,** "You see, we
13.14 You, then, should wash **one another's** feet.
13.22 disciples looked at **one another,** completely puzzled about whom
13.34 love **one another.**
13.34 As I have loved you, so you must love **one another.**
13.35 If you have love for **one another,** then everyone will
15.12 love **one another,** just as I love you.
15.17 love **one another.**
19.24 The soldiers said to **one another,** "Let's not tear it;
Acts 2.44 in close fellowship and shared their belongings with **one another.**
4.32 but they all shared with **one another** everything they had.
21. 6 Then we said good-bye to **one another,** and we went on board
28. 4 Paul's hand and said to **one another,** "This man must be a

Rom 1.30 They gossip [30] and speak evil of **one another;**
12.10 Love **one another** warmly as Christian brothers,
12.10 and be eager to show respect for **one another.**
13. 8 the only obligation you have is to love **one another.**
14.13 So then, let us stop judging **one another.**
14.19 things that bring peace and that help to strengthen **one another.**
15. 7 Accept **one another,** then, for the glory of God, as Christ
15.14 all knowledge, and that you are able to teach **one another.**
16.16 Greet **one another** with a brotherly kiss.
1 Cor 3. 3 and you quarrel with **one another,** doesn't this prove that you
6. 8 Instead, you yourselves wrong **one another**
6. 8 and rob **one another,** even your own brothers!
11.33 together to eat the Lord's Supper, wait for **one another.**
12.25 its different parts have the same concern for **one another.**
16.20 Greet **one another** with a brotherly kiss.
2 Cor 13.11 agree with **one another;**
13.12 Greet **one another** with a brotherly kiss.
Gal 5.13 Instead, let love make you serve **one another.**
5.15 then watch out, or you will completely destroy **one another.**
5.26 not be proud or irritate **one another**
5.26 or be jealous of **one another.**
6. 2 Help to carry **one another's** burdens, and in this way you
Eph 4. 2 Show your love by being tolerant with **one another.**
4.32 be kind and tender-hearted to **one another,**
4.32 and forgive **one another,** as God has forgiven you
5.19 Speak to **one another** with the words of psalms, hymns,
5.21 Submit yourselves to **one another** because of your reverence for Christ.
Phil 2. 1 and you have kindness and compassion for **one another.**
2. 3 be humble towards **one another,** always considering others better
2. 4 And look out for **one another's** interests, not just for your own.
Col 3. 9 Do not lie to **one another,** for you have taken off the
3.13 Be tolerant with **one another** and forgive one another
3.13 You must forgive **one another** just as the Lord has forgiven you.
1 Thes 3.12 Lord make your love for **one another** and for all people grow
4. 9 have been taught by God how you should love **one another.**
4.18 So then, encourage **one another** with these words.
5.11 And so encourage **one another** and help one another,
5.15 your aim to do good to **one another** and to all people.
Heb 3.13 you must help **one another** every day, as long as
10.24 Let us be concerned for **one another,**
10.24 to help **one another** to show love and to
10.25 Instead, let us encourage **one another** all the more,
13. 1 Keep on loving **one another** as Christian brothers.
13.16 do good and to help **one another,** because these are the
Jas 4.11 Do not criticize **one another,** my brothers.
5. 9 Do not complain against **one another,** my brothers, so that God
5.16 confess your sins to **one another** and pray for one another,
1 Pet 1.22 love **one another** earnestly with all your heart.
3. 8 love **one another** as brothers,
3. 8 and be kind and humble with **one another.**
4. 8 love **one another** earnestly, because love covers over many sins.
5. 5 you must put on the apron of humility, to serve **one another;**
5.14 Greet **one another** with the kiss of Christian love.
1 Jn 1. 7 we have fellowship with **one another,** and the blood of Jesus,
3.11 we must love **one another.**
3.23 and love **one another,** just as Christ commanded us.
4. 7 friends, let us love **one another,** because love comes from God.
4.11 this is how God loved us, then we should love **one another.**
4.12 but if we love **one another,** God lives in union with
2 Jn 5 let us all love **one another.**

ONE-FIFTH see FIVE

ONE-TENTH see TEN

ONE-THIRD see THIRD

ONIONS

Num 11. 5 water-melons, the leeks, the **onions,** and the garlic we had?

ONLOOKERS

Song 6.13 want to watch me as I dance between the rows of **onlookers?**

ONRUSHING see RUSH (2)

ONYCHA

Ex 30.34 spices—stacte, **onycha,** galbanum, and pure frankincense.

ONYX
A semi-precious stone of various colours.

Rev 21.20 the fourth emerald, [20] the fifth **onyx,** the sixth carnelian,

OPEN
[RE-OPENED]

Gen 4.11 blood as if it had **opened** its mouth to receive it when
7.11 water beneath the earth burst **open,** all the floodgates of
7.11 floodgates of the sky were **opened,** [12] and rain fell
8. 6 After forty days Noah **opened** a window [7] and sent out a raven.
21.19 Then God **opened** her eyes, and she saw a well.
28.17 it must be the gate that **opens** into heaven."
29. 2 from this well, which had a large stone over the **opening.**

Gen	41.56	the whole country, so Joseph **opened** all the storehouses and
	42.27	the night, one of them **opened** his sack to feed his donkey
	43.21	on the way home, we **opened** our sacks, and each man found
	44.11	their sacks to the ground, and each man **opened** his sack.
Ex	2. 6	The princess **opened** it and saw a baby boy.
	9. 9	will produce boils that become **open** sores on the people and
	9.10	they produced boils that became **open** sores on the people and
	9.19	else you have in the **open** to be put under shelter.
	9.21	Lord's warning and left their slaves and animals out in the **open.**
	9.25	struck down everything in the **open,** including all the people
	33.22	will put you in an **opening** in the rock and cover you
Lev	1.17	wings and tear its body **open,** without tearing the wings off,
	13.14	But from the moment an **open** sore appears, he is unclean.
	13.15	and if he sees an **open** sore, he shall pronounce him unclean.
	13.15	An **open** sore means a dreaded skin-disease,
	14. 7	He shall let the live bird fly away over the **open** fields.
	14.53	live bird fly away outside the city over the **open** fields.
	17. 5	Lord the animals which they used to kill in the **open** country.
Num	13.19	the people live in **open** towns or in fortified cities.
	16.30	and the earth **opens** up and swallows them
	16.31	Dathan and Abiram split **open** [32] and swallowed them
	26.10	The ground **opened** and swallowed them, and they died with
Deut	11. 6	sight of everyone the earth **opened** up and swallowed them,
	20.11	If they **open** the gates and surrender, they are all to
Josh	8.17	the city was left wide **open,** with no one to defend it.
	10.22	Then Joshua said, **"Open** the entrance to the cave and
	10.23	So the cave was **opened,** and the kings of Jerusalem,
Judg	3.25	when he still did not **open** the door,
	3.25	they took the key and **opened** it.
	4.19	She **opened** a leather bag of milk, gave him a drink, and
	15.19	Then God **opened** a hollow place in the ground there at Lehi,
	19.27	that morning, and when he **opened** the door to go on his
	20.31	killing some Israelites in the **open** country on the road to
	20.42	ran towards the **open** country, but they could not escape.
	20.45	and ran towards the **open** country to the Rock of Rimmon.
	20.47	able to escape to the **open** country to the Rock of Rimmon,
1 Sam	3.15	then he got up and **opened** the doors of the house of
2 Sam	10. 8	Tob and Maacah, took up their position in the **open** countryside.
	11.11	commander Joab and his officers are camping out in the **open.**
	11.23	to fight us in the **open,** but we drove them back to
	17.19	covering, spread it over the **opening** of the well and
1 Kgs	2.34	Joab, and he was buried at his home in the **open** country.
	6. 4	walls of the Temple had **openings** in them, narrower on the
	11.29	from Shiloh, met him alone on the road in the **open** country.
	14.11	any who die in the **open** country will be eaten by vultures.
	16. 4	who die in the **open** country will be eaten by vultures."
	21.24	who die in the **open** country will be eaten by vultures."
2 Kgs	4.35	The boy sneezed seven times, and then **opened** his eyes.
	6.17	Then he prayed, "O Lord, **open** his eyes and let him see!"
	6.20	entered the city, Elisha prayed, **"Open** their eyes, Lord,
	8.12	children to death, and rip **open** their pregnant women."
	13.17	the king **opened** the window that faced towards Syria.
	15.16	He even ripped **open** the bellies of all the pregnant women.
1 Chr	4.40	in a stretch of **open** country that was quiet and peaceful.
	9.27	their duty to guard it and to **open** the gates every morning.
	19. 9	to help took up their position in the **open** countryside.
2 Chr	26.10	fortified towers in the **open** country and dug many cisterns,
	29. 3	Hezekiah became king, he **re-opened** the gates of the Temple
	32. 6	them to assemble in the **open** square at the city gate.
Ezra	10.13	We can't stand here in the **open** like this.
Neh	7. 3	have the gates of Jerusalem **opened** in the morning until well
	8. 5	As soon as he **opened** the book, they all stood up.
	13.19	fall, and not to be **opened** again until the Sabbath was over.
Job	26. 6	The world of the dead lies **open** to God;
	36.15	God teaches men through suffering and uses distress to **open** their eyes.
	41.14	Who can make him **open** his jaws,
Ps	22.13	They **open** their mouths like lions,
	24. 7	Fling wide the gates, **open** the ancient doors, and the
	24. 9	Fling wide the gates, **open** the ancient doors, and the
	60. 2	You have made the land tremble, and you have cut it **open;**
	78.15	He split rocks **open** in the desert and gave them water
	78.23	he spoke to the sky above and commanded its doors to **open;**
	81.10	**Open** your mouth, and I will feed you.
	105.41	He **opened** a rock, and water gushed out, flowing through
	106.17	Then the earth **opened** up and swallowed Dathan and buried
	118.19	**Open** to me the gates of the Temple;
	119.18	**Open** my eyes, so that I may see the wonderful truths in
	119.131	In my desire for your commands I pant with **open** mouth.
Prov	8.28	in the sky, when he **opened** the springs of the ocean [29] and
	10.10	trouble, but one who **openly** criticizes works for peace.
	24. 2	time they **open** their mouth someone is going to be hurt.
	25.28	are as helpless as a city without walls, **open** to attack.
	27. 5	Better to correct someone **openly** than to let him think you
	29.11	Stupid people express their anger **openly,** but sensible
Song	5. 6	I **opened** the door for my lover, but he had already gone.
	7.12	are **opening** and the pomegranate-trees are in bloom.
Is	1. 6	You are covered with bruises and sores and **open** wounds.
	3. 8	they **openly** insult God himself.
	3. 9	They sin as **openly** as the people of Sodom did.
	5.14	the dead is hungry for them, and it **opens** its mouth wide.
	9.12	Philistia on the west have **opened** their mouths to devour Israel.
	10.14	no beak **opened** to scream at me!"
	22.22	what he **opens,** no one will shut,
	22.22	and what he shuts, no one will **open.**
	24.19	The earth will crack and shatter and split **open.**
	26. 2	**Open** the city gates and let the faithful nation enter, the
	29.18	have been living in darkness, will **open** their eyes and see.
	32. 3	eyes and ears will be **open** to the needs of the people.
	42. 7	You will **open** the eyes of the blind and set free those
	45. 1	the Lord will **open** the gates of cities for him.
Is	45. 8	the earth will **open** to receive it and will blossom with
	46. 6	People **open** their purses and pour out gold;
	48.16	the beginning I have spoken **openly,** and have always made my
	48.21	he split the rock **open,** and water flowed out.
	58. 7	with the hungry and **open** your homes to the homeless poor.
	60.11	night your gates will be **open,** So that the kings of the
Jer	12. 5	can't even stand up in **open** country, how will you manage in
	17. 3	on the hill-tops [3] and on the mountains in the **open** country.
	32.11	conditions, and the **open** copy—[12] and gave them to Baruch,
	32.14	deed of purchase and the **open** copy, and to place them in
	50.25	I have **opened** the place where my weapons are stored, and
	50.26	from every side and break **open** the places where its grain is
Lam	3. 4	He has left my flesh **open** and raw, and has broken my
	3.41	Let us **open** our hearts to God in heaven and pray,
	3.53	me alive into a pit and closed the **opening** with a stone.
Ezek	1. 1	The sky **opened,** and I saw a vision of God.
	2. 8	**Open** your mouth and eat what I am going to give you."
	3. 2	So I **opened** my mouth, and he gave me the scroll to
	16. 5	You were thrown out in an **open** field.
	16.63	will remember them and be too ashamed to **open** your mouth."
	37.12	that I, the Sovereign Lord, am going to **open** their graves.
	37.13	When I **open** the graves where my people are buried and
	39. 5	They will fall dead in the **open** field.
	40.11	and the space between the **open** gates was five metres.
	40.16	There were small **openings** in the outside walls of all
	40.38	It **opened** into the entrance room that faced the courtyard,
	40.44	There were two rooms **opening** on the inner courtyard, one
	41. 8	the priests there was an **open** space ten metres across, along
	41.12	the far end of the **open** space on the west side of
	41.13	of the Temple, across the **open** space to the far side of
	41.14	of the Temple, including the **open** space on either side, was
	41.24	They were double doors that swung **open** in the middle.
	44. 2	me, "This gate will stay closed and will never be **opened.**
	45. 2	surrounded by an **open** space twenty-five metres wide.
	46. 1	but it is to be **opened** on the Sabbath and at the
	46.12	the east gate to the inner courtyard will be **opened** for him.
	48.17	on each side there will be an **open** space 125 metres across.
Dan	4.25	ox, and sleep in the **open** air, where the dew will fall
	5.21	ox, and slept in the **open** air with nothing to protect him
	6.10	he knelt down at the **open** windows and prayed to God three
	7.10	The court began its session, and the books were **opened.**
Hos	12.11	there will become piles of stone in the **open** fields."
	13. 8	bear that has lost her cubs, and I will tear you **open.**
	13.16	to the ground, and pregnant women will be ripped **open."**
Amos	1.13	territory they even ripped **open** pregnant women in Gilead.
Mic	1. 6	ruins in the **open** country, a place for planting grapevines.
	2.13	God will **open** the way for them and lead them out of
	4.10	will have to leave the city and live in the **open** country.
Nah	2. 6	The gates by the river burst **open;**
Hab	3. 9	Your lightning split **open** the earth.
Zeph	2. 6	by the sea will become **open** fields with shepherds' huts and
Zech	11. 1	**Open** your doors, Lebanon, so that fire can burn down your cedar-trees!
	13. 1	Almighty, "a fountain will be **opened** to purify the
Mal	3.10	will see that I will **open** the windows of heaven and pour
Mt	3.16	Then heaven was **opened** to him, and he saw the Spirit of
	7. 7	knock, and the door will be **opened** to you.
	7. 8	and the door will be **opened** to him who knocks.
	11.10	send my messenger ahead of you to **open** the way for you.'
	26.43	they could not keep their eyes **open.**
	27.52	the graves broke **open,** and many of God's people who
Mk	1.10	he saw heaven **opening** and the Spirit coming down on
	2. 4	When they had made an **opening,** they let the man down, lying
	4.22	be brought out into the **open,** and whatever is covered up
	7.34	and said to the man, "Ephphatha," which means, **"Open** up!"
	14.40	they could not keep their eyes **open.**
Lk	3.21	heaven was **opened,** [22] and the Holy Spirit came down
	5.19	on the roof, made an **opening** in the tiles, and let him
	7.27	send my messenger ahead of you to **open** the way for you.'
	8.17	be brought out into the **open,** and whatever is covered up
	11. 9	knock, and the door will be **opened** to you.
	11.10	and the door will be **opened** to anyone who knocks.
	11.52	have kept the key that **opens** the door to the house of
	12.36	comes and knocks, they will **open** the door for him at once.
	13.25	knock on the door and say, **'Open** the door for us, sir!'
	24.31	Then their eyes were **opened** and they recognized him,
	24.45	Then he **opened** their minds to understand the Scriptures,
Jn	1.20	did not refuse to answer, but spoke out **openly** and clearly,
	1.51	you will see heaven **open** and God's angels going up and
	7.10	however, he did not go **openly,** but secretly.
	7.13	no one talked about him **openly,** because they were afraid of
	10. 3	The gatekeeper **opens** the gate for him;
	11.54	So Jesus did not travel **openly** in Judaea, but left and
	12.42	did not talk about it **openly,** so as not to be expelled
	13.21	deeply troubled and declared **openly,** "I am telling you the truth:
Acts	1.18	he burst **open** and all his bowels spilt out.
	5.19	an angel of the Lord **opened** the prison gates, led the
	5.23	but when we **opened** the gates, we found no one inside!"
	7.56	"I see heaven **opened** and the Son of Man standing at the
	9. 8	up from the ground and **opened** his eyes, but could not see
	9.25	let him down through an **opening** in the wall, lowering him in
	9.40	She **opened** her eyes, and when she saw Peter, she sat up.
	10.11	He saw heaven **opened** and something coming down that looked
	12.10	The gate **opened** for them by itself, and they went out.
	12.14	she ran back in without **opening** the door, and announced that
	12.16	At last they **opened** the door, and when they saw him,
	14.27	and how he had **opened** the way for the Gentiles
	16.14	worshipped God, and the Lord **opened** her mind to pay
	16.26	At once all the doors **opened,** and the chains fell off all
	16.27	he saw the prison doors **open,** he thought that the prisoners

Acts	17.11	people there were more **open-minded** than the people in Thessalonica.
	26.18	You are to **open** their eyes and turn them from the
Rom	12.13	your needy fellow-Christians, and **open** your homes to strangers.
	16.26	brought out into the **open** through the writings of the prophets;
1 Cor	14.25	will be brought into the **open**, and he will bow down
2 Cor	2.12	found that the Lord had **opened** the way for the work there.
	6.11	we have **opened** our hearts wide.
	6.13	**Open** your hearts wide!
	11.33	in a basket through an **opening** in the wall and escaped from
Eph	1.18	that your minds may be **opened** to see his light,
Phil	2.11	and all will **openly** proclaim that Jesus Christ is Lord,
Col	2. 3	He is the key that **opens** all the hidden treasures of God's
2 Tim	2.17	Such teaching is like an **open** sore that eats away the flesh.
Heb	4.13	all creation is exposed and lies **open** before his eyes.
	9. 8	Place has not yet been **opened** as long as the outer Tent
	10.20	He **opened** for us a new way, a living way,
	11.13	and welcomed them, and admitted **openly** that they were foreigners
Jas	3.11	pours out sweet water and bitter water from the same **opening.**
1 Pet	4. 9	**Open** your homes to each other without complaining.
Rev	3. 5	of his angels I will declare **openly** that they belong to me.
	3. 7	and when he **opens** a door, no one can close
	3. 7	and when he closes it, no one can **open** it.
	3. 8	I have **opened** a door in front of you, which no one
	3.20	anyone hears my voice and **opens** the door, I will come into
	4. 1	I had another vision and saw an **open** door in heaven.
	5. 2	"Who is worthy to break the seals and **open** the scroll?"
	5. 3	world below who could **open** the scroll and look inside it.
	5. 4	found who was worthy to **open** the scroll or look inside it.
	5. 5	and he can break the seven seals and **open** the scroll."
	5. 9	are worthy to take the scroll and to break **open** its seals.
	6. 1	I saw the Lamb break **open** the first of the seven seals,
	6. 3	Then the Lamb broke **open** the second seal;
	6. 5	Then the Lamb broke **open** the third seal;
	6. 7	Then the Lamb broke **open** the fourth seal;
	6. 9	Then the Lamb broke **open** the fifth seal.
	6.12	And I saw the Lamb break **open** the sixth seal.
	8. 1	When the Lamb broke **open** the seventh seal, there was
	9. 2	The star **opened** the abyss, and smoke poured out of it,
	10. 2	He had a small scroll **open** in his hand.
	10. 8	saying, "Go and take the **open** scroll which is in the hand
	11.19	God's temple in heaven was **opened,** and the Covenant Box was
	12.16	it **opened** its mouth and swallowed the water that had come
	15. 5	saw the temple in heaven **open,** with the Tent of God's
	19.11	Then I saw heaven **open,** and there was a white horse.
	20.12	Books were **opened,**
	20.12	and then another book was **opened,** the book of the living.
	21.25	The gates of the city will stand **open** all day;

OPINION

Lev	13. 5	day, and if in his **opinion** the sore looks the same and
	13.37	But if in the priest's **opinion** the sore has not spread
2 Sam	19.22	David said to Abishai and his brother Joab, "Who asked your **opinion?**
Esth	1.13	to ask for expert **opinion** on questions of law and order,
Prov	25. 9	neighbour have a difference of **opinion,** settle it between
	26.16	seven men who can give good reasons for their **opinions.**
	28.26	It is foolish to follow your own **opinions.**
Mt	17.25	Jesus spoke up first, "Simon, what is your **opinion?**
Lk	10.36	Jesus concluded, "In your **opinion,** which one of these three acted
Acts	15.19	"It is my **opinion,"** James went on, "that we should
Rom	14. 1	but do not argue with him about his personal **opinions.**
1 Cor	7.25	but I give my **opinion** as one who by the Lord's
	7.40	That is my **opinion,** and I think that I too have God's
2 Cor	8.10	My **opinion** is that it is better for you to finish now
	12. 6	anyone to have a higher **opinion** of me than he has

OPPONENT

2 Sam	2.16	Each man caught his **opponent** by the head
	2.16	plunged his sword into his **opponent's** side, so that all
	3. 1	his **opponents** became weaker and weaker.
Job	31.35	If the charges my **opponent** brings against me were written
Ps	55.12	if it were an **opponent** boasting over me, I could hide myself
	56. 2	All day long my **opponents** attack me.
Prov	18.17	seems right until his **opponent** begins to question him.
Lk	18. 3	and pleading for her rights, saying, 'Help me against my **opponent!'**
Acts	25.18	His **opponents** stood up, but they did not accuse him of
1 Cor	16. 9	for great and worthwhile work, even though there are many **opponents.**
2 Tim	2.25	gentle as he corrects his **opponents,** for it may be that God

OPPORTUNITY

Lk	20.20	So they looked for an **opportunity.**
Acts	5.31	people of Israel the **opportunity** to repent and have their sins
	11.18	given to the Gentiles also the **opportunity** to repent and live!"
1 Cor	16. 9	There is a real **opportunity** here for great and worthwhile work,
Eph	5.16	Make good use of every **opportunity** you have,
Col	4. 3	will give us a good **opportunity** to preach his message about
	4. 5	are not believers, making good use of every **opportunity** you have.
2 Tim	2.25	God will give them the **opportunity** to repent and come to
2 Pet	3.15	our Lord's patience as the **opportunity** he is giving you to

OPPOSE

Ex	23.27	"I will make the people who **oppose** you afraid of me;
Num	22.34	not know that you were standing in the road to **oppose** me;
Deut	2.15	The Lord kept on **opposing** them until he had destroyed them all.
	32.39	wound and I heal, and no one can **oppose** what I do.
	32.42	with their blood, and my sword will kill all who **oppose** me.
1 Sam	15. 2	of Amalek because their ancestors **opposed** the Israelites
2 Sam	15.34	And do all you can to **oppose** any advice that Ahithophel gives.
	19. 6	You **oppose** those who love you and support those who hate you!
2 Kgs	10. 4	"How can we **oppose** Jehu," they said, "when neither King
2 Chr	13. 3	and Jeroboam **opposed** him with an army of 800,000.
	20. 6	You are powerful and mighty, and no one can **oppose** you.
	28.12	Amasa son of Hadlai also **opposed** the actions of the army.
	28.20	Assyrian emperor, instead of helping Ahaz, **opposed** him
	35.21	on my side, so don't **oppose** me, or he will destroy you."
Ezra	10.15	No one was **opposed** to the plan except Jonathan son of
Job	6.10	I have never **opposed** what he commands.
	9.13	enemies who helped Rahab, the sea-monster, **oppose** him.
	23.13	No one can **oppose** him or stop him from doing what he
	27. 7	May all who **oppose** me and fight against me be punished
Ps	8. 2	you stop anyone who **opposes** you.
	17.13	**Oppose** my enemies and defeat them!
	34.16	but he **opposes** those who do evil, so that when they die,
	35. 1	**Oppose** those who oppose me, Lord, and fight those who
	109. 4	They **oppose** me, even though I love them and have prayed
	138. 7	You **oppose** my angry enemies and save me by your power.
Prov	18.18	If two powerful men are **opposing** each other in court,
Is	31. 6	"People of Israel, you have sinned against me and **opposed** me.
Jer	49.19	What ruler could **oppose** me?
	50.44	What ruler could **oppose** me?
Ezek	14. 8	I will **oppose** him.
Dan	4.35	No one can **oppose** his will or question what he does.
	10.13	of the kingdom of Persia **opposed** me for twenty-one days.
	11.16	The Syrian invader will do with them as he pleases, without **opposition.**
	11.22	Anyone who **opposes** him, even God's High Priest, will be
	11.30	come in ships and **oppose** him, and he will be frightened.
Mic	7. 6	their fathers like fools, daughters **oppose** their mothers,
Nah	1. 2	he punishes those who **oppose** him.
	1. 8	he sends to their death those who **oppose** him.
	1. 9	No one **opposes** him more than once.
Acts	6. 9	But he was **opposed** by some men who were members of the
	13. 8	But they were **opposed** by the magician Elymas
	18. 6	they **opposed** him and said evil things about him, he protested
	28.19	But when the Jews **opposed** this, I was forced to appeal
Rom	13. 2	Whoever **opposes** the existing authority opposes what God has ordered;
1 Cor	11.18	I have been told that there are **opposing** groups in your meetings;
Gal	2.11	Peter came to Antioch, I **opposed** him in public, because he
	5.17	our human nature wants is **opposed** to what the Spirit wants,
	5.17	the Spirit wants is **opposed** to what our human nature wants.
1 Thes	2. 2	even though there was much **opposition,** our God gave us courage
2 Thes	2. 4	He will **oppose** every so-called god or object of worship
2 Tim	3. 8	As Jannes and Jambres were **opposed** to Moses,
	3. 8	so also these people are **opposed** to the truth—
	4.15	because he was violently **opposed** to our message.
Tit	1. 9	also to show the error of those who are **opposed** to it.
Heb	10.27	and the fierce fire which will destroy those who **oppose** God!
1 Pet	3.12	but he **opposes** those who do evil."

OPPOSITE

Gen	15.10	half, and placed the halves **opposite** each other in two rows;
Ex	40.24	Tent, on the south side, **opposite** the table, [25] and there
Num	22. 1	the plains of Moab east of the Jordan and **opposite** Jericho.
	34.15	on the eastern side of the Jordan, **opposite** Jericho."
Deut	3.29	"So we remained in the valley **opposite** the town of Bethpeor."
	4.45	east of the River Jordan, **opposite** the town of Bethpeor,
	32.49	Abarim Mountains in the land of Moab **opposite** the city of Jericho;
	34. 6	in a valley in Moab, **opposite** the town of Bethpeor, but to
Josh	18.17	to Enshemesh and then on to Geliloth, **opposite** Adummim Pass.
Judg	2. 2	You have done just the **opposite!**
1 Sam	20.25	Abner sat next to him, and Jonathan sat **opposite** him.
2 Sam	2.13	side of the pool and the other group on the **opposite** side.
1 Kgs	7. 5	three rows of windows in each wall faced the **opposite** rows.
Neh	3.27	second one, from a point **opposite** the large tower guarding
Ezek	46. 9	same way as he entered, but must leave by the **opposite** gate.
Jon	1. 3	however, set out in the **opposite** direction in order to get

OPPRESS

Ex	1.12	But the more the Egyptians **oppressed** the Israelites, the
	3. 9	my people, and I see how the Egyptians are **oppressing** them.
	22.21	"Do not ill-treat or **oppress** a foreigner;
Deut	28.29	You will be constantly **oppressed** and robbed, and there will
	28.33	receive nothing but constant **oppression** and harsh treatment.
	28.48	The Lord will **oppress** you harshly until you are destroyed.
	30. 7	enemies, who hated you and **oppressed** you, [8] and you will
Judg	2.18	because they groaned under their suffering and **oppression.**
	10. 8	For eighteen years they **oppressed** and persecuted all the
	10.12	the Amalekites, and the Maonites **oppressed** you in the past,
1 Sam	10.18	Egyptians and all the other peoples who were **oppressing** you.
	12. 3	Have I cheated or **oppressed** anyone?
	12. 4	"No, you have not cheated us or **oppressed** us;
	12. 8	to Egypt and the Egyptians **oppressed** them, your ancestors
	22. 2	People who were **oppressed** or in debt or dissatisfied went to him,
2 Sam	7.10	where they will live without being **oppressed** any more.
2 Kgs	13. 4	of Syria was **oppressing** the Israelites, answered his prayer.
	13.22	King Hazael of Syria **oppressed** the Israelites
1 Chr	16.21	But God let no one **oppress** them;
	17. 9	where they will live without being **oppressed** any more.
2 Chr	15. 6	One nation **oppressed** another nation, and one city oppressed another city,
Neh	5. 7	people and told them, "You are **oppressing** your brothers!"

Neh	5.15	Even their servants had **oppressed** the people.
	9.10	his land, because you knew how they **oppressed** your people.
	9.32	the time when Assyrian kings **oppressed** us, even till now,
Job	5.15	he saves the needy from **oppression.**
	15.20	A wicked man who **oppresses** others will be in torment as
	20.19	enjoy his wealth, [19] because he **oppressed** and neglected the
	34.30	could do to keep godless **oppressors** from ruling them.
	35. 9	When men are **oppressed,** they groan;
	37.17	suffer in the heat when the south wind **oppresses** the land.
Ps	9. 9	is a refuge for the **oppressed,** a place of safety in times
	10.18	You will hear the cries of the **oppressed** and the orphans;
	12. 5	"because the needy are **oppressed** and the persecuted groan in pain.
	34. 2	may all who are **oppressed** listen and be glad!
	34. 5	The **oppressed** look to him and are glad;
	35.10	You protect the weak from the strong, the poor from the **oppressor."**
	55. 3	of my enemies, crushed by the **oppression** of the wicked.
	55.11	the streets are full of **oppression** and fraud.
	57. 3	he will defeat my **oppressors.**
	69.32	When the **oppressed** see this, they will be glad;
	72. 2	with justice and govern the **oppressed** with righteousness.
	72. 4	may he help the needy and defeat their **oppressors.**
	72.14	He rescues them from **oppression** and violence;
	73. 8	they are proud and make plans to **oppress** others.
	74.21	Don't let the **oppressed** be put to shame;
	76. 9	to pronounce judgement, to save all the **oppressed** on earth.
	94. 5	they **oppress** those who belong to you.
	103. 6	Lord judges in favour of the **oppressed**
	105.14	But God let no one **oppress** them;
	106.42	They were **oppressed** by their enemies and were in
	106.46	He made all their **oppressors** feel sorry for them.
	107.39	defeated and humiliated by cruel **oppression** and suffering,
	107.40	he showed contempt for their **oppressors** and made them
	119.122	don't let arrogant men **oppress** me!
	119.134	Save me from those who **oppress** me, so that I may obey
	119.157	I have many enemies and **oppressors,** but I do not fail
	123. 4	too long by the rich and scorned by proud **oppressors.**
	143.12	and destroy all my **oppressors,** for I am your servant.
	146. 7	in favour of the **oppressed** and gives food to the hungry.
Prov	14.31	If you **oppress** poor people, you insult the God who made them;
	22. 8	will spring up, and your **oppression** of others will end.
	22.16	gifts to rich people or **oppress** the poor to get rich, you
	28. 3	A man in authority who **oppresses** poor people is like a
	29.13	A poor man and his **oppressor** have this in common—the
Ecc	4. 1	The **oppressed** were weeping, and no one would help them.
	4. 1	help them, because their **oppressors** had power on their side.
	5. 8	you see that the government **oppresses** the poor and denies
Is	1.17	those who are **oppressed,** give orphans their rights,
	3.12	Money-lenders **oppress** my people, and their creditors cheat them.
	9. 4	the nation that **oppressed** and exploited your people,
	10. 1	You make unjust laws that **oppress** my people.
	10.24	the Assyrians, even though they **oppress** you as the Egyptians
	14. 2	of Israel will rule over those who once **oppressed** them.
	14. 4	He will never **oppress** anyone again!
	14. 6	the evil rulers [6] who angrily **oppressed** the peoples and
	16. 4	**(Oppression** and destruction will end, and those who are
	19.20	When the people there are **oppressed** and call out to the Lord
	23.12	Sidon, your happiness has ended, and your people are **oppressed.**
	26. 6	Those who were **oppressed** walk over it now and trample it
	29.20	end of those who **oppress** others and show contempt for God.
	49.26	I will make your **oppressors** kill each other;
	51.13	the fury of those who **oppress** you, of those who are ready
	51.23	give it to those who **oppressed** you, to those who made you
	54.14	You will be safe from **oppression** and terror.
	58. 3	you pursue your own interests and **oppress** your workers.
	58. 6	Remove the chains of **oppression** and the yoke of injustice,
	58. 6	and let the **oppressed** go free.
	58. 9	you put an end to **oppression,** to every gesture of contempt,
	59. 9	know why God does not save us from those who **oppress** us.
	59.11	God to save us from **oppression** and wrong, but nothing happens.
	59.13	We have **oppressed** others and turned away from you.
	59.16	to see that there is no one to help the **oppressed.**
	60.14	The sons of those who **oppressed** you will come And bow
	60.17	Your rulers will no longer **oppress** you;
	61. 8	"I love justice and I hate **oppression** and crime.
Jer	5.28	give orphans their rights or show justice to the **oppressed.**
	6. 6	"I will punish this city because it is full of **oppression.**
	20.13	He rescues the **oppressed** from the power of evil men.
	22. 3	Do not ill-treat or **oppress** foreigners, orphans, or widows;
	22.17	you kill the innocent and violently **oppress** your people.
	30.16	All who **oppress** you will be oppressed, and all who plunder
	30.20	I will punish all who **oppress** them.
	50.33	Lord Almighty says, "The people of Israel and of Judah are **oppressed.**
Ezek	18.16	He doesn't seduce another man's wife [16] or **oppress** anyone
	45. 8	that he will no longer **oppress** the people, but will let the
	45. 9	Stop your violence and **oppression.**
	46.18	so that he will not **oppress** any of my people by taking
Dan	7.25	He will speak against the Supreme God and **oppress** God's people.
	11.20	will send an officer to **oppress** the people with taxes in
Hos	5.11	Israel is suffering **oppression;**
	8.10	writhe in pain, when the emperor of Assyria **oppresses** them.
Amos	4. 1	Bashan, who ill-treat the weak, **oppress** the poor, and demand
	5.11	You have **oppressed** the poor and robbed them of their grain.
	6.14	It will **oppress** you from Hamath Pass in the north to the
Hab	3.14	us, gloating like those who secretly **oppress** the poor.
Zeph	3. 1	that corrupt, rebellious city that **oppresses** its own people.
	3.19	I will punish your **oppressors;**
Zech	7.10	Do not **oppress** widows, orphans, foreigners who live among you,
	9. 8	I will not allow tyrants to **oppress** my people any more.
Lk	4.18	to set free the **oppressed** [19] and announce that the time has
2 Cor	5. 4	in this earthly tent, we groan with a feeling of **oppression;**
Jas	2. 6	Who are the ones who **oppress** you and drag you before the

ORAL TRANSLATION

Neh	8. 8	They gave an **oral translation** of God's Law and explained

ORCHARD

Ex	23.16	when you gather the fruit from your vineyards and **orchards.**
Deut	6.11	and vineyards and olive **orchards** that you did not plant.
Judg	15. 5	was still in the fields, and the olive **orchards** as well.
Ecc	2. 5	I planted gardens and **orchards,** with all kinds of fruit-trees
Song	4.13	They grow like an **orchard** of pomegranate-trees
Hos	2.12	I will turn her vineyards and **orchards** into a wilderness;
Hag	1.11	and olive **orchards**—on every crop the ground produces,

ORDAIN

[ORDINATION]

Ex	28.41	Then **ordain** them and dedicate them by anointing them with olive-oil,
	29. 9	That is how you are to **ordain** Aaron and his sons.
	29.27	"When a priest is **ordained,** the breast and the thigh of
	29.27	ram being used for the **ordination** are to be dedicated to me
	29.29	after his death, for them to wear when they are **ordained.**
	29.31	the ram used for the **ordination** of Aaron and his sons and
	29.33	was used in the ritual of forgiveness at their **ordination.**
	29.35	"Perform the rites of **ordination** for Aaron and his sons
	30.30	Aaron and his sons, and **ordain** them as priests in my service.
Lev	6.20	regulations [20] for the **ordination** of an Aaronite priest.
	6.20	On the day he is **ordained,** he shall present as an offering
	7.35	Aaron and his sons on the day they were **ordained** as priests.
	7.37	the **ordination-offerings,** and the fellowship-offerings.
	8.12	He **ordained** Aaron by pouring some of the anointing oil
	8.22	ram, which was for the **ordination** of priests, and Aaron and
	8.28	on top of the burnt-offering, as an **ordination** offering.
	8.29	It was Moses' part of the **ordination** ram.
	8.31	basket of **ordination** offerings, just as the Lord commanded.
	8.33	until your **ordination** rites are completed.
	9. 1	The day after the **ordination** rites were completed,
	16.32	The High Priest, properly **ordained** and consecrated
Num	3. 3	They were anointed and **ordained** as priests, [4] but Nadab
1 Kgs	13.33	He **ordained** as priest anyone who wanted to be one.
2 Kgs	23. 5	the kings of Judah had **ordained** to offer sacrifices on the

AV ORDAIN

1 Chr	17. 9	I have **chosen** a place for my people Israel and have
2 Chr	11.15	Jeroboam **appointed** priests of his own to serve at the pagan
Esth	9.27	the Jews made it a **rule** for themselves, their descendants,
Ps	7.13	takes up his deadly weapons and **aims** his burning arrows.
	132.17	here I will preserve the **rule** of my chosen king.
Is	30.33	Long ago a place was **prepared** where a huge fire will
Jer	1. 5	before you were born I **selected** you to be a prophet to
Dan	2.24	whom the king had **commanded** to execute the royal advisers.
Hab	1.12	God and protector, you have **chosen** the Babylonians and made
Mk	3.14	came to him, [14] and he **chose** twelve, whom he named apostles.
Jn	15.16	I chose you and **appointed** you to go and bear much fruit,
Acts	10.42	the one whom God has **appointed** judge of the living and the
	13.48	those who had been **chosen** for eternal life became believers.
	14.23	In each church they **appointed** elders, and with prayers
	16. 4	the believers the rules **decided** upon by the apostles and elders
	17.31	whole world with justice by means of a man he has **chosen.**
1 Cor	2. 7	but which he had already **chosen** for our glory even before
	7.17	This is the rule I **teach** in all the churches.
	9.14	same way, the Lord has **ordered** that those who preach the
Gal	3.19	The Law was **handed down** by angels, with a man acting as
Eph	2.10	of good deeds, which he has already **prepared** for us to do.
1 Tim	2. 7	that is why I was **sent** as an apostle and teacher of
Tit	1. 5	things that still needed doing and **appoint** church elders
Heb	5. 1	from his fellow-men and **appointed** to serve God on their behalf,
	8. 3	Every High Priest is **appointed** to present offerings and animal
	9. 6	This is how those things have been **arranged.**
Jude	4	the Scriptures **predicted** the condemnation they have received.

ORDER (1)

Gen	12.20	The king gave **orders** to his men, so they took Abram and
	19. 3	Lot **ordered** his servants to bake some bread and prepare a
	32.17	He **ordered** the first servant, "When my brother Esau
	32.19	He gave the same **order** to the second, the third, and to
	38.24	Judah **ordered,** "Take her out and burn her to death."
	41.35	**Order** them to collect all the food during the good years
	41.40	of my country, and all my people will obey your **orders.**
	41.55	So he **ordered** them to go to Joseph and do what he
	42.25	Joseph gave **orders** to fill his brothers' packs with corn,
	43.31	and controlling himself, he **ordered** the meal to be served.
	45. 1	of his servants, so he **ordered** them all to leave the room.
	45.21	wagons, as the king had **ordered,** and food for the journey.
	50. 2	Then Joseph gave **orders** to embalm his father's body.
Ex	4.28	the miracles which the Lord had **ordered** him to perform.
	5.16	are given no straw, but we are still **ordered** to make bricks!
	6.13	of Egypt that I have **ordered** you to lead the Israelites out
	9.19	Now give **orders** for your livestock and everything else
	38.21	The list was **ordered** by Moses and made by the Levites who
Lev	13.54	on the object, [54] he shall **order** it to be washed and put
	14. 4	is healed, [4] the priest shall **order** two ritually clean birds
	14. 5	Then the priest shall **order** one of the birds to be killed
	14.36	The priest shall **order** everything to be moved out of the

Lev 14.40 mildew has spread, [40]he shall **order** the stones on which
24. 2 Moses [2]to give the following **orders** to the people of Israel:
Deut 9.23 you from Kadesh Barnea with **orders** to go and take possession
19. 7 This is why I **order** you to set aside three cities.
20.17 Hivites, and the Jebusites, as the Lord **ordered** you to do.
Josh 1.10 Then Joshua **ordered** the leaders to [11]go through the
1.18 or disobeys any of your **orders** will be put to death.
2. 1 the camp at Acacia with **orders** to go and secretly explore
4. 8 The men followed Joshua's **orders.**
4.10 been done that the Lord **ordered** Joshua to tell the people to
6. 7 Then he **ordered** his men to start marching round the city,
6. 8 So, just as Joshua had **ordered,** an advance guard
6.10 But Joshua had **ordered** his men not to shout,
6.10 not to say a word until he gave the **order.**
6.16 to sound the trumpets, Joshua **ordered** his men to shout, and
7. 1 man named Achan disobeyed that **order,** and so the Lord was
7. 2 near Bethaven, with **orders** to go and explore the land.
7.11 broken the agreement with me that I **ordered** them to keep.
7.12 unless you destroy the things you were **ordered** not to take!
7.13 your possession some things that I **ordered** you to destroy!
8. 4 best troops and sent them out at night [4]with these **orders:**
8. 8 These are your **orders."**
8.29 At sunset Joshua gave **orders** for the body to be removed, and
9.22 Joshua **ordered** the people of Gibeon to be brought to him,
10.24 of Israel to him and **ordered** the officers who had gone with
10.27 At sunset Joshua gave **orders,** and their bodies were
22. 2 that Moses the Lord's servant **ordered** you to do, and you
Judg 3.19 So the king **ordered** his servants, "Leave us alone!"
6.14 Then the Lord **ordered** him, "Go with all your great
6.20 The angel **ordered** him, "Put the meat and the bread on
9.28 And Zebul takes **orders** from him, but why should we serve him?
9.54 his weapons and **ordered,** "Draw your sword and kill me.
21.10 men with the **orders,** "Go and kill everyone in Jabesh,
Ruth 2. 9 I have **ordered** my men not to molest you.
2.15 on picking up corn, Boaz **ordered** the workers, "Let her pick
1 Sam 14.24 day, because Saul, with a solemn oath, had given the **order:**
14.34 Then he gave another **order:**
15.16 "Stop," Samuel **ordered,** "and I will tell you what
15.18 he sent you out with **orders** to destroy those wicked people
15.32 "Bring King Agag here to me," Samuel **ordered.**
16.16 So give us the **order,** sir, and we will look for a
16.17 Saul **ordered** them, "Find me a man who plays well and
17.56 "Then go and find out," Saul **ordered.**
18.22 He **ordered** his officials to speak privately to David
18.25 and Saul **ordered** them to tell David:
19.15 He **ordered** them, "Carry him here in his bed, and I will
20.29 feast in town, and my brother **ordered** me to be there.
21. 8 The king's **orders** made me leave in such a hurry that I
22.19 Saul also **ordered** all the other inhabitants of Nob, the
25. 5 sent ten young men with **orders** to go to Carmel, find Nabal,
25.13 he **ordered,** and they all did.
28. 7 Then Saul **ordered** his officials, "Find me a woman who is
2 Sam 1.18 and his son Jonathan, [18]and **ordered** it to be taught to the
2.26 will it be before you **order** your men to stop chasing us?"
3.31 Then David **ordered** Joab and his men to tear their clothes,
4.12 David gave the **order,** and his soldiers killed Rechab and
13.28 much to drink, and then when I give the **order,** kill him.
14.24 The king, however, gave **orders** that Absalom should not
18. 5 He gave **orders** to Joab, Abishai, and Ittai:
18.16 Joab **ordered** the trumpet to be blown to stop the fighting,
24. 2 So David gave **orders** to Joab, the commander of his army:
24. 4 But the king made Joab and his officers obey his **order;**
1 Kgs 2. 3 and do what the Lord your God **orders** you to do.
2.25 So King Solomon gave **orders** to Benaiah, who went out
2.30 and said to Joab, "The king **orders** you to come out."
2.46 Then the king gave **orders** to Benaiah, who went out and
13. 4 he pointed at him and **ordered,** "Seize that man!"
13.22 meal in a place he had **ordered** you not to eat in.
15.22 King Asa sent out an **order** throughout all Judah
18.14 So how can you **order** me to go and tell the king
18.19 Now **order** all the people of Israel to meet me at Mount
18.40 Elijah **ordered,** "Seize the prophets of Baal;
18.44 Elijah **ordered** his servant, "Go to King Ahab and tell him
20.12 He **ordered** his men to get ready to attack the city, so
20.18 He **ordered,** "Take them alive, no matter whether they
20.33 "Bring him to me," Ahab **ordered.**
20.35 of a group of prophets **ordered** a fellow-prophet to hit him.
20.42 to escape whom I had **ordered** to be killed, you will pay
22.26 Then King Ahab **ordered** one of his officers, "Arrest
22.31 The king of Syria had **ordered** his thirty-two chariot
22.36 Near sunset the **order** went out through the Israelite ranks:
2 Kgs 1. 9 to him, "Man of God, the king **orders** you to come down."
1.11 "Man of God, the king **orders** you to come down at once!"
2. 2 the Lord has **ordered** me to go to Bethel."
2. 4 the Lord has **ordered** me to go to Jericho."
2. 6 the Lord has **ordered** me to go to the River Jordan."
2.20 salt in a new bowl, and bring it to me," he **ordered.**
4.15 "Tell her to come here," Elisha **ordered.**
4.24 had the donkey saddled, and **ordered** the servant, "Make the
6. 7 "Take it out," he **ordered,** and the man bent down and
6.13 he is," the king **ordered,** "and I will capture him."
9.21 "Get my chariot ready," King Joram **ordered.**
9.26 So take Joram's body," Jehu **ordered** his aide, "and throw
9.27 Jehu **ordered** his men, and they wounded him as he drove his
10. 6 are ready to follow my **orders,** bring the heads of King
10. 8 descendants had been brought, he **ordered** them to be piled up
10.14 Jehu **ordered** his men, "Take them alive!"
10.20 Then Jehu **ordered,** "Proclaim a day of worship in honour of Baal!"
10.22 Then Jehu **ordered** the priest in charge of the sacred robes
11. 1 her son's murder, she gave **orders** for all the members of the
11. 5 King Ahaziah's son Joash [5]and gave them the following **orders:**
2 Kgs 11.15 Athaliah killed in the temple area, so he **ordered** the army officers:
12. 4 Joash called the priests and **ordered** them to save up the
13.15 "Get a bow and some arrows," Elisha **ordered** him.
13.17 Elisha **ordered.**
16.15 Then he **ordered** Uriah:
17.35 The Lord had made a covenant with them and had **ordered** them:
22. 3 Azaliah and grandson of Meshullam, to the Temple with the **order:**
22. 8 Shaphan delivered the king's **order** to Hilkiah, and
22.12 and gave the following **order** to Hilkiah the priest,
23. 4 Then Josiah **ordered** the High Priest Hilkiah, his assistant priests,
23.18 "Leave it as it is," Josiah **ordered.**
23.21 King Josiah **ordered** the people to celebrate the
1 Chr 14.12 idols behind, and David gave **orders** for them to be burnt.
21. 2 David gave **orders** to Joab and the other officers,
21. 4 But the king made Joab obey the **order.**
21.17 I am the one who **ordered** the census.
22. 2 King David gave **orders** for all the foreigners living in
25. 6 And Asaph, Jeduthun, and Heman were under **orders** from the king.
2 Chr 1. 2 King Solomon gave an **order** to all the officers in charge
3.10 The king also **ordered** his workmen to make two winged
16. 6 men from throughout Judah and **ordered** them to carry off the
18.25 Then King Ahab **ordered** one of his officers, "Arrest
18.30 The king of Syria had **ordered** his chariot commanders to
20. 3 Then he gave **orders** for a fast to be observed throughout the
20.21 with the people, the king **ordered** some musicians to put on
22.10 her son's murder, she gave **orders** for all the members of the
24. 5 He **ordered** the priests and the Levites to go to the cities
24. 8 The king **ordered** the Levites to make a box for
24.21 Zechariah, and on the king's **orders** the people stoned
29.27 Hezekiah gave the **order** for the burnt-offering to be presented;
31. 5 As soon as the **order** was given, the people of Israel
31.11 On the king's **orders** they prepared storerooms in the
32. 1 the fortified cities and gave **orders** for his army to break
32. 6 command of army officers and **ordered** them to assemble in the
34.20 dismay [20]and gave the following **order** to Hilkiah, to
35.23 He **ordered** his servants, "Take me away;
Ezra 4.15 so we suggest [15]that you **order** a search to be made in
4.19 I gave **orders** for an investigation to be made, and it
4.21 Therefore you are to issue **orders** that those men are to
5. 3 "Who gave you **orders** to build this Temple and equip it?"
5.13 Babylonia, Cyrus issued **orders** for the Temple to be rebuilt.
5.17 whether or not Cyrus gave **orders** for this Temple in
6. 1 So Darius the emperor issued **orders** for a search to be
6.11 that if anyone disobeys this **order,** a wooden beam is to be
6.12 I, Darius, have given this **order.**
8.21 the Ahava Canal I gave **orders** for us all to fast and
10. 8 meet in Jerusalem [8]by **order** of the leaders of the people.
Neh 8.14 the Lord gave through Moses, **ordered** the people of Israel to
13. 9 I gave **orders** for the rooms to be ritually purified and
13.19 So I gave **orders** for the city gates to be shut at
13.22 I **ordered** the Levites to purify themselves and to go and
Esth 1. 8 the king had given **orders** to the palace servants that
1.11 He **ordered** them to bring in Queen Vashti, wearing her royal crown.
1.19 **Order** it to be written into the laws of Persia and Media,
2. 3 province of the empire and **order** them to bring all these
2.23 The king **ordered** an account of this to be written down in
3. 2 The king **ordered** all the officials in his service to show
3. 7 of Nisan, Haman **ordered** the lots to be cast ("purim,"
4. 8 been issued in Susa, **ordering** the destruction of the Jews.
5. 5 The king then **ordered** Haman to come quickly, so that they
6. 1 get to sleep, so he **ordered** the official records of the
6. 7 So he answered the king, **"Order** royal robes to be brought
6. 7 **Order** a royal ornament to be put on your own horse.
8. 5 prevent Haman's **orders** from being carried out—
8. 5 those **orders** that the son of Hammedatha
9.13 And **order** the bodies of Haman's ten sons to be hung from
9.14 The king **ordered** this to be done, and the proclamation
9.25 and the king issued written **orders** with the result that
Job 38.13 Have you **ordered** the dawn to seize the earth and shake
38.34 Can you shout **orders** to the clouds and make them drench
Ps 73. 9 in heaven and give arrogant **orders** to men on earth, [10]so
81. 4 is the law in Israel, an **order** from the God of Jacob.
Prov 8.29 springs of the ocean [29]and **ordered** the waters of the sea
Is 20. 1 Under the **orders** of Sargon, emperor of Assyria, the
23.11 He has **ordered** the Phoenician centres of commerce to be destroyed.
36. 2 Then he **ordered** his chief official to go from Lachish to
44.28 you will **order** Jerusalem to be rebuilt and the Temple
Jer 6. 6 The Lord Almighty has **ordered** these kings to cut down
14.14 did I give them any **orders** or speak one word to them.
15.17 In obedience to your **orders** I stayed by myself and was
20. 2 me proclaim these things, [2]he **ordered** me to be beaten and
23.32 did not send them or **order** them to go, and they are
32.14 the God of Israel, has **ordered** you to take these deeds, both
32.23 they did nothing that you had **ordered** them to do.
32.25 you are the one who **ordered** me to buy the field in
34.22 I will give the **order,** and they will return to this city.
36.26 Then he **ordered** Prince Jerahmeel, together with Seraiah
37.15 were furious with me and **ordered** me to be beaten and locked
37.21 So King Zedekiah **ordered** me to be locked up in the
38.10 Then the king **ordered** Ebedmelech to take with him three
39.11 the commanding officer, to give the following **order:**
Ezek 9.11 reported to the Lord, "I have carried out your **orders."**
38. 8 After many years I will **order** him to invade a country
Dan 1. 3 The king **ordered** Ashpenaz, his chief official, to select
1. 5 The king also gave **orders** that every day they were to be
2.12 flew into a rage and **ordered** the execution of all the royal
2.13 So the **order** was issued for all of them to be killed,
2.14 bodyguard, who had been **ordered** to carry out the execution.

Dan 2.15 he asked Arioch why the king had issued such a harsh **order.**
2.46 to the ground and gave **orders** for sacrifices and offerings
3. 2 Then the king gave **orders** for all his officials to come
3.10 Your Majesty has issued an **order** that as soon as the
3.12 Meshach, and Abednego—who are disobeying Your Majesty's **orders.**
3.13 flew into a rage and **ordered** the three men to be brought
3.19 So he **ordered** his men to heat the furnace seven times hotter
3.22 the king had given strict **orders** for the furnace to be made
3.28 They disobeyed my **orders** and risked their lives rather than
4. 6 I **ordered** all the royal advisers in Babylon to be brought
4.26 The angel **ordered** the stump to be left in the ground.
5. 2 they were drinking, Belshazzar gave **orders** to bring in the
5.29 Immediately Belshazzar **ordered** his servants to dress
6. 7 Your Majesty should issue an **order** and enforce it strictly.
6. 7 Give **orders** that for thirty days no one be permitted to
6. 7 Anyone who violates this **order** is to be thrown into a pit
6. 8 let Your Majesty issue this **order** and sign it, and it will
6. 9 And so King Darius signed the **order.**
6.10 When Daniel learnt that the **order** had been signed, he
6.12 "Your Majesty, you signed an **order** that for the next thirty
6.12 king replied, "Yes, a strict **order,** a law of the Medes and
6.13 does not respect Your Majesty or obey the **order** you issued.
6.15 the Medes and Persians no **order** which the king issues can be
6.16 So the king gave **orders** for Daniel to be arrested and he
6.23 king was overjoyed and gave **orders** for Daniel to be pulled
6.24 Then the king gave **orders** to arrest all the men who had
Joel 1.14 Give **orders** for a fast;
2.15 give **orders** for a fast and call an assembly!
Amos 2.12 the Nazirites drink wine, and **ordered** the prophets not to
7.15 work as a shepherd and **ordered** me to come and prophesy to
9. 4 by their enemies, I will **order** them to be put to death.
Jon 2.10 Then the Lord **ordered** the fish to spew Jonah up on the
3. 7 "This is an **order** from the king and his officials:
Mt 2.16 He gave **orders** to kill all the boys in Bethlehem and its
4. 3 "If you are God's Son, **order** these stones to turn into bread."
4. 6 says, 'God will give **orders** to his angels about you;
8. 4 that you are cured, offer the sacrifice that Moses **ordered."**
8. 8 Just give the **order,** and my servant will get well.
8. 9 I **order** this one, 'Go!'
8. 9 and I **order** that one, 'Come!'
8. 9 and I **order** my slave, 'Do this!'
8.18 the crowd round him, he **ordered** his disciples to go to the
8.26 Then he got up and **ordered** the winds and the waves to
12.16 and gave them **orders** not to tell others about him.
14. 3 Herod had earlier **ordered** John's arrest, and he had him chained
14. 9 of all his guests he gave **orders** that her wish be granted.
14.19 He **ordered** the people to sit down on the grass;
14.28 if it is really you, **order** me to come out on the
15.35 So Jesus **ordered** the crowd to sit down on the ground.
16.20 Then Jesus **ordered** his disciples not to tell anyone that
17. 9 came down the mountain, Jesus **ordered** them, "Don't tell
18.25 his debt, so the king **ordered** him to be sold as a
27.58 Pilate gave **orders** for the body to be given to Joseph.
27.64 Give **orders,** then, for his tomb to be carefully guarded
Mk 1.25 Jesus **ordered** the spirit, "Be quiet, and come out of the man!"
1.27 man has authority to give **orders** to the evil spirits,
1.44 you are cured, offer the sacrifice that Moses **ordered."**
3.12 Jesus sternly **ordered** the evil spirits not to tell
5.43 But Jesus gave them strict **orders** not to tell anyone,
6. 8 over the evil spirits [8]and **ordered** them, "Don't take
6.17 Herod himself had **ordered** John's arrest, and he had him chained
6.27 sent off a guard at once with **orders** to bring John's head.
7.36 Then Jesus **ordered** the people not to speak of it to anyone;
7.36 but the more he **ordered** them not to, the more they spoke.
8. 6 He **ordered** the crowd to sit down on the ground.
8.26 him home with the **order,** "Don't go back into the village."
8.30 Then Jesus **ordered** them, "Do not tell anyone about me."
9. 9 came down the mountain, Jesus **ordered** them, "Don't tell anyone
9.10 obeyed his **order,** but among themselves they started discussing
9.25 dumb spirit," he said, "I **order** you to come out of the
Lk 2. 1 the Emperor Augustus **ordered** a census to be taken throughout
4. 3 "If you are God's Son, **order** this stone to turn into bread."
4.10 the scripture says, 'God will **order** his angels to take good
4.35 Jesus **ordered** the spirit, "Be quiet and come out of the man!"
4.36 and power this man gives **orders** to the evil spirits,
4.39 and stood at her bedside and **ordered** the fever to leave her.
4.41 Jesus gave the demons an **order** and would not let them speak,
5.14 Jesus **ordered** him, "Don't tell anyone, but go straight to
5.14 that you are cured, offer the sacrifice as Moses **ordered."**
7. 7 Just give the **order,** and my servant will get well.
7. 8 I **order** this one, 'Go!'
7. 8 I **order** that one, 'Come!'
7. 8 and I **order** my slave, 'Do this!'
8.24 got up and gave an **order** to the wind and the stormy
8.25 He gives **orders** to the winds and waves, and they obey him!"
8.29 said this because Jesus had **ordered** the evil spirit to go
8.55 up at once, and Jesus **ordered** them to give her something to
9.21 Then Jesus gave them strict **orders** not to tell this to anyone.
14.22 Soon the servant said, 'Your **order** has been carried out, sir,
15.29 you like a slave, and I have never disobeyed your **orders.**
17. 9 The servant does not deserve thanks for obeying **orders,**
18.40 So Jesus stopped and **ordered** the blind man to be brought
19.15 At once he **ordered** his servants to appear before him,
Jn 2.16 and he **ordered** the men who sold the pigeons, "Take them
7.22 Moses **ordered** you to circumcise your sons
11.39 Jesus **ordered.**
11.57 the Pharisees had given **orders** that if anyone knew where Jesus
Acts 1. 4 And when they came together, he gave them this **order:**
3. 6 I **order** you to get up and walk!"
5.21 then they sent **orders** to the prison to have the apostles
Acts 5.28 "We gave you strict **orders** not to teach in the name of
5.34 He **ordered** the apostles to be taken out for a while,
5.40 had them whipped, and **ordered** them never again to speak in
8.38 The official **ordered** the carriage to stop, and both Philip and
10.48 So he **ordered** them to be baptized in the name of Jesus
12.19 Herod gave **orders** to search for him, but they could not
12.19 the guards questioned and **ordered** them to be put to death.
16.18 name of Jesus Christ I **order** you to come out of her!"
16.22 clothes off Paul and Silas and **ordered** them to be whipped.
16.23 into jail, and the jailer was **ordered** to lock them up tight.
16.24 receiving this **order,** the jailer threw them into the inner cell
16.35 sent police officers with the **order,** "Let those men go."
16.36 "The officials have sent an **order** for you and Silas to be
18. 2 the Emperor Claudius had **ordered** all the Jews to leave Rome.
21.33 to Paul, arrested him, and **ordered** him to be bound with two
21.34 what had happened, so he **ordered** his men to take Paul up
22.24 The Roman commander **ordered** his men to take Paul into the fort,
22.30 Paul's chains taken off and **ordered** the chief priests and the
23. 2 High Priest Ananias **ordered** those who were standing close to Paul
23. 3 yet you break the Law by **ordering** them to strike me!"
23.10 So he **ordered** his soldiers to go down into the group,
23.31 The soldiers carried out their **orders.**
23.35 Then he gave **orders** for Paul to be kept under guard
24.23 He **ordered** the officer in charge of Paul to keep him
25. 6 in the court of judgement and **ordered** Paul to be brought in.
25.17 sat in the court and **ordered** the man to be brought in.
25.21 So I gave **orders** for him to be kept under guard
25.23 Festus gave the **order,** and Paul was brought in.
26.12 went to Damascus with authority and **orders** from the chief priests.
27.43 Instead, he **ordered** all the men who could swim to jump
Rom 13. 2 Whoever opposes the existing authority opposes what God has **ordered;**
1 Cor 7. 6 tell you this not as an **order,** but simply as a concession.
9.14 same way, the Lord has **ordered** that those who preach the
9.16 After all, I am under **orders** to do so.
2 Cor 11.20 You tolerate anyone who **orders** you about or takes advantage
1 Tim 1. 1 apostle of Christ Jesus by **order** of God our Saviour and
1. 3 are teaching false doctrines, and you must **order** them to stop.
1. 5 The purpose of this **order** is to arouse the love that comes
6.14 command you [14]to obey your **orders** and keep them faithfully
Tit 1. 3 to me, and I proclaim it by **order** of God our Saviour.
Phlm 8 your brother in Christ, to **order** you to do what should be
Heb 11.23 and they were not afraid to disobey the king's **order.**
11.28 establish the Passover and **order** the blood to be sprinkled on
12.20 they could not bear the **order** which said, "If even an
13.17 Obey your leaders and follow their **orders.**

ORDER (2)

Gen 25.13 had the following sons, listed in the **order** of their birth:
43.33 table, facing Joseph, in the **order** of their age from the
Ex 28.10 sons of Jacob, [10]in the **order** of their birth, with six on
Num 2.17 shall march in the same **order** as they camp, each in position
7.12 They presented their offerings in the following **order:**
10.14 and each time they moved, they were in the same **order.**
10.28 This, then, was the **order** of march, company by company,
Josh 6.12 marched round the city in the same **order** as the day before:
2 Sam 3. 2 following six sons, in the **order** of their birth, were born
17.23 After putting his affairs in **order,** he hanged himself.
2 Kgs 20. 1 to put everything in **order,** because you will not recover.
1 Chr 2.13 In **order** of age they were:
3. 1 The following, in **order** of age, are David's sons who
8. 1 In **order** of age they were Bela, Ashbel, Aharah, [2]Nohah, and
12. 9 They were ranked in the following **order:**
23.10 Jahath, Zina, Jeush, and Beriah, in **order** of age.
24. 7 This is the **order** in which the twenty-four family
24.23 sons of Hebron, in **order** of age;
25. 9 This is the **order** in which they were on duty:
26. 2 He had seven sons, listed in **order** of age:
26. 4 God blessed by giving him eight sons, listed in **order** of age:
Esth 1.13 questions of law and **order,** so he called for his advisers,
Ps 122. 3 Jerusalem is a city restored in beautiful **order** and harmony.
Prov 29.18 A nation without God's guidance is a nation without **order.**
Is 38. 1 are to put everything in **order** because you will not recover.
Jer 31.36 as long as the natural **order** lasts, so long will Israel be
Ezek 48. 1 Mediterranean Sea, in the following **order** from north to south:
48.23 Mediterranean Sea, in the following **order** from north to south:
Lk 1. 3 it would be good to write an **orderly** account for you.
1 Cor 14.40 Everything must be done in a proper and **orderly** way.
2 Thes 3.12 and warn them to lead **orderly** lives and work to earn their
1 Tim 3. 2 have only one wife, be sober, self-controlled, and **orderly;**
Tit 1. 5 that you could put in **order** the things that still needed
Heb 9.10 only until the time when God will establish the new **order.**

ORDER (3)
[PRIESTLY ORDER]

Ps 110. 4 a priest for ever in the **priestly order** of Melchizedek."
Lk 1. 5 named Zechariah, who belonged to the **priestly order** of Abijah.
Heb 5. 6 a priest for ever, in the **priestly order** of Melchizedek."
5.10 to be high priest, in the **priestly order** of Melchizedek.
6.20 a high priest for ever, in the **priestly order** of Melchizedek.
7.11 one who is in the **priestly order** of Melchizedek, not of
7.17 a priest for ever, in the **priestly order** of Melchizedek."

ORDINANCE

Ex 24. 3 Lord's commands and all the **ordinances,**

AV **ORDINANCE**
see also **REGULATION, RULE**

Ex 13.10 Celebrate this **festival** at the appointed time each year.
15.25 There the Lord gave them **laws** to live by, and there he
18.20 You should teach them God's **commands** and explain to them
Lev 18. 4 Obey my laws and do what I **command.**
18.30 the Lord said, "Obey the **commands** I give and do not follow
Num 9.14 The same **law** applies to everyone, whether native or foreigner."
18. 8 to your descendants as the part **assigned** to you for ever.
2 Chr 33. 8 Israel will obey all my **commands** and keep the whole Law that
35.25 It has become a **custom** in Israel for the singers, both men
Ezra 3.10 the Lord according to the **instructions** handed down from the
Job 38.33 Do you know the **laws** that govern the skies, and can you
Ps 99. 7 they obeyed the laws and **commands** that he gave them.
119.91 of your **command,** because they are all your servants.
Is 58. 2 that they are eager to know my ways and obey my **laws.**
58. 2 me to give them just **laws** and that they take pleasure in
Jer 31.36 as long as the natural **order** lasts, so long will Israel be
Ezek 11.20 Then they will keep my laws and faithfully obey all my **commands.**
43.11 its shape, the **arrangement** of everything, and all its rules
43.11 how everything is arranged and can carry out all the **rules.**
Mal 3. 7 you, have turned away from my **laws** and have not kept them.
Lk 1. 6 and obeyed fully all the Lord's laws and **commands.**
Rom 13. 2 Whoever opposes the existing authority opposes what God has **ordered;**
1 Cor 11. 2 remember me and follow the **teachings** that I have handed on
1 Pet 2.13 For the sake of the Lord submit to every human **authority:**

ORDINARY

Ex 30.32 must not be poured on **ordinary** men, and you must not use
Lev 19. 8 be guilty of treating as **ordinary** what is dedicated to me,
1 Sam 21. 4 The priest said, "I haven't any **ordinary** bread,
21. 5 ritually pure even when we go out on an **ordinary** mission;
1 Kgs 10.27 as plentiful as **ordinary** sycomore in the foothills of Judah.
13.33 continued to choose priests from **ordinary** families to serve
2 Chr 1.15 and cedar was as plentiful as **ordinary** sycomore.
9.27 as plentiful as **ordinary** sycomore in the foothills of Judah.
Neh 7.73 the musicians, many of the **ordinary** people, the temple
Prov 12. 9 is better to be an **ordinary** man working for a living than
Mt 5.47 to your friends, have you done anything out of the **ordinary?**
Lk 17.10 you have been told to do, say, 'We are **ordinary** servants;
Jn 2.10 have had plenty to drink, he serves the **ordinary** wine.
Acts 4.13 and to learn that they were **ordinary** men of no education.
Rom 9.21 one for special occasions and the other for **ordinary** use.
1 Cor 14.16 how can an **ordinary** person taking part in the meeting
14.23 and if some **ordinary** people or unbelievers come in,
14.24 message when some unbeliever or **ordinary** person comes in, he will
2 Tim 2.20 some are for special occasions, others for **ordinary** use.

ORDINATION see **ORDAIN**

ORDINATION OFFERING

Lev 7.37 the **ordination-offerings,** and the fellowship-offerings.
8.28 on top of the burnt-offering, as an **ordination offering.**
8.31 basket of **ordination offerings,** just as the Lord commanded.

ORE

Ezek 22.20 the same way that the **ore** of silver, copper, iron, lead, and
22.20 My anger and rage will melt them just as fire melts **ore.**

ORGAN

Ex 12. 9 including the head, the legs, and the internal **organs.**
29.13 covers the internal **organs,** the best part of the liver,
29.17 wash its internal **organs** and its hind legs, and put them on
29.22 covering the internal **organs,** the best part of the liver,
Lev 1. 9 man must wash the internal **organs** and the hind legs, and the
1.13 man must wash the internal **organs** and the hind legs, and the
3. 3 the fat on the internal **organs,** [4] the kidneys and the fat on
3. 9 the fat covering the internal **organs,** [10] the kidneys and
3.14 the fat on the internal **organs,** [15] the kidneys and the fat
4. 8 the fat on the internal **organs,** [9] the kidneys and the fat on
4.11 its legs, and its internal **organs** including the intestines,
7. 3 the fat covering the internal **organs,** [4] the kidneys and the
8.16 the fat on the internal **organs,** the best part of the liver,
8.20 washed the internal **organs** and the hind legs with water,
8.25 covering the internal **organs,** the best part of the liver,
9.14 Then he washed the internal **organs** and the hind legs and
Num 5.21 May he cause your genital **organs** to shrink and your stomach
5.22 cause it to swell up and your genital **organs** to shrink."
5.27 stomach will swell up and her genital **organs** will shrink.

ORGANIZE

1 Kgs 10. 5 quarters for his officials, the **organization** of his palace
1 Chr 24. 3 King David **organized** the descendants of Aaron into groups
24. 4 The descendants of Eleazar were **organized** into sixteen groups,
24. 4 while the descendants of Ithamar were **organized** into eight;
28.13 gave him the plans for **organizing** the priests and Levites to
2 Chr 8.14 he **organized** the daily work of the priests
8.14 He also **organized** the temple guards in sections for
9. 4 living-quarters for his officials, the **organization** of his
25. 5 King Amaziah **organized** all the men of the tribes of Judah
31. 2 King Hezekiah re-established the **organization** of the priests
Ezra 6.18 They also **organized** the priests and the Levites for the
Neh 12.24 Binnui, and Kadmiel, the Levites were **organized** into groups.
Esth 8.11 Jews in every city to **organize** themselves for self-defence.
9. 2 in the empire the Jews **organized** themselves to attack anyone
9.16 The Jews in the provinces also **organized** and defended themselves.

ORGY

Ex 32. 6 to a feast, which turned into an **orgy** of drinking and sex.
Rom 13.13 no **orgies** or drunkenness, no immorality or indecency,
1 Cor 10. 7 to a feast which turned into an **orgy** of drinking and sex."
Gal 5.21 get drunk, have **orgies,** and do other things like these.
1 Pet 4. 3 spent in indecency, lust, drunkenness, **orgies,** drinking parties,

ORIGIN

Gen 36.20 The **original** inhabitants of the land of Edom were
Lev 5. 3 touches anything of human **origin** that is unclean,
25.10 shall be restored to the **original** owner or his descendants,
25.13 that has been sold shall be restored to its **original** owner.
25.24 sold, the right of the **original** owner to buy it back must
25.28 In that year it will be returned to its **original** owner.
25.31 the **original** owner has the right to buy them back, and they
27.24 be returned to the **original** owner or to his descendants.
Num 36. 4 sold is restored to its **original** owners, the property of
Deut 2.23 had destroyed the Avvim, the **original** inhabitants, and had
17.18 made from the **original** copy kept by the levitical priests.
Judg 11.39 This was the **origin** of the custom in Israel [40] that the
19.16 He was **originally** from the hill-country of Ephraim, but he
1 Sam 10.12 This is how the saying **originated,** "Has even Saul become a prophet?"
19.24 (This is how the saying **originated,** "Has even Saul become a prophet?")
2 Sam 4. 3 Its **original** inhabitants had fled to Gittaim, where they
1 Chr 1.38 The **original** inhabitants of Edom were descended
11. 4 and the Jebusites, the **original** inhabitants of the land,
2 Chr 24.13 the Temple to its **original** condition, as solid as ever.
Ezra 4. 9 other officials, who are men **originally** from Erech, Babylon,
5.11 rebuilding the Temple which was **originally** built and
Ezek 29.14 and I will let them live in southern Egypt, their **original** home.
Acts 5.38 and done is of human **origin,** it will disappear, [39] but if
Gal 1.11 brothers, that the gospel I preach is not of human **origin.**
Heb 9.23 are copies of the heavenly **originals,** had to be purified in
Rev 3.14 true witness, who is the **origin** of all that God has created.

ORION
A group of bright stars that can be seen during winter evenings.

Job 9. 9 the sky—the Great Bear, **Orion,** the Pleiades, and the stars
38.31 the Pleiades together or loosen the bonds that hold **Orion?**
Amos 5. 8 The Lord made the stars, the Pleiades and **Orion.**

ORNAMENT

Ex 28.36 "Make an **ornament** of pure gold and engrave on it
32.24 to bring me their gold **ornaments,** and those who had any took
32.24 I threw the **ornaments** into the fire and out came this bull-calf!"
39.30 They made the **ornament,** the sacred sign of dedication,
Lev 8. 9 it he put the gold **ornament,** the sacred sign of dedication,
Num 31.50 we are bringing the gold **ornaments,** armlets, bracelets,
31.51 the gold, all of which was in the form of **ornaments.**
Judg 8.21 killed them and took the **ornaments** that were on the necks of
8.26 this did not include the **ornaments,** necklaces, and purple
Esth 6. 7 Order a royal **ornament** to be put on your own horse.
Ps 45. 9 throne stands the queen, wearing **ornaments** of finest gold.
Song 1.11 will make for you a chain of gold with **ornaments** of silver.
Is 3.18 are so proud of—the **ornaments** they wear on their ankles, on
Ezek 16.13 You had **ornaments** of gold and silver, and you always
28.13 You had **ornaments** of gold.
1 Tim 2. 9 hair styles or with gold **ornaments** or pearls or expensive dresses,
Rev 17. 4 and covered with gold **ornaments,** precious stones, and pearls.
18.16 cover herself with gold **ornaments,** precious stones, and pearls!

ORPHAN
see also **FATHERLESS**

Ex 22.22 Do not ill-treat any widow or **orphan.**
Deut 10.18 He makes sure that **orphans** and widows are treated fairly;
14.29 property, and for the foreigners, **orphans,** and widows who
16.11 servants, and the Levites, foreigners, **orphans,** and widows
16.14 servants, and the Levites, foreigners, **orphans,** and widows
24.17 "Do not deprive foreigners and **orphans** of their rights;
24.19 be left for the foreigners, **orphans,** and widows, so that the
24.20 they are for the foreigners, **orphans,** and widows.
24.21 the grapes that are left are for the foreigners, **orphans,**
26.12 the Levites, the foreigners, the **orphans,** and the widows, so
26.13 the Levites, the foreigners, the **orphans,** and the widows, as
27.19 deprives foreigners, **orphans,** and widows of their rights.'
Job 6.27 would even throw dice for **orphan** slaves and make yourselves
22. 9 help widows, but you also robbed and ill-treated **orphans.**
24. 3 take donkeys that belong to **orphans,** and keep a widow's ox
29.12 I gave help to **orphans** who had nowhere to turn.
31.17 live in despair [17] or let **orphans** go hungry while I ate.
31.21 I have ever cheated an **orphan,** knowing I could win in court,
Ps 10.18 You will hear the cries of the oppressed and the **orphans;**
68. 5 his sacred Temple, cares for **orphans** and protects widows.
82. 3 Defend the rights of the poor and the **orphans;**
94. 6 They kill widows and **orphans,** and murder the strangers who
109. 9 May his children become **orphans,** and his wife a widow!
109.12 be kind to him or care for the **orphans** he leaves behind.
146. 9 he helps widows and **orphans,** but takes the wicked to their ruin.

Prov 23.10 Never move an old boundary-mark or take over land owned by **orphans.**
Is 1.17 oppressed, give **orphans** their rights, and defend widows."
1.23 They never defend **orphans** in court or listen when widows
9.17 any of the widows and **orphans,** because all the people are
10. 2 you take the property that belongs to widows and **orphans.**
Jer 5.28 They do not give **orphans** their rights or show justice to the
7. 6 Stop taking advantage of aliens, **orphans,** and widows.
22. 3 Do not ill-treat or oppress foreigners, **orphans,** or widows;
49.11 Leave your **orphans** with me, and I will take care of them.
Ezek 22. 7 You cheat foreigners and take advantage of widows and **orphans.**
Zech 7.10 Do not oppress widows, **orphans,** foreigners who live among you,
Mal 3. 5 who take advantage of widows, **orphans,** and
Jas 1.27 to take care of **orphans** and widows in their suffering and to

OSTRICH

Lev 11.13 **ostriches;** seagulls, storks,
Deut 14.12 **ostriches;** seagulls, storks,
Job 30.29 sad and lonely as the cries of a jackal or an **ostrich.**
39.13 How fast the wings of an **ostrich** beat!
39.13 But no **ostrich** can fly like a stork.
39.14 The **ostrich** leaves her eggs on the ground for the heat
Is 13.21 **Ostriches** will live there, and wild goats will prance through the ruins.
43.20 jackals and **ostriches** will praise me when I make rivers
Lam 4. 3 but my people are like **ostriches,** cruel to their young.
Mic 1. 8 I will howl like a jackal and wail like an **ostrich.**

OTHERS

Mt 5. 7 "Happy are those who are merciful to **others;**
5.19 of the commandments and teaches **others** to do the same, will
5.19 obeys the Law and teaches **others** to do the same, will be
6.12 as we forgive the wrongs that **others** have done to us.
6.14 "If you forgive **others** the wrongs they have done to you,
6.15 if you do not forgive **others,** then your Father will not
6.18 so that **others** cannot know that you are fasting
7. 1 "Do not judge **others,** so that God will not judge you,
7. 2 same way as you judge **others,**
7. 2 he will apply to you the same rules you apply to **others.**
7.12 "Do for **others** what you want them to do for you:
12.16 and gave them orders not to tell **others** about him.
13. 8 a hundred grains, **others** sixty, and others thirty."
13.23 some as much as a hundred, others sixty, and **others** thirty."
13.41 people to sin and all **others** who do evil things, [42]and
15.16 them, "You are still no more intelligent than the **others.**
15.19 to rob, lie, and slander **others.**
16.14 **"Others** say Elijah, while others say Jeremiah or some other prophet."
19.12 **others,** because men made them that way;
19.12 and **others** do not marry for the sake of the Kingdom of
21. 8 cloaks on the road while **others** cut branches from the trees
22. 6 another to his shop, [6]while **others** grabbed the servants,
23.23 These you should practise, without neglecting the **others.**
23.34 kill some of them, crucify **others,**
23.34 and whip **others** in the synagogues and chase them
25.33 righteous people on his right and the **others** on his left.
27.42 "He saved **others,** but he cannot save himself!
27.49 But the **others** said, "Wait, let us see if Elijah is
Mk 4. 8 had thirty grains, **others** sixty, and others a hundred."
4.11 "But the **others,** who are on the outside, hear all things by
4.24 rules you use to judge **others** will be used by God to
6.15 **Others,** however, said, "He is Elijah."
6.15 **Others** said, "He is a prophet, like one of the prophets of
7.13 teaching you pass on to **others** cancels out the word of God.
7.18 "You are no more intelligent than the **others,"** Jesus said
8.28 **"others** say that you are Elijah, while others say that you
9. 6 He and the **others** were so frightened that he did not know
11. 8 cloaks on the road, while **others** cut branches in the fields
12. 5 and they treated many **others** the same
12. 5 beating some and killing **others.**
12.43 poor widow put more in the offering box than all the **others.**
12.44 For the **others** put in what they had to spare of their
15.31 "He saved **others,** but he cannot save himself!
16.13 returned and told the **others,** but they would not believe it.
Lk 1.14 and how happy many **others** will be when he is born!
5. 9 He and the **others** with him were all amazed at the large
6.31 Do for **others** just what you want them to do for you.
6.37 "Do not judge **others,** and God will not judge you;
6.37 do not condemn **others,** and God will not condemn you;
6.37 forgive **others,** and God will forgive you.
6.38 Give to **others,** and God will give to you.
6.38 The measure you use for **others** is the one that God will
7.49 The **others** sitting at the table began to say to themselves,
9. 8 **Others** were saying that Elijah had appeared,
9. 8 and still **others** that one of the prophets of
9.19 **"Others** say that you are Elijah,
9.19 while **others** say that one of the prophets
11.16 **Others** wanted to trap Jesus, so they asked him to
11.42 These you should practise, without neglecting the **others.**
11.49 they will kill some of them and persecute **others.'**
21. 3 this poor widow put in more than all the **others.**
21. 4 For the **others** offered their gifts from what they had to
21.24 killed by the sword, and **others** will be taken as prisoners
23.35 "He saved **others;**
24.33 disciples gathered together with the **others** [34]and saying,
Jn 4.38 **others** worked there, and you profit from their work."
7.12 "No," **others** said, "he is misleading the people."
7.41 **Others** said, "He is the Messiah!"
7.41 But **others** said, "The Messiah will not come from Galilee!
Jn 7.50 said to the **others,** [51]"According to our Law we cannot condemn
9. 9 Some said, "He is the one," but **others** said, "No he
9.16 **Others,** however, said, "How could a man who is a sinner
10. 8 All **others** who came before me are thieves and robbers,
10.21 But **others** were saying, "A man with a demon could not
12.29 was thunder, while **others** said, "An angel spoke to him!"
13.28 None of the **others** at the table understood why Jesus
18. 8 "If, then, you are looking for me, let these **others** go."
18.25 So the **others** said to him, "Aren't you also one of the
18.34 question come from you or have **others** told you about me?"
21. 3 Simon Peter said to the **others,** "I am going fishing."
21.15 son of John, do you love me more than these **others** do?"
Acts 2.13 **others** made fun of the believers, saying, "These people are drunk!"
4. 6 John, Alexander, and the **others** who belonged to the High Priest's
5.11 church and all the **others** who heard of this were terrified.
14. 4 some were for the Jews, **others** for the apostles.
15. 2 Barnabas and some of the **others** in Antioch should go to
15.35 and together with many **others** they taught and preached the word
16.32 the Lord to him and to all the **others** in his house.
17. 9 authorities made Jason and the **others** pay the required amount
17.18 **Others** answered, "He seems to be talking about foreign gods."
17.32 made fun of him, but **others** said, "We want to hear you
19.25 called them all together with **others** whose work was like theirs
19.32 people were shouting one thing, **others** were shouting something else,
21.12 heard this, we and the **others** there begged Paul not to go
21.34 Some in the crowd shouted one thing, **others** something else.
23. 6 group were Sadducees and the **others** were Pharisees, he called out
26.16 You are to tell **others** what you have seen of me today
26.30 governor, Bernice, and all the **others** got up,
28.24 were convinced by his words, but **others** would not believe.
Rom 1.31 promises, and they show no kindness or pity for **others.**
1.32 very things, but they even approve of **others** who do them.
2. 1 Do you, my friend, pass judgement on **others?**
2. 1 For when you judge **others** and then do the same things which
2. 3 do those very things for which you pass judgement on **others!**
2.21 You teach **others**—why don't you teach yourself?
12. 8 if it is to encourage **others,** we should do so.
12. 8 Whoever shares with **others** should do it generously;
12. 8 whoever shows kindness to **others** should do it cheerfully.
13. 9 all these, and any **others** besides, are summed up in the
14.18 in this way, he pleases God and is approved by **others.**
1 Cor 3.12 **others** will use wood or grass or straw.
4. 7 Who made you superior to **others?**
6.10 are drunkards or who slander **others** or are thieves—none of
7.12 To the **others** I say (I, myself, not the Lord):
9. 2 Even if **others** do not accept me as an apostle, surely you
9.12 If **others** have the right to expect this from you,
9.27 from being disqualified after having called **others** to the contest.
10.11 to them as examples for **others,** and they were written down
10.24 to his own interests, but to the interests of **others.**
11.21 own meal, so that some are hungry while **others** get drunk.
12.28 to heal or to help **others** or to direct them or to
14. 2 tongues does not speak to **others** but to God, because no one
14.19 understood, in order to teach **others,** than speak thousands of
14.29 should speak, while the **others** are to judge what they say.
2 Cor 1. 4 we are able to help **others** who have all kinds of troubles,
2.17 are not like so many **others,** who handle God's message as if
5.11 means to fear the Lord, and so we try to persuade **others.**
5.18 and gave us the task of making **others** his friends also.
7. 5 There were troubles everywhere, quarrels with **others,**
8. 8 But by showing how eager **others** are to help, I am trying
8.13 am not trying to relieve **others** by putting a burden on you;
10.15 boast about the work that **others** have done beyond the limits
13. 2 you who have sinned in the past, and to all the **others;**
Gal 1.23 They knew only what **others** were saying:
Eph 2.22 built together with all the **others** into a place where God
4.11 appointed some to be apostles, **others** to be prophets,
4.11 others to be evangelists, **others** to be pastors and teachers.
4.14 of deceitful men, who lead **others** into error by the tricks
Phil 1.13 palace guard and all the **others** here know that I am in
1.15 are jealous and quarrelsome, but **others** from genuine goodwill.
1.17 The **others** do not proclaim Christ sincerely,
2. 3 always considering **others** better than yourselves.
Col 2. 1 Laodicea and for all **others** who do not know me personally.
1 Thes 2. 6 either from you or from **others,** [7]even though as apostles
2.19 After all, it is you—you, no less than **others!**
5. 6 So then, we should not be sleeping like the **others;**
2 Thes 1. 3 the love each of you has for the **others** is becoming greater.
1 Tim 2. 2 for kings and all **others** who are in authority, that we may
5.22 Take no part in the sins of **others;**
5.24 but the sins of **others** are seen only later.
6.18 good works, to be generous and ready to share with **others.**
2 Tim 2. 2 to reliable people, who will be able to teach **others** also.
2.20 some are made of silver and gold, **others** of wood and clay;
2.20 some are for special occasions, **others** for ordinary use.
3.13 going from bad to worse, deceiving **others** and being deceived
Tit 1. 9 will be able to encourage **others** with the true teaching
1.10 especially converts from Judaism, who rebel and deceive **others**
3. 3 **others** hated us and we hated them.
Heb 4. 6 There are, then, **others** who are allowed to receive it.
7.20 There was no such vow when the **others** were made priests.
11.35 **Others,** refusing to accept freedom, died under torture
11.36 were mocked and whipped, and **others** were put in chains and
Jas 3. 1 we teachers will be judged with greater strictness than **others.**
1 Pet 4.10 use for the good of **others** the special gift he has received
2 Pet 2. 2 because of what they do, **others** will speak evil of the Way
1 Jn 4.14 we have seen and tell **others** that the Father sent his Son
Jude 16 These people are always grumbling and blaming **others;**

Jude 16 boast about themselves and flatter **others** in order to get their
23 save **others** by snatching them out of the fire;
23 and to **others** show mercy mixed with fear, but hate their
Rev 2.24 not learnt what the **others** call 'the deep secrets of Satan.'
18.17 passengers, the sailors and all **others** who earn their living on

OTHNIEL

Caleb's nephew who led Israel to victory over the king of Mesopotamia.

Josh 15.17 **Othniel,** the son of Caleb's brother Kenaz, captured the city,
15.18 On the wedding day **Othniel** urged her to ask her father
Judg 1.13 **Othniel,** the son of Caleb's younger brother Kenaz, captured the city,
1.14 On the wedding day **Othniel** urged her to ask her father
3. 9 This was **Othniel,** the son of Caleb's younger brother Kenaz.
3.10 **Othniel** went to war, and the Lord gave him victory over the
3.11 peace in the land for forty years, and then **Othniel** died.
1 Chr 4.13 Kenaz had two sons, **Othniel** and Seraiah.
4.13 **Othniel** also had two sons, Hathath and Meonothai.
27. 2 Heldai from Netophah (he was a descendant of **Othniel)**

OUGHT

Lev 21.15 Otherwise, his children, who **ought** to be holy, will be ritually unclean.
Ruth 4. 4 Elimelech, [4]and I think you **ought** to know about it.
2 Sam 12. 5 the living Lord that the man who did this **ought** to die!
Neh 5. 9 You **ought** to obey God and do what's right.
Job 32. 7 I told myself that you **ought** to speak, that you older men
Prov 20.16 responsible for a stranger's debts **ought** to have his own
30.17 mother in her old age **ought** to be eaten by vultures or
Ecc 3.16 you find wickedness where justice and right **ought** to be.
7.11 Everyone who lives **ought** to be wise;
Is 45.11 about my children or to tell me what I **ought** to do!
Jer 26. 8 seized me and shouted, "You **ought** to be killed for this!
Mt 3.14 "I **ought** to be baptized by you," John said, "and yet you
Jn 19. 7 a law that says he **ought** to die, because he claimed to
Acts 24.19 themselves **ought** to come before you and make their accusations
Rom 8.26 For we do not know how we **ought** to pray;
15. 1 are strong in the faith **ought** to help the weak to carry
15.27 the Gentiles **ought** to use their material blessings to
1 Cor 7.36 and he feels that they **ought** to marry, then they should get
8. 2 he knows something really doesn't know as he **ought** to know.
2 Cor 12.11 You are the ones who **ought** to show your approval of me.
Eph 5.28 Men **ought** to love their wives just as they love their
1 Jn 3.16 We too, then, **ought** to give our lives for our brothers!

OUR FATHER see FATHER (2)

OUR LORD see LORD

OUTCAST

In other Bibles this word is translated "sinners". In the Gospels it refers to Jews who were not allowed to attend synagogue worship because they had broken rules about foods that should not be eaten, and about being friendly with people who were not Jews. Such outcasts were looked down on by many of their fellow-Jews, and Jesus was criticized for being friendly with them.

Jer 30.17 your wounds, though your enemies say, 'Zion is an **outcast;**
Mt 9.10 many tax collectors and other **outcasts** came and joined Jesus
9.13 I have not come to call respectable people, but **outcasts."**
11.19 and a drinker, a friend of tax collectors and other **outcasts!'**
Mk 2.15 of tax collectors and other **outcasts** were following Jesus,
2.16 Jesus was eating with these **outcasts** and tax collectors,
2.17 I have not come to call respectable people, but **outcasts."**
Lk 5.30 "Why do you eat and drink with tax collectors and other **outcasts?"**
5.32 have not come to call respectable people to repent, but **outcasts."**
7.34 and a drinker, a friend of tax collectors and other **outcasts!'**
15. 1 many tax collectors and other **outcasts** came to listen to Jesus,
15. 2 "This man welcomes **outcasts** and even eats with them!"

OUTDOOR

Gen 25.27 a man who loved the **outdoor** life, but Jacob was a quiet

OUTER

Ex 26.14 and the other of fine leather, to serve as the **outer** cover.
35.11 covering and its **outer** covering, its hooks and its frames,
36.19 and the other of fine leather, to serve as an **outer** cover.
40.19 the Tent and put the **outer** covering over it, just as the
Num 3.25 inner cover, its **outer** cover, the curtain for the entrance,
3.37 for the posts, bases, pegs, and ropes for the **outer** court.
4.25 Tent, its inner cover, its **outer** cover, the fine leather
2 Sam 18.24 in the space between the inner and **outer** gates of the city.
20.15 ramps of earth against the **outer** wall and also began to dig
1 Kgs 7. 9 measure, with their inner and **outer** sides trimmed with saws.
7.24 All round the **outer** edge of the rim of the tank were
7.50 the Most Holy Place and of the **outer** doors of the Temple.
2 Chr 4. 3 All round the **outer** edge of the rim of the tank were
4. 9 courtyard for the priests, and also an **outer** courtyard.
4.22 The **outer** doors of the Temple and the doors to the Most
32. 5 the wall, building towers on it, and building an **outer** wall.
33.14 increased the height of the **outer** wall on the east side of
Job 41.13 one can tear off his **outer** coat or pierce the armour he
Ezek 8. 7 to the entrance of the **outer** courtyard and showed me a hole
9. 2 six men came from the **outer** north gate of the Temple, each
10. 5 the creatures' wings was heard even in the **outer** courtyard.
40.17 thirty rooms built against the **outer** wall, and in front of
40.18 This **outer** courtyard was at a lower level than the inner courtyard.
40.20 gateway on the north side that led into the **outer** courtyard.
40.28 it was the same size as the gateways in the **outer** wall.
40.34 The entrance room faced the **outer** courtyard.
40.37 The entrance room faced the **outer** courtyard.
40.38 In the **outer** courtyard there was an annexe attached to
41. 6 The Temple's **outer** wall on each floor was thinner than on
41. 7 Against the Temple's **outer** wall, on the outside of the rooms,
42. 1 man took me into the **outer** courtyard and led me to a
42. 3 on the other side it faced the pavement of the **outer** court.
42. 7 At the lower level the **outer** wall of the building was
42. 9 began, there was an entrance into the **outer** courtyard.
42.14 want to go to the **outer** courtyard, they must leave in these
44. 1 man led me to the **outer** gate at the east side of
44.19 Before they go to the **outer** courtyard where the people are,
46. 2 prince will go from the **outer** courtyard into the entrance
46.20 holy is carried to the **outer** courtyard, where it might harm
46.21 he led me to the **outer** courtyard and showed me that in
Jn 13. 4 the table, took off his **outer** garment, and tied a towel
13.12 their feet, he put his **outer** garment back on and returned to
21. 7 he wrapped his **outer** garment round him (for he had
Heb 9. 2 Tent was put up, the **outer** one, which was called the Holy
9. 6 The priests go into the **outer** Tent every day to perform
9. 8 not yet been opened as long as the **outer** Tent still stands.
Rev 11. 2 But do not measure the **outer** courts, because they have been

OUTLAW

1 Kgs 11.24 Zobah, [24]and had become the leader of a gang of **outlaws.**
Mt 26.55 swords and clubs to capture me, as though I were an **outlaw?**
Mk 14.48 swords and clubs to capture me, as though I were an **outlaw?**
Lk 22.52 to come with swords and clubs, as though I were an **outlaw?**

OUTLET

Gen 7.11 the second month all the **outlets** of the vast body of water
8. 2 The **outlets** of the water beneath the earth and the
2 Chr 32.30 King Hezekiah who blocked the **outlet** for the Spring of Gihon

OUTLINE

Is 44.13 He **outlines** a figure with chalk, carves it out with his tools,
Heb 10. 1 it is only a faint **outline** of the good things to come.

OUTLIVE

2 Chr 25.25 King Amaziah of Judah **outlived** King Jehoash of Israel

OUTNUMBER

Num 3.46 Since the first-born Israelite sons **outnumber** the Levites
22. 6 They **outnumber** us, so please come and put a curse on them
Deut 7. 7 you and choose you because you **outnumbered** other peoples;
7.17 tell yourselves that these peoples **outnumber** you and that
20. 1 horses and an army that **outnumbers** yours, do not be afraid
Jer 46.23 their soldiers **outnumber** the locusts.

OUTPOURING see POUR

OUTRAGE

Ezek 5.13 spoken to you because I am **outraged** at your unfaithfulness.
8. 3 Temple, where there was an idol that was an **outrage** to God.
8. 5 the gateway I saw the idol that was an **outrage** to God.

OUTSIDE

Gen 15. 5 The Lord took him **outside** and said, "Look at the sky and
19. 6 Lot went **outside** and closed the door behind him.
19.11 they struck all the men **outside** with blindness, so that they
24.11 he made the camels kneel down at the well **outside** the city.
24.29 named Laban, and he ran **outside** to go to the well where
39.12 But he escaped and ran **outside,** leaving his robe in her hand.
39.15 me scream, he ran **outside,** leaving his robe beside me."
39.18 But when I screamed, he ran **outside,** leaving his robe beside me."
Ex 9.19 animals left **outside** unprotected, and they will all die.' "
12.46 it must not be taken **outside.**
16.25 the Lord, and you will not find any food **outside** the camp.
21.18 to get up and walk **outside** with the help of a stick,
26. 4 blue cloth on the edge of the **outside** piece in each set.
26.35 **Outside** the Most Holy Place put the table against the
27.21 the Tent of my presence **outside** the curtain which is in
29.14 bull's flesh, its skin, and its intestines **outside** the camp.
30. 6 Put this altar **outside** the curtain which hangs in front of
36.11 blue cloth on the edge of the **outside** piece in each set.
40.22 Tent, on the north side **outside** the curtain, [23]and placed
Lev 4.12 the intestines, [12]carry it all **outside** the camp to the
4.21 he shall take the bull **outside** the camp and burn it, just
6.11 clothes and take the ashes **outside** the camp to a ritually
8.17 and intestines, and burnt it **outside** the camp, just as the
9.11 But he burnt the meat and the skin **outside** the camp.
10. 4 away from the sacred Tent and put them **outside** the camp."
10. 5 the corpses and carried them **outside** the camp, just as Moses
13.46 and he must live **outside** the camp, away from others.
14. 3 and the priest shall take him **outside** the camp and examine him.

Lev 14. 8 the camp, but he must live **outside** his tent for seven days.
14.40 removed and thrown into some unclean place **outside** the city.
14.41 and the plaster dumped in an unclean place **outside** the city.
14.53 live bird fly away **outside** the city over the open fields.
15.25 of blood for several days **outside** her monthly period or if
16.27 take away sin, shall be carried **outside** the camp and burnt.
24. 3 there in the Lord's presence **outside** the curtain in front of
24.23 Israel, they took the man **outside** the camp and stoned him to
Num 15.35 whole community is to stone him to death **outside** the camp."
15.36 the whole community took him **outside** the camp and stoned him
19. 3 It is to be taken **outside** the camp and killed in his
19. 9 in a ritually clean place **outside** the camp, where they are
31.19 touched a corpse must stay **outside** the camp for seven days.
Deut 17. 5 Israel, [5]then take that person **outside** the town and stone
22.24 You are to take them **outside** the town and stone them to
23.10 the night, he is to go **outside** the camp and stay there.
23.12 are to have a place **outside** the camp where you can go
24.11 wait **outside** and let him bring it to you himself.
25. 5 widow is not to be married to someone **outside** the family;
Judg 3.23 Then Ehud went **outside,** closed the doors behind him,
9.34 their move at night and hid **outside** Shechem in four groups.
12. 9 gave his daughters in marriage **outside** the clan
12. 9 and brought thirty girls from **outside** the clan for his sons
19.23 But the old man went **outside** and said to them, "No, my
19.25 So the Levite took his concubine and put her **outside** with them.
1 Kgs 6. 4 in them, narrower on the **outside** than on the inside.
6. 5 Against the **outside** walls, on the sides and the back of
6.10 high, was built against the **outside** walls of the Temple, and
21.13 and so he was taken **outside** the city and stoned to death.
22.10 at the threshing-place just **outside** the gate of Samaria,
2 Kgs 7. 3 a dreaded skin-disease were **outside** the gates of Samaria,
10.24 He had stationed eighty men **outside** the temple
10.25 swords, killed them all, and dragged the bodies **outside.**
23. 4 king burnt all these objects **outside** the city near the
25. 1 They set up camp **outside** the city, built siege walls round it,
2 Chr 18. 9 at the threshing-place just **outside** the gate of Samaria,
23. 6 people must obey the Lord's instructions and stay **outside.**
29.16 the Levites took it all **outside** the city to the valley of
32. 3 off the supply of water **outside** the city in order to prevent
33.15 took all these things **outside** the city and threw them away.
Neh 11.16 prominent Levites in charge of the work **outside** the Temple.
13.20 kinds of goods spent Friday night **outside** the city walls.
Esth 5. 2 king saw Queen Esther standing **outside,** she won his favour,
7. 7 fury, left the room, and went **outside** to the palace gardens.
Job 8.11 they are never found **outside** a swamp.
31. 9 neighbour's wife, and waited, hidden, **outside** her door,
Prov 22.13 he says a lion might get him if he goes **outside.**
Jer 22.19 be dragged away and thrown **outside** Jerusalem's gates."
52. 4 They set up camp **outside** the city, built siege walls round it,
Ezek 5. 2 it up with your sword as you move about **outside** the city.
5.12 a third will be cut down by swords **outside** the city;
40.15 of the gateway from the **outside** wall of the gate to the
40.16 were small openings in the **outside** walls of all the rooms
40.40 **Outside** the room there were four similar tables, two on
41. 7 walls, when seen from the **outside,** seemed to have the same
41. 7 Temple's outer wall, on the **outside** of the rooms, two wide
41. 8 The **outside** wall of these rooms was two and a half
41.13 The man measured the **outside** of the Temple, and it was
41.25 a wooden covering over the **outside** of the doorway of the
42.15 the east gate and then measured the **outside** of the area.
43.13 with a rim at the **outside** edge twenty-five centimetres high.
43.17 with a rim at the **outside** edge twenty-five centimetres high.
43.21 and burn it at the specified place **outside** the temple area.
Mal 1. 5 "The Lord is mighty even **outside** the land of Israel!"
Mt 7.15 looking like sheep on the **outside,** but on the inside they
12.46 They stood **outside,** asking to speak with him.
12.47 mother and brothers are standing **outside,** and they want to speak
22.13 him up hand and foot, and throw him **outside** in the dark.
23.25 You clean the **outside** of your cup and plate, while the
23.26 the cup first, and then the **outside** will be clean too!
23.27 which look fine on the **outside** but are full of bones
23.28 the same way, on the **outside** you appear good to everybody,
25.30 As for this useless servant—throw him **outside** in the darkness;
26.69 Peter was sitting **outside** in the courtyard when one of the
Mk 3.31 They stood **outside** the house and sent in a message,
3.32 and your brothers and sisters are **outside,** and they want you."
4.11 others, who are on the **outside,** hear all things by means of
7.15 person from the **outside** which can make him ritually unclean.
7.18 into a person from the **outside** can really make him unclean,
Lk 1.10 while the crowd of people **outside** prayed during the hour when
8.20 mother and brothers are standing **outside** and want to see you."
11.39 then, you Pharisees clean the **outside** of your cup and plate,
11.40 Did not God, who made the **outside,** also make the inside?
13.25 then when you stand **outside** and begin to knock on the door
Jn 18.16 High Priest's house, [16]while Peter stayed **outside** by the gate.
18.29 So Pilate went **outside** to them and asked, "What do you
18.38 Then Pilate went back **outside** to the people and said to them,
19.13 these words, he took Jesus **outside** and sat down on the
20.11 Mary stood crying **outside** the tomb.
Acts 5.13 Nobody **outside** the group dared to join them,
12.13 Peter knocked at the **outside** door, and a servant-girl
12.14 opening the door, and announced that Peter was standing **outside.**
14.13 Zeus, whose temple stood just **outside** the town,
Rom 2.28 Jew on the **outside,** whose circumcision is a physical thing.
1 Cor 9.21 I live like a Gentile, **outside** the Jewish Law, in order to
Gal 5. 4 You are **outside** God's grace.
1 Tim 3. 7 is respected by the people **outside** the church, so that he
Heb 13.11 but the bodies of the animals are burnt **outside** the camp.
13.12 this reason Jesus also died **outside** the city, in order to
13.13 us, then, go to him **outside** the camp and share his shame.
Rev 14.20 out in the winepress **outside** the city, and blood came out
22.15 **outside** the city are the perverts and those who practise magic,

OUTSIDER

Jer 8.13 I have allowed **outsiders** to take over the land."
1 Cor 5.12 After all, it is none of my business to judge **outsiders.**

OUTSKIRTS

2 Sam 17.17 spring of Enrogel, on the **outskirts** of Jerusalem, because

OUTSPREAD see SPREAD

OUTSTANDING

2 Sam 23.23 He was **outstanding** among them,
1 Chr 5.24 They were all **outstanding** soldiers,
7.40 famous fighting men, **outstanding** leaders.
8.40 Ulam's sons were **outstanding** soldiers and archers.
11.25 He was **outstanding** among "The Thirty,"
11.26 These are the other **outstanding** soldiers:
12.21 because they were all **outstanding** soldiers.
26.30 hundred of his relatives, all **outstanding** men, were put in
26.31 line of Hebron's descendants, and **outstanding** soldiers
26.32 chose two thousand seven hundred **outstanding** heads of families
2 Chr 17.13 In Jerusalem he stationed **outstanding** officers,
17.17 Eliada, an **outstanding** soldier, in command of 200,000 men
Neh 11. 6 descendants of Perez, 468 **outstanding** men lived in Jerusalem.
11.14 128 members of this clan who were **outstanding** soldiers.
Dan 6. 3 Because he was so **outstanding,** the king considered putting
Rom 16.13 greetings to Rufus, that **outstanding** worker in the Lord's service,

OUTSTRETCHED see STRETCH

OUTWARD

1 Sam 16. 7 Man looks at the **outward** appearance, but I look at the heart."
2 Cor 10. 7 You are looking at the **outward** appearance of things.
Gal 2. 6 God does not judge by **outward** appearances—
2 Tim 3. 5 they will hold to the **outward** form of our religion, but
Heb 9.10 These are all **outward** rules, which apply only until the time
Jas 2. 1 people in different ways according to their **outward** appearance.
2. 9 treat people according to their **outward** appearance, you are guilty
1 Pet 3. 3 You should not use **outward** aids to make yourselves beautiful,

OUTWARDS

Num 35. 4 pasture land is to extend **outwards** from the city walls 450
1 Kgs 7.25 bulls that faced **outwards,** three facing in each direction.
7.26 rim of a cup, curving **outwards** like the petals of a lily.
2 Chr 4. 4 bulls that faced **outwards,** three facing in each direction.
4. 5 rim of a cup, curving **outwards** like the petals of a flower.

OVEN

[TOWER OF THE OVENS]

Ex 8. 3 and your people, and even into your **ovens** and baking-pans.
Lev 2. 4 is bread baked in an **oven,** it must be made without yeast.
7. 9 has been baked in an **oven** or prepared in a pan or
11.35 a clay stove or **oven** shall be broken, [36]but a spring or
26.26 women will need only one **oven** to bake all the bread they
Neh 3.11 Moab built both the next section and the **Tower of the Ovens.**
12.38 past the **Tower of the Ovens** to the Broad Wall, [39]and from
Lam 5.10 burn with fever, until our skin is as hot as an **oven.**
Hos 7. 4 like the fire in an **oven,** which is not stirred by the
7. 6 Yes, they burned like an **oven** with their plotting.
Mt 6.30 that is here today and gone tomorrow, burnt up in the **oven.**
Lk 12.28 that is here today and gone tomorrow, burnt up in the **oven.**

OVER- *Where not listed below, see under main part of word, e.g. for "overjoyed" see JOY*

OVERBOARD

Jon 1. 5 order to lessen the danger, they threw the cargo **overboard.**
Acts 27.18 some of the ship's cargo **overboard,** [19]and on the following day
27.19 following day they threw part of the ship's equipment **overboard.**
27.43 men who could swim to jump **overboard** first and swim ashore;

OVERCHARGE see CHARGE (2)

OVERCOME

Gen 4. 7 It wants to rule you, but you must **overcome** it."
2 Sam 18.33 The king was **overcome** with grief.
22.30 to attack my enemies and power to **overcome** their defences.
Neh 9.24 you **overcame** the people living there.
Esth 6.13 He is a Jew, and you cannot **overcome** him.
Job 30.15 I am **overcome** with terror;
Ps 18.29 to attack my enemies and power to **overcome** their defences.
39. 3 I was **overcome** with anxiety.
55. 5 I am **overcome** with horror.
57. 6 I am **overcome** with distress.
119.28 I am **overcome** by sorrow;
119.133 don't let me be **overcome** by evil.

Ps 129. 2 have persecuted me cruelly, but they have not **overcome** me.
Is 13. 8 will all be terrified and **overcome** with pain, like the pain
28.18 When disaster sweeps down, you will be **overcome.**
Jer 46. 5 **overcome** with fear, they run as fast as they can and do
Ezek 3.15 seven days I stayed there, **overcome** by what I had seen and
Mal 4. 3 when I act, you will **overcome** the wicked, and they will be
Mt 16.18 church, and not even death will ever be able to **overcome** it.
Lk 10.19 and scorpions and **overcome** all the power of the Enemy,
1 Cor 15.24 Christ will **overcome** all spiritual rulers, authorities,

OVERFLOW

1 Chr 12.15 River Jordan **overflowed** its banks, they crossed the river,
Is 8. 7 waters of the River Euphrates, **overflowing** all its banks.
Lam 1.16 "That is why my eyes are **overflowing** with tears.
Joel 2.24 the pits beside the presses will **overflow** with wine and olive-oil.
Mt 7.25 rain poured down, the rivers **overflowed,** and the wind blew hard
7.27 rain poured down, the rivers **overflowed,** the wind blew hard
Lk 6.48 The river **overflowed** and hit that house but could not shake it,

OVERGROWN

Prov 24.31 They were full of thorn bushes and **overgrown** with weeds.
Is 5. 6 I will let it be **overgrown** with weeds.
7.23 of silver, will be **overgrown** with thorn-bushes and briars.
7.25 to grow will be so **overgrown** with thorns that no one will
Ezek 36.34 by your fields saw how **overgrown** and wild they were, but I
Hos 9. 6 once stood will be **overgrown** with weeds and thorn-bushes.
Zeph 2. 9 of salt pits and everlasting ruin, **overgrown** with weeds.

OVERHEAR
see also **HEAR**

Job 15. 8 Did you **overhear** the plans God made?
Jer 38.27 could do, because no one had **overheard** the conversation.

OVERLAY

1 Kgs 10.16 had each one **overlaid** with almost seven kilogrammes of gold.
10.17 made three hundred smaller shields, **overlaying** each one of
2 Chr 3. 4 The inside of the room was **overlaid** with pure gold.
3. 5 was panelled with cedar and **overlaid** with fine gold, in
3. 7 He used the gold to **overlay** the temple walls, the rafters,
4.22 the doors to the Most Holy Place were **overlaid** with gold.

OVERLOOK (1)

Num 23.28 took Balaam to the top of Mount Peor **overlooking** the desert.
Josh 15. 6 and went north of the ridge **overlooking** the Jordan Valley.
18.16 foot of the mountain that **overlooks** the Valley of Hinnom, at
18.18 and passed north of the ridge **overlooking** the Jordan Valley.
Judg 16. 3 them all the way to the top of the hill **overlooking** Hebron.
1 Sam 13.18 one went to the border **overlooking** the Valley of Zeboim and

OVERLOOK (2)

Prov 10.12 Hate stirs up trouble, but love **overlooks** all offences.
Is 65. 6 I will not **overlook** what they have done, but will repay them
Acts 17.30 God has **overlooked** the times when people did not know him,
Rom 3.25 In the past he was patient and **overlooked** people's sins;

OVERNIGHT see NIGHT

OVERPOWER

Judg 2.14 He let enemies all around **overpower** them, and the Israelites
16. 5 strong and how we can **overpower** him, tie him up, and make
2 Sam 13.14 stronger than she was, he **overpowered** her and raped her.
2 Chr 13.16 and God let the Judaeans **overpower** them.
14.13 They were **overpowered** by the Lord and his army, and the army
Job 14.20 You **overpower** a man and send him away for ever;
33. 7 I will not **overpower** you.
Is 28. 2 a rushing, **overpowering** flood, and will overwhelm the land.
Jer 20. 7 You are stronger than I am, and you have **overpowered** me.
Acts 19.16 attacked them with such violence that he **overpowered** them all.

OVERRULE

Jer 38.22 'The king's best friends misled him, they **overruled** him.

OVERRUN

Ps 105.30 Their country was **overrun** with frogs, even the palace
Is 23.13 not the Assyrians, who let the wild animals **overrun** Tyre.

OVERSEAS

Ezek 27.33 merchandise went **overseas,** You filled the needs of every nation.

OVERTAKE

Gen 19.19 the disaster will **overtake** me, and I will die before I get
Ps 69.24 let your indignation **overtake** them.
140.11 may evil **overtake** violent men and destroy them.
Jer 41.12 him with their men and **overtook** him near the large pool at
42.16 war that you fear will **overtake** you, and the hunger you

OVERTHROW

Ex 15. 7 In majestic triumph you **overthrow** your foes;
Ezra 6.12 he is to be worshipped **overthrow** any king or nation that
Job 34.25 what they do he **overthrows** them and crushes them by night.
Is 13.19 But I, the Lord, will **overthrow** Babylon as I did Sodom and
23.11 stretched out his hand over the sea and **overthrown** kingdoms.
Jer 1.10 down, to destroy and to **overthrow,** to build and to plant."
31.28 pull down, to **overthrow,** to destroy, and to demolish them,
Dan 7.24 from the earlier ones and will **overthrow** three kings.
Hag 2. 7 I will **overthrow** all the nations, and their treasures will
2.22 and earth [22] and **overthrow** kingdoms and end their power.
Zech 1.21 have come to terrify and **overthrow** the nations that
Jn 12.31 now the ruler of this world will be **overthrown.**

OVERTURN

Hag 2.22 I will **overturn** chariots and their drivers;
Mt 21.12 He **overturned** the tables of the money-changers and the stools of
Mk 11.15 He **overturned** the tables of the money-changers and the stools of
Jn 2.15 he **overturned** the tables of the money-changers and scattered their

OVERWHELM

Deut 28.65 the Lord will **overwhelm** you with anxiety, hopelessness, and
Job 22.11 so dark that you cannot see, and a flood **overwhelms** you.
Is 28. 2 a rushing, overpowering flood, and will **overwhelm** the land.
43. 2 your troubles will not **overwhelm** you.

OVERWORKED
see also **WORK**

2 Cor 6. 5 we have been **overworked** and have gone without sleep or food.

OWE

Deut 15. 1 you are to cancel the debts of those who **owe** you money.
15. 3 may collect what a foreigner **owes** you,
15. 3 you must not collect what any of your own people **owe** you.
2 Kgs 4. 1 but now a man he **owed** money to has come to take
Neh 5.11 Cancel all the debts they **owe** you—money or corn or wine
Job 22. 6 repay you the money he **owed,** you took away his clothes and
Amos 2. 8 wine which they have taken from those who **owe** them money.
Mt 18.24 one of them was brought in who **owed** him millions of pounds.
18.28 met one of his fellow-servants who **owed** him a few pounds.
18.28 'Pay back what you **owe** me!'
18.32 you the whole amount you **owed** me, just because you asked me
Lk 7.41 "There were two men who **owed** money to a money-lender,"
7.41 "One **owed** him five hundred silver coins,
7.41 and the other **owed** him fifty.
16. 5 He asked the first one, 'How much do you **owe** my master?'
16. 7 Then he asked another one, 'And you—how much do you **owe?'**
Rom 13. 7 Pay, then, what you **owe** them;
Phlm 18 done you any wrong or **owes** you anything, charge it to my
19 remind you, of course, that you **owe** your very self to me.)

OWL

Lev 11.13 eagles, **owls,** hawks, falcons;
Deut 14.12 eagles, **owls,** hawks, falcons;
Ps 102. 6 a wild bird in the desert, like an **owl** in abandoned ruins.
Is 13.21 where desert animals live and where **owls** build their nests.
14.23 I will turn Babylon into a marsh, and **owls** will live there.
34.11 **Owls** and ravens will take over the land.
34.13 and walled towns, and jackals and **owls** will live in them.
34.15 **Owls** will build their nests, lay eggs, hatch their young,
Zeph 2.14 **Owls** will live among its ruins and hoot from the windows.

OWN

Gen 12.20 country, together with his wife and everything he **owned.**
13. 1 his wife and everything he **owned,** and Lot went with him.
23. 9 your presence, so that I can **own** it as a burial-ground."
24.36 was old, and my master has given everything he **owns** to him.
25. 5 Abraham left everything he **owned** to Isaac;
31. 1 All his wealth has come from what our father **owned."**
31.21 He took everything he **owned** and left in a hurry.
32. 5 I **own** cattle, donkeys, sheep, goats, and slaves.
32.17 Who **owns** these animals in front of you?'
32.23 sent across all that he **owned,** [24] but he stayed behind,
34.10 live anywhere you wish, trade freely, and **own** property."
34.23 Won't all their livestock and everything else they **own** be ours?
38.25 "I am pregnant by the man who **owns** these things.
39. 4 he put him in charge of his house and everything he **owned.**
47. 1 Canaan with their flocks, their herds, and all that they **own.**
47.19 We will be the king's slaves, and he will **own** our land.
Ex 20.17 his cattle, his donkeys, or anything else that he **owns."**
21.28 but its **owner** is not to be punished.
21.29 of attacking people and its **owner** had been warned, but did
21.29 to be stoned, and its **owner** is to be put to death
21.30 However, if the **owner** is allowed to pay a fine to save
21.32 its owner shall pay the **owner** of the slave thirty pieces of
21.34 pay the money to the **owner** and may keep the dead animal.
21.36 habit of attacking and its **owner** did not keep it penned up,
22. 2 If he **owns** nothing, he shall be sold as a slave to
22.11 animal was not stolen, the **owner** shall accept the loss, and
22.12 but if the animal was stolen, the man must repay the **owner.**
22.14 injured or dies when its **owner** is not present, the man must
22.15 if that happens when the **owner** is present, the man need not
Lev 6. 4 he must repay the **owner** in full, plus an additional twenty

Lev	13.57	it is spreading again, and the **owner** shall burn the object.
	25.10	be restored to the original **owner** or his descendants, and
	25.13	that has been sold shall be restored to its original **owner.**
	25.23	be sold on a permanent basis, because you do not **own** it;
	25.24	the right of the original **owner** to buy it back must be
	25.28	In that year it will be returned to its original **owner.**
	25.31	the original **owner** has the right to buy them back, and they
	25.33	the houses which the Levites **own** in their cities are their
	27.24	be returned to the original **owner** or to his descendants.
	27.33	The **owner** may not arrange the animals so that the poor
Num	16.30	swallows them with all they **own,** so that they go down alive
	36. 4	is restored to its original **owners,** the property of
Deut	5.21	his cattle, his donkeys, or anything else that he **owns.'**
	14.29	Levites, since they **own** no property, and for the foreigners,
	18. 2	They are to **own** no land, as the other tribes do;
	22. 2	But if its **owner** lives a long way off
	22. 2	if you don't know who **owns** it, then take it home with
	22. 2	When its **owner** comes looking for it, give it to him.
	23.15	runs away from his **owner** and comes to you for protection,
Josh	7.15	his family and everything he **owns,** for he has brought
	7.24	donkeys, and sheep, his tent, and everything else he **owned;**
1 Sam	25. 2	town of Maon, and who **owned** land near the town of Carmel.
	25. 2	a very rich man, the **owner** of three thousand sheep and one
1 Kgs	16.24	it Samaria, after Shemer, the former **owner** of the hill.
	20. 4	he can have me and everything I **own,"** Ahab answered.
	21. 1	in Jezreel there was a vineyard **owned** by a man named Naboth.
2 Kgs	25.12	of the poorest people, who **owned** no property, and put them
Neh	5.13	and everything you **own,** and will leave you with nothing."
Job	1. 3	and **owned** seven thousand sheep, three thousand camels,
	1.10	You have always protected him and his family and everything he **owns.**
	15.28	cities and seized houses whose **owners** had fled, but war will
	15.29	nothing he **owns** will last.
	22.20	All that the wicked **own** is destroyed, and fire burns up
	24. 6	to harvest fields they don't **own,** and gather grapes in
	24.18	away by floods, and the land he **owns** is under God's curse;
	31.38	taken it from its rightful **owners—** [39] if I have eaten the
	42.12	Job **owned** fourteen thousand sheep, six thousand camels, two
Ps	37.16	little that a good man **owns** is worth more than the wealth
	60. 8	throw my sandals on Edom, as a sign that I **own** it.
	108. 9	throw my sandals on Edom, as a sign that I **own** it.
Prov	13. 7	Others pretend to be poor, but **own** a fortune.
	23.10	Never move an old boundary-mark or take over land **owned** by orphans.
	29.21	on, some day he will take over everything you **own.**
Ecc	2. 7	I **owned** more livestock than anyone else who had ever lived
	2.19	Yet he will **own** everything I have worked for, everything my
Is	1. 3	Cattle know who **owns** them, and donkeys know where their
Jer	8.10	their fields to new **owners** and their wives to other men.
	35. 9	we live in tents—and we **own** no vineyards, fields, or corn.
	39.10	of the poorest people, who **owned** no property, and he gave
	48.36	song on a flute, because everything they **owned** is gone.
	52.16	of the poorest people, who **owned** no property, and he put
Ezek	46.16	any of the land he **owns** to one of his sons as
	46.17	to him, and only he and his sons can **own** it permanently.
Zech	11. 5	Their **owners** kill them and go unpunished.
Mt	9.38	Pray to the **owner** of the harvest that he will send out
	13.52	of heaven is like the **owner** of a house who takes new
	20. 8	evening came, the **owner** told his foreman, 'Call the workers
	20.13	friend,' the **owner** answered one of them, 'I have not cheated
	21.38	the son, they said to themselves, 'This is the **owner's** son.
	21.40	"Now, when the **owner** of the vineyard comes, what will
	24.43	If the **owner** of a house knew the time when the thief
Mk	12. 4	Then the **owner** sent another slave;
	12. 5	The **owner** sent another slave, and they killed him;
	12. 7	But those tenants said to one another, 'This is the **owner's** son.
	12. 9	"What, then, will the **owner** of the vineyard do?"
	14.14	the house he enters, and say to the **owner** of the house:
Lk	10. 2	Pray to the **owner** of the harvest that he will send out
	11.22	away all the weapons the **owner** was depending on and divides
	12.15	up of the things he **owns,** no matter how rich he may
	12.39	be sure that if the **owner** of a house knew the time
	19.33	were untying the colt, its **owners** said to them, "Why are
	20.13	Then the **owner** of the vineyard said, 'What shall I do?
	20.14	saw him, they said to one another, 'This is the **owner's** son.
	20.15	"What, then, will the **owner** of the vineyard do to the tenants?"
	22.11	house that he enters, [11] and say to the **owner** of the house:
Jn	10.12	a shepherd and does not **own** the sheep, sees a wolf coming,
Acts	4.34	Those who **owned** fields or houses would sell them, bring the
	4.37	sold a field he **owned,** brought the money, and handed it
	13.19	land of Canaan and made his people the **owners** of the land.
	16.16	She earned a lot of money for her **owners** by telling fortunes.
	16.19	her **owners** realized that their chance of making money was gone,
	21.11	The **owner** of this belt will be tied up in this way
	26.14	by hitting back, like an ox kicking against its **owner's** stick.'
	27.11	what the captain and the **owner** of the ship said, and not
1 Cor	7.30	those who buy, as though they did not **own** what they bought;
2 Cor	1.22	has placed his mark of **ownership** upon us, and who has given
Gal	4. 1	while he is young, even though he really **owns** everything.
Eph	1.13	God put his stamp of **ownership** on you by giving you the
	4.30	Spirit is God's mark of **ownership** on you, a guarantee that
Rev	18.14	good things you longed to **own** have disappeared,

OX

Num	7. 3	six wagons and twelve **oxen,** a wagon for every two leaders
	7. 3	and an **ox** for each leader.
	7. 6	So Moses gave the wagons and the **oxen** to the Levites.
	7. 7	gave two wagons and four **oxen** to the Gershonites,
	7. 8	and four wagons and eight **oxen** to the Merarites.
	7. 9	Moses gave no wagons or **oxen** to the Kohathites, because the
Num	23.22	He fights for them like a wild **ox.**
	24. 8	He fights for them like a wild **ox.**
Deut	22.10	"Do not hitch an **ox** and a donkey together for ploughing.
	25. 4	"Do not muzzle an **ox** when you are using it to thresh
	33.17	has the strength of a bull, The horns of a wild **ox.**
1 Sam	11. 5	from the field with his **oxen,** and he asked, "What's wrong?
	11. 7	He took two **oxen,** cut them in pieces, and sent messengers
	11. 7	Saul and Samuel into battle will have this done to his **oxen!"**
2 Sam	6. 6	the threshing-place of Nacon, the **oxen** stumbled, and Uzzah
	24.22	Here are these **oxen** to burn as an offering on the altar;
	24.24	the threshing-place and the **oxen** for fifty pieces of silver.
1 Kgs	19.19	Elijah left and found Elisha ploughing with a team of **oxen;**
	19.20	Elisha then left his **oxen,** ran after Elijah, and said,
	19.21	went to his team of **oxen,** killed them, and cooked the meat,
1 Chr	12.40	donkeys, camels, mules, and **oxen** loaded with food—flour,
	13. 9	the threshing-place of Chidon, the **oxen** stumbled, and Uzzah
	21.23	Here are these **oxen** to burn as an offering on the altar,
Neh	5.18	Every day I served one **ox,** six of the best sheep, and
Job	1.14	ploughing the fields with the **oxen,"** he said, "and the
	24. 3	to orphans, and keep a widow's **ox** till she pays her debts.
	39. 9	Will a wild **ox** work for you?
Ps	92.10	You have made me as strong as a wild **ox;**
Prov	7.22	going with her like an **ox** on the way to be slaughtered,
	14. 4	Without any **oxen** to pull the plough your barn will be empty,
Is	30.24	The **oxen** and donkeys that plough your fields will eat
	34. 7	people will fall like wild **oxen** and young bulls, and the
Dan	4.25	will eat grass like an **ox,** and sleep in the open air,
	4.32	with wild animals, and eat grass like an **ox** for seven years.
	4.33	was driven out of human society and ate grass like an **ox.**
	5.21	donkeys, ate grass like an **ox,** and slept in the open air
Amos	6.12	Do men plough the sea with **oxen?**
Zech	1.18	In another vision I saw four **ox** horns.
Lk	13.15	of you would untie his **ox** or his donkey from the stall
	14. 5	had a son or an **ox** that happened to fall in a
	14.19	have bought five pairs of **oxen** and am on my way to
Acts	26.14	by hitting back, like an **ox** kicking against its owner's stick.'
1 Cor	9. 9	"Do not muzzle an **ox** when you are using it to
	9. 9	Now, is God concerned about **oxen?**
1 Tim	5.18	"Do not muzzle an **ox** when you are using it to

OX-GOAD

Judg	3.31	did so by killing six hundred Philistines with an **ox-goad.**
1 Sam	13.21	sharpening axes and for repairing **ox-goads,** and two coins

PACK (1)

Gen	42.25	orders to fill his brothers' **packs** with corn, to put each
	43.11	of the land in your **packs** as a present for the governor:
	46. 1	Jacob **packed** up all he had and went to Beersheba, where he
Judg	19.10	way, with their servant and two donkeys with **pack** saddles.
1 Sam	9. 7	no food left in our **packs,** and we haven't anything to give
2 Kgs	3. 9	and there was none left for the men or the **pack-animals.**
	3.17	livestock, and your **pack-animals** will have plenty to drink.'
Ezra	1. 4	silver and gold, supplies and **pack animals,** as well as
	1. 6	utensils, gold, supplies, **pack animals,** other valuables,
Ezek	12. 3	"Now, mortal man, **pack** a bundle just as a refugee would,
	12. 4	While it is still daylight, **pack** your bundle for exile, so
	12. 5	the wall of your house and take your **pack** out through it.
	12. 6	them watch you putting your **pack** on your shoulder and going
	12. 7	That day I **packed** a bundle as a refugee would, and that
	12. 7	While everyone watched, I put the **pack** on my shoulder and left.
	12.12	ruling them will shoulder his **pack** in the dark and escape
Mt	5.41	forces you to carry his **pack** one kilometre, carry it two

PACK (2)

Ps	22.16	like a **pack** of dogs they close in on me;
Mt	10.16	am sending you out just like sheep to a **pack** of wolves.

PACT

2 Chr	23. 1	He made a **pact** with five army officers:

PAGAN

Ex	34.15	when they worship their **pagan** gods and sacrifice to them,
	34.16	to be unfaithful to me and to worship their **pagan** gods.
Lev	18.24	for that is how the **pagans** made themselves unclean,
	18.24	those **pagans** who lived in the land before
	18.28	you, as it rejected the **pagans** who lived there before you.
	20.23	I am driving out those **pagans** so that you can enter the
Deut	31.16	abandon me and worship the **pagan** gods of the land they are
2 Sam	1.20	do not let the daughters of **pagans** rejoice.
1 Kgs	13. 2	serving at the **pagan** altars who offer sacrifices on you,
	14.24	who served as prostitutes at those **pagan** places of worship.
	15.12	female prostitutes serving at the **pagan** places of worship,
	15.14	did not destroy all the **pagan** places of worship, he remained
	22.43	but the **pagan** places of worship were not destroyed, and the
	22.46	female prostitutes serving at the **pagan** altars who were
2 Kgs	12. 3	However, the **pagan** places of worship were not destroyed,
	14. 4	did not tear down the **pagan** places of worship, and the
	15. 4	But the **pagan** places of worship were not destroyed, and
	15.35	But the **pagan** places of worship were not destroyed, and
	16. 4	At the **pagan** places of worship, on the hills, and under
	17. 9	They built **pagan** places of worship in all their towns, from
	17.11	burnt incense on all the **pagan** altars, following the
	17.17	sons and daughters as burnt-offerings to **pagan** gods;
	17.32	serve as priests at the **pagan** places of worship and to offer
	18. 4	He destroyed the **pagan** places of worship, broke the stone pillars,
	21. 3	He rebuilt the **pagan** places of worship that his father

2 Kgs 21. 4 He built **pagan** altars in the Temple, the place that the
23. 5 to offer sacrifices on the **pagan** altars in the cities of
23.10 Josiah also desecrated Topheth, the **pagan** place of worship
23.19 Josiah tore down all the **pagan** places of worship which had
23.20 He killed all the **pagan** priests on the altars where they served,
23.24 gods, idols, and all other **pagan** objects of worship.
2 Chr 11.15 own to serve at the **pagan** places of worship and to worship
14. 3 the foreign altars and the **pagan** places of worship, broke
14. 5 Because he abolished the **pagan** places of worship and the
15.17 did not destroy all the **pagan** places of worship in the land,
17. 6 Lord and destroyed all the **pagan** places of worship and the
20.33 but the **pagan** places of worship were not destroyed.
21.11 He even built **pagan** places of worship in the Judaean
28. 4 At the **pagan** places of worship, on the hills, and under
28.25 town in Judah, he built **pagan** places of worship, where
31. 1 and destroyed the altars and the **pagan** places of worship.
33. 3 He rebuilt the **pagan** places of worship that his father
33. 4 He built **pagan** altars in the Temple, the place that the
33.15 had placed there, and the **pagan** altars that were on the hill
33.19 the evil he did, the **pagan** places of worship and the symbols
34. 3 he began to destroy the **pagan** places of worship, the symbols
34. 5 burnt the bones of the **pagan** priests on the altars where
34. 8 and the Temple by ending **pagan** worship, King Josiah sent
Ezra 6.21 who had given up the **pagan** ways of the other people who
Ps 106.35 but they intermarried with them and adopted their **pagan** ways.
Is 27. 9 when the stones of **pagan** altars are ground up like chalk,
65. 3 They offer **pagan** sacrifices in sacred gardens
65. 3 and burn incense on **pagan** altars.
65. 4 and drink broth made from meat offered in **pagan** sacrifices.
65. 7 They have burnt incense at **pagan** hill shrines and spoken
66.17 those who purify themselves for **pagan** worship, who go in
Jer 3.23 not helped at all by our **pagan** worship on the hill-tops.
13.27 has seen you go after **pagan** gods on the hills and in
Ezek 18.12 He goes to **pagan** shrines, worships disgusting idols,
Hos 4.14 and together with them you offer **pagan** sacrifices.
4.19 wind, and they will be ashamed of their **pagan** sacrifices.
7.14 When they pray for corn and wine, they gash themselves like **pagans.**
9. 1 People of Israel, stop celebrating your festivals like **pagans.**
Zeph 1. 4 no one will even remember the **pagan** priests who serve him.
1. 9 punish all who worship like **pagans** and who steal and kill in
Mt 5.47 Even the **pagans** do that!
6. 7 of meaningless words, as the **pagans** do, who think that their
6.32 (These are the things the **pagans** are always concerned about.)
18.17 treat him as though he were a **pagan** or a tax collector.
Lk 12.30 the **pagans** of this world are always concerned about all these
22.25 "The kings of the **pagans** have power over their people,
1 Cor 5.10 Now I did not mean **pagans** who are immoral or greedy or
7.14 If this were not so, their children would be like **pagan** children;
10.20 that what is sacrificed on **pagan** altars is offered to demons,
2 Cor 6.16 How can God's temple come to terms with **pagan** idols?

PAIN

Gen 3.16 your trouble in pregnancy and your **pain** in giving birth.
35.17 When her labour **pains** were at their worst, the midwife
Num 5.24 may then cause her bitter **pain,** [25] the priest shall take
5.27 If she has committed adultery, the water will cause bitter **pain;**
Deut 28.35 The Lord will cover your legs with incurable, **painful**
Josh 23.13 or a pit and as **painful** as a whip on your back
Judg 11.35 Why must it be you that causes me **pain?**
1 Chr 4. 9 him the name Jabez, because his birth had been very **painful.**
4.10 and keep me from anything evil that might cause me **pain."**
2 Chr 21.15 You yourself will suffer a **painful** disease of the
21.18 Lord brought on the king a **painful** disease of the intestines.
Neh 9.21 never wore out, and their feet were not swollen with **pain.**
Job 6.10 would, I would leap for joy, no matter how great my **pain.**
7.13 I look for relief from my **pain.**
9.27 and try to forget my **pain,** all my suffering comes back to
14.22 He feels only the **pain** of his own body and the grief
16. 6 I say helps, and being silent does not calm my **pain.**
30.17 the **pain** that gnaws me never stops.
30.27 I am torn apart by worry and **pain;**
33.19 a man by sending sickness and filling his body with **pain.**
Ps 12. 5 "because the needy are oppressed and the persecuted groan in **pain.**
38. 3 Because of your anger, I am in great **pain;**
38. 8 my heart is troubled, and I groan with **pain.**
38.17 I am about to fall and am in constant **pain.**
69.29 But I am in **pain** and despair;
73. 4 They do not suffer **pain;**
78.41 to the test and brought **pain** to the Holy God of Israel.
116.15 How **painful** it is to the Lord when one of his people
Prov 1.27 fierce winds of trouble, and you are in **pain** and misery.
3. 8 good medicine, healing your wounds and easing your **pains.**
5. 4 is all over, she leaves you nothing but bitterness and **pain.**
20.30 Sometimes it takes a **painful** experience to make us change our ways.
Ecc 11.10 Don't let anything worry you or cause you **pain.**
Is 13. 6 Howl in **pain!**
13. 8 and overcome with pain, like the **pain** of a woman in labour.
14. 3 of Israel relief from their **pain** and suffering, and from the
17.11 There would be only trouble and incurable **pain.**
21. 3 filled me with terror and **pain,** pain like that of a woman
26.17 us cry out, as a woman in labour cries out in **pain.**
26.18 We were in **pain** and agony, but we gave birth to nothing.
38.13 night I cried out with **pain,** As if a lion were breaking
53. 3 he endured suffering and **pain.**
53. 4 should have been ours, the **pain** that we should have borne.
Jer 4.19 The **pain!**
4.19 I can't bear the **pain!**
Jer 6.24 we are seized by anguish and **pain** like a woman in labour.
13.21 You will be in **pain** like a woman giving birth.
20.16 May he hear cries of **pain** in the morning and the battle
22.23 how pitiful you'll be when **pains** strike you,
22.23 **pains** like those of a woman in
49.24 They are in **pain** and misery like a woman in labour.
50.43 He is seized by anguish, by **pain** like a woman in labour.
Lam 1.12 "No one has ever had **pain** like mine,
1.12 **Pain** that the Lord brought on me
1.13 Then he abandoned me and left me in constant **pain.**
1.18 look at me in my **pain.**
3.19 The thought of my **pain,** my homelessness, is bitter poison;
3.33 He takes no pleasure in causing us grief or **pain.**
Ezek 5.16 You will feel the **pains** of hunger like sharp arrows sent to
Hos 8.10 Soon they will writhe in **pain,** when the emperor of Assyria
Zech 9. 5 The city of Gaza will see it and suffer great **pain.**
Mt 24. 8 All these things are like the first **pains** of childbirth.
Mk 13. 8 These things are like the first **pains** of childbirth.
Lk 16.23 where he was in great **pain,** he looked up and saw Abraham,
16.24 cool my tongue, because I am in great **pain** in this fire!'
16.25 But now he is enjoying himself here, while you are in **pain.**
16.28 that they, at least, will not come to this place of **pain.'**
Rom 2. 9 There will be suffering and **pain** for all those who do what
8.22 all of creation groans with **pain,** like the pain of childbirth.
9. 2 my sorrow, how endless the **pain** in my heart [3] for my people,
2 Cor 12. 7 I was given a **painful** physical ailment, which acts as Satan's
Gal 4.19 feel the same kind of **pain** for you until Christ's nature is
4.27 cry with joy, you who never felt the **pains** of childbirth!
1 Thes 5. 3 come as suddenly as the **pains** that come upon a woman in
1 Pet 2.19 if you endure the **pain** of undeserved suffering because you are
4.12 not be surprised at the **painful** test you are suffering,
Rev 9. 5 The **pain** caused by the torture is like
9. 5 the **pain** caused by a scorpion's sting.
12. 2 to give birth, and the **pains** and suffering of childbirth
16. 2 Terrible and **painful** sores appeared on those who had the
16.10 their tongues because of their **pain,** [11] and they cursed the God
16.11 and they cursed the God of heaven for their **pains** and sores.
21. 4 will be no more death, no more grief or crying or **pain.**

PAINT

Jer 4.30 Why do you put on jewellery and **paint** your eyes?
22.14 in his house, panels it with cedar, and **paints** it red.
Ezek 23.14 carved into the wall and **painted** bright red, with sashes

PAIR

Gen 7. 2 Take with you seven **pairs** of each kind of ritually clean animal,
7. 2 but only one **pair** of each kind of unclean animal.
7. 3 Take also seven **pairs** of each kind of bird.
Ex 25.35 to be one bud below each of the three **pairs** of branches.
37.21 There was one bud below each of the three **pairs** of branches.
Is 6. 6 that he had taken from the altar with a **pair** of tongs.
Amos 2. 6 men who cannot repay even the price of a **pair** of sandals.
8. 6 even the price of a **pair** of sandals, and we'll buy him
Lk 2.24 offer a sacrifice of a **pair** of doves or two young pigeons,
14.19 said, 'I have bought five **pairs** of oxen and am on my
Rev 6. 5 Its rider held a **pair** of scales in his hand.

PALACE

Gen 12.15 so she was taken to his **palace.**
12.17 terrible diseases on him and on the people of his **palace.**
20.17 for any woman in Abimelech's **palace** to have children.
37.36 king's officers, who was the captain of the **palace** guard.
39. 1 king's officers, who was the captain of the **palace** guard.
45. 2 Egyptians heard it, and the news was taken to the king's **palace.**
45.16 When the news reached the **palace** that Joseph's brothers had come,
47.14 Joseph collected all the money and took it to the **palace.**
Ex 7.23 and went back to his **palace** without paying any attention
8. 3 it and go into your **palace,** your bedroom, your bed, the
8.24 into the king's **palace** and the houses of his officials.
10. 6 They will fill your **palaces** and the houses of all your
Num 22.18 silver and gold in his **palace,** I could not disobey the
24.13 silver and gold in your **palace,** I could not disobey the
2 Sam 5.11 logs and with carpenters and stone-masons to build a **palace.**
7. 1 David was settled in his **palace,** and the Lord kept him safe
11. 2 David got up from his nap and went to the **palace** roof.
11. 9 instead he slept at the **palace** gate with the king's guards.
11.13 instead he slept on his blanket in the **palace** guardroom.
11.27 mourning was over, David sent for her to come to the **palace;**
12.20 When he returned to the **palace,** he asked for food and ate
13. 7 So David sent word to Tamar in the **palace:**
14.24 gave orders that Absalom should not live in the **palace.**
15.16 concubines, whom he left behind to take care of the **palace.**
15.35 tell them everything you hear in the king's **palace.**
16.21 concubines whom he left behind to take care of the **palace.**
16.22 tent for Absalom on the **palace** roof, and in the sight of
19.11 be the last to help bring the king back to his **palace?**
20. 3 When David arrived at his **palace** in Jerusalem, he took
20. 3 left to take care of the **palace,** and put them under guard.
1 Kgs 1.22 She was still speaking, when Nathan arrived at the **palace.**
3. 1 he had finished building his **palace,** the Temple, and the
4. 6 In charge of the **palace** servants:
4.27 Solomon needed for himself and for all who ate in the **palace;**
7. 1 Solomon also built a **palace** for himself, and it took him
7.12 The **palace** court, the inner court of the Temple, and the
9. 1 building the Temple and the **palace** and everything else he
9.10 It took Solomon twenty years to build the Temple and his **palace.**
9.15 build the Temple and the **palace,** to fill in land on the

1 Kgs 9.24 from David's City to the **palace** Solomon built for her.
10. 4 Sheba heard Solomon's wisdom and saw the **palace** he had built.
10. 5 organization of his **palace** staff and the uniforms they wore,
10.12 in the Temple and the **palace,** and also to make harps and
11.20 by the queen in the **palace,** where he lived with the king's
14.26 the Temple and in the **palace,** including the gold shields
14.27 to the officers responsible for guarding the **palace** gates.
15.18 in the Temple and the **palace,** and sent it by some of
16. 9 in the home of Arza, who was in charge of the **palace.**
16.18 he went into the **palace's** inner fortress,
16.18 set the **palace** on fire, and died
18. 3 so Ahab called in Obadiah, who was in charge of the **palace.**
20. 6 to search your **palace** and the homes of your officials,
21. 1 Near King Ahab's **palace** in Jezreel there was a vineyard
21. 2 it is close to my **palace,** and I want to use the
22.39 including an account of his **palace** decorated with ivory and
2 Kgs 1. 2 the roof of his **palace** in Samaria and was seriously injured.
7.11 The guards announced the news, and it was reported in the **palace.**
9.30 looking down at the street from a window in the **palace.**
9.32 Two or three **palace** officials looked down at him from a window,
9.34 over her body, [34]entered the **palace,** and had a meal.
10. 5 officer in charge of the **palace** and the official in charge
11. 4 royal bodyguard and of the **palace** guards, and told them to
11. 5 on the Sabbath, one third of you are to guard the **palace;**
11.16 her, took her to the **palace,** and there at the Horse Gate
11.19 the royal bodyguard, and the **palace** guards escorted the king
11.19 from the Temple to the **palace,** followed by all the people.
11.20 was quiet, now that Athaliah had been killed in the **palace.**
12.18 of the Temple and the **palace,** and sent them all as a
14.14 temple equipment and all the **palace** treasures, and carried
15.25 Pekahiah in the **palace's** inner fortress in Samaria,
16. 8 from the Temple and the **palace** treasury and sent it as a
18.15 him all the silver in the Temple and in the **palace** treasury;
18.18 Eliakim son of Hilkiah, who was in charge of the **palace;**
19. 2 in charge of the **palace,** Shebna, the court secretary,
20. 4 the central courtyard of the **palace** the Lord told him [5]to
20.15 "What did they see in the **palace?"**
20.17 coming when everything in your **palace,** everything that your
20.18 eunuchs to serve in the **palace** of the king of Babylonia."
21.18 and was buried in the **palace** garden, the garden of Uzza, and
21.23 plotted against him and assassinated him in the **palace.**
23.12 Judah had built on the **palace** roof above King Ahaz'
24.12 and the **palace** officials, surrendered to the Babylonians.
24.13 to Babylon all the treasures in the Temple and the **palace.**
25. 9 burnt down the Temple, the **palace,** and the houses of all the
1 Chr 14. 1 logs and with stone-masons and carpenters to build a **palace.**
17. 1 King David was now living in his **palace.**
28. 1 his sons—indeed all the **palace** officials, leading soldiers,
29. 1 because this is not a **palace** for men but a temple for
2 Chr 2. 1 Lord would be worshipped, and also to build a **palace** for himself.
2. 3 King David, when you sold him cedar logs for building his **palace.**
2.12 to build a temple for the Lord and a **palace** for himself.
7.11 finished the Temple and the **palace,** successfully completing
8. 1 It took Solomon twenty years to build the Temple and his **palace.**
8.11 must not live in the **palace** of King David of Israel, because
9. 3 Sheba heard Solomon's wisdom and saw the **palace** he had built.
9. 4 organization of his **palace** staff and the uniforms they wore,
9.11 the Temple and for his **palace,** and to make harps and lyres
12. 9 took the treasures from the Temple and from the **palace.**
12.10 to the officers responsible for guarding the **palace** gates.
16. 2 of the Temple and the **palace** and sent it to Damascus, to
19. 1 King Jehoshaphat of Judah returned safely to his **palace**
21.17 invaded Judah, looted the royal **palace,** and carried off as
23. 5 third will guard the royal **palace,** and the rest will be
23.15 her, took her to the **palace,** and there at the Horse Gate
23.20 that brought the king from the Temple to the **palace.**
25.24 by the descendants of Obed Edom, and the **palace** treasures.
28. 7 King Ahaz' son Maaseiah, the **palace** administrator Azrikam,
28.21 gold from the Temple, the **palace,** and the homes of the
33.20 and was buried at the **palace,** and his son Amon succeeded him
33.24 plotted against him and assassinated him in the **palace.**
36. 7 of the Temple and put them in his **palace** in Babylon.
36.19 the city, with all its **palaces** and its wealth, and broke
Neh 3.25 the tower of the upper **palace** near the court of the guard;
12.37 to David's City, past David's **palace,** and back to the wall
Esth 1. 5 whole week and was held in the gardens of the royal **palace.**
1. 8 had given orders to the **palace** servants that everyone could
1. 9 Meanwhile, inside the royal **palace** Queen Vashti was giving
2. 8 was put in the royal **palace** in the care of Hegai, who
2. 9 girls specially chosen from the royal **palace** to serve her.
2.13 the harem to the **palace,** she could wear whatever she wanted.
2.16 Esther was brought to King Xerxes in the royal **palace.**
2.21 Mordecai held office in the **palace,** Bigthana and Teresh,
2.21 two of the **palace** eunuchs who guarded the entrance to
4. 2 and bitterly, [2]until he came to the entrance of the **palace.**
4. 5 called Hathach, one of the **palace** eunuchs appointed as her
4. 6 Mordecai in the city square at the entrance of the **palace.**
4.13 than any other Jew just because you are in the royal **palace.**
5. 1 the inner courtyard of the **palace,** facing the throne room.
5. 9 at the entrance of the **palace,** and when Mordecai did not
5.13 I see that Jew Mordecai sitting at the entrance of the **palace."**
6. 2 Bigthana and Teresh, the two **palace** eunuchs who had guarded
6. 4 "Are any of my officials in the **palace?"**
6.10 You will find him sitting at the entrance of the **palace."**
6.12 went back to the **palace** entrance while Haman hurried home,
6.14 they were still talking, the **palace** eunuchs arrived in a
7. 7 fury, left the room, and went outside to the **palace** gardens.
7. 8 the queen right here in front of me, in my own **palace?"**
8.15 Mordecai left the **palace,** wearing royal robes of blue and white,
9. 4 a powerful man in the **palace** and was growing more powerful.
Job 3.14 sleeping like the kings and rulers who rebuilt ancient **palaces.**
Ps 45. 8 musicians entertain you in **palaces** decorated with ivory.
45.13 The princess is in the **palace**—how beautiful she is!
45.15 With joy and gladness they come and enter the king's **palace.**
101. 6 are faithful to God and will let them live in my **palace.**
101. 7 No liar will live in my **palace;**
105.30 overrun with frogs, even the **palace** was filled with them.
122. 7 May there be peace inside your walls and safety in your **palaces."**
144.12 like stately pillars which adorn the corners of a **palace.**
Prov 30.28 hold one in your hand, but you can find them in **palaces.**
Song 1. 5 Kedar, but beautiful as the curtains in Solomon's **palace.**
Is 13.22 The towers and **palaces** will echo with the cries of
25. 2 The **palaces** which our enemies built are gone for ever.
32.14 Even the **palace** will be abandoned
34.13 grow up in all the **palaces** and walled towns, and jackals and
36. 3 official in charge of the **palace,** Eliakim son of Hilkiah;
37. 2 in charge of the **palace,** Shebna, the court secretary,
39. 4 "What did they see in the **palace?"**
39. 6 coming when everything in your **palace,** everything that your
39. 7 eunuchs to serve in the **palace** of the king of Babylonia."
Jer 9.21 Death has come in through our windows and entered our **palaces;**
17.27 Fire will burn down the **palaces** of Jerusalem, and no one
21.14 I will set your **palace** on fire, and the fire will burn
22. 1 me to go to the **palace** of the king of Judah, the
22. 4 through the gates of this **palace** in chariots and on horses.
22. 5 then I swear to you that this **palace** will fall into ruins.
22. 6 "To me, Judah's royal **palace** is as beautiful as the land
26.10 they hurried from the royal **palace** to the Temple and took
27.18 Temple and in the royal **palace** to be taken to Babylonia."
27.21 are left in the Temple and in the royal **palace** in Jerusalem:
29. 2 King Jehoiachin, his mother, the **palace** officials, the
30.18 Jerusalem will be rebuilt, and its **palace** restored.
32. 2 and I was locked up in the courtyard of the royal **palace.**
33. 4 of Jerusalem and the royal **palace** of Judah will be torn down
34.18 of Jerusalem, together with the **palace** officials, the
36.12 he went to the royal **palace,** to the room of the court
36.22 king was sitting in his winter **palace** in front of the fire.
37.17 me, and there in the **palace** he asked me privately, "Is
37.21 King Zedekiah ordered me to be locked up in the **palace** courtyard.
38. 6 Prince Malchiah's well, which was in the **palace** courtyard.
38. 7 who worked in the royal **palace,** heard that they had put me
38.11 with the men to the **palace** storeroom and got some worn-out
38.22 women left in Judah's royal **palace** being led out to the king
38.28 I was kept in the **palace** courtyard until the day Jerusalem
39. 8 Babylonians burnt down the royal **palace** and the houses of
39.14 king of Babylonia, [14]brought me from the **palace** courtyard.
39.15 was still imprisoned in the **palace** courtyard, the Lord told
49.27 Damascus on fire and will burn down King Benhadad's **palaces.**
52.13 burnt down the Temple, the **palace,** and the houses of all the
Lam 2. 5 He has left her forts and **palaces** in ruins.
Ezek 43. 8 thresholds and door-posts of their **palace** right against the
Dan 4. 4 "I was living comfortably in my **palace,** enjoying great prosperity.
4.29 the roof of his royal **palace** in Babylon, [30]he said, "Look
5. 5 the plaster wall of the **palace,** where the light from the
6.18 the king returned to the **palace** and spent a sleepless night,
Hos 8.14 people of Israel have built **palaces,** but they have forgotten
8.14 fire that will burn down their **palaces** and their cities."
Amos 1. 4 will send fire upon the **palace** built by King Hazael and I
3. 9 Announce to those who live in the **palaces** of Egypt and Ashdod:
8. 3 day the songs in the **palace** will become cries of mourning.
Nah 2. 6 the **palace** is filled with terror.
Mt 11. 8 People who dress like that live in **palaces!**
26. 3 elders met together in the **palace** of Caiaphas, the High Priest,
27.27 took Jesus into the governor's **palace,** and the whole company
Mk 15.16 courtyard of the governor's **palace** and called together the rest
Lk 7.25 who dress like that and live in luxury are found in **palaces!**
Jn 18.28 Jesus was taken from Caiaphas' house to the governor's **palace.**
18.28 did not go inside the **palace,** for they wanted to keep
18.33 Pilate went back into the **palace** and called Jesus.
19. 9 He went back into the **palace** and asked Jesus, "Where do
Acts 12.20 the man in charge of the **palace,** that he should help them.
Phil 1.13 As a result, the whole **palace guard** and all the others
4.22 send greetings, especially those who belong to the Emperor's **palace.**

PALE

Is 29.22 longer, and your faces will no longer be **pale** with shame.
Jer 30. 6 Why is everyone so **pale?**
Dan 5. 6 He turned **pale** and was so frightened that his knees began
5. 9 distress King Belshazzar grew even **paler,** and his noblemen
5.10 Please do not be so disturbed and look so **pale.**
7.28 that I turned **pale,** and I kept everything to myself.
Joel 2. 6 every face turns **pale.**
Nah 2.10 faces grow **pale.**
Rev 6. 8 I looked, and there was a **pale-coloured** horse.

PALM (1)

Ex 15.27 where there were twelve springs and seventy **palm-trees;**
Lev 23.40 fruit from your trees, take **palm** branches and the branches
Num 24. 6 Like long rows of **palms** Or gardens beside a river,
33. 9 were twelve springs of water and seventy **palm-trees** there.
Deut 34. 3 that reaches from Zoar to Jericho, the city of **palm-trees.**
Judg 1.16 from Jericho, the city of **palm-trees,** into the barren
3.13 Israel and captured Jericho, the city of **palm-trees.**
4. 5 to sit under a certain **palm-tree** between Ramah and Bethel in
1 Kgs 6.29 with carved figures of winged creatures, **palm-trees,**
6.32 with carved figures of winged creatures, **palm-trees,**
6.32 and the **palm-trees** were covered with gold.
6.35 carved figures of winged creatures, **palm-trees,** and flowers,

1 Kgs 7.36 lions, and **palm-trees,** wherever there was space for them,
2 Chr 3. 5 which were worked designs of **palm-trees** and chain patterns.
28.15 to Judaean territory at Jericho, the city of **palm-trees.**
Neh 8.15 branches from pines, olives, myrtles, **palms,** and other trees
Ps 92.12 The righteous will flourish like **palm-trees;**
Song 7. 7 are as graceful as a **palm-tree,** and your breasts are
7. 8 I will climb the **palm-tree** and pick its fruit.
Ezek 40.16 There were **palm-trees** carved on the inner walls
40.22 the windows, and the carved **palm-trees** were like those in
40.26 There were **palm-trees** carved on the inner walls
40.31 faced the other courtyard, and **palm-trees** were carved on the
40.34 **Palm-trees** were carved on the walls along the passage.
40.37 **Palm-trees** were carved on the walls along the passage.
41.18 with carvings [18]of **palm-trees** and winged creatures.
41.18 **Palm-trees** alternated with creatures, one following the other,
41.19 that was turned towards the **palm-tree** on one side, and a
41.25 There were **palm-trees** and winged creatures carved on the
41.26 were windows, and the walls were decorated with **palm-trees.**
Jn 12.13 So they took branches of **palm-trees** and went out to meet him,
Rev 7. 9 dressed in white robes and holding **palm** branches in their hands.

PALM (2)

Lev 14.15 and pour it in the **palm** of his own left hand,
14.17 oil that is in the **palm** of his hand and some of
14.18 oil that is in the **palm** of his hand on the man's
14.26 of the oil into the **palm** of his own left hand
14.29 oil that is in his **palm** he shall put on the man's
Is 49.16 I have written your name on the **palms** of my hands.

PAN

[BAKING-PANS, FIRE-PAN]

Ex 8. 3 and your people, and even into your ovens and **baking-pans.**
12.34 the people filled their **baking-pans** with unleavened dough,
27. 3 Make **pans** for the greasy ashes, and make shovels, bowls,
27. 3 the greasy ashes, and make shovels, bowls, hooks, and **firepans.**
38. 3 **pans,** the shovels, the bowls,
38. 3 the hooks, and the **firepans.**
Lev 2. 7 is bread cooked in a **pan,** it is to be made of
7. 9 oven or prepared in a **pan** or on a griddle belongs to
10. 1 and Abihu, each took his **fire-pan,** put live coals in it,
16.12 he shall take a **fire-pan** full of burning coals from the
Num 4.14 **firepans,** hooks, shovels, and basins.
16. 6 and your followers take **firepans,** put live coals and incense
16.17 of you will take his **firepan,** put incense on it, and then
16.18 So every man took his **firepan,** put live coals and incense
16.37 priest to remove the bronze **firepans** from the remains of the
16.37 scatter the coals from the **firepans** somewhere else,
16.37 because the **firepans** are holy.
16.38 So take the **firepans** of these men who were put to death
16.39 Eleazar the priest took the **firepans** and had them beaten into
16.46 to Aaron, "Take your **firepan,** put live coals from the altar
16.47 Aaron obeyed, took his **firepan** and ran into the middle of
2 Sam 13. 9 emptied them out of the **pan** for him to eat, but he
1 Kgs 7.50 for incense, and the **pans** used for carrying live coals;
2 Kgs 25.15 the small bowls and the **pans** used for carrying live coals.
2 Chr 4.22 for incense, and the **pans** used for carrying live coals.
35.13 offerings in pots, cauldrons, and **pans,** and quickly
Jer 52.19 the small bowls, the **pans** used for carrying live coals, the
Ezek 4. 3 Take an iron **pan** and set it up like a wall between

PANEL

1 Kgs 6.15 covered with cedar **panels** from the floor to the ceiling,
6.18 The cedar **panels** were decorated with carvings of gourds
6.20 The altar was covered with cedar **panels.**
7. 7 had cedar **panels** from the floor to the rafters.
7.28 They were made of square **panels** which were set in frames,
7.29 figures of lions, bulls, and winged creatures on the **panels;**
7.32 they were under the **panels,** and the axles were of one piece
7.35 its supports and the **panels** were of one piece with the cart.
7.36 The supports and **panels** were decorated with figures
2 Chr 3. 5 The main room was **panelled** with cedar and overlaid with fine gold,
Ps 74. 6 They smashed all the wooden **panels** with their axes
Song 8. 9 she is a gate, we will protect her with **panels** of cedar.
Jer 22.14 puts windows in his house, **panels** it with cedar, and paints
Ezek 41.16 Most Holy Place [16]were all **panelled** with wood from the

PANIC

Ex 14.24 and cloud at the Egyptian army and threw them into a **panic.**
23.28 I will throw your enemies into a **panic;**
Deut 7.20 He will even cause **panic** among them and will destroy
7.23 in your power and make them **panic** until they are destroyed.
20. 3 Do not be afraid of your enemies, or lose courage, or **panic.**
Josh 10.10 The Lord made the Amorites **panic** at the sight of Israel's army.
24.12 advanced, I threw them into **panic** in order to drive out the
Judg 8.12 and captured them, and caused their whole army to **panic.**
20.41 Benjaminites were thrown into a **panic** because they realized
1 Sam 5. 9 the Lord punished that city too and caused a great **panic.**
5.11 There was **panic** throughout the city because God was
7.10 They became completely confused and fled in **panic.**
14.15 the earth shook, and there was great **panic.**
2 Chr 20.22 to sing, the Lord threw the invading armies into a **panic.**
Is 22. 5 This is a time of **panic,** defeat, and confusion in the
Jer 51.32 The Babylonian soldiers have **panicked.**

PANT

Ps 119.131 In my desire for your commands I **pant** with open mouth.
Jer 14. 6 stand on the hill-tops and **pant** for breath like jackals;

PAPER

Deut 24. 1 So he writes out divorce **papers,** gives them to her, and
24. 3 he also writes out divorce **papers,** gives them to her, and
Is 50. 1 Where, then, are the **papers** of divorce?
2 Jn 12 but I would rather not do it with **paper** and ink;

PARABLE

A story which teaches spiritual truth. It was often used by Jesus.

Ezek 17. 2 "tell the Israelites a **parable** [3]to let them know what I,
17.12 "Ask these rebels if they know what the **parable** means.
24. 3 Tell my rebellious people this **parable** that I, the Sovereign Lord,
Mt 13. 3 He used **parables** to tell them many things.
13.10 "Why do you use **parables** when you talk to the people?"
13.13 The reason I use **parables** in talking to them is that
13.18 "Listen, then, and learn what the **parable** of the sower means.
13.24 Jesus told them another **parable:**
13.31 Jesus told them another **parable:**
13.33 Jesus told them still another **parable:**
13.34 Jesus used **parables** to tell all these things to the crowds;
13.34 he would not say a thing to them without using a **parable.**
13.35 said come true, "I will use **parables** when I speak to them;
13.36 said, "Tell us what the **parable** about the weeds in the
13.53 When Jesus finished telling these **parables,** he left that
21.33 "Listen to another **parable,"** Jesus said.
21.45 the Pharisees heard Jesus' **parables** and knew that he was talking
22. 1 Jesus again used **parables** in talking to the people.
Mk 3.23 So Jesus called them to him and spoke to them in **parables:**
4. 2 He used **parables** to teach them many things, saying to them:
4.10 with the twelve disciples and asked him to explain the **parables.**
4.11 all things by means of **parables,** [12]so that, 'They may look
4.13 Then Jesus asked them, "Don't you understand this **parable?**
4.13 How, then, will you ever understand any **parable?**
4.30 "What **parable** shall we use to explain it?
4.33 preached his message to the people, using many other **parables**
4.34 speak to them without using **parables,** but when he was alone
12. 1 Then Jesus spoke to them in **parables:**
12.12 because they knew that he had told this **parable** against them.
Lk 5.36 Jesus also told them this **parable:**
6.39 And Jesus told them this **parable:**
8. 4 and when a great crowd gathered, Jesus told this **parable:**
8. 9 disciples asked Jesus what this **parable** meant, [10]and he answered,
8.10 it comes by means of **parables,** so that they may look
8.11 "This is what the **parable** means:
12.16 Then Jesus told them this **parable:**
12.41 Peter said, "Lord, does this **parable** apply to us, or do
13. 6 Then Jesus told them this **parable:**
14. 7 the best places, so he told this **parable** to all of them:
15. 3 So Jesus told them this **parable:**
18. 1 Jesus told his disciples a **parable** to teach them that they
18. 9 Jesus also told this **parable** to people who were sure of
19.11 were listening to this, Jesus continued and told them a **parable.**
20. 9 Then Jesus told the people this **parable:**
20.19 because they knew that he had told this **parable** against them;
21.29 Then Jesus told them this **parable:**
Jn 10. 6 Jesus told them this **parable,** but they did not understand what

AV **PARACLETE** see **HELPER (2)**

PARADE

Is 45.20 The people who **parade** with their idols of wood and pray to

PARADISE

Lk 23.43 "I promise you that today you will be in **Paradise** with me."
2 Cor 12. 3 this man was snatched to **Paradise** (again, I do not know

AV **PARADISE** see **GARDEN**

PARALYSE

1 Sam 25.37 He suffered a stroke and was completely **paralysed.**
1 Kgs 13. 4 once the king's arm became **paralysed** so that he couldn't
Ezek 3.26 I will **paralyse** your tongue so that you won't be able to
Mt 4.24 and epileptics, and **paralytics**—and Jesus healed them all.
9. 2 some people brought to him a **paralysed** man, lying on a bed.
9. 2 faith they had, he said to the **paralysed** man, "Courage, my
9. 6 So he said to the **paralysed** man, "Get up, pick up your
12.10 where there was a man who had a **paralysed** hand.
12.13 the man with the **paralysed** hand, "Stretch out your hand."
Mk 2. 3 when four men arrived, carrying a **paralysed** man to Jesus.
2. 5 Jesus said to the **paralysed** man, "My son, your sins are
2. 9 easier to say to this **paralysed** man, 'Your sins are forgiven',
2.10 So he said to the **paralysed** man, [11]"I tell you, get up,
3. 1 synagogue, where there was a man who had a **paralysed** hand.
Lk 5.18 Some men came carrying a **paralysed** man on a bed, and
5.24 So he said to the **paralysed** man, "I tell you, get up,
6. 6 A man was there whose right hand was **paralysed.**
Jn 5. 3 lying in the porches—the blind, the lame, and the **paralysed.**
Acts 8. 7 a loud cry, and many **paralysed** and lame people were healed.
9.33 man named Aeneas, who was **paralysed** and had not been able to

PARAN

Desert area in the Sinai peninsula.

Gen 21.20 in the wilderness of **Paran** and became a skilful hunter.
Num 10.12 The cloud came to rest in the wilderness of **Paran.**
12.16 left Hazeroth and set up camp in the wilderness of **Paran.**
13. 3 and from the wilderness of **Paran** he sent out leaders, as
13.26 community of Israel at Kadesh in the wilderness of **Paran.**
Deut 1. 1 Suph, between the town of **Paran** on one side and the towns
33. 2 the sun over Edom and shone on his people from Mount **Paran.**
1 Sam 25. 1 After this, David went to the wilderness of **Paran.**
1 Kgs 11.18 Midian and went to **Paran,** where some other men joined them.
Hab 3. 3 the holy God is coming from the hills of **Paran.**

PARCHMENT

2 Tim 4.13 the books too, and especially the ones made of **parchment.**

PARDON

Gen 40.13 the king will release you, **pardon** you, and restore you to
Ex 23.21 for I have sent him, and he will not **pardon** such rebellion.
Job 7.21 Can't you **pardon** the wrong I do?
Ps 32. 1 Happy are those whose sins are forgiven, whose wrongs are **pardoned.**
85. 2 You have forgiven your people's sins and **pardoned** all their wrongs.
Ecc 10. 4 serious wrongs may be **pardoned** if you keep calm.
Jer 18.23 Do not forgive their evil or **pardon** their sin.
Rom 4. 7 "Happy are those whose wrongs are forgiven, whose sins are **pardoned!**

PARENT

Ex 34. 7 and fourth generation for the sins of their **parents."**
Num 14.18 third and fourth generation for the sins of their **parents.'**
Deut 21.13 stay in your home and mourn for her **parents** for a month;
21.18 who will not obey his **parents,** even though they punish him.
21.19 His **parents** are to take him before the leaders of the
22.15 "If this happens, the girl's **parents** are to take the
24.16 **"Parents** are not to be put to death for crimes
24.16 to be put to death for crimes committed by their **parents;**
33. 9 They showed greater loyalty to you Than to **parents,**
Judg 14. 4 His **parents** did not know that it was the Lord who was
14. 6 But he did not tell his **parents** what he had done.
1 Sam 22. 4 So David left his **parents** with the king of Moab, and they
2 Sam 19.37 Then let me go back home and die near my **parents'** grave.
2 Kgs 14. 6 **"Parents** are not to be put to death for crimes committed by
14. 6 to be put to death for crimes committed by their **parents;**
2 Chr 25. 4 **"Parents** are not to be put to death for crimes committed by
25. 4 to be put to death for crimes committed by their **parents;**
Esth 2. 7 At the death of her **parents,** Mordecai had adopted her and
Prov 4. 3 only a little boy, my **parents'** only son, [4] my father would
19.14 house and money from his **parents,** but only the Lord can give
20.20 If you curse your **parents,** your life will end like a
28.24 wrong to steal from his **parents** is no better than a common
Is 45.10 dare to say to his **parents,** "Why did you make me like
Jer 16. 3 to the children who are born here and to their **parents.**
31.29 'The **parents** ate the sour grapes, But the children got the
32.18 but you also punish people for the sins of their **parents.**
Ezek 5.10 As a result, **parents** in Jerusalem will eat their children,
5.10 and children will eat their **parents.**
18. 2 'The **parents** ate the sour grapes, But the children got the
18. 4 me, the life of the **parent** as well as that of the
22. 7 No one in the city honours his **parents.**
44.25 it is one of his **parents,** one of his children or a
Amos 8.10 and you will be like **parents** mourning for their only son.
Mt 10.21 will turn against their **parents** and have them put to death.
Mk 13.12 will turn against their **parents** and have them put to death.
Lk 2.27 When the **parents** brought the child Jesus into the Temple to
2.41 Every year the **parents** of Jesus went to Jerusalem for the
2.43 His **parents** did not know this;
2.48 His **parents** were astonished when they saw him, and his mother
8.56 Her **parents** were astounded, but Jesus commanded them not to
18.29 or wife or brothers or **parents** or children for the sake of
21.16 be handed over by your **parents,** your brothers, your relatives,
Jn 3. 6 born physically of human **parents,** but he is born spiritually of
9. 2 Was it his own or his **parents'** sin?"
9. 3 blindness has nothing to do with his sins or his **parents'**
9.18 until they called his **parents** [19] and asked them, "Is this your
9.20 His **parents** answered, "We know that he is our son,
9.22 His **parents** said this because they were afraid of the Jewish
9.23 That is why his **parents** said, "He is old enough;
Rom 1.30 they disobey their **parents;**
2 Cor 12.14 have to provide for their **parents,**
12.14 but **parents** should provide for their children.
Eph 6. 1 Christian duty to obey your **parents,** for this is the right
6. 4 **Parents,** do not treat your children in such a way as to
Col 3.20 duty to obey your **parents** always, for that is what pleases
3.21 **Parents,** do not irritate your children, or they will become discouraged.
1 Tim 5. 4 in this way repay their **parents** and grandparents, because that is
2 Tim 3. 2 they will be insulting, disobedient to their **parents,** ungrateful, and
Heb 11.23 was faith that made the **parents** of Moses hide him for three
1 Pet 1.23 again as the children of a **parent** who is immortal, not

PART (1)

Gen 4. 4 killed it, and gave the best **parts** of it as an offering.
12. 9 place to place, going towards the southern **part** of Canaan.
13. 1 of Egypt to the southern **part** of Canaan with his wife and
Gen 13. 9 Choose any **part** of the land you want.
18. 1 his tent during the hottest **part** of the day, [2] he looked up
20. 1 from Mamre to the southern **part** of Canaan and lived between
21.10 woman must not get any **part** of your wealth, which my son
24.62 Who Sees Me" and was staying in the southern **part** of Canaan.
27.16 goats on his arms and on the hairless **part** of his neck.
33.19 He bought that **part** of the field from the descendants of
47. 6 settle in the region of Goshen, the best **part** of the land.
49. 6 talks, Nor will I take **part** in their meetings, For they
Ex 15. 8 the deepest **part** of the sea became solid.
16.20 of them did not listen to Moses and saved **part** of it.
28.27 attach them to the lower **part** of the front of the two
29.13 the internal organs, the best **part** of the liver, and the two
29.22 the internal organs, the best **part** of the liver, the two
29.26 This **part** of the animal will be yours,
30.34 to Moses, "Take an equal **part** of each of the following
30.36 Beat **part** of it into a fine powder, take it into the
34. 3 no one is to be seen on any **part** of the mountain;
34.25 until the following morning any **part** of the animal killed at
39.20 attached them to the lower **part** of the front of the two
Lev 1.12 on the fire all the **parts,** including the head and the fat.
2. 9 The priest will take **part** of it as a token that it
2.16 The priest will burn that **part** of the meal and oil that
3. 3 altar [3] and present the following **parts** of the animal as a
3. 4 and the fat on them, and the best **part** of the liver.
3. 9 altar [9] and present the following **parts** of the animal as a
3.10 and the fat on them, and the best **part** of the liver.
3.14 and present the following **parts** as a food-offering to the Lord:
3.15 and the fat on them, and the best **part** of the liver.
4. 9 and the fat on them, and the best **part** of the liver.
6.16 given it to the priests as their **part** of the food-offerings.
6.23 No **part** of a grain-offering that a priest makes may be eaten;
7. 4 and the fat on them, and the best **part** of the liver.
7.14 He shall present one **part** of each kind of bread as a
7.29 offers a fellowship-offering must bring **part** of it as a
7.35 This is the **part** of the food offered to the Lord that
7.36 the people of Israel to give them this **part** of the offering.
8.16 the internal organs, the best **part** of the liver, and the
8.25 the internal organs, the best **part** of the liver, the kidneys
8.29 It was Moses' **part** of the ordination ram.
9.10 the kidneys, and the best **part** of the liver, just as the
9.19 Aaron put the fat **parts** of the bull and the ram [20] on
9.24 consumed the burnt-offering and the fat **parts** on the altar.
10.13 it is the **part** that belongs to you and your sons from
10.14 and your children as the **part** that belongs to you from the
10.15 These **parts** belong to you and your children for ever, just
11.40 And if anyone eats any **part** of the animal, he must wash
13.45 hair uncombed, cover the lower **part** of his face, and call
21. 1 himself ritually unclean by taking **part** in the funeral
21. 5 "No priest shall shave any **part** of his head or trim his
24. 9 this is a very holy **part** of the food offered to the
25.51 He must refund a **part** of the purchase price
26. 9 I will keep my **part** of the covenant that I made with
27.16 If a man dedicates **part** of his land to the Lord, the
Num 13.17 from here into the southern **part** of the land of Canaan and
13.22 went first into the southern **part** of the land and came to
13.29 Amalekites live in the southern **part** of the land;
18. 8 to your descendants as the **part** assigned to you for ever.
18.20 can be inherited, and no **part** of the land of Israel will
18.30 you have presented the best **part,** you may keep the rest,
18.32 by eating any of the gifts before the best **part** is offered;
21. 1 of Arad in the southern **part** of Canaan heard that the
22.41 from where Balaam could see a **part** of the people of Israel.
31.27 was taken into two equal **parts,**
31.27 one **part** for the soldiers
31.27 and the other **part** for the rest of the community.
31.28 From the **part** that belongs to the soldiers, withhold as
31.30 From the **part** given to the rest of the people, take one
Deut 3.12 near the River Arnon and **part** of the hill-country of Gilead,
3.16 the River Jabbok, **part** of which formed the Ammonite border.
19. 2 divide the territory into three **parts,** each with a
23.13 Carry a stick as **part** of your equipment, so that when
26. 2 in a basket the first **part** of each crop that you harvest
26.10 to the Lord the first **part** of the harvest that he has
34. 3 the southern **part** of Judah;
Josh 1. 7 Do not neglect any **part** of it and you will succeed wherever
7. 1 to the clan of Zerah, a **part** of the tribe of Judah.)
13.15 Moses had given a **part** of the land to the families of
13.24 Moses had also given a **part** of the land to the families
13.29 Moses had given a **part** of the land to the families of
15. 1 of Judah received a **part** of the land described as follows:
15.13 As the Lord commanded Joshua, **part** of the territory of
17. 1 A **part** of the land west of the Jordan was assigned to
17. 4 well as our male relatives, a **part** of the land to possess."
17.14 you given us only one **part** of the land to possess as
18. 5 The land will be divided among them in seven **parts;**
18. 9 divided it into seven **parts,** making a list of the towns.
18.10 the remaining tribes of Israel a certain **part** of the land.
19. 9 was larger than was needed, **part** of its territory was given
19.49 Joshua son of Nun a **part** of the land as his own.
19.51 tribes of Israel assigned these **parts** of the land by drawing
23. 6 Do not neglect any **part** of it, [7] and then you will not
24.28 away, and everyone returned to his own **part** of the land.
Judg 2. 9 was buried in his own **part** of the land at Timnath Serah
6.35 throughout the territory of both **parts** of Manasseh to call
7.23 Naphtali, Asher, and both **parts** of Manasseh were called out,
1 Sam 1. 1 to the family of Tohu, a **part** of the clan of Zuph.
2.29 fatten themselves on the best **parts** of all the sacrifices my
9. 1 to the family of Becorath, a **part** of the clan of Aphiah.
23.19 Horesh on Mount Hachilah, in the southern **part** of the Judaean wilderness.

1 Sam 23.24 valley in the southern **part** of the Judaean wilderness.
27.10 had gone to the southern **part** of Judah or to the territory
30.14 the Cherethites in the southern **part** of Judah and the
30.26 returned to Ziklag, he sent **part** of the loot to his friends,
30.27 in Ramah in the southern **part** of Judah, and to the people
2 Sam 4. 2 (Beeroth is counted as **part** of Benjamin.
8.12 and Amalek—as well as **part** of the loot he had taken
13.24 Will you and your officials come and take **part** in the festivities?"
24. 7 and finally to Beersheba, in the southern **part** of Judah.
1 Kgs 8.64 he also consecrated the central **part** of the courtyard, the
10.18 **Part** of it was covered with ivory and the rest of it
13.34 This sin on his **part** brought about the ruin and total
18. 6 They agreed on which **part** of the land each one would explore,
2 Kgs 19.23 and that you reached the deepest **parts** of the forests.
22.14 Huldah, a prophet who lived in the newer **part** of Jerusalem.
1 Chr 5.10 and occupied their land in the eastern **part** of Gilead.
27. 2 the clan of Perez, a **part** of the tribe of Judah)
27. 2 the clan of Zerah, a **part** of the tribe of Judah)
2 Chr 4. 6 be used to rinse the **parts** of the animals that were burnt
7. 7 Solomon consecrated the central **part** of the courtyard,
9.17 **Part** of it was covered with ivory and the rest of it
20.34 of Hanani, which is a **part** of The History of the Kings
28.24 the Temple and set up altars in every **part** of Jerusalem.
31. 2 the fellowship-offerings, taking **part** in the temple worship,
31. 2 giving praise and thanks in the various **parts** of the Temple.
32. 5 filled in on the east side of the old **part** of Jerusalem.
34.22 Huldah, a prophet who lived in the newer **part** of Jerusalem.
Neh 2.16 or anyone else who would be taking **part** in the work.
3.25 (This was near that **part** of the city called Ophel, where the
8.18 to the last they read a **part** of God's Law every day.
11.21 temple workmen lived in the **part** of Jerusalem called Ophel
Esth 6. 2 The **part** they read included the account of how Mordecai
Job 42.12 The Lord blessed the last **part** of Job's life even more
Ps 16. 4 I will not take **part** in their sacrifices;
22.27 From every **part** of the world they will turn to him;
69.27 don't let them have any **part** in your salvation.
139.13 You created every **part** of me;
141. 4 May I never take **part** in their feasts.
Prov 9.14 a seat in the highest **part** of the town, [15]and calls out
12. 9 living than to play the **part** of a great man but go
17. 2 worthless son and receive a **part** of the inheritance.
Ecc 9. 6 They will never again take **part** in anything that happens in
Is 8. 9 Listen, you distant **parts** of the earth.
14.15 brought down to the deepest **part** of the world of the dead.
24.16 From the most distant **parts** of the world we will hear
37.24 and that you reached the deepest **parts** of the forests.
43. 6 return from distant lands, from every **part** of the world.
44.15 A man uses **part** of a tree for fuel
44.15 and **part** of it for making an idol.
44.15 With one **part** he builds a fire to warm himself and bake
44.15 with the other **part** he makes a god and worships it.
56. 3 cannot have children, he can never be **part** of God's people.
56. 6 to those foreigners who become **part** of his people, who love
Jer 12.16 they will also be a **part** of my people and will prosper.
44. 1 and Memphis, and in the southern **part** of the country.
Ezek 5. 1 Then weigh the hair on scales and divide it into three **parts.**
16.61 you, even though this was not **part** of my covenant with you.
32.23 graves are in the deepest **parts** of the world of the dead.
45. 1 each tribe a share, one **part** is to be dedicated to the
45. 4 It will be a holy **part** of the country, set aside for
46.16 will belong to that son as a **part** of his family property.
47. 1 down from under the south **part** of the temple past the south
48.14 the Lord is the best **part** of all the land, and none
48.15 The **part** of the special area that is left, twelve and a
Dan 2.33 of iron, and its feet **partly** of iron and partly of clay.
2.41 that the feet and the toes were **partly** clay and partly iron.
2.42 The toes—**partly** iron and partly clay—mean that
2.42 part of the empire will be strong and **part** of it weak.
11. 4 his empire will break up and be divided into four **parts.**
Zeph 1.10 hear wailing in the newer **part** of the city and a great
1.11 that live in the lower **part** of the city, because all the
Zech 9. 7 All the survivors will become **part** of my people and be like
9. 7 Ekron will become **part** of my people, as the Jebusites did.
11. 4 said to me, "Act the **part** of the shepherd of a flock
11.15 me, "Once again act the **part** of a shepherd, this time a
Mt 5.29 for you to lose a **part** of your body than to have
9.26 The news about this spread all over that **part** of the country.
9.31 the news about Jesus all over that **part** of the country.
Lk 2. 8 some shepherds in that **part** of the country who were spending
11.36 full of light, with no **part** of it in darkness, it will
15.13 the younger son sold his **part** of the property and left home
Jn 19.23 clothes and divided them into four **parts,**
19.23 one **part** for each soldier.
Acts 1.17 for he had been chosen to have a **part** in our work."
2.42 learning from the apostles, taking **part** in the fellowship,
5. 2 his wife's agreement he kept **part** of the money for himself
5. 3 the Holy Spirit by keeping **part** of the money you received
7. 5 not then give Abraham any **part** of it as his own,
8.21 You have no **part** or share in our work, because your
27.19 following day they threw **part** of the ship's equipment overboard.
27.41 the front **part** of the ship got stuck and could not move,
27.41 while the back **part** was being broken to pieces
Rom 6.13 Nor must you surrender any **part** of yourselves to sin
7. 4 also have died because you are **part** of the body of Christ;
12. 4 We have many **parts** in the one body,
12. 4 and all these **parts** have different functions.
12. 5 are all joined to each other as different **parts** of one body.
12.18 Do everything possible on your **part** to live in peace with
1 Cor 6.15 You know that your bodies are **parts** of the body of Christ.
6.15 Shall I take a **part** of Christ's body
6.15 and make it **part** of the body of a prostitute?
1 Cor 9.24 know that many runners take **part** in a race, but only one
11.18 and this I believe is **partly** true.
12.12 Christ is like a single body, which has many **parts;**
12.12 one body, even though it is made up of different **parts.**
12.14 is not made up of only one **part,** but of many parts.
12.15 that would not keep it from being a **part** of the body.
12.16 that would not keep it from being a **part** of the body.
12.18 however, God put every different **part** in the body just as he
12.19 would not be a body if it were all only one **part!**
12.20 As it is, there are many **parts** but one body.
12.22 we cannot do without the **parts** of the body that seem to
12.23 and those **parts** that we think aren't worth very much are
12.23 while the **parts** of the body which don't look very nice are
12.24 special modesty, [24]which the more beautiful **parts** do not need.
12.24 way as to give greater honour to those **parts** that need it.
12.25 but all its different **parts** have the same concern for one
12.26 If one **part** of the body suffers,
12.26 all the other **parts** suffer with it;
12.26 **part** is praised, all the other parts share its happiness.
12.27 you are Christ's body, and each one is a **part** of it.
14.14 my spirit prays indeed, but my mind has no **part** in it.
14.16 an ordinary person taking **part** in the meeting say "Amen"
2 Cor 1.13 now understand us only in **part,** I hope that you will come
2. 5 it to me but to all of you—in **part** at least.
8. 4 of having a **part** in helping God's people in Judaea.
Gal 4.30 not have a **part** of the father's property along with
Eph 2.12 You had no **part** in the covenants, which were based on God's
3. 6 the Gentiles have a **part** with the Jews in God's blessings;
4.16 his control all the different **parts** of the body fit together,
4.16 So when each separate **part** works as it should, the whole
4.18 They have no **part** in the life that God gives, for they
Phil 1.30 Now you can take **part** with me in the battle.
1 Thes 3. 3 know that such persecutions are **part** of God's will for us.
1 Tim 5.22 Take no **part** in the sins of others;
2 Tim 1. 8 Instead, take your **part** in suffering for the Good News, as
2. 3 Take your **part** in suffering, as a loyal soldier of Christ Jesus.
Heb 9.11 that is, it is not a **part** of this created world.
Rev 13.10 This calls for endurance and faith on the **part** of God's people."
14.12 calls for endurance on the **part** of God's people, those who
16.19 city was split into three **parts,** and the cities of all
18. 4 You must not take **part** in her sins;
18. 9 of the earth who took **part** in her immorality and lust will

PART (2)

Gen 13.11 That is how the two men **parted.**
26.31 Isaac said good-bye to them, and they **parted** as friends.

PARTIAL

1 Cor 13. 9 our gifts of knowledge and of inspired messages are only **partial;**
13.10 when what is perfect comes, then what is **partial** will disappear.
13.12 What I know now is only **partial;**

PARTIALITY

Ex 23. 3 Do not show **partiality** to a poor man at his trial.
Deut 1.17 Show no **partiality** in your decisions;
10.17 He does not show **partiality,** and he does not accept bribes.
16.19 They are not to be unjust or show **partiality** in their judgements;
21.16 he is not to show **partiality** to the son of his favourite
2 Chr 19. 7 God does not tolerate fraud or **partiality** or the taking of bribes."
Ps 82. 2 you must no longer be **partial** to the wicked!

PARTICIPATE

Mal 2.12 and never again let them **participate** in the offerings our

PARTICULAR

1 Cor 12. 6 the same God gives ability to all for their **particular** service.

PARTITIONED

1 Kgs 6.16 nine metres long and was **partitioned** off by cedar boards

PARTNER

Prov 29.24 A thief's **partner** is his own worst enemy.
Mal 2.14 She was your **partner,** and you have broken your promise to her,
Lk 5. 4 water, and you and your **partners** let down your nets for a
5. 7 So they motioned to their **partners** in the other boat to
5.10 same was true of Simon's **partners,** James and John, the sons
1 Cor 3. 9 For we are **partners** working together for God, and you are
7.15 a believer wishes to leave the Christian **partner,** let it be
7.15 In such cases the Christian **partner,** whether husband or wife,
10.20 And I do not want you to be **partners** with demons.
2 Cor 6.14 How can right and wrong be **partners?**
8.23 for Titus, he is my **partner** and works with me to help
Gal 2. 9 with Barnabas and me, as a sign that we were all **partners.**
Phil 4. 3 And you too, my faithful **partner,** I want you to help these
Phlm 17 think of me as your **partner,** welcome him back just as you
Heb 3.14 For we are all **partners** with Christ if we hold firmly to
2 Jn 11 him peace becomes his **partner** in the evil things he does.
Rev 1. 9 I am your **partner** in patiently enduring the suffering that

PARTY (1)

2 Sam 4. 2 of raiding **parties,** Baanah and Rechab, sons of Rimmon,
19.18 river to escort the royal **party** across and to do whatever
Mt 22.16 some of their disciples and some members of Herod's **party.**

Mk 3. 6 with some members of Herod's **party,** and they made plans to
12.13 and some members of Herod's **party** were sent to Jesus to trap
Jn 3. 1 named Nicodemus, who belonged to the **party** of the Pharisees.
Acts 5.17 of the local **party** of the Sadducees, became extremely jealous
15. 5 believers who belonged to the **party** of the Pharisees stood up
23. 9 Law who belonged to the **party** of the Pharisees stood up
24. 5 the world and is a leader of the **party** of the Nazarenes.
26. 5 a member of the strictest **party** of our religion, the Pharisees.
28.22 everywhere people speak against this **party** to which you belong."
Gal 5.20 They separate into **parties** and groups;

PARTY (2)

Esth 9.22 these days with feasts and **parties,** giving gifts of food to
Ecc 7. 2 one where there is a **party,** because the living should always
Mt 9.15 the guests at a wedding **party** to be sad as long as
Mk 2.19 you expect the guests at a wedding **party** to go without food?
Lk 5.34 the guests at a wedding **party** go without food as long as
1 Pet 4. 3 orgies, drinking **parties,** and the disgusting worship of idols.

PASS (1)

Num 13.21 south all the way to Rehob, near Hamath **Pass** in the north.
34. 4 will turn southwards towards Akrabbim **Pass** and continue on
34. 8 Mediterranean to Mount Hor [8]and from there to Hamath **Pass.**
Josh 10.10 pursued them down the mountain **pass** at Beth Horon, keeping
10.11 Amorites were running down the **pass** from the Israelite army,
13. 5 Baalgad, which is south of Mount Hermon, to Hamath **Pass.**
15. 3 went southwards from the Akrabbim **Pass** and on to Zin.
15. 7 towards Gilgal, which faces Adummim **Pass** on the south side
18.17 to Enshemesh and then on to Geliloth, opposite Adummim **Pass.**
Judg 1.36 North of Sela, the Edomite border ran through Akrabbim **Pass.**
3. 3 Lebanon Mountains from Mount Baal Hermon as far as Hamath **Pass.**
8.13 battle by way of Heres **Pass,** [14]he captured a young man
1 Sam 13.23 sent a group of soldiers to defend the **pass** of Michmash.
14. 4 In the **pass** of Michmash, which Jonathan had to go through
14. 4 were two large jagged rocks, one on each side of the **pass:**
14. 5 the north side of the **pass,** facing Michmash, and the other
14.13 climbed up out of the **pass** on his hands and knees, and
1 Kgs 8.65 as far away as Hamath **Pass** in the north and the Egyptian
2 Kgs 14.25 belonged to Israel, from Hamath **Pass** in the north to the
1 Chr 13. 5 in the south to Hamath **Pass** in the north, in order to
2 Chr 7. 8 as far away as Hamath **Pass** in the north and the Egyptian
20.16 Attack them tomorrow as they come up the **pass** at Ziz.
Is 10.29 They have crossed the **pass** and are spending the night at Geba!
Ezek 47.15 city of Hethlon, to Hamath **Pass,** to the city of Zedad,
47.20 Mediterranean and runs north to a point west of Hamath **Pass.**
48. 1 city of Hethlon, to Hamath **Pass,** to the city of Enon, to
Amos 6.14 will oppress you from Hamath **Pass** in the north to the brook

PASS (2)

Gen 15.17 appeared and **passed** between the pieces of the animals.
18. 3 he said, "Sirs, please do not **pass** by my home without stopping;
Ex 12.13 see the blood, I will **pass** over you and will not harm
12.27 honour the Lord, because he **passed** over the houses of the
33.19 will make all my splendour **pass** before you and in your
33.22 dazzling light of my presence **passes** by, I will put you in
33.22 rock and cover you with my hand until I have **passed** by.
34. 6 The Lord then **passed** in front of him and called out, "I,
Num 20.17 Please permit us to **pass** through your land.
20.18 Edomites answered, "We refuse to let you **pass** through our country!
20.19 we will pay for it—all we want is to **pass** through."
20.21 would not let the Israelites **pass** through their territory,
21.22 "Let us **pass** through your land.
21.23 permit the people of Israel to **pass** through his territory.
22.26 where there was no room at all to **pass** on either side.
31.22 tin, or lead, is to be purified by **passing** it through fire.
33. 8 They left Pi Hahiroth and **passed** through the Red Sea into
Deut 2.18 us, [18]'Today you are to **pass** through the territory of Moab
2.24 "After we had **passed** through Moab, the Lord said to us,
2.27 'Let us **pass** through your country.
2.28 want to do is to **pass** through your country, [29]until we
2.29 live in Ar, allowed us to **pass** through their territory.'
2.30 "But King Sihon would not let us **pass** through his country.
Josh 16. 2 Bethel it went to Luz, **passing** on to Ataroth Addar, where
18.18 a son of Reuben) [18]and **passed** north of the ridge
18.19 went down into the valley, [19]**passing** north of the ridge of
24.17 we went among all the nations through which we **passed.**
Judg 9.25 and they robbed everyone who **passed** their way.
19.12 We'll **pass** on and go a little farther and spend the night
2 Sam 15.18 to him as the royal bodyguard **passed** by in front of him.
15.18 followed him from Gath also **passed** by, [19]and the king said
18.23 through the Jordan Valley, and soon he **passed** the slave.
20.14 Sheba **passed** through the territory of all the tribes of
1 Kgs 9. 8 and everyone who **passes** by will be shocked and amazed.
13.25 Some men **passed** by and saw the body on the road, with
19.11 Then the Lord **passed** by and sent a furious wind that split
20.38 stood by the road, waiting for the king of Israel to **pass.**
20.39 As the king was **passing** by, the prophet called out to
2 Kgs 3.25 As they **passed** a fertile field, every Israelite would throw
14. 9 A wild animal **passed** by and trampled the bush down.
20. 4 king, but before he had **passed** through the central courtyard
1 Chr 29.15 O Lord, that we **pass** through life like exiles and strangers,
29.15 Our days are like a **passing** shadow, and we cannot escape death.
2 Chr 7.21 honoured, but then everyone who **passes** by it will be amazed
25.18 A wild animal **passed** by and trampled the bush down.
Esth 5. 9 sign of respect as he **passed,** Haman was furious with him.
Job 7. 6 My days **pass** by without hope, pass faster than a weaver's shuttle.
Job 8. 9 we **pass** like shadows across the earth.
9.11 God **passes** by, but I cannot see him.
Ps 37.36 but later I **passed** by, and he wasn't there;
80.12 Now anyone **passing** by can steal its grapes;
84. 6 As they **pass** through the dry valley of Baca, it becomes a
89.41 All who **pass** by steal his belongings;
104. 9 a boundary they can never **pass,** to keep them from covering
129. 8 No one who **passes** by will say, "May the Lord bless you!
144. 4 his days are like a **passing** shadow.
Prov 7. 8 He was **passing** near her house [9]in the evening after it was
9.15 and calls out to people **passing** by, who are minding
Is 6. 5 doomed because every word that **passes** my lips is sinful, and
10.28 They have **passed** through Migron!
35. 9 no fierce animals will **pass** that way.
43. 2 When you **pass** through deep waters, I will be with you;
43. 2 When you **pass** through fire, you will not be burnt;
Jer 18.16 All who **pass** by will be shocked at what they see;
19. 8 city that everyone who **passes** by will be shocked and amazed.
22. 4 their people, will continue to **pass** through the gates of
22. 8 many foreigners will **pass** by and ask one another why I,
49.17 that everyone who **passes** by will be shocked and terrified.
50.13 in ruins, and all who **pass** by will be shocked and amazed.
Lam 1.12 she cries to everyone who **passes** by.
2.15 People **passing** by the city look at you in scorn.
Ezek 5.14 the nations around you who **passes** by will sneer at you and
16. 6 "Then I **passed** by and saw you squirming in your own blood.
16. 8 "As I **passed** by again, I saw that the time had come
26.10 shake your walls as they **pass** through the gates of the
43. 4 The dazzling light **passed** through the east gate and went
Zeph 2.15 Everyone who **passes** by will shrink back in horror.
Zech 9. 8 I will guard my land and keep armies from **passing** through it.
10.11 When they **pass** through their sea of trouble, I, the
Mt 20.30 heard that Jesus was **passing** by, so they began to shout,
27.39 People **passing** by shook their heads and hurled insults at
Mk 6.48 He was going to **pass** them by, [49]but they saw him walking
15.29 People **passing** by shook their heads and hurled insults at
Lk 18.36 When he heard the crowd **passing** by, he asked, "What is this?"
18.37 "Jesus of Nazareth is **passing** by," they told him.
19. 1 Jesus went on into Jericho and was **passing** through.
19. 4 sycomore tree to see Jesus, who was going to **pass** that way.
Jn 5.24 not be judged, but has already **passed** from death to life.
Acts 5.15 Peter's shadow might fall on some of them as he **passed** by.
12.10 They **passed** by the first guard post and then the second,
14.22 "We must **pass** through many troubles to enter the Kingdom of God,"
17.17 square every day with the people who happened to **pass** by.
27. 7 sheltered side of the island of Crete, **passing** by Cape Salmone.
27.16 got some shelter when we **passed** to the south of the little
1 Cor 10. 1 and all **passed** safely through the Red Sea.
16. 7 I want to see you more than just briefly in **passing;**

PASS (3)

1 Tim 3.10 first, and then, if they **pass** the test, they are to serve.
Jas 1.12 because when he succeeds in **passing** such a test, he will

PASS (4)

Num 27. 7 Let his inheritance **pass** on to them.
36. 9 and the property will not **pass** from one tribe to another.
Ruth 2.14 with the workers, and Boaz **passed** some roasted grain to her.
Ezra 9.12 to enjoy the land and **pass** it on to our descendants for
Ecc 5.14 and end up with nothing left to **pass** on to their children.
Ezek 3.17 You will **pass** on to them the warnings I give you.
33. 7 You must **pass** on to them the warnings I give you.
Mk 7.13 this way the teaching you **pass** on to others cancels out the
Acts 7.38 and he received God's living messages to **pass** on to us.
1 Cor 11.23 received from the Lord the teaching that I **passed** on to you:
15. 3 I **passed** on to you what I received, which is of the
Heb 7.24 and his work as priest does not **pass** on to someone else.

PASS (5)

Lk 23.24 Pilate **passed** the sentence on Jesus that they were asking for.
Jn 8.15 I **pass judgement** on no one.
Acts 7. 7 But I will **pass judgement** on the people that they will serve,
13.28 could find no reason to **pass** the death sentence on him,
Rom 2. 1 Do you, my friend, **pass judgement** on others?
2. 3 do those very things for which you **pass judgement** on others!
14. 3 only vegetables is not to **pass judgement** on the one who will
14.10 only vegetables—why do you **pass judgement** on your brother?
1 Cor 4. 3 I don't even **pass judgement** on myself.
4. 4 The Lord is the one who **passes judgement** on me.
4. 5 you should not **pass judgement** on anyone before the right time
5. 3 of our Lord Jesus already **passed judgement** on the man who
2 Cor 1. 9 We felt that the death sentence had been **passed** on us.

PASS (6)

Gen 1. 5 Evening **passed** and morning came—that was the first day.
1. 8 Evening **passed** and morning came—that was the second day.
1.13 Evening **passed** and morning came—that was the third day.
1.19 Evening **passed** and morning came—that was the fourth day.
1.23 Evening **passed** and morning came—that was the fifth day.
1.31 Evening **passed** and morning came—that was the sixth day.
41. 1 After two years had **passed,** the king of Egypt dreamt that
Ex 7.25 Seven days **passed** after the Lord struck the river.
Job 9.26 My life **passes** like the swiftest boat, as fast as an
16.22 My years are **passing** now, and I walk the road of no
17.11 My days have **passed;**
Ecc 6.12 short, useless life of his—a life that **passes** like a shadow?

Ecc 12. 2 grow dim for you, and the rain clouds will never **pass away.**
Ezek 3.16 After the seven days had **passed,** the Lord spoke to me.
Dan 4.34 "When the seven years had **passed,"** said the king, "I
9.25 God's chosen leader comes, seven times seven years will **pass.**
12.11 is, from the time of The Awful Horror, 1,290 days will **pass.**
Mt 24.35 Heaven and earth will **pass away,**
24.35 but my words will never **pass away.**
Mk 13.31 Heaven and earth will **pass away,**
13.31 but my words will never **pass away.**
Lk 21.33 Heaven and earth will **pass away,**
21.33 but my words will never **pass away.**
Acts 7.30 "After forty years had **passed,** an angel appeared to Moses
24.27 two years had **passed,** Porcius Festus succeeded Felix as governor.
1 Cor 13. 8 there is knowledge, but it will **pass.**
Jas 1.10 For the rich will **pass away** like the flower of a wild
1 Jn 2. 8 For the darkness is **passing away,** and the real light is
2.17 The world and everything in it that people desire is **passing away;**

PASSAGE (1)

Ezek 8.16 the altar and the **passage,** were about twenty-five men.
40. 7 Beyond it there was a **passage,** which had three guardrooms
40. 7 the guardrooms there was a **passage** three metres long that
40.10 on each side of the **passage** were all the same size, and
40.11 Next, the man measured the width of the **passage** in the gateway.
40.13 of the room across the **passage** from it, and it was twelve
40.16 There were palm-trees carved on the inner walls that faced the **passage.**
40.21 on each side of the **passage,** the walls between them, and the
40.26 palm-trees carved on the inner walls that faced the **passage.**
40.31 and palm-trees were carved on the walls along the **passage.**
40.34 Palm-trees were carved on the walls along the **passage.**
40.37 Palm-trees were carved on the walls along the **passage.**
41. 1 He measured the **passage** leading into it:
41. 3 He measured the **passage** leading into it:
41.23 at the end of the **passage** leading to the Holy Place and
41.23 at the end of the **passage** leading to the Most Holy Place.
42. 4 of this building was a **passage** five metres wide and fifty
42.11 the rooms there was a **passage** just like the one on the
Mk 14.68 talking about," he answered, and went out into the **passage.**

PASSAGE (2)

Neh 13. 1 people, they came to the **passage** that said that no Ammonite
Mk 12.26 in the Book of Moses the **passage** about the burning bush?
Lk 4.21 to them, "This **passage** of scripture has come true today,
20.37 In the **passage** about the burning bush he speaks of the Lord
Acts 8.32 The **passage** of scripture which he was reading was this:
8.35 starting from this **passage** of scripture, he told him the
13.35 he says in another **passage,** 'You will not allow your devoted
Rom 11. 2 the scripture says in the **passage** where Elijah pleads with God
2 Cor 3.17 Now, "the Lord" in this **passage** is the Spirit;
2 Pet 3.16 explain falsely, as they do with other **passages** of the Scriptures.

Am **PASSAGEWAY** see **PASSAGE (1)**

PASSENGER

Rev 18.17 All the ships' captains and **passengers,** the sailors and all

PASSION

Ecc 9. 6 Their loves, their hates, their **passions,** all died with them.
Song 2. 5 I am weak from **passion.**
5. 8 find my lover, you will tell him I am weak from **passion.**
8. 6 **passion** is as strong as death itself.
Rom 1.26 Because they do this, God has given them over to shameful **passions.**
1.27 sexual relations with women and burn with **passion** for each other.
1 Cor 7. 9 and marry—it is better to marry than to burn with **passion.**
7.36 the girl and if his **passions** are too strong and he feels
Gal 5.24 death their human nature with all its **passions** and desires.
Eph 4.31 Get rid of all bitterness, **passion,** and anger.
Col 2.23 they have no real value in controlling physical **passions.**
3. 5 sexual immorality, indecency, lust, evil **passions,** and greed
3. 8 anger, **passion,** and hateful feelings.
2 Tim 2.22 Avoid the **passions** of youth, and strive for righteousness,
Tit 2.12 ungodly living and worldly **passions,** and to live self-controlled,
3. 3 We were slaves to **passions** and pleasures of all kinds.
1 Pet 2.11 not give in to bodily **passions,** which are always at war

PASSOVER

The Israelite festival, on the 14th day of the month Nisan (about April 1st), which celebrated the freeing of the Hebrews from their captivity in Egypt. The Angel of Death killed the first-born in the Egyptian homes but passed over the Hebrew homes. The Jewish name for this festival is Pesach.

Ex 12.11 It is the **Passover** Festival to honour me, the Lord.
12.13 see the blood, I will **pass over** you and will not harm
12.21 and kill it, so that your families can celebrate **Passover.**
12.27 'It is the sacrifice of **Passover** to honour the Lord,
12.27 because he **passed over** the houses of the Israelites
12.43 "These are the **Passover** regulations:
12.43 No foreigner shall eat the **Passover** meal, [44] but any slave
12.48 you and wants to celebrate **Passover** to honour the Lord, you
34.25 any part of the animal killed at the **Passover** Festival.
Lev 23. 5 The **Passover,** celebrated to honour the Lord, begins at
Num 9. 2 Israel are to observe the **Passover** according to all the
Num 9. 4 the people to observe the **Passover,** [5] and on the evening of
9. 6 and they were not able to keep the **Passover** on that day.
9.10 still want to keep the **Passover,** [11] you are permitted to
9.12 Observe the **Passover** according to all the regulations.
9.13 who does not observe the **Passover,** shall no longer be
9.14 you wants to keep the **Passover,** he must observe it according
28.16 The **Passover** Festival in honour of the Lord is to be
33. 3 first month of the year, the day after the first **Passover.**
Deut 16. 1 Lord your God by celebrating **Passover** in the month of Abib;
16. 2 sheep or cattle for the **Passover** meal to honour the Lord
16. 5 "Slaughter the **Passover** animals at the one place of
16.16 at **Passover,** Harvest Festival, and the Festival of Shelters.
Josh 5.10 plain near Jericho, they observed **Passover** on the evening of
2 Kgs 23.21 the people to celebrate the **Passover** in honour of the Lord
23.22 No **Passover** like this one had ever been celebrated by
23.23 reign of Josiah, the **Passover** was celebrated in Jerusalem.
2 Chr 30. 1 able to celebrate the **Passover** Festival at the proper time,
30. 1 Jerusalem to celebrate the **Passover** in honour of the Lord,
30. 5 Jerusalem and celebrate the **Passover** according to the Law,
30.15 the month they killed the lambs for the **Passover** sacrifice.
30.17 they could not kill the **Passover** lambs, so the Levites did
30.18 and so they were observing **Passover** improperly.
35. 1 King Josiah celebrated the **Passover** at Jerusalem
35. 6 You are to kill the **Passover** lambs and goats.
35. 7 of the people at the **Passover,** King Josiah contributed from
35.10 everything was arranged for the **Passover,** the priests and
35.13 The Levites roasted the **Passover** sacrifices over the fire,
35.15 because the other Levites prepared the **Passover** for them.
35.16 Lord, the keeping of the **Passover** Festival, and the offering
35.17 the **Passover** and the Festival of Unleavened Bread.
35.18 Samuel, the **Passover** had never been celebrated like this.
35.18 kings had ever celebrated a **Passover** like this one
Ezra 6.19 had returned from exile celebrated **Passover** on the
6.20 killed the animals for the **Passover** sacrifices for all the
Ezek 45.21 you will begin the celebration of the **Passover** Festival.
Mt 26. 2 it will be the **Passover** Festival, and the Son of Man
26.17 do you want us to get the **Passover** meal ready for you?"
26.18 and I will celebrate the **Passover** at your house.'"
26.19 did as Jesus had told them and prepared the **Passover** meal.
27.15 At every **Passover** Festival the Roman governor was in the habit
Mk 14. 1 days before the Festival of **Passover** and Unleavened Bread.
14.12 day the lambs for the **Passover** meal were killed, Jesus' disciples
14.12 want us to go and get the **Passover** meal ready for you?"
14.14 room where my disciples and I will eat the **Passover** meal?'
14.16 and they prepared the **Passover** meal.
15. 6 every **Passover** Festival Pilate was in the habit of setting free
Lk 2.41 the parents of Jesus went to Jerusalem for the **Passover** Festival.
22. 1 for the Festival of Unleavened Bread, which is called the **Passover.**
22. 7 when the lambs for the **Passover** meal were to be killed.
22. 8 "Go and get the **Passover** meal ready for us to eat."
22.11 room where my disciples and I will eat the **Passover** meal?'
22.13 Jesus had told them, and they prepared the **Passover** meal.
22.15 so much to eat this **Passover** meal with you before I suffer!
Jn 2.13 almost time for the **Passover** Festival, so Jesus went to Jerusalem.
2.23 in Jerusalem during the **Passover** Festival, many believed in him
4.45 they had gone to the **Passover** Festival in Jerusalem and had
6. 4 The time for the **Passover** Festival was near.
11.55 The time for the **Passover** Festival was near, and many people
12. 1 Six days before the **Passover,** Jesus went to Bethany,
12.12 that had come to the **Passover** Festival heard that Jesus was
13. 1 It was now the day before the **Passover** Festival.
18.28 clean, in order to be able to eat the **Passover** meal.
18.39 I always set free a prisoner for you during the **Passover.**
19.14 It was then almost noon of the day before the **Passover.**
Acts 12. 4 Herod planned to put him on trial in public after **Passover.**
1 Cor 5. 7 For our **Passover** Festival is ready,
5. 7 now that Christ, our **Passover** lamb, has been sacrificed.
5. 8 celebrate our **Passover,** then, not with bread having the old
Heb 11.28 that made him establish the **Passover** and order the blood to

PAST

Deut 4.32 "Search the **past,** the time before you were born, all
8. 2 journey through the desert these **past** forty years, sending
32. 7 "Think of the **past,** of the time long ago;
32. 7 you what happened, ask the old men to tell of the **past.**
Judg 10.12 Maonites oppressed you in the **past,** and you cried out to me.
1 Sam 2.30 of Israel, promised in the **past** that your family and your
2 Sam 5. 2 In the **past,** even when Saul was still our king, you led
1 Kgs 3. 4 He had offered hundreds of burnt-offerings there in the **past.**
1 Chr 11. 2 In the **past,** even when Saul was still our king, you led
Job 11.16 memory, like floods that are **past** and remembered no more.
42. 5 In the **past** I knew only what others had told me, but
Ps 42. 4 breaks when I remember the **past,** when I went with the crowds
77.11 I will recall the wonders you did in the **past.**
78. 2 mysteries from the **past,** [3] things we have heard and known,
Ecc 1.11 what has happened in the **past,** and no one in days to
Is 14.12 In the **past** you conquered nations, but now you have been
41.22 court the events of the **past,** and tell us what they mean.
43.18 cling to events of the **past** or dwell on what happened long
48. 7 nothing like this took place in the **past.**
63. 9 care of them in the **past,** [10] but they rebelled against him
63.11 But then they remembered the **past,** the days of Moses,
65. 7 So I will punish them as their **past** deeds deserve."
65.16 The troubles of the **past** will be gone and forgotten."
65.17 The events of the **past** will be completely forgotten.
Jer 46.26 people will live in Egypt again, as they did in times **past.**
Lam 1. 6 The splendour of Jerusalem is a thing of the **past.**
Ezek 33.13 he starts thinking that his **past** goodness is enough and
Dan 9.16 have defended us in the **past,** so do not be angry with

Dan 9.27 when half this time is **past,** he will put an end to
10. 3 any wine, or comb my hair until the three weeks were **past.**
Hos 13. 1 In the **past,** when the tribe of Ephraim spoke, the other
Zech 8.13 In the **past** foreigners have cursed one another by saying,
14. 3 fight against those nations, as he has fought in times **past.**
Mal 3. 4 be pleasing to him, as they used to be in the **past.**
Mt 5.21 that people were told in the **past,** 'Do not commit murder;
5.33 people were told in the **past,** 'Do not break your promise,
Acts 14.16 In the **past** he allowed all people to go their own way.
27. 9 voyage, for by now the Day of Atonement was already **past.**
Rom 3.25 In the **past** he was patient and overlooked people's sins;
11.30 As for you Gentiles, you disobeyed God in the **past;**
16.25 the secret truth which was hidden for long ages in the **past.**
2 Cor 3.10 now the glory that was so bright in the **past** is gone.
11. 9 As in the **past,** so in the future:
12.21 many who sinned in the **past** and have not repented of the
13. 2 you who have sinned in the **past,** and to all the others;
Gal 2. 2 want my work in the **past** or in the present to be
4. 8 In the **past** you did not know God, and so you were
Eph 2. 1 In the **past** you were spiritually dead because of your disobedience
2.11 remember what you were in the **past.**
3. 5 In **past** times mankind was not told this secret, but God
3. 9 secret hidden through all the **past** ages, [10] in order that
Phil 1.30 saw me fighting in the **past,** and as you hear, the one
Col 1.26 secret he hid through all **past** ages from all mankind but has
1 Tim 1.13 even though in the **past** I spoke evil of him
1.18 the words of prophecy spoken in the **past** about you.
Heb 1. 1 In the **past,** God spoke to our ancestors many times and in
10.32 Remember how it was with you in the **past.**
1 Pet 3. 5 the devout women of the **past** who placed their hope in God
4. 3 spent enough time in the **past** doing what the heathen like to
2 Pet 1. 9 has forgotten that he has been purified from his **past** sins.
2. 1 False prophets appeared in the **past** among the people,
Jude 17 you were told in the **past** by the apostles of our Lord
25 and authority, from all ages **past,** and now, and for ever

PASTE

2 Kgs 20. 7 put on his boil a **paste** made of figs, and he would
Is 38. 6 the king to put a **paste** made of figs on his boil,

PASTOR

Eph 4.11 others to be evangelists, others to be **pastors** and teachers.

PASTRIES

Gen 40.17 there were all kinds of **pastries** for the king, and the birds

PASTURE

Gen 13. 6 so there was not enough **pasture** land for the two of them
29. 7 why don't you water them and take them back to **pasture?"**
47. 4 famine is so severe that there is no **pasture** for our flocks.
Lev 25.34 But the **pasture** land round the Levite cities shall never be sold;
Num 22. 4 round us, like a bull eating the grass in a **pasture."**
35. 2 Levites some cities to live in and **pasture** land round the cities.
35. 3 The **pasture** land will be for their cattle and all their
35. 4 The **pasture** land is to extend outwards from the city walls
35. 7 with their **pasture** land, making a total of forty-eight.
Josh 21. 2 in, as well as **pasture** land round them for our livestock."
21. 3 certain cities and **pasture** lands out of their own territories.
21. 8 these cities and their **pasture** lands to the Levites,
21.11 of Judah, along with the **pasture** land surrounding it.
21.16 Ain, Juttah, and Beth Shemesh, with their **pasture** lands:
21.18 Geba, [18] Anathoth, and Almon, with their **pasture** lands.
21.19 in all, with their **pasture** lands, were given to the priests,
21.21 Shechem and its **pasture** lands in the hill-country of Ephraim
21.22 Kibzaim, and Beth Horon, with their **pasture** lands.
21.24 Aijalon, and Gathrimmon, with their **pasture** lands.
21.25 Taanach and Gathrimmon, with their **pasture** lands.
21.26 Kohath received ten cities in all, with their **pasture** lands.
21.27 and Beeshterah, with their **pasture** lands.
21.29 Jarmuth, and Engannim, with their **pasture** lands.
21.31 Abdon, [31] Helkath, and Rehob, with their **pasture** lands.
21.32 Kedesh in Galilee, with its **pasture** lands
21.32 Hammoth Dor, and Kartan, with their **pasture** lands.
21.33 Gershon received a total of thirteen cities with their **pasture** lands.
21.35 Kartah, [35] Dimnah, and Nahalal, with their **pasture** lands.
21.37 Jahaz, [37] Kedemoth, and Mephaath, with their **pasture** lands.
21.38 Ramoth in Gilead, with its **pasture** lands (one of the cities
21.39 Mahanaim, [39] Heshbon, and Jazer, with their **pasture** lands.
21.41 of forty-eight cities, with the **pasture** lands round them,
1 Kgs 4.23 ten stall-fed cattle, twenty **pasture-fed** cattle,
1 Chr 4.39 westwards almost to Gerar and **pastured** their sheep on the
4.40 They found plenty of fertile **pasture** lands there in a
4.41 because there was plenty of **pasture** for their sheep.
5.16 in the towns there and all over the **pasture** lands of Sharon.
6.55 Hebron in the territory of Judah and the **pasture** lands round it.
6.57 Debir, Ashan, and Beth Shemesh, with their **pasture** lands.
6.60 assigned the following towns with their **pasture** lands:
6.64 together with the **pasture** lands round the towns.
6.66 Kohath were assigned towns and **pasture** lands
6.70 of Aner and Bileam with the surrounding **pasture** lands.
6.71 the following towns, with the surrounding **pasture** lands:
6.77 the following towns with the surrounding **pasture** lands:
2 Chr 11.14 The Levites abandoned their **pastures** and other land and
31.19 or in the **pasture** lands belonging to these cities,
Job 1.14 oxen," he said, "and the donkeys were in a nearby **pasture.**
5.25 as many children as there are blades of grass in a **pasture.**
Job 39. 8 The mountains are the **pastures** where they feed, where they
Ps 65.12 The **pastures** are filled with flocks;
78.70 he took him from the **pastures,** [71] where he looked after his flocks,
Song 1. 8 find **pasture** for your goats near the tents of the shepherds.
Is 5.17 lambs will eat grass and young goats will find **pasture.**
7.19 and they will cover every thorn-bush and every **pasture.**
13.20 there, and no shepherd will ever **pasture** his flock there.
17. 2 They will be a **pasture** for sheep and cattle, and no one
27.10 It has become a **pasture** for cattle, where they can rest and
30.23 harvest, and your livestock will have plenty of **pasture.**
32.14 Wild donkeys will roam there, and sheep will find **pasture** there.
32.20 and safe **pasture** everywhere for the donkeys and cattle.
65.10 their sheep and cattle to **pasture** in the Plain of Sharon in
Jer 9.10 and weep for the **pastures,** because they have dried up,
23.10 the Lord's curse the land mourns and the **pastures** are dry.
33.12 once again be **pastures** where shepherds can take their sheep.
49.19 Jordan up to the green **pasture** land, I will come and make
50.44 Jordan up to the green **pasture** land, I, the Lord, will come
Ezek 34.13 streams of Israel and will feed them in pleasant **pastures.**
34.14 valleys and in all the green **pastures** of the land of Israel.
36. 5 they captured my land and took possession of its **pastures.**
Joel 1.18 bellowing in distress because there is no **pasture** for them;
1.19 to you, Lord, because the **pastures** and trees are dried up,
2.22 The **pastures** are green;
Amos 1. 2 The **pastures** dry up, and the grass on Mount Carmel turns brown."
Mic 2.12 Like a **pasture** full of sheep, your land will once again be
5. 8 like a lion hunting for food in a forest or a **pasture:**
7.14 and feed in the rich **pastures** of Bashan and Gilead, as they
Zeph 2. 7 They will **pasture** their flocks there and sleep in the houses
Lk 15. 4 other ninety-nine sheep in the **pasture** and goes looking for
Jn 10. 9 he will come in and go out and find **pasture.**

PATCH

Josh 9. 4 their donkeys with worn-out sacks and **patched-up** wineskins.
Mt 9.16 "No one **patches** up an old coat with a piece of new
9.16 new cloth, for the new **patch** will shrink and make an even
Mk 2.21 piece of new cloth to **patch** up an old coat,
2.21 because the new **patch** will shrink and tear off some
Lk 5.36 a piece off a new coat to **patch** up an old coat.

PATH

Gen 49.17 A poisonous snake beside the **path,**
Deut 23.24 "When you walk along a **path** in someone else's vineyard,
23.25 When you walk along a **path** in someone else's cornfield,
2 Sam 22.33 he makes my **pathway** safe.
Neh 2.14 riding could not find any **path** through the rubble, [15] so I
9.11 the sea you made a **path** for your people and led them
9.19 or the fire that showed them the **path** by day and night.
Job 18.10 a trap has been set in his **path.**
19. 8 he has hidden my **path** in darkness.
22.15 to walk in the **paths** that evil men have always followed?
22.28 succeed in all you do, and light will shine on your **path.**
28.26 would fall, And the **path** that the thunderclouds travel;
31. 7 have turned from the right **path** or let myself be attracted
41.32 He leaves a shining **path** behind him and turns the sea to
Ps 16.11 You will show me the **path** that leads to life;
17. 4 I have obeyed your command and have not followed **paths** of violence.
18.32 is the God who makes me strong, who makes my **pathway** safe.
23. 3 He guides me in the right **paths,** as he has promised.
25. 8 and good, he teaches sinners the **path** they should follow.
25.12 the Lord will learn from him the **path** they should follow.
27.11 and lead me along a safe **path,** because I have many enemies.
35. 6 May their **path** be dark and slippery while the angel of the
57. 6 They dug a pit in my **path,** but fell into it themselves.
58. 7 may they be crushed like weeds on a **path.**
85.13 Righteousness will go before the Lord and prepare the **path** for him.
119.105 is a lamp to guide me and a light for my **path.**
140. 5 their snares and along the **path** they have set traps to catch
142. 3 In the **path** where I walk, my enemies have hidden a trap
143.10 Be good to me, and guide me on a safe **path.**
Prov 8.20 I follow the **paths** of justice, [21] giving wealth to those
12.26 his friend, but the **path** of the wicked leads them astray.
20.24 The Lord has determined our **path;**
21. 8 Guilty people walk a crooked **path;**
Is 2. 3 we will walk in the **paths** he has chosen.
8.11 me not to follow the **path** which the people were following.
26. 7 Lord, you make the **path** smooth for good men;
30.11 Get out of our way and stop blocking our **path.**
43.16 a road through the sea, a **path** through the swirling waters.
50.10 words of his servant, the **path** you walk may be dark indeed,
51.10 the sea and made a **path** through the water, so that those
57.14 Remove every obstacle from their **path!**
59. 8 You follow a crooked **path,**
59. 8 and no one who walks that **path** will ever be safe.
Jer 6.16 Ask for the ancient **paths** and where the best road is.
18.15 they walk on unmarked **paths.**
23.12 The **paths** they follow will be slippery and dark;
Hos 13. 7 Like a leopard I will lie in wait along your **path.**
Mic 4. 2 we will walk in the **paths** he has chosen.
Mal 2. 8 "But now you priests have turned away from the right **path.**
Mt 3. 3 make a straight **path** for him to travel!'"
13. 4 of it fell along the **path,** and the birds came and ate
13.19 understand it are like the seeds that fell along the **path.**
21.32 showing you the right **path** to take, and you would not
Mk 1. 3 make a straight **path** for him to travel!'"
4. 4 of it fell along the **path,** and the birds came and ate

Mk 4.15 Some people are like the seeds that fall along the **path;**
Lk 1.79 of death, to guide our steps into the **path** of peace."
3. 4 make a straight **path** for him to travel!
3. 5 roads must be made straight, and the rough **paths** made smooth.
8. 5 of it fell along the **path,** where it was stepped on,
8.12 The seeds that fell along the **path** stand for those who hear;
Jn 1.23 Make a straight **path** for the Lord to travel!' "
Acts 2.28 You have shown me the **paths** that lead to life,
Rom 3.17 They have not known the **path** of peace,
Gal 2.14 were not walking a straight **path** in line with the truth of
Phil 2. 8 was humble and walked the **path** of obedience all the way to
Heb 12.13 Keep walking on straight **paths,** so that the lame foot
2 Pet 2.15 They have left the straight **path** and have lost their way;
2.15 they have followed the **path** taken by Balaam son of Beor,

PATIENT

Num 14.22 but they have tried my **patience** over and over again and have
21. 4 lost their **patience** [5] and spoke against God and Moses.
Ruth 3.18 said to her, "Now be **patient,** Ruth, until you see how this
Neh 9.30 Year after year you **patiently** warned them.
Job 32.11 I listened **patiently** while you were speaking and waited
35.14 but wait **patiently**—your case is before him.
36. 1 Be **patient** and listen a little longer to what I am
Ps 37. 7 Be **patient** and wait for the Lord to act;
40. 1 I waited **patiently** for the Lord's help;
62. 1 I wait **patiently** for God to save me;
86.15 and loving God, always **patient,** always kind and faithful.
Prov 15.18 Hot tempers cause arguments, but **patience** brings peace.
16.32 It is better to be **patient** than powerful.
25.15 **Patient** persuasion can break down the strongest
29.11 openly, but sensible people are **patient** and hold it back.
Ecc 7. 8 **Patience** is better than pride.
Is 7.13 the patience of men—must you wear out God's **patience** too?
28.16 are written the words, 'Faith that is firm is also **patient.'**
Jer 15.15 Do not be so **patient** with them that they succeed in killing
Lam 3.26 for us to wait in **patience**—to wait for him to save
3.27 And it is best to learn this **patience** in our youth.
3.28 When we suffer, we should sit alone in silent **patience;**
Hos 12. 6 Be loyal and just, and wait **patiently** for your God to act.
Joel 2.13 he is **patient** and keeps his promise;
Jon 4. 2 loving and merciful God, always **patient,** always kind, and
Mic 2. 7 Has the Lord lost his **patience?**
Zech 11. 8 I lost **patience** with three other shepherds, who hated me,
Mal 3.15 prosper, but they test God's **patience** with their evil deeds
Mt 18.26 'Be **patient** with me,' he begged, 'and I will pay you everything!'
18.29 down and begged him, 'Be **patient** with me, and I will pay
Acts 18.14 it would be reasonable for me to be **patient** with you Jews.
26. 3 I ask you, then, to listen to me with **patience.**
Rom 2. 4 perhaps you despise his great kindness, tolerance, and **patience.**
3.25 In the past he was **patient** and overlooked people's sins;
8.25 for what we do not see, we wait for it with **patience.**
9.22 But he was very **patient** in enduring those who were the
12.12 hope keep you joyful, be **patient** in your troubles, and pray
15. 4 hope through the **patience** and encouragement which the Scriptures
15. 5 may God, the source of **patience** and encouragement, enable you to
1 Cor 13. 4 Love is **patient** and kind;
13. 7 and its faith, hope, and **patience** never fail.
2 Cor 1. 6 the strength to endure with **patience** the same sufferings that we
6. 4 that we are God's servants by **patiently** enduring troubles,
6. 6 By our purity, knowledge, **patience,** and kindness we have shown
12.12 I am an apostle were performed among you with much **patience.**
Gal 5.22 Spirit produces love, joy, peace, **patience,** kindness, goodness,
Eph 4. 2 Be always humble, gentle, and **patient.**
Col 1.11 so that you may be able to endure everything with **patience.**
3.12 clothe yourselves with compassion, kindness, humility, gentleness, and **patience.**
1 Thes 5.14 encourage the timid, help the weak, be **patient** with everyone.
1 Tim 1.16 Jesus might show his full **patience** in dealing with me, the
2 Tim 2.24 towards all, a good and **patient** teacher, [25] who is gentle
3.10 have observed my faith, my **patience,** my love, my endurance,
4. 2 convince, reproach, and encourage, as you teach with all **patience.**
Heb 6.12 those who believe and are **patient,** and so receive what God
6.15 Abraham was **patient,** and so he received what God had promised.
10.36 You need to be **patient,** in order to do the will of
13.22 beg you, my brothers, to listen **patiently** to this message
Jas 5. 7 Be **patient,** then, my brothers, until the Lord comes.
5. 7 See how **patient** a farmer is as he waits for his land
5. 7 He waits **patiently** for the autumn and spring rains.
5. 8 You also must be **patient.**
5.10 Take them as examples of **patient** endurance under suffering.
5.11 You have heard of Job's **patience,** and you know how the Lord
1 Pet 3.20 obeyed God when he waited **patiently** during the days that
2 Pet 3. 9 Instead, he is **patient** with you, because he does not want
3.15 Look on our Lord's **patience** as the opportunity he is giving
Rev 1. 9 I am your partner in **patiently** enduring the suffering that comes
2. 2 know how hard you have worked and how **patient** you have been.
2. 3 You are **patient,** you have suffered for my sake, and you
2.19 I know your love, your faithfulness, your service, and your **patience.**

AV **PATRIARCHS** see **ANCESTORS**

PATRIOT

Lk 6.15 Simon (who was called the **Patriot**), [16] Judas son of James,

PATROL

Neh 7. 3 posts and others to **patrol** the area round their own houses.
Song 3. 3 The watchmen **patrolling** the city saw me.
5. 7 The watchmen **patrolling** the city found me;

PATTERN

Num 8. 4 according to the **pattern** that the Lord had shown Moses.
2 Chr 3. 5 which were worked designs of palm-trees and chain **patterns.**
4. 7 lampstands according to the usual **pattern,** and ten tables,
Acts 7.44 make it, according to the **pattern** that Moses had been shown.
Heb 8. 5 according to the **pattern** you were shown on the mountain."

PAUL

(SAUL until Acts 13.9)
Pharisee who came from Tarsus and after his sudden conversion became a leader of the early Church.

Acts 7.54–8.1a **The stoning of Stephen**
8.1b-3 **Saul persecutes the church**
9.1-19a **The conversion of Saul**
19b-25 **Saul preaches in Damascus**
26-31 **Saul in Jerusalem**
11.19-30 **The church at Antioch**
12.20-25 **The death of Herod**
13.1-3 **Barnabas and Saul are chosen and sent**
4-12 **In Cyprus**
13-52 **In Antioch in Pisidia**
14.1-7 **In Iconium**
8-20 **In Lystra and Derbe**
21-28 **The return to Antoich in Syria**
15.1-21 **The meeting at Jerusalem**
22-35 **The letter to the Gentile believers**
36-41 **Paul and Barnabas separate**
16.1-5 **Timothy goes with Paul and Silas**
6-10 **In Troas: Paul's vision**
11-15 **In Philippi: the conversion of Lydia**
16-40 **In prison at Philippi**
17.1-9 **In Thessalonica**
10-15 **In Berea**
16-34 **In Athens**
18.1-17 **In Corinth**
18-23 **The return to Antioch**
19.1-10 **Paul in Ephesus**
11-20 **The sons of Sceva**
21-41 **The riot in Ephesus**
20.1-6 **To Macedonia and Achaia**
7-12 **Paul's last visit to Troas**
13-16 **From Troas to Miletus**
17-38 **Paul's farewell speech to the elders of Ephesus**
21.1-16 **Paul goes to Jerusalem**
17-26 **Paul visits James**
27-36 **Paul is arrested in the Temple**
21.37–22.5 **Paul defends himself**
22.6-16 **Paul tells of his conversion**
17-29 **Paul's call to preach to the Gentiles**
22.30–23.11 **Paul before the Council**
23.12-22 **The plot against Paul's life**
23-35 **Paul is sent to governor Felix**
24.1-9 **Paul is accused by the Jews**
10-23 **Paul's defence before Felix**
24-27 **Paul before Felix and Drusilla**
25.1-12 **Paul appeals to the Emperor**
13-27 **Paul before Agrippa and Bernice**
26.1-11 **Paul defends himself before Agrippa**
12-18 **Paul tells of his conversion**
19-32 **Paul tells of his work**
27.1-12 **Paul sails for Rome**
13-38 **The storm at sea**
39-44 **The shipwreck**
28.1-10 **In Malta**
11-15 **From Malta to Rome**
16-31 **In Rome**

Rom 1. 1 From **Paul,** a servant of Christ Jesus and an apostle chosen
1 Cor 1. 1 From **Paul,** who was called by the will of God to be
1.12 One says, "I follow **Paul"**;
1.13 Was it **Paul** who died on the cross for you?
1.13 Were you baptized as **Paul's** disciples?
3. 4 of you says, "I follow **Paul,"** and another, "I follow Apollos"—
3. 5 And who is **Paul?**
3.22 **Paul,** Apollos, and Peter;
16.21 Greetings from **Paul.**
2 Cor 1. 1 From **Paul,** an apostle of Christ Jesus by God's will,
10. 1 I, **Paul,** make a personal appeal to you—I who am said
10.10 Someone will say, **"Paul's** letters are severe and strong,
Gal 1. 1 From **Paul,** whose call to be an apostle did not come from
5. 2 I, **Paul,** tell you that if you allow yourselves to be circumcised,
Eph 1. 1 From **Paul,** who by God's will is an apostle of Christ Jesus
3. 1 For this reason I, **Paul,** the prisoner of Christ Jesus for
Phil 1. 1 From **Paul** and Timothy, servants of Christ Jesus— To all
Col 1. 1 From **Paul,** who by God's will is an apostle of Christ Jesus,
1.23 of this gospel that I, **Paul,** became a servant—this gospel
4.18 Greetings from **Paul.**
1 Thes 1. 1 From **Paul,** Silas, and Timothy— To the people of the church
2 Thes 1. 1 From **Paul,** Silas, and Timothy— To the people of the church
3.17 Greetings from **Paul.**
1 Tim 1. 1 From **Paul,** an apostle of Christ Jesus by order of God our
2 Tim 1. 1 From **Paul,** an apostle of Christ Jesus by God's will,
Tit 1. 1 From **Paul,** a servant of God and an apostle of Jesus Christ.
Phlm 1 From **Paul,** a prisoner for the sake of Christ Jesus,

Phlm 9 this even though I am **Paul,** the ambassador of Christ Jesus,
19 I, **Paul,** will pay you back.
2 Pet 3.15 just as our dear brother **Paul** wrote to you, using the wisdom

PAVED

Esth 1. 6 in the courtyard, which was **paved** with white marble, red
Ezek 40.17 them there was an area **paved** with stones, [18]which extended

PAVEMENT
[THE STONE PAVEMENT]

Ex 24.10 was what looked like a **pavement** of sapphire, as blue as the
2 Chr 7. 3 fell face downwards on the **pavement,** worshipping God and
Jer 43. 9 in the mortar of the **pavement** in front of the entrance to
Ezek 42. 3 on the other side it faced the **pavement** of the outer court.
Jn 19.13 the judge's seat in the place called **"The Stone Pavement."**

PAVILION

1 Chr 26.18 Near the western **pavilion** there were four guards by the road
26.18 and two at the **pavilion** itself.

PAW

Lev 11.24 they chew the cud, and all four-footed animals with **paws.**
Job 39.21 They eagerly **paw** the ground in the valley;
Lam 4. 5 those raised in luxury are **pawing** through refuse for food.
Hab 1. 8 their horses **paw** the ground.

PAY
[PAID]
see also **REPAY**

Gen 4.24 seven lives are taken to **pay** for killing Cain, Seventy-seven
23.13 Accept my **payment,** and I will bury my wife there."
29.15 How much **pay** do you want?"
30.16 because I have **paid** for you with my son's mandrakes."
30.28 Name your wages, and I will **pay** them."
30.31 "What shall I **pay** you?"
31.15 now he has spent all the money he was **paid** for us.
34.12 you want, and set the **payment** for the bride as high as
38.23 I did try to **pay** her, but you couldn't find her."
42.22 And now we are being **paid** back for his death."
43.23 I received your **payment."**
50.15 hates us and plans to **pay** us back for all the harm
Ex 2. 9 this baby and nurse him for me, and I will **pay** you."
21. 2 year he is to be set free without having to **pay** anything.
21.11 to her, he must set her free and not receive any **payment.**
21.18 who hit him is to **pay** for his lost time and take
21.26 it, he is to free the slave as **payment** for the eye.
21.27 tooth, he is to free the slave as **payment** for the tooth.
21.30 the owner is allowed to **pay** a fine to save his life,
21.30 he must **pay** the full amount required.
21.32 female slave, its owner shall **pay** the owner of the slave
21.34 or a donkey falls into it, [34]he must **pay** for the animal.
21.34 He is to **pay** the money to the owner and may keep
22. 1 or sells it, he must **pay** five cows for one cow and
22. 2 He must **pay** for what he stole.
22. 2 be sold as a slave to **pay** for what he has stolen.
22. 2 is found alive in his possession, he shall **pay** two for one.
22. 6 the one who started the fire is to **pay** for the damage.
22. 9 God declares to be guilty shall **pay** double to the other man.
22.13 he need not **pay** for what has been killed by wild animals.
22.14 when its owner is not present, the man must **pay** for it.
22.16 is not engaged, he must **pay** the bride-price for her and
22.17 him marry her, he must **pay** the father a sum of money
22.25 not act like a money-lender and require him to **pay** interest.
22.26 a pledge that he will **pay** you, you must give it back
30.12 Israel, each man is to **pay** me a price for his life,
30.13 in the census must **pay** the required amount of money,
30.13 Everyone must **pay** this as an offering to me.
30.14 man twenty years old or older, is to **pay** me this amount.
30.15 rich man is not to **pay** more, nor the poor man less,
30.15 when they **pay** this amount for their lives.
30.16 This tax will be the **payment** for their lives, and I will
38.26 This amount equalled the total **paid** by all persons
38.26 in the census, each one **paying** the required amount, weighed
Lev 5. 7 to the Lord as the **payment** for his sin two doves or
5.15 to hand over the **payments** that are sacred to the Lord,
5.16 He must make the **payments** he has failed to hand over and
5.16 to hand over and must **pay** an additional twenty per cent.
5.17 the Lord's commands, he is guilty and must **pay** the penalty.
19.20 and she has not been **paid** for and freed, then if another
20.20 his uncle, and he and the woman will **pay** the penalty;
25.27 In that case he must **pay** to the man who bought it
25.37 Do not make him **pay** interest on the money you lend him,
25.50 release on the basis of the wages **paid** to a hired man.
26.41 are humbled and they have **paid** the penalty for their sin and
26.43 complete rest, and they must **pay** the full penalty for having
27. 2 be set free by the **payment** of the following sums of money,
27. 8 vow is too poor to **pay** the standard price, he shall bring
27. 8 a lower price, according to the ability of the man to **pay.**
27.13 buy it back, he must **pay** the price plus an additional twenty
27.15 buy it back, he must **pay** the price plus an additional twenty
27.19 buy it back, he must **pay** the price plus an additional twenty
27.23 Restoration, and the man must **pay** the price that very day;
27.31 of it back, he must **pay** the standard price plus an
Num 3.47 For each one **pay** five pieces of silver, according to the
5. 8 no near relative to whom **payment** can be made, it shall be
5. 8 This **payment** is in addition to the ram used to perform the
Num 18.15 But you must accept **payment** to buy back every first-born child,
18.15 and must also accept **payment** for every first-born animal that is
18.21 This is in **payment** for their service in taking care of the
20.19 of your water, we will **pay** for it—all we want is
22. 7 took with them the **payment** for the curse, went to Balaam,
31.50 to the Lord as a **payment** for our lives, so that he
35.31 He cannot escape this penalty by the **payment** of money.
35.32 allow him to make a **payment** in order to return home before
Deut 2.28 We will **pay** for the food we eat and the water we
22.29 He is to **pay** the girl's father the bride price of fifty
24.15 Each day before sunset **pay** him for that day's work;
24.15 If you do not **pay** him, he will cry out against you
Judg 9.24 to murder Gideon's seventy sons, would **pay** for their crime.
9.56 In this way God **paid** Abimelech back for the crime that
15. 7 I swear that I won't stop until I **pay** you back!"
18. 4 with Micah, who **pays** me to serve as his priest."
1 Sam 6. 3 send with it a gift to him to **pay** for your sin.
6. 8 are sending to him as a gift to **pay** for your sins.
6.17 Lord as a gift to **pay** for their sins, one each for
12. 3 any of these things, I will **pay** back what I have taken."
17.25 and will not require his father's family to **pay** taxes."
18.25 king wants from you as **payment** for the bride is the
25.21 and this is how he **pays** me back for the help I
2 Sam 3.14 I **paid** a hundred Philistine foreskins in order to marry her."
8. 2 So the Moabites became his subjects and **paid** taxes to him.
8. 6 and they became his subjects and **paid** taxes to him.
12. 6 a cruel thing, he must **pay** back four times as much as
19.42 He hasn't **paid** for our food nor has he given us anything."
24.24 But the king answered, "No, I will **pay** you for it.
1 Kgs 2.23 if I don't make Adonijah **pay** with his life for asking this!
4.21 They **paid** him taxes and were subject to him all his life.
5. 6 work with them, and I will **pay** your men whatever you decide.
10.15 in addition to the taxes **paid** by merchants,
10.15 profits from trade, and tribute **paid** by the Arabian kings and
20.39 if he escapes, you will **pay** for it with your life
20.39 or else **pay** a fine of three thousand pieces
20.40 your own sentence, and you will have to **pay** the penalty."
20.42 to be killed, you will **pay** for it with your life, and
21. 2 it, or, if you prefer, I will **pay** you a fair price."
2 Kgs 4. 1 my two sons as slaves in **payment** for my husband's debt."
4. 7 her, "Sell the olive-oil and **pay** all your debts, and there
5.20 "My master has let Naaman get away without **paying** a thing!
10.24 lets one of them escape will **pay** for it with his life!"
12. 4 to save up the money **paid** in connection with the sacrifices
12. 4 the Temple, both the dues **paid** for the regular sacrifices
12.11 would **pay** the carpenters, the builders, [12]the masons,
12.12 used in the repairs, and **pay** all other necessary expenses.
12.13 money, however, was used to **pay** for making silver cups,
12.14 It was all used to **pay** the workmen and to buy the
17. 3 Hoshea surrendered to Shalmaneser and **paid** him tribute every year.
17. 4 his help, and stopped **paying** the annual tribute to Assyria.
18.14 stop your attack, and I will **pay** whatever you demand."
22. 5 They are to **pay** [6]the carpenters, the builders, and the masons,
23.33 of Hamath, and made Judah **pay** 3,400 kilogrammes of silver
23.35 raise the amount needed to **pay** the tribute demanded by the
1 Chr 18. 2 Moabites, who became his subjects and **paid** taxes to him.
18. 6 and they became his subjects and **paid** taxes to him.
19. 6 David their enemy, so they **paid** thirty-four thousand
21.24 But the king answered, "No, I will **pay** you the full price.
21.25 he **paid** Araunah six hundred gold coins for the threshing-place.
2 Chr 9.14 in addition to the taxes **paid** by the traders and merchants.
24. 6 Lord, required the people to **pay** for support of the Tent of
25. 9 "But what about all that silver I have already **paid** for them?"
26. 8 The Ammonites **paid** tribute to Uzziah, and he became so
27. 5 he forced the Ammonites to **pay** him the following tribute
36. 3 him prisoner and made Judah **pay** 3,400 kilogrammes of silver
Ezra 3. 7 The people gave money to **pay** the stonemasons and the
4.13 completed, the people will stop **paying** taxes, and your royal
6. 4 All expenses are to be **paid** by the royal treasury.
6. 8 Their expenses are to be **paid** promptly out of the royal
Neh 5. 4 had to borrow money to **pay** the royal tax on our fields
7.70 contributed to help **pay** the cost of restoring the Temple:
10.32 grammes of silver to help **pay** the expenses of the Temple.
13. 2 Instead, they **paid** money to Balaam to curse Israel, but our
Job 7. 2 like a worker waiting for his **pay.**
21.31 accuse a wicked man or **pay** him back for all he has
24. 3 to orphans, and keep a widow's ox till she **pays** her debts.
24. 9 and take the poor man's children in **payment** for debts.
Ps 35.12 They **pay** me back evil for good, and I sink in despair.
37.21 wicked man borrows and never **pays** back, but the good man is
38.20 Those who **pay** back evil for good are against me because
41.10 and restore my health, and I will **pay** my enemies back.
49. 7 he cannot **pay** God the price for his life,
49. 8 for his life, [8]because the **payment** for a human life is too
49. 8 What he could **pay** would never be enough [9]to keep him from
79.12 Lord, **pay** the other nations back seven times for all the
109. 5 They **pay** me back evil for good and hatred for love.
137. 8 Happy is the man who **pays** you back for what you have
Prov 6.31 he is caught, he must **pay** back seven times more—he must
6.35 He will not accept any **payment;**
11.15 If you promise to **pay** a stranger's debt, you will regret it.
17.26 It is not right to make an innocent person **pay** a fine;
19.17 like lending to the Lord, and the Lord will **pay** you back.
20.16 ought to have his own property held to guarantee **payment.**
22.27 you should be unable to **pay,** they will take away even your
23.23 good sense—these are worth **paying** for, but too valuable for
27.13 to have his own property held to guarantee **payment.**
Song 8.11 each one **pays** a thousand silver coins.
Is 24. 6 Its people are **paying** for what they have done.
52. 3 people, "When you became slaves, no money was **paid** for you;

Is	52. 3	in the same way nothing will be **paid** to set you free.
	52. 4	however, took you away by force and **paid** nothing for you.
	52. 5	you are captives, and nothing was **paid** for you.
	57. 8	large beds with your lovers, whom you **pay** to sleep with you.
Jer	14.16	I will make them **pay** for their wickedness."
	16.18	I will make them **pay** double for their sin and wickedness,
	18.20	Is evil the **payment** for good?
	22.13	countrymen work for nothing and does not **pay** their wages.
	25.14	I will **pay** the Babylonians back for what they have done,
	50.29	**Pay** it back for all it has done, and treat it as
	51.36	and will make your enemies **pay** for what they did to you.
Lam	4.22	Zion has **paid** for her sin;
	5. 4	We must **pay** for the water we drink;
Ezek	7. 3	I will **pay** you back for all your disgusting conduct.
	7. 8	have done, and I will **pay** you back for all your disgusting
	16.33	A prostitute is **paid,** but you gave presents to all your
	16.34	You didn't get **paid;**
	16.34	you **paid** them!
	16.43	That is why I have made you **pay** for them all.
	22.12	Some of your people murder for **pay.**
	27.12	iron, tin, and lead in **payment** for your abundant goods.
	27.16	fine linen, coral, and rubies in **payment** for your wares.
	27.17	Judah and Israel **paid** for your goods with wheat, honey,
	27.18	your merchandise and your products, **paying** for them with
	27.21	of the land of Kedar **paid** for your merchandise with lambs,
	29.19	and carry off all the wealth of Egypt as his army's **pay.**
	29.20	am giving him Egypt in **payment** for his services, because his
	35.11	the living God, I will **pay** you back for your anger, your
Hos	3. 2	So I **paid** fifteen pieces of silver
	4. 9	will punish you and make you **pay** for the evil you do.
	8. 9	from Assyria, and have **paid** other nations to protect them.
	9. 1	Baal and have loved the corn you thought he **paid** you with!
	12. 2	He will **pay** them back for what they have done.
Joel	3. 3	and girls into slavery to **pay** for prostitutes and wine.
	3. 4	Are you trying to **pay** me back for something?
	3. 4	If you are, I will quickly **pay** you back!
Amos	2. 6	honest men who cannot **pay** their debts,
	5.16	to mourn the dead along with those who are **paid** to mourn.
	7.12	Let them **pay** you for it.
	7.14	"I am not the kind of prophet who prophesies for **pay.**
	8. 6	a poor man who can't **pay** his debts, not even the price
Jon	1. 3	He **paid** his fare and went aboard with the crew to sail
Mic	3. 5	promise peace to those who **pay** them, but threaten war for
	3.11	priests interpret the Law for **pay,** the prophets give their
	6. 7	Shall I offer him my first-born child to **pay** for my sins?
Nah	1. 2	In his anger he **pays** them back.
Hab	2. 6	you go on getting rich by forcing your debtors to **pay** up?"
	2. 7	will be in debt yourselves and be forced to **pay** interest.
Zech	11.12	So they **paid** me thirty pieces of silver as my wages.
Mt	5.26	I tell you, until you **pay** the last penny of your fine.
	6. 2	I assure you, they have already been **paid** in full.
	6. 5	I assure you, they have already been **paid** in full.
	6.16	I assure you, they have already been **paid** in full.
	10. 8	You have received without paying, so give without being **paid.**
	17.24	came to Peter and asked, "Does your teacher **pay** the temple-tax?"
	17.25	Who **pays** duties or taxes to the kings of this world?
	17.26	replied Jesus, "that means that the citizens don't have to **pay.**
	17.27	Take it and **pay** them our taxes."
	18.25	did not have enough to **pay** his debt, so the king ordered
	18.25	children and all that he had, in order to **pay** the debt.
	18.26	'Be patient with me,' he begged, 'and I will **pay** you everything!'
	18.28	'**Pay** back what you owe me!'
	18.29	begged him, 'Be patient with me, and I will **pay** you back!'
	18.30	he had him thrown into jail until he should **pay** the debt.
	18.34	to be punished until he should **pay** back the whole amount."
	20. 2	He agreed to **pay** them the regular wage, a silver coin
	20. 4	work in the vineyard, and I will **pay** you a fair wage.'
	20. 8	'Call the workers and **pay** them their wages,
	20. 9	begun to work at five o'clock were **paid** a silver coin each.
	20.10	be hired came to be **paid,** they thought they would get more;
	20.12	hot sun—yet you paid them the same as you **paid** us!'
	20.14	Now take your **pay** and go home.
	22.17	it against our Law to **pay** taxes to the Roman Emperor,
	22.19	Show me the coin for **paying** the tax!"
	22.21	said to them, "Well, then, **pay** the Emperor
	22.21	belongs to the Emperor, and **pay** God what belongs to God."
	27. 9	of Israel had agreed to **pay** for him, [10] and used the money
Mk	12.14	is it against our Law to **pay** taxes to the Roman Emperor?
	12.14	Should we **pay** them or not?"
	12.17	So Jesus said, "Well, then, **pay** the Emperor
	12.17	belongs to the Emperor, and **pay** God what belongs to God."
Lk	3.14	Be content with your **pay."**
	7.42	Neither of them could **pay** him back, so he cancelled the
	10. 7	they offer you, for a worker should be given his **pay.**
	10.35	back this way, I will **pay** you whatever else you spend on
	12.59	I tell you, until you **pay** the last penny of your fine."
	14.12	and in this way you will be **paid** for what you did.
	14.14	will be blessed, because they are not able to **pay** you back.
	19. 8	cheated anyone, I will **pay** him back four times as much."
	20.22	our Law for us to **pay** taxes to the Roman Emperor,
	20.25	So Jesus said, "Well, then, **pay** the Emperor
	20.25	belongs to the Emperor, and **pay** God what belongs to God."
	22. 5	They were pleased and offered to **pay** him money.
	23. 2	telling them not to **pay** taxes to the Emperor and claiming
Jn	4.36	reaps the harvest is being **paid** and gathers the crops
Acts	17. 9	made Jason and the others **pay** the required amount of money
	21.24	join them in the ceremony of purification and **pay** their expenses;
	22.28	said, "I became one by **paying** a large amount of money."
	25.13	Bernice came to Caesarea to **pay** a visit of welcome to Festus.
Rom	4. 4	A person who works is **paid** his wages,
	6.23	For sin **pays** its wage—death;
Rom	11.35	ever given him anything, so that he had to **pay** it back?"
	12.19	"I will take revenge, I will **pay** back, says the Lord."
	13. 6	That is also why you **pay** taxes, because the authorities are
	13. 7	**Pay,** then, what you owe them;
	13. 7	**pay** them your personal and property taxes, and show respect
1 Cor	9. 7	What soldier ever has to **pay** his own expenses in the army?
	9.17	a matter of free choice, then I could expect to be **paid;**
	9.18	What **pay** do I get, then?
	14.38	he does not pay attention to this, **pay** no attention to him.
2 Cor	11. 8	While I was working among you, I was **paid** by other churches.
1 Thes	5.12	beg you, our brothers, to **pay** proper respect to those who
	5.15	See that no one **pays** back wrong for wrong, but at all
2 Thes	3. 8	We did not accept anyone's support without **paying** for it.
1 Tim	5.17	worthy of receiving double **pay,** especially those who work hard
	5.18	and "A worker should be given his **pay."**
Phlm	19	I, Paul, will **pay** you back.
Heb	7. 9	so to speak, when Abraham **paid** the tenth,
	7. 9	Levi (whose descendants collect the tenth) also **paid** it.
Jas	5. 4	You have not **paid** any wages to the men who work in
1 Pet	1.18	For you know what was **paid** to set you free
	3. 9	Do not **pay** back evil with evil or cursing with cursing;
	3. 9	instead, **pay** back with a blessing,
	5. 2	your work, not for mere **pay,** but from a real desire to
2 Pet	2.13	and they will be **paid** with suffering for the suffering they
Rev	18. 6	**pay** her back double for all she has done.
	21. 6	from the spring of the water of life without **paying** for it.

PAY ATTENTION see ATTENTION

PEACE

Gen	15.15	live to a ripe old age, die in **peace,** and be buried.
	26.29	We were kind to you and let you leave **peacefully.**
Lev	26. 6	"I will give you **peace** in your land, and you will sleep
Num	6.26	May the Lord look on you with favour and give you **peace.**
	23.10	Let me die in **peace** like the righteous."
Deut	2.26	to King Sihon of Heshbon with the following offer of **peace:**
	3.20	lets them live there in **peace,** as he has already done here
	12. 9	Lord your God is giving you, where you can live in **peace.**
	12.10	you safe from all your enemies, and you will live in **peace.**
	28.65	You will find no **peace** anywhere, no place to call your own;
	33.28	So Jacob's descendants live in **peace,** secure in a land
Josh	10. 1	people of Gibeon had made **peace** with the Israelites
	10. 4	its people have made **peace** with Joshua and the Israelites."
	11.19	The only city that made **peace** with the people of Israel
	14.15	There was now **peace** in the land.
	21.44	The Lord gave them **peace** throughout the land,
	22. 4	the Lord your God has given your fellow-Israelites **peace.**
Judg	3.11	There was **peace** in the land for forty years,
	3.30	Moab, and there was **peace** in the land for eighty years.
	4.17	King Jabin of Hazor was at **peace** with Heber's family.
	5.31	And there was **peace** in the land for forty years.
	6.23	But the Lord said to him, **"Peace.**
	6.24	altar to the Lord there and named it "The Lord is **Peace."**
	8.28	The land was at **peace** for forty years, until Gideon died.
	11.13	Now you must give it back **peacefully."**
	18. 7	They were a **peaceful,** quiet people, with no disputes with anyone;
	18.27	attacked Laish, that town of **peaceful,** quiet people
1 Sam	1.17	"Go in **peace,"** Eli said, "and may the God of Israel
	7.14	there was **peace** also between the Israelites and the Canaanites.
	16. 4	trembling to meet him and asked, "Is this a **peaceful** visit,
	29. 7	So go back home in **peace,** and don't do anything that would
2 Sam	10.19	they made **peace** with them and became their subjects.
	15. 9	"Go in **peace,"** the king said.
	15.27	Abiathar's son Jonathan and go back to the city in **peace.**
	20.19	a great city, one of the most **peaceful** and loyal in Israel.
1 Kgs	2. 5	murdered them in time of **peace** in revenge for deaths
	4.24	and he was at **peace** with all the neighbouring countries.
	5. 4	the Lord my God has given me **peace** on all my borders.
	5.12	There was **peace** between Hiram and Solomon,
	8.56	Lord who has given his people **peace,** as he promised he would.
	20.18	whether they are coming to fight or to ask for **peace."**
	22. 1	There was **peace** between Israel and Syria for the next two years,
	22.17	let them go home in **peace.' "**
	22.44	Jehoshaphat made **peace** with the king of Israel.
2 Kgs	5.19	"Go in **peace,"** Elisha said.
	9.22	"Are you coming in **peace?"**
	9.22	"How can there be **peace,"** Jehu answered, "when we still
	13. 5	from the Syrians, and so the Israelites lived in **peace,**
	20.19	that there would be **peace** and security during his lifetime,
	22.20	I will let you die in **peace."**
1 Chr	4.40	in a stretch of open country that was quiet and **peaceful.**
	19.19	Israel, they made **peace** with David and became his subjects.
	22. 9	son who will rule in **peace,**
	22. 9	because I will give him **peace** from all his enemies.
	22. 9	during his reign I will give Israel **peace** and security.
	22.18	God has been with you and given you **peace** on all sides.
	23.25	God of Israel has given **peace** to his people, and he himself
2 Chr	14. 1	as king, and under Asa the land enjoyed **peace** for ten years.
	14. 5	cities of Judah, the kingdom was at **peace** under his rule.
	14. 6	years there was no war, because the Lord gave him **peace.**
	15.15	and he accepted them and gave them **peace** on every side.
	18.16	let them go home in **peace.' "**
	20.30	so Jehoshaphat ruled in **peace,**
	32.22	He let the people live in **peace** with all the neighbouring countries.
	34.28	I will let you die in **peace."**
Ezra	5. 7	"To Emperor Darius, may you rule in **peace.**
Neh	9.28	When **peace** returned, they sinned again,
Esth	9.30	It wished the Jews **peace** and security [31] and directed them

Job	3.18	Even prisoners enjoy **peace,** free from shouts and harsh commands.
	3.26	I have no **peace,** no rest, and my troubles never end.
	5.24	Then you will live at **peace** in your tent;
	12. 6	and godless men live in **peace,** though their only god is
	16.12	I was living in **peace,** but God took me by the throat
	21.13	They live out their lives in **peace** and quietly die
	22.21	Now, Job, make **peace** with God and stop treating him like
	25. 1	he keeps his heavenly kingdom in **peace.**
	36.11	him, they live out their lives in **peace** and prosperity.
Ps	4. 8	When I lie down, I go to sleep in **peace;**
	29.11	The Lord gives strength to his people and blesses them with **peace.**
	34.14	strive for **peace** with all your heart.
	35.20	instead they invent all kinds of lies about **peace-loving** people.
	37.11	the humble will possess the land and enjoy prosperity and **peace.**
	37.37	a **peaceful** man has descendants,
	85. 8	he promises **peace** to us, his own people,
	85.10	righteousness and **peace** will embrace.
	120. 6	I have lived too long with people who hate **peace!**
	120. 7	When I speak of **peace,** they are for war.
	122. 6	Pray for the **peace** of Jerusalem:
	122. 7	May there be **peace** inside your walls and safety in your palaces."
	122. 8	and friends I say to Jerusalem, **"Peace** be with you!"
	125. 5	**Peace** be with Israel!
	128. 6	**Peace** be with Israel!
	131. 2	Instead, I am content and at **peace.**
Prov	10.10	trouble, but one who openly criticizes works for **peace.**
	13.17	those who can be trusted bring **peace.**
	14.30	**Peace** of mind makes the body healthy,
	15.18	Hot tempers cause arguments, but patience brings **peace.**
	17. 1	dry crust of bread with **peace** of mind than to have a
	27. 9	you feel happier, but trouble shatters your **peace** of mind.
Ecc	3. 8	time for hate, the time for war and the time for **peace.**
	4. 6	have only a little, with **peace** of mind, than to be busy
Song	8.10	My lover knows that with him I find contentment and **peace.**
Is	9. 6	"Mighty God," "Eternal Father," "Prince of **Peace."**
	9. 7	his kingdom will always be at **peace.**
	11. 6	sheep will live together in **peace,** and leopards will lie
	11. 7	together, and their calves and cubs will lie down in **peace.**
	14. 7	world enjoys rest and **peace,** and everyone sings for joy.
	26. 3	You, Lord, give perfect **peace** to those who keep their
	27. 5	my people want my protection, let them make **peace** with me.
	27. 5	Yes, let them make **peace** with me."
	32.17	do what is right, there will be **peace** and security for ever.
	32.18	be free from worries, and their homes **peaceful** and safe.
	33. 7	ambassadors who tried to bring about **peace** are crying bitterly.
	38.17	My bitterness will turn into **peace.**
	39. 8	that there would be **peace** and security during his lifetime,
	52. 7	the mountains, bringing good news, the news of **peace!**
	54.10	I will keep for ever my promise of **peace."**
	54.13	"I myself will teach your people, and give them prosperity and **peace.**
	55.12	you will be led out of the city in **peace.**
	57. 2	Those who live good lives find **peace** and rest in death.
	57.19	I offer **peace** to all, both near and far!
	60.17	I will make them rule with justice and **peace.**
Jer	4.10	have said there would be **peace,** but a sword is at their
	6.16	Walk on it, and you will live in **peace."**
	8.15	We hoped for **peace** and a time of healing,
	12.12	no one can live in **peace.**
	14.13	they say, that there will be only **peace** in our land."
	14.19	We looked for **peace,** but nothing good happened;
	16. 5	bless my people with **peace** or show them love and mercy.
	23. 6	will be safe, and the people of Israel will live in **peace.**
	25.36	your nation and left your **peaceful** country in ruins.
	28. 9	But a prophet who predicts **peace** can only be recognized as
	30. 5	a cry of terror, a cry of fear and not of **peace.**
	30.10	You will come back home and live in **peace;**
	33. 6	I will show them abundant **peace** and security.
	34. 5	You will die in **peace,** and as people burnt incense when
	46.27	You will come back home and live in **peace;**
	50.34	their cause and will bring **peace** to the earth, but trouble
Lam	3.17	I have forgotten what health and **peace** and happiness are.
Ezek	7.25	You will look for **peace** and never find it.
	16.49	to eat and lived in **peace** and quiet, but they did not
	38.11	where the people live in **peace** and security in unwalled
Dan	11. 8	After several years of **peace** [9] the king of Syria will invade Egypt,
Hos	2.18	and bows, and will let my people live in **peace** and safety.
Obad	7	People who were at **peace** with you have now conquered you.
Mic	3. 5	by prophets who promise **peace** to those who pay them,
	4. 4	Everyone will live in **peace** among his own vineyards and fig-trees,
	5. 5	will acknowledge his greatness, [5] and he will bring **peace.**
Hag	2. 9	one, and there I will give my people prosperity and **peace."**
Zech	1.15	I am very angry with the nations that enjoy quiet and **peace.**
	3.10	neighbour to come and enjoy **peace** and security, surrounded
	6.13	throne, and they will work together in **peace** and harmony.'
	8.12	They will sow their crops in **peace.**
	8.16	In the courts, give real justice—the kind that brings **peace.**
	8.19	You must love truth and **peace."**
	9.10	Your king will make **peace** among the nations;
Mt	5. 9	"Happy are those who work for **peace;**
	5.24	go at once and make **peace** with your brother, and then come
	10.12	When you go into a house, say, **'Peace** be with you.'
	10.13	in that house welcome you, let your greeting of **peace** remain;
	10.34	not think that I have come to bring **peace** to the world.
	10.34	No, I did not come to bring **peace,** but a sword.
	26.49	straight to Jesus and said, **"Peace** be with you, Teacher,"
	28. 9	Suddenly Jesus met them and said, **"Peace** be with you."
Mk	5.34	Go in **peace,** and be healed of your trouble."
Mk	9.50	of friendship among yourselves, and live in **peace** with one another."
Lk	1.28	The angel came to her and said, **"Peace** be with you!
	1.79	of death, to guide our steps into the path of **peace."**
	2.14	in the highest heaven, and **peace** on earth to those with whom
	2.29	your promise, and you may let your servant go in **peace.**
	7.50	go in **peace."**
	8.48	Go in **peace."**
	10. 5	you go into a house, first say, **'Peace** be with this house.'
	10. 6	If a **peace-loving** man lives there,
	10. 6	let your greeting of **peace** remain on him;
	10. 6	if not, take back your greeting of **peace.**
	12.51	Do you suppose that I came to bring **peace** to the world?
	12.51	No, not **peace,** but division.
	14.32	to ask for terms of **peace** while he is still a long
	19.38	**Peace** in heaven and glory to God!"
	19.42	saying, "If you only knew today what is needed for **peace!**
	24.36	stood among them and said to them, **"Peace** be with you."
Jn	14.27	**"Peace** is what I leave with you;
	14.27	it is my own **peace** that I give you.
	16.33	so that you will have **peace** by being united to me.
	20.19	**"Peace** be with you," he said.
	20.21	Jesus said to them again, **"Peace** be with you.
	20.26	Jesus came and stood among them and said, **"Peace** be with you."
Acts	7.26	two Israelites fighting, and he tried to make **peace** between them.
	9.31	throughout Judaea, Galilee, and Samaria had a time of **peace.**
	10.36	proclaiming the Good News of **peace** through Jesus Christ,
	12.20	Herod and asked him for **peace,** because their country got its
	15.33	they were sent off in **peace** by the believers and went back
	16.36	You may leave, then, and go in **peace."**
	24. 2	a long period of **peace,** and many necessary reforms are being
Rom	1. 7	Father and the Lord Jesus Christ give you grace and **peace.**
	2.10	will give glory, honour, and **peace** to all who do what is
	3.17	not known the path of **peace,** [18] nor have they learnt reverence
	5. 1	through faith, we have **peace** with God through our Lord Jesus
	8. 6	to be controlled by the Spirit results in life and **peace.**
	12.18	everything possible on your part to live in **peace** with everybody.
	14.17	but of the righteousness, **peace,** and joy which the Holy Spirit
	14.19	at those things that bring **peace** and that help to strengthen
	15.13	you with all joy and **peace** by means of your faith in
	15.33	May God, our source of **peace,** be with all of you.
	16.20	And God, our source of **peace,** will soon crush Satan under
1 Cor	1. 3	Father and the Lord Jesus Christ give you grace and **peace.**
	7.15	God has called you to live in **peace.**
	14.33	not want us to be in disorder but in harmony and **peace.**
	16.11	to continue his trip in **peace,** so that he will come back
2 Cor	1. 2	Father and the Lord Jesus Christ give you grace and **peace.**
	13.11	live in **peace.**
	13.11	And the God of love and **peace** will be with you.
Gal	1. 3	Father and the Lord Jesus Christ give you grace and **peace.**
	5.22	the Spirit produces love, joy, **peace,** patience, kindness,
	6.16	rule in their lives, may **peace** and mercy be with them—
Eph	1. 2	Father and the Lord Jesus Christ give you grace and **peace.**
	2.14	Christ himself has brought us **peace** by making Jews and
	2.15	new people in union with himself, in this way making **peace.**
	2.17	preached the Good News of **peace** to all—to you Gentiles,
	4. 3	Spirit gives by means of the **peace** that binds you together.
	6.15	your shoes the readiness to announce the Good News of **peace.**
	6.23	Christ give to all Christian brothers **peace** and love with faith.
Phil	1. 2	Father and the Lord Jesus Christ give you grace and **peace.**
	4. 7	And God's **peace,** which is far beyond human understanding,
	4. 9	And the God who gives us **peace** will be with you.
Col	1. 2	May God our Father give you grace and **peace.**
	1.20	God made **peace** through his Son's sacrificial death on the cross
	3.15	The **peace** that Christ gives is to guide you in the
	3.15	for it is to this **peace** that God has called you together
1 Thes	1. 1	May grace and **peace** be yours.
	5.13	Be at **peace** among yourselves.
	5.23	the God who gives us **peace** make you holy in every way
2 Thes	1. 2	Father and the Lord Jesus Christ give you grace and **peace.**
	3.16	who is our source of **peace,** give you peace at all times
1 Tim	1. 2	Father and Christ Jesus our Lord give you grace, mercy, and **peace.**
	2. 2	may live a quiet and **peaceful** life with all reverence
	3. 3	not be a drunkard or a violent man, but gentle and **peaceful;**
2 Tim	1. 2	Father and Christ Jesus our Lord give you grace, mercy, and **peace.**
	2.22	for righteousness, faith, love, and **peace,** together with those
Tit	1. 4	Father and Christ Jesus our Saviour give you grace and **peace.**
	3. 2	of anyone, but to be **peaceful** and friendly, and always to
Phlm	3	Father and the Lord Jesus Christ give you grace and **peace.**
Heb	7. 2	was king of Salem, his name also means "King of **Peace."**)
	12.11	by such punishment reap the **peaceful** reward of a righteous life.
	12.14	Try to be at **peace** with everyone, and try to live a
	13.20	May the God of **peace** provide you with every good thing you
Jas	3.17	it is also **peaceful,** gentle, and friendly;
	3.18	that is produced from the seeds the peacemakers plant in **peace.**
1 Pet	1. 2	May grace and **peace** be yours in full measure.
	3.11	he must strive for **peace** with all his heart.
	5.14	May **peace** be with all of you who belong to Christ.
2 Pet	1. 2	May grace and **peace** be yours in full measure
	3.14	and faultless in God's sight and to be at **peace** with him.
2 Jn	3	Jesus Christ, the Father's Son, give us grace, mercy, and **peace;**
	10	do not even say, **"Peace** be with you."
	11	anyone who wishes him **peace** becomes his partner in the evil
3 Jn	15	**Peace** be with you.
Jude	2	May mercy, **peace,** and love be yours in full measure.
Rev	1. 4	Grace and **peace** be yours from God, who is, who was,

PEAK

Deut 3.27 Go to the **peak** of Mount Pisgah and look to the north
Job 39.28 the highest rocks and makes the sharp **peaks** its fortress.
Ps 68.15 What a mighty mountain is Bashan, a mountain of many **peaks!**
68.16 Why from your mighty **peaks** do you look with scorn on the

PEAL OF THUNDER

Rev 4. 5 came flashes of lightning, rumblings, and **peals of thunder.**
8. 5 There were rumblings and **peals of thunder,** flashes of lightning,
11.19 lightning, rumblings and **peals of thunder,** an earthquake, and heavy hail.
14. 2 like a roaring waterfall, like a loud **peal of thunder.**
16.18 rumblings and **peals of thunder,** and a terrible earthquake.
19. 6 sound of a roaring waterfall, like loud **peals of thunder.**

PEARL

Mt 7. 6 Do not throw your **pearls** in front of pigs—they will only
13.45 man is looking for fine **pearls,** [46]and when he finds one
13.46 he goes and sells everything he has, and buys that **pearl.**
1 Tim 2. 9 gold ornaments or **pearls** or expensive dresses, [10]but with good
Rev 17. 4 and covered with gold ornaments, precious stones, and **pearls.**
18.12 no one buys their gold, silver, precious stones, and **pearls;**
18.16 and cover herself with gold ornaments, precious stones, and **pearls!**
21.21 The twelve gates were twelve **pearls;**
21.21 each gate was made from a single **pearl.**

PEAS

2 Sam 17.28 grain, beans, **peas,** honey, cheese, cream, and some sheep.
23.11 Philistines had gathered at Lehi, where there was a field of **peas.**
Ezek 4. 9 "Now take some wheat, barley, beans, **peas,** millet, and

PEG

Ex 27.19 the Tent and all the **pegs** for the Tent and for the
35.18 the **pegs** and ropes for the Tent and the enclosure;
38.20 All the **pegs** for the Tent and for the surrounding
38.31 the enclosure, and all the **pegs** for the Tent and the
39.40 the **pegs** for the Tent;
Num 3.37 for the posts, bases, **pegs,** and ropes for the outer court.
4.32 Tent, [32]and the posts, bases, **pegs,** and ropes of the court
Judg 4.21 killed him by driving the **peg** right through the side of his
5.26 She took a tent **peg** in one hand, a workman's hammer in
16.13 make it tight with a **peg,** I'll be as weak as anybody
16.14 She made it tight with a **peg** and shouted, "Samson!
Is 22.23 firmly in place like a **peg,** and he will be a source
22.24 will hang on him like pots and bowls hanging from a **peg!**
22.25 When that happens, the **peg** that was firmly fastened will
33.20 that is never moved, whose **pegs** are never pulled up and
54. 2 lengthen its ropes and strengthen the **pegs!**
Ezek 15. 3 Can you even make a **peg** out of it to hang things

PEKAH

One of the last kings of the n. kingdom (Israel), who was assassinated by Hoshea.

2 Kgs 15.25 An officer of Pekahiah's forces, **Pekah** son of Remaliah,
15.27 of King Uzziah of Judah, **Pekah** son of Remaliah became king
15.29 It was while **Pekah** was king that Tiglath Pileser, the
15.30 of Elah plotted against King **Pekah,** assassinated him, and
15.31 Everything else that **Pekah** did is recorded in The
15.32 year of the reign of **Pekah** son of Remaliah as king of
15.37 King Rezin of Syria and King **Pekah** of Israel to attack Judah.
16. 1 year of the reign of **Pekah** son of Remaliah as king of
16. 5 Rezin of Syria and King **Pekah** of Israel attacked Jerusalem
2 Chr 28. 5 let the king of Israel, **Pekah** son of Remaliah, defeat Ahaz
Is 7. 1 king of Syria, and **Pekah** son of Remaliah, king of Israel,
7. 4 his Syrians and of King **Pekah** is no more dangerous than the
7. 9 capital city, and Samaria is no stronger than King **Pekah.**
8. 6 before King Rezin and King **Pekah,** [7]I, the Lord, will bring

PELICAN

Lev 11.13 seagulls, storks, herons, **pelicans,** cormorants;
Deut 14.12 sea-gulls, storks, herons, **pelicans,** cormorants;

PEN (1)

Ex 21.29 but did not keep it **penned** up—then if it gores someone
21.36 owner did not keep it **penned** up, he must make good the
1 Sam 24. 3 cave close to some sheep **pens** by the road and went in
Ps 68.13 of you stay among the sheep **pens** on the day of battle?)
Zeph 2. 6 will become open fields with shepherds' huts and sheep **pens.**

PEN (2)

Ps 45. 1 Like the **pen** of a good writer my tongue is ready
Jer 17. 1 "People of Judah, your sin is written with an iron **pen;**
3 Jn 13 but I do not want to do it with **pen** and ink.

PENALTY

Lev 5. 6 the sin, [6]and as the **penalty** for his sin he must bring
5.17 the Lord's commands, he is guilty and must pay the **penalty.**
20.20 his uncle, and he and the woman will pay the **penalty;**
26.41 and they have paid the **penalty** for their sin and rebellion,
26.43 they must pay the full **penalty** for having rejected my laws
Num 18.22 and in this way bring on themselves the **penalty** of death.
35.31 He cannot escape this **penalty** by the payment of money.
1 Kgs 20.40 your own sentence, and you will have to pay the **penalty."**
Neh 10.29 leaders in an oath, under **penalty** of a curse if we break
Acts 25.11 which I deserve the death **penalty,** I do not ask to escape

PENIS

Lev 15. 2 has a discharge from his **penis,** the discharge is unclean,
15. 3 discharge is unclean, [3]whether the **penis** runs with it or is
Deut 23. 1 has been castrated or whose **penis** has been cut off may be

PENNY

Mt 5.26 I tell you, until you pay the last **penny** of your fine.
10.29 For only a **penny** you can buy two sparrows, yet not one
Mk 12.42 and dropped in two little copper coins, worth about a **penny.**
Lk 12. 6 "Aren't five sparrows sold for two **pennies?**
12.59 I tell you, until you pay the last **penny** of your fine."

PENTECOST

The Greek name for the Israelite festival of wheat harvest (see Harvest Festival). The name Pentecost (meaning "fiftieth") comes from the fact that the feast was held fifty days after Passover.

Acts 2. 1 When the day of **Pentecost** came, all the believers were gathered
20.16 in Jerusalem by the day of **Pentecost,** if at all possible.
1 Cor 16. 8 I will stay here in Ephesus until the day of **Pentecost.**

PEOPLE

see also **GOD'S PEOPLE**

Gen 10. 2 Tiras—were the ancestors of the **peoples** who bear their names.
10. 6 Canaan—were the ancestors of the **peoples** who bear their names.
10.15 Heth—were the ancestors of the **peoples** who bear their names.
10.22 Aram—were the ancestors of the **peoples** who bear their names.
10.32 All these **peoples** are the descendants of Noah, nation by nation,
11. 6 "Now then, these are all **one people** and they speak one language;
25.23 You will give birth to two rival **peoples.**
27.29 May nations be your servants, and may **peoples** bow down before you.
34. 9 there will be intermarriage between **our people** and yours.
34.16 We will settle among you and become **one people** with you.
34.22 live among us and be **one people** with us only on condition
Ex 19. 6 will be my chosen people, [6]**a people** dedicated to me alone,
Num 22.11 them to tell me [11]that **a people** who came from Egypt has
Deut 4.19 God has given these to all other **peoples** for them to worship.
4.34 dared to go and take **a people** from another nation and make
6.14 other gods, any of the gods of the **peoples** around you.
7. 6 From all the **peoples** on earth he chose you to be his
7. 7 you and choose you because you outnumbered other **peoples;**
7.17 not tell yourselves that these **peoples** outnumber you and
9.27 to the stubbornness, wickedness, and sin of **this people.**
10.18 the foreigners who live with **our people,** and gives them food
14. 2 own people from among all the **peoples** who live on earth.
22.21 done a shameful thing among **our people** by having intercourse
28.10 Then all the **peoples** on earth will see that the Lord has
32. 8 he determined where **peoples** should live.
Josh 13. 6 I will drive all these **peoples** out as the people of Israel
14. 8 The men who went with me, however, made **our people** afraid.
22.27 instead, as a sign for **our people** and yours, and for the
22.28 or for sacrifice, but as a sign for **our people** and yours.'
23. 7 will not associate with these **peoples** left among you or
Judg 2.12 to worship other gods, the gods of the **peoples** round them.
9.29 I wish I were leading **this people!**
14. 3 you find a girl in our own clan, among all **our people?"**
Ruth 2.11 you came to live among **a people** you had never known before.
1 Sam 10.18 Egyptians and all the other **peoples** who were oppressing you.
14.29 "What a terrible thing my father has done to **our people!**
14.30 would have been today if **our people** had eaten the food they
15. 6 a warning to the Kenites, **a people** whose ancestors had been
2 Sam 10.12 Let's fight hard for **our people** and for the cities of our
17.13 he retreats into a city, **our people** will all bring ropes and
1 Kgs 3. 8 chosen to be your own, **a people** who are so many that
8.43 do, so that all the **peoples** of the world may know you
8.53 chose them from all the **peoples** to be your own people, as
12. 7 "If you want to serve **this people** well, give a favourable
18.37 Lord, answer me, so that **this people** will know that you, the
2 Kgs 19. 4 So pray to God for those of **our people** who survive."
1 Chr 1. 5 Tiras—were the ancestors of the **peoples** who bear their names.
1. 8 Canaan—were the ancestors of the **peoples** who bear their names.
1.13 Heth—were the ancestors of the **peoples** who bear their names.
1.17 Meshek—were the ancestors of the **peoples** who bear their names.
16.24 Proclaim his glory to the nations, his mighty deeds to all **peoples.**
19.13 Let's fight hard for **our people** and for the cities of our
2 Chr 1. 9 have made me king over **a people** who are so many that
6.33 do, so that all the **peoples** of the world may know you
32.19 the gods of the other **peoples,** idols made by human hands.
Ezra 4.10 Elam, [10]together with the other **peoples** whom the great and
Neh 5.19 to my credit everything that I have done for **this people.**
6. 6 the neighbouring **peoples** that you and the Jewish people
9.32 our ancestors, and all **our people** have suffered.
13.16 goods into the city to sell to **our people** on the Sabbath.
Ps 7. 7 so bring together all the **peoples** round you, and rule over
33. 8 Honour him, all **peoples** of the world!
47. 1 Clap your hands for joy, all **peoples!**
47. 3 He gave us victory over the **peoples;**
57. 9 I will praise you among the **peoples.**
65. 7 you calm the uproar of the **peoples.**
67. 3 May the **peoples** praise you, O God;

Ps 67. 3 may all the **peoples** praise you!
67. 4 joy, because you judge the **peoples** with justice and guide
67. 5 May the **peoples** praise you, O God;
67. 5 may all the **peoples** praise you!
72. 9 The **peoples** of the desert will bow down before him;
87. 6 write a list of the **peoples** and include them all as citizens
96. 3 Proclaim his glory to the nations, his mighty deeds to all **peoples.**
96.10 he will judge the **peoples** with justice."
96.13 He will rule the **peoples** of the world with justice and fairness.
98. 9 He will rule the **peoples** of the world with justice and fairness.
105.44 them the lands of other **peoples** and let them take over their
108. 3 I will praise you among the **peoples.**
117. 1 Praise him, all **peoples!**
148.11 Praise him, kings and all **peoples,** princes and all other rulers;
149. 7 hands [7] to defeat the nations and to punish the **peoples;**
Is 6. 5 and I live among **a people** whose every word is sinful.
14. 6 rulers [6] who angrily oppressed the **peoples** and never stopped
26.19 Those of **our people** who have died will live again!
28.14 rule here in Jerusalem over **this people,** listen to what the
37. 4 So pray to God for those of **our people** who survive."
42. 6 Through you I will make a covenant with all **peoples;**
49. 8 you and through you make a covenant with all **peoples.**
53. 8 He was put to death for the sins of **our people.**
61. 9 will know That they are **a people** whom I have blessed."
Jer 10.21 This is why they have failed, and **our people** have been scattered.
12. 4 because of the wickedness of **our people,** people who say,
19.11 had said, "I will break **this people** and this city, and it
25. 9 to send for all the **peoples** from the north and for my
36. 7 because the Lord has threatened **this people** with his
37.18 you or your officials or **this people,** to make you put me
44.18 we have had nothing, and **our people** have died in war and
46.16 Let's go home to **our people** and escape the enemy's sword!'
Ezek 29.12 They will flee to every country and live among other **peoples."**
36.15 to the nations mocking it or see the **peoples** sneer at it.
Hos 4.14 As the proverb says, **'A people** without sense will be ruined.'
13.14 I will not save **this people** from the world of the dead
13.14 I will no longer have pity for **this people.**
Zech 8.22 Many **peoples** and powerful nations will come to Jerusalem
Mt 1.21 him Jesus—because he will save his **people** from their sins."
2. 6 you will come a leader who will guide my **people** Israel.' "
10.26 "So do not be afraid of **people.**
11.16 "Now, to what can I compare the **people** of this day?
12.21 and in him all **peoples** will put their hope."
12.39 "How evil and godless are the **people** of this day!"
12.45 This is what will happen to the evil **people** of this day."
13.14 'This **people** will listen and listen, but not understand;
15. 8 'These **people,** says God, honour me with their words,
16. 4 How evil and godless are the **people** of this day!
19. 4 in the beginning the Creator made **people** male and female?
21.43 and given to a **people** who will produce the proper fruits."
23.36 for all these murders will fall on the **people** of this day!
24.22 of his chosen **people,** however, God will reduce the days.
24.24 in order to deceive even God's chosen **people,** if possible.
24.30 and all the **peoples** of earth will weep as they see the
24.31 they will gather his chosen **people** from one end of the world
25.32 his royal throne, [32] and the **people** of all the nations will
28.19 Go, then, to all **peoples** everywhere and make them my disciples:
Mk 6. 2 Many **people** were there;
7. 6 'These **people,** says God, honour me with their words, but
8.12 and said, "Why do the **people** of this day ask for a
8.12 No such proof will be given to these **people!"**
8.24 said, "Yes, I can see **people,** but they look like trees
9.19 Jesus said to them, "How unbelieving you **people** are!
11.32 (They were afraid of the **people,** because everyone was convinced
13.10 the end comes, the gospel must be preached to all **peoples.**
Lk 1.17 he will get the Lord's **people** ready for him."
1.68 come to the help of his **people** and has set them free.
1.77 to tell his **people** that they will be
2.10 news for you, which will bring great joy to all the **people.**
2.31 salvation, [31] which you have prepared in the presence of all **peoples:**
2.32 to the Gentiles and bring glory to your **people** Israel."
4.19 that the time has come when the Lord will save his **people."**
7. 5 He loves our **people** and he himself built a synagogue for us."
7.16 "God has come to save his **people!"**
7.31 "Now to what can I compare the **people** of this day?
11.29 went on to say, "How evil are the **people** of this day!
11.30 of Man will be a sign for the **people** of this day.
11.31 stand up and accuse the **people** of today, because she
11.50 So the **people** of this time will be punished for the
11.51 Yes, I tell you, the **people** of this time will be punished
16. 8 because the **people** of this world are much more shrewd
16. 8 handling their affairs than the **people** who belong to the light."
17.25 must suffer much and be rejected by the **people** of this day.
20.19 but they were afraid of the **people.**
22.25 and the rulers claim the title 'Friends of the **People.'**
23. 2 this man misleading our **people,** telling them not to pay taxes
Jn 1.11 to his own country, but his own **people** did not receive him.
5.42 I know what kind of **people** you are,
10.35 those people gods, the **people** to whom his message was given.
10.41 Many **people** came to him.
11.50 one man die for the **people,** instead of having the whole
11.51 to die for the Jewish **people,** [52] and not only for them,
12.36 have it, so that you will be the **people** of the light."
16. 8 he will prove to the **people** of the world that they are
18.14 it was better that one man should die for all the **people.**
18.35 It was your own **people** and the chief priests who handed you
Acts 3.22 he sent me, and he will be one of your own **people.**
4.25 why did **people** make their useless plots?
7.25 (He thought that his own **people** would understand that God was
7.34 I have seen the cruel suffering of my **people** in Egypt.
Acts 7.37 he sent me, and he will be one of your own **people.'**
13.17 our ancestors and made the **people** a great nation during the
13.19 land of Canaan and made his **people** the owners of the land.
15.14 Gentiles by taking from among them a **people** to belong to him.
18. 9 able to harm you, for many in this city are my **people."**
20.32 up and give you the blessings God has for all his **people.**
24.17 to take some money to my own **people** and to offer sacrifices.
26. 7 the twelve tribes of our **people** hope to receive, as they
28.17 I did nothing against our **people** or the customs that we
28.19 though I had no accusation to make against my own **people.**
28.21 nor have any of our **people** come from there with any news
28.26 For he said, 'Go and say to this **people:**
28.27 but not see, [27] because this **people's** minds are dull, and
Rom 1.14 have an obligation to all **peoples,** to the civilized and to
8.17 blessings he keeps for his **people,** and we will also possess
8.27 God on behalf of his **people** and in accordance with his will.
9. 3 pain in my heart [3] for my **people,** my own flesh and blood!
9.24 For we are the **people** he called, not only from among the
9.25 "The **people** who were not mine I will call 'My People.'
9.26 told, 'You are not my **people,'** there they will be called the
10. 1 wish with all my heart that my own **people** might be saved!
10.19 "I will use a so-called nation to make my **people** jealous;
10.19 means of a nation of fools I will make my **people** angry."
10.21 I held out my hands to welcome a disobedient and rebellious **people."**
11. 2 God has not rejected his **people,** whom he chose from the beginning.
15.11 praise him, all **peoples!"**
1 Cor 3. 3 because you still live as the **people** of this world live.
10. 7 As the scripture says, "The **people** sat down to a feast
14.21 strange languages I will speak to my **people,** says the Lord.
14.21 foreigners, but even then my **people** will not listen to me."
2 Cor 6.16 "I will make my home with my **people** and live among them;
6.16 I will be their God, and they shall be my **people."**
Eph 2.14 has brought us peace by making Jews and Gentiles one **people.**
2.15 the two races one new **people** in union with himself,
5. 7 So have nothing at all to do with such **people.**
Col 1.27 this rich and glorious secret which he has for all **peoples.**
2 Tim 2.14 Remind your **people** of this, and give them a solemn
Tit 2.14 to make us a pure **people** who belong to him alone and
3. 1 Remind your **people** to submit to rulers and authorities,
3.14 Our **people** must learn to spend their time doing good,
Heb 1. 8 You rule over your **people** with justice.
8. 8 with the people of Israel and with the **people** of Judah.
8.10 I will be their God, and they will be my **people.**
10.30 and who also said, "The Lord will judge his **people."**
10.38 My righteous **people,** however, will believe and live;
Jas 4. 4 Unfaithful **people!**
1 Pet 1. 2 and were made a holy **people** by his Spirit, to obey Jesus
1 Jn 3.13 surprised, my brothers, if the **people** of the world hate you.
Rev 1. 7 All **peoples** on earth will mourn over him.
11.18 and all your **people,** all who have reverence for you,
14. 6 News to announce to the **peoples** of the earth, to every race,
14. 8 She made all **peoples** drink her wine—the strong wine of her
17.15 on which the prostitute is sitting, are nations, **peoples,** races,
18. 4 I heard another voice from heaven, saying, "Come out, my **people!**
18.23 false magic you deceived all the **peoples** of the world!"
21.24 The **peoples** of the world will walk by its light,

PEOPLE OF GOD see GOD'S PEOPLE

PEOPLE OF ISRAEL see ISRAEL (2)

PEOPLE'S GATE

Jer 17.19 message at the **People's Gate,** through which the kings of Judah

PEOR

District in Moab where the Israelites worshipped the Baal of Peor, also called Mount Peor.

Num 23.28 took Balaam to the top of Mount **Peor** overlooking the desert.
25. 3 The Israelites ate the food and worshipped the god [3] Baal of **Peor.**
25. 5 your tribe who has become a worshipper of Baal of **Peor."**
25.18 when they deceived you at **Peor,** and because of Cozbi,
25.18 who was killed at the time of the epidemic at **Peor."**
31.16 followed Balaam's instructions and at **Peor** led the people to
Deut 4. 3 You yourselves saw what the Lord did at Mount **Peor.**
Josh 22.17 Remember our sin at **Peor,** when the Lord punished his own people
Ps 106.28 Then at **Peor,** God's people joined in the worship of Baal,
Hos 9.10 when they came to Mount **Peor,** they began to worship Baal,

PERCEIVE

Mt 9. 4 Jesus **perceived** what they were thinking, so he said,
Rom 1.20 they are **perceived** in the things that God has made.

PERCH

Ezek 31.13 The birds will come and **perch** on the fallen tree, and

AV PERDITION

Jn 17.12 was bound to be **lost**—so that the scripture might come
Phil 1.28 to them that they will **lose** and that you will win, because
2 Thes 2. 3 place and the Wicked One appears, who is destined for **hell.**
1 Tim 6. 9 and harmful desires, which pull them down to ruin and **destruction.**

Heb 10.39 We are not people who turn back and are **lost.**
2 Pet 3. 7 the day when godless people will be judged and **destroyed.**
Rev 17. 8 come up from the abyss and will go off to be **destroyed.**
17.11 is one of the seven and is going off to be **destroyed.**

PEREZ

Judah's son and ancestor of David.

Gen 38.29 So he was named **Perez.**
46.12 Shelah, **Perez,** and Zerah.
46.12 **Perez'** sons were Hezron and Hamul.
Num 26.19 the clans of Shelah, **Perez,** Zerah, Hezron, and Hamul.
Ruth 4.12 like the family of **Perez,** the son of Judah and Tamar."
4.18 This is the family line from **Perez** to David:
4.18 **Perez,** Hezron, Ram, Amminadab, Nahshon, Salmon, Boaz, Obed,
1 Chr 2. 4 By his daughter-in-law Tamar, Judah had two more sons, **Perez** and Zerah.
2. 5 **Perez** had two sons, Hezron and Hamul.
4. 1 **Perez,** Hezron, Carmi, Hur, and Shobal.
9. 4 The descendants of Judah's son **Perez** had as their leader Uthai,
27. 2 member of the clan of **Perez,** a part of the tribe of
Neh 11. 4 and Mahalalel, descendants of Judah's son **Perez.**
11. 6 Of the descendants of **Perez,** 468 outstanding men lived in Jerusalem.
Mt 1. 2 then **Perez** and Zerah (their mother was Tamar), Hezron, Ram,
Lk 3.33 of Hezron, the son of **Perez,** the son of Judah, [34] the son

PERFECT

Lev 22.23 that is stunted or not **perfectly** formed, but it is not
Deut 32. 4 Lord is your mighty defender, **perfect** and just in all his ways;
2 Sam 22.26 to you, and completely good to those who are **perfect.**
22.31 This God—how **perfect** are his deeds, how dependable his words!
2 Chr 5.11 The singers were accompanied in **perfect** harmony by trumpets,
Ps 4. 8 you alone, O Lord, keep me **perfectly** safe.
18.25 completely good to those who are **perfect.**
18.30 This God—how **perfect** are his deeds!
19. 7 The law of the Lord is **perfect;**
19.13 Then I shall be **perfect** and free from the evil of sin.
50. 2 God shines from Zion, the city **perfect** in its beauty.
64. 6 They make evil plans and say, "We have planned a **perfect** crime."
119.45 I will live in **perfect** freedom, because I try to obey
119.80 May I **perfectly** obey your commandments and be spared the
119.96 but your commandment is **perfect.**
119.165 who love your law have **perfect** security, and there is
Song 4. 2 they are all **perfectly** matched.
4. 7 how **perfect** you are!
6. 6 they are all **perfectly** matched.
Is 26. 3 You, Lord, give **perfect** peace to those who keep their
Jer 17.14 rescue me and I will be **perfectly** safe.
Ezek 16.14 in every nation for your **perfect** beauty, because I was the
27. 3 Tyre, you boasted of your **perfect** beauty.
28.12 You were once an example of **perfection.**
28.15 Your conduct was **perfect** from the day you were created
Mt 5.48 You must be **perfect**—just as your Father in heaven is perfect!
19.21 "If you want to be **perfect,** go and sell all you have
21.16 'You have trained children and babies to offer **perfect** praise.'"
Acts 23. 1 My conscience is **perfectly** clear about the way in which I
Rom 12. 2 God—what is good and is pleasing to him and is **perfect.**
1 Cor 13.10 when what is **perfect** comes, then what is partial will disappear.
2 Cor 13. 9 And so we also pray that you will become **perfect.**
13.11 Strive for **perfection;**
Phil 1. 9 together with true knowledge and **perfect** judgement,
2.15 innocent and pure as God's **perfect** children, who live in a
3.12 claim that I have already succeeded or have already become **perfect.**
Col 3.14 add love, which binds all things together in **perfect** unity.
1 Thes 3.13 and you will be **perfect** and holy in the presence of
Heb 2.10 should make Jesus **perfect** through suffering, in order to bring
5. 9 When he was made **perfect,** he became the source of eternal
7.11 levitical priests had been **perfect,** there would have been no need
7.19 For the Law of Moses could not make anything **perfect.**
7.28 Law, appoints the Son, who has been made **perfect** for ever.
9. 9 cannot make the worshipper's heart **perfect,** [10] since they have
9.11 The tent in which he serves is greater and more **perfect;**
9.14 eternal Spirit he offered himself as a **perfect** sacrifice to God.
10. 1 of these sacrifices make **perfect** the people who come to God?
10.14 then, he has made **perfect** for ever those who are purified
11.40 that only in company with us would they be made **perfect.**
12.23 all mankind, and to the spirits of good people made **perfect.**
Jas 1. 4 so that you may be **perfect** and complete, lacking nothing.
1.17 Every good gift and every **perfect** present comes from heaven;
1.25 whoever looks closely into the **perfect** law that sets people free,
2.22 his faith was made **perfect** through his actions.
3. 2 what he says, he is **perfect** and is also able to control
1 Pet 5.10 union with Christ, will himself **perfect** you and give you firmness,
1 Jn 2. 5 is the one whose love for God has really been made **perfect.**
4.12 in union with us, and his love is made **perfect** in us.
4.17 Love is made **perfect** in us in order that we may have
4.18 **perfect** love drives out all fear.
4.18 love has not been made **perfect** in anyone who is afraid,
Rev 3. 2 have done is not yet **perfect** in the sight of my God.
21.16 The city was **perfectly** square, as wide as it was long.

PERFORM

Gen 50.10 and Joseph **performed** mourning ceremonies for seven days.
Ex 4.17 for with it you will **perform** miracles."
4.21 to Egypt, be sure to **perform** before the king all the
4.28 the miracles which the Lord had ordered him to **perform.**
Ex 4.30 to Moses, and then Moses **performed** all the miracles in front
7. 9 that you prove yourselves by **performing** a miracle, tell
10. 1 in order that I may **perform** these miracles among them [2] and
10. 2 I made fools of the Egyptians when I **performed** the miracles.
11.10 Moses and Aaron **performed** all these miracles before the king,
12.25 Lord has promised to give you, you must **perform** this ritual.
29.35 "**Perform** the rites of ordination for Aaron and his sons
30.10 a year Aaron is to **perform** the ritual for purifying the
Lev 12. 7 offering to the Lord and **perform** the ritual to take away her
12. 8 sin-offering, and the priest shall **perform** the ritual to
14.18 In this way he shall **perform** the ritual of purification.
14.19 the sin-offering and **perform** the ritual of purification.
14.20 way the priest shall **perform** the ritual of purification,
14.29 head and in this way **perform** the ritual of purification.
14.31 In this way the priest shall **perform** the ritual of purification.
14.53 In this way he shall **perform** the ritual of purification for
15.15 In this way he will **perform** the ritual of purification for
15.30 way he will **perform** the ritual of purification for her.
16.16 In this way he will **perform** the ritual to purify the
16.17 the Most Holy Place to **perform** the ritual of purification
16.17 When he has **performed** the ritual for himself, his family,
16.20 When Aaron has finished **performing** the ritual to purify
16.30 the ritual is to be **performed** to purify them from all their
16.32 his father, is to **perform** the ritual of purification.
16.33 on the priestly garments [33] and **perform** the ritual to
16.34 This ritual must be **performed** once a year to purify the
19.22 with it the priest shall **perform** the ritual of purification
23.26 annual ritual is to be **performed** to take away the sins of
23.28 it is the day for **performing** the ritual to take away sin.
Num 3. 7 Tent of my presence and **perform** duties for the priests and
3. 8 equipment of the Tent and **perform** the duties for the rest of
3.38 for carrying out the services **performed** in the Holy Place
4.26 They shall **perform** all the tasks required for these things.
4.27 to it that the Gershonites **perform** all the duties and carry
5. 8 to the ram used to **perform** the ritual of purification for
5.29 of the altar, and the priest shall **perform** this ritual.
6.11 other as a burnt-offering, to **perform** the ritual of
6.13 When a Nazirite completes his vow, he shall **perform** the ritual.
8.12 a burnt-offering, in order to **perform** the ritual of
8.21 He also **performed** the ritual of purification for them.
8.24 of twenty-five each Levite shall **perform** his duties in the
8.26 his fellow-Levites in **performing** their duties in the Tent,
8.26 but he must not **perform** any service by himself.
14.11 even though I have **performed** so many miracles among them?
14.22 miracles that I **performed** in Egypt and in the wilderness,
15.25 The priest shall **perform** the ritual of purification
15.28 the altar the priest shall **perform** the ritual of
16. 9 can approach him, **perform** your service in the Lord's Tent,
16.46 the people and **perform** the ritual of purification for them.
16.47 incense on the coals and **performed** the ritual of
19. 9 This ritual is **performed** to remove sin.
28.22 sin-offering, and in this way **perform** the ritual of
28.30 sin-offering, and in this way **perform** the ritual of
29. 5 sin-offering, and in this way **perform** the ritual of
35.33 there is no way to **perform** the ritual of purification for
Deut 29. 3 the miracles, and the great wonders that the Lord **performed.**
34.11 the Lord sent Moses to **perform** against the king of Egypt,
Josh 3. 5 tomorrow the Lord will **perform** miracles among you."
24.17 slavery in Egypt, and we saw the miracles that he **performed.**
1 Kgs 8.11 and they could not go back in to **perform** their duties.
1 Chr 16.12 that God **performed** and the judgements that he gave.
16.37 They were to **perform** their duties there day by day.
24.19 going to the Temple and **performing** the duties established by
25. 1 with the type of service that each group **performed:**
28.13 the priests and Levites to **perform** their duties, to do the
28.21 Levites have been assigned duties to **perform** in the Temple.
2 Chr 8.14 in sections for **performing** their daily duties at each gate,
13.10 Priests descended from Aaron **perform** their duties,
19. 9 "You must **perform** your duties in reverence for the Lord,
30.18 and Zebulun had not **performed** the ritual of purification,
31.18 to be ready to **perform** their sacred duties at any time.
35. 2 the duties they were to **perform** in the Temple and encouraged
Neh 9.17 they forgot the miracles you had **performed.**
12.30 The priests and the Levites **performed** ritual purification
12.45 and the Levites, [45] because they **performed** the ceremonies
12.45 and the temple guards also **performed** their duties in
Ps 78.11 what he had done, the miracles they had seen him **perform.**
78.12 While their ancestors watched, God **performed** miracles in
78.43 them from their enemies [43] and **performed** his mighty acts
88.10 Do you **perform** miracles for the dead?
105. 5 that God **performed** and the judgements that he gave.
105.27 They did God's mighty acts and **performed** miracles in Egypt.
135. 9 There he **performed** miracles and wonders to punish the king
136. 4 He alone **performs** great miracles;
Jer 21. 2 Maybe the Lord will **perform** one of his miracles for us and
32.20 Long ago, you **performed** miracles and wonders in Egypt,
32.20 and you have continued to **perform** them to this day, both in
Ezek 44.11 of the gates and by **performing** the work of the Temple.
Dan 4. 3 How powerful are the miracles he **performs!**
6.27 he **performs** wonders and miracles in heaven and on earth.
Zech 3. 7 you obey my laws and **perform** the duties I have assigned to
Mt 6. 1 "Make certain you do not **perform** your religious duties in public
7.22 name we drove out many demons and **performed** many miracles!'
11.20 the towns where Jesus had **performed** most of his miracles did
11.21 If the miracles which were **performed** in you
11.21 had been **performed** in Tyre and Sidon, the people
11.23 If the miracles which were **performed** in you
11.23 had been **performed** in Sodom, it would still be
12.38 "Teacher," they said, "we want to see you **perform** a miracle."
13.58 did not have faith, he did not **perform** many miracles there.
14. 2 "That is why he has this power to **perform** miracles."

Mt 16. 1 so they asked him to **perform** a miracle for them, to show
24.24 they will **perform** great miracles and wonders in order to deceive
Mk 6. 2 How does he **perform** miracles?
6. 5 He was not able to **perform** any miracles there, except that
6.14 That is why he has this power to **perform** miracles."
8.11 so they asked him to **perform** a miracle to show that God
9.39 "because no one who **performs** a miracle in my name will
13.22 They will **perform** miracles and wonders in order to deceive even
16.17 Believers will be given the power to **perform** miracles:
16.20 that their preaching was true by the miracles that were **performed.**
Lk 2.22 for Joseph and Mary to **perform** the ceremony of purification,
10.13 If the miracles which were **performed** in you
10.13 had been **performed** in Tyre and Sidon, the people
11.16 so they asked him to **perform** a miracle to show that God
13.32 am driving out demons and **performing** cures today and tomorrow,
23. 8 He was hoping to see Jesus **perform** some miracle.
Jn 2.11 Jesus **performed** this first miracle in Cana in Galilee;
2.18 "What miracle can you **perform** to show us that you have
2.23 many believed in him as they saw the miracles he **performed.**
3. 2 No one could **perform** the miracles you are doing unless God
4.54 the second miracle that Jesus **performed** after coming from Judaea
6.14 this miracle that Jesus had **performed,** the people there said,
6.30 replied, "What miracle will you **perform** so that we may see
7.21 "I **performed** one miracle, and you were all surprised.
7.31 Messiah comes, will he **perform** more miracles than this man has?"
9.16 a man who is a sinner **perform** such miracles as these?"
10.41 "John **performed** no miracles," they said, "but everything he said
11.47 Look at all the miracles this man is **performing!**
11.55 the country to Jerusalem to **perform** the ritual of purification
12.18 met him—because they heard that he had **performed** this miracle.
12.37 though he had **performed** all these miracles in their presence,
20.30 In his disciples' presence Jesus **performed** many other miracles
Acts 2.19 I will **perform** miracles in the sky above and wonders on
2.22 by all the miracles and wonders which God **performed** through him.
4.16 this extraordinary miracle has been **performed** by them,
4.22 miracle of healing had been **performed** was over forty years old.
4.30 wonders and miracles may be **performed** through the name of your
5.12 and wonders were being **performed** among the people by the apostles.
6. 8 and full of power, **performed** great miracles and wonders among
7.36 the people out of Egypt, **performing** miracles and wonders in Egypt
8. 6 they listened to him and saw the miracles that he **performed.**
8.13 he saw the great wonders and miracles that were being **performed.**
14. 3 by giving them the power to **perform** miracles and wonders.
15.12 wonders that God had **performed** through them among the Gentiles.
19.11 God was **performing** unusual miracles through Paul.
21.26 and the next day **performed** the ceremony of purification with them.
1 Cor 12. 6 are different abilities to **perform** service, but the same God gives
12.28 those who **perform** miracles, followed by those who are given the
2 Cor 9.12 For this service you **perform** not only meets the needs of
12.12 I am an apostle were **performed** among you with much patience.
Col 1.25 by God, who gave me this task to **perform** for your good.
2 Thes 2. 9 the power of Satan and **perform** all kinds of false miracles
1 Tim 5.10 **performed** humble duties for fellow-Christians, helped people
2 Tim 4. 5 of the Good News, and **perform** your whole duty as a servant
Heb 2. 4 his witness to theirs by **performing** all kinds of miracles
9. 6 outer Tent every day to **perform** their duties, [7]but only the
10.11 Every Jewish priest **performs** his services every day
Jas 3.13 by his good deeds **performed** with humility and wisdom.
Jude 15 godless deeds they have **performed** and for all the terrible words
Rev 13.13 This second beast **performed** great miracles;
13.14 which it was allowed to **perform** in the presence of the first
16.14 They are the spirits of demons that **perform** miracles.
19.20 with the false prophet who had **performed** miracles in his presence.

PERFUME

Gen 2.12 (Pure gold is found there and also rare **perfume**
Ex 30.25 and make a sacred anointing oil, mixed like **perfume.**
30.35 Use them to make incense, mixed like **perfume.**
30.38 like it for use as **perfume,** he will no longer be considered
37.29 and the pure sweet-smelling incense, mixed like **perfume.**
Ruth 3. 3 wash yourself, put on some **perfume,** and get dressed in your
1 Sam 8.13 daughters will have to make **perfumes** for him and work as his
2 Kgs 20.13 his spices and **perfumes,** and all his military equipment.
2 Chr 16.14 They used spices and **perfumed** oils to prepare his body for burial,
Neh 3. 8 Hananiah, a maker of **perfumes,** built the next section, as
Ps 45. 8 The **perfume** of myrrh and aloes is on your clothes;
Prov 7.17 I've **perfumed** it with myrrh, aloes, and cinnamon.
27. 9 **Perfume** and fragrant oils make you feel happier, but
Ecc 7. 1 A good reputation is better than expensive **perfume;**
10. 1 make a whole bottle of **perfume** stink, and a little stupidity
Song 1.12 on his couch, and my **perfume** filled the air with fragrance.
4.10 your **perfume** more fragrant than any spice.
4.14 Myrrh and aloes grow there with all the most fragrant **perfumes.**
Is 3.24 Instead of using **perfumes,** they will stink;
28. 1 Their proud heads are well **perfumed,** but there they lie,
39. 2 his spices and **perfumes,** and all his military equipment.
57. 9 You put on your **perfumes** and ointments and go to worship
Amos 6. 6 bowlful and use the finest **perfumes,** but you do not mourn
Mt 26. 7 filled with an expensive **perfume,** which she poured on his head.
26. 9 "This **perfume** could have been sold for a large amount
26.12 did was to pour this **perfume** on my body to get me
Mk 14. 3 jar full of a very expensive **perfume** made of pure nard.
14. 3 She broke the jar and poured the **perfume** on Jesus' head.
14. 4 to one another, "What was the use of wasting the **perfume?**
14. 8 she poured **perfume** on my body to prepare it ahead of time
Lk 7.37 an alabaster jar full of **perfume** [38]and stood behind Jesus,
7.38 with her hair, kissed them, and poured the **perfume** on them.
7.46 for my head, but she has covered my feet with **perfume.**
23.56 home and prepared the spices and **perfumes** for the body.
Jn 11. 2 the one who poured the **perfume** on the Lord's feet and wiped
12. 3 litre of a very expensive **perfume** made of pure nard, poured
12. 3 The sweet smell of the **perfume** filled the whole house.
12. 5 "Why wasn't this **perfume** sold for three hundred silver coins

PERIOD (1)

Num 6.12 The previous **period** of time doesn't count, because his
7.11 that each day for a **period** of twelve days one of the
2 Kgs 8.22 During this same **period** the city of Libnah also revolted.
1 Chr 26.16 Guard duty was divided into assigned **periods,** one after another.
2 Chr 21.10 During this same **period,** the city of Libnah also revolted,
Lk 1.23 his **period** of service in the Temple was over, Zechariah went
Acts 21.26 until the end of the **period** of purification, when a sacrifice
24. 2 has brought us a long **period** of peace, and many necessary

PERIOD (2)

[MONTHLY PERIOD]

Gen 18.11 were very old, and Sarah had stopped having her **monthly periods.**
31.35 I am having my **monthly period."**
Lev 12. 2 is ritually unclean, as she is during her **monthly period.**
12. 5 is ritually unclean, as she is during her **monthly period.**
15.19 When a woman has her **monthly period,** she remains unclean
15.20 which she sits or lies during her **monthly period** is unclean.
15.24 intercourse with her during her **period,** he is contaminated
15.25 for several days outside her **monthly period** or if her flow
15.25 continues beyond her regular **period,** she remains unclean as long
15.25 flow continues, just as she is during her **monthly period.**
15.33 semen, [33]a woman during her **monthly period,** or a man who
18.19 during her **monthly period,** because she is ritually unclean.
20.18 with a woman during her **monthly period,** both of them are to
Ezek 18. 6 wife or have intercourse with a woman during her **period.**
22.10 Some force women to have intercourse with them during their **period.**
36.17 ritually unclean as a woman is during her **monthly period.**

PERISH

Num 24.20 nation of all, But at the end it will **perish** for ever."
24.24 Assyria and Eber, But they, in turn, will **perish** for ever."
Job 34.20 God strikes men down and they **perish;**
36.20 Don't wish for night to come, the time when nations will **perish.**
Ps 68. 2 of the fire, so do the wicked **perish** in God's presence.
73.27 Those who abandon you will certainly **perish;**
1 Cor 8.11 whom Christ died, will **perish** because of your "knowledge"!
2 Thes 2.10 and use every kind of wicked deceit on those who will **perish.**
2.10 They will **perish** because they did not welcome and love the

PERMANENT

Ex 18.22 Let them serve as judges for the people on a **permanent** basis.
18.26 for the people on a **permanent** basis, bringing the difficult
28.43 This is a **permanent** rule for Aaron and his descendants.
31.17 It is a **permanent** sign between the people of Israel and me,
Lev 25.23 not be sold on a **permanent** basis, because you do not own
25.30 and the house becomes the **permanent** property of the
25.33 are their **permanent** property among the people of Israel.
25.55 An Israelite cannot be a **permanent** slave, because the
27.21 the field will become the Lord's **permanent** property;
27.28 It belongs **permanently** to the Lord.
Num 15.14 on a temporary or a **permanent** basis, makes a food-offering,
18.23 This is a **permanent** rule that applies also to your descendants.
18.23 The Levites shall have no **permanent** property in Israel,
18.24 I told them that they would have no **permanent** property in Israel."
25.13 He and his descendants are **permanently** established as priests,
35.15 for foreigners who are temporary or **permanent** residents.
36. 4 of Zelophehad's daughters will be **permanently** added to the
Josh 12. 7 the tribes and gave it to them as a **permanent** possession.
1 Sam 28. 2 I will make you my **permanent** bodyguard."
1 Kgs 8.36 which you gave to your people as a **permanent** possession.
1 Chr 4.41 people out and settled there **permanently** because there was
5.26 East Manasseh and settled them **permanently** in Halah, Habor,
16.37 Asaph and his fellow-Levites in **permanent** charge of the
28. 2 I wanted to build a **permanent** home for the Covenant Box, the
2 Chr 6.27 which you gave to your people as a **permanent** possession.
28.18 Gimzo with their villages, and settled there **permanently.**
30.25 foreigners who had settled **permanently** in Israel and Judah.
Ps 89. 2 time, that your faithfulness is as **permanent** as the sky.
89.29 His dynasty will be as **permanent** as the sky;
89.37 It will be as **permanent** as the moon, that faithful
119.151 are near to me, Lord, and all your commands are **permanent.**
Prov 6.33 he will be **permanently** disgraced.
27.24 carefully as you can, [24]because wealth is not **permanent.**
Is 30. 8 that there would be a **permanent** record of how evil they are.
Jer 3.18 that I gave your ancestors as a **permanent** possession."
5.22 of the sea, a **permanent** boundary that it cannot cross.
7. 7 land which I gave your ancestors as a **permanent** possession.
25. 5 Lord gave you and your ancestors as a **permanent** possession.

Jer 32.41 them, and I will establish them **permanently** in this land.
Ezek 46.17 to him, and only he and his sons can own it **permanently.**
47.22 it is to be your **permanent** possession.
Jn 8.35 not belong to a family **permanently,** but a son belongs there
Rom 11.25 people of Israel is not **permanent,** but will last only until
Heb 11.10 God has designed and built, the city with **permanent** foundations.
13.14 For there is no **permanent** city for us here on earth;
2 Pet 1.10 God's call and his choice of you a **permanent** experience;

PERMIT

Gen 41.44 so much as lift a hand or a foot without your **permission."**
47. 4 Please give us **permission** to live in the region of Goshen."
Lev 20.14 such a thing must not be **permitted** among you.
22.24 This is not **permitted** in your land.
Num 9.11 keep the Passover, [11] you are **permitted** to observe it one
20.17 Please **permit** us to pass through your land.
21.23 But Sihon would not **permit** the people of Israel to pass
31.24 ritually clean and will be **permitted** to enter the camp."
Judg 11.17 the king of Edom to ask **permission** to go through his land.
11.19 Heshbon, and asked him for **permission** to go through his
12. 5 was trying to escape asked **permission** to cross, the men of
1 Sam 20. 6 that I begged your **permission** to hurry home to Bethlehem,
1 Kgs 20.31 Give us **permission** to go to the king of Israel with
2 Kgs 6. 2 Give us **permission** to go to the Jordan and cut down some
25.29 So Jehoiachin was **permitted** to change from his prison
2 Chr 28. 5 the God of their ancestors, **permitted** this to happen,
Ezra 3. 7 All this was done with the **permission** of Cyrus, emperor of Persia.
7.13 Levites that so desire be **permitted** to go with you to Jerusalem.
9. 9 of Persia favour us and **permit** us to go on living and
Neh 13. 1 Ammonite or Moabite was ever to be **permitted** to join God's people.
13. 6 I received his **permission** [7] and returned to Jerusalem.
Jer 7.21 completely on the altar, and some you are **permitted** to eat.
52.33 So Jehoiachin was **permitted** to change from his prison
Ezek 40.46 tribe of Levi who are **permitted** to go into the Lord's
Dan 2.16 at once and obtained royal **permission** for more time, so that
6. 7 thirty days no one be **permitted** to request anything from any
7.12 taken away, but they were **permitted** to go on living for a
Mt 16.19 and what you permit on earth will be **permitted** in heaven."
18.18 and what you permit on earth will be **permitted** in heaven.
19. 8 "Moses gave you **permission** to divorce your wives because you
Mk 10. 4 Their answer was, "Moses gave **permission** for a man to
Lk 22.31 Satan has received **permission** to test all of you, to separate
Acts 21.40 The commander gave him **permission,** so Paul stood on the steps
26. 1 Paul, "You have **permission** to speak on your own behalf."
Rom 13. 1 no authority exists without God's **permission,**
Rev 13. 5 and it was **permitted** to have authority for forty-two months.

PERSECUTE

Judg 10. 8 eighteen years they oppressed and **persecuted** all the
Esth 7. 6 "Our enemy, our **persecutor,** is this evil man Haman!"
Job 19.22 Why must you **persecute** me as God does?
30.21 you **persecute** me with all your power.
Ps 10. 2 The wicked are proud and **persecute** the poor;
12. 5 "because the needy are oppressed and the **persecuted** groan in pain.
31.15 save me from my enemies, from those who **persecute** me.
56. 1 my enemies **persecute** me all the time.
69.26 They **persecute** those whom you have punished;
74.19 don't forget your **persecuted** people!
109.16 he **persecuted** and killed the poor, the needy, and the helpless.
109.28 May my **persecutors** be defeated, and may I, your servant,
119.84 When will you punish those who **persecute** me?
119.86 men **persecute** me with lies—help me!
119.150 My cruel **persecutors** are coming closer, people who never keep your law.
129. 1 your enemies have **persecuted** you ever since you were young.
129. 2 was young, my enemies have **persecuted** me cruelly, but they
Is 14. 6 never stopped **persecuting** the nations they had conquered.
Jer 15.15 Let me have revenge on those who **persecute** me.
17.18 Bring disgrace on those who **persecute** me, but spare me,
20.11 strong and mighty, and those who **persecute** me will fail.
Dan 12. 7 When the **persecution** of God's people ends, all these things
Amos 5.12 You **persecute** good men, take bribes, and prevent the poor
Mt 5.10 "Happy are those who are **persecuted** because they do what God requires;
5.11 when people insult you and **persecute** you and tell all kinds
5.12 This is how the prophets who lived before you were **persecuted.**
5.44 and pray for those who **persecute** you, [45] so that you may
10.23 When they **persecute** you in one town, run away to another one.
13.21 So when trouble or **persecution** comes because of the message,
Mk 4.17 So when trouble or **persecution** comes because of the message,
10.30 sisters, mothers, children and fields—and **persecutions** as well;
Lk 11.49 they will kill some of them and **persecute** others.'
21.12 however, you will be arrested and **persecuted;**
Jn 5.16 they began to **persecute** Jesus, because he had done this healing
15.20 If they persecuted me, they will **persecute** you too;
Acts 7.52 Was there any prophet that your ancestors did not **persecute?**
8. 1 very day the church in Jerusalem began to suffer cruel **persecution.**
9. 4 Why do you **persecute** me?"
9. 5 "I am Jesus, whom you **persecute,"** the voice said.
11.19 scattered by the **persecution** which took place when Stephen was
12. 1 King Herod began to **persecute** some members of the church.
13.50 They started a **persecution** against Paul and Barnabas
22. 4 I **persecuted** to the death the people who followed this Way.
22. 7 Why do you **persecute** me?'
22. 8 'I am Jesus of Nazareth, whom you **persecute,'** he said to me.
26.11 that I even went to foreign cities to **persecute** them.
Acts 26.14 Why are you **persecuting** me?
26.15 And the Lord answered, 'I am Jesus, whom you **persecute.**
Rom 8.35 or hardship or **persecution** or hunger or poverty or danger
12.14 God to bless those who **persecute** you—yes, ask him to bless,
1 Cor 4.12 when we are **persecuted,** we endure;
15. 9 to be called an apostle, because I **persecuted** God's church.
2 Cor 12.10 hardships, **persecutions,** and difficulties for Christ's sake.
Gal 1.13 how I **persecuted** without mercy the church of God
1.23 "The man who used to **persecute** us is now preaching the
4.29 born in the usual way **persecuted** the one who was born
5.11 that circumcision is necessary, why am I still being **persecuted?**
6.12 so that they may not be **persecuted** for the cross of Christ.
Phil 3. 6 Pharisee, [6] and I was so zealous that I **persecuted** the church.
1 Thes 2.14 You suffered the same **persecutions** from your own countrymen that
2.15 who killed the Lord Jesus and the prophets, and **persecuted** us.
3. 3 so that none of you should turn back because of these **persecutions.**
3. 3 You yourselves know that such **persecutions** are part of God's will
3. 4 we told you beforehand that we were going to be **persecuted;**
2 Thes 1. 4 endure and believe through all the **persecutions** and sufferings
1 Tim 1.13 past I spoke evil of him and **persecuted** and insulted him.
2 Tim 3.11 my love, my endurance, [11] my **persecutions,** and my sufferings.
3.11 Antioch, Iconium, and Lystra, the terrible **persecutions** I endured!
3.12 a godly life in union with Christ Jesus will be **persecuted;**
Heb 11.37 in skins of sheep or goats—poor, **persecuted,** and ill-treated.
Rev 7.14 the people who have come safely through the terrible **persecution.**

PERSEVERE

1 Tim 2.15 through having children, if she **perseveres** in faith and love

PERSIA

[EMPEROR OF PERSIA]
Empire which at the height of its power extended from India to Greece.

2 Chr 36.20 descendants as slaves until the rise of the **Persian** Empire.
36.22 first year that Cyrus of **Persia** was emperor, the Lord made
36.23 "This is the command of Cyrus, **Emperor of Persia.**
Ezra 1. 1 first year that Cyrus of **Persia** was emperor, the Lord made
1. 2 "This is the command of Cyrus, **Emperor of Persia.**
3. 7 All this was done with the permission of Cyrus, **emperor of Persia.**
4. 3 just as Cyrus, **emperor of Persia,** commanded us."
4. 5 They also bribed **Persian** government officials to work against them.
4. 7 the reign of Artaxerxes, **emperor of Persia,** Bishlam,
4.24 the second year of the reign of Darius, **emperor of Persia.**
5. 5 the Jewish leaders, and the **Persian** officials decided to
6.14 by Cyrus, Darius, and Artaxerxes, emperors of **Persia.**
7. 1 later, when Artaxerxes was **emperor of Persia,** there was a
9. 9 You made the emperors of **Persia** favour us and permit us to
Neh 1. 1 year that Artaxerxes was **emperor of Persia,** I, Nehemiah, was
11.24 represented the people of Israel at the **Persian** court.
12.22 This record was finished when Darius was **emperor of Persia.**
Esth 1. 1 From his royal throne in **Persia's** capital city of Susa,
1. 3 The armies of **Persia** and Media were present, as well as the
1.14 and Memucan—seven officials of **Persia** and Media who held the
1.18 of the royal officials of **Persia** and Media hear about the
1.19 written into the laws of **Persia** and Media, so that it can
3. 6 He made plans to kill every Jew in the whole **Persian** Empire.
8.12 to take effect throughout the **Persian** Empire on the day set
9.20 near and far, throughout the **Persian** Empire, [21] telling
9.30 were sent to all the 127 provinces of the **Persian** Empire.
10. 2 in the official records of the kings of **Persia** and Media.
Ezek 27.10 "Soldiers from **Persia,** Lydia, and Libya served in your army.
38. 5 Men from **Persia,** Sudan, and Libya are with him, and all
Dan 1.21 until Cyrus the **emperor of Persia** conquered Babylonia.
5.28 is divided up and given to the Medes and **Persians."**
6. 8 a law of the Medes and **Persians,** which cannot be changed."
6.12 a law of the Medes and **Persians,** which cannot be changed."
6.15 laws of the Medes and **Persians** no order which the king
6.28 the reign of Darius and the reign of Cyrus the **Persian.**
8.20 had two horns represents the kingdoms of Media and **Persia.**
10. 1 year that Cyrus was **emperor of Persia,** a message was
10.13 of the kingdom of **Persia** opposed me for twenty-one days.
10.13 to help me, because I had been left there alone in **Persia.**
10.20 I have to go back and fight the guardian angel of **Persia.**
11. 2 more kings will rule over **Persia,** followed by a fourth, who
Hag 1. 1 year that Darius was **emperor of Persia,** on the first day of
Zech 1. 1 year that Darius was **emperor of Persia,** the Lord gave this

PERSIST

Mt 12.20 He will **persist** until he causes justice to triumph,
Lk 8.15 good and obedient heart, and they **persist** until they bear fruit.
Col 4. 2 Be **persistent** in prayer, and keep alert as you pray,

PERSON

Gen 7.21 the earth died—every bird, every animal, and every **person.**
Ex 12. 4 number of people and the amount that each **person** can eat.
16.22 gathered twice as much food, four litres for each **person.**
23. 7 do not put an innocent **person** to death, for I will condemn
38.26 the total paid by all **persons** enrolled in the census, each
Lev 5. 5 When a **person** is guilty, he must confess the sin, [6] and as
13. 3 and the priest shall pronounce the **person** unclean.
13. 4 white, the priest shall isolate the **person** for seven days.
13. 6 The **person** shall wash his clothes and be ritually clean.
13.12 spreads and covers the **person** from head to foot,
13.13 whole body, he shall pronounce the **person** ritually clean.

Lev	13.15	a dreaded skin-disease, and the **person** is unclean.
	13.16	and becomes white again, the **person** shall go to the priest,
	13.24	In the case of a **person** who has been burnt, if the
	13.30	skin-disease, and he shall pronounce the **person** unclean.
	13.33	than the surrounding skin, [33] the **person** shall shave the
	13.34	The **person** shall wash his clothes, and he will be clean.
	13.36	the **person** is obviously unclean.
	13.39	spots on the skin, [39] the priest shall examine that **person.**
	13.39	the **person** is ritually clean.
	13.45	A **person** who has a dreaded skin-disease must wear torn clothes,
	14. 2	purification of a **person** cured of a dreaded skin-disease.
	14. 7	blood seven times on the **person** who is to be purified from
	14. 8	The **person** shall wash his clothes, shave off all his hair,
	15. 8	who is ritually clean, that **person** must wash his clothes and
	15.11	having washed his hands, that **person** must wash his clothes
	17.15	Any **person,** Israelite or foreigner, who eats meat from
	20.27	**person** who does this is responsible for his own death."
	21.11	where there is a dead **person,** even if it is his own
	22. 5	or if he has touched an unclean animal or **person.**
	22.14	"If any **person** who is not a member of a priestly family
	22.16	offerings [16] by letting any unauthorized **person** eat them;
	22.16	this would bring guilt and punishment on such a **person.**
	24.19	"If anyone injures another **person,** whatever he has done
	24.20	Whatever injury he causes another **person** shall be done to
	27. 2	When a **person** has been given to the Lord in fulfilment of
	27. 2	a special vow, that **person** may be set free by the
	27. 8	price, he shall bring the **person** to the priest, and the
Num	5. 7	an additional twenty per cent, to the **person** he has wronged.
	5. 8	But if that **person** has died and has no near relative to
	5. 8	to perform the ritual of purification for the guilty **person.**
	15.30	But any **person** who sins deliberately, whether he is a
	18. 4	in the Tent, but no unqualified **person** may work with you.
	18. 7	Any unqualified **person** who comes near the sacred objects
	19.16	If someone touches a **person** who has been killed or has
	19.19	and on the seventh the **person** who is ritually clean is to
	19.19	to sprinkle the water on the unclean **person.**
	19.21	The **person** who sprinkles the water for purification must
	19.22	Whatever an unclean **person** touches is unclean, and
Deut	17. 5	in Israel, [5] then take that **person** outside the town and
	17. 7	and then the rest of the people are to stone that **person;**
	23. 2	descendant of such a **person,** even in the tenth generation,
	24.16	a **person** is to be put to death only for a crime
	27.25	" 'God's curse on anyone who accepts money to murder an innocent **person.'**
Josh	8.25	not put it down until every **person** there had been killed.
	10.30	They spared no one, but killed every **person** in it.
	10.32	they spared no one, but killed every **person** in the city.
	11.14	But they put every **person** to death;
	20. 3	A **person** who kills someone accidentally can go there and
	20. 5	he killed the **person** accidentally and not out of anger.
	20. 9	Anyone who killed a **person** accidentally could find
Judg	11.31	as an offering the first **person** that comes out of my house
	11.31	I will offer that **person** to you as a sacrifice."
	18.10	it has everything a **person** could want, and God has given it
1 Sam	10. 6	dancing and shouting and will become a different **person.**
1 Kgs	8.31	"When a **person** is accused of wronging another and is
	8.39	Deal with each **person** as he deserves, [40] so that your
2 Kgs	8. 5	Elisha had brought a dead **person** back to life, the woman
	14. 6	a **person** is to be put to death only for a crime
1 Chr	25. 1	This is the list of **persons** chosen to lead the worship, with
2 Chr	6.22	"When a **person** is accused of wronging another and is
	6.30	Deal with each **person** as he deserves, [31] so that your
	25. 4	a **person** is to be put to death only for a crime
Esth	4.11	sees the king without being summoned, that **person** must die.
	4.11	gold sceptre to someone, then that **person's** life is spared.
Job	5.17	Happy is the **person** whom God corrects!
	33.30	he saves a **person's** life, and gives him the joy of living.
	34.34	Any sensible **person** will surely agree;
Ps	15. 2	A **person** who obeys God in everything and always does what
	49. 7	A **person** can never redeem himself;
	94.12	Lord, how happy is the **person** you instruct, the one to
	112. 1	Happy is the **person** who honours the Lord, who takes pleasure
	112. 5	Happy is the **person** who is generous with his loans, who
	112. 6	A good **person** will never fail;
Prov	1. 4	They can make an inexperienced **person** clever and teach
	13. 1	him, but an arrogant **person** never admits he is wrong.
	13. 4	matter how much a lazy **person** may want something, he will
	14. 8	Why is a clever **person** wise?
	14. 8	Why is a stupid **person** foolish?
	16.21	A wise, mature **person** is known for his understanding.
	17. 3	tested by fire, and a **person's** heart is tested by the Lord.
	17.10	An intelligent **person** learns more from one rebuke than a
	17.24	An intelligent **person** aims at wise action, but a fool
	17.26	It is not right to make an innocent **person** pay a fine;
	18. 4	A **person's** words can be a source of wisdom, deep as the
	18. 9	A lazy **person** is as bad as someone who is destructive.
	18.16	Do you want to meet an important **person?**
	19.26	Only a shameful, disgraceful **person** would ill-treat his
	20. 5	A **person's** thoughts are like water in a deep well, but
	21.11	his punishment, even an unthinking **person** learns a lesson.
	21.24	Show me a conceited **person** and I will show you someone
	22. 3	avoid it, but an unthinking **person** will walk right into it
	22.10	Get rid of a conceited **person,** and then there will be no
	24. 7	Wise sayings are too deep for a stupid **person** to understand.
	24. 9	People hate a **person** who has nothing but scorn for others.
	24.20	A wicked **person** has no future—nothing to look forward to.
	24.24	If he pronounces a guilty **person** innocent, he will be
	25.12	warning given by an experienced **person** to someone willing to
	25.19	Depending on an unreliable **person** in a crisis is like
	25.20	Singing to a **person** who is depressed is like taking off
	25.26	A good **person** who gives in to someone who is evil
	26. 4	question, you are just as silly as the **person** who asked it.
	27.12	avoid it, but an unthinking **person** will walk right into it
	27.21	a **person's** reputation can also be tested.
	28. 1	chasing them, but an honest **person** is as brave as a lion.
	28.10	If you trick an honest **person** into doing evil, you will
	28.11	are wise, but a poor **person** who has insight into character
	29. 7	A good **person** knows the rights of the poor, but wicked
	29.10	righteous people will protect the life of such a **person.**
Ecc	7. 4	A wise **person** thinks about death.
	7.19	Wisdom does more for a **person** than ten rulers can do for
Is	6.13	Even if one **person** out of ten remains in the land, he
	11. 4	the people will be punished, and evil **persons** will die.
	32. 7	A stupid **person** is evil and does evil things;
	32. 8	But an honourable **person** acts honestly and stands firm for
	38.11	I would never again see the Lord Or any living **person.**
Jer	5. 1	Can you find one **person** who does what is right and tries
	10.23	no **person** has control over his own life.
	17. 5	"I will condemn the **person** who turns away from me and puts
	17. 7	"But I will bless the **person** who puts his trust in me.
	17.11	The **person** who gets money dishonestly is like a bird
	21.11	Protect the **person** who is being cheated from the one who is
	22. 3	Protect the **person** who is being cheated from the one who is
Ezek	18. 4	The life of every **person** belongs to me, the life of the
	18. 4	The **person** who sins is the one who will die.
	24.16	blow I am going to take away the **person** you love most.
	44. 5	Note carefully which **persons** are allowed to go in
	44. 5	and out of the Temple and which **persons** are not.
Jon	3. 7	**persons,** cattle, and sheep are forbidden to eat or drink.
	3. 8	All **persons** and animals must wear sackcloth.
Mic	7. 2	There is not an honest **person** left in the land, no one
Mal	3. 8	I ask you, is it right for a **person** to cheat God?
	3.18	to the wicked, to the **person** who serves me and the one

PERSONAL

Gen	39. 4	Potiphar was pleased with him and made him his **personal** servant;
2 Sam	13.17	he called in his **personal** servant and said, "Get this
	17.11	the sea-shore, and that you lead them **personally** in battle.
2 Kgs	7. 2	The **personal** attendant of the king said to Elisha, "That
	7.17	the command of the officer who was his **personal** attendant.
	25.19	troops, five of the king's **personal** advisers who were still
1 Chr	29. 3	silver and gold from my **personal** property because of my love
Esth	1.10	seven eunuchs who were his **personal** servants, Mehuman,
Jer	51.59	King Zedekiah's **personal** attendant was Seraiah, the son
	52.25	troops, seven of the king's **personal** advisers who were still
Acts	10. 7	a religious man who was one of his **personal** attendants.
Rom	13. 7	pay them your **personal** and property taxes, and show respect
	14. 1	but do not argue with him about his **personal** opinions.
2 Cor	10. 1	I, Paul, make a **personal** appeal to you—I who am said

PERSONALLY

[IN PERSON]

Jer	32. 4	see him face to face and will speak to him **in person.**
	34. 3	will see him face to face and talk to him **in person;**
Lk	7. 7	neither do I consider myself worthy to come to you **in person.**
	23.49	All those who knew Jesus **personally,** including the women who
Acts	15.27	who will tell you **in person** the same things we are writing.
2 Cor	10.10	he is with us **in person,** he is weak, and his words
Gal	1.22	of the churches in Judaea did not know me **personally.**
Col	2. 1	Laodicea and for all others who do not know me **personally.**
	4.13	I can **personally** testify to his hard work for you and
1 Thes	3.10	to let us see you **personally** and supply what is needed in
2 Jn	12	and talk with you **personally,** so that we shall be completely
3 Jn	14	I hope to see you soon, and then we will talk **personally.**
	15	Greet all our friends **personally.**

PERSPIRE

Ezek	44.18	So that they won't **perspire,** they are to wear linen

PERSUADE

Deut	13. 8	But do not let him **persuade** you;
Judg	19. 3	go after her and try to **persuade** her to return to him.
2 Kgs	18.30	And don't let him **persuade** you to rely on the Lord.
2 Chr	18. 2	He tried to **persuade** Jehoshaphat to join him in attacking
	24.17	dead, the leaders of Judah **persuaded** King Joash to listen to
Ezra	7.28	I have been able to **persuade** many of the heads of the
Job	2. 3	You **persuaded** me to let you attack him for no reason at
Prov	16.21	The more pleasant his words, the more **persuasive** he is.
	16.23	what they say is then more **persuasive.**
	25.15	Patient **persuasion** can break down the strongest
Is	36.15	And don't let him **persuade** you to rely on the Lord.
Mt	27.20	chief priests and the elders **persuaded** the crowd to ask Pilate
Acts	10.23	the men in and **persuaded** them to spend the night there.
	16.15	And she **persuaded** us to go.
	18.13	they said, "is trying to **persuade** people to worship God in
2 Cor	5.11	means to fear the Lord, and so we try to **persuade** others.
Gal	5. 7	How did he **persuade** you?
Rev	2.14	of Israel into sin by **persuading** them to eat food that had

PERVERT

Ex	23. 2	do wrong or when they give evidence that **perverts** justice.
Lev	18.23	that **perversion** makes you ritually unclean.
Judg	19.22	of a sudden some sexual **perverts** from the town surrounded
	20.13	Now hand over those **perverts** in Gibeah, so that we can
Prov	6.14	in their **perverted** minds, stirring up trouble everywhere.
	17.26	justice is **perverted** when good people are punished.

Jer 23.36 The people have **perverted** the words of their God, the living God,
Lam 3.36 When justice is **perverted** in court, he knows.
Hab 1. 4 the better of the righteous, and so justice is **perverted.**
Rom 1.26 Even the women **pervert** the natural use of their sex by
1 Cor 6. 9 or are adulterers or homosexual **perverts** [10] or who steal
1 Tim 1.10 for the immoral, for sexual **perverts,** for kidnappers,
Jude 7 those angels did and indulged in sexual immorality and **perversion:**
Rev 17. 5 the mother of all the prostitutes and **perverts** in the world."
21. 8 But cowards, traitors, **perverts,** murderers, the immoral,
22.15 outside the city are the **perverts** and those who practise magic,

PET

Job 41. 5 tie him up like a **pet** bird, like something to amuse your

PETAL

Ex 25.31 decorative flowers, including buds and **petals,** are to form
25.33 flowers shaped like almond blossoms with buds and **petals.**
25.34 flowers shaped like almond blossoms with buds and **petals.**
37.17 including buds and **petals,** formed one piece with it.
37.19 flowers shaped like almond blossoms with buds and **petals.**
37.20 flowers shaped like almond blossoms with buds and **petals.**
1 Kgs 7.26 rim of a cup, curving outwards like the **petals** of a lily.
2 Chr 4. 5 rim of a cup, curving outwards like the **petals** of a flower.

PETER

[SIMON PETER]
Simon Peter, leader of the apostles, also known as Cephas. Both Cephas and Peter mean 'rock'.

Mt 4.18-22 **Jesus calls four fishermen**
8.14-17 **Jesus heals many people**
10.1-4 **The twelve apostles**
14.22-33 **Jesus walks on the water**
15.10-20 **The things that make a person unclean**
16.13-20 **Peter's declaration about Jesus**
21-28 **Jesus speaks about his suffering and death**
17.1-13 **The Transfiguration**
24-27 **Payment of the Temple-tax**
18.21-35 **The parable of the unforgiving servant**
19.16-30 **The rich young man**
26.31-35 **Jesus predicts Peter's denial**
36-46 **Jesus prays in Gethsemane**
57-68 **Jesus before the Council**
69-75 **Peter denies Jesus**
Mk 1.14-20 **Jesus calls four fishermen**
29-34 **Jesus heals many people**
35-39 **Jesus preaches in Galilee**
3.13-19 **Jesus chooses the twelve apostles**
5.21-43 **Jairus' daughter and the woman who touched Jesus' cloak**
8.27-30 **Peter's declaration about Jesus**
8.31-9.1 **Jesus speaks about his suffering and death**
9.2-13 **The Transfiguration**
10.17-31 **The rich man**
11.20-26 **The lesson from the fig-tree**
13.3-13 **Troubles and persecutions**
14.27-31 **Jesus predicts Peter's denial**
32-42 **Jesus prays in Gethsemane**
53-65 **Jesus before the Council**
66-72 **Peter denies Jesus**
16.1-8 **The Resurrection**
16.9-10 **Another old ending to the Gospel**
Lk 4.38-41 **Jesus heals many people**
5.1-11 **Jesus calls the first disciples**
6.12-16 **Jesus chooses the twelve apostles**
8.40-56 **Jairus' daughter and the woman who touched Jesus' cloak**
9.18-20 **Peter's declaration about Jesus**
28-36 **The Transfiguration**
12.41-48 **The faithful or the unfaithful servant**
18.18-30 **The rich man**
22.7-13 **Jesus prepares to eat the Passover meal**
31-34 **Jesus predicts Peter's denial**
54-62 **Peter denies Jesus**
24.1-12 **The Resurrection**
13-35 **The walk to Emmaus**
Jn 1.35-42 **The first disciples of Jesus**
43-51 **Jesus calls Philip and Nathanael**
6.1-15 **Jesus feeds five thousand men**
60-71 **The words of eternal life**
13.1-20 **Jesus washes his disciples' feet**
21-30 **Jesus predicts his betrayal**
36-38 **Jesus predicts Peter's denial**
18.1-11 **The arrest of Jesus**
15-18 **Peter denies Jesus**
25-27 **Peter denies Jesus again**
20.1-10 **The empty tomb**
21.1-14 **Jesus appears to seven disciples**
15-19 **Jesus and Peter**
20-24 **Jesus and the other disciple**
Acts 1.12-26 **Judas' successor**
2.14-42 **Peter's message**
3.1-10 **A lame man is healed**
11-26 **Peter's message in the Temple**
4.1-22 **Peter and John before the Council**
5.1-11 **Ananias and Sapphira**
12-16 **Miracles and wonders**
17-42 **The apostles are persecuted**
8.4-25 **The Gospel is preached in Samaria**
9.32-43 **Peter in Lydda and Joppa**
Acts 10.1-33 **Peter and Cornelius**
34-43 **Peter's speech**
44-48 **The Gentiles receive the Holy Spirit**
11.1-18 **Peter's report to the church at Jerusalem**
12.1-5 **More persecution**
6-19 **Peter is set free from prison**
15.1-21 **The meeting at Jerusalem**
1 Cor 1.12 another, "I follow **Peter";**
3.22 Paul, Apollos, and **Peter;**
9. 5 and the Lord's brothers and **Peter,** by taking a Christian wife
15. 5 that he appeared to **Peter** and then to all twelve apostles.
Gal 1.18 Jerusalem to obtain information from **Peter,** and I stayed with him
2. 7 just as he had given **Peter** the task of preaching the gospel
2. 8 to the Gentiles, just as **Peter** was made an apostle to the
2. 9 James, **Peter,** and John, who seemed to be the leaders, recognized
2.11 But when **Peter** came to Antioch, I opposed him in public,
2.12 arrived there, **Peter** had been eating with the Gentile
2.13 Jewish brothers also started acting like cowards along with **Peter;**
2.14 the gospel, I said to **Peter** in front of them all, "You
1 Pet 1. 1 From **Peter,** apostle of Jesus Christ— To God's chosen
2 Pet 1. 1 From **Simon Peter,** a servant and apostle of Jesus Christ—

PETITION

1 Kgs 8.59 times this prayer and these **petitions** I have made to him.
1 Tim 2. 1 I urge that **petitions,** prayers, requests, and thanksgivings be

PHARAOH

see also **KING (OF EGYPT)**

Song 1. 9 men as a mare excites the stallions of **Pharaoh's** chariots.

PHARISEES

Jewish religious party who were strict in obeying the Law and other regulations added to it.

Mt 3. 7 When John saw many **Pharisees** and Sadducees coming to him
5.20 of the Law and the **Pharisees** in doing what God requires.
9.11 **Pharisees** saw this and asked his disciples, "Why does your teacher
9.14 we and the **Pharisees** fast often, but your disciples don't
9.34 But the **Pharisees** said, "It is the chief of the demons
12. 2 When the **Pharisees** saw this, they said to Jesus, "Look,
12.14 Then the **Pharisees** left and made plans to kill Jesus.
12.24 **Pharisees** heard this, they replied, "He drives out demons only
12.38 Then some teachers of the Law and some **Pharisees** spoke up.
15. 1 Then some **Pharisees** and teachers of the Law came from Jerusalem
15.12 "Do you know that the **Pharisees** had their feelings hurt by
16. 1 **Pharisees** and Sadducees who came to Jesus wanted to trap him,
16. 6 guard against the yeast of the **Pharisees** and Sadducees."
16.11 Guard yourselves from the yeast of the **Pharisees** and Sadducees!"
16.12 but from the teaching of the **Pharisees** and Sadducees.
19. 3 Some **Pharisees** came to him and tried to trap him by asking,
19. 7 The **Pharisees** asked him, "Why, then, did Moses give the law
21.45 chief priests and the **Pharisees** heard Jesus' parables and knew
22.15 The **Pharisees** went off and made a plan to trap Jesus
22.34 When the **Pharisees** heard that Jesus had silenced the Sadducees,
22.41 When some **Pharisees** gathered together, Jesus asked them,
23. 2 and the **Pharisees** are the authorized interpreters of Moses'
23.13 "How terrible for you, teachers of the Law and **Pharisees!**
23.15 "How terrible for you, teachers of the Law and **Pharisees!**
23.23 "How terrible for you, teachers of the Law and **Pharisees!**
23.25 "How terrible for you, teachers of the Law and **Pharisees!**
23.26 Blind **Pharisee!**
23.27 "How terrible for you, teachers of the Law and **Pharisees!**
23.29 "How terrible for you, teachers of the Law and **Pharisees!**
27.62 the chief priests and the **Pharisees** met with Pilate [63] and said,
Mk 2.16 of the Law, who were **Pharisees,** saw that Jesus was eating
2.18 the followers of John the Baptist and the **Pharisees** were fasting.
2.18 and the disciples of the **Pharisees** fast, but yours do not?"
2.24 So the **Pharisees** said to Jesus, "Look, it is against
3. 6 So the **Pharisees** left the synagogue and met at once with
7. 1 **Pharisees** and teachers of the Law who had come from Jerusalem
7. 2 washed them in the way the **Pharisees** said people should.
7. 3 (For the **Pharisees,** as well as the rest of the Jews,
7. 5 So the **Pharisees** and the teachers of the Law asked Jesus,
8.11 Some **Pharisees** came to Jesus and started to argue with him.
8.15 against the yeast of the **Pharisees** and the yeast of Herod."
10. 2 Some **Pharisees** came to him and tried to trap him.
12.13 **Pharisees** and some members of Herod's party were sent to Jesus
Lk 5.17 when Jesus was teaching, some **Pharisees** and teachers of the Law
5.21 of the Law and the **Pharisees** began to say to themselves,
5.30 Some **Pharisees** and some teachers of the Law who belonged to
5.33 offer prayers, and the disciples of the **Pharisees** do the same;
6. 2 Some **Pharisees** asked, "Why are you doing what our Law
6. 7 of the Law and some **Pharisees** wanted a reason to accuse
7.30 the **Pharisees** and the teachers of the Law rejected God's purpose
7.36 A **Pharisee** invited Jesus to have dinner with him,
7.37 Jesus was eating in the **Pharisee's** house, so she brought
7.39 When the **Pharisee** saw this, he said to himself, "If
11.37 Jesus finished speaking, a **Pharisee** invited him to eat with him;
11.38 **Pharisee** was surprised when he noticed that Jesus had not washed
11.39 "Now then, you **Pharisees** clean the outside of your cup
11.42 "How terrible for you **Pharisees!**
11.43 "How terrible for you **Pharisees!**
11.53 of the Law and the **Pharisees** began to criticize him bitterly

Lk 12. 1 guard against the yeast of the **Pharisees**—I mean their hypocrisy.
13.31 At that same time some **Pharisees** came to Jesus and said
14. 1 eat a meal at the home of one of the leading **Pharisees;**
14. 3 of the Law and the **Pharisees,** "Does our Law allow healing
15. 2 to listen to Jesus, [2]the **Pharisees** and the teachers of the
16.14 When the **Pharisees** heard all this, they sneered at Jesus,
17.20 Some **Pharisees** asked Jesus when the Kingdom of God would come.
18.10 one was a **Pharisee,** the other a tax collector.
18.11 **Pharisee** stood apart by himself and prayed, 'I thank you, God,
18.14 tax collector, and not the **Pharisee,** was in the right with
19.39 Then some of the **Pharisees** in the crowd spoke to Jesus.
Jn 1.24 had been sent by the **Pharisees,** [25]then asked John, "If
3. 1 leader named Nicodemus, who belonged to the party of the **Pharisees.**
4. 1 **Pharisees** heard that Jesus was winning and baptizing more disciples
7.32 **Pharisees** heard the crowd whispering these things about Jesus,
7.45 the chief priests and **Pharisees** asked them, "Why did you not
7.47 the **Pharisees** asked them.
7.48 one of the authorities or one **Pharisee** to believe in him?
7.50 One of the **Pharisees** there was Nicodemus, the man who
8. 3 of the Law and the **Pharisees** brought in a woman who had
8.12 Jesus spoke to the **Pharisees** again.
8.13 The **Pharisees** said to him, "Now you are testifying on your
9.13 Then they took to the **Pharisees** the man who had been blind.
9.15 The **Pharisees,** then, asked the man again how he had received
9.16 Some of the **Pharisees** said, "The man who did this
9.17 So the **Pharisees** asked the man once more, "You say he
9.40 Some **Pharisees** who were there with him heard him say this
11.46 of them returned to the **Pharisees** and told them what Jesus
11.47 So the **Pharisees** and the chief priests met with the Council
11.57 chief priests and the **Pharisees** had given orders that if anyone
12.19 The **Pharisees** then said to one another, "You see, we
12.42 because of the **Pharisees** they did not talk about it openly,
18. 3 some temple guards sent by the chief priests and the **Pharisees;**
Acts 5.34 But one of them, a **Pharisee** named Gamaliel, who was a
15. 5 to the party of the **Pharisees** stood up and said, "The
23. 6 and the others were **Pharisees,** he called out in the Council,
23. 6 I am a **Pharisee,** the son of Pharisees.
23. 7 as he said this, the **Pharisees** and Sadducees started to quarrel,
23. 8 but the **Pharisees** believe in all three.)
23. 9 belonged to the party of the **Pharisees** stood up and protested
26. 5 of the strictest party of our religion, the **Pharisees.**
Phil 3. 5 is concerned, I was a **Pharisee,** [6]and I was so zealous that

PHILIP (1)
Philip the Tetrarch, who married Herodias' daughter and ruled over parts of n. Palestine.

Lk 3. 1 and his brother **Philip** was ruler of the territory

PHILIP (2)
Herod Antipas' half-brother and first husband of Herodias.

Mt 14. 3 He had done this because of Herodias, his brother **Philip's** wife.
Mk 6.17 married, even though she was the wife of his brother **Philip.**

PHILIP (3)
One of the twelve apostles.

Mt 10. 3 **Philip** and Bartholomew;
Mk 3.18 Andrew, **Philip,** Bartholomew, Matthew, Thomas, James
Lk 6.14 James and John, **Philip** and Bartholomew, [15]Matthew and Thomas,
Jn 1.43 He found **Philip** and said to him, "Come with me!"
1.44 **(Philip** was from Bethsaida, the town where Andrew and Peter lived.)
1.45 **Philip** found Nathanael and told him, "We have found the one
1.46 "Come and see," answered **Philip.**
1.48 when you were under the fig-tree before **Philip** called you."
6. 5 so he asked **Philip,** "Where can we buy enough food
6. 6 (He said this to test **Philip;**
6. 7 **Philip** answered, "For everyone to have even a little, it would
12.21 They went to **Philip** (he was from Bethsaida in Galilee)
12.22 **Philip** went and told Andrew, and the two of them went
14. 8 **Philip** said to him, "Lord, show us the Father;
14. 9 yet you do not know me, **Philip?**
14.10 Do you not believe, **Philip,** that I am in the Father
Acts 1.13 Peter, John, James and Andrew, **Philip** and Thomas, Bartholomew

PHILIP (4)
Philip the Evangelist.

Acts 6. 5 and **Philip,** Prochorus, Nicanor, Timon, Parmenas, and Nicolaus,
8. 5 **Philip** went to the principal city in Samaria and preached
8. 6 paid close attention to what **Philip** said, as they listened
8.12 But when they believed **Philip's** message about the good news
8.13 he stayed close to **Philip** and was astounded when he saw
8.26 of the Lord said to **Philip,** "Get ready and go south to
8.27 So **Philip** got ready and went.
8.29 The Holy Spirit said to **Philip,** "Go over to that carriage
8.30 **Philip** ran over and heard him reading from the book of
8.31 And he invited **Philip** to climb up and sit in the carriage
8.34 official asked **Philip,** "Tell me, of whom is the prophet saying
8.35 Then **Philip** began to speak;
8.38 carriage to stop, and both **Philip** and the official
8.38 went down into the water, and **Philip** baptized him.
8.39 out of the water, the Spirit of the Lord took **Philip** away.
8.40 **Philip** found himself in Azotus;
21. 8 stayed at the house of **Philip** the evangelist, one of the

PHILISTIA
Area in s.w. Palestine occupied by the Philistines.

Gen 21.32 at Beersheba, Abimelech and Phicol went back to **Philistia.**
21.34 Abraham lived in **Philistia** for a long time.
Ex 13.17 up the coast to **Philistia,** although it was the shortest way.
Josh 13. 2 all the territory of **Philistia** and Geshur, [3]as well as
Judg 10. 6 of Syria, of Sidon, of Moab, of Ammon, and of **Philistia.**
1 Sam 6. 1 Covenant Box had been in **Philistia** for seven months, [2]the
27. 1 The best thing for me to do is to escape to **Philistia.**
27. 7 David lived in **Philistia** for sixteen months.
27.11 This is what David did the whole time he lived in **Philistia.**
29.11 morning to go back to **Philistia,** and the Philistines went on
30.16 amount of loot they had captured from **Philistia** and Judah.
31. 9 sent messengers with them throughout **Philistia** to tell the
2 Sam 1.20 Do not make the women of **Philistia** glad;
8.12 had conquered—[12]Edom, Moab, Ammon, **Philistia,** and
1 Kgs 4.21 the River Euphrates to **Philistia** and the Egyptian border.
15.27 Nadab and his army were besieging the city of Gibbethon in **Philistia.**
16.15 the city of Gibbethon in **Philistia,** [16]and when they heard
2 Kgs 8. 2 with her family to live in **Philistia** for the seven years.
1 Chr 10. 9 sent messengers with them throughout **Philistia** to tell the
18.11 from the nations he conquered—Edom, Moab, Ammon, **Philistia,**
2 Chr 9.26 the River Euphrates to **Philistia** and the Egyptian border.
26. 6 fortified cities near Ashdod and in the rest of **Philistia.**
Ps 83. 7 the people of Gebal, Ammon, and Amalek, and of **Philistia** and Tyre.
87. 4 among the inhabitants of Jerusalem the people of **Philistia,**
Is 2. 6 full of magic practices from the east and from **Philistia.**
9.12 Syria on the east and **Philistia** on the west have opened
14.29 People of **Philistia,** the rod that beat you is broken,
14.32 How shall we answer the messengers that come to us from **Philistia?**
20. 6 live along the coast of **Philistia** will say, 'Look at what
Jer 47. 1 Egypt attacked Gaza, the Lord spoke to me about **Philistia.**
47. 4 time has come to destroy **Philistia,** to cut off from Tyre and
47. 5 How long will the rest of **Philistia** mourn?
Joel 3. 4 to do to me, Tyre, Sidon, and all the regions of **Philistia?**
Obad 19 those from the western foothills will capture **Philistia;**

PHILISTINES
Inhabitants of Palestine with whom the Israelites were frequently at war.

Gen 10.14 and of Crete from whom the **Philistines** are descended.
26. 1 Isaac went to Abimelech, king of the **Philistines,** at Gerar.
26.14 and many servants, the **Philistines** were jealous of him.
26.18 which the **Philistines** had stopped up after Abraham's death.
Ex 15.14 the **Philistines** are seized with terror.
Josh 13. 3 the kings of the **Philistines** lived at Gaza, Ashdod,
Judg 3. 3 land were the five **Philistine** cities, all the Canaanites,
3.31 did so by killing six hundred **Philistines** with an ox-goad.
10. 7 and let the **Philistines** and the Ammonites conquer them.
10.11 the **Philistines,** [12]the Sidonians, the Amalekites,
13. 1 Lord again, and he let the **Philistines** rule them for forty years.
13. 5 He will begin the work of rescuing Israel from the **Philistines."**
14. 1 Timnah, where he noticed a certain **Philistine** girl.
14. 2 and mother, "There is a **Philistine** girl down at Timnah who
14. 3 you have to go to those heathen **Philistines** to get a wife?
14. 4 the Lord was looking for a chance to fight the **Philistines.**
14. 4 At this time the **Philistines** were ruling Israel.
14.11 When the **Philistines** saw him, they sent thirty young men
14.17 Then she told the **Philistines.**
15. 3 going to be responsible for what I do to the **Philistines!"**
15. 5 and turned the foxes loose in the **Philistine** cornfields.
15. 6 When the **Philistines** asked who had done this, they learnt
15. 6 So the **Philistines** went and burnt the woman to death and
15. 9 The **Philistines** came and made camp in Judah, and attacked
15.11 "Don't you know that the **Philistines** are our rulers?
15.14 he got to Lehi, the **Philistines** came running towards him,
15.18 of thirst and be captured by these heathen **Philistines?"**
15.20 Samson led Israel for twenty years while the **Philistines** ruled
16. 1 day Samson went to the **Philistine** city of Gaza, where he met
16. 5 The five **Philistine** kings went to her and said, "Trick
16. 8 So the **Philistine** kings brought Delilah seven new
16. 9 The **Philistines** are coming!"
16.12 The **Philistines** are coming!"
16.14 The **Philistines** are coming!"
16.18 sent a message to the **Philistine** kings and said, "Come back
16.20 The **Philistines** are coming!"
16.21 The **Philistines** captured him and put his eyes out.
16.23 The **Philistine** kings met together to celebrate and
16.27 All five **Philistine** kings were there, and there were about
16.28 get even with the **Philistines** for putting out my two eyes."
16.30 them [30]and shouted, "Let me die with the **Philistines!"**
1 Sam 4. 1 At that time the **Philistines** gathered to go to war against Israel,
4. 1 set up their camp at Ebenezer and the **Philistines** at Aphek.
4. 2 The **Philistines** attacked, and after fierce fighting they
4. 3 "Why did the Lord let the **Philistines** defeat us today?
4. 6 The **Philistines** heard the shouting and said, "Listen to
4. 9 Be brave, **Philistines!**
4.10 The **Philistines** fought hard and defeated the Israelites,
4.17 The messenger answered, "Israel ran away from the **Philistines;**
5. 1 After the **Philistines** captured the Covenant Box, they
5. 8 together all five of the **Philistine** kings and asked them,
5. 8 so they took it to Gath, another **Philistine** city.
5.10 So they sent the Covenant Box to Ekron, another **Philistine** city;

1 Sam 5.11 they sent for all the **Philistine** kings and said, "Send the
6. 4 and five gold mice, one of each for each **Philistine** king.
6.12 The five **Philistine** kings followed them as far as the border
6.16 The five **Philistine** kings watched them do this and then
6.17 The **Philistines** sent the five gold tumours to the Lord
6.18 cities ruled by the five **Philistine** kings, both the
6.21 "The **Philistines** have returned the Lord's Covenant Box.
7. 3 and he will rescue you from the power of the **Philistines."**
7. 7 When the **Philistines** heard that the Israelites had gathered
7. 7 at Mizpah, the five **Philistine** kings started out with their men
7. 8 to the Lord our God to save us from the **Philistines."**
7.10 the **Philistines** moved forward to attack;
7.11 Mizpah and pursued the **Philistines** almost as far as Bethcar,
7.13 So the **Philistines** were defeated, and the Lord prevented
7.14 All the cities which the **Philistines** had captured
9.16 people Israel, and he will rescue them from the **Philistines.**
10. 5 the Hill of God in Gibeah, where there is a **Philistine** camp.
12. 9 and so he let the **Philistines** and the king of Moab and
13. 3 Jonathan killed the **Philistine** commander in Geba,
13. 3 and all the **Philistines** heard about it.
13. 4 Saul had killed the **Philistine** commander
13. 4 and that the **Philistines** hated them.
13. 5 The **Philistines** assembled to fight the Israelites;
13.11 besides that, the **Philistines** are gathering at Michmash.
13.12 So I thought, 'The **Philistines** are going to attack me
13.16 the **Philistine** camp was at Michmash.
13.17 The **Philistine** soldiers went out on raids from their
13.19 blacksmiths in Israel because the **Philistines** were
13.20 had to go to the **Philistines** to get their ploughs, hoes,
13.23 The **Philistines** sent a group of soldiers to defend the
14. 1 his weapons, "Let's go across to the **Philistine** camp."
14. 4 to get over to the **Philistine** camp, there were two large
14. 6 "Let's cross over to the camp of those heathen **Philistines.**
14. 8 "We will go across and let the **Philistines** see us.
14.11 So they let the **Philistines** see them, and the Philistines said,
14.13 Jonathan attacked the **Philistines** and knocked them down, and
14.15 All the **Philistines** in the countryside were terrified;
14.16 saw the **Philistines** running in confusion.
14.19 the confusion in the **Philistine** camp got worse and worse,
14.20 marched into battle against the **Philistines,** who were
14.21 who had been on the **Philistine** side and had gone with them
14.22 of Ephraim, heard that the **Philistines** were running away, so
14.22 the **Philistines,** [23]fighting all the way beyond Bethaven.
14.30 Just think how many more **Philistines** they would have killed!"
14.31 day the Israelites defeated the **Philistines,** fighting all
14.36 go down and attack the **Philistines** in the night, plunder
14.37 So Saul asked God, "Shall I attack the **Philistines?**
14.46 that, Saul stopped pursuing the **Philistines,** and they went
14.47 Ammon, and of Edom, the kings of Zobah, and the **Philistines.**
14.52 lived, Saul had to fight fiercely against the **Philistines.**
17. 1 The **Philistines** gathered for battle in Socoh, a town in Judah;
17. 2 Valley of Elah, where they got ready to fight the **Philistines.**
17. 3 **Philistines** lined up on one hill and the Israelites on another,
17. 4 out from the **Philistine** camp to challenge the Israelites.
17. 8 I am a **Philistine,** you slaves of Saul!
17.19 Israelites are in the Valley of Elah fighting the **Philistines."**
17.21 **Philistine** and the Israelite armies took up positions for battle,
17.26 kills this **Philistine** and frees Israel from this disgrace?
17.26 who is this heathen **Philistine** to defy the army
17.32 "Your Majesty, no one should be afraid of this **Philistine!**
17.36 the same to this heathen **Philistine,** who has defied the army
17.37 he will save me from this **Philistine."**
17.41 The **Philistine** started walking towards David, with his
17.46 give the bodies of the **Philistine** soldiers to the birds and
17.48 David ran quickly towards the **Philistine** battle line to fight him.
17.51 When the **Philistines** saw that their hero was dead, they ran
17.52 The **Philistines** fell wounded all along the road that leads to Shaaraim,
17.53 came back from pursuing the **Philistines,** they looted their camp.
18.17 that in this way the **Philistines** would kill David,
18.21 her to trap him, and he will be killed by the **Philistines."**
18.25 of a hundred dead **Philistines,** as revenge on his enemies."
18.25 (This was how Saul planned to have David killed by the **Philistines.)**
18.27 David and his men went and killed two hundred **Philistines.**
18.30 The **Philistine** armies would come and fight, but in
19. 8 War with the **Philistines** broke out again.
21. 9 the sword of Goliath the **Philistine,** whom you killed in the
22.10 David some food and the sword of Goliath the **Philistine."**
23. 1 David heard that the **Philistines** were attacking the town
23. 2 So he asked the Lord, "Shall I go and attack the **Philistines?"**
23. 3 worse if we go to Keilah and attack the **Philistine** forces!"
23. 4 because I will give you victory over the **Philistines."**
23. 5 So David and his men went to Keilah and attacked the **Philistines;**
23.27 The **Philistines** are invading the country!"
23.28 So Saul stopped pursuing David and went to fight the **Philistines.**
24. 1 came back from fighting the **Philistines,** he was told that
28. 1 the **Philistines** gathered their troops to fight Israel,
28. 4 The **Philistine** troops assembled and camped near the town of Shunem;
28. 5 When Saul saw the **Philistine** army, he was terrified, [6]and
28.15 The **Philistines** are at war with me, and God has abandoned me.
28.19 He will hand you and Israel over to the **Philistines.**
28.19 Lord will also hand the army of Israel over to the **Philistines."**
29. 1 The **Philistines** brought all their troops together at Aphek,
29. 2 The five **Philistine** kings marched out with their units of
29. 3 The **Philistine** commanders saw them and asked, "What are
29. 4 But the **Philistine** commanders were angry with Achish
29.11 back to Philistia, and the **Philistines** went on to Jezreel.
31. 1 **Philistines** fought a battle against the Israelites on Mount Gilboa.
31. 2 But the **Philistines** caught up with them and killed three
1 Sam 31. 4 me, so that these godless **Philistines** won't gloat over me
31. 7 Then the **Philistines** came and occupied them.
31. 8 the battle the **Philistines** went to plunder the corpses,
31.11 in Gilead heard what the **Philistines** had done to Saul,
2 Sam 3.14 I paid a hundred **Philistine** foreskins in order to marry her."
3.18 Israel from the **Philistines** and from all their other enemies.' "
5.17 The **Philistines** were told that David had been made king of Israel,
5.18 The **Philistines** arrived at the Valley of Rephaim and occupied it.
5.19 David asked the Lord, "Shall I attack the **Philistines?**
5.20 So David went to Baal Perazim and there he defeated the **Philistines.**
5.21 When the **Philistines** fled, they left their idols behind,
5.22 Then the **Philistines** went back to the Valley of Rephaim
5.24 I will be marching ahead of you to defeat the **Philistine** army."
5.25 was able to drive the **Philistines** back from Geba all the way
8. 1 later King David attacked the **Philistines** again, defeated
19. 9 "He rescued us from the **Philistines,** but now he has fled
21.12 in Beth Shan, where the **Philistines** had hanged the bodies on
21.15 was another war between the **Philistines** and Israel,
21.15 and David and his men went and fought the **Philistines.**
21.18 was a battle with the **Philistines** at Gob, during which
21.19 was another battle with the **Philistines** at Gob, and Elhanan
23. 9 David challenged the **Philistines** who had gathered for battle.
23.10 his ground and fought the **Philistines** until his hand was so
23.11 The **Philistines** had gathered at Lehi, where there was a
23.11 The Israelites fled from the **Philistines,** [12]but Shammah
23.12 in the field, defended it, and killed the **Philistines.**
23.13 was, while a band of **Philistines** was camping in the Valley
23.14 hill, and a group of **Philistines** had occupied Bethlehem.
23.16 forced their way through the **Philistine** camp, drew some
2 Kgs 1. 2 Baalzebub, the god of the **Philistine** city of Ekron, in order
18. 8 He defeated the **Philistines,** and raided their settlements,
1 Chr 1.12 Crete (from whom the **Philistines** were descended).
10. 1 **Philistines** fought a battle against the Israelites on Mount Gilboa.
10. 2 But the **Philistines** caught up with them and killed three
10. 4 to keep these godless **Philistines** from gloating over me."
10. 7 Then the **Philistines** came and occupied them.
10. 8 the battle, the **Philistines** went to plunder the corpses,
10.11 in Gilead heard what the **Philistines** had done to Saul,
11.13 David's side against the **Philistines** at the battle of Pas Dammim.
11.14 stand in the middle of the field and fought the **Philistines.**
11.15 Adullam, while a band of **Philistines** was camping in the
11.16 hill, and a group of **Philistines** had occupied Bethlehem.
11.18 forced their way through the **Philistine** camp, drew some
12.19 he was marching out with the **Philistines** to fight King Saul.
12.19 he did not help the **Philistines,** for their kings were afraid
14. 8 When the **Philistines** heard that David had now been made
14. 9 The **Philistines** arrived at the Valley of Rephaim
14.10 David asked God, "Shall I attack the **Philistines?**
14.12 When the **Philistines** fled, they left their idols behind,
14.13 the **Philistines** returned to the valley and started plundering it
14.15 I will be marching ahead of you to defeat the **Philistine** army."
14.16 and so he drove the **Philistines** back from Gibeon all the way
18. 1 King David attacked the **Philistines** again and defeated them.
20. 4 Later on, war broke out again with the **Philistines** at Gezer.
20. 4 killed a giant named Sippai, and the **Philistines** were defeated.
20. 5 was another battle with the **Philistines,** and Elhanan son of
2 Chr 17.11 Some of the **Philistines** brought Jehoshaphat a large
21.16 Some **Philistines** and Arabs lived near where some
26. 6 Uzziah went to war against the **Philistines.**
26. 7 him to defeat the **Philistines,** the Arabs living at Gurbaal,
28.18 At this same time the **Philistines** were raiding the towns
Ps 60. 8 Did the **Philistines** think they would shout in triumph over me?"
108. 9 I will shout in triumph over the **Philistines."**
Is 11.14 Together they will attack the **Philistines** on the west
14.30 a terrible famine on you **Philistines,** and it will not leave
14.31 Howl and cry for help, all you **Philistine** cities!
20. 1 of the Assyrian army attacked the **Philistine** city of Ashdod.
Jer 25.19 all the kings of the **Philistine** cities of Ashkelon, Gaza,
47. 4 the Lord, will destroy the **Philistines,** all who came from
Ezek 16.27 handed you over to the **Philistines,** who hate you and are
16.57 joke to the Edomites, the **Philistines,** and your other
25.15 The Sovereign Lord said, "The **Philistines** have taken
25.16 that I will attack the **Philistines** and wipe them out.
25.16 I will destroy everyone left living there on the **Philistine** Plain.
Amos 1. 8 of Ekron, and all the **Philistines** who are left will die."
6. 2 city of Hamath and on down to the **Philistine** city of Gath.
9. 7 I brought the **Philistines** from Crete and the Syrians from Kir,
Zeph 2. 5 You **Philistines** are doomed, you people who live along the coast.
Zech 9. 6 The Lord says, "I will humble all these proud **Philistines.**

PHILOSOPHER

Ecc 1. 1 are the words of the **Philosopher,** David's son, who was king
1. 2 It is useless, useless, said the **Philosopher.**
1.12 I, the **Philosopher,** have been king over Israel in Jerusalem.
7.27 Yes, said the **Philosopher,** I found this out little by
12. 8 Useless, useless, said the **Philosopher.**
12. 9 But because the **Philosopher** was wise, he kept on teaching
12.10 The **Philosopher** tried to find comforting words, but the
Dan 1.17 young men knowledge and skill in literature and **philosophy.**

PHINEHAS (1)

Eleazar's son and Aaron's grandson.

Ex 6.25 one of Putiel's daughters, who bore him **Phinehas.**
Num 25. 7 **Phinehas,** the son of Eleazar and grandson of Aaron the priest,
25.11 to Moses, [11]"Because of what **Phinehas** has done, I am no
31. 6 war under the command of **Phinehas** son of Eleazar the priest,
Josh 22.13 of Israel sent **Phinehas,** the son of Eleazar the priest,
22.14 Ten leading men went with **Phinehas,** one from each of the

Josh 22.30 **Phinehas** the priest and the ten leading men of the
22.31 **Phinehas,** the son of Eleazar the priest, said to them,
22.32 Then **Phinehas** and the leaders left the people of Reuben
24.33 of Ephraim which had been given to his son **Phinehas.**
Judg 20.27 Bethel in those days, and **Phinehas,** the son of Eleazar and
1 Chr 6. 4 **Phinehas,** Abishua, [5]Bukki, Uzzi, [6]Zerahiah, Meraioth,
6.50 Eleazar, **Phinehas,** Abishua, [51]Bukki, Uzzi, Zerahiah,
9.20 **Phineas** son of Eleazar—may the Lord be with him!—
Ezra 7. 5 son of Abishua, son of **Phinehas,** son of Eleazar, son of
8. 2 Gershom, of the clan of **Phinehas** Daniel, of the clan
Ps 106.30 But **Phinehas** stood up and punished the guilty, and the

PHRASE

Job 32.11 speaking and waited while you searched for wise **phrases.**

AV PHYLACTERIES see STRAP

PHYSICAL

Gen 17.13 and this will be a **physical** sign to show that my covenant
Lev 21.17 your descendants who has any **physical** defect may present the
21.18 No man with any **physical** defect may make the offering:
21.21 the priest who has any **physical** defect may present the
21.23 but because he has a **physical** defect, he shall not come
Dan 1. 4 to learn, and free from **physical** defects, so that they would
Jn 3. 6 A person is born **physically** of human parents, but he is
Rom 2.27 obey the Law, even though they are not **physically** circumcised.
2.28 Jew on the outside, whose circumcision is a **physical** thing.
1 Cor 6.16 joins his body to a prostitute becomes **physically** one with her?
15.44 When buried, it is a **physical** body;
15.44 There is, of course, a **physical** body, so there has to be
15.46 that comes first, but the **physical,** and then the spiritual.
2 Cor 4.16 Even though our **physical** being is gradually decaying,
12. 7 I was given a painful **physical** ailment, which acts as Satan's
Gal 4.14 But even though my **physical** condition was a great trial to you,
5.13 become an excuse for letting your **physical** desires control you.
6.13 they can boast that you submitted to this **physical** ceremony.
Col 1.22 now, by means of the **physical** death of his Son, God has
1.24 for by means of my **physical** sufferings I am helping to
2.23 they have no real value in controlling **physical** passions.
1 Tim 4. 8 **Physical** exercise has some value, but spiritual exercise is
1 Pet 3.18 He was put to death **physically,** but made alive spiritually,
4. 1 Christ suffered **physically,** you too must strengthen yourselves
4. 1 whoever suffers **physically** is no longer involved with sin.
4. 6 had been judged in their **physical** existence as everyone is judged;

PICK

Gen 18. 7 ran to the herd and **picked** out a calf that was tender
21.18 Get up, go and **pick** him up, and comfort him.
22.10 Then he **picked** up the knife to kill him.
27. 9 Go to the flock and **pick** out two fat young goats, so
42.24 speak again, he came back, **picked** out Simeon, and had him
Ex 4. 4 said to Moses, "Bend down and **pick** it up by the tail."
10.19 very strong west wind, which **picked** up the locusts and blew
17. 9 Moses said to Joshua, **"Pick** out some men to go and fight
Lev 19.10 that were missed or to **pick** up the grapes that have fallen;
26. 5 when it is time to **pick** grapes,
26. 5 and you will still be **picking** grapes when it is time to
Deut 24.20 When you have **picked** your olives once, do not go back
Josh 7.14 The tribe that I **pick** out will then come forward,
7.14 The clan that I **pick** out will come forward, family by family.
7.14 The family that I **pick** out will come forward, man by man.
7.15 The one who is then **picked** out and found with the
7.16 tribe by tribe, and the tribe of Judah was **picked** out.
7.17 forward, clan by clan, and the clan of Zerah was **picked** out.
7.17 family by family, and the family of Zabdi was **picked** out.
7.18 the son of Carmi and grandson of Zabdi, was **picked** out.
8. 3 He **picked** out thirty thousand of his best troops and sent
Judg 1. 7 and big toes cut off have **picked** up scraps under my table.
9.27 their vineyards and **picked** the grapes, made wine from them,
15.15 He bent down and **picked** it up, and killed a thousand men
Ruth 2. 3 behind the workers, **picking** up the corn which they left.
2. 7 me to let her follow the workers and **pick** up the corn.
2. 8 Don't **pick** up corn anywhere except in this field.
2.15 had left to go on **picking** up corn, Boaz ordered the workers,
2.15 "Let her **pick** it up even where the bundles
2.15 corn from the bundles and leave it for her to **pick** up."
2.21 he told me to keep **picking** up corn with his workers until
1 Sam 10.20 come forward, and the Lord **picked** the tribe of Benjamin.
10.21 Benjamin come forward, and the family of Matri was **picked** out.
10.21 of Matri came forward, and Saul son of Kish was **picked** out.
13. 2 2 Saul **picked** three thousand men, keeping two thousand of
17.10 I dare you to **pick** someone to fight me!"
17.40 his shepherd's stick and then **picked** up five smooth stones
17.54 David **picked** up Goliath's head and took it to Jerusalem,
20.38 The boy **picked** up the arrow and returned to his master,
2 Sam 4. 4 from the city of Jezreel, his nurse **picked** him up and fled;
15.24 set it down and didn't **pick** it up again until all the
1 Kgs 13.29 The old prophet **picked** up the body, put it on the donkey,
2 Kgs 2.13 Then he **picked** up Elijah's cloak that had fallen from him,
4.39 found a wild vine, and **picked** as many gourds as he could
6. 7 out," he ordered, and the man bent down and **picked** it up.
2 Chr 25. 5 They were **picked** troops, ready for battle, skilled in using
Ps 102. 9 You **picked** me up and threw me away.
Prov 26. 9 a drunk man trying to **pick** a thorn out of his hand.
30.17 by vultures or have his eyes **picked** out by wild ravens.
Song 7. 8 I will climb the palm-tree and **pick** its fruit.
Is 17. 5 field in the valley of Rephaim when it has been **picked** bare.
Is 17. 6 all the olives have been **picked** except two or three at the
22.17 important, but the Lord will **pick** you up and throw you away.
22.18 He will **pick** you up like a ball and throw you into
24.13 off every tree and the last grapes **picked** from the vines.
28. 4 first figs of the season, **picked** and eaten as soon as they
30.14 no piece big enough to **pick** up hot coals with, or to
Jer 6. 9 like a vineyard from which every grape has been **picked.**
23.39 them that [39]I will certainly **pick** them up and throw them
43.12 As a shepherd **picks** his clothes clean of lice,
43.12 the king of Babylonia will **pick** the land of Egypt clean
49. 9 When men **pick** grapes, they leave a few on the vines, and
Ezek 10. 7 that was there among them, **picked** up some coals, and put
Hos 11. 4 I **picked** them up and held them to my cheek;
Jon 1.15 Then they **picked** Jonah up and threw him into the sea,
Mic 7. 1 All the grapes and all the tasty figs have been **picked.**
Zech 5. 9 They **picked** up the basket and flew off with it.
Mt 9. 6 the paralysed man, "Get up, **pick** up your bed, and go
12. 1 hungry, so they began to **pick** ears of corn and eat the
27. 6 The chief priests **picked** up the coins and said,
Mk 2. 9 or to say, 'Get up, **pick** up your mat, and walk'?
2.11 "I tell you, get up, **pick** up your mat, and go home!"
2.12 the man got up, **picked** up his mat, and hurried away.
2.23 walked along with him, they began to **pick** the ears of corn.
16.18 if they **pick** up snakes or drink any poison, they will
Lk 5.24 "I tell you, get up, **pick** up your bed, and go home!"
6. 1 His disciples began to **pick** the ears of corn, rub them in
6.44 you do not **pick** figs from thorn bushes or gather grapes from
Jn 5. 8 Jesus said to him, "Get up, **pick** up your mat, and walk."
5. 9 he **picked** up his mat and started walking.
5.11 made me well told me to **pick** up my mat and walk."
8.59 Then they **picked** up stones to throw at him, but Jesus
10.31 Then the people again **picked** up stones to throw at him.
Acts 20. 9 When they **picked** him up, he was dead.
Rev 18.21 Then a mighty angel **picked** up a stone the size of a

PIECE

[HALF-PIECE]

Gen 15.17 appeared and passed between the **pieces** of the animals.
20.16 your brother a thousand **pieces of silver** as proof to all who
23.15 only four hundred **pieces of silver**—what is that between us?
23.16 the people—four hundred **pieces of silver,** according to the
33.19 of Hamor father of Shechem for a hundred **pieces of silver.**
37.28 sold him for twenty **pieces of silver** to the Ishmaelites, who
37.33 My son Joseph has been torn to **pieces!"**
44.28 must have been torn to **pieces** by wild animals, because I
45.22 Benjamin three hundred **pieces of silver**
Ex 15. 6 it breaks the enemy in **pieces.**
15.25 the Lord showed him a **piece** of wood, which he threw into
21.32 of the slave thirty **pieces of silver,** and the bull shall be
25.19 Make them so that they form one **piece** with the lid.
25.31 including buds and petals, are to form one **piece** with it.
25.36 lamp-stand are to be a single **piece** of pure hammered gold.
26. 1 presence, out of ten **pieces** of fine linen woven with blue,
26. 2 Make each **piece** the same size, twelve metres long and two
26. 4 blue cloth on the edge of the outside **piece** in each set.
26. 5 fifty loops on the first **piece** of the first set
26. 5 loops matching them on the last **piece** of the second set.
26. 6 gold hooks with which to join the two sets into one **piece.**
26. 7 the Tent out of eleven **pieces** of cloth made of goats' hair.
26. 9 Fold the sixth **piece** double over the front of the Tent.
26.10 the edge of the last **piece** of one set, and fifty loops
26.12 Hang the extra **half-piece** over the back of the Tent.
27. 2 They are to form one **piece** with the altar, and the whole
28. 8 attached to the ephod so as to form one **piece** with it.
29.17 Cut the ram in **pieces;**
29.17 and put them on top of the head and the other **pieces.**
30. 2 at the four corners are to form one **piece** with it.
36. 8 made it out of ten **pieces** of fine linen woven with blue,
36. 9 Each **piece** was the same size, twelve metres long and two
36.11 blue cloth on the edge of the outside **piece** in each set.
36.12 fifty loops on the first **piece** of the first set
36.12 loops matching them on the last **piece** of the second set.
36.13 gold hooks, with which to join the two sets into one **piece.**
36.14 the Tent out of eleven **pieces** of cloth made of goats' hair.
36.17 the edge of the last **piece** of one set and fifty loops
37. 8 He made them so that they formed one **piece** with the lid.
37.17 including buds and petals, formed one **piece** with it.
37.22 the lamp-stand were a single **piece** of pure hammered gold.
37.25 Its projections at the four corners formed one **piece** with it.
38. 2 four corners, so that they formed one **piece** with the altar.
39. 5 so as to form one **piece** with it, as the Lord had
Lev 1. 8 put on the fire the **pieces** of the animal, including the head
8.20 He cut the ram in **pieces,** washed the internal
9.13 the head and the other **pieces** of the animal, and he burnt
13.48 wool or linen, [48]or on any **piece** of linen or wool cloth
14. 4 be brought, together with a **piece** of cedar-wood, a red cord,
27. 3 50 **pieces of silver**
27. 3 30 **pieces of silver**
27. 3 20 **pieces of silver**
27. 3 10 **pieces of silver**
27. 3 5 **pieces of silver**
27. 3 3 **pieces of silver**
27. 3 15 **pieces of silver**
27. 3 10 **pieces of silver**
27.16 the rate of ten **pieces of silver** for every twenty kilogrammes
Num 3.47 five **pieces of silver,** according to the official standard,
3.50 and took [50]the 1,365 **pieces of silver** [51]and gave them to
18.16 five **pieces of silver,** according to the official standard.
31.20 You must also purify every **piece** of clothing and
33.54 drawing lots, giving a large **piece** of property to a large

Deut 7. 5 their sacred stone pillars in **pieces,** cut down the symbols
9.17 you I threw the stone tablets down and broke them to **pieces.**
9.21 Then I broke it in **pieces,** ground it to dust, and threw
12. 3 Tear down their altars and smash their sacred stone pillars to **pieces.**
22. 3 you find a donkey, a **piece** of clothing, or anything else
22.19 fine him a hundred **pieces of silver** and give the money to
22.29 bride price of fifty **pieces of silver,** and she is to become
Josh 24.32 buried at Shechem, in the **piece** of land that Jacob had
24.32 the father of Shechem, for a hundred **pieces of silver.**
Judg 5.30 for Sisera, embroidered **pieces** for the neck of the queen."
9. 4 They gave him seventy **pieces of silver** from the temple
14.12 each one of you a **piece** of fine linen and a change
16. 5 Each one of us will give you eleven hundred **pieces of silver."**
17. 2 stole those eleven hundred **pieces of silver** from you, you
17. 3 So now I will give the **pieces of silver** back to you."
17. 4 two hundred of the **pieces of silver** and gave them to a
17.10 will give you ten **pieces of silver** a year, some clothes, and
19.29 body, cut it into twelve **pieces,**
19.29 and sent one **piece** to each of the twelve tribes
20. 6 her body, cut it in **pieces,**
20. 6 and sent one **piece** to each of the twelve tribes
Ruth 2.14 Ruth, "Come and have a **piece** of bread, and dip it in
1 Sam 9.23 to the cook, "Bring the **piece** of meat I gave you, which
9.24 the cook brought the choice **piece** of the leg and placed it
9.24 Samuel said, "Look, here is the **piece** that was kept for you.
11. 7 two oxen, cut them in **pieces,** and sent messengers
11. 7 to carry the **pieces** throughout the land of Israel
15.33 And he cut Agag to **pieces** in front of the altar in
24. 4 over and cut off a **piece** of Saul's robe without Saul's
24.11 my father, look at the **piece** of your robe I am holding!
2 Sam 6.19 a loaf of bread, a **piece** of roasted meat, and some raisins.
18.11 would have given you ten **pieces of silver** and a belt."
18.12 gave me a thousand **pieces of silver,** I wouldn't lift a
24.24 the threshing-place and the oxen for fifty **pieces of silver.**
1 Kgs 7.24 been cast all in one **piece** with the rest of the tank.
7.32 the panels, and the axles were of one **piece** with the carts.
7.34 corners of each cart, which were of one **piece** with the cart.
7.35 its supports and the panels were of one **piece** with the cart.
10.29 selling chariots for 600 **pieces of silver** each and horses
11.30 tore it into twelve **pieces,** [31] and said to Jeroboam,
11.31 "Take ten **pieces** for yourself, because the Lord,
16.24 Samaria for six thousand **pieces of silver** from a man named Shemer.
18.23 kill it, cut it in **pieces,** and put it on the wood
18.33 altar, cut the bull in **pieces,** and laid it on the wood.
20.39 life or else pay a fine of three thousand **pieces of silver.'**
2 Kgs 2.24 out of the woods and tore forty-two of the boys to **pieces.**
5. 5 thousand **pieces of silver,**
5. 5 six thousand **pieces** of gold,
5.22 give them three thousand **pieces of silver** and two changes of
5.23 "Please take six thousand **pieces of silver,"** Naaman replied.
6.25 donkey's head cost eighty **pieces of silver,**
6.25 two hundred grammes of dove's dung cost five **pieces of silver.**
7. 1 or six kilogrammes of barley for one **piece of silver."**
7.16 kilogrammes of barley were sold for one **piece of silver.**
7.18 in Samaria for one **piece of silver,** [19] to which the officer
15.20 Israel by forcing each one to contribute fifty **pieces of silver.**
18. 4 He also broke in **pieces** the bronze snake that Moses had made,
23.14 broke the stone pillars to **pieces,** cut down the symbols of
23.15 broke its stones into **pieces,** and pounded them to dust;
25.13 The Babylonians broke in **pieces** the bronze columns and
1 Chr 16. 3 a loaf of bread, a **piece** of roasted meat, and some raisins.
2 Chr 1.17 chariots for six hundred **pieces of silver** each and horses
4. 3 been cast all in one **piece** with the rest of the tank.
15.16 it up, and burnt the **pieces** in the valley of the Kidron.
28.24 he took all the temple equipment and broke it in **pieces.**
34. 7 idols to dust, and broke in **pieces** all the incense-altars.
Job 2. 8 rubbish heap and took a **piece** of broken pottery to scrape
13.25 you are attacking a **piece** of dry straw.
41.29 him a club is a **piece** of straw, and he laughs when
41.30 The scales on his belly are like jagged **pieces** of pottery;
Ps 2. 9 you will shatter them in **pieces** like a clay pot.' "
7. 2 one can save me, and there they will tear me to **pieces.**
17.12 like lions, waiting for me, wanting to tear me to **pieces.**
107.14 their gloom and darkness and broke their chains in **pieces.**
Prov 30. 4 Or wrapped up water in a **piece** of cloth?
Is 7.23 each worth a thousand **pieces of silver,** will be overgrown
8. 1 to me, "Take a large **piece** of writing material and write on
30.14 broken that there is no **piece** big enough to pick up hot
44.12 The metalworker takes a **piece** of metal and works with it
51. 9 It was you that cut the sea-monster Rahab to **pieces.**
Jer 4.20 their curtains are torn to **pieces.**
5. 6 desert will tear them to **pieces,** and leopards will prowl
17.18 Bring disaster on them and break them to **pieces.**
18. 4 Whenever a **piece** of pottery turned out imperfect, he would
23.29 like a fire, and like a hammer that breaks rocks in **pieces.**
28.10 my neck, broke it in **pieces,** [11] and said in the presence of
32. 9 the price came to seventeen **pieces of silver.**
48.12 They will empty its wine-jars and break them in **pieces.**
50.23 the whole world to **pieces,** and now that hammer is shattered!
52.17 The Babylonians broke in **pieces** the bronze columns and
Lam 2. 6 He smashed to **pieces** the Temple where we worshipped him;
2. 9 The gates lie buried in rubble, their bars smashed to **pieces.**
3.11 chased me off the road, tore me to **pieces,** and left me.
Ezek 6. 6 smashed to **pieces,** their incense-altars will be shattered,
13.19 get a few handfuls of barley and a few **pieces** of bread.
16.40 you, and they will cut you to **pieces** with their swords.
23.34 drain it dry, and with its broken **pieces** tear your breast.
24. 4 Put in the best **pieces** of meat— the shoulders
24. 4 and the legs— fill it with choice bony **pieces** too.
Ezek 24. 6 **Piece after piece** of meat is taken out, and not one is
Hos 3. 2 So I paid fifteen **pieces of silver** and 150 kilogrammes of
4.12 They ask for revelations from a **piece** of wood!
5.14 I myself will tear them to **pieces** and then leave them.
8. 6 The gold bull worshipped in Samaria will be smashed to **pieces!**
13. 8 the spot, and will tear you to **pieces** like a wild animal.
Amos 6.11 command, houses large and small will be smashed to **pieces.**
Mic 1. 7 idols will be smashed to **pieces,** everything given to its
5. 8 them, and tears them to **pieces**—and there is no hope of
Nah 2.12 prey and tore it to **pieces** for his mate and her cubs;
Hab 2.19 You say to a **piece** of wood, "Wake up!"
Hag 2.12 Suppose someone takes a **piece** of consecrated meat from a
Zech 11.12 So they paid me thirty **pieces of silver** as my wages.
11.13 I took the thirty **pieces of silver**—the magnificent sum they
Mt 9.16 an old coat with a **piece** of new cloth, for the new
15.37 the disciples took up seven baskets full of **pieces** left over.
24.51 master will cut him in **pieces** and make him share the fate
26.26 were eating, Jesus took a **piece** of bread, gave a prayer of
Mk 2.21 "No one uses a **piece** of new cloth to patch up an
8. 8 the disciples took up seven baskets full of **pieces** left over.
8.19 How many baskets full of leftover **pieces** did you take up?"
8.20 "how many baskets full of leftover **pieces** did you take up?"
14.22 were eating, Jesus took a **piece** of bread, gave a prayer of
15.24 throwing dice to see who would get which **piece** of clothing.
Lk 5.36 "No one tears a **piece** off a new coat to patch up
5.36 the new coat, and the **piece** of new cloth will not match
12.46 master will cut him in **pieces** and make him share the fate
20.18 Everyone who falls on that stone will be cut to **pieces;**
22.19 Then he took a **piece** of bread, gave thanks to God, broke
24.42 They gave him a **piece** of cooked fish, [43] which he took
Jn 6.12 he said to his disciples, "Gather the **pieces** left over;
6.13 filled twelve baskets with the **pieces** left over from the five
13.26 So he took a **piece** of bread, dipped it, and gave it
19.23 which was made of one **piece** of woven cloth without any seams
Acts 23.10 the commander was afraid that Paul would be torn to **pieces.**
27.41 was being broken to **pieces** by the violence of the waves.
27.44 on to the planks or to some broken **pieces** of the ship.
Rom 11.16 If the first **piece** of bread is given to God, then the
1 Cor 11.23 was betrayed, took a **piece** of bread, [24] gave thanks to God,
Rev 2.26 an iron rod and to break them to **pieces** like clay pots.

PIERCE

Ex 21. 6 stand against the door or the door-post and **pierce** his ear.
Deut 15.17 him to the door of your house and there **pierce** his ear;
Judg 5.26 she **pierced** him through the head.
2 Kgs 9.24 arrow that struck Joram in the back and **pierced** his heart.
Job 6. 4 Almighty God has **pierced** me with arrows, and their poison
16.13 at me from every side— arrows that **pierce** and wound me;
41. 7 hide with fishing-spears or **pierce** his head with a harpoon?
41.13 can tear off his outer coat or **pierce** the armour he wears.
Ps 45. 5 Your arrows are sharp, they **pierce** the hearts of your enemies;
Prov 7.23 into a trap [23] where an arrow would **pierce** its heart.
Ezek 29. 7 leaned on you, you broke, **pierced** their armpits, and made
Hab 3.14 Your arrows **pierced** the commander of his army when it
Jn 19.37 scripture that says, "People will look at him whom they **pierced."**
Rev 1. 7 Everyone will see him, including those who **pierced** him.

PIG

Lev 11. 7 Do not eat **pigs.**
Deut 14. 8 Do not eat **pigs.**
Ps 80.13 wild **pigs** trample it down, and wild animals feed on it.
Prov 11.22 good judgement is like a gold ring in a **pig's** snout.
Is 66. 3 whether they present a grain-offering or offer **pigs'** blood;
Mt 7. 6 in front of **pigs**—they will only trample them underfoot.
8.30 Not far away there was a large herd of **pigs** feeding.
8.31 going to drive us out, send us into that herd of **pigs."**
8.32 so they left and went off into the **pigs.**
8.33 been taking care of the **pigs** ran away and went into the
Mk 5.11 was a large herd of **pigs** near by, feeding on a hillside.
5.12 "Send us to the **pigs,** and let us go into them."
5.13 the evil spirits went out of the man and entered the **pigs.**
5.13 whole herd—about two thousand **pigs** in all—rushed down the
5.14 been taking care of the **pigs** ran away and spread the news
5.16 happened to the man with the demons, and about the **pigs.**
Lk 8.32 was a large herd of **pigs** near by, feeding on a hillside.
8.32 Jesus to let them go into the **pigs,** and he let them.
8.33 They went out of the man and into the **pigs.**
8.34 been taking care of the **pigs** saw what happened, so they ran
15.15 sent him out to his farm to take care of the **pigs.**
15.16 with the bean pods the **pigs** ate, but no one gave him
2 Pet 2.22 and "A **pig** that has been washed goes back

PIGEON

Gen 15. 9 each of them three years old, and a dove and a **pigeon."**
Lev 1.14 bird as a burnt-offering, it must be a dove or a **pigeon.**
5. 7 sin two doves or two **pigeons,** one for a sin-offering and the
5.11 afford two doves or two **pigeons,** he shall bring one
12. 6 a burnt-offering and a **pigeon** or a dove for a sin-offering.
12. 8 bring two doves or two **pigeons,** one for a burnt-offering and
14.22 bring two doves or two **pigeons,** one for the sin-offering and
14.30 one of the doves or **pigeons** [31] as the sin-offering and the
15.14 take two doves or two **pigeons** to the entrance of the Tent
15.29 take two doves or two **pigeons** to the priest at the entrance
Num 6.10 bring two doves or two **pigeons** to the priest at the entrance
Hos 7.11 Israel flits about like a silly **pigeon;**
Mt 21.12 stools of those who sold **pigeons,** [13] and said to them, "It
Mk 11.15 stools of those who sold **pigeons,** [16] and he would not let
Lk 2.24 of doves or two young **pigeons,** as required by the law

Jn 2.14 men selling cattle, sheep, and **pigeons,**
2.16 the men who sold the **pigeons,** "Take them out of here!

PIGHEADED

1 Sam 25.17 He is so **pigheaded** that he won't listen to anybody!"

PILATE

[PONTIUS PILATE]
Pontius Pilate, Roman governor of Judaea, who handed Jesus over to the Jews for punishment.

Mt 27. 2 him off, and handed him over to **Pilate,** the Roman governor.
27.13 So **Pilate** said to him, "Don't you hear all these things
27.17 when the crowd gathered, **Pilate** asked them, "Which one do you
27.19 While **Pilate** was sitting in the judgement hall, his wife sent
27.20 persuaded the crowd to ask **Pilate** to set Barabbas free
27.21 But **Pilate** asked the crowd, "Which one of these two do
27.22 **Pilate** asked them.
27.23 But **Pilate** asked, "What crime has he committed?"
27.24 When **Pilate** saw that it was no use to go on,
27.26 Then **Pilate** set Barabbas free for them;
27.27 Then **Pilate's** soldiers took Jesus into the governor's palace,
27.58 went into the presence of **Pilate** and asked for the body of
27.58 **Pilate** gave orders for the body to be given to Joseph.
27.62 the Pharisees met with **Pilate** [63] and said, "Sir, we remember
27.65 "Take a guard," **Pilate** told them;
Mk 15. 1 Jesus in chains, led him away, and handed him over to **Pilate.**
15. 2 **Pilate** questioned him, "Are you the king of the Jews?"
15. 4 so **Pilate** questioned him again, "Aren't you going
15. 5 Again Jesus refused to say a word, and **Pilate** was amazed.
15. 6 every Passover Festival **Pilate** was in the habit of setting free
15. 8 gathered and began to ask **Pilate** for the usual favour,
15.11 to ask, instead, for **Pilate** to set Barabbas free for them.
15.12 **Pilate** spoke again to the crowd, "What, then, do you
15.14 **Pilate** asked.
15.15 **Pilate** wanted to please the crowd, so he set Barabbas free
15.42 boldly into the presence of **Pilate** and asked him for the
15.44 **Pilate** was surprised to hear that Jesus was already dead.
15.45 hearing the officer's report, **Pilate** told Joseph he could have
Lk 3. 1 **Pontius Pilate** was governor of Judaea, Herod was ruler of Galilee,
13. 1 the Galileans whom **Pilate** had killed while they were offering
23. 1 and took Jesus before **Pilate,** [2] where they began to accuse him:
23. 3 **Pilate** asked him, "Are you the king of the Jews?"
23. 4 Then **Pilate** said to the chief priests and the crowds, "I
23. 6 When **Pilate** heard this, he asked, "Is this man a Galilean?"
23.11 put a fine robe on him and sent him back to **Pilate.**
23.12 On that very day Herod and **Pilate** became friends;
23.13 **Pilate** called together the chief priests, the leaders,
23.20 **Pilate** wanted to set Jesus free, so he appealed to the
23.22 **Pilate** said to them the third time, "But what crime has
23.24 **Pilate** passed the sentence on Jesus that they were asking for.
23.52 went into the presence of **Pilate** and asked for the body of
Jn 18.29 So **Pilate** went outside to them and asked, "What do you
18.31 **Pilate** said to them, "Then you yourselves take him and
18.33 **Pilate** went back into the palace and called Jesus.
18.35 **Pilate** replied, "Do you think I am a Jew?
18.37 So **Pilate** asked him, "Are you a king, then?"
18.38 **Pilate** asked.
18.38 Then **Pilate** went back outside to the people and said to them,
19. 1 Then **Pilate** took Jesus and had him whipped.
19. 4 **Pilate** went out once more and said to the crowd, "Look, I
19. 5 **Pilate** said to them, "Look!
19. 6 **Pilate** said to them, "You take him, then, and crucify him.
19. 8 When **Pilate** heard this, he was even more afraid.
19.10 **Pilate** said to him, "You will not speak to me?
19.12 When **Pilate** heard this, he tried to find a way to set
19.13 When **Pilate** heard these words, he took Jesus outside and sat
19.14 **Pilate** said to the people, "Here is your king!"
19.15 **Pilate** asked them, "Do you want me to crucify your king?"
19.16 Then **Pilate** handed Jesus over to them to be crucified.
19.19 **Pilate** wrote a notice and had it put on the cross.
19.21 The chief priests said to **Pilate,** "Do not write 'The
19.22 **Pilate** answered, "What I have written stays written."
19.31 the Jewish authorities asked **Pilate** to allow them to break the
19.38 the town of Arimathea, asked **Pilate** if he could take Jesus'
19.38 **Pilate** told him he could have the body, so Joseph went
Acts 3.13 and you rejected him in **Pilate's** presence,
3.13 even after **Pilate** had decided to set him free.
3.14 and instead you asked **Pilate** to do you the favour of
4.27 For indeed Herod and **Pontius Pilate** met together in this city
13.28 sentence on him, they asked **Pilate** to have him put to death.
1 Tim 6.13 firmly professed his faith before **Pontius Pilate,**

Am **PILE**
see also **HEAP**

PILE

Gen 31.44 Let us make a **pile** of stones to remind us of our
31.46 He told his men to gather some rocks and **pile** them up.
31.46 Then they ate a meal beside the **pile** of rocks.
31.48 Laban said to Jacob, "This **pile** of rocks will be a
31.51 the rocks that I have **piled** up between us, and here is
31.52 Both this **pile** and this memorial stone are reminders.
31.52 will never go beyond this **pile** to attack you, and you must
Ex 8.14 The Egyptians **piled** them up in great heaps, until the
15. 8 You blew on the sea and the water **piled** up high;
Deut 13.16 people who live there and **pile** them up in the town square.
Josh 3.13 the water coming downstream will **pile** up in one place."
3.16 the water stopped flowing and **piled** up, far upstream at Adam,
7.26 They put a huge **pile** of stones over him, which is there
8.29 covered it with a huge **pile** of stones, which is still there
Judg 9.49 Abimelech and **piled** the wood up against the stronghold.
15.16 With the jaw-bone of a donkey I **piled** them up in piles."
Ruth 3. 7 He went to the **pile** of barley and lay down to sleep.
1 Sam 20.19 the other time, and hide behind the **pile** of stones there.
20.41 got up from behind the **pile** of stones, fell on his knees
2 Sam 18.17 in the forest, and covered it with a huge **pile** of stones.
1 Kgs 9. 8 This Temple will become a **pile** of ruins, and everyone who
2 Kgs 10. 8 he ordered them to be **piled** up in two heaps at the
19.25 you the power to turn fortified cities into **piles** of rubble.
2 Chr 31. 7 month and continued to **pile** up for the next four months.
Ezra 9. 6 Our sins **pile** up, high above our heads;
Job 22.25 be your gold, and let him be silver, **piled** high for you.
36.16 your table was **piled** high with food.
Ecc 2. 8 I also **piled** up silver and gold from the royal treasuries
Is 17. 1 it will be only a **pile** of ruins.
30. 1 sign treaties against my will, **piling** one sin on another.
30.33 It is deep and wide, and **piled** high with wood.
37.26 you the power to turn fortified cities into **piles** of rubble.
Jer 9.11 "I will make Jerusalem a **pile** of ruins, a place where
9.22 scattered everywhere, like **piles** of manure on the fields,
16. 4 Their bodies will lie like **piles** of manure on the ground.
21. 4 I will **pile** up your soldiers' weapons in the centre of the
25.33 They will lie on the ground like **piles** of manure.
26.18 field, Jerusalem will become a **pile** of ruins, and the Temple
27.17 Why should this city become a **pile** of ruins?
50.26 **Pile** up the loot like piles of grain!
51.37 That country will become a **pile** of ruins where wild animals live.
Ezek 24. 5 **pile** the wood under the pot.
24. 9 I myself will **pile** up the firewood.
Dan 2. 5 torn limb from limb and make your houses a **pile** of ruins.
3.29 limb, and his house is to be made a **pile** of ruins.
Hos 12.11 there will become **piles** of stone in the open fields."
Mic 1. 6 "I will make Samaria a **pile** of ruins in the open country,
3.12 field, Jerusalem will become a **pile** of ruins, and the Temple
Nah 3. 3 Corpses are **piled** high, dead bodies without number— men
Hab 1.10 fortress can stop them—they **pile** up earth against it and
Zech 9. 3 fortifications for herself and has **piled** up so much silver
Lk 12.21 it is with those who **pile** up riches for themselves but are
Jas 5. 3 You have **piled** up riches in these last days.
Rev 18. 5 For her sins are **piled** up as high as heaven,

PILGRIMAGE

Ps 84. 5 you, who are eager to make the **pilgrimage** to Mount Zion.

PILLAR

Gen 19.26 Lot's wife looked back and was turned into a **pillar** of salt.
Ex 13.21 front of them in a **pillar** of cloud to show them the
13.21 front of them in a **pillar** of fire to give them light,
13.22 The **pillar** of cloud was always in front of the people
13.22 during the day, and the **pillar** of fire at night.
14.19 The **pillar** of cloud also moved until it was [20] between the
14.24 Lord looked down from the **pillar** of fire and cloud at the
23.24 Destroy their gods and break down their sacred stone **pillars.**
33. 9 Moses had gone in, the **pillar** of cloud would come down and
33.10 as the people saw the **pillar** of cloud at the door of
34.13 their altars, destroy their sacred **pillars,** and cut down the
Lev 26. 1 set up statues, stone **pillars,** or carved stones to worship.
Num 12. 5 Lord came down in a **pillar** of cloud, stood at the entrance
14.14 go before us in a **pillar** of cloud by day
14.14 and a **pillar** of fire by night.
Deut 1.33 front of you in a **pillar** of fire by night
1.33 and in a **pillar** of cloud by day.
7. 5 altars, break their sacred stone **pillars** in pieces, cut down
12. 3 smash their sacred stone **pillars** to pieces.
16.22 And do not set up any stone **pillar** for idol worship;
31.15 to them there in a **pillar** of cloud that stood by the
Judg 16.24 him entertain them and made him stand between the **pillars.**
16.26 hand, "Let me touch the **pillars** that hold up the building.
16.29 Samson took hold of the two middle **pillars** holding up the building.
16.29 Putting one hand on each **pillar,** he pushed against them
1 Kgs 7. 2 had three rows of cedar **pillars,** fifteen in each row, with
7. 2 over store-rooms, which were supported by the **pillars.**
14.23 gods, and put up stone **pillars** and symbols of Asherah to
2 Kgs 10.26 temple, [26] brought out the sacred **pillar** that was there,
10.27 So they destroyed the sacred **pillar** and the temple, and
17.10 they put up stone **pillars** and images of the goddess Asherah,
18. 4 of worship, broke the stone **pillars,** and cut down the images
23.14 King Josiah broke the stone **pillars** to pieces, cut down
2 Chr 31. 1 Judah and broke the stone **pillars,** cut down the symbols of
Job 9. 6 he rocks the **pillars** that support the earth.
26.11 When he threatens the **pillars** that hold up the sky, they
38. 6 What holds up the **pillars** that support the earth?
Ps 99. 7 He spoke to them from the **pillar** of cloud;
144.12 our daughters be like stately **pillars** which adorn the
Prov 9. 1 Wisdom has built her house and made seven **pillars** for it.
Is 19.19 of Egypt and a stone **pillar** dedicated to him at the Egyptian
Jer 1.18 be like a fortified city, an iron **pillar,** and a bronze wall.
22. 7 its beautiful cedar **pillars,** and throw them into the fire.
Ezek 26.11 Your mighty **pillars** will be thrown to the ground.
Hos 3. 4 without sacrifices or sacred stone **pillars,** without idols or
10. 1 beautiful they made the sacred stone **pillars** they worship.
10. 2 God will break down their altars and destroy their sacred **pillars.**
Mic 5.13 I will destroy your idols and sacred stone **pillars;**
1 Tim 3.15 of the living God, the **pillar** and support of the truth.

Rev 3.12 him who is victorious a **pillar** in the temple of my God,
10. 1 was like the sun, and his legs were like **pillars** of fire.

PILLOW

1 Sam 19.13 on the bed, put a **pillow** made of goats'-hair at its head,
19.16 idol in the bed and the goats'-hair **pillow** at its head.
Ps 6. 6 my **pillow** is soaked with tears.
Mk 4.38 the back of the boat, sleeping with his head on a **pillow.**

PILOT

Jas 3. 4 small rudder, and it goes wherever the **pilot** wants it to go.

PIN

Ex 35.22 men and women, brought decorative **pins,** earrings, rings,
1 Sam 18.11 "I'll **pin** him to the wall," Saul said to himself, and
19.10 Saul tried to **pin** David to the wall with his spear, but
26. 8 own spear through him and **pin** him to the ground with just

PINE

1 Kgs 5. 8 I will provide the cedars and the **pine-trees.**
5.10 with all the cedar and **pine** logs that he wanted, [11] and
6.15 the floor to the ceiling, and the floor was made of **pine.**
6.34 two folding doors made of **pine** [35] and decorated with carved
9.11 with all the cedar and **pine** and with all the gold he
Neh 8.15 hills and get branches from **pines,** olives, myrtles, palms,
Is 41.19 in barren land, forests of **pine** and juniper and cypress.
60.13 "The wood of the **pine,** the juniper, and the cypress,
Ezek 27. 6 made your deck out of **pine** from Cyprus And inlaid it with

PIPES

Zech 4.12 beside the two gold **pipes** from which the olive-oil pours?"

PISTACHIO

A small greenish nut.

Gen 43.11 a little resin, a little honey, spices, **pistachio** nuts, and

PIT

Gen 14.10 valley was full of tar **pits,** and when the kings of Sodom
14.10 tried to run away from the battle, they fell into the **pits;**
Ex 21.33 takes the cover off a **pit** or if he digs one and
Josh 23.13 as a trap or a **pit** and as painful as a whip
1 Sam 13. 6 caves and holes or among the rocks or in **pits** and wells;
2 Sam 18.17 threw it into a deep **pit** in the forest, and covered it
23.20 once went down into a **pit** on a snowy day and killed
2 Kgs 10.14 seized them, and he put them to death near a **pit** there.
1 Chr 11.22 once went down into a **pit** on a snowy day and killed
Job 9.31 God throws me into a **pit** of filth, and even my clothes
28. 4 There they work in loneliness, Clinging to ropes in the **pits.**
Ps 9.15 The heathen have dug a **pit** and fallen in;
40. 2 me out of a dangerous **pit,** out of the deadly quicksand.
57. 6 They dug a **pit** in my path, but fell into it themselves.
88. 6 the depths of the tomb, into the darkest and deepest **pit.**
94.13 days of trouble until a **pit** is dug to trap the wicked.
119.85 who do not obey your law, have dug **pits** to trap me.
140.10 may they be thrown into a **pit** and never get out.
Ecc 10. 8 If you dig a **pit,** you fall in it;
Is 5. 2 a tower to guard them, dug a **pit** for treading the grapes.
14.19 thrown with them into a rocky **pit,** and trampled down.
24.17 There are terrors, **pits,** and traps waiting for you.
24.18 terror will fall into a **pit,**
24.18 anyone who escapes from the **pit** will be caught in a trap.
24.22 God will crowd kings together like prisoners in a **pit.**
Jer 18.20 Yet they have dug a **pit** for me to fall in.
18.22 They have dug a **pit** for me to fall in and have
48.43 Terror, **pits,** and traps are waiting for the people of Moab.
48.44 terror will fall into the **pits,**
48.44 whoever climbs out of the **pits** will be caught in the traps,
Lam 3.53 threw me alive into a **pit** and closed the opening with a
3.55 "From the bottom of the **pit,** O Lord, I cried out to
Ezek 19. 4 The nations heard about him and trapped him in a **pit.**
Dan 6. 7 this order is to be thrown into a **pit** filled with lions.
6.12 except you, would be thrown into a **pit** filled with lions."
6.16 arrested and he was thrown into the **pit** filled with lions.
6.17 over the mouth of the **pit,** and the king placed his own
6.19 At dawn the king got up and hurried to the **pit.**
6.23 gave orders for Daniel to be pulled up out of the **pit.**
6.24 wives and their children, into the **pit** filled with lions.
6.24 reached the bottom of the **pit,** the lions pounced on them and
Hos 5. 2 on Mount Tabor, [2] a deep **pit** at Acacia City, and I will
Joel 2.24 the **pits** beside the presses will overflow with wine and olive-oil.
Zeph 2. 9 of salt **pits** and everlasting ruin, overgrown with weeds.
Zech 9.11 set your people free— free from the waterless **pit** of exile.
Lk 16.26 there is a deep **pit** lying between us, so that those

AV **PIT** see **ABYSS, GRAVE, TRAP, WORLD OF THE DEAD**

PITCH (1)

[HIGH-PITCHED, LOW-PITCHED]

1 Chr 15.17 chose the following Levites to play the **high-pitched** harps:
15.17 To play the **low-pitched** harps they chose the following Levites:

PITCH (2)

Is 13.20 No wandering Arab will ever **pitch** his tent there, and no
Jer 6. 3 They will **pitch** their tents round the city, and each one

PITFALL

Job 22.10 So now there are **pitfalls** all round you, and suddenly

PITIFUL

Jer 22.23 but how **pitiful** you'll be when pains strike you, pains
Gal 4. 9 want to turn back to those weak and **pitiful** ruling spirits?
Rev 3.17 But you do not know how miserable and **pitiful** you are!

PITY

Gen 19.16 The Lord, however, had **pity** on him;
43.14 cause the man to have **pity** on you, so that he will
Ex 33.19 the Lord, and I show compassion and **pity** on those I choose.
34. 6 is full of compassion and **pity,** who is not easily angered
Num 11.15 treat me like this, take **pity** on me and kill me, so
Deut 13. 8 Show him no mercy or **pity,** and do not protect him.
2 Chr 30. 9 away as prisoners will take **pity** on them and let them come
Job 16.13 and even then he shows no **pity.**
19.21 Take **pity** on me!
27.22 blow down on them without **pity** while they try their best to
30.24 a ruined man, one who can do nothing but beg for **pity?**
Ps 6. 2 have **pity** on me!
17.10 they have no **pity** and speak proudly.
72.13 He has **pity** on the weak and poor;
90.13 Have **pity,** O Lord, on your servants!
102.13 You will rise and take **pity** on Zion;
102.14 they have **pity** on her, even though she is in ruins.
135.14 he will take **pity** on his servants.
Prov 20.26 out who is doing wrong, and will punish him without **pity.**
Is 9.17 and he will not show **pity** to any of the widows and
13.18 will show no mercy to babies and take no **pity** on children.
27.11 God their Creator will not **pity** them or show them any mercy.
30.18 He is ready to take **pity** on you because he always does
49.13 he will have **pity** on his suffering people.
Jer 13.14 No **pity,** compassion, or mercy will stop me from killing them."
15. 5 "Who will **pity** you, people of Jerusalem, and who will
21. 7 any of you or show mercy or **pity** to any of you.
48. 1 **"Pity** the people of Nebo— their town is destroyed!
48.46 **Pity** the people of Moab!
Ezek 9.10 But I will not have **pity** on them;
16. 5 No one took enough **pity** on you to do any of these
20.17 "But then I took **pity** on them.
24.14 I will not ignore your sins or show **pity** or be merciful.
Hos 13.14 I will no longer have **pity** for this people.
Joel 2.17 "Have **pity** on your people, Lord.
Jon 4.11 more, then, should I have **pity** on Nineveh, that great city.
Zech 11. 5 Even their own shepherds have no **pity** on them."
11. 6 (The Lord said, "I will no longer **pity** anyone on earth.
Mt 9.27 "Take **pity** on us, Son of David!"
9.36 his heart was filled with **pity** for them, because they were
14.14 his heart was filled with **pity** for them, and he healed those
20.30 Take **pity** on us, sir!"
20.31 Take **pity** on us, sir!"
20.34 Jesus had **pity** on them and touched their eyes;
Mk 1.41 Jesus was filled with **pity,** and stretched out his hand
6.34 his heart was filled with **pity** for them, because they were
9.22 Have **pity** on us and help us, if you possibly can!"
10.47 Take **pity** on me!"
10.48 shouted even more loudly, "Son of David, take **pity** on me!"
Lk 7.13 his heart was filled with **pity** for her, and he said to
10.33 and when he saw him, his heart was filled with **pity.**
15.20 his heart was filled with **pity,** and he ran, threw his arms
16.24 Take **pity** on me, and send Lazarus to dip his finger in
17.13 Take **pity** on us!"
18.13 on his breast and said, 'God, have **pity** on me, a sinner!'
18.38 Take **pity** on me!"
18.39 Take **pity** on me!"
Rom 1.31 promises, and they show no kindness or **pity** for others.
9.15 I will take **pity** on anyone I wish."
1 Cor 15.19 then we deserve more **pity** than anyone else in all the
Phil 2.27 But God had **pity** on him, and not only on him

PLACE (1)

[HIDING-PLACE, HIGH PLACES, RESTING-PLACE, THE PLACE OF THE SKULL]

see also **HOLY PLACE, PLACE OF WORSHIP**

Gen 1. 6 and to keep it in two separate **places"**—and it was done.
1. 9 come together in one **place,** so that the land will appear"
1.17 He **placed** the lights in the sky to shine on the earth,
2.15 Then the Lord God **placed** the man in the Garden of Eden
4.11 You are **placed** under a curse and can no longer farm the
8. 9 all the land, the dove did not find a **place** to alight.
9. 2 They are all **placed** under your power.
12. 6 came to the sacred tree of Moreh, the holy **place** at Shechem.
12. 9 moved on from place to **place,** going towards the southern
13. 3 there and moved from **place** to place, going towards Bethel.
13. 3 He reached the **place** between Bethel and Ai where he had
15.10 cut them in half, and **placed** the halves opposite each other
18.16 left and went to a **place** where they could look down at
19.13 out of here, [13] because we are going to destroy this **place.**
19.14 the Lord is going to destroy this **place."**
19.20 see it is just a small **place**—and I will be safe."
19.27 morning Abraham hurried to the **place** where he had stood in

Gen 21.31 And so the **place** was called Beersheba, because it was
22. 3 They started out for the **place** that God had told him about.
22. 4 On the third day Abraham saw the **place** in the distance.
22. 9 When they came to the **place** which God had told him about,
22. 9 tied up his son and **placed** him on the altar, on top
22.14 Abraham named that **place** "The Lord Provides."
23. 3 He left the **place** where his wife's body was lying, went to
24. 2 of all that he had, **"Place** your hand between my thighs and
24.25 at our house, and there is a **place** for you to stay."
24.31 you in my house, and there is a **place** for your camels."
28.11 At sunset he came to a holy **place** and camped there.
28.16 He is in this **place,** and I didn't know it!"
28.17 He was afraid and said, "What a terrifying **place** this is!
28.19 He named the **place** Bethel.
28.22 set up will be the **place** where you are worshipped, and I
29. 3 Then they would put the stone back in **place.**
30. 2 angry with Rachel and said, "I can't take the **place** of God.
30.38 He **placed** these branches in front of the flocks
31.48 That is why that **place** was named Galeed.
31.49 So the **place** was also named Mizpah.
32. 2 so he called the **place** Mahanaim.
32.30 so he named the **place** Peniel.
33.17 That is why the **place** was named Sukkoth.
35. 7 altar there and named the **place** after the God of Bethel,
35.15 He named the **place** Bethel.
38.22 The men of the **place** said that there had never been a
40. 3 of the guard, in the same **place** where Joseph was being kept.
41.42 linen robe on him, and **placed** a gold chain round his neck.
42.27 At the **place** where they spent the night, one of them
44.33 I will stay here as your slave in **place** of the boy;
47.29 Joseph and said to him, **"Place** your hand between my thighs
49.15 But he sees that the **resting-place** is good And that the
50.11 That is why the **place** was named Abel Mizraim.
50.19 I can't put myself in the **place** of God.
Ex 2. 3 baby in it and then **placed** it in the tall grass at
4.24 At a camping **place** on the way to Egypt, the Lord met
9.26 Israelites lived, was the only **place** where there was no hail.
13. 3 on which you left Egypt, the **place** where you were slaves.
13.13 first-born male donkey by offering a lamb in its **place.**
13.14 Lord brought us out of Egypt, the **place** where we were slaves.
13.19 you, you must carry my body with you from this **place."**
15.17 them on your mountain, the **place** that you, Lord, have chosen
15.23 Then they came to a **place** called Marah, but the water
16.33 of manna in it, and **place** it in the Lord's presence to
17. 1 of Sin, moving from one **place** to another at the command of
17. 7 The **place** was named Massah and Meribah, because the
20.24 In every **place** that I set aside for you to worship me,
21.13 he can escape to a **place** which I will choose for you,
23.20 travel and to bring you to the **place** which I have prepared.
25.27 poles for carrying the table are to be **placed** near the rim.
25.30 The table is to be **placed** in front of the Covenant Box,
26.33 **Place** the curtain under the row of hooks in the roof of
29.31 of Aaron and his sons and boil it in a holy **place.**
29.43 the dazzling light of my presence will make the **place** holy.
30. 6 That is the **place** where I will meet you.
30.18 **Place** it between the Tent and the altar, and put water in
32.34 Now go, lead the people to the **place** I told you about.
33. 1 said to Moses, "Leave this **place,** you and the people you
33.15 you do not go with us, don't make us leave this **place.**
33.21 alive, [21] but here is a **place** beside me where you can stand
34.20 every first-born donkey by offering a lamb in its **place.**
37.14 the poles for carrying the table were **placed** near the rim.
40. 3 **Place** in it the Covenant Box containing the Ten
40. 4 Bring in the table and **place** the equipment on it.
40.23 side outside the curtain, [23] and **placed** on it the bread
40.29 of the curtain he **placed** the altar for burning offerings.
40.36 moved their camp to another **place** only when the cloud lifted
Lev 4.12 to the ritually clean **place** where the ashes are poured out,
6.11 take the ashes outside the camp to a ritually clean **place.**
6.16 and eaten in a holy **place,** the courtyard of the Tent of
6.26 eat it in a holy **place,** the courtyard of the Tent of
6.27 with the animal's blood, it must be washed in a holy **place.**
7. 6 must be eaten in a holy **place,** because it is very holy.
8. 9 He **placed** the turban on his head, and on the front of
10.13 Eat it in a holy **place;**
10.14 You may eat them in any ritually clean **place.**
10.17 "Why didn't you eat the sin-offering in a sacred **place?**
14.13 kill the lamb in the **place** where the animals for the
14.28 of the oil on the same **places** as he put the blood:
14.40 removed and thrown into some unclean **place** outside the city.
14.41 and the plaster dumped in an unclean **place** outside the city.
14.45 plaster must be carried out of the city to an unclean **place.**
16.24 must bathe in a holy **place** and put on his own clothes.
19.30 Keep the Sabbath, and honour the **place** where I am worshipped.
24. 7 food-offering to the Lord to take the **place** of the bread.
24. 8 come, the bread must be **placed** in the presence of the Lord.
24. 9 eat it in a holy **place,** because this is a very holy
26. 2 and honour the **place** where I am worshipped.
Num 1.51 Tent down and set it up again at each new camping **place.**
3.40 But in **place** of them I claim all the Levites as mine!
3.40 livestock of the Levites in **place** of all the first-born of
3.45 Levites as mine in **place** of all the first-born Israelite sons,
3.45 of the Levites in **place** of the first-born of the Israelites'
4.10 in a fine leather cover and **place** it on a carrying-frame.
4.12 leather cover over them, and **place** them on a carrying-frame.
8. 2 on the lamp-stand, he should **place** them so that the light
8. 3 Aaron obeyed and **placed** the lamps facing the front
8.10 people of Israel are to **place** their hands on the heads of
8.16 have claimed them in the **place** of all the first-born sons of
9.17 set up camp again in the **place** where the cloud came down.
10.29 to start out for the **place** which the Lord said he would
Num 10.33 went ahead of them to find a **place** for them to camp.
11. 3 So the **place** was named Taberah, because there the fire of
11.24 He assembled seventy of the leaders and **placed** them round the Tent.
11.34 That **place** was named Kibroth Hattaavah
13.24 (That **place** was named the Valley of Eshcol because of
14.40 ready to go to the **place** which the Lord told us about.
18.10 these things in a holy **place,** and only males may eat them;
19. 9 them in a ritually clean **place** outside the camp, where they
20. 5 of Egypt into this miserable **place** where nothing will grow?
21. 3 destroyed them and their cities, and named the **place** Hormah.
21.11 After leaving that **place,** they camped at the ruins of
21.16 they went on to a **place** called Wells, where the Lord said
22. 6 you pronounce a curse, they are **placed** under a curse."
22.26 he stood in a narrow **place** where there was no room at
23.13 "Come with me to another **place** from which you can see only
23.27 said, "Come with me, and I will take you to another **place.**
24.21 "The **place** where you live is secure, Safe as a nest set
27.18 of Nun, a capable man, and **place** your hands on his head.
32.14 you have taken your fathers' **place,** a new generation of
33. 1 gives the names of the **places** where the Israelites set up
33. 2 down the name of the **place** each time they set up camp.
33.15 Rephidim to Mount Hor they set up camp at the following **places:**
33.41 plains of Moab the Israelites set up camp at the following **places:**
Deut 1.15 chose from your tribes, and I **placed** them in charge of you.
1.31 all the way to this **place,** just as a father would carry
1.33 went ahead of you to find a **place** for you to camp.
2.24 I am **placing** in your power Sihon, the Amorite king of Heshbon,
2.37 hill-country or to any other **place** where the Lord our God
3. 3 "So the Lord also **placed** King Og and his people in our
7. 2 When the Lord your God **places** these people in your power
7.16 that the Lord your God **places** in your power, and do not
10. 7 to Gudgodah and then on to Jotbathah, a well-watered **place.**
12. 2 are taking, destroy all the **places** where the people worship
12. 3 that they will never again be worshipped at those **places.**
12. 5 Lord will choose the one **place** where the people are to come
12.11 Lord will choose a single **place** where he is to be worshipped,
12.14 them only in the one **place** that the Lord will choose in
12.17 the Lord is to be eaten in the **places** where you live:
14.23 Then go to the one **place** where the Lord your God has
16. 3 the day you came out of Egypt, that **place** of suffering.
21. 2 measure the distance from the **place** where the body was found
21. 6 from the town nearest the **place** where the murdered man was
23.12 "You are to have a **place** outside the camp where you
26. 2 there, [2] each of you must **place** in a basket the first part
26. 4 the basket from you and **place** it before the altar of the
26.15 Look down from your holy **place** in heaven and bless your
28.65 You will find no peace anywhere, no **place** to call your own;
29. 7 when we came to this **place,** King Sihon of Heshbon and King
31.26 book of God's Law and **place** it beside the Covenant Box of
34. 6 to this day no one knows the exact **place** of his burial.
Josh 2. 7 as far as the **place** where the road crosses the Jordan.
3.13 the water coming downstream will pile up in one **place."**
4. 3 Jordan, from the very **place** where the priests were standing.
4. 8 carried them to the camping **place,** and put them down there.
5. 3 the Israelites at a **place** called Circumcision Hill.
5. 9 That is why the **place** was named Gilgal, the name it still
7.26 That is why that **place** is still called Trouble Valley.
8. 9 and they went to their **hiding place** and waited there, west
8.14 the Israelites at the same **place** as before, not knowing that
9.27 do this work in the **place** where the Lord has chosen to
10.18 **Place** some guards there, [19] but don't stay there yourselves.
10.27 Large stones were **placed** at the entrance to the cave, and
20. 4 these cities, go to the **place** of judgement at the entrance
20. 4 city and give him a **place** to live in, so that he
Judg 2. 5 began to cry, [5] and that is why the **place** is called Bochim.
3.28 Ehud down and captured the **place** where the Moabites were to
6. 2 hid from them in caves and other safe **places** in the hills.
7.21 Every man stood in his **place** round the camp, and the
9.35 at the city gate, they got up from their **hiding places.**
12. 5 Gileadites captured the **places** where the Jordan could be crossed.
15.17 The **place** where this happened was named Ramath Lehi.
15.19 Then God opened a hollow **place** in the ground there at Lehi,
16. 2 there, so they surrounded the **place** and waited for him all
17. 4 It was **placed** in Micah's house.
18.12 That is why the **place** is still called Camp of Dan.
20.20 the army of Benjamin, and **placed** the soldiers in position
20.22 army was encouraged, and they **placed** their soldiers in the
20.30 the army of Benjamin and **placed** their soldiers in battle
20.33 rushed out of their **hiding places** in the rocky country
Ruth 4. 1 Boaz went to the meeting **place** at the town gate and sat
1 Sam 1. 9 Eli the priest was sitting in his **place** by the door.
2. 8 companions of princes and puts them in **places** of honour.
2.20 this woman to take the **place** of the one you dedicated to
5. 3 So they lifted it up and put it back in its **place.**
5. 5 in Ashdod step over that **place** and do not walk on it.)
5.11 Israel back to its own **place,** so that it won't kill us
6. 8 it on the wagon, and **place** in a box beside it the
6.15 the gold models in it, and **placed** them on the large rock.
6.18 Beth Shemesh, on which they **placed** the Lord's Covenant Box,
7.16 and Mizpah, and in these **places** he would settle disputes.
9.22 room and gave them a **place** at the head of the table
9.24 the choice piece of the leg and **placed** it before Saul.
10.25 wrote them in a book, which he deposited in a holy **place.**
11.15 and there at the holy **place** they proclaimed Saul king.
17. 1 at a **place** called Ephes Dammim, between Socoh and Azekah.
19. 2 hide in some secret **place** and stay there.
20.19 so go to the **place** where you hid the other time, and
20.25 to the meal [25] and sat in his usual **place** by the wall.
20.25 David's **place** was empty, [26] but Saul said nothing that day,
20.27 the New Moon Festival, David's **place** was still empty, and

1 Sam	20.29	That is why he isn't in his **place** at your table."
	20.37	When the boy reached the **place** where the arrow had fallen,
	21. 2	men, I have told them to meet me at a certain **place.**
	23.23	Find out exactly the **places** where he hides, and be sure
	23.28	That is why that **place** is called Separation Hill.
	24.22	and David and his men went back to their **hiding place.**
	26. 5	once and located the exact **place** where Saul and Abner son of
	30.31	sent it to all the **places** where he and his men had
2 Sam	2.16	And so that **place** in Gibeon is called "Field of Swords."
	2.23	everyone who came to the **place** where he was lying stopped
	5. 9	round it, starting at the **place** where land was filled in on
	5.17	When David heard of it, he went down to a fortified **place.**
	5.20	And so that **place** is called Baal Perazim.
	6. 3	Abinadab's home on the hill and **placed** it on a new cart.
	6. 8	Covenant Box, [8]and so that **place** has been called Perez
	6.17	and put it in its **place** in the Tent that David had
	7.10	I have chosen a **place** for my people Israel and
	10.10	He **placed** the rest of his troops under the command of
	11.16	he sent Uriah to a **place** where he knew the enemy was
	15.25	me come back to see it and the **place** where it stays.
	16.12	and give me some blessings to take the **place** of his curse."
	17. 9	now he is probably hiding in a cave or some other **place.**
	17.25	put Amasa in command of the army in the **place** of Joab.
	18. 1	and of a hundred, and **placed** officers in command of them.
	18.33	If only I had died in your **place,** my son!
	19.13	am putting you in charge of the army in **place** of Joab.
1 Kgs	2.35	Joab's place and put Zadok the priest in Abiathar's **place.**
	3. 6	love by giving him a son who today rules in his **place.**
	5. 9	rafts to float them down the coast to the **place** you choose.
	5.16	to carry it, [16]and he **placed** 3,300 foremen in charge of
	6.19	was built, where the Lord's Covenant Box was to be **placed.**
	6.21	gold, and gold chains were **placed** across the entrance of the
	6.23	made of olive wood and **placed** in the Most Holy Place, each
	6.27	They were **placed** side by side in the Most Holy Place, so
	6.31	olive wood was set in **place** at the entrance of the Most
	7.15	5.3 metres in circumference, and **placed** them at the entrance
	7.16	one 2.2 metres tall, to be **placed** on top of the columns.
	7.20	1.8 metres tall, [20]and were **placed** on a rounded section
	7.21	Huram **placed** these two bronze columns in front of the
	7.39	He **placed** five of the carts on the south side of the
	7.39	the tank he **placed** at the south-east corner.
	7.51	work on the Temple, he **placed** in the temple storerooms all
	8. 9	stone tablets which Moses had **placed** there at Mount Sinai,
	8.12	"You, Lord, have **placed** the sun in the sky, yet you have
	8.13	majestic temple for you, a **place** for you to live in for
	8.21	I have also provided a **place** in the Temple for the
	8.29	Temple day and night, this **place** where you have chosen to be
	8.30	prayers of your people when they face this **place** and pray.
	8.43	I have built is the **place** where you are to be worshipped.
	9. 3	you have built as the **place** where I shall be worshipped for
	9. 7	I have consecrated as the **place** where I am to be worshipped.
	10.17	He had all these shields **placed** in the Hall of the Forest
	11. 7	of Jerusalem he built a **place** to worship Chemosh, the
	11. 7	god of Moab, and a **place** to worship Molech, the disgusting
	11.36	the city I have chosen as the **place** where I am worshipped.
	12. 4	Solomon treated us harshly and **placed** heavy burdens on us.
	12.11	Tell them, 'My father **placed** heavy burdens on you;
	12.14	He said, "My father **placed** heavy burdens on you;
	12.29	He **placed** one of the gold bull-calves in Bethel and the
	12.32	he had made, and he **placed** there in Bethel the priests
	13.22	ate a meal in a **place** he had ordered you not to
	14.14	The Lord is going to **place** a king over Israel who will
	14.21	of Israel as the **place** where he was to be worshipped.
	15.15	He **placed** in the Temple all the objects his father had
	17. 3	said to Elijah, [3]"Leave this **place** and go east and hide
	18.12	carries you off to some unknown **place** as soon as I leave?
	18.33	Then he **placed** the wood on the altar, cut the bull in
	21. 9	the people together, and give Naboth the **place** of honour.
	21.12	the people together, and gave Naboth the **place** of honour.
	21.19	'In the very **place** that the dogs licked up Naboth's blood
2 Kgs	4.34	lay down on the boy, **placing** his mouth, eyes, and hands on
	6. 1	complained to him, "The **place** where we live is too small!
	6. 2	down some trees, so that we can build a **place** to live."
	6. 6	The man showed him the **place,** and Elisha cut off a stick,
	6. 8	consulted his officers and chose a **place** to set up his camp.
	6. 9	not to go near that **place,** because the Syrians were waiting
	6.10	the men who lived in that **place,** and they were on guard.
	10.12	On the way, at a **place** called "Shepherds' Camp," [13]he
	11.12	Then Jehoiada led Joash out, **placed** the crown on his head,
	11.19	entered by the Guard Gate and took his **place** on the throne.
	12. 9	hole in the lid, and **placed** the box by the altar, on
	13.16	did so, and Elisha **placed** his hands on the king's hands.
	16.17	twelve bronze bulls, and **placed** it on a stone foundation.
	17.24	in the cities of Samaria, in **place** of the exiled Israelites.
	17.29	their own idols, and they **placed** them in the shrines that
	18.20	that words can take the **place** of military skill and might?
	19.14	he went to the Temple, **placed** the letter there in the
	21. 4	altars in the Temple, the **place** that the Lord had said was
	21. 7	He **placed** the symbol of the goddess Asherah in the Temple,
	21. 7	the **place** about which the Lord had said
	21. 7	in this Temple, is the **place** that I have chosen out of
	21. 7	tribes of Israel as the **place** where I am to be worshipped.
	22.19	it a terrifying sight, a **place** whose name people will use as
	23. 5	cities of Judah and in **places** near Jerusalem—all the priests
	23.27	chose, and the Temple, the **place** I said was where I should
	23.30	His officials **placed** his body in a chariot and took it
	25. 7	had Zedekiah's eyes put out, **placed** him in chains, and took
	25.22	Shaphan, governor of Judah, and **placed** him in charge of all
1 Chr	4.32	They also lived in five other **places:**
	4.33	kept of their families and of the **places** where they lived.
	7.29	All these are the **places** where the descendants of Joseph
1 Chr	11. 8	the city, starting at the **place** where land was filled in on
	12.23	help make him king in **place** of Saul, as the Lord had
	13.11	God's presence, [11]and so that **place** has been called Perez
	14.11	So that **place** is called Baal Perazim.
	15. 1	He also prepared a **place** for God's Covenant Box and put up
	15. 3	bring the Covenant Box to the **place** he had prepared for it.
	15.12	Lord God of Israel to the **place** I have prepared for it.
	16.30	The earth is set firmly in **place** and cannot be moved.
	16.37	that was held at the **place** where the Covenant Box was kept.
	17. 5	I have always lived in tents and moved from **place to place.**
	17. 9	I have chosen a **place** for my people Israel and have
	19.11	He **placed** the rest of his troops under the command of
	19.16	River Euphrates and **placed** them under the command of Shobach,
	22.19	Temple, so that you can **place** in it the Covenant Box of
	28.16	gold table on which were **placed** the loaves of bread offered
2 Chr	2. 4	It will be a holy **place** where my people and I will
	2. 6	would be anything more than a **place** to burn incense to God?
	3. 1	Solomon's father, had already prepared a **place** for the Temple.
	3. 1	Lord appeared to David, the **place** which Araunah the Jebusite
	3.10	cover them with gold, and **place** them in the Most Holy Place,
	3.15	a half metres tall, and **placed** them in front of the Temple.
	4. 6	ten basins, five to be **placed** on the south side of the
	4. 7	pattern, and ten tables, and **placed** them in the main room of
	4.10	The tank was **placed** near the south-east corner of the Temple.
	5. 1	work on the Temple, he **placed** in the temple storerooms all
	5.10	stone tablets which Moses had **placed** there at Mount Sinai,
	6. 2	majestic temple for you, a **place** for you to live in for
	6. 5	land of Israel as the **place** to build a temple where I
	6. 6	chosen Jerusalem as the **place** where I will be worshipped,
	6.11	I have **placed** in the Temple the Covenant Box, which
	6.21	of your people Israel when they face this **place** and pray.
	6.40	look on us and listen to the prayers offered in this **place.**
	7. 6	The priests stood in the **places** that were assigned to them,
	7.12	accept this Temple as the **place** where sacrifices are to be
	7.16	and consecrated it as the **place** where I will be worshipped
	7.20	I have consecrated as the **place** where I am to be worshipped.
	8.11	David of Israel, because any **place** where the Covenant Box
	9.16	He had them all **placed** in the Hall of the Forest of
	10. 4	"Your father **placed** heavy burdens on us.
	10.11	Tell them, 'My father **placed** heavy burdens on you;
	10.14	He said, "My father **placed** heavy burdens on you;
	11.11	and in each one he **placed** supplies of food, olive-oil, and
	12.13	of Israel as the **place** where he was to be worshipped.
	13. 9	In their **place** you appointed priests in the same way that
	15.18	He **placed** in the Temple all the objects his father
	21. 3	and other valuable possessions, and **placed** each one in
	23.11	Then Jehoiada led Joash out, **placed** the crown on his head,
	23.20	the main gate, and the king took his **place** on the throne.
	24. 8	a box for contributions and to **place** it at the temple gate.
	24.11	would take the money out and return the box to its **place.**
	25. 5	clans they belonged to, and **placed** officers in command of
	26.18	Leave this holy **place.**
	29. 6	him and turned their backs on the **place** where he dwells.
	30.16	They took their **places** in the Temple according to the
	31.12	They **placed** a Levite named Conaniah in charge and made his
	32. 6	He **placed** all the men in the city under the command of
	33. 4	altars in the Temple, the **place** that the Lord had said was
	33. 7	He **placed** an image in the Temple,
	33. 7	the **place** about which God had said to
	33. 7	in this Temple, is the **place** that I have chosen out of
	33. 7	tribes of Israel as the **place** where I am to be worshipped.
	33.15	the image that he had **placed** there, and the pagan altars
	33.15	where the Temple stood and in other **places** in Jerusalem;
	35. 3	longer to carry it from **place to place,** but you are to
	35. 4	Take your **places** in the Temple by clans, according to the
	35.10	and the Levites took their **places,** as commanded by the king.
	35.15	of Asaph were in the **places** assigned to them by King David's
	35.24	him out of his chariot, **placed** him in a second chariot which
Ezra	3.10	their robes took their **places** with trumpets in their hands,
	5.14	Temple in Jerusalem and had **placed** in the temple in Babylon.
	6. 3	Jerusalem be rebuilt as a **place** where sacrifices are made
	6. 5	returned to their proper **place** in the Jerusalem Temple."
	6.12	who chose Jerusalem as the **place** where he is to be
	9. 8	escape from slavery and live in safety in this holy **place.**
Neh	1. 9	bring you back to the **place** where I have chosen to be
	3. 1	the Sheep Gate, dedicated it, and put the gates in **place.**
	3. 3	beams and the gates in **place,** and put in the bolts and
	3. 6	beams and the gates in **place,** and put in the bolts and
	3.13	They put the gates in **place,** put in the bolts and the
	3.14	He put the gates in **place,** and put in the bolts and
	3.15	gateway, put the gates in **place,** and put in the bolts and
	3.19	of the armoury, as far as the **place** where the wall turns;
	7. 1	had all been put in **place,** and the temple guards, the
	8. 2	Ezra brought it to the **place** where the people had gathered—men,
	8. 7	rose and stood in their **places,** and the following Levites
Esth	1. 6	gold and silver had been **placed** in the courtyard, which was
	1.19	Then give her **place** as queen to some better woman.
	2. 4	girl you like best and make her queen in Vashti's **place."**
	2. 9	He gave her the best **place** in the harem and assigned seven
	2.17	He **placed** the royal crown on her head
	2.17	and made her queen in **place** of Vashti.
Job	8.19	others now come and take their **places.**
	12.22	He sends light to **places** dark as death.
	16. 4	If you were in my **place** and I in yours, I could
	20. 4	times, when man was first **placed** on earth, [5]no wicked man
	20. 9	He will disappear from the **place** where he used to live;
	21.22	Can a man teach God, who judges even those in high **places?**
	25. 3	Is there any **place** where God's light does not shine?
	28. 1	There are **places** where gold is refined.
	28.23	knows the way, Knows the **place** where wisdom is found,
	29. 7	met and I took my **place** among them, [8]young men stepped

Job 30. 3 would gnaw dry roots— at night, in wild, desolate **places.**
31.36 proudly on my shoulder and **place** them on my head like a
38.13 seize the earth and shake the wicked from their **hiding places?**
38.24 Have you been to the **place** where the sun comes up,
38.24 or the **place** from which the east wind blows?
Ps 8. 3 which you set in their **places**— [4]what is man, that you
8. 6 you **placed** him over all creation:
9. 9 for the oppressed, a **place** of safety in times of trouble.
10. 9 he waits in his **hiding place** like a lion.
26. 8 where you live, O Lord, the **place** where your glory dwells.
31. 5 I **place** myself in your care.
32. 7 You are my **hiding place;**
33. 7 He gathered all the seas into one **place;**
56. 6 They gather in **hiding-places** and watch everything I do,
59. 4 any fault of mine, O Lord, that they hurry to their **places.**
62. 4 You only want to bring him down from his **place** of honour;
64. 5 they plan where to **place** their traps.
65. 6 You set the mountains in **place** by your strength, showing
66.11 us fall into a trap and **placed** heavy burdens on our backs.
66.12 flood, but now you have brought us to a **place** of safety.
68.17 chariots the Lord comes from Sinai into the holy **place.**
73.18 them in slippery **places** and make them fall to destruction!
74. 4 they have **placed** their flags there as signs of victory.
74. 7 they desecrated the **place** where you are worshipped.
74. 8 they burnt down every holy **place** in the land.
74.16 you set the sun and the moon in their **places;**
77. 9 Has anger taken the **place** of his compassion?"
80. 9 You cleared a **place** for it to grow;
81. 7 From my **hiding-place** in the storm, I answered you.
84. 6 the dry valley of Baca, it becomes a **place** of springs;
87. 2 more than any other **place** in Israel he loves the city of
88.11 the grave or your faithfulness in the **place** of destruction?
88.12 your miracles seen in that **place** of darkness or your
90. 8 You **place** our sins before you, our secret sins where you
93. 1 The earth is set firmly in **place** and cannot be moved.
96.10 The earth is set firmly in **place** and cannot be moved;
102.19 looked down from his holy **place** on high, he looked down from
103.19 The Lord **placed** his throne in heaven;
103.22 Praise the Lord, all his creatures in all the **places** he rules.
104. 6 You **placed** the ocean over it like a robe, and the water
104. 8 and into the valleys, to the **place** you had made for them.
119.81 I **place** my trust in your word.
119.90 you have set the earth in **place,** and it remains.
119.147 I **place** my hope in your promise.
127. 5 when he meets his enemies in the **place** of judgement.
132. 5 sleep, [5]until I provide a **place** for the Lord, a home for
139. 9 or lived in the farthest **place** in the west, [10]you would be
141. 3 Lord, **place** a guard at my mouth, a sentry at the door
148. 6 fixed in their **places** for ever, and they cannot disobey.
Prov 3.19 by his knowledge he set the sky in **place.**
8.25 the hills were set in **place,** [26]before God made the earth
8.27 he set the sky in **place,** when he stretched the horizon
8.28 across the ocean, [28]when he **placed** the clouds in the sky,
9. 3 to call out from the highest **place** in the town:
11. 7 Confidence **placed** in riches comes to nothing.
18. 3 Lose your honour, and you will get scorn in its **place.**
25. 7 to be told to give your **place** to someone more important.
26. 1 a fool is out of **place,** like snow in summer or rain
30.23 **place** of her mistress.
31.14 She brings home food from out-of-the-way **places,**
Ecc 3.20 They are both going to the same **place**—the dust.
4.15 them there is a young man who will take the king's **place.**
6. 6 After all, both of them are going to the same **place.**
8. 3 don't stay in such a dangerous **place.**
11. 2 Put your investments in several **places**—
11. 2 many **places,** in fact—because you never know
12. 5 You will be afraid of high **places,** and walking will be dangerous.
12. 5 are going to our final **resting place,** and then there will be
Song 1. 8 Don't you know the **place,** loveliest of women?
3.11 the crown that his mother **placed** on his head on his wedding
8. 5 apple-tree I woke you, in the **place** where you were born.
8.11 Solomon has a vineyard in a **place** called Baal Hamon.
Is 4. 6 day and make it a **place** of safety, sheltered from the rain
7.25 It will be a **place** where cattle and sheep graze."
8.17 his people, but I trust him and **place** my hope in him.
13.13 be shaken out of its **place** on that day when I, the
13.21 It will be a **place** where desert animals live and where
14.13 to heaven and to **place** your throne above the highest stars.
14.29 When one snake dies, a worse one comes in its **place.**
22. 9 You found the **places** where the walls of Jerusalem needed repair.
22.23 will fasten him firmly in **place** like a peg, and he will
28.16 "I am **placing** in Zion a foundation that is firm and strong.
30.33 Long ago a **place** was prepared where a huge fire will
32. 2 a shelter from the wind and a **place** to hide from storms.
33.20 What a safe **place** it will be to live in!
34.14 The night monster will come there looking for a **place** to rest.
36. 5 that words can take the **place** of military skill and might?
37.14 he went to the Temple, **placed** the letter there in the
41. 7 is good'— and they fasten the idol in **place** with nails.
44.13 a man, a handsome human figure, to be **placed** in his house.
44.23 Shout, deep **places** of the earth!
45. 3 I will give you treasures from dark, secret **places;**
45.18 it a desolate waste, but a **place** for people to live in.
46. 7 they put it in **place,** and there it stands, unable to move
53. 9 He was **placed** in a grave with evil men, he was buried
53.12 I will give him a **place** of honour,
53.12 a **place** among great and powerful men.
53.12 He took the **place** of many sinners and prayed that they might
55.13 myrtle-trees will come up in **place** of thorns.
57.15 in a high and holy **place,** but I also live with people
Is 59.14 Truth stumbles in the public square, and honesty finds no **place** there.
60.15 you great and beautiful, A **place** of joy for ever and ever.
62. 6 On your walls, Jerusalem, I have **placed** sentries;
64.11 sacred and beautiful **place** where our ancestors praised you,
64.11 All the **places** we loved are in ruins.
66. 1 build for me, what kind of **place** for me to live in?
Jer 3. 2 Is there any **place** where you have not acted like a prostitute?
4. 7 a lion coming from its **hiding place,** a destroyer of nations
5.22 I **placed** the sand as the boundary of the sea, a permanent
6. 8 turn your city into a desert, a **place** where no one lives."
7.11 Do you think that my Temple is a **hiding place** for robbers?
7.12 Go to Shiloh, the first **place** where I chose to be worshipped,
7.14 Here in this **place** that I gave to your ancestors and to
7.30 They have **placed** their idols, which I hate, in my Temple and
8. 3 survive, who live in the **places** where I have scattered them,
9. 2 I wish I had a **place** to stay in the desert where
9.11 make Jerusalem a pile of ruins, a **place** where jackals live;
9.11 Judah will become a desert, a **place** where no one lives."
10.22 of Judah into a desert, a **place** where jackals live."
11. 3 Lord God of Israel, have **placed** a curse on everyone who does
11.20 I have **placed** my cause in your hands;
13. 7 and when I found the **place** where I had hidden them, I
14.21 disgrace on Jerusalem, the **place** of your glorious throne.
16. 2 "Do not marry or have children in a **place** like this.
17.17 you are my **place** of safety when trouble comes.
19. 3 such a disaster on this **place** that everyone who hears about
19. 4 abandoned me and defiled this **place** by offering sacrifices
19. 4 They have filled this **place** with the blood of innocent people,
19. 6 time will come when this **place** will no longer be called
19. 7 In this **place** I will frustrate all the plans of the people
20. 2 me to be beaten and **placed** in chains near the upper Benjamin
20.12 on my enemies, for I have **placed** my cause in your hands.
22. 3 and do not kill innocent people in this holy **place.**
22. 6 but I will make it a desolate **place** where no one lives.
23.23 am a God who is everywhere and not in one **place** only.
24. 1 showed me two baskets of figs **placed** in front of the Temple.
26.10 palace to the Temple and took their **places** at the New Gate.
27. 6 am the one who has **placed** all these nations under the power
27.22 Then I will bring them back and restore them to this **place.**
28. 3 will bring back to this **place** all the temple treasures that
29.14 country and from every **place** to which I have scattered you,
29.26 made you a priest in **place** of Jehoiada, and you are now
29.26 to be a prophet is **placed** in chains with an iron collar
31.23 sacred hill of Jerusalem, the holy **place** where he lives.'
32.14 the open copy, and to **place** them in a clay jar, so
32.34 They even **placed** their disgusting idols in the Temple
32.37 bring them back to this **place** and let them live here in
33. 2 earth, who formed it and set it in **place,** spoke to me.
33.10 "People are saying that this **place** is like a desert, that
33.10 But in these **places** you will hear again [11]the shouts of
35. 5 Then I **placed** cups and bowls full of wine before the Rechabites,
37. 1 Josiah king of Judah in the **place** of Jehoiachin son of Jehoiakim.
39. 3 Babylonia came and took their **places** at the Middle Gate,
39. 7 put out and had him **placed** in chains to be taken to
40. 7 of the land and had **placed** him in charge of all those
40.12 So they left the **places** where they had been scattered,
41.10 the commanding officer had **placed** under the care of Gedaliah.
42.18 You will never see this **place** again.' "
43.10 Nebuchadnezzar of Babylonia to this **place,** and he will put
44.29 will punish you in this **place** and that my promise to bring
48.18 Dibon, come down from your **place** of honour and sit on the
49.10 descendants completely and uncovered their **hiding places,**
49.33 be made a desert for ever, a **place** where only jackals live.
50.25 I have opened the **place** where my weapons are stored, and
50.26 side and break open the **places** where its grain is stored!
51.12 **Place** men in ambush!"
51.51 foreigners have taken over the holy **places** in the Temple.'
51.62 that you would destroy this **place,** so that there would be no
52.11 put out and had him **placed** in chains and taken to Babylon.
Lam 1. 3 in other lands, with no **place** to call their own— Surrounded
5.15 grief has taken the **place** of our dances.
Ezek 4. 4 left side, and I will **place** on you the guilt of the
6. 3 a sword to destroy the **places** where people worship idols.
6.13 every large oak, in every **place** where they burnt sacrifices
6.14 not sparing any **place** where the Israelites live.
7.24 when I let the nations profane the **places** where you worship.
8. 6 driving me farther and farther away from my holy **place.**
10.18 of the Temple and moved to a **place** above the creatures.
12. 3 Let everyone see you leaving and going to another **place.**
13. 5 They don't guard the **places** where the walls have crumbled,
16.24 you built **places** to worship idols and practise prostitution.
16.31 On every street you built **places** to worship idols
16.39 they will tear down the **places** where you engage in
17. 4 to a land of commerce, and **placed** in a city of merchants.
20.29 What are these high **places** where you go?
20.29 So they have been called **'High Places'** ever since.
21. 2 Denounce the **places** where people worship.
21.22 the battle-cry, to **place** battering-rams against the gates,
21.30 will judge you in the **place** where you were created, in the
22. 8 respect for the holy **places,** and you don't keep the Sabbath.
22.30 who could stand in the **places** where the walls have crumbled
25. 5 city of Rabbah into a **place** to keep camels, and the whole
25. 5 country of Ammon into a **place** to keep sheep, so that you
26.20 be inhabited and take your **place** in the land of the living.
31. 4 They watered the **place** where the tree was growing And sent
32.27 of the dead, their swords **placed** under their heads and their
34.12 them back from all the **places** where they were scattered on
34.15 of my sheep, and I will find them a **place** to rest.
36. 4 brooks and valleys, to you **places** that were left in ruins,
37.28 When I **place** my Temple there to be among them for ever,

Ezek 38.15 will set out [15]from your **place** in the far north, leading a
40.43 meat to be offered in sacrifice was **placed** on the tables.
42.13 holy, the priests will **place** the holiest offerings there:
43. 7 gods or by burying the corpses of their kings in this **place.**
43.21 and burn it at the specified **place** outside the temple area.
45. 3 it will contain the Temple, the holiest **place** of all.
46.19 He pointed out a **place** on the west side of the rooms
46.20 and said, "This is the **place** where the priests are to
Dan 1.11 the guard whom Ashpenaz had **placed** in charge of him and his
5.20 removed from his royal throne and lost his **place** of honour.
6.17 the pit, and the king **placed** his own royal seal and the
7. 9 While I was looking, thrones were put in **place.**
8. 8 In its **place** four prominent horns came up, each pointing in
9.27 The Awful Horror will be **placed** on the highest point of the
11. 4 him will rule in his **place,** but they will not have the
Hos 4.13 At sacred **places** on the mountain-tops they offer sacrifices,
6. 9 on the road to the holy **place** at Shechem they commit murder.
8.11 the more **places** they have for sinning!
9. 6 treasures of silver and the **places** where their homes once
Joel 3. 7 bring them out of the **places** to which you have sold them.
Amos 4. 4 Israel, go to the holy **place** in Bethel and sin, if you
7. 9 The **places** where Isaac's descendants worship will be destroyed.
7. 9 The holy **places** of Israel will be left in ruins.
Obad 17 Mount Zion some will escape, and it will be a sacred **place.**
Mic 1. 3 The Lord is coming from his holy **place;**
1. 6 ruins in the open country, a **place** for planting grapevines.
2.10 Your sins have doomed this **place** to destruction.
Nah 2.11 a den of lions, the **place** where young lions were fed, where
Zeph 2. 9 They will become a **place** of salt pits and everlasting ruin,
2.14 It will be a **place** where flocks, herds, and animals of
2.15 What a desolate **place** it will become, a place where wild
Zech 3. 9 I am **placing** in front of Joshua a single stone with seven
4. 2 are seven lamps, each one with **places** for seven wicks.
4. 7 in **place,** the people will shout, 'Beautiful, beautiful!' "
5.11 the basket will be **placed** there to be worshipped."
7.14 land was left a desolate **place,** with no one living in it."
9.12 return to your **place** of safety.
10. 9 the nations, yet in far-off **places** they will remember me.
Mal 3.12 happy, because your land will be a good **place** to live in.
Mt 2. 9 of them until it stopped over the **place** where the child was.
5.35 nor by earth, for it is the resting **place** for his feet;
9. 9 Jesus left that **place,** and as he walked along, he saw a
9.18 but come and **place** your hands on her, and she will live."
9.27 Jesus left that **place,** and as he walked along, two blind
10.11 welcome you, and stay with him until you leave that **place.**
10.14 then leave that **place** and shake the dust off your
11. 1 twelve disciples, he left that **place** and went off to teach
12. 9 Jesus left that **place** and went to a synagogue,
12.15 about the plot against him, he went away from that **place;**
12.43 it travels over dry country looking for a **place** to rest.
13.53 these parables, he left that **place** [54]and went back to his
14.13 there in a boat and went to a lonely **place** by himself.
14.15 said, "It is already very late, and this is a lonely **place.**
15.21 Jesus left that **place** and went off to the territory near
15.30 and many other sick people, whom they **placed** at Jesus' feet;
19.13 to Jesus for him to **place** his hands on them and to
19.15 He **placed** his hands on them and then went away.
20.23 These **places** belong to those for whom my Father has prepared them."
23. 6 They love the best **places** at feasts and the reserved seats
24. 2 not a single stone here will be left in its **place;**
24.15 It will be standing in the holy **place."**
24.45 one that his master has **placed** in charge of the other
26.36 with his disciples to a **place** called Gethsemane, and he said
26.52 "Put your sword back in its **place,"** Jesus said to him.
27.29 out of thorny branches and **placed** it on his head,
27.33 a place called Golgotha, which means, "The **Place** of the Skull."
27.60 a new linen sheet, [60]and **placed** it in his own tomb,
28. 6 Come here and see the **place** where he was lying.
Mk 1.35 went out of the town to a lonely **place,** where he prayed.
1.45 he stayed out in lonely **places,** and people came to him from
2. 4 a hole in the roof right above the **place** where Jesus was.
5.23 Please come and **place** your hands on her, so that she will
6. 1 Jesus left that **place** and went back to his home town,
6. 5 miracles there, except that he **placed** his hands on a few
6.10 welcomed, stay in the same house until you leave that **place.**
6.31 off by ourselves to some **place** where we will be alone
6.32 started out in a boat by themselves for a lonely **place.**
6.33 and arrived at the **place** ahead of Jesus and his disciples.
6.35 said, "It is already very late, and this is a lonely **place.**
7.32 speak, and they begged Jesus to **place** his hands on him.
8.23 on the man's eyes, Jesus **placed** his hands on him and asked
8.25 Jesus again **placed** his hands on the man's eyes.
9.30 Jesus and his disciples left that **place** and went on
9.35 wants to be first must **place** himself last of all and be
10. 1 Then Jesus left that **place,** went to the province of Judaea,
10.13 to Jesus for him to **place** his hands on them,
10.16 the children in his arms, **placed** his hands on each of them,
10.40 God who will give these **places** to those for whom he has
12.39 reserved seats in the synagogues and the best **places** at feasts.
13. 2 Not a single stone here will be left in its **place;**
13.14 'The Awful Horror' standing in the **place** where he should not be."
14.32 They came to a **place** called Gethsemane, and Jesus said
15.22 a place called Golgotha, which means **"The Place of the Skull."**
15.46 it in the sheet, and **placed** it in a tomb which had
15.47 Joseph were watching and saw where the body of Jesus was **placed.**
16. 6 Look, here is the **place** where they put him.
16.18 will **place** their hands on sick people, who will get well."
Lk 4.17 the scroll and found the **place** where it is written,
4.40 he **placed** his hands on every one of them and healed them
Lk 4.42 daybreak Jesus left the town and went off to a lonely **place.**
5.16 But he would go away to lonely **places,** where he prayed.
6.17 he stood on a level **place** with a large number of his
7. 8 I, too, am a man **placed** under the authority of superior officers,
9.12 and find food and lodging, because this is a lonely **place."**
10. 1 him to every town and **place** where he himself was about to
11. 1 One day Jesus was praying in a certain **place.**
11.24 it travels over dry country looking for a **place** to rest.
11.53 When Jesus left that **place,** the teachers of the Law and
13.13 **placed** his hands on her, and at once she straightened herself
14. 7 guests were choosing the best **places,** so he told this
14. 8 to a wedding feast, do not sit down in the best **place.**
14. 9 have to come and say to you, 'Let him have this **place.'**
14. 9 would be embarrassed and have to sit in the lowest **place.**
14.10 and sit in the lowest **place,** so that your host will come
14.10 and say, 'Come on up, my friend, to a better **place.'**
16.28 that they, at least, will not come to this **place** of pain.'
18.15 their babies to Jesus for him to **place** his hands on them.
19. 5 When Jesus came to that **place,** he looked up and said to
19.37 came near Jerusalem, at the **place** where the road went down
19.44 will they leave in its **place,** because you did not recognize
20.46 reserved seats in the synagogues and the best **places** at feasts;
21. 6 when not a single stone here will be left in its **place;**
22.14 came, Jesus took his **place** at the table with the apostles.
22.40 When he arrived at the **place,** he said to them, "Pray
23.33 they came to the **place** called "The Skull," they crucified Jesus
23.46 In your hands I **place** my spirit!"
23.53 in a linen sheet, and **placed** it in a tomb which had
23.55 and saw the tomb and how Jesus' body was **placed** in it.
Jn 3.23 from Salim, because there was plenty of water in that **place.**
4.20 Jews say that Jerusalem is the **place** where we should worship God."
5.13 was a crowd in that **place,** and Jesus had slipped away.
6.21 the boat reached land at the **place** they were heading for.
6.23 came to shore near the **place** where the crowd had eaten the
6.62 of Man go back up to the **place** where he was before?
7. 3 said to him, "Leave this **place** and go to Judaea, so that
8.20 Temple, in the room where the offering boxes were **placed.**
10.40 the River Jordan to the **place** where John had been baptizing,
11.30 but was still in the **place** where Martha had met him.)
11.38 tomb, which was a cave with a stone **placed** at the entrance.
11.54 left and went to a **place** near the desert, to a town
13.12 garment back on and returned to his **place** at the table.
14. 2 Father's house, and I am going to prepare a **place** for you.
14. 3 I go and prepare a **place** for you, I will come back
14. 4 know the way that leads to the **place** where I am going."
14.31 "Come, let us go from this **place.**
18. 1 was a garden in that **place,** and Jesus and his disciples went
18.11 Jesus said to Peter, "Put your sword back in its **place!**
19.13 on the judge's seat in the **place** called "The Stone Pavement."
19.17 and came to **"The Place of the Skull,"** as it is
19.20 because the **place** where Jesus was crucified was not
19.41 was a garden in the **place** where Jesus had been put to
19.42 and because the tomb was close by, they **placed** Jesus' body
Acts 1.20 It is also written, 'May someone else take his **place** of service.'
1.25 as an apostle in the **place** of Judas,
1.25 Judas, who left to go to the **place** where he belongs."
2. 1 all the believers were gathered together in one **place.**
4.31 finished praying, the **place** where they were meeting was shaken.
5.15 out into the streets and **placed** on beds and mats so that
6. 6 to the apostles, who prayed and **placed** their hands on them.
7. 7 come out of that country and will worship me in this **place.'**
7.33 your sandals off, for the **place** where you are standing is
7.46 allow him to provide a dwelling **place** for the God of Jacob.
7.49 Where is the **place** for me to live in?
8.17 Peter and John **placed** their hands on them, and they received
8.18 to the believers when the apostles **placed** their hands on them.
8.19 so that anyone I **place** my hands on will receive the
8.36 they came to a **place** where there was some water,
9.12 named Ananias come in and **place** his hands on him so that
9.17 the house where Saul was, and **placed** his hands on him.
13. 3 They fasted and prayed, **placed** their hands on them,
13.29 took him down from the cross and **placed** him in a tomb.
14.26 sailed back to Antioch, the **place** where they had been commended
16. 3 Jews who lived in those **places** knew that Timothy's father was
16.13 there would be a **place** where Jews gathered for prayer.
16.16 we were going to the **place** of prayer, we were met by
17.26 times and the limits of the **places** where they would live.
19. 6 Paul **placed** his hands on them, and the Holy Spirit came
20.28 all the flock which the Holy Spirit has **placed** in your care.
21.28 brought some Gentiles into the Temple and defiled this holy **place!"**
26.18 sins forgiven and receive their **place** among God's chosen people.'
27. 8 great difficulty came to a **place** called Safe Harbours,
28. 7 Not far from that **place** were some fields that belonged to Publius,
28. 8 went into his room, prayed, **placed** his hands on him, and
28.23 of them came that day to the **place** where Paul was staying.
28.30 years Paul lived in a **place** he rented for himself, and there
Rom 9.26 And in the very **place** where they were told, 'You are not
9.33 "Look, I **place** in Zion a stone that will make people stumble,
11.20 believe, while you remain in **place** because you do believe.
11.23 they will be put back in the **place** where they were;
15.20 proclaim the Good News in **places** where Christ has not been
1 Cor 3.11 For God has already **placed** Jesus Christ as the one and
4. 9 has given the very last **place** to us apostles, like men
4.11 we wander from **place to place;**
12.28 In the church God has put all in **place:**
15.28 when all things have been **placed** under Christ's rule,
15.28 he himself, the Son, will **place** himself under God,
15.28 God, who **placed** all things under him;

2 Cor 1.10 and we have **placed** our hope in him that he will save
1.22 us apart, [22] who has **placed** his mark of ownership upon us,
11.32 the governor under King Aretas **placed** guards at the city gates
Gal 1.21 Afterwards I went to **places** in Syria and Cilicia.
Eph 2.22 the others into a **place** where God lives through his Spirit.
Phil 2. 9 raised him to the highest **place** above and gave him the name
Col 1.17 and in union with him all things have their proper **place.**
1.18 that he alone might have the first **place** in all things.
1 Tim 4.10 hard, because we have **placed** our hope in the living God,
5. 5 take care of her, has **placed** her hope in God and continues
6.17 to be proud, but to **place** their hope, not in such an
Phlm 13 the gospel's sake, so that he could help me in your **place.**
Heb 2. 5 God has not **placed** the angels as rulers over the new world
5. 6 He also said in another **place,** "You will be a priest for
6.18 greatly encouraged to hold firmly to the hope **placed** before us.
9. 1 rules for worship and a man-made **place** for worship as well.
9. 5 with their wings spread over the **place** where sins were forgiven.
10. 9 sacrifices and puts the sacrifice of Christ in their **place.**
Jas 1.18 so that we should have first **place** among all his creatures.
3. 6 world of wrong, occupying its **place** in our bodies
4. 5 says, "The spirit that God **placed** in us is filled with
1 Pet 2. 6 stone, which I am **placing** as the cornerstone in Zion;
2.23 he did not threaten, but **placed** his hopes in God, the
3. 5 women of the past who **placed** their hope in God used to
2 Pet 1.19 lamp shining in a dark **place** until the Day dawns and the
2.17 God has reserved a **place** for them in the deepest darkness.
Jude 6 of their proper authority, but abandoned their own dwelling **place:**
13 God has reserved a **place** for ever in the deepest darkness.
Rev 1.17 He **placed** his right hand on me and said, "Don't be afraid!
2. 5 I will come to you and take your lamp-stand from its **place.**
6.14 and every mountain and island was moved from its **place.**
12. 6 to the desert, to a **place** God had prepared for her,
12.14 order to fly to her **place** in the desert, where she will
13. 6 curse God, his name, the **place** where he lives, and all those
13.16 to have a mark **placed** on their right hands or on
16.16 kings together in the **place** that in Hebrew is called Armageddon.
17.17 For God has **placed** in their hearts the will to carry out
21. 8 idols, and all liars—the **place** for them is the lake burning

PLACE (2)
[TAKE PLACE]

Ex 8.23 This miracle will **take place** tomorrow.'"
1 Chr 20. 6 Another battle **took place** at Gath, where there was a
Is 41.22 will happen, so that we will know it when it **takes place.**
48. 3 "Long ago I predicted what would **take place;**
48. 5 announcing events before they **took place,** to prevent you
48. 6 "All I foretold has now **taken place;**
48. 7 nothing like this **took place** in the past.
Jer 32.44 This will **take place** in the territory of Benjamin, in the
Lam 3.38 Good and evil alike **take place** at his command.
Amos 5.17 All this will **take place** because I am coming to punish you."
7. 3 his mind and said, "What you saw will not **take place."**
7. 6 mind again and said, "This will not **take place** either."
Hab 2. 3 it will certainly **take place,** and it will not be delayed.
Mt 1.18 This was how the birth of Jesus Christ **took place.**
Mk 13. 4 that the time has come for all these things to **take place."**
Lk 1. 1 write a report of the things that have **taken place** among us.
2. 2 When this first census **took place,** Quirinius was the governor
21. 7 to show that the time has come for it to **take place?"**
21.12 all these things **take place,** however, you will be arrested
21.32 these things will **take place** before the people now living have
23.19 a riot that had **taken place** in the city, and for murder.)
Acts 10.37 the great event that **took place** throughout the land of Israel,
11.19 by the persecution which **took place** when Stephen was killed
Rom 4.10 When did this **take place?**
1 Cor 15.54 So when this **takes place,** and the mortal has been
2 Thes 2. 3 until the final Rebellion **takes place** and the Wicked One appears,
2 Tim 2.18 by saying that our resurrection has already **taken place.**

PLACE OF WORSHIP

Ex 21. 6 then his master shall take him to the **place of worship.**
22. 8 be brought to the **place of worship** and there he must take
22. 9 the property shall be taken to the **place of worship.**
22.11 must go to the **place of worship** and take an oath that
Lev 26.30 I will destroy your **places of worship** on the hills, tear
26.31 into ruins, destroy your **places of worship,** and refuse to
Num 33.52 their stone and metal idols and all their **places of worship.**
Deut 12.18 God, in the one **place of worship** chosen by the Lord your
12.21 If the one **place of worship** is too far away, then,
12.26 Take to the one **place of worship** your offerings and the
14.24 If the **place of worship** is too far from your home for
14.25 and take the money with you to the one **place of worship.**
15.20 eat them in the Lord's presence at the one **place of worship.**
16. 2 Go to the one **place of worship** and slaughter there one of
16. 5 animals at the one **place of worship**—and nowhere else in the
16. 7 Boil the meat and eat it at the one **place of worship;**
16.11 Do this at the one **place of worship.**
16.15 this festival for seven days at the one **place of worship.**
16.16 the Lord three times a year at the one **place of worship:**
17. 8 go to the one **place of worship** chosen by the Lord your
18. 6 Israel to the one **place of worship** [7] and may serve there as
19.17 go to the one **place of worship** and be judged by the
26. 2 you must take it with you to the one **place of worship.**
31.11 to worship the Lord your God at the one **place of worship.**
Judg 17. 5 This man Micah had his own **place of worship.**
20.18 Israelites went to the **place of worship** at Bethel, and there
20.22 Israelites went to the **place of worship** and mourned in the
1 Sam 9.14 coming out towards them on his way to the **place of worship.**
9.19 Go on ahead of me to the **place of worship.**
1 Sam 9.25 went down from the **place of worship** to the town, they made
2 Sam 15.32 where there was a **place of worship,** his trusted friend
1 Kgs 11. 8 He also built **places of worship** where all his foreign
12.31 Jeroboam also built **places of worship** on hilltops, and
12.32 Bethel the priests serving at the **places of worship** he had built.
13.32 and against all the **places of worship** in the towns of
14.23 They built **places of worship** for false gods, and put up
14.24 who served as prostitutes at those pagan **places of worship.**
15.12 serving at the pagan **places of worship,** and he removed all
15.14 destroy all the pagan **places of worship,** he remained
22.43 but the pagan **places of worship** were not destroyed, and the
2 Kgs 12. 3 However, the pagan **places of worship** were not destroyed,
14. 4 tear down the pagan **places of worship,** and the people
15. 4 But the pagan **places of worship** were not destroyed, and
15.35 But the pagan **places of worship** were not destroyed, and
16. 4 At the pagan **places of worship,** on the hills, and under
17. 9 They built pagan **places of worship** in all their towns, from
17.32 priests at the pagan **places of worship** and to offer
18. 4 He destroyed the pagan **places of worship,** broke the stone pillars,
21. 3 He rebuilt the pagan **places of worship** that his father
23.10 also desecrated Topheth, the pagan **place of worship** in the
23.15 also tore down the **place of worship** in Bethel which had been
23.19 down all the pagan **places of worship** which had been built by
1 Chr 6.31 the music at the **place of worship** in Jerusalem after the
6.48 were assigned all the other duties at the **place of worship.**
16.39 the worship of the Lord at the **place of worship** in Gibeon.
21.29 were still at the **place of worship** at Gibeon at this time;
2 Chr 1. 3 them to go with him to the **place of worship** at Gibeon.
1.13 So Solomon left the **place of worship** at Gibeon, where
11.15 serve at the pagan **places of worship** and to worship demons
14. 3 altars and the pagan **places of worship,** broke down the
14. 5 he abolished the pagan **places of worship** and the
15.17 destroy all the pagan **places of worship** in the land, he
17. 6 destroyed all the pagan **places of worship** and the symbols of
20.33 but the pagan **places of worship** were not destroyed.
21.11 He even built pagan **places of worship** in the Judaean
28. 4 At the pagan **places of worship,** on the hills, and under
28.25 Judah, he built pagan **places of worship,** where incense was
31. 1 and destroyed the altars and the pagan **places of worship.**
33. 3 He rebuilt the pagan **places of worship** that his father
33.17 offer sacrifices at other **places of worship,** they offered
33.19 he did, the pagan **places of worship** and the symbols of the
34. 3 to destroy the pagan **places of worship,** the symbols of the
Ps 78.58 him with their heathen **places of worship,** and with their
Jer 48.35 making burnt-offerings at their **places of worship** and from
Ezek 16.16 decorate your **places of worship,** and just like a prostitute,
28.18 and selling that your **places of worship** were corrupted.
Amos 2. 8 At every **place of worship** men sleep on clothing that they
7.13 This is the king's **place of worship,** the national temple."
Acts 17.23 city and looked at the **places** where you worship, I found an
Heb 13.10 who serve in the Jewish **place** of worship have no right to

PLAGUE

Num 16.47 When he saw that the **plague** had already begun, he put the
16.48 This stopped the **plague,** and he was left standing
16.50 When the **plague** had stopped, Aaron returned to Moses at
Deut 4.34 he brought **plagues** and war, worked miracles and wonders, and
7.19 Remember the terrible **plagues** that you saw with your own eyes,
29. 3 You saw the terrible **plagues,** the miracles, and the great
1 Sam 6. 4 The same **plague** was sent on all of you and on the
6. 9 doesn't, then we will know that he did not send the **plague;**
Ps 78.50 anger or spare their lives, but killed them with a **plague.**
91. 6 during the day [6] or the **plagues** that strike in the dark or
106.30 Phinehas stood up and punished the guilty, and the **plague** was stopped.
Hos 13.14 Bring on your **plagues,** death!
Amos 4.10 "I sent a **plague** on you like the one I sent on
Lk 21.11 There will be terrible earthquakes, famines, and **plagues** everywhere;
Rev 9.18 A third of mankind was killed by those three **plagues:**
9.20 not been killed by these **plagues,** did not turn away from
11. 6 the earth with every kind of **plague** as often as they wish.
15. 1 were seven angels with seven **plagues,** which are the last ones,
15. 6 angels who had the seven **plagues** came out of the temple,
15. 8 the temple until the seven **plagues** brought by the seven angels
16. 9 the name of God, who has authority over these **plagues.**
16.21 God on account of the **plague** of hail,
16.21 because it was such a terrible **plague.**
18. 8 she will be struck with **plagues**— disease, grief, and famine.
21. 9 full of the seven last **plagues** came to me and said, "Come,
22.18 God will add to his punishment the **plagues** described in this book.

PLAIN (1)

Num 14.14 with us, that you are **plainly** seen when your cloud stops
2 Kgs 5. 7 It's **plain** that he is trying to start a quarrel with me!"
Ps 5. 8 make your way **plain** for me to follow.
19. 1 How **plainly** it shows what he has done!
50.21 But now I reprimand you and make the matter **plain** to you.
Prov 8. 9 to the well-informed, it is all **plain.**
Ecc 7.29 God made us **plain** and simple, but we have made ourselves
Hos 6. 5 What I want from you is **plain** and clear:
Mt 16.21 on Jesus began to say **plainly** to his disciples, "I must go
Lk 1.66 For it was **plain** that the Lord's power was upon him.
Jn 10.24 Tell us the **plain** truth:
11.14 Jesus told them **plainly,** "Lazarus is dead, [15] but for your sake
16.25 of speech, but will speak to you **plainly** about the Father.
16.29 "Now you are speaking **plainly,** without using figures of speech.
Acts 2.29 I must speak to you **plainly** about our famous ancestor King David.
Rom 1.19 about God is plain to them, for God himself made it **plain.**

1 Cor 1.11 have told me quite **plainly,** my brothers, that there are quarrels
6.16 The scripture says quite **plainly,** "The two will become one body."
2 Cor 7.12 I wrote it to make **plain** to you, in God's sight, how
Gal 5.19 What human nature does is quite **plain.**
1 Tim 5.24 sins of some people are **plain** to see, and their sins go
5.25 same way good deeds are **plainly** seen,
5.25 and even those that are not so **plain** cannot be hidden.
Heb 7.15 The matter becomes even **plainer;**
12.27 The words "once more" **plainly** show that the created things
2 Pet 1.14 this mortal body, as our Lord Jesus Christ **plainly** told me.
Jude 7 the punishment of eternal fire as a **plain** warning to all.

PLAIN (2)

Gen 11. 2 East, they came to a **plain** in Babylonia and settled there.
14. 5 Ham, the Emim in the **plain** of Kiriathaim, [6]and the Horites
Num 22. 1 set up camp in the **plains** of Moab east of the Jordan
26. 3 They assembled in the **plains** of Moab across the River Jordan
26.63 of the Israelites in the **plains** of Moab across the River
31.12 at the camp on the **plains** of Moab across the Jordan from
33.41 From Mount Hor to the **plains** of Moab the
33.41 Mount Nebo, and in the **plains** of Moab across the River
33.50 There in the **plains** of Moab across the Jordan from
35. 1 In the **plains** of Moab across the Jordan from Jericho the
36.13 Israelites through Moses in the **plains** of Moab across the
Deut 34. 1 Moses went up from the **plains** of Moab to Mount Nebo, to
34. 3 and the **plain** that reaches from Zoar to Jericho, the city of
34. 8 Israel mourned for him for thirty days in the **plains** of Moab.
Josh 4.13 men ready for war crossed over to the **plain** near Jericho.
5.10 camping at Gilgal on the **plain** near Jericho, they observed
9. 1 and all along the coastal **plain** of the Mediterranean Sea as
13.32 Jericho and the Jordan when he was in the **plains** of Moab.
17.16 but the Canaanites in the **plains** have iron chariots, both
Judg 1.34 hill-country and did not let them come down to the **plain.**
1 Kgs 20.23 will certainly defeat them if we fight them in the **plains.**
20.25 fight the Israelites in the **plains,** and this time we will
20.28 hills and not of the **plains,** I will give you victory over
2 Kgs 25. 5 Zedekiah, captured him in the **plains** near Jericho, and all
1 Chr 27.25 Joash Cattle in the **Plain** of Sharon:
2 Chr 26.10 herds of livestock in the western foothills and **plains.**
35.22 himself and went into battle on the **plain** of Megiddo.
Neh 6. 2 with them in one of the villages in the **Plain** of Ono.
Job 39. 6 to be their home, and let them live on the salt **plains.**
Ps 78.12 God performed miracles in the **plain** of Zoan in the land of
78.43 acts and miracles in the **plain** of Zoan in the land of
Is 40. 4 The hills will become a **plain,** and the rough country will be
65.10 cattle to pasture in the **Plain** of Sharon in the west and
Jer 21.13 high above the valleys, like a rock rising above the **plain.**
39. 5 pursued them and captured Zedekiah in the **plains** near Jericho.
48. 8 both valley and **plain** will be ruined.
52. 8 Zedekiah, captured him in the **plains** near Jericho, and all
Ezek 25.16 I will destroy everyone left living there on the Philistine **Plain.**
Dan 3. 1 it set up in the **plain** of Dura in the province of
Zech 12.11 as the mourning for Hadad-rimmon in the **plain** of Megiddo.

PLAN

Gen 27.42 Rebecca heard about Esau's **plan,** she sent for Jacob and said,
27.42 "Listen, your brother Esau is **planning** to get even with you
37.22 He said this, **planning** to save him from them and send him
41.37 his officials approved this **plan,** [38]and he said to them,
50.15 Joseph still hates us and **plans** to pay us back for all
Ex 25. 9 its furnishings according to the **plan** that I will show you.
25.40 make them according to the **plan** that I showed you on the
26.30 the Tent according to the **plan** that I showed you on the
27. 8 it hollow, according to the **plan** that I showed you on the
31. 4 kind of artistic work—[4]for **planning** skilful designs and
32.12 your people out of Egypt, **planning** to kill them in the
33.13 you are, tell me your **plans,** so that I may serve you
35.32 kind of artistic work, [32]for **planning** skilful designs and
Num 33.56 out, I will destroy you, as I **planned** to destroy them."
Judg 9.42 people of Shechem were **planning** to go out into the fields,
20.32 But the Israelites had **planned** to retreat and lead them
1 Sam 18.25 (This was how Saul **planned** to have David killed by the Philistines.)
19. 1 Jonathan and all his officials that he **planned** to kill David.
20. 3 let you know what he **plans** to do, because you would be
23. 9 David heard that Saul was **planning** to attack him, he said to
23.10 have heard that Saul is **planning** to come to Keilah and
23.13 that David had escaped from Keilah, he gave up his **plan.**
2 Sam 17.21 told him what Ahithophel had **planned** against him and said,
20.21 That is not our **plan.**
20.22 of the city with her **plan,** and they cut off Sheba's head
1 Kgs 6.38 Temple was completely finished exactly as it had been **planned.**
8.17 Solomon continued, "My father David **planned** to build a
20.22 your forces, and make careful **plans,** because the king of
2 Kgs 7.12 officials, "I'll tell you what the Syrians are **planning!**
11. 4 he made them agree under oath to what he **planned** to do.
19.25 "Have you never heard that I **planned** all this long ago?
1 Chr 28.11 David gave Solomon the **plans** for all the temple buildings,
28.12 He also gave him the **plans** for all he had in mind
28.13 David also gave him the **plans** for organizing the priests
28.19 this is contained in the **plan** written according to the
2 Chr 2.12 understanding and skill, who now **plans** to build a temple for
4.20 to burn in front of the Most Holy Place, according to **plan;**
6. 7 Solomon continued, "My father David **planned** to build a
7.11 palace, successfully completing all his **plans** for them,
8. 6 He carried out all his **plans** for building in Jerusalem, in
30. 4 with their **plan,** [5]so they invited all the Israelites,
Ezra 10.15 one was opposed to the **plan** except Jonathan son of Asahel
10.16 The returned exiles accepted the **plan,** so Ezra the
Neh 2.19 Geshem heard what we were **planning** to do, they laughed at us
4.12 to warn us of the **plans** our enemies were making against us.
4.15 and they realized that God had defeated their **plans.**
6. 6 He also says you **plan** to make yourself king [7]and that you
Esth 3. 6 He made **plans** to kill every Jew in the whole Persian Empire.
9.24 he had **planned** to wipe them out.
9.25 suffered the fate he had **planned** for the Jews—he and his
Job 5.12 He upsets the **plans** of cunning men, and traps wise
10.13 that all that time you were secretly **planning** to harm me.
10.17 you always **plan** some new attack.
15. 8 Did you overhear the **plans** God made?
15.35 These are the men who **plan** trouble and do evil;
17.11 my **plans** have failed;
23.14 He will fulfil what he has **planned** for me;
23.14 that **plan** is just one of the many he has;
27.11 is God's power, and explain what Almighty God has **planned.**
Ps 2. 1 Why do the nations **plan** rebellion?
2. 4 in heaven the Lord laughs and mocks their feeble **plans.**
7.14 they **plan** trouble and practise deception.
14. 6 Evildoers frustrate the **plans** of the humble man, but the
20. 4 give you what you desire and make all your **plans** succeed.
21.11 They make their **plans,** and plot against him, but they
31.13 They are making **plans** against me, plotting to kill me.
33.10 he keeps them from carrying out their **plans.**
33.11 But his **plans** endure for ever;
36. 4 He makes evil **plans** as he lies in bed;
37. 7 those who prosper or those who succeed in their evil **plans.**
40. 5 You have made many wonderful **plans** for us.
52. 2 You make **plans** to ruin others;
56. 5 they are always **planning** how to hurt me!
64. 5 they **plan** where to place their traps.
64. 6 They make evil **plans** and say,
64. 6 "We have **planned** a perfect crime."
73. 8 they are proud and make **plans** to oppress others.
83. 3 They are making secret **plans** against your people;
83. 5 They agree on their **plan** and form an alliance against you:
103. 7 He revealed his **plans** to Moses and let the people of
146. 4 on that day all their **plans** come to an end.
Prov 3.29 Don't **plan** anything that will hurt your neighbour;
4.26 **Plan** carefully what you do, and whatever you do will
6.14 all the while **planning** evil in their perverted minds,
6.16 a mind that thinks up wicked **plans,**
7.10 she was dressed like a prostitute and was making **plans.**
8.14 I make **plans** and carry them out.
12. 2 Lord is pleased with good people, but condemns those who **plan** evil.
12.20 Those who **plan** evil are in for a rude surprise, but
16. 1 We may make our **plans,** but God has the last word.
16. 3 the Lord to bless your **plans,** and you will be successful in
16. 9 You may make your **plans,** but God directs your actions.
19.21 People may **plan** all kinds of things, but the Lord's will
20.18 don't go charging into battle without a **plan.**
21. 5 **Plan** carefully and you will have plenty;
24. 6 all, you must make careful **plans** before you fight a battle,
24. 8 If you are always **planning** evil, you will earn a
30.32 foolish enough to be arrogant and **plan** evil, stop and think!
Ecc 10.10 It is more sensible to **plan** ahead.
Is 5.19 Let Israel's holy God carry out his **plans;**
8.10 Make your **plans!**
10. 7 But the Assyrian emperor has his own violent **plans** in mind.
14.24 "What I have **planned** will happen.
14.26 This is my **plan** for the world, and my arm is stretched
19. 3 am going to frustrate the **plans** of the Egyptians and destroy
19.12 can tell you what **plans** the Lord Almighty has for Egypt.
22.11 no attention to God, who **planned** all this long ago and who
23. 8 Who was it that **planned** to bring all this on Tyre, that
23. 9 The Lord Almighty **planned** it.
23. 9 He **planned** it in order to put an end to their pride
25. 1 you have faithfully carried out the **plans** you made long ago.
28.29 The **plans** God makes are wise, and they always succeed!
29.15 Those who try to hide their **plans** from the Lord are doomed!
30. 1 They follow **plans** that I did not make, and sign treaties
30.16 you **plan** to escape from your enemies by riding fast horses.
30.28 nations to destruction and puts an end to their evil **plans.**
33.11 You make worthless **plans** and everything you do is useless.
33.15 Don't join with those who **plan** to commit murder or to do
37.26 "Have you never heard that I **planned** all this long ago?
44.26 a messenger to reveal my **plans,**
44.26 I make those **plans** and predictions come true.
46.10 I said that my **plans** would never fail, that I would do
46.11 swoop down like a hawk and accomplish what I have **planned.**
55.11 it will not fail to do what I **plan** for it;
59. 4 You carry out your **plans** to hurt others.
59. 7 You are always **planning** something evil, and you can hardly
Jer 11.19 that it was against me that they were **planning** evil things.
18.11 Jerusalem that I am making **plans** against them and getting
19. 7 I will frustrate all the **plans** of the people of Judah and
26. 3 mind about the destruction I **plan** to bring on them for all
29.11 I alone know the **plans** I have for you,
29.11 **plans** to bring you prosperity
29.11 and not disaster, **plans** to bring about the future
32.19 You make wise **plans** and do mighty things;
49.20 So listen to the **plan** that I have made against the
50.45 So listen to the **plan** that I have made against the city
51.29 Lord is carrying out his **plan** to make Babylonia a desert,
Lam 3.62 All day long they talk about me and make their **plans.**
Ezek 11. 2 man, these men make evil **plans** and give bad advice in this
11. 5 I know what you are saying and what you are **planning.**
38.10 "When that time comes, you will start thinking up an evil **plan.**
43.10 of Israel about the Temple, and let them study its **plan.**
43.11 what they have done, explain the **plan** of the Temple to them:

Dan 11.17 "The king of Syria will **plan** an expedition, using his whole army.
11.17 but his **plan** will not succeed.
11.24 He will make **plans** to attack fortresses, but his time will
11.36 God will do exactly what he has **planned.**
Amos 3. 7 does anything without revealing his **plan** to his servants,
Mic 2. 1 terrible it will be for those who lie awake and **plan** evil!
2. 1 soon as they have the chance, they do the evil they **planned.**
2. 3 the Lord says, "I am **planning** to bring disaster on you, and
6. 5 what King Balak of Moab **planned** to do to you and how
Zech 7.10 And do not **plan** ways of harming one another.'
8.14 ancestors made me angry, I **planned** disaster for them
8.14 and did not change my mind, but carried out my **plans.**
8.15 But now I am **planning** to bless the people of Jerusalem
8.17 Do not **plan** ways of harming one another.
Mt 1.19 so he made **plans** to break the engagement privately.
12.14 Then the Pharisees left and made **plans** to kill Jesus.
22.15 Pharisees went off and made a **plan** to trap Jesus with questions.
22.18 aware of their evil **plan,** and so he said, "You hypocrites!
26. 4 and made **plans** to arrest Jesus secretly and put
27. 1 and the elders made their **plans** against Jesus to put him to
28.12 The chief priests met with the elders and made their **plan;**
Mk 3. 6 of Herod's party, and they made **plans** to kill Jesus.
15. 1 of the Law, and the whole Council, and made their **plans.**
Lk 1.51 mighty arm and scattered the proud with all their **plans.**
14.28 "If one of you is **planning** to build a tower, he sits
19.12 to be made king, after which he **planned** to come back home.
Jn 11. 8 and are you **planning** to go back?"
11.53 From that day on the Jewish authorities made **plans** to kill Jesus.
12.10 So the chief priests made **plans** to kill Lazarus too,
Acts 2.23 In accordance with his own **plan** God had already decided that
5.38 If what they have **planned** and done is of human origin,
8.22 Repent, then, of this evil **plan** of yours, and pray to
9.23 Jews met together and made **plans** to kill Saul,
9.24 but he was told of their **plan.**
12. 4 Herod **planned** to put him on trial in public after Passover.
23.12 The next morning some Jews met together and made a **plan.**
23.13 There were more than forty who **planned** this together.
27.13 they could carry out their **plan,** so they pulled up the
27.42 The soldiers made a **plan** to kill all the prisoners,
Rom 1.13 that many times I have **planned** to visit you, but something
2 Cor 1.15 all this that I made **plans** at first to visit you,
1.16 For I **planned** to visit you on my way to Macedonia
1.17 In **planning** this, did I appear fickle?
1.17 When I make my **plans,** do I make them from selfish motives,
2.11 for we know what his **plans** are.
8.11 it as you were to **plan** it, and do it with what
Eph 1. 9 known to us the secret **plan** he had already decided to
1.10 This **plan,** which God will complete when the time is right,
1.11 All things are done according to God's **plan** and decision;
3. 3 God revealed his secret **plan** and made it known to me.
3. 9 people see how God's secret **plan** is to be put into effect.
Col 1.27 God's **plan** is to make known his secret to his people,
1 Tim 1. 4 they do not serve God's **plan,** which is known by faith.
Heb 11.40 because God had decided on an even better **plan** for us.
Rev 10. 7 God will accomplish his secret **plan,** as he announced

PLANE-TREE

Gen 30.37 branches of poplar, almond, and **plane trees** and stripped off
Ezek 31. 8 No fir-tree ever had such branches, And no **plane-tree** such boughs.

PLANET

2 Kgs 23. 5 to Baal, to the sun, the moon, the **planets,** and the stars.

PLANK

Acts 27.44 follow, holding on to the **planks** or to some broken pieces of

Am

PLANT

see also **SOW**

PLANT

[REPLANT]

Gen 1.11 earth produce all kinds of **plants,** those that bear grain and
1.12 earth produced all kinds of **plants,** and God was pleased with
1.30 provided grass and leafy **plants** for food"—and it was done.
2. 5 the universe, [5] there were no **plants** on the earth and no
2. 8 Then the Lord God **planted** a garden in Eden, in the East,
3.18 weeds and thorns, and you will have to eat wild **plants.**
8.22 there will be a time for **planting** and a time for harvest.
9. 3 Now you can eat them, as well as green **plants;**
9.20 who was a farmer, was the first man to **plant** a vineyard.
21.33 Then Abraham **planted** a tamarisk-tree in Beersheba
Ex 9.22 the people, the animals, and all the **plants** in the fields."
9.25 It beat down all the **plants** in the fields and broke all
10.15 left on any tree or **plant** in all the land of Egypt.
15.17 You bring them in and **plant** them on your mountain,
Lev 19.19 Do not **plant** two kinds of seed in the same field.
19.23 the land of Canaan and **plant** any kind of fruit tree,
25.22 to eat until the crops you **plant** that year are harvested.
Num 24. 6 beside a river, Like aloes **planted** by the Lord Or cedars
24. 7 abundant rainfall And **plant** their seed in well-watered fields.
Deut 6.11 and vineyards and olive orchards that you did not **plant.**
20. 6 man here who has just **planted** a vineyard, but has not yet
21. 4 has never been ploughed or **planted,** and there they are to
22. 9 "Do not **plant** any crop in the same field as your grapevines;
28.30 You will **plant** a vineyard—but never eat its grapes.
Deut 28.39 You will **plant** vineyards and take care of them, but you
29.18 like a root that grows to be a bitter and poisonous **plant.**
29.23 nothing will be **planted,** and not even weeds will grow there.
32. 2 showers on young **plants,** like gentle rain on tender grass.
Josh 24.13 vines that you did not **plant,**
24.13 and olives from trees that you did not **plant.'"**
1 Kgs 4.33 He spoke of trees and **plants,** from the Lebanon cedars to
2 Kgs 19.29 your corn and harvest it, and **plant** vines and eat grapes.
19.30 who survive will flourish like **plants** that send roots deep
2 Chr 26.10 he encouraged the people to **plant** vineyards in the
Job 14. 9 the ground, [9] with water it will sprout like a young **plant.**
30. 4 They pulled up the **plants** of the desert and ate them, even
Ps 37. 2 they will die like **plants** that wither.
65.10 the soil with showers and cause the young **plants** to grow.
80. 8 you drove out other nations and **planted** it in their land.
80.15 save this grapevine that you **planted,** this young vine you
92.13 They are like trees **planted** in the house of the Lord,
104.14 grow for the cattle and **plants** for man to use, so that
104.16 get plenty of rain— the Lord's own trees, which he **planted.**
105.35 they ate all the **plants** in the land;
107.37 They sowed the fields and **planted** grapevines
144.12 our sons in their youth be like **plants** that grow up strong.
Prov 2.22 and pull sinners out of it like **plants** from the ground.
31.16 it, and with money she has earned she **plants** a vineyard.
Ecc 2. 4 I built myself houses and **planted** vineyards.
2. 5 I **planted** gardens and orchards, with all kinds of fruit-trees
3. 2 death, the time for **planting** and the time for pulling up,
Song 4.13 there the **plants** flourish.
6.11 almond-trees to see the young **plants** in the valley, to see
Is 1.29 that you ever worshipped trees and **planted** sacred gardens.
4. 2 the Lord will make every **plant** and tree in the land grow
5. 2 he **planted** the finest vines.
5. 7 the people of Judah are the vines he **planted.**
17.10 you **plant** sacred gardens in order to worship a foreign god.
17.11 blossomed the very morning you **planted** them, there would
37.30 your corn and harvest it, and **plant** vines and eat grapes.
37.31 who survive will flourish like **plants** that send roots deep
40.24 They are like young **plants,** just set out and barely rooted.
44.14 Or he might **plant** a laurel-tree and wait for the rain to
51. 3 will make it a garden, like the garden I **planted** in Eden.
53. 2 servant should grow like a **plant** taking root in dry ground.
60.21 I **planted** them, I made them, To reveal my greatness to all.
61. 3 They will be like trees That the Lord himself has **planted.**
65.21 They will **plant** vineyards and enjoy the wine—it will not be
Jer 1.10 down, to destroy and to overthrow, to build and to **plant."**
2.21 I **planted** you like a choice vine from the very best seed.
9.15 give my people bitter **plants** to eat and poison to drink.
11.17 "I, the Lord Almighty, **planted** Israel and Judah;
12. 2 You **plant** them, and they take root;
12.14 their countries like an uprooted **plant,** and I will rescue
18. 9 that I am going to **plant** or build up any nation or
23.15 I will give them bitter **plants** to eat and poison to drink,
24. 6 I will **plant** them and not pull them up.
29. 5 **Plant** gardens and eat what you grow in them.
29.28 settle down, **plant** gardens, and eat what they grow."
31. 5 Once again you will **plant** vineyards on the hills of Samaria,
31. 5 and those who **plant** them will eat what the vineyards
31.28 I will take care to **plant** them and to build them up.
35. 7 or farm the land, and not to **plant** vineyards or buy them.
42.10 I will **plant** you and not pull you up.
45. 4 down what I have built and pulling up what I have **planted.**
Ezek 16. 7 I made you grow like a healthy **plant.**
17. 5 Then he took a young **plant** from the land of Israel
17. 5 and **planted** it in a fertile field,
17. 6 The **plant** sprouted and became a low, wide-spreading grapevine.
17. 8 the vine had already been **planted** in a fertile, well-watered
17.10 Yes, it is **planted,** but will it live and grow?
17.22 I will **plant** it on a high mountain,
19.10 Your mother was like a grapevine **planted** near a stream.
19.13 Now it is **planted** in the desert, in a dry and waterless
28.26 They will build houses and **plant** vineyards.
36.36 I, the Lord, rebuild ruined cities and **replant** waste fields.
Dan 4.15 this man, and let him live with the animals and the **plants.**
Hos 9.16 of Israel are like a **plant** whose roots have dried up and
10.12 'Plough new ground for yourselves, **plant** righteousness, and
10.13 But instead you **planted** evil and reaped its harvest.
Joel 2. 3 Like fire they eat up the **plants.**
Amos 5.11 build or drink wine from the beautiful vineyards you **plant.**
9.14 they will **plant** vineyards and drink the wine;
9.14 they will **plant** gardens and eat what they grow.
9.15 I will **plant** my people on the land I gave them, and
Jon 4. 6 the Lord God made a **plant** grow up over Jonah to give
4. 6 Jonah was extremely pleased with the **plant.**
4. 7 day, at God's command, a worm attacked the **plant,** and it
4. 9 him, "What right have you to be angry about the **plant?"**
4.10 Lord said to him, "This **plant** grew up in one night and
Mic 1. 6 ruins in the open country, a place for **planting** grapevines.
5. 7 the Lord for many nations, like showers on growing **plants.**
Zeph 1.13 or drink wine from the vineyards they are **planting."**
Mt 13. 6 But when the sun came up, it burnt the young **plants;**
13. 6 roots had not grown deep enough, the **plants** soon dried up.
13. 7 among thorn bushes, which grew up and choked the **plants.**
13. 8 But some seeds fell in good soil, and the **plants** produced corn;
13.26 When the **plants** grew and the ears of corn began to form,
13.32 but when it grows up, it is the biggest of all **plants.**
15.13 "Every **plant** which my Father in heaven did not plant
21.33 was once a landowner who **planted** a vineyard, put a fence
Mk 4. 6 Then, when the sun came up, it burnt the young **plants;**
4. 6 roots had not grown deep enough, the **plants** soon dried up.
4. 7 up and choked the **plants,** and they didn't produce any corn.
4. 8 in good soil, and the **plants** sprouted, grew, and produced corn:

Mk 4.28 The soil itself makes the **plants** grow and bear fruit;
4.31 the smallest seed in the world, and **plants** it in the ground.
4.32 a while it grows up and becomes the biggest of all **plants.**
12. 1 there was a man who **planted** a vineyard, put a fence round
Lk 8. 6 rocky ground, and when the **plants** sprouted, they dried up
8. 7 thorn bushes, which grew up with the **plants** and choked them.
8. 8 the **plants** grew and produced corn, a hundred grains each."
13.19 The **plant** grows and becomes a tree, and the birds make their
17. 6 'Pull yourself up by the roots and **plant** yourself in the sea!'
17.28 Everybody kept on eating and drinking, buying and selling, **planting**
20. 9 was once a man who **planted** a vineyard, let it out to
1 Cor 3. 6 the seed, Apollos watered the **plant,**
3. 6 but it was God who made the **plant** grow.
3. 7 It is God who matters, because he makes the **plant** grow.
15.37 other grain, not the full-bodied **plant** that will later grow up.
Heb 6. 7 on it and which grows **plants** that are useful to those for
12.15 one become like a bitter **plant** that grows up and causes many
Jas 1.10 the rich will pass away like the flower of a wild **plant.**
1.11 The sun rises with its blazing heat and burns the **plant;**
1.21 accept the word that he **plants** in your hearts, which is able
3.18 that is produced from the seeds the peacemakers **plant** in peace.
Rev 9. 4 not to harm the grass or the trees or any other **plant;**

PLASTER
[REPLASTERED]

Lev 14.41 walls scraped and the **plaster** dumped in an unclean place
14.42 that were removed, and new **plaster** will be used to cover the
14.43 scraped and **plastered,** [44]the priest shall go and look.
14.45 its wood, and all its **plaster** must be carried out of the
14.48 after the house has been **replastered,** he shall pronounce the
Deut 27. 2 large stones, cover them with **plaster,** [3]and write on them
27. 4 as I am instructing you today, and cover them with **plaster.**
27. 8 On the stones covered with **plaster** write clearly every
Dan 5. 5 and began writing on the **plaster** wall of the palace, where

PLATE
see also **DISH**

PLATE (1)

Ex 25.29 **plates,** cups, jars, and bowls to be used for the wine-offerings.
37.16 the **plates,** the cups, the jars, and the bowls to be used
2 Kgs 21.13 people, as clean as a **plate** that has been wiped and turned
Mt 23.25 outside of your cup and **plate,** while the inside is full of
Lk 11.39 outside of your cup and **plate,** but inside you are full of
11.41 is in your cups and **plates** to the poor, and everything will

PLATE (2)

Num 16.38 sin, beat them into thin **plates,** and make a covering for the
16.39 had them beaten into thin **plates** to make a covering for the
Is 30.22 You will take your idols **plated** with silver and your

PLATEAU

Deut 3.10 cities on the **plateau,** the regions of Gilead and of Bashan,
4.43 Reuben there was the city of Bezer, on the desert **plateau;**
Josh 13. 9 valley and included all the **plateau** from Medeba to Dibon.
13.16 of that valley and included all the **plateau** round Medeba.
13.17 It included Heshbon and all the cities on the **plateau:**
13.21 all the cities of the **plateau** and the whole kingdom of the
20. 8 the Jordan, on the desert **plateau** east of Jericho, they
1 Chr 6.78 Bezer on the **plateau,** Jahzah, [79]Kedemoth, and Mephaath.
Jer 48.21 "Judgement has come on the cities of the **plateau:**

PLATFORM

2 Kgs 16.18 removed from the Temple the **platform** for the royal throne
2 Chr 6.13 (Solomon had made a bronze **platform** and put it in the
6.13 He mounted this **platform,** knelt down where everyone could see him,
Neh 8. 4 was standing on a wooden **platform** that had been built for
8. 5 Ezra stood there on the **platform** high above the people, they
9. 4 There was a **platform** for the Levites, and on it stood Jeshua,

PLAY (1)

Gen 4.21 ancestor of all musicians who **play** the harp and the flute.
Ex 15.20 all the women followed her, **playing** tambourines and dancing.
Judg 5. 3 I will sing, I will **play** music to Israel's God, the Lord.
11.34 coming out to meet him, dancing and **playing** the tambourine.
1 Sam 10. 5 from the altar on the hill, **playing** harps, drums, flutes,
16.16 will look for a man who knows how to **play** the harp.
16.16 on you, the man can **play** his harp, and you will be
16.17 "Find me a man who **plays** well and bring him to me."
16.23 God came on Saul, David would get his harp and **play** it.
18. 6 dancing, and **playing** tambourines and lyres.
18.10 David was **playing** the harp, as he did every day, and Saul
19. 9 spear in his hand, and David was there, **playing** his harp.
2 Sam 6. 5 They were **playing** harps, lyres, drums, rattles, and
1 Kgs 1.40 back, shouting for joy and **playing** flutes, making enough
2 Kgs 3.15 As the musician **played** his harp, the power of the Lord came
1 Chr 13. 8 They sang and **played** musical instruments—harps, drums,
15.16 Levites to sing and to **play** joyful music on harps and cymbals.
15.17 they chose the following men to **play** the brass cymbals:
15.17 chose the following Levites to **play** the high-pitched harps:
15.17 To **play** the low-pitched harps they chose the following Levites:
16. 5 Eliab, Benaiah, Obed Edom, and Jeiel were to **play** harps.
1 Chr 16.42 the other instruments which were **played** when the songs of
25. 6 All his sons **played** cymbals and harps
2 Chr 5.11 them were a hundred and twenty priests **playing** trumpets.
29.27 and the musicians began to **play** the trumpets and all the
Neh 12.36 musical instruments of the kind **played** by King David, the
Ps 33. 3 a new song to him, **play** the harp with skill, and shout
43. 4 I will **play** my harp and sing praise to you, O God,
49. 4 to proverbs and explain their meaning as I **play** the harp.
71.22 On my harp I will **play** hymns to you, the Holy One
71.23 I will shout for joy as I **play** for you;
81. 2 **play** pleasant music on the harps and the lyres.
98. 5 **Play** music on the harps!
137. 5 I never be able to **play** the harp again if I forget
144. 9 I will **play** the harp and sing to you.
147. 7 **play** music on the harp to our God.
149. 3 **play** drums and harps in praise of him.
Ecc 12. 4 grinds or music as it **plays,** but even the song of a
Is 23.16 **Play** and sing your songs again to bring men back once more.
38.20 We will **play** harps and sing your praise, Sing praise in your
Jer 48.36 Kir Heres, like someone **playing** a funeral song on a flute,
Ezek 33.32 than an entertainer singing love songs or **playing** a harp.
Dan 3. 5 the trumpets, followed by the **playing** of oboes, lyres,
Amos 6. 5 like to compose songs, as David did, and **play** them on harps.
Mt 11.17 shouts to the other, [17]'We **played** wedding music for you, but
Lk 7.32 shouts to the other, 'We **played** wedding music for you, but
1 Cor 14. 7 tune that is being **played** unless the notes are sounded distinctly?
14. 8 And if the man who **plays** the bugle does not sound a
Rev 14. 2 It sounded like the music made by musicians **playing** their harps.
18.22 of human voices, of **players** of the flute and the trumpet,

PLAY (2)

Gen 21. 9 Egyptian had borne to Abraham, was **playing** with Sarah's son Isaac.
Job 21.11 Their children run and **play** like lambs [12]and dance to
40.20 Grass to feed him grows on the hills where wild beasts **play.**
Ps 104.26 and in it **plays** Leviathan, that sea-monster which you made.
Prov 12. 9 for a living than to **play** the part of a great man
26.18 only joking is like a madman **playing** with a deadly weapon.
Is 11. 8 baby will not be harmed if it **plays** near a poisonous snake.
Ezek 23.21 girl in Egypt, where men **played** with your breasts and you
Zech 8. 5 And the streets will again be full of boys and girls **playing.**

PLEAD

Gen 27.38 Esau continued to **plead** with his father:
Ex 32.11 But Moses **pleaded** with the Lord his God and said,
1 Sam 15.11 Samuel was angry, and all night long he **pleaded** with the Lord.
1 Kgs 20.32 "Your servant Benhadad **pleads** with you for his life."
2 Kgs 1.13 in front of Elijah, and **pleaded,** "Man of God, be merciful
16. 9 Pileser, in answer to Ahaz' **plea,** marched out with his army
Esth 4. 8 ask her to go and **plead** with the king and beg him
Job 8. 5 But turn now and **plead** with Almighty God;
16.21 I want someone to **plead** with God for me,
16.21 as a man **pleads** for his friend.
30.28 I stand up in public and **plead** for help.
41. 3 Will he **plead** with you for mercy?
Ps 17. 1 Listen, O Lord, to my **plea** for justice;
35.23 rise up, my God, and **plead** my cause.
55. 1 don't turn away from my **plea!**
142. 1 I **plead** with him.
143. 1 In your righteousness listen to my **plea;**
Prov 2. 3 **plead** for insight.
Jer 3.21 people of Israel crying and **pleading,** because they have
7.16 do not **plead** with me, for I will not listen to you.
11.14 don't pray to me or **plead** with me on behalf of these
15. 1 and Samuel were standing here **pleading** with me, I would not
15.11 well, if I have not **pleaded** with you on behalf of my
Dan 9. 3 the Lord God, **pleading** with him, fasting, wearing sackcloth,
9.17 O God, hear my prayer and **pleading.**
9.20 of my people Israel, and **pleading** with the Lord my God to
9.23 When you began to **plead** with God, he answered you.
Hos 2. 2 My children, **plead** with your mother—though she is no
2. 2 **Plead** with her to stop her adultery and prostitution.
Lk 18. 3 kept coming to him and **pleading** for her rights, saying,
Rom 8.26 the Spirit himself **pleads** with God for us in groans that
8.27 because the Spirit **pleads** with God on behalf of his people
8.34 is at the right-hand side of God, **pleading** with him for us!
11. 2 says in the passage where Elijah **pleads** with God against Israel:
2 Cor 5.20 We **plead** on Christ's behalf:
8. 4 they begged us and **pleaded** for the privilege of having a
Heb 7.25 because he lives for ever to **plead** with God for them.
1 Jn 2. 1 we have someone who **pleads** with the Father on our behalf

PLEASANT

Gen 27.27 He said, "The **pleasant** smell of my son is like the smell
Ps 81. 2 play **pleasant** music on the harps and the lyres.
106.24 Then they rejected the **pleasant** land, because they did
133. 1 How wonderful it is, how **pleasant,** for God's people to
147. 1 it is **pleasant** and right to praise him.
Prov 3.17 Wisdom can make your life **pleasant** and lead you safely through it.
3.22 They will provide you with life—a **pleasant** and happy life.
16.21 The more **pleasant** his words, the more persuasive he is.
Ecc 11. 7 is good to be able to enjoy the **pleasant** light of day.
Song 7.13 mandrakes, and all the **pleasant** fruits are near our door.
Is 27. 2 Lord will say of his **pleasant** vineyard, [3]"I watch over it
Ezek 34.13 streams of Israel and will feed them in **pleasant** pastures.
Hos 4.13 tall, spreading trees, because the shade is so **pleasant!**
Col 4. 6 Your speech should always be **pleasant** and interesting,

PLEASE

Gen 1. 4 God was **pleased** with what he saw.
1.10 And God was **pleased** with what he saw.
1.12 all kinds of plants, and God was **pleased** with what he saw.
1.18 And God was **pleased** with what he saw.
1.21 And God was **pleased** with what he saw.
1.25 God made them all, and he was **pleased** with what he saw.
1.31 God looked at everything he had made, and he was very **pleased.**
4. 4 The Lord was **pleased** with Abel and his offering, [5]but he
6. 8 But the Lord was **pleased** with Noah.
8.21 The odour of the sacrifice **pleased** the Lord, and he said
15. 6 of this the Lord was **pleased** with him and accepted him.
39. 4 Potiphar was **pleased** with him and made him his personal servant;
39.21 Joseph and blessed him, so that the jailer was **pleased** with him.
45.16 Joseph's brothers had come, the king and his officials were **pleased.**
Ex 29.18 The odour of this offering **pleases** me.
29.25 The odour of this offering **pleases** me.
29.41 a food offering to me, the Lord, and its odour **pleases** me.
33.12 have said that you know me well and are **pleased** with me.
33.13 plans, so that I may serve you and continue to **please** you.
33.16 anyone know that you are **pleased** with your people and with
33.17 because I know you very well and I am **pleased** with you."
34. 9 "Lord, if you really are **pleased** with me, I ask you to
Lev 1. 9 The smell of this food-offering is **pleasing** to the Lord.
1.13 The smell of this food-offering is **pleasing** to the Lord.
1.17 The smell of this food-offering is **pleasing** to the Lord.
2. 2 The smell of this food-offering is **pleasing** to the Lord.
2. 9 The smell of this food-offering is **pleasing** to the Lord.
3. 5 The smell of this food-offering is **pleasing** to the Lord.
3.16 this on the altar as a food-offering **pleasing** to the Lord.
4.31 burn it on the altar so that the smell **pleases** the Lord.
6.15 The smell of this offering is **pleasing** to the Lord.
6.21 presented as a grain-offering, a smell **pleasing** to the Lord.
8.20 a food-offering, and the smell was **pleasing** to the Lord.
8.28 This was a food-offering, and the smell was **pleasing** to the Lord.
17. 6 the fat to produce a smell that is **pleasing** to the Lord.
23.13 The smell of this offering is **pleasing** to the Lord.
23.18 The smell of this offering is **pleasing** to the Lord.
Num 14. 8 If the Lord is **pleased** with us, he will take us there
15. 3 the smell of these food-offerings is **pleasing** to the Lord.
15. 7 The smell of these sacrifices is **pleasing** to the Lord.
15.10 The smell of this sacrifice is **pleasing** to the Lord.
15.13 he presents a food-offering, a smell **pleasing** to the Lord.
15.14 a food-offering, a smell that **pleases** the Lord, he is to
15.24 a burnt-offering, a smell that **pleases** the Lord, with the
18.17 burn their fat as a food-offering, a smell **pleasing** to me.
28. 2 times the required food-offerings that are **pleasing** to him.
28. 6 Mount Sinai as a food-offering, a smell **pleasing** to the Lord.
28. 8 It also is a food-offering, a smell **pleasing** to the Lord.
28.13 food-offerings, a smell **pleasing** to the Lord.
28.24 offer to the Lord a food-offering, a smell **pleasing** to him.
28.27 Offer a burnt-offering as a smell **pleasing** to the Lord:
29. 2 Present a burnt-offering to the Lord, a smell **pleasing** to him:
29. 6 These food-offerings are a smell **pleasing** to the Lord.
29. 8 Offer a burnt-offering to the Lord, a smell **pleasing** to him:
29.13 offer a food-offering to the Lord, a smell **pleasing** to him:
29.36 as a food-offering to the Lord, a smell **pleasing** to him:
Deut 6.25 that God has commanded us, he will be **pleased** with us.'
12. 8 all been worshipping as you **please,** [9]because you have not
12.25 command, the Lord will be **pleased,** and all will go well for
12.28 be doing what is right and what **pleases** the Lord your God.
24.13 grateful, and the Lord your God will be **pleased** with you.
33.11 Be **pleased** with what they do.
Judg 6.17 Gideon replied, "If you are **pleased** with me, give me
17. 6 everyone did just as he **pleased.**
21.25 Everyone did just as he **pleased.**
1 Sam 18. 5 This **pleased** all of Saul's officers and men.
18.20 with David, and when Saul heard of this, he was **pleased.**
18.22 tell him, "The king is **pleased** with you and all his
29. 6 and I would be **pleased** to let you go with me and
2 Sam 3.36 They took note of this and were **pleased.**
3.36 Indeed, everything the king did **pleased** the people.
11.27 But the Lord was not **pleased** with what David had done.
14.22 I know that you are **pleased** with me, because you have
15.25 If the Lord is **pleased** with me, some day he will let
15.26 But if he isn't **pleased** with me—well, then, let him do
16. 4 "May I always **please** Your Majesty!"
22.20 he saved me because he was **pleased** with me.
1 Kgs 3.10 The Lord was **pleased** that Solomon had asked for this,
5. 7 Hiram was extremely **pleased** when he received Solomon's message,
10. 9 He has shown how **pleased** he is with you by making you
14.13 only one with whom the Lord, the God of Israel, is **pleased.**
15. 5 because David had done what **pleased** him and had never
15.11 Asa did what **pleased** the Lord, as his ancestor David had done.
2 Kgs 12. 2 his life he did what **pleased** the Lord, because Jehoiada the
14. 3 He did what was **pleasing** to the Lord, but he was not
15. 3 example of his father, he did what was **pleasing** to the Lord.
15.34 his father Uzziah, Jotham did what was **pleasing** to the Lord.
16. 2 he did what was not **pleasing** to the Lord his God
16.18 And in order to **please** the Assyrian emperor, Ahaz also
18. 3 ancestor King David, he did what was **pleasing** to the Lord.
22. 2 Josiah did what was **pleasing** to the Lord;
1 Chr 13. 4 The people were **pleased** with the suggestion and agreed to it.
29.17 everyone's heart and are **pleased** with people of integrity.
2 Chr 9. 8 He has shown how **pleased** he is with you by making you
10. 7 and try to **please** them by giving a considerate answer,
14. 2 Asa **pleased** the Lord, his God, by doing what was right and
2 Chr 24. 2 He did what was **pleasing** to the Lord as long as Jehoiada
24.10 This **pleased** the people and their leaders, and they
25. 2 He did what was **pleasing** to the Lord, but did it reluctantly.
26. 4 example of his father, he did what was **pleasing** to the Lord.
27. 2 He did what was **pleasing** to the Lord, just as his father
28. 1 he did what was not **pleasing** to the Lord [2]and followed the
29. 2 ancestor King David, he did what was **pleasing** to the Lord.
30. 4 king and the people were **pleased** with their plan, [5]so they
31.20 what was right and what was **pleasing** to the Lord his God.
34. 2 He did what was **pleasing** to the Lord;
Ezra 5.17 "Now, if it **please** Your Majesty, let a search be made
10.11 Lord, the God of your ancestors, and do what **pleases** him.
Neh 2. 5 emperor, "If Your Majesty is **pleased** with me and is willing
9.24 power to do as they **pleased** with the people and kings of
9.37 They do as they **please** with us and our livestock, and we
12.44 of Judah were **pleased** with the priests and the Levites,
Esth 1.19 If it **please** Your Majesty, issue a royal proclamation
3. 9 If it **please** Your Majesty, issue a decree that they are to
5. 4 Esther replied, "If it **please** Your Majesty, I would like
7. 3 Queen Esther answered, "If it **please** Your Majesty to
8. 5 up and said, [5]"If it **please** Your Majesty, and if you care
9.13 Esther answered, "If it **please** Your Majesty, let the
Job 14.15 I will answer, and you will be **pleased** with me, your creature.
31.29 enemies suffered, or **pleased** when they met with disaster;
Ps 5. 4 You are not a God who is **pleased** with wrongdoing;
18.19 he saved me because he was **pleased** with me.
20. 3 all your offerings and be **pleased** with all your sacrifices.
35.27 He is **pleased** with the success of his servant."
37.23 in the way he should go and protects those who **please** him.
41.11 over me, and I will know that you are **pleased** with me.
51.16 you are not **pleased** with burnt-offerings.
51.19 Then you will be **pleased** with proper sacrifices
69.31 This will **please** the Lord more than offering him cattle,
77. 7 Will he never again be **pleased** with us?
104.34 May he be **pleased** with my song, for my gladness comes
Prov 3. 4 you do this, both God and man will be **pleased** with you.
8.31 happy with the world and **pleased** with the human race.
8.35 finds me finds life, and the Lord will be **pleased** with him.
12. 2 The Lord is **pleased** with good people, but condemns those
12.22 Lord hates liars, but is **pleased** with those who keep their word.
14.35 Kings are **pleased** with competent officials, but they
15. 8 The Lord is **pleased** when good men pray, but hates the
15.26 The Lord hates evil thoughts, but he is **pleased** with friendly words.
16. 7 When you **please** the Lord, you can make your enemies into friends.
21. 3 that **pleases** the Lord more than bringing him sacrifices.
Ecc 2.26 to those who **please** him, but he makes sinners work,
2.26 that what they get can be given to those who **please** him.
7.26 A man who **pleases** God can get away, but she will catch
Is 42. 1 strengthen— the one I have chosen, with whom I am **pleased.**
53.11 servant, with whom I am **pleased,** will bear the punishment of
56. 4 if you do what **pleases** me and faithfully keep my covenant,
56.11 one of them does as he **pleases** and seeks his own advantage.
57. 6 Do you think I am **pleased** with all this?
58. 5 Do you think I will be **pleased** with that?
60. 7 as sacrifices And offered on the altar to **please** the Lord.
62. 4 Your new name will be "God Is **Pleased** with Her."
62. 4 Married," Because the Lord is **pleased** with you
66. 2 I am **pleased** with those who are humble and repentant, who
66. 3 "The people do as they **please.**
Jer 2.31 you will do as you **please,** that you will never come back
6.20 not accept their offerings or be **pleased** with their sacrifices.
9.24 These are the things that **please** me.
14.10 So I am not **pleased** with them.
14.12 and grain-offerings, I will not be **pleased** with them.
34.15 few days ago you changed your minds and did what **pleased** me.
42. 6 Whether it **pleases** us or not, we will obey the Lord our
Ezek 20.39 "And now, all you Israelites, **please** yourselves!
20.40 I will be **pleased** with you and will expect you to bring
31.16 gone to the world below will be **pleased** at its downfall.
43.27 Then I will be **pleased** with all of you.
Dan 8. 4 He did as he **pleased** and grew arrogant.
9.13 we have not tried to **please** you by turning from our sins
11.16 The Syrian invader will do with them as he **pleases,**
11.28 He will do as he **pleases** and then return to his own
11.36 "The king of Syria will do as he **pleases.**
Hos 8.13 I, the Lord, am not **pleased** with them, and now I will
Jon 4. 6 Jonah was extremely **pleased** with the plant.
Mic 6. 7 Will the Lord be **pleased** if I bring him thousands of sheep
Hag 1. 8 then I will be **pleased** and will be worshipped as I should
Mal 1. 8 Would he be **pleased** with you or grant you any favours?"
1.10 I am not **pleased** with you;
3. 4 to the Lord will be **pleasing** to him, as they used to
Mt 3.17 "This is my own dear Son, with whom I am **pleased."**
7. 4 you say to your brother, **'Please,** let me take that speck out
12.18 have chosen, the one I love, and with whom I am **pleased.**
14. 6 Herod was so **pleased** [7]that he promised her, "I swear that
17. 5 my own dear Son, with whom I am **pleased**—listen to him!"
17.12 did not recognize him, but treated him just as they **pleased.**
Mk 1.11 I am **pleased** with you."
5.23 **Please** come and place your hands on her, so that she will
6.22 Herodias came in and danced, and **pleased** Herod and his guests.
9.13 him just as they **pleased,** as the Scriptures say about him."
14.11 They were **pleased** to hear what he had to say, and
15.15 Pilate wanted to **please** the crowd, so he set Barabbas free
Lk 2.14 and peace on earth to those with whom he is **pleased!"**
3.22 I am **pleased** with you."
6.42 you say to your brother, **'Please,** brother, let me take that
12.32 flock, for your Father is **pleased** to give you the Kingdom.
14.18 **please** accept my apologies.'
14.19 **please** accept my apologies.'

Lk 22. 5 They were **pleased** and offered to pay him money.
23. 8 Herod was very **pleased** when he saw Jesus, because he had
Jn 8.29 not left me alone, because I always do what **pleases** him."
Acts 6. 5 The whole group was **pleased** with the apostles' proposal,
7.10 God gave him a **pleasing** manner and wisdom, and the king
8.24 said to Peter and John, **"Please** pray to the Lord for me,
9.38 to him with the message, **"Please** hurry and come to us."
10. 4 The angel answered, "God is **pleased** with your prayers and works
12. 3 When he saw that this **pleased** the Jews, he went on to
21.39 **Please** let me speak to the people."
Rom 8. 8 Those who obey their human nature cannot **please** God.
12. 1 sacrifice to God, dedicated to his service and **pleasing** to him.
12. 2 God—what is good and is **pleasing** to him and is perfect.
14.18 in this way, he **pleases** God and is approved by others.
15. 1 We should not **please** ourselves.
15. 2 Instead, we should all **please** our brothers for their own good,
15. 3 For Christ did not **please** himself.
1 Cor 7.32 the Lord's work, because he is trying to **please** the Lord.
7.33 with worldly matters, because he wants to **please** his wife;
7.34 with worldly matters, because she wants to **please** her husband.
10. 5 even then God was not **pleased** with most of them, and so
10.33 I try to **please** everyone in all that I do, not thinking
2 Cor 5. 9 however, we want to **please** him, whether in our home here
11. 1 **Please** do!
12.13 **Please** forgive me for being so unfair!
Eph 5. 2 as a sweet-smelling offering and sacrifice that **pleases** God.
5.10 Try to learn what **pleases** the Lord.
Phil 4. 2 Euodia and Syntyche, **please,** I beg you, try to agree as
4.18 to God, a sacrifice which is acceptable and **pleasing** to him.
Col 1.10 live as the Lord wants and will always do what **pleases** him.
3.20 to obey your parents always, for that is what **pleases** God.
1 Thes 2. 4 We do not try to **please** men, but to please God,
2.12 the kind of life that **pleases** God, who calls you to share
4. 1 learnt from us how you should live in order to **please** God.
1 Tim 2. 3 This is good and it **pleases** God our Saviour,
5. 4 repay their parents and grandparents, because that is what **pleases** God.
2 Tim 2. 4 on active service wants to **please** his commanding officer and so
Tit 2. 9 to submit to their masters and **please** them in all things.
Phlm 20 So, my brother, **please** do me this favour for the Lord's sake;
Heb 10. 6 You are not **pleased** with animals burnt whole on the altar
10. 8 neither want nor are you **pleased** with sacrifices and offerings
10.38 any of them turns back, I will not be **pleased** with him."
11. 5 says that before Enoch was taken up, he had **pleased** God.
11. 6 No one can **please** God without faith, for whoever comes to
12.28 God in a way that will **please** him, with reverence and awe;
13.16 because these are the sacrifices that **please** God.
13.20 and may he, through Jesus Christ, do in us what **pleases** him.
2 Pet 1.17 saying, "This is my own dear Son, with whom I am **pleased!"**
1 Jn 3.22 ask, because we obey his commands and do what **pleases** him.
3 Jn 6 **Please** help them to continue their journey
6 to continue their journey in a way that will **please** God.

PLEASURE

2 Sam 19.35 eighty years old, and nothing gives me **pleasure** any more.
1 Chr 28. 4 that family it was his **pleasure** to take me and make me
Ps 16. 3 My greatest **pleasure** is to be with them.
16.11 your presence fills me with joy and brings me **pleasure** for ever.
62. 4 you take **pleasure** in lies.
112. 1 the Lord, who takes **pleasure** in obeying his commands.
119.16 I take **pleasure** in your laws;
119.24 Your instructions give me **pleasure;**
119.47 I find **pleasure** in obeying your commands, because I love them.
119.70 These men have no understanding, but I find **pleasure** in your law.
119.77 me, and I will live because I take **pleasure** in your law.
147.10 His **pleasure** is not in strong horses, nor his delight in
147.11 but he takes **pleasure** in those who honour him, in those
149. 4 The Lord takes **pleasure** in his people;
Prov 2.10 You will become wise, and your knowledge will give you **pleasure.**
2.14 of sin, [14]men who find **pleasure** in doing wrong and who
10.23 Intelligent people take **pleasure** in wisdom.
17. 5 You will be punished if you take **pleasure** in someone's misfortune.
Ecc 2. 2 that laughter is foolish, that **pleasure** does you no good.
2.10 I did not deny myself any **pleasure.**
4. 8 For whom is he working so hard and denying himself any **pleasure?**
8.15 enjoy himself, because the only **pleasure** he has in this life
Is 11. 3 have reverence for him, [3]and find **pleasure** in obeying him.
47. 8 to this, you lover of **pleasure,** you that think you are safe
58. 2 just laws and that they take **pleasure** in worshipping me."
66. 3 They take **pleasure** in disgusting ways of worship.
Jer 32.41 I will take **pleasure** in doing good things for them, and
Lam 3.33 He takes no **pleasure** in causing us grief or pain.
Mic 7.18 but you take **pleasure** in showing us your constant love.
Lk 8.14 the worries and riches and **pleasures** of this life crowd in
Eph 1. 5 he would make us his sons—this was his **pleasure** and purpose.
2 Thes 2.12 but have taken **pleasure** in sin, will be condemned.
1 Tim 5. 6 widow who gives herself to **pleasure** has already died,
2 Tim 3. 4 they will love **pleasure** rather than God;
Tit 3. 3 We were slaves to passions and **pleasures** of all kinds.
Jas 4. 1 your desires for **pleasure,** which are constantly fighting within
4. 3 you ask for things to use for your own **pleasures.**
5. 5 Your life here on earth has been full of luxury and **pleasure.**
2 Pet 2.13 **Pleasure** for them is to do anything in broad daylight that

PLEDGE

Gen 38.17 me something to keep as a **pledge** until you send the goat."
38.18 "What shall I give you as a **pledge?"**
38.20 the articles he had **pledged,** but Hirah could not find her.
43. 9 I will **pledge** my own life, and you can hold me responsible
44.32 What is more, I **pledged** my life to my father for the
Ex 22.26 take someone's cloak as a **pledge** that he will pay you, you
Josh 24.23 have," he demanded, "and **pledge** your loyalty to the Lord,
2 Sam 15.13 "The Israelites are **pledging** their loyalty to Absalom."

PLEIADES

A small group of stars visible during winter evenings.

Job 9. 9 Great Bear, Orion, the **Pleiades,** and the stars of the south.
38.31 Can you tie the **Pleiades** together or loosen the bonds
Amos 5. 8 The Lord made the stars, the **Pleiades** and Orion.

PLENTY

Gen 13.10 the way to Zoar, had **plenty** of water, like the Garden of
24.25 "There is **plenty** of straw and fodder at our house, and
27.28 May he give you **plenty** of corn and wine!
41.29 be seven years of great **plenty** in all the land of Egypt.
41.31 The time of **plenty** will be entirely forgotten, because
41.34 take a fifth of the crops during the seven years of **plenty.**
41.47 During the seven years of **plenty** the land produced abundant crops,
41.53 The seven years of **plenty** that the land of Egypt had
Lev 26. 5 Your crops will be so **plentiful** that you will still be
26.10 Your harvests will be so **plentiful** that they will last
Num 11.33 While there was still **plenty** of meat for them to eat,
Deut 28.38 "You will sow **plenty** of seed, but reap only a small harvest,
32.14 Their cows and goats gave **plenty** of milk;
Ruth 1.21 I left here, I had **plenty,** but the Lord has brought me
1 Kgs 10.27 stone, and cedar was as **plentiful** as ordinary sycomore in
2 Kgs 3.17 livestock, and your pack-animals will have **plenty** to drink.'
1 Chr 4.40 They found **plenty** of fertile pasture lands there in a
4.41 because there was **plenty** of pasture for their sheep.
2 Chr 1.15 and cedar was as **plentiful** as ordinary sycomore.
9.27 stone, and cedar was as **plentiful** as ordinary sycomore in
Job 29. 6 My cows and goats gave **plenty** of milk, and my olive-trees
Ps 65.11 Wherever you go there is **plenty.**
72.16 May there be **plenty** of corn in the land;
73.12 They have **plenty** and are always getting more.
104.16 The cedars of Lebanon get **plenty** of rain— the Lord's own
144.14 May our cattle reproduce **plentifully** without miscarriage or loss.
Prov 7.20 He took **plenty** of money with him and won't be back for
12.11 A hard-working farmer has **plenty** to eat, but it is
13.23 Unused fields could yield **plenty** of food for the poor,
20.13 Keep busy and you will have **plenty** to eat.
21. 5 Plan carefully and you will have **plenty;**
28.19 A hard-working farmer has **plenty** to eat.
Is 30.23 harvest, and your livestock will have **plenty** of pasture.
32.20 happy everyone will be with **plenty** of water for the crops
58.11 like a garden that has **plenty** of water, like a spring of
65.13 and obey me will have **plenty** to eat and drink, but you
Jer 44.17 Then we had **plenty** of food, we were prosperous, and had no
Ezek 16.49 were proud because they had **plenty** to eat and lived in peace
19.10 Because there was **plenty** of water, the vine was covered with
36.29 command the corn to be **plentiful,** so that you will not have
Joel 2.22 bear their fruit, and there are **plenty** of figs and grapes.
2.26 Now you will have **plenty** to eat, and be satisfied.
3.18 there will be **plenty** of water for all the streams of Judah.
Zech 8.12 earth will produce crops, and there will be **plenty** of rain.
Mal 3.10 to the Temple, so that there will be **plenty** of food there.
Jn 2.10 after the guests have had **plenty** to drink, he serves the
3.23 from Salim, because there was **plenty** of water in that place.
2 Cor 8.13 but since you have **plenty** at this time, it is only fair
8.13 you are in need and they have **plenty,** they will help you.

PLOT (1)

Gen 37.18 before he reached them, they **plotted** against him and decided
50.20 You **plotted** evil against me, but God turned it into good,
Ex 10.10 It is clear that you are **plotting** to revolt.
1 Sam 22. 8 Is that why you are **plotting** against me?
22.13 Saul asked him, "Why are you and David **plotting** against me?
22.15 As for **plotting** against you, Your Majesty must not accuse me
2 Sam 15.11 they knew nothing of the **plot** and went in all good faith.
15.12 The **plot** against the king gained strength, and Absalom's
1 Kgs 15.27 of the tribe of Issachar, **plotted** against Nadab and killed
16. 9 in charge of half the king's chariots, **plotted** against him.
16.16 Zimri had **plotted** against the king and assassinated him,
2 Kgs 9.14 Then Jehu **plotted** against King Joram, who was in Jezreel,
10. 9 "I was the one who **plotted** against King Joram and killed him;
12.20 King Joash's officials **plotted** against him, and two of them,
14.19 There was a **plot** in Jerusalem to assassinate Amaziah,
15.25 Pekah son of Remaliah, **plotted** with fifty men from Gilead,
15.30 Hoshea son of Elah **plotted** against King Pekah, assassinated him,
21.23 Amon's officials **plotted** against him and assassinated him
2 Chr 24.25 two of his officials **plotted** against him and killed him
24.26 (Those who **plotted** against him were Zabad, the son of an
25.17 King Amaziah of Judah and his advisers **plotted** against Israel.
25.27 the Lord, there had been a **plot** against him in Jerusalem.
33.24 Amon's officials **plotted** against him and assassinated him
Neh 4. 8 So they all **plotted** together to come and attack Jerusalem
4.15 found out what they were **plotting,** and they realized that
Esth 2.21 hostile to King Xerxes and **plotted** to assassinate him.
3. 7 find out the right day and month to carry out his **plot.**
6. 2 how Mordecai had uncovered a **plot** to assassinate the king—
6. 2 the **plot** made by Bigthana and Teresh,
8. 3 to stop the evil **plot** that Haman, the descendant of Agag,
8. 7 have hanged Haman for his **plot** against the Jews, and I have
Ps 2. 1 Why do people make their useless **plots?**
2. 2 Their kings revolt, their rulers **plot** together against the

Ps 5.10 may their own **plots** cause their ruin.
21.11 They make their plans, and **plot** against him, but they
31.13 They are making plans against me, **plotting** to kill me.
31.20 them in the safety of your presence from the **plots** of men;
35. 4 May those who **plot** against me be turned back and confused!
37.12 The wicked man **plots** against the good man and glares at
38.12 they never stop **plotting** against me.
64. 2 Protect me from the **plots** of the wicked, from mobs of evil
64. 5 They encourage each other in their evil **plots;**
71.10 they talk and **plot** against me.
83. 3 they are **plotting** against those you protect.
94.21 who make injustice legal, [21] who **plot** against good men and
119.23 The rulers meet and **plot** against me, but I will study
140. 2 They are always **plotting** evil, always stirring up quarrels.
140. 4 keep me safe from violent men who **plot** my downfall.
140. 8 don't let their **plots** succeed.
Is 7. 5 Syria, together with Israel and its king, has made a **plot.**
32. 7 he **plots** to ruin the poor with lies and to prevent them
50.11 All of you that **plot** to destroy others
50.11 will be destroyed by your own **plots.**
59. 5 The evil **plots** you make are as deadly as the eggs of
59. 5 But your **plots** will do you no good—they are as useless
Jer 11. 9 "The people of Judah and of Jerusalem are **plotting** against me.
11.18 Lord informed me of the **plots** that my enemies were making
18.23 But, Lord, you know all their **plots** to kill me.
48. 2 captured Heshbon and **plot** to destroy the nation of Moab.
49.30 King Nebuchadnezzar of Babylonia has **plotted** against you,
Lam 3.60 know how my enemies hate me and how they **plot** against me.
3.61 you know all their **plots.**
Hos 7. 3 "People deceive the king and his officers by their evil **plots.**
7. 6 Yes, they burned like an oven with their **plotting.**
7.15 them up and made them strong, they **plotted** against me.
Amos 7.10 "Amos is **plotting** against you among the people.
Nah 1. 9 What are you **plotting** against the Lord?
1.11 a man full of wicked schemes, who **plotted** against the Lord.
Mt 12.15 When Jesus heard about the **plot** against him, he went away
Acts 4.25 why did people make their useless **plots?**
20. 3 when he discovered that the Jews were **plotting** against him;
20.19 times that came to me because of the **plots** of the Jews.
23.16 But the son of Paul's sister heard about the **plot;**
23.30 informed that there was a **plot** against him, at once I
25. 3 for they had made a **plot** to kill him on the way.

PLOT (2)

Ezek 45. 2 is to be a square **plot** of land for the Temple, 250

PLOUGH

Gen 45. 6 years in which there will be neither **ploughing** nor reaping.
Ex 34.21 the seventh day, not even during **ploughing** time or harvest.
Deut 21. 4 the ground has never been **ploughed** or planted, and there
22.10 "Do not hitch an ox and a donkey together for **ploughing.**
Judg 14.18 "If you hadn't been **ploughing** with my cow, You wouldn't
1 Sam 8.12 Your sons will have to **plough** his fields, harvest his crops,
13.20 Philistines to get their **ploughs,** hoes, axes, and sickles sharpened;
13.21 ox-goads, and two coins for sharpening **ploughs** or hoes.)
1 Kgs 19.19 Elijah left and found Elisha **ploughing** with a team of oxen;
19.19 teams ahead of him, and he was **ploughing** with the last one.
Job 1.14 "We were **ploughing** the fields with the oxen," he said,
4. 8 I have seen people **plough** fields of evil and sow
5.23 The fields you **plough** will be free of rocks;
39.10 Can you hold one with a rope and make him **plough?**
Ps 65.10 rain on the **ploughed** fields and soak them with water;
129. 3 deep wounds in my back and made it like a **ploughed** field.
Prov 14. 4 any oxen to pull the **plough** your barn will be empty, but
20. 4 who is too lazy to **plough** his fields at the right time
Is 2. 4 They will hammer their swords into **ploughs**
28.24 No farmer goes on constantly **ploughing** his fields and
30.24 The oxen and donkeys that **plough** your fields will eat
Jer 4. 3 of Judah and Jerusalem, **"Plough** up your unploughed fields;
26.18 'Zion will be **ploughed** like a field, Jerusalem will become a
51.23 and their flocks, to slaughter **ploughmen** and their horses,
Ezek 36. 9 sure that your land is **ploughed** again and that seeds are
Hos 10. 4 injustice, growing like poisonous weeds in a **ploughed** field.
10.11 I made Judah pull the **plough** and Israel pull the harrow.
10.12 I said, **'Plough** new ground for yourselves, plant righteousness,
Joel 3.10 Hammer the points of your **ploughs** into swords
Amos 6.12 Do men **plough** the sea with oxen?
Mic 3.12 Zion will be **ploughed** like a field,
4. 3 They will hammer their swords into **ploughs**
Lk 9.62 "Anyone who starts to **plough** and then keeps looking back is
17. 7 has a servant who is **ploughing** or looking after the sheep.
1 Cor 9.10 The man who **ploughs** and the man who reaps should do their

PLUMAGE

Ezek 17. 7 "There was another giant eagle with huge wings and thick **plumage.**

PLUMB LINE

see also **LINE (3)**

Is 28.17 for the foundation, and honesty will be its **plumb-line."**
Amos 7. 7 with the help of a **plumb-line,**
7. 7 and there was a **plumb-line** in his hand.
7. 8 "A **plumb-line,"** I answered.

PLUNDER

Num 31. 9 their cattle and their flocks, **plundered** all their wealth,
Deut 2.35 We took the livestock and **plundered** the towns.
3. 7 We took the livestock and **plundered** the towns.
1 Sam 14.36 the Philistines in the night, **plunder** them until dawn, and
31. 8 battle the Philistines went to **plunder** the corpses, and they
2 Kgs 21.14 their enemies, who will conquer them and **plunder** their land.
1 Chr 10. 8 battle, the Philistines went to **plunder** the corpses, and
14. 9 The Philistines arrived at the Valley of Rephaim and began **plundering.**
14.13 returned to the valley and started **plundering** it again.
2 Chr 14.14 The army **plundered** all those cities
Is 3.14 "You have **plundered** vineyards, and your houses are full of
8. 1 'Quick Loot, Fast **Plunder.'**
11.14 Philistines on the west and **plunder** the people who live to
17.14 That is the fate of everyone who **plunders** our land.
42.22 But now his people have been **plundered;**
42.22 They were robbed and **plundered,** with no one to come to their
Jer 12.12 Across all the desert highlands men have come to **plunder.**
18.22 Send a mob to **plunder** their homes without warning;
20. 5 will also let their enemies **plunder** all the wealth of this
30.16 and all who **plunder** you will be plundered.
50.11 The Lord says, "People of Babylonia, you **plundered** my nation.
50.37 **plunder** and loot.
Ezek 25. 7 you over to other nations who will rob you and **plunder** you.
26. 5 The nations will **plunder** Tyre, [6] and with their swords they
29.19 He will loot and **plunder** it and carry off all the wealth
30. 4 The country will be **plundered** And left in ruins.
34.28 The heathen nations will not **plunder** them any more, and
36. 3 nations captured and **plundered** the mountains of Israel,
36. 4 you deserted cities which were **plundered** and mocked by all
38.12 You will **plunder** and loot the people who live in cities
38.13 your army and attacked in order to loot and **plunder?**
39.10 They will loot and **plunder** those who looted and plundered them."
Amos 3.11 land, destroy their defences, and **plunder** their mansions."
Nah 2. 2 of Israel, as it was before her enemies **plundered** her.)
2. 9 **Plunder** the silver!
2. 9 **Plunder** the gold!
3. 1 murderous city, full of wealth to be looted and **plundered!**
Hab 2. 7 They will **plunder** you!
2. 8 You have **plundered** the people of many nations, but now
2. 8 those who have survived will **plunder** you because of the
Zeph 1. 7 his people and has invited enemies to **plunder** Judah.
2. 9 people who survive will **plunder** them and take their land."
Zech 2. 8 this message for the nations that had **plundered** his people:
2. 9 you, and you will be **plundered** by the people who were once
Mt 12.29 then he can **plunder** his house.
Mk 3.27 then he can **plunder** his house.

PLUNGE

Judg 3.21 from his right side and **plunged** it into the king's belly.
1 Sam 26. 8 Now let me **plunge** his own spear through him and pin him
2 Sam 2.16 by the head and **plunged** his sword into his opponent's side,
18.14 He took three spears and **plunged** them into Absalom's chest
Ps 107.26 lifted high in the air and **plunged** down into the depths.
Ezek 32. 8 the lights of heaven and **plunge** your world into darkness.
Jn 19.34 One of the soldiers, however, **plunged** his spear into Jesus'

PLURAL

Gal 3.16 scripture does not use the **plural** "descendants," meaning many

POCKET

Mt 10. 9 Do not carry any gold, silver, or copper money in your **pockets;**
Mk 6. 8 a stick—no bread, no beggar's bag, no money in your **pockets.**

PODS

[BEAN PODS]

Lk 15.16 fill himself with the **bean pods** the pigs ate,

POETRY

[POEM]

Num 21.27 That is why the **poets** sing,
Ps 45. 1 pen of a good writer my tongue is ready with a **poem.**
Acts 17.28 is as some of your **poets** have said, 'We too are his

POINT (1)

Josh 15. 1 south to the southernmost **point** of the wilderness of Zin,
16. 1 Jordan near Jericho, at a **point** east of the springs of Jericho,
Judg 20.43 them as far as a **point** east of Gibeah, killing them as
2 Chr 32.30 through a tunnel to a **point** inside the walls of Jerusalem.
33.14 of David's City, from a **point** in the valley near the spring
Neh 3.25 the next section, to a **point** on the east near the Water
3.27 their second one, from a **point** opposite the large tower
Ezek 47.18 boundary runs south from a **point** between the territory of
47.20 Mediterranean and runs north to a **point** west of Hamath Pass.
Dan 9.27 be placed on the highest **point** of the Temple and will remain
Mt 4. 5 set him on the highest **point** of the Temple, [6] and said
Lk 4. 9 set him on the highest **point** of the Temple, and said to

POINT (2)

Josh 8.18 Then the Lord said to Joshua, **"Point** your spear at Ai;
8.25 Joshua kept his spear **pointed** at Ai and did not
1 Kgs 13. 4 King Jeroboam heard this, he **pointed** at him and ordered,

Jer	4. 6	**Point** the way to Zion!
Ezek	16. 2	"Mortal man," he said, "**point** out to Jerusalem what
	30.25	him my sword and he **points** it towards Egypt, everyone will
	46.19	He **pointed** out a place on the west side of the rooms
Dan	8. 8	horns came up, each **pointing** in a different direction.
Mt	12.49	Then he **pointed** to his disciples and said, "Look!
Heb	9. 9	This is an illustration which **points** to the present time.
1 Pet	1.11	Christ's Spirit in them was **pointing**, in predicting the sufferings
	3.21	which was a symbol **pointing** to baptism, which now saves you.

POINT (3)

1 Kgs	6.31	the top of the doorway was a **pointed** arch.
Job	20.25	its shiny **point** drips with his blood, and terror grips his heart.
Jer	17. 1	your hearts with a diamond **point** and carved on the corners
Joel	3.10	Hammer the **points** of your ploughs into swords

POINT (4)

Mt	5.18	earth last, not the least **point** nor the smallest detail of

POISON

Gen	49.17	side of the road, A **poisonous** snake beside the path, That
Num	21. 6	Then the Lord sent **poisonous** snakes among the people, and
Deut	8.15	desert where there were **poisonous** snakes and scorpions.
	29.18	like a root that grows to be a bitter and **poisonous** plant.
	32.24	animals to attack them, and **poisonous** snakes to bite them.
	32.32	vines that bear bitter and **poisonous** grapes, [33] like wine
2 Kgs	4.40	they tasted it they exclaimed to Elisha, "It's **poisoned**!"—
Job	6. 4	me with arrows, and their **poison** spreads through my body.
	20.14	the food turns bitter, as bitter as any **poison** could be.
	20.16	What the evil man swallows is like **poison;**
Ps	58. 4	They are full of **poison** like snakes;
	69.21	When I was hungry, they gave me **poison;**
	91.13	lions and snakes, fierce lions and **poisonous** snakes.
	140. 3	their words are like a cobra's **poison.**
Prov	23.32	will feel as if you had been bitten by a **poisonous** snake.
	25.26	evil reminds you of a polluted spring or a **poisoned** well.
Is	11. 8	baby will not be harmed if it plays near a **poisonous** snake.
	30. 6	and where there are **poisonous** snakes and flying dragons.
	59. 5	you make are as deadly as the eggs of a **poisonous** snake.
Jer	8.14	he has given us **poison** to drink, because we have sinned
	8.17	snakes among you, **poisonous** snakes that cannot be charmed,
	9.15	give my people bitter plants to eat and **poison** to drink.
	23.15	bitter plants to eat and **poison** to drink, because they have
Lam	3.19	The thought of my pain, my homelessness, is bitter **poison;**
Hos	10. 4	injustice, growing like **poisonous** weeds in a ploughed field.
Amos	6.12	Yet you have turned justice into **poison,** and right into wrong.
Mk	16.18	pick up snakes or drink any **poison,** they will not be harmed;
Rom	3.13	and dangerous threats, like snake's **poison,** from their lips;
Heb	12.15	that grows up and causes many troubles with its **poison.**
Jas	3. 8	It is evil and uncontrollable, full of deadly **poison.**

POLE

Gen	40.19	hang your body on a **pole,** and the birds will eat your
Ex	25.15	The **poles** are to be left in the rings and must not
	25.27	The rings to hold the **poles** for carrying the table are
	25.28	Make the **poles** of acacia-wood and cover them with gold.
	30. 4	two sides to hold the **poles** with which it is to be
	30. 5	Make these **poles** of acacia-wood and cover them with gold.
	35.12	the Covenant Box, its **poles,** its lid, and the curtain to
	35.13	the table, its **poles,** and all its equipment;
	35.15	the altar for burning incense and its **poles;**
	35.16	bronze grating attached, its **poles,** and all its equipment;
	37.14	The rings to hold the **poles** for carrying the table were
	37.15	He made the **poles** of acacia-wood and covered them with gold.
	37.27	two sides, to hold the **poles** with which it was to be
	37.28	He made the **poles** of acacia-wood and covered them with gold.
	39.35	the Covenant Box containing the stone tablets, its **poles,**
	39.39	with its bronze grating, its **poles,** and all its equipment;
	40.20	He put the **poles** in the rings of the box and put
Num	13.23	it took two men to carry it on a **pole** between them.
	21. 8	and put it on a **pole,** so that anyone who was bitten
	21. 9	So Moses made a bronze snake and put it on a **pole.**
1 Kgs	8. 7	wings covered the box and the **poles** it was carried by.
	8. 8	The ends of the **poles** could be seen by anyone standing
	8. 8	(The **poles** are still there today.)
1 Chr	15.15	The Levites carried it on **poles** on their shoulders, as
2 Chr	5. 9	The ends of the **poles** could be seen by anyone standing
	5. 9	(The **poles** are still there today.)
Jn	3.14	the bronze snake on a **pole** in the desert, in the same

POLICE

Mt	5.25	hand you over to the **police,** and you will be put in
Lk	12.58	hand you over to the **police,** and you will be put in
Acts	16.35	the Roman authorities sent **police** officers with the order,
	16.37	Paul said to the **police** officers, "We were not found guilty
	16.38	**police** officers reported these words to the Roman officials;

POLICIES

2 Chr	27. 7	reign, his wars, and his **policies,** are all recorded in The
Mic	6.16	You have continued their **policies,** and so I will bring you

POLISHED

2 Sam	1.21	the shield of Saul is no longer **polished** with oil.
1 Kgs	7.40	which Huram made for King Solomon, was of **polished** bronze.
2 Chr	4.11	out of **polished** bronze, as King Solomon had commanded,
Job	37.18	stretch out the sky and make it as hard as **polished** metal?
Ezek	1. 7	They shone like **polished** bronze.
	8. 2	and from the waist up he was shining like **polished** bronze.
	21. 9	A sword, a sword is sharpened and **polished.**
	21.10	It is sharpened to kill, **polished** to flash like lightning.
	21.11	The sword is being **polished,** to make it ready for use.
	21.11	It is sharpened and **polished,** to be put in the hands of
	21.28	It is **polished** to kill, to flash like lightning.
Dan	10. 6	arms and legs shone like **polished** bronze, and his voice
Rev	1.15	that has been refined and **polished,** and his voice sounded
	2.18	whose eyes blaze like fire, whose feet shine like **polished** brass.

POLITE

Prov	18.23	he has to beg **politely,** but when the rich man answers,

POLITICIAN

Is	3. 3	military and civilian leaders, their **politicians** and
Jer	24. 8	King Zedekiah of Judah, the **politicians** round him, and the

POLLUTE

Prov	25.26	evil reminds you of a **polluted** spring or a poisoned well.
Ezek	32. 2	You muddy the water with your feet and **pollute** the rivers.

POMEGRANATE

A reddish fruit about the size of a large apple. It has a hard rind and is full of tasty seeds.

Ex	28.33	round its lower hem put **pomegranates** of blue, purple, and
	39.24	lower hem they put **pomegranates** of fine linen and of blue,
Num	13.23	They also brought back some **pomegranates** and figs.
	20. 5	There's no corn, no figs, no grapes, no **pomegranates.**
Deut	8. 8	that produces wheat and barley, grapes, figs, **pomegranates,**
1 Sam	14. 2	who was camping under a **pomegranate-tree** in Migron,
1 Kgs	7.18	interwoven chains, [18] and two rows of bronze **pomegranates.**
	7.20	There were two hundred **pomegranates** in two rows round each capital.
	7.40	The four hundred bronze **pomegranates,** in two rows of
2 Kgs	25.17	bronze grating decorated with **pomegranates** made of bronze.
2 Chr	3.16	of interwoven chains and one hundred bronze **pomegranates.**
	4.11	The four hundred bronze **pomegranates** arranged in two
Song	4.13	They grow like an orchard of **pomegranate-trees**
	6.11	on the vines and the blossoms on the **pomegranate-trees.**
	7.12	are opening and the **pomegranate-trees** are in bloom.
	8. 2	I would give you spiced wine, my **pomegranate** wine to drink.
Jer	52.21	was a grating decorated with **pomegranates,** all of which was
	52.23	column there were a hundred **pomegranates** in all, and
Hag	2.19	**pomegranates,** and olive-trees have not yet produced,

POMP

Acts	25.23	and Bernice came with great **pomp** and ceremony and entered the

POND

2 Kgs	18.17	work, by the ditch that brings water from the upper **pond.**
Ecc	2. 6	I dug **ponds** to irrigate them.
Is	36. 2	work, by the ditch that brings water from the upper **pond.**
Ezek	47.11	water in the marshes and **ponds** along the shore will not be

POOL

Ex	7.19	hold it out over all the rivers, canals, and **pools** in Egypt.
	8. 5	rivers, the canals, and the **pools,** and make frogs come up
Josh	15.19	She answered, "I want some **pools** of water.
Judg	1.15	She answered, "I want some **pools** of water.
2 Sam	2.13	officials met them at the **pool,** where they all sat down, one
	2.13	on one side of the **pool** and the other group on the
	4.12	hands and feet, which they hung up near the **pool** in Hebron.
1 Kgs	22.38	was cleaned up at the **pool** of Samaria, where dogs licked up
Neh	2.14	city I went north to the Fountain Gate and the King's **Pool.**
	3.15	At the **Pool** of Shelah he built the wall next to the
	3.16	as far as David's tomb, the **pool,** and the barracks.
Ps	23. 2	of green grass and leads me to quiet **pools** of fresh water.
	84. 6	the autumn rain fills it with **pools.**
	107.35	He changed deserts into **pools** of water and dry land into
	114. 8	Jacob, [8] who changes rocks into **pools** of water and solid
Song	7. 4	Your eyes are like the **pools** in the city of Heshbon, near
Is	7. 3	the end of the ditch that brings water from the upper **pool.**
	22.11	the city to hold the water flowing down from the old **pool.**
	41.18	will turn the desert into **pools** of water and the dry land
	42.15	river valleys into deserts and dry up the **pools** of water.
Jer	41.12	their men and overtook him near the large **pool** at Gibeon.
Jn	5. 2	Sheep Gate in Jerusalem there is a **pool** with five porches;
	5. 7	to put me in the **pool** when the water is stirred up;
	9. 7	and said, "Go and wash your face in the **Pool** of Siloam."

POOR

[POVERTY]

Gen	41.19	They were the **poorest** cows I have ever seen anywhere in Egypt.
Ex	4.10	I am a **poor** speaker, slow and hesitant."
	6.12	I am such a **poor** speaker."
	6.30	But Moses answered, "You know that I am such a **poor** speaker;
	22.25	of my people who are **poor,** do not act like a money-lender
	23. 3	Do not show partiality to a **poor** man at his trial.
	23. 6	not deny justice to a **poor** man when he appears in court.

Ex	23.11	The **poor** may eat what grows there, and the wild animals can
	30.15	to pay more, nor the **poor** man less, when they pay this
Lev	14.21	If the man is **poor** and cannot afford any more, he shall
	19.10	leave them for **poor** people and foreigners.
	19.15	do not show favouritism to the **poor** or fear the rich.
	23.22	leave them for **poor** people and foreigners.
	25.25	If an Israelite becomes **poor** and is forced to sell his land,
	25.35	living near you becomes **poor** and cannot support himself,
	25.39	living near you becomes so **poor** that he sells himself to you
	25.47	rich, while a fellow-Israelite becomes **poor** and sells
	27. 8	made the vow is too **poor** to pay the standard price, he
	27.33	the animals so that the **poor** animals are chosen, and he may
Deut	15. 4	of your people will be **poor** [5] if you obey him and carefully
	15.11	be some Israelites who are **poor** and in need, and so I
	24.12	If he is a **poor** man, do not keep it overnight;
	24.14	"Do not cheat a **poor** and needy hired servant, whether
	28.18	only a few children, **poor** crops, and few cattle and sheep.
Ruth	3.10	for a young man, either rich or **poor,** but you didn't.
1 Sam	2. 7	He makes some men **poor** and others rich;
	2. 8	He lifts the **poor** from the dust and raises the needy from
	18.23	too great for someone **poor** and insignificant like me."
2 Sam	5. 8	the water tunnel and attack those **poor** blind cripples."
	12. 1	one was rich and the other **poor.**
	12. 3	cattle and sheep, [3] while the **poor** man had only one lamb,
	12. 4	instead, he took the **poor** man's lamb and cooked a meal for
	14. 5	"I am a **poor** widow, sir," she answered.
	24.17	What have these **poor** people done?
2 Kgs	23. 2	and all the rest of the people, rich and **poor** alike.
	24.14	leaving only the **poorest** of the people behind in Judah.
	25.12	in Judah some of the **poorest** people, who owned no property,
	25.26	rich and **poor** alike, together with the army officers,
1 Chr	21.17	What have these **poor** people done?
2 Chr	34.30	Levites and all the rest of the people, rich and **poor** alike.
Esth	1. 5	the men in the capital city of Susa, rich and **poor** alike.
	1.20	husband with proper respect, whether he's rich or **poor."**
	9.22	giving gifts of food to one another and to the **poor.**
Job	5.15	But God saves the **poor** from death;
	5.16	He gives hope to the **poor** and silences the wicked.
	20.10	and his sons will make good what he stole from the **poor.**
	20.19	he oppressed and neglected the **poor** and seized houses
	24. 4	They prevent the **poor** from getting their rights and force
	24. 5	So the **poor,** like wild donkeys, search for food in the dry
	24. 9	and take the **poor** man's children in payment for debts.
	24.10	But the **poor** must go out with no clothes to protect them;
	24.14	and goes out to kill the **poor,** and at night he steals.
	26. 1	help you are to me— **poor,** weak man that I am!
	29.12	When the **poor** cried out, I helped them;
	29.16	like a father to the **poor** and took the side of strangers
	30. 3	They were so **poor** and hungry that they would gnaw dry
	31.16	I have never refused to help the **poor;**
	31.19	found someone in need, too **poor** to buy clothes, [20] I would
	34.19	favour the rich against the **poor,** for he created everyone.
	34.28	They forced the **poor** to cry out to God, and he heard
	36. 6	live on, and he always treats the **poor** with justice.
Ps	9.18	the hope of the **poor** will not be crushed for ever.
	10. 2	The wicked are proud and persecute the **poor;**
	10. 9	He lies in wait for the **poor;**
	22.24	He does not neglect the **poor** or ignore their suffering;
	22.26	The **poor** will eat as much as they want;
	35.10	You protect the weak from the strong, the **poor** from the oppressor."
	37.14	their bows to kill the **poor** and needy, to slaughter those
	40.17	I am weak and **poor,** O Lord, but you have not forgotten
	41. 1	Happy are those who are concerned for the **poor;**
	49. 2	great and small alike, rich and **poor** together.
	68.10	in your goodness you provided for the **poor.**
	70. 5	I am weak and **poor;**
	72. 4	May the king judge the **poor** fairly;
	72.12	He rescues the **poor** who call to him, and those who are
	72.13	He has pity on the weak and **poor;**
	74.21	let those **poor** and needy people praise you.
	82. 3	Defend the rights of the **poor** and the orphans;
	109.16	he persecuted and killed the **poor,** the needy, and the helpless.
	109.22	I am **poor** and needy;
	109.31	people, [31] because he defends the **poor** man and saves him
	113. 7	He raises the **poor** from the dust;
	132.15	I will satisfy her **poor** with food.
	140.12	defend the cause of the **poor** and the rights of the needy.
Prov	6.11	But while he sleeps, **poverty** will attack him like an armed robber.
	10. 4	Being lazy will make you **poor,** but hard work will make you
	10.15	poverty destroys the **poor.**
	11.24	Others are cautious, and yet grow **poorer.**
	13. 7	Others pretend to be **poor,** but own a fortune.
	13. 8	money to save his life, but no one threatens a **poor** man.
	13.18	Someone who will not learn will be **poor** and disgraced.
	13.23	plenty of food for the **poor,** but unjust men keep them from
	14.20	even his neighbour, likes a **poor** man, but the rich have many
	14.21	If you want to be happy, be kind to the **poor;**
	14.23	if you sit around talking you will be **poor.**
	14.31	If you oppress **poor** people, you insult the God who made them;
	14.31	but kindness shown to the **poor** is an act of worship.
	15.15	The life of the **poor** is a constant struggle, but happy
	15.16	Better to be **poor** and fear the Lord than to be rich
	16.19	to be humble and stay **poor** than to be one of the
	17. 5	If you laugh at **poor** people, you insult the God who made
	18.23	When the **poor** man speaks, he has to beg politely, but
	19. 1	It is better to be **poor** but honest than to be a
	19. 4	new friends, but the **poor** cannot keep the few they have.
	19. 7	Even the brothers of a **poor** man have no use for him;
	19.17	When you give to the **poor,** it is like lending to the
	19.22	**poor** people are better off than liars.
Prov	20.13	If you spend your time sleeping, you will be **poor.**
	21.13	to the cry of the **poor,** your own cry for help will
	22. 2	The rich and the **poor** have this in common:
	22. 7	**Poor** people are the rich man's slaves.
	22. 9	Be generous and share your food with the **poor.**
	22.16	the poor to get rich, you will become **poor** yourself.
	22.22	Don't take advantage of the **poor** just because you can;
	23.21	Drunkards and gluttons will be reduced to **poverty.**
	24.34	but while you are asleep, **poverty** will attack you like
	28. 3	man in authority who oppresses **poor** people is like a driving
	28. 6	Better to be **poor** and honest than rich and dishonest.
	28. 8	your wealth will go to someone who is kind to the **poor.**
	28.11	they are wise, but a **poor** person who has insight into
	28.15	**Poor** people are helpless against a wicked ruler;
	28.19	People who waste time will always be **poor.**
	28.22	rich that they do not know when **poverty** is about to strike.
	28.27	Give to the **poor** and you will never be in need.
	28.27	close your eyes to the **poor,** many people will curse you.
	29. 7	knows the rights of the **poor,** but wicked people cannot
	29.13	A **poor** man and his oppressor have this in common—the
	29.14	defends the rights of the **poor,** he will rule for a long
	30. 8	keep me from lying, and let me be neither rich nor **poor.**
	30. 9	But if I am **poor,** I might steal and bring disgrace on
	30.14	There are people who take cruel advantage of the **poor** and needy;
	31. 7	Let them drink and forget their **poverty** and unhappiness.
	31. 9	Protect the rights of the **poor** and needy."
	31.11	puts his confidence in her, and he will never be **poor.**
	31.20	She is generous to the **poor** and needy.
Ecc	4.13	A man may rise from **poverty** to become king of his country,
	4.13	as well off as a young man who is **poor** but intelligent.
	5. 8	that the government oppresses the **poor** and denies them
	6. 8	good does it do a **poor** man to know how to face
	9.15	man lived there who was **poor,** but so clever that he could
	9.16	no one thinks of a **poor** man as wise or pays any
Is	3.14	your houses are full of what you have taken from the **poor.**
	3.15	no right to crush my people and take advantage of the **poor.**
	10. 2	is how you prevent the **poor** from having their rights and
	11. 4	he will judge the **poor** fairly and defend the rights of
	14.30	be a shepherd to the **poor** of his people and will let
	17. 4	come to an end, and its wealth will be replaced by **poverty.**
	19.15	Egypt, rich or **poor,** important or unknown, can offer help.
	23.16	Take your harp, go round the town, you **poor** forgotten whore!
	24. 2	buyers and sellers, lenders and borrowers, rich and **poor.**
	25. 4	The **poor** and the helpless have fled to you and have been
	29.19	**Poor** and humble people will once again find the
	32. 7	he plots to ruin the **poor** with lies and to prevent them
	33.15	Don't use your power to cheat the **poor** and don't accept bribes.
	58. 7	with the hungry and open your homes to the homeless **poor.**
	61. 1	bring good news to the **poor,** To heal the broken-hearted, To
Jer	2.34	with the blood of the **poor** and innocent, not with the blood
	5. 4	Then I thought, "These are only the **poor** and ignorant.
	16. 6	The rich and the **poor** will die in this land, but no
	22.16	He gave the **poor** a fair trial, and all went well with
	39.10	of Judah some of the **poorest** people, who owned no property,
	40. 7	been taken away to Babylonia—the **poorest** people in the land.
	52.16	in Judah some of the **poorest** people, who owned no property,
Ezek	16.49	they did not take care of the **poor** and the underprivileged.
	18.12	He cheats the **poor,** he robs, he keeps what a borrower
	21.26	Raise the **poor** to power!
	22.29	They ill-treat the **poor** and take advantage of foreigners.
Dan	4.27	Stop sinning, do what is right, and be merciful to the **poor.**
Amos	2. 6	who cannot pay their debts, **poor** men who cannot repay even
	2. 7	the weak and helpless and push the **poor** out of the way.
	2. 8	that they have taken from the **poor** as security for debts.
	4. 1	ill-treat the weak, oppress the **poor,** and demand that your
	5.11	You have oppressed the **poor** and robbed them of their grain.
	5.12	and prevent the **poor** from getting justice in the courts.
	8. 4	on the needy and try to destroy the **poor** of the country.
	8. 6	We'll find a **poor** man who can't pay his debts, not even
Mic	6.12	Your rich men exploit the **poor,** and all of you are liars.
Hab	3.14	us, gloating like those who secretly oppress the **poor.**
Mt	5. 3	"Happy are those who know they are spiritually **poor;**
	7.17	tree bears good fruit, but a **poor** tree bears bad fruit.
	7.18	bear bad fruit, and a **poor** tree cannot bear good fruit.
	11. 5	back to life, and the Good News is preached to the **poor.**
	12.33	if you have a **poor** tree, you will have bad fruit.
	19.21	give the money to the **poor,** and you will have riches in
	26. 9	sold for a large amount and the money given to the **poor!"**
	26.11	You will always have **poor** people with you, but you will
Mk	10.21	give the money to the **poor,** and you will have riches in
	12.42	then a **poor** widow came along and dropped in two little
	12.43	"I tell you that this **poor** widow put more in the offering
	12.44	but she, **poor** as she is, put in all she had—
	14. 5	three hundred silver coins and the money given to the **poor!"**
	14. 7	You will always have **poor** people with you, and any time
Lk	4.18	because he has chosen me to bring good news to the **poor.**
	6.20	Jesus looked at his disciples and said, "Happy are you **poor;**
	6.43	not bear bad fruit, nor does a **poor** tree bear good fruit.
	7.22	raised to life, and the Good News is preached to the **poor.**
	11.41	cups and plates to the **poor,** and everything will be ritually
	12.33	Sell all your belongings and give the money to the **poor.**
	14.13	give a feast, invite the **poor,** the crippled, the lame,
	14.21	town, and bring back the **poor,** the crippled, the blind,
	16.20	There was also a **poor** man named Lazarus, covered with sores,
	16.22	"The **poor** man died and was carried by the angels to sit
	18.22	give the money to the **poor,** and you will have riches in
	19. 8	my belongings to the **poor,** and if I have cheated anyone,
	21. 2	he also saw a very **poor** widow dropping in two little copper
	21. 3	"I tell you that this **poor** widow put in more than all
	21. 4	but she, **poor** as she is, gave all she had to live
Jn	12. 5	three hundred silver coins and the money given to the **poor?"**

Jn 12. 6 because he cared about the **poor,** but because he was a thief.
12. 8 You will always have **poor** people with you, but you will
13.29 needed for the festival, or to give something to the **poor.**
Acts 9.36 She spent all her time doing good and helping the **poor.**
10. 2 much to help the Jewish **poor** people and was constantly
Rom 8.35 hardship or persecution or hunger or **poverty** or danger or death?
11.12 their spiritual **poverty** brought rich blessings to the Gentiles.
15.26 offering to help the **poor** among God's people in Jerusalem.
2 Cor 6.10 we seem **poor,** but we make many people rich;
8. 2 extremely generous in their giving, even though they are very **poor.**
8. 9 he made himself **poor** for your sake,
8. 9 in order to make you rich by means of his **poverty.**
Eph 4.28 honest living for himself and to be able to help the **poor.**
Heb 11.37 in skins of sheep or goats—**poor,** persecuted, and ill-treated.
Jas 1. 9 The Christian who is **poor** must be glad when God lifts him
2. 2 your meeting, and a **poor** man in ragged clothes also comes.
2. 3 but say to the **poor** man, "Stand over there, or sit
2. 5 God chose the **poor** people of this world to be rich in
2. 6 But you dishonour the **poor!**
Rev 2. 9 I know that you are **poor**—but really you are rich!
3.17 You are **poor,** naked, and blind.
13.16 small and great, rich and **poor,** slave and free, to have a

POPLAR

Gen 30.37 Jacob got green branches of **poplar,** almond, and plane

POPULAR

Gal 1.10 Am I trying to be **popular** with men?

POPULATION

Josh 8.25 The whole **population** of Ai was killed that day—twelve
14. 1 of the Israelite tribes divided it among the **population.**
1 Chr 5.23 and their **population** increased greatly.
Ezek 36.10 I will make your **population** grow.
37.26 establish them and increase their **population,** and put my

Am **PORCH see PASSAGE (1)**

PORCH

1 Kgs 7. 6 It had a covered **porch,** supported by columns.
Amos 9. 1 the temple columns so hard that the whole **porch** will shake.
Jn 5. 2 Sheep Gate in Jerusalem there is a pool with five **porches;**
5. 3 people were lying in the **porches**—the blind, the lame,

PORK

Is 65. 4 They eat **pork** and drink broth made from meat offered in
66.17 and who eat **pork** and mice and other disgusting foods.

PORT
[SEAPORTS]

2 Chr 8.17 went to Eziongeber and Elath, **ports** on the shore of the Gulf
20.36 At the **port** of Eziongeber they built ocean-going ships.
Ps 107.30 the calm, and he brought them safe to the **port** they wanted.
Is 23. 1 Your home **port** of Tyre has been destroyed;
Acts 27. 2 ready to leave for the **seaports** of the province of Asia,

PORTION

Josh 11.23 their own and divided it into **portions,** one for each tribe.
12. 8 This **portion** included the hill-country, the western foothills,
14. 3 However, Moses gave the Levites no **portion** of the territory.
Neh 12.47 and the Levites gave the required **portion** to the priests.
Ezek 48.10 The priests are to have a **portion** of this holy area.
48.10 From east to west their **portion** is to measure
48.28 the south side of the **portion** given to the tribe of Gad,

POSITION

Gen 40.13 release you, pardon you, and restore you to your **position.**
40.21 to his former **position,** [22] but he executed the chief baker.
41.13 restored me to my **position,** but you executed the baker."
44.15 that a man in my **position** could find you out by practising
Num 2.17 same order as they camp, each in **position** under its banner.
Judg 20.20 and placed the soldiers in **position** facing the city.
20.22 their soldiers in the same **position** as they had been the day
20.30 placed their soldiers in battle **position** facing Gibeah, as
1 Sam 17.21 Israelite armies took up **positions** for battle, facing each other.
2 Sam 10. 8 out and took up their **position** at the entrance to Rabbah,
10. 8 Tob and Maacah, took up their **position** in the open countryside.
10. 9 Israel's soldiers and put them in **position** facing the Syrians.
10.10 Abishai, who put them in **position** facing the Ammonites.
10.17 Helam, where the Syrians took up their **position** facing him.
1 Kgs 15.13 his grandmother Maacah from her **position** as queen mother,
20.12 get ready to attack the city, so they moved into **position.**
2 Kgs 25.28 kindly, and gave him a **position** of greater honour than he
1 Chr 9.22 Samuel who had put their ancestors in these responsible **positions.**
18.17 and King David's sons held high **positions** in his service.
19. 9 out and took up their **position** at the entrance to Rabbah,
19. 9 to help took up their **position** in the open countryside.
19.10 Israel's soldiers and put them in **position** facing the Syrians.
19.11 Abishai, who put them in **position** facing the Ammonites.
19.17 the Jordan, and put them in **position** facing the Syrians.
2 Chr 14.10 both sides took up their **positions** in the Valley of
15.16 his grandmother Maacah from her **position** as queen mother,
17. 1 Asa as king and strengthened his **position** against Israel.
20.17 Just take up your **positions** and wait;
31.16 in the Temple in accordance with their **positions.**
Esth 2.19 Mordecai had been appointed by the king to an administrative **position.**
3. 1 Xerxes promoted a man named Haman to the **position** of prime minister.
Job 22. 8 your power and your **position** to take over the whole land.
Prov 25. 7 asked to take a higher **position** than to be told to give
Ecc 9.11 rich, and capable men do not always rise to high **positions.**
10. 6 Stupid people are given **positions** of authority
Is 22.19 from office and bring you down from your high **position."**
Jer 52.32 kindly and gave him a **position** of greater honour than he
Dan 2.48 Daniel a high **position,** presented him with many splendid gifts,
3.30 Abednego to higher **positions** in the province of Babylon.
2 Pet 3.17 errors of lawless people and fall from your safe **position.**

POSSESS

Gen 14.12 living in Sodom, so they took him and all his **possessions.**
14.16 his nephew Lot and his **possessions,** together with the women
28. 4 Abraham, and may you take **possession** of this land, in which
36. 6 his livestock and all the **possessions** he had acquired in the
45.20 They are not to worry about leaving their **possessions** behind;
46. 6 took their livestock and the **possessions** they had acquired
48. 4 land to your descendants as their **possession** for ever.' "
Ex 6. 8 and I will give it to you as your own **possession.**
22. 2 is found alive in his **possession,** he shall pay two for one.
23.30 there are enough of you to take **possession** of the land.
32.13 that land you promised would be their **possession** for ever."
Lev 14.34 which the Lord was going to give them as their **possession.)**
20.24 and fertile land as your **possession,** and I will give it to
Num 14.24 explored, and his descendants will **possess** the land [25] in
16.14 fields and vineyards as our **possession,** and now you are
16.32 with all of Korah's followers and their **possessions.**
16.33 down alive to the world of the dead, with their **possessions.**
18.24 given to them as their **possession** the tithe which the
18.26 Lord gives you as your **possession,** you must present a tenth
32.18 Israelites have taken **possession** of the land assigned to them.
32.19 We will not take **possession** of any property among them
32.22 the Lord defeats them [22] and takes **possession** of the land.
36. 9 Each tribe will continue to **possess** its own property."
Deut 3.12 "When we took **possession** of the land, I assigned to
6.18 will be able to take **possession** of the fertile land that the
8.13 gold, and all your other **possessions** have increased,
9. 4 brought you in to **possess** this land because you deserved it.
9.23 orders to go and take **possession** of the land that he was
10.11 so that you could take **possession** of the land that he had
13.16 Bring together all the **possessions** of the people who
17.14 "After you have taken **possession** of the land that the
21.17 a double share of his **possessions** to his first son, even
30. 5 that you may again take **possession** of the land where your
33. 4 Law that Moses gave us, our nation's most treasured **possession.**
Josh 7.13 'Israel, you have in your **possession** some things that I
7.25 they also stoned and burnt his family and **possessions.**
12. 6 Gad and to half the tribe of Manasseh, to be their **possession.**
12. 7 the tribes and gave it to them as a permanent **possession.**
13. 7 the tribe of Manasseh, for them to **possess** as their own."
13.14 were to receive as their **possession** a share of the
13.15 to the families of the tribe of Reuben as their **possession.**
13.23 to the families of the tribe of Reuben as their **possession.**
13.24 to the families of the tribe of Gad as their **possession.**
13.28 to the families of the tribe of Gad as their **possession.**
13.29 families of half the tribe of Manasseh as their **possession.**
13.33 He told them that their **possession** was to be a share of
14. 9 receive as our **possession** the land which I walked over.
14.13 Jephunneh and gave him the city of Hebron as his **possession.**
15.20 families of the tribe of Judah received as their **possession.**
16. 4 Ephraim and West Manasseh, received this land as their **possession.**
16. 8 tribe of Ephraim as their **possession,** [9] along with some
17. 4 well as our male relatives, a part of the land to **possess."**
17.11 Issachar and Asher, Manasseh **possessed** Beth Shan and Ibleam,
17.14 us only one part of the land to **possess** as our own?
17.18 will clear it and take **possession** of it from one end to
18. 4 territory that they would like to have as their **possession.**
18.20 of the tribe of Benjamin received as their **possession.**
18.28 of the tribe of Benjamin received as their **possession.**
19. 8 of the tribe of Simeon received as their **possession.**
19.16 of the tribe of Zebulun received as their **possession.**
19.23 of the tribe of Issachar received as their **possession.**
19.31 of the tribe of Asher received as their **possession.**
19.39 of the tribe of Naphtali received as their **possession.**
19.48 families of the tribe of Dan received as their **possession.**
21.12 been given to Caleb son of Jephunneh as his **possession.**
21.41 people of Israel **possessed,** a total of forty-eight cities,
21.43 When they had taken **possession** of it, they settled down there.
23. 4 I have assigned as the **possession** of your tribes the land
24. 4 hill-country of Edom as his **possession,** but your ancestor
Judg 1.18 of Judah, and they took **possession** of the hill-country.
2. 6 each man went to take **possession** of his own share of the
11.21 So the Israelites took **possession** of all the territory of
1 Kgs 8.36 which you gave to your people as a permanent **possession.**
9.20 Israelites had not killed when they took **possession** of their land.
21.15 Now go and take **possession** of the vineyard which he refused
21.16 At once Ahab went to the vineyard to take **possession** of it.
21.18 him in Naboth's vineyard, about to take **possession** of it.
2 Kgs 17.24 They took **possession** of these cities and lived there.
1 Chr 16.18 "It will be your own **possession."**
28. 8 that you may continue to **possess** this good land and so that

2 Chr 6.27 which you gave to your people as a permanent **possession.**
8. 7 Israelites had not killed when they took **possession** of the land.
21. 3 gold, silver, and other valuable **possessions,** and placed
21.14 children, and your wives, and will destroy your **possessions.**
Ezra 8.21 and protect us and our children and all our **possessions.**
Esth 8.11 slaughter them to the last man and take their **possessions.**
Ps 25.13 and their children will **possess** the land.
37. 9 trust in the Lord will **possess** the land, but the wicked will
37.11 the humble will **possess** the land and enjoy prosperity and peace.
37.22 blessed by the Lord will **possess** the land, but those who are
37.29 The righteous will **possess** the land and live in it for ever.
47. 4 we live, the proud **possession** of his people, whom he loves.
69.35 His people will live there and **possess** the land;
105.11 "It will be your own **possession."**
114. 2 Judah became the Lord's holy people, Israel became his own **possession.**
119.111 Your commandments are my eternal **possession;**
Is 15. 7 Valley of Willows, trying to escape with all their **possessions.**
60.21 all do what is right, And will **possess** the land for ever.
65. 9 and their descendants will **possess** my land of mountains.
Jer 2. 3 you were my sacred **possession.**
3.18 that I gave your ancestors as a permanent **possession."**
7. 7 land which I gave your ancestors as a permanent **possession.**
20. 5 city and seize all its **possessions** and property, even the
25. 5 Lord gave you and your ancestors as a permanent **possession.**
30. 3 I gave their ancestors, and they will take **possession** of it again.
32.23 into this land and took **possession** of it, they did not obey
37.12 territory of Benjamin to take **possession** of my share of the
Ezek 11.15 He has given us **possession** of the land.'
13.18 You want to **possess** the power of life and death over my
35.10 you and that you would **possess** them, even though I, the
35.15 just as you rejoiced at the devastation of Israel, my own **possession.**
36. 5 they captured my land and took **possession** of its pastures.
45. 5 be set aside as the **possession** of the Levites, who do the
47.14 ancestors that I would give them **possession** of this land;
47.22 it is to be your permanent **possession.**
48.29 into sections for the tribes of Israel to **possess."**
Dan 11.43 Egypt's hidden treasures of gold and silver and its other prized **possessions.**
Obad 17 The people of Jacob will **possess** the land that is theirs by
19 Israelites will **possess** the territory of Ephraim and Samaria;
Zech 2.12 Judah will be the special **possession** of the Lord in his
Mt 5.28 a woman and wants to **possess** her is guilty of committing
25.34 Come and **possess** the kingdom which has been prepared for you
Acts 2.45 sell their property and **possessions,** and distribute the money
Rom 8.17 are his children, we will **possess** the blessings he keeps for
8.17 and we will also **possess** with Christ what God has kept
1 Cor 6. 9 Surely you know that the wicked will not **possess** God's Kingdom.
6.10 or are thieves—none of these will **possess** God's Kingdom.
15.50 and what is mortal cannot **possess** immortality.
2 Cor 6.10 we seem to have nothing, yet we really **possess** everything.
Gal 5.21 who do these things will not **possess** the Kingdom of God.
1 Thes 5. 9 but to **possess** salvation through our Lord Jesus Christ,
2 Thes 2.14 he called you to **possess** your share of the glory of our
1 Tim 6.21 For some have claimed to **possess** it, and as a result
Tit 3. 7 with God and come into **possession** of the eternal life we
Heb 1. 2 one whom God has chosen to **possess** all things at the end.
10.34 you knew that you still **possessed** something much better,
Jas 2. 5 rich in faith and to **possess** the kingdom which he promised
1 Pet 1. 4 we look forward to **possessing** the rich blessings that God keeps

POSSIBLE

Gen 29.31 than Rachel, he made it **possible** for her to have children,
30.22 her prayer and made it **possible** for her to have children.
Deut 5.24 have seen that it is **possible** for a man to continue to
Ruth 1. 9 may the Lord make it **possible** for each of you to marry
Lam 2.13 there is no **possible** hope.
Ezek 41. 7 built, so that it was **possible** to go from the lower storey
Mt 19.26 "This is impossible for man, but for God everything is **possible."**
24.24 in order to deceive even God's chosen people, if **possible.**
26.39 "My Father, if it is **possible,** take this cup of suffering
Mk 9.22 Have pity on us and help us, if you **possibly** can!"
9.23 Everything is **possible** for the person who has faith."
10.27 everything is **possible** for God."
13.22 in order to deceive even God's chosen people, if **possible.**
14.35 and prayed that, if **possible,** he might not have to go
14.36 All things are **possible** for you.
Lk 18.27 "What is impossible for man is **possible** for God."
Jn 6.65 unless the Father makes it **possible** for him to do so."
Acts 5.39 but if it comes from God, you cannot **possibly** defeat them.
17.15 Paul that Silas and Timothy should join him as soon as **possible.**
20.16 in Jerusalem by the day of Pentecost, if at all **possible.**
27.12 trying to reach Phoenix, if **possible,** in order to spend the
27.13 and sailed as close as **possible** along the coast of Crete.
27.39 and decided that, if **possible,** they would run the ship aground
Rom 1.10 may at last make it **possible** for me to visit you now.
12.18 Do everything **possible** on your part to live in peace with
1 Cor 9.19 slave in order to win as many people as **possible.**
9.22 I may save some of them by whatever means are **possible.**
Phil 1.18 in every way **possible,** whether from wrong or right motives.
Col 1.28 With all **possible** wisdom we warn and teach them in order to

POST (1)

2 Chr 35.15 not need to leave their **posts,** because the other Levites
Neh 7. 3 some of them to specific **posts** and others to patrol the area
Is 21. 6 said to me, "Go and **post** a sentry, and tell him to
21. 8 "Sir, I have been standing guard at my **post** day and night."
Jer 51.12 **Post** the sentries!
Acts 12.10 passed by the first guard **post** and then the second, and came

POST (2)

[CORNER-POSTS, DOOR-POST]

Ex 12. 7 and put it on the **door-posts** and above the doors of the
12.13 The blood on the **door-posts** will be a sign to mark the
12.22 and wipe the blood on the **door-posts** and the beam above the
12.23 on the beams and the **door-posts** and will not let the Angel
21. 6 stand against the door or the **door-post** and pierce his ear.
26.32 Hang it on four **posts** of acacia-wood covered with gold,
26.37 For this curtain make five **posts** of acacia-wood covered
26.37 make five bronze bases for these **posts.**
27.10 supported by twenty bronze **posts** in twenty bronze bases,
27.12 to be curtains 22 metres long, with ten **posts** and ten bases.
27.14 be 6.6 metres of curtains, with three **posts** and three bases.
27.16 It is to be supported by four **posts** in four bases.
27.17 All the **posts** round the enclosure are to be connected
35.11 its hooks and its frames, its cross-bars, its **posts,** and its
35.17 the curtains for the enclosure, its **posts** and bases;
36.36 They made four **posts** of acacia-wood to hold the curtain,
36.36 Then they made four silver bases to hold the **posts.**
36.38 this curtain they made five **posts** fitted with hooks, covered
36.38 rods with gold, and made five bronze bases for the **posts.**
38.10 supported by twenty bronze **posts** in twenty bronze bases,
38.12 22 metres long, with ten **posts** and ten bases and with hooks
38.14 6.6 metres of curtains, with three **posts** and three bases.
38.17 The bases for the **posts** were made of bronze, and the
38.17 the covering of the tops of the **posts** were made of silver.
38.17 All the **posts** round the enclosure were connected with silver rods.
38.19 It was supported by four **posts** in four bronze bases.
38.28 the hooks for the **posts,** and the covering for their tops.
39.33 equipment, its hooks, its frames, its cross-bars, its **posts,**
39.40 the curtains for the enclosure and its **posts** and bases;
40.18 its frames, attached its cross-bars, and put up its **posts.**
Num 3.36 for the Tent, its bars, **posts,** bases, and all its fittings.
3.37 were also responsible for the **posts,** bases, pegs, and ropes
4.31 for carrying the frames, bars, **posts,** and bases of the Tent,
4.32 and the **posts,** bases, pegs, and ropes of the
Deut 6. 9 Write them on the **door-posts** of your houses and on your gates.
11.20 Write them on the **door-posts** of your houses and on your gates.
21.22 body is hung on a **post,** [23] it is not to remain there
21.23 dead body hanging on a **post** brings God's curse on the land.
Judg 16. 3 the city gate and pulled it up—doors, **posts,** lock, and all.
2 Kgs 18.16 he himself had covered the **doorposts,** and he sent it all to
Song 3.10 Its **posts** are covered with silver;
Ezek 41.21 The **door-posts** of the Holy Place were square.
41.22 Its **corner-posts,** its base, and its sides were all made of wood.
43. 8 kings built the thresholds and **door-posts** of their palace
43. 8 right against the thresholds and **door-posts** of my Temple,
45.19 and put it on the **door-posts** of the Temple, on the four
45.19 the altar, and on the **posts** of the gateways to the inner
46. 2 gateway and stand beside the **posts** of the gate while the

POT

[COOKING-POT, FIRE-POT]

Gen 15.17 a smoking **fire-pot** and a flaming torch suddenly appeared
Lev 6.28 Any clay **pot** in which the meat is boiled must be broken,
6.28 and if a metal **pot** is used, it must be scrubbed
11.33 bodies fall into a clay **pot,** everything that is in it
11.33 shall be unclean, and you must break the **pot.**
11.34 water from such a **pot** has been poured, will be unclean,
11.34 and anything drinkable in such a **pot** is unclean.
15.12 Any clay **pot** that the man touches must be broken, and
Num 19.15 Every jar and **pot** in the tent that has no lid on
19.17 shall be taken and put in a **pot,** and fresh water added.
Judg 6.19 and the broth in a **pot,** brought them to the Lord's angel
1 Sam 2.14 stick the fork into the **cooking-pot,** and whatever the fork
2 Sam 17.28 They brought bowls, clay **pots,** and bedding, and
1 Kgs 7.40 Huram also made **pots,** shovels, and bowls.
7.40 bulls supporting the tank The **pots,** shovels, and bowls
2 Kgs 4.38 servant to put a big **pot** on the fire and make some
4.41 meal, threw it into the **pot,** and said, "Pour out some more
1 Chr 4.23 They were **potters** in the service of the king and lived
2 Chr 4.11 Huram also made **pots,** shovels, and bowls.
4.11 The **pots,** shovels, and forks
35.13 boiled the sacred offerings in **pots,** cauldrons, and pans,
Job 2. 8 heap and took a piece of broken **pottery** to scrape his sores.
41.20 out of his nose, like smoke from weeds burning under a **pot.**
41.30 The scales on his belly are like jagged pieces of **pottery;**
41.31 like boiling water and makes it bubble like a **pot** of oil.
Ps 2. 9 you will shatter them in pieces like a clay **pot.' "**
Prov 26.23 really thinking is like a fine glaze on a cheap clay **pot.**
Is 22.24 will hang on him like **pots** and bowls hanging from a peg!
29.16 Which is more important, the **potter** or the clay?
30.14 be shattered like a clay **pot,** so badly broken that there is
41.25 rulers as if they were mud, like a **potter** trampling clay.
45. 9 Does a clay **pot** dare to argue with its maker,
45. 9 a **pot** that is like all the others?
45. 9 Does the clay ask the **potter** what he is doing?
45. 9 Does the **pot** complain that its maker has no skill?
64. 8 We are like clay, and you are like the **potter.**
Jer 1.13 I answered, "I see a **pot** boiling in the north,
18. 2 me, [2] "Go down to the **potter's** house, where I will give you
18. 3 So I went there and saw the **potter** working at his wheel.
18. 4 Whenever a piece of **pottery** turned out imperfect, he would
18. 6 with you people of Israel what the **potter** did with the clay?
18. 6 You are in my hands just like clay in the **potter's** hands.
Lam 4. 2 us as gold, but now they are treated like common clay **pots.**

Ezek 11. 3 The city is like a **cooking-pot,** and we are like the meat
11. 7 This city is indeed a **cooking-pot,** but what is the meat?
11.11 will not protect you as a **pot** protects the meat in it.
24. 3 Set the **pot** on the fire and fill it up with water.
24. 5 pile the wood under the **pot.**
24. 6 It is like a corroded **pot** that is never cleaned.
24.11 Now set the empty bronze **pot** on the coals and let it
24.11 Then the **pot** will be ritually pure again after the corrosion
Hos 8. 8 like any other nation and is as useless as a broken **pot.**
Mic 3. 3 break their bones, and chop them up like meat for the **pot.**
Zech 14.20 The **cooking-pots** in the Temple will be as sacred as the
14.21 Every **cooking-pot** in Jerusalem and in all Judah will be
Mk 7. 4 as the proper way to wash cups, **pots,** copper bowls, and
Rom 9.20 A clay **pot** does not ask the man who made it, "Why
9.21 the man who makes the **pots** has the right to use the
9.21 and to make two **pots** from the same lump of clay,
2 Cor 4. 7 treasure are like common clay **pots,** in order to show that
Rev 2.26 an iron rod and to break them to pieces like clay **pots.**

POTSHERD GATE

Jer 19. 2 priests, [2]and to go through **Potsherd Gate** out to the Valley

POTTER'S FIELD

Mt 27. 7 the money to buy **Potter's Field,** as a cemetery for foreigners.
27.10 the money to buy the **potter's field,** as the Lord had

POULTRY

1 Kgs 4.23 sheep, besides deer, gazelles, roebucks, and **poultry.**

POUNCE

Is 33. 4 Their belongings are **pounced** upon and taken as loot.
Lam 3.10 he **pounced** on me like a lion.
Dan 6.24 of the pit, the lions **pounced** on them and broke all their
Mic 5. 8 gets in among the sheep, **pounces** on them, and tears them to

POUND (1)

Num 11. 8 gather it, grind it or **pound** it into flour, and then boil
Deut 28.67 Your hearts will **pound** with fear at everything you see.
2 Kgs 23. 6 of the Kidron, burnt it, **pounded** its ashes to dust, and
23.15 broke its stones into pieces, and **pounded** them to dust;
Ps 38.10 My heart is **pounding,** my strength is gone, and my eyes
Is 44.12 His strong arm swings a hammer to **pound** the metal into shape.
Ezek 26. 9 They will **pound** in your walls with battering-rams and tear

POUND (2)

Mt 18.24 one of them was brought in who owed him millions of **pounds.**
18.28 met one of his fellow-servants who owed him a few **pounds.**

POUR
[OUTPOURINGS]

Gen 28.18 Then he **poured** olive-oil on it to dedicate it to God.
31.13 stone as a memorial by **pouring** olive-oil on it and where you
35.14 and consecrated it by **pouring** wine and olive-oil on it.
Ex 4. 9 take some water from the Nile and **pour** it on the ground.
29. 7 Then take the anointing oil, **pour** it on his head, and
29.12 Then **pour** out the rest of the blood at the base of
29.40 **Pour** out one litre of wine as an offering.
30. 9 grain-offering, and do not **pour** out any wine-offering on it.
30.32 It must not be **poured** on ordinary men, and you must not
32. 4 the earrings, melted them, **poured** the gold into a mould,
Lev 2. 6 Crumble it up and **pour** the oil on it when you present
4. 7 He shall **pour** out the rest of the blood at the base
4.12 place where the ashes are **poured** out, and there he shall
4.18 incense-altar inside the Tent and **pour** out the rest of it at
4.25 corners of the altar, and **pour** out the rest of it at
4.30 corners of the altar, and **pour** out the rest of it at
4.34 corners of the altar, and **pour** out the rest of it at
8.12 He ordained Aaron by **pouring** some of the anointing oil
8.15 He then **poured** out the rest of the blood at the base
9. 9 corners of the altar, and **poured** out the rest of it at
11.34 such a pot has been **poured,** will be unclean, and anything
14.15 some of the olive-oil and **pour** it in the palm of his
14.26 The priest shall **pour** some of the oil into the palm of
17.11 commanded that all blood be **poured** out on the altar to take
17.13 is ritually clean, he must **pour** out its blood on the ground
21.10 has had the anointing oil **poured** on his head and has been
Num 5.15 flour, but he shall not **pour** any olive-oil on it or put
5.17 He shall **pour** some holy water into a clay bowl and take
19. 7 to wash his clothes and **pour** water over himself, and then he
19. 8 also wash his clothes and **pour** water over himself, but he
19.19 after washing his clothes and **pouring** water over himself,
28. 7 wine-offering with the first lamb, **pour** out at the altar one
Deut 12.16 you must **pour** it out on the ground like water.
12.24 instead **pour** it out on the ground like water.
12.27 you eat the meat and **pour** the blood out on the altar.
15.23 instead, you must **pour** it out on the ground like water.
Judg 5. 4 Yes, water **poured** down from the clouds.
6.20 and the bread on this rock, and **pour** the broth over them."
Ruth 3.15 She did, and he **poured** out nearly twenty kilogrammes of
1 Sam 1.15 I have been praying, **pouring** out my troubles to the Lord.
7. 6 They drew some water and **poured** it out as an offering to
10. 1 a jar of olive-oil and **poured** it on Saul's head, kissed him,
2 Sam 22. 9 Smoke **poured** out of his nostrils, a consuming flame and
23.16 instead he **poured** it out as an offering to the Lord [17]and
1 Kgs 18.33 four jars with water and **pour** it on the offering and the
2 Kgs 4. 4 house, close the door, and start **pouring** oil into the jars.
4. 5 small jar of olive-oil, and **poured** oil into the jars as her
4.40 The stew was **poured** out for the men to eat, but as
4.41 the pot, and said, "**Pour** out some more stew for them."
9. 3 away from his companions, [3]**pour** this olive-oil on his head,
9. 6 indoors, and the young prophet **poured** the olive-oil on
16.13 and grain-offerings on it, and **poured** a wine-offering and
16.15 **Pour** on it the blood of all the animals that are sacrificed.
1 Chr 11.18 instead he **poured** it out as an offering to the Lord [19]and
2 Chr 29.24 priests killed the goats and **poured** their blood on the altar
29.35 the people ate, and for **pouring** out the wine that was
Job 16.20 my eyes **pour** out tears to God.
30.14 They **pour** through the holes in my defences and come
36.28 He lets the rain **pour** from the clouds in showers for all
38.25 dug a channel for the **pouring** rain and cleared the way for
38.37 and tilt them over to **pour** out the rain, [38]rain that
40.11 **pour** out your anger and humble them.
41.20 Smoke comes **pouring** out of his nose, like smoke from
Ps 18. 8 Smoke **poured** out of his nostrils, a consuming flame and
45. 7 has chosen you and has **poured** out more happiness on you than
68. 8 earth shook, and the sky **poured** down rain, because of the
69.24 **Pour** out your anger on them;
73. 7 their hearts **pour** out evil, and their minds are busy with
75. 8 He **pours** it out, and all the wicked drink it;
77.17 The clouds **poured** down rain;
78.49 great distress by **pouring** out his anger and fierce rage,
104.32 he touches the mountains, and they **pour** out smoke.
119.136 My tears **pour** down like a river, because people do not
144. 5 touch the mountains, and they will **pour** out smoke.
Prov 1.22 How long will you enjoy **pouring** scorn on knowledge?
Is 24.18 Torrents of rain will **pour** from the sky, and earth's
44. 3 I will **pour** out my spirit on your children and my blessing
46. 6 People open their purses and **pour** out gold;
57. 6 You **pour** out wine as offerings to them
63. 6 I **poured** out their life-blood on the ground."
Jer 6.11 the Lord said to me, "**Pour** out my anger on the children
7.18 They also **pour** out wine-offerings to other gods, in order to
7.20 I, the Sovereign Lord, will **pour** out my fierce anger on this
7.20 I will **pour** it out on people and animals alike, and even
19.13 and where wine has been **poured** out as an offering to other
32.29 and by **pouring** out wine-offerings to other gods.
42.18 anger and fury were **poured** out on the people of Jerusalem,
42.18 so my fury will be **poured** out on you if you go
44. 6 So I **poured** out my anger and fury on the towns of
44.17 of Heaven, and we will **pour** out wine-offerings to her, just
44.18 Queen of Heaven and stopped **pouring** out wine-offerings to her,
44.19 sacrifices to her, and **poured** out wine-offerings to her,
44.24 offer sacrifices to her and **pour** out wine-offerings to her,
48.11 left to settle undisturbed and never **poured** from jar to jar.
48.12 coming when I will send people to **pour** Moab out like wine.
52.19 and the bowls used for **pouring** out offerings of wine.
Lam 2.19 **Pour** out your heart and beg him for mercy on your children
3.49 "My tears will **pour** out in a ceaseless stream [50]Until
Ezek 7.19 nor gold can save them when the Lord **pours** out his fury.
7.26 another, and a steady stream of bad news will **pour** in.
13.11 I will send a **pouring** rain.
13.13 will send a strong wind, **pouring** rain, and hailstones to
32. 6 I will **pour** out your blood until it spreads over the
38.22 with fire and sulphur, will **pour** down on him and his army
39.29 I will **pour** out my spirit on the people of Israel and
Dan 7.10 with fire, [10]and a stream of fire was **pouring** out from it.
Hos 5.10 So I will **pour** out punishment on them like a flood.
10.12 your Lord, and I will come and **pour** out blessings upon you.'
Joel 2.23 he has **poured** down the winter rain for you and the spring
2.28 "Afterwards I will **pour** out my spirit on everyone:
2.29 At that time I will **pour** out my spirit even on servants,
Amos 5. 8 the waters of the sea and **pours** them out on the earth.
9. 6 the waters of the sea and **pours** them out on the earth.
Mic 1. 4 they will **pour** down into the valleys
1. 4 like water **pouring** down a hill.
1. 6 I will **pour** the rubble of the city down into the valley,
Nah 1. 6 He **pours** out his flaming anger;
Hab 3.10 water **poured** down from the skies.
Zeph 1.17 now their blood will be **poured** out like water, and their
Zech 4.12 beside the two gold pipes from which the olive-oil **pours?"**
9.15 the blood of a sacrifice **poured** on the altar from a bowl.
Mal 3.10 the windows of heaven and **pour** out on you in abundance all
Mt 7.25 The rain **poured** down, the rivers overflowed, and the wind blew
7.27 The rain **poured** down, the rivers overflowed, the wind blew
9.17 Nor does anyone **pour** new wine into used wineskins,
9.17 will burst, the wine will **pour** out, and the skins will be
9.17 Instead, new wine is **poured** into fresh wineskins,
26. 7 filled with an expensive perfume, which she **poured** on his head.
26.12 What she did was to **pour** this perfume on my body to
26.28 seals God's covenant, my blood **poured** out for many
Mk 2.22 Nor does anyone **pour** new wine into used wineskins,
2.22 Instead, new wine must be **poured** into fresh wineskins."
14. 3 She broke the jar and **poured** the perfume on Jesus' head.
14. 8 she **poured** perfume on my body to prepare it ahead of time
14.24 is my blood which is **poured** out for many, my blood which
Lk 5.37 Nor does anyone **pour** new wine into used wineskins,
5.37 the wine will **pour** out, and the skins will be
5.38 Instead, new wine must be **poured** into fresh wineskins!
6.38 full measure, a generous helping, **poured** into your hands—
7.38 with her hair, kissed them, and **poured** the perfume on them.
10.34 He went over to him, **poured** oil and wine on his wounds
22.20 covenant sealed with my blood, which is **poured** out for you.
Jn 7.38 streams of life-giving water will **pour** out from his heart.' "
11. 2 Mary was the one who **poured** the perfume on the Lord's feet
12. 3 perfume made of pure nard, **poured** it on Jesus' feet, and

Jn 13. 5 Then he **poured** some water into a basin and began to wash
19.34 into Jesus' side, and at once blood and water **poured** out.
Acts 2.17 I will **pour** out my Spirit on everyone.
2.18 men and women, I will **pour** out my Spirit in those days,
2.33 is his gift that he has **poured** out on us.
4.33 and God **poured** rich blessings on them all.
10.38 and how God **poured** out on him the Holy Spirit
10.45 were amazed that God had **poured** out his gift of the Holy
Rom 2. 8 on them God will **pour** out his anger and fury.
5. 5 for God has **poured** out his love into our hearts
9.23 his abundant glory, which was **poured** out on us who are the
2 Cor 9.12 but also produces an **outpouring** of gratitude to God.
Phil 2.17 life's blood is to be **poured** out like an offering on the
1 Tim 1.14 And our Lord **poured** out his abundant grace on me
Tit 3. 6 God **poured** out the Holy Spirit abundantly on us through
Heb 9.22 and sins are forgiven only if blood is **poured** out.
Jas 3.10 Words of thanksgiving and cursing **pour** out from the same mouth.
3.11 No spring of water **pours** out sweet water and bitter water
5.18 he prayed, and the sky **poured** out its rain and the earth
1 Jn 2.20 have had the Holy Spirit **poured** out on you by Christ,
2.27 But as for you, Christ has **poured** out his Spirit on you.
Rev 8. 7 Hail and fire, mixed with blood, came **pouring** down on the earth.
9. 2 opened the abyss, and smoke **poured** out of it, like the smoke
12.15 from his mouth the dragon **poured** out a flood of water after
14.10 his fury, which he has **poured** at full strength into the cup
16. 1 "Go and **pour** out the seven bowls of God's anger on the
16. 2 The first angel went and **poured** out his bowl on the earth.
16. 3 Then the second angel **poured** out his bowl on the sea.
16. 4 Then the third angel **poured** out his bowl on the rivers
16. 6 They **poured** out the blood of God's people and of the prophets,
16. 8 Then the fourth angel **poured** out his bowl on the sun,
16.10 Then the fifth angel **poured** out his bowl on the throne
16.12 Then the sixth angel **poured** out his bowl on the great
16.17 Then the seventh angel **poured** out his bowl in the air.

POVERTY see POOR

POWDER

Ex 30.36 of it into a fine **powder,** take it into the Tent of
32.20 it, ground it into fine **powder,** and mixed it with water.

POWER

[ALL-POWERFUL, GOD'S POWER, LORD'S POWER, SPIRIT'S POWER, SUPREME POWER]

Gen 1. 2 in total darkness, and the **power of God** was moving over the
1.26 They will have **power** over the fish, the birds, and all animals,
9. 2 They are all placed under your **power.**
26.16 You have become more **powerful** than we are."
31.29 I have the **power** to do you harm, but last night the
45.13 Tell my father how **powerful** I am here in Egypt and tell
49.24 are made strong By the **power** of the Mighty God of Jacob,
Ex 1. 8 king, who knew nothing about Joseph, came to **power** in Egypt.
3.20 But I will use my **power** and will punish Egypt by doing
4.21 all the miracles which I have given you the **power** to do.
9.16 But to show you my **power** I have let you live so
13. 3 is the day the Lord brought you out by his great **power.**
13. 9 the Lord brought you out of Egypt by his great **power.**
13.14 answer him, 'By using great **power** the Lord brought us out of
13.16 the Lord brought us out of Egypt by his great **power.'"**
14.31 the Israelites saw the great **power** with which the Lord had
15. 6 "Your right hand, Lord, is awesome in **power;**
23.31 I will give you **power** over the inhabitants of the land, and
29.37 touches it will be harmed by the **power** of its holiness.
30.29 touches them will be harmed by the **power** of its holiness.
31. 3 the tribe of Judah, [3]and I have filled him with my **power.**
32.11 whom you rescued from Egypt with great might and **power?**
35.31 has filled him with his **power** and given him skill, ability,
Lev 6.18 food-offering will be harmed by the **power** of its holiness.
6.27 of the animal will be harmed by the **power** of its holiness.
26.13 I broke the **power** that held you down and I let you
26.45 showed all the nations my **power** by bringing my people out of
Num 11.23 "Is there a limit to my **power?"**
13.28 people who live there are **powerful,** and their cities are
13.31 the people there are more **powerful** than we are."
14.12 a nation that is larger and more **powerful** than they are!"
14.13 Lord, "You brought these people out of Egypt by your **power.**
14.17 I pray, show us your **power** and do what you promised when
20.12 to acknowledge my holy **power** before the people of Israel,
20.20 they marched out with a **powerful** army to attack the people
22.28 Lord gave the donkey the **power** of speech, and it said to
22.38 But now, what **power** have I got?
24.20 "Amalek was the most **powerful** nation of all, But at the end
27.14 you refused to acknowledge my holy **power** before them."
33. 4 Lord showed that he was more **powerful** than the gods of Egypt.
Deut 2.24 I am placing in your **power** Sihon, the Amorite king of Heshbon,
2.33 God put him in our **power,** and we killed him, his sons,
3. 3 Og and his people in our **power,** and we slaughtered them all.
4.34 Before your very eyes he used his great **power** and strength;
4.37 you, and by his great **power** he himself brought you out of
4.38 out nations greater and more **powerful** than you, so that he
5.15 Lord your God, rescued you by my great **power** and strength.
6.21 king of Egypt, and the Lord rescued us by his great **power.**
7. 1 drive out seven nations larger and more **powerful** than you:
7. 2 places these people in your **power** and you defeat them, you
7.16 your God places in your **power,** and do not show them any
7.19 and wonders, and the great **power** and strength by which the
7.23 put your enemies in your **power** and make them panic until
7.24 He will put their kings in your **power.**
Deut 8.17 have made yourselves wealthy by your own **power** and strength.
8.18 the Lord your God who gives you the **power** to become rich.
9. 1 belonging to nations greater and more **powerful** than you.
9.14 father of a nation larger and more **powerful** than they are.'
9.26 and brought out of Egypt by your great strength and **power.**
9.29 you brought out of Egypt by your great **power** and might.'
10.17 Lord your God is supreme over all gods and over all **powers.**
11. 2 You saw the Lord's greatness, his **power,** his might,
11.23 belonging to nations greater and more **powerful** than you.
26. 5 went there, but they became a large and **powerful** nation.
26. 8 By his great **power** and strength he rescued us from Egypt.
28.43 gain more and more **power,** while you gradually lose yours.
Josh 4.24 will know how great the **Lord's power** is, and you will honour
9.25 Now we are in your **power;**
11.10 (At that time Hazor was the most **powerful** of all those kingdoms.)
17.17 "There are indeed many of you, and you are very **powerful.**
23. 9 Lord has driven great and **powerful** nations out as you
Judg 8. 3 After all, through the **power of God** you killed the two
13.25 And the **Lord's power** began to strengthen him while he
14. 6 Suddenly the **power of the Lord** made Samson strong, and he
14.19 Suddenly the **power of the Lord** made him strong, and he
15.14 Suddenly the **power of the Lord** made him strong, and he broke
1 Sam 2.10 he will give **power** to his king, he will make his chosen
4. 8 Who can save us from those **powerful** gods?
7. 3 and he will rescue you from the **power** of the Philistines."
10.26 Some **powerful** men, whose hearts God had touched, went with
17.46 This very day the Lord will put you in my **power;**
17.47 in battle, and he will put all of you in our **power."**
23. 7 to Keilah, and he said, "God has put him in my **power.**
24. 4 put your enemy in your **power** and you could do to him
24.10 just now in the cave the Lord put you in my **power.**
24.18 not kill me, even though the Lord put me in your **power.**
26. 8 to David, "God has put your enemy in your **power** tonight.
26.23 he put you in my **power,** but I did not harm you,
2 Sam 3. 6 Abner became more and more **powerful** among Saul's followers.
22.18 He rescued me from my **powerful** enemies and from all
22.30 to attack my enemies and **power** to overcome their defences.
1 Kgs 2.12 David as king, and his royal **power** was firmly established.
11.34 and I will keep him in **power** as long as he lives.
15.16 at war with each other as long as they were in **power.**
15.32 at war with each other as long as they were in **power.**
18.46 The **power of the Lord** came on Elijah;
2 Kgs 2. 9 the share of your **power** that will make me your successor,"
2.15 Jericho saw him and said, "The **power** of Elijah is on Elisha!"
3.15 played his harp, the **power of the Lord** came on Elisha,
5. 7 think that I am God, with the **power** of life and death?
8.13 "How could I ever be that **powerful?"**
14. 5 as Amaziah was firmly in **power,** he executed the officials
15.19 support in strengthening Menahem's **power** over the country.
17.36 who brought you out of Egypt with great **power** and strength;
19.25 I gave you the **power** to turn fortified cities into piles of
19.26 The people who lived there were **powerless;**
1 Chr 16.27 Glory and majesty surround him, **power** and joy fill his Temple.
25. 5 as he had promised, in order to give **power** to Heman.
29.11 You are great and **powerful,** glorious, splendid, and
29.12 you rule everything by your strength and **power;**
29.30 tell how he ruled, how **powerful** he was, and all the things
2 Chr 1. 1 the Lord his God blessed him and made him very **powerful.**
6.32 land hears how great and **powerful** you are and how you are
6.41 Box, the symbol of your **power,** enter the Temple and stay
12.13 Rehoboam ruled in Jerusalem and increased his **power** as king.
13.20 Jeroboam never regained his **power** during Abijah's reign.
13.21 Abijah, however, grew more **powerful.**
14.11 you can help a weak army as easily as a **powerful** one.
17.12 So Jehoshaphat continued to grow more and more **powerful.**
20. 6 You are **powerful** and mighty, and no one can oppose you.
25. 3 as he was firmly in **power,** he executed the officials who had
25. 8 is God who has the **power** to give victory or defeat, and
25.15 could not even save their own people from your **power?"**
26. 8 Uzziah, and he became so **powerful** that his fame spread even
26.15 everywhere, and he became very **powerful** because of the help
27. 6 Jotham grew **powerful** because he faithfully obeyed the Lord his God.
32. 7 We have more **power** on our side than he has on his.
32. 8 He has human **power,** but we have the Lord our God to
32.11 will save you from our **power,** but Hezekiah is deceiving you
32.17 saved their people from my **power,** and neither will
32.22 Jerusalem from the **power** of Sennacherib, the emperor of Assyria,
Ezra 4.10 peoples whom the great and **powerful** Ashurbanipal moved from
4.20 **Powerful** kings have reigned there and have ruled over
5.11 and equipped many years ago by a **powerful** king of Israel.
7.28 of his counsellors, and of all his **powerful** officials;
Neh 1.10 You rescued them by your great **power** and strength.
9. 6 The heavenly **powers** bow down and worship you.
9.24 You gave your people the **power** to do as they pleased with
9.32 How terrifying, how **powerful!**
Esth 6.13 said to him, "You are beginning to lose **power** to Mordecai.
9. 1 enemies of the Jews were hoping to get them in their **power.**
9. 4 that Mordecai was now a **powerful** man in the palace
9. 4 and was growing more **powerful.**
Job 1.12 he has is in your **power,** but you must not hurt Job
2. 6 right, he is in your **power,** but you are not to kill
9. 4 God is so wise and **powerful;**
11. 7 the limits and bounds of the greatness and **power of God?**
12.10 every man's life is in his **power.**
12.12 Old men have wisdom, but God has wisdom and **power.**
12.12 God has insight and **power** to act.
12.16 both deceived and deceiver are in his **power.**
12.19 he humbles priests and men of **power.**
12.21 He disgraces those in **power** and puts an end to the
13.11 reprimand you, [11]and his **power** will fill you with terror.

Job 15.24 disaster, like a **powerful** king, is waiting to attack him.
22. 8 You used your **power** and your position to take over the
25. 1 God is **powerful;**
26.14 are only hints of his **power,** only the whispers that we have
27.11 you how great is **God's power,** and explain what Almighty God
27.23 them as they run, frightening them with destructive **power.**
28.25 God gave the wind its **power** And determined the size of the
29.17 I destroyed the **power** of cruel men and rescued their victims.
30.21 you persecute me with all your **power.**
34.13 Did God get his **power** from someone else?
36.22 Remember how great is **God's power;**
37.23 **God's power** is so great that we cannot come near him;
38.11 Here your **powerful** waves must stop."
40.16 is in his body, and what **power** there is in his muscles!
41.22 His neck is so **powerful** that all who meet him are terrified.
42. 2 I know, Lord, that you are **all-powerful;**
Ps 3. 7 You punish all my enemies and leave them **powerless** to harm me.
10.15 Break the **power** of wicked and evil men;
16.10 secure, [10]because you protect me from the **power** of death.
18.17 He rescued me from my **powerful** enemies and from all
18.29 to attack my enemies and **power** to overcome their defences.
18.35 care has made me great, and your **power** has kept me safe.
20. 6 his holy heaven and by his **power** gives him great victories.
20. 7 horses, but we trust in the **power of the Lord** our God.
21.13 We will sing and praise your **power.**
29. 1 praise his glory and **power.**
33.16 A king does not win because of his **powerful** army;
37.33 abandon him to his enemy's **power** or let him be condemned
41. 2 he will not abandon them to the **power** of their enemies.
44. 3 they did not win it by their own **power;**
44. 3 it was by your **power** and your strength, by the assurance of
44. 5 to your people, [5]and by your **power** we defeat our enemies.
47. 9 More **powerful** than all armies is he;
49.15 he will save me from the **power** of death.
54. 1 Save me by your **power,** O God;
62.11 have heard God say that **power** belongs to him [12]and that
65. 6 in place by your strength, showing your mighty **power.**
66. 3 Your **power** is so great that your enemies bow down in fear
68.28 your power, O God, the **power** you have used on our behalf
68.34 Proclaim **God's power;**
68.35 He gives strength and **power** to his people.
71. 4 me from wicked men, from the **power** of cruel and evil men.
71.16 I will praise your **power,** Sovereign Lord;
71.18 me while I proclaim your **power** and might to all generations
75.10 He will break the **power** of the wicked,
75.10 but the **power** of the righteous will be increased.
77.10 hurts me most is this— that God is no longer **powerful."**
77.15 By your **power** you saved your people, the descendants of
78. 4 the next generation about the **Lord's power** and his great
78.26 to blow, and by his **power** he stirred up the south wind;
78.42 They forgot his great **power** and the day when he saved
78.61 the Covenant Box, the symbol of his **power** and glory.
79.11 prisoners, and by your great **power** free those who are
82. 4 Rescue them from the **power** of evil men.
83.16 with shame, O Lord, and make them acknowledge your **power.**
89. 9 You rule over the **powerful** sea;
89.13 How **powerful** you are!
89.21 will always be with him, my **power** will make him strong.
90.11 Who has felt the full **power** of your anger?
93. 4 roar of the ocean, more **powerful** than the waves of the sea.
96. 6 **power** and beauty fill his Temple.
97.10 he rescues them from the **power** of the wicked.
98. 1 By his own **power** and holy strength he has won the victory.
98. 2 he made his saving **power** known to the nations.
102.15 all the kings of the earth will fear his **power.**
103.21 the Lord, all you heavenly **powers,** you servants of his, who
105.22 over all the land, [22]with **power** over the king's officials
106. 8 them, as he had promised, in order to show his great **power.**
106.41 He abandoned them to the **power** of the heathen, and their
110. 2 From Zion the Lord will extend your royal **power.**
111. 6 He has shown his **power** to his people by giving them the
112. 2 The good man's children will be **powerful** in the land;
112. 9 he will be **powerful** and respected.
118.10 but I destroyed them by the **power of the Lord!**
118.11 but I destroyed them by the **power of the Lord!**
118.12 by the **power of the Lord** I destroyed them.
118.14 The Lord makes me **powerful** and strong;
118.15 "The **Lord's mighty power** has done it!
118.16 His **power** has brought us victory— his mighty power in battle!"
119.161 **Powerful** men attack me unjustly, but I respect your law.
132. 8 Covenant Box, the symbol of your **power,** and stay here for ever.
135.10 He destroyed many nations and killed **powerful** kings:
136.12 with his strong hand, his **powerful** arm;
136.17 He killed **powerful** kings;
138. 7 You oppose my angry enemies and save me by your **power.**
139. 5 you protect me with your **power.**
140. 4 Protect me, Lord, from the **power** of the wicked;
144. 7 save me from the **power** of foreigners, [8]who never tell the
144.11 rescue me from the **power** of foreigners, who never tell the
145.11 the glory of your royal **power** and tell of your might, [12]so
Prov 6. 3 you are in that man's **power,** but this is how to get
12.24 Hard work will give you **power;**
16.32 It is better to be patient than **powerful.**
18.18 If two **powerful** men are opposing each other in court,
20.28 A king will remain in **power** as long as his rule is
23.11 The Lord is their **powerful** defender, and he will argue
28.12 When good men come to **power,** everybody celebrates, but
28.28 People stay in hiding when bad men come to **power.**
28.28 But when they fall from **power,** righteous men will rule again.
29.16 When evil men are in **power,** crime increases.
Ecc 4. 1 help them, because their oppressors had **power** on their side.

Ecc 8. 9 world where some men have **power** and others have to suffer
9.14 A **powerful** king attacked it.
Song 8. 6 Love is as **powerful** as death;
Is 1.24 listen to what the Lord Almighty, Israel's **powerful** God,
1.31 fire by a spark, so **powerful** men will be destroyed by their
2.10 from the Lord's anger and to hide from his **power** and glory!
2.12 who is **powerful,** everyone who is proud and conceited.
2.19 and to hide from his **power** and glory, when he comes to
2.21 escape from his anger and to hide from his **power** and glory.
4. 4 By his **power** the Lord will judge and purify the nation and
8.11 With his great **power** the Lord warned me not to follow
9. 7 His royal **power** will continue to grow;
9. 7 King David's successor, basing his **power** on right and justice,
10.27 will free you from the **power** of Assyria, and their yoke will
11.11 will once again use his **power** and bring back home those of
12. 2 The Lord gives me **power** and strength;
14. 5 The Lord has ended the **power** of the evil rulers [6]who
14. 9 The ghosts of those who were **powerful** on earth are stirring about.
17.12 **Powerful** nations are in commotion with a sound like the
18. 2 rivers, to your strong and **powerful** nation, to your tall and
18. 7 and **powerful** nation, this tall and smooth-skinned people,
19. 2 fight each other, and rival kings will struggle for **power.**
24.21 the Lord will punish the **powers** above and the rulers of the
25. 3 The people of **powerful** nations will praise you;
27. 1 Lord will use his **powerful** and deadly sword to punish Leviathan,
28. 2 Lord has someone strong and **powerful** ready to attack them,
30. 3 But the king will be **powerless** to help them, and Egypt's
30.27 The **Lord's power** and glory can be seen in the distance.
31. 8 Assyria will be destroyed in war, but not by human **power.**
33.10 I will show how **powerful** I am.
33.13 and far hear what I have done and acknowledge my **power."**
33.15 Don't use your **power** to cheat the poor and don't accept bribes.
35. 2 Everyone will see the Lord's splendour, see his greatness and **power.**
37.26 I gave you the **power** to turn fortified cities into piles of
37.27 The people who lived there were **powerless;**
40.10 is coming to rule with **power,** bringing with him the people
40.23 He brings down **powerful** rulers and reduces them to nothing.
40.26 His **power** is so great— not one of them is ever
41.29 do nothing at all— these idols are weak and **powerless."**
42. 6 called you and given you **power** to see that justice is done
42.13 he shows his **power** against his enemies.
43.13 No one can escape from my **power;**
44. 8 Is there some **powerful** god I never heard of?"
45. 1 he sends him to strip kings of their **power;**
45.12 By my **power** I stretched out the heavens;
47. 6 I put them in your **power,** and you showed them no mercy;
47.13 You are **powerless** in spite of the advice you get.
48.16 (Now the Sovereign Lord has given me his **power** and sent me.)
49.26 They will know that I am Israel's **powerful** God."
51. 9 Use your **power** and save us;
52.10 The Lord will use his holy **power;**
53.12 a place of honour, a place among great and **powerful** men.
55. 4 of nations, and through him I showed them my **power.**
59.16 he will use his own **power** to rescue them and to win
59.17 like a coat of armour and saving **power** like a helmet.
59.19 From east to west everyone will fear him and his great **power.**
59.21 I have given you my **power** and my teachings to be yours
60.22 humblest family Will become as great as a **powerful** nation.
62. 8 a solemn promise, And by his **power** he will carry it out:
63. 1 dressed in red, marching along in **power** and strength?"
63. 1 "It is the Lord, **powerful** to save, coming to announce his victory."
63.12 the Lord, who by his **power** did great things through Moses,
63.15 Where is your **power?**
64. 2 Come and reveal your **power** to your enemies, and make the
66.18 they will see what my **power** can do [19]and will know that
66.19 have not heard of my fame or seen my greatness and **power:**
66.22 heavens will endure by my **power,** so your descendants and
Jer 5. 5 I will go to the people in **power,** and talk with them.
5.27 That is why they are **powerful** and rich, [28]why they are fat
10. 6 you are mighty, and your name is great and **powerful.**
10.12 The Lord made the earth by his **power;**
12. 7 given the people I love into the **power** of their enemies.
14. 9 a man taken by surprise, like a soldier **powerless** to help?
15.21 I will rescue you from the **power** of wicked and violent men.
16.21 all I will make the nations know my **power** and my might;
17.25 of Jerusalem and have the same royal **power** that David had.
20. 4 people of Judah under the **power** of the king of Babylonia;
20.13 He rescues the oppressed from the **power** of evil men.
23.10 they live wicked lives and misuse their **power.**
26.14 As for me, I am in your **power!**
27. 5 "By my great **power** and strength I created the world,
27. 6 all these nations under the **power** of my servant, King
27. 7 Then his nation will serve **powerful** nations and great kings.
28. 2 "I have broken the **power** of the king of Babylonia.
28. 4 Yes, I will break the **power** of the king of Babylonia.
28. 8 disease would come to many nations and **powerful** kingdoms.
29.21 them over to the **power** of King Nebuchadnezzar of Babylonia,
30.20 I will restore the nation's ancient **power** and establish it
32.17 made the earth and the sky by your great **power** and might;
32.18 You are a great and **powerful** God;
32.21 our enemies, you used your **power** and might to bring your
42.11 I am with you, and I will rescue you from his **power.**
43. 3 that the Babylonians will gain **power** over us and can either
48.17 Say, 'Its **powerful** rule has been broken;
48.25 its **power** has been destroyed.
49. 4 do you trust in your **power** and say that no one would
49.35 "I will kill all the bowmen who have made Elam so **powerful.**
51.15 The Lord made the earth by his **power;**
Lam 1. 5 they hold her in their **power.**
5. 8 than slaves, and no one can save us from their **power.**

Ezek 1. 3 I heard the Lord speak to me and I felt his **power.**
3.14 The **power of the Lord** came on me with great force, and
3.22 I felt the **powerful** presence of the Lord and heard him
3.27 and give you back the **power** of speech, you will tell them
8. 1 Suddenly the **power of the Sovereign Lord** came on me.
13.18 so that they can have **power** over other people's lives.
13.18 You want to possess the **power** of life and death over my
13.21 and let my people escape from your **power** once and for all.
13.23 rescuing my people from your **power,** so that you will know
16.39 will put you in their **power,** and they will tear down the
17.17 Even the **powerful** army of the king of Egypt will not be
20.33 will rule over you with a strong hand, with all my **power.**
20.34 I will show you my **power** and my anger when I gather
21.26 Raise the poor to **power!**
24.27 you will get back the **power** of speech which you had lost,
26. 2 Her commercial **power** is gone!
30.12 up the Nile and put Egypt under the **power** of evil men.
30.18 Tahpanhes when I break the **power** of Egypt and put an end
31. 2 How **powerful** you are!
32.18 them down with the other **powerful** nations to the world of
32.27 These heroes were once **powerful** enough to terrify the living.
32.29 They were **powerful** soldiers, but now they lie in the world
32.30 Their **power** once spread terror, but now they go down in
33.22 he came, I had felt the **powerful** presence of the Lord.
33.22 next morning, the Lord gave me back the **power** of speech.
33.28 a desolate waste, and the **power** they were so proud of will
37. 1 I felt the **powerful** presence of the Lord, and his spirit
38.15 a large, **powerful** army of soldiers from many nations,
39.21 them how I use my **power** to carry out my just decisions.
40. 1 that day I felt the **powerful** presence of the Lord, and he
Dan 2.10 even the greatest and most **powerful,** has ever made such a
2.20 "God is wise and **powerful!**
2.37 heaven has made you emperor and given you **power,** might, and
3.17 us from the blazing furnace and from your **power,** then he
4. 3 How **powerful** are the miracles he performs!
4.17 that the Supreme God has **power** over human kingdoms and that
4.22 reach the sky, and your **power** extends over the whole world.
4.30 city to display my **power** and might, my glory and majesty."
4.31 Your royal **power** is now taken away from you.
4.32 that the Supreme God has **power** over human kingdoms and that
4.36 back my royal **power,** with even greater honour than before.
5. 7 round his neck, and be the third in **power** in the kingdom."
5.16 your neck, and be the third in **power** in the kingdom."
5.29 And he made him the third in **power** in the kingdom.
5.31 who was then sixty-two years old, seized the royal **power.**
6.26 be destroyed, and his **power** will never come to an end.
7. 7 It was **powerful,** horrible, terrifying.
7.12 The other beasts had their **power** taken away, but they
7.14 given authority, honour, and royal **power,** so that the people
7.18 Supreme God will receive royal **power** and keep it for ever
7.22 The time had arrived for God's people to receive royal **power.**
7.25 people will be under his **power** for three and a half years.
7.26 judgement, take away his **power,** and destroy him completely.
7.27 The **power** and greatness of all the kingdoms on earth
7.27 Their royal **power** will never end and all rulers on earth
8. 4 No animal could stop him or escape his **power.**
8. 8 but at the height of his **power** his horn was broken.
8. 9 grew a little horn, whose **power** extended towards the south
8.24 He will grow strong—but not by his own **power.**
8.24 He will bring destruction on **powerful** men and on God's own people.
8.25 but he will be destroyed without the use of any human **power.**
9.15 you showed your **power** by bringing your people out
9.15 of Egypt, and your **power** is still remembered.
9.26 Temple will be destroyed by the invading army of a **powerful** ruler.
11. 2 At the height of his **power** and wealth he will challenge the
11. 4 at the height of his **power** his empire will break up and
11. 4 his place, but they will not have the **power** that he had.
11.16 in the Promised Land and have it completely in his **power.**
11.21 but he will come unexpectedly and seize **power** by trickery.
11.25 will prepare to fight back with a huge and **powerful** army.
11.40 with all his **power,** using chariots, horses, and many ships.
Hos 1. 5 I will at that time destroy Israel's military **power."**
2.10 and no one will be able to save her from my **power.**
5. 4 Idolatry has a **powerful** hold on them, and they do not
7.16 keep on turning away from me to a god that is **powerless.**
13.14 world of the dead or rescue them from the **power** of death.
Joel 1. 6 they are **powerful** and too many to count;
Mic 3. 8 me with his spirit and **power,** and gives me a sense of
4. 3 among the nations, among the great **powers** near and far.
Nah 1. 3 become angry, but he is **powerful** and never lets the guilty
1.13 I will now end Assyria's **power** over you and break the
2. 1 The **power** that will shatter you has come.
3. 9 She ruled Sudan and Egypt, there was no limit to her **power;**
Hab 1. 6 I am bringing the Babylonians to **power,**
1.11 wind and are gone, these men whose **power** is their god."
3. 4 light flashes from his hand, there where his **power** is hidden.
Zeph 2.13 The Lord will use his **power** to destroy Assyria.
2.15 is so proud of its own **power** and thinks it is safe.
3.17 his **power** gives you victory.
Hag 2.22 and earth [22] and overthrow kingdoms and end their **power.**
Zech 1.19 "They stand for the world **powers** that have scattered the
5. 9 flying towards me with **powerful** wings like those of a stork.
8.22 Many peoples and **powerful** nations will come to Jerusalem
10. 3 They will be my **powerful** war-horses.
10.11 Proud Assyria will be humbled, and mighty Egypt will lose her **power.**
11. 6 myself will put all the people in the **power** of their rulers.
11. 6 the earth, and I will not save it from their **power.")**
11.17 War will totally destroy his **power.**
Mal 4. 2 who obey me, my saving **power** will rise on you like the
Mt 9.34 of the demons who gives him the **power** to drive out demons."
12.24 only because their ruler Beelzebul gives him **power** to do so."
12.27 out demons because Beelzebul gives me the **power** to do so.
12.27 Well, then, who gives your followers the **power** to drive them out?
12.28 Spirit, who gives me the **power** to drive out demons, which
14. 2 "That is why he has this **power** to perform miracles."
20.25 rulers of the heathen have **power** over them, and the leaders
22.29 It is because you don't know the Scriptures or **God's power.**
24.29 from heaven, and the **powers in space** will be driven from
24.30 Man coming on the clouds of heaven with **power** and great glory.
26.45 of Man to be handed over to the **power** of sinful men.
Mk 3.22 of the demons who gives him the **power** to drive them out."
5.30 At once Jesus knew that **power** had gone out of him,
6.14 That is why he has this **power** to perform miracles."
9. 1 until they have seen the Kingdom of God come with **power."**
10.42 rulers of the heathen have **power** over them, and the leaders
12.24 It is because you don't know the Scriptures or **God's power.**
13.25 from heaven, and the **powers in space** will be driven from
13.26 Man will appear, coming in the clouds with great **power** and glory.
14.41 Man is now being handed over to the **power** of sinful men.
16.17 Believers will be given the **power** to perform miracles:
Lk 1.35 Spirit will come on you, and **God's power** will rest upon you.
1.66 For it was plain that the **Lord's power** was upon him.
1.71 from our enemies, from the **power** of all those who hate us.
4. 6 will give you all this **power** and all this wealth," the
4.14 to Galilee, and the **power of the Holy Spirit** was with him.
4.36 With authority and **power** this man gives orders to the evil spirits,
5.17 The **power of the Lord** was present for Jesus to heal the
6.19 tried to touch him, for **power** was going out from him
8.46 touched me, for I knew it when **power** went out of me."
9. 1 disciples together and gave them **power** and authority to drive out
9.43 All the people were amazed at the mighty **power of God.**
9.44 Man is going to be handed over to the **power** of men."
10.19 and overcome all the **power** of the Enemy, and nothing will
11.15 of the demons, who gives him the **power** to drive them out."
11.18 out demons because Beelzebul gives me the **power** to do so.
11.20 rather by means of **God's power** that I drive out demons,
20.20 him over to the authority and **power** of the Roman Governor.
21.26 whole earth, for the **powers in space** will be driven from
21.27 Man will appear, coming in a cloud with great **power** and glory.
22.25 kings of the pagans have **power** over their people, and the
22.53 is your hour to act, when the **power** of darkness rules."
24.19 all the people to be **powerful** in everything he said and did.
24.49 the city until the **power** from above comes down upon you."
Jn 3.35 The Father loves his Son and has put everything in his **power.**
4.23 here, when by the **power of God's Spirit** people will worship
4.24 and only by the **power** of his Spirit can people worship
6.63 man's **power** is of no use at all.
9. 3 is blind so that **God's power** might be seen at work
12.38 To whom did the Lord reveal his **power?"**
13. 3 Jesus knew that the Father had given him complete **power;**
14.30 He has no **power** over me, [31] but the world must know that
17.11 Keep them safe by the **power** of your name, the name you
17.12 kept them safe by the **power** of your name, the name you
Acts 1. 2 instructions by the **power of the Holy Spirit** to the men
1. 8 you will be filled with **power,** and you will be witnesses for
2.24 setting him free from its **power,** because it was impossible that
3.12 by means of our own **power** or godliness that we made this
3.16 It was the **power** of his name that gave strength to this
4. 7 What **power** have you got or whose name did you use?"
4.10 completely well through the **power** of the name of Jesus Christ
4.28 everything that you by your **power** and will had already decided
4.33 With great **power** the apostles gave witness to the resurrection
6. 8 by God and full of **power,** performed great miracles and wonders
8.10 "He is that **power of God** known as 'The Great Power',"
8.19 and said, "Give this **power** to me too, so that anyone
9.22 Saul's preaching became even more **powerful,** and his proofs that
10.38 and how God poured out on him the Holy Spirit and **power.**
10.38 all who were under the **power** of the Devil, for God was
10.43 will have his sins forgiven through the **power** of his name."
11.21 The **Lord's power** was with them, and a great number of
11.28 and by the **power of the Spirit** predicted that a severe
12.11 rescue me from Herod's **power** and from everything the Jewish people
13.17 of Egypt by his great **power,** [18] and for forty years he
14. 3 by giving them the **power** to perform miracles and wonders.
19.20 In this **powerful** way the word of the Lord kept spreading
21. 4 By the **power of the Spirit** they told Paul not to go
26.18 the light and from the **power** of Satan to God, so that
Rom 1. 4 he was shown with great **power** to be the Son of God
1.16 it is **God's power** to save all who believe, first the Jews
1.20 invisible qualities, both his eternal **power** and his divine nature,
3. 9 that Jews and Gentiles alike are all under the **power** of sin.
4.20 his faith filled him with **power,** and he gave praise to God.
6. 4 from death by the glorious **power** of the Father, so also we
6. 6 in order that the **power** of the sinful self might be
6. 7 a person dies, he is set free from the **power** of sin.
6.10 And so, because he died, sin has no **power** over him;
8.15 and by the **Spirit's power** we cry out to God, "Father!
8.38 heavenly rulers or **powers,** neither the present nor the future,
9.17 use you to show my **power** and to spread my fame over
9.22 He wanted to show his anger and to make his **power** known.
13. 4 then be afraid of him, because his **power** to punish is real.
15.13 hope will continue to grow by the **power of the Holy Spirit.**
15.19 by the **power** of miracles and wonders,
15.19 and by the **power of the Spirit** of God.
1 Cor 1.17 Christ's death on the cross is not robbed of its **power.**
1.18 but for us who are being saved it is **God's power.**
1.24 Christ, who is the **power of God** and the wisdom of God.
1.26 few of you were wise or **powerful** or of high social standing.

1 Cor 1.27 the world considers weak in order to shame the **powerful.**
2. 4 but with convincing proof of the **power of God's Spirit.**
2. 5 then, does not rest on human wisdom but on **God's power.**
2. 6 this world or to the **powers** that rule this world—
2. 6 **powers** that are losing their power.
4.19 find out for myself the **power** which these proud people have,
4.20 Kingdom of God is not a matter of words but of **power.**
5. 3 in my spirit, by the **power of our Lord** Jesus present with
6.14 Lord from death, and he will also raise us by his **power.**
10.13 not allow you to be tested beyond your **power** to remain firm;
12. 9 while to another person he gives the **power** to heal.
12.10 The Spirit gives one person the **power** to work miracles;
12.28 those who are given the **power** to heal or to help others
12.29 Not everyone has the **power** to work miracles
14. 2 He is speaking secret truths by the **power of the Spirit.**
15.24 rulers, authorities, and **powers,** and will hand over the Kingdom
15.55 Where, Death, is your **power** to hurt?"
15.56 Death gets its **power** to hurt from sin,
15.56 and sin gets its **power** from the Law.
2 Cor 1.12 frankness and sincerity, by the **power** of God's grace, and
4. 7 to show that the supreme **power** belongs to God, not to us.
6. 7 by our message of truth, and by the **power of God.**
10. 4 but God's **powerful** weapons, which we use to destroy
12. 9 all you need, for my **power** is greatest when you are weak."
12. 9 in order to feel the protection of Christ's **power** over me.
13. 3 instead, he shows his **power** among you.
13. 4 death on the cross, it is by **God's power** that he lives.
13. 4 relations with you we shall share **God's power** in his life.
Gal 2. 8 For by **God's power** I was made an apostle to the Gentiles,
3. 3 do you now want to finish by your own **power?**
3.22 says that the whole world is under the **power** of sin;
5. 5 for by the **power of God's Spirit** working through our faith.
Eph 1.19 how very great is his **power** at work in us who believe.
1.19 This **power** working in us is the same as the mighty strength
1.21 rules there above all heavenly rulers, authorities, **powers,** and
2. 2 ruler of the spiritual **powers in space,** the spirit who now
3. 7 gift, which he gave me through the working of his **power.**
3.10 the angelic rulers and **powers** in the heavenly world might learn
3.16 his glory to give you **power** through his Spirit to be strong
3.18 God's people, may have the **power** to understand how broad and long,
3.20 who by means of his **power** working in us is able to
6.10 in union with the Lord and by means of his mighty **power.**
6.12 the rulers, authorities, and cosmic **powers** of this dark age.
Phil 3.10 and to experience the **power** of his resurrection, to share in
3.21 own glorious body, using that **power** by which he is able to
4.13 to face all conditions by the **power** that Christ gives me.
Col 1.11 which comes from his glorious **power,** so that you may be able
1.13 He rescued us from the **power** of darkness and brought us
1.16 seen and the unseen things, including spiritual **powers,** lords,
2.11 consists of being freed from the **power** of this sinful self.
2.12 faith in the active **power of God,** who raised him from death.
2.15 Christ freed himself from the **power** of the spiritual rulers and
1 Thes 1. 5 words only, but also with **power** and the Holy Spirit, and
2 Thes 1.11 May he fulfil by his **power** all your desire for goodness
2. 9 One will come with the **power** of Satan and perform all kinds
2.11 And so God sends the **power** of error to work in them
2.13 be saved by the **Spirit's power** to make you his holy people
1 Tim 1.20 I have punished by handing them over to the **power** of Satan;
2 Tim 1. 7 his Spirit fills us with **power,** love, and self-control.
1.10 He has ended the **power** of death and through the gospel has
1.14 Through the **power of the Holy Spirit,** who lives in us,
3. 5 the outward form of our religion, but reject its real **power.**
Heb 1. 3 God's own being, sustaining the universe with his **powerful** word.
1. 3 in heaven at the right-hand side of God, the **Supreme Power.**
2.14 the Devil, who has the **power** over death, [15] and in this way
6. 5 and they had felt the **powers** of the coming age.
7.16 and regulations, but through the **power** of a life which has
Jas 5.16 The prayer of a good person has a **powerful** effect.
1 Pet 1. 5 are kept safe by **God's power** for the salvation which is
1.12 Good News by the **power of the Holy Spirit** sent from heaven.
3.22 of God, ruling over all angels and heavenly authorities and **powers.**
4.11 Jesus Christ, to whom belong glory and **power** for ever and ever.
5.11 To him be the **power** for ever!
2 Pet 1. 3 **God's divine power** has given us everything we need to live
1 Jn 3.14 Whoever does not love is still under the **power** of death.
4. 4 is in you is more **powerful** than the spirit in those who
Jude 20 Pray in the **power of the Holy Spirit,** [21] and keep
Rev 1. 6 To Jesus Christ be the glory and **power** for ever and ever!
3. 8 I know that you have a little **power;**
4.11 You are worthy to receive glory, honour, and **power.**
5.12 is worthy to receive **power,** wealth, wisdom, and strength, honour,
6. 4 Its rider was given the **power** to bring war on the earth,
6.15 chiefs, the rich and the **powerful,** and all other men,
7. 2 whom God had given the **power** to damage the earth and the
7.12 wisdom, thanksgiving, honour, **power,** and might belong to our God
9. 3 they were given the same kind of **power** that scorpions have.
9.10 they have the **power** to hurt people for five months.
9.19 For the **power** of the horses is in their mouths and also
11.15 in heaven, saying, "The **power** to rule over the world belongs
11.17 you have taken your great **power** and have begun to rule!
12.10 Now God has shown his **power** as King!
13. 2 the beast his own **power,** his throne, and his vast authority.
15. 8 from the glory and **power of God,** and no one could go
17.13 and they give their **power** and authority to the beast.
17.17 and giving the beast their **power** to rule until God's words
18.23 Your businessmen were the most **powerful** in all the world,
19. 1 Salvation, glory, and **power** belong to our God!
20. 4 and those who sat on them were given the **power** to judge.
20. 6 The second death has no **power** over them;

PRACTICE

Gen 44.15 my position could find you out by **practising** divination?"
Ex 22.18 "Put to death any woman who **practises** magic.
23.24 or worship them, and do not adopt their religious **practices.**
Lev 18. 3 Do not follow the **practices** of the people of Egypt, where
18. 5 Follow the **practices** and the laws that I give you;
18.30 and do not follow the **practices** of the people who lived in
19.26 Do not **practise** any kind of magic.
20.23 They have disgusted me with all their evil **practices.**
Deut 12.30 their religious **practices,** because that would be fatal.
18. 9 the disgusting **practices** of the nations that are there.
18.10 and don't let your people **practise** divination or look for
18.14 advice of those who **practise** divination and look for omens,
1 Kgs 14.24 The people of Judah **practised** all the shameful things done
2 Kgs 16. 3 to idols, imitating the disgusting **practice** of the people
17.11 the pagan altars, following the **practice** of the people whom
17.22 Jeroboam and continued to **practise** all the sins he had committed,
21. 2 Following the disgusting **practices** of the nations whom the
21. 6 He **practised** divination and magic
23. 3 to put into **practice** the demands attached to the covenant,
2 Chr 28. 3 to idols, imitating the disgusting **practice** of the people
33. 2 Following the disgusting **practices** of the nations whom the
33. 6 He **practised** divination and magic
34.31 to put into **practice** the demands attached to the covenant,
36. 8 Jehoiakim did, including his disgusting **practices**
Ezra 7.10 Law of the Lord, to **practising** it, and to teaching all its
Job 21.28 house of the great man now, the man who **practised** evil?"
Ps 7.14 they plan trouble and **practise** deception.
Is 2. 6 full of magic **practices** from the east and from Philistia.
Jer 44. 5 not give up your evil **practice** of sacrificing to other gods.
44.22 Lord could no longer endure your wicked and evil **practices.**
Ezek 16.24 you built places to worship idols and **practise** prostitution.
16.31 you built places to worship idols and **practise** prostitution.
18.14 sins his father **practised,** but does not follow his example.
23.45 adultery and murder, because they **practise** adultery and
Mic 6.16 you have followed the evil **practices** of King Omri and of his
Zeph 1. 8 the king's sons, and all who **practise** foreign customs.
Mal 3. 5 once against those who **practise** magic, against adulterers,
Mt 23. 3 because they don't **practise** what they preach.
23.23 These you should **practise,** without neglecting the others.
Lk 11.42 These you should **practise,** without neglecting the others.
Jn 13.17 truth, how happy you will be if you put it into **practice!**
Acts 16.21 and we cannot accept these customs or **practise** them."
19.19 Many of those who had **practised** magic brought their books
Gal 1.14 of my age in my **practice** of the Jewish religion,
6.13 Even those who **practise** circumcision do not obey the Law;
Phil 4. 9 Put into **practice** what you learnt and received from me,
1 Thes 1. 3 you put your faith into **practice,** how your love made you
1 Tim 4.15 **Practise** these things and devote yourself to them,
Heb 5.14 adults, who through **practice** are able to distinguish between good
Jas 1.22 instead, put it into **practice.**
1.23 does not put it into **practice** is like a man who looks
1.25 but puts it into **practice**—that person will be blessed by
Rev 2.14 that had been offered to idols and to **practise** sexual immorality.
2.20 she misleads my servants into **practising** sexual immorality
17. 2 The kings of the earth **practised** sexual immorality with her,
18. 3 The kings of the earth **practised** sexual immorality with her,
21. 8 the immoral, those who **practise** magic, those who worship idols,
22.15 the perverts and those who **practise** magic, the immoral

PRAISE

Gen 9.26 Give **praise** to the Lord, the God of Shem!
14.20 Most High God, who gave you victory over your enemies, be **praised!"**
24.27 He said, **"Praise** the Lord, the God of my master Abraham,
24.48 I **praised** the Lord, the God of my master Abraham, who had
29.35 She said, "This time I will **praise** the Lord";
49. 8 "Judah, your brothers will **praise** you.
Ex 15. 2 my God, and I will **praise** him, my father's God, and I
18.10 he was happy [10] and said, **"Praise** the Lord, who saved you
18.10 **Praise** the Lord, who saved his people from slavery!
Deut 10.21 **Praise** him—he is your God, and you have seen with your
26.19 created, and you will bring **praise** and honour to his name.
32. 3 I will **praise** the name of the Lord, and his people will
32.43 "Nations, you must **praise** the Lord's people— he
33.20 **"Praise** God, who made their territory large.
Josh 22.33 The Israelites were satisfied and **praised** God.
Judg 5. 2 **Praise** the Lord!
5. 9 **Praise** the Lord!
16.24 When the people saw him, they sang **praise** to their god:
Ruth 4.14 The women said to Naomi, **"Praise** the Lord!
1 Sam 19. 4 Jonathan **praised** David to Saul and said, "Sir, don't do
25.32 David said to her, **"Praise** the Lord, the God of Israel,
25.39 When David heard that Nabal had died, he said, **"Praise** the Lord!
2 Sam 18.28 ground before him, and said, **"Praise** the Lord your God, who
22. 4 **Praise** the Lord!
22.47 **Praise** my defender!
22.50 And so I **praise** you among the nations;
22.50 I sing **praises** to you.
1 Kgs 1.48 and prayed, 'Let us **praise** the Lord, the God of Israel,
5. 7 Solomon's message, and he said, **"Praise** the Lord today for
8.15 He said, **"Praise** the Lord God of Israel!
8.56 He said, [56] **"Praise** the Lord who has given his people peace,
8.66 They all **praised** him and went home happy because of all the
10. 9 **Praise** the Lord your God!
1 Chr 16. 4 in front of the Covenant Box, by singing and **praising** him.
16. 7 the responsibility for singing **praises** to the Lord.
16. 9 Sing **praise** to the Lord;
16.25 The Lord is great and is to be highly **praised;**

1 Chr 16.28 **Praise** the Lord, all people on earth, praise his glory and might.
16.29 **Praise** the Lord's glorious name;
16.35 so that we may be thankful and **praise** your holy name."
16.36 **Praise** the Lord, the God of Israel!
16.36 **Praise** him now and for ever!
16.36 Then all the people said, "Amen," and **praised** the Lord.
16.41 were specifically chosen to sing **praises** to the Lord for his
16.42 which were played when the songs of **praise** were sung.
23. 5 duty, and four thousand to **praise** the Lord, using the
23.30 and to **praise** and glorify the Lord every morning and
25. 3 the music of harps, and sang **praise** and thanks to the Lord.
29.10 There in front of the whole assembly King David **praised** the Lord.
29.10 of our ancestor Jacob, may you be **praised** for ever and ever!
29.13 God, we give you thanks, and we **praise** your glorious name.
29.20 Then David commanded the people, **"Praise** the Lord your God!"
29.20 And the whole assembly **praised** the Lord,
2 Chr 2.12 **Praise** the Lord God of Israel, Creator of heaven and earth!
5.11 cymbals, and other instruments, as they **praised** the Lord,
5.11 **"Praise** the Lord, because he is good, And his love is eternal."
6. 4 He said, **"Praise** the Lord God of Israel!
7. 3 the pavement, worshipping God and **praising** him for his
7. 6 facing them stood the Levites, **praising** the Lord with the
9. 8 **Praise** the Lord your God!
20.19 and with a loud shout **praised** the Lord, the God of Israel.
20.21 **"Praise** the Lord!
20.26 the Valley of Beracah and **praised** the Lord for all he had
29.27 offering began, the people sang **praise** to the Lord, and the
29.30 the Lord the songs of **praise** that were written by David and
30.21 Levites and the priests **praised** the Lord with all their strength.
30.22 Hezekiah **praised** the Levites for their skill in
30.22 which they offered sacrifices in **praise** of the Lord, the God
31. 2 the temple worship, and giving **praise** and thanks in the
31. 8 given, they praised the Lord and **praised** his people Israel.
Ezra 3.10 They **praised** the Lord according to the instructions handed
3.11 They sang the Lord's **praises,** repeating the refrain:
3.11 shouted with all his might, **praising** the Lord, because the
7.27 Ezra said, **"Praise** the Lord, the God of our ancestors!
Neh 5.13 and **praised** the Lord.
8. 6 Ezra said, **"Praise** the Lord, the great God!"
9. 5 "Stand up and **praise** the Lord your God;
9. 5 **praise** him for ever and ever!
9. 5 Let everyone **praise** his glorious name,
9. 5 although no human **praise** is great enough."
11. 2 **praised** anyone else who volunteered to live in Jerusalem.
12.24 Two groups at a time **praised** God responsively and gave
12.46 musicians have led songs of **praise** and thanksgiving to God.
Job 1.21 May his name be **praised!"**
29.13 who were in deepest misery **praised** me, and I helped widows
29.20 Everyone was always **praising** me, and my strength never failed me.
31.20 Then he would **praise** me with all his heart.
36.24 He has always been **praised** for what he does;
36.24 you also must **praise** him.
40.14 will be the first to **praise** you and admit that you won
Ps 6. 5 no one can **praise** you there.
7.17 for his justice, I sing **praises** to the Lord, the Most High.
8. 1 Your **praise** reaches up to the heavens;
9. 1 I will **praise** you, Lord, with all my heart;
9. 2 I will sing **praise** to you, Almighty God.
9.11 Sing **praise** to the Lord, who rules in Zion!
9.14 Jerusalem and tell them all the things for which I **praise** you.
12. 7 Wicked men are everywhere, and everyone **praises** what is evil.
16. 7 I **praise** the Lord, because he guides me, and in the night
18. 3 **Praise** the Lord!
18.46 **Praise** my defender!
18.49 And so I **praise** you among the nations;
18.49 I sing **praises** to you.
20. 5 victory and celebrate your triumph by **praising** our God.
21.13 We **praise** you, Lord, for your great strength!
21.13 We will sing and **praise** your power.
22. 3 are enthroned as the Holy One, the one whom Israel **praises.**
22.22 I will **praise** you in their assembly:
22.23 **"Praise** him, you servants of the Lord!
22.25 the full assembly I will **praise** you for what you have done;
22.26 those who come to the Lord will **praise** him.
26.12 in the assembly of his people I **praise** the Lord.
27. 6 I will sing, I will **praise** the Lord.
28. 6 Give **praise** to the Lord;
28. 7 I **praise** him with joyful songs.
29. 1 **Praise** the Lord, you heavenly beings;
29. 1 **praise** his glory and power.
29. 2 **Praise** the Lord's glorious name;
30. 1 I **praise** you, Lord, because you have saved me and kept my
30. 4 Sing **praise** to the Lord, all his faithful people!
30. 9 Are dead people able to **praise** you?
30.12 I will sing **praise** to you.
31.21 **Praise** the Lord!
33. 1 **praise** him, all you that obey him.
34. 1 I will never stop **praising** him.
34. 2 I will **praise** him for what he has done;
34. 3 let us **praise** his name together!
35.18 I will **praise** you before them all.
35.28 your righteousness, and I will **praise** you all day long.
40. 3 to sing a new song, a song of **praise** to our God.
41.13 **Praise** the Lord, the God of Israel!
41.13 **Praise** him now and for ever!
42. 4 along, a happy crowd, singing and shouting **praise** to God.
42. 5 and once again I will **praise** him, my saviour and my God.
42.11 and once again I will **praise** him, my saviour and my God.
43. 4 play my harp and sing **praise** to you, O God, my God.
43. 5 and once again I will **praise** him, my saviour and my God.

Ps 44. 8 We will always **praise** you and give thanks to you for ever.
45.17 ever, and everyone will **praise** you for all time to come.
47. 1 **Praise** God with loud songs!
47. 6 Sing **praise** to God;
47. 6 sing **praise** to our king!
47. 7 **praise** him with songs!
48. 1 and is to be highly **praised** in the city of our God,
48.10 You are **praised** by people everywhere, and your fame
49.18 with this life and is **praised** because he is successful,
50.15 I will save you, and you will **praise** me."
51.15 Help me to speak, Lord, and I will **praise** you.
56. 4 I **praise** him for what he has promised.
56.10 God is on my side— [10]the Lord, whose promises I **praise.**
57. 7 I will sing and **praise** you!
57. 9 I will **praise** you among the peoples.
59.17 I will **praise** you, my defender.
61. 8 So I will always sing **praises** to you, as I offer you
63. 3 love is better than life itself, and so I will **praise** you.
63. 5 be satisfied, and I will sing glad songs of **praise** to you.
63.11 promises in God's name will **praise** him, but the mouths of
64.10 all good people will **praise** him.
65. 1 is right for us to **praise** you in Zion and keep our
66. 1 **Praise** God with shouts of joy, all people!
66. 2 offer him glorious **praise!**
66. 4 they sing **praises** to you, they sing praises to your name."
66. 8 **Praise** our God, all nations;
66. 8 let your **praise** be heard.
66.17 I **praised** him with songs.
66.20 I **praise** God, because he did not reject my prayer or
67. 3 May the peoples **praise** you, O God;
67. 3 may all the peoples **praise** you!
67. 5 May the peoples **praise** you, O God;
67. 5 may all the peoples **praise** you!
68. 4 Sing to God, sing **praises** to his name;
68.19 **Praise** the Lord, who carries our burdens day after day;
68.26 **"Praise** God in the meeting of his people;
68.26 **praise** the Lord, all you descendants of Jacob!"
68.32 kingdoms of the world, sing **praise** to the Lord, [33]to him
68.35 **Praise** God!
69.30 I will **praise** God with a song;
69.34 **Praise** God, O heaven and earth, seas and all creatures in them.
71. 6 I will always **praise** you.
71. 8 All day long I **praise** you and proclaim your glory.
71.14 I will **praise** you more and more.
71.16 I will **praise** your power, Sovereign Lord;
71.22 I will indeed **praise** you with the harp;
71.22 I will **praise** your faithfulness, my God.
72.18 **Praise** the Lord, the God of Israel!
72.19 **Praise** his glorious name for ever!
74.21 let those poor and needy people **praise** you.
75. 9 speaking of the God of Jacob or singing **praises** to him.
76.10 Men's anger only results in more **praise** for you;
79.13 thank you for ever and **praise** you for all time to come.
80.18 keep us alive, and we will **praise** you.
81. 1 sing **praise** to the God of Jacob!
84. 4 who live in your Temple, always singing **praise** to you.
85. 6 Make us strong again, and we, your people, will **praise** you.
86. 9 they will **praise** your greatness.
86.12 I will **praise** you with all my heart, O Lord my God;
88.10 Do they rise up and **praise** you?
89.16 all day long, and they **praise** you for your goodness.
89.52 **Praise** the Lord for ever!
95. 1 Come, let us **praise** the Lord!
95. 2 him with thanksgiving and sing joyful songs of **praise.**
96. 2 Sing to the Lord, and **praise** him!
96. 4 The Lord is great and is to be highly **praised;**
96. 7 **Praise** the Lord, all people on earth;
96. 7 **praise** his glory and might.
96. 8 **Praise** the Lord's glorious name;
98. 4 **praise** him with songs and shouts of joy!
98. 5 Sing **praises** to the Lord!
99. 3 Everyone will **praise** his great and majestic name.
99. 5 **Praise** the Lord our God;
99. 9 **Praise** the Lord our God, and worship at his sacred hill!
100. 4 Enter the temple gates with thanksgiving, go into its courts with **praise.**
100. 4 Give thanks to him and **praise** him.
102.18 Lord has done, so that people not yet born will **praise** him.
102.21 Zion, and he will be **praised** in Jerusalem [22]when nations
103. 1 **Praise** the Lord, my soul!
103. 1 All my being, **praise** his holy name!
103. 2 **Praise** the Lord, my soul, and do not forget how kind he
103.20 **Praise** the Lord, you strong and mighty angels, who obey his commands,
103.21 **Praise** the Lord, all you heavenly powers, you servants of his,
103.22 **Praise** the Lord, all his creatures in all the places he rules.
103.22 **Praise** the Lord, my soul!
104. 1 **Praise** the Lord, my soul!
104.33 as long as I live I will sing **praises** to my God.
104.35 **Praise** the Lord, my soul!
104.35 **Praise** the Lord!
105. 2 Sing **praise** to the Lord;
105.45 **Praise** the Lord!
106. 1 **Praise** the Lord!
106. 2 Who can **praise** him enough?
106.12 Then his people believed his promises and sang **praises** to him.
106.47 so that we may be thankful and **praise** your holy name.
106.48 **Praise** the Lord, the God of Israel;
106.48 **praise** him now and for ever!
106.48 **Praise** the Lord!
107. 2 Repeat these words in **praise** to the Lord, all you whom he

Ps 107.32 assembly of the people and **praise** him before the council of
108. 1 I will sing and **praise** you!
108. 3 I will **praise** you among the peoples.
109. 1 I **praise** you, God;
109.30 I will **praise** him in the assembly of the people,
111. 1 **Praise** the Lord!
111.10 He is to be **praised** for ever.
112. 1 **Praise** the Lord!
113. 1 **Praise** the Lord!
113. 1 You servants of the Lord, **praise** his name!
113. 2 May his name be **praised,** now and for ever.
113. 3 From the east to the west **praise** the name of the Lord!
113. 9 **Praise** the Lord!
115.17 The Lord is not **praised** by the dead, by any who go
115.18 **Praise** the Lord!
116.18 **Praise** the Lord!
117. 1 **Praise** the Lord, all nations!
117. 1 **Praise** him, all peoples!
117. 2 **Praise** the Lord!
118.21 I **praise** you, Lord, because you heard me, because you
119. 7 righteous judgements, I will **praise** you with a pure heart.
119.12 I **praise** you, O Lord;
119.62 I wake up to **praise** you for your righteous judgements.
119.171 I will always **praise** you, because you teach me your laws.
119.175 Give me life, so that I may **praise** you;
134. 1 Come, **praise** the Lord, all his servants, all who serve in
134. 2 Raise your hands in prayer in the Temple, and **praise** the Lord!
135. 1 **Praise** the Lord!
135. 1 **Praise** his name, you servants of the Lord, [2]who stand in
135. 3 **Praise** the Lord, because he is good;
135. 3 sing **praises** to his name, because he is kind.
135.19 **Praise** the Lord, people of Israel;
135.19 **praise** him, you priests of God!
135.20 **Praise** the Lord, you Levites;
135.20 **praise** him, all you that worship him!
135.21 **Praise** the Lord in Zion, in Jerusalem, his home.
135.21 **Praise** the Lord!
138. 1 I sing **praise** to you before the gods.
138. 2 holy Temple, bow down, and **praise** your name because of your
138. 4 kings in the world will **praise** you, Lord, because they have
139.14 I **praise** you because you are to be feared;
140.13 The righteous will **praise** you indeed;
142. 7 of your people I will **praise** you because of your goodness to
144. 1 **Praise** the Lord, my protector!
145. 2 I will **praise** you for ever and ever.
145. 3 The Lord is great and is to be highly **praised;**
145. 4 have done will be **praised** from one generation to the next;
145.10 All your creatures, Lord, will **praise** you, and all your
145.21 I will always **praise** the Lord;
145.21 let all his creatures **praise** his holy name for ever.
146. 1 **Praise** the Lord!
146. 1 **Praise** the Lord, my soul!
146. 2 I will **praise** him as long as I live;
146.10 **Praise** the Lord!
147. 1 **Praise** the Lord!
147. 1 It is good to sing **praise** to our God;
147. 1 it is pleasant and right to **praise** him.
147. 7 Sing hymns of **praise** to the Lord;
147.12 **Praise** the Lord, O Jerusalem!
147.12 **Praise** your God, O Zion!
147.20 **Praise** the Lord!
148. 1 **Praise** the Lord!
148. 1 **Praise** the Lord from heaven, you that live in the heights above.
148. 2 **Praise** him, all his angels, all his heavenly armies.
148. 3 **Praise** him, sun and moon;
148. 3 **praise** him, shining stars.
148. 4 **Praise** him, highest heavens, and the waters above the sky.
148. 5 Let them all **praise** the name of the Lord!
148. 7 **Praise** the Lord from the earth, sea-monsters and all ocean depths;
148. 9 **Praise** him, hills and mountains, fruit-trees and forests;
148.11 **Praise** him, kings and all peoples, princes and all other rulers;
148.13 Let them all **praise** the name of the Lord!
148.14 so that all his people **praise** him— the people of Israel,
148.14 **Praise** the Lord!
149. 1 **Praise** the Lord!
149. 1 **praise** him in the assembly of his faithful people!
149. 3 **Praise** his name with dancing;
149. 3 play drums and harps in **praise** of him.
149. 6 them shout aloud as they **praise** God, with their sharp swords
149. 9 **Praise** the Lord!
150. 1 **Praise** the Lord!
150. 1 **Praise** God in his Temple!
150. 1 **Praise** his strength in heaven!
150. 2 **Praise** him for the mighty things he has done.
150. 2 **Praise** his supreme greatness.
150. 3 **Praise** him with trumpets.
150. 3 **Praise** him with harps and lyres.
150. 4 **Praise** him with drums and dancing.
150. 4 **Praise** him with harps and flutes.
150. 5 **Praise** him with cymbals.
150. 5 **Praise** him with loud cymbals.
150. 6 **Praise** the Lord, all living creatures!
150. 6 **Praise** the Lord!
Prov 11.26 a higher price, but they **praise** the one who puts it up
12. 8 If you are intelligent, you will be **praised;**
25.27 bad for you, and so is trying to win too much **praise.**
26. 1 **Praise** for a fool is out of place, like snow in summer
26. 8 **Praising** someone who is stupid makes as much sense as
27. 2 Let other people **praise** you—even strangers;
31.28 Her children show their appreciation, and her husband **praises** her.
Prov 31.30 but a woman who honours the Lord should be **praised.**
Ecc 7. 5 reprimand you than to have stupid people sing your **praises.**
8.10 back from the cemetery people **praise** them in the very city
Song 6. 9 All women look at her and **praise** her;
6. 9 queens and concubines sing her **praises.**
Is 12. 1 "I **praise** you, Lord!
24.15 the Lord is, [15]and those in the east will **praise** him.
24.15 live along the sea will **praise** the Lord, the God of Israel.
24.16 will hear songs in **praise** of Israel, the righteous nation.
25. 1 I will honour you and **praise** your name.
25. 3 The people of powerful nations will **praise** you;
38. 9 Hezekiah recovered from his illness, he wrote this song of **praise:**
38.18 No one in the world of the dead can **praise** you;
38.19 It is the living who **praise** you, As I praise you now.
38.20 play harps and sing your **praise,** Sing praise in your Temple
41.16 you will **praise** me, the holy God of Israel.
42. 8 I will not let idols share my **praise.**
42.10 sing his **praise,** all the world!
42.10 **Praise** him, you that sail the sea;
42.10 **praise** him, all creatures of the sea!
42.11 Let the desert and its towns **praise** God;
42.11 let the people of Kedar **praise** him!
42.12 live in distant lands give **praise** and glory to the Lord!
43.20 jackals and ostriches will **praise** me when I make rivers
43.21 people I made for myself, and they will sing my **praises!"**
45.25 all the descendants of Jacob, and they will give me **praise.**
48. 9 "In order that people will **praise** my name, I am holding
49. 3 because of you, people will **praise** me."
51. 3 will be there, and songs of **praise** and thanks to me.
60.18 You will **praise** me because I have saved you.
61. 3 instead of grief, A song of **praise** instead of sorrow.
61. 3 is right, And God will be **praised** for what he has done.
61.11 Lord will save his people, And all the nations will **praise** him.
62. 7 Jerusalem And makes it a city the whole world **praises.**
62. 9 harvested the corn Will eat the bread and **praise** the Lord.
63. 7 I **praise** him for all he has done for us.
64.11 where our ancestors **praised** you, has been destroyed by fire.
Jer 4. 2 will ask me to bless them, and they will **praise** me."
13.11 be my people and would bring **praise** and honour to my name;
17.14 You are the one I **praise!**
20.13 **Praise** the Lord!
30.19 The people who live there will sing **praise;**
31. 7 Sing your song of **praise,** 'The Lord has saved his people;
51.41 "The city that the whole world **praised** has been captured!
Ezek 3.12 of a voice that said, **"Praise** the glory of the Lord in
28.22 people will **praise** me because of what I do to you.
Dan 2.19 to Daniel in a vision, and he **praised** the God of heaven:
2.20 **praise** him for ever and ever.
2.23 I **praise** you and honour you, God of my ancestors.
3.28 The king said, **"Praise** the God of Shadrach, Meshach,
4.34 I **praised** the Supreme God and gave honour and glory to the
4.37 I, Nebuchadnezzar, **praise,** honour, and glorify the King of Heaven.
5. 4 wine out of them [4]and **praised** gods made of gold, silver,
5.23 wine out of them and **praised** gods made of gold, silver,
Hos 14. 2 our prayer, and we will **praise** you as we have promised.
Joel 2.26 You will **praise** the Lord your God, who has done wonderful
Jon 2. 9 But I will sing **praises** to you;
Hab 3. 3 and the earth is full of his **praise.**
Zeph 3.19 their shame to honour, and all the world will **praise** them.
Zech 11. 5 They sell the meat and say, **'Praise** the Lord!
Mt 5.16 the good things you do and **praise** your Father in heaven.
6. 2 They do it so that people will **praise** them.
9. 8 they were afraid, and **praised** God for giving such authority
15.31 and they **praised** the God of Israel.
21. 9 and those walking behind began to shout, **"Praise** to David's Son!
21. 9 **Praise** God!"
21.15 the children shouting in the Temple, **"Praise** to David's Son!"
21.16 'You have trained children and babies to offer perfect **praise.'"**
Mk 2.12 completely amazed and **praised** God, saying, "We have never seen
11. 9 and those who followed behind began to shout, **"Praise** God!
11.10 **Praise** God!"
Lk 1.46 Mary said, "My heart **praises** the Lord;
1.64 Zechariah was able to speak again, and he started **praising** God.
1.68 "Let us **praise** the Lord, the God of Israel!
2.13 heaven's angels appeared with the angel, singing **praises** to God:
2.20 The shepherds went back, singing **praises** to God for all they
4.15 He taught in the synagogues and was **praised** by everyone.
5.25 the bed he had been lying on, and went home, **praising** God.
5.26 Full of fear, they **praised** God, saying, "What marvellous things
7.16 They all were filled with fear and **praised** God.
13.13 and at once she straightened herself up and **praised** God.
16. 8 master of this dishonest manager **praised** him for doing such
17.15 he was healed, he came back, **praising** God in a loud voice.
18.43 When the crowd saw it, they all **praised** God.
19.37 began to thank God and **praise** him in loud voices for all
23.47 what had happened, and he **praised** God, saying, "Certainly he
Jn 5.41 "I am not looking for human **praise.**
5.44 You like to receive **praise** from one another, but you do
5.44 try to win **praise** from the one who alone is
12.13 of palm-trees and went out to meet him, shouting, **"Praise** God!
Acts 2.47 glad and humble hearts, [47]**praising** God, and enjoying the good
3. 8 into the Temple with them, walking and jumping and **praising** God.
3. 9 saw him walking and **praising** God, [10]and when they recognized
4.21 because the people were all **praising** God for what had happened.
10.46 speaking in strange tongues and **praising** God's greatness.
11.18 they stopped their criticism and **praised** God, saying,
13.48 heard this, they were glad and **praised** the Lord's message;
21.20 After hearing him, they all **praised** God.
Rom 1.25 of the Creator himself, who is to be **praised** for ever!
2.29 Such a person receives his **praise** from God, not from man.

Rom 4.20 his faith filled him with power, and he gave **praise** to God.
9. 5 May God, who rules over all, be **praised** for ever!
13. 3 is good, and he will **praise** you, [4]because he is God's
15. 6 all of you together may **praise** with one voice the God
15. 9 and to enable even the Gentiles to **praise** God for his mercy.
15. 9 says, "And so I will **praise** you among the Gentiles;
15. 9 I will sing **praises** to you."
15.11 And again, **"Praise** the Lord, all Gentiles;
15.11 **praise** him, all peoples!"
1 Cor 4. 5 And then everyone will receive from God the **praise** he deserves.
11. 2 I **praise** you because you always remember me and follow the
11.17 however, I do not **praise** you, because your meetings for worship
11.22 Shall I **praise** you?
12.26 part is **praised,** all the other parts share its happiness.
2 Cor 6. 8 we are insulted and **praised.**
Gal 1.24 And so they **praised** God because of me.
Eph 1. 6 Let us **praise** God for his glorious grace, for the free
1.12 who were the first to hope in Christ, **praise** God's glory!
1.14 Let us **praise** his glory!
5.19 hymns and psalms to the Lord with **praise** in your hearts.
Phil 1.11 Jesus Christ can produce, for the glory and **praise** of God.
4. 8 with those things that are good and that deserve **praise:**
1 Thes 2. 6 did not try to get **praise** from anyone, either from you or
Heb 2.12 I will **praise** you in their meeting."
13.15 Let us, then, always offer **praise** to God as our sacrifice
Jas 5.13 He should sing **praises.**
1 Pet 1. 7 Then you will receive **praise** and glory and honour on the Day
2.12 your good deeds and so **praise** God on the Day of his
2.14 to punish the evildoers and to **praise** those who do good.
4.11 so that in all things **praise** may be given to God through
Rev 5.12 power, wealth, wisdom, and strength, honour, glory, and **praise!"**
5.13 and to the Lamb, be **praise** and honour, glory and might,
7.12 **Praise,** glory, wisdom, thanksgiving, honour, power, and might
11.13 the people were terrified and **praised** the greatness of the God
14. 7 He said in a loud voice, "Honour God and **praise** his greatness!
16. 9 But they would not turn from their sins and **praise** his greatness.
19. 1 roar of a large crowd of people in heaven, saying, **"Praise**
19. 3 Again they shouted, **"Praise** God!
19. 4 **Praise** God!"
19. 5 sound of a voice, saying, **"Praise** our God, all his servants
19. 6 I heard them say, **"Praise** God!
19. 7 let us **praise** his greatness!

PRANCE

Prov 7.22 be slaughtered, like a deer **prancing** into a trap
Is 13.21 and wild goats will **prance** through the ruins.
Nah 2. 3 Their horses **prance!**

PRAY

Gen 20. 7 a prophet, and he will **pray** for you, so that you will
20.17 So Abraham **prayed** for Abimelech, and God healed him.
24.12 He **prayed,** "Lord, God of my master Abraham, give me
24.15 Before he had finished **praying,** Rebecca arrived with a
24.42 the well today, I **prayed,** 'Lord, God of my master Abraham,
25.21 Because Rebecca had no children, Isaac **prayed** to the Lord for her.
32. 9 Then Jacob **prayed,** "God of my grandfather Abraham and God
32.11 Save me, I **pray,** from my brother Esau.
Ex 8. 8 Moses and Aaron and said, **"Pray** to the Lord to take away
8. 9 Moses replied, "I will be glad to **pray** for you.
8. 9 time when I am to **pray** for you, your officers, and your
8.10 The king answered, **"Pray** for me tomorrow."
8.12 left the king, and Moses **prayed** to the Lord to take away
8.28 **Pray** for me."
8.29 as I leave, I will **pray** to the Lord that tomorrow the
8.30 Moses left the king and **prayed** to the Lord, [31]and the
9.28 **Pray** to the Lord!
10.17 my sin this once and **pray** to the Lord your God to
10.18 Moses left the king and **prayed** to the Lord.
12.32 Also **pray** for a blessing on me."
15.25 Moses **prayed** earnestly to the Lord, and the Lord showed
17. 4 Moses **prayed** earnestly to the Lord and said, "What can I
23.13 Do not **pray** to other gods;
Num 11. 2 he **prayed** to the Lord, and the fire died down.
14.17 So now Lord, I **pray,** show us your power and do what
14.19 unchanging love, forgive, I **pray,** the sin of these people,
16. 4 When Moses heard this, he threw himself on the ground and **prayed.**
21. 7 Now **pray** to the Lord to take these snakes away."
21. 7 So Moses **prayed** for the people.
27.15 Moses **prayed,** [16]"Lord God, source of all life, appoint, I pray,
27.16 of all life, appoint, I **pray,** a man who can lead the
Deut 3.23 "At that time I earnestly **prayed,** [24]'Sovereign Lord,
9.20 to kill him, so I **prayed** for Aaron at the same time.
9.26 And I **prayed,** 'Sovereign Lord, don't destroy your own people,
Judg 13. 8 Then Manoah **prayed** to the Lord, "Please, Lord, let the
16.28 Then Samson **prayed,** "Sovereign Lord, please remember me;
1 Sam 1. 9 and she cried bitterly as she **prayed** to the Lord.
1.12 Hannah continued to **pray** to the Lord for a long time,
1.13 She was **praying** silently;
1.15 desperate, and I have been **praying,** pouring out my troubles
1.16 I have been **praying** like this because I'm so miserable."
1.26 I am the woman you saw standing here, **praying** to the Lord.
2. 1 Hannah **prayed:**
7. 5 Mizpah, saying, "I will **pray** to the Lord for you there."
7. 8 and said to Samuel, "Keep **praying** to the Lord our God to
7. 9 Then he **prayed** to the Lord to help Israel, and the Lord
8. 6 so he **prayed** to the Lord, [7]and the Lord said, "Listen to
12.17 But I will **pray,** and the Lord will send thunder and rain.
1 Sam 12.18 So Samuel **prayed,** and on that same day the Lord sent
12.19 said to Samuel, "Please, sir, **pray** to the Lord your God for
12.23 that I should sin against him by no longer **praying** for you.
2 Sam 7.18 Lord's presence, sat down and **prayed,** "I am not worthy of
7.27 I have the courage to **pray** this prayer to you, because you
12.16 David **prayed** to God that the child would get well.
14.11 She said, "Your Majesty, please **pray** to the Lord your God,
15.31 had joined Absalom's rebellion, he **prayed,** "Please, Lord,
1 Kgs 1.48 worship on his bed [48]and **prayed,** 'Let us praise the Lord,
8.12 Then Solomon **prayed:**
8.23 he raised his arms [23]and **prayed,** "Lord God of Israel,
8.25 Lord God of Israel, I **pray** that you will also keep the
8.29 Hear me when I face this Temple and **pray.**
8.30 prayers of your people when they face this place and **pray.**
8.33 come to this Temple, humbly **praying** to you for forgiveness,
8.35 and face this Temple, humbly **praying** to you, [36]listen to
8.41 to worship you and to **pray** at this Temple, [43]listen to his
8.44 their enemies and they **pray** to you, wherever they are,
8.47 that land they repent and **pray** to you, confessing how sinful
8.48 truly and sincerely repent, and **pray** to you as they face
8.54 After Solomon had finished **praying** to the Lord, he
13. 6 said to the prophet, "Please **pray** for me to the Lord your
13. 6 The prophet **prayed** to the Lord, and the king's arm was healed.
17.20 Then he **prayed** aloud, "O Lord my God, why have you done
17.21 the boy three times and **prayed,** "O Lord my God, restore
18.24 let the prophets of Baal **pray** to their god,
18.24 and I will **pray** to the Lord, and the one
18.25 **Pray** to your god, but don't set fire to the wood."
18.26 brought to them, prepared it, and **prayed** to Baal until noon.
18.27 **"Pray** louder!
18.28 So the prophets **prayed** louder and cut themselves
18.36 Elijah approached the altar and **prayed,** "O Lord,
19. 4 "It's too much, Lord," he **prayed.**
2 Kgs 4.33 He closed the door and **prayed** to the Lord.
5.11 least come out to me, **pray** to the Lord his God, wave
6.17 Then he **prayed,** "O Lord, open his eyes and let him see!"
6.18 Elisha **prayed,** "O Lord, strike these men blind!"
6.20 had entered the city, Elisha **prayed,** "Open their eyes,
13. 4 Then Jehoahaz **prayed** to the Lord, and the Lord, seeing how
19. 4 So **pray** to God for those of our people who survive."
19.15 of the Lord, [15]and **prayed,** "O Lord, the God of Israel,
20. 2 Hezekiah turned his face to the wall and **prayed:**
20.11 Isaiah **prayed** to the Lord, and the Lord made the shadow
1 Chr 4.10 But Jabez **prayed** to the God of Israel, "Bless me, God,
4.10 And God gave him what he **prayed** for.
5.20 their trust in God and **prayed** to him for help, and God
17.16 Lord's presence, sat down, and **prayed,** "I am not worthy of
17.25 I have the courage to **pray** this prayer to you, my God,
21.17 David **prayed,** "O God, I am the one who did wrong.
21.26 He **prayed,** and the Lord answered him by sending fire from
2 Chr 6. 1 Then King Solomon **prayed,**
6.14 He **prayed,** "Lord God of Israel, in all heaven and earth
6.20 be worshipped, so hear me when I face this Temple and **pray.**
6.21 prayers of your people Israel when they face this place and **pray.**
6.24 come to this Temple, humbly **praying** to you for forgiveness,
6.26 and face this Temple, humbly **praying** to you, [27]O Lord,
6.32 and then he comes to **pray** at this Temple, [33]listen to his
6.34 their enemies and they **pray** to you, wherever they are,
6.37 that land they repent and **pray** to you, confessing how sinful
6.38 truly and sincerely repent and **pray** to you as they face
7.14 on my people, [14]if they **pray** to me and repent and turn
14.11 Asa **prayed** to the Lord his God, "O Lord, you can help
20. 3 Jehoshaphat was frightened and **prayed** to the Lord for guidance.
20. 6 and stood before them [6]and **prayed** aloud, "O Lord God of
20. 9 They could **pray** to you in their trouble, and you would hear
32.20 prophet Isaiah son of Amoz **prayed** to God and cried out to
32.24 He **prayed,** and the Lord gave him a sign that he would
Ezra 6.10 the God of Heaven and **pray** for his blessing on me and
8.23 So we fasted and **prayed** for God to protect us, and he
Neh 1. 4 I **prayed** to God, [5]"Lord God of Heaven!
1. 6 hear my prayer, as I **pray** day and night for your servants,
2. 4 I **prayed** to the God of Heaven, [5]and then I said to
4. 4 I **prayed,** "Listen to them mocking us, O God!
4. 9 and create confusion, [9]but we **prayed** to our God and kept
5.19 I **pray** you, O God, remember to my credit everything that
6. 9 I **prayed,** "But now, God, make me strong!"
6.14 I **prayed,** "God, remember what Tobiah and Sanballat have
9. 4 They **prayed** aloud to the Lord their God.
9. 6 And then the people of Israel **prayed** this prayer:
Esth 4.16 hold a fast and **pray** for me.
Job 15. 4 no one would **pray** to him.
21.15 no need to serve God nor any advantage in **praying** to him.
22.27 When you **pray,** he will answer you, and you will keep the
27.10 they should have constantly **prayed** to him.
30.20 and when I **pray,** you pay no attention.
31.30 I never sinned by **praying** for their death.
33.26 when he **prays,** God will answer him;
36.13 angry, and even when punished, they don't **pray** for help.
42. 8 Job will **pray** for you, and I will answer his prayer and
42.10 Then, after Job had **prayed** for his three friends, the
Ps 4. 1 Answer me when I **pray,** O God, my defender!
4. 6 There are many who **pray:**
5. 2 I **pray** to you, O Lord;
14. 4 They live by robbing my people, and they never **pray** to me."
14. 7 How I **pray** that victory will come to Israel from Zion.
17. 6 I **pray** to you, O God, because you answer me;
31. 1 save me, I **pray!**
32. 6 all your loyal people should **pray** to you in times of need;
34. 4 I **prayed** to the Lord, and he answered me;
35.13 I **prayed** with my head bowed low, [14]as I would pray for
35.14 bowed low, [14]as I would **pray** for a friend or a brother.

Ps	44.20	stopped worshipping our God and **prayed** to a foreign god,
	53. 4	They live by robbing my people, and they never **pray** to me."
	53. 6	How I **pray** that victory will come to Israel from Zion.
	69.13	But as for me, I will **pray** to you, Lord;
	77. 2	In times of trouble I **pray** to the Lord;
	78.34	they would repent and **pray** earnestly to him.
	79. 6	not worship you, on the people who do not **pray** to you.
	86. 3	I **pray** to you all day long.
	86. 5	forgiving, full of constant love for all who **pray** to you.
	88.13	every morning I **pray** to you.
	99. 6	Aaron were his priests, and Samuel was one who **prayed** to him;
	109. 4	me, even though I love them and have **prayed** for them.
	122. 6	**Pray** for the peace of Jerusalem:
	122. 9	the house of the Lord our God I **pray** for your prosperity.
	141. 5	men, because I am always **praying** against their evil deeds.
Prov	15. 8	is pleased when good men **pray**, but hates the sacrifices that
	15.29	When good people **pray**, the Lord listens, but he ignores
Is	1.15	No matter how much you **pray**, I will not listen, for your
	16.12	and to their temples to **pray**, but it will do them no
	26.16	You punished your people, Lord, and in anguish they **prayed** to you.
	37. 4	So **pray** to God for those of our people who survive."
	37.15	presence of the Lord, [15]and **prayed**, [16]"Almighty Lord,
	38. 2	Hezekiah turned his face to the wall and **prayed:**
	44.17	He **prays** to it and says, "You are my god—save me!"
	45.20	their idols of wood and **pray** to gods that cannot save them
	46. 7	If anyone **prays** to it, it cannot answer or save him from
	53.12	of many sinners and **prayed** that they might be forgiven."
	55. 6	Turn to the Lord and **pray** to him, now that he is
	58. 9	When you **pray**, I will answer you.
	65. 1	ready to answer my people's prayers, but they did not **pray**.
	65. 1	The nation did not **pray** to me, even though I was always
	65.24	Even before they finish **praying** to me, I will answer their prayers.
	66. 3	whether they offer incense or **pray** to an idol.
Jer	7.16	The Lord said, "Jeremiah, do not **pray** for these people.
	7.16	Do not cry or **pray** on their behalf;
	11.14	Jeremiah, don't **pray** to me or plead with me on behalf of
	11.20	Then I **prayed**, "Almighty Lord, you are a just judge;
	18.19	So I **prayed**, "Lord, hear what I am saying and listen to
	29. 7	**Pray** to me on their behalf, because if they are prosperous,
	29.12	You will come and **pray** to me, and I will answer you.
	31. 9	My people will return weeping, **praying** as I lead them back.
	32.16	of purchase to Baruch, I **prayed**, [17]"Sovereign Lord, you
	36. 7	Perhaps they will **pray** to the Lord and turn from their
	37. 3	Maaseiah to ask me to **pray** to the Lord our God on
	42. 2	**Pray** to the Lord our God for us.
	42. 2	**Pray** for all of us who have survived.
	42. 3	**Pray** that the Lord our God will show us the way we
	42. 4	I will **pray** to the Lord our God, just as you have
	42. 6	the Lord our God, to whom we are asking you to **pray**.
	42.20	You asked me to **pray** to the Lord our God for you,
	51.62	Then **pray**, 'Lord, you have said that you would destroy this place,
Lam	3.41	God in heaven and **pray**, [42]"We have sinned and rebelled,
Dan	2.18	He told them to **pray** to the God of heaven for mercy
	6.10	at the open windows and **prayed** to God three times a day.
	6.11	When Daniel's enemies observed him **praying** to God,
	6.13	He **prays** regularly three times a day."
	9. 3	And I **prayed** earnestly to the Lord God, pleading with him,
	9. 4	I **prayed** to the Lord my God and confessed the sins of
	9.18	We are **praying** to you because you are merciful, not because
	9.20	I went on **praying**, confessing my sins and the sins of
	9.21	While I was **praying**, Gabriel, whom I had seen in the
Hos	7. 7	one after another, but no one **prays** to me for help."
	7.14	They have not **prayed** to me sincerely, but instead they
	7.14	When they **pray** for corn and wine, they gash themselves like pagans.
Joel	2.17	altar and the entrance of the Temple, must weep and **pray:**
Jon	1. 6	Get up and **pray** to your god for help.
	1.14	the Lord, "O Lord, we **pray**, don't punish us with death for
	2. 1	From deep inside the fish Jonah **prayed** to the Lord his God:
	2. 7	away, then, O Lord, I **prayed** to you, and in your holy
	3. 8	Everyone must **pray** earnestly to God and must give up his
	4. 2	So he **prayed**, "Lord, didn't I say before I left home that
Zeph	3. 9	the nations, and they will **pray** to me alone and not to
Zech	7. 2	of the Lord Almighty to **pray** for the Lord's blessing [3]and
	7.13	not listen when I spoke, I did not answer when they **prayed.**
	8.21	to worship the Lord Almighty and **pray** for his blessing.
	8.22	Jerusalem to worship the Lord Almighty, and to **pray** for his blessing.
	13. 9	Then they will **pray** to me, and I will answer them.
Mt	5.44	love your enemies and **pray** for those who persecute you,
	6. 5	"When you **pray**, do not be like the hypocrites!
	6. 5	love to stand up and **pray** in the houses of worship
	6. 6	But when you **pray**, go to your room, close the door,
	6. 6	and **pray** to your Father, who is unseen.
	6. 7	"When you **pray**, do not use a lot of meaningless words,
	6. 9	This, then, is how you should **pray:**
	9.38	**Pray** to the owner of the harvest that he will send out
	14.23	the people away, he went up a hill by himself to **pray**.
	18.19	agree about anything you **pray** for, it will be done
	19.13	hands on them and to **pray** for them, but the disciples
	24.20	**Pray** to God that you will not have to run away during
	26.36	said to them, "Sit here while I go over there and **pray.**"
	26.39	on the ground, and **prayed**, "My Father, if it is possible,
	26.41	Keep watch and **pray** that you will not fall into temptation.
	26.42	Jesus went away and **prayed**, "My Father, if this cup of
	26.44	left them, went away, and **prayed** the third time, saying the
Mk	1.35	went out of the town to a lonely place, where he **prayed.**
	6.46	good-bye to the people he went away to a hill to **pray.**
	11.24	you **pray** and ask for something, believe that you have received
	11.25	when you stand and **pray**, forgive anything you may have against
Mk	13.18	**Pray** to God that these things will not happen in the winter!
	14.32	and Jesus said to his disciples, "Sit here while I **pray.**"
	14.35	on the ground, and **prayed** that, if possible, he might not
	14.36	"Father," he **prayed**, "my Father!
	14.38	"Keep watch, and **pray** that you will not fall into
	14.39	He went away once more and **prayed**, saying the same words.
Lk	1.10	crowd of people outside **prayed** during the hour when the incense
	2.36	day and night she worshipped God, fasting and **praying.**
	3.21	While he was **praying**, heaven was opened, [22]and the Holy Spirit
	5.16	But he would go away to lonely places, where he **prayed.**
	6.12	went up a hill to **pray**
	6.12	and spent the whole night there **praying** to God.
	6.28	bless those who curse you, and **pray** for those who ill-treat you.
	9.18	when Jesus was **praying** alone, the disciples came to him.
	9.28	John, and James with him and went up a hill to **pray.**
	9.29	While he was **praying**, his face changed its appearance,
	10. 2	**Pray** to the owner of the harvest that he will send out
	11. 1	One day Jesus was **praying** in a certain place.
	11. 1	"Lord, teach us to **pray**, just as John taught his disciples."
	11. 2	Jesus said to them, "When you **pray**, say this:
	18. 1	that they should always **pray** and never become discouraged.
	18.10	there were two men who went up to the Temple to **pray:**
	18.11	stood apart by himself and **prayed**, 'I thank you, God, that I
	21.36	Be on the alert and **pray** always that you will have the
	22.32	But I have **prayed** for you, Simon, that your faith will
	22.40	he said to them, "**Pray** that you will not fall into
	22.41	the distance of a stone's throw and knelt down and **prayed.**
	22.44	In great anguish he **prayed** even more fervently;
	22.46	Get up and **pray** that you will not fall into temptation."
Jn	17. 9	"I **pray** for them.
	17. 9	I do not **pray** for the world but for those you gave
	17.20	"I **pray** not only for them, but also for those who
	17.21	I **pray** that they may all be one.
Acts	1.14	gathered frequently to **pray** as a group, together with the women
	1.24	Then they **prayed**, "Lord, you know the thoughts of everyone, so
	4.31	finished **praying**, the place where they were meeting was shaken.
	6. 6	to the apostles, who **prayed** and placed their hands on them.
	8.15	they **prayed** for the believers that they might receive
	8.22	evil plan of yours, and **pray** to the Lord that he will
	8.24	to Peter and John, "Please **pray** to the Lord for me,
	9.11	He is **praying**, [12]and in a vision he has seen a man
	9.40	put them all out of the room, and knelt down and **prayed;**
	10. 2	the Jewish poor people and was constantly **praying** to God.
	10. 9	on the roof of the house about noon in order to **pray.**
	10.30	days ago that I was **praying** in my house at three o'clock
	11. 5	"While I was **praying** in the city of Joppa, I had a
	12. 5	people of the church were **praying** earnestly to God for him.
	12.12	where many people had gathered and were **praying.**
	13. 3	They fasted and **prayed**, placed their hands on them,
	16.25	midnight Paul and Silas were **praying** and singing hymns to God,
	20.36	When Paul finished, he knelt down with them and **prayed.**
	21. 5	of the city to the beach, where we all knelt and **prayed.**
	22.16	baptized and have your sins washed away by **praying** to him.'
	22.17	Jerusalem, and while I was **praying** in the Temple, I had a
	27.29	anchors from the back of the ship and **prayed** for daylight.
	28. 8	Paul went into his room, **prayed**, placed his hands on him,
Rom	1.10	God knows that I remember you [10]every time I **pray.**
	8.26	For we do not know how we ought to **pray;**
	10. 1	How I **pray** to God for them!
	12.12	be patient in your troubles, and **pray** at all times.
	15.30	join me in **praying** fervently to God for me.
	15.31	**Pray** that I may be kept safe from the unbelievers in
1 Cor	11. 4	So a man who **prays** or proclaims God's message in public
	11. 5	any woman who **prays** or proclaims God's message in public worship
	11.13	proper for a woman to **pray** to God in public worship
	14.13	in strange tongues, then, must **pray** for the gift to explain
	14.14	For if I **pray** in this way, my spirit prays indeed,
	14.15	I will **pray** with my spirit,
	14.15	but I will **pray** also with my mind;
2 Cor	9.14	with deep affection they will **pray** for you
	12. 8	Three times I **prayed** to the Lord about this and asked him
	13. 7	We **pray** to God that you will do no wrong—
	13. 9	And so we also **pray** that you will become perfect.
Eph	3. 1	of Christ Jesus for the sake of you Gentiles, **pray** to God.
	3.17	and I **pray** that Christ will make his home
	3.17	I **pray** that you may have your roots and foundation in love,
	6.18	**Pray** on every occasion, as the Spirit leads.
	6.18	**pray** always for all God's people.
	6.19	And **pray** also for me, that God will give me a message
	6.20	**Pray** that I may be bold in speaking about the gospel
Phil	1. 4	and every time I **pray** for you all, I pray with joy
	1. 9	I **pray** that your love will keep on growing more and more,
Col	1. 3	the Father of our Lord Jesus Christ, when we **pray** for you.
	1. 9	this reason we have always **prayed** for you, ever since we
	4. 2	and keep alert as you **pray**, giving thanks to God.
	4. 3	At the same time **pray** also for us, so that God will
	4. 4	**Pray**, then, that I may speak, as I should, in such a
	4.12	He always **prays** fervently for you, asking God to make you
1 Thes	5.17	**pray** at all times, [18]be thankful in all circumstances.
	5.25	**Pray** also for us, brothers.
2 Thes	1.11	That is why we always **pray** for you.
	3. 1	our brothers, **pray** for us, that the Lord's message may continue
	3. 2	**Pray** also that God will rescue us from wicked and evil people;
1 Tim	2. 8	I want the men to **pray**, men who are dedicated to God
	5. 5	in God and continues to **pray** and ask him for his help
Phlm	4	Philemon, every time I **pray**, I mention you and give thanks
Heb	13.18	Keep on **praying** for us.
	13.19	even more earnestly to **pray** that God will send me back
Jas	1. 5	lacks wisdom, he should **pray** to God, who will give it
	1. 6	But when you **pray**, you must believe and not doubt at all.

Jas	5.13	He should **pray.**
	5.14	the church elders, who will **pray** for him and rub olive-oil
	5.16	sins to one another and **pray** for one another, so that you
	5.17	He **prayed** earnestly that there would be no rain,
	5.18	Once again he **prayed,** and the sky poured out its rain
1 Pet	1.17	call him Father, when you **pray** to God, who judges all people
	4. 7	You must be self-controlled and alert, to be able to **pray.**
1 Jn	5.16	lead to death, you should **pray** to God, who will give him
	5.16	I do not say that you should **pray** to God about that.
3 Jn	2	My dear friend, I **pray** that everything may go well with
Jude	20	**Pray** in the power of the Holy Spirit, [21] and keep

PRAYER

Gen	24.45	I had finished my silent **prayer,** Rebecca came with a
	25.21	The Lord answered his **prayer,** and Rebecca became pregnant.
	30. 6	He has heard my **prayer** and has given me a son";
	30.17	God answered Leah's **prayer,** and she became pregnant and
	30.22	he answered her **prayer** and made it possible for her to have
Ex	9.29	city, I will lift up my hands in **prayer** to the Lord.
	9.33	the city, and lifted up his hands in **prayer** to the Lord.
1 Sam	1.19	with his wife Hannah, and the Lord answered her **prayer.**
	7. 9	the Lord to help Israel, and the Lord answered his **prayer.**
2 Sam	7.27	the courage to pray this **prayer** to you, because you have
	21.14	And after that, God answered their **prayers** for the country.
	24.25	Lord answered his **prayer,** and the epidemic in Israel was stopped.
1 Kgs	8.28	Listen to my **prayer,** and grant the requests I make to you
	8.30	Hear my **prayers** and the prayers of your people when they
	8.38	disease or sickness among them, [38] listen to their **prayers.**
	8.38	stretch out their hands in **prayer** towards this Temple,
	8.39	hear their **prayer.**
	8.43	you and to pray at this Temple, [43] listen to his **prayer.**
	8.45	Temple which I have built for you, [45] listen to their **prayers.**
	8.47	that land is far away, [47] listen to your people's **prayers.**
	8.47	sinful and wicked they have been, hear their **prayers** O Lord.
	8.49	Temple which I have built for you, [49] then listen to their **prayers.**
	8.52	their king, and hear their **prayer** whenever they call to you
	8.59	remember at all times this **prayer** and these petitions I have
	9. 3	The Lord said to him, "I have heard your **prayer.**
	17.22	The Lord answered Elijah's **prayer;**
2 Kgs	6.17	The Lord answered his **prayer,** and Elisha's servant looked up
	6.18	The Lord answered his **prayer** and struck them blind.
	6.20	The Lord answered his **prayer;**
	13. 4	of Syria was oppressing the Israelites, answered his **prayer.**
	19.20	in answer to the king's **prayer** [21] the Lord had said, "The
	20. 5	ancestor David, have heard your **prayer** and seen your tears.
	22.19	But I have heard your **prayer,** [20] and the punishment which I
1 Chr	5.20	help, and God answered their **prayers** and made them
	17.25	the courage to pray this **prayer** to you, my God, because you
	21.28	the Lord had answered his **prayer,** so he offered sacrifices
2 Chr	6.12	stood in front of the altar and raised his arms in **prayer.**
	6.19	Listen to my **prayer** and grant the requests I make to you.
	6.21	Hear my **prayers** and the prayers of your people Israel
	6.29	disease or sickness among them, [29] listen to their **prayers.**
	6.29	stretch out their hands in **prayer** towards this Temple,
	6.30	hear their **prayer.**
	6.33	he comes to pray at this Temple, [33] listen to his **prayer.**
	6.35	Temple which I have built for you, [35] listen to their **prayers.**
	6.37	that land is far away, [37] listen to your people's **prayers.**
	6.37	how sinful and wicked they have been, hear their **prayers,**
	6.39	Temple which I have built for you, [39] then listen to their **prayers.**
	6.40	look on us and listen to the **prayers** offered in this place.
	7. 1	When King Solomon finished his **prayer,** fire came down from
	7.12	him, "I have heard your **prayer,** and I accept this Temple as
	7.15	ready to hear all the **prayers** that are offered here,
	30.18	King Hezekiah offered this **prayer** for them:
	30.20	The Lord answered Hezekiah's **prayer;**
	30.27	In his home in heaven God heard their **prayers** and accepted them.
	33.13	God accepted Manasseh's **prayer** and answered it by
	33.18	else that Manasseh did, the **prayer** he made to his God, and
	33.19	The king's **prayer** and God's answer to it, and an account
	34.27	I have heard your **prayer,** [28] and the punishment which I am
Ezra	8.23	prayed for God to protect us, and he answered our **prayers.**
	9. 5	torn clothes, I knelt in **prayer** and stretched out my hands
	10. 1	While Ezra was bowing in **prayer** in front of the Temple,
Neh	1. 6	me, Lord, and hear my **prayer,** as I pray day and night
	1.11	Listen now to my **prayer**
	1.11	and to the **prayers** of all your other servants
	9. 6	And then the people of Israel prayed this **prayer:**
	11.17	He led the temple choir in singing the **prayer** of thanksgiving.
Job	6. 8	Why won't he answer my **prayer?**
	12. 4	but there was a time when God answered my **prayers.**
	16.17	guilty of any violence, and my **prayer** to God is sincere.
	24.12	wounded and dying cry out, but God ignores their **prayers.**
	42. 8	and I will answer his **prayer** and not disgrace you as you
	42. 9	Lord had told them to do, and the Lord answered Job's **prayer.**
Ps	4. 1	Be kind to me now and hear my **prayer.**
	5. 3	at sunrise I offer my **prayer** and wait for your answer.
	6. 9	he listens to my cry for help and will answer my **prayer.**
	10.17	You will listen, O Lord, to the **prayers** of the lowly;
	17. 1	Listen to my honest **prayer.**
	25. 1	To you, O Lord, I offer my **prayer;**
	39.12	Hear my **prayer,** Lord, and listen to my cry;
	42. 8	a song at night, a **prayer** to the God of my life.
	54. 2	Hear my **prayer,** O God;
	55. 1	Hear my **prayer,** O God;
	60. 5	our **prayer,** so that the people you love may be rescued.
	61. 1	listen to my **prayer!**
	63. 4	I will raise my hands to you in **prayer.**
	64. 1	I am in trouble, God—listen to my **prayer!**

Ps	65. 2	Zion and keep our promises to you, [2] because you answer **prayers.**
	66.19	he has listened to my **prayer.**
	66.20	he did not reject my **prayer** or keep back his constant love
	68.31	the Sudanese will raise their hands in **prayer** to God.
	72.15	may **prayers** be said for him at all times;
	72.20	This is the end of the **prayers** of David son of Jesse.
	77. 2	long I lift my hands in **prayer,** but I cannot find comfort.
	80. 4	Lord God Almighty, will you be angry with your people's **prayers?**
	84. 8	Hear my **prayer,** Lord God Almighty.
	86. 4	your servant glad, O Lord, because my **prayers** go up to you.
	86. 6	Listen, Lord, to my **prayer;**
	86. 7	to you in times of trouble, because you answer my **prayers.**
	88. 2	Hear my **prayer;**
	88. 9	I call to you and lift my hands to you in **prayer.**
	102. 1	Listen to my **prayer,** O Lord, and hear my cry for help!
	102.17	He will hear his forsaken people and listen to their **prayer.**
	108. 6	my **prayer,** so that the people you love may be rescued.
	109. 7	may even his **prayer** be considered a crime!
	116. 1	he listens to my **prayers.**
	116.17	you a sacrifice of thanksgiving and offer my **prayer** to you.
	119.108	Accept my **prayer** of thanks, O Lord, and teach me your commands.
	119.170	Listen to my **prayer,** and save me according to your promise!
	134. 2	Raise your hands in **prayer** in the Temple, and praise the Lord!
	141. 2	Receive my **prayer** as incense,
	143. 1	Lord, hear my **prayer!**
	143. 6	I lift up my hands to you in **prayer;**
	143. 8	My **prayers** go up to you;
Prov	28. 9	the law, God will find your **prayers** too hateful to hear.
	31. 2	"You are my own dear son, the answer to my **prayers.**
Is	1.15	you lift your hands in **prayer,** I will not look at you.
	19.22	turn to him, and he will hear their **prayers** and heal them.
	37.21	in answer to the king's **prayer** [22] the Lord had said, "The
	38. 5	ancestor David, have heard your **prayer** and seen your tears;
	41.17	with thirst, then I, the Lord, will answer their **prayer;**
	56. 7	joy in my house of **prayer,** and accept the sacrifices you
	56. 7	called a house of **prayer** for the people of all nations."
	58. 4	this kind of fasting will make me listen to your **prayers?**
	64. 7	No one turns to you in **prayer;**
	65. 1	ready to answer my people's **prayers,** but they did not pray.
	65.24	Even before they finish praying to me, I will answer their **prayers.**
Lam	3.44	a cloud of fury too thick for our **prayers** to get through.
Ezek	8.18	They will shout **prayers** to me as loud as they can, but
Dan	2.23	you have answered my **prayer** and shown us what to tell the
	9.17	O God, hear my **prayer** and pleading.
	10.12	God has heard your **prayers** ever since the first day you
	10.12	I have come in answer to your **prayer.**
Hos	2.21	At that time I will answer the **prayers** of my people Israel.
	14. 2	to the Lord, and let this **prayer** be your offering to him:
	14. 2	our sins and accept our **prayer,** and we will praise you as
	14. 8	I will answer their **prayers** and take care of them;
Mic	3. 4	He will not listen to your **prayers,** for you have done evil.
Hab	3. 1	This is a **prayer** of the prophet Habakkuk:
Zech	3. 7	and I will hear your **prayers,**
	3. 7	just as I hear the **prayers** of the angels
	10. 6	I will answer their **prayers.**
	12.10	Jerusalem with the spirit of mercy and the spirit of **prayer.**
Mal	1. 9	He will not answer your **prayer,** and it will be your fault.
Mt	6. 7	that their gods will hear them because their **prayers** are long.
	21.13	that God said, 'My Temple will be called a house of **prayer.'**
	21.22	If you believe, you will receive whatever you ask for in **prayer."**
	26.26	piece of bread, gave a **prayer** of thanks, broke it, and gave
Mk	9.29	"Only **prayer** can drive this kind out," answered Jesus;
	11.17	be called a house of **prayer** for the people of all nations.'
	12.40	and then make a show of saying long **prayers.**
	14.22	piece of bread, gave a **prayer** of thanks, broke it, and gave
Lk	1.13	God has heard your **prayer,** and your wife Elizabeth will bear
	5.33	fast frequently and offer **prayers,** and the disciples of the
	19.46	that God said, 'My Temple will be called a house of **prayer.'**
	20.47	and then make a show of saying long **prayers!**
	22.45	Rising from his **prayer,** he went back to the disciples
Jn	18. 1	After Jesus had said this **prayer,** he left with his disciples
Acts	2.42	and sharing in the fellowship meals and the **prayers.**
	3. 1	Temple at three o'clock in the afternoon, the hour for **prayer.**
	4.24	heard it, they all joined together in **prayer** to God:
	6. 4	give our full time to **prayer** and the work of preaching."
	10. 4	"God is pleased with your **prayers** and works of charity,
	10.31	God has heard your **prayer** and has taken notice of your works
	14.23	appointed elders, and with **prayers** and fasting they commended
	16.13	there would be a place where Jews gathered for **prayer.**
	16.16	going to the place of **prayer,** we were met by a slave-girl
	26.29	Paul answered, "my **prayer** to God is that you
1 Cor	7. 5	for a while in order to spend your time in **prayer;**
	14.16	in the meeting say "Amen" to your **prayer** of thanksgiving?
	14.17	Even if your **prayer** of thanks to God is quite good,
2 Cor	1.11	as you help us by means of your **prayers** for us.
	1.11	will be that the many **prayers** for us will be answered,
	4.15	offer to the glory of God more **prayers** of thanksgiving.
Eph	1.16	I remember you in my **prayers** [17] and ask the God of our
	6.18	Do all this in **prayer,** asking for God's help.
Phil	1.19	that by means of your **prayers** and the help which comes from
	4. 6	but in all your **prayers** ask God for what you need,
Col	4. 2	Be persistent in **prayer,** and keep alert as you pray,
1 Thes	1. 2	thank God for you all and always mention you in our **prayers.**
1 Tim	2. 1	that petitions, **prayers,** requests, and thanksgivings be offered
	2. 8	can lift up their hands in **prayer** without anger or argument.
	4. 3	to be eaten, after a **prayer** of thanks, by those who are
	4. 4	to be received with a **prayer** of thanks, [5] because the word
	4. 5	the word of God and the **prayer** make it acceptable to God.
2 Tim	1. 3	as I remember you always in my **prayers** night and day.
Phlm	6	My **prayer** is that our fellowship with you as believers will

Phlm 22 that God will answer the **prayers** of all of you and give
Heb 5. 7 on earth Jesus made his **prayers** and requests with loud cries
Jas 5.15 This **prayer** made in faith will heal the sick person;
5.16 The **prayer** of a good person has a powerful effect.
1 Pet 3. 7 Do this so that nothing will interfere with your **prayers.**
3.12 the Lord watches over the righteous and listens to their **prayers;**
Rev 5. 8 bowls filled with incense, which are the **prayers** of God's people.
8. 3 incense to add to the **prayers** of all God's people
8. 4 incense went up with the **prayers** of God's people from the

PREACH

Lam 2.14 Their **preaching** deceived you by never exposing your sin.
Amos 7.12 Go on back to Judah and do your **preaching** there.
Mic 2. 6 The people preach at me and say, "Don't **preach** at us.
2. 6 Don't **preach** about all that.
Mt 3. 1 John the Baptist came to the desert of Judaea and started **preaching.**
4.17 From that time Jesus began to **preach** his message:
4.23 in the synagogues, **preaching** the Good News about the Kingdom,
9.35 He taught in the synagogues, **preached** the Good News
10. 7 Go and **preach,** 'The Kingdom of heaven is near!'
11. 1 and went off to teach and **preach** in the towns near there.
11. 5 back to life, and the Good News is **preached** to the poor.
11.12 From the time John **preached** his message until this very day
12.41 because they turned from their sins when they heard Jonah **preach;**
23. 3 because they don't practise what they **preach.**
24.14 about the Kingdom will be **preached** through all the world for
26.13 that wherever this gospel is **preached** all over the world,
Mk 1. 4 So John appeared in the desert, baptizing and **preaching.**
1.14 Jesus went to Galilee and **preached** the Good News from God.
1.38 I have to **preach** in them also, because that is why I
1.39 he travelled all over Galilee, **preaching** in the synagogues
2. 2 Jesus was **preaching** the message to them [3] when four men arrived,
3.14 also send you out to **preach,** [15] and you will have authority
4.33 Jesus **preached** his message to the people, using many other
6.12 they went out and **preached** that people should turn away from
13.10 the end comes, the gospel must be **preached** to all peoples.
14. 9 that wherever the gospel is **preached** all over the world,
16.15 "Go throughout the whole world and **preach** the gospel to all
16.20 disciples went and **preached** everywhere, and the Lord worked with
16.20 and proved that their **preaching** was true by the miracles that
Lk 3. 3 of the River Jordan, **preaching,** "Turn away from your sins
3.18 In many different ways John **preached** the Good News to
4.43 said to them, "I must **preach** the Good News about the
4.44 So he **preached** in the synagogues throughout the country.
7.22 raised to life, and the Good News is **preached** to the poor.
8. 1 travelled through towns and villages, **preaching** the Good News
9. 2 he sent them out to **preach** the Kingdom of God and to
9. 6 travelled through all the villages, **preaching** the Good News
11.32 because they turned from their sins when they heard Jonah **preach;**
20. 1 Temple teaching the people and **preaching** the Good News,
24.47 forgiveness of sins must be **preached** to all nations, beginning
Acts 1.21 beginning from the time John **preached** his message of baptism
5.42 they continued to teach and **preach** the Good News about Jesus
6. 2 for us to neglect the **preaching** of God's word in order to
6. 4 give our full time to prayer and the work of **preaching."**
8. 4 believers who were scattered went everywhere, **preaching** the message.
8. 5 principal city in Samaria and **preached** the Messiah to the people
8.25 On their way they **preached** the Good News in many villages of
8.40 and on the way he **preached** the Good News in every town.
9.20 the synagogues and began to **preach** that Jesus was the Son of
9.22 But Saul's **preaching** became even more powerful, and his proofs
9.27 them how boldly Saul had **preached** in the name of Jesus in
9.28 and went all over Jerusalem, **preaching** boldly in the name of
10.37 beginning in Galilee after John **preached** his message of baptism.
10.42 And he commanded us to **preach** the gospel to the people
13. 5 they arrived at Salamis, they **preached** the word of God in
13.24 Jesus began his work, John **preached** to all the people of
13.38 that the message about forgiveness of sins is **preached** to you;
14. 7 There they **preached** the Good News.
14.21 Paul and Barnabas **preached** the Good News in Derbe and
14.25 they **preached** the message in Perga and then went to Attalia,
15. 7 from among you to **preach** the Good News to the Gentiles,
15.21 and his words are **preached** in every town."
15.35 many others they taught and **preached** the word of the Lord.
15.36 in every town where we **preached** the word of the Lord,
16. 6 Spirit did not let them **preach** the message in the province
16.10 God had called us to **preach** the Good News to the people
16.32 Then they **preached** the word of the Lord to him and to
17.13 heard that Paul had **preached** the word of God in Berea
17.18 because Paul was **preaching** about Jesus and the resurrection.
18. 5 his whole time to **preaching** the message, testifying to the Jews
19.13 "I command you in the name of Jesus, whom Paul **preaches."**
20.20 help to you as I **preached** and taught in public and in
20.25 gone about among all of you, **preaching** the Kingdom of God.
26.20 and among the Gentiles, I **preached** that they must repent of
28.31 He **preached** about the Kingdom of God and taught about
Rom 1. 1 apostle chosen and called by God to **preach** his Good News.
1. 9 with all my heart by **preaching** the Good News about his Son.
1.15 then, I am eager to **preach** the Good News to you also
2.16 to the Good News I **preach,** this is how it will be
2.21 You **preach,** "Do not steal"—but do you yourself steal?
10. 8 your heart"—that is, the message of faith that we **preach.**
10.17 and the message comes through **preaching** Christ.
15.16 serve like a priest in **preaching** the Good News from God,
16.25 to the Good News I **preach** about Jesus Christ and according
1 Cor 1.21 the so-called "foolish" message we **preach,** God decided to save
2. 1 to you, my brothers, to **preach** God's secret truth, I did not
9.14 ordered that those who **preach** the gospel should get their living
9.16 I have no right to boast just because I **preach** the gospel.
9.16 it would be for me if I did not **preach** the gospel!
9.18 It is the privilege of **preaching** the Good News without charging
13. 2 I may have the gift of inspired **preaching;**
15. 1 the Good News which I **preached** to you, which you received,
15. 2 That is the gospel, the message that I **preached** to you.
15.11 this is what we all **preach,** and this is what you believe.
15.14 we have nothing to **preach** and you have nothing to believe.
2 Cor 1.19 Son of God, who was **preached** among you by Silas, Timothy,
2.12 I arrived in Troas to **preach** the Good News about Christ,
4. 3 For if the gospel we **preach** is hidden, it is hidden only
4. 5 For it is not ourselves that we **preach;**
4. 5 we **preach** Jesus Christ as Lord, and ourselves as your servants
8.18 in all the churches for his work in **preaching** the gospel.
10.16 Then we can **preach** the Good News in other countries
11. 4 who comes to you and **preaches** a different Jesus,
11. 4 not the one we **preached;**
11. 7 you a thing when I **preached** the Good News of God to
Gal 1. 8 an angel from heaven should **preach** to you a gospel that is
1. 8 different from the one we **preached** to you, may he be
1. 9 if anyone **preaches** to you a gospel that is different from
1.11 brothers, that the gospel I **preach** is not of human origin.
1.16 so that I might **preach** the Good News about him to
1.23 to persecute us is now **preaching** the faith that he once
2. 2 I explained the gospel message that I **preach** to the Gentiles.
2. 7 given me the task of **preaching** the gospel to the Gentiles,
2. 7 given Peter the task of **preaching** the gospel to the Jews.
4.13 You remember why I **preached** the gospel to you the first time;
5.11 brothers, if I continue to **preach** that circumcision is necessary,
5.11 that were true, then my **preaching** about the cross of Christ
Eph 2.17 So Christ came and **preached** the Good News of peace to
Phil 1.14 they grow bolder all the time to **preach** the message fearlessly.
1.15 Of course some of them **preach** Christ because they are jealous
1.18 so long as Christ is **preached** in every way possible,
4.15 in the early days of **preaching** the Good News, you were the
Col 1.23 this gospel which has been **preached** to everybody in the world.
1.28 So we **preach** Christ to everyone.
4. 3 a good opportunity to **preach** his message about the secret of
1 Thes 2. 9 trouble to you as we **preached** to you the Good News from
2.16 tried to stop us from **preaching** to the Gentiles the message
3. 2 with us for God in **preaching** the Good News about Christ.
2 Thes 2. 2 said this while prophesying or **preaching,** or that we wrote
2.14 called you to this through the Good News we **preached** to you;
2.15 we taught you, both in our **preaching** and in our letter.
1 Tim 3.16 He was **preached** among the nations, was believed in throughout
4.13 public reading of the Scriptures and to **preaching** and teaching.
5.17 especially those who work hard at **preaching** and teaching.
6. 2 You must teach and **preach** these things.
2 Tim 2. 8 descendant of David, as is taught in the Good News I **preach.**
2. 9 Because I **preach** the Good News, I suffer and I am even
4. 2 I solemnly urge you [2] to **preach** the message,
4. 5 do the work of a **preacher** of the Good News, and perform
1 Pet 3.19 he went and **preached** to the imprisoned spirits.
4. 6 why the Good News was **preached** also to the dead, to those
4. 6 it was **preached** to them so that in their spiritual existence
4.11 Whoever **preaches** must preach God's messages;
2 Pet 2. 5 ones he saved were Noah, who **preached** righteousness, and seven

AV PREACHER

see also **PHILOSOPHER**

Rom 10.14 And how can they hear if the message is not **proclaimed?**
1 Tim 2. 7 sent as an apostle and **teacher** of the Gentiles, to proclaim
2 Tim 1.11 me as an apostle and **teacher** to proclaim the Good News,

PRECIOUS

Gen 2.12 (Pure gold is found there and also rare perfume and **precious stones.)**
Ex 28.17 Mount four rows of **precious stones** on it;
39.10 They mounted four rows of **precious stones** on it:
1 Sam 25.29 God will keep you safe, as a man guards a **precious** treasure.
1 Chr 29. 2 iron, timber, **precious stones** and gems, stones for mosaics,
29. 8 Those who had **precious stones** gave them to the temple treasury,
2 Chr 3. 6 decorated the Temple with beautiful **precious stones** and with
32.27 built for his gold, silver, **precious stones,** spices,
Job 28.10 As they tunnel through the rocks, They discover **precious stones.**
Ps 36. 7 How **precious,** O God, is your constant love!
72.14 their lives are **precious** to him.
133. 2 It is like the **precious** anointing oil running down from
Is 43. 4 your life, because you are **precious** to me and because I love
54.11 you, I will rebuild your foundations with **precious stones.**
Lam 4. 2 Zion's young men were as **precious** to us as gold, but now
Ezek 1.16 each one shone like a **precious stone,** and each had another
10. 9 The wheels shone like **precious stones,** and each one had
Mic 1. 7 All its **precious** idols will be smashed to pieces,
Zech 2. 8 Anyone who strikes you strikes what is most **precious** to me."
1 Cor 3.12 or silver or **precious stones** in building on the foundation;
Jas 5. 7 is as he waits for his land to produce **precious** crops.
1 Pet 1. 7 which is much more **precious** than gold, must also be tested,
2 Pet 1. 1 Saviour Jesus Christ have been given a faith as **precious** as ours:
1. 4 us the very great and **precious** gifts he promised, so that by
Rev 4. 3 His face gleamed like such **precious stones** as jasper and carnelian,
17. 4 scarlet, and covered with gold ornaments, **precious stones,**
18.12 no one buys their gold, silver, **precious stones,** and
18.16 and cover herself with gold ornaments, **precious stones,**

Rev 21.11 The city shone like a **precious stone,** like a jasper, clear
21.19 city wall were adorned with all kinds of **precious stones.**

PREDECESSOR

1 Kgs 15.12 and he removed all the idols his **predecessors** had made.
16.19 Like his **predecessor** Jeroboam he displeased the Lord by his
16.25 Omri sinned against the Lord more than any of his **predecessors.**
16.30 He sinned against the Lord more than any of his **predecessors.**
2 Kgs 12.18 all the offerings that his **predecessors** Jehoshaphat,
14.24 example of his **predecessor** King Jeroboam son of Nebat,
15. 9 He, like his **predecessors,** sinned against the Lord.

PREDICT

1 Kgs 13. 5 as the prophet had **predicted** in the name of the Lord.
2 Kgs 7.17 and died, as Elisha had **predicted** when the king went to see
23.16 doing what the prophet had **predicted** long before during the
23.16 saw the tomb of the prophet who had made this **prediction.**
23.17 who came from Judah and **predicted** these things that you have
Ps 105.19 round his neck, [19]until what he had **predicted** came true.
Is 41.22 Come here and **predict** what will happen, so that we will
41.26 Which of you **predicted** that this would happen, so that
42. 9 The things I **predicted** have now come true.
43. 9 Which of their gods can **predict** the future?
43.12 I **predicted** what would happen, and then I came to your aid.
44. 7 Who could have **predicted** all that would happen from the
44. 8 times until now I have **predicted** all that would happen, and
44.25 and frustrate the **predictions** of astrologers.
44.26 when my servant makes a **prediction,** when I send a messenger
44.26 my plans, I make those plans and **predictions** come true.
45.21 Who **predicted** long ago what would happen?
46.10 From the beginning I **predicted** the outcome;
48. 3 "Long ago I **predicted** what would take place;
48. 5 And so I **predicted** your future long ago, announcing events
48. 6 you have to admit my **predictions** were right.
48.14 None of the gods could **predict** that the man I have chosen
Jer 14.14 **predictions** are worthless things that they have imagined.
27. 9 anyone who claims he can **predict** the future, either by
28. 8 before my time and yours, **predicted** that war, starvation,
28. 9 But a prophet who **predicts** peace can only be recognized as
28. 9 Lord has truly sent when that prophet's **predictions** come true."
29. 8 you or by any others who claim they can **predict** the future.
Ezek 12.22 'Time goes by, and **predictions** come to nothing'?
12.23 The time has come, and the **predictions** are coming true!
13. 6 Their visions are false, and their **predictions** are lies.
13. 7 you see are false, and the **predictions** you make are lies.
13. 9 who have false visions and make misleading **predictions.**
13.17 look at the women among your people who make up **predictions.**
13.23 So now your false visions and misleading **predictions** are over.
21.23 But this **prediction** is to remind them of their sins and to
21.29 you see are false, and the **predictions** you make are lies.
22.28 They see false visions and make false **predictions.**
Mic 3. 6 visions, and you will not be able to **predict** anything."
3. 7 Those who **predict** the future will be disgraced by their failure.
Mt 11.14 to believe their message, John is Elijah, whose coming was **predicted.**
16. 3 You can **predict** the weather by looking at the sky,
Lk 12.56 can look at the earth and the sky and **predict** the weather;
Acts 1.16 speaking through David, made a **prediction** about Judas,
11.28 the power of the Spirit **predicted** that a severe famine was
16.16 had an evil spirit that enabled her to **predict** the future.
Gal 3. 8 scripture **predicted** that God would put the Gentiles right with
1 Pet 1.11 was pointing, in **predicting** the sufferings that Christ would have
Jude 4 the Scriptures **predicted** the condemnation they have received.

PREFER

Gen 25.28 Isaac **preferred** Esau, because he enjoyed eating the animals
25.28 but Rebecca **preferred** Jacob.
Judg 9. 2 them [2]to ask the men of Shechem, "Which would you **prefer?**
1 Sam 15.22 Samuel said, "Which does the Lord **prefer:**
1 Kgs 21. 2 for it, or, if you **prefer,** I will pay you a fair
21. 6 his vineyard, or, if he **preferred,** to give him another one
2 Kgs 20. 9 Now, would you **prefer** the shadow on the stairway to go
Job 3.21 they **prefer** a grave to any treasure.
Prov 5.20 Why should you **prefer** the charms of another man's wife?
Jer 8. 3 I have scattered them, will **prefer** to die rather than to go
Ezek 6. 9 faithless hearts deserted me and they **preferred** idols to me.
20.16 profaned the Sabbath—they **preferred** to worship their idols.
Hos 4.18 in their prostitution, **preferring** disgrace to honour.
1 Cor 4.21 Which do you **prefer?**
7. 7 Actually I would **prefer** that all of you were as I am;
2 Cor 5. 8 of courage and would much **prefer** to leave our home in the
1 Tim 5.14 So I would **prefer** that the younger widows get married,
Heb 11.25 **preferred** to suffer with God's people rather than to enjoy sin

PREGNANT

Gen 3.16 your trouble in **pregnancy** and your pain in giving birth.
4. 1 Then Adam had intercourse with his wife, and she became **pregnant.**
16. 4 Abram had intercourse with Hagar, and she became **pregnant.**
16. 4 that she was **pregnant,** she became proud and despised Sarai.
16. 5 she found out that she was **pregnant,** she has despised me.
19.36 both of Lot's daughters became **pregnant** by their own father.
21. 2 had promised, [2]and she became **pregnant** and bore a son to
25.21 The Lord answered his prayer, and Rebecca became **pregnant.**
29.32 Leah became **pregnant** and gave birth to a son.
29.33 She became **pregnant** again and gave birth to another son.
29.34 Once again she became **pregnant** and gave birth to another son.
Gen 29.35 Then she became **pregnant** again and gave birth to another son.
30. 5 Bilhah became **pregnant** and bore Jacob a son.
30. 7 Bilhah became **pregnant** again and bore Jacob a second son.
30.17 and she became **pregnant** and bore Jacob a fifth son.
30.19 Leah became **pregnant** again and bore Jacob a sixth son.
30.23 She became **pregnant** and gave birth to a son.
38. 4 She became **pregnant** again and bore another son and named him Onan.
38.18 Then they had intercourse, and she became **pregnant.**
38.24 Tamar has been acting like a whore, and now she is **pregnant."**
38.25 "I am **pregnant** by the man who owns these things.
Ex 21.22 are fighting and hurt a **pregnant** woman so that she loses her
Judg 13. 3 have children, but you will soon be **pregnant** and have a son.
13. 7 did tell me that I would become **pregnant** and have a son.
Ruth 4.13 The Lord blessed her, and she became **pregnant** and had a son.
1 Sam 1.20 it was that she became **pregnant** and gave birth to a son.
4.19 the wife of Phinehas, was **pregnant,** and it was almost time
2 Sam 11. 5 she discovered that she was **pregnant** and sent a message to
2 Kgs 8.12 children to death, and rip open their **pregnant** women."
15.16 He even ripped open the bellies of all the **pregnant** women.
1 Chr 7.23 with his wife again, and she became **pregnant** and had a son.
Ecc 11. 5 how new life begins in the womb of a **pregnant** woman.
Is 7.14 a young woman who is **pregnant** will have a son and will
8. 3 Some time later my wife became **pregnant.**
Jer 31. 8 lame will come with them, **pregnant** women and those about to
Hos 1. 8 her daughter, she became **pregnant** again and had another son.
9.11 to them, no more women **pregnant,** no more children conceived.
13.16 to the ground, and **pregnant** women will be ripped open."
Amos 1.13 territory they even ripped open **pregnant** women in Gilead.
Mt 1.23 true, [23]"A virgin will become **pregnant** and have a son,
24.19 for women who are **pregnant** and for mothers with little babies!
Mk 13.17 for women who are **pregnant** and for mothers with little babies!
Lk 1.24 his wife Elizabeth became **pregnant** and did not leave the house
1.26 sixth month of Elizabeth's **pregnancy** God sent the angel Gabriel
1.31 You will become **pregnant** and give birth to a son,
1.36 is now six months **pregnant,** even though she is very old.
2. 5 She was **pregnant,** [6]and while they were in Bethlehem, the time
21.23 for women who are **pregnant** and for mothers with little babies!

PREJUDICE

Job 13.10 Even though your **prejudice** is hidden, he will reprimand you,
Prov 24.23 It is wrong for a judge to be **prejudiced.**
28.21 **Prejudice** is wrong.
Is 3. 9 Their **prejudices** will be held against them.
1 Tim 5.21 without showing any **prejudice** or favour to anyone in anything
Jas 3.17 it is free from **prejudice** and hypocrisy.

PREPARATION DAY

The sixth day of the week (Friday), on which the Jews got ready to keep the Sabbath (Saturday).
see also **FRIDAY**

Mk 15.42 It was **Preparation day** (that is, the day before the Sabbath),

PREPARE

Gen 19. 3 to bake some bread and **prepare** a fine meal for the guests.
26.30 Isaac **prepared** a feast for them, and they ate and drank.
33.12 Esau said, "Let's **prepare** to leave.
43.16 eat with me at noon, so kill an animal and **prepare** it."
50. 5 in the tomb which he had **prepared** in the land of Canaan.
Ex 12.16 is to be done on those days, but you may **prepare** food.
12.39 time to get their food ready or to **prepare** leavened dough.
12.46 meal must be eaten in the house in which it was **prepared;**
16. 5 are to bring in twice as much as usual and **prepare** it."
23.20 travel and to bring you to the place which I have **prepared.**
39. 6 They **prepared** the carnelians and mounted them in gold settings;
Lev 7. 9 baked in an oven or **prepared** in a pan or on a
Num 4.20 and see the priests **preparing** the sacred objects for moving, they
19. 9 to use in **preparing** the water for removing ritual uncleanness.
28.17 which only bread **prepared** without yeast is to be eaten.
Deut 16. 3 When you eat this meal, do not eat bread **prepared** with yeast.
16. 3 you are to eat bread **prepared** without yeast, as you did when
16. 8 you are to eat bread **prepared** without yeast, and on the
24. 6 away the family's means of **preparing** food to keep alive.
28. 5 bless your corn crops and the food you **prepare** from them.
28.17 curse your corn crops and the food you **prepare** from them.
Josh 8. 2 **Prepare** to attack the city by surprise from the rear."
Judg 10.17 Then the Ammonite army **prepared** for battle
12. 1 The men of Ephraim **prepared** for battle;
13.15 But if you want to **prepare** it, burn it as an offering
1 Sam 6. 7 So **prepare** a new wagon and two cows that have never been
28.22 Let me **prepare** some food for you.
28.24 Then she took some flour, **prepared** it, and baked some bread
2 Sam 12. 4 kill one of his own animals to **prepare** a meal for him;
13. 5 I want her to **prepare** the food here where I can see
13. 7 "Go to Amnon's house and **prepare** some food for him."
13. 8 She took some dough, **prepared** it, and made some cakes there
13.27 Absalom **prepared** a banquet fit for a king
1 Kgs 5.18 from the city of Byblos **prepared** the stones and the timber
6. 7 Temple was built had been **prepared** at the quarry, so that
7. 9 The stones were **prepared** at the quarry and cut to measure,
7.10 were made of large stones **prepared** at the quarry, some of
17.12 to take back home and **prepare** what little I have for my
17.13 "Go ahead and **prepare** your meal.
17.13 it to me, and then **prepare** the rest for you and your
18.25 so many of you, you take a bull and **prepare** it first.
18.26 that was brought to them, **prepared** it, and prayed to Baal
1 Chr 9.31 Korah, was responsible for **preparing** the baked offerings.
9.32 of Kohath were responsible for **preparing** the sacred bread

1 Chr	12.39	drink which their fellow-countrymen had **prepared** for them.
	15. 1	He also **prepared** a place for God's Covenant Box and put up
	15. 3	bring the Covenant Box to the place he had **prepared** for it.
	15.12	Lord God of Israel to the place I have **prepared** for it.
	16. 1	the tent which David had **prepared** for it and put it inside.
	22. 2	Some of them **prepared** stone blocks for building the Temple.
	22. 5	and inexperienced, so I must make **preparations** for it."
	28. 2	I have made **preparations** for building a temple to honour him,
	29. 2	made every effort to **prepare** materials for the Temple—gold,
	29.19	the Temple for which I have made these **preparations."**
2 Chr	2. 9	to assist yours [9] in **preparing** large quantities of timber,
	3. 1	Solomon's father, had already **prepared** a place for the Temple.
	16.14	spices and perfumed oils to **prepare** his body for burial, and
	29.17	sixteenth of the month, **preparing** the Temple for worship.
	31.11	On the king's orders they **prepared** storerooms in the
	35. 6	make yourselves ritually clean and **prepare** the sacrifices in
	35.15	because the other Levites **prepared** the Passover for them.
Neh	13.30	I **prepared** regulations for the priests and the Levites so
Esth	3.14	so that everyone would be **prepared** when that day came.
	5. 4	be my guests tonight at a banquet I am **preparing** for you."
	5. 8	tomorrow at another banquet that I will **prepare** for you.
Job	30.12	they **prepare** their final assault.
	33. 5	**Prepare** your arguments.
Ps	23. 5	You **prepare** a banquet for me, where all my enemies can see
	68. 4	**prepare** a way for him who rides on the clouds.
	85.13	Righteousness will go before the Lord and **prepare** the path for him.
	144. 1	He trains me for battle and **prepares** me for war.
Prov	31.15	gets up before daylight to **prepare** food for her family
Ecc	9.14	He surrounded it and **prepared** to break through the walls.
Is	2. 4	Nations will never again go to war, never **prepare** for battle again.
	13. 4	The Lord of Armies is **preparing** his troops for battle.
	19.17	of the fate that the Lord Almighty has **prepared** for them.
	21. 5	**Prepare** your shields!"
	25. 6	Zion the Lord Almighty will **prepare** a banquet for all the
	26.11	let them suffer the punishment you have **prepared.**
	28.25	Once he has **prepared** the soil, he sows the seeds of
	30.33	Long ago a place was **prepared** where a huge fire will
	34. 5	The Lord has **prepared** his sword in heaven, and now it will
	40. 3	A voice cries out, **"Prepare** in the wilderness a road for
	45. 2	"I myself will **prepare** your way, levelling mountains and hills.
	49.11	highway across the mountains and **prepare** a road for my
	62.10	**Prepare** a highway;
Jer	6. 4	They will say, **"Prepare** to attack Jerusalem!
	6.22	a mighty nation far away is **preparing** for war.
	50.41	many kings are **preparing** for war.
	51.27	**Prepare** the nations for war against Babylonia!
	51.28	**Prepare** the nations for war against Babylonia.
	51.39	I will **prepare** them a feast and make them drunk and happy.
Ezek	39.17	from all round to eat the sacrifice I am **preparing** for them.
	40.42	the annexe, used to **prepare** the offerings to be burnt whole,
Dan	9.14	O Lord our God, were **prepared** to punish us, and you did,
	9.26	bringing the war and destruction which God has **prepared.**
	9.27	it there meets the end which God has **prepared** for him."
	11.10	the king of Syria will **prepare** for war and gather a large
	11.25	king of Egypt, who will **prepare** to fight back with a huge
Joel	2.16	**prepare** them for a sacred meeting;
	3. 9	**'Prepare** for war;
Amos	7. 4	In it I saw him **preparing** to punish his people with fire.
Mic	4. 3	Nations will never again go to war, never **prepare** for battle again.
Nah	1.14	I am **preparing** a grave for the Assyrians—they don't deserve
	2. 1	**Prepare** for battle!
	2. 3	They are **preparing** to attack!
	3.14	Draw water to **prepare** for a siege, and strengthen your fortresses!
Zeph	1. 7	The Lord is **preparing** to sacrifice his people and has
Mal	3. 1	"I will send my messenger to **prepare** the way for me.
Mt	3. 3	"Someone is shouting in the desert, **'Prepare** a road for the Lord;
	20.23	These places belong to those for whom my Father has **prepared** them."
	22. 2	there was a king who **prepared** a wedding feast for his son.
	25.34	kingdom which has been **prepared** for you ever since the creation
	25.41	fire which has been **prepared** for the Devil and his angels!
	26.19	did as Jesus had told them and **prepared** the Passover meal.
Mk	10.40	give these places to those for whom he has **prepared** them."
	14. 8	perfume on my body to **prepare** it ahead of time for burial.
	14.15	a large upstairs room, **prepared** and furnished, where you will get
	14.16	and they **prepared** the Passover meal.
Lk	1.76	ahead of the Lord to **prepare** his road for him, [77] to tell
	2.31	salvation, [31] which you have **prepared** in the presence of all
	22.13	Jesus had told them, and they **prepared** the Passover meal.
	23.56	they went back home and **prepared** the spices and perfumes for
	24. 1	went to the tomb, carrying the spices they had **prepared.**
Jn	12. 2	**prepared** a dinner for him there, which Martha helped to serve;
	14. 2	Father's house, and I am going to **prepare** a place for you.
	14. 3	And after I go and **prepare** a place for you, I will
	19.40	according to the Jewish custom of **preparing** a body for burial.
Acts	4.26	The kings of the earth **prepared** themselves, and the rulers met
	10.10	while the food was being **prepared,** he had a vision.
Rom	9.23	those of us whom he has **prepared** to receive his glory.
1 Cor	2. 9	is the very thing God **prepared** for those who love him."
	14. 8	does not sound a clear call, who will **prepare** for battle?
2 Cor	5. 5	is the one who has **prepared** us for this change,
Eph	2.10	of good deeds, which he has already **prepared** for us to do.
	4.12	He did this to **prepare** all God's people for the work of
1 Thes	3.11	himself and our Lord Jesus **prepare** the way for us to come
Heb	10. 5	sacrifices and offerings, but you have **prepared** a body for me.
	11.16	him their God, because he has **prepared** a city for them.
Rev	8. 6	the seven angels with the seven trumpets **prepared** to blow them.
	12. 6	to a place God had **prepared** for her, where she will be
	18. 6	a drink twice as strong as the drink she **prepared** for you.
Rev	19. 7	of the Lamb, and his bride has **prepared** herself for it.
	21. 2	out of heaven from God, **prepared** and ready, like a bride

PRESENCE

see also **TENT (2) (Tent of God's Presence)**

Gen	4.14	You are driving me off the land and away from your **presence.**
	4.16	Cain went away from the Lord's **presence** and lived in a land
	19.27	the place where he had stood in the **presence** of the Lord.
	21.23	a vow here in the **presence** of God that you will not
	23. 9	full price, here in your **presence,** so that I can own it
	23.11	Here in the **presence** of my own people, I will give it
	27. 7	you my blessing in the **presence** of the Lord before I die.'
	31.35	sir, but I am not able to stand up in your **presence;**
	41.14	and changed his clothes, he came into the king's **presence.**
	43. 3	not be admitted to his **presence** unless we had our brother
	43. 5	admitted to his **presence** unless our brother was with us."
	44.23	not be admitted to my **presence** again unless your youngest
	44.26	be admitted to the man's **presence** unless our youngest
Ex	7.20	In the **presence** of the king and his officers, Aaron raised
	10.11	With that, Moses and Aaron were driven out of the king's **presence.**
	16. 7	you will see the dazzling light of the Lord's **presence.**
	16.33	and place it in the Lord's **presence** to be kept for our
	17. 6	Moses did so in the **presence** of the leaders of Israel.
	24.16	The dazzling light of the Lord's **presence** came down
	27.21	There in my **presence** it is to burn from evening until morning.
	28.30	Aaron will carry them when he comes into my holy **presence.**
	28.35	When he comes into my **presence** in the Holy Place or when
	29.11	bull there in my holy **presence** at the entrance of the Tent.
	29.42	to be offered in my **presence** at the entrance of the Tent
	29.43	the dazzling light of my **presence** will make the place holy.
	33.16	Your **presence** with us will distinguish us from any other
	33.18	"Please, let me see the dazzling light of your **presence."**
	33.19	you and in your **presence** I will pronounce my sacred name.
	33.22	the dazzling light of my **presence** passes by, I will put you
	34.10	In their **presence** I will do great things such as have never
	40.25	and there in the Lord's **presence** he lit the lamps,
	40.34	Tent and the dazzling light of the Lord's **presence** filled it.
	40.38	see the cloud of the Lord's **presence** over the Tent during
Lev	4. 4	hand on its head, and kill it there in the Lord's **presence.**
	9. 6	that the dazzling light of his **presence** can appear to you."
	9.23	light of the Lord's **presence** appeared to all the people.
	10. 2	it burnt them to death there in the **presence** of the Lord.
	14.16	some of it seven times there in the Lord's **presence.**
	14.27	some of it seven times there in the Lord's **presence.**
	16.13	There in the Lord's **presence** he shall put the incense on
	24. 3	until morning, there in the Lord's **presence** outside the
	24. 4	must see that they burn regularly in the Lord's **presence.**
	24. 6	covered with pure gold, which is in the Lord's **presence.**
	24. 8	come, the bread must be placed in the **presence** of the Lord.
Num	14.10	dazzling light of the Lord's **presence** appear over the tent.
	14.21	and as surely as my **presence** fills the earth, [72] none of
	14.22	the dazzling light of my **presence** and the miracles that I
	16.19	of the Lord's **presence** appeared to the whole community,
	16.42	that the dazzling light of the Lord's **presence** had appeared.
	19. 3	is to be taken outside the camp and killed in his **presence.**
	19. 5	intestines, is to be burnt in the **presence** of the priest.
	20. 6	the dazzling light of the Lord's **presence** appeared to them.
	32.20	say, then here in the **presence** of the Lord get ready to
Deut	4.10	day you stood in the **presence** of the Lord your God at
	9.18	lay face downwards in the Lord's **presence** for forty days and
	9.25	in the Lord's **presence** those forty days and nights,
	12. 5	the people are to come into his **presence** and worship him.
	12. 7	There, in the **presence** of the Lord your God, who has
	12.12	Be joyful there in his **presence,** together with your children,
	12.18	these offerings only in the **presence** of the Lord your God,
	14.23	and there in his **presence** eat the tithes of your corn, wine,
	14.26	beer—and there, in the **presence** of the Lord your God, you
	15.20	to eat them in the Lord's **presence** at the one place of
	16.11	Be joyful in the Lord's **presence,** together with your children,
	18.16	or to see his fiery **presence** any more, because you were
	25. 9	up to him in the **presence** of the town leaders, take off
	26. 5	Then, in the Lord's **presence** you will recite these words:
	26.10	"Then set the basket down in the Lord's **presence** and worship there.
	27. 7	and be grateful in the **presence** of the Lord your God.
	29.10	you are standing in the **presence** of the Lord your God, all
	29.15	who stand here in his **presence** today and also with our
	31. 7	said to him in the **presence** of all the people of Israel,
	32.51	unfaithful to me in the **presence** of the people of Israel.
	32.51	of Zin, you dishonoured me in the **presence** of the people.
Josh	4.13	In the **presence** of the Lord about forty thousand men
	7.23	Israelites, and laid them down in the **presence** of the Lord.
	10.12	In the **presence** of the Israelites he said,
	24. 1	officers of Israel, and they came into the **presence** of God.
Judg	11.11	Jephthah stated his terms at Mizpah in the **presence** of the Lord.
	20. 1	They gathered in one body in the Lord's **presence** at Mizpah.
	20.22	and mourned in the **presence** of the Lord until evening.
	20.26	They sat there in the Lord's **presence** and did not eat until
	20.26	burnt some sacrifices whole—all in the **presence** of the Lord.
	21. 2	Bethel and sat there in the **presence** of God until evening.
	21. 5	not go to the gathering in the Lord's **presence** at Mizpah?"
Ruth	4. 4	want it, buy it in the **presence** of these men sitting here.
1 Sam	2.35	who will always serve in the **presence** of my chosen king.
	12. 3	accuse me now in the **presence** of the Lord and the king
	16. 6	man standing here in the Lord's **presence** is surely the one
	19.24	danced and shouted in Samuel's **presence,** and lay naked all
2 Sam	24. 4	they left his **presence** and went out to count the people of
1 Kgs	8.11	the dazzling light of the Lord's **presence,** and they could
	8.22	Then in the **presence** of the people Solomon went and

1 Kgs 10. 8 who are always in your **presence** and are privileged to hear
2 Kgs 19.14 letter there in the **presence** of the Lord, [15]and prayed,
1 Chr 13.10 He died there in God's **presence,** [11]and so that place has
28. 8 now, my people, in the **presence** of our God and of this
29.22 happy as they ate and drank in the **presence** of the Lord.
2 Chr 5.11 the dazzling light of the Lord's **presence,** and they could
6.12 Then in the **presence** of the people Solomon went and
7. 1 the dazzling light of the Lord's **presence** filled the Temple.
9. 7 who are always in your **presence** and are privileged to hear
Ezra 9. 6 God, I am too ashamed to raise my head in your **presence.**
9.15 we have no right to come into your **presence."**
Esth 8. 1 then on Mordecai was allowed to enter the king's **presence.**
Job 2. 7 Then Satan left the Lord's **presence** and made sores break
31.37 I have done, and hold my head high in his **presence.**
Ps 5. 4 you allow no evil in your **presence.**
5.10 Drive them out of your **presence** because of their many sins
11. 7 those who do them will live in his **presence.**
16. 8 I am always aware of the Lord's **presence;**
16.11 your **presence** fills me with joy and brings me pleasure for ever.
17.15 and when I awake, your **presence** will fill me with joy.
21. 6 are with him for ever and your **presence** fills him with joy.
22.25 in the **presence** of those who worship you I will offer the
24. 6 to God, who come into the **presence** of the God of Jacob.
31.20 them in the safety of your **presence** from the plots of men;
31.22 and thought that he had driven me out of his **presence.**
41.12 you will keep me in your **presence** for ever.
42. 2 when can I go and worship in your **presence?**
44. 3 of your **presence,** which showed that you loved them.
51.11 Do not banish me from your **presence;**
52. 9 in the **presence** of your people I will proclaim that you
56.13 so I walk in the **presence** of God, in the light that
61. 7 May he rule for ever in your **presence,** O God;
68. 2 of the fire, so do the wicked perish in God's **presence.**
68. 3 But the righteous are glad and rejoice in his **presence;**
68. 4 His name is the Lord—be glad in his **presence!**
76. 7 No one can stand in your **presence** when you are angry.
85. 9 him, and his saving **presence** will remain in our land.
101. 7 no hypocrite will remain in my **presence.**
114. 7 the Lord's coming, at the **presence** of the God of Jacob,
116. 9 so I walk in the **presence** of the Lord in the world
119.135 Bless me with your **presence** and teach me your laws.
139. 7 Where could I get away from your **presence?**
140.13 they will live in your **presence.**
Prov 8.30 joy, always happy in his **presence—** [31]happy with the world
Ecc 8. 3 The king can do anything he likes, so depart from his **presence;**
Is 19.20 They will be symbols of the Lord Almighty's **presence** in Egypt.
37.14 letter there in the **presence** of the Lord, [15]and prayed,
58. 8 my **presence** will protect you on every side.
60. 2 The brightness of his **presence** will be with you.
64. 2 your enemies, and make the nations tremble at your **presence!**
Jer 7.10 come and stand in my **presence,** in my own Temple, and say,
28. 1 In the **presence** of the priests and of the people he told
28. 5 Then in the **presence** of the priests and of all the people
28.11 in pieces, [11]and said in the **presence** of all the people:
32.12 them to him in the **presence** of Hanamel and of the witnesses
32.25 buy the field in the **presence** of witnesses, even though the
34.15 made a covenant in my **presence,** in the Temple where I am
Ezek 1.28 This was the dazzling light that shows the **presence** of the Lord.
3.22 I felt the powerful **presence** of the Lord and heard him
8. 4 dazzling light that shows the **presence** of Israel's God, just
9. 3 the dazzling light of the **presence** of the God of Israel rose
10. 4 The dazzling light of the Lord's **presence** rose up from the
10.18 the dazzling light of the Lord's **presence** left the entrance
11.22 The dazzling light of the **presence** of the God of Israel was
20. 9 my name, for in the **presence** of the people among whom they
33.22 he came, I had felt the powerful **presence** of the Lord.
37. 1 I felt the powerful **presence** of the Lord, and his spirit
40. 1 day I felt the powerful **presence** of the Lord, and he carried
40.46 are permitted to go into the Lord's **presence** to serve him.
41.22 "This is the table which stands in the **presence** of the Lord."
42.13 who enter the Lord's **presence** eat the holiest offerings.
43. 2 the dazzling light of the **presence** of the God of Israel.
43.19 only ones who are to come into my **presence** to serve me.
44. 3 however, may go there to eat a holy meal in my **presence.**
44. 4 the Lord was filled with the dazzling light of his **presence.**
44.15 me and come into my **presence** to offer me the fat and
Dan 2.25 Daniel into King Nebuchadnezzar's **presence** and told the king,
5.13 at once into the king's **presence,** and the king said to him,
Hos 6. 2 days he will revive us, and we will live in his **presence.**
Jon 2. 4 had been banished from your **presence** and would never see
Nah 1. 5 Mountains quake in the **presence** of the Lord;
Hab 2.20 let everyone on earth be silent in his **presence.**
Zeph 1. 7 so be silent in his **presence.**
Zech 2.13 Be silent, everyone, in the **presence** of the Lord, for he
3. 7 I hear the prayers of the angels who are in my **presence.**
6. 5 have just come from the **presence** of the Lord of all the
Mal 3.16 In his **presence,** there was written down in a book a record
Mt 18.10 tell you, are always in the **presence** of my Father in heaven.
27.58 He went into the **presence** of Pilate and asked for the
Mk 15.42 Joseph went boldly into the **presence** of Pilate and asked him
Lk 1.19 "I stand in the **presence** of God, who sent me to speak
2.31 salvation, [31]which you have prepared in the **presence** of all
14.10 bring you honour in the **presence** of all the other guests.
19.27 their king, bring them here and kill them in my **presence!'"**
23.14 examined him here in your **presence,** and I have not found him
23.52 He went into the **presence** of Pilate and asked for the
24.43 cooked fish, [43]which he took and ate in their **presence.**
Jn 10.32 many good deeds in your **presence** which the Father gave me to
12.37 miracles in their **presence,** they did not believe in him,
17. 5 Give me glory in your **presence** now, the same glory I had
20.30 In his disciples' **presence** Jesus performed many other miracles
Acts 2.28 that lead to life, and your **presence** will fill me with joy.'
3.13 rejected him in Pilate's **presence,** even after Pilate had decided
10.33 are all here in the **presence** of God, waiting to hear
Rom 3.23 everyone has sinned and is far away from God's saving **presence.**
8.11 to your mortal bodies by the **presence** of his Spirit in you.
1 Cor 1.29 This means that no one can boast in God's **presence.**
12. 7 The Spirit's **presence** is shown in some way in each person
2 Cor 2.10 I do it in Christ's **presence** because of you, [11]in order to
2.17 we speak with sincerity in his **presence,** as servants of Christ.
4.14 Jesus and take us, together with you, into his **presence.**
12.19 us to speak in the **presence** of God, and everything we do,
12.21 will humiliate me in your **presence,** and I shall weep over
Eph 2.18 to come in the one Spirit into the **presence** of the Father.
3.12 have the boldness to go into God's **presence** with all confidence.
4.10 beyond the heavens, to fill the whole universe with his **presence.**
Col 1.22 to bring you, holy, pure, and faultless, into his **presence.**
1.28 bring each one into God's **presence** as a mature individual
1 Thes 2.19 of our victory in the **presence** of our Lord Jesus when he
3. 9 for the joy we have in his **presence** because of you.
3.13 perfect and holy in the **presence** of our God and Father when
2 Thes 1. 9 eternal destruction, separated from the **presence** of the Lord
2. 8 breath from his mouth and destroy him with his dazzling **presence.**
1 Tim 5.21 In the **presence** of God and of Christ Jesus and of the
2 Tim 2. 2 heard me proclaim in the **presence** of many witnesses,
2.14 a solemn warning in God's **presence** not to fight over words.
4. 1 In the **presence** of God and of Christ Jesus, who will judge
Heb 4.14 has gone into the very **presence** of God—Jesus, the Son of
9. 5 creatures representing God's **presence,** with their wings spread
9.24 where he now appears on our behalf in the **presence** of God.
2 Pet 2.11 do not accuse them with insults in the **presence** of the Lord.
1 Jn 3.19 this is how we will be confident in God's **presence.**
3.21 conscience does not condemn us, we have courage in God's **presence.**
5.14 We have courage in God's **presence,** because we are sure that
Jude 24 and joyful before his glorious **presence—**[25]to the only God
Rev 3. 5 In the **presence** of my Father and of his angels I will
7.15 He who sits on the throne will protect them with his **presence.**
13.12 It used the vast authority of the first beast in its **presence.**
13.14 was allowed to perform in the **presence** of the first beast.
19.20 with the false prophet who had performed miracles in his **presence.**
20.11 Earth and heaven fled from his **presence** and were seen no more.

PRESENT (1)

Gen 43.15 There they **presented** themselves to Joseph.
43.25 got their gifts ready to **present** to Joseph when he arrived
47. 2 He then **presented** his brothers to the king.
47. 7 Then Joseph brought his father Jacob and **presented** him to the king.
Lev 1. 3 He must **present** it at the entrance of the Tent of the
1. 5 and the Aaronite priests shall **present** the blood to the Lord
1.13 legs, and the priest will **present** the sacrifice to the Lord
1.15 The priest shall **present** it at the altar, wring its neck,
2. 1 When anyone **presents** an offering of grain to the Lord, he
2. 6 pour the oil on it when you **present** it as an offering.
2. 8 offering to the Lord and **present** it to the priest, who will
2.11 of the grain-offerings which you **present** to the Lord may be
3. 3 sides of the altar [3]and **present** the following parts of the
3. 9 sides of the altar [9]and **present** the following parts of the
3.14 sides of the altar [14]and **present** the following parts as a
4. 3 on the people, he shall **present** a young bull without any
6.14 An Aaronite priest shall **present** the grain-offering to the
6.20 he is ordained, he shall **present** as an offering to the Lord
6.21 griddle and then crumbled and **presented** as a grain-offering,
7.11 regulations for the fellowship-offerings **presented** to the Lord.
7.12 thank-offering to God, he shall **present,** together with the
7.14 He shall **present** one part of each kind of bread as a
7.30 animal with its breast and **present** it as a special gift to
8.27 and his sons, and they **presented** it as a special gift to
8.29 Moses took the breast and **presented** it as a special gift to
9. 7 **Present** this offering to take away the sins of the people,
9.15 After that, he **presented** the people's offerings.
9.17 He **presented** the grain-offering and took a handful of
9.21 fat on the altar [21]and **presented** the breasts and the right
10. 1 coals in it, added incense, and **presented** it to the Lord.
10. 1 holy, because the Lord had not commanded them to **present** it.
10.14 the hind leg that are **presented** as the special gift and the
10.15 time the fat is **presented** as a food-offering to the Lord.
10.19 The people **presented** their sin-offering to the Lord today,
12. 7 The priest shall **present** her offering to the Lord and
14.12 He shall **present** them as a special gift to the Lord for
14.24 lamb and the olive-oil and **present** them as a special gift to
16.10 chosen for Azazel shall be **presented** alive to the Lord and
16.20 and the altar, he shall **present** to the Lord the live goat
21. 8 priest holy, because he **presents** the food-offerings to me.
21.17 has any physical defect may **present** the food-offering to me.
21.21 has any physical defect may **present** the food-offering to me.
22.18 any foreigner living in Israel **presents** a burnt-offering,
22.21 When anyone **presents** a fellowship-offering to the Lord,
23.11 He shall **present** it as a special offering to the Lord,
23.11 The priest shall **present** it the day after the Sabbath.
23.12 On the day you **present** the offering of corn, also
23.13 With it you shall **present** two kilogrammes of flour mixed
23.13 You shall also **present** with it an offering of one litre of
23.15 which you bring your sheaf of corn to **present** to the Lord.
23.16 day after the seventh Sabbath, **present** to the Lord another
23.17 two loaves of bread and **present** them to the Lord as a
23.17 with yeast and shall be **presented** to the Lord as an offering
23.18 bread the community is to **present** seven one-year-old lambs,
23.20 The priest shall **present** the bread with the two lambs as

Lev 23.25 **Present** a food-offering to the Lord and do none of your
23.26 for worship, and **present** a food-offering to the Lord.
23.36 Each day for seven days you shall **present** a food-offering.
23.36 come together again for worship and **present** a food-offering.
23.37 **presenting** food-offerings, burnt-offerings, grain-offerings, sacrifices, and wine-offerings,
Num 5. 9 to the Lord belongs to the priest to whom they **present** it.
5.10 Each priest shall keep the offerings **presented** to him.
5.25 out in dedication to the Lord, and **present** it on the altar.
6.14 entrance of the Tent [14] and **present** to the Lord three
6.16 The priest shall **present** all these to the Lord and offer
6.17 he shall also **present** the offerings of corn and wine.
6.20 Next, the priest shall **present** them as a special gift to
7. 3 After they had **presented** them, [4] the Lord said to Moses,
7.10 When they were ready to **present** their gifts at the altar,
7.11 of the leaders is to **present** his gifts for the dedication of
7.12 They **presented** their offerings in the following order:
9. 7 should we be excluded from **presenting** the Lord's offering
9.13 people, because he did not **present** the offering to me at the
10.10 **present** your burnt-offerings and your fellowship-offerings.
15. 3 or a goat may be **presented** to the Lord as a burnt-offering
15. 4 Whoever **presents** a sheep or a goat as a burnt-offering
15. 6 of olive-oil are to be **presented** as a grain-offering,
15. 9 is to be **presented,** [10] together with two litres of wine.
15.13 to do this when he **presents** a food-offering, a smell
15.20 new corn is to be **presented** as a special contribution to the
15.20 This is to be **presented** in the same way as the special
16.17 put incense on it, and then **present** it at the altar."
16.35 out and burnt up the 250 men who had **presented** the incense.
16.38 They became holy when they were **presented** at the Lord's altar.
18. 9 Everything that is **presented** to me as a sacred offering
18.11 that the Israelites **present** to me shall be yours.
18.15 or animal that the Israelites **present** to me belongs to you.
18.19 special contributions which the Israelites **present** to me.
18.21 Levites every tithe that the people of Israel **present** to me.
18.24 the Israelites **present** to me as a special contribution.
18.26 as your possession, you must **present** a tenth of it as a
18.28 this way you also will **present** the special contribution that
18.30 When you have **presented** the best part, you may keep the rest,
18.32 as long as you have **presented** the best of it to the
27. 5 Moses **presented** their case to the Lord, [6] and the Lord
28. 2 to instruct the Israelites to **present** to God at the
28. 3 These are the food-offerings that are to be **presented** to the Lord:
28.11 **Present** a burnt-offering to the Lord at the beginning of each month:
28.26 the Harvest Festival, when you **present** the offering of new
29. 2 **Present** a burnt-offering to the Lord, a smell pleasing to him:
Deut 17. 9 the Lord your God, [9] and **present** your case to the levitical
Josh 8.31 Lord, and they also **presented** their fellowship-offerings.
2 Sam 4. 8 They **presented** the head to King David at Hebron and said
1 Kgs 3.16 two prostitutes came and **presented** themselves before King Solomon.
10.10 She **presented** to King Solomon the gifts she had brought:
18. 1 said to Elijah, "Go and **present** yourself to King Ahab, and
18.15 I promise that I will **present** myself to the king today."
2 Kgs 10.25 As soon as Jehu had **presented** the offerings, he said to
1 Chr 6.49 Aaron and his descendants **presented** the offerings of
2 Chr 2. 4 fragrant spices, where we will **present** offerings of sacred
9. 9 She **presented** to King Solomon the gifts she had brought:
13.11 They **present** the offerings of bread on a table that is
29.27 Hezekiah gave the order for the burnt-offering to be **presented;**
29.35 out the wine that was **presented** with the burnt-offerings.
Ezra 1. 4 as well as offerings to **present** in the Temple of God in
7.19 You are to **present** to God in Jerusalem all the utensils
Job 5. 8 you, I would turn to God and **present** my case to him.
23. 4 case before him and **present** all the arguments in my favour.
Is 1.23 orphans in court or listen when widows **present** their case.
41. 1 Get ready to **present** your case in court;
41.21 "You gods of the nations, **present** your case.
43.26 **Present** your case to prove you are in the right!
45.20 **present** yourselves for the trial!
45.21 Come and **present** your case in court;
48.13 I summon earth and sky, they come at once and **present** themselves.
66. 3 whether they **present** a grain-offering or offer pigs' blood;
Dan 2.48 Daniel a high position, **presented** him with many splendid gifts,
7.13 one who had been living for ever and was **presented** to him.
Mic 4.13 got by violence you will **present** to me, the Lord of the
6. 1 Arise, O Lord, and **present** your case;
Mt 2.11 gold, frankincense, and myrrh, and **presented** them to him.
Lk 2.22 the child to Jerusalem to **present** him to the Lord,
Acts 6. 6 The group **presented** them to the apostles, who prayed and
9.41 including the widows, and **presented** her alive to them.
Eph 5.27 in order to **present** the church to himself in all
Heb 8. 3 is appointed to **present** offerings and animal sacrifices to God,
9. 9 the offerings and animal sacrifices **presented** to God cannot
13.15 Jesus, which is the offering **presented** by lips that confess him

PRESENT (2)

Gen 19.37 He was the ancestor of the **present-day** Moabites.
19.38 He was the ancestor of the **present-day** Ammonites.
Ex 22.14 when its owner is not **present,** the man must pay for it.
22.15 happens when the owner is **present,** the man need not repay.
Deut 6.15 Lord your God, who is **present** with you, tolerates no rivals.
Judg 20. 2 of Israel were **present** at this gathering of God's people,
1 Kgs 3.18 of us were there in the house—no one else was **present.**
9.20 descendants continue to be slaves down to the **present** time.
2 Kgs 10.19 to Baal, and whoever is not **present** will be put to death."
10.23 only worshippers of Baal are **present** and that no worshipper
2 Chr 5.11 priests **present,** regardless of the group to which they belonged,
8. 7 descendants continue to be slaves down to the **present** time.
20.14 the Lord came upon a Levite who was **present** in the crowd.
34.32 of Benjamin and everyone else **present** in Jerusalem promise
35.17 people of Israel who were **present** celebrated the Passover
Ezra 5.16 continued from then until the **present,** but the Temple is
Neh 5.13 Everyone who was **present** said, "Amen!"
Esth 1. 3 of Persia and Media were **present,** as well as the governors
Ps 27.13 I will live to see the Lord's goodness in this **present** life.
Jer 36. 2 first spoke to you, when Josiah was king, up to the **present.**
44.23 This **present** disaster has come on you because you
Ezek 11.16 time being I will be **present** with them in the lands where
Mk 10.30 for the gospel, [30] will receive much more in this **present** age.
13.19 very beginning when God created the world until the **present** time.
Lk 5.17 power of the Lord was **present** for Jesus to heal the sick.
12.56 why, then, don't you know the meaning of this **present** time?
18.30 receive much more in this **present** age and eternal life in
Acts 21.18 and all the church elders were **present.**
Rom 3.25 but in the **present** time he deals with their sins, in order
8.18 what we suffer at this **present** time cannot be compared at
8.22 know that up to the **present** time all of creation groans with
8.38 rulers or powers, neither the **present** nor the future,
1 Cor 3.22 world, life and death, the **present** and the future—all these
5. 3 power of our Lord Jesus **present** with us, [5] you are to hand
7.26 Considering the **present** distress, I think it is better for
14. 5 unless there is someone **present** who can explain what he says,
2 Cor 3.17 where the Spirit of the Lord is **present,** there is freedom.
Gal 1. 4 set us free from this **present** evil age, Christ gave himself
2. 2 work in the past or in the **present** to be a failure.
4.25 is a figure of the **present** city of Jerusalem, in slavery
Eph 3.10 in order that at the **present** time, by means of the church,
1 Tim 4. 8 it promises life both for the **present** and for the future.
2 Tim 4.10 fell in love with this **present** world and has deserted me,
Phlm 9 Christ Jesus, and at **present** also a prisoner for his sake.
Heb 9. 9 This is an illustration which points to the **present** time.

PRESENT (3)

Gen 25. 6 was still alive, he gave **presents** to the sons his other
32.13 Jacob chose from his livestock as a **present** for his brother Esau:
32.18 He sends them as a **present** to his master Esau.
34.12 Tell me what **presents** you want, and set the payment for
43.11 of the land in your packs as a **present** for the governor:
1 Sam 25.27 Please, sir, accept this **present** I have brought you, and
30.26 the message, "Here is a **present** for you from the loot we
2 Sam 8.10 Joram took David **presents** made of gold, silver, and bronze.
11. 8 Uriah left, and David sent a **present** to his home.
1 Kgs 9.16 gave it as a wedding **present** to his daughter when she
15.19 This silver and gold is a **present** for you.
2 Kgs 16. 8 the palace treasury and sent it as a **present** to the emperor.
20.12 had been ill, so he sent him a letter and a **present.**
1 Chr 18.10 Joram brought David **presents** made of gold, silver, and
2 Chr 16. 3 This silver and gold is a **present** for you.
Is 16. 1 send a lamb as a **present** to the one who rules in
39. 1 had been ill, so he sent him a letter and a **present.**
Jer 40. 5 Then he gave me a **present** and some food to take with
Ezek 16.33 is paid, but you gave **presents** to all your lovers and bribed
46.16 of his sons as a **present,** it will belong to that son
Jas 1.17 Every good gift and every perfect **present** comes from heaven;
Rev 11.10 They will celebrate and send **presents** to each other,

PRESERVE

Gen 50.20 into good, in order to **preserve** the lives of many people who
2 Sam 7.26 And you will **preserve** my dynasty for all time.
1 Chr 17.24 And you will **preserve** my dynasty for all time.
2 Chr 9. 8 people Israel and wants to **preserve** them for ever, he has
Ps 12. 7 Keep us always safe, O Lord, and **preserve** us from such people.
25.21 May my goodness and honesty **preserve** me, because I trust in you.
34.20 the Lord **preserves** him completely;
41. 2 The Lord will protect them and **preserve** their lives;
80.17 **Preserve** and protect the people you have chosen, the
89. 4 I will **preserve** your dynasty for ever.'"
119.149 show your mercy, and **preserve** my life!
132.17 here I will **preserve** the rule of my chosen king.
Prov 18.21 What you say can **preserve** life or destroy it;
Is 8.16 disciples are to guard and **preserve** the messages that God
Jer 32.14 clay jar, so that they may be **preserved** for years to come.
Eph 4. 3 Do your best to **preserve** the unity which the Spirit gives
Heb 2.10 that God, who creates and **preserves** all things, should make Jesus
2 Pet 3. 7 now exist are being **preserved** by the same command of God,

PRESIDE

Ps 82. 1 God **presides** in the heavenly council;

PRESS

Deut 16.13 threshed all your corn and **pressed** all your grapes,
Judg 4.24 They **pressed** harder and harder against him
Neh 13.15 I saw people in Judah **pressing** juice from grapes on the Sabbath.
Job 24.11 They **press** olives for oil, and grapes for wine, but they
Joel 2.24 the pits beside the **presses** will overflow with wine and olive-oil.
Mic 6.15 You will **press** oil from olives, but never be able to use
Nah 2. 5 they stumble as they **press** forward.

PRESSURE

2 Cor 11.28 I am under the **pressure** of my concern for all the

PRETEND

Josh 8.15 Joshua and his men **pretended** that they were retreating,
1 Sam 21.13 whenever they were around, David **pretended** to be insane and
2 Sam 13. 5 Jonadab said to him, **"Pretend** that you are ill and go to
13. 6 So Amnon **pretended** that he was ill and went to bed.
14. 2 arrived, he said to her, **"Pretend** that you are in mourning;
1 Kgs 14. 5 When Jeroboam's wife arrived, she **pretended** to be someone else.
14. 6 Why are you **pretending** to be someone else?
Prov 13. 7 Some people **pretend** to be rich, but have nothing.
13. 7 Others **pretend** to be poor, but own a fortune.
21.29 the wicked have to **pretend** as best they can.
25. 6 king, don't try to impress him and **pretend** to be important.
Jer 3.10 Israel's unfaithful sister, only **pretended** to return to me;
29.26 see that every madman who **pretends** to be a prophet is placed
Ezek 28. 2 You may **pretend** to be a god, but, no, you are mortal,
Lk 20.20 They bribed some men to **pretend** they were sincere, and they
Acts 23.15 bring Paul down to you, **pretending** that you want to get more
23.20 Paul down to the Council, **pretending** that the Council wants to
27.30 boat into the water and **pretended** that they were going to
Gal 2. 4 **Pretending** to be fellow-believers, these men slipped into our group

PRETTY

Judg 15. 2 But her younger sister is **prettier**, anyway.
Prov 5.19 with the girl you married—[19]**pretty** and graceful as a deer.
Song 7. 6 How **pretty** you are, how beautiful;

PREVAIL

Amos 5.15 what is right, and see that justice **prevails** in the courts.

PREVENT

Ex 8.29 not deceive us again and **prevent** the people from going to
Num 4.19 To **prevent** this happening, Aaron and his sons shall go in
22.16 "Please don't let anything **prevent** you from coming to me!
30.12 her, because her husband **prevented** her from keeping her vow.
1 Sam 7.13 were defeated, and the Lord **prevented** them from invading
2 Chr 32. 3 the city in order to **prevent** the Assyrians from having any
Esth 8. 5 please issue a proclamation to **prevent** Haman's orders from
Job 24. 4 They **prevent** the poor from getting their rights and force
Ps 106.23 against God and **prevented** his anger from destroying them.
Prov 2.12 protect you [12]and **prevent** you from doing the wrong thing.
18. 5 the guilty and **prevent** the innocent from receiving justice.
Is 5.23 go free, and you **prevent** the innocent from getting justice.
10. 2 That is how you **prevent** the poor from having their rights
29.21 others, those who **prevent** the punishment of criminals,
32. 7 the poor with lies and to **prevent** them getting their rights.
48. 5 before they took place, to **prevent** you from claiming that
Jer 11.15 Do they think they can **prevent** disaster by making promises
Ezek 13.22 You **prevent** evil people from giving up evil and saving their lives.
Hos 5. 4 people have done **prevents** them from returning to their God.
Amos 5.12 good men, take bribes, and **prevent** the poor from getting
Mal 1.10 temple doors so as to **prevent** you from lighting useless
Rom 1.18 people whose evil ways **prevent** the truth from being known.
15.22 And so I have been **prevented** many times from coming to you.

PREY

Nah 2.12 The lion killed his **prey** and tore it to pieces for his
Hab 1. 8 They come swooping down like eagles attacking their **prey.**

PRICE

[BRIDE-PRICE]

Gen 23. 9 to me for its full **price**, here in your presence, so that
Ex 22.16 engaged, he must pay the **bride-price** for her and marry her.
22.17 a sum of money equal to the **bride-price** for a virgin.
30.12 is to pay me a **price** for his life, so that no
Lev 25.15 The **price** is to be fixed according to the number of
25.16 there are many years, the **price** shall be higher, but if
25.16 only a few years, the **price** shall be lower, because what is
25.50 Restoration and must set the **price** for his release on the
25.51 a part of the purchase **price** according to the number of
27. 8 poor to pay the standard **price,** he shall bring the person to
27. 8 priest will set a lower **price,** according to the ability of
27.12 The priest shall fix a **price** for it,
27.12 to its good or bad qualities, and the **price** will be final.
27.13 he must pay the **price** plus an additional twenty per cent.
27.14 the priest shall fix the **price** according to its good or bad
27.14 and the **price** will be final.
27.15 he must pay the **price** plus an additional twenty per cent.
27.16 land to the Lord, the **price** shall be fixed according to the
27.17 after a Year of Restoration, the full **price** applies.
27.18 until the next Year of Restoration, and fix a reduced **price.**
27.19 he must pay the **price** plus an additional twenty per cent.
27.23 Restoration, and the man must pay the **price** that very day;
27.25 All **prices** shall be fixed according to the official standard.
27.27 at the standard **price** plus an additional twenty per cent.
27.27 back, it may be sold to someone else at the standard **price.**
27.31 pay the standard **price** plus an additional twenty per cent.
Num 18.16 one month for the fixed **price** of five pieces of silver,
Deut 22.29 the girl's father the **bride price** of fifty pieces of silver,
1 Kgs 21. 2 it, or, if you prefer, I will pay you a fair **price."**
1 Chr 21.22 I'll give you the full **price."**
21.24 But the king answered, "No, I will pay you the full **price.**
Ps 44.12 people for a small **price** as though they had little value.
49. 7 he cannot pay God the **price** for his life, [8]because the
Prov 6.26 hire a prostitute for the **price** of a loaf of bread, but
Prov 11.26 grain, waiting for a higher **price,** but they praise the one
20.14 customer always complains that the **price** is too high, but
Jer 32. 9 the **price** came to seventeen pieces of silver.
Amos 2. 6 men who cannot repay even the **price** of a pair of sandals.
8. 6 We can sell worthless wheat at a high **price.**
8. 6 his debts, not even the **price** of a pair of sandals, and
Acts 19.19 They added up the **price** of the books, and the total came
1 Cor 6.20 he bought you for a **price.**
7.23 God bought you for a **price;**
2 Cor 9.15 Let us thank God for his **priceless** gift!

PRIDE see PROUD

PRIEST

[FELLOW-PRIESTS]

see also **CHIEF PRIEST, HIGH PRIEST**

Gen 14.18 of Salem and also a **priest** of the Most High God, brought
41.45 daughter of Potiphera, a **priest** in the city of Heliopolis.
46.20 Asenath, the daughter of Potiphera, a **priest** in Heliopolis.
47.22 he did not buy was the land that belonged to the **priests.**
47.26 Only the lands of the **priests** did not become the king's property.
Ex 2.15 seven daughters of Jethro, the **priest** of Midian, came to
3. 1 of his father-in-law Jethro, the **priest** of Midian, he led
18. 1 Moses' father-in-law Jethro, the **priest** of Midian, heard
19. 6 dedicated to me alone, and you will serve me as **priests."**
19.22 Even the **priests** who come near me must purify themselves,
19.24 But the **priests** and the people must not cross the boundary
28. 1 the people of Israel, so that they may serve me as **priests.**
28. 2 Make **priestly** garments for your brother Aaron, to provide
28. 3 so that he may be dedicated as a **priest** in my service.
28. 4 They are to make these **priestly** garments for your brother
28. 4 Aaron and his sons, so that they can serve me as **priests.**
28.35 Aaron is to wear this robe when he serves as **priest.**
28.41 them with olive-oil, so that they may serve me as **priests.**
28.43 the altar to serve as **priests** in the Holy Place, so that
29. 1 Aaron and his sons to dedicate them as **priests** in my service.
29. 5 Then dress Aaron in the **priestly** garments—the shirt, the
29. 9 They and their descendants are to serve me as **priests** for ever.
29.14 This is an offering to take away the sins of the **priests.**
29.27 "When a **priest** is ordained, the breast and the thigh of
29.27 to me as a special gift and set aside for the **priests.**
29.28 breast and the thigh of the animal belong to the **priests.**
29.29 "Aaron's **priestly** garments are to be handed on to his
29.30 Aaron who succeeds him as **priest** and who goes into the Tent
29.33 Only **priests** may eat this food, because it is sacred.
29.44 will set Aaron and his sons apart to serve me as **priests.**
30.30 Aaron and his sons, and ordain them as **priests** in my service.
30.33 anyone who is not a **priest** will no longer be considered one
31.10 and its base, [10]the magnificent **priestly** garments for
31.10 use when they serve as **priests,** [11]the anointing oil, and
32.29 you have consecrated yourselves as **priests** in the service of
35.19 and the magnificent garments the **priests** are to wear
35.19 the sacred clothes for Aaron the **priest** and for his sons."
35.21 for use in worship and for making the **priestly** garments.
38.21 under the direction of Ithamar son of Aaron the **priest.**
39. 1 the magnificent garments which the **priests** were to wear when
39. 1 They made the **priestly** garments for Aaron, as the Lord had
39.41 and the magnificent garments the **priests** were to wear in
39.41 the sacred clothes for Aaron the **priest** and for his sons.
40.13 Dress Aaron in the **priestly** garments, anoint him, and in
40.13 this way consecrate him, so that he can serve me as **priest.**
40.15 anointed their father, so that they can serve me as **priests.**
40.15 This anointing will make them **priests** for all time to come."
Lev 1. 5 bull there, and the Aaronite **priests** shall present the blood
1. 7 cut it up, [7]and the **priests** shall arrange fire-wood on the
1. 9 hind legs, and the officiating **priest** will burn the whole
1.11 of the altar, and the **priests** shall throw its blood on all
1.12 cuts it up, the officiating **priest** shall put on the fire all
1.13 the hind legs, and the **priest** will present the sacrifice to
1.15 The **priest** shall present it at the altar, wring its neck,
2. 2 and incense on it [2]and bring it to the Aaronite **priests.**
2. 2 The officiating **priest** shall take a handful of the flour and
2. 3 The rest of the grain-offering belongs to the **priests;**
2. 8 and present it to the **priest,** who will take it to the
2. 9 The **priest** will take part of it as a token that it
2.10 The rest of the offering belongs to the **priests;**
2.16 The **priest** will burn that part of the meal and oil that
3. 2 The Aaronite **priests** shall throw the blood against all four
3. 5 The **priests** shall burn all this on the altar along with
3. 8 The **priests** shall throw its blood against all four sides of
3.11 The officiating **priest** shall burn all this on the altar
3.13 The **priests** shall throw its blood against all four sides of
3.16 The **priest** shall burn all this on the altar as a
4.10 The **priest** shall take this fat and burn it on the altar
4.25 The **priest** shall dip his finger in the blood of the animal,
4.26 In this way the **priest** shall offer the sacrifice for the sin
4.30 The **priest** shall dip his finger in the blood of the animal,
4.31 In this way the **priest** shall offer the sacrifice for the
4.34 The **priest** shall dip his finger in the blood of the animal,
4.35 In this way the **priest** shall offer the sacrifice for the
5. 6 The **priest** shall offer the sacrifice for the man's sin.
5. 8 shall bring them to the **priest,** who will first offer the
5.10 In this way the **priest** shall offer the sacrifice for the
5.12 shall bring it to the **priest,** who will take a handful of
5.13 In this way the **priest** shall offer the sacrifice for the
5.13 the flour belongs to the **priest,** just as in the case of
5.16 shall give it to the **priest,** and the priest shall offer the
5.18 He must bring to the **priest** as a repayment-offering a
5.18 The **priest** shall offer the sacrifice for the sin which the

Lev 6. 6 He shall bring to the **priest** as his repayment-offering to
6. 7 The **priest** shall offer the sacrifice for the man's sin,
6.10 Then the **priest,** wearing his linen robe and linen shorts,
6.12 Every morning the **priest** shall put firewood on it, arrange
6.14 An Aaronite **priest** shall present the grain-offering to the
6.16 The **priests** shall eat the rest of it.
6.16 given it to the **priests** as their part of the food-offerings.
6.20 regulations [20] for the ordination of an Aaronite **priest.**
6.23 No part of a grain-offering that a **priest** makes may be eaten;
6.26 The **priest** who sacrifices the animal shall eat it in a
6.29 Any male of the **priestly** families may eat this offering;
7. 5 The **priest** shall burn all the fat on the altar as a
7. 6 Any male of the **priestly** families may eat it, but it must
7. 7 the meat belongs to the **priest** who offers the sacrifice.
7. 8 belongs to the **priest** who offers the sacrifice.
7. 9 a griddle belongs to the **priest** who has offered it to God.
7.10 belong to all the Aaronite **priests** and must be shared
7.14 it belongs to the **priest** who takes the blood of the animal
7.31 The **priest** shall burn the fat on the altar,
7.31 but the breast shall belong to the **priests.**
7.33 a special contribution [33] to the **priest** who offers the
7.34 taken from the people of Israel and given to the **priests.**
7.34 of Israel must give to the **priests** for all time to come.
7.35 Aaron and his sons on the day they were ordained as **priests.**
8. 2 presence and bring the **priestly** garments, the anointing oil,
8.22 was for the ordination of **priests,** and Aaron and his sons
9.21 gift to the Lord for the **priests,** as Moses had commanded.
10.14 and the special contribution to the Lord for the **priests.**
12. 6 she shall bring to the **priest** at the entrance of the Tent
12. 7 The **priest** shall present her offering to the Lord and
12. 8 for a sin-offering, and the **priest** shall perform the ritual
13. 2 skin-disease, he shall be brought to the Aaronite **priest.**
13. 3 The **priest** shall examine the sore, and if the hairs in it
13. 3 and the **priest** shall pronounce the person unclean.
13. 4 have not turned white, the **priest** shall isolate the person
13. 5 The **priest** shall examine him again on the seventh day, and
13. 6 The **priest** shall examine him again on the seventh day, and
13. 7 the sore spreads after the **priest** has examined him and
13. 7 him clean, he must appear before the **priest** again.
13. 8 The **priest** will examine him again, and if it has spread,
13. 9 he shall be brought to the **priest,** [10] who will examine him.
13.11 The **priest** shall pronounce him unclean;
13.13 from head to foot, [13] the **priest** shall examine him again.
13.15 The **priest** shall examine him again, and if he sees an
13.16 shall go to the **priest,** [17] who will examine him again.
13.17 ritually clean, and the **priest** shall pronounce him clean.
13.19 spot appears where the boil was, he shall go to the **priest.**
13.20 The **priest** shall examine him, and if the spot seems to
13.21 But if the **priest** examines it and finds that the hairs
13.21 light in colour, the **priest** shall isolate him for seven days.
13.22 If the spot spreads, the **priest** shall pronounce him unclean;
13.23 boil, and the **priest** shall pronounce him ritually clean.
13.25 white or reddish-white, [25] the **priest** shall examine him.
13.25 in the burn, and the **priest** shall pronounce him unclean.
13.26 in colour, the **priest** shall isolate him for seven days.
13.27 The **priest** shall examine him again on the seventh day,
13.27 skin-disease, and the **priest** shall pronounce him unclean.
13.28 The **priest** shall pronounce him ritually clean, because it is
13.30 on the head or the chin, [30] the **priest** shall examine it.
13.31 If, when the **priest** examines him, the sore does not
13.32 The **priest** shall examine the sore again on the seventh day,
13.33 The **priest** shall then isolate him for another seven days.
13.34 On the seventh day the **priest** shall again examine the sore,
13.36 pronounced clean, [36] the **priest** shall examine him again.
13.37 But if in the **priest's** opinion the sore has not spread
13.37 healed, and the **priest** shall pronounce him ritually clean.
13.39 spots on the skin, [39] the **priest** shall examine that person.
13.43 The **priest** shall examine him, and if there is a reddish-white sore,
13.44 sore, [44] the **priest** shall pronounce him unclean,
13.49 it is a spreading mildew and must be shown to the **priest.**
13.50 The **priest** shall examine it and put the object away for
13.52 The **priest** shall burn it, because it is a spreading
13.53 when he examines it, the **priest** finds that the mildew has
13.56 But if, when the **priest** examines it again, the mildew has faded,
14. 2 shall be brought to the **priest,**
14. 3 and the **priest** shall take him outside the camp
14. 4 the disease is healed, [4] the **priest** shall order two ritually
14. 5 Then the **priest** shall order one of the birds to be killed
14.11 The **priest** shall take the man and these offerings to the
14.12 Then the **priest** shall take one of the male lambs and
14.12 present them as a special gift to the Lord for the **priest.**
14.13 the sin-offering, belongs to the **priest** and is very holy.
14.14 The **priest** shall take some of the blood of the lamb and
14.15 The **priest** shall take some of the olive-oil and pour it
14.19 Then the **priest** shall offer the sin-offering and perform
14.20 In this way the **priest** shall perform the ritual of purification,
14.21 a special gift to the Lord for the **priest.**
14.23 shall bring them to the **priest** at the entrance of the Tent.
14.24 The **priest** shall take the lamb and the olive-oil and
14.24 present them as a special gift to the Lord for the **priest.**
14.26 The **priest** shall pour some of the oil into the palm of
14.31 In this way the **priest** shall perform the ritual of purification.
14.34 his house, then he must go and tell the **priest** about it.
14.36 The **priest** shall order everything to be moved out of the
14.44 scraped and plastered, [44] the **priest** shall go and look.
14.48 If, when the **priest** comes to look, the mildew has not
15.14 the Tent of the Lord's presence and give them to the **priest.**
15.15 The **priest** shall offer one of them as a sin-offering and
15.29 or two pigeons to the **priest** at the entrance of the Tent
15.30 The **priest** shall offer one of them as a sin-offering and
16. 4 Place, he must have a bath and put on the **priestly** garments:

Lev 16.23 the Tent, take off the **priestly** garments that he had put on
16.32 He shall put on the **priestly** garments [33] and perform the
16.33 Lord's presence, the altar, the **priests,** and all the people
17. 5 now bring them to the **priest** at the entrance of the Tent
17. 6 The **priest** shall throw the blood against the sides of the
19.22 repayment-offering, [22] and with it the **priest** shall perform
21. 1 to say to the Aaronite **priests,** "No priest is to make
21. 1 to the Aaronite priests, "No **priest** is to make himself
21. 5 "No **priest** shall shave any part of his head or trim his
21. 7 A **priest** shall not marry a woman who has been a prostitute
21. 8 The people must consider the **priest** holy, because he
21. 9 If a **priest's** daughter becomes a prostitute, she disgraces her father;
21.10 been consecrated to wear the **priestly** garments, so he must
21.21 No descendant of Aaron the **priest** who has any physical
22. 4 Any **priest** is unclean if he touches anything which is
22. 6 Any **priest** who becomes unclean remains unclean until evening,
22. 9 "All **priests** shall observe the regulations that I have given.
22.10 "Only a member of a **priestly** family may eat any of the
22.10 them—not even someone staying with a **priest** or hired by him.
22.11 But a **priest's** slaves, bought with his own money or born
22.11 or born in his home, may eat the food the **priest** receives.
22.12 A **priest's** daughter who marries someone who is not a priest
22.13 dependant may eat the food her father receives as a **priest.**
22.13 Only a member of a **priestly** family may eat any of it.
22.14 not a member of a **priestly** family eats any of the sacred
22.14 to, he must repay the **priest** its full value plus an
22.15 The **priests** shall not profane the sacred offerings
23. 9 you harvest your corn, take the first sheaf to the **priest.**
23.11 The **priest** shall present it the day after the Sabbath.
23.20 The **priest** shall present the bread with the two lambs
23.20 as a special gift to the Lord for the **priests.**
24. 9 holy part of the food offered to the Lord for the **priests.**
27. 8 bring the person to the **priest,**
27. 8 and the **priest** will set a lower price,
27.11 to the Lord, the man shall take the animal to the **priest.**
27.12 The **priest** shall fix a price for it, according to its
27.14 house to the Lord, the **priest** shall fix the price according
27.18 he dedicates it later, the **priest** shall estimate the cash
27.21 it shall belong to the **priests.**
27.23 that he has bought, [23] the **priest** shall estimate its value

Num 3. 3 were anointed and ordained as **priests,** [4] but Nadab and Abihu
3. 4 Eleazar and Ithamar served as **priests** during Aaron's lifetime.
3. 6 of Levi and appoint them as servants of Aaron the **priest.**
3. 7 perform duties for the **priests** and for the whole community.
3.10 Aaron and his sons to carry out the duties of the **priesthood;**
3.31 the altars, the utensils the **priests** use in the Holy Place,
3.32 The chief of the Levites was Eleazar son of Aaron the **priest.**
4.16 Eleazar son of Aaron the **priest** shall be responsible for
4.20 Tent and see the **priests** preparing the sacred objects for moving,
4.28 out under the direction of Ithamar son of Aaron the **priest.**
4.33 out under the direction of Ithamar son of Aaron the **priest.**
5. 8 be made, it shall be given to the Lord for the **priest.**
5. 9 to the Lord belongs to the **priest** to whom they present it.
5.10 Each **priest** shall keep the offerings presented to him.
5.15 In either case the man shall take his wife to the **priest.**
5.16 The **priest** shall bring the woman forward and make her
5.18 In his hands the **priest** shall hold the bowl containing the
5.19 Then the **priest** shall make the woman agree
5.19 to this oath spoken by the **priest:**
5.23 Then the **priest** shall write this curse down and wash the
5.25 cause her bitter pain, [25] the **priest** shall take the
5.29 of the altar, and the **priest** shall perform this ritual.
6.10 or two pigeons to the **priest** at the entrance of the Tent
6.11 The **priest** shall offer one as a sin-offering and the
6.16 The **priest** shall present all these to the Lord and offer
6.19 the ram is boiled, the **priest** shall take it and put it,
6.20 Next, the **priest** shall present them as a special gift to
6.20 a sacred offering for the **priest,** in addition to the breast
6.20 the leg of the ram which by law belong to the **priest.**
10. 8 The trumpets are to be blown by Aaron's sons, the **priests.**
15.25 The **priest** shall perform the ritual of purification
15.28 At the altar the **priest** shall perform the ritual of
16.10 honour—and now you are trying to get the **priesthood** too!
16.37 Eleazar son of Aaron the **priest** to remove the bronze
16.39 So Eleazar the **priest** took the firepans and had them
18. 1 will suffer the consequences of service in the **priesthood.**
18. 7 all the responsibilities of the **priesthood** that concern the
18. 7 because I have given you the gift of the **priesthood.**
18.28 this special contribution for the Lord to Aaron the **priest.**
19. 3 put to work, [3] and they will give it to Eleazar the **priest.**
19. 5 intestines, is to be burnt in the presence of the **priest.**
20.26 and there remove Aaron's **priestly** robes and put them on Eleazar.
20.28 and Moses removed Aaron's **priestly** robes and put them on Eleazar.
25. 7 and grandson of Aaron the **priest,** saw this, he got up and
25.13 descendants are permanently established as **priests,** because
27. 2 stood before Moses, Eleazar the **priest,** the leaders, and the
27.19 in front of Eleazar the **priest** and the whole community, and
27.21 will depend on Eleazar the **priest,** who will learn my will by
27.22 He made Joshua stand before Eleazar the **priest**
31. 6 Phinehas son of Eleazar the **priest,** who took charge of the
31.21 Eleazar the **priest** said to the men who had returned from battle,
31.29 Give them to Eleazar the **priest** as a special
33.38 At the command of the Lord, Aaron the **priest** climbed Mount Hor.
34.17 said to Moses, [17] "Eleazar the **priest** and Joshua son of

Deut 10. 6 and was buried, and his son Eleazar succeeded him as **priest.**
10. 8 Box, to serve him as **priests,** and to pronounce blessings in
10. 9 privilege of being the Lord's **priests,** as the Lord your God promised.)
17. 9 your case to the levitical **priests** and to the judge who is

Deut	17.12	either the judge or the **priest** on duty is to be put
	17.18	made from the original copy kept by the levitical **priests.**
	18. 1	"The **priestly** tribe of Levi is not to receive any share
	18. 2	privilege of being the Lord's **priests,** as the Lord has promised.
	18. 3	are sacrificed, the **priests** are to be given the shoulder,
	18. 5	tribes the tribe of Levi to serve him as **priests** for ever.
	18. 7	may serve there as a **priest** of the Lord his God, like
	18. 8	of food as the other **priests,** and he may keep whatever his
	19.17	and be judged by the **priests** and judges who are then in
	20. 2	Before you start fighting, a **priest** is to come forward and
	21. 5	The levitical **priests** are to go there also, because they
	24. 8	be sure to do exactly what the levitical **priests** tell you;
	26. 3	Go to the **priest** in charge at that time and say to
	26. 4	"The **priest** will take the basket from you and place it
	27. 9	Moses, together with the levitical **priests,** said to all the
	31. 9	gave it to the levitical **priests,** who were in charge of the
	31.25	he said to the levitical **priests,** who were in charge of the
Josh	3. 3	people, "When you see the **priests** carrying the Covenant Box
	3. 6	Then he told the **priests** to take the Covenant Box and go
	3. 8	Tell the **priests** carrying the Covenant Box that when they
	3.13	When the **priests** who carry the Covenant Box of the Lord
	3.14	to cross the Jordan, the **priests** went ahead of them,
	3.14	As soon as the **priests** stepped into the river, [16] the water
	3.17	across on dry ground, the **priests** carrying the Lord's
	4. 3	Jordan, from the very place where the **priests** were standing.
	4. 9	where the **priests** carrying the Covenant Box had stood.
	4.10	The **priests** stood in the middle of the Jordan until
	4.11	on the other side, the **priests** with the Lord's Covenant Box
	4.16	told Joshua [16] to command the **priests** carrying the Covenant
	4.18	did so, [18] and when the **priests** reached the river bank, the
	6. 4	Seven **priests,** each carrying a trumpet, are to go in front
	6. 4	the city seven times while the **priests** blow the trumpets.
	6. 6	Joshua called the **priests** and said to them, "Take the Covenant Box,
	6. 8	started out ahead of the **priests** who were blowing trumpets;
	6. 8	these came the **priests** who were carrying the Covenant Box,
	6.12	for the second time the **priests** and soldiers marched round
	6.12	next, the seven **priests** blowing the seven trumpets;
	6.12	then, the **priests** carrying the Lord's Covenant Box;
	6.16	round, when the **priests** were about to sound the trumpets,
	6.20	So the **priests** blew the trumpets.
	8.33	Lord's Covenant Box, facing the levitical **priests** who carried it.
	14. 1	Eleazar the **priest,** Joshua son of Nun, and the leaders of
	17. 4	They went to Eleazar the **priest** and to Joshua son of Nun
	18. 7	you, because their share is to serve as the Lord's **priests.**
	19.51	Eleazar the **priest,** Joshua son of Nun, and the leaders
	21. 1	families went to Eleazar the **priest,** Joshua son of Nun, and
	21. 4	were descended from Aaron the **priest** were assigned thirteen
	21.13	cities were assigned to the descendants of Aaron the **priest:**
	21.19	lands, were given to the **priests,** the descendants of Aaron.
	22.13	the son of Eleazar the **priest,** to the people of the tribes
	22.30	Phinehas the **priest** and the ten leading men of the
	22.31	the son of Eleazar the **priest,** said to them, "Now we know
Judg	17. 5	and an ephod, and appointed one of his sons as his **priest.**
	17.10	Be my adviser and **priest,** and I will give you ten pieces
	17.12	Micah appointed him as his **priest,** and he lived in Micah's home.
	17.13	have a Levite as my **priest,** I know that the Lord will
	18. 4	with Micah, who pays me to serve as his **priest."**
	18. 6	The **priest** answered, "You have nothing to worry about.
	18.17	and the ephod, while the **priest** stayed at the gate with the
	18.18	objects, the **priest** asked them, "What are you doing?"
	18.19	Come with us and be our **priest** and adviser.
	18.19	Wouldn't you rather be a **priest** for a whole Israelite tribe
	18.20	This made the **priest** very happy, so he took the sacred
	18.24	You take my **priest** and the gods that I made, and walk
	18.27	from Dan had taken the **priest** and the things that Micah had
	18.30	of Moses, served as a **priest** for the tribe of Dan, and
	18.30	his descendants served as their **priests** until the people
1 Sam	1. 3	and Phinehas, the two sons of Eli, were **priests** of the Lord.
	1. 9	Eli the **priest** was sitting in his place by the door.
	2.11	Samuel stayed in Shiloh and served the Lord under the **priest** Eli.
	2.13	concerning what the **priests** could demand from the people.
	2.13	was offering his sacrifice, the **priest's** servant would come
	2.14	and whatever the fork brought out belonged to the **priest.**
	2.15	taken off and burnt, the **priest's** servant would come and say
	2.15	the sacrifice, "Give me some meat for the **priest** to roast;
	2.16	then take what you want," the **priest's** servant would say,
	2.28	his family to be my **priests,** to serve at the altar, to
	2.30	family and your clan would serve me as **priests** for all time.
	2.33	of your descendants alive, and he will serve me as **priest.**
	2.35	I will choose a **priest** who will be faithful to me and
	2.36	have to go to that **priest** and ask him for money and
	2.36	be allowed to help the **priests,** in order to have something
	5. 5	is why even today the **priests** of Dagon and all his
	6. 2	the people called the **priests** and the magicians and asked,
	14. 3	(The **priest** carrying the ephod was Ahijah, the son of
	14. 3	Phinehas and grandson of Eli, the **priest** of the Lord in Shiloh.)
	14.18	"Bring the ephod here," Saul said to Ahijah the **priest.**
	14.19	Saul was speaking to the **priest,** the confusion in the
	14.36	But the **priest** said, "Let's consult God first."
	21. 1	David went to the **priest** Ahimelech in Nob.
	21. 4	The **priest** said, "I haven't any ordinary bread,
	21. 6	So the **priest** gave David the sacred bread,
	22.11	King Saul sent for the **priest** Ahimelech and all his relatives,
	22.11	who were also **priests** in Nob, and they came
	22.17	to the guards standing near him, "Kill the Lord's **priests!**
	22.17	guards refused to lift a hand to kill the Lord's **priests.**
	22.18	that day he killed eighty-five **priests** who were qualified to
	22.19	inhabitants of Nob, the city of **priests,** to be put to death:
	22.21	He told him how Saul had slaughtered the **priests** of the Lord.
	23. 9	he said to the **priest** Abiathar, "Bring the ephod here."
1 Sam	30. 7	David said to the **priest** Abiathar son of Ahimelech,
2 Sam	8.17	Zadok son of Ahitub and Ahimelech son of Abiathar were **priests;**
	8.18	in charge of David's bodyguard and David's sons were **priests.**
	15.24	Zadok the **priest** was there, and with him were the Levites,
	15.24	The **priest** Abiathar was there too.
	15.35	The **priests** Zadok and Abiathar will be there;
	17.15	Then Hushai told the **priests** Zadok and Abiathar what
	19.11	So he sent the **priests** Zadok and Abiathar to ask the leaders
	20.25	Zadok and Abiathar were the **priests,**
	20.26	Ira from the town of Jair was also one of David's **priests.**
1 Kgs	1. 7	Zeruiah) and with Abiathar the **priest,** and they agreed to
	1. 8	But Zadok the **priest,** Benaiah son of Jehoiada, Nathan the prophet,
	1.19	your sons, and Abiathar the **priest,** and Joab the commander
	1.25	your army, and Abiathar the **priest,** and just now they are
	1.26	not invite me, sir, or Zadok the **priest,** or Benaiah, or
	1.42	Jonathan, the son of the **priest** Abiathar, arrived.
	2.22	and Abiathar the **priest** and Joab are on his side!"
	2.26	Solomon said to Abiathar the **priest,** "Go to your country
	2.27	Abiathar from serving as a **priest** of the Lord, and so he
	2.27	Shiloh about the **priest** Eli and his descendants come true.
	2.35	Joab's place and put Zadok the **priest** in Abiathar's place.
	4. 2	The **priest: Azariah son of Zadok**
	4. 4	**Priests: Zadok and Abiathar**
	4. 5	**priest Zabud son of Nathan**
	8. 3	the leaders had gathered, the **priests** lifted the Covenant Box
	8. 4	The Levites and the **priests** also moved the Tent
	8. 6	Then the **priests** carried the Covenant Box into the Temple
	8.10	As the **priests** were leaving the Temple, it was suddenly
	12.31	on hilltops, and he chose **priests** from families who were not
	12.32	placed there in Bethel the **priests** serving at the places of
	13. 2	will slaughter on you the **priests** serving at the pagan
	13.33	ways, but continued to choose **priests** from ordinary families
	13.33	He ordained as **priest** anyone who wanted to be one.
2 Kgs	10.11	living in Jezreel, and all his officers, close friends, and **priests;**
	10.19	prophets of Baal, all his worshippers, and all his **priests.**
	10.22	Then Jehu ordered the **priest** in charge of the sacred
	11. 4	the seventh year Jehoiada the **priest** sent for the officers
	11.17	The **priest** Jehoiada made King Joash and the people
	11.18	idols, and killed Mattan, the **priest** of Baal, in front of
	12. 2	the Lord, because Jehoiada the **priest** instructed him.
	12. 4	Joash called the **priests** and ordered them to save up the
	12. 5	Each **priest** was to be responsible for the money brought by
	12. 6	year of Joash's reign the **priests** still had not made any
	12. 7	in Jehoiada and the other **priests** and asked them, "Why
	12. 8	The **priests** agreed to this and also agreed not to make the
	12. 9	The **priests** on duty at the entrance put in the box all
	12.16	it belonged to the **priests.**
	16.10	sent back to Uriah the **priest** an exact model of it, down
	17.27	"Send back one of the **priests** we brought as prisoners;
	17.28	So an Israelite **priest** who had been deported from
	17.32	of people to serve as **priests** at the pagan places of worship
	19. 2	court secretary, and the senior **priests** to the prophet
	22. 4	amount of money that the **priests** on duty at the entrance to
	22.12	order to Hilkiah the **priest,** to Ahikam son of Shaphan,
	23. 2	the Temple, accompanied by the **priests** and the prophets and
	23. 4	High Priest Hilkiah, his assistant **priests,** and the guards
	23. 5	He removed from office the **priests** that the kings of Judah
	23. 5	Jerusalem—all the **priests** who offered sacrifices to Baal,
	23. 8	He brought to Jerusalem the **priests** who were in the cities
	23. 9	Those **priests** were not allowed to serve in the Temple, but
	23. 9	eat the unleavened bread provided for their **fellow-priests.**
	23.20	He killed all the pagan **priests** on the altars where they served,
	25.18	Zephaniah the **priest** next in rank, and the three
1 Chr	9. 2	Israelite laymen, **priests,** Levites, and temple workmen.
	9.10	The following **priests** lived in Jerusalem:
	9.13	Meshullam, Meshillemith, and Immer [13] The **priests** who were
	9.30	the responsibility for mixing the spices belonged to the **priests.**
	13. 2	countrymen and to the **priests and Levites** in their towns,
	15.11	David called in the **priests** Zadok and Abiathar and the six Levites,
	15.14	Then the **priests and the Levites** purified themselves in
	15.23	The **priests** Shebaniah, Joshaphat, Nethanel, Amasai,
	16. 6	sound the cymbals, [6] and two **priests,** Benaiah and Jahaziel,
	16.39	Zadok the **priest** and his fellow-priests, however, were
	18.16	Zadok son of Ahitub and Ahimelech son of Abiathar were **priests;**
	23. 2	all the Israelite leaders and all the **priests and Levites.**
	23.28	the **priests** descended from Aaron with the temple worship,
	23.32	assisting their relatives, the **priests** descended from Aaron,
	24. 2	so their brothers Eleazar and Ithamar became **priests.**
	24. 6	The king, his officials, the **priest** Zadok,
	24. 6	heads of the **priestly** families and of the Levite families,
	24.31	just as their relatives, the **priests** descended from Aaron,
	24.31	families of the **priests** and of the Levites were witnesses.
	27. 2	Benaiah son of Jehoiada the **priest;**
	28.13	organizing the **priests and Levites** to perform their duties,
	28.21	The **priests and the Levites** have been assigned duties to
	29.22	Lord they anointed him as their ruler and Zadok as **priest.**
2 Chr	4. 6	in the large tank was for the **priests** to use for washing.
	4. 9	courtyard for the **priests,** and also an outer courtyard.
	5. 5	The **priests and the Levites** also moved the Tent of the
	5. 7	Then the **priests** carried the Covenant Box of the Lord into
	5.11	**priests** present, regardless of the group to which they belonged,
	5.11	with them were a hundred and twenty **priests** playing trumpets.
	5.11	As the **priests** were leaving the Temple, it was suddenly filled
	6.41	Bless your **priests** in all they do, and may all your people
	7. 2	full of the dazzling light, the **priests** could not enter it.
	7. 6	The **priests** stood in the places that were assigned to them,
	7. 6	The **priests** blew trumpets while all the people stood.
	8.14	the daily work of the **priests** and of the Levites
	8.14	who assisted the **priests** in singing hymns
	8.15	David had given the **priests and the Levites** concerning the

2 Chr	11.13	territory of Israel **priests and Levites** came south to Judah.
	11.14	successors would not let them serve as **priests** of the Lord.
	11.15	Jeroboam appointed **priests** of his own to serve at the
	13. 9	You drove out the Lord's **priests,** the descendants of Aaron,
	13. 9	In their place you appointed **priests** in the same way that
	13. 9	consecrated as a **priest** of those so-called gods of yours.
	13.10	**Priests** descended from Aaron perform their duties,
	13.12	is our leader and his **priests** are here with trumpets, ready
	13.14	to the Lord for help, and the **priests** blew the trumpets.
	15. 3	without the true God, without **priests** to teach them, and
	17. 8	They were accompanied by nine Levites and two **priests.**
	17. 8	and the **priests** were Elishama and Jehoram.
	19. 8	In Jerusalem Jehoshaphat appointed Levites, **priests,** and
	22.11	Jehosheba, who was married to a **priest** named Jehoiada.
	23. 1	waiting six years Jehoiada the **priest** decided that it was
	23. 4	When the **priests and Levites** come on duty on the Sabbath,
	23. 6	except the **priests and the Levites** who are on duty.
	23.11	Jehoiada the **priest** and his sons anointed Joash,
	23.16	The **priest** Jehoiada got King Joash and the people to
	23.17	there and killed Mattan, the **priest** of Baal, in front of the
	23.18	Jehoiada put the **priests and Levites** in charge of the
	24. 2	to the Lord as long as Jehoiada the **priest** was alive.
	24. 5	He ordered the **priests and the Levites** to go to the cities
	24.20	of God took control of Zechariah son of Jehoiada the **priest.**
	24.25	bed to avenge the murder of the son of Jehoiada the **priest.**
	26.17	Azariah the **priest,**
	26.17	eighty strong and courageous **priests,** followed the king
	26.18	Only the **priests** who are descended from Aaron have been
	26.19	He became angry with the **priests,** and immediately a dreaded
	26.20	Azariah and the other **priests** stared at the king's forehead
	29. 4	assembled a group of **priests and Levites** in the east
	29.16	The **priests** went inside the Temple to purify it, and
	29.21	The king told the **priests,** who were descendants of Aaron, to
	29.22	The **priests** killed the bulls first, then the sheep, and
	29.24	Then the **priests** killed the goats and poured their blood
	29.26	The **priests** also stood there with trumpets.
	29.34	Since there were not enough **priests** to kill all these animals,
	29.34	By then more **priests** had made themselves ritually clean.
	29.34	Levites were more faithful in keeping ritually clean than the **priests**
	29.35	that were burnt whole, the **priests** were responsible for
	30. 1	first month, because not enough **priests** were ritually clean
	30.15	The **priests and Levites** who were not ritually clean were so
	30.16	sacrifices to the **priests,** who sprinkled it on the altar.
	30.21	day the Levites and the **priests** praised the Lord with all
	30.24	A large number of **priests** went through the ritual of purification.
	30.25	the people of Judah, the **priests,** the Levites, the people
	30.27	The **priests and the Levites** asked the Lord's blessing
	31. 2	the organization of the **priests and Levites,** under which
	31. 4	to which the **priests and the Levites** were entitled,
	31. 9	king spoke to the **priests and the Levites** about these gifts,
	31.15	In the other cities where **priests** lived, he was
	31.17	The **priests** were assigned their duties by clans, and the
	31.19	Among the **priests** who lived in the cities
	31.19	all the males in the **priestly** families and to everyone who
	34. 5	the bones of the pagan **priests** on the altars where they had
	34.30	Temple, accompanied by the **priests and the Levites** and all
	35. 2	He assigned to the **priests** the duties they were to perform
	35. 8	for the people, the **priests, and the Levites** to use.
	35. 8	Zechariah, and Jehiel—gave the **priests** two thousand six
	35.10	the Passover, the **priests and the Levites** took their places,
	35.11	and the **priests** sprinkled the blood on the altar.
	35.14	for themselves and for the **priests** descended from Aaron,
	35.14	for the **priests** were kept busy until night, burning
	35.18	celebrated by King Josiah, the **priests,** the Levites, and the
	36.14	the leaders of Judah, the **priests,** and the people followed
Ezra	1. 5	Judah and Benjamin, the **priests and Levites,** and everyone
	2.36	This is the list of the **priestly** clans that returned from exile:
	2.61	The following **priestly** clans could find no record
	2.61	(The ancestor of the **priestly** clan of Barzillai had married
	2.61	who their ancestors were, they were not accepted as **priests.**
	2.63	God until there was a **priest** who could use the Urim and
	2.69	2,800 kilogrammes of silver, and 100 robes for **priests.**
	2.70	The **priests,** the Levites, and some of the people settled
	3. 2	Joshua son of Jehozadak, his **fellow-priests,** and Zerubbabel
	3. 8	of their fellow-countrymen, the **priests, and the Levites,** in
	3.10	foundation of the Temple, the **priests** in their robes took
	3.12	Many of the older **priests,** Levites, and heads of clans
	6. 9	you are to give the **priests** in Jerusalem whatever they tell
	6.16	the people of Israel—the **priests,** the Levites, and all the
	6.18	They also organized the **priests and the Levites** for the
	6.20	All the **priests and the Levites** had purified themselves
	6.20	who had returned, for the **priests,** and for themselves.
	7. 6	Israelites which included **priests,** Levites, temple musicians,
	7.11	following document to Ezra, the **priest** and scholar, who had
	7.12	the emperor to Ezra the **priest,** scholar in the Law of the
	7.13	all the Israelite people, **priests, and Levites** that so
	7.13	empire all the Israelite people, **priests,** and Levites that
	7.16	the Israelite people and their **priests** give for the Temple
	7.21	provide promptly for Ezra, the **priest** and scholar in the Law
	7.24	collect any taxes from the **priests,** Levites, musicians,
	8.15	I found that there were **priests** in the group, but no Levites.
	8.24	From among the leading **priests** I chose Sherebiah, Hashabiah,
	8.25	be used in the Temple, and I gave it to the **priests.**
	8.29	There in the **priests'** room weigh them and hand them over
	8.29	to the leaders of the **priests** and of the Levites,
	8.30	So the **priests and the Levites** took charge of the silver,
	8.33	utensils, and handed them over to Meremoth the **priest,** son
	9. 1	that the people, the **priests, and the Levites** had not kept
	9. 7	we, our kings, and our **priests** have fallen into the hands of
	10. 5	making the leaders of the **priests,** of the Levites, and of
Ezra	10.10	Ezra the **priest** stood up and spoke to them.
	10.16	the plan, so Ezra the **priest** appointed men from among the
	10.18	**Priests,** listed by clans:
Neh	2.16	any of my fellow-Jews—the **priests,** the leaders, the
	3. 1	Eliashib and his **fellow-priests** rebuilt the Sheep Gate, dedicated it,
	3.22	following **priests** rebuilt the next several sections of the wall:
	3.22	**Priests** from the area around Jerusalem built the next section;
	3.28	A group of **priests** built the next section, going north
	5.12	I called in the **priests** and made the leaders swear in front
	7.39	This is the list of the **priestly** clans that returned from exile:
	7.63	The following **priestly** clans could find no record
	7.63	(The ancestor of the **priestly** clan of Barzillai had married
	7.63	who their ancestors were, they were not accepted as **priests.**
	7.65	God until there was a **priest** who could use the Urim and
	7.70	530 robes for **priests**
	7.70	67 robes for **priests**
	7.73	The **priests,** the Levites, the temple guards, the
	8. 1	They asked Ezra, the **priest** and scholar of the Law which the
	8. 9	was the governor, Ezra, the **priest** and scholar of the Law,
	8.13	clans, together with the **priests and the Levites,** went to
	9.32	Our kings, our leaders, our **priests** and prophets, our
	9.34	our kings, leaders, and **priests** have not kept your Law.
	9.38	our Levites, and our **priests** put their seals to it.
	10.28	of Israel, the **priests,** the Levites, the temple guards,
	10.34	We, the people, **priests, and Levites,** will draw lots
	10.36	we will take to the **priests** in the Temple and there, as
	10.37	We will take to the **priests** in the Temple the dough made
	10.38	**Priests** who are descended from Aaron are to be with the
	10.39	are kept and where the **priests** who are on duty, the temple
	11. 3	of Israel, the **priests,** the Levites, the temple workmen,
	11.20	Israel and the remaining **priests and Levites** lived on their
	12. 1	a list of the **priests and Levites** who returned from exile
	12. 2	among all their **fellow-priests** in the days of Joshua.
	12.12	the following priests were the heads of the **priestly** clans:
	12.22	Levite families and of the **priestly** families during the
	12.26	the time of Ezra, the **priest** who was a scholar of the
	12.30	The **priests and the Levites** performed ritual purification
	12.33	The following **priests,** blowing trumpets, marched
	12.41	my group included the following **priests,** blowing trumpets:
	12.44	for the **priests and the Levites** which the Law required.
	12.44	were pleased with the **priests and the Levites,** [45] because
	12.47	and the Levites gave the required portion to the **priests.**
	13. 4	The **priest** Eliashib, who was in charge of the temple storerooms,
	13. 5	the offerings for the **priests,** and the tithes of corn,
	13.13	Shelemiah, a **priest;**
	13.29	defiled both the office of **priest**
	13.29	and the covenant you made with the **priests and the Levites.**
	13.30	prepared regulations for the **priests and the Levites** so that
Job	12.19	he humbles **priests** and men of power.
Ps	78.64	**Priests** died by violence, and their widows were not allowed to mourn.
	99. 6	Moses and Aaron were his **priests,** and Samuel was one who
	110. 4	a priest for ever in the **priestly order** of Melchizedek."
	115.10	Trust in the Lord, you **priests** of God.
	115.12	will bless the people of Israel and all the **priests** of God.
	118. 3	Let the **priests** of God say, "His love is eternal."
	132. 9	May your **priests** do always what is right;
	132.16	I will bless her **priests** in all they do, and her people
	135.19	praise him, you **priests** of God!
Ecc	5. 6	that you have to tell God's **priest** that you didn't mean it.
Is	8. 2	Get two reliable men, the **priest** Uriah and Zechariah
	24. 2	same fate—the **priests** and the people, slaves and masters,
	28. 7	Even the prophets and the **priests** are so drunk that they stagger.
	28. 7	that God sends, and the **priests** are too drunk to decide the
	37. 2	court secretary, and the senior **priests** to the prophet
	61. 6	will be known as the **priests** of the Lord, The servants of
	66.21	I will make some of them **priests and Levites.**
Jer	1. 1	of Hilkiah, one of the **priests** of the town of Anathoth in
	1.18	of Judah, the officials, the **priests,** and the people—will be
	2. 8	The **priests** did not ask, 'Where is the Lord?'
	2. 8	My own **priests** did not know me.
	2.26	Israel will be disgraced—your kings and officials, your **priests**
	4. 9	**priests** will be shocked and prophets will be astonished."
	5.31	**priests** rule as the prophets command,
	6.13	even prophets and **priests** cheat the people.
	8. 1	as the bones of the **priests,** of the prophets, and of the
	8.10	Even prophets and **priests** cheat the people.
	13.13	who are David's descendants, the **priests,** the prophets, and
	14.18	Prophets and **priests** carry on their work, but they don't
	18.18	There will always be **priests** to instruct us, wise men to
	19. 1	and some of the older **priests,** [2] and to go through Potsherd
	20. 1	When the **priest** Pashhur son of Immer, who was the chief
	21. 1	son of Malchiah and the **priest** Zephaniah son of Maaseiah to
	23.11	"The prophets and the **priests** are godless;
	23.33	or a prophet or a **priest** asks you, 'What is the Lord's
	23.34	or a prophet or a **priest** even uses the words 'the Lord's
	26. 7	The **priests,** the prophets, and all the people heard me
	26.11	Then the **priests** and the prophets said to the leaders
	26.16	the people said to the **priests** and the prophets, "This man
	27.16	Then I told the **priests** and the people that the Lord had
	28. 1	In the presence of the **priests** and of the people he told
	28. 5	in the presence of the **priests** and of all the people who
	29. 1	wrote a letter to the **priests,** the prophets, the leaders of
	29.24	priest Zephaniah son of Maaseiah and to all the other **priests.**
	29.26	"The Lord made you a **priest** in place of Jehoiada, and
	31.14	I will fill the **priests** with the richest food and
	32.32	with their kings and leaders, their **priests** and prophets.
	33.18	that there will always be **priests** from the tribe of Levi to
	33.21	made a covenant with the **priests** from the tribe of Levi that
	33.22	David and the number of **priests** from the tribe of Levi, so
	34.18	with the palace officials, the **priests,** and all the leaders,

Jer 37. 3 son of Shelemiah and the **priest** Zephaniah son of Maaseiah to
48. 7 Chemosh will go into exile, along with his princes and **priests.**
49. 3 Molech will be taken into exile, together with his **priests**
52.24 Zephaniah the **priest** next in rank, and the three
Lam 1. 4 The girls who sang there suffer, and the **priests** can only groan.
1.19 The **priests** and the leaders died in the city streets,
2. 6 King and **priest** alike have felt the force of his anger.
2.20 **Priests** and prophets are being killed in the Temple itself!
4.13 her prophets sinned and her **priests** were guilty of causing
4.16 He showed no regard for our **priests** and leaders.
Ezek 1. 1 thirtieth year, I, Ezekiel the **priest,** son of Buzi, was
7.26 The **priests** will have nothing to teach the people, and the
22.26 The **priests** break my law and have no respect for what is
40.45 faced south was for the **priests** who served in the Temple,
40.46 faced north was for the **priests** who served at the altar.
40.46 All the **priests** are descended from Zadok;
41. 8 the buildings used by the **priests** there was an open space
42.13 In them the **priests** who enter the Lord's presence eat the
42.13 holy, the **priests** will place the holiest offerings there:
42.14 When **priests** have been in the Temple and want to go to
43.19 Those **priests** belonging to the tribe of Levi who are
43.24 The **priests** will sprinkle salt on them and burn them as an
43.26 For seven days the **priests** are to consecrate the altar
43.27 the week is over, the **priests** are to begin offering on the
44.13 not to serve me as **priests** or to go near anything that
44.15 The Sovereign Lord said, "Those **priests** belonging to
44.20 **"Priests** must neither shave their heads nor let their hair grow long.
44.21 **Priests** must not drink any wine before going into the inner courtyard.
44.22 No **priest** may marry a divorced woman;
44.22 only an Israelite virgin or the widow of another **priest.**
44.23 "The **priests** are to teach my people the difference
44.24 a legal dispute arises, the **priests** are to decide the case
44.25 "A **priest** is not to become ritually unclean by touching a corpse,
44.28 "The **priests** have the priesthood as their share of what
44.29 the repayment-offerings will be the **priests'** food, and they
44.30 The **priests** are to have the best of all the first
44.30 they are to give the **priests** the first loaf as an offering,
44.31 The **priests** must not eat any bird or animal that dies a
45. 4 country, set aside for the **priests** who serve the Lord in his
45.19 The **priest** will take some of the blood of this
46. 2 of the gate while the **priests** burn his sacrifices whole and
46.19 These are holy rooms for the **priests.**
46.20 is the place where the **priests** are to boil the meat offered
48.10 The **priests** are to have a portion of this holy area.
48.11 area is to be for the **priests** who are descendants of Zadok.
48.13 are to have a special area, south of that of the **priests.**
48.21 which contains the Temple, the **priests'** land, the Levites'
Hos 4. 4 or reprimand them—my complaint is against you **priests.**
4. 6 You **priests** have refused to acknowledge me
4. 6 I reject you and will not acknowledge your sons as my **priests.**
4. 7 "The more of you **priests** there are, the more you sin
5. 1 "Listen to this, you **priests!**
6. 9 The **priests** are like a gang of robbers who wait in ambush
10. 5 They and the **priests** who serve the idol will weep over it.
Joel 1. 9 the **priests** mourn because they have no offerings for the Lord.
1.13 Put on sackcloth and weep, you **priests** who serve at the altar!
2.17 The **priests,** serving the Lord between the altar and the
Amos 7.10 Amaziah, the **priest** of Bethel, then sent a report to
Mic 3.11 govern for bribes, the **priests** interpret the Law for pay,
Zeph 1. 4 no one will even remember the pagan **priests** who serve him.
3. 4 the **priests** defile what is sacred, and twist the law of God
Hag 2.11 He said, "Ask the **priests** for a ruling on this question:
2.12 When the question was asked, the **priests** answered, "No."
2.13 The **priests** answered, "Yes."
Zech 3. 8 and listen, you **fellow-priests** of his, you that are the sign
6.13 A **priest** will stand by his throne, and they will work
7. 3 and to ask the **priests** and the prophets this question:
7. 5 of the land and the **priests** that when they fasted and
Mal 1. 6 Lord Almighty says to the **priests,** "A son honours his father,
1. 9 Now, you **priests,** try asking God to be good to us.
2. 1 The Lord Almighty says to the **priests,** "This command is for you:
2. 4 that my covenant with the **priests,** the descendants of Levi,
2. 7 It is the duty of **priests** to teach the true knowledge of
2. 8 "But now you **priests** have turned away from the right path.
3. 3 Lord's messenger will purify the **priests,** so that they will
Mt 8. 4 but go straight to the **priest** and let him examine you;
12. 4 to eat it—only the **priests** were allowed to eat that bread.
12. 5 that every Sabbath the **priests** in the Temple actually break the
Mk 1.44 But go straight to the **priest** and let him examine you;
2.26 to our Law only the **priests** may eat this bread—but David
Lk 1. 5 there was a **priest** named Zechariah,
1. 5 who belonged to the **priestly order** of Abijah.
1. 5 she also belonged to a **priestly** family.
1. 8 doing his work as a **priest** in the Temple, taking his turn
1. 9 the custom followed by the **priests,** he was chosen by lot
5.14 but go straight to the **priest** and let him examine you;
6. 4 our Law for anyone except the **priests** to eat that bread."
10.31 It so happened that a **priest** was going down that road;
17.14 and said to them, "Go and let the **priests** examine you."
Jn 1.19 authorities in Jerusalem sent some **priests** and Levites to John,
Acts 4. 1 to the people when some **priests,** the officer in charge of
6. 7 and a great number of **priests** accepted the faith.
14.13 The **priest** of the god Zeus, whose temple stood just
Rom 15.16 I serve like a **priest** in preaching the Good News from God,
Heb 5. 6 "You will be a **priest** for ever,
5. 6 in the **priestly order** of Melchizedek."
5.10 to be high priest, in the **priestly order** of Melchizedek.
6.20 a high priest for ever, in the **priestly order** of Melchizedek.
7. 1 was king of Salem and a **priest** of the Most High God.
Heb 7. 3 he remains a **priest** for ever.
7. 5 descendants of Levi who are **priests** are commanded by the Law
7. 8 In the case of the **priests** the tenth is collected by men
7.11 the basis of the levitical **priesthood** that the Law was given
7.11 the work of the levitical **priests** had been perfect, there would
7.11 for a different kind of **priest** to appear, one who is in
7.11 one who is in the **priestly order** of Melchizedek, not of
7.12 For when the **priesthood** is changed, there also has to be
7.13 and no member of his tribe ever served as a **priest.**
7.14 Moses did not mention this tribe when he spoke of **priests.**
7.15 a different **priest** has appeared, who is like Melchizedek.
7.16 He was made a **priest,** not by human rules and regulations,
7.17 "You will be a **priest** for ever,
7.17 a priest for ever, in the **priestly order** of Melchizedek."
7.20 There was no such vow when the others were made **priests.**
7.21 But Jesus became a **priest** by means of a vow when God
7.21 'You will be a **priest** for ever.'"
7.23 were many of those other **priests,** because they died and
7.24 and his work as **priest** does not pass on to someone
8. 4 he would not be a **priest** at all,
8. 4 since there are **priests** who offer the gifts required by
8. 5 The work they do as **priests** is really only a copy
8. 6 Jesus has been given **priestly** work which is superior to theirs,
9. 6 The **priests** go into the outer Tent every day to perform
10.11 Every Jewish **priest** performs his services every day
10.21 We have a great **priest** in charge of the house of God.
13.10 The **priests** who serve in the Jewish place of worship
1 Pet 2. 5 serve as holy **priests** to offer spiritual and acceptable sacrifices
2. 9 the chosen race, the King's **priests,** the holy nation,
Rev 1. 6 made us a kingdom of **priests** to serve his God and Father.
5.10 made them a kingdom of **priests** to serve our God, and they
20. 6 they shall be **priests** of God and of Christ, and they will
also Neh 10.2 Neh 11.10 Neh 12.2 Neh 12.12

PRIME

1 Sam 9. 2 a son named Saul, a handsome man in the **prime** of life.
Esth 3. 1 Xerxes promoted a man named Haman to the position of **prime** minister.
Is 38.10 I thought that in the **prime** of life I was going to
Jer 15. 8 young men in their **prime** and made their mothers suffer.
17.11 In the **prime** of life he will lose his riches,

PRINCE

Gen 17.20 be the father of twelve **princes,** and I will make a great
Num 21.18 The well dug by **princes** And by leaders of the people,
1 Sam 2. 8 He makes them companions of **princes** and puts them in places
1 Kgs 22.26 him to Amon, the governor of the city, and to **Prince** Joash.
2 Kgs 24.14 Jerusalem, all the royal **princes,** and all the leading men,
2 Chr 18.25 him to Amon, the governor of the city, and to **Prince** Joash.
22.11 him away from the other **princes** who were about to be
Job 3.15 I would be sleeping like **princes** who filled their houses
Ps 76.12 he humbles proud **princes** and terrifies great kings.
82. 7 your life will end like that of any **prince."**
113. 8 misery [8]and makes them companions of **princes,**
113. 8 the **princes** of his people.
148.11 Praise him, kings and all peoples, **princes** and all other rulers;
Is 9. 6 "Mighty God," "Eternal Father," **"Prince** of Peace."
23. 8 that imperial city, whose merchant **princes** were the most
49. 7 **princes** also will see it, and they will bow low to honour
Jer 17.25 Then their kings and **princes** will enter the gates of
30.21 from their own nation, their **prince** from their own people.
36.26 Then he ordered **Prince** Jerahmeel, together with Seraiah
38. 6 me down by ropes into **Prince** Malchiah's well, which was in
48. 7 Chemosh will go into exile, along with his **princes** and priests.
49. 3 Molech will be taken into exile, together with his priests and **princes.**
Lam 4. 7 Our **princes** were undefiled and pure as snow, vigorous and strong,
Ezek 7.27 The king will mourn, the **prince** will give up hope, and
12.10 This message is for the **prince** ruling in Jerusalem and for
12.12 The **prince** who is ruling them will shoulder his pack in
19. 1 me to sing this song of sorrow for two **princes** of Israel:
32.30 "All the **princes** of the north are there, and so are the
44. 3 The ruling **prince,** however, may go there to eat a holy
45. 7 Land is also to be set aside for the ruling **prince.**
45. 8 be the share the ruling **prince** will have in the land of
45.16 must take these offerings to the ruling **prince** of Israel.
45.22 of the festival the ruling **prince** must offer a bull as a
45.25 of the seventh month, the **prince** will offer on each of the
46. 2 The ruling **prince** will go from the outer courtyard into
46. 4 On the Sabbath the **prince** is to bring to the Lord, as
46. 7 the offering is to be whatever the **prince** wants to give.
46. 8 The **prince** must leave the entrance room of the gateway and
46.10 The **prince** is to come in when the people come, and leave
46.12 "When the ruling **prince** wants to make a voluntary
46.16 "If the ruling **prince** gives any of the land he owns to
46.17 But if the ruling **prince** gives any of his land to anyone
46.17 service, it will become the **prince's** property again when the
46.18 The ruling **prince** must not take any of the people's
48.21 the city, the remaining land belongs to the ruling **prince.**
Dan 3. 2 come together—the **princes,** governors, lieutenant-governors,
3.27 All the **princes,** governors, lieutenant-governors, and
8.11 It even defied the **Prince** of the heavenly army, stopped
10.13 The angel **prince** of the kingdom of Persia opposed me for

PRINCESS

Ex 2. 6 The **princess** opened it and saw a baby boy.
2. 9 The **princess** told the woman, "Take this baby and nurse

2 Sam 13.18 the usual clothing for an unmarried **princess** in those days.
1 Kgs 11. 3 Solomon married seven hundred **princesses**
Ps 45.13 The **princess** is in the palace—how beautiful she is!

PRINCIPAL

Acts 8. 5 Philip went to the **principal** city in Samaria and preached

AV PRINCIPALITY see RULER

PRINCIPLE

Lev 24.18 The **principle** is a life for a life.
1 Cor 4.17 will remind you of the **principles** which I follow in the new

PRISON
[IMPRISONMENT]

Gen 14.16 together with the women and the other **prisoners.**
39.20 arrested and put in the **prison**
39.20 where the king's **prisoners** were kept, and there he stayed.
39.22 charge of all the other **prisoners** and made him responsible
39.22 responsible for everything that was done in the **prison.**
40. 3 officials [3]and put them in **prison** in the house of the
40. 4 spent a long time in **prison,** and the captain assigned Joseph
40. 5 One night there in **prison** the wine steward and the chief
40.14 to the king and help me to get out of this **prison.**
40.15 Egypt I didn't do anything to deserve being put in **prison."**
41.10 and you put us in **prison** in the house of the captain
41.14 for Joseph, and he was immediately brought from the **prison.**
42.17 Then he put them in **prison** for three days.
42.19 of you will stay in the **prison** where you have been kept;
Ex 12.29 to the throne, to the son of the **prisoner** in the dungeon;
Num 31.11 they had captured, including the **prisoners** and the animals,
31.26 has been captured, including the **prisoners** and the animals.
31.28 out of every five hundred **prisoners** and the same proportion
31.30 one out of every fifty **prisoners** and the same proportion of
31.47 one out of every fifty **prisoners** and animals, and as the
Deut 21.10 in battle and you take **prisoners,** [11]you may see among them
28.41 them, because they will be taken away as **prisoners** of war.
32.42 even the wounded and **prisoners** will die.'
Judg 15.10 "We came to take Samson **prisoner** and to treat him as he
16.21 and put him to work grinding at the mill in the **prison.**
16.24 brought Samson out of the **prison,** they made him entertain
2 Sam 8. 2 He made the **prisoners** lie down on the ground and put two
1 Kgs 8.46 them and take them as **prisoners** to some other land, even if
22.27 them to throw him in **prison** and to put him on bread
2 Kgs 14.13 Jehoash took Amaziah **prisoner,** advanced on Jerusalem,
15.29 and Naphtali, and took the people to Assyria as **prisoners.**
16. 9 killed King Rezin, and took the people to Kir as **prisoners.**
17. 4 Shalmaneser learnt of this, he had Hoshea arrested and put in **prison.**
17. 6 the Israelites to Assyria as **prisoners,** and settled some of
17.27 "Send back one of the priests we brought as **prisoners;**
18.11 the Israelites to Assyria as **prisoners** and settled some of
23.33 Neco of Egypt took him **prisoner** in Riblah, in the land of
24.12 Nebuchadnezzar's reign he took Jehoiachin **prisoner** [13]and
24.14 Nebuchadnezzar carried away as **prisoners** the people of Jerusalem,
24.15 Jehoiachin to Babylon as a **prisoner,**
25.18 officer, took away as **prisoners** Seraiah the High Priest,
25.27 to King Jehoiachin of Judah by releasing him from **prison.**
25.27 year after Jehoiachin had been taken away as **prisoner.**
25.29 permitted to change from his **prison** clothes and to dine at
1 Chr 3.17 King Jehoiachin, who was taken **prisoner** by the Babylonians.
5.21 and 2,000 donkeys, and took 100,000 **prisoners** of war.
2 Chr 6.36 them and take them as **prisoners** to some other land, even if
18.26 them to throw him in **prison** and to put him on bread
21.17 palace, and carried off as **prisoners** all the king's wives
25.12 They took the **prisoners** to the top of the cliff at the
28. 5 a large number of Judaeans back to Damascus as **prisoners.**
28. 8 women and children as **prisoners** and took them back to Samaria,
28. 9 Israelite army with its Judaean **prisoners** as it was about to
28.11 These **prisoners** are your brothers and sisters.
28.13 They said, "Don't bring those **prisoners** here!
28.14 then the army handed the **prisoners** and the loot over to the
28.15 provide the **prisoners** with clothing from the captured loot.
28.15 on donkeys, and all the **prisoners** were taken back to Judaean
28.16 captured many **prisoners,** so King Ahaz asked Tiglath Pileser,
29. 9 our wives and children have been taken away as **prisoners.**
30. 9 taken your relatives away as **prisoners** will take pity on
36. 3 Neco of Egypt took him **prisoner** and made Judah pay 3,400
36.10 Jehoiachin to Babylonia as a **prisoner,** and carried off the
Ezra 2. 1 ever since King Nebuchadnezzar had taken them there as **prisoners.**
7.26 by exile or by confiscation of his property or by **imprisonment."**
9. 7 been slaughtered, robbed, and carried away as **prisoners.**
Neh 4. 4 have, and let them be taken as **prisoners** to a foreign land.
7. 6 ever since King Nebuchadnezzar had taken them there as **prisoners.**
Job 3.18 Even **prisoners** enjoy peace, free from shouts and harsh commands.
12.14 who can rebuild, and who can free the man God **imprisons?**
12.18 He dethrones kings and makes them **prisoners;**
Ps 68. 6 to live in and leads **prisoners** out into happy freedom, but
69.33 to those in need and does not forget his people in **prison.**
79.11 to the groans of the **prisoners,** and by your great power free
102.20 He heard the groans of **prisoners** and set free those who
107.10 living in gloom and darkness, **prisoners** suffering in chains,
143. 3 put me in a dark **prison,** and I am like those who
Ps 146. 7 The Lord sets **prisoners** free [8]and gives sight to the blind.
Ecc 4.13 his country, or go from **prison** to the throne, but if in
Is 5.13 Lord is doing, [13]and so you will be carried away as **prisoners.**
10. 4 You will be killed in battle or dragged off as **prisoners.**
14.17 the man who never freed his **prisoners** or let them go home?'
20. 4 naked the **prisoners** he captures from those two countries.
24.22 God will crowd kings together like **prisoners** in a pit.
24.22 He will shut them in **prison** until the time of their
28.13 You will be wounded, trapped, and taken **prisoner.**
42. 7 of the blind and set free those who sit in dark **prisons.**
42.22 they are locked up in dungeons and hidden away in **prisons.**
49. 9 I will say to the **prisoners,** 'Go free!'
49.24 Can you rescue the **prisoners** of a tyrant?
49.25 The soldier's **prisoners** will be taken away, and the tyrant's
51.14 Those who are **prisoners** will soon be set free;
61. 1 To announce release to captives And freedom to those in **prison.**
Jer 15. 2 to be taken away as **prisoners**— that's where they will go!
20. 4 will take some away as **prisoners** to his country and put
22.22 wind, your allies taken as **prisoners** of war, your city
24. 1 Jehoiachin of Judah, as a **prisoner** from Jerusalem to Babylonia,
28. 6 and all the people who were taken away as **prisoners.**
29. 1 Nebuchadnezzar had taken away as **prisoners** from Jerusalem
29. 4 allowed Nebuchadnezzar to take away as **prisoners** from Jerusalem
29. 7 good of the cities where I have made you go as **prisoners.**
29.16 relatives who were not taken away as **prisoners** with you.
29.22 who were taken away as **prisoners** from Jerusalem to Babylonia
29.28 Babylonia that they would be **prisoners** there a long time and
29.31 to send to all the **prisoners** in Babylon this message
30.10 that distant land, from the land where you are **prisoners.**
30.16 and all your enemies will be taken away as **prisoners.**
32. 3 King Zedekiah had **imprisoned** me there and had accused me of
33. 1 While I was still in **prison** in the courtyard, the Lord's
37. 4 not yet been put in **prison** and was still moving about freely
37.15 court secretary, whose house had been made into a **prison.**
37.18 your officials or this people, to make you put me in **prison?**
37.20 Please do not send me back to the **prison** in Jonathan's house.
38.23 You will be taken **prisoner** by the king of Babylonia, and
38.26 begging me not to send you back to **prison** to die there."
39. 9 commanding officer, took away as **prisoners** to Babylonia the
39.15 While I was still **imprisoned** in the palace courtyard,
40. 1 who were being taken away as **prisoners** to Babylonia.
41.10 Then he made **prisoners** of the king's daughters and all
41.10 Ishmael took them **prisoner** and started off in the direction
41.13 When Ishmael's **prisoners** saw Johanan and the leaders of
41.16 Ishmael had taken away as **prisoners** from Mizpah
43.11 be taken away as **prisoners** will be taken away as prisoners,
46.19 Get ready to be taken **prisoner,** you people of Egypt!
46.27 that distant land, from the land where you are **prisoners.**
48.46 their sons and daughters have been taken away as **prisoners.**
52.11 Zedekiah remained in **prison** in Babylon until the day he died.
52.24 officer, took away as **prisoners** Seraiah the High Priest,
52.28 of the people that Nebuchadnezzar took away as **prisoners:**
52.31 to King Jehoiachin of Judah by releasing him from **prison.**
52.31 year after Jehoiachin had been taken away as a **prisoner.**
52.33 permitted to change from his **prison** clothes and to dine at
Lam 3. 5 He has shut me in a **prison** of misery and anguish.
3. 7 I am a **prisoner** with no hope of escape.
3.34 The Lord knows when our spirits are crushed in **prison;**
Ezek 30.17 die in the war, and the other people will be taken **prisoner.**
30.18 and the people of all her cities will be taken **prisoner.**
Dan 1. 2 He took some **prisoners** back with him to the temple of his
11.33 burnt to death, and some will be robbed and made **prisoners.**
Amos 1. 5 Syria will be taken away as **prisoners** to the land of Kir."
Mt 4.12 that John had been put in **prison,** he went away to Galilee.
11. 2 John the Baptist heard in **prison** about the things that Christ
14. 3 John's arrest, and he had him chained and put in **prison.**
14.10 So he had John beheaded in **prison.**
25.36 and you took care of me, in **prison** and you visited me.'
25.39 did we ever see you sick or in **prison,** and visit you?'
25.43 I was sick and in **prison** but you would not take care
25.44 or naked or sick or in **prison,** and would not help you?'
27.15 habit of setting free any one **prisoner** the crowd asked for.
27.16 there was a well-known **prisoner** named Jesus Barabbas.
Mk 1.14 John had been put in **prison,** Jesus went to Galilee and
6.17 John's arrest, and he had him chained and put in **prison.**
6.27 The guard left, went to the **prison,** and cut John's head off;
15. 6 habit of setting free any one **prisoner** the people asked for.
15. 7 named Barabbas was in **prison** with the rebels who had committed
Lk 3.20 Then Herod did an even worse thing by putting John in **prison.**
8.29 though he was kept a **prisoner,** his hands and feet fastened
21.12 handed over to be tried in synagogues and be put in **prison;**
21.24 and others will be taken as **prisoners** to all countries;
22.33 am ready to go to **prison** with you and to die with
23.19 (Barabbas had been put in **prison** for a riot that had
23.25 who had been put in **prison** for riot and murder, and he
Jn 3.24 (This was before John had been put in **prison.)**
18.39 I always set free a **prisoner** for you during the Passover.
Acts 2.24 because it was impossible that death should hold him **prisoner.**
5.19 of the Lord opened the **prison** gates, led the apostles out,
5.21 sent orders to the **prison** to have the apostles brought before
5.22 not find the apostles in **prison,** so they returned to the
5.25 The men you put in **prison** are in the Temple teaching the
8.23 you are full of bitter envy and are a **prisoner** of sin."
12. 6 chains, and there were guards on duty at the **prison** gate.
12. 9 followed him out of the **prison,** not knowing, however, if
12.17 to them how the Lord had brought him out of **prison.**
16.25 singing hymns to God, and the other **prisoners** were listening
16.26 a violent earthquake, which shook the **prison** to its foundations.
16.26 the doors opened, and the chains fell off all the **prisoners.**
16.27 and when he saw the **prison** doors open,

Acts 16.27 he thought that the **prisoners** had escaped;
16.37 Then they threw us in **prison.**
16.39 led them out of the **prison** and asked them to leave the
16.40 Paul and Silas left the **prison** and went to Lydia's house.
20.23 Holy Spirit has warned me that **prison** and troubles wait for me.
22. 4 I arrested men and women and threw them into **prison.**
23.18 and said, "The **prisoner** Paul called me and asked me
23.29 anything for which he deserved to die or be put in **prison;**
24.27 to gain favour with the Jews so he left Paul in **prison.**
25. 4 "Paul is being kept a **prisoner** in Caesarea, and I myself
25.14 "There is a man here who was left a **prisoner** by Felix;
25.27 to send a **prisoner** without clearly indicating the charges against
26.10 the chief priests and put many of God's people in **prison;**
26.31 done anything for which he should die or be put in **prison."**
27. 1 handed Paul and some other **prisoners** over to Julius, an officer
27.42 plan to kill all the **prisoners,** in order to keep them from
28.17 I was made a **prisoner** in Jerusalem and handed over to
Rom 7. 6 because we died to that which once held us **prisoners.**
7.23 It makes me a **prisoner** to the law of sin which is
11.32 God has made all people **prisoners** of disobedience,
16. 7 to Andronicus and Junias, fellow-Jews who were in **prison** with me;
2 Cor 2.14 are always led by God as **prisoners** in Christ's victory procession.
6. 5 We have been beaten, **imprisoned,** and mobbed;
11.23 I have been in **prison** more times, I have been whipped
Gal 3.23 us all locked up as **prisoners** until this coming faith should
Eph 3. 1 this reason I, Paul, the **prisoner** of Christ Jesus for the
4. 1 I who am a **prisoner** because I serve the Lord:
6.20 this gospel I am an ambassador, though now I am in **prison.**
Phil 1. 7 now that I am in **prison** and also while I was free
1.13 know that I am in **prison** because I am a servant of
1.14 And my being in **prison** has given most of the brothers
1.17 they will make more trouble for me while I am in **prison.**
Col 4. 3 For that is why I am now in **prison.**
4.10 Aristarchus, who is in **prison** with me, sends you greetings,
2 Tim 1. 8 nor be ashamed of me, a **prisoner** for Christ's sake.
1.16 ashamed that I am in **prison,** [17] but as soon as he arrived
Phlm 1 From Paul, a **prisoner** for the sake of Christ Jesus,
9 Christ Jesus, and at present also a **prisoner** for his sake.
10 for while in **prison** I have become his spiritual father.
13 while I am in **prison** for the gospel's sake, so that
23 Epaphras, who is in **prison** with me for the sake of
Heb 10.34 shared the sufferings of **prisoners,** and when all your belongings
11.36 and others were put in chains and taken off to **prison.**
13. 3 Remember those who are in **prison,**
13. 3 as though you were in **prison** with them.
13.23 to know that our brother Timothy has been let out of **prison.**
1 Pet 3.19 he went and preached to the **imprisoned** spirits.
Rev 2.10 some of you thrown into **prison,** and your troubles will last
19.20 The beast was taken **prisoner,** together with the false prophet
20. 7 be let loose from his **prison,** [8] and he will go out to

PRIVATE

1 Sam 18.22 his officials to speak **privately** to David and tell him,
2 Sam 3.27 though he wanted to speak **privately** with him, and there he
2 Kgs 6.12 Israel what you say even in the **privacy** of your own room."
9. 2 Take him to a **private** room away from his companions, [3] pour
16.18 and closed up the king's **private** entrance to the Temple.
Ecc 10.20 criticize the rich, even in the **privacy** of your bedroom.
Song 4.12 is a secret garden, a walled garden, a **private** spring;
Jer 37.17 the palace he asked me **privately,** "Is there any message
40.15 Then Johanan said **privately** to him, "Let me go and kill Ishmael,
Mt 1.19 so he made plans to break the engagement **privately.**
6. 4 Then it will be a **private** matter.
6. 4 Father, who sees what you do in **private,** will reward you.
6. 6 Father, who sees what you do in **private,** will reward you.
6.18 Father, who sees what you do in **private,** will reward you.
10.27 you have heard in **private** you must announce from the housetops.
17.19 disciples came to Jesus in **private** and asked him, "Why couldn't
18.15 But do it **privately,** just between yourselves.
20.17 disciples aside and spoke to them **privately,** as they walked along.
24. 3 the Mount of Olives, the disciples came to him in **private.**
Mk 9.28 his disciples asked him **privately,** "Why couldn't we drive the
13. 3 Temple, when Peter, James, John, and Andrew came to him in **private.**
Lk 10.23 disciples and said to them **privately,** "How fortunate you are
12. 3 whatever you have whispered in **private** in a closed room will
Jn 11.28 she went back and called her sister Mary **privately.**
Gal 2. 2 In a **private** meeting with the leaders I explained the gospel

PRIVILEGE
[UNDERPRIVILEGED]

Deut 10. 9 they received was the **privilege** of being the Lord's priests,
18. 2 their share is the **privilege** of being the Lord's priests, as
1 Kgs 10. 8 your presence and are **privileged** to hear your wise sayings!
2 Chr 9. 7 your presence and are **privileged** to hear your wise sayings!
Ezek 16.49 they did not take care of the poor and the **underprivileged.**
Rom 1. 5 God gave me the **privilege** of being an apostle for the
15.15 been bold because of the **privilege** God has given me [16] of
1 Cor 9.18 It is the **privilege** of preaching the Good News without charging
2 Cor 8. 4 and pleaded for the **privilege** of having a part in helping
Eph 3. 8 yet God gave me this **privilege** of taking to the Gentiles the
Phil 1. 7 shared with me in this **privilege** that God has given me,
1.29 you have been given the **privilege** of serving Christ, not

PRIZE

Is 44. 9 worthless, and the gods they **prize** so highly are useless.
Dan 11.43 treasures of gold and silver and its other **prized** possessions.
Mt 22. 4 my bullocks and **prize** calves have been butchered, and everything
Lk 15.23 Then go and get the **prize** calf and kill it, and let
15.27 your father has killed the **prize** calf, because he got him
15.30 when he comes back home, you kill the **prize** calf for him!'
1 Cor 9.24 part in a race, but only one of them wins the **prize.**
9.24 Run, then, in such a way as to win the **prize.**
Phil 3.12 keep striving to win the **prize** for which Christ Jesus has
3.14 in order to win the **prize,** which is God's call through
2 Tim 2. 5 in a race cannot win the **prize** unless he obeys the rules.
4. 8 for me the victory **prize** of being put right with God,
Rev 2.10 and I will give you life as your **prize** of victory.
3.11 so that no one will rob you of your victory **prize.**

PROBLEM

Neh 5. 7 assembly to deal with the **problem** [8] and said, "As far as we
Ps 73.16 I tried to think this **problem** through, but it was too
Prov 1. 6 meanings of proverbs and the **problems** that wise men raise.
Dan 1.20 the king asked, or what **problem** he raised, these four knew

PROCESSION

2 Chr 23.20 people joined Jehoiada in a **procession** that brought the king
Neh 12.36 Ezra the scholar led this group in the **procession.**
Job 21.33 tomb, [33] thousands join the funeral **procession,** and even
Ps 68.24 is seen by all, the **procession** of God, my king, into his
Is 66.17 pagan worship, who go in **procession** to sacred gardens, and
Lk 7.12 the gate of the town, a funeral **procession** was coming out.
2 Cor 2.14 are always led by God as prisoners in Christ's victory **procession.**
Col 2.15 by leading them as captives in his victory **procession.**

PROCLAIM

Lev 23. 4 **Proclaim** the following festivals at the appointed times.
25.10 the fiftieth year apart and **proclaim** freedom to all the
Num 23.21 They **proclaim** that he is their king.
27.19 and there before them all **proclaim** him as your successor.
27.23 hands on Joshua's head and **proclaimed** him as his successor.
Deut 11.29 to occupy, you are to **proclaim** the blessing from Mount
1 Sam 11.14 all go to Gilgal and once more **proclaim** Saul as our king."
11.15 and there at the holy place they **proclaimed** Saul king.
2 Sam 22.47 **Proclaim** the greatness of the strong God who saves me!
1 Kgs 16.16 they all **proclaimed** their commander Omri king of Israel.
21. 9 **"Proclaim** a day of fasting, call the people together, and
21.12 They **proclaimed** a day of fasting, called the people together,
2 Kgs 9. 3 head, and say, 'The Lord **proclaims** that he anoints you king
9. 6 and said to him, "The Lord, the God of Israel, **proclaims:**
9.12 "He told me that the Lord **proclaims:**
10.20 Then Jehu ordered, **"Proclaim** a day of worship in honour of Baal!"
10.20 The **proclamation** was made, [21] and Jehu sent word throughout
11.12 Then Joash was anointed and **proclaimed** king.
1 Chr 16. 8 Give thanks to the Lord, **proclaim** his greatness;
16.23 **Proclaim** every day the good news that he has saved us.
16.24 **Proclaim** his glory to the nations, his mighty deeds to all peoples.
25. 1 They were to **proclaim** God's messages, accompanied by the
25. 2 who **proclaimed** God's messages whenever the king commanded.
25. 3 direction of their father they **proclaimed** God's message,
29.22 For a second time they **proclaimed** Solomon king.
Neh 6. 7 arranged for some prophets to **proclaim** in Jerusalem that you
Esth 1.19 Your Majesty, issue a royal **proclamation** that Vashti may
1.20 When your **proclamation** is made known all over this huge empire,
2. 1 what Vashti had done and about his **proclamation** against her.
2. 8 king had issued his new **proclamation** and many girls were
2.18 He **proclaimed** a holiday for the whole empire and distributed
3.10 was used to stamp **proclamations** and make them official,
3.12 king's secretaries and dictated a **proclamation** to be
3.13 Runners took this **proclamation** to every province of the empire.
3.14 The contents of the **proclamation** were to be made public
4. 3 provinces, wherever the king's **proclamation** was made known,
4. 8 Hathach a copy of the **proclamation** that had been issued in Susa,
8. 5 to you, please issue a **proclamation** to prevent Haman's
8. 8 But a **proclamation** issued in the king's name and stamped
8.13 It was to be **proclaimed** as law and made known to
8.17 and province, wherever the king's **proclamation** was read, the
9. 1 day on which the royal **proclamation** was to take effect, the
9.14 this to be done, and the **proclamation** was issued in Susa.
Ps 18.46 **Proclaim** the greatness of the God who saves me.
30. 9 Can they **proclaim** your unfailing goodness?
34. 3 **Proclaim** with me the Lord's greatness;
35.28 Then I will **proclaim** your righteousness, and I will
50. 6 The heavens **proclaim** that God is righteous,
51.14 O God, and save me, and I will gladly **proclaim** your righteousness.
52. 9 presence of your people I will **proclaim** that you are good.
68.34 **Proclaim** God's power;
69.30 I will **proclaim** his greatness by giving him thanks.
71. 8 All day long I praise you and **proclaim** your glory.
71.16 I will **proclaim** your goodness, yours alone.
71.18 Be with me while I **proclaim** your power and might to all
73.28 the Sovereign Lord and to **proclaim** all that he has done!
75. 1 We **proclaim** how great you are and tell of the wonderful
86.12 I will **proclaim** your greatness for ever.
89. 1 I will **proclaim** your faithfulness for ever.
92. 2 O Most High God, [2] to **proclaim** your constant love every
96. 2 **Proclaim** every day the good news that he has saved us.
96. 3 **Proclaim** his glory to the nations, his mighty deeds to all peoples.
97. 6 The heavens **proclaim** his righteousness,
102.21 so his name will be **proclaimed** in Zion, and he will be
105. 1 Give thanks to the Lord, **proclaim** his greatness;

Ps 107.32 They must **proclaim** his greatness in the assembly of the
118.17 instead, I will live and **proclaim** what the Lord has done.
118.28 I will **proclaim** your greatness.
135.13 Lord, you will always be **proclaimed** as God;
145. 1 I will **proclaim** your greatness, my God and king;
145. 4 they will **proclaim** your mighty acts.
145. 6 of your mighty deeds, and I will **proclaim** your greatness.
Is 14.28 is a message that was **proclaimed** in the year that King Ahaz
40. 6 A voice cries out, **"Proclaim** a message!"
40. 6 "What message shall I **proclaim?"**
40. 6 **"Proclaim** that all mankind are like grass;
40. 9 Jerusalem, go up on a high mountain and **proclaim** the good news!
61. 2 He has sent me to **proclaim** That the time has come When
66.19 Among these nations they will **proclaim** my greatness.
Jer 2. 2 Lord told me [2]to **proclaim** this message to everyone in Jerusalem.
11. 6 **Proclaim** my message there and tell the people to listen to
11.21 would kill me if I kept on **proclaiming** the Lord's message.
15.19 of talking nonsense you **proclaim** a worthwhile message,
18.18 to give us counsel, and prophets to **proclaim** God's message.
19. 2 There I was to **proclaim** the message that he would give me.
19.14 Topheth, where the Lord had sent me to **proclaim** his message.
20. 1 of the Temple, heard me **proclaim** these things, [2]he ordered
20. 8 and scorned all the time because I **proclaim** your message.
23.22 thoughts, then they could have **proclaimed** my message to my
23.28 prophet who has heard my message should **proclaim** that message
23.30 who take each other's words and **proclaim** them as my message.
25.30 "You, Jeremiah, must **proclaim** everything I have said.
26. 2 court of the Temple and **proclaim** all I have commanded you to
26.12 "The Lord sent me to **proclaim** everything that you heard me
31.10 "Nations, listen to me, and **proclaim** my words on the far-off shores.
46.14 **"Proclaim** it in the towns of Egypt, in Migdol, Memphis, and Tahpanhes:
50. 2 **Proclaim** it!
Dan 4.14 He **proclaimed** in a loud voice, 'Cut the tree down and
Joel 2.28 your sons and daughters will **proclaim** my message;
Amos 3. 8 When the Sovereign Lord speaks, who can avoid **proclaiming**
Jon 3. 2 Nineveh, that great city, and **proclaim** to the people the
3. 4 walking a whole day, he **proclaimed,** "In forty days Nineveh
3. 7 He sent out a **proclamation** to the people of Nineveh:
Zech 1.14 angel told me to **proclaim** what the Lord Almighty had said:
1.17 The angel also told me to **proclaim:**
Mal 3. 1 The messenger you long to see will come and **proclaim** my covenant."
Lk 1. 2 saw these things from the beginning and who **proclaimed** the message.
4.18 He has sent me to **proclaim** liberty to the captives and
9.60 You go and **proclaim** the Kingdom of God."
Acts 2.17 Your sons and daughters will **proclaim** my message;
2.18 my Spirit in those days, and they will **proclaim** my message.
4.31 with the Holy Spirit and began to **proclaim** God's message
8.25 had given their testimony and **proclaimed** the Lord's message,
10.36 to the people of Israel, **proclaiming** the Good News of peace
11.20 went to Antioch and **proclaimed** the message to Gentiles also,
17.23 you do not know it, is what I now **proclaim** to you.
18.25 and with great enthusiasm he **proclaimed** and taught correctly
19. 6 spoke in strange tongues and also **proclaimed** God's message.
21. 9 He had four unmarried daughters who **proclaimed** God's message.
Rom 10.14 And how can they hear if the message is not **proclaimed?**
10.15 how can the message be **proclaimed** if the messengers are not
15.19 I have **proclaimed** fully the Good News about Christ.
15.20 ambition has always been to **proclaim** the Good News in places
1 Cor 1.23 As for us, we **proclaim** the crucified Christ, a message that
2. 6 Yet I do **proclaim** a message of wisdom to those who are
2. 7 The wisdom I **proclaim** is God's secret wisdom, which is hidden
11. 4 a man who prays or **proclaims** God's message in public worship
11. 5 any woman who prays or **proclaims** God's message in public worship
11.26 from this cup you **proclaim** the Lord's death until he comes.
14. 1 spiritual gifts, especially the gift of **proclaiming** God's message.
14. 3 the one who **proclaims** God's message speaks to people and gives
14. 4 but the one who **proclaims** God's message helps the whole church.
14. 5 I would rather that you had the gift of **proclaiming** God's message.
14. 5 For the person who **proclaims** God's message is of greater value
14.22 the gift of **proclaiming** God's message is proof for believers,
14.24 if everyone is **proclaiming** God's message when some unbeliever
14.31 All of you may **proclaim** God's message, one by one,
14.32 **proclaiming** God's message should be under the speaker's control,
14.39 set your heart on **proclaiming** God's message, but do not forbid
Phil 1.17 others do not **proclaim** Christ sincerely, but from a spirit of
2.11 and all will openly **proclaim** that Jesus Christ is Lord,
Col 1.25 task of fully **proclaiming** his message, [26]which is the secret
1 Tim 2. 7 of the Gentiles, to **proclaim** the message of faith and truth.
2 Tim 1. 1 by God's will, sent to **proclaim** the promised life which we
1.11 an apostle and teacher to **proclaim** the Good News,
2. 2 teachings that you heard me **proclaim** in the presence of many
4. 2 the message, to insist upon **proclaiming** it (whether the time is
4.17 that I was able to **proclaim** the full message for all the
Tit 1. 3 entrusted to me, and I **proclaim** it by order of God our
Heb 9.19 First, Moses **proclaimed** to the people all the commandments
1 Pet 1.25 This word is the Good News that was **proclaimed** to you.
2. 9 God's own people, chosen to **proclaim** the wonderful acts of God,
2 Pet 1.19 even more confident of the message **proclaimed** by the prophets.
Rev 1. 9 of Patmos because I had **proclaimed** God's word and the truth
6. 9 been killed because they had **proclaimed** God's word and had been
10.11 "Once again you must **proclaim** God's message about many nations,
11. 3 and they will **proclaim** God's message during those 1,260 days."
11. 6 will be no rain during the time they **proclaim** God's message.
Rev 11. 7 they finish **proclaiming** their message, the beast that comes up out
12.11 blood of the Lamb and by the truth which they **proclaimed;**
20. 4 because they had **proclaimed** the truth that Jesus revealed

PRODUCE

Gen 1.11 he commanded, "Let the earth **produce** all kinds of plants,
1.12 So the earth **produced** all kinds of plants, and God was
1.24 "Let the earth **produce** all kinds of animal life:
2. 9 kinds of beautiful trees grow there and **produce** good fruit.
3.17 hard all your life to make it **produce** enough food for you.
3.18 It will **produce** weeds and thorns, and you will have to
3.19 sweat to make the soil **produce** anything, until you go back
4.12 If you try to grow crops, the soil will not **produce** anything;
30.39 of the branches, they **produced** young that were streaked,
31. 8 be your wages,' all the flocks **produced** speckled young.
31. 8 shall be your wages,' all the flocks **produced** striped young.
41.47 years of plenty the land **produced** abundant crops, [48]all of
43.11 be, then take the best **products** of the land in your packs
49.20 "Asher's land will **produce** rich food.
Ex 9. 9 Egypt, and everywhere they will **produce** boils that become
9.10 into the air, and they **produced** boils that became open sores
23.10 "For six years sow your field and gather in what it **produces.**
Lev 17. 6 and burn the fat to **produce** a smell that is pleasing to
25. 7 Everything that it **produces** may be eaten.
25.12 you shall eat only what the fields **produce** of themselves.
25.15 of years the land can **produce** crops before the next Year of
25.16 is being sold is the number of crops the land can **produce.**
25.19 The land will **produce** its crops, and you will have all
25.21 year so that it will **produce** enough food for two years.
26. 4 so that the land will **produce** crops and the trees will bear
26.20 because your land will not **produce** crops and the trees will
27.30 One-tenth of all the **produce** of the land, whether grain or fruit,
Num 13.32 said, "That land doesn't even **produce** enough to feed the
15.19 When any food **produced** there is eaten, some of it is to
17. 8 It had budded, blossomed, and **produced** ripe almonds!
18.12 the best of the first **produce** which the Israelites give me
21.17 "Wells, **produce** your water;
Deut 8. 8 a land that **produces** wheat and barley, grapes, figs,
14.22 a tithe—a tenth of all that your fields **produce** each year.
14.24 there the tithe of the **produce** that the Lord has blessed you
14.25 Sell your **produce** and take the money with you to the one
22. 9 to use either the grapes or the **produce** of the other crop.
30. 9 of livestock, and your fields will **produce** abundant crops.
Judg 9. 9 I would have to stop **producing** my oil, which is used to
9.11 you, I would have to stop **producing** my good sweet fruit.'
9.13 I would have to stop **producing** my wine, that makes gods and
2 Kgs 8. 6 crops that her fields had **produced** during the seven years
8. 9 kinds of the finest **products** of Damascus and went to Elisha.
19.30 that send roots deep into the ground and **produce** fruit.
2 Chr 31. 5 olive-oil, honey, and other farm **produce,** and they also
Neh 9.37 What the land **produces** goes to the kings that you put
Ps 67. 6 The land has **produced** its harvest;
85.12 and our land will **produce** rich harvests.
104.15 can grow his crops [15]and **produce** wine to make him happy,
Prov 3. 9 an offering from the best of all that your land **produces.**
25. 4 out of silver and the artist can **produce** a thing of beauty.
Is 1.19 obey me, you will eat the good things the land **produces.**
4. 2 take delight and pride in the crops that the land **produces.**
5. 4 Then why did it **produce** sour grapes and not the good grapes
5.10 litres of seed will **produce** only eighteen litres of corn."
27. 6 The earth will be covered with the fruit they **produce.**
32.15 land will become fertile, and fields will **produce** rich crops.
37.31 that send roots deep into the ground and **produce** fruit.
Jer 31. 5 those who plant them will eat what the vineyards **produce.**
Ezek 7.11 Violence **produces** more wickedness.
27.16 The people of Syria bought your merchandise and your many **products.**
27.18 bought your merchandise and your **products,** paying for them
34.27 bear fruit, the fields will **produce** crops, and everyone will
Hos 2.21 and the earth will **produce** corn and grapes and olives.
8. 7 A field of corn that doesn't ripen can never **produce** any bread.
10. 1 The more **productive** their land was, the more beautiful they
10.12 reap the blessings that your devotion to me will **produce.**
10.13 You have eaten the fruit **produced** by your lies.
Nah 3.16 You **produced** more merchants than there are stars in the sky!
Hab 3.17 olive-crop fails and the fields **produce** no corn, even though
Hag 1.11 on every crop the ground **produces,** on men and animals, on
2.14 to the people of this nation and to everything they **produce;**
2.19 and olive-trees have not yet **produced,** yet from now on I
Zech 8.12 bear grapes, the earth will **produce** crops, and there will be
Mt 13. 8 But some seeds fell in good soil, and the plants **produced** corn;
13. 8 **produced** a hundred grains, others sixty, and others thirty."
21.43 and given to a people who will **produce** the proper fruits."
Mk 4. 7 up and choked the plants, and they didn't **produce** any corn.
4. 8 in good soil, and the plants sprouted, grew, and **produced** corn:
Lk 8. 8 the plants grew and **produced** corn, a hundred grains each."
Jn 12.24 If it does die, then it **produces** many grains.
Rom 5. 3 because we know that trouble **produces** endurance,
2 Cor 9.10 make it grow and **produce** a rich harvest from your generosity.
9.12 but also **produces** an outpouring of gratitude to God.
Gal 5.22 But the Spirit **produces** love, joy, peace, patience, kindness,
Phil 1.11 which only Jesus Christ can **produce,** for the glory and
Col 1.10 Your lives will **produce** all kinds of good deeds, and you
1 Tim 1. 4 and those long lists of ancestors, which only **produce** arguments;
Jas 3.12 nor can a salty spring **produce** sweet water.
3.17 is full of compassion and **produces** a harvest of good deeds;
3.18 the harvest that is **produced** from the seeds the peacemakers plant
5. 7 is as he waits for his land to **produce** precious crops.
5.18 sky poured out its rain and the earth **produced** its crops.

PROFANE

Lev 21.23 He must not **profane** these holy things, because I am the Lord
22.15 The priests shall not **profane** the sacred offerings
Num 18.32 But be sure not to **profane** the sacred gifts of the
Neh 13.18 of God's anger down on Israel by **profaning** the Sabbath."
Is 43.28 and your rulers **profaned** my sanctuary.
Ezek 7.22 when my treasured Temple is **profaned,** when robbers break
7.24 when I let the nations **profane** the places where you worship.
20.13 They completely **profaned** the Sabbath.
20.16 commands, broken my laws, and **profaned** the Sabbath—they
20.21 They **profaned** the Sabbath.
20.24 my commands, broken my laws, **profaned** the Sabbath, and
23.38 They **profaned** my Temple and broke the Sabbath,
23.39 to idols, they came to my Temple and **profaned** it!
24.21 and to visit it, but the Lord is going to **profane** it.
25. 3 delighted to see my Temple **profaned,** to see the land of
44. 7 They have **profaned** my Temple by letting uncircumcised foreigners,
Amos 2. 7 with the same slave-girl, and so **profane** my holy name.
Eph 5. 4 for you to use language which is obscene, **profane,** or vulgar.
1 Tim 6.20 Avoid the **profane** talk and foolish arguments of what some people
2 Tim 2.16 Keep away from **profane** and foolish discussions,

PROFESS

2 Cor 9.13 gospel of Christ, which you **profess,** and for your generosity
1 Tim 6.12 God called you when you firmly **professed** your faith before many
6.13 Jesus, who firmly **professed** his faith before Pontius Pilate,
Heb 3. 1 God sent to be the High Priest of the faith we **profess.**
4.14 Let us, then, hold firmly to the faith we **profess.**
10.23 firmly to the hope we **profess,** because we can trust God

PROFIT

Lev 25.37 and do not make a **profit** on the food you sell him.
1 Kgs 10.15 taxes paid by merchants, the **profits** from trade, and tribute
Ps 30. 9 What **profit** from my going to the grave?
Prov 3.14 There is more **profit** in it than there is in silver;
9.12 are the one who will **profit** if you have wisdom, and if
15.27 you try to make a **profit** dishonestly, you will get your
Ecc 11. 1 foreign trade, and one of these days you will make a **profit.**
Ezek 18. 8 He doesn't lend money for **profit.**
18.13 worships disgusting idols, [13]and lends money for **profit.**
18.17 He refuses to do evil and doesn't lend money for **profit.**
28. 5 You made clever business deals and kept on making **profits.**
Jn 4.38 others worked there, and you **profit** from their work."
Acts 19.24 his business brought a great deal of **profit** to the workers.
Phil 3. 7 that I might count as **profit** I now reckon as loss for
4.15 you were the only ones who shared my **profits** and losses.
4.17 rather, I want to see **profit** added to your account.
2 Pet 2. 3 false teachers will make a **profit** out of telling you made-up

AV PROFIT

Gen 25.32 what **good** will my rights do me then?"
37.26 "What will we **gain** by killing our brother and covering
1 Sam 12.21 they cannot **help** you or save you, for they are not real.
Esth 3. 8 so it is not in your best **interests** to tolerate them.
Job 21.15 no need to serve God nor any **advantage** in praying to him.
35. 3 What have I **gained** by not sinning?"
35. 8 who suffers from your sins, and the good you do **helps** him.
Prov 10. 2 will do you no **good,** but honesty can save your life.
11. 4 Riches will do you no **good** on the day you face death,
Ecc 2.11 It was like chasing the wind—of no **use** at all.
3. 9 What do we **gain** from all our work?
Is 30. 5 a nation that fails them when they expect **help."**
30. 6 expensive gifts for a nation that cannot give them any **help.**
47.12 Perhaps they will be of some **help** to you;
48.17 wants to teach you **for your own good** and direct you in
57.12 your conduct, and your idols will not be able to **help** you.
Jer 23.32 and they are of no **help** at all to the people.
Mal 3.14 What's the **use** of doing what he says or of trying to
Mk 8.36 Does a person **gain** anything if he wins the whole world
Rom 3. 1 Or is there any **value** in being circumcised?
1 Cor 7.35 I am saying this because I want to **help** you.
10.33 not thinking of my own **good,** but of the good of all,
12. 7 shown in some way in each person for the **good** of all.
14. 6 to you, my brothers, what **use** will I be to you if
Gal 5. 2 it means that Christ is of no **use** to you at all.
2 Tim 2.14 It does no **good,** but only ruins the people who listen.
Heb 4. 2 but it did them no **good,** because when they heard it, they
12.10 does it for our own **good,** so that we may share his
Jas 2.14 My brothers, what **good** is it for someone to say that he
2.16 What **good** is there in your saying to them, "God bless you!

PROGRESS

Ezra 6.14 The Jewish leaders made good **progress** with the building
Neh 4. 7 heard that we were making **progress** in rebuilding the wall of
Zech 4.10 They are disappointed because so little **progress** is being made.
Phil 1.12 to me have really helped the **progress** of the gospel.
1.25 to add to your **progress** and joy in the faith,
1 Tim 4.15 to them, in order that your **progress** may be seen by all.

PROHIBIT

Mt 16.19 what you **prohibit** on earth will be prohibited in heaven,
18.18 what you **prohibit** on earth will be prohibited in heaven,

PROJECT (1)

Ex 1.13 them work on their building **projects** and in their fields,
1 Kgs 9.23 labour working on Solomon's various building **projects.**
2 Chr 8.10 the forced labour working on the various building **projects.**
8.16 By this time all Solomon's **projects** had been completed.
Prov 12.11 to eat, but it is stupid to waste time on useless **projects.**
17.12 her cubs than to meet some fool busy with a stupid **project.**

PROJECT (2)

Ex 26.17 centimetres wide, [17]with two matching **projections,** so that
26.17 All the frames are to have these **projections.**
26.19 two bases under each frame to hold its two **projections.**
27. 2 Make **projections** at the top of the four corners.
29.12 and with your finger put it on the **projections** of the altar.
30. 2 Its **projections** at the four corners are to form one piece
30. 3 all four sides, and its **projections** with pure gold, and put
30.10 by putting on its four **projections** the blood of the animal
36.22 centimetres wide, [22]with two matching **projections,** so that
36.22 All the frames had these **projections.**
36.24 two bases under each frame to hold its two **projections.**
37.25 Its **projections** at the four corners formed one piece with it.
37.26 all four sides, and its **projections** with pure gold and put a
38. 2 He made the **projections** at the top of the four corners, so
Lev 4. 7 of the blood on the **projections** at the corners of the
4.18 of the blood on the **projections** at the corners of the
4.25 put it on the **projections** at the corners of the altar,
4.30 put it on the **projections** at the corners of the altar,
4.34 put it on the **projections** at the corners of the altar,
8.15 put it on the **projections** at the corners of the altar,
9. 9 some of it on the **projections** at the corners of the altar,
16.18 put it all over the **projections** at the corners of the altar.
1 Kgs 7.31 It **projected** upwards 45 centimetres from the top of the cart
Ezek 43.15 The **projections** on the four corners were higher than the
43.20 and put it on the **projections** on the top corners of the

PROMINENT

1 Chr 2.10 Amminadab, Nahshon (a **prominent** man of the tribe of Judah),
Neh 11.16 Shabbethai and Jozabad, **prominent** Levites in charge of
Dan 8. 5 He had one **prominent** horn between his eyes.
8. 8 In its place four **prominent** horns came up, each pointing in
8.21 kingdom of Greece, and the **prominent** horn between his eyes

PROMISE

[LAND WHICH THE LORD PROMISED]

Gen 9.11 I **promise** that never again will all living beings be
9.15 appears, [15]I will remember my **promise** to you and to all
9.17 is the sign of the **promise** which I am making to all
15.18 He said, "I **promise** to give your descendants all this land
17. 4 I **promise** that you will be the ancestor of many nations.
17. 7 "I will keep my **promise** to you and to your descendants in
18.19 do, I will do everything for him that I have **promised."**
21. 1 blessed Sarah, as he had **promised,** [2]and she became pregnant
21.12 Isaac that you will have the descendants I have **promised.**
21.23 been loyal to you, so **promise** that you will also be loyal
21.24 Abraham said, "I **promise."**
22.17 only son from me, [17]I **promise** that I will give you as
24. 7 my relatives, and he solemnly **promised** me that he would give
24. 8 to come with you, you will be free from this **promise.**
24.12 give me success today and keep your **promise** to my master.
24.14 I will know that you have kept your **promise** to my master."
24.27 Abraham, who has faithfully kept his **promise** to my master.
24.37 My master made me **promise** with a vow to obey his command.
26. 3 I will keep the **promise** I made to your father Abraham.
26.24 descendants because of my **promise** to my servant Abraham."
26.28 We want you to **promise** [29]that you will not harm us, just
26.31 morning each man made his **promise** and sealed it with a vow.
28.15 leave you until I have done all that I have **promised** you."
31.53 Isaac worshipped, Jacob solemnly vowed to keep this **promise.**
32.12 Remember that you **promised** to make everything go well
50. 5 to die, he made me **promise** him that I would bury him
50. 6 "Go and bury your father, as you **promised** you would."
50.24 this land to the **land he solemnly promised** to Abraham,
50.25 **"Promise** me," he said, "that when God leads you to that land,
Ex 6. 4 made my covenant with them, **promising** to give them the land
6. 8 you to the **land that I solemnly promised** to give to Abraham,
9.28 I **promise** to let you go;
12.25 land that the Lord has **promised** to give you, you must
13. 5 The Lord solemnly **promised** your ancestors to give you the
13.11 which he solemnly **promised** to you and your ancestors.
13.19 as Joseph had made the Israelites solemnly **promise** to do.
15.13 Faithful to your **promise,** you led the people you had rescued;
32.13 Remember the solemn **promise** you made to them to give them as
32.13 their descendants all that **land you promised** would be their
33. 1 and go to the **land that I promised** to give to Abraham,
34. 7 I keep my **promise** for thousands of generations and forgive
Lev 19.12 Do not make a **promise** in my name if you do not
20.24 But I have **promised** you this rich and fertile land as
26.42 and I will renew my **promise** to give my people the land.
Num 6.21 but if a Nazirite **promises** an offering beyond what his vow
6.21 him to give, he must fulfil exactly the **promise** he made.
10.29 He has **promised** to make Israel prosperous, so come with us,
11.12 all the way to the **land you promised** to their ancestors?
14.16 able to bring them into the **land you promised** to give them.
14.17 power and do what you **promised** when you said, [18]'I, the
14.21 But I **promise** that as surely as I live and as surely
14.23 They will never enter the land which I **promised** to their ancestors.

Num 14.30 I **promised** to let you live there, but not one of you
20.12 not lead them into the **land that I promised** to give them."
20.24 going to enter the land which I **promised** to give to Israel;
23.19 Whatever he **promises,** he does;
24.11 I **promised** to reward you, but the Lord has kept you from
30. 2 he must not break his **promise,** but must do everything that
30. 3 something to the Lord or **promises** to abstain from something,
30. 4 everything that she vowed or **promised** unless her father
30. 6 or carelessly, or **promises** to abstain from something,
30. 7 everything that she vowed or **promised** unless her husband
30. 9 vow she makes and every **promise** to abstain from something.
30.10 woman makes a vow or **promises** to abstain from something,
30.11 everything that she vowed or **promised** unless her husband
30.13 affirm or to annul any vow or **promise** that she has made.
30.14 she must do everything that she has vowed or **promised.**
32.10 The Lord was angry that day and made a **promise:**
32.11 Egypt will enter the **land that I promised** to Abraham, Isaac,
32.23 you do not keep your **promise,** I warn you that you will
32.24 enclosures for your sheep, but do what you have **promised!"**
Deut 1. 8 land which I, the Lord, **promised** to give to your ancestors,
1.11 thousand times more and make you prosperous, as he **promised!**
1.35 the fertile **land that I promised** to give your ancestors.
6. 3 just as the Lord, the God of our ancestors, has **promised.**
6.10 as the Lord your God **promised** your ancestors, Abraham,
6.13 worship only him, and make your **promises** in his name alone.
6.18 of the fertile **land that the Lord promised** your ancestors,
6.19 and you will drive out your enemies, as he **promised.**
6.23 us this land, as he had **promised** our ancestors he would.
7. 8 wanted to keep the **promise** that he made to your ancestors.
7.12 show you his constant love, as he **promised** your ancestors.
7.13 these blessings in the **land that he promised** your ancestors
8. 1 occupy the **land which the Lord promised** to your ancestors.
9. 3 drive them out and destroy them quickly, as he **promised.**
9. 5 intends to keep the **promise** that he made to your ancestors,
9.28 take your people into the **land that you had promised** them.
10. 9 being the Lord's priests, as the Lord your God **promised.)**
10.11 possession of the **land that he had promised** to give to your
10.20 Be faithful to him and make your **promises** in his name alone.
11. 9 rich and fertile **land that the Lord promised** to give your
11.21 that the Lord your God **promised** to give to your ancestors.
11.25 fear you, as he has **promised,** and no one will be able
12. 6 gifts that you **promise** to the Lord, your freewill offerings,
12.11 and those special gifts that you have **promised** to the Lord.
12.17 gifts that you **promise** to the Lord, your freewill offerings,
12.20 your territory, as he has **promised,** you may eat meat
12.26 offerings and the gifts that you have **promised** the Lord.
13. 1 an interpreter of dreams may **promise** a miracle or a wonder,
13. 2 Even if what he **promises** comes true, [3]do not pay any
13.17 a numerous people, as he **promised** your ancestors, [18]if you
15. 6 The Lord will bless you, as he has **promised.**
18. 2 of being the Lord's priests, as the Lord has **promised.**
19. 8 gives you all the **land he has promised,** [9]then you are to
23.21 the Lord your God, do not put off doing what you **promised;**
26. 3 I have entered the **land that he promised** our ancestors to
26.15 that you have given us, as you **promised** our ancestors.'
26.17 you have **promised** to obey him, to keep all his laws, and
26.18 Lord has accepted you as his own people, as he **promised** you;
26.19 You will be his own people, as he **promised."**
27. 3 the God of your ancestors, **promised** you, [4]and you are on
28. 9 he will make you his own people, as he has **promised.**
28.11 abundant crops in the **land that he promised** your ancestors
29.13 be your God, as he **promised** you and your ancestors, Abraham,
30.20 long in the **land that he promised** to give your ancestors,
31. 7 occupy the **land that the Lord promised** to their ancestors.
31.20 this rich and fertile land, as I **promised** their ancestors.
31.21 take them into the **land that I promised** to give them, I
31.23 of Israel into the **land that I promised** them, and I will
34. 4 Moses, "This is the **land that I promised** Abraham, Isaac,
Josh 1. 6 as they occupy this land which I **promised** their ancestors.
2.13 **Promise** me that you will save my father and mother, my
2.14 we have been doing, we **promise** you that when the Lord gives
2.17 her, "We will keep the **promise** that you have made us give.
2.20 not have to keep our **promise** which you have made us give
5. 4 rich and fertile **land that he had promised** their ancestors.
6.22 and bring her and her family out, as you **promised** her."
9.15 of Israel gave their solemn **promise** to keep the treaty.
9.18 leaders had made a solemn **promise** to them in the name of
9.19 "We have made our solemn **promise** to them in the name of
9.20 We must let them live because of our **promise;**
14. 9 Because I did, Moses **promised** me that my children and I
14.10 and the Lord, as he **promised,** has kept me alive ever since.
14.12 the hill-country that the Lord **promised** me on that day when
21.43 he had solemnly **promised** their ancestors he would give them.
21.44 the land, just as he had **promised** their ancestors.
21.45 kept every one of the **promises** that he had made to the
22. 4 Now, as he **promised,** the Lord your God has given your
23. 5 have their land, as the Lord your God has **promised** you.
23.10 the Lord your God is fighting for you, just as he **promised.**
23.14 your God has given you all the good things that he **promised.**
23.14 Every **promise** he made has been kept;
23.15 just as he kept every **promise** that he made to you, so
Judg 2. 1 brought you to the **land that I promised** to your ancestors.
11.30 Jephthah **promised** the Lord:
11.35 I have made a solemn **promise** to the Lord, and I cannot
11.36 "If you have made a **promise** to the Lord, do what you
11.39 He did what he had **promised** the Lord, and she died still
21. 1 at Mizpah, they had made a solemn **promise** to the Lord:
21. 7 We have made a solemn **promise** to the Lord that we will
21.22 to us, you are not guilty of breaking your **promise.'"**
Ruth 2.20 "The Lord always keeps his **promises** to the living and the dead."
1 Sam 1.11 Hannah made a solemn **promise:**
1 Sam 1.11 give me a son, I **promise** that I will dedicate him to
1.21 Lord the yearly sacrifice and the special sacrifice he had **promised.**
1.23 And may the Lord make your **promise** come true."
2.30 the Lord God of Israel, **promised** in the past that your
12.22 Lord has made a solemn **promise,** and he will not abandon you,
14.39 I **promise** by the living Lord, who gives Israel victory,
14.45 We **promise** by the living Lord that he will not lose even
17.25 King Saul has **promised** to give a big reward to the man
20. 8 me this favour, and keep the sacred **promise** you made to me.
20.14 alive, please keep your sacred **promise** and be loyal to me;
20.16 may our **promise** to each other still be unbroken.
20.17 Once again Jonathan made David **promise** to love him, for
20.23 As for the **promise** we have made to each other, the Lord
20.42 ever keep the sacred **promise** we have made to each other."
23.18 of them made a sacred **promise** of friendship to each other.
24.21 But **promise** me in the Lord's name that you will spare my
24.22 David **promised** that he would.
25.30 the good things he has **promised** you and has made you king
28.10 "By the living Lord I **promise** that you will not be punished
30.15 answered, "I will if you **promise** me in God's name that you
2 Sam 3. 9 The Lord **promised** David that he would take the
3.35 but he made a solemn **promise,** "May God strike me dead if
5. 2 in battle, and the Lord **promised** you that you would lead his
7.10 I **promise** to keep you safe from all your enemies and to
7.19 made **promises** about my descendants in the years to come.
7.25 fulfil for all time the **promise** you made about me and my
7.28 keep your **promises,** and you have made this wonderful promise
7.28 promises, and you have made this wonderful **promise** to me.
7.29 You, Sovereign Lord, have **promised** this, and your blessing
9. 3 I can show loyalty and kindness, as I **promised** God I would?"
14.11 "I **promise** by the living Lord," David replied, "that
14.17 said to myself that your **promise,** sir, would make me safe,
15. 7 go to Hebron and keep a **promise** I made to the Lord.
15. 8 in Geshur in Syria, I **promised** the Lord that if he would
21. 2 Amorites whom the Israelites had **promised** to protect, but
21. 7 But because of the sacred **promise** that he and Jonathan
21.17 Then David's men made David **promise** that he would never
23. 5 will not be broken, a **promise** that will not be changed.
1 Kgs 1.13 'Your Majesty, didn't you solemnly **promise** me that my son
1.17 you made me a solemn **promise** in the name of the Lord
1.29 he said to her, "I **promise** you by the living Lord, who
1.30 today I will keep the **promise** I made to you in the
2. 4 the Lord will keep the **promise** he made when he told me
2. 8 I gave him my solemn **promise** in the name of the Lord
2.23 Then Solomon made a solemn **promise** in the Lord's name,
2.24 he has kept his **promise** and given the kingdom to me and
2.42 and said, "I made you **promise** in the Lord's name not to
2.43 Why, then, have you broken your **promise** and disobeyed my command?
5. 5 The Lord **promised** my father David, 'Your son, whom I will
5.12 The Lord kept his **promise** and gave Solomon wisdom.
6.12 I will do for you what I **promised** your father David.
8.15 He has kept the **promise** he made to my father David, when
8.20 "And now the Lord has kept his **promise.**
8.24 You have kept the **promise** you made to my father David;
8.25 will also keep the other **promise** you made to my father when
8.26 everything come true that you **promised** to my father David,
8.56 Lord who has given his people peace, as he **promised** he would.
8.56 all the generous **promises** he made through his servant Moses.
9. 5 you, [5]I will keep the **promise** I made to your father David
11.11 and disobeyed my commands, I **promise** that I will take the
17.16 As the Lord had **promised** through Elijah, the bowl did
18.15 Lord, whom I serve, I **promise** that I will present myself to
22.14 "By the living Lord I **promise** that I will say what he
2 Kgs 8.19 destroy Judah, because he had **promised** his servant David
9.26 And I **promise** that I will punish you here in this same
9.26 belonged to Naboth, so as to fulfil the Lord's **promise."**
10.10 The Lord has done what he **promised** through his prophet Elijah."
10.30 So I **promise** you that your descendants,
14.25 God of Israel, had **promised** through his servant the prophet
15.12 So the **promise** was fulfilled which the Lord had made to
19.34 and because of the **promise** I made to my servant David.'"
20. 6 and because of the **promise** I made to my servant David."
20. 9 give you a sign to prove that he will keep his **promise.**
23. 3 And all the people **promised** to keep the covenant.
1 Chr 11. 2 and the Lord your God **promised** you that you would lead his
11. 3 of Israel, just as the Lord had **promised** through Samuel.
11.10 as the Lord had **promised,** and they kept his kingdom strong.
12.23 make him king in place of Saul, as the Lord had **promised.**
16.16 the covenant he made with Abraham, the **promise** he made to Isaac.
17. 9 I **promise** to defeat all your enemies and to give you descendants.
17.17 made **promises** about my descendants in the years to come,
17.23 fulfil for all time the **promise** you made about me and my
17.26 are God, and you have made this wonderful **promise** to me.
22. 9 He did, however, make me a **promise.**
22.11 and may he keep his **promise** to make you successful in
25. 5 three daughters, as he had **promised,** in order to give power
27.23 twenty, because of the Lord's **promise** to make the people of
29.24 all of David's other sons **promised** to be loyal to Solomon as
2 Chr 1. 9 O Lord God, fulfil the **promise** you made to my father.
2.15 us the wheat, barley, wine, and olive-oil that you **promised.**
4.11 the objects that he had **promised** King Solomon he would make
6. 4 He has kept the **promise** he made to my father David when
6.10 "Now the Lord has kept his **promise:**
6.15 You have kept the **promise** you made to my father David;
6.16 of Israel, keep the other **promise** you made to my father when
6.17 come true that you **promised** to your servant David.
6.20 You have **promised** that this is where you will be worshipped,
7.18 you, [18]I will keep the **promise** I made to your father David

2 Chr	21. 7	a covenant with David and **promised** that his descendants
	23. 3	as the Lord **promised** that King David's descendants would be.
	34.32	everyone else present in Jerusalem **promise** to keep the covenant.
Ezra	10. 3	we must make a solemn **promise** to our God that we will
	10.19	They **promised** to divorce their wives, and they offered a
Neh	5.12	in front of them to keep the **promise** they had just made.
	5.13	will shake any of you who don't keep your **promise,"** I said.
	5.13	And the leaders kept their **promise.**
	9. 8	You **promised** to give him the land of the Canaanites, the
	9. 8	You kept your **promise,** because you are faithful.
	9.15	control of the land which you had **promised** to give them.
	9.23	land that you had **promised** their ancestors to give them.
	9.32	You faithfully keep your covenant **promises.**
Esth	4. 7	how much money Haman had **promised** to put into the royal
Job	31. 1	I have made a solemn **promise** never to look with lust at
	34.31	confessed your sins to God and **promised** not to sin again?
	41. 4	an agreement with you and **promise** to serve you for ever?
Ps	12. 6	The **promises** of the Lord can be trusted;
	15. 4	He always does what he **promises,** no matter how much it may
	22.25	who worship you I will offer the sacrifices I **promised.**
	23. 3	He guides me in the right paths, as he has **promised.**
	24. 4	thought, who do not worship idols or make false **promises.**
	25.11	Keep your **promise,** Lord, and forgive my sins, for they are many.
	31. 3	guide me and lead me as you have **promised.**
	35. 3	**Promise** that you will save me.
	50.14	to God, and give the Almighty all that you **promised.**
	55.20	he broke his **promises.**
	56. 4	I praise him for what he has **promised.**
	56.10	God is on my side— [10] the Lord, whose **promises** I praise.
	56.12	O God, I will offer you what I have **promised;**
	61. 5	You have heard my **promises,** O God, and you have given me
	61. 8	praises to you, as I offer you daily what I have **promised.**
	63.11	Those who make **promises** in God's name will praise him, but
	65. 1	Zion and keep our **promises** to you, [2] because you answer prayers.
	66.13	I will offer you what I **promised.**
	69.13	of your great love, because you keep your **promise** to save.
	76.11	Give the Lord your God what you **promised** him;
	77. 8	Does his **promise** no longer stand?
	85. 8	he **promises** peace to us, his own people, if we do not
	89. 3	I have **promised** my servant David, [4] 'A descendant of yours
	89.28	I will always keep my **promise** to him, and my covenant
	89.33	not stop loving David or fail to keep my **promise** to him.
	89.34	covenant with him or take back even one **promise** I made him.
	89.35	"Once and for all I have **promised** by my holy name:
	89.49	Where are the **promises** you made to David?
	95.11	I was angry and made a solemn **promise:**
	98. 3	He kept his **promise** to the people of Israel with loyalty
	105. 8	covenant for ever, his **promises** for a thousand generations.
	105. 9	agreement he made with Abraham and his **promise** to Isaac.
	105.42	He remembered his sacred **promise** to Abraham his servant.
	106. 8	saved them, as he had **promised,** in order to show his great
	106.12	Then his people believed his **promises** and sang praises to him.
	106.24	pleasant land, because they did not believe God's **promise.**
	109.21	help me as you have **promised,** and rescue me because of the
	110. 4	The Lord made a solemn **promise** and will not take it back:
	116.14	of all his people I will give him what I have **promised.**
	116.18	Temple in Jerusalem, I will give you what I have **promised.**
	119.25	revive me, as you have **promised.**
	119.28	strengthen me, as you have **promised.**
	119.37	be good to me, as you have **promised.**
	119.38	Keep your **promise** to me, your servant—
	119.38	the **promise** you make to those who obey
	119.41	you love me, Lord, and save me according to your **promise.**
	119.49	Remember your **promise** to me, your servant;
	119.50	I was comforted because your **promise** gave me life.
	119.57	I **promise** to obey your laws.
	119.58	all my heart to have mercy on me, as you have **promised!**
	119.59	I **promise** to follow your instructions.
	119.65	You have kept your **promise,** Lord, and you are good to me,
	119.74	be glad when they see me, because I trust in your **promise.**
	119.76	your constant love comfort me, as you have **promised** me, your
	119.82	from watching for what you **promised,** while I ask, "When
	119.106	I will keep my solemn **promise** to obey your just instructions.
	119.107	keep me alive, as you have **promised.**
	119.114	I put my hope in your **promise.**
	119.116	Give me strength, as you **promised,** and I shall live;
	119.122	**Promise** that you will help your servant;
	119.123	for your saving help, for the deliverance you **promised.**
	119.133	As you have **promised,** keep me from falling;
	119.140	How certain your **promise** is!
	119.147	I place my hope in your **promise.**
	119.154	save me, as you have **promised.**
	119.162	I am because of your **promises**— as happy as someone who
	119.169	Give me understanding, as you have **promised.**
	119.170	Listen to my prayer, and save me according to your **promise!**
	132. 2	Remember, Lord, what he **promised,** the vow he made to you,
	132.10	You made a **promise** to your servant David;
	132.11	solemn promise to David— a **promise** you will not take back:
	133. 3	is where the Lord has **promised** his blessing— life that never
	138. 4	praise you, Lord, because they have heard your **promises.**
	138. 8	You will do everything you have **promised;**
	143.11	Rescue me, Lord, as you have **promised;**
	145.13	Lord is faithful to his **promises,** and he is merciful in all
	146. 6	He always keeps his **promises;**
Prov	6. 1	Have you **promised** to be responsible for someone else's debts,
	6. 2	been caught by your own words, trapped by your own **promises?**
	11.15	If you **promise** to pay a stranger's debt, you will regret it.
	17.18	man with no sense would **promise** to be responsible for
	20.16	Anyone stupid enough to **promise** to be responsible for a
	20.25	Think carefully before you **promise** an offering to God.
	22.26	Don't **promise** to be responsible for someone else's debts.
Prov	25.14	People who **promise** things that they never give are like
	27.13	Anyone stupid enough to **promise** to be responsible for a
	30. 5	"God keeps every **promise** he makes.
Ecc	5. 2	Think before you speak, and don't make any rash **promises** to God.
	5. 4	So when you make a **promise** to God, keep it as quickly
	5. 4	Do what you **promise** to do.
	5. 5	Better not to **promise** at all
	5. 5	than to make a **promise** and not keep it.
	8. 2	what the king says, and don't make any rash **promises** to God.
Song	2. 7	**Promise** me, women of Jerusalem;
	3. 5	**Promise** me, women of Jerusalem;
	5. 8	**Promise** me, women of Jerusalem, that if you find my lover,
	5. 9	so wonderful about him that we should give you our **promise?**
	8. 4	**Promise** me, women of Jerusalem, that you will not interrupt our love.
Is	19.21	They will make solemn **promises** to him and do what they promise.
	19.21	They will make solemn promises to him and do what they **promise.**
	37.35	and because of the **promise** I made to my servant David.' "
	38. 7	give you a sign to prove that he will keep his **promise.**
	40. 5	The Lord himself has **promised** this."
	42.16	These are my **promises,** and I will keep them without fail.
	45.23	My **promise** is true, and it will not be changed.
	45.23	I solemnly **promise** by all that I am:
	49. 7	the holy God of Israel keeps his **promises.**
	54. 9	the time of Noah I **promised** never again to flood the earth.
	54. 9	Now I **promise** not to be angry with you again;
	54.10	I will keep for ever my **promise** of peace."
	55. 3	with you and give you the blessings I **promised** to David.
	56. 8	Israel home from exile, has **promised** that he will bring
	62. 6	the Lord of his **promises** And never let him forget them.
	62. 8	Lord has made a solemn **promise,** And by his power he will
Jer	11. 5	Then I would keep the **promise** I made to their ancestors
	11.15	by making **promises** and by offering animal sacrifices?
	14. 7	our sins accuse us, help us, Lord, as you have **promised.**
	14.13	or starvation, because you have **promised,** they say, that
	14.21	Remember your **promises** and do not despise us;
	19.12	I **promise** that I will make this city and its inhabitants
	29.10	concern for you and keep my **promise** to bring you back home.
	31.36	He **promises** that as long as the natural order lasts, so
	32.22	rich and fertile land, as you had **promised** their ancestors.
	32.42	going to give them all the good things that I have **promised.**
	33.14	when I will fulfil the **promise** that I made to the people
	33.17	I, the Lord, **promise** that there will always be a
	35.17	Judah and of Jerusalem all the destruction that I **promised.**
	35.19	Almighty, the God of Israel, **promise** that Jonadab son of
	38.16	So King Zedekiah **promised** me in secret, "I swear by the
	38.25	They will **promise** not to put you to death if you tell
	42.20	God for you, and you **promised** that you would do everything
	44.24	your wives have made solemn **promises** to the Queen of Heaven.
	44.24	You **promised** that you would offer sacrifices to her and pour
	44.24	and you have kept your **promises.**
	44.24	Keep your **promises!**
	44.29	this place and that my **promise** to bring destruction on you
	48.40	The Lord has **promised** that a nation will swoop down on
Lam	1.21	Bring the day you **promised;**
Ezek	16. 8	your naked body with my coat and **promised** to love you.
	16.59	because you ignored your **promises** and broke the covenant.
	20. 5	When I chose Israel, I made them a **promise.**
	20. 6	It was then that I **promised** to take them out of Egypt
	20.15	So I made a **promise** in the desert that I would not
	20.16	I made the **promise** because they had rejected my commands,
	20.23	So I made another **promise** in the desert.
	20.28	I brought them to the **land I had promised** to give them.
	20.42	back to Israel, the **land that I promised** I would give to
	33.13	I may **promise** life to a good man, but if he starts
	36. 7	I, the Sovereign Lord, solemnly **promise** that the
	36.36	I, the Lord, have **promised** that I would do this—and I
	37.14	I have **promised** that I would do this— and I will.
	47.14	I solemnly **promised** your ancestors that I would give
Dan	8. 9	the south and the east and towards the **Promised Land.**
	11.16	He will stand in the **Promised Land** and have it completely in
	11.41	He will even invade the **Promised Land** and kill tens of thousands,
	12. 7	sky and made a solemn **promise** in the name of the Eternal
Hos	2.20	I will keep my **promise** and make you mine, and you will
	4. 2	They make **promises** and break them;
	4.15	Gilgal or Bethaven, or make **promises** there in the name of
	10. 4	They utter empty words and make false **promises** and useless treaties.
	14. 2	our prayer, and we will praise you as we have **promised.**
Joel	2.13	he is patient and keeps his **promise;**
Amos	4. 2	Lord is holy, he has **promised,** "The days will come when
Jon	1.16	Lord that they offered a sacrifice and **promised** to serve him.
	2. 9	I will offer you a sacrifice and do what I have **promised.**
Mic	3. 5	by prophets who **promise** peace to those who pay them,
	4. 4	The Lord Almighty has **promised** this.
	7.20	Abraham and of Jacob, as you **promised** our ancestors long ago.
Nah	1.15	your festivals and give God what you solemnly **promised** him.
Hag	1.13	"I will be with you—that is my **promise."**
	2. 5	came out of Egypt, I **promised** that I would always be with
Zech	2. 5	The Lord has **promised** that he himself will be a wall of
Mal	1.14	in his flock a good animal that he **promised** to give me!
	2. 5	"In my covenant I **promised** them life and well-being, and
	2.10	why do we break our **promises** to one another, and why do
	2.11	of Judah have broken their **promise** to God and done a
	2.14	knows you have broken your **promise** to the wife you married
	2.14	you have broken your **promise** to her,
	2.14	although you **promised** before God
	2.15	make sure that none of you breaks his **promise** to his wife.
	2.16	do not break your **promise** to be faithful to your wife."

Mt 5. 5 they will receive what God has **promised!**
5.33 'Do not break your **promise,** but do what you have vowed
5.34 do not use any vow when you make a **promise.**
14. 7 was so pleased [7]that he **promised** her, "I swear that I will
14. 9 sad, but because of the **promise** he had made in front of
20.21 She answered, "**Promise** me that these two sons of mine will
Mk 14.11 hear what he had to say, and **promised** to give him money.
Lk 1.20 remain silent until the day my **promise** to you comes true."
1.27 a message for a girl **promised** in marriage to a man named
1.54 He has kept the **promise** he made to our ancestors,
1.70 He **promised** through his holy prophets long ago
1.73 to our ancestor Abraham he **promised** to rescue us from our
2. 5 to register with Mary, who was **promised** in marriage to him.
2.26 not die before he had seen the Lord's **promised** Messiah.
2.29 Lord, you have kept your **promise,** and you may let your
23.43 Jesus said to him, "**I promise** you that today you will
24.49 And I myself will send upon you what my Father has **promised.**
Jn 9.24 and said to him, "**Promise** before God that you will tell
Acts 1. 4 for the gift I told you about, the gift my Father **promised.**
2.30 He was a prophet, and he knew what God had **promised** him:
2.33 has received from him the Holy Spirit, as he had **promised.**
2.39 For God's **promise** was made to you and your children,
3.25 The **promises** of God through his prophets are for you,
7. 5 metre of ground, but God **promised** to give it to him,
7. 5 At the time God made this **promise,** Abraham had no children.
7.17 for God to keep the **promise** he had made to Abraham,
13.23 the Saviour of the people of Israel, as he had **promised.**
13.32 what God **promised** our ancestors he would do, he has now done
13.34 you the sacred and sure blessings that I **promised** to David.'
26. 6 hope I have in the **promise** that God made to our ancestors
Rom 1. 2 The Good News was **promised** long ago by God through his prophets,
1.31 they do not keep their **promises,** and they show no kindness
4.13 God **promised** Abraham and his descendants that the world would
4.14 For if what God **promises** is to be given to those who
4.14 then man's faith means nothing and God's **promise** is worthless.
4.16 And so the **promise** was based on faith,
4.16 in order that the **promise** should be guaranteed as God's free
4.17 So the **promise** is good in the sight of God, in whom
4.20 faith did not leave him, and he did not doubt God's **promise;**
4.21 sure that God would be able to do what he had **promised.**
9. 4 they have received God's **promises;**
9. 6 I am not saying that the **promise** of God has failed;
9. 7 through Isaac that you will have the descendants I **promised** you."
9. 8 of God's **promise** are regarded as the true descendants.
9. 9 For God's **promise** was made in these words:
15. 8 is faithful, to make his **promises** to their ancestors come true,
1 Cor 10.13 But God keeps his **promise,** and he will not allow you to
2 Cor 1.18 God speaks the truth, my **promise** to you was not a "Yes"
1.20 for it is he who is the "Yes" to all God's **promises.**
7. 1 All these **promises** are made to us, my dear friends.
9. 5 and get ready in advance the gift you **promised** to make.
11. 2 virgin whom I have **promised** in marriage to one man only,
11.10 Christ's truth in me, I **promise** that this boast of mine will
Gal 3.14 that the blessing which God **promised** to Abraham might be
3.14 through faith we might receive the Spirit **promised** by God.
3.16 Now, God made his **promises** to Abraham and to his descendant.
3.17 God made a covenant with Abraham and **promised** to keep it.
3.17 years later, cannot break that covenant and cancel God's **promise.**
3.18 on the Law, then it no longer depends on his **promise.**
3.18 it was because of his **promise** that God gave that gift to
3.19 the coming of Abraham's descendant, to whom the **promise** was made.
3.21 Does this mean that the Law is against God's **promises?**
3.22 so the gift which is **promised** on the basis of faith in
3.29 the descendants of Abraham and will receive what God has **promised.**
4.23 by the free woman was born as a result of God's **promise.**
4.28 God's children as a result of his **promise,** just as Isaac was.
Eph 1.13 on you by giving you the Holy Spirit he had **promised.**
1.14 shall receive what God has **promised** his people, and this assures
1.18 are the wonderful blessings he **promises** his people,
2.12 which were based on God's **promises** to his people, and you
3. 6 and share in the **promise** that God made through Christ Jesus.
6. 2 and mother" is the first commandment that has a **promise** added:
1 Tim 4. 8 in every way, because it **promises** life both for the present
5.12 and so become guilty of breaking their earlier **promise** to him.
2 Tim 1. 1 sent to proclaim the **promised** life which we have in union
Tit 1. 2 God, who does not lie, **promised** us this life before the
Heb 3.11 I was angry and made a solemn **promise:**
3.18 God made his solemn **promise,** "They will never enter the land
4. 1 God has offered us the **promise** that we may receive that rest
4. 1 will be found to have failed to receive that **promised** rest.
4. 3 We who believe, then, do receive that rest which God **promised.**
4. 3 just as he said, "I was angry and made a solemn **promise:**
4. 8 the rest that God had **promised,** God would not have spoken
4.10 that rest which God **promised** will rest from his own work,
6.12 and are patient, and so receive what God has **promised.**
6.13 When God made his **promise** to Abraham, he made a vow to
6.13 to Abraham, he made a vow to do what he had **promised.**
6.14 He said, "I **promise** you that I will bless you and give
6.15 Abraham was patient, and so he received what God had **promised.**
6.17 were to receive what he **promised,** God wanted to make it very
6.17 so he added his vow to the **promise.**
7. 6 from Abraham and blessed him, the man who received God's **promises.**
7.21 Lord has made a solemn **promise** and will not take it back:
7.28 but God's **promise** made with the vow, which came later than
8. 6 one, because it is based on **promises** of better things.
9.15 may receive the eternal blessings that God has **promised.**
10.23 we profess, because we can trust God to keep his **promise.**
Heb 10.36 order to do the will of God and receive what he **promises.**
11. 8 go out to a country which God had **promised** to give him.
11. 9 as a foreigner in the country that God had **promised** him.
11. 9 did Isaac and Jacob, who received the same **promise** from God.
11.11 He trusted God to keep his **promise.**
11.13 receive the things God had **promised,** but from a long way off
11.17 whom God had made the **promise,** yet he was ready to offer
11.18 "It is through Isaac that you will have the descendants I **promised.**"
11.20 faith that made Isaac **promise** blessings for the future to Jacob
11.33 They did what was right and received what God had **promised.**
11.39 not receive what God had **promised,** [40]because God had decided
12.24 to the sprinkled blood that **promises** much better things than
12.26 but now he has **promised,** "I will once more shake not
Jas 1.12 the life which God has **promised** to those who love him.
2. 5 possess the kingdom which he **promised** to those who love him.
5.12 my brothers, do not use an oath when you make a **promise.**
1 Pet 3. 9 a blessing is what God **promised** to give you when he called
3.21 of bodily dirt, but the **promise** made to God from a good
4.19 to their Creator, who always keeps his **promise.**
2 Pet 1. 4 great and precious gifts he **promised,** so that by means of
2.19 They **promise** them freedom while they themselves are slaves
3. 4 will mock you [4]and will ask, "He **promised** to come, didn't
3. 9 is not slow to do what he has **promised,** as some think.
3.13 But we wait for what God has **promised:**
1 Jn 1. 9 to God, he will keep his **promise** and do what is right:
2.25 this is what Christ himself **promised** to give us—eternal life.

PROMOTE

Esth 3. 1 Some time later King Xerxes **promoted** a man named Haman to
5.11 had, how the king had **promoted** him to high office, and how
10. 2 whole story of how he **promoted** Mordecai to high office, are
Dan 3.30 And the king **promoted** Shadrach, Meshach, and Abednego

PROMPTED

2 Chr 36.22 He **prompted** Cyrus to issue the following command and send it
Ezra 1. 1 He **prompted** Cyrus to issue the following command and send it

PROMPTLY

2 Chr 24. 5 He told them to act **promptly,** but the Levites delayed, [6]so
Ezra 6. 8 expenses are to be paid **promptly** out of the royal funds
7.21 of West Euphrates to provide **promptly** for Ezra, the priest
7.26 or the laws of the empire, he is to be punished **promptly:**

PRONOUNCE

Gen 48.20 "The Israelites will use your names when they **pronounce** blessings.
Ex 33.19 you and in your presence I will **pronounce** my sacred name.
34. 5 cloud, stood with him there, and **pronounced** his holy name,
Lev 13. 3 and the priest shall **pronounce** the person unclean.
13. 6 and has not spread, he shall **pronounce** him ritually clean;
13. 7 priest has examined him and **pronounced** him clean, he must
13. 8 again, and if it has spread, he shall **pronounce** him unclean;
13.11 The priest shall **pronounce** him unclean;
13.13 whole body, he shall **pronounce** the person ritually clean.
13.15 and if he sees an open sore, he shall **pronounce** him unclean.
13.17 ritually clean, and the priest shall **pronounce** him clean.
13.20 in it have turned white, he shall **pronounce** him unclean.
13.22 If the spot spreads, the priest shall **pronounce** him unclean;
13.23 boil, and the priest shall **pronounce** him ritually clean.
13.25 in the burn, and the priest shall **pronounce** him unclean.
13.27 skin-disease, and the priest shall **pronounce** him unclean.
13.28 The priest shall **pronounce** him ritually clean, because it is
13.30 skin-disease, and he shall **pronounce** the person unclean.
13.34 the surrounding skin, he shall **pronounce** him ritually clean.
13.35 spreads after he has been **pronounced** clean, [36]the priest
13.37 healed, and the priest shall **pronounce** him ritually clean.
13.44 sore, [44]the priest shall **pronounce** him unclean,
14. 2 day he is to be **pronounced** clean, he shall be brought to
14. 7 his skin-disease, and then he shall **pronounce** him clean.
14.48 replastered, he shall **pronounce** the house ritually clean,
Num 6.27 the Lord said, "If they **pronounce** my name as a blessing
22. 6 I know that when you **pronounce** a blessing, people are blessed,
22. 6 and when you **pronounce** a curse, they are placed under
Deut 10. 8 him as priests, and to **pronounce** blessings in his name.
21. 5 them to serve him and to **pronounce** blessings in his name.
27.12 Mount Gerizim when the blessings are **pronounced** on the people:
27.13 will stand on Mount Ebal when the curses are **pronounced:**
33. 1 Moses, the man of God, **pronounced** on the people of Israel
Judg 12. 6 "Sibboleth," because he could not **pronounce** it correctly.
1 Kgs 20.40 The king answered, "You have **pronounced** your own sentence,
2 Chr 19. 6 "Be careful in **pronouncing** judgement;
Ps 9.19 Bring the heathen before you and **pronounce** judgement on them.
76. 9 when you rose up to **pronounce** judgement, to save all the
Prov 24.24 If he **pronounces** a guilty person innocent, he will be
Is 9. 8 The Lord has **pronounced** judgement on the kingdom of Israel,
24. 6 So God has **pronounced** a curse on the earth.
Jer 4.12 It is the Lord himself who is **pronouncing** judgement on his people.
Dan 7.22 living for ever came and **pronounced** judgement in favour of

PROOF see PROVE

PROP

1 Kgs 22.35 raged on, King Ahab remained **propped** up in his chariot,
2 Chr 18.34 raged on, King Ahab remained **propped** up in his chariot,

PROPER

Lev 16. 2 Aaron that only at the **proper** time is he to go behind
16.32 The High Priest, **properly** ordained and consecrated
Num 15.24 the Lord, with the **proper** grain-offering and wine-offering.
28.14 The **proper** wine-offering is two litres of wine with each bull,
28.20 Offer the **proper** grain-offering of flour mixed with olive-oil:
28.28 Offer the **proper** grain-offering of flour mixed with olive-oil:
29. 3 Offer the **proper** grain-offering of flour mixed with olive-oil:
29. 9 Offer the **proper** grain-offering of flour mixed with olive-oil:
29.14 Offer the **proper** grain-offering of flour mixed with olive-oil:
Judg 9.16 Gideon's memory and treat his family **properly,**
1 Kgs 14.13 Jeroboam's family who will be **properly** buried, because he is
2 Chr 30. 1 Passover Festival at the **proper** time, in the first month,
Ezra 6. 5 returned to their **proper** place in the Jerusalem Temple."
Neh 13.31 to be brought at the **proper** times, and for the people to
Esth 1.20 husband with **proper** respect, whether he's rich or poor."
9.27 a Jew, that at the **proper** time each year these two days
9.31 days of Purim at the **proper** time, just as they had adopted
Ps 51.19 Then you will be pleased with **proper** sacrifices
Prov 5. 2 will know how to behave **properly,** and your words will show
Ecc 10.17 leaders who eat at the **proper** time, who control themselves
Is 28.27 instead he uses light sticks of the **proper** size.
Jer 33.20 the night, so that they always come at their **proper** times;
Ezek 44.20 They are to keep it a **proper** length.
Dan 8.12 there instead of offering the **proper** daily sacrifices, and
11.13 When the **proper** time comes, he will return with a large,
Mt 15. 2 They don't wash their hands in the **proper** way before they eat!"
21.43 and given to a people who will produce the **proper** fruits."
24.45 other servants to give them their food at the **proper** time.
Mk 7. 3 do not eat unless they wash their hands in the **proper** way;
7. 4 such as the **proper** way to wash cups, pots, copper
Lk 12.42 other servants their share of the food at the **proper** time.
Rom 13.13 conduct ourselves **properly,** as people who live in the light
1 Cor 4. 6 you may learn what the saying means, "Observe the **proper** rules."
7.35 do what is right and **proper,** and to give yourselves
7.36 that he is not acting **properly** towards the girl and if his
11.13 for yourselves whether it is **proper** for a woman to pray to
14.40 Everything must be done in a **proper** and orderly way.
15.23 But each one will be raised in his **proper** order:
15.38 he gives each seed its own **proper** body.
Col 1.17 and in union with him all things have their **proper** place.
1 Thes 5.12 you, our brothers, to pay **proper** respect to those who work
2 Thes 2. 6 At the **proper** time, then, the Wicked One will appear.
1 Tim 2. 2 life with all reverence towards God and with **proper** conduct.
2. 9 and sensible about their clothes and to dress **properly;**
2.10 with good deeds, as is **proper** for women who claim to be
1 Pet 3. 7 your wives with the **proper** understanding that they are the weaker
Jude 6 within the limits of their **proper** authority, but abandoned their

PROPERTY

Gen 15. 3 children, and one of my slaves will inherit my **property."**
15. 4 "This slave Eliezer will not inherit your **property;**
23.17 the **property** which had belonged to Ephron at Machpelah,
23.17 the trees in the field up to the edge of the **property.**
23.18 It was recognized as Abraham's **property** by all the
23.20 in it, became the **property** of Abraham for a burial-ground.
24.10 was in charge of Abraham's **property,** took ten of his
34.10 live anywhere you wish, trade freely, and own **property."**
47.11 brothers in Egypt, giving them **property** in the best of the
47.20 and all the land became the king's **property.**
47.26 Only the lands of the priests did not become the king's **property.**
Ex 21.21 The loss of his **property** is punishment enough.
22. 8 an oath that he has not stolen the other man's **property.**
22. 9 of a dispute about **property,** whether it involves cattle,
22. 9 the two men claiming the **property** shall be taken to the
Lev 25.10 During this year all **property** that has been sold shall be
25.13 In this year all **property** that has been sold shall be
25.30 the permanent **property** of the purchaser and his descendants;
25.32 at any time their **property** in the cities assigned to them.
25.33 are their permanent **property** among the people of Israel.
25.34 it is their **property** for ever.
25.41 return to his family and to the **property** of his ancestors.
25.45 your land may become your **property,** [46]and you may leave
27.21 the field will become the Lord's permanent **property;**
Num 18.20 "You will not receive any **property** that can be inherited,
18.23 Levites shall have no permanent **property** in Israel,
18.24 I told them that they would have no permanent **property** in Israel."
24.18 make their land his **property,** While Israel continues victorious.
26.62 because they were not given any **property** in Israel.
27. 4 Give us **property** among our father's relatives."
27. 7 give them **property** among their father's relatives.
27. 8 leaving a son, his daughter is to inherit his **property.**
27.11 relative is to inherit it and hold it as his own **property.**
32. 5 us this land as our **property,** and do not make us cross
32.19 not take possession of any **property** among them on the other
32.29 land, then give them the land of Gilead as their **property.**
32.30 receive their share of the **property** in the land of Canaan,
32.32 that we can retain our **property** here east of the Jordan."
33.54 giving a large piece of **property** to a large clan and a
34.14 Manasseh have received their **property,**
34.29 Lord assigned to divide the **property** for the people of
35. 2 the Israelites that from the **property** they receive they must
36. 2 commanded you to give the **property** of our relative
36. 3 tribe, their **property** will then belong to that tribe,
36. 4 when all **property** that has been sold is restored
36. 4 the **property** of Zelophehad's daughters will be permanently
36. 7 The **property** of every Israelite will remain attached to his tribe.
Num 36. 8 Every woman who inherits **property** in an Israelite tribe
36. 8 each Israelite will inherit the **property** of his ancestors,
36. 9 and the **property** will not pass from one tribe
36. 9 Each tribe will continue to possess its own **property."**
36.12 and their **property** remained in their father's tribe.
Deut 14.27 they have no **property** of their own.
14.29 Levites, since they own no **property,** and for the foreigners,
17. 8 such as certain cases of **property** rights or of bodily injury
21.16 is going to divide his **property** among his children, he is
25. 5 brothers live on the same **property** and one of them dies,
Judg 21.24 back to his own tribe and family and to his own **property.**
Ruth 4. 7 sale or an exchange of **property,** it was the custom for the
4.10 This will keep the **property** in the dead man's family, and
1 Sam 25.21 I ever protect that fellow's **property** out here in the wilderness?
2 Sam 19.29 I have decided that you and Ziba will share Saul's **property."**
1 Kgs 21.19 'After murdering the man, are you taking over his **property** as well?'
2 Kgs 25.12 poorest people, who owned no **property,** and put them to work
1 Chr 9. 2 to their **property** in the cities included Israelite laymen,
27.25 This is the list of those who administered the royal **property:**
28. 1 clans, the supervisors of the **property** and livestock that
29. 3 and gold from my personal **property** because of my love for
29. 6 the administrators of the royal **property** volunteered to give
Ezra 7.26 or by confiscation of his **property** or by imprisonment."
10. 8 within three days, all his **property** would be confiscated,
Neh 2.20 have no right to any **property** in Jerusalem, and you have no
5.12 We'll give the **property** back and not try to collect the debts."
5.16 into rebuilding the wall and did not acquire any **property.**
11. 3 Solomon's servants lived on their own **property** in their own towns.
11.20 Levites lived on their own **property** in the other cities and
Esth 8. 1 gave Queen Esther all the **property** of Haman, the enemy of
8. 2 Esther put Mordecai in charge of Haman's **property.**
8. 7 plot against the Jews, and I have given Esther his **property.**
Ps 109.11 creditors take away all his **property,** and may strangers get
Prov 15.25 of arrogant men, but he will protect a widow's **property.**
20.16 ought to have his own **property** held to guarantee payment.
27.13 to have his own **property** held to guarantee payment.
Ecc 5.19 gives a man wealth and **property** and lets him enjoy them, he
6. 2 wealth, honour, and **property,** yes, everything he wants,
Is 10. 2 you take the **property** that belongs to widows and orphans.
Jer 20. 5 seize all its possessions and **property,** even the treasures
37.12 Benjamin to take possession of my share of the family **property.**
39.10 poorest people, who owned no **property,** and he gave them
52.16 poorest people, who owned no **property,** and he put them to
Lam 5. 2 Our **property** is in the hands of strangers;
Ezek 22.25 take all the money and **property** they can get, and by their
38.12 now they have livestock and **property** and live at the
38.13 silver and gold, livestock and **property,** and to march off
44.28 They are not to hold **property** in Israel;
46.16 will belong to that son as a part of his family **property.**
46.17 it will become the prince's **property** again when the Year of
46.18 must not take any of the people's **property** away from them.
Dan 11.24 his followers the goods and **property** he has captured in war.
Mic 2. 2 No man's family or **property** is safe.
Mt 21.38 Come on, let's kill him, and we will get his **property!'**
24.47 master will put that servant in charge of all his **property.**
25.14 called his servants and put them in charge of his **property.**
Mk 12. 7 Come on, let's kill him, and his **property** will be ours!'
Lk 12.13 brother to divide with me the **property** our father left us."
12.14 right to judge or to divide the **property** between you two?"
12.44 master will put that servant in charge of all his **property.**
15.12 said to him, 'Father, give me my share of the **property** now.'
15.12 So the man divided his **property** between his two sons.
15.13 sold his part of the **property** and left home with the money.
15.30 wasted all your **property** on prostitutes, and when he comes
16. 1 once a rich man who had a servant who managed his **property.**
16. 2 of your handling of my **property,** because you cannot be my
20.14 Let's kill him, and his **property** will be ours!'
Acts 2.45 They would sell their **property** and possessions, and distribute
5. 1 with his wife Sapphira sold some **property** that belonged to them.
5. 3 by keeping part of the money you received for the **property?**
5. 4 Before you sold the **property,** it belonged to you;
5. 8 the full amount you and your husband received for your **property?"**
Rom 13. 7 pay them your personal and **property** taxes, and show respect
Gal 4. 1 will receive his father's **property** is treated just like a slave
4.30 a part of the father's **property** along with the son of the

Am **PROPERTY LINE** see **BOUNDARY (stone), BOUNDARY (mark)**

PROPHECY

Num 23. 7 Balaam uttered this **prophecy:**
23.18 and Balaam uttered this **prophecy:**
24. 3 of God took control of him, [3]and he uttered this **prophecy:**
24.15 Then he uttered this **prophecy:**
24.20 Balaam saw the Amalekites and uttered this **prophecy:**
24.21 In his vision he saw the Kenites, and uttered this **prophecy:**
24.23 Balaam uttered this **prophecy:**
1 Kgs 22. 8 But I hate him, because he never **prophesies** anything good for me;
22.10 and all the prophets were **prophesying** in front of them.
22.13 "All the other prophets have **prophesied** success for the king,
22.18 "Didn't I tell you that he never **prophesies** anything good for me?
2 Chr 9.29 Nathan the Prophet, in The **Prophecy** of Ahijah of Shiloh, and
15. 8 When Asa heard the **prophecy** that Azariah son of Oded had spoken,
18. 7 But I hate him because he never **prophesies** anything good for me;
18. 9 and all the prophets were **prophesying** in front of them.

2 Chr 18.12 “All the other prophets have **prophesied** success for the king,
18.17 “I told you that he never **prophesies** anything good for me;
24.27 the sons of Joash, the **prophecies** spoken against him, and
Jer 28. 6 hope he will make your **prophecy** come true and will bring
Ezek 4. 7 Shake your fist at the city and **prophesy** against it.
11.13 While I was **prophesying,** Pelatiah dropped dead.
12.24 Israel there will be no more false visions or misleading **prophecies.**
12.27 that your visions and **prophecies** are about the distant future.
13. 2 “denounce the prophets of Israel who make up their own **prophecies.**
20.46 **prophesy** against the forest of the south.
21. 9 The Lord said to me, [9]“Mortal man, **prophesy.**
21.14 “Now, mortal man, **prophesy.**
21.28 “Mortal man, **prophesy.**
30. 2 “Mortal man,” he said, **“prophesy** and announce what I,
34. 2 **Prophesy** to them, and tell them what I, the Sovereign Lord,
36. 3 **“Prophesy,** then, and announce what I, the Sovereign Lord,
36. 6 “So **prophesy** to the land of Israel;
37. 4 He said, **“Prophesy** to the bones.
37. 7 So I **prophesied** as I had been told.
37. 9 God said to me, “Mortal man, **prophesy** to the wind.
37.10 So I **prophesied** as I had been told.
37.12 So **prophesy** to my people Israel and tell them that I,
Dan 9.22 “Daniel, I have come here to help you understand the **prophecy.**
9.24 that the vision and the **prophecy** will come true, and the
Amos 7.13 Don’t **prophesy** here at Bethel any more.
7.14 “I am not the kind of prophet who **prophesies** for pay.
7.15 and ordered me to come and **prophesy** to his people Israel.
7.16 You tell me to stop **prophesying,** to stop raving against the
Obad 1 This is the **prophecy** of Obadiah—what the Sovereign Lord
Mic 2.11 and deceit and says, ‘I **prophesy** that wine and liquor will
Zech 13. 3 if anyone still insists on **prophesying,** his own father and
13. 3 When he **prophesies,** his own father and mother will stab him
Mt 13.14 So the **prophecy** of Isaiah applies to them:
15. 7 How right Isaiah was when he **prophesied** about you!
26.68 and those who slapped him [68]said, **“Prophesy** for us,
Mk 7. 6 “How right Isaiah was when he **prophesied** about you!
Jn 11.51 Priest that year, he was **prophesying** that Jesus was going to
2 Thes 2. 2 that we said this while **prophesying** or preaching, or that we
1 Tim 1.18 with the words of **prophecy** spoken in the past about you.
1 Pet 1.10 and they **prophesied** about this gift which God would
2 Pet 1.20 no one can explain by himself a **prophecy** in the Scriptures.
Jude 14 descendant from Adam, who long ago **prophesied** this about them:

PROPHET

[FALSE PROPHET, FELLOW-PROPHET, GROUP OF PROPHETS]
A person who proclaims a message from God. The word usually refers to certain men in the Old Testament, but the New Testament speaks of prophets in the early church. John the Baptist is also called a prophet.
see also **AMOS (1), DANIEL (1), ELIJAH, ELISHA, EZEKIEL, HABAKKUK, HAGGAI, HOSEA, ISAIAH, JEREMIAH, JOEL, JONAH, MALACHI, MICAH, NAHUM, OBADIAH, ZECHARIAH, ZEPHANIAH**

Gen 20. 7 He is a **prophet,** and he will pray for you, so that
Ex 7. 1 and your brother Aaron will speak to him as your **prophet.**
15.20 The **prophet** Miriam, Aaron’s sister, took her tambourine,
Num 11.25 them, they began to shout like **prophets,** but not for long.
11.26 came on them, and they too began to shout like **prophets.**
11.29 all his people and make all of them shout like **prophets!”**
12. 6 When there are **prophets** among you, I reveal myself to them
Deut 13. 1 “A **prophet** or an interpreter of dreams may promise a
13. 5 any interpreter of dreams or **prophet** that tells you to rebel
18.15 he will send you a **prophet** like me from among your own
18.18 I will send them a **prophet** like you from among their own
18.20 But if any **prophet** dares to speak a message in my name
18.20 and so must any **prophet** who speaks in the name
18.21 you can tell when a **prophet’s** message does not come from the
18.22 If a **prophet** speaks in the name of the Lord
18.22 That **prophet** has spoken on his own authority,
34.10 There has never been a **prophet** in Israel like Moses;
34.11 No other **prophet** has ever done miracles and wonders like
34.12 No other **prophet** has been able to do the great and
Judg 4. 4 wife of Lappidoth, was a **prophet,** and she was serving as a
6. 8 and he sent them a **prophet** who brought them this message
1 Sam 2.27 A **prophet** came to Eli with this message from the Lord:
3.20 other, knew that Samuel was indeed a **prophet** of the Lord.
9. 9 (At that time a **prophet** was called a seer, and so whenever
10. 5 you will meet a **group of prophets** coming down from the altar
10.10 his servant arrived at Gibeah, a **group of prophets** met him.
10.11 Has Saul become a **prophet?”**
10.12 asked, “How about these other **prophets**—who do you think
10.12 This is how the saying originated, “Has even Saul become a **prophet?”**
19.20 They saw the **group of prophets** dancing and shouting, with
19.24 (This is how the saying originated, “Has even Saul become a **prophet?”)**
22. 5 Then the **prophet** Gad came to David and said, “Don’t stay here;
28. 6 dreams or by the use of Urim and Thummim or by **prophets.**
28.15 He doesn’t answer me any more, either by **prophets** or by dreams.
2 Sam 7. 2 the king said to the **prophet** Nathan, “Here I am living in
12. 1 The Lord sent the **prophet** Nathan to David.
12.25 and commanded the **prophet** Nathan to name the boy Jedidiah,
24.11 Lord said to Gad, David’s **prophet,** “Go and tell David that
1 Kgs 1. 8 son of Jehoiada, Nathan the **prophet,** Shimei, Rei, and
1.10 Solomon or Nathan the **prophet,** or Benaiah, or the king’s bodyguard.
1.23 king was told that the **prophet** was there, and Nathan went in
11.29 was travelling from Jerusalem, the **prophet** Ahijah, from
1 Kgs 12.15 Jeroboam son of Nebat through the **prophet** Ahijah from Shiloh.
12.22 But God told the **prophet** Shemaiah [23]to give this
13. 1 At the Lord’s command a **prophet** from Judah went to Bethel
13. 2 Following the Lord’s command, the **prophet** denounced the altar:
13. 3 And the **prophet** went on to say, “This altar will fall apart,
13. 5 to the ground, as the **prophet** had predicted in the name of
13. 6 King Jeroboam said to the **prophet,** “Please pray for me to
13. 6 The **prophet** prayed to the Lord, and the king’s arm was healed.
13. 7 the king said to the **prophet,** “Come home with me and have
13. 8 The **prophet** answered, “Even if you gave me half your wealth,
13.11 At that time there was an old **prophet** living in Bethel.
13.11 and told him what the **prophet** from Judah had done in Bethel
13.12 the old **prophet** asked them.
13.14 down the road after the **prophet** from Judah and found him
13.14 “Are you the **prophet** from Judah?”
13.16 But the **prophet** from Judah answered, “I can’t go home
13.18 Then the old **prophet** from Bethel said to him,
13.18 “I, too, am a **prophet** just like you,
13.18 But the old **prophet** was lying.
13.19 So the **prophet** from Judah went home with the old prophet
13.20 Lord came to the old **prophet,**
13.21 he cried out to the **prophet** from Judah, “The Lord says that
13.23 the old **prophet** saddled the donkey for the prophet
13.26 When the old **prophet** heard about it, he said,
13.26 “That is the **prophet** who disobeyed the Lord’s command!
13.28 rode off and found the **prophet’s** body lying on the road,
13.29 The old **prophet** picked up the body, put it on the donkey,
13.31 After the burial, the **prophet** said to his sons, “When I
14. 2 go to Shiloh, where the **prophet** Ahijah lives, the one who
14.18 the Lord had said through his servant, the **prophet** Ahijah.
15.29 said through his servant, the **prophet** Ahijah from Shiloh,
16. 1 The Lord spoke to the **prophet** Jehu son of Hanani and gave
16. 7 family was given by the **prophet** Jehu because of the sins
16.12 said against Baasha through the **prophet** Jehu, Zimri killed
17. 1 A **prophet** named Elijah, from Tishbe in Gilead, said to King Ahab,
18. 4 Jezebel was killing the Lord’s **prophets,**
18.13 when Jezebel was killing the **prophets** of the Lord I hid a
18.19 Bring along the 450 **prophets** of Baal
18.19 and the 400 **prophets** of the goddess Asherah who are
18.20 all the Israelites and the **prophets** of Baal to meet at Mount
18.22 said, “I am the only **prophet** of the Lord still left,
18.22 but there are 450 **prophets** of Baal.
18.23 let the **prophets** of Baal take one, kill it, cut it in
18.24 Then let the **prophets** of Baal pray to their god, and I
18.25 Then Elijah said to the **prophets** of Baal, “Since there
18.28 So the **prophets** prayed louder and cut themselves
18.36 the **prophet** Elijah approached the altar and prayed,
18.40 Elijah ordered, “Seize the **prophets** of Baal;
19. 1 and how he had put all the **prophets** of Baal to death.
19. 2 do the same thing to you that you did to the **prophets.”**
19.10 you, torn down your altars, and killed all your **prophets.**
19.14 you, torn down your altars, and killed all your **prophets.**
19.16 Elisha son of Shaphat from Abel Meholah to succeed you as **prophet.**
20.13 Meanwhile, a **prophet** went to King Ahab and said,
20.14 The **prophet** answered, “The Lord says that the young
20.14 “You,” the **prophet** answered.
20.22 Then the **prophet** went to King Ahab and said, “Go back
20.28 A **prophet** went to King Ahab and said, “This is what
20.35 a member of a **group of prophets**
20.35 ordered a **fellow-prophet** to hit him.
20.37 Then this same **prophet** went to another man and said,
20.38 The **prophet** bandaged his face with a cloth, to disguise himself,
20.39 king was passing by, the **prophet** called out to him and said,
20.41 The **prophet** tore the cloth from his face,
20.41 and at once the king recognized him as one of the **prophets.**
20.42 The **prophet** then said to the king, “This is the word of
21.17 Lord said to Elijah, the **prophet** from Tishbe, [18]“Go to
21.28 The Lord said to the **prophet** Elijah, [29]“Have you
22. 6 So Ahab called in the **prophets,** about four hundred of them,
22. 7 Jehoshaphat asked, “Isn’t there another **prophet** through
22.10 and all the **prophets** were prophesying in front of them.
22.12 All the other **prophets** said the same thing.
22.13 “All the other **prophets** have prophesied success for the king,
22.22 replied, ‘I will go and make all Ahab’s **prophets** tell lies.’
22.23 The Lord has made these **prophets** of yours lie to you.
22.24 Then the **prophet** Zedekiah went up to Micaiah, slapped his face,
2 Kgs 1. 3 the Lord commanded Elijah, the **prophet** from Tishbe, to go
2. 3 A **group of prophets** who lived there went to Elisha and
2. 5 A **group of prophets** who lived there went to Elisha and
2. 7 on, [7]and fifty of the **prophets** followed them to the Jordan.
2. 7 river, and the fifty **prophets** stood a short distance away.
2.15 The fifty **prophets** from Jericho saw him and said, “The
3.11 Jehoshaphat asked, “Is there a **prophet** here through whom we
3.12 “He is a true **prophet,”** King Jehoshaphat said.
3.13 consult those **prophets** that your father and mother consulted.”
4. 1 a member of a **group of prophets** went to Elisha and said,
4. 7 went back to Elisha, the **prophet,** who said to her, “Sell
4.22 I need to go to the **prophet** Elisha.
4.38 he was teaching a **group of prophets,** he told his servant to
4.42 feed the **group of prophets** with this, [43]but he answered,
5. 3 that my master could go to the **prophet** who lives in Samaria!
5. 8 When the **prophet** Elisha heard what had happened, he sent word
5. 8 and I’ll show him that there is a **prophet** in Israel!”
5.13 and said, “Sir, if the **prophet** had told you to do something
5.22 two members of the **group of prophets** in the hill-country of
6. 1 One day the **group of prophets** that Elisha was in charge of
6.12 The **prophet** Elisha tells the king of Israel what you say
8. 8 “Take a gift to the **prophet,** and ask him to consult the
9. 1 Meanwhile the **prophet** Elisha called one of the young prophets
9. 4 So the young **prophet** went to Ramoth, [5]where he found the

2 Kgs 9. 6 went indoors, and the young **prophet** poured the olive-oil on
9. 7 I may punish Jezebel for murdering my **prophets**
9.10 After saying this, the young **prophet** left the room and fled.
10.10 The Lord has done what he promised through his **prophet** Elijah."
10.19 Call together all the **prophets** of Baal, all his worshippers,
13.14 The **prophet** Elisha fell ill with a fatal disease, and
13.17 Then, following the **prophet's** instructions, the king
13.17 arrow, the **prophet** exclaimed, "You are the Lord's arrow,
14.25 promised through his servant the **prophet** Jonah son of Amittai,
17.13 Lord had sent his messengers and **prophets** to warn Israel and Judah:
17.13 which I handed on to you through my servants the **prophets."**
17.23 warned through his servants the **prophets** that he would do.
19. 2 and the senior priests to the **prophet** Isaiah son of Amoz.
20. 1 The **prophet** Isaiah son of Amoz went to see him and said
20.14 Then the **prophet** Isaiah went to King Hezekiah and asked,
21.10 Through his servants the **prophets** the Lord said,
22.14 a woman named Huldah, a **prophet** who lived in the newer part
23. 2 by the priests and the **prophets** and all the rest of the
23.16 the altar, doing what the **prophet** had predicted long before
23.16 saw the tomb of the **prophet** who had made this prediction.
23.17 is the tomb of the **prophet** who came from Judah and predicted
23.18 were those of the **prophet** who had come from Samaria.
24. 2 Lord had said through his servants the **prophets** that he would do.
1 Chr 9.22 was King David and the **prophet** Samuel who had put their
16.22 do not touch my **prophets."**
17. 1 day he sent for the **prophet** Nathan and said to him, "Here
21. 9 Lord said to Gad, David's **prophet,** [10]"Go and tell David
25. 5 gave to Heman, the king's **prophet,** these fourteen sons and
26.28 the gifts brought by the **prophet** Samuel, by King Saul, by
29.29 recorded in the records of the three **prophets,** Samuel,
2 Chr 9.29 The History of Nathan the **Prophet,** in The Prophecy of Ahijah
9.29 The Visions of Iddo the **Prophet,** which also deal with the
10.15 Jeroboam son of Nebat through the **prophet** Ahijah from Shiloh.
11. 2 But the Lord told the **prophet** Shemaiah [3]to give this
12. 5 Shemaiah the **prophet** went to King Rehoboam and the Judaean
12.15 The History of Shemaiah the **Prophet**
12.15 and The History of Iddo the **Prophet.**
13.22 what he did, is written in The History of Iddo the **Prophet.**
16. 7 At that time the **prophet** Hanani went to King Asa and said,
16.10 Asa so angry with the **prophet** that he had him put in
18. 5 So Ahab called in the **prophets,** about four hundred of them,
18. 6 Jehoshaphat asked, "Isn't there another **prophet** through
18. 9 and all the **prophets** were prophesying in front of them.
18.11 All the other **prophets** said the same thing.
18.12 "All the other **prophets** have prophesied success for the king,
18.21 replied, 'I will go and make all Ahab's **prophets** tell lies.'
18.22 The Lord has made these **prophets** of yours lie to you.
18.23 Then the **prophet** Zedekiah went up to Micaiah, slapped his face,
19. 2 A **prophet,** Jehu son of Hanani, went to meet the king and
20.20 Believe what his **prophets** tell you, and you will succeed."
21.12 The **prophet** Elijah sent Jehoram a letter, which read as follows:
24.19 The Lord sent **prophets** to warn them to return to him,
25. 7 But a **prophet** went to the king and said to him, "Don't
25. 9 Amaziah asked the **prophet,** "But what about all that silver
25. 9 The **prophet** replied, "The Lord can give you back more than that!"
25.15 This made the Lord angry, so he sent a **prophet** to Amaziah.
25.15 The **prophet** demanded, "Why have you worshipped foreign gods
25.16 The **prophet** stopped, but not before saying, "Now I know
26.22 The **prophet** Isaiah son of Amoz recorded all the other
28. 9 A man named Oded, a **prophet** of the Lord, lived in the
29.25 King David through Gad, the king's **prophet,**
29.25 and through the **prophet** Nathan;
29.30 praise that were written by David and by Asaph the **prophet.**
32.20 Then King Hezekiah and the **prophet** Isaiah son of Amoz
32.32 in The Vision of the **Prophet** Isaiah Son of Amoz and in
33.18 and the messages of the **prophets** who spoke to him in the
33.19 worshipped—are all recorded in The History of the **Prophets.**
34.22 a woman named Huldah, a **prophet** who lived in the newer part
35.15 Asaph, Heman, and Jeduthun, the king's **prophet.**
35.18 Since the days of the **prophet** Samuel, the Passover had
35.25 The **prophet** Jeremiah composed a lament for King Josiah.
36.12 not listen humbly to the **prophet** Jeremiah, who spoke the
36.15 had continued to send **prophets** to warn his people,
36.16 words and laughing at his **prophets,** until at last the Lord's
36.21 Lord had foretold through the **prophet** Jeremiah was fulfilled:
36.22 Lord made what he had said through the **prophet** Jeremiah come true.
Ezra 1. 1 Lord made what he had said through the **prophet** Jeremiah come true.
5. 1 At that time two **prophets,** Haggai and Zechariah son of Iddo,
5. 2 the Temple in Jerusalem, and the two **prophets** helped them.
6.14 the Temple, encouraged by the **prophets** Haggai and Zechariah.
9.11 that you gave us through your servants, the **prophets.**
Neh 6. 7 you have arranged for some **prophets** to proclaim in Jerusalem
6.14 Nodiah and all the other **prophets** who tried to frighten me."
9.26 They killed the **prophets** who warned them, who told them to
9.30 You inspired your **prophets** to speak, but your people were deaf,
9.32 our leaders, our priests and **prophets,** our ancestors, and
Ps 74. 9 there are no **prophets** left, and no one knows how long this
105.15 do not touch my **prophets."**
Is 3. 2 their **prophets,** their fortune-tellers and their statesmen,
9.15 head—and the tail is the **prophets** whose teachings are lies!
28. 7 Even the **prophets** and the priests are so drunk that they stagger.
28. 7 The **prophets** are too drunk to understand the visions that God sends,
29.10 The **prophets** should be the eyes of the people,
29.11 The meaning of every **prophetic** vision will be hidden from you;
30.10 They tell the **prophets** to keep quiet.
37. 2 and the senior priests to the **prophet** Isaiah son of Amoz.
Is 38. 1 The **prophet** Isaiah son of Amoz went to see him and said
39. 3 Then the **prophet** Isaiah went to King Hezekiah and asked,
Jer 1. 5 were born I selected you to be a **prophet** to the nations."
2. 8 the **prophets** spoke in the name of Baal and worshipped useless idols.
2.26 disgraced—your kings and officials, your priests and **prophets.**
2.30 Like a raging lion, you have murdered your **prophets.**
4. 9 priests will be shocked and **prophets** will be astonished."
5.13 They have said that the **prophets** are nothing but
5.31 **prophets** speak nothing but lies;
5.31 as the **prophets** command, and my people offer no objections.
6.13 even **prophets** and priests cheat the people.
7.25 day, I have kept on sending my servants, the **prophets,** to
8. 1 of the priests, of the **prophets,** and of the other people who
8.10 Even **prophets** and priests cheat the people.
13.13 the priests, the **prophets,** and all the people of Jerusalem.
14.13 Lord, you know that the **prophets** are telling the people that
14.14 But the Lord replied, "The **prophets** are telling lies in my name;
14.15 going to do to those **prophets** whom I did not send but
14.18 **Prophets** and priests carry on their work, but they don't
15.19 proclaim a worthwhile message, you will be my **prophet** again.
18.18 to give us counsel, and **prophets** to proclaim God's message.
23.11 "The **prophets** and the priests are godless;
23.13 I have seen the sin of Samaria's **prophets:**
23.14 But I have seen the **prophets** in Jerusalem do even worse:
23.15 I, the Lord Almighty, say about the **prophets** of Jerusalem:
23.16 of Jerusalem, "Do not listen to what the **prophets** say;
23.18 I said, "None of these **prophets** has ever known the
23.21 "I did not send these **prophets,** but even so they went.
23.25 I know what those **prophets** have said who speak lies in
23.26 How much longer will those **prophets** mislead my people
23.28 The **prophet** who has had a dream should say it is only a dream,
23.28 but the **prophet** who has heard my message
23.30 I am against those **prophets** who take each other's words
23.31 I am also against those **prophets** who speak their own
23.32 I am against the **prophets** who tell their dreams that are
23.33 of my people or a **prophet** or a priest asks you, 'What
23.34 of my people or a **prophet** or a priest even uses the
23.37 Jeremiah, ask the **prophets,** 'What answer did the Lord give you?
25. 4 Lord has continued to send you his servants the **prophets.**
26. 5 words of my servants, the **prophets,** whom I have kept on
26. 7 The priests, the **prophets,** and all the people heard me
26.11 Then the priests and the **prophets** said to the leaders
26.16 to the priests and the **prophets,** "This man spoke to us in
26.18 was king of Judah, the **prophet** Micah of Moresheth told all
27. 9 Do not listen to your **prophets** or to anyone who claims he
27.14 Do not listen to the **prophets** who tell you not to
27.15 you and the **prophets** who are telling you these lies."
27.16 "Do not listen to the **prophets** who say that the temple
27.18 If they are really **prophets** and if they have my message,
28. 1 Hananiah son of Azzur, a **prophet** from the town of Gibeon,
28. 8 The **prophets** who spoke long ago, before my time and yours,
28. 9 But a **prophet** who predicts peace can only be recognized
28. 9 as a **prophet** whom the Lord has truly sent
28. 9 when that **prophet's** predictions come true."
29. 1 to the priests, the **prophets,** the leaders of the people,
29. 8 yourselves be deceived by the **prophets** who live among you or
29.15 "You say that the Lord has given you **prophets** in Babylonia.
29.19 I kept on sending to them through my servants the **prophets.**
29.26 who pretends to be a **prophet** is placed in chains with an
29.27 Anathoth, who has been speaking as a **prophet** to the people?
29.31 as if he were a **prophet,** and he made you believe lies.
32.32 with their kings and leaders, their priests and **prophets.**
35. 4 room of the disciples of the **prophet** Hanan son of Igdaliah.
35.15 you all my servants the **prophets,** and they have told you to
37.19 What happened to your **prophets** who told you that the
44. 4 sending you my servants the **prophets,** who told you not to do
50.36 Death to its lying **prophets—** what fools they are!
Lam 2. 9 taught, and the **prophets** have no visions from the Lord.
2.14 Your **prophets** had nothing to tell you but lies;
2.20 Priests and **prophets** are being killed in the Temple itself!
4.13 But it happened because her **prophets** sinned and her
Ezek 2. 5 or not, they will know that a **prophet** has been among them.
7.26 You will beg the **prophets** to reveal what they foresee.
13. 2 man," he said, "denounce the **prophets** of Israel who make
13. 3 "These foolish **prophets** are doomed!
13. 4 People of Israel, your **prophets** are as useless as foxes
13. 9 am about to punish you **prophets** who have false visions and
13.10 "The **prophets** mislead my people by saying that all is well.
13.10 loose stones, and then the **prophets** have come and covered it
13.11 Tell the **prophets** that their wall is going to fall down.
13.16 those who whitewashed it— [16]those **prophets** who assured
14. 4 then comes to consult a **prophet,** will get an answer from me
14. 7 then goes to consult a **prophet,** I, the Lord, will give him
14. 9 "If a **prophet** is deceived into giving a false answer, it
14.10 Both the **prophet** and the one who consults him will get
22.28 The **prophets** have hidden these sins like men covering a
33.33 they will know that a **prophet** has been among them."
38.17 announced through my servants, the **prophets** of Israel, that
Dan 9. 2 according to what the Lord had told the **prophet** Jeremiah.
9. 6 listened to your servants the **prophets,** who spoke in your
9.10 laws which you gave us through your servants the **prophets.**
Hos 4. 5 day you blunder on, and the **prophets** do no better than you.
6. 5 why I have sent my **prophets** to you with my message of
9. 7 "This **prophet,"** you say, "is a fool.
9. 8 God has sent me as a **prophet** to warn his people Israel.
9. 8 Even in God's Temple the people are the **prophet's** enemies.
12.10 "I spoke to the **prophets** and gave them many visions,
12.10 and through the **prophets** I gave my people warnings.
12.13 The Lord sent a **prophet** to rescue the people of Israel
Amos 2.11 of your sons to be **prophets,** and some of your young men

Amos 2.12 and ordered the **prophets** not to speak my message.
3. 7 without revealing his plan to his servants, the **prophets.**
7.12 Amaziah then said to Amos, "That's enough, **prophet!**
7.14 "I am not the kind of **prophet** who prophesies for pay.
Mic 2.11 people want the kind of **prophet** who goes about full of lies
3. 5 My people are deceived by **prophets** who promise peace to
3. 5 To these **prophets** the Lord says,
3. 6 **"Prophets,** your day is almost over;
3. 6 you will have no more **prophetic** visions, and you will not be
3.11 the Law for pay, the **prophets** give their revelations for
7. 4 as he warned them through their watchmen, the **prophets.**
Hab 1. 1 the message that the Lord revealed to the **prophet** Habakkuk.
3. 1 This is a prayer of the **prophet** Habakkuk:
Zeph 3. 4 The **prophets** are irresponsible and treacherous;
Hag 1. 1 the sixth month, the Lord spoke through the **prophet** Haggai.
1. 3 message to the people through the **prophet** Haggai:
1.12 They were afraid and obeyed the **prophet** Haggai,
2. 1 same year, the Lord spoke again through the **prophet** Haggai.
2.10 the Lord Almighty spoke again to the **prophet** Haggai.
Zech 1. 1 gave this message to the **prophet** Zechariah, the son of
1. 4 Long ago the **prophets** gave them my message, telling them not
1. 5 Your ancestors and those **prophets** are no longer alive.
1. 6 Through my servants the **prophets** I gave your ancestors commands
7. 3 and to ask the priests and the **prophets** this question:
7. 7 Lord said through the earlier **prophets** at the time when
7.12 which I sent through the **prophets** who lived long ago, I
8. 9 hearing the same words the **prophets** spoke at the time the
13. 2 who claims to be a **prophet** and will take away the desire
13. 4 When that time comes, no **prophet** will be proud of his visions,
13. 4 or act like a **prophet,**
13. 4 or wear a **prophet's** coarse garment in order to deceive
13. 5 Instead, he will say, 'I am not a **prophet.**
Mal 4. 5 day of the Lord comes, I will send you the **prophet** Elijah.
Mt 1.22 Lord had said through the **prophet** come true, [23] "A virgin will
2. 5 "For this is what the **prophet** wrote:
2.15 Lord had said through the **prophet** come true, "I called my
2.17 In this way what the **prophet** Jeremiah had said came true:
2.23 And so what the **prophets** had said came true:
3. 3 John was the man the **prophet** Isaiah was talking about when
4.14 done to make what the **prophet** Isaiah had said come true,
5.12 This is how the **prophets** who lived before you were persecuted.
5.17 with the Law of Moses and the teachings of the **prophets.**
7.12 of the Law of Moses and of the teachings of the **prophets.**
7.15 "Be on your guard against **false prophets;**
7.20 So then, you will know the **false prophets** by what they do.
8.17 this to make what the **prophet** Isaiah had said come true,
11. 9 A **prophet?**
11. 9 Yes indeed, but you saw much more than a **prophet.**
11.13 time of John all the **prophets** and the Law of Moses spoke
12.17 what God had said through the **prophet** Isaiah come true:
12.39 you will be given is the miracle of the **prophet** Jonah.
13.17 assure you that many **prophets** and many of God's people wanted
13.35 this to make what the **prophet** had said come true, "I will
13.57 Jesus said to them, "A **prophet** is respected everywhere except
14. 5 Jewish people, because they considered John to be a **prophet.**
16.14 "Others say Elijah, while others say Jeremiah or some other **prophet."**
21. 4 in order to make what the **prophet** had said come true:
21.11 "This is the **prophet** Jesus, from Nazareth in Galilee,"
21.26 because they are all convinced that John was a **prophet."**
21.46 afraid of the crowds, who considered Jesus to be a **prophet.**
22.40 the teachings of the **prophets** depend on these two commandments."
23.29 make fine tombs for the **prophets** and decorate the monuments of
23.30 would not have done what they did and killed the **prophets.**
23.31 that you are the descendants of those who murdered the **prophets!**
23.34 that I will send you **prophets** and wise men and teachers;
23.37 You kill the **prophets** and stone the messengers God has sent you!
24.11 Then many **false prophets** will appear and deceive many people.
24.15 "You will see 'The Awful Horror' of which the **prophet** Daniel spoke.
24.24 For false Messiahs and **false prophets** will appear;
26.56 to make what the **prophets** wrote in the Scriptures come true."
27. 9 Then what the **prophet** Jeremiah had said came true:
Mk 1. 2 It began as the **prophet** Isaiah had written:
6. 4 Jesus said to them, "A **prophet** is respected everywhere except
6.15 "He is a prophet, like one of the **prophets** of long ago."
8.28 Elijah, while others say that you are one of the **prophets."**
11.32 because everyone was convinced that John had been a **prophet.)**
13.22 For false Messiahs and **false prophets** will appear.
Lk 1.17 of the Lord, strong and mighty like the **prophet** Elijah.
1.70 He promised through his holy **prophets** long ago
1.76 my child, will be called a **prophet** of the Most High God.
2.36 There was a very old **prophetess,** a widow named Anna,
3. 4 As it is written in the book of the **prophet** Isaiah:
4.17 and was handed the book of the **prophet** Isaiah.
4.24 Jesus added, "a **prophet** is never welcomed in his home
4.27 who lived in Israel during the time of the **prophet** Elisha;
6.23 For their ancestors did the very same things to the **prophets.**
6.26 said the very same things about the **false prophets.**
7.16 "A great **prophet** has appeared among us!"
7.26 A **prophet?**
7.26 Yes indeed, but you saw much more than a **prophet.**
7.39 this man really were a **prophet,** he would know who this woman
9. 8 others that one of the **prophets** of long ago had come back
9.19 say that one of the **prophets** of long ago has come back
10.24 I tell you that many **prophets** and kings wanted to see
11.30 the same way that the **prophet** Jonah was a sign for the
11.47 make fine tombs for the **prophets**—
11.47 the very **prophets** your ancestors murdered.
Lk 11.48 they murdered the **prophets,** and you build their tombs.
11.49 Wisdom of God said, 'I will send them **prophets** and messengers;
11.50 the murder of all the **prophets** killed since the creation of
13.28 and Jacob, and all the **prophets** in the Kingdom of God,
13.33 is not right for a **prophet** to be killed anywhere except in
13.34 You kill the **prophets,** you stone the messengers God has sent you!
16.16 and the writings of the **prophets** were in effect up to the
16.29 'Your brothers have Moses and the **prophets** to warn them;
16.31 listen to Moses and the **prophets,** they will not be convinced
18.31 where everything the **prophets** wrote about the Son of Man
20. 6 us, because they are convinced that John was a **prophet."**
24.19 "This man was a **prophet** and was considered by God and by
24.25 how slow you are to believe everything the **prophets** said!
24.27 the books of Moses and the writings of all the **prophets.**
24.44 the writings of the **prophets,** and the Psalms had to come
Jn 1.21 "Are you the **Prophet?"**
1.23 John answered by quoting the **prophet** Isaiah:
1.25 Messiah nor Elijah nor the **Prophet,** why do you baptize?"
1.45 the book of the Law and whom the **prophets** also wrote about.
4.19 "I see you are a **prophet,** sir," the woman said.
4.44 he himself had said, "A **prophet** is not respected in his own
6.14 said, "Surely this is the **Prophet** who was to come into the
6.45 The **prophets** wrote, 'Everyone will be taught by God.'
7.40 him say this and said, "This man is really the **Prophet!"**
7.52 and you will learn that no **prophet** ever comes from Galilee."
8.52 Abraham died, and the **prophets** died, yet you say that whoever
8.53 And the **prophets** also died.
9.17 "He is a **prophet,"** the man answered.
12.38 so that what the **prophet** Isaiah had said might come true:
Acts 2.16 Instead, this is what the **prophet** Joel spoke about:
2.30 He was a **prophet,** and he knew what God had promised him:
3.18 ago through all the **prophets** that his Messiah had to suffer;
3.21 as God announced through his holy **prophets** who lived long ago.
3.22 God will send you a **prophet,** just as he sent me,
3.23 does not obey that **prophet** shall be separated from God's people
3.24 And all the **prophets** who had a message, including Samuel
3.25 promises of God through his **prophets** are for you, and you
7.37 'God will send you a **prophet,** just as he sent me,
7.42 of heaven, as it is written in the book of the **prophets:**
7.48 as the **prophet** says, [49] 'Heaven is my throne, says the Lord,
7.52 Was there any **prophet** that your ancestors did not persecute?
8.27 along, he was reading from the book of the **prophet** Isaiah.
8.30 and heard him reading from the book of the **prophet** Isaiah.
8.34 "Tell me, of whom is the **prophet** saying this?
10.43 the **prophets** spoke about him, saying that everyone who believes
11.27 About that time some **prophets** went from Jerusalem to Antioch.
13. 1 In the church at Antioch there were some **prophets** and teachers:
13. 6 magician named Bar-Jesus, a Jew who claimed to be a **prophet.**
13.15 the writings of the **prophets,** the officials of the synagogue sent
13.20 he gave them judges until the time of the **prophet** Samuel.
13.27 understand the words of the **prophets** that are read every Sabbath.
13.27 Yet they made the **prophets'** words come true by condemning Jesus.
13.40 so that what the **prophets** said may not happen to you:
15.15 The words of the **prophets** agree completely with this.
15.32 and Silas, who were themselves **prophets,** spoke a long time with
21.10 for several days when a **prophet** named Agabus arrived from Judaea.
24.14 written in the Law of Moses and the books of the **prophets.**
26.22 very same thing which the **prophets** and Moses said was going
26.27 King Agrippa, do you believe the **prophets?**
28.23 from the Law of Moses and the writings of the **prophets.**
28.25 Holy Spirit spoke through the **prophet** Isaiah to your ancestors!
Rom 1. 2 by God through his **prophets,** as written in the Holy Scriptures.
3.21 the Law of Moses and the **prophets** gave their witness to it.
11. 3 "Lord, they have killed your **prophets** and torn down your altars;
16.26 brought out into the open through the writings of the **prophets;**
1 Cor 12.28 in the second place **prophets,** and in the third place teachers;
12.29 They are not all apostles or **prophets** or teachers.
Eph 2.20 laid by the apostles and **prophets,** the cornerstone being Christ
3. 5 it now by the Spirit to his holy apostles and **prophets.**
4.11 be apostles, others to be **prophets,** others to be evangelists,
1 Thes 2.15 who killed the Lord Jesus and the **prophets,** and persecuted us.
1 Tim 4.14 given to you when the **prophets** spoke and the elders laid
Tit 1.12 himself, one of their own **prophets,** who spoke the truth when
Heb 1. 1 in many ways through the **prophets,** [2] but in these last days
11.32 Gideon, Barak, Samson, Jephthah, David, Samuel, and the **prophets.**
Jas 5.10 My brothers, remember the **prophets** who spoke in the name of
1 Pet 1.10 concerning this salvation that the **prophets** made careful search
1.12 God revealed to these **prophets** that their work was not for
2 Pet 1.19 are even more confident of the message proclaimed by the **prophets.**
1.21 For no **prophetic** message ever came just from the will of man,
2. 1 **False prophets** appeared in the past among the people, and
2.16 spoke with a human voice and stopped the **prophet's** insane action.
3. 2 long ago by the holy **prophets,** and the command from the Lord
1 Jn 4. 1 For many **false prophets** have gone out everywhere.
4. 4 children, and have defeated the **false prophets,** because the
4. 5 Those **false prophets** speak about matters of the world, and
Rev 1. 3 to the words of this **prophetic** message and obey what is
10. 7 his secret plan, as he announced to his servants, the **prophets."**
11.10 because those two **prophets** brought much suffering upon mankind.
11.12 Then the two **prophets** heard a loud voice say to them
11.18 to reward your servants, the **prophets,** and all your people,
16. 6 God's people and of the **prophets,** and so you have given them
16.13 the mouth of the beast, and the mouth of the **false prophet.**
18.20 Be glad, God's people and the apostles and **prophets!**
18.24 because the blood of **prophets** and of God's people was found
19.10 For the truth that Jesus revealed is what inspires the **prophets.**

Rev 19.20 taken prisoner, together with the **false prophet** who had
19.20 The beast and the **false prophet** were both thrown alive into
20.10 the beast and the **false prophet** had already been thrown;
22. 6 gives his Spirit to the **prophets**, has sent his angel to show
22. 7 Happy are those who obey the **prophetic** words in this book!"
22. 9 and of your brothers the **prophets** and of all those who obey
22.10 "Do not keep the **prophetic** words of this book a secret,
22.18 solemnly warn everyone who hears the **prophetic** words of this book:
22.19 takes anything away from the **prophetic** words of this book,

AV **PROPITIATION** see **FORGIVE**

PROPORTION

1 Cor 16. 2 put aside some money, in **proportion** to what he has earned,
Eph 4. 7 received a special gift in **proportion** to what Christ has given.

PROPOSE

Gen 34.24 Hamor and Shechem **proposed,** and all the males were circumcised.
1 Sam 25.39 Then David sent a **proposal** of marriage to Abigail.
1 Kgs 15.20 King Benhadad agreed to Asa's **proposal** and sent his
2 Chr 13. 8 Now you **propose** to fight against the royal authority that
16. 4 Benhadad agreed to Asa's **proposal** and sent his commanding
Ezra 10. 5 take an oath that they would do what Shecaniah had **proposed.**
Acts 1.23 So they **proposed** two men:
6. 5 was pleased with the apostles' **proposal,** so they chose Stephen,

PROSPER

Gen 26.13 He continued to **prosper** and became a very rich man.
26.22 to live in the land, and we will be **prosperous** here."
30.29 for you and how your flocks have **prospered** under my care.
Lev 25.26 it back may later become **prosperous** and have enough to buy
Num 10.29 has promised to make Israel **prosperous,**
10.29 come with us, and we will share our **prosperity** with you."
Deut 1.11 thousand times more and make you **prosperous,** as he promised!
6.10 with large and **prosperous** cities which you did not build.
6.24 he will always watch over our nation and keep it **prosperous.**
22. 7 bird go, so that you will live a long and **prosperous** life.
23. 6 anything to help these nations or to make them **prosperous.**
28.13 you will always **prosper** and never fail if you obey
28.29 You will not **prosper** in anything you do.
28.63 took delight in making you **prosper** and in making you
30. 3 he has scattered you, and he will make you **prosperous** again.
30. 5 he will make you more **prosperous** and more numerous than your
30. 9 The Lord will make you **prosperous** in all that you do;
30. 9 as glad to make you **prosperous** as he was
30. 9 to make your ancestors **prosperous,** [10] but you will have to obey
30.16 his laws, then you will **prosper** and become a nation of many
33.18 "May Zebulun be **prosperous** in their trade on the sea, And
Josh 1. 8 Then you will be **prosperous** and successful.
2 Sam 5.12 making his kingdom **prosperous** for the sake of his people.
1 Kgs 1.37 and make his reign even more **prosperous** than yours."
1.47 and may Solomon's reign be even more **prosperous** than yours.'
2. 3 that wherever you go you may **prosper** in everything you do.
1 Chr 14. 2 making his kingdom **prosperous** for the sake of his people.
2 Chr 7.14 forgive their sins, and make their land **prosperous** again.
14. 7 And so they built and **prospered.**
Ezra 9.12 and never to help them **prosper** or succeed if we wanted to
Job 20.21 nothing left over, but now his **prosperity** comes to an end.
21. 7 does God let evil men live, let them grow old and **prosper?**
22.18 was God who made them **prosperous**— I can't understand the
24.24 a while the wicked man **prospers,** but then he withers like a
29. 4 when I was **prosperous,** and the friendship of God protected
30.15 gone like a puff of wind, and my **prosperity** like a cloud.
36.11 him, they live out their lives in peace and **prosperity.**
42.10 friends, the Lord made him **prosperous** again and gave him
Ps 14. 7 Israel will be when the Lord makes them **prosperous** again!
22.26 May they **prosper** for ever!
25.13 They will always be **prosperous,**
37. 7 be worried about those who **prosper** or those who succeed in
37.11 the humble will possess the land and enjoy **prosperity** and peace.
44. 2 punished the other nations and caused your own to **prosper.**
53. 6 of Israel will be when God makes them **prosperous** again!
72. 3 May the land enjoy **prosperity;**
72. 7 in his lifetime, and may **prosperity** last as long as the moon
85. 1 you have made Israel **prosperous** again.
85.12 The Lord will make us **prosperous,** and our land will produce
92. 7 the wicked may grow like weeds, those who do wrong may **prosper;**
106. 5 Let me see the **prosperity** of your people and share in the
112. 3 be wealthy and rich, and he will be **prosperous** for ever.
122. 6 "May those who love you **prosper.**
122. 9 the house of the Lord our God I pray for your **prosperity.**
126. 4 Lord, make us **prosperous** again, just as the rain brings
128. 2 you will be happy and **prosperous.**
128. 5 May you see Jerusalem **prosper** all the days of your life!
132.18 with shame, but his kingdom will **prosper** and flourish."
Prov 3. 2 My teaching will give you a long and **prosperous** life.
8.18 I have riches and honour to give, **prosperity** and success.
11.25 Be generous, and you will be **prosperous.**
11.28 but the righteous will **prosper** like the leaves of summer.
19. 8 then remember what you learn and you will **prosper.**
24.25 however, will be **prosperous** and enjoy a good reputation.
Is 26.12 You will give us **prosperity,** Lord;
54.13 "I myself will teach your people, and give them **prosperity**
66.11 You will enjoy her **prosperity,** like a child at its mother's breast.
Is 66.12 The Lord says, "I will bring you lasting **prosperity;**
Jer 12. 1 Why are wicked men so **prosperous?**
12.16 they will also be a part of my people and will **prosper.**
22.15 just and fair, and he **prospered** in everything he did.
22.21 to you when you were **prosperous,** but you refused to listen.
29. 7 because if they are **prosperous,** you will be prosperous too.
29.11 you, plans to bring you **prosperity** and not disaster, plans
33. 7 will make Judah and Israel **prosperous,** and I will rebuild
33. 9 the **prosperity** that I bring to the city."
33.11 I will make this land as **prosperous** as it was before.
33.26 I will be merciful to my people and make them **prosperous** again."
39.16 I am going to bring upon this city destruction and not **prosperity.**
44.17 had plenty of food, we were **prosperous,** and had no troubles.
44.27 see to it that you will not **prosper,** but will be destroyed.
48.47 But in days to come the Lord will make Moab **prosperous** again.
49. 6 "But later on I will make Ammon **prosperous** again.
49.39 But later on I will make the people of Elam **prosperous** again.
Ezek 16.53 Jerusalem, "I will make them **prosperous** again—Sodom and her
16.53 Yes, I will make you **prosperous** too.
16.55 They will become **prosperous** again, and you and your
36.11 used to live, and I will make you more **prosperous** than ever.
39.25 the people of Israel, and make them **prosperous** again.
Dan 4. 4 "I was living comfortably in my palace, enjoying great **prosperity.**
4.27 Then you will continue to be **prosperous."**
6.28 Daniel **prospered** during the reign of Darius and the
Hos 1.11 and once again they will grow and **prosper** in their land.
2.23 I will establish my people in the land and make them **prosper.**
7. 1 people Israel and make them **prosperous** again, all I can see
10. 1 The more **prosperous** they were, the more altars they built.
Joel 3. 1 "At that time I will restore the **prosperity** of Judah and Jerusalem.
Zeph 2. 7 Lord their God will be with them and make them **prosper** again.
3.13 They will be **prosperous** and secure, afraid of no one."
3.20 throughout the world and make you **prosperous** once again."
Hag 2. 9 one, and there I will give my people **prosperity** and peace."
Zech 1.17 that his cities will be **prosperous** again and that he will
7. 7 the time when Jerusalem was **prosperous** and filled with
Mal 3.15 Evil men not only **prosper,** but they test God's patience with
Acts 19.25 "Men, you know that our **prosperity** comes from this work.

PROSTITUTE

Gen 38.15 that she was a **prostitute,** because she had her face covered.
38.21 "Where is the **prostitute** who was here by the road?"
38.21 "There has never been a **prostitute** here," they answered.
38.22 place said that there had never been a **prostitute** there."
Lev 19.29 "Do not disgrace your daughters by making them temple **prostitutes;**
21. 7 woman who has been a **prostitute** or a woman who is not
21. 9 priest's daughter becomes a **prostitute,** she disgraces her father;
21.14 or a divorced woman or a woman who has been a **prostitute.**
Deut 23.17 "No Israelite, man or woman, is to become a temple **prostitute.**
23.18 The Lord hates temple **prostitutes.**
Josh 2. 1 to spend the night in the house of a **prostitute** named Rahab.
6.17 Only the **prostitute** Rahab and her household will be spared,
6.22 as spies, "Go into the **prostitute's** house and bring her and
6.25 the lives of the **prostitute** Rahab and all her relatives,
Judg 11. 1 Jephthah, a brave soldier from Gilead, was the son of a **prostitute.**
16. 1 Gaza, where he met a **prostitute** and went to bed with her.
1 Kgs 3.16 two **prostitutes** came and presented themselves before King Solomon.
14.24 who served as **prostitutes** at those pagan places of worship.
15.12 all the male and female **prostitutes** serving at the pagan
22.38 licked up his blood and **prostitutes** washed themselves, as
22.46 all the male and female **prostitutes** serving at the pagan
2 Kgs 23. 7 living-quarters in the Temple occupied by the temple **prostitutes.**
Prov 6.26 A man can hire a **prostitute** for the price of a loaf
7.10 she was dressed like a **prostitute** and was making plans.
23.27 **Prostitutes** and immoral women are a deadly trap.
29. 3 It is a foolish waste to spend money on **prostitutes.**
Is 23.15 are over, Tyre will be like the **prostitute** in the song:
57. 3 You are no better than sorcerers, adulterers, and **prostitutes.**
Jer 3. 2 Is there any place where you have not acted like a **prostitute?**
3. 2 You have defiled the land with your **prostitution.**
3. 3 You even look like a **prostitute;**
3. 6 and under every green tree she has acted like a **prostitute.**
3. 8 because she had turned from me and had become a **prostitute.**
3. 8 She too became a **prostitute** [9] and was not at all ashamed.
5. 7 committed adultery and spent their time with **prostitutes.**
Ezek 16.16 and just like a **prostitute,** you gave yourself to everyone.
16.22 your disgusting life as a **prostitute** you never once
16.24 you built places to worship idols and practise **prostitution.**
16.25 who came by, and you were more of a **prostitute** every day.
16.26 with you, and you used your **prostitution** to make me angry.
16.28 You were their **prostitute,** but they didn't satisfy you either.
16.29 You were also a **prostitute** for the Babylonians,
16.30 "You have done all this like a shameless **prostitute.**
16.31 you built places to worship idols and practise **prostitution.**
16.31 But you are not out for money like a common **prostitute.**
16.33 A **prostitute** is paid, but you gave presents to all your
16.34 You are a special kind of **prostitute.**
16.36 your clothes and, like a **prostitute,** you gave yourself to
16.39 places where you engage in **prostitution** and worship idols.
16.41 make you stop being a **prostitute** and make you stop giving
23. 3 in Egypt, they lost their virginity and became **prostitutes.**
23. 5 Oholah continued to be a **prostitute** and was full of lust for
23. 8 she had begun as a **prostitute** in Egypt, where she lost her
23. 8 girl, men slept with her and treated her like a **prostitute.**
23.11 wilder and more of a **prostitute** than Oholah had ever been.
23.19 She became more of a **prostitute** than ever, acting just as
23.19 she did as a girl, when she was a **prostitute** in Egypt.
23.29 for and leave you stripped naked, exposed like a **prostitute.**

Ezek 23.29 Your lust and your **prostitution** [30]have brought this on you.
23.30 You were a **prostitute** for the nations and defiled yourself
23.35 me, you will suffer for your lust and your **prostitution."**
23.43 were using as a **prostitute** a woman worn out by adultery.
23.44 They went back to these **prostitutes** again and again.
Hos 2. 2 Plead with her to stop her adultery and **prostitution.**
2. 4 they are the children of a shameless **prostitute.**
3. 3 for me without being a **prostitute** or committing adultery;
4.12 a woman who becomes a **prostitute,** they have given themselves
4.13 as **prostitutes,** and your daughters-in-law commit adultery.
4.14 yourselves go off with temple **prostitutes,** and together with
4.18 in their **prostitution,** preferring disgrace to honour.
9. 1 you have sold yourselves like **prostitutes** to the god Baal
Joel 3. 3 and girls into slavery to pay for **prostitutes** and wine.
Amos 7.17 'Your wife will become a **prostitute** on the streets, and your
Mic 1. 7 given to its temple **prostitutes** will be destroyed by fire,
1. 7 will carry them off for temple **prostitutes** elsewhere."
Mt 21.31 the tax collectors and the **prostitutes** are going into the Kingdom
21.32 but the tax collectors and the **prostitutes** believed him.
Lk 15.30 wasted all your property on **prostitutes,** and when he comes back
1 Cor 6.15 Christ's body and make it part of the body of a **prostitute?**
6.16 joins his body to a **prostitute** becomes physically one with her?
Heb 11.31 faith that kept the **prostitute** Rahab from being killed with those
Jas 2.25 It was the same with the **prostitute** Rahab.
Rev 17. 1 show you how the famous **prostitute** is to be punished,
17. 5 the mother of all the **prostitutes** and perverts in the world."
17.15 on which the **prostitute** is sitting, are nations, peoples, races,
17.16 The ten horns you saw, and the beast, will hate the **prostitute;**
19. 2 He has condemned the **prostitute** who was corrupting the earth

PROTECT
[UNPROTECTED]

Gen 19. 8 they are guests in my house, and I must **protect** them."
28.15 will be with you and **protect** you wherever you go, and I
28.20 will be with me and **protect** me on the journey I am
49.24 Mighty God of Jacob, By the Shepherd, the **Protector** of Israel.
Ex 9.19 animals left outside **unprotected,** and they will all die.' "
23.20 angel ahead of you to **protect** you as you travel and to
30.16 for their lives, and I will remember to **protect** them."
Num 8.19 people of Israel and to **protect** the Israelites from the
14. 9 Lord is with us and has defeated the gods who **protected** them;
31.50 as a payment for our lives, so that he will **protect** us."
31.54 Tent, so that the Lord would **protect** the people of Israel.
33. 3 Under the Lord's **protection** they left the city of Rameses in
Deut 7.15 The Lord will **protect** you from all sickness, and he will
13. 8 Show him no mercy or pity, and do not **protect** him.
19. 2 will be able to escape to one of them for **protection.**
19.11 and then escapes to one of those cities for **protection.**
23.14 you in your camp to **protect** you and to give you victory
23.15 owner and comes to you for **protection,** do not send him back.
32.10 He **protected** them and cared for them,
32.10 as he would **protect** himself.
33. 3 The Lord loves his people and **protects** those who belong to him.
33.12 "This is the tribe the Lord loves and **protects;**
33.25 May his towns be **protected** with iron gates, And may he
Josh 7. 9 And then what will you do to **protect** your honour?"
9.26 he **protected** them and did not allow the people of Israel to
20. 5 They must **protect** him because he killed the person
20. 9 a person accidentally could find **protection** there from the
Judg 2.14 them, and the Israelites could no longer **protect** themselves.
Ruth 2.12 Lord God of Israel, to whom you have come for **protection!"**
1 Sam 2. 2 there is none like him, no **protector** like our God.
2. 9 "He **protects** the lives of his faithful people, but the
10. 1 You will rule his people and **protect** them from all their enemies.
17. 6 His legs were also **protected** by bronze armour, and he
23.16 of God's **protection,** [17]saying to him, "Don't be afraid.
25.16 They **protected** us day and night the whole time we were
25.21 thinking, "Why did I ever **protect** that fellow's property
26.15 So why aren't you **protecting** your master, the king?
26.16 die, because you have not **protected** your master, whom the
2 Sam 21. 2 the Israelites had promised to **protect,** but Saul had tried
21.10 and at night she would **protect** them from wild animals.
22. 2 The Lord is my **protector;**
22. 3 My God is my **protection,** and with him I am safe.
22. 3 He **protects** me like a shield;
22. 3 he **protects** me and saves me from violence.
22.19 I was in trouble, they attacked me, but the Lord **protected** me.
22.31 He is like a shield for all who seek his **protection.**
22.36 O Lord, you **protect** me and save me;
22.49 me victory over my enemies and **protect** me from violent men.
23. 3 the **protector** of Israel said to me:
1 Kgs 9. 3 I will watch over it and **protect** it for all time.
2 Kgs 11. 7 Sabbath are to stand guard at the Temple to **protect** the king.
11.11 all round the front of the Temple, to **protect** the king.
19.34 will defend this city and **protect** it, for the sake of my
1 Chr 16.21 to **protect** them, he warned the kings:
2 Chr 7.16 I will watch over it and **protect** it for all time.
14. 7 He has **protected** us and given us security on every side."
23.10 all round the front of the Temple, to **protect** the king.
Ezra 8.21 us on our journey and **protect** us and our children and all
8.23 prayed for God to **protect** us, and he answered our prayers.
8.31 God was with us and **protected** us from enemy attacks and from
Job 1.10 You have always **protected** him and his family
5.20 he will keep you alive, and in war **protect** you from death.
11.18 God will **protect** you and give you rest.
24.10 But the poor must go out with no clothes to **protect** them;
29. 4 I was prosperous, and the friendship of God **protected** my home.
36. 7 He **protects** those who are righteous;
Ps 1. 6 The righteous are guided and **protected** by the Lord, but
2.12 Happy are all who go to him for **protection.**
Ps 3. 5 down and sleep, and all night long the Lord **protects** me.
5.11 **Protect** those who love you;
5.12 your love **protects** them like a shield.
7. 1 O Lord, my God, I come to you for **protection;**
7.10 God is my **protector;**
14. 6 plans of the humble man, but the Lord is his **protection.**
16. 1 **Protect** me, O God;
16.10 secure, [10]because you **protect** me from the power of death.
17. 8 **Protect** me as you would your very eyes;
18. 2 The Lord is my **protector;**
18. 2 My God is my **protection,** and with him I am safe.
18. 2 He **protects** me like a shield;
18.18 I was in trouble, they attacked me, but the Lord **protected** me.
18.30 He is like a shield for all who seek his **protection.**
18.35 O Lord, you **protect** me and save me;
18.48 me victory over my enemies and **protect** me from violent men.
20. 1 May the God of Jacob **protect** you!
23. 4 Your shepherd's rod and staff **protect** me.
25.20 **Protect** me and save me;
27. 1 The Lord **protects** me from all danger;
28. 7 The Lord **protects** and defends me;
28. 8 The Lord **protects** his people;
30. 7 you **protected** me like a mountain fortress.
31. 1 I come to you, Lord, for **protection;**
31. 2 Be my refuge to **protect** me;
31.19 good you are, how securely you **protect** those who trust you.
31.23 The Lord **protects** the faithful, but punishes the proud
32. 7 I sing aloud of your salvation, because you **protect** me.
32.10 who trust in the Lord are **protected** by his constant love.
33.20 he is our **protector** and our help.
34.22 those who go to him for **protection** will be spared.
35.10 You **protect** the weak from the strong, the poor from the oppressor."
36. 7 We find **protection** under the shadow of your wings.
37.17 the strength of the wicked, but **protect** those who are good.
37.23 in the way he should go and **protects** those who please him.
37.28 He **protects** them for ever, but the descendants of the wicked
37.39 The Lord saves righteous men and **protects** them
37.40 from the wicked, because they go to him for **protection.**
41. 2 The Lord will **protect** them and preserve their lives;
43. 2 You are my **protector;**
57. 1 wings I find **protection** until the raging storms are over.
59. 1 **protect** me from those who attack me!
59.11 Scatter them by your strength and defeat them, O Lord, our **protector.**
61. 3 for you are my **protector,** my strong defence against my enemies.
61. 7 **protect** him with your constant love and faithfulness.
62. 2 He alone **protects** and saves me;
62. 6 He alone **protects** and saves me;
62. 7 he is my strong **protector;**
64. 2 **Protect** me from the plots of the wicked, from mobs of evil
68. 5 his sacred Temple, cares for orphans and **protects** widows.
71. 1 Lord, I have come to you for **protection;**
71. 3 Be my secure shelter and a strong fortress to **protect** me;
71. 6 you have **protected** me since the day I was born.
73.28 be near God, to find **protection** with the Sovereign Lord and
78.35 remembered that God was their **protector,** that the Almighty
80.17 Preserve and **protect** the people you have chosen, the
83. 3 they are plotting against those you **protect.**
84.11 The Lord is our **protector** and glorious king, blessing us
89.18 You, O Lord, chose our **protector;**
89.26 you are my **protector** and saviour.'
91. 1 whoever remains under the **protection** of the Almighty,
91. 2 can say to him, "You are my defender and **protector.**
91. 4 his faithfulness will **protect** and defend you.
91. 9 defender, the Most High your **protector,** [10]and so no
91.11 his angels in charge of you to **protect** you wherever you go.
91.14 love me and will **protect** those who acknowledge me as Lord.
92.15 the Lord is just, that there is no wrong in my **protector.**
94.22 my God **protects** me.
95. 1 Let us sing for joy to God, who **protects** us!
97.10 he **protects** the lives of his people;
102.28 and under your **protection** their descendants will be secure.
105.14 to **protect** them, he warned the kings:
115. 9 He helps you and **protects** you.
115.10 He helps you and **protects** you.
115.11 He helps you and **protects** you.
116. 6 The Lord **protects** the helpless;
119.114 You are my defender and **protector;**
121. 3 your **protector** is always awake.
121. 4 The **protector** of Israel never dozes or sleeps.
121. 5 he is by your side to **protect** you.
121. 7 The Lord will **protect** you from all danger;
121. 8 He will **protect** you as you come and go now and for
127. 1 if the Lord does not **protect** the city, it is useless for
139. 5 you **protect** me with your power.
140. 4 **Protect** me, Lord, from the power of the wicked;
140. 7 My Sovereign Lord, my strong defender, you have **protected** me
141. 8 I seek your **protection;**
141. 9 **Protect** me from the traps they have set for me, from the
142. 4 there is no one to help me, no one to **protect** me.
142. 5 you, Lord, are my **protector;**
143. 9 I go to you for **protection,** Lord;
144. 1 Praise the Lord, my **protector!**
144. 2 He is my **protector** and defender, my shelter and saviour,
145.20 He **protects** everyone who loves him, but he will destroy the wicked.
146. 9 He **protects** the strangers who live in our land;
Prov 2. 7 He provides help and **protection** for righteous, honest men.
2. 8 He **protects** those who treat others fairly, and guards
2.11 Your insight and understanding will **protect** you [12]and

Prov 4. 6 Do not abandon wisdom, and she will **protect** you;
6.22 lead you when you travel, **protect** you at night, and advise
7. 2 to follow my teaching as you are to **protect** your eyes.
10.15 Wealth **protects** the rich;
10.29 The Lord **protects** honest people, but destroys those who do wrong.
11. 8 The righteous are **protected** from trouble;
13. 3 Be careful what ou say and **protect** your life.
13. 6 Righteousness **protects** the innocent;
14. 3 a wise man's words **protect** him.
14.32 deeds, but good people are **protected** by their integrity.
15.25 of arrogant men, but he will **protect** a widow's property.
18.11 however, imagine that their wealth **protects** them like high,
18.19 brother and he will **protect** you like a strong city wall,
29.10 righteous people will **protect** the life of such a person.
30. 5 He is like a shield for all who seek his **protection.**
31. 8 **Protect** the rights of all who are helpless.
31. 9 **Protect** the rights of the poor and needy."
Ecc 5. 8 Every official is **protected** by the one over him,
5. 8 and both are **protected** by still higher officials.
12. 3 Then your arms, that have **protected** you, will tremble, and
Song 8. 9 she is a gate, we will **protect** her with panels of cedar.
Is 4. 5 God's glory will cover and **protect** the whole city.
5. 5 break down the wall that **protects** it, and let wild animals
8. 8 His outspread wings **protect** the land.
16. 3 **Protect** us like a tree that casts a cool shadow in the
16. 4 **Protect** us from those who want to destroy us."
17.10 God who rescues you and who **protects** you like a mighty rock.
20. 6 we relied on to **protect** us from the emperor of Assyria!
23.10 There is no one to **protect** you any more.
25.10 The Lord will **protect** Mount Zion, but the people of Moab
26. 4 he will always **protect** us.
27. 5 my people want my **protection,** let them make peace with me.
30. 2 They want Egypt to **protect** them, so they put their trust in
30. 3 to help them, and Egypt's **protection** will end in disaster.
31. 2 his threats to punish evil men and those who **protect** them.
31. 4 can keep me, the Lord Almighty, from **protecting** Mount Zion.
31. 5 hovers over its nest to **protect** its young,
31. 5 so I, the Lord Almighty, will **protect** Jerusalem and defend it."
33. 2 **Protect** us day by day and save us in times of trouble.
33. 6 He always **protects** his people and gives them wisdom and knowledge.
33.22 he will rule over us and **protect** us.
37.35 will defend this city and **protect** it, for the sake of my
38. 6 of Assyria, and I will continue to **protect** the city."
41.10 I will **protect** you and save you.
44. 6 The Lord, who rules and **protects** Israel, the Lord Almighty,
49. 2 With his own hand he **protected** me.
49. 8 I will guard and **protect** you and through you make a covenant
51.16 given you my teaching, and I **protect** you with my hand.' "
52.12 Lord your God will lead you and **protect** you on every side.
58. 8 my presence will **protect** you on every side.
60.18 I will **protect** and defend you like a wall;
Jer 1. 8 afraid of them, for I will be with you to **protect** you.
1.18 not defeat you, for I will be with you to **protect** you.
15.20 I will be with you to **protect** you and keep you safe.
16.19 Lord, you are the one who **protects** me and gives me strength;
21.11 **Protect** the person who is being cheated from the one who is
22. 3 **Protect** the person who is being cheated from the one who is
31.22 and different, as different as a woman **protecting** a man."
39.17 But I, the Lord, will **protect** you, and you will not be
48.45 Helpless refugees try to find **protection** in Heshbon, the
49.31 Their city has no gates or locks and is completely **unprotected.'**
Lam 4.20 the one we had trusted to **protect** us from every invader.
Ezek 11. 3 meat in it, but at least it **protects** us from the fire.'
11.11 This city will not **protect** you
11.11 as a pot **protects** the meat in it.
20.44 When I act to **protect** my honour, you Israelites will
23.24 **Protected** by shields and helmets, they will surround you.
34.30 Everyone will know that I **protect** Israel and that they
39.25 I will **protect** my holy name.
Dan 5.21 in the open air with nothing to **protect** him from the dew.
11.38 Instead, he will honour the god who **protects** fortresses.
Hos 8. 9 from Assyria, and have paid other nations to **protect** them.
14. 3 Assyria can never save us, and war-horses cannot **protect** us.
14. 7 Once again they will live under my **protection.**
Nah 1. 7 he **protects** his people in times of trouble;
3. 8 too had a river to **protect** her like a wall—the Nile
Hab 1.12 Lord, my God and **protector,** you have chosen the Babylonians
Zech 2. 5 fire round the city to **protect** it and that he will live
9.15 The Lord Almighty will **protect** his people, and they will
12. 8 that time the Lord will **protect** those who live in Jerusalem,
Jn 17.12 I **protected** them, and not one of them was lost, except the
1 Cor 10. 1 They were all under the **protection** of the cloud, and all
2 Cor 12. 9 in order to feel the **protection** of Christ's power over me.
Jude 1 love of God the Father and the **protection** of Jesus Christ:
Rev 7.15 He who sits on the throne will **protect** them with his presence.

PROTEST

Num 16.42 they had all gathered to **protest** to Moses and Aaron, they
Judg 21.22 brothers come to you and **protest,** you can say, 'Please let
Job 19. 7 I **protest** against his violence, but no one is listening;
Ezek 20.49 But I **protested,** "Sovereign Lord, don't make me do it!
Acts 13.51 dust off their feet in **protest** against them and went on to
18. 6 evil things about him, he **protested** by shaking the dust from
23. 9 the party of the Pharisees stood up and **protested** strongly:

PROUD

[PRIDE]

Gen 16. 4 that she was pregnant, she became **proud** and despised Sarai.
49. 3 of my manhood, The **proudest** and strongest of all my sons.
Lev 26.19 I will break your stubborn **pride;**
Deut 1.43 him, and in your **pride** you marched into the hill-country.
8.14 that you do not become **proud** and forget the Lord your God
1 Sam 2. 3 silence your **proud** words.
2 Sam 22.28 those who are humble, but you humble those who are **proud.**
2 Kgs 14.10 have defeated the Edomites, and you are filled with **pride.**
19.28 of that rage and that **pride** of yours, and now I will
2 Chr 17. 6 He took **pride** in serving the Lord and destroyed all the
32.25 But Hezekiah was too **proud** to show gratitude for what
Neh 9.16 But our ancestors grew **proud** and stubborn and refused to
9.17 In their **pride** they chose a leader to take them back to
9.29 obey your teachings, but in **pride** they rejected your laws,
Job 15.26 That man is **proud** and rebellious;
22.29 God brings down the **proud** and saves the humble.
31.25 I have never trusted in riches [25] or taken **pride** in my wealth.
31.36 them, [36] I would wear them **proudly** on my shoulder and place
33.17 stop their sinning and to save them from becoming **proud.**
35.12 but God doesn't answer, for they are **proud** and evil men.
36. 9 have done, [9] God shows them their sins and their **pride.**
40.10 If so, stand up in your honour and **pride;**
40.11 Look at those who are **proud;**
41.34 He looks down on even the **proudest** animals;
Ps 5. 5 You cannot stand the sight of **proud** men;
10. 2 The wicked are **proud** and persecute the poor;
10. 3 The wicked man is **proud** of his evil desires;
10. 4 in his **pride** he thinks that God doesn't matter.
17.10 they have no pity and speak **proudly.**
18.27 those who are humble, but you humble those who are **proud.**
22.29 All **proud** men will bow down to him;
31.18 those liars— all the **proud** and arrogant who speak with
31.23 The Lord protects the faithful, but punishes the **proud**
36.11 Do not let **proud** men attack me or wicked men make me
47. 4 land where we live, the **proud** possession of his people, whom
54. 3 **Proud** men are coming to attack me;
59.12 may they be caught in their **pride!**
73. 3 I was jealous of the **proud** when I saw that things go
73. 6 And so they wear **pride** like a necklace and violence like a
73. 8 they are **proud** and make plans to oppress others.
76.12 he humbles **proud** princes and terrifies great kings.
86.14 **Proud** men are coming against me, O God;
94. 2 rise and give the **proud** what they deserve!
94. 4 How much longer will criminals be **proud** and boast
101. 5 I will not tolerate a man who is **proud** and arrogant.
106. 5 your nation, in the glad **pride** of those who belong to you.
119.21 You reprimand the **proud;**
119.51 The **proud** are always scornful of me, but I have not
119.69 **Proud** men have told lies about me, but with all my heart
119.78 May the **proud** be ashamed for falsely accusing me;
119.85 **Proud** men, who do not obey your law, have dug pits to
123. 4 too long by the rich and scorned by **proud** oppressors.
131. 1 I have given up my **pride** and turned away from my arrogance.
138. 6 you care for the lowly, and the **proud** cannot hide from you.
140. 5 **Proud** men have set a trap for me;
Prov 3.12 loves, as a father corrects a son of whom he is **proud.**
6.16 A **proud** look,
8.13 I hate **pride** and arrogance, evil ways and false words.
10. 1 A wise son makes his father **proud** of him;
11. 2 People who are **proud** will soon be disgraced.
12. 4 A good wife is her husband's **pride** and joy;
14. 3 A fool's **pride** makes him talk too much;
16.18 **Pride** leads to destruction, and arrogance to downfall.
17. 6 Old men are **proud** of their grandchildren,
17. 6 just as boys are **proud** of their fathers.
21.24 I will show you someone who is arrogant, **proud,** and inconsiderate.
23.16 I will be **proud** when I hear you speaking words of wisdom.
23.24 You can take **pride** in a wise son.
23.25 Make your father and mother **proud** of you;
29. 3 If you appreciate wisdom, your father will be **proud** of you.
29.17 Discipline your son and you can always be **proud** of him.
Ecc 2.10 I was **proud** of everything I had worked for, and all this
7. 8 Patience is better than **pride.**
Is 2.11 day is coming when human **pride** will be ended and human
2.12 who is powerful, everyone who is **proud** and conceited.
2.17 Human **pride** will be ended, and human arrogance will be destroyed.
3.16 The Lord said, "Look how **proud** the women of Jerusalem are!
3.18 Jerusalem everything they are so **proud** of—the ornaments they
4. 2 survive will take delight and **pride** in the crops that the
5.15 Everyone will be disgraced, and all who are **proud** will be humbled.
9. 9 Now they are **proud** and arrogant.
10.12 of Assyria for all his boasting and all his **pride."**
10.33 The **proudest** and highest of them will be cut down and humiliated.
13. 2 the signal for them to attack the gates of the **proud** city.
13. 3 Lord has called out his **proud** and confident soldiers to
13.11 will humble everyone who is **proud** and punish everyone who is
13.19 it is the **pride** of its people.
16. 6 Judah say, "We have heard how **proud** the people of Moab are.
22.18 You will die there beside the chariots you were so **proud** of.
23. 9 put an end to their **pride** in what they had done and
26. 5 He has humbled those who were **proud;**
28. 1 Their **proud** heads are well perfumed, but there they lie,
28. 3 The **pride** of those drunken leaders will be trampled underfoot.
28. 4 The fading glory of those **proud** leaders will disappear
37.29 of that rage and that **pride** of yours, and now I will

Is 48. 2 And yet you are **proud** to say that you are citizens of
49.18 proud of your people, as **proud** as a bride is of her
61. 6 the wealth of the nations And be **proud** that it is yours.
Jer 13. 9 destroy the pride of Judah and the great **pride** of Jerusalem.
13.17 not listen, I will cry in secret because of your **pride;**
13.20 entrusted to your care, your people you were so **proud** of?
33. 9 Jerusalem will be a source of joy, honour, and **pride** to me;
48.29 Moab is very **proud!**
48.29 I have heard how **proud,** arrogant, and conceited the people are,
49.16 Your **pride** has deceived you.
50.29 others, because it acted with **pride** against me, the Holy One
50.31 "Babylonia, you are filled with **pride,**
50.32 Your **proud** nation will stumble and fall, and no one will
Lam 2.15 Is this the **pride** of the world?"
5.16 Nothing is left of all we were **proud** of.
Ezek 7.10 **Pride** is at its height.
7.20 Once they were **proud** of their beautiful jewels, but they
16.49 She and her daughters were **proud** because they had plenty
16.50 They were **proud** and stubborn and did the things that I hate,
16.56 those days when you were **proud** [57] and before the evil you
24.21 You are **proud** of the strength of the Temple.
24.25 strong Temple that was their **pride** and joy, which they liked
28. 2 Puffed up with **pride,** you claim to be a god.
28. 5 How **proud** you are of your wealth!
28.17 You were **proud** of being handsome, and your fame made you
30. 6 Egypt's **proud** army will be destroyed.
30.18 and put an end to the strength they were so **proud** of.
31.10 As it grew taller it grew **proud;**
32.12 and everything else that you are **proud** of will be destroyed.
33.28 the power they were so **proud** of will come to an end.
Dan 4.37 and just, and he can humble anyone who acts **proudly."**
5.20 But because he became **proud,** stubborn, and cruel, he was
7. 8 This horn had human eyes and a mouth that was boasting **proudly.**
7.20 It had eyes and a mouth and was boasting **proudly.**
8.25 He will be **proud** of himself and destroy many people without warning.
11.12 He will be **proud** of his victory and of the many soldiers
Hos 13. 6 full and satisfied, and then you grew **proud** and forgot me.
Amos 6. 8 "I hate the **pride** of the people of Israel;
Obad 3 Your **pride** has deceived you.
Mic 2. 3 in trouble, and then you will not walk so **proudly** any more.
Hab 1. 7 terror, and in their **pride** they are a law to themselves.
2. 5 Greedy men are **proud** and restless—like death itself they are
Zeph 2.10 will be punished for their **pride** and arrogance and for
2.15 the city that is so **proud** of its own power and thinks
3.11 will remove everyone who is **proud** and arrogant, and you will
Zech 9. 6 The Lord says, "I will humble all these **proud** Philistines.
10.11 **Proud** Assyria will be humbled, and mighty Egypt will lose her power.
13. 4 comes, no prophet will be **proud** of his visions, or act like
Mal 3.15 As we see it, **proud** people are the ones who are happy.
4. 1 day is coming when all **proud** and evil people will burn like
Mk 7.22 slander, **pride,** and folly—[23] all these evil things come
Lk 1.51 mighty arm and scattered the **proud** with all their plans.
Rom 1.30 they are hateful to God, insolent, **proud,** and boastful;
11.13 an apostle to the Gentiles, I will take **pride** in my work.
11.18 How can you be **proud?**
11.20 But do not be **proud** of it;
12.16 Do not be **proud,** but accept humble duties.
15.17 Christ Jesus, then, I can be **proud** of my service for God.
1 Cor 4. 6 None of you should be **proud** of one person and despise another.
4.18 Some of you have become **proud** because you have thought
4.19 myself the power which these **proud** people have, and not just
5. 2 How, then, can you be **proud?**
5. 6 It is not right for you to be **proud!**
8. 1 Such knowledge, however, puffs a person up with **pride;**
13. 4 it is not jealous or conceited or **proud;**
15.31 The **pride** I have in you, in our life in union with
2 Cor 1.12 We are **proud** that our conscience assures us that our
1.13 Jesus you can be as **proud** of us as we shall be
5.12 a good reason to be **proud** of us, so that you will
7. 4 I take such **pride** in you!
10. 5 we pull down every **proud** obstacle that is raised against the
12. 7 being puffed up with **pride** because of the many wonderful things
12. 7 Satan's messenger to beat me and keep me from being **proud.**
12. 9 most happy, then, to be **proud** of my weaknesses, in order to
12.20 and selfishness, insults and gossip, **pride** and disorder.
Gal 5.26 We must not be **proud** or irritate one another or be
6. 4 then he can be **proud** of what he himself has done,
Phil 1.26 even more reason to be **proud** of me in your life in
2.16 shall have reason to be **proud** of you on the Day of
3.19 They are **proud** of what they should be ashamed of,
4. 1 How happy you make me, and how **proud** I am of you!
1 Thes 2.20 Indeed, you are our **pride** and our joy!
1 Tim 3. 6 will not swell up with **pride** and be condemned, as the Devil
6. 4 of our religion [4] is swollen with **pride** and knows nothing.
6.17 this life not to be **proud,** but to place their hope,
2 Tim 3. 4 they will be treacherous, reckless, and swollen with **pride;**
Jas 4. 6 "God resists the **proud,** but gives grace to the humble."
4.16 But now you are **proud,** and you boast;
1 Pet 5. 5 "God resists the **proud,** but shows favour to the humble."
2 Pet 2.18 They make **proud** and stupid statements, and use immoral bodily
1 Jn 2.16 world that people are so **proud** of—none of this comes from
Rev 13. 5 allowed to make **proud** claims which were insulting to God,

PROVE

[DISPROVE, PROOF]

Gen 20.16 thousand pieces of silver as **proof** to all who are with you
42.19 To **prove** that you are honest, one of you will stay in
42.20 This will **prove** that you have been telling the truth, and I
Ex 3.12 That will be the **proof** that I have sent you."
4. 5 Lord said, "Do this to **prove** to the Israelites that the Lord,
7. 9 demands that you **prove** yourselves by performing a miracle,
Deut 4.35 has shown you this, to **prove** to you that he alone is
19.15 two witnesses are necessary to **prove** that a man is guilty.
22.15 wedding sheet that **proves** the girl was a virgin,
22.17 But here is the **proof** that my daughter was a virgin;
22.20 true and there is no **proof** that the girl was a virgin,
33. 8 the test at Massah And **proved** them true at the waters of
Judg 6.17 with me, give me some **proof** that you are really the Lord.
1 Sam 10. 1 And this is the **proof** to you that the Lord has chosen
1 Kgs 18.36 of Abraham, Isaac, and Jacob, **prove** now that you are the God
2 Kgs 10.10 This **proves** that everything that the Lord said about the
20. 8 "What is the sign to **prove** that the Lord will heal me
20. 9 give you a sign to **prove** that he will keep his promise.
Ezra 2.59 could not **prove** that they were descendants of Israelites.
2.61 priestly clans could find no record to **prove** their ancestry:
2.61 Since they were unable to **prove** who their ancestors were,
Neh 7.61 could not **prove** that they were descendants of Israelites.
7.63 priestly clans could find no record to **prove** their ancestry:
7.63 Since they were unable to **prove** who their ancestors were,
Job 16. 8 skin and bones, and people take that as **proof** of my guilt.
19. 5 than I am, and regard my troubles as **proof** of my guilt.
24.25 Can anyone **prove** that my words are not true?
32.12 you have not **disproved** what Job has said.
40. 8 Are you trying to **prove** that I am unjust— to put
Ps 86.17 Show me **proof** of your goodness, Lord;
89.49 Lord, where are the former **proofs** of your love?
105.19 The word of the Lord **proved** him right.
Prov 22.12 that truth is kept safe by **disproving** the words of liars.
25. 8 If another witness later **proves** you wrong, what will you do then?
Is 38. 7 give you a sign to **prove** that he will keep his promise.
38.22 "What is the sign to **prove** that I will be able to
43. 9 bring in their witnesses to **prove** that they are right, to
43.26 Present your case to **prove** you are in the right!
48. 4 I knew that you would **prove** to be stubborn, as rigid as
50. 8 for God is near, and he will **prove** me innocent.
50. 9 Lord himself defends me— who, then, can **prove** me guilty?
Jer 3.11 from him, she had **proved** to be better than unfaithful Judah.
12. 1 I argued my case with you, you would **prove** to be right.
44.29 the Lord, will give you **proof** that I will punish you in
46.11 All your medicine has **proved** useless;
Mt 8. 4 then in order to **prove** to everyone that you are cured, offer
9. 6 I will **prove** to you, then, that the Son of Man has
12.27 What your own followers do **proves** that you are wrong!
12.28 to drive out demons, which **proves** that the Kingdom of God
Mk 1.44 then in order to **prove** to everyone that you are cured, offer
2.10 I will **prove** to you, then, that the Son of Man has
8.12 No such **proof** will be given to these people!"
16.20 Lord worked with them and **proved** that their preaching was true
Lk 2.12 And this is what will **prove** it to you:
5.14 then to **prove** to everyone that you are cured, offer the
5.24 I will **prove** to you, then, that the Son of Man has
7.47 great love she has shown **proves** that her many sins have been
11.19 Your own followers **prove** that you are wrong!
11.20 drive out demons, and this **proves** that the Kingdom of God
13. 2 do you think it **proves** that they were worse sinners than
13. 4 Do you suppose this **proves** that they were worse than all the
20.37 And Moses clearly **proves** that the dead are raised to life.
Jn 5.31 what I say is not to be accepted as real **proof.**
8.13 what you say **proves** nothing."
8.46 Which one of you can **prove** that I am guilty of sin?
16. 8 when he comes, he will **prove** to the people of the world
Acts 1. 3 times in ways that **proved** beyond doubt that he was alive.
2.22 divine authority was clearly **proven** to you by all the miracles
4. 2 had risen from death, which **proved** that the dead will rise
9.22 even more powerful, and his **proofs** that Jesus was the Messiah
14. 3 about the Lord, who **proved** that their message about his grace
17. 3 explaining the Scriptures and **proving** from them that the Messiah
17.31 He has given **proof** of this to everyone by raising that man
18.28 in public debates by **proving** from the Scriptures that Jesus is
22. 5 and the whole Council can **prove** that I am telling the truth.
24.13 Nor can they give you **proof** of the accusations they now
25. 7 serious charges against him, which they were not able to **prove.**
Rom 16.10 Greetings to Apelles, whose loyalty to Christ has been **proved.**
1 Cor 1.22 Jews want miracles for **proof,** and Greeks look for wisdom.
2. 4 but with convincing **proof** of the power of God's Spirit.
3. 3 doesn't this **prove** that you belong to this world,
4. 4 is clear, but that does not **prove** that I am really innocent.
9. 2 the Lord you yourselves are **proof** of the fact that I am
14.22 speaking in strange tongues is **proof** for unbelievers,
14.22 gift of proclaiming God's message is **proof** for believers,
2 Cor 7.11 earnest it has made you, how eager to **prove** your innocence!
7.14 the same way the boast we made to Titus has **proved** true.
9.13 And because of the **proof** which this service of yours brings,
10. 6 after you have **proved** your complete loyalty, we will be ready
12.12 many miracles and wonders that **prove** that I am an apostle
13. 3 You will have all the **proof** you want that Christ speaks
Phil 1.28 be courageous, and this will **prove** to them that they will
2.22 yourselves know how he has **proved** his worth, how he and I,
2 Thes 1. 5 All of this **proves** that God's judgement is just
1 Tim 2. 6 That was the **proof** at the right time that God wants everyone
Tit 3.11 a person is corrupt, and his sins **prove** that he is wrong.
Heb 2. 3 and those who heard him **proved** to us that it is true.
9.16 it is necessary to **prove** that the person who made it
Jas 2.14 say that he has faith if his actions do not **prove** it?
3.13 He is to **prove** it by his good life, by his good
1 Pet 1. 7 Their purpose is to **prove** that your faith is genuine.

PROVERB

1 Kgs 4.32 He composed three thousand **proverbs**
Job 13.12 Your **proverbs** are as useless as ashes;
17. 5 In the old **proverb** a man betrays his friends for money,
17. 6 And now people use this **proverb** against me;
Ps 49. 4 will turn my attention to **proverbs** and explain their meaning
Prov 1. 1 The **proverbs** of Solomon, son of David and king of Israel.
1. 2 Here are **proverbs** that will help you to recognize wisdom
1. 5 These **proverbs** can even add to the knowledge of wise men
1. 6 understand the hidden meanings of **proverbs** and the problems
10. 1 These are Solomon's **proverbs:**
25. 1 Here are more of Solomon's **proverbs,** copied by men at the
26. 7 A fool can use a **proverb** about as well as a crippled
Ecc 12. 9 He studied **proverbs** and honestly tested their truth.
12.11 to guide sheep, and collected **proverbs** are as lasting as
Is 28.20 like the man in the **proverb,** who tries to sleep in a
Ezek 12.22 he said, "why do the people of Israel repeat this **proverb:**
12.23 I will put an end to that **proverb.**
16.44 The Lord said, "People will use this **proverb** about you,
18. 2 and said, "What is this **proverb** people keep repeating in
18. 3 "you will not repeat this **proverb** in Israel any more.
Hos 4.14 As the **proverb** says, 'A people without sense will be ruined.'
Lk 4.23 that you will quote this **proverb** to me, 'Doctor, heal yourself.'
2 Pet 2.22 What happened to them shows that the **proverbs** are true:

PROVIDE
[THE LORD PROVIDES]

Gen 1.29 I have **provided** all kinds of grain and all kinds of
1.30 the birds I have **provided** grass and leafy plants for food"
22. 8 Abraham answered, "God himself will **provide** one."
22.14 Abraham named that place **"The Lord Provides."**
22.14 And even today people say, "On the Lord's mountain he **provides."**
47.12 Joseph **provided** food for his father, his brothers, and
49.20 He will **provide** food fit for a king.
Ex 10.25 "Then you would have to **provide** us with animals for
28. 2 your brother Aaron, to **provide** him with dignity and beauty.
28.40 for Aaron's sons, to **provide** them with dignity and beauty.
Lev 25. 6 during that year, it will **provide** food for you, your slaves,
25.35 cannot support himself, you must **provide** for him as you
Deut 23. 4 They refused to **provide** you with food and water when you
29. 6 to drink, but the Lord **provided** for your needs in order to
Judg 20.10 the men in Israel will **provide** food for the army, and the
21. 7 What shall we do to **provide** wives for the men of Benjamin
21.16 What shall we do to **provide** wives for the men who are
2 Sam 5.11 he **provided** him with cedar logs and with carpenters and
9.10 Saul's family and bring in the harvest, to **provide** food for them.
15. 1 After this, Absalom **provided** a chariot and horses for himself,
20. 3 He **provided** for their needs, but did not have intercourse with them.
1 Kgs 1. 5 He **provided** for himself chariots, horses,
4. 7 They were to **provide** food from their districts for the king
5. 8 I will **provide** the cedars and the pine-trees.
5.11 that he wanted, [11] and Solomon **provided** Hiram with two
8.21 I have also **provided** a place in the Temple for the
8.25 ruling as king of Israel, **provided** they obeyed you as
9.11 King Hiram of Tyre had **provided** him with all the cedar
11.18 gave Hadad some land and a house and **provided** him with food.
18. 4 two groups of fifty, and **provided** them with food and water.)
2 Kgs 4.13 for all the trouble she has had in **providing** for our needs.
6.23 So the king of Israel **provided** a great feast for them;
6.27 "If the Lord won't help you, what help can I **provide?**
23. 9 eat the unleavened bread **provided** for their fellow-priests.
1 Chr 5. 2 the strongest and **provided** a ruler for all the tribes.)
7. 4 were able to **provide** 36,000 men for military service.
14. 1 he **provided** him with cedar logs and with stone-masons and
23. 5 musical instruments **provided** by the king for this purpose.
28. 4 the tribe of Judah to **provide** leadership, and out of Judah
29. 3 all this that I have **provided,** I have given silver and gold
2 Chr 2.10 As **provisions** for your workmen, I will send you two
6.16 ruling as king of Israel, **provided** that they carefully
7. 6 that King David had **provided** and singing the hymn,
11.23 He **provided** generously for them and also secured many wives
28.15 four men were appointed to **provide** the prisoners with
31. 3 own flocks and herds he **provided** animals for the
35.14 this was done, the Levites **provided** meat for themselves and
Ezra 1. 4 They are to **provide** them with silver and gold, supplies and
7.21 province of West Euphrates to **provide** promptly for Ezra, the
7.23 You must be careful to **provide** everything which the God
Neh 5.18 and every ten days I **provided** a fresh supply of wine.
9.21 in the desert you **provided** all that they needed;
10.33 We will **provide** for the temple worship the following:
10.34 determine which clans are to **provide** wood to burn the
Esth 6.10 the horse, and **provide** these honours for Mordecai the Jew.
Job 36.31 how he feeds the people and **provides** an abundance of food.
Ps 36. 8 We feast on the abundant food you **provide;**
65. 9 you **provide** the earth with crops.
65.11 What a rich harvest your goodness **provides!**
68.10 in your goodness you **provided** for the poor.
78.20 but can he also **provide** us with bread and give his people
95. 7 the people he cares for, the flock for which he **provides.**
104.11 They **provide** water for the wild animals;
104.21 while they hunt, looking for the food that God **provides.**
104.28 you **provide** food, and they are satisfied.
111. 5 He **provides** food for those who honour him;
127. 2 For the Lord **provides** for those he loves, while they are asleep.
128. 2 Your work will **provide** for your needs;
132. 5 rest or sleep, [5] until I **provide** a place for the Lord, a
132.15 I will richly **provide** Zion with all she needs;
147. 8 he **provides** rain for the earth and makes grass grow on the
Prov 2. 7 He **provides** help and protection for righteous, honest men.
3.22 They will **provide** you with life—a pleasant and happy life.
27.27 rest of the goats will **provide** milk for you and your family,
Is 55.10 make the crops grow and **provide** seed for sowing and food to
Jer 31.35 The Lord **provides** the sun for light by day, the moon and
Ezek 13. 3 They **provide** their own inspiration and invent their own visions.
45.17 will be his duty to **provide** the animals to be burnt whole,
45.17 He is to **provide** the sin-offerings, the grain-offerings, the
47.12 of the stream all kinds of trees will grow to **provide** food.
47.12 The trees will **provide** food, and their leaves will be used
Dan 1.16 to eat vegetables instead of what the king **provided.**
Hab 1.16 their nets **provide** them with the best of everything.
Mt 6.33 and he will **provide** you with all these other things.
Lk 1.69 He has **provided** for us a mighty Saviour, a descendant of
7.46 You **provided** no olive-oil for my head, but she has
12.31 with his Kingdom, and he will **provide** you with these things.
12.33 **Provide** for yourselves purses that don't wear out, and save your
Jn 4.14 a spring which will **provide** him with life-giving water and give
Acts 7.46 God to allow him to **provide** a dwelling place for the God
20.34 these hands of mine to **provide** everything that my companions
23.24 **Provide** some horses for Paul to ride and get him safely
24.23 freedom and allow his friends to **provide** for his needs.
1 Cor 6.13 and the Lord **provides** for the body.
10.13 strength to endure it, and so **provide** you with a way out.
15.38 God **provides** that seed with the body he wishes;
2 Cor 12.14 children should not have to **provide** for their parents,
12.14 but parents should **provide** for their children.
Eph 4.16 is held together by every joint with which it is **provided.**
4.29 kind that build up and **provide** what is needed, so that what
Tit 3.14 their time doing good, in order to **provide** for real needs;
Heb 7.19 a better hope has been **provided** through which we come near
13.20 May the God of peace **provide** you with every good thing you
Jas 5.11 and you know how the Lord **provided** for him in the end.
2 Pet 1.15 do my best, then, to **provide** a way for you to remember
Rev 16.12 The river dried up, to **provide** a way for the kings who

PROVINCE

Ezra 2. 1 of the exiles left the **province** of Babylon and returned to
4. 8 Shimshai, the secretary of the **province,** wrote the following
4. 9 Shimshai, secretary of the **province,** from their associates,
4.10 Samaria and elsewhere in the **province** of West Euphrates."
4.15 it has given trouble to kings and to rulers of **provinces.**
4.16 longer be able to control the **province** of West Euphrates."
4.17 to Shimshai, secretary of the **province,** and to their
4.20 have ruled over the entire **province** of West Euphrates,
5. 8 that we went to the **province** of Judah and found that the
6. 2 city of Ecbatana in the **province** of Media that a scroll was
7.16 which you collect throughout the **province** of Babylon and the
7.21 in the **province** of West Euphrates to provide promptly
8.36 governors and officials of the **province** of West Euphrates,
Neh 2. 7 the governors of West Euphrates **Province,** instructing them
2.10 Tobiah, an official in the **province** of Ammon, heard that
7. 6 of the exiles left the **province** of Babylon and returned to
11. 3 citizens of the **province** of Judah who lived in Jerusalem:
Esth 1. 1 King Xerxes ruled over 127 **provinces,** all the way from India
1. 3 as well as the governors and noblemen of the **provinces.**
1.22 To each of the royal **provinces** he sent a message in the
1.22 system of writing of that **province,** saying that every
2. 3 can appoint officials in every **province** of the empire and
3. 8 scattered all over your empire and found in every **province.**
3.13 Runners took this proclamation to every **province** of the empire.
3.14 be made public in every **province,** so that everyone would be
3.15 city of Susa, and runners carried the news to the **provinces.**
4. 3 the **provinces,** wherever the king's proclamation was made known,
4.11 from the king's advisers to the people in the **provinces,**
8. 9 and officials of all the 127 **provinces** from India to Sudan.
8. 9 letters were written to each **province** in its own language
8.11 of any nationality in any **province** attacked the Jewish men,
8.13 known to everyone in every **province,** so that the Jews would
8.17 city and **province,** wherever the king's proclamation was read,
9. 3 In fact, all the **provincial** officials—governors, administrators,
9.12 What must they have done out in the **provinces!**
9.16 The Jews in the **provinces** also organized and defended themselves.
9.28 every future generation in every **province** and every city
9.30 were sent to all the 127 **provinces** of the Persian Empire.
Dan 2.48 him in charge of the **province** of Babylon, and made him the
2.49 Abednego in charge of the affairs of the **province** of Babylon;
3. 1 set up in the plain of Dura in the **province** of Babylon.
3. 2 magistrates, and all the other officials of the **provinces.**
3.12 put in charge of the **province** of Babylon—Shadrach, Meshach,
3.30 Abednego to higher positions in the **province** of Babylon.
8. 2 myself in the walled city of Susa in the **province** of Elam.
11.24 He will invade a wealthy **province** without warning and
Mt 2.22 so he went to the **province** of Galilee [23] and made his home
3. 5 from Jerusalem, from the whole **province** of Judaea, and from all
Mk 1. 5 people from the **province** of Judaea and the city of Jerusalem
1. 9 came from Nazareth in the **province** of Galilee, and was baptized
1.28 about Jesus spread quickly everywhere in the **province** of Galilee.
10. 1 went to the **province** of Judaea, and crossed the River
Jn 3.22 his disciples went to the **province** of Judaea, where he spent
Acts 6. 9 other Jews from the **provinces** of Cilicia and Asia started arguing
8. 1 were scattered throughout the **provinces** of Judaea and Samaria.
16. 6 did not let them preach the message in the **province** of Asia.
16. 7 tried to go into the **province** of Bithynia, but the Spirit of
19. 1 Paul travelled through the interior of the **province** and arrived
19.10 who lived in the **province** of Asia, both Jews and Gentiles,
19.22 Macedonia, while he spent more time in the **province** of Asia.
19.26 here in Ephesus and in nearly the whole **province** of Asia.

Acts	19.31	of the **provincial authorities,** who were his friends, also sent
	20. 4	Tychicus and Trophimus, from the **province** of Asia;
	20.16	so as not to lose any time in the **province** of Asia.
	20.18	from the first day I arrived in the **province** of Asia.
	21.27	some Jews from the **province** of Asia saw Paul in the
	23.34	read the letter and asked Paul what **province** he was from.
	24.19	But some Jews from the **province** of Asia were there;
	25. 1	after Festus arrived in the **province,** he went from Caesarea to
	27. 2	the seaports of the **province** of Asia, and we sailed away.
Rom	16. 5	the first man in the **province** of Asia to believe in Christ.
1 Cor	16.19	The churches in the **province** of Asia send you their greetings;
2 Cor	1. 8	brothers, of the trouble we had in the **province** of Asia.
2 Tim	1.15	know that everyone in the **province** of Asia, including Phygelus
1 Pet	1. 1	refugees scattered throughout the **provinces** of Pontus, Galatia,
Rev	1. 4	From John to the seven churches in the **province** of Asia:

PROWL

Prov	28.15	he is as dangerous as a growling lion or a **prowling** bear.
Jer	5. 6	to pieces, and leopards will **prowl** through their towns.
Lam	5.18	lonely and deserted, and wild jackals **prowl** through its ruins.
Ezek	19. 6	When he was full-grown, he **prowled** with the other lions.

PRUNE
[UNPRUNED]

Lev	25. 3	You shall sow your fields, **prune** your vineyards, and
	25. 4	Do not sow your fields or **prune** your vineyards.
	25. 5	sown, and do not gather the grapes from your **unpruned** vines;
	25.11	by itself or gather the grapes in your **unpruned** vineyards.
Is	2. 4	their swords into ploughs and their spears into **pruning-knives.**
	5. 6	I will not **prune** the vines or hoe the ground;
Joel	3.10	ploughs into swords and your **pruning-knives** into spears.
Mic	4. 3	their swords into ploughs and their spears into **pruning-knives.**
Jn	15. 2	bear fruit, and he **prunes** every branch that does bear fruit,

PSALM

Lk	20.42	says in the book of **Psalms,** 'The Lord said to my Lord:
	24.44	writings of the prophets, and the **Psalms** had to come true."
Acts	1.20	written in the book of **Psalms,** 'May his house become empty;
	13.32	As it is written in the second **Psalm,** 'You are my Son;
Eph	5.19	another with the words of **psalms,** hymns, and sacred songs;
	5.19	hymns and **psalms** to the Lord with praise in your hearts.
Col	3.16	Sing **psalms,** hymns, and sacred songs;

PUBLIC

Lev	20.17	or half-sister, they shall be **publicly** disgraced and driven
Num	35.12	is not to be put to death without a **public** trial.
Deut	24. 5	be drafted into military service or any other **public** duty;
	25. 3	more than that would humiliate him **publicly.**
Josh	20. 6	until he has received a **public** trial and until the death of
	20. 9	not be killed unless he had first received a **public** trial.
2 Sam	13.13	How could I ever hold up my head in **public** again?
	21.12	had stolen them from the **public** square in Beth Shan, where
1 Kgs	21.13	The two scoundrels **publicly** accused him of cursing God
2 Kgs	23. 6	to dust, and scattered it over the **public** burial-ground.
Neh	5. 7	I called a **public** assembly to deal with the problem [8] and said,
	8.16	temple courtyard, and in the **public** squares by the Water
Esth	3.14	proclamation were to be made **public** in every province, so
	3.15	the decree was made **public** in the capital city of Susa,
	8.14	The decree was also made **public** in Susa, the capital city.
	9.14	The bodies of Haman's ten sons were **publicly** displayed.
Job	30.28	I stand up in **public** and plead for help.
	33.27	He will say in **public,** "I have sinned.
Prov	5.14	And suddenly I found myself **publicly** disgraced."
Is	59.14	Truth stumbles in the **public** square,
Jer	26.23	killed and his body thrown into the **public** burial-ground.)
	48.38	in all its **public** squares there is nothing but mourning,
Ezek	3.25	man, and you will not be able to go out in **public.**
	23.18	She exposed herself **publicly** and let everyone know she was a whore.
Dan	11.20	king will be killed, but not **publicly** and not in battle."
Mt	1.19	was right, but he did not want to disgrace Mary **publicly;**
	6. 1	perform your religious duties in **public** so that people will see
	6. 1	If you do these things **publicly,** you will not have any
	10.32	"If anyone declares **publicly** that he belongs to me, I
	10.33	But if anyone rejects me **publicly,** I will reject him
Mk	1.45	talked so much that Jesus could not go into a town **publicly.**
Lk	1.25	"He has taken away my **public** disgrace!"
	1.80	the day when he appeared **publicly** to the people of Israel.
	12. 8	assure you that whoever declares **publicly** that he belongs to me,
	12. 9	But whoever rejects me **publicly,** the Son of Man will also
Jn	7.26	He is talking in **public,** and they say nothing against him!
	18.20	Jesus answered, "I have always spoken **publicly** to everyone;
Acts	5.18	They arrested the apostles and put them in the **public** jail.
	12. 4	Herod planned to put him on trial in **public** after Passover.
	16.19	and dragged them to the authorities in the **public** square.
	16.37	yet they whipped us in **public**—and we are Roman citizens!
	17.17	and also in the **public** square every day with the people
	18.28	defeated the Jews in **public** debates by proving from the Scriptures
	19.18	of the believers came, **publicly** admitting and revealing what they
	19.19	brought their books together and burnt them in **public.**
	20.20	as I preached and taught in **public** and in your homes.
1 Cor	4. 9	men condemned to die in **public** as a spectacle for the whole
	11. 4	proclaims God's message in **public** worship with his head covered
	11. 5	proclaims God's message in **public** worship with nothing on her head
	11.13	to pray to God in **public** worship with nothing on her head.
Gal	2.11	I opposed him in **public,** because he was clearly wrong.
Col	2.15	he made a **public** spectacle of them by leading them as
1 Tim	4.13	time and effort to the **public** reading of the Scriptures and
	5.20	Rebuke **publicly** all those who commit sins, so that the rest
Heb	6. 6	crucifying the Son of God and exposing him to **public** shame.
	10.33	You were at times **publicly** insulted and ill-treated,
Rev	16.15	he will not walk around naked and be ashamed in **public!"**

AV **PUBLICAN see TAX-COLLECTOR**

PUFF

Job	30.15	dignity is gone like a **puff** of wind, and my prosperity like
Ps	39. 5	is no more than a **puff** of wind, [6] no more than a
	39.11	Indeed a man is no more than a **puff** of wind!
	62. 9	Men are all like a **puff** of breath;
	144. 4	He is like a **puff** of wind;
Is	57.13	A **puff** of wind will carry them off!
Ezek	28. 2	**Puffed** up with pride, you claim to be a god.
1 Cor	8. 1	Such knowledge, however, **puffs** a person up with pride;
2 Cor	12. 7	to keep me from being **puffed** up with pride because of the
Col	2.18	such a person is all **puffed** up by his human way of
Jas	4.14	You are like a **puff** of smoke, which appears for a moment

PULL

Gen	19.10	two men inside reached out, **pulled** Lot back into the house,
	37.28	traders came by, the brothers **pulled** Joseph out of the well
	38.29	But he **pulled** his arm back, and his brother was born first.
Ex	2.10	She said to herself, "I **pulled** him out of the water, and
Lev	5. 8	will break its neck without **pulling** off its head [9] and
Deut	23.25	all the corn you can **pull** off with your hands, but you
	25.10	as 'the family of the man who had his sandal **pulled** off.'
Judg	3.22	Ehud did not **pull** it out of the king's belly, and it
	16. 3	of the city gate and **pulled** it up—doors, posts, lock, and
	16.14	But he woke up and **pulled** his hair loose from the loom.
	20.33	of the Israelites **pulled** back and regrouped at Baaltamar,
Ruth	2.15	Besides that, **pull** out some corn from the bundles and leave
2 Sam	17.13	bring ropes and just **pull** the city into the valley below.
	22.17	he **pulled** me out of the deep waters.
1 Kgs	13. 4	arm became paralysed so that he couldn't **pull** it back.
	15.19	that he will have to **pull** his troops out of my territory."
	22.34	"Turn round and **pull** out of the battle!"
2 Kgs	2.11	suddenly a chariot of fire **pulled** by horses of fire came
	3. 2	he **pulled** down the image his father had made for the worship
	23.15	Josiah **pulled** down the altar, broke its stones into pieces,
2 Chr	16. 3	that he will have to **pull** his troops out of my territory."
	18.33	"Turn round and **pull** out of the battle!"
Neh	13.25	down curses on them, beat them, and **pulled** out their hair.
Job	8.18	But then **pull** them up— no one will ever know they
	30. 4	They **pulled** up the plants of the desert and ate them, even
	39.10	Or make him **pull** a harrow in your fields?
	41.17	so firmly together that nothing can ever **pull** them apart.
Ps	17.11	wherever I turn, watching for a chance to **pull** me down.
	18.16	he **pulled** me out of the deep waters.
	40. 2	He **pulled** me out of a dangerous pit, out of the deadly
	144. 7	Reach down from above, **pull** me out of the deep water, and
Prov	2.22	men from the land and **pull** sinners out of it like plants
	14. 4	Without any oxen to **pull** the plough your barn will be empty,
Ecc	3. 2	planting and the time for **pulling** up, [3] the time for killing
Is	33.20	whose pegs are never **pulled** up and whose ropes never break.
	50. 6	they insulted me, when they **pulled** out the hairs of my beard
Jer	1.10	to uproot and to **pull** down, to destroy and to overthrow,
	22.24	my right hand, I would **pull** you off [25] and give you to
	24. 6	I will plant them and not **pull** them up.
	31.28	took care to uproot, to **pull** down, to overthrow, to destroy,
	38.10	him three men and to **pull** me out of the well before
	38.13	I did this, [13] and they **pulled** me up out of the well.
	41. 2	men with him **pulled** out their swords and killed Gedaliah.
	42.10	I will plant you and not **pull** you up.
	45. 4	down what I have built and **pulling** up what I have planted.
Ezek	17. 9	Won't the first eagle **pull** it up by its roots,
	17. 9	**pull** off the grapes, and break off
	17. 9	not take much strength or a mighty nation to **pull** it up.
	19.12	But angry hands **pulled** it up by the roots and threw it
	26.10	The noise of their horses **pulling** wagons and chariots will
	26.12	They will **pull** down your walls and shatter your luxurious houses.
	29. 4	Then I will **pull** you up out of the Nile, with all
Dan	6.23	gave orders for Daniel to be **pulled** up out of the pit.
	6.23	So they **pulled** him up and saw that he had not been
Hos	10.11	I made Judah **pull** the plough and Israel pull the harrow.
Amos	9.15	land I gave them, and they will not be **pulled** up again."
Obad	3	and so you say to yourself, 'Who can ever **pull** me down?'
	4	seems to be among the stars, yet I will **pull** you down.
Mic	5.14	I will **pull** down the images of the goddess Asherah in
Zech	6. 2	The first chariot was **pulled** by red horses, the second by
	6. 6	The chariot **pulled** by the black horses was going north
Mt	13.28	'Do you want us to go and **pull** up the weeds?'
	13.29	gather the weeds you might **pull** up some of the wheat along
	13.30	tell the harvest workers to **pull** up the weeds first, tie
	13.48	the net is full, they **pull** it to shore and sit down
	15.13	Father in heaven did not plant will be **pulled** up," answered Jesus.
	17.27	**Pull** up the first fish you hook, and in its mouth you
Lk	5. 2	He saw two boats **pulled** up on the beach;
	5.11	**pulled** the boats up on the beach, left everything, and followed
	14. 5	a Sabbath, would you not **pull** him out at once on the
	17. 6	say to this mulberry tree, '**Pull** yourself up by the roots
Jn	21. 6	net out and could not **pull** it back in, because they had
	21. 8	came to shore in the boat, **pulling** the net full of fish.
Acts	16.27	so he **pulled** out his sword and was about to kill himself.
	27.13	out their plan, so they **pulled** up the anchor and sailed

Acts 27.17 They **pulled** it aboard and then fastened some ropes tight
1 Cor 7.34 and so he is **pulled** in two directions.
2 Cor 10. 5 we **pull** down every proud obstacle that is raised against the
Phil 1.23 I am **pulled** in two directions.
1 Tim 6. 9 and harmful desires, which **pull** them down to ruin and destruction.
Jude 12 trees that have been **pulled** up by the roots and are

PUNCH

1 Cor 9.26 why I am like a boxer who does not waste his **punches.**

PUNISH

[UNPUNISHED]

Gen 3.14 Lord God said to the snake, "You will be **punished** for this;
4.13 said to the Lord, "This **punishment** is too hard for me
9. 5 If anyone takes human life, he will be **punished.**
9. 5 I will **punish** with death any animal that takes a human life.
15.14 But I will **punish** the nation that enslaves them,
15.16 Amorites until they become so wicked that they must be **punished."**
18.25 If you did, the innocent would be **punished** along with the guilty.
Ex 3.20 and will **punish** Egypt by doing terrifying things there.
5.21 you have done and will **punish** you for making the king and
6. 6 mighty arm to bring terrible **punishment** upon them,
7. 3 Then I will bring severe **punishment** on Egypt
8. 2 If you refuse, I will **punish** your country by covering it
8.21 if you refuse, I will **punish** you by sending flies on you,
9. 3 let them go, [3] I will **punish** you by sending a terrible
9.14 This time I will **punish** not only your officials and your people,
9.14 but I will **punish** you as well,
10.17 Lord your God to take away this fatal **punishment** from me."
11. 1 will send only one more **punishment** on the king of Egypt and
12.12 both human and animal, and **punishing** all the gods of Egypt.
12.13 over you and will not harm you when I **punish** the Egyptians.
15.26 my commands, I will not **punish** you with any of the diseases
19.22 near me must purify themselves, or I will **punish** them."
19.24 the boundary to come up to me, or I will **punish** them."
20. 5 I bring **punishment** on those who hate me and on their
20. 7 the Lord your God, will **punish** anyone who misuses my name.
21.18 fist, but does not kill him, he is not to be **punished.**
21.20 the slave dies on the spot, the man is to be **punished.**
21.21 for a day or two, the master is not to be **punished.**
21.21 The loss of his property is **punishment** enough.
21.23 herself is injured, the **punishment** shall be life for life,
21.28 but its owner is not to be **punished.**
32.34 is coming when I will **punish** these people for their sin."
34. 7 I will not fail to **punish** children and grandchildren to the
Lev 18.25 and so the Lord is **punishing** the land and making it reject
19.20 with her, they will be **punished** but not put to death, since
22.16 this would bring guilt and **punishment** on such a person.
26.14 "If you will not obey my commands, you will be **punished.**
26.16 the covenant I have made with you, [16] I will **punish** you.
26.18 do not obey me, I will increase your **punishment** seven times.
26.21 obey me, I will again increase your **punishment** seven times.
26.23 "If after all this **punishment** you still do not listen to me,
26.24 turn on you and **punish** you seven times harder than before.
26.25 bring war on you to **punish** you for breaking our covenant,
26.28 again make your **punishment** seven times worse than before.
Num 12.11 do not make us suffer this **punishment** for our foolish sin.
14.18 I will not fail to **punish** children and grandchildren
16.29 a natural death without some **punishment** from God,
31. 2 The Lord said to Moses, [2] **"Punish** the Midianites
31. 3 you can attack Midian and **punish** them for what they did
32.23 you will be **punished** for your sin.
Deut 5. 9 I bring **punishment** on those who hate me and on their
5.11 the Lord your God, will **punish** anyone who misuses my name.
7.10 but he will not hesitate to **punish** those who hate him.
8. 5 Lord your God corrects and **punishes** you just as a father
18.19 my name, and I will **punish** anyone who refuses to obey him.
19.19 receive the **punishment** the accused man would have received.
19.21 the **punishment** is to be a life for a life,
21.18 who will not obey his parents, even though they **punish** him.
32.34 he waits for the right time to **punish** them.
32.35 The Lord will take revenge and **punish** them;
32.41 take revenge on my enemies and **punish** those who hate me.
32.43 praise the Lord's people— he **punishes** all who kill them.
Josh 9.20 if we don't, God will **punish** us.
22.17 when the Lord **punished** his own people with an epidemic?
22.20 the whole community of Israel was **punished** for that.
22.23 or fellowship-offerings, let the Lord himself **punish** us.
22.31 saved the people of Israel from the Lord's **punishment."**
23.16 in his anger he will **punish** you, and soon none of you
24.20 serve foreign gods, he will turn against you and **punish** you.
Judg 8.16 the desert and used them to **punish** the leaders of Sukkoth.
20.10 the others will go and **punish** Gibeah for this immoral act
Ruth 1.17 May the Lord's worst **punishment** come upon me if I let
1 Sam 3.13 that I am going to **punish** his family for ever because his
3.17 God will **punish** you severely if you don't tell me everything
5. 6 The Lord **punished** the people of Ashdod severely and terrified them.
5. 6 He **punished** them and the people in the surrounding territory
5. 7 said, "The God of Israel is **punishing** us and our god Dagon.
5. 9 it arrived there, the Lord **punished** that city too and caused
5. 9 He **punished** them with tumours which developed in all the
5.11 the city because God was **punishing** them so severely.
6. 3 and you will find out why he has kept on **punishing** you."
6. 5 Perhaps he will stop **punishing** you, your gods, and your
15. 2 He is going to **punish** the people of Amalek because their
20.16 If it is broken, the Lord will **punish** you."
1 Sam 24.12 May he **punish** you for your action against me, for I will
25.26 and all who want to harm you will be **punished** like Nabal.
25.39 The Lord has **punished** Nabal for his evil."
26. 9 The Lord will certainly **punish** whoever harms his chosen king.
28.10 that you will not be **punished** for doing this," he told
2 Sam 3.29 May the **punishment** for it fall on Joab and all his family!
3.39 May the Lord **punish** these criminals as they deserve!"
6. 8 David was furious because the Lord had **punished** Uzzah in anger.
7.14 he does wrong, I will **punish** him
7.14 as a father **punishes** his son.
16. 8 and now the Lord is **punishing** you for murdering so many of
24.14 But I don't want to be **punished** by men.
24.14 Lord himself be the one to **punish** us, for he is merciful."
24.16 Lord changed his mind about **punishing** the people and said to
24.17 You should **punish** me and my family."
1 Kgs 2. 9 But you must not let him go **unpunished.**
2.32 The Lord will **punish** Joab for those murders, which he
2.33 The **punishment** for their murders will fall on Joab and
2.44 The Lord will **punish** you for it.
8.32 **Punish** the guilty one as he deserves, and acquit the one who
11.39 of Solomon's sin I will **punish** the descendants of David, but
14.15 The Lord will **punish** Israel, and she will shake like a
2 Kgs 7. 9 wait until morning to tell it, we are sure to be **punished.**
9. 7 Ahab, so that I may **punish** Jezebel for murdering my prophets
9.26 I promise that I will **punish** you here in this same field.'
17.20 Lord rejected all the Israelites, **punishing** them and handing
19. 3 we are being **punished** and are in disgrace.
19. 4 God hear these insults and **punish** those who spoke them.
21.13 I will **punish** Jerusalem as I did Samaria, as I did King
22.16 "I am going to **punish** Jerusalem and all its people, as
22.19 heard how I threatened to **punish** Jerusalem and its people.
22.20 heard your prayer, [20] and the **punishment** which I am going
1 Chr 9. 1 Judah had been deported to Babylon as **punishment** for their sins.
12.17 the God of our ancestors will know it and **punish** you."
13.11 David was furious because the Lord had **punished** Uzzah in anger.
15.13 time, the Lord our God **punished** us for not worshipping him
21. 7 God was displeased with what had been done, so he **punished** Israel.
21.13 But I don't want to be **punished** by men.
21.13 Lord himself be the one to **punish** me, because he is merciful."
21.17 my God, **punish** me and my family, and spare your people."
27.24 God **punished** Israel because of this census, so the final
2 Chr 6.23 **Punish** the guilty one as he deserves and acquit the one who
12. 2 Rehoboam's reign their disloyalty to the Lord was **punished.**
20. 9 any disaster struck them to **punish** them—a war, an epidemic,
20.12 **Punish** them, for we are helpless in the face of this large
21.14 result, the Lord will severely **punish** your people, your
24.22 "May the Lord see what you are doing and **punish** you!"
24.24 In this way King Joash was **punished.**
26.20 He hurried to get out, because the Lord had **punished** him.
28.11 Let them go, or the Lord will **punish** you in his anger."
28.13 against the Lord and made him angry enough to **punish** us.
30. 7 As you can see, he **punished** them severely.
32.26 Lord did not **punish** the people until after Hezekiah's death.
34.24 "I am going to **punish** Jerusalem and all its people with the
34.27 heard how I threatened to **punish** Jerusalem and its people.
34.28 heard your prayer, [28] and the **punishment** which I am going
Ezra 7.26 or the laws of the empire, he is to be **punished** promptly:
8.22 displeased with and **punishes** anyone who turns away from him.
9.13 has happened to us in **punishment** for our sins and wrongs, we
9.13 that you, our God, have **punished** us less than we deserve and
Neh 6.14 "God, remember what Tobiah and Sanballat have done and **punish** them.
9.33 You have done right to **punish** us;
13.18 This is exactly why God **punished** your ancestors when he
Esth 3. 6 was a Jew, he decided to do more than **punish** Mordecai alone.
7. 7 the king was determined to **punish** him for this, so he stayed
Job 8. 4 against God, and so he **punished** them as they deserved.
9.34 Stop **punishing** me, God!
11. 6 God is **punishing** you less than you deserve.
13.21 stop **punishing** me, and don't crush me with terror.
20.23 God will **punish** him in fury and anger.
21.17 Did God ever **punish** the wicked in anger [18] and blow them
21.19 You claim God **punishes** a child for the sins of his father.
21.19 Let God **punish** the sinners themselves;
21.20 Let sinners bear their own **punishment;**
21.30 day God is angry and **punishes,** it is the wicked man who
22.19 and innocent men laugh when they see the wicked **punished.**
27. 7 fight against me be **punished** like wicked, unrighteous men.
27.13 This is how Almighty God **punishes** wicked, violent men.
31.11 Such wickedness should be **punished** by death.
31.23 Because I fear God's **punishment,** I could never do such a thing.
31.28 Such a sin should be **punished** by death;
32.22 how to flatter, and God would quickly **punish** me if I did.
34.26 He **punishes** sinners where all can see it, [27] because
35.15 think that God does not **punish,** that he pays little
36.13 angry, and even when **punished,** they don't pray for help.
36.17 But now you are being **punished** as you deserve.
37.13 he may send it to **punish** men, or to show them his
Ps 3. 7 You **punish** all my enemies and leave them powerless to harm me.
5.10 Condemn and **punish** them, O God;
6. 1 Don't **punish** me in your anger!
7.16 So they are **punished** by their own evil and are hurt by
9.12 not forget their cry, and he **punishes** those who wrong them.
10.12 O Lord, **punish** those wicked men!
10.13 despise God and say to himself, "He will not **punish** me"?
10.15 **punish** them for the wrong they have done until they do it
11. 6 he **punishes** them with scorching winds.
17.14 **Punish** them with the sufferings you have stored up for them;
28. 4 **Punish** them for what they have done,
28. 4 **Punish** them for all their deeds;

Ps 28. 5 so he will **punish** them and destroy them for ever.
31.23 The Lord protects the faithful, but **punishes** the proud
32. 4 Day and night you **punished** me, Lord;
34.21 those who hate the righteous will be **punished.**
38. 1 O Lord, don't **punish** me in your anger!
39.10 Don't **punish** me any more!
39.11 You **punish** a man's sins by your rebukes, and like a moth
44. 2 **punished** the other nations and caused your own to prosper.
54. 5 May God use their own evil to **punish** my enemies.
56. 7 **Punish** them, O God, for their evil;
58.10 The righteous will be glad when they see sinners **punished;**
59. 5 Wake up and **punish** the heathen;
69.26 They persecute those whom you have **punished;**
73.14 every morning you have **punished** me.
79. 8 Do not **punish** us for the sins of our ancestors.
79.10 Let us see you **punish** the nations for shedding the blood of
81.15 their **punishment** would last for ever.
88.15 I am worn out from the burden of your **punishments.**
89.32 commandments, [32] then I will **punish** them for their sins;
91. 8 You will look and see how the wicked are **punished.**
94. 1 Lord, you are a God who **punishes;**
94.10 He scolds the nations—won't he **punish** them?
94.23 He will **punish** them for their wickedness and destroy
99. 8 God who forgives, even though you **punished** them for their sins.
103.10 He does not **punish** us as we deserve or repay us
106.30 But Phinehas stood up and **punished** the guilty, and the
109.20 Lord, **punish** my enemies in that way— those who say such
118.18 He has **punished** me severely, but he has not let me die.
119.67 Before you **punished** me, I used to go wrong, but now I
119.71 My **punishment** was good for me, because it made me learn
119.75 Lord, and that you **punished** me because you are faithful.
119.84 When will you **punish** those who persecute me?
120. 3 How will he **punish** you?
125. 5 But when you **punish** the wicked,
125. 5 **punish** also those who abandon your ways.
135. 9 and wonders to **punish** the king and all his officials.
141. 5 A good man may **punish** me and rebuke me in kindness, but
149. 7 hands [7] to defeat the nations and to **punish** the peoples;
149. 9 to **punish** the nations as God has commanded.
Prov 10.13 Intelligent people talk sense, but stupid people need to be **punished.**
11.21 evil men will be **punished,** but righteous men will escape.
11.31 can be sure that wicked and sinful people will be **punished.**
13.24 If you don't **punish** your son, you don't love him.
14.35 competent officials, but they **punish** those who fail them.
15.10 If you do what is wrong, you will be severely **punished;**
16. 5 he will never let them escape **punishment.**
17. 5 You will be **punished** if you take pleasure in someone's misfortune.
17.26 justice is perverted when good people are **punished.**
19. 5 in court, you will be **punished**—there will be no escape.
19. 9 No one who tells lies in court can escape **punishment;**
19.25 Arrogance should be **punished,** so that people who don't
20.26 out who is doing wrong, and will **punish** him without pity.
21.11 who is conceited gets his **punishment,** even an unthinking
24.18 and then he might not **punish** him.
24.25 Judges who **punish** the guilty, however, will be
28.20 in a hurry to get rich, you are going to be **punished.**
29.24 He will be **punished** if he tells the truth in court, and
Ecc 8.11 Because crime is not **punished** quickly enough.
8.14 sometimes righteous men get the **punishment** of the wicked,
Is 1. 5 Do you want to be **punished** even more?
3.17 But I will **punish** them—I will shave their heads and
5.25 his people and has stretched out his hand to **punish** them.
5.25 ended, but his hand will still be stretched out to **punish.**
9.12 his hand is still stretched out to **punish.**
9.13 though the Lord Almighty has **punished** them, they have not
9.14 day the Lord will **punish** Israel's leaders and its people;
9.17 ended, but his hand will still be stretched out to **punish.**
9.19 Lord Almighty is angry, his **punishment** burns like a fire
9.21 his hand is still stretched out to **punish.**
10. 3 What will you do when God **punishes** you?
10. 4 his hand will still be stretched out to **punish.**
10. 5 Assyria like a club to **punish** those with whom I am angry.
10.10 out my hand to **punish** those kingdoms that worship idols,
10.12 and in Jerusalem, I will **punish** the emperor of Assyria for
10.16 going to send disease to **punish** those who are now well-fed.
10.25 little while I will finish **punishing** you, and then I will
10.26 I will **punish** Assyria as I punished Egypt.
11. 4 the people will be **punished,** and evil persons will die.
13. 3 to fight a holy war and **punish** those he is angry with.
13.11 on the earth and **punish** all wicked people for their sins.
13.11 who is proud and **punish** everyone who is arrogant and cruel.
14.26 world, and my arm is stretched out to **punish** the nations."
14.27 stretched out his arm to **punish,** and no one can stop him.
19.16 the Lord Almighty has stretched out his hand to **punish** them.
19.22 The Lord will **punish** the Egyptians, but then he will heal them.
24.21 coming when the Lord will **punish** the powers above and the
24.22 them in prison until the time of their **punishment** comes.
26.11 Your enemies do not know that you will **punish** them.
26.11 let them suffer the **punishment** you have prepared.
26.14 not rise, for you have **punished** them and destroyed them.
26.16 You **punished** your people, Lord, and in anguish they prayed to you.
26.21 from his heavenly dwelling-place to **punish** the people of the
27. 1 sword to **punish** Leviathan, that wriggling, twisting dragon,
27. 7 Israel has not been **punished** by the Lord as severely as
27. 8 The Lord **punished** his people by sending them into exile.
29.21 others, those who prevent the **punishment** of criminals, and
30.31 hear the Lord's voice and feel the force of his **punishment.**
31. 2 carries out his threats to **punish** evil men and those who
35. 4 God is coming to your rescue, coming to **punish** your enemies."
Is 37. 3 we are being **punished** and are in disgrace.
37. 4 Lord your God hear these insults and **punish** those who spoke them.
40. 2 I have **punished** them in full for all their sins."
51.17 have drunk the cup of **punishment** that the Lord in his anger
53. 4 we thought that his suffering was **punishment** sent by God.
53. 5 We are healed by the **punishment** he suffered, made whole by
53. 6 But the Lord made the **punishment** fall on him,
53. 6 the **punishment** all of us deserved.
53.11 am pleased, will bear the **punishment** of many and for his
54. 9 I will not reprimand or **punish** you.
57.17 sin and greed, and so I **punished** them and abandoned them.
59.17 set things right and to **punish** and avenge the wrongs that
59.18 He will **punish** his enemies according to what they have done,
60.10 In my anger I **punished** you, But now I will show you
63. 4 it was time to **punish** their enemies.
65. 6 on their **punishment,** and their sentence is written down.
65. 7 So I will **punish** them as their past deeds deserve."
65.20 die before that would be a sign that I had **punished** them.
66. 6 the Temple, is the sound of the Lord **punishing** his enemies!
66.15 the wings of a storm to **punish** those he is angry with.
66.16 fire and sword he will **punish** all the people of the world
66.19 do [19] and will know that I am the one who **punishes** them.
Jer 1.16 I will **punish** my people because they have sinned;
2.19 Your own evil will **punish** you, and your turning from me
2.30 I **punished** you, but it did no good;
2.35 But I, the Lord, will **punish** you because you deny that you
5. 9 Shouldn't I **punish** them for these things and take revenge
5.29 "But I, the Lord, will **punish** them for these things;
6. 6 He has said, "I will **punish** this city because it is full
6.12 I am going to **punish** the people of this land.
6.15 when I **punish** them, that will be the end of them.
6.19 As **punishment** for all their schemes I am bringing ruin on
7.28 obey me, the Lord their God, or learn from their **punishment.**
8.12 when I **punish** you, that will be the end of you.
9. 9 Will I not **punish** them for these things?
9.25 is coming when I will **punish** the people of Egypt, Judah,
10.24 be too hard on us or **punish** us when you are angry;
11. 8 So I brought on them all the **punishments** described in it."
11.22 So the Lord Almighty said, "I will **punish** them!
14.10 they have done and **punish** them because of their sins."
15.13 my people, in order to **punish** them for the sins they have
16.10 will ask you why I have decided to **punish** them so harshly.
18.11 I am making plans against them and getting ready to **punish** them.
19.15 every nearby town all the **punishment** that I said I would,
21.14 But I will **punish** you for what you have done.
23. 2 Now I am going to **punish** you for the evil you have
23. 4 be afraid or terrified, and I will not **punish** them again.
23.12 the time of their **punishment** is coming.
23.34 words 'the Lord's burden,' I will **punish** him and his family.
25. 6 had obeyed the Lord, then he would not have **punished** you.
25. 7 your idols and have brought his **punishment** on yourselves.
25.12 After that I will **punish** Babylonia and its king for their sin.
25.13 I will **punish** Babylonia with all the disasters that I
25.29 Do they think they will go **unpunished?**
25.29 No, they will be **punished,** for I am going to send war
27. 8 his rule, then I will **punish** that nation by war, starvation,
29.31 "I, the Lord, will **punish** Shemaiah and all his descendants.
30.11 I will not let you go **unpunished;**
30.11 but when I **punish** you, I will be fair.
30.14 your **punishment** has been harsh because your sins are many
30.15 I **punished** you like this because your sins are many and your
30.20 I will **punish** all who oppress them.
31.19 After you had **punished** us, we hung our heads in grief.
32.18 to thousands, but you also **punish** people for the sins of
36.31 I will **punish** you, your descendants, and your officials
44.13 I will **punish** those who live in Egypt,
44.13 just as I **punished** Jerusalem—with war, starvation,
44.29 you proof that I will **punish** you in this place and that
46.10 today he will **punish** his enemies.
46.25 says, "I am going to **punish** Amon, the god of Thebes,
46.28 I will not let you go **unpunished;**
46.28 but when I **punish** you, I will be fair.
49. 8 because the time has come for me to **punish** them.
49.12 did not deserve to be **punished** had to drink from the cup
49.12 from the cup of **punishment,** do you think that you will
49.12 cup of punishment, do you think that you will go **unpunished?**
50.18 God of Israel, will **punish** King Nebuchadnezzar and his country,
50.18 just as I **punished** the emperor of Assyria.
50.27 The time has come for them to be **punished!"**
50.31 The time has come for me to **punish** you.
51. 6 I am now taking my revenge and **punishing** it as it deserves.
51. 9 God has **punished** Babylonia with all his might and has
51.44 I will **punish** Bel, the god of Babylonia, and make him
51.56 I am a God who **punishes** evil, and I will treat Babylon
Lam 1.22 **Punish** them as you punished me for my sins.
3. 1 am one who knows what it is to be **punished** by God.
3.39 Why should we ever complain when we are **punished** for our sin?
3.64 **"Punish** them for what they have done, O Lord;
4. 6 people have been **punished** even more than the inhabitants of Sodom,
4.22 But Edom, the Lord will **punish** you;
Ezek 4. 4 you to one day for each year their **punishment** will last.
4. 6 Judah for forty days—one day for each year of their **punishment.**
5. 9 that I hate, I will **punish** Jerusalem as I have never done
5.10 I will **punish** you and scatter in every direction any who are
5.15 and furious with you and **punish** you, all the nations around
6. 9 and know that I have **punished** them and disgraced them,
7. 4 I am going to **punish** you for the disgusting things you have
7. 9 I am going to **punish** you for the disgusting things you have
7. 9 am the Lord, and that I am the one who **punishes** you."

Ezek	7.12	because God's **punishment** will fall on everyone alike.
	7.27	I will **punish** you for all you have done, and will judge
	9. 1	"Come here, you men who are going to **punish** the city.
	11.11	I will **punish** you wherever you may be in the land of
	11.21	But I will **punish** the people who love to worship filthy,
	11.21	I will **punish** them for what they have done."
	13. 9	I am about to **punish** you prophets who have false visions
	14.10	and the one who consults him will get the same **punishment.**
	14.21	will send my four worst **punishments** on Jerusalem—war,
	14.22	and be convinced that the **punishment** I am bringing on
	15. 7	the people who live in Jerusalem [7] and will **punish** them.
	15. 7	When I **punish** them, you will know that I am the Lord.
	16.27	have raised my hand to **punish** you and to take away your
	16.38	and in my anger and fury I will **punish** you with death.
	16.41	houses down and let crowds of women see your **punishment.**
	17.15	He cannot break the treaty and go **unpunished!**
	17.19	the living God, I will **punish** him for breaking the treaty
	17.20	take him to Babylonia and **punish** him there, because he was
	20.26	This was to **punish** them and show them that I am the
	21.10	my people have disregarded every warning and **punishment.**
	21.25	of Israel, your day, the day of your final **punishment,** is
	21.27	the one whom I have chosen to **punish** the city has come.
	21.29	and your day is coming, the day of your final **punishment.**
	22.24	land is unholy, and so I am **punishing** it in my anger.
	23.31	so I will give you the same cup of **punishment** to drink."
	23.49	you two sisters—I will **punish** you for your immorality and
	24.14	You will be **punished** for what you have done."
	25.11	I will **punish** Moab, and they will know that I am the
	25.13	I announce that I will **punish** Edom and kill every man and
	25.17	I will **punish** them severely and take full revenge on them.
	28.22	show how holy I am by **punishing** those who live in you.
	28.26	I will **punish** all their neighbours who treated them with scorn,
	29. 2	him how he and all the land of Egypt will be **punished.**
	30.14	I will **punish** the capital city of Thebes.
	30.19	When I **punish** Egypt in this way, they will know that I
	33.12	doing evil, he won't be **punished,** and if a good man starts
	33.29	When I **punish** the people for their sins and make the
	35. 5	of her disaster, the time of final **punishment** for her sins.
	35.11	will know that I am **punishing** you for what you did to
	38.22	I will **punish** him with disease and bloodshed.
	44.10	said to me, "I am **punishing** those Levites who, together
	44.12	Sovereign Lord, solemnly swear that they must be **punished.**
	44.13	This is the **punishment** for the disgusting things they have done.
Dan	2. 9	all of you the same **punishment** if you don't tell me the
	8.23	wicked that they must be **punished,** there will be a stubborn,
	9.12	You **punished** Jerusalem more severely than any other city on earth,
	9.13	giving us all the **punishment** described in the Law of Moses.
	9.14	our God, were prepared to **punish** us, and you did, because
	11.36	be able to do this until the time when God **punishes** him.
Hos	1. 4	not be long before I **punish** the king of Israel for the
	2.13	I will **punish** her for the times that she forgot me when
	4. 9	You will suffer the same **punishment** as the people!
	4. 9	I will **punish** you and make you pay for the evil you
	4.14	Yet I will not **punish** them for this, because you
	5. 2	deep pit at Acacia City, and I will **punish** all of you.
	5. 9	The day of **punishment** is coming, and Israel will be ruined.
	5.10	So I will pour out **punishment** on them like a flood.
	6.11	have set a time to **punish** you also for what you are
	7.12	I will **punish** them for the evil they have done.
	8.10	But now I am going to gather them together and **punish** them.
	8.13	and now I will remember their sin and **punish** them for it;
	9. 7	The time for **punishment** has come, the time when people
	9. 9	God will remember their sin and **punish** them for it.
	10.10	I will attack this sinful people and **punish** them.
	10.10	them, and they will be **punished** for their many sins.
	11. 9	I will not **punish** you in my anger;
	12. 2	he is also going to **punish** Israel for the way her people
	12.14	The Lord will **punish** them for the disgrace they have brought
	13.16	Samaria must be **punished** for rebelling against me.
Joel	2.13	he is always ready to forgive and not **punish.**
Amos	1. 3	again and again, and for this I will certainly **punish** them.
	1. 6	again and again, and for this I will certainly **punish** them.
	1. 8	I will **punish** the city of Ekron, and all the Philistines who
	1. 9	again and again, and for this I will certainly **punish** them.
	1.11	again and again, and for this I will certainly **punish** them.
	1.13	again and again, and for this I will certainly **punish** them.
	2. 1	again and again, and for this I will certainly **punish** them.
	2. 4	again and again, and for this I will certainly **punish** them.
	2. 6	again and again, and for this I will certainly **punish** them.
	3. 2	so terrible, and that is why I must **punish** you for them."
	3.14	"On the day when I **punish** the people of Israel for
	4.12	"So then, people of Israel, I am going to **punish** you.
	5.17	All this will take place because I am coming to **punish** you."
	7. 4	In it I saw him preparing to **punish** his people with fire.
	7. 8	I will not change my mind again about **punishing** them.
	8. 1	I will not change my mind again about **punishing** them.
Obad	8	"On the day I **punish** Edom, I will destroy their clever
	16	have drunk a bitter cup of **punishment** on my sacred hill.
	16	nations will drink a still more bitter cup of **punishment;**
Jon	1.14	"O Lord, we pray, don't **punish** us with death for taking
	3.10	his mind and did not **punish** them as he had said he
	4. 2	kind, and always ready to change your mind and not **punish.**
Mic	4. 6	the people I **punished,** those who have suffered in exile.
	4.12	been gathered together to be **punished** in the same way that
	4.13	The Lord says, "People of Jerusalem, go and **punish** your enemies!
	7. 4	has come when God will **punish** the people, as he warned them
Nah	1. 2	he **punishes** those who oppose him.
	1. 3	but he is powerful and never lets the guilty go **unpunished.**
	3. 4	Nineveh the whore is being **punished.**
	3. 5	"I will **punish** you, Nineveh!
Hab	1.12	Babylonians and made them strong so that they can **punish** us.
	2.16	drink your own cup of **punishment,** and your honour will be
	3.16	the time to come when God will **punish** those who attack us.
Zeph	1. 4	"I will **punish** the people of Jerusalem and of all Judah.
	1. 8	the Lord, "I will **punish** the officials, the king's sons,
	1. 9	I will **punish** all who worship like pagans and who steal
	1.12	I will **punish** the people who are self-satisfied and confident,
	2. 3	Perhaps you will escape **punishment** on the day when the Lord
	2.10	Moab and Ammon will be **punished** for their pride and
	3.15	The Lord has ended your **punishment;**
	3.19	I will **punish** your oppressors;
Zech	1. 6	I, the Lord Almighty, had **punished** them as they deserved and
	9. 1	He has decreed **punishment** for the land of Hadrach and for
	10. 3	who rule my people, and I am going to **punish** them.
	11. 5	Their owners kill them and go **unpunished.**
	14.19	This will be the **punishment** that will fall on Egypt and
Mal	2. 3	I will **punish** your children and rub your faces in the dung
Mt	3. 7	you could escape from the **punishment** God is about to send?
	3. 9	don't think you can escape **punishment** by saying that Abraham is
	8.29	Have you come to **punish** us before the right time?"
	18.34	servant to jail to be **punished** until he should pay back the
	23.35	As a result, the **punishment** for the murder of all innocent
	23.36	the **punishment** for all these murders will fall on the people
	24. 9	arrested and handed over to be **punished** and be put to death.
	25.46	be sent off to eternal **punishment,** but the righteous will go
	26.74	May God **punish** me if I am not!
Mk	5. 7	For God's sake, I beg you, don't **punish** me!"
	12.40	Their **punishment** will be all the worse!"
	14.71	May God **punish** me if I am not!
Lk	3. 7	you could escape from the **punishment** God is about to send?
	8.28	I beg you, don't **punish** me!"
	11.50	of this time will be **punished** for the murder of all the
	11.51	the people of this time will be **punished** for them all!
	12.47	ready and do it, will be **punished** with a heavy whipping.
	12.48	he deserves a whipping, will be **punished** with a light whipping.
	20.47	Their **punishment** will be all the worse!"
	21.22	will be 'The Days of **Punishment,**' to make all that the
	21.23	upon this land, and God's **punishment** will fall on this people.
Jn	3.36	Son will not have life, but will remain under God's **punishment.**
Acts	2.40	"Save yourselves from the **punishment** coming on this wicked people!"
	4.21	it was impossible to **punish** them, because the people were all
	22. 5	and bring them back in chains to Jerusalem to be **punished.**
	26.11	Many times I had them **punished** in the synagogues and
Rom	1.19	God **punishes** them, because what can be known about God is
	1.27	they bring upon themselves the **punishment** they deserve for their
	2. 5	you are making your own **punishment** even greater on the Day
	3. 5	Can we say that God does wrong when he **punishes** us?
	11. 9	may they fall, may they be **punished!**
	13. 4	then be afraid of him, because his power to **punish** is real.
	13. 4	and carries out God's **punishment** on those who do evil.
	13. 5	not just because of God's **punishment,** but also as a matter
1 Cor	11.32	But we are judged and **punished** by the Lord, so that we
2 Cor	2. 6	that this person has been **punished** in this way by most of
	6. 9	Although **punished,** we are not killed;
	7.11	such devotion, such readiness to **punish** wrongdoing!
	10. 6	we will be ready to **punish** any act of disloyalty.
	13. 2	the next time I come nobody will escape **punishment.**
Gal	5.10	is upsetting you, whoever he is, will be **punished** by God.
1 Thes	4. 6	warned you that the Lord will **punish** those who do that.
2 Thes	1. 8	with a flaming fire, to **punish** those who reject God and
	1. 9	They will suffer the **punishment** of eternal destruction,
1 Tim	1.20	and Alexander, whom I have **punished** by handing them over to
Heb	2. 2	follow it or obey it received the **punishment** he deserved.
	10.29	Just think how much worse is the **punishment** he will deserve!
	12. 6	corrects everyone he loves, and **punishes** everyone he accepts as
	12. 7	Endure what you suffer as being a father's **punishment;**
	12. 7	Was there ever a son who was not **punished** by his father?
	12. 8	If you are not **punished,** as all his sons are, it means
	12. 9	our human fathers, they **punished** us and we respected them.
	12.10	Our human fathers **punished** us for a short time, as it
	12.11	When we are **punished,** it seems to us at the time
	12.11	have been disciplined by such **punishment** reap the peaceful reward
1 Pet	2.14	been appointed by him to **punish** the evildoers and to praise
2 Pet	2. 9	to keep the wicked under **punishment** for the Day of Judgement,
1 Jn	4.18	who is afraid, because fear has to do with **punishment.**
Jude	7	they suffer the **punishment** of eternal fire as a plain
Rev	3.19	I rebuke and **punish** all whom I love.
	6.10	judge the people on earth and **punish** them for killing us?"
	17. 1	famous prostitute is to be **punished,** that great city that is
	18. 4	you must not share in her **punishment!**
	18.10	In just one hour you have been **punished!"**
	18.24	Babylon was **punished** because the blood of prophets and of
	19. 2	God has **punished** her because she killed his servants."
	22.18	God will add to his **punishment** the plagues described in this book.

PUPIL

Mt	10.24	"No **pupil** is greater than his teacher;
	10.25	So a **pupil** should be satisfied to become like his teacher,
Lk	6.40	No **pupil** is greater than his teacher;
	6.40	but every **pupil,** when he has completed his training, will be

PURCHASE

[REPURCHASE]

Lev	25.30	he loses the right of **repurchase,** and the house becomes the
	25.30	the permanent property of the **purchaser** and his descendants;
	25.51	refund a part of the **purchase** price according to the number

Jer 32.11 copies of the deed of **purchase**—the sealed copy containing
32.12 had signed the deed of **purchase** and of the men who were
32.14 both the sealed deed of **purchase** and the open copy, and to
32.16 deed of **purchase** to Baruch, I prayed, [17] "Sovereign Lord,

PURE

[PURIFICATION, PURIFY, PURITY]

Gen 2.12 (**Pure** gold is found there and also rare perfume and precious stones.)
35. 2 **purify** yourselves and put on clean clothes.
Ex 19.10 spend today and tomorrow **purifying** themselves for worship.
19.22 near me must **purify** themselves, or I will punish them."
25.11 Cover it with **pure** gold inside and out and put a gold
25.17 "Make a lid of **pure** gold, 110 centimetres long and 66
25.24 Cover it with **pure** gold and put a gold border round it.
25.29 All of these are to be made of **pure** gold.
25.31 "Make a lamp-stand of **pure** gold.
25.36 lamp-stand are to be a single piece of **pure** hammered gold.
25.38 Make its tongs and trays of **pure** gold.
25.39 Use thirty-five kilogrammes of **pure** gold to make the
28.14 settings [14] and two chains of **pure** gold twisted like cords,
28.22 For the breast-piece make chains of **pure** gold, twisted like cords.
28.36 "Make an ornament of **pure** gold and engrave on it
29.36 This will **purify** the altar.
29.40 of fine wheat flour mixed with one litre of **pure** olive-oil.
30. 3 sides, and its projections with **pure** gold, and put a gold
30.10 to perform the ritual for **purifying** the altar by putting on
30.34 spices—stacte, onycha, galbanum, and **pure** frankincense.
30.35 Add salt to keep it **pure** and holy.
31. 8 the lamp-stand of **pure** gold and all its equipment,
37. 2 He covered it with **pure** gold inside and out and put a
37. 6 He made a lid of **pure** gold, 110 centimetres long and 66
37.11 He covered it with **pure** gold and put a gold border round
37.16 He made the dishes of **pure** gold for the table:
37.17 He made the lamp-stand of **pure** gold.
37.22 the lamp-stand were a single piece of **pure** hammered gold.
37.23 lamp-stand, and he made its tongs and trays of **pure** gold.
37.24 He used 35 kilogrammes of **pure** gold to make the
37.26 sides, and its projections with **pure** gold and put a gold
37.29 and the **pure** sweet-smelling incense, mixed like perfume.
39.15 For the breast-piece they made chains of **pure** gold,
39.24 wool, alternating with bells of **pure** gold, just as the Lord
39.30 sign of dedication, out of **pure** gold, and they engraved on
39.37 the lamp-stand of **pure** gold, its lamps, all its equipment,
Lev 8.15 In this way he dedicated it and **purified** it.
12. 4 Tent until the time of her **purification** is completed.
12. 6 When the time of her **purification** is completed, whether
14. 2 following regulations about the ritual **purification** of a
14. 7 person who is to be **purified** from his skin-disease, and then
14.18 In this way he shall perform the ritual of **purification.**
14.19 the sin-offering and perform the ritual of **purification.**
14.20 shall perform the ritual of **purification,** and the man will
14.21 he shall bring for his **purification** only one male lamb as
14.23 the eighth day of his **purification** he shall bring them to
14.29 head and in this way perform the ritual of **purification.**
14.31 In this way the priest shall perform the ritual of **purification.**
14.32 afford the normal offerings required for his **purification.**
14.49 To **purify** the house, he shall take two birds, some cedar-wood,
14.52 In this way he shall **purify** the house with the bird's blood,
14.53 shall perform the ritual of **purification** for the house, and
15.15 way he will perform the ritual of **purification** for the man.
15.30 way he will perform the ritual of **purification** for her.
16.16 will perform the ritual to **purify** the Most Holy Place from
16.17 to perform the ritual of **purification** until he comes out,
16.18 then go out to the altar for burnt-offerings and **purify** it.
16.19 this way he is to **purify** it from the sins of the
16.20 performing the ritual to **purify** the Most Holy Place,
16.30 is to be performed to **purify** them from all their sins, so
16.32 his father, is to perform the ritual of **purification.**
16.33 and perform the ritual to **purify** the Most Holy Place,
16.34 performed once a year to **purify** the people of Israel from
19.22 perform the ritual of **purification** to remove the man's sin,
24. 2 Bring **pure** olive-oil of the finest quality for the lamps in
24. 4 lamps on the lampstand of **pure** gold and must see that they
24. 6 on the table covered with **pure** gold, which is in the Lord's
24. 7 Put some **pure** incense on each row, as a token
Num 5. 8 to perform the ritual of **purification** for the guilty person.
6.11 to perform the ritual of **purification** for him because of his
8. 6 the people of Israel and **purify** them [7] in the following way:
8. 7 them with the water of **purification** and tell them to shave
8.12 to perform the ritual of **purification** for the Levites.
8.15 After you have **purified** and dedicated the Levites, they
8.21 The Levites **purified** themselves and washed their clothes,
8.21 He also performed the ritual of **purification** for them.
11.18 Now tell the people, '**Purify** yourselves for tomorrow;
15.25 shall perform the ritual of **purification** for the community,
15.28 shall perform the ritual of **purification**
15.28 to **purify** the man from his sin,
16.46 the people and perform the ritual of **purification** for them.
16.47 and performed the ritual of **purification** for the people.
19.12 He must **purify** himself
19.12 with the water for **purification** on the third day
19.12 But if he does not **purify** himself on both the third and
19.13 a corpse and does not **purify** himself remains unclean,
19.13 the water for **purification** has not been thrown over him.
19.19 seventh day he is to **purify** the man, who, after washing his
19.20 unclean and does not **purify** himself remains unclean,
19.20 the water for **purification** has not been thrown over him.
19.21 the water for **purification** must also wash his clothes;
28.22 this way perform the ritual of **purification** for the people.
Num 28.30 this way perform the ritual of **purification** for the people.
29. 5 this way perform the ritual of **purification** for the people.
29.11 offered in the ritual of **purification** for the people, and
31.19 and on the seventh day **purify** yourselves and the women you
31.20 You must also **purify** every piece of clothing and
31.22 tin, or lead, is to be **purified** by passing it through fire.
31.22 Everything else is to be **purified**
31.22 by the water for **purification.**
35.33 to perform the ritual of **purification** for the land where a
Josh 3. 5 Joshua said to the people, "**Purify** yourselves, because
7.13 **Purify** the people and get them ready to come before me.
1 Sam 16. 5 **Purify** yourselves and come with me."
16. 5 Jesse and his sons to **purify** themselves, and he invited them
20.26 "Something has happened to him, and he is not ritually **pure."**
21. 5 men always keep themselves ritually **pure** even when we go out
2 Sam 11. 4 (She had just finished her monthly ritual of **purification.)**
22.27 You are **pure** to those who are pure, but hostile to those
1 Kgs 5.11 four hundred thousand litres of **pure** olive-oil every year to
6.20 wide, and nine metres high, all covered with **pure** gold.
10.21 in the Hall of the Forest of Lebanon were of **pure** gold.
2 Kgs 2.21 'I make this water **pure,** and it will not cause any more
2.22 And that water has been **pure** ever since, just as Elisha
1 Chr 15.12 **Purify** yourselves and your fellow-Levites, so that you can
15.14 the priests and the Levites **purified** themselves in order to
28.17 instructions as to how much **pure** gold was to be used in
28.18 making dishes, [18] and how much **pure** gold in making the
29. 4 and forty metric tons of **pure** silver for decorating the
2 Chr 3. 4 The inside of the room was overlaid with **pure** gold.
4.22 All these objects were made of **pure** gold.
9.17 with ivory and the rest of it was covered with **pure** gold.
9.20 in the Hall of the Forest of Lebanon were of **pure** gold.
29. 5 to consecrate yourselves and **purify** the Temple of the Lord,
29.16 went inside the Temple to **purify** it, and they carried out
29.18 "We have completed the ritual **purification** of the whole Temple,
29.21 of Judah and to **purify** the Temple, they took seven bulls,
30.18 not performed the ritual of **purification,** and so they were
30.24 A large number of priests went through the ritual of **purification.**
34. 8 his reign, after he had **purified** the land and the Temple by
Ezra 6.20 the Levites had **purified** themselves and were ritually clean.
8.35 they also offered 12 goats to **purify** themselves from sin.
Neh 12.30 the Levites performed ritual **purification** for themselves,
12.45 they performed the ceremonies of **purification** and the other
13. 9 **purified** and for the temple equipment, grain-offerings,
13.22 I ordered the Levites to **purify** themselves and to go and
13.30 I **purified** the people from everything foreign;
Job 1. 5 sacrifices for each of his children in order to **purify** them.
4.17 in the sight of God or be **pure** before his Creator?
8. 6 you are so honest and **pure,** then God will come and help
11. 4 you claim you are **pure** in the sight of God.
15.14 Can any man be really **pure?**
15.15 even they are not **pure** in his sight.
23.10 if he tests me, he will find me **pure.**
25. 4 Can anyone be righteous or **pure** in God's sight?
25. 5 his eyes even the moon is not bright, nor the stars **pure.**
28.19 The finest topaz and the **purest** gold Cannot compare with
Ps 18.26 You are **pure** to those who are pure, but hostile to those
19.10 they are sweeter than the **purest** honey.
24. 4 Those who are **pure** in act and in thought, who do not
51.10 Create a **pure** heart in me, O God, and put a new
66.10 as silver is **purified** by fire so you have tested us.
73. 1 God is indeed good to Israel, to those who have **pure** hearts.
73.13 that I have kept myself **pure** and have not committed sin?
101. 2 I will live a **pure** life in my house, [3] and will never
119. 7 righteous judgements, I will praise you with a **pure** heart.
119. 9 How can a young man keep his life **pure?**
Prov 8.19 better than the finest gold, better than the **purest** silver.
10.20 A good man's words are like **pure** silver;
22.11 If you love **purity** of heart and graciousness of speech,
30.12 people who think they are **pure** when they are as filthy as
Ecc 10.13 He starts out with silly talk and ends up with **pure** madness.
Is 1.25 I will **purify** you just as metal is refined, and will remove
4. 4 the Lord will judge and **purify** the nation and wash away the
66.17 is near for those who **purify** themselves for pagan worship,
Jer 13.27 When will you ever be **pure?**
33. 8 I will **purify** them from the sins that they have committed
Lam 4. 7 Our princes were undefiled and **pure** as snow, vigorous and strong,
Ezek 16.52 bear your shame, because you make your sisters look **pure."**
24.11 the pot will be ritually **pure** again after the corrosion is
24.13 Although I tried to **purify** you, you remained defiled.
24.13 You will not be **pure** again until you have felt the full
37.23 I will **purify** them;
43.20 In this way you will **purify** the altar and consecrate it.
43.22 **Purify** the altar with its blood in the same way as you
44.27 offer a sacrifice for his **purification,** so that he can serve
45.18 sacrifice a bull without any defects and **purify** the Temple.
Dan 7. 9 clothes were white as snow, and his hair was like **pure** wool.
11.35 killed, but as a result of this the people will be **purified.**
12.10 Many people will be **purified.**
Zech 13. 1 fountain will be opened to **purify** the descendants of David
13. 9 that survives and will **purify** them
13. 9 as silver is **purified** by fire.
Mal 3. 3 He will come to judge like one who refines and **purifies** silver.
3. 3 so the Lord's messenger will **purify** the priests, so that
Mt 5. 8 "Happy are the **pure** in heart;
Mk 9.49 "Everyone will be **purified** by fire
9.49 as a sacrifice is **purified** by salt.
14. 3 jar full of a very expensive perfume made of **pure** nard.
Lk 2.22 to perform the ceremony of **purification,** as the Law of Moses
Jn 8.15 You make judgements in a **purely** human way;
11.55 to perform the ritual of **purification** before the festival.

Jn 12. 3 expensive perfume made of **pure** nard, poured it on Jesus' feet,
Acts 21.24 join them in the ceremony of **purification** and pay their expenses;
21.26 and the next day performed the ceremony of **purification** with them.
21.26 end of the period of **purification,** when a sacrifice would be
24.18 in the Temple after I had completed the ceremony of **purification.**
1 Cor 5. 7 the old yeast of sin so that you will be entirely **pure.**
5. 8 the bread that has no yeast, the bread of **purity** and truth.
6.11 But you have been **purified** from sin;
2 Cor 6. 6 By our **purity,** knowledge, patience, and kindness we have shown
7. 1 So then, let us **purify** ourselves from everything that makes body
11. 2 you are like a **pure** virgin whom I have promised in marriage
11. 3 will abandon your full and **pure** devotion to Christ—in the
Eph 5.27 in all its beauty—**pure** and faultless, without spot or wrinkle
Phil 2.15 you may be innocent and **pure** as God's perfect children, who
3. 5 by birth, of the tribe of Benjamin, a **pure-blooded** Hebrew.
4. 8 that are true, noble, right, **pure,** lovely, and honourable.
Col 1.22 to bring you, holy, **pure,** and faultless, into his presence.
1 Thes 2.10 our conduct towards you who believe was **pure,** right, and without
1 Tim 1. 5 love that comes from a **pure** heart, a clear conscience,
4.12 in your speech, your conduct, your love, faith, and **purity.**
5. 2 as mothers, and the younger women as sisters, with all **purity.**
5.22 keep yourself **pure.**
2 Tim 2.22 with those who with a **pure** heart call out to the Lord
Tit 1.15 Everything is **pure** to those who are themselves pure;
1.15 but nothing is **pure** to those who are defiled and unbelieving,
2. 5 to be self-controlled and **pure,** and to be good housewives
2.14 and to make us a **pure** people who belong to him alone
Heb 2.11 He **purifies** people from their sins, and both he and
2.11 he and those who are made **pure** all have the same Father.
9.10 to do only with food, drink, and various **purification** ceremonies.
9.13 are ritually unclean, and this **purifies** them by taking away their
9.14 His blood will **purify** our consciences from useless rituals,
9.22 almost everything is **purified** by blood, and sins are forgiven
9.23 of the heavenly originals, had to be **purified** in that way.
10. 2 worshipping God had really been **purified** from their sins,
10.10 we are all **purified** from sin by the offering that
10.14 has made perfect for ever those who are **purified** from sin.
10.22 with hearts that have been **purified** from a guilty conscience
10.29 the blood of God's covenant which **purified** him from sin?
13.12 the city, in order to **purify** the people from sin with his
Jas 1.27 God the Father considers to be **pure** and genuine religion is this:
3.17 But the wisdom from above is **pure** first of all;
4. 8 **Purify** your hearts, you hypocrites!
1 Pet 1. 2 Spirit, to obey Jesus Christ and be **purified** by his blood.
1.22 to the truth you have **purified** yourselves and have come to
2. 2 always thirsty for the **pure** spiritual milk, so that by drinking
3. 2 because they will see how **pure** and reverent your conduct is.
2 Pet 1. 9 has forgotten that he has been **purified** from his past sins.
3. 1 I have tried to arouse **pure** thoughts in your minds by
3.14 do your best to be **pure** and faultless in God's sight
1 Jn 1. 7 the blood of Jesus, his Son, **purifies** us from every sin.
1. 9 forgive us our sins and **purify** us from all our wrongdoing.
3. 3 hope in Christ keeps himself **pure,** just as Christ is pure.
Rev 3.18 to buy gold from me, **pure** gold, in order to be rich.
14. 4 men who have kept themselves **pure** by not having sexual relations
21.18 the city itself was made of **pure** gold, as clear as glass.
21.21 The street of the city was of **pure** gold, transparent as glass.

AV PURGE

1 Sam 3.14 be able to **remove** the consequences of this terrible sin."
2 Chr 34. 3 years later he began to **destroy** the pagan places of worship,
34. 8 his reign, after he had **purified** the land and the Temple by
Ps 51. 7 **wash** me, and I will be whiter than snow.
65. 3 Our faults defeat us, but you **forgive** them.
79. 9 rescue us and **forgive** our sins for the sake of your own
Prov 16. 6 Be loyal and faithful, and God will **forgive** your sin.
Is 1.25 I will **purify** you just as metal is refined, and will remove
4. 4 the Lord will judge and **purify** the nation and wash away the
6. 7 and now your guilt is gone, and your sins are **forgiven."**
22.14 "This evil will never be **forgiven** them as long as they live.
27. 9 Israel's sins will be **forgiven** only when the stones of pagan
Ezek 24.13 Although I tried to **purify** you,
24.13 you remained **defiled.**
24.13 You will not be **pure** again until you have felt the full
43.20 In this way you will **purify** the altar and consecrate it.
43.26 days the priests are to **consecrate** the altar and make it
Dan 11.35 killed, but as a result of this the people will be **purified.**
Mal 3. 3 As a metal-worker **refines** silver and gold, so the Lord's
Mt 3.12 his winnowing shovel with him to **thresh** out all the grain.
Lk 3.17 winnowing shovel with him, to **thresh** out all the grain and
1 Cor 5. 7 You must **remove** the old yeast of sin so that you will
2 Tim 2.21 If anyone makes himself **clean** from all those evil things,
Heb 1. 3 After achieving **forgiveness** for the sins of mankind, he sat
9.14 His blood will **purify** our consciences from useless rituals,
9.22 almost everything is **purified** by blood, and sins are forgiven
10. 2 worshipping God had really been **purified** from their sins,
2 Pet 1. 9 has forgotten that he has been **purified** from his past sins.

PURIFICATION see PURE

PURIFY see PURE

PURIM

The Jewish religious holiday held on the 14th day of the month Adar (about March 1st), celebrating the deliverance of the Jews from Haman by Esther and Mordecai.

Esth 3. 7 the lots to be cast **("purim,"** they were called) to find
9.24 people—had cast lots (or **"purim,"** as they were called) to
9.26 That is why the holidays are called **Purim.**
9.28 and observe the days of **Purim** for all time to come.
9.29 the letter about **Purim,** which Mordecai had written earlier.
9.31 to observe the days of **Purim** at the proper time, just as
9.32 the rules for **Purim,** was written down on a scroll.

PURITY see PURE

PURPLE

Ex 25. 4 blue, **purple,** and red wool;
26. 1 ten pieces of fine linen woven with blue, **purple,** and red
26.31 a curtain of fine linen woven with blue, **purple,** and red
26.36 fine linen woven with blue, **purple,** and red wool and
27.16 fine linen woven with blue, **purple,** and red wool, and
28. 5 craftsmen are to use blue, **purple,** and red wool, gold
28. 6 make the ephod of blue, **purple,** and red wool, gold thread,
28.33 hem put pomegranates of blue, **purple,** and red wool,
35. 6 blue, **purple,** and red wool;
35.23 blue, **purple,** or red wool;
35.25 thread and thread of blue, **purple,** and red wool, which they
35.35 blue, **purple,** and red wool;
36. 8 fine linen woven with blue, **purple,** and red wool and
36.35 fine linen, woven with blue, **purple,** and red wool and
36.37 fine linen woven with blue, **purple,** and red wool and
38.18 fine linen woven with blue, **purple,** and red wool and
38.23 a weaver of fine linen and of blue, **purple,** and red wool.
39. 1 With the blue, **purple,** and red wool they made the
39. 2 blue, **purple,** and red wool;
39. 3 into the fine linen and into the blue, **purple,** and red wool.
39.24 fine linen and of blue, **purple,** and red wool, alternating
39.29 of blue, **purple,** and red wool, decorated with embroidery,
Num 4.13 ashes from the altar and spread a **purple** cloth over it.
Judg 8.26 include the ornaments, necklaces, and **purple** clothes that
2 Chr 2. 7 bronze, and iron, and in making blue, **purple** and red cloth.
2.14 He can work with blue, **purple,** and red cloth, and with linen.
3.14 material, which was dyed blue, **purple,** and red, with designs
Esth 1. 6 tied by cords of fine **purple** linen to silver rings on marble
8.15 a cloak of fine **purple** linen, and a magnificent gold crown.
Prov 31.22 She makes bedspreads and wears clothes of fine **purple** linen.
Song 3.10 Its cushions are covered with **purple** cloth, lovingly woven
Jer 10. 9 in violet and **purple** cloth woven by skilled weavers.
Ezek 23. 6 They were soldiers in uniforms of **purple,**
27. 7 made of finest cloth, Of **purple** from the island of Cyprus.
27.16 They gave emeralds, **purple** cloth, embroidery, fine linen,
27.24 They sold you luxurious clothing, **purple** cloth, and embroidery,
Dan 5. 7 dressed in robes of royal **purple,** wear a gold chain of
5.16 dressed in robes of royal **purple,** wear a gold chain of
5.29 in a robe of royal **purple** and to hang a gold chain
Mk 15.17 They put a **purple** robe on Jesus, made a crown out of
15.20 they took off the **purple** robe and put his own clothes
Jn 19. 2 then they put a **purple** robe on him [3]and came to him
19. 5 Jesus came out, wearing the crown of thorns and the **purple** robe.
Acts 16.14 Lydia from Thyatira, who was a dealer in **purple** cloth.
Rev 17. 4 woman was dressed in **purple** and scarlet, and covered with gold
18.12 their goods of linen, **purple** cloth, silk, and scarlet cloth;
18.16 to dress herself in linen, **purple,** and scarlet, and cover herself

PURPOSE

Ex 20. 7 use my name for evil **purposes,** for I, the Lord your God,
Lev 7.24 not be eaten, but it may be used for any other **purpose.**
Deut 5.11 use my name for evil **purposes,** for I, the Lord your God,
Judg 20.11 in Israel assembled with one **purpose**—to attack the town.
2 Sam 7.21 It was your will and **purpose** to do this;
2 Kgs 14.27 it was not the Lord's **purpose** to destroy Israel completely
1 Chr 12.38 of the people of Israel were united in the same **purpose.**
17.19 It was your will and **purpose** to do this for me and
23. 5 musical instruments provided by the king for this **purpose.**
Ps 33.10 The Lord frustrates the **purposes** of the nations;
33.11 his **purposes** last eternally.
Is 26. 3 to those who keep their **purpose** firm and put their trust in
45.13 Cyrus to action to fulfil my **purpose** and put things right.
45.19 I have not spoken in secret or kept my **purpose** hidden.
53.10 live a long life, and through him my **purpose** will succeed.
Jer 32.39 I will give them a single **purpose** in life:
Mal 2.15 What was his **purpose** in this?
Lk 7.30 of the Law rejected God's **purpose** for themselves and refused to
9.31 he would soon fulfil God's **purpose** by dying in Jerusalem.
Jn 2. 6 ritual washing, and for this **purpose** six stone water jars were
18.37 the world for this one **purpose,** to speak about the truth.
Acts 9.21 come here for the very **purpose** of arresting those people
13.36 For David served God's **purposes** in his own time, and
20.27 held back from announcing to you the whole **purpose** of God.
26.12 was for this **purpose** that I went to Damascus with authority
Rom 6.13 part of yourselves to sin to be used for wicked **purposes.**
6.13 your whole being to him to be used for righteous **purposes.**
6.19 as slaves to impurity and wickedness for wicked **purposes.**
6.19 yourselves entirely as slaves of righteousness for holy **purposes.**
8.20 was condemned to lose its **purpose,** not of its own will,
8.28 love him, those whom he has called according to his **purpose.**
9.11 the result of God's own **purpose,** God said to her, "The
1 Cor 1.10 Be completely united, with only one thought and one **purpose.**

1 Cor 1.27 God **purposely** chose what the world considers nonsense in order to
2.10 searches everything, even the hidden depths of God's **purposes.**
4. 5 the dark secrets and expose the hidden **purposes** of people's minds.
4.17 For this **purpose** I am sending to you Timothy, who is my
2 Cor 2. 4 my **purpose** was not to make you sad, but to make you
8.21 Our **purpose** is to do what is right, not only in the
Gal 3.19 What, then, was the **purpose** of the Law?
4.18 a deep interest if the **purpose** is good—this is true always,
Eph 1. 5 he would make us his sons—this was his pleasure and **purpose.**
1. 9 God did what he had **purposed,** and made known to us the
1.11 Christ because of his own **purpose,** based on what he had
3.11 his eternal **purpose,** which he achieved through Christ Jesus
Phil 1.27 firm with one common **purpose** and that with only one desire
2.13 to make you willing and able to obey his own **purpose.**
1 Tim 1. 5 The **purpose** of this order is to arouse the love that comes
2 Tim 1. 9 what we have done, but because of his own **purpose** and grace.
2.21 be used for special **purposes,** because he is dedicated and useful
3.10 followed my teaching, my conduct, and my **purpose** in life;
Tit 1.11 not, and all for the shameful **purpose** of making money.
Heb 6.17 make it very clear that he would never change his **purpose;**
10.26 take away sins if we **purposely** go on sinning after the truth
11.40 His **purpose** was that only in company with us would they be
Jas 1.20 Man's anger does not achieve God's righteous **purpose.**
1 Pet 1. 2 were chosen according to the **purpose** of God the Father and
1. 7 Their **purpose** is to prove that your faith is genuine.
1. 9 of your souls, which is the **purpose** of your faith in him.
2 Pet 3. 5 They **purposely** ignore the fact that long ago God gave a command,
Rev 17.13 ten all have the same **purpose,** and they give their
17.17 will to carry out his **purpose** by acting together and giving

PURSE

Is 3.22 all their fine robes, gowns, cloaks, and **purses;**
46. 6 People open their **purses** and pour out gold;
Lk 10. 4 Don't take a **purse** or a beggar's bag or shoes;
12.33 Provide for yourselves **purses** that don't wear out,
22.35 you out that time without **purse,** bag, or shoes, did you lack
22.36 Jesus said, "whoever has a **purse** or a bag must take it;

PURSUE

Gen 14. 6 in the mountains of Edom, **pursuing** them as far as Elparan on
14.14 camp, 318 in all, and **pursued** the four kings all the way
31.23 his men with him and **pursued** Jacob for seven days until he
35. 5 people of the nearby towns, and they did not **pursue** them.
49.19 by a band of robbers, But he will turn and **pursue** them.
49.23 him fiercely And **pursue** him with their bows and arrows.
Ex 14. 4 him stubborn, and he will **pursue** you, and my victory over
14. 8 he **pursued** the Israelites, who were leaving triumphantly.
14. 9 the horses, chariots, and drivers, **pursued** them and caught
14.23 The Egyptians **pursued** them and went after them into the
15. 9 The enemy said, 'I will **pursue** them and catch them;
Lev 26.36 as if you were being **pursued** in battle, and you will fall
Num 14.45 and defeated them, and **pursued** them as far as Hormah.
Deut 11. 4 by drowning them in the Red Sea when they were **pursuing** you.
Josh 8. 6 They will **pursue** us until we have led them away from the
8.16 after them, and as they **pursued** Joshua, they kept getting
10.10 slaughtered them at Gibeon and **pursued** them down the
11. 8 the Israelites attacked and **pursued** them as far north as
24. 6 and the Egyptians **pursued** them with chariots and cavalry.
Judg 4.16 Barak **pursued** the chariots and the army
7.23 Manasseh were called out, and they **pursued** the Midianites.
7.25 They continued to **pursue** the Midianites and brought the
8. 4 They were exhausted, but were still **pursuing** the enemy.
8. 5 I am **pursuing** Zebah and Zalmunna, the Midianite kings."
8.12 Zalmunna, ran away, but he **pursued** them and captured them,
9.40 Gaal fled, and Abimelech **pursued** him.
20.43 trapped, and without stopping they **pursued** them as far as a
20.45 The Israelites continued to **pursue** the rest to Gidom,
1 Sam 7.11 marched out from Mizpah and **pursued** the Philistines almost
14.46 After that, Saul stopped **pursuing** the Philistines, and
17.52 shouted and ran after them, **pursuing** them all the way to
17.53 Israelites came back from **pursuing** the Philistines,
23.28 So Saul stopped **pursuing** David and went to fight the Philistines.
26.18 And he added, "Why, sir, are you still **pursuing** me,
2 Sam 2.28 as a signal for his men to stop **pursuing** the Israelites;
18.16 and his troops came back from **pursuing** the Israelites.
20.13 from the road, everyone followed Joab in **pursuit** of Sheba.
22.38 I **pursue** my enemies and defeat them;
1 Kgs 20.20 Israelites in hot **pursuit,** but Benhadad escaped on horseback,
2 Kgs 3.24 The Israelites kept up the **pursuit,** slaughtering the Moabites
9.27 chariot towards the town of Beth Haggan, **pursued** by Jehu.
25. 5 But the Babylonian army **pursued** King Zedekiah, captured
2 Chr 13.19 Abijah **pursued** Jeroboam's army and occupied some of his cities:
14.13 and Asa and his troops **pursued** them as far as Gerar.
18.32 he was not the king of Israel, so they stopped **pursuing** him.
Neh 9.11 Those who **pursued** them drowned in deep water, as a stone
Ps 7. 1 save me from all who **pursue** me, [2] or else like a lion
7. 5 then let my enemies **pursue** me and catch me, let them
18.37 I **pursue** my enemies and catch them;
35. 3 Lift up your spear and your axe against those who **pursue** me.
35. 5 blown by the wind as the angel of the Lord **pursues** them!
Is 30.16 are fast enough, but those who **pursue** you will be faster!
41. 3 He follows in **pursuit** and marches safely on, so fast that
58. 3 time as you fast, you **pursue** your own interests and oppress
58.13 as sacred and do not **pursue** your own interests on that day;
Jer 29.18 I will **pursue** them with war, starvation, and disease,
39. 5 But the Babylonian army **pursued** them and captured Zedekiah
Jer 52. 8 But the Babylonian army **pursued** King Zedekiah, captured
Lam 3.43 "You **pursued** us and killed us;
Ezek 5. 2 third to the winds, and I will **pursue** it with my sword.
5.12 the last third to the winds and **pursue** them with a sword.
Hos 8. 3 Because of this their enemies will **pursue** them.
Rev 12.13 the earth, he began to **pursue** the woman who had given birth

PUS

Lev 13.10 white and is full of **pus,** [11] it is a chronic skin-disease.
Job 7. 5 **pus** runs out of my sores.

PUSH

Gen 19. 9 They **pushed** Lot back and moved up to break down the door.
Num 35.20 someone and kills him by **pushing** him down or by throwing
35.22 does not hate, whether by **pushing** him down or by throwing
Deut 33.17 he gores the nations And **pushes** them to the ends of the
Judg 16.29 hand on each pillar, he **pushed** against them [30] and shouted,
16.30 He **pushed** with all his might, and the building fell down on
2 Kgs 4.27 Gehazi was about to **push** her away, but Elisha said, "Leave
Ezek 31.14 tall as that again or **push** its top through the clouds and
34.21 You **pushed** the sick ones aside and butted them away from
Amos 2. 7 the weak and helpless and **push** the poor out of the way.
Zech 5. 8 Then he **pushed** her down into the basket and put the lid
Mk 3.10 those who were ill kept **pushing** their way to him in order
Lk 5. 1 Lake Gennesaret while the people **pushed** their way up to him
5. 3 Simon—and asked him to **push** off a little from the shore.
5. 4 speaking, he said to Simon, **"Push** the boat out further to
Acts 7.27 But the one who was ill-treating the other **pushed** Moses aside.
7.39 they **pushed** him aside and wished that they could go back to

PUT ASIDE

Mk 7. 8 "You **put aside** God's command and obey the teachings of men."
1 Cor 16. 2 Sunday each of you must **put aside** some money, in proportion
2 Cor 4. 2 We **put aside** all secret and shameful deeds;

PUT OFF

Deut 23.21 the Lord your God, do not **put off** doing what you promised;
Ecc 8. 8 keep himself from dying or **put off** the day of his death.
2 Pet 1.14 know that I shall soon **put off** this mortal body, as our

PUT ON

Gen 35. 2 purify yourselves and **put on** clean clothes.
37.34 Jacob tore his clothes in sorrow and **put on** sackcloth.
Ex 32.27 every one of you to **put on** his sword and go through
34.35 Then he would **put the veil back on** until the next time
Lev 16. 4 Place, he must have a bath and **put on** the priestly garments:
16.23 priestly garments that he had **put on** before entering the
16.24 must bathe in a holy place and **put on** his own clothes.
16.32 He shall **put on** the priestly garments [33] and perform the
Josh 9. 5 They **put on** ragged clothes and worn-out sandals
Ruth 3. 3 So wash yourself, **put on** some perfume, and get dressed in
1 Sam 28. 8 he **put on** different clothes, and after dark he went with two
2 Sam 14. 2 **put on** your mourning clothes, and don't comb your hair.
1 Kgs 21.27 Ahab tore his clothes, took them off, and **put on** sackcloth.
2 Kgs 9.30 what had happened, **put on** eyeshadow, arranged her hair,
19. 1 tore his clothes in grief, **put on** sackcloth, and went to the
2 Chr 20.21 king ordered some musicians to **put on** the robes they wore on
Esth 4. 3 wailed, and most of them **put on** sackcloth and lay in ashes.
4. 4 Mordecai some clothes to **put on** instead of the sackcloth,
5. 1 day of her fast Esther **put on** her royal robes and went
Is 37. 1 tore his clothes in grief, **put on** sackcloth, and went to the
57. 9 You **put on** your perfumes and ointments and go to worship
Jer 4. 8 So **put on** sackcloth, and weep and wail because the fierce
4.30 Why do you **put on** jewellery and paint your eyes?
6.26 Lord says to his people, **"Put on** sackcloth and roll in ashes.
13. 1 go and buy myself some linen shorts and to **put them on;**
13. 2 So I bought them and **put them on.**
46. 4 Fall in line and **put on** your helmets!
46. 4 **Put on** your armour!'
49. 3 **Put on** sackcloth and mourn.
51. 3 time to shoot their arrows or to **put on** their armour.
Ezek 7.18 They will **put on** sackcloth and they will tremble all over.
23.40 The two sisters would bathe and **put on** eye-shadow and jewellery.
42.14 They must **put on** other clothes before going out to the area
44.17 courtyard of the Temple, they are to **put on** linen clothing.
44.19 They are to **put on** other clothing in order to keep their
Hos 2.13 burnt incense to Baal and **put on** her jewellery to go chasing
Joel 1.13 **Put on** sackcloth and weep, you priests who serve at the altar!
Jon 3. 5 the greatest to the least, **put on** sackcloth to show that
3. 6 throne, took off his robe, **put on** sackcloth, and sat down in
Mt 6.16 when you fast, do not **put on** a sad face as the
11.21 there would long ago have **put on** sackcloth and sprinkled
Lk 10.13 long ago have sat down, **put on** sackcloth, and sprinkled
17. 8 'Get my supper ready, then **put on** your apron and wait on
Acts 12. 8 Then the angel said, "Fasten your belt and **put on** your sandals."
12.21 On a chosen day Herod **put on** his royal robes, sat on
2 Cor 5. 2 our home which comes from heaven should be **put on** over us;
5. 4 to have the heavenly one **put on** over us, so that what
Eph 4.24 completely new, [24] and you must **put on** the new self, which
6.11 **Put on** all the armour that God gives you, so that you
6.13 So **put on** God's armour now!
Col 3.10 old self with its habits [10] and have **put on** the new self.
1 Pet 3. 3 hair, or the jewellery you **put on,** or the dresses you wear.
5. 5 And all of you must **put on** the apron of humility,

PUT OUT

Job 18. 5 The wicked man's light will still be **put out;**
21.17 Was a wicked man's light ever **put out?**
Song 8. 7 Water cannot **put it out;**
Is 42. 3 not break off a bent reed or **put out** a flickering lamp.
66.24 die, and the fire that burns them will never be **put out.**
Jer 4. 4 will burn, and there will be no one to **put it out."**
7.20 anger will be like a fire that no one can **put out.**
17.27 of Jerusalem, and no one will be able to **put it out."**
21.11 make my anger burn like a fire that cannot be **put out.**
Ezek 20.47 Nothing will be able to **put it out.**
20.48 set it on fire and that no one can **put it out."**
32. 8 I will **put out** all the lights of heaven and plunge your
Amos 5. 6 of Bethel, and no one will be able to **put it out.**
Mt 12.20 not break off a bent reed, or **put out** a flickering lamp.
Mk 9.48 never die, and the fire that burns them is never **put out.'**
Jn 1. 5 in the darkness, and the darkness has never **put it out.**
Eph 6.16 you will be able to **put out** all the burning arrows shot
Heb 11.34 shut the mouths of lions, [34]**put out** fierce fires, escaped

PUT UP WITH

Mt 17.17 How long do I have to **put up with** you?
20.12 they said, 'while we **put up with** a whole day's work in
Mk 9.19 How long do I have to **put up with** you?
Lk 9.41 How long do I have to **put up with** you?"
Heb 12. 3 how he **put up with** so much hatred from sinners!

PUZZLED

Dan 8.27 to me, but I was **puzzled** by the vision and could not
Lk 24. 4 They stood there **puzzled** about this, when suddenly two men
Jn 13.22 looked at one another, completely **puzzled** about whom he meant.

QUAIL

Ex 16.13 evening a large flock of **quails** flew in, enough to cover the
Num 11.31 sent a wind that brought **quails** from the sea, flying less
11.32 and all the next day, the people worked catching **quails;**
Ps 105.40 They asked, and he sent **quails;**

QUAKE

Judg 5. 5 The mountains **quaked** before the Lord of Sinai, before the Lord,
Amos 8. 8 And so the earth will **quake,** and everyone in the land will
9. 5 The Sovereign Lord Almighty touches the earth, and it **quakes;**
Nah 1. 5 Mountains **quake** in the presence of the Lord;

QUALIFIED
[UNQUALIFIED]

Num 4. 3 thirty and fifty who were **qualified** to work in the Tent of
4.23 thirty and fifty who were **qualified** to work in the Tent of
4.30 thirty and fifty who were **qualified** to work in the Tent of
4.34 thirty and fifty who were **qualified** to work in the Tent of
8.15 the Levites, they will be **qualified** to work in the Tent.
8.22 And so the Levites were **qualified** to work in the Tent under
18. 4 in the Tent, but no **unqualified** person may work with you.
18. 7 Any **unqualified** person who comes near the sacred objects
Judg 18. 2 people of Dan chose five **qualified** men out of all the
1 Sam 22.18 eighty-five priests who were **qualified** to carry the ephod.
2 Kgs 10. 3 are to choose the best **qualified** of the king's descendants,
1 Chr 26. 8 a total of sixty-two highly **qualified** men for this work.
26. 9 Meshelemiah's family furnished eighteen **qualified** men.
Dan 1. 4 so that they would be **qualified** to serve in the royal court.
2 Tim 3.17 serves God may be fully **qualified** and equipped to do every

QUALITY

Lev 24. 2 olive-oil of the finest **quality** for the lamps in the Tent,
27.12 to its good or bad **qualities,** and the price will be final.
Rom 1.20 his invisible **qualities,** both his eternal power and his
1 Cor 3.13 And the **quality** of each person's work will be seen when
3.13 the fire will test it and show its real **quality.**
Phil 1.11 with the truly good **qualities** which only Jesus Christ can produce,
Col 3.14 to all these **qualities** add love, which binds all things together
2 Pet 1. 8 These are the **qualities** you need, and if you have them in

QUANTITY

Lev 19.35 by using false measures of length, weight, or **quantity.**
2 Sam 8. 8 He also took a great **quantity** of bronze from Betah and Berothai,
1 Chr 18. 8 He also took a great **quantity** of bronze from Tibhath and Kun,
29. 2 and gems, stones for mosaics, and **quantities** of marble.
2 Chr 2. 9 assist yours [9]in preparing large **quantities** of timber,
25.13 killed three thousand men, and captured **quantities** of loot.
31. 6 and they also brought large **quantities** of gifts,

QUARREL

Gen 13. 7 So **quarrels** broke out between the men who took care of
13. 8 "We are relatives, and your men and my men shouldn't be **quarrelling.**
26.20 The shepherds of Gerar **quarrelled** with Isaac's shepherds
26.20 So Isaac named the well **"Quarrel."**
26.21 well, and there was a **quarrel** about that one also, so he
45.24 they left, he said to them, "Don't **quarrel** on the way."
Lev 24.10 There in the camp this man **quarrelled** with an Israelite.
24.10 During the **quarrel** he cursed God, so they took him to Moses,
Judg 11.12 the king of Ammon to say, "What is your **quarrel** with us?
Judg 12. 2 "My people and I had a serious **quarrel** with the Ammonites.
2 Sam 14. 6 day they got into a **quarrel** out in the fields, where there
19. 9 All over the country they started **quarrelling** among themselves.
21. 4 They answered, "Our **quarrel** with Saul and his family
2 Kgs 5. 7 It's plain that he is trying to start a **quarrel** with me!"
Job 9.32 we could go to court to decide our **quarrel.**
21. 4 My **quarrel** is not with mortal men;
Ps 140. 2 They are always plotting evil, always stirring up **quarrels.**
Prov 18.19 city wall, but if you **quarrel** with him, he will close his
22.10 be no more arguments, **quarrelling,** or calling of names.
26.20 without gossip, **quarrelling** stops.
29.22 People with quick tempers cause a lot of **quarrelling** and trouble.
Is 58. 4 Your fasting makes you violent, and you **quarrel** and fight.
Jer 15.10 I have to **quarrel** and argue with everyone in the land.
Mic 7. 6 mothers, and young women **quarrel** with their mothers-in-law;
Hab 1. 3 round me, and there is fighting and **quarrelling** everywhere.
Acts 6. 1 there was a **quarrel** between the Greek-speaking Jews and the
23. 7 the Pharisees and Sadducees started to **quarrel,** and the group was
1 Cor 1.11 quite plainly, my brothers, that there are **quarrels** among you.
3. 3 jealousy among you and you **quarrel** with one another, doesn't this
2 Cor 7. 5 There were troubles everywhere, **quarrels** with others, fears
12.20 afraid that I will find **quarrelling** and jealousy, hot tempers
Phil 1.15 because they are jealous and **quarrelsome,** but others from genuine
1 Tim 6. 4 unhealthy desire to argue and **quarrel** about words,
2 Tim 2.23 you know that they end up in **quarrels.**
2.24 The Lord's servant must not **quarrel.**
Tit 3. 9 long lists of ancestors, **quarrels,** and fights about the Law.
Jas 4. 1 Where do all the fights and **quarrels** among you come from?
4. 2 things, but you cannot get them, so you **quarrel** and fight.
Jude 9 In his **quarrel** with the Devil, when they argued about who

QUARRY

Josh 7. 5 gate as far as some **quarries** and killed about thirty-six of
1 Kgs 5.15 80,000 men in the hill-country **quarrying** stone, with 70,000
5.17 At King Solomon's command they **quarried** fine large
6. 7 had been prepared at the **quarry,** so that there was no noise
7. 9 stones were prepared at the **quarry** and cut to measure, with
7.10 large stones prepared at the **quarry,** some of them three and
1 Chr 22.15 in the stone **quarries,** and there are masons and carpenters,
2 Chr 2. 2 materials, and eighty thousand men to work **quarrying** stone.
Ecc 10. 9 If you work in a stone **quarry,** you get hurt by stones.
Is 51. 1 from which you came, the **quarry** from which you were dug.

QUARTER (1)

1 Sam 14.14 twenty men in an area of about a **quarter** of a hectare.
Rev 6. 8 were given authority over a **quarter** of the earth, to kill by

QUARTER (2)
[LIVING-QUARTERS]

1 Kgs 7. 8 Solomon's own **quarters,** in another court
10. 5 served at his table, the **living quarters** for his officials,
2 Kgs 23. 7 He destroyed the **living-quarters** in the Temple
23.11 from the **living-quarters** of Nathan Melech, a high official.)
23.12 roof above King Ahaz' **quarters,** King Josiah tore down,
2 Chr 9. 4 served at his table, the **living-quarters** for his officials,
Ezra 10. 6 Temple into the **living-quarters** of Jehohanan son of Eliashib,
Neh 10.39 and the members of the temple choir have their **quarters.**
Esth 9. 2 In the Jewish **quarter** of every city in the empire the Jews

QUARTZ
A semi-precious stone of various colours, but usually clear.

Rev 21.20 sixth carnelian, the seventh yellow **quartz,** the eighth beryl,

QUEEN

Judg 5.30 for Sisera, embroidered pieces for the neck of the **queen."**
1 Kgs 10. 1 The **queen of Sheba** heard of Solomon's fame, and she
10. 4 The **queen of Sheba** heard Solomon's wisdom and saw the
10.13 King Solomon gave the **queen of Sheba** everything she asked for,
11.19 the sister of **Queen** Tahpenes, to Hadad in marriage.
11.20 was brought up by the **queen** in the palace, where he lived
15.13 Maacah from her position as **queen** mother, because she had
18.19 prophets of the goddess Asherah who are supported by **Queen** Jezebel."
2 Kgs 10.13 respects to the children of **Queen** Jezebel and to the rest of
11. 3 him hidden in the Temple, while Athaliah ruled as **queen.**
11.13 **Queen** Athaliah heard the noise being made by the guards
2 Chr 9. 1 The **queen of Sheba** heard of King Solomon's fame, and she
9. 3 The **queen of Sheba** heard Solomon's wisdom and saw the
9. 9 fine as those that the **queen of Sheba** gave to King Solomon.
9.12 King Solomon gave the **queen of Sheba** everything she asked for.
15.16 Maacah from her position as **queen** mother, because she had
22.12 he remained there in hiding, while Athaliah ruled as **queen.**
Esth 1. 9 Meanwhile, inside the royal palace **Queen** Vashti was giving
1.11 He ordered them to bring in **Queen** Vashti, wearing her royal crown.
1.11 The **queen** was a beautiful woman, and the king wanted to show
1.12 But when the servants told **Queen** Vashti of the king's command,
1.15 Xerxes, sent my servants to **Queen** Vashti with a command, and
1.16 **"Queen** Vashti has insulted not only the king but also his
1.17 her husband as soon as she hears what the **queen** has done.
1.17 They'll say, 'King Xerxes commanded **Queen** Vashti to come to him,
1.18 and Media hear about the **queen's** behaviour they will be

Esth 1.19 Then give her place as **queen** to some better woman.
2. 4 girl you like best and make her **queen** in Vashti's place."
2.17 crown on her head and made her **queen** in place of Vashti.
2.22 learnt about it and told **Queen** Esther, who then told the
4.14 it was for a time like this that you were made **queen!"**
5. 2 When the king saw **Queen** Esther standing outside, she won his favour,
5. 3 "What is it, **Queen** Esther?"
5.12 is more," Haman went on, **"Queen** Esther gave a banquet for
7. 2 king asked her again, "Now, **Queen** Esther, what do you want?
7. 3 **Queen** Esther answered, "If it please Your Majesty to
7. 5 Then King Xerxes asked **Queen** Esther, "Who dares to do
7. 6 Haman stared at the king and **queen** in terror.
7. 7 this, so he stayed behind to beg **Queen** Esther for his life.
7. 8 man going to rape the **queen** right here in front of me,
8. 1 day King Xerxes gave **Queen** Esther all the property of Haman,
8. 7 King Xerxes then said to **Queen** Esther and Mordecai, the
9.12 He then said to **Queen** Esther, "In Susa alone the Jews
9.29 Then **Queen** Esther, the daughter of Abihail, along with Mordecai,
9.31 This was commanded by both Mordecai and **Queen** Esther.
Ps 45. 9 throne stands the **queen,** wearing ornaments of finest gold.
Song 6. 8 Let the king have sixty **queens,** eighty concubines,
6. 9 **queens** and concubines sing her praises.
Is 47. 5 no more will they call you the **queen** of nations!
47. 7 you would always be a **queen,** and did not take these things
49.23 **queens** will be like mothers.
Jer 7.18 to bake cakes for the goddess they call the **Queen of Heaven.**
44.17 to our goddess, the **Queen of Heaven,** and we will pour out
44.18 stopped sacrificing to the **Queen of Heaven** and stopped
44.19 shaped like the **Queen of Heaven,** offered sacrifices to her,
44.24 your wives have made solemn promises to the **Queen of Heaven.**
Ezek 16.13 Your beauty was dazzling, and you became a **queen.**
Dan 5.10 The **queen** mother heard the noise made by the king
Nah 2. 7 The **queen** is taken captive;
Mt 12.42 On Judgement Day the **Queen of Sheba** will stand up
Lk 11.31 On Judgement Day the **Queen of Sheba** will stand up
Acts 8.27 of the treasury of the **queen** of Ethiopia, was on his way
Rev 18. 7 'Here I sit, a **queen!**

QUENCH

Ps 104.11 there the wild donkeys **quench** their thirst.

AV QUENCH

Num 11. 2 he prayed to the Lord, and the fire **died** down.
2 Sam 14. 7 They will **destroy** my last hope and leave my husband without
2 Kgs 22.17 My anger is aroused against Jerusalem, and it will not **die** down.
2 Chr 34.25 My anger is aroused against Jerusalem, and it will not **die** down.
Ps 118.12 me like bees, but they **burnt** out as quickly as a fire
Song 8. 7 Water cannot **put it out;**
Is 1.31 deeds, and no one will be able to **stop** the destruction.
34.10 It will **burn** day and night, and smoke will rise from it
42. 3 not break off a bent reed or **put out** a flickering lamp.
43.17 they fell, never to rise, **snuffed** out like the flame of a
66.24 die, and the fire that burns them will never be **put out.**
Jer 4. 4 will burn, and there will be no one to **put it out."**
7.20 anger will be like a fire that no one can **put out.**
17.27 of Jerusalem, and no one will be able to **put it out."**
21.11 make my anger burn like a fire that cannot be **put out.**
Ezek 20.47 Nothing will be able to **put it out.**
20.48 set it on fire and that no one can **put it out."**
Amos 5. 6 of Bethel, and no one will be able to **put it out.**
Mt 12.20 not break off a bent reed, or **put out** a flickering lamp.
Mk 9.48 never die, and the fire that burns them is never **put out.'**
Eph 6.16 you will be able to **put out** all the burning arrows shot
1 Thes 5.19 Do not **restrain** the Holy Spirit;
Heb 11.34 shut the mouths of lions, [34] **put out** fierce fires, escaped

QUESTION

Gen 43. 7 We had to answer his **questions.**
Josh 1.18 Whoever **questions** your authority or disobeys any of your
Judg 8.14 he captured a young man from Sukkoth and **questioned** him.
1 Sam 9. 9 wanted to ask God a **question,** he would say, "Let's go to
9.19 I will answer all your **questions** and send you on your way.
17.29 "Can't I even ask a **question?"**
17.30 and asked him the same **question,** and every time he asked, he
20.12 tomorrow and on the following day I will **question** my father.
2 Sam 14.18 going to ask you a **question,** and you must tell me the
14.19 Your Majesty, that there is no way to avoid answering your **question.**
1 Kgs 10. 1 travelled to Jerusalem to test him with difficult **questions.**
10. 2 she asked him all the **questions** that she could think of.
2 Kgs 8. 6 In answer to the king's **question,** she confirmed Gehazi's story,
9.19 Another messenger was sent out, who asked Jehu the same **question.**
2 Chr 9. 1 travelled to Jerusalem to test him with difficult **questions.**
9. 1 she asked him all the **questions** that she could think of.
Esth 1.13 ask for expert opinion on **questions** of law and order, so he
Job 9. 3 He can ask a thousand **questions** that no one could ever answer.
38. 2 Who are you to **question** my wisdom with your ignorant,
38. 3 up now like a man and answer the **questions** I ask you.
40. 7 Stand up now like a man, and answer my **questions.**
42. 3 You ask how I dare **question** your wisdom when I am so
42. 4 listen while you spoke and to try to answer your **questions.**
Prov 18.17 seems right until his opponent begins to **question** him.
26. 4 If you answer a silly **question,** you are just as silly as
26. 5 silly answer to a silly **question,** and the one who asked it
Ecc 7.10 It's not an intelligent **question.**
7.25 and the answers to my **questions,** and to learn how wicked and
Is 41.28 not one could answer the **questions** I asked.
45.11 "You have no right to **question** me about my children or to
Jer 12. 1 Yet I must **question** you about matters of justice.
38.14 going to ask you a **question,** and I want you to tell
38.27 all the officials came and **questioned** me, and I told them
Dan 1.20 No matter what **question** the king asked, or what problem he raised,
4.35 No one can oppose his will or **question** what he does.
Hag 2.11 He said, "Ask the priests for a ruling on this **question:**
2.12 When the **question** was asked, the priests answered, "No."
Zech 7. 3 and to ask the priests and the prophets this **question:**
Mt 21.24 will ask you just one **question,** and if you give me
22.15 Pharisees went off and made a plan to trap Jesus with **questions.**
22.35 a teacher of the Law, tried to trap him with a **question.**
22.46 that day on no one dared to ask him any more **questions.**
27.11 Jesus stood before the Roman governor, who **questioned** him.
Mk 10. 3 Jesus answered with a **question,** "What law did Moses give you?"
11.29 will ask you just one **question,** and if you give me an
12.13 Herod's party were sent to Jesus to trap him with **questions.**
12.28 Sadducees a good answer, so he came to him with a **question:**
12.34 After this nobody dared to ask Jesus any more **questions.**
12.35 the Temple, he asked the **question,** "How can the teachers of
14.60 front of them all and **questioned** Jesus, "Have you no answer
14.61 Again the High Priest **questioned** him, "Are you the Messiah,
15. 2 Pilate **questioned** him, "Are you the king of the Jews?"
15. 4 so Pilate **questioned** him again, "Aren't you going to
Lk 2.46 with the Jewish teachers, listening to them and asking **questions.**
11.53 and ask him **questions** about many things, [54] trying to lay
20. 3 Jesus answered them, "Now let me ask you a **question.**
20.20 to trap Jesus with **questions,** so that they could hand him
20.40 For they did not dare ask him any more **questions.**
22.68 and if I ask you a **question,** you will not answer.
23. 9 So Herod asked Jesus many **questions,** but Jesus made no answer.
Jn 2.18 Jewish authorities replied with a **question,** "What miracle can
8. 7 they stood there asking him **questions,** he straightened himself up
16.19 knew that they wanted to **question** him, so he said to them,
16.30 you do not need someone to ask you **questions.**
18.19 The High Priest **questioned** Jesus about his disciples and about
18.21 Why, then, do you **question** me?
18.21 **Question** the people who heard me.
18.34 answered, "Does this **question** come from you or have others told
Acts 4. 9 if we are being **questioned** today about the good deed done
5.27 before the Council, and the High Priest **questioned** them.
12.19 So he had the guards **questioned** and ordered them to be put
15. 6 The apostles and the elders met together to consider this **question.**
22.29 the men who were going to **question** Paul drew back from him;
23.29 against him had to do with **questions** about their own law.
24. 8 If you **question** this man, you yourself will be able to
28.18 After **questioning** me, the Romans wanted to release me,
Rom 3. 5 (This would be the natural **question** to ask.)
1 Cor 10.25 in the meat-market, without asking any **questions** because of your
10.27 is set before you, without asking any **questions** because of your

QUICK

Gen 18. 6 tent and said to Sarah, **"Quick,** take a sack of your best
19.15 **"Quick!"**
24.18 She said, "Drink, sir," and **quickly** lowered her jar
24.20 She **quickly** emptied her jar into the animals'
24.46 She **quickly** lowered her jar from her shoulder and said,
27.20 Isaac said, "How did you find it so **quickly,** my son?"
44.11 So they **quickly** lowered their sacks to the ground, and
Ex 12.11 You are to eat it **quickly,** for you are to be dressed
34. 8 Moses **quickly** bowed down to the ground and worshipped.
Deut 9. 3 drive them out and destroy them **quickly,** as he promised.
28.20 you do, until you are **quickly** and completely destroyed.
Josh 2. 4 but if you start after them **quickly,** you can catch them."
8.14 When the king of Ai saw Joshua's men, he acted **quickly.**
8.19 had been hiding got up **quickly,** ran into the city and
Judg 9.48 He told his men to be **quick** and do the same thing.
9.54 Then he **quickly** called the young man who was carrying
20.37 These men ran **quickly** towards Gibeah;
1 Sam 17.48 David again, and David ran **quickly** towards the Philistine
25.18 Abigail **quickly** collected two hundred loaves of bread,
25.23 When Abigail saw David, she **quickly** dismounted and
25.42 She rose **quickly** and mounted her donkey.
28.24 The woman **quickly** killed a calf which she had been fattening.
2 Sam 17.16 Hushai added, **"Quick,** now!
1 Chr 12. 8 as fierce-looking as lions and as **quick** as mountain deer.
2 Chr 29.36 because God had helped them to do all this so **quickly.**
35.13 and pans, and **quickly** distributed the meat to the people.
Esth 5. 5 then ordered Haman to come **quickly,** so that they could be
Job 14. 2 We grow and wither as **quickly** as flowers;
32.22 how to flatter, and God would **quickly** punish me if I did.
Ps 2.12 anger will be **quickly** aroused, and you will suddenly die.
10. 7 he is **quick** to speak hateful, evil words.
22.19 Come **quickly** to my rescue!
25. 3 in you, but to those who are **quick** to rebel against you.
49.14 over them, as their bodies **quickly** decay in the world of the
55. 8 I would **quickly** find myself a shelter from the raging wind
64. 4 They are **quick** to spread their shameless lies;
70. 5 come to me **quickly,** O God.
81.14 I would **quickly** defeat their enemies and conquer all their foes.
94.17 me, I would have gone **quickly** to the land of silence.
102. 2 Listen to me, and answer me **quickly** when I call!
106.13 But they **quickly** forgot what he had done and acted
118.12 bees, but they burnt out as **quickly** as a fire among thorns;
147.15 a command to the earth, and what he says is **quickly** done.
Prov 12.16 When a fool is annoyed, he **quickly** lets it be known.
14.16 but stupid people are careless and act too **quickly.**
15.28 Evil people have a **quick** reply, but it causes trouble.

Prov 21. 5 if you act too **quickly,** you will never have enough.
25. 8 Don't be too **quick** to go to court about something you have
29.22 People with **quick** tempers cause a lot of quarrelling and trouble.
Ecc 5. 4 you make a promise to God, keep it as **quickly** as possible.
8.11 Because crime is not punished **quickly** enough.
Is 5.26 And here they come, swiftly, **quickly!**
8. 1 **'Quick** Loot, Fast Plunder.'
16. 5 He will be **quick** to do what is right, and he will
51. 5 I will come **quickly** and save them;
55. 7 he is merciful and **quick** to forgive.
58. 8 the morning sun, and your wounds will be **quickly** healed.
60.22 When the right time comes, I will make this happen **quickly.**
Jer 48. 6 **'Quick,** run for your lives!'
Dan 1. 4 to be handsome, intelligent, well-trained, **quick** to learn,
Hos 6. 4 Your love for me disappears as **quickly** as morning mist;
Joel 3. 4 If you are, I will **quickly** pay you back!
Hab 2. 3 But the time is coming **quickly,** and what I show you will
Mt 21.20 "How did the fig-tree dry up so **quickly?"**
26.50 Jesus answered, "Be **quick** about it, friend!"
28. 7 Go **quickly** now, and tell his disciples, 'He has been raised
Mk 1.28 the news about Jesus spread **quickly** everywhere in the province
9. 8 They took a **quick** look round but did not see anyone else;
Lk 18. 8 tell you, he will judge in their favour and do it **quickly.**
Jn 13.27 Jesus said to him, "Be **quick** about what you are doing!"
Acts 22.18 'Hurry and leave Jerusalem **quickly,** because the people here will
Rom 3.15 They are **quick** to hurt and kill;
9.28 the Lord will **quickly** settle his full account with the world."
1 Cor 15.51 changed in an instant, as **quickly** as the blinking of an eye.
Jas 1.19 Everyone must be **quick** to listen, but slow to speak

AV QUICK

Num 16.30 so that they go down **alive** to the world of the dead,
Ps 55.15 may they go down **alive** into the world of the dead!
124. 3 they would have swallowed us **alive** in their furious anger
Heb 4.12 The word of God is **alive** and active,

QUICK-LOOT-FAST-PLUNDER

Is 8. 3 the Lord said to me, "Name him **'Quick-Loot-Fast-Plunder.'**

QUICK-TEMPERED see TEMPER

AV QUICKEN

Ps 71.20 and suffering on me, but you will **restore** my strength;
80.18 keep us **alive,** and we will praise you.
119.25 **revive** me, as you have promised.
119.93 your instructions, because by them you have kept me **alive.**
119.107 keep me **alive,** as you have promised.
119.154 **save** me, as you have promised.
119.156 show your mercy and **save** me!
119.159 Your love never changes, so **save** me!
143.11 **Rescue** me, Lord, as you have promised;
1 Pet 3.18 to death physically, but made **alive** spiritually,

QUICKSAND

Ps 40. 2 me out of a dangerous pit, out of the deadly **quicksand.**

QUIET

Gen 25.27 outdoor life, but Jacob was a **quiet** man who stayed at home.
Judg 4.21 tent-peg, went up to him **quietly,** and killed him by driving
16. 2 They were **quiet** all night, thinking to themselves,
18. 7 They were a peaceful, **quiet** people, with no disputes with anyone;
18.19 They said, "Keep **quiet.**
18.27 Laish, that town of peaceful, **quiet** people which was in the
Ruth 3. 7 Ruth slipped over **quietly,** lifted the covers and lay down at
2 Sam 19. 3 went back into the city **quietly,** like soldiers who are
2 Kgs 11.20 happiness, and the city was **quiet,** now that Athaliah had
18.36 The people kept **quiet,** just as King Hezekiah had told them to;
1 Chr 4.40 in a stretch of open country that was **quiet** and peaceful.
2 Chr 23.21 and the city was **quiet,** now that Athaliah had been killed.
Esth 4.14 If you keep **quiet** at a time like this, help will come
7. 4 I would have kept **quiet** and not bothered you about it;
Job 4. 1 I can't keep **quiet** any longer.
4.12 Once a message came **quietly,**
4.12 so **quietly** I could hardly hear it.
6. 5 when eating grass, and a cow is **quiet** when eating hay.
6.24 I will be **quiet** and listen to you.
7.11 I can't be **quiet!**
13.13 Be **quiet** and give me a chance to speak, and let the
18. 1 Job, can't people like you ever be **quiet?**
21.13 They live out their lives in peace and **quietly** die
31.34 I have never kept **quiet** or stayed indoors because I feared
33.31 be **quiet** and let me speak.
33.33 But if not, be **quiet** and listen to me, and I will
Ps 23. 2 of green grass and leads me to **quiet** pools of fresh water.
39. 2 I kept **quiet,** not saying a word, not even about anything good!
39. 9 I will keep **quiet,** I will not say a word, for you
83. 1 do not be still, do not be **quiet!**
107.29 He calmed the raging storm, and the waves became **quiet.**
131. 2 As a child lies **quietly** in its mother's arms,
131. 2 so my heart is **quiet** within me.
Prov 10.19 If you are wise, you will keep **quiet.**
11.12 If you are sensible, you will keep **quiet.**
12.23 Sensible people keep **quiet** about what they know, but
15. 1 A gentle answer **quietens** anger, but a harsh one stirs it up.
17.28 and intelligent if he stays **quiet** and keeps his mouth shut.
Prov 27.16 How can you keep her **quiet?**
Ecc 9.17 better to listen to the **quiet** words of a wise man than
Is 8. 6 have rejected the **quiet** waters from the brook of Shiloah,
18. 4 look down from heaven as **quietly** as the dew forms in the
30.10 They tell the prophets to keep **quiet.**
30.15 says to the people, "Come back and **quietly** trust in me.
36.21 The people kept **quiet,** just as King Hezekiah had told them to;
Jer 4.19 I can't keep **quiet;**
Ezek 16.49 and lived in peace and **quiet,** but they did not take care
Amos 5.13 And so, keeping **quiet** in such evil times is the clever
6.10 Then the relative will say, "Be **quiet!**
Hab 3.16 I will **quietly** wait for the time to come when God will
Zech 1.15 I am very angry with the nations that enjoy **quiet** and peace.
Mt 20.31 The crowd scolded them and told them to be **quiet.**
26.63 But Jesus kept **quiet.**
Mk 1.25 Jesus ordered the spirit, "Be **quiet,** and come out of the man!"
4.39 Jesus stood up and commanded the wind, "Be **quiet!"**
10.48 Many of the people scolded him and told him to be **quiet.**
14.61 But Jesus kept **quiet** and would not say a word.
Lk 4.35 Jesus ordered the spirit, "Be **quiet** and come out of the man!"
9.36 The disciples kept **quiet** about all this, and told no one
18.39 The people in front scolded him and told him to be **quiet.**
19.39 "Teacher," they said, "command your disciples to be **quiet!"**
19.40 if they keep **quiet,** the stones themselves will start shouting."
20.26 out in anything, so they kept **quiet,** amazed at his answer.
Acts 12.17 hand for them to be **quiet,** and he explained to them how
21.40 When they were **quiet,** Paul spoke to them in Hebrew:
22. 2 heard him speaking to them in Hebrew, they became even **quieter;**
1 Cor 14.28 in strange tongues must be **quiet** and speak only to himself
14.34 the women should keep **quiet** in the meetings.
1 Thes 4.11 your aim to live a **quiet** life, to mind your own business,
5. 3 "Everything is **quiet** and safe," then suddenly destruction will
1 Tim 2. 2 that we may live a **quiet** and peaceful life with all
2.12 they must keep **quiet.**
1 Pet 3. 4 beauty of a gentle and **quiet** spirit, which is of the

Am QUIT see GIVE UP

QUIVER

2 Sam 22. 8 the foundations of the sky rocked and **quivered**
Ps 18. 7 the foundations of the mountains rocked and **quivered,**
Hab 3.16 my lips **quiver** with fear.

QUOTE

Deut 30.14 You know it and can **quote** it, so now obey it.
Prov 22.18 you will be glad if you remember them and can **quote** them.
26. 9 A fool **quoting** a wise saying reminds you of a drunk man
Lk 4.23 am sure that you will **quote** this proverb to me, 'Doctor,
Jn 1.23 John answered by **quoting** the prophet Isaiah:
Acts 17. 2 with the people, **quoting** [3] and explaining the Scriptures
28.23 convince them about Jesus by **quoting** from the Law of Moses
Rom 4. 9 For we have **quoted** the scripture, "Abraham believed God,
Heb 4. 7 spoke of it through David in the scripture already **quoted:**

RABBAH (1)

Chief city in Ammon.

Deut 3.11 It can still be seen in the Ammonite city of **Rabbah.)**
Josh 13.25 land of Ammon as far as Aroer, which is east of **Rabbah;**
2 Sam 10. 8 entrance to **Rabbah,** their capital city, while the others,
11. 1 they defeated the Ammonites and besieged the city of **Rabbah.**
12.26 Joab continued his campaign against **Rabbah,**
12.27 "I have attacked **Rabbah** and have captured its water supply.
12.29 David gathered his forces, went to **Rabbah,** attacked it,
17.27 Nahash, from the city of **Rabbah** in Ammon, and by Machir son
1 Chr 19. 9 position at the entrance to **Rabbah,** their capital city, and
20. 1 They besieged the city of **Rabbah,** attacked it, and destroyed it.
Jer 49. 2 of the capital city of **Rabbah** hear the noise of battle, and
49. 3 Women of **Rabbah,** go into mourning!
Ezek 21.20 to the Ammonite city of **Rabbah,** and the other the way to
25. 5 will turn the city of **Rabbah** into a place to keep camels,
Amos 1.14 upon the city walls of **Rabbah** and burn down its fortresses.

RABBI

A Hebrew word which means "my teacher".

Jn 1.38 They answered, "Where do you live, **Rabbi?"**
3. 2 Jesus and said to him, **"Rabbi,** we know that you are a

RABBIT

Lev 11. 4 but you must not eat camels, rock-badgers, or **rabbits.**
Deut 14. 7 You may not eat camels, **rabbits,** or rock-badgers.
Job 9.26 boat, as fast as an eagle swooping down on a **rabbit.**

RABBONI

Jn 20.16 She turned towards him and said in Hebrew, **"Rabboni!"**

RACE (1)

Num 13.22 the descendants of a **race** of giants called the Anakim,
Deut 2.10 (A mighty **race** of giants called the Emim used to live
2.10 They were as tall as the Anakim, another **race** of giants.
2.21 There were many of them, and they were a mighty **race.**
Josh 11.21 Joshua went and destroyed the **race** of giants called the
14.12 told you then that the **race** of giants called the Anakim were

Neh 5. 5 We are of the same **race** as our fellow-Jews.
Esth 3. 8 king, "There is a certain **race** of people scattered all over
Ps 22.27 all **races** will worship him.
Prov 8.31 happy with the world and pleased with the human **race.**
Jer 34. 1 from all the nations and **races** that were subject to him,
Dan 3. 4 announced in a loud voice, "People of all nations, **races,**
3. 7 people of all the nations, **races,** and languages bowed down
3.29 if anyone of any nation, **race,** or language speaks
4. 1 people of all nations, **races,** and languages in the world:
5.19 that people of all nations, **races,** and languages were afraid
6.25 the people of all nations, **races,** and languages on earth:
7.14 people of all nations, **races,** and languages would serve him.
Zech 9. 6 People of mixed **race** will live in Ashdod.
Acts 7. 8 Jacob circumcised his twelve sons, the famous ancestors of our **race.**
10.35 is acceptable to him, no matter what **race** he belongs to.
17.26 one man he created all **races** of mankind and made them live
Rom 4. 1 What shall we say, then, of Abraham, the father of our **race?**
5.12 spread to the whole human **race** because everyone has sinned.
9. 5 and Christ, as a human being, belongs to their **race.**
11.14 the people of my own **race** jealous, and so be able to
Eph 2.15 create out of the two **races** one new people in union with
2.16 the cross he united both **races** into one body and brought
1 Pet 2. 9 But you are the chosen **race,** the King's priests, the holy nation,
Rev 5. 9 bought for God people from every tribe, language, nation, and **race.**
7. 9 were from every **race,** tribe, nation, and language, and they stood
10.11 must proclaim God's message about many nations, **races,** languages,
11. 9 nations, tribes, languages, and **races** will look at their bodies
13. 7 it was given authority over every tribe, nation, language, and **race.**
14. 6 peoples of the earth, to every **race,** tribe, language, and nation.
17.15 on which the prostitute is sitting, are nations, peoples, **races,**

RACE (2)

Job 9.25 My days **race** by, not one of them good.
39.24 Trembling with excitement, the horses **race** ahead;
Ps 19. 5 a happy bridegroom, like an athlete eager to run a **race.**
Ecc 9.11 do not always win the **race,** and the brave do not always
Song 2. 8 He comes running over the mountains, **racing** across the hills
Jer 12. 5 "Jeremiah, if you get tired **racing** against men,
12. 5 how can you **race** against horses?
1 Cor 9.24 runners take part in a **race,** but only one of them wins
1 Tim 6.12 Run your best in the **race** of faith, and win eternal life
2 Tim 2. 5 athlete who runs in a **race** cannot win the prize unless he
4. 7 done my best in the **race,** I have run the full distance,
Heb 12. 1 let us run with determination the **race** that lies before us.

RACHEL

Laban's daughter, Jacob's wife and Joseph and Benjamin's mother.

Gen 29.1-14 **Jacob arrives at Laban's home**
15-30 **Jacob serves Laban for Rachel and Leah**
29.31-30.24 **The children born to Jacob**
31.1-21 **Jacob flees from Laban**
22-42 **Laban pursues Jacob**
33.1-20 **Jacob meets Esau**
35.16-21 **The death of Rachel**

Gen 35.24 The sons of **Rachel** were Joseph and Benjamin.
35.25 The sons of **Rachel's** slave Bilhah were Dan and Naphtali.
44.27 us, 'You know that my wife **Rachel** bore me only two sons.
46.19 Jacob's wife **Rachel** bore him two sons:
46.22 These fourteen are the descendants of Jacob by **Rachel.**
46.25 by Bilhah, the slave-girl whom Laban gave to his daughter **Rachel.**
48. 7 I am doing this because of your mother **Rachel.**
Ruth 4.11 make your wife become like **Rachel** and Leah, who bore many
1 Sam 10. 2 will meet two men near **Rachel's** tomb at Zelzah in the
Jer 31.15 **Rachel** is crying for her children;
Mt 2.18 **Rachel** is crying for her children;

RAFT

1 Kgs 5. 9 will tie them together in **rafts** to float them down the coast
2 Chr 2.16 need, bind them together in **rafts,** and float them by sea as

RAFTERS

1 Kgs 7. 7 had cedar panels from the floor to the **rafters.**
2 Chr 3. 7 to overlay the temple walls, the **rafters,** the thresholds,
Hab 2.11 walls cry out against you, and the **rafters** echo the cry.

RAGE

Gen 1. 2 The **raging** ocean that covered everything was engulfed in total
49. 4 You are like a **raging** flood, But you will not be the
Deut 9. 3 Lord your God will go ahead of you like a **raging** fire.
1 Sam 20.34 from the table in a **rage** and ate nothing that day—the
1 Kgs 22.35 While the battle **raged** on, King Ahab remained propped
2 Kgs 5.11 But Naaman left in a **rage,** saying, "I thought that he
19.27 I know how you **rage** against me.
19.28 received the report of that **rage** and that pride of yours,
2 Chr 18.34 While the battle **raged** on, King Ahab remained propped up
Neh 9.11 drowned in deep water, as a stone sinks in the **raging** sea.
Job 19.11 God is angry and **rages** against me;
30.22 you toss me about in a **raging** storm.
Ps 46. 3 if the seas roar and **rage,** and the hills are shaken by
50. 3 a **raging** fire is in front of him, a furious storm is
55. 8 find myself a shelter from the **raging** wind and the storm.
57. 1 wings I find protection until the **raging** storms are over.
78.49 anger and fierce **rage,** which came as messengers of death.
85. 3 You stopped being angry with them and held back your furious **rage.**
107.29 He calmed the **raging** storm, and the waves became quiet.
124. 5 covered us, [5] the **raging** torrent would have drowned us."
Song 8. 6 It bursts into flame and burns like a **raging** fire.
Is 29. 6 He will send tempests and **raging** fire;
37.28 I know how you **rage** against me.
37.29 received the report of that **rage** and that pride of yours,
49.26 they will be drunk with murder and **rage.**
Jer 2.30 Like a **raging** lion, you have murdered your prophets.
4.21 I see the battle **raging** and hear the blasts of trumpets?
23.19 a furious wind that will **rage** over the heads of the wicked,
30.23 a furious wind that will **rage** over the heads of the wicked.
Lam 2. 3 He **raged** against us like fire, destroying everything.
Ezek 5.13 all the force of my anger and **rage** until I am satisfied.
22.20 My anger and **rage** will melt them just as fire melts ore.
Dan 2.12 the king flew into a **rage** and ordered the execution of all
3.13 the king flew into a **rage** and ordered the three men to
11.30 will turn back in a **rage** and try to destroy the religion
Amos 1.14 the day of battle, and the fighting will **rage** like a storm.
Lk 6.11 They were filled with **rage** and began to discuss among themselves
21.25 afraid of the roar of the sea and the **raging** tides.
Rev 11.18 The heathen were filled with **rage,**
12.12 and he is filled with **rage,** because he knows that he has

RAGS

[RAGGED]

Josh 9. 5 They put on **ragged** clothes and worn-out sandals
Prov 23.21 you do is eat and sleep, you will soon be wearing **rags.**
Is 3.24 instead of fine clothes, they will be dressed in **rags;**
32.11 Strip off your clothes and tie **rags** round your waist.
Jer 38.12 told me to put the **rags** under my arms, so that the
1 Cor 4.11 we are clothed in **rags;**
Jas 2. 2 your meeting, and a poor man in **ragged** clothes also comes.

RAHAB (1)

A prostitute in Jericho who helped the Israelite spies.

Josh 2. 1 to spend the night in the house of a prostitute named **Rahab.**
2. 3 night to spy out the country, [3] so he sent word to **Rahab:**
2. 4 (Now **Rahab** had taken the two spies up on the roof
2. 8 settled down for the night, **Rahab** went up on the roof
2.15 **Rahab** lived in a house built into the city wall,
6.17 Only the prostitute **Rahab** and her household will be spared,
6.23 So they went and brought **Rahab** out,
6.25 the lives of the prostitute **Rahab** and all her relatives,
Heb 11.31 faith that kept the prostitute **Rahab** from being killed
Jas 2.25 It was the same with the prostitute **Rahab.**

RAHAB (2)

Legendary sea-monster.

Job 9.13 He crushed his enemies who helped **Rahab,** the sea-monster,
26.12 by his skill he destroyed the monster **Rahab.**
Ps 89.10 You crushed the monster **Rahab** and killed it;
Is 51. 9 It was you that cut the sea-monster **Rahab** to pieces.

RAID

Ex 22.10 is carried off in a **raid,** and if there was no witness,
Judg 2.14 became furious with Israel and let **raiders** attack and rob them.
2.16 Lord gave the Israelites leaders who saved them from the **raiders.**
1 Sam 13.17 Philistine soldiers went out on **raids** from their camp
14.15 the **raiders** and the soldiers in the camp trembled with fear;
27. 8 He would **raid** their land as far as Shur, all the way
27.10 would ask him, "Where did you go on a **raid** this time?"
30. 1 The Amalekites had **raided** southern Judah and attacked Ziklag.
30. 8 David asked the Lord, "Shall I go after those **raiders?**
30.14 We had **raided** the territory of the Cherethites
30.15 "Will you lead me to those **raiders?"**
30.16 The **raiders** were scattered all over the place, eating,
30.23 He kept us safe and gave us victory over the **raiders.**
2 Sam 3.22 other officials returned from a **raid,** bringing a large
4. 2 who were leaders of **raiding** parties, Baanah and Rechab,
2 Kgs 5. 2 In one of their **raids** against Israel, the Syrians had
6.23 From then on the Syrians stopped **raiding** the land of Israel.
18. 8 He defeated the Philistines, and **raided** their settlements,
2 Chr 22. 1 Some Arabs had led a **raid** and killed all King Jehoram's
28.16 Edomites began to **raid** Judah again and captured many prisoners, so
28.18 same time the Philistines were **raiding** the towns in the
Job 1.17 "Three bands of Chaldean **raiders** attacked us,

RAILING

Deut 22. 8 be sure to put a **railing** round the edge of the roof.
1 Kgs 10.12 the wood to build **railings** in the Temple and the palace,

RAIN

Gen 2. 5 he had not sent any **rain,** and there was no one to
7. 4 I am going to send **rain** that will fall for forty days
7.12 the sky were opened, [12] and **rain** fell on the earth for
8. 2 The **rain** stopped, [3] and the water gradually went down for a
19.24 Suddenly the Lord **rained** burning sulphur on the cities
49.25 blesses you With blessings of **rain** from above And of deep
Ex 9.33 The thunder, the hail, and the **rain** all stopped.
16. 4 am going to make food **rain** down from the sky for all

Lev 26. 4 commands, [4]I will send you **rain** at the right time, so that
26.19 there will be no **rain,** and your land will be dry and
Num 24. 7 They will have abundant **rainfall** And plant their seed
Deut 11.11 is a land of mountains and valleys, a land watered by **rain.**
11.14 you do, he will send **rain** on your land when it is
11.17 He will hold back the **rain,** and your ground will become too
28.12 He will send **rain** in season from his rich storehouse in
28.23 No **rain** will fall, and your ground will become as hard
28.24 Instead of **rain,** the Lord will send down duststorms and
32. 2 will fall like drops of **rain** and form on the earth like
32. 2 showers on young plants, like gentle **rain** on tender grass.
33.13 Lord bless their land with **rain** And with water from under
Judg 5. 4 of Edom, the earth shook, and **rain** fell from the sky.
1 Sam 12.17 But I will pray, and the Lord will send thunder and **rain.**
12.18 prayed, and on that same day the Lord sent thunder and **rain.**
2 Sam 1.21 "May no **rain** or dew fall on Gilboa's hills;
21.10 from the beginning of harvest until the autumn **rains** came.
23. 4 dawn, the sun that makes the grass sparkle after **rain."**
1 Kgs 8.35 "When you hold back the **rain** because your people have
8.36 Then, O Lord, send **rain** on this land of yours, which you
17. 1 will be no dew or **rain** for the next two or three
17. 7 a while the brook dried up because of the lack of **rain.**
17.14 out of oil before the day that I, the Lord, send **rain.'"**
18. 1 "Go and present yourself to King Ahab, and I will send **rain."**
18.41 I hear the roar of **rain** approaching."
18.44 his chariot and go back home before the **rain** stops him."
18.45 the wind began to blow, and heavy **rain** began to fall.
2 Kgs 3.17 you will not see any **rain** or wind, this stream bed will
2 Chr 6.26 "When you hold back the **rain** because your people have
6.27 Then, O Lord, send **rain** on this land of yours, which you
7.13 Whenever I hold back the **rain** or send locusts to eat up
Ezra 10. 9 It was **raining** hard, and because of the weather and the
10.13 But they added, "The crowd is too big, and it's **raining** hard.
Job 5.10 He sends **rain** on the land and he waters the fields.
6.15 you deceive me like streams that go dry when no **rain** comes.
12.15 Drought comes when God withholds **rain;**
14.19 wear down rocks, and heavy **rain** will wash away the soil;
24. 8 They are drenched by the **rain** that falls on the mountains,
28.26 When God decided where the **rain** would fall, And the path
29.22 My words sank in like drops of **rain;**
29.23 everyone welcomed them just as farmers welcome **rain** in spring.
36.27 takes water from the earth and turns it into drops of **rain.**
36.28 He lets the **rain** pour from the clouds in showers for all
37. 6 to fall on the earth, and sends torrents of drenching **rain.**
37.13 God sends **rain** to water the earth;
38.25 a channel for the pouring **rain** and cleared the way for the
38.26 Who makes **rain** fall where no one lives?
38.28 Does either the **rain** or the dew have a father?
38.34 orders to the clouds and make them drench you with **rain?**
38.36 Nile will flood, or who tells the cock that **rain** will fall?
38.37 over to pour out the **rain,**
38.38 **rain** that hardens the dust into lumps?
Ps 65. 9 You show your care for the land by sending **rain;**
65.10 you send abundant **rain** on the ploughed fields and soak
68. 8 and the sky poured down **rain,** because of the coming of the
68. 9 caused abundant **rain** to fall and restored your worn-out land;
72. 6 May the king be like **rain** on the fields, like showers
77.17 The clouds poured down **rain;**
84. 6 the autumn **rain** fills it with pools.
104.13 From the sky you send **rain** on the hills, and the earth
104.16 of Lebanon get plenty of **rain**— the Lord's own trees, which
105.32 He sent hail and lightning on their land instead of **rain;**
126. 4 just as the **rain** brings water back to dry river-beds.
147. 8 he provides **rain** for the earth and makes grass grow on the
Prov 3.20 rivers to flow and the clouds to give **rain** to the earth.
16.15 the clouds that bring **rain** in the springtime—life is there.
19.12 the roar of a lion, but his favour is like welcome **rain.**
25.14 never give are like clouds and wind that bring no **rain.**
25.23 Gossip brings anger just as surely as the north wind brings **rain.**
26. 1 out of place, like snow in summer or **rain** at harvest time.
27.15 A nagging wife is like water going drip-drip-drip on a **rainy** day.
28. 3 poor people is like a driving **rain** that destroys the crops.
30.16 dry ground that needs **rain,**
Ecc 11. 3 When the clouds are full, it **rains.**
12. 2 grow dim for you, and the **rain** clouds will never pass away.
Song 2.11 the **rains** have stopped;
Is 4. 6 it a place of safety, sheltered from the **rain** and storm.
5. 6 I will even forbid the clouds to let **rain** fall on it."
24.18 Torrents of **rain** will pour from the sky, and earth's
28. 2 like a torrent of **rain,** like a rushing, overpowering flood,
30.23 seeds, the Lord will send **rain** to make them grow and will
30.30 will be flames, cloudbursts, hailstones, and torrents of **rain.**
44.14 plant a laurel-tree and wait for the **rain** to make it grow.
45. 8 I will send victory from the sky like **rain;**
55.10 like the snow and the **rain** that come down from the sky
Jer 3. 3 That is why the **rains** were held back, and the spring
5.24 though I send the autumn **rains** and the spring rains and give
10.13 makes lightning flash in the **rain** and sends the wind from
14. 4 Because there is no **rain** and the ground is dried up, the
14.22 None of the idols of the nations can send **rain;**
17. 8 it has no worries when there is no **rain;**
51.16 makes lightning flash in the **rain** and sends the wind from
Ezek 13.11 I will send a pouring **rain.**
13.13 wind, pouring **rain,** and hailstones to destroy the wall.
34.26 I will bless them with showers of **rain** when they need it.
38.22 Torrents of **rain** and hail, together with fire and sulphur,
Hos 2.21 I will make **rain** fall on the earth, and the earth will
6. 3 as surely as the spring **rains** that water the earth."
14. 5 be to the people of Israel like **rain** in a dry land.
Joel 2.23 He has given you the right amount of autumn **rain;**
2.23 has poured down the winter **rain** for you and the spring rain
Amos 4. 7 I held back the **rain** when your crops needed it most.
4. 7 I sent **rain** on one city, but not on another.
4. 7 **Rain** fell on one field, but another field dried up.
Hag 1.10 That is why there is no **rain** and nothing can grow.
Zech 8.12 earth will produce crops, and there will be plenty of **rain.**
10. 1 Ask the Lord for **rain** in the spring of the year.
10. 1 is the Lord who sends **rain** clouds and showers, making the
14.17 Lord Almighty as king, then **rain** will not fall on their land.
Mt 5.45 good people alike, and gives **rain** to those who do good
7.25 The **rain** poured down, the rivers overflowed,
7.27 The **rain** poured down, the rivers overflowed, the wind
16. 3 say, 'It is going to **rain,** because the sky is red
Lk 4.25 Elijah, when there was no **rain** for three and a half years
12.54 once you say that it is going to **rain**—and it does.
17.29 left Sodom, fire and sulphur **rained** down from heaven
Acts 14.17 he gives you **rain** from heaven and crops at the right times;
28. 2 It had started to **rain** and was cold, so they lit a
Heb 6. 7 soil which drinks in the **rain** that often falls on it
Jas 5. 7 He waits patiently for the autumn and spring **rains.**
5.17 that there would be no **rain,** and no rain fell on the
5.18 sky poured out its **rain** and the earth produced its crops.
Jude 12 like clouds carried along by the wind, but bringing no **rain.**
Rev 11. 6 that there will be no **rain** during the time they proclaim

RAINBOW

Gen 9.14 sky with clouds and the **rainbow** appears, [15]I will remember
9.16 When the **rainbow** appears in the clouds, I will see it
Ezek 1.28 light [28]that had in it all the colours of the **rainbow.**
Rev 4. 3 the throne there was a **rainbow** the colour of an emerald.
10. 1 was wrapped in a cloud and had a **rainbow** round his head;

Am RAISE

see also **BRING UP, REAR (2)**

RAISE

Gen 4.20 the ancestor of those who **raise** livestock and live in tents.
Ex 6. 6 I will **raise** my mighty arm to bring terrible punishment
7. 5 am the Lord, when I **raise** my hand against them and bring
7.20 king and his officers, Aaron **raised** his stick and struck the
9.15 If I had **raised** my hand to strike you and your people
9.22 the Lord said to Moses, **"Raise** your hand towards the sky,
9.23 So Moses **raised** his stick towards the sky, and the Lord
10.12 the Lord said to Moses, **"Raise** your hand over the land of
10.13 So Moses **raised** his stick, and the Lord caused a wind
10.21 Lord then said to Moses, **"Raise** your hand towards the sky,
10.22 Moses **raised** his hand towards the sky, and there was
Lev 9.22 finished all the sacrifices, he **raised** his hands over the
Num 20.11 Then Moses **raised** the stick and struck the rock twice with it,
30. 4 or promised unless her father **raises** an objection when he
30. 7 or promised unless her husband **raises** an objection when he
30.11 or promised unless her husband **raises** an objection when he
30.14 of the vow, he has **raised** no objection, she must do
Deut 32.40 am the living God, I **raise** my hand and I vow [41]that
1 Sam 2. 8 poor from the dust and **raises** the needy from their misery.
1 Kgs 8.22 of the altar, where he **raised** his arms [23]and prayed,
2 Kgs 4.28 Didn't I tell you not to **raise** my hopes?"
23.35 their wealth, in order to **raise** the amount needed to pay the
2 Chr 6.12 stood in front of the altar and **raised** his arms in prayer.
6.13 could see him, and **raised** his hands towards heaven.)
13. 3 Abijah **raised** an army of 400,000 soldiers, and Jeroboam
Ezra 9. 6 God, I am too ashamed to **raise** my head in your presence.
Neh 8. 6 All the people **raised** their arms in the air and answered,
Job 5.11 Yes, it is God who **raises** the humble and gives joy to
Ps 63. 4 I will **raise** my hands to you in prayer.
68.31 the Sudanese will **raise** their hands in prayer to God.
93. 3 The ocean depths **raise** their voice, O Lord;
93. 3 they **raise** their voice and roar.
113. 7 He **raises** the poor from the dust;
134. 2 **Raise** your hands in prayer in the Temple, and praise the Lord!
147. 6 He **raises** the humble, but crushes the wicked to the ground.
Prov 1. 6 meanings of proverbs and the problems that wise men **raise.**
Song 2. 4 his banqueting hall and **raised** the banner of love over me.
Is 11.12 The Lord will **raise** a signal flag to show the nations
13. 2 On the top of a barren hill **raise** the battle flag!
13. 2 Shout to the soldiers and **raise** your arm as the signal for
18. 3 a signal flag to be **raised** on the tops of the mountains!
42. 2 He will not shout or **raise** his voice or make loud speeches
Jer 50.15 **Raise** the war cry all round the city!
Lam 4. 5 those **raised** in luxury are pawing through refuse for food.
Ezek 1.11 wings of each creature were **raised** so that they touched the
2. 2 God's spirit entered me and **raised** me to my feet,
3.24 but God's spirit entered me and **raised** me to my feet.
16.27 "Now I have **raised** my hand to punish you
21.26 **Raise** the poor to power!
26.10 The clouds of dust **raised** by their horses will cover you.
Dan 1.20 asked, or what problem he **raised,** these four knew ten times
8.18 he took hold of me, **raised** me to my feet, [19]and said,
10.10 took hold of me and **raised** me to my hands and knees;
11.25 "He will boldly **raise** a large army to attack the king
12. 7 The angel **raised** both hands towards the sky
Hos 5. 8 **Raise** the war-cry at Bethaven!
Nah 1. 3 the clouds are the dust **raised** by his feet!
Zech 5. 7 I watched, the lid was **raised,** and there in the basket sat
Mt 16.21 to death, but three days later I will be **raised** to life."
17. 9 have seen until the Son of Man has been **raised** from death."
17.23 but three days later he will be **raised** to life."
20.19 but three days later he will be **raised** to life."
26.32 But after I am **raised** to life, I will go to Galilee

Mt 27.52 and many of God's people who had died were **raised** to life.
27.63 alive he said, 'I will be **raised** to life three days later.'
27.64 and then tell the people that he was **raised** from death.
28. 6 he has been **raised,** just as he said.
28. 7 'He has been **raised** from death,
Mk 12.26 Now, as for the dead being **raised:**
14.28 But after I am **raised** to life, I will go to Galilee
16. 6 He is not here—he has been **raised!**
Lk 7.22 the dead are **raised** to life,
9.22 to death, but three days later he will be **raised** to life."
18.13 and would not even **raise** his face to heaven,
20.37 And Moses clearly proves that the dead are **raised** to life.
21.28 stand up and **raise** your heads, because your salvation is
24. 6 he has been **raised.**
24.50 far as Bethany, where he **raised** his hands and blessed them.
Jn 2.22 So when he was **raised** from death, his disciples remembered
5.21 Just as the Father **raises** the dead and gives them life,
6.39 but that I should **raise** them all to life
6.40 And I will **raise** them to life on the last day."
6.44 and I will **raise** him to life on the last day.
6.54 eternal life, and I will **raise** him to life on the last
7.39 yet been given, because Jesus had not been **raised** to glory.
12. 1 Bethany, the home of Lazarus, the man he had **raised** from death.
12. 9 Jesus but also to see Lazarus, whom Jesus had **raised** from death.
12.16 but when Jesus had been **raised** to glory, they remembered
12.17 out of the grave and **raised** him from death had reported what
21.14 Jesus appeared to the disciples after he was **raised** from death.
Acts 2.24 But God **raised** him from death, setting him free from its power,
2.32 God has **raised** this very Jesus from death,
2.33 He has been **raised** to the right-hand side of God, his
3.15 leads to life, but God **raised** him from death—and we are
4.10 of Nazareth—whom you crucified and whom God **raised** from death.
5.30 The God of our ancestors **raised** Jesus from death, after
5.31 God **raised** him to his right-hand side as Leader and Saviour,
10.40 But God **raised** him from death three days later and
13.30 God **raised** him from death, [31]and for many days he appeared
13.32 for us, who are their descendants, by **raising** Jesus to life.
13.34 is what God said about **raising** him from death, never to rot
13.37 this did not happen to the one whom God **raised** from death.
17.31 proof of this to everyone by **raising** that man from death!"
17.32 heard Paul speak about a **raising** from death, some of them
26. 8 find it impossible to believe that God **raises** the dead?
27.40 Then they **raised** the sail at the front of the ship
Rom 1. 4 power to be the Son of God by being **raised** from death.
4.24 who believe in him who **raised** Jesus our Lord from death.
4.25 to die, and he was **raised** to life in order to put
6. 4 that, just as Christ was **raised** from death by the glorious
6. 5 be one with him by being **raised** to life as he was.
6. 9 know that Christ has been **raised** from death
7. 4 belong to him who was **raised** from death in order that we
8.11 the Spirit of God, who **raised** Jesus from death, lives in
8.11 then he who **raised** Christ from death will also give
8.34 died, or rather, who was **raised** to life and is at the
10. 9 Lord and believe that God **raised** him from death, you will be
15.28 the money that has been **raised** for them, I shall leave for
1 Cor 6.14 God **raised** the Lord from death,
6.14 and he will also **raise** us by his power.
15. 4 buried and that he was **raised** to life three days later,
15.12 is that Christ has been **raised** from death, how can some
15.12 of you say that the dead will not be **raised** to life?
15.13 If that is true, it means that Christ was not **raised;**
15.14 if Christ has not been **raised** from death, then we have
15.15 because we said that he **raised** Christ from death—
15.15 that the dead are not **raised** to life,
15.15 then he did not **raise** Christ.
15.16 For if the dead are not raised, neither has Christ been **raised.**
15.17 if Christ has not been **raised,** then your faith is a delusion
15.20 is that Christ has been **raised** from death, as the guarantee
15.20 that those who sleep in death will also be **raised.**
15.22 same way all will be **raised** to life because of their union
15.23 But each one will be **raised** in his proper order:
15.29 that the dead are not **raised** to life, why are those people
15.32 if the dead are not **raised** to life, then, as the saying
15.35 Someone will ask, "How can the dead be **raised** to life?
15.42 is how it will be when the dead are **raised** to life.
15.42 when **raised,** it will be immortal.
15.43 when **raised,** it will be beautiful and strong.
15.44 when **raised,** it will be a spiritual body.
15.51 the dead will be **raised,** never to die again,
16. 1 about the money to be **raised** to help God's people in Judaea.
2 Cor 1. 9 not on ourselves, but only on God, who **raises** the dead.
1.11 many will **raise** their voices to him in thanksgiving for us.
4.14 We know that God, who **raised** the Lord Jesus to life,
4.14 will also **raise** us up with Jesus
5.15 for him who died and was **raised** to life for their sake.
10. 5 every proud obstacle that is **raised** against the knowledge of God;
Gal 1. 1 Jesus Christ and God the Father, who **raised** him from death.
Eph 1.20 which he used when he **raised** Christ from death
2. 6 union with Christ Jesus he **raised** us up with him to rule
Phil 2. 9 For this reason God **raised** him to the highest place above
3.11 the hope that I myself will be **raised** from death to life.
Col 1.18 the first-born Son, who was **raised** from death, in order that
2.12 in baptism you were also **raised** with Christ through your faith
2.12 faith in the active power of God, who **raised** him from death.
3. 1 You have been **raised** to life with Christ, so set your
1 Thes 1.10 his Son Jesus, whom he **raised** from death and who rescues us
2 Tim 2. 8 Remember Jesus Christ, who was **raised** from death,
Heb 7.26 been set apart from sinners and **raised** above the heavens.
11.19 that God was able to **raise** Isaac from death—
11.35 women received their dead relatives **raised** back to life.
Heb 11.35 died under torture in order to be **raised** to a better life.
13.20 God has **raised** from death our Lord Jesus,
1 Pet 1. 3 he gave us new life by **raising** Jesus Christ from death.
1.21 you believe in God, who **raised** him from death
Rev 1. 5 the first to be **raised** from death
10. 5 sea and on the land **raised** his right hand to heaven
20. 5 This is the first **raising** of the dead.
20. 6 those who are included in this first **raising** of the dead.

RAISINS

Num 6. 3 kind of drink made from grapes or eat any grapes or **raisins.**
1 Sam 25.18 grain, a hundred bunches of **raisins,** and two hundred cakes
30.12 and water, [12]some dried figs, and two bunches of **raisins.**
2 Sam 6.19 a loaf of bread, a piece of roasted meat, and some **raisins.**
16. 1 bunches of **raisins,** a hundred bunches of fresh fruit,
1 Chr 12.40 mules, and oxen loaded with food—flour, figs, **raisins,** wine,
16. 3 a loaf of bread, a piece of roasted meat, and some **raisins.**
Song 2. 5 Restore my strength with **raisins** and refresh me with apples!
Hos 3. 1 gods and like to take offerings of **raisins** to idols."

RALLY

2 Chr 14.13 were killed that the army was unable to **rally** and fight.

RAM (1)

Gen 15. 9 cow, a goat, and a **ram,** each of them three years old,
22.13 looked round and saw a **ram** caught in a bush by its
31.38 reproduce, and I have not eaten any **rams** from your flocks.
Ex 25. 5 **rams'** skin dyed red;
26.14 two more coverings, one of **rams'** skin dyed red and the other
29. 1 Take one young bull and two **rams** without any defects.
29. 3 them to me when you sacrifice the bull and the two **rams.**
29.15 "Take one of the **rams** and tell Aaron and his sons to
29.17 Cut the **ram** in pieces;
29.18 Burn the whole **ram** on the altar as a food offering.
29.19 "Take the other **ram**—the ram used for dedication—and
29.22 "Cut away the **ram's** fat, the fat tail, the fat covering
29.26 "Take the breast of this **ram** and dedicate it to me as
29.27 and the thigh of the **ram** being used for the ordination are
29.31 "Take the meat of the **ram** used for the ordination of
35. 7 **rams'** skin dyed red;
35.23 **rams'** skin dyed red;
36.19 two more coverings, one of **rams'** skin dyed red and the other
39.34 the covering of **rams'** skin dyed red;
Lev 8. 2 the two **rams,** and the basket of unleavened bread.
8.18 Next, Moses brought the **ram** for the burnt-offering, and
8.20 He cut the **ram** in pieces, washed the internal
8.20 all the rest of the **ram** on the altar, just as the
8.22 Then Moses brought the second **ram,** which was for the
8.29 It was Moses' part of the ordination **ram.**
9. 2 a young bull and a **ram** without any defects and offer them
9. 2 bull for a sin-offering and the **ram** for a burnt-offering.
9. 4 and a bull and a **ram** for a fellowship-offering.
9.18 bull and the **ram** as a fellowship-offering for the people.
9.19 of the bull and the **ram** [20]on top of the breasts of
16. 3 bull for a sin-offering and a **ram** for a burnt-offering."
16. 5 goats for a sin-offering and a **ram** for a burnt-offering.
19.21 The man shall bring a **ram** to the entrance of the Tent
23.18 lambs, one bull, and two **rams,** none of which may have any
Num 5. 8 is in addition to the **ram** used to perform the ritual of
6.14 for a sin-offering, and a **ram** for a fellowship-offering.
6.17 He shall sacrifice the **ram** to the Lord as a fellowship-offering,
6.19 when the shoulder of the **ram** is boiled, the priest shall
6.20 and the leg of the **ram** which by law belong to the
7.12 one **ram,** and a one-year-old lamb, for the burnt-offering;
7.12 and two bulls, five **rams,** five goats, and five one-year-old
7.84 twelve bulls, twelve **rams,** and twelve one-year-old lambs, together with the grain-offerings
7.84 sixty **rams,** sixty goats, sixty one-year-old lambs,
15. 3 A bull, a **ram,** a sheep, or a goat may be presented
15. 6 When a **ram** is offered, two kilogrammes of flour mixed with
15.11 is what shall be offered with each bull, **ram,** sheep, or
23. 1 here for me, and bring me seven bulls and seven **rams."**
23. 2 he and Balaam offered a bull and a **ram** on each altar.
23. 4 the seven altars and offered a bull and a **ram** on each."
23.14 altars and offered a bull and a **ram** on each of them.
23.29 for me here and bring me seven bulls and seven **rams."**
23.30 was told, and offered a bull and a **ram** on each altar.
28.11 two young bulls, one **ram,** seven one-year-old male lambs, all
28.12 with the **ram,** two kilogrammes;
28.14 a half litres with the **ram,** and one litre with each lamb.
28.19 two young bulls, one **ram,** and seven one-year-old male lambs,
28.20 two kilogrammes with the **ram,** [21]and one kilogramme
28.27 two young bulls, one **ram,** and seven one-year-old male lambs,
28.28 two kilogrammes with the **ram,** [29]and one kilogramme
29. 2 one young bull, one **ram,** and seven one-year-old male lambs,
29. 3 two kilogrammes with the **ram,** [4]and one kilogramme
29. 8 one young bull, one **ram,** and seven one-year-old male lambs,
29. 9 two kilogrammes with the **ram,** [10]and one kilogramme
29.13 young bulls, two **rams,** and fourteen one-year-old male lambs,
29.14 two kilogrammes with each **ram,** [15]and one kilogramme
29.17 young bulls, two **rams,** and fourteen one-year-old male lambs,
29.20 young bulls, two **rams,** and fourteen one-year-old male lambs,
29.23 young bulls, two **rams,** and fourteen one-year-old male lambs,
29.26 young bulls, two **rams,** and fourteen one-year-old male lambs,
29.29 young bulls, two **rams,** and fourteen one-year-old male lambs,
29.32 young bulls, two **rams,** and fourteen one-year-old male lambs,
29.36 one young bull, one **ram,** and seven one-year-old male lambs,
1 Chr 29.21 a thousand bulls, a thousand **rams,** and a thousand lambs,

Ezra 7.17 money carefully and buy bulls, **rams,** lambs, corn, and wine
8.35 They offered 12 bulls for all Israel, 96 **rams,** and 77 lambs;
10.19 and they offered a **ram** as a sacrifice for their sins.
Job 42. 8 take seven bulls and seven **rams** to Job and offer them as
Jer 25.34 you to be slaughtered, and you will be butchered like **rams.**
51.40 I will take them to be slaughtered, like lambs, goats, and **rams.**
Ezek 39.18 whom will be killed like **rams** or lambs or goats or fat
43.23 bull and a young **ram,** both of them without any defects,
43.25 offer a goat, a bull, and a **ram** as sacrifices for sin.
45.23 Lord seven bulls and seven **rams** without any defects and burn
45.24 For each bull and each **ram** that is sacrificed, there is
46. 4 burnt whole, six lambs and one **ram,** all without any defects.
46. 5 With each **ram** he is to bring an offering of seventeen and
46. 6 a young bull, six lambs, and a **ram,** all without any defects.
46. 7 With each bull and each **ram** the offering is to be
46.11 litres with each bull or **ram,** and whatever the worshipper
Dan 8. 3 the river I saw a **ram** that had two long horns,
8. 4 I watched the **ram** butting with his horns to the west, the
8. 6 He came towards the **ram,** which I had seen standing beside
8. 7 I watched him attack the **ram.**
8. 7 The **ram** had no strength to resist.
8.20 "The **ram** you saw that had two horns represents the

RAMAH (1)
City in Benjamin.

Josh 18.25 There were also Gibeon, **Ramah,** Beeroth, [26]Mizpah,
Judg 4. 5 under a certain palm-tree between **Ramah** and Bethel in the
19.12 a little farther and spend the night at Gibeah or **Ramah."**
1 Kgs 15.17 Judah and started to fortify **Ramah** in order to cut off all
15.21 happened, he stopped fortifying **Ramah** and went to Tirzah.
15.22 to help carry away from **Ramah** the stones and timber that
1 Chr 27.25 Shimei from **Ramah**
2 Chr 16. 1 Judah and started to fortify **Ramah** in order to cut off all
16. 5 he stopped fortifying **Ramah** and abandoned the work.
16. 6 Baasha had been using at **Ramah,** and they used them to
Ezra 2.21 **Ramah** and Geba - 621
Neh 7.26 **Ramah** and Geba - 621
11.33 villages, [32]Anathoth, Nob, Ananiah, [33]Hazor, **Ramah,**
Is 10.29 people in the town of **Ramah** are terrified, and the people in
Jer 31.15 "A sound is heard in **Ramah,** the sound of bitter weeping.
40. 1 the commanding officer, had set me free at **Ramah.**
Hos 5. 8 Sound the alarm in **Ramah!**
Mt 2.18 "A sound is heard in **Ramah,** the sound of bitter weeping.

RAMAH (2)
City in Ephraim, the home of Samuel.

1 Sam 1. 1 lived in the town of **Ramah** in the hill-country of Ephraim.
1. 3 Every year Elkanah went from **Ramah** to worship and offer
1.19 after worshipping the Lord, they went back home to **Ramah.**
2.11 Elkanah went back home to **Ramah,** but the boy Samuel stayed
7.17 back to his home in **Ramah,** where also he would serve as
7.17 In **Ramah** he built an altar to the Lord.
8. 4 together, went to Samuel in **Ramah,** [5]and said to him,
15.34 Then Samuel went to **Ramah,** and King Saul went home to Gibeah.
16.13 Then Samuel returned to **Ramah.**
19.18 and went to Samuel in **Ramah** and told him everything that
19.19 David was in Naioth in **Ramah,** [20]so he sent some men to
19.22 Then he himself started out for **Ramah.**
20. 1 Then David fled from Naioth in **Ramah** and went to Jonathan.
25. 1 Then they buried him at his home in **Ramah.**
28. 3 for him and had buried him in his own city of **Ramah.**

RAMOTH (1)
Important city in Gilead, e. of R. Jordan.

Deut 4.43 tribe of Gad there was **Ramoth,** in the territory of Gilead;
Josh 20. 8 **Ramoth** in Gilead, in the territory of Gad;
21.38 **Ramoth** in Gilead, with its pasture lands (one of the cities
1 Kgs 4.13 the city of **Ramoth** in Gilead, and the villages in Gilead
22. 3 done anything to get back **Ramoth** in Gilead from the king of
22. 4 Ahab asked Jehoshaphat, "Will you go with me to attack **Ramoth?"**
22. 6 them, and asked them, "Should I go and attack **Ramoth,** or
22.12 "March against **Ramoth** and you will win," they said.
22.15 "Micaiah, should King Jehoshaphat and I go and attack **Ramoth,**
22.20 deceive Ahab so that he will go and be killed at **Ramoth?'**
22.29 Jehoshaphat of Judah went to attack the city of **Ramoth** in Gilead.
2 Kgs 8.28 The armies clashed at **Ramoth** in Gilead, and Joram was
9. 1 and said to him, "Get ready and go to **Ramoth** in Gilead.
9. 4 the young prophet went to **Ramoth,** [5]where he found the army
9.14 in the battle at **Ramoth** against King Hazael of Syria.
9.14 no one slips out of **Ramoth** to go and warn the people
1 Chr 6.80 **Ramoth** in Gilead, Mahanaim, [81]Heshbon, and Jazer.
2 Chr 18. 2 to join him in attacking the city of **Ramoth** in Gilead.
18. 3 He asked, "Will you go with me to attack **Ramoth?"**
18. 5 and asked them, "Should I go and attack **Ramoth,** or not?"
18.11 "March against **Ramoth** and you will win," they said.
18.14 "Micaiah, should King Jehoshaphat and I go and attack **Ramoth,**
18.19 deceive Ahab so that he will go and get killed at **Ramoth?'**
18.28 Jehoshaphat of Judah went to attack the city of **Ramoth** in Gilead.
22. 5 The armies clashed at **Ramoth** in Gilead, and Joram was

RAMP

2 Sam 20.15 They built **ramps** of earth against the outer wall

RANG see RING (2)

RANGE

Gen 8. 4 the boat came to rest on a mountain in the Ararat **range.**

RANK
[HIGH-RANKING]

1 Sam 23.17 of Israel and that I will be next in **rank** to you."
1 Kgs 22.36 Near sunset the order went out through the Israelite **ranks:**
2 Kgs 18.24 match for even the lowest **ranking** Assyrian official, and yet
25.18 Zephaniah the priest next in **rank,** and the three other
1 Chr 12. 9 They were **ranked** in the following order:
2 Chr 17.15 Second in **rank** was Jehohanan, with 280,000 soldiers,
Esth 10. 3 Mordecai the Jew was second in **rank** only to King Xerxes himself.
Is 14.31 the north—it is an army with no cowards in its **ranks.**
19.24 that time comes, Israel will **rank** with Egypt and Assyria,
36. 9 match for even the lowest **ranking** Assyrian official, and yet
Jer 52.24 Zephaniah the priest next in **rank,** and the three other
Ezek 23. 6 in uniforms of purple, noblemen and **high-ranking** officers;
23.23 those important officials and **high-ranking** cavalry officers.
Joel 2.20 Their front **ranks** will be driven into the Dead Sea,
2.20 their rear **ranks** into the Mediterranean.
Lk 19.12 once a man of high **rank** who was going to a country

RANSOM

Job 33.24 Here is the **ransom** to set him free."

RANTING

1 Kgs 18.29 kept on **ranting** and raving until the middle of the afternoon;

RAPE

Gen 34. 2 chief of that region, saw her, he took her and **raped** her.
34. 7 insulted the people of Israel by **raping** Jacob's daughter.
39.14 my room and tried to **rape** me, but I screamed as loud
Deut 22.25 man out in the countryside **rapes** a girl who is engaged to
22.27 The man **raped** the engaged girl in the countryside, and
22.28 "Suppose a man is caught **raping** a girl who is not engaged.
Judg 19.25 They **raped** her and abused her all night long and didn't stop
20. 5 instead they **raped** my concubine, and she died.
2 Sam 13.14 stronger than she was, he overpowered her and **raped** her.
13.22 Amnon so much for having **raped** his sister Tamar that he
13.32 to do this from the time that Amnon **raped** his sister Tamar.
Esth 7. 8 "Is this man going to **rape** the queen right here in front
Is 13.16 houses will be looted, and their wives will be **raped."**
Jer 13.22 off and you have been **raped**—it is because your sin is
Lam 5.11 Our wives have been **raped** on Mount Zion itself;
Zech 14. 2 The city will be taken, the houses looted, and the women **raped.**

RAPID

2 Thes 3. 1 message may continue to spread **rapidly** and be received with honour,

RARE

Gen 2.12 (Pure gold is found there and also **rare** perfume
1 Sam 3. 1 from the Lord, and visions from him were quite **rare.**
Rev 18.12 all kinds of **rare** woods and all kinds of objects made of

RASH

Ecc 5. 2 Think before you speak, and don't make any **rash** promises to God.
8. 2 what the king says, and don't make any **rash** promises to God.

RATE

2 Cor 10.12 or compare ourselves with those who **rate** themselves so highly.

RATION

Lev 26.26 They will **ration** it out, and when you have eaten it all,

RATS

Lev 11.29 Moles, **rats,** mice, and lizards must be considered unclean.

RATTLE

2 Sam 6. 5 They were playing harps, lyres, drums, **rattles,** and
Job 39.23 weapons which their riders carry **rattle** and flash in the sun.
Ezek 37. 7 was speaking, I heard a **rattling** noise, and the bones began
Joel 2. 5 on the tops of the mountains, they **rattle** like chariots;
Nah 3. 2 of the whip, the **rattle** of wheels, the gallop of horses,

RAVAGE

1 Sam 6. 5 of the mice that are **ravaging** your country, and you must

RAVE

1 Sam 18.10 control of Saul, and he **raved** in his house like a madman.
1 Kgs 18.29 kept on ranting and **raving** until the middle of the afternoon;
Amos 7.16 prophesying, to stop **raving** against the people of Israel.

RAVEN

Gen 8. 7 After forty days Noah opened a window [7]and sent out a **raven.**
1 Kgs 17. 4 and I have commanded **ravens** to bring you food there."

1 Kgs 17. 6 water from the brook, and **ravens** brought him bread and meat
Job 38.41 is it that feeds the **ravens** when they wander about hungry,
Ps 147. 9 their food and feeds the young **ravens** when they call.
Prov 30.17 by vultures or have his eyes picked out by wild **ravens.**
Song 5.11 his hair is wavy, black as a **raven.**
Is 34.11 Owls and **ravens** will take over the land.

RAVINE

Jer 48.28 the dove that makes its nest in the sides of a **ravine.**

RAW

Ex 12. 9 not eat any of it **raw** or boiled, but eat it roasted
Lev 13.24 been burnt, if the **raw** flesh becomes white or reddish-white,
23.14 of the new corn, whether **raw,** roasted, or baked into bread,
1 Sam 2.15 he won't accept boiled meat from you, only **raw** meat."
Lam 3. 4 has left my flesh open and **raw,** and has broken my bones.
Ezek 29.18 and their shoulders were worn **raw,** but neither the king nor

RAY

Mal 4. 2 on you like the sun and bring healing like the sun's **rays.**

RAZOR

Ps 52. 2 your tongue is like a sharp **razor.**

RE- *Where not listed below, see under main part of word, e.g. for "reappear" see APPEAR*

Am **REACH** see **STRETCH**

REACH

Gen 8. 9 back to the boat, and Noah **reached** out and took it in.
10.19 out, [19] until the Canaanite borders **reached** from Sidon
11. 4 city with a tower that **reaches** the sky, so that we can
13. 3 He **reached** the place between Bethel and Ai where he had
19.10 But the two men inside **reached** out, pulled Lot back into
19.23 The sun was rising when Lot **reached** Zoar.
28.12 that he saw a stairway **reaching** from earth to heaven, with
37.18 the distance, and before he **reached** them, they plotted
45.16 the news **reached** the palace that Joseph's brothers had come,
49.13 His territory will **reach** as far as Sidon.
Ex 16.35 next forty years, until they **reached** the land of Canaan,
27. 5 rim of the altar, so that it **reaches** half-way up the altar.
28.42 linen shorts for them, **reaching** from the waist to the thighs,
38. 4 rim of the altar, so that it **reached** half-way up the altar.
Deut 1.19 When we **reached** Kadesh Barnea, [20-21] I said, 'You have
1.28 and that they live in cities with walls that **reach** the sky.
9. 1 Their cities are large, with walls that **reach** the sky.
19. 2 three parts, each with a city that can be easily **reached.**
30.11 giving you today is not too difficult or beyond your **reach.**
32.22 It will **reach** to the world below and consume the roots of
33.23 Their land **reaches** to the south from Lake Galilee."
34. 3 and the plain that **reaches** from Zoar to Jericho, the city of
Josh 1. 4 Your borders will **reach** from the desert in the south to
3. 8 Covenant Box that when they **reach** the river, they must wade
4.18 so, [18] and when the priests **reached** the river bank, the
11. 1 the news of Israel's victories **reached** King Jabin of Hazor,
15. 1 The land **reached** south to the southernmost point of the
15.47 with their towns and villages, **reaching** to the stream on the
16. 7 to Ataroth and Naarah, **reaching** Jericho and ending at the Jordan.
17. 7 The territory of Manasseh **reached** from Asher to Michmethath,
19.10 The land which they received **reached** as far as Sarid.
19.29 border then turned to Ramah, **reaching** the fortified city of Tyre;
Judg 6.21 Then the Lord's angel **reached** out and touched the meat
19.27 in front of the house with her hands **reaching** for the door.
1 Sam 14.27 so he **reached** out with the stick he was carrying, dipped it
20.37 When the boy **reached** the place where the arrow had fallen,
2 Sam 6. 6 the oxen stumbled, and Uzzah **reached** out and took hold of
15. 5 down before him, Absalom would **reach** out, take hold of him,
15.32 When David **reached** the top of the hill, where there was
16.14 out when they **reached** the Jordan, and there they rested.
17.24 David had **reached** the town of Mahanaim by the time
19.11 The news of what the Israelites were saying **reached** King David.
20. 8 When they **reached** the large rock at Gibeon, Amasa met them.
22.17 The Lord **reached** down from above and took hold of me;
1 Kgs 2.29 When the news **reached** King Solomon that Joab had fled to
6.16 off by cedar boards **reaching** from the floor to the ceiling.
11.21 When the news **reached** Hadad in Egypt that David had
2 Kgs 3.24 But when they **reached** the camp, the Israelites attacked
5.24 When they **reached** the hill where Elisha lived, Gehazi
6.14 They **reached** the town at night and surrounded it.
7. 5 the Syrian camp, but when they **reached** it, no one was there.
7. 8 When the four men **reached** the edge of the camp, they went
9.18 the messenger had **reached** the group but was not returning.
9.20 the messenger had **reached** the group but was not returning.
9.27 to keep going until he **reached** the city of Megiddo, where he
19. 9 Word **reached** the Assyrians that the Egyptian army, led by
19.23 and that you **reached** the deepest parts of the forests.
1 Chr 23.27 registered for service when they **reached** the age of twenty,
2 Chr 3.11 centre of the room and **reached** the wall on either side of
20.24 When the Judaean army **reached** a tower that was in the desert,
20.28 When they **reached** the city, they marched to the Temple,
24.15 After **reaching** the very old age of a hundred and thirty,
Ezra 8.29 Guard them carefully until you **reach** the Temple.
8.32 When we **reached** Jerusalem, we rested for three days.
Ezra 9. 6 they **reach** as high as the heavens.
Neh 12.40 that were giving thanks to God **reached** the temple area.
Job 11. 8 sky is no limit for God, but it lies beyond your **reach.**
11.13 **Reach** out to God.
20. 6 so great that his head **reaches** the clouds, [7] but he will be
Ps 8. 1 Your praise **reaches** up to the heavens;
18.16 The Lord **reached** down from above and took hold of me;
32. 6 flood of trouble comes rushing in, it will not **reach** them.
36. 5 Lord, your constant love **reaches** the heavens;
57.10 Your constant love **reaches** the heavens;
71.19 Your righteousness, God, **reaches** the skies.
72. 8 His kingdom will **reach** from sea to sea, from the Euphrates
85.11 Man's loyalty will **reach** up from the earth, and God's
108. 4 Your constant love **reaches** above the heavens;
119.169 Let my cry for help **reach** you, Lord!
144. 7 **Reach** down from above, pull me out of the deep water, and
Is 7. 2 When word **reached** the king of Judah that the armies of
28.15 a treaty with death and **reached** an agreement with the world
35.10 They will **reach** Jerusalem with gladness, singing and shouting
37. 9 Word **reached** the Assyrians that the Egyptian army, led by
37.24 and that you **reached** the deepest parts of the forests.
51.11 whom you have rescued will **reach** Jerusalem with gladness,
Jer 37.13 But when I **reached** the Benjamin Gate, the officer in
48.32 like a vine whose branches **reach** across the Dead Sea and go
Ezek 19.11 The vine grew tall enough to **reach** the clouds;
31. 3 A tree so tall it **reaches** the clouds.
31. 7 Its roots **reached** down to the deep-flowing streams.
31.10 happen to that tree that grew until it **reached** the clouds.
31.14 or push its top through the clouds and **reach** such a height.
Dan 4.11 bigger and bigger until it **reached** the sky and could be seen
4.20 tree, so tall that it **reached** the sky, could be seen by
4.22 grown so great that you **reach** the sky, and your power
6.24 Before they even **reached** the bottom of the pit, the lions
Mic 1. 9 **reached** the gates of Jerusalem itself,
Zech 14.10 city will **reach** from the Benjamin Gate to the Corner Gate,
Mt 14.31 At once Jesus **reached** out and grabbed hold of him and said,
27. 7 After **reaching** an agreement about it, they used the money
Jn 6.21 and immediately the boat **reached** land at the place they were
20. 4 disciple ran faster than Peter and **reached** the tomb first.
20. 8 the other disciple, who had **reached** the tomb first, also
Acts 9.41 Peter **reached** over and helped her get up.
11.22 The news about this **reached** the church in Jerusalem,
16. 7 When they **reached** the border of Mysia, they tried to go
20.15 we came to Samos, and the following day we **reached** Miletus.
21. 1 the next day we **reached** Rhodes, and from there we went on
27.12 to sea and trying to **reach** Phoenix, if possible, in order to
Rom 10.18 their words **reached** the ends of the earth."
2 Cor 4.15 and as God's grace **reaches** more and more people, they will
Gal 4. 3 spirits of the universe before we **reached** spiritual maturity.
Eph 4.13 we shall become mature people, **reaching** to the very height
Phil 3.13 is behind me and do my best to **reach** what is ahead.
Jas 5. 4 gather in your crops have **reached** the ears of God, the Lord
Rev 1.13 being, wearing a robe that **reached** to his feet, and a gold

READ

Ex 24. 7 Lord's commands were written, and **read** it aloud to the people.
Deut 17.19 this book near him and **read** from it all his life, so
31.10 debts are cancelled comes round, **read** this aloud at the
31.11 **Read** it to the people of Israel when they come to
Josh 1. 8 that the book of the Law is always **read** in your worship.
8.34 Joshua then **read** aloud the whole Law, including the
8.35 of Moses was **read** by Joshua to the whole gathering,
2 Kgs 5. 6 The letter that he took **read:**
5. 7 When the king of Israel **read** the letter, he tore his
10. 1 The letter **read:**
19.14 King Hezekiah took the letter from the messengers and **read** it.
22. 8 Hilkiah gave him the book, and Shaphan **read** it.
22.10 And he **read** it aloud to the king.
22.11 heard the book being **read,** he tore his clothes in dismay,
22.16 its people, as written in the book that the king has **read.**
23. 2 Before them all, the king **read** aloud the whole book of the
2 Chr 21.12 The prophet Elijah sent Jehoram a letter, which **read** as follows:
34.18 And he **read** it aloud to the king.
34.19 king heard the book being **read,** he tore his clothes in
34.24 the curses written in the book that was **read** to the king.
34.30 Before them all, the king **read** aloud the whole book of the
36.22 out in writing to be **read** aloud everywhere in his empire:
Ezra 1. 1 out in writing to be **read** aloud everywhere in his empire:
4. 7 was written in Aramaic and was to be translated when **read.**
4.18 "The letter which you sent has been translated and **read** to me.
4.23 Artaxerxes was **read** to Rehum, Shimshai,
Neh 6. 6 It **read:**
8. 3 square by the gate he **read** the Law to them from dawn
8.12 others, because they understood what had been **read** to them.
8.18 festival to the last they **read** a part of God's Law every
9. 3 the Lord their God was **read** to them, and for the next
13. 1 Law of Moses was being **read** aloud to the people, they came
13. 3 of Israel heard this law **read,** they excluded all foreigners
Esth 6. 1 records of the empire to be brought and **read** to him.
6. 2 The part they **read** included the account of how Mordecai
8.17 wherever the king's proclamation was **read,** the Jews held a
Is 29.11 someone who knows how to **read** and ask him to read it
29.12 it to someone who can't **read** and ask him to read it
29.18 to hear a book being **read** aloud, and the blind, who have
34.16 the Lord's book of living creatures and **read** what it says.
37.14 King Hezekiah took the letter from the messengers and **read** it.
Jer 29.29 Zephaniah **read** the letter to me, [30] and then the Lord
36. 6 You are to **read** the scroll aloud, so that they will hear
36. 8 So Baruch **read** the Lord's words in the Temple exactly as I
36.10 the people were listening, Baruch **read** from the scroll

Jer 36.11 grandson of Shaphan, heard Baruch **read** from the scroll what
36.13 them everything that he had heard Baruch **read** to the people.
36.14 Baruch to bring the scroll that he had **read** to the people.
36.15 "Sit down," they said, "and **read** the scroll to us."
36.16 After he had **read** it, they turned to one another in alarm,
36.21 the room of Elishama and **read** it to the king and all
36.23 As soon as Jehudi finished **reading** three or four columns,
51.61 to Babylon, be sure to **read** aloud to the people everything
51.63 Seraiah, when you finish **reading** this book to the people,
Dan 1. 4 was to teach them to **read** and write the Babylonian language.
5. 7 to them, "Anyone who can **read** this writing and tell me what
5. 8 but none of them could **read** the writing or tell the king
5.15 magicians were brought in to **read** this writing and tell me
5.16 If you can **read** this writing and tell me what it means,
5.17 I will **read** for Your Majesty what has been written and tell
Hab 2. 2 reveal to you, so that it can be **read** at a glance.
Mt 12. 3 Jesus answered, "Have you never **read** what David did that time
12. 5 Or have you not **read** in the Law of Moses that every
19. 4 Jesus answered, "Haven't you **read** the scripture that says that
21.16 "Haven't you ever **read** this scripture?
21.42 said to them, "Haven't you ever **read** what the Scriptures say?
22.31 haven't you ever **read** what God has told you?
24.15 (Note to the **reader:**
Mk 2.25 Jesus answered, "Have you never **read** what David did that time
12.10 Surely you have **read** this scripture?
12.26 haven't you ever **read** in the Book of Moses the passage about
13.14 (Note to the **reader:**
Lk 4.16 He stood up to **read** the Scriptures [17]and was handed the
4.21 scripture has come true today, as you heard it being **read."**
6. 3 Jesus answered them, "Haven't you **read** what David did when he
Jn 19.20 Many people **read** it, because the place where Jesus was crucified
Acts 8.27 he rode along, he was **reading** from the book of the prophet
8.30 ran over and heard him **reading** from the book of the prophet
8.30 He asked him, "Do you understand what you are **reading?"**
8.32 The passage of scripture which he was **reading** was this:
13.15 After the **reading** from the Law of Moses and from the
13.27 understand the words of the prophets that are **read** every Sabbath.
15.21 Law of Moses has been **read** for a very long time
15.31 When the people **read** it, they were filled with joy
23.34 The governor **read** the letter and asked Paul what province he
1 Cor 9. 9 We **read** in the Law of Moses, "Do not muzzle an ox
2 Cor 1.13 We write to you only what you can **read** and understand.
3. 2 have, written on our hearts for everyone to know and **read.**
3.14 the same veil as they **read** the books of the old covenant.
3.15 Even today, whenever they **read** the Law of Moses, the
Eph 3. 4 and if you will **read** what I have written, you can
Col 4.16 After you **read** this letter,
4.16 make sure that it is **read** also in the church at Laodicea.
4.16 same time, you are to **read** the letter that the brothers in
1 Thes 5.27 of the Lord to **read** this letter to all the believers.
1 Tim 4.13 effort to the public **reading** of the Scriptures and to preaching
Rev 1. 3 Happy is the one who **reads** this book, and happy are those

READY

Gen 18. 7 and gave it to a servant, who hurried to get it **ready.**
19. 3 When it was **ready,** they ate it.
24.31 I have a room **ready** for you in my house, and there
24.61 and her young women got **ready** and mounted the camels to go
31.13 Now get **ready** to go back to the land where you were
31.17 So Jacob got **ready** to go back to his father in the
31.44 children, [44]I am **ready** to make an agreement with you.
37.13 Joseph answered, "I am **ready."**
43.25 They got their gifts **ready** to present to Joseph when he
46.30 said to Joseph, "I am **ready** to die, now that I have
Ex 12.39 time to get their food **ready** or to prepare leavened dough.
14. 6 The king got his war chariot and his army **ready.**
17. 4 They are almost **ready** to stone me."
19.11 must wash their clothes [11]and be **ready** the day after tomorrow.
19.14 the mountain and told the people to get **ready** for worship.
19.15 Moses said to them, "Be **ready** by the day after tomorrow and
24.13 and his helper Joshua got **ready,** and Moses began to go up
30. 7 comes to get the lamps **ready,** he is to burn sweet-smelling
34. 2 Be **ready** tomorrow morning, and come up Mount Sinai to meet
Num 7.10 When they were **ready** to present their gifts at the altar,
14.40 hill-country, saying, "Now we are **ready** to go to the place
22.20 to go with them, get **ready** to go, but do only what
24.25 Then Balaam got **ready** and went back home, and Balak went
31. 3 said to the people, "Get **ready** for war, so that you can
31. 5 each tribe, a total of twelve thousand men **ready** for battle.
32.14 new generation of sinful men **ready** to bring down the fierce
32.17 Then we will be **ready** to go with our fellow-Israelites
32.20 in the presence of the Lord get **ready** to go into battle.
32.27 But all of us are **ready** to go into battle under the
32.29 and Reuben cross the Jordan **ready** for battle at the Lord's
Deut 1.41 each one of you got **ready** to fight, thinking it would be
Josh 1. 2 Get **ready** now, you and all the people of Israel, and cross
1.11 the people, "Get some food **ready,** because in three days you
4.12 half the tribe of Manasseh, **ready** for battle, crossed ahead
4.13 Lord about forty thousand men **ready** for war crossed over to
7.13 Purify the people and get them **ready** to come before me.
7.13 Tell them to be **ready** tomorrow, because I, the Lord God of
8. 3 So Joshua got **ready** to go to Ai with all his soldiers.
8. 4 be **ready** to attack.
9.11 us to get some food **ready** for a journey and to go
Judg 5.13 the Lord's people came to him **ready** to fight.
18.11 the tribe of Dan left Zorah and Eshtaol, **ready** for battle.
18.16 six hundred soldiers from Dan, **ready** for battle, were
19. 5 the fourth day they woke up early and got **ready** to go.
Ruth 1. 6 so she got **ready** to leave Moab with her daughters-in-law.
1 Sam 14.43 Here I am—I am **ready** to die."
1 Sam 17. 2 Valley of Elah, where they got **ready** to fight the Philistines.
17.40 With his catapult **ready,** he went out to meet Goliath.
25.41 said, "I am his servant, **ready** to wash the feet of his
2 Sam 5.23 but go round and get **ready** to attack them from the other
15.15 "We are **ready** to do whatever you say."
19.18 As the king was getting **ready** to cross, Shimei threw
1 Kgs 5. 8 received your message and I am **ready** to do what you ask.
20.12 ordered his men to get **ready** to attack the city, so they
22. 4 "I am **ready** when you are," Jehoshaphat answered, "and so
2 Kgs 9. 1 and said to him, "Get **ready** and go to Ramoth in Gilead.
9.21 "Get my chariot **ready,"** King Joram ordered.
10. 5 are your servants and we are **ready** to do anything you say.
10. 6 are with me, and are **ready** to follow my orders, bring the
13.16 Jehoash got them, [16]and Elisha told him to get **ready** to shoot.
19. 3 like a woman who is **ready** to give birth, but is too
20. 1 Get **ready** to die."
1 Chr 12.23 50,000 loyal and reliable men **ready** to fight, trained to use
12.23 40,000 men **ready** for battle;
12.38 All these soldiers, **ready** for battle, went to Hebron,
14.14 but go round and get **ready** to attack them from the other
19. 7 too came out from all their cities and got **ready** to fight.
21.16 holding his sword in his hand, **ready** to destroy Jerusalem.
22. 5 David got large amounts of the materials **ready** before he died.
22.14 I also have wood and stone **ready,** but you must get more.
2 Chr 2. 8 I am **ready** to send my men to assist yours [9]in preparing
6.32 and how you are always **ready** to act, and then he comes
7.15 over this Temple and be **ready** to hear all the prayers that
13.12 priests are here with trumpets, **ready** to blow them and call
18. 3 Jehoshaphat replied, "I am **ready** when you are, and so is
25. 5 They were picked troops, **ready** for battle, skilled in using
26.11 He had a large army **ready** for battle.
31.18 they were required to be **ready** to perform their sacred
Ezra 1. 5 heart God had moved got **ready** to go and rebuild the Lord's
Neh 2.18 And they got **ready** to start the work.
Esth 6. 4 to have Mordecai hanged on the gallows that was now **ready.**
8.13 that the Jews would be **ready** to take revenge on their
Job 13.14 I am **ready** to risk my life.
13.18 I am **ready** to state my case, because I know I am
13.19 If you do, I am **ready** to be silent and die.
33. 2 I am **ready** to say what's on my mind.
38.23 I keep them **ready** for times of trouble, for days of
Ps 7.12 He bends his bow and makes it **ready;**
10.14 of trouble and suffering and are always **ready** to help.
26.10 do evil all the time and are always **ready** to take bribes.
45. 1 pen of a good writer my tongue is **ready** with a poem.
46. 1 and strength, always **ready** to help in times of trouble.
50.19 "You are always **ready** to speak evil;
50.20 You are **ready** to accuse your own brothers and to find
85. 9 Surely he is **ready** to save those who honour him, and his
119.109 I am always **ready** to risk my life;
119.173 Always be **ready** to help me, because I follow your commands.
142. 3 When I am **ready** to give up, he knows what I should
143. 4 So I am **ready** to give up;
Prov 1.16 They're always **ready** to kill.
6. 8 up their food during the summer, getting **ready** for winter.
10. 5 A sensible man gathers the crops when they are **ready;**
18.15 Intelligent people are always eager and **ready** to learn.
21.31 You can get horses **ready** for battle, but it is the Lord
24.27 home until your fields are **ready,** and you are sure that you
Ecc 8.11 Why do people commit crimes so **readily?**
Song 5. 5 I was **ready** to let him come in.
Is 3.13 The Lord is **ready** to state his case;
3.13 he is **ready** to judge his people.
5.28 Their arrows are sharp, and their bows are **ready** to shoot.
8. 9 Get **ready** to fight, but be afraid!
8. 9 Yes, get **ready,** but be afraid!
14. 9 the dead is getting **ready** to welcome the king of Babylonia.
21. 5 In the vision a banquet is **ready;**
21.15 escape from swords that are **ready** to kill them,
21.15 from bows that are **ready** to shoot, from all the dangers
22. 6 Soldiers from the land of Kir had their shields **ready.**
28. 2 has someone strong and powerful **ready** to attack them,
28.24 ploughing his fields and getting them **ready** for sowing.
29.10 Lord has made you drowsy, **ready** to fall into a deep sleep.
30.18 He is **ready** to take pity on you because he always does
37. 3 like a woman who is **ready** to give birth, but is too
38. 1 Get **ready** to die."
41. 1 Get **ready** to present your case in court;
42.13 he is **ready** and eager for battle.
49. 2 He made me like an arrow, sharp and **ready** for use.
51.13 who oppress you, of those who are **ready** to destroy you?
57.14 Build the road, and make it **ready!**
65. 1 The Lord said, "I was **ready** to answer my people's prayers,
65. 1 I was **ready** for them to find me, but they did not
65. 1 me, even though I was always **ready** to answer, 'Here I am;
65. 2 I have always been **ready** to welcome my people, who
Jer 1.17 Get **ready,** Jeremiah;
6. 4 Get **ready!**
6.23 They are **ready** for battle against Jerusalem."
9. 3 They are always **ready** to tell lies;
18.11 I am making plans against them and getting **ready** to punish them.
31.18 we are **ready** to return to you, the Lord our God.
46. 3 officers shout, 'Get your shields **ready** and march into battle!
46.14 'Get **ready** to defend yourselves;
46.19 Get **ready** to be taken prisoner, you people of Egypt!
49.14 to assemble their armies and to get **ready** to attack you.
50.42 They are **ready** for battle against Babylonia.
51.11 Get your shields **ready!**
Ezek 7.14 The trumpet sounds, and everyone gets **ready.**
20. 4 "Are you **ready** to pass sentence on them, mortal man?
20. 8 I was **ready** to let them feel the full force of my

Ezek 20.13 I was **ready** to let them feel the force of my anger
20.21 I was **ready** to let them feel the force of my anger
21.11 The sword is being polished, to make it **ready** for use.
21.15 a sword that flashes like lightning and is **ready** to kill.
21.28 'A sword is **ready** to destroy;
22. 2 man," he said, "are you **ready** to judge the city that is
23.36 "Mortal man, are you **ready** to judge Oholah and Oholibah?
32.20 A sword is **ready** to kill them all.
38. 7 Tell him to get **ready** and have all his troops ready at
43.26 are to consecrate the altar and make it **ready** for use.
Hos 7. 4 not stirred by the baker until the dough is **ready** to bake.
10.11 a well-trained young cow, **ready** and willing to thresh grain.
Joel 2. 5 They are lined up like a great army **ready** for battle.
2.13 he is always **ready** to forgive and not punish.
3.12 "The nations must get **ready** and come to the Valley of Judgement.
Amos 4.12 I am going to do this, get **ready** to face my judgement!"
Obad 1 "Get **ready!**
Jon 4. 2 patient, always kind, and always **ready** to change your mind
Nah 3.14 Trample the clay to make bricks, and get the brick moulds **ready!**
Hab 3. 9 You got **ready** to use your bow, ready to shoot your arrows.
Zech 3. 1 Joshua stood Satan, **ready** to bring an accusation
Mt 3.10 The axe is **ready** to cut down the trees at the roots;
4.21 in their boat with their father Zebedee, getting their nets **ready.**
8.19 "Teacher," he said, "I am **ready** to go with you wherever
17.11 coming first," answered Jesus, "and he will get everything **ready.**
22. 4 'My feast is **ready** now;
22. 4 prize calves have been butchered, and everything is **ready.**
22. 8 'My wedding feast is **ready,** but the people I invited did
24.33 things, you will know that the time is near, **ready** to begin.
24.44 you also must always be **ready,** because the Son of Man will
25.10 The five girls who were **ready** went in with him to the
26.12 pour this perfume on my body to get me **ready** for burial.
26.17 do you want us to get the Passover meal **ready** for you?"
Mk 1. 3 shouting in the desert, 'Get the road **ready** for the Lord;
1.19 They were in their boat getting their nets **ready.**
3. 9 disciples to get a boat **ready** for him, so that the people
9.12 "Elijah is indeed coming first in order to get everything **ready.**
13.29 you will know that the time is near, **ready** to begin.
14.12 want us to go and get the Passover meal **ready** for you?"
14.15 room, prepared and furnished, where you will get everything **ready**
Lk 1.17 he will get the Lord's people **ready** for him."
1.39 Soon afterwards Mary got **ready** and hurried off to a town
3. 4 'Get the road **ready** for the Lord;
3. 9 The axe is **ready** to cut down the trees at the roots;
9.52 into a village in Samaria to get everything **ready** for him.
11.21 man, with all his weapons **ready,** guards his own house, all
12.35 "Be **ready** for whatever comes, dressed for action
12.37 servants whose master finds them awake and **ready** when he returns!
12.38 are if he finds them **ready,** even if he should come at
12.40 And you, too, must be **ready,** because the Son of Man will
12.47 but does not get himself **ready** and do it, will be punished
14.17 sent his servant to tell his guests, 'Come, everything is **ready!'**
17. 8 to him, 'Get my supper **ready,** then put on your apron
22. 8 "Go and get the Passover meal **ready** for us to eat."
22. 9 "Where do you want us to get it **ready?"**
22.12 large furnished room upstairs, where you will get everything **ready."**
22.33 Peter answered, "Lord, I am **ready** to go to prison with
Jn 4.35 the crops are now ripe and **ready** to be harvested!
13.37 "I am **ready** to die for you!"
13.38 Jesus answered, "Are you really **ready** to die for me?
21.18 young, you used to get **ready** and go anywhere you wanted to;
Acts 8.26 Lord said to Philip, "Get **ready** and go south to the road
8.27 So Philip got **ready** and went.
9.11 Lord said to him, "Get **ready** and go to Straight Street,
9.39 So Peter got **ready** and went with them.
10. 4 prayers and works of charity, and is **ready** to answer you.
10.20 So get **ready** and go down, and do not hesitate to go
10.23 The next day he got **ready** and went with them;
16.10 had this vision, we got **ready** to leave for Macedonia,
20. 3 He was getting **ready** to go to Syria when he discovered that
21.13 I am **ready** not only to be tied up in Jerusalem
21.15 time there, we got our things **ready** and left for Jerusalem.
23.15 But we will be **ready** to kill him before he ever gets
23.21 They are now **ready** to do it and are waiting for your
23.23 "Get two hundred soldiers **ready** to go to Caesarea, together with
23.23 hundred spearmen, and be **ready** to leave by nine o'clock tonight.
27. 2 ship from Adramyttium, which was **ready** to leave for the seaports
1 Cor 3. 2 milk, not solid food, because you were not **ready** for it.
3. 2 even now you are not **ready** for it, [3] because you still live
5. 7 Passover Festival is **ready,** now that Christ, our Passover lamb,
2 Cor 1.17 from selfish motives, **ready** to say "Yes, yes" and "No,
2. 9 and whether you are always **ready** to obey my instructions.
7. 7 how sorry you are, how **ready** you are to defend me;
7.11 such feelings, such devotion, such **readiness** to punish wrongdoing!
7.15 how all of you were **ready** to obey his instructions, how you
9. 2 Achaia," I said, "have been **ready** to help since last year."
9. 3 But, just as I said, you will be **ready** with your help.
9. 4 out that you are not **ready,** how ashamed we would be—
9. 5 ahead of me and get **ready** in advance the gift you promised
9. 5 Then it will be **ready** when I arrive, and it will show
10. 6 we will be **ready** to punish any act of disloyalty.
12.14 third time that I am **ready** to come to visit you—
Eph 6.14 So stand **ready,** with truth as a belt tight round your waist,
6.15 and as your shoes the **readiness** to announce the Good News
6.19 a message when I am **ready** to speak, so that I may
1 Thes 2. 8 love for you we were **ready** to share with you not only
1 Tim 6.18 good works, to be generous and **ready** to share with others.
2 Tim 2.21 and useful to his Master, **ready** to be used for every good
Tit 3. 1 obey them, and to be **ready** to do good in every way.
Phlm 22 same time, get a room **ready** for me, because I hope that
Heb 10.33 at other times you were **ready** to join those who were being
11.17 the promise, yet he was **ready** to offer his only son
Jas 4. 2 things, but you cannot have them, so you are **ready** to kill;
5. 9 The Judge is near, **ready** to appear.
1 Pet 1. 5 for the salvation which is **ready** to be revealed at the end
1.13 So then, have your minds **ready** for action.
3.15 Be **ready** at all times to answer anyone who asks you to
4. 5 themselves to God, who is **ready** to judge the living and the
2 Pet 2. 3 now their Judge has been **ready,** and their Destroyer has been
Rev 9. 7 The locusts looked like horses **ready** for battle;
9.15 year they had been kept **ready** to kill a third of all
21. 2 heaven from God, prepared and **ready,** like a bride dressed to

REAL

Deut 32.17 to gods that are not **real,** new gods their ancestors had
32.39 no other god is **real.**
1 Sam 12.21 they cannot help you or save you, for they are not **real.**
1 Kgs 3.26 The **real** mother, her heart full of love for her son,
3.27 Give it to the first woman—she is its **real** mother."
20.11 "Tell King Benhadad that a **real** soldier does his boasting
Ps 127. 3 they are a **real** blessing.
Prov 17.27 People who stay calm have **real** insight.
Jer 2.11 has ever changed its gods, even though they were not **real.**
5. 7 They have abandoned me and have worshipped gods that are not **real.**
23.36 anyone does, I will make my message a **real** burden to him.
Zech 8.16 In the courts, give **real** justice—the kind that brings peace.
Mk 6.52 they had not understood the **real** meaning of the feeding of
Jn 1. 9 This was the **real** light—the light that comes into the
1.47 to him, he said about him, "Here is a **real** Israelite;
5.31 behalf, what I say is not to be accepted as **real** proof.
6.32 it is my Father who gives you the **real** bread from heaven.
6.55 For my flesh is the **real** food;
6.55 my blood is the **real** drink.
15. 1 "I am the **real** vine, and my Father is the gardener.
Acts 12. 9 not knowing, however, if what the angel was doing was **real;**
Rom 2.28 After all, who is a **real** Jew, truly circumcised?
2.29 Rather, the **real** Jew is the person who is a Jew on
11. 6 on what people do, then his grace would not be **real** grace.
13. 4 then be afraid of him, because his power to punish is **real.**
1 Cor 3.13 the fire will test it and show its **real** quality.
16. 9 There is a **real** opportunity here for great and worthwhile work,
2 Cor 8. 8 I am trying to find out how **real** your own love is.
11.13 and disguise themselves to look like **real** apostles of Christ.
Gal 3. 7 realize then, that the **real** descendants of Abraham are the people
Col 2.17 the **reality** is Christ.
2.23 they have no **real** value in controlling physical passions.
3. 4 Your **real** life is Christ and when he appears, then you too
3.24 For Christ is the **real** Master you serve.
2 Tim 3. 5 the outward form of our religion, but reject its **real** power.
Tit 3.14 their time doing good, in order to provide for **real** needs;
Heb 8. 2 Place, that is, in the **real** tent which was put up by
9.24 a man-made Holy Place, which was a copy of the **real** one.
10. 1 Law is not a full and faithful model of the **real** things;
12. 8 his sons are, it means you are not **real** sons, but bastards.
1 Pet 5. 2 work, not for mere pay, but from a **real** desire to serve.
1 Jn 2. 8 darkness is passing away, and the **real** light is already shining.

REALIZE

Gen 3. 7 were given understanding and **realized** that they were naked;
30. 9 When Leah **realized** that she had stopped having children,
41. 7 The king woke up and **realized** that he had been dreaming.
Ex 5.19 The foremen **realized** that they were in trouble when they
10. 7 Don't you **realize** that Egypt is ruined?"
Lev 5. 2 unclean and guilty as soon as he **realizes** what he has done.
5. 3 he is guilty as soon as he **realizes** what he has done.
5. 4 he is guilty as soon as he **realizes** what he has done.
Deut 31.17 and then they will **realize** that these things are happening
Josh 3. 7 great man, and they will **realize** that I am with you as
Judg 6.22 Gideon then **realized** that it was the Lord's angel he had seen,
13.20 Manoah **realized** then that the man had been the Lord's angel,
16.18 When Delilah **realized** that he had told her the truth,
20.34 The Benjaminites had not **realized** that they were about to be
20.36 day, [36] and the Benjaminites **realized** they were defeated.
20.41 into a panic because they **realized** that they were about to
1 Sam 3. 8 Then Eli **realized** that it was the Lord who was calling the
12.17 When this happens, you will **realize** that you committed a
12.19 We now **realize** that, besides all our other sins, we have
18.28 Saul **realized** clearly that the Lord was with David and
20.31 Don't you **realize** that as long as David is alive, you
20.33 kill him, and Jonathan **realized** that his father was really
2 Sam 3.38 to his officials, "Don't you **realize** that this day a great
5.12 And so David **realized** that the Lord had established him
10. 6 The Ammonites **realized** that they had made David their enemy,
10.15 Syrians **realized** that they had been defeated by the Israelites,
10.19 who were subject to Hadadezer **realized** that they had been
11.20 Didn't you **realize** that they would shoot arrows from the walls?
12.19 to each other, he **realized** that the child had died.
1 Kgs 3.15 Solomon woke up and **realized** that God had spoken to him
22.33 when he cried out, [33] they **realized** that he was not the
2 Kgs 3.26 When the king of Moab **realized** that he was losing the battle,
1 Chr 14. 2 And so David **realized** that the Lord had established him as
19. 6 King Hanun and the Ammonites **realized** that they had made
19.16 Syrians **realized** that they had been defeated by the Israelites,
19.19 who were subject to Hadadezer **realized** that they had been
28.10 You must **realize** that the Lord has chosen you to build

Neh 4.15 and they **realized** that God had defeated their plans.
6.12 I thought it over, I **realized** that God had not spoken to
6.16 nations heard this, they **realized** that they had lost face,
Esth 3. 5 Haman was furious when he **realized** that Mordecai was not
Prov 5. 6 but wanders off, and does not **realize** what is happening.
24.22 Do you **realize** the disaster that God or the king can cause?
26. 5 one who asked it will **realize** that he's not as clever as
Ecc 2.11 worked doing it, and I **realized** that it didn't mean a thing.
2.24 And yet, I **realized** that even this comes from God.
3.12 So I **realized** that all we can do is to be happy
3.22 So I **realized** then that the best thing we can do is
4.15 in this world, and I **realized** that somewhere among them
8.16 on in the world, I **realized** that you could stay awake night
9.11 I **realized** another thing, that in this world fast
Ezek 12.16 among the nations they will **realize** how disgusting their
18.28 He **realizes** what he is doing and stops sinning, so he
Hos 7. 9 around them [9]and do not **realize** that this reliance on
Mic 4.12 They do not **realize** that they have been gathered together to
6. 5 these things and you will **realize** what I did in order to
Mt 2.16 Herod **realized** that the visitors from the east had tricked him,
24.39 they did not **realize** what was happening until the flood came
Mk 5.33 The woman **realized** what had happened to her, so she came,
Jn 6.22 other side of the lake **realized** that there had been only one
11.50 Don't you **realize** that it is better for you to let one
Acts 4.13 They **realized** then that they had been companions of Jesus.
10.34 "I now **realize** that it is true that God treats everyone on
12.11 Then Peter **realized** what had happened to him, and said,
16.19 her owners **realized** that their chance of making money was gone,
22.29 was frightened when he **realized** that Paul was a Roman citizen
1 Cor 14.37 a spiritual gift, he must **realize** that what I am writing to
2 Cor 2. 4 but to make you **realize** how much I love you all.
Gal 3. 7 You should **realize** then, that the real descendants of Abraham
Rev 12.13 When the dragon **realized** that he had been thrown down to

REALLY

Gen 3. 1 asked the woman, "Did God **really** tell you not to eat fruit
16.13 Hagar asked herself, "Have I **really** seen God and lived
18.13 laugh and say, 'Can I **really** have a child when I am
18.23 Lord and asked, "Are you **really** going to destroy the
20.12 She **really** is my sister.
27.21 Are you **really** Esau?"
27.24 his blessing, [24]but asked again, "Are you **really** Esau?"
45. 5 It was **really** God who sent me ahead of you to save
45. 8 So it was not **really** you who sent me here, but God.
45.12 you, and you too, Benjamin, can see that I am **really** Joseph.
Ex 16. 8 you are **really** complaining against the Lord."
34. 9 He said, "Lord, if you **really** are pleased with me, I ask
Num 16.11 complain against Aaron, it is **really** against the Lord that
32.20 Moses answered, "If you **really** mean what you say, then
Deut 32.21 with their so-called gods, gods that are **really** not gods.
Josh 7.22 found that the condemned things **really** were buried there,
9.24 we learnt that it was **really** true that the Lord your God
Judg 6.17 with me, give me some proof that you are **really** the Lord.
9.15 thorn-bush answered, 'If you **really** want to make me your king,
9.16 then," Jotham continued, "were you **really** honest and
15. 2 He said to Samson, "I **really** thought that you hated her,
Ruth 1.19 and the women there exclaimed, "Is this **really** Naomi?"
1 Sam 20.33 realized that his father was **really** determined to kill David.
23.11 Will Saul **really** come, as I have heard?
24.16 speaking, Saul said, "Is that **really** you, David my son?"
27.11 to Gath and report what he and his men had **really** done.
2 Sam 3. 8 Do you **really** think I'm serving Judah?"
1 Kgs 8.27 "But can you, O God, **really** live on earth?
17.24 a man of God and that the Lord **really** speaks through you!"
18. 7 him, bowed low before him, and asked, "Is it **really** you,
1 Chr 29.14 my people and I cannot **really** give you anything, because
2 Chr 2. 6 Yet no one can **really** build a temple for God, because even
6.18 "But can you, O God, **really** live on earth among men
Job 15.14 Can any man be **really** pure?
21.21 over, does he **really** care whether his children are happy?
Ps 60.10 Have you **really** rejected us?
108.11 Have you **really** rejected us?
Prov 11.18 Wicked people do not **really** gain anything, but if you do
20. 6 faithful he is, but just try to find someone who **really** is!
20. 9 Can anyone **really** say that his conscience is clear, that
22.21 advice, [21]and will teach you what the truth **really** is.
23. 7 What he thinks is what he **really** is.
26.23 that hides what you are **really** thinking is like a fine glaze
Ecc 1.16 I know what wisdom and knowledge **really** are."
8. 1 Only a wise man knows what things **really** mean.
Is 42.20 You have ears to hear with, but what have you **really** heard?"
Jer 5.12 denied him and have said, "He won't **really** do anything.
7.19 But am I **really** the one they are hurting?
9. 8 to his neighbour, but is **really** setting a trap for him.
12. 2 speak well of you, yet they do not **really** care about you.
16.20 No, if he did, they would not **really** be gods."
22. 4 If you **really** do as I have commanded, then David's
27.18 If they are **really** prophets and if they have my message,
32. 8 So I knew that the Lord had **really** spoken to me.
Ezek 16.45 You **really** are your mother's daughter.
Amos 5.14 Then the Lord God Almighty **really** will be with you, as you
Mic 2. 7 Would he **really** do such things?
Mt 14.28 "Lord, if it is **really** you, order me to come out on
27.54 were terrified and said, "He **really** was the Son of God!"

REAP

Gen 45. 6 years in which there will be neither ploughing nor **reaping.**
Deut 28.38 sow plenty of seed, but **reap** only a small harvest, because
Ruth 2. 9 watch them to see where they are **reaping** and stay with them.
Ps 107.37 and planted grapevines and **reaped** an abundant harvest.
Jer 9.22 and left behind by the **reapers,** corn that no one gathers.
Hos 8. 7 When they sow the wind, they will **reap** a storm!
10.12 for yourselves, plant righteousness, and **reap** the blessings
10.13 But instead you planted evil and **reaped** its harvest.
Mt 25.24 you **reap** harvests where you did not sow, and you gather
25.26 knew, did you, that I **reap** harvests where I did not sow,
Lk 19.21 take what is not yours and **reap** what you did not sow.'
19.22 taking what is not mine and **reaping** what I have not sown.
Jn 4.36 The man who **reaps** the harvest is being paid and gathers
4.36 man who sows and the man who **reaps** will be glad together.
4.37 The saying is true, 'One man sows, another man **reaps.'**
4.38 I have sent you to **reap** a harvest in a field where
1 Cor 9.10 ploughs and the man who **reaps** should do their work in the
9.11 Is it too much if we **reap** material benefits from you?
Gal 6. 7 A person will **reap** exactly what he sows.
6. 9 the time will come when we will **reap** the harvest.
Heb 12.11 been disciplined by such punishment **reap** the peaceful reward of
Rev 14.15 "Use your sickle and **reap** the harvest, because the time has
14.16 sickle on the earth, and the earth's harvest was **reaped.**

REAR (1)

Gen 33. 2 Leah and her children, and finally Rachel and Joseph at the **rear.**
Ex 14.19 front of the army of Israel, moved and went to the **rear.**
Num 10.25 of Dan, serving as the **rearguard** of all the divisions, would
Deut 25.18 you from the **rear** when you were tired and exhausted,
Josh 6. 8 who were carrying the Covenant Box, followed by a **rearguard.**
6.12 and finally, the **rearguard.**
8. 2 Prepare to attack the city by surprise from the **rear."**
8.14 not knowing that he was about to be attacked from the **rear.**
10.19 Keep on after the enemy and attack them from the **rear;**
1 Sam 29. 2 David and his men marched in the **rear** with King Achish.
2 Sam 10. 9 in front and from the **rear,** so he chose the best of
1 Kgs 6.16 the Most Holy Place, was built in the **rear** of the Temple.
6.19 In the **rear** of the Temple an inner room was built,
1 Chr 19.10 in front and from the **rear,** so he chose the best of
2 Chr 13.13 the Judaean army from the **rear,** while the rest faced them
Joel 2.20 into the Dead Sea, their **rear** ranks into the Mediterranean.

REAR (2)

Lam 2.22 They murdered my children, whom I had **reared** and loved.
Ezek 19. 2 She **reared** her cubs among the fierce male lions.
19. 3 She **reared** a cub and taught him to hunt;
19. 5 Then she **reared** another of her cubs, and he grew into a

REASON

Deut 29.24 What was the **reason** for his fierce anger?'
1 Sam 19. 5 to an innocent man and kill David for no **reason** at all?"
27. 6 of Ziklag, and for this **reason** Ziklag has belonged to the
2 Sam 14.15 Now, Your Majesty, the **reason** I have come to speak to
1 Kgs 9.13 For this **reason** the area is still called Cabul.
Neh 5. 9 give our enemies, the Gentiles, any **reason** to ridicule us.
Job 2. 3 you attack him for no **reason** at all, but Job is still
9.17 storms to batter and bruise me without any **reason** at all.
17. 4 You have closed their minds to **reason;**
21. 4 I have good **reason** to be impatient.
23. 7 I could **reason** with God;
33. 7 So you have no **reason** to fear me;
Ps 35. 7 Without any **reason** they laid a trap for me and dug a
35.19 hate me for no **reason** smirk with delight over my sorrow.
38.19 there are many who hate me for no **reason.**
69. 4 who hate me for no **reason** are more numerous than the hairs
94.11 he knows how senseless their **reasoning** is.
109. 3 and they say evil things about me, attacking me for no **reason.**
Prov 1.33 He will be safe, with no **reason** to be afraid."
3.30 argue with someone for no **reason** when he has never done you
8. 1 **Reason** is making herself heard.
23.24 A righteous man's father has good **reason** to be happy.
24.28 without good **reason,** or say misleading things about him.
26.16 seven men who can give good **reasons** for their opinions.
29.17 He will never give you **reason** to be ashamed.
Is 14.29 beat you is broken, but you have no **reason** to be glad.
Ezek 14.23 will know that there was good **reason** for everything I did."
Dan 11.34 though many who join them will do so for selfish **reasons.**
Mic 7. 8 Our enemies have no **reason** to gloat over us.
Zeph 3.15 there is no **reason** now to be afraid.
Mt 13.13 The **reason** I use parables in talking to them is that
19. 3 a man to divorce his wife for whatever **reason** he wishes?"
19. 5 And God said, 'For this **reason** a man will leave his father
19.12 For there are different **reasons** why men cannot marry:
Mk 10. 7 'And for this **reason** a man will leave his father and
11.24 For this **reason** I tell you:
Lk 1.35 For this **reason** the holy child will be called the Son of
6. 7 Pharisees wanted a **reason** to accuse Jesus of doing wrong,
11.49 For this **reason** the Wisdom of God said, 'I will send
14.20 'I have just got married, and for that **reason** I cannot come.'
23. 4 and the crowds, "I find no **reason** to condemn this man."
Jn 6.65 added, "This is the very **reason** I told you that no one
15.25 'They hated me for no **reason** at all.'
18.38 and said to them, "I cannot find any **reason** to condemn him.
19. 4 let you see that I cannot find any **reason** to condemn him."
19. 6 I find no **reason** to condemn him."
Acts 13.28 though they could find no **reason** to pass the death sentence
18.14 been committed, it would be **reasonable** for me to be patient
19.40 we would not be able to give a good **reason** for it."
24.26 and for this **reason** he would often send for him and talk
26.21 It was for this **reason** that the Jews seized me while I
Rom 3.27 And what is the **reason** for this?

Rom 4.18 even when there was no **reason** for hoping, and so became
13. 5 For this **reason** you must obey the authorities—not just because
16.19 to the gospel, and for this **reason** I am happy about you.
2 Cor 4.16 For this **reason** we never become discouraged.
5.12 to give you a good **reason** to be proud of us, so
11.12 other "apostles" from having any **reason** for boasting and saying
11.18 many who boast for merely human **reasons,** I will do the same.
Eph 1.15 For this **reason,** ever since I heard of your faith in the
3. 1 For this **reason** I, Paul, the prisoner of Christ Jesus for
3.14 For this **reason** I fall on my knees before the Father,
5.31 the scripture says, "For this **reason** a man will leave his
6.18 For this **reason** keep alert and never give up;
Phil 1.26 you will have even more **reason** to be proud of me in
2. 9 For this **reason** God raised him to the highest place above
2.16 do so, I shall have **reason** to be proud of you on
3. 4 ceremonies, I have even more **reason** to feel that way.
Col 1. 9 For this **reason** we have always prayed for you, ever since
2.18 For no **reason** at all, such a person is all puffed up
1 Thes 2.13 And there is another **reason** why we always give thanks to God.
2.19 hope, our joy, and our **reason** for boasting of our victory in
2 Tim 1. 6 For this **reason** I remind you to keep alive the gift that
1.12 and it is for this **reason** that I suffer these things.
Tit 1.12 For this **reason** you must rebuke them sharply, so that they
Phlm 8 For this **reason** I could be bold enough, as your brother in
Heb 9.15 For this **reason** Christ is the one who arranges a new covenant,
10. 5 For this **reason,** when Christ was about to come into the world,
13.12 For this **reason** Jesus also died outside the city, in
2 Pet 1. 5 For this very **reason** do your best to add goodness to your
1 Jn 3. 8 God appeared for this very **reason,** to destroy what the Devil

REASSURE

Gen 50.21 So he **reassured** them with kind words that touched their hearts.
2 Sam 19. 7 Now go and **reassure** your men.

REBECCA

Isaac's wife.

Gen 22.23 Hazo, Pildash, Jidlaph, and Bethuel, [23]**Rebecca's** father.
24.15 Before he had finished praying, **Rebecca** arrived
24.29 Now **Rebecca** had a brother named Laban,
24.45 had finished my silent prayer, **Rebecca** came with a water-jar
24.51 Here is **Rebecca;**
24.53 and silver and gold jewellery, and gave them to **Rebecca.**
24.55 But **Rebecca's** brother and her mother said, "Let the
24.58 So they called **Rebecca** and asked, "Do you want to go
24.59 So they let **Rebecca** and her old family servant go
24.60 And they gave **Rebecca** their blessing in these words:
24.61 Then **Rebecca** and her young women got ready and mounted
24.64 When **Rebecca** saw Isaac, she got down from her camel
24.67 Then Isaac brought **Rebecca** into the tent that his mother
24.67 Isaac loved **Rebecca,** and so he was comforted for the loss of
25.20 years old when he married **Rebecca,** the daughter of Bethuel
25.21 Because **Rebecca** had no children, Isaac prayed to the Lord
25.21 The Lord answered his prayer, and **Rebecca** became pregnant.
25.28 the animals Esau killed, but **Rebecca** preferred Jacob.
26. 7 there would kill him to get **Rebecca,** who was very beautiful.
26. 8 down from his window and saw Isaac and **Rebecca** making love.
26.35 They made life miserable for Isaac and **Rebecca.**
27. 5 While Isaac was talking to Esau, **Rebecca** was listening.
27. 8 Now, my son," **Rebecca** continued, "listen to me and do
27.42 But when **Rebecca** heard about Esau's plan, she sent for
27.46 **Rebecca** said to Isaac, "I am sick and tired of Esau's
28. 5 and the brother of **Rebecca,** the mother of Jacob and Esau.
29.12 He told her, "I am your father's relative, the son of **Rebecca."**
35. 8 **Rebecca's** nurse Deborah died and was buried beneath the
49.31 that is where they buried Isaac and his wife **Rebecca;**
Rom 9.10 For **Rebecca's** two sons had the same father, our ancestor Isaac.

REBEL

Gen 14. 4 years, but in the thirteenth year they **rebelled** against him.
27.40 Yet when you **rebel,** You will break away from his control."
Ex 23.21 Do not **rebel** against him,
23.21 for I have sent him, and he will not pardon such **rebellion.**
Lev 16.21 all the evils, sins, and **rebellions** of the people of Israel,
26.40 ancestors, who resisted me and **rebelled** against me, [41]and
26.41 penalty for their sin and **rebellion,** [42]I will remember my
Num 14. 9 Do not **rebel** against the Lord and don't be afraid of the
14.18 I show great love and faithfulness and forgive sin and **rebellion.**
16. 1 Levite clan of Kohath, **rebelled** against the leadership of Moses.
16.11 the Lord that you and your followers are **rebelling."**
16.49 14,700, not counting those who died in Korah's **rebellion.**
17.10 as a warning to the **rebel** Israelites that they will die
20.10 in front of the rock, and Moses said, "Listen, you **rebels!**
20.24 the two of you **rebelled** against my command at Meribah.
26. 9 the followers of Korah when they **rebelled** against the Lord.
27. 3 among the followers of Korah, who **rebelled** against the Lord;
27.14 did, [14]because both of you **rebelled** against my command in
Deut 1.26 "But you **rebelled** against the command of the Lord your God,
1.43 You **rebelled** against him, and in your pride you marched into
2.30 had made him stubborn and **rebellious,** so that we could
9. 7 until the day you arrived here, you have **rebelled** against him.
9.23 the land that he was giving you, you **rebelled** against him;
9.24 Ever since I have known you, you have **rebelled** against the Lord.
13. 5 prophet that tells you to **rebel** against the Lord, who
21.18 son who is stubborn and **rebellious,** a son who will not obey
21.20 'Our son is stubborn and **rebellious** and refuses to obey us;
31.27 I know how stubborn and **rebellious** they are.
31.27 They have **rebelled** against the Lord during my lifetime,
31.27 and they will **rebel** even more after I am dead.
Deut 32.15 "The Lord's people grew rich, but **rebellious;**
Josh 22.16 You have **rebelled** against the Lord by building this altar
22.18 If you **rebel** against the Lord today, he will be angry with
22.19 But don't **rebel** against the Lord
22.19 or make **rebels** out of us
22.22 If we **rebelled** and did not keep faith with the Lord, do
22.29 We would certainly not **rebel** against the Lord or stop
22.31 You have not **rebelled** against him, and so you have saved the
24.27 against you, to keep you from **rebelling** against your God."
Judg 9.23 Shechem hostile to each other, and they **rebelled** against him.
1 Sam 15.23 **Rebellion** against him is as bad as witchcraft, and
20.30 said to him, "How **rebellious** and faithless your mother was!
24.11 I have no thought of **rebelling** against you or of harming you.
2 Sam 15.31 that Ahithophel had joined Absalom's **rebellion,** he prayed,
18.28 victory over the men who **rebelled** against Your Majesty!"
18.31 Lord has given you victory over all who **rebelled** against you!"
18.32 all your enemies, sir, and to all who **rebel** against you."
20.21 of Ephraim, started a **rebellion** against King David.
22.44 You saved me from my **rebellious** people and maintained my
1 Kgs 8.50 all their sins and their **rebellion** against you, and make
12.16 So the people of Israel **rebelled,** [17]leaving Rehoboam as
12.19 Israel have been in **rebellion** against the dynasty of David.
2 Kgs 1. 1 the country of Moab **rebelled** against Israel.
3. 5 when King Ahab of Israel died, Mesha **rebelled** against Israel.
3. 7 "The king of Moab has **rebelled** against me;
18. 7 He **rebelled** against the emperor of Assyria and refused to
18.20 Who do you think will help you **rebel** against Assyria?
24. 1 then he **rebelled.**
25. 1 Zedekiah **rebelled** against King Nebuchadnezzar of Babylonia,
2 Chr 10.16 So the people of Israel **rebelled,** [17]leaving Rehoboam as
10.19 Israel have been in **rebellion** against the dynasty of David.
13. 6 Jeroboam son of Nebat **rebelled** against Solomon, his king.
25.27 since the time when he **rebelled** against the Lord, there had
36.13 Zedekiah **rebelled** against King Nebuchadnezzar, who had
Ezra 4.12 Jerusalem and are rebuilding that evil and **rebellious** city.
4.15 this city has always been **rebellious** and that from ancient
4.19 and that it has been full of **rebels** and troublemakers.
Neh 2.19 Are you going to **rebel** against the emperor?"
9.26 "But your people **rebelled** and disobeyed you;
Job 15.26 That man is proud and **rebellious;**
23. 1 I still **rebel** and complain against God;
34.37 To his sins he adds **rebellion;**
Ps 2. 1 Why do the nations plan **rebellion?**
5.10 because of their many sins and their **rebellion** against you.
18.43 You saved me from a **rebellious** people and made me ruler
25. 3 in you, but to those who are quick to **rebel** against you.
66. 7 Let no **rebels** rise against him.
68. 6 out into happy freedom, but **rebels** will have to live in a
68.18 he receives gifts from **rebellious** men.
78. 8 like their ancestors, a **rebellious** and disobedient people,
78.17 God, and in the desert they **rebelled** against the Most High.
78.40 How often they **rebelled** against him in the desert;
78.56 they **rebelled** against Almighty God and put him to the test.
78.57 but were **rebellious** and disloyal like their fathers,
83. 2 Your enemies are in revolt, and those who hate you are **rebelling.**
106. 7 them his love, and they **rebelled** against the Almighty at the
106.43 people, but they chose to **rebel** against him and sank deeper
107.11 in chains, [11]because they had **rebelled** against the
139.21 How I despise those who **rebel** against you!
Prov 24.21 Have nothing to do with people who **rebel** against them;
Is 1. 2 The children I brought up have **rebelled** against me.
1. 5 Why do you keep on **rebelling?**
1.23 Your leaders are **rebels** and friends of thieves;
1.28 But he will crush everyone who sins and **rebels** against him;
30. 1 "Those who rule Judah are doomed because they **rebel** against me.
30. 9 They are always **rebelling** against God, always lying,
36. 5 Who do you think will help you **rebel** against Assyria?
48. 8 be trusted, that you have always been known as a **rebel.**
50. 5 and I have not **rebelled** or turned away from him.
59.13 We have **rebelled** against you, rejected you, and refused
63.10 in the past, [10]but they **rebelled** against him and made his
66.24 see the dead bodies of those who have **rebelled** against me.
Jer 2. 8 The rulers **rebelled** against me;
2.29 Why have you **rebelled** against me?
3.13 are guilty and that you have **rebelled** against the Lord, your
4.17 a field, because her people have **rebelled** against the Lord.
5.23 You are stubborn and **rebellious;**
6.28 They are all stubborn **rebels,** hard as bronze and iron.
7.26 became more stubborn and **rebellious** than your ancestors.
28.16 you have told the people to **rebel** against the Lord."
29.31 do for my people, because he told them to **rebel** against me.
33. 8 me, and I will forgive their sins and their **rebellion.**
48.26 "Make Moab drunk, because it has **rebelled** against me.
48.42 will no longer be a nation, because it **rebelled** against me.
52. 3 Zedekiah **rebelled** against King Nebuchadnezzar of Babylonia,
Lam 3.42 pray, [42]"We have sinned and **rebelled,** and you, O Lord,
Ezek 2. 3 They have **rebelled** and turned against me
2. 3 and are still **rebels,** just as their ancestors were.
2. 5 Whether those **rebels** listen to you or not, they will know
2. 6 don't be afraid of those **rebels** or of anything they say.
2. 7 Remember what **rebels** they are.
2. 8 Don't be **rebellious** like them.
3. 9 don't be afraid of those **rebels."**
3.26 so that you won't be able to warn these **rebellious** people.
3.27 some will ignore you, for they are a nation of **rebels."**
5. 6 But Jerusalem **rebelled** against my commands and showed that
12. 2 he said, "you are living among **rebellious** people.
12. 2 ears, but they hear nothing, because they are **rebellious.**
12. 3 Maybe those **rebels** will notice you.
12. 9 that those Israelite **rebels** are asking you what you're doing,

Ezek 12.25 In your own lifetime, you **rebels,** I will do what I have
17.12 said to me, [12]"Ask these **rebels** if they know what the
17.15 But the king of Judah **rebelled** and sent agents to Egypt
20.38 away from among you those who are **rebellious** and sinful.
24. 3 Tell my **rebellious** people this parable that I, the Sovereign
44. 6 "Tell those **rebellious** people of Israel that I, the Sovereign
Dan 9. 9 merciful and forgiving, although we have **rebelled** against you.
11.14 Then many people will **rebel** against the king of Egypt.
11.14 from your nation, Daniel, will **rebel** because of a vision
Hos 7.13 They have left me and **rebelled** against me.
7.14 What **rebels** they are!
8. 1 I made with them and have **rebelled** against my teaching.
9.15 all their leaders have **rebelled** against me.
11.12 people of Judah are still **rebelling** against me, the faithful
13.16 Samaria must be punished for **rebelling** against me.
Mic 1. 5 the people of Israel have sinned and **rebelled** against God.
1. 5 Who is to blame for Israel's **rebellion?**
Zeph 3. 1 Jerusalem is doomed, that corrupt, **rebellious** city
3.11 no longer need to be ashamed that you **rebelled** against me.
3.11 you will never again **rebel** against me on my sacred hill.
Mk 15. 7 was in prison with the **rebels** who had committed murder in
Jn 19.12 who claims to be a king is a **rebel** against the Emperor!"
Rom 10.21 held out my hands to welcome a disobedient and **rebellious** people."
2 Thes 2. 3 not come until the final **Rebellion** takes place and the
Tit 1.10 especially converts from Judaism, who **rebel** and deceive others
Heb 3. 8 your ancestors were when they **rebelled** against God,
3.15 stubborn, as your ancestors were when they **rebelled** against God."
3.16 were the people who heard God's voice and **rebelled** against him?
3.18 Of those who **rebelled.**
Jude 11 They have **rebelled** as Korah rebelled, and like him they are

REBUILD

Num 21.27 We want to see it **rebuilt** and restored.
32.34 The tribe of Gad **rebuilt** the fortified towns of Dibon,
32.37 The tribe of Reuben **rebuilt** Heshbon, Elealeh,
32.38 They gave new names to the towns they **rebuilt.**
Deut 13.16 must be left in ruins for ever and never again be **rebuilt.**
Josh 6.26 "Anyone who tries to **rebuild** the city of Jericho will be
19.50 He **rebuilt** the city and settled there.
Judg 18.27 The men from Dan **rebuilt** the town and settled down there.
21.23 their own territory, **rebuilt** their towns, and lived there.
1 Kgs 9.15 He also used it to **rebuild** the cities of Hazor, Megiddo, and
9.17 when she married Solomon, [17]and Solomon **rebuilt** it.)
9.17 his forced labour, Solomon also **rebuilt** Lower Beth Horon,
16.34 During his reign Hiel from Bethel **rebuilt** Jericho.
18.32 With these stones he **rebuilt** the altar for the worship
2 Kgs 14.22 Uzziah reconquered and **rebuilt** Elath after his father's death.
21. 3 He **rebuilt** the pagan places of worship that his father
1 Chr 11. 8 He **rebuilt** the city, starting at the place where land was
2 Chr 8. 2 He also **rebuilt** the cities that King Hiram had given him,
8. 4 He **rebuilt** all the cities in Hamath that were centres for
8. 5 Solomon also **rebuilt** the following cities:
24.27 against him, and the record of how he **rebuilt** the Temple.
26. 2 Amaziah that Uzziah recaptured Elath and **rebuilt** the city.)
33. 3 He **rebuilt** the pagan places of worship that his father
Ezra 1. 3 to go to Jerusalem and **rebuild** the Temple of the Lord, the
1. 5 got ready to go and **rebuild** the Lord's Temple in Jerusalem.
2.68 offerings to help **rebuild** the Temple on its old site.
3. 2 Shealtiel, together with his relatives, **rebuilt** the altar of
3. 3 living in the land, they **rebuilt** the altar where it had
3. 6 had not yet started to **rebuild** the Temple, they began on the
3. 8 were put in charge of the work of **rebuilding** the Temple.
3. 9 together in taking charge of the **rebuilding** of the Temple.
4. 1 returned from exile were **rebuilding** the Temple of the Lord,
4.12 Jerusalem and are **rebuilding** that evil and rebellious city.
4.12 They have begun to **rebuild** the walls and will soon finish them.
4.13 if this city is **rebuilt** and its walls are completed,
4.16 that if this city is **rebuilt** and its walls are completed,
4.21 those men are to stop **rebuilding** the city until I give
4.23 Jerusalem and forced the Jews to stop **rebuilding** the city.
5. 2 messages, they began to **rebuild** the Temple in Jerusalem,
5. 8 the great God is being **rebuilt** with large stone blocks and
5. 9 given them authority to **rebuild** the Temple and to equip it.
5.11 and earth, and we are **rebuilding** the Temple which was
5.13 Babylonia, Cyrus issued orders for the Temple to be **rebuilt.**
5.15 Temple in Jerusalem, and to **rebuild** the Temple where it had
5.17 Temple in Jerusalem to be **rebuilt,** and then inform us what
6. 3 the Temple in Jerusalem be **rebuilt** as a place where
6. 7 Judah and the Jewish leaders **rebuild** the Temple of God where
6. 8 I hereby command you to help them **rebuild** it.
6.22 them in their work of **rebuilding** the Temple of the God of
9. 9 go on living and to **rebuild** your Temple, which was in ruins,
Neh 2. 5 my ancestors are buried, so that I can **rebuild** the city."
2.17 Let's **rebuild** the city walls and put an end to our disgrace."
2.18 They responded, "Let's start **rebuilding!"**
3. 1 This is how the city wall was **rebuilt.**
3. 1 Priest Eliashib and his fellow-priests **rebuilt** the Sheep Gate,
3. 6 and Meshullam son of Besodeiah **rebuilt** Jeshanah Gate.
3.13 inhabitants of the city of Zanoah **rebuilt** the Valley Gate.
3.14 of the Beth Haccherem District, **rebuilt** the Rubbish Gate.
3.15 ruler of the Mizpah District, **rebuilt** the Fountain Gate.
3.17 Levites **rebuilt** the next several sections of the wall:
3.22 priests **rebuilt** the next several sections of the wall:
4. 1 that we Jews had begun **rebuilding** the wall, he was furious
4. 2 Do they intend to **rebuild** the city?
4. 6 So we went on **rebuilding** the wall, and soon it was half
4. 7 we were making progress in **rebuilding** the wall of Jerusalem
4.15 Then all of us went back to **rebuilding** the wall.
Neh 4.17 full support to the people [17]who were **rebuilding** the wall.
5.16 put all my energy into **rebuilding** the wall and did not
5.16 Everyone who worked for me joined in the **rebuilding.**
6. 6 to revolt and that this is why you are **rebuilding** the wall.
7. 1 now the wall had been **rebuilt,** the gates had all been put
Job 3.14 sleeping like the kings and rulers who **rebuilt** ancient palaces.
12.14 God tears down, who can **rebuild,** and who can free the man
Ps 51.18 **rebuild** the walls of Jerusalem.
69.35 He will save Jerusalem and **rebuild** the towns of Judah.
102.16 When the Lord **rebuilds** Zion, he will reveal his greatness.
Is 44.26 again, and the cities of Judah that they will be **rebuilt.**
44.28 will order Jerusalem to be **rebuilt** and the Temple
45.13 will **rebuild** my city, Jerusalem, and set my captive people free.
49.17 "Those who will **rebuild** you are coming soon, and those
54.11 you, I will **rebuild** your foundations with precious stones.
58.12 Your people will **rebuild** what has long been in ruins,
58.12 known as the people who **rebuilt** the walls, who restored the
60.10 says to Jerusalem, "Foreigners will **rebuild** your walls, And
60.13 Lebanon, Will be brought to **rebuild** you, Jerusalem, To make
61. 4 They will **rebuild** cities that have long been in ruins.
Jer 30.18 Jerusalem will be **rebuilt,** and its palace restored.
31. 4 Once again I will **rebuild** you.
31.38 "when all Jerusalem will be **rebuilt** as my city, from
33. 7 Israel prosperous, and I will **rebuild** them as they were before.
Ezek 13. 5 have crumbled, nor do they **rebuild** the walls, and so Israel
26.14 The city will never be **rebuilt.**
36.10 in the cities and **rebuild** everything that was left in ruins.
36.33 you live in your cities again and let you **rebuild** the ruins.
36.36 I, the Lord, **rebuild** ruined cities and replant waste fields.
Dan 9.25 given to **rebuild** Jerusalem, until God's chosen leader comes,
9.25 Jerusalem will be **rebuilt** with streets and strong defences,
Amos 9.11 I will **rebuild** it and make it as it was long ago.
9.14 They will **rebuild** their ruined cities and live there;
Mic 7.11 Jerusalem, the time to **rebuild** the city walls is coming.
Hag 1. 2 say that this is not the right time to **rebuild** the Temple."
1. 8 Now go up into the hills, get timber, and **rebuild** the Temple;
2.15 Before you started to **rebuild** the Temple, [16]you would go
Zech 1.16 My Temple will be restored, and the city will be **rebuilt."**
4. 7 You will **rebuild** the Temple, and as you put the last stone
6.12 Branch will flourish where he is and **rebuild** the Lord's Temple.
6.15 away will come and help to **rebuild** the Temple of the Lord.
6.15 And when it is **rebuilt,** you will know that the Lord Almighty
8. 9 time the foundation was being laid for **rebuilding** my Temple.
Mal 1. 4 but we will **rebuild** them," then the Lord will reply,
1. 4 "Let them **rebuild**—I will tear them down again.
Acts 15.16 I will **rebuild** its ruins and make it strong again.
Gal 2.18 If I start to **rebuild** the system of Law that I tore

REBUKE

2 Sam 22.16 were uncovered when the Lord **rebuked** his enemies and roared
Job 5.17 Do not resent it when he **rebukes** you.
Ps 6. 1 Lord, don't be angry and **rebuke** me!
18.15 earth were uncovered, when you **rebuked** your enemies, Lord,
39.11 a man's sins by your **rebukes,** and like a moth you destroy
68.30 **Rebuke** Egypt, that wild animal in the reeds;
68.30 **rebuke** the nations, that herd of bulls with their calves,
103. 9 He does not keep on **rebuking;**
104. 7 When you **rebuked** the waters, they fled;
141. 5 man may punish me and **rebuke** me in kindness, but I will
Prov 17.10 person learns more from one **rebuke** than a fool learns from
Mt 16.22 Peter took him aside and began to **rebuke** him.
Mk 8.32 So Peter took him aside and began to **rebuke** him.
8.33 Jesus turned round, looked at his disciples, and **rebuked** Peter.
Lk 9.55 Jesus turned and **rebuked** them.
17. 3 "If your brother sins, **rebuke** him, and if he repents,
23.40 other one, however, **rebuked** him, saying, "Don't you fear God?
1 Tim 5. 1 Do not **rebuke** an older man, but appeal to him as if
5.20 **Rebuke** publicly all those who commit sins, so that the
2 Tim 3.16 useful for teaching the truth, **rebuking** error, correcting faults,
Tit 1.12 For this reason you must **rebuke** them sharply, so that they
2.15 use your full authority as you encourage and **rebuke** your hearers.
Heb 12. 5 Lord corrects you, and do not be discouraged when he **rebukes** you.
2 Pet 2.16 would get for doing wrong [16]and was **rebuked** for his sin.
Jude 9 the Devil with insulting words, but said, "The Lord **rebuke** you!"
Rev 3.19 I **rebuke** and punish all whom I love.

RECALL

Deut 11. 6 You **recall** what he did to Dathan and Abiram, the sons of
Ps 77.11 I will **recall** the wonders you did in the past.
Song 1. 3 the sound of your name **recalls** it.
Lam 1. 7 A lonely ruin now, Jerusalem **recalls** her ancient splendour.

RECEIPT

Phil 4.18 Here, then, is my **receipt** for everything you have given me—

RECEIVE

Gen 4.11 it had opened its mouth to **receive** it when you killed him.
43.23 I **received** your payment."
50.17 Joseph cried when he **received** this message.
50.23 He also lived to **receive** the children of Machir son of
Ex 21.11 to her, he must set her free and not **receive** any payment.
25. 2 **Receive** whatever offerings any man wishes to give.
36. 3 They **received** from him all the offerings which the
Lev 22.11 or born in his home, may eat the food the priest **receives.**
22.13 dependant may eat the food her father **receives** as a priest.
Num 9. 8 "Wait until I **receive** instructions from the Lord."

Num 18.20 "You will not **receive** any property that can be inherited,
18.26 "When you **receive** from the Israelites the tithe that the
18.28 Lord from all the tithes which you **receive** from the Israelites.
18.29 Give it from the best that you **receive.**
24.16 what God is saying And **receive** the knowledge that comes from
31.51 Moses and Eleazar **received** the gold, all of which was in
32.19 the Jordan, because we have **received** our share here east of
32.30 with you, they are to **receive** their share of the property in
34.13 the land that you will **receive** by drawing lots, the land
34.14 eastern half of Manasseh have **received** their property,
35. 2 that from the property they **receive** they must give the
Deut 9. 9 went up the mountain to **receive** the stone tablets on which
10. 9 why the tribe of Levi **received** no land as the other tribes
10. 9 they **received** was the privilege of being the Lord's priests,
18. 1 of Levi is not to **receive** any share of land in Israel;
18. 4 They are to **receive** the first share of the corn, wine,
18. 8 He is to **receive** the same amount of food as the other
19.19 he is to receive the punishment the accused man would have **received.**
28.33 hard to grow, while you **receive** nothing but constant
Josh 8.33 do this when the time came for them to **receive** the blessing.
13. 8 tribe of Manasseh had already **received** the land that Moses,
13.14 told Moses, they were to **receive** as their possession a share
14. 3 Instead, they **received** cities to live in, with fields for
14. 9 children and I would certainly **receive** as our possession the
15. 1 of the tribe of Judah **received** a part of the land described
15.13 He **received** Hebron, the city belonging to Arba, father of Anak.
15.20 families of the tribe of Judah **received** as their possession.
16. 4 Ephraim and West Manasseh, **received** this land
17. 5 That is why Manasseh **received** ten shares in addition to
18. 7 The Levites, however, will not **receive** a share of the land
18. 7 Manasseh have already **received** their land east of the Jordan,
18.20 of the tribe of Benjamin **received** as their possession.
18.28 of the tribe of Benjamin **received** as their possession.
19. 8 of the tribe of Simeon **received** as their possession.
19.10 The land which they **received** reached as far as Sarid.
19.16 of the tribe of Zebulun **received** as their possession.
19.23 of the tribe of Issachar **received** as their possession.
19.31 of the tribe of Asher **received** as their possession.
19.39 of the tribe of Naphtali **received** as their possession.
19.48 families of the tribe of Dan **received** as their possession.
20. 6 the city until he has **received** a public trial and until the
20. 9 not be killed unless he had first **received** a public trial.
21.26 of the clan of Kohath **received** ten cities in all, with their
21.27 Levites, the clan of Gershon, **received** from the territory of
21.28 From the territory of Issachar they **received** four cities:
21.30 From the territory of Asher they **received** four cities:
21.32 From the territory of Naphtali they **received** three cities:
21.33 of the clan of Gershon **received** a total of thirteen cities
21.34 Levites, the clan of Merari, **received** from the territory of
21.36 From the territory of Reuben they **received** four cities:
21.38 From the tribe of Gad they **received** four cities:
Judg 8.26 The gold earrings that Gideon **received** weighed nearly twenty
18. 1 because they had not yet **received** any land of their own
1 Sam 11. 9 When the people of Jabesh **received** the message, they were
25. 8 on a feast day, and David asks you to **receive** us kindly.
2 Sam 15.28 crossings in the wilderness until I **receive** news from you."
1 Kgs 5. 7 was extremely pleased when he **received** Solomon's message,
5. 8 "I have **received** your message and I am ready to do what
10.10 was by far the greatest that he ever **received** at any time.
10.14 Every year King Solomon **received** almost twenty-three
20.12 Benhadad **received** Ahab's answer as he and his allies,
21.15 As soon as Jezebel **received** the message, she said to Ahab,
2 Kgs 2. 9 "Let me **receive** the share of your power that will make me
2.10 "But you will **receive** it if you see me as I am
2.10 if you don't see me, you won't **receive** it."
9.14 the wounds which he had **received** in the battle at Ramoth
10. 2 then, as soon as you **receive** this letter, [3] you are to
10. 7 When Jehu's letter was **received,** the leaders of Samaria
12. 7 From now on you are not to keep the money you **receive;**
19. 5 When Isaiah **received** King Hezekiah's message, [6] he sent back
19.28 I have **received** the report of that rage and that pride
1 Chr 6.54 **received** the first share of the land assigned to the Levites.
2 Chr 9.13 Every year King Solomon **received** almost twenty-three
26.15 very powerful because of the help he **received** from God.
31.14 Temple, was in charge of **receiving** the gifts offered to the
Ezra 5. 5 action until they could write to Darius and **receive** a reply.
6. 8 of the royal funds **received** from taxes in West Euphrates,
Neh 13. 6 I **received** his permission [7] and returned to Jerusalem.
Esth 4.12 When Mordecai **received** Esther's message, [13] he sent her
Ps 68.18 he **receives** gifts from rebellious men.
73.24 instruction and at the end you will **receive** me with honour.
112. 7 He is not afraid of **receiving** bad news;
141. 2 **Receive** my prayer as incense, my uplifted hands as an evening
Prov 10. 6 A good man will **receive** blessings.
15.33 You must be humble before you can ever **receive** honours.
17. 2 worthless son and **receive** a part of the inheritance.
18. 5 the guilty and prevent the innocent from **receiving** justice.
Ecc 6. 3 of happiness and does not **receive** a decent burial, then I
7.11 it is as good as **receiving** an inheritance [12] and will give
Is 13. 1 about Babylon, which Isaiah son of Amoz **received** from God.
18. 7 when the Lord Almighty will **receive** offerings from this land
37. 5 When Isaiah **received** King Hezekiah's message, [6] he sent back
37.29 I have **received** the report of that rage and that pride
45. 8 the earth will open to **receive** it and will blossom with
53. 5 he suffered, made whole by the blows he **received.**
Jer 25. 1 was king of Judah, I **received** a message from the Lord
49.14 I said, "Edom, I have **received** a message from the Lord.
Ezek 44.29 food, and they are to **receive** everything in Israel that is
47.13 tribes, with the tribe of Joseph **receiving** two sections.
47.22 born here are also to **receive** their share of the land when
Ezek 47.23 Each foreign resident will **receive** his share with the
48. 1 Each tribe is to **receive** one section of land extending from
48.23 the remaining tribes is to **receive** one section of land
Dan 7.18 of the Supreme God will **receive** royal power and keep it for
7.22 The time had arrived for God's people to **receive** royal power.
11.34 going on, God's people will **receive** a little help, even
12.13 but you will rise to **receive** your reward at the end of
Hos 3. 5 Then they will fear the Lord and will **receive** his good gifts.
Zech 6.13 who will build it and **receive** the honour due to a king,
8.13 to one another, 'May you **receive** the same blessings that
12. 7 the people of Jerusalem will **receive** will be no greater than
Mal 2. 2 will put a curse on the things you **receive** for your support.
Mt 5. 5 they will **receive** what God has promised!
7. 7 "Ask, and you will **receive;**
7. 8 everyone who asks will **receive,** and anyone who seeks will find,
10. 8 You have **received** without paying, so give without being paid.
10.42 because he is my follower, will certainly **receive** a reward."
13.20 ground stand for those who **receive** the message gladly as
19.16 "what good thing must I do to **receive** eternal life?"
19.29 fields for my sake, will **receive** a hundred times more and
21.22 If you believe, you will **receive** whatever you ask for
21.34 slaves to the tenants to **receive** his share of the harvest.
25.16 The servant who had **received** five thousand coins went at once
25.17 servant who had **received** two thousand coins earned another two
25.18 But the servant who had **received** one thousand coins went off,
25.20 servant who had **received** five thousand coins came in and handed
25.24 "Then the servant who had **received** one thousand coins came in
25.27 bank, and I would have **received** it all back with interest
25.35 was a stranger and you **received** me in your homes,
Mk 4.16 As soon as they hear the message, they **receive** it gladly.
7. 3 the Jews, follow the teaching they **received** from their ancestors:
7. 4 other rules which they have **received,** such as the proper way
9.41 water because you belong to me will certainly **receive** his reward.
10.15 that whoever does not **receive** the Kingdom of God like a
10.17 "Good Teacher, what must I do to **receive** eternal life?"
10.30 for the gospel, [30] will **receive** much more in this present age.
10.30 He will **receive** a hundred times more houses, brothers, sisters,
10.30 and in the age to come he will **receive** eternal life.
11.24 believe that you have **received** it, and you will be given
12. 2 slave to the tenants to **receive** from them his share of the
Lk 6.32 the people who love you, why should you **receive** a blessing?
6.33 those who do good to you, why should you **receive** a blessing?
6.34 you hope to get it back, why should you **receive** a blessing?
6.38 Indeed, you will **receive** a full measure, a generous helping,
8.13 stand for those who hear the message and **receive** it gladly.
9.53 the people there would not **receive** him, because it was clear
10.25 "Teacher," he asked, "what must I do to **receive** eternal life?"
11. 9 Ask, and you will **receive;**
11.10 For everyone who asks will **receive,** and he who seeks will find,
12.50 I have a baptism to **receive,** and how distressed I am
18.17 Whoever does not **receive** the Kingdom of God like a child
18.18 "Good Teacher, what must I do to **receive** eternal life?"
18.30 the Kingdom of God [30] will **receive** much more in this
19.23 Then I would have **received** it back with interest when I returned.'
20.10 slave to the tenants to **receive** from them his share of the
22.31 Satan has **received** permission to test all of you, to separate
23.40 You **received** the same sentence he did.
Jn 1.11 to his own country, but his own people did not **receive** him.
1.12 Some, however, did **receive** him and believed in him;
1.14 the glory which he **received** as the Father's only Son.
5.43 come with my Father's authority, but you have not **received** me;
5.43 someone comes with his own authority, you will **receive** him.
5.44 You like to **receive** praise from one another, but you do
7.39 Spirit, which those who believed in him were going to **receive.**
9.15 asked the man again how he had **received** his sight.
10.17 up my life, in order that I may **receive** it back again.
11. 4 be the means by which the Son of God will **receive** glory."
11. 6 Yet when he **received** the news that Lazarus was ill, he
12.23 has now come for the Son of Man to **receive** great glory.
13.20 whoever **receives** anyone I send receives me also;
13.20 and whoever **receives** me receives him who sent me."
14.17 The world cannot **receive** him, because it cannot see him or
16.24 you will **receive,** so that your happiness may be complete.
17. 8 them the message that you gave me, and they **received** it;
20.22 Then he breathed on them and said, **"Receive** the Holy Spirit.
Acts 2.33 God, his Father, and has **received** from him the Holy Spirit,
2.38 and you will **receive** God's gift, the Holy Spirit.
4.34 sell them, bring the money **received** from the sale, [35] and hand
5. 3 by keeping part of the money you **received** for the property?
5. 8 the full amount you and your husband **received** for your property?"
7.38 on Mount Sinai, and he **received** God's living messages to
7.45 our ancestors who **received** the tent from their fathers carried
7.53 You are the ones who **received** God's law, that was handed
7.59 called out to the Lord, "Lord Jesus, **receive** my spirit!"
8.14 the people of Samaria had **received** the word of God, so they
8.15 prayed for the believers that they might **receive** the Holy Spirit.
8.17 placed their hands on them, and they **received** the Holy Spirit.
8.19 anyone I place my hands on will **receive** the Holy Spirit."
10.47 "These people have **received** the Holy Spirit, just as we also
11. 1 heard that the Gentiles also had **received** the word of God.
15.24 they had not, however, **received** any instruction from us.
16.24 **receiving** this order, the jailer threw them into the inner cell
19. 2 asked them, "Did you **receive** the Holy Spirit when you became
19. 3 "Well, then, what kind of baptism did you **receive?"**
20.35 'There is more happiness in giving than in **receiving.'"**
22. 3 I **received** strict instruction in the Law of our ancestors
22. 5 I **received** from them letters written to fellow-Jews in Damascus,
26. 7 of our people hope to **receive,** as they worship God day
26.10 I **received** authority from the chief priests and put many of
26.18 sins forgiven and **receive** their place among God's chosen people.'

Acts 28.17 or the customs that we **received** from our ancestors, I was
28.21 "We have not **received** any letters from Judaea about you,
Rom 2.29 Such a person **receives** his praise from God, not from man.
5.17 All who **receive** God's abundant grace and are freely put right
6.17 your heart the truths found in the teaching you **received.**
9. 4 they have **received** God's promises;
9.23 those of us whom he has prepared to **receive** his glory.
11.30 you have **received** God's mercy because the Jews were disobedient.
11.31 the mercy that you have **received,** the Jews now disobey God,
11.31 God, in order that they also may now **receive** God's mercy.
16. 2 **Receive** her in the Lord's name, as God's people should,
16.17 and go against the teaching which you have **received.**
1 Cor 1. 7 you have not failed to **receive** a single blessing, as you
2.12 We have not **received** this world's spirit;
2.12 instead, we have **received** the Spirit sent by God, so that we
2.14 not have the Spirit cannot **receive** the gifts that come from
3.14 foundation survives the fire, the builder will **receive** a reward.
4. 5 And then everyone will **receive** from God the praise he deserves.
11.23 For I **received** from the Lord the teaching that I passed
14.30 someone sitting in the meeting **receives** a message from God,
15. 1 preached to you, which you **received,** and on which your faith
15. 3 to you what I **received,** which is of the greatest importance:
2 Cor 1. 4 using the same help that we ourselves have **received** from God.
1. 7 in our sufferings, you also share in the help we **receive.**
5.10 Each one will **receive** what he deserves, according to everything
6. 1 we beg you who have **received** God's grace not to let it
6. 2 This is the hour to **receive** God's favour;
9.11 will thank God for your gifts which they **receive** from us.
11. 4 different from the Spirit and the gospel you **received** from us!
Gal 1.12 I did not **receive** it from any man, nor did anyone teach
3. 2 did you **receive** God's Spirit by doing what the Law requires
3.14 that through faith we might **receive** the Spirit promised by God.
3.21 For if mankind had **received** a law that could bring life,
3.29 the descendants of Abraham and will **receive** what God has promised.
4. 1 the son who will **receive** his father's property is treated just
4.14 Instead, you **received** me as you would an angel from heaven;
4.14 you **received** me as you would Christ Jesus.
Eph 1.14 guarantee that we shall **receive** what God has promised his people,
3.15 every family in heaven and on earth **receives** its true name.
4. 7 Each one of us has **received** a special gift in proportion
5. 5 form of idolatry) will ever **receive** a share in the Kingdom
Phil 2.29 **Receive** him, then, with joy, as a brother in the Lord.
3. 3 we, not they, who have **received** the true circumcision,
4. 9 practice what you learnt and **received** from me, both from my
4.17 It is not that I just want to **receive** gifts;
Col 4.10 (You have already **received** instructions to welcome Mark
1 Thes 1. 6 though you suffered much, you **received** the message with the joy
1. 9 people speak about how you **received** us when we visited you,
2 Thes 1.10 comes on that Day to **receive** glory from all his people
1.12 of our Lord Jesus will **receive** glory from you, and you from
3. 1 to spread rapidly and be **received** with honour, just as it
1 Tim 1.16 those who would later believe in him and **receive** eternal life.
4. 4 but everything is to be **received** with a prayer of thanks,
5.10 brought up her children well, **received** strangers in her home,
5.17 should be considered worthy of **receiving** double pay,
Heb 1.14 are sent by him to help those who are to **receive** salvation.
2. 2 follow it or obey it **received** the punishment he deserved.
3. 3 builds a house **receives** more honour than the house itself.
4. 1 the promise that we may **receive** that rest he spoke about.
4. 1 will be found to have failed to **receive** that promised rest.
4. 3 We who believe, then, do **receive** that rest which God promised.
4. 6 the Good News did not **receive** that rest, because they did
4. 6 There are, then, others who are allowed to **receive** it.
4.10 whoever **receives** that rest which God promised will rest from his
4.11 then, do our best to **receive** that rest, so that no one
4.16 There we will **receive** mercy and find grace to help us
6. 4 tasted heaven's gift and **received** their share of the Holy Spirit;
6.12 and are patient, and so **receive** what God has promised.
6.15 Abraham was patient, and so he **received** what God had promised.
6.17 To those who were to **receive** what he promised, God
7. 6 from Abraham and blessed him, the man who **received** God's promises.
9.15 been called by God may **receive** the eternal blessings that
10.36 order to do the will of God and **receive** what he promises.
11. 7 world was condemned, and Noah **received** from God the righteousness
11. 9 did Isaac and Jacob, who **received** the same promise from God.
11.13 They did not **receive** the things God had promised, but from a
11.19 and, so to speak, Abraham did **receive** Isaac back from death.
11.33 They did what was right and **received** what God had promised.
11.35 Through faith women **received** their dead relatives raised back to
11.39 Yet they did not **receive** what God had promised, [40] because God
12.17 Afterwards, you know, he wanted to **receive** his father's blessing;
12.28 then, because we **receive** a kingdom that cannot be shaken.
13. 9 It is good to **receive** inner strength from God's grace,
Jas 1. 7 must not think that he will **receive** anything from the Lord.
1.12 such a test, he will **receive** as his reward the life which
4. 3 ask, you do not **receive** it, because your motives are bad;
1 Pet 1. 7 Then you will **receive** praise and glory and honour on the Day
1. 9 because you are **receiving** the salvation of your souls, which
2.10 not know God's mercy, but now you have **received** his mercy.
3. 7 because they also will **receive,** together with you, God's gift of
4.10 good of others the special gift he has **received** from God.
5. 4 Chief Shepherd appears, you will **receive** the glorious crown
2 Pet 1.12 them and are firmly grounded in the truth you have **received.**
1 Jn 3.22 **receive** from him whatever we ask, because we obey his commands
2 Jn 8 we have worked for, but will **receive** your reward in full.
3 Jn 10 he will not **receive** the Christian brothers when they come,
10 stops those who want to **receive** them and tries to drive them
Jude 4 the Scriptures predicted the condemnation they have **received.**
Rev 2.17 new name that no one knows except the one who **receives** it.
2.26 I will give the same authority that I **received** from my Father:
4.11 You are worthy to **receive** glory, honour, and power.
5.12 is worthy to **receive** power, wealth, wisdom, and strength, honour,
14. 9 beast and its image and **receives** the mark on his forehead
20. 4 its image, nor had they **received** the mark of the beast on
21. 7 Whoever wins the victory will **receive** this from me:

RECITE

Ex 13. 9 remind you to continue to **recite** and study the Law of the
Deut 26. 5 Then, in the Lord's presence you will **recite** these words:
31.30 Then Moses **recited** the entire song while all the people
32.44 and Joshua son of Nun **recited** this song, so that the people
Ps 50.16 God says to the wicked, "Why should you **recite** my commandments?

RECKLESS

Ecc 2.12 about what it meant to be wise or **reckless** or foolish.
Lk 15.13 far away, where he wasted his money in **reckless** living.
Acts 19.36 So then, you must calm down and not do anything **reckless.**
2 Tim 3. 4 they will be treacherous, **reckless,** and swollen with pride;
1 Pet 4. 4 the same wild and **reckless** living, and so they insult you.

RECKON

Acts 20.24 But I **reckon** my own life to be worth nothing to me;
2 Cor 10. 7 Is there someone there who **reckons** himself to belong to Christ?
Phil 3. 7 count as profit I now **reckon** as loss for Christ's sake.
3. 8 I **reckon** everything as complete loss for the sake of what is
Heb 11.19 Abraham **reckoned** that God was able to raise Isaac from death—
11.26 He **reckoned** that to suffer scorn for the Messiah was worth

RECLINE

Amos 3.12 of Samaria's people, who now **recline** on luxurious couches.

RECOGNIZE

Gen 23.18 It was **recognized** as Abraham's property by all the
27.23 He did not **recognize** Jacob, because his arms were hairy
37.33 He **recognized** it and said, "Yes, it is his!
38.26 Judah **recognized** them and said, "She is in the right.
42. 7 Joseph saw his brothers, he **recognized** them, but he acted as
42. 8 Joseph **recognized** his brothers, they did not recognize him.
Lev 19.20 "If a slave-girl is the **recognized** concubine of a man
25.24 of the original owner to buy it back must be **recognized.**
Num 11.16 respected men who are **recognized** as leaders of the people,
Judg 18. 3 they **recognized** the accent of the young Levite,
1 Sam 26.17 Saul **recognized** David's voice and asked, "David, is
1 Kgs 14. 2 so that no one will **recognize** you, and go to Shiloh, where
18. 7 He **recognized** him, bowed low before him, and asked, "Is it
20.41 and at once the king **recognized** him as one of the prophets.
2 Chr 24.16 tombs in David's City in **recognition** of the service he had
Job 2.12 a long way off they saw Job, but did not **recognize** him.
Ps 51. 3 I **recognize** my faults;
Prov 1. 2 that will help you to **recognize** wisdom and good advice, and
Is 26.10 they refuse to **recognize** your greatness.
Jer 28. 9 predicts peace can only be **recognized** as a prophet whom the
Ezek 10.20 I **recognized** them as the same creatures which I had seen
27. 7 Embroidered linen from Egypt, Easily **recognized** from afar.
Dan 10. 8 my face was so changed that no one could have **recognized** me.
Mt 14.35 to land at Gennesaret, [35] where the people **recognized** Jesus.
17.12 come and people did not **recognize** him, but treated him just
Mk 6.54 As they left the boat, people **recognized** Jesus at once.
Lk 19.44 because you did not **recognize** the time when God came to
24.16 they saw him, but somehow did not **recognize** him.
24.31 eyes were opened and they **recognized** him, but he disappeared
24.35 road, and how they had **recognized** the Lord when he broke the
Jn 1.10 the world through him, yet the world did not **recognize** him.
Acts 3.10 and when they **recognized** him as the beggar who had
12.14 She **recognized** Peter's voice and was so happy that she ran
19.34 But when they **recognized** that he was a Jew, they all
27.39 the sailors did not **recognize** the coast, but they noticed
1 Cor 11.29 For if he does not **recognize** the meaning of the Lord's
2 Cor 5.14 Christ, now that we **recognize** that one man died for everyone,
Gal 2. 9 seemed to be the leaders, **recognized** that God had given me
1 Pet 2.12 they will have to **recognize** your good deeds and so praise

RECOMMEND

Rom 16. 1 I **recommend** to you our sister Phoebe, who serves the
2 Cor 3. 1 we need letters of **recommendation** to you or from you?
5.12 We are not trying again to **recommend** ourselves to you;

AV RECOMPENCE

Deut 32.35 The Lord will take revenge and **punish** them;
Job 15.31 enough to trust in evil, then evil will be his **reward.**
Prov 12.14 Your **reward** depends on what you say and what you do;
Is 35. 4 God is coming to your rescue, coming to **punish** your enemies."
59.18 He will **punish** his enemies according to what they have done,
66. 6 the Temple, is the sound of the Lord **punishing** his enemies!
Jer 51. 6 I am now taking my **revenge** and punishing it as it deserves.
Lam 3.64 "**Punish** them for what they have done, O Lord;
Hos 9. 7 The time for **punishment** has come, the time when people

Rom 1.27 they bring upon themselves the **punishment** they deserve for their
11. 9 may they fall, may they be **punished!**
2 Cor 6.13 **show** us the same feelings that we have for you.
Heb 2. 2 follow it or obey it received the **punishment** he deserved.
10.35 your courage, then, because it brings with it a great **reward.**
11.26 of Egypt, for he kept his eyes on the future **reward.**

AV RECOMPENSE

Num 5. 7 and make full **repayment,** plus an additional twenty per cent,
Ruth 2.12 May the Lord **reward** you for what you have done.
2 Sam 19.36 I don't deserve such a great **reward.**
22.21 The Lord **rewards** me because I do what is right;
22.25 And so he **rewards** me because I do what is right, because
Ps 18.20 The Lord **rewards** me because I do what is right;
18.24 And so he **rewards** me because I do what is right, because
Prov 11.31 Those who are good are **rewarded** here on earth, so you
Is 65. 6 they have done, but will **repay** them [7] for their sins and the
Ezek 7. 4 I am going to **punish** you for the disgusting things you have
7. 9 I am going to **punish** you for the disgusting things you have
11.21 I will **punish** them for what they have done."
17.19 the living God, I will **punish** him for breaking the treaty
23.49 you two sisters—I will **punish** you for your immorality and
Lk 14.14 God will **repay** you on the day the good people rise from

RECONCILE

1 Cor 7.11 she must remain single or else be **reconciled** to her husband;

AV RECONCILE

Lev 6.30 used in the ritual to **take away** sin, the animal must not
8.15 In this way he dedicated it and **purified** it.
16.20 performing the ritual to **purify** the Most Holy Place,
1 Sam 29. 4 to win back his master's **favour** than by the death of our
2 Chr 29.24 on the altar as a **sacrifice** to take away the sin of
Ezek 45.15 for fellowship-offerings, so that your sins will be **forgiven.**
45.17 whole, and the fellowship-offerings, to **take away** the sins
45.20 In this way, you will keep the Temple **holy.**
Dan 9.24 Sin will be **forgiven** and eternal justice established,
Mt 5.24 go at once and make **peace** with your brother, and then come
Rom 5.10 but he made us his **friends** through the death of his Son.
5.10 Now that we are God's **friends,** how much more will we be
11.15 mankind was changed from God's enemies into his **friends.**
2 Cor 5.18 us from enemies into his **friends**
5.18 and gave us the task of making others his **friends** also.
5.19 that God was making all mankind his **friends** through Christ.
5.19 us the message which tells how he makes them his **friends.**
5.20 let God change you from enemies into his **friends!**
Eph 2.16 both races into one body and **brought** them back to God.
Col 1.20 God decided to **bring** the whole universe back to himself.
1.22 God has made you his **friends,** in order to bring you, holy,
Heb 2.17 service to God, so that the people's sins would be **forgiven.**

RECORD

Num 1.18 years old or older were **recorded** and counted, [19] as the
2 Sam 1.18 (It is **recorded** in The Book of Jashar.)
8.16 Jehoshaphat son of Ahilud was in charge of the **records;**
20.24 Jehoshaphat son of Ahilud was in charge of the **records;**
1 Kgs 4. 3 In charge of the **records:** Jehoshaphat
11.41 and his wisdom, are all **recorded** in The History of Solomon.
14.19 how he ruled, are all **recorded** in The History of the Kings
14.29 that King Rehoboam did is **recorded** in The History of the
15. 7 else that Abijah did is **recorded** in The History of the Kings
15.23 towns he fortified, are all **recorded** in The History of the
15.31 else that Nadab did is **recorded** in The History of the Kings
16. 5 all his brave deeds are **recorded** in The History of the Kings
16.14 else that Elah did is **recorded** in The History of the Kings
16.20 account of his conspiracy, is **recorded** in The History of the
16.27 and all his accomplishments are **recorded** in The History of
22.39 the cities he built, is **recorded** in The History of the Kings
22.45 bravery and his battles, are **recorded** in The History of the
2 Kgs 1.18 that King Ahaziah did is **recorded** in The History of the
8.23 else that Jehoram did is **recorded** in The History of the
10.34 including his brave deeds, is **recorded** in The History of the
12.11 After **recording** the exact amount, they would hand the
12.19 that King Joash did is **recorded** in The History of the Kings
13. 8 all his brave deeds are **recorded** in The History of the Kings
13.12 King Amaziah of Judah, is **recorded** in The History of the
14.15 King Amaziah of Judah, is **recorded** in The History of the
14.18 else that Amaziah did is **recorded** in The History of the
14.28 Hamath to Israel, are all **recorded** in The History of the
15. 6 else that Uzziah did is **recorded** in The History of the Kings
15.11 else that Zechariah did is **recorded** in The History of the
15.15 account of his conspiracy, is **recorded** in The History of the
15.21 else that Menahem did is **recorded** in The History of the
15.26 else that Pekahiah did is **recorded** in The History of the
15.31 else that Pekah did is **recorded** in The History of the Kings
15.36 else that Jotham did is **recorded** in The History of the Kings
16.19 that King Ahaz did is **recorded** in The History of the Kings
18.18 and Joah son of Asaph, who was in charge of the **records.**
20.20 into the city, are all **recorded** in The History of the Kings
21.17 the sins he committed, is **recorded** in The History of the
21.25 else that Amon did is **recorded** in The History of the Kings
23.28 that King Josiah did is **recorded** in The History of the Kings
24. 5 else that Jehoiakim did is **recorded** in The History of the
25.19 charge of military **records,** and sixty other important men.
1 Chr 4.33 These are the **records** which they kept of their families and
5. 7 The family **records** list the following clan leaders in the
1 Chr 5.17 (These **records** were compiled in the days of King Jotham
7. 5 The official **records** of all the families of the tribe of
7. 9 The official **record** of their descendants by families
9. 1 families, and this information was **recorded** in The Book of
18.15 Jehoshaphat son of Ahilud was in charge of the **records;**
23. 4 Temple, six thousand to keep **records** and decide disputes,
26.29 **records** and settling disputes for the people
27.24 were never **recorded** in King David's official records.
29.29 is recorded in the **records** of the three prophets, Samuel,
29.30 The **records** tell how he ruled, how powerful he was, and
2 Chr 9.29 from beginning to end is **recorded** in The History of Nathan
12.15 to end and his family **records** are found in The History of
16.11 from beginning to end are **recorded** in The History of the
20.34 reign to its end, is **recorded** in The History of Jehu Son
24.27 against him, and the **record** of how he rebuilt the Temple.
25.26 end of his reign are **recorded** in The History of the Kings
26.11 Its **records** were kept by his secretaries Jeiel and Maaseiah
26.22 prophet Isaiah son of Amoz **recorded** all the other things
27. 7 and his policies, are all **recorded** in The History of the
28.26 from beginning to end, are **recorded** in The History of the
32.32 devotion to the Lord are **recorded** in The Vision of the
33.18 God of Israel, are all **recorded** in The History of the Kings
33.19 worshipped—are all **recorded** in The History of the Prophets.
34.13 various jobs, and others kept **records** or served as guards.
35.27 beginning to end—is all **recorded** in The History of the Kings
36. 8 the evil he committed, is **recorded** in The History of the
Ezra 2.61 priestly clans could find no **record** to prove their ancestry:
4.15 a search to be made in the **records** your ancestors kept.
5.17 be made in the royal **records** in Babylon to find whether or
6. 1 to be made in the royal **records** that were kept in Babylon.
6. 2 Media that a scroll was found, containing the following **record:**
8. 2 of his clan (there were **records** of their ancestry)
8.34 weighed, and a complete **record** was made at the same time.
10.16 from among the heads of the clans and **recorded** their names.
Neh 7. 5 leaders and officials and to check their family **records.**
7. 5 the **records** of those who had first returned from captivity,
7.63 priestly clans could find no **record** to prove their ancestry:
12.22 A **record** was kept of the heads of the Levite families
12.22 This **record** was finished when Darius was emperor of Persia.
12.23 Levite families, however, were **recorded** in the official records
Esth 2.23 to be written down in the official **records** of the empire.
6. 1 so he ordered the official **records** of the empire to be
10. 2 Mordecai to high office, are **recorded** in the official records
10. 2 are recorded in the official **records** of the kings of Persia
Job 19.23 someone would remember my words and **record** them in a book!
Ps 56. 8 you have kept a **record** of my tears.
69.27 Keep a **record** of all their sins;
130. 3 If you kept a **record** of our sins, who could escape being
139.16 to me had all been **recorded** in your book, before any of
Is 30. 8 that there would be a permanent **record** of how evil they are.
36. 3 the official in charge of the **records,** Joah son of Asaph.
Jer 25.13 I spoke through Jeremiah—all the disasters **recorded** in this book.
52.25 charge of military **records,** and sixty other important men.
52.28 This is the **record** of the people that Nebuchadnezzar
Dan 7. 1 down, and this is the **record** [2] of what I saw that night:
Hos 13.12 sin and guilt are on **record,**
13.12 and the **records** are safely stored away.
Mal 3.16 down in a book a **record** of those who feared the Lord
1 Cor 13. 5 love does not keep a **record** of wrongs;
Col 2.14 he cancelled the unfavourable **record** of our debts
Heb 7. 3 There is no **record** of Melchizedek's father or mother or of
7. 3 no **record** of his birth or of his death.
11.39 What a **record** all of these have won by their faith!
Rev 1. 1 This book is the **record** of the events that Jesus Christ revealed.
20.12 according to what they had done, as **recorded** in the books.

RECOVER

Gen 14.16 of Damascus, [16] and **recovered** the loot that had been taken.
14.20 Abram gave Melchizedek a tenth of all the loot he had **recovered.**
45.27 had sent to take him to Egypt, he **recovered** from the shock.
Lev 25.27 Year of Restoration, when he would in any event **recover** his land.
Deut 28.60 you experienced in Egypt, and you will never **recover.**
1 Sam 30.20 He also **recovered** all the flocks and herds;
2 Kgs 1. 2 Ekron, in order to find out whether or not he would **recover.**
1. 4 the Lord says, 'You will not **recover** from your injuries;
1. 6 You will not **recover** from your injuries;
8. 9 ask you whether or not he will **recover** from his illness."
8.10 but go to him and tell him that he will **recover."**
8.29 the city of Jezreel to **recover** from his wounds, and Ahaziah
9.14 where he had gone to **recover** from the wounds which he had
9.16 Joram had still not **recovered,** and King Ahaziah of Judah was
20. 1 to put everything in order, because you will not **recover.**
2 Chr 22. 6 the city of Jezreel to **recover** from his wounds, and Ahaziah
32.24 prayed, and the Lord gave him a sign that he would **recover.**
Prov 29. 1 corrected, one day you will be crushed and never **recover.**
Is 38. 1 are to put everything in order because you will not **recover.**
38. 9 After Hezekiah **recovered** from his illness, he wrote this song
Amos 3.12 Lord says, "As a shepherd **recovers** only two legs or an ear
Lk 4.18 liberty to the captives and **recovery** of sight to the blind;

RECTANGULAR

1 Kgs 6.33 main room a **rectangular** door-frame of olive wood was made.
7. 5 doorways and the windows had **rectangular** frames, and the

RED
[BLOOD-RED]

Gen 25.25 The first one was **reddish,** and his skin was like a hairy
25.30 give me some of that **red** stuff."

Gen 38.28 midwife caught it, tied a **red** thread round it, and said,
38.30 brother was born with the **red** thread on his arm, and he
49.11 He washes his clothes in **blood-red** wine.
Ex 25. 4 blue, purple, and **red** wool;
25. 5 rams' skin dyed **red;**
26. 1 pieces of fine linen woven with blue, purple, and **red** wool.
26.14 one of rams' skin dyed **red** and the other of fine leather,
26.31 curtain of fine linen woven with blue, purple, and **red** wool.
26.36 blue, purple, and **red** wool and decorated with embroidery.
27.16 blue, purple, and **red** wool, and decorated with embroidery.
28. 5 blue, purple, and **red** wool, gold thread, and fine linen.
28. 6 of blue, purple, and **red** wool, gold thread, and fine linen,
28.33 of blue, purple, and **red** wool, alternating with gold bells.
35. 6 blue, purple, and **red** wool;
35. 7 rams' skin dyed **red;**
35.23 blue, purple, or **red** wool;
35.23 rams' skin dyed **red;**
35.25 thread of blue, purple, and **red** wool, which they had made.
35.35 blue, purple, and **red** wool;
36. 8 woven with blue, purple, and **red** wool and embroidered with
36.19 one of rams' skin dyed **red** and the other of fine leather,
36.35 woven with blue, purple, and **red** wool and embroidered it
36.37 blue, purple, and **red** wool and decorated with embroidery.
38.18 blue, purple, and **red** wool and decorated with embroidery.
38.23 a weaver of fine linen and of blue, purple, and **red** wool.
39. 1 With the blue, purple, and **red** wool they made the
39. 2 blue, purple, and **red** wool;
39. 3 into the fine linen and into the blue, purple, and **red** wool.
39.24 and of blue, purple, and **red** wool, alternating with bells of
39.29 of blue, purple, and **red** wool, decorated with embroidery,
39.34 the covering of rams' skin dyed **red;**
Lev 13.19 swelling or a **reddish-white** spot appears where the boil was,
13.24 white or **reddish-white,**
13.42 But if a **reddish-white** sore appears on the bald spot, it
13.43 and if there is a **reddish-white** sore, [44]the priest shall
13.49 leather, [49]if it is greenish or **reddish,** it is a spreading
14. 4 a piece of cedar-wood, a **red** cord, and a sprig of hyssop.
14. 6 together with the cedar-wood, the **red** cord, and the hyssop,
14.37 If there are greenish or **reddish** spots that appear to be
14.49 birds, some cedar-wood, a **red** cord, and a sprig of hyssop.
14.51 the cedar-wood, the hyssop, the **red** cord, and the live bird
14.52 the live bird, the cedar-wood, the hyssop, and the **red** cord.
Num 4. 8 They shall spread a **red** cloth over all this, put a fine
19. 2 to Moses and Aaron a **red** cow which has no defects and
19. 6 sprig of hyssop, and a **red** cord and throw them into the
19.17 uncleanness, some ashes from the **red** cow which was burnt to
Josh 2.18 invade your land, tie this **red** cord to the window you let
2.21 When they had gone, she tied the **red** cord to the window.
2 Kgs 3.22 was shining on the water, making it look as **red** as blood.
2 Chr 2. 7 bronze, and iron, and in making blue, purple and **red** cloth.
2.14 He can work with blue, purple, and **red** cloth, and with linen.
3.14 was dyed blue, purple, and **red,** with designs of the winged
Esth 1. 6 **red** feldspar, shining mother-of-pearl, and blue turquoise.
Job 16.16 cried until my face is **red,** and my eyes are swollen and
Ps 120. 4 With a soldier's sharp arrows, with **red-hot** charcoal!
140.10 May **red-hot** coals fall on them;
Prov 23.31 even though it is rich **red,** though it sparkles in the cup,
Is 1.18 You are stained **red** with sin, but I will wash you as
1.18 Although your stains are deep **red,** you will be as white as
15. 9 of Dibon the river is **red** with blood, and God has something
34. 3 and the mountains will be **red** with blood.
34. 7 and the earth will be **red** with blood and covered with fat.
63. 1 dressed in **red,** marching along in power and strength?"
63. 2 "Why is his clothing so **red,** like that of a man who
Jer 22.14 in his house, panels it with cedar, and paints it **red.**
Ezek 23.14 the wall and painted bright **red,** with sashes round their
24.11 the empty bronze pot on the coals and let it get **red-hot.**
Dan 3.19 temper, and his face turned **red** with anger at Shadrach,
Joel 2.31 and the moon will turn **red** as blood before the great and
Nah 2. 3 The enemy soldiers carry **red** shields and wear uniforms of red.
Zech 1. 8 I saw an angel of the Lord riding a **red** horse.
1. 8 a valley, and behind him were other horses—**red,** dappled, and
6. 2 was pulled by **red** horses, the second by black horses,
Mt 16. 2 'We are going to have fine weather, because the sky is **red.'**
16. 3 'It is going to rain, because the sky is **red** and dark.'
Acts 2.20 and the moon will turn **red** as blood, before the great
Heb 9.19 all the people, using a sprig of hyssop and some **red** wool.
Rev 6. 4 Another horse came out, a **red** one.
6.12 coarse black cloth, and the moon turned completely **red** like blood.
9.17 they had breastplates **red** as fire, blue as sapphire, and yellow
12. 3 There was a huge **red** dragon with seven heads and ten horns
17. 3 a woman sitting on a **red** beast that had names insulting to

RED SEA

Sea crossed by the Israelites in their escape from Egypt.

Ex 13.18 in a roundabout way through the desert towards the **Red Sea.**
14. 2 Pi Hahiroth, between Migdol and the **Red Sea,** near Baal Zephon.
14. 9 they were camped by the **Red Sea** near Pi Hahiroth
15. 4 the best of its officers were drowned in the **Red Sea.**
15.22 of Israel away from the **Red Sea** into the desert of Shur.
Num 33. 8 and passed through the **Red Sea** into the desert of Shur;
Deut 11. 4 by drowning them in the **Red Sea** when they were pursuing you.
Josh 2.10 the Lord dried up the **Red Sea** in front of you
4.23 had crossed, just as he dried up the **Red Sea** for us.
24. 6 your ancestors got to the **Red Sea** [7]they cried out to me
Neh 9. 9 you heard their call for help at the **Red Sea.**
Ps 106. 7 and they rebelled against the Almighty at the **Red Sea.**
106. 9 He gave a command to the **Red Sea,** and it dried up;
106.22 What amazing things at the **Red Sea!**
114. 3 The **Red Sea** looked and ran away;
136.13 He divided the **Red Sea;**
Acts 7.36 in Egypt and at the **Red Sea** and for forty years in
1 Cor 10. 1 of the cloud, and all passed safely through the **Red Sea.**
Heb 11.29 Israelites able to cross the **Red Sea** as if on dry land;

REDEEM

Ps 19.14 be acceptable to you, O Lord, my refuge and my **redeemer!**
49. 7 A person can never **redeem** himself;
Mt 20.28 but to serve and to give his life to **redeem** many people."
Mk 10.45 came to serve and to give his life to **redeem** many people."
Gal 3.13 curse for us Christ has **redeemed** us from the curse
4. 5 the Jewish Law, [5]to **redeem** those who were under the Law,
1 Tim 2. 6 the man Christ Jesus, [6]who gave himself to **redeem** all mankind.
2 Pet 2. 1 will deny the Master who **redeemed** them,
Rev 14. 3 Of all mankind they are the only ones who have been **redeemed.**
14. 4 They have been **redeemed** from the rest of mankind

AV REDEEM

see also **BUY, RESCUE, SAVE**

Ex 21. 8 like her, then she is to be **sold** back to her father;
Lev 19.20 and she has not been **paid** for and freed, then if another
25.49 cousin or another of his close relatives may **buy** him back;
25.49 or if he himself earns enough, he may **buy** his own freedom.
25.51 refund a part of the **purchase** price according to the number
25.54 If he is not **set free** in any of these ways, he
Num 18.15 But you must accept **payment** to buy back every first-born child,
18.15 and must also accept **payment** for every first-born animal that is
Deut 7. 8 great might and **set you free** from slavery to the king of
15.15 were slaves in Egypt and the Lord your God **set you free;**
24.18 slaves in Egypt and that the Lord your God **set you free;**
Ruth 4. 4 then, if you want it, **buy** it in the presence of these
4. 4 so, because the right to **buy** it belongs first to you and
4. 4 The man said, "I will **buy** it."
4. 6 give up my right to **buy** the field, because it would mean
4. 6 You **buy** it;
4. 7 those days, to settle a **sale** or an exchange of property, it
2 Sam 7.23 the people whom you **set free** from Egypt to be your own.
Job 5.20 when famine comes, he will **keep** you alive,
Ps 49. 8 for his life, [8]because the **payment** for a human life is too
74. 2 yourself long ago, whom you **brought** out of slavery to be
103. 4 He **keeps me from** the grave and blesses me with love
111. 9 He set his people **free** and made an eternal covenant with them.
136.24 he **freed** us from our enemies;
Jer 31.11 I have set Israel's people **free** and have saved them from
32. 7 his nearest relative and had the right to **buy** it for myself.
Lk 1.68 come to the help of his people and has **set them free.**
2.38 to all who were waiting for God to **set Jerusalem free.**
21.28 stand up and raise your heads, because your **salvation** is near."
24.21 he would be the one who was going to **set Israel free!**
Rom 3.24 put right with him through Christ Jesus, who **sets them free.**
8.23 God to make us his sons and **set our whole being free.**
1 Cor 1.30 we become God's holy people and are **set free.**
Eph 1. 7 death of Christ we are **set free,** that is, our sins are
1.14 us that God will give complete **freedom** to those who are his.
4.30 guarantee that the Day will come when God will **set you free.**
5.16 Make good **use** of every opportunity you have,
Col 1.14 Son, [14]by whom we are **set free,** that is, our sins are
4. 5 are not believers, making good **use** of every opportunity you have.
Heb 9.12 he took his own blood and obtained eternal **salvation** for us.
9.15 been a death which **sets people free** from the wrongs they did
1 Pet 1.18 what was paid to **set you free** from the worthless manner of
Rev 5. 9 your sacrificial death you **bought** for God people from every tribe,

AV REDEEMER

Job 19.25 is someone in heaven who will come at last to my **defence.**
Ps 78.35 God was their protector, that the Almighty came to their **aid.**
Prov 23.11 The Lord is their powerful **defender,**
Is 41.14 I, the holy God of Israel, am the one who **saves** you.
43.14 Israel's holy God, the Lord who **saves** you, says,
44. 6 The Lord, who rules and **protects** Israel, the Lord Almighty,
44.24 "I am the Lord, your **saviour;**
47. 4 God of Israel **sets us free**— his name is the Lord
48.17 The holy God of Israel, the Lord who **saves** you, says:
49. 7 Israel's holy God and **saviour** says to the one who is
49.26 am the Lord, the one who saves you and **sets you free.**
54. 5 holy God of Israel will **save** you— he is the ruler
54. 8 So says the Lord who **saves** you.
59.20 will come to Jerusalem to **defend** you and to save all of
60.16 saved you, That the mighty God of Israel **sets you free.**
63.16 Lord, are our father, the one who has always **rescued** us.
Jer 50.34 But the one who will **rescue** them is strong—his name is

REDUCE

Lev 27.18 until the next Year of Restoration, and fix a **reduced** price.
Num 36. 3 to that tribe, and the total allotted to us will be **reduced.**
2 Kgs 10.32 the Lord began to **reduce** the size of Israel's territory.
Prov 23.21 Drunkards and gluttons will be **reduced** to poverty.
Is 40.23 He brings down powerful rulers and **reduces** them to nothing.
Ezek 28.18 All who look at you now see you **reduced** to ashes.
Zeph 2.11 He will **reduce** the gods of the earth to nothing,
Mt 24.22 But God has already **reduced** the number of days;
24.22 of his chosen people, however, God will **reduce** the days.
Mk 13.20 But the Lord has **reduced** the number of those days;
13.20 sake of his chosen people, however, he has **reduced** those days.

REED

Ex 2. 3 took a basket made of **reeds** and covered it with tar to
1 Kgs 14.15 Israel, and she will shake like a **reed** shaking in a stream.
2 Kgs 18.21 would be like using a **reed** as a walking-stick—it would break
Job 8.11 "**Reeds** can't grow where there is no water;
8.13 Godless men are like those **reeds**;
40.21 the thorn-bushes, and hides among the **reeds** in the swamp.
Ps 68.30 Rebuke Egypt, that wild animal in the **reeds**;
Is 18. 2 land ambassadors come down the Nile in boats made of **reeds.**
19. 6 **Reeds** and rushes will wither, [7] and all the crops sown along
35. 7 Where jackals used to live, marsh grass and **reeds** will grow.
36. 6 would be like using a **reed** as a walking-stick—it would break
42. 3 not break off a bent **reed** or put out a flickering lamp.
Mt 12.20 not break off a bent **reed,** or put out a flickering lamp.

REFER

Eph 2.11 call themselves "the circumcised" (which **refers** to what men do
Col 2.22 these **refer** to things which become useless once they are used;

REFINE

Deut 28.54 Even the most **refined** man of noble birth will
28.56 Even the most **refined** woman of noble birth, so
Job 28. 1 There are places where gold is **refined.**
Ps 12. 6 as genuine as silver **refined** seven times in the furnace.
Is 1.25 just as metal is **refined,** and will remove all your impurity.
48.10 the fire of suffering, as silver is **refined** in a furnace.
Jer 6.29 is useless to go on **refining** my people, because those who
9. 7 Lord Almighty says, "I will **refine** my people like metal and
Ezek 22.18 lead—left over after silver has been **refined** in a furnace.
22.20 copper, iron, lead, and tin is put in a **refining** furnace.
Mal 3. 2 He will be like strong soap, like a fire that **refines** metal.
3. 3 He will come to judge like one who **refines** and purifies silver.
3. 3 As a metal-worker **refines** silver and gold, so the Lord's
Rev 1.15 like brass that has been **refined** and polished, and his voice

REFLECT

Prov 27.19 own face that you see **reflected** in the water and it is
1 Cor 11. 7 his head, because he **reflects** the image and glory of God.
11. 7 But woman **reflects** the glory of man;
2 Cor 3.18 All of us, then, **reflect** the glory of the Lord with
Heb 1. 3 **reflects** the brightness of God's glory and is the exact likeness

REFORM

Acts 24. 2 of peace, and many necessary **reforms** are being made for the

REFRAIN

Ezra 3.11 They sang the Lord's praises, repeating the **refrain:**

REFRESH

Prov 25.13 A reliable messenger is **refreshing** to the one who sends him,
Song 2. 5 Restore my strength with raisins and **refresh** me with apples!
Is 26.19 As the sparkling dew **refreshes** the earth, so the Lord will
Jer 31.25 I will **refresh** those who are weary and will satisfy with
31.26 people will say, 'I went to sleep and woke up **refreshed.'**
Mic 5. 7 who survive will be like **refreshing** dew sent by the Lord for
Rom 15.32 if it is God's will, and enjoy a **refreshing** visit to you.

REFUGE

[CITIES OF REFUGE]

Num 35. 6 give the Levites six **cities of refuge** to which a man can
35.11 you are to choose **cities of refuge** to which a man can
35.15 These will serve as **cities of refuge** for Israelites and
35.25 return him to the **city of refuge** to which he had escaped.
35.26 of manslaughter leaves the **city of refuge** to which he has
35.28 must remain in the **city of refuge** until the death of the
35.32 has fled to a **city of refuge,** do not allow him to
Josh 20. 2 of Israel, "Choose the **cities of refuge** that I commanded
20. 9 These were the **cities of refuge** chosen for all the people
2 Sam 22.33 This God is my strong **refuge;**
1 Kgs 20.30 into the city and took **refuge** in the back room of a
1 Chr 6.57 Hebron, a **city of refuge,** Jattir, and the towns of Libnah,
6.67 Shechem, the **city of refuge** in the hills of Ephraim,
Ps 9. 9 The Lord is a **refuge** for the oppressed, a place of safety
19.14 be acceptable to you, O Lord, my **refuge** and my redeemer!
31. 2 Be my **refuge** to protect me;
31. 3 You are my **refuge** and defence;
46. 7 the God of Jacob is our **refuge.**
46.11 the God of Jacob is our **refuge.**
59. 9 you are my **refuge,** O God.
59.16 You have been a **refuge** for me, a shelter in my time
59.17 My **refuge** is God, the God who loves me.
61. 2 Take me to a safe **refuge,** [3] for you are my protector, my
62. 8 Tell him all your troubles, for he is our **refuge.**
71. 3 you are my **refuge** and defence.
Mic 1.11 Bethezel mourn, you will know that there is no **refuge** there.
also Josh 21.13 Josh 21.21 Josh 21.27 Josh 21.32 Josh 21.38

REFUGEE

Num 21.29 god let the men become **refugees,** And the women became
2 Sam 15.19 You are a foreigner, a **refugee** away from your own country.
Is 16. 3 We are **refugees;**
21.14 You people of the land of Tema, give food to the **refugees.**
Jer 44.14 No one will return except a few **refugees."**
48.45 Helpless **refugees** try to find protection in Heshbon, the
49.36 until there is no country where her **refugees** have not gone.
50.28 (**Refugees** escape from Babylonia and come to Jerusalem,
Ezek 12. 3 just as a **refugee** would, and start out before nightfall.
12. 7 packed a bundle as a **refugee** would, and that evening as it
12.11 what will happen to them—they will be **refugees** and captives.
29.12 I will make the Egyptians **refugees.**
Heb 11.13 admitted openly that they were foreigners and **refugees** on earth.
11.38 wandered like **refugees** in the deserts and hills, living in caves
1 Pet 1. 1 people who live as **refugees** scattered throughout the provinces
2.11 to you, my friends, as strangers and **refugees** in this world!

REFUND

Lev 25.51 He must **refund** a part of the purchase price

REFUSE (1)

Gen 24.41 my relatives and they **refuse** you, then you will be free.'
37.35 to comfort him, but he **refused** to be comforted and said,
39. 8 He **refused** and said to her, "Look, my master does not
48.19 His father **refused,** saying, "I know, my son, I know.
Ex 4. 9 believe you, and if they **refuse** to listen to what you say,
4.23 my son go, so that he might worship me, but you **refused.**
7.14 "The king is very stubborn and **refuses** to let the people go.
7.22 Lord had said, the king **refused** to listen to Moses and Aaron.
8. 2 If you **refuse,** I will punish your country by covering it
8.21 warn you that if you **refuse,** I will punish you by sending
9. 2 If you again **refuse** to let them go, [3] I will punish you
9.17 Yet you are still arrogant and **refuse** to let my people go.
10. 3 says 'How much longer will you **refuse** to submit to me?
10. 4 If you keep on **refusing,** then I will bring locusts into
11. 9 "The king will continue to **refuse** to listen to you, in
13.15 of Egypt was stubborn and **refused** to let us go, the Lord
16.28 "How much longer will you people **refuse** to obey my commands?
22.17 But if her father **refuses** to let him marry her, he must
Lev 6. 2 sins against the Lord by **refusing** to return what a
26.15 If you **refuse** to obey my laws and commands and break the
26.21 continue to resist me and **refuse** to obey me, I will again
26.27 continue to defy me and **refuse** to obey me, [28] then in my
26.31 places of worship, and **refuse** to accept your sacrifices.
Num 14.11 How much longer will they **refuse** to trust in me, even though
14.22 my patience over and over again and have **refused** to obey me.
14.43 not be with you, because you have **refused** to follow him."
20.18 But the Edomites answered, "We **refuse** to let you pass
20.20 The Edomites repeated, "We **refuse!"**
22.13 the Lord has **refused** to let me go with you."
22.14 Balak and told him that Balaam had **refused** to come with them.
23.25 said to Balaam, "You **refuse** to curse the people of Israel,
25.11 He **refused** to tolerate the worship of any god but me, and
27.14 against me at Meribah, you **refused** to acknowledge my holy
30. 5 forgive her, because her father **refused** to let her keep it.
32.15 people of Reuben and Gad **refuse** to follow him now, he will
Deut 15. 7 in need, then do not be selfish and **refuse** to help him.
15. 9 Do not **refuse** to lend him something, just because the year
15. 9 If you **refuse** to make the loan, he will cry out to
18.19 my name, and I will punish anyone who **refuses** to obey him.
21.20 'Our son is stubborn and rebellious and **refuses** to obey us;
23. 4 They **refused** to provide you with food and water when you
25. 7 he **refuses** to give his brother a descendant among the people
25. 8 If he still **refuses** to marry her, [9] his brother's widow is
25. 9 to the man who **refuses** to give his brother a descendant.'
30.17 But if you disobey and **refuse** to listen, and are led
31.18 And I will **refuse** to help them then, because they have
Josh 22.18 Are you going to **refuse** to follow him now?
22.20 how Achan son of Zerah **refused** to obey the command about the
Judg 2.19 and worship other gods, and **refused** to give up their own
8.15 of Sukkoth and said, "Remember when you **refused** to help me?
1 Sam 1. 7 Hannah so much that she would cry and **refuse** to eat anything.
22.17 But the guards **refused** to lift a hand to kill the Lord's
28.23 Saul **refused** and said he would not eat anything.
2 Sam 12.16 He **refused** to eat anything, and every night he went into his
12.17 him get up, but he **refused** and would not eat anything with
14.29 Again Absalom sent for him, and again Joab **refused** to come.
23.17 So he **refused** to drink it.
1 Kgs 2.16 please do not **refuse** me."
2.17 Solomon—I know he won't **refuse** you—to let me have Abishag,
2.20 please do not **refuse** me."
2.20 "I will not **refuse** you."
20.35 But he **refused,** [36] so he said to him, "Because you have
21.15 of the vineyard which he **refused** to sell to you."
21.27 He **refused** food, slept in the sackcloth, and went about
22.49 with Jehoshaphat's men, but Jehoshaphat **refused** the offer.
2 Kgs 14.11 But Amaziah **refused** to listen, so King Jehoash marched
17.15 They **refused** to obey his instructions, they did not keep
18. 7 against the emperor of Assyria and **refused** to submit to him.
1 Chr 11.19 So he **refused** to drink it.
2 Chr 24.19 them to return to him, but the people **refused** to listen.
25.20 But Amaziah **refused** to listen.
33.10 Lord warned Manasseh and his people, they **refused** to listen.
35.22 He **refused** to listen to what God was saying through King Neco,
36.13 He stubbornly **refused** to repent and return to the Lord, the
Neh 3. 5 leading men of the town **refused** to do the manual labour
9.16 grew proud and stubborn and **refused** to obey your commands.
9.17 They **refused** to obey;
9.29 Obstinate and stubborn, they **refused** to obey.
Esth 1.12 Queen Vashti of the king's command, she **refused** to come.
1.15 to Queen Vashti with a command, and she **refused** to obey it!
1.17 Xerxes commanded Queen Vashti to come to him, and she **refused.'**

Esth 3. 2 They all did so, except for Mordecai, who **refused** to do it.
Job 10.14 if I would sin, so that you could **refuse** to forgive me.
22. 7 You **refused** water to those who were tired,
22. 7 and **refused** to feed those who were hungry.
22. 9 You not only **refused** to help widows, but you also robbed
27. 1 the living Almighty God, who **refuses** me justice and makes my
31.16 I have never **refused** to help the poor;
34. 5 that he is innocent, that God **refuses** to give him justice.
Ps 50.17 You **refuse** to let me correct you;
55.19 for they **refuse** to change, and they do not fear him.
74.11 Why have you **refused** to help us?
78.10 they **refused** to obey his law.
84.11 He does not **refuse** any good thing to those who do what
95.10 They **refuse** to obey my commands.'
Prov 1. 7 Stupid people have no respect for wisdom and **refuse** to learn.
1.29 use for knowledge and have always **refused** to obey the Lord.
3. 7 simply obey the Lord and **refuse** to do wrong.
4.15 **Refuse** it and go on your way.
13.13 If you **refuse** good advice, you are asking for trouble;
13.19 Stupid people **refuse** to turn away from evil.
15.32 If you **refuse** to learn, you are hurting yourself.
21. 7 they **refuse** to do what is right.
21.13 If you **refuse** to listen to the cry of the poor, your
21.25 A lazy man who **refuses** to work is only killing himself;
27. 7 are full, you will **refuse** honey, but when you are hungry,
Is 7.12 I **refuse** to put the Lord to the test."
26.10 they **refuse** to recognize your greatness.
28.12 comfort to all of you, but you **refused** to listen to him.
30. 9 lying, always **refusing** to listen to the Lord's teachings.
30.15 But you **refuse** to do it!
58. 7 to wear, and do not **refuse** to help your own relatives.
59.13 rebelled against you, rejected you, and **refused** to follow you.
Jer 2.20 you **refused** to obey me and worship me.
5. 3 he crushed you, but you **refused** to learn.
5. 5 have rejected the Lord's authority and **refuse** to obey him.
6.10 They are stubborn and **refuse** to listen to your message;
7.13 I spoke to you over and over again, you **refused** to listen.
8. 5 You cling to your idols and **refuse** to return to me.
11. 8 I had commanded them to keep the covenant, but they **refused.**
11.10 the sins of their ancestors, who **refused** to do what I said;
13.10 These evil people have **refused** to obey me.
22.21 to you when you were prosperous, but you **refused** to listen.
23.17 To the people who **refuse** to listen to what I have said,
25. 7 But the Lord himself says that you **refused** to listen to him.
25.28 And if they **refuse** to take the cup from your hand and
29.19 They **refused** to listen.
31.15 they are gone, and she **refuses** to be comforted.
35.12 Lord, ask you why you **refuse** to listen to me and to
38.21 me in a vision what will happen if you **refuse** to surrender.
42.13 disobey the Lord your God and **refuse** to live in this land.
44.16 all—said to me, [16]"We **refuse** to listen to what you have
Lam 1.19 "I called to my allies, but they **refused** to help me.
2. 3 He **refused** to help us when the enemy came.
3. 8 I cry aloud for help, but God **refuses** to listen;
Ezek 5. 6 Jerusalem rejected my commands and **refused** to keep my laws.
18. 8 He **refuses** to do evil and gives an honest decision in any
18.17 He **refuses** to do evil and doesn't lend money for profit.
20. 8 But they defied me and **refused** to listen.
21.13 my people, and if they **refuse** to repent, all these things
Dan 3.14 is it true that you **refuse** to worship my god and to
9.11 Israel broke your laws and **refused** to listen to what you said.
Hos 4. 6 You priests have **refused** to acknowledge me and have rejected
11. 5 "They **refuse** to return to me, and so they must return to
13.13 about to be born, who **refuses** to come out of the womb.
Amos 6. 3 You **refuse** to admit that a day of disaster is coming, but
Zech 7.11 "But my people stubbornly **refused** to listen.
14.17 If any nation **refuses** to go and worship the Lord
14.18 If the Egyptians **refuse** to celebrate the Festival of Shelters,
14.18 that the Lord will send on every nation that **refuses** to go.
Mt 2.18 she **refuses** to be comforted, for they are dead."
18.30 But he **refused;**
25.45 'I tell you, whenever you **refused** to help one of these least
25.45 one of these least important ones, you **refused** to help me.'
27.14 But Jesus **refused** to answer a single word, with the result
Mk 6.26 sad, but he could not **refuse** her because of the vows he
15. 5 Again Jesus **refused** to say a word, and Pilate was amazed.
Lk 7.30 rejected God's purpose for themselves and **refused** to be baptized
18. 4 a long time the judge **refused** to act, but at last he
Jn 1.20 John did not **refuse** to answer, but spoke out openly
Acts 7.39 "But our ancestors **refused** to obey him;
Rom 1.28 those people **refuse** to keep in mind the true knowledge about
14. 6 Whoever **refuses** to eat certain things does so in honour of
Gal 2.21 I **refuse** to reject the grace of God.
2 Thes 3.10 to say to you, "Whoever **refuses** to work is not allowed to
Heb 3.10 'They are always disloyal and **refuse** to obey my commands.'
11.24 when he had grown up, **refuse** to be called the son of
11.27 As though he saw the invisible God, he **refused** to turn back.
11.35 Others, **refusing** to accept freedom, died under torture in order
12.25 Be careful, then, and do not **refuse** to hear him who speaks.
12.25 Those who **refused** to hear the one who gave the divine
Rev 15. 4 Who will **refuse** to declare your greatness?

REFUSE (2)

Jer 31.40 the dead are buried and **refuse** is thrown, and all the fields
Lam 3.45 You have made us the **refuse** heap of the world.
4. 5 those raised in luxury are pawing through **refuse** for food.
Ezek 7.19 away in the streets like **refuse,** because neither silver nor
1 Cor 4.13 We are no more than this world's **refuse;**
Phil 3. 8 consider it all as mere **refuse,** so that I may gain Christ

REFUTE

Is 44.25 words of the wise I **refute** and show that their wisdom is
Lk 21.15 enemies will be able to **refute** or contradict what you say.
Acts 6.10 Stephen such wisdom that when he spoke, they could not **refute** him.

REGAIN

2 Kgs 16. 6 the king of Edom **regained** control of the city of Elath,
2 Chr 13.20 Jeroboam never **regained** his power during Abijah's reign.
Mt 16.26 There is nothing he can give to **regain** his life.
Mk 8.37 There is nothing he can give to **regain** his life.

REGARD

2 Sam 16.21 will know that your father **regards** you as his enemy, and
Job 19. 5 better than I am, and **regard** my troubles as proof of my
Ps 139.22 I **regard** them as my enemies.
Prov 28. 4 If you have no **regard** for the law, you are on the
29. 8 People with no **regard** for others can throw whole cities
Ecc 9.13 saw, a good example of how wisdom is **regarded** in this world.
Lam 4.16 He showed no **regard** for our priests and leaders.
Ezek 36.17 I **regarded** their behaviour as being as ritually unclean as a
Rom 2.26 Law, will God not **regard** him as though he were circumcised?
4. 4 is paid his wages, but they are not **regarded** as a gift;
9. 8 of God's promise are **regarded** as the true descendants.
14.16 Do not let what you **regard** as good get a bad name.
1 Pet 5.12 of Silas, whom I **regard** as a faithful Christian brother.

REGIMENT

Acts 10. 1 was a captain in the Roman regiment called "The Italian **Regiment."**
27. 1 an officer in the Roman **regiment** called "The Emperor's Regiment."

REGION

Gen 34. 2 who was chief of that **region,** saw her, he took her and
36.31 from Bozrah Husham from the **region** of Teman Hadad son of
45.10 You can live in the **region** of Goshen, where you can be
46.34 this way he will let you live in the **region** of Goshen."
47. 1 They are now in the **region** of Goshen."
47. 4 Please give us permission to live in the **region** of Goshen."
47. 6 Let them settle in the **region** of Goshen, the best part of
47.27 lived in Egypt in the **region** of Goshen, where they became
48.22 am giving Shechem, that fertile **region** which I took from the
50. 8 sheep, goats, and cattle stayed in the **region** of Goshen.
Ex 8.22 But I will spare the **region** of Goshen, where my people live,
9.26 The **region** of Goshen, where the Israelites lived, was
Num 32. 3 the community and said, [3-4]"This **region** which the Lord
Deut 1. 7 and to all the surrounding **regions**—to the Jordan Valley, to
1. 7 to the southern **region,** and to the Mediterranean coast.
3. 1 we moved north towards the **region** of Bashan, and King Og
3. 4 captured sixty towns—the whole **region** of Argob, where King
3.10 cities on the plateau, the **regions** of Gilead and of Bashan,
3.13 where Og had ruled, that is, the entire Argob **region."**
3.14 of Manasseh, took the entire **region** of Argob, that is,
4.49 It also included all the **region** east of the River Jordan
Josh 13.11 It included Gilead, the **regions** of Geshur and Maacah,
Judg 5. 4 you came out of the **region** of Edom, the earth shook, and
1 Sam 9. 4 hill-country of Ephraim and the **region** of Shalishah, but did
9. 4 they went on through the **region** of Shaalim, but the donkeys
9. 5 When they came into the **region** of Zuph, Saul said to his
23.23 he is still in the **region,** I will hunt him down, even
23.29 left and went to the **region** of Engedi, where he stayed in
27. 8 Amalek, who had been living in the **region** a very long time.
1 Kgs 4.11 the whole **region** of Dor
4.12 Taanach, Megiddo, and all the **region** near Beth Shan, near
4.13 descendant of Manasseh, and the **region** of Argob in Bashan,
4.16 the **region** of Asher and the town of Bealoth
4.19 the **region** of Gilead, which had been ruled by King Sihon of
9.11 King Solomon gave Hiram twenty towns in the **region** of Galilee.
1 Chr 1.43 Husham from the **region** of Teman
Esth 10. 1 the people of the coastal **regions** of his empire as well as
Is 9. 1 will bring honour to this **region,** from the Mediterranean
Jer 50.19 Mount Carmel and in the **region** of Bashan, and they will eat
Ezek 47.17 of Enon, with the border **regions** of Damascus and Hamath to
Joel 3. 4 to do to me, Tyre, Sidon, and all the **regions** of Philistia?
Mic 7.12 in the south, from the **region** of the Euphrates, from distant
Zech 7. 7 also in the southern **region** and in the western foothills.
14.10 The whole **region,** from Geba in the north to Rimmon in
Mt 15.22 A Canaanite woman who lived in that **region** came to him.
Mk 3. 8 the Jordan, and from the **region** round the cities of Tyre
5.10 Jesus not to send the evil spirits out of that **region.**
6.55 So they ran throughout the whole **region;**
7.26 was a Gentile, born in the **region** of Phoenicia in Syria.
Lk 4.37 And the report about Jesus spread everywhere in that **region.**
23. 7 that Jesus was from the **region** ruled by Herod, he sent him
Acts 2.10 and Pamphylia, from Egypt and the **regions** of Libya near Cyrene.
13.49 The word of the Lord spread everywhere in that **region.**
13.50 against Paul and Barnabas and threw them out of their **region.**
16. 6 They travelled through the **region** of Phrygia and Galatia
18.23 went through the **region** of Galatia and Phrygia, strengthening all
20. 2 He went through those **regions** and encouraged the people
Rom 15.23 finished my work in these **regions** and since I have been

REGISTER

Num 1.18 of the second month and **registered** all the people by clans
1.19 In the Sinai Desert, Moses **registered** the people.
1.20 fit for military service were **registered** by name according
1.47 The Levites were not **registered** with the other tribes,
2.33 Levites were not **registered** with the rest of the Israelites.
3.15 Lord commanded Moses [15] to **register** the Levites by clans
3.40 So **register** by name every first-born male Israelite, one
3.42 Moses obeyed, and **registered** all the first-born males
4. 3 sub-clans and families, [3] and to **register** all the men
4.23 sub-clans and families, [23] and to **register** all the men
4.30 sub-clans and families, [30] and to **register** all the men
4.34 by sub-clans and families and **registered** all the men between
4.49 Each man was **registered** as the Lord had commanded Moses;
1 Chr 9.22 They were **registered** according to the villages where they lived.
23.24 by clans and families, every one of them **registered** by name.
23.27 final instructions all Levites were **registered** for service
24. 6 Then they were **registered** by Shemaiah son of Nethanel,
24.19 Maaziah [19] These men were **registered** according to their
2 Chr 31.18 They were all **registered** together with their wives, children,
Lk 2. 3 Everyone, then, went to **register** himself, each to his own town.
2. 5 He went to **register** with Mary, who was promised in

REGRET

Gen 6. 6 He was so filled with **regret** [7] that he said, "I will wipe
1 Sam 25.31 will not have to feel **regret** or remorse, sir, for having
Prov 11.15 If you promise to pay a stranger's debt, you will **regret** it.
17.25 grief to his father and bitter **regrets** to his mother.
20.25 You might **regret** it later.
22. 3 person will walk right into it and **regret** it later.
27.12 person will walk right into it and **regret** it later.
Ecc 2.20 So I came to **regret** that I had worked so hard.
Is 30. 5 the people of Judah will **regret** that they ever trusted
2 Cor 7.10 that leads to salvation—and there is no **regret** in that!
9. 7 he has decided, not with **regret** or out of a sense of

REGROUP

Judg 20.33 the Israelites pulled back and **regrouped** at Baaltamar, the

REGULAR

Lev 15.25 her flow continues beyond her **regular** period, she remains
23.38 are in addition to the **regular** Sabbaths, and these offerings
23.38 are in addition to your **regular** gifts, your offerings in
24. 2 in the Tent, so that a light may be kept burning **regularly.**
24. 4 must see that they burn **regularly** in the Lord's presence.
Num 15. 3 or as an offering at your **regular** religious festivals;
28.23 Offer these in addition to the **regular** morning burnt-offering.
29. 6 these in addition to the **regular** burnt-offering for the
2 Sam 17.17 servant-girl would **regularly** go and tell them what was happening,
2 Kgs 3.20 at the time of the **regular** morning sacrifice, water came
12. 4 the dues paid for the **regular** sacrifices and the money given
25.30 he lived, he was given a **regular** allowance for his needs.
1 Chr 6.32 They took **regular** turns of duty at the Tent of the
16. 6 to blow trumpets **regularly** in front of the Covenant Box.
2 Chr 19. 4 lived in Jerusalem, he travelled **regularly** among the people,
24.14 sacrifices were offered **regularly** at the Temple.
Ezra 3. 3 to burn on it the **regular** morning and evening sacrifices.
3. 5 in addition they offered the **regular** sacrifices to be burnt
3. 5 and at all the other **regular** assemblies at which the Lord is
Neh 5.17 I **regularly** fed at my table a hundred and fifty of the
Esth 2.12 The **regular** beauty treatment for the women lasted a
9.27 be **regularly** observed according to Mordecai's instructions.
Jer 52.34 he lived, he was given a **regular** allowance for his needs.
Dan 6.13 He prays **regularly** three times a day."
Mt 20. 2 agreed to pay them the **regular** wage, a silver coin a day,
Acts 19.38 we have the authorities and the **regular** days for court;

REGULATION

Ex 12.43 Lord said to Moses and Aaron, "These are the Passover **regulations:**
12.49 The same **regulations** apply to native-born Israelites and
Lev 5.10 bird as a burnt-offering, according to the **regulations.**
5.14 The Lord gave the following **regulations** to Moses.
6. 1 The Lord gave the following **regulations** to Moses.
6. 9 and his sons the following **regulations** for burnt-offerings.
6.14 The following are the **regulations** for grain-offerings.
6.19 Lord gave Moses the following **regulations** [20] for the
6.25 Aaron and his sons the following **regulations** for sin-offerings.
7. 1 The following are the **regulations** for repayment-offerings,
7. 7 There is one **regulation** that applies to both the
7.11 **regulations** for the fellowship-offerings presented to the Lord.
7.22 The Lord gave Moses the following **regulations**
7.28 The Lord gave Moses the following **regulations**
7.36 It is a **regulation** that the people of Israel must obey for
7.37 These, then, are the **regulations** for the burnt-offerings,
9.16 burnt-offering and offered it according to the **regulations.**
11. 1 Moses and Aaron the following **regulations**
12. 1 The Lord gave Moses the following **regulations**
13. 1 The Lord gave Moses and Aaron these **regulations.**
14. 2 Lord gave Moses [2] the following **regulations** about the ritual
14.34 **regulations** about houses affected by spreading mildew.
15. 1 Moses and Aaron the following **regulations**
15.32 These are the **regulations** about a man who has a
16.29 following **regulations** are to be observed for all time to come.
16.31 These **regulations** are to be observed for all time to come.
Lev 16.34 These **regulations** are to be observed for all time to come.
17. 2 sons and all the people of Israel the following **regulations.**
17. 7 of Israel must keep this **regulation** for all time to come.
18. 6 The Lord gave the following **regulations.**
19. 5 keep the **regulations** that I have given you,
20. 9 The Lord gave the following **regulations.**
20.18 they have broken the **regulations** about ritual uncleanness.
22. 9 "All priests shall observe the **regulations** that I have given.
22. 9 and die, because they have disobeyed the sacred **regulations.**
22.18 sons and all the people of Israel the following **regulations.**
23. 2 the following **regulations** for the religious festivals,
23.14 This **regulation** is to be observed by all your descendants
23.21 are to observe this **regulation** for all time to come,
23.31 This **regulation** applies to all your descendants,
23.41 This **regulation** is to be kept by your descendants for all
23.44 the people of Israel the **regulations** for observing the
24. 3 This **regulation** is to be observed for all time to come.
25. 2 to give the following **regulations** to the people of Israel.
27. 2 The Lord gave Moses [2] the following **regulations**
Num 6.21 These are the **regulations** for Nazirites;
8.26 This is how you are to **regulate** the duties of the Levites."
9. 2 Passover according to all the rules and **regulations** for it."
9.12 Observe the Passover according to all the **regulations.**
9.14 must observe it according to all the rules and **regulations.**
15. 2 Lord gave Moses [2] the following **regulations** for the people
15.14 pleases the Lord, he is to observe the same **regulations.**
15.16 the same laws and **regulations** apply to you and to them.
15.18 Lord gave Moses [18] the following **regulations** for the people
15.22 some of these **regulations** which the Lord has given Moses.
15.29 **regulation** applies to everyone who unintentionally commits a sin,
19. 2 Moses and Aaron [2] to give the Israelites the following **regulations.**
19.10 This **regulation** is valid for all time to come, both for the
28.14 This is the **regulation** for the burnt-offering for the first
29.39 These are the **regulations** concerning the burnt-offerings,
31.21 from battle, "These are the **regulations** that the Lord has
36.13 These are the rules and **regulations** that the Lord gave
1 Sam 2.13 the Lord [13] or to the **regulations** concerning what the
2 Chr 35.13 the fire, according to the **regulations,** and boiled the
Ezra 3. 4 celebrated the Festival of Shelters according to the **regulations;**
7.10 all its laws and **regulations** to the people of Israel.
Neh 11.23 There were royal **regulations** stating how the clans
12.45 duties in accordance with the **regulations** made by King David
13.30 I prepared **regulations** for the priests and the Levites so
Ezek 43.11 of everything, and all its rules and **regulations.**
44. 5 going to tell you the rules and **regulations** for the Temple.
44.24 according to my rules and **regulations,** and they are to keep
Heb 7.16 not by human rules and **regulations,** but through the power of

REHOBOAM

Solomon's son and first king of the s. kingdom (Judah).

1 Kgs 12.1-20 **The Northern tribes revolt**
21-24 **Shemaiah's prophecy**
25-31 **Jeroboam turns away from the LORD**
14.21-31 **King Rehoboam of Judah**
1 Chr 3.10-16 **The descendants of King Solomon**
2 Chr 10.1-19 **The Northern tribes revolt**
11.1-4 **Shemaiah's prophecy**
5-12 **Rehoboam fortifies the cities**
13-17 **Priests and Levites come to Judah**
18-23 **Rehoboam's family**
12.1-12 **An Egyptian invasion of Judah**
13-16 **Summary of Rehoboam's reign**

1 Kgs 11.43 David's City, and his son **Rehoboam** succeeded him as king.
15. 6 war which had begun between **Rehoboam** and Jeroboam continued
2 Chr 9.31 David's City, and his son **Rehoboam** succeeded him as king.
13. 7 they forced their will on **Rehoboam** son of Solomon, who was
Mt 1. 6 **Rehoboam,** Abijah, Asa, Jehoshaphat, Jehoram, Uzziah, Jotham,

REIGN

Deut 17.20 Then he will **reign** for many years, and his descendants will
2 Sam 21. 1 During David's **reign** there was a severe famine which
1 Kgs 1.37 and make his **reign** even more prosperous than yours."
1.47 and may Solomon's **reign** be even more prosperous than yours.'
6. 1 year of Solomon's **reign** over Israel, in the second month,
6.37 the month of Ziv, in the fourth year of Solomon's **reign.**
6.38 the eleventh year of Solomon's **reign,** the Temple was
10.27 During his **reign** silver was as common in Jerusalem as stone,
11.12 do this in your lifetime, but during the **reign** of your son.
14.25 Rehoboam's **reign** King Shishak of Egypt attacked Jerusalem.
15. 1 the eighteenth year of the **reign** of King Jeroboam of Israel,
15. 9 the twentieth year of the **reign** of King Jeroboam of Israel,
15.25 the second year of the **reign** of King Asa of Judah, King
15.28 during the third year of the **reign** of King Asa of Judah.
15.33 the third year of the **reign** of King Asa of Judah, Baasha
16. 8 the twenty-sixth year of the **reign** of King Asa of Judah,
16.10 the twenty-seventh year of the **reign** of King Asa of Judah.
16.15 the twenty-seventh year of the **reign** of King Asa of Judah,
16.23 the thirty-first year of the **reign** of King Asa of Judah,
16.29 the thirty-eighth year of the **reign** of King Asa of Judah,
16.34 During his **reign** Hiel from Bethel rebuilt Jericho.
22.41 the fourth year of the **reign** of King Ahab of Israel,
22.51 seventeenth year of the **reign** of King Jehoshaphat of Judah,
2 Kgs 1.17 the second year of the **reign** of Jehoram son of Jehoshaphat,
3. 1 eighteenth year of the **reign** of King Jehoshaphat of Judah,
8.16 the fifth year of the **reign** of Joram son of Ahab as
8.20 During Jehoram's **reign** Edom revolted against Judah
8.25 the twelfth year of the **reign** of Joram son of Ahab as
12. 1 the seventh year of the **reign** of King Jehu of Israel, Joash

2 Kgs 12. 6 the twenty-third year of Joash's **reign** the priests still had
13. 1 the twenty-third year of the **reign** of Joash son of Ahaziah
13.10 the thirty-seventh year of the **reign** of King Joash of Judah,
13.22 Israelites during all of Jehoahaz' **reign,** [23]but the Lord
13.25 Benhadad during the **reign** of Jehoahaz, the father of Jehoash.
14. 1 the second year of the **reign** of Jehoash son of Jehoahaz as
14.23 the fifteenth year of the **reign** of Amaziah son of Joash as
15. 1 year of the **reign** of King Jeroboam II of Israel,
15. 8 the thirty-eighth year of the **reign** of King Uzziah of Judah,
15.13 the thirty-ninth year of the **reign** of King Uzziah of Judah,
15.17 the thirty-ninth year of the **reign** of King Uzziah of Judah,
15.23 the fiftieth year of the **reign** of King Uzziah of Judah,
15.27 the fifty-second year of the **reign** of King Uzziah of Judah,
15.30 the twentieth year of the **reign** of Jotham son of Uzziah as
15.32 the second year of the **reign** of Pekah son of Remaliah as
16. 1 the seventeenth year of the **reign** of Pekah son of Remaliah
17. 1 the twelfth year of the **reign** of King Ahaz of Judah, Hoshea
17. 6 the ninth year of the **reign** of Hoshea, the Assyrian emperor
18. 1 the third year of the **reign** of Hoshea son of Elah as
18. 9 the fourth year of Hezekiah's **reign**—which was the seventh
18. 9 seventh year of King Hoshea's **reign** over Israel—Emperor
18.10 the sixth year of Hezekiah's **reign,**
18.10 and the ninth year of Hoshea's **reign.**
18.13 the fourteenth year of the **reign** of King Hezekiah,
22. 3 the eighteenth year of his **reign,** King Josiah sent the court
23.23 the eighteenth year of the **reign** of Josiah, the Passover was
23.33 His **reign** ended when King Neco of Egypt took him
24.10 It was during his **reign** that the Babylonian army,
24.12 the eighth year of Nebuchadnezzar's **reign** he took Jehoiachin
25. 1 of the tenth month of the ninth year of Zedekiah's **reign.**
1 Chr 22. 9 be Solomon, because during his **reign** I will give Israel
2 Chr 1.15 During his **reign** silver and gold became as common in
9.27 During his **reign** silver was as common in Jerusalem as stone,
9.29 which also deal with the **reign** of King Jeroboam of Israel.
12. 2 the fifth year of Rehoboam's **reign** their disloyalty to the
13. 1 the eighteenth year of the **reign** of King Jeroboam of Israel,
13.20 Jeroboam never regained his power during Abijah's **reign.**
15.19 There was no more war until the thirty-fifth year of his **reign.**
16. 1 the thirty-sixth year of the **reign** of King Asa of Judah,
16.11 All the events of Asa's **reign** from beginning to end are
17. 7 the third year of his **reign** he sent out the following
20.34 from the beginning of his **reign** to its end, is recorded in
21. 8 During Jehoram's **reign** Edom revolted against Judah
25.26 to the end of his **reign** are recorded in The History of
26.22 all the other things that King Uzziah did during his **reign.**
27. 7 The other events of Jotham's **reign,** his wars, and his policies,
28.26 the other events of his **reign,** from beginning to end, are
34. 8 the eighteenth year of his **reign,** after he had purified the
35.19 and Jerusalem [19]in the eighteenth year of Josiah's **reign.**
Ezra 4. 5 on doing this throughout the **reign** of Cyrus
4. 5 and into the **reign** of Darius.
4. 6 At the beginning of the **reign** of Xerxes the emperor, the
4. 7 Again, in the **reign** of Artaxerxes, emperor of Persia,
4.20 Powerful kings have **reigned** there and have ruled over
4.24 the second year of the **reign** of Darius, emperor of Persia.
5.13 the first year of the **reign** of King Cyrus as emperor of
6. 3 the first year of his **reign** Cyrus the emperor commanded that
6.15 Adar in the sixth year of the **reign** of Darius the emperor.
7. 6 the seventh year of the **reign** of Artaxerxes, Ezra set out
7.23 is never angry with me or with those who **reign** after me.
Esth 1. 3 the third year of his **reign** he gave a banquet for all
Ps 146.10 Your God, O Zion, will **reign** for all time.
Jer 1. 3 the eleventh year of the **reign** of Zedekiah son of Josiah.
52. 4 of the tenth month of the ninth year of Zedekiah's **reign.**
Dan 6.28 Daniel prospered during the **reign** of Darius
6.28 and the **reign** of Cyrus the Persian.
9. 2 the first year of his **reign,** I was studying the sacred books

REINFORCE

Ex 28.32 this hole is to be **reinforced** with a woven binding to keep
39.23 hole for the head was **reinforced** with a woven binding to
Judg 9.29 I would say to him, '**Reinforce** your army, come on out and

REJECT

Gen 4. 5 Abel and his offering, [5]but he **rejected** Cain and his offering.
Ex 32. 7 whom you led out of Egypt, have sinned and **rejected** me.
Lev 18.25 the land and making it **reject** the people who lived there.
18.28 then the land will not **reject** you,
18.28 as it **rejected** the pagans who lived there
20.22 that you will not be **rejected** by the land of Canaan, into
26.43 full penalty for having **rejected** my laws and my commands.
Num 11.20 will happen because you have **rejected** the Lord who is here
14.11 said to Moses, "How much longer will these people **reject** me?
14.23 None of those who have **rejected** me will ever enter it.
14.31 into the land that you **rejected,** and it will be their home.
15.31 to death, [31]because he has **rejected** what the Lord said and
16.30 you will know that these men have **rejected** the Lord."
Deut 28.20 "If you do evil and **reject** the Lord, he will bring on
31.20 They will **reject** me and break my covenant, [21]and many
31.29 will become wicked and **reject** what I have taught them.
32.15 abandoned God their Creator and **rejected** their mighty saviour.
32.19 Lord saw this, he was angry and **rejected** his sons and daughters.
1 Sam 8. 7 You are not the one they have **rejected;**
8. 7 I am the one they have **rejected** as their king.
10.19 difficulties, but today you have **rejected** me and have asked
12.12 about to attack you, you **rejected** the Lord as your king and
15.23 you **rejected** the Lord's command, he has rejected you as king."
15.26 "You **rejected** the Lord's command,
15.26 and he has **rejected** you as king of Israel."
1 Sam 16. 1 I have **rejected** him as king of Israel.
16. 7 I have **rejected** him, because I do not judge as man judges.
1 Kgs 11.33 Solomon has **rejected** me and has worshipped foreign gods:
14. 9 You have **rejected** me and have aroused my anger by making
2 Kgs 17.20 The Lord **rejected** all the Israelites, punishing them and
21.22 He **rejected** the Lord, the God of his ancestors, and
22.17 have **rejected** me and have offered sacrifices to other gods, and
23.27 my sight, and I will **reject** Jerusalem, the city I chose, and
2 Chr 6.42 Lord God, do not **reject** the king you have chosen.
34.25 have **rejected** me and have offered sacrifices to other gods, and
Neh 9.29 teachings, but in pride they **rejected** your laws, although
Job 15.11 why still **reject** it?
22.17 These are the men who **rejected** God and believed that he
24.13 There are men who **reject** the light;
Ps 1. 1 Happy are those who **reject** the advice of evil men, who do
9.17 the destiny of all the wicked, of all those who **reject** God.
10. 3 the greedy man curses and **rejects** the Lord.
15. 4 He despises those whom God **rejects,** but honours those who
36. 1 he **rejects** God and has no reverence for him.
36. 4 nothing he does is good, and he never **rejects** anything evil.
44. 9 But now you have **rejected** us and let us be defeated;
44.23 Don't **reject** us for ever!
50.17 you **reject** my commands.
51.17 you will not **reject** a humble and repentant heart.
53. 5 God has **rejected** them, and so Israel will totally defeat them.
60. 1 You have **rejected** us, God, and defeated us;
60.10 Have you really **rejected** us?
66.20 God, because he did not **reject** my prayer or keep back his
71. 9 Do not **reject** me now that I am old;
77. 7 "Will the Lord always **reject** us?
78.59 angry when he saw it, so he **rejected** his people completely.
78.67 But he **rejected** the descendants of Joseph;
88.14 Why do you **reject** me, Lord?
89.38 you have deserted and **rejected** him.
106.24 Then they **rejected** the pleasant land, because they did
107.11 commands of Almighty God and had **rejected** his instructions.
108.11 Have you really **rejected** us?
118.22 The stone which the builders **rejected** as worthless
119.118 You **reject** everyone who disobeys your laws;
132.10 do not **reject** your chosen king, Lord.
Prov 1.32 Inexperienced people die because they **reject** wisdom.
9.12 have wisdom, and if you **reject** it, you are the one who
Is 1. 4 You have **rejected** the Lord, the holy God of Israel, and have
5.24 blow away, because you have **rejected** what the Lord Almighty,
8. 6 said, "Because these people have **rejected** the quiet waters
41. 9 I did not **reject** you, but chose you.
53. 3 We despised him and **rejected** him;
59.13 We have rebelled against you, **rejected** you, and refused
Jer 2.20 "Israel, long ago you **rejected** my authority;
2.37 I, the Lord, have **rejected** those you trust;
4.30 Your lovers have **rejected** you and want to kill you.
5. 5 But all of them have **rejected** the Lord's authority and
6.19 these people, because they have **rejected** my teaching and
6.30 worthless dross, because I, the Lord, have **rejected** them."
7.29 because I, the Lord, am angry, and have **rejected** my people.
8. 9 They have **rejected** my words;
9. 5 The Lord says that his people **reject** him.
10.25 that do not worship you and on the people who **reject** you.
12. 7 I have **rejected** my chosen nation.
14.19 Lord, have you completely **rejected** Judah?
15. 6 You people have **rejected** me;
31.37 explored, only then would he **reject** the people of Israel
33.24 are saying that I have **rejected** Israel and Judah, the two
Lam 2. 7 The Lord **rejected** his altar and deserted his holy Temple;
3.31 The Lord is merciful and will not **reject** us for ever.
5.22 Or have you **rejected** us for ever?
Ezek 5. 6 Jerusalem **rejected** my commands and refused to keep my laws.
20.13 They broke my laws and **rejected** my commands, which bring
20.16 because they had **rejected** my commands, broken my laws,
20.24 this because they had **rejected** my commands, broken my laws,
31.11 so I have **rejected** it and will let a foreign ruler have
Dan 9. 5 We have **rejected** what you commanded us to do and have turned
Hos 4. 6 and have **rejected** my teaching,
4. 6 and so I **reject** you and will not acknowledge
8. 3 and that they know me, [3]they have **rejected** what is good.
8.12 for the people, but they **reject** them as strange and foreign.
9.17 The God I serve will **reject** his people, because they
Zech 10. 6 They will be as though I had never **rejected** them.
Mt 10.33 But if anyone **rejects** me publicly,
10.33 I will **reject** him before my Father in heaven.
13.57 And so they **rejected** him.
21.42 'The stone which the builders **rejected** as worthless turned
Mk 6. 3 And so they **rejected** him.
7. 9 have a clever way of **rejecting** God's law in order to uphold
8.31 much and be **rejected** by the elders, the chief priests,
9.12 say that the Son of Man will suffer much and be **rejected?**
12.10 'The stone which the builders **rejected** as worthless turned out
Lk 6.22 when people hate you, **reject** you, insult you, and say that
7.30 the teachers of the Law **rejected** God's purpose for themselves
9.22 much and be **rejected** by the elders, the chief priests,
10.16 whoever **rejects** you rejects me;
10.16 and whoever **rejects** me rejects the one who sent me."
12. 9 But whoever **rejects** me publicly,
12. 9 Son of Man will also **reject** him before the angels of God.
17.25 must suffer much and be **rejected** by the people of this day.
20.17 'The stone which the builders **rejected** as worthless turned out
Jn 12.11 his account many Jews were **rejecting** them and believing in
Jesus.
12.48 Whoever **rejects** me and does not accept my message has
Acts 3.13 to the authorities, and you **rejected** him in Pilate's presence,
3.14 holy and good, but you **rejected** him, and instead you asked

Acts 7.35 "Moses is the one who was **rejected** by the people of Israel.
13.46 But since you **reject** it and do not consider yourselves
Rom 2. 8 Other people are selfish and **reject** what is right, in
11. 1 Did God **reject** his own people?
11. 2 God has not **rejected** his people, whom he chose from the beginning.
11.15 when they were **rejected,** mankind was changed from God's enemies
11.28 Because they **reject** the Good News, the Jews are God's enemies
Gal 2.21 I refuse to **reject** the grace of God.
4.14 a great trial to you, you did not despise or **reject** me.
1 Thes 4. 8 whoever **rejects** this teaching is not rejecting man, but God,
2 Thes 1. 8 fire, to punish those who **reject** God and who do not obey
1 Tim 4. 4 nothing is to be **rejected,** but everything is to be received
2 Tim 3. 5 the outward form of our religion, but **reject** its real power.
Tit 1.14 commandments which come from people who have **rejected** the truth.
1 Pet 2. 4 the Lord, the living stone **rejected** by man as worthless
2. 7 "The stone which the builders **rejected** as worthless turned out
1 Jn 2.22 the Enemy of Christ—he **rejects** both the Father and the Son.
2.23 For whoever **rejects** the Son also rejects the Father;
Jude 4 their immoral ways, and who **reject** Jesus Christ, our only Master

REJOICE

Gen 31.27 you on your way with **rejoicing** and singing to the music of
2 Sam 1.20 do not let the daughters of pagans **rejoice.**
1 Chr 16.10 let all who worship him **rejoice!**
Ps 5.11 But all who find safety in you will **rejoice;**
9.14 I will **rejoice** because you saved me.
21. 1 he **rejoices** because you made him victorious.
31. 7 I will be glad and **rejoice** because of your constant love.
32.11 are righteous, be glad and **rejoice** because of what the Lord
63.11 Because God gives him victory, the king will **rejoice.**
64.10 All righteous people will **rejoice** because of what the Lord
66. 6 There we **rejoiced** because of what he did.
68. 3 But the righteous are glad and **rejoice** in his presence;
89.16 Because of you they **rejoice** all day long, and they
97. 1 **Rejoice,** you islands of the seas!
97. 8 and the cities of Judah **rejoice** because of your judgements,
105. 3 let all who worship him **rejoice.**
149. 2 **rejoice,** people of Zion, because of your king!
149. 5 Let God's people **rejoice** in their triumph and sing
Prov 24.17 enemy meets disaster, and don't **rejoice** when he stumbles.
Is 9. 3 They **rejoice** in what you have done,
9. 3 as people **rejoice** when they harvest their corn or
12. 3 the thirsty, so God's people **rejoice** when he saves them."
14. 8 and the cedars of Lebanon **rejoice** over the fallen king,
35. 1 desert will **rejoice,** and flowers will bloom in the wilderness.
61.10 Jerusalem **rejoices** because of what the Lord has done.
65.18 Be glad and **rejoice** for ever in what I create.
66. 5 his greatness and save you, so that we may see you **rejoice.'**
66.10 **Rejoice** with Jerusalem;
66.10 **Rejoice** with her now, all you that have mourned for her!
Jer 31.13 dance and be happy, and men, young and old, will **rejoice.**
Ezek 21.10 There can be no **rejoicing,** for my people have disregarded
35.14 that the whole world will **rejoice** at your downfall,
35.15 just as you **rejoiced** at the devastation of Israel,
Joel 2.23 "Be glad, people of Zion, **rejoice** at what the Lord your
Zeph 3.14 **Rejoice** with all your heart, Jerusalem!
Zech 9. 9 **Rejoice,** rejoice, people of Zion!
Lk 1.58 the Lord had been to her, and they all **rejoiced** with her.
13.17 while the people **rejoiced** over all the wonderful things that
15.10 the angels of God **rejoice** over one sinner who repents."
Jn 8.56 Your father Abraham **rejoiced** that he was to see the time
Rom 5.11 we **rejoice** because of what God has done through our Lord
15.10 Again it says, **"Rejoice,** Gentiles, with God's people!"
Phil 3. 3 means of his Spirit and **rejoice** in our life in union with
4. 4 **rejoice!**
1 Pet 1. 8 So you **rejoice** with a great and glorious joy which words
Rev 19. 7 Let us **rejoice** and be glad;

RELATE

Jn 20.18 had seen the Lord and **related** to them what he had told

RELATIONS

Ex 22.19 "Put to death any man who has sexual **relations** with an animal.
Lev 18.22 No man is to have sexual **relations** with another man;
18.23 No man or woman is to have sexual **relations** with an animal;
19.20 if another man has sexual **relations** with her, they will be
20.13 If a man has sexual **relations** with another man, they
20.15 If a man has sexual **relations** with an animal, he and the
20.16 woman tries to have sexual **relations** with an animal, she and
Deut 27.21 " 'God's curse on anyone who has sexual **relations** with an animal'
1 Sam 21. 4 it if your men haven't had sexual **relations** recently."
1 Kgs 3. 6 he was good, loyal, and honest in his **relations** with you.
Mt 1.25 But he had no sexual **relations** with her before she gave
Rom 1.27 men give up natural sexual **relations** with women
1 Cor 7. 5 but then resume normal marital **relations.**
8. 8 Food, however, will not improve our **relations** with God;
2 Cor 1.12 and especially our **relations** with you, have been ruled by
13. 4 but in our **relations** with you we shall share God's power in
Rev 14. 4 kept themselves pure by not having sexual **relations** with women;

RELATIVE

Gen 12. 1 "Leave your country, your **relatives,** and your father's home,
13. 8 said to Lot, "We are **relatives,** and your men and my men
16.12 He will live apart from all his **relatives."**
19.12 daughters, sons-in-law, or any other **relatives** living in the
24. 4 and get a wife for my son Isaac from among my **relatives."**
24. 7 from the land of my **relatives,** and he solemnly promised me
24.27 The Lord has led me straight to my master's **relatives."**
24.38 people, to my **relatives,** and choose a wife for him.'
24.41 if you go to my **relatives** and they refuse you, then you
24.48 me straight to my master's **relative,** where I found his
27.29 you rule over all your **relatives,** and may your mother's
27.37 over you, and I have made all his **relatives** his slaves.
29.12 "I am your father's **relative,** the son of Rebecca."
29.15 work for me for nothing just because you are my **relative.**
31. 3 "Go back to the land of your fathers and to your **relatives.**
32. 9 my land and to my **relatives,** and you would make everything
Ex 4.18 me go back to my **relatives** in Egypt to see if they
Lev 18. 6 Do not have sexual intercourse with any of your **relatives.**
18.17 they may be **related** to you, and that would be incest.
21. 1 ceremonies when a **relative** dies, [2]unless it is his mother,
21. 4 unclean at the death of those **related** to him by marriage.
25.25 to sell his land, his closest **relative** is to buy it back.
25.26 A man who has no **relative** to buy it back may later
25.49 cousin or another of his close **relatives** may buy him back;
Num 5. 8 died and has no near **relative** to whom payment can be made,
18. 2 Bring in your **relatives,** the tribe of Levi, to work with
18. 6 one who has chosen your **relatives** the Levites from among the
27. 4 Give us property among our father's **relatives."**
27. 7 give them property among their father's **relatives.**
27.11 or uncles, then his nearest **relative** is to inherit it and
35.12 will be safe from the dead man's **relative** who seeks revenge.
35.19 The dead man's nearest **relative** has the responsibility
35.21 The dead man's nearest **relative** has the responsibility for
35.24 in favour of the dead man's **relative** who is seeking revenge.
35.25 manslaughter from the dead man's **relative,** and they are to
35.27 and if the dead man's **relative** finds him and kills him,
36. 2 the property of our **relative** Zelophehad to his daughters.
Deut 2. 4 of your distant **relatives,** the descendants of Esau.
19. 6 be too great, and the **relative** who is responsible for taking
19.12 hand him over to the **relative** responsible for taking revenge
23. 7 they are your **relatives.**
Josh 6.25 prostitute Rahab and all her **relatives,** because she had
17. 4 as well as our male **relatives,** a part of the land to
17. 4 they were given land along with their male **relatives.**
Judg 9. 1 Shechem, where all his mother's **relatives** lived, and told
9. 3 His mother's **relatives** talked to the men of Shechem about
9. 3 Shechem decided to follow Abimelech because he was their **relative.**
9.18 by his servant-girl, is your **relative,** you have made him
Ruth 2. 1 Naomi had a **relative** named Boaz, a rich and influential
2.20 "That man is a close **relative** of ours, one of those
3. 2 whose women you have been working with, is our **relative.**
3. 9 "Because you are a close **relative,** you are responsible for
3.12 that I am a close **relative** and am responsible for you, but
3.12 there is a man who is a closer **relative** than I am.
4. 1 Elimelech's nearest **relative,** the man whom Boaz had mentioned,
4. 3 seated, [3]he said to his **relative,** "Now that Naomi has come
4. 3 field that belonged to our **relative** Elimelech, [4]and I think
1 Sam 20.29 if you are my friend, let me go and see my **relatives.'**
22.11 Ahimelech and all his **relatives,** who were also priests in Nob,
22.16 king said, "Ahimelech, you and all your **relatives** must die."
22.22 So I am responsible for the death of all your **relatives.**
2 Sam 14. 7 And now, sir, all my **relatives** have turned against me and
14.11 your God, so that my **relative** who is responsible for
16. 5 at Bahurim, one of Saul's **relatives,** Shimei son of Gera,
19.12 You are my **relatives,** my own flesh and blood;
19.13 David also told them to say to Amasa, "You are my **relative.**
1 Kgs 16.11 Every male **relative** and friend was put to death.
21.24 Any of your **relatives** who die in the city will be eaten
2 Kgs 8.27 Since Ahaziah was **related** to King Ahab by marriage, he
10.11 to death all the other **relatives** of Ahab living in Jezreel,
10.13 "Shepherds' Camp," [13]he met some **relatives** of the late
10.13 "Ahaziah's **relatives,"** they answered.
10.17 Jehu killed all of Ahab's **relatives,** not sparing even one.
1 Chr 4.27 and six daughters, but his **relatives** had fewer children, and
7.22 them for many days, and his **relatives** came to comfort him.
9.25 guards were assisted by their **relatives,** who lived in the
12.23 **Relatives** of Zadok, an able young fighter:
15.17 Heman son of Joel, his **relative** Asaph son of Berechiah, and
23.32 assisting their **relatives,** the priests descended from Aaron,
24.31 just as their **relatives,** the priests descended from Aaron,
26.25 Through Gershom's brother Eliezer he was **related** to Shelomith.
26.30 and seventeen hundred of his **relatives,** all outstanding men,
26.32 heads of families from Jeriah's **relatives** and put them in
2 Chr 30. 9 those who have taken your **relatives** away as prisoners will
Ezra 3. 2 of Shealtiel, together with his **relatives,** rebuilt the altar
3. 9 Jeshua and his sons and **relatives,** and Kadmiel and his sons
8.19 Jeshaiah of the clan of Merari, with twenty of their **relatives.**
Neh 5.14 his thirty-second year, neither my **relatives** nor I ate the
11. 8 Gabbai and Sallai, close **relatives** of Sallu.
11.19 Akkub, Talmon, and their **relatives,** 172 in all.
Esth 8. 1 the king that Mordecai was **related** to her, and from then on
8. 6 comes on my people, and my own **relatives** are killed?"
Job 19.14 my **relatives** and friends are gone.
Ps 45.10 to what I say— forget your people and your **relatives.**
122. 8 For the sake of my **relatives** and friends I say to Jerusalem,
Is 22.24 all his **relatives** and dependants will become a burden to him.
58. 7 to wear, and do not refuse to help your own **relatives.**
Jer 7.15 sight as I drove out your **relatives,** the people of Israel.
23.35 friends and his **relatives,** 'What answer has the Lord given?
29.16 this city, that is, your **relatives** who were not taken away
32. 7 because I was his nearest **relative** and had the right to buy
Dan 11. 7 Soon afterwards, one of her **relatives** will become king.
Amos 6.10 The dead man's **relative,** the one in charge of the funeral,

Amos 6.10 The **relative** will call to whoever is still left in the house,
6.10 Then the **relative** will say, "Be quiet!
Mk 6. 4 in his own home town and by his **relatives** and his family."
Lk 1.36 Remember your **relative** Elizabeth.
1.58 Her neighbours and **relatives** heard how wonderfully good
1.61 They said to her, "But you have no **relatives** with that name!"
2.44 then started looking for him among their **relatives** and friends.
14.12 or your brothers or your **relatives** or your rich neighbours—
21.16 handed over by your parents, your brothers, your **relatives,**
Jn 18.26 the High Priest's slaves, a **relative** of the man whose ear
Acts 10.24 waiting for him, together with **relatives** and close friends
1 Tim 5. 8 not take care of his **relatives,** especially the members of
Heb 11.35 women received their dead **relatives** raised back to life.

RELEASE

Gen 40.13 three days the king will **release** you, pardon you, and
40.19 three days the king will **release** you—and have your head cut
40.20 he **released** his wine steward and his chief baker and brought
Lev 25.50 set the price for his **release** on the basis of the wages
Deut 15.12 a slave, you are to **release** him after he has served you
2 Kgs 25.27 to King Jehoiachin of Judah by **releasing** him from prison.
Job 33.24 In mercy the angel will say, **"Release** him!
Ps 105.20 Then the king of Egypt had him **released;**
Prov 6. 3 hurry to him, and beg him to **release** you.
Is 49. 7 "Kings will see you **released** and will rise to show their respect;
61. 1 heal the broken-hearted, To announce **release** to captives And
Jer 20. 3 next morning, after Pashhur had **released** me from the chains,
52.31 to King Jehoiachin of Judah by **releasing** him from prison.
Lk 13.16 should she not be **released** on the Sabbath?"
Acts 16.36 have sent an order for you and Silas to be **released.**
17. 9 amount of money to be **released,** and then let them go.
26.32 "This man could have been **released** if he had not appealed
28.18 the Romans wanted to **release** me, because they found that I
Rev 9.14 said to the sixth angel, **"Release** the four angels who are
9.15 The four angels were **released;**

RELENT

Ps 106.45 his covenant, and because of his great love he **relented.**

RELIABLE see RELY

RELIANCE see RELY

RELIEF

1 Kgs 7.29 the lions and bulls, there were spiral figures in **relief.**
7.30 the supports were decorated with spiral figures in **relief.**

RELIEVE (1)

Gen 5.29 this child will bring us **relief** from all our hard work";
2 Kgs 15. 5 a house on his own, **relieved** of all duties, while his son
2 Chr 26.21 lived in his own house, **relieved** of all duties, while his
Esth 8.16 Jews there was joy and **relief,** happiness and a sense of victory.
Job 7.13 I look for **relief** from my pain.
30.16 there is no **relief** for my suffering.
Ps 25.17 **Relieve** me of my worries and save me from all my troubles.
Is 14. 3 the people of Israel **relief** from their pain and suffering,
Mic 1.12 of Maroth wait anxiously for **relief,** because the Lord has
2 Cor 8.13 I am not trying to **relieve** others by putting a
2 Thes 1. 7 and he will give **relief** to you who suffer and to
Rev 14.11 There is no **relief** day or night for those who worship the

RELIEVE (2)

Deut 23.12 camp where you can go when you need to **relieve yourselves.**
Judg 3.24 only thought that the king was inside, **relieving himself.**
1 Sam 24. 3 some sheep pens by the road and went in to **relieve himself.**
1 Kgs 18.27 Maybe he is day-dreaming or **relieving himself,** or perhaps

RELIGION

Gen 1.14 the time when days, years, and **religious** festivals begin;
Ex 12.14 celebrate this day as a **religious** festival to remind you of
23.24 or worship them, and do not adopt their **religious** practices.
Lev 23. 2 the following regulations for the **religious** festivals,
23.37 (These are the **religious** festivals on which you honour
23.40 leafy trees, and begin a **religious** festival to honour the
23.44 Israel the regulations for observing the **religious** festivals
26. 2 Keep the **religious** festivals and honour the place
Num 10.10 Moon Festivals and your other **religious** festivals—you are to
15. 3 or as an offering at your regular **religious** festivals;
28.17 On the fifteenth day a **religious** festival begins which lasts
Deut 12.30 their **religious** practices, because that would be fatal.
1 Sam 10. 6 you will join in their **religious** dancing and shouting and
10.17 the people together for a **religious** gathering at Mizpah
21. 7 that day, because he had to fulfil a **religious** obligation.)
1 Kgs 12.32 Jeroboam also instituted a **religious** festival on the
1 Chr 26.30 of the administration of all **religious** and civil matters in
26.32 in charge of administering all **religious** and civil matters
2 Chr 19.11 in all **religious** cases, and Zebadiah son of Ishmael,
26. 5 As long as Zechariah, his **religious** adviser, was living,
Ecc 9. 2 bad, to those who are **religious** and those who are not, to
Is 1.13 Moon Festivals, your Sabbaths, and your **religious** gatherings;
29.13 Their **religion** is nothing but human rules and traditions,
33.20 Zion, the city where we celebrate our **religious** festivals.
Jer 10. 3 The **religion** of these people is worthless.
Jer 12.16 they will accept the **religion** of my people and will swear,
Ezek 44.24 They are to keep the **religious** festivals according to my
Dan 6. 5 Daniel unless it is something in connection with his **religion."**
7.25 will try to change their **religious** laws and festivals, and
8.12 sacrifices, and true **religion** was thrown to the ground.
11.28 determined to destroy the **religion** of God's people.
11.30 in a rage and try to destroy the **religion** of God's people.
11.30 will follow the advice of those who have abandoned that **religion.**
11.32 who have already abandoned their **religion,** but those who
Hos 2.11 and her Sabbath celebrations—all her **religious** meetings.
Amos 5.21 The Lord says, "I hate your **religious** festivals;
Mt 6. 1 you do not perform your **religious** duties in public so that
Jn 5. 1 After this, Jesus went to Jerusalem for a **religious** festival.
Acts 2. 5 were Jews living in Jerusalem, **religious** men who had come from
10. 2 He was a **religious** man;
10. 7 servants and a soldier, a **religious** man who was one of his
10.28 not allowed by his **religion** to visit or associate with Gentiles.
17.22 "I see that in every way you Athenians are very **religious.**
22.12 a man named Ananias, a **religious** man who obeyed our Law
25.19 him about their own **religion** and about a man named Jesus,
26. 5 as a member of the strictest party of our **religion,** the
Gal 1.13 devoted to the Jewish **religion,** how I persecuted without mercy
1.14 my practice of the Jewish **religion,** and was much more
1 Tim 1. 9 for those who are not **religious** or spiritual, for those who
2.10 deeds, as is proper for women who claim to be **religious.**
3.16 No one can deny how great is the secret of our **religion:**
5. 4 to carry out their **religious** duties towards their own family
6. 3 with the teaching of our **religion** [4] is swollen with pride
6. 5 They think that **religion** is a way to become rich.
6. 6 Well, **religion** does make a person very rich, if he is
2 Tim 3. 5 the outward form of our **religion,** but reject its real power.
Tit 1. 1 the truth taught by our **religion,** [2] which is based on the
Jas 1.26 Does anyone think he is **religious?**
1.26 not control his tongue, his **religion** is worthless
1.27 God the Father considers to be pure and genuine **religion** is this:
2 Pet 1. 3 need to live a truly **religious** life through our knowledge of

RELUCTANT

2 Chr 25. 2 He did what was pleasing to the Lord, but did it **reluctantly.**

RELY

[RELIABLE, RELIANCE, UNRELIABLE]

Judg 20.36 the Benjaminites because they were **relying** on the men that
2 Kgs 18.21 what the king of Egypt is like when anyone **relies** on him."
18.22 you tell me that you are **relying** on the Lord your God?
18.30 And don't let him persuade you to **rely** on the Lord.
1 Chr 12. 1 was joined by many experienced, **reliable** soldiers, [2] members
12.23 50,000 loyal and **reliable** men ready to fight, trained to use
2 Chr 13.18 victorious over Israel, because they **relied** on the Lord, the
14.11 our God, because we are **relying** on you, and in your name
16. 7 Asa and said, "Because you **relied** on the king of Syria
16. 7 instead of **relying** on the Lord your God,
16. 8 But because you **relied** on the Lord, he gave you victory over
Neh 7. 2 Hananiah was a **reliable** and God-fearing man without an equal.
Job 39.11 Can you **rely** on his great strength and expect him to do
Ps 13. 5 **I rely** on your constant love;
22. 8 "You **relied** on the Lord," they say.
22.10 I have **relied** on you since the day I was born, and
71. 6 I have **relied** on you all my life;
78.57 disloyal like their fathers, **unreliable** as a crooked arrow.
Prov 2.15 senseless evil, [15] **unreliable** men who cannot be trusted.
3. 5 Never **rely** on what you think you know.
13.17 **Unreliable** messengers cause trouble,
14. 5 A **reliable** witness always tells the truth,
14. 5 but an **unreliable** one tells nothing but lies.
21.22 by strong men, and destroy the walls they **relied** on.
25.13 A **reliable** messenger is refreshing to the one who sends him,
25.19 Depending on an **unreliable** person in a crisis is like
Is 8. 2 Get two **reliable** men, the priest Uriah and Zechariah son of Jeberechiah,
10.20 have survived will no longer **rely** on the nation that almost
17. 8 They will no longer **rely** on the altars they made with
20. 6 happened to the people we **relied** on to protect us from the
23.14 The city you **relied** on has been destroyed.
30. 5 that they ever trusted that **unreliable** nation, a nation that
30.12 "You ignore what I tell you and **rely** on violence and deceit.
31. 1 They are **relying** on Egypt's vast military strength—horses,
31. 1 But they do not **rely** on the Lord, the holy God of
36. 6 what the king of Egypt is like when anyone **relies** on him."
36. 7 you tell me that you are **relying** on the Lord your God?
36.15 And don't let him persuade you to **rely** on the Lord.
50.10 be dark indeed, but trust in the Lord, **rely** on your God.
Ezek 29. 6 "The Israelites **relied** on you Egyptians for support,
29.16 fate will remind Israel how wrong it was to **rely** on them.
33.26 You **rely** on your swords.
Dan 6. 4 they couldn't, because Daniel was **reliable** and did not do
Hos 7. 8 They **rely** on the nations around them [9] and do not realize
7. 9 do not realize that this **reliance** on foreigners has robbed
7.16 They are as **unreliable** as a crooked bow.
2 Cor 1. 9 happened so that we should **rely,** not on ourselves, but only
2 Tim 2. 2 witnesses, and entrust them to **reliable** people, who will be able

REMAIN

see also **REMAINS**

Gen 18.22 went on towards Sodom, but the Lord **remained** with Abraham.
29.31 for her to have children, but Rachel **remained** childless.
38.11 to your father's house and **remain** a widow until my son
47.26 This law still **remains** in force today.

Gen	49.24	But his bow **remains** steady, And his arms are made strong
Ex	7.13	king, however, **remained** stubborn and, just as the Lord had said,
	8.31	not one fly **remained.**
	9.34	He and his officials **remained** as stubborn as ever [35]and,
	38.28	With the **remaining** 30 kilogrammes of silver Bezalel made
Lev	7.17	Any meat that still **remains** on the third day must be burnt.
	10. 3	But Aaron **remained** silent.
	10.12	to Aaron and his two **remaining** sons, Eleazar and Ithamar,
	11.32	dipped in water, but it will **remain** unclean until evening.
	11.36	a spring or a cistern **remains** clean, although anything else
	11.37	on seed that is going to be sown, the seed **remains** clean.
	13.23	But if it **remains** unchanged and does not spread, it is
	13.28	But if the spot **remains** unchanged and does not spread
	13.46	He **remains** unclean as long as he has the disease, and he
	15. 6	and have a bath, and he **remains** unclean until evening.
	15. 7	and have a bath, and he **remains** unclean until evening.
	15. 8	and have a bath, and he **remains** unclean until evening.
	15.10	and have a bath, and he **remains** unclean until evening.
	15.11	and have a bath, and he **remains** unclean until evening.
	15.16	bathe his whole body, and he **remains** unclean until evening.
	15.17	falls must be washed, and it **remains** unclean until evening.
	15.18	must have a bath, and they **remain** unclean until evening.
	15.19	has her monthly period, she **remains** unclean for seven days.
	15.21	and have a bath, and he **remains** unclean until evening.
	15.24	by her impurity and **remains** unclean for seven days,
	15.25	beyond her regular period, she **remains** unclean as long as
	15.27	he **remains** unclean until evening.
	22. 6	Any priest who becomes unclean **remains** unclean until evening,
	25.27	for the years **remaining** until the next Year of Restoration,
	25.28	buy the land back, it **remains** under the control of the man
Num	9.20	Sometimes the cloud **remained** over the Tent for only a few days;
	9.20	in any case, they **remained** in camp or moved, according to
	9.21	Sometimes the cloud **remained** only from evening until morning,
	9.22	as long as the cloud **remained** over the Tent, they did not
	14.24	a different attitude and has **remained** loyal to me, I will
	19. 7	but he **remains** ritually unclean until evening.
	19. 8	over himself, but he also **remains** unclean until evening.
	19.10	must wash his clothes, but he **remains** unclean until evening.
	19.13	and does not purify himself **remains** unclean, because the
	19.20	and does not purify himself **remains** unclean, because the
	19.21	touches the water **remains** ritually unclean until evening.
	19.22	anyone else who touches it **remains** unclean until evening.
	32.11	that because they did not **remain** loyal to me, none of the
	32.12	they **remained** loyal to the Lord.
	32.26	cattle and sheep will **remain** here in the towns of Gilead.
	35.28	man guilty of manslaughter must **remain** in the city of refuge
	36. 7	property of every Israelite will **remain** attached to his tribe.
	36.12	and their property **remained** in their father's tribe.
Deut	1.36	He has **remained** faithful to me, and I will give him and
	3.19	a lot of livestock—will **remain** behind in the towns that I
	3.29	"So we **remained** in the valley opposite the town of Bethpeor."
	21.23	is hung on a post, [23]it is not to **remain** there overnight.
	31.26	God, so that it will **remain** there as a witness against his
Josh	18.10	and assigned each of the **remaining** tribes of Israel a
Judg	2.23	So the Lord allowed those nations to **remain** in the land;
	5.17	of the Jordan, and the tribe of Dan **remained** by the ships.
	5.17	they **remained** along the shore.
	18.31	Micah's idol **remained** there all the time that the Tent
	18.31	Tent where God was worshipped **remained** at Shiloh.
1 Sam	20.14	And if I **remain** alive, please keep your sacred promise
2 Sam	20. 2	but the men of Judah **remained** loyal and followed David from
1 Kgs	11.15	He and his men **remained** in Edom six months, and during that
	12.20	Only the tribe of Judah **remained** loyal to David's descendants.
	15.14	pagan places of worship, he **remained** faithful to the Lord
	22.35	raged on, King Ahab **remained** propped up in his chariot,
2 Kgs	13. 6	and the image of the goddess Asherah **remained** in Samaria.
	25.11	left in the city, the **remaining** skilled workmen, and those
1 Chr	6.77	The **remaining** families of the clan of Merari were
	12.23	(most of the people of Benjamin had **remained** loyal to Saul);
2 Chr	11. 5	Rehoboam **remained** in Jerusalem and had fortifications
	15.17	worship in the land, he **remained** faithful to the Lord all
	18.34	raged on, King Ahab **remained** propped up in his chariot,
	22.12	For six years he **remained** there in hiding, while
	24.14	the repairs were finished, the **remaining** gold and silver was
	32.10	people the confidence to **remain** in Jerusalem under siege.
	34.21	me and for the people who still **remain** in Israel and Judah.
Ezra	4.24	had been stopped and had **remained** at a standstill until the
Neh	11.20	people of Israel and the **remaining** priests and Levites lived
Job	15.29	He will not **remain** rich for long;
	17.12	say that light is near, but I know I **remain** in darkness.
	36.30	through all the sky, but the depths of the sea **remain** dark.
Ps	78. 8	God was never firm and who did not **remain** faithful to him.
	85. 9	him, and his saving presence will **remain** in our land.
	91. 1	whoever **remains** under the protection of the Almighty,
	101. 7	no hypocrite will **remain** in my presence.
	102.26	They will disappear, but you will **remain;**
	109. 1	don't **remain** silent!
	119.90	you have set the earth in place, and it **remains.**
	119.91	All things **remain** to this day because of your command,
Prov	14.17	wiser people **remain** calm.
	20.28	A king will **remain** in power as long as his rule is
Is	1.21	filled with righteous men, but now only murderers **remain.**
	6.13	one person out of ten **remains** in the land, he too will
	24. 6	Fewer and fewer **remain** alive.
Jer	2.19	the Lord your God, and no longer to **remain** loyal to me.
	25.19	cities of Ashkelon, Gaza, Ekron, and what **remains** of Ashdod;
	27.18	to allow the treasures that **remain** in the Temple and in the
	27.22	taken to Babylonia and will **remain** there until I turn my
	32. 5	Babylonia, and he will **remain** there until I deal with him.
	35. 7	tents, so that we might **remain** in this land where we live
	43. 4	obey the Lord's command to **remain** in the land of Judah.
Jer	47. 4	to cut off from Tyre and Sidon all the help that **remains.**
	50. 7	and they themselves should have **remained** faithful to him.'
	51.30	soldiers have stopped fighting and **remain** in their forts.
	52.11	Zedekiah **remained** in prison in Babylon until the day he died.
	52.15	left in the city, the **remaining** skilled workmen, and those
Ezek	5. 2	Scatter the **remaining** third to the winds, and I will pursue
	7.11	Nothing of theirs will **remain,** nothing of their wealth, their splendour,
	24.13	Although I tried to purify you, you **remained** defiled.
	39.14	find and bury those bodies **remaining** on the ground, so that
	42. 7	and there were rooms in the **remaining** twenty-five metres.
	44. 2	It is to **remain** closed.
	47.11	They will **remain** there as a source of salt.
	48.21	the city, the **remaining** land belongs to the ruling prince.
	48.23	special section, each of the **remaining** tribes is to receive
Dan	1.21	Daniel **remained** at the royal court until Cyrus the
	2.49	Daniel, however, **remained** at the royal court.
	9.27	of the Temple and will **remain** there until the one who put
	12.12	Happy are those who **remain** faithful until 1,335 days are over!
Hos	9. 3	people of Israel will not **remain** in the Lord's land, but
Zech	5. 4	It will **remain** in their houses and leave them in ruins."
	12. 6	The people of Jerusalem will **remain** safe in the city.
Mt	10.13	that house welcome you, let your greeting of peace **remain;**
Lk	1.20	you will **remain** silent until the day my promise to you comes
	10. 6	peace-loving man lives there, let your greeting of peace **remain**
Jn	3.36	will not have life, but will **remain** under God's punishment.
	12.24	a grain of wheat **remains** no more than a single grain unless
	12.46	everyone who believes in me should not **remain** in the darkness.
	14.10	The Father, who **remains** in me, does his own work.
	14.17	you know him, because he **remains** with you and is in you.
	15. 4	**Remain** united to me, and I will remain united to you.
	15. 4	it can do so only if it **remains** in the vine.
	15. 4	the same way you cannot bear fruit unless you **remain** in me.
	15. 5	Whoever **remains** in me, and I in him, will bear much fruit;
	15. 6	Whoever does not **remain** in me is thrown out like a branch
	15. 7	If you **remain** in me and my words remain in you,
	15. 9	**remain** in my love.
	15.10	obey my commands, you will **remain** in my love, just as
	15.10	I have obeyed my Father's commands and **remain** in his love.
Acts	3.21	He must **remain** in heaven until the time comes for all
	14.22	the believers and encouraged them to **remain** true to the faith.
Rom	11.20	believe, while you **remain** in place because you do believe.
1 Cor	7.11	if she does, she must **remain** single or else be reconciled to
	7.20	Everyone should **remain** as he was when he accepted God's call.
	7.24	My brothers, each one should **remain** in fellowship with God
	10.13	not allow you to be tested beyond your power to **remain** firm;
	13.13	Meanwhile these three **remain:**
Phil	1.24	for your sake it is much more important that I **remain** alive.
Col	1.24	to complete what still **remains** of Christ's sufferings on behalf
2 Tim	1.13	for you to follow, and **remain** in the faith and love that
	2.13	we are not faithful, he **remains** faithful, because he cannot be
Heb	1.11	They will disappear, but you will **remain;**
	4. 9	it is, however, there still **remains** for God's people a rest
	7. 3	he **remains** a priest for ever.
	12.27	so that the things that cannot be shaken will **remain.**
Jas	1.12	Happy is the person who **remains** faithful under trials,
1 Pet	1.25	fall, [25]but the word of the Lord **remains** for ever."
1 Jn	2. 6	whoever says that he **remains** in union with God should live
	2.27	As long as his Spirit **remains** in you, you do not need
	2.27	Obey the Spirit's teaching, then, and **remain** in union with Christ.
	2.28	Yes, my children, **remain** in union with him, so that when
2 Jn	2	love you, [2]because the truth **remains** in us and will be with

REMAINS

Ex	22.13	wild animals, the man is to bring the **remains** as evidence;
Num	16.37	the bronze firepans from the **remains** of the men who have
2 Kgs	9.37	Her **remains** will be scattered there like dung, so that

REMEDY

Jer	30.13	take care of you, no **remedy** for your sores, no hope of
Nah	3.19	There is no **remedy** for your injuries, and your wounds

REMEMBER

Gen	9.15	the rainbow appears, [15]I will **remember** my promise to you
	9.16	I will see it and **remember** the everlasting covenant between
	28.15	**Remember,** I will be with you and protect you wherever you go,
	30.22	Then God **remembered** Rachel;
	31.50	I don't know about it, **remember** that God is watching us.
	32.12	**Remember** that you promised to make everything go well
	40.14	But please **remember** me when everything is going well for you,
	42. 9	He **remembered** the dreams he had dreamt about them and said,
Ex	2.24	heard their groaning and **remembered** his covenant with Abraham,
	6. 5	Egyptians have enslaved, and I have **remembered** my covenant.
	13. 3	Moses said to the people, **"Remember** this day—the day on
	16.29	**Remember** that I, the Lord, have given you a day of rest,
	17.14	"Write an account of this victory, so that it will be **remembered.**
	22.21	**remember** that you were foreigners in Egypt.
	28.12	so that I, the Lord, will always **remember** my people.
	28.29	Israel, so that I, the Lord, will always **remember** my people.
	30.16	for their lives, and I will **remember** to protect them."
	32.13	**Remember** your servants Abraham, Isaac, and Jacob.
	32.13	**Remember** the solemn promise you made to them to give them as
	32.34	**Remember** that my angel will guide you, but the time is
	33.13	**Remember** also that you have chosen this nation to be your own."
Lev	19.34	**Remember** that you were once foreigners in the land of Egypt.
	23. 3	to do your work, but **remember** that the seventh day, the
	26.42	sin and rebellion, [42]I will **remember** my covenant with

Book	Ref	Context
Num	11. 5	**Remember** the cucumbers, the water-melons, the leeks, the
Num	15.39	see them you will **remember** all my commands and obey them;
Num	18. 8	The Lord said to Aaron, **“Remember** that I am giving you
Num	31.16	**Remember** that it was the women who followed Balaam's
Num	36. 3	But **remember,** if they marry men of another tribe, their
Deut	2. 7	**“Remember** how the Lord your God has blessed you in
Deut	4.39	So **remember** today and never forget:
Deut	5.15	**Remember** that you were slaves in Egypt, and that I, the
Deut	6. 4	“Israel, **remember** this!
Deut	7. 9	**Remember** that the Lord your God is the only God and that
Deut	7.18	**remember** what the Lord your God did to the king of Egypt
Deut	7.19	**Remember** the terrible plagues that you saw with your own eyes,
Deut	8. 2	**Remember** how the Lord your God led you on this long
Deut	8. 5	**Remember** that the Lord your God corrects and punishes you
Deut	8.18	**Remember** that it is the Lord your God who gives you the
Deut	9.14	destroy them so that no one will **remember** them any longer.
Deut	9.27	**Remember** your servants, Abraham, Isaac, and Jacob, and
Deut	11. 2	**Remember** today what you have learned about the Lord
Deut	11.18	**“Remember** these commands and cherish them.
Deut	12.12	**remember** that the Levites will have no land of their own.
Deut	15.15	**Remember** that you were slaves in Egypt and the Lord your
Deut	16. 3	as you live you will **remember** the day you came out of
Deut	24. 9	**Remember** what the Lord your God did to Miriam as you were
Deut	24.18	**Remember** that you were slaves in Egypt and that the Lord
Deut	25.17	**“Remember** what the Amalekites did to you as you were
Deut	25.19	Amalekites, so that no one will **remember** them any longer.
Deut	29.16	“You **remember** what life was like in Egypt and what it
Deut	30. 1	God has scattered you, you will **remember** the choice I gave you.
Deut	32.26	them completely, so that no one would **remember** them.
Deut	32.34	“The Lord **remembers** what their enemies have done;
Josh	1. 9	**Remember** that I have commanded you to be determined and confident!
Josh	1.13	of Manasseh, [13]**“Remember** how Moses, the Lord's servant,
Josh	22.17	**Remember** our sin at Peor, when the Lord punished his own
Josh	22.20	**Remember** how Achan son of Zerah refused to obey the
Judg	8.15	of Sukkoth and said, **“Remember** when you refused to help me?
Judg	9. 2	**Remember** that Abimelech is your own flesh and blood.”
Judg	9.17	**Remember** that my father fought for you.
Judg	16.28	Then Samson prayed, “Sovereign Lord, please **remember** me;
Ruth	3. 2	**Remember** that this man Boaz, whose women you have been working
1 Sam	1.11	See my trouble and **remember** me!
1 Sam	1.26	Do you **remember** me?
1 Sam	12.24	**Remember** the great things he has done for you.
2 Sam	3.18	**Remember** that the Lord has said, ‘I will use my servant
2 Sam	11.21	Don't you **remember** how Abimelech son of Gideon was killed?
1 Kgs	2. 5	You **remember** what Joab did to me by killing the two
1 Kgs	2. 5	You **remember** how he murdered them in time of peace in
1 Kgs	8.59	May the Lord our God **remember** at all times this prayer
1 Kgs	18.12	**Remember** that I have been a devout worshipper of the Lord
2 Kgs	9.25	**Remember** that when you and I were riding together behind
2 Kgs	20. 3	**“Remember,** Lord, that I have served you faithfully and loyally,
1 Chr	16.12	of Israel, whom God chose, **remember** the miracles that God
2 Chr	6.42	**Remember** the love you had for your servant David.”
Neh	1. 8	**Remember** now what you told Moses:
Neh	4.14	**Remember** how great and terrifying the Lord is, and fight for
Neh	5.19	I pray you, O God, **remember** to my credit everything that
Neh	6.14	I prayed, “God, **remember** what Tobiah and Sanballat have
Neh	6.14	**Remember** that woman Nodiah and all the other prophets who
Neh	9.32	**Remember** how much we have suffered!
Neh	13.14	**Remember,** my God, all these things that I have done for
Neh	13.22	**Remember** me, O God, for this also, and spare me because of
Neh	13.29	**Remember,** O God, how those people defiled both the
Neh	13.31	**Remember** all this, O God, and give me credit for it.
Esth	9.28	province and every city should **remember** and observe the days
Job	3. 4	Never again **remember** that day;
Job	7. 7	**Remember,** O God, my life is only a breath;
Job	10. 9	**Remember** that you made me from clay;
Job	11.16	memory, like floods that are past and **remembered** no more.
Job	14.13	your anger is over, and then set a time to **remember** me.
Job	18.17	no one **remembers** him any more.
Job	19.23	I wish that someone would **remember** my words and record them
Job	24.20	Not even his mother **remembers** him now;
Job	36.22	**Remember** how great is God's power;
Ps	4. 3	**Remember** that the Lord has chosen the righteous for his own,
Ps	6. 5	In the world of the dead you are not **remembered;**
Ps	9. 5	they will be **remembered** no more.
Ps	9.12	God **remembers** those who suffer;
Ps	10.12	**Remember** those who are suffering!
Ps	22.27	All nations will **remember** the Lord.
Ps	25. 6	**Remember,** O Lord, your kindness and constant love which
Ps	25. 7	In your constant love and goodness, **remember** me, Lord!
Ps	30. 4	**Remember** what the Holy One has done, and give him thanks!
Ps	42. 4	My heart breaks when I **remember** the past, when I went with
Ps	63. 6	As I lie in bed, I **remember** you;
Ps	74. 2	**Remember** your people, whom you chose for yourself long ago,
Ps	74. 2	**Remember** Mount Zion, where once you lived.
Ps	74.18	But **remember,** O Lord, that your enemies laugh at you,
Ps	74.20	**Remember** the covenant you made with us.
Ps	74.22	**Remember** that godless people laugh at you all day long.
Ps	77. 5	I think of days gone by and **remember** years of long ago.
Ps	77.11	I will **remember** your great deeds, Lord;
Ps	78.35	They **remembered** that God was their protector, that the
Ps	78.39	He **remembered** that they were only mortal beings, like a
Ps	89.47	**Remember** how short my life is;
Ps	89.47	**remember** that you created all of us mortal!
Ps	97.12	**Remember** what the holy God has done, and give thanks to him.
Ps	102.12	all generations will **remember** you.
Ps	103.14	he **remembers** that we are dust.
Ps	105. 5	**remember** the miracles that God performed and the judgements
Ps	105.42	He **remembered** his sacred promise to Abraham his servant.
Ps	106. 4	**Remember** me, Lord, when you help your people;
Ps	106.31	This has been **remembered** in his favour ever since and
Ps	106.45	For their sake he **remembered** his covenant, and because
Ps	109.14	May the Lord **remember** the evil of his ancestors and
Ps	109.15	May the Lord always **remember** their sins, but may they
Ps	112. 6	he will always be **remembered.**
Ps	115.12	The Lord **remembers** us and will bless us;
Ps	119.49	**Remember** your promise to me, your servant;
Ps	119.52	I **remember** your judgements of long ago, and they bring me
Ps	119.55	In the night I **remember** you, Lord, and I think about
Ps	132. 2	**Remember,** Lord, what he promised, the vow he made to you,
Ps	135.13	all generations will **remember** you.
Ps	137. 1	there we wept when we **remembered** Zion.
Ps	137. 6	again if I do not **remember** you, if I do not think
Ps	137. 7	**Remember,** Lord, what the Edomites did the day Jerusalem was
Ps	137. 7	**Remember** how they kept saying, “Tear it down to the ground!”
Ps	143. 5	I **remember** the days gone by;
Prov	3. 1	Always **remember** what I tell you to do.
Prov	3. 6	**Remember** the Lord in everything you do, and he will show
Prov	4. 2	What I am teaching you is good, so **remember** it all.
Prov	4. 4	He would say, **“Remember** what I say and never forget it.
Prov	4.13	Always **remember** what you have learnt.
Prov	4.21	**Remember** them and keep them in your heart.
Prov	7. 1	**Remember** what I say, my son, and never forget what I tell
Prov	10. 7	Good people will be **remembered** as a blessing, but the
Prov	17. 9	**Remembering** wrongs can break up a friendship.
Prov	19. 8	then **remember** what you learn and you will prosper.
Prov	21. 2	is right, but **remember** that the Lord judges your motives.
Prov	22. 6	how he should live, and he will **remember** it all his life.
Prov	22.18	you will be glad if you **remember** them and can quote them.
Prov	23.35	“I must have been beaten up, but I don't **remember** it.
Ecc	1.11	No one **remembers** what has happened in the past, and no
Ecc	1.11	to come will **remember** what happens between now and then.
Ecc	2.16	No one **remembers** wise men, and no one remembers fools.
Ecc	7.14	for you, be glad, and when trouble comes, just **remember:**
Ecc	11. 8	matter how long you live, **remember** that you will be dead
Ecc	11. 9	But **remember** that God is going to judge you for whatever you
Ecc	12. 1	So **remember** your Creator while you are still young, before
Is	8.13	**Remember** that I, the Lord Almighty, am holy;
Is	16. 7	will all weep when they **remember** the fine food they used to
Is	26.14	No one **remembers** them any more.
Is	38. 3	**“Remember,** Lord, that I have served you faithfully and loyally,
Is	44.21	“Israel, **remember** this;
Is	44.21	**remember** that you are my servant.
Is	46. 8	**“Remember** this, you sinners;
Is	46. 9	**Remember** what happened long ago;
Is	56. 5	then your name will be **remembered** in my Temple and among
Is	63.11	But then they **remembered** the past, the days of Moses,
Is	64. 5	what is right, those who **remember** how you want them to live.
Jer	2. 2	“I **remember** how faithful you were when you were young, how
Jer	3.16	They will no longer think about it or **remember** it;
Jer	11.19	let's kill him so that no one will **remember** him any more.”
Jer	14.10	I will **remember** the wrongs they have done and punish them
Jer	14.21	**Remember** your promises and do not despise us;
Jer	15.15	**Remember** me and help me.
Jer	15.15	**Remember** that it is for your sake that I am insulted.
Jer	18.20	**Remember** how I came to you and spoke on their behalf, so
Jer	31.34	their sins and I will no longer **remember** their wrongs.
Jer	42.22	So then, **remember** this:
Jer	48.27	Moab, **remember** how you jeered at the people of Israel?
Jer	51.50	home, think about me, your Lord, and **remember** Jerusalem.
Lam	3.21	Yet hope returns when I **remember** this one thing:
Lam	5. 1	**Remember,** O Lord, what has happened to us.
Lam	5.20	Will you ever **remember** us again?
Ezek	2. 7	**Remember** what rebels they are.
Ezek	3.10	pay close attention and **remember** everything I tell you.
Ezek	3.20	his sins—I will not **remember** the good he did—and I
Ezek	6. 9	There they will **remember** me and know that I have punished
Ezek	16.22	never once **remembered** your childhood—when you were naked,
Ezek	16.61	You will **remember** how you have acted, and be ashamed of
Ezek	16.63	have done, but you will **remember** them and be too ashamed to
Ezek	18.24	None of the good he did will be **remembered.**
Ezek	20.43	Then you will **remember** all the disgraceful things you
Ezek	21.32	your own country, and no one will **remember** you any more.’ ”
Ezek	33.13	to sin, I will not **remember** any of the good he did.
Ezek	36.31	You will **remember** your evil conduct and the wrongs that you
Dan	9.15	people out of Egypt, and your power is still **remembered.**
Hos	7. 2	It never enters their heads that I will **remember** all this evil;
Hos	8.13	them, and now I will **remember** their sin and punish them for
Hos	9. 9	God will **remember** their sin and punish them for it.
Mic	6. 5	My people, **remember** what King Balak of Moab planned to do
Mic	6. 5	**Remember** the things that happened on the way from the camp
Mic	6. 5	**Remember** these things and you will realize what I did in
Zeph	1. 4	no one will even **remember** the pagan priests who serve him.
Hag	2. 3	among you who can still **remember** how splendid the Temple
Zech	10. 7	Their descendants will **remember** this victory and be glad
Zech	10. 9	the nations, yet in far-off places they will **remember** me.
Zech	13. 2	idols from the land, and no one will **remember** them any more.
Mal	4. 4	**“Remember** the teachings of my servant Moses, the laws and
Mt	5.18	**Remember** that as long as heaven and earth last, not the
Mt	5.23	and there you **remember** that your brother has something against
Mt	16. 9	Don't you **remember** when I broke the five loaves for the five
Mt	24.34	**Remember** that all these things will happen before the people
Mt	26.75	a cock crowed, [75]and Peter **remembered** what Jesus had told him:
Mt	27.63	and said, “Sir, we **remember** that while that liar was still
Mt	28. 7	**Remember** what I have told you.”
Mk	8.18	Don't you **remember** [19]when I broke the five loaves for the
Mk	11.21	Peter **remembered** what had happened and said to Jesus,
Mk	13.30	**Remember** that all these things will happen before the people
Mk	14.72	second time, and Peter **remembered** how Jesus had said to him,
Lk	1.36	**Remember** your relative Elizabeth.

Lk	1.48	God my Saviour, [48] for he has **remembered** me, his lowly servant!
	1.55	He has **remembered** to show mercy to Abraham and to all
	1.72	show mercy to our ancestors and **remember** his sacred covenant.
	2.19	Mary **remembered** all these things and thought deeply about them.
	10.11	But **remember** that the Kingdom of God has come near you!'
	16.25	"But Abraham said, '**Remember,** my son, that in your lifetime
	17.32	**Remember** Lot's wife!
	18.17	**Remember** this!
	21.32	"**Remember** that all these things will take place before the
	22.61	straight at Peter, and Peter **remembered** that the Lord had said
	23.42	And he said to Jesus, "**Remember** me, Jesus, when you come
	24. 6	**Remember** what he said to you while he was in Galilee:
	24. 8	Then the women **remembered** his words, [9] returned from the tomb,
Jn	2.17	**remembered** that the scripture says, "My devotion to
	2.22	raised from death, his disciples **remembered** that he had said this,
	3.26	John and said, "Teacher, you **remember** the man who was with
	4.53	Then the father **remembered** that it was at that very hour
	12.16	been raised to glory, they **remembered** that the scripture said
	14.26	everything and make you **remember** all that I have told you.
	15.18	world hates you, just **remember** that it has hated me first.
	15.20	**Remember** what I told you:
	16. 4	them to do these things, you will **remember** that I told you.
	19.10	**Remember,** I have the authority to set you free and also to
Acts	5.36	You **remember** that Theudas appeared some time ago, claiming
	7.60	Do not **remember** this sin against them!"
	11.16	Then I **remembered** what the Lord had said:
	20.31	Watch, then, and **remember** that with many tears, day and night,
	20.35	we must help the weak, **remembering** the words that the Lord
Rom	1. 9	God knows that I **remember** you [10] every time I pray.
	1.13	You must **remember,** my brothers, that many times I have planned
1 Cor	1.16	but I can't **remember** whether I baptized anyone else.)
	1.26	Now **remember** what you were, my brothers, when God called you.
	10. 1	want you to **remember,** my brothers, what happened to our ancestors
	11. 2	because you always **remember** me and follow the teachings that
2 Cor	7.15	you grows stronger, as he **remembers** how all of you were
	9. 6	**Remember** that the person who sows few seeds will have a
Gal	2.10	asked was that we should **remember** the needy in their group,
	4.13	You **remember** why I preached the gospel to you the first time;
Eph	1.16	I **remember** you in my prayers [17] and ask the God of our
	2.11	men do to their bodies)—**remember** what you were in the past.
	6. 8	**Remember** that the Lord will reward everyone, whether slave or free,
	6. 9	**Remember** that you and your slaves belong to the same Master
Col	3.24	**Remember** that the Lord will give you as a reward what he
	4. 1	**Remember** that you too have a Master in heaven.
1 Thes	1. 3	For we **remember** before our God and Father how you put your
	2. 9	Surely you **remember,** our brothers, how we worked and toiled!
2 Thes	2. 5	Don't you **remember?**
1 Tim	1. 9	It must be **remembered,** of course, that laws are made, not
2 Tim	1. 3	I thank him as I **remember** you always in my prayers
	1. 4	I **remember** your tears, and I want to see you very much,
	1. 5	I **remember** the sincere faith you have, the kind of faith
	2. 8	**Remember** Jesus Christ, who was raised from death,
	3. 1	**Remember** that there will be difficult times in the last days.
	3.15	your teachers were, [15] and you **remember** that ever since you were
Tit	1. 5	**Remember** my instructions:
Heb	8.12	forgive their sins and will no longer **remember** their wrongs."
	10.17	he says, "I will not **remember** their sins and evil deeds
	10.32	**Remember** how it was with you in the past.
	13. 2	**Remember** to welcome strangers in your homes.
	13. 3	**Remember** those who are in prison, as though you were in
	13. 3	**Remember** those who are suffering, as though you were suffering as
	13. 7	**Remember** your former leaders, who spoke God's message to you.
Jas	1.19	**Remember** this, my dear brothers!
	5.10	My brothers, **remember** the prophets who spoke in the name of
	5.20	and another one brings him back again, [20] **remember** this:
2 Pet	1.15	a way for you to **remember** these matters at all times after
	1.20	Above all else, however, **remember** that no one can explain by
	3. 2	I want you to **remember** the words that were spoken long ago
Jude	6	**Remember** the angels who did not stay within the limits of
	7	**Remember** Sodom and Gomorrah, and the nearby towns, whose people
	17	But **remember,** my friends, what you were told in the past
Rev	3. 3	**Remember,** then, what you were taught and what you heard;
	16.19	God **remembered** great Babylon and made her drink the wine
	18. 5	up as high as heaven, and God **remembers** her wicked ways.

REMIND

Gen	31.44	us make a pile of stones to **remind** us of our agreement."
	31.48	"This pile of rocks will be a **reminder** for both of us."
	31.52	Both this pile and this memorial stone are **reminders.**
Ex	12.14	as a religious festival to **remind** you of what I, the Lord,
	13. 9	This observance will be a **reminder,** like something tied on
	13. 9	it will **remind** you to continue to recite and study the Law
	13.16	This observance will be a **reminder,** like something tied
	13.16	it will **remind** us that the Lord brought us out of Egypt
Num	15.39	The tassels will serve as **reminders,** and each time you
	15.40	The tassels will **remind** you to keep all my commands, and
Deut	6. 8	on your arms and wear them on your foreheads as a **reminder.**
	11.18	on your arms and wear them on your foreheads as a **reminder.**
Josh	4. 6	These stones will **remind** the people of what the Lord has done.
	4. 7	These stones will always **remind** the people of Israel of what
1 Sam	12. 7	you before the Lord by **reminding** you of all the mighty
1 Kgs	17.18	Did you come here to **remind** God of my sins and so
Job	33.23	of God's thousands of angels, who **remind** men of their duty.
Ps	143. 8	**Remind** me each morning of your constant love, for I put my
Prov	25.26	to someone who is evil **reminds** you of a polluted spring or
	26. 9	fool quoting a wise saying **reminds** you of a drunk man trying
Ecc	7. 2	because the living should always **remind** themselves that
Is	19.17	Judah every time they are **reminded** of the fate that the Lord
	55.13	will last for ever, a **reminder** of what I, the Lord, have
	62. 6	They must **remind** the Lord of his promises And never let him
Ezek	20. 4	**Remind** them of the disgusting things their fathers did.
	20.12	the agreement between us, to **remind** them that I, the Lord,
	20.20	covenant we made, and will **remind** you that I am the Lord
	21.23	But this prediction is to **remind** them of their sins and to
	29.16	Egypt's fate will **remind** Israel how wrong it was to rely on
Rom	15.15	quite bold about certain subjects of which I have **reminded** you.
1 Cor	4.17	He will **remind** you of the principles which I follow in the
	15. 1	And now I want to **remind** you, my brothers, of the Good
2 Cor	1. 8	We want to **remind** you, brothers, of the trouble we had in
2 Tim	1. 6	For this reason I **remind** you to keep alive the gift that
	2.14	**Remind** your people of this, and give them a solemn warning
Tit	3. 1	**Remind** your people to submit to rulers and authorities,
Phlm	19	(I should not have to **remind** you, of course, that you owe
Heb	10. 3	sacrifices serve year after year to **remind** people of their sins.
2 Pet	1.12	And so I will always **remind** you of these matters, even
	3. 1	arouse pure thoughts in your minds by **reminding** you of these
Jude	5	all this, I want to **remind** you of how the Lord once

AV **REMISSION** see **FORGIVE**

REMORSE

1 Sam	25.31	have to feel regret or **remorse,** sir, for having killed

REMOVE

Gen	8.13	Noah **removed** the covering of the boat, looked round, and saw
	30.35	But that day Laban **removed** the male goats that had
	30.35	he also **removed** all the black sheep.
	41.42	The king **removed** from his finger the ring engraved with
Ex	32.32	but if you won't, then **remove** my name from the book in
	32.33	sinned against me whose names I will **remove** from my book.
Lev	1.16	He shall **remove** the crop and its contents and throw them
	4.31	Then he shall **remove** all its fat,
	4.31	just as the fat is **removed** from the animals killed
	4.35	Then he shall **remove** all its fat,
	4.35	just as the fat is **removed** from the sheep killed
	6.10	robe and linen shorts, shall **remove** the greasy ashes left on
	7. 3	All its fat shall be **removed** and offered on the altar:
	14.40	mildew is found to be **removed** and thrown into some unclean
	14.42	replace the stones that were **removed,** and new plaster will
	14.43	after the stones have been **removed** and the house has been
	14.48	clean, because the mildew has been completely **removed.**
	16.24	and offer the burnt-offering to **remove** his own sins and
	19.22	the ritual of purification to **remove** the man's sin, and God
Num	4.13	They shall **remove** the greasy ashes from the altar and
	16.37	Aaron the priest to **remove** the bronze firepans from the remains
	19. 9	to use in preparing the water for **removing** ritual uncleanness.
	19. 9	This ritual is performed to **remove** sin.
	19.17	To **remove** the uncleanness, some ashes from the red cow
	19.17	which was burnt to **remove** sin shall be taken
	20.26	up Mount Hor, [26] and there **remove** Aaron's priestly robes
	20.28	the whole community, [28] and Moses **removed** Aaron's priestly
Deut	17.12	in this way you will **remove** this evil from Israel.
Josh	5. 9	to Joshua, "Today I have **removed** from you the disgrace of
	8.29	for the body to be **removed,** and it was thrown down at
Judg	20.13	so that we can kill them and **remove** this evil from Israel."
1 Sam	3.14	be able to **remove** the consequences of this terrible sin."
	21. 6	to God, which had been **removed** from the sacred table and
2 Sam	7.15	did from Saul, whom I **removed** so that you could be king.
	14.16	son and me and so **remove** us from the land God gave
	20.13	After the body had been **removed** from the road, everyone
1 Kgs	9. 7	other gods, [7] then I will **remove** my people Israel from the
	15.12	places of worship, and he **removed** all the idols his
	15.13	**removed** his grandmother Maacah from her position as queen mother,
	20.24	Now, **remove** the thirty-two rulers from their commands
2 Kgs	16.17	used in the Temple and **removed** the basins that were on them;
	16.18	the Assyrian emperor, Ahaz also **removed** from the Temple the
	23. 5	He **removed** from office the priests that the kings of Judah
	23. 6	He **removed** from the Temple the symbol of the goddess Asherah,
	23.11	He also **removed** the horses that the kings of Judah had
	23.24	in the Temple, King Josiah **removed** from Jerusalem and the
1 Chr	17.13	did from Saul, whom I **removed** so that you could be king.
2 Chr	7.20	other gods, [20] then I will **remove** you from the land that I
	14. 3	He **removed** the foreign altars and the pagan places of worship,
	15.16	King Asa **removed** his grandmother Maacah from her position
	19. 3	You have **removed** all the symbols of the goddess Asherah
	29. 5	**Remove** from the Temple everything that defiles it.
	33.15	He **removed** from the Temple the foreign gods and the
Job	34.24	to **remove** leaders and replace them with others.
Ps	51. 7	**Remove** my sin, and I will be clean;
	52. 5	he will **remove** you from the world of the living.
	103.12	from the west, so far does he **remove** our sins from us.
Is	1.25	just as metal is refined, and will **remove** all your impurity.
	22.19	The Lord will **remove** you from office and bring you down
	25. 7	Here he will suddenly **remove** the cloud of sorrow that has
	49.19	those who left you in ruins will be far **removed** from you.
	57.14	**Remove** every obstacle from their path!
	58. 6	**Remove** the chains of oppression and the yoke of injustice,
Jer	4. 1	are faithful to me and **remove** the idols I hate, [2] it will

Jer 13.23 the colour of his skin, or a leopard **remove** its spots?
30. 8 is round their necks and **remove** their chains, and they will
Ezek 14. 8 I will **remove** him from the community of my people, so that
14. 9 I will **remove** him from the people of Israel.
43. 9 other gods and **remove** the corpses of their kings.
Dan 5.20 stubborn, and cruel, he was **removed** from his royal throne
Hos 2.18 I will also **remove** all weapons of war from the land, all
8.11 people of Israel build for **removing** sin, the more places
Joel 2.20 I will **remove** the locust army that came from the north
Amos 1. 5 city gates of Damascus and **remove** the inhabitants of the
1. 8 I will **remove** the rulers of the cities of Ashdod and Ashkelon.
9. 9 them among the nations to **remove** all who are worthless.
Zeph 3.11 I will **remove** everyone who is proud and arrogant, and you
3.15 he has **removed** all your enemies.
Zech 5. 3 it says that every thief will be **removed** from the land;
9.10 "I will **remove** the war-chariots from Israel and take the
13. 2 At that time I will **remove** the names of the idols from
Mal 2.12 May the Lord **remove** from the community of Israel those
Mk 7.35 his speech impediment was **removed,** and he began to talk without
Acts 13.22 After **removing** him, God made David their king.
Rom 11.26 come from Zion and **remove** all wickedness from the descendants
1 Cor 5. 7 You must **remove** the old yeast of sin so that you will
5.12 As the scripture says, **"Remove** the evil man from your group."
7.18 God's call, he should not try to **remove** the marks of circumcision;
2 Cor 3.14 The veil is **removed** only when a person is joined to Christ.
3.16 But it can be **removed,** as the scripture says about Moses:
3.16 "His veil was **removed** when he turned to the Lord."
Heb 9.26 and for all, to **remove** sin through the sacrifice of himself.
12.27 things will be shaken and **removed,** so that the things that
Rev 3. 5 and I will not **remove** their names from the book

RENAMED see NAME (1)

AV RENDER

Deut 32.41 I will take **revenge** on my enemies and punish those who hate
32.43 He takes **revenge** on his enemies and forgives the sins of his
Judg 9.57 men of Shechem **suffer** for their wickedness, just as Jotham,
1 Sam 26.23 The Lord **rewards** those who are faithful and righteous.
2 Chr 6.30 **Deal** with each person as he deserves, [31] so that your
Job 33.26 God will set things **right** for him again.
34.11 He **rewards** people for what they do and treats them as
Ps 28. 4 **Punish** them for all their deeds;
38.20 Those who **pay** back evil for good are against me because
56.12 O God, I will **offer** you what I have promised;
79.12 Lord, **pay** the other nations back seven times for all the
94. 2 rise and **give** the proud what they deserve!
116.12 What can I **offer** the Lord for all his goodness to me?
Prov 24.12 And he will **reward** you according to what you do.
24.29 I'll get **even** with him!"
Is 66.15 the wings of a storm to **punish** those he is angry with.
Jer 51.24 says, "You will see me **repay** Babylonia and its people for
Hos 14. 2 our prayer, and we will **praise** you as we have promised.
Joel 3. 4 Are you trying to **pay** me back for something?
Zech 9.12 tell you now, I will **repay** you twice over with blessing for
Mt 21.41 to other tenants, who will **give** him his share of the harvest
22.21 said to them, "Well, then, **pay** the Emperor
Mk 12.17 So Jesus said, "Well, then, **pay** the Emperor
Lk 20.25 So Jesus said, "Well, then, **pay** the Emperor
Rom 2. 6 For God will **reward** every person according to what he has done.
13. 7 **Pay,** then, what you owe them;
1 Cor 7. 3 A man should **fulfil** his duty as a husband,
1 Thes 5.15 See that no one **pays** back wrong for wrong, but at all

RENEW

Lev 26.42 with Abraham, and I will **renew** my promise to give my people
26.45 I will **renew** the covenant that I made with their
Is 40.31 in the Lord for help will find their strength **renewed.**
Ezek 16.62 I will **renew** my covenant with you, and you will know
2 Cor 4.16 yet our spiritual being is **renewed** day after day.
Col 3.10 God, its Creator, is constantly **renewing** in his own image,

Am RENT see LET

RENT

Song 8.11 There are farmers who **rent** it from him;
Acts 28.30 lived in a place he **rented** for himself, and there he

REPAIR

1 Sam 13.21 for sharpening axes and for **repairing** ox-goads, and two
1 Kgs 11.27 on the east side of Jerusalem and **repairing** the city walls.
18.30 He set about **repairing** the altar of the Lord which had been
2 Kgs 12. 5 the money was to be used to **repair** the Temple, as needed.
12. 6 the priests still had not made any **repairs** to the Temple.
12. 7 and asked them, "Why aren't you **repairing** the Temple?
12. 7 you must hand it over, so that the **repairs** can be made."
12. 8 this and also agreed not to make the **repairs** in the Temple.
12.12 used in the **repairs,** and pay all other necessary expenses.
12.14 the workmen and to buy the materials used in the **repairs.**
22. 5 the men who are in charge of the **repairs** in the Temple.
22. 6 and buy the timber and the stones used in the **repairs.**
22. 9 have handed it over to the men in charge of the **repairs."**
2 Chr 15. 8 He also **repaired** the altar of the Lord that stood in the
24. 4 king for a while, Joash decided to have the Temple **repaired.**
24. 5 enough money to make the annual **repairs** on the Temple.
24.12 charge of **repairing** the Temple, and they hired stonemasons,
2 Chr 24.12 carpenters, and metalworkers to make the **repairs.**
24.14 When the **repairs** were finished, the remaining gold and
29. 3 he re-opened the gates of the Temple and had them **repaired.**
32. 5 defences by **repairing** the wall, building towers on it,
32. 5 In addition, he **repaired** the defences built on the land that
33.16 He also **repaired** the altar where the Lord was worshipped,
34. 8 Josiah sent three men to **repair** the Temple of the Lord God:
34.10 in charge of the temple **repairs,** and they gave it to [11] the
34.11 and the timber used to **repair** the buildings that the kings
Neh 3.13 for locking the gate, and **repaired** the wall for 440 metres,
Ecc 10.18 man is too lazy to **repair** his roof, it will leak, and
Is 22. 9 You found the places where the walls of Jerusalem needed **repair.**
22. 9 some of them down to get stones to **repair** the city walls.
Amos 9.11 I will **repair** its walls and restore it.

REPAY
see also **REPAYMENT-OFFERING**

Ex 22. 7 his house, the thief, if he is found, shall **repay** double.
22.11 shall accept the loss, and the other man need not **repay** him;
22.12 but if the animal was stolen, the man must **repay** the owner.
22.15 happens when the owner is present, the man need not **repay.**
Lev 6. 4 ways, he must **repay** whatever he got by dishonest means.
6. 4 is found guilty, he must **repay** the owner in full, plus an
22.14 without intending to, he must **repay** the priest its full
Num 5. 7 and make full **repayment,** plus an additional twenty per cent,
2 Chr 20.11 This is how they **repay** us—they come to drive us out
Neh 5.10 Now let's give up all our claims to **repayment.**
Job 22. 6 To make your brother **repay** you the money he owed, you took
31. 2 How does he **repay** human deeds?
Ps 103.10 us as we deserve or **repay** us according to our sins and
Prov 17.13 If you **repay** good with evil, you will never get evil out
20.22 Don't take it on yourself to **repay** a wrong.
Is 65. 6 they have done, but will **repay** them [7] for their sins and the
Jer 51.24 says, "You will see me **repay** Babylonia and its people for
Amos 2. 6 debts, poor men who cannot **repay** even the price of a pair
Zech 9.12 tell you now, I will **repay** you twice over with blessing for
Lk 14.14 God will **repay** you on the day the good people rise from
Rom 12.17 someone has done you wrong, do not **repay** him with a wrong.
Col 3.25 every wrongdoer will be **repaid** for the wrong things he does,
1 Tim 5. 4 family and in this way **repay** their parents and grandparents,
Heb 10.30 For we know who said, "I will take revenge, I will **repay";**
Rev 2.23 I will **repay** each one of you according to what he has

REPAYMENT-OFFERING

Lev 5.15 he shall bring as his **repayment-offering** to the Lord a male
5.18 to the priest as a **repayment-offering** a male sheep or goat
5.19 **repayment-offering** for the sin he committed against the Lord.
6. 6 to the priest as his **repayment-offering** to the Lord a male
6.16 very holy, like the sin-offerings and the **repayment-offerings.**
7. 1 the regulations for **repayment-offerings,** which are very holy.
7. 5 It is a **repayment-offering.**
7. 7 applies to both the sin-offering and the **repayment-offering:**
7.37 the grain-offerings, the sin-offerings, the **repayment-offerings,**
14.12 of a litre of oil he shall offer it as a **repayment-offering.**
14.13 this because the **repayment-offering,** like the sin-offering,
14.21 one male lamb as his **repayment-offering,** a special gift to
19.21 of my presence as his **repayment-offering,** [22] and with it
Num 6.12 As a **repayment offering** he shall bring a one-year-old lamb.
18. 9 the sin-offerings, and the **repayment offerings.**
2 Kgs 12.16 The money given for the **repayment offerings** and for the
Ezek 40.39 whole or to be sacrifices for sin or as **repayment-offerings.**
42.13 the sacrifices offered for sin or as **repayment-offerings.**
44.29 and the **repayment-offerings** will be the priests'
46.20 sacrifices for sin or as **repayment-offerings,** and to bake

REPEAT

Gen 41.32 The **repetition** of your dream means that the matter is
44. 6 When the servant caught up with them, he **repeated** these words.
Num 20.20 The Edomites **repeated,** "We refuse!"
Deut 6. 7 **Repeat** them when you are at home and when you are away,
32.46 **Repeat** them to your children, so that they may faithfully
Ezra 3.11 They sang the Lord's praises, **repeating** the refrain:
Ps 19. 2 each night **repeats** it to the next.
107. 2 **Repeat** these words in praise to the Lord, all you whom he
119.13 I will **repeat** aloud all the laws you have given.
Ezek 12.22 he said, "why do the people of Israel **repeat** this proverb:
12.23 It won't be **repeated** in Israel any more.
18. 2 "What is this proverb people keep **repeating** in the land of Israel?
18. 3 "you will not **repeat** this proverb in Israel any more.
23.21 (Oholibah, you wanted to **repeat** the immorality you were
33.10 he said, **"repeat** to the Israelites what they are saying:
Mt 10.27 in the dark you must **repeat** in broad daylight, and what you
19.24 I **repeat:**
Mk 14.69 him there and began to **repeat** to the bystanders, "He is one
2 Cor 11.16 I **repeat:**
12. 3 I **repeat,** I know that this man was snatched to Paradise
Phil 3. 1 I don't mind **repeating** what I have written before, and you
3.18 you this many times before, and now I **repeat** it with tears:

REPENT

1 Kgs 8.35 you, and then when they **repent** and face this Temple, humbly
8.47 there in that land they **repent** and pray to you, confessing
8.48 land they truly and sincerely **repent,** and pray to you as
2 Kgs 22.19 book, [19] and you **repented** and humbled yourself before me,
2 Chr 6.26 you and then when they **repent** and face this Temple, humbly
6.37 there in that land they **repent** and pray to you, confessing
6.38 land they truly and sincerely **repent** and pray to you as they

2 Chr 7.14 they pray to me and **repent** and turn away from the evil
33.19 sins he committed before he **repented**—the evil he did, the
34.27 book, [27]and you **repented** and humbled yourself before me,
36.13 He stubbornly refused to **repent** and return to the Lord, the
Neh 9.28 Yet when they **repented** and asked you to save them, in heaven
Job 42. 6 ashamed of all I have said and **repent** in dust and ashes.
Ps 51.17 you will not reject a humble and **repentant** heart.
78.34 they would **repent** and pray earnestly to him.
Is 1.27 he will save Jerusalem and everyone there who **repents.**
9.13 The people of Israel have not **repented;**
57.15 people who are humble and **repentant,** so that I can restore
66. 2 who are humble and **repentant,** who fear me and obey me.
Lam 2.14 They made you think you did not need to **repent.**
Ezek 18.23 "No, I would rather see him **repent** and live.
21.13 and if they refuse to **repent,** all these things will happen
Joel 2.12 even now," says the Lord, **"repent** sincerely and return to
Jon 3. 5 the least, put on sackcloth to show that they had **repented.**
Hag 2.17 everything you tried to grow, but still you did not **repent.**
Zech 1. 6 Then they **repented** and acknowledged that I, the Lord Almighty,
Mt 3.11 to show that you have **repented,** but the one who will come
27. 3 had been condemned, he **repented** and took back the thirty silver
Lk 5.32 have not come to call respectable people to **repent,** but outcasts."
15. 7 heaven over one sinner who **repents** than over
15. 7 ninety-nine respectable people who do not need to **repent.**
15.10 the angels of God rejoice over one sinner who **repents."**
17. 3 your brother sins, rebuke him, and if he **repents,** forgive him.
17. 4 he comes to you saying, 'I **repent,'** you must forgive him."
24.47 his name the message about **repentance** and the forgiveness of sins
Acts 3.19 **Repent,** then, and turn to God, so that he will forgive
5.31 of Israel the opportunity to **repent** and have their sins forgiven.
8.22 **Repent,** then, of this evil plan of yours, and pray to
11.18 given to the Gentiles also the opportunity to **repent** and live!"
26.20 I preached that they must **repent** of their sins and turn to
26.20 to God and do the things that would show they had **repented.**
Rom 2. 4 God is kind, because he is trying to lead you to **repent.**
2 Cor 12.21 the past and have not **repented** of the immoral things they
2 Tim 2.25 them the opportunity to **repent** and come to know the truth.
Heb 6. 4 who abandon their faith be brought back to **repent** again?
6. 6 to bring them back to **repent** again, because they are again
Rev 2.21 have given her time to **repent** of her sins, but she does
2.22 do this now unless they **repent** of the wicked things they did
9.21 Nor did they **repent** of their murders, their magic,

AV REPENT

see also **CHANGE (mind), TURN (from)**

Gen 6. 6 all the time, [6]he was **sorry** that he had ever made them
6. 7 the birds, because I am **sorry** that I made any of them."
Deut 32.36 He will have **mercy** on those who serve him, when he sees
Judg 2.18 The Lord would have **mercy** on them because they groaned under
21. 6 The people of Israel felt **sorry** for their brothers the
21.15 The people felt **sorry** for the Benjaminites because the
1 Sam 15.11 Lord said to Samuel, [11]"I am **sorry** that I made Saul king;
15.35 The Lord was **sorry** that he had made Saul king of Israel.
Ps 90.13 Have **pity,** O Lord, on your servants!
106.45 his covenant, and because of his great love he **relented.**
110. 4 The Lord made a solemn promise and will not **take** it back:
135.14 he will take **pity** on his servants.
Jer 8. 6 Not one of you has been **sorry** for his wickedness;
20.16 May he be like those cities that the Lord destroyed without **mercy.**
31.19 We turned away from you, but soon we wanted to **return.**
42.10 The destruction I brought on you has caused me great **sorrow.**
Ezek 24.14 I will not ignore your sins or show pity or be **merciful.**
2 Cor 7. 8 of mine made you sad, I am not **sorry** I wrote it.
7. 8 I could have been **sorry** when I saw that it made you
Heb 7.21 Lord has made a solemn promise and will not **take** it back:

AV REPENTANCE

Hos 13.14 I will no longer have **pity** for this people.
2 Cor 7. 9 you sad, but because your sadness made you **change** your ways.
7.10 used by God brings a **change** of heart that leads to salvation
7.10 that leads to salvation—and there is no **regret** in that!
Heb 12.17 not find any way to **change** what he had done, even though

REPHAIM (1)

Inhabitants of Canaan before its conquest by Israel.

Gen 14. 5 their armies and defeated the **Rephaim** in Ashteroth Karnaim,
15.20 the Hittites, the Perizzites, the **Rephaim,**
Deut 2.11 Like the Anakim they were also known as **Rephaim;**
2.20 as the land of the **Rephaim,** the name of the people who
3.11 (King Og was the last of the **Rephaim.**
3.13 (Bashan was known as the land of the **Rephaim.**
Josh 12. 4 Og of Bashan, who was one of the last of the **Rephaim;**
13.12 Og, the last of the **Rephaim,** who had ruled at Ashtaroth
17.15 yourselves in the land of the Perizzites and the **Rephaim."**

REPLACE

Gen 4.25 "God has given me a son to **replace** Abel, whom Cain killed."
Lev 14.42 are to be used to **replace** the stones that were removed, and
24.18 kills an animal belonging to someone else must **replace** it.
24.21 Whoever kills an animal shall **replace** it, but whoever
1 Sam 21. 6 removed from the sacred table and **replaced** by fresh bread.
1 Kgs 14.27 To **replace** them, King Rehoboam made bronze shields and
20.24 from their commands and **replace** them with field commanders.
2 Chr 12.10 To **replace** them, Rehoboam made bronze shields and
Job 34.24 to remove leaders and **replace** them with others.
Is 9.10 fallen down, but we will **replace** them with stone buildings.
Is 9.10 cut down, but we will **replace** them with the finest cedar."
17. 4 come to an end, and its wealth will be **replaced** by poverty.
Jer 28.13 a wooden yoke, but he will **replace** it with an iron yoke.
Ezek 47. 8 into the Dead Sea, it **replaces** the salt water of that sea
Dan 8.13 How long will an awful sin **replace** the daily sacrifices?

REPLY

2 Kgs 14. 9 But King Jehoash sent back the following **reply:**
2 Chr 2.11 King Hiram sent Solomon a letter in **reply.**
Ezra 5. 5 action until they could write to Darius and receive a **reply.**
6. 6 Then Darius sent the following **reply:**
Neh 6. 4 four times, and each time I sent them the same **reply.**
6. 8 I sent a **reply** to him:
Esth 4.15 Esther sent Mordecai this **reply:**
Job 20. 3 said is an insult, but I know how to **reply** to you.
Prov 15.28 Evil people have a quick **reply,** but it causes trouble.

REPORT

Gen 14.13 But a man escaped and **reported** all this to Abram, the
32. 4 "I, Jacob, your obedient servant, **report** to my master Esau
37. 2 He brought bad **reports** to his father about what his brothers
Ex 19. 8 the Lord has said," and Moses **reported** this to the Lord.
36. 5 doing the work went [5]and **reported** to Moses, "The people
Num 13.26 They **reported** what they had seen and showed them the fruit
13.32 So they spread a false **report** among the Israelites about
14.36 land brought back a false **report** which caused the people to
22. 8 here, and tomorrow I will **report** to you whatever the Lord
31.49 army went to Moses [49]and **reported,** "Sir, we have counted
Deut 1.25 fruit they found there, and **reported** that the land which the
17. 4 If you hear such a **report,** then investigate it thoroughly.
Josh 7. 3 When they had done so, [3]they **reported** back to Joshua:
14. 7 I brought an honest **report** back to him.
14.12 Lord promised me on that day when my men and I **reported.**
22.32 to Canaan, to the people of Israel, and **reported** to them.
1 Sam 11. 5 They told him what the messengers from Jabesh had **reported.**
18.26 Saul's officials **reported** to David what Saul had said,
23.23 and be sure to bring back a **report** to me straight away.
27.11 go back to Gath and **report** what he and his men had
2 Sam 11.18 Then Joab sent a **report** to David telling him about the battle,
12.27 He sent messengers to David to **report:**
13.34 He went to the king and **reported** what he had seen.
15.13 A messenger **reported** to David, "The Israelites are
17.21 up out of the well and went and **reported** to King David.
18.10 David's men saw him and **reported** to Joab, "Sir, I saw
24. 9 They **reported** to the king the total number of men capable
1 Kgs 13.25 They went on into Bethel and **reported** what they had seen.
18.10 the ruler of a country **reported** that you were not in his
20.17 Scouts sent out by Benhadad **reported** to him that a group of
2 Kgs 7.11 guards announced the news, and it was **reported** in the palace.
7.15 Then they returned and **reported** to the king.
9.18 The guard on the watch-tower **reported** that the messenger
9.20 Once more the guard **reported** that the messenger had
9.36 When they **reported** this to Jehu, he said, "This is what
18.37 in grief, and went and **reported** to the king what the
19. 1 King Hezekiah heard their **report,** he tore his clothes in grief,
19.28 I have received the **report** of that rage and that pride
22. 4 Priest Hilkiah and get a **report** on the amount of money that
22. 9 Then he went back to the king and **reported:**
1 Chr 21. 5 He **reported** to King David the total number of men capable
2 Chr 29.18 The Levites made the following **report** to King Hezekiah:
34.16 He **reported,** "We have done everything that you commanded.
Ezra 5. 6 This is the **report** that they sent to the emperor:
Neh 13. 6 was king of Babylon I had gone back to **report** to him.
Esth 2.23 it was discovered that the **report** was true, so both men were
9.11 number of people killed in Susa was **reported** to the king.
Job 21.29 Don't you know the **reports** they bring back?
Is 21. 6 and post a sentry, and tell him to **report** what he sees.
36.22 in grief and went and **reported** to the king what the Assyrian
37. 1 King Hezekiah heard their **report,** he tore his clothes in grief,
37.29 I have received the **report** of that rage and that pride
53. 1 "Who would have believed what we now **report?**
Jer 20.10 So let's **report** him to the authorities!"
36.16 and said to Baruch, "We must **report** this to the king."
36.20 king's court, where they **reported** everything to the king.
Ezek 9.11 wearing linen clothes returned and **reported** to the Lord,
Amos 7.10 of Bethel, then sent a **report** to King Jeroboam of Israel:
Zech 1.11 They **reported** to the angel:
Mt 28.15 And so that is the **report** spread round by the Jews to
Mk 15.45 After hearing the officer's **report,** Pilate told Joseph
Lk 1. 1 their best to write a **report** of the things that have taken
4.37 And the **report** about Jesus spread everywhere in that region.
Jn 3.11 of what we know and **report** what we have seen, yet none
11.57 where Jesus was, he must **report** it, so that they could
12.17 grave and raised him from death had **reported** what had happened.
21.23 a **report** spread among the followers of Jesus that this disciple
Acts 5.22 to the Council and **reported,** [23]"When we arrived at the jail,
15. 3 Phoenicia and Samaria, they **reported** how the Gentiles had turned
15.12 they heard Barnabas and Paul **report** all the miracles and wonders
16.38 police officers **reported** these words to the Roman officials;
21.19 and gave a complete **report** of everything that God had done
21.31 to kill Paul, when a **report** was sent up to the commander
23.22 commander said, "Don't tell anyone that you have **reported** this
2 Cor 7. 7 cheered us, but also his **report** of how you encouraged him.
Rev 1. 2 This is his **report** concerning the message from God and the

REPRESENT

Ex 18.19 is right for you to **represent** the people before God and
28.12 of the ephod to **represent** the twelve tribes of Israel.
28.21 one of the sons of Jacob, to **represent** the tribes of Israel.
39. 7 of the ephod to **represent** the twelve tribes of Israel,
39.14 of Jacob, in order to **represent** the twelve tribes of Israel.
Lev 2.13 because salt **represents** the covenant between you and God.
Num 17. 3 and then write Aaron's name on the stick **representing** Levi.
17. 8 he saw that Aaron's stick, **representing** the tribe of Levi,
2 Sam 2.15 twelve men, **representing** Ishbosheth and the tribe of Benjamin,
15. 3 side, but there is no **representative** of the king to hear
2 Chr 24.11 secretary and the High Priest's **representative** would take
Neh 11.24 and the tribe of Judah, **represented** the people of Israel at
Esth 9. 3 administrators, and royal **representatives**—helped the Jews because they were
Is 6.13 (The stump **represents** a new beginning for God's people.)
Jer 40.10 and be your **representative** when the Babylonians come here.
Ezek 4. 1 and scratch lines on it to **represent** the city of Jerusalem.
4. 2 Then, to **represent** a siege, put trenches, earthworks,
4.13 The Lord said, "This **represents** the way the Israelites
23. 4 one was named Oholah (she **represents** Samaria),
23. 4 the younger one was named Oholibah (she **represents** Jerusalem).
37.19 going to take the stick **representing** Israel
37.19 and put it with the one that **represents** Judah.
Dan 8.20 had two horns **represents** the kingdoms of Media and Persia.
8.21 The goat **represents** the kingdom of Greece, and the
8.22 the first horn was broken **represent** the four kingdoms into
Zech 5. 8 The angel said, "This woman **represents** wickedness."
2 Cor 8.23 going with him, they **represent** the churches and bring glory to
Gal 4.24 the two women **represent** two covenants.
4.24 is Hagar, and she **represents** the covenant made at Mount Sinai.
Heb 9. 5 Box were the winged creatures **representing** God's presence, with
Rev 15. 2 and over the one whose name is **represented** by a number.

REPRIMAND

Num 20.12 But the Lord **reprimanded** Moses and Aaron.
1 Kgs 1. 5 David had never **reprimanded** him about anything, and he was
Neh 13.11 I **reprimanded** the officials for letting the Temple be neglected.
13.17 I **reprimanded** the Jewish leaders and said, "Look at the
13.25 I **reprimanded** the men, called down curses on them, beat
Job 13.10 prejudice is hidden, he will **reprimand** you, [11]and his
22. 4 awe of God that he **reprimands** you and brings you to trial.
Ps 50. 8 I do not **reprimand** you because of your sacrifices and the
50.21 But now I **reprimand** you and make the matter plain to you.
119.21 You **reprimand** the proud;
Prov 1.23 Listen when I **reprimand** you;
9. 7 If you **reprimand** an evil man, you will only get hurt.
30. 6 he never said, he will **reprimand** you and show that you are
Ecc 7. 5 better to have wise people **reprimand** you than to have stupid
Is 17.13 rushing waves, but God **reprimands** them and they retreat,
54. 9 I will not **reprimand** or punish you.
Hos 4. 4 one accuse the people or **reprimand** them—my complaint is
Lk 3.19 John **reprimanded** Herod, the governor, because he had married

REPROACH

Mt 11.20 did not turn from their sins, so he **reproached** those towns.
2 Tim 4. 2 to convince, **reproach,** and encourage, as you teach with

AV REPROBATE

Jer 6.30 They will be called **worthless** dross, because I, the
Rom 1.28 has given them over to **corrupted** minds, so that they do the
2 Tim 3. 8 minds do not function and who are **failures** in the faith.
Tit 1.16 They are hateful and disobedient, not **fit** to do anything good.

REPRODUCE

Gen 1.22 live in the water to **reproduce,** and to fill the sea, and
7. 3 and bird will be kept alive to **reproduce** again on the earth.
8.17 so that they may **reproduce** and spread over all the earth."
31.38 goats have not failed to **reproduce,** and I have not eaten any
Ps 144.14 May our cattle **reproduce** plentifully without miscarriage

REPTILE

Deut 4.18 man or woman, [17]animal or bird, [18]**reptile** or fish.
1 Kgs 4.33 he talked about animals, birds, **reptiles,** and fish.
Ps 148.10 all animals, tame and wild, **reptiles** and birds.
Acts 10.12 In it were all kinds of animals, **reptiles,** and wild birds.
11. 6 and saw domesticated and wild animals, **reptiles,** and wild birds.
Rom 1.23 to look like mortal man or birds or animals or **reptiles.**
Jas 3. 7 has tamed all other creatures—wild animals and birds, **reptiles**

REPULSIVE

Ps 88. 8 you have made me **repulsive** to them.
Ezek 7.20 That is why the Lord has made their wealth **repulsive** to them.

REPUTATION

Neh 6.13 so that they could ruin my **reputation** and humiliate me.
Job 19. 9 He has taken away all my wealth and destroyed my **reputation.**
Prov 3.35 men will gain an honourable **reputation,** but stupid men will
22. 1 to choose between a good **reputation** and great wealth,
22. 1 choose a good **reputation.**
24. 8 planning evil, you will earn a **reputation** as a troublemaker.
24.25 however, will be prosperous and enjoy a good **reputation.**
27.21 a person's **reputation** can also be tested.
Ecc 7. 1 A good **reputation** is better than expensive perfume;
Mk 6.14 Herod heard about all this, because Jesus' **reputation** had spread
1 Tim 5.10 been married only once [10]and have a **reputation** for good deeds:
Tit 1. 6 and not have the **reputation** of being wild or disobedient.
Rev 3. 1 know that you have the **reputation** of being alive, even

REQUEST

Gen 17.20 I have heard your **request** about Ishmael, so I will bless
Ex 33.18 Then Moses **requested,** "Please, let me see the dazzling
Num 27. 7 "What the daughters of Zelophehad **request** is right;
Deut 18.17 So the Lord said to me, 'They have made a wise **request.**
Judg 8. 8 Penuel and made the same **request** of the people there, but
1 Sam 8. 6 Samuel was displeased with their **request** for a king;
2 Sam 14.22 are pleased with me, because you have granted my **request."**
1 Kgs 2.16 And now I have one **request** to make;
8.28 to my prayer, and grant the **requests** I make to you today.
12. 7 a favourable answer to their **request,** and they will always
2 Kgs 2.10 "That is a difficult **request** to grant," Elijah replied.
2 Chr 6.19 Listen to my prayer and grant the **requests** I make to you.
Neh 2. 5 is willing to grant my **request,** let me go to the land
2. 6 emperor, with the empress sitting at his side, approved my **request.**
Esth 5. 6 I will grant your **request,** even if you ask for half my
5. 8 kind enough to grant my **request,** I would like you and Haman
7. 3 Majesty to grant my humble **request,** my wish is that I may
Ps 20. 5 May the Lord answer all your **requests.**
21. 2 you have answered his **request.**
Jer 21. 1 priest Zephaniah son of Maaseiah to me with this **request:**
32. 7 come to me with the **request** to buy his field at Anathoth
42. 9 you sent me with your **request** has said, [10]'If you are
Dan 2.49 At Daniel's **request** the king put Shadrach, Meshach, and
6. 7 no one be permitted to **request** anything from any god or from
6.12 next thirty days anyone who **requested** anything from any god
Jn 19.31 They **requested** this because it was Friday, and they did not
2 Cor 8.17 Not only did he welcome our **request;**
1 Tim 2. 1 petitions, prayers, **requests,** and thanksgivings be offered to God
Phlm 9 But because I love you, I make a **request** instead.
10 So I make a **request** to you on behalf of Onesimus,
Heb 5. 7 Jesus made his prayers and **requests** with loud cries and tears

REQUIRE

Ex 5. 8 But still **require** them to make the same number of bricks
21.30 fine to save his life, he must pay the full amount **required.**
22.25 not act like a money-lender and **require** him to pay interest.
30.13 the census must pay the **required** amount of money, weighed
38.26 census, each one paying the **required** amount, weighed
Lev 5. 1 Sin-offerings are **required** in the following cases.
14.32 afford the normal offerings **required** for his purification.
23.37 sacrifices, and wine-offerings, as **required** day by day.
Num 3. 7 They shall do the work **required** for the Tent of my
4.26 They shall perform all the tasks **required** for these things.
5.15 He shall also take the **required** offering of one kilogramme
6.15 and in addition the **required** offerings of corn and wine.
6.21 offering beyond what his vow **requires** him to give, he must
8. 8 the **required** grain-offering of flour mixed with olive-oil;
27.11 observe this as a legal **requirement,** just as I, the Lord,
28. 2 times the **required** food-offerings that are pleasing to him.
29.15 one kilogramme with each lamb, with the **required** wine-offerings.
29.18 all the other offerings **required** for the first day.
29.21 all the other offerings **required** for the first day.
29.24 all the other offerings **required** for the first day.
29.27 all the other offerings **required** for the first day.
29.30 all the other offerings **required** for the first day.
29.33 all the other offerings **required** for the first day.
29.37 all the other offerings **required** for the first day.
30. 5 when he hears about it, she is not **required** to keep it.
30. 8 when he hears about it, she is not **required** to keep it.
30.12 when he hears about it, she is not **required** to keep it.
Deut 13.18 that I have given you today, and do what he **requires.**
21. 9 by doing what the Lord **requires,** you will not be held
1 Sam 2.29 the sacrifices and offerings which I **require** from my people?
17.25 and will not **require** his father's family to pay taxes."
1 Kgs 15.22 throughout all Judah **requiring** everyone, without exception,
18.10 in his country, Ahab would **require** that ruler to swear that
2 Kgs 12.15 there was no need to **require** them to account for the funds.
22. 7 is no need to **require** them to account for the funds."
2 Chr 8.13 offered burnt-offerings according to the **requirements** of the
24. 6 the servant of the Lord, **required** the people to pay for
31. 3 other festivals which are **required** by the Law of the Lord.
31. 4 all their time to the **requirements** of the Law of the Lord.
31.18 other dependants, because they were **required** to be ready to
34.32 people of Jerusalem obeyed the **requirements** of the covenant
34.33 long as he lived, he **required** the people to serve the Lord,
Ezra 3. 4 each day they offered the sacrifices **required** for that day;
7.23 which the God of Heaven **requires** for his Temple, and so make
Neh 8. 9 people heard what the Law **required,** they were so moved that
8.18 day there was a closing ceremony, as **required** in the Law.
10.29 and that we will keep all his laws and **requirements.**
10.34 the Lord our God, according to the **requirements** of the Law.
10.36 the Temple and there, as **required** by the Law, dedicate him
12.44 for the priests and the Levites which the Law **required.**
12.47 and the Levites gave the **required** portion to the priests.
Ps 51. 6 Sincerity and truth are what you **require;**
Is 45.19 I did not **require** the people of Israel to look for me
Jer 5. 4 don't know what their God **requires,** what the Lord wants them
5. 5 they know what their God **requires,** what the Lord wants them
Mic 6. 8 What he **requires** of us is this:
Mt 3.15 For in this way we shall do all that God **requires."**

Mt 5. 6 "Happy are those whose greatest desire is to do what God **requires;**
5.10 "Happy are those who are persecuted because they do what God **requires;**
5.20 of the Law and the Pharisees in doing what God **requires.**
6.33 God and with what he **requires** of you, and he will provide
Lk 2.24 or two young pigeons, as **required** by the law of the Lord.
2.27 for him what the Law **required,** [28] Simeon took the child in
2.39 finished doing all that was **required** by the law of the Lord,
12.48 Much is **required** from the person to whom much is given;
12.48 much more is **required** from the person to whom much more is
Acts 15. 1 unless you are circumcised as the Law of Moses **requires."**
17. 9 the others pay the **required** amount of money to be released,
Rom 3.20 is put right in God's sight by doing what the Law **requires;**
1 Cor 4. 2 The one thing **required** of such a servant is that he be
Gal 2.16 faith in Jesus Christ, never by doing what the Law **requires.**
2.16 our faith in Christ, and not by doing what the Law **requires.**
2.16 one is put right with God by doing what the Law **requires.**
3. 2 by doing what the Law **requires** or by hearing the gospel
3. 5 you do what the Law **requires** or because you hear the gospel
3.12 says, "Whoever does everything the Law **requires** will live."
Phil 1.27 as the gospel of Christ **requires,** so that, whether or not I
Heb 8. 4 are priests who offer the gifts **required** by the Jewish Law.
9.23 But the heavenly things themselves **require** much better sacrifices.

RESCUE

Gen 45. 7 me ahead of you to **rescue** you in this amazing way and
48.16 May the angel, who has **rescued** me from all harm, bless
Ex 2.17 Moses went to their **rescue** and watered their animals for them.
2.19 "An Egyptian **rescued** us from the shepherds," they
3. 7 heard them cry out to be **rescued** from their slave-drivers.
3. 8 I have come down to **rescue** them from the Egyptians and to
6. 6 I will **rescue** you and set you free from your slavery to
13.19 Joseph had said, "When God **rescues** you, you must carry my
15.13 Faithful to your promise, you led the people you had **rescued;**
18. 8 and the people of Egypt in order to **rescue** the Israelites.
32.11 with your people, whom you **rescued** from Egypt with great
Num 35.25 The community is to **rescue** the man guilty of
Deut 4.20 you are the people he **rescued** from Egypt, that blazing furnace.
5. 6 the Lord your God, who **rescued** you from Egypt, where you
5.15 I, the Lord your God, **rescued** you by my great power and
6.12 not forget the Lord who **rescued** you from Egypt, where you
6.21 king of Egypt, and the Lord **rescued** us by his great power.
8.14 the Lord your God who **rescued** you from Egypt, where you were
9.26 own people, the people you **rescued** and brought out of Egypt
13. 5 rebel against the Lord, who **rescued** you from Egypt, where
13.10 the Lord your God, who **rescued** you from Egypt, where you
16. 1 on a night in that month that he **rescued** you from Egypt.
20. 1 The Lord your God, who **rescued** you from Egypt, will be with
21. 8 Lord, forgive your people Israel, whom you **rescued** from Egypt.
26. 8 By his great power and strength he **rescued** us from Egypt.
32.36 The Lord will **rescue** his people when he sees that their
32.38 let them run to your **rescue.**
Josh 24.10 he blessed you, and in this way I **rescued** you from Balak.
Judg 3.31 He too **rescued** Israel, and did so by killing six hundred
6. 9 I **rescued** you from the Egyptians and from the people who
6.14 all your great strength and **rescue** Israel from the Midianites.
6.15 Gideon replied, "But Lord, how can I **rescue** Israel?
6.36 "You say that you have decided to use me to **rescue** Israel.
6.37 will know that you are going to use me to **rescue** Israel."
7. 7 said to Gideon, "I will **rescue** you and give you victory
10.13 other gods, so I am not going to **rescue** you again.
10.14 Let them **rescue** you when you get into trouble."
12. 2 I did call you, but you would not **rescue** me from them.
13. 5 begin the work of **rescuing** Israel from the Philistines."
1 Sam 7. 3 only him, and he will **rescue** you from the power of the
9.16 people Israel, and he will **rescue** them from the Philistines.
10.18 you out of Egypt and **rescued** you from the Egyptians and all
10.19 your God, the one who **rescues** you from all your troubles and
11. 9 "Tell your people that before noon tomorrow they will be **rescued."**
11.13 death today, for this is the day the Lord **rescued** Israel."
12.10 **Rescue** us from our enemies, and we will worship you!'
12.11 Each of us **rescued** you from your enemies, and you lived in
17.35 a lamb, [35] I go after it, attack it, and **rescue** the lamb.
30. 8 you will catch them and **rescue** the captives."
30.18 David **rescued** everyone and everything the Amalekites had taken,
2 Sam 3.18 use my servant David to **rescue** my people Israel from the
7. 6 From the time I **rescued** the people of Israel from Egypt
7.23 earth like Israel, whom you **rescued** from slavery to make
12. 7 'I made you king of Israel and **rescued** you from Saul.
19. 9 "He **rescued** us from the Philistines, but now he has fled
22.18 He **rescued** me from my powerful enemies and from all
1 Kgs 1.29 the living Lord, who has **rescued** me from all my troubles,
2 Kgs 11. 2 with the others, but was **rescued** by his aunt Jehosheba, who
11.15 rows of guards, and kill anyone who tries to **rescue** her."
14.27 and for ever, so he **rescued** them through King Jeroboam II.
16. 7 Come and **rescue** me from the kings of Syria and of Israel,
17. 7 Lord their God, who had **rescued** them from the king of Egypt
17.39 Lord your God, and I will **rescue** you from your enemies."
18.32 Hezekiah fool you into thinking that the Lord will **rescue** you.
19.19 Now, Lord our God, **rescue** us from the Assyrians, so that
20. 6 I will **rescue** you and this city of Jerusalem from the
1 Chr 16.35 **rescue** us from the nations, so that we may be thankful and
17. 5 From the time I **rescued** the people of Israel from Egypt
17.21 earth like Israel, whom you **rescued** from slavery to make
17.21 You **rescued** your people from Egypt and drove out other
2 Chr 18.31 shout, and the Lord God **rescued** him and turned the attack
2 Chr 20. 9 in their trouble, and you would hear them and **rescue** them.
22.11 She secretly **rescued** one of Ahaziah's sons, Joash, took him
23.14 rows of guards, and kill anyone who tries to **rescue** her."
32.22 In this way the Lord **rescued** King Hezekiah and the
Neh 1.10 You **rescued** them by your great power and strength.
9.27 you sent them leaders who **rescued** them from their foes.
9.28 and time after time you **rescued** them in your great mercy.
Job 5.21 God will **rescue** you from slander;
22.30 He will **rescue** you if you are innocent, if what you do
29.17 I destroyed the power of cruel men and **rescued** their victims.
Ps 6. 4 in your mercy **rescue** me from death.
7. 1 **rescue** me and save me from all who pursue me, [2] or else
9.13 **Rescue** me from death, O Lord, [14] that I may stand before
13. 5 I will be glad, because you will **rescue** me.
18.17 He **rescued** me from my powerful enemies and from all
22.19 Come quickly to my **rescue!**
22.21 **Rescue** me from these lions;
25.15 Lord for help at all times, and he **rescues** me from danger.
34. 7 those who honour the Lord and **rescues** them from danger.
34.17 he **rescues** them from all their troubles.
35. 2 Take your shield and armour and come to my **rescue.**
35.17 **Rescue** me from their attacks;
37.40 He helps them and **rescues** them;
49.15 But God will **rescue** me;
54. 7 You have **rescued** me from all my troubles, and I have seen
56.13 of thanksgiving, [13] because you have **rescued** me from death
59. 2 **rescue** me from those murderers!
60. 5 our prayer, so that the people you love may be **rescued.**
68.20 he is the Lord, our Lord, who **rescues** us from death.
69.18 **rescue** me from my enemies.
71. 2 Because you are righteous, help me and **rescue** me.
71. 4 My God, **rescue** me from wicked men, from the power of cruel
71.11 there is no one to **rescue** him."
72.12 He **rescues** the poor who call to him, and those who are
72.14 He **rescues** them from oppression and violence;
79. 9 **rescue** us and forgive our sins for the sake of your own
82. 4 **Rescue** them from the power of evil men.
91.15 I will **rescue** them and honour them.
97.10 he **rescues** them from the power of the wicked.
106.10 he **rescued** them from their enemies.
106.43 Many times the Lord **rescued** his people, but they chose
107. 2 He has **rescued** you from your enemies [3] and has brought you
107.41 But he **rescued** the needy from their misery and made
108. 6 my prayer, so that the people you love may be **rescued.**
109.21 as you have promised, and **rescue** me because of the goodness
143. 9 **rescue** me from my enemies.
143.11 **Rescue** me, Lord, as you have promised;
144. 7 from above, pull me out of the deep water, and **rescue** me;
144.10 You give victory to kings and **rescue** your servant David.
144.11 **rescue** me from the power of foreigners, who never tell the
Prov 11. 6 Righteousness **rescues** the honest man, but someone who
12. 6 the words of the righteous **rescue** those who are threatened.
24.11 to **rescue** someone who is about to be executed unjustly.
Is 17.10 have forgotten the God who **rescues** you and who protects you
19.20 to the Lord for help, he will send someone to **rescue** them.
25. 9 We have put our trust in him, and he has **rescued** us.
29. 6 the Lord Almighty will **rescue** you with violent thunderstorms
29.22 the God of Israel, who **rescued** Abraham from trouble, says,
34. 8 time when the Lord will **rescue** Zion and take vengeance on
35. 4 God is coming to your **rescue,** coming to punish your enemies."
35. 9 Those whom the Lord has **rescued** will travel home by that road.
36.18 Hezekiah fool you into thinking that the Lord will **rescue** you.
37.20 Now, Lord our God, **rescue** us from the Assyrians, so that
38. 6 I will **rescue** you and this city of Jerusalem from the
38.14 Lord, **rescue** me from all this trouble.
40.10 with power, bringing with him the people he has **rescued.**
42.22 robbed and plundered, with no one to come to their **rescue.**
45.25 I, the Lord, will **rescue** all the descendants of Jacob,
46. 4 I will give you help and **rescue** you.
49.24 Can you **rescue** the prisoners of a tyrant?
49.25 whoever fights you, and I will **rescue** your children.
51.11 Those whom you have **rescued** will reach Jerusalem with gladness,
52. 9 The Lord will **rescue** his city and comfort his people.
59.16 use his own power to **rescue** them and to win the victory.
62.11 to save you, Bringing with him the people he has **rescued."**
63. 9 In his love and compassion he **rescued** them.
63.16 Lord, are our father, the one who has always **rescued** us.
Jer 2. 6 about me, even though I **rescued** them from Egypt and led them
6. 9 So you must **rescue** everyone you can while there is still time."
12.14 like an uprooted plant, and I will **rescue** Judah from them.
15.21 I will **rescue** you from the power of wicked and violent men.
17.14 **rescue** me and I will be perfectly safe.
20.13 He **rescues** the oppressed from the power of evil men.
30.10 I will **rescue** you from that distant land, from the land
31. 7 he has **rescued** all who are left.'
33.16 Judah and of Jerusalem will be **rescued** and will live in safety.
34.13 with your ancestors when I **rescued** them from Egypt and set
42.11 I am with you, and I will **rescue** you from his power.
46.27 I will **rescue** you from that distant land, from the land
50.34 But the one who will **rescue** them is strong—his name is
Lam 3.58 "You came to my **rescue,** Lord, and saved my life.
Ezek 13.23 I am **rescuing** my people from your power, so that you will
34.10 I will **rescue** my sheep from you and not let you eat
34.22 But I will **rescue** my sheep and not let them be
Dan 3.28 He sent his angel and **rescued** these men who serve and trust
3.29 There is no other god who can **rescue** like this."
6.14 upset and did his best to find some way to **rescue** Daniel.
6.16 to Daniel, "May your God, whom you serve so loyally, **rescue**
6.17 noblemen on the stone, so that no one could **rescue** Daniel.
6.27 He saves and **rescues;**

Hos 12.13 Lord sent a prophet to **rescue** the people of Israel from
13.14 world of the dead or **rescue** them from the power of death.
Mic 5. 8 and tears them to pieces—and there is no hope of **rescue.**
6. 4 I **rescued** you from slavery;
Zeph 3.19 I will **rescue** all the lame and bring the exiles home.
Zech 8. 7 I will **rescue** my people from the lands where they have
10. 6 I will **rescue** the people of Israel.
10. 8 I will **rescue** them and make them as numerous as they used
Lk 1.73 he promised to **rescue** us from our enemies and allow
Acts 12.11 Lord sent his angel to **rescue** me from Herod's power and from
23.27 a Roman citizen, so I went with my soldiers and **rescued** him.
26.17 I will **rescue** you from the people of Israel and from the
Rom 7.24 Who will **rescue** me from this body that is taking me to
Col 1.13 He **rescued** us from the power of darkness and brought us
1 Thes 1.10 raised from death and who **rescues** us from God's anger that
2 Thes 3. 2 Pray also that God will **rescue** us from wicked and evil people;
2 Tim 3.11 But the Lord **rescued** me from them all.
4.17 and I was **rescued** from being sentenced to death.
4.18 And the Lord will **rescue** me from all evil and take me
Tit 2.14 gave himself for us, to **rescue** us from all wickedness and to
2 Pet 2. 7 He **rescued** Lot, a good man, who was distressed by the
2. 9 the Lord knows how to **rescue** godly people from their trials
Jude 5 how the Lord once **rescued** the people of Israel from Egypt,

RESEMBLE

Gen 1.26 they will be like us and **resemble** us.

RESENT

Deut 15.18 Do not be **resentful** when you set a slave free;
Job 5. 2 worry yourself to death with **resentment** would be a foolish,
5.17 Do not **resent** it when he rebukes you.

RESERVATION

1 Cor 7.35 yourselves completely to the Lord's service without any **reservation.**

RESERVE

Gen 41.36 The food will be a **reserve** supply for the country during
2 Chr 23.13 entrance, standing by the column **reserved** for kings and
Mt 23. 6 best places at feasts and the **reserved seats** in the synagogues;
Mk 12.39 who choose the **reserved seats** in the synagogues and the
Lk 11.43 You love the **reserved seats** in the synagogues and to be
20.46 choose the **reserved seats** in the synagogues and the best places
Col 1.11 share of what God has **reserved** for his people in the kingdom
2 Pet 2.17 God has **reserved** a place for them in the deepest darkness.
Jude 13 stars, for whom God has **reserved** a place for ever in the

RESERVOIR

2 Kgs 20.20 of how he built a **reservoir** and dug a tunnel to bring
Is 22.11 store water, [11] you built a **reservoir** inside the city to

RESETTLES see SETTLE (1)

RESIDE

Ex 12.45 No temporary **resident** or hired worker may eat it.
Num 15.29 whether he is a native Israelite or a **resident** foreigner.
35.15 and for foreigners who are temporary or permanent **residents.**
2 Chr 2.17 There were 153,600 **resident** foreigners.
Neh 3. 7 as far as the **residence** of the governor of West Euphrates.
Ezek 47.23 Each foreign **resident** will receive his share with the

RESIGNATION

Ecc 10. 4 becomes angry with you, do not hand in your **resignation;**

RESIN

A fragrant, gummy substance produced from the sap of certain trees and shrubs.

Gen 37.25 Their camels were loaded with spices and **resins.**
43.11 a little **resin,** a little honey, spices, pistachio nuts,

RESIST

Lev 26.21 "If you still continue to **resist** me and refuse to obey me,
26.40 of their ancestors, who **resisted** me and rebelled against me,
2 Chr 13. 7 Solomon, who was too young and inexperienced to **resist** them.
26.18 and courageous priests, followed the king [18] to **resist** him.
Prov 2.16 You will be able to **resist** any immoral woman who tries
25.15 down the strongest **resistance** and can even convince rulers.
Ecc 4.12 Two men can **resist** an attack that would defeat one man alone.
Jer 1.18 But today I am giving you the strength to **resist** them;
Dan 8. 7 The ram had no strength to **resist.**
Acts 7.51 you too have always **resisted** the Holy Spirit!
Rom 9.19 Who can **resist** God's will?"
Eph 6.13 day comes, you will be able to **resist** the enemy's attacks;
Heb 12. 4 have not yet had to **resist** to the point of being killed.
Jas 4. 6 As the scripture says, "God **resists** the proud, but gives grace
4. 7 **Resist** the Devil, and he will run away from you.
5. 6 have condemned and murdered innocent people, and they do not **resist**
1 Pet 5. 5 for the scripture says, "God **resists** the proud, but shows favour
5. 9 firm in your faith and **resist** him, because you know that

RESOLUTE

Col 2. 5 glad as I see the **resolute** firmness with which you stand

RESOLVED

Esth 9.28 It was **resolved** that every Jewish family of every future

RESOURCE

Prov 1. 4 person clever and teach young men how to be **resourceful.**
Lk 8. 3 used their own **resources** to help Jesus and his disciples.

RESPECT

[DISRESPECT, DISRESPECTFUL]

Ex 3.21 "I will make the Egyptians **respect** you so that when my
11. 3 The Lord made the Egyptians **respect** the Israelites.
12.36 The Lord made the Egyptians **respect** the people and give
20.12 "**Respect** your father and your mother, so that you may
Lev 10. 3 when he said, 'All who serve me must **respect** my holiness;
19. 3 Each of you must **respect** his mother and his father, and
19.32 "Show **respect** for old people and honour them.
22. 2 holy name, so treat with **respect** the sacred offerings that
Num 11.16 said to Moses, "Assemble seventy **respected** men who are
Deut 5.16 "'**Respect** your father and your mother, as I, the Lord your God,
Judg 9.16 Did you **respect** Gideon's memory and treat his family properly,
1 Sam 2.17 because they treated the offerings to the Lord with such **disrespect.**
9. 6 is highly **respected** because everything he says comes true.
15.30 "But at least show me **respect** in front of the leaders of
22.14 and highly **respected** by everyone in the royal court.
24. 8 down to the ground in **respect** [9] and said, "Why do you
28.14 that it was Samuel, and he bowed to the ground in **respect.**
2 Sam 1. 2 He went to David and bowed to the ground in **respect.**
9. 6 of Saul, arrived, he bowed down before David in **respect.**
14. 4 the ground in **respect,** and said, "Help me, Your Majesty!"
14.22 in front of David in **respect,** and said, "God bless you,
1 Kgs 1.47 went in to pay their **respects** to His Majesty King David, and
3.28 were all filled with deep **respect** for him, because they knew
2 Kgs 3.14 you if I didn't **respect** your ally King Jehoshaphat of Judah.
5. 1 the Syrian army, was highly **respected** and esteemed by the
10.13 to Jezreel to pay our **respects** to the children of Queen
19.22 You have been **disrespectful** to me, the holy God of Israel.
1 Chr 4. 9 Jabez, who was the most **respected** member of his family.
29.28 ripe old age, wealthy and **respected,** and his son Solomon
2 Chr 22. 9 body out of **respect** for his grandfather King Jehoshaphat,
Esth 1.18 Wives everywhere will have no **respect** for their husbands,
1.20 husband with proper **respect,** whether he's rich or poor."
3. 2 his service to show their **respect** for Haman by kneeling and
5. 9 or show any sign of **respect** as he passed, Haman was furious
Job 17. 9 Those who claim to be **respectable** are more and more
29. 8 they saw me, and old men stood up to show me **respect.**
34. 7 He never shows **respect** for God.
Ps 112. 9 he will be powerful and **respected.**
119.48 I **respect** and love your commandments;
119.161 Powerful men attack me unjustly, but I **respect** your law.
Prov 1. 7 Stupid people have no **respect** for wisdom and refuse to learn.
5. 9 do, others will gain the **respect** that you once had, and you
9. 8 But if you correct a wise man, he will **respect** you.
11.16 A gracious lady is **respected,** but a woman without virtue
11.27 are good, you will be **respected,** but if you are looking for
13.15 Intelligence wins **respect,** but those who can't be
13.18 Anyone who listens to correction is **respected.**
14.22 will earn the trust and **respect** of others if you work for
17. 7 **Respected** people do not tell lies, and fools have nothing
18.12 No one is **respected** unless he is humble;
20.29 the strength of youth and **respect** the grey hair of age.
21.21 others will **respect** you and treat you fairly.
29.23 downfall, but if you are humble, you will be **respected.**
31.25 She is strong and **respected** and not afraid of the future.
31.31 She deserves the **respect** of everyone.
Ecc 7.28 man in a thousand that I could **respect,** but not one woman.
Is 3. 5 Young people will not **respect** their elders,
3. 5 and worthless people will not **respect** their superiors.
33. 8 No one is **respected** any more.
37.23 You have been **disrespectful** to me, the holy God of Israel.
49. 7 "Kings will see you released and will rise to show their **respect;**
49.23 they will humbly show their **respect** for you.
60.14 oppressed you will come And bow low to show their **respect.**
Jer 49.15 is going to make you weak, and no one will **respect** you.
Lam 5.12 our old men are shown no **respect.**
Ezek 2. 4 are stubborn and do not **respect** me, so I am sending you
22. 8 You have no **respect** for the holy places, and you don't
22.26 priests break my law and have no **respect** for what is holy.
22.26 As a result the people of Israel do not **respect** me.
Dan 3.29 speaks **disrespectfully** of the God of Shadrach, Meshach,
6.13 exiles from Judah, does not **respect** Your Majesty or obey the
6.26 my empire everyone should fear and **respect** Daniel's God.
Mal 1. 6 I am your master—why don't you **respect** me?
1. 7 Then you ask, 'How have we failed to **respect** you?'
2. 5 this is what I gave them, so that they might **respect** me.
2. 5 In those days they did **respect** and fear me.
3. 5 orphans, and foreigners—against all who do not **respect** me.
3.16 a record of those who feared the Lord and **respected** him.
Mt 9.13 I have not come to call **respectable** people, but outcasts."
13.57 "A prophet is **respected** everywhere except in his home town
15. 4 For God said, '**Respect** your father and your mother,'
19.19 **respect** your father and your mother;
21.37 'Surely they will **respect** my son,' he said.
23. 7 love to be greeted with **respect** in the market-places and to

Mk 2.17 I have not come to call **respectable** people, but outcasts."
6. 4 "A prophet is **respected** everywhere except in his own home
7.10 For Moses commanded, '**Respect** your father and your mother,'
10.19 **respect** your father and your mother.' "
12. 6 'I am sure they will **respect** my son,' he said.
12.38 and be greeted with **respect** in the market-place,
15.42 He was a **respected** member of the Council, who was waiting
Lk 5.32 have not come to call **respectable** people to repent, but outcasts."
11.43 and to be greeted with **respect** in the market-places.
15. 7 who repents than over ninety-nine **respectable** people who do not
18. 2 there was a judge who neither feared God nor **respected** man.
18. 4 I don't fear God or **respect** man, [5] yet because of all the
18.20 **respect** your father and your mother.' "
20.13 surely they will **respect** him!'
20.46 and love to be greeted with **respect** in the market-place;
Jn 4.44 had said, "A prophet is not **respected** in his own country."
9.31 does listen to people who **respect** him and do what he wants
Acts 5.34 and was highly **respected** by all the people, stood up
10.22 God and is highly **respected** by all the Jewish people.
15.22 two men who were highly **respected** by the believers, Judas,
22.12 Law and was highly **respected** by all the Jews living there.
Rom 12.10 Christian brothers, and be eager to show **respect** for one another.
13. 7 and property taxes, and show **respect** and honour for them all.
2 Cor 8.18 the brother who is highly **respected** in all the churches for
Eph 5.33 wife as himself, and every wife must **respect** her husband.
6. 2 "**Respect** your father and mother" is the first commandment that
Phil 2.29 Show **respect** to all such people as he, [30] because he risked
1 Thes 4.12 way you will win the **respect** of those who are not believers,
5.12 brothers, to pay proper **respect** to those who work among you,
5.13 Treat them with the greatest **respect** and love because of the
1 Tim 3. 4 family well and make his children obey him with all **respect.**
3. 7 be a man who is **respected** by the people outside the church,
5. 3 Show **respect** for widows who really are all alone.
6. 1 their masters worthy of all **respect,** so that no one will
Heb 12. 9 of our human fathers, they punished us and we **respected** them.
Jas 2. 3 If you show more **respect** to the well-dressed man and say
1 Pet 2.17 **Respect** everyone, love your fellow-believers,
2.17 honour God, and **respect** the Emperor.
2.18 masters and show them complete **respect,** not only to those
3. 7 Treat them with **respect,** because they also will receive,
3.16 you have in you, [16] but do it with gentleness and **respect.**
2 Pet 2.10 and arrogant, and show no **respect** for the glorious beings above;

RESPOND

Num 5.22 The woman shall **respond,** "I agree;
Judg 21. 9 the roll call of the army no one from Jabesh had **responded.**
Neh 2.18 They **responded,** "Let's start rebuilding!"
12. 9 The following formed the choir that sang the **responses:**
12.24 at a time praised God **responsively** and gave thanks to him,
Is 50. 2 did my people fail to **respond** when I went to them to
58. 9 When you call to me, I will **respond.**
Hos 2.15 She will **respond** to me there as she did when she was
Mt 27.12 he said nothing in **response** to the accusations of the chief

RESPONSIBLE

Gen 24.49 you intend to fulfil your **responsibility** towards my master
26.10 wife, and you would have been **responsible** for our guilt."
39.22 other prisoners and made him **responsible** for everything that
39.23 anything for which Joseph was **responsible,** because the Lord
43. 9 pledge my own life, and you can hold me **responsible** for him.
Lev 20. 9 he is **responsible** for his own death.
20.11 They are **responsible** for their own death.
20.12 have committed incest and are **responsible** for their own death.
20.13 They are **responsible** for their own death.
20.16 They are **responsible** for their own death.
20.27 person who does this is **responsible** for his own death."
Num 3. 9 The only **responsibility** the Levites have is to serve Aaron
3.25 They were **responsible** for the Tent, its inner cover, its outer cover,
3.26 **responsible** for all the service connected with these items.
3.31 They were **responsible** for the Covenant Box, the table,
3.31 **responsible** for all the service connected with these items.
3.36 They were assigned **responsibility** for the frames for the Tent,
3.36 **responsible** for all the service connected with these items.
3.37 They were also **responsible** for the posts, bases, pegs,
3.38 They were **responsible** for carrying out the services
4.15 These are the **responsibilities** of the clan of Kohath
4.16 Aaron the priest shall be **responsible** for the whole Tent and
4.24 They shall be **responsible** for carrying the following objects:
4.28 These are the **responsibilities** of the Gershon clan in the Tent;
4.31 They shall be **responsible** for carrying the frames, bars,
4.32 Each man will be **responsible** for carrying specific items.
4.33 These are the **responsibilities** of the Merari clan in
4.49 Moses, each man was assigned **responsibility** for his task of
11.11 Why have you given me the **responsibility** for all these people?
11.14 I can't be **responsible** for all these people by myself;
11.17 help you to bear the **responsibility** for these people, and
15.31 He is **responsible** for his own death.
18. 3 duties to you and their **responsibilities** for the Tent, but
18. 4 and fulfil their **responsibilities** for all the service in the
18. 5 sons alone must fulfil the **responsibilities** for the Holy
18. 7 shall fulfil all the **responsibilities** of the priesthood
18. 7 These things are your **responsibility,** because I have given
18.23 care of the Tent and bear the full **responsibility** for it.
32.15 and you will be **responsible** for their destruction."
35.19 has the **responsibility** for putting the murderer to death.
35.21 has the **responsibility** for putting the murderer to death.
Deut 1. 9 Sinai, I told you, 'The **responsibility** for leading you is
1.12 I alone bear the heavy **responsibility** for settling your disputes?
Deut 1.15 Some were **responsible** for a thousand people, some for a hundred,
19. 6 and the relative who is **responsible** for taking revenge for
19.12 the relative **responsible** for taking revenge for the murder,
21. 8 and do not hold us **responsible** for the murder of an innocent
21. 9 Lord requires, you will not be held **responsible** for the murder.
22. 8 Then you will not be **responsible** if someone falls off and is
Josh 2.19 death will be his own fault, and we will not be **responsible;**
2.19 the house with you is harmed, then we will be **responsible.**
Judg 15. 3 I'm not going to be **responsible** for what I do to the
Ruth 2.20 of ours, one of those **responsible** for taking care of us."
3. 9 a close relative, you are **responsible** for taking care of me.
3.12 a close relative and am **responsible** for you, but there is a
3.13 find out whether or not he will take **responsibility** for you.
3.13 I swear by the living Lord that I will take the **responsibility.**
1 Sam 22.22 So I am **responsible** for the death of all your relatives.
2 Sam 13.28 I will take the **responsibility** myself.
14.11 that my relative who is **responsible** for avenging the death
1 Kgs 2. 5 and now I bear the **responsibility** for what he did, and I
2.31 will any longer be held **responsible** for what Joab did when
4. 7 his household, each man being **responsible** for one month out
14.27 to the officers **responsible** for guarding the palace gates.
2 Kgs 10. 9 you are not **responsible** for that.
12. 5 Each priest was to be **responsible** for the money brought by
1 Chr 6.49 They were **responsible** for all the worship in the Most Holy
9.19 the clan of Korah, was **responsible** for guarding the entrance
9.22 who had put their ancestors in these **responsible** positions.
9.26 four chief guards were Levites and had the final **responsibility.**
9.26 They were also **responsible** for the rooms in the Temple and
9.28 Other Levites were **responsible** for the utensils used in worship.
9.30 **responsibility** for mixing the spices belonged to the priests.
9.31 Korah, was **responsible** for preparing the baked offerings.
9.32 the clan of Kohath were **responsible** for preparing the sacred
9.33 Some Levite families were **responsible** for the temple music.
16. 7 and his fellow-Levites the **responsibility** for singing praises
23.29 to be **responsible** for the bread offered to God, the
23.32 They were given the **responsibility** of taking care of the
26.13 drew lots to see which gate it would be **responsible** for.
26.24 was the chief official **responsible** for the temple treasury.
2 Chr 2. 2 three thousand six hundred men **responsible** for supervising
11.23 Rehoboam wisely assigned **responsibilities** to his sons,
12.10 to the officers **responsible** for guarding the palace gates.
19.11 The Levites have the **responsibility** of seeing that the
29.35 burnt whole, the priests were **responsible** for burning the
31.16 or older who had daily **responsibilities** in the Temple in
31.19 to these cities, there were **responsible** men who distributed
35. 4 by clans, according to the **responsibilities** assigned to you
36.23 and has given me the **responsibility** of building a temple for
Ezra 1. 2 and has given me the **responsibility** of building a temple for
10. 4 It is your **responsibility** to act.
Neh 11.22 Asaph, the clan that was **responsible** for the music in the
12.44 These men were **responsible** for collecting from the farms
Prov 6. 1 Have you promised to be **responsible** for someone else's debts,
17.18 would promise to be **responsible** for someone else's debts.
20.16 enough to promise to be **responsible** for a stranger's debts
22.26 Don't promise to be **responsible** for someone else's debts.
27.13 enough to promise to be **responsible** for a stranger's debts
Jer 51.35 "May Babylonia be held **responsible** for the violence done to us!"
51.35 "May Babylonia be held **responsible** for what we have suffered!"
Ezek 3.18 a sinner, and I will hold you **responsible** for his death.
3.20 good he did—and I will hold you **responsible** for his death.
33. 6 but I will hold the watchman **responsible** for their death.
33. 8 a sinner, and I will hold you **responsible** for his death.
Dan 11. 1 He is **responsible** for helping and defending me.
Jon 1.14 You, O Lord, are **responsible** for all this;
Mt 27.24 and said, "I am not **responsible** for the death of this man!
27.25 crowd answered, "Let the **responsibility** for his death fall on us
Acts 5.28 and you want to make us **responsible** for his death!"
18. 6 I am not **responsible.**
19.33 concluded that Alexander was **responsible,** since the Jews made him
20.26 if any of you should be lost, I am not **responsible.**

REST (1)
[DAY OF REST]

Gen 18. 4 you can **rest** here beneath this tree.
28.11 He lay down to sleep, **resting** his head on a stone.
49.15 But he sees that the **resting-place** is good And that the
Ex 16.23 that tomorrow is a holy **day of rest,** dedicated to him.
16.25 is the Sabbath, a **day of rest** dedicated to the Lord, and
16.26 on the seventh day, the **day of rest,** there will be none."
16.29 have given you a **day of rest,** and that is why on
20.10 but the seventh day is a **day of rest** dedicated to me.
20.11 and everything in them, but on the seventh day I **rested.**
23.11 the seventh year let it **rest,** and do not harvest anything
23.12 foreigners who work for you and even your animals can **rest.**
31.13 "Keep the Sabbath, my **day of rest,** because it is a sign
31.14 You must keep the **day of rest,** because it is sacred.
31.15 the seventh day is a solemn **day of rest** dedicated to me.
31.17 and on the seventh day I stopped working and **rested."**
35. 2 be sacred, a solemn **day of rest** dedicated to me, the Lord.
39.21 cord, so that the breast-piece **rested** above the belt and did
Lev 23. 3 that the seventh day, the Sabbath, is a **day of rest.**
23.23 month observe a special **day of rest,** and come together for
23.32 day as a special **day of rest,** during which nothing may be
23.39 The first day shall be a special **day of rest.**
25. 4 be a year of complete **rest** for the land, a year dedicated
25. 5 it is a year of complete **rest** for the land.
26.34 enjoy the years of complete **rest** that you would not give it;
26.34 lie abandoned and get its **rest** while you are in exile in

Lev 26.43 it can enjoy its complete **rest,** and they must pay the full
Num 23.24 It doesn't **rest** until it has torn and devoured, Until it has
Deut 5.14 but the seventh day is a **day of rest** dedicated to me.
5.14 Your slaves must **rest** just as you do.
6. 7 you are away, when you are **resting** and when you are working.
11.19 you are away, when you are **resting** and when you are working.
Josh 11.23 So the people **rested** from war.
Ruth 2. 7 just now stopped to **rest** for a while under the shelter."
3.18 Boaz will not **rest** today until he settles the matter."
2 Sam 4. 5 there about noon, while he was taking his midday **rest.**
11. 8 Then he said to Uriah, "Go home and **rest** a while."
16.14 out when they reached the Jordan, and there they **rested.**
1 Kgs 7. 2 fifteen in each row, with cedar beams **resting** on them.
7.25 The tank **rested** on the backs of twelve bronze bulls that
2 Kgs 4.11 Elisha returned to Shunem and went up to his room to **rest.**
2 Chr 4. 4 The tank **rested** on the backs of twelve bronze bulls that
36.21 make up for the Sabbath **rest** that has not been observed."
Ezra 8.32 When we reached Jerusalem, we **rested** for three days.
Job 3.13 then, I would be at **rest** now, [14] sleeping like the kings
3.17 men stop their evil, and tired workmen find **rest** at last.
3.26 I have no peace, no **rest,** and my troubles never end.
7.13 I lie down and try to **rest;**
11.18 God will protect you and give you **rest.**
Ps 22. 2 I call at night, but get no **rest.**
23. 2 He lets me **rest** in fields of green grass and leads me
55. 6 I would fly away and find **rest.**
94.13 You give him **rest** from days of trouble until a pit is
95.11 never enter the land where I would have given you **rest.'** "
132. 4 I will not **rest** or sleep, [5] until I provide a place for
139. 3 You see me, whether I am working or **resting;**
Prov 6. 4 Don't let yourself go to sleep or even stop to **rest.**
6.10 "I'll fold my hands and **rest** a while."
24.33 Fold your hands and **rest** awhile, [34] but while you are asleep,
Ecc 2.23 Even at night your mind can't **rest.**
6. 5 at least it has found **rest**—[6] more so than the man who
12. 5 are going to our final **resting place,** and then there will be
Song 1. 7 Where will they **rest** from the noonday sun?
Is 14. 7 last the whole world enjoys **rest** and peace, and everyone
16. 3 in the heat of noon, and let us **rest** in your shade.
27.10 become a pasture for cattle, where they can **rest** and graze.
28.12 He offered **rest** and comfort to all of you, but you
34.14 The night monster will come there looking for a place to **rest.**
57. 2 Those who live good lives find peace and **rest** in death.
57.20 evil men are like the **restless** sea, whose waves never stop
62. 7 They must give him no **rest** until he restores Jerusalem And
63.14 led into a fertile valley, so the Lord gave his people **rest.**
Jer 22.23 You **rest** secure among the cedars brought from Lebanon;
31. 2 people of Israel longed for **rest,** [3] I appeared to them from
45. 3 I am worn out from groaning, and I can't find any **rest!'**
47. 6 Go back to your scabbard, stay there and **rest!'**
47. 7 But how can it **rest,** when I have given it work to
49.23 Anxiety rolls over them like a sea, and they cannot **rest.**
Lam 5. 5 donkeys or camels, we are tired, but are allowed no **rest.**
Ezek 31. 6 The nations of the world **rested** in its shade.
32.30 disgrace with those killed in battle and are laid to **rest,**
32.32 be killed and laid to **rest** with all the uncircumcised who
34.15 of my sheep, and I will find them a place to **rest.**
Dan 4.12 Wild animals **rested** in its shade, birds built nests
4.21 Wild animals **rested** under it, and birds made their nests in
Hab 1. 6 the Babylonians to power, those fierce, **restless** people.
2. 5 Greedy men are proud and **restless**—like death itself they are
Zeph 2.15 place it will become, a place where wild animals will **rest!**
Mt 5.35 nor by earth, for it is the **resting place** for his feet;
8.20 but the Son of Man has nowhere to lie down and **rest."**
11.28 tired from carrying heavy loads, and I will give you **rest.**
11.29 and you will find **rest.**
12.43 it travels over dry country looking for a place to **rest.**
26.45 to the disciples and said, "Are you still sleeping and **resting?**
Mk 6.31 where we will be alone and you can **rest** for a while."
14.41 time, he said to them, "Are you still sleeping and **resting?**
Lk 9.58 but the Son of Man has nowhere to lie down and **rest."**
11.24 it travels over dry country looking for a place to **rest.**
23.56 On the Sabbath they **rested,** as the Law commanded.
2 Cor 7. 5 Even after we arrived in Macedonia, we had no **rest.**
Heb 3.11 never enter the land where I would have given them **rest!'** "
3.18 I would have given them **rest"**—of whom was he speaking?
4. 1 the promise that we may receive that **rest** he spoke about.
4. 1 will be found to have failed to receive that promised **rest.**
4. 3 We who believe, then, do receive that **rest** which God promised.
4. 3 never enter the land where I would have given them **rest!'** "
4. 4 "God **rested** on the seventh day from all his work."
4. 5 never enter that land where I would have given them **rest."**
4. 6 Good News did not receive that **rest,** because they did not believe.
4. 8 had given the people the **rest** that God had promised, God
4. 9 remains for God's people a **rest**
4. 9 like God's **resting** on the seventh day.
4.10 For whoever receives that **rest** which God promised
4.10 will rest from his own work, just as God **rested** from his.
4.11 our best to receive that **rest,** so that no one of us
13.17 watch over your souls without **resting,** since they must give God
Rev 6.11 and they were told to **rest** a little while longer, until the
14.13 "They will enjoy **rest** from their hard work, because the results

REST (2)

Mt 20.26 wants to be great, he must be the servant of the **rest;**
26.33 "I will never leave you, even though all the **rest** do!"
Mk 7. 3 Pharisees, as well as the **rest** of the Jews, follow the
9.14 When they joined the **rest** of the disciples, they saw a
10.43 wants to be great, he must be the servant of the **rest;**
12.22 happened to the third brother, [22] and then to the **rest:**
14.29 "I will never leave you, even though all the **rest** do!"
15.16 governor's palace and called together the **rest** of the company.
Lk 8.10 to you, but to the **rest** it comes by means of parables,
24. 9 all these things to the eleven disciples and all the **rest.**
Jn 1.39 where he lived, and spent the **rest** of that day with him.
Acts 5. 2 money for himself and handed the **rest** over to the apostles.
12.17 "Tell this to James and the **rest** of the believers," he
15.17 And so all the **rest** of mankind will come to me,
26.29 that you and all the **rest** of you who are listening to
27.44 the **rest** were to follow, holding on to the planks or to
Rom 11. 7 the **rest** grew deaf to God's call.
1 Tim 5.20 all those who commit sins, so that the **rest** may be afraid.
1 Pet 1.17 so then, spend the **rest** of your lives here on earth in
4. 2 then, you must live the **rest** of your earthly lives
Rev 2.24 "But the **rest** of you in Thyatira have not followed this
9.20 The **rest** of mankind, all those who had not been killed
11.13 The **rest** of the people were terrified and praised the greatness
12.17 off to fight against the **rest** of her descendants, all those
14. 4 have been redeemed from the **rest** of mankind and are the
20. 5 (The **rest** of the dead did not come to life until the

REST (3)

Gen 8. 4 month the boat came to **rest** on a mountain in the Ararat
49.26 May these blessings **rest** on the head of Joseph, On the brow
Ex 28.28 cord, so that the breast-piece **rests** above the belt and does
Num 10.12 The cloud came to **rest** in the wilderness of Paran.
2 Sam 7.29 and your blessing will **rest** on my descendants for ever."
1 Kgs 6. 6 so that the rooms could **rest** on the wall without having
1 Chr 17.27 them, and your blessing will **rest** on them for ever."
Ezek 41. 6 so that the rooms could **rest** on the wall without being
44.30 as an offering, and my blessing will **rest** on their homes.
Lk 1.35 Spirit will come on you, and God's power will **rest** upon you.
Acts 2.26 mortal though I am, will **rest** assured in hope, [27] because you
1 Cor 2. 5 Your faith, then, does not **rest** on human wisdom but on
1 Pet 4.14 the glorious Spirit, the Spirit of God, is **resting** on you.

AV RESTITUTION

Ex 22. 2 He must **pay** for what he stole.
22. 5 man's field, he must make **good** the loss with the crops from
22. 6 the one who started the fire is to **pay** for the damage.
22.12 but if the animal was stolen, the man must **repay** the owner.
Acts 3.21 all things to be made **new,** as God announced through his holy

RESTORATION

[YEAR OF RESTORATION]

The year, coming every fifty years, when the ancient Israelites returned to the original owner any property they were holding. They also freed their Israelite slaves, and did not cultivate their fields.

Lev 25.15 land can produce crops before the next **Year of Restoration.**
25.27 until the next **Year of Restoration,** when he would in any
25.28 of the man who bought it until the next **Year of Restoration.**
25.30 it will not be returned in the **Year of Restoration.**
25.31 and they are to be returned in the **Year of Restoration.**
25.33 returned in the **Year of Restoration,** because the houses
25.40 hired man and serve you until the next **Year of Restoration.**
25.50 until the next **Year of Restoration** and must set the price
25.54 children must be set free in the next **Year of Restoration.**
27.17 after a **Year of Restoration,** the full price applies.
27.18 until the next **Year of Restoration,** and fix a reduced price.
27.21 At the next **Year of Restoration** the field will become
27.23 until the next **Year of Restoration,** and the man must pay the
27.24 At the **Year of Restoration** the field shall be returned
Num 36. 4 In the **Year of Restoration,** when all property that has
Ezek 46.17 property again when the **Year of Restoration** comes round.

RESTORE

Gen 40.13 release you, pardon you, and **restore** you to your position.
40.21 He **restored** the wine steward to his former position,
41.13 **restored** me to my position, but you executed the baker."
Lev 25.10 has been sold shall be **restored** to the original owner or his
25.13 that has been sold shall be **restored** to its original owner.
Num 21.27 We want to see it rebuilt and **restored.**
36. 4 that has been sold is **restored** to its original owners, the
1 Sam 2. 6 The Lord kills and **restores** to life;
2 Sam 8. 3 was on his way to **restore** his control over the territory by
16. 3 that the Israelites will now **restore** to him the kingdom of
1 Kgs 12.21 to go to war and **restore** his control over the northern
17.21 and prayed, "O Lord my God, **restore** this child to life!"
20.34 said to him, "I will **restore** to you the towns my father
2 Kgs 6.20 **restored** their sight, and they saw that they were inside Samaria.
8. 3 ask for her house and her land to be **restored** to her.
14.28 battles, and how he **restored** Damascus and Hamath to Israel,
1 Chr 11. 8 side of the hill, and Joab **restored** the rest of the city.
2 Chr 11. 1 to go to war and **restore** his control over the northern
24.13 and they **restored** the Temple to its original condition,
Ezra 5.14 He **restored** the gold and silver temple utensils which
Neh 1. 3 gates had not been **restored** since the time they were burnt.
7.70 contributed to help pay the cost of **restoring** the Temple:
Job 8. 6 and help you and **restore** your household as your reward.
Ps 3. 3 you give me victory and **restore** my courage.
13. 3 **Restore** my strength;
30. 3 on my way to the depths below, but you **restored** my life.
41. 3 them when they are sick and will **restore** them to health.
41.10 merciful to me, Lord, and **restore** my health, and I will pay
68. 9 caused abundant rain to fall and **restored** your worn-out land;
71.20 and suffering on me, but you will **restore** my strength;

Ps 122. 3 Jerusalem is a city **restored** in beautiful order and harmony.
147. 2 The Lord is **restoring** Jerusalem;
Song 2. 5 **Restore** my strength with raisins and refresh me with apples!
Is 49. 6 Not only will you **restore** to greatness the people of
57.15 repentant, so that I can **restore** their confidence and hope.
58.12 who rebuilt the walls, who **restored** the ruined houses."
62. 7 him no rest until he **restores** Jerusalem And makes it a city
Jer 27.22 Then I will bring them back and **restore** them to this place.
29.14 you will find me, and I will **restore** you to your land.
30. 3 is coming when I will **restore** my people, Israel and Judah.
30.18 "I will **restore** my people to their land and have mercy on
30.18 Jerusalem will be rebuilt, and its palace **restored.**
30.20 I will **restore** the nation's ancient power and establish it
31.23 of Israel, says, "When I **restore** the people to their land,
32.44 I will **restore** the people to their land.
33. 6 heal this city and its people and **restore** them to health.
50.19 I will **restore** the people of Israel to their land.
Lam 5.21 **Restore** our ancient glory.
Ezek 16.55 again, and you and your villages will also be **restored.**
Dan 8.14 Then the Temple will be **restored."**
9.17 **Restore** your Temple, which has been destroyed;
9.17 **restore** it so that everyone will know that you are God.
9.20 pleading with the Lord my God to **restore** his holy Temple.
Joel 3. 1 I will **restore** the prosperity of Judah and Jerusalem.
Amos 9.11 is coming when I will **restore** the kingdom of David, which is
9.11 I will repair its walls and **restore** it.
Nah 2. 2 (The Lord is about to **restore** the glory of Israel, as it
Zech 1.16 My Temple will be **restored,** and the city will be rebuilt."
Mt 9.30 and their sight was **restored.**
Acts 15.16 I will return, says the Lord, and **restore** the kingdom of David.
Jas 5.15 the Lord will **restore** him to health, and the sins he has

AV RESTORE

Gen 20. 7 But now, **give** the woman back to her husband.
20. 7 But if you do not **give** her back, I warn you that
Ex 22. 1 or sells it, he must **pay** five cows for one cow and
22. 2 is found alive in his possession, he shall **pay** two for one.
Lev 6. 4 ways, he must **repay** whatever he got by dishonest means.
6. 4 is found guilty, he must **repay** the owner in full, plus an
24.21 Whoever kills an animal shall **replace** it, but whoever
25.27 In that case he must **pay** to the man who bought it
25.28 not have enough money to **buy** the land back, it remains under
Num 35.25 relative, and they are to **return** him to the city of refuge
Deut 22. 2 When its owner comes looking for it, **give** it to him.
2 Sam 9. 7 I will **give** you back all the land that belonged to your
12. 6 a cruel thing, he must **pay** back four times as much as
2 Kgs 8. 6 official and told him to **give** back to her everything that
Neh 5.11 And **give** them back their fields, vineyards, olive-groves,
5.12 We'll **give** the property back and not try to collect the debts."
Ps 23. 3 He **gives** me new strength.
51.12 **Give** me again the joy that comes from your salvation,
Prov 6.31 he is caught, he must **pay** back seven times more—he must
Is 1.26 I will **give** you rulers and advisers like those you had
42.22 robbed and plundered, with no one to come to their **rescue.**
57.18 I will lead them and **help** them, and I will comfort those
Jer 30.17 I will make you **well** again;
Ezek 33.15 good—[15] for example, if he **returns** the security he took for
Dan 9.25 given to **rebuild** Jerusalem, until God's chosen leader comes,
Joel 2.25 I will **give** you back what you lost in the years when
Mt 17.11 coming first," answered Jesus, "and he will get everything **ready.**
Lk 19. 8 I will **give** half my belongings to the poor, and if I
Acts 1. 6 "Lord, will you at this time **give** the Kingdom back to Israel?"
Gal 6. 1 those of you who are spiritual should set him **right;**

RESTRAIN

1 Sam 21.13 and acted like a madman when they tried to **restrain** him;
Job 38.15 for the wicked and **restrains** them from deeds of violence.
Ps 78.38 Many times he held back his anger and **restrained** his fury.
78.50 He did not **restrain** his anger or spare their lives, but
Prov 23. 2 If you have a big appetite, **restrain** yourself.
1 Cor 7. 9 But if you cannot **restrain** your desires, go ahead and marry—
Eph 4.19 vice and do all sorts of indecent things without **restraint.**
1 Thes 5.19 Do not **restrain** the Holy Spirit;

RESTRICTIONS

1 Cor 7.35 I am not trying to put **restrictions** on you.

RESULT

Mt 11.19 God's wisdom, however, is shown to be true by its **results."**
23.35 As a **result,** the punishment for the murder of all
27.14 with the **result** that the Governor was greatly surprised.
Lk 16. 8 "As a **result** the master of this dishonest manager praised him
Jn 11. 4 he said, "The final **result** of this illness will not be
Acts 5.15 As a **result** of what the apostles were doing, sick people
Rom 1.27 and as a **result** they bring upon themselves the punishment
5.12 As a **result,** death has spread to the whole human race
5.17 how much greater is the **result** of what was done by the
5.19 made sinners as the **result** of the disobedience of one man,
5.19 right with God as the **result** of the obedience of the one
6.16 either of sin, which **results** in death,
6.16 or of obedience, which **results** in being put right with God.
6.21 The **result** of those things is death!
6.22 life fully dedicated to him, and the **result** is eternal life.
8. 6 To be controlled by human nature **results** in death;
8. 6 to be controlled by the Spirit **results** in life and peace.
9. 8 the children born as a **result** of God's promise are regarded
9.11 son might be completely the **result** of God's own purpose, God
1 Cor 9. 1 And aren't you the **result** of my work for the Lord?
2 Cor 12. 6 than he has as a **result** of what he has seen me
Gal 4.23 by the free woman was born as a **result** of God's promise.
4.28 are God's children as a **result** of his promise, just as Isaac
Eph 2. 8 It is not the **result** of your own efforts, but God's gift,
Phil 1.13 As a **result,** the whole palace guard and all the others
Col 3.11 As a **result,** there is no longer any distinction between
2 Thes 1. 5 is just and as a **result** you will become worthy of his
2.12 The **result** is that all who have not believed the truth,
1 Tim 6.21 possess it, and as a **result** they have lost the way of
Heb 11. 7 As a **result,** the world was condemned, and Noah received from
13.20 of the sheep as the **result** of his sacrificial death, by
Jas 1. 3 in facing such trials, the **result** is the ability to endure.
Rev 14.13 hard work, because the **results** of their service go with them."
17. 4 full of obscene and filthy things, the **result** of her immorality.

RESUME

1 Cor 7. 5 but then **resume** normal marital relations.

RESURRECTION

see also **RAISE, RISE**

Mk 12.23 to life on the day of **resurrection,** whose wife will she be?
Jn 11.25 Jesus said to her, "I am the **resurrection** and the life.
Acts 1.21 join us as a witness to the **resurrection** of the Lord Jesus.
2.31 he spoke about the **resurrection** of the Messiah when he said,
4.33 apostles gave witness to the **resurrection** of the Lord Jesus,
17.18 because Paul was preaching about Jesus and the **resurrection.**
Phil 3.10 experience the power of his **resurrection,** to share in his
2 Tim 2.18 by saying that our **resurrection** has already taken place.
Heb 6. 2 of the **resurrection** of the dead and the eternal judgement.
1 Pet 3.21 It saves you through the **resurrection** of Jesus Christ,

RETAIN

Num 32.32 battle, so that we can **retain** our property here east of the
Lk 8.15 who hear the message and **retain** it in a good and obedient

RETIRE

Num 8.25 of my presence, [25] and at the age of fifty he shall **retire.**

RETREAT

Josh 7. 4 Israelites made the attack, but they were forced to **retreat.**
7. 8 I say, O Lord, now that Israel has **retreated** from the enemy?
7.12 They **retreat** from them because they themselves have now been
8.15 men pretended that they were **retreating,** and ran away
23. 5 your God will make them **retreat** from you, and he will drive
Judg 20.32 the Israelites had planned to **retreat** and lead them away
20.36 of the Israelite army had **retreated** from the Benjaminites
20.42 **retreated** from the Israelites and ran towards the open country,
2 Sam 10.14 they fled from Abishai and **retreated** into the city.
11.15 fighting is heaviest, then **retreat** and let him be killed."
17.13 If he **retreats** into a city, our people will all bring
1 Chr 19.15 they fled from Abishai and **retreated** into the city.
Is 17.13 God reprimands them and they **retreat,** driven away like dust
Jer 21. 2 his miracles for us and force Nebuchadnezzar to **retreat."**
37. 5 Egyptian army had crossed the Egyptian border, they **retreated.**
37.11 Babylonian army **retreated** from Jerusalem because the Egyptian
Dan 11. 9 Syria will invade Egypt, but he will be forced to **retreat.**

RETURN

Gen 8.11 It **returned** to him in the evening with a fresh olive
18.14 months from now I will **return,** and Sarah will have a son."
18.33 Abraham, the Lord went away, and Abraham **returned** home.
28.21 clothing, [21] and if I **return** safely to my father's home,
30.25 said to Laban, "Let me go, so that I can **return** home.
32. 4 with Laban and that I have delayed my **return** until now.
33.18 On his **return** from Mesopotamia Jacob arrived safely at
35. 9 When Jacob **returned** from Mesopotamia, God appeared to him
37.30 He **returned** to his brothers and said, "The boy is not there!
38.11 said to his daughter-in-law Tamar, **"Return** to your father's
38.22 He **returned** to Judah and said, "I couldn't find her.
42.28 "My money has been **returned** to me," he called to his brothers.
43.12 back the money that was **returned** in the top of your sacks.
43.13 Take your brother and **return** at once.
43.18 of the money that was **returned** in our sacks the first time.
44.13 in sorrow, loaded their donkeys, and **returned** to the city.
44.25 Then he told us to **return** and buy a little food.
45.17 to load their animals and to **return** to the land of Canaan.
48. 7 not far from Ephrath, as I was **returning** from Mesopotamia.
49. 9 lion, Killing his victim and **returning** to his den,
50.14 had buried his father, he **returned** to Egypt with his
Ex 2.18 When they **returned** to their father, he asked, "Why have
4.28 the Lord had said when he told him to **return** to Egypt;
13.17 to change their minds and **return** to Egypt when they see that
14.27 sea, and at daybreak the water **returned** to its normal level.
14.28 The water **returned** and covered the chariots, the
32.31 Moses then **returned** to the Lord and said, "These people
33.11 Then Moses would **return** to the camp.
Lev 6. 2 the Lord by refusing to **return** what a fellow-Israelite has
14.39 On the seventh day he shall **return** and examine it again.
16.28 wash his clothes and have a bath before he **returns** to camp.
22.13 no children and who has **returned** to live in her father's
24.20 he causes another person shall be done to him in **return.**
25.10 who has been sold as a slave shall **return** to his family.
25.28 In that year it will be **returned** to its original owner.
25.30 it will not be **returned** in the Year of Restoration.

Lev	25.31	and they are to be **returned** in the Year of Restoration.
	25.33	bought back, it must be **returned** in the Year of Restoration,
	25.41	children shall leave you and **return** to his family and to the
	27.24	Restoration the field shall be **returned** to the original
Num	10.36	it stopped, he would say, **"Return,** Lord, to the thousands
	13.25	for forty days, the spies **returned** [26] to Moses, Aaron, and
	16.50	the plague had stopped, Aaron **returned** to Moses at the
	22.14	So they **returned** to Balak and told him that Balaam had
	22.34	it is wrong for me to go on, I will **return** home."
	31.14	of battalions and companies, who had **returned** from the war.
	31.21	to the men who had **returned** from battle, "These are the
	32. 9	the land, but when they **returned,** they discouraged the
	32.18	We will not **return** to our homes until all the other
	32.22	After that, you may **return,** because you will have fulfilled
	35.25	relative, and they are to **return** him to the city of refuge
	35.28	death of the High Priest, but after that he may **return** home.
	35.32	a payment in order to **return** home before the death of the
Deut	3.20	After that, you may **return** to this land which I have
	5.27	Then **return** and tell us what he said to you.
	5.30	Go and tell them to **return** to their tents.
	16. 7	and the next morning **return** home.
	17.16	the Lord has said that his people are never to **return** there.
	24.13	**return** it to him each evening, so that he can have it
	28.32	your eyes, looking in vain for your children to **return.**
Josh	2.22	but they did not find them, so they **returned** to Jericho.
	6.14	again marched round the city once and then **returned** to camp.
	24.28	the people away, and everyone **returned** to his own part of
Judg	2.19	died, the people used to **return** to the old ways and behave
	5.28	"Why are his horses so slow to **return?"**
	8.13	Gideon was **returning** from the battle by way of Heres Pass,
	11.29	through Gilead and Manasseh and **returned** to Mizpah in Gilead
	18. 8	When the five men **returned** to Zorah and Eshtaol, their
	19. 3	go after her and try to persuade her to **return** to him.
Ruth	3.15	Then she **returned** to the town with it.
1 Sam	6. 3	They answered, "If you **return** the Covenant Box of the
	6.21	"The Philistines have **returned** the Lord's Covenant Box.
	7.14	between Ekron and Gath were **returned** to Israel, and so
	16.13	Then Samuel **returned** to Ramah.
	17.57	So when David **returned** to camp after killing Goliath,
	18. 6	As David was **returning** after killing Goliath and as the
	20.38	picked up the arrow and **returned** to his master, [39] not
	23.24	So they left and **returned** to Ziph ahead of Saul.
	26.25	So David went on his way, and Saul **returned** home.
	30.12	After he had eaten, his strength **returned;**
	30.26	When David **returned** to Ziklag, he sent part of the loot
2 Sam	3.22	Joab and David's other officials **returned** from a raid,
	8.13	even more famous when he **returned** from killing eighteen
	10. 5	They were too ashamed to **return** home.
	10. 5	Jericho and not **return** until their beards had grown again.
	11.10	he asked him, "You have just **returned** after a long absence;
	12.20	When he **returned** to the palace, he asked for food and ate
	12.31	Then he and his men **returned** to Jerusalem.
	14.13	allowed your own son to **return** from exile, and so you have
	15.34	you can help me by **returning** to the city and telling Absalom
	15.37	So Hushai, David's friend, **returned** to the city just as
	17. 3	all his men to you, like a bride **returning** to her husband.
	17.20	but could not find them, and so they **returned** to Jerusalem.
	19.14	and they sent him word to **return** with all his officials.
	19.24	time the king left Jerusalem until he **returned** victorious.
	20.22	And Joab **returned** to Jerusalem to the king.
	23.10	it was over, the Israelites **returned** to where Eleazar was
	24. 8	months and twenty days they **returned** to Jerusalem, having
1 Kgs	10.13	Then she and her attendants **returned** to the land of Sheba.
	10.22	three years his fleet would **return,** bringing gold, silver,
	12. 2	from King Solomon, heard this news, he **returned** from Egypt.
	12.12	Jeroboam and all the people **returned** to King Rehoboam, as he
	12.20	Israel heard that Jeroboam had **returned** from Egypt, they
	13. 9	a thing, and not to **return** home the same way I came."
	13.17	a thing, and not to **return** home the same way I came."
	13.22	Instead, you **returned** and ate a meal in a place he had
	14.28	the shields, and then **returned** them to the guard-room.
	18.43	The servant went and **returned,** saying, "I didn't see anything."
	18.44	The seventh time he **returned** and said, "I saw a little
	19. 7	The Lord's angel **returned** and woke him up a second time,
	19.15	The Lord said, **"Return** to the wilderness near Damascus,
	20. 9	The messengers left and then **returned** with another message
	22.27	and to put him on bread and water until I **return** safely."
	22.28	"If you **return** safely," Micaiah exclaimed, "then the
2 Kgs	1. 5	Lord commanded, [5] and the messengers **returned** to the king.
	2.18	Then they **returned** to Elisha, who had waited at Jericho,
	2.25	Elisha went on to Mount Carmel, and later **returned** to Samaria.
	3.27	drew back from the city and **returned** to their own country.
	4.11	One day Elisha **returned** to Shunem and went up to his
	4.13	can do for her in **return** for all the trouble she has
	4.38	was a famine throughout the land, Elisha **returned** to Gilgal.
	5.15	He **returned** to Elisha with all his men and said, "Now I
	6.22	to eat and drink, and let them **return** to their king."
	7. 8	they **returned,** entered another tent, and did the same thing.
	7.15	Then they **returned** and reported to the king.
	8. 3	of the seven years, she **returned** to Israel and went to the
	8.29	He **returned** to the city of Jezreel to recover from his wounds,
	9.18	the messenger had reached the group but was not **returning.**
	9.20	the messenger had reached the group but was not **returning.**
	16.11	an altar just like it, and finished it before Ahaz **returned.**
	16.12	On his **return** from Damascus, Ahaz saw that the altar was
	19.36	Assyrian emperor Sennacherib withdrew and **returned** to Nineveh.
	22.20	The men **returned** to King Josiah with this message.
	23.20	Then he **returned** to Jerusalem.
1 Chr	9. 2	The first to **return** to their property in the cities
	12.20	Manasseh who went over to David's side when he was **returning:**
1 Chr	14.13	the Philistines **returned** to the valley and started plundering
	19. 5	They were too ashamed to **return** home.
	19. 5	Jericho and not **return** until their beards had grown again.
	20. 3	Then he and his men **returned** to Jerusalem.
	21. 4	the whole country of Israel, and then **returned** to Jerusalem.
2 Chr	1.13	Tent of the Lord's presence was, and **returned** to Jerusalem.
	9.12	Then she and her attendants **returned** to the land of Sheba.
	9.21	three years his fleet would **return,** bringing gold, silver,
	10. 2	to escape from King Solomon, heard this news, he **returned** home.
	10.12	Jeroboam and all the people **returned** to King Rehoboam, as he
	12.11	carried the shields and then **returned** them to the guardroom.
	14.15	Then they **returned** to Jerusalem.
	18.26	and to put him on bread and water until I **return** safely."
	18.27	"If you **return** safely," Micaiah exclaimed, "then the
	19. 1	Jehoshaphat of Judah **returned** safely to his palace in Jerusalem.
	22. 6	He **returned** to the city of Jezreel to recover from his wounds,
	24.11	would take the money out and **return** the box to its place.
	24.19	prophets to warn them to **return** to him, but the people
	25.14	When Amaziah **returned** from defeating the Edomites, he
	28. 9	He met the **returning** Israelite army with its Judaean
	28.15	Then the Israelites **returned** home to Samaria.
	30. 6	Now **return** to the Lord, the God of Abraham,
	30. 6	and he will **return** to you.
	30. 9	If you **return** to the Lord, then those who have taken your
	30. 9	merciful, and if you **return** to him, he will accept you."
	31. 1	then they all **returned** home.
	34. 7	Then he **returned** to Jerusalem.
	34.28	The men **returned** to King Josiah with this message.
	36.13	stubbornly refused to repent and **return** to the Lord, the God
Ezra	1. 4	in exile need help to **return,** their neighbours are to give
	2. 1	the province of Babylon and **returned** to Jerusalem and Judah,
	2. 2	the number of those from each clan who **returned** from exile:
	2.21	whose ancestors had lived in the following towns also **returned:**
	2.36	This is the list of the priestly clans that **returned** from exile:
	2.40	Clans of Levites who **returned** from exile:
	2.43	Clans of temple workmen who **returned** from exile:
	2.55	Clans of Solomon's servants who **returned** from exile:
	2.58	and of Solomon's servants who **returned** from exile was 392.
	2.59	Tobiah, and Nekoda who **returned** from the towns of Tel Melah,
	2.64	Total number of exiles who **returned** – 42,360
	3. 3	Even though the **returning** exiles were afraid of the people
	4. 1	heard that those who had **returned** from exile were rebuilding
	5.15	him to take them and **return** them to the Temple in Jerusalem,
	6. 5	in Jerusalem are to be **returned** to their proper place in the
	6.16	who had **returned** from exile—joyfully dedicated the Temple.
	6.19	The people who had **returned** from exile celebrated
	6.20	who had **returned,** for the priests, and for themselves.
	6.21	all the Israelites who had **returned** from exile and by all
	7.28	of the heads of the clans of Israel to **return** with me."
	8. 1	exile in Babylonia and who **returned** with Ezra to Jerusalem
	8. 2	Adonikam, with 60 men (they **returned** at a later date)
	8.35	All those who had **returned** from exile then brought
	9. 4	said about the sins of those who had **returned** from exile.
	10. 7	that all those who had **returned** from exile were to meet in
	10.16	The **returned** exiles accepted the plan, so Ezra the
Neh	1. 2	about our fellow-Jews who had **returned** from exile in Babylonia.
	2. 6	would be gone and when I would **return,** and I told him.
	2.15	Then I **returned** the way I had come and went back into
	7. 5	of those who had first **returned** from captivity, and this is
	7. 6	the province of Babylon and **returned** to Jerusalem and Judah,
	7. 8	the number of those from each clan who **returned** from exile:
	7.26	whose ancestors had lived in the following towns also **returned:**
	7.39	This is the list of the priestly clans that **returned** from exile:
	7.43	Clans of Levites who **returned** from exile:
	7.46	Clans of temple workmen who **returned** from exile:
	7.57	Clans of Solomon's servants who **returned** from exile:
	7.60	and of Solomon's servants who **returned** from exile was 392.
	7.61	Tobiah, and Nekoda who **returned** from the towns of Tel Melah,
	7.66	Total number of exiles who **returned** – 42,360
	9.28	When peace **returned,** they sinned again, and again you
	12. 1	the priests and Levites who **returned** from exile with
	13. 7	I received his permission [7] and **returned** to Jerusalem.
Job	7. 9	cloud that fades and is gone, a man dies and never **returns;**
	16.22	years are passing now, and I walk the road of no **return.**
	22.23	Yes, you must humbly **return** to God and put an end to
Ps	76. 4	How majestic, as you **return** from the mountains where you
	90. 3	You tell man to **return** to what he was;
	146. 4	When they die, they **return** to the dust;
Prov	2.19	He never **returns** to the road to life.
Ecc	1. 7	The water **returns** to where the rivers began, and starts all
	12. 7	Our bodies will **return** to the dust of the earth, and the
Song	2.17	**Return,** my darling, like a gazelle, like a stag on the
Is	9.13	Lord Almighty has punished them, they have not **returned** to him.
	14. 2	the people of Israel to **return** to the land which the Lord
	23. 1	As your ships **return** from Cyprus, you learn the news.
	37.37	Assyrian emperor Sennacherib withdrew and **returned** to Nineveh.
	43. 6	Let my people **return** from distant lands, from every part of
	52. 8	see with their own eyes the **return** of the Lord to Zion!
	57.14	The Lord says, "Let my people **return** to me.
	60. 8	that skim along like clouds, Like doves **returning** home?
	62.10	out of the city And build a road for your **returning** people!
Jer	3. 1	have had many lovers, and now you want to **return** to me!
	3. 7	after she had done all this, she would surely **return** to me.
	3. 7	But she did not **return,** and her unfaithful sister Judah saw
	3.10	Israel's unfaithful sister, only pretended to **return** to me;
	3.18	in the north and will **return** to the land that I gave
	3.22	**Return,** all of you who have turned away from the Lord;
	8. 5	You cling to your idols and refuse to **return** to me.
	8. 7	Even storks know when it is time to **return;**
	15.19	the Lord replied, "If you **return,** I will take you back, and

Jer	22.10	taking him away, never to **return,** never again to see the
	22.11	of Judah, "He has gone away from here, never to **return.**
	22.27	to see this country again, but you will never **return."**
	24. 7	God, because they will **return** to me with all their heart.
	31. 9	My people will **return** weeping, praying as I lead them back.
	31.16	they will **return** from the enemy's land.
	31.18	we are ready to **return** to you, the Lord our God.
	31.19	We turned away from you, but soon we wanted to **return.**
	34.22	I will give the order, and they will **return** to this city.
	37. 7	is on its way to help you, but it will **return** home.
	40.12	places where they had been scattered, and **returned** to Judah.
	43. 5	all the people who had **returned** from the nations where they
	44.14	Not one of them will **return** to Judah, where they long to
	44.14	No one will **return** except a few refugees."
	44.28	few of you will escape death and **return** from Egypt to Judah.
Lam	3.21	Yet hope **returns** when I remember this one thing:
Ezek	9.11	man wearing linen clothes **returned** and reported to the Lord,
	11.18	When they **return,** they are to get rid of all the filthy,
	13. 9	you will never **return** to your land.
	18. 7	He **returns** what a borrower gives him as security;
	18.16	He **returns** what a borrower gives him as security.
	20.38	but I will not let them **return** to the land of Israel.
	33.15	good—[15] for example, if he **returns** the security he took for
Dan	4.34	the king, "I looked up at the sky, and my sanity **returned.**
	4.36	"When my sanity **returned,** my honour, my majesty, and
	6.18	the king **returned** to the palace and spent a sleepless night,
	11.13	time comes, he will **return** with a large, well-equipped army.
	11.19	The king will **return** to the fortresses of his own land,
	11.28	The king of Syria will **return** home with all the loot he
	11.28	will do as he pleases and then **return** to his own land.
Hos	5. 4	people have done prevents them from **returning** to their God.
	6. 1	The people say, "Let's **return** to the Lord!
	7.10	happened, they have not **returned** to me, the Lord their God.
	11. 5	"They refuse to **return** to me,
	11. 5	and so they must **return** to Egypt, and Assyria will rule
	12. 6	descendants of Jacob, trust in your God and **return** to him.
	14. 1	**Return** to the Lord your God, people of Israel.
	14. 2	**Return** to the Lord, and let this prayer be your offering
Joel	2.12	the Lord, "repent sincerely and **return** to me with fasting
Amos	5. 3	Israel sends out a thousand soldiers, but only a hundred **return;**
Obad	20	exiles from northern Israel will **return** and conquer
Mic	2. 8	Men **return** from battle, thinking they are safe at home, but
	2.12	I will bring you together like sheep **returning** to the fold.
	7.12	Your people will **return** to you from everywhere—from
Hag	1.12	all the people who had **returned** from the exile in Babylonia,
	1.14	High Priest, and all the people who had **returned** from the exile.
Zech	1. 3	say to you, 'Return to me, and I will **return** to you.
	2. 6	now, you exiles, escape from Babylonia and **return** to Jerusalem.
	6.10	All these men have **returned** from exile in Babylonia.
	8. 3	I will **return** to Jerusalem, my holy city, and live there.
	9.12	**Return,** you exiles who now have hope;
	9.12	**return** to your place of safety.
	10. 9	They and their children will survive and **return** home together.
Mt	2.12	Then they **returned** to their country by another road,
	17.14	When they **returned** to the crowd, a man came to Jesus,
	25.27	I would have received it all back with interest when I **returned.**
	26.40	Then he **returned** to the three disciples and found them asleep;
	26.43	He **returned** once more and found the disciples asleep;
	26.45	he **returned** to the disciples and said, "Are you still sleeping
Mk	6.30	The apostles **returned** and met with Jesus, and told him all
	8.25	his eyesight **returned,** and he saw everything clearly.
	14.37	Then he **returned** and found the three disciples asleep.
	16.13	They **returned** and told the others, but they would not believe
Lk	2.39	law of the Lord, they **returned** to their home town of
	4. 1	Jesus **returned** from the Jordan full of the Holy Spirit and
	4.14	Jesus **returned** to Galilee, and the power of the Holy Spirit
	8.40	When Jesus **returned** to the other side of the lake, the
	8.55	Her life **returned,** and she got up at once, and Jesus
	12.37	servants whose master finds them awake and ready when he **returns!**
	19.23	Then I would have received it back with interest when I **returned.'**
	24. 9	women remembered his words, [9] **returned** from the tomb, and told
Jn	4.27	moment Jesus' disciples **returned,** and they were greatly surprised
	11.46	But some of them **returned** to the Pharisees and told them
	13.12	garment back on and **returned** to his place at the table.
	20.17	tell them that I am **returning** to him who is my Father
Acts	4.23	John were set free, they **returned** to their group and told
	5.22	apostles in prison, so they **returned** to the Council and reported,
	12.25	Saul finished their mission and **returned** from Jerusalem,
	15.16	'After this I will **return,** says the Lord, and restore the
	17.15	as Athens and then **returned** to Berea with instructions from Paul
	23.32	The next day the foot-soldiers **returned** to the fort and left
Gal	1.17	I went at once to Arabia, and then I **returned** to Damascus.
1 Thes	2.18	We wanted to **return** to you.
Heb	11.15	if they had, they would have had the chance to **return.**

REUBEN

Jacob and Leah's eldest son, the tribe descended from him and its territory e. of R. Jordan.

Gen	29.32	so she named him **Reuben.**
	30.14	**Reuben** went into the fields and found mandrakes,
	35.22	in that land, **Reuben** had sexual intercourse with Bilhah,
	35.23	The sons of Leah were **Reuben** (Jacob's eldest son),
	37.21	**Reuben** heard them and tried to save Joseph.
	37.29	When **Reuben** came back to the well and found that Joseph
	42.22	**Reuben** said, "I told you not to harm the boy, but you
	42.37	**Reuben** said to his father, "If I do not bring Benjamin
	46. 8	Egypt with him were his eldest son **Reuben** [9] and Reuben's sons:
	48. 5	and Manasseh are just as much my sons as **Reuben** and Simeon.
Gen	49. 3	**"Reuben,** my first-born, you are my strength And the first
Ex	1. 2	each with his family, were [2] **Reuben,** Simeon, Levi, Judah,
	6.14	**Reuben,** Jacob's first-born, had four sons:
Num	1.20	beginning with the tribe of **Reuben,** Jacob's eldest son.
	2.10	banner of the division of **Reuben** shall camp in their groups,
	2.10	The division of **Reuben** shall march second.
	10.18	by the tribe of **Reuben** would start out, company by company,
	16. 1	members of the tribe of **Reuben**—Dathan and Abiram, the sons
	26. 5	The tribe of **Reuben** (Reuben was the eldest son of Jacob):
	32. 1	The tribes of **Reuben** and Gad had a lot of livestock.
	32.15	If you people of **Reuben** and Gad refuse to follow him now,
	32.25	The men of Gad and **Reuben** said, "Sir, we will do as
	32.29	the men of Gad and **Reuben** cross the Jordan ready for battle
	32.31	The men of Gad and **Reuben** answered, "Sir, we will do as
	32.33	the tribes of Gad and **Reuben** and to half the tribe of
	32.37	The tribe of **Reuben** rebuilt Heshbon, Elealeh,
	34.14	The tribes of **Reuben** and Gad and the eastern half of
Deut	3.12	assigned to the tribes of **Reuben** and Gad the territory north
	3.16	And to the tribes of **Reuben** and Gad I assigned the
	4.43	For the tribe of **Reuben** there was the city of Bezer, on
	11. 6	Dathan and Abiram, the sons of Eliab of the tribe of **Reuben.**
	27.13	**Reuben,** Gad, Asher, Zebulun, Dan, and Naphtali.
	29. 8	it among the tribes of **Reuben** and Gad, and half the tribe
	33. 6	Moses said about the tribe of **Reuben:**
	33. 6	"May **Reuben** never die out, Although their people are few."
Josh	1.12	said to the tribes of **Reuben** and Gad and to half the
	4.12	men of the tribes of **Reuben** and Gad and of half the
	12. 6	land to the tribes of **Reuben** and Gad and to half the
	13. 8	The tribes of **Reuben** and Gad and the other half of the
	13.15	to the families of the tribe of **Reuben** as their possession.
	13.23	The Jordan was the western border of the tribe of **Reuben.**
	13.23	to the families of the tribe of **Reuben** as their possession.
	15. 6	(Bohan was a son of **Reuben),** [7] from Trouble Valley up to Debir,
	18. 7	course, the tribes of Gad, **Reuben,** and East Manasseh have
	18.17	(Bohan was a son of **Reuben)** [18] and passed north of the
	20. 8	of Jericho, they chose Bezer in the territory of **Reuben;**
	21. 7	were assigned twelve cities from the territories of **Reuben,**
	21.36	From the territory of **Reuben** they received four cities:
	22. 1	the people of the tribes of **Reuben,** Gad, and East Manasseh.
	22. 9	people of the tribes of **Reuben,** Gad, and East Manasseh went
	22.10	tribes of **Reuben,** Gad, and East Manasseh arrived at Geliloth,
	22.11	people of the tribes of **Reuben,** Gad, and East Manasseh have
	22.13	people of the tribes of **Reuben,** Gad, and East Manasseh in
	22.15	Gilead, to the people of **Reuben,** Gad, and East Manasseh,
	22.21	people of the tribes of **Reuben,** Gad, and East Manasseh
	22.25	Jordan a boundary between us and you people of **Reuben** and Gad.
	22.30	people of the tribes of **Reuben,** Gad, and East Manasseh had
	22.32	leaders left the people of **Reuben** and Gad in the land of
	22.33	the land where the people of **Reuben** and Gad had settled.
	22.34	The people of **Reuben** and Gad said, "This altar is a
Judg	5.15	But the tribe of **Reuben** was divided;
	5.16	Yes, the tribe of **Reuben** was divided;
2 Kgs	10.33	where the tribes of Gad, **Reuben,** and East Manasseh lived.
1 Chr	2. 1	**Reuben,** Simeon, Levi, Judah, Issachar, Zebulun, [2] Dan,
	5. 1	the descendants of **Reuben,** the eldest of Jacob's sons.
	5. 3	**Reuben,** the eldest of Jacob's sons, had four sons:
	5. 7	list the following clan leaders in the tribe of **Reuben:**
	5.10	King Saul the tribe of **Reuben** attacked the Hagrites, killed
	5.11	lived to the north of **Reuben** in the land of Bashan as
	5.18	In the tribes of **Reuben,** Gad, and East Manasseh there
	5.26	He deported the tribes of **Reuben,** Gad, and East Manasseh and
	6.63	towns in the territories of **Reuben,** Gad, and Zebulun were
	6.78	In the territory of **Reuben,** east of the River Jordan
	11.26	member of the tribe of **Reuben,** with his own group of thirty
	12.23	Tribes east of the Jordan—**Reuben,** Gad, and East Manasseh:
	26.32	River Jordan—the territories of **Reuben,** Gad, and East Manasseh.
	27.16	**Reuben** Eliezer son of Zichri
Ezek	48. 1	Dan Asher Naphtali Manasseh Ephraim **Reuben** Judah
	48.30	gates in the north wall are named after **Reuben,** Judah, and
Rev	7. 5	Judah, **Reuben,** Gad, Asher, Naphtali, Manasseh, Simeon, Levi,
	also	Num 1.5 Num 1.20 Num 2.10 Num 7.12 Num 13.3

REVEAL

Gen	35. 7	of Bethel, because God had **revealed** himself to him there
Ex	3.18	'The Lord, the God of the Hebrews, has **revealed** himself to us.
	5. 3	"The God of the Hebrews has **revealed** himself to us.
Lev	10. 3	I will **reveal** my glory to my people.' "
Num	12. 6	are prophets among you, I **reveal** myself to them in visions
	23. 3	I will tell you whatever he **reveals** to me."
Deut	29.29	but he has **revealed** his Law, and we and our descendants are
	33. 8	"You, Lord, **reveal** your will by the Urim and Thummim
1 Sam	2.27	slaves of the king of Egypt, I **revealed** myself to Aaron.
	3.21	The Lord continued to **reveal** himself at Shiloh, where he
2 Sam	7.17	Nathan told David everything that God had **revealed** to him.
	7.27	to you, because you have **revealed** all this to me, your
2 Kgs	8.10	"The Lord has **revealed** to me that he will die;
1 Chr	17.15	Nathan told David everything that God had **revealed** to him.
	17.25	my God, because you have **revealed** all this to me, your
Job	20.27	Heaven **reveals** this man's sin, and the earth gives testimony
Ps	9.16	The Lord has **revealed** himself by his righteous judgements,
	17. 7	**Reveal** your wonderful love and save me;
	19. 1	How clearly the sky **reveals** God's glory!
	80. 2	**reveal** yourself to the tribes of Ephraim,
	94. 1	**reveal** your anger!
	102.16	When the Lord rebuilds Zion, he will **reveal** his greatness.
	103. 7	He **revealed** his plans to Moses and let the people of
Prov	25. 9	settle it between yourselves and do not **reveal** any secrets.
Is	1. 1	Judah and Jerusalem which God **revealed** to Isaiah son of Amoz
	5.16	is right, and he **reveals** his holiness by judging his people.
	19.21	The Lord will **reveal** himself to the Egyptian people, and

Is	26.21	on the earth will be **revealed,** and the ground will no longer
	40. 5	of the Lord will be **revealed,** and all mankind will see it.
	44.26	I send a messenger to **reveal** my plans, I make those plans
	48. 6	of new things to come, events that I did not **reveal** before.
	60.21	I planted them, I made them, To **reveal** my greatness to all.
	64. 2	Come and **reveal** your power to your enemies, and make the
Ezek	7.26	You will beg the prophets to **reveal** what they foresee.
	20. 5	I **revealed** myself to them in Egypt and told them:
Dan	2.19	same night the mystery was **revealed** to Daniel in a vision,
	2.22	He **reveals** things that are deep and secret;
	2.28	But there is a God in heaven, who **reveals** mysteries.
	2.29	who **reveals** mysteries, showed you what is going to happen.
	2.30	Now, this mystery was **revealed** to me, not because I am
	2.47	the Lord over kings, and the one who **reveals** mysteries.
	10. 1	of Persia, a message was **revealed** to Daniel, who is also
	10.20	It is to **reveal** to you what is written in the Book
Hos	4.12	They ask for **revelations** from a piece of wood!
Amos	1. 1	was king of Israel, God **revealed** to Amos all these things
	3. 7	Lord never does anything without **revealing** his plan
Mic	1. 1	The Lord **revealed** to Micah all these things about Samaria
	3.11	pay, the prophets give their **revelations** for money—and they
Hab	1. 1	the message that the Lord **revealed** to the prophet Habakkuk.
	2. 2	on clay tablets what I **reveal** to you, so that it can
	2.19	Can an idol **reveal** anything to you?
Zech	3. 8	I will **reveal** my servant, who is called The Branch!
Mt	11.27	the Son and those to whom the Son chooses to **reveal** him.
Lk	2.32	A light to **reveal** your will to the Gentiles and bring
	2.35	people will speak against [35] and so **reveal** their secret thoughts.
	10.22	the Son and those to whom the Son chooses to **reveal** him."
	17.30	it will be on the day the Son of Man is **revealed.**
Jn	2.11	he **revealed** his glory, and his disciples believed in him.
	12.38	To whom did the Lord **reveal** his power?"
	13.31	Jesus said, "Now the Son of Man's glory is **revealed;**
	13.31	now God's glory is **revealed** through him.
	13.32	And if God's glory is **revealed** through him,
	13.32	then God will **reveal** the glory of the Son of
	14.17	He is the Spirit who **reveals** the truth about God.
	14.21	I too will love him and **reveal** myself to him."
	14.22	it be that you will **reveal** yourself to us and not to
	15.26	will come—the Spirit, who **reveals** the truth about God and
	16.13	the Spirit comes, who **reveals** the truth about God, he will
Acts	19.18	believers came, publicly admitting and **revealing** what they had
Rom	1.17	For the gospel **reveals** how God puts people right with himself:
	1.18	God's anger is **revealed** from heaven against all the sin
	2. 5	the Day when God's anger and righteous judgements will be **revealed.**
	3.21	God's way of putting people right with himself has been **revealed.**
	7.13	in order that its true nature as sin might be **revealed.**
	8.18	all with the glory that is going to be **revealed** to us.
	8.19	creation waits with eager longing for God to **reveal** his sons.
	9. 4	he made them his sons and **revealed** his glory to them;
	9.23	he also wanted to **reveal** his abundant glory, which was poured
	16.25	and according to the **revelation** of the secret truth which was
1 Cor	1. 7	as you wait for our Lord Jesus Christ to be **revealed.**
	3.13	For on that Day fire will **reveal** everyone's work;
	14. 6	unless I bring you some **revelation** from God or some knowledge
	14.26	another a teaching, another a **revelation** from God,
2 Cor	12. 1	now talk about visions and **revelations** given me by the Lord.
Gal	1.12	It was Jesus Christ himself who **revealed** it to me.
	1.16	And when he decided [16] to **reveal** his Son to me, so that
	2. 2	I went because God **revealed** to me that I should go.
	3.23	locked up as prisoners until this coming faith should be **revealed.**
Eph	1.17	will make you wise and **reveal** God to you, so that you
	3. 3	God **revealed** his secret plan and made it known to me.
	3. 5	this secret, but God has **revealed** it now by the Spirit to
	4.24	created in God's likeness and **reveals** itself in the true life
	5.13	out to the light, then their true nature is clearly **revealed;**
	5.14	for anything that is clearly **revealed** becomes light.
	5.32	is a deep secret truth **revealed** in this scripture,
Col	1.26	ages from all mankind but has now **revealed** to his people.
2 Thes	2. 8	Wicked One will be **revealed,** but when the Lord Jesus comes,
1 Tim	3. 9	they should hold to the **revealed** truth of the faith with
2 Tim	1.10	but now it has been **revealed** to us through the coming of
	1.10	power of death and through the gospel has **revealed** immortal life.
Tit	1. 3	and at the right time he **revealed** it in his message.
	2.11	God has **revealed** his grace for the salvation of all mankind.
	3. 4	kindness and love of God our Saviour was **revealed,** [5] he
1 Pet	1. 5	salvation which is ready to be **revealed** at the end of time.
	1. 7	glory and honour on the Day when Jesus Christ is **revealed.**
	1.12	God **revealed** to these prophets that their work was not for
	1.13	which will be given you when Jesus Christ is **revealed.**
	1.20	of the world and was **revealed** in these last days for your
	4.13	that you may be full of joy when his glory is **revealed.**
	5. 1	and I will share in the glory that will be **revealed.**
Rev	1. 1	This book is the record of the events that Jesus Christ **revealed.**
	1. 1	God gave him this **revelation** in order to show his servants
	1. 2	concerning the message from God and the truth **revealed** by Jesus
	1. 9	I had proclaimed God's word and the truth that Jesus **revealed.**
	12.17	and are faithful to the truth **revealed** by Jesus.
	19.10	all those who hold to the truth that Jesus **revealed.**
	19.10	For the truth that Jesus **revealed** is what inspires the prophets.
	20. 4	the truth that Jesus **revealed** and the word of God.

AV REVEAL

1 Sam	3. 6	the Lord, because the Lord had never **spoken** to him before.
	3.21	at Shiloh, where he had **appeared** to Samuel and had spoken to
Is	22.14	The Sovereign Lord Almighty himself **spoke** to me and said,
	23. 1	As your ships return from Cyprus, you **learn** the news.
	53. 1	Who could have **seen** the Lord's hand in this?
Dan	2.47	I know this because you have been able to **explain** this mystery."
Mt	10.26	now covered up will be **uncovered,** and every secret will be
	11.25	thank you because you have **shown** to the unlearned what you
	16.17	human being, but it was **given** to you directly by my Father
Lk	2.26	was with him [26] and had **assured** him that he would not die
	10.21	thank you because you have **shown** to the unlearned what you
	12. 2	is covered up will be **uncovered,** and every secret will be
1 Cor	2.10	to us that God made **known** his secret by means of his
	14.30	in the meeting receives a **message** from God, the one who is
Phil	3.15	have a different attitude, God will make this **clear** to you.
2 Thes	1. 7	when the Lord Jesus **appears** from heaven with his mighty angels,
	2. 3	and the Wicked One **appears,** who is destined for hell.
	2. 6	At the proper time, then, the Wicked One will **appear.**

REVEALING

Is	3.23	their **revealing** garments, their linen handkerchiefs,

REVENGE

Gen	4.10	out to me from the ground, like a voice calling for **revenge.**
	4.15	If anyone kills you, seven lives will be taken in **revenge."**
	34.27	looted the town to take **revenge** for their sister's disgrace.
Lev	19.18	Do not take **revenge** on anyone or continue to hate him,
Num	35.12	will be safe from the dead man's relative who seeks **revenge.**
	35.24	in favour of the dead man's relative who is seeking **revenge.**
	35.27	finds him and kills him, this act of **revenge** is not murder.
Deut	19. 6	who is responsible for taking **revenge** for the killing might
	19.12	the relative responsible for taking **revenge** for the murder,
	32.35	The Lord will take **revenge** and punish them;
	32.41	I will take **revenge** on my enemies and punish those who hate
	32.43	He takes **revenge** on his enemies and forgives the sins of his
Josh	20. 3	can go there and escape the man who is looking for **revenge.**
	20. 5	If the man looking for **revenge** follows him there, the
	20. 9	find protection there from the man looking for **revenge;**
Judg	11.36	Lord has given you **revenge** on your enemies, the Ammonites."
1 Sam	14.24	eats any food today before I take **revenge** on my enemies."
	18.25	of a hundred dead Philistines, as **revenge** on his enemies."
	25.26	who has kept you from taking **revenge** and killing your enemies.
	25.31	killed without cause or for having taken your own **revenge.**
	25.33	me from the crime of murder and from taking my own **revenge.**
	25.39	He has taken **revenge** on Nabal for insulting me and has kept
2 Sam	3.30	and his brother Abishai took **revenge** on Abner for killing
	4. 8	Your Majesty to take **revenge** on Saul and his descendants."
	4.11	I will now take **revenge** on you for murdering him and will
1 Kgs	2. 5	in time of peace in **revenge** for deaths they had caused in
Esth	8.13	would be ready to take **revenge** on their enemies when that
Prov	6.34	his **revenge** knows no limits.
Is	1.24	"I will take **revenge** on you, my enemies, and you will cause
Jer	5. 9	for these things and take **revenge** on a nation such as this?
	5.29	I will take **revenge** on this nation.
	9. 9	Will I not take **revenge** on a nation like this?
	11.20	so let me watch you take **revenge** on these people."
	15.15	Let me have **revenge** on those who persecute me.
	20.10	"then we can catch him and get **revenge."**
	20.12	let me see you take **revenge** on my enemies, for I have
	46.10	today he will take **revenge;**
	50.15	I am taking my **revenge** on the Babylonians.
	50.15	So take your **revenge** on them, and treat them as they have
	50.28	the Lord our God took **revenge** for what the Babylonians had
	51. 6	I am now taking my **revenge** and punishing it as it deserves.
	51.11	how he will take **revenge** for the destruction of his Temple.
Ezek	24. 8	it cannot be hidden, where it demands angry **revenge."**
	25.12	people of Edom took cruel **revenge** on Judah,
	25.12	and that **revenge** has brought lasting guilt on Edom.
	25.14	My people Israel will take **revenge** on Edom for me, and
	25.14	will know what it means to be the object of my **revenge."**
	25.15	"The Philistines have taken cruel **revenge** on their age-long
	25.17	I will punish them severely and take full **revenge** on them.
Mic	5.15	great anger I will take **revenge** on all nations that have not
Mt	5.39	do not take **revenge** on someone who wrongs you.
Acts	7.24	to his help and took **revenge** on the Egyptian by killing him.
Rom	12.19	Never take **revenge,** my friends, but instead let God's anger
	12.19	scripture says, "I will take **revenge,** I will pay back, says
Heb	10.30	For we know who said, "I will take **revenge,** I will repay";

REVENUE

Ezra	4.13	stop paying taxes, and your royal **revenues** will decrease.
	4.20	province of West Euphrates, collecting taxes and **revenue.**

REVERENCE

Gen	20.11	no one here who has **reverence** for God and that they would
Lev	19.32	**Reverently** obey me;
2 Chr	19. 9	must perform your duties in **reverence** for the Lord,
Job	28.28	to men, "To be wise, you must have **reverence** for the Lord.
	31.27	to honour them by kissing my hand in **reverence** to them.
Ps	5. 7	in your holy Temple and bow down to you in **reverence.**
	19. 9	**Reverence** for the Lord is good;
	25.12	Those who have **reverence** for the Lord will learn from
	36. 1	he rejects God and has no **reverence** for him.
	60. 4	show you **reverence,** so that they might escape destruction.
Prov	1. 7	To have knowledge, you must first have **reverence** for the Lord.
	9.10	To be wise you must first have **reverence** for the Lord.
	14. 2	Be honest and you show that you have **reverence** for the Lord;
	14.26	**Reverence** for the Lord gives confidence and security to
	14.27	**Reverence** for the Lord is a fountain of life.
	15.33	**Reverence** for the Lord is an education in itself.
	23.17	let **reverence** for the Lord be the concern of your life.
	24.21	Have **reverence** for the Lord, my son, and honour the king.

Ecc 7.18 If you have **reverence** for God, you will be successful anyway.
12.13 Have **reverence** for God, and obey his commands, because this
Is 11. 2 the Lord's will and have **reverence** for him, [3]and find
33. 6 Their greatest treasure is their **reverence** for the Lord.
Zeph 3. 7 people would have **reverence** for me and accept my discipline,
Acts 9.31 and grew in numbers, as it lived in **reverence** for the Lord.
Rom 3.18 the path of peace, [18]nor have they learnt **reverence** for God."
Eph 5.21 Submit yourselves to one another because of your **reverence** for Christ.
Col 3.22 with a sincere heart because of your **reverence** for the Lord.
1 Tim 2. 2 life with all **reverence** towards God and with proper conduct.
Heb 12.28 God in a way that will please him, with **reverence** and awe;
1 Pet 1.17 the rest of your lives here on earth in **reverence** for him.
3. 2 because they will see how pure and **reverent** your conduct is.
3.15 But have **reverence** for Christ in your hearts, and honour him
Rev 11.18 all who have **reverence** for you, great and small alike.
19. 5 people, both great and small, who have **reverence** for him!"

REVIVE

1 Kgs 17.22 the child started breathing again and **revived.**
Ps 119.25 **revive** me, as you have promised.
Is 26.19 so the Lord will **revive** those who have long been dead.
Hos 6. 2 or three days he will **revive** us, and we will live in

REVOKE

Esth 8. 8 name and stamped with the royal seal cannot be **revoked.**

REVOLT

Ex 10.10 It is clear that you are plotting to **revolt.**
1 Kgs 11.27 This is the story of the **revolt.**
2 Kgs 8.20 During Jehoram's reign Edom **revolted** against Judah
8.22 During this same period the city of Libnah also **revolted.**
2 Chr 21. 8 During Jehoram's reign Edom **revolted** against Judah
21.10 Libnah also **revolted,** because Jehoram had abandoned the Lord,
Ezra 4.19 from ancient times Jerusalem has **revolted** against royal
Neh 6. 6 the Jewish people intend to **revolt** and that this is why you
Ps 2. 2 Their kings **revolt,** their rulers plot together against the
83. 2 Your enemies are in **revolt,** and those who hate you

REVOLTING

Job 33.20 his appetite, and even the finest food looks **revolting.**

REVOLUTION

Lk 21. 9 Don't be afraid when you hear of wars and **revolutions;**
Acts 21.38 started a **revolution** and led four thousand armed terrorists

REWARD

[UNREWARDED]

Gen 15. 1 I will shield you from danger and give you a great **reward."**
15. 2 Lord, what good will your **reward** do me, since I have no
30.18 "God has given me my **reward,** because I gave my slave to
Num 22.17 I will **reward** you richly and do anything you say.
22.37 Did you think I wasn't able to **reward** you enough?"
24.11 I promised to **reward** you,
24.11 but the Lord has kept you from getting the **reward."**
Ruth 2.12 May the Lord **reward** you for what you have done.
2.12 May you have a full **reward** from the Lord God of Israel,
1 Sam 17.25 promised to give a big **reward** to the man who kills him;
26.23 The Lord **rewards** those who are faithful and righteous.
2 Sam 4.10 That was the **reward** I gave him for his good news!
18.22 "You will get no **reward** for it."
19.36 I don't deserve such a great **reward.**
22.21 The Lord **rewards** me because I do what is right;
22.25 And so he **rewards** me because I do what is right, because
1 Kgs 13. 7 I will **reward** you for what you have done."
2 Chr 15. 7 The work that you do will be **rewarded."**
Esth 6. 3 "How have we honoured and **rewarded** Mordecai for this?"
6. 9 'See how the king **rewards** a man he wishes to honour!' "
6.11 "See how the king **rewards** a man he wishes to honour!"
Job 8. 6 and help you and restore your household as your **reward.**
15.31 enough to trust in evil, then evil will be his **reward.**
34.11 He **rewards** people for what they do and treats them as
Ps 7. 9 Stop the wickedness of evil men and **reward** those who are good.
18.20 The Lord **rewards** me because I do what is right;
18.24 And so he **rewards** me because I do what is right, because
19.11 I am **rewarded** for obeying them.
58.11 People will say, "The righteous are indeed **rewarded;**
62.12 You yourself, O Lord, **reward** everyone according to his deeds.
91.16 I will **reward** them with long life;
Prov 10.16 The **reward** for doing good is life, but sin leads only to
11.18 if you do what is right, you are certain to be **rewarded.**
11.31 Those who are good are **rewarded** here on earth, so you
12.14 Your **reward** depends on what you say and what you do;
13. 2 Good people will be **rewarded** for what they say, but those
13.21 but righteous people will be **rewarded** with good things.
14.14 Good people will be **rewarded** for their deeds.
14.18 deserves, but the clever are **rewarded** with knowledge.
14.24 Wise people are **rewarded** with wealth, but fools are
16.31 Long life is the **reward** of the righteous;
24.12 And he will **reward** you according to what you do.
25.22 make him burn with shame, and the Lord will **reward** you.
28.10 The innocent will be well **rewarded.**
Ecc 2.10 of everything I had worked for, and all this was my **reward.**
8.14 the wicked, and wicked men get the **reward** of the righteous.
9. 5 They have no further **reward;**
Is 49. 4 he will **reward** me for what I do.
61. 8 I will faithfully **reward** my people And make an eternal
Jer 31.16 All that you have done for your children will not go **unrewarded;**
32.19 people do, and you **reward** them according to their actions.
Ezek 18.20 A good man will be **rewarded** for doing good, and an evil
Dan 2. 6 its meaning, I will **reward** you with gifts and great honour.
11.39 put them into high offices, and give them land as a **reward.**
12.13 you will rise to receive your **reward** at the end of time."
Mt 5.12 and glad, for a great **reward** is kept for you in heaven.
5.46 Why should God **reward** you if you love only the people
6. 1 you will not have any **reward** from your Father in heaven.
6. 4 Father, who sees what you do in private, will **reward** you.
6. 6 Father, who sees what you do in private, will **reward** you.
6.18 Father, who sees what you do in private, will **reward** you.
10.41 because he is God's messenger, will share in his **reward.**
10.41 a good man because he is good, will share in his **reward.**
10.42 because he is my follower, will certainly receive a **reward."**
16.27 and then he will **reward** each one according to his deeds.
Mk 9.41 because you belong to me will certainly receive his **reward.**
Lk 6.23 for joy, because a great **reward** is kept for you in heaven.
6.35 will then have a great **reward,** and you will be sons of
Rom 2. 6 For God will **reward** every person according to what he has done.
1 Cor 3. 8 God will **reward** each one according to the work he has done.
3.14 foundation survives the fire, the builder will receive a **reward.**
Eph 6. 8 that the Lord will **reward** everyone, whether slave or free,
Col 3.24 will give you as a **reward** what he has kept for his
2 Tim 4.14 the Lord will **reward** him according to what he has done.
Heb 10.35 your courage, then, because it brings with it a great **reward.**
11. 6 have faith that God exists and **rewards** those who seek him.
11.26 of Egypt, for he kept his eyes on the future **reward.**
12.11 by such punishment reap the peaceful **reward** of a righteous life.
Jas 1.12 he will receive as his **reward** the life which God has
2 Jn 8 we have worked for, but will receive your **reward** in full.
Rev 11.18 The time has come to **reward** your servants, the prophets, and
22.12 I will bring my **rewards** with me, to give to each one

RIB

Gen 2.21 took out one of the man's **ribs** and closed up the flesh.
2.22 formed a woman out of the **rib** and brought her to him.
Dan 7. 5 It was holding three **ribs** between its teeth, and a voice

RIBBON

Song 4. 3 Your lips are like a scarlet **ribbon;**

RICH

Gen 13. 2 Abram was a very **rich** man, with sheep, goats, and cattle,
14.23 you can never say, 'I am the one who made Abram **rich.'**
22.16 own name—the Lord is speaking—that I will **richly** bless you.
24.35 Lord has greatly blessed my master and made him a **rich** man.
26.13 He continued to prosper and became a very **rich** man.
47.27 of Goshen, where they became **rich** and had many children.
49.20 "Asher's land will produce **rich** food.
Ex 3. 8 spacious land, one which is **rich** and fertile and in which
3.17 will take them to a **rich** and fertile land—the land of
13. 5 he brings you into that **rich** and fertile land, you must
30.15 The **rich** man is not to pay more, nor the poor man
33. 3 You are going to a **rich** and fertile land.
Lev 19.15 do not show favouritism to the poor or fear the **rich.**
20.24 promised you this **rich** and fertile land as your possession,
25.47 foreigner living with you becomes **rich,** while a
Num 13.27 "We explored the land and found it to be **rich** and fertile;
14. 8 will take us there and give us that **rich** and fertile land.
22.17 I will reward you **richly** and do anything you say.
Deut 6. 3 nation and live in that **rich** and fertile land, just as the
7.14 No people in the world will be as **richly** blessed as you.
8.18 the Lord your God who gives you the power to become **rich.**
11. 9 a long time in the **rich** and fertile land that the Lord
17.17 and he is not to make himself **rich** with silver and gold.
26. 9 He brought us here and gave us this **rich** and fertile land.
26.15 bless also the **rich** and fertile land that you have given us,
27. 3 When you have entered the **rich** and fertile land that the Lord,
28.12 rain in season from his **rich** storehouse in the sky and bless
28.56 woman of noble birth, so **rich** that she has never had to
31.20 will take them into this **rich** and fertile land, as I
32.15 "The Lord's people grew **rich,** but rebellious;
33.14 be blessed with sun-ripened fruit, **Rich** with the best fruits
33.23 "Naphtali is **richly** blessed by the Lord's good favour;
33.24 of his brothers, And may his land be **rich** with olive-trees.
Josh 5. 4 not allowed to see the **rich** and fertile land that he had
22. 6 are going back home very **rich,** with a lot of livestock,
Judg 5.30 or two for every soldier, **rich** cloth for Sisera, embroidered
Ruth 2. 1 a relative named Boaz, a **rich** and influential man who
3.10 for a young man, either **rich** or poor, but you didn't.
4.11 May you become **rich** in the clan of Ephrath and famous in
1 Sam 2. 7 He makes some men poor and others **rich;**
25. 2 He was a very **rich** man, the owner of three thousand sheep
2 Sam 1.24 He clothed you in **rich** scarlet dresses and adorned you
12. 1 one was **rich** and the other poor.
12. 2 The **rich** man had many cattle and sheep, [3]while the poor
12. 4 One day a visitor arrived at the **rich** man's home.
12. 4 The **rich** man didn't want to kill one of his own animals
12. 5 was very angry with the **rich** man and said, "I swear by
19.32 He was very **rich** and had supplied the king with food while
1 Kgs 10.23 King Solomon was **richer** and wiser than any other king,
2 Kgs 4. 8 One day Elisha went to Shunem, where a **rich** woman lived.
15.20 got the money from the **rich** men of Israel by forcing each
23. 2 and all the rest of the people, **rich** and poor alike.
25.26 Then all the Israelites, **rich** and poor alike, together

2 Chr	9.22	King Solomon was **richer** and wiser than any other king
	18. 1	King Jehoshaphat of Judah became **rich** and famous, he
	34.30	Levites and all the rest of the people, **rich** and poor alike.
Esth	1. 5	the men in the capital city of Susa, **rich** and poor alike.
	1.20	husband with proper respect, whether he's **rich** or poor."
	5.11	He boasted to them how **rich** he was, how many sons he
Job	1. 3	number of servants and was the **richest** man in the East.
	6.27	slaves and make yourselves **rich** off your closest friends!
	15.29	He will not remain **rich** for long;
	18.12	He used to be **rich,** but now he goes hungry;
	27.19	time they will lie down **rich,** and when they wake up, they
	34.19	of rulers nor favour the **rich** against the poor, for he
Ps	45.12	**rich** people will try to win your favour.
	49. 2	great and small alike, **rich** and poor together.
	49.16	a man becomes **rich,** when his wealth grows even greater;
	65. 9	you make it **rich** and fertile.
	65.11	What a **rich** harvest your goodness provides!
	85.12	make us prosperous, and our land will produce **rich** harvests.
	107.34	He made **rich** soil become a salty wilderness because of
	112. 3	family will be wealthy and **rich,** and he will be prosperous
	119.36	me the desire to obey your laws rather than to get **rich.**
	119.162	your promises— as happy as someone who finds **rich** treasure.
	123. 4	too long by the **rich** and scorned by proud oppressors.
	132.15	I will **richly** provide Zion with all she needs;
Prov	10. 4	lazy will make you poor, but hard work will make you **rich.**
	10.15	Wealth protects the **rich;**
	10.22	Hard work can make you no **richer.**
	11.16	will never have money, but an aggressive man will get **rich.**
	11.24	Some people spend their money freely and still grow **richer.**
	13. 7	Some people pretend to be **rich,** but have nothing.
	13. 8	A **rich** man has to use his money to save his life,
	14.20	likes a poor man, but the **rich** have many friends.
	15.16	poor and fear the Lord than to be **rich** and in trouble.
	18.11	**Rich** people, however, imagine that their wealth protects them
	18.23	to beg politely, but when the **rich** man answers, he is rude.
	19. 4	**Rich** people are always finding new friends, but the poor
	21.17	luxuries, wine, and **rich** food will never make you wealthy.
	22. 2	The **rich** and the poor have this in common:
	22. 7	Poor people are the **rich** man's slaves.
	22.16	If you make gifts to **rich** people
	22.16	oppress the poor to get **rich,** you will become poor yourself.
	23. 4	Be wise enough not to wear yourself out trying to get **rich.**
	23.31	you, even though it is **rich** red, though it sparkles in the
	28. 6	Better to be poor and honest than **rich** and dishonest.
	28. 8	If you get **rich** by charging interest and taking advantage
	28.11	**Rich** people always think they are wise, but a poor
	28.20	in a hurry to get **rich,** you are going to be punished.
	28.22	such a hurry to get **rich** that they do not know when
	30. 8	keep me from lying, and let me be neither **rich** nor poor.
Ecc	5.10	if you long to be **rich,** you will never get all you
	5.11	The **richer** you are, the more mouths you must feed.
	5.11	All you gain is the knowledge that you are **rich.**
	5.12	A **rich** man, however, has so much that he stays awake worrying.
	9.11	men do not always get **rich,** and capable men do not always
	10. 6	are given positions of authority while **rich** men are ignored.
	10.20	silently, and don't criticize the **rich,** even in the privacy
Is	10.18	The **rich** forests and farmlands will be totally destroyed,
	19.15	No one in Egypt, **rich** or poor, important or unknown, can
	24. 2	buyers and sellers, lenders and borrowers, **rich** and poor.
	25. 6	the world—a banquet of the **richest** food and the finest wine.
	30.23	and will give you a **rich** harvest, and your livestock will
	32.15	land will become fertile, and fields will produce **rich** crops.
	53. 9	he was buried with the **rich,** even though he had never
	63. 7	He has **richly** blessed the people of Israel because of his
Jer	5.27	why they are powerful and **rich,** [28] why they are fat and
	9.23	strong men of their strength, nor **rich** men of their wealth.
	11. 5	I would give them the **rich** and fertile land which they now
	14. 3	The **rich** people send their servants for water;
	16. 6	The **rich** and the poor will die in this land, but no
	31.14	fill the priests with the **richest** food and satisfy all the
	32.22	You gave them this **rich** and fertile land, as you had
	51.13	has many rivers and **rich** treasures, but its time is up,
Ezek	20. 6	had chosen for them, a **rich** and fertile land, the finest
	20.15	I had given them, a **rich** and fertile land, the finest land
	22.12	fellow-Israelites and get **rich** by taking advantage of them.
	22.27	They commit murder in order to get **rich.**
	27.33	Kings were made **rich** By the wealth of your goods.
	28. 4	and skill made you **rich** with treasures of gold and silver.
Dan	10. 3	I did not eat any **rich** food or any meat, drink any
	11. 2	by a fourth, who will be **richer** than all the others.
	11.38	gold, silver, jewels, and other **rich** gifts to a god his
Hos	4. 8	You grow **rich** from the sins of my people, and so you
	12. 8	'We are **rich,'** they say.
	12. 8	And no one can accuse us of getting **rich** dishonestly.'
Joel	3. 5	and gold and carried my **rich** treasures into your temples.
Mic	6.12	Your **rich** men exploit the poor, and all of you are liars.
	7.14	go and feed in the **rich** pastures of Bashan and Gilead, as
Hab	2. 6	will you go on getting **rich** by forcing your debtors to pay
	2. 9	You have made your family **rich** with what you took by violence,
Zech	11. 5	We are **rich!'**
Mt	19.22	man heard this, he went away sad, because he was very **rich.**
	19.23	will be very hard for **rich** people to enter the Kingdom of
	19.24	is much harder for a **rich** person to enter the Kingdom of
	27.57	When it was evening, a **rich** man from Arimathea arrived;
Mk	10.22	his face, and he went away sad, because he was very **rich.**
	10.23	hard it will be for **rich** people to enter the Kingdom of
	10.25	is much harder for a **rich** person to enter the Kingdom of
	12.41	Many **rich** men dropped in a lot of money;
Lk	1.53	with good things, and sent the **rich** away with empty hands.
	6.24	"But how terrible for you who are **rich** now;
	12.15	of the things he owns, no matter how **rich** he may be."
Lk	12.16	"There was once a **rich** man who had land which bore good
	12.21	up riches for themselves but are not **rich** in God's sight."
	14.12	your relatives or your **rich** neighbours—for they will invite you
	16. 1	disciples, "There was once a **rich** man who had a servant who
	16. 1	The **rich** man was told that the manager was wasting his
	16.19	"There was once a **rich** man who dressed in the most
	16.20	to be brought to the **rich** man's door, [21] hoping to eat the
	16.21	eat the bits of food that fell from the **rich** man's table.
	16.22	The **rich** man died and was buried, [23] and in Hades, where he
	16.27	**rich** man said, 'Then I beg you, father Abraham, send Lazarus
	16.30	The **rich** man answered, 'That is not enough, father Abraham!
	18.23	heard this, he became very sad, because he was very **rich.**
	18.24	"How hard it is for **rich** people to enter the Kingdom of
	18.25	is much harder for a **rich** person to enter the Kingdom of
	19. 2	was a chief tax collector there named Zacchaeus, who was **rich.**
	21. 1	Jesus looked round and saw **rich** men dropping their gifts
Acts	4.33	the Lord Jesus, and God poured **rich** blessings on them all.
	6. 8	Stephen, a man **richly** blessed by God and full of power,
Rom	10.12	same Lord of all and **richly** blesses all who call to him.
	11.12	sin of the Jews brought **rich** blessings to the world, and
	11.12	their spiritual poverty brought **rich** blessings to the Gentiles.
1 Cor	1. 5	with Christ you have become **rich** in all things, including all
	4. 8	Are you already **rich?**
2 Cor	6.10	we seem poor, but we make many people **rich;**
	8. 7	You are so **rich** in all you have:
	8. 9	**rich** as he was, he made himself poor for your sake,
	8. 9	in order to make you **rich** by means of his poverty.
	9.10	it grow and produce a **rich** harvest from your generosity.
	9.11	He will always make you **rich** enough to be generous at
Eph	1.18	has called you, how **rich** are the wonderful blessings he promises
	5. 9	light that brings a **rich** harvest of every kind of goodness,
Col	1.27	secret to his people, this **rich** and glorious secret which he
	3.16	Christ's message in all its **richness** must live in your hearts.
1 Tim	6. 5	They think that religion is a way to become **rich.**
	6. 6	does make a person very **rich,** if he is satisfied with what
	6. 9	those who want to get **rich** fall into temptation and are
	6.17	Command those who are **rich** in the things of this life
	6.18	to do good, to be **rich** in good works, to be generous
Jas	1.10	lifts him up, [10] and the **rich** Christian must be glad when
	1.10	For the **rich** will pass away like the flower of a wild
	1.11	In the same way the **rich** man will be destroyed while he
	2. 2	Suppose a **rich** man wearing a gold ring and fine clothes
	2. 5	of this world to be **rich** in faith and to possess the
	2. 6	The **rich!**
	5. 1	And now, you **rich** people, listen to me!
1 Pet	1. 4	look forward to possessing the **rich** blessings that God keeps for
1 Jn	3.17	If a **rich** person sees his brother in need, yet closes
Rev	2. 9	I know that you are poor—but really you are **rich!**
	3.17	You say, 'I am **rich** and well off;
	3.18	to buy gold from me, pure gold, in order to be **rich.**
	6.15	and the military chiefs, the **rich** and the powerful, and all
	13.16	the people, small and great, **rich** and poor, slave and free,
	18. 3	the businessmen of the world grew **rich** from her unrestrained lust."
	18.15	businessmen, who became **rich** from doing business in that city,
	18.19	who have ships sailing the seas became **rich** on her wealth!

RICHES

1 Kgs	3.11	life for yourself or **riches** or the death of your enemies,
1 Chr	29.12	All **riches** and wealth come from you;
Esth	1. 4	made a show of the **riches** of the imperial court with all
Job	31.24	I have never trusted in **riches** [25] or taken pride in my wealth.
	36.18	not to let bribes deceive you, or **riches** lead you astray.
Ps	49. 6	who trust in their **riches** and boast of their great wealth.
	49.10	They all leave their **riches** to their descendants.
	62.10	even if your **riches** increase, don't depend on them.
Prov	1.13	We'll find all kinds of **riches** and fill our houses with loot!
	8.18	I have **riches** and honour to give, prosperity and success.
	11. 4	**Riches** will do you no good on the day you face death,
	11. 7	Confidence placed in **riches** comes to nothing.
	21. 6	The **riches** you get by dishonesty soon disappear, but not
	22. 4	humble, and you will get **riches,** honour, and a long life.
Is	60. 5	From across the sea their **riches** will come.
Jer	17.11	life he will lose his **riches,** and in the end he is
Obad	13	and to seize their **riches** on the day of their disaster.
Mt	6.19	"Do not store up **riches** for yourselves here on earth,
	6.20	Instead, store up **riches** for yourselves in heaven,
	6.21	For your heart will always be where your **riches** are.
	13.22	life and the love for **riches** choke the message, and they
	19.21	the money to the poor, and you will have **riches** in heaven;
Mk	4.19	this life, the love for **riches,** and all other kinds of
	10.21	the money to the poor, and you will have **riches** in heaven;
	12.44	the others put in what they had to spare of their **riches;**
Lk	8.14	but the worries and **riches** and pleasures of this life crowd
	12.21	with those who pile up **riches** for themselves but are not
	12.33	wear out, and save your **riches** in heaven, where they will
	12.34	For your heart will always be where your **riches** are.
	18.22	the money to the poor, and you will have **riches** in heaven;
	21. 4	their gifts from what they had to spare of their **riches;**
Rom	11.33	How great are God's **riches!**
Eph	3. 8	Good News about the infinite **riches** of Christ, [9] and of making
1 Tim	6.17	such an uncertain thing as **riches,** but in God, who generously
Jas	5. 2	Your **riches** have rotted away, and your clothes have been eaten
	5. 3	You have piled up **riches** in these last days.

RID

Gen	35. 2	who were with him, "Get **rid** of the foreign gods that you
Ex	8. 9	Then you will be **rid** of the frogs, and there will be
	8.11	and your people will be **rid** of the frogs, and there will

Ex 12.15 day you are to get **rid** of all the yeast in your
Lev 26. 6 I will get **rid** of the dangerous animals in the land, and
26.43 however, the land must be **rid** of its people, so that it
Deut 13. 5 be put to death, in order to **rid** yourselves of this evil.
17. 7 in this way you will get **rid** of this evil.
19.13 **Rid** Israel of this murderer, so that all will go well with
19.19 In this way you will get **rid** of this evil.
21.21 him to death, and so you will get **rid** of this evil.
22.21 In this way you will get **rid** of this evil.
22.22 In this way you will get **rid** of this evil.
22.24 In this way you will get **rid** of this evil.
24. 7 In this way you will get **rid** of this evil.
Josh 7.13 against your enemies until you get **rid** of these things!'
24.14 Get **rid** of the gods which your ancestors used to worship in
24.23 "Then get **rid** of those foreign gods that you have," he
Judg 9.29 I would get **rid** of Abimelech!
10.16 So they got **rid** of their foreign gods and worshipped the Lord;
1 Sam 7. 3 your hearts, you must get **rid** of all the foreign gods and
7. 4 So the Israelites got **rid** of their idols of Baal and Astarte,
1 Kgs 14.10 I will get **rid** of your family;
21.21 away with you and get **rid** of every male in your family,
22.46 He got **rid** of all the male and female prostitutes
2 Kgs 9. 8 I will get **rid** of every male in his family, young and
Ezra 10.11 living in our land and get **rid** of your foreign wives."
Esth 9.16 They **rid** themselves of their enemies by killing seventy-five
9.22 days on which the Jews had **rid** themselves of their enemies;
Ps 35.25 Don't let them say to themselves, "We are **rid** of him!
101. 5 I will get **rid** of anyone who whispers evil things about
Prov 20. 9 his conscience is clear, that he has got **rid** of his sin?
22.10 Get **rid** of a conceited person, and then there will be no
Jer 23.33 to the Lord, and he is going to get **rid** of you.'
28.16 Lord himself says that he is going to get **rid** of you.
Ezek 11.18 return, they are to get **rid** of all the filthy, disgusting
34.25 I will get **rid** of all the dangerous animals in the land,
Zech 11. 8 hated me, and I got **rid** of them all in a single
13. 2 I will get **rid** of anyone who claims to be a prophet
1 Cor 7.27 Then don't try to get **rid** of her.
2 Cor 5. 4 that we want to get **rid** of our earthly body, but that
Eph 4.22 So get **rid** of your old self, which made you live as
4.31 Get **rid** of all bitterness, passion, and anger.
Col 3. 8 But now you must get **rid** of all these things:
Heb 12. 1 So then, let us **rid** ourselves of everything that gets in the
Jas 1.21 So get **rid** of every filthy habit and all wicked conduct.
1 Pet 2. 1 **Rid** yourselves, then, of all evil;

RIDDLE

Num 12. 8 I speak to him face to face, clearly and not in **riddles;**
Judg 14.12 Samson said to them, "Let me ask you a **riddle.**
14.12 "Tell us your **riddle,**" they said.
14.14 Three days later they had still not solved the **riddle.**
14.15 "Trick your husband into telling us what the **riddle** means.
14.16 You asked my friends a **riddle** and didn't tell me what it
14.17 he told her what the **riddle** meant, for she nagged him about
14.19 their fine clothes to the men who had solved the **riddle.**
Ezek 20.49 Everyone is already complaining that I always speak in **riddles."**
Dan 5.12 dreams, solving **riddles,** and explaining mysteries;

RIDE
[RODE]

Gen 41.43 the second royal chariot to **ride** in, and his guard of honour
49.17 horse's heel, So that the **rider** is thrown off backwards.
Ex 15. 1 he has thrown the horses and their **riders** into the sea.
15.21 he has thrown the horses and their **riders** into the sea."
Num 22.22 going, and as Balaam was **riding** along on his donkey,
22.30 not the same donkey on which you have **ridden** all your life?
Deut 33.26 god is like your God, **riding** in splendour across the sky,
33.26 **riding** through the clouds
Judg 5.10 Tell of it, you that **ride** on white donkeys, sitting on saddles,
10. 4 He had thirty sons who **rode** thirty donkeys.
12.14 forty sons and thirty grandsons, who **rode** on seventy donkeys.
1 Sam 25.20 She was **riding** her donkey round a bend on a hillside
2 Sam 16. 2 for Your Majesty's family to **ride,** the bread and the fruit
18. 9 Absalom was **riding** a mule, and as it went under a large
19.26 donkey so that I could **ride** along with you, but he betrayed
1 Kgs 1.33 let my son Solomon **ride** my own mule, and escort him down
1.44 They made him **ride** on the king's mule, [45]and Zadok and
13.13 They did so, and he **rode** off [14]down the road after the
13.24 the donkey for the prophet from Judah, [24]who **rode** off.
13.28 They did so, [28]and he **rode** off and found the prophet's
2 Kgs 9.17 "I see some men **riding** up!"
9.18 The messenger **rode** out to Jehu and said to him, "The
9.21 and he and King Ahaziah **rode** out, each in his own chariot,
9.25 and I were **riding** together behind King Joram's father Ahab,
10.16 And they **rode** on together to Samaria.
18.23 thousand horses if you can find that many men to **ride** them!
Neh 2.12 The only animal we took was the donkey that I **rode** on.
2.14 The donkey I was **riding** could not find any path through the
2.15 valley of the Kidron and **rode** along, looking at the wall.
Esth 8.10 They were delivered by **riders** mounted on fast horses from
8.14 At the king's command the **riders** mounted royal horses
8.14 and **rode** off at top speed.
Job 39.18 she begins to run, she can laugh at any horse and **rider.**
39.23 weapons which their **riders** carry rattle and flash in the sun.
Ps 45. 4 **Ride** on in majesty to victory for the defence of truth and
68. 4 prepare a way for him who **rides** on the clouds.
68.33 the Lord, [33]to him who **rides** in the sky, the ancient sky.
76. 6 O God of Jacob, the horses and their **riders** fell dead.
104. 3 clouds as your chariot and **ride** on the wings of the wind.
Is 19. 1 The Lord is coming to Egypt, **riding** swiftly on a cloud.
Is 21. 7 two by two, and men **riding** on donkeys and camels, he is
22. 6 the land of Elam came **riding** on horseback, armed with bows
30.16 you plan to escape from your enemies by **riding** fast horses.
36. 8 thousand horses if you can find that many men to **ride** them.
66.15 He will **ride** on the wings of a storm to punish those
Jer 6.23 They sound like the roaring sea, as they **ride** their horses.
17.25 and of Jerusalem, they will **ride** in chariots and on horses,
50.42 They sound like the roaring sea, as they **ride** their horses.
51.21 to shatter horses and **riders,** to shatter chariots
Ezek 38. 4 with its horses and uniformed **riders,** is enormous, and every
39.20 of horses and their **riders** and of soldiers and fighting men.
Hab 1. 8 Their horsemen come **riding** from distant lands;
3. 8 You **rode** upon the clouds;
Hag 2.22 the horses will die, and their **riders** will kill one another.
Zech 1. 8 I saw an angel of the Lord **riding** a red horse.
9. 9 and victorious, but humble and **riding** on a donkey— on a
12. 4 terrify all their horses and make all their **riders** go mad.
Mt 21. 5 He is humble and **rides** on a donkey and on a colt,
Mk 11. 2 you will find a colt tied up that has never been **ridden.**
Lk 19.30 you will find a colt tied up that has never been **ridden.**
19.36 As he **rode** on, people spread their cloaks on the road.
Jn 12.14 Jesus found a donkey and **rode** on it, just as the
12.15 Here comes your king, **riding** on a young donkey."
Acts 8.27 As he **rode** along, he was reading from the book of the
23.24 some horses for Paul to **ride** and get him safely through to
Rev 6. 2 Its **rider** held a bow, and he was given a crown.
6. 2 He **rode** out as a conqueror to conquer.
6. 4 Its **rider** was given the power to bring war on the earth,
6. 5 Its **rider** held a pair of scales in his hand.
6. 8 Its **rider** was named Death, and Hades followed close behind.
9.17 And in my vision I saw the horses and their **riders:**
19.11 Its **rider** is called Faithful and True;
19.14 armies of heaven followed him, **riding** on white horses and dressed
19.18 flesh of horses and their **riders,** the flesh of all people,
19.19 the one who was **riding** the horse and against his army.
19.21 out of the mouth of the one who was **riding** the horse;

RIDGE

Josh 15. 6 and went north of the **ridge** overlooking the Jordan Valley.
18.16 Valley of Hinnom, south of the Jebusite **ridge,** towards Enrogel.
18.18 Reuben) [18]and passed north of the **ridge** overlooking the Jordan Valley.
18.19 valley, [19]passing north of the **ridge** of Beth Hoglah, and

RIDICULE

Deut 28.37 they will make fun of you and **ridicule** you.
1 Kgs 9. 7 everywhere will **ridicule** Israel and treat her with contempt.
2 Kgs 19.22 Whom do you think you have been insulting and **ridiculing?**
2 Chr 7.20 People everywhere will **ridicule** it and treat it with contempt.
30.10 of Zebulun, but people laughed at them and **ridiculed** them.
36.16 But they **ridiculed** God's messengers, ignoring his words
Neh 4. 1 the wall, he was furious and began to **ridicule** us.
4. 4 Let their **ridicule** fall on their own heads.
5. 9 give our enemies, the Gentiles, any reason to **ridicule** us.
Is 37.23 Whom do you think you have been insulting and **ridiculing?**
Jer 20. 8 Lord, I am **ridiculed** and scorned all the time because I
24. 9 them, make jokes about them, **ridicule** them, and use their

RIGGING

Prov 23.34 sea-sick, swinging high up in the **rigging** of a tossing ship.
Is 33.22 All the **rigging** on those ships is useless;

RIGHT (1)
see also **RIGHT WITH GOD, RIGHTEOUS**

Gen 4. 7 If you had done the **right** thing, you would be smiling;
7. 1 the only one in all the world who does what is **right.**
16. 5 May the Lord judge which of us is **right,** you or me!"
17. 1 Obey me and always do what is **right.**
18.19 descendants to obey me and to do what is **right** and just.
31.37 see it, and let them decide which one of us is **right.**
38.26 Judah recognized them and said, "She is in the **right.**
Ex 8.26 "It would not be **right** to do that," Moses answered,
9.27 the Lord is in the **right,** and my people and I are
10.29 "You are **right,"** Moses answered.
15.26 by doing what I consider **right** and by keeping my commands, I
18.16 which one of them is **right,** and I tell them God's commands
18.17 Then Jethro said, "You are not doing it the **right** way.
18.19 It is **right** for you to represent the people before God and
23. 8 people blind to what is **right** and ruins the cause of those
Lev 26. 4 send you rain at the **right** time, so that the land will
Num 27. 7 "What the daughters of Zelophehad request is **right;**
36. 5 tribe of Manasseh says is **right,** [6]and so the Lord says that
Deut 1.39 still too young to know **right** from wrong, will enter the
5.28 'I have heard what these people said, and they are **right.**
6.18 what the Lord says is **right** and good, and all will go
9. 5 good and do what is **right** that the Lord is letting you
12.28 will be doing what is **right** and what pleases the Lord your
32. 4 he does what is **right** and fair.
32.34 he waits for the **right** time to punish them.
33.19 to their mountain And offer the **right** sacrifices there.
Josh 9.25 do with us what you think is **right."**
1 Sam 2.16 answered, "Let us do what is **right** and burn the fat first;
12.23 will teach you what is good and **right** for you to do.
24.17 Then he said to David, "You are **right,** and I am wrong.
2 Sam 19.27 you are like God's angel, so do what seems **right** to you.
22.21 The Lord rewards me because I do what is **right;**

2 Sam 22.25 because I do what is **right,** because he knows that I am
1 Kgs 8.18 said to him, 'You were **right** in wanting to build a temple
8.36 Teach them to do what is **right.**
22.43 him, he did what was **right** in the sight of the Lord;
2 Chr 1.11 God replied to Solomon, "You have made the **right** choice.
6. 8 said to him, 'You were **right** in wanting to build a temple
6.27 the people of Israel, and teach them to do what is **right.**
14. 2 pleased the Lord, his God, by doing what was **right** and good.
19. 2 "Do you think it is **right** to help those who are wicked
19.11 and may the Lord be on the side of the **right!"**
20.32 him, he did what was **right** in the sight of the Lord;
31.20 King Hezekiah did what was **right** and what was pleasing to
Neh 5. 9 You ought to obey God and do what's **right.**
9.33 You have done **right** to punish us;
Esth 3. 7 called) to find out the **right** day and month to carry out
8. 5 me and if it seems **right** to you, please issue a proclamation
Job 6.29 I'm in the **right.**
6.30 I am lying— you think I can't tell **right** from wrong.
8. 3 he never fails to do what is **right.**
10. 3 Is it **right** for you to be so cruel?
10.15 trouble with you, but when I do **right,** I get no credit.
11. 1 Does talking so much put a man in the **right?**
11.13 Put your heart **right,** Job.
13.18 to state my case, because I know I am in the **right.**
17. 9 be respectable are more and more convinced they are **right.**
22. 3 Does your doing **right** benefit God, or does your being good
22.30 rescue you if you are innocent, if what you do is **right.**
27. 5 I will never say that you men are **right;**
27. 6 I will never give up my claim to be **right;**
31. 7 I have turned from the **right** path or let myself be attracted
32. 9 that makes men wise or helps them to know what is **right.**
33.26 God will set things **right** for him again.
33.27 I have not done **right,** but God spared me.
33.32 I would gladly admit you are in the **right.**
35. 1 It is not **right,** Job, for you to say that you are
40. 8 to put me in the wrong and yourself in the **right?**
Ps 1. 3 that bear fruit at the **right** time, and whose leaves do not
4. 5 Offer the **right** sacrifices to the Lord, and put your trust
14. 1 there is no one who does what is **right.**
14. 3 Not one of them does what is **right,** not a single one.
15. 2 always does what is **right,** whose words are true and sincere,
17. 2 You will judge in my favour, because you know what is **right.**
18.20 The Lord rewards me because I do what is **right;**
18.24 because I do what is **right,** because he knows that I am
19. 8 laws of the Lord are **right,** and those who obey them are
23. 3 He guides me in the **right** paths, as he has promised.
25. 9 the humble in the **right** way and teaches them his will.
26. 1 O Lord, because I do what is **right** and trust you completely.
26.11 As for me, I do what is **right;**
37.14 poor and needy, to slaughter those who do what is **right;**
37.28 the Lord loves what is **right** and does not abandon his
38.20 evil for good are against me because I try to do **right.**
41.12 You will help me, because I do what is **right;**
45. 7 you love what is **right** and hate what is evil.
48.11 You give **right** judgements;
51. 4 So you are **right** in judging me;
53. 1 there is no one who does what is **right.**
53. 3 Not one of them does what is **right,** not a single one.
65. 1 O God, it is **right** for us to praise you in Zion
84.11 not refuse any good thing to those who do what is **right.**
99. 4 Mighty king, you love what is **right;**
102.13 this is the **right** time.
105.19 The word of the Lord proved him **right.**
106. 3 those who obey his commands, who always do what is **right.**
119.121 I have done what is **right** and good;
119.138 The rules that you have given are completely fair and **right.**
132. 9 May your priests do always what is **right;**
147. 1 it is pleasant and **right** to praise him.
Prov 2. 9 listen to me, you will know what is **right,** just, and fair.
3. 6 in everything you do, and he will show you the **right** way.
4.11 I have taught you wisdom and the **right** way to live.
4.26 what you do, and whatever you do will turn out **right.**
4.27 Don't go one step off the **right** way.
8. 6 all I tell you is **right.**
11.18 if you do what is **right,** you are certain to be rewarded.
11.19 who is determined to do **right** will live, but anyone who
11.20 The Lord hates evil-minded people, but loves those who do **right.**
12.15 Stupid people always think they are **right.**
14.12 What you think is the **right** road may lead to death.
15. 9 ways of evil people, but loves those who do what is **right.**
15.21 with their foolishness, but the wise will do what is **right.**
15.23 it is to find just the **right** word for the right occasion!
16. 2 you do is **right,** but the Lord judges your motives.
16.10 his decisions are always **right.**
16.25 What you think is the **right** road may lead to death.
17.26 It is not **right** to make an innocent person pay a fine;
18. 1 they will disagree with what everyone else knows is **right.**
18. 5 It is not **right** to favour the guilty and prevent the
18.17 speak in court always seems **right** until his opponent begins
20. 4 his fields at the **right** time will have nothing to harvest.
20. 7 they have a father who is honest and does what is **right.**
20.22 Trust the Lord and he will make it **right.**
21. 2 that everything you do is **right,** but remember that the Lord
21. 3 Do what is **right** and fair;
21. 7 they refuse to do what is **right.**
21. 8 the innocent do what is **right.**
22.21 sent to find it out, you will bring back the **right** answer.
Ecc 2.21 It is useless, and it isn't **right!**
3.11 He has set the **right** time for everything.
3.16 you find wickedness where justice and **right** ought to be.
5. 1 foolish people do, people who don't know **right** from wrong.
Ecc 5.16 It isn't **right!**
7.20 earth who does what is **right** all the time and never makes
8. 6 There is a **right** time and a right way to do everything,
10. 2 wise man to do the **right** thing and for a fool to
11. 4 and the weather are just **right,** you will never sow anything
Is 1.17 Yes, stop doing evil [17] and learn to do **right.**
5. 7 them to do what was **right,** but their victims cried out for
5.16 greatness by doing what is **right,** and he reveals his
9. 7 successor, basing his power on **right** and justice, from now
16. 5 quick to do what is **right,** and he will see that justice
26. 2 nation enter, the nation whose people do what is **right.**
26.10 kind to wicked men, they never learn to do what is **right.**
30.10 They say, "Don't talk to us about what's **right.**
30.16 And you are **right**—escape is what you will have to do!
30.18 to take pity on you because he always does what is **right.**
32. 8 person acts honestly and stands firm for what is **right.**
32.17 everyone will do what is **right,** there will be peace and
33.15 You can survive if you say and do what is **right.**
41. 1 Let us come together to decide who is **right.**
41.26 would happen, so that we could say that you were **right?**
43. 9 to prove that they are **right,** to testify to the truth of
43.26 Present your case to prove you are in the **right!**
45.13 Cyrus to action to fulfil my purpose and put things **right.**
45.19 I make known what is **right."**
48. 6 you have to admit my predictions were **right.**
51. 7 you that know what is **right,** who have my teaching fixed in
54.14 Justice and **right** will make you strong.
56. 1 "Do what is just and **right,** for soon I will save you.
57.12 that what you do is **right,** but I will expose your conduct,
59.14 Justice is driven away, and **right** cannot come near.
59.17 strong desire to set things **right** and to punish and avenge
60.21 will all do what is **right,** And will possess the land for
60.22 When the **right** time comes, I will make this happen quickly.
61. 3 will all do what is **right,** And God will be praised for
64. 5 joy in doing what is **right,** those who remember how you want
Jer 1.12 "You are **right,"** the Lord said, "and I am watching to
4. 2 I hate, [2] it will be **right** for you to swear by my
5. 1 person who does what is **right** and tries to be faithful to
9.24 my love is constant, and I do what is just and **right.**
12. 1 I argued my case with you, you would prove to be **right.**
13.23 that do nothing but evil could learn to do what is **right.**
22. 3 "I, the Lord, command you to do what is just and **right.**
23. 5 wisely and do what is **right** and just throughout the land.
26.14 Do with me whatever you think is fair and **right.**
33.10 And they are **right;**
33.15 That king will do what is **right** and just throughout the land.
35.15 to give up your evil ways and to do what is **right.**
51.10 people shout, 'The Lord has shown that we are in the **right.**
Ezek 18.19 The answer is that the son did what was **right** and good.
18.21 if he does what is **right** and good, he will not die;
18.22 be forgiven, and he will live, because he did what is **right.**
18.25 "But you say, 'What the Lord does isn't **right.'**
18.25 Do you think my way of doing things isn't **right?**
18.25 It is your way that isn't **right.**
18.27 and does what is **right** and good, he saves his life.
18.29 And you Israelites say, 'What the Lord does isn't **right.'**
18.29 You think my way isn't **right,** do you?
18.29 It is your way that isn't **right.**
33.14 and does what is **right** and good—[15] for example, if he
33.16 he will live because he has done what is **right** and good.
33.17 "And your people say that what I do isn't **right!**
33.17 No, it's their way that isn't **right.**
33.19 and does what is **right** and good,
33.20 But Israel, you say that what I do isn't **right.**
34.16 destroy, because I am a shepherd who does what is **right.**
45. 9 Do what is **right** and just.
Dan 4.27 Stop sinning, do what is **right,** and be merciful to the poor.
4.37 Everything he does is **right** and just, and he can humble
9. 5 do and have turned away from what you showed us was **right.**
9. 7 Lord, always do what is **right,** but we have always brought
9.14 you always do what is **right,** and we did not listen to
9.18 because you are merciful, not because we have done **right.**
12. 3 people to do what is **right** will shine like the stars for
Hos 14. 9 Lord's ways are **right,** and righteous people live by following them,
Joel 2.23 He has given you the **right** amount of autumn rain;
Amos 5.14 aim to do what is **right,** not what is evil, so that
5.15 is evil, love what is **right,** and see that justice prevails
6.12 Yet you have turned justice into poison, and **right** into wrong.
Mic 2. 7 Doesn't he speak kindly to those who do **right?"**
3. 9 of Israel, you that hate justice and turn **right** into wrong.
7. 9 he will defend us and **right** the wrongs that have been done
Zeph 2. 3 Do what is **right,** and humble yourselves before the Lord.
3. 5 he does what is **right** and never what is wrong.
Hag 1. 2 say that this is not the **right** time to rebuild the Temple."
Mal 2. 6 They taught what was **right,** not what was wrong.
2. 6 not only did what was **right** themselves, but they also helped
2. 8 "But now you priests have turned away from the **right** path.
3. 3 they will bring to the Lord the **right** kind of offerings.
3. 8 I ask you, is it **right** for a person to cheat God?
Mt 1.19 who always did what was **right,** but he did not want to
8.29 Have you come to punish us before the **right** time?"
14. 4 had told Herod, "It isn't **right** for you to be married to
15. 7 How **right** Isaiah was when he prophesied about you!
15.26 Jesus answered, "It isn't **right** to take the children's food
21.32 to you showing you the **right** path to take, and you would
21.41 will give him his share of the harvest at the **right** time."
Mk 1.15 "The **right** time has come," he said, "and the Kingdom
5.15 He was sitting there, clothed and in his **right** mind;
6.18 kept telling Herod, "It isn't **right** for you to be married
7. 6 Jesus answered them, "How **right** Isaiah was when he prophesied
7.27 It isn't **right** to take the children's food and throw it to

Mk 11.13 only leaves, because it was not the **right** time for figs.
Lk 1.20 believed my message, which will come true at the **right** time.
7.43 "You are **right,**" said Jesus.
8.35 sitting at the feet of Jesus, clothed and in his **right** mind;
10.28 "You are **right,**" Jesus replied;
10.42 Mary has chosen the **right** thing, and it will not be taken
12.57 "Why do you not judge for yourselves the **right** thing to do?
13.33 it is not **right** for a prophet to be killed anywhere except
16.15 ones who make yourselves look **right** in other people's sight,
20.21 Jesus, "Teacher, we know that what you say and teach is **right.**
23.41 is only **right,** because we are getting what we deserve
Jn 4.17 Jesus replied, "You are **right** when you say you haven't got
5.30 so my judgement is **right,** because I am not trying to
7. 6 Jesus said to them, "The **right** time for me has not yet
7. 6 Any time is **right** for you.
7. 8 this festival, because the **right** time has not come for me."
8.48 asked Jesus, "Were we not **right** in saying that you are a
13.13 and Lord, and it is **right** that you do so, because that
16. 8 about sin and about what is **right** and about God's judgement.
16.10 are wrong about what is **right,** because I am going to the
18.23 But if I am **right** in what I have said, why do
Acts 4.19 "You yourselves judge which is **right** in God's sight—to obey
6. 2 and said, "It is not **right** for us to neglect the preaching
8.21 in our work, because your heart is not **right** in God's sight.
10.35 him and does what is **right** is acceptable to him, no matter
14.17 he gives you rain from heaven and crops at the **right** times;
15.38 did not think it was **right** to take him, because he had
Rom 2. 2 We know that God is **right** when he judges the people
2. 8 selfish and reject what is **right,** in order to follow what is
2.18 and you have learnt from the Law to choose what is **right;**
3. 4 says, "You must be shown to be **right** when you speak;
3. 5 wrong serves to show up more clearly God's doing **right?**
3.12 no one does what is **right,** not even one.
7.12 Law itself is holy, and the commandment is holy, **right,** and
7.16 to do, this shows that I agree that the Law is **right.**
9. 9 "At the **right** time I will come back, and Sarah will have
14.21 The **right** thing to do is to keep from eating meat,
14.22 not feel guilty when he does something he judges is **right!**
1 Cor 4. 5 should not pass judgement on anyone before the **right** time comes.
5. 6 It is not **right** for you to be proud!
7.35 to do what is **right** and proper, and to give yourselves
11.19 that the ones who are in the **right** may be clearly seen.)
15.34 Come back to your **right** senses and stop your sinful ways.
2 Cor 6.14 How can **right** and wrong be partners?
8.21 is to do what is **right,** not only in the sight of
8.24 of it and know that we are **right** in boasting about you.
13. 7 you may do what is **right,** even though we may seem to
Gal 4. 4 But when the **right** time finally came, God sent his own Son.
6. 1 those of you who are spiritual should set him **right;**
Eph 1.10 when the time is **right,** is to bring all creation together,
5. 3 it is not **right** that any matters of sexual immorality
6. 1 to obey your parents, for this is the **right** thing to do.
Phil 1. 7 And so it is only **right** for me to feel as I
1.18 in every way possible, whether from wrong or **right** motives.
3.17 to those who follow the **right** example that we have set for
4. 8 that are true, noble, **right,** pure, lovely, and honourable.
Col 4. 6 you should know how to give the **right** answer to everyone.
1 Thes 2.10 our conduct towards you who believe was pure, **right,**
2 Thes 1. 3 It is **right** for us to do so, because your faith is
1. 6 God will do what is **right:**
1 Tim 2. 6 was the proof at the **right** time that God wants everyone to
3.16 was shown to be **right** by the Spirit, and was seen
6.15 be brought about at the **right** time by God, the blessed
2 Tim 3.16 and giving instruction for **right** living, [17] so that the person
4. 2 (whether the time is **right** or not), to convince, reproach,
Tit 1. 3 of time, [3] and at the **right** time he revealed it in his
Heb 1. 9 You love what is **right** and hate what is wrong.
2.10 It was only **right** that God, who creates and preserves all
5.13 without any experience in the matter of **right** and wrong.
11.33 They did what was **right** and received what God had promised.
12.10 punished us for a short time, as it seemed **right** to them;
13. 9 all kinds of strange teachings lead you from the **right** way.
13.18 because we want to do the **right** thing at all times.
Jas 2. 8 You will be doing the **right** thing if you obey the law
1 Pet 2.20 even when you have done **right,** God will bless you for it.
3.14 should suffer for doing what is **right,** how happy you are!
2 Pet 1.13 I think it only **right** for me to stir up your memory
1 Jn 1. 9 to God, he will keep his promise and do what is **right:**
2.29 then, that everyone who does what is **right** is God's child.
3. 7 Whoever does what is **right** is righteous, just as Christ is
3.10 does not do what is **right** or does not love his brother
3.12 did were wrong, but the things his brother did were **right.**
Rev 15. 3 King of the nations, how **right** and true are your ways!

RIGHT (2)

Gen 48.13 Joseph put Ephraim at Jacob's left and Manasseh at his **right.**
48.14 his hands, and put his **right hand** on the head of Ephraim,
48.17 that his father had put his **right hand** on Ephraim's head;
48.18 put your **right hand** on his head."
Ex 15. 6 "Your **right hand,** Lord, is awesome in power;
15.12 You stretched out your **right hand,** and the earth swallowed
29.20 on the lobes of the **right** ears of Aaron and his sons,
29.20 on the thumbs of their **right hands**
29.20 and on the big toes of their **right** feet.
29.22 the two kidneys with the fat on them, and the **right** thigh.
Lev 7.32 The **right** hind leg of the animal shall be given as a
7.34 a special gift, and the **right** hind leg is a special
8.23 on the lobe of Aaron's **right** ear,
8.23 on the thumb of his **right hand,**
8.23 and on the big toe of his **right** foot.
Lev 8.24 on the lobes of their **right** ears,
8.24 on the thumbs of their **right hands,**
8.24 and on the big toes of their **right** feet.
8.25 the kidneys with the fat on them, and the **right** hind leg.
8.26 put them on top of the fat and the **right** hind leg.
9.21 presented the breasts and the **right** hind legs as the special
14.14 on the lobe of the **right** ear,
14.14 on the thumb of the **right hand,**
14.14 the big toe of the **right** foot of the man who is
14.16 dip a finger of his **right hand** in it, and sprinkle some
14.17 on the lobe of the **right** ear,
14.17 on the thumb of the **right hand,**
14.17 the big toe of the **right** foot of the man who is
14.25 the lobe of the man's **right** ear,
14.25 on the thumb of his **right hand,**
14.25 and on the big toe of his **right** foot.
14.27 with a finger of his **right hand** sprinkle some of it seven
14.28 the lobe of the man's **right** ear,
14.28 on the thumb of his **right hand,**
14.28 and on the big toe of his **right** foot.
Num 18.18 the breast and the **right** hind leg of the special offering.
Deut 33. 2 angels were with him, a flaming fire at his **right hand.**
Judg 3.16 He had it fastened on his **right** side under his clothes.
3.21 took the sword from his **right** side and plunged it into the
7.20 hands, the trumpets in their **right,** and shouted, "A sword
1 Sam 11. 2 I will put out everyone's **right** eye and so bring disgrace on
2 Sam 20. 9 of his beard with his **right hand** in order to kiss him.
1 Kgs 2.19 had another one brought in on which she sat at his **right.**
2 Kgs 12. 9 by the altar, on the **right** side as one enters the Temple.
1 Chr 12. 2 They could shoot arrows and sling stones either **right-handed** or left-handed.
Neh 8. 4 The following men stood at his **right:**
12.31 first group went to the **right** on top of the wall towards
Ps 45. 9 of kings, and on the **right** of your throne stands the queen,
110. 1 king, "Sit here at my **right** until I put your enemies under
110. 5 The Lord is at your **right** side;
Song 2. 6 left hand is under my head, and his **right hand** caresses me.
8. 3 hand is under my head, and your **right hand** caresses me.
Is 30.21 off the road to the **right** or the left, you will hear
Jer 22.24 were the signet-ring on my **right hand,** I would pull you off
Ezek 1.10 a lion's face at the **right,** a bull's face at the left,
4. 6 that, turn over on your **right** side and suffer for the guilt
21.16 Cut to the **right** and the left, you sharp sword!
21.22 His **right hand** holds the arrow marked 'Jerusalem'!
39. 3 of his left hand and his arrows out of his **right hand.**
Zech 11.17 His arm will wither, and his **right** eye will go blind."
Mt 5.29 So if your **right** eye causes you to sin, take it out
5.30 If your **right hand** causes you to sin, cut it off
5.39 anyone slaps you on the **right** cheek, let him slap your left
20.21 mine will sit at your **right** and your left when you are
20.23 right to choose who will sit at my **right** and my left.
22.44 Sit here on my **right** until I put your enemies under your
25.33 righteous people on his **right** and the others on his left.
25.34 to the people on his **right,** 'Come, you that are blessed by
26.64 of Man sitting on the **right** of the Almighty and coming on
27.29 it on his head, and put a stick in his **right hand;**
*27.38 with Jesus, one on his **right** and the other on his left.
Mk 10.37 sit with you, one at your **right** and one at your left."
10.40 to choose who will sit at my **right** and my left.
12.36 Sit here on my **right** until I put your enemies under your
14.62 of Man seated on the **right** of the Almighty and coming with
15.27 with Jesus, one on his **right** and the other on his left.
16. 5 young man sitting on the **right,** wearing a white robe—
16.19 taken up to heaven and sat at the **right side** of God.
Lk 1.11 standing on the **right** of the altar where the incense
6. 6 A man was there whose **right hand** was paralysed.
20.42 Sit here on my **right** [43] until I put your enemies as a
22.50 struck the High Priest's slave and cut off his **right** ear.
22.69 Son of Man will be seated on the **right** of Almighty God."
23.33 two criminals, one on his **right** and the other on his left.
Jn 18.10 and struck the High Priest's slave, cutting off his **right** ear.
21. 6 your net out on the **right side** of the boat, and you
Acts 2.33 has been raised to the **right-hand side** of God, his Father,
2.34 Sit here at my **right** [35] until I put your enemies as a
3. 7 Then he took him by his **right hand** and helped him up.
5.31 God raised him to his **right-hand side** as Leader and Saviour,
7.55 God's glory and Jesus standing at the **right-hand side** of God.
7.56 and the Son of Man standing at the **right-hand side** of God!"
Rom 8.34 and is at the **right-hand side** of God, pleading with him
Eph 1.20 and seated him at his **right side** in the heavenly world.
Col 3. 1 Christ sits on his throne at the **right-hand side** of God.
Heb 1. 3 in heaven at the **right-hand side** of God, the Supreme Power.
1.13 "Sit here on my **right** until I put your enemies as a
8. 1 Priest, who sits at the **right** of the throne of the Divine
10.12 and then he sat down at the **right-hand side** of God.
12. 2 he is now seated at the **right-hand side** of God's throne.
1 Pet 3.22 heaven and is at the **right-hand side** of God, ruling over all
Rev 1.16 held seven stars in his **right hand,** and a sharp two-edged
1.17 He placed his **right hand** on me and said, "Don't be afraid!
1.20 that you see in my **right hand,** and of the seven gold
2. 1 the seven stars in his **right hand** and who walks among the
5. 1 saw a scroll in the **right hand** of the one who sits
5. 7 took the scroll from the **right hand** of the one who sits
10. 2 He put his **right** foot on the sea and his left foot
10. 5 on the land raised his **right hand** to heaven [6] and took a
13.16 a mark placed on their **right hands** or on their foreheads.

RIGHT (3)

Gen 18.27 I am only a man and have no **right** to say anything.
25.31 to you if you give me your **rights** as the first-born son."

Gen 25.32 what good will my **rights** do me then?"
25.33 "First make a vow that you will give me your **rights."**
25.33 Esau made the vow and gave his **rights** to Jacob.
25.34 That was all Esau cared about his **rights** as the first-born son.
27.36 He took my **rights** as the first-born son, and now he has
31.36 have I broken that gives you the **right** to hunt me down?
Ex 21.10 food and clothing and the same **rights** that she had before.
Lev 25.24 When land is sold, the **right** of the original owner to
25.29 walled city, he has the **right** to buy it back during the
25.30 the year, he loses the **right** of repurchase, and the house
25.31 the original owner has the **right** to buy them back, and they
25.32 However, Levites have the **right** to buy back at any time
25.48 he is sold, he still has the **right** to be bought back.
27.20 back from the Lord, he loses the **right** to buy it back.
Num 30.13 Her husband has the **right** to affirm or to annul any vow
Deut 17. 8 as certain cases of property **rights** or of bodily injury or
24.17 "Do not deprive foreigners and orphans of their **rights;**
27.19 deprives foreigners, orphans, and widows of their **rights.'**
Ruth 4. 4 it, say so, because the **right** to buy it belongs first to
4. 6 I will give up my **right** to buy the field, because it
1 Sam 2.28 And I gave them the **right** to keep a share of the
10.25 explained to the people the **rights** and duties of a king, and
2 Sam 16.10 him to, who has the **right** to ask why he does it?"
19.28 Majesty, but you gave me the **right** to eat at your table.
19.28 I have no **right** to ask for any more favours
19.41 Judah, think they had the **right** to take you away and escort
1 Chr 5. 1 he lost the **rights** belonging to the first-born son,
5. 1 and those **rights** were given to Joseph.
2 Chr 26.18 You have no **right** to burn incense to the Lord.
28.19 of Judah had violated the **rights** of his people and had
Ezra 9.15 we have no **right** to come into your presence."
10. 8 and he would lose his **right** to be a member of the
Neh 2.20 But you have no **right** to any property in Jerusalem, and you
Job 24. 4 the poor from getting their **rights** and force the needy to
31.38 and taken it from its **rightful** owners— [39] if I have eaten
Ps 24. 3 Who has the **right** to go up the Lord's hill?
82. 3 Defend the **rights** of the poor and the orphans;
103. 6 Lord judges in favour of the oppressed and gives them their **rights.**
140.12 defend the cause of the poor and the **rights** of the needy.
Prov 29. 7 A good person knows the **rights** of the poor, but wicked
29.14 If a king defends the **rights** of the poor, he will rule
31. 5 forget the laws and ignore the **rights** of people in need.
31. 8 Protect the **rights** of all who are helpless.
31. 9 Protect the **rights** of the poor and needy."
Ecc 5. 8 oppresses the poor and denies them justice and their **rights.**
Is 1.17 oppressed, give orphans their **rights,** and defend widows."
3.15 You have no **right** to crush my people and take advantage
10. 2 the poor from having their **rights** and from getting justice.
11. 4 the poor fairly and defend the **rights** of the helpless.
22.16 What **right** have you to carve a tomb for yourself out of
32. 7 the poor with lies and to prevent them getting their **rights.**
45.11 "You have no **right** to question me about my children or to
Jer 5.28 give orphans their **rights** or show justice to the oppressed.
11.15 What **right** have they to be in my Temple?
18. 6 to me, [6] "Haven't I the **right** to do with you people of
32. 7 his nearest relative and had the **right** to buy it for myself.
Lam 3.35 He knows when we are denied the **rights** he gave us;
Dan 11.21 evil man who has no **right** to be king, but he will
Hos 5.11 has lost land that was **rightfully** hers, because she insisted
Amos 5. 7 that twist justice and cheat people out of their **rights!**
Obad 17 of Jacob will possess the land that is theirs by **right.**
Jon 4. 4 The Lord answered, "What **right** have you to be angry?"
4. 9 God said to him, "What **right** have you to be angry
4. 9 Jonah replied, "I have every **right** to be angry—
Mt 20.15 Don't I have the **right** to do as I wish with my
20.23 I do not have the **right** to choose who will sit at
21.23 to him and asked, "What **right** have you to do these things?
21.23 Who gave you this **right?"**
21.24 I will tell you what **right** I have to do these things.
21.25 Where did John's **right** to baptize come from:
21.27 will I tell you, then, by what **right** I do these things.
Mk 10.40 I do not have the **right** to choose who will sit at
11.28 and asked him, "What **right** have you to do these things?
11.28 Who gave you this **right?"**
11.29 I will tell you what **right** I have to do these things.
11.30 Tell me, where did John's **right** to baptize come from:
11.33 will I tell you, then, by what **right** I do these things."
Lk 12.14 who gave me the **right** to judge or to divide the
18. 3 pleading for her **rights,** saying, 'Help me against my opponent!'
18. 5 giving me, I will see to it that she gets her **rights.**
20. 2 to him, "Tell us, what **right** have you to do these things?
20. 2 Who gave you this **right?"**
20. 4 Tell me, [4] did John's **right** to baptize come from God or from
20. 8 will I tell you, then, by what **right** I do these things."
22.29 Father has given me the **right** to rule,
22.29 so I will give you the same **right.**
Jn 1.12 so he gave them the **right** to become God's children.
2.18 perform to show us that you have the **right** to do this?"
5.22 given his Son the full **right** to judge, [23] so that all will
5.27 has given the Son the **right** to judge, because he is the
10.18 I have the **right** to give it up,
10.18 and I have the **right** to take it back.
Rom 9.21 makes the pots has the **right** to use the clay as he
1 Cor 9. 4 Haven't I the **right** to be given food and drink for my
9. 5 Haven't I the **right** to follow the example of the other
9.12 If others have the **right** to expect this from you,
9.12 haven't we an even greater **right?**
9.12 But we haven't made use of this **right.**
9.15 use of any of these **rights,** nor am I writing this now
9.15 in order to claim such **rights** for myself.
9.15 Nobody is going to turn my **rightful** boast into empty words!
1 Cor 9.16 I have no **right** to boast just because I preach the gospel.
9.18 it, without claiming my **rights** in my work for the gospel.
2 Thes 3. 9 this, not because we have no **right** to demand our support;
Heb 12.16 who for a single meal sold his **rights** as the elder son.
13.10 place of worship have no **right** to eat any of the sacrifice
2 Pet 1.11 will be given the full **right** to enter the eternal Kingdom of
Rev 2. 7 victory I will give the **right** to eat the fruit of the
3.21 victory I will give the **right** to sit beside me on my
21. 6 thirsty I will give the **right** to drink from the spring of
22.14 clean and so have the **right** to eat the fruit from the

RIGHT WITH GOD

see also **RIGHTEOUS**

Job 15.14 Can anyone be **right with God?**
Lk 18.14 the Pharisee, was in the **right with God** when he went home.
Rom 1.17 For the gospel reveals how God puts people **right with himself:**
1.17 "The person who is put **right with God** through faith shall live."
2.13 that people are put **right with God,** but by doing what the
3.20 For no one is put **right** in God's sight by doing what
3.21 God's way of putting people **right with himself** has been revealed.
3.22 God puts people **right** through their faith in Jesus Christ.
3.24 grace all are put **right with him** through Christ Jesus, who
3.25 and that he puts **right** everyone who believes in Jesus.
3.28 a person is put **right with God** only through faith, and not
3.30 will put the Jews **right with himself** on the basis of their
3.30 their faith, and will put the Gentiles **right** through their faith.
4. 2 If he was put **right with God** by the things he did,
4. 5 God takes into account in order to put him **right with himself.**
4.25 was raised to life in order to put us **right with God.**
5. 1 we have been put **right with God** through faith, we have peace
5. 9 By his sacrificial death we are now put **right with God;**
5.17 and are freely put **right with him** will rule in life through
5.19 will all be put **right with God** as the result of the
6.16 or of obedience, which results in being put **right with God.**
8.10 you have been put **right with God,** even though your bodies
8.30 he called, he put **right with himself,** and he shared his
9.30 trying to put themselves **right with God,**
9.30 were put **right with him** through faith;
9.31 law that would put them **right with God,** did not find it.
10. 3 which God puts people **right with himself,** and instead, they have
10. 3 did not submit themselves to God's way of putting people **right.**
10. 4 so that everyone who believes is put **right with God.**
10. 5 this about being put **right with God** by obeying the Law:
10. 6 scripture says about being put **right with God** through faith is
10.10 it is by our faith that we are put **right with God;**
1 Cor 1.30 By him we are put **right with God;**
6.11 you have been put **right with God** by the Lord Jesus Christ
Gal 2.16 a person is put **right with God** only through faith in Jesus
2.16 order to be put **right with God** through our faith in Christ,
2.16 no one is put **right with God** by doing what the Law
2.17 try to be put **right with God** by our union with Christ,
2.21 a person is put **right with God** through the Law, it means
3. 8 that God would put the Gentiles **right with himself** through faith.
3.11 no one is put **right with God** by means of the Law,
3.11 person who is put **right with God** through faith shall live."
3.21 then everyone could be put **right with God** by obeying it.
3.24 that we might then be put **right with God** through faith.
5. 4 try to be put **right with God** by obeying the Law have
5. 5 our hope is that God will put us **right with him;**
2 Tim 4. 8 prize of being put **right with God,** which the Lord, the
Tit 3. 7 we might be put **right with God** and come into possession of
Jas 2.21 How was our ancestor Abraham put **right with God?**
2.24 a person is put **right with God,** and not by his faith
2.25 She was put **right with God** through her actions, by welcoming

RIGHTEOUS

[UNRIGHTEOUS]
see also **RIGHT WITH GOD**

Num 23.10 Let me die in peace like the **righteous."**
1 Sam 26.23 The Lord rewards those who are faithful and **righteous.**
Job 4. 7 Name a single case where a **righteous** man met with disaster.
4.17 "Can anyone be **righteous** in the sight of God or be pure
12. 4 they laugh, although I am **righteous** and blameless;
25. 4 Can anyone be **righteous** or pure in God's sight?
27. 7 fight against me be punished like wicked, **unrighteous** men.
34.17 Are you condemning the **righteous** God?
35. 7 Do you help God by being so **righteous?**
36. 7 He protects those who are **righteous;**
37.23 he is **righteous** and just in his dealings with men.
Ps 1. 6 The **righteous** are guided and protected by the Lord, but
4. 3 the Lord has chosen the **righteous** for his own, and he hears
7. 9 You are a **righteous** God and judge our thoughts and desires.
7.11 God is a **righteous** judge and always condemns the wicked.
9. 8 He rules the world with **righteousness;**
9.16 has revealed himself by his **righteous** judgements, and the
11. 7 The Lord is **righteous** and loves good deeds;
25. 8 Because the Lord is **righteous** and good, he teaches sinners
31. 1 You are a **righteous** God;
31.18 and arrogant who speak with contempt about **righteous** men.
32.11 You that are **righteous,** be glad and rejoice because of
33. 1 All you that are **righteous,** shout for joy for what the
33. 5 The Lord loves what is **righteous** and just;
34.15 The Lord watches over the **righteous** and listens to their cries;
34.17 The **righteous** call to the Lord, and he listens;
34.21 those who hate the **righteous** will be punished.
35.24 You are **righteous,** O Lord, so declare me innocent;
35.28 Then I will proclaim your **righteousness,** and I will
36. 6 Your **righteousness** is towering like the mountains;
36.10 who know you and to do good to those who are **righteous.**

Ps 37. 6 he will make your **righteousness** shine like the noonday sun.
37.29 The **righteous** will possess the land and live in it for ever.
37.37 Notice the good man, observe the **righteous** man;
37.39 The Lord saves **righteous** men and protects them
49.14 The **righteous** will triumph over them, as their bodies
50. 6 The heavens proclaim that God is **righteous,**
51.14 O God, and save me, and I will gladly proclaim your **righteousness.**
52. 6 **Righteous** people will see this and be afraid;
58.10 The **righteous** will be glad when they see sinners punished;
58.11 People will say, "The **righteous** are indeed rewarded;
64.10 **righteous** people will rejoice because of what the Lord has done.
68. 3 But the **righteous** are glad and rejoice in his presence;
71. 2 Because you are **righteous,** help me and rescue me.
71.19 Your **righteousness,** God, reaches the skies.
71.24 I will speak of your **righteousness** all day long, because
72. 1 Teach the king to judge with your **righteousness,** O God;
72. 2 with justice and govern the oppressed with **righteousness.**
72. 3 may it experience **righteousness.**
72. 7 May **righteousness** flourish in his lifetime, and may
75.10 wicked, but the power of the **righteous** will be increased.
85.10 **righteousness** and peace will embrace.
85.11 earth, and God's **righteousness** will look down from heaven.
85.13 **Righteousness** will go before the Lord and prepare the path for him.
89.14 Your kingdom is founded on **righteousness** and justice;
92.12 The **righteous** will flourish like palm-trees;
94.15 in the courts, and all **righteous** people will support it.
97. 2 he rules with **righteousness** and justice.
97. 6 The heavens proclaim his **righteousness,**
97.11 Light shines on the **righteous,** and gladness on the good.
97.12 All you that are **righteous** be glad because of what the
99. 4 you have brought **righteousness** and fairness.
107.42 The **righteous** see this and are glad, but all the wicked
111. 3 his **righteousness** is eternal.
111. 8 they were given in truth and **righteousness.**
118.20 only the **righteous** can come in.
119. 7 As I learn your **righteous** judgements, I will praise you
119.40 give me new life, for you are **righteous.**
119.62 I wake up to praise you for your **righteous** judgements.
119.75 know that your judgements are **righteous,** Lord, and that you
119.137 You are **righteous,** Lord, and your laws are just.
119.142 Your **righteousness** will last for ever,
119.160 is truth, and all your **righteous** judgements are eternal.
119.164 Seven times each day I thank you for your **righteous** judgements.
125. 3 The wicked will not always rule over the land of the **righteous;**
125. 3 if they did, the **righteous** themselves might do evil.
129. 4 But the Lord, the **righteous** one, has freed me from slavery."
140.13 The **righteous** will praise you indeed;
143. 1 In your **righteousness** listen to my plea;
145.17 The Lord is **righteous** in all he does, merciful in all
146. 8 he loves his **righteous** people.
Prov 2. 7 He provides help and protection for **righteous,** honest men.
2.13 men who have abandoned a **righteous** life to live in the
2.20 follow the example of good men and live a **righteous** life.
2.21 **Righteous** men—men of integrity—will live in this land of ours.
3.32 who do evil, but he takes **righteous** men into his confidence.
3.33 homes of wicked men, but blesses the homes of the **righteous.**
4.18 The road the **righteous** travel is like the sunrise,
8.20 I walk the way of **righteousness;**
9. 9 Whatever you tell a **righteous** man will add to his knowledge.
10.24 The **righteous** get what they want, but the wicked will
10.30 **Righteous** people will always have security, but the
10.31 **Righteous** people speak wisdom, but the tongue that
10.32 **Righteous** people know the kind thing to say, but the
11. 6 **Righteousness** rescues the honest man, but someone who
11. 8 The **righteous** are protected from trouble;
11. 9 people, but the wisdom of the **righteous** can save you.
11.11 A city becomes great when **righteous** men give it their blessing;
11.21 evil men will be punished, but **righteous** men will escape.
11.28 leaves of autumn, but the **righteous** will prosper like the
11.30 **Righteousness** gives life, but violence takes it away.
12. 3 Wickedness does not give security, but **righteous** people stand firm.
12. 6 the words of the **righteous** rescue those who are threatened.
12. 7 no descendants, but the families of **righteous** men live on.
12.12 is to find evil things to do, but the **righteous** stand firm.
12.21 Nothing bad happens to **righteous** people, but the wicked
12.26 The **righteous** man is a guide to his friend, but the path
12.28 **Righteousness** is the road to life;
13. 6 **Righteousness** protects the innocent;
13. 9 The **righteous** are like a light shining brightly;
13.21 Trouble follows sinners everywhere, but **righteous** people
13.22 but the wealth of sinners will go to **righteous** men.
13.25 The **righteous** have enough to eat, but the wicked are always hungry.
14.19 to bow down to the **righteous** and humbly beg their favour.
14.34 **Righteousness** makes a nation great;
15. 6 **Righteous** men keep their wealth, but wicked men lose
16.31 Long life is the reward of the **righteous;**
18.10 like a strong tower, where the **righteous** can go and be safe.
21.12 God, the **righteous** one, knows what goes on in the homes
21.26 A **righteous** man, however, can give, and give generously.
21.29 **Righteous** people are sure of themselves;
23.24 A **righteous** man's father has good reason to be happy.
28.28 But when they fall from power, **righteous** men will rule again.
29. 2 Show me a **righteous** ruler and I will show you a happy
29.10 hate anyone who's honest, but **righteous** people will protect
29.16 But the **righteous** will live to see the downfall of such men.
29.27 The **righteous** hate the wicked, and the wicked hate the righteous.
31. 9 Speak for them and be a **righteous** judge.
Ecc 3.17 is going to judge the **righteous** and the evil alike,
8.14 sometimes **righteous** men get the punishment of the wicked,
8.14 and wicked men get the reward of the **righteous.**
9. 1 the actions of wise and **righteous** men, even their love and
9. 2 same fate comes to the **righteous** and the wicked,
Is 1.21 filled with **righteous** men, but now only murderers remain.
1.26 Then Jerusalem will be called the **righteous,** faithful city."
1.27 Because the Lord is **righteous,** he will save Jerusalem
3.10 **Righteous** men will be happy, and things will go well for them.
24.16 will hear songs in praise of Israel, the **righteous** nation.
26.10 Even here in a land of **righteous** people they still do wrong;
32.16 Everywhere in the land **righteousness** and justice will be done.
Jer 23. 5 when I will choose as king a **righteous** descendant of David.
33.15 time I will choose as king a **righteous** descendant of David.
Ezek 18. 5 "Suppose there is a truly good man, **righteous** and honest.
18. 9 He is **righteous,** and he will live," says the Sovereign Lord.
18.24 "But if a **righteous** man stops doing good and starts
18.26 When a **righteous** man stops doing good and starts doing
23.45 **Righteous** men will condemn them on the charge of adultery and murder,
33.18 When a **righteous** man stops doing good and starts doing evil,
Hos 10.12 new ground for yourselves, plant **righteousness,** and reap the
14. 9 Lord's ways are right, and **righteous** people live by following them,
Amos 5.24 flow like a stream, and **righteousness** like a river that
Hab 1. 4 the better of the **righteous,** and so justice is perverted.
1.13 they destroy people who are more **righteous** than they are?
2. 4 survive, but those who are **righteous** will live because they
Zeph 3. 5 And yet the **unrighteous** people there keep on doing wrong and
Mal 3.18 between what happens to the **righteous** and to the wicked, to
Mt 25.33 He will put the **righteous** people on his right and the
25.37 "The **righteous** will then answer him, 'When, Lord, did we ever
25.46 to eternal punishment, but the **righteous** will go to eternal life."
Lk 1.17 disobedient people back to the way of thinking of the **righteous;**
1.75 we might be holy and **righteous** before him all the days
7.29 ones who had obeyed God's **righteous** demands and had been baptized
Jn 17.25 **Righteous** Father!
Acts 7.52 who long ago announced the coming of his **righteous** Servant.
22.14 his will, to see his **righteous** Servant, and to hear him
Rom 2. 5 Day when God's anger and **righteous** judgements will be revealed.
3.10 is no one who is **righteous,** [11] no one who is wise
3.25 God did this in order to demonstrate that he is **righteous.**
3.25 he deals with their sins, in order to demonstrate his **righteousness.**
3.25 shows that he himself is **righteous**
4. 3 and because of his faith God accepted him as **righteous."**
4. 6 person whom God accepts as **righteous,** apart from anything that
4. 9 and because of his faith God accepted him as **righteous."**
4.11 God had accepted him as **righteous** before he had been circumcised.
4.11 God and are accepted as **righteous** by him, even though they
4.13 but because he believed and was accepted as **righteous** by God.
4.22 why Abraham, through faith, "was accepted as **righteous** by God."
4.23 "he was accepted as **righteous"** were not written for him alone.
4.24 are to be accepted as **righteous,** who believe in him who
5. 7 a difficult thing for someone to die for a **righteous** person.
5.18 the same way the one **righteous** act sets all mankind free
5.21 grace rules by means of **righteousness,** leading us to eternal life
6.13 your whole being to him to be used for **righteous** purposes.
6.18 You were set free from sin and became the slaves of **righteousness.**
6.19 must now surrender yourselves entirely as slaves of **righteousness**
6.20 When you were the slaves of sin, you were free from **righteousness.**
8. 4 did this so that the **righteous** demands of the Law might be
14.17 but of the **righteousness,** peace, and joy which the Holy
2 Cor 5.21 in union with him we might share the **righteousness** of God.
6. 7 We have **righteousness** as our weapon, both to attack and to
11.15 disguise themselves to look like servants of **righteousness.**
Gal 3. 6 and because of his faith God accepted him as **righteous."**
Eph 5. 9 brings a rich harvest of every kind of goodness, **righteousness,**
6.14 tight round your waist, with **righteousness** as your breastplate,
Phil 3. 6 as a person can be **righteous** by obeying the commands of the
3. 9 I no longer have a **righteousness** of my own, the kind that
3. 9 now have the **righteousness** that is given through faith in Christ,
3. 9 the **righteousness** that comes from God
1 Tim 6.11 Strive for **righteousness,** godliness, faith, love, endurance, and gentleness.
2 Tim 2.22 and strive for **righteousness,** faith, love, and peace,
4. 8 God, which the Lord, the **righteous** Judge, will give me on
Heb 7. 2 first meaning of Melchizedek's name is "King of **Righteousness";**
10.38 My **righteous** people, however, will believe and live;
11. 4 won God's approval as a **righteous** man, because God himself
11. 7 and Noah received from God the **righteousness** that comes by faith.
12.11 by such punishment reap the peaceful reward of a **righteous** life.
Jas 1.20 Man's anger does not achieve God's **righteous** purpose.
2.23 and because of his faith God accepted him as **righteous."**
1 Pet 2.23 not threaten, but placed his hopes in God, the **righteous** Judge.
2.24 so that we might die to sin and live for **righteousness.**
3.12 the Lord watches over the **righteous** and listens to their prayers;
2 Pet 1. 1 those who through the **righteousness** of our God and Saviour Jesus
2. 5 ones he saved were Noah, who preached **righteousness,** and seven
2.21 have known the way of **righteousness** than to know it and then
3.13 and a new earth, where **righteousness** will be at home.
1 Jn 2. 1 with the Father on our behalf—Jesus Christ, the **righteous** one.
2.29 You know that Christ is **righteous;**
3. 7 Whoever does what is right is **righteous,**
3. 7 just as Christ is **righteous.**

AV RIGHTEOUS
see also **GOOD, INNOCENT, JUST, RIGHT (1), RIGHT WITH GOD**

Deut 1.16 Judge every dispute **fairly,** whether it concerns only your
4. 8 Laws so **just** as those that I have taught you
16.19 eyes even of wise and **honest** men, and cause them to give
2 Chr 12. 6 sinned, and they said, "What the Lord is doing is **just."**
Ezra 9.15 God of Israel, you are **just,** but you have let us survive.
Neh 9. 8 You kept your promise, because you are **faithful.**
Job 17. 9 Those who claim to be **respectable** are more and more
23. 7 I am **honest;**
Ps 1. 5 be condemned by God and kept apart from **God's own people.**
5.12 You bless those who **obey** you, Lord;
14. 5 they will be terrified, for God is with those who **obey** him.
19. 9 The judgements of the Lord are **just;**
35.27 who want to see me **acquitted** shout for joy and say again
55.22 he never lets **honest** men be defeated.
67. 4 you judge the peoples with **justice**
96.10 he will judge the peoples with **justice."**
112. 4 for good men, for those who are merciful, kind, and **just.**
118.15 to the glad shouts of victory in the tents of **God's people:**
119.106 I will keep my solemn promise to obey your **just** instructions.
Prov 10.25 the wicked are blown away, but **honest** people are always safe.
11.10 A city is happy when **honest** people have good fortune,
12. 5 **Honest** people will treat you fairly;
13. 5 **Honest** people hate lies, but the words of wicked people are
15.19 but if you are **honest,** you will have no trouble.
16.13 king wants to hear the **truth** and will favour those who speak
24.15 who scheme to rob an **honest** man or to take away his
28. 1 is chasing them, but an **honest** person is as brave as a
28.10 If you trick an **honest** person into doing evil,
29. 6 in their own sins, while **honest** people are happy and free.
Is 53.11 My **devoted** servant, with whom I am pleased,
Jer 11.20 Then I prayed, "Almighty Lord, you are a **just** judge;
Lam 1.18 "But the Lord is **just,** for I have disobeyed him.
Amos 2. 6 They sell into slavery **honest** men who cannot pay their debts,
Mt 9.13 I have not come to call **respectable** people, but outcasts."
13.17 many prophets and many of **God's people** wanted very much to
13.43 Then **God's people** will shine like the sun in their Father's
Mk 2.17 I have not come to call **respectable** people, but outcasts."
Lk 5.32 have not come to call **respectable** people to repent, but outcasts."
Jn 7.24 Stop judging by external standards, and judge by **true** standards."
2 Thes 1. 5 proves that God's judgement is **just** and as a result you will
Tit 2.12 to live self-controlled, **upright,** and godly lives in this world,
Rev 16. 5 judgements you have made are **just,** O Holy One, you who are
16. 7 True and **just** indeed are your judgements!"
19. 2 True and **just** are his judgements!

AV RIGHTEOUSNESS

Gen 30.33 the future you can easily find out if I have been **honest.**
Lev 19.15 "Be honest and **just** when you make decisions in legal cases;
Deut 9. 4 brought you in to possess this land because you **deserved** it.
9. 6 Lord is not giving you this fertile land because you **deserve** it.
24.13 grateful, and the Lord your God will be **pleased** with you.
Job 29.14 I have always acted **justly** and fairly.
35. 8 who suffers from your sins, and the **good** you do helps him.
36. 3 use what I know to show that God, my Creator, is **just.**
Ps 4. 1 Answer me when I pray, O God, my **defender!**
5. 8 Lead me to do your **will;**
7.17 thank the Lord for his **justice,** I sing praises to the Lord,
11. 7 The Lord is righteous and loves **good** deeds;
22.31 "The Lord **saved** his people."
24. 5 God will declare them **innocent.**
36.10 who know you and to do **good** to those who are righteous.
40.10 I have not kept the news of **salvation** to myself;
45. 4 in majesty to victory for the defence of truth and **justice!**
48.10 You rule with **justice;**
51.19 Then you will be pleased with **proper** sacrifices
52. 3 You love evil more than good and falsehood more than **truth.**
58. 1 Do you rulers ever give a **just** decision?
69.27 don't let them have any part in your **salvation.**
71.15 I will tell of your **goodness;**
71.16 I will proclaim your **goodness,** yours alone.
88.12 of darkness or your **goodness** in the land of the forgotten?
89.16 all day long, and they praise you for your **goodness.**
94.15 **Justice** will again be found in the courts,
96.13 He will rule the peoples of the world with **justice**
98. 2 he made his **saving** power known to the nations.
98. 9 He will rule the peoples of the world with **justice**
103.17 lasts for ever, and his **goodness** endures for all generations
118.19 Open to me the gates of the **Temple;**
119.123 watching for your saving help, for the **deliverance** you promised.
119.144 Your instructions are always **just;**
119.172 I will sing about your law, because your commands are **just.**
Prov 8. 8 Everything I say is **true;**
12.17 When you tell the truth, **justice** is done,
25. 5 the king and his government will be known for its **justice.**
Ecc 7.15 A **good** man may die while another man lives on, even though
Is 11. 4 he will judge the poor **fairly** and defend the rights of
11. 5 He will rule his people with **justice** and integrity.
26. 9 earth and its people, they will all learn what **justice** is.
32. 1 king who rules with **integrity,** and national leaders who govern
42. 6 and given you power to see that **justice** is done on earth.
45.19 I am the Lord, and I speak the **truth;**
51. 1 you that want to be **saved,** you that come to me for
58. 8 I will always be with you to **save** you;
62. 1 be silent until she is **saved,** And her victory shines like a
Jer 23. 6 He will be called 'The Lord Our **Salvation.'**
33.16 The city will be called 'The Lord Our **Salvation.'**
Ezek 33.12 a good man sins, the **good** he has done will not save
33.13 thinking that his past **goodness** is enough and begins to sin,
33.13 to sin, I will not remember any of the **good** he did.
33.18 a righteous man stops doing **good** and starts doing evil, he
Hos 2.19 I will be **true** and faithful;
10.12 your Lord, and I will come and pour out **blessings** upon you.'
Mic 6. 5 and you will realize what I did in order to **save** you."
7. 9 we will live to see him **save** us.
Zech 8. 8 I will be their God, ruling over them faithfully and **justly.**
Mal 4. 2 you who obey me, my **saving** power will rise on you like
Mt 3.15 For in this way we shall do all **that God requires."**
5. 6 "Happy are those whose greatest desire is to do **what God requires;**
5.10 "Happy are those who are persecuted because they do **what God requires;**
5.20 of the Law and the Pharisees in doing **what God requires.**
6.33 God and with **what he requires** of you, and he will provide
Acts 13.10 You are the enemy of everything that is **good.**
17.31 judge the whole world with **justice** by means of a man he
24.25 Paul went on discussing about **goodness,** self-control,
Rom 2.26 is not circumcised, obeys the **commands** of the Law, will God
2 Cor 3. 9 much more glorious is the activity which brings **salvation!**
9. 9 his **kindness** lasts for ever."
9.10 grow and produce a rich harvest from your **generosity.**
Eph 4.24 reveals itself in the true life that is **upright** and holy.
Phil 1.11 be filled with the truly **good** qualities which only Jesus Christ
Tit 3. 5 not because of any **good** deeds that we ourselves had done,
Heb 1. 8 You rule over your people with **justice.**
Jas 3.18 And **goodness** is the harvest that is produced from the seeds
Rev 19. 8 (The linen is the **good** deeds of God's people.)
19.11 it is with **justice** that he judges and fights his battles.

RIGID

Is 48. 4 to be stubborn, as **rigid** as iron and unyielding as bronze.

RIM

Ex 25.25 Make a **rim** 75 millimetres wide round it
25.25 and a gold border round the **rim.**
25.27 poles for carrying the table are to be placed near the **rim.**
27. 5 Put the grating under the **rim** of the altar, so that it
37.12 He made a **rim** 75 millimetres wide round it
37.12 and put a gold border round the **rim.**
37.14 the poles for carrying the table were placed near the **rim.**
38. 4 and put it under the **rim** of the altar, so that it
1 Kgs 7.24 the outer edge of the **rim** of the tank were two rows
7.26 Its **rim** was like the rim of a cup, curving outwards like
7.33 their axles, **rims,** spokes, and hubs were all of bronze.
2 Chr 4. 3 the outer edge of the **rim** of the tank were two rows
4. 5 Its **rim** was like the rim of a cup, curving outwards
Ezek 1.18 The **rims** of the wheels were covered with eyes.
43.13 fifty centimetres wide, with a **rim** at the outside edge
43.17 on each side, with a **rim** at the outside edge

RING (1)
[NOSE-RING, SIGNET-RING]

Gen 24.22 man took an expensive gold **ring** and put it in her nose
24.30 Laban had seen the **nose-ring** and the bracelets on his
24.47 Then I put the **ring** in her nose and the bracelets on
41.42 removed from his finger the **ring** engraved with the royal
Ex 25.12 attach them to its four legs, with two **rings** on each side.
25.14 and put them through the **rings** on each side of the box.
25.15 to be left in the **rings** and must not be taken out.
25.27 The **rings** to hold the poles for carrying the table are
26.29 and fit them with gold **rings** to hold the cross-bars, which
27. 7 and put them in the **rings** on each side of the altar
28.23 Make two gold **rings** and attach them to the upper corners
28.24 and fasten the two gold cords to the two **rings.**
28.26 Then make two **rings** of gold and attach them to the lower
28.27 Make two more gold **rings** and attach them to the lower
28.28 Tie the **rings** of the breast-piece to
35.22 women, brought decorative pins, earrings, **rings,** necklaces,
36.34 and fitted them with gold **rings** to hold the cross-bars,
37. 3 attached them to its four feet, with two **rings** on each side.
37. 5 and put them through the **rings** on each side of the box.
37.14 The **rings** to hold the poles for carrying the table were
38. 7 and put them in the **rings** on each side of the altar.
39.16 gold settings and two gold **rings**
39.16 and attached the two **rings** to the upper corners
39.17 gold cords to the two **rings** [18] and fastened the other two
39.19 They made two **rings** of gold and attached them to the
39.20 They made two more gold **rings** and attached them to the
39.21 they tied the **rings** of the breast-piece
39.21 to the **rings** of the ephod
40.20 put the poles in the **rings** of the box and put the
Num 31.50 the gold ornaments, armlets, bracelets, **rings,** earrings, and
Esth 1. 6 of fine purple linen to silver **rings** on marble columns.
3.10 The king took off his **ring,** which was used to stamp
3.12 issued in the name of King Xerxes and stamped with his **ring.**
8. 2 The king took off his **ring** with his seal on it (which
Job 41.14 open his jaws, **ringed** with those terrifying teeth?
42.11 Each of them gave him some money and a gold **ring.**
Prov 11.22 good judgement is like a gold **ring** in a pig's snout.
25.12 is more valuable than gold **rings** or jewellery made of the
Song 5.14 His hands are well-formed, and he wears **rings** set with gems.
Is 3.21 the **rings** they wear on their fingers and in their noses;
Jer 22.24 even if you were the **signet-ring** on my right hand, I would
Ezek 16.12 I gave you a **nose-ring** and earrings and a beautiful
Lk 15.22 Put a **ring** on his finger and shoes on his feet.
Jas 2. 2 rich man wearing a gold **ring** and fine clothes comes to your

RING (2)
[RANG]

Esth	8.15	Then the streets of Susa **rang** with cheers and joyful shouts.
Is	21. 5	Suddenly the command **rings** out:
Nah	2. 8	the cry **rings** out— but no one turns back.
Mt	25. 6	already midnight when the cry **rang** out, 'Here is the bridegroom!

RINSE

Lev	6.28	pot is used, it must be scrubbed and **rinsed** with water.
2 Chr	4. 6	were to be used to **rinse** the parts of the animals that

RIOT

Ps	55. 9	I see violence and **riots** in the city, [10]surrounding it day
Mt	26. 5	during the festival," they said, "or the people will **riot."**
	27.24	go on, but that a **riot** might break out, he took some
Mk	14. 2	during the festival," they said, "or the people might **riot."**
	15. 7	prison with the rebels who had committed murder in the **riot.**
Lk	23. 5	he is starting a **riot** among the people all through Judaea.
	23.19	put in prison for a **riot** that had taken place in the
	23.25	been put in prison for **riot** and murder, and he handed Jesus
Acts	19.40	there is the danger that we will be accused of a **riot.**
	21.31	of the Roman troops that all Jerusalem was **rioting.**
	24. 5	he starts **riots** among the Jews all over the world and is

RIP

Gen	37.23	up to his brothers, they **ripped** off his long robe
2 Kgs	8.12	children to death, and **rip** open their pregnant women."
	15.16	He even **ripped** open the bellies of all the pregnant women.
Ezek	13.20	I will **rip** them off your arms and set free the people
	13.21	I will **rip** off your scarves and let my people escape
Hos	13.16	and pregnant women will be **ripped** open."
Amos	1.13	they even **ripped** open pregnant women in Gilead.

RIPE
[SUN-RIPENED, UNRIPE]

Gen	15.15	yourself will live to a **ripe** old age, die in peace, and
	25. 7	Abraham died at the **ripe** old age of a hundred and seventy-five.
	35.29	hundred and eighty years old [29]and died at a **ripe** old age;
	40.10	came out, the blossoms appeared, and the grapes **ripened.**
	41. 5	Seven ears of corn, full and **ripe,** were growing on one stalk.
	41.22	ears of corn which were full and **ripe,** growing on one stalk.
Ex	9.31	because the barley was **ripe,** and the flax was budding.
	9.32	But none of the wheat was ruined, because it **ripens** later.
Num	13.20	(It was the season when grapes were beginning to **ripen.)**
	17. 8	It had budded, blossomed, and produced **ripe** almonds!
Deut	33.14	their land be blessed with **sun-ripened** fruit, Rich with the
Judg	8.32	of Joash died at a **ripe** old age and was buried in
1 Chr	29.28	He died at a **ripe** old age, wealthy and respected, and
Neh	10.35	we harvest and of the first fruit that **ripens** on our trees.
	12.44	tithes and the first corn and fruit that **ripened** each year.
	13.31	of the first corn and the first fruits that **ripened.**
Job	5.26	Like wheat that **ripens** till harvest time,
	5.26	you will live to a **ripe** old age.
	15.33	He will be like a vine that loses its **unripe** grapes;
Song	2.13	Figs are beginning to **ripen;**
Is	5. 2	He waited for the grapes to **ripen,** but every grape was sour.
	18. 5	fallen and the grapes are **ripening,** the enemy will destroy
	28. 4	of the season, picked and eaten as soon as they are **ripe.**
Jer	24. 2	The first basket contained good figs, those that **ripen** early;
Hos	8. 7	A field of corn that doesn't **ripen** can never produce any bread.
	9.10	it was like seeing the first **ripe** figs of the season.
Nah	3.12	All your fortresses will be like fig-trees with **ripe** figs:
Zech	12. 6	or in a field of **ripe** corn—they will destroy all the
Mk	4.29	When the corn is **ripe,** the man starts cutting it with
Lk	8.14	life crowd in and choke them, and their fruit never **ripens.**
Jn	4.35	the crops are now **ripe** and ready to be harvested!
Rev	6.13	down to the earth, like **unripe** figs falling from the tree
	14.15	the earth is **ripe** for the harvest!"
	14.18	from the vineyard of the earth, because the grapes are **ripe!"**

RISE
[ROSE]

Gen	7.20	it went on **rising** until it was about seven metres above
	19.23	The sun was **rising** when Lot reached Zoar.
	19.28	whole valley and saw smoke **rising** from the land, like smoke
	32.31	The sun **rose** as Jacob was leaving Peniel, and he was
Deut	33. 2	he **rose** like the sun over Edom and shone on his people
	33.11	Let them never **rise** again."
Josh	8.20	of Ai looked back, they saw the smoke **rising** to the sky.
Judg	5.31	O Lord, but may your friends shine like the **rising** sun!
1 Sam	25.42	She **rose** quickly and mounted her donkey.
2 Sam	22.39	I strike them down, and they cannot **rise;**
2 Chr	6.41	**Rise** up now, Lord God, and with the Covenant Box, the
	36.20	descendants as slaves until the **rise** of the Persian Empire.
Neh	8. 7	Then they **rose** and stood in their places, and the
Esth	5. 9	and when Mordecai did not **rise** or show any sign of respect
Job	9. 7	can keep the sun from **rising,** and the stars from shining at
	14.12	and lakes that go dry, [12]people die, never to **rise.**
	41.18	when he sneezes, and his eyes glow like the **rising** sun.
	41.25	When he **rises** up, even the strongest are frightened;
Ps	7. 6	**Rise** in your anger, O Lord!
	18.38	I strike them down, and they cannot **rise;**
	20. 8	will stumble and fall, but we will **rise** and stand firm.
	35.23	**rise** up, my God, and plead my cause.
	36.12	There they lie, unable to **rise.**
Ps	59. 5	**Rise,** Lord God Almighty, and come to my aid;
	66. 7	Let no rebels **rise** against him.
	68. 1	God **rises** up and scatters his enemies.
	76. 9	and kept silent, [9]when you **rose** up to pronounce judgement,
	88.10	Do they **rise** up and praise you?
	94. 2	**rise** and give the proud what they deserve!
	102.13	You will **rise** and take pity on Zion;
	104.22	When the sun **rises,** they go back and lie down in their
Prov	8.29	the waters of the sea to **rise** no further than he said.
Ecc	1. 5	The sun still **rises,** and it still goes down, going wearily
	4.13	A man may **rise** from poverty to become king of his country,
	9.11	rich, and capable men do not always **rise** to high positions.
Is	8. 8	Judah in a flood, **rising** shoulder high and covering everything."
	13.10	will be dark when it **rises,** and the moon will give no
	14. 9	The ghosts of kings are **rising** from their thrones.
	24.20	it will collapse and never **rise** again.
	26.14	their ghosts will not **rise,** for you have punished them and
	34.10	burn day and night, and smoke will **rise** from it for ever.
	40.31	They will **rise** on wings like eagles;
	43.17	Down they fell, never to **rise,** snuffed out like the flame of
	44.26	Those cities will **rise** from the ruins.
	49. 7	"Kings will see you released and will **rise** to show their respect;
	52. 2	**Rise** from the dust and sit on your throne!
Jer	21.13	high above the valleys, like a rock **rising** above the plain.
	46. 7	Who is this that **rises** like the Nile, like a river
	46. 8	It is Egypt, **rising** like the Nile, like a river flooding
	46. 8	Egypt said, 'I will **rise** and cover the world;
	47. 2	Waters are **rising** in the north and will rush like a river
	51.64	it will sink and never **rise** again, because of the
Ezek	1.19	them, and if the creatures **rose** up from the earth, so did
	1.21	creatures moved or stopped or **rose** in the air, the wheels
	8.11	an incense-burner, and smoke was **rising** from the incense.
	8.16	bowing low towards the east, worshipping the **rising** sun.
	9. 3	of the God of Israel **rose** up from the winged creatures,
	10. 4	light of the Lord's presence **rose** up from the creatures and
	10.15	When the creatures **rose** in the air [16]and moved, the wheels
	17.14	to keep the nation from **rising** again and to make sure
Dan	12.13	will die, but you will **rise** to receive your reward at the
Amos	5. 2	Virgin Israel has fallen, Never to **rise** again!
	8. 8	it will **rise** and fall like the River Nile.
	8.14	of Beersheba'—those people will fall and not **rise** again."
	9. 5	The whole world **rises** and falls like the River Nile.
Jon	4. 8	After the sun had **risen,** God sent a hot east wind, and
Mic	7. 8	We have fallen, but we will **rise** again.
Hab	3.10	The waters under the earth roared, and their waves **rose** high.
Zeph	3. 8	"Wait for the day when I **rise** to accuse the nations.
Mal	4. 2	me, my saving power will **rise** on you like the sun and
Mt	13.33	litres of flour until the whole batch of dough **rises."**
	22.23	to Jesus and claimed that people will not **rise** from death.
	22.28	the day when the dead **rise** to life, whose wife will she
	22.30	For when the dead **rise** to life, they will be like the
	22.31	Now, as for the dead **rising** to life:
	27.53	the graves, and after Jesus **rose** from death, they went into
Mk	8.31	put to death, but three days later he will **rise** to life."
	9. 9	you have seen, until the Son of Man has **risen** from death."
	9.10	"What does this **'rising** from death' mean?"
	9.27	by the hand and helped him to **rise,** and he stood up.
	9.31	Three days later, however, he will **rise** to life."
	10.34	but three days later he will **rise** to life."
	12.18	say that people will not **rise** from death, came to Jesus
	12.23	Now, when all the dead **rise** to life on the day of
	12.25	For when the dead **rise** to life, they will be like the
	16. 9	After Jesus **rose** from death early on Sunday, he appeared first
Lk	1.78	bright dawn of salvation to **rise** on us [79]and to shine from
	3.15	People's hopes began to **rise,** and they began to wonder whether
	4.29	They **rose** up, dragged Jesus out of the town, and took
	13.21	litres of flour until the whole batch of dough **rises."**
	14.14	will repay you on the day the good people **rise** from death."
	16.30	But if someone were to **rise** from death and go to them,
	16.31	not be convinced even if someone were to **rise** from death.' "
	18.33	and kill him, but three days later he will **rise** to life."
	20.27	say that people will not **rise** from death, came to Jesus
	20.33	the day when the dead **rise** to life, whose wife will she
	20.35	women who are worthy to **rise** from death and live in the
	20.36	They are the sons of God, because they have **risen** from death.
	22.45	**Rising** from his prayer, he went back to the disciples
	23. 1	The whole group **rose** up and took Jesus before Pilate,
	24. 7	men, be crucified, and three days later **rise** to life.' "
	24.34	with the others [34]and saying, "The Lord is **risen** indeed!
	24.46	Messiah must suffer and must **rise** from death three days later,
Jn	5.29	who have done good will **rise** and live,
	5.29	and those who have done evil will **rise** and be condemned.
	11.23	"Your brother will **rise** to life," Jesus told her.
	11.24	she replied, "that he will **rise** to life on the last day."
	13. 4	So he **rose** from the table, took off his outer garment,
	20. 9	understand the scripture which said that he must **rise** from death.)
	21. 4	As the sun was **rising,** Jesus stood at the water's edge,
Acts	4. 2	the people that Jesus had **risen** from death,
	4. 2	which proved that the dead will **rise** to life.
	10.26	But Peter made him **rise.**
	10.41	us who ate and drank with him after he **rose** from death.
	17. 3	them that the Messiah had to suffer and **rise** from death.
	23. 6	of the hope I have that the dead will **rise** to life!"
	23. 8	say that people will not **rise** from death and that there are
	24.15	all people, both the good and the bad, will **rise** from death.
	24.21	you today for believing that the dead will **rise** to life.' "
	26.23	be the first one to **rise** from death, to announce the light
Rom	14. 9	For Christ died and **rose** to life in order to be the
1 Cor	5. 6	"A little bit of yeast makes the whole batch of dough **rise."**
	15.21	in the same way the **rising** from death comes by means of
Gal	5. 9	yeast to make the whole batch of dough **rise,"** as they say.

Eph 5.14 "Wake up, sleeper, and **rise** from death, and Christ will shine
1 Thes 4.14 believe that Jesus died and **rose** again, and so we believe
4.16 Those who have died believing in Christ will **rise** to life first;
Jas 1.11 The sun **rises** with its blazing heat and burns the plant;

RISK

Deut 5.25 But why should we **risk** death again?
Judg 5.18 Zebulun and Naphtali **risked** their lives on the battlefield.
9.17 He **risked** his life to save you from the Midianites.
12. 3 were not going to, I **risked** my life and crossed the border
1 Sam 19. 5 He **risked** his life when he killed Goliath, and the Lord
28.21 to him, "Please, sir, I **risked** my life by doing what you
2 Sam 23.17 drinking the blood of these men who **risked** their lives!"
1 Chr 11.19 drinking the blood of these men who **risked** their lives!"
Job 13.14 I am ready to **risk** my life.
Ps 119.109 I am always ready to **risk** my life;
Lam 5. 9 we **risk** our lives when we look for food.
Dan 3.28 They disobeyed my orders and **risked** their lives rather than
Acts 15.26 Barnabas and Paul, [26] who have **risked** their lives in the service
Rom 16. 4 they **risked** their lives for me.
1 Cor 15.30 for us—why would we run the **risk** of danger every hour?
Phil 2.30 people as he, [30] because he **risked** his life and nearly died

RITE

Ex 4.25 Because of the **rite** of circumcision she said to Moses, "You
29.35 "Perform the **rites** of ordination for Aaron and his sons
Lev 8.33 Tent for seven days, until your ordination **rites** are completed.
9. 1 The day after the ordination **rites** were completed, Moses
Mic 1. 7 these things for its fertility **rites**, and now her enemies

RITUAL

Ex 12.25 Lord has promised to give you, you must perform this **ritual**.
12.26 When your children ask you, 'What does this **ritual** mean?'
29. 4 Tent of my presence, and tell them to take a **ritual** bath.
29.33 was used in the **ritual** of forgiveness at their ordination.
30.10 Aaron is to perform the **ritual** for purifying the altar by
40.12 entrance of the Tent, and tell them to take a **ritual** bath.
Lev 6.30 Tent and used in the **ritual** to take away sin, the animal
8. 6 and his sons forward and told them to take a **ritual** bath.
12. 7 the Lord and perform the **ritual** to take away her impurity,
12. 8 priest shall perform the **ritual** to take away her impurity,
14. 2 the following regulations about the **ritual** purification of
14.18 In this way he shall perform the **ritual** of purification.
14.19 the sin-offering and perform the **ritual** of purification.
14.20 the priest shall perform the **ritual** of purification, and the
14.29 head and in this way perform the **ritual** of purification.
14.31 In this way the priest shall perform the **ritual** of purification.
14.53 he shall perform the **ritual** of purification for the house,
15.15 way he will perform the **ritual** of purification for the man.
15.30 way he will perform the **ritual** of purification for her.
16.16 way he will perform the **ritual** to purify the Most Holy Place
16.17 to perform the **ritual** of purification until he comes out,
16.17 When he has performed the **ritual** for himself, his family,
16.20 finished performing the **ritual** to purify the Most Holy Place,
16.30 On that day the **ritual** is to be performed to purify them
16.32 his father, is to perform the **ritual** of purification.
16.33 and perform the **ritual** to purify the Most Holy Place,
16.34 This **ritual** must be performed once a year to purify the
19.22 the priest shall perform the **ritual** of purification to
20.18 they have broken the regulations about **ritual** uncleanness.
23.26 the day when the annual **ritual** is to be performed to take
23.28 it is the day for performing the **ritual** to take away sin.
Num 5. 8 to perform the **ritual** of purification for the guilty person.
5.29 of the altar, and the priest shall perform this **ritual**.
6.11 a burnt-offering, to perform the **ritual** of purification for
6.13 When a Nazirite completes his vow, he shall perform the **ritual**.
8.12 to perform the **ritual** of purification for the Levites.
8.21 He also performed the **ritual** of purification for them.
15.25 The priest shall perform the **ritual** of purification
15.28 the priest shall perform the **ritual** of purification to
16.46 the people and perform the **ritual** of purification for them.
16.47 and performed the **ritual** of purification for the people.
19. 9 to use in preparing the water for removing **ritual** uncleanness.
19. 9 This **ritual** is performed to remove sin.
28.22 this way perform the **ritual** of purification for the people.
28.30 this way perform the **ritual** of purification for the people.
29. 5 this way perform the **ritual** of purification for the people.
29.11 goat offered in the **ritual** of purification for the people,
35.33 no way to perform the **ritual** of purification for the land
2 Sam 11. 4 (She had just finished her monthly **ritual** of purification.)
1 Kgs 18.28 and daggers, according to their **ritual**, until blood flowed.
2 Chr 29.18 "We have completed the **ritual** purification of the whole Temple,
30.18 Zebulun had not performed the **ritual** of purification, and so
30.24 A large number of priests went through the **ritual** of purification.
Neh 12.30 the Levites performed **ritual** purification for themselves,
12.45 purification and the other **rituals** that God had commanded.
Ezek 44. 8 taken charge of the sacred **rituals** in my Temple, but instead
Jn 2. 6 The Jews have rules about **ritual** washing, and for this purpose
3.25 began arguing with a Jew about the matter of **ritual** washing.
11.55 to perform the **ritual** of purification before the festival.
Heb 9.13 and this purifies them by taking away their **ritual** impurity.
9.14 purify our consciences from useless **rituals**, so that we may serve

RITUALLY CLEAN, UNCLEAN see CLEAN, UNCLEAN

RIVAL

Gen 25.23 You will give birth to two **rival** peoples.
Ex 20. 5 because I am the Lord your God and I tolerate no **rivals**.
34.14 any other god, because I, the Lord, tolerate no **rivals**.
Num 25.13 he did not tolerate any **rivals** to me and brought about
Deut 4.24 he tolerates no **rivals**.
5. 9 for I am the Lord your God and I tolerate no **rivals**.
6.15 Lord your God, who is present with you, tolerates no **rivals**.
Josh 24.19 He will tolerate no **rivals**, [20] and if you leave him to
1 Sam 1. 6 Peninnah, her **rival**, would torment and humiliate her,
Is 19. 2 **Rival** cities will fight each other,
19. 2 and **rival** kings will struggle for power.
Ezek 26. 2 She won't be our **rival** any more!'
Nah 1. 2 The Lord God tolerates no **rivals**;

RIVER
see also **EUPHRATES, JORDAN**

Gen 2.10 beyond Eden it divided into four **rivers**.
2.11 The first **river** is the Pishon;
2.13 The second **river** is the Gihon;
2.14 The third **river** is the Tigris, which flows east of Assyria,
2.14 and the fourth **river** is the Euphrates.
32.22 and his eleven children, and crossed the **River** Jabbok.
41. 1 he was standing by the **River** Nile, [2] when seven cows, fat
41. 2 came up out of the **river** and began to feed on the
41. 3 the other cows on the **river-bank**, [4] and the thin cows ate up
41.18 came up out of the **river** and began feeding on the grass.
Ex 2. 3 placed it in the tall grass at the edge of the **river**.
2. 5 daughter came down to the **river** to bathe, while her servants
7.15 a snake, and wait for him on the bank of the **river**.
7.17 strike the surface of the **river** with this stick, and the
7.18 fish will die, and the **river** will stink so much that the
7.19 hold it out over all the **rivers**, canals, and pools in Egypt.
7.20 struck the surface of the **river**, and all the water in it
7.21 The fish in the **river** died, and it smelt so bad that
7.24 along the bank of the **river** for drinking water,
7.24 because they were not able to drink water from the **river**.
7.25 Seven days passed after the Lord struck the **river**.
8. 5 out his stick over the **rivers**, the canals, and the pools,
8.20 as he goes to the **river**, and tell him that the Lord
Num 21.13 the north side of the **River** Arnon, in the wilderness which
21.14 the **River** Arnon, [15] and the slope of the valleys that
21.24 their land from the **River** Arnon north to the Jabbok,
21.26 and had captured all his land as far as the **River** Arnon.
22.36 Ar, a city on the **River** Arnon at the border of Moab.
24. 6 palms Or gardens beside a **river**, Like aloes planted by the
Deut 2.13 "Then we crossed the **River** Zered as the Lord told us
2.24 Lord said to us, 'Now, start out and cross the **River** Arnon.
2.37 to the banks of the **River** Jabbok or to the towns of
3. 8 from the **River** Arnon to Mount Hermon.
3.12 town of Aroer near the **River** Arnon and part of the
3.16 Gad I assigned the territory from Gilead to the **River** Arnon.
3.16 The middle of the **river** was their southern boundary, and
3.16 their northern boundary was the **River** Jabbok, part of which
4.22 land and never cross the **river**, but you are about to go
4.48 on the edge of the **River** Arnon, all the way north to
8. 7 land—a land that has **rivers** and springs, and underground
11. 8 be able to cross the **river** and occupy the land that you
Josh 2.23 from the hills, crossed the **river**, and went back to Joshua.
3. 8 that when they reach the **river**, they must wade in and stand
3.14 It was harvest time, and the **river** was in flood.
3.14 the priests stepped into the **river**, [16] the water stopped
4. 7 Jordan stopped flowing when the Lord's Covenant Box crossed the **river**.
4.10 The people hurried across the **river**.
4.18 when the priests reached the **river bank**,
4.18 the **river** began flowing once more and flooded
12. 2 valley, as far as the **River** Jabbok, the border of Ammon;
22.10 they built a large, impressive altar there by the **river**.
Judg 4. 7 of Jabin's army, to fight against you at the **River** Kishon.
4.13 them from Harosheth-of-the-Gentiles to the **River** Kishon.
5.21 in the Kishon swept them away— the onrushing **River** Kishon.
11.13 to the **River** Jabbok and the River Jordan.
11.18 east side of Moab, on the other side of the **River** Arnon.
11.26 them, and all the cities on the banks of the **River** Arnon.
11.32 So Jephthah crossed the **river** to fight the Ammonites,
1 Sam 15. 5 the city of Amalek and waited in ambush in a dry **river-bed**.
2 Sam 15.28 I will wait at the **river crossings** in the wilderness until I
17.16 spend the night at the **river crossings** in the wilderness,
17.20 "They crossed the **river**," she answered.
17.21 against him and said, "Hurry up and cross the **river**."
19.15 who had come to Gilgal to escort him across the **river**.
19.18 They crossed the **river** to escort the royal party across
1 Kgs 18. 5 at every spring and every **river-bed** in the land to see if
18.40 Elijah led them down to the **River** Kishon and killed them.
2 Kgs 2. 7 and Elisha stopped by the **river**, and the fifty prophets
5.12 Besides, aren't the **rivers** Abana and Pharpar, back in Damascus,
5.12 better than any **river** in Israel?
10.33 town of Aroer on the **River** Arnon—this included the
17. 6 Halah, some near the **River** Habor in the district of Gozan,
18.11 Halah, some near the **River** Habor in the district of Gozan,
19.24 that the feet of your soldiers tramped the **River** Nile dry.
1 Chr 5.26 in Halah, Habor, and Hara, and by the **River** Gozan.
12.15 they crossed the **river**, scattering the people
12.15 who lived in the valleys both east and west of the **river**.
Job 14.11 Like **rivers** that stop running, and lakes that go dry,
20.17 will not live to see **rivers** of olive-oil or streams that
28.11 dig to the sources of **rivers** And bring to light what is
40.23 He is not afraid of a rushing **river**;

Ps	36. 8	you let us drink from the **river** of your goodness.
	46. 4	There is a **river** that brings joy to the city of God,
	66. 6	our ancestors crossed the **river** on foot.
	74.15	you dried up large **rivers.**
	78.16	come out of the rock and made water flow like a **river.**
	78.44	He turned the **rivers** into blood, and the Egyptians had
	83. 9	Midianites, and to Sisera and Jabin at the **River** Kishon.
	98. 8	Clap your hands, you **rivers;**
	104.10	flow in the valleys, and **rivers** run between the hills.
	105.29	He turned their **rivers** into blood and killed all their fish.
	105.41	water gushed out, flowing through the desert like a **river.**
	107.33	The Lord made **rivers** dry up completely
	119.136	tears pour down like a **river,** because people do not obey
	126. 4	just as the rain brings water back to dry **river-beds.**
	137. 1	By the **rivers** of Babylon we sat down;
Prov	3.20	His wisdom caused the **rivers** to flow and the clouds to
Ecc	1. 7	Every **river** flows into the sea, but the sea is not yet
	1. 7	to where the **rivers** began, and starts all over again.
Is	15. 9	the town of Dibon the **river** is red with blood, and God
	16. 2	on the banks of the **River** Arnon and move aimlessly to and
	18. 1	Beyond the **rivers** of Sudan there is a land where the sound
	18. 2	land divided by **rivers,** to your strong and powerful nation,
	18. 7	land divided by **rivers,** this strong and powerful nation,
	19. 5	be low in the Nile, and the **river** will gradually dry up.
	19. 6	The channels of the **river** will stink as they slowly go dry.
	33.21	We will live beside broad **rivers** and streams, but hostile
	34. 9	The **rivers** of Edom will turn into tar, and the soil will
	37.25	that the feet of your soldiers tramped the **River** Nile dry.
	41.18	I will make **rivers** flow among barren hills and springs
	42.15	I will turn the **river** valleys into deserts and dry up the
	43.20	praise me when I make **rivers** flow in the desert to give
	50. 2	with a command and turn **rivers** into a desert, so that the
	59.19	He will come like a rushing **river,** like a strong wind.
	66.12	nations will flow to you like a **river** that never goes dry.
Jer	46. 7	that rises like the Nile, like a **river** flooding its banks?
	46. 8	rising like the Nile, like a **river** flooding its banks.
	47. 2	rising in the north and will rush like a **river** in flood.
	48.20	Announce along the **River** Arnon that Moab is destroyed!'
	50.38	Bring a drought on its land and dry up its **rivers.**
	51.13	That country has many **rivers** and rich treasures, but its
	51.32	The enemy have captured the **river-crossing** and have set
	51.36	the source of Babylonia's water and make its **rivers** go dry.
Lam	2.18	Let your tears flow like **rivers** night and day;
	3.48	My eyes flow with **rivers** of tears at the destruction
Ezek	1. 1	with the Jewish exiles by the **River** Chebar in Babylonia.
	1. 3	There in Babylonia beside the **River** Chebar, I heard the
	3.15	Tel Abib beside the **River** Chebar, where the exiles were living,
	3.23	the Lord, just as I had seen it beside the **River** Chebar.
	8. 4	as I had seen it when I was by the **River** Chebar.
	10.15	the same creatures that I had seen by the **River** Chebar.)
	10.20	I had seen beneath the God of Israel at the **River** Chebar.
	10.22	exactly like the faces I had seen by the **River** Chebar.
	29. 3	I am your enemy, you monster crocodile, lying in the **river.**
	29. 4	jaw and make the fish in your **river** stick fast to you.
	31. 4	water to make it grow, And underground **rivers** to feed it.
	31.15	I will hold back the **rivers** and not let the many streams
	32. 2	but you are more like a crocodile splashing through a **river.**
	32. 2	You muddy the water with your feet and pollute the **rivers.**
	32.14	waters settle and become clear and let your **rivers** run calm.
	43. 3	to destroy Jerusalem, and the one I saw by the **River** Chebar.
	47. 6	to the bank of the **river,** [7]and when I got there I
Dan	8. 2	I was standing by the **River** Ulai,
	8. 3	Ulai, [3]and there beside the **river** I saw a ram that had
	8. 6	had seen standing beside the **river,** and rushed at him with
	8.16	voice call out over the **River** Ulai, "Gabriel, explain to
	10. 4	year, I was standing on the bank of the mighty **River** Tigris.
	12. 5	I saw two men standing by a **river,** one on each bank.
Amos	5.24	stream, and righteousness like a **river** that never goes dry.
	8. 8	it will rise and fall like the **River** Nile.
	9. 5	The whole world rises and falls like the **River** Nile.
Nah	1. 4	He makes the **rivers** go dry.
	2. 6	The gates by the **river** burst open;
	3. 8	She too had a **river** to protect her like a wall—the
Hab	3. 8	Was it the **rivers** that made you angry, Lord?
Mt	3. 5	of Judaea, and from all the country near the **River** Jordan.
	7.25	The rain poured down, the **rivers** overflowed, and the wind blew
	7.27	The rain poured down, the **rivers** overflowed, the wind blew
	19. 1	territory of Judaea on the other side of the **River** Jordan.
Mk	1. 5	confessed their sins, and he baptized them in the **River** Jordan.
	10. 1	went to the province of Judaea, and crossed the **River** Jordan.
Lk	3. 3	whole territory of the **River** Jordan, preaching, "Turn away from
	6.48	The **river** overflowed and hit that house but could not shake it,
Jn	1.28	east side of the **River** Jordan, where John was baptizing.
	10.40	went back again across the **River** Jordan to the place where
Acts	16.13	of the city to the **river-side,** where we thought there would
Rev	8.10	on a third of the **rivers** and on the springs of water.
	9.14	the four angels who are bound at the great **river** Euphrates!"
	16. 4	out his bowl on the **rivers** and the springs of water,
	16.12	angel poured out his bowl on the great **river** Euphrates.
	16.12	The **river** dried up, to provide a way for the kings
	17. 1	be punished, that great city that is built near many **rivers.**
	22. 1	angel also showed me the **river** of the water of life,
	22. 2	On each side of the **river** was the tree of life,

ROAD

Gen	16. 7	in the desert on the **road** to Shur [8]and said, "Hagar, slave
	35.19	buried beside the **road** to Ephrath, now known as Bethlehem.
	38.14	at the entrance to Enaim, a town on the **road** to Timnah.
	38.16	at the side of the **road** and said, "All right, how much
	38.21	"Where is the prostitute who was here by the **road?"**
	48. 7	I buried her there beside the **road** to Ephrath."
	49.17	at the side of the **road,** A poisonous snake beside the path,
Ex	13.17	not take them by the **road** that goes up the coast to
Lev	26.22	and leave so few of you that your **roads** will be deserted.
Num	20.17	cattle will not leave the **road** or go into your fields or
	20.17	will stay on the main **road** until we are out of your
	20.19	will stay on the main **road,** and if we or our animals
	21. 4	left Mount Hor by the **road** that leads to the Gulf of
	21.22	cattle will not leave the **road** and go into your fields or
	21.22	will stay on the main **road** until we are out of your
	21.33	Israelites turned and took the **road** to Bashan, and King Og
	22.22	angel of the Lord stood in the **road** to bar his way.
	22.23	a sword, it left the **road** and turned into the fields.
	22.23	Balaam beat the donkey and brought it back on to the **road.**
	22.24	the angel stood where the **road** narrowed between two
	22.34	not know that you were standing in the **road** to oppose me;
Deut	1.40	back into the desert along the **road** to the Gulf of Aqaba.'
	2. 1	into the desert, along the **road** to the Gulf of Aqaba, as
	2. 8	moved on and left the **road** that goes from the towns of
	2.27	We will go straight through and not leave the **road.**
Josh	2. 7	as far as the place where the **road** crosses the Jordan.
Judg	5. 6	went through the land, and travellers used the side **roads.**
	8.11	Gideon went along the **road** by the edge of the desert,
	9.37	along the **road** from the oak-tree of the fortune-tellers!"
	14. 8	the way he left the **road** to look at the lion he
	19.15	They turned off the **road** to go and spend the night there.
	20.31	country on the road to Bethel and on the **road** to Gibeah.
	20.32	retreat and lead them away from the city on to the **roads.**
	20.45	Five thousand of them were killed along the **road.**
	21.19	Lebonah, and east of the **road** between Bethel and Shechem.)
1 Sam	4.13	the Covenant Box, was sitting on a seat beside the **road,**
	6.12	cows started off on the **road** to Beth Shemesh
	6.12	and headed straight towards it, without turning off the **road.**
	17.52	fell wounded all along the **road** that leads to Shaaraim, as
	24. 3	some sheep pens by the **road** and went in to relieve himself.
	26. 3	look for David, [3]and camped by the **road** on Mount Hachilah.
2 Sam	2.24	the east of Giah on the **road** to the wilderness of Gibeon.
	6.10	instead, he turned off the **road** and took it to the house
	13.34	large crowd coming down the hill on the **road** from Horonaim.
	15. 2	early and go and stand by the **road** at the city gate.
	16.13	So David and his men continued along the **road.**
	18.23	Ahimaaz ran off down the **road** through the Jordan Valley, and
	20.12	covered with blood, was lying in the middle of the **road.**
	20.12	dragged the body from the **road** into the field and threw a
	20.13	had been removed from the **road,** everyone followed Joab in
1 Kgs	11.29	from Shiloh, met him alone on the **road** in the open country.
	13.10	go back the same way he had come, but by another **road.**
	13.12	They showed him the **road** [13]and he told them to saddle his
	13.14	he rode off [14]down the **road** after the prophet from Judah
	13.24	His body lay on the **road,** and the donkey and the lion
	13.25	saw the body on the **road,** with the lion standing near by.
	13.28	prophet's body lying on the **road,** with the donkey and the
	20.38	went and stood by the **road,** waiting for the king of Israel
2 Kgs	6.19	Elisha went to them and said, "You are on the wrong **road;**
	7.15	Jordan, and all along the **road** they saw the clothes and
	9.27	drove his chariot on the **road** up to Gur, near the town
	12.20	east side of Jerusalem, on the **road** that goes down to Silla.
	18.17	they occupied the **road** where the clothmakers work,
	19.28	your mouth, and take you back by the same **road** you came."
	19.33	back by the same **road** he came, without entering this city.
1 Chr	26.16	the west gate and the Shallecheth Gate on the upper **road.**
	26.18	were four guards by the **road** and two at the pavilion itself.
Job	16.22	years are passing now, and I walk the **road** of no return.
	23.11	I follow faithfully the **road** he chooses, and never
	28. 7	No hawk sees the **roads** to the mines, And no vulture ever
	28. 8	No lion or other fierce beast Ever travels those lonely **roads.**
Ps	107. 7	led them by a straight **road** to a city where they could
	110. 7	by the **road,** and strengthened, he will stand victorious.
Prov	2.18	you go to her house, you are travelling the **road** to death.
	2.19	He never returns to the **road** to life.
	4.18	The **road** the righteous travel is like the sunrise,
	4.19	The **road** of the wicked, however, is dark as night.
	5. 5	the **road** she walks is the road to death.
	5. 6	She does not stay on the **road** to life;
	8. 2	On the hilltops near the **road** and at the cross-roads she stands.
	12.28	Righteousness is the **road** to life;
	12.28	wickedness is the **road** to death.
	13.15	but those who can't be trusted are on the **road** to ruin.
	14.12	What you think is the right **road** may lead to death.
	15.24	Wise people walk the **road** that leads upwards to life,
	15.24	not the **road** that leads downwards to death.
	16.17	Those who are good travel a **road** that avoids evil;
	16.25	What you think is the right **road** may lead to death.
Is	7. 3	will find him on the **road** where the cloth makers work, at
	15. 5	Some climb the **road** to Luhith, weeping as they go;
	26. 7	the **road** they travel is level.
	30.21	If you wander off the **road** to the right or the left,
	30.21	will hear his voice behind you saying, "Here is the **road.**
	35. 8	There will be a highway there, called "The **Road of Holiness."**
	35. 8	No sinner will ever travel that **road;**
	35. 9	Those whom the Lord has rescued will travel home by that **road.**
	36. 2	The official occupied the **road** where the clothmakers work,
	37.29	and will take you back by the **road** on which you came."
	37.34	will go back by the **road** on which he came, without entering
	40. 3	cries out, "Prepare in the wilderness a **road** for the Lord!
	42.16	"I will lead my blind people by **roads** they have never travelled.
	43.16	ago the Lord made a **road** through the sea, a path through
	43.19	I will make a **road** through the wilderness and give you
	45.13	I will straighten every **road** that he travels.
	49.11	the mountains and prepare a **road** for my people to travel.
	57.14	Build the **road,** and make it ready!

Is 62.10 out of the city And build a **road** for your returning people!
Jer 3. 2 waited for lovers along the **roadside,** as an Arab waits for
6.16 Ask for the ancient paths and where the best **road** is.
6.25 countryside or walk on the **roads,** because our enemies are
8. 4 If someone misses the **road,** doesn't he turn back?
31. 9 of water, on a smooth **road** where they will not stumble.
31.21 Set up signs and mark the **road;**
48. 5 of their sobs along the **road** up to Luhith, the cries of
48.19 You that live in Aroer, stand by the **road** and wait;
Lam 3.11 He chased me off the **road,** tore me to pieces, and left
Ezek 16.24 by the side of every **road** you built places to worship
21.19 he said, "mark out two **roads** by which the king of Babylonia
21.19 Put up a signpost where the **roads** fork.
21.21 of Babylonia stands by the signpost at the fork of the **road.**
Hos 6. 9 Even on the **road** to the holy place at Shechem they commit
Nah 2. 1 Guard the **road!**
Mt 2.12 to their country by another **road,** since God had warned them
3. 3 "Someone is shouting in the desert, 'Prepare a **road** for the Lord;
4.15 land of Naphtali, on the **road** to the sea, on the other
7.13 hell is wide and the **road** that leads to it is easy,
8.28 and were so fierce that no one dared travel on that **road.**
20.30 were sitting by the **road** heard that Jesus was passing by,
21. 8 spread their cloaks on the **road** while others
21. 8 cut branches from the trees and spread them on the **road.**
21.19 by the side of the **road** and went to it, but found
Mk 1. 3 shouting in the desert, 'Get the **road** ready for the Lord;
9.33 asked his disciples, "What were you arguing about on the **road?"**
9.34 because on the **road** they had been arguing among themselves
10.32 his disciples were now on the **road** going up to Jerusalem.
10.46 beggar named Bartimaeus son of Timaeus was sitting by the **road.**
10.52 once he was able to see and followed Jesus on the **road.**
11. 8 spread their cloaks on the **road,** while others
11. 8 cut branches in the fields and spread them on the **road.**
11.20 as they walked along the **road,** they saw the fig-tree.
Lk 1.76 the Lord to prepare his **road** for him, [77] to tell his people
3. 4 'Get the **road** ready for the Lord;
3. 5 The winding **roads** must be made straight, and the rough paths
10. 4 don't stop to greet anyone on the **road.**
10.31 It so happened that a priest was going down that **road;**
14.23 'Go out to the country **roads** and lanes and make people come
18.35 near Jericho, there was a blind man sitting by the **road,**
19.36 As he rode on, people spread their cloaks on the **road.**
19.37 at the place where the **road** went down the Mount of Olives,
24.32 to us on the **road** and explained the Scriptures to us?"
24.35 what had happened on the **road,** and how they had recognized
Acts 8.26 and go south to the **road** that goes from Jerusalem to Gaza."
8.26 (This **road** is not used nowadays.)
8.36 As they travelled down the **road,** they came to a place
9.17 who appeared to you on the **road** as you were coming here.
9.27 seen the Lord on the **road** and that the Lord had spoken
26.13 It was on the **road** at midday, Your Majesty, that I saw
Jas 2.25 Israelite spies and helping them to escape by a different **road.**

ROAM

1 Sam 30.31 it to all the places where he and his men had **roamed.**
Job 1. 7 "I have been walking here and there, **roaming** round the earth."
2. 2 "I have been walking here and there, **roaming** round the earth."
39. 5 Who turned them loose and let them **roam?**
Ps 59.15 about the city, [15] like dogs **roaming** about for food and
Is 32.14 Wild donkeys will **roam** there, and sheep will find pasture there.
34.14 Wild animals will **roam** there, and demons will call to each other.
Lam 5. 9 Murderers **roam** through the countryside;
1 Pet 5. 8 Your enemy, the Devil, **roams** round like a roaring lion,

ROAR

Judg 14. 5 through the vineyards there, he heard a young lion **roaring.**
2 Sam 22.16 the Lord rebuked his enemies and **roared** at them in anger.
1 Kgs 18.41 I hear the **roar** of rain approaching."
1 Chr 16.32 **Roar,** sea, and every creature in you;
Job 4.10 The wicked **roar** and growl like lions, but God silences
36.29 or how the thunder **roars** through the sky, where God dwells.
37. 4 Then the **roar** of his voice is heard, the majestic sound of
Ps 18.15 rebuked your enemies, Lord, and **roared** at them in anger.
22.13 They open their mouths like lions, **roaring** and tearing at me.
42. 6 chaos **roars** at me like a flood, like waterfalls thundering
46. 3 even if the seas **roar** and rage, and the hills are shaken
65. 7 You calm the **roar** of the seas and the noise of the
68.33 Listen to him shout with a mighty **roar.**
93. 3 they raise their voice and **roar.**
93. 4 in heaven, greater than the **roar** of the ocean, more powerful
96.11 **Roar,** sea, and every creature in you;
98. 7 **Roar,** sea, and every creature in you;
104.21 The young lions **roar** while they hunt, looking for the
Prov 19.12 king's anger is like the **roar** of a lion, but his favour
Is 5.29 The soldiers **roar** like lions that have killed an animal
5.30 that day comes, they will **roar** over Israel as loudly as the
17.12 with a sound like the **roar** of the sea, like the crashing
51.15 I stir up the sea and make its waves **roar.**
Jer 2.15 They have **roared** at him like lions;
5.22 the waves may **roar,** but they cannot break through.
6.23 They sound like the **roaring** sea, as they ride their horses.
10.13 At his command the waters above the sky **roar;**
11.16 but now, with a **roar** like thunder I will set its leaves
12. 8 in the forest they have **roared** at me, and so I hate
25.30 'The Lord will **roar** from heaven and thunder from the heights
25.30 He will **roar** against his people;
31.35 He stirs up the sea and makes it **roar;**
50.42 They sound like the **roaring** sea, as they ride their horses.
51.16 At his command the waters above the sky **roar;**
Jer 51.38 The Babylonians all **roar** like lions and growl like lion cubs.
51.42 The sea has rolled over Babylon and covered it with **roaring** waves.
51.55 The armies rush in like **roaring** waves and attack with noisy shouts.
Ezek 1.24 it sounded like the **roar** of the sea, like the noise of
3.12 heard behind me the loud **roar** of a voice that said, "Praise
19. 7 The people of the land were terrified every time he **roared.**
19. 9 under guard, so that his **roar** would never be heard again on
22.25 leaders are like lions **roaring** over the animals they have killed.
43. 2 God's voice sounded like the **roar** of the sea, and the earth
Dan 10. 6 and his voice sounded like the **roar** of a great crowd.
Hos 11.10 will follow me when I **roar** like a lion at their enemies.
Joel 3.16 The Lord **roars** from Mount Zion;
Amos 1. 2 "The Lord **roars** from Mount Zion;
3. 4 Does a lion **roar** in the forest unless he has found a
3. 8 When a lion **roars,** who can avoid being afraid?
Hab 3.10 The waters under the earth **roared,** and their waves rose high.
Zeph 3. 3 Its officials are like **roaring** lions;
Zech 11. 3 Listen to the **roaring** of the lions;
Lk 21.25 in despair, afraid of the **roar** of the sea and the raging
1 Pet 5. 8 Devil, roams round like a **roaring** lion, looking for someone to
Rev 1.15 and his voice sounded like a **roaring** waterfall.
10. 3 out in a loud voice that sounded like the **roar** of lions.
10. 3 After he had called out, the seven thunders answered with a **roar.**
14. 2 heaven that sounded like a **roaring** waterfall, like a loud peal
19. 1 heard what sounded like the **roar** of a large crowd of people
19. 6 sound of a **roaring** waterfall, like loud peals of thunder.

ROAST

Ex 12. 8 the meat is to be **roasted,** and eaten with bitter herbs and
12. 9 or boiled, but eat it **roasted** whole, including the head, the
Lev 2.14 first corn harvested, offer **roasted** grain or ground meal.
23.14 the new corn, whether raw, **roasted,** or baked into bread,
Josh 5.11 **roasted** grain and bread made without yeast.
Ruth 2.14 with the workers, and Boaz passed some **roasted** grain to her.
1 Sam 2.15 the sacrifice, "Give me some meat for the priest to **roast;**
17.17 "Take ten kilogrammes of this **roasted** grain and these ten
25.18 five **roasted** sheep, seventeen kilogrammes of roasted grain,
2 Sam 6.19 a loaf of bread, a piece of **roasted** meat, and some raisins.
17.28 wheat, barley, meal, **roasted** grain, beans, peas, honey,
1 Chr 16. 3 a loaf of bread, a piece of **roasted** meat, and some raisins.
2 Chr 35.13 The Levites **roasted** the Passover sacrifices over the fire,
Is 44.16 he **roasts** meat, eats it, and is satisfied.
44.19 some bread on the embers and I **roasted** meat and ate it.
Jer 29.22 Zedekiah and Ahab, whom the king of Babylonia **roasted** alive!'

ROB

Gen 49.19 attacked by a band of **robbers,** But he will turn and pursue
Lev 19.13 "Do not take advantage of anyone or **rob** him.
Deut 28.29 will be constantly oppressed and **robbed,** and there will be
Judg 2.14 became furious with Israel and let raiders attack and **rob** them.
9.25 and they **robbed** everyone who passed their way.
14.15 You two invited us so that you could **rob** us, didn't you?"
2 Sam 17. 8 they are as fierce as a mother bear **robbed** of her cubs.
Ezra 9. 7 been slaughtered, **robbed,** and carried away as prisoners.
Neh 4. 4 Let them be **robbed** of everything they have, and let them be
Job 15.21 scream in his ears, and **robbers** attack when he thinks he is
22. 9 help widows, but you also **robbed** and ill-treated orphans.
Ps 14. 4 They live by **robbing** my people, and they never pray to me."
53. 4 They live by **robbing** my people, and they never pray to me."
62.10 don't hope to gain anything by **robbery;**
Prov 1.19 **Robbery** always claims the life of the robber—
6.11 But while he sleeps, poverty will attack him like an armed **robber.**
12.25 Worry can **rob** you of happiness, but kind words will
17.12 to meet a mother bear **robbed** of her cubs than to meet
23.28 They wait for you like **robbers** and cause many men to be
24.15 the wicked who scheme to **rob** an honest man or to take
24.34 poverty will attack you like an armed **robber.**
Is 33. 1 They have **robbed** and betrayed,
33. 1 although no one has **robbed** them or betrayed them.
33. 1 But their time to **rob** and betray will end, and they
33. 1 themselves will become victims of **robbery** and treachery.
42.22 They were **robbed** and plundered, with no one to come to their
Jer 7.11 Do you think that my Temple is a hiding place for **robbers?**
48.27 them as though they had been caught with a gang of **robbers.**
49. 9 on the vines, and when **robbers** come at night, they take only
Lam 1.10 Her enemies **robbed** her of all her treasures.
Ezek 7.21 "I will let foreigners **rob** them," says the Lord, "and
7.22 Temple is profaned, when **robbers** break into it and defile it.
18. 7 He doesn't cheat or **rob** anyone.
18.10 man has a son who **robs** and kills, who does any of
18.12 He cheats the poor, he **robs,** he keeps what a borrower
18.16 or oppress anyone or **rob** anyone.
18.18 hand, cheated and **robbed,** and always did evil to everyone.
22.13 "I will bring my fist down on your **robberies** and murders.
22.29 The wealthy cheat and **rob.**
23.46 "Bring a mob to terrorize them and **rob** them.
25. 7 you over to other nations who will **rob** you and plunder you.
36.13 and they say that it **robs** the nation of its children.
36.14 will no longer be a man-eater who **robs** you of your children.
36.15 The land will no longer **rob** the nation of its children.
Dan 11.33 burnt to death, and some will be **robbed** and made prisoners.
Hos 4.11 "Wine, both old and new, is **robbing** my people of their senses!
6. 9 are like a gang of **robbers** who wait in ambush for a
7. 1 they **rob** people in the streets.
7. 9 reliance on foreigners has **robbed** them of their strength.
Amos 5.11 You have oppressed the poor and **robbed** them of their grain.
Obad 10 "Because you **robbed** and killed your brothers,

Mic	2. 9	they love, and you have **robbed** their children of my
Mt	6.19	where moths and rust destroy, and **robbers** break in and steal.
	6.20	rust cannot destroy, and **robbers** cannot break in and steal.
	15.19	to **rob**, lie, and slander others.
Mk	7.21	to do immoral things, to **rob**, kill, [22] commit adultery,
	12.40	take advantage of widows and **rob** them of their homes,
Lk	10.30	from Jerusalem to Jericho when **robbers** attacked him, stripped him,
	10.36	acted like a neighbour towards the man attacked by the **robbers?"**
	20.47	take advantage of widows and **rob** them of their homes,
Jn	10. 1	but climbs in some other way, is a thief and a **robber.**
	10. 8	before me are thieves and **robbers,** but the sheep did not
Acts	19.37	even though they have not **robbed** temples or said evil things
Rom	2.22	You detest idols—but do you **rob** temples?
1 Cor	1.17	Christ's death on the cross is not **robbed** of its power.
	6. 7	Would it not be better for you to be **robbed?**
	6. 8	wrong one another and **rob** one another, even your own brothers!
2 Cor	11. 8	I was **robbing** them, so to speak, in order to help you.
	11.26	danger from floods and from **robbers,** in danger from fellow-Jews
Eph	4.28	The man who used to **rob** must stop robbing and start working,
Rev	3.11	so that no one will **rob** you of your victory prize.

ROBE

Gen	9.23	Shem and Japheth took a **robe** and held it behind them on
	25.25	his skin was like a hairy **robe**, so he was named Esau.
	37. 3	He made a long **robe** with full sleeves for him.
	37.23	brothers, they ripped off his long **robe** with full sleeves.
	37.31	Then they killed a goat and dipped Joseph's **robe** in its blood.
	37.32	They took the **robe** to their father and said, "We found this.
	39.12	She caught him by his **robe** and said, "Come to bed with
	39.12	But he escaped and ran outside, leaving his **robe** in her hand.
	39.13	that he had left his **robe** and had run out of the
	39.15	me scream, he ran outside, leaving his **robe** beside me."
	39.16	She kept his **robe** with her until Joseph's master came home.
	39.18	But when I screamed, he ran outside, leaving his **robe** beside me."
	41.42	He put a fine linen **robe** on him, and placed a gold
Ex	4. 6	The Lord spoke to Moses again, "Put your hand inside your **robe."**
	4. 7	Then the Lord said, "Put your hand inside your **robe** again."
	28. 4	a breast-piece, an ephod, a **robe,** an embroidered shirt, a
	28.31	"The **robe** that goes under the ephod is to be made
	28.35	Aaron is to wear this **robe** when he serves as priest.
	29. 5	garments—the shirt, the **robe** that goes under the ephod,
	39.22	The **robe** that goes under the ephod was made entirely of
Lev	6.10	the priest, wearing his linen **robe** and linen shorts, shall
	8. 7	put the shirt and the **robe** on Aaron and the sash round
	16. 4	the linen **robe** and shorts, the belt, and the turban.
Num	20.26	and there remove Aaron's priestly **robes** and put them on Eleazar.
	20.28	and Moses removed Aaron's priestly **robes** and put them on Eleazar.
1 Sam	2.19	mother would make a little **robe** and take it to him when
	18. 4	He took off the **robe** he was wearing and gave it to
	24. 4	cut off a piece of Saul's **robe** without Saul's knowing it.
	24.11	my father, look at the piece of your **robe** I am holding!
2 Sam	13.18	Tamar was wearing a long **robe** with full sleeves, the usual
	13.19	on her head, tore her **robe,** and with her face buried in
1 Kgs	10.25	gift—articles of silver and gold, **robes,** weapons, spices,
	11.30	Ahijah took off the new **robe** he was wearing, tore it
	22.10	kings, dressed in their royal **robes,** were sitting on their
2 Kgs	10.22	in charge of the sacred **robes** to bring the robes out and
	22.14	Tikvah and grandson of Harhas, was in charge of the temple **robes.)**
	23. 7	there that women wove **robes** used in the worship of Asherah.)
1 Chr	15.27	David was wearing a **robe** made of the finest linen, and
2 Chr	9.24	gifts—articles of silver and gold, **robes,** weapons, spices,
	18. 9	kings, dressed in their royal **robes,** were sitting on their
	20.21	musicians to put on the **robes** they wore on sacred occasions
	34.22	Tikvah and grandson of Harhas, was in charge of the temple **robes.)**
Ezra	2.69	2,800 kilogrammes of silver, and 100 **robes** for priests.
	3.10	Temple, the priests in their **robes** took their places with
Neh	7.70	530 **robes** for priests
	7.70	67 **robes** for priests
Esth	5. 1	Esther put on her royal **robes** and went and stood in the
	6. 7	answered the king, "Order royal **robes** to be brought
	6. 7	for this man—**robes** that you yourself wear.
	6. 9	dress the man in these **robes** and lead him, mounted on the
	6.10	Haman, "Hurry and get the **robes** and the horse, and provide
	6.11	So Haman got the **robes** and the horse,
	6.11	and he put the **robes** on Mordecai.
	8.15	left the palace, wearing royal **robes** of blue and white, a
Ps	73. 6	they wear pride like a necklace and violence like a **robe;**
	104. 6	over it like a **robe,** and the water covered the mountains.
	109.29	may they wear their shame like a **robe.**
	133. 2	Aaron's head and beard, down to the collar of his **robes.**
Is	3.22	all their fine **robes,** gowns, cloaks, and purses;
	6. 1	high and exalted, and his **robe** filled the whole Temple.
	22.21	I will put your official **robe** and belt on him and give
Ezek	26.16	They will take off their **robes** and their embroidered clothes
Dan	3.21	them up, fully dressed—shirts, **robes,** caps, and all—and
	5. 7	means will be dressed in **robes** of royal purple, wear a gold
	5.16	you will be dressed in **robes** of royal purple, wear a gold
	5.29	to dress Daniel in a **robe** of royal purple and to hang
Jon	3. 6	his throne, took off his **robe,** put on sackcloth, and sat
Hag	2.12	from a sacrifice and carries it in a fold of his **robe.**
	2.12	If he then lets his **robe** touch any bread, cooked food, wine,
Mt	27.28	They stripped off his clothes and put a scarlet **robe** on him.
	27.31	mocking him, they took the **robe** off and put his own clothes
Mk	12.38	walk around in their long **robes** and be greeted with respect
	14.63	The High Priest tore his **robes** and said, "We don't need
	15.17	They put a purple **robe** on Jesus, made a crown out of
	15.20	they took off the purple **robe** and put his own clothes back
	16. 5	on the right, wearing a white **robe**—and they were alarmed.
Lk	15.22	'Bring the best **robe** and put it on him.
	20.46	walk about in their long **robes** and love to be greeted with
	23.11	then they put a fine **robe** on him and sent him back
Jn	19. 2	then they put a purple **robe** on him [3] and came to him
	19. 5	Jesus came out, wearing the crown of thorns and the purple **robe.**
	19.23	They also took the **robe,** which was made of one piece of
	19.24	"They divided my clothes among themselves and gambled for my **robe."**
Acts	12.21	Herod put on his royal **robes,** sat on his throne, and made
Rev	1.13	a human being, wearing a **robe** that reached to his feet,
	6.11	them was given a white **robe,** and they were told to rest
	7. 9	dressed in white **robes** and holding palm branches in their
	7.13	dressed in white **robes,** and where do they come from?"
	7.14	They have washed their **robes** and made them white with the
	19.13	The **robe** he wore was covered with blood.
	19.16	On his **robe** and on his thigh was written the name:
	22.14	are those who wash their **robes** clean and so have the right

ROCK (1)

Gen	31.46	He told his men to gather some **rocks** and pile them up.
	31.46	Then they ate a meal beside the pile of **rocks.**
	31.48	to Jacob, "This pile of **rocks** will be a reminder for both
	31.51	Here are the **rocks** that I have piled up between us, and
Ex	17. 6	I will stand before you on a **rock** at Mount Sinai.
	17. 6	Strike the **rock,** and water will come out of it for the
	33.21	is a place beside me where you can stand on a **rock.**
	33.22	in an opening in the **rock** and cover you with my hand
Num	20. 8	them all speak to that **rock** over there, and water will gush
	20. 8	bring water out of the **rock** for the people, for them and
	20.10	community in front of the **rock,** and Moses said, "Listen,
	20.10	Do we have to get water out of this **rock** for you?"
	20.11	the stick and struck the **rock** twice with it, and a great
	23. 9	From the high **rocks** I can see them;
Deut	8. 9	Its **rocks** have iron in them, and from its hills you can
	8.15	waterless land he made water flow out of solid **rock** for you.
	32.13	They found wild honey among the **rocks;**
Judg	6.20	and the bread on this **rock,** and pour the broth over them."
	6.21	Fire came out of the **rock** and burnt up the meat and
	7.25	they killed Oreb at Oreb **Rock,** and Zeeb at the Winepress of
	13.19	and offered them on the **rock** altar to the Lord who works
	20.33	of their hiding places in the **rocky** country round the city.
	20.45	and ran towards the open country to the **Rock** of Rimmon.
	20.47	the open country to the **Rock** of Rimmon, and they stayed
	21.13	Benjaminites who were at the **Rock** of Rimmon and offered to
1 Sam	6.14	in Beth Shemesh, and it stopped there near a large **rock.**
	6.15	the gold models in it, and placed them on the large **rock.**
	6.18	The large **rock** in the field of Joshua of Beth Shemesh, on
	13. 6	caves and holes or among the **rocks** or in pits and wells;
	14. 4	there were two large jagged **rocks,** one on each side of the
	23.25	it and went to a **rocky** hill in the wilderness of Maon
	24. 2	went looking for David and his men east of Wild Goat **Rocks.**
2 Sam	20. 8	When they reached the large **rock** at Gibeon, Amasa met them.
	21.10	shelter for herself on the **rock** where the corpses were, and
1 Kgs	1. 9	fattened calves at Snake **Rock,** near the spring of Enrogel.
	19.11	the hills and shattered the **rocks**—but the Lord was not in
1 Chr	11.15	leading soldiers went to a **rock** where David was staying near
2 Chr	16.14	and was buried in the **rock** tomb which he had carved out
	25.12	them off, so that they were killed on the **rocks** below.
Neh	9.15	from heaven, and water from a **rock** when they were thirsty.
Job	5.23	The fields you plough will be free of **rocks;**
	8.17	Their roots wrap round the stones and hold fast to every **rock.**
	14.19	Water will wear down **rocks,** and heavy rain will wash
	24. 8	mountains, and they huddle beside the **rocks** for shelter.
	28. 3	the depths of the earth And dig for **rocks** in the darkness.
	28. 9	Men dig the hardest **rocks,** Dig mountains away at their base.
	28.10	As they tunnel through the **rocks,** They discover precious stones.
	29. 6	of milk, and my olive-trees grew in the **rockiest** soil.
	39.28	its home on the highest **rocks** and makes the sharp peaks its
	41.28	**rocks** thrown at him are like bits of straw.
Ps	27. 5	safe in his Temple and make me secure on a high **rock.**
	40. 2	He set me safely on a **rock** and made me secure.
	78.15	He split **rocks** open in the desert and gave them water
	78.16	to come out of the **rock** and made water flow like a
	78.20	true that he struck the **rock,** and water flowed out in a
	105.41	He opened a **rock,** and water gushed out, flowing through
	114. 8	God of Jacob, [8] who changes **rocks** into pools of water and
	137. 9	who takes your babies and smashes them against a **rock.**
	141. 6	rulers are thrown down from **rocky** cliffs, the people will
Prov	30.19	a snake moving on a **rock,**
	30.26	strong either, but they make their homes among the **rocks.**
Song	2.14	are like a dove that hides in the crevice of a **rock.**
Is	2.10	hide in caves in the **rocky** hills or dig holes in the
	2.19	hide in caves in the **rocky** hills or dig holes in the
	2.21	holes and caves in the **rocky** hills to try to escape from
	7.19	in the caves in the **rocks,** and they will cover every
	10.26	as I beat the people of Midian at the **Rock** of Oreb.
	14.19	thrown with them into a **rocky** pit, and trampled down.
	17.10	God who rescues you and who protects you like a mighty **rock.**
	22.16	you to carve a tomb for yourself out of the **rocky** hillside?
	32. 2	desert, like the shadow of a giant **rock** in a barren land.
	33.12	You will crumble like **rocks** burnt to make lime, like
	48.21	He made water come from a **rock** for them;
	48.21	he split the **rock** open, and water flowed out.
	51. 1	Think of the **rock** from which you came, the quarry from which
	57. 5	children as sacrifices in the **rocky** caves near the bed of a
Jer	2.27	a tree is your father and that a **rock** is your mother.
	4.29	run to the forest, others will climb up among the **rocks.**
	13. 4	River Euphrates and hide the shorts in a hole in the **rocks."**

Jer	16.16	on every mountain and hill and in the caves among the **rocks.**
	18.14	Are Lebanon's **rocky** heights ever without snow?
	21.13	high above the valleys, like a **rock** rising above the plain.
	23.29	like a fire, and like a hammer that breaks **rocks** in pieces.
	49.16	You live on the **rocky** cliffs, high on top of the mountain;
Ezek	3. 9	make you as firm as a **rock,** as hard as a diamond;
	20.32	who live in other countries and worship trees and **rocks.**
	24. 7	it was spilt on a bare **rock.**
	26. 4	will sweep away all the dust and leave only a bare **rock.**
	26.14	leave only a bare **rock** where fishermen can dry their nets.
Amos	6.12	Do horses gallop on **rocks?**
Obad	3	Your capital is a fortress of solid **rock;**
Nah	1. 6	**rocks** crumble to dust before him.
Zech	7.12	They closed their minds [12]and made their hearts as hard as **rock.**
Mt	7.24	is like a wise man who built his house on **rock.**
	7.25	But it did not fall, because it was built on **rock.**
	13. 5	Some of it fell on **rocky** ground, where there was little soil.
	13.20	The seeds that fell on **rocky** ground stand for those who
	16.18	you are a **rock,**
	16.18	and on this **rock** foundation I will build my church,
	27.51	The earth shook, the **rocks** split apart, [52]the graves broke open,
	27.60	own tomb, which he had just recently dug out of solid **rock.**
Mk	4. 5	Some of it fell on **rocky** ground, where there was little soil.
	4.16	Other people are like the seeds that fall on **rocky** ground.
	15.46	it in a tomb which had been dug out of solid **rock.**
Lk	6.48	his house, dug deep and laid the foundation on **rock.**
	8. 6	Some of it fell on **rocky** ground, and when the plants sprouted,
	8.13	The seeds that fell on **rocky** ground stand for those who
	23.53	been dug out of solid **rock** and which had never been used.
Jn	1.42	(This is the same as Peter and means "a **rock.**")
Acts	27.29	ship would go on the **rocks,** so they lowered four anchors
Rom	9.33	will make people stumble, a **rock** that will make them fall.
1 Cor	10. 4	They drank from the spiritual **rock** that went with them;
	10. 4	and that **rock** was Christ himself.
1 Pet	2. 8	make people stumble, the **rock** that will make them fall."
Rev	6.15	hid themselves in caves and under **rocks** on the mountains.
	6.16	the mountains and to the **rocks,** "Fall on us and hide us

ROCK (2)

2 Sam	22. 8	the foundations of the sky **rocked** and quivered
Job	9. 6	he **rocks** the pillars that support the earth.
Ps	18. 7	the foundations of the mountains **rocked** and quivered,
Jer	4.24	were shaking, and the hills were **rocking** to and fro.

ROCK-BADGER

Lev	11. 4	the cud, [4-6]but you must not eat camels, **rock-badgers,**
Deut	14. 7	You may not eat camels, rabbits, or **rock-badgers.**
Ps	104.18	high mountains, and the **rock-badgers** hide in the cliffs.
Prov	30.26	**Rock-badgers:**

ROD
[MEASURING-ROD]

Ex	27.10	in twenty bronze bases, with hooks and **rods** made of silver.
	27.17	to be connected with silver **rods,** and their hooks are to be
	36.38	covered their tops and their **rods** with gold, and made five
	38.10	in twenty bronze bases, with hooks and **rods** made of silver.
	38.12	posts and ten bases and with hooks and **rods** made of silver.
	38.17	bronze, and the hooks, the **rods,** and the covering of the
	38.17	All the posts round the enclosure were connected with silver **rods.**
	38.19	covering of their tops, and their **rods** were made of silver.
	38.28	of silver Bezalel made the **rods,** the hooks for the posts,
Ps	2. 9	You will break them with an iron **rod;**
	23. 4	Your shepherd's **rod** and staff protect me.
Is	9. 4	that burdened them and the **rod** that beat their shoulders.
	14.29	People of Philistia, the **rod** that beat you is broken,
Ezek	40. 3	and a **measuring-rod** and was standing by a gateway.
	40. 5	The man took his **measuring-rod,** which was three metres long,
	42.16	He took the **measuring-rod** and measured the east side,
	47. 3	With his **measuring-rod** the man measured five hundred
Rev	2.26	rule them with an iron **rod** and to break them to pieces
	11. 1	stick that looked like a **measuring-rod,** and was told, "Go and
	12. 5	a son, who will rule over all nations with an iron **rod.**
	19.15	rule over them with a **rod** of iron, and he will trample
	21.15	to me had a gold **measuring-rod** to measure the city,
	21.16	The angel measured the city with his **measuring-rod:**

ROEBUCK

1 Kgs	4.23	and a hundred sheep, besides deer, gazelles, **roebucks,**

Am **ROLL (dice)** see **THROW**

ROLL (1)

Gen	29. 3	the shepherds would **roll** the stone back and water them.
	29. 8	all the flocks are here and the stone has been **rolled** back;
	29.10	he went to the well, **rolled** the stone back, and watered the
Josh	10.18	He said, "**Roll** some big stones in front of the entrance
	24. 7	I made the sea come **rolling** over the Egyptians and drown them.
Judg	7.13	a loaf of barley bread **rolled** into our camp and hit a
1 Sam	14.33	"**Roll** a big stone over here to me."
2 Sam	22. 5	the waves of destruction **rolled** over me.
1 Kgs	3.19	Then one night she accidentally **rolled** over on her baby
2 Kgs	2. 8	Elijah took off his cloak, **rolled** it up, and struck the
Ps	18. 4	the waves of destruction **rolled** over me.
	77.18	The crash of your thunder **rolled** out, and flashes of
	78.53	but the sea came **rolling** over their enemies.
Is	34. 4	disappear like a scroll being **rolled** up, and the stars will
	48.18	have come to you like the waves that **roll** on the shore.
	57.20	whose waves never stop **rolling** in, bringing filth and muck.
Jer	6.26	Lord says to his people, "Put on sackcloth and **roll** in ashes.
	25.34	Mourn and **roll** in the dust.
	46. 9	Command the horses to go and the chariots to **roll!**
	48.26	Moab will **roll** in its own vomit, and people will laugh.
	49.23	Anxiety **rolls** over them like a sea, and they cannot rest.
	51.42	The sea has **rolled** over Babylon and covered it with roaring waves.
Ezek	27.30	for you, Throwing dust on their heads and **rolling** in ashes.
Jon	2. 3	all round me, and all your mighty waves **rolled** over me.
Mic	1.10	People of Beth Leaphrah, show your despair by **rolling** in the dust!
Mt	27.60	Then he **rolled** a large stone across the entrance to the tomb
	28. 2	Lord came down from heaven, **rolled** the stone away, and sat
Mk	9.20	fell on the ground and **rolled** round, foaming at the mouth.
	15.46	Then he **rolled** a large stone across the entrance to the tomb.
	16. 3	to one another, "Who will **roll** away the stone for us from
	16. 3	up and saw that the stone had already been **rolled** back.
Lk	4.20	Jesus **rolled** up the scroll, gave it back to the attendant,
	24. 2	They found the stone **rolled** away from the entrance to the tomb,
Jn	20. 7	lying with the linen wrappings but was **rolled** up by itself.
Rom	3.13	wicked lies **roll** off their tongues, and dangerous threats,
2 Pet	2.22	pig that has been washed goes back to **roll** in the mud."
Rev	6.14	disappeared like a scroll being **rolled** up, and every mountain

ROLL (2)

Judg	21. 9	at the **roll call** of the army no one from Jabesh had
2 Chr	31.19	and to everyone who was on the **rolls** of the Levite clans.

ROME
[ROMAN]

The greatest city in the w. world at the time of the New Testament: its empire extended from one end of the Mediterranean Sea to the other.

Dan	11.30	The **Romans** will come in ships and oppose him,
Mt	8. 5	When Jesus entered Capernaum, a **Roman** officer met him and begged
	22.17	against our Law to pay taxes to the **Roman** Emperor, or not?"
	27. 2	him off, and handed him over to Pilate, the **Roman** governor.
	27.11	Jesus stood before the **Roman** governor, who questioned him.
	27.15	At every Passover Festival the **Roman** governor was in the habit
Mk	12.14	is it against our Law to pay taxes to the **Roman** Emperor?
Lk	2. 1	Augustus ordered a census to be taken throughout the **Roman** Empire.
	7. 2	A **Roman** officer there had a servant who was very dear to
	20.20	him over to the authority and power of the **Roman** Governor.
	20.22	Law for us to pay taxes to the **Roman** Emperor, or not?"
Jn	11.48	and the **Roman** authorities will take action and destroy
	18. 3	with him a group of **Roman** soldiers, and some temple guards
	18.12	Then the **Roman** soldiers with their commanding officer and
Acts	2.10	Some of us are from **Rome,** [11]both Jews and Gentiles
	10. 1	was a captain in the **Roman** regiment called "The Italian Regiment."
	16.12	it is also a **Roman** colony.
	16.20	They brought them before the **Roman** officials and said,
	16.21	we are **Roman** citizens, and we cannot accept these customs
	16.35	the **Roman** authorities sent police officers with the order,
	16.37	yet they whipped us in public—and we are **Roman** citizens!
	16.37	The **Roman** officials themselves must come here and let us out."
	16.38	police officers reported these words to the **Roman** officials;
	16.38	heard that Paul and Silas were **Roman** citizens, they were afraid.
	18. 2	the Emperor Claudius had ordered all the Jews to leave **Rome.**
	18.12	When Gallio was made the **Roman** governor of Achaia, the Jews
	19.21	"After I go there," he said, "I must also see **Rome.**"
	21.31	the commander of the **Roman** troops that all Jerusalem was rioting.
	22.24	The **Roman** commander ordered his men to take Paul into the fort,
	22.25	for you to whip a **Roman** citizen who hasn't even been tried
	22.26	That man is a **Roman** citizen!"
	22.27	to Paul and asked him, "Tell me, are you a **Roman** citizen?"
	22.29	realized that Paul was a **Roman** citizen and that he had put
	23.11	here in Jerusalem, and you must also do the same in **Rome.**"
	23.15	Council send word to the **Roman** commander to bring Paul down
	23.27	learnt that he was a **Roman** citizen, so I went with my
	25. 8	Jews or against the Temple or against the **Roman** Emperor."
	25.16	I told them that we **Romans** are not in the habit of
	27. 1	an officer in the **Roman** regiment called "The Emperor's Regiment."
	28.14	And so we came to **Rome.**
	28.15	The believers in **Rome** heard about us and came as far
	28.16	When we arrived in **Rome,** Paul was allowed to live by
	28.17	made a prisoner in Jerusalem and handed over to the **Romans.**
	28.18	After questioning me, the **Romans** wanted to release me,
Rom	1. 6	includes you who are in **Rome,** whom God has called to belong
	1. 7	to all of you in **Rome** whom God loves and has called
	1.15	to preach the Good News to you also who live in **Rome.**
2 Cor	11.25	three times I was whipped by the **Romans;**
2 Tim	1.17	soon as he arrived in **Rome,** he started looking for me until

ROOF

Gen	6.16	Make a **roof** for the boat and leave a space
	6.16	of 44 centimetres between the **roof** and the sides.
Ex	26.33	row of hooks in the **roof** of the Tent, and behind the
Deut	22. 8	be sure to put a railing round the edge of the **roof.**
Josh	2. 4	two spies up on the **roof** and hidden them under some stalks
	2. 8	Rahab went up on the **roof** [9]and said to them, "I know

Judg 3.20 his cool room on the **roof,** Ehud went over to him and
9.51 They locked themselves in and went up to the **roof.**
16.27 men and women on the **roof,** watching Samson entertain them.
1 Sam 9.25 up a bed for Saul on the **roof,** [26] and he slept there.
9.26 called to Saul on the **roof,** "Get up, and I will send
2 Sam 11. 2 David got up from his nap and went to the palace **roof.**
16.22 for Absalom on the palace **roof,** and in the sight of everyone
18.24 top of the wall and stood on the **roof** of the gateway;
2 Kgs 1. 2 off the balcony on the **roof** of his palace in Samaria and
4.10 a small room on the **roof,** put a bed, a table, a
19.26 or weeds growing on a **roof** when the hot east wind blasts
23.12 had built on the palace **roof** above King Ahaz' quarters, King
Neh 8.16 shelters on the flat **roofs** of their houses, in their yards,
Ps 22.15 as dust, and my tongue sticks to the **roof** of my mouth.
Prov 21. 9 Better to live on the **roof** than share the house with a
25.24 Better to live on the **roof** than share the house with a
Ecc 10.18 too lazy to repair his **roof,** it will leak, and the house
Is 22. 1 people of the city celebrating on the **roofs** of the houses?
37.27 or weeds growing on a **roof** when the hot east wind blasts
Jer 19.13 all the houses on whose **roofs** incense has been burnt to the
32.29 incense to Baal on the **roof-tops** and by pouring out
Dan 4.29 walking about on the **roof** of his royal palace in Babylon,
Zeph 1. 5 who goes up on the **roof** and worships the sun, the moon,
Mt 24.17 man who is on the **roof** of his house must not take
Mk 2. 4 made a hole in the **roof** right above the place where Jesus
13.15 man who is on the **roof** of his house must not lose
Lk 5.19 carried him up on the **roof,** made an opening in the tiles,
17.31 man who is on the **roof** of his house must not go
Acts 10. 9 Peter went up on the **roof** of the house about noon

Am **ROOF TOP** see **HOUSE-TOP**

ROOM
[BEDROOM, STOREROOM]

Gen 6.14 make **rooms** in it and cover it with tar inside and out.
24.23 Is there **room** in his house for my men and me to
24.31 I have a **room** ready for you in my house, and there
39.14 He came into my **room** and tried to rape me, but I
39.17 that you brought here came into my **room** and insulted me.
43.30 about to break down, so he went to his **room** and cried.
45. 1 of his servants, so he ordered them all to leave the **room.**
Ex 8. 3 go into your palace, your **bedroom,** your bed, the houses of
Lev 26.10 is left of the old harvest to make **room** for the new.
Num 22.26 place where there was no **room** at all to pass on either
Judg 3.20 there alone in his cool **room** on the roof, Ehud went over
14.18 before Samson went into the **bedroom,** the men of the city
15. 1 said to her father, "I want to go to my wife's **room."**
16. 9 She had some men waiting in another **room,** so she shouted,
16.12 The men were waiting in another **room.**
1 Sam 3. 2 Eli, who was now almost blind, was sleeping in his own **room;**
9.22 his servant into the large **room** and gave them a place at
2 Sam 4. 7 they went to Ishbosheth's **bedroom,** where he was sound asleep,
12.16 night he went into his **room** and spent the night lying on
18.33 He went up to the **room** over the gateway and wept.
1 Kgs 1.15 So Bathsheba went to see the king in his **bedroom.**
6. 3 The entrance **room** was 4.5 metres deep and 9 metres wide,
6. 6 Each **room** in the lowest storey was 2.2 metres wide, in the
6. 6 floor below so that the **rooms** could rest on the wall without
6.16 An inner **room,** called the Most Holy Place, was built in
6.17 The **room** in front of the Most Holy Place was eighteen
6.19 of the Temple an inner **room** was built, where the Lord's
6.20 This inner **room** was nine metres long, nine metres wide,
6.21 of the inner **room,** which was also covered with gold.
6.27 in the middle of the **room,** and the other two wings touched
6.29 The walls of the main **room** and of the inner room were
6.33 the entrance to the main **room** a rectangular door-frame of
7. 2 over **store-rooms,** which were supported by the pillars.
7. 7 The Throne **Room,** also called the Hall of Judgement, where
7.12 the Temple, and the entrance **room** of the Temple had walls
7.51 he placed in the temple **storerooms** all the things that his
17.19 carried him upstairs to the **room** where he was staying, and
20.30 the city and took refuge in the back **room** of a house.
22.25 when you go into some back **room** to hide," Micaiah replied.
2 Kgs 4.10 Let's build a small **room** on the roof, put a bed, a
4.11 Elisha returned to Shunem and went up to his **room** to rest.
4.21 carried him up to Elisha's **room,** put him on the bed and
4.32 he went alone into the **room** and saw the boy lying dead
4.35 got up, walked about the **room,** and then went back and again
6.12 Israel what you say even in the privacy of your own **room."**
9. 2 Take him to a private **room** away from his companions, [3] pour
9.10 After saying this, the young prophet left the **room** and fled.
11. 2 and his nurse into a **bedroom** in the Temple and hid him
20.13 There was nothing in his **storerooms** or anywhere in his
20.15 There is nothing in the **storerooms** that I didn't show them."
1 Chr 9.26 were also responsible for the **rooms** in the Temple and for
23.28 of its courtyards and its **rooms,** and to keep undefiled
26.15 gate, and his sons were allotted to guard the **storerooms.**
26.17 Four guards were stationed at the **storerooms** daily, two at each storeroom.
26.20 treasury and the **storerooms** for gifts dedicated to God.
26.22 Zetham and Joel, had charge of the temple treasury and **storerooms.**
27.25 Royal **storerooms:**
27.25 Local **storerooms:**
28.11 buildings, for the **storerooms** and all the other rooms,
28.11 and all the other **rooms,** and for the Most Holy Place,
28.12 for the courtyards and the **rooms** around them,
28.12 and for the **storerooms** for the temple equipment
2 Chr 3. 4 The entrance **room** was the full width of the Temple, nine
2 Chr 3. 4 The inside of the **room** was overlaid with pure gold.
3. 5 The main **room** was panelled with cedar and overlaid with fine gold,
3. 8 The inner **room,** called the Most Holy Place, was nine
3. 9 the walls of the upper **rooms** were also covered with gold.
3.11 in the centre of the **room** and reached the wall
3.11 on either side of the **room,** stretching across the full width
4. 7 placed them in the main **room** of the Temple, five lampstands
5. 1 he placed in the temple **storerooms** all the things that his
18.24 when you go into some back **room** to hide," Micaiah replied.
22.11 and hid him and a nurse in a **bedroom** at the Temple.
29.17 finished it all, including the entrance **room** to the Temple.
31.11 the king's orders they prepared **storerooms** in the Temple
32.27 He had **storerooms** built for his gold, silver, precious stones,
34.14 being taken out of the **storeroom,** Hilkiah found the book of
Ezra 8.29 There in the priests' **room** weigh them and hand them over to
Neh 3.31 the Miphkad Gate, near the **room** on top of the north-east
3.32 the last section, from the **room** at the corner as far as
10.38 to take to the temple **storerooms** one tenth of all the tithes
10.39 wine, and olive-oil to the **storerooms** where the utensils for
12.25 of guarding the **storerooms** by the gates to the Temple:
12.44 put in charge of the **storerooms** where contributions for the
13. 4 in charge of the temple **storerooms,** had for a long time been
13. 5 Tobiah to use a large **room** that was intended only for
13. 7 Eliashib had allowed Tobiah to use a **room** in the Temple.
13. 9 I gave orders for the **rooms** to be ritually purified and
13.12 bringing to the temple **storerooms** their tithes of corn,
13.13 I put the following men in charge of the **storerooms:**
Esth 2.21 the entrance to the king's **rooms,** became hostile to King
5. 1 the inner courtyard of the palace, facing the throne **room.**
6. 2 the two palace eunuchs who had guarded the king's **rooms.**
7. 7 in a fury, left the **room,** and went outside to the palace
7. 8 when the king came back into the **room** from the gardens.
Job 38.22 Have you ever visited the **storerooms,** where I keep the
Ps 33. 7 he shut up the ocean depths in **storerooms.**
135. 7 the storms, and he brings out the wind from his **storeroom.**
Prov 24. 4 Where there is knowledge, the **rooms** are furnished with valuable,
27.20 like the world of the dead—there is always **room** for more.
Ecc 10.20 criticize the rich, even in the privacy of your **bedroom.**
Song 1. 4 be my king and take me to your **room.**
3. 4 him to my mother's house, to the **room** where I was born.
Is 39. 2 There was nothing in his **storerooms** or anywhere in his
39. 4 There is nothing in the **storerooms** that I didn't show them."
49.20 land is too small— we need more **room** to live in!'
Jer 10.13 flash in the rain and sends the wind from his **storeroom.**
22.14 "I will build myself a mansion with spacious **rooms** upstairs."
35. 2 them into one of the **rooms** in the Temple and offer them
35. 4 I took them into the **room** of the disciples of the prophet
35. 4 This **room** was above the room of Maaseiah son of Shallum, an
35. 4 in the Temple, and near the **rooms** of the other officials.
36.10 in the Temple, from the **room** of Gemariah son of Shaphan, the
36.10 His **room** was in the upper court near the entrance of the
36.12 the royal palace, to the **room** of the court secretary, where
36.20 put the scroll in the **room** of Elishama, the court secretary,
36.21 He took it from the **room** of Elishama and read it to
38.11 the men to the palace **storeroom** and got some worn-out
51.16 flash in the rain and sends the wind from his **storeroom.**
Ezek 8.12 They are all worshipping in a **room** full of images.
40. 7 Each of the **rooms** was square, three metres on each side, and
40. 7 long that led to an entrance **room** which faced the Temple.
40. 8 He measured this **room,** and found it was four metres deep.
40.12 (The **rooms** were three metres square.)
40.13 the back wall of one **room**
40.13 the back wall of the **room** across the passage from it,
40.14 The **room** at the far end led out to a courtyard.
40.14 He measured that **room** and found it was ten metres wide.
40.15 to the far side of the last **room** was twenty-five metres.
40.16 outside walls of all the **rooms**
40.16 and also in the inner walls between the **rooms.**
40.17 There were thirty **rooms** built against the outer wall, and in
40.21 and the entrance **room** all had the same measurements
40.22 The entrance **room,** the windows, and the carved
40.22 and the entrance **room** was at the end
40.24 inner walls and its entrance **room,** and they were the same as
40.25 There were windows in the **rooms** of this gateway just as
40.26 to it, and its entrance **room** was also at the end facing
40.29 Its guardrooms, its entrance **room,** and its inner
40.29 There were also windows in the **rooms** of this gateway.
40.31 Its entrance **room** faced the other courtyard, and
40.33 Its guardrooms, its entrance **room,** and its inner walls
40.33 There were windows all round, and in the entrance **room** also.
40.34 The entrance **room** faced the outer courtyard.
40.36 inner walls, an entrance **room,** and windows all round.
40.37 The entrance **room** faced the outer courtyard.
40.38 It opened into the entrance **room** that faced the courtyard,
40.39 In this entrance **room** there were four tables,
40.39 two on each side of the **room.**
40.40 Outside the **room** there were four similar tables, two on
40.41 four inside the **room** and four out in the courtyard.
40.44 There were two **rooms** opening on the inner courtyard, one
40.45 man told me that the **room** which faced south was for the
40.46 in the Temple, [46] and the **room** which faced north was for
40.48 Then he took me into the entrance **room** of the Temple.
40.49 led up to the entrance **room,** which was ten metres wide and
41. 1 Next, the man took me into the central **room,** the Holy Place.
41. 2 He measured the **room** itself:
41. 3 Then he went to the innermost **room.**
41. 4 He measured the **room** itself, and it was ten metres square.
41. 4 This **room** was beyond the central room.
41. 5 the Temple, was a series of small **rooms** two metres wide.

Ezek 41. 6 These **rooms** were in three storeys, with thirty rooms on each floor.
41. 6 floor below, so that the **rooms** could rest on the wall
41. 7 on the outside of the **rooms,** two wide stairways were built,
41. 8 The outside wall of these **rooms** was two and a half
41. 8 was one door into the **rooms** on the north side of the
41. 8 level with the foundation of the **rooms** by the temple walls.
41.15 The entrance **room** of the Temple, the Holy Place, and the
41.18 one following the other, all the way round the **room.**
41.25 over the outside of the doorway of the entrance **room.**
41.26 At the sides of this **room** there were windows, and the
42. 5 The **rooms** at the upper level of the building were narrower
42. 6 The **rooms** at all three levels were on terraces and were
42. 7 and there were **rooms** in the remaining twenty-five metres.
42. 7 the top level there were **rooms** in the entire length of the
42. 9 Below these two **rooms** at the east end of the building,
42.11 In front of the **rooms** there was a passage just like the
42.12 was a door under the **rooms** on the south side of the
42.13 Because the **rooms** are holy, the priests will place the
42.14 they must leave in these **rooms** the holy clothing they wore
44. 3 the gateway through the entrance **room** at the inner end."
44.19 on duty in the Temple and leave them in the holy **rooms.**
46. 2 outer courtyard into the entrance **room** by the gateway and
46. 8 prince must leave the entrance **room** of the gateway and go
46.19 to the entrance of the **rooms** facing north near the gate on
46.19 These are holy **rooms** for the priests.
46.19 the west side of the **rooms** [20] and said, "This is the place
Dan 1. 2 and put the captured treasures in the temple **storerooms.**
6.10 In an upstairs **room** of his house there were windows that
Joel 2.16 Even newly married couples must leave their **room** and come.
Mt 6. 6 you pray, go to your **room,** close the door, and pray to
9.25 Jesus went into the girl's **room** and took hold of her hand,
13.52 a house who takes new and old things out of his **storeroom."**
Mk 2. 2 together that there was no **room** left, not even out in front
5.40 disciples, and went into the **room** where the child was lying.
14.14 Teacher says, Where is the **room** where my disciples and I
14.15 show you a large upstairs **room,** prepared and furnished, where you
Lk 2. 7 a manger—there was no **room** for them to stay in the
12. 3 in a closed **room** will be shouted from the housetops.
12.24 they don't have **store-rooms** or barns;
14.22 has been carried out, sir, but there is **room** for more.'
22.11 to you, Where is the **room** where my disciples and I will
22.12 show you a large furnished **room** upstairs, where you will get
Jn 8.20 Temple, in the **room** where the offering boxes were placed.
14. 2 There are many **rooms** in my Father's house, and I am going
Acts 1.13 the city and went up to the **room** where they were staying:
4.15 them to leave the Council **room,** and then they started discussing
9.37 Her body was washed and laid in a **room** upstairs.
9.39 he was taken to the **room** upstairs, where all the widows
9.40 put them all out of the **room,** and knelt down and prayed;
20. 8 lamps were burning in the upstairs **room** where we were meeting.
28. 8 Paul went into his **room,** prayed, placed his hands on him,
Rom 11.19 "Yes, but the branches were broken off to make **room** for me."
2 Cor 7. 2 Make **room** for us in your hearts.
Phlm 22 the same time, get a **room** ready for me, because I hope

Am **ROOSTER** see **COCK**

ROOT

Deut 29.18 This would be like a **root** that grows to be a bitter
32.22 to the world below and consume the **roots** of the mountains.
2 Kgs 19.30 flourish like plants that send **roots** deep into the ground
Job 8.17 Their **roots** wrap round the stones and hold fast to every rock.
14. 8 Even though its **roots** grow old, and its stump dies in the
18.16 His **roots** and branches are withered and dry.
29.19 was like a tree whose **roots** always have water and whose
30. 3 that they would gnaw dry **roots**— at night, in wild, desolate
30. 4 and ate them, even the tasteless **roots** of the broom-tree!
Ps 80. 9 its **roots** went deep, and it spread out over the whole land.
Is 5.24 burn in the fire, your **roots** will rot and your blossoms will
27. 6 descendants of Jacob, will take **root** like a tree, and they
37.31 flourish like plants that send **roots** deep into the ground
40.24 They are like young plants, just set out and barely **rooted.**
53. 2 servant should grow like a plant taking **root** in dry ground.
Jer 12. 2 You plant them, and they take **root;**
17. 8 growing near a stream and sending out **roots** to the water.
Ezek 17. 6 The branches grew upward towards the eagle, and the **roots** grew deep.
17. 7 now the vine sent its **roots** towards him and turned its
17. 9 pull it up by its **roots,** pull off the grapes, and break
19.12 pulled it up by the **roots** and threw it to the ground.
31. 7 Its **roots** reached down to the deep-flowing streams.
Hos 9.16 are like a plant whose **roots** have dried up and which bears
14. 5 they will be firmly **rooted** like the trees of Lebanon.
Jon 2. 6 went down to the very **roots** of the mountains, into the land
Mt 3.10 The axe is ready to cut down the trees at the **roots;**
13. 6 and because the **roots** had not grown deep enough, the plants
Mk 4. 6 and because the **roots** had not grown deep enough, the plants
11.20 It was dead all the way down to its **roots.**
Lk 3. 9 The axe is ready to cut down the trees at the **roots;**
17. 6 'Pull yourself up by the **roots** and plant yourself in the sea!'
Rom 11.16 and if the **roots** of a tree are offered to God,
11.18 you don't support the **roots**—the roots support you.
Eph 3.17 that you may have your **roots** and foundation in love,
Col 2. 7 Keep your **roots** deep in him, build your lives on him,
Jude 12 have been pulled up by the **roots** and are completely dead.

AV **ROOT**

Deut 29.28 in his great anger he **uprooted** them from their land and
1 Kgs 14.15 He will **uproot** the people of Israel from this good land
2 Chr 7.20 other gods, [20] then I will **remove** you from the land that I
Job 5. 3 have seen fools who looked **secure,** but I called down a
18.14 He is **torn** from the tent where he lived secure, and is
28. 9 Men dig the hardest rocks, Dig mountains away at their **base.**
31. 8 then let my crops be **destroyed,** or let others eat the food
31.12 like a destructive, hellish fire, **consuming** everything I have.
Ps 52. 5 he will **remove** you from the world of the living.
Prov 2.22 men from the land and **pull** sinners out of it like plants
12. 3 but righteous people **stand firm.**
12.12 is to find evil things to do, but the righteous **stand firm.**
Is 11. 1 new branches sprout from a **stump,** so a new king will arise
11.10 is coming when the new **king** from the royal line of David
Jer 1.10 over nations and kingdoms to **uproot** and to pull down, to
Dan 4.15 But leave the **stump** in the ground with a band of iron
4.23 tree down and destroy it, but leave the **stump** in the ground.
4.26 The angel ordered the **stump** to be left in the ground.
7. 8 It **tore** out three of the horns that were already there.
11. 7 Soon afterwards, one of her **relatives** will become king.
Zeph 2. 4 and the people of Ekron will be **driven** from their city.
Mal 4. 1 they will burn up, and there will be **nothing** left of them.
Mt 13.21 But it does not **sink** deep into them, and they don't last
13.29 gather the weeds you might **pull** up some of the wheat along
15.13 Father in heaven did not plant will be **pulled** up," answered Jesus.
Mk 4.17 But it does not **sink** deep into them, and they don't last
Lk 8.13 But it does not **sink** deep into them;
Rom 11.17 and now you share the strong **spiritual** life of the Jews.
15.12 And again, Isaiah says, "A **descendant** of Jesse will appear;
1 Tim 6.10 the love of money is a **source** of all kinds of evil.
Heb 12.15 one become like a bitter **plant** that grows up and causes many
Rev 5. 5 the great **descendant of David,** has won the victory,
22.16 I am **descended** from the family of David;

ROPE

Ex 35.18 the pegs and **ropes** for the Tent and the enclosure;
39.40 the curtain for the entrance of the enclosure and its **ropes;**
Num 3.37 for the posts, bases, pegs, and **ropes** for the outer court.
4.26 the entrance, [26] the curtains and **ropes** for the court that
4.32 posts, bases, pegs, and **ropes** of the court round the Tent,
Josh 2.15 so she let the men down from the window by a **rope.**
Judg 15.13 him up with two new **ropes** and brought him back from the
15.14 strong, and he broke the **ropes** round his arms and hands as
16.11 they tie me with new **ropes** that have never been used, I'll
16.12 So Delilah got some new **ropes** and tied him up.
16.12 But he snapped the **ropes** off his arms like thread.
2 Sam 17.13 our people will all bring **ropes** and just pull the city into
1 Kgs 20.31 sackcloth round our waists and **ropes** round our necks, and
20.32 sackcloth round their waists and **ropes** round their necks,
Job 28. 4 There they work in loneliness, Clinging to **ropes** in the pits.
39.10 Can you hold one with a **rope** and make him plough?
41. 1 Leviathan with a fish-hook or tie his tongue down with a **rope?**
41. 2 Can you put a **rope** through his snout or put a hook
Ecc 4.12 A **rope** made of three cords is hard to break.
12. 6 the **rope** at the well will break, and the water jar will
Is 3.24 instead of fine belts, they will wear coarse **ropes;**
33.20 whose pegs are never pulled up and whose **ropes** never break.
54. 2 lengthen its **ropes** and strengthen the pegs!
Jer 10.20 the **ropes** that held them have broken.
38. 6 and let me down by **ropes** into Prince Malchiah's well, which
38.11 got some worn-out clothing which he let down to me by **ropes.**
38.12 the rags under my arms, so that the **ropes** wouldn't hurt me.
Ezek 3.25 You will be tied with **ropes,** mortal man, and you will
27.24 brightly coloured carpets, and well-made cords and **ropes.**
Acts 27.17 it aboard and then fastened some **ropes** tight round the ship.
27.32 So the soldiers cut the **ropes** that held the boat and let
27.40 same time they untied the **ropes** that held the steering oars.

ROSE see **RISE**

ROT

Ex 16.20 of worms and smelt **rotten,** and Moses was angry with them.
Lev 13.55 burn the object, whether the **rot** is on the front or the
Job 13.28 As a result, I crumble like **rotten** wood, like a moth-eaten coat.
18.13 spreads over his body and causes his arms and legs to **rot.**
41.27 is as flimsy as straw, and bronze as soft as **rotten** wood.
Ps 38. 5 Because I have been foolish, my sores stink and **rot.**
83.10 You defeated them at Endor, and their bodies **rotted** on the ground.
Is 5.24 the fire, your roots will **rot** and your blossoms will dry up
14.19 you have no tomb, and your corpse is thrown out to **rot.**
34. 3 will not be buried, but will lie there **rotting** and stinking;
40.20 afford silver or gold chooses wood that will not **rot.**
Jer 2.21 You are like a **rotten,** worthless vine.
29.17 will make them like figs that are too **rotten** to be eaten.
Ezek 32. 5 I will cover mountains and valleys with your **rotting** corpse.
Zeph 1.17 and their dead bodies will lie **rotting** on the ground."
Zech 14.12 Their flesh will **rot** away while they are still alive;
14.12 their eyes and their tongues will **rot** away.
Acts 2.27 you will not allow your faithful servant to **rot** in the grave.
2.31 his body did not **rot** in the grave.'
13.34 raising him from death, never to **rot** away in the grave:
13.35 'You will not allow your devoted servant to **rot** in the grave.'
13.36 buried with his ancestors, and his body **rotted** in the grave.
Jas 5. 2 Your riches have **rotted** away, and your clothes have been eaten

ROUGH

Is 40. 4 become a plain, and the **rough** country will be made smooth.
42.16 into light and make **rough** country smooth before them.
Lk 3. 5 roads must be made straight, and the **rough** paths made smooth.

ROUND

1 Kgs 7.20 and were placed on a **rounded** section which was above the
7.23 Huram made a **round** tank of bronze, 2.2 metres deep,
2 Chr 4. 2 He also made a **round** tank of bronze, 2.2 metres deep,

ROUNDABOUT

Ex 13.18 he led them in a **roundabout** way through the desert towards

ROUSE

Ps 7. 6 **rouse** yourself and help me!
35.23 **Rouse** yourself, O Lord, and defend me;
44.23 **Rouse** yourself!
73.20 when you **rouse** yourself, O Lord, they disappear.
74.22 **Rouse** yourself, God, and defend your cause!
Is 51.17 **Rouse** yourself and get up!
Zech 4. 1 to me came again and **roused** me as if I had been

ROUTE

Deut 1.22 can tell us the best **route** to take and what kind of
2 Kgs 3. 8 What **route** shall we take for the attack?"

ROW (1)

Jon 1.13 tried to get the ship to shore, **rowing** with all their might.
Mk 6.48 straining at the oars, because they were **rowing** against the wind;
Jn 6.19 disciples had **rowed** about five or six kilometres when they saw

ROW (2)

Gen 15.10 half, and placed the halves opposite each other in two **rows;**
Ex 26.33 Place the curtain under the **row** of hooks in the roof of
28.17 Mount four **rows** of precious stones on it;
28.17 in the first **row** mount a ruby, a topaz, and a garnet;
28.18 in the second **row,** an emerald, a sapphire, and a
28.19 in the third **row,** a turquoise, an agate, and an amethyst;
28.20 and in the fourth **row,** a beryl, a carnelian, and a
39.10 They mounted four **rows** of precious stones on it:
39.10 in the first **row** they mounted a ruby, a topaz, and a
39.11 in the second **row,** an emerald, a sapphire, and a
39.12 in the third **row,** a turquoise, an agate, and an amethyst;
39.13 and in the fourth **row,** a beryl, a carnelian, and a
Lev 24. 6 Put the loaves in two **rows,**
24. 6 six in each **row,** on the table
24. 7 some pure incense on each **row,** as a token food-offering to
Num 24. 6 Israel are beautiful, [6] Like long **rows** of palms Or gardens
1 Kgs 7. 2 It had three **rows** of cedar pillars,
7. 2 fifteen in each **row,** with cedar beams resting on them.
7. 4 each of the two side walls there were three **rows** of windows.
7. 5 three rows of windows in each wall faced the opposite **rows.**
7.18 interwoven chains, [18] and two **rows** of bronze pomegranates.
7.20 two hundred pomegranates in two **rows** round each capital.
7.24 of the tank were two **rows** of bronze gourds, which had been
7.40 hundred bronze pomegranates, in two **rows** of a hundred each
2 Kgs 11.15 "Take her out between the **rows** of guards, and kill anyone
2 Chr 4. 3 the tank were two **rows** of decorations, one above the other.
4.11 bronze pomegranates arranged in two **rows** round the design of
23.14 "Take her out between the **rows** of guards, and kill anyone
Job 41.15 His back is made of **rows** of shields, fastened together
Song 6.13 want to watch me as I dance between the **rows** of onlookers?
Is 28.25 He sows **rows** of wheat and barley, and at the edges of
Mk 6.40 the people sat down in **rows,** in groups of a hundred

ROYAL

Gen 41.42 the ring engraved with the **royal** seal and put it on Joseph's
41.43 He gave him the second **royal** chariot to ride in, and his
49.10 Judah will hold the **royal** sceptre,
Num 21.18 people, Dug with a **royal** sceptre And with their sticks."
1 Sam 22.14 and highly respected by everyone in the **royal** court.
2 Sam 14. 9 you and the **royal** family are innocent."
14.26 two kilogrammes according to the **royal** standard of weights.
15.18 next to him as the **royal** bodyguard passed by in front of
19.18 the river to escort the **royal** party across and to do
20. 7 So Joab's men, the **royal** bodyguard, and all the other
1 Kgs 1.38 Zadok, Nathan, Benaiah, and the **royal** bodyguard put Solomon
1.44 He sent Zadok, Nathan, Benaiah, and the **royal** bodyguard
2.12 David as king, and his **royal** power was firmly established.
4. 5 **Royal** adviser: the priest Zabud
11.14 Lord caused Hadad, of the **royal** family of Edom, to turn
14.31 and was buried in the **royal** tombs in David's City, and his
15.24 and was buried in the **royal** tombs in David's City, and his
22.10 two kings, dressed in their **royal** robes, were sitting on
22.30 I will disguise myself, but you wear your **royal** garments."
22.50 and was buried in the **royal** tombs in David's City, and his
2 Kgs 8.24 and was buried in the **royal** tombs in David's City, and his
9.28 chariot and buried him in the **royal** tombs in David's City.
10.13 of Queen Jezebel and to the rest of the **royal** family."
11. 1 orders for all the members of the **royal** family to be killed.
11. 4 in charge of the **royal** bodyguard and of the palace guards,
11.19 then he, the officers, the **royal** bodyguard, and the palace
12.10 money in the box, the **royal** secretary and the High Priest
2 Kgs 12.20 Joash was buried in the **royal** tombs in David's City, and his
13.13 and was buried in the **royal** tombs in Samaria, and his son
14.16 and was buried in the **royal** tombs in Samaria, and his son
14.20 a horse and was buried in the **royal** tombs in David's City.
14.29 and was buried in the **royal** tombs, and his son Zechariah
15. 7 and was buried in the **royal** burial ground in David's City,
15.38 and was buried in the **royal** tombs in David's City, and his
16.18 Temple the platform for the **royal** throne and closed up the
16.20 and was buried in the **royal** tombs in David's City, and his
23. 3 He stood by the **royal** column and made a covenant with the
23.30 back to Jerusalem, where he was buried in the **royal** tombs.
24.14 Jerusalem, all the **royal** princes, and all the leading men,
25. 4 left by way of the **royal** garden, went through the gateway
25.25 Elishama, a member of the **royal** family, went to Mizpah with
1 Chr 27.25 This is the list of those who administered the **royal** property:
27.25 **Royal** storerooms: Azmaveth son of Adiel
27.34 Joab was commander of the **royal** army.
29. 6 and the administrators of the **royal** property volunteered to
2 Chr 12.16 and was buried in the **royal** tombs in David's City and his
13. 8 propose to fight against the **royal** authority that the Lord
14. 1 Abijah died and was buried in the **royal** tombs in David's City.
18. 9 two kings, dressed in their **royal** robes, were sitting on
18.29 I will disguise myself, but you wear your **royal** garments."
21. 1 and was buried in the **royal** tombs in David's City and his
21.17 They invaded Judah, looted the **royal** palace, and carried
21.20 They buried him in David's City, but not in the **royal** tombs.
22.10 all the members of the **royal** family of Judah to be killed.
23. 5 another third will guard the **royal** palace, and the rest
24.11 take the box to the **royal** official who was in charge of
24.11 Whenever it was full, the **royal** secretary and the High
24.16 They buried him in the **royal** tombs in David's City in
24.25 He was buried in David's City, but not in the **royal** tombs.
25.28 and he was buried in the **royal** tombs in David's City.
26.23 and was buried in the **royal** burial-ground,
26.23 because of his disease he was not buried in the **royal** tombs.
28.27 and was buried in Jerusalem, but not in the **royal** tombs.
29.21 away the sins of the **royal** family and of the people of
32.33 died and was buried in the upper section of the **royal** tombs.
34.31 He stood by the **royal** column and made a covenant with
35.24 There he died and was buried in the **royal** tombs.
Ezra 1. 8 to Mithredath, chief of the **royal** treasury, who made an
4.13 stop paying taxes, and your **royal** revenues will decrease.
4.19 times Jerusalem has revolted against **royal** authority and
5.17 search be made in the **royal** records in Babylon to find
6. 1 to be made in the **royal** records that were kept in Babylon.
6. 4 All expenses are to be paid by the **royal** treasury.
6. 8 paid promptly out of the **royal** funds received from taxes in
7.20 need for the Temple, you may get from the **royal** treasury.
Neh 2. 8 to Asaph, keeper of the **royal** forests, instructing him to
3.15 the wall next to the **royal** garden, as far as the steps
5. 4 money to pay the **royal** tax on our fields and vineyards.
11.23 There were **royal** regulations stating how the clans
Esth 1. 1 From his **royal** throne in Persia's capital city of Susa,
1. 5 whole week and was held in the gardens of the **royal** palace.
1. 7 them alike, and the king was generous with the **royal** wine.
1. 9 Meanwhile, inside the **royal** palace Queen Vashti was giving
1.11 He ordered them to bring in Queen Vashti, wearing her **royal** crown.
1.18 When the wives of the **royal** officials of Persia and
1.19 please Your Majesty, issue a **royal** proclamation that Vashti
1.22 To each of the **royal** provinces he sent a message in the
2. 8 too was put in the **royal** palace in the care of Hegai,
2. 9 girls specially chosen from the **royal** palace to serve her.
2.16 Esther was brought to King Xerxes in the **royal** palace.
2.17 He placed the **royal** crown on her head and made her queen
3. 3 The other officials in the **royal** service asked him why he
3. 9 kilogrammes of silver into the **royal** treasury for the
4. 7 promised to put into the **royal** treasury if all the Jews were
4.13 than any other Jew just because you are in the **royal** palace.
5. 1 fast Esther put on her **royal** robes and went and stood in
5. 1 The king was inside, seated on the **royal** throne,
6. 7 he answered the king, "Order **royal** robes to be brought for
6. 7 Order a **royal** ornament to be put on your own horse.
8. 8 name and stamped with the **royal** seal cannot be revoked.
8. 8 write it in my name and stamp it with the **royal** seal."
8.10 of King Xerxes, and he stamped them with the **royal** seal.
8.10 by riders mounted on fast horses from the **royal** stables.
8.14 king's command the riders mounted **royal** horses and rode off
8.15 Mordecai left the palace, wearing **royal** robes of blue and white,
9. 1 the day on which the **royal** proclamation was to take effect,
9. 3 provincial officials—governors, administrators, and **royal**
Ps 60. 7 Ephraim is my helmet and Judah my **royal** sceptre.
89.44 You have taken away his **royal** sceptre and hurled his
108. 8 Ephraim is my helmet and Judah my **royal** sceptre.
110. 2 From Zion the Lord will extend your **royal** power.
145.11 of the glory of your **royal** power and tell of your might,
Ecc 2. 8 and gold from the **royal** treasuries of the lands I ruled.
Is 7.17 people, and on the whole **royal** family, days of trouble worse
9. 7 His **royal** power will continue to grow;
11. 1 The **royal** line of David is like a tree that has been
11.10 the new king from the **royal** line of David will be a
11.10 They will gather in his **royal** city and give him honour.
22.15 Shebna, the manager of the **royal** household, and say to him,
Jer 17.25 of Jerusalem and have the same **royal** power that David had.
21.11 give this message to the **royal** house of Judah, the
22. 6 "To me, Judah's **royal** palace is as beautiful as the land
26.10 happened, they hurried from the **royal** palace to the Temple
27.18 Temple and in the **royal** palace to be taken to Babylonia."
27.21 are left in the Temple and in the **royal** palace in Jerusalem:
32. 2 and I was locked up in the courtyard of the **royal** palace.
33. 4 houses of Jerusalem and the **royal** palace of Judah will be

Jer 36.12 Then he went to the **royal** palace, to the room of the
38. 7 eunuch who worked in the **royal** palace, heard that they had
38.22 the women left in Judah's **royal** palace being led out to the
39. 4 left by way of the **royal** garden, went through the gateway
39. 8 the Babylonians burnt down the **royal** palace and the houses
41. 1 Elishama, a member of the **royal** family and one of the king's
43.10 that you buried, and will spread the **royal** tent over them.
52. 7 left by way of the **royal** garden, went through the gateway
Ezek 19.11 Its branches were strong, and grew to be **royal** sceptres.
19.14 branches will never again be strong, will never be **royal** sceptres.
Dan 1. 3 young men of the **royal** family and of the noble families.
1. 4 so that they would be qualified to serve in the **royal** court.
1. 5 the same food and wine as the members of the **royal** court.
1. 8 drinking the wine of the **royal** court, so he asked Ashpenaz
1.13 eating the food of the **royal** court, and base your decision
1.15 stronger than all those who had been eating the **royal** food.
1.21 Daniel remained at the **royal** court until Cyrus the
2.12 ordered the execution of all the **royal** advisers in Babylon.
2.16 went at once and obtained **royal** permission for more time, so
2.24 whom the king had commanded to execute the **royal** advisers.
2.48 of Babylon, and made him the head of all the **royal** advisers.
2.49 Daniel, however, remained at the **royal** court.
4. 6 I ordered all the **royal** advisers in Babylon to be brought
4.18 None of my **royal** advisers could tell me, but you can,
4.29 on the roof of his **royal** palace in Babylon, [30] he said,
4.31 Your **royal** power is now taken away from you.
4.36 I was given back my **royal** power, with even greater honour
5. 7 be dressed in robes of **royal** purple, wear a gold chain of
5. 8 The **royal** advisers came forward, but none of them could
5.16 be dressed in robes of **royal** purple, wear a gold chain of
5.20 he was removed from his **royal** throne and lost his place of
5.29 Daniel in a robe of **royal** purple and to hang a gold
5.31 who was then sixty-two years old, seized the **royal** power.
6.17 the king placed his own **royal** seal and the seal of his
7.14 was given authority, honour, and **royal** power, so that the
7.18 the Supreme God will receive **royal** power and keep it for
7.22 The time had arrived for God's people to receive **royal** power.
7.27 Their **royal** power will never end and all rulers on earth
11.45 even set up his huge **royal** tents between the sea and the
Hos 5. 1 Listen, you that belong to the **royal** family!
Zech 14.10 and from the Tower of Hananel to the **royal** winepresses.
Mt 25.31 he will sit on his **royal** throne, [32] and the people of all
Acts 7.10 made Joseph governor over the country and the **royal** household.
12.21 Herod put on his **royal** robes, sat on his throne,

RUB

Prov 25.20 clothes on a cold day or like **rubbing** salt in a wound.
Lam 3.16 He **rubbed** my face in the ground and broke my teeth on
Ezek 16. 4 cord or washed you or **rubbed** you with salt or wrapped you
16. 9 I **rubbed** olive-oil on your skin.
29.18 loads that their heads were **rubbed** bald and their shoulders
Mal 2. 3 will punish your children and **rub** your faces in the dung of
Mk 6.13 drove out many demons, and **rubbed** olive-oil on many sick people
Lk 6. 1 pick the ears of corn, **rub** them in their hands, and eat
Jn 9. 6 he **rubbed** the mud on the man's eyes [7] and said, "Go
9.11 called Jesus made some mud, **rubbed** it on my eyes, and told
Jas 5.14 will pray for him and **rub** olive-oil on him in the name

RUBBISH

Ezra 6.11 And his house is to be made a **rubbish** heap.
Job 2. 8 went and sat by the **rubbish** heap and took a piece of
Ps 119.119 treat all the wicked like **rubbish,**
Is 5.25 of those who die will be left in the streets like **rubbish.**

RUBBISH GATE

Neh 2.13 and went south past Dragon's Fountain to the **Rubbish Gate.**
3.13 the wall for 440 metres, as far as the **Rubbish Gate.**
3.14 of the Beth Haccherem District, rebuilt the **Rubbish Gate.**
12.31 to the right on top of the wall towards the **Rubbish Gate.**

RUBBLE

1 Kgs 20.10 this city of yours and carry off the **rubble** in their hands.
2 Kgs 19.25 you the power to turn fortified cities into piles of **rubble.**
Neh 2.14 find any path through the **rubble,** [15] so I went down into
4. 2 Can they make building-stones out of heaps of burnt **rubble?"**
4.10 There's so much **rubble** to take away.
Is 37.26 you the power to turn fortified cities into piles of **rubble.**
Lam 2. 9 The gates lie buried in **rubble,** their bars smashed to pieces.
Ezek 26.12 and wood and all the **rubble,** and dump them into the sea.
Mic 1. 6 I will pour the **rubble** of the city down into the valley,

RUBY

Ex 28.17 in the first row mount a **ruby,** a topaz, and a garnet;
39.10 the first row they mounted a **ruby,** a topaz, and a garnet;
Job 28.18 The value of wisdom is more Than coral or crystal or **rubies.**
Is 54.12 will build your towers with **rubies,** your gates with stones
Ezek 27.16 fine linen, coral, and **rubies** in payment for your wares.
28.13 **rubies** and diamonds;

RUDDER

Jas 3. 4 steered by a very small **rudder,** and it goes wherever the

RUDE

Prov 18.23 to beg politely, but when the rich man answers, he is **rude.**

RUE

Lk 11.42 herbs, such as mint and **rue** and all the other herbs, but

RUG

Is 21. 5 **rugs** are spread for the guests to sit on.

RUGGED

Is 7.19 They will swarm in the **rugged** valleys and in the caves

RUIN

Gen 41.30 will be forgotten, because the famine will **ruin** the country.
Ex 8.24 The whole land of Egypt was brought to **ruin** by the flies.
9.31 and the barley were **ruined,** because the barley was ripe,
9.32 But none of the wheat was **ruined,** because it ripens later.
10. 7 Don't you realize that Egypt is **ruined?"**
23. 8 to what is right and **ruins** the cause of those who are
Lev 26.31 turn your cities into **ruins,** destroy your places of worship,
26.33 Your land will be deserted, and your cities left in **ruins.**
Num 21.11 place, they camped at the **ruins** of Abarim in the wilderness
21.29 You worshippers of Chemosh are brought to **ruin!**
33.41 Punon, Oboth, the **ruins** of Abarim in the territory of Moab,
Deut 13.16 It must be left in **ruins** for ever and never again be
28.63 take delight in destroying you and in bringing **ruin** on you.
Josh 8.28 Joshua burnt Ai and left it in **ruins.**
2 Sam 16. 8 to your son Absalom, and you are **ruined,** you murderer!"
20.19 Do you want to **ruin** what belongs to the Lord?"
20.20 "I will never **ruin** or destroy your city!
1 Kgs 9. 8 will become a pile of **ruins,** and everyone who passes by will
13.34 about the **ruin** and total destruction of his dynasty.
20. 7 country and said, "You see that this man wants to **ruin** us.
2 Kgs 3.19 stop all their springs, and **ruin** all their fertile fields by
Ezra 9. 9 your Temple, which was in **ruins,** and to find safety here in
Neh 2. 3 ancestors are buried is in **ruins** and its gates have been
2.17 because Jerusalem is in **ruins** and its gates are destroyed!
6.13 so that they could **ruin** my reputation and humiliate me.
Job 30.24 Why do you attack a **ruined** man, one who can do nothing
31. 3 He sends disaster and **ruin** to those who do wrong.
Ps 5.10 may their own plots cause their **ruin.**
38.12 me, and those who want to hurt me threaten to **ruin** me;
52. 2 You make plans to **ruin** others;
52. 5 So God will **ruin** you for ever;
69.22 May their banquets cause their **ruin;**
74. 3 Walk over these total **ruins;**
78.45 that tormented them, and frogs that **ruined** their land.
79. 1 They have desecrated your holy Temple and left Jerusalem in **ruins.**
79. 7 they have **ruined** your country.
89.40 down the walls of his city and left his forts in **ruins.**
102. 6 a wild bird in the desert, like an owl in abandoned **ruins.**
102.14 they have pity on her, even though she is in **ruins.**
109.10 may they be driven from the **ruins** they live in!
146. 9 he helps widows and orphans, but takes the wicked to their **ruin.**
Prov 7.26 She has been the **ruin** of many men and caused the death
10. 8 People who talk foolishly will come to **ruin.**
11. 9 You can be **ruined** by the talk of godless people, but the
11.11 a city is brought to **ruin** by the words of the wicked.
13.15 but those who can't be trusted are on the road to **ruin.**
13.20 If you make friends with stupid people, you will be **ruined.**
18. 7 When a fool speaks, he is **ruining** himself;
18.12 arrogant people are on the way to **ruin.**
19. 3 Some people **ruin** themselves by their own stupid actions
19.13 A stupid son can bring his father to **ruin.**
21.12 of the wicked, and he will bring the wicked down to **ruin.**
24.22 such men could be **ruined** in a moment.
26.28 Insincere talk brings nothing but **ruin.**
28.14 If you are stubborn, you will be **ruined.**
29. 4 he is only concerned with money, he will **ruin** his country.
Ecc 7. 7 If you take a bribe, you **ruin** your character.
Song 2.15 the little foxes, before they **ruin** our vineyard in bloom.
Is 1. 7 foreigners take over your land and bring everything to **ruin.**
5. 9 Lord Almighty say, "All these big, fine houses will be empty **ruins.**
5.17 In the **ruins** of the cities lambs will eat grass and
6.11 answered, "Until the cities are **ruined** and empty—until the
13.21 and wild goats will prance through the **ruins.**
14.20 Because you **ruined** your country and killed your own people,
14.22 Lord Almighty says, "I will attack Babylon and bring it to **ruin.**
17. 1 it will be only a pile of **ruins.**
17. 9 be deserted and left in **ruins** like the cities that the
23. 1 its houses and its harbour are in **ruins.**
23.13 the fortifications of Tyre, and left the city in **ruins.**
24. 3 The earth will lie shattered and **ruined.**
24.12 The city is in **ruins,** and its gates have been broken down.
25. 2 You have turned cities into **ruins**
27.10 The fortified city lies in **ruins.**
28.28 He does not **ruin** the wheat by threshing it endlessly,
32. 7 he plots to **ruin** the poor with lies and to prevent them
32.14 and the forts that guarded them will be in **ruins** for ever.
44.26 Those cities will rise from the **ruins.**
47.11 **Ruin** will come on you suddenly— ruin you never dreamt of!
49.19 "Your country was **ruined** and desolate— but now it will
49.19 those who left you in **ruins** will be far removed from you.
51. 3 show compassion to Jerusalem, to all who live in her **ruins.**
52. 9 Break into shouts of joy, you **ruins** of Jerusalem!
58.12 long been in **ruins,** building again on the old foundations.
58.12 who rebuilt the walls, who restored the **ruined** houses."
59. 7 You leave **ruin** and destruction wherever you go, [8] and no one
61. 4 They will rebuild cities that have long been in **ruins.**

Is 64.10 Jerusalem is a deserted **ruin,** [11] and our Temple, the sacred
64.11 All the places we loved are in **ruins.**
Jer 2. 7 But instead they **ruined** my land;
2.15 a desert, and his towns lie in **ruins,** completely abandoned.
4. 7 Judah will be left in **ruins,** and no one will live in
4.20 the whole country is left in **ruins.**
4.26 its cities were in **ruins** because of the Lord's fierce anger.
6.19 their schemes I am bringing **ruin** on these people, because
9.11 make Jerusalem a pile of **ruins,** a place where jackals live;
9.19 "We are **ruined!**
10.20 Our tents are **ruined;**
10.25 they have destroyed us completely and left our country in **ruins.**
12.14 about Israel's neighbours who have **ruined** the land I gave to
13. 7 I saw that they were **ruined** and were no longer any good.
22. 5 then I swear to you that this palace will fall into **ruins.**
25. 9 neighbours and leave them in **ruins** for ever, a terrible and
25.11 land will be left in **ruins** and will be a shocking sight,
25.12 I will destroy that country and leave it in **ruins** for ever.
25.36 your nation and left your peaceful country in **ruins.**
26.18 will become a pile of **ruins,** and the Temple hill will become
27.17 Why should this city become a pile of **ruins?**
44. 2 now they are still in **ruins,** and no one lives in them
44. 6 They were left in **ruins** and became a horrifying sight, as
44.22 day your land lies in **ruins** and no one lives in it.
46.19 Memphis will be made a desert, a **ruin** where no one lives.
48. 8 both valley and plain will be **ruined.**
48. 9 towns will be left in **ruins,** and no one will live there
48.11 Its flavour has never been **ruined,** and it tastes as good as
48.16 its **ruin** is coming soon.
48.18 Moab's destroyer is here and has left its forts in **ruins.**
48.39 It is in **ruins,** and all the surrounding nations jeer at it.
49. 2 it will be left in **ruins** and its villages burnt to the
49.13 All the near-by villages will be in **ruins** for ever.
50.13 it will be left in **ruins,** and all who pass by will
51.26 of the stones from your **ruins** will ever be used again for
51.37 That country will become a pile of **ruins** where wild animals live.
Lam 1. 7 A lonely **ruin** now, Jerusalem recalls her ancient splendour.
2. 1 Its heavenly splendour he has turned into **ruins.**
2. 5 He has left her forts and palaces in **ruins.**
2. 8 The towers and walls now lie in **ruins** together.
2.15 They shake their heads and laugh at the **ruins** of Jerusalem.
3.47 We have been through disaster and **ruin;**
5.18 and wild jackals prowl through its **ruins.**
Ezek 13. 4 are as useless as foxes living among the **ruins** of a city.
19. 7 He wrecked forts, he **ruined** towns.
21.27 **Ruin, ruin!**
21.27 Yes, I will make the city a **ruin.**
23.33 that cup of fear and **ruin,** your sister Samaria's cup.
26.10 walls as they pass through the gates of the **ruined** city.
26.19 make you as desolate as **ruined** cities where no one lives.
26.20 world among eternal **ruins,** keeping company with the dead.
29.12 of Egypt will lie in **ruins,** ruins worse than those of any
30. 4 The country will be plundered And left in **ruins.**
30. 7 in the world, and its cities will be left totally in **ruins.**
33.24 who are living in the **ruined** cities of the land of Israel
33.27 the people who live in the **ruined** cities will be killed.
35. 4 I will leave your cities in **ruins** And your land desolate;
36. 4 places that were left in **ruins,** and to you deserted cities
36.10 in the cities and rebuild everything that was left in **ruins.**
36.33 you live in your cities again and let you rebuild the **ruins.**
36.35 looted, and left in **ruins,** are now inhabited and fortified.
36.36 I, the Lord, rebuild **ruined** cities and replant waste fields.
36.38 cities that are now in **ruins** will then be as full of
38.12 loot the people who live in cities that were once in **ruins.**
Dan 2. 5 torn limb from limb and make your houses a pile of **ruins.**
3.29 limb, and his house is to be made a pile of **ruins.**
9. 2 that Jerusalem would be in **ruins,** according to what the Lord
11.26 His closest advisers will **ruin** him.
Hos 4.14 As the proverb says, 'A people without sense will be **ruined.'**
5. 9 The day of punishment is coming, and Israel will be **ruined.**
5.12 destruction on Israel and **ruin** on the people of Judah.
Joel 1.17 to be stored, and so the empty granaries are in **ruins.**
3.19 a desert, and Edom a **ruined** waste, because they attacked the
Amos 3.15 The houses decorated with ivory will fall in **ruins;**
6. 6 perfumes, but you do not mourn over the **ruin** of Israel.
7. 9 The holy places of Israel will be left in **ruins.**
9.11 kingdom of David, which is like a house fallen into **ruins.**
9.14 They will rebuild their **ruined** cities and live there;
Obad 12 You should not have been glad on the day of their **ruin.**
Mic 1. 6 make Samaria a pile of **ruins** in the open country, a place
2. 4 We are completely **ruined!**
3.12 will become a pile of **ruins,** and the Temple hill will become
4.11 We will see this city in **ruins!"**
6.13 I have already begun your **ruin** and destruction because of your sins.
6.16 so I will bring you to **ruin,** and everyone will despise you.
Nah 3. 7 They will say, 'Nineveh lies in **ruins!**
Hab 2.10 many nations you have only brought **ruin** on yourself.
Zeph 1.15 and distress, a day of **ruin** and destruction, a day of
2. 9 of salt pits and everlasting **ruin,** overgrown with weeds.
2.13 the city of Nineveh a deserted **ruin,** a waterless desert.
2.14 Owls will live among its **ruins** and hoot from the windows.
3. 6 their cities and left their walls and towers in **ruins.**
Hag 1. 4 living in well-built houses while my Temple lies in **ruins?**
1. 9 Because my Temple lies in **ruins** while every one of you is
2.17 winds and hail to **ruin** everything you tried to grow,
Zech 5. 4 It will remain in their houses and leave them in **ruins."**
Mt 9.17 burst, the wine will pour out, and the skins will be **ruined.**
Mk 2.22 the skins, and both the wine and the skins will be **ruined.**
Lk 5.37 skins, the wine will pour out, and the skins will be **ruined.**
Acts 15.16 I will rebuild its **ruins** and make it strong again.
Rom 3.16 they leave **ruin** and destruction wherever they go.
11.11 When the Jews stumbled, did they fall to their **ruin?**
14.15 the food that you eat **ruin** the person for whom Christ died!
1 Cor 15.33 "Bad companions **ruin** good character."
2 Cor 7. 2 have **ruined** no one, nor tried to take advantage of anyone.
Eph 5.18 Do not get drunk with wine, which will only **ruin** you;
1 Tim 1.19 to their conscience and have made a **ruin** of their faith.
6. 9 and harmful desires, which pull them down to **ruin** and destruction.
2 Tim 2.14 It does no good, but only **ruins** the people who listen.

RULE

[RULING SPIRITS]

Gen 1.16 larger lights, the sun to **rule** over the day
1.16 and the moon to **rule** over the night;
1.18 shine on the earth, [18] to **rule** over the day and the night,
4. 7 It wants to **rule** you, but you must overcome it."
27.29 May you **rule** over all your relatives, and may your mother's
36.31 in Israel, the following kings **ruled** over the land of Edom
37. 8 think you are going to be a king and **rule** over us?"
45. 8 I am the **ruler** of all Egypt.
45. 9 'God has made me **ruler** of all Egypt;
45.26 "He is the **ruler** of all Egypt!"
49.10 And his descendants will always **rule.**
49.16 "Dan will be a **ruler** for his people.
Ex 2.14 The man answered, "Who made you our **ruler** and judge?
12.24 You and your children must obey these **rules** for ever.
21.31 the bull kills a boy or a girl, the same **rule** applies.
28.43 This is a permanent **rule** for Aaron and his descendants.
30.21 This is a **rule** which they and their descendants are to
Lev 1. 1 and gave him the following **rules** [2] for the Israelites to
3.17 this is a **rule** to be kept for ever by all Israelites
4. 2 would have to observe the following **rules.**
4.22 If it is a **ruler** who sins and becomes guilty of breaking
4.26 for the sin of the **ruler,** and he will be forgiven.
22.29 to the Lord, follow the **rules** so that you will be accepted;
26.17 will be defeated, and those who hate you will **rule** over you;
Num 9. 2 Passover according to all the **rules** and regulations for it."
9.14 must observe it according to all the **rules** and regulations.
10. 8 "The following **rule** is to be observed for all time to come.
15.15 time to come, the same **rules** are binding on you and on
18.23 This is a permanent **rule** that applies also to your descendants.
19.21 You are to observe this **rule** for all time to come.
21.34 you did to Sihon, the Amorite king who **ruled** at Heshbon."
24. 7 than Agag, And his **rule** shall be extended far and wide.
30.16 These are the **rules** that the Lord gave Moses concerning
35.29 These **rules** apply to you and your descendants
36.13 These are the **rules** and regulations that the Lord gave
Deut 1. 4 Sihon of the Amorites, who **ruled** in the town of Heshbon, and
1. 4 King Og of Bashan, who **ruled** in the towns of Ashtaroth and
3. 2 as you did to Sihon the Amorite king who **ruled** in Heshbon.'
3. 4 whole region of Argob, where King Og of Bashan **ruled.**
3.13 where Og had **ruled,** that is, the entire Argob region."
4.45 Sihon of the Amorites, who had **ruled** in the town of Heshbon.
17.20 and his descendants will **rule** Israel for many generations.
23.20 Obey this **rule,** and the Lord your God will bless everything
28.44 In the end they will be your **rulers.**
32.13 "He let them **rule** the highlands, and they ate what grew
Josh 12. 2 One was Sihon, the Amorite king who **ruled** at Heshbon.
12. 4 he **ruled** at Ashtaroth and Edrei.
13.10 the cities that had been **ruled** by the Amorite king Sihon
13.10 who had **ruled** at Heshbon.
13.12 last of the Rephaim, who had **ruled** at Ashtaroth and Edrei.
13.21 kingdom of the Amorite king Sihon, who had **ruled** at Heshbon.
13.21 Moses defeated him, as well as the **rulers** of Midian:
13.21 All of them had **ruled** the land for King Sihon.
24.25 and there at Shechem he gave them laws and **rules** to follow.
Judg 1.35 Manasseh kept them under their **rule** and forced them to work
3. 8 Mesopotamia conquer them, and he **ruled** over them for eight years.
4. 2 by Jabin, a Canaanite king who **ruled** in the city of Hazor.
4. 3 hundred iron chariots, and he **ruled** the people of Israel
5. 3 Pay attention, you **rulers!**
6. 1 so he let the people of Midian **rule** them for seven years.
8.22 Gideon, "Be our **ruler**—you and your descendants after you.
8.23 Gideon answered, "I will not be your **ruler,** nor will my son.
8.23 The Lord will be your **ruler."**
9.22 Abimelech **ruled** Israel for three years.
9.30 Zebul, the **ruler** of the city, became angry when he
11. 9 Ammonites and the Lord gives me victory, I will be your **ruler."**
11.11 of Gilead, and the people made him their **ruler** and leader.
13. 1 and he let the Philistines **rule** them for forty years.
14. 4 At this time the Philistines were **ruling** Israel.
15.11 "Don't you know that the Philistines are our **rulers?**
15.20 for twenty years while the Philistines **ruled** the land.
1 Sam 6.18 for each of the cities **ruled** by the five Philistine kings,
7.15 Samuel **ruled** Israel as long as he lived.
8. 5 then, appoint a king to **rule** over us, so that we will
8.20 with our own king to **rule** us and to lead us out
9.16 anoint him as **ruler** of my people Israel, and he will rescue
9.17 He will **rule** my people."
10. 1 said, "The Lord anoints you as **ruler** of his people Israel.
10. 1 You will **rule** his people and protect them from all their enemies.
10. 1 the Lord has chosen you to be the **ruler** of his people:
11. 1 a treaty with us, and we will accept you as our **ruler."**
12. 1 given you a king to **rule** you, [2] and now you have him
12.12 king and said to me, 'We want a king to **rule** us.'
13.13 have let you and your descendants **rule** over Israel for ever.
13.14 But now your **rule** will not continue.
13.14 kind of man he wants and make him **ruler** of his people."

1 Sam 24.20 Israel and that the kingdom will continue under your **rule.**
30.25 David made this a **rule,** and it has been followed in
2 Sam 2.10 he was made king of Israel, and he **ruled** for two years.
2.11 loyal to David, [11]and he **ruled** in Hebron over Judah for
3.12 was at Hebron, to say, "Who is going to **rule** this land?
3.21 what you have wanted and will **rule** over the whole land."
5. 2 you that you would lead his people and be their **ruler."**
5. 4 years old when he became king, and he **ruled** for forty years.
5. 5 He **ruled** in Hebron over Judah for seven and a half years,
7. 8 in the fields and made you the **ruler** of my people Israel.
8. 8 bronze from Betah and Berothai, cities **ruled** by Hadadezer.
8.15 David **ruled** over all Israel and made sure that his
22.44 rebellious people and maintained my **rule** over the nations;
23. 3 "The king who **rules** with justice, who rules in obedience to God,
1 Kgs 1.35 one I have chosen to be the **ruler** of Israel and Judah."
2. 4 me that my descendants would **rule** Israel as long as they
2.11 of Israel for forty years, **ruling** seven years in Hebron and
3. 6 love by giving him a son who today **rules** in his place.
3. 7 even though I am very young and don't know how to **rule.**
3. 9 the wisdom I need to **rule** your people with justice and to
3. 9 would I ever be able to **rule** this great people of yours?"
3.11 asked for the wisdom to **rule** justly, instead of long life
4.19 of Gilead, which had been **ruled** by King Sihon of the
4.24 Solomon **ruled** over all the land west of the River Euphrates,
8.16 But I chose you, David, to **rule** my people.' "
8.25 be one of his descendants **ruling** as king of Israel, provided
9. 5 I told him that Israel would always be **ruled** by his descendants.
11.36 descendant of my servant David **ruling** in Jerusalem, the city
11.37 of Israel, and you will **rule** over all the territory that you
11.38 make sure that your descendants **rule** after you, just as I
14. 7 among the people and made you the **ruler** of my people Israel.
14. 9 You have committed far greater sins than those who **ruled** before you.
14.19 he fought and how he **ruled,** are all recorded in The History
14.20 Jeroboam **ruled** as king for twenty-two years.
14.21 of Judah, and he **ruled** for seventeen years in Jerusalem,
15. 2 king of Judah, [2]and he **ruled** for three years in Jerusalem.
15. 4 gave Abijah a son to **rule** after him in Jerusalem and to
15.10 of Judah, [10]and he **ruled** for forty-one years in Jerusalem.
15.25 son Nadab became king of Israel, and he **ruled** for two years.
15.33 of all Israel, and he **ruled** in Tirzah for twenty-four years.
16. 8 became king of Israel, and he **ruled** in Tirzah for two years.
16.15 King Asa of Judah, Zimri **ruled** in Tirzah over Israel for
16.23 Omri became king of Israel, and he **ruled** for twelve years.
16.23 The first six years he **ruled** in Tirzah, [24]and then he
16.29 of Israel, and he **ruled** in Samaria for twenty-two years.
18.10 Whenever the **ruler** of a country reported that you were not
18.10 country, Ahab would require that **ruler** to swear that you
20. 1 by thirty-two other **rulers** with their horses and chariots,
20.12 his allies, the other **rulers,** were drinking in their tents.
20.24 Now, remove the thirty-two **rulers** from their commands
22.42 and he **ruled** in Jerusalem for twenty-five years.
22.47 it was **ruled** by a deputy appointed by the king of Judah.
22.51 king of Israel, and he **ruled** in Samaria for two years.
2 Kgs 3. 1 king of Israel, and he **ruled** in Samaria for twelve years.
8.17 of thirty-two, and he **ruled** in Jerusalem for eight years.
8.19 David that his descendants would always continue to **rule.**
8.26 age of twenty-two, and he **ruled** in Jerusalem for one year.
10. 1 and sent copies to the **rulers** of the city, to the leading
10. 4 The **rulers** of Samaria were terrified.
10.36 Jehu had **ruled** in Samaria as king of Israel
11. 3 him hidden in the Temple, while Athaliah **ruled** as queen.
12. 1 king of Judah, and he **ruled** in Jerusalem for forty years.
13. 1 king of Israel, and he **ruled** in Samaria for seventeen years.
13.10 king of Israel, and he **ruled** in Samaria for sixteen years.
14. 2 and he **ruled** in Jerusalem for twenty-nine years.
14.23 king of Israel, and he **ruled** in Samaria for forty-one years.
15. 2 of sixteen, and he **ruled** in Jerusalem for fifty-two years.
15. 8 king of Israel, and he **ruled** in Samaria for six months.
15.13 king of Israel, and he **ruled** in Samaria for one month.
15.17 king of Israel, and he **ruled** in Samaria for ten years.
15.23 king of Israel, and he **ruled** in Samaria for two years.
15.27 king of Israel, and he **ruled** in Samaria for twenty years.
15.33 of twenty-five, and he **ruled** in Jerusalem for sixteen years.
16. 2 age of twenty, and he **ruled** in Jerusalem for sixteen years.
17. 1 king of Israel, and he **ruled** in Samaria for nine years.
17. 2 not as much as the kings who had **ruled** Israel before him.
18. 2 and he **ruled** in Jerusalem for twenty-nine years.
19.15 you alone are God, **ruling** all the kingdoms of the world.
20. 5 to go back to Hezekiah, **ruler** of the Lord's people, and
21. 1 of Judah, and he **ruled** in Jerusalem for fifty-five years.
21.19 king of Judah, and he **ruled** in Jerusalem for two years.
22. 1 of Judah, and he **ruled** in Jerusalem for thirty-one years.
23.22 Israel or of Judah, since the time when judges **ruled** the nation.
23.31 king of Judah, and he **ruled** in Jerusalem for three months.
23.36 king of Judah, and he **ruled** in Jerusalem for eleven years.
24. 1 for three years Jehoiakim was forced to submit to his **rule;**
24. 8 king of Judah, and he **ruled** in Jerusalem for three months.
24.18 king of Judah, and he **ruled** in Jerusalem for eleven years.
1 Chr 1.43 The following kings **ruled** the land of Edom one after the other,
2.22 Jair **ruled** twenty-three cities in the territory of Gilead.
3. 4 Hebron during the seven and a half years that David **ruled** there.
3. 4 In Jerusalem he **ruled** as king for thirty-three years, [5]and
5. 2 the strongest and provided a **ruler** for all the tribes.)
10. 6 all died together and none of his descendants ever **ruled.**
11. 2 you that you would lead his people and be their **ruler."**
16.33 will shout for joy when the Lord comes to **rule** the earth.
17. 7 in the fields and made you the **ruler** of my people Israel.
18. 8 of bronze from Tibhath and Kun, cities **ruled** by Hadadezer.
18.14 David **ruled** over all Israel and made sure that his
22. 9 have a son who will **rule** in peace, because I will give

1 Chr 22.10 His dynasty will **rule** Israel for ever.' "
23.31 **Rules** were made specifying the number of Levites assigned to
28. 4 Israel, chose me and my descendants to **rule** Israel for ever.
28. 5 he chose Solomon to **rule** over Israel, the Lord's kingdom.
29.11 earth is yours, and you are king, supreme **ruler** over all.
29.12 you **rule** everything by your strength and power;
29.22 Lord they anointed him as their **ruler** and Zadok as priest.
29.25 more glorious than any other king that had **ruled** Israel.
29.26 David son of Jesse **ruled** over all Israel [27]for forty years.
29.27 He **ruled** in Hebron for seven years
29.30 The records tell how he **ruled,** how powerful he was, and
2 Chr 1.10 give me the wisdom and knowledge I need to **rule** over them.
1.10 would I ever be able to **rule** this great people of yours?"
1.11 knowledge so that you can **rule** my people, over whom I have
1.13 There he **ruled** over Israel.
6. 6 I will be worshipped, and you, David, to **rule** my people.' "
6.16 be one of his descendants **ruling** as king of Israel, provided
7.18 I told him that Israel would always be **ruled** by his descendants.
8. 6 in Lebanon, and throughout the territory that he **ruled** over.
8.14 Following the **rules** laid down by his father David, he
9. 8 is with you by making you king, to **rule** in his name.
9.26 He was supreme **ruler** of all the kings in the territory
9.30 Solomon **ruled** in Jerusalem over all Israel for forty years.
11.17 as they had under the **rule** of King David and King Solomon.
12. 8 difference between serving me and serving earthly **rulers."**
12.13 Rehoboam **ruled** in Jerusalem and increased his power as king.
12.13 became king, and he **ruled** for seventeen years in Jerusalem,
13. 2 king of Judah, [2]and he **ruled** for three years in Jerusalem.
14. 5 cities of Judah, the kingdom was at peace under his **rule.**
20. 6 God of our ancestors, you **rule** in heaven over all the
20.30 enemies was terrified, [30]so Jehoshaphat **ruled** in peace,
20.31 and had **ruled** in Jerusalem for twenty-five years.
21. 5 of thirty-two, and he **ruled** in Jerusalem for eight years.
21. 7 promised that his descendants would always continue to **rule.**
21.20 of thirty-two and had **ruled** in Jerusalem for eight years.
22. 2 age of twenty-two, and he **ruled** in Jerusalem for one year.
22. 9 No member of Ahaziah's family was left who could **rule** the kingdom.
22.12 he remained there in hiding, while Athaliah **ruled** as queen.
24. 1 the age of seven, and he **ruled** in Jerusalem for forty years.
25. 1 and he **ruled** in Jerusalem for twenty-nine years.
26. 3 of sixteen, and he **ruled** in Jerusalem for fifty-two years.
27. 1 of twenty-five, and he **ruled** in Jerusalem for sixteen years.
27. 8 he became king, and he **ruled** in Jerusalem for sixteen years.
28. 1 age of twenty, and he **ruled** in Jerusalem for sixteen years.
29. 1 and he **ruled** in Jerusalem for twenty-nine years.
33. 1 of Judah, and he **ruled** in Jerusalem for fifty-five years.
33.13 it by letting him go back to Jerusalem and **rule** again.
33.21 king of Judah, and he **ruled** in Jerusalem for two years.
34. 1 of Judah, and he **ruled** in Jerusalem for thirty-one years.
36. 2 king of Judah, and he **ruled** in Jerusalem for three months.
36. 5 king of Judah, and he **ruled** in Jerusalem for eleven years.
36. 9 king of Judah, and he **ruled** in Jerusalem for three months
36.11 king of Judah, and he **ruled** in Jerusalem for eleven years.
36.23 of Heaven, has made me **ruler** over the whole world and has
Ezra 1. 2 of Heaven, has made me **ruler** over the whole world and has
4.15 it has given trouble to kings and to **rulers** of provinces.
4.20 have reigned there and have **ruled** over the entire province
5. 7 "To Emperor Darius, may you **rule** in peace.
Neh 3. 9 Rephaiah son of Hur, **ruler** of half the Jerusalem District,
3.12 Shallum son of Hallohesh, **ruler** of the other half of the
3.14 Malchijah son of Rechab, **ruler** of the Beth Haccherem District,
3.15 Shallum son of Colhozeh, **ruler** of the Mizpah District,
3.16 Nehemiah son of Azbuk, **ruler** of half the Bethzur District,
3.17 Hashabiah, **ruler** of half the Keilah District, built the
3.18 Bavvai son of Henadad, **ruler** of the other half of the
3.19 Ezer son of Jeshua, **ruler** of Mizpah, built the next
9.22 land of Heshbon, where Sihon **ruled,** and the land of Bashan,
9.27 time, [27]so you let their enemies conquer and **rule** them.
9.35 With your blessing, kings **ruled** your people when they
Esth 1. 1 city of Susa, King Xerxes **ruled** over 127 provinces, all the
3. 7 twelfth year of King Xerxes' **rule,** in the first month, the
3.12 empire and to be sent to all the **rulers,** governors, and
9.27 the Jews made it a **rule** for themselves, their descendants,
9.31 just as they had adopted **rules** for the observance of fasts
9.32 Esther's command, confirming the **rules** for Purim, was
Job 3.14 sleeping like the kings and **rulers** who rebuilt ancient palaces.
12.17 away the wisdom of **rulers** and makes leaders act like fools.
12.21 those in power and puts an end to the strength of **rulers.**
34.18 God condemns kings and **rulers** when they are worthless or wicked.
34.19 not take the side of **rulers** nor favour the rich against the
34.30 could do to keep godless oppressors from **ruling** them.
36. 7 he allows them to **rule** like kings and lets them be
Ps 2. 2 Their kings revolt, their **rulers** plot together against the
2. 3 "Let us free ourselves from their **rule,"** they say;
2.10 learn this lesson, you **rulers** of the world:
7. 7 all the peoples round you, and **rule** over them from above.
8. 6 You appointed him **ruler** over everything you made;
9. 8 He **rules** the world with righteousness;
9.11 Sing praise to the Lord, who **rules** in Zion!
18.43 a rebellious people and made me **ruler** over the nations;
19.13 don't let them **rule** over me.
22.28 The Lord is king, and he **rules** the nations.
29.10 The Lord **rules** over the deep waters;
29.10 he **rules** as king for ever.
33.14 From where he **rules,** he looks down on all who live on
45. 6 You **rule** over your people with justice;
45.16 kings, and you will make them **rulers** over the whole earth.
47. 2 he is a great king, **ruling** over all the world.
47. 3 he made us **rule** over the nations.

Ps	47. 8	he **rules** over the nations.
	47. 9	The **rulers** of the nations assemble with the people of the
	47. 9	he **rules** supreme.
	48.10	You **rule** with justice;
	55.19	God, who has **ruled** from eternity, will hear me and defeat them;
	58. 1	Do you **rulers** ever give a just decision?
	59.13	everyone will know that God **rules** in Israel,
	59.13	that his **rule** extends over all the earth.
	61. 7	May he **rule** for ever in your presence, O God;
	66. 7	He **rules** for ever by his might and keeps his eyes on
	72. 2	justice, [2]so that he will **rule** over your people with
	82. 8	Come, O God, and **rule** the world;
	83.11	defeat all their **rulers** as you did Zebah and Zalmunna,
	83.18	you alone are the Lord, supreme **ruler** over all the earth.
	89. 9	You **rule** over the powerful sea;
	93. 4	The Lord **rules** supreme in heaven, greater than the roar of
	95. 4	He **rules** over the whole earth, from the deepest caves to
	95. 5	He **rules** over the sea, which he made;
	96.13	shout for joy [13]when the Lord comes to **rule** the earth.
	96.13	He will **rule** the peoples of the world with justice and fairness.
	97. 2	he **rules** with righteousness and justice.
	97. 9	Lord Almighty, you are **ruler** of all the earth;
	98. 9	joy before the Lord, [9]because he comes to **rule** the earth.
	98. 9	He will **rule** the peoples of the world with justice and fairness.
	103.22	Praise the Lord, all his creatures in all the places he **rules.**
	105.20	the **ruler** of nations set him free.
	105.21	his government and made him **ruler** over all the land,
	106.41	power of the heathen, and their enemies **ruled** over them.
	110. 2	**"Rule** over your enemies," he says.
	113. 4	The Lord **rules** over all nations;
	119.23	The **rulers** meet and plot against me, but I will study
	119.138	The **rules** that you have given are completely fair and right.
	123. 1	Lord, I look up to you, up to heaven, where you **rule.**
	125. 3	The wicked will not always **rule** over the land of the righteous;
	132.11	make one of your sons king, and he will **rule** after you.
	132.14	this is where I want to **rule.**
	132.17	here I will preserve the **rule** of my chosen king.
	136. 8	the sun to **rule** over the day;
	136. 9	the moon and the stars to **rule** over the night;
	141. 6	When their **rulers** are thrown down from rocky cliffs, the
	145.13	Your **rule** is eternal, and you are king for ever.
	148.11	Praise him, kings and all peoples, princes and all other **rulers;**
Prov	6. 7	have no leader, chief, or **ruler,** [8]but they store up their
	8.15	I help kings to govern and **rulers** to make good laws.
	8.16	Every **ruler** on earth governs with my help,
	14.28	A king's greatness depends on how many people he **rules;**
	19.10	live in luxury, and slaves should not **rule** over noblemen.
	20.28	in power as long as his **rule** is honest, just, and fair.
	25.15	down the strongest resistance and can even convince **rulers.**
	28. 2	When a nation sins, it will have one **ruler** after another.
	28.12	celebrates, but when bad men **rule,** people stay in hiding.
	28.15	Poor people are helpless against a wicked **ruler;**
	28.16	A **ruler** without good sense will be a cruel tyrant.
	28.16	One who hates dishonesty will **rule** a long time.
	28.28	But when they fall from power, righteous men will **rule** again.
	29. 2	Show me a righteous **ruler** and I will show you a happy
	29. 2	Show me a wicked **ruler** and I will show you a miserable
	29.12	If a **ruler** pays attention to false information, all his
	29.14	the rights of the poor, he will **rule** for a long time.
	29.26	the good will of the **ruler,** but only from the Lord can
Ecc	1.16	man, far wiser than anyone who **ruled** Jerusalem before me.
	2. 8	and gold from the royal treasuries of the lands I **ruled.**
	4.16	may be no limit to the number of people a king **rules;**
	7.19	more for a person than ten **rulers** can do for a city.
	9.17	than to the shouts of a **ruler** at a council of fools.
	10. 4	If your **ruler** becomes angry with you, do not hand in your
	10. 5	I have seen in the world—an injustice caused by **rulers.**
Is	1.10	Jerusalem, your **rulers** and your people are like those of
	1.26	I will give you **rulers** and advisers like those you had
	7. 1	son of Jotham and grandson of Uzziah, **ruled** Judah, war broke
	9. 6	And he will be our **ruler.**
	9. 7	He will **rule** as King David's successor, basing his power on
	11. 2	him wisdom, and the knowledge and skill to **rule** his people.
	11. 5	He will **rule** his people with justice and integrity.
	14. 2	of Israel will **rule** over those who once oppressed them.
	14. 5	the power of the evil **rulers** [6]who angrily oppressed the
	14.21	None of them will ever **rule** the earth or cover it with
	16. 1	a lamb as a present to the one who **rules** in Jerusalem.
	16. 5	and he will **rule** the people with faithfulness and love.
	16. 8	whose wine used to make the **rulers** of the nations drunk.
	19. 4	over to a tyrant, to a cruel king who will **rule** them.
	24.21	Lord will punish the powers above and the **rulers** of the earth.
	24.23	He will **rule** in Jerusalem on Mount Zion, and the leaders of
	26.13	our God, we have been **ruled** by others, but you alone are
	28.14	Now you arrogant men who **rule** here in Jerusalem over this people,
	29.13	religion is nothing but human **rules** and traditions, which
	30. 1	"Those who **rule** Judah are doomed because they rebel against me.
	32. 1	will be a king who **rules** with integrity, and national
	33. 5	He **rules** over everything.
	33.17	you will see a king **ruling** in splendour over a land that
	33.22	he will **rule** over us and protect us.
	34.12	will be no king to **rule** the country, and the leaders will
	37.16	you alone are God, **ruling** all the kingdoms of the world.
	40.10	Sovereign Lord is coming to **rule** with power, bringing with
	40.23	He brings down powerful **rulers** and reduces them to nothing.
	41.25	He tramples on **rulers** as if they were mud, like a potter
	43.28	and your **rulers** profaned my sanctuary.
	44. 6	The Lord, who **rules** and protects Israel, the Lord Almighty,
	44.28	say to Cyrus, 'You are the one who will **rule** for me;
Is	49. 7	who is hated by the nations and is the servant of **rulers:**
	51. 5	I myself will **rule** over the nations.
	52. 5	Those who **rule** over you boast and brag and constantly show
	54. 5	will save you— he is the **ruler** of all the world.
	60.17	Your **rulers** will no longer oppress you;
	60.17	I will make them **rule** with justice and peace.
	63.19	you had never been our **ruler,** as though we had never been
Jer	2. 8	The **rulers** rebelled against me;
	3.15	I will give you **rulers** who obey me,
	3.15	and they will **rule** you with wisdom and understanding.
	5.31	**rule** as the prophets command, and my people offer no objections.
	8. 7	people, you do not know the laws by which I **rule** you.
	9. 3	dishonesty instead of truth **rules** the land.
	12.10	Many foreign **rulers** have destroyed my vineyard;
	13.21	thought were your friends conquer you and **rule** over you?
	22.30	descendants who will **rule** in Judah as David's successors.
	23. 1	judgement on those **rulers** who destroy and scatter his people!
	23. 2	of Israel, says about the **rulers** who were supposed to take
	23. 4	I will appoint **rulers** to take care of them.
	23. 5	That king will **rule** wisely and do what is right and just
	27. 8	will not submit to his **rule,** then I will punish that nation
	29.16	says about the king who **rules** the kingdom that David ruled
	30.21	Their **ruler** will come from their own nation, their
	33.26	David's descendants to **rule** over the descendants of Abraham,
	36.30	no descendant of yours will ever **rule** over David's kingdom.
	48.17	Say, 'Its powerful **rule** has been broken;
	48.45	the city that King Sihon once **ruled,** but it is in flames.
	49.19	Then the leader I choose will **rule** the nation.
	49.19	What **ruler** could oppose me?
	50.35	Death to its people, to its **rulers,** to its men of wisdom.
	50.44	Then the leader I choose will **rule** the nation.
	50.44	What **ruler** could oppose me?
	51.23	and their horses, to crush **rulers** and high officials."
	51.57	I will make its **rulers** drunk— men of wisdom, leaders,
	52. 1	king of Judah, and he **ruled** in Jerusalem for eleven years.
Lam	2. 2	He brought disgrace on the kingdom and its **rulers.**
	4.12	No one anywhere, not even **rulers** of foreign nations,
	5. 8	We are **ruled** by men who are no better than slaves, and
	5.19	are king for ever, and will **rule** to the end of time.
Ezek	12.10	message is for the prince **ruling** in Jerusalem and for all
	12.12	The prince who is **ruling** them will shoulder his pack in
	20.33	in my anger I will **rule** over you with a strong hand,
	21.25	"You wicked, unholy **ruler** of Israel, your day, the day
	21.26	Bring down those who are **ruling!**
	26.17	The people of this city **ruled** the seas And terrified all who
	27.21	The Arabians and the **rulers** of the land of Kedar paid
	28. 2	man," he said, "tell the **ruler** of Tyre what I, the
	29.15	of all, and they will never again **rule** over other nations.
	30.13	will be no one to **rule** over Egypt, and I will terrify
	31.11	I have rejected it and will let a foreign **ruler** have it.
	32.29	"Edom is there with her kings and **rulers.**
	34. 2	"Mortal man," he said, "denounce the **rulers** of Israel.
	34.24	God, and a king like my servant David will be their **ruler.**
	37.22	will have one king to **rule** over them, and they will no
	37.24	be united under one **ruler** and will obey my laws faithfully.
	37.25	A king like my servant David will **rule** over them for ever.
	38. 2	he said, "denounce Gog, chief **ruler** of the nations of
	39. 1	man, denounce Gog, the chief **ruler** of the nations of Meshech
	39.18	drink the blood of the **rulers** of the earth, all of whom
	43. 7	here among the people of Israel and **rule** over them for ever.
	43.11	of everything, and all its **rules** and regulations.
	43.11	how everything is arranged and can carry out all the **rules.**
	44. 3	The **ruling** prince, however, may go there to eat a holy
	44. 5	going to tell you the **rules** and regulations for the Temple.
	44.24	religious festivals according to my **rules** and regulations,
	45. 7	Land is also to be set aside for the **ruling** prince.
	45. 8	will be the share the **ruling** prince will have in the land
	45. 9	"You have sinned too long, you **rulers** of Israel!
	45.16	must take these offerings to the **ruling** prince of Israel.
	45.22	day of the festival the **ruling** prince must offer a bull as
	46. 2	The **ruling** prince will go from the outer courtyard into
	46.12	"When the **ruling** prince wants to make a voluntary
	46.14	The **rules** for this offering to the Lord are to be in
	46.16	"If the **ruling** prince gives any of the land he owns to
	46.17	But if the **ruling** prince gives any of his land to anyone
	46.18	The **ruling** prince must not take any of the people's
	48.21	the city, the remaining land belongs to the **ruling** prince.
Dan	2.38	He has made you **ruler** of all the inhabited earth
	2.38	and **ruler** over all the animals and birds.
	2.39	third, an empire of bronze, which will **rule** the whole earth.
	2.43	This means that the **rulers** of that empire will try to unite
	2.44	At the time of those **rulers** the God of heaven will
	4. 3	he will **rule** for all time.
	4.26	again when you acknowledge that God **rules** all the world.
	4.34	"He will **rule** for ever, and his kingdom will last for all
	6.26	"He is a living God, and he will **rule** for ever.
	7.24	The ten horns are ten kings who will **rule** that empire.
	7.27	will never end and all **rulers** on earth will serve and obey
	9. 1	was the son of Xerxes, **ruled** over the kingdom of Babylonia.
	9. 6	our kings, our **rulers,** our ancestors, and our whole nation.
	9. 8	Our kings, our **rulers,** and our ancestors have acted
	9.12	did what you said you would do to us and our **rulers.**
	9.26	Temple will be destroyed by the invading army of a powerful **ruler.**
	9.27	That **ruler** will have a firm agreement with many people
	11. 2	"Three more kings will **rule** over Persia, followed by a fourth,
	11. 3	He will **rule** over a huge empire and do whatever he wants.
	11. 4	not descended from him will **rule** in his place, but they will
	11. 5	however, will be even stronger and **rule** a greater kingdom.
	11.23	and stronger, even though he **rules** only a small nation.
	11.39	those who accept him as **ruler,** put them into high offices,

Hos 7. 7 "In the heat of their anger they murdered their **rulers.**
11. 5 so they must return to Egypt, and Assyria will **rule** them.
Amos 1. 5 inhabitants of the Valley of Aven and the **ruler** of Betheden.
1. 8 I will remove the **rulers** of the cities of Ashdod and Ashkelon.
2. 3 I will kill the **ruler** of Moab and all the leaders of
Obad 21 The victorious men of Jerusalem will attack Edom and **rule** over it.
Mic 3. 1 Listen, you **rulers** of Israel!
3. 9 Listen to me, you **rulers** of Israel, you that hate justice
3.11 The city's **rulers** govern for bribes, the priests
4. 7 I will **rule** over them on Mount Zion from that time on
5. 2 you I will bring a **ruler** for Israel, whose family line goes
5. 4 When he comes, he will **rule** his people with the strength
Nah 3. 9 She **ruled** Sudan and Egypt, there was no limit to her power;
Hab 1.14 like a swarm of insects that have no **ruler** to direct them?
Hag 2.11 He said, "Ask the priests for a **ruling** on this question:
2.23 my servant, and I will appoint you to **rule** in my name.
Zech 6.13 the honour due to a king, and he will **rule** his people.
8. 8 I will be their God, **ruling** over them faithfully and justly.
9.10 he will **rule** from sea to sea, from the River Euphrates to
10. 3 angry with those foreigners who **rule** my people, and I am
10. 4 From among them will come **rulers,** leaders, and commanders
11. 3 The **rulers** cry out in grief;
11. 6 myself will put all the people in the power of their **rulers.**
11. 6 Those **rulers** will devastate the earth, and I will not save
Mt 7. 2 he will apply to you the same **rules** you apply to others.
10.18 be brought to trial before **rulers** and kings, to tell the
12.24 out demons only because their **ruler** Beelzebul gives him power to
14. 1 At that time Herod, the **ruler** of Galilee, heard about Jesus.
15. 9 because they teach man-made **rules** as though they were my laws!' "
19.28 also sit on thrones, to **rule** the twelve tribes of Israel.
20.25 said, "You know that the **rulers** of the heathen have power
Mk 4.24 The same **rules** you use to judge others will be used by
7. 4 And they follow many other **rules** which they have received,
7. 7 because they teach man-made **rules** as though they were God's laws!'
10.42 the men who are considered **rulers** of the heathen have power
13. 9 you will stand before **rulers** and kings for my sake to tell
Lk 3. 1 It was the fifteenth year of the **rule** of the Emperor Tiberius;
3. 1 governor of Judaea, Herod was **ruler** of Galilee,
3. 1 and his brother Philip was **ruler** of the territory of Iturea
3. 1 Lysanias was **ruler** of Abilene, [2]and Annas and Caiaphas were high
9. 7 When Herod, the **ruler** of Galilee, heard about all the things
12.11 synagogues or before governors or **rulers,** do not be worried about
21.12 you will be brought before kings and **rulers** for my sake.
22.25 over their people, and the **rulers** claim the title 'Friends
22.29 given me the right to **rule,** so I will give you the
22.30 sit on thrones to **rule** over the twelve tribes of Israel.
22.53 is your hour to act, when the power of darkness **rules."**
23. 7 Jesus was from the region **ruled** by Herod, he sent him to
24.20 Our chief priests and **rulers** handed him over to be sentenced
Jn 2. 6 The Jews have **rules** about ritual washing, and for this purpose
12.31 now the **ruler** of this world will be overthrown.
14.30 you much longer, because the **ruler** of this world is coming.
16.11 wrong about judgement, because the **ruler** of this world has already
Acts 4.26 prepared themselves, and the **rulers** met together against the Lord
7.18 king who did not know about Joseph began to **rule** in Egypt.
7.27 'Who made you **ruler** and judge over us?'
7.35 'Who made you **ruler** and judge over us?'
7.35 one whom God sent to **rule** the people and set them free
15.28 put any other burden on you besides these necessary **rules:**
16. 4 delivered to the believers the **rules** decided upon by the apostles
16. 4 and elders in Jerusalem, and told them to obey those **rules.**
23. 5 'You must not speak evil of the **ruler** of your people.' "
Rom 5.14 the time of Moses death **ruled** over all mankind, even over
5.17 of one man death began to **rule** because of that one man.
5.17 freely put right with him will **rule** in life through Christ.
5.21 So then, just as sin **ruled** by means of death,
5.21 so also God's grace **rules** by means of righteousness, leading us
6. 9 and will never die again—death will no longer **rule** over him.
6.12 Sin must no longer **rule** in your mortal bodies, so that
7. 1 The law **rules** over people only as long as they live.
8.38 neither angels nor other heavenly **rulers** or powers,
9. 1 My conscience, **ruled** by the Holy Spirit, also assures me
9. 5 May God, who **rules** over all, be praised for ever!
13. 3 For **rulers** are not to be feared by those who do good,
15.12 he will come to **rule** the Gentiles, and they will put their
1 Cor 2. 6 or to the powers that **rule** this world—powers that are losing
2. 8 None of the **rulers** of this world knew this wisdom.
4. 6 you may learn what the saying means, "Observe the proper **rules."**
7.17 This is the **rule** I teach in all the churches.
15.24 Christ will overcome all spiritual **rulers,** authorities,
15.25 Christ must **rule** until God defeats all enemies and puts them
15.28 have been placed under Christ's **rule,** then he himself, the Son,
15.28 and God will **rule** completely over all.
2 Cor 1.12 relations with you, have been **ruled** by God-given frankness and
5.14 We are **ruled** by the love of Christ, now that we
8. 8 I am not laying down any **rules.**
Gal 4. 3 too were slaves of the **ruling spirits** of the universe before
4. 9 want to turn back to those weak and pitiful **ruling spirits?**
6.16 for those who follow this **rule** in their lives, may peace
Eph 1.21 Christ **rules** there above all heavenly rulers, authorities, powers,
2. 2 you obeyed the **ruler** of the spiritual powers in space,
2. 6 us up with him to **rule** with him in the heavenly world.
2.15 Law with its commandments and **rules,** in order to create out
3.10 the church, the angelic **rulers** and powers in the heavenly world
Eph 6.12 in the heavenly world, the **rulers,** authorities, and cosmic powers
Phil 3.16 according to the same **rules** we have followed until now.
3.21 by which he is able to bring all things under his **rule.**
Col 1.16 and the unseen things, including spiritual powers, lords, **rulers,**
2. 8 by men and from the **ruling spirits** of the universe, and not
2.10 He is supreme over every spiritual **ruler** and authority.
2.14 our debts with its binding **rules** and did away with it
2.15 Christ freed himself from the power of the spiritual **rulers** and
2.16 So let no one make **rules** about what you eat or drink
2.20 Christ and are set free from the **ruling spirits** of the universe.
2.20 Why do you obey such **rules** as [21]"Don't handle this,"
2.22 they are only man-made **rules** and teachings.
2.23 Of course such **rules** appear to be based on wisdom in
1 Tim 6.15 God, the blessed and only **Ruler,** the King of kings and the
2 Tim 2. 5 in a race cannot win the prize unless he obeys the **rules.**
2.12 If we continue to endure, we shall also **rule** with him.
4. 1 because he is coming to **rule** as King, I solemnly urge you
Tit 3. 1 your people to submit to **rulers** and authorities, to obey them,
Heb 1. 8 You **rule** over your people with justice.
2. 5 not placed the angels as **rulers** over the new world to come
2. 8 glory and honour, [8]and made him **ruler** over all things."
2. 8 It says that God made man **"ruler** over all things";
2. 8 We do not, however, see man **ruling** over all things now.
7.16 priest, not by human **rules** and regulations, but through the power
7.18 The old **rule,** then, is set aside, because it was weak
9. 1 The first covenant had **rules** for worship and a man-made place
9.10 These are all outward **rules,** which apply only until the time
13. 9 strength from God's grace, and not by obeying **rules** about foods;
13. 9 those who obey these **rules** have not been helped by them.
1 Pet 3.22 the right-hand side of God, **ruling** over all angels and heavenly
5. 3 Do not try to **rule** over those who have been put in
1 Jn 5.19 though the whole world is under the **rule** of the Evil One.
Rev 1. 5 and who is also the **ruler** of the kings of the world.
2.26 authority over the nations, to **rule** them with an iron rod
5.10 of priests to serve our God, and they shall **rule** on earth."
6.15 kings of the earth, the **rulers** and the military chiefs, the
9.11 They have a king **ruling** over them, who is the angel in
11.15 heaven, saying, "The power to **rule** over the world belongs
11.15 Lord and his Messiah, and he will **rule** for ever and ever!"
11.17 you have taken your great power and have begun to **rule!**
12. 5 to a son, who will **rule** over all nations with an iron
17.10 them have fallen, one still **rules,** and the other one has not
17.10 when he comes, he must **rule** only a little while.
17.12 have not yet begun to **rule,** but who
17.12 will be given authority to **rule** as kings for one hour with
17.17 the beast their power to **rule** until God's words come true.
17.18 is the great city that **rules** over the kings of the earth."
19.15 He will **rule** over them with a rod of iron, and he
20. 4 They came to life and **ruled** as kings with Christ
20. 6 Christ, and they will **rule** with him for a thousand years.
22. 5 their light, and they will **rule** as kings for ever and ever.

RUMBLE

Jer 47. 3 of horses, the clatter of chariots, the **rumble** of wheels.
Rev 4. 5 From the throne came flashes of lightning, **rumblings,** and peals
8. 5 There were **rumblings** and peals of thunder, flashes of lightning,
11.19 there were flashes of lightning, **rumblings** and peals of thunder,
16.18 There were flashes of lightning, **rumblings** and peals of thunder,

RUMOUR

Ex 23. 1 "Do not spread false **rumours,** and do not help a guilty
Deut 13.14 If you hear such a **rumour,** investigate it thoroughly;
2 Kgs 19. 7 the emperor to hear a **rumour** that will make him go back
Neh 6. 6 "Geshem tells me that a **rumour** is going round among the
Job 28.22 Even death and destruction Admit they have heard only **rumours.**
Ps 15. 3 to his friends nor spreads **rumours** about his neighbours.
Is 37. 7 the emperor to hear a **rumour** that will make him go back
Jer 51.46 lose courage or be afraid because of the **rumours** you hear.
51.46 Every year a different **rumour** spreads—
51.46 **rumours** of violence in the land

RUN

[RAN]

Gen 14.10 Sodom and Gomorrah tried to **run** away from the battle, they
16. 6 Then Sarai treated Hagar so cruelly that she **ran** away.
16. 8 She answered, "I am **running** away from my mistress."
18. 2 As soon as he saw them, he **ran** out to meet them.
18. 7 Then he **ran** to the herd and picked out a calf that
19.17 Then one of the angels said, **"Run** for your lives!
19.17 **Run** to the hills, so that you won't be killed."
19.22 **Run!**
24.17 The servant **ran** to meet her and said, "Please give me a
24.20 into the animals' drinking-trough and **ran** to the well to get
24.28 The girl **ran** to her mother's house and told the whole story.
24.29 brother named Laban, and he **ran** outside to go to the well
29.12 She **ran** to tell her father;
29.13 about his nephew Jacob, he **ran** to meet him, hugged him and
33. 4 But Esau **ran** to meet him, threw his arms round him, and
35. 1 to you when you were **running** away from your brother Esau."
35. 7 to him there when he was **running** away from his brother.
39.12 But he escaped and **ran** outside, leaving his robe in her hand.
39.13 left his robe and had **run** out of the house, [14]she called
39.15 me scream, he **ran** outside, leaving his robe beside me."
39.18 when I screamed, he **ran** outside, leaving his robe beside me."
49.21 "Naphtali is a deer that **runs** free, Who bears lovely fawns.
Ex 4. 3 down, it turned into a snake, and he **ran** away from it.
21.14 to death, even if he has **run** to my altar for safety.
23. 4 enemy's cow or donkey **running** loose, take it back to him.

Ex 23.27 and I will make all your enemies turn and **run** from you.
Lev 15. 3 is unclean, [3]whether the penis **runs** with it or is stopped
22.22 mutilated, or that has a **running** sore or a skin eruption or
26.17 so terrified that you will **run** when no one is chasing you.
26.36 sound of a leaf blowing in the wind will make you **run.**
26.36 You will **run** as if you were being pursued in battle, and
Num 11.27 A young man **ran** out to tell Moses what Eldad and Medad
16.34 They shouted, **"Run!**
16.47 obeyed, took his firepan and **ran** into the middle of the
Deut 19. 5 kills the other, he can **run** to one of those three cities
21. 4 near a stream that never **runs** dry and where the ground has
22. 1 cow or sheep **running** loose, do not ignore it;
23.15 "If a slave **runs** away from his owner and comes to you
28. 7 direction, but they will **run** from you in all directions.
28.25 one direction, but you will **run** from them in all directions,
32.38 let them **run** to your rescue.
Josh 7.22 Joshua sent some men, who **ran** to the tent and found that
8. 5 us, we will turn and **run,** just as we did the first
8. 6 will think that we are **running** away from them, as we did
8.15 were retreating, and **ran** away towards the barren country.
8.19 hiding got up quickly, **ran** into the city and captured it.
8.20 because the Israelites who had **run** towards the barren
10.11 While the Amorites were **running** down the pass
15. 2 This southern border **ran** from the south end of the Dead Sea,
15. 3 It **ran** south of Kadesh Barnea, past Hezron and up to Addar,
16. 5 border **ran** from Ataroth Addar eastwards to Upper Beth Horon,
20. 4 He can **run** away to one of these cities, go to the
20. 6 back home to his own town, from which he had **run** away."
23.10 can make a thousand men **run** away, because the Lord your God
Judg 1. 6 He **ran** away, but they chased him, caught him, and cut off
1.36 North of Sela, the Edomite border **ran** through Akrabbim Pass.
4.17 Sisera **ran** away to the tent of Jael, the wife of Heber
7.21 round the camp, and the whole enemy army **ran** away yelling.
7.22 They **ran** towards Zerethan as far as Beth Shittah, as far as
8.12 Midianite kings, Zebah and Zalmunna, **ran** away, but he
9.21 of his brother Abimelech, Jotham **ran** away and went to live
9.51 man and woman in the city, including the leaders, **ran** to it.
9.54 So the young man **ran** him through, and he died.
13.10 not with her, [10]so she **ran** at once and said to him,
15.14 the Philistines came **running** towards him, shouting at him.
20.37 These men **ran** quickly towards Gibeah;
20.42 from the Israelites and **ran** towards the open country,
20.45 The others turned and **ran** towards the open country to
1 Sam 3. 5 and **ran** to Eli and said, "You called me, and here I
4.10 defeated the Israelites, who went **running** to their homes.
4.12 from the tribe of Benjamin **ran** all the way from the
4.16 from the battle and have **run** all the way here today."
4.17 The messenger answered, "Israel **ran** away from the Philistines;
8.11 in his cavalry, and others will **run** before his chariots.
10.23 So they **ran** and brought Saul out to the people, and
11.11 The survivors scattered, each man **running** off by himself.
14.16 saw the Philistines **running** in confusion.
14.22 heard that the Philistines were **running** away, so they also
17.22 in charge of the supplies, **ran** to the battle line, went to
17.24 When the Israelites saw Goliath, they **ran** away in terror.
17.48 towards David again, and David **ran** quickly towards the
17.51 He **ran** to him, stood over him, took Goliath's sword out
17.51 the Philistines saw that their hero was dead, they **ran** away.
17.52 Israel and Judah shouted and **ran** after them, pursuing them
19.10 David **ran** away and escaped.
19.12 let him down from a window, and he **ran** away and escaped.
20.36 him [36]and said to him, **"Run** and find the arrows I'm going
20.36 The boy **ran,** and Jonathan shot an arrow beyond him.
22.17 tell me that he had **run** away, even though they knew it
25.10 The country is full of **runaway** slaves nowadays!
2 Sam 1. 4 "Our army **ran** away from the battle," he replied, "and
2.18 Asahel, who could **run** as fast as a wild deer, [19]started
2.19 deer, [19]started chasing Abner, **running** straight for him.
2.21 **"Run** after one of the soldiers and take what he has."
10.14 the Ammonites saw the Syrians **running** away, they fled from
17. 2 He will be frightened, and all his men will **run** away.
18. 3 rest of us turn and **run,** or even if half of us
18. 9 The mule **ran** on and Absalom was left hanging in mid air.
18.19 said to Joab, "Let me **run** to the king with the good
18.21 The slave bowed and **ran** off.
18.23 So Ahimaaz **ran** off down the road through the Jordan Valley,
18.24 he looked out and saw a man **running** alone.
18.25 The **runner** came nearer and nearer.
18.26 the watchman saw another man **running** alone, and he called
18.26 There's another man **running!"**
18.27 said, "I can see that the first man **runs** like Ahimaaz."
19. 3 who are ashamed because they are **running** away from battle.
22.15 with flashes of lightning he sent them **running.**
22.41 You make my enemies **run** from me;
24.13 land or three months of **running** away from your enemies or
1 Kgs 2.39 two of Shimei's slaves **ran** away to the king of Gath,
17.14 'The bowl will not **run** out of flour
17.14 or the jar **run** out of oil before the day
17.16 the bowl did not **run** out of flour
17.16 nor did the jar **run** out of oil.
18.35 The water **ran** down round the altar and filled the trench.
18.46 tight round his waist and **ran** ahead of Ahab all the way
19.20 Elisha then left his oxen, **ran** after Elijah, and said,
22.35 The blood from his wound **ran** down and covered the bottom of
2 Kgs 3. 9 marching for seven days, they **ran** out of water, and there
5.20 the living Lord, I will **run** after him and get something from
5.21 When Naaman saw a man **running** after him, he got down from
13.21 the people threw the corpse into Elisha's tomb and **ran** off.
1 Chr 10. 7 his sons had died, they abandoned their towns and **ran** off.
11.13 when the Israelites started to **run** away, [14]so he and his
19.15 the Ammonites saw the Syrians **running** away, they fled from

1 Chr 21.12 Or three months of **running** away from the armies of your enemies?
21.20 wheat, and when they saw the angel, the sons **ran** and hid.
Ezra 8.15 group by the canal that **runs** to the town of Ahava, and
Neh 6.11 I answered, "I'm not the kind of man that **runs** and hides.
Esth 3.13 **Runners** took this proclamation to every province of the empire.
3.15 city of Susa, and **runners** carried the news to the provinces.
Job 1.14 their eldest brother, [14]a messenger came **running** to Job.
7. 5 pus **runs** out of my sores.
14.11 Like rivers that stop **running,** and lakes that go dry,
21.11 Their children **run** and play like lambs [12]and dance to
24. 4 getting their rights and force the needy to **run** and hide.
27.23 them as they **run,** frightening them with destructive power.
30.12 they send me **running;**
39.18 But when she begins to **run,** she can laugh at any horse
41.28 There is no arrow that can make him **run;**
Ps 18.14 with flashes of lightning he sent them **running.**
18.40 You make my enemies **run** from me;
19. 5 a happy bridegroom, like an athlete eager to **run** a race.
21.12 will shoot his arrows at them and make them turn and **run.**
31.11 when they see me in the street, they **run** away.
36.11 let proud men attack me or wicked men make me **run** away.
44.10 You made us **run** from our enemies, and they took for
48. 5 they were afraid and **ran** away.
68. 1 Those who hate him **run** away in defeat.
68.12 "Kings and their armies are **running** away!"
78. 9 armed with bows and arrows, **ran** away on the day of battle.
104.10 flow in the valleys, and rivers **run** between the hills.
112. 5 is generous with his loans, who **runs** his business honestly.
114. 3 The Red Sea looked and **ran** away;
114. 5 What happened, Sea, to make you **run** away?
133. 2 anointing oil **running** down from Aaron's head and beard,
144. 6 shoot your arrows and send them **running.**
Prov 4.12 if you walk wisely, and you will not stumble when you **run.**
28. 1 The wicked **run** when no one is chasing them, but an honest
Ecc 9.11 that in this world fast **runners** do not always win the race,
Song 1. 4 Take me with you, and we'll **run** away;
2. 8 He comes **running** over the mountains, racing across the hills to me.
7. 2 A bowl is there, that never **runs** out of spiced wine.
Is 10. 3 Where will you **run** to find help?
10.29 and the people in King Saul's town of Gibeah have **run** away.
10.31 The people of Madmenah and Gebim are **running** for their lives.
13.14 living in Babylon will **run** away to their own countries,
22. 3 All your leaders **ran** away and were captured before they
30.13 You are like a high wall with a crack **running** down it;
30.17 A thousand of you will **run** away when you see one enemy
30.17 and five soldiers will be enough to make you all **run** away.
31. 8 The Assyrians will **run** from battle, and their young men will
31. 9 Their emperor will **run** away in terror, and the officers
33. 3 you fight for us, nations **run** away from the noise of battle.
40.31 they will **run** and not get weary;
41.18 among barren hills and springs of water **run** in the valleys.
44. 4 grass, like willows by streams of **running** water.
55. 5 not know you, but now they will come **running** to join you!
58.11 plenty of water, like a spring of water that never **runs** dry.
Jer 2.23 on heat, **running** about loose, [24]rushing into the desert.
4. 5 of Judah and Jerusalem to **run** to the fortified cities.
4. 6 **Run** for safety!
4.29 At the noise of the horsemen and bowmen everyone will **run** away.
4.29 Some will **run** to the forest, others will climb up among the
5. 1 People of Jerusalem, **run** through your streets!
6. 1 People of Benjamin, **run** for safety!
6.29 fiercely, but the waste metals do not melt and **run** off.
8.14 "Come on, we will **run** to the fortified cities, and die
14.10 these people, "They love to **run** away from me, and they will
18.14 Do its cool mountain streams ever **run** dry?
41.14 with him, they were glad, [14]and turned and **ran** to them.
46. 5 overcome with fear, they **run** as fast as they can and do
46. 6 Those who **run** fast cannot get away;
46.21 all of them turned and **ran.**
46.22 Egypt **runs** away, hissing like a snake,
48. 6 'Quick, **run** for your lives!'
48. 6 '**Run** like a wild desert donkey!'
48.19 ask those who are **running** away, find out from them what
49. 3 **Run** about in confusion.
49. 5 You will all **run** away.
49. 5 Each one will **run** for his life,
49. 8 People of Dedan, turn and **run!**
49.19 and make the Edomites **run** away suddenly from their country.
49.30 Hazor, I, the Lord, warn you to **run** far away and hide.
50. 3 Men and animals will **run** away, and no one will live there."
50. 8 "People of Israel, **run** away from Babylonia!
50.44 and make the Babylonians **run** away suddenly from their city.
51. 6 **Run** away from Babylonia!
51. 6 **Run** for your lives!
51.31 Messenger after messenger **runs** to tell the king of
51.45 People of Israel, **run** away from there!
51.45 **Run** for your life from my fierce anger.
Lam 1. 2 tears **run** down her cheeks.
Ezek 4.17 They will **run** out of bread and water;
16.28 by the others, you went **running** after the Assyrians.
20.30 same sins your fathers did and go **running** after their idols?
32.14 waters settle and become clear and let your rivers **run** calm.
40.43 Ledges seventy-five millimetres wide **ran** round the edge
47.15 "The northern boundary **runs** eastwards from the
47.17 So the northern boundary **runs** from the Mediterranean
47.18 "The eastern boundary **runs** south from a point between
47.19 "The southern boundary **runs** south-west from Tamar to
47.20 formed by the Mediterranean and **runs** north to a point west
48. 1 northern boundary of the land **runs** eastwards from the

Ezek 48.23 receive one section of land **running** from the eastern
48.28 tribe of Gad, the boundary **runs** south-west from Tamar to the
Dan 10. 7 not see anything, but they were terrified and **ran** and hid.
11.24 plans to attack fortresses, but his time will soon **run** out.
Hos 2. 7 She will **run** after her lovers but will not catch them.
7.11 people call on Egypt for help, and then they **run** to Assyria!
Joel 2. 4 they **run** like war-horses.
2. 9 they **run** over the walls;
3.13 are crushed in a full winepress until the wine **runs** over."
Amos 2.14 Not even fast **runners** will escape;
2.15 not stand their ground, fast **runners** will not get away, and
2.16 even the bravest soldiers will drop their weapons and **run."**
5.19 be like a man who **runs** from a lion and meets a
Jon 1.10 on to tell them that he was **running** away from the Lord.
4. 2 That's why I did my best to **run** away to Spain!
Zech 2. 4 one said to the other, **"Run** and tell that young man with
Mt 8.33 taking care of the pigs **ran** away and went into the town,
10.23 When they persecute you in one town, **run** away to another one.
24.16 "Then those who are in Judaea must **run** away to the hills.
24.20 you will not have to **run** away during the winter or on
26.31 night all of you will **run** away and leave me, for the
26.56 Then all the disciples left him and **ran** away.
27.48 One of them **ran** up at once, took a sponge, soaked it
28. 8 and yet filled with joy, and **ran** to tell his disciples.
Mk 5. 6 so he **ran,** fell on his knees before him, [7]and screamed
5.14 taking care of the pigs **ran** away and spread the news in
6.33 from all the towns and **ran** ahead by land and arrived at
6.55 So they **ran** throughout the whole region;
9.15 they were greatly surprised, and **ran** to him and greeted him.
10.17 his way again, a man **ran** up, knelt before him, and asked
13.14 "Then those who are in Judaea must **run** away to the hills.
14.27 "All of you will **run** away and leave me, for the
14.50 Then all the disciples left him and **ran** away.
14.52 arrest him, [52]but he **ran** away naked, leaving the cloth behind.
15.36 One of them **ran** up with a sponge, soaked it in cheap
16. 8 So they went out and **ran** from the tomb, distressed and terrified.
Lk 8.34 saw what happened, so they **ran** off and spread the news in
12.42 will put in charge, to **run** the household and give the other
15.20 filled with pity, and he **ran,** threw his arms round his son,
19. 4 So he **ran** ahead of the crowd and climbed a sycomore tree
21.21 Then those who are in Judaea must **run** away to the hills;
24.12 But Peter got up and **ran** to the tomb;
Jn 10. 5 instead, they will **run** away from such a person, because they
10.12 sees a wolf coming, he leaves the sheep and **runs** away;
10.13 The hired man **runs** away because he is only a hired man
20. 2 She went **running** to Simon Peter and the other disciple,
20. 4 The two of them were **running,** but the other disciple ran
Acts 3.11 as it was called, the people were amazed and **ran** to them.
8.30 Philip **ran** over and heard him reading from the book of
12.14 was so happy that she **ran** back in without opening the door,
14.14 tore their clothes and **ran** into the middle of the crowd,
19.16 They **ran** away from his house, wounded and with their clothes
21.30 and the people all **ran** together, seized Paul, and dragged him
27.17 were afraid that they might **run** into the sandbanks off the
27.39 decided that, if possible, they would **run** the ship aground there.
1 Cor 9.24 Surely you know that many **runners** take part in a race,
9.24 **Run,** then, in such a way as to win the prize.
9.26 That is why I **run** straight for the finishing-line;
15.30 for us—why would we **run** the risk of danger every hour?
2 Cor 7. 4 I am **running** over with joy.
Phil 3.14 So I **run** straight towards the goal in order to win the
1 Tim 6.12 **Run** your best in the race of faith, and win eternal life
2 Tim 2. 5 An athlete who **runs** in a race cannot win the prize unless
4. 7 in the race, I have **run** the full distance, and I have
Heb 12. 1 and let us **run** with determination the race that lies
Jas 4. 7 Resist the Devil, and he will **run** away from you.

RUSH (1)

Is 19. 6 Reeds and **rushes** will wither, [7]and all the crops sown along

RUSH (2)
[ONRUSHING]

Judg 5.21 in the Kishon swept them away— the **onrushing** River Kishon.
20.33 the men surrounding Gibeah suddenly **rushed** out of their
1 Sam 11.11 groups, and at dawn they **rushed** into the enemy camp and
14.32 with hunger, [32]and so they **rushed** over to what they had
15.19 Why did you **rush** to seize the loot, and so do what
2 Kgs 7.16 The people of Samaria **rushed** out and looted the Syrian camp.
Job 15.26 he stubbornly holds up his shield and **rushes** to fight against God.
39.21 they **rush** into battle with all their strength.
40.23 He is not afraid of a **rushing** river;
Ps 16. 4 Those who **rush** to other gods bring many troubles on themselves.
32. 6 flood of trouble comes **rushing** in, it will not reach them.
104. 7 they **rushed** away when they heard your shout of command.
Is 17.13 The nations advance like **rushing** waves, but God
28. 2 torrent of rain, like a **rushing,** overpowering flood, and
59.19 He will come like a **rushing** river, like a strong wind.
Jer 2.24 on heat, running about loose, [24]**rushing** into the desert.
8. 6 on going his own way, like a horse **rushing** into battle.
47. 2 rising in the north and will **rush** like a river in flood.
51.55 The armies **rush** in like roaring waves and attack
Dan 8. 5 this meant, a goat came **rushing** out of the west, moving so
8. 6 beside the river, and **rushed** at him with all his force.
Joel 2. 9 They **rush** against the city;
Nah 1. 8 Like a great **rushing** flood he completely destroys his enemies;
2. 4 dash wildly through the streets, **rushing** to and fro through
2. 5 The attackers **rush** to the wall and set up the shield for
2. 8 Like water from a broken dam the people **rush** from Nineveh!
Mt 8.32 The whole herd **rushed** down the side of the cliff into the
Mk 5.13 two thousand pigs in all—**rushed** down the side of the cliff
Lk 8.33 The whole herd **rushed** down the side of the cliff into the
Acts 7.57 Then they all **rushed** at him at once, [58]threw him out of
16.29 jailer called for a light, **rushed** in, and fell trembling
19.29 were travelling with Paul, and **rushed** with them to the theatre.
21.32 took some officers and soldiers and **rushed** down to the crowd.
Rev 9. 9 like the noise of many horse-drawn chariots **rushing** into battle.

RUST

Mt 6.19 on earth, where moths and **rust** destroy, and robbers break in
6.20 heaven, where moths and **rust** cannot destroy, and robbers cannot
Jas 5. 3 and silver are covered with **rust,**
5. 3 and this **rust** will be a witness against you

RUTH
Naomi's daughter-in-law who married Boaz and was David's great-grandmother.

Ruth 1. 4 her two sons, [4]who married Moabite girls, Orpah and **Ruth.**
1.14 good-bye and went back home, but **Ruth** held on to her.
1.15 So Naomi said to her, **"Ruth,** your sister-in-law has
1.16 But **Ruth** answered, "Don't ask me to leave you!
1.18 When Naomi saw that **Ruth** was determined to go with her,
1.22 Naomi came back from Moab with **Ruth,** her Moabite daughter-in-law.
2. 2 One day **Ruth** said to Naomi, "Let me go to the fields
2. 3 So **Ruth** went out to the fields and walked behind the workers,
2. 8 Then Boaz said to **Ruth,** "Let me give you some advice.
2.10 **Ruth** bowed down with her face touching the ground, and
2.13 **Ruth** answered, "You are very kind to me, sir.
2.14 At meal-time Boaz said to **Ruth,** "Come and have a piece
2.17 So **Ruth** went on gathering corn in the field until evening,
2.19 So **Ruth** told Naomi that she had been working in a field
2.21 Then **Ruth** said, "Best of all, he told me to keep
2.22 Naomi said to **Ruth,** "Yes, my daughter, it will be
2.23 So **Ruth** worked with them and gathered corn until all the
3. 1 time later Naomi said to **Ruth,** "I must find a husband for
3. 5 **Ruth** answered, "I will do everything you say."
3. 6 So **Ruth** went to the threshing-place and did just what her
3. 7 **Ruth** slipped over quietly, lifted the covers and lay down at
3. 9 "It's **Ruth,** sir," she answered.
3.11 Now don't worry, **Ruth.**
3.16 **Ruth** told her everything that Boaz had done for her.
3.18 to her, "Now be patient, **Ruth,** until you see how this all
4. 5 then you are also buying **Ruth,** the Moabite widow, so that
4.10 In addition, **Ruth** the Moabite, Mahlon's widow, becomes my wife.
4.13 So Boaz took **Ruth** home as his wife.
Mt 1. 2 Obed (his mother was **Ruth),** Jesse, and King David.

RUTHLESS

Deut 28.50 They will be **ruthless** and show no mercy to anyone, young
Ezek 28. 7 as a god, [7]I will bring **ruthless** enemies to attack you.
30.11 He and his **ruthless** army will come to devastate the land.
31.12 **Ruthless** foreigners will cut it down and leave it.

SABBATH
The seventh day of the week (from sunset on Friday to sunset on Saturday), a holy day on which no work was permitted.
see also **SATURDAY, SEVENTH (day)**

Ex 16.25 today, because today is the **Sabbath,** a day of rest dedicated
20. 8 "Observe the **Sabbath** and keep it holy.
20.11 is why I, the Lord, blessed the **Sabbath** and made it holy.
31.13 people of Israel, "Keep the **Sabbath,** my day of rest,
35. 3 Do not even light a fire in your homes on the **Sabbath."**
Lev 19. 3 his father, and must keep the **Sabbath,** as I have commanded.
19.30 Keep the **Sabbath,** and honour the place where I am worshipped.
23. 3 that the seventh day, the **Sabbath,** is a day of rest.
23. 3 The **Sabbath** belongs to the Lord, no matter where you live.
23.11 The priest shall present it the day after the **Sabbath.**
23.15 from the day after the **Sabbath** on which you bring your sheaf
23.16 the day after the seventh **Sabbath,** present to the Lord
23.38 in addition to the regular **Sabbaths,** and these offerings are
24. 8 Every **Sabbath,** for all time to come, the bread must be
Num 15.32 a man was found gathering firewood on the **Sabbath.**
28. 9 On the **Sabbath** day offer two one-year-old male lambs
28.10 is to be offered every **Sabbath** in addition to the daily
Deut 5.12 " 'Observe the **Sabbath** and keep it holy, as I, the Lord
5.15 That is why I command you to observe the **Sabbath.**
2 Kgs 4.23 "It's neither a **Sabbath** nor a New Moon Festival."
11. 5 come on duty on the **Sabbath,** one third of you are to
11. 7 go off duty on the **Sabbath** are to stand guard at the
11. 9 those going off duty on the **Sabbath** and those going on duty.
1 Chr 9.32 preparing the sacred bread for the Temple every **Sabbath.**
23.31 Lord are burnt on the **Sabbath,** the New Moon Festival, and
2 Chr 2. 4 evening, as well as on **Sabbaths,** New Moon Festivals, and
8.13 **Sabbaths,** New Moon Festivals, and the three annual
23. 4 come on duty on the **Sabbath,** one third of them will guard
23. 8 went off duty on the **Sabbath,** so the commanders had
31. 3 for those offered on the **Sabbath,** at the New Moon Festival,
36.21 make up for the **Sabbath** rest that has not been observed."
Neh 9.14 taught them to keep your **Sabbaths** holy, and through your
10.31 sell to us on the **Sabbath** or on any other holy day,
10.33 for **Sabbaths,** New Moon Festivals, and other festivals,
13.15 I saw people in Judah pressing juice from grapes on the **Sabbath.**
13.15 I warned them not to sell anything on the **Sabbath.**
13.16 goods into the city to sell to our people on the **Sabbath.**
13.17 You're making the **Sabbath** unholy.
13.18 of God's anger down on Israel by profaning the **Sabbath."**

Neh 13.19 at the beginning of every **Sabbath,** as soon as evening began
13.19 and not to be opened again until the **Sabbath** was over.
13.19 sure that nothing was brought into the city on the **Sabbath.**
13.21 From then on they did not come back on the **Sabbath.**
13.22 the gates to make sure that the **Sabbath** was kept holy.
Is 1.13 New Moon Festivals, your **Sabbaths,** and your religious gatherings;
56. 2 those who always observe the **Sabbath** and do not misuse it.
56. 4 honour me by observing the **Sabbath** and if you do what
56. 6 who observe the **Sabbath** and faithfully keep his covenant:
58.13 says, "If you treat the **Sabbath** as sacred and do not pursue
66.23 New Moon Festival and every **Sabbath,** people of every nation
Jer 17.21 their lives, they must not carry any load on the **Sabbath;**
17.22 Jerusalem [22] or carry anything out of their houses on the **Sabbath.**
17.22 They must not work on the **Sabbath;**
17.24 any load in through the gates of this city on the **Sabbath.**
17.24 They must observe the **Sabbath** as a sacred day and must not
17.27 they must obey me and observe the **Sabbath** as a sacred day.
Lam 2. 6 He has put an end to holy days and **Sabbaths.**
Ezek 20.12 made the keeping of the **Sabbath** a sign of the agreement
20.13 They completely profaned the **Sabbath.**
20.16 profaned the **Sabbath**—they preferred to worship their idols.
20.20 Make the **Sabbath** a holy day, so that it will be a
20.21 They profaned the **Sabbath.**
20.24 broken my laws, profaned the **Sabbath,** and worshipped the
22. 8 respect for the holy places, and you don't keep the **Sabbath.**
22.26 clean and unclean things, and they ignore the **Sabbath.**
23.38 They profaned my Temple and broke the **Sabbath,**
44.24 and regulations, and they are to keep the **Sabbaths** holy.
45.17 New Moon Festivals, the **Sabbaths,** and the other festivals.
46. 1 to be opened on the **Sabbath** and at the New Moon Festival.
46. 3 Each **Sabbath** and each New Moon Festival all the people are
46. 4 On the **Sabbath** the prince is to bring to the Lord, as
46.12 as he does on the **Sabbath,** and the gate is to be
Hos 2.11 and her **Sabbath** celebrations—all her religious meetings.
Amos 8. 5 When will the **Sabbath** end, so that we can start selling again?
Mt 12. 1 Jesus was walking through some cornfields on the **Sabbath.**
12. 2 our Law for your disciples to do this on the **Sabbath!"**
12. 5 Law of Moses that every **Sabbath** the priests in the Temple
12. 5 actually break the **Sabbath** law, yet they are not guilty?
12. 8 for the Son of Man is Lord of the **Sabbath."**
12.10 asked him, "Is it against our Law to heal on the **Sabbath?"**
12.11 a sheep and it falls into a deep hole on the **Sabbath?**
12.12 our Law does allow us to help someone on the **Sabbath."**
24.20 not have to run away during the winter or on a **Sabbath!**
27.62 next day, which was a **Sabbath,** the chief priests and the
28. 1 After the **Sabbath,** as Sunday morning was dawning, Mary Magdalene
Mk 1.21 Capernaum, and on the next **Sabbath** Jesus went to the synagogue
2.23 Jesus was walking through some cornfields on the **Sabbath.**
2.24 our Law for your disciples to do that on the **Sabbath!"**
2.27 Jesus concluded, "The **Sabbath** was made for the good of man;
2.27 man was not made for the **Sabbath.**
2.28 So the Son of Man is Lord even of the **Sabbath."**
3. 2 closely to see whether he would heal the man on the **Sabbath.**
3. 4 "What does our Law allow us to do on the **Sabbath?**
6. 2 On the **Sabbath** he began to teach in the synagogue.
15.42 the day before the **Sabbath),** so Joseph went boldly into the
16. 1 After the **Sabbath** was over, Mary Magdalene, Mary the mother
Lk 4.16 brought up, and on the **Sabbath** he went as usual to the
4.31 town in Galilee, where he taught the people on the **Sabbath.**
6. 1 Jesus was walking through some cornfields on the **Sabbath.**
6. 2 doing what our Law says you cannot do on the **Sabbath?"**
6. 5 And Jesus concluded, "The Son of Man is Lord of the **Sabbath."**
6. 6 On another **Sabbath** Jesus went into a synagogue and taught.
6. 7 watched him closely to see if he would heal on the **Sabbath.**
6. 9 What does our Law allow us to do on the **Sabbath?**
13.10 One **Sabbath** Jesus was teaching in a synagogue.
13.14 Jesus had healed on the **Sabbath,** so he spoke up and said
13.14 during those days and be healed, but not on the **Sabbath!"**
13.15 and take it out to give it water on the **Sabbath.**
13.16 should she not be released on the **Sabbath?"**
14. 1 One **Sabbath** Jesus went to eat a meal at the home of
14. 3 "Does our Law allow healing on the **Sabbath** or not?"
14. 5 in a well on a **Sabbath,** would you not
14. 5 pull him out at once on the **Sabbath** itself?"
23.54 It was Friday, and the **Sabbath** was about to begin.
23.56 On the **Sabbath** they rested, as the Law commanded.
Jn 5. 9 day this happened was a **Sabbath,** [10] so the Jewish authorities
5.10 been healed, "This is a **Sabbath,** and it is against our Law
5.16 Jesus, because he had done this healing on a **Sabbath.**
5.18 only had he broken the **Sabbath** law, but he had said that
7.22 and so you circumcise a boy on the **Sabbath.**
7.23 boy is circumcised on the **Sabbath** so that Moses' Law is not
7.23 with me because I made a man completely well on the **Sabbath?**
9.14 made the mud and cured him of his blindness was a **Sabbath.**
9.16 cannot be from God, for he does not obey the **Sabbath** law."
19.31 on the crosses on the **Sabbath,** since
19.31 the coming **Sabbath** was especially holy.
19.42 was the day before the **Sabbath** and because the tomb was
Acts 13.14 in Pisidia, and on the **Sabbath** they went into the synagogue
13.27 understand the words of the prophets that are read every **Sabbath.**
13.42 to come back the next **Sabbath** and tell them more about these
13.44 The next **Sabbath** nearly everyone in the town came to
15.21 time in the synagogues every **Sabbath,** and his words are preached
16.13 On the **Sabbath** we went out of the city to the river-side,
17. 2 There during three **Sabbaths** he held discussions with the people,
18. 4 discussions in the synagogue every **Sabbath,** trying to convince
Col 2.16 or about holy days or the New Moon Festival or the **Sabbath.**

SACK

Gen 18. 6 to Sarah, "Quick, take a **sack** of your best flour, and bake
42.25 man's money back in his **sack,** and to give them food for
42.27 one of them opened his **sack** to feed his donkey
42.27 and found his money at the top of the **sack.**
42.28 "Here it is in my **sack!"**
42.35 when they emptied out their **sacks,** every one of them found
43.12 back the money that was returned in the top of your **sacks.**
43.18 of the money that was returned in our **sacks** the first time.
43.21 way home, we opened our **sacks,** and each man found his money
43.21 his money in the top of his **sack**—every bit of it.
43.22 We do not know who put our money back in our **sacks."**
43.23 your father, must have put the money in your **sacks** for you.
44. 1 his house, "Fill the men's **sacks** with as much food as they
44. 1 carry, and put each man's money in the top of his **sack.**
44. 2 top of the youngest brother's **sack,** together with the money
44. 8 of Canaan the money we found in the top of our **sacks.**
44.11 So they quickly lowered their **sacks** to the ground,
44.11 and each man opened his **sack.**
44.12 with the youngest, and the cup was found in Benjamin's **sack.**
Lev 11.32 of wood, cloth, leather, or **sacking,** no matter what it is
Josh 9. 4 their donkeys with worn-out **sacks** and patched-up wineskins.
Lk 16. 7 'A thousand **sacks** of wheat,' he answered.

SACKCLOTH

A coarse cloth made of goats' hair, which was worn as a sign of mourning or distress.

Gen 37.34 Jacob tore his clothes in sorrow and put on **sackcloth.**
2 Sam 3.31 to tear their clothes, wear **sackcloth,** and mourn for Abner.
21.10 the daughter of Aiah, used **sackcloth** to make a shelter for
1 Kgs 20.31 the king of Israel with **sackcloth** round our waists and ropes
20.32 So they wrapped **sackcloth** round their waists
21.27 Ahab tore his clothes, took them off, and put on **sackcloth.**
21.27 in the **sackcloth,** and went about gloomy
2 Kgs 6.30 could see that he was wearing **sackcloth** under his clothes.
19. 1 clothes in grief, put on **sackcloth,** and went to the Temple
19. 2 They also were wearing **sackcloth.**
1 Chr 21.16 all of whom were wearing **sackcloth**—bowed low, with their
Neh 9. 1 They wore **sackcloth** and put dust on their heads as signs of
Esth 4. 1 Then he dressed in **sackcloth,** covered his head with ashes,
4. 2 go in because no one wearing **sackcloth** was allowed inside.
4. 3 wailed, and most of them put on **sackcloth** and lay in ashes.
4. 4 on instead of the **sackcloth,** but he would not accept them.
Job 16.15 and wear clothes made of **sackcloth,** and I sit here in the
Is 15. 3 The people in the streets are dressed in **sackcloth;**
20. 2 Amoz to take off his sandals and the **sackcloth** he was wearing.
22.12 to weep and mourn, to shave your heads and wear **sackcloth.**
37. 1 clothes in grief, put on **sackcloth,** and went to the Temple
37. 2 They also were wearing **sackcloth.**
58. 5 of grass, and spread out **sackcloth** and ashes to lie on.
Jer 4. 8 So put on **sackcloth,** and weep and wail because the fierce
6.26 Lord says to his people, "Put on **sackcloth** and roll in ashes.
48.37 gashes on their hands, and everyone is wearing **sackcloth.**
49. 3 Put on **sackcloth** and mourn.
Lam 2.10 With dust on their heads and **sackcloth** on their bodies.
Ezek 7.18 They will put on **sackcloth** and they will tremble all over.
27.31 They shave their heads for you And dress themselves in **sackcloth.**
Dan 9. 3 fasting, wearing **sackcloth,** and sitting in ashes.
Joel 1.13 Put on **sackcloth** and weep, you priests who serve at the altar!
Amos 8.10 shave your heads and wear **sackcloth,** and you will be like
Jon 3. 5 the least, put on **sackcloth** to show that they had repented.
3. 6 took off his robe, put on **sackcloth,** and sat down in ashes.
3. 8 All persons and animals must wear **sackcloth.**
Mt 11.21 long ago have put on **sackcloth** and sprinkled ashes on themselves,
Lk 10.13 sat down, put on **sackcloth,** and sprinkled ashes on themselves,
Rev 11. 3 two witnesses dressed in **sackcloth,** and they will proclaim God's

SACRED

Gen 12. 6 until he came to the **sacred** tree of Moreh, the holy place
13.18 camp and settled near the **sacred** trees of Mamre at Hebron,
14.13 living near the **sacred** trees belonging to Mamre the Amorite.
18. 1 The Lord appeared to Abraham at the **sacred** trees of Mamre.
Ex 15.13 by your strength you guided them to your **sacred** land.
18.12 with him to eat the **sacred** meal as an act of worship.
19.23 us to consider the mountain **sacred** and to mark a boundary
23.24 Destroy their gods and break down their **sacred** stone pillars.
25. 8 The people must make a **sacred** tent for me, so that I
25.30 table there is always to be the **sacred** bread offered to me.
26. 1 "Make the interior of the **sacred** Tent, the Tent of my presence,
29. 6 and tie on it the **sacred** sign of dedication engraved
29.33 Only priests may eat this food, because it is **sacred.**
29.34 it is not to be eaten, for it is **sacred.**
30.25 and make a **sacred** anointing oil, mixed like perfume.
31.14 You must keep the day of rest, because it is **sacred.**
33. 7 camp, Moses would take the **sacred** Tent and put it up some
33.19 you and in your presence I will pronounce my **sacred** name.
34.13 down their altars, destroy their **sacred** pillars, and cut
35. 2 seventh day is to be **sacred,** a solemn day of rest dedicated
35.19 in the Holy Place—the **sacred** clothes for Aaron the priest
36. 1 everything needed to build the **sacred** Tent, are to make
36. 3 the Israelites had brought for constructing the **sacred** Tent.
36. 6 was to make any further contribution for the **sacred** Tent;
37.29 He also made the **sacred** anointing oil
38.24 the Lord for the **sacred** Tent weighed a thousand kilogrammes,
38.27 the hundred bases for the **sacred** Tent and for the curtain,
39.30 They made the ornament, the **sacred** sign of dedication,
39.41 in the Holy Place—the **sacred** clothes for Aaron the priest

Ex	40. 9	by anointing it with the **sacred** oil, and it will be holy.
Lev	4. 6	and sprinkle it in front of the **sacred** curtain seven times.
	5.15	over the payments that are **sacred** to the Lord, he shall
	8. 9	put the gold ornament, the **sacred** sign of dedication, just
	10. 4	cousins' bodies away from the **sacred** Tent and put them
	10.17	"Why didn't you eat the sin-offering in a **sacred** place?
	10.18	was not brought into the **sacred** tent, you should have eaten
	12. 4	is holy or enter the **sacred** Tent until the time of her
	20. 3	to Molech and makes my **sacred** Tent unclean and disgraces my
	21.11	is he to defile my **sacred** Tent by leaving it and entering
	21.23	not come near the **sacred** curtain or approach the altar.
	22. 2	so treat with respect the **sacred** offerings that the people
	22. 3	ritually unclean, comes near the **sacred** offerings which the
	22. 4	eat any of the **sacred** offerings until he is ritually clean.
	22. 6	not eat any of the **sacred** offerings until he has had a
	22. 7	then he may eat the **sacred** offerings, which are his food.
	22. 9	and die, because they have disobeyed the **sacred** regulations.
	22.10	of a priestly family may eat any of the **sacred** offerings;
	22.12	is not a priest may not eat any of the **sacred** offerings.
	22.14	eats any of the **sacred** offerings without intending to,
	22.15	priests shall not profane the **sacred** offerings
	25.12	The whole year shall be **sacred** for you;
	26.11	live among you in my **sacred** tent, and I will never turn
	27. 9	made to the Lord is **sacred,** [10]and the man who made the
Num	4.15	shall come to carry the **sacred** objects only after Aaron and
	4.15	Kohath must not touch the **sacred** objects, or they will die.
	4.19	Kohath [19]be killed by coming near these most **sacred** objects.
	4.20	preparing the **sacred** objects for moving, they will die."
	6.20	they are a **sacred** offering for the priest, in addition to
	7. 9	to the Kohathites, because the **sacred** objects they took care
	10.21	clan of Kohath would start out, carrying the **sacred** objects.
	18. 3	not have any contact with **sacred** objects in the Holy Place
	18. 7	who comes near the **sacred** objects shall be put to death."
	18. 9	Of the most **sacred** offerings not burnt on the altar, the
	18. 9	presented to me as a **sacred** offering belongs to you and your
	18.32	sure not to profane the **sacred** gifts of the Israelites by
	31. 6	who took charge of the **sacred** objects and the trumpets for
Deut	7. 5	their altars, break their **sacred** stone pillars in pieces,
	11.30	west, not far from the **sacred** trees of Moreh near the town
	12. 3	Tear down their altars and smash their **sacred** stone pillars
	26.13	the Lord, 'None of the **sacred** tithe is left in my house;
Josh	22.27	worship the Lord before his **sacred** Tent with our offerings
Judg	9. 6	together and went to the **sacred** oak-tree at Shechem, where
	18.18	Micah's house and took the **sacred** objects, the priest asked them,
	18.20	so he took the **sacred** objects and went along with them.
1 Sam	2.18	Samuel continued to serve the Lord, wearing a **sacred** linen apron.
	3. 3	sleeping in the sanctuary, where the **sacred** Covenant Box was.
	10. 3	until you come to the **sacred** tree at Tabor, where you will
	14.41	Lord, God of Israel, answer me by the **sacred** stones.
	20. 8	me this favour, and keep the **sacred** promise you made to me.
	20.14	alive, please keep your **sacred** promise and be loyal to me;
	20.42	will for ever keep the **sacred** promise we have made to each
	21. 4	"I haven't any ordinary bread, only **sacred** bread;
	21. 6	the priest gave David the **sacred** bread, because the only
	21. 6	removed from the **sacred** table and replaced by fresh bread.
	23.18	of them made a **sacred** promise of friendship to each other.
	28.10	Then Saul made a **sacred** vow.
2 Sam	5. 3	He made a **sacred** alliance with them, they anointed him, and
	6.16	and jumping around in the **sacred** dance, and she was
	11.11	By all that's **sacred,** I swear that I could never do such
	14.19	swear by all that is **sacred,** Your Majesty, that there is no
	15.24	with him were the Levites, carrying the **sacred** Covenant Box.
	21. 7	But because of the **sacred** promise that he and Jonathan
2 Kgs	10.22	priest in charge of the **sacred** robes to bring the robes out
	10.26	temple, [26]brought out the **sacred** pillar that was there,
	10.27	So they destroyed the **sacred** pillar and the temple, and
1 Chr	9.29	in charge of the other **sacred** equipment, and of the flour,
	9.32	preparing the **sacred** bread for the Temple every Sabbath.
	11. 3	He made a **sacred** alliance with them, they anointed him, and
	22.19	and all the other **sacred** objects used in worshipping him."
	23.13	be in charge of the **sacred** objects for ever, to burn incense
	23.28	its rooms, and to keep undefiled everything that is **sacred;**
2 Chr	2. 4	will present offerings of **sacred** bread to him continuously,
	14. 3	of worship, broke down the **sacred** stone columns, and cut
	20.21	the robes they wore on **sacred** occasions and to march ahead
	24. 7	used many of the **sacred** objects in the worship of Baal.)
	29.18	the table for the **sacred** bread, and all their equipment.
	31.18	to be ready to perform their **sacred** duties at any time.
	35. 3	"Put the **sacred** Covenant Box in the Temple that King Solomon,
	35.13	the regulations, and boiled the **sacred** offerings in pots,
Ezra	8.28	said to them, "You are **sacred** to the Lord, the God of
Neh	7. 1	guards, the members of the **sacred** choir, and the other
	10.33	the **sacred** bread, the daily grain-offering,
	10.33	the **sacred** offerings for Sabbaths, New Moon Festivals,
	10.33	and other festivals, the other **sacred** offerings,
	12.47	The people gave a **sacred** offering to the Levites, and the
Ps	2. 6	"On Zion, my **sacred** hill," he says, "I have installed my king."
	3. 4	the Lord for help, and from his **sacred** hill he answers me.
	15. 1	Who may worship on Zion, your **sacred** hill?
	43. 3	me back to Zion, your **sacred** hill, and to your Temple, where
	46. 4	the city of God, to the **sacred** house of the Most High.
	47. 8	God sits on his **sacred** throne;
	48. 1	highly praised in the city of our God, on his **sacred** hill.
	65. 4	things of your house, the blessings of your **sacred** Temple.
	68. 5	God, who lives in his **sacred** Temple, cares for orphans and
	69.22	may their **sacred** feasts cause their downfall.
	74. 9	All our **sacred** symbols are gone;
	87. 1	The Lord built his city on the **sacred** hill;
	99. 9	Praise the Lord our God, and worship at his **sacred** hill!
	105.42	He remembered his **sacred** promise to Abraham his servant.
	110. 3	your young men will come to you on the **sacred** hills.
Prov	2.17	who is faithless to her own husband and forgets her **sacred** vows.
Is	1.29	that you ever worshipped trees and planted **sacred** gardens.
	11. 9	On Zion, God's **sacred** hill, there will be nothing harmful or evil.
	17.10	you plant **sacred** gardens in order to worship a foreign god.
	27.13	come and worship the Lord in Jerusalem, on his **sacred** hill.
	30.29	and sing as you do on the night of a **sacred** festival.
	56. 7	bring you to Zion, my **sacred** hill, give you joy in my
	57. 5	gods by having sex under those **sacred** trees of yours.
	58.13	you treat the Sabbath as **sacred** and do not pursue your own
	64.10	Your **sacred** cities are like a desert;
	64.11	ruin, [11]and our Temple, the **sacred** and beautiful place
	65. 3	They offer pagan sacrifices in **sacred** gardens and burn
	65.11	who ignore Zion, my **sacred** hill, and worship Gad and Meni,
	65.25	On Zion, my **sacred** hill, there will be nothing harmful or evil."
	66.17	who go in procession to **sacred** gardens, and who eat pork and
	66.20	will bring them to my **sacred** hill in Jerusalem on horses,
Jer	2. 3	you were my **sacred** possession.
	17.22	observe it as a **sacred** day, as I commanded their ancestors.
	17.24	observe the Sabbath as a **sacred** day and must not do any
	17.27	they must obey me and observe the Sabbath as a **sacred** day.
	31.23	'May the Lord bless the **sacred** hill of Jerusalem, the holy
	31.40	as the Horse Gate to the east, will be **sacred** to me.
	43.13	He will destroy the **sacred** stone monuments at Heliopolis
Ezek	34.26	"I will bless them and let them live round my **sacred** hill.
	43.12	it on the top of the mountain is **sacred** and holy."
	44. 8	not taken charge of the **sacred** rituals in my Temple, but
	44.19	to keep their **sacred** clothing from harming the people.
Dan	9. 2	reign, I was studying the **sacred** books and thinking about
	9.16	It is your city, your **sacred** hill.
Hos	3. 4	or leaders, without sacrifices or **sacred** stone pillars,
	4.13	At **sacred** places on the mountain-tops they offer sacrifices,
	10. 1	beautiful they made the **sacred** stone pillars they worship.
	10. 2	God will break down their altars and destroy their **sacred** pillars.
Joel	2. 1	sound the alarm on Zion, God's **sacred** hill.
	2.16	prepare them for a **sacred** meeting;
	3.17	I live on Zion, my **sacred** hill.
	3.17	Jerusalem will be a **sacred** city;
Obad	16	have drunk a bitter cup of punishment on my **sacred** hill.
	17	Mount Zion some will escape, and it will be a **sacred** place.
Mic	5.13	I will destroy your idols and **sacred** stone pillars;
Zeph	3. 4	the priests defile what is **sacred,** and twist the law of God
	3.11	you will never again rebel against me on my **sacred** hill.
Zech	2.12	of the Lord in his **sacred** land, and Jerusalem will be the
	8. 3	hill of the Lord Almighty will be called the **sacred** hill.
	14.20	the Temple will be as **sacred** as the bowls before the altar.
Mk	16.10	east to the west the **sacred** and ever-living message of eternal
Lk	1.72	show mercy to our ancestors and remember his **sacred** covenant.
Acts	6.13	"is always talking against our **sacred** Temple and the Law of Moses.
	13.34	'I will give you the **sacred** and sure blessings that I
	19.35	Artemis and of the **sacred** stone that fell down from heaven.
Eph	2.21	makes it grow into a **sacred** temple dedicated to the Lord.
	5.19	another with the words of psalms, hymns, and **sacred** songs;
Col	3.16	Sing psalms, hymns, and **sacred** songs;
2 Pet	2.21	then turn away from the **sacred** command that was given them.
Jude	20	keep on building yourselves up on your most **sacred** faith.

SACRIFICE

Gen	8.20	and bird, and burnt them whole as a **sacrifice** on the altar.
	8.21	The odour of the **sacrifice** pleased the Lord, and he said
	22. 2	that I will show you, offer him as a **sacrifice** to me."
	22. 3	cut some wood for the **sacrifice,** loaded his donkey, and took
	22. 6	carry the wood for the **sacrifice,** and he himself carried a
	22. 7	and the wood, but where is the lamb for the **sacrifice?"**
	31.54	which he offered as a **sacrifice** on the mountain, and he
	46. 1	to Beersheba, where he offered **sacrifices** to the God of his
Ex	3.18	days into the desert to offer **sacrifices** to the Lord, our
	5. 3	into the desert to offer **sacrifices** to the Lord our God.
	5. 8	asking me to let them go and offer **sacrifices** to their God!
	5.17	ask me to let you go and offer **sacrifices** to the Lord.
	8. 8	people go, so that they can offer **sacrifices** to the Lord."
	8.25	and said, "Go and offer **sacrifices** to your God here in this
	8.26	would be offended by our **sacrificing** the animals that we
	8.26	the Egyptians by **sacrificing** them where they can see us,
	8.27	into the desert to offer **sacrifices** to the Lord our God,
	8.28	will let you go to **sacrifice** to the Lord, your God, in
	8.29	prevent the people from going to **sacrifice** to the Lord."
	10.25	provide us with animals for **sacrifices** and burnt-offerings
	10.26	there, we will not know what animals to **sacrifice** to him."
	12.27	answer, 'It is the **sacrifice** of Passover to honour the Lord,
	13.15	That is why we **sacrifice** every first-born male animal to the Lord,
	18.12	to be burnt whole and other **sacrifices** to be offered to God;
	20.24	for me, and on it **sacrifice** your sheep and your cattle as
	22.20	death anyone who offers **sacrifices** to any god except to me,
	23.18	bread made with yeast when you **sacrifice** an animal to me.
	23.18	The fat of animals **sacrificed** to me during these festivals
	24. 5	and they burnt **sacrifices** to the Lord
	24. 5	and **sacrificed** some cattle as fellowship-offerings.
	29. 3	them to me when you **sacrifice** the bull and the two rams.
	29.36	offer a bull as a **sacrifice,** so that sin may be forgiven.
	29.38	time to come, **sacrifice** on the altar two one-year-old lambs.
	29.39	**Sacrifice** one of the lambs in the morning and the other
	29.41	**Sacrifice** the second lamb in the evening, and offer with
	30.10	four projections the blood of the animal **sacrificed** for sin.
	32. 6	as **sacrifices** and others to eat as fellowship-offerings.
	32. 8	gold and have worshipped it and offered **sacrifices** to it.
	34.15	worship their pagan gods and **sacrifice** to them, they will
	34.25	bread made with yeast when you **sacrifice** an animal to me.
	40.29	On it he **sacrificed** the burnt-offering and the grain-offering,
Lev	1. 2	for the Israelites to observe when they offer their **sacrifices.**

Lev 1. 2 When anyone offers an animal **sacrifice,** it may be one of
1. 4 it will be accepted as a **sacrifice** to take away his sins.
1. 9 priest will burn the whole **sacrifice** on the altar.
1.13 the priest will present the **sacrifice** to the Lord and burn
4. 3 bull without any defects and **sacrifice** it to the Lord for
4. 7 the altar used for burning **sacrifices,** which is at the
4.18 the altar used for burning **sacrifices,** which is at the
4.20 way he shall make the **sacrifice** for the people's sin, and
4.26 priest shall offer the **sacrifice** for the sin of the ruler,
4.31 the priest shall offer the **sacrifice** for the man's sin, and
4.35 the priest shall offer the **sacrifice** for the man's sin, and
5. 6 The priest shall offer the **sacrifice** for the man's sin.
5.10 the priest shall offer the **sacrifice** for the man's sin, and
5.13 the priest shall offer the **sacrifice** for the man's sin, and
5.16 offer the animal as a **sacrifice** for the man's sin, and he
5.18 The priest shall offer the **sacrifice** for the sin which the
6. 7 The priest shall offer the **sacrifice** for the man's sin,
6.22 It shall be completely burnt as a **sacrifice** to the Lord.
6.26 The priest who **sacrifices** the animal shall eat it in a
7. 7 the meat belongs to the priest who offers the **sacrifice.**
7. 8 belongs to the priest who offers the **sacrifice.**
7.12 with the animal to be **sacrificed,** an offering of bread made
7.15 of the animal must be eaten on the day it is **sacrificed;**
9. 4 They are to **sacrifice** them to the Lord with the
9.22 Aaron had finished all the **sacrifices,** he raised his hands
10.18 you should have eaten the **sacrifice** there, as I commanded."
16. 6 offer a bull as a **sacrifice** to take away his own sins
16. 9 Aaron shall **sacrifice** the goat chosen by lot for the Lord
16.11 When Aaron **sacrifices** the bull as the sin-offering for
17. 7 animals in the fields as **sacrifices** to the goat-demons.
17. 8 a burnt-offering or any other **sacrifice** [9]as an offering to
22.28 Do not **sacrifice** a cow and its calf or a sheep and
22.29 When you offer a **sacrifice** of thanksgiving to the Lord,
23.12 the offering of corn, also **sacrifice** as a burnt-offering a
23.37 grain-offerings, **sacrifices,** and wine-offerings,
26.31 places of worship, and refuse to accept your **sacrifices.**
Num 6.17 He shall **sacrifice** the ram to the Lord as a fellowship-offering,
15. 3 a burnt-offering or as a **sacrifice** in fulfilment of a vow or
15. 7 The smell of these **sacrifices** is pleasing to the Lord.
15. 8 a burnt-offering or as a **sacrifice** in fulfilment of a vow or
15.10 The smell of this **sacrifice** is pleasing to the Lord.
18. 8 contributions made to me that are not burnt as **sacrifices.**
18.17 they belong completely to me and are to be **sacrificed.**
25. 2 These women invited them to **sacrificial** feasts,
Deut 12. 6 you are to offer your **sacrifices** that are to be burnt
12. 6 and your other **sacrifices,** your tithes and your offerings,
12.11 your **sacrifices** that are to be burnt
12.11 and your other **sacrifices,** your tithes and your offerings,
12.13 You are not to offer your **sacrifices** wherever you choose;
12.14 are you to offer your **sacrifices** that are to be burnt and
12.27 Offer there the **sacrifices** which are to be completely burnt
12.27 Also offer those **sacrifices** in which you eat the meat and
12.31 They even **sacrifice** their children in the fires on their altars.
15.21 defect, you must not **sacrifice** them to the Lord your God.
17. 1 "Do not **sacrifice** to the Lord your God cattle or sheep
18. 1 on the offerings and other **sacrifices** given to the Lord.
18. 3 "Whenever cattle or sheep are **sacrificed,** the priests
18.10 Don't **sacrifice** your children in the fires on your altars;
27. 6 you are to offer the **sacrifices** that are to be burnt, [7]and
27. 7 and there you are to **sacrifice** and eat your
32.17 They **sacrificed** to gods that are not real, new gods
32.38 the fat of your **sacrifices** and offered them wine to drink.
33.10 They will offer **sacrifices** on your altar.
33.19 And offer the right **sacrifices** there.
Josh 8.31 On it they offered burnt **sacrifices** to the Lord, and they
13.14 possession a share of the **sacrifices** burnt on the altar to
22.23 our own altar to burn **sacrifices** on or to use for
22.26 not to burn **sacrifices** or make offerings, [27]but instead,
22.27 with our offerings to be burnt and with **sacrifices**
22.28 for burning offerings or for **sacrifice,** but as a sign for
22.29 to burn offerings on or for grain-offerings or **sacrifices.**
Judg 2. 5 There they offered **sacrifices** to the Lord.
11.31 I will offer that person to you as a **sacrifice."**
16.23 to celebrate and offer a great **sacrifice** to their god Dagon.
20.26 They offered fellowship **sacrifices**
20.26 and burnt some **sacrifices** whole—
21. 4 built an altar there, offered fellowship **sacrifices**
21. 4 and burnt some **sacrifices** whole.
1 Sam 1. 3 offer **sacrifices** to the Lord Almighty at Shiloh,
1. 4 Each time Elkanah offered his **sacrifice,** he would give one
1.21 to the Lord the yearly **sacrifice**
1.21 and the special **sacrifice** he had promised.
2.13 a man was offering his **sacrifice,** the priest's servant would
2.14 Israelites who came to Shiloh to offer **sacrifices**
2.15 to the man offering the **sacrifice,** "Give me some meat for
2.19 she accompanied her husband to offer the yearly **sacrifice.**
2.28 right to keep a share of the **sacrifices** burnt on the altar.
2.29 look with greed at the **sacrifices** and offerings which I
2.29 the best parts of all the **sacrifices** my people offer to me?
3.14 family of Eli that no **sacrifice** or offering will ever be
6.15 offered burnt-sacrifices and other **sacrifices** to the Lord.
7. 9 young lamb and burnt it whole as a **sacrifice** to the Lord.
7.10 While Samuel was offering the **sacrifice,** the Philistines moved
9.12 are going to offer a **sacrifice** on the altar on the hill.
9.12 he gets there, because he has to bless the **sacrifice** first.
10. 3 men on their way to offer a **sacrifice** to God at Bethel.
13.12 So I felt I had to offer a **sacrifice."**
15.15 cattle to offer as a **sacrifice** to the Lord your God, and
15.21 to Gilgal to offer as a **sacrifice** to the Lord your God."
15.22 obedience or offerings and **sacrifices?**
15.22 better to obey him than to **sacrifice** the best sheep to him.
1 Sam 16. 2 say that you are there to offer a **sacrifice** to the Lord.
16. 3 Invite Jesse to the **sacrifice,** and I will tell you what to
16. 5 "I have come to offer a **sacrifice** to the Lord.
16. 5 to purify themselves, and he invited them to the **sacrifice.**
16.11 "We won't offer the **sacrifice** until he comes."
20. 6 the time for the annual **sacrifice** there for my whole family.
20.29 our family is celebrating the **sacrificial** feast in town,
2 Sam 6.13 he offered the Lord a **sacrifice** of a bull and a fattened
6.17 Then he offered **sacrifices** and fellowship-offerings to the Lord.
6.18 he had finished offering the **sacrifices,** he blessed the
15.12 And while he was offering **sacrifices,** Absalom also sent
24.24 to the Lord my God **sacrifices** that have cost me nothing."
1 Kgs 1. 9 One day Adonijah offered a **sacrifice** of sheep, bulls, and
1. 9 Judah to come to this **sacrificial** feast,
1.19 He has offered a **sacrifice** of many bulls,
1.25 has gone and offered a **sacrifice** of many bulls, sheep, and
3. 2 were still offering **sacrifices** at many different altars.
3. 3 animals and offered them as **sacrifices** on various altars.
3. 4 went to Gibeon to offer **sacrifices** because that was where
8. 5 of the Covenant Box and **sacrificed** a large number of sheep
8.62 and all the people there offered **sacrifices** to the Lord.
8.63 He **sacrificed** 22,000 head of cattle and 120,000 sheep
8.64 there the **sacrifices** burnt whole, the grain-offerings,
10. 5 him at feasts, and the **sacrifices** he offered in the Temple.
11. 8 could burn incense and offer **sacrifices** to their own gods.
12.26 go to Jerusalem and offer **sacrifices** to the Lord in the
12.32 altar in Bethel he offered **sacrifices** to the gold
12.33 to Bethel and offered a **sacrifice** on the altar in
13. 1 there as Jeroboam stood at the altar to offer the **sacrifice.**
13. 2 the pagan altars who offer **sacrifices** on you, and he will
18.36 the hour of the afternoon **sacrifice** the prophet Elijah
18.38 and it burnt up the **sacrifice,** the wood, and the stones,
22.43 people continued to offer **sacrifices** and burn incense there.
2 Kgs 3.20 time of the regular morning **sacrifice,** water came flowing
3.27 on the city wall as a **sacrifice** to the god of Moab.
5.17 on I will not offer **sacrifices** or burnt-offerings to any god
10.19 going to offer a great **sacrifice** to Baal, and whoever is not
10.24 Jonadab went in to offer **sacrifices** and burnt-offerings to Baal.
12. 3 continued to offer **sacrifices** and burn incense there.
12. 4 paid in connection with the **sacrifices** in the Temple, both
12. 4 dues paid for the regular **sacrifices** and the money given as
14. 4 continued to offer **sacrifices** and burn incense there.
15. 4 people continued to offer **sacrifices** and burn incense there.
15.35 people continued to offer **sacrifices** and burn incense there.
16. 3 He even **sacrificed** his own son as a burnt-offering to idols,
16. 4 shady tree, Ahaz offered **sacrifices** and burnt incense.
16.13 so he burnt animal **sacrifices** and grain-offerings on it,
16.15 Pour on it the blood of all the animals that are **sacrificed.**
17.17 They **sacrificed** their sons and daughters as burnt-offerings
17.31 and the people of Sepharvaim **sacrificed** their children as
17.32 places of worship and to offer **sacrifices** for them there.
17.35 bow down to them or serve them or offer **sacrifices** to them.
17.36 you are to bow down to me and offer **sacrifices** to me.
21. 6 He **sacrificed** his son as a burnt-offering.
22.17 rejected me and have offered **sacrifices** to other gods, and
23. 5 Judah had ordained to offer **sacrifices** on the pagan altars
23. 5 all the priests who offered **sacrifices** to Baal, to the sun,
23. 8 he desecrated the altars where they had offered **sacrifices.**
23.10 so that no one could **sacrifice** his son or daughter as a
25.14 from the **sacrifices,** the bowls used for burning incense,
1 Chr 6.49 and offered the **sacrifices** that were burnt on the altar.
6.49 for the **sacrifices** by which God forgives Israel's sins.
15.26 They **sacrificed** seven bulls and seven sheep, to make
16. 1 Then they offered **sacrifices** and fellowship-offerings to God.
16. 2 David had finished offering the **sacrifices,** he blessed the
16.40 evening they were to burn **sacrifices** whole on the altar in
21.26 fire from heaven to burn the **sacrifices** on the altar.
21.28 **sacrifices** on the altar at Araunah's threshing-place.
21.29 and the altar on which **sacrifices** were burnt were still at
29.21 killed animals as **sacrifices,** dedicating them to the Lord,
29.21 In addition, they **sacrificed** a thousand bulls, a thousand rams,
2 Chr 1. 6 the Lord by offering **sacrifices** on the bronze altar;
4. 6 the parts of the animals that were burnt as **sacrifices.**
5. 6 of the Covenant Box and **sacrificed** a large number of sheep
7. 1 heaven and burnt up the **sacrifices** that had been offered,
7. 4 Then Solomon and all the people offered **sacrifices** to the Lord.
7. 5 He **sacrificed** 22,000 head of cattle and 120,000 sheep
7. 7 there the **sacrifices** burnt whole, the grain-offerings,
7.12 Temple as the place where **sacrifices** are to be offered to me.
8.12 Solomon offered **sacrifices** to the Lord on the altar
9. 4 him at feasts, and the **sacrifices** he offered in the Temple.
11.16 so that they could offer **sacrifices** to the Lord, the God of
13.11 they offer him incense and animal **sacrifices** burnt whole.
15.11 On that day they offered **sacrifices** to the Lord from the
23.18 David and to burn the **sacrifices** offered to the Lord in
24.14 **sacrifices** were offered regularly at the Temple.
28. 3 Valley of Hinnom, and even **sacrificed** his own sons as
28. 4 every shady tree Ahaz offered **sacrifices** and burnt incense.
28.23 He offered **sacrifices** to the gods of the Syrians, who
28.23 of Syria, so if I **sacrifice** to them, they may help me
29.21 of Aaron, to offer the animals as **sacrifices** on the altar.
29.22 and sprinkled the blood of each **sacrifice** on the altar.
29.24 on the altar as a **sacrifice** to take away the sin of
29.28 the music continued until all the **sacrifices** had been burnt.
29.31 you are ritually clean, bring **sacrifices** as offerings of
29.31 brought animals to be **sacrificed** as burnt-offerings.
29.33 three thousand sheep as **sacrifices** for the people to eat.
29.35 In addition to offering the **sacrifices** that were burnt whole,
29.35 that was offered from the **sacrifices** which the people ate,
30.14 used in Jerusalem for offering **sacrifices** and burning
30.15 the month they killed the lambs for the Passover **sacrifice.**

2 Chr 30.15 and now they could **sacrifice** burnt-offerings in the Temple.
30.16 gave the blood of the **sacrifices** to the priests, who
30.22 during which they offered **sacrifices** in praise of the Lord,
33. 6 He **sacrificed** his sons in the Valley of Hinnom as burnt-offerings.
33.16 he **sacrificed** fellowship-offerings and thanksgiving-offerings
33.17 continued to offer **sacrifices** at other places of worship,
34. 4 dust on the graves of the people who had **sacrificed** to them.
34.25 rejected me and have offered **sacrifices** to other gods, and
35. 6 ritually clean and prepare the **sacrifices** in order that your
35. 8 and three hundred bulls for **sacrifices** during the festival.
35. 9 five hundred bulls for the Levites to offer as **sacrifices.**
35.13 The Levites roasted the Passover **sacrifices** over the fire,
35.14 animals that were burnt whole and the fat of the **sacrifices.**
Ezra 3. 2 so that they could burn **sacrifices** on it according to the
3. 3 to burn on it the regular morning and evening **sacrifices.**
3. 4 each day they offered the **sacrifices** required for that day;
3. 5 addition they offered the regular **sacrifices** to be burnt
3. 6 day of the seventh month to burn **sacrifices** to the Lord.
4. 2 have been offering **sacrifices** to him ever since Esarhaddon,
6. 3 a place where **sacrifices** are made and offerings are burnt.
6.10 so that they can offer **sacrifices** that are acceptable to the
6.17 and four hundred lambs as **sacrifices,** and twelve goats as
6.20 the animals for the Passover **sacrifices** for all the people
6.21 The **sacrifices** were eaten by all the Israelites who had
8.35 offerings to be burnt as **sacrifices** to the God of Israel.
8.35 All these animals were burnt as **sacrifices** to the Lord.
9. 4 the time for the evening **sacrifice** to be offered, and people
9. 5 time came for the evening **sacrifice,** I got up from where I
10.19 and they offered a ram as a **sacrifice** for their sins.
Neh 4. 2 they think that by offering **sacrifices** they can finish the
10.33 each day as **sacrifices,** the sacred offerings for Sabbaths,
10.34 wood to burn the **sacrifices** offered to the Lord our God,
12.43 That day many **sacrifices** were offered, and the people
Job 1. 5 get up early and offer **sacrifices** for each of his children
42. 8 rams to Job and offer them as a **sacrifice** for yourselves.
Ps 4. 5 Offer the right **sacrifices** to the Lord, and put your trust
16. 4 I will not take part in their **sacrifices;**
20. 3 all your offerings and be pleased with all your **sacrifices.**
22.25 who worship you I will offer the **sacrifices** I promised.
27. 6 With shouts of joy I will offer **sacrifices** in his Temple;
40. 6 You do not want **sacrifices** and offerings;
40. 6 whole on the altar or for **sacrifices** to take away sins.
50. 5 who made a covenant with me by offering a **sacrifice."**
50. 8 reprimand you because of your **sacrifices** and the
50.14 giving of thanks be your **sacrifice** to God, and give the
50.23 Giving thanks is the **sacrifice** that honours me, and I
51.16 You do not want **sacrifices,** or I would offer them;
51.17 My **sacrifice** is a humble spirit, O God;
51.19 Then you will be pleased with proper **sacrifices**
51.19 and bulls will be **sacrificed** on your altar.
54. 6 I will gladly offer you a **sacrifice,** O Lord;
66.15 I will **sacrifice** bulls and goats, and the smoke will go up
69.31 more than **sacrificing** a full-grown bull.
106.28 of Baal, and ate **sacrifices** offered to lifeless gods.
106.37 sons and daughters as **sacrifices** to the idols of Canaan.
107.22 They must thank him with **sacrifices,** and with songs of
116.17 I will give you a **sacrifice** of thanksgiving and offer my
141. 2 my prayer as incense, my uplifted hands as an evening **sacrifice.**
Prov 7.14 "I made my offerings today and have the meat from the **sacrifices.**
15. 8 pray, but hates the **sacrifices** that wicked men bring him.
21. 3 that pleases the Lord more than bringing him **sacrifices.**
21.27 when wicked men offer him **sacrifices,** especially if they do
Ecc 5. 1 to learn than to offer **sacrifices** as foolish people do,
9. 2 are not, to those who offer **sacrifices** and those who do not.
Is 1.11 think I want all these **sacrifices** you keep offering to me?
1.11 the sheep you burn as **sacrifices** and of the fat
19.21 and worship him, and bring him **sacrifices** and offerings.
31. 9 in Jerusalem and whose fire burns there for **sacrifices.**
34. 6 the blood and fat of lambs and goats that are **sacrificed.**
34. 6 The Lord will offer this **sacrifice** in the city of Bozrah;
40.16 are not enough for a **sacrifice** to our God, and its trees
43.23 you did not honour me with your **sacrifices.**
53.10 his death was a **sacrifice** to bring forgiveness.
56. 7 of prayer, and accept the **sacrifices** you offer on my altar.
57. 5 You offer your children as **sacrifices** in the rocky caves
57. 7 You go to the high mountains to offer **sacrifices** and have sex.
60. 7 be brought to you as **sacrifices** And offered on the altar to
65. 3 They offer pagan **sacrifices** in sacred gardens and burn
65. 4 and drink broth made from meat offered in pagan **sacrifices.**
66. 3 they kill a bull as a **sacrifice** or sacrifice a human being;
66. 3 whether they **sacrifice** a lamb or break a dog's neck;
Jer 1.16 have abandoned me, have offered **sacrifices** to other gods,
6.20 I will not accept their offerings or be pleased with their **sacrifices.**
7. 9 tell lies under oath, offer **sacrifices** to Baal, and worship
7.21 "My people, some **sacrifices** you burn completely on the altar,
7.22 or any other kinds of **sacrifices,** when I brought them out of
7.31 Topheth, so that they can **sacrifice** their sons and daughters
11.12 gods to whom they offer **sacrifices** and will cry out to them
11.13 up as many altars for **sacrifices** to that disgusting god Baal
11.15 by making promises and by offering animal **sacrifices?**
11.17 they have made me angry by offering **sacrifices** to Baal."
17.26 burnt-offerings and **sacrifices,** grain-offerings and incense,
19. 4 defiled this place by offering **sacrifices** here to other
19. 5 Baal in order to burn their children in the fire as **sacrifices.**
32.35 the Valley of Hinnom, to **sacrifice** their sons and daughters
33.18 to offer burnt-offerings, grain-offerings, and **sacrifices."**
44. 3 They offered **sacrifices** to other gods and served gods that
44. 5 not give up your evil practice of **sacrificing** to other gods.
44. 8 idols and by **sacrificing** to other gods here in Egypt,
44.15 knew that their wives offered **sacrifices** to other gods, and

Jer 44.17 We will offer **sacrifices** to our goddess, the Queen of Heaven,
44.18 But ever since we stopped **sacrificing** to the Queen of
44.19 the Queen of Heaven, offered **sacrifices** to her, and poured
44.21 "As for the **sacrifices** which you and your ancestors,
44.23 on you because you offered **sacrifices** to other gods and
44.24 promised that you would offer **sacrifices** to her and pour out
46.10 Today the Almighty **sacrifices** his victims in the north,
48.35 of worship and from offering **sacrifices** to their gods.
52.18 from the **sacrifices,** the bowls used for burning incense,
52.19 from the **sacrifices,** the ash containers, the lampstands,
Ezek 6.13 in every place where they burnt **sacrifices** to their idols.
16.19 you offered it as a **sacrifice** to win the favour of idols."
16.20 you had borne me and offered them as **sacrifices** to idols.
16.21 without taking my children and **sacrificing** them to idols?
16.36 idols, and you killed your children as **sacrifices** to idols.
18. 6 or eat the **sacrifices** offered at forbidden shrines.
18.11 He eats **sacrifices** offered at forbidden shrines
18.15 or eat the **sacrifices** offered at forbidden shrines.
20.26 offerings, and I let them **sacrifice** their first-born sons.
20.28 and green trees, they offered **sacrifices** at all of them.
20.28 made me angry by the **sacrifices** they burnt and by the wine
20.31 with the same idols by **sacrificing** your children to them in
20.40 you to bring me your **sacrifices,** your best offerings, and
20.41 together, I will accept the **sacrifices** that you burn, and
21.21 he examines the liver of a **sacrificed** animal.
22. 9 Some of them eat **sacrifices** offered to idols.
23.37 They **sacrificed** my sons to their idols.
23.39 they killed my children as **sacrifices** to idols, they came to
36.38 of the sheep which were offered as **sacrifices** at a festival.
39.17 from all round to eat the **sacrifice** I am preparing for them.
39.19 I kill these people like **sacrifices,** the birds and animals
40.38 carcasses of the animals to be burnt whole as **sacrifices.**
40.39 animals to be offered as **sacrifices,** either to be burnt
40.39 whole or to be **sacrifices** for sin or as repayment-offerings.
40.41 tables on which the animals to be **sacrificed** were killed:
40.42 in killing the **sacrificial** animals was kept on these tables.
40.43 meat to be offered in **sacrifice** was placed on the tables.
42.13 the **sacrifices** offered for sin or as repayment-offerings.
43.15 top section, on which the **sacrifices** were burnt, was also
43.18 to dedicate it by burning **sacrifices** on it and by sprinkling
43.18 on it the blood of the animals that were **sacrificed.**
43.19 give them a young bull to offer as a **sacrifice** for sin.
43.21 that is offered as a **sacrifice** for sin and burn it at
43.22 without any defects and offer it as a **sacrifice** for sin.
43.25 offer a goat, a bull, and a ram as **sacrifices** for sin.
44. 7 fat and the blood of the **sacrifices** are being offered to me.
44.11 offer for burnt-offerings and for **sacrifices,** and they are
44.15 to offer me the fat and the blood of the **sacrifices.**
44.27 the Temple and offer a **sacrifice** for his purification, so
45.18 first month you are to **sacrifice** a bull without any defects
45.22 offer a bull as a **sacrifice** for his sins and for those
45.23 the festival he is to **sacrifice** to the Lord seven bulls and
45.23 He is also to **sacrifice** a male goat each day as a
45.24 and each ram that is **sacrificed,** there is to be an offering
45.25 the seven days the same **sacrifice** for sin, the same
46. 2 his **sacrifices** whole and offer his fellowship-offerings.
46. 4 bring to the Lord, as **sacrifices** to be burnt whole, six
46.20 offered as **sacrifices** for sin or as repayment-offerings,
46.24 servants are to boil the **sacrifices** the people offer."
Dan 2.46 ground and gave orders for **sacrifices** and offerings to be
8.11 heavenly army, stopped the daily **sacrifices** offered to him,
8.12 of offering the proper daily **sacrifices,** and true religion
8.13 How long will an awful sin replace the daily **sacrifices?**
8.14 during which evening and morning **sacrifices** will not be offered.
8.26 about the evening and morning **sacrifices** which has been
9.21 It was the time for the evening **sacrifice** to be offered.
9.27 is past, he will put an end to **sacrifices** and offerings.
11.31 They will stop the daily **sacrifices** and set up The Awful Horror.
12.11 "From the time the daily **sacrifices** are stopped, that
Hos 3. 4 or leaders, without **sacrifices** or sacred stone pillars,
4.10 You will eat your share of the **sacrifices,** but still be hungry.
4.13 on the mountain-tops they offer **sacrifices,** and on the hills
4.14 and together with them you offer pagan **sacrifices.**
4.19 wind, and they will be ashamed of their pagan **sacrifices.**
5. 6 and cattle to offer as **sacrifices** to the Lord, but it does
6. 6 I want your constant love, not your animal **sacrifices.**
8.13 They offer sacrifices to me and eat the meat of the **sacrifices.**
9. 4 of wine to the Lord, or bring their **sacrifices** to him.
11. 2 My people **sacrificed** to Baal;
12.11 Bulls are **sacrificed** in Gilgal, and the altars there will
13. 2 And then they say, "Offer **sacrifices** to them!"
Amos 4. 4 and bring animals to be **sacrificed** morning after morning,
5.25 Israel, I did not demand **sacrifices** and offerings during
Jon 1.16 Lord that they offered a **sacrifice** and promised to serve him.
2. 9 I will offer you a **sacrifice** and do what I have promised.
Hab 1.16 worship their nets and offer **sacrifices** to them, because
Zeph 1. 7 The Lord is preparing to **sacrifice** his people and has
Hag 2.12 of consecrated meat from a **sacrifice** and carries it in a
Zech 9.11 sealed by the blood of **sacrifices,** I will set your people
9.15 like the blood of a **sacrifice** poured on the altar from a
14.21 The people who offer **sacrifices** will use them
14.21 for boiling the meat of the **sacrifices.**
Mal 1. 8 sick or lame animal to **sacrifice** to me, do you think there's
1.11 Everywhere they burn incense to me and offer acceptable **sacrifices.**
1.14 curse on the cheat who **sacrifices** a worthless animal to me,
2. 3 dung of the animals you **sacrifice**—and you will be taken out
Mt 8. 4 that you are cured, offer the **sacrifice** that Moses ordered."
9.13 'It is kindness that I want, not animal **sacrifices.'**
12. 7 scripture says, 'It is kindness that I want, not animal **sacrifices.'**
Mk 1.44 that you are cured, offer the **sacrifice** that Moses ordered."

Mk 9.49 be purified by fire as a **sacrifice** is purified by salt.
12.33 commandments than to offer animals and other **sacrifices** to God."
Lk 2.24 also went to offer a **sacrifice** of a pair of doves
5.14 that you are cured, offer the **sacrifice** as Moses ordered."
13. 1 whom Pilate had killed while they were offering **sacrifices** to God.
Acts 7.41 shape of a bull, offered **sacrifice** to it, and had a feast
7.42 you slaughtered and **sacrificed** animals for forty years in the
14.13 and the crowds wanted to offer **sacrifice** to the apostles.
14.18 apostles could hardly keep the crowd from offering a **sacrifice** to
20.28 he made his own through the **sacrificial death** of his Son.
21.26 period of purification, when a **sacrifice** would be offered for
24.17 to take some money to my own people and to offer **sacrifices.**
Rom 3.25 so that by his **sacrificial death** he should become the means
5. 9 By his **sacrificial death** we are now put right with God;
12. 1 Offer yourselves as a living **sacrifice** to God, dedicated to his
1 Cor 5. 7 is ready, now that Christ, our Passover lamb, has been **sacrificed.**
9.13 that those who offer the **sacrifices** on the altar
9.13 get a share of the **sacrifices.**
10.18 eat what is offered in **sacrifice** share in the altar's
10.20 saying is that what is **sacrificed** on pagan altars is offered
Eph 1. 7 For by the **sacrificial death** of Christ we are set free,
2.13 have been brought near by the **sacrificial death** of Christ.
5. 2 as a sweet-smelling offering and **sacrifice** that pleases God.
Phil 2.17 an offering on the **sacrifice** that your faith offers to God.
4.18 sweet-smelling offering to God, a **sacrifice** which is acceptable
Col 1.20 made peace through his Son's **sacrificial death** on the cross
2 Tim 4. 6 As for me, the hour has come for me to be **sacrificed;**
Heb 5. 1 serve God on their behalf, to offer **sacrifices** and offerings
5. 3 himself weak, he must offer **sacrifices** not only for the sins
7.27 does not need to offer **sacrifices** every day for his own sins
7.27 offered one **sacrifice,** once and for all, when he offered himself.
8. 3 present offerings and animal **sacrifices** to God, and so our High
9. 9 the offerings and animal **sacrifices** presented to God cannot make
9.12 take the blood of goats and bulls to offer as a **sacrifice;**
9.14 eternal Spirit he offered himself as a perfect **sacrifice** to God.
9.23 But the heavenly things themselves require much better **sacrifices.**
9.26 and for all, to remove sin through the **sacrifice** of himself.
9.28 Christ also was offered in **sacrifice** once to take away the
10. 1 The same **sacrifices** are offered for ever, year after year.
10. 1 by means of these **sacrifices** make perfect the people who come
10. 2 feel guilty of sin any more, and all **sacrifices** would stop.
10. 3 however, the **sacrifices** serve year after year to remind
10. 5 "You do not want **sacrifices** and offerings,
10. 6 whole on the altar or with **sacrifices** to take away sins.
10. 8 nor are you pleased with **sacrifices** and offerings
10. 8 burnt on the altar and the **sacrifices** to take away sins."
10. 8 even though all these **sacrifices** are offered according to the Law.
10. 9 old sacrifices and puts the **sacrifice** of Christ in their place.
10.11 every day and offers the same **sacrifices** many times;
10.11 but these **sacrifices** can never take away sins.
10.12 Christ, however, offered one **sacrifice** for sins, an offering
10.14 With one **sacrifice,** then, he has made perfect for ever those
10.26 there is no longer any **sacrifice** that will take away sins if
11. 4 that made Abel offer to God a better **sacrifice** than Cain's.
11.17 his son Isaac as a **sacrifice** when God put Abraham to the
11.17 yet he was ready to offer his only son as a **sacrifice.**
13.10 have no right to eat any of the **sacrifice** on our altar.
13.11 the Most Holy Place to offer it as a **sacrifice** for sins;
13.15 praise to God as our **sacrifice** through Jesus, which is
13.16 because these are the **sacrifices** that please God.
13.20 as the result of his **sacrificial death,** by which the eternal
1 Pet 1.19 it was the costly **sacrifice** of Christ, who was like a
2. 5 offer spiritual and acceptable **sacrifices** to God through Jesus Christ.
Rev 1. 5 loves us, and by his **sacrificial death** he has freed us from
5. 9 and by your **sacrificial death** you bought for God people

SAD

1 Sam 1. 8 Why are you always so **sad?**
1.18 Then she went away, ate some food, and was no longer **sad.**
2 Sam 13. 4 the king's son, yet day after day I see you looking **sad.**
13.20 So Tamar lived in Absalom's house, **sad** and lonely.
19. 2 was turned into **sadness** for all David's troops that day,
Neh 2. 1 had never seen me look **sad** before,
2. 2 so he asked, "Why are you looking so **sad?**
2. 3 How can I help looking **sad** when the city where my ancestors
8.10 Today is holy to our Lord, so don't be **sad.**
8.11 and telling them not to be **sad** on such a holy day.
Job 30.29 My voice is as **sad** and lonely as the cries of a
Ps 30.11 You have changed my **sadness** into a joyful dance;
42. 5 Why am I so **sad?**
42.11 Why am I so **sad?**
43. 5 Why am I so **sad?**
78.40 how many times they made him **sad!**
90.15 as much happiness as the **sadness** you gave us during all our
Prov 14.13 Laughter may hide **sadness.**
15.13 they smile, but when they are **sad,** they look depressed.
17.21 There is nothing but **sadness** and sorrow for a father
Ecc 7. 3 may **sadden** your face, but it sharpens your understanding.
Is 16.11 I groan with **sadness** for Moab, with grief for Kir Heres.
24. 7 was once happy is now **sad,** [8]and the joyful music of their
63.10 but they rebelled against him and made his holy spirit **sad.**
Mt 6.16 fast, do not put on a **sad** face as the hypocrites do.
9.15 a wedding party to be **sad** as long as the bridegroom is
14. 9 The king was **sad,** but because of the promise he had made
17.23 The disciples became very **sad.**
19.22 man heard this, he went away **sad,** because he was very rich.
Mk 6.26 This made the king very **sad,** but he could not refuse her
10.22 and he went away **sad,** because he was very rich.
Lk 18.23 heard this, he became very **sad,** because he was very rich.
18.24 Jesus saw that he was **sad** and said, "How hard it is
24.17 They stood still, with **sad** faces.
Jn 16. 6 now that I have told you, your hearts are full of **sadness.**
16.20 you will be **sad,** but your sadness will turn into gladness.
16.21 to give birth, she is **sad** because her hour of suffering has
16.22 now you are **sad,** but I will see you again, and your
21.17 Peter was **sad** because Jesus asked him the third time,
Acts 20.38 They were especially **sad** because he had said that they would
1 Cor 5. 2 you should be filled with **sadness,** and the man who has done
7.30 those who weep, as though they were not **sad;**
2 Cor 2. 1 my mind not to come to you again to make you **sad.**
2. 2 I were to make you **sad,** who would be left to cheer
2. 2 Only the very persons I had made **sad.**
2. 3 to you and be made **sad** by the very people who should
2. 4 was not to make you **sad,** but to make you realize how
2. 5 if anyone has made somebody **sad,** he has not done it to
2. 7 to keep him from becoming so **sad** as to give up completely.
6.10 although **saddened,** we are always glad;
7. 8 letter of mine made you **sad,** I am not sorry I wrote
7. 8 sorry when I saw that it made you **sad** for a while.
7. 9 not because I made you **sad,**
7. 9 but because your **sadness** made you change your ways.
7. 9 That **sadness** was used by God, and so we caused you no
7.10 For the **sadness** that is used by God brings a change of
7.10 But **sadness** that is merely human causes death.
7.11 See what God did with this **sadness** of yours:
Eph 4.30 And do not make God's Holy Spirit **sad;**
1 Thes 4.13 that you will not be **sad,** as are those who have no
Heb 12.11 to us at the time something to make us **sad,** not glad.
13.17 they will do it with **sadness,** and that would be of no
1 Pet 1. 6 necessary for you to be **sad** for a while because of the

SADDLE

Gen 31.34 and put them in a camel's **saddlebag** and was sitting on them.
49.14 a donkey That lies stretched out between its **saddlebags.**
Lev 15. 9 Any **saddle** or seat on which the man with the discharge
Num 22.21 So the next morning Balaam **saddled** his donkey and went
Judg 5.10 on white donkeys, sitting on **saddles,** and you that must walk
19.10 way, with their servant and two donkeys with pack **saddles.**
2 Sam 17.23 had not been followed, he **saddled** his donkey and went back
19.26 I told my servant to **saddle** my donkey so that I could
1 Kgs 2.40 they were in Gath, [40]he **saddled** his donkey and went to
13.13 the road [13]and he told them to **saddle** his donkey for him.
13.23 finished eating, the old prophet **saddled** the donkey for the
13.27 Then he said to his sons, **"Saddle** my donkey for me."
2 Kgs 4.24 Then she had the donkey **saddled,** and ordered the servant,
Ezek 27.20 The people of Dedan exchanged **saddle-cloths** for your goods.

SADDUCEES

Small Jewish religious party.

Mt 3. 7 John saw many Pharisees and **Sadducees** coming to him to be baptized,
16. 1 Some Pharisees and **Sadducees** who came to Jesus wanted to trap him,
16. 6 on your guard against the yeast of the Pharisees and **Sadducees."**
16.11 Guard yourselves from the yeast of the Pharisees and **Sadducees!"**
16.12 in bread but from the teaching of the Pharisees and **Sadducees.**
22.23 That same day some **Sadducees** came to Jesus and claimed that
22.34 Jesus had silenced the **Sadducees,** they came together,
Mk 12.18 some **Sadducees,** who say that people will not rise from death,
12.28 that Jesus had given the **Sadducees** a good answer,
Lk 20.27 some **Sadducees,** who say that people will not rise from death,
Acts 4. 1 in charge of the temple guards, and some **Sadducees** arrived.
5.17 party of the **Sadducees,** became extremely jealous of the apostles;
23. 6 some of the group were **Sadducees** and the others were Pharisees,
23. 7 said this, the Pharisees and **Sadducees** started to quarrel,
23. 8 (For the **Sadducees** say that people will not rise from death

SAFE

Gen 19.20 see it is just a small place—and I will be **safe."**
19.29 kept Abraham in mind and allowed Lot to escape to **safety.**
28.21 clothing, [21]and if I return **safely** to my father's home,
33.18 return from Mesopotamia Jacob arrived **safely** at the city of
37.14 see if your brothers are **safe** and if the flock is all
43. 9 bring him back to you **safe** and sound, I will always bear
44.17 rest of you may go back **safe** and sound to your father."
Ex 21.13 which I will choose for you, and there he will be **safe.**
21.14 to death, even if he has run to my altar for **safety.**
Lev 25.18 and commands, so that you may live in **safety** in the land.
25.19 will have all you want to eat and will live in **safety.**
26. 5 want to eat, and you will live in **safety** in your land.
26.25 gather in your cities for **safety,** I will send incurable
Num 24.21 where you live is secure, **Safe** as a nest set high on
32.17 in the fortified towns, **safe** from the people of this land.
35.12 There he will be **safe** from the dead man's relative who
Deut 1.31 saw how he brought you **safely** all the way to this place,
4.42 man could escape and be **safe** if he had accidentally killed
12.10 He will keep you **safe** from all your enemies, and you will
19. 4 enemy, he may escape to any of these cities and be **safe.**
19. 5 he can run to one of those three cities and be **safe.**
25.19 the land and made you **safe** from all your enemies who live
32.11 young to fly, catching them **safely** on its spreading wings,
Josh 1.15 When he has given **safety** to all the tribes of Israel, then
6.23 all, family and slaves, to **safety** near the Israelite camp.
10.20 although some managed to find **safety** inside their city walls

Josh	10.21	of Joshua's men came back **safe** to him at the camp at
	24.17	He kept us **safe** wherever we went among all the nations
Judg	6. 2	hid from them in caves and other **safe** places in the hills.
	8. 9	am going to come back **safe** and sound, and when I do,
	9.46	heard about this, they sought **safety** in the stronghold of
	18. 7	They saw how **safely** the people there were living,
1 Sam	12.11	rescued you from your enemies, and you lived in **safety**.
	20. 7	If he says, 'All right,' I will be **safe**;
	20.13	I don't let you know about it and get you **safely** away.
	20.21	get them,' that means that you are **safe** and can come out.
	22.23	kill both you and me, but you will be **safe** with me."
	25.29	your God will keep you **safe**, as a man guards a precious
	26.13	top of the hill, a **safe** distance away, [14]and shouted to
	27. 1	give up looking for me in Israel, and I will be **safe**."
	30.23	He kept us **safe** and gave us victory over the raiders.
2 Sam	3.21	gave Abner a guarantee of **safety** and sent him on his way.
	3.22	because David had sent him away with a guarantee of **safety**.
	3.23	King David and had been sent away with a guarantee of **safety**.
	7. 1	his palace, and the Lord kept him **safe** from all his enemies.
	7.10	I promise to keep you **safe** from all your enemies and to
	14.17	promise, sir, would make me **safe**, because the king is like
	17. 3	the rest of the people will be **safe**."
	18.29	"Is the young man Absalom **safe**?"
	18.32	"Is the young man Absalom **safe**?"
	19.30	"It's enough for me that Your Majesty has come home **safely**."
	22. 3	My God is my protection, and with him I am **safe**.
	22. 3	he defends me and keeps me **safe**.
	22.33	he makes my pathway **safe**.
	22.34	he keeps me **safe** on the mountains.
1 Kgs	4.25	Judah and Israel lived in **safety**, each family with its own
	22.27	and to put him on bread and water until I return **safely**."
	22.28	"If you return **safely**," Micaiah exclaimed, "then the
2 Chr	15. 5	could come and go in **safety**, because there was trouble and
	18.26	and to put him on bread and water until I return **safely**."
	18.27	"If you return **safely**," Micaiah exclaimed, "then the
	19. 1	King Jehoshaphat of Judah returned **safely** to his palace
	31.12	and put all the gifts and tithes in them for **safe-keeping**.
Ezra	9. 8	escape from slavery and live in **safety** in this holy place.
	9. 9	in ruins, and to find **safety** here in Judah and Jerusalem.
Esth	4.13	"Don't imagine that you are **safer** than any other Jew just
Job	5. 4	Their sons can never find **safety**;
	5.24	when you look at your sheep, you will find them **safe**.
	15.21	in his ears, and robbers attack when he thinks he is **safe**.
	41.11	Who can attack him and still be **safe**?
Ps	4. 8	you alone, O Lord, keep me perfectly **safe**.
	5.11	But all who find **safety** in you will rejoice;
	8. 2	You are **safe** and secure from all your enemies;
	9. 9	for the oppressed, a place of **safety** in times of trouble.
	11. 1	I trust in the Lord for **safety**.
	12. 7	Keep us always **safe**, O Lord, and preserve us from such people.
	16. 1	I trust in you for **safety**.
	17. 7	at your side I am **safe** from my enemies.
	18. 2	My God is my protection, and with him I am **safe**.
	18. 2	he defends me and keeps me **safe**.
	18.32	is the God who makes me strong, who makes my pathway **safe**.
	18.33	he keeps me **safe** on the mountains.
	18.35	care has made me great, and your power has kept me **safe**.
	19.13	Keep me **safe**, also, from wilful sins;
	22. 9	was you who brought me **safely** through birth,
	22. 9	and when I was a baby, you kept me **safe**.
	25.20	I come to you for **safety**.
	26.12	I am **safe** from all dangers;
	27. 5	he will keep me **safe** in his Temple and make me secure
	27.11	and lead me along a **safe** path, because I have many enemies.
	31. 4	Keep me **safe** from the trap that has been set for me;
	31.20	You hide them in the **safety** of your presence from the
	31.20	in a **safe** shelter you hide them from the insults of their
	34. 8	Happy are those who find **safety** with him.
	37. 3	live in the land and be **safe**.
	40. 2	He set me **safely** on a rock and made me secure.
	40.11	Your love and loyalty will always keep me **safe**.
	48. 3	has shown that there is **safety** with him inside the
	48. 8	he will keep the city **safe** for ever.
	52. 7	not depend on God for **safety**, but trusted instead in his
	55.18	He will bring me **safely** back from the battles that I
	57. 1	me, O God, be merciful, because I come to you for **safety**.
	61. 2	Take me to a **safe** refuge, [3]for you are my protector, my
	61. 4	let me find **safety** under your wings.
	63. 8	I cling to you, and your hand keeps me **safe**.
	64.10	They will find **safety** in him;
	66.12	flood, but now you have brought us to a place of **safety**.
	69.14	keep me **safe** from my enemies, safe from the deep water.
	78.53	He led them **safely**, and they were not afraid;
	91. 1	goes to the Lord for **safety**, whoever remains under the
	91. 3	He will keep you **safe** from all hidden dangers and from all
	91. 4	you will be **safe** in his care;
	102.28	Our children will live in **safety**,
	107.30	the calm, and he brought them **safe** to the port they wanted.
	119.73	You created me, and you keep me **safe**;
	119.117	me, and I will be **safe**, and I will always pay attention
	121. 7	he will keep you **safe**.
	122. 7	May there be peace inside your walls and **safety** in your palaces."
	138. 7	When I am surrounded by troubles, you keep me **safe**.
	140. 1	keep me **safe** from violent men.
	140. 4	keep me **safe** from violent men who plot my downfall.
	143.10	Be good to me, and guide me on a **safe** path.
	144. 2	my shelter and saviour, in whom I trust for **safety**.
	147.14	He keeps your borders **safe** and satisfies you with the finest wheat.
Prov	1.33	He will be **safe**, with no reason to be afraid."
	3.17	Wisdom can make your life pleasant and lead you **safely** through it.
Prov	3.23	You can go **safely** on your way and never even stumble.
	3.26	The Lord will keep you **safe**.
	4. 6	love her, and she will keep you **safe**.
	10. 9	Honest people are **safe** and secure, but the dishonest will be caught.
	10.25	wicked are blown away, but honest people are always **safe**.
	13.13	follow it and you are **safe**.
	18.10	like a strong tower, where the righteous can go and be **safe**.
	19.23	and you will live a long life, content and **safe** from harm.
	22.12	that truth is kept **safe** by disproving the words of liars.
	28.18	Be honest and you will be **safe**.
	28.26	Be **safe**, and follow the teachings of wiser people.
	29.25	think of you, but if you trust the Lord, you are **safe**.
Ecc	7.12	Wisdom keeps you **safe**—this is the advantage of knowledge.
	8. 5	obey his commands, you are **safe**, and a wise man knows how
Is	4. 6	it a place of **safety**, sheltered from the rain and storm.
	14.30	the poor of his people and will let them live in **safety**.
	14.32	Zion and that his suffering people will find **safety** there.
	23.12	Even if they escape to Cyprus, they will still not be **safe**.
	24.10	and people lock themselves in their houses for **safety**.
	25. 4	have fled to you and have been **safe** in times of trouble.
	28.15	because you depend on lies and deceit to keep you **safe**.
	32.18	be free from worries, and their homes peaceful and **safe**.
	32.20	water for the crops and **safe** pasture everywhere for the
	33.16	Then you will be **safe**;
	33.20	What a **safe** place it will be to live in!
	41. 3	follows in pursuit and marches **safely** on, so fast that he
	47. 8	lover of pleasure, you that think you are **safe** and secure.
	48.22	"There is no **safety** for sinners," says the Lord.
	54.14	You will be **safe** from oppression and terror.
	57.21	There is no **safety** for sinners," says the Lord.
	59. 8	wherever you go, [8]and no one is **safe** when you are about.
	59. 8	path, and no one who walks that path will ever be **safe**.
Jer	4. 6	Run for **safety**!
	6. 1	People of Benjamin, run for **safety**!
	7. 4	Stop believing those deceitful words, 'We are **safe**!
	7.10	in my presence, in my own Temple, and say, 'We are **safe**!'
	15.20	I will be with you to protect you and keep you **safe**.
	17.14	rescue me and I will be perfectly **safe**.
	17.17	you are my place of **safety** when trouble comes.
	23. 6	people of Judah will be **safe**, and the people of Israel will
	32.37	them back to this place and let them live here in **safety**.
	33.16	Judah and of Jerusalem will be rescued and will live in **safety**.
	39.14	grandson of Shaphan, who was to see that I got home **safely**.
	39.18	I will keep you **safe**, and you will not be put to
	49.31	We'll attack those people that feel **safe** and secure!
Ezek	28.26	They will live there in **safety**.
	34.14	will let them graze in **safety** in the mountain meadows and
	34.25	that my sheep can live **safely** in the fields
	34.27	crops, and everyone will live in **safety** on his own land.
	34.28	They will live in **safety**, and no one will terrify them.
	38. 8	so long, but where all the people now live in **safety**.
	39.26	are once more living in **safety** in their own land, with no
Hos	2.18	and bows, and will let my people live in peace and **safety**.
	13.12	guilt are on record, and the records are **safely** stored away.
Amos	6. 1	and for you that feel **safe** in Samaria—you great men of
Mic	2. 2	No man's family or property is **safe**.
	2. 8	battle, thinking they are **safe** at home, but there you are,
	2.10	there is no **safety** here any more.
	5. 4	His people will live in **safety** because people all over the
Nah	2.11	lion and the lioness would go and their cubs would be **safe**?
Hab	2. 9	have tried to make your own home **safe** from harm and danger!
	3.19	sure-footed as a deer, and keeps me **safe** on the mountains.
Zeph	2.15	is so proud of its own power and thinks it is **safe**.
Zech	8.10	either men or animals, and no one was **safe** from his enemies.
	9.12	return to your place of **safety**.
	12. 6	The people of Jerusalem will remain **safe** in the city.
	14.11	The people will live there in **safety**,
Mt	6.13	us to hard testing, but keep us **safe** from the Evil One.'
Mk	6.20	was a good and holy man, and so he kept him **safe**.
Lk	11.21	weapons ready, guards his own house, all his belongings are **safe**.
	15.27	the prize calf, because he got him back **safe** and sound.'
	21.36	have the strength to go **safely** through all those things
Jn	17.11	Keep them **safe** by the power of your name,
	17.12	I kept them **safe** by the power of your name,
	17.15	I do ask you to keep them **safe** from the Evil One.
Acts	7.10	God was with him [10]and brought him **safely** through all his troubles.
	23.24	Paul to ride and get him **safely** through to the governor Felix."
	27.44	And this was how we all got **safely** ashore.
	28. 1	When we were **safely** ashore, we learnt that the island was
Rom	15.31	that I may be kept **safe** from the unbelievers in Judaea
1 Cor	10. 1	of the cloud, and all passed **safely** through the Red Sea.
Gal	2. 5	the truth of the gospel **safe** for you, we did not give
Phil	3. 1	have written before, and you will be **safer** if I do so.
	4. 7	keep your hearts and minds **safe** in union with Christ Jesus.
Col	1. 5	what you hope for, which is kept **safe** for you in heaven.
	1.13	of darkness and brought us **safe** into the kingdom of his dear
1 Thes	5. 3	"Everything is quiet and **safe**," then suddenly destruction will
2 Thes	3. 3	he will strengthen you and keep you **safe** from the Evil One.
1 Tim	6.20	Timothy, keep **safe** what has been entrusted to your care.
2 Tim	1.12	he is able to keep **safe** until that Day what he has
	4.18	from all evil and take me **safely** into his heavenly Kingdom.
Heb	6.18	So we who have found **safety** with him are greatly encouraged
	6.19	It is **safe** and sure, and goes through the curtain of the
1 Pet	1. 5	who through faith are kept **safe** by God's power for the
2 Pet	3.17	errors of lawless people and fall from your **safe** position.
1 Jn	5.18	Son of God keeps him **safe**, and the Evil One cannot harm
	5.21	My children, keep yourselves **safe** from false gods!
Rev	3.10	I will also keep you **safe** from the time of trouble
	3.11	Keep **safe** what you have, so that no one will rob you

Rev	7.14	“These are the people who have come **safely** through the terrible persecution.
	12.14	for three and a half years, **safe** from the dragon's attack.

SAFE HARBOURS

Acts	27. 8	came to a place called **Safe Harbours,** not far from the town

SAFFRON

Song	4.14	of henna and nard, [14]of **saffron,** calamus, and cinnamon, or

SAIL

Num	24.24	Invaders will **sail** from Cyprus;
1 Kgs	9.28	They **sailed** to the land of Ophir, and brought back to
	10.22	He had a fleet of ocean-going ships **sailing** with Hiram's fleet.
	22.48	Jehoshaphat built ocean-going ships to **sail** to the land of
	22.48	but they were wrecked at Eziongeber and never **sailed.**
	22.49	offered to let his men **sail** with Jehoshaphat's men, but
2 Chr	8.18	They **sailed** with Solomon's officers to the land of Ophir and
	9.21	a fleet of ocean-going ships **sailing** with King Hiram's fleet.
	20.37	And the ships were wrecked and never **sailed.**
Ps	104.26	The ships **sail** on it, and in it plays Leviathan, that
	107.23	Some **sailed** over the ocean in ships, earning their
Is	33.21	and streams, but hostile ships will not **sail** on them.
	33.22	the **sails** cannot be spread!
	42.10	Praise him, you that **sail** the sea;
Ezek	27. 7	Your **sails** were made of linen, Embroidered linen from Egypt,
Jon	1. 3	aboard with the crew to **sail** to Spain, where he would be
Mt	23.15	You **sail** the seas and cross whole countries to win one convert;
Lk	8.23	As they were **sailing,** Jesus fell asleep.
	8.26	Jesus and his disciples **sailed** on over to the territory of Gerasa,
Acts	13. 4	Saul went to Seleucia and **sailed** from there to the island
	13.13	Paul and his companions **sailed** from Paphos and came to Perga,
	14.26	and from there they **sailed** back to Antioch,
	15.39	Barnabas took Mark and **sailed** off for Cyprus, [40]while Paul
	16.11	by ship from Troas and **sailed** straight across to Samothrace,
	18.18	then left them and **sailed** off with Priscilla and Aquila
	18.18	Before **sailing** from Cenchreae he had his head shaved
	18.21	And so he **sailed** from Ephesus.
	20. 6	We **sailed** from Philippi after the Festival of Unleavened Bread,
	20.13	ahead to the ship and **sailed** off to Assos, where we were
	20.15	We **sailed** from there and arrived off Chios the next day.
	20.16	Paul had decided to **sail** on past Ephesus,
	21. 1	After **sailing** straight across, we came to Cos;
	21. 2	was going to Phoenicia, so we went aboard and **sailed** away.
	21. 3	could see Cyprus, and then **sailed** south of it on to Syria.
	21. 7	We continued our voyage, **sailing** from Tyre to Ptolemais,
	27. 1	was decided that we should **sail** to Italy, they handed Paul
	27. 2	the seaports of the province of Asia, and we **sailed** away.
	27. 4	were blowing against us, we **sailed** on the sheltered side
	27. 6	Alexandria that was going to **sail** for Italy, so he put us
	27. 7	We **sailed** slowly for several days and with great
	27. 7	in that direction, so we **sailed** down the sheltered side
	27.13	pulled up the anchor and **sailed** as close as possible
	27.17	so they lowered the **sail** and let the ship be carried
	27.21	should have listened to me and not have **sailed** from Crete;
	27.24	has spared the lives of all those who are **sailing** with you.'
	27.40	Then they raised the **sail** at the front of the ship
	28.10	many gifts, and when we **sailed,** they put on board what we
	28.11	After three months we **sailed** away on a ship from Alexandria,
	28.13	From there we **sailed** on and arrived in the city of Rhegium.
Rev	18.19	where all who have ships **sailing** the seas became rich

SAILOR

2 Chr	8.18	of his own officers and manned by experienced **sailors.**
Is	23. 1	Howl with grief, you **sailors** out on the ocean!
	23.14	Howl with grief, you **sailors** out on the ocean!
Ezek	27. 8	Your own skilful men were the **sailors.**
	27. 9	**Sailors** from every sea-going ship Did business in your shops.
	27.27	wealth of merchandise, All the **sailors** in your crew, Your
	27.28	The shouts of the drowning **sailors** Echoed on the shore.
	27.29	“Every ship is now deserted, And every **sailor** has gone ashore.
Jon	1. 5	The **sailors** were terrified and cried out for help, each
	1. 7	The **sailors** said to one another, “Let's draw lots and
	1.10	The **sailors** were terrified, and said to him, “That was an
	1.11	all the time, so the **sailors** asked him, “What should we do
	1.13	Instead, the **sailors** tried to get the ship to shore,
	1.16	This made the **sailors** so afraid of the Lord that they
Acts	27.27	About midnight the **sailors** suspected that we were getting close to land.
	27.30	Then the **sailors** tried to escape from the ship;
	27.31	officer and soldiers, “If the **sailors** don't stay on board,
	27.39	When day came, the **sailors** did not recognize the coast,
Rev	18.17	ships' captains and passengers, the **sailors** and all others

AV SAINT

see also **GOD'S PEOPLE**

Deut	33. 2	Ten thousand **angels** were with him, a flaming fire at his
	33. 3	Lord loves his people and protects those who **belong** to him.
Job	5. 1	Is there any **angel** to whom you can turn?
	15.15	Why, God does not trust even his **angels;**
Ps	16. 3	How excellent are the Lord's **faithful** people!
	79. 2	the bodies of your **servants** for wild animals to eat.
	85. 8	promises peace to us, his **own people,** if we do not go
	89. 5	the **holy ones** sing of your faithfulness, Lord.
	89. 7	You are feared in the council of the **holy ones;**
	106.16	were jealous of Moses and of Aaron, the Lord's **holy** servant.
Ps	149. 1	praise him in the assembly of his **faithful** people!
Prov	2. 8	others fairly, and guards those who are **devoted** to him.
Dan	7.21	that horn made war on **God's people** and conquered them.
	8.13	Then I heard one **angel** ask another, “How long
Zech	14. 5	The Lord my God will come, bringing all the **angels** with him.
Acts	9.41	Then he called all the **believers,** including the widows,
Rom	12.13	needy **fellow-Christians,** and open your homes to strangers.
1 Thes	3.13	when our Lord Jesus comes with all who **belong** to him.
1 Tim	5.10	duties for **fellow-Christians,** helped people in trouble,
Heb	6.10	you gave and are still giving to your **fellow-Christians.**
Jude	14	thousands of his **holy** angels [15]to bring judgement on all,
Rev	15. 3	King of the **nations,** how right and true are your ways!

SAKE

Gen	18.26	in Sodom, I will spare the whole city for their **sake.”**
2 Sam	5.12	making his kingdom prosperous for the **sake** of his people.
	9. 1	I would like to show him kindness for Jonathan's **sake.”**
	9. 7	will be kind to you for the **sake** of your father Jonathan.
	18. 5	“For my **sake** don't harm the young man Absalom.”
	18.12	Abishai and Ittai, ‘For my **sake** don't harm the young man Absalom.’
1 Kgs	11.12	However, for the **sake** of your father David I will not do
	11.13	him one tribe for the **sake** of my servant David
	11.13	and for the **sake** of Jerusalem,
	11.32	keep one tribe, for the **sake** of my servant David
	11.32	and for the **sake** of Jerusalem, the city I have
	11.34	I will do for the **sake** of my servant David,
	15. 4	But for David's **sake,** the Lord his God gave Abijah a son
2 Kgs	19.34	and protect it, for the **sake** of my own honour and because
	20. 6	defend this city, for the **sake** of my own honour and because
1 Chr	14. 2	making his kingdom prosperous for the **sake** of his people.
Ps	69. 7	It is for your **sake** that I have been insulted and that
	79. 9	us and forgive our sins for the **sake** of your own honour.
	106.45	For their **sake** he remembered his covenant, and because
	122. 8	For the **sake** of my relatives and friends I say to Jerusalem,
	122. 9	For the **sake** of the house of the Lord our God I
Is	37.35	and protect it, for the **sake** of my own honour and because
	48.11	is done for my own **sake**— I will not let my
	53.11	punishment of many and for his **sake** I will forgive them.
	63.17	Come back, for the **sake** of those who serve you,
	63.17	for the **sake** of the people
Jer	15.15	Remember that it is for your **sake** that I am insulted.
Ezek	36.22	do is not for the **sake** of you Israelites,
	36.22	but for the **sake** of my holy name,
	36.32	to know that I am not doing all this for your **sake.**
Amos	2. 9	it was for your **sake** that I totally destroyed the Amorites,
Mt	10.18	For my **sake** you will be brought to trial before rulers
	10.39	but whoever loses his life for my **sake** will gain it.
	16.25	but whoever loses his life for my **sake** will find it.
	19.12	others do not marry for the **sake** of the Kingdom of heaven.
	19.29	children or fields for my **sake,** will receive a hundred times
	24.22	For the **sake** of his chosen people, however, God will reduce
Mk	5. 7	For God's **sake,** I beg you, don't punish me!”
	13. 9	rulers and kings for my **sake** to tell them the Good News.
	13.20	For the **sake** of his chosen people, however, he has reduced
Lk	9.24	but whoever loses his life for my **sake** will save it.
	18.29	parents or children for the **sake** of the Kingdom of God
	21.12	you will be brought before kings and rulers for my **sake.**
Jn	11.15	but for your **sake** I am glad
	11.42	I say this for the **sake** of the people here,
	12.30	“It was not for my **sake** that this voice spoke,
	17.19	And for their **sake** I dedicate myself to you,
Acts	5.41	worthy to suffer disgrace for the **sake** of Jesus.
	9.16	will show him all that he must suffer for my **sake.”**
	21.13	but even to die there for the **sake** of the Lord Jesus.”
	28.20	chains like this for the **sake** of him
Rom	1. 5	being an apostle for the **sake** of Christ,
	8.36	the scripture says, “For your **sake** we are in danger of
	9. 3	For their **sake** I could wish that I myself were under God's
	11.28	the Jews are God's enemies for the **sake** of you Gentiles.
1 Cor	4. 6	For your **sake,** my brothers, I have applied all this to
	4.10	For Christ's **sake** we are fools;
	9.23	I do for the gospel's **sake,** in order to share in its
	10.28	eat that food, for the **sake** of the one who told you
	10.28	for conscience' **sake**—[29]that is, not your own conscience,
	11. 9	created for woman's sake, but woman was created for man's **sake.**
2 Cor	4. 5	Jesus Christ as Lord, and ourselves as your servants for Jesus' **sake.**
	4.11	danger of death for Jesus' **sake,** in order that his life may
	4.15	All this is for your **sake;**
	5.13	It is for God's **sake.**
	5.13	Then it is for your **sake.**
	5.15	for him who died and was raised to life for their **sake.**
	5.21	without sin, but for our **sake** God made him share our sin
	8. 9	made himself poor for your **sake,** in order to make you rich
	8.19	service of love for the **sake** of the Lord's glory, and in
	12.10	hardships, persecutions, and difficulties for Christ's **sake.**
Eph	3. 1	of Christ Jesus for the **sake** of you Gentiles, pray to God.
	6.20	For the **sake** of this gospel I am an ambassador,
Phil	1.24	but for your **sake** it is much more important that I
	2.22	his father, have worked together for the **sake** of the gospel.
	2.30	and nearly died for the **sake** of the work of Christ,
	3. 7	count as profit I now reckon as loss for Christ's **sake.**
	3. 8	as complete loss for the **sake** of what is so much more
	3. 8	For his **sake** I have thrown everything away;
2 Tim	1. 8	nor be ashamed of me, a prisoner for Christ's **sake.**
	2.10	I endure everything for the **sake** of God's chosen people,
Phlm	1	Paul, a prisoner for the **sake** of Christ Jesus,
	9	Christ Jesus, and at present also a prisoner for his **sake.**
	13	in prison for the gospel's **sake,** so that he could help me

Phlm 20 So, my brother, please do me this favour for the Lord's **sake;**
23 prison with me for the **sake** of Christ Jesus, sends you his
1 Pet 1.20 the world and was revealed in these last days for your **sake.**
2.13 For the **sake** of the Lord submit to every human authority:
1 Jn 2.12 because your sins are forgiven for the **sake** of Christ.
Jude 11 For the **sake** of money they have given themselves over to the
Rev 2. 3 you have suffered for my **sake,** and you have not given up.

SALE see SELL

SALT (1)
[UNSALTED]

Gen 19.26 Lot's wife looked back and was turned into a pillar of **salt.**
Ex 30.35 Add **salt** to keep it pure and holy.
Lev 2.13 Put **salt** on every grain-offering,
2.13 because **salt** represents the covenant between you and
2.13 (You must put **salt** on all your offerings.)
Deut 29.23 The fields will be a barren waste, covered with sulphur and **salt;**
Judg 9.45 its people, tore it down, and covered the ground with **salt.**
2 Kgs 2.20 "Put some **salt** in a new bowl, and bring it to me,"
2.21 to the spring, threw the **salt** in the water, and said, "This
Ezra 6. 9 offerings to the God of Heaven, or wheat, **salt,** wine, or
7.22 2,000 litres of olive-oil, and as much **salt** as necessary.
Job 6. 6 But who can eat tasteless, **unsalted** food?
39. 6 to be their home, and let them live on the **salt** plains.
Ps 107.34 made rich soil become a **salty** wilderness because of the
Prov 25.20 clothes on a cold day or like rubbing **salt** in a wound.
Jer 17. 6 dry wilderness, on **salty** ground where nothing else grows.
Ezek 16. 4 washed you or rubbed you with **salt** or wrapped you in cloth.
43.24 The priests will sprinkle **salt** on them and burn them as an
47. 8 Dead Sea, it replaces the **salt** water of that sea with fresh
47.11 They will remain there as a source of **salt.**
Zeph 2. 9 will become a place of **salt** pits and everlasting ruin,
Mt 5.13 "You are like **salt** for all mankind.
5.13 But if **salt** loses its saltiness,
5.13 there is no way to make it **salty** again.
Mk 9.49 be purified by fire as a sacrifice is purified by **salt.**
9.50 **"Salt** is good;
9.50 if it loses its saltiness, how can you make it **salty** again?
9.50 "Have the **salt** of friendship among yourselves, and live in peace
Lk 14.34 **"Salt** is good, but if it loses its saltiness,
14.34 there is no way to make it **salty** again.
Jas 3.12 bear figs, nor can a **salty** spring produce sweet water.

SALT (2)

Josh 15.62 Beth Arabah, Middin, Secacah, [62]Nibshan, the city of **Salt,**

SALT VALLEY
[VALLEY OF SALT]

2 Sam 8.13 killing eighteen thousand Edomites in the **Valley of Salt.**
2 Kgs 14. 7 Amaziah killed ten thousand Edomite soldiers in **Salt Valley;**
1 Chr 18.12 the Edomites in the **Valley of Salt** and killed eighteen
2 Chr 25.11 up his courage and led his army to the **Valley of Salt.**

SALUTE

Mk 15.18 Then they began to **salute** him:

SALVATION
see also **SAVE**

Ps 27. 1 The Lord is my light and my **salvation;**
32. 7 I sing aloud of your **salvation,** because you protect me.
40.10 I have not kept the news of **salvation** to myself;
40.16 who are thankful for your **salvation** always say, "How great
51.12 joy that comes from your **salvation,** and make me willing to
62. 7 My **salvation** and honour depend on God;
67. 2 so that all nations may know your **salvation.**
69.27 don't let them have any part in your **salvation.**
70. 4 for your **salvation** always say, "How great is God!"
71.15 I will speak of your **salvation,** though it is more than I
Is 61.10 God has clothed her with **salvation** and victory.
Jer 23. 6 He will be called 'The Lord Our **Salvation.'**
33.16 The city will be called 'The Lord Our **Salvation.'**
Jon 2. 9 **Salvation** comes from the Lord!"
Mk 16.10 the sacred and ever-living message of eternal **salvation.**
Lk 1.78 cause the bright dawn of **salvation** to rise on us
2.30 I have seen your **salvation,** [31] which you have prepared
2.34 for the destruction and the **salvation** of many in Israel.
3. 6 All mankind will see God's **salvation!'"**
19. 9 Jesus said to him, **"Salvation** has come to this house today,
21.28 stand up and raise your heads, because your **salvation** is near."
Jn 4.22 because it is from the Jews that **salvation** comes.
Acts 4.12 **Salvation** is to be found through him alone;
13.26 it is to us that this message of **salvation** has been sent!
26.23 to announce the light of **salvation** to the Jews and to the
28.28 that God's message of **salvation** has been sent to the Gentiles.
Rom 11.11 Because they sinned, **salvation** has come to the Gentiles,
2 Cor 1. 6 If we suffer, it is for your help and **salvation;**
3. 9 much more glorious is the activity which brings **salvation!**
7.10 of heart that leads to **salvation**—and there is no regret in
Eph 1.13 the true message, the Good News that brought you **salvation.**
6.17 And accept **salvation** as a helmet, and the word of God as
Phil 2.12 to complete your **salvation,** [13] because God is always at work
1 Thes 2.16 preaching to the Gentiles the message that would bring them **salvation.**
5. 8 as a breastplate, and our hope of **salvation** as a helmet.
1 Thes 5. 9 but to possess **salvation** through our Lord Jesus Christ,
2 Tim 2.10 they too may obtain the **salvation** that comes through Christ Jesus
3.15 the wisdom that leads to **salvation** through faith in Christ Jesus.
Tit 2.11 For God has revealed his grace for the **salvation** of all mankind.
Heb 1.14 sent by him to help those who are to receive **salvation.**
2. 3 if we pay no attention to such a great **salvation?**
2. 3 Lord himself first announced this **salvation,**
2.10 For Jesus is the one who leads them to **salvation.**
5. 9 the source of eternal **salvation** for all those who obey him,
6. 9 you have the better blessings that belong to your **salvation.**
9.12 he took his own blood and obtained eternal **salvation** for us.
1 Pet 1. 5 by God's power for the **salvation** which is ready to be
1. 9 because you are receiving the **salvation** of your souls,
1.10 It was concerning this **salvation** that the prophets made careful search
Jude 3 write to you about the **salvation** we share in common,
Rev 7.10 **"Salvation** comes from our God, who sits on the throne,
12.10 a loud voice in heaven saying, "Now God's **salvation** has come!
19. 1 **Salvation,** glory, and power belong to our God!

AV SALVATION

Gen 49.18 "I wait for your **deliverance,** Lord.
Deut 32.15 They abandoned God their Creator and rejected their mighty **saviour.**
1 Sam 2. 1 how joyful I am because God has **helped** me!
11.13 death today, for this is the day the Lord **rescued** Israel."
14.45 who won this great **victory** for Israel, be put to death?
19. 5 killed Goliath, and the Lord won a great **victory** for Israel.
2 Sam 22.51 God gives great **victories** to his king;
23. 5 that will be my **victory,** and God will surely bring it about.
1 Chr 16.35 Say to him, "Save us, O God our **Saviour;**
2 Chr 6.41 **Bless** your priests in all they do, and may all your people
20.17 you will see the Lord give you **victory.**
Ps 3. 8 **Victory** comes from the Lord— may he bless his people.
13. 5 I will be glad, because you will **rescue** me.
14. 7 How I pray that **victory** will come to Israel from Zion.
18. 2 he **defends** me and keeps me safe.
20. 5 shout for joy over your **victory** and celebrate your triumph
21. 1 he rejoices because you made him **victorious.**
21. 5 His glory is great because of your **help;**
27. 9 don't leave me, don't abandon me, O God, my **saviour.**
38.22 Help me now, O Lord my **saviour!**
40.10 I have always spoken of your faithfulness and **help.**
53. 6 How I pray that **victory** will come to Israel from Zion.
85. 4 back, O God our **saviour,** and stop being displeased with us!
88. 1 Lord God, my **saviour,** I cry out all day, and at night
89.26 you are my protector and **saviour.'**
95. 1 Let us sing for joy to God, who **protects** us!
98. 2 The Lord announced his **victory;**
98. 3 All people everywhere have seen the **victory** of our God.
118.15 to the glad shouts of **victory** in the tents of God's people:
118.21 because you heard me, because you have given me **victory.**
132.16 I will **bless** her priests in all they do, and her people
140. 7 My Sovereign Lord, my strong **defender,** you have protected me
144.10 You give **victory** to kings and rescue your servant David.
149. 4 he honours the humble with **victory.**
Is 12. 2 God is my **saviour;**
12. 2 he is my **saviour.**
17.10 have forgotten the God who **rescues** you and who protects you
26. 1 God himself **defends** its walls!
33. 6 He always **protects** his people and gives them wisdom and knowledge.
45. 8 open to receive it and will blossom with **freedom** and justice.
45.17 Israel is saved by the Lord, and her **victory** lasts for ever;
46.13 My **triumph** will not be delayed.
51. 6 But the **deliverance** I bring will last for ever;
51. 8 my **victory** will endure for all time."
52. 7 He announces **victory** and says to Zion, "Your God is king!"
59.16 use his own power to **rescue** them and to win the victory.
62. 1 she is saved, And her **victory** shines like a torch in the
63. 5 But my anger made me strong, and I won the **victory** myself.
Jer 3.23 **Help** for Israel comes only from the Lord our God.
Hab 3. 8 was your chariot, as you brought **victory** to your people.
3.18 be joyful and glad, because the Lord God is my **saviour.**
Zech 9. 9 He comes triumphant and **victorious,** but humble and riding on
Lk 1.69 for us a mighty **Saviour,** a descendant of his servant David.
Phil 1.19 comes from the Spirit of Jesus Christ I shall be **set free.**
1.28 and that you will **win,** because it is God who gives

SAMARIA

Capital of the n. kingdom (Israel), sometimes used as a name for the territory of n. Israel.
In the New Testament it denotes the territory between Galilee in the n. and Judaea in the s. Because of differences in politics, race, customs and religion, there was much bad feeling between the Samaritans and the Jews.

1 Kgs 13.32 of worship in the towns of **Samaria** will surely come true."
16.24 bought the hill of **Samaria** for six thousand pieces of silver
16.24 and named it **Samaria,** after Shemer, the former owner
16.28 died and was buried in **Samaria,** and his son Ahab succeeded
16.29 of Israel, and he ruled in **Samaria** for twenty-two years.
16.32 a temple to Baal in **Samaria,** made an altar for him, and
18. 2 The famine in **Samaria** was at its worst, [3] so Ahab called in
20. 1 up, laid siege to **Samaria,** and launched attacks against it.
20.17 to him that a group of soldiers was coming out of **Samaria.**
20.34 yourself in Damascus, just as my father did in **Samaria."**
20.43 The king went back home to **Samaria,** worried and depressed.
21.18 the prophet from Tishbe, [18] "Go to King Ahab of **Samaria.**
22.10 just outside the gate of **Samaria,** and all the prophets were

1 Kgs 22.37 His body was taken to **Samaria** and buried.
22.38 up at the pool of **Samaria,** where dogs licked up his blood
22.51 king of Israel, and he ruled in **Samaria** for two years.
2 Kgs 1. 2 the roof of his palace in **Samaria** and was seriously injured.
2.25 Elisha went on to Mount Carmel, and later returned to **Samaria.**
3. 1 king of Israel, and he ruled in **Samaria** for twelve years.
3. 6 At once King Joram left **Samaria** and gathered all his troops.
5. 3 that my master could go to the prophet who lives in **Samaria!**
6.19 And he led them to **Samaria.**
6.20 their sight, and they saw that they were inside **Samaria.**
6.24 army against Israel and laid siege to the city of **Samaria.**
7. 1 be able to buy in **Samaria** three kilogrammes of the best
7. 3 outside the gates of **Samaria,** and they said to one another,
7.10 Syrian camp, went back to **Samaria** and called out to the
7.16 The people of **Samaria** rushed out and looted the Syrian camp.
7.18 barley would be sold in **Samaria** for one piece of silver,
10. 1 descendants of King Ahab living in the city of **Samaria.**
10. 4 The rulers of **Samaria** were terrified.
10. 6 the leading citizens of **Samaria,** who were bringing them up.
10. 7 leaders of **Samaria** killed all seventy of Ahab's descendants,
10.12 Jehu left Jezreel to go to **Samaria.**
10.16 And they rode on together to **Samaria.**
10.18 Jehu called the people of **Samaria** together and said,
10.35 died and was buried in **Samaria,** and his son Jehoahaz
10.36 Jehu had ruled in **Samaria** as king of Israel for twenty-eight years.
13. 1 king of Israel, and he ruled in **Samaria** for seventeen years.
13. 6 and the image of the goddess Asherah remained in **Samaria.**
13. 9 died and was buried in **Samaria,** and his son Jehoash
13.10 king of Israel, and he ruled in **Samaria** for sixteen years.
13.13 in the royal tombs in **Samaria,** and his son Jeroboam II
14.14 all the palace treasures, and carried them back to **Samaria.**
14.16 in the royal tombs in **Samaria,** and his son Jeroboam II
14.23 king of Israel, and he ruled in **Samaria** for forty-one years.
15. 8 king of Israel, and he ruled in **Samaria** for six months.
15.13 king of Israel, and he ruled in **Samaria** for one month.
15.14 Gadi went from Tirzah to **Samaria,** assassinated Shallum, and
15.17 king of Israel, and he ruled in **Samaria** for ten years.
15.23 king of Israel, and he ruled in **Samaria** for two years.
15.25 inner fortress in **Samaria,** and succeeded him as king.
15.27 king of Israel, and he ruled in **Samaria** for twenty years.
17. 1 king of Israel, and he ruled in **Samaria** for nine years.
17. 5 Then Shalmaneser invaded Israel and besieged **Samaria.**
17. 6 Hoshea, the Assyrian emperor captured **Samaria,** took the
17. 7 **Samaria** fell because the Israelites sinned against the Lord their God,
17.24 in the cities of **Samaria,** in place of the exiled Israelites.
17.26 settled in the cities of **Samaria** did not know the law of
17.28 who had been deported from **Samaria** went and lived in Bethel,
17.29 who settled in **Samaria** continued to make their own idols,
18. 9 Israel—Emperor Shalmaneser of Assyria invaded Israel and besieged **Samaria.**
18.10 In the third year of the siege, **Samaria** fell;
18.12 **Samaria** fell because the Israelites did not obey the Lord their God,
18.34 Did anyone save **Samaria?**
21.13 punish Jerusalem as I did **Samaria,** as I did King Ahab of
23.18 were those of the prophet who had come from **Samaria.**
2 Chr 18. 2 later Jehoshaphat went to the city of **Samaria** to visit Ahab.
18. 9 just outside the gate of **Samaria,** and all the prophets were
22. 9 was made for Ahaziah, and he was found hiding in **Samaria.**
25.13 attacked the Judaean cities between **Samaria** and Beth Horon,
25.24 He took back to **Samaria** as loot all the gold and silver
28. 8 them back to **Samaria,** along with large amounts of loot.
28. 9 Oded, a prophet of the Lord, lived in the city of **Samaria.**
28.15 Then the Israelites returned home to **Samaria.**
Ezra 4.10 settled in the city of **Samaria** and elsewhere in the province
4.17 their associates who live in **Samaria** and in the rest of West
Neh 4. 2 of his companions and the **Samaritan** troops he said, "What
Is 7. 9 Israel is no stronger than **Samaria,** its capital city,
7. 9 and **Samaria** is no stronger than King Pekah.
8. 4 and all the loot of **Samaria** will be carried off by the
9. 9 lives in the city of **Samaria,** will know that he has done
10. 9 I conquered **Samaria** and Damascus.
10.10 idols more numerous than those of Jerusalem and **Samaria.**
10.11 I have destroyed **Samaria** and all its idols, and I will
36.19 Did anyone save **Samaria?**
Jer 23.13 I have seen the sin of **Samaria's** prophets:
31. 5 vineyards on the hills of **Samaria,** and those who plant them
41. 5 eighty men arrived from Shechem, Shiloh, and **Samaria.**
Ezek 16.46 "Your elder sister is **Samaria,** in the north, with her villages.
16.51 "**Samaria** did not sin half as much as you have.
16.53 again—Sodom and her villages and **Samaria** and her villages.
23. 4 was named Oholah (she represents **Samaria),** and the younger
23.33 that cup of fear and ruin, your sister **Samaria's** cup.
Hos 8. 5 gold bull worshipped by the people of the city of **Samaria.**
8. 6 The gold bull worshipped in **Samaria** will be smashed to pieces!
10. 5 live in the city of **Samaria** will be afraid and will mourn
13.16 **Samaria** must be punished for rebelling against me.
Amos 3. 9 together in the hills surrounding **Samaria** and see the great
3.12 a few will survive of **Samaria's** people, who now recline on
4. 1 to this, you women of **Samaria,** who grow fat like the
6. 1 you that feel safe in **Samaria**—you great men of this great
8.14 swear by the idols of **Samaria,** who say, 'By the god of
Obad 19 Israelites will possess the territory of Ephraim and **Samaria;**
Mic 1. 1 The Lord revealed to Micah all these things about **Samaria**
1. 5 **Samaria,** the capital city itself!
1. 6 Lord says, "I will make **Samaria** a pile of ruins in the
1. 7 **Samaria** acquired these things for its fertility rites, and
1. 9 **Samaria's** wounds cannot be healed, and Judah is about to
Mt 10. 5 "Do not go to any Gentile territory or any **Samaritan** towns.
Lk 9.52 into a village in **Samaria** to get everything ready for him.
10.33 But a **Samaritan** who was travelling that way came upon the man,
17.11 he went along the border between **Samaria** and Galilee.
17.16 The man was a **Samaritan.**
Jn 4. 4 on his way there he had to go through **Samaria.**
4. 5 In **Samaria** he came to a town named Sychar,
4. 7 A **Samaritan** woman came to draw some water,
4. 9 and I am a **Samaritan**—so how can you ask me
4. 9 (Jews will not use the same cups and bowls that **Samaritans** use.)
4.20 "My **Samaritan** ancestors worshipped God on this mountain,
4.22 You **Samaritans** do not really know whom you worship;
4.39 Many of the **Samaritans** in that town believed in Jesus
4.40 So when the **Samaritans** came to him, they begged him to
8.48 saying that you are a **Samaritan** and have a demon in you?"
Acts 1. 8 Jerusalem, in all Judaea and **Samaria,** and to the ends of the
8. 1 were scattered throughout the provinces of Judaea and **Samaria.**
8. 5 to the principal city in **Samaria** and preached the Messiah
8. 9 who for some time had astounded the **Samaritans** with his magic.
8.14 that the people of **Samaria** had received the word of God,
8.25 they preached the Good News in many villages of **Samaria.**
9.31 throughout Judaea, Galilee, and **Samaria** had a time of peace.
15. 3 they went through Phoenicia and **Samaria,**

SAME

Ex 12.49 The **same** regulations apply to native-born Israelites and
Lev 22.30 eat it the **same** day and leave none of it until the
Num 9.14 The **same** law applies to everyone, whether native or foreigner."
15.15 all time to come, the **same** rules are binding on you and
15.16 the **same** laws and regulations apply to you and to them.
15.29 The **same** regulation applies to everyone who unintentionally
Deut 1.17 judge everyone on the **same** basis, no matter who he is.
16. 4 the evening of the first day must be eaten that **same** night.
Ezra 4. 2 We worship the **same** God you worship, and we have been
Neh 5. 5 We are of the **same** race as our fellow-Jews.
Job 10. 8 formed and shaped me, and now those **same** hands destroy me.
14. 1 All lead the **same** short, troubled life.
28. 5 the earth, But underneath the **same** earth All is torn up and
31.15 The **same** God who created me created my servants also.
33. 6 You and I are the **same** in God's sight, both of us
Ps 102.27 But you are always the **same,** and your life never ends.
139.12 Darkness and light are the **same** to you.
Ecc 1. 4 Generations come and generations go, but the world stays just the **same.**
2.14 I also know that the **same** fate is waiting for us all.
2.15 I thought to myself, "I will suffer the **same** fate as fools.
3.15 God makes the **same** thing happen again and again.
3.19 After all, the **same** fate awaits man and animal alike.
3.20 They are both going to the **same** place—the dust.
6. 6 After all, both of them are going to the **same** place.
9. 2 The **same** fate comes to the righteous and the wicked, to the
Is 10.11 and I will do the **same** to Jerusalem and the images that
24. 2 Everyone will meet the **same** fate—the priests and the people,
Ezek 7.27 will judge you in the **same way** as you have judged others.
21.26 Nothing will be the **same** again.
Dan 5.30 That **same** night Belshazzar, the king of Babylonia, was
Zech 14. 9 will worship him as God and know him by the **same** name.
Mal 2.10 Don't we all have the **same** father?
2.10 Didn't the **same** God create us all?
Mt 2. 9 they saw the **same** star they had seen
5.19 teaches others to do the **same,** will be least in the Kingdom
5.19 teaches others to do the **same,** will be great in the Kingdom
7. 2 will judge you in the **same way** as you judge others,
7. 2 he will apply to you the **same** rules you apply to others.
10.21 and fathers will do the **same** to their children;
10.32 I will do the **same** for him before my Father
13. 1 That **same** day Jesus left the house and went to the lake-side,
13.40 so the **same** thing will happen at the end
20. 5 and again at three o'clock he did the **same** thing.
20.12 yet you paid them the **same** as you paid us!'
21.30 the father went to the other son and said the **same** thing.
22.23 That **same** day some Sadducees came to Jesus
22.26 The **same** thing happened to the second brother,
26.35 And all the other disciples said the **same** thing.
26.44 went away, and prayed the third time, saying the **same** words.
Mk 4.24 The **same** rules you use to judge others will be used by
4.35 On the evening of that **same** day Jesus said to his disciples,
6.10 stay in the **same** house until you leave that place.
12.21 The **same** thing happened to the third brother,
13.12 and fathers will do the **same** to their children.
14.31 And all the other disciples said the **same** thing.
14.39 He went away once more and prayed, saying the **same** words.
Lk 2.38 That very **same** hour she arrived and gave thanks to God
4.23 in my home town the **same** things you heard were done in
5.10 The **same** was true of Simon's partners, James and John,
5.33 and the disciples of the Pharisees do the **same;**
6.23 For their ancestors did the very **same** things to the prophets.
6.26 said the very **same** things about the false prophets.
6.34 Even sinners lend to sinners, to get back the **same** amount!
9. 4 stay in the **same** house until you leave that town;
10. 7 Stay in that **same** house, eating and drinking whatever they offer you,
10.37 Jesus replied, "You go, then, and do the **same.**"
12. 8 of Man will do the **same** for him before the angels of
17.10 It is the **same** with you;
17.34 there will be two people sleeping in the **same** bed:
18. 3 was a widow in that **same** town who kept coming to him
20.31 The **same** thing happened to all seven—
22.29 the right to rule, so I will give you the **same** right.
23.40 You received the **same** sentence he did.
24.13 On that **same** day two of Jesus' followers were going
Jn 1. 1 he was with God, and he was the **same** as God.

Jn 1.18 only Son, who is the **same** as God
1.42 (This is the **same** as Peter and means "a rock.")
4. 9 (Jews will not use the **same** cups and bowls that Samaritans use.)
5.23 honour the Son in the **same way** as they honour the Father.
6.11 He did the **same** with the fish,
8.39 Jesus replied, "you would do the **same** things that he did.
17. 5 in your presence now, the **same** glory I had with you before
17.22 I gave them the **same** glory you gave me,
21.13 he did the **same** with the fish.
Acts 1.11 will come back in the **same way** that you saw him go
10.34 it is true that God treats everyone on the **same** basis.
11.17 God gave those Gentiles the **same** gift that he gave us
14. 1 The **same** thing happened in Iconium:
15.27 will tell you in person the **same** things we are writing.
19.34 they all shouted together the **same** thing for two hours:
23.11 and you must also do the **same** in Rome."
24.15 I have the **same** hope in God that these themselves have,
26.22 I say is the very **same** thing which the prophets and Moses
27.28 little later they did the **same** and found that it was thirty
Rom 2. 1 others and then do the **same** things which they do, you
2.11 For God judges everyone by the **same** standard.
4.12 being circumcised, also live the **same** life of faith that our
5.14 did not sin in the **same way** that Adam did
5.15 the two are not the **same,** because God's free gift is not
9.10 For Rebecca's two sons had the **same** father, our ancestor Isaac.
9.21 make two pots from the **same** lump of clay, one for special
9.22 And the **same** is true of what God has done.
10.12 God is the **same** Lord of all and richly blesses all who
11. 5 It is the **same way** now:
12.16 Have the **same** concern for everyone.
14. 5 while someone else thinks that all days are the **same.**
15. 5 enable you to have the **same** point of view among yourselves
1 Cor 7.24 fellowship with God in the **same** condition as he was
9. 8 these everyday examples, because the Law says the **same** thing.
10. 3 All ate the **same** spiritual bread
10. 4 and drank the **same** spiritual drink.
10.17 though many, are one body, for we all share the **same** loaf.
12. 4 different kinds of spiritual gifts, but the **same** Spirit gives them.
12. 5 There are different ways of serving, but the **same** Lord is served.
12. 6 to perform service, but the **same** God gives ability to all
12. 8 while to another person the **same** Spirit gives a message full
12. 9 One and the **same** Spirit gives faith to one person,
12.11 But it is one and the **same** Spirit who does all this;
12.13 the one body by the **same** Spirit, and we have all been
12.25 its different parts have the **same** concern for one another.
15.39 flesh of living beings is not all the **same** kind of flesh;
2 Cor 1. 4 using the **same** help that we ourselves have received
1. 6 to endure with patience the **same** sufferings that we also endure.
3.14 minds are covered with the **same** veil as they read the books
3.18 that **same** glory, coming from the Lord, who is the Spirit,
4. 6 is the **same** God who made his light shine in our hearts,
4.13 In the **same** spirit of faith, we also speak because we believe.
6.13 show us the **same** feelings that we have for you.
11. 3 in the **same way** that Eve was deceived
11.12 saying that they work in the **same way** that we do.
11.18 many who boast for merely human reasons, I will do the **same.**
12.18 act from the very same motives and behave in the **same way?**
Gal 4.17 that you will have the **same** interest in them as they have
4.19 in childbirth, I feel the **same** kind of pain for you until
4.29 and it is the **same** now.
Eph 1.19 working in us is the **same** as the mighty strength
3. 6 they are members of the **same** body and share in the promise
4.10 who came down is the **same** one who went up, above and
6. 9 Masters, behave in the **same way** towards your slaves
6. 9 your slaves belong to the **same** Master in heaven,
6. 9 who judges everyone by the **same** standard.
Phil 1.30 It is the **same** battle you saw me fighting in the past,
2. 2 completely happy by having the **same** thoughts,
2. 2 sharing the **same** love, and being one in soul
3.15 All of us who are spiritually mature should have this **same** attitude.
3.16 according to the **same** rules we have followed until now.
Col 3.25 because God judges everyone by the **same** standard.
1 Thes 2.14 Our brothers, the **same** things happened to you
2.14 You suffered the **same** persecutions from your own countrymen
Heb 1.12 But you are always the **same,** and your life never ends."
2.11 he and those who are made pure all have the **same** Father.
4. 5 This **same** matter is spoken of again:
8. 5 It is the **same** as it was with Moses.
9.28 In the **same** manner Christ also was offered in sacrifice once
10. 1 The **same** sacrifices are offered for ever, year after year.
10.11 every day and offers the **same** sacrifices many times;
11. 9 did Isaac and Jacob, who received the **same** promise from God.
13. 8 Jesus Christ is the **same** yesterday, today, and for ever.
Jas 2.11 For the **same** one who said, "Do not commit adultery,"
2.25 It was the **same** with the prostitute Rahab.
3.10 Words of thanksgiving and cursing pour out from the **same** mouth.
3.11 pours out sweet water and bitter water from the **same** opening.
5.17 Elijah was the **same** kind of person as we are.
1 Pet 1.17 judges all people by the **same** standard,
3. 8 you must all have the **same** attitude and the same feelings;
4. 1 strengthen yourselves with the **same way** of thinking that he had;
4. 4 not join them in the **same** wild and reckless living,
5. 9 all the world are going through the **same** kind of sufferings.
2 Pet 3. 4 but everything is still the **same** as it was since the
3. 7 are being preserved by the **same** command of God,
3. 8 to him the two are the **same.**
1 Jn 4.17 because our life in this world is the **same** as Christ's.
5. 8 and all three give the **same** testimony.
Rev 2.26 I will give the **same** authority that I received
9. 3 they were given the **same** kind of power that scorpions have.
17.13 These ten all have the **same** purpose, and they give their

SAMSON

Leader of Israel before the monarchy.

Judg 13.1-25 **The birth of Samson**
14.1-15.8 **Samson and the girl from Timnah**
15.9-20 **Samson defeats the Philistines**
16.1-3 **Samson at Gaza**
4-22 **Samson and Delilah**
23-31 **The death of Samson**
Heb 11.32 Gideon, Barak, **Samson,** Jephthah, David, Samuel, and the prophets.

SAMUEL

Prophet who appointed Saul as king of Israel.

1 Sam 1.19-28 **Samuel's birth and dedication**
2.1-11 **Hannah's prayer**
18-21 **Samuel at Shiloh**
22-26 **Eli and his sons**
3.1-21 **The LORD appears to Samuel**
7.2-17 **Samuel rules Israel**
8.1-22 **The people ask for a king**
9.1-26a **Saul meets Samuel**
9.26b-10.16 **Samuel anoints Saul as ruler**
10.17-27 **Saul is acclaimed as king**
11.1-15 **Saul defeats the Ammonites**
12.1-25 **Samuel addresses the people**
13.1-23 **War against the Philistines**
15.1-9 **War against the Amalekites**
10-35 **Saul is rejected as king**
16.1-13 **David is anointed king**
19.1-24 **David is persecuted by Saul**
25.1a **The death of Samuel**
28.3-25 **Saul consults a medium**
1 Chr 6.28 **Samuel** had two sons:
6.33 Heman, Joel, **Samuel,** [34] Elkanah, Jeroham, Eliel, Toah,
9.22 King David and the prophet **Samuel** who had put their
11. 3 of Israel, just as the Lord had promised through **Samuel.**
26.28 gifts brought by the prophet **Samuel,** by King Saul, by Abner
29.29 the records of the three prophets, **Samuel,** Nathan, and Gad.
2 Chr 35.18 the days of the prophet **Samuel,** the Passover had never been
Ps 99. 6 Aaron were his priests, and **Samuel** was one who prayed to him;
Jer 15. 1 "Even if Moses and **Samuel** were standing here pleading with me,
Acts 3.24 including **Samuel** and those who came after him,
13.20 he gave them judges until the time of the prophet **Samuel.**
Heb 11.32 Gideon, Barak, Samson, Jephthah, David, **Samuel,** and the prophets.

AV SANCTIFY

see also **HOLY**

Gen 2. 3 seventh day and set it **apart** as a special day, because by
Ex 13. 2 **"Dedicate** all the first-born males to me,
19.10 spend today and tomorrow **purifying** themselves for worship.
19.14 the mountain and told the people to get **ready** for worship.
19.22 near me must **purify** themselves, or I will punish them."
19.23 us to consider the mountain **sacred** and to mark a boundary
28.41 ordain them and **dedicate** them by anointing them with olive-oil,
29.27 the ordination are to be **dedicated** to me as a special gift
30.29 **Dedicate** these things in this way,
31.13 to show that I, the Lord, have made you **my own people.**
40.10 **dedicate** the altar and all its equipment by anointing it,
40.11 Also **dedicate** the wash-basin and its base in the same way.
40.13 him, and in this way **consecrate** him, so that he can serve
Lev 8.10 it, and in this way he **dedicated** it all to the Lord.
8.11 basin and its base, in order to **dedicate** them to the Lord.
8.15 In this way he **dedicated** it and purified it.
8.30 In this way he **consecrated** them and their clothes to the Lord.
11.44 and you must keep yourselves **holy,** because I am holy.
20. 7 Keep yourselves **holy,** because I am the Lord your God.
21.15 and I have set him apart as the **High Priest."**
27.14 When someone **dedicates** his house to the Lord,
27.15 If the one who **dedicated** the house wishes to buy it back,
27.16 If a man **dedicates** part of his land to the Lord,
27.17 If he **dedicates** the land immediately after a Year of
27.18 If he **dedicates** it later, the priest shall estimate
27.19 If the man who **dedicated** the field wishes to buy it back,
27.22 If a man **dedicates** to the Lord a field that he has
27.26 so no one may **dedicate** it to him as a freewill
Num 7. 1 he anointed and **dedicated** the Tent and all its equipment,
8.17 the first-born in Egypt, I **consecrated** as my own the eldest
11.18 Now tell the people, **'Purify** yourselves for tomorrow;
20.12 not have enough faith to **acknowledge** my holy power
27.14 you refused to **acknowledge** my holy power before them."
Deut 5.12 the Sabbath and keep it **holy,** as I, the Lord your God,
15.19 **"Set aside** for the Lord your God all the first-born
32.51 the wilderness of Zin, you **dishonoured** me in the presence
Josh 3. 5 Joshua said to the people, **"Purify** yourselves, because
7.13 **Purify** the people and get them ready to come before me.
1 Sam 7. 1 They **consecrated** his son Eleazar to be in charge of it.
16. 5 **Purify** yourselves and come with me."
16. 5 Jesse and his sons to **purify** themselves, and he invited them
1 Chr 15.12 **Purify** yourselves and your fellow-Levites, so that you can
15.14 the priests and the Levites **purified** themselves in order to
23.13 set apart to be in **charge** of the sacred objects for ever,
2 Chr 5.11 group to which they belonged, had **consecrated** themselves.
7.16 I have chosen it and **consecrated** it as the place where I
7.20 this Temple that I have **consecrated** as the place where I am
29. 5 said, "You Levites are to **consecrate** yourselves and purify
29.15 and they all made themselves ritually **clean.**
29.17 sixteenth of the month, **preparing** the Temple for worship.

2 Chr 29.19 years he was unfaithful to God, and we have **rededicated** it.
29.34 By then more priests had made themselves ritually **clean.**
29.34 Levites were more faithful in keeping ritually **clean** than the priests were.)
30. 1 not enough priests were ritually **clean** and not many people
30. 8 Lord your God has made **holy** for ever, and worship him so
30.15 were so ashamed that they **dedicated** themselves to the Lord,
30.17 the people were not ritually **clean,** they could not kill the
30.17 Levites did it for them, and **dedicated** the lambs to the Lord.
30.24 A large number of priests went through the ritual of **purification.**
31.18 they were required to be **ready** to perform their sacred
35. 6 Now make yourselves ritually **clean** and prepare the
Neh 3. 1 fellow-priests rebuilt the Sheep Gate, **dedicated** it,
3. 1 They **dedicated** the wall as far as the Tower of the Hundred
12.47 The people gave a **sacred** offering to the Levites, and the
13.22 the gates to make sure that the Sabbath was kept **holy.**
Job 1. 5 sacrifices for each of his children in order to **purify** them.
Is 8.13 Remember that I, the Lord Almighty, am **holy;**
13. 3 Lord has called out his **proud** and confident soldiers to
29.23 then you will **acknowledge** that I am the holy God
Ezek 20.12 between us, to remind them that I, the Lord, make them **holy.**
36.23 demonstrate to the nations the **holiness** of my great name—
36.23 I will use you to show the nations that I am **holy.**
37.28 that I, the Lord, have **chosen** Israel to be my own people."
44.19 to keep their **sacred** clothing from harming the people.
46.20 so that nothing **holy** is carried to the outer courtyard,
Joel 1.14 Give **orders** for a fast;
2.15 give **orders** for a fast and call an assembly!
2.16 **prepare** them for a sacred meeting;
Jn 17.19 And for their sake I **dedicate** myself to you, in order
17.19 in order that they, too, may be truly **dedicated** to you.
Acts 20.32 up and give you the blessings God has for all **his people.**
26.18 sins forgiven and receive their place among God's **chosen people.'**
Rom 15.16 offering acceptable to God, **dedicated** to him by the Holy Spirit.
1 Cor 1. 2 God's holy people, who **belong** to him in union with Christ
6.11 you have been **dedicated** to God;
7.14 unbelieving husband is made **acceptable** to God by being united
7.14 the unbelieving wife is made **acceptable** to God by being united
1 Tim 4. 5 the word of God and the prayer make it **acceptable** to God.
2 Tim 2.21 because he is **dedicated** and useful to his Master, ready
Heb 2.11 He **purifies** people from their sins, and both he and
2.11 he and those who are made **pure** all have the same Father.
10.10 we are all **purified** from sin by the offering that
10.14 has made perfect for ever those who are **purified** from sin.
10.29 the blood of God's covenant which **purified** him from sin?
Jude 1 been called by God, who **live** in the love of God the

SANCTUARY

A building dedicated to the worship of God. Sometimes the word refers to the central place of worship and not to the whole building.

Josh 9.23 wood and carrying water for the **sanctuary** of my God."
24.26 and set it up under the oak-tree in the Lord's **sanctuary.**
1 Sam 3. 3 Samuel was sleeping in the **sanctuary,**
1 Kgs 6. 3 deep and 9 metres wide, as wide as the **sanctuary** itself.
2 Kgs 10.25 went on into the inner **sanctuary** of the temple, [26] brought
Ps 60. 6 From his **sanctuary** God has said, "In triumph I will
61. 4 Let me live in your **sanctuary** all my life;
63. 2 Let me see you in the **sanctuary;**
65. 4 whom you choose, whom you bring to live in your **sanctuary.**
68.24 by all, the procession of God, my king, into his **sanctuary.**
68.35 God as he comes from his **sanctuary**— the God of Israel!
108. 7 From his **sanctuary** God has said, "In triumph I will
116.18 your people, in the **sanctuary** of your Temple in Jerusalem,
Is 43.28 and your rulers profaned my **sanctuary.**
63.18 they trampled down your **sanctuary.**
Ezek 8.16 of the **sanctuary,** between the altar and the passage,
8.16 turned their backs to the **sanctuary** and were bowing low
Heb 6.19 the curtain of the heavenly temple into the inner **sanctuary.**

AV SANCTUARY

see also **TEMPLE**

Ex 25. 8 people must make a sacred **tent** for me, so that I may
Lev 12. 4 holy or enter the sacred **Tent** until the time of her
16.33 ritual to purify the **Most Holy Place,** the rest of the Tent
19.30 Keep the Sabbath, and honour the **place** where I am worshipped.
20. 3 makes my sacred **Tent** unclean and disgraces my holy name,
21.11 he to defile my sacred **Tent** by leaving it and entering a
21.23 He must not profane these **holy** things,
26. 2 and honour the **place** where I am worshipped.
26.31 into ruins, destroy your **places of worship,** and refuse to
Num 3.38 services performed in the **Holy Place** for the people of Israel.
10.21 clan of Kohath would start out, carrying the **sacred** objects.
18. 1 any guilt connected with serving in the **Tent** of my presence;
19.20 He defiles the Lord's **Tent** and will no longer be considered
2 Chr 26.18 Leave this **holy** place.
Is 8.14 Because of my awesome **holiness** I am like a stone that
Jer 51.51 foreigners have taken over the **holy** places in the Temple.'

SAND

Gen 22.17 are stars in the sky or grains of **sand** along the seashore.
32.12 count, as many as the grains of **sand** along the seashore."
41.49 Joseph stopped measuring it—it was like the **sand** of the sea.
Ex 2.12 he killed the Egyptian and hid his body in the **sand.**
Deut 28.24 will send down duststorms and **sandstorms** until you are destroyed.
33.19 wealth from the sea And from the **sand** along the shore."
Josh 11. 4 as many men as there are grains of **sand** on the seashore.
Judg 7.12 many camels as there were grains of **sand** on the seashore.
1 Sam 13. 5 many soldiers as there are grains of **sand** on the seashore.
2 Sam 17.11 many as the grains of **sand** on the sea-shore, and that you
1 Kgs 4.20 Israel were as numerous as the grains of **sand** on the seashore;
Job 6. 3 would weigh more than the **sands** of the sea,
Ps 78.27 down birds, as many as the grains of **sand** on the shore;
139.18 I counted them, they would be more than the grains of **sand.**
Prov 20.17 but sooner or later it will be like a mouthful of **sand.**
27. 3 The weight of stone and **sand** is nothing compared to the
Is 10.22 as there are grains of **sand** by the sea, only a few
35. 7 the burning **sand** will become a lake, and dry land will
48.19 as numerous as grains of **sand,** and I would have made sure
Jer 2. 6 a land of deserts and **sand-dunes,** a dry and dangerous land
5.22 I placed the **sand** as the boundary of the sea, a permanent
15. 8 more widows in your land than grains of **sand** by the sea.
33.22 stars in the sky or the grains of **sand** on the sea-shore."
Hos 1.10 Israel will become like the **sand** of the sea, more than can
Hab 1. 9 Their captives are as numerous as grains of **sand.**
Mt 7.26 like a foolish man who built his house on **sand.**
Acts 27.17 they might run into the **sandbanks** off the coast of Libya,
27.41 But the ship hit a **sandbank** and went aground;
Rom 9.27 many as the grains of **sand** by the sea,
Heb 11.12 as many as the numberless grains of **sand** on the sea-shore.
Rev 20. 8 as many as the grains of **sand** on the sea-shore.

SANDAL

Gen 14.23 keep anything of yours, not even a thread or a **sandal** strap.
Ex 3. 5 Take off your **sandals,** because you are standing on holy ground.
12.11 dressed for travel, with your **sandals** on your feet and your
Deut 25. 9 take off one of his **sandals,** spit in his face, and say,
25.10 as 'the family of the man who had his **sandal** pulled off.'
29. 5 the desert, and your clothes and **sandals** never wore out.
Josh 5.15 of the Lord's army told him, "Take your **sandals** off;
9. 5 ragged clothes and worn-out **sandals** that had been mended.
9.13 Our clothes and **sandals** are worn out from the long journey."
Ruth 4. 7 seller to take off his **sandal** and give it to the buyer.
4. 8 buy it," he took off his **sandal** and gave it to Boaz.
2 Chr 28.15 They gave them clothes and **sandals** to wear, gave them enough
Ps 60. 8 and I will throw my **sandals** on Edom, as a sign that
108. 9 and I will throw my **sandals** on Edom, as a sign that
Song 7. 1 How beautiful are your feet in **sandals.**
Is 5.27 not a **sandal** strap is broken.
20. 2 Amoz to take off his **sandals** and the sackcloth he was wearing.
Amos 2. 6 men who cannot repay even the price of a pair of **sandals.**
8. 6 price of a pair of **sandals,** and we'll buy him as a
Mt 3.11 and I am not good enough even to carry his **sandals.**
Mk 1. 7 not good enough even to bend down and untie his **sandals.**
6. 9 Wear **sandals,** but don't carry an extra shirt."
Lk 3.16 I am not good enough even to untie his **sandals.**
Jn 1.27 but I am not good enough even to untie his **sandals."**
Acts 7.33 said to him, 'Take your **sandals** off, for the place where you
12. 8 Then the angel said, "Fasten your belt and put on your **sandals."**
13.25 I am not good enough to take his **sandals** off his feet.'

SANE

[SANITY]

Dan 4.34 "I looked up at the sky, and my **sanity** returned.
4.36 "When my **sanity** returned, my honour, my majesty, and
2 Cor 5.13 Or are we **sane?**

SAPPHIRE

A very valuable stone, usually blue in colour.

Ex 24.10 what looked like a pavement of **sapphire,** as blue as the sky.
28.18 in the second row, an emerald, a **sapphire,** and a
39.11 in the second row, an emerald, a **sapphire,** and a
Job 28. 6 The stones of the earth contain **sapphires,** And its dust contains gold.
Song 5.14 His body is like smooth ivory, with **sapphires** set in it.
Ezek 1.26 like a throne made of **sapphire,** and sitting on the throne
10. 1 was something that seemed to be a throne made of **sapphire.**
28.13 **sapphires,** emeralds, and garnets.
Rev 9.17 breastplates red as fire, blue as **sapphire,** and yellow as sulphur.
21.19 foundation-stone was jasper, the second **sapphire,**

SARAH

(SARAI until GEN. 17.15)
Abraham's wife and Isaac's mother.

Gen 11.29 Abram married **Sarai,** and Nahor married Milcah,
11.30 **Sarai** was not able to have children.
11.31 of Haran, and his daughter-in-law **Sarai,** Abram's wife, and
12. 5 Abram took his wife **Sarai,** his nephew Lot, and all the
12.11 he said to his wife **Sarai,** "You are a beautiful woman.
12.17 because the king had taken **Sarai,** the Lord sent terrible
16. 1 Abram's wife **Sarai** had not borne him any children.
16. 2 Abram agreed with what **Sarai** said.
16. 4 that she was pregnant, she became proud and despised **Sarai.**
16. 5 Then **Sarai** said to Abram, "It's your fault that Hagar despises me.
16. 6 Then **Sarai** treated Hagar so cruelly that she ran away.
16. 8 and said, "Hagar, slave of **Sarai,** where have you come
17.15 God said to Abraham, "You must no longer call your wife **Sarai;**
17.15 from now on her name is **Sarah.**
17.17 Can **Sarah** have a child at ninety?"
17.19 Your wife **Sarah** will bear you a son and you will name
17.21 who will be born to **Sarah** about this time next year."
18. 6 the tent and said to **Sarah,** "Quick, take a sack of your
18. 9 Then they asked him, "Where is your wife **Sarah?"**
18.10 I will come back, and your wife **Sarah** will have a son."

Gen 18.10 **Sarah** was behind him, at the door of the tent, listening.
18.11 Abraham and **Sarah** were very old,
18.11 and **Sarah** had stopped having her monthly periods.
18.12 So **Sarah** laughed to herself and said, "Now that I am
18.13 Lord asked Abraham, "Why did **Sarah** laugh and say, 'Can I
18.14 months from now I will return, and **Sarah** will have a son."
18.15 Because **Sarah** was afraid, she denied it.
20. 2 in Gerar, [2]he said that his wife **Sarah** was his sister.
20. 2 So King Abimelech of Gerar had **Sarah** brought to him.
20.14 Then Abimelech gave **Sarah** back to Abraham, and at the
20.16 He said to **Sarah,** "I am giving your brother a thousand
20.17 of what had happened to **Sarah,** Abraham's wife, the Lord had
21. 1 The Lord blessed **Sarah,** as he had promised, [2]and she
21. 6 **Sarah** said, "God has brought me joy and laughter.
21. 7 "Who would have said to Abraham that **Sarah** would nurse children?
21. 9 was playing with **Sarah's** son Isaac.
21.10 **Sarah** saw them and said to Abraham, "Send this
21.12 Do whatever **Sarah** tells you, because it is through Isaac
23. 1 **Sarah** lived to be a hundred and twenty-seven years old.
23.19 Then Abraham buried his wife **Sarah** in that cave in the
24.36 **Sarah,** my master's wife, bore him a son when she was old,
24.67 the tent that his mother **Sarah** had lived in, and she became
25.10 both Abraham and his wife **Sarah** were buried there.
25.12 Hagar, the Egyptian slave of **Sarah,** bore to Abraham, [13]had
49.31 That is where they buried Abraham and his wife **Sarah;**
Is 51. 2 Abraham, and of **Sarah,** from whom you are descended.
Rom 4.19 or of the fact that **Sarah** could not have children.
9. 9 right time I will come back, and **Sarah** will have a son."
Heb 11.11 he was too old and **Sarah** herself could not have children.
1 Pet 3. 6 **Sarah** was like that;

SASH

Ex 28. 4 ephod, a robe, an embroidered shirt, a turban, and a **sash.**
28.39 of fine linen and also a **sash** decorated with embroidery.
28.40 "Make shirts, **sashes,** and caps for Aaron's sons, to
29. 9 put **sashes** round their waists and tie caps on their heads.
39.29 linen shorts, [29]and the **sash** of fine linen and of blue,
Lev 8. 7 shirt and the robe on Aaron and the **sash** round his waist.
8.13 put shirts on them, put **sashes** round their waists, and tied
Neh 5.13 Then I took off the **sash** I was wearing round my waist
Ezek 23.14 and painted bright red, with **sashes** round their waists and

SATAN

Accuser or tempter. In the New Testament Satan is regarded as the chief of the spiritual powers opposed to God.

1 Chr 21. 1 **Satan** wanted to bring trouble on the people of Israel, so
Job 1. 6 to appear before the Lord, **Satan** was there among them.
1. 7 **Satan** answered, "I have been walking here and there,
1. 9 **Satan** replied, "Would Job worship you if he got nothing
1.12 the Lord said to **Satan,** "everything he has is in
1.12 So **Satan** left.
2. 1 to appear before the Lord again, **Satan** was there among them.
2. 2 **Satan** answered, "I have been walking here and there,
2. 4 **Satan** replied, "A man will give up everything in order to
2. 6 So the Lord said to **Satan,** "All right, he is in your
2. 7 Then **Satan** left the Lord's presence and made sores break
Zech 3. 1 And there beside Joshua stood **Satan,** ready to bring an
3. 2 the Lord said to **Satan,** "May the Lord condemn you, Satan!
Mt 4.10 Then Jesus answered, "Go away, **Satan!**
12.26 group is fighting another in **Satan's** kingdom, this means
16.23 Jesus turned around and said to Peter, "Get away from me, **Satan!**
Mk 1.13 where he stayed forty days, being tempted by **Satan.**
3.23 "How can **Satan** drive out Satan?
3.26 So if **Satan's** kingdom divides into groups, it cannot last,
4.15 as they hear the message, **Satan** comes and takes it away.
8.33 "Get away from me, **Satan,**" he said.
Lk 10.18 Jesus answered them, "I saw **Satan** fall like lightning from heaven.
11.18 So if **Satan's** kingdom has groups fighting each other,
13.16 this descendant of Abraham whom **Satan** has kept bound up
22. 3 Then **Satan** entered Judas, called Iscariot, who was one of
22.31 **Satan** has received permission to test all of you, to
Jn 13.27 As soon as Judas took the bread, **Satan** entered him.
Acts 5. 3 "Ananias, why did you let **Satan** take control of you and
26.18 and from the power of **Satan** to God, so that through their
Rom 16.20 God, our source of peace, will soon crush **Satan** under your feet.
1 Cor 5. 5 hand this man over to **Satan** for his body to be destroyed,
7. 5 kept from giving in to **Satan's** temptation
2 Cor 2.11 you, [11]in order to keep **Satan** from getting the upper hand
11.14 Even **Satan** can disguise himself to look like an angel of light!
12. 7 physical ailment, which acts as **Satan's** messenger to beat me
1 Thes 2.18 to go back more than once, but **Satan** would not let us.
2 Thes 2. 9 come with the power of **Satan** and perform all kinds of false
1 Tim 1.20 I have punished by handing them over to the power of **Satan;**
5.15 For some widows have already turned away to follow **Satan.**
Rev 2. 9 they are a group that belongs to **Satan!**
2.13 I know where you live, there where **Satan** has his throne.
2.13 Antipas, my faithful witness, was killed there where **Satan** lives.
2.24 not learnt what the others call 'the deep secrets of **Satan.**'
3. 9 that group that belongs to **Satan,** those liars
12. 9 called the Devil, or **Satan,** that deceived the whole world.
20. 2 that is, the Devil, or **Satan**—and chained him up
20. 7 the thousand years are over, **Satan** will be let loose
20. 8 **Satan** will bring them all together for battle,

SATIN

Song 7. 5 Your braided hair shines like the finest **satin;**

SATISFY

[DISSATISFIED, SELF-SATISFIED]

Lev 10.20 When Moses heard this, he was **satisfied.**
Num 11.22 Could enough cattle and sheep be killed to **satisfy** them?
Josh 22.30 Gad, and East Manasseh had to say, and they were **satisfied.**
22.33 The Israelites were **satisfied** and praised God.
Ruth 2.14 She ate until she was **satisfied,** and she still had some food
1 Sam 22. 2 oppressed or in debt or **dissatisfied** went to him,
2 Kgs 14.10 Be **satisfied** with your fame and stay at home.
Job 18. 4 Will God move mountains to **satisfy** you?
20.20 His greed is never **satisfied.**
38.39 for lions to eat, and **satisfy** hungry young lions [40]when
Ps 49.13 fate of those who are **satisfied** with their wealth— [14]they
49.18 Even if a man is **satisfied** with this life and is praised
63. 5 soul will feast and be **satisfied,** and I will sing glad songs
65. 4 We shall be **satisfied** with the good things of your house,
78.29 So the people ate and were **satisfied;**
78.30 But they had not yet **satisfied** their craving and were still eating,
81.16 with the finest wheat and **satisfy** you with wild honey."
104.28 you provide food, and they are **satisfied.**
105.40 he gave them food from heaven to **satisfy** them.
107. 9 He **satisfies** those who are thirsty and fills the hungry
132.15 I will **satisfy** her poor with food.
145.16 You give them enough and **satisfy** the needs of all.
147.14 He keeps your borders safe and **satisfies** you with the finest wheat.
Prov 6.35 no amount of gifts will **satisfy** his anger.
15.14 stupid people are **satisfied** with ignorance.
16.26 him work harder, because he wants to **satisfy** his hunger.
30.15 There are four things that are never **satisfied:**
Ecc 1. 8 Our eyes can never see enough to be **satisfied;**
3.11 us the **satisfaction** of fully understanding what he does.
4. 8 is always working, never **satisfied** with the wealth he has.
5.10 If you love money, you will never be **satisfied;**
6. 9 It is better to be **satisfied** with what you have than to
Is 9.20 of food they can find, but their hunger is never **satisfied.**
32.10 You may be **satisfied** now, but this time next year you
43.24 buy incense for me or **satisfy** me with the fat of your
44.16 he roasts meat, eats it, and is **satisfied.**
55. 2 Why spend money on what does not **satisfy?**
57. 8 And there you **satisfy** your lust.
58.10 food to the hungry and **satisfy** those who are in need, then
58.11 And I will always guide you and **satisfy** you with good things.
Jer 31.14 the richest food and **satisfy** all the needs of my people.
31.25 who are weary and will **satisfy** with food everyone who is
46.10 it is full, and drink their blood until it is **satisfied.**
Ezek 5.13 all the force of my anger and rage until I am **satisfied.**
7.19 They cannot use it to **satisfy** their desires or fill their stomachs.
8.17 people of Judah are not **satisfied** with merely doing all the
16.28 "Because you were not **satisfied** by the others, you went
16.28 You were their prostitute, but they didn't **satisfy** you either.
16.29 of businessmen, but they didn't **satisfy** you either."
22. 9 Some are always **satisfying** their lusts.
34.18 Some of you are not **satisfied** with eating the best grass;
Hos 9. 4 It will be used only to **satisfy** their hunger;
13. 6 land, you became full and **satisfied,** and then you grew proud
Joel 2.19 you corn and wine and olive-oil, and you will be **satisfied.**
2.26 Now you will have plenty to eat, and be **satisfied.**
Mic 6.14 will eat, but not be **satisfied**—in fact you will still be
Hab 2. 5 and restless—like death itself they are never **satisfied.**
Zeph 1.12 punish the people who are **self-satisfied** and confident, who say
Zech 7. 6 And when they ate and drank, it was for their own **satisfaction."**
Mt 5. 6 God will **satisfy** them fully!
10.25 So a pupil should be **satisfied** to become like his teacher,
Rom 8. 4 the Law might be fully **satisfied** in us who live according to
13.14 stop paying attention to your sinful nature and **satisfying** its desires.
1 Cor 7. 3 duty as a wife, and each should **satisfy** the other's needs.
Gal 5.16 and you will not **satisfy** the desires of the human nature.
Phil 4.11 for I have learnt to be **satisfied** with what I have.
1 Tim 6. 6 a person very rich, if he is **satisfied** with what he has.
Heb 13. 5 from the love of money, and be **satisfied** with what you have.
2 Pet 2.13 in broad daylight that will **satisfy** their bodily appetites;
2.14 their appetite for sin is never **satisfied.**

AV SATISFY

Ex 15. 9 I will divide their wealth and **take** all I want;
Lev 26.26 and when you have eaten it all, you will still be **hungry.**
Deut 14.29 They are to come and get all they **need.**
33.23 "Naphtali is richly **blessed** by the Lord's good favour;
Job 19.22 Haven't you tormented me **enough?**
27.14 their children never have **enough** to eat.
38.27 Who **waters** the dry and thirsty land, so that grass springs up?
Ps 17.15 and when I awake, your presence will **fill** me with joy.
22.26 The poor will **eat** as much as they want;
36. 8 We feast on the **abundant** food you provide;
37.19 they will have **enough** in time of famine.
59.15 about for food and growling if they do not find **enough.**
90.14 **Fill** us each morning with your constant love, so that we
91.16 I will **reward** them with long life;
104.13 on the hills, and the earth is **filled** with your blessings.
Prov 5.19 Let her charms keep you **happy;**
12.11 A hard-working farmer has **plenty** to eat, but it is
13.25 The righteous have **enough** to eat, but the wicked are always hungry.
14.14 Good people will be **rewarded** for their deeds.
19.23 and you will live a long life, **content** and safe from harm.
20.13 Keep busy and you will have **plenty** to eat.
Is 53.11 After a life of suffering, he will again have **joy;**
66.11 You will **enjoy** her prosperity,

Jer 50.10 and those who loot it will take everything they **want.**
50.19 they will eat all they **want** of the crops that grow in
Lam 5. 6 To get food **enough** to stay alive, we went begging to Egypt
Amos 4. 8 they hoped to find water, but there was not **enough** to drink.
Mk 8. 4 can anyone find enough food to **feed** all these people?"
Col 2.23 they have no real value in **controlling** physical passions.

SATURDAY

Acts 20. 7 On **Saturday** evening we gathered together for the fellowship meal.

SAUCE

Ruth 2.14 and have a piece of bread, and dip it in the **sauce."**
Jn 13.26 will dip some bread in the **sauce** and give it to him;

SAUL

First king of Israel.

1 Sam 9.1-26a **Saul meets Samuel**
9.26b–10.16 **Samuel anoints Saul as ruler**
10.17-27 **Saul is acclaimed as king**
11.1-15 **Saul defeats the Ammonites**
13.1-23 **War against the Philistines**
14.1-15 **Jonathan's daring deed**
16-23 **The defeat of the Philistines**
24-46 **Events after the battle**
47-52 **Saul's reign and family**
15.1-9 **War against the Amalekites**
10-35 **Saul is rejected as king**
16.1-13 **David is anointed king**
14-23 **David in Saul's court**
17.1-11 **Goliath challenges the Israelites**
12-40 **David in Saul's camp**
17.55–18.5 **David is presented to Saul**
18.6-16 **Saul becomes jealous of David**
17-30 **David marries Saul's daughter**
19.1-24 **David is persecuted by Saul**
20.1-42 **Jonathan helps David**
21.1-15 **David flees from Saul**
22.1-23 **The slaughter of the priests**
23.1-13 **David saves the town of Keilah**
14-29 **David in the hill-country**
24.1-22 **David spares Saul's life**
25.1b-44 **David and Abigail**
26.1-25 **David spares Saul's life again**
27.1–28.2 **David among the Philistines**
28.3-25 **Saul consults a medium**
29.1-11 **David is rejected by the Philistines**
31.1-13 **The death of Saul and his sons**
2 Sam 1.1-16 **David learns of Saul's death**
17-27 **David's lament for Saul and Jonathan**
1 Chr 8.33-40 **The family of King Saul**
9.35-44 **The ancestors and descendants of King Saul**
10.1-14 **The death of King Saul**

2 Sam 2. 4 Jabesh in Gilead had buried **Saul,** [5] he sent some men there
2. 7 **Saul** your king is dead, and the people of Judah have
2. 8 The commander of **Saul's** army, Abner son of Ner,
2. 8 had fled with **Saul's** son Ishbosheth across the
3. 1 fighting between the forces supporting **Saul's** family and
3. 6 and the forces loyal to **Saul's** family,
3. 6 Abner became more and more powerful among **Saul's** followers.
3. 7 One day Ishbosheth son of **Saul** accused Abner of
3. 7 sleeping with **Saul's** concubine Rizpah, the daughter of Aiah.
3. 8 "Do you think that I would betray **Saul?**
3. 8 cause of your father **Saul,** his brothers, and his friends,
3. 9 take the kingdom away from **Saul** and his descendants and
3.13 you must bring **Saul's** daughter Michal to me when you come to
4. 1 When **Saul's** son Ishbosheth heard that Abner had been killed in Hebron,
4. 4 Another descendant of **Saul** was Jonathan's son Mephibosheth,
4. 4 who was five years old when **Saul** and Jonathan were killed.
4. 8 the son of your enemy **Saul,** who tried to kill you.
4. 8 Your Majesty to take revenge on **Saul** and his descendants."
4.10 Ziklag and told me of **Saul's** death thought he was bringing
5. 2 In the past, even when **Saul** was still our king, you led
6.16 brought into the city, Michal, **Saul's** daughter, looked out
6.23 Michal, **Saul's** daughter, never had any children.
7.15 him as I did from **Saul,** whom I removed so that you
9. 1 One day David asked, "Is there anyone left of **Saul's** family?
9. 2 There was a servant of **Saul's** family named Ziba, and he
9. 3 "Is there anyone left of **Saul's** family to whom I can show
9. 6 of Jonathan and grandson of **Saul,** arrived, he bowed down
9. 7 that belonged to your grandfather **Saul,** and you will always
9. 9 Then the king called Ziba, **Saul's** servant, and said, "I
9. 9 grandson, everything that belonged to **Saul** and his family.
9.10 land for your master **Saul's** family and bring in the harvest,
12. 7 'I made you king of Israel and rescued you from **Saul.**
16. 3 "Where is Mephibosheth, the grandson of your master **Saul?"**
16. 3 Israelites will now restore to him the kingdom of his grandfather **Saul."**
16. 5 at Bahurim, one of **Saul's** relatives, Shimei son of Gera,
16. 8 You took **Saul's** kingdom, and now the Lord is punishing you
16. 8 for murdering so many of **Saul's** family.
19.17 And Ziba, the servant of **Saul's** family, also came with his
19.24 Then Mephibosheth, **Saul's** grandson, came down to meet the king.
19.29 I have decided that you and Ziba will share **Saul's** property."
21. 1 it, and the Lord said, **"Saul** and his family are guilty of
21. 2 had promised to protect, but **Saul** had tried to destroy them
21. 4 They answered, "Our quarrel with **Saul** and his family
2 Sam 21. 5 They answered, **"Saul** wanted to destroy us and leave none
21. 6 Lord at Gibeah, the town of **Saul,** the Lord's chosen king."
21. 7 David spared Jonathan's son Mephibosheth, the grandson of **Saul.**
21. 8 two sons that Rizpah the daughter of Aiah had borne to **Saul;**
21. 8 took the five sons of **Saul's** daughter Merab, whom she had
21.10 Then **Saul's** concubine Rizpah, the daughter of Aiah,
21.12 and got the bones of **Saul** and of his son Jonathan from
21.12 the bodies on the day they killed **Saul** on Mount Gilboa.)
21.13 David took the bones of **Saul** and Jonathan and also
21.14 they buried the bones of **Saul** and Jonathan
21.14 in the grave of **Saul's** father Kish, in Zela in the
22. 1 the Lord saved David from **Saul** and his other enemies, David
1 Chr 5.10 In the time of King **Saul** the tribe of Reuben attacked
11. 2 In the past, even when **Saul** was still our king, you led
12. 1 in Ziklag, where he had gone to escape from King **Saul.**
12. 2 members of the tribe of Benjamin, to which **Saul** belonged.
12.19 he was marching out with the Philistines to fight King **Saul.**
12.19 them to his former master **Saul,** so they sent him back to
12.23 make him king in place of **Saul,** as the Lord had promised.
12.23 Benjamin **(Saul's** own tribe):
12.23 (most of the people of Benjamin had remained loyal to **Saul);**
13. 3 God's Covenant Box, which was ignored while **Saul** was king."
15.29 brought into the city, Michal, **Saul's** daughter, looked out
17.13 him as I did from **Saul,** whom I removed so that you
26.28 the prophet Samuel, by King **Saul,** by Abner son of Ner, and
Is 10.29 and the people in King **Saul's** town of Gibeah have run away.
Acts 13.21 God gave them **Saul** son of Kish from the tribe

SAVAGE

2 Chr 20.23 it, and then they turned on each other in **savage** fighting.
Amos 1. 3 They treated the people of Gilead with **savage** cruelty.
Rom 1.14 the civilized and to the **savage,** to the educated and to the
Col 3.11 barbarians, **savages,** slaves, and free men, but Christ

SAVE

see also **SALVATION, SAVIOUR**

Gen 18.24 Won't you spare it in order to **save** the fifty?
19.19 You have done me a great favour and **saved** my life.
27.36 Haven't you **saved** a blessing for me?"
32.11 **Save** me, I pray, from my brother Esau.
37.21 Reuben heard them and tried to **save** Joseph.
37.22 He said this, planning to **save** him from them and send him
45. 5 really God who sent me ahead of you to **save** people's lives.
47.25 They answered, "You have **saved** our lives;
Ex 6. 6 to bring terrible punishment upon them, and I will **save** you.
14.13 you will see what the Lord will do to **save** you today;
14.30 On that day the Lord **saved** the people of Israel from the
15. 2 he is the one who has **saved** me.
16.20 of them did not listen to Moses and **saved** part of it.
16.32 Lord has commanded us to **save** some manna, to be kept for
18. 4 my father helped me and **saved** me from being killed by the
18. 8 had faced on the way and how the Lord had **saved** them.
18.10 said, "Praise the Lord, who **saved** you from the king and the
18.10 Praise the Lord, who **saved** his people from slavery!
21.30 to pay a fine to **save** his life, he must pay the
Lev 18. 5 you will **save** your life by doing so.
Num 10. 9 Lord your God, will help you and **save** you from your enemies.
Deut 7. 8 That is why he **saved** you by his great might and set
33.29 There is no one like you, a nation **saved** by the Lord.
Josh 2.13 Promise me that you will **save** my father and mother, my
10. 6 **Save** us!
22.31 him, and so you have **saved** the people of Israel from the
Judg 2.16 Lord gave the Israelites leaders who **saved** them from the raiders.
2.18 would help him and would **save** the people from their enemies
8.22 You have **saved** us from the Midianites."
8.34 Lord their God, who had **saved** them from all their enemies
9.17 He risked his life to **save** you from the Midianites.
10.12 Did I not **save** you from them?
10.15 Do whatever you like, but please, **save** us today."
18.27 There was no one to **save** them, because Laish was a long
1 Sam 4. 3 that he will go with us and **save** us from our enemies."
4. 8 Who can **save** us from those powerful gods?
7. 8 to the Lord our God to **save** us from the Philistines."
9.24 I **saved** it for you to eat at this time with the
12. 7 mighty actions the Lord did to **save** you and your ancestors.
12.21 they cannot help you or **save** you, for they are not real.
14.23 The Lord **saved** Israel that day.
14.45 So the people **saved** Jonathan from being put to death.
14.48 He **saved** the Israelites from all attacks.
17.37 The Lord has **saved** me from lions and bears;
17.37 he will **save** me from this Philistine."
17.47 the Lord does not need swords or spears to **save** his people.
23. 2 "Attack them and **save** Keilah."
23. 5 And that was how David **saved** the town.
24.15 he look into the matter, defend me, and **save** me from you."
2 Sam 3. 8 friends, and I have **saved** you from being defeated by David;
4. 9 vow by the living Lord, who has **saved** me from all dangers!
14.16 would listen to me and **save** me from the one who is
18.19 good news that the Lord has **saved** him from his enemies."
19. 5 your men—the men who **saved** your life and the lives of
19. 9 "King David **saved** us from our enemies," they said to one another.
22. 1 When the Lord **saved** David from Saul and his other enemies,
22. 3 he protects me and **saves** me from violence.
22. 4 I call to the Lord, and he **saves** me from my enemies.
22.20 he **saved** me because he was pleased with me.
22.28 You **save** those who are humble, but you humble those who
22.36 O Lord, you protect me and **save** me;
22.42 They look for help, but no one **saves** them;
22.44 You **saved** me from my rebellious people and maintained my

2 Sam 22.47 Proclaim the greatness of the strong God who **saves** me!
22.49 he subdues the nations under me [49] and **saves** me from my foes.
1 Kgs 1.12 If you want to **save** your life and the life of your
2 Kgs 12. 4 priests and ordered them to **save** up the money paid in
18.29 Hezekiah can't **save** you.
18.30 think that the Lord will **save** you, and that he will stop
18.33 gods of any other nations **save** their countries from the
18.34 Did anyone **save** Samaria?
18.35 these countries ever **save** their country from our emperor?
18.35 Then what makes you think the Lord can **save** Jerusalem?"
19. 6 Assyrians frighten you with their claims that he cannot **save** you.
19.12 lived in Telassar, and none of their gods could **save** them.
1 Chr 16.23 Proclaim every day the good news that he has **saved** us.
16.35 Say to him, "**Save** us, O God our Saviour;
2 Chr 22.11 By keeping him hidden, she **saved** him from death at the hands
25.15 could not even **save** their own people from your power?"
32.11 the Lord your God will **save** you from our power, but Hezekiah
32.13 gods of any other nation **save** their people from the emperor
32.14 gods of all those countries ever **save** their country from us?
32.14 Then what makes you think that your god can **save** you?
32.15 ever been able to **save** his people from any Assyrian emperor.
32.15 So certainly this god of yours can't **save** you!"
32.17 of the nations have not **saved** their people from my power,
32.17 and neither will Hezekiah's god **save** his people from me."
Neh 6.11 think I would try to **save** my life by hiding in the
9.28 repented and asked you to **save** them, in heaven you heard,
Esth 4.14 Jews, and they will be **saved**, but you will die and your
7. 9 that he could hang Mordecai, who **saved** Your Majesty's life.
Job 5.15 But God **saves** the poor from death;
5.15 he **saves** the needy from oppression.
5.19 Time after time he will **save** you from harm;
5.21 he will **save** you when destruction comes.
6.13 I have no strength left to **save** myself;
6.23 on my behalf [23] or to **save** me from some enemy or tyrant?
10. 7 I am not guilty, that no one can **save** me from you.
13.16 be that my boldness will **save** me, since no wicked man would
20.26 Everything he has **saved** is destroyed;
22.29 God brings down the proud and **saves** the humble.
33.17 stop their sinning and to **save** them from becoming proud.
33.18 he **saves** them from death itself.
33.30 he **saves** a person's life, and gives him the joy of living.
35. 9 they cry for someone to **save** them.
Ps 3. 7 **Save** me, my God!
6. 4 Come and **save** me, Lord;
7. 1 rescue me and **save** me from all who pursue me, [2] or else
7. 2 off where no one can **save** me, and there they will tear
7.10 he **saves** those who obey him.
9.14 I will rejoice because you **saved** me.
17. 7 Reveal your wonderful love and **save** me;
17.13 **Save** me from the wicked by your sword;
17.14 **save** me from those who in this life have all they want.
18. 3 I call to the Lord, and he **saves** me from my enemies.
18.19 he **saved** me because he was pleased with me.
18.27 You **save** those who are humble, but you humble those who
18.35 O Lord, you protect me and **save** me;
18.41 They cry for help, but no one **saves** them;
18.43 You **saved** me from a rebellious people and made me ruler
18.46 Proclaim the greatness of the God who **saves** me.
18.48 he subdues the nations under me [48] and **saves** me from my foes.
22. 4 they trusted you, and you **saved** them.
22. 8 "Why doesn't he **save** you?
22.20 **Save** me from the sword;
22.20 **save** my life from these dogs.
22.31 "The Lord **saved** his people."
24. 5 The Lord will bless them and **save** them;
25. 2 **Save** me from the shame of defeat;
25. 5 according to your truth, for you are my God, who **saves** me.
25.17 Relieve me of my worries and **save** me from all my troubles.
25.20 Protect me and **save** me;
25.22 From all their troubles, O God, **save** your people Israel!
26.11 be merciful to me and **save** me!
28. 8 he defends and **saves** his chosen king.
28. 9 **Save** your people, Lord, and bless those who are yours.
30. 1 you, Lord, because you have **saved** me and kept my enemies
31. 1 **save** me, I pray!
31. 2 **Save** me now!
31. 2 my defence to **save** me.
31. 5 You will **save** me, Lord;
31.15 **save** me from my enemies, from those who persecute me.
31.16 **save** me in your constant love.
32. 7 you will **save** me from trouble.
33.17 their great strength cannot **save**.
33.19 He **saves** them from death;
34. 6 he **saves** them from all their troubles.
34.18 he **saves** those who have lost all hope.
34.19 many troubles, but the Lord **saves** him from them all;
34.22 The Lord will **save** his people;
35. 3 Promise that you will **save** me.
35. 9 I will be happy because he **saved** me.
35.17 **save** my life from these lions!
37.39 The Lord **saves** righteous men and protects them
37.40 he **saves** them from the wicked, because they go to him for
39. 8 **Save** me from all my sins, and don't let fools laugh at
40. 9 your people, Lord, I told the good news that you **save** us.
40.13 **Save** me, Lord!
44. 6 not trust in my bow or in my sword to **save** me;
44. 7 but you have **saved** us from our enemies and defeated those
44.26 Because of your constant love **save** us!
49.12 A man's greatness cannot **save** him from death;
49.15 he will **save** me from the power of death.
49.20 A man's greatness cannot **save** him from death;

Ps 50.15 I will **save** you, and you will praise me."
50.22 will destroy you, and there will be no one to **save** you.
50.23 that honours me, and I will surely **save** all who obey me."
51.14 my life, O God, and **save** me, and I will gladly proclaim
54. 1 **Save** me by your power, O God;
55.16 call to the Lord God for help, and he will **save** me.
57. 3 He will answer from heaven and **save** me;
59. 1 **Save** me from my enemies, my God;
59. 2 **Save** me from those evil men;
60. 5 **Save** us by your might;
62. 1 I wait patiently for God to **save** me;
62. 2 He alone protects and **saves** me;
62. 6 He alone protects and **saves** me;
64. 1 I am afraid of my enemies—**save** my life!
65. 5 giving us victory and you do wonderful things to **save** us.
68.19 he is the God who **saves** us.
68.20 Our God is a God who **saves**;
69. 1 **Save** me, O God!
69.13 of your great love, because you keep your promise to **save.**
69.14 **Save** me from sinking in the mud;
69.18 Come to me and **save** me;
69.29 lift me up, O God, and **save** me!
69.35 He will **save** Jerusalem and rebuild the towns of Judah.
70. 1 **Save** me, O God!
71. 2 Listen to me and **save** me!
71.23 with my whole being I will sing because you have **saved** me.
72.13 he **saves** the lives of those in need.
74.12 you have **saved** us many times.
76. 9 to pronounce judgement, to **save** all the oppressed on earth.
77.15 By your power you **saved** your people, the descendants of
78.22 faith in him and did not believe that he would **save** them.
78.42 and the day when he **saved** them from their enemies [43] and
79. 9 Help us, O God, and **save** us;
80. 2 come and **save** us!
80. 3 Show us your mercy, and we will be **saved!**
80. 7 Show us your mercy, and we will be **saved!**
80.14 come and **save** your people!
80.15 Come and **save** this grapevine that you planted, this
80.19 Show us your mercy, and we will be **saved.**
81. 7 you were in trouble, you called to me, and I **saved** you.
85. 7 your constant love, O Lord, and give us your **saving** help.
85. 9 Surely he is ready to **save** those who honour him,
85. 9 and his **saving** presence will remain in our land.
86. 2 **Save** me from death, because I am loyal to you;
86. 2 **save** me, for I am your servant and I trust in you.
86.13 You have **saved** me from the grave itself.
86.16 strengthen me and **save** me, because I serve you, just as my
91.14 God says, "I will **save** those who love me and will
91.16 I will **save** them."
96. 2 Proclaim every day the good news that he has **saved** us.
98. 2 he made his **saving** power known to the nations.
106. 4 include me when you **save** them.
106. 8 But he **saved** them, as he had promised, in order to show
106.10 He **saved** them from those who hated them;
106.21 forgot the God who had **saved** them by his mighty acts in
106.47 **Save** us, O Lord our God, and bring us back from among
107. 2 words in praise to the Lord, all you whom he has **saved.**
107. 6 called to the Lord, and he **saved** them from their distress.
107.13 called to the Lord, and he **saved** them from their distress.
107.19 called to the Lord, and he **saved** them from their distress.
107.20 He healed them with his command and **saved** them from the grave.
107.28 called to the Lord, and he **saved** them from their distress.
108. 6 **Save** us by your might;
109.26 because of your constant love, **save** me!
109.27 Make my enemies know that you are the one who **saves** me.
109.31 defends the poor man and **saves** him from those who condemn
116. 4 Then I called to the Lord, "I beg you, Lord, **save** me!"
116. 6 when I was in danger, he **saved** me.
116. 8 The Lord **saved** me from death;
116.13 a wine-offering to the Lord, to thank him for **saving** me.
116.16 You have **saved** me from death.
118.14 he has **saved** me.
118.25 **Save** us, Lord, save us!
119.39 **Save** me from the insults I fear;
119.41 you love me, Lord, and **save** me according to your promise.
119.81 I am worn out, Lord, waiting for you to **save** me;
119.94 I am yours—**save** me!
119.123 for your **saving** help, for the deliverance you promised.
119.134 **Save** me from those who oppress me, so that I may obey
119.146 **save** me, and I will keep your laws.
119.153 Look at my suffering, and **save** me,
119.154 **save** me, as you have promised.
119.155 The wicked will not be **saved,** for they do not obey
119.156 show your mercy and **save** me!
119.159 Your love never changes, so **save** me!
119.166 I wait for you to **save** me, Lord, and I do what
119.170 Listen to my prayer, and **save** me according to your promise!
119.174 How I long for your **saving** help, O Lord!
120. 2 **Save** me, Lord, from liars and deceivers.
130. 7 his love is constant and he is always willing to **save.**
130. 8 He will **save** his people Israel from all their sins.
138. 7 You oppose my angry enemies and **save** me by your power.
140. 1 **Save** me, Lord, from evil men;
142. 6 **Save** me from my enemies;
143.11 in your goodness **save** me from my troubles!
144. 7 **save** me from the power of foreigners, [8] who never tell the
144.11 **Save** me from my cruel enemies;
145.19 he hears their cries and **saves** them.
146. 3 no human being can **save** you.
Prov 10. 2 will do you no good, but honesty can **save** your life.

Prov	11. 4	on the day you face death, but honesty can **save** your life.
	11. 9	people, but the wisdom of the righteous can **save** you.
	13. 8	to use his money to **save** his life, but no one threatens
	14.25	A witness **saves** lives when he tells the truth;
	16.17	so watch where you are going—it may **save** your life.
	23.14	As a matter of fact, it may **save** his life.
Ecc	2.26	makes sinners work, earning and **saving,** so that what they
	3. 6	losing, the time for **saving** and the time for throwing away,
	5.13	people **save** up their money for a time when they may need
	9.15	was poor, but so clever that he could have **saved** the town.
Is	1.27	he will **save** Jerusalem and everyone there who repents.
	7.21	farmer has been able to **save** only one young cow and two
	12. 3	the thirsty, so God's people rejoice when he **saves** them."
	25. 9	and now we are happy and joyful because he has **saved** us."
	33. 2	Protect us day by day and **save** us in times of trouble.
	36.14	Hezekiah can't **save** you.
	36.15	think that the Lord will **save** you and that he will stop
	36.18	gods of any other nations **save** their countries from the
	36.19	Did anyone **save** Samaria?
	36.20	these countries ever **save** their country from our emperor?
	36.20	Then what makes you think the Lord can **save** Jerusalem?"
	37. 6	Assyrians frighten you by their claims that he cannot **save** you.
	37.12	lived in Telassar, and none of their gods could **save** them.
	38.17	You **save** my life from all danger;
	41.10	I will protect you and **save** you.
	41.14	I, the holy God of Israel, am the one who **saves** you.
	42.21	God who is eager to **save,** so he exalted his laws and
	43. 1	"Do not be afraid—I will **save** you.
	43. 3	the Lord your God, the holy God of Israel, who **saves** you.
	43. 4	give up whole nations to **save** your life, because you are
	43.11	"I alone am the Lord, the only one who can **save** you.
	43.14	Israel's holy God, the Lord who **saves** you, says,
	43.14	"To **save** you, I will send an army against Babylon;
	44.17	He prays to it and says, "You are my god—**save** me!"
	44.22	I am the one who **saves** you."
	44.23	The Lord has shown his greatness by **saving** his people Israel.
	45.15	The God of Israel, who **saves** his people, is a God who
	45.17	But Israel is **saved** by the Lord, and her victory lasts
	45.20	pray to gods that cannot **save** them— those people know
	45.21	Was it not I, the Lord, the God who **saves** his people?
	45.22	"Turn to me now and be **saved,** people all over the world!
	46. 2	The idols cannot **save** themselves;
	46. 7	prays to it, it cannot answer or **save** him from disaster.
	46.13	I will **save** Jerusalem and bring honour to Israel there."
	47.13	your astrologers come forward and **save** you— those people who
	47.14	not even be able to **save** themselves— the flames will be
	47.15	go their own way, and none will be left to **save** you."
	48.17	The holy God of Israel, the Lord who **saves** you, says:
	48.20	"The Lord has **saved** his servant Israel!"
	49. 6	to the nations— so that all the world may be **saved."**
	49. 8	"When the time comes to **save** you, I will show you favour
	49.26	am the Lord, the one who **saves** you and sets you free.
	50. 2	people fail to respond when I went to them to **save** them?
	50. 2	Am I too weak to **save** them?
	51. 1	you that want to be **saved,** you that come to me for
	51. 5	I will come quickly and **save** them;
	51. 5	they wait with hope for me to **save** them.
	51. 9	Use your power and **save** us;
	51.10	the water, so that those you were **saving** could cross.
	52.10	he will **save** his people, and all the world will see it.
	54. 5	holy God of Israel will **save** you— he is the ruler
	54. 8	So says the Lord who **saves** you.
	56. 1	"Do what is just and right, for soon I will **save** you.
	57.13	When you cry for help, let those idols of yours **save** you!
	58. 8	I will always be with you to **save** you;
	59. 1	Lord is too weak to **save** you or too deaf to hear
	59. 9	know why God does not **save** us from those who oppress us.
	59.11	We long for God to **save** us from oppression and wrong, but
	59.17	like a coat of armour and **saving** power like a helmet.
	59.20	to defend you and to **save** all of you that turn from
	60.16	that I, the Lord, have **saved** you, That the mighty God of
	60.18	You will praise me because I have **saved** you.
	61. 2	When the Lord will **save** his people And defeat their enemies.
	61.11	grow, The Sovereign Lord will **save** his people, And all the
	62. 1	be silent until she is **saved,** And her victory shines like a
	62.11	the Lord is coming to **save** you, Bringing with him the people
	62.12	"God's Holy People," "The People the Lord Has **Saved."**
	63. 1	"It is the Lord, powerful to **save,** coming to announce his victory."
	63. 4	I decided that the time to **save** my people had come;
	63. 8	And so he **saved** them [9] from all their suffering.
	63. 9	It was not an angel, but the Lord himself who **saved** them.
	63.11	now is the Lord, who **saved** the leaders of his people from
	65. 8	I destroy all my people—I will **save** those who serve me.
	66. 5	Lord show his greatness and **save** you, so that we may see
Jer	2.27	you are in trouble, you ask me to come and **save** you.
	2.28	When you are in trouble, let them **save** you—if they can!
	4.14	wash the evil from your heart, so that you may be **saved.**
	8.20	is gone, the harvest is over, but we have not been **saved."**
	11.12	will not be able to **save** them when this destruction comes.
	14. 8	you are the one who **saves** us from disaster.
	30.11	I will come to you and **save** you.
	31. 7	Sing your song of praise, 'The Lord has **saved** his people;
	31.11	Israel's people free and have **saved** them from a mighty nation.
	46.28	I will come to you and **save** you.
Lam	3.26	to wait for him to **save** us— [27] And it is best
	3.58	"You came to my rescue, Lord, and **saved** my life.
	5. 8	than slaves, and no one can **save** us from their power.
Ezek	3.18	ways so that he can **save** his life, he will die, still
	7.19	neither silver nor gold can **save** them when the Lord pours
	13.22	You prevent evil people from giving up evil and **saving** their lives.
	14.14	there, their goodness would **save** only their own lives."
Ezek	14.16	God—they would not be able to **save** even their own children.
	14.16	They would **save** only their own lives, and the land would
	14.18	would not be able to **save** even their children, but only
	14.20	God—they would not be able to **save** even their own children.
	14.20	Their goodness would **save** only their own lives."
	14.22	If anyone does survive and **save** his children, look at
	18.27	sinning and does what is right and good, he **saves** his life.
	33. 8	ways so that he can **save** his life, then he will die,
	33.12	good man sins, the good he has done will not **save** him.
	33.19	and does what is right and good, he has **saved** his life.
	36.29	I will **save** you from everything that defiles you.
Dan	3.15	Do you think there is any god who can **save** you?"
	3.17	we serve is able to **save** us from the blazing furnace and
	6.20	God you serve so loyally able to **save** you from the lions?"
	6.27	He **saves** and rescues;
	6.27	He **saved** Daniel from being killed by the lions."
	8. 7	and trampled on, and there was no one who could **save** him.
	12. 1	nation whose names are written in God's book will be **saved.**
Hos	1. 7	the Lord their God, will **save** them, but I will not do
	2.10	and no one will be able to **save** her from my power.
	5.14	I drag them off, no one will be able to **save** them.
	7.13	I wanted to **save** them, but their worship of me was false.
	13.10	a king and for leaders, but how can they **save** the nation?
	13.14	I will not **save** this people from the world of the dead
	14. 3	Assyria can never **save** us, and war-horses cannot protect us.
Joel	2.32	But all who ask the Lord for help will be **saved.**
Amos	2.14	and soldiers will not be able to **save** their own lives.
	4.11	who survived were like a burning stick **saved** from a fire.
Mic	4.10	Babylon, but there the Lord will **save** you from your enemies.
	5. 6	of Nimrod, and they will **save** us from the Assyrians when
	6. 5	and you will realize what I did in order to **save** you."
	6.14	carry things off, but you will not be able to **save** them;
	6.14	anything you do **save** I will destroy in war.
	7. 7	I will wait confidently for God, who will **save** me.
	7. 9	we will live to see him **save** us.
Hab	1. 2	help before you listen, before you **save** us from violence?
	3.13	You went out to **save** your people,
	3.13	to **save** your chosen king.
Zeph	1.18	his fury, not even all their silver and gold will **save** them.
Zech	8.13	But I will **save** you, and then those foreigners will say to
	9.16	the Lord will **save** his people,
	9.16	as a shepherd **saves** his flock from danger.
	11. 6	the earth, and I will not **save** it from their power.")
Mal	4. 2	you who obey me, my **saving** power will rise on you like
Mt	1.21	him Jesus—because he will **save** his people from their sins."
	8.25	**"Save** us, Lord!"
	10.22	But whoever holds out to the end will be **saved.**
	14.30	**"Save** me, Lord!"
	16.25	For whoever wants to **save** his own life will lose it;
	19.25	"Who, then, can be **saved?"**
	24.13	But whoever holds out to the end will be **saved.**
	27.40	**Save** yourself if you are God's Son!
	27.42	"He **saved** others, but he cannot save himself!
	27.43	Well, then, let us see if God wants to **save** him now!"
	27.49	said, "Wait, let us see if Elijah is coming to **save** him!"
Mk	3. 4	To **save** a man's life or to destroy it?"
	8.35	For whoever wants to **save** his own life will lose it;
	8.35	loses his life for me and for the gospel will **save** it.
	10.26	amazed and asked one another, "Who, then, can be **saved?"**
	13.13	But whoever holds out to the end will be **saved.**
	15.30	Now come down from the cross and **save** yourself!"
	15.31	each other, "He **saved** others, but he cannot save himself!
	16.16	Whoever believes and is baptized will be **saved;**
Lk	1.71	long ago [71] that he would **save** us from our enemies,
	1.77	they will be **saved** by having their sins forgiven.
	2.25	God-fearing man and was waiting for Israel to be **saved.**
	4.19	that the time has come when the Lord will **save** his people."
	6. 9	To **save** a man's life or destroy it?"
	7.16	"God has come to **save** his people!"
	7.50	But Jesus said to the woman, "Your faith has **saved** you;
	8.12	hearts in order to keep them from believing and being **saved.**
	9.24	For whoever wants to **save** his own life will lose it,
	9.24	but whoever loses his life for my sake will **save** it.
	12.33	that don't wear out, and **save** your riches in heaven,
	13.23	Someone asked him, "Sir, will just a few people be **saved?"**
	17.33	Whoever tries to **save** his own life will lose it;
	17.33	whoever loses his life will **save** it.
	18.26	The people who heard him asked, "Who, then, can be **saved?"**
	19.10	The Son of Man came to seek and to **save** the lost."
	19.44	you did not recognize the time when God came to **save** you!"
	21.19	Stand firm, and you will **save** yourselves.
	23.35	"He **saved** others;
	23.35	let him **save** himself if he is the Messiah
	23.37	him cheap wine, [37] and said, **"Save** yourself if you are the
	23.39	**Save** yourself and us!"
Jn	5.34	I say this only in order that you may be **saved.**
	10. 9	Whoever comes in by me will be **saved;**
	12.47	I came, not to judge the world, but to **save** it.
Acts	2.21	whoever calls out to the Lord for help will be **saved.'**
	2.40	words he urged them, saying, **"Save** yourselves from the
	2.47	the Lord added to their group those who were being **saved.**
	4.12	is no one else whom God has given who can **save** us."
	11.14	by which you and all your family will be **saved.'**
	13.47	for the Gentiles, so that all the world may be **saved.' "**
	15. 1	"You cannot be **saved** unless you are circumcised
	15.11	We believe and are **saved** by the grace of the Lord Jesus,
	16.17	They announce to you how you can be **saved!"**
	16.30	and asked, "Sirs, what must I do to be **saved?"**
	16.31	the Lord Jesus, and you will be **saved**—you and your family."
	27.20	We finally gave up all hope of being **saved.**
	27.31	don't stay on board, you have no hope of being **saved."**

Acts 27.43 the army officer wanted to **save** Paul, so he stopped them
Rom 1.16 it is God's power to **save** all who believe, first the Jews
3.23 everyone has sinned and is far away from God's **saving** presence.
5. 9 much more, then, will we be **saved** by him from God's anger!
5.10 how much more will we be **saved** by Christ's life!
8.24 For it was by hope that we were **saved;**
9.27 yet only a few of them will be **saved;**
10. 1 wish with all my heart that my own people might be **saved!**
10. 9 believe that God raised him from death, you will be **saved.**
10.10 it is by our confession that we are **saved.**
10.13 "Everyone who calls out to the Lord for help will be **saved."**
11.14 own race jealous, and so be able to **save** some of them.
11.26 And this is how all Israel will be **saved.**
13.11 moment when we will be **saved** is closer now than it was
1 Cor 1.18 but for us who are being **saved** it is God's power.
1.21 message we preach, God decided to **save** those who believe.
3.15 but he himself will be **saved,** as if he had escaped
5. 5 that his spirit may be **saved** in the Day of the Lord.
7.16 Christian wife, that you will not **save** your husband?
7.16 Christian husband, that you will not **save** your wife?
9.22 all men, that I may **save** some of them by whatever means
10.33 but of the good of all, so that they might be **saved.**
15. 2 You are **saved** by the gospel if you hold firmly to it
16. 2 what he has earned, and **save** it up, so that there will
2 Cor 1.10 terrible dangers of death he **saved** us, and will save us;
1.10 in him that he will **save** us again, [11] as you help us
2.15 those who are being **saved** and those who are being lost.
2.16 for those who are being **saved,** it is a fragrance that brings
6. 2 when the day arrived for me to **save** you I helped you."
6. 2 today is the day to be **saved!**
Eph 2. 5 It is by God's grace that you have been **saved.**
2. 8 it is by God's grace that you have been **saved** through faith.
2 Thes 2.10 did not welcome and love the truth so as to be **saved.**
2.13 as the first to be **saved** by the Spirit's power to make
1 Tim 1.15 Christ Jesus came into the world to **save** sinners.
2. 4 who wants everyone to be **saved** and to come to know the
2. 6 God wants everyone to be **saved,** [7] and that is why I was
2.15 But a woman will be **saved** through having children, if
4.16 if you do, you will **save** both yourself and those who hear
2 Tim 1. 9 He **saved** us and called us to be his own people,
Tit 3. 5 love of God our Saviour was revealed, [5] he **saved** us.
3. 5 his own mercy that he **saved** us, through the Holy Spirit,
Heb 5. 7 loud cries and tears to God, who could **save** him from death.
7.25 able, now and always, to **save** those who come to God
9.28 deal with sin, but to **save** those who are waiting for him.
10.39 Instead, we have faith and are **saved.**
11. 7 and built a boat in which he and his family were **saved.**
Jas 1.21 that he plants in your hearts, which is able to **save** you.
2.14 Can that faith **save** him?
4.12 He alone can **save** and destroy.
5.20 from his wrong way will **save** that sinner's soul from death
1 Pet 2. 2 so that by drinking it you may grow up and be **saved.**
3.20 boat—eight in all—were **saved** by the
3.21 which was a symbol pointing to baptism, which now **saves** you.
3.21 It **saves** you through the resurrection of Jesus Christ,
4.18 says, "It is difficult for good people to be **saved;**
2 Pet 2. 5 only ones he **saved** were Noah, who preached righteousness,
3.15 is giving you to be **saved,** just as our dear brother Paul
Jude 23 **save** others by snatching them out of the fire;

SAVIOUR
see also **SAVE**

Deut 32.15 They abandoned God their Creator and rejected their mighty **saviour.**
32.18 forgot their God, their mighty **saviour,**
2 Sam 22. 3 He is my **saviour;**
1 Chr 16.35 Say to him, "Save us, O God our **Saviour;**
Ps 27. 9 don't leave me, don't abandon me, O God, my **saviour.**
38.22 Help me now, O Lord my **saviour!**
40.17 You are my **saviour** and my God— hurry to my aid!
42. 5 and once again I will praise him, my **saviour** and my God.
42.11 and once again I will praise him, my **saviour** and my God.
43. 5 and once again I will praise him, my **saviour** and my God.
70. 5 You are my **saviour,** O Lord— hurry to my aid!
85. 4 back, O God our **saviour,** and stop being displeased with us!
88. 1 Lord God, my **saviour,** I cry out all day, and at night
89.26 you are my protector and **saviour.'**
144. 2 my shelter and **saviour,** in whom I trust for safety.
Is 12. 2 God is my **saviour;**
12. 2 he is my **saviour.**
44.24 "I am the Lord, your **saviour;**
49. 7 Israel's holy God and **saviour** says to the one who is
Hos 13. 4 I alone am your **saviour.**
Hab 3.18 be joyful and glad, because the Lord God is my **saviour.**
Lk 1.47 glad because of God my **Saviour,** [48] for he has remembered me,
1.69 for us a mighty **Saviour,** a descendant of his servant David.
2.11 day in David's town your **Saviour** was born—Christ the Lord!
Jn 3.17 into the world to be its judge, but to be its **saviour.**
4.42 and we know that he really is the **Saviour** of the world."
Acts 5.31 right-hand side as Leader and **Saviour,** to give the people of
13.23 whom God made the **Saviour** of the people of Israel,
13.27 know that he is the **Saviour,** nor did they understand
Rom 11.26 As the scripture says, "The **Saviour** will come from Zion and
Eph 5.23 and Christ is himself the **Saviour** of the church, his body.
Phil 3.20 we eagerly wait for our **Saviour,** the Lord Jesus Christ, to
1 Tim 1. 1 by order of God our **Saviour** and Christ Jesus our hope—
2. 3 and it pleases God our **Saviour,** [4] who wants everyone to be
4.10 living God, who is the **Saviour** of all
2 Tim 1.10 been revealed to us through the coming of our **Saviour,**
Tit 1. 3 to me, and I proclaim it by order of God our **Saviour.**
1. 4 Father and Christ Jesus our **Saviour** give you grace and peace.
2.10 to the teaching about God our **Saviour** in all they do.
2.13 glory of our great God and **Saviour** Jesus Christ will appear.
3. 4 kindness and love of God our **Saviour** was revealed,
3. 6 us through Jesus Christ our **Saviour,** [7] so that by his grace
2 Pet 1. 1 righteousness of our God and **Saviour** Jesus Christ
1.11 the eternal Kingdom of our Lord and **Saviour** Jesus Christ.
2.20 knowledge of our Lord and **Saviour** Jesus Christ,
3. 2 command from the Lord and **Saviour** which was given you
3.18 grace and knowledge of our Lord and **Saviour** Jesus Christ.
1 Jn 4.14 the Father sent his Son to be the **Saviour** of the world.
Jude 25 to the only God our **Saviour,** through Jesus Christ our Lord,

SAW
see also **SEE**

2 Sam 12.31 its people to work with **saws,** iron hoes, and iron axes, and
1 Kgs 7. 9 measure, with their inner and outer sides trimmed with **saws.**
1 Chr 20. 3 city and put them to work with **saws,** iron hoes, and axes.
Is 10.15 Is a saw more important than the man who **saws** with it?
Heb 11.37 They were stoned, they were **sawn** in two, they were

SAY

Ps 12. 5 now I will come," **says the Lord,** "because the needy are
Is 46. 5 **says the Lord.**
48.22 "There is no safety for sinners," **says the Lord.**
54. 8 So **says the Lord** who saves you.
54.10 So **says the Lord** who loves you.
55. 8 "My thoughts," **says the Lord,** "are not like yours, and
57.21 There is no safety for sinners," **says the Lord.**
66.23 will come to worship me here in Jerusalem," **says the Lord.**
Jer 16.21 "So then," **says the Lord,** "once and for all I will
23. 7 "The time is coming," **says the Lord,** "when people will
31.38 "The time is coming," **says the Lord,** "when all
Ezek 7.21 let foreigners rob them," **says the Lord,** "and law-breakers
12.25 I have spoken," **says the Sovereign Lord.**
17.16 am the living God," **says the Sovereign Lord,** "this king
18. 3 am the living God," **says the Sovereign Lord,** "you will not
18. 9 He is righteous, and he will live," **says the Sovereign Lord.**
18.32 I do not want anyone to die," **says the Sovereign Lord.**
20.36 I condemned your fathers in the Sinai Desert," **says the Sovereign Lord.**
31.18 I have spoken," **says the Sovereign Lord.**
32.31 the king of Egypt and his army," **says the Sovereign Lord.**
34.31 my people, and I am your God," **says the Sovereign Lord.**
Joel 2.12 "But even now," **says the Lord,** "repent sincerely and
Amos 3.13 descendants of Jacob," **says the Sovereign Lord** Almighty.
4.11 Still you did not come back to me," **says the Lord.**
5.27 Damascus," **says the Lord,** whose name is Almighty God.
9.12 that were once mine," **says the Lord,** who will cause this to
9.13 "The days are coming," **says the Lord,** "when corn will
Mic 4. 6 "The time is coming," **says the Lord,** "when I will
Nah 2.13 **says the Lord** Almighty.
Zeph 1. 8 slaughter," **says the Lord,** "I will punish the officials,
1.10 "On that day," **says the Lord,** "you will hear the
Zech 13. 1 "When that time comes," **says the Lord** Almighty, "a
Mal 2.16 "I hate divorce," **says the Lord** God of Israel.
3.13 "You have said terrible things about me," **says the Lord.**
3.17 "They will be my people," **says the Lord** Almighty.
Mt 10.19 what you are going to **say** or how you will say it;
10.19 when the time comes, you will be given what you will **say.**
12.31 people can be forgiven any sin and any evil thing they **say;**
12.31 but whoever **says evil things** against the Holy Spirit will
13.34 he would not **say** a thing to them without using a parable.
15.23 But Jesus did not **say** a word to her.
16.13 his disciples, "Who do people **say** the Son of Man is?"
16.15 "Who do you **say** I am?"
21.25 They started to argue among themselves, "What shall we **say?**
26.25 Jesus answered, "So you **say."**
26.64 Jesus answered him, "So you **say.**
27.11 "So you **say,"** answered Jesus.
Mk 1.34 would not let the demons **say** anything, because they knew who
3. 4 But they did not **say** a thing.
3.28 all their sins and all the evil things they may **say.**
3.29 But whoever **says evil things** against the Holy Spirit
8.27 way he asked them, "Tell me, who do people **say** I am?"
8.29 "Who do you **say** I am?"
9. 6 others were so frightened that he did not know what to **say.**
11.31 "What shall we **say?**
13.11 do not worry beforehand about what you are going to **say;**
13.11 when the time comes, **say** whatever is then given to you.
13.37 What I **say** to you, then, I say to all:
14.40 And they did not know what to **say** to him.
14.61 But Jesus kept quiet and would not **say** a word.
15. 2 Jesus answered, "So you **say."**
15. 5 Again Jesus refused to **say** a word, and Pilate was amazed.
Lk 1.22 Unable to **say** a word, he made signs to them with his
7.49 at the table began to **say** to themselves, "Who is this, who
9.18 "Who do the crowds **say** I am?"
9.20 "Who do you **say** I am?"
11. 9 "And so I **say** to you:
12.10 but whoever **says evil things** against the Holy Spirit will
12.11 about how you will defend yourself or what you will **say.**
12.12 Holy Spirit will teach you at that time what you should **say."**
14. 4 But they would not **say** anything.
16.29 your brothers should listen to what they **say.'**
20. 5 They started to argue among themselves, "What shall we **say?**
20.21 Jesus, "Teacher, we know that what you **say** and teach is right.
21.15 enemies will be able to refute or contradict what you **say.**
22.70 He answered them, "You **say** that I am."

Lk 23. 3 "So you **say,**" answered Jesus.
Jn 1.22 What do you **say** about yourself?"
5.31 my own behalf, what I **say** is not to be accepted as
5.34 I **say** this only in order that you may be saved.
5.47 not believe what he wrote, how can you believe what I **say?"**
6.42 How, then, does he now **say** he came down from heaven?"
7.26 He is talking in public, and they **say** nothing against him!
8. 5 Now, what do you **say?"**
8.13 what you **say** proves nothing."
8.14 my own behalf, what I **say** is true, because I know where
8.17 Law that when two witnesses agree, what they **say** is true.
8.26 I have much to **say** about you, much to condemn you for.
8.28 but I say only what the Father has instructed me to **say.**
8.43 Why do you not understand what I **say?**
8.52 the prophets died, yet you **say** that whoever obeys your
8.54 me is my Father—the very one you **say** is your God.
8.55 If I were to **say** that I do not know him, I
9.17 you of your blindness—well, what do you **say** about him?"
11.42 listen to me, but I **say** this for the sake of the
11.51 Actually, he did not **say** this of his own accord;
12.27 "Now my heart is troubled—and what shall I **say?**
12.49 who sent me has commanded me what I must **say** and speak.
12.50 I say, then, is what the Father has told me to **say."**
16.14 because he will take what I **say** and tell it to you.
Acts 4.14 was nothing that they could **say,** because they saw the man
8.32 when its wool is cut off, he did not **say** a word.
10.33 to hear anything that the Lord has instructed you to **say."**
18. 6 they opposed him and **said evil things** about him, he
19. 9 the whole group they **said evil things** about the Way of the
19.37 not robbed temples or **said evil things** about our goddess.
21.37 "May I **say** something to you?"
23.18 young man to you, because he has something to **say** to you."
26.22 What I **say** is the very same thing which the prophets and
28.26 For he said, 'Go and **say** to this people:
Rom 4. 1 What shall we **say,** then, of Abraham, the father of our race?
6. 1 What shall we **say,** then?
8.31 In view of all this, what can we **say?**
9.19 But one of you will **say** to me, "If this is so,
1 Cor 1.10 to agree in what you **say,** so that there will be no
4.19 which these proud people have, and not just what they **say.**
7.12 To the others I **say** (I, myself, not the Lord):
10.15 judge for yourselves what I **say.**
11.22 What do you expect me to **say** to you about this?
14.29 should speak, while the others are to judge what they **say.**
2 Cor 11.17 saying now is not what the Lord would like me to **say;**
12. 6 result of what he has seen me do and heard me **say.**
Gal 1. 9 We have said it before, and now I **say** it again:
Eph 4.29 needed, so that what you **say** will do good to those who
Col 3.17 Everything you do or **say,** then, should be done in the
1 Thes 1. 8 There is nothing, then, that we need to **say.**
2 Thes 2.17 you and strengthen you to always do and **say** what is good.
Jas 4.15 What you should **say** is this:
1 Pet 3. 1 be necessary for you to **say** a word, [2]because they will see
3.16 as followers of Christ will be ashamed of what they **say.**
3 Jn 9 be their leader, will not pay any attention to what I **say.**
12 add our testimony, and you know that what we **say** is true.

SAYING

1 Sam 10.12 the **saying** originated, "Has even Saul become a prophet?"
19.24 the **saying** originated, "Has even Saul become a prophet?")
24.13 You know the old **saying,** 'Evil is done only by evil men.'
1 Kgs 10. 8 your presence and are privileged to hear your wise **sayings!**
2 Chr 9. 7 your presence and are privileged to hear your wise **sayings!**
Ps 78. 2 to use wise **sayings** and explain mysteries from the past,
Prov 1. 2 and good advice, and understand **sayings** with deep meaning.
22.20 I have written down thirty **sayings** for you.
24. 7 Wise **sayings** are too deep for a stupid person to understand.
26. 9 A fool quoting a wise **saying** reminds you of a drunk man
Ecc 12.11 The **sayings** of wise men are like the sharp sticks that
Is 29.17 the **saying** goes, before long the dense forest will become farmland,
Mt 15.15 Peter spoke up, "Explain this **saying** to us."
Mk 7.17 the house, his disciples asked him to explain this **saying.**
Jn 4.35 You have a **saying,** 'Four more months and then the harvest.'
4.37 The **saying** is true, 'One man sows, another man reaps.'
5.18 This **saying** made the Jewish authorities all the more
1 Cor 4. 6 learn what the **saying** means, "Observe the proper rules."
5. 6 You know the **saying,** "A little bit of yeast makes the whole
15.32 to life, then, as the **saying** goes, "Let us eat and drink,
1 Tim 1.15 This is a true **saying,** to be completely accepted and believed:
3. 1 This is a true **saying:**
4. 9 This is a true **saying,** to be completely accepted and believed.
2 Tim 2.11 This is a true **saying:**
Tit 3. 8 This is a true **saying.**

SCAB

Lev 22.22 or that has a running sore or a skin eruption or **scabs.**
Deut 28.27 You will be covered with **scabs,** and you will itch, but there
Job 7. 5 it is covered with **scabs;**

SCABBARD

Jer 47. 6 Go back to your **scabbard,** stay there and rest!'

SCALE (1)
[FISH SCALES]

Lev 11. 9 fish that has fins and **scales,** [10]but anything living in
11.10 water that does not have fins and **scales** must not be eaten.
11.12 that lives in the water and does not have fins and **scales.**
Deut 14. 9 fish that has fins and **scales,** [10]but anything living in
14.10 water that does not have fins and **scales** may not be eaten;
Job 41.30 The **scales** on his belly are like jagged pieces of pottery;
Acts 9.18 At once something like **fish scales** fell from Saul's eyes,

SCALE (2)

Lev 19.36 Use honest **scales,** honest weights, and honest measures.
Job 6. 1 and griefs were weighed on **scales,** [3]they would weigh more
31. 6 God weigh me on honest **scales,** and he will see how innocent
Ps 62. 9 Put them on the **scales,** and they weigh nothing;
Prov 11. 1 The Lord hates people who use dishonest **scales.**
20.23 The Lord hates people who use dishonest **scales** and weights.
Is 40.12 earth in a cup or weigh the mountains and hills on **scales?**
46. 6 they weigh out silver on the **scales.**
Jer 32.10 deed, had it witnessed, and weighed out the money on **scales.**
Ezek 5. 1 Then weigh the hair on **scales** and divide it into three parts.
Dan 5.27 have been weighed on the **scales** and found to be too light;
Hos 12. 7 they love to cheat their customers with false **scales.**
Amos 8. 5 measures, and tamper with the **scales** to cheat our customers.
Mic 6.11 How can I forgive men who use false **scales** and weights?
Rev 6. 5 Its rider held a pair of **scales** in his hand.

SCALP

Deut 33.20 waits like a lion To tear off an arm or a **scalp.**

SCAR

Lev 13.23 spread, it is only the **scar** left from the boil, and the
13.28 ritually clean, because it is only a **scar** from the burn.
Jn 20.25 "Unless I see the **scars** of the nails in his hands
20.25 put my finger on those **scars** and my hand in his side,
Gal 6.17 any more trouble, because the **scars** I have on my body show

SCARCE

Is 13.12 Those who survive will be **scarcer** than gold.
24. 7 The grapevines wither, and wine is becoming **scarce.**

SCARE

Deut 28.26 your bodies, and there will be no one to **scare** them off.
Is 10.14 Not a wing fluttered to **scare** me off;
31. 4 yell and shout, they can't **scare** away a lion from an animal
Jer 7.33 wild animals, and there will be no one to **scare** them off.

SCARECROW

Jer 10. 5 Such idols are like **scarecrows** in a field of melons;

SCARF

Gen 24.65 So she took her **scarf** and covered her face.
Is 3.23 their linen handkerchiefs, and the **scarves** and long veils
Ezek 13.18 for everyone and make magic **scarves** for everyone to wear on
13.21 I will rip off your **scarves** and let my people escape

SCARLET

2 Sam 1.24 He clothed you in rich **scarlet** dresses and adorned you
Song 4. 3 Your lips are like a **scarlet** ribbon;
Jer 4.30 Why do you dress in **scarlet?**
Mt 27.28 They stripped off his clothes and put a **scarlet** robe on him.
Rev 17. 4 was dressed in purple and **scarlet,** and covered with gold ornaments,
18.12 their goods of linen, purple cloth, silk, and **scarlet** cloth;
18.16 purple, and **scarlet,** and cover herself with gold ornaments,

SCATTER

Gen 11. 4 for ourselves and not be **scattered** all over the earth."
11. 8 So the Lord **scattered** them all over the earth, and they
11. 9 and from there he **scattered** them all over the earth.
49. 7 I will **scatter** them throughout the land of Israel.
Lev 26.33 I will bring war on you and **scatter** you in foreign lands.
Num 10.35 **scatter** your enemies and put to flight those who hate you!"
14.29 You will die and your corpses will be **scattered**
16.37 who have been burnt, and **scatter** the coals from the firepans
Deut 4.27 The Lord will **scatter** you among other nations, where
28.37 to which the Lord will **scatter** you, the people will be
28.64 "The Lord will **scatter** you among all the nations, from
30. 1 the Lord your God has **scattered** you, you will remember the
30. 3 the nations where he has **scattered** you, and he will make you
30. 4 Even if you are **scattered** to the farthest corners of the earth,
1 Sam 11.11 The survivors **scattered,** each man running off by himself.
30.16 The raiders were **scattered** all over the place, eating,
2 Sam 17.19 opening of the well and **scattered** grain over it, so that no
22.15 He shot his arrows and **scattered** his enemies;
1 Kgs 13. 3 will fall apart, and the ashes on it will be **scattered.**
14.15 and he will **scatter** them beyond the River Euphrates,
22.17 see the army of Israel **scattered** over the hills like sheep
2 Kgs 8.21 out and escape, and his soldiers **scattered** to their homes.
9.37 Her remains will be **scattered** there like dung, so that
23. 6 to dust, and **scattered** it over the public burial-ground.
1 Chr 12.15 banks, they crossed the river, **scattering** the people who
2 Chr 18.16 see the army of Israel **scattered** over the hills like sheep
34. 4 the other idols and then **scattered** the dust on the graves of
Neh 1. 8 to me, I will **scatter** you among the other nations.
1. 9 even though you are **scattered** to the ends of the earth.'

Esth	3. 8	a certain race of people **scattered** all over your empire and
Job	4.11	and eat, they die, and all their children are **scattered.**
Ps	18.14	He shot his arrows and **scattered** his enemies;
	44.11	you **scattered** us in foreign countries.
	53. 5	been before, for God will **scatter** the bones of the enemies
	59.11	**Scatter** them by your strength and defeat them, O Lord, our protector.
	68. 1	God rises up and **scatters** his enemies.
	68.14	When Almighty God **scattered** the kings on Mount Zalmon,
	68.30	**Scatter** those people who love to make war!
	83.13	**Scatter** them like dust, O God, like straw blown away by
	106.27	desert [27] and **scatter** their descendants among the heathen,
	141. 7	so their bones are **scattered** at the edge of the grave.
	144. 6	Send flashes of lightning and **scatter** your enemies;
	147.16	He spreads snow like a blanket and **scatters** frost like dust.
Is	11.12	is gathering together again the **scattered** people of Israel
	13.14	own countries, **scattering** like deer escaping from hunters,
	24. 1	He will twist the earth's surface and **scatter** its people.
	41. 2	His arrows **scatter** them like straw before the wind.
	41.16	carry them off, and they will be **scattered** by the storm.
	49. 5	his people, to bring back the **scattered** people of Israel.
Jer	8. 3	the places where I have **scattered** them, will prefer to die
	9.16	I will **scatter** them among nations that neither they nor
	9.22	Dead bodies are **scattered** everywhere,
	10.21	This is why they have failed, and our people have been **scattered.**
	13.24	The Lord will **scatter** you like straw that is blown away
	16.15	out of all the other countries where I had **scattered** them.
	18.17	I will **scatter** my people before their enemies, like dust
	23. 1	judgement on those rulers who destroy and **scatter** his people!
	23. 2	you have **scattered** them and driven them away.
	23. 3	the countries where I have **scattered** them, and I will bring
	23. 8	out of all the other countries where I had **scattered** them.
	24. 9	and use their name as a curse everywhere I **scatter** them.
	25.33	Lord has killed will lie **scattered** from one end of the earth
	29.14	place to which I have **scattered** you, and I will bring you
	29.18	Everywhere I **scatter** them, people will be shocked and
	30.11	the nations where I have **scattered** you, but I will not
	31.10	I **scattered** my people, but I will gather them and guard them
	32.37	countries where I have **scattered** them in my anger and fury,
	40.12	places where they had been **scattered,** and returned to Judah.
	40.15	gathered round you to be **scattered,** and it would bring
	43. 5	had returned from the nations where they had been **scattered:**
	46.28	the nations where I have **scattered** you, but I will not
	49.32	I will **scatter** in every direction those people who cut their
	49.36	all directions, and I will **scatter** her people everywhere,
	50.17	"The people of Israel are like sheep, chased and **scattered** by lions.
Lam	4. 1	the stones of the Temple lie **scattered** in the streets.
	4.16	he **scattered** them himself.
Ezek	4.13	Law forbids, when I **scatter** them to foreign countries."
	5. 2	**Scatter** the remaining third to the winds, and I will pursue
	5.10	I will punish you and **scatter** in every direction any who are
	5.12	and I will **scatter** the last third to the winds and pursue
	6. 5	I will **scatter** the corpses of the people of Israel;
	6. 5	I will **scatter** their bones all round the altars.
	6. 8	escape the slaughter and be **scattered** among the nations,
	6.13	Corpses will be **scattered** among the idols and round the altars,
	6.13	**scattered** on every high hill,
	10. 2	Then **scatter** the coals over the city."
	11.16	in far-off nations and **scattered** them in other countries.
	11.17	of the countries where I **scattered** them, and will give the
	12.14	I will **scatter** in every direction all the members of his
	12.15	"When I **scatter** them among the other nations
	17.21	and the survivors will be **scattered** in every direction.
	20.23	I vowed that I would **scatter** them all over the world.
	20.34	back from all the countries where you have been **scattered.**
	20.41	where you have been **scattered** and gather you together,
	22.15	I will **scatter** your people to every country and nation
	28.25	from the nations where I **scattered** them, and all the nations
	29.13	the nations where I have **scattered** them, [14] and I will let
	30.23	I am going to **scatter** the Egyptians throughout the world.
	30.26	I will **scatter** the Egyptians throughout the world.
	31.17	live under its shadow will be **scattered** among the nations.
	34. 5	had no shepherd, they were **scattered,** and wild animals
	34. 6	They were **scattered** over the face of the earth, and no one
	34.12	sheep that were **scattered** and are brought together again.
	34.12	where they were **scattered** on that dark, disastrous day.
	36.19	and acted, and I **scattered** them through foreign countries.
Dan	4.14	strip off its leaves and **scatter** its fruit.
	9. 7	all the Israelites whom you **scattered** in countries near and
Hos	9. 6	comes and the people are **scattered,** the Egyptians will
Joel	3. 2	They have **scattered** the Israelites in foreign countries
Nah	3.18	Your people are **scattered** on the mountains, and there is no
Hab	3.14	came like a storm to **scatter** us, gloating like those who
Zeph	3.10	from distant Sudan my **scattered** people will bring offerings
	3.20	I will bring your **scattered** people home;
Zech	1.19	the world powers that have **scattered** the people of Judah,
	1.21	crushed the land of Judah and **scattered** its people."
	2. 6	The Lord said to his people, "I **scattered** you in all directions.
	10. 9	Though I have **scattered** them among the nations, yet in
	13. 7	Kill him, and the sheep will be **scattered.**
Mt	12.30	anyone who does not help me gather is really **scattering.**
	13. 4	As he **scattered** the seed in the field,
	25.24	and you gather crops where you did not **scatter** seed.
	25.26	and gather crops where I did not **scatter** seed?
	26.31	the shepherd, and the sheep of the flock will be **scattered.'**
Mk	4. 4	As he **scattered** the seed in the field,
	4.26	A man **scatters** seed in his field.
	14.27	'God will kill the shepherd, and the sheep will all be **scattered.'**
Lk	1.51	mighty arm and **scattered** the proud with all their plans.
	8. 5	As he **scattered** the seed in the field,
Lk	11.23	anyone who does not help me gather is really **scattering.**
Jn	2.15	the tables of the money-changers and **scattered** their coins;
	10.12	so the wolf snatches the sheep and **scatters** them.
	11.52	together into one body all the **scattered** people of God.
	16.32	all of you will be **scattered,** each one to his own home,
Acts	5.36	all his followers were **scattered,** and his movement died out.
	5.37	but he also was killed, and all his followers were **scattered.**
	8. 1	believers, except the apostles, were **scattered** throughout the provinces
	8. 4	The believers who were **scattered** went everywhere, preaching the message.
	11.19	of the believers who were **scattered** by the persecution which
1 Cor	10. 5	and so their dead bodies were **scattered** over the desert.
Jas	1. 1	Greetings to all God's people **scattered** over the whole world.
1 Pet	1. 1	people who live as refugees **scattered** throughout the provinces
Rev	20. 8	out to deceive the nations **scattered** over the whole world,

SCENT

Song	1.13	My lover has the **scent** of myrrh as he lies upon my
	7.13	You can smell the **scent** of mandrakes, and all the

SCEPTRE

Gen	49.10	Judah will hold the royal **sceptre,** And his descendants will always rule.
Num	21.18	people, Dug with a royal **sceptre** And with their sticks."
Esth	4.11	king holds out his gold **sceptre** to someone, then that
	5. 2	won his favour, and he held out to her the gold **sceptre.**
	8. 4	king held out the gold **sceptre** to her, so she stood up
Ps	60. 7	Ephraim is my helmet and Judah my royal **sceptre.**
	89.44	have taken away his royal **sceptre** and hurled his throne to
	108. 8	Ephraim is my helmet and Judah my royal **sceptre.**
Ezek	19.11	Its branches were strong, and grew to be royal **sceptres.**
	19.14	The branches will never again be strong, will never be royal **sceptres.**

SCHEME

Job	5.12	men in their own **schemes,** so that nothing they do succeeds;
	10. 3	And then to smile on the **schemes** of wicked men?
Ps	73. 7	out evil, and their minds are busy with wicked **schemes.**
	119.118	their deceitful **schemes** are useless.
Prov	24. 9	Any **scheme** a fool thinks up is sinful.
	24.15	be like the wicked who **scheme** to rob an honest man or
Is	8.12	"Do not join in the **schemes** of the people and do not
	29.15	They carry out their **schemes** in secret and think no one will
Jer	6.19	As punishment for all their **schemes** I am bringing ruin on
Mic	7. 3	man tells them what he wants, and so they **scheme** together.
Nah	1.11	a man full of wicked **schemes,** who plotted against the Lord.
Hab	2.10	But your **schemes** have brought shame on your family;

SCHOLAR

1 Chr	27.32	Jonathan, King David's uncle, was a skilful adviser and a **scholar.**
Ezra	7. 6	Ezra was a **scholar** with a thorough knowledge of the
	7.11	to Ezra, the priest and **scholar,** who had a thorough
	7.12	emperor to Ezra the priest, **scholar** in the Law of the God
	7.21	for Ezra, the priest and **scholar** in the Law of the God
Neh	8. 1	asked Ezra, the priest and **scholar** of the Law which the Lord
	8. 9	governor, Ezra, the priest and **scholar** of the Law, and the
	12.26	time of Ezra, the priest who was a **scholar** of the Law.
	12.36	Ezra the **scholar** led this group in the procession.
	13.13	Zadok, a **scholar** of the Law;
Is	19.11	that they are successors to the ancient **scholars** and kings?
1 Cor	1.19	the wise and set aside the understanding of the **scholars."**
	1.20	or the **scholars?**

SCOFF

Acts	13.41	'Look, you **scoffers!**

SCOLD

Gen	37.10	told the dream to his father, and his father **scolded** him:
Ps	94.10	He **scolds** the nations—won't he punish them?
Mt	19.13	to pray for them, but the disciples **scolded** the people.
	20.31	The crowd **scolded** them and told them to be quiet.
Mk	10.13	his hands on them, but the disciples **scolded** the people.
	10.48	Many of the people **scolded** him and told him to be quiet.
	16.14	He **scolded** them, because they did not have faith
Lk	18.15	The disciples saw them and **scolded** them for doing so,
	18.39	The people in front **scolded** him and told him to be quiet.

SCOOP

Judg	7. 6	were three hundred men who **scooped** up water in their hands
Is	30.14	pick up hot coals with, or to **scoop** water from a cistern."

SCORCH

Gen	41. 6	of corn sprouted, thin and **scorched** by the desert wind,
	41.23	of corn sprouted, thin and **scorched** by the desert wind,
	41.27	seven thin ears of corn **scorched** by the desert wind are
Deut	28.22	will send drought and **scorching** winds to destroy your crops.
1 Kgs	8.37	crops are destroyed by **scorching** winds or swarms of locusts,
	18.38	the wood, and the stones, **scorched** the earth and dried up
2 Chr	6.28	crops are destroyed by **scorching** winds or swarms of locusts,
Ps	11. 6	he punishes them with **scorching** winds.
Jer	4.11	will be told that a **scorching** wind is blowing in from the
Amos	4. 9	"I sent a **scorching** wind to dry up your crops.

Hag 2.17 I sent **scorching** winds and hail to ruin everything you
Rev 7.16 nor any **scorching** heat will burn them, [17]because the Lamb,

SCORN

Judg 9.27 where they ate and drank and spoke **scornfully** of Abimelech.
9.38 These are the men you were treating so **scornfully.**
1 Sam 17.42 David, he was filled with **scorn** for him because he was just
Job 16.20 My friends **scorn** me;
31.34 kept quiet or stayed indoors because I feared their **scorn.**
Ps 22. 6 I am a worm, despised and **scorned** by everyone!
44.14 they shake their heads at us in **scorn.**
68.16 peaks do you look with **scorn** on the mountain on which God
109.25 they shake their heads in **scorn.**
119.22 their insults and **scorn,** because I have kept your laws.
119.51 The proud are always **scornful** of me, but I have not
123. 4 too long by the rich and **scorned** by proud oppressors.
Prov 1.22 How long will you enjoy pouring **scorn** on knowledge?
11.12 It is foolish to speak **scornfully** of others.
18. 3 Lose your honour, and you will get **scorn** in its place.
24. 9 People hate a person who has nothing but **scorn** for others.
Jer 20. 8 Lord, I am ridiculed and **scorned** all the time because I
42.18 people will treat you with **scorn** and use your name as a
44. 8 earth will treat you with **scorn** and use your name as a
44.12 people will treat them with **scorn** and use their name as a
Lam 2.15 People passing by the city look at you in **scorn.**
Ezek 23.32 Everyone will **scorn** and mock you;
28.24 nations that treated Israel with **scorn** will ever again be
28.26 who treated them with **scorn,** and Israel will be secure.
Hab 2. 6 will taunt their conquerors and show their **scorn** for them.
Heb 11.26 He reckoned that to suffer **scorn** for the Messiah was

SCORPION

Deut 8.15 desert where there were poisonous snakes and **scorpions.**
Ezek 2. 6 it will be like living among **scorpions.**
Lk 10.19 can walk on snakes and **scorpions** and overcome all the power
11.12 would you give him a **scorpion** when he asks for an egg?
Rev 9. 3 they were given the same kind of power that **scorpions** have.
9. 5 is like the pain caused by a **scorpion's** sting.
9.10 stings like those of a **scorpion,**

SCOUNDREL

Judg 9. 4 money he hired a bunch of worthless **scoundrels** to join him.
1 Sam 2.12 The sons of Eli were **scoundrels.**
1 Kgs 21.10 Get a couple of **scoundrels** to accuse him to his face of
21.13 two **scoundrels** publicly accused him of cursing God and the king,
2 Chr 13. 7 together a group of worthless **scoundrels,** and they forced
Is 32. 5 that a fool is honourable or say that a **scoundrel** is honest.

SCOUT

1 Kgs 20.17 **Scouts** sent out by Benhadad reported to him that a group of

SCOWL

Gen 4. 5 Cain became furious, and he **scowled** in anger.
4. 6 Why that **scowl** on your face?

SCRAPE

Lev 14.41 have all the interior walls **scraped** and the plaster dumped
14.43 and the house has been **scraped** and plastered, [44]the priest
Judg 14. 9 He **scraped** the honey out into his hands and ate it as
Job 2. 8 heap and took a piece of broken pottery to **scrape** his sores.

SCRAPS

Judg 1. 7 and big toes cut off have picked up **scraps** under my table.

SCRATCH

Jer 6.14 They act as if my people's wounds were only **scratches.**
8.11 They act as if my people's wounds were only **scratches.**
Ezek 4. 1 in front of you, and **scratch** lines on it to represent the

SCREAM

Gen 39.14 tried to rape me, but I **screamed** as loud as I could.
39.15 When he heard me **scream,** he ran outside, leaving his
39.18 But when I **screamed,** he ran outside, leaving his robe beside me."
1 Sam 28.12 the woman saw Samuel, she **screamed** and said to Saul, "Why
Job 15.21 Voices of terror will **scream** in his ears, and robbers
Is 10.14 no beak opened to **scream** at me!"
Jer 4.31 a woman in labour, a **scream** like a woman bearing her first
Ezek 26.15 be terrified at the **screams** of those who are slaughtered.
Mt 8.29 At once they **screamed,** "What do you want with us, you
14.26 they said, and **screamed** with fear.
Mk 1.23 the synagogue and **screamed,** [24]"What do you want with us,
1.26 gave a loud **scream,** and came out of him.
3.11 fall down before him and **scream,** "You are the Son of God!"
5. 5 the hills, **screaming** and cutting himself with stones.
5. 7 and **screamed** in a loud voice, "Jesus,
6.49 they thought, and **screamed.**
9.26 The spirit **screamed,** threw the boy into a bad fit,
Lk 4.33 he **screamed** out in a loud voice, [34]"Ah!
4.41 out from many people, **screaming,** "You are the Son of God!"
Acts 21.36 They were all coming after him and **screaming,** "Kill
22.23 They were **screaming,** waving their clothes, and throwing dust
Acts 22.24 find out why the Jews were **screaming** like this against him.
25.24 They **scream** that he should not live any longer.

SCREEN

Ex 35.12 Box, its poles, its lid, and the curtain to **screen** it off;
40.21 In this way he **screened** off the Covenant Box, just as the

SCRIBBLE

1 Sam 21.13 would **scribble** on the city gates and dribble down his beard.

SCRIBES

Jer 8. 8 Look, the laws have been changed by dishonest **scribes.**

AV **SCRIBES** see **TEACHER(S) OF THE LAW**

SCRIPTURE

In the New Testament the word refers to the Hebrew sacred writings, known to Christians as the Old Testament. The singular "scripture" refers to a single passage of the Old Testament.

Mt 4. 4 But Jesus answered, "The **scripture** says, 'Man cannot live on bread alone,
4. 6 throw yourself down, for the **scripture** says, 'God will give orders
4. 7 Jesus answered, "But the **scripture** also says, 'Do not put
4.10 The **scripture** says, 'Worship the Lord your God and serve only him!' "
9.13 Go and find out what is meant by the **scripture** that says:
11.10 For John is the one of whom the **scripture** says:
12. 7 The **scripture** says, 'It is kindness that I want, not animal sacrifices.'
18.16 testimony of two or more witnesses,' as the **scripture** says.
19. 4 answered, "Haven't you read the **scripture** that says that in
21.13 "It is written in the **Scriptures** that God said, 'My Temple
21.16 "Haven't you ever read this **scripture?**
21.42 Jesus said to them, "Haven't you ever read what the **Scriptures** say?
22.29 It is because you don't know the **Scriptures** or God's power.
23. 5 Look at the straps with **scripture** verses on them which they
26.24 Man will die as the **Scriptures** say he will, but how terrible
26.31 me, for the **scripture** says, 'God will kill the shepherd,
26.54 that case, how could the **Scriptures** come true which say that
26.56 make what the prophets wrote in the **Scriptures** come true."
Mk 9.12 Yet why do the **Scriptures** say that the Son of Man will
9.13 him just as they pleased, as the **Scriptures** say about him."
10. 6 'God made them male and female,' as the **scripture** says.
11.17 "It is written in the **Scriptures** that God said, 'My Temple
12.10 Surely you have read this **scripture?**
12.24 It is because you don't know the **Scriptures** or God's power.
14.21 The Son of Man will die as the **Scriptures** say he will;
14.27 me, for the **scripture** says, 'God will kill the shepherd,
14.49 But the **Scriptures** must come true."
Lk 4. 4 But Jesus answered, "The **scripture** says, 'Man cannot live on bread alone.' "
4. 8 Jesus answered, "The **scripture** says, 'Worship the Lord
4.10 For the **scripture** says, 'God will order his angels to
4.12 But Jesus answered, "The **scripture** says, 'Do not put
4.16 stood up to read the **Scriptures** [17]and was handed the book
4.21 "This passage of **scripture** has come true today,
7.27 For John is the one of whom the **scripture** says:
10.26 Jesus answered him, "What do the **Scriptures** say?
19.46 "It is written in the **Scriptures** that God said, 'My Temple
20.17 Jesus looked at them and asked, "What, then, does this **scripture** mean?
21.22 Days of Punishment,' to make all that the **Scriptures** say come true.
22.37 I tell you that the **scripture** which says, 'He shared the
24.27 about himself in all the **Scriptures,** beginning with the
24.32 to us on the road and explained the **Scriptures** to us?"
24.45 minds to understand the **Scriptures,** [46]and said to them,
Jn 2.17 His disciples remembered that the **scripture** says, "My devotion to your house,
2.22 and they believed the **scripture** and what Jesus had said.
5.39 You study the **Scriptures,** because you think that in them
5.39 And these very **Scriptures** speak about me!
6.31 just as the **scripture** says, 'He gave them bread from
7.38 As the **scripture** says, 'Whoever believes in me, streams
7.42 The **scripture** says that the Messiah will be a descendant
7.52 Study the **Scriptures** and you will learn that no prophet ever
10.35 We know that what the **scripture** says is true for ever;
12.14 just as the **scripture** says, [15]"Do not be afraid, city
12.16 they remembered that the **scripture** said this about him
13.18 But the **scripture** must come true that says, 'The man who
17.12 was bound to be lost—so that the **scripture** might come true.
19.24 This happened in order to make the **scripture** come true:
19.28 in order to make the **scripture** come true, he said,
19.36 This was done to make the **scripture** come true:
19.37 And there is another **scripture** that says, "People will
20. 9 still did not understand the **scripture** which said that he
Acts 1.16 "My brothers," he said, "the **scripture** had to come
4.11 the one of whom the **scripture** says, 'The stone that you
8.32 The passage of **scripture** which he was reading was this:
8.35 starting from this passage of **scripture,** he told him the
13.29 had done everything that the **Scriptures** say about him, they
15.15 As the **scripture** says, [16]'After this I will return, says
17. 3 quoting [3]and explaining the **Scriptures** and proving from them
17.11 every day they studied the **Scriptures** to see if what Paul
18.24 speaker and had a thorough knowledge of the **Scriptures.**

Acts	18.28	by proving from the **Scriptures** that Jesus is the Messiah.
	23. 5	The **scripture** says, 'You must not speak evil of the ruler
Rom	1. 2	God through his prophets, as written in the Holy **Scriptures.**
	1.17	As the **scripture** says, "The person who is put right with
	2.24	The **scripture** says, "Because of you Jews, the Gentiles
	3. 4	As the **scripture** says, "You must be shown to be right when
	3.10	As the **Scriptures** say:
	4. 3	The **scripture** says, "Abraham believed God, and because of
	4. 9	For we have quoted the **scripture,** "Abraham believed God,
	4.17	as the **scripture** says, "I have made you father of many nations."
	4.18	Just as the **scripture** says, "Your descendants will be as
	8.36	As the **scripture** says, "For your sake we are in danger
	9.13	As the **scripture** says, "I loved Jacob, but I hated Esau."
	9.17	For the **scripture** says to the king of Egypt, "I made
	9.33	the "stumbling stone" [33] that the **scripture** speaks of:
	10. 6	But what the **scripture** says about being put right with God
	10.11	The **scripture** says, "Whoever believes in him will not be disappointed."
	10.13	As the **scripture** says, "Everyone who calls out to the Lord
	10.15	As the **scripture** says, "How wonderful is the coming of
	10.18	Of course they did—for as the **scripture** says:
	11. 2	You know what the **scripture** says in the passage where Elijah
	11. 8	As the **scripture** says, "God made their minds and hearts dull;
	11.26	As the **scripture** says, "The Saviour will come from Zion and
	11.34	As the **scripture** says, "Who knows the mind of the Lord?
	12.19	For the **scripture** says, "I will take revenge, I will pay back,
	12.20	Instead, as the **scripture** says:
	14.11	For the **scripture** says, "As surely as I am the living God,
	15. 3	Instead, as the **scripture** says, "The insults which are
	15. 4	Everything written in the **Scriptures** was written to teach us,
	15. 4	the patience and encouragement which the **Scriptures** give us.
	15. 9	As the **scripture** says, "And so I will praise you among the
	15.21	As the **scripture** says, "Those who were not told about
1 Cor	1.19	The **scripture** says, "I will destroy the wisdom of the wise
	1.31	So then, as the **scripture** says, "Whoever wants to boast
	2. 9	However, as the **scripture** says, "What no one ever saw or heard,
	2.16	As the **scripture** says, "Who knows the mind of the Lord?
	3.19	As the **scripture** says, "God traps the wise in their cleverness";
	3.20	and another **scripture** says, "The Lord knows that the
	5.12	As the **scripture** says, "Remove the evil man from your group."
	6.16	The **scripture** says quite plainly, "The two will become one body."
	10. 7	As the **scripture** says, "The people sat down to a feast
	10.26	For, as the **scripture** says, "The earth and everything
	14.21	In the **Scriptures** it is written, "By means of men
	15. 3	Christ died for our sins, as written in the **Scriptures;**
	15. 4	to life three days later, as written in the **Scriptures;**
	15.27	For the **scripture** says, "God put all things under his feet."
	15.45	For the **scripture** says, "The first man, Adam, was
	15.54	into the immortal, then the **scripture** will come true:
2 Cor	3.16	But it can be removed, as the **scripture** says about Moses:
	4.13	The **scripture** says, "I spoke because I believed."
	8.15	As the **scripture** says, "The one who gathered much did
	9. 9	As the **scripture** says, "He gives generously to the needy;
	10.17	But as the **scripture** says, "Whoever wants to boast must
	13. 1	evidence of two or more witnesses"—as the **scripture** says.
Gal	3. 6	as the **scripture** says, "He believed God, and because of his
	3. 8	The **scripture** predicted that God would put the Gentiles
	3. 8	And so the **scripture** announced the Good News to Abraham:
	3.10	For the **scripture** says, "Whoever does not always obey
	3.11	of the Law, because the **scripture** says, "Only the person
	3.12	Instead, as the **scripture** says, "Whoever does everything
	3.13	for the **scripture** says, "Anyone who is hanged on a tree is
	3.16	The **scripture** does not use the plural "descendants," meaning many people,
	3.22	But the **scripture** says that the whole world is under the
	4.27	For the **scripture** says, "Be happy, you childless woman!
	4.30	But what does the **scripture** say?
Eph	4. 8	As the **scripture** says, "When he went up to the very heights,
	5.31	As the **scripture** says, "For this reason a man will
	5.32	secret truth revealed in this **scripture,** which I understand
1 Tim	4.13	reading of the **Scriptures** and to preaching and teaching.
	5.18	For the **scripture** says, "Do not muzzle an ox when you
2 Tim	3.15	you have known the Holy **Scriptures,** which are able to give
	3.16	All **Scripture** is inspired by God and is useful for teaching
Heb	2. 6	Instead, as it is said somewhere in the **Scriptures:**
	2.16	Instead, as the **scripture** says, "He helps the descendants of Abraham."
	3.13	long as the word "Today" in the **scripture** applies to us.
	3.15	This is what the **scripture** says:
	4. 4	For somewhere in the **Scriptures** this is said about the seventh day:
	4. 7	spoke of it through David in the **scripture** already quoted:
	7. 8	tenth was collected by one who lives, as the **scripture** says.
	7.17	For the **scripture** says, "You will be a priest for ever,
	10.37	For, as the **scripture** says, "Just a little while longer,
	11. 5	The **scripture** says that before Enoch was taken up, he had
Jas	2. 8	which is found in the **scripture,** "Love your neighbour as
	2.23	And the **scripture** came true that said, "Abraham believed God,
	4. 5	is no truth in the **scripture** that says, "The spirit that
	4. 6	As the **scripture** says, "God resists the proud, but gives
1 Pet	1.16	The **scripture** says, "Be holy because I am holy."
	1.24	As the **scripture** says, "All mankind are like grass,
	2. 3	As the **scripture** says, "You have found out for yourselves
	2. 6	For the **scripture** says, "I chose a valuable stone,
	2. 8	And another **scripture** says, "This is the stone that will
	3.10	As the **scripture** says, "Whoever wants to enjoy life
	4.18	As the **scripture** says, "It is difficult for good people
	5. 5	for the **scripture** says, "God resists the proud, but shows
2 Pet	1.20	no one can explain by himself a prophecy in the **Scriptures.**
	3.16	falsely, as they do with other passages of the **Scriptures.**
Jude	4	Long ago the **Scriptures** predicted the condemnation they have received.

SCROLL

Ezra	6. 2	Media that a **scroll** was found, containing the following record:
Esth	9.32	the rules for Purim, was written down on a **scroll.**
Is	29.11	it will be like a sealed **scroll.**
	34. 4	sky will disappear like a **scroll** being rolled up, and the
Jer	36. 2	said to me, [2] "Get a **scroll** and write on it everything that
	36. 4	And Baruch wrote it all down on a **scroll.**
	36. 6	You are to read the **scroll** aloud, so that they will hear
	36.10	Baruch read from the **scroll** everything that I had said.
	36.11	heard Baruch read from the **scroll** what the Lord had said.
	36.14	tell Baruch to bring the **scroll** that he had read to the
	36.14	Baruch brought them the **scroll.**
	36.15	"Sit down," they said, "and read the **scroll** to us."
	36.18	to me, and I wrote it down in ink on this **scroll."**
	36.20	The officials put the **scroll** in the room of Elishama,
	36.21	Then the king sent Jehudi to get the **scroll.**
	36.23	He kept doing this until the entire **scroll** was burnt up.
	36.25	king not to burn the **scroll,** he paid no attention to them.
	36.27	King Jehoiakim had burnt the **scroll** that I had dictated to Baruch,
	36.28	told me [28] to take another **scroll** and write on it
	36.29	king, "You have burnt the **scroll,** and you have asked
	36.32	Then I took another **scroll** and gave it to my secretary Baruch,
	36.32	had been on the first **scroll** and similar messages that I
Ezek	2. 9	hand stretched out towards me, and it was holding a **scroll.**
	2.10	The hand unrolled the **scroll,** and I saw that there was
	3. 1	God said, "Mortal man, eat this **scroll;**
	3. 2	I opened my mouth, and he gave me the **scroll** to eat.
	3. 3	He said, "Mortal man, eat this **scroll** that I give you;
Zech	5. 1	again, and this time I saw a **scroll** flying through the air.
	5. 2	I answered, "A **scroll** flying through the air;
	5. 3	On one side of the **scroll** it says that every thief will
Lk	4.17	He unrolled the **scroll** and found the place where it is written,
	4.20	Jesus rolled up the **scroll,** gave it back to the attendant,
Rev	5. 1	I saw a **scroll** in the right hand of the one
	5. 2	"Who is worthy to break the seals and open the **scroll?"**
	5. 3	who could open the **scroll** and look inside it.
	5. 4	found who was worthy to open the **scroll** or look inside it.
	5. 5	and he can break the seven seals and open the **scroll."**
	5. 7	Lamb went and took the **scroll** from the right hand
	5. 9	are worthy to take the **scroll** and to break open its seals.
	6.14	The sky disappeared like a **scroll** being rolled up,
	10. 2	He had a small **scroll** open in his hand.
	10. 8	"Go and take the open **scroll** which is in the hand of
	10. 9	to the angel and asked him to give me the little **scroll.**
	10.10	I took the little **scroll** from his hand and ate it,

SCRUB

Lev	6.28	pot is used, it must be **scrubbed** and rinsed with water.

SCUM

1 Cor	4.13	we are the **scum** of the earth to this very moment!

SEA

Gen	1.10	"Earth," and the water which had come together he named **"Sea."**
	1.21	So God created the great **sea-monsters,** all kinds of
	1.22	reproduce, and to fill the **sea,** and he told the birds to
	14. 3	forces in the Valley of Siddim, which is now the Dead **Sea.**
	22.17	are stars in the sky or grains of sand along the **seashore.**
	32.12	count, as many as the grains of sand along the **seashore."**
	41.49	Joseph stopped measuring it—it was like the sand of the **sea.**
	49.13	"Zebulun will live beside the **sea.**
Ex	13.18	in a roundabout way through the desert towards the Red **Sea.**
	14. 2	Pi Hahiroth, between Migdol and the Red **Sea,** near Baal Zephon.
	14. 9	camped by the Red **Sea** near Pi Hahiroth and Baal Zephon.
	14.16	Lift up your stick and hold it out over the **sea.**
	14.16	Israelites will be able to walk through the **sea** on dry ground.
	14.21	out his hand over the **sea,**
	14.21	and the Lord drove the **sea** back with a strong east wind.
	14.21	It blew all night and turned the **sea** into dry land.
	14.22	the Israelites went through the **sea** on dry ground, with
	14.23	went after them into the **sea** with all their horses,
	14.26	out your hand over the **sea,** and the water will come back
	14.27	out his hand over the **sea,** and at daybreak the water
	14.27	escape from the water, but the Lord threw them into the **sea.**
	14.28	Egyptian army that had followed the Israelites into the **sea;**
	14.29	the Israelites walked through the **sea** on dry ground, with
	14.30	and the Israelites saw them lying dead on the **seashore.**
	15. 1	he has thrown the horses and their riders into the **sea.**
	15. 4	"He threw Egypt's army and its chariots into the **sea;**
	15. 4	the best of its officers were drowned in the Red **Sea.**
	15. 5	The deep **sea** covered them;
	15. 8	You blew on the **sea** and the water piled up high;
	15. 8	the deepest part of the **sea** became solid.
	15.19	The Israelites walked through the **sea** on dry ground.
	15.19	drivers went into the **sea,** the Lord brought the water back,
	15.21	he has thrown the horses and their riders into the **sea."**
	15.22	of Israel away from the Red **Sea** into the desert of Shur.
	20.11	the earth, the sky, the **sea,** and everything in them, but on
	23.31	of Aqaba to the Mediterranean **Sea** and from the desert to the
Num	11.22	Are all the fish in the **sea** enough for them?"
	11.31	that brought quails from the **sea,** flying less than a metre
	13.29	live by the Mediterranean **Sea** and along the River Jordan."
	33. 8	Hahiroth and passed through the Red **Sea** into the desert of Shur;
	34. 3	begin on the east at the southern end of the Dead **Sea.**

Num 34. 6 “The western border will be the Mediterranean **Sea.**
34.12 then south along the River Jordan to the Dead **Sea.**
Deut 2. 8 Eziongeber to the Dead **Sea,** and we turned north-east towards Moab.
3.17 north down to the Dead **Sea** in the south and to the
4.49 far south as the Dead **Sea** and east to the foot of
11. 4 by drowning them in the Red **Sea** when they were pursuing you.
11.24 River Euphrates in the east to the Mediterranean **Sea** in the west.
33.18 in their trade on the **sea,** And may Issachar's wealth
33.19 get their wealth from the **sea** And from the sand along the
34. 2 the territory of Judah as far west as the Mediterranean **Sea;**
Josh 1. 4 the Hittite country, to the Mediterranean **Sea** in the west.
2.10 Lord dried up the Red **Sea** in front of you when you
3.16 flow downstream to the Dead **Sea** was completely cut off, and
4.23 had crossed, just as he dried up the Red **Sea** for us.
5. 1 Canaanite kings along the Mediterranean **Sea** heard that the
9. 1 plain of the Mediterranean **Sea** as far north as Lebanon;
11. 4 as many men as there are grains of sand on the **seashore.**
12. 3 Jeshimoth (east of the Dead **Sea)** and on towards the foot of
15. 2 south end of the Dead **Sea,** [3]went southwards from the
15. 4 of Egypt to the Mediterranean **Sea,** where the border ended.
15. 5 eastern border was the Dead **Sea,** all the way up to the
15.11 It ended at the Mediterranean **Sea,**
15.46 and towns near Ashdod, from Ekron to the Mediterranean **Sea.**
15.47 the border of Egypt and the coast of the Mediterranean **Sea.**
16. 3 on from there to Gezer and ended at the Mediterranean **Sea.**
16. 6 Upper Beth Horon, [6]and from there to the Mediterranean **Sea.**
16. 8 Tappuah to the stream of Kanah and ended at the Mediterranean **Sea.**
17. 9 north side of the stream and ended at the Mediterranean **Sea.**
17.10 north, with the Mediterranean **Sea** as their western border.
18.19 northern inlet on the Dead **Sea,** where the River Jordan
19.29 then it turned to Hosah and ended at the Mediterranean **Sea.**
23. 4 River Jordan in the east to the Mediterranean **Sea** in the west.
24. 6 ancestors got to the Red **Sea** [7]they cried out to me for
24. 7 I made the **sea** come rolling over the Egyptians and drown them.
Judg 5.17 The tribe of Asher stayed by the **sea-coast;**
7.12 many camels as there were grains of sand on the **seashore.**
1 Sam 13. 5 many soldiers as there are grains of sand on the **seashore.**
2 Sam 17.11 grains of sand on the **sea-shore,** and that you lead them
1 Kgs 4.20 Israel were as numerous as the grains of sand on the **seashore;**
5. 9 down from Lebanon to the **sea,** and will tie them together in
9.27 King Hiram sent some experienced **seamen** from his fleet
18.43 He said to his servant, “Go and look towards the **sea.**”
18.44 no bigger than a man's hand, coming up from the **sea.**”
2 Kgs 14.25 Hamath Pass in the north to the Dead **Sea** in the south.
1 Chr 16.32 Roar, **sea,** and every creature in you;
2 Chr 2.16 together in rafts, and float them by **sea** as far as Joppa.
20. 2 come from the other side of the Dead **Sea** to attack you.
Ezra 3. 7 from Lebanon, which were to be brought by **sea** to Joppa.
Neh 9. 6 You made land and **sea** and everything in them;
9. 9 you heard their call for help at the Red **Sea.**
9.11 Through the **sea** you made a path for your people and led
9.11 drowned in deep water, as a stone sinks in the raging **sea.**
Job 6. 3 than the sands of the **sea,** so my wild words should not
7.12 Do you think I am a **sea-monster?**
9. 8 God spread out the heavens or trample the **sea-monster's** back.
9.13 He crushed his enemies who helped Rahab, the **sea-monster,**
11. 9 God's greatness is broader than the earth, wider than the **sea.**
12. 8 ask the creatures of earth and **sea** for their wisdom.
26.10 from darkness by a circle drawn on the face of the **sea.**
26.12 It is his strength that conquered the **sea;**
28.14 depths of the oceans and **seas** Say that wisdom is not found
28.25 gave the wind its power And determined the size of the **sea;**
36.30 through all the sky, but the depths of the **sea** remain dark.
38. 8 gates to hold back the **sea** when it burst from the womb
38. 9 was I who covered the **sea** with clouds and wrapped it in
38.10 a boundary for the **sea** and kept it behind bolted gates.
38.16 Have you been to the springs in the depths of the **sea?**
38.30 turn the waters to stone and freeze the face of the **sea?**
41.31 He churns up the **sea** like boiling water and makes it
41.32 a shining path behind him and turns the **sea** to white foam.
Ps 8. 8 the birds and the fish and the creatures in the **seas.**
29. 3 The voice of the Lord is heard on the **seas;**
33. 7 He gathered all the **seas** into one place;
36. 6 your justice is like the depths of the **sea.**
46. 3 even if the **seas** roar and rage, and the hills are shaken
65. 5 over the world and across the distant **seas** trust in you.
65. 7 calm the roar of the **seas** and the noise of the waves;
66. 6 He changed the **sea** into dry land;
69.34 Praise God, O heaven and earth, **seas** and all creatures in them.
72. 8 His kingdom will reach from **sea** to sea, from the Euphrates
74.13 mighty strength you divided the **sea**
74.13 and smashed the heads of the **sea-monsters;**
77.16 O God, they were afraid, and the depths of the **sea** trembled.
77.19 you crossed the deep **sea,** but your footprints could not be seen.
78.13 He divided the **sea** and took them through it;
78.53 but the **sea** came rolling over their enemies.
80.11 its branches to the Mediterranean **Sea** and as far as the
89. 9 You rule over the powerful **sea;**
93. 4 roar of the ocean, more powerful than the waves of the **sea.**
95. 5 He rules over the **sea,** which he made;
96.11 Roar, **sea,** and every creature in you;
97. 1 Rejoice, you islands of the **seas!**
98. 7 Roar, **sea,** and every creature in you;
104.26 and in it plays Leviathan, that **sea-monster** which you made.
106. 7 and they rebelled against the Almighty at the Red **Sea.**
106. 9 He gave a command to the Red **Sea,** and it dried up;
106.22 What amazing things at the Red **Sea!**
107.23 over the ocean in ships, earning their living on the **seas.**
107.24 saw what the Lord can do, his wonderful acts on the **seas.**
Ps 114. 3 The Red **Sea** looked and ran away;
114. 5 What happened, **Sea,** to make you run away?
135. 6 heaven and on earth, in the **seas** and in the depths below.
136.13 He divided the Red **Sea;**
146. 6 Creator of heaven, earth, and **sea,** and all that is in them.
148. 7 Praise the Lord from the earth, **sea-monsters** and all ocean depths;
Prov 8.29 ordered the waters of the **sea** to rise no further than he
23.34 were out on the ocean, **sea-sick,** swinging high up in the
30.19 a ship finding its way over the **sea,**
Ecc 1. 7 Every river flows into the **sea,**
1. 7 but the **sea** is not yet full.
Is 5.30 day comes, they will roar over Israel as loudly as the **sea.**
10.22 grains of sand by the **sea,** only a few will come back.
11. 9 of knowledge of the Lord as the **seas** are full of water.
11.11 Hamath, and in the coastlands and on the islands of the **sea.**
16. 8 the desert, and westwards to the other side of the Dead **Sea.**
17.12 like the roar of the **sea,** like the crashing of huge waves.
23. 3 You sent men [3]across the **sea** to buy and sell the corn
23. 4 The **sea** and the great ocean depths disown you and say, “I
23. 7 that sent settlers across the **sea** to establish colonies?
23.11 Lord has stretched out his hand over the **sea**
24.15 people who live along the **sea** will praise the Lord, the God
27. 1 dragon, and to kill the monster that lives in the **sea.**
42.10 Praise him, you that sail the **sea;**
42.10 praise him, all creatures of the **sea!**
43.16 a road through the **sea,** a path through the swirling waters.
50. 2 I can dry up the **sea** with a command and turn rivers
51. 9 It was you that cut the **sea-monster** Rahab to pieces.
51.10 also who dried up the **sea** and made a path through the
51.15 I stir up the **sea** and make its waves roar.
57.20 like the restless **sea,** whose waves never stop rolling in,
60. 5 From across the **sea** their riches will come.
63.11 the Lord, who saved the leaders of his people from the **sea?**
63.12 dividing the waters of the **sea** and leading his people
Jer 5.22 as the boundary of the **sea,** a permanent boundary that it
5.22 The **sea** may toss, but it cannot go beyond it;
6.23 They sound like the roaring **sea,** as they ride their horses.
15. 8 more widows in your land than grains of sand by the **sea.**
31.35 He stirs up the **sea** and makes it roar;
33.22 stars in the sky or the grains of sand on the **sea-shore.**”
46.18 Carmel stands high above the **sea,** so will be the strength of
48.32 branches reach across the Dead **Sea** and go as far as Jazer.
49.23 Anxiety rolls over them like a **sea,** and they cannot rest.
50.42 They sound like the roaring **sea,** as they ride their horses.
51.42 The **sea** has rolled over Babylon and covered it
Ezek 1.24 like the roar of the **sea,** like the noise of a huge
26. 3 attack you, and they will come like the waves of the **sea.**
26. 5 dry their nets on it, there where it stands in the **sea.**
26.12 and wood and all the rubble, and dump them into the **sea.**
26.16 All the kings of the **seafaring** nations will come down
26.17 Her ships have been swept from the **seas.**
26.17 of this city ruled the **seas** And terrified all who lived on
27. 3 at the edge of the **sea** and does business
27. 3 with the people living on every **seacoast.**
27. 4 Your home is the **sea.**
27. 9 Sailors from every **sea-going** ship Did business in your shops.
27.25 You were like a ship at **sea** Loaded with heavy cargo.
27.26 oarsmen brought you out to **sea,** An east wind wrecked you far
27.27 All, all were lost at **sea** When your ship was wrecked.
27.32 can be compared to Tyre, To Tyre now silent in the **sea?**
27.34 Now you are wrecked in the **sea;**
27.34 all who worked for you Have vanished with you in the **sea.**’
28. 2 like a god you sit on a throne, surrounded by the **seas.**
39.11 in Israel, in Travellers' Valley, east of the Dead **Sea.**
43. 2 like the roar of the **sea,** and the earth shone with the
45. 7 the holy area it will extend west to the Mediterranean **Sea;**
47. 8 east and down into the Jordan Valley and to the Dead **Sea.**
47. 8 it flows into the Dead **Sea,**
47. 8 it replaces the salt water of that **sea** with fresh water.
47. 9 the water of the Dead **Sea** fresh, and wherever it flows, it
47.10 on the shore of the **sea,** and they will spread out their
47.10 kinds of fish there as there are in the Mediterranean **Sea.**
47.15 eastwards from the Mediterranean **Sea** to the city of Hethlon,
47.18 Gilead on the east, as far as Tamar on the Dead **Sea.**
47.19 along the Egyptian border to the Mediterranean **Sea.**
48. 1 eastwards from the Mediterranean **Sea** to the city of Hethlon,
48. 1 boundary westwards to the Mediterranean **Sea,** in the
48.21 and westwards to the Mediterranean **Sea,** and is bounded on
48.23 boundary westwards to the Mediterranean **Sea,** in the
48.28 along the Egyptian border to the Mediterranean **Sea.**
Dan 11.18 will attack the nations by the **sea** and conquer many of them.
11.45 huge royal tents between the **sea** and the mountain on which
Hos 1.10 like the sand of the **sea,** more than can be counted or
Joel 2.20 into the Dead **Sea,** their rear ranks into the Mediterranean.
Amos 5. 8 for the waters of the **sea** and pours them out on the
6.12 Do men plough the **sea** with oxen?
8.12 will wander from the Dead **Sea** to the Mediterranean and then
9. 3 at the bottom of the **sea,**
9. 3 I will command the **sea-monster** to bite them.
9. 6 for the waters of the **sea** and pours them out on the
Jon 1. 4 a strong wind on the **sea,** and the storm was so violent
1. 9 the Lord, the God of heaven, who made land and **sea.**”
1.12 Jonah answered, “Throw me into the **sea,** and it will calm down.
1.15 and threw him into the **sea,** and it calmed down at once.
2. 3 the very bottom of the **sea,** where the waters were all round
2. 5 the **sea** covered me completely,
Mic 7.12 of the Euphrates, from distant **seas** and far-off mountains.
7.19 our sins underfoot and send them to the bottom of the **sea!**
Nah 1. 4 He commands the **sea,** and it dries up!
Hab 2.14 of the Lord's glory as the **seas** are full of water.

Hab 3. 8 Was it the **sea** that made you furious?
3.15 You trampled the **sea** with your horses,
Zeph 2. 6 Your land by the **sea** will become open fields
Hag 2. 6 "Before long I will shake heaven and earth, land and **sea.**
Zech 9. 4 throw her wealth into the **sea,** and the city will be burnt
9.10 he will rule from **sea** to sea, from the River Euphrates to
10.11 When they pass through their **sea** of trouble, I, the
14. 8 of it to the Dead **Sea** and the other half to the
Mt 4.15 on the road to the **sea,** on the other side of the
18. 6 tied round his neck and be drowned in the deep **sea.**
21.21 hill, 'Get up and throw yourself in the **sea,'** and it will.
23.15 You sail the **seas** and cross whole countries to win one convert;
Mk 9.42 millstone tied round his neck and be thrown into the **sea.**
11.23 and throw itself in the **sea** and does not doubt in his
Lk 17. 2 he were thrown into the **sea** than for him to cause one
17. 6 'Pull yourself up by the roots and plant yourself in the **sea!'**
21.25 despair, afraid of the roar of the **sea** and the raging tides.
Acts 4.24 Creator of heaven, earth, and **sea,** and all that is in them!
7.36 Egypt and at the Red **Sea** and for forty years
10. 6 a tanner of leather named Simon, who lives by the **sea."**
10.32 home of Simon the tanner of leather, who lives by the **sea.'**
14.15 God, who made heaven, earth, **sea,** and all that is in them.
27. 5 We crossed over the **sea** off Cilicia and Pamphylia
27.12 favour of putting out to **sea** and trying to reach Phoenix,
27.38 lightened the ship by throwing all the wheat into the **sea.**
27.40 let them sink in the **sea,** and at the same time
28. 4 not let him live, even though he escaped from the **sea."**
Rom 9.27 grains of sand by the **sea,** yet only a few of them
1 Cor 10. 1 of the cloud, and all passed safely through the Red **Sea.**
10. 2 the cloud and in the **sea** they were all baptized as followers
2 Cor 11.26 dangers on the high **seas,** and dangers from false friends.
Heb 11.12 as many as the numberless grains of sand on the **sea-shore.**
11.29 Israelites able to cross the Red **Sea** as if on dry land;
Jas 1. 6 like a wave in the **sea** that is driven and blown about
Jude 13 like wild waves of the **sea,** with their shameful deeds
Rev 4. 6 was what looked like a **sea** of glass, clear as crystal.
5.13 world below, and in the **sea**—all living beings in the
7. 1 should blow on the earth or the **sea** or against any tree.
7. 2 God had given the power to damage the earth and the **sea.**
7. 3 not harm the earth, the **sea,** or the trees, until we mark
8. 8 looked like a huge mountain on fire was thrown into the **sea.**
8. 8 A third of the **sea** was turned into blood,
8. 9 the living creatures in the **sea** died, and a third of the
10. 2 his right foot on the **sea** and his left foot on the
10. 5 I saw standing on the **sea** and on the land
10. 6 who created heaven, earth, and the **sea,** and everything in them.
10. 8 hand of the angel standing on the **sea** and on the land."
12.12 But how terrible for the earth and the **sea!**
12.18 And the dragon stood on the **sea-shore.**
13. 1 Then I saw a beast coming up out of the **sea.**
14. 7 Worship him who made heaven, earth, **sea,** and the springs of water!"
15. 2 I saw what looked like a **sea** of glass mixed with fire.
15. 2 They were standing by the **sea** of glass, holding harps
16. 3 Then the second angel poured out his bowl on the **sea.**
16. 3 and every living creature in the **sea** died.
18.17 earn their living on the **sea,** stood a long way off,
18.19 who have ships sailing the **seas** became rich on her wealth!
18.21 and threw it into the **sea,** saying, "This is how the great
20. 8 for battle, as many as the grains of sand on the **sea-shore.**
20.13 Then the **sea** gave up its dead.
21. 1 The first heaven and the first earth disappeared, and the **sea** vanished.

Am SEACOAST see COAST

SEAGULL

Lev 11.13 **seagulls,** storks, herons, pelicans, cormorants;
Deut 14.12 **sea-gulls,** storks, herons, pelicans, cormorants;

SEAL
[UNSEALED]

Gen 26.31 morning each man made his promise and **sealed** it with a vow.
38.18 She answered, "Your **seal** with its cord and the stick you
38.25 whose they are—this **seal** with its cord and this stick."
41.42 engraved with the royal **seal** and put it on Joseph's finger.
Ex 24. 8 "This is the blood that **seals** the covenant which the Lord
1 Kgs 21. 8 signed them with Ahab's name, **sealed** them with his seal, and
Neh 6. 5 fifth message, this one in the form of an **unsealed** letter.
9.38 our Levites, and our priests put their **seals** to it.
Esth 8. 2 off his ring with his **seal** on it (which he had taken
8. 8 name and stamped with the royal **seal** cannot be revoked.
8. 8 write it in my name and stamp it with the royal **seal."**
8.10 of King Xerxes, and he stamped them with the royal **seal.**
Job 38.14 of a garment, clear as the imprint of a **seal** on clay.
Is 29.11 it will be like a **sealed** scroll.
29.11 he will say he can't because it is **sealed.**
Jer 32.10 I signed and **sealed** the deed, had it witnessed, and
32.11 the deed of purchase—the **sealed** copy containing the contract
32.14 take these deeds, both the **sealed** deed of purchase and the
32.44 will buy them, and the deeds will be signed, **sealed,** and
Dan 6.17 king placed his own royal **seal**
6.17 and the **seal** of his noblemen on the stone,
12. 4 the book and put a **seal** on it until the end of
Zech 9.11 with you that was **sealed** by the blood of sacrifices,
Mt 26.28 "this is my blood, which **seals** God's covenant, my blood
27.66 tomb secure by putting a **seal** on the stone
Mk 14.24 is poured out for many, my blood which **seals** God's covenant.
Lk 22.20 cup is God's new covenant **sealed** with my blood,
1 Cor 11.25 "This cup is God's new covenant, **sealed** with my blood.
Heb 9.20 "This is the blood which **seals** the covenant that God has
13.20 his sacrificial death, by which the eternal covenant is **sealed.**
Rev 5. 1 with writing on both sides and was **sealed** with seven seals.
5. 2 "Who is worthy to break the **seals** and open the scroll?"
5. 5 and he can break the seven **seals** and open the scroll."
5. 9 are worthy to take the scroll and to break open its **seals.**
6. 1 the first of the seven **seals,** and I heard one of the
6. 3 Then the Lamb broke open the second **seal;**
6. 5 Then the Lamb broke open the third **seal;**
6. 7 Then the Lamb broke open the fourth **seal;**
6. 9 Then the Lamb broke open the fifth **seal.**
6.12 And I saw the Lamb break open the sixth **seal.**
7. 2 coming up from the east with the **seal** of the living God.
7. 3 the servants of our God with a **seal** on their foreheads."
7. 4 who were marked with God's **seal** on their foreheads was 144,000.
8. 1 Lamb broke open the seventh **seal,** there was silence in
9. 4 who did not have the mark of God's **seal** on their foreheads.
20. 3 the abyss, locked it, and **sealed** it, so that he could not

SEAM

Ex 28.27 of the ephod near the **seam** and above the finely woven belt.
39.20 of the ephod, near the **seam** and above the finely woven belt.
Jn 19.23 made of one piece of woven cloth without any **seams** in it.

SEAPORTS see PORT

SEARCH

Gen 31.33 Laban went and **searched** Jacob's tent;
31.34 Laban **searched** through the whole tent, but did not find them.
31.35 Laban **searched** but did not find his household gods.
31.37 Now that you have **searched** through all my belongings,
44.12 Joseph's servant **searched** carefully, beginning with the
Deut 4.29 your God, and if you **search** for him with all your heart,
4.32 **"Search** the past, the time before you were born, all
4.32 **Search** the entire earth.
1 Sam 23.23 down, even if I have to **search** the whole land of Judah."
1 Kgs 1. 3 A **search** was made all over Israel for a beautiful girl,
18.10 the king has made a **search** for you in every country in
20. 6 will send my officers to **search** your palace and the homes of
2 Chr 15. 4 They **searched** for him and found him.
22. 9 A **search** was made for Ahaziah, and he was found hiding in
Ezra 4.15 suggest [15] that you order a **search** to be made in the
5.17 please Your Majesty, let a **search** be made in the royal
6. 1 emperor issued orders for a **search** to be made in the royal
Esth 2. 2 "Why don't you make a **search** to find some beautiful young virgins?
Job 6.19 Caravans from Sheba and Tema **search,** [20] but their hope
23. 8 I have **searched** in the east, but God is not there;
23. 8 I have not found him when I **searched** in the west.
24. 5 like wild donkeys, **search** for food in the dry wilderness;
28. 3 They **search** the depths of the earth And dig for rocks in
32.11 speaking and waited while you **searched** for wise phrases.
39. 8 they feed, where they **search** for anything green to eat.
Is 30.20 you, and you will not have to **search** for him any more.
34.16 **Search** in the Lord's book of living creatures and read
Jer 5. 1 **Search** the market-places!
17.10 I, the Lord, **search** the minds and test the hearts of men.
Ezek 12.14 bodyguard, and people will **search** for them to kill them.
Amos 9. 3 top of Mount Carmel, I will **search** for them and catch them.
Zeph 1.12 "At that time I will take a lamp and **search** Jerusalem.
Mt 2. 8 "Go and make a careful **search** for the child,
Mk 1.36 and his companions went out **searching** for him, [37] and when
Acts 12.19 Herod gave orders to **search** for him, but they could not
1 Cor 2.10 The Spirit **searches** everything, even the hidden depths of God's purposes.
1 Pet 1.10 that the prophets made careful **search** and investigation,

AV SEARCH
see also EXPLORE

Lev 27.33 The owner may not **arrange** the animals so that the poor
Num 10.33 went ahead of them to **find** a place for them to camp.
14. 6 of Jephunneh, two of the **spies,** tore their clothes in sorrow
14.38 Of the twelve **spies** only Joshua and Caleb survived.
Deut 1.22 men ahead of us to **spy** out the land, so that they
1.33 went ahead of you to **find** a place for you to camp.
Josh 2. 2 had come that night to **spy** out the country, [3] so he sent
2. 3 men in your house have come to **spy** out the whole country!
2 Kgs 10.23 to the people there, "Make **sure** that only worshippers of
Job 5.27 Job, we have **learnt** this by long study.
11. 7 Can you **discover** the limits and bounds of the greatness
13. 9 If God **looks** at you closely, will he find anything good?
28.27 then he saw wisdom and **tested** its worth— He gave it
36.26 fully know his greatness or **count** the number of his years.
Ps 44.21 you would surely have **discovered** it, because you know
139. 1 Lord, you have **examined** me and you know me.
139.23 **Examine** me, O God, and know my mind;
Prov 20.27 we cannot **hide** from ourselves.
25. 2 we honour kings for what they **explain.**
25.27 bad for you, and so is **trying** to win too much praise.
Ecc 1.13 I determined that I would **examine** and study all the
7.25 I was determined to **find** wisdom and the answers to my questions,
Is 40.28 No one **understands** his thoughts.
Jer 29.13 because you will **seek** me with all your heart.
46.23 Their men are too many to **count;**
Lam 3.40 Let us **examine** our ways and turn back to the Lord.

Ezek 34. 6 the earth, and no one **looked for** them or tried to find
34. 8 My shepherds did not try to **find** the sheep.
34.11 you that I myself will **look for** my sheep and take care
39.14 the land in order to **find** and bury those bodies remaining on
Jn 5.39 You **study** the Scriptures, because you think that in them
7.52 **Study** the Scriptures and you will learn that no prophet ever
Acts 17.11 and every day they **studied** the Scriptures to see if what
1 Pet 1.11 They tried to **find out** when the time would be and how

SEASON

Gen 31.10 "During the breeding **season** I had a dream, and I saw
Num 13.20 (It was the **season** when grapes were beginning to ripen.)
Deut 28.12 He will send rain in **season** from his rich storehouse in
33.14 fruit, Rich with the best fruits of each **season.**
1 Sam 12.17 It's the dry **season,** isn't it?
Job 38.32 Can you guide the stars **season** by season and direct the
Is 28. 4 the first figs of the **season,** picked and eaten as soon as
Jer 5.24 the spring rains and give you the harvest **season** each year.
Dan 2.21 He controls the times and the **seasons;**
Hos 9.10 it was like seeing the first ripe figs of the **season.**
Zech 14. 8 the year round, in the dry **season** as well as the wet.
Gal 4.10 You pay special attention to certain days, months, **seasons,**

SEASONING HERBS

Mt 23.23 a tenth even of the **seasoning herbs,** such as mint, dill,
Lk 11.42 God a tenth of the **seasoning herbs,** such as mint and rue

SEAT

Gen 43.33 The brothers had been **seated** at table, facing Joseph,
43.33 saw how they had been **seated,** they looked at one another
Lev 15. 9 Any saddle or **seat** on which the man with the discharge
Ruth 4. 2 When they were **seated,** [3]he said to his relative, "Now that
1 Sam 4.13 the Covenant Box, was sitting on a **seat** beside the road,
4.18 Covenant Box, Eli fell backwards from his **seat** beside the gate.
9.22 table where the guests, about thirty in all, were **seated.**
Esth 5. 1 The king was inside, **seated** on the royal throne,
Ps 80. 1 **Seated** on your throne above the winged creatures, [2]reveal
Prov 9.14 her house or on a **seat** in the highest part of the
Mt 23. 6 places at feasts and the reserved **seats** in the synagogues;
Mk 12.39 who choose the reserved **seats** in the synagogues
14.62 see the Son of Man **seated** on the right of the Almighty
Lk 11.43 You love the reserved **seats** in the synagogues and to be
20.46 who choose the reserved **seats** in the synagogues and the best
22.69 Son of Man will be **seated** on the right of Almighty God."
Jn 19.13 sat down on the judge's **seat** in the place called "The Stone
Eph 1.20 raised Christ from death and **seated** him at his right side
Heb 12. 2 and he is now **seated** at the right-hand side of God's
Jas 2. 3 to him, "Have this best **seat here,**" but say to the poor
Rev 4. 4 other thrones, on which were **seated** twenty-four elders dressed in white
19. 4 fell down and worshipped God, who was **seated** on the throne.

SEAWEED

Jon 2. 5 and **seaweed** was wrapped round my head.

SECOND (1)

Gen 1. 8 Evening passed and morning came—that was the **second** day.
2.13 The **second** river is the Gihon;
7.11 the seventeenth day of the **second** month all the outlets of
8.14 day of the **second** month the earth was completely dry.
22.15 to Abraham from heaven a **second** time, [16]"I make a vow by
25.26 The **second** one was born holding on tightly to the heel
27.36 Esau said, "This is the **second** time that he has cheated me.
30. 7 Bilhah became pregnant again and bore Jacob a **second** son.
32.19 the same order to the **second,** the third, and to all the
41.40 Your authority will be **second** only to mine.
41.43 He gave him the **second** royal chariot to ride in, and his
41.52 so he named his **second** son Ephraim.
45. 6 This is only the **second** year of famine in the land;
Ex 16. 1 fifteenth day of the **second** month after they had left Egypt,
21.10 If a man takes a **second** wife, he must continue to give
26. 5 loops matching them on the last piece of the **second** set.
28.18 in the **second** row, an emerald, a sapphire, and a
29.41 Sacrifice the **second** lamb in the evening, and offer with
36.12 loops matching them on the last piece of the **second** set.
39.11 in the **second** row, an emerald, a sapphire, and a
40.17 the first month of the **second** year after they left Egypt,
Lev 5.10 Then he shall offer the **second** bird as a burnt-offering,
8.22 Then Moses brought the **second** ram, which was for the
Num 1. 1 the first day of the **second** month in the second year after
1.18 the first day of the **second** month and registered all the
2.10 The division of Reuben shall march **second.**
9. 1 the first month of the **second** year after the people of
9.11 on the evening of the fourteenth day of the **second** month.
10. 6 short blasts are sounded a **second** time, the tribes on the
10.11 the twentieth day of the **second** month
10.11 in the **second** year after the people left Egypt,
19.18 In the **second** case, someone who is ritually clean is to
28. 4 in the morning, and the **second** in the evening, [5]each with a
28. 8 In the evening offer the **second** lamb in the same way as
29.17 On the **second** day offer twelve young bulls, two rams,
Deut 24. 3 Or suppose her **second** husband dies.
24.21 grapes once, do not go back over the vines a **second** time;
Josh 6.12 next morning, and for the **second** time the priests and
6.14 On this **second** day they again marched round the city
10.32 Israelites victory over Lachish on the **second** day of the battle.
Josh 19. 1 The **second** assignment made was for the families of the
Judg 6.26 Then take the **second** bull and burn it whole as an offering,
6.28 cut down, and that the **second** bull had been burnt on the
20.24 They marched against the army of Benjamin a **second** time.
20.25 And for the **second** time the Benjaminites came out of Gibeah,
1 Sam 18.21 So for the **second** time Saul said to David, "You will be
20.34 nothing that day—the **second** day of the New Moon Festival.
2 Sam 23. 9 The **second** of the famous three was Eleazar son of Dodo, of
1 Kgs 6. 1 reign over Israel, in the **second** month, the month of Ziv,
6. 8 with stairs leading up to the **second** and third storeys.
6.37 Temple was laid in the **second** month, the month of Ziv, in
15.25 In the **second** year of the reign of King Asa of Judah,
19. 7 and woke him up a **second** time, saying, "Get up and eat,
20. 9 to his first demand, but I cannot agree to the **second."**
2 Kgs 1.17 him as king in the **second** year of the reign of Jehoram
14. 1 In the **second** year of the reign of Jehoash son of Jehoahaz
15.32 In the **second** year of the reign of Pekah son of
1 Chr 2.51 his **second** son Salma founded Bethlehem,
5.12 leading clan, and Shapham of the **second** most important clan.
6.39 Asaph was leader of the **second** choir.
7.15 Machir's **second** son was Zelophehad, and he had only daughters.
23.18 Kohath's **second** son, Izhar, had a son, Shelomith, the
23.23 Merari's **second** son, Mushi, had three sons:
27. 2 **Second** month:
27. 2 a descendant of Ahohi (Mikloth was his **second** in command)
29.22 For a **second** time they proclaimed Solomon king.
2 Chr 3. 2 began the construction [2]in the **second** month of the fourth
17.15 **Second** in rank was Jehohanan, with 280,000 soldiers,
17.18 His **second** in command was Jehozabad with 180,000 men,
28. 7 Azrikam, and Elkanah, who was **second** in command to the king.
30. 1 to celebrate it in the **second** month, and the king sent word
30.13 gathered in Jerusalem in the **second** month to celebrate the
35.24 chariot, placed him in a **second** chariot which he had there,
Ezra 3. 8 So in the **second** month of the year after they came back
4.24 a standstill until the **second** year of the reign of Darius,
Neh 3.27 built the next section, their **second** one, from a point
3.30 son of Zalaph, built the next section, their **second** one.
11. 9 Judah son of Hassenuah was the **second** senior official in the city.
Esth 7. 2 king and Haman went to eat with Esther [2]for a **second** time.
10. 3 Mordecai the Jew was **second** in rank only to King Xerxes himself.
Job 42.14 Jemimah, the **second** Keziah, and the youngest Keren Happuch.
Prov 26.11 doing some stupid thing a **second** time is like a dog going
Ezek 10.14 face of a bull, the **second** a human face, the third the
18.14 "Now suppose this **second** man has a son.
23.13 was completely immoral, that the **second** sister was as bad as
40.27 distance to this **second** gateway, and it was fifty metres.
Dan 2. 1 In the **second** year that Nebuchadnezzar was king, he had a dream.
7. 5 The **second** beast looked like a bear standing on its hind legs.
8. 1 third year that Belshazzar was king, I saw a **second** vision.
Hos 1. 6 Gomer had a **second** child—this time it was a girl.
Hag 1. 1 During the **second** year that Darius was emperor of Persia,
1.15 the sixth month of the **second** year that Darius was emperor.
2.10 the ninth month of the **second** year that Darius was emperor,
2.20 the Lord gave Haggai a **second** message [21]for Zerubbabel,
Zech 1. 1 the eighth month of the **second** year that Darius was emperor
1. 7 In the **second** year that Darius was emperor, on the
6. 2 pulled by red horses, the **second** by black horses, [3]the
11.14 Then I broke the **second** stick, the one called "Unity,"
Mt 22.26 same thing happened to the **second** brother, to the third,
22.39 The **second** most important commandment is like it:
Mk 12.21 Then the **second** one married the woman, and he also died
12.31 The **second** most important commandment is this:
14.72 then a cock crowed a **second** time, and Peter remembered how
Lk 19.18 The **second** servant came and said, 'Sir, I have earned
20.30 Then the **second** one married the woman, [31]and then the third.
Jn 3. 4 cannot enter his mother's womb and be born a **second** time!"
4.54 This was the **second** miracle that Jesus performed after
9.24 A **second** time they called back the man
21.16 A **second** time Jesus said to him, "Simon son of John, do
Acts 7.13 On the **second** visit Joseph made himself known to his brothers,
12.10 guard post and then the **second,** and came at last to the
13.32 As it is written in the **second** Psalm, 'You are my Son;
1 Cor 12.28 first place apostles, in the **second** place prophets, and in
15.47 the **second** Adam came from heaven.
2 Cor 13. 2 said it before during my **second** visit to you, but I will
Heb 8. 7 covenant, there would have been no need for a **second** one.
9. 3 Behind the **second** curtain was the Tent called the Most Holy Place.
9.28 He will appear a **second** time, not to deal with sin, but
2 Pet 3. 1 this is now the **second** letter I have written to you.
Rev 2.11 who win the victory will not be hurt by the **second** death.
4. 7 the **second** looked like a bull;
6. 3 Then the Lamb broke open the **second** seal;
6. 3 and I heard the **second** living creature say, "Come!"
8. 8 Then the **second** angel blew his trumpet.
11.14 The **second** horror is over, but the third horror will come soon!
13.13 This **second** beast performed great miracles;
13.15 The **second** beast was allowed to breathe life into the
14. 8 A **second** angel followed the first one, saying, "She has fallen!
16. 3 Then the **second** angel poured out his bowl on the sea.
20. 6 The **second** death has no power over them;
20.14 (This lake of fire is the **second** death.)
21. 8 burning with fire and sulphur, which is the **second** death."
21.19 first foundation-stone was jasper, the **second** sapphire, the third agate,

SECOND (2)

Lk 4. 5 and showed him in a **second** all the kingdoms of the world.

SECRET

Gen 49. 6 will not join in their **secret** talks, Nor will I take part
Num 5.12 wife may have kept it **secret**—there was no witness, and she
Deut 13. 6 friend may **secretly** encourage you to worship other gods,
27.15 an idol of stone, wood, or metal and **secretly** worships it;
27.24 " 'God's curse on anyone who **secretly** commits murder.'
28.56 for food that she will **secretly** eat her newborn child and
29.29 "There are some things that the Lord our God has kept **secret**;
Josh 2. 1 with orders to go and **secretly** explore the land of Canaan,
Judg 3.19 said, "Your Majesty, I have a **secret** message for you."
6.11 Gideon was threshing some wheat **secretly** in a winepress, so
16. 9 So they still did not know the **secret** of his strength.
1 Sam 19. 2 hide in some **secret** place and stay there.
2 Sam 12.12 You sinned in **secret**, but I will make this happen in
2 Chr 22.11 She **secretly** rescued one of Ahaziah's sons, Joash, took him
Esth 2.10 of Mordecai, Esther had kept it **secret** that she was Jewish.
Job 10.13 that all that time you were **secretly** planning to harm me.
15.18 learnt from their fathers, and they kept no **secrets** hidden.
Ps 44.21 surely have discovered it, because you know our **secret** thoughts.
83. 3 They are making **secret** plans against your people;
90. 8 sins before you, our **secret** sins where you can see them.
139.15 I was growing there in **secret**, you knew that I was there
Prov 11.13 can be trusted with a **secret**, but you can put confidence in
17.23 Corrupt judges accept **secret** bribes,
20.19 A gossip can never keep a **secret**.
21.14 angry with you, a gift given **secretly** will calm him down.
25. 9 settle it between yourselves and do not reveal any **secrets**.
25.10 that you can't keep a **secret**, and you will never live down
Ecc 12.14 we do, whether good or bad, even things done in **secret**.
Song 4.12 sweetheart, my bride, is a **secret** garden, a walled garden, a
Is 26.21 The murders that were **secretly** committed on the earth
29.15 carry out their schemes in **secret** and think no one will see
45. 3 I will give you treasures from dark, **secret** places;
45.19 I have not spoken in **secret** or kept my purpose hidden.
Jer 13.17 not listen, I will cry in **secret** because of your pride;
23.18 "None of these prophets has ever known the Lord's **secret** thoughts.
23.22 If they had known my **secret** thoughts, then they could
38.16 King Zedekiah promised me in **secret**, "I swear by the living God,
50. 2 Do not keep it a **secret**!
Ezek 8.12 do you see what the Israelite leaders are doing in **secret**?
28. 3 are wiser than Danel, that no **secret** can be kept from you.
Dan 2.22 He reveals things that are deep and **secret**;
8.26 But keep it **secret** now, because it will be a long time
12. 9 words are to be kept **secret** and hidden until the end comes.
Hab 3.14 us, gloating like those who **secretly** oppress the poor.
Mt 2. 7 from the east to a **secret** meeting and found out from them
10.26 up will be uncovered, and every **secret** will be made known.
13.11 answered, "The knowledge about the **secrets** of the Kingdom of heaven
26. 4 and made plans to arrest Jesus **secretly** and put him to death.
Mk 4.11 "You have been given the **secret** of the Kingdom of God,"
14. 1 for a way to arrest Jesus **secretly** and put him to death.
Lk 2.35 will speak against [35] and so reveal their **secret** thoughts.
8.10 answered, "The knowledge of the **secrets** of the Kingdom of God
12. 2 up will be uncovered, and every **secret** will be made known.
22. 2 trying to find a way of putting Jesus to death **secretly**.
Jn 7.10 however, he did not go openly, but **secretly**.
18.20 I have never said anything in **secret**.
19.38 follower of Jesus, but in **secret**, because he was afraid of
Acts 16.37 And now they want to send us away **secretly**.
Rom 2.16 God through Jesus Christ will judge the **secret** thoughts of all.
11.25 There is a **secret** truth, my brothers, which I want you
16.25 to the revelation of the **secret** truth which was hidden for
1 Cor 2. 1 my brothers, to preach God's **secret** truth, I did not use big
2. 7 I proclaim is God's **secret** wisdom, which is hidden from mankind,
2.10 God made known his **secret** by means of his Spirit.
4. 1 Christ's servants, who have been put in charge of God's **secret** truths.
4. 5 bring to light the dark **secrets** and expose the hidden purposes
13. 2 I may have all knowledge and understand all **secrets**;
14. 2 He is speaking **secret** truths by the power of the Spirit.
14.25 his **secret** thoughts will be brought into the
15.51 Listen to this **secret** truth:
2 Cor 4. 2 We put aside all **secret** and shameful deeds;
Eph 1. 9 made known to us the **secret** plan he had already decided
3. 3 God revealed his **secret** plan and made it known to me.
3. 4 you can learn about my understanding of the **secret** of Christ.)
3. 5 mankind was not told this **secret**, but God has revealed it
3. 6 The **secret** is that by means of the gospel the Gentiles
3. 9 all people see how God's **secret** plan is to be put into
3. 9 kept his **secret** hidden through all the past ages,
5.12 shameful even to talk about the things they do in **secret**.)
5.32 There is a deep **secret** truth revealed in this scripture,
6.19 that I may speak boldly and make known the gospel's **secret**.
Phil 4.12 I have learnt this **secret**, so that anywhere, at any time,
Col 1.26 his message, [26] which is the **secret** he hid through all past
1.27 is to make known his **secret** to his people,
1.27 this rich and glorious **secret** which he has
1.27 And the **secret** is that Christ is in you,
2. 2 In this way they will know God's **secret**, which is Christ himself.
4. 3 to preach his message about the **secret** of Christ.
1 Tim 3.16 No one can deny how great is the **secret** of our religion:
Rev 1.20 This is the **secret** meaning of the seven stars that you
2.24 not learnt what the others call 'the deep **secrets** of Satan.'
10. 4 heaven, "Keep **secret** what the seven thunders have said;
10. 7 then God will accomplish his **secret** plan,
17. 5 On her forehead was written a name that has a **secret** meaning:
17. 7 "I will tell you the **secret** meaning of the woman
22.10 words of this book a **secret**, because the time is near when

SECRETARY

2 Sam 8.17 Seraiah was the court **secretary**;
20.25 Sheva was the court **secretary**;
1 Kgs 4. 3 The court **secretaries**: Elihoreph and Ahijah
2 Kgs 12.10 the box, the royal **secretary** and the High Priest would come,
18.18 Shebna, the court **secretary**;
19. 2 the palace, Shebna, the court **secretary**, and the senior
22. 3 King Josiah sent the court **secretary** Shaphan, the son of
22.12 the court **secretary**, and to Asaiah, the king's attendant:
1 Chr 18.16 Seraiah was court **secretary**;
24. 6 were registered by Shemaiah son of Nethanel, a Levite **secretary**.
2 Chr 24.11 it was full, the royal **secretary** and the High Priest's
26.11 records were kept by his **secretaries** Jeiel and Maaseiah
34.20 the court **secretary**, and to Asaiah, the king's attendant:
Ezra 4. 8 the governor, and Shimshai, the **secretary** of the province,
4. 9 Shimshai, **secretary** of the province, from their associates,
4.17 Rehum, the governor, to Shimshai, **secretary** of the province,
Esth 3.12 month Haman called the king's **secretaries** and dictated a
8. 9 Mordecai called the king's **secretaries** and dictated letters
Is 36. 3 the court **secretary**, Shebna;
37. 2 the palace, Shebna, the court **secretary**, and the senior
Jer 36.10 the room of Gemariah son of Shaphan, the court **secretary**.
36.12 the room of the court **secretary**, where all the officials
36.12 Elishama, the court **secretary**, Delaiah son of Shemaiah,
36.20 Elishama, the court **secretary**, and went to the king's court,
36.26 Shelemiah son of Abdeel, to arrest me and my **secretary** Baruch.
36.32 and gave it to my **secretary** Baruch, and he wrote down
37.15 house of Jonathan, the court **secretary**, whose house had been

SECTION

1 Kgs 7.20 on a rounded **section** which was above the chain design.
2 Chr 8.14 organized the temple guards in **sections** for performing their
32.33 died and was buried in the upper **section** of the royal tombs.
Neh 3. 2 The men of Jericho built the next **section**.
3. 2 Zaccur son of Imri built the next **section**.
3. 4 of Uriah and grandson of Hakkoz, built the next **section**.
3. 4 and grandson of Meshezabel, built the next **section**.
3. 4 Zadok son of Baana built the next **section**.
3. 5 of Tekoa built the next **section**, but the leading men of the
3. 7 and Mizpah built the next **section**, as far as the residence
3. 8 Uzziel son of Harhaiah, a goldsmith, built the next **section**.
3. 8 of perfumes, built the next **section**, as far as Broad Wall.
3. 9 of half the Jerusalem District, built the next **section**.
3.10 Harumaph built the next **section**, which was near his own house.
3.10 Hattush son of Hashabneiah built the next **section**.
3.11 Moab built both the next **section** and the Tower of the Ovens.
3.12 half of the Jerusalem District, built the next **section**.
3.16 Bethzur District, built the next **section**, as far as David's tomb,
3.17 Levites rebuilt the next several **sections** of the wall:
3.17 Rehum son of Bani built the next **section**;
3.17 built the next **section** on behalf of his district;
3.18 other half of the Keilah District, built the next **section**;
3.19 of Mizpah, built the next **section** in front of the armoury,
3.20 of Zabbai built the next **section**, as far as the entrance to
3.21 of Hakkoz, built the next **section**, up to the far end of
3.22 priests rebuilt the next several **sections** of the wall:
3.22 Priests from the area around Jerusalem built the next **section**;
3.23 and Hasshub built the next **section**, which was in front of
3.23 of Ananiah, built the next **section**, which was in front of
3.24 of Henadad built the next **section**, from Azariah's house to
3.25 of Uzai built the next **section**, beginning at the corner of
3.25 of Parosh built the next **section**, to a point on the east
3.27 of Tekoa built the next **section**, their second one, from a
3.28 built the next **section**, going north from the Horse Gate,
3.29 of Immer built the next **section**, which was in front of his
3.29 Shecaniah, keeper of the East Gate, built the next **section**.
3.30 son of Zalaph, built the next **section**, their second one.
3.30 of Berechiah built the next **section**, which was in front of
3.31 a goldsmith, built the next **section**, as far as the building
3.32 the merchants built the last **section**, from the room at the
Ezek 43.14 The lowest **section** of the altar, from the top of the base,
43.14 The next **section** was set back from the edge fifty
43.14 The **section** after that was also set back from the edge fifty
43.15 This top **section**, on which the sacrifices were burnt,
43.17 The middle **section** was also a square, seven metres on each side,
43.20 the corners of the middle **section** of the altar, and all
45. 3 Half of this area, a **section** twelve and a half kilometres
45. 4 contain their houses and the **section** of land for the Temple.
45. 6 to the holy area, another **section**, twelve and a half
47.13 tribes, with the tribe of Joseph receiving two **sections**.
48. 1 tribe is to receive one **section** of land extending from the
48. 8 The next **section** of the land is to be set apart for
48. 8 from east to west as the **sections** given to the tribes.
48. 8 The Temple will be in this **section**.
48. 9 In the centre of this **section**, a special area twelve and a
48.20 in the centre of the **section** which was set apart will be
48.21 on the north by the **section** belonging to Judah
48.21 and on the south by the **section** belonging to Benjamin.
48.23 South of this special **section**, each of the
48.23 tribes is to receive one **section** of land running from the
48.29 is to be divided into **sections** for the tribes of Israel to

SECURE

Num 24.21 place where you live is **secure**, Safe as a nest set high
Deut 24. 6 are not to take as **security** his millstones used for grinding
24.10 to get the garment he is going to give you as **security**;
24.17 and do not take a widow's garment as **security** for a loan.
33.25 protected with iron gates, And may he always live **secure**."

Deut 33.28 Jacob's descendants live in peace, **secure** in a land full of
Josh 23. 1 the Lord gave Israel **security** from their enemies around them.
Ruth 4.15 new life to you and give you **security** in your old age."
1 Kgs 2.45 me and he will make David's kingdom **secure** for ever."
15. 4 to rule after him in Jerusalem and to keep Jerusalem **secure.**
2 Kgs 20.19 there would be peace and **security** during his lifetime, so he
1 Chr 22. 9 during his reign I will give Israel peace and **security.**
2 Chr 11.23 He provided generously for them and also **secured** many wives
14. 7 He has protected us and given us **security** on every side."
20.30 Jehoshaphat ruled in peace, and God gave him **security**
Esth 9.30 wished the Jews peace and **security** [31] and directed them and
10. 3 his people and for the **security** of all their descendants.
Job 5. 3 have seen fools who looked **secure,** but I called down a
11.18 You will live **secure** and full of hope;
18.14 the tent where he lived **secure,** and is dragged off to face
24.23 God may let him live **secure,** but keeps an eye on him
29.13 misery praised me, and I helped widows find **security.**
36.16 God brought you out of trouble, and let you enjoy **security;**
Ps 8. 2 You are safe and **secure** from all your enemies;
12. 5 I will give them the **security** they long for."
15. 5 Whoever does these things will always be **secure.**
16. 9 glad, and I feel completely **secure,** [10] because you protect
21. 7 and because of the Lord's constant love he will always be **secure.**
27. 5 safe in his Temple and make me **secure** on a high rock.
30. 6 I felt **secure** and said to myself, "I will never be defeated."
31.19 good you are, how **securely** you protect those who trust you.
40. 2 He set me safely on a rock and made me **secure.**
52. 7 his great wealth and looked for **security** in being wicked."
71. 3 Be my **secure** shelter and a strong fortress to protect me;
78.69 he made it firm like the earth itself, **secure** for all time.
102.28 and under your protection their descendants will be **secure.**
119.165 love your law have perfect **security,** and there is nothing
Prov 1.33 But whoever listens to me will have **security.**
10. 9 Honest people are safe and **secure,** but the dishonest will be
10.30 Righteous people will always have **security,** but the
11.14 Many advisers mean **security.**
12. 3 Wickedness does not give **security,** but righteous people stand
14.26 Lord gives confidence and **security** to a man and his family.
Ecc 7.12 and will give you as much **security** as money can.
Is 28.17 lies you depend on, and floods will destroy your **security.**
30.15 Then you will be strong and **secure."**
32.17 do what is right, there will be peace and **security** for ever.
33.16 you will be as **secure** as if you were in a strong
39. 8 there would be peace and **security** during his lifetime, so he
47. 8 lover of pleasure, you that think you are safe and **secure.**
Jer 22.23 You rest **secure** among the cedars brought from Lebanon;
30.10 you will be **secure,** and no one will make you afraid.
33. 6 I will show them abundant peace and **security.**
46.27 you will be **secure,** and no one will make you afraid.
48.11 said, "Moab has always lived **secure** and has never been
49.31 We'll attack those people that feel safe and **secure!**
Ezek 18. 7 He returns what a borrower gives him as **security;**
18.12 he robs, he keeps what a borrower gives him as **security.**
18.16 He returns what a borrower gives him as **security.**
28.26 who treated them with scorn, and Israel will be **secure.**
33.15 example, if he returns the **security** he took for a loan or
34.25 I will make a covenant with them that guarantees their **security.**
37.26 covenant with them that guarantees their **security** for ever.
38.11 people live in peace and **security** in unwalled towns that
38.14 my people Israel live in **security,** you will set out [15] from
Amos 2. 8 that they have taken from the poor as **security** for debts.
Zeph 3.13 They will be prosperous and **secure,** afraid of no one."
Zech 3.10 and **security,** surrounded by your vineyards and fig-trees."
Mt 27.65 "go and make the tomb as **secure** as you can."
27.66 left and made the tomb **secure** by putting a seal on
Acts 27.16 There, with some difficulty, we managed to make the ship's boat **secure.**

SEDUCE

Ex 22.16 "If a man **seduces** a virgin who is not engaged, he must
Prov 2.16 immoral woman who tries to **seduce** you with her smooth talk,
6.24 bad women, from the **seductive** words of other men's wives.
7. 5 from other men's wives, from women with **seductive** words.
Ezek 18. 6 He doesn't **seduce** another man's wife or have intercourse
18.11 offered at forbidden shrines and **seduces** other men's wives.
18.15 He doesn't **seduce** another man's wife [16] or oppress anyone
22.11 and others **seduce** their daughters-in-law or their half-sisters.

SEE

[SAW]
see also **SIGHT**

Gen 1. 4 God was pleased with what he **saw.**
1.10 And God was pleased with what he **saw.**
1.12 all kinds of plants, and God was pleased with what he **saw.**
1.18 And God was pleased with what he **saw.**
1.21 And God was pleased with what he **saw.**
1.25 God made them all, and he was pleased with what he **saw.**
2.19 brought them to the man to **see** what he would name them;
3. 6 The woman **saw** how beautiful the tree was and how good its
6. 2 some of the heavenly beings **saw** that these girls were beautiful,
6. 5 When the Lord **saw** how wicked everyone on earth was and how
6.12 looked at the world and **saw** that it was evil, for the
8. 8 sent out a dove to **see** if the water had gone down,
8.13 boat, looked round, and **saw** that the ground was getting dry.
9.16 in the clouds, I will **see** it and remember the everlasting
9.22 Ham, the father of Canaan, **saw** that his father was naked, he
9.23 keeping their faces turned away so as not to **see** him naked.
11. 5 the Lord came down to **see** the city and the tower which
12.12 When the Egyptians **see** you, they will assume that you
Gen 12.14 Egypt, the Egyptians did **see** that his wife was beautiful.
12.15 Some of the court officials **saw** her and told the king
13.10 Lot looked round and **saw** that the whole Jordan Valley,
13.15 all the land that you **see,** and it will be yours for
16.13 asked herself, "Have I really **seen** God and lived to tell
16.13 called the Lord who had spoken to her "A God Who **Sees."**
16.14 Kadesh and Bered "The Well of the Living One Who **Sees** Me."
18. 2 of the day, [2] he looked up and **saw** three men standing there.
18. 2 As soon as he **saw** them, he ran out to meet them.
19. 1 As soon as he **saw** them, he got up and went to
19.20 Do you **see** that little town?
19.20 go over there—you can **see** it is just a small place
19.28 and the whole valley and **saw** smoke rising from the land,
21.10 Sarah **saw** them and said to Abraham, "Send this
21.16 She said to herself, "I can't bear to **see** my child die."
21.19 Then God opened her eyes, and she **saw** a well.
22. 4 On the third day Abraham **saw** the place in the distance.
22. 7 Isaac asked, "I **see** that you have the coals and the wood,
22.13 Abraham looked round and **saw** a ram caught in a bush by
24.21 watching her in silence, to **see** if the Lord had given him
24.30 Laban had **seen** the nose-ring and the bracelets on his sister's
24.62 of the Living One Who **Sees** Me" and was staying in the
24.63 evening to take a walk in the fields and **saw** camels coming.
24.64 When Rebecca **saw** Isaac, she got down from her camel
25.11 who lived near "The Well of the Living One Who **Sees** Me."
26. 8 down from his window and **saw** Isaac and Rebecca making love.
26.26 adviser and Phicol the commander of his army to **see** Isaac.
26.27 have you now come to **see** me, when you were so unfriendly
27. 2 Isaac said, "You **see** that I am old and may die soon.
28.12 He dreamt that he **saw** a stairway reaching from earth to heaven,
29.10 When Jacob **saw** Rachel with his uncle Laban's flock, he
29.31 When the Lord **saw** that Leah was loved less than Rachel,
29.32 She said, "The Lord has **seen** my trouble, and now my husband
31. 2 He also **saw** that Laban was no longer as friendly as he
31.10 had a dream, and I **saw** that the male goats that were
31.12 this happen because I have **seen** all that Laban is doing to
31.37 your men and mine can **see** it, and let them decide which
31.42 But God has **seen** my trouble and the work I have done,
31.43 In fact, everything you **see** here belongs to me.
32. 2 When he **saw** them, he said, "This is God's camp";
32.25 When the man **saw** that he was not winning the struggle,
32.30 Jacob said, "I have **seen** God face to face, and I am
33. 1 Jacob **saw** Esau coming with his four hundred men, so he
33. 5 When Esau looked round and **saw** the women and the children,
33.10 To **see** your face is for me
33.10 like **seeing** the face of God,
34. 2 was chief of that region, **saw** her, he took her and raped
37. 4 When his brothers **saw** that their father loved Joseph more
37. 9 another dream, in which I **saw** the sun, the moon, and eleven
37.14 His father said, "Go and **see** if your brothers are safe
37.15 the country when a man **saw** him and asked him, "What are
37.18 They **saw** him in the distance, and before he reached them,
37.20 Then we will **see** what becomes of his dreams."
37.25 they were eating, they suddenly **saw** a group of Ishmaelites
38.15 When Judah **saw** her, he thought that she was a prostitute,
38.25 Look at them and **see** whose they are—this seal with its
39. 3 of his Egyptian master, [3] who **saw** that the Lord was with
39.13 When she **saw** that he had left his robe and had run
40. 6 came to them in the morning, he **saw** that they were upset.
40.16 When the chief baker **saw** that the interpretation of the
41.19 They were the poorest cows I have ever **seen** anywhere in Egypt.
41.22 I also dreamt that I **saw** seven ears of corn which were
42. 7 When Joseph **saw** his brothers, he recognized them, but he
42.21 we **saw** the great trouble he was in when he begged for
42.35 and when they **saw** the money, they and their father Jacob
43.16 When Joseph **saw** Benjamin with them, he said to the
43.29 When Joseph **saw** his brother Benjamin, he said, "So this
43.33 When they **saw** how they had been seated, they looked at one
44.21 here, so that you could **see** him, [22] and we answered that
44.30 boy, as soon as he **sees** that the boy is not with
44.34 I cannot bear to **see** this disaster come upon my father."
45.12 you, and you too, Benjamin, can **see** that I am really Joseph.
45.13 in Egypt and tell him about everything that you have **seen.**
45.27 to them, and when he **saw** the wagons which Joseph had sent
45.28 I must go and **see** him before I die."
46.30 die, now that I have **seen** you and know that you are
48. 1 his two sons, Manasseh and Ephraim, and went to **see** Jacob.
48. 2 son Joseph had come to **see** him, he gathered his strength and
48. 8 When Jacob **saw** Joseph's sons, he asked, "Who are these boys?"
48.10 failing because of his age, and he could not **see** very well.
48.11 Joseph, "I never expected to **see** you again,
48.11 and now God has even let me **see** your children."
48.17 Joseph was upset when he **saw** that his father had put his
48.21 said to Joseph, "As you **see,** I am about to die, but
49.15 But he **sees** that the resting-place is good And that the
50.11 When the citizens of Canaan **saw** those people mourning at Atad,
50.23 He lived to **see** Ephraim's children and grandchildren.
Ex 2. 2 When she **saw** what a fine baby he was, she hid him
2. 4 stood some distance away to **see** what would happen to him.
2. 6 The princess opened it and **saw** a baby boy.
2.11 people, the Hebrews, and he **saw** how they were forced to do
2.11 He even **saw** an Egyptian kill a Hebrew, one of Moses' own
2.12 all round, and when he **saw** that no one was watching, he
2.13 The next day he went back and **saw** two Hebrew men fighting.
2.25 He **saw** the slavery of the Israelites and was concerned for them.
3. 2 Moses **saw** that the bush was on fire but that it was
3. 3 I will go closer and **see."**
3. 4 When the Lord **saw** that Moses was coming closer, he called
3. 7 the Lord said, "I have **seen** how cruelly my people are being
3. 9 my people, and I **see** how the Egyptians are oppressing them.
3.16 come to them and have **seen** what the Egyptians are doing to

Ex 4.14 now coming to meet you and will be glad to **see** you.
4.18 to my relatives in Egypt to **see** if they are still alive."
4.31 to them and had **seen** how they were being treated cruelly,
5.21 and Aaron, "The Lord has **seen** what you have done and will
6. 1 "Now you are going to **see** what I will do to the
8.15 When the king **saw** that the frogs were dead, he became
8.26 sacrificing them where they can **see** us, they will stone us
9.34 When the king **saw** what had happened, he sinned again.
10. 1 Then the Lord said to Moses, "Go and **see** the king.
10. 6 They will be worse than anything your ancestors ever **saw.'** "
10.14 locusts that had ever been **seen** or that ever would be seen
10.23 The Egyptians could not **see** each other, and no one left
10.28 Don't let me ever **see** you again!
10.29 "You will never **see** me again."
12.13 When I **see** the blood, I will pass over you and will
12.23 kill the Egyptians, he will **see** the blood on the beams and
13.17 return to Egypt when they **see** that they are going to have
14.10 When the Israelites **saw** the king and his army marching
14.13 your ground, and you will **see** what the Lord will do to
14.13 you will never **see** these Egyptians again.
14.30 and the Israelites **saw** them lying dead on the seashore.
14.31 When the Israelites **saw** the great power with which the
15.16 They **see** your strength, O Lord, and stand helpless with fear
16. 7 In the morning you will **see** the dazzling light of the
16.15 When the Israelites **saw** it, they didn't know what it was
16.32 descendants, so that they can **see** the food which he gave us
18.14 When Jethro **saw** everything that Moses had to do, he
19. 4 "You **saw** what I, the Lord, did to the Egyptians and how
19.11 come down on Mount Sinai, where all the people can **see** me.
20.18 blast and **saw** the lightning and the smoking mountain,
20.22 "You have **seen** how I, the Lord, have spoken to you from
23. 4 "If you happen to **see** your enemy's cow or donkey running loose,
24.10 Israel went up the mountain [10]and they **saw** the God of Israel.
24.11 they **saw** God, and then they ate and drank together.
32. 1 When the people **saw** that Moses had not come down from the
32.19 enough to the camp to **see** the bull-calf
32.19 and to **see** the people dancing, he was furious.
32.25 Moses **saw** that Aaron had let the people get out of
33.10 As soon as the people **saw** the pillar of cloud at the
33.18 "Please, let me **see** the dazzling light of your presence."
33.20 I will not let you **see** my face,
33.20 because no one can **see** me and stay alive, [21] but here
33.23 hand away, and you will **see** my back but not my face."
34. 3 no one is to be **seen** on any part of the mountain;
34.10 All the people will **see** what great things I, the Lord, can
34.30 people looked at Moses and **saw** that his face was shining,
34.35 to say, [35]and they would **see** that his face was shining.
39.43 Moses examined everything and **saw** that they had made it
40.38 all their wanderings they could **see** the cloud of the Lord's
Lev 5. 1 information about something he has **seen** or heard, he must suffer
9.24 When the people **saw** it, they all shouted and bowed down with
13.15 him again, and if he **sees** an open sore, he shall pronounce
16.13 the Covenant Box so that he will not **see** it and die.
24. 4 of pure gold and must **see** that they burn regularly in the
Num 4.20 Kohathites enter the Tent and **see** the priests preparing the
11.23 "You will soon **see** whether what I have said will happen or
12. 8 he has even **seen** my form!
12.10 Aaron looked at her and **saw** that she was covered with the
13.26 They reported what they had **seen** and showed them the fruit
13.28 Even worse, we **saw** the descendants of the giants there.
13.32 Everyone we **saw** was very tall,
13.33 and we even **saw** giants there, the descendants of Anak.
14.10 death, but suddenly the people **saw** the dazzling light of the
14.14 us, that you are plainly **seen** when your cloud stops over us,
14.22 They have **seen** the dazzling light of my presence and the
15.39 reminders, and each time you **see** them you will remember all
16. 6 Then we will **see** which of us the Lord has chosen.
16.42 turned towards the Tent and **saw** that the cloud was covering
16.47 When he **saw** that the plague had already begun, he put the
17. 8 went into the Tent, he **saw** that Aaron's stick, representing
17. 9 They **saw** what had happened, and each leader took his own
21.27 We want to **see** it rebuilt and restored.
22.23 When the donkey **saw** the angel standing there holding a sword,
22.25 When the donkey **saw** the angel, it moved over against the
22.27 This time, when the donkey **saw** the angel, it lay down.
22.31 Then the Lord let Balaam **see** the angel standing there
22.33 But your donkey **saw** me and turned aside three times.
22.41 Baal, from where Balaam could **see** a part of the people of
23. 3 burnt-offering, while I go to **see** whether or not the Lord
23. 9 From the high rocks I can **see** them;
23.13 place from which you can **see** only some of the Israelites.
24. 2 turned towards the desert [2]and **saw** the people of Israel
24. 3 of the man who can **see** clearly, [4] Who can hear what God
24. 4 With staring eyes I **see** in a trance A vision from Almighty
24.15 of the man who can **see** clearly, [16] Who can hear what God
24.16 With staring eyes I **see** in a trance A vision from Almighty
24.17 I look into the future, And I **see** the nation of Israel.
24.20 Then in his vision Balaam **saw** the Amalekites
24.21 In his vision he **saw** the Kenites, and uttered this prophecy:
25. 7 grandson of Aaron the priest, **saw** this, he got up and left
27.13 After you have **seen** it, you will die, as your brother
32. 1 When they **saw** how suitable the land of Jazer and Gilead was
32. 9 Valley of Eshcol and **saw** the land, but when they returned,
Deut 1.28 They **saw** giants there!'
1.30 for you, just as you **saw** him do in Egypt
1.31 You **saw** how he brought you safely all the way to this
3.11 It can still be **seen** in the Ammonite city of Rabbah.)
3.21 'You have **seen** all that the Lord your God did to those
3.25 the River Jordan, Lord, and **see** the fertile land on the
3.27 Look carefully at what you **see,** because you will never go
3.28 lead the people across to occupy the land that you **see.'**
Deut 4. 3 You yourselves **saw** what the Lord did at Mount Peor.
4. 9 long as you live, what you have **seen** with your own eyes.
4.12 him speaking but did not **see** him in any form at all.
4.15 from the fire on Mount Sinai, you did not **see** any form.
4.19 worship and serve what you **see** in the sky—the sun, the
4.28 wood and stone, gods that cannot **see** or hear, eat or smell.
4.36 on earth he let you **see** his holy fire, and he spoke
5.24 Today we have **seen** that it is possible for a man to
6.22 With our own eyes we **saw** him work miracles and do
7.19 the terrible plagues that you **saw** with your own eyes, the
9. 3 But now you will **see** for yourselves that the Lord your God
9.16 I **saw** that you had already disobeyed the command that
10.21 your God, and you have **seen** with your own eyes the great
11. 2 You **saw** the Lord's greatness, his power, his might,
11. 3 You **saw** what he did to the king of Egypt
11. 4 You **saw** how the Lord completely wiped out the Egyptian army,
11. 7 are the ones who have **seen** all these great things that the
13. 3 him to test you, to **see** if you love the Lord with
18.16 Lord speak again or to **see** his fiery presence any more,
20. 1 against your enemies and you **see** chariots and horses and an
21.11 you take prisoners, [11] you may **see** among them a beautiful
22. 1 "If you **see** a fellow-Israelite's cow or sheep running loose,
26. 7 He heard us and **saw** our suffering, hardship, and misery.
28.10 the peoples on earth will **see** that the Lord has chosen you
28.25 earth will be terrified when they **see** what happens to you.
28.67 Your hearts will pound with fear at everything you **see.**
29. 2 and said to them, "You **saw** for yourselves what the Lord did
29. 3 You **saw** the terrible plagues, the miracles, and the great
29.17 You **saw** their disgusting idols made of wood, stone,
29.22 foreigners from distant lands will **see** the disasters and
32.19 "When the Lord **saw** this, he was angry and rejected his
32.20 will **see** what happens to them, those stubborn, unfaithful people.
32.29 They fail to **see** why they were defeated;
32.36 rescue his people when he **sees** that their strength is gone.
32.36 on those who serve him, when he **sees** how helpless they are.
34. 4 I have let you **see** it, but I will not let you
Josh 3. 3 to the people, "When you **see** the priests carrying the
5. 4 they were not allowed to **see** the rich and fertile land that
5.13 was near Jericho, he suddenly **saw** a man standing in front of
7.21 the things we seized I **saw** a beautiful Babylonian cloak,
8.14 When the king of Ai **saw** Joshua's men, he acted quickly.
8.20 of Ai looked back, they **saw** the smoke rising to the sky.
8.21 When Joshua and his men **saw** that the others had taken
23. 3 You have **seen** everything that the Lord your God has done
24.17 slavery in Egypt, and we **saw** the miracles that he performed.
24.31 leaders were alive who had **seen** for themselves everything that
Judg 1.24 spies to the city, [24] who **saw** a man leaving and said to
2. 7 leaders were alive who had **seen** for themselves all the great
3.24 The servants came and **saw** that the doors were locked, but
6.11 in a winepress, so that the Midianites would not **see** him.
6.22 the Lord's angel he had **seen,** and he said in terror,
6.22 I have **seen** your angel face to face!"
9.35 When Abimelech and his men **saw** Gaal come out and stand
9.36 Gaal **saw** them and said to Zebul, "Look!
9.43 When he **saw** the people coming out of the city, he came
9.55 When the Israelites **saw** that Abimelech was dead,
11.35 When he **saw** her, he tore his clothes in sorrow and said,
12. 3 When I **saw** that you were not going to, I risked my
13.20 altar, Manoah and his wife **saw** the Lord's angel go up
13.20 They never **saw** the angel again.
13.22 his wife, "We are sure to die, because we have **seen** God!"
14.11 When the Philistines **saw** him, they sent thirty young men
16.24 When the people **saw** him, they sang praise to their god:
18. 7 They **saw** how safely the people there were living,
18. 9 We **saw** the land, and it's very good.
18.26 Micah **saw** that they were too strong for him, so he turned
19. 3 house, and when her father **saw** him, he gave him a warm
19.30 Everyone who **saw** it said, "We have never heard of such
20.38 When they **saw** a big cloud of smoke going up from the
20.40 them and were amazed to **see** the whole city going up in
Ruth 1.18 When Naomi **saw** that Ruth was determined to go with her,
2. 9 watch them to **see** where they are reaping and stay with them.
3.14 enough for her to be **seen,** because Boaz did not want anyone
3.18 "Now be patient, Ruth, until you **see** how this all turns out.
1 Sam 1.11 **See** my trouble and remember me!
1.26 I am the woman you **saw** standing here, praying to the Lord.
5. 3 morning the people of Ashdod **saw** that the statue of Dagon
5. 4 Early the following morning they **saw** that the statue had
5. 7 When they **saw** what was happening, they said, "The God of
6.13 when suddenly they looked up and **saw** the Covenant Box.
9.14 they were going in, they **saw** Samuel coming out towards them
9.16 I have **seen** the suffering of my people and have heard their
10.11 who had known him before **saw** him doing this and asked one
10.14 Saul's uncle **saw** him and the servant, and he asked them,
10.23 the people, and they could **see** that he was a head taller
12.12 But when you **saw** that King Nahash of Ammon was about to
12.16 you are, and you will **see** the great thing which the Lord
14. 8 "We will go across and let the Philistines **see** us.
14.11 So they let the Philistines **see** them, and the Philistines said,
14.16 **saw** the Philistines running in confusion.
15.35 As long as Samuel lived, he never again **saw** the king;
16. 6 When they arrived, Samuel **saw** Jesse's son Eliab
17.18 something to show that you **saw** them and that they are well.
17.24 When the Israelites **saw** Goliath, they ran away in terror.
17.47 God, [47]and everyone here will **see** that the Lord does not
17.51 When the Philistines **saw** that their hero was dead, they ran
17.55 When Saul **saw** David going out to fight Goliath, he asked Abner,
19. 5 When you **saw** it, you were glad.
19.20 They **saw** the group of prophets dancing and shouting, with
22. 9 officers, and he said, "I **saw** David when he went to
22.22 said to him, "When I **saw** Doeg there that day, I knew

1 Sam 23.15 David **saw** that Saul was out to kill him.
23.22 out for certain where he is and who has **seen** him there.
24.10 You can **see** for yourself that just now in the cave the
25.23 When Abigail **saw** David, she quickly dismounted and
26.12 No one **saw** it or knew what had happened or even woke
28. 2 servant, and you will **see** for yourself what I can do." [6]and
28. 5 When Saul **saw** the Philistine army, he was terrified, [6]and
28.12 When the woman **saw** Samuel, she screamed and said to Saul,
28.13 "What do you **see?"**
28.13 "I **see** a spirit coming up from the earth," she answered.
28.21 went over to him and **saw** that he was terrified, so she
29. 3 The Philistine commanders **saw** them and asked, "What are
31. 5 The young man **saw** that Saul was dead, so he too threw
2 Sam 1. 6 on Mount Gilboa, and I **saw** that Saul was leaning on his
1. 7 Then he turned round, **saw** me, and called to me.
2.26 Can't you **see** that in the end there will be nothing but
6.16 out of the window and **saw** King David dancing and jumping
7.19 And you let a man **see** this, Sovereign Lord!
10. 9 Joab **saw** that the enemy troops would attack him in front
10.11 said to him, "If you **see** that the Syrians are defeating me,
10.14 When the Ammonites **saw** the Syrians running away, they
11. 2 he walked about up there, he **saw** a woman having a bath.
12.11 You will **see** it when I take your wives from you and
12.12 this happen in broad daylight for all Israel to **see.'"**
13. 5 food here where I can **see** her, and then serve it to
13. 6 cakes here where I can **see** her, and then serve them to
13. 8 it, and made some cakes there where he could **see** her.
13.20 When her brother Absalom **saw** her, he asked,
13.34 the soldier on sentry duty **saw** a large crowd coming down the
13.34 He went to the king and reported what he had **seen.**
14.24 "I don't want to **see** him," the king said.
15.25 let me come back to **see** it and the place where it
17.17 because they did not dare to be **seen** entering the city.
17.18 one day a boy happened to **see** them, and he told Absalom;
17.23 When Ahithophel **saw** that his advice had not been followed,
18.10 One of David's men **saw** him and reported to Joab,
18.10 "Sir, I **saw** Absalom hanging in an oak-tree!"
18.11 Joab answered, "If you **saw** him, why didn't you kill
18.21 Sudanese slave, "Go and tell the king what you have **seen."**
18.24 he looked out and **saw** a man running alone.
18.26 Then the watchman **saw** another man running alone, and he
18.27 The watchman said, "I can **see** that the first man runs
18.29 officer Joab sent me, I **saw** a great commotion, but I
20.12 Joab's man **saw** that everybody was stopping, so he dragged
24. 3 they are now, and may you live to **see** him do it.
24.17 David **saw** the angel who was killing the people, and
24.20 Araunah looked down and **saw** the king and his officials
1 Kgs 1.48 succeed me as king, and has let me live to **see** it!'"
3.21 was going to feed my baby, I **saw** that it was dead.
3.21 at it more closely and **saw** that it was not my child."
6.18 cedar, so that the stones of the walls could not be **seen.**
8. 8 of the poles could be **seen** by anyone standing directly in
10. 4 Sheba heard Solomon's wisdom and **saw** the palace he had built.
10. 5 She **saw** the food that was served at his table, the living
10. 7 believe it until I had come and **seen** it all for myself.
10.12 none like it has ever been **seen** again.)
12.16 When the people **saw** that the king would not listen to them,
13.25 Some men passed by and **saw** the body on the road, with
13.25 They went on into Bethel and reported what they had **seen.**
16.18 When Zimri **saw** that the city had fallen, he went into
17.10 to the gate of the town, he **saw** a widow gathering firewood.
18.17 When Ahab **saw** him, he said, "So there you are—the worst
18.39 When the people **saw** this, they threw themselves on the
18.43 The servant went and returned, saying, "I didn't **see** anything."
18.44 he returned and said, "I **saw** a little cloud no bigger than
19. 6 He looked round, and **saw** a loaf of bread and a jar
21.20 When Ahab **saw** Elijah, he said, "Have you caught up with me,
22.17 Micaiah answered, "I can **see** the army of Israel scattered
22.19 I **saw** the Lord sitting on his throne in heaven, with all
22.32 So when they **saw** King Jehoshaphat, they all thought that
2 Kgs 2.10 will receive it if you **see** me as I am being taken
2.10 if you don't **see** me, you won't receive it."
2.12 Elisha **saw** it and cried out to Elijah, "My father,
2.12 And he never **saw** Elijah again.
2.15 The fifty prophets from Jericho **saw** him and said, "The
3.17 Even though you will not **see** any rain or wind, this
4.25 Elisha **saw** her coming while she was still some distance away,
4.32 alone into the room and **saw** the boy lying dead on the
5.21 When Naaman **saw** a man running after him, he got down from
6.15 out of the house, and **saw** the Syrian troops with their
6.17 Then he prayed, "O Lord, open his eyes and let him **see!"**
6.17 Elisha's servant looked up and **saw** the hillside covered with
6.20 Elisha prayed, "Open their eyes, Lord, and let them **see."**
6.20 their sight, and they **saw** that they were inside Samaria.
6.21 When the king of Israel **saw** the Syrians, he asked Elisha,
6.30 close to the wall could **see** that he was wearing sackcloth
7. 2 "You will **see** it happen, but you will never eat any of
7.10 "We went to the Syrian camp and didn't **see** or hear anybody;
7.15 all along the road they **saw** the clothes and equipment that
7.19 Elisha had replied, "You will **see** it happen, but you will
9.17 the watch-tower at Jezreel **saw** Jehu and his men approaching.
9.17 "I **see** some men riding up!"
9.26 'I **saw** the murder of Naboth and his sons yesterday.
9.27 King Ahaziah **saw** what happened, so he fled in his
10.16 saying, "Come with me and **see** for yourself how devoted
11.14 There she **saw** the new king standing by the column at the
13.21 one of those bands was **seen,** and the people threw the corpse
14.26 The Lord **saw** the terrible suffering of the Israelites;
16.10 meet Emperor Tiglath Pileser, he **saw** the altar there and
16.12 return from Damascus, Ahaz **saw** that the altar was finished,
20. 5 ancestor David, have heard your prayer and **seen** your tears.

2 Kgs 20.15 "What did they **see** in the palace?"
20.15 "They **saw** everything.
23.16 Then Josiah looked round and **saw** some tombs there on the hill;
23.16 King Josiah looked round and **saw** the tomb of the prophet who
1 Chr 10. 5 The young man **saw** that Saul was dead, so he too threw
15.29 out of the window and **saw** King David dancing and leaping for
19.10 Joab **saw** that the enemy troops would attack him in
19.12 said to him, "If you **see** that the Syrians are defeating me,
19.15 When the Ammonites **saw** the Syrians running away, they
21.16 David **saw** the angel standing in mid air, holding his
21.20 threshing wheat, and when they **saw** the angel, the sons ran
21.21 As soon as Araunah **saw** King David approaching, he left
21.28 David **saw** by this that the Lord had answered his prayer,
29.17 to you, and I have **seen** how your people who are gathered
2 Chr 5. 9 of the poles could be **seen** by anyone standing directly in
6.13 knelt down where everyone could **see** him, and raised his hands
7. 3 When the people of Israel **saw** the fire fall from heaven
9. 3 Sheba heard Solomon's wisdom and **saw** the palace he had built.
9. 4 She **saw** the food that was served at his table, the
9. 6 believe what they told me until I came and **saw** for myself.
9.11 like that had ever been **seen** before in the land of Judah.)
10.16 When the people **saw** that the king would not listen to them,
12. 7 When the Lord **saw** this, he spoke again to Shemaiah and
13.14 The Judaeans looked round and **saw** that they were surrounded.
15. 9 kingdom, because they had **seen** that the Lord was with him.
18.16 Micaiah answered, "I can **see** the army of Israel
18.18 I **saw** the Lord sitting on his throne in heaven, with all
18.31 So when they **saw** King Jehoshaphat, they all thought that
18.32 The chariot commanders **saw** that he was not the king of Israel,
20.17 you will **see** the Lord give you victory.
20.24 looked towards the enemy and **saw** that they were all lying on
23.13 There she **saw** the new king at the temple entrance,
24.20 stood where the people could **see** him and called out, "The
24.22 called out, "May the Lord **see** what you are doing and punish
31. 8 King Hezekiah and his officials **saw** how much had been given,
32. 2 When Hezekiah **saw** that Sennacherib intended to attack Jerusalem
Ezra 3.12 and heads of clans had **seen** the first Temple, and as they
Neh 2. 1 He had never **seen** me look sad before, [2]so he asked, "Why
2.17 now I said to them, **"See** what trouble we are in because
4.11 enemies thought we would not **see** them or know what was
4.14 I **saw** that the people were worried, so I said to them
9. 9 "You **saw** how our ancestors suffered in Egypt;
13.15 At that time I **saw** people in Judah pressing juice from
Esth 2.15 Esther—admired by everyone who **saw** her.
4.11 to the inner courtyard and **sees** the king without being summoned,
5. 2 When the king **saw** Queen Esther standing outside,
5. 9 But then he **saw** Mordecai at the entrance of the palace, and
5.13 me as long as I **see** that Jew Mordecai sitting at the
6. 9 '**See** how the king rewards a man he wishes to honour!'"
6.11 **"See** how the king rewards a man he wishes to honour!"
Job 2.12 a long way off they **saw** Job, but did not recognize him.
2.13 saying a word, because they **saw** how much he was suffering.
4. 8 I have **seen** people plough fields of evil and sow
4.16 I could **see** something standing there;
5. 3 I have **seen** fools who looked secure, but I called down a
6.21 those streams to me, you **see** my fate and draw back in
7. 8 You **see** me now, but never again.
9.11 God passes by, but I cannot **see** him.
10. 4 Do you **see** things as we do?
10.18 I should have died before anyone **saw** me.
11.11 he **sees** all their evil deeds.
17.15 Who **sees** any?
19. 6 Can't you **see** it is God who has done this?
19.18 Children despise me and laugh when they **see** me.
19.26 eaten by disease, while still in this body I will **see** God.
19.27 I will **see** him with my own eyes, and he will not
20. 8 a dream, like a vision at night, and never be **seen** again.
20.17 He will not live to **see** rivers of olive-oil or streams
22.11 so dark that you cannot **see,** and a flood overwhelms you.
22.14 thick clouds keep him from **seeing,** as he walks on the dome
22.19 and innocent men laugh when they **see** the wicked punished.
23. 9 the north and the south, but still I have not **seen** him.
24.15 he covers his face so that no one can **see** him.
27.12 But no, after all, you have **seen** for yourselves;
28. 7 No hawk **sees** the roads to the mines, And no vulture ever
28.21 No living creature can **see** it, Not even a bird in flight.
28.24 **sees** the ends of the earth, **Sees** everything under the sky.
28.27 It was then he **saw** wisdom and tested its worth— He
29. 8 aside as soon as they **saw** me, and old men stood up
29.11 Everyone who **saw** me or heard of me had good things to
31. 4 he **sees** every step I take.
31. 6 me on honest scales, and he will **see** how innocent I am.
31.35 down so that I could **see** them, [36]I would wear them proudly
32. 5 When he **saw** that the three men could not answer Job, he
33.21 you can **see** all his bones;
34. 7 Have you ever **seen** anyone like this man Job?
34.26 punishes sinners where all can **see** it,
35. 5 **See** how high the clouds are!
35.13 Almighty God does not **see** or hear them.
35.14 Job, you say you can't **see** God;
36. 4 you **see** before you a truly wise man.
36.25 Everyone has **seen** what he has done;
37.22 A golden glow is **seen** in the north, and the glory of
41. 9 Anyone who **sees** Leviathan loses courage and falls to the ground.
42. 5 told me, but now I have **seen** you with my own eyes.
42.16 forty years after this, long enough to **see** his grandchildren
Ps 6. 7 I can hardly **see;**
7.14 **See** how wicked people think up evil;
8. 1 O Lord, our Lord, your greatness is **seen** in all the world!
8. 9 O Lord, our Lord, your greatness is **seen** in all the world!

Ps 9.13 **See** the sufferings my enemies cause me!
10.11 He has closed his eyes and will never **see** me!"
10.14 But you do **see;**
17.15 But I will **see** you, because I have done no wrong;
19.12 No one can **see** his own errors;
22. 7 All who **see** me jeer at me;
22.17 All my bones can be **seen.**
23. 5 prepare a banquet for me, where all my enemies can **see** me;
25.19 **See** how many enemies I have;
25.19 **see** how much they hate me.
27.13 that I will live to **see** the Lord's goodness in this present
31. 7 You **see** my suffering;
31.11 when they **see** me in the street, they run away.
33.13 The Lord looks down from heaven and **sees** all mankind.
35.21 They accuse me, shouting, "We **saw** what you did!"
35.22 But you, O Lord, have **seen** this.
35.27 May those who want to **see** me acquitted shout for joy and
36. 9 of all life, and because of your light we **see** the light.
36.12 **See** where evil men have fallen.
37.25 time, but I have never **seen** a good man abandoned by the
37.34 you the land, and you will **see** the wicked driven out.
40. 3 Many who **see** this will take warning and will put their trust
40.12 sins have caught up with me, and I can no longer **see;**
44.13 Our neighbours **see** what you did to us, and they mock us
46. 8 Come and **see** what the Lord has done.
46. 8 **See** what amazing things he has done on earth.
48. 5 But when they **saw** it, they were amazed;
48. 8 done, and now we have **seen** it in the city of our
49.10 Anyone can **see** that even wise men die, as well as
49.13 **See** what happens to those who trust in themselves, the
50. 4 heaven and earth as witnesses to **see** him judge his people.
50.18 of every thief you **see** and you associate with adulterers.
52. 6 Righteous people will **see** this and be afraid;
54. 7 from all my troubles, and I have **seen** my enemies defeated.
55. 9 I **see** violence and riots in the city, [10] surrounding it day
58. 8 they be like a baby born dead that never **sees** the light.
58.10 The righteous will be glad when they **see** sinners punished;
59. 5 **see** for yourself, God of Israel!
59.10 he will let me **see** my enemies defeated.
63. 2 Let me **see** you in the sanctuary;
63. 2 let me **see** how mighty and glorious you are.
64. 5 "No one can **see** them," they say.
64. 8 all who **see** them will shake their heads.
66. 5 Come and **see** what God has done, his wonderful acts among men.
68.24 your march of triumph is **seen** by all, the procession of God,
69.19 you **see** all my enemies.
69.32 When the oppressed **see** this, they will be glad;
73. 3 of the proud when I **saw** that things go well for the
77.16 When the waters **saw** you, O God, they were afraid, and
77.19 you crossed the deep sea, but your footprints could not be **seen.**
78.11 what he had done, the miracles they had **seen** him perform.
78.59 God was angry when he **saw** it, so he rejected his people
79.10 Let us **see** you punish the nations for shedding the blood of
84. 7 they will **see** the God of gods on Zion.
86.17 will be ashamed when they **see** that you have given me comfort
88.12 Are your miracles **seen** in that place of darkness or your
90. 8 sins before you, our secret sins where you can **see** them.
90.16 Let us, your servants, **see** your mighty deeds;
90.16 let our descendants **see** your glorious might.
91. 8 You will look and **see** how the wicked are punished.
92.11 I have **seen** the defeat of my enemies and heard the cries
94. 7 They say, "The Lord does not **see** us;
94. 9 He made our eyes—can't he **see?**
95. 9 and tried me, although they had **seen** what I did for them.
97. 4 the earth **sees** it and trembles.
97. 6 proclaim his righteousness, and all the nations **see** his glory.
98. 3 All people everywhere have **seen** the victory of our God.
103. 7 let the people of Israel **see** his mighty deeds.
103.16 on it, and it is gone— no one **sees** it again.
106. 5 Let me **see** the prosperity of your people and share in the
107.24 They **saw** what the Lord can do, his wonderful acts on the
107.42 The righteous **see** this and are glad, but all the wicked
109.25 When people **see** me, they laugh at me;
112. 8 he is certain to **see** his enemies defeated.
112.10 The wicked **see** this and are angry;
113. 6 but he bends down to **see** the heavens and the earth.
115. 5 They have mouths, but cannot speak, and eyes, but cannot **see.**
118. 7 the Lord who helps me, and I will **see** my enemies defeated.
119.18 eyes, so that I may **see** the wonderful truths in your law.
119.53 When I **see** the wicked breaking your law, I am filled
119.74 will be glad when they **see** me, because I trust in your
119.159 **See** how I love your instructions, Lord.
119.168 you **see** everything I do.
128. 5 May you **see** Jerusalem prosper all the days of your life!
128. 6 May you live to **see** your grandchildren!
135.16 They have mouths, but cannot speak, and eyes, but cannot **see.**
139. 3 You **see** me, whether I am working or resting;
139.16 that I was there— [16] you **saw** me before I was born.
142. 4 I look beside me, I **see** that there is no one to
Prov 4.19 They fall, but cannot **see** what they have stumbled over.
5.21 The Lord **sees** everything you do.
7. 7 of my house, [7] and I **saw** many inexperienced young men, but
15. 3 The Lord **sees** what happens everywhere;
20. 8 The king sits in judgement and knows evil when he **sees** it.
20.12 has given us eyes to **see** with and ears to listen with.
22. 3 Sensible people will **see** trouble coming and avoid it,
25. 8 be too quick to go to court about something you have **seen.**
26.26 his hatred, but everyone will **see** the evil things he does.
27.12 Sensible people will **see** trouble coming and avoid it,
27.19 your own face that you **see** reflected in the water
27.19 and it is your own self that you **see** in your heart.
Prov 29.16 But the righteous will live to **see** the downfall of such men.
Ecc 1. 8 Our eyes can never **see** enough to be satisfied;
1.14 I have **seen** everything done in this world, and I tell you,
2.14 Wise men can **see** where they are going, and fools cannot."
4. 3 been born, who have never **seen** the injustice that goes on in
5.13 Here is a terrible thing that I have **seen** in this world:
6. 5 It never **sees** the light of day or knows what life is
7.15 My life has been useless, but in it I have **seen** everything.
8. 9 I **saw** all this when I thought about the things that are
8.10 Yes, I have **seen** wicked men buried and in their graves,
9. 1 hard about all this and **saw** that God controls the actions of
9.13 There is something else I **saw,** a good example of how
10. 5 is an injustice I have **seen** in the world—an injustice caused
10. 7 I have **seen** slaves on horseback while noblemen go on foot
12. 3 to chew your food, and your eyes too dim to **see** clearly.
Song 2.14 Let me **see** your lovely face and hear your enchanting voice.
3. 3 The watchmen patrolling the city **saw** me.
3.11 Women of Zion, come and **see** King Solomon.
6.11 among the almond-trees to **see** the young plants in the valley,
6.11 to **see** the new leaves on the vines
7.12 look at the vines to **see** whether they've started to grow,
Is 1.16 Stop all this evil that I **see** you doing.
5.19 do what he says he will, so that we can **see** it.
6. 1 In the year that King Uzziah died, I **saw** the Lord.
6. 5 my own eyes, I have **seen** the King, the Lord Almighty!"
6.10 eyes blind, so that they cannot **see** or hear or understand.
8.22 the ground, but they will **see** nothing but trouble and darkness,
9. 2 The people who walked in darkness have **seen** a great light.
19.16 tremble in terror when they **see** that the Lord Almighty
21. 2 I have **seen** a vision of cruel events, a vision of betrayal
21. 3 What I **saw** and heard in the vision has filled me with
21. 6 and post a sentry, and tell him to report what he **sees.**
21. 7 If he **sees** men coming on horseback, two by two, and men
24.23 Mount Zion, and the leaders of the people will **see** his glory.
29.15 and think no one will **see** them or know what they are
29.18 have been living in darkness, will open their eyes and **see.**
29.23 When you **see** the children that I will give you, then you
30.17 will run away when you **see** one enemy soldier, and five
30.27 The Lord's power and glory can be **seen** in the distance.
33.17 Once again you will **see** a king ruling in splendour over
33.19 You will no longer **see** any arrogant foreigners who speak a
35. 2 Everyone will **see** the Lord's splendour, see his greatness
35. 5 The blind will be able to **see,** and the deaf will hear.
38. 5 ancestor David, have heard your prayer and **seen** your tears;
38.11 I would never again **see** the Lord Or any living person.
39. 4 "What did they **see** in the palace?"
39. 4 "They **saw** everything.
40. 5 of the Lord will be revealed, and all mankind will **see** it.
40.26 Who created the stars you **see?**
41. 5 "The people of distant lands have **seen** what I have done;
41.20 People will **see** this and know that I, the Lord, have
42.20 Israel, you have **seen** so much, but what has it meant to
43.19 It is happening already—you can **see** it now!
47. 3 People will **see** you naked;
47. 3 they will **see** you humbled and shamed.
47.10 you thought that no one could **see** you.
49. 7 "Kings will **see** you released and will rise to show their respect;
49. 7 princes also will **see** it, and they will bow low to honour
49.18 Look around and **see** what is happening!
52. 7 How wonderful it is to **see** a messenger coming
52. 8 They can **see** with their own eyes the return of the Lord
52.10 he will save his people, and all the world will **see** it.
52.14 Many people were shocked when they **saw** him;
52.15 They will **see** and understand something they had never known."
53. 1 Who could have **seen** the Lord's hand in this?
53.10 And so he will **see** his descendants;
57.18 "I have **seen** how they acted, but I will heal them.
59.15 The Lord has **seen** this, and he is displeased that there is
59.16 He is astonished to **see** that there is no one to help
60. 4 Look around you and **see** what is happening:
60. 5 You will **see** this and be filled with joy;
61. 9 Everyone who **sees** them will know That they are a people whom
62. 2 Jerusalem, the nations will **see** you victorious!
62. 2 All their kings will **see** your glory.
63. 5 amazed when I looked and **saw** that there was no one to
64. 1 The mountains would **see** you and shake with fear.
64. 3 the mountains **saw** you and shook with fear.
64. 4 No one has ever **seen** or heard of a God like you,
66. 5 his greatness and save you, so that we may **see** you rejoice.'
66. 8 Has anyone ever **seen** or heard of such a thing?
66.14 When you **see** this happen, you will be glad;
66.18 they come together, they will **see** what my power can do
66.19 have not heard of my fame or **seen** my greatness and power:
66.24 "As they leave, they will **see** the dead bodies of those
Jer 1.11 The Lord asked me, "Jeremiah, what do you **see?"**
1.12 said, "and I am watching to **see** that my words come true."
1.13 "What else do you **see?"**
1.13 I answered, "I **see** a pot boiling in the north,
2.10 You will **see** that nothing like this has ever happened before.
2.22 strongest soap, I would still **see** the stain of your guilt.
2.23 **see** what you have done.
3. 6 to me, "Have you **seen** what Israel, that unfaithful woman,
3. 7 did not return, and her unfaithful sister Judah **saw** it all.
3. 8 Judah also **saw** that I divorced Israel and sent her away
4.21 How long must I **see** the battle raging and hear the
4.25 I **saw** that there were no people;
5. 1 **See** for yourselves!
5.21 have eyes, but cannot **see,** and have ears, but cannot hear.
6. 7 sickness and wounds are all I **see.**
7.11 I have **seen** what you are doing.
7.12 chose to be worshipped, and **see** what I did to it because

Jer 7.17 Don't you **see** what they are doing in the cities of Judah
12. 3 you **see** what I do, and how I love you.
12. 4 people who say, 'God doesn't **see** what we are doing.' "
13. 7 I had hidden them, I **saw** that they were ruined and were
13.27 He has **seen** you do the things he hates.
13.27 He has **seen** you go after pagan gods on the hills and
14.18 I **see** the bodies of men killed
14.18 when I go into the towns, I **see** people starving to death.
16. 9 The people here will live to **see** this happen.
16.17 I **see** everything they do.
18. 3 So I went there and **saw** the potter working at his wheel.
18.16 All who pass by will be shocked at what they **see**;
20. 4 your friends, and you will **see** them all killed by the swords
20.12 So let me **see** you take revenge on my enemies,
22.10 to return, never again to **see** the land where he was born.
22.12 have taken him, and he will never again **see** this land."
22.17 But you can only **see** your selfish interests;
22.27 You will long to **see** this country again, but you will
23.13 I have **seen** the sin of Samaria's prophets:
23.14 But I have **seen** the prophets in Jerusalem do even worse:
23.24 No one can hide where I cannot **see** him.
24. 3 Then the Lord said to me, "Jeremiah, what do you **see?"**
29.18 the nations of the world will be horrified at what they **see.**
29.31 He will not live to **see** the good things that I am
30. 6 Why then do I **see** every man with his hands on his
32. 4 he will **see** him face to face and will speak to him
32.19 you **see** everything that people do, and you reward them
32.24 You can **see** that all you have said has come true.
34. 3 You will **see** him face to face and talk to him in
38.22 In it I **saw** all the women left in Judah's royal palace
39. 4 Zedekiah and all his soldiers **saw** what was happening, they
39.16 And when this happens, you will be there to **see** it.
41.13 When Ishmael's prisoners **saw** Johanan and the leaders of
42.18 You will never **see** this place again.' "
43. 9 the city, and let some of the Israelites **see** you do it.
44. 2 yourselves have **seen** the destruction I brought on Jerusalem
46. 5 "But what do I **see?"**
51.24 The Lord says, "You will **see** me repay Babylonia and its
51.37 one will live there, and all who **see** it will be terrified.
Lam 1. 9 Her uncleanness was easily **seen,** but she showed no concern
1.10 She **saw** them enter the Temple itself, Where the Lord had
1.11 "**see** me in my misery."
3.50 Until the Lord looks down from heaven and **sees** us.
3.51 heart is grieved when I **see** what has happened to the women
5. 1 Look at us, and **see** our disgrace.
5.17 very hearts and can hardly **see** through our tears, [18]because Mount
Ezek 1. 1 The sky opened, and I **saw** a vision of God.
1. 4 I looked up and **saw** a storm coming from the north.
1. 5 centre of the storm, I **saw** what looked like four living
1.15 the four creatures, I **saw** four wheels touching the ground,
1.28 When I **saw** this, I fell face downwards on the ground.
2. 9 I **saw** a hand stretched out towards me, and it was holding
2.10 unrolled the scroll, and I **saw** that there was writing on
3.15 days I stayed there, overcome by what I had **seen** and heard.
3.23 the valley, and there I **saw** the glory of the Lord,
3.23 just as I had **seen** it beside the River Chebar.
4.12 bread on the fire, and eat it where everyone can **see** you."
5. 8 will pass judgement on you where all the nations can **see** it.
8. 2 I looked up and **saw** a vision of a fiery human form.
8. 4 There I **saw** the dazzling light that shows the presence of
8. 4 God, just as I had **seen** it when I was by the
8. 5 entrance of the gateway I **saw** the idol that was an outrage
8. 6 God said to me, "Mortal man, do you **see** what is happening?
8. 6 You will **see** even more disgraceful things than this."
8.12 me, "Mortal man, do you **see** what the Israelite leaders are
8.12 'The Lord doesn't **see** us!
8.13 me, "You are going to **see** them do even more disgusting
8.15 He asked, "Mortal man, do you **see** that?
8.15 You will **see** even more disgusting things."
8.17 The Lord said to me, "Mortal man, do you **see** that?
8.17 disgusting things you have **seen** here and with spreading violence
9. 9 have abandoned their country and that I don't **see** them.
10. 8 I **saw** that each creature had what looked like a human hand
10. 9 I also **saw** that there were four wheels, all alike,
10.13 were the same as those I had **seen** in my first vision.
10.15 the same creatures that I had **seen** by the River Chebar.)
10.20 same creatures which I had **seen** beneath the God of Israel at
10.22 exactly like the faces I had **seen** by the River Chebar.
11. 1 There near the gate I **saw** twenty-five men, including
12. 2 They have eyes, but they **see** nothing;
12. 3 Let everyone **see** you leaving and going to another place.
12. 4 exile, so that they can **see** you, and then let them watch
12. 6 eyes covered, so that you can't **see** where you are going.
12.12 He will cover his eyes and not **see** where he is going.
12.13 city of Babylon, where he will die without having **seen** it.
13. 7 Those visions you **see** are false, and the predictions you
14.22 **See** how evil they are, and be convinced that the punishment
16. 6 "Then I passed by and **saw** you squirming in your own blood.
16. 8 I passed by again, I **saw** that the time had come for
16.37 I will strip off your clothes and let them **see** you naked.
16.41 houses down and let crowds of women **see** your punishment.
18.14 He **sees** all the sins his father practised, but does not
18.23 "No, I would rather **see** him repent and live.
19. 5 She waited until she **saw** all hope was gone.
19.11 everyone **saw** how leafy and tall it was.
20.14 the nations which had **seen** me lead Israel out of Egypt.
20.22 the nations which had **seen** me bring Israel out of Egypt.
20.28 When they **saw** the high hills and green trees, they offered
20.41 that you burn, and the nations will **see** that I am holy.
20.48 They will all **see** that I, the Lord, set it on fire
21.29 The visions that you **see** are false, and the predictions you
Ezek 22.28 They **see** false visions and make false predictions.
23.11 "Even though her sister Oholibah **saw** this, she was
23.13 I **saw** that she was completely immoral, that the second
23.16 As soon as she **saw** them, she was filled with lust and
25. 3 You were delighted to **see** my Temple profaned,
25. 3 to **see** the land of Israel devastated,
25. 3 to **see** the people of Judah go into
28.18 All who look at you now **see** you reduced to ashes.
33. 3 When he **sees** the enemy approaching, he sounds the alarm to
33. 6 If, however, the watchman **sees** the enemy coming and does
33.11 I would rather **see** him stop sinning and live.
36.15 to the nations mocking it or **see** the peoples sneer at it.
36.34 to walk by your fields **saw** how overgrown and wild they were,
37. 2 the valley, and I could **see** that there were very many bones
37.20 in your hand the two sticks and let the people **see** them.
39.21 "I will let the nations **see** my glory and show them how
40. 2 I **saw** in front of me a group of buildings that looked
40. 3 took me closer, and I **saw** a man who shone like bronze.
40. 4 You are to tell the people of Israel everything you **see."**
40. 5 What I **saw** was the Temple, and there was a wall round
40.24 took me to the south side, and there we **saw** another gateway.
41. 7 so the temple walls, when **seen** from the outside, seemed to
41. 8 I **saw** that there was a terrace two and a half metres
43. 2 faces east, [2]and there I **saw** coming from the east the
43. 3 like the one I had **seen** when God came to destroy Jerusalem,
43. 3 and the one I **saw** by the River Chebar.
43. 5 the inner courtyard, where I **saw** that the Temple was filled
43.11 them so that they can **see** how everything is arranged and can
44. 4 As I looked, I **saw** that the Temple of the Lord was
44. 5 "Mortal man, pay attention to everything you **see** and hear.
47. 7 when I got there I **saw** that there were very many trees
Dan 2.31 in your vision you **saw** standing before you a giant statue,
2.41 You also **saw** that the feet and the toes were partly clay
2.43 You also **saw** that the iron was mixed with the clay.
2.45 You **saw** how a stone broke loose from a cliff without
3.25 "Then why do I **see** four men walking about in the fire?"
4. 5 dream and **saw** terrifying visions while I was asleep.
4.11 reached the sky and could be **seen** by everyone in the world.
4.13 about the vision, I **saw** coming down from heaven an angel,
4.20 it reached the sky, could be **seen** by everyone in the world.
5. 5 And the king **saw** the hand as it was writing.
5.23 and stone—gods that cannot **see** or hear and that do not
6.23 they pulled him up and **saw** that he had not been hurt
7. 1 Babylonia, I had a dream and **saw** a vision in the night.
7. 2 down, and this is the record [2]of what I **saw** that night:
7. 8 staring at the horns, I **saw** a little horn coming up among
7.13 vision in the night, I **saw** what looked like a human being.
7.15 The visions I **saw** alarmed me, and I was deeply disturbed.
8. 1 third year that Belshazzar was king, I **saw** a second vision.
8. 3 there beside the river I **saw** a ram that had two long
8. 6 the ram, which I had **seen** standing beside the river, and
8.13 "How long will these things that were **seen** in the vision continue?
8.16 River Ulai, "Gabriel, explain to him the meaning of what he **saw."**
8.20 "The ram you **saw** that had two horns represents the
9.18 look at us, and **see** the trouble we are in and the
9.21 Gabriel, whom I had **seen** in the earlier vision,
10. 5 I looked up and **saw** someone who was wearing linen clothes
10. 7 I was the only one who **saw** the vision.
10. 7 were with me did not **see** anything, but they were terrified
11.14 of a vision they have **seen,** but they will be defeated.
12. 5 Then I **saw** two men standing by a river, one on each
Hos 5.13 "When Israel **saw** how sick she was
5.13 and when Judah **saw** her own wounds,
6.10 I have **seen** a horrible thing in Israel:
7. 1 prosperous again, all I can **see** is their wickedness and the
7. 2 their sins surround them, and I cannot avoid **seeing** them."
9.10 When I first **saw** your ancestors,
9.10 it was like **seeing** the first ripe figs
9.13 Lord, I can **see** their children being hunted down and killed.
Joel 2.28 men will have dreams, and your young men will **see** visions.
Amos 3. 9 the hills surrounding Samaria and **see** the great disorder and the
7. 1 In it I **saw** him create a swarm of locusts just after
7. 2 In my vision I **saw** the locusts eat up every green thing
7. 3 his mind and said, "What you **saw** will not take place."
7. 4 In it I **saw** him preparing to punish his people with fire.
7. 7 In it I **saw** him standing beside a wall that had been
7. 8 He asked me, "Amos, what do you **see?"**
8. 1 In it I **saw** a basket of fruit.
8. 1 The Lord asked, "Amos, what do you **see?"**
9. 1 I **saw** the Lord standing by the altar.
Jon 2. 4 your presence and would never **see** your holy Temple again.
3.10 God **saw** what they did;
3.10 he **saw** that they had given up their wicked behaviour.
Mic 1.10 don't let them **see** you weeping.
4.11 We will **see** this city in ruins!"
7. 9 we will live to **see** him save us.
7.10 Then our enemies will **see** this and be disgraced—
7.10 We will **see** them defeated, trampled down like mud in the streets.
7.16 The nations will **see** this and be frustrated in spite of
Nah 1. 1 the account of a vision **seen** by Nahum, who was from Elkosh.
3. 5 and let the nations see you, **see** you in all your shame.
3. 7 All who **see** you will shrink back.
Hab 1. 3 Why do you make me **see** such trouble?
1. 5 round you, and you will be astonished at what you **see.**
3. 7 I **saw** the people of Cushan afraid and the people of Midian
3.10 When the mountains **saw** you, they trembled;
Hag 1. 5 Don't you **see** what is happening to you?
1. 7 Can't you **see** why this has happened?
2.15 The Lord says, "Can't you **see** what has happened to you?
2.18 **See** what is going to happen from now on.
Zech 1. 8 I **saw** an angel of the Lord riding a red horse.

Zech 1.18 In another vision I **saw** four ox horns.
2. 1 In another vision I **saw** a man with a measuring-line in his
2. 3 Then I **saw** the angel who had been speaking to me step
4. 2 "What do you **see?**"
4.10b the seven eyes of the Lord, which **see** all over the earth."
4.10 But they will **see** Zerubbabel continuing to build the Temple,
5. 1 again, and this time I **saw** a scroll flying through the air.
5. 2 The angel asked me what I **saw.**
5. 9 I looked up and **saw** two women flying towards me with
6. 1 This time I **saw** four chariots coming out from between two
9. 5 The city of Ashkelon will **see** this and be afraid.
9. 5 The city of Gaza will **see** it and suffer great pain.
9. 8 I have **seen** how my people have suffered."
Mal 1. 5 of Israel are going to **see** this with their own eyes, and
3. 1 messenger you long to **see** will come and proclaim my covenant."
3.15 As we **see** it, proud people are the ones who are happy.
3.18 Once again my people will **see** the difference between
Mt 2. 2 We **saw** his star when it came up in the east,
2. 9 they saw the same star they had **seen** in the east.
2. 9 When they **saw** it, how happy they were, what joy was theirs!
2.11 the house, and when they **saw** the child with his mother Mary,
3. 7 When John **saw** many Pharisees and Sadducees coming to him
3.16 opened to him, and he **saw** the Spirit of God coming down
4.16 The people who live in darkness will **see** a great light.
4.18 of Lake Galilee, he **saw** two brothers who were fishermen,
4.21 He went on and **saw** two other brothers, James and John,
5. 1 Jesus **saw** the crowds and went up a hill, where he sat
5. 8 they will **see** God!
5.16 so that they will **see** the good things you do
6. 1 duties in public so that people will **see** what you do.
6. 4 And your Father, who **sees** what you do in private, will
6. 5 and on the street corners, so that everyone will **see** them.
6. 6 And your Father, who **sees** what you do in private, will
6.16 appearance so that everyone will **see** that they are fasting.
6.18 And your Father, who **sees** what you do in private, will
7. 5 you will be able to **see** clearly to take the speck out
8.14 Peter's home, and there he **saw** Peter's mother-in-law sick in
8.34 they **saw** him, they begged him to leave their territory.
9. 2 When Jesus **saw** how much faith they had, he said to the
9. 8 When the people **saw** it, they were afraid, and praised God
9. 9 as he walked along, he **saw** a tax collector, named Matthew,
9.11 Some Pharisees **saw** this and asked his disciples, "Why
9.22 Jesus turned round and **saw** her, and said, "Courage, my
9.23 When he **saw** the musicians for the funeral and the people
9.33 "We have never **seen** anything like this in Israel!"
9.36 As he **saw** the crowds, his heart was filled with pity
11. 4 "Go back and tell John what you are hearing and **seeing:**
11. 5 the blind can **see,** the lame can walk, those who suffer
11. 7 out to John in the desert, what did you expect to **see?**
11. 8 What did you go out to **see?**
11. 9 Tell me, what did you go out to **see?**
11. 9 Yes indeed, but you **saw** much more than a prophet.
12. 2 When the Pharisees **saw** this, they said to Jesus, "Look,
12.22 healed the man, so that he was able to talk and **see.**
12.38 "Teacher," they said, "we want to **see** you perform a miracle."
13.13 they look, but do not **see,** and they listen, but do not
13.14 and look, but not **see,** [15]because their minds are dull,
13.15 Otherwise, their eyes would **see,** their ears would hear,
13.16 Your eyes **see** and your ears hear.
13.17 people wanted very much to **see** what you see, but they could
14.14 the boat, and when he **saw** the large crowd, his heart was
14.26 When they **saw** him walking on the water, they were terrified.
15.31 people were amazed as they **saw** the dumb speaking, the
15.31 the crippled made whole, the lame walking, and the blind **seeing;**
16.28 not die until they have **seen** the Son of Man come as
17. 3 Then the three disciples **saw** Moses and Elijah talking with Jesus.
17. 8 So they looked up and **saw** no one there but Jesus.
17. 9 about this vision you have **seen** until the Son of Man has
18.31 When the other servants **saw** what had happened, they were
20. 3 nine o'clock and **saw** some men standing there doing nothing,
20. 6 market-place and **saw** some other men still standing there.
20.34 at once they were able to **see,** and they followed him.
21.15 Law became angry when they **saw** the wonderful things he was
21.19 He **saw** a fig-tree by the side of the road and went
21.20 The disciples **saw** this and were astounded.
21.32 Even when you **saw** this, you did not later change your minds
21.38 But when the tenants **saw** the son, they said to themselves,
22.11 look at the guests and **saw** a man who was not wearing
23. 5 They do everything so that people will **see** them.
23.39 tell you, you will never **see** me again until you say, 'God
24.15 "You will **see** 'The Awful Horror' of which the prophet Daniel spoke.
24.30 earth will weep as they **see** the Son of Man coming on
24.33 the same way, when you **see** all these things, you will know
25.37 'When, Lord, did we ever **see** you hungry and feed you, or
25.38 When did we ever **see** you a stranger and welcome you in
25.39 When did we ever **see** you sick or in prison, and visit
25.44 'When, Lord, did we ever **see** you hungry or thirsty or a
26. 8 The disciples **saw** this and became angry.
26.58 down with the guards to **see** how it would all come out.
26.64 this time on you will **see** the Son of Man sitting on
26.71 Another servant-girl **saw** him and said to the men there, "He
27.24 When Pilate **saw** that it was no use to go on,
27.43 Well, then, let us **see** if God wants to save him now!"
27.49 others said, "Wait, let us **see** if Elijah is coming to save
27.53 they went into the Holy City, where many people **saw** them.
27.54 him who were watching Jesus **saw** the earthquake and
28. 6 Come here and **see** the place where he was lying.
28. 7 there you will **see** him!'
28.10 my brothers to go to Galilee, and there they will **see** me."
28.17 When they **saw** him, they worshipped him,
Mk 1.10 out of the water, he **saw** heaven opening and the Spirit
1.16 he **saw** two fishermen, Simon and his brother
1.19 farther on and **saw** two other brothers, James and John,
1.20 As soon as Jesus **saw** them, he called them;
2. 5 **Seeing** how much faith they had, Jesus said to the paralysed man,
2.12 God, saying, "We have never **seen** anything like this!"
2.14 As he walked along, he **saw** a tax collector, Levi
2.16 the Law, who were Pharisees, **saw** that Jesus was eating with
3. 2 they watched him closely to **see** whether he would heal the
3.11 had evil spirits in them **saw** him, they would fall down
4.12 so that, 'They may look and look, yet not **see;**
5. 6 He was some distance away when he **saw** Jesus;
5.14 People went out to **see** what had happened, [15]and when they
5.15 they came to Jesus, they **saw** the man who used to have
5.16 Those who had **seen** it told the people what had happened
5.22 synagogue, arrived, and when he **saw** Jesus, he threw himself
5.31 His disciples answered, "You **see** how the people are crowding you;
5.32 But Jesus kept looking round to **see** who had done it.
5.38 at Jairus' house, where Jesus **saw** the confusion and heard
6.33 Many people, however, **saw** them leave and knew at once
6.34 out of the boat, he **saw** this large crowd, and his heart
6.38 Go and **see."**
6.48 He **saw** that his disciples were straining at the oars,
6.49 to pass them by, [49]but they **saw** him walking on the water.
6.50 They were all terrified when they **saw** him.
8.18 You have eyes—can't you **see?**
8.23 his hands on him and asked him, "Can you **see** anything?"
8.24 and said, "Yes, I can **see** people, but they look like trees
8.25 his eyesight returned, and he **saw** everything clearly.
9. 1 not die until they have **seen** the Kingdom of God come with
9. 4 Then the three disciples **saw** Elijah and Moses talking with Jesus.
9. 8 They took a quick look round but did not **see** anyone else;
9. 9 tell anyone what you have **seen,** until the Son of Man has
9.14 rest of the disciples, they **saw** a large crowd round them and
9.15 When the people **saw** Jesus, they were greatly surprised,
9.20 As soon as the spirit **saw** Jesus, it threw the boy into
9.38 said to him, "Teacher, we **saw** a man who was driving out
10.51 "Teacher," the blind man answered, "I want to **see** again."
10.52 once he was able to **see** and followed Jesus on the road.
11.13 He **saw** in the distance a fig-tree covered with leaves,
11.13 so he went to **see** if he could find any figs
11.20 as they walked along the road, they **saw** the fig-tree.
12.15 But Jesus **saw** through their trick and answered, "Why
12.15 Bring a silver coin, and let me **see** it."
12.28 He **saw** that Jesus had given the Sadducees a good answer, so
13. 2 Jesus answered, "You **see** these great buildings?
13.14 "You will **see** 'The Awful Horror' standing in the place
13.29 the same way, when you **see** these things happening, you will
14.62 Jesus, "and you will all **see** the Son of Man seated on
14.67 When she **saw** Peter warming himself, she looked straight
14.69 The servant-girl **saw** him there and began to repeat to the bystanders,
15.32 Let us **see** the Messiah, the king of Israel, come down
15.36 Let us **see** if Elijah is coming to bring him down from
15.39 standing there in front of the cross **saw** how Jesus had died.
15.47 of Joseph were watching and **saw** where the body of Jesus was
16. 3 Then they looked up and **saw** that the stone had already been
16. 5 entered the tomb, where they **saw** a young man sitting on the
16. 7 there you will **see** him, just as he told you.' "
16.11 alive and that she had **seen** him, they did not believe her.
16.14 were too stubborn to believe those who had **seen** him alive.
Lk 1. 2 been told by those who **saw** these things from the beginning
1.12 When Zechariah **saw** him, he was alarmed and felt afraid.
1.22 so they knew that he had **seen** a vision in the Temple.
2.15 "Let's go to Bethlehem and **see** this thing that has happened,
2.16 found Mary and Joseph and **saw** the baby lying in the manger.
2.17 When the shepherds **saw** him, they told them what the
2.20 singing praises to God for all they had heard and **seen;**
2.26 not die before he had **seen** the Lord's promised Messiah.
2.30 my own eyes I have **seen** your salvation, [31]which you have
2.48 parents were astonished when they **saw** him, and his mother
3. 6 All mankind will **see** God's salvation!' "
5. 2 He **saw** two boats pulled up on the beach;
5. 8 When Simon Peter **saw** what had happened, he fell on his
5.12 When he **saw** Jesus, he threw himself down and begged him,
5.20 When Jesus **saw** how much faith they had, he said to the
5.26 God, saying, "What marvellous things we have **seen** today!"
5.27 this, Jesus went out and **saw** a tax collector named Levi,
6. 7 they watched him closely to **see** if he would heal on the
6.42 your eye,' yet cannot even **see** the log in your own eye?
6.42 you will be able to **see** clearly to take the speck out
7.13 When the Lord **saw** her, his heart was filled with pity
7.22 "Go back and tell John what you have **seen** and heard:
7.22 the blind can **see,** the lame can walk, those who suffer from
7.24 out to John in the desert, what did you expect to **see?**
7.25 What did you go out to **see?**
7.26 Tell me, what did you go out to **see?**
7.26 Yes indeed, but you **saw** much more than a prophet.
7.39 When the Pharisee **saw** this, he said to himself, "If
7.44 to the woman and said to Simon, "Do you **see** this woman?
8.10 they may look but not **see,** and listen but not understand.
8.16 so that people will **see** the light as they come in.
8.20 "Your mother and brothers are standing outside and want to **see** you."
8.28 When he **saw** Jesus, he gave a loud cry, threw himself
8.34 taking care of the pigs **saw** what happened, so they ran off
8.35 People went out to **see** what had happened, and when they
8.36 Those who had **seen** it told the people how the man had
8.47 The woman **saw** that she had been found out, so she came
9. 9 And he kept trying to **see** Jesus.

Lk 9.27 who will not die until they have **seen** the Kingdom of God."
9.32 but they woke up and **saw** Jesus' glory and the two men
9.36 this, and told no one at that time anything they had **seen.**
9.49 John spoke up, "Master, we **saw** a man driving out demons
9.54 the disciples James and John **saw** this, they said, "Lord, do
10.18 Jesus answered them, "I **saw** Satan fall like lightning from heaven.
10.23 "How fortunate you are to **see** the things you see!
10.24 prophets and kings wanted to **see** what you see, but they
10.31 but when he **saw** the man, he walked on by, on the
10.33 the man, and when he **saw** him, his heart was filled with
11.33 lampstand, so that people may **see** the light as they come in.
12.54 to the people, "When you **see** a cloud coming up in the
13.12 When Jesus **saw** her, he called out to her, "Woman, you
13.28 grind your teeth when you **see** Abraham, Isaac, and Jacob, and
13.35 you that you will not **see** me until the time comes when
14.28 what it will cost, to **see** if he has enough money to
14.29 and all who **see** what happened will laugh at him.
15.20 was still a long way from home when his father **saw** him;
16.23 pain, he looked up and **saw** Abraham, far away, with Lazarus
17.14 Jesus **saw** them and said to them, "Go and let the
17.15 When one of them **saw** that he was healed, he came back,
17.20 God does not come in such a way as to be **seen.**
17.22 you will wish you could **see** one of the days
17.22 of the Son of Man, but you will not **see** it.
18.15 The disciples **saw** them and scolded them for doing so,
18.24 Jesus **saw** that he was sad and said, "How hard it is
18.41 "Sir," he answered, "I want to **see** again."
18.42 Jesus said to him, "Then **see!**
18.43 once he was able to **see,** and he followed Jesus, giving
18.43 When the crowd **saw** it, they all praised God.
19. 3 He was trying to **see** who Jesus was, but he was a
19. 3 a little man and could not **see** Jesus because of the crowd.
19. 4 climbed a sycomore tree to **see** Jesus, who was going to pass
19. 7 All the people who **saw** it started grumbling, "This man
19.13 gold coin and told them, '**See** what you can earn with this
19.37 in loud voices for all the great things that they had **seen:**
19.41 the city, and when he **saw** it, he wept over it, [42]saying,
19.42 But now you cannot **see** it!
20.14 But when the tenants **saw** him, they said to one another,
20.23 But Jesus **saw** through their trick and said to them,
21. 1 Jesus looked round and **saw** rich men dropping their gifts
21. 2 temple treasury, [2]and he also **saw** a very poor widow
21. 6 Jesus said, [6]"All this you **see**—the time will come when not
21.20 "When you **see** Jerusalem surrounded by armies, then you
21.30 When you **see** their leaves beginning to appear, you know
21.31 the same way, when you **see** these things happening, you will
22.49 disciples who were with Jesus **saw** what was going to happen,
22.56 When one of the servant-girls **saw** him sitting there at the fire,
23. 8 was very pleased when he **saw** Jesus, because he had heard
23. 8 him and had been wanting to **see** him for a long time.
23. 8 He was hoping to **see** Jesus perform some miracle.
23.47 The army officer **saw** what had happened, and he praised God,
23.48 there to watch the spectacle **saw** what happened, they all
23.55 Galilee went with Joseph and **saw** the tomb and how Jesus'
24.12 he bent down and **saw** the linen wrappings but nothing else.
24.16 they **saw** him, but somehow did not recognize him.
24.23 came back saying they had **seen** a vision of angels who told
24.24 exactly as the women had said, but they did not **see** him."
24.37 They were terrified, thinking that they were **seeing** a ghost.
24.39 my hands and my feet, and **see** that it is I myself.
24.39 ghost doesn't have flesh and bones, as you can **see** I have."
Jn 1.14 We **saw** his glory, the glory which he received as the
1.18 No one has ever **seen** God.
1.29 The next day John **saw** Jesus coming to him, and said,
1.32 "I **saw** the Spirit come down like a dove from heaven and
1.33 said to me, 'You will **see** the Spirit come down and stay
1.34 I have **seen** it," said John, "and I tell you that he
1.36 with two of his disciples, [36]when he **saw** Jesus walking by.
1.38 Jesus turned, **saw** them following him, and asked, "What
1.39 "Come and **see,**" he answered.
1.39 they went with him and **saw** where he lived, and spent the
1.46 "Come and **see,**" answered Philip.
1.47 When Jesus **saw** Nathanael coming to him, he said about him,
1.48 Jesus answered, "I **saw** you when you were under the
1.50 because I told you I **saw** you when you were under the
1.50 You will **see** much greater things than this!"
1.51 you will **see** heaven open and God's angels going up and
2.23 Festival, many believed in him as they **saw** the miracles he performed.
3. 3 no one can **see** the Kingdom of God unless he is born
3.11 and report what we have **seen,** yet none of you is willing
3.32 He tells what he has **seen** and heard, yet no one accepts
4.19 "I **see** you are a prophet, sir," the woman said.
4.29 the people there, [29]"Come and **see** the man who told me
4.45 Festival in Jerusalem and had **seen** everything that he had
4.48 "None of you will ever believe unless you **see** miracles and wonders."
5. 6 Jesus **saw** him lying there, and he knew that the man had
5.19 he does only what he **sees** his Father doing.
5.37 never heard his voice or **seen** his face, [38]and you do not
6. 2 followed him, because they had **seen** his miracles of healing
6. 5 Jesus looked round and **saw** that a large crowd was coming
6.14 **Seeing** this miracle that Jesus had performed, the people there said,
6.19 or six kilometres when they **saw** Jesus walking on the water,
6.24 When the crowd **saw** that Jesus was not there, nor his disciples,
6.30 will you perform so that we may **see** it and believe you?
6.36 I told you that you have **seen** me but will not believe.
6.40 wants is that all who **see** the Son and believe in him
6.46 This does not mean that anyone has **seen** the Father;
6.46 is from God is the only one who has **seen** the Father.

Jn 6.62 Suppose, then, that you should **see** the Son of Man go
7. 3 that your followers will **see** the things that you are doing.
7.50 was Nicodemus, the man who had gone to **see** Jesus before.
8.56 Abraham rejoiced that he was to **see** the time of my coming;
8.56 he **saw** it and was glad."
8.57 "You are not even fifty years old—and you have **seen** Abraham?"
9. 1 Jesus was walking along, he **saw** a man who had been born
9. 3 blind so that God's power might be **seen** at work in him.
9. 7 So the man went, washed his face, and came back **seeing.**
9. 8 and the people who had **seen** him begging before this, asked,
9.10 "How is it that you can now **see?**"
9.11 So I went, and as soon as I washed, I could **see.**"
9.15 I washed my face, and now I can **see.**"
9.18 been blind and could now **see,** until they called his parents
9.19 how is it, then, that he can now **see?**"
9.21 he is now able to **see,** nor do we know who cured
9.25 I was blind, and now I **see.**"
9.37 to him, "You have already **seen** him, and he is the one
9.39 blind should see and those who **see** should become blind."
9.41 you claim that you can **see,** this means that you are still
10.12 does not own the sheep, **sees** a wolf coming, he leaves the
11. 9 does not stumble, for he **sees** the light of this world.
11.19 many Judaeans had come to **see** Martha and Mary to comfort
11.31 her, followed her when they **saw** her get up and hurry out.
11.32 and as soon as she **saw** him, she fell at his feet.
11.33 Jesus **saw** her weeping, and he saw how the people who
11.34 "Come and **see,** Lord," they answered.
11.36 "**See** how much he loved him!"
11.40 I tell you that you would **see** God's glory if you believed?"
11.45 had come to visit Mary **saw** what Jesus did, and they believed
12. 9 of Jesus but also to **see** Lazarus, whom Jesus had raised from
12.19 to one another, "You **see,** we are not succeeding at all!
12.21 Bethsaida in Galilee) and said, "Sir, we want to **see** Jesus."
12.40 eyes would not **see,** and their minds would not understand,
12.41 Isaiah said this because he **saw** Jesus' glory and spoke about him.
12.45 Whoever **sees** me sees also him who sent me.
14. 7 from now on you do know him and you have **seen** him."
14. 9 Whoever has **seen** me has seen the Father.
14.17 cannot receive him, because it cannot **see** him or know him.
14.19 the world will see me no more, but you will **see** me;
15.24 as it is, they have **seen** what I did, and they hate
16.10 going to the Father and you will not **see** me any more;
16.16 little while you will not **see** me any more,
16.16 and then a little while later you will **see** me."
16.17 little while we will not **see** him,
16.17 and then a little while later we will **see** him;
16.19 little while you will not **see** me,
16.19 and then a little while later you will **see** me.'
16.22 are sad, but I will **see** you again, and your hearts will
17.24 am, so that they may **see** my glory, the glory you gave
18.26 "Didn't I **see** you with him in the garden?"
19. 4 to you to let you **see** that I cannot find any reason
19. 6 chief priests and the temple guards **saw** him, they shouted,
19.24 let's throw dice to **see** who will get it."
19.26 Jesus **saw** his mother and the disciple he loved standing there;
19.33 they came to Jesus, they **saw** that he was already dead,
19.35 (The one who **saw** this happen has spoken of it,
19.39 at first had gone to **see** Jesus at night, went with Joseph,
20. 1 went to the tomb and **saw** that the stone had been taken
20. 5 He bent over and **saw** the linen wrappings, but he did not
20. 6 He **saw** the linen wrappings lying there [7]and the cloth which
20. 8 he **saw** and believed.
20.12 in the tomb [12]and **saw** two angels there dressed in white,
20.14 Then she turned round and **saw** Jesus standing there;
20.18 the disciples that she had **seen** the Lord and related to them
20.20 The disciples were filled with joy at **seeing** the Lord.
20.25 So the other disciples told him, "We have **seen** the Lord!"
20.25 said to them, "Unless I **see** the scars of the nails in
20.29 Jesus said to him, "Do you believe because you **see** me?
20.29 How happy are those who believe without **seeing** me!"
21. 9 When they stepped ashore, they **saw** a charcoal fire there
21.20 Peter turned round and **saw** behind him that other disciple,
21.21 When Peter **saw** him, he asked Jesus, "Lord, what about this man?"
Acts 1. 3 They **saw** him, and he talked with them about the Kingdom of
1.11 back in the same way that you **saw** him go to heaven."
2. 3 Then they **saw** what looked like tongues of fire which
2.17 your young men will **see** visions, and your old men will
2.25 David said about him, 'I **saw** the Lord before me at all
2.31 David **saw** what God was going to do in the future, and
2.33 What you now **see** and hear is his gift that he has
3. 3 When he **saw** Peter and John going in, he begged them to
3. 9 The people there **saw** him walking and praising God,
3.12 When Peter **saw** the people, he said to them, "Fellow-Israelites,
3.16 What you **see** and know was done by faith in his name;
3.16 in Jesus that has made him well, as you can all **see.**
4.13 the Council were amazed to **see** how bold Peter and John were
4.14 they could say, because they **saw** the man who had been healed
4.20 stop speaking of what we ourselves have **seen** and heard."
4.21 They **saw** that it was impossible to punish them, because the
5.10 young men came in and **saw** that she was dead, so they
5.28 "but **see** what you have done!
6.15 their eyes on Stephen and **saw** that his face looked like the
7.24 He **saw** one of them being ill-treated by an Egyptian, so
7.26 The next day he **saw** two Israelites fighting, and he
7.31 was amazed by what he **saw,** and went near the bush to
7.34 I have **seen** the cruel suffering of my people in Egypt.
7.55 looked up to heaven and **saw** God's glory and Jesus standing
7.56 "I **see** heaven opened and the Son of Man standing at the
8. 6 they listened to him and **saw** the miracles that he performed.
8.13 and was astounded when he **saw** the great wonders and miracles

Acts 8.18 Simon **saw** that the Spirit had been given to the
8.23 For I **see** that you are full of bitter envy and are
8.39 The official did not **see** him again, but continued on his way,
9. 7 they heard the voice but could not **see** anyone.
9. 8 the ground and opened his eyes, but could not **see** a thing.
9. 9 he was not able to **see**, and during that time he did
9.12 in a vision he has **seen** a man named Ananias come in
9.12 and place his hands on him so that he might **see** again."
9.17 me so that you might **see** again and be filled with the
9.18 scales fell from Saul's eyes, and he was able to **see** again.
9.27 to them how Saul had **seen** the Lord on the road and
9.35 living in Lydda and Sharon **saw** him, and they turned to the
9.40 She opened her eyes, and when she **saw** Peter, she sat up.
10. 3 vision, in which he clearly **saw** an angel of God come in
10.11 He **saw** heaven opened and something coming down that
11. 5 I **saw** something coming down that looked like a large sheet
11. 6 I looked closely inside and **saw** domesticated and wild animals,
11.13 told us how he had **seen** an angel standing in his house,
11.23 When he arrived and **saw** how God had blessed the people,
12. 3 When he **saw** that this pleased the Jews, he went on to
12. 9 he thought he was **seeing** a vision.
12.16 opened the door, and when they **saw** him, they were amazed.
12.20 Tyre and Sidon, so they went in a group to **see** him.
13.11 be blind and will not **see** the light of day for a
13.12 When the governor **saw** what had happened, he believed;
13.45 When the Jews **saw** the crowds, they were filled with jealousy;
14. 9 Paul **saw** that he believed and could be healed, so he looked
14.11 When the crowds **saw** what Paul had done, they started
15. 2 should go to Jerusalem and **see** the apostles and elders about
16. 9 in which he **saw** a Macedonian standing and begging him,
16.27 woke up, and when he **saw** the prison doors open, he thought
17.11 they studied the Scriptures to **see** if what Paul said was
17.22 city council and said, "I **see** that in every way you
18. 2 Paul went to **see** them, [3]and stayed and worked with them,
19.21 "After I go there," he said, "I must also **see** Rome."
19.26 Now, you can **see** and hear for yourselves what this
20.25 now I know that none of you will ever **see** me again.
20.38 sad because he had said that they would never **see** him again.
21. 3 came to where we could **see** Cyprus, and then sailed south of
21.18 The next day Paul went with us to **see** James;
21.20 said, "Brother Paul, you can **see** how many thousands of Jews
21.27 some Jews from the province of Asia **saw** Paul in the Temple.
21.29 said this because they had **seen** Trophimus from Ephesus with
21.32 When the people **saw** him with the soldiers, they stopped beating Paul.
22. 9 The men with me **saw** the light, but did not hear the
22.13 came to me, stood by me, and said, 'Brother Saul, **see**
22.13 At that very moment I **saw** again and looked at him.
22.14 to know his will, to **see** his righteous Servant, and to hear
22.15 for him to tell everyone what you have **seen** and heard.
22.18 a vision, [18]in which I **saw** the Lord, as he said to
23. 6 When Paul **saw** that some of the group were Sadducees and
25.24 You **see** this man against whom all the Jewish people, both
26.13 midday, Your Majesty, that I **saw** a light much brighter than
26.16 tell others what you have **seen** of me today and what I
27. 3 allowed him to go and **see** his friends, to be given what
27.10 "Men, I **see** that our voyage from here on will be dangerous;
27.20 many days we could not **see** the sun or the stars, and
28. 4 The natives **saw** the snake hanging on Paul's hand and said
28. 6 and not **seeing** anything unusual happening to him,
28.15 When Paul **saw** them, he thanked God and was greatly encouraged.
28.20 That is why I asked to **see** you and talk with you.
28.26 look, but not **see**, [27]because this people's minds are dull,
28.27 Otherwise, their eyes would **see**, their ears would hear,
28.30 for himself, and there he welcomed all who came to **see** him.
Rom 1.11 I want very much to **see** you, in order to share a
1.20 eternal power and his divine nature, have been clearly **seen;**
7.23 But I **see** a different law at work in my body—a
8.24 but if we **see** what we hope for, then it is not
8.24 For who hopes for something he **sees?**
8.25 for what we do not **see**, we wait for it with patience.
8.27 And God, who **sees** into our hearts, knows what the
11. 8 to this very day they cannot **see** or hear."
11.10 May their eyes be blinded so that they cannot **see;**
11.22 Here we **see** how kind and how severe God is.
15.21 not told about him will **see**, and those who have not heard
15.23 many years to come to **see** you, [24]I hope to do so
15.24 I would like to **see** you on my way to Spain, and
1 Cor 2. 9 says, "What no one ever **saw** or heard, what no one ever
3.13 each person's work will be **seen** when the Day of Christ
8.10 in this matter **sees** you, who have so-called "knowledge,"
9. 1 Haven't I **seen** Jesus our Lord?
11.19 that the ones who are in the right may be clearly **seen.)**
13.12 What we **see** now is like a dim image in a mirror;
13.12 then we shall **see** face to face.
16. 7 I want to **see** you more than just briefly in passing;
2 Cor 3.13 of Israel would not **see** the brightness fade and disappear.
4. 4 He keeps them from **seeing** the light shining on them,
4.10 Jesus, so that his life also may be **seen** in our bodies.
4.11 that his life may be **seen** in this mortal body of ours.
4.18 not on things that are **seen**, but on things that are unseen.
4.18 What can be **seen** lasts only for a time,
4.18 but what cannot be **seen** lasts for ever.
6. 9 as though we were dead, but, as you **see**, we live on.
7. 7 how much you want to **see** me, how sorry you are, how
7. 8 have been sorry when I **saw** that it made you sad for
7.11 **See** what God did with this sadness of yours:
12. 6 result of what he has **seen** me do and heard me say.
12. 7 the many wonderful things I **saw**, I was given a painful
Gal 1.17 I go to Jerusalem to **see** those who were apostles before me.
Gal 1.19 I did not **see** any other apostle except James, the Lord's brother.
2. 7 On the contrary, they **saw** that God had given me the task
2.14 When I **saw** that they were not walking a straight path in
6.11 **See** what big letters I make as I write to you now
Eph 1.18 minds may be opened to **see** his light, so that you will
3. 9 and of making all people **see** how God's secret plan is to
Phil 1.27 am able to go and **see** you, I will hear that you
1.30 is the same battle you **saw** me fighting in the past, and
2.26 He is anxious to **see** you all and is very upset because
2.28 be glad again when you **see** him, and my own sorrow will
4.17 rather, I want to **see** profit added to your account.
Col 1.16 heaven and on earth, the **seen** and the unseen things,
2. 5 I am glad as I **see** the resolute firmness with which you
1 Thes 2.17 we missed you and how hard we tried to **see** you again!
3. 6 and that you want to **see** us
3. 6 just as much as we want to **see** you.
3.10 our heart to let us **see** you personally and supply what is
1 Tim 3.14 this letter to you, I hope to come and **see** you soon.
3.16 shown to be right by the Spirit, and was **seen** by angels.
4.15 to them, in order that your progress may be **seen** by all.
5.24 some people are plain to **see**, and their sins go ahead of
5.24 but the sins of others are **seen** only later.
5.25 way good deeds are plainly **seen**, and even those that are not
6.16 No one has ever **seen** him;
6.16 no one can ever **see** him.
2 Tim 1. 4 tears, and I want to **see** you very much, so that I
3. 9 get very far, because everyone will **see** how stupid they are.
Heb 2. 8 We do not, however, **see** man ruling over all things now.
2. 9 But we do **see** Jesus, who for a little while was made
2. 9 We **see** him now crowned with glory and honour because of the
3. 9 God, although they had **seen** what I did for forty years.
3.19 We **see**, then, that they were not able to enter the land,
7. 4 You **see**, then, how great he was.
10.25 all the more, since you **see** that the Day of the Lord
11. 1 we hope for, to be certain of the things we cannot **see.**
11. 3 what can be seen was made out of what cannot be **seen.**
11. 7 God's warnings about things in the future that he could not **see.**
11.13 a long way off they **saw** them and welcomed them, and admitted
11.23 They **saw** that he was a beautiful child, and they were not
11.27 As though he **saw** the invisible God, he refused to turn back.
12.14 a holy life, because no one will **see** the Lord without it.
13.23 soon enough, I will have him with me when I **see** you.
Jas 1.23 man who looks in a mirror and **sees** himself as he is.
2.22 Can't you **see?**
2.24 You **see**, then, that it is by his actions that a person
5. 7 **See** how patient a farmer is as he waits for his land
1 Pet 1. 8 him, although you have not **seen** him,
1. 8 and you believe in him, although you do not now **see** him.
3. 2 a word, [2]because they will **see** how pure and reverent your
3.10 enjoy life and wishes to **see** good times, must keep from
2 Pet 1. 9 so short-sighted that he cannot **see** and has forgotten that
1.16 With our own eyes we **saw** his greatness.
2. 8 he suffered agony as he **saw** and heard their evil actions.
1 Jn 1. 1 We have heard it, and we have **seen** it with our eyes;
1. 1 yes, we have **seen** it, and our hands have touched it.
1. 2 When this life became visible, we **saw** it;
1. 3 What we have **seen** and heard we announce to you also, so
2. 8 new, because its truth is **seen** in Christ and also in you.
2.16 sinful self desires, what people **see** and want, and
3. 1 **See** how much the Father has loved us!
3. 2 be like him, because we shall **see** him as he really is.
3. 6 whoever continues to sin has never **seen** him or known him.
3.17 If a rich person **sees** his brother in need, yet closes
4.12 No one has ever **seen** God, but if we love one another,
4.14 And we have **seen** and tell others that the Father sent
4.20 God, whom he has not **seen,**
4.20 if he does not love his brother, whom he has **seen.**
5.16 If you **see** your brother commit a sin that does not lead
3 Jn 11 whoever does what is bad has not **seen** God.
14 I hope to **see** you soon, and then we will talk personally.
Rev 1. 2 angel to him, [2]and John has told all that he has **seen.**
1. 7 Everyone will **see** him, including those who pierced him.
1.11 said, "Write down what you **see**, and send the book to the
1.12 I turned round to **see** who was talking to me, and I
1.12 talking to me, and I **saw** seven gold lamp-stands, [13]and
1.17 When I **saw** him, I fell down at his feet like a
1.19 Write, then, the things you **see**, both the things that
1.20 the seven stars that you **see** in my right hand, and of
3.18 some ointment to put on your eyes, so that you may **see.**
4. 1 point I had another vision and **saw** an open door in heaven.
5. 1 I **saw** a scroll in the right hand of the one who
5. 2 And I **saw** a mighty angel, who announced in a loud voice,
5. 6 Then I **saw** a Lamb standing in the centre of the throne,
6. 1 Then I **saw** the Lamb break open the first of the seven
6. 9 I **saw** underneath the altar the souls of those who had been
6.12 And I **saw** the Lamb break open the sixth seal.
7. 1 After this I **saw** four angels standing at the four corners
7. 2 And I **saw** another angel coming up from the east with the
8. 2 Then I **saw** the seven angels who stand before God, and they
9. 1 I **saw** a star which had fallen down to the earth, and
9.17 And in my vision I **saw** the horses and their riders:
9.20 gold, silver, bronze, stone, and wood, which cannot **see,**
10. 1 Then I **saw** another mighty angel coming down out of heaven.
10. 5 Then the angel that I **saw** standing on the sea and on
11.11 and all who **saw** them were terrified.
11.19 in heaven was opened, and the Covenant Box was **seen** there.
13. 1 Then I **saw** a beast coming up out of the sea.
13.11 Then I **saw** another beast, which came up out of the earth.
14. 6 Then I **saw** another angel flying high in the air, with an
14.17 Then I **saw** another angel come out of the temple in heaven,

Rev 15. 1 Then I **saw** in the sky another mysterious sight, great and amazing.
15. 2 Then I **saw** what looked like a sea of glass mixed with
15. 2 I also **saw** those who had won the victory over the beast
15. 4 worship you, because your just actions are **seen** by all."
15. 5 After this I **saw** the temple in heaven open, with the Tent
16.13 Then I **saw** three unclean spirits that looked like frogs.
17. 3 There I **saw** a woman sitting on a red beast that had
17. 6 And I **saw** that the woman was drunk with the blood of
17. 6 When I **saw** her, I was completely amazed.
17.12 "The ten horns you **saw** are ten kings who have not yet
17.15 "The waters you **saw**, on which the prostitute is sitting,
17.16 The ten horns you **saw**, and the beast, will hate the prostitute;
17.18 "The woman you **saw** is the great city that rules over
18. 1 After this I **saw** another angel coming down out of heaven.
18. 9 over the city when they **see** the smoke from the flames that
18.18 and cried out as they **saw** the smoke from the flames that
18.21 Babylon will be violently thrown down and will never be **seen** again.
18.23 Never again will the light of a lamp be **seen** in you;
19.11 Then I **saw** heaven open, and there was a white horse.
19.17 Then I **saw** an angel standing on the sun.
19.19 Then I **saw** the beast and the kings of the earth and
20. 1 Then I **saw** an angel coming down from heaven, holding in
20. 4 Then I **saw** thrones, and those who sat on them were given
20. 4 I also **saw** the souls of those who had been executed because
20.11 Then I **saw** a great white throne and the one who sits
20.11 Earth and heaven fled from his presence and were **seen** no more.
20.12 And I **saw** the dead, great and small alike, standing
21. 1 Then I **saw** a new heaven and a new earth.
21. 2 And I **saw** the Holy City, the new Jerusalem, coming down
21.22 I did not **see** a temple in the city, because its temple
22. 4 They will **see** his face, and his name will be written on
22. 8 I, John, have heard and **seen** all these things.
22. 8 when I finished hearing and **seeing** them, I fell down at the

SEED

Gen 2. 5 on the earth and no **seeds** had sprouted, because he had not
26.12 Isaac sowed **seed** in that land, and that year he
47.19 corn to keep us alive and **seed** to sow in our fields."
47.23 Here is **seed** for you to sow in your fields.
47.24 can use the rest for **seed** and for food for yourselves and
Ex 16.31 was like a small white **seed**, and tasted like biscuits made
Lev 11.37 on seed that is going to be sown, the **seed** remains clean.
11.38 But if the **seed** is soaking in water
11.38 and one of them falls on it, the **seed** is unclean.
19.19 Do not plant two kinds of **seed** in the same field.
26.16 You will sow your **seed**, but it will do you no good,
27.16 according to the amount of **seed** it takes to sow it, at
Num 6. 4 from a grapevine, not even the **seeds** or skins of grapes.
11. 7 (Manna was like small **seeds**, whitish yellow in colour.
24. 7 They will have abundant rainfall And plant their **seed**
Deut 11.10 There, when you sowed **seed**, you had to work hard to irrigate
28.38 "You will sow plenty of **seed**, but reap only a small harvest,
Judg 6. 3 Whenever the Israelites sowed any **seed**, the Midianites
Job 4. 8 seen people plough fields of evil and sow wickedness like **seed**;
Ps 126. 5 wept as they sowed their **seed**, gather the harvest with joy!
126. 6 went out carrying the **seed** will come back singing for joy,
Prov 22. 8 If you sow the **seeds** of injustice, disaster will spring up,
Is 5.10 hundred and eighty litres of **seed** will produce only eighteen
28.25 the soil, he sows the **seeds** of herbs such as dill and
28.27 uses a heavy club to beat out dill **seeds** or cumin seeds;
30.23 Whenever you sow your **seeds**, the Lord will send rain to
55.10 the crops grow and provide **seed** for sowing and food to eat.
61.11 As surely as **seeds** sprout and grow, The Sovereign Lord
Jer 2.21 I planted you like a choice vine from the very best **seed**.
4. 3 do not sow your **seeds** among thorns.
50.16 Do not let **seeds** be sown in that country or let a
Ezek 17.23 grow branches and bear **seed** and become a magnificent cedar.
36. 9 your land is ploughed again and that **seeds** are sown there.
Joel 1.17 The **seeds** die in the dry earth.
Mt 6.26 they do not sow **seeds**, gather a harvest and put it in
13. 4 As he scattered the **seed** in the field, some of it fell
13. 5 The **seeds** soon sprouted, because the soil wasn't deep.
13. 7 Some of the **seed** fell among thorn bushes,
13. 8 But some **seeds** fell in good soil, and the plants produced corn;
13.19 understand it are like the **seeds** that fell along the path.
13.20 The **seeds** that fell on rocky ground stand for those who
13.22 The **seeds** that fell among thorn bushes stand for those
13.23 And the **seeds** sown in the good soil stand for those who
13.24 A man sowed good **seed** in his field.
13.27 'Sir, it was good **seed** you sowed in your field;
13.31 A man takes a mustard **seed** and sows it in his field.
13.32 is the smallest of all **seeds**, but when it grows up,
13.37 "The man who sowed the good **seed** is the Son of Man;
13.38 the good **seed** is the people who belong to the Kingdom;
17.20 as big as a mustard **seed**, you can say to this hill,
25.24 and you gather crops where you did not scatter **seed**.
25.26 and gather crops where I did not scatter **seed?**
Mk 4. 4 As he scattered the **seed** in the field, some of it fell
4. 5 The **seeds** soon sprouted, because the soil wasn't deep.
4. 7 Some of the **seed** fell among thorn bushes,
4. 8 But some **seeds** fell in good soil, and the plants sprouted,
4.15 Some people are like the **seeds** that fall along the path;
4.16 Other people are like the **seeds** that fall on rocky ground.
4.18 Other people are like the **seeds** sown among the thorn bushes.
4.20 But other people are like the **seeds** sown in good soil.
4.26 A man scatters **seed** in his field.
4.27 and all the while the **seeds** are sprouting and growing.
4.31 A man takes a mustard **seed**, the smallest seed in the world,
Lk 8. 5 As he scattered the **seed** in the field, some of it fell
8. 7 Some of the **seed** fell among thorn bushes,
8. 8 And some **seeds** fell in good soil;
8.11 the **seed** is the word of God.
8.12 The **seeds** that fell along the path stand for those who hear;
8.13 The **seeds** that fell on rocky ground stand for those who
8.14 The **seeds** that fell among thorn bushes stand for those who hear;
8.15 The **seeds** that fell in good soil stand for those who
12.24 they don't sow **seeds** or gather a harvest;
13.19 A man takes a mustard **seed** and sows it in his field.
17. 6 as big as a mustard **seed**, you could say to this mulberry
1 Cor 3. 6 I sowed the **seed**, Apollos watered the plant, but it was
9.11 We have sown spiritual **seed** among you.
15.36 When you sow a **seed** in the ground, it does not sprout
15.37 you sow is a bare **seed**, perhaps a grain of wheat
15.38 God provides that **seed** with the body he wishes;
15.38 he gives each **seed** its own proper body.
2 Cor 9. 6 that the person who sows few **seeds** will have a small crop;
9. 6 the one who sows many **seeds** will have a large crop.
9.10 And God, who supplies **seed** to sow and bread to eat,
9.10 supply you with all the **seed** you need and will make it
Jas 3.18 is produced from the **seeds** the peacemakers plant in peace.

AV **SEED** see **CHILD, DESCENDANT, FAMILY**

SEEK
[SOUGHT]

Num 35.12 will be safe from the dead man's relative who **seeks** revenge.
35.24 in favour of the dead man's relative who is **seeking** revenge.
Judg 9.46 Shechem heard about this, they **sought** safety in the
2 Sam 22.31 He is like a shield for all who **seek** his protection.
Ps 18.30 He is like a shield for all who **seek** his protection.
37. 4 **Seek** your happiness in the Lord, and he will give you your
141. 8 I **seek** your protection;
Prov 30. 5 He is like a shield for all who **seek** his protection.
Is 56.11 one of them does as he pleases and **seeks** his own advantage.
Jer 29.13 You will **seek** me, and you will find me
29.13 because you will **seek** me with all your heart.
Hos 8. 9 They have gone off to **seek** help from Assyria, and have paid
Mt 7. 7 **seek**, and you will find;
7. 8 and anyone who **seeks** will find,
Lk 11. 9 **seek**, and you will find;
11.10 and he who **seeks** will find,
19.10 The Son of Man came to **seek** and to save the lost."
Jn 8.50 I am not **seeking** honour for myself.
8.50 there is one who is **seeking** it and who judges
Rom 2. 7 on doing good, and **seek** glory, honour, and immortal life;
9.31 while God's people, who were **seeking** a law that would
Heb 11. 6 have faith that God exists and rewards those who **seek** him.
Rev 9. 6 five months they will **seek** death, but will not find it;

SEEM

Acts 17.18 Others answered, "He **seems** to be talking about foreign gods."
25.27 For it **seems** unreasonable to me to send a prisoner
1 Cor 1.25 For what **seems** to be God's foolishness is wiser than human wisdom,
1.25 and what **seems** to be God's weakness is stronger
4. 9 For it **seems** to me that God has given the very last
12.22 do without the parts of the body that **seem** to be weaker;
16. 4 If it **seems** worth while for me to go,
2 Cor 6.10 we **seem** poor, but we make many people rich;
6.10 we **seem** to have nothing, yet we really possess everything.
13. 7 do what is right, even though we may **seem** to be failures.
Gal 2. 6 But those who **seemed** to be the leaders—
2. 9 James, Peter, and John, who **seemed** to be the leaders,
Col 2. 4 with false arguments, no matter how good they **seem** to be.
Heb 12.10 punished us for a short time, as it **seemed** right to them;
12.11 When we are punished, it **seems** to us at the time
Rev 9. 7 they had what **seemed** to be crowns of gold,
13. 3 the heads of the beast **seemed** to have been fatally wounded,

SEER

1 Sam 9. 9 They asked the girls, "Is the **seer** in town?"
9. 9 a prophet was called a **seer**, and so whenever someone wanted
9. 9 God a question, he would say, "Let's go to the **seer**.")
9.18 the gate, and asked, "Tell me, where does the **seer** live?"
9.19 Samuel answered, "I am the **seer**.
16. 4 to meet him and asked, "Is this a peaceful visit, **seer?"**

SEIZE

Gen 21.25 Abimelech about a well which the servants of Abimelech had **seized.**
Ex 15.14 the Philistines are **seized** with terror.
Deut 1.39 land—the children you said would be **seized** by your enemies.
Josh 7.21 Among the things we **seized** I saw a beautiful Babylonian cloak,
7.24 all the people of Israel, **seized** Achan, the silver, the
Judg 12. 6 Then they would **seize** him and kill him there at one of
1 Sam 15.19 Why did you rush to **seize** the loot, and so do what
2 Sam 4.10 I **seized** him and had him put to death.
10. 4 Hanun **seized** David's messengers, shaved off one side of
1 Kgs 13. 4 he pointed at him and ordered, **"Seize** that man!"
18.40 Elijah ordered, **"Seize** the prophets of Baal;
18.40 The people **seized** them all, and Elijah led them down to the
2 Kgs 10.14 They **seized** them, and he put them to death near a pit
11.16 They **seized** her, took her to the palace, and there at
1 Chr 19. 4 Hanun **seized** David's messengers, shaved off their beards, cut

2 Chr 23.15 They **seized** her, took her to the palace, and there at
Job 15.28 man who captured cities and **seized** houses whose owners had fled,
16. 8 You have **seized** me;
20.19 neglected the poor and **seized** houses someone else had built.
30.18 God **seizes** me by my collar and twists my clothes out of
36.32 He **seizes** the lightning with his hands and commands it
38.13 you ordered the dawn to **seize** the earth and shake the wicked
Ps 48. 6 There they were **seized** with fear and anguish, like a woman
Is 33.22 We will **seize** all the wealth of enemy armies, and there will
49.25 will be taken away, and the tyrant's loot will be **seized.**
Jer 6.24 we are **seized** by anguish and pain like a woman in labour.
20. 5 wealth of this city and **seize** all its possessions and property,
26. 8 commanded me to speak, they **seized** me and shouted, "You
49.29 **Seize** their tents and their flocks, their tent curtains and
50.43 He is **seized** by anguish, by pain like a woman in labour.
Ezek 8. 3 what seemed to be a hand and **seized** me by the hair.
23.10 They stripped her naked, **seized** her sons and daughters, and
Dan 1. 2 King Jehoiakim and **seize** some of the temple treasures.
5.31 who was then sixty-two years old, **seized** the royal power.
11.21 but he will come unexpectedly and **seize** power by trickery.
Obad 13 over their suffering and to **seize** their riches on the day of
Mic 2. 2 When they want fields, they **seize** them;
Zeph 2. 8 my people, and boasting that they would **seize** their land.
Zech 14.13 and afraid that everyone will **seize** the man next to him and
Mt 11.12 suffered violent attacks, and violent men try to **seize** it.
21.35 The tenants **seized** his slaves, beat one, killed another,
21.39 So they **seized** him, threw him out of the vineyard,
Mk 12. 3 The tenants **seized** the slave, beat him, and sent him back
12. 8 So they **seized** the son and killed him
Lk 8.29 Many times it had **seized** him, and even though he was kept
23.26 They **seized** him, put the cross on him, and made him carry
Jn 6.15 were about to come and **seize** him in order to make him
7.30 Then they tried to **seize** him, but no one laid a hand
7.44 Some wanted to **seize** him, but no one laid a hand on
10.39 Once more they tried to **seize** Jesus, but he slipped out
Acts 6.12 They **seized** Stephen and took him before the Council.
16.19 they **seized** Paul and Silas
18.12 the Jews got together, **seized** Paul, and took him into court.
18.17 They all **seized** Sosthenes, the leader of the synagogue,
19.29 The mob **seized** Gaius and Aristarchus, two Macedonians
21.27 They stirred up the whole crowd and **seized** Paul.
21.30 the people all ran together, **seized** Paul, and dragged him
23.27 The Jews **seized** this man and were about to kill him.
26.21 this reason that the Jews **seized** me while I was in the
Heb 10.34 when all your belongings were **seized,** you endured your loss gladly,
Rev 20. 2 He **seized** the dragon, that ancient serpent—that is, the Devil,

SELECT

Ex 10.26 We ourselves must **select** the animals with which to worship
31. 6 I have also **selected** Oholiab son of Ahisamach, from the
Deut 1.23 thing to do, so I **selected** twelve men, one from each tribe.
19. 9 he has promised, [9]then you are to **select** three more cities.
21. 3 body was found are to **select** a young cow that has never
2 Chr 2. 7 the craftsmen of Judah and Jerusalem whom my father David **selected.**
Ps 78.67 he did not **select** the tribe of Ephraim.
Jer 1. 5 before you were born I **selected** you to be a prophet to
Dan 1. 3 Ashpenaz, his chief official, to **select** from among the Israelite

SELF

Prov 27.19 and it is your own **self** that you see in your heart.
Mt 16.24 he must forget **self,** carry his cross, and follow me.
Mk 8.34 "he must forget **self,** carry his cross, and follow me.
Lk 9.23 he must forget **self,** take up his cross every day,
Rom 6. 6 the power of the sinful **self** might be destroyed,
6.12 so that you obey the desires of your natural **self.**
6.19 (I use everyday language because of the weakness of your natural **selves.)**
Eph 3.16 be strong in your inner **selves,**
4.22 get rid of your old **self,** which made you live as you
4.22 the old **self** that was being destroyed
4.24 put on the new **self,** which is created in God's likeness
Col 2.11 consists of being freed from the power of this sinful **self.**
3. 9 have taken off the old **self** with its habits
3.10 and have put on the new **self.**
Phlm 19 remind you, of course, that you owe your very **self** to me.)
1 Pet 3. 4 consist of your true inner **self,** the ageless beauty of a
1 Jn 2.16 what the sinful **self** desires, what people see and want,

SELF-CONTROL

Prov 5.23 He dies because he has no **self-control.**
Acts 24.25 discussing about goodness, **self-control,** and the coming Day of Judgement,
1 Cor 7. 5 giving in to Satan's temptation because of your lack of **self-control.**
Gal 5.23 goodness, faithfulness, [23]humility, and **self-control.**
1 Tim 3. 2 he must have only one wife, be sober, **self-controlled,**
2 Tim 1. 7 his Spirit fills us with power, love, and **self-control.**
Tit 1. 8 He must be **self-controlled,** upright, holy, and disciplined.
2. 2 Instruct the older men to be sober, sensible, and **self-controlled;**
2. 5 husbands and children, [5]to be **self-controlled** and pure,
2. 6 In the same way urge the young men to be **self-controlled.**
2.12 and to live **self-controlled,** upright, and godly lives
1 Pet 4. 7 You must be **self-controlled** and alert, to be able to pray.
2 Pet 1. 6 to your knowledge add **self-control;**
1. 6 to your **self-control** add endurance;

SELF-DEFENCE
see also **DEFEND**

Esth 8.11 Jews in every city to organize themselves for **self-defence.**

SELF-SATISFIED
see also **SATISFY**

Zeph 1.12 punish the people who are **self-satisfied** and confident, who say

SELFISH
[UNSELFISH]

Deut 15. 7 in need, then do not be **selfish** and refuse to help him.
15.10 Give to him freely and **unselfishly,** and the Lord will
Ps 78.72 of them with **unselfish** devotion and led them with skill.
Prov 28.22 **Selfish** people are in such a hurry to get rich that they
28.25 **Selfishness** only causes trouble.
Jer 22.17 But you can only see your **selfish** interests;
Dan 11.34 though many who join them will do so for **selfish** reasons.
Mt 23.25 full of what you have obtained by violence and **selfishness.**
Rom 2. 8 Other people are **selfish** and reject what is right,
7. 8 its chance to stir up all kinds of **selfish** desires in me.
1 Cor 13. 5 love is not ill-mannered or **selfish** or irritable;
2 Cor 1.17 do I make them from **selfish** motives,
12.20 hot tempers and **selfishness,** insults and gossip,
Phil 1.17 not proclaim Christ sincerely, but from a spirit of **selfish** ambition;
2. 3 Don't do anything from **selfish** ambition
2 Tim 3. 2 People will be **selfish,** greedy, boastful, and conceited;
Jas 3.14 you are jealous, bitter, and **selfish,** don't sin against the truth
3.16 Where there is jealousy and **selfishness,** there is also disorder

SELL
[SALE, SOLD]

Gen 23. 4 **sell** me some land, so that I can bury my wife."
23. 9 Ephron son of Zohar [9]to **sell** me Machpelah Cave, which is
23. 9 Ask him to **sell** it to me for its full price, here
31.15 He **sold** us, and now he has spent all the money he
37.27 Let's **sell** him to these Ishmaelites.
37.28 out of the well and **sold** him for twenty pieces of silver
37.36 in Egypt, the Midianites had **sold** Joseph to Potiphar, one of
39. 1 taken Joseph to Egypt and **sold** him to Potiphar, one of the
41.56 opened all the storehouses and **sold** corn to the Egyptians.
42. 6 the land of Egypt, was **selling** corn to people from all over
45. 4 said, "I am your brother Joseph, whom you **sold** into Egypt.
45. 5 not be upset or blame yourselves because you **sold** me here.
47.20 Every Egyptian was forced to **sell** his land, because the
47.22 They did not have to **sell** their lands, because the king gave
Ex 21. 7 "If a man **sells** his daughter as a slave, she is not
21. 8 If she is **sold** to someone who intends to make her his
21. 8 like her, then she is to be **sold** back to her father;
21. 8 her master cannot **sell** her to foreigners, because he has
21.16 kidnaps a man, either to **sell** him or to keep him as
21.35 bull, the two men shall **sell** the live bull and divide the
22. 1 sheep and kills it or **sells** it, he must pay five cows
22. 2 owns nothing, he shall be **sold** as a slave to pay for
Lev 25.10 all property that has been **sold** shall be restored to the
25.10 and anyone who has been **sold** as a slave shall return to
25.13 all property that has been **sold** shall be restored to its
25.14 So when you **sell** land to your fellow-Israelite or buy
25.16 lower, because what is being **sold** is the number of crops the
25.23 Your land must not be **sold** on a permanent basis, because
25.24 When land is **sold,** the right of the original owner to
25.25 poor and is forced to **sell** his land, his closest relative is
25.29 If a man **sells** a house in a walled city, he has
25.29 it back during the first full year from the date of **sale.**
25.33 one of these cities is **sold** by a Levite and is not
25.34 But the pasture land round the Levite cities shall never be **sold;**
25.37 and do not make a profit on the food you **sell** him.
25.39 becomes so poor that he **sells** himself to you as a slave,
25.42 they must not be **sold** into slavery.
25.47 a fellow-Israelite becomes poor and **sells** himself as a slave to
25.48 After he is **sold,** he still has the right to be bought
25.50 years from the time he **sold** himself until the next Year of
27.20 If he **sells** the field to someone else without first
27.27 bought back, it may be **sold** to someone else at the standard
27.28 No one may **sell** or buy back what he has unconditionally
Num 36. 4 that has been **sold** is restored to its original owners,
Deut 14.21 among you eat it, or you may **sell** it to other foreigners.
14.25 **Sell** your produce and take the money with you to the one
15.12 man or woman, **sells** himself to you as a slave,
21.14 with you, you cannot treat her as a slave and **sell** her.
24. 7 makes him his slave or **sells** him into slavery is to be
28.68 There you will try to **sell** yourselves to your enemies as slaves,
Ruth 4. 3 from Moab, she wants to **sell** the field that belonged to our
4. 7 those days, to settle a **sale** or an exchange of property, it
4. 7 was the custom for the **seller** to take off his sandal and
1 Kgs 10.29 kings with horses and chariots, **selling** chariots for 600 pieces
21.15 of the vineyard which he refused to **sell** to you."
2 Kgs 4. 7 prophet, who said to her, "**Sell** the olive-oil and pay all
7.16 kilogrammes of barley were **sold** for one piece of silver.
7.18 kilogrammes of barley would be **sold** in Samaria for one piece
1 Chr 21.22 David said to him, "**Sell** me your threshing-place, so that
2 Chr 1.17 kings with horses and chariots, **selling** chariots for six hundred
2. 3 father, King David, when you **sold** him cedar logs for
Neh 5. 5 Some of our daughters have already been **sold** as slaves.
5. 8 buying back our Jewish brothers who had to **sell** themselves
5. 8 are forcing your own brothers to **sell** themselves to you,
10.31 corn or anything else to **sell** to us on the Sabbath or
13.15 I warned them not to **sell** anything on the Sabbath.

Neh 13.16 goods into the city to **sell** to our people on the Sabbath.
13.20 Once or twice merchants who **sold** all kinds of goods
Esth 7. 4 My people and I have been **sold** for slaughter.
7. 4 nothing more serious than being **sold** into slavery, I would
Job 41. 6 Will merchants cut him up to **sell?**
Ps 44.12 You **sold** your own people for a small price as though
105.17 man ahead of them, Joseph, who had been **sold** as a slave.
Prov 11.26 price, but they praise the one who puts it up for **sale.**
16.11 and measures to be honest and every **sale** to be fair.
23.23 are worth paying for, but too valuable for you to **sell.**
27.26 land with the money you get from **selling** some of your goats.
31.24 She makes clothes and belts, and **sells** them to merchants.
Song 3. 6 with incense and myrrh, the incense **sold** by the traders?
Is 23. 3 the sea to buy and **sell** the corn that grew in Egypt
24. 2 and masters, buyers and **sellers,** lenders and borrowers,
50. 1 Do you think I **sold** you into captivity
50. 1 like a man who **sells** his children as slaves?
Ezek 7.12 is near when buying and **selling** will have no more meaning,
27.14 You **sold** your goods for draught-horses, war-horses,
27.24 They **sold** you luxurious clothing, purple cloth, and embroidery,
28.16 You were busy buying and **selling,** and this led you to
28.18 such evil in buying and **selling** that your places of worship
48.14 none of it may be **sold** or exchanged or transferred to anyone
Hos 9. 1 over the land you have **sold** yourselves like prostitutes to
Joel 3. 3 They **sold** boys and girls into slavery to pay for prostitutes
3. 6 far from their own country and **sold** them to the Greeks.
3. 7 bring them out of the places to which you have **sold** them.
3. 8 let your sons and daughters be **sold** to the people of Judah;
3. 8 they will **sell** them to the far-off Sabeans.
Amos 1. 6 off a whole nation and **sold** them as slaves to the people
2. 6 They **sell** into slavery honest men who cannot pay their debts,
8. 5 holy days to be over so that we can **sell** our corn.
8. 5 When will the Sabbath end, so that we can start **selling** again?
8. 6 We can **sell** worthless wheat at a high price.
Zech 11. 5 They **sell** the meat and say, 'Praise the Lord!
11. 7 Those who bought and **sold** the sheep hired me, and I became
11.11 Those who bought and **sold** the sheep were watching me, and
Mt 13.44 he goes and **sells** everything he has,
13.46 he goes and **sells** everything he has,
18.25 king ordered him to be **sold** as a slave, with his wife
19.21 to be perfect, go and **sell** all you have
21.12 Temple and drove out all those who were buying and **selling** there.
21.12 the stools of those who **sold** pigeons, [13]and said to them,
26. 9 "This perfume could have been **sold** for a large amount and
Mk 10.21 Go and **sell** all you have and give the money
11.15 began to drive out all those who were buying and **selling.**
11.15 the stools of those who **sold** pigeons, [16]and he would not
14. 5 It could have been **sold** for more than three hundred silver
Lk 12. 6 "Aren't five sparrows **sold** for two pennies?
12.33 **Sell** all your belongings and give the money to the poor.
15.13 few days the younger son **sold** his part of the property and
17.28 Everybody kept on eating and drinking, buying and **selling,**
18.22 **Sell** all you have and give the money to the poor,
22.36 and whoever has no sword must **sell** his coat and buy one.
Jn 2.14 the Temple he found men **selling** cattle, sheep, and pigeons,
2.16 he ordered the men who **sold** the pigeons, "Take them out of
12. 5 said, [5]"Why wasn't this perfume **sold** for three hundred
Acts 2.45 They would **sell** their property and possessions, and distribute the money
4.34 owned fields or houses would **sell** them, bring the money
4.34 the money received from the **sale,** [35]and hand it over to
4.37 (which means "One who Encourages"), [37]**sold** a field he owned,
5. 1 his wife Sapphira **sold** some property that belonged to them.
5. 4 Before you **sold** the property, it belonged to you;
5. 4 and after you **sold** it, the money was yours.
7. 9 of their brother Joseph and **sold** him to be a slave in
Rom 7.14 but I am a mortal man, **sold** as a slave to sin.
1 Cor 10.25 are free to eat anything **sold** in the meat-market, without
Heb 12.16 who for a single meal **sold** his rights as the elder son.
Rev 13.17 No one could buy or **sell** unless he had this mark,

SEMEN

Gen 38. 9 brother's widow, he let the **semen** spill on the ground, so
Lev 15.16 man has an emission of **semen,** he must bathe his whole body,
15.17 or leather on which the **semen** falls must be washed, and it
15.32 discharge or an emission of **semen,** [33]a woman during her monthly
22. 4 he has an emission of **semen** [5]or if he has touched an

SEND

Gen 2. 5 sprouted, because he had not **sent** any rain, and there was no
3.23 So the Lord God **sent** him out of the Garden of Eden
6.17 I am going to **send** a flood on the earth to destroy
7. 4 now I am going to **send** rain that will fall for forty
8. 7 After forty days Noah opened a window [7]and **sent** out a raven.
8. 8 Meanwhile, Noah **sent** out a dove to see if the water had
8.10 He waited another seven days and **sent** out the dove again.
8.12 waited another seven days and **sent** out the dove once more;
12.17 had taken Sarai, the Lord **sent** terrible diseases on him and
12.18 Then the king **sent** for Abram and asked him, "What have
18.16 Sodom, and Abraham went with them to **send** them on their way.
19.13 against these people and has **sent** us to destroy Sodom."
20.13 So when God **sent** me from my father's house into foreign lands,
21.10 said to Abraham, **"Send** this slave-girl and her son away.
21.14 He put the child on her back and **sent** her away.
24. 5 Shall I **send** your son back to the land you came from?"
24. 6 Abraham answered, "Make sure that you don't **send** my son back
24. 7 He will **send** his angel before you, so that you can get
24.40 I have always obeyed, will **send** his angel with you and give
Gen 25. 6 Then he **sent** these sons to the land of the East, away
26. 9 Abimelech **sent** for Isaac and said, "So she is your wife!
27. 1 He **sent** for his elder son Esau and said to him, "My
27.42 heard about Esau's plan, she **sent** for Jacob and said, "Listen,
27.45 Then I will **send** someone to bring you back.
28. 5 Isaac **sent** Jacob away to Mesopotamia, to Laban, who was
28. 6 Isaac had blessed Jacob and **sent** him away to Mesopotamia to
31. 4 So Jacob **sent** word to Rachel and Leah to meet him in
31.27 told me, I would have **sent** you on your way with rejoicing
31.42 with me, you would have already **sent** me away empty-handed.
32. 3 Jacob **sent** messengers ahead of him to his brother Esau in
32. 5 I am **sending** you word, sir, in the hope of gaining your
32.18 He **sends** them as a present to his master Esau.
32.21 He **sent** the gifts on ahead of him and spent that night
32.23 After he had **sent** them across,
32.23 he also **sent** across all that he owned,
37.14 So his father **sent** him on his way
37.22 to save him from them and **send** him back to his father.
38.17 He answered, "I will **send** you a young goat from my flock."
38.17 me something to keep as a pledge until you **send** the goat."
38.20 Judah **sent** his friend Hirah to take the goat and get
38.25 As she was being taken out, she **sent** word to her father-in-law:
41. 8 he was worried, so he **sent** for all the magicians and wise
41.14 The king **sent** for Joseph, and he was immediately brought
42. 4 Egypt, [4]but Jacob did not **send** Joseph's full-brother Benjamin
43. 4 If you are willing to **send** our brother with us, we will
43. 8 Judah said to his father, **"Send** the boy with me, and we
44. 3 the brothers were **sent** on their way with their donkeys.
45. 5 It was really God who **sent** me ahead of you to save
45. 7 God **sent** me ahead of you to rescue you in this amazing
45. 8 So it was not really you who **sent** me here, but God.
45.23 He **sent** his father ten donkeys loaded with the best Egyptian
45.24 He **sent** his brothers off and as they left, he said to
45.27 the wagons which Joseph had **sent** to take him to Egypt, he
46. 5 their wives in the wagons which the king of Egypt had **sent.**
46.28 Jacob **sent** Judah ahead to ask Joseph to meet them in Goshen.
50.16 So they **sent** a message to Joseph:
Ex 1.18 So the king **sent** for the midwives and asked them, "Why
2. 5 basket in the tall grass and **sent** a slave-girl to get it.
3.10 Now I am **sending** you to the king of Egypt so that
3.12 That will be the proof that I have **sent** you."
3.13 'The God of your ancestors **sent** me to you,' they will ask
3.14 'The one who is called I AM has **sent** me to you.'
3.15 the God of Abraham, Isaac, and Jacob, have **sent** you to them.
4.10 But Moses said, "No, Lord, don't **send** me.
4.13 But Moses answered, "No, Lord, please **send** someone else."
5.22 Why did you **send** me here?
7.16 the God of the Hebrews, **sent** me to tell you to let
8.21 I will punish you by **sending** flies on you, your officials,
8.24 The Lord **sent** great swarms of flies into the king's
9. 3 I will punish you by **sending** a terrible disease on all
9.23 the sky, and the Lord **sent** thunder and hail,
9.23 The Lord **sent** [24]a heavy hailstorm,
9.27 The king **sent** for Moses and Aaron and said, "This time
11. 1 said to Moses, "I will **send** only one more punishment on the
12.31 That same night the king **sent** for Moses and Aaron and said,
18. 6 He had **sent** word to Moses that they were coming, [7]so
23.20 "I will **send** an angel ahead of you to protect you as
23.21 against him, for I have **sent** him, and he will not pardon
24. 5 Then he **sent** young men, and they burnt sacrifices to the
32.35 So the Lord **sent** a disease on the people, because they
33. 2 I will **send** an angel to guide you, and I will drive
33.12 but you did not tell me whom you would **send** with me.
36. 6 So Moses **sent** a command throughout the camp that no one
Lev 9.24 the Lord **sent** a fire, and it consumed the burnt-offering
10. 2 Suddenly the Lord **sent** fire, and it burnt them to death
10. 6 to mourn this death caused by the fire which the Lord **sent.**
14.34 finds that the Lord has **sent** mildew on his house, then he
16.10 alive to the Lord and **sent** off into the desert to Azazel,
25. 9 month, the Day of Atonement, **send** a man to blow a trumpet
26. 4 obey my commands, [4]I will **send** you rain at the right time,
26.22 I will **send** dangerous animals among you, and they will kill
26.25 cities for safety, I will **send** incurable diseases among you,
26.41 me turn against them and **send** them into exile in the land
Num 5. 3 **Send** all these ritually unclean people out, so that they
11. 1 Lord heard them, he was angry and **sent** fire on the people.
11.31 the Lord **sent** a wind that brought quails from the sea,
13. 2 of the twelve tribes and **send** them as spies to explore the
13. 3 and from the wilderness of Paran he **sent** out leaders, as
13.16 These are the spies Moses **sent** to explore the land.
13.17 When Moses **sent** them out, he said to them, "Go north
14.12 I will **send** an epidemic and destroy them, but I will
14.36 The men Moses had **sent** to explore the land brought
16.12 Then Moses **sent** for Dathan and Abiram, but they said,
16.28 know that the Lord has **sent** me to do all these things
16.29 some punishment from God, then the Lord did not **send** me.
16.35 Then the Lord **sent** a fire that blazed out and burnt up
20.14 Moses **sent** messengers from Kadesh to the king of Edom.
20.16 He heard our cry and **sent** an angel, who led us out
21. 6 Then the Lord **sent** poisonous snakes among the people, and
21.21 Then the people of Israel **sent** messengers to the Amorite king
21.32 of the Amorites, [32]and Moses **sent** men to find the best way
22. 5 So King Balak [5]**sent** messengers to summon Balaam son of Beor,
22.10 "King Balak of Moab has **sent** them to tell me [11]that a
22.15 Then Balak **sent** a larger number of leaders, who were more
22.37 "Why didn't you come when I **sent** for you the first time?
23. 5 Balaam what to say and **sent** him back to Balak to give
23.16 him what to say, and **sent** him back to Balak to give
24.12 "I told the messengers you **sent** to me that [13]even if you
31. 4 From each tribe of Israel **send** a thousand men to war."
31. 6 Moses **sent** them to war under the command of Phinehas son

Num 32. 8 your fathers did when I **sent** them from Kadesh Barnea to
Deut 1.22 to me and said, 'Let's **send** men ahead of us to spy
1.28 The men we **sent** tell us that the people there are stronger
2.26 "Then I **sent** messengers from the desert of Kedemoth to King
3.18 arm your fighting men and **send** them across the Jordan ahead
8. 2 desert these past forty years, **sending** hardships to test you,
8.16 He **sent** hardships on you to test you, so that in the
9.23 And when he **sent** you from Kadesh Barnea with orders to
11.14 If you do, he will **send** rain on your land when it
15.13 When you set him free, do not **send** him away empty-handed.
17.16 and he is not to **send** people to Egypt to buy horses,
18. 8 priests, and he may keep whatever his family **sends** him.
18.15 Instead, he will **send** you a prophet like me from among
18.18 I will **send** them a prophet like you from among their own
19.12 his own town are to **send** for him and hand him over
23.15 owner and comes to you for protection, do not **send** him back.
24. 1 papers, gives them to her, and **sends** her away from his home.
24. 3 papers, gives them to her, and **sends** her away from his home.
28.12 He will **send** rain in season from his rich storehouse in
28.21 He will **send** disease after disease on you until there is
28.22 will **send** drought and scorching winds to destroy your crops.
28.24 the Lord will **send** down duststorms and sandstorms until you
28.27 The Lord will **send** boils on you, as he did on the
28.48 the enemies that the Lord is going to **send** against you.
28.59 Lord your God, [59]he will **send** on you and on your
28.61 He will also **send** all kinds of diseases and epidemics
28.68 The Lord will **send** you back to Egypt in ships, even
32.24 I will **send** wild animals to attack them, and poisonous
34.11 like those that the Lord **sent** Moses to perform against the
Josh 1.16 you have told us and will go wherever you **send** us.
2. 1 Then Joshua **sent** two spies from the camp at Acacia with
2. 3 night to spy out the country, [3]so he **sent** word to Rahab:
2.21 She agreed and **sent** them away.
6.25 she had hidden the two spies that he had **sent** to Jericho.
7. 2 Joshua **sent** some men from Jericho to Ai, a city east of
7. 3 **Send** only about two or three thousand men.
7. 3 Don't **send** the whole army up there to fight;
7.22 So Joshua **sent** some men, who ran to the tent and found
8. 3 of his best troops and **sent** them out at night
8. 9 So Joshua **sent** them out, and they went to their hiding
10. 3 Adonizedek **sent** the following message to King Hoham of Hebron,
10. 6 The men of Gibeon **sent** word to Joshua at the camp in
11. 1 King Jabin of Hazor, he **sent** word to King Jobab of Madon,
11. 3 He also **sent** word to the Canaanites on both sides of the
14. 7 when the Lord's servant Moses **sent** me from Kadesh Barnea to
14.11 just as strong today as I was when Moses **sent** me out.
18. 4 I will **send** them out over the whole country to map out
22. 6 Joshua **sent** them home with his blessing
22.13 Then the people of Israel **sent** Phinehas, the son of
24. 5 Later I **sent** Moses and Aaron, and I brought great trouble
24. 9 He **sent** word to Balaam son of Beor and asked him to
24.28 Then Joshua **sent** the people away, and everyone returned
Judg 1.22 They **sent** spies to the city, [24]who saw a man leaving
2. 6 Joshua **sent** the people of Israel on their way, and each
3. 9 out to the Lord, and he **sent** a man who freed them.
3.15 out to the Lord, and he **sent** a man to free them.
3.15 The people of Israel **sent** Ehud to King Eglon of Moab
4. 6 One day she **sent** for Barak son of Abinoam from the city
4.13 and all his men, and **sent** them from Harosheth-of-the-Gentiles
6. 8 against the Midianites, [8]and he **sent** them a prophet who brought
6.14 I myself am **sending** you."
6.35 He **sent** messengers throughout the territory of both parts
6.35 He **sent** messengers to the tribes of Asher, Zebulun,
7. 8 Gideon **sent** all the Israelites home, except the three hundred,
7.24 Gideon **sent** messengers through all the hill-country of Ephraim
9.31 He **sent** messengers to Abimelech at Arumah to say,
11.12 Then Jephthah **sent** messengers to the king of Ammon
11.14 Jephthah **sent** messengers back to the king of Ammon
11.17 Then they **sent** messengers to the king of Edom to ask
11.19 Then the Israelites **sent** messengers to Sihon,
11.38 He told her to go and **sent** her away for two months.
13. 8 man of God that you **sent** come back to us and tell
14.11 the Philistines saw him, they **sent** thirty young men to stay
16.18 told her the truth, she **sent** a message to the Philistine
18. 2 families in the tribe and **sent** them from the towns of Zorah
19.29 it into twelve pieces, and **sent** one piece to each of the
20. 6 cut it in pieces, and **sent** one piece to each of the
20.12 The Israelite tribes **sent** messengers all through the territory
21.10 So the assembly **sent** twelve thousand of their bravest men with
21.13 Then the whole assembly **sent** word to the Benjaminites who
Ruth 1.21 when the Lord Almighty has condemned me and **sent** me trouble?"
1 Sam 2. 6 he **sends** people to the world of the dead and brings them
4. 4 So they **sent** messengers to Shiloh and fetched the Covenant Box
5. 8 So they **sent** messengers and called together all five of
5.10 So they **sent** the Covenant Box to Ekron, another Philistine city;
5.11 So again they **sent** for all the Philistine kings and said,
5.11 "**Send** the Covenant Box of Israel back
6. 2 If we **send** it back where it belongs,
6. 2 what shall we **send** with it?"
6. 3 Israel, you must, of course, **send** with it a gift to him
6. 4 "What gift shall we **send** him?"
6. 4 The same plague was **sent** on all of you and on the
6. 8 gold models that you are **sending** to him as a gift to
6. 9 God of the Israelites who has **sent** this terrible disaster on us.
6. 9 doesn't, then we will know that he did not **send** the plague;
6.17 The Philistines **sent** the five gold tumours to the Lord
6.18 They also **sent** gold mice, one for each of the cities
6.20 Where can we **send** him to get him away from us?"
6.21 They **sent** messengers to the people of Kiriath Jearim to say,
7. 5 Then Samuel **sent** for all the Israelites to meet at Mizpah,
1 Sam 9.16 about this time I will **send** you a man from the tribe
9.19 I will answer all your questions and **send** you on your way.
9.26 the roof, "Get up, and I will **send** you on your way."
10.25 Then he **sent** everyone home.
11. 3 "Give us seven days to **send** messengers throughout the land
11. 7 cut them in pieces, and **sent** messengers to carry the pieces
12. 8 Lord for help, and he **sent** Moses and Aaron, who brought them
12.11 And the Lord **sent** Gideon, Barak, Jephthah, and finally me.
12.17 But I will pray, and the Lord will **send** thunder and rain.
12.18 prayed, and on that same day the Lord **sent** thunder and rain.
13. 2 and **sending** one thousand with his son Jonathan
13. 2 The rest of the men Saul **sent** home.
13. 3 Then Saul **sent** messengers to call the Hebrews to war by
13.23 The Philistines **sent** a group of soldiers to defend the pass
15. 1 the one whom the Lord **sent** to anoint you king of his
15. 6 He **sent** a warning to the Kenites, a people whose ancestors
15.18 king of Israel, [18]and he **sent** you out with orders to
16.12 So Jesse **sent** for him.
16.14 Saul, and an evil spirit **sent** by the Lord tormented him.
16.15 "We know that an evil spirit **sent** by God is tormenting you.
16.19 So Saul **sent** messengers to Jesse to say,
16.19 "**Send** me your son David,
16.20 Jesse **sent** David to Saul with a young goat, a donkey
16.22 Then Saul **sent** a message to Jesse:
16.23 on, whenever the evil spirit **sent** by God came on Saul, David
17.31 what David had said, and they told Saul, who **sent** for him.
18. 5 the missions on which Saul **sent** him, and so Saul made him
18.13 So Saul **sent** him away and put him in command of a
19.11 That same night Saul **sent** some men to watch David's
19.15 But Saul **sent** them back to see David for themselves.
19.20 in Naioth in Ramah, [20]so he **sent** some men to arrest him.
19.21 Saul heard of this, he **sent** more messengers, and they also
19.21 He **sent** messengers the third time, and the same thing
20.12 If his attitude towards you is good, I will **send** you word.
20.22 of you,' then leave, because the Lord is **sending** you away.
21. 2 me not to let anyone know what he **sent** me to do.
22.11 So King Saul **sent** for the priest Ahimelech and all his
25. 5 heard about it, [5]so he **sent** ten young men with orders to
25. 6 "David **sends** you greetings, my friend, with his best wishes for
25.14 David **sent** some messengers from the wilderness with greetings
25.32 Lord, the God of Israel, who **sent** you today to meet me!
25.39 Then David **sent** a proposal of marriage to Abigail.
25.40 and said to her, "David **sent** us to take you to him
26. 4 to look for him, [4]he **sent** spies and found out that Saul
26.12 because the Lord had **sent** a heavy sleep on them all.
29. 4 Achish and said to him, "**Send** that fellow back to the town
30.26 David returned to Ziklag, he **sent** part of the loot to his
30.27 He **sent** it to the people in Bethel, to the people in
30.31 He **sent** it to all the places where he and his men
31. 9 stripped off his armour, and **sent** messengers with them
2 Sam 2. 5 had buried Saul, [5]he **sent** some men there with the message:
3.12 Abner **sent** messengers to David, who at that time was at Hebron,
3.14 And David also **sent** messengers to Ishbosheth to say, "Give me
3.21 gave Abner a guarantee of safety and **sent** him on his way.
3.22 with David, because David had **sent** him away with a guarantee
3.23 King David and had been **sent** away with a guarantee of safety.
3.26 After leaving David, Joab **sent** messengers to get Abner,
5.11 King Hiram of Tyre **sent** a trade mission to David;
8. 5 the Syrians of Damascus **sent** an army to help King Hadadezer,
8.10 So he **sent** his son Joram to greet King David and
9. 5 So King David **sent** for him.
10. 2 So David **sent** messengers to express his sympathy.
10. 3 that David has **sent** these men to express sympathy
10. 3 He has **sent** them here as spies to explore the city, so
10. 4 cut off their clothes at the hips, and **sent** them away.
10. 5 about what had happened, he **sent** word that they should stay
10. 7 David heard of it and **sent** Joab against them with the
10.16 King Hadadezer **sent** for the Syrians who were on the east
11. 1 usually go to war, David **sent** out Joab with his officers and
11. 3 So he **sent** a messenger to find out who she was, and
11. 4 David **sent** messengers to fetch her;
11. 5 that she was pregnant and **sent** a message to David to tell
11. 6 David then **sent** a message to Joab:
11. 6 "**Send** me Uriah the Hittite."
11. 6 So Joab **sent** him to David.
11. 8 Uriah left, and David **sent** a present to his home.
11.12 here the rest of the day, and tomorrow I'll **send** you back."
11.14 morning David wrote a letter to Joab and **sent** it by Uriah.
11.16 was besieging the city, he **sent** Uriah to a place where he
11.18 Then Joab **sent** a report to David telling him about the battle,
11.27 of mourning was over, David **sent** for her to come to the
12. 1 The Lord **sent** the prophet Nathan to David.
12.27 He **sent** messengers to David to report:
13. 7 So David **sent** word to Tamar in the palace:
13. 9 He said, "**Send** everyone away"—and they all left.
13.16 "To **send** me away like this is a greater crime than what
14. 2 Absalom very much, [2]so he **sent** for a clever woman who lived
14.29 Then he **sent** for Joab, to ask him to go to the
14.29 Again Absalom **sent** for him, and again Joab refused to come.
14.32 answered, "Because you wouldn't come when I **sent** for you.
14.33 The king **sent** for Absalom, who went to him and bowed down
15.10 But he **sent** messengers to all the tribes of Israel to say,
15.12 was offering sacrifices, Absalom also **sent** to the town of
15.36 with them, and you can **send** them to me with all the
17.16 **Send** a message to David not to spend the night at the
18. 2 Then he **sent** them out in three groups, with Joab and
18. 3 better if you stay here in the city and **send** us help."
18.29 "Sir, when your officer Joab **sent** me, I saw a great commotion,
19.11 So he **sent** the priests Zadok and Abiathar to ask the leaders
19.14 men of Judah, and they **sent** him word to return with all
22.15 with flashes of lightning he **sent** them running.

2 Sam 24.15 So the Lord **sent** an epidemic on Israel, which lasted
1 Kgs 1.32 Then King David **sent** for Zadok, Nathan, and Benaiah.
1.44 He **sent** Zadok, Nathan, Benaiah, and the royal bodyguard
1.53 King Solomon then **sent** for Adonijah and had him brought
2.29 was by the altar, Solomon **sent** a messenger to Joab to ask
2.29 So King Solomon **sent** Benaiah to kill Joab.
2.36 Then the king **sent** for Shimei and said to him, "Build
2.42 what Shimei had done, [42] he **sent** for him and said, "I made
3.24 He **sent** for a sword, and when it was brought, [25] he
4.34 world heard of his wisdom and **sent** people to listen to him.
5. 1 his father David as king he **sent** ambassadors to him.
5. 2 Solomon **sent** back this message to Hiram:
5. 6 So **send** your men to Lebanon to cut down cedars for me.
5. 8 Then Hiram **sent** Solomon the following message:
7.13 King Solomon **sent** for a man named Huram, a craftsman living
8.36 Then, O Lord, **send** rain on this land of yours, which you
8.66 On the eighth day Solomon **sent** the people home.
9.14 Hiram had **sent** Solomon more than four thousand kilogrammes
9.27 King Hiram **sent** some experienced seamen from his fleet
12. 3 people of the northern tribes **sent** for him, and then they
12.18 Then King Rehoboam **sent** Adoniram, who was in charge
13.26 And so the Lord **sent** the lion to attack and kill him,
15.18 Temple and the palace, and **sent** it by some of his officials
15.20 agreed to Asa's proposal and **sent** his commanding officers and
15.22 Then King Asa **sent** out an order throughout all Judah
17.14 out of oil before the day that I, the Lord, **send** rain.' "
18. 1 "Go and present yourself to King Ahab, and I will **send** rain."
18.24 Lord, and the one who answers by **sending** fire—he is God."
18.38 The Lord **sent** fire down, and it burnt up the sacrifice,
19. 2 She **sent** a message to Elijah:
19.11 the Lord passed by and **sent** a furious wind that split the
20. 2 He **sent** messengers into the city to King Ahab of Israel to
20. 5 "I **sent** you word that you were to hand over to me
20. 6 Now, however, I will **send** my officers to search your
20. 7 He **sent** me a message demanding my wives and children, my
20.17 Scouts **sent** out by Benhadad reported to him that a group of
21. 8 them with his seal, and **sent** them to the officials and
21.14 The message was **sent** to Jezebel:
2 Kgs 1. 2 So he **sent** some messengers to consult Baalzebub, the god of
1. 6 'Why are you **sending** messengers to consult Baalzebub, the god
1. 9 Then he **sent** an officer with fifty men to get Elijah.
1.11 The king **sent** another officer with fifty men, who went
1.13 Once more the king **sent** an officer with fifty men.
1.16 'Because you **sent** messengers to consult Baalzebub, the god
3. 7 He **sent** word to King Jehoshaphat of Judah:
4.22 and said to him, "**Send** a servant here with a donkey.
5. 8 Elisha heard what had happened, he **sent** word to the king:
5. 8 **Send** the man to me, and I'll show him that there is
5.10 Elisha **sent** a servant out to tell him to go and wash
5.22 "But my master **sent** me to tell you that just now two
5.23 to two of his servants, and **sent** them on ahead of Gehazi.
5.24 Then he **sent** Naaman's servants back.
6. 9 But Elisha **sent** word to the king of Israel, warning him
6.14 Elisha was in Dothan, [14] he **sent** a large force there with
6.23 had eaten and drunk, he **sent** them back to the king of
6.32 And he **sent** a messenger to get Elisha.
6.32 the elders, "That murderer is **sending** someone to kill me!
7. 2 not even if the Lord himself were to **send** grain at once!"
7.13 So let's **send** some men with five of the horses that are
7.14 some men, and the king **sent** them in two chariots with
7.19 not even if the Lord himself were to **send** grain at once!"
8. 1 life, that the Lord was **sending** a famine on the land, which
8. 9 "Your servant King Benhadad has **sent** me to ask you whether
9.17 Joram replied, "**Send** a horseman to find out if they are
9.19 Another messenger was **sent** out, who asked Jehu the same
10. 1 Jehu wrote a letter and **sent** copies to the rulers of the
10. 5 leading citizens and the guardians, **sent** this message to Jehu:
10. 7 their heads in baskets, and **sent** them to Jehu at Jezreel.
10.21 proclamation was made, [21] and Jehu **sent** word throughout all
11. 4 seventh year Jehoiada the priest **sent** for the officers in charge
12.18 Temple and the palace, and **sent** them all as a gift to
13. 5 The Lord **sent** Israel a leader, who freed them from the Syrians,
14. 8 Then Amaziah **sent** messengers to King Jehoash of Israel,
14. 9 But King Jehoash **sent** back the following reply:
14. 9 bush on the Lebanon Mountains **sent** a message to a cedar:
15.37 king that the Lord first **sent** King Rezin of Syria and King
16. 7 Ahaz **sent** men to Tiglath Pileser, the emperor of Assyria,
16. 8 and the palace treasury and **sent** it as a present to the
16.10 saw the altar there and **sent** back to Uriah the priest an
17. 4 But one year Hoshea **sent** messengers to So, king of Egypt,
17.13 The Lord had **sent** his messengers and prophets to warn Israel
17.25 the Lord, and so he **sent** lions, which killed some of them.
17.26 and so the god had **sent** lions, which were killing them.
17.27 "**Send** back one of the priests we brought as prisoners;
18.14 Hezekiah **sent** a message to Sennacherib, who was in Lachish:
18.14 Hezekiah should **send** him ten thousand kilogrammes of silver
18.15 Hezekiah **sent** him all the silver in the Temple and in
18.16 had covered the doorposts, and he **sent** it all to Sennacherib.
18.17 The Assyrian emperor **sent** a large army from Lachish to
18.18 Then they **sent** for King Hezekiah, and three of his officials
18.24 you expect the Egyptians to **send** you chariots and horsemen!
18.27 the only ones the emperor **sent** me to say all these things
19. 2 He **sent** Eliakim, the official in charge of the palace, Shebna,
19. 4 The Assyrian emperor has **sent** his chief official to insult
19. 6 When Isaiah received King Hezekiah's message, [6] he **sent** back
19. 9 the emperor heard this, he **sent** a letter to King Hezekiah
19.20 Then Isaiah **sent** a message telling King Hezekiah that
19.23 You **sent** your messengers to boast to me that with all
19.30 will flourish like plants that **send** roots deep into the
20.12 had been ill, so he **sent** him a letter and a present.
22. 3 of his reign, King Josiah **sent** the court secretary Shaphan,
2 Kgs 24. 2 The Lord **sent** armed bands of Babylonians, Syrians, Moabites,
1 Chr 6.15 of Judah and Jerusalem whom the Lord **sent** into exile.
10. 9 and **sent** messengers with them throughout Philistia
12.19 to his former master Saul, so they **sent** him back to Ziklag.
13. 2 Lord our God, let us **send** messengers to the rest of our
14. 1 King Hiram of Tyre **sent** a trade mission to David;
15. 4 Next he **sent** for the descendants of Aaron and for the Levites.
17. 1 One day he **sent** for the prophet Nathan and said to him,
18. 5 When the Syrians of Damascus **sent** an army to help King Hadadezer,
18.10 So he **sent** his son Joram to greet King David and
19. 2 So David **sent** messengers to express his sympathy.
19. 3 that David has **sent** these men to express sympathy
19. 3 He has **sent** them here as spies to explore the land, so
19. 4 cut off their clothes at the hips, and **sent** them away.
19. 5 heard what had happened, he **sent** word for them to stay in
19. 8 what was happening, he **sent** out Joab and the whole army,
21.12 you with his sword and **sends** an epidemic on your land, using
21.14 So the Lord **sent** an epidemic on the people of Israel,
21.15 Then he **sent** an angel to destroy Jerusalem, but he
21.26 the Lord answered him by **sending** fire from heaven to burn
22. 6 He **sent** for his son Solomon and commanded him to build a
2 Chr 2. 3 Solomon **sent** a message to King Hiram of Tyre:
2. 7 Now **send** me a man with skill in engraving, in working gold,
2. 8 skilful your woodmen are, so **send** me cedar, cypress, and juniper
2. 8 I am ready to **send** my men to assist yours [9] in preparing
2.10 for your workmen, I will **send** you two thousand metric tons
2.11 King Hiram **sent** Solomon a letter in reply.
2.13 I am **sending** you a wise and skilful master craftsman
2.15 So now **send** us the wheat, barley, wine, and olive-oil
6.27 Then, O Lord, **send** rain on this land of yours, which you
7.10 of the seventh month, Solomon **sent** the people home.
7.13 hold back the rain or **send** locusts to eat up the crops
7.13 crops or **send** an epidemic on my
8. 2 King Hiram had given him, and **sent** Israelites to settle in them.
8.18 King Hiram **sent** him ships under the command of his own
10. 3 people of the northern tribes **sent** for him, and they all
10.18 Then King Rehoboam **sent** Adoniram, who was in charge
13.13 Meanwhile Jeroboam had **sent** some of his troops to ambush
16. 2 Temple and the palace and **sent** it to Damascus, to King
16. 4 agreed to Asa's proposal and **sent** his commanding officers and
17. 7 year of his reign he **sent** out the following officials to
21.12 The prophet Elijah **sent** Jehoram a letter, which read as follows:
24. 9 They **sent** word throughout Jerusalem and Judah for everyone
24.19 The Lord **sent** prophets to warn them to return to him,
25.10 So Amaziah **sent** the hired troops away and told them to
25.15 This made the Lord angry, so he **sent** a prophet to Amaziah.
25.17 He then **sent** a message to King Jehoash of Israel, who was
25.18 Jehoash **sent** this answer to Amaziah:
25.18 bush in the Lebanon Mountains **sent** a message to a cedar:
28.16 asked Tiglath Pileser, the emperor of Assyria, to **send** help.
30. 1 second month, and the king **sent** word to all the people of
30. 1 He took special care to **send** letters to the tribes of
32. 9 were still at Lachish, he **sent** the following message to Hezekiah
32.21 The Lord **sent** an angel that killed the soldiers and officers
34. 8 ending pagan worship, King Josiah **sent** three men to repair
35.21 Josiah tried to stop him, [21] but Neco **sent** Josiah this message:
36.15 had continued to **send** prophets to warn his people,
36.22 issue the following command and **send** it out in writing to be
Ezra 1. 1 issue the following command and **send** it out in writing to be
3. 7 drink, and olive-oil to be **sent** to the cities of Tyre and
4. 2 since Esarhaddon, emperor of Assyria, **sent** us here to live."
4.17 The emperor **sent** this answer:
4.18 "The letter which you **sent** has been translated and read to me.
5. 6 This is the report that they **sent** to the emperor:
6. 6 Then Darius **sent** the following reply:
7.14 together with my seven counsellors, **send** you to investigate
8.16 I **sent** for nine of the leaders:
8.17 I **sent** them to Iddo, head of the community at Casiphia,
8.17 associates, the temple workmen, to **send** us people to serve
8.18 Through God's grace they **sent** us Sherebiah, an able man,
8.19 They also **sent** Hashabiah and Jeshaiah of the clan of Merari,
10. 3 God that we will **send** these women and their children away.
10. 7 A message was **sent** throughout Jerusalem and Judah that all
10.44 They divorced them and **sent** them and their children away.
Neh 2. 9 The emperor **sent** some army officers and a troop of
6. 2 So Sanballat and Geshem **sent** me a message, suggesting that
6. 3 I **sent** messengers to say to them, "I am doing important
6. 4 They **sent** me the same message four times,
6. 4 and each time I **sent** them the same reply.
6. 5 Then Sanballat **sent** one of his servants to me with a fifth
6. 8 I **sent** a reply to him:
6.19 And he kept **sending** me letters to try to frighten me.
8.15 the following instructions and **sent** them all through Jerusalem
9.27 In your great mercy you **sent** them leaders who rescued them
Esth 1.15 these men, "I, King Xerxes, **sent** my servants to Queen
1.22 of the royal provinces he **sent** a message in the language and
3.12 the empire and to be **sent** to all the rulers, governors, and
4. 4 **sent** Mordecai some clothes to put on instead of the sackcloth,
4.11 But it has been a month since the king **sent** for me."
4.13 Mordecai received Esther's message, [13] he **sent** her this warning:
4.15 Esther **sent** Mordecai this reply:
9.20 these events written down and **sent** letters to all the Jews,
9.30 the Jews, and copies were **sent** to all the 127 provinces of
Job 2.10 When God **sends** us something good, we welcome it.
2.10 How can we complain when he **sends** us trouble?"
5.10 He **sends** rain on the land and he waters the fields.
7.14 you **send** me visions and nightmares [15] until I would rather
9. 6 God **sends** earthquakes and shakes the ground;
9.17 He **sends** storms to batter and bruise me without any
12.22 He **sends** light to places dark as death.

Job 14.20 You overpower a man and **send** him away for ever;
19.12 He **sends** his army to attack me;
30.12 they **send** me running;
31. 3 He **sends** disaster and ruin to those who do wrong.
33.19 God corrects a man by **sending** sickness and filling his body
36.21 your suffering was **sent** to keep you from it.
36.30 He **sends** lightning through all the sky, but the depths
37. 3 He **sends** the lightning across the sky, from one end of the
37. 6 to fall on the earth, and **sends** torrents of drenching rain.
37.13 God **sends** rain to water the earth;
37.13 he may **send** it to punish men, or to show them his
38.20 you show them how far to go, or **send** them back again?
Ps 11. 6 He **sends** down flaming coals and burning sulphur on the wicked;
18.14 with flashes of lightning he **sent** them running.
20. 2 May he **send** you help from his Temple and give you aid
42. 6 He has **sent** waves of sorrow over my soul;
43. 3 **Send** your light and your truth;
65. 9 You show your care for the land by **sending** rain;
65.10 you **send** abundant rain on the ploughed fields and soak them
71.20 You have **sent** troubles and suffering on me, but you will
78.24 grain from heaven, by **sending** down manna for them to eat.
78.27 and to his people he **sent** down birds, as many as the
78.45 He **sent** flies among them, that tormented them, and frogs
78.46 He **sent** locusts to eat their crops and to destroy their fields.
104.13 From the sky you **send** rain on the hills, and the earth
105.16 The Lord **sent** famine to their country and took away all
105.17 But he **sent** a man ahead of them, Joseph, who had been
105.26 Then he **sent** his servant Moses, and Aaron, whom he had chosen.
105.28 God **sent** darkness on the country, but the Egyptians did
105.32 He **sent** hail and lightning on their land instead of rain;
105.40 They asked, and he **sent** quails;
106.15 asked for, but also **sent** a terrible disease among them.
144. 6 **Send** flashes of lightning and scatter your enemies;
144. 6 shoot your arrows and **send** them running.
147.17 He **sends** hail like gravel;
147.17 no one can endure the cold he **sends!**
147.18 he **sends** the wind, and the water flows.
Prov 5.23 His utter stupidity will **send** him to his grave.
9. 3 She has **sent** her servant-girls to call out from the
22.21 Then when you are **sent** to find it out, you will bring
25.13 refreshing to the one who **sends** him, like cold water in the
Ecc 7.14 God **sends** both happiness and trouble;
Is 4. 5 gathered there, the Lord will **send** a cloud in the daytime
6. 8 Then I heard the Lord say, "Whom shall I **send?**
6. 8 **Send** me!"
6.12 I will **send** the people far away and make the whole land
7.10 The Lord **sent** another message to Ahaz:
8.18 is on Mount Zion, has **sent** us as living messages to the
9.18 It burns like a forest fire that **sends** up columns of smoke.
10. 6 I **sent** Assyria to attack a godless nation,
10. 6 I **sent** them to loot and steal and trample on the people
10.16 Lord Almighty is going to **send** disease to punish those who
14.30 But he will **send** a terrible famine on you Philistines, and
16. 1 desert the people of Moab **send** a lamb as a present to
19.20 to the Lord for help, he will **send** someone to rescue them.
22. 5 and the Sovereign Lord Almighty has **sent** it on us.
22.20 "When that happens, I will **send** for my servant Eliakim son
23. 2 You **sent** men [3]across the sea to buy and sell the corn
23. 7 Is this the city that **sent** settlers across the sea to
26. 5 they lived in, and **sent** its walls crashing into the dust.
27. 8 The Lord punished his people by **sending** them into exile.
28. 7 understand the visions that God **sends,** and the priests
29. 6 He will **send** tempests and raging fire;
30.23 your seeds, the Lord will **send** rain to make them grow and
30.28 He **sends** the wind in front of him like a flood that
31. 2 He **sends** disaster.
32.15 But once more God will **send** us his spirit.
36. 9 you expect the Egyptians to **send** you chariots and cavalry.
36.12 the only ones the emperor **sent** me to say all these things
37. 2 He **sent** Eliakim, the official in charge of the palace, Shebna,
37. 4 The Assyrian emperor has **sent** his chief official to insult
37. 6 When Isaiah received King Hezekiah's message, [6]he **sent** back
37. 9 the emperor heard this, he **sent** a letter to King Hezekiah
37.21 Then Isaiah **sent** a message telling King Hezekiah that
37.24 You **sent** your servants to boast to me that with all your
37.31 will flourish like plants that **send** roots deep into the
39. 1 had been ill, so he **sent** him a letter and a present.
40. 7 fade, when the Lord **sends** the wind blowing over them.
40.24 When the Lord **sends** a wind, they dry up and blow away
41.27 **sent** a messenger to Jerusalem to say, 'Your people are coming!
42.19 blind than my servant, more deaf than the messenger I **send?**
43.14 "To save you, I will **send** an army against Babylon;
44.26 a prediction, when I **send** a messenger to reveal my plans,
45. 1 he **sends** him to strip kings of their power;
45. 8 I will **send** victory from the sky like rain;
48.16 (Now the Sovereign Lord has given me his power and **sent** me.)
50. 1 "Do you think I **sent** my people away like a man who
50. 1 you were **sent** away because of your crimes.
53. 4 we thought that his suffering was punishment **sent** by God.
55.11 it will do everything I **send** it to do.
57. 9 find gods to worship, you **send** messengers far and wide, even
61. 1 He has chosen me and **sent** me To bring good news to
61. 2 He has **sent** me to proclaim That the time has come When
61. 2 He has **sent** me to comfort all who mourn, [3]To give to
66.19 spare some of them and **send** them to the nations and the
Jer 1. 7 go to the people I **send** you to, and tell them everything
2. 3 I **sent** suffering and disaster on everyone who hurt you.
2.10 the island of Cyprus, and **send** someone eastwards to the land
3. 8 that I divorced Israel and **sent** her away because she had
5.10 I will **send** enemies to cut down my people's vineyards,
5.24 honour me, even though I **send** the autumn rains and the

Jer 7. 1 The Lord **sent** me to the gate of the Temple where the
7.25 day, I have kept on **sending** my servants, the prophets, to
8.17 Lord says, "I am **sending** snakes among you, poisonous snakes
9.16 heard about, and I will **send** armies against them until I
10.13 flash in the rain and **sends** the wind from his storeroom.
12.12 I have **sent** war to destroy the entire land;
14. 3 The rich people **send** their servants for water;
14.14 I did not **send** them, nor did I give them any orders
14.15 prophets whom I did not **send** but who speak in my name
14.22 None of the idols of the nations can **send** rain;
15.13 said to me, "I will **send** enemies to carry away the wealth
16.16 The Lord says, "I am **sending** for many fishermen to come
16.16 Then I will **send** for many hunters to hunt them down on
17. 8 growing near a stream and **sending** out roots to the water.
18.22 **Send** a mob to plunder their homes without warning;
19.14 Topheth, where the Lord had **sent** me to proclaim his message.
21. 1 King Zedekiah of Judah **sent** Pashhur son of Malchiah
21. 3 the men who had been **sent** to me [4]to tell Zedekiah that
22. 7 I am **sending** men to destroy it.
23.21 Lord said, "I did not **send** these prophets, but even so they
23.32 I did not **send** them or order them to go, and they
25. 4 Lord has continued to **send** you his servants the prophets.
25. 9 says, [9]'I am going to **send** for all the peoples from the
25.15 the nations to whom I **send** you, and make them drink from
25.16 their minds because of the war I am **sending** against them."
25.17 to whom the Lord had **sent** me, and made them drink from
25.27 get up, because of the war that I am **sending** against them.
25.29 for I am going to **send** war on all the people on
26. 5 servants, the prophets, whom I have kept on **sending** to you.
26.12 Then I said, "The Lord **sent** me to proclaim everything
26.15 it is the Lord who **sent** me to give you this warning."
26.22 King Jehoiakim, however, **sent** Elnathan son of Achbor and
27. 3 the Lord told me to **send** a message to the kings of
27.15 said that he did not **send** them and that they are lying
28. 9 Lord has truly **sent** when that prophet's predictions come true."
28.15 The Lord did not **send** you, and you are making these people
29. 3 whom King Zedekiah of Judah was **sending** to King Nebuchadnezzar
29. 9 I did not **send** them.
29.14 to the land from which I had **sent** you away into exile.
29.19 message that I kept on **sending** to them through my servants
29.20 All of you whom I **sent** into exile in Babylonia, listen
29.24 Shemaiah of Nehelam, who had **sent** a letter in his own name
29.31 the Lord told me [31-32]to **send** to all the prisoners in
29.31 I did not **send** him, but he spoke to you as if
35.15 I have continued to **send** you all my servants the prophets,
36.14 Then the officials **sent** Jehudi (the son of Nethaniah,
36.21 Then the king **sent** Jehudi to get the scroll.
37. 3 Zedekiah **sent** Jehucal son of Shelemiah and the priest Zephaniah
37.17 Later on King Zedekiah **sent** for me, and there in the
37.20 Please do not **send** me back to the prison in Jonathan's house.
38.26 were begging me not to **send** you back to prison to die
40.14 that King Baalis of Ammon has **sent** Ishmael to murder you?"
42. 9 of Israel, to whom you **sent** me with your request has said,
42.21 everything that the Lord our God **sent** me to tell you.
43. 1 everything that the Lord their God had **sent** me to tell them.
43. 2 Lord our God did not **send** you to tell us not to
44. 4 I kept **sending** you my servants the prophets, who told you
46. 9 **Send** out the soldiers:
48.12 is coming when I will **send** people to pour Moab out like
49.14 He has **sent** a messenger to tell the nations to assemble
49.37 the people of Elam and **send** armies against them until I have
50.29 **Send** out everyone who knows how to use the bow and arrow.
51. 2 I will **send** foreigners to destroy Babylonia like a wind that
51.16 flash in the rain and **sends** the wind from his storeroom.
51.28 **Send** for the kings of Media, their leaders and officials,
51.53 fortress there, I would still **send** people to destroy it.
Lam 1.13 "He **sent** fire from above, a fire that burnt inside me.
1.15 He **sent** an army to destroy my young men.
Ezek 2. 3 "Mortal man, I am **sending** you to the people of Israel.
2. 4 respect me, so I am **sending** you to tell them what I,
3. 5 I am not **sending** you to a nation that speaks a difficult
3. 6 If I **sent** you to great nations that spoke difficult languages
5.16 the pains of hunger like sharp arrows **sent** to destroy you.
5.17 I will **send** hunger and wild animals to kill your children,
5.17 and will **send** sickness, violence, and war
6. 3 I will **send** a sword to destroy the places where people
11.16 I am the one who **sent** them to live in far-off nations
13. 6 that they are speaking my message, but I have not **sent** them.
13.11 I will **send** a pouring rain.
13.13 "In my anger I will **send** a strong wind, pouring rain, and
14.13 I will **send** a famine and kill people and animals alike.
14.15 "Or I might **send** wild animals to kill the people,
14.17 war on that country and **send** destructive weapons to wipe out
14.19 "If I **send** an epidemic on that country and in my anger
14.21 "I will **send** my four worst punishments on Jerusalem—war, famine,
17. 7 And now the vine **sent** its roots towards him and turned its
17.15 king of Judah rebelled and **sent** agents to Egypt to get
23.16 filled with lust and **sent** messengers to them in Babylonia.
23.40 "Again and again they **sent** messengers to invite men to come
26.20 I will **send** you down to the world of the dead to
28. 8 They will kill you and **send** you to a watery grave.
28.23 I will **send** diseases on you and make blood flow in your
30. 9 Egypt is destroyed, I will **send** messengers in ships to
31. 4 the tree was growing And **sent** streams to all the trees of
31.16 When I **send** it down to the world of the dead, the
32.18 **Send** them down with the other powerful nations to the world
38.14 So the Sovereign Lord **sent** me to tell Gog what he was
38.16 the time comes, I will **send** you to invade my land in
39.28 will know this, because I **sent** them into captivity and now

Dan	2. 2	he couldn't sleep, [2]so he **sent** for his fortune-tellers,
	3.28	He **sent** his angel and rescued these men who serve and trust
	4. 1	King Nebuchadnezzar **sent** the following message to the people of
	5. 2	The king **sent** for them so that he, his noblemen, his wives,
	5.12	**send** for this man Daniel, whom the king named Belteshazzar,
	5.24	That is why God has **sent** the hand to write these words.
	6.22	God **sent** his angel to shut the mouths of the lions so
	10.11	I have been **sent** to you."
	11.20	by another king, who will **send** an officer to oppress the
Hos	6. 5	That is why I have **sent** my prophets to you with my
	8.13	I will **send** them back to Egypt!
	8.14	But I will **send** fire that will burn down their palaces and
	9. 8	God has **sent** me as a prophet to warn his people Israel.
	12.13	The Lord **sent** a prophet to rescue the people of Israel
	13.15	flourishes like weeds, I will **send** a hot east wind from the
Joel	2.25	It was I who **sent** this army against you.
	3.11	**Send** down, O Lord, your army to attack them.
Amos	1. 4	So I will **send** fire upon the palace built by King Hazael
	1. 7	So I will **send** fire upon the city walls of Gaza and
	1.10	So I will **send** fire upon the city walls of Tyre and
	1.12	So I will **send** fire upon the city of Teman and burn
	1.14	So I will **send** fire upon the city walls of Rabbah and
	2. 2	I will **send** fire upon the land of Moab and burn down
	2. 5	So I will **send** fire upon Judah and burn down the
	3. 6	Does disaster strike a city unless the Lord **sends** it?
	4. 7	I **sent** rain on one city, but not on another.
	4. 9	"I **sent** a scorching wind to dry up your crops.
	4.10	sent a plague on you like the one I **sent** on Egypt.
	5. 3	says, "A city in Israel **sends** out a thousand soldiers, but
	5. 3	another city **sends** out a hundred, but only ten come back."
	6.14	Israel, I am going to **send** a foreign army to occupy your
	7.10	the priest of Bethel, then **sent** a report to King Jeroboam of
	8.11	"The time is coming when I will **send** famine on the land.
Obad	15	The Lord has **sent** his messenger to the nations, and we have
Jon	1. 4	But the Lord **sent** a strong wind on the sea, and the
	3. 7	He **sent** out a proclamation to the people of Nineveh:
	4. 8	the sun had risen, God **sent** a hot east wind, and Jonah
Mic	5. 5	we will **send** our strongest leaders to fight them.
	5. 7	be like refreshing dew **sent** by the Lord for many nations,
	6. 4	I **sent** Moses, Aaron, and Miriam to lead you.
	7.19	trample our sins underfoot and **send** them to the bottom of
Nah	1. 8	he **sends** to their death those who oppose him.
Hab	3. 5	He **sends** disease before him and commands death to follow him.
Hag	2.17	I **sent** scorching winds and hail to ruin everything you tried
Zech	1.10	The Lord **sent** them to go and inspect the earth."
	2. 8	So the Lord Almighty **sent** me with this message for the
	2. 9	everyone will know that the Lord Almighty **sent** me.
	2.11	you, and you will know that he has **sent** me to you.
	4. 9	people will know that it is I who **sent** you to them.
	5. 4	Almighty says that he will **send** this curse out, and it will
	6.15	you will know that the Lord Almighty **sent** me to you.
	7. 2	The people of Bethel had **sent** Sharezer and Regemmelech and
	7.12	to the teaching which I **sent** through the prophets who lived
	10. 1	It is the Lord who **sends** rain clouds and showers, making the
	14.18	disease that the Lord will **send** on every nation that refuses
Mal	3. 1	Lord Almighty answers, "I will **send** my messenger to prepare
	4. 5	day of the Lord comes, I will **send** you the prophet Elijah.
Mt	2. 8	Then he **sent** them to Bethlehem with these instructions:
	3. 7	you could escape from the punishment God is about to **send?**
	8.31	going to drive us out, **send** us into that herd of pigs."
	9.38	the harvest that he will **send** out workers to gather in his
	10. 5	These twelve men were **sent** out by Jesus with the following instructions:
	10.16	I am **sending** you out just like sheep
	10.40	and whoever welcomes me welcomes the one who **sent** me.
	11. 2	he **sent** some of his disciples to him.
	11.10	'God said, I will **send** my messenger ahead of you to open
	12.18	I will **send** my Spirit upon him, and he will announce my
	13.41	the Son of Man will **send** out his angels to gather
	14.15	**Send** the people away and let them go to the villages
	14.22	the other side of the lake, while he **sent** the people away.
	14.23	After **sending** the people away, he went up a hill by
	14.35	So they **sent** for the sick people in all the surrounding
	15.23	His disciples came to him and begged him, "**Send** her away!
	15.24	Jesus replied, "I have been **sent** only to the lost sheep
	15.32	I don't want to **send** them away without feeding them,
	15.39	Then Jesus **sent** the people away, got into a boat, and
	18.34	was very angry, and he **sent** the servant to jail
	19. 7	to hand his wife a divorce notice and **send** her away?"
	20. 2	silver coin a day, and **sent** them to work in his vineyard.
	21. 1	There Jesus **sent** two of the disciples on ahead [2]with these instructions:
	21.34	to gather the grapes, he **sent** his slaves to the tenants
	21.36	Again the man **sent** other slaves, more than the first time,
	21.37	Last of all he **sent** his son to them.
	22. 3	He **sent** his servants to tell the invited guests to come
	22. 4	So he **sent** other servants with this message for the guests:
	22. 7	so he **sent** his soldiers, who killed those murderers
	22.16	Then they **sent** to him some of their disciples
	23.34	tell you that I will **send** you prophets and wise men
	23.37	You kill the prophets and stone the messengers God has **sent** you!
	24.31	and he will **send** out his angels to the four
	25.46	These, then, will be **sent** off to eternal punishment,
	26.47	with swords and clubs and **sent** by the chief priests
	26.53	and at once he would **send** me more than twelve armies
	27.19	judgement hall, his wife **sent** him a message:
Mk	1. 2	"God said, 'I will **send** my messenger ahead of you
	1.43	spoke sternly to him and **sent** him away at once,
	3.14	"I will also **send** you out to preach,
	3.31	outside the house and **sent** in a message, asking for him.
	5.10	kept begging Jesus not to **send** the evil spirits out
Mk	5.12	So the spirits begged Jesus, "**Send** us to the pigs,
	6. 7	the twelve disciples together and **sent** them out two by two.
	6.27	So he **sent** off a guard at once with orders to bring
	6.36	**Send** the people away, and let them go to the nearby
	6.45	the other side of the lake, while he **sent** the crowd away.
	8. 3	If I **send** them home without feeding them, they will faint
	8. 8	Jesus **sent** the people away [10]and at once got into a boat
	8.26	Jesus then **sent** him home with the order, "Don't go back
	9.37	welcomes not only me but also the one who **sent** me."
	10. 4	to write a divorce notice and **send** his wife away."
	11. 1	Jesus **sent** two of his disciples on ahead [2]with these instructions:
	11. 3	the Master needs it and will **send** it back at once."
	12. 2	to gather the grapes, he **sent** a slave to the tenants
	12. 3	the slave, beat him, and **sent** him back without a thing.
	12. 4	Then the owner **sent** another slave;
	12. 5	The owner **sent** another slave, and they killed him;
	12. 6	The only one left to **send** was the man's own dear son.
	12. 6	Last of all, then, he **sent** his son to the tenants.
	12.13	members of Herod's party were **sent** to Jesus to trap him
	13.27	He will **send** the angels out to the four corners of the
	14.13	Then Jesus **sent** two of them with these instructions:
	14.43	with swords and clubs, and **sent** by the chief priests,
	16.10	After this, Jesus himself **sent** out through his disciples
Lk	1.19	the presence of God, who **sent** me to speak to you
	1.26	God **sent** the angel Gabriel to a town
	1.53	and **sent** the rich away with empty hands.
	3. 7	you could escape from the punishment God is about to **send?**
	4.18	He has **sent** me to proclaim liberty to the captives
	4.26	Yet Elijah was not **sent** to anyone in Israel,
	4.43	other towns also, because that is what God **sent** me to do."
	7. 3	officer heard about Jesus, he **sent** some Jewish elders
	7. 6	the officer **sent** friends to tell him, "Sir, don't
	7.19	called two of them [19]and **sent** them to the Lord
	7.20	they said, "John the Baptist **sent** us to ask if you are
	7.27	'God said, I will **send** my messenger ahead of you
	8.31	The demons begged Jesus not to **send** them into the abyss.
	8.38	But Jesus **sent** him away, saying, [39]"Go back home
	9. 2	Then he **sent** them out to preach the Kingdom of God
	9.12	came to him and said, "**Send** the people away
	9.48	whoever welcomes me, also welcomes the one who **sent** me.
	9.52	He **sent** messengers ahead of him, who went into a village
	10. 1	chose another seventy-two men and **sent** them out two by two,
	10. 2	the harvest that he will **send** out workers to gather in his
	10. 3	I am **sending** you like lambs among wolves.
	10.16	and whoever rejects me rejects the one who **sent** me."
	11.49	Wisdom of God said, 'I will **send** them prophets and messengers;
	13.34	You kill the prophets, you stone the messengers God has **sent** you!
	14. 4	Jesus took the man, healed him, and **sent** him away.
	14.17	time for the feast, he **sent** his servant to tell his guests,
	14.32	If he isn't, he will **send** messengers to meet the other king,
	15.15	citizens of that country, who **sent** him out to his farm
	16.24	Take pity on me, and **send** Lazarus to dip his finger
	16.27	father Abraham, **send** Lazarus to my father's house,
	19.14	hated him, and so they **sent** messengers after him to say, 'We
	19.29	Mount of Olives, he **sent** two disciples ahead [30]with these instructions:
	20.10	to gather the grapes, he **sent** a slave to the tenants
	20.10	tenants beat the slave and **sent** him back without a thing.
	20.11	So he **sent** another slave;
	20.11	treated him shamefully, and **sent** him back without a thing.
	20.12	Then he **sent** a third slave;
	20.13	I will **send** my own dear son;
	20.20	sincere, and they **sent** them to trap Jesus with questions,
	22. 8	Jesus **sent** off Peter and John with these instructions:
	22.35	disciples, "When I **sent** you out that time without purse,
	23. 7	region ruled by Herod, he **sent** him to Herod, who was also
	23.11	put a fine robe on him and **sent** him back to Pilate.
	23.15	did Herod find him guilty, for he **sent** him back to us.
	24.49	And I myself will **send** upon you what my Father has promised.
Jn	1. 6	God **sent** his messenger, a man named John, [7]who came to
	1.19	The Jewish authorities in Jerusalem **sent** some priests and Levites to John,
	1.22	"We have to take an answer back to those who **sent** us.
	1.24	The messengers, who had been **sent** by the Pharisees, [25]then asked John,
	1.33	the one, but God, who **sent** me to baptize with water, had
	3. 2	him, "Rabbi, we know that you are a teacher **sent** by God.
	3.17	For God did not **send** his Son into the world to be
	3.28	am not the Messiah, but I have been **sent** ahead of him.'
	3.34	The one whom God has **sent** speaks God's words, because
	4.34	will of the one who **sent** me and to finish the work
	4.38	I have **sent** you to reap a harvest in a field where
	5.23	not honour the Son does not honour the Father who **sent** him.
	5.24	my words and believes in him who **sent** me has eternal life.
	5.30	do what I want, but only what he who **sent** me wants.
	5.33	the one to whom you **sent** your messengers, and he spoke on
	5.36	speak on my behalf and show that the Father has **sent** me.
	5.37	And the Father, who **sent** me, also testifies on my behalf.
	5.38	hearts, for you do not believe in the one whom he **sent.**
	6.29	wants you to do is to believe in the one he **sent."**
	6.38	not my own will but the will of him who **sent** me.
	6.39	the will of him who **sent** me that I should not lose
	6.44	to me unless the Father who **sent** me draws him to me;
	6.57	The living Father **sent** me, and because of him I live also.
	7.16	not my own teaching, but it comes from God, who **sent** me.
	7.18	glory for the one who **sent** him is honest, and there is
	7.28	He who **sent** me, however, is truthful.
	7.29	I know him, because I come from him and he **sent** me."
	7.32	they and the chief priests **sent** some guards to arrest him.
	7.33	longer, and then I shall go away to him who **sent** me.
	8.16	the Father who **sent** me is with me.

Jn 8.18 and the Father who **sent** me also testifies on my behalf."
8.26 The one who **sent** me, however, is truthful, and I tell the
8.29 And he who **sent** me is with me;
8.42 I did not come on my own authority, but he **sent** me.
9. 4 we must keep on doing the work of him who **sent** me;
9. 7 (This name means **"Sent."**)
10.36 for me, the Father chose me and **sent** me into the world.
11. 3 The sisters **sent** Jesus a message:
11.42 people here, so that they will believe that you **sent** me."
12.44 believes not only in me but also in him who **sent** me.
12.45 Whoever sees me sees also him who **sent** me.
12.49 authority, but the Father who **sent** me has commanded me what
13.16 and no messenger is greater than the one who **sent** him.
13.20 whoever receives anyone I **send** receives me also;
13.20 and whoever receives me receives him who **sent** me."
14.24 heard is not mine, but comes from the Father, who **sent** me.
14.26 Spirit, whom the Father will **send** in my name, will teach you
15.21 for they do not know the one who **sent** me.
15.26 I will **send** him to you from the Father,
16. 5 am going to him who **sent** me, yet none of you asks
16. 7 if I do go away, then I will **send** him to you.
17. 3 the only true God, and knowing Jesus Christ, whom you **sent.**
17. 8 that I came from you, and they believe that you **sent** me.
17.18 I **sent** them into the world, just as you sent me into
17.21 be one, so that the world will believe that you **sent** me.
17.23 world may know that you **sent** me and that you love them
17.25 you, but I know you, and these know that you **sent** me.
18. 3 soldiers, and some temple guards **sent** by the chief priests
18.24 Then Annas **sent** him, still bound, to Caiaphas the High Priest.
20.21 As the Father sent me, so I **send** you."
Acts 3.20 and he will **send** Jesus, who is the Messiah
3.22 'The Lord your God will **send** you a prophet,
3.22 just as he **sent** me,
3.26 God chose his Servant and **sent** him first to you, to bless
5.21 then they **sent** orders to the prison to have the apostles
7.12 was corn in Egypt, he **sent** his sons, our ancestors, on their
7.14 So Joseph **sent** a message to his father Jacob, telling
7.34 I will **send** you to Egypt.'
7.35 is the one whom God **sent** to rule the people and set
7.37 people of Israel, 'God will **send** you a prophet,
7.37 just as he **sent** me,
7.43 And so I will **send** you into exile beyond Babylon.'
8.14 the word of God, so they **sent** Peter and John to them.
9.17 he said, "the Lord has **sent** me—Jesus himself, who appeared
9.17 He **sent** me so that you might see again and be filled
9.30 they took Saul to Caesarea and **sent** him away to Tarsus.
9.38 Peter was in Lydda, they **sent** two men to him with the
10. 5 And now **send** some men to Joppa for a certain man
10. 8 He told them what had happened and **sent** them off to Joppa.
10.17 of this vision, the men **sent** by Cornelius had learnt where
10.20 do not hesitate to go with them, for I have **sent** them."
10.22 "Captain Cornelius **sent** us," they answered.
10.29 And so when you **sent** for me, I came without any objection.
10.29 I ask you, then, why did you **send** for me?"
10.32 **Send** someone to Joppa for a man whose full name is Simon
10.33 And so I **sent** for you at once, and you have been
10.36 You know the message he **sent** to the people of Israel,
11.11 three men who had been **sent** to me from Caesarea arrived at
11.13 who said to him, **'Send** someone to Joppa for a man
11.22 the church in Jerusalem, so they **sent** Barnabas to Antioch.
11.29 that each of them would **send** as much as he could to
11.30 They did this, then, and **sent** the money to the church
12.11 The Lord **sent** his angel to rescue me from Herod's power and
13. 3 and prayed, placed their hands on them, and **sent** them off.
13. 4 Having been **sent** by the Holy Spirit, Barnabas and Saul
13.15 the officials of the synagogue **sent** them a message:
13.26 it is to us that this message of salvation has been **sent!**
15. 3 They were **sent** on their way by the church;
15.22 men from the group and **send** them to Antioch with Paul
15.23 Barsabbas, and Silas, [23] and they **sent** the following letter by them:
15.23 and the elders, your brothers, **send greetings** to all our brothers
15.25 agreed to choose some messengers and **send** them to you.
15.27 We **send** you, then, Judas and Silas,
15.30 The messengers were **sent** off and went to Antioch, where
15.33 they were **sent** off in peace by the believers
15.33 and went back to those who had **sent** them.
16.35 the Roman authorities **sent** police officers with the order,
16.36 told Paul, "The officials have **sent** an order for you and
16.37 And now they want to **send** us away secretly.
17.10 as night came, the believers **sent** Paul and Silas to Berea.
17.14 At once the believers **sent** Paul away to the coast;
19.22 So he **sent** Timothy and Erastus, two of his helpers, to
19.31 who were his friends, also **sent** him a message begging him
20.17 From Miletus Paul **sent** a message to Ephesus, asking the
21.25 have become believers, we have **sent** them a letter telling
21.31 Paul, when a report was **sent** up to the commander of the
22.21 'for I will **send** you far away to the Gentiles.'"
23.15 you and the Council **send** word to the Roman commander
23.22 And he **sent** the young man away.
23.30 at once I decided to **send** him to you.
24.24 He **sent** for Paul and listened to him as he talked about
24.26 this reason he would often **send** for him and talk with him.
25.21 be kept under guard until I could **send** him to the Emperor."
25.25 made an appeal to the Emperor, I have decided to **send** him.
25.27 seems unreasonable to me to **send** a prisoner without clearly indicating
26.17 of Israel and from the Gentiles to whom I will **send** you.
28.28 God's message of salvation has been **sent** to the Gentiles.
Rom 8. 3 sin in human nature by **sending** his own Son,
10.15 message be proclaimed if the messengers are not **sent** out?
16. 3 I **send greetings** to Priscilla and Aquila, my fellow-workers
Rom 16.13 I **send greetings** to Rufus, that outstanding worker in the Lord's service,
16.16 All the churches of Christ **send you their greetings.**
16.21 Timothy, my fellow-worker, **sends you his greetings;**
16.22 I, Tertius, the writer of this letter, **send you Christian greetings.**
16.23 Gaius, in whose house the church meets, **sends you his greetings;**
16.23 Erastus, the city treasurer, and our brother Quartus **send you their greetings.**
1 Cor 1.17 Christ did not **send** me to baptize.
1.17 He **sent** me to tell the Good News, and to tell it
2.12 we have received the Spirit **sent** by God, so that we may
4.17 For this purpose I am **sending** to you Timothy,
16. 3 men you have approved, and **send** them to take your gift
16.19 The churches in the province of Asia **send you their greetings;**
16.19 that meets in their house **send warm Christian greetings.**
16.20 All the brothers here **send greetings.**
2 Cor 2.17 but because God has **sent** us, we speak with sincerity in his
3. 3 that Christ himself wrote this letter and **sent** it by us.
8.18 With him we are **sending** the brother who is highly respected
8.22 So we are **sending** our brother with them;
9. 1 to you about the help being **sent** to God's people in Judaea.
9. 3 Now I am **sending** these brothers, so that our boasting
12.17 I take advantage of you through any of the messengers I **sent?**
12.18 Titus to go, and I **sent** the other Christian brother with him.
13.12 All God's people **send you their greetings.**
Gal 1. 2 join me in **sending greetings** to the churches of Galatia:
2.12 some men who had been **sent** by James arrived there, Peter had
4. 4 But when the right time finally came, God **sent** his own Son.
4. 6 you are his sons, God **sent** the Spirit of his Son into
4.30 It says, **"Send** the slave-woman and her son away;
Eph 6.22 That is why I am **sending** him to you—to tell you
Phil 2.19 I will be able to **send** Timothy to you soon,
2.23 So I hope to **send** him to you
2.25 thought it necessary to **send** you our brother Epaphroditus,
2.28 the more eager, then, to **send** him to you,
4.16 once when I needed help in Thessalonica, you **sent** it to me.
4.21 The brothers here with me **send you their greetings.**
4.22 All God's people here **send greetings,**
Col 4. 8 That is why I am **sending** him to you, in order to
4.10 in prison with me, **sends you greetings,** and so does Mark,
4.11 Joshua, also called Justus, **sends greetings** too.
4.14 Luke, our dear doctor, and Demas **send you their greetings.**
4.16 read the letter that the brothers in Laodicea will **send** you.
1 Thes 3. 2 alone in Athens [2] while we **sent** Timothy, our brother who
3. 2 We **sent** him to strengthen you and help your faith, [3] so that
3. 5 That is why I had to **send** Timothy.
3. 5 it any longer, so I **sent** him to find out about your
2 Thes 2.11 And so God **sends** the power of error to work in them
3.14 will not obey the message we **send** you in this letter.
1 Tim 2. 7 that is why I was **sent** as an apostle and teacher of
2 Tim 1. 1 Christ Jesus by God's will, **sent** to proclaim the promised
4.12 I **sent** Tychicus to Ephesus.
4.19 I **send greetings** to Priscilla and Aquila
4.21 Pudens, Linus, and Claudia **send their greetings,**
Tit 1. 1 I was chosen and **sent** to help the faith of God's chosen
3.12 When I **send** Artemas or Tychicus to you,
3.15 All who are with me **send you greetings.**
Phlm 12 I am **sending** him back to you now, and with him goes
23 sake of Christ Jesus, **sends you his greetings,**
Heb 1. 6 God was about to **send** his first-born Son into the world,
1.14 who serve God and are **sent** by him to help those who
3. 1 Think of Jesus, whom God **sent** to be the High Priest of
13.19 to pray that God will **send** me back to you soon.
13.24 The brothers from Italy **send you their greetings.**
Jas 5.14 He should **send** for the church elders, who will pray for him
1 Pet 1.12 Good News by the power of the Holy Spirit **sent** from heaven.
5.13 also chosen by God, **sends you greetings,** and so does my son
1 Jn 4. 9 his love for us by **sending** his only Son into the world,
4.10 that he loved us and **sent** his Son to be the means
4.14 tell others that the Father **sent** his Son to be the Saviour
2 Jn 13 The children of your dear Sister **send you their greetings.**
3 Jn 15 All your friends **send greetings.**
Rev 1. 1 to his servant John by **sending** his angel to him,
1.11 and **send** the book to the churches
5. 6 of God that have been **sent** throughout the whole earth.
11. 3 I will **send** my two witnesses dressed in sackcloth,
11.10 They will celebrate and **send** presents to each other,
22. 6 Spirit to the prophets, has **sent** his angel to show his
22.16 "I, Jesus, have **sent** my angel to announce these things

SENIOR

Gen 50. 7 All the king's officials, the **senior** men of his court, and
2 Kgs 19. 2 court secretary, and the **senior** priests to the prophet Isaiah
1 Chr 12.14 the tribe of Gad were **senior** officers in command of a
Neh 11. 9 Judah son of Hassenuah was the second **senior** official
Is 37. 2 court secretary, and the **senior** priests to the prophet Isaiah

SENNACHERIB

Emperor of Assyria who failed to capture Jerusalem.

2 Kgs 18.13 reign of King Hezekiah, **Sennacherib,** the emperor of Assyria,
18.14 Hezekiah sent a message to **Sennacherib,** who was in Lachish:
18.16 covered the doorposts, and he sent it all to **Sennacherib.**
19.16 to all the things that **Sennacherib** is saying to insult you,
19.21 city of Jerusalem laughs at you, **Sennacherib,** and despises you.
19.36 Then the Assyrian emperor **Sennacherib** withdrew and returned
2 Chr 32. 1 **Sennacherib,** the emperor of Assyria, invaded Judah.
32. 2 When Hezekiah saw that **Sennacherib** intended to attack
32. 9 while **Sennacherib** and his army were still at Lachish,
32.10 "I, **Sennacherib,** Emperor of Assyria, ask what gives you people

2 Chr 32.22 Jerusalem from the power of **Sennacherib,** the emperor of Assyria,
Is 36. 1 Hezekiah was king of Judah, **Sennacherib,** the emperor of Assyria,
37.17 to all the things that **Sennacherib** is saying to insult you,
37.22 city of Jerusalem laughs at you, **Sennacherib,** and despises you.
37.37 Then the Assyrian emperor **Sennacherib** withdrew and returned

SENSE

Deut 32. 6 you should treat the Lord, you foolish, **senseless** people?
32.28 "Israel is a nation without **sense;**
1 Sam 25.33 Thank God for your good **sense** and for what you have done
Esth 8.16 Jews there was joy and relief, happiness and a **sense** of victory.
Job 5. 2 with resentment would be a foolish, **senseless** thing to do.
7.16 My life makes no **sense.**
12. 3 But I have as much **sense** as you have;
34.34 Any **sensible** person will surely agree;
34.35 is speaking from ignorance and that nothing he says makes **sense.**
Ps 94.11 he knows how **senseless** their reasoning is.
Prov 2.14 doing wrong and who enjoy **senseless** evil, [15]unreliable men who
6.32 But a man who commits adultery hasn't any **sense.**
8. 5 Learn to have **sense.**
10. 5 A **sensible** man gathers the crops when they are ready;
10. 8 **Sensible** people accept good advice.
10.13 Intelligent people talk **sense,** but stupid people need
11.12 If you are **sensible,** you will keep quiet.
12.16 **Sensible** people will ignore an insult.
12.23 **Sensible** people keep quiet about what they know, but stupid
13.16 **Sensible** people always think before they act, but stupid
14.15 **sensible** people watch their step.
17.16 money on an education, because he has no common **sense.**
17.18 Only a man with no **sense** would promise to be responsible
19.11 If you are **sensible,** you will control your temper.
19.14 parents, but only the Lord can give him a **sensible** wife.
21.16 Death is waiting for anyone who wanders away from good **sense.**
22. 3 **Sensible** people will see trouble coming and avoid it, but
23. 9 Don't try to talk **sense** to a fool;
23.23 Truth, wisdom, learning, and good **sense**—these are worth
26. 8 is stupid makes as much **sense** as tying a stone in a
27.12 **Sensible** people will see trouble coming and avoid it, but
28. 2 and endure when it has intelligent, **sensible** leaders.
28.16 A ruler without good **sense** will be a cruel tyrant.
29.11 express their anger openly, but **sensible** people are patient
30. 2 I do not have the **sense** a man should have.
Ecc 10.10 It is more **sensible** to plan ahead.
Is 28. 6 He will give a **sense** of justice to those who serve as
44.19 hasn't the wit or the **sense** to say, "Some of the wood
44.20 It makes as much **sense** as eating ashes.
Jer 10.14 At the sight of this, men feel stupid and **senseless;**
51.17 At the sight of this, men feel stupid and **senseless;**
Dan 5.11 king, this man showed good **sense,** knowledge, and wisdom like
Hos 4.11 "Wine, both old and new, is robbing my people of their **senses!**
4.14 As the proverb says, 'A people without **sense** will be ruined.'
Mic 3. 8 power, and gives me a **sense** of justice and the courage to
Zeph 2. 1 Shameless nation, come to your **senses** [2]before you are driven
Lk 15.17 he came to his **senses** and said, 'All my father's hired
1 Cor 10.15 I speak to you as **sensible** people;
15.34 Come back to your right **senses** and stop your sinful ways.
2 Cor 9. 7 not with regret or out of a **sense** of duty;
1 Tim 2. 9 women to be modest and **sensible** about their clothes
2 Tim 2.26 they will come to their **senses** and escape from the trap
Tit 2. 2 Instruct the older men to be sober, **sensible,** and self-controlled;

SENTENCE

Deut 25. 2 If the guilty man is **sentenced** to be beaten, the judge is
1 Kgs 20.40 "You have pronounced your own **sentence,** and you will have
2 Kgs 25. 6 of Riblah, and there Nebuchadnezzar passed **sentence** on him.
2 Chr 19. 6 of the Lord, and he is with you when you pass **sentence.**
22. 8 Jehu was carrying out God's **sentence** on the dynasty, he came
Ps 94.21 who plot against good men and **sentence** the innocent to death.
Is 53. 8 He was arrested and **sentenced** and led off to die, and no
65. 6 decided on their punishment, and their **sentence** is written down.
Jer 26.11 "This man deserves to be **sentenced** to death because he has
39. 5 of Hamath, and there Nebuchadnezzar passed **sentence** on him.
52. 9 of Hamath, and there Nebuchadnezzar passed **sentence** on him.
Ezek 4. 4 I have **sentenced** you to one day for each year their
11. 9 I have **sentenced** you to death, [10]and you will be killed in
20. 4 "Are you ready to pass **sentence** on them, mortal man?
Zeph 2. 5 The Lord has passed **sentence** on you.
Lk 23.24 So Pilate passed the **sentence** on Jesus that they were asking for.
23.40 You received the same **sentence** he did.
24.20 him over to be **sentenced** to death, and he was crucified.
Acts 13.28 reason to pass the death **sentence** on him, they asked Pilate
25.25 had done anything for which he deserved the death **sentence.**
26.10 they were **sentenced** to death, I also voted against them.
2 Cor 1. 9 We felt that the death **sentence** had been passed on us.
2 Tim 4.17 and I was rescued from being **sentenced** to death.

SENTRY

2 Sam 13.34 Just then the soldier on **sentry** duty saw a large crowd
Ps 127. 1 the city, it is useless for the **sentries** to stand guard.
141. 3 guard at my mouth, a **sentry** at the door of my lips.
Is 21. 6 me, "Go and post a **sentry,** and tell him to report what
21. 8 The **sentry** calls out, "Sir, I have been standing guard at
21. 9 The **sentry** gives the news, "Babylon has fallen!
21.11 calls to me from Edom, **"Sentry,** how soon will the night be
62. 6 On your walls, Jerusalem, I have placed **sentries;**
Jer 51.12 Post the **sentries!**

SEPARATE

Gen 1. 4 Then he **separated** the light from the darkness, [5]and he
1. 6 and to keep it in two **separate** places"—and it was done.
1. 6 made a dome, and it **separated** the water under it from the
1.14 appear in the sky to **separate** day from night and to show
1.18 the day and the night, and to **separate** light from darkness.
13. 9 So let's **separate.**
21.28 Abraham **separated** seven lambs from his flock,
30.40 Jacob kept the sheep **separate** from the goats and made them
31.49 keep an eye on us while we are **separated** from each other."
43.32 eating there were served **separately,** because they considered
Ex 26.33 curtain will **separate** the Holy Place from the Most Holy Place.
28. 1 **Separate** them from the people of Israel, so that they may
Num 8. 6 The Lord said to Moses, [6]**"Separate** the Levites from the rest
8.14 **Separate** the Levites in this way from the rest of the Israelites,
26.62 They were listed **separately** from the rest of the Israelites,
Judg 7. 4 down to the water, and I will **separate** them for you there.
7. 5 the Lord said to him, **"Separate** everyone who laps up the
Ruth 1.17 upon me if I let anything but death **separate** me from you!"
1 Sam 23.26 one side of the hill, **separated** from David and his men, who
2 Sam 14. 6 there was no one to **separate** them, and one of them killed
2 Kgs 17.21 After the Lord had **separated** Israel from Judah, the Israelites
Ezra 9. 1 Levites had not kept themselves **separate** from the people in
10.11 **Separate** yourselves from the foreigners living in our land and
Neh 4.19 that we are widely **separated** from one another on the wall.
9. 1 They had already **separated** themselves from all foreigners.
10.28 obedience to God's Law have **separated** themselves from
Is 7.17 since the kingdom of Israel **separated** from Judah—he is going
27.12 by one, like someone **separating** the wheat from the chaff.
59. 2 It is your sins that **separate** you from God when you try
Ezek 34.17 judge each of you and **separate** the good from the bad, the
34.22 judge each of my sheep and **separate** the good from the bad.
42.20 The wall served to **separate** what was holy from what was not.
Zech 12.12 men of each family will mourn **separately** from the women.
Mt 19. 6 Man must not **separate,** then, what God has joined together."
25.32 just as a shepherd **separates** the sheep from the goats.
Mk 10. 9 Man must not **separate,** then, what God has joined together."
Lk 22.31 test all of you, to **separate** the good from the bad,
22.31 as a farmer **separates** the wheat from the chaff.
Acts 3.23 prophet shall be **separated** from God's people and destroyed.'
15.39 There was a sharp argument, and they **separated:**
Rom 8.35 Who, then, can **separate** us from the love of Christ?
8.38 For I am certain that nothing can **separate** us from his love:
8.39 will ever be able to **separate** us from the love of God
9. 3 I myself were under God's curse and **separated** from Christ.
2 Cor 6.17 Lord says, "You must leave them and **separate** yourselves from them.
Gal 4.17 All they want is to **separate** you from me, so that you
5.20 They **separate** into parties and groups;
Eph 2.14 down the wall that **separated** them and kept them enemies.
4.16 So when each **separate** part works as it should, the whole
1 Thes 2.17 us, brothers, when we were **separated** from you for a little
2 Thes 1. 9 the punishment of eternal destruction, **separated** from the

SEPARATION HILL

1 Sam 23.28 That is why that place is called **Separation Hill.**

SERENE

Is 18. 4 nights of harvest time, as **serenely** as the sun shines in the

SERIES

Ezek 41. 5 the Temple, was a **series** of small rooms two metres wide.

SERIOUS

Gen 44. 5 You have committed a **serious** crime!' "
Deut 15.21 blind or have any other **serious** defect, you must not sacrifice
Judg 12. 2 "My people and I had a **serious** quarrel with the Ammonites.
1 Sam 2.17 sons of Eli was extremely **serious** in the Lord's sight,
2 Kgs 1. 2 the roof of his palace in Samaria and was **seriously** injured.
Esth 7. 4 If it were nothing more **serious** than being sold into slavery,
Prov 4.10 Take **seriously** what I am telling you, and you will live a
23.19 son, be wise and give **serious** thought to the way you live.
Ecc 6. 1 I have noticed that in this world a **serious** injustice is done.
10. 4 **serious** wrongs may be pardoned if you keep calm.
Mal 2. 2 curse on them, because you do not take my command **seriously.**
Acts 19.23 this time that there was **serious** trouble in Ephesus because
25. 7 him and started making many **serious** charges against him,
Tit 2. 7 Be sincere and **serious** in your teaching.

SERPENT

A name given to the dragon, which appears in the New Testament as a picture of the Devil.

Rev 12. 9 was thrown out—that ancient **serpent,** called the Devil, or
20. 2 seized the dragon, that ancient **serpent**—that is, the Devil,

AV **SERPENT** see **DRAGON, MONSTER, SNAKE**

SERVANT

[FELLOW-SERVANT]

Gen 13. 5 goats, and cattle, as well as his own family and **servants.**
18. 7 and gave it to a **servant,** who hurried to get it ready.
19. 3 Lot ordered his **servants** to bake some bread and prepare a
21.25 about a well which the **servants** of Abimelech had seized.

Gen 22. 3 loaded his donkey, and took Isaac and two **servants** with him.
22. 5 Then he said to the **servants,** "Stay here with the donkey.
22.19 Abraham went back to his **servants,** and they went together
24. 2 He said to his oldest **servant,** who was in charge of all
24. 5 But the **servant** asked, "What if the girl will not leave
24. 9 So the **servant** put his hand between the thighs of Abraham,
24.10 The **servant,** who was in charge of Abraham's property, took ten
24.14 she be the one that you have chosen for your **servant** Isaac.
24.17 The **servant** ran to meet her and said, "Please give me a
24.29 ran outside to go to the well where Abraham's **servant** was.
24.30 He went to Abraham's **servant,** who was standing by his camels
24.32 he brought water for Abraham's **servant** and his men to wash
24.34 "I am the **servant** of Abraham," he began.
24.52 When the **servant** of Abraham heard this, he bowed down and
24.54 Then Abraham's **servant** and the men with him ate and drank,
24.59 Rebecca and her old family **servant**
24.59 go with Abraham's **servant** and his men.
24.61 to go with Abraham's **servant,** and they all started out.
24.65 her camel [65] and asked Abraham's **servant,** "Who is that man
24.65 "He is my master," the **servant** answered.
24.66 The **servant** told Isaac everything he had done.
26.14 sheep and cattle and many **servants,** the Philistines were jealous
26.15 all the wells which the **servants** of his father Abraham had
26.19 Isaac's **servants** dug a well in the valley and found water.
26.21 Isaac's **servants** dug another well, and there was a quarrel
26.24 many descendants because of my promise to my **servant** Abraham."
26.25 set up his camp there, and his **servants** dug another well.
26.32 On that day Isaac's **servants** came and told him about the
27.29 May nations be your **servants,** and may peoples bow down
32. 4 "I, Jacob, your obedient **servant,** report to my master Esau
32.10 and faithfulness that you have shown me, your **servant.**
32.16 herds and put one of his **servants** in charge of each herd.
32.17 He ordered the first **servant,** "When my brother Esau meets you
32.18 you must answer, 'They belong to your **servant** Jacob.
32.20 You must say, 'Yes, your **servant** Jacob is just behind us.' "
39. 4 Potiphar was pleased with him and made him his personal **servant;**
39.11 house to do his work, none of the house **servants** was there.
39.14 she called to her house **servants** and said, "Look at this!
40. 4 prison, and the captain assigned Joseph as their **servant.**
43.16 them, he said to the **servant** in charge of his house, "Take
43.17 The **servant** did as he was commanded and took the
43.19 they said to the **servant** in charge, [20] "If you please, sir,
43.23 The **servant** said, "Don't worry.
43.24 The **servant** took the brothers into the house.
43.28 "Your humble **servant,** our father, is still alive and well."
44. 1 Joseph commanded the **servant** in charge of his house,
44. 4 city, Joseph said to the **servant** in charge of his house,
44. 6 When the **servant** caught up with them, he repeated these words.
44.12 Joseph's **servant** searched carefully, beginning with the eldest
45. 1 feelings in front of his **servants,** so he ordered them all to
50.17 the wrong that we, the **servants** of your father's God, have
Ex 2. 5 river to bathe, while her **servants** walked along the bank.
14.31 and they had faith in the Lord and in his **servant** Moses.
32.13 Remember your **servants** Abraham, Isaac, and Jacob.
Num 3. 6 of Levi and appoint them as **servants** of Aaron the priest.
12. 7 It is different when I speak with my **servant** Moses;
12. 8 How dare you speak against my **servant** Moses?"
14.24 But because my **servant** Caleb has a different attitude and has
22.22 donkey, accompanied by his two **servants,** the angel of the Lord
Deut 9.27 Remember your **servants,** Abraham, Isaac, and Jacob, and do not
11. 6 families, their tents, and all their **servants** and animals.
12.12 your children, your **servants,** and the Levites who live in
12.18 your children, together with your **servants** and the Levites who
15.18 you for six years at half the cost of a hired **servant.**
16.11 together with your children, your **servants,** and the Levites,
16.14 your children, your **servants,** and the Levites, foreigners,
24.14 a poor and needy hired **servant,** whether he is a fellow-Israelite
33. 8 the Urim and Thummim Through your faithful **servants,** the Levites;
34. 5 So Moses, the Lord's **servant,** died there in the land of Moab,
Josh 1. 1 death of the Lord's **servant** Moses, the Lord spoke to Moses'
1. 2 He said, "My **servant** Moses is dead.
1. 7 that you obey the whole Law that my **servant** Moses gave you.
1.13 "Remember how Moses, the Lord's **servant,** told you that
1.15 the Jordan, which Moses, the Lord's **servant,** gave to you."
5.14 on the ground in worship and said, "I am your **servant,** sir.
8.31 instructions that Moses, the Lord's **servant,** had given
8.33 The Lord's **servant** Moses had commanded them to do this when
9.24 your God had commanded his **servant** Moses to give you the
11.12 putting everyone to death, just as Moses, the Lord's **servant,**
11.15 given his commands to his **servant** Moses, Moses had given
12. 6 Moses, the Lord's **servant,** gave their land to the tribes of
13. 8 the land that Moses, the Lord's **servant,** had given them;
14. 7 years old when the Lord's **servant** Moses sent me from Kadesh
18. 7 Jordan, which Moses, the Lord's **servant,** gave to them."
22. 2 everything that Moses the Lord's **servant** ordered you to do,
22. 4 east side of the Jordan, that Moses, the Lord's **servant,**
24.29 After that, the Lord's **servant** Joshua son of Nun died at
Judg 2. 8 The Lord's **servant** Joshua son of Nun died at the age of
3.19 So the king ordered his **servants,** "Leave us alone!"
3.24 The **servants** came and saw that the doors were locked, but
6.27 Gideon took ten of his **servants** and did what the Lord had
7.10 to attack, go down to the camp with your **servant** Purah.
7.11 So Gideon and his **servant** Purah went down to the edge of
9.18 Abimelech, his son by his **servant-girl,** is your relative,
19. 3 He took his **servant** and two donkeys with him.
19. 9 his concubine, and the **servant** once more started to leave,
19.10 way, with their **servant** and two donkeys with pack saddles.
19.10 so the **servant** said to his master,

Judg 19.19 bread and wine for my concubine and me and for my **servant.**
Ruth 2.13 even though I am not the equal of one of your **servants."**
1 Sam 1.11 "Almighty Lord, look at me, your **servant!**
2.13 offering his sacrifice, the priest's **servant** would come with
2.15 off and burnt, the priest's **servant** would come and say to
2.16 then take what you want," the priest's **servant** would say,
3. 9 you again, say, 'Speak, Lord, your **servant** is listening.' "
3.10 your **servant** is listening."
8.16 He will take your **servants** and your best cattle and donkeys,
9. 3 Saul, "Take one of the **servants** with you and go and look
9. 5 Zuph, Saul said to his **servant,** "Let's go back home, or my
9. 6 The **servant** answered, "Wait!
9. 8 The **servant** answered, "I have a small silver coin.
9.14 So Saul and his **servant** went on to the town, and as
9.22 Samuel led Saul and his **servant** into the large room and gave
9.27 said to Saul, "Tell the **servant** to go on ahead of us."
9.27 The **servant** left, and Samuel continued,
10.10 When Saul and his **servant** arrived at Gibeah, a group of
10.14 uncle saw him and the **servant,** and he asked them, "Where
16.15 His **servants** said to him, "We know that an evil spirit
17.58 "I am the son of your **servant** Jesse from Bethlehem," David
19. 4 Saul and said, "Sir, don't do wrong to your **servant** David.
20.21 Then I will tell my **servant** to go and find them.
23.10 to Keilah and destroy it on account of me, your **servant.**
25. 8 can to us your **servants** and to your dear friend David."
25.14 One of Nabal's **servants** said to Nabal's wife Abigail,
25.19 Then she said to the **servants,** "You go on ahead and I
25.25 I wasn't there when your **servants** arrived, sir.
25.39 insulting me and has kept me his **servant** from doing wrong.
25.40 His **servants** went to her at Carmel and said to her,
25.41 and said, "I am his **servant,**
25.41 ready to wash the feet of his **servants."**
25.42 maids, she went with David's **servants** and became his wife.
26.18 And he added, "Why, sir, are you still pursuing me, your **servant?**
28. 2 "I am your **servant,** and you will see for yourself what I
2 Sam 3.18 said, 'I will use my **servant** David to rescue my people
6.20 fool in the sight of the **servant-girls** of his officials!"
7. 5 Nathan, [5] "Go and tell my **servant** David that I say to him,
7. 8 "So tell my **servant** David that I, the Lord Almighty, say
7.20 You know me, your **servant.**
7.27 all this to me, your **servant,** and have told me that you
9. 2 There was a **servant** of Saul's family named Ziba, and he
9. 9 the king called Ziba, Saul's **servant,** and said, "I am giving
9.10 You, your sons, and your **servants** will farm the land for
9.10 (Ziba had fifteen sons and twenty **servants.)**
9.12 All the members of Ziba's family became **servants** of Mephibosheth.
13.17 he called in his personal **servant** and said, "Get this
13.18 The **servant** put her out and locked the door.
13.28 prepared a banquet fit for a king [28] and instructed his **servants:**
13.29 the **servants** followed Absalom's instructions and killed Amnon.
13.31 The **servants** who were there with him tore their clothes also.
14.30 So Absalom said to his **servants,** "Look, Joab's field is next
14.31 demanded, "Why did your **servants** set fire to my field?"
16. 1 suddenly met by Ziba, the **servant** of Mephibosheth, who had
16. 4 "I am your **servant,**" Ziba replied.
17.17 **servant-girl** would regularly go and tell them what was happening,
19.17 And Ziba, the **servant** of Saul's family, also came with his
19.17 fifteen sons and twenty **servants,** and they arrived at the Jordan
19.26 I told my **servant** to saddle my donkey so that I could
1 Kgs 1. 1 old man, and although his **servants** covered him with blankets,
3. 6 for my father David, your **servant,** and he was good, loyal,
4. 6 In charge of the palace **servants:** Ahishar
8.26 true that you promised to my father David, your **servant.**
8.28 Lord my God, I am your **servant.**
8.32 O Lord, listen in heaven and judge your **servants.**
8.53 you told them through your **servant** Moses when you brought our
8.56 kept all the generous promises he made through his **servant** Moses.
8.66 the Lord had given his **servant** David and his people Israel.
10. 5 they wore, the **servants** who waited on him at feasts,
10. 8 how fortunate your **servants,** who are always in your presence
11.13 for the sake of my **servant** David and for the sake of
11.17 Hadad and some of his father's Edomite **servants,** who escaped
11.32 for the sake of my **servant** David and for the sake of
11.34 for the sake of my **servant** David, whom I chose and who
11.36 have a descendant of my **servant** David ruling in Jerusalem,
11.38 what I command, as my **servant** David did, I will always be
14. 8 have not been like my **servant** David, who was completely
14.18 the Lord had said through his **servant,** the prophet Ahijah.
15.29 Lord had said through his **servant,** the prophet Ahijah
18.36 and that I am your **servant** and have done all this at
18.43 He said to his **servant,** "Go and look towards the sea."
18.43 The **servant** went and returned, saying, "I didn't see anything."
18.44 Elijah ordered his **servant,** "Go to King Ahab and tell him
19. 3 he took his **servant** and went to Beersheba in Judah.
19. 3 Leaving the **servant** there, [4] Elijah walked a whole day
20.32 to Ahab and said, "Your **servant** Benhadad pleads with you
2 Kgs 4.12 He told his **servant** Gehazi to go and call the woman.
4.19 "Carry the boy to his mother," the father said to a **servant.**
4.20 The **servant** carried the boy back to his mother, who held
4.22 and said to him, "Send a **servant** here with a donkey.
4.24 donkey saddled, and ordered the **servant,** "Make the donkey go as
4.25 away, and said to his **servant** Gehazi, "Look—there comes the
4.38 of prophets, he told his **servant** to put a big pot on
4.42 Elisha told his **servant** to feed the group of prophets with this,
4.44 So the **servant** set the food before them, and, as the
5. 2 Israelite girl, who became a **servant** of Naaman's wife.
5.10 Elisha sent a **servant** out to tell him to go and wash
5.13 His **servants** went up to him and said, "Sir, if the

2 Kgs 5.20 when Elisha's **servant** Gehazi said to himself,
5.23 clothes to two of his **servants,** and sent them on ahead of
5.24 Then he sent Naaman's **servants** back.
5.26 olive-groves and vineyards, sheep and cattle, or **servants!**
6.15 Early the next morning Elisha's **servant** got up, went out
6.17 answered his prayer, and Elisha's **servant** looked up and saw
8. 4 She found the king talking with Gehazi, Elisha's **servant;**
8. 9 met him, he said, "Your **servant** King Benhadad has sent me
8.19 because he had promised his **servant** David that his descendants
9. 7 punish Jezebel for murdering my prophets and my other **servants.**
9.36 Lord said would happen, when he spoke through his **servant** Elijah:
10. 5 "We are your **servants** and we are ready to do anything you
14.25 promised through his **servant** the prophet Jonah son of Amittai,
16. 7 "I am your devoted **servant.**
17.13 which I handed on to you through my **servants** the prophets."
17.23 warned through his **servants** the prophets that he would do.
18.12 all the laws given by Moses, the **servant** of the Lord.
19.34 and because of the promise I made to my **servant** David.' "
20. 6 and because of the promise I made to my **servant** David."
21. 8 the whole Law that my **servant** Moses gave them, then I will
21.10 Through his **servants** the prophets the Lord said,
22. 9 "Your **servants** have taken the money that was in the Temple
24. 2 Lord had said through his **servants** the prophets that he would do.
1 Chr 2.34 He had an Egyptian **servant** named Jarha, [35] to whom he gave
6.49 in accordance with the instructions given by Moses, God's **servant.**
16.12 You descendants of Jacob, God's **servant,**
16.22 "Don't harm my chosen **servants;**
17. 4 Nathan, [4] "Go and tell my **servant** David that I say to him,
17. 7 "So tell my **servant** David that I, the Lord Almighty, say
17.18 You know me well, and yet you honour me, your **servant.**
17.25 all this to me, your **servant,** and have told me that you
21. 3 Your Majesty, they are all your **servants.**
2 Chr 1. 3 which Moses, the Lord's **servant,** had made in the wilderness.
6.17 everything come true that you promised to your **servant** David.
6.19 Lord my God, I am your **servant.**
6.23 O Lord, listen in heaven and judge your **servants.**
6.27 forgive the sins of your **servants,** the people of Israel, and
6.42 Remember the love you had for your **servant** David."
9. 4 the clothing of the **servants** who waited on him at feasts,
24. 6 the tax which Moses, the **servant** of the Lord, required the
24. 9 the tax which Moses, God's **servant,** had first collected in
32.16 things about the Lord God and Hezekiah, the Lord's **servant.**
33. 8 the whole Law that my **servant** Moses gave them, then I will
35.23 He ordered his **servants,** "Take me away;
Ezra 2.55 Clans of Solomon's **servants** who returned from exile:
2.58 temple workmen and of Solomon's **servants** who returned from exile
2.64 Their male and female **servants** – 7,337
4.11 Emperor Artaxerxes from his **servants,** the men of West Euphrates.
5.11 "They answered, 'We are **servants** of the God of heaven and earth,
9.11 that you gave us through your **servants,** the prophets.
Neh 1. 6 I pray day and night for your **servants,** the people of Israel.
1. 7 kept the laws which you gave us through Moses, your **servant.**
1.10 "Lord, these are your **servants,** your own people.
1.11 prayers of all your other **servants** who want to honour you.
2.20 We are his **servants,** and we are going to start building.
4.23 did any of my companions nor my **servants** nor my bodyguard.
5.15 Even their **servants** had oppressed the people.
6. 5 Sanballat sent one of his **servants** to me with a fifth message,
7.57 Clans of Solomon's **servants** who returned from exile:
7.60 temple workmen and of Solomon's **servants** who returned from exile
7.66 Their male and female **servants** – 7,337
9.14 and through your **servant** Moses you gave them your laws.
10.29 according to God's Law, which God gave through his **servant** Moses;
11. 3 descendants of Solomon's **servants** lived on their own property
Esth 1. 8 given orders to the palace **servants** that everyone could have
1.10 eunuchs who were his personal **servants,** Mehuman, Biztha,
1.12 But when the **servants** told Queen Vashti of the king's command,
1.15 "I, King Xerxes, sent my **servants** to Queen Vashti with a command,
4. 4 When Esther's **servant-girls** and eunuchs told her what Mordecai
4. 5 palace eunuchs appointed as her **servant** by the king, and
4.16 My **servant-girls** and I will be doing the same.
6. 3 His **servants** answered, "Nothing has been done for him."
6. 5 So the **servants** answered, "Haman is here, waiting to see you."
Job 1. 3 had a large number of **servants** and was the richest man in
1. 8 "Did you notice my **servant** Job?"
1.15 They killed every one of your **servants** except me.
1.16 another **servant** came and said, "Lightning struck the
1.17 another **servant** came and said, "Three bands of
1.17 away the camels, and killed all your **servants** except me.
1.18 another **servant** came and said, "Your children were
2. 3 "Did you notice my **servant** Job?"
4.18 God does not trust his heavenly **servants;**
19.15 my **servant-girls** treat me like a stranger and a foreigner.
19.16 When I call a **servant,** he doesn't answer— even when I
31.13 When one of my **servants** complained against me, I would listen
31.15 The same God who created me created my **servants** also.
41. 5 a pet bird, like something to amuse your **servant-girls?**
42. 7 did not speak the truth about me, as my **servant** Job did.
Ps 19.11 They give knowledge to me, your **servant;**
22.23 "Praise him, you **servants** of the Lord!
27. 9 don't turn your **servant** away.
31.16 Look on your **servant** with kindness;
35.27 He is pleased with the success of his **servant."**
69.17 Don't hide yourself from your **servant;**
69.36 the descendants of his **servants** will inherit it, and those
Ps 78.70 He chose his **servant** David;
79. 2 the bodies of your **servants** for wild animals to eat.
79.10 punish the nations for shedding the blood of your **servants.**
86. 2 save me, for I am your **servant** and I trust in you.
86. 4 Make your **servant** glad, O Lord, because my prayers go up
89. 3 I have promised my **servant** David, [4] 'A descendant of yours will
89.19 you said to your faithful **servants,** "I have given help to a
89.20 I have made my **servant** David king by anointing him with
89.39 broken your covenant with your **servant** and thrown his crown
89.50 Don't forget how I, your **servant,** am insulted, how I
90.13 Have pity, O Lord, on your **servants!**
90.16 Let us, your **servants,** see your mighty deeds;
102.14 Your **servants** love her, even though she is destroyed;
103.21 you heavenly powers, you **servants** of his, who do his will!
104. 4 your messengers and flashes of lightning as your **servants.**
105. 5 You descendants of Abraham, his **servant;**
105.15 "Don't harm my chosen **servants;**
105.25 Egyptians hate his people and treat his **servants** with deceit.
105.26 Then he sent his **servant** Moses, and Aaron, whom he had chosen.
105.42 He remembered his sacred promise to Abraham his **servant.**
106.16 jealous of Moses and of Aaron, the Lord's holy **servant.**
106.23 his chosen **servant,** Moses, stood up against God
109.28 May my persecutors be defeated, and may I, your **servant,**
113. 1 You **servants** of the Lord, praise his name!
116.16 I am your **servant,** Lord;
119.17 Be good to me, your **servant,** so that I may live and
119.38 your promise to me, your **servant**— the promise you make to
119.49 Remember your promise to me, your **servant;**
119.65 your promise, Lord, and you are good to me, your **servant.**
119.76 love comfort me, as you have promised me, your **servant.**
119.91 of your command, because they are all your **servants.**
119.122 Promise that you will help your **servant;**
119.125 I am your **servant;**
119.176 and look for me, your **servant,** because I have not neglected
123. 2 As a **servant** depends on his master, as a maid depends on
132.10 You made a promise to your **servant** David;
134. 1 praise the Lord, all his **servants,** all who serve in his
135. 1 Praise his name, you **servants** of the Lord,
135.14 he will take pity on his **servants.**
136.22 he gave them to Israel, his **servant;**
143. 2 Don't put me, your **servant,** on trial;
143.12 and destroy all my oppressors, for I am your **servant.**
144.10 You give victory to kings and rescue your **servant** David.
Prov 9. 3 She has sent her **servant-girls** to call out from the
11.29 Foolish men will always be **servants** to the wise.
17. 2 shrewd **servant** will gain authority over a master's worthless son
27.18 A **servant** who takes care of his master will be honoured.
27.27 you and your family, and for your **servant-girls** as well.
29.19 You cannot correct a **servant** just by talking to him.
29.21 If you give your **servant** everything he wants from childhood on,
30.10 Never criticize a **servant** to his master.
30.23 and a **servant-girl** who takes the
31.15 for her family and to tell her **servant-girls** what to do.
Ecc 7.21 say—you may hear your **servant** insulting you, [22] and you know
Is 20. 3 the Lord said, "My **servant** Isaiah has been going about naked
22.20 happens, I will send for my **servant** Eliakim son of Hilkiah.
37.24 You sent your **servants** to boast to me that with all your
37.35 and because of the promise I made to my **servant** David.' "
41. 8 "But you, Israel my **servant,** you are the people that I
41. 9 its farthest corners and said to you, 'You are my **servant.'**
42. 1 "Here is my **servant,** whom I strengthen— the one I have
42. 5 Lord God says to his **servant,** [6] "I, the Lord, have called
42.19 anyone more blind than my **servant,** more deaf than the
43.10 chose you to be my **servant,** so that you would know me
44. 1 "Listen now, Israel, my **servant,** my chosen people,
44. 2 you are my **servant,** my chosen people whom I love.
44.21 remember that you are my **servant.**
44.21 created you to be my **servant,** and I will never forget you.
44.26 But when my **servant** makes a prediction, when I send a
45. 4 appoint you to help my **servant** Israel, the people that I
48.20 "The Lord has saved his **servant** Israel!"
49. 1 born, the Lord chose me and appointed me to be his **servant.**
49. 3 He said to me, "Israel, you are my **servant;**
49. 5 he made me his **servant** to bring back his people, to bring
49. 6 "I have a greater task for you, my **servant.**
49. 7 who is hated by the nations and is the **servant** of rulers:
49. 7 This will happen because the Lord has chosen his **servant;**
50.10 obey the words of his **servant,** the path you walk may be
52.13 "My **servant** will succeed in his task;
53. 2 of the Lord that his **servant** should grow like a plant taking
53.11 My devoted **servant,** with whom I am pleased, will bear the
54.17 I will defend my **servants** and give them victory."
61. 6 known as the priests of the Lord, The **servants** of our God.
63.11 the days of Moses, the **servant** of the Lord, and they asked,
Jer 7.25 day, I have kept on sending my **servants,** the prophets, to
14. 3 The rich people send their **servants** for water;
15.19 I will take you back, and you will be my **servant** again.
25. 4 Lord has continued to send you his **servants** the prophets.
25. 9 peoples from the north and for my **servant,** King Nebuchadnezzar
26. 5 to the words of my **servants,** the prophets, whom I have kept
27. 6 under the power of my **servant,** King Nebuchadnezzar of Babylonia,
29.19 I kept on sending to them through my **servants** the prophets.
33.21 made a covenant with my **servant** David that he would always
33.22 number of descendants of my **servant** David and the number of
33.26 my covenant with Jacob's descendants and with my **servant** David.
35.15 to send you all my **servants** the prophets, and they have told
43.10 am going to bring my **servant** King Nebuchadnezzar of
44. 4 I kept sending you my **servants** the prophets, who told you
Ezek 28.25 their own land, the land that I gave to my **servant** Jacob.

Ezek 34.23 them a king like my **servant** David to be their one shepherd,
34.24 God, and a king like my **servant** David will be their ruler.
37.24 A king like my **servant** David will be their king.
37.25 land I gave to my **servant** Jacob, the land where their
37.25 A king like my **servant** David will rule over them for ever.
38.17 when I announced through my **servants,** the prophets of Israel,
46.24 the kitchens where the temple **servants** are to boil the sacrifices
Dan 3.26 **Servants** of the Supreme God!
5.29 Immediately Belshazzar ordered his **servants** to dress Daniel
6.20 he called out anxiously, "Daniel, **servant** of the living God!
9. 6 have not listened to your **servants** the prophets, who spoke
9.10 laws which you gave us through your **servants** the prophets.
9.11 that are written in the Law of Moses, your **servant.**
11. 6 husband, her child, and the **servants** who went with her will
Joel 2.29 pour out my spirit even on **servants,** both men and women.
Amos 3. 7 without revealing his plan to his **servants,** the prophets.
Nah 2. 7 her **servants** moan like doves and beat their breasts in sorrow.
Hag 2.23 will take you, Zerubbabel my **servant,** and I will appoint you
Zech 1. 6 Through my **servants** the prophets I gave your ancestors commands
2. 9 be plundered by the people who were once your **servants."**
3. 8 I will reveal my **servant,** who is called The Branch!
Mal 1. 6 "A son honours his father, and a **servant** honours his master.
4. 4 "Remember the teachings of my **servant** Moses, the laws and
Mt 8. 6 "Sir, my **servant** is sick in bed at home, unable to move
8. 8 Just give the order, and my **servant** will get well.
8.13 And the officer's **servant** was healed that very moment.
12.18 "Here is my **servant,** whom I have chosen, the one I love,
13.27 The man's **servants** came to him and said, 'Sir, it was
18.23 there was a king who decided to check on his **servants'**
18.25 The **servant** did not have enough to pay his debt, so the
18.26 The **servant** fell on his knees before the king.
18.28 met one of his **fellow-servants** who owed him a few pounds.
18.29 His **fellow-servant** fell down and begged him, 'Be patient with me,
18.31 When the other **servants** saw what had happened, they were
18.32 So he called the **servant** in.
18.33 have had mercy on your **fellow-servant,** just as I had mercy
18.34 angry, and he sent the **servant** to jail to be punished until
20.26 wants to be great, he must be the **servant** of the rest;
22. 3 He sent his **servants** to tell the invited guests to come to
22. 4 So he sent other **servants** with this message for the guests:
22. 6 while others grabbed the **servants,** beat them, and killed them.
22. 8 Then he called his **servants** and said to them, 'My wedding
22.10 So the **servants** went out into the streets and gathered
22.13 Then the king told the **servants,** 'Tie him up hand and foot,
23.11 The greatest one among you must be your **servant.**
24.45 "Who, then, is a faithful and wise **servant?**
24.45 in charge of the other **servants** to give them their food at
24.46 How happy that **servant** is if his master finds him doing
24.47 master will put that **servant** in charge of all his property.
24.48 if he is a bad **servant,** he will tell himself that his
24.49 will begin to beat his **fellow-servants** and to eat and drink
24.50 Then that **servant's** master will come back
24.50 one day when the **servant** does not expect him
25.14 called his **servants** and put them in charge of his property.
25.16 The **servant** who had received five thousand coins went at
25.17 In the same way the **servant** who had received two
25.18 But the **servant** who had received one thousand coins went off,
25.19 time the master of those **servants** came back and settled
25.20 The **servant** who had received five thousand coins came in
25.21 'Well done, you good and faithful **servant!'**
25.22 "Then the **servant** who had been given two thousand coins
25.23 'Well done, you good and faithful **servant!'**
25.24 "Then the **servant** who had received one thousand coins
25.26 'You bad and lazy **servant!'**
25.30 As for this useless **servant**—throw him outside in the darkness;
26.69 one of the High Priest's **servant-girls** came to him and said,
26.71 Another **servant-girl** saw him and said to the men there, "He
Mk 9.35 must place himself last of all and be the **servant** of all."
10.43 wants to be great, he must be the **servant** of the rest;
13.34 a journey and leaves his **servants** in charge, after giving to
14.66 when one of the High Priest's **servant-girls** came by.
14.69 The **servant-girl** saw him there and began to repeat to the bystanders,
Lk 1.38 "I am the Lord's **servant,"** said Mary;
1.48 God my Saviour, [48]for he has remembered me, his lowly **servant!**
1.54 ancestors, and has come to the help of his **servant** Israel.
1.69 for us a mighty Saviour, a descendant of his **servant** David.
2.29 your promise, and you may let your **servant** go in peace.
7. 2 Roman officer there had a **servant** who was very dear to him;
7. 3 some Jewish elders to ask him to come and heal his **servant.**
7. 7 Just give the order, and my **servant** will get well.
7.10 back to the officer's house and found his **servant** well.
12.36 with your lamps lit, [36]like **servants** who are waiting for
12.37 How happy are those **servants** whose master finds them
12.42 The Lord answered, "Who, then, is the faithful and wise **servant?**
12.42 household and give the other **servants** their share of the
12.43 How happy that **servant** is if his master finds him doing
12.44 master will put that **servant** in charge of all his property.
12.45 But if that **servant** says to himself that his master is
12.45 to beat the other **servants,** both the men and the women,
12.46 back one day when the **servant** does not expect him and at
12.47 "The **servant** who knows what his master wants him to do,
12.48 But the **servant** who does not know what his master wants,
14.17 the feast, he sent his **servant** to tell his guests, 'Come,
14.18 The first one told the **servant,** 'I have bought a field and
14.21 "The **servant** went back and told all this to his master.
14.21 furious and said to his **servant,** 'Hurry out to the streets
14.22 Soon the **servant** said, 'Your order has been carried out,
14.23 the master said to the **servant,** 'Go out to the country roads
15.22 But the father called his **servants.**
Lk 15.26 called one of the **servants** and asked him, 'What's going on?'
15.27 has come back home,' the **servant** answered, 'and your father
16. 1 once a rich man who had a **servant** who managed his property.
16. 3 The **servant** said to himself, 'My master is going to
16.13 "No **servant** can be the slave of two masters;
17. 7 one of you has a **servant** who is ploughing or looking after
17. 9 The **servant** does not deserve thanks for obeying orders,
17.10 you have been told to do, say, 'We are ordinary **servants;**
19.13 left, he called his ten **servants** and gave them each a gold
19.15 At once he ordered his **servants** to appear before him, in
19.17 'you are a good **servant!**
19.18 The second **servant** came and said, 'Sir, I have earned
19.20 "Another **servant** came and said, 'Sir, here is your gold coin;
19.22 He said to him, 'You bad **servant!**
19.24 from him and give it to the **servant** who has ten coins.'
22.26 like the youngest, and the leader must be like the **servant.**
22.56 When one of the **servant-girls** saw him sitting there at the fire,
Jn 2. 5 Jesus' mother then told the **servants,** "Do whatever he tells you."
2. 7 Jesus said to the **servants,** "Fill these jars with water."
2. 9 from (but, of course, the **servants** who had drawn out the
4.51 On his way home his **servants** met him with the news,
12.26 follow me, so that my **servant** will be with me where I
15.15 I do not call you **servants** any longer,
15.15 because a **servant** does not know what his master
18.18 It was cold, so the **servants** and guards had built a
Acts 2.18 Yes, even on my **servants,** both men and women, I will
2.27 you will not allow your faithful **servant** to rot in the grave.
3.13 God of our ancestors, has given divine glory to his **Servant** Jesus.
3.26 And so God chose his **Servant** and sent him first to you,
4.25 through our ancestor David, your **servant,** when he said, 'Why
4.27 Israel against Jesus, your holy **Servant,** whom you made Messiah.
4.29 made, and allow us, your **servants,** to speak your message
4.30 be performed through the name of your holy **Servant** Jesus."
7.52 God's messengers, who long ago announced the coming of his righteous **Servant.**
10. 7 called two of his house **servants** and a soldier, a religious
12.13 door, and a **servant-girl** named Rhoda came to answer it.
13.35 'You will not allow your devoted **servant** to rot in the grave.'
16.17 us, shouting, "These men are **servants** of the Most High God!
20.19 my work as the Lord's **servant** during the hard times that
22.14 will, to see his righteous **Servant,** and to hear him speaking
26.16 I have appeared to you to appoint you as my **servant.**
Rom 1. 1 From Paul, a **servant** of Christ Jesus and an apostle chosen
13. 4 because he is God's **servant** working for your own good.
13. 4 He is God's **servant** and carries out God's punishment on
14. 4 Who are you to judge the **servant** of someone else?
15.16 given me [16]of being a **servant** of Christ Jesus to work for
1 Cor 3. 5 We are simply God's **servants,** by whom you were led to believe.
4. 1 think of us as Christ's **servants,** who have been put in
4. 2 thing required of such a **servant** is that he be faithful to
2 Cor 2.17 with sincerity in his presence, as **servants** of Christ.
4. 5 Jesus Christ as Lord, and ourselves as your **servants** for Jesus'
6. 4 that we are God's **servants** by patiently enduring troubles,
6. 6 shown ourselves to be God's **servants**—by the Holy Spirit, by
11.15 servants disguise themselves to look like **servants** of righteousness.
11.23 Are they Christ's **servants?**
11.23 like a madman—but I am a better **servant** than they are!
Gal 1.10 trying to do so, I would not be a **servant** of Christ.
Eph 3. 7 I was made a **servant** of the gospel by God's special gift,
6.21 our dear brother and faithful **servant** in the Lord's work,
Phil 1. 1 From Paul and Timothy, **servants** of Christ Jesus— To all
1.13 that I am in prison because I am a **servant** of Christ.
2. 7 gave up all he had, and took the nature of a **servant.**
Col 1. 7 grace from Epaphras, our dear **fellow-servant,** who is
1.23 that I, Paul, became a **servant**—this gospel which has been
1.25 I have been made a **servant** of the church by God, who
4. 7 is a faithful worker and **fellow-servant** in the Lord's work,
4.12 Epaphras, another member of your group and a **servant** of Christ Jesus.
1 Tim 4. 6 you will be a good **servant** of Christ Jesus, as you feed
2 Tim 2.24 The Lord's **servant** must not quarrel.
4. 5 Good News, and perform your whole duty as a **servant** of God.
Tit 1. 1 From Paul, a **servant** of God and an apostle of Jesus Christ.
Heb 1. 7 "God makes his angels winds, and his **servants** flames of fire."
3. 5 in God's house as a **servant,** and he spoke of the things
Jas 1. 1 From James, a **servant** of God and of the Lord Jesus Christ:
1 Pet 2.18 You **servants** must submit to your masters and show them complete respect,
2 Pet 1. 1 From Simon Peter, a **servant** and apostle of Jesus Christ—
Jude 1 From Jude, **servant** of Jesus Christ, and brother of James— To
Rev 1. 1 in order to show his **servants** what must happen very soon.
1. 1 these things known to his **servant** John by sending his angel
2.20 her teaching she misleads my **servants** into practising sexual
6.11 of their **fellow-servants** and brothers had been killed,
7. 3 trees, until we mark the **servants** of our God with a seal
10. 7 plan, as he announced to his **servants,** the prophets."
11.18 to reward your **servants,** the prophets, and all your people,
15. 3 the song of Moses, the **servant** of God, and the song of
19. 2 God has punished her because she killed his **servants."**
19. 5 "Praise our God, all his **servants** and all people, both
19.10 I am a **fellow-servant** of yours and of your brothers, all
22. 3 Lamb will be in the city, and his **servants** will worship him.
22. 6 his angel to show his **servants** what must happen very soon."
22. 9 I am a **fellow-servant** of yours and of your brothers the

SERVE

Gen 18. 3 I am here to **serve** you.
18. 5 honoured me by coming to my home, so let me **serve** you."
18. 8 There under the tree he **served** them himself, and they ate.

Gen 19. 2 down before them [2]and said, "Sirs, I am here to **serve** you.
25.23 The older will **serve** the younger."
30.26 You know how well I have **served** you."
41.45 thirty years old when he began to **serve** the king of Egypt.
43.31 and controlling himself, he ordered the meal to be **served.**
43.32 Joseph was **served** at one table and his brothers at another.
43.32 who were eating there were **served** separately,
43.34 Food was **served** to them from Joseph's table,
43.34 and Benjamin was **served** five times as much
48.15 God whom my fathers Abraham and Isaac **served** bless these boys!
Ex 1.11 Pithom and Rameses to **serve** as supply centres for the king.
18.22 Let them **serve** as judges for the people on a permanent basis.
18.26 They **served** as judges for the people on a permanent basis,
19. 6 dedicated to me alone, and you will **serve** me as priests."
21. 2 you buy a Hebrew slave, he shall **serve** you for six years.
26.14 and the other of fine leather, to **serve** as the outer cover.
28. 1 the people of Israel, so that they may **serve** me as priests.
28. 4 Aaron and his sons, so that they can **serve** me as priests.
28.35 Aaron is to wear this robe when he **serves** as priest.
28.41 them with olive-oil, so that they may **serve** me as priests.
28.43 or approach the altar to **serve** as priests in the Holy Place,
29. 9 They and their descendants are to **serve** me as priests for ever.
29.30 Tent of my presence to **serve** in the Holy Place is to
29.44 will set Aaron and his sons apart to **serve** me as priests.
31.10 to use when they **serve** as priests, [11]the anointing oil,
33.13 plans, so that I may **serve** you and continue to please you.
35.19 are to wear when they **serve** in the Holy Place—the sacred
36.19 and the other of fine leather, to **serve** as an outer cover.
38. 8 belonging to the women who **served** at the entrance of the
39. 1 the priests were to wear when they **served** in the Holy Place.
40.13 this way consecrate him, so that he can **serve** me as priest.
40.15 anointed their father, so that they can **serve** me as priests.
Lev 2.16 and oil that is to **serve** as a token, and also all
6.22 by every descendant of Aaron who is **serving** as High Priest.
10. 3 when he said, 'All who **serve** me must respect my holiness;
22. 3 have dedicated to me, he can never again **serve** at the altar.
25.40 as a hired man and **serve** you until the next Year of
25.46 to your sons, whom they must **serve** as long as they live.
Num 1.50 carry it and its equipment, **serve** in it, and set up their
3. 4 so Eleazar and Ithamar **served** as priests during Aaron's lifetime.
3. 9 responsibility the Levites have is to **serve** Aaron and his sons.
4.49 responsibility for his task of **serving** or carrying.
10.25 by the tribe of Dan, **serving** as the rearguard of all the
15.39 The tassels will **serve** as reminders, and each time you
16. 9 Lord's Tent, and minister to the community and **serve** them?
18. 1 any guilt connected with **serving** in the Tent of my presence;
18. 2 help you while you and your sons are **serving** at the Tent.
35.15 These will **serve** as cities of refuge for Israelites and for
Deut 4.19 be tempted to worship and **serve** what you see in the sky
4.28 There you will **serve** gods made by human hands, gods of
8.19 your God or turn to other gods to worship and **serve** them.
10. 8 of the Covenant Box, to **serve** him as priests, and to
10.12 Love him, **serve** him with all your heart, [13]and obey all
11.13 love the Lord your God and **serve** him with all your heart.
11.16 be led away from the Lord to worship and **serve** other gods.
13. 2 lead you to worship and **serve** gods that you have not
15.12 are to release him after he has **served** you for six years.
15.18 after all, he has **served** you for six years at half the
17. 3 his covenant [3]by worshipping and **serving** other gods or the
18. 5 tribes the tribe of Levi to **serve** him as priests for ever.
18. 7 place of worship [7]and may **serve** there as a priest of the
18. 7 Lord his God, like the other Levites who are **serving** there.
21. 5 God has chosen them to **serve** him and to pronounce blessings
28.14 disobey them in any way, or worship and **serve** other gods.
28.36 there you will **serve** gods made of wood and stone.
28.47 but you would not **serve** him with glad and joyful hearts.
28.48 So then, you will **serve** the enemies that the Lord is
28.64 other, and there you will **serve** gods made of wood and stone,
29.26 They **served** other gods that they had never worshipped before,
32.36 have mercy on those who **serve** him, when he sees how helpless
Josh 6.22 the two men who had **served** as spies, "Go into the
18. 7 you, because their share is to **serve** as the Lord's priests.
22. 5 be faithful to him, and **serve** him with all your heart and
23.16 to keep and if you **serve** and worship other gods, then in
24.14 Joshua continued, "honour the Lord and **serve** him sincerely
24.14 in Mesopotamia and in Egypt, and **serve** only the Lord.
24.15 you are not willing to **serve** him,
24.15 decide today whom you will **serve,**
24.15 As for my family and me, we will **serve** the Lord."
24.16 "We would never leave the Lord to **serve** other gods!
24.18 So we also will **serve** the Lord;
24.19 the people, "But you may not be able to **serve** the Lord.
24.20 if you leave him to **serve** foreign gods, he will turn against
24.21 We will **serve** the Lord."
24.22 to the fact that you have chosen to **serve** the Lord."
24.24 then said to Joshua, "We will **serve** the Lord our God.
24.31 lived, the people of Israel **served** the Lord, and after his
Judg 2. 7 lived, the people of Israel **served** the Lord, and after his
2.11 Israel sinned against the Lord and began to **serve** the Baals.
2.13 They stopped worshipping the Lord and **served** the Baals
2.19 They would **serve** and worship other gods, and refused to give
4. 4 a prophet, and she was **serving** as a judge for the Israelites
8.34 their god, [34]and no longer **served** the Lord their God, who
9.28 Why are we **serving** Abimelech?
9.28 And Zebul takes orders from him, but why should we **serve** him?
9.38 the one who asked why we should **serve** this man Abimelech.
18. 4 with Micah, who pays me to **serve** as his priest."
18.30 Gershom and grandson of Moses, **served** as a priest for the
18.30 of Dan, and his descendants **served** as their priests until
1 Sam 2.11 Samuel stayed in Shiloh and **served** the Lord under the priest Eli.
2.18 the boy Samuel continued to **serve** the Lord, wearing a sacred

1 Sam 2.28 to be my priests, to **serve** at the altar, to burn the
2.30 family and your clan would **serve** me as priests for all time.
2.33 of your descendants alive, and he will **serve** me as priest.
2.35 him descendants, who will always **serve** in the presence of my
3. 1 when the boy Samuel was **serving** the Lord under the direction
7.17 to his home in Ramah, where also he would **serve** as judge.
8.11 some of them will **serve** in his war chariots, others in his
12.14 honour the Lord your God, **serve** him, listen to him, and obey
12.20 turn away from the Lord, but **serve** him with all your heart.
12.24 Obey the Lord and **serve** him faithfully with all your heart.
18.17 wife on condition that you **serve** me as a brave and loyal
19. 7 him to Saul, and David **served** the king as he had before.
27.12 Israelites that he will have to **serve** me all his life."
29. 8 since the day I started **serving** you, why shouldn't I go with
2 Sam 3. 8 Do you really think I'm **serving** Judah?"
12.20 asked for food and ate it as soon as it was **served.**
13. 5 where I can see her, and then **serve** it to me herself.' "
13. 6 where I can see her, and then **serve** them to me herself."
13.10 the cakes here to my bed and **serve** them to me yourself."
15.34 will now serve him as faithfully as you **served** his father.
16.19 After all, whom should I **serve,** if not my master's son?
16.19 As I **served** your father, so now I will serve you."
19.37 Here is my son Chimham, who will **serve** you;
1 Kgs 2.27 Solomon dismissed Abiathar from **serving** as a priest of the Lord,
9. 4 If you will **serve** me in honesty and integrity, as your
9.22 **served** as his soldiers, officers, commanders, chariot captains,
9.27 experienced seamen from his fleet to **serve** with Solomon's men.
10. 5 saw the food that was **served** at his table, the living
12. 6 the older men who had **served** as his father Solomon's advisers.
12. 7 replied, "If you want to **serve** this people well,
12. 7 and they will always **serve** you loyally."
12.32 there in Bethel the priests **serving** at the places of worship
13. 2 slaughter on you the priests **serving** at the pagan altars who
13.33 from ordinary families to **serve** at the altars he had built.
14.24 were men and women who **served** as prostitutes at those pagan
15.12 prostitutes **serving** at the pagan places of worship,
17. 1 God of Israel, whom I **serve,** I tell you that there will
18.15 the living Lord, whom I **serve,** I promise that I will present
19.10 "Lord God Almighty, I have always **served** you—you alone.
19.14 "Lord God Almighty, I have always **served** you—you alone.
22.46 male and female prostitutes **serving** at the pagan altars
22.53 He worshipped and **served** Baal, and like his father before him,
2 Kgs 3.14 the living Lord, whom I **serve,** I swear that I would have
5.16 the living Lord, whom I **serve,** I swear that I will not
10.18 together and said, "King Ahab **served** the god Baal a little,
10.18 but I will **serve** him much more.
12. 5 money brought by those he **served,** and the money was to be
17.16 goddess Asherah, worshipped the stars, and **served** the god Baal.
17.32 all sorts of people to **serve** as priests at the pagan places
17.35 bow down to them or **serve** them or offer sacrifices to them.
20. 3 "Remember, Lord, that I have **served** you faithfully and loyally,
20.18 away and made eunuchs to **serve** in the palace of the king
23. 9 priests were not allowed to **serve** in the Temple, but they
23.20 on the altars where they **served,** and he burnt human bones on
23.25 like him before, who **served** the Lord with all his heart,
25.24 Settle in this land, **serve** the king of Babylonia, and all
1 Chr 6.10 Azariah (the one who **served** in the Temple which King Solomon
12.21 They **served** David as officers over his troops, because
15. 2 the Lord chose to carry it and to **serve** him for ever."
22.19 Now **serve** the Lord your God with all your heart and soul.
23.13 worship of the Lord, to **serve** him, and to bless the people
26. 1 of work for the Levites who **served** as temple guards.
28. 9 your father's God and to **serve** him with an undivided heart
28.20 The Lord God, whom I **serve,** will be with you.
2 Chr 7.17 If you **serve** me faithfully as your father David did, obeying
8. 9 used in forced labour, but **served** as soldiers, officers,
9. 4 saw the food that was **served** at his table, the
9. 7 fortunate are the men who **serve** you, who are always in your
10. 6 the older men who had **served** as his father Solomon's advisers.
10. 7 a considerate answer, they will always **serve** you loyally."
11.14 successors would not let them **serve** as priests of the Lord.
11.15 priests of his own to **serve** at the pagan places of worship
12. 8 the difference between **serving** me and serving earthly rulers."
13.10 "But we still **serve** the Lord our God and have not
17. 4 He **served** his father's God, obeyed God's commands, and did not
17. 6 He took pride in **serving** the Lord and destroyed all the
17.16 (Amasiah had volunteered to **serve** the Lord.)
17.19 These men **served** the king in Jerusalem, and in addition
22. 9 King Jehoshaphat, who had done all he could to **serve** the Lord.
26. 5 religious adviser, was living, he **served** the Lord faithfully,
32. 1 in which King Hezekiah **served** the Lord faithfully, Sennacherib,
34.13 and others kept records or **served** as guards.
34.33 he required the people to **serve** the Lord, the God of their
35. 3 place, but you are to **serve** the Lord your God and his
36.20 survivors to Babylonia, where they **served** him and his descendants
Ezra 8.17 workmen, to send us people to **serve** God in the Temple.
Neh 5.18 Every day I **served** one ox, six of the best sheep, and
9.35 but they failed to turn from sin and **serve** you.
11.12 In all, 822 members of this clan **served** in the Temple.
Esth 1. 7 Drinks were **served** in gold cups, no two of them alike, and
2. 9 seven girls specially chosen from the royal palace to **serve** her.
Job 21.15 there is no need to **serve** God nor any advantage in praying
24. 1 time for judging, a day of justice for those who **serve** him?
25. 3 Can anyone count the angels who **serve** him?
36.11 If they obey God and **serve** him, they live out their
41. 4 an agreement with you and promise to **serve** you for ever?
Ps 2.11 **Serve** the Lord with fear;
16.10 I have **served** you faithfully, and you will not abandon me
22.30 Future generations will **serve** him;
72.11 all nations will **serve** him.

Ps 86.11 teach me to **serve** you with complete devotion.
86.16 and save me, because I **serve** you, just as my mother did.
101. 6 Those who are completely honest will be allowed to **serve** me.
116.16 I **serve** you, just as my mother did.
119.10 With all my heart I try to **serve** you;
119.63 a friend of all who **serve** you, of all who obey your
134. 1 all his servants, all who **serve** in his Temple at night.
Prov 23. 3 Don't be greedy for the fine food he **serves;**
23. 6 a stingy man or be greedy for the fine food he **serves.**
Is 8. 2 Uriah and Zechariah son of Jeberechiah, to **serve** as witnesses."
14. 2 and there the nations will **serve** Israel as slaves.
28. 6 of justice to those who **serve** as judges, and courage to
38. 3 "Remember, Lord, that I have **served** you faithfully and loyally,
39. 7 away and made eunuchs to **serve** in the palace of the king
56. 6 people, who love him and **serve** him, who observe the Sabbath
58.14 then you will find the joy that comes from **serving** me.
60.10 will rebuild your walls, And their kings will **serve** you.
60.12 But nations that do not **serve** you Will be completely destroyed.
61. 5 My people, foreigners will **serve** you.
63.17 the sake of those who **serve** you, for the sake of the
65. 8 I destroy all my people—I will save those who **serve** me.
65. 9 My chosen people, who **serve** me, will live there.
Jer 5.19 away from me and **served** foreign gods in their own land,
5.19 so they will **serve** strangers in a land
8. 2 people have loved and **served,** and which they have consulted
13.10 and wicked as ever, and have worshipped and **served** other gods.
15.11 true if I have not **served** you well, if I have not
15.14 I will make them **serve** their enemies in a land they know
16.11 turned away from me and worshipped and **served** other gods.
16.13 And there you will **serve** other gods day and night, and I
17. 4 and I will make you **serve** your enemies in a land you
22. 9 with me, your God, and have worshipped and **served** other gods."
25. 6 you not to worship and **serve** other gods and not to make
25.11 neighbouring nations will **serve** the king of Babylonia
27. 6 Babylonia, and I have made even the wild animals **serve** him.
27. 7 All nations will **serve** him,
27. 7 and they will **serve** his son and his grandson
27. 7 Then his nation will **serve** powerful nations and great kings.
27.11 the king of Babylonia and **serves** him, then I will let it
27.12 **Serve** him and his people, and you will live.
28.14 they will **serve** King Nebuchadnezzar of Babylonia.
28.14 he will make even the wild animals **serve** Nebuchadnezzar."
30. 9 Instead, they will **serve** me, the Lord their God, and a
33.18 the tribe of Levi to **serve** me and to offer burnt-offerings,
33.21 from the tribe of Levi that they would always **serve** me;
34.14 set free any Hebrew slave who had **served** them for six years.
35.15 you not to worship and **serve** other gods, so that you could
35.19 of Rechab will always have a male descendant to **serve** me."
40. 9 Settle down in this land, **serve** the king of Babylonia, and
44. 3 sacrifices to other gods and **served** gods that neither they
Ezek 20.24 and worshipped the same idols their ancestors had **served.**
20.39 Go on and **serve** your idols!
27.10 "Soldiers from Persia, Lydia, and Libya **served** in your army.
40.45 was for the priests who **served** in the Temple, [46] and the
40.46 faced north was for the priests who **served** at the altar.
40.46 are permitted to go into the Lord's presence to **serve** him.
42.14 rooms the holy clothing they wore while **serving** the Lord.
42.20 The wall **served** to separate what was holy from what was not.
43.19 only ones who are to come into my presence to **serve** me.
44.11 They may **serve** me in the Temple by taking charge of the
44.11 sacrifices, and they are to be on duty to **serve** the people.
44.13 They are not to **serve** me as priests or to go near
44.15 however, continued to **serve** me faithfully in the Temple
44.15 the ones who are to **serve** me and come into my presence
44.16 alone will enter my Temple, **serve** at my altar, and conduct
44.27 his purification, so that he can **serve** in the Temple again.
45. 4 set aside for the priests who **serve** the Lord in his Temple.
48.11 They **served** me faithfully and did not join the rest of the
Dan 1. 4 so that they would be qualified to **serve** in the royal court.
3.17 If the God whom we **serve** is able to save us from
3.28 his angel and rescued these men who **serve** and trust him.
6.16 to Daniel, "May your God, whom you **serve** so loyally, rescue
6.20 Was the God you **serve** so loyally able to save you from
7.10 thousands of people there to **serve** him, and millions of
7.14 people of all nations, races, and languages would **serve** him.
7.27 end and all rulers on earth will **serve** and obey them."
11.37 ignore the god his ancestors **served,** and also the god that
Hos 2.12 which she said her lovers gave her for **serving** them.
4.13 your daughters **serve** as prostitutes, and your daughters-in-law
9.17 The God I **serve** will reject his people, because they
10. 5 They and the priests who **serve** the idol will weep over it.
Joel 1.13 Put on sackcloth and weep, you priests who **serve** at the altar!
2.17 The priests, **serving** the Lord between the altar and the
Amos 2. 4 astray by the same false gods that their ancestors **served.**
Jon 1.16 Lord that they offered a sacrifice and promised to **serve** him.
Zeph 1. 4 no one will even remember the pagan priests who **serve** him.
Zech 4.14 has chosen and anointed to **serve** him, the Lord of the whole
Mal 3.14 You have said, 'It's useless to **serve** God.
3.17 them, as a father is merciful to the son who **serves** him.
3.18 wicked, to the person who **serves** me and the one who does
Mt 4.10 The scripture says, 'Worship the Lord your God and **serve** only him!' "
6.24 You cannot **serve** both God and money.
20.28 did not come to be **served,** but to serve and to give
Mk 10.45 For even the Son of Man did not come to be **served;**
10.45 he came to **serve** and to give his life to redeem many
Lk 1.73 enemies and allow us to **serve** him without fear, [75] so that
4. 8 "The scripture says, 'Worship the Lord your God and **serve** only him!' "
16.13 You cannot **serve** both God and money."
22.27 one who sits down to eat or the one who **serves** him?
Lk 22.27 But I am among you as one who **serves.**
Jn 2.10 said to him, "Everyone else **serves** the best wine first, and
2.10 have had plenty to drink, he **serves** the ordinary wine.
12. 2 They prepared a dinner for him there, which Martha helped to **serve;**
12.26 Whoever wants to **serve** me must follow me, so that my
12.26 And my Father will honour anyone who **serves** me.
16. 2 kills you will think that by doing this he is **serving** God.
Acts 1.25 two you have chosen [25] to **serve** as an apostle in the place
7. 7 the people that they will **serve,** and afterwards they will
9.15 I have chosen him to **serve** me, to make my name known
13. 2 While they were **serving** the Lord and fasting, the Holy
13.36 For David **served** God's purposes in his own time, and
Rom 1. 9 true—the God whom I **serve** with all my heart by preaching
1.25 they worship and **serve** what God has created instead of the
3. 5 what if our doing wrong **serves** to show up more clearly God's
3. 7 But what if my untruth **serves** God's glory by making his
7. 6 No longer do we **serve** in the old way of a written
7.25 on my own I can **serve** God's law only with my mind,
7.25 while my human nature **serves** the law of sin.
9.11 God said to her, "The elder will **serve** the younger."
12. 7 if it is to **serve,** we should serve;
12.11 **Serve** the Lord with a heart full of devotion.
14.18 And when someone **serves** Christ in this way, he pleases
15.16 I **serve** like a priest in preaching the Good News from God,
16. 1 you our sister Phoebe, who **serves** the church at Cenchreae.
16.18 do such things are not **serving** Christ our Lord, but their
1 Cor 6.13 not to be used for sexual immorality, but to **serve** the Lord;
11.15 Her long hair has been given her to **serve** as a covering.
12. 5 There are different ways of **serving,** but the same Lord is served.
16.16 these, and of anyone else who works and **serves** with them.
2 Cor 3. 6 who made us capable of **serving** the new covenant, which
Gal 1.15 me even before I was born, and called me to **serve** him.
2.17 are—does this mean that Christ is **serving** the cause of sin?
5.13 Instead, let love make you **serve** one another.
Eph 4. 1 you, then—I who am a prisoner because I **serve** the Lord:
6. 5 it with a sincere heart, as though you were **serving** Christ.
6. 7 as though you **served** the Lord, and not merely men.
Phil 1.29 been given the privilege of **serving** Christ, not only by
2.25 my side and who has **served** as your messenger in helping me.
Col 3.24 For Christ is the real Master you **serve.**
1 Thes 1. 9 from idols to God, to **serve** the true and living God [10] and
1 Tim 1. 4 they do not **serve** God's plan, which is known by faith.
1.12 worthy and appointing me to **serve** him, [13] even though in
3.10 first, and then, if they pass the test, they are to **serve.**
6. 2 Instead, they are to **serve** them even better, because those
2 Tim 1. 3 thanks to God, whom I **serve** with a clear conscience, as my
3.17 so that the person who **serves** God may be fully qualified
Heb 1.14 They are spirits who **serve** God and are sent by him to
5. 1 his fellow-men and appointed to **serve** God on their behalf,
7.13 tribe, and no member of his tribe ever **served** as a priest.
8. 2 He **serves** as High Priest in the Most Holy Place, that is,
9.11 The tent in which he **serves** is greater and more perfect;
9.14 from useless rituals, so that we may **serve** the living God.
10. 3 however, the sacrifices **serve** year after year
13.10 The priests who **serve** in the Jewish place of worship
1 Pet 2. 5 spiritual temple, where you will **serve** as holy priests to
4.11 whoever serves must **serve** with the strength that God gives him,
5. 2 work, not for mere pay, but from a real desire to **serve.**
5. 5 you must put on the apron of humility, to **serve** one another;
Rev 1. 6 made us a kingdom of priests to **serve** his God and Father.
5.10 a kingdom of priests to **serve** our God, and they shall rule
7.15 stand before God's throne and **serve** him day and night

SERVICE

[ARMY SERVICE, MILITARY SERVICE]

Ex 28. 3 so that he may be dedicated as a priest in my **service.**
29. 1 Aaron and his sons to dedicate them as priests in my **service.**
30.30 Aaron and his sons, and ordain them as priests in my **service.**
30.31 is to be used in my **service** for all time to come.
32.29 yourselves as priests in the **service** of the Lord by killing
Num 1. 3 twenty years old or older who are fit for **military service.**
1.20 older who were fit for **military service** were registered by
1.49 of the men fit for **military service,** do not include the
3.26 responsible for all the **service** connected with these items.
3.31 responsible for all the **service** connected with these items.
3.36 responsible for all the **service** connected with these items.
3.38 for carrying out the **services** performed in the Holy Place
4. 4 Their **service** involves the most holy things.
4.14 on it all the equipment used in the **service** at the altar:
4.33 responsibilities of the Merari clan in their **service** in the Tent:
8.26 in the Tent, but he must not perform any **service** by himself.
16. 9 approach him, perform your **service** in the Lord's Tent,
18. 1 sons will suffer the consequences of **service** in the priesthood.
18. 4 responsibilities for all the **service** in the Tent,
18.21 is in payment for their **service** in taking care of the Tent
18.31 because it is your wages for your **service** in the Tent.
26. 2 years old or older who are fit for **military service."**
Deut 24. 5 be drafted into **military service** or any other public duty;
Josh 9. 8 They said to Joshua, "We are at your **service."**
9.11 to put ourselves at your **service** and ask you to make a
1 Sam 2.21 The boy Samuel grew up in the **service** of the Lord.
16.21 David came to Saul and entered his **service.**
16.22 Let him stay here in my **service."**
22.12 "At your **service,** sir," he answered.
2 Sam 9. 2 "At your **service,** sir," he answered.
9. 6 "Mephibosheth," and he answered, "At your **service,** sir."
24. 9 king the total number of men capable of **military service:**
2 Kgs 25.14 all the other bronze articles used in the temple **service.**
1 Chr 4.23 They were potters in the **service** of the king and lived

1 Chr 7. 4 were able to provide 36,000 men for **military service.**
7. 5 Issachar listed 87,000 men eligible for **military service.**
7. 7 descendants included 22,034 men eligible for **military service.**
7. 9 families listed 20,200 men eligible for **military service.**
7.11 descendants included 17,200 men eligible for **military service.**
7.40 descendants included 26,000 men eligible for **military service.**
18.17 and King David's sons held high positions in his **service.**
21. 5 King David the total number of men capable of **military service:**
23.27 Levites were registered for **service** when they reached the age
25. 1 chose the following Levite clans to lead the **services** of worship:
25. 1 the worship, with the type of **service** that each group performed:
2 Chr 5.11 and they could not continue the **service** of worship.
24.16 City in recognition of the **service** he had done for the
24.22 king forgot about the loyal **service** that Zechariah's father
Ezra 6.18 the Levites for the temple **services** in Jerusalem, according to
7.19 that have been given to you for use in the temple **services.**
Neh 11.22 that was responsible for the music in the temple **services.**
Esth 3. 2 all the officials in his **service** to show their respect for
3. 3 officials in the royal **service** asked him why he was disobeying
Job 7. 1 life is like forced **army service,** like a life of hard manual
38.35 to flash, will it come to you and say, "At your **service"?**
Jer 52.18 all the other bronze articles used in the temple **service.**
Ezek 29.20 Egypt in payment for his **services,** because his army was working
46.17 anyone who is in his **service,** it will become the prince's
Lk 1. 8 priest in the Temple, taking his turn in the daily **service.**
1.23 When his period of **service** in the Temple was over,
Acts 1.20 It is also written, 'May someone else take his place of **service.'**
15.26 risked their lives in the **service** of our Lord Jesus Christ.
Rom 7. 4 in order that we might be useful in the **service** of God.
12. 1 to God, dedicated to his **service** and pleasing to him.
15. 8 you that Christ's life of **service** was on behalf of the Jews,
15.17 Christ Jesus, then, I can be proud of my **service** for God.
15.25 I am going to Jerusalem in the **service** of God's people there.
15.31 in Judaea and that my **service** in Jerusalem may be acceptable
16. 3 Priscilla and Aquila, my fellow-workers in the **service** of Christ Jesus;
16. 9 Urbanus, our fellow-worker in Christ's **service,** and to Stachys, my dear friend.
16.12 work in the Lord's **service,** and to my dear friend Persis,
16.13 outstanding worker in the Lord's **service,** and to his mother,
1 Cor 7.35 completely to the Lord's **service** without any reservation.
10.18 is offered in sacrifice share in the altar's **service** to God.
12. 6 are different abilities to perform **service,** but the same God
12. 6 same God gives ability to all for their particular **service.**
15.58 that nothing you do in the Lord's **service** is ever useless.
16.15 Achaia and have given themselves to the **service** of God's people.
2 Cor 8. 6 it and help you complete this special **service** of love.
8. 7 we want you to be generous also in this **service** of love.
8.19 as we carry out this **service** of love for the sake of
9.12 For this **service** you perform not only meets the needs of
9.13 of the proof which this **service** of yours brings, many will
Eph 4.12 for the work of Christian **service,** in order to build up the
Col 4.17 to finish the task you were given in the Lord's **service."**
1 Tim 2. 8 In every church **service** I want the men to pray, men who
5.22 lay hands on someone to dedicate him to the Lord's **service.**
2 Tim 2. 4 A soldier on active **service** wants to please his commanding
Heb 2.17 merciful High Priest in his **service** to God, so that the
10.11 Every Jewish priest performs his **services** every day and
13.17 since they must give God an account of their **service.**
3 Jn 7 on their journey in the **service** of Christ without accepting
Rev 2.19 I know your love, your faithfulness, your **service,** and your patience.
14.13 those who from now on die in the **service** of the Lord!"
14.13 work, because the results of their **service** go with them."

AV SERVICE

see also **WORK**

Ex 12.25 Lord has promised to give you, you must perform this **ritual.**
12.26 When your children ask you, 'What does this **ritual** mean?'
13. 5 land, you must celebrate this **festival** in the first month of
Num 4.19 and assign each man his **task** and tell him what to carry.
4.28 These are the **responsibilities** of the Gershon clan in the Tent;
8.24 Levite shall perform his **duties** in the Tent of my presence,
18. 6 me, so that they can carry out their **duties** in the Tent.
Josh 22.27 us, that we do indeed **worship** the Lord before his sacred
1 Kgs 12. 4 If you make these **burdens** lighter and make life easier for us,
1 Chr 24. 3 descendants of Aaron into groups according to their **duties.**
28.21 Levites have been assigned duties to **perform** in the Temple.
29. 5 else is willing to give a generous **offering** to the Lord?"
2 Chr 31. 2 priests and Levites, under which they each had specific **duties.**
35. 2 assigned to the priests the **duties** they were to perform
Neh 10.32 grammes of silver to help pay the **expenses** of the Temple.
Ps 104.14 and plants for man to **use,** so that he can grow his
Rom 9. 4 they have the true **worship;**
12. 1 This is the true **worship** that you should offer.
Gal 4. 8 God, and so you were **slaves** of beings who are not gods.
Phil 2.17 an offering on the **sacrifice** that your faith offers to God.
Heb 9. 1 first covenant had rules for **worship**
9. 6 every day to perform their **duties,** [7] but only the High Priest
9. 9 cannot make the **worshipper's** heart perfect,

SESSION

Jer 36.12 court secretary, where all the officials were in **session.**
Dan 7.10 The court began its **session,** and the books were opened.

SET (1)

Ex 26. 3 of them together in one **set,** and do the same with the
26. 4 blue cloth on the edge of the outside piece in each **set.**
Ex 26. 5 first piece of the first **set** and fifty loops matching them
26. 5 on the last piece of the second **set.**
26. 6 gold hooks with which to join the two **sets** into one piece.
26. 9 together in one set, and the other six in another **set.**
26.10 the last piece of one **set,**
26.10 and fifty loops on the edge of the other **set.**
26.11 loops to join the two **sets** so as to form one cover.
36.10 of them together in one **set** and did the same with the
36.11 blue cloth on the edge of the outside piece in each **set.**
36.12 first piece of the first **set** and fifty loops matching them
36.12 on the last piece of the second **set.**
36.13 gold hooks, with which to join the two **sets** into one piece.
36.16 together in one set and the other six in another **set.**
36.17 the last piece of one **set**
36.17 and fifty loops on the edge of the other **set.**
36.18 hooks to join the two **sets,** so as to form one cover.

SET (2)

Gen 12. 8 the city of Bethel and **set up** his camp between Bethel on
18. 8 some milk, and the meat, and **set** the food before the men.
26.17 So Isaac left and **set up** his camp in the Valley of
26.25 Then he **set up** his camp there, and his servants dug another
28.18 that was under his head, and **set it up** as a memorial.
28.22 memorial stone which I have **set up** will be the place where
31.25 Jacob had **set up** his camp on a mountain,
31.25 and Laban **set up** his camp with his kinsmen
31.45 So Jacob took a stone and **set it up** as a memorial.
33.18 the land of Canaan and **set up** his camp in a field
34.12 what presents you want, and **set** the payment for the bride as
35.14 had spoken to him, Jacob **set up** a memorial stone and
35.20 Jacob **set up** a memorial stone there, and it still marks
35.21 Jacob moved on and **set up** his camp on the other side
43.21 When we **set up** camp on the way home, we opened our
Ex 8. 9 Just **set** the time when I am to pray for you, your
9. 5 I, the Lord, have **set** tomorrow as the time when I will
19. 1 There they **set up** camp at the foot of Mount Sinai, [3] and
20.24 In every place that I **set aside** for you to worship me,
24. 4 foot of the mountain and **set up** twelve stones, one for each
25. 7 and other jewels to be **set** in the ephod of the High
25.37 for the lamp-stand and **set them up** so that they shine
26.28 The middle cross-bar, **set** half-way up the frames,
26.30 **Set up** the Tent according to the plan that I showed you
26.32 fitted with hooks, and **set** in four silver bases.
27.21 and his sons are to **set up** the lamp in the Tent
28.11 and mount the stones in gold **settings.**
28.13 Make two gold **settings** [14] and two chains
28.14 gold twisted like cords, and attach them to the **settings.**
28.20 These are to be mounted in gold **settings.**
28.25 the cords to the two **settings,** and in this way attach them
29.27 to me as a special gift and **set aside** for the priests.
31. 5 for cutting jewels to be **set;**
33. 7 Whenever the people of Israel **set up** camp, Moses would
35. 9 and other jewels to be **set** in the High Priest's ephod
35.27 and other jewels to be **set** in the ephod and the breast-piece
35.33 for cutting jewels to be **set;**
36.33 The middle cross-bar, **set** half-way up the frames,
39. 6 They prepared the carnelians and mounted them in gold **settings;**
39.13 These were mounted in gold **settings.**
39.16 They made two gold **settings** and two gold rings
39.18 the cords to the two **settings** and in this way attached them
40. 2 day of the first month **set up** the Tent of the Lord's
40. 4 Also bring in the lamp-stand and **set up** the lamps on it.
40.17 they left Egypt, the Tent of the Lord's presence was **set up.**
40.18 Moses put down its bases, **set up** its frames, attached its
40.33 Moses **set up** the enclosure round the Tent and the altar
Lev 25.50 Year of Restoration and must **set** the price for his release
26. 1 "Do not make idols or **set up** statues, stone pillars, or
27. 8 priest, and the priest will **set** a lower price, according to
Num 1.50 its equipment, serve in it, and **set up** their camp round it.
1.51 the Tent down and **set it up** again at each new camping
1.52 of the Israelites shall **set up** camp, company by company,
2. 2 When the Israelites **set up** camp, each man will camp under
2. 2 The camp is to be **set up** all round the Tent.
4.26 and all the fittings used in **setting up** these objects.
4.32 the Tent, with all the fittings used in **setting them up.**
7. 1 On the day Moses finished **setting up** the Tent of the
9.15 of the Lord's presence was **set up,** a cloud came and covered
9.17 Israel broke camp, and they **set up** camp again in the place
9.18 command of the Lord, and at his command they **set up** camp.
9.23 They **set up** camp and broke camp in obedience to the
10.21 arrived at the next camp, the Tent had been **set up** again.
12.16 Then they left Hazeroth and **set up** camp in the
15.19 of it is to be **set aside** as a special contribution to
16. 3 Moses, do you **set** yourself above the Lord's community?"
22. 1 The Israelites moved on and **set up** camp in the plains of
24.21 secure, Safe as a nest **set** high on a cliff,
33. 1 the places where the Israelites **set up** camp after they left
33. 2 down the name of the place each time they **set up** camp.
33. 5 The people of Israel left Rameses and **set up** camp at Sukkoth.
33.15 Rephidim to Mount Hor they **set up** camp at the following places:
33.41 of Moab the Israelites **set up** camp at the following places:
Deut 4.41 Then Moses **set aside** three cities east of the River Jordan
14.22 **"Set aside** a tithe—a tenth of all that your fields
15.19 **"Set aside** for the Lord your God all the first-born
16.22 And do not **set up** any stone pillar for idol worship;
19. 7 This is why I order you to **set aside** three cities.
26.10 **set** the basket down in the Lord's presence and worship there.
27. 2 giving you, you are to **set up** some large stones, cover them
27. 4 other side of the Jordan, **set up** these stones on Mount Ebal,
Josh 4. 9 Joshua also **set up** twelve stones in the middle of the Jordan,

Josh 4.20 There Joshua **set up** the twelve stones taken from the Jordan.
8.11 entrance to the city and **set up** camp on the north side,
11. 5 forces and came together and **set up** camp at Merom Brook to
18. 1 Israel assembled at Shiloh and **set up** the Tent of the Lord's
18. 9 all over the land and **set** down in writing how they divided
20. 7 side of the Jordan they **set aside** Kedesh in Galilee, in the
24.26 a large stone and **set it up** under the oak-tree in the
Judg 4.11 meantime Heber the Kenite had **set up** his tent close to
18.30 The men from Dan **set up** the idol to be worshipped, and
1 Sam 4. 1 The Israelites **set up** their camp at Ebenezer and the Philistines
5. 2 temple of their god Dagon, and **set it up** beside his statue.
7.12 Samuel took a stone, **set it up** between Mizpah and Shen, and
9.23 of meat I gave you, which I told you to **set aside."**
18.26 Before the day **set** for the wedding, [27] David and his men
28.25 She **set** the food before Saul and his officers, and they
2 Sam 6.17 its place in the Tent that David had **set up** for it.
8. 6 Then he **set up** military camps in their territory, and they
8.14 He **set up** military camps throughout Edom, and the people there
15.24 They **set** it down and didn't pick it up again until all
16.22 So they **set up** a tent for Absalom on the palace roof,
20. 5 he did not get back by the time the king had **set.**
22. 6 death was round me, and the grave **set** its trap for me.
1 Kgs 6.31 made of olive wood was **set** in place at the entrance of
7.28 of square panels which were **set** in frames, [29] with the
12.33 day that he himself had **set,** he went to Bethel and offered
20.34 your father, and you may **set up** a commercial centre for
2 Kgs 4. 4 **Set each one aside** as soon as it is full."
4.44 So the servant **set** the food before them, and, as the
6. 8 consulted his officers and chose a place to **set up** his camp.
10.29 the gold bull-calves he **set up** in Bethel and in Dan.
20.11 go back ten steps on the stairway **set up** by King Ahaz.
25. 1 They **set up** camp outside the city, built siege walls round it,
1 Chr 16.30 The earth is **set** firmly in place and cannot be moved.
18. 6 Then he **set up** military camps in their territory, and they
18.13 He **set up** military camps throughout Edom, and the people there
2 Chr 1. 4 tent which King David had **set up** when he brought the Box
3.17 The columns were **set** at the sides of the temple entrance:
25.14 idols back with him, **set them up,** worshipped them, and burnt
28.24 He closed the Temple and **set up** altars in every part of
Ezra 5. 8 large stone blocks and with wooden beams **set** in the wall.
10.14 foreign wife come at a **set** time, together with the leaders
Neh 6. 1 although we still had not **set up** the gates in the gateways.
Esth 8.12 Persian Empire on the day **set** for the slaughter of the Jews,
Job 14.13 your anger is over, and then **set** a time to remember me.
18.10 a trap has been **set** in his path.
19. 6 He has **set** a trap to catch me.
24. 1 Why doesn't God **set** a time for judging, a day of justice
33.26 God will **set** things right for him again.
34.23 God does not need to **set** a time for men to go
Ps 7.15 in the traps they **set** for others, they themselves get caught.
8. 3 and the stars, which you **set** in their places—
9. 7 he has **set up** his throne for judgement.
18. 5 death was round me, and the grave **set** its trap for me.
21. 3 him with great blessings and **set** a crown of gold on his
31. 4 Keep me safe from the trap that has been **set** for me;
40. 2 He **set** me safely on a rock and made me secure.
65. 6 You **set** the mountains in place by your strength,
74.16 you **set** the sun and the moon in their places;
74.17 you **set** the limits of the earth;
75. 2 "I have **set** a time for judgement," says God,
93. 1 The earth is **set** firmly in place and cannot be moved.
96.10 The earth is **set** firmly in place and cannot be moved;
104. 5 You have **set** the earth firmly on its foundations,
104. 9 You **set** a boundary they can never pass,
119.90 you have **set** the earth in place, and it remains.
140. 5 Proud men have **set** a trap for me;
140. 5 they have **set** traps to catch me.
141. 9 from the traps they have **set** for me, from the snares of
Prov 1.18 but men like that are **setting** a trap for themselves,
3.19 by his knowledge he **set** the sky in place.
8.25 before the hills were **set** in place,
8.27 I was there when he **set** the sky in place,
25.11 An idea well-expressed is like a design of gold, **set** in silver.
26.27 People who **set** traps for others get caught themselves.
29. 5 If you flatter your friends, you **set** a trap for yourself.
Ecc 3. 2 He **sets** the time for birth and the time for death,
3. 4 He **sets** the time for sorrow and the time for joy,
3. 6 He **sets** the time for finding and the time for losing,
3. 8 He **sets** the time for love and the time for hate,
3.11 He has **set** the right time for everything.
3.17 every action, will happen at its own **set** time."
Song 5.14 His hands are well-formed, and he wears rings **set** with gems.
5.14 His body is like smooth ivory, with sapphires **set** in it.
5.15 His thighs are columns of alabaster **set** in sockets of gold.
Is 40.19 metalworkers cover with gold and **set** in a base of silver.
40.24 They are like young plants, just **set** out and barely rooted.
57. 8 You **set up** your obscene idols just inside your front doors.
Jer 1.15 Their kings will **set up** their thrones at the gates of
5.26 to catch birds, but they have **set** their traps to catch men.
9. 8 to his neighbour, but is really **setting** a trap for him.
11.13 the inhabitants of Jerusalem have **set up** as many altars
11.23 I have **set** a time for bringing disaster on the people of
17. 2 the symbols that have been **set up** for the goddess Asherah by
18.22 for me to fall in and have **set** traps to catch me.
31.21 **Set up** signs and mark the road;
31.30 eats sour grapes will have his own teeth **set** on edge;
33. 2 earth, who formed it and **set** it in place, spoke to me.
48. 9 **Set up** a tombstone for Moab;
48.44 because the Lord has **set** the time for Moab's destruction.
49.38 destroy their kings and leaders, and **set up** my throne there.
50.24 caught in the trap I **set** for you,
Jer 52. 4 They **set up** camp outside the city, built siege walls round it,
Lam 1.13 He **set** a trap for me and brought me to the ground.
Ezek 4. 3 an iron pan and **set it up** like a wall between you
21.22 to go and **set up** battering-rams, to shout the battle-cry,
24. 3 **Set** the pot on the fire and fill it up with water.
24.11 Now **set** the empty bronze pot on the coals
25. 4 They will **set up** their camps in your country and settle there.
37. 1 his spirit took me and **set** me down in a valley where
42. 3 on three levels, each one **set** further back than the one
42. 5 the middle and lower levels because they were **set** further back.
43.14 The next section was **set** back from the edge
43.14 section after that was also **set** back from the edge
45. 4 holy part of the country, **set aside** for the priests who
45. 5 the area is to be **set aside** as the possession of the
45. 6 kilometres wide, is to be **set aside** for a city where any
45. 7 Land is also to be **set aside** for the ruling prince.
Dan 1.18 the end of three years **set** by the king, Ashpenaz took all
3. 1 wide, and he had it **set up** in the plain of Dura
3. 2 the dedication of the statue which King Nebuchadnezzar had **set up.**
3. 5 and worship the gold statue that King Nebuchadnezzar has **set up.**
3. 7 and worshipped the gold statue which King Nebuchadnezzar had **set up.**
3.12 worship your god or bow down to the statue you **set up."**
3.14 and to bow down to the gold statue I have **set up?**
3.18 not bow down to the gold statue that you have **set up."**
9.24 length of time God has **set** for freeing your people and your
11.31 They will stop the daily sacrifices and **set up** The Awful Horror.
11.35 continue until the end comes, the time that God has **set.**
11.45 He will even **set up** his huge royal tents between the sea
Hos 6.11 people of Judah, I have **set** a time to punish you also
Amos 3. 5 Does a trap spring unless something **sets** it off?
Nah 2. 5 to the wall and **set up** the shield for the battering-ram.
Mt 4. 5 to Jerusalem, the Holy City, **set** him on the highest point of
10.35 I came to **set** sons against their fathers, daughters against their mothers,
Mk 3.21 family heard about it, they **set** out to take charge of him,
Lk 4. 9 took him to Jerusalem and **set** him on the highest point of
9.51 made up his mind and **set** out on his way to Jerusalem.
10. 8 made welcome, eat what is **set** before you, [9] heal the sick in
12.49 "I came to **set** the earth on fire, and how I wish
Jn 13.15 I have **set** an example for you, so that you will do
Acts 1. 7 "The times and occasions are **set** by my Father's own authority,
13. 2 Holy Spirit said to them, **"Set apart** for me Barnabas and Saul,
17. 5 They **set** the whole city in an uproar and attacked the home
Rom 8.29 had already chosen he also **set apart** to become like his Son,
8.30 And so those whom God **set apart,** he called;
10. 3 and instead, they have tried to **set** up their own way;
1 Cor 1.19 the wise and **set aside** the understanding of the scholars."
10.27 to go, eat what is **set** before you, without asking any
12.31 **Set** your hearts, then, on the more important gifts.
14. 1 **Set** your hearts on spiritual gifts, especially the gift of
14.39 So then, my brothers, **set** your heart on proclaiming God's message,
2 Cor 1.21 God himself who has **set us apart,** [22] who has placed his
10.13 the work which God has **set** for us, and this includes our
10.15 work that others have done beyond the limits God **set** for us.
10.15 work among you, always within the limits that God has **set.**
Gal 4. 2 him and manage his affairs until the time **set** by his father.
6. 1 those of you who are spiritual should **set** him right;
Eph 4. 1 that measures up to the standard God **set** when he called you.
Phil 3.17 those who follow the right example that we have **set** for you.
Col 3. 1 to life with Christ, so **set** your hearts on the things that
Heb 4. 7 fact that God **sets** another day, which is called "Today."
7.18 The old rule, then, is **set aside,** because it was weak
7.26 been **set apart** from sinners and raised above the heavens.
9.19 to the people all the commandments as **set forth** in the Law.
Jas 3. 5 large a forest can be **set** on fire by a tiny flame!
3. 6 It **sets** on fire the entire course of our existence with the
1 Pet 1.13 Keep alert and **set** your hope completely on the blessing
3 Jn 7 For they **set** out on their journey in the service of Christ

SET (3)
see also **SUNSET**

Gen 15.17 When the sun had **set** and it was dark, a smoking fire-pot
Ex 22.26 to him before the sun **sets,** [27] because it is the only
Lev 22. 7 After the sun **sets** he is clean, and then he may eat
Ps 104.19 the sun knows the time to **set.**
Mt 16. 2 answered, "When the sun is **setting,** you say, 'We are going
Mk 1.32 After the sun had **set** and evening had come, people
Lk 9.12 the sun was beginning to **set,** the twelve disciples came to

SET FREE see FREE

SETTLE (1)
[RESETTLES]

Gen 11. 2 East, they came to a plain in Babylonia and **settled** there.
11.31 They went as far as Haran and **settled** there.
13.12 land of Canaan, and Lot **settled** among the cities in the
13.18 Abram moved his camp and **settled** near the sacred trees of
22.19 and they went together to Beersheba, where Abraham **settled.**
34.16 We will **settle** among you and become one people with you.
47. 6 Let them **settle** in the region of Goshen, the best part of
47.11 Then Joseph **settled** his father and his brothers in Egypt,
Ex 10.14 They came in swarms and **settled** over the whole country.
12.48 If a foreigner has **settled** among you and wants to celebrate
12.49 Israelites and to foreigners who **settle** among you."
16.35 until they reached the land of Canaan, where they **settled.**

Num 11.31 They **settled** on the camp and all round it for many
21.25 Heshbon and all the surrounding towns, and **settled** in them.
21.31 the people of Israel **settled** in the territory of the Amorites,
32. 5 do not make us cross the River Jordan and **settle** there."
32.17 the attack until we have **settled** them in the land that will
33.53 Occupy the land and **settle** in it, because I am giving it
Deut 2.12 destroyed their nation, and **settled** there themselves, just as
2.21 that the Ammonites took over their land and **settled** there.
2.22 Edomites took over their land and **settled** there,
2.23 Mediterranean coast had been **settled** by people from the island
11.31 When you take it and **settle** there, [32]be sure to obey all
12.29 invade their land, and you will occupy it and **settle** there.
17.14 to give you and have **settled** there, then you will decide you
19. 1 cities and houses and **settled** there, [2-3]divide the territory
20.15 cities that are far away from the land you will **settle** in.
26. 1 is giving you and have **settled** there, [2]each of you must
Josh 1.15 you may come back and **settle** here in your own land east
2. 8 Before the spies **settled** down for the night, Rahab went up
19.47 They **settled** there and changed the name of the city from
19.50 He rebuilt the city and **settled** there.
21.43 When they had taken possession of it, they **settled** down there.
22.33 the land where the people of Reuben and Gad had **settled.**
Judg 1.16 There they **settled** among the Amalekites.
3. 5 people of Israel **settled** down among the Canaanites,
18.27 The men from Dan rebuilt the town and **settled** down there.
1 Sam 12. 8 who brought them out of Egypt and **settled** them in this land.
27. 3 David and his men **settled** there in Gath with their families.
2 Sam 2. 3 their families, and they **settled** in the towns round Hebron.
7. 1 King David was **settled** in his palace, and the Lord kept
7.10 my people Israel and have **settled** them there, where they
2 Kgs 16. 6 The Edomites **settled** in Elath, and still live there.)
17. 6 to Assyria as prisoners, and **settled** some of them in the
17.24 and Sepharvaim, and **settled** them in the cities of Samaria,
17.25 When they first **settled** there, they did not worship the Lord,
17.26 that the people he had **settled** in the cities of Samaria did
17.29 But the people who **settled** in Samaria continued to make their
18. 8 and raided their **settlements,** from the smallest village to the
18.11 to Assyria as prisoners and **settled** some of them in the city
18.32 own wells—[32]until the emperor **resettles** you in a country
25.24 **Settle** in this land, serve the king of Babylonia, and all
1 Chr 4.22 who married Moabite women and then **settled** in Bethlehem.
4.41 drove the people out and **settled** there permanently
5.23 The people of East Manasseh **settled** in the territory of Bashan
5.26 Gad, and East Manasseh and **settled** them permanently in
7.28 territory which they took and **settled** in included Bethel and the
8.13 were heads of families that **settled** in the city of Aijalon
8.29 Jeiel founded the city of Gibeon and **settled** there.
9.35 Jeiel founded the city of Gibeon and **settled** there.
17. 9 my people Israel and have **settled** them there, where they
2 Chr 8. 2 King Hiram had given him, and sent Israelites to **settle** in them.
21.16 Arabs lived near where some Sudanese had **settled** along the coast.
28.18 and Gimzo with their villages, and **settled** there permanently.
30.25 the foreigners who had **settled** permanently in Israel and Judah.
Ezra 2.70 and some of the people **settled** in or near Jerusalem;
2.70 and the temple workmen **settled** in nearby towns;
2.70 the rest of the Israelites **settled** in the towns
3. 1 month the people of Israel were all **settled** in their towns.
4.10 moved from their homes and **settled** in the city of Samaria
4.12 other territories have **settled** in Jerusalem and are rebuilding
Neh 7.73 all the people of Israel—**settled** in the towns and cities of
8. 1 month the people of Israel were all **settled** in their towns.
11. 1 The leaders **settled** in Jerusalem, and the rest of the people
12.28 the area where they had **settled** round Jerusalem and from the
Ps 105.23 Then Jacob went to Egypt and **settled** in that country.
107.36 He let hungry people **settle** there, and they built a city
Prov 26. 2 They are like birds that fly by and never **settle.**
Is 23. 7 city that sent **settlers** across the sea to establish colonies?
36.17 own wells—[17]until the emperor **resettles** you in a country
49. 8 I will let you **settle** once again in your land that is
Jer 29. 5 'Build houses and **settle** down.
29.28 time and should build houses, **settle** down, plant gardens, and
40. 9 **Settle** down in this land, serve the king of Babylonia, and
48.11 is like wine left to **settle** undisturbed and never poured
49. 1 Molech take the territory of the tribe of Gad and **settle** there?
Ezek 25. 4 They will set up their camps in your country and **settle** there.
32.14 I will let your waters **settle** and become clear and let
Joel 1. 4 Swarm after swarm of locusts **settled** on the crops;
Zech 10.10 I will bring them home and **settle** them in their own country.
10.10 I will **settle** them in Gilead and Lebanon also;

SETTLE (2)

Ex 18.13 The next day Moses was **settling** disputes among the people,
18.23 all these people can go home with their disputes **settled."**
24.14 and so whoever has a dispute to **settle** can go to them."
Lev 19.17 a grudge against anyone, but **settle** your differences with him,
Deut 1.12 bear the heavy responsibility for **settling** your disputes?
25. 1 Israelites go to court to **settle** a dispute, and one is
Ruth 3.18 Boaz will not rest today until he **settles** the matter."
4. 7 Now in those days, to **settle** a sale or an exchange of
4. 7 In this way the Israelites showed that the matter was **settled.**
1 Sam 7. 6 at Mizpah that Samuel **settled** disputes among the Israelites.)
7.16 and Mizpah, and in these places he would **settle** disputes.
2 Sam 15. 2 he wanted the king to **settle,** Absalom would call him over
21. 4 and his family can't be **settled** with silver or gold, nor do
1 Kgs 3.28 God had given him the wisdom to **settle** disputes fairly.
1 Chr 26.29 records and **settling** disputes for the people of Israel.
Job 14. 5 You have **settled** it, and it can't be changed.
Prov 18.18 opposing each other in court, casting lots can **settle** the issue.
25. 9 have a difference of opinion, **settle** it between yourselves
Is 1.18 The Lord says, "Now, let's **settle** the matter.
2. 4 He will **settle** disputes among great nations.
Mic 4. 3 He will **settle** disputes among the nations,
Mt 5.25 and takes you to court, **settle** the dispute with him while
25.19 of those servants came back and **settled** accounts with them.
Lk 12.58 court, do your best to **settle** the dispute with him before
Acts 18.15 and names and your own law, you yourselves must **settle** it.
19.39 it will have to be **settled** in a legal meeting of citizens.
Rom 9.28 for the Lord will quickly **settle** his full account with the world."
1 Cor 6. 1 judges instead of letting God's people **settle** the matter?
6. 4 to take them to be **settled** by people who have no standing
6. 5 who can **settle** a dispute between fellow-Christians.
11.34 As for the other matters, I will **settle** them when I come.
Heb 6.16 greater than himself, and the vow **settles** all arguments.

SEVEN

see also **SABBATH**

Gen 2. 2 By the **seventh day** God finished what he had been doing and
2. 3 He blessed the **seventh day** and set it apart as a special
4.15 If anyone kills you, **seven** lives will be taken in revenge."
4.24 If **seven** lives are taken to pay for killing
7. 2 Take with you **seven** pairs of each kind of ritually clean animal,
7. 3 Take also **seven** pairs of each kind of bird.
7. 4 **Seven days** from now I am going to send rain that will
7.10 **Seven days** later the flood came.
7.20 rising until it was about **seven** metres above the tops of the
8. 4 the seventeenth day of the **seventh** month the boat came to
8.10 He waited another **seven days** and sent out the dove again.
8.12 Then he waited another **seven days** and sent out the dove
21.28 Abraham separated **seven** lambs from his flock,
21.30 Abraham answered, "Accept these **seven** lambs.
29.18 he said, "I will work **seven years** for you, if you will
29.20 Jacob worked **seven years** so that he could have Rachel,
29.27 you Rachel, if you will work for me another **seven years."**
29.30 Then he worked for Laban another **seven years.**
31.23 him and pursued Jacob for **seven days** until he caught up with
33. 3 down to the ground **seven** times as he approached his brother.
41. 2 by the River Nile, [2]when **seven** cows, fat and sleek, came up
41. 3 Then **seven** other cows came up;
41. 5 **Seven** ears of corn, full and ripe, were growing on one stalk.
41. 6 Then **seven** other ears of corn sprouted, thin and scorched
41.18 bank of the Nile, [18]when **seven** cows, fat and sleek, came
41.19 Then **seven** other cows came up which were thin and bony.
41.22 also dreamt that I saw **seven** ears of corn which were full
41.23 Then **seven** ears of corn sprouted, thin and scorched
41.26 The **seven** fat cows are seven years,
41.26 and the seven full ears of corn are also **seven years;**
41.27 The **seven** thin cows which came up later
41.27 and the **seven** thin ears of corn
41.27 scorched by the desert wind are **seven** years of famine.
41.29 There will be **seven years** of great plenty in all the
41.30 After that, there will be **seven years** of famine, and all
41.34 take a fifth of the crops during the **seven years** of plenty.
41.36 for the country during the **seven years** of famine which are
41.47 During the **seven years** of plenty the land produced abundant
41.53 The **seven years** of plenty that the land of Egypt had
41.54 to an end, [54]and the **seven years** of famine began, just as
46.25 These **seven** are the descendants of Jacob by Bilhah,
50.10 and Joseph performed mourning ceremonies for **seven days.**
Ex 2.15 **seven** daughters of Jethro, the priest
7.25 **Seven days** passed after the Lord struck the river.
12.15 The Lord said, "For **seven days** you must not eat any bread
12.15 if anyone during those **seven days** eats bread made with yeast,
12.16 day and again on the **seventh day** you are to meet for
12.19 For **seven days** no yeast must be found in your houses,
13. 6 For **seven days** you must eat unleavened bread
13. 6 and on the **seventh day** there is to be
13. 7 For **seven days** you must not eat any bread made with yeast;
16.26 six days, but on the **seventh day,** the day of rest, there
16.27 On the **seventh day** some of the people went out to gather
16.29 where he is on the **seventh day** and not leave his home."
16.30 So the people did no work on the **seventh day.**
20.10 do your work, [10]but the **seventh day** is a day of rest
20.11 and everything in them, but on the **seventh day** I rested.
21. 2 In the **seventh** year he is to be set free without having
22.30 stay with its mother for **seven days,** and on the eighth day
23.11 But in the **seventh year** let it rest, and do not harvest
23.12 do no work on the **seventh day,** so that your slaves and
23.15 made with yeast during the **seven days** of this festival.
24.16 six days, and on the **seventh day** the Lord called to Moses
25.37 Make **seven** lamps for the lamp-stand and set them up so
29.30 in the Holy Place is to wear these garments for **seven days.**
29.35 Aaron and his sons for **seven days** exactly as I have
29.37 Do this every day for **seven days.**
31.15 do your work, but the **seventh day** is a solemn day of
31.17 and on the **seventh day** I stopped working and rested."
34.18 eat unleavened bread for **seven days** in the month of Abib,
34.21 do not work on the **seventh day,** not even during ploughing
35. 2 do your work, but the **seventh day** is to be sacred, a
37.23 He made **seven** lamps for the lamp-stand, and he made its
Lev 4. 6 and sprinkle it in front of the sacred curtain **seven** times.
4.17 in it, and sprinkle it in front of the curtain **seven** times.
8.11 the oil and sprinkled it **seven** times on the altar and its
8.33 entrance of the Tent for **seven days,** until your ordination rites
8.35 Tent day and night for **seven days,** doing what the Lord has
12. 2 For **seven days** after a woman gives birth to a son, she
13. 4 white, the priest shall isolate the person for **seven days.**
13. 5 examine him again on the **seventh day,** and if in his opinion
13. 5 has not spread, he shall isolate him for another **seven days.**
13. 6 examine him again on the **seventh day,** and if the sore has

Lev 13.21 in colour, the priest shall isolate him for **seven days.**
13.26 in colour, the priest shall isolate him for **seven days.**
13.27 him again on the **seventh day,** and if it is spreading,
13.31 no healthy hairs in it, he shall isolate him for **seven days.**
13.32 the sore again on the **seventh day,** and if it has not
13.33 The priest shall then isolate him for another **seven days.**
13.34 On the **seventh day** the priest shall again examine the sore,
13.50 shall examine it and put the object away for **seven days.**
13.51 examine it again on the **seventh day,** and if the mildew has
13.54 order it to be washed and put away for another **seven days.**
14. 7 He shall sprinkle the blood **seven** times on the person who
14. 8 the camp, but he must live outside his tent for **seven days.**
14. 9 On the **seventh day** he shall again shave his head, his
14.16 some of it **seven** times there in the Lord's presence.
14.27 some of it **seven** times there in the Lord's presence.
14.38 he shall leave the house and lock it up for **seven days.**
14.39 On the **seventh day** he shall return and examine it again.
14.51 And he shall sprinkle the house **seven** times.
15.13 his discharge, he must wait **seven days** and then wash his
15.19 has her monthly period, she remains unclean for **seven days.**
15.24 impurity and remains unclean for **seven days,** and any bed on
15.28 flow stops, she must wait **seven days,** and then she will be
16.14 then sprinkle some of it **seven** times in front of the
16.19 he must sprinkle some of the blood on the altar **seven** times.
16.29 tenth day of the **seventh** month the Israelites and the foreigners
22.26 taken from its mother for **seven days,** but after that it is
23. 3 work, but remember that the **seventh day,** the Sabbath, is a
23. 6 Unleavened Bread begins, and for **seven days** you must not eat
23. 8 Offer your food-offerings to the Lord for **seven days.**
23. 8 On the **seventh day** you shall again gather for worship, but
23.15 Count **seven** full weeks from the day after the Sabbath on
23.16 day, the day after the **seventh** Sabbath, present to the Lord
23.18 the community is to present **seven** one-year-old lambs, one bull,
23.23 the first day of the **seventh** month observe a special day of
23.26 The tenth day of the **seventh** month is the day when
23.33 day of the seventh month and continues for **seven days.**
23.36 Each day for **seven days** you shall present a food-offering.
23.39 celebrate this festival for **seven days,**
23.39 beginning on the fifteenth day of the **seventh** month.
23.41 Celebrate it for **seven days.**
23.42 live in shelters for **seven days,** [43]so that your descendants
25. 2 honour the Lord by not cultivating the land every **seventh year.**
25. 4 But the **seventh year** is to be a year of complete rest
25. 8 Count **seven times seven years,** a total of forty-nine years.
25. 9 the tenth day of the **seventh** month, the Day of Atonement,
25.20 be to eat during the **seventh year,** when no fields are sown
26.18 do not obey me, I will increase your punishment **seven** times.
26.21 obey me, I will again increase your punishment **seven** times.
26.24 turn on you and punish you **seven** times harder than before.
26.28 again make your punishment **seven** times worse than before.
Num 6. 9 suddenly dies, he must wait **seven days** and then shave off
8. 2 that when he puts the **seven** lamps on the lamp-stand, he
12.14 face, she would have to bear her disgrace for **seven days.**
12.15 out of the camp for **seven days,** and the people did not
13.22 (Hebron was founded **seven years** before Zoan in Egypt.)
19. 4 with his finger sprinkle it **seven** times in the direction of
19.11 Whoever touches a corpse is ritually unclean for **seven days.**
19.12 third day and on the **seventh day,** and then he will be
19.12 both the third and the **seventh day,** he will not be clean.
19.14 or who enters it becomes ritually unclean for **seven days.**
19.16 a human bone or a grave, he becomes unclean for **seven days.**
19.19 third day and on the **seventh** the person who is ritually
19.19 On the **seventh day** he is to purify the man, who, after
23. 1 He said to Balak, "Build **seven** altars here for me,
23. 1 and bring me **seven** bulls and seven rams."
23. 4 him, "I have built the **seven** altars and offered a bull and
23.14 There also he built **seven** altars and offered a bull and a
23.29 Balaam said to him, "Build **seven** altars for me here
23.29 and bring me **seven** bulls and seven rams."
28.11 two young bulls, one ram, **seven** one-year-old male lambs,
28.17 religious festival begins which lasts **seven days,** during which
28.19 one ram, and **seven** one-year-old male lambs,
28.24 In the same way, for **seven days** offer to the Lord a
28.25 Meet for worship on the **seventh day** and do no work.
28.27 one ram, and **seven** one-year-old male lambs,
29. 1 the first day of the **seventh** month you are to gather for
29. 2 one ram, and **seven** one-year-old male lambs,
29. 7 Gather for worship on the tenth day of the **seventh** month;
29. 8 one ram, and **seven** one-year-old male lambs,
29.12 Gather for worship on the fifteenth day of the **seventh** month.
29.12 in honour of the Lord for **seven days** and do no work.
29.32 On the **seventh day** offer seven young bulls, two rams,
29.36 one ram, and **seven** one-year-old male lambs,
31.19 touched a corpse must stay outside the camp for **seven days.**
31.19 third day and on the **seventh day** purify yourselves and the
31.24 On the **seventh day** you must wash your clothes;
Deut 5.14 do your work, [14]but the **seventh day** is a day of rest
7. 1 he will drive out **seven** nations larger and more powerful
15. 1 "At the end of every **seventh year** you are to cancel the
15.12 When the **seventh year** comes, you must let him go free.
16. 3 For **seven days** you are to eat bread prepared without yeast,
16. 4 For **seven days** no one in your land is to have any
16. 8 without yeast, and on the **seventh day** assemble to worship
16. 9 "Count **seven** weeks from the time that you begin to
16.13 celebrate the Festival of Shelters for **seven days.**
16.15 by celebrating this festival for **seven days** at the one place
31.10 "At the end of every **seven years,** when the year that debts
Josh 6. 4 **Seven** priests, each carrying a trumpet, are to go in front
6. 4 On the **seventh day** you and your soldiers are to march
6. 4 march round the city **seven** times while the priests blow
6. 6 "Take the Covenant Box, and **seven** of you go in front of
Josh 6.12 next, the **seven** priests blowing the seven trumpets;
6.15 On the **seventh day** they got up at daybreak
6.15 and marched **seven** times round the city
6.15 was the only day that they marched round it **seven** times.
6.16 The **seventh** time round, when the priests were about to sound
18. 2 There were still **seven** tribes of the people of Israel who
18. 5 The land will be divided among them in **seven** parts;
18. 6 a description of these **seven** divisions and bring it to me.
18. 9 how they divided it into **seven** parts, making a list
19.40 The **seventh** assignment made was for the families of the tribe
Judg 6. 1 so he let the people of Midian rule them for **seven years.**
6.25 father's bull and another bull **seven years** old, tear down your
12. 9 Ibzan led Israel for **seven years,** [10]then he died and was
14.12 me its meaning before the **seven days** of the wedding feast
14.17 She cried about it for the whole **seven days** of the feast.
14.17 But on the **seventh day** he told her what the riddle meant,
14.18 So on the **seventh day,** before Samson went into the bedroom,
16. 7 they tie me up with **seven** new bowstrings that are not dried
16. 8 the Philistine kings brought Delilah **seven** new bowstrings
16.13 answered, "If you weave my **seven** locks of hair into a loom,
16.14 him to sleep, took his **seven** locks of hair, and wove them
16.19 then called a man, who cut off Samson's **seven** locks of hair.
Ruth 4.15 loves you, and has done more for you than **seven** sons.
1 Sam 2. 5 childless wife has borne **seven** children, but the mother of many
6. 1 in Philistia for **seven** months, [2]the people called the priests
10. 8 Wait there **seven days** until I come and tell you what to
11. 3 "Give us **seven days** to send messengers throughout the
13. 8 He waited **seven days** for Samuel, as Samuel had instructed
16.10 In this way Jesse brought **seven** of his sons to Samuel.
17. 7 and its iron head weighed about **seven** kilogrammes.
31.13 the tamarisk-tree in the town, and fasted for **seven days.**
2 Sam 2.11 he ruled in Hebron over Judah for **seven** and a half years.
5. 5 in Hebron over Judah for **seven** and a half years, and in
21. 6 So hand over **seven** of his male descendants, and we will
21. 9 before the Lord—and all **seven** of them died together.
21.13 gathered up the bones of the **seven** men who had been hanged.
1 Kgs 2.11 forty years, ruling **seven years** in Hebron and thirty-three years
6.38 It had taken Solomon **seven years** to build it.
8. 2 Festival of Shelters in the **seventh** month,
8.65 Israel celebrated the Festival of Shelters for **seven days.**
10.16 and had each one overlaid with almost **seven** kilogrammes of gold.
16.15 Asa of Judah, Zimri ruled in Tirzah over Israel for **seven days.**
18.43 **Seven** times in all Elijah told him to go and look.
18.44 The **seventh** time he returned and said, "I saw a little
20.29 For **seven days** the Syrians and the Israelites stayed in their
20.29 On the **seventh day** they started fighting, and the Israelites
2 Kgs 3. 9 After marching for **seven days,** they ran out of water, and
4.35 The boy sneezed **seven** times, and then opened his eyes.
5.10 to go and wash himself **seven** times in the River Jordan,
5.14 dipped himself in it **seven** times, as Elisha had instructed,
8. 1 land, which would last for **seven years,** and that she should
8. 2 with her family to live in Philistia for the **seven years.**
8. 3 At the end of the **seven years,** she returned to Israel and
8. 6 had produced during the **seven years** she had been away.
11. 4 But in the **seventh year** Jehoiada the priest sent for
11.21 Joash became king of Judah at the age of **seven.**
12. 1 In the **seventh year** of the reign of King Jehu of Israel,
18. 9 was the **seventh year** of King Hoshea's reign over
25. 8 On the **seventh day** of the fifth month of the nineteenth
25.25 But in the **seventh** month of that year, Ishmael, the son
1 Chr 2.13 Jesse had **seven** sons.
3. 4 born in Hebron during the **seven** and a half years that David
3.17 Jehoiachin had **seven** sons:
3.24 Elioenai had **seven** sons:
5.13 members of the tribe belonged to the following **seven** clans:
7.10 Jediael had one son, Bilhan, and Bilhan had **seven** sons:
8. 8 the country of Moab, he married Hodesh and had **seven** sons:
9.25 to take turns at guard duty for **seven days** at a time.
10.12 They buried them there under an oak and fasted for **seven days.**
15.26 They sacrificed **seven** bulls and seven sheep,
26. 2 He had **seven** sons, listed in order of age:
27. 2 **Seventh** month:
29.27 He ruled in Hebron for **seven years** and in Jerusalem
2 Chr 7. 8 Israel celebrated the Festival of Shelters for **seven days.**
7. 9 They had spent **seven days** for the dedication of the altar
7. 9 and then **seven** more days for the festival.
7.10 twenty-third day of the **seventh** month, Solomon sent the people
9.15 which was covered with about **seven** kilogrammes of beaten gold,
13. 9 along with a bull or **seven** sheep can get himself consecrated
24. 1 Judah at the age of **seven,** and he ruled in Jerusalem for
29.21 they took seven bulls, **seven** sheep, seven lambs, and seven goats.
30.21 For **seven days** the people who had gathered in Jerusalem
30.22 After the **seven days** during which they offered sacrifices
30.23 they all decided to celebrate for another **seven days.**
35.17 For **seven days** all the people of Israel who were present
Ezra 3. 1 By the **seventh** month the people of Israel were all settled
3. 6 the first day of the **seventh** month to burn sacrifices to the
6.22 For **seven days** they joyfully celebrated the Festival
7. 6 In the **seventh year** of the reign of Artaxerxes, Ezra set out
7.14 I, together with my **seven** counsellors, send you to investigate
Neh 8. 1 By the **seventh** month the people of Israel were all settled
8.18 They celebrated for **seven days,** and on the eighth day there
10.31 Every **seventh year** we will not farm the land, and we will
Esth 1.10 On the **seventh day** of his banquet the king was drinking
1.10 called in the **seven** eunuchs who were his personal servants,
1.14 **seven** officials of Persia and Media
2. 9 in the harem and assigned **seven** girls specially chosen
2.16 So in Xerxes' **seventh year** as king, in the tenth month,
Job 1. 2 He had **seven** sons and three daughters,
2.13 the ground with him for **seven days** and nights without saying
42. 8 Now take **seven** bulls and seven rams to Job and offer them

Job 42.13 He was the father of **seven** sons and three daughters.
Ps 12. 6 as genuine as silver refined **seven** times in the furnace.
79.12 pay the other nations back **seven** times for all the insults
119.164 **Seven** times each day I thank you for your righteous judgements.
Prov 6.16 There are **seven** things that the Lord hates and cannot tolerate:
6.31 he must pay back **seven** times more—
9. 1 Wisdom has built her house and made **seven** pillars for it.
26.16 he is more intelligent than **seven** men who can give good
Is 4. 1 When that time comes, **seven** women will grab hold of one
11.15 the Euphrates, leaving only **seven** tiny streams,
30.26 and the sun will be **seven** times brighter than usual,
30.26 like the light of **seven** days in one.
Jer 15. 9 The mother who lost her **seven** children has fainted,
28.17 And Hananiah died in the **seventh** month of that same year.
34.14 I told them that [14]every **seven years** they were to set free
41. 1 In the **seventh** month of that year, Ishmael, the son of
52.25 in command of the troops, **seven** of the king's personal advisers
52.28 in his **seventh year** as king he carried away 3,023;
Ezek 3.15 exiles were living, and for **seven days** I stayed there,
3.16 After the **seven days** had passed, the Lord spoke to me.
20. 1 day of the fifth month of the **seventh year** of our exile.
30.20 On the **seventh day** of the first month of the eleventh
39. 9 and clubs, and will have enough to last for **seven years.**
39.12 It will take the Israelites **seven** months to bury all the
39.14 After the **seven** months are over, men will be chosen
40.22 Here **seven** steps led up to the gate,
40.26 **Seven** steps led up to it,
40.48 a half metres deep and **seven** metres wide, with walls
43.17 section was also a square, **seven** metres on each side,
43.25 Each day for **seven days** you are to offer a goat, a
43.26 For **seven days** the priests are to consecrate the altar and
44.26 clean again, he must wait **seven days** [27]and then go into
45.20 On the **seventh day** of the month you are to do the
45.21 For **seven days** everyone will eat bread made without yeast.
45.23 On each of the **seven days** of the festival he is to
45.23 sacrifice to the Lord **seven** bulls and seven rams
45.25 the fifteenth day of the **seventh** month, the prince will
45.25 offer on each of the **seven days** the same sacrifice for sin,
Dan 3.19 his men to heat the furnace **seven** times hotter than usual.
4.16 For **seven years** he will not have a human mind, but the
4.23 and let him live there with the animals for **seven years.'**
4.25 For **seven years** you will eat grass like an ox, and sleep
4.32 with wild animals, and eat grass like an ox for **seven years.**
4.34 "When the **seven years** had passed," said the king,
9.24 **"Seven** times seventy years is the length of time God
9.25 God's chosen leader comes, **seven times seven** years will pass.
9.25 and will stand for **seven** times sixty-two years,
9.27 agreement with many people for **seven years,** and when half
Hag 2. 1 the twenty-first day of the **seventh** month of that same year,
Zech 3. 9 placing in front of Joshua a single stone with **seven** facets.
4. 2 seven lamps, each one with places for **seven** wicks.
4.10b "The seven lamps are the **seven** eyes of the Lord,
7. 5 mourned in the fifth and **seventh** months during these seventy
8.19 fourth, fifth, **seventh,** and tenth months will become festivals
Mt 12.45 and brings along **seven** other spirits even worse than itself,
15.34 **"Seven** loaves," they answered, "and a few small fish."
15.36 Then he took the **seven** loaves and the fish, gave thanks
15.37 Then the disciples took up **seven** baskets full of pieces left over.
16.10 And what about the **seven** loaves for the four thousand men?
18.21 **Seven** times?"
18.22 "No, not **seven** times," answered Jesus, "but seventy times seven,
22.25 Now, there were **seven** brothers who used to live here.
22.26 the second brother, to the third, and finally to all **seven.**
Mk 8. 5 **"Seven** loaves," they answered.
8. 6 Then he took the **seven** loaves, gave thanks to God, broke
8. 8 Then the disciples took up **seven** baskets full of pieces left over.
8.20 "And when I broke the **seven** loaves for the four thousand people,"
8.20 **"Seven,"** they answered.
12.20 Once there were **seven** brothers;
12.22 **seven** brothers married the woman and died without having children.
12.23 All **seven** of them had married her."
16. 9 to Mary Magdalene, from whom he had driven out **seven** demons.
Lk 2.36 had been married for only **seven** years and was now
8. 2 (who was called Magdalene), from whom **seven** demons had been driven out;
11.26 out and brings **seven** other spirits even worse than itself,
17. 4 If he sins against you **seven** times in one day, and each
20.29 Once there were **seven** brothers;
20.31 The same thing happened to all **seven**—they died without having children.
20.33 All **seven** of them had married her."
Acts 6. 3 So then, brothers, choose **seven** men among you who are
13.19 He destroyed **seven** nations in the land of Canaan and
19.14 **Seven** brothers, who were the sons of a Jewish High
21. 8 the evangelist, one of the **seven** men who had been chosen as
21.27 But just when the **seven days** were about to come to an
Heb 4. 4 For somewhere in the Scriptures this is said about the **seventh day:**
4. 4 "God rested on the **seventh day** from all his work."
4. 9 God's people a rest like God's resting on the **seventh day.**
11.30 after the Israelites had marched round them for **seven days.**
2 Pet 2. 5 Noah, who preached righteousness, and **seven** other people.
Rev 1. 4 From John to the **seven** churches in the province of Asia:
1. 4 to come, and from the **seven** spirits in front of his throne,
1.11 and send the book to the churches in these **seven** cities:
1.12 to me, and I saw **seven** gold lamp-stands, [13]and among them
1.16 He held **seven** stars in his right hand, and a sharp
1.20 the secret meaning of the **seven** stars
1.20 and of the **seven** gold lamp-stands:
1.20 the **seven** stars are the angels of the seven churches,
Rev 1.20 and the seven lamp-stands are the **seven** churches.
2. 1 the one who holds the **seven** stars in his right hand
2. 1 and who walks among the **seven** gold lamp-stands.
3. 1 one who has the seven spirits of God and the **seven** stars.
4. 5 In front of the throne **seven** lighted torches were burning,
4. 5 which are the **seven** spirits of God.
5. 1 with writing on both sides and was sealed with **seven** seals.
5. 5 and he can break the **seven** seals and open the scroll."
5. 6 It had **seven** horns and seven eyes,
5. 6 which are the **seven** spirits of God
6. 1 open the first of the **seven** seals,
8. 1 the Lamb broke open the **seventh** seal, there was silence in
8. 2 Then I saw the **seven** angels who stand before God,
8. 2 and they were given **seven** trumpets.
8. 6 Then the **seven** angels with the seven trumpets prepared to blow them.
10. 3 After he had called out, the **seven** thunders answered with a roar.
10. 4 "Keep secret what the **seven** thunders have said;
10. 7 But when the **seventh** angel blows his trumpet, then God
11.15 Then the **seventh** angel blew his trumpet, and there were
12. 3 a huge red dragon with **seven** heads and ten horns
13. 1 It had ten horns and **seven** heads;
15. 1 There were **seven** angels with seven plagues,
15. 6 The **seven** angels who had the seven plagues came out
15. 7 four living creatures gave the **seven** angels seven gold bowls
15. 8 seven plagues brought by the **seven** angels had come to an end.
16. 1 a loud voice speaking from the temple to the **seven** angels:
16. 1 "Go and pour out the **seven** bowls of God's anger on the
16.17 Then the **seventh** angel poured out his bowl in the air.
17. 1 Then one of the **seven** angels who had the seven bowls came
17. 3 the beast had **seven** heads and ten horns.
17. 7 the beast with **seven** heads and ten horns.
17. 9 The **seven** heads are seven hills, on which the woman sits.
17. 9 They are also **seven** kings:
17.11 who is one of the **seven** and is going off to be
21. 9 One of the **seven** angels who had the seven bowls
21. 9 full of the **seven** last plagues came to me
21.20 the sixth carnelian, the **seventh** yellow quartz,
also Num 7.12 1 Chr 24.7 1 Chr 25.9

SEVERAL

Acts 16.12 We spent **several** days there.
21.10 We had been there for **several** days when a prophet named
24.17 being away from Jerusalem for **several** years, I went there to
25.14 After they had been there **several** days, Festus explained Paul's situation
27. 7 We sailed slowly for **several** days and with great
1 Cor 11.30 why many of you are weak and ill, and **several** have died.

SEVERE

Gen 41.57 buy corn from Joseph, because the famine was **severe** everywhere.
47. 4 Canaan the famine is so **severe** that there is no pasture for
47.13 The famine was so **severe** that there was no food anywhere,
47.20 forced to sell his land, because the famine was so **severe;**
Ex 7. 3 Then I will bring **severe** punishment on Egypt and lead the
1 Sam 3.17 God will punish you **severely** if you don't tell me everything
5. 6 The Lord punished the people of Ashdod **severely** and terrified
5.11 throughout the city because God was punishing them so **severely.**
2 Sam 21. 1 David's reign there was a **severe** famine which lasted for
1 Kgs 20.21 and inflicted a **severe** defeat on the Syrians.
2 Kgs 6.25 in the city was so **severe** that a donkey's head cost eighty
2 Chr 16.12 that Asa was king, he was crippled by a **severe** foot disease;
21.14 the Lord will **severely** punish your people, your children, and
24.25 He was **severely** wounded, and when the enemy withdrew,
30. 7 As you can see, he punished them **severely.**
Ps 118.18 He has punished me **severely,** but he has not let me die.
Prov 15.10 If you do what is wrong, you will be **severely** punished;
Is 27. 7 punished by the Lord as **severely** as its enemies, nor has she
Ezek 25.17 I will punish them **severely** and take full revenge on them.
38.19 day there will be a **severe** earthquake in the land of Israel.
Dan 9.12 You punished Jerusalem more **severely** than any other city
Mt 9.20 woman who had suffered from **severe** bleeding for twelve years
Mk 4.24 be used by God to judge you—but with even greater **severity.**
5.25 who had suffered terribly from **severe** bleeding for twelve years,
Lk 4.25 a **severe** famine spread throughout the whole land.
8.43 who had suffered from **severe** bleeding for twelve years;
15.14 Then a **severe** famine spread over that country,
Acts 11.28 the Spirit predicted that a **severe** famine was about to come
16.23 After a **severe** beating, they were thrown into jail,
Rom 11.22 Here we see how kind and how **severe** God is.
11.22 He is **severe** towards those who have fallen, but kind to you
2 Cor 8. 2 They have been **severely** tested by the troubles they went through;
10.10 "Paul's letters are **severe** and strong,
Col 2.23 false humility, and **severe** treatment of the body;

SEW

Gen 3. 7 so they **sewed** fig leaves together and covered themselves.
Ex 26. 3 **Sew** five of them together in one set, and do the same
26. 9 **Sew** five of them together in one set, and the other six
36.10 They **sewed** five of them together in one set and did the
36.16 They **sewed** five of them together in one set and the
Deut 22.12 **"Sew** tassels on the four corners of your clothes.
Ezek 13.18 You **sew** magic wristbands for everyone and make magic scarves

SEX
[OVERSEXED]

Gen 18.12 that I am old and worn out, can I still enjoy **sex?**
19. 5 The men of Sodom wanted to have **sex** with them.
35.22 in that land, Reuben had **sexual** intercourse with Bilhah, one
Ex 19.15 don't have **sexual** intercourse in the meantime."
22.19 "Put to death any man who has **sexual** relations with an animal.
32. 6 to a feast, which turned into an orgy of drinking and **sex.**
Lev 15.18 After **sexual** intercourse both the man and the woman must have
15.24 If a man has **sexual** intercourse with her during her period,
15.33 or a man who has **sexual** intercourse with a woman who is
18. 6 Do not have **sexual** intercourse with any of your relatives.
18.22 No man is to have **sexual** relations with another man;
18.23 No man or woman is to have **sexual** relations with an animal;
19.20 then if another man has **sexual** relations with her, they will
20.13 If a man has **sexual** relations with another man, they
20.15 If a man has **sexual** relations with an animal, he and the
20.16 a woman tries to have **sexual** relations with an animal, she
Num 25. 1 the men began to have **sexual** intercourse with the Moabite
31.17 every woman who has had **sexual** intercourse, [18]but keep alive
Deut 27.21 " 'God's curse on anyone who has **sexual** relations with an animal.'
Judg 19.22 all of a sudden some **sexual** perverts from the town surrounded
19.22 We want to have **sex** with him!"
1 Sam 21. 4 it if your men haven't had **sexual** relations recently."
Prov 31. 3 spend all your energy on **sex** and all your money on women;
Is 57. 5 gods by having **sex** under those sacred trees of yours.
57. 7 You go to the high mountains to offer sacrifices and have **sex.**
Ezek 16.43 add **sexual** immorality to all the other disgusting things
23.17 The Babylonians came to have **sex** with her.
23.20 was filled with lust for **oversexed** men who had all the
Mt 1.25 But he had no **sexual** relations with her before she gave
Acts 15.20 to keep themselves from **sexual** immorality;
15.29 and keep yourselves from **sexual** immorality.
21.25 and that they must keep themselves from **sexual** immorality."
Rom 1.26 pervert the natural use of their **sex** by unnatural acts.
1.27 the men give up natural **sexual** relations with women and burn
1 Cor 5. 1 being said that there is **sexual** immorality among you so
6.13 not to be used for **sexual** immorality, but to serve the Lord;
6.18 is guilty of **sexual** immorality sins against his own body.
10. 7 to a feast which turned into an orgy of drinking and **sex."**
10. 8 must not be guilty of **sexual** immorality, as some of them
2 Cor 12.21 things they have done—their lust and their **sexual** sins.
Eph 5. 3 right that any matters of **sexual** immorality or indecency or
Col 3. 5 work in you, such as **sexual** immorality, indecency, lust,
1 Thes 4. 3 God wants you to be holy and completely free from **sexual** immorality.
1 Tim 1.10 for the immoral, for **sexual** perverts, for kidnappers,
1 Pet 3. 7 with the proper understanding that they are the weaker **sex.**
Jude 7 angels did and indulged in **sexual** immorality and perversion:
Rev 2.14 had been offered to idols and to practise **sexual** immorality.
2.20 misleads my servants into practising **sexual** immorality and
9.21 their magic, their **sexual** immorality, or their stealing.
14. 4 themselves pure by not having **sexual** relations with women;
17. 2 kings of the earth practised **sexual** immorality with her, and
18. 3 kings of the earth practised **sexual** immorality with her, and

SHADE

Judg 9.15 make me your king, then come and take shelter in my **shade.**
1 Kgs 14.23 of Asherah to worship on the hills and under **shady** trees.
19. 4 and sat down in the **shade** of a tree and wished he
2 Kgs 16. 4 and under every **shady** tree, Ahaz offered sacrifices and burnt
17.10 the hills and under every **shady** tree they put up stone
2 Chr 28. 4 and under every **shady** tree Ahaz offered sacrifices and burnt
Job 7. 2 hard manual labour, [2]like a slave longing for cool **shade;**
40.22 the willows by the stream give him shelter in their **shade.**
Ps 80.10 It covered the hills with its **shade;**
Is 4. 6 His glory will **shade** the city from the heat of the day
16. 3 in the heat of noon, and let us rest in your **shade.**
25. 4 give them shelter from storms and **shade** from the burning heat.
Ezek 17.23 every kind will live there and find shelter in its **shade.**
31. 3 cedar in Lebanon, With beautiful, **shady** branches, A tree so tall
31. 6 The nations of the world rested in its **shade.**
31.12 the nations that have been living in its **shade** will go away.
Dan 4.12 Wild animals rested in its **shade,** birds built nests in its
Hos 4.13 tall, spreading trees, because the **shade** is so pleasant!
Jon 4. 5 himself and sat in its **shade,** waiting to see what would
4. 6 Jonah to give him some **shade,** so that he would be more
Mk 4.32 that the birds come and make their nests in its **shade."**

SHADOW
[OVERSHADOWED]
see also **EYESHADOW**

Judg 9.36 "They are just **shadows** on the mountains."
2 Kgs 20. 9 Now, would you prefer the **shadow** on the stairway to go
20.10 "It's easy to make the **shadow** go forward ten steps!
20.11 and the Lord made the **shadow** go back ten steps on the
1 Chr 29.15 Our days are like a passing **shadow,** and we cannot escape death.
Job 8. 9 we pass like **shadows** across the earth.
10.22 a land of darkness, **shadows,** and confusion, where the light
14. 2 we disappear like **shadows.**
15.29 Even his **shadow** will vanish, [30]and he will not escape
16.16 are swollen and circled with **shadows,** [17]but I am not
17. 7 my arms and legs are as thin as **shadows.**
Ps 11. 2 aimed their arrows to shoot from the **shadows** at good men.
17. 8 hide me in the **shadow** of your wings [9]from the attacks of
36. 7 We find protection under the **shadow** of your wings.
39. 6 no more than a puff of wind, [6]no more than a **shadow.**
57. 1 In the **shadow** of your wings I find protection until the
63. 7 In the **shadow** of your wings I sing for joy.
80.10 its branches **overshadowed** the giant cedars.
102.11 My life is like the evening **shadows;**
109.23 Like an evening **shadow** I am about to vanish;
144. 4 his days are like a passing **shadow.**
Ecc 6.12 short, useless life of his—a life that passes like a **shadow?**
8.13 Their life is like a **shadow** and they will die young, because
Song 2. 3 love to sit in its **shadow,** and its fruit is sweet to
Is 9. 2 lived in a land of **shadows,** but now light is shining on
16. 3 tree that casts a cool **shadow** in the heat of noon, and
32. 2 in a desert, like the **shadow** of a giant rock in a
38. 8 King Ahaz, the Lord will make the **shadow** go back ten steps."
38. 8 And the **shadow** moved back ten steps.
Jer 6. 4 is almost over, and the evening **shadows** are growing long.
Ezek 31.17 live under its **shadow** will be scattered among the nations.
Mk 9. 7 and covered them with its **shadow,** and a voice came from the
Lk 1.79 who live in the dark **shadow** of death, to guide our steps
9.34 speaking, a cloud appeared and covered them with its **shadow;**
Acts 5.15 so that at least Peter's **shadow** might fall on some of them
Col 2.17 All such things are only a **shadow** of things in the future;
Heb 8. 5 really only a copy and a **shadow** of what is in heaven.

SHADRACH
One of Daniel's three companions, also known as Hananiah.

Dan 1. 7 Belteshazzar, **Shadrach,** Meshach, and Abednego.
2.49 the king put **Shadrach,** Meshach, and Abednego in charge
3.12 Babylon—**Shadrach,** Meshach, and Abednego—who are disobeying
3.14 He said to them, **"Shadrach,** Meshach, and Abednego, is it true
3.16 **Shadrach,** Meshach, and Abednego answered, "Your Majesty,
3.19 face turned red with anger at **Shadrach,** Meshach, and Abednego.
3.23 Then **Shadrach,** Meshach, and Abednego, still tied up, fell into
3.26 the door of the blazing furnace and called out, **"Shadrach!**
3.28 "Praise the God of **Shadrach,** Meshach, and Abednego!
3.29 disrespectfully of the God of **Shadrach,** Meshach, and Abednego,
3.30 And the king promoted **Shadrach,** Meshach, and Abednego

SHAFT (1)

Ex 25.31 Make its base and its **shaft** of hammered gold;
25.34 The **shaft** of the lamp-stand is to have four decorative flowers
37.17 He made its base and its **shaft** of hammered gold;
37.20 The **shaft** of the lamp-stand had four decorative flowers shaped
2 Sam 21.19 Gath, whose spear had a **shaft** as thick as the bar on
1 Chr 20. 5 Gath, whose spear had a **shaft** as thick as the bar on

SHAFT (2)

Job 28. 4 Or human feet ever travel, Men dig the **shafts** of mines.

SHAKE
[SHOOK]

Gen 27.33 Isaac began to tremble and **shake** all over, and he asked,
Judg 5. 4 of Edom, the earth **shook,** and rain fell from the sky.
1 Sam 4. 5 Israelites gave such a loud shout of joy that the earth **shook.**
14.15 the earth **shook,** and there was great panic.
2 Sam 22. 8 Then the earth trembled and **shook;**
1 Kgs 1.40 playing flutes, making enough noise to **shake** the ground.
14.15 Israel, and she will shake like a reed **shaking** in a stream.
Neh 5.13 the sash I was wearing round my waist and **shook** it out.
5.13 "This is how God will **shake** any of you who don't keep
Job 4.14 my whole body **shook** with fear.
9. 6 God sends earthquakes and **shakes** the ground;
15.25 fate of the man who **shakes** his fist at God and defies
16. 4 I could **shake** my head wisely and drown you with a flood
21. 6 has happened to me, I am stunned, and I tremble and **shake.**
26.11 that hold up the sky, they **shake** and tremble with fear.
38.13 the earth and **shake** the wicked from their hiding places?
Ps 16. 8 he is near, and nothing can **shake** me.
18. 7 Then the earth trembled and **shook;**
22. 7 they stick out their tongues and **shake** their heads.
29. 8 His voice makes the desert **shake;**
29. 8 he **shakes** the desert of Kadesh.
29. 9 The Lord's voice **shakes** the oaks and strips the leaves
44.14 they **shake** their heads at us in scorn.
46. 2 even if the earth is **shaken** and mountains fall into the
46. 3 roar and rage, and the hills are **shaken** by the violence.
46. 6 Nations are terrified, kingdoms are **shaken;**
64. 8 all who see them will **shake** their heads.
68. 8 the desert, [8]the earth **shook,** and the sky poured down rain,
75. 3 earth itself be **shaken,** I will keep its foundations firm.
77.18 the earth trembled and **shook.**
99. 1 He is enthroned above the winged creatures and the earth **shakes.**
109.25 they **shake** their heads in scorn.
125. 1 like Mount Zion, which can never be **shaken,** never be moved.
Is 2.19 from his power and glory, when he comes to **shake** the earth.
2.21 When the Lord comes to **shake** the earth, people will hide
5.25 The mountains will **shake,** and the bodies of those who die
6. 4 the foundation of the Temple **shake,** and the Temple itself was
7. 2 so terrified that they trembled like trees **shaking** in the wind.
10.32 Nob, and there they are **shaking** their fists at Mount Zion,
13.13 and the earth will be **shaken** out of its place on that
14.16 'Is this the man who **shook** the earth and made kingdoms tremble?
24.18 will pour from the sky, and earth's foundations will **shake.**
52. 2 **Shake** yourself free, Jerusalem!
64. 1 The mountains would see you and **shake** with fear.
64. 3 the mountains saw you and **shook** with fear.
Jer 2.12 I command the sky to **shake** with horror, to be amazed and
4.24 at the mountains—they were **shaking,** and the hills were
18.16 they will **shake** their heads in amazement.

Jer 49.21 that the entire earth will **shake,** and the cries of alarm
50.46 that the entire earth will **shake,** and the cries of alarm
51.29 The earth trembles and **shakes** because the Lord is carrying out
Lam 2.15 They **shake** their heads and laugh at the ruins of Jerusalem.
Ezek 4. 7 **Shake** your fist at the city and prophesy against it.
7.17 Everyone's hands will be weak, and their knees will **shake.**
7.27 will give up hope, and the people will **shake** with fear.
12.18 "tremble when you eat, and **shake** with fear when you drink.
12.19 tremble when they eat and **shake** with fear when they drink.
21.21 To discover which way to go, he **shakes** the arrows;
26.10 pulling wagons and chariots will **shake** your walls as they pass
31.16 the dead, the noise of its downfall will **shake** the nations.
Dan 5. 6 pale and was so frightened that his knees began to **shake.**
Joel 2.10 The earth **shakes** as they advance;
Amos 8. 8 The whole country will be **shaken;**
9. 1 the temple columns so hard that the whole porch will **shake.**
9. 9 will give the command and **shake** the people of Israel like
9. 9 I will **shake** them among the nations to remove all who are
Nah 1. 5 The earth **shakes** when the Lord appears;
3.12 **shake** the trees, and the fruit falls right into your mouth!
Hab 3. 6 When he stops, the earth **shakes;**
Hag 2. 6 "Before long I will **shake** heaven and earth, land and sea.
2.21 "I am about to **shake** heaven and earth [22]and overthrow kingdoms
Mt 10.14 you, then leave that place and **shake** the dust off your feet.
27.39 People passing by **shook** their heads and hurled insults at Jesus:
27.51 The earth **shook,** the rocks split apart, [52]the graves broke open,
Mk 1.26 The evil spirit **shook** the man hard, gave a loud scream,
6.11 listen to you, leave it and **shake** the dust off your feet.
15.29 People passing by **shook** their heads and hurled insults at Jesus:
Lk 6.48 house but could not **shake** it, because it was well built.
9. 5 you, leave that town and **shake** the dust off your feet as
Acts 4.31 they finished praying, the place where they were meeting was **shaken.**
12. 7 The angel **shook** Peter by the shoulder, woke him up, and
13.51 The apostles **shook** the dust off their feet in protest
16.26 earthquake, which **shook** the prison to its foundations.
18. 6 about him, he protested by **shaking** the dust from his clothes
28. 5 But Paul **shook** the snake off into the fire without being
2 Cor 1. 7 So our hope in you is never **shaken;**
Gal 2. 9 so they **shook** hands with Barnabas and me,
Col 1.23 not allow yourselves to be **shaken** from the hope you gained
2 Tim 2.19 But the solid foundation that God has laid cannot be **shaken;**
Heb 12.26 His voice **shook** the earth at that time,
12.26 promised, "I will once more **shake** not only the earth but
12.27 the created things will be **shaken** and removed,
12.27 so that the things that cannot be **shaken** will remain.
12.28 thankful, then, because we receive a kingdom that cannot be **shaken.**
Rev 6.13 figs falling from the tree when a strong wind **shakes** it.

SHALLECHETH GATE

1 Chr 26.16 the west gate and the **Shallecheth Gate** on the upper road.

SHAME

see also **ASHAMED**

Deut 22.21 done a **shameful** thing among our people by having intercourse
Josh 7.15 for he has brought terrible **shame** on Israel and has broken
1 Kgs 14.24 of Judah practised all the **shameful** things done by the
21.26 He committed the most **shameful** sins by worshipping idols,
Job 10.15 I am miserable and covered with **shame.**
19. 3 insult me and show no **shame** for the way you abuse me.
Ps 6.10 My enemies will know the bitter **shame** of defeat;
25. 2 Save me from the **shame** of defeat;
35.26 to be better than I am be covered with **shame** and disgrace.
44.15 I am covered with **shame** [16]from hearing the sneers and insults
64. 4 They are quick to spread their **shameless** lies;
69. 6 Don't let me bring **shame** on those who trust in you,
69. 7 that I have been insulted and that I am covered with **shame.**
71.13 May those who try to hurt me be **shamed** and disgraced.
74.21 Don't let the oppressed be put to **shame;**
78.66 He drove his enemies back in lasting and **shameful** defeat.
83.16 Cover their faces with **shame,** O Lord, and make them acknowledge
97. 7 Everyone who worships idols is put to **shame;**
109.29 may they wear their **shame** like a robe.
119. 6 to all your commands, then I will not be put to **shame.**
119.31 don't let me be put to **shame.**
119.80 obey your commandments and be spared the **shame** of defeat.
132.18 will cover his enemies with **shame,** but his kingdom will prosper
Prov 4.25 don't hang your head in **shame.**
7.11 a bold and **shameless** woman who always walked the streets
9.13 Stupidity is like a loud, ignorant, **shameless** woman.
12. 4 but a wife who brings **shame** on her husband is like a
13. 5 but the words of wicked people are **shameful** and disgraceful.
18. 3 Sin and **shame** go together.
19.26 Only a **shameful,** disgraceful person would ill-treat his father
25.10 keep a secret, and you will never live down the **shame.**
25.22 make him burn with **shame,** and the Lord will reward you.
Is 3.24 their beauty will be turned to **shame!**
4. 1 we won't have to endure the **shame** of being unmarried."
13. 8 at each other in fear, and their faces will burn with **shame.**
20. 4 with their buttocks exposed, bringing **shame** on Egypt.
26.11 Lord, put them to **shame** and let them suffer;
29.22 longer, and your faces will no longer be pale with **shame.**
41.11 "Those who are angry with you will know the **shame** of defeat.
47. 3 they will see you humbled and **shamed.**
61. 7 Your **shame** and disgrace are ended.
65. 3 They **shamelessly** keep on making me angry.
Jer 2.37 You will turn away from Egypt, hanging your head in **shame.**
Jer 3. 3 you have no **shame.**
3.24 of Baal, the god of **shame,** has made us lose flocks
3.25 We should lie down in **shame** and let our disgrace cover us.
7.19 are hurting themselves and bringing **shame** on themselves.
8. 9 Your wise men are put to **shame;**
13.26 Lord himself will strip off your clothes and expose you to **shame.**
17.13 all who abandon you will be put to **shame.**
22.22 city disgraced and put to **shame** because of all the evil you
23.40 will bring on them everlasting **shame** and disgrace
46.12 Nations have heard of your **shame;**
46.24 The people of Egypt are put to **shame;**
48. 1 its mighty fortress torn down, and its people put to **shame;**
50. 2 Babylon's idols are put to **shame,** her disgusting images
51.47 country will be put to **shame,** and all its people will be
Lam 1. 8 She groans and hides her face in **shame.**
4.21 you too will stagger naked in **shame.**
Ezek 16.30 "You have done all this like a **shameless** prostitute.
16.52 Now blush and bear your **shame,** because you make your sisters
36.32 want you to feel the **shame** and disgrace of what you are
Dan 9. 8 ancestors have acted **shamefully** and sinned against you, Lord.
Hos 2. 4 they are the children of a **shameless** prostitute.
10. 6 and put to **shame** because of the advice she followed.
Nah 3. 5 and let the nations see you, see you in all your **shame.**
Hab 2.10 But your schemes have brought **shame** on your family;
2.16 You in turn will be covered with **shame** instead of honour.
Zeph 2. 1 **Shameless** nation, come to your senses [2]before you are driven
3.19 I will turn their **shame** to honour, and all the world will
Mk 12. 4 tenants beat him over the head and treated him **shamefully.**
Lk 20.11 beat him also, treated him **shamefully,** and sent him back
Rom 1.24 their hearts desire, and they do **shameful** things with each other.
1.26 they do this, God has given them over to **shameful** passions.
1.27 Men do **shameful** things with each other,
2.23 law—but do you bring **shame** on God by breaking his law?
12.20 for by doing this you will make him burn with **shame."**
1 Cor 1.27 considers nonsense in order to **shame** the wise,
1.27 what the world considers weak in order to **shame** the powerful.
6. 5 **Shame** on you!
11. 6 And since it is a **shameful** thing for a woman
11.22 of God and put to **shame** the people who are in need?
15.34 I declare to your **shame** that some of you do not know
2 Cor 4. 2 We put aside all secret and **shameful** deeds;
9. 4 not to speak of your **shame**—for feeling so sure of you!
Eph 4.19 They have lost all feeling of **shame;**
5.12 (It is really too **shameful** even to talk about the things
Tit 1.11 not, and all for the **shameful** purpose of making money.
2. 8 enemies may be put to **shame** by not having anything bad to
Heb 6. 6 crucifying the Son of God and exposing him to public **shame.**
13.13 us, then, go to him outside the camp and share his **shame.**
2 Pet 2.13 they are a **shame** and a disgrace as they join you in
1 Jn 2.28 and need not hide in **shame** from him on the Day he
Jude 12 With their **shameless** carousing they are like dirty spots
13 of the sea, with their **shameful** deeds showing up like foam.
Rev 3.18 clothing to dress yourself and cover up your **shameful** nakedness.
21.27 the city, nor anyone who does **shameful** things or tells lies.

Am

SHAPE

see also **STATE**

SHAPE

Gen 29.17 Leah had lovely eyes, but Rachel was **shapely** and beautiful.
Ex 25.33 to have three decorative flowers **shaped** like almond blossoms
25.34 to have four decorative flowers **shaped** like almond blossoms
37.19 had three decorative flowers **shaped** like almond blossoms with buds and
37.20 had four decorative flowers **shaped** like almond blossoms with buds and
1 Kgs 6.24 Both were of the same size and **shape.**
7.19 The capitals were **shaped** like lilies, 1.8 metres tall,
7.37 they were all alike, having the same size and **shape.**
2 Chr 4. 3 The decorations were in the **shape** of bulls, which had been
Neh 9.18 made an idol in the **shape** of a bull-calf and said it
Job 10. 8 Your hands formed and **shaped** me, and now those same hands
30.18 seizes me by my collar and twists my clothes out of **shape.**
Prov 4.23 your life is **shaped** by your thoughts.
Is 44.12 His strong arm swings a hammer to pound the metal into **shape.**
45.11 the holy God of Israel, the one who **shapes** the future,
Jer 44.19 added, "When we baked cakes **shaped** like the Queen of Heaven,
Ezek 43.11 entrances and exits, its **shape,** the arrangement of everything,
Hos 13. 2 How can men kiss those idols—idols in the **shape** of bulls!
Acts 7.41 made an idol in the **shape** of a bull,
17.29 gold or silver or stone, **shaped** by the art and skill of
1 Pet 1.14 allow your lives to be **shaped** by those desires you had when

SHAPHAN (1)

Court secretary in Josiah's time.

2 Kgs 22. 3 Josiah sent the court secretary **Shaphan,** the son of Azaliah
22. 8 **Shaphan** delivered the king's order to Hilkiah,
22. 8 Hilkiah gave him the book, and **Shaphan** read it.
22.12 to **Shaphan,** the court secretary,
22.14 Hilkiah, Ahikam, Achbor, **Shaphan,** and Asaiah went to consult
2 Chr 34. 8 **Shaphan** son of Azaliah, Maaseiah, the governor of Jerusalem,
34.15 He said to **Shaphan,** "I have found the book of the Law
34.15 He gave **Shaphan** the book, [16]and Shaphan took it to the king.
34.20 to Ahikam son of **Shaphan,** to Abdon son of Micaiah,
34.20 to **Shaphan,** the court secretary,

SHARE
[HALF-SHARE]

Gen 14.24 But let my allies, Aner, Eshcol, and Mamre, take their **share."**
Ex 12. 4 and his next-door neighbour may **share** an animal, in proportion
18.22 That will make it easier for you, as they **share** your burden.
Lev 6.18 eat it as their continuing **share** of the food offered to the
7.10 the Aaronite priests and must be **shared** equally among them.
Num 10.29 come with us, and we will **share** our prosperity with you."
10.32 come with us, we will **share** with you all the blessings that
26.54 lots, and give a large **share** to a large tribe and a
31.36 The **half-share** of the soldiers was 337,500 sheep and goats,
31.42 The **share** of the community was the same as that
31.47 From this **share** Moses took one out of every fifty prisoners
32.19 we have received our **share** here east of the Jordan."
32.30 they are to receive their **share** of the property in the land
Deut 18. 1 of Levi is not to receive any **share** of land in Israel;
18. 2 their **share** is the privilege of being the Lord's priests, as
18. 4 are to receive the first **share** of the corn, wine, olive-oil,
21.16 by giving him the **share** that belongs to the first-born son.
21.17 is to give a double **share** of his possessions to his first
21.17 first son and give him the **share** he is legally entitled to.
28.56 She will not **share** them with the husband she loves or with
33.21 A leader's **share** was assigned to them.
Josh 13.14 receive as their possession a **share** of the sacrifices burnt
13.33 possession was to be a **share** of the offerings to the Lord
17. 5 Manasseh received ten **shares** in addition to Gilead and Bashan
17.17 You shall have more than one **share.**
18. 2 Israel who had not yet been assigned their **share** of the land.
18. 7 will not receive a **share** of the land with the rest
18. 7 because their **share** is to serve as the Lord's
22. 6 **Share** with your fellow-tribesmen what you took from your enemies."
Judg 2. 6 man went to take possession of his own **share** of the land.
1 Sam 1. 4 he would give one **share** of the meat to Peninnah
1. 4 and one **share** to each of her children.
1. 5 would give her only one **share,** because the Lord had kept her
2.28 the right to keep a **share** of the sacrifices burnt on the
30.24 All must **share** alike:
30.24 the supplies gets the same **share** as the one who goes into
2 Sam 19.29 I have decided that you and Ziba will **share** Saul's property."
1 Kgs 2.26 with my father David, and you **shared** in all his troubles."
4.28 Each governor also supplied his **share** of barley and straw,
2 Kgs 2. 9 "Let me receive the **share** of your power that will make me
1 Chr 6.54 received the first **share** of the land assigned to the Levites.
23.24 age or older, had a **share** in the work of the Lord's
2 Chr 31.16 They gave a **share** to all males thirty years of age or
Neh 2.20 in Jerusalem, and you have no **share** in its traditions."
8.10 **Share** your food and wine with those who haven't enough.
8.12 ate and drank joyfully and **shared** what they had with others,
Job 26. 3 give such good advice and **share** your knowledge with a fool
32. 7 to speak, that you older men should **share** your wisdom.
42.15 Their father gave them a **share** of the inheritance along with
Ps 41. 9 most, the one who **shared** my food, has turned against me.
72. 1 **share** with him your own justice, [2]so that he will rule
106. 5 of your people and **share** in the happiness of your nation,
Prov 1.14 Come and join us, and we'll all **share** what we steal."
1.23 I will give you good advice and **share** my knowledge with you.
14.10 No one can **share** them with you.
16.19 be one of the arrogant and get a **share** of their loot.
17.17 What are brothers for if not to **share** trouble?
21. 9 live on the roof than **share** the house with a nagging wife.
22. 9 Be generous and **share** your food with the poor.
25.24 live on the roof than **share** the house with a nagging wife.
Ecc 6. 3 he does not get his **share** of happiness and does not receive
Song 8.12 coins, and the farmers to two hundred as their **share;**
Is 33.22 will be so much that even lame men can have a **share.**
34.17 divide the land among them and give each of them a **share.**
42. 8 No other god may **share** my glory;
42. 8 I will not let idols **share** my praise.
48.11 dishonoured or let anyone else **share** the glory that should
53.12 He willingly gave his life and **shared** the fate of evil men.
58. 7 **Share** your food with the hungry and open your homes to the
Jer 37.12 Benjamin to take possession of my **share** of the family property.
Ezek 16.27 to punish you and to take away your **share** of my blessing.
27.36 world are terrified, afraid that they will **share** your fate."
28.19 you are terrified, afraid that they will **share** your fate."
32.25 they lie dead and disgraced, **sharing** the fate of those
32.30 They **share** the disgrace of those who go down to the world
44.28 have the priesthood as their **share** of what I have given
45. 1 to give each tribe a **share,** one part is to be dedicated
45. 8 This area will be the **share** the ruling prince will have in
47.22 are also to receive their **share** of the land when you divide
47.22 are to draw lots for **shares** of the land along with the
47.23 foreign resident will receive his **share** with the people of
Dan 11.33 Wise leaders of the people will **share** their wisdom with many
Hos 4.10 You will eat your **share** of the sacrifices, but still be hungry.
Amos 7. 1 locusts just after the king's **share** of the hay had been cut
Mic 2. 5 the Lord's people, there will be no **share** for any of you.
Zech 8.23 and say, 'We want to **share** in your destiny, because we have
Mt 10.41 because he is God's messenger, will **share** in his reward.
10.41 because he is good, will **share** in his reward.
21.34 to the tenants to receive his **share** of the harvest.
21.41 who will give him his **share** of the harvest
24.51 and make him **share** the fate of the hypocrites.
25.21 Come on in and **share** my happiness!'
25.23 Come on in and **share** my happiness!'
Mk 12. 2 the tenants to receive from them his **share** of the harvest.
Lk 3.11 and whoever has food must **share** it."
12.42 give the other servants their **share** of the food
12.46 and make him **share** the fate of the disobedient.
Lk 15.12 'Father, give me my **share** of the property now.'
20.10 the tenants to receive from them his **share** of the harvest.
22.17 "Take this and **share** it among yourselves.
22.37 the scripture which says, 'He **shared** the fate of criminals,'
Jn 13.18 that says, 'The man who **shared** my food turned against me.'
Acts 2.42 part in the fellowship, and **sharing** in the fellowship meals
2.44 fellowship and **shared** their belongings with one another.
3.25 for you, and you **share** in the covenant which God made
4.32 but they all **shared** with one another everything they had.
8.21 You have no part or **share** in our work,
Rom 1.11 in order to **share** a spiritual blessing with you
5. 2 so we boast of the hope we have of **sharing** God's glory!
6. 4 were buried with him and **shared** his death, in order that,
8.17 for if we **share** Christ's suffering,
8.17 we will also **share** his glory.
8.21 and would **share** the glorious freedom of the children
8.30 put right with himself, and he **shared** his glory with them.
11.17 and now you **share** the strong spiritual life
12. 8 Whoever **shares** with others should do it generously;
12.13 **Share** your belongings with your needy fellow-Christians,
15.27 Since the Jews **shared** their spiritual blessings with the Gentiles,
1 Cor 9.10 in the hope of getting a **share** of the crop.
9.13 the sacrifices on the altar get a **share** of the sacrifices.
9.23 for the gospel's sake, in order to **share** in its blessings.
10.16 we drink from it, we are **sharing** in the blood of Christ.
10.16 when we eat it, we are **sharing** in the body of Christ.
10.17 though many, are one body, for we all **share** the same loaf.
10.18 is offered in sacrifice **share** in the altar's service to God.
12.26 part is praised, all the other parts **share** its happiness.
15.50 of flesh and blood cannot **share** in God's Kingdom,
2 Cor 1. 5 Just as we have a **share** in Christ's many sufferings,
1. 5 so also through Christ we **share** in God's great help.
1. 7 know that just as you **share** in our sufferings,
1. 7 you also **share** in the help we receive.
5.14 died for everyone, which means that all **share** in his death.
5.21 God made him **share** our sin
5.21 in union with him we might **share** the righteousness of God.
9.13 for your generosity in **sharing** with them and everyone else.
13. 4 relations with you we shall **share** God's power in his life.
Gal 6. 6 taught the Christian message should **share** all the good things
Eph 3. 6 of the same body and **share** in the promise that God made
5. 5 will ever receive a **share** in the Kingdom of Christ
Phil 1. 7 For you have all **shared** with me in this privilege that God
2. 2 by having the same thoughts, **sharing** the same love,
2.17 I am glad and **share** my joy with you all.
2.18 you too must be glad and **share** your joy with me.
2.20 is the only one who **shares** my feelings and who really cares
3.10 power of his resurrection, to **share** in his sufferings
4.15 you were the only ones who **shared** my profits and losses.
Col 1.11 fit to have your **share** of what God has reserved
1.27 which means that you will **share** in the glory of God.
3. 4 then you too will appear with him and **share** his glory!
1 Thes 2. 8 we were ready to **share** with you not only the Good
2.12 God, who calls you to **share** in his own Kingdom and glory.
2 Thes 2.14 called you to possess your **share** of the glory of our Lord
1 Tim 6.18 to be generous and ready to **share** with others.
2 Tim 2. 6 the hard work should have the first **share** of the harvest.
Heb 2.10 in order to bring many sons to **share** his glory.
2.14 Jesus himself became like them and **shared** their human nature.
6. 4 heaven's gift and received their **share** of the Holy Spirit;
10.34 You **shared** the sufferings of prisoners,
12.10 it for our own good, so that we may **share** his holiness.
13.13 go to him outside the camp and **share** his shame.
1 Pet 4.13 be glad that you are **sharing** Christ's sufferings,
5. 1 Christ's sufferings, and I will **share** in the glory that will
5.10 who calls you to **share** his eternal glory
2 Pet 1. 3 one who called us to **share** in his own glory and goodness.
1. 4 is in the world, and may come to **share** the divine nature.
3 Jn 8 people, so that we may **share** in their work for the truth.
Jude 3 you about the salvation we **share** in common, when I felt the
Rev 18. 4 you must not **share** in her punishment!
18.10 because they are afraid of **sharing** in her suffering.
18.15 because they are afraid of **sharing** in her suffering.
22.19 take away from him his **share** of the fruit of the tree

SHARP

Ex 4.25 Zipporah, his wife, took a **sharp** stone, cut off the foreskin
Deut 32.41 I vow [41] that I will **sharpen** my flashing sword and see that
1 Sam 13.20 to get their ploughs, hoes, axes, and sickles **sharpened;**
13.21 one small coin for **sharpening** axes and for repairing ox-goads,
13.21 and two coins for **sharpening** ploughs or hoes.)
Ezra 6.11 torn out of his house, **sharpened** at one end, and then driven
Job 39.28 the highest rocks and makes the **sharp** peaks its fortress.
Ps 7.12 If they do not change their ways, God will **sharpen** his sword.
45. 5 Your arrows are **sharp,** they pierce the hearts of your enemies;
52. 2 your tongue is like a **sharp** razor.
55.21 were as soothing as oil, but they cut like **sharp** swords.
57. 4 their tongues are like **sharp** swords.
64. 3 They **sharpen** their tongues like swords and aim cruel words
120. 4 With a soldier's **sharp** arrows, with red-hot charcoal!
149. 6 they praise God, with their **sharp** swords in their hands
Prov 25.18 is as deadly as a sword, a club, or a **sharp** arrow.
27.17 People learn from one another, just as iron **sharpens** iron.
Ecc 7. 3 may sadden your face, but it **sharpens** your understanding.
10.10 is blunt and you don't **sharpen** it, you have to work harder
12.11 wise men are like the **sharp** sticks that shepherds use to
Is 5.28 Their arrows are **sharp,** and their bows are ready to shoot.
41.15 like a threshing-board, with spikes that are new and **sharp.**
49. 2 He made my words as **sharp** as a sword.
49. 2 He made me like an arrow, **sharp** and ready for use.

Jer 46. 4 **Sharpen** your spears!
51.11 The attacking officers command, "**Sharpen** your arrows!
Ezek 5. 1 said, "Mortal man, take a **sharp** sword and use it to shave
5.16 the pains of hunger like **sharp** arrows sent to destroy you.
21. 9 A sword, a sword is **sharpened** and polished.
21.10 It is **sharpened** to kill, polished to flash like lightning.
21.11 It is **sharpened** and polished, to be put in the hands of
21.16 Cut to the right and the left, you **sharp** sword!
Joel 1. 6 their teeth are as **sharp** as those of a lion.
Lk 2.35 And sorrow, like a **sharp** sword, will break your own heart."
Acts 15.39 There was a **sharp** argument, and they separated:
Tit 1.12 reason you must rebuke them **sharply,** so that they may have a
Heb 4.12 God is alive and active, **sharper** than any double-edged sword.
Rev 1.16 his right hand, and a **sharp** two-edged sword came out
2.12 the message from the one who has the **sharp** two-edged sword.
14.14 of gold on his head and a **sharp** sickle in his hand.
14.17 and he also had a **sharp** sickle.
14.18 the angel who had the **sharp** sickle, "Use your sickle, and
19.15 of his mouth came a **sharp** sword, with which he will defeat

SHATTER

1 Kgs 19.11 that split the hills and **shattered** the rocks—but the Lord
Ps 2. 9 you will **shatter** them in pieces like a clay pot.' "
Prov 27. 9 make you feel happier, but trouble **shatters** your peace of mind.
Ecc 12. 6 at the well will break, and the water jar will be **shattered.**
Is 7. 8 years it will be too **shattered** to survive as a nation.
20. 5 boasted about Egypt will be disillusioned, their hopes **shattered.**
21. 9 All the idols they worshipped lie **shattered** on the ground."
24. 3 The earth will lie **shattered** and ruined.
24.19 The earth will crack and **shatter** and split open.
30.14 You will be **shattered** like a clay pot, so badly broken
60.18 Destruction will not **shatter** your country again.
63. 6 In my anger I trampled whole nations and **shattered** them.
Jer 48.39 Moab has been **shattered!**
50. 2 Her god Marduk has been **shattered!**
50.23 the whole world to pieces, and now that hammer is **shattered!**
51.21 **shatter** horses and riders, to **shatter** chariots and their drivers,
Lam 2. 3 In his fury he **shattered** the strength of Israel;
Ezek 6. 6 their incense-altars will be **shattered,** and everything they made
13.14 wall they whitewashed, to **shatter** it, and to leave the foundation
26. 2 They shout, 'Jerusalem is **shattered!**
26.12 They will pull down your walls and **shatter** your luxurious houses.
Dan 2.34 the iron and clay feet of the statue, and **shattered** them.
2.40 a fourth empire, as strong as iron, which **shatters** and breaks
2.40 And just as iron **shatters** everything, it will shatter and crush
Nah 2. 1 The power that will **shatter** you has come.
Hab 3. 6 The eternal mountains are **shattered;**
Zech 9. 5 So will Ekron, and her hopes will be **shattered.**
11.14 "Unity," and the unity of Judah and Israel was **shattered.**

SHAVE

Gen 41.14 After he had **shaved** and changed his clothes, he came into
Lev 13.33 surrounding skin, [33] the person shall **shave** the head except
14. 8 person shall wash his clothes, **shave** off all his hair, and
14. 9 seventh day he shall again **shave** his head, his beard, his
21. 5 "No priest shall **shave** any part of his head or trim his
Num 6. 5 under the Nazirite vow, he must not cut his hair or **shave.**
6. 9 must wait seven days and then **shave** off his hair and beard;
6.18 the Tent the Nazirite shall **shave** off his hair and put it
8. 7 purification and tell them to **shave** their whole bodies and
Deut 14. 1 dead, don't gash yourselves or **shave** the front of your head,
21.12 your home, where she will **shave** her head, cut her fingernails,
2 Sam 10. 4 seized David's messengers, **shaved** off one side of their beards,
1 Chr 19. 4 Hanun seized David's messengers, **shaved** off their beards,
Job 1.20 **shaved** his head and threw himself face downwards on the ground.
Is 3.17 punish them—I will **shave** their heads and leave them bald."
7.20 and he will **shave** off your beards, and the hair on your
15. 2 they have **shaved** their heads and their beards in grief.
22.12 to weep and mourn, to **shave** your heads and wear sackcloth.
Jer 16. 6 one will gash himself or **shave** his head to show his grief.
41. 5 They had **shaved** off their beards, torn their clothes, and gashed
48.37 All of them have **shaved** their heads and cut off their beards.
Ezek 5. 1 sword and use it to **shave** off your beard and all your
7.18 Their heads will be **shaved,** and they will all be disgraced.
27.31 They **shave** their heads for you And dress themselves in sackcloth.
44.20 "Priests must neither **shave** their heads nor let their hair
Amos 8.10 I will make you **shave** your heads and wear sackcloth, and you
Acts 18.18 he had his head **shaved** because of a vow
21.24 then they will be able to **shave** their heads.
1 Cor 11. 5 between her and a woman whose head has been **shaved.**
11. 6 for a woman to **shave** her head or cut her hair,

SHE-BEARS see BEAR (5)

SHEAF

Gen 37. 7 sheaves of wheat, when my **sheaf** got up and stood up straight.
Lev 23. 9 you harvest your corn, take the first **sheaf** to the priest.
23.15 on which you bring your **sheaf** of corn to present to the
Song 7. 2 A **sheaf** of wheat is there, surrounded by lilies.

SHEAR
[SHORN]

Gen 31.19 Laban had gone to **shear** his sheep, and during his absence
38.12 of Adullam went to Timnah, where his sheep were being **sheared.**
38.13 her father-in-law was going to Timnah to **shear** his sheep.
Deut 15.19 of these cattle for work and don't **shear** any of these sheep.
1 Sam 25. 2 Nabal was **shearing** his sheep in Carmel, [4] and David, who
25. 7 He heard that you were **shearing** your sheep, and he wants
25.11 I have slaughtered for my **shearers,** and give them to men who
2 Sam 13.23 Absalom was having his sheep **sheared** at Baal Hazor, near the
13.24 King David and said, "Your Majesty, I am having my sheep
sheared.
Song 4. 2 are as white as sheep that have just been **shorn** and washed.
Is 53. 7 like a sheep about to be **sheared,** he never said a word.

SHEATH

1 Sam 17.51 Goliath's sword out of its **sheath,** and cut off his head and
2 Sam 20. 8 for battle, with a sword in its **sheath** fastened to his belt.

SHEBA (1)
Ancient kingdom in s. Arabia, inhabited by the Sabeans.

Gen 10. 7 The descendants of Raamah were the people of **Sheba** and Dedan.
10.28 Hadoram, Uzal, Diklah, [28] Obal, Abimael, **Sheba,** [29] Ophir,
25. 3 Jokshan was the father of **Sheba** and Dedan, and the descendants
1 Kgs 10. 1 The queen of **Sheba** heard of Solomon's fame, and she
10. 4 The queen of **Sheba** heard Solomon's wisdom and saw the
10.13 Solomon gave the queen of **Sheba** everything she asked for,
10.13 Then she and her attendants returned to the land of **Sheba.**
1 Chr 1. 9 The descendants of Raamah were the people of **Sheba** and Dedan.
1.22 Hadoram, Uzal, Diklah, [22] Ebal, Abimael, **Sheba,** [23] Ophir,
1.32 **Sheba** and Dedan.
2 Chr 9. 1 The queen of **Sheba** heard of King Solomon's fame, and she
9. 3 The queen of **Sheba** heard Solomon's wisdom and saw the
9. 9 fine as those that the queen of **Sheba** gave to King Solomon.
9.12 King Solomon gave the queen of **Sheba** everything she asked for.
9.12 Then she and her attendants returned to the land of **Sheba.**
Job 6.19 Caravans from **Sheba** and Tema search, [20] but their hope dies
Ps 72.10 the kings of **Sheba** and Seba will bring him offerings.
Is 60. 6 They will come from **Sheba,** bringing gold and incense.
Jer 6.20 incense they bring me from **Sheba,** or the spices from a
Ezek 27.22 your goods the merchants of **Sheba** and Raamah exchanged
jewels,
27.23 and Eden, the merchants of **Sheba,** the cities of Asshur and
38.13 The people of **Sheba** and Dedan and the merchants from the
Mt 12.42 the Queen of **Sheba** will stand up and accuse you,
Lk 11.31 the Queen of **Sheba** will stand up and accuse the

SHEBA (2)
Member of tribe of Benjamin who led a revolt against David.

2 Sam 20. 1 a worthless character named **Sheba** son of Bikri, of the tribe
20. 2 deserted David and went with **Sheba,** but the men of Judah
20. 6 the king said to Abishai, "**Sheba** will give us more trouble
20. 7 soldiers left Jerusalem with Abishai to go after **Sheba.**
20.10 Then Joab and his brother Abishai went on after **Sheba.**
20.13 everyone followed Joab in pursuit of **Sheba.**
20.14 **Sheba** passed through the territory of all the tribes of Israel
20.15 Joab's men heard that **Sheba** was there, and so they went
20.21 A man named **Sheba** son of Bikri, who is from the hill-country
20.22 plan, and they cut off **Sheba's** head and threw it over the

SHEBAT
Eleventh month of the Hebrew calendar.

Zech 1. 7 eleventh month (the month of **Shebat**), the Lord gave me a

SHEBNA
Official at King Hezekiah's court.

2 Kgs 18.18 **Shebna,** the court secretary;
18.26 Eliakim, **Shebna,** and Joah told the official, "Speak Aramaic
18.37 Then Eliakim, **Shebna,** and Joah tore their clothes in grief,
19. 2 in charge of the palace, **Shebna,** the court secretary,
Is 22.15 told me to go to **Shebna,** the manager of the royal household,
22.20 The Lord said to **Shebna,** "When that happens, I will
36. 3 the court secretary, **Shebna;**
36.11 Eliakim, **Shebna,** and Joah said to the official, "Speak Aramaic
36.22 Then Eliakim, **Shebna,** and Joah tore their clothes in grief
37. 2 in charge of the palace, **Shebna,** the court secretary,

SHECHEM (1)
Important city in central Palestine.

Gen 12. 6 came to the sacred tree of Moreh, the holy place at **Shechem.**
33.18 safely at the city of **Shechem** in the land of Canaan and
35. 4 He buried them beneath the oak-tree near **Shechem.**
37.12 Joseph's brothers had gone to **Shechem** to take care of their
37.13 want you to go to **Shechem,** where your brothers are taking
37.14 Joseph arrived at **Shechem** [15] and was wandering about
48.22 brothers that I am giving **Shechem,** that fertile region which
Josh 17. 7 of Manasseh reached from Asher to Michmethath, east of
Shechem.
20. 7 **Shechem,** in the hill-country of Ephraim;
21.21 **Shechem** and its pasture lands in the hill-country of Ephraim
24. 1 Joshua gathered all the tribes of Israel together at **Shechem.**
24.25 that day, and there at **Shechem** he gave them laws and rules
24.32 from Egypt, was buried at **Shechem,** in the piece of land that
Judg 8.31 He also had a concubine in **Shechem;**
9. 1 town of **Shechem,** where all his mother's relatives lived,
9. 2 them [2] to ask the men of **Shechem,** "Which would you prefer?
9. 3 talked to the men of **Shechem** about this for him,
9. 3 and the men of **Shechem** decided to follow Abimelech
9. 6 Then all the men of **Shechem** and Bethmillo got together
9. 6 the sacred oak-tree at **Shechem,** where they made Abimelech
king.

Judg	9. 7	to me, you men of **Shechem,** and God may listen to you!
	9.18	is your relative, you have made him king of **Shechem.**
	9.20	from Abimelech and burn up the men of **Shechem** and Bethmillo.
	9.20	the men of **Shechem** and Bethmillo and burn Abimelech up."
	9.23	Abimelech and the men of **Shechem** hostile to each other, and
	9.24	Abimelech and the men of **Shechem,** who encouraged him to murder
	9.25	The men of **Shechem** put men in ambush against Abimelech
	9.26	son of Ebed came to **Shechem** with his brothers,
	9.26	and the men of **Shechem** put their confidence in him.
	9.28	Gaal said, "What kind of men are we in **Shechem?**
	9.31	his brothers have come to **Shechem,** and they are not going to
	9.34	their move at night and hid outside **Shechem** in four groups.
	9.39	Gaal led the men of **Shechem** out and fought Abimelech.
	9.41	and his brothers out of **Shechem,** so that they could no
	9.42	the people of **Shechem** were planning to go out
	9.46	men in the fort at **Shechem** heard about this, they sought
	9.57	also made the men of **Shechem** suffer for their wickedness,
	21.19	Lebonah, and east of the road between Bethel and **Shechem.)**
1 Kgs	12. 1	Rehoboam went to **Shechem,** where all the people of northern
	12.25	Israel fortified the town of **Shechem** in the hill-country
1 Chr	6.67	**Shechem,** the city of refuge in the hills of Ephraim, Gezer,
	7.28	also included the cities of **Shechem** and Ayyah, and the towns
2 Chr	10. 1	Rehoboam went to **Shechem,** where all the people of northern
Ps	60. 6	"In triumph I will divide **Shechem** and distribute the Valley
	108. 7	"In triumph I will divide **Shechem** and distribute the Valley
Jer	41. 5	eighty men arrived from **Shechem,** Shiloh, and Samaria.
Hos	6. 9	on the road to the holy place at **Shechem** they commit murder.
Acts	7.16	Their bodies were taken to **Shechem,** where they were buried

SHECHEM (2)

Hamor's son, killed for raping Dinah, Jacob's daughter.

Gen	33.19	of Hamor father of **Shechem** for a hundred pieces of silver.
	34. 2	When **Shechem** son of Hamor the Hivite, who was chief of
	34. 6	**Shechem's** father Hamor went out to talk with Jacob,
	34. 7	were shocked and furious that **Shechem** had done such a thing
	34. 8	said to him, "My son **Shechem** has fallen in love with your
	34.11	Then **Shechem** said to Dinah's father and brothers,
	34.13	Because **Shechem** had disgraced their sister Dinah,
	34.13	Jacob's sons answered **Shechem** and his father Hamor
	34.18	to Hamor and his son **Shechem,** [19]and the young man lost no
	34.20	Hamor and his son **Shechem** went to the meeting-place at
	34.24	agreed with what Hamor and **Shechem** proposed, and all the males
	34.26	and killed all the men, [26]including Hamor and his son **Shechem.**
	34.26	Then they took Dinah from **Shechem's** house and left.
Josh	24.32	the father of **Shechem,** for a hundred pieces of silver.

SHED (1)

[BLOODSHED]

Lev	17. 3	He has **shed** blood and shall no longer be considered one of
1 Chr	22. 8	so, because of all the **bloodshed** I have caused, he would not
	28. 3	it, because I am a soldier and have **shed** too much blood.
Ps	79. 3	They **shed** your people's blood like water;
	79.10	punish the nations for **shedding** the blood of your servants.
Is	4. 4	guilt of Jerusalem and the blood that has been **shed** there.
Ezek	21.32	Your blood will be **shed** in your own country, and no one
	24.16	You are not to complain or cry or **shed** any tears.
	38.22	I will punish him with disease and **bloodshed.**
Joel	2.30	there will be **bloodshed,** fire, and clouds of smoke.
Zech	9.15	like drunken men and will **shed** the blood of their enemies;

SHED (2)

Is	1. 8	watchman's hut in a vineyard or a **shed** in a cucumber field.

SHEEP

see also **SHEEP GATE, SHEEPFOLD**

Gen	4. 4	born to one of his **sheep,** killed it, and gave the best
	12.16	and gave him flocks of **sheep** and goats, cattle, donkeys, slaves,
	13. 2	a very rich man, with **sheep,** goats, and cattle, as well as
	13. 5	Lot also had **sheep,** goats, and cattle, as well as his own
	20.14	and at the same time he gave him **sheep,** cattle, and slaves.
	21.27	Then Abraham gave some **sheep** and cattle to Abimelech, and the
	24.35	has given him flocks of **sheep** and goats, cattle, silver,
	26.14	he had many herds of **sheep** and cattle and many servants, the
	29. 2	out in the fields with three flocks of **sheep** lying round it.
	29.10	to the well, rolled the stone back, and watered the **sheep.**
	30.33	speckled or spotted or any **sheep** that isn't black, you will
	30.35	he also removed all the black **sheep.**
	30.40	Jacob kept the **sheep** separate from the goats and made
	31.19	had gone to shear his **sheep,** and during his absence Rachel
	31.38	your **sheep** and your goats have not failed to reproduce, and
	31.39	Whenever a **sheep** was killed by wild animals, I always
	32. 5	I own cattle, donkeys, **sheep,** goats, and slaves.
	32. 7	who were with him, and also his **sheep,** goats, cattle, and
	32.13	twenty males, two hundred female **sheep** and twenty males, thirty
	33.13	I must think of the **sheep** and livestock with their young.
	37. 2	seventeen, took care of the **sheep** and goats with his brothers,
	38.12	of Adullam went to Timnah, where his **sheep** were being sheared.
	38.13	that her father-in-law was going to Timnah to shear his **sheep.**
	45.10	your children, your grandchildren, your **sheep,** your goats, your
	47.17	food in exchange for their horses, **sheep,** goats, cattle,
	50. 8	their small children and their **sheep,** goats, and cattle stayed
Ex	2.15	and fill the troughs for their father's **sheep** and goats.
	3. 1	care of the **sheep** and goats of his father-in-law Jethro,
	9. 3	animals—your horses, donkeys, camels, cattle, **sheep,** and goats.
	10. 9	our sons and daughters, our **sheep** and goats, and our cattle,
Ex	10.24	But your **sheep,** goats, and cattle must stay here."
	12. 5	You may choose either a **sheep** or a goat, but it must
	12.32	Take your **sheep,** goats, and cattle, and leave.
	12.38	of other people and many **sheep,** goats, and cattle also went
	20.24	and on it sacrifice your **sheep** and your cattle as offerings
	22. 1	steals a cow or a **sheep** and kills it or sells it,
	22. 1	pay five cows for one cow and four **sheep** for one sheep.
	22. 2	cow, a donkey, or a **sheep,** is found alive in his possession,
	22. 9	cattle, donkeys, **sheep,** clothing, or any other lost object,
	22.10	keep another man's donkey, cow, **sheep,** or other animal for him,
	22.30	Give me the first-born of your cattle and your **sheep.**
	23.19	"Do not cook a young **sheep** or goat in its mother's milk.
	34. 3	and no **sheep** or cattle are to graze at the foot of
	34.26	"Do not cook a young **sheep** or goat in its mother's milk."
Lev	1. 2	be one of his cattle or one of his **sheep** or goats.
	1.10	is offering one of his **sheep** or goats, it must be a
	3. 6	If a **sheep** or goat is used as a fellowship-offering, it
	3. 7	If a man offers a **sheep,** [8]he shall put his hand on
	4.32	If a man brings a **sheep** as a sin-offering, it must be
	4.35	removed from the **sheep** killed for the fellowship-offerings,
	5. 6	bring to the Lord a female **sheep** or goat as an offering.
	5. 7	a man cannot afford a **sheep** or a goat, he shall bring
	5.15	to the Lord a male **sheep** or goat without any defects.
	5.18	a repayment-offering a male **sheep** or goat without any defects.
	6. 6	to the Lord a male **sheep** or goat without any defects.
	7.23	No fat of cattle, **sheep,** or goats shall be eaten.
	17. 3	kills a cow or a **sheep** or a goat as an offering
	22.28	and its calf or a **sheep** and its lamb or a goat
Num	11.22	Could enough cattle and **sheep** be killed to satisfy them?
	15. 3	A bull, a ram, a **sheep,** or a goat may be presented
	15. 4	Whoever presents a **sheep** or a goat as a burnt-offering
	15.11	is what shall be offered with each bull, ram, **sheep,** or
	18.17	But the first-born of cows, **sheep,** and goats are not to
	22.40	where Balak slaughtered cattle and **sheep** and gave some of the
	27.17	your community will not be like **sheep** without a shepherd."
	31.28	the same proportion of the cattle, donkeys, **sheep,** and goats.
	31.30	the same proportion of the cattle, donkeys, **sheep,** and goats.
	31.32	**sheep** and goats, 72,000 cattle, 61,000 donkeys,
	31.36	of the soldiers was 337,500 **sheep** and goats, of which 675
	31.42	**sheep** and goats, 36,000 cattle, 30,500 donkeys,
	32.16	stone enclosures here for our **sheep** and fortified towns
	32.24	enclosures for your **sheep,** but do what you have promised!"
	32.26	children and our cattle and **sheep** will remain here in the
Deut	7.13	will bless you by giving you a lot of livestock and **sheep.**
	8.13	and when your cattle and **sheep,** your silver and gold,
	12. 6	freewill offerings, and the first-born of your cattle and **sheep.**
	12.17	first-born of your cattle and **sheep,** the gifts that you
	12.21	any of the cattle or **sheep** that the Lord has given you,
	14. 4	cattle, **sheep,** goats, [5]deer, wild sheep, wild goats,
	14.21	"Do not cook a young **sheep** or goat in its mother's milk.
	14.23	and olive-oil, and the first-born of your cattle and **sheep.**
	15.14	from what the Lord has blessed you with—**sheep,** corn, and
	15.19	Lord your God all the first-born males of your cattle and **sheep;**
	15.19	of these cattle for work and don't shear any of these **sheep.**
	16. 2	slaughter there one of your **sheep** or cattle for the Passover
	17. 1	to the Lord your God cattle or **sheep** that have any defects;
	18. 3	"Whenever cattle or **sheep** are sacrificed, the priests are to
	22. 1	fellow-Israelite's cow or **sheep** running loose, do not ignore
	28. 4	children, with abundant crops, and with many cattle and **sheep.**
	28.18	only a few children, poor crops, and few cattle and **sheep.**
	28.31	Your **sheep** will be given to your enemies, and there will be
	28.51	will not leave you any corn, wine, olive-oil, livestock, or **sheep;**
	32.14	they had the best **sheep,** goats, and cattle, the finest wheat,
Josh	6.21	They also killed the cattle, **sheep,** and donkeys.
	7.24	daughters, his cattle, donkeys, and **sheep,** his tent, and
Judg	5.16	Why did they stay behind with the **sheep?**
	6. 4	They would take all the **sheep,** cattle, and donkeys, and leave
1 Sam	14.32	captured from the enemy, took **sheep** and cattle, slaughtered them
	14.34	and tell them all to bring their cattle and **sheep** here.
	15. 3	the cattle, **sheep,** camels, and donkeys."
	15. 9	did not kill the best **sheep** and cattle, the best calves and
	15.14	"Why, then, do I hear cattle mooing and **sheep** bleating?"
	15.15	They kept the best **sheep** and cattle to offer as a sacrifice
	15.21	did not kill the best **sheep** and cattle that they captured;
	15.22	better to obey him than to sacrifice the best **sheep** to him.
	16.11	the youngest, but he is out taking care of the **sheep."**
	16.19	me your son David, the one who takes care of the **sheep."**
	17.15	Bethlehem from time to time, to take care of his father's **sheep.**
	17.20	else in charge of the **sheep,** took the food, and went as
	17.28	is taking care of those **sheep** of yours out there in the
	17.34	"Your Majesty," David said, "I take care of my father's **sheep.**
	22.19	and babies, cattle, donkeys, and **sheep**—they were all killed.
	24. 3	a cave close to some **sheep** pens by the road and went
	25. 2	the owner of three thousand **sheep** and one thousand goats.
	25. 2	Nabal was shearing his **sheep** in Carmel, [4]and David, who
	25. 7	that you were shearing your **sheep,** and he wants you to know
	25.18	five roasted **sheep,** seventeen kilogrammes of roasted grain,
	27. 9	and women and taking the **sheep,** cattle, donkeys, camels, and
2 Sam	7. 8	took you from looking after **sheep** in the fields and made you
	12. 2	man had many cattle and **sheep,** [3]while the poor man had only
	13.23	later Absalom was having his **sheep** sheared at Baal Hazor,
	13.24	and said, "Your Majesty, I am having my **sheep** sheared.
	17.28	roasted grain, beans, peas, honey, cheese, cream, and some **sheep.**
1 Kgs	1. 9	Adonijah offered a sacrifice of **sheep,** bulls, and fattened
	1.19	a sacrifice of many bulls, **sheep,** and fattened calves,
	1.25	offered a sacrifice of many bulls, **sheep,** and fattened calves.
	4.23	pasture-fed cattle, and a hundred **sheep,** besides deer, gazelles,
	8. 5	a large number of **sheep** and cattle—too many to count.
	8.63	22,000 head of cattle and 120,000 **sheep** as fellowship-offerings.
	22.17	Israel scattered over the hills like **sheep** without a shepherd.

2 Kgs 3. 4 King Mesha of Moab bred **sheep,** and every year he gave as
3. 4 of Israel 100,000 lambs, and the wool from 100,000 **sheep.**
5.26 olive-groves and vineyards, **sheep** and cattle, or servants!
1 Chr 4.39 to Gerar and pastured their **sheep** on the eastern side of the
4.41 permanently because there was plenty of pasture for their **sheep.**
5.21 the enemy 50,000 camels, 250,000 **sheep,** and 2,000 donkeys,
12.40 They also brought cattle and **sheep** to kill and eat.
15.26 sacrificed seven bulls and seven **sheep,** to make sure that
17. 7 took you from looking after **sheep** in the fields and made you
27.25 **Sheep** and goats:
2 Chr 5. 6 a large number of **sheep** and cattle—too many to count.
7. 5 22,000 head of cattle and 120,000 **sheep** as fellowship-offerings.
13. 9 with a bull or seven **sheep** can get himself consecrated as a
14.15 of some shepherds, capturing large numbers of **sheep** and camels.
15.11 seven hundred head of cattle and seven thousand **sheep.**
17.11 and some Arabs brought him 7,700 **sheep** and 7,700 goats.
18. 2 a large number of **sheep** and cattle slaughtered for a feast.
18.16 Israel scattered over the hills like **sheep** without a shepherd.
29.21 took seven bulls, seven **sheep,** seven lambs, and seven goats.
29.22 the bulls first, then the **sheep,** and then the lambs, and
29.32 a hundred **sheep,** and two hundred lambs as burnt-offerings
29.33 and three thousand **sheep** as sacrifices for the people to
30.24 thousand bulls and seven thousand **sheep** for the people to
30.24 officials gave them another thousand bulls and ten thousand **sheep.**
31. 6 tithes of their cattle and **sheep,** and they also brought
32.28 and enclosures for his **sheep.**
32.29 all this, God gave him **sheep** and cattle and so much other
35. 7 herds and flocks thirty thousand **sheep,** lambs, and young goats,
Ezra 6. 9 young bulls, **sheep,** or lambs to be burnt as offerings to the
6.17 a hundred bulls, two hundred **sheep,** and four hundred lambs as
Neh 5.18 ox, six of the best **sheep,** and many chickens, and every ten
10.36 first lamb or kid born to each of our **sheep** or goats.
Job 1. 3 and owned seven thousand **sheep,** three thousand camels,
1.16 "Lightning struck the **sheep** and the shepherds and killed them
5.24 when you look at your **sheep,** you will find them safe.
24. 2 they steal **sheep** and put them with their own flocks.
30. 1 that I wouldn't let them help my dogs guard **sheep.**
31.20 made of wool that had come from my own flock of **sheep.**
42.12 Job owned fourteen thousand **sheep,** six thousand camels,
Ps 8. 7 **sheep** and cattle, and the wild animals too;
44.11 You allowed us to be slaughtered like **sheep;**
44.22 the time, that we are treated like **sheep** to be slaughtered.
49.14 doomed to die like **sheep,** and Death will be their shepherd.
65.13 The fields are covered with **sheep;**
66.15 I will offer **sheep** to be burnt on the altar;
68.13 of you stay among the **sheep** pens on the day of battle?)
79.13 Then we, your people, the **sheep** of your flock, will
119.176 I wander about like a lost **sheep;**
144.13 May the **sheep** in our fields bear young by the tens of
Prov 27.23 Look after your **sheep** and cattle as carefully as you can,
27.26 from the wool of your **sheep** and buy land with the money
Ecc 12.11 that shepherds use to guide **sheep,** and collected proverbs are
Song 4. 2 teeth are as white as **sheep** that have just been shorn and
6. 6 as white as a flock of **sheep** that have just been washed.
Is 1.11 more than enough of the **sheep** you burn as sacrifices and of
1.11 I am tired of the blood of bulls and **sheep** and goats.
7.25 It will be a place where cattle and **sheep** graze."
11. 6 Wolves and **sheep** will live together in peace, and leopards will
13.14 like deer escaping from hunters, like **sheep** without a shepherd.
17. 2 will be a pasture for **sheep** and cattle, and no one will
22.13 You killed **sheep** and cattle to eat, and you drank wine.
32.14 Wild donkeys will roam there, and **sheep** will find pasture there.
43.23 You did not bring me your burnt-offerings of **sheep;**
49. 9 They will be like **sheep** that graze on the hills;
53. 6 All of us were like **sheep** that were lost, each of us
53. 7 to be slaughtered, like a **sheep** about to be sheared, he
60. 7 All the **sheep** of Kedar and Nebaioth Will be brought to you
65.10 me and will lead their **sheep** and cattle to pasture in the
Jer 12. 3 Drag these evil men away like **sheep** to be butchered;
31.12 of corn and wine and olive-oil, gifts of **sheep** and cattle.
33.12 will once again be pastures where shepherds can take their **sheep.**
33.13 towns of Judah, shepherds will once again count their **sheep.**
50. 6 "My people are like **sheep** whose shepherds have let them
50. 6 They have wandered like **sheep** from one mountain to another,
50.17 "The people of Israel are like **sheep,** chased and scattered
Ezek 24. 5 Use the meat of the finest **sheep;**
25. 5 into a place to keep **sheep,** so that you will know that
27.21 land of Kedar paid for your merchandise with lambs, **sheep,** and
34. 2 You take care of yourselves, but never tend the **sheep.**
34. 3 made from the wool, and kill and eat the finest **sheep.**
34. 3 But you never tend the **sheep.**
34. 5 Because the **sheep** had no shepherd, they were scattered,
34. 6 So my **sheep** wandered over the high hills and the mountains.
34. 8 My **sheep** have been attacked by wild animals that killed and
34. 8 My shepherds did not try to find the **sheep.**
34. 8 They were taking care of themselves and not the **sheep.**
34.10 I will take my **sheep** away from you and never again let
34.10 I will rescue my **sheep** from you and not let you eat
34.11 myself will look for my **sheep** and take care of them [12]in
34.12 shepherd takes care of his **sheep** that were scattered and
34.15 be the shepherd of my **sheep,** and I will find them a
34.17 separate the good from the bad, the **sheep** from the goats.
34.19 My other **sheep** have to eat the grass you trample down
34.20 I will judge between you strong **sheep** and the weak sheep.
34.22 But I will rescue my **sheep** and not let them be
34.22 will judge each of my **sheep** and separate the good from the
34.25 the land, so that my **sheep** can live safely in the fields
34.31 "You, my **sheep,** the flock that I feed, are my people,
36.37 I will let them increase in numbers like a flock of **sheep.**
36.38 was once full of the **sheep** which were offered as sacrifices
45.13 **Sheep:**
Ezek 45.13 1 **sheep** out of every 200 from the meadows of Israel
Hos 5. 6 They take their **sheep** and cattle to offer as sacrifices to
12.12 wife, he worked for another man and took care of his **sheep.**
Joel 1.18 the flocks of **sheep** also suffer.
Amos 3.12 or an ear of a **sheep** that a lion has eaten, so
Jon 3. 7 persons, cattle, and **sheep** are forbidden to eat or drink.
Mic 2.12 I will bring you together like **sheep** returning to the fold.
2.12 Like a pasture full of **sheep,** your land will once again be
5. 8 he gets in among the **sheep,** pounces on them, and tears them
6. 7 I bring him thousands of **sheep** or endless streams of olive-oil?
Hab 3.17 no corn, even though the **sheep** all die and the cattle-stalls
Zeph 2. 6 sea will become open fields with shepherds' huts and **sheep** pens.
Zech 10. 2 So the people wander about like lost **sheep.**
11. 4 shepherd of a flock of **sheep** that are going to be butchered.
11. 7 who bought and sold the **sheep** hired me, and I
11. 7 the shepherd of the **sheep** that were going to be butchered.
11.11 who bought and sold the **sheep** were watching me, and they
11.16 does not help the **sheep** that are threatened by destruction;
11.16 the meat of the fattest **sheep** and tears off their hoofs.
13. 7 Kill him, and the **sheep** will be scattered.
Mt 7.15 come to you looking like **sheep** on the outside,
9.36 they were worried and helpless, like **sheep** without a shepherd.
10. 6 are to go to the lost **sheep** of the people of Israel.
10.16 am sending you out just like **sheep** to a pack of wolves.
12.11 one of you has a **sheep** and it falls
12.12 And a man is worth much more than a **sheep!**
15.24 been sent only to the lost **sheep** of the people of Israel."
18.12 who has a hundred **sheep** and one of them gets lost?
18.12 grazing on the hillside and go and look for the lost **sheep.**
18.13 far happier over this one **sheep** than over the ninety-nine
25.32 just as a shepherd separates the **sheep** from the goats.
26.31 the shepherd, and the **sheep** of the flock will be scattered.'
Mk 6.34 for them, because they were like **sheep** without a shepherd.
14.27 'God will kill the shepherd, and the **sheep** will all be scattered.'
Lk 15. 4 has a hundred **sheep** and loses one of them—
15. 4 He leaves the other ninety-nine **sheep** in the pasture and
15. 6 says to them, 'I am so happy I found my lost **sheep.**
17. 7 a servant who is ploughing or looking after the **sheep.**
Jn 2.14 he found men selling cattle, **sheep,** and pigeons,
2.15 out of the Temple, both the **sheep** and the cattle;
10. 2 who goes in through the gate is the shepherd of the **sheep.**
10. 3 the **sheep** hear his voice
10. 3 as he calls his own **sheep** by name, and he leads them
10. 4 and the **sheep** follow him, because they know
10. 7 I am the gate for the **sheep.**
10. 8 thieves and robbers, but the **sheep** did not listen to them.
10.11 the good shepherd, who is willing to die for the **sheep.**
10.12 and does not own the **sheep,** sees a wolf coming,
10.12 he leaves the **sheep** and runs away;
10.12 so the wolf snatches the **sheep** and scatters them.
10.13 only a hired man and does not care about the **sheep.**
10.14 in the same way I know my **sheep** and they know me.
10.16 There are other **sheep** which belong to me
10.26 but you will not believe, for you are not my **sheep.**
10.27 My **sheep** listen to my voice;
21.16 Jesus said to him, "Take care of my **sheep."**
21.17 Jesus said to him, "Take care of my **sheep.**
Acts 8.32 "Like a **sheep** that is taken to be slaughtered,
Rom 8.36 we are treated like **sheep** that are going to be slaughtered."
1 Cor 9. 7 What shepherd does not use the milk from his own **sheep?**
Heb 11.37 clothed in skins of **sheep** or goats—poor, persecuted,
13.20 the Great Shepherd of the **sheep**
1 Pet 2.25 You were like **sheep** that had lost their way,
Rev 18.13 flour and wheat, cattle and **sheep,** horses and carriages,

SHEEP GATE

Neh 3. 1 and his fellow-priests rebuilt the **Sheep Gate,** dedicated it, and
3.32 from the room at the corner as far as the **Sheep Gate.**
12.39 of Hananel, and the Tower of the Hundred, to the **Sheep Gate.**
Jn 5. 2 Near the **Sheep Gate** in Jerusalem there is a pool with five

SHEEPFOLD

[FOLD]

Mic 2.12 I will bring you together like sheep returning to the **fold.**
Jn 10. 1 who does not enter the **sheepfold** by the gate, but climbs in
10.16 sheep which belong to me that are not in this **sheepfold.**

SHEET (1)

Deut 22.15 to take the blood-stained wedding **sheet** that proves the girl
22.17 look at the bloodstains on the wedding **sheet!"**
Prov 7.16 I've covered my bed with **sheets** of coloured linen from Egypt.
Mt 27.59 in a new linen **sheet,** [60]and placed it in his own
Mk 15.46 Joseph bought a linen **sheet,** took the body down,
15.46 wrapped it in the **sheet,** and placed it in a tomb
Lk 23.53 wrapped it in a linen **sheet,** and placed it in a tomb
Acts 10.11 that looked like a large **sheet** being lowered
11. 5 that looked like a large **sheet** being lowered

SHEET (2)

Ex 39. 3 They hammered out **sheets** of gold

SHEKEL

Israelite unit of weight.

Ezek 45.12 20 gerahs = 1 **shekel** 60 shekels = 1 mina

SHELAH (1)
Judah's son.

Gen 38. 5 Again she had a son and named him **Shelah.**
38.11 and remain a widow until my son **Shelah** grows up."
38.11 because he was afraid that **Shelah** would be killed,
38.14 Judah's youngest son **Shelah** had now grown up,
38.26 her—I should have given her to my son **Shelah** in marriage."
46.12 **Shelah,** Perez, and Zerah.
Num 26.19 the clans of **Shelah,** Perez, Zerah, Hezron, and Hamul.
1 Chr 2. 3 Er, Onan, and **Shelah.**
4.21 **Shelah** was one of Judah's sons.
9. 4 The descendants of Judah's son **Shelah** had as their leader Asaiah,
Neh 11. 5 Adaiah, Joiarib, and Zechariah, descendants of Judah's son **Shelah.**

SHELTER
[FESTIVAL OF SHELTERS]
The Festival of Shelters was celebrated by the Israelites in the autumn after the harvest was complete. In order to help them remember the years when their ancestors wandered through the wilderness, the Israelites built rough shelters to live in during the festival. The Jewish name for this festival is Sukkoth. It is also called the Feast of Tabernacles or the Feast of Booths.

Gen 33.17 he built a house for himself and **shelters** for his livestock.
Ex 9.19 else you have in the open to be put under **shelter.**
9.20 and they brought their slaves and animals indoors for **shelter.**
23.16 "Celebrate the **Festival of Shelters** in the autumn,
34.22 and keep the **Festival of Shelters** in the autumn when you
Lev 23.33 The **Festival of Shelters** begins on the fifteenth day
23.42 of Israel shall live in **shelters** for seven days, [43]so that
23.43 of Israel live in simple **shelters** when he led them out of
Deut 16.13 celebrate the **Festival of Shelters** for seven days.
16.16 at Passover, Harvest Festival, and the **Festival of Shelters.**
31.10 read this aloud at the **Festival of Shelters.**
Judg 9.15 make me your king, then come and take **shelter** in my shade.
Ruth 2. 7 just now stopped to rest for a while under the **shelter."**
2 Sam 21.10 used sackcloth to make a **shelter** for herself on the rock
1 Kgs 8. 2 assembled during the **Festival of Shelters** in the seventh month,
8.65 Israel celebrated the **Festival of Shelters** for seven days.
2 Chr 5. 3 They all assembled at the time of the **Festival of Shelters.**
7. 8 Israel celebrated the **Festival of Shelters** for seven days.
8.13 the Harvest Festival, and the **Festival of Shelters.**
Ezra 3. 4 They celebrated the **Festival of Shelters** according to the
Neh 8.14 live in temporary **shelters** during the Festival of Shelters.
8.15 and other trees to make **shelters** according to the instructions
8.16 people got branches and built **shelters** on the flat roofs of
8.17 come back from captivity built **shelters** and lived in them.
Job 24. 8 mountains, and they huddle beside the rocks for **shelter.**
40.22 the willows by the stream give him **shelter** in their shade.
Ps 27. 5 In times of trouble he will **shelter** me;
31. 4 **shelter** me from danger.
31.20 in a safe **shelter** you hide them from the insults of their
46. 1 God is our **shelter** and strength, always ready to help in
55. 8 would quickly find myself a **shelter** from the raging wind and
59.16 been a refuge for me, a **shelter** in my time of trouble.
62. 7 he is my **shelter.**
71. 3 Be my secure **shelter** and a strong fortress to protect me;
144. 2 my protector and defender, my **shelter** and saviour, in whom I
Is 4. 6 it a place of safety, **sheltered** from the rain and storm.
25. 4 give them **shelter** from storms and shade from the burning heat.
32. 2 them will be like a **shelter** from the wind and a place
Ezek 17.23 every kind will live there and find **shelter** in its shade.
31. 6 The wild animals bore their young in its **shelter;**
45.25 "For the **Festival of Shelters,** which begins on the fifteenth
Hos 14. 8 Like an evergreen tree I will **shelter** them;
Jon 4. 5 He made a **shelter** for himself and sat in its shade, waiting
Zech 14.16 Lord Almighty as king, and to celebrate the **Festival of Shelters.**
14.18 to celebrate the **Festival of Shelters,** then they will be
14.19 nations if they do not celebrate the **Festival of Shelters.**
Jn 7. 2 The time for the **Festival of Shelters** was near, [3]so
Acts 27. 4 we sailed on the **sheltered side** of the island of Cyprus.
27. 7 so we sailed down the **sheltered side** of the island of Crete,
27.16 We got some **shelter** when we passed to the south
2 Cor 11.27 I have often been without enough food, **shelter,** or clothing.

SHEM
Noah's son.

Gen 5.32 was 500 years old, he had three sons, **Shem,** Ham, and Japheth.
6. 9 He had three sons, **Shem,** Ham, and Japheth.
7.13 with their three sons, **Shem,** Ham, and Japheth, and their wives.
9.18 Noah who went out of the boat were **Shem,** Ham, and Japheth.
9.23 Then **Shem** and Japheth took a robe and held it behind
9.26 Give praise to the Lord, the God of **Shem!**
9.26 Canaan will be the slave of **Shem.**
9.27 May his descendants live with the people of **Shem!**
10. 1 These are the descendants of Noah's sons, **Shem,** Ham, and Japheth.
10.21 **Shem,** the elder brother of Japheth, was the ancestor of
10.22 **Shem's** sons—Elam, Asshur, Arpachshad, Lud, and Aram—
10.31 These are the descendants of **Shem,** living in their different
11.10 These are the descendants of **Shem.**
11.10 years after the flood, when **Shem** was 100 years old, he had
1 Chr 1. 4 **Shem,** Ham, and Japheth.
1.17 **Shem's** sons—Elam, Asshur, Arpachshad, Lud, Aram, Uz, Hul,
1.24 The family line from **Shem** to Abram is as follows:
1.24 **Shem,** Arpachshad, Shelah, [25]Eber, Peleg, Reu, [26]Serug, Nahor,
Lk 3.36 the son of **Shem,** the son of Noah,

SHEPHERD

Gen 4. 2 Abel became a **shepherd,** but Cain was a farmer.
26.20 The **shepherds** of Gerar quarrelled with Isaac's shepherds
29. 3 flocks came together there, the **shepherds** would roll the
29. 4 Jacob asked the **shepherds,** "My friends, where are you from?"
46.32 tell him that you are **shepherds** and take care of livestock
46.34 because Egyptians will have nothing to do with **shepherds.**
47. 3 "We are **shepherds,** sir, just as our ancestors were,"
49.24 Mighty God of Jacob, By the **Shepherd,** the Protector of Israel.
Ex 2.17 But some **shepherds** drove Jethro's daughters away.
2.19 Egyptian rescued us from the **shepherds,"** they answered,
Num 27.17 your community will not be like sheep without a **shepherd."**
Judg 5.16 to listen to **shepherds** calling the flocks?
1 Sam 17.40 He took his **shepherd's** stick and then picked up five
25. 7 you to know that your **shepherds** have been with us and we
1 Kgs 22.17 Israel scattered over the hills like sheep without a **shepherd.**
2 Chr 14.15 camps of some **shepherds,** capturing large numbers of sheep
18.16 Israel scattered over the hills like sheep without a **shepherd.**
Job 1.16 "Lightning struck the sheep and the **shepherds** and killed them
Ps 23. 1 The Lord is my **shepherd;**
23. 4 Your **shepherd's** rod and staff protect me.
28. 9 Be their **shepherd,** and take care of them for ever.
49.14 doomed to die like sheep, and Death will be their **shepherd.**
77.20 people like a **shepherd,** with Moses and Aaron
78.52 out like a **shepherd** and guided them through the desert.
78.71 made him king of Israel, the **shepherd** of the people of God.
80. 1 Listen to us, O **Shepherd** of Israel;
Ecc 12.11 like the sharp sticks that **shepherds** use to guide sheep, and
12.11 They have been given by God, the one **Shepherd** of us all.
Song 1. 7 to look for you among the flocks of the other **shepherds?**
1. 8 find pasture for your goats near the tents of the **shepherds.**
Is 13.14 deer escaping from hunters, like sheep without a **shepherd.**
13.20 there, and no **shepherd** will ever pasture his flock there.
14.30 The Lord will be a **shepherd** to the poor of his people
31. 4 to me, "No matter how **shepherds** yell and shout, they can't
40.11 He will take care of his flock like a **shepherd;**
Jer 25.34 Cry, you leaders, you **shepherds** of my people, cry out
31.10 gather them and guard them as a **shepherd** guards his flock.
31.24 and there will be farmers, and **shepherds** with their flocks.
33.12 once again be pastures where **shepherds** can take their sheep.
33.13 towns of Judah, **shepherds** will once again count their sheep.
43.12 As a **shepherd** picks his clothes clean of lice, so the king
50. 6 people are like sheep whose **shepherds** have let them get lost
51.23 to slaughter **shepherds** and their flocks,
Ezek 34. 2 You are doomed, you **shepherds** of Israel!
34. 5 Because the sheep had no **shepherd,** they were scattered,
34. 7 "Now, you **shepherds,** listen to what I, the Lord, am telling you.
34. 8 that killed and ate them because there was no **shepherd.**
34. 8 My **shepherds** did not try to find the sheep.
34. 9 So listen to me, you **shepherds.**
34.10 sheep away from you and never again let you be their **shepherds;**
34.12 the same way as a **shepherd** takes care of his sheep
34.15 I myself will be the **shepherd** of my sheep,
34.16 destroy, because I am a **shepherd** who does what is right.
34.23 David to be their one **shepherd,** and he will take care of
Amos 1. 1 are the words of Amos, a **shepherd** from the town of Tekoa.
3.12 The Lord says, "As a **shepherd** recovers only two legs
7.15 from my work as a **shepherd** and ordered me to come and
Mic 4. 8 where God, like a **shepherd,** watches over his people,
7.14 Be a **shepherd** to your people, Lord, the people you have chosen.
Zeph 2. 6 will become open fields with **shepherds'** huts and sheep pens.
Zech 9.16 save his people, as a **shepherd** saves his flock from danger.
11. 4 "Act the part of the **shepherd** of a flock of sheep
11. 5 Even their own **shepherds** have no pity on them."
11. 7 and I became the **shepherd** of the sheep
11. 8 lost patience with three other **shepherds,** who hated me,
11. 9 said to the flock, "I will not be your **shepherd** any longer.
11.15 again act the part of a **shepherd,** this time a worthless one.
11.16 I have put a **shepherd** in charge of my flock,
11.17 That worthless **shepherd** is doomed!
13. 7 "Wake up, sword, and attack the **shepherd** who works for me!
Mt 9.36 because they were worried and helpless, like sheep without a **shepherd.**
25.32 just as a **shepherd** separates the sheep from the goats.
26.31 says, 'God will kill the **shepherd,** and the sheep
Mk 6.34 pity for them, because they were like sheep without a **shepherd.**
14.27 says, 'God will kill the **shepherd,** and the sheep will all be
Lk 2. 8 There were some **shepherds** in that part of the country
2.15 the **shepherds** said to one another, "Let's go
2.17 When the **shepherds** saw him, they told them
2.18 All who heard it were amazed at what the **shepherds** said.
2.20 The **shepherds** went back, singing praises to God
Jn 10. 2 who goes in through the gate is the **shepherd** of the sheep.
10.11 "I am the good **shepherd,**
10.12 man, who is not a **shepherd** and does not own the sheep,
10.14 I am the good **shepherd.**
10.16 and they will become one flock with one **shepherd.**
Acts 20.28 Be **shepherds** of the church of God,
1 Cor 9. 7 What **shepherd** does not use the milk from his own sheep?
Heb 13.20 Jesus, who is the Great **Shepherd** of the sheep
1 Pet 2.25 to follow the **Shepherd** and Keeper of your souls.
5. 2 appeal to you [2]to be **shepherds** of the flock that God gave
5. 4 And when the Chief **Shepherd** appears, you will receive
Rev 7.17 will be their **shepherd,** and he will guide them

SHEPHERDS' CAMP

2 Kgs 10.12 way, at a place called **"Shepherds' Camp,"** [13]he met some

SHIBBOLETH
Word used to test which tribe Israelites belonged to in Jephthah's time.

Judg 12. 6 If he said, "No," [6]they would tell him to say **"Shibboleth."**

SHIELD

Gen 15. 1 I will **shield** you from danger and give you a great reward."
Deut 33.29 The Lord himself is your **shield** and your sword, to defend
Judg 5. 8 thousand men in Israel, did anyone carry **shield** or spear?
1 Sam 17. 7 A soldier walked in front of him carrying his **shield.**
17.41 David, with his **shield-bearer** walking in front of him.
2 Sam 1.21 For the **shields** of the brave lie there in disgrace;
1.21 the **shield** of Saul is no longer polished with oil.
8. 7 David captured the gold **shields** carried by Hadadezer's
22. 3 He protects me like a **shield;**
22.31 He is like a **shield** for all who seek his protection.
1 Kgs 10.16 Solomon made two hundred large **shields,** and had each
10.17 also made three hundred smaller **shields,** overlaying each one
10.17 He had all these **shields** placed in the Hall of the Forest
14.26 and in the palace, including the gold **shields** Solomon had made.
14.27 them, King Rehoboam made bronze **shields** and entrusted them
14.28 Temple, the guards carried the **shields,** and then returned
2 Kgs 11.10 the officers the spears and **shields** that had belonged to
19.32 No soldiers with **shields** will come near the city, and no
1 Chr 5.18 were 44,760 soldiers, well-trained in the use of **shields,**
12. 8 They were experts with **shields** and spears, as fierce-looking
12.23 6,800 well-equipped men, armed with **shields** and spears;
12.23 together with 37,000 men armed with **shields** and spears;
18. 7 David captured the gold **shields** carried by Hadadezer's
2 Chr 9.15 Solomon made two hundred large **shields,** each of which
9.16 gold, [16]and three hundred smaller **shields,** each covered
11.12 food, olive-oil, and wine, [12]and also **shields** and spears.
12. 9 including the gold **shields** that King Solomon had made.
12.10 replace them, Rehoboam made bronze **shields** and entrusted
12.11 Temple, the guards carried the **shields** and then returned
14. 8 men from Judah, armed with **shields** and spears,
14. 8 and 280,000 men from Benjamin, armed with **shields** and bows.
17.17 in command of 200,000 men armed with **shields** and bows.
23. 9 the officers the spears and **shields** that had belonged to
25. 5 ready for battle, skilled in using spears and **shields.**
26.14 Uzziah supplied the army with **shields,** spears, helmets,
32. 5 He also had a large number of spears and **shields** made.
32.27 stones, spices, **shields,** and other valuable objects.
Neh 4.16 wearing coats of armour and armed with spears, **shields,**
Job 15.26 stubbornly holds up his **shield** and rushes to fight against God.
26. 6 no covering **shields** it from his sight.
41.15 of rows of **shields,** fastened together and hard as stone.
Ps 3. 3 But you, O Lord, are always my **shield** from danger;
5.12 your love protects them like a **shield.**
18. 2 He protects me like a **shield;**
18.30 He is like a **shield** for all who seek his protection.
35. 2 Take your **shield** and armour and come to my rescue.
46. 9 he breaks bows, destroys spears, and sets **shields** on fire.
76. 3 enemy, their **shields** and swords, yes, all their weapons.
Prov 30. 5 He is like a **shield** for all who seek his protection.
Song 4. 4 with a necklace like a thousand **shields** hung round it.
Is 21. 5 Prepare your **shields!"**
22. 6 Soldiers from the land of Kir had their **shields** ready.
37.33 No soldiers with **shields** will come near the city, and no
Jer 46. 3 officers shout, 'Get your **shields** ready and march into battle!
46. 9 men from Sudan and Libya, carrying **shields,** and skilled bowmen
51.11 Get your **shields** ready!
Ezek 23.24 Protected by **shields** and helmets, they will surround you.
26. 8 earthworks, and make a solid wall of **shields** against you.
27.10 They hung their **shields** and their helmets in your barracks.
27.11 They hung their **shields** on your walls.
32.27 under their heads and their **shields** over their bodies.
38. 4 every soldier carries a **shield** and is armed with a sword.
38. 5 and Libya are with him, and all have **shields** and helmets.
39. 9 will build fires with the **shields,** bows, arrows, spears, and
Nah 2. 3 The enemy soldiers carry red **shields** and wear uniforms of red.
2. 5 to the wall and set up the **shield** for the battering-ram.
Eph 6.16 At all times carry faith as a **shield;**

SHIFTING

Eph 4.14 blown about by every **shifting** wind of the teaching

SHILOH
Important city and a religious sanctuary in c. Israel.
see also TAANATH SHILOH

Josh 18. 1 community of Israel assembled at **Shiloh** and set up the Tent
18. 8 And then here in **Shiloh** I will consult the Lord for you
18. 9 Then they went back to Joshua in the camp at **Shiloh.**
19.51 to consult the Lord at **Shiloh,** at the entrance of the Tent
21. 2 There at **Shiloh** in the land of Canaan they said to them,
22. 9 the people of Israel at **Shiloh** in the land of Canaan
22.12 whole community came together at **Shiloh** to go to war against
Judg 18.31 that the Tent where God was worshipped remained at **Shiloh.**
21.12 them to the camp at **Shiloh,** which is in the land of
21.19 "The yearly festival of the Lord at **Shiloh** is coming soon."
21.19 **(Shiloh** is north of Bethel, south of Lebonah,
21.21 When the girls of **Shiloh** come out to dance during the festival,
21.23 the girls who were dancing at **Shiloh** and carried her away.
1 Sam 1. 3 to the Lord Almighty at **Shiloh,** where Hophni and Phinehas,
1. 9 meal in the house of the Lord at **Shiloh,** Hannah got up.
1.21 his family to go to **Shiloh** and offer to the Lord
1.24 she took him to **Shiloh,** taking along a three-year-old bull,
1 Sam 1.24 young as he was, to the house of the Lord at **Shiloh.**
2.11 the boy Samuel stayed in **Shiloh** and served the Lord
2.14 the Israelites who came to **Shiloh** to offer sacrifices were
3.21 continued to reveal himself at **Shiloh,** where he had appeared
4. 3 the Lord's Covenant Box from **Shiloh,** so that he will go with
4. 4 So they sent messengers to **Shiloh** and fetched the Covenant
4.12 the battlefield to **Shiloh** and arrived there the same day.
14. 3 Phinehas and grandson of Eli, the priest of the Lord in **Shiloh.)**
1 Kgs 2.27 the Lord had said in **Shiloh** about the priest Eli
11.29 the prophet Ahijah, from **Shiloh,** met him alone
12.15 Jeroboam son of Nebat through the prophet Ahijah from **Shiloh.**
14. 2 you, and go to **Shiloh,** where the prophet Ahijah lives,
14. 4 So she went to Ahijah's home in **Shiloh.**
15.29 Ahijah from **Shiloh,** all Jeroboam's family were killed;
2 Chr 9.29 The Prophecy of Ahijah of **Shiloh,**
10.15 Jeroboam son of Nebat through the prophet Ahijah from **Shiloh.**
Ps 78.60 He abandoned his tent in **Shiloh,**
Jer 7.12 Go to **Shiloh,** the first place where I chose to be worshipped,
7.14 so, what I did to **Shiloh** I will do to this Temple
7.14 I will do the same thing that I did to **Shiloh.**
26. 6 Temple what I did to **Shiloh,** and all the nations
26. 9 this Temple will become like **Shiloh**
41. 5 Gedaliah's murder, [5]eighty men arrived from Shechem, **Shiloh,**

SHIMEI (1)
Saul's relative who opposed David during Absalom's rebellion.

2 Sam 16. 5 one of Saul's relatives, **Shimei** son of Gera, came
16. 6 **Shimei** started throwing stones at David and his officials,
16. 7 **Shimei** cursed him and said, "Get out!
16.13 **Shimei** kept up with them, walking on the hillside;
19.16 the same time the Benjaminite **Shimei** son of Gera
19.18 was getting ready to cross, **Shimei** threw himself down
19.21 **"Shimei** should be put to death because he cursed the one
19.23 And he said to **Shimei,** "I give you my word
1 Kgs 2. 8 "There is also **Shimei** son of Gera,
2.36 Then the king sent for **Shimei** and said to him, "Build
2.38 "Very well, Your Majesty," **Shimei** answered.
2.39 years later, however, two of **Shimei's** slaves ran away
2.39 When **Shimei** heard that they were in Gath,
2.41 When Solomon heard what **Shimei** had done, [42]he sent for
2.46 king gave orders to Benaiah, who went out and killed **Shimei.**

SHINE
[SHONE]

Gen 1.15 they will **shine** in the sky to give light to the earth"
1.17 lights in the sky to **shine** on the earth, [18]to rule over
Ex 25.37 and set them up so that they **shine** towards the front.
34.29 Ten Commandments, his face was **shining** because he had been
34.30 saw that his face was **shining,** and they were afraid to go
34.35 to say, [35]and they would see that his face was **shining.**
Num 8. 2 place them so that the light **shines** towards the front."
Deut 33. 2 the sun over Edom and **shone** on his people from Mount Paran.
Judg 5.31 O Lord, but may your friends **shine** like the rising sun!
2 Sam 23. 4 God, [4]is like the sun **shining** on a cloudless dawn, the sun
1 Kgs 8.11 suddenly filled with a cloud [11]**shining** with the dazzling
2 Kgs 3.22 following morning, the sun was **shining** on the water, making
2 Chr 5.11 suddenly filled with a cloud **shining** with the dazzling light
Esth 1. 6 red feldspar, **shining** mother-of-pearl, and blue turquoise.
Job 3. 4 never again let light **shine** on it.
3. 9 Keep the morning star from **shining;**
9. 7 the sun from rising, and the stars from **shining** at night.
11.17 at noon, and life's darkest hours will **shine** like the dawn.
20.25 its **shiny** point drips with his blood, and terror grips his heart.
22.28 succeed in all you do, and light will **shine** on your path.
25. 3 Is there any place where God's light does not **shine?**
41.32 He leaves a **shining** path behind him
Ps 37. 6 he will make your righteousness **shine** like the noonday sun.
50. 2 God **shines** from Zion, the city perfect in its beauty.
56.13 presence of God, in the light that **shines** on the living.
72. 5 as long as the sun **shines,** as long as the moon gives
89.36 I will watch over his kingdom as long as the sun **shines.**
97.11 Light **shines** on the righteous, and gladness on the good.
112. 4 Light **shines** in the darkness for good men,
148. 3 praise him, **shining** stars.
Prov 6.23 Their instructions are a **shining** light;
13. 9 The righteous are like a light **shining** brightly;
Song 1.15 how your eyes **shine** with love!
4. 1 How your eyes **shine** with love behind your veil.
7. 5 Your braided hair **shines** like the finest satin;
Is 9. 2 in a land of shadows, but now light is **shining** on them.
13.10 and every constellation will stop **shining,** the sun will be
18. 4 as serenely as the sun **shines** in the heat of the day.
24.23 the sun will no longer **shine,** for the Lord Almighty will be
58. 8 "Then my favour will **shine** on you like the morning sun,
60. 1 Arise, Jerusalem, and **shine** like the sun;
60. 1 The glory of the Lord is **shining** on you!
60. 2 by darkness, But on you the light of the Lord will **shine;**
60.19 The light of my glory will **shine** on you.
62. 1 is saved, And her victory **shines** like a torch in the night.
Jer 31.35 light by day, the moon and the stars to **shine** at night.
Ezek 1. 4 Where the lightning was flashing, something **shone** like bronze.
1. 7 They **shone** like polished bronze.
1.16 each one **shone** like a precious stone, and each had another
1.27 The figure seemed to be **shining** like bronze in the
1.27 It **shone** all over with a bright light [28]that had in it
8. 2 and from the waist up he was **shining** like polished bronze.
10. 9 The wheels **shone** like precious stones, and each one had
40. 3 took me closer, and I saw a man who **shone** like bronze.
43. 2 of the sea, and the earth **shone** with the dazzling light.

Dan 2.31 giant statue, bright and **shining,** and terrifying to look at.
5. 5 where the light from the lamps was **shining** most brightly.
10. 6 His body **shone** like a jewel.
10. 6 His arms and legs **shone** like polished bronze, and his voice
12. 3 The wise leaders will **shine** with all the brightness of the sky.
12. 3 to do what is right will **shine** like the stars for ever."
Joel 2.10 sun and the moon grow dark, and the stars no longer **shine.**
3.15 sun and the moon grow dark, and the stars no longer **shine.**
Hab 3.11 and the gleam of your **shining** spear, the sun and the moon
Zech 9.16 They will **shine** in his land like the jewels of a crown.
Mt 4.16 who live in the dark land of death the light will **shine."**
5.16 your light must **shine** before people,
5.45 he makes his sun to **shine** on bad and good people alike,
13.43 Then God's people will **shine** like the sun in their Father's Kingdom.
17. 2 his face was **shining** like the sun, and his clothes were
17. 5 While he was talking, a **shining** cloud came over them,
24.29 moon will no longer **shine,** the stars will fall from heaven,
Mk 9. 3 and his clothes became **shining** white—
13.24 will no longer **shine,** [25]the stars will fall from heaven,
Lk 1.79 rise on us [79]and to **shine** from heaven on all those who
2. 9 appeared to them, and the glory of the Lord **shone** over them.
11.36 as when a lamp **shines** on you with its brightness."
23.44 the sun stopped **shining** and darkness covered the whole country
24. 4 suddenly two men in bright **shining** clothes stood by them.
Jn 1. 5 The light **shines** in the darkness,
1. 9 light that comes into the world and **shines** on all mankind.
5.35 like a lamp, burning and **shining,**
Acts 10.30 Suddenly a man dressed in **shining** clothes stood in front of
12. 7 of the Lord stood there, and a light **shone** in the cell.
26.13 coming from the sky and **shining** round me
2 Cor 4. 4 them from seeing the light **shining** on them, the light that
4. 6 The God who said, "Out of darkness the light shall **shine!"**
4. 6 God who made his light **shine** in our hearts, to bring us
4. 6 the knowledge of God's glory **shining** in the face of Christ.
Eph 5.14 rise from death, and Christ will **shine** on you."
Phil 2.15 You must **shine** among them like stars lighting up the sky,
Heb 10.32 God's light had **shone** on you, you suffered many things,
2 Pet 1.19 it is like a lamp **shining** in a dark place
1.19 the light of the morning star **shines** in your hearts.
1 Jn 2. 8 is passing away, and the real light is already **shining.**
Rev 1.15 his feet **shone** like brass that has been refined and polished,
2.18 whose eyes blaze like fire, whose feet **shine** like polished brass.
15. 6 the temple, dressed in clean **shining** linen and with gold
19. 8 She has been given clean **shining** linen to wear."
21.11 of heaven from God [11]and **shining** with the glory of God.
21.11 The city **shone** like a precious stone, like a jasper, clear
21.23 sun or the moon to **shine** on it,
21.23 because the glory of God **shines** on it,

SHIP

Gen 49.13 His shore will be a haven for **ships.**
Deut 28.68 you back to Egypt in **ships,** even though he said that you
Judg 5.17 of the Jordan, and the tribe of Dan remained by the **ships.**
1 Kgs 9.26 built a fleet of **ships** at Eziongeber, which is near Elath,
10.22 He had a fleet of ocean-going **ships** sailing with Hiram's fleet.
22.48 King Jehoshaphat built ocean-going **ships** to sail to the
2 Chr 8.18 King Hiram sent him **ships** under the command of his own
9.21 a fleet of ocean-going **ships** sailing with King Hiram's fleet.
20.36 At the port of Eziongeber they built ocean-going **ships.**
20.37 And the **ships** were wrecked and never sailed.
Ps 48. 7 to bear a child, [7]like **ships** tossing in a furious storm.
104.26 The **ships** sail on it, and in it plays Leviathan, that
107.23 over the ocean in **ships,** earning their living on the seas.
107.26 The **ships** were lifted high in the air and plunged down
Prov 23.34 sea-sick, swinging high up in the rigging of a tossing **ship.**
30.19 a **ship** finding its way over the sea,
31.14 food from out-of-the-way places, as merchant **ships** do.
Is 2.16 He will sink even the largest and most beautiful **ships.**
23. 1 As your **ships** return from Cyprus, you learn the news.
33.21 and streams, but hostile **ships** will not sail on them.
33.22 All the rigging on those **ships** is useless;
60. 8 What are these **ships** that skim along like clouds, Like
60. 9 **ships** coming from distant lands, Bringing God's people home.
Ezek 26.17 Her **ships** have been swept from the seas.
27. 4 Your builders made you like a beautiful **ship;**
27. 9 The **ship's** carpenters Were well-trained men from Byblos.
27. 9 Sailors from every sea-going **ship** Did business in your shops.
27.25 Your merchandise was carried in fleets of the largest cargo **ships.**
27.25 You were like a **ship** at sea Loaded with heavy cargo.
27.27 in your crew, Your **ship's** carpenters and your merchants,
27.27 Every soldier on board the **ship**—
27.27 All, all were lost at sea When your **ship** was wrecked.
27.29 "Every **ship** is now deserted, And every sailor has gone ashore.
30. 9 I will send messengers in **ships** to arouse the unsuspecting
Dan 11.30 The Romans will come in **ships** and oppose him, and he
11.40 with all his power, using chariots, horses, and many **ships.**
Jon 1. 3 to Joppa, where he found a **ship** about to go to Spain.
1. 4 was so violent that the **ship** was in danger of breaking up.
1. 5 had gone below and was lying in the **ship's** hold, sound
1.13 sailors tried to get the **ship** to shore, rowing with all
Acts 16.11 We left by **ship** from Troas and sailed straight across to Samothrace,
20.13 went on ahead to the **ship** and sailed off to Assos,
20.38 And so they went with him to the **ship.**
21. 2 There we found a **ship** that was going to Phoenicia,
21. 3 at Tyre, where the **ship** was going to unload its cargo.
21. 6 and we went on board the **ship** while they went back home.
27. 2 We went aboard a **ship** from Adramyttium, which was ready to
27. 6 There the officer found a **ship** from Alexandria
Acts 27.10 the cargo and to the **ship,** and loss of life as well."
27.11 and the owner of the **ship** said, and not by what Paul
27.15 It hit the **ship,** and since it was impossible
27.15 impossible to keep the **ship** headed into the wind,
27.16 There, with some difficulty, we managed to make the **ship's** boat secure.
27.17 and then fastened some ropes tight round the **ship.**
27.17 lowered the sail and let the **ship** be carried by the wind.
27.18 to throw some of the **ship's** cargo overboard,
27.19 they threw part of the **ship's** equipment overboard.
27.22 only the **ship** will be lost.
27.29 They were afraid that the **ship** would go on the rocks,
27.29 anchors from the back of the **ship** and prayed for daylight.
27.30 Then the sailors tried to escape from the **ship;**
27.30 going to put out some anchors from the front of the **ship.**
27.38 they lightened the **ship** by throwing all the wheat
27.39 if possible, they would run the **ship** aground there.
27.40 at the front of the **ship** so that the wind
27.40 would blow the **ship** forward, and we headed for shore.
27.41 But the **ship** hit a sandbank and went aground;
27.41 the front part of the **ship** got stuck and could not move,
27.44 on to the planks or to some broken pieces of the **ship.**
28.11 away on a **ship** from Alexandria, called "The Twin Gods,"
2 Cor 11.25 I have been in three **shipwrecks,**
Jas 3. 4 Or think of a **ship:**
Rev 8. 9 and a third of the **ships** were destroyed.
18.17 All the **ships'** captains and passengers,
18.19 city where all who have **ships** sailing the seas became rich

SHIRT

Ex 28. 4 an ephod, a robe, an embroidered **shirt,** a turban,
28.39 "Weave Aaron's **shirt** of fine linen and make a turban
28.40 "Make **shirts,** sashes, and caps for Aaron's sons,
29. 5 in the priestly garments—the **shirt,** the robe that goes under
29. 8 "Bring his sons and put **shirts** on them;
39.27 They made the **shirts** for Aaron and his sons, [28]and the turban,
40.14 Bring his sons and put the **shirts** on them.
Lev 8. 7 He put the **shirt** and the robe on Aaron and the sash
8.13 of Aaron forward and put **shirts** on them, put sashes round
Dan 3.21 tied them up, fully dressed—**shirts,** robes, caps, and all—
Mt 5.40 to sue you for your **shirt,** let him have your coat
10.10 for the journey or an extra **shirt** or shoes or a stick.
Mk 6. 9 Wear sandals, but don't carry an extra **shirt."**
Lk 3.11 He answered, "Whoever has two **shirts** must give one to
6.29 if someone takes your coat, let him have your **shirt** as well.
9. 3 no beggar's bag, no food, no money, not even an extra **shirt.**
Acts 9.39 and showing him all the **shirts** and coats that Dorcas had

SHOCK

Gen 34. 7 heard about it, they were **shocked** and furious that Shechem
45.27 had sent to take him to Egypt, he recovered from the **shock.**
Lev 26.32 enemies who occupy it will be **shocked** at the destruction.
Deut 28.37 you, the people will be **shocked** at what has happened to you;
1 Kgs 9. 8 and everyone who passes by will be **shocked** and amazed.
2 Chr 29. 8 he has done to them has **shocked** and frightened everyone.
Neh 13. 7 There I was **shocked** to find that Eliashib had allowed Tobiah
Job 17. 8 claim to be honest are **shocked,** and they all condemn me as
21. 5 Isn't that enough to make you stare in **shocked** silence?
Is 23. 5 Even the Egyptians will be **shocked** and dismayed when they
52.14 Many people were **shocked** when they saw him;
Jer 4. 9 priests will be **shocked** and prophets will be astonished."
5.30 A terrible and **shocking** thing has happened in the land:
18.16 All who pass by will be **shocked** at what they see;
19. 8 city that everyone who passes by will be **shocked** and amazed.
25. 9 leave them in ruins for ever, a terrible and **shocking** sight.
25.11 ruins and will be a **shocking** sight, and the neighbouring
25.18 a desert, a terrible and **shocking** sight, and so that people
29.18 scatter them, people will be **shocked** and terrified at what
49.17 that everyone who passes by will be **shocked** and terrified.
50.13 in ruins, and all who pass by will be **shocked** and amazed.
50.23 All the nations are **shocked** at what has happened to that country.
Ezek 26.18 And their people are **shocked** at such destruction."
27.35 "Everyone who lives along the coast is **shocked** at your fate.
32.10 What I do to you will **shock** many nations.
Mk 10.24 The disciples were **shocked** at these words, but Jesus went on

SHOES

Ezek 16.10 embroidered gowns and gave you **shoes** of the best leather, a
Mt 10.10 for the journey or an extra shirt or **shoes** or a stick.
Lk 10. 4 Don't take a purse or a beggar's bag or **shoes;**
15.22 Put a ring on his finger and **shoes** on his feet.
22.35 without purse, bag, or **shoes,** did you lack anything?"
Eph 6.15 your breastplate, [15]and as your **shoes** the readiness to

Am **SHOOT** see **PIERCE**

SHOOT

[SHOT]

Ex 19.13 be stoned or **shot** with arrows, without anyone touching him.
1 Sam 20.20 I will then **shoot** three arrows at it, as though it were
20.36 said to him, "Run and find the arrows I'm going to **shoot."**
20.36 The boy ran, and Jonathan **shot** an arrow beyond him.
2 Sam 11.20 Didn't you realize that they would **shoot** arrows from the walls?
11.24 Then they **shot** arrows at us from the wall, and some of
22.15 He **shot** his arrows and scattered his enemies;
1 Kgs 22.34 chance, however, a Syrian soldier **shot** an arrow which struck

2 Kgs	9.24	and with all his strength **shot** an arrow that struck Joram in
	13.16	Jehoash got them, [16] and Elisha told him to get ready to **shoot.**
	13.17	**"Shoot** the arrow!"
	13.17	As soon as the king **shot** the arrow, the prophet exclaimed,
	19.32	will not enter this city or **shoot** a single arrow against it.
1 Chr	12. 2	They could **shoot** arrows and sling stones either right-handed
2 Chr	18.33	chance, however, a Syrian soldier **shot** an arrow which struck
	26.15	his inventors made equipment for **shooting** arrows and for
Job	16.13	uses me for target-practice [13] and **shoots** arrows at me from
	20.24	from an iron sword, a bronze bow will **shoot** him down.
Ps	11. 2	aimed their arrows to **shoot** from the shadows at good men.
	18.14	He **shot** his arrows and scattered his enemies;
	21.12	He will **shoot** his arrows at them and make them turn and
	64. 7	God **shoots** his arrows at them, and suddenly they are wounded.
	144. 6	**shoot** your arrows and send them running.
Is	5.28	Their arrows are sharp, and their bows are ready to **shoot.**
	21.15	bows that are ready to **shoot,** from all the dangers of war.
	22. 3	ran away and were captured before they **shot** a single arrow.
	37.33	will not enter this city or **shoot** a single arrow against it.
Jer	50. 9	skilful hunters, **shooting** arrows that never miss the mark.
	50.14	**Shoot** all your arrows at Babylon, because it has sinned
	51. 3	give its soldiers time to **shoot** their arrows or to put on
Lam	3.13	He **shot** his arrows deep into my body.
Ezek	1.13	The fire would blaze up and **shoot** out flashes of lightning.
Hab	3. 9	You got ready to use your bow, ready to **shoot** your arrows.
Zech	9.14	he will **shoot** his arrows like lightning.
Eph	6.16	to put out all the burning arrows **shot** by the Evil One.

SHOP

Ezek	27. 9	Sailors from every sea-going ship Did business in your **shops.**
Mt	22. 5	another to his **shop,** [6] while others grabbed the servants,
	25. 9	Go to the **shop** and buy some for yourselves.'

SHORE

[SEA-SHORE]
see also **ASHORE**

Gen	22.17	are stars in the sky or grains of sand along the **seashore.**
	32.12	count, as many as the grains of sand along the **seashore."**
	49.13	His **shore** will be a haven for ships.
Ex	14.30	and the Israelites saw them lying dead on the **seashore.**
Num	34.11	the hills on the eastern **shore** of Lake Galilee, [12] then
Deut	33.19	wealth from the sea And from the sand along the **shore."**
Josh	11. 4	as many men as there are grains of sand on the **seashore.**
Judg	5.17	they remained along the **shore.**
	7.12	many camels as there were grains of sand on the **seashore.**
1 Sam	13. 5	many soldiers as there are grains of sand on the **seashore.**
2 Sam	17.11	grains of sand on the **sea-shore,** and that you lead them
1 Kgs	4.20	Israel were as numerous as the grains of sand on the **seashore;**
	9.26	is near Elath, on the **shore** of the Gulf of Aqaba, in
2 Chr	8.17	and Elath, ports on the **shore** of the Gulf of Aqaba, in
Ps	78.27	down birds, as many as the grains of sand on the **shore;**
Is	48.18	have come to you like the waves that roll on the **shore.**
Jer	31.10	listen to me, and proclaim my words on the far-off **shores.**
	33.22	stars in the sky or the grains of sand on the **sea-shore."**
	47. 4	the Philistines, all who came from the **shores** of Crete.
Ezek	27.28	The shouts of the drowning sailors Echoed on the **shore.**
	47.10	will be fishermen on the **shore** of the sea, and they will
	47.11	marshes and ponds along the **shore** will not be made fresh.
Jon	1.13	tried to get the ship to **shore,** rowing with all their might.
Mt	4.18	As Jesus walked along the **shore** of Lake Galilee, he saw
	13. 2	while the crowd stood on the **shore.**
	13.48	full, they pull it to **shore** and sit down to divide the
Mk	1.16	As Jesus walked along the **shore** of Lake Galilee, he saw
	2.13	Jesus went back again to the **shore** of Lake Galilee.
	4. 1	water, and the crowd stood on the **shore** at the water's edge.
Lk	5. 1	Jesus was standing on the **shore** of Lake Gennesaret while the
	5. 3	Simon—and asked him to push off a little from the **shore.**
Jn	6.23	were from Tiberias, came to **shore** near the place where the
	21. 8	The other disciples came to **shore** in the boat, pulling the
Acts	27.40	wind would blow the ship forward, and we headed for **shore.**
Heb	11.12	as many as the numberless grains of sand on the **sea-shore.**
Rev	12.18	And the dragon stood on the **sea-shore.**
	20. 8	for battle, as many as the grains of sand on the **sea-shore.**

SHORN see SHEAR

SHORT

Gen	44. 4	they had gone only a **short** distance from the city, Joseph
Ex	13.17	up the coast to Philistia, although it was the **shortest** way.
Num	10. 5	When **short** blasts are sounded, the tribes camped on the
	10. 6	When **short** blasts are sounded a second time, the tribes on
	10. 6	So **short** blasts are to be sounded to break camp, [7] but in
Judg	7.19	edge of the camp a **short** while before midnight, just after
2 Sam	15.20	have lived here only a **short** time, so why should I make
2 Kgs	2. 7	river, and the fifty prophets stood a **short** distance away.
	5.19	He had gone only a **short** distance, [20] when Elisha's
	6.25	of the siege the food **shortage** in the city was so severe
Ezra	9. 8	Now for a **short** time, O Lord our God, you have been
Job	8. 9	Our life is **short,** we know nothing at all;
	10. 5	Is your life as **short** as ours?
	14. 1	All lead the same **short,** troubled life.
Ps	31.10	I am exhausted by sorrow, and weeping has **shortened** my life.
	39. 5	How **short** you have made my life!
	89.47	Remember how **short** my life is;
	90. 4	yesterday, already gone, like a **short** hour in the night.
	90. 9	Our life is cut **short** by your anger;
	90.12	Teach us how **short** our life is, so that we may become
Ps	102.23	he has **shortened** my life.
Prov	6.10	"I'll just take a **short** nap," he says;
	7.27	It is a **short cut** to death.
	12.19	A lie has a **short** life, but truth lives on for ever.
Ecc	2. 3	the best way people can spend their **short** lives on earth.
	5.18	has worked for during the **short** life that God has given him;
	5.20	happy, he will not worry too much about how **short** life is.
	6.12	for a man in this **short,** useless life of his—a life
Is	28.20	sleep in a bed too **short** to stretch out on, with a
Jer	9.25	Moab, and the desert people, who have their hair cut **short.**
	25.19	all the people who cut their hair **short;**
	49.32	people who cut their hair **short,** and I will bring disaster
Dan	11.20	In a **short** time that king will be killed, but not publicly
Jn	11. 8	the disciples answered, "just a **short** time ago the people
Acts	26.28	said to Paul, "In this **short** time do you think you will
	26.29	"Whether a **short** time or a long time," Paul answered,
Phlm	15	away from you for a **short** time so that you might have
Heb	12.10	fathers punished us for a **short** time, as it seemed right to
3 Jn	9	I wrote a **short** letter to the church;

SHORT-SIGHTED see SIGHT

SHORTS

Ex	28.42	Make linen **shorts** for them, reaching from the waist
	39.28	turban, the caps, the linen **shorts,** [29] and the sash of fine
Lev	6.10	his linen robe and linen **shorts,** shall remove the greasy
	16. 4	the linen robe and **shorts,** the belt, and the turban.
Jer	13. 1	go and buy myself some linen **shorts** and to put them on;
	13. 4	River Euphrates and hide the **shorts** in a hole in the rocks."
	13. 6	told me to go back to the Euphrates and get the **shorts.**
	13.10	will become like these **shorts** that are no longer any good.
	13.11	Just as **shorts** fit tightly round the waist, so I

SHOT see SHOOT

SHOULDER

Gen	9.23	Japheth took a robe and held it behind them on their **shoulders.**
	24.15	praying, Rebecca arrived with a water-jar on her **shoulder.**
	24.18	her jar from her **shoulder** and held it while he drank.
	24.45	with a water-jar on her **shoulder** and went down to the well
	24.46	lowered her jar from her **shoulder** and said, 'Drink, and I
Ex	12.34	them in clothing, and carried them on their **shoulders.**
	28. 7	Two **shoulder-straps,** by which it can be fastened, are to
	28.12	Put them on the **shoulder-straps** of the ephod to
	28.12	carry their names on his **shoulders,** so that I, the Lord,
	28.25	attach them in front to the **shoulder-straps** of the ephod.
	28.27	the front of the two **shoulder-straps** of the ephod near the
	39. 4	They made two **shoulder-straps** for the ephod and attached
	39. 7	They put them on the **shoulder-straps** of the ephod to
	39.18	attached them in front to the **shoulder-straps** of the ephod.
	39.20	the front of the two **shoulder straps** of the ephod, near the
Num	6.19	Then, when the **shoulder** of the ram is boiled, the priest
	7. 9	they took care of had to be carried on their **shoulders.**
Deut	18. 3	are to be given the **shoulder,** the jaw, and the stomach.
Josh	4. 5	take a stone on your **shoulder,** one for each of the tribes
Judg	9.48	cut a branch off a tree, and put it on his **shoulder.**
	16. 3	He put them on his **shoulders** and carried them all the way
Ruth	3.15	of barley and helped her to lift it on her **shoulder.**
1 Sam	17. 6	and he carried a bronze javelin slung over his **shoulder.**
1 Chr	15.15	it on poles on their **shoulders,** as the Lord had commanded
Job	31.22	may they be torn from my **shoulders.**
	31.36	wear them proudly on my **shoulder** and place them on my head
Prov	27. 6	But when an enemy puts his arm round your **shoulder—**watch out!
Is	8. 8	Judah in a flood, rising **shoulder** high and covering everything."
	9. 4	that burdened them and the rod that beat their **shoulders.**
	10.27	their yoke will no longer be a burden on your **shoulders."**
	46. 7	They lift it to their **shoulders** and carry it;
Ezek	12. 6	putting your pack on your **shoulder** and going out into the
	12. 7	While everyone watched, I put the pack on my **shoulder** and left.
	12.12	who is ruling them will **shoulder** his pack in the dark and
	24. 4	pieces of meat—the **shoulders** and the legs— fill it
	29.18	were rubbed bald and their **shoulders** were worn raw, but
Lk	15. 5	that he puts it on his **shoulders** [6] and carries it back home.
Acts	12. 7	angel shook Peter by the **shoulder,** woke him up, and said,

SHOUT

Ex	32.17	Joshua heard the people **shouting** and said to Moses, "I
	32.18	"That doesn't sound like a **shout** of victory or a cry of
	32.26	gate of the camp and **shouted,** "Everyone who is on the
Lev	9.24	people saw it, they all **shouted** and bowed down with their
Num	11.25	them, they began to **shout** like prophets, but not for long.
	11.26	came on them, and they too began to **shout** like prophets.
	11.29	all his people and make all of them **shout** like prophets!"
	16.34	They **shouted,** "Run!
Josh	6. 5	are to give a loud **shout,** and the city walls will collapse.
	6.10	ordered his men not to **shout,** not to say a word until
	6.16	Joshua ordered his men to **shout,** and he said, "The Lord has
	6.20	heard it, they gave a loud **shout,** and the walls collapsed.
Judg	7.18	round the camp and **shout,** 'For the Lord and for Gideon!' "
	7.20	trumpets in their right, and **shouted,** "A sword for the Lord
	9. 7	of Mount Gerizim and **shouted** out to them, "Listen to me,
	15.14	the Philistines came running towards him, **shouting** at him.
	16. 9	She had some men waiting in another room, so she **shouted,**
	16.12	Then she **shouted,** "Samson!
	16.14	She made it tight with a peg and **shouted,** "Samson!
	16.20	Then she **shouted,** "Samson!

Judg 16.30 them [30]and **shouted,** "Let me die with the Philistines!"
18.23 They caught up with the men from Dan [23]and **shouted** at them.
1 Sam 4. 5 Israelites gave such a loud **shout** of joy that the earth shook.
4. 6 The Philistines heard the **shouting**
4. 6 and said, "Listen to all that **shouting** in the Hebrew camp!
10. 5 They will be dancing and **shouting.**
10. 6 dancing and **shouting** and will become a different person.
10.10 him, and he joined in their ecstatic dancing and **shouting.**
10.13 finished his ecstatic dancing and **shouting,** he went to the
10.24 All the people **shouted,** "Long live the king!"
17. 8 Goliath stood and **shouted** at the Israelites, "What are you
17.20 were going out to their battle line, **shouting** the war-cry.
17.52 men of Israel and Judah **shouted** and ran after them, pursuing
19.20 prophets dancing and **shouting,** with Samuel as their leader.
19.20 of Saul's men, and they also began to dance and **shout.**
19.21 more messengers, and they also began to dance and **shout.**
19.23 him also, and he danced and **shouted** all the way to Naioth.
19.24 his clothes and danced and **shouted** in Samuel's presence, and
20.37 the arrow had fallen, Jonathan **shouted** to him, "The arrow
26.14 away, [14]and **shouted** to Saul's troops and to Abner,
26.14 "Who is that **shouting** and waking up the king?"
2 Sam 6.15 Box up to Jerusalem with **shouts** of joy and the sound of
15.10 of trumpets, **shout,** 'Absalom has become king at Hebron!' "
16.16 trusted friend, met Absalom, he **shouted,** "Long live the king!
20.16 a wise woman in the city who **shouted** from the wall,
1 Kgs 1.25 feasting with him and **shouting,** 'Long live King Adonijah!'
1.34 Then blow the trumpet and **shout,** 'Long live King Solomon!'
1.39 and all the people **shouted,** "Long live King Solomon!"
1.40 all followed him back, **shouting** for joy and playing flutes,
1.45 they went into the city, **shouting** for joy, and the people
12.16 to them, they **shouted,** "Down with David and his family!
18.24 The people **shouted** their approval.
18.26 They **shouted,** "Answer us, Baal!"
2 Kgs 2.23 they **shouted.**
9.13 Jehu to stand on, blew trumpets, and **shouted,** "Jehu is king!"
9.32 Jehu looked up and **shouted,** "Who is on my side?"
11.12 people clapped their hands and **shouted,** "Long live the king!"
11.14 the people were all **shouting** joyfully and blowing trumpets.
11.14 Athaliah tore her clothes in distress and **shouted,**
18.28 the official stood up and **shouted** in Hebrew, "Listen to
1 Chr 15.28 Box up to Jerusalem with **shouts** of joy, the sound of trumpets,
16.33 trees in the woods will **shout** for joy when the Lord comes
2 Chr 10.16 to them, they **shouted,** "Down with David and his family!
13.15 The Judaeans gave a loud **shout,** and led by Abijah, they
15.14 keep the covenant, and then they **shouted** and blew trumpets.
18.31 But Jehoshaphat gave a **shout,** and the Lord God rescued him
20.19 up and with a loud **shout** praised the Lord, the God of
23.11 Joash, and everyone **shouted,** "Long live the king!"
23.13 All the people were **shouting** joyfully and blowing trumpets,
23.13 She tore her clothes in distress and **shouted,** "Treason!
32.18 The officials **shouted** this in Hebrew in order to
Ezra 3.11 Everyone **shouted** with all his might, praising the Lord,
3.12 But the others who were there **shouted** for joy.
3.13 could distinguish between the joyful **shouts** and the crying,
10.12 The people **shouted** in answer, "We will do whatever you say."
Esth 8.15 Then the streets of Susa rang with cheers and joyful **shouts.**
Job 3.18 Even prisoners enjoy peace, free from **shouts** and harsh commands.
8.21 will let you laugh and **shout** again, [22]but he will bring
30. 5 Everyone drove them away with **shouts,**
30. 5 as if they were **shouting** at thieves.
38. 7 sang together, and the heavenly beings **shouted** for joy.
38.34 Can you **shout** orders to the clouds and make them drench
39.25 get near, and they hear the officers **shouting** commands.
Ps 20. 5 Then we will **shout** for joy over your victory and celebrate
27. 6 With **shouts** of joy I will offer sacrifices in his Temple;
29. 9 while everyone in his Temple **shouts,** "Glory to God!"
32.11 You that obey him, **shout** for joy!
33. 1 All you that are righteous, **shout** for joy for what the
33. 3 song to him, play the harp with skill, and **shout** for joy!
35.21 They accuse me, **shouting,** "We saw what you did!"
35.27 want to see me acquitted **shout** for joy and say again and
42. 4 along, a happy crowd, singing and **shouting** praise to God.
47. 5 There are **shouts** of joy and the blast of trumpets, as the
60. 8 Did the Philistines think they would **shout** in triumph over me?"
65. 8 Your deeds bring **shouts** of joy from one end of the earth
65.13 Everything **shouts** and sings for joy.
66. 1 Praise God with **shouts** of joy, all people!
68. 3 they are happy and **shout** for joy.
68.33 Listen to him **shout** with a mighty roar.
71.23 I will **shout** for joy as I play for you;
74. 4 Your enemies have **shouted** in triumph in your Temple;
74.23 Don't forget the angry **shouts** of your enemies, the
81. 1 **Shout** for joy to God our defender;
96.12 trees in the woods will **shout** for joy [13]when the Lord
98. 4 praise him with songs and **shouts** of joy!
98. 6 Blow trumpets and horns, and **shout** for joy to the Lord,
104. 7 they rushed away when they heard your **shout** of command.
105.43 his chosen people out, and they sang and **shouted** for joy.
108. 9 I will **shout** in triumph over the Philistines."
118.15 Listen to the glad **shouts** of victory in the tents of
132. 9 may your people **shout** for joy!
132.16 all they do, and her people will sing and **shout** for joy.
149. 6 Let them **shout** aloud as they praise God, with their sharp
Prov 11.10 fortune, and there are joyful **shouts** when wicked men die.
Ecc 9.17 wise man than to the **shouts** of a ruler at a council
Is 10.30 **Shout,** people of Gallim!
12. 6 Let everyone who lives in Zion **shout** and sing!
13. 2 **Shout** to the soldiers and raise your arm as the signal for
16.10 No one **shouts** or sings in the vineyards.
16.10 the **shouts** of joy are ended.
Is 24.11 People **shout** in the streets because there is no more wine.
25. 5 you silence the **shouts** of cruel men, as a cloud cools a
30.22 throw them away like filth, **shouting,** "Out of my sight!"
31. 4 matter how shepherds yell and **shout,** they can't scare away a
35. 2 The desert will sing and **shout** for joy;
35. 6 and dance, and those who cannot speak will **shout** for joy.
35.10 reach Jerusalem with gladness, singing and **shouting** for joy.
36.13 the official stood up and **shouted** in Hebrew, "Listen to
42. 2 He will not **shout** or raise his voice or make loud speeches
42.11 in the city of Sela **shout** for joy from the tops of
43.14 the city gates, and the **shouts** of her people will turn into
44.23 **Shout** for joy, you heavens!
44.23 **Shout,** deep places of the earth!
44.23 **Shout** for joy, mountains, and every tree of the forest!
48.20 **Shout** the news gladly;
49.13 **Shout** for joy, earth!
51.11 Jerusalem with gladness, singing and **shouting** for joy.
52. 8 Those who guard the city are **shouting,** shouting together for joy!
52. 9 Break into **shouts** of joy, you ruins of Jerusalem!
54. 1 a childless woman, but now you can sing and **shout** for joy.
55.12 will burst into singing, and the trees will **shout** for joy.
58. 1 The Lord says, **"Shout** as loud as you can!
Jer 4. 5 **Shout** loud and clear!
4.16 These enemies will **shout** against the cities of Judah [17]and
4.19 I hear the trumpets and the **shouts** of battle.
20. 8 Whenever I speak, I have to cry out and **shout,** "Violence!
22.20 Jerusalem, go to Lebanon and **shout,** go to the land of Bashan
25.10 I will silence their **shouts** of joy and gladness and the
25.30 he will **shout** like a man treading grapes.
26. 8 speak, they seized me and **shouted,** "You ought to be killed
30.19 they will **shout** for joy.
33.11 you will hear again [11]the **shouts** of gladness and joy and
46. 3 "The Egyptian officers **shout,** 'Get your shields ready and march
48.33 there is no one to make the wine and **shout** for joy.
51.10 The Lord says, "My people **shout,** 'The Lord has shown
51.14 like a swarm of locusts, and they will **shout** with victory.
51.48 and in the sky will **shout** for joy when Babylonia falls to
51.55 The armies rush in like roaring waves and attack with noisy **shouts.**
Lam 2. 7 They **shouted** in victory where once we had worshipped in joy.
4.15 "Go away!" people **shouted.**
Ezek 8.18 They will **shout** prayers to me as loud as they can, but
9. 1 Then I heard God **shout,** "Come here, you men who are going
9. 8 downwards on the ground and **shouted,** "Sovereign Lord, are
11.13 downwards on the ground and **shouted,** "No, Sovereign Lord!
21.22 and set up battering-rams, to **shout** the battle-cry, to place
26. 2 They **shout,** 'Jerusalem is shattered!
27.28 The **shouts** of the drowning sailors Echoed on the shore.
30. 2 You are to **shout** these words:
32.21 They **shout:** 'The ungodly who were killed in battle
Dan 5. 7 He **shouted** for someone to bring in the magicians, wizards,
Amos 1.14 Then there will be **shouts** on the day of battle, and the
2. 2 while soldiers are **shouting** and trumpets are sounding.
Hab 1.15 drag them off in nets and **shout** for joy over their catch!
Zeph 3.14 Sing and **shout** for joy, people of Israel!
Zech 4. 7 in place, the people will **shout,** 'Beautiful, beautiful!' "
9. 9 **Shout** for joy, you people of Jerusalem!
9.15 They will **shout** in battle like drunken men and will shed the
Mt 3. 3 "Someone is **shouting** in the desert, 'Prepare a road
9.27 "Take pity on us, Son of David!" they **shouted.**
11.16 One group **shouts** to the other, [17]'We played wedding music for you,
12.19 He will not argue or **shout,** or make loud speeches
20.30 Jesus was passing by, so they began to **shout,** "Son of David!
20.31 But they **shouted** even more loudly, "Son of David!
21. 9 and those walking behind began to **shout,** "Praise to David's Son!
21.15 and the children **shouting** in the Temple, "Praise to David's
27.23 Then they started **shouting** at the top of their voices:
27.46 Jesus cried out with a loud **shout,** "Eli, Eli, lema sabachthani?"
Mk 1. 3 Someone is **shouting** in the desert, 'Get the road ready
10.47 heard that it was Jesus of Nazareth, he began to **shout,**
10.48 But he **shouted** even more loudly, "Son of David, take pity
11. 9 and those who followed behind began to **shout,** "Praise God!
15.13 They **shouted** back, "Crucify him!"
15.14 They **shouted** all the louder, "Crucify him!"
15.34 Jesus cried out with a loud **shout,** "Eloi, Eloi, lema sabachthani?"
Lk 3. 4 "Someone is **shouting** in the desert:
7.32 One group **shouts** to the other, 'We played wedding music for you,
8.28 down at his feet, and **shouted,** "Jesus, Son of the Most High
9.38 A man **shouted** from the crowd, "Teacher!
9.39 attacks him with a sudden **shout** and throws him into a fit,
12. 3 in a closed room will be **shouted** from the housetops.
17.13 They stood at a distance [13]and **shouted,** "Jesus!
18.39 But he **shouted** even more loudly, "Son of David!
19.40 if they keep quiet, the stones themselves will start **shouting."**
23.21 But they **shouted** back, "Crucify him!
23.23 But they kept on **shouting** at the top of their voices
23.23 that Jesus should be crucified, and finally their **shouting** succeeded.
Jn 1.23 "I am 'the voice of someone **shouting** in the desert:
12.13 and went out to meet him, **shouting,** "Praise God!
18.40 They answered him with a **shout,** "No, not him!
19. 6 chief priests and the temple guards saw him, they **shouted,**
19.12 But the crowd **shouted** back, "If you set him free, that
19.15 They **shouted** back, "Kill him!
Acts 12.22 isn't a man speaking, but a god!" they **shouted.**
14.11 they started **shouting** in their own Lycaonian language, "The
14.14 middle of the crowd, **shouting,** [15]"Why are you doing this?
16.17 She followed Paul and us, **shouting,** "These men are
16.28 But Paul **shouted** at the top of his voice, "Don't harm yourself!
17. 6 and **shouted,** "These men have caused trouble everywhere!

Acts	19.28	they became furious and started **shouting,** "Great is Artemis of Ephesus!"
	19.32	some people were **shouting** one thing,
	19.32	others were **shouting** something else,
	19.34	they all **shouted** together the same thing
	21.28	"Men of Israel!" they **shouted.**
	21.34	Some in the crowd **shouted** one thing, others something else.
	22.22	but then they started **shouting** at the top of their voices,
	23. 9	The **shouting** became louder, and some of the teachers of
	26.24	Festus **shouted** at him, "You are mad, Paul!
Gal	4.27	**Shout** and cry with joy, you who never felt the pains of
Eph	4.31	No more **shouting** or insults, no more hateful feelings of any sort.
1 Thes	4.16	There will be the **shout** of command, the archangel's voice,
Rev	6.10	They **shouted** in a loud voice, "Almighty Lord, holy and
	14.18	He **shouted** in a loud voice to the angel
	19. 3	Again they **shouted,** "Praise God!
	19.17	He **shouted** in a loud voice to all the birds flying in

SHOVEL

[WINNOWING SHOVEL]

Ex	27. 3	pans for the greasy ashes, and make **shovels,** bowls, hooks,
	38. 3	pans, the **shovels,** the bowls, the hooks, and the firepans.
Num	4.14	firepans, hooks, **shovels,** and basins.
1 Kgs	7.40	Huram also made pots, **shovels,** and bowls.
	7.40	The pots, **shovels,** and bowls
2 Kgs	25.14	They also took away the **shovels** and the ash containers
2 Chr	4.11	Huram also made pots, **shovels,** and bowls.
	4.11	The twelve bulls supporting the tank The pots, **shovels,**
Jer	52.18	They also took away the **shovels** and the ash containers
Mt	3.12	He has his **winnowing shovel** with him to thresh out all
Lk	3.17	He has his **winnowing shovel** with him, to thresh out all

SHOW

see also **SHOW OFF**

for SHOW MERCY, SHOW LOVE etc. see under next word

Gen	1.14	day from night and to **show** the time when days, years, and
	12. 1	and go to a land that I am going to **show** you.
	17.11	This will **show** that there is a covenant between you and me.
	17.13	be a physical sign to **show** that my covenant with you is
	20.13	said to her, 'You can **show** how loyal you are to me
	22. 2	a mountain that I will **show** you, offer him as a sacrifice
	31.39	take it to you to **show** that it was not my fault.
	32.10	all the kindness and faithfulness that you have **shown** me,
	41.28	I told you—God has **shown** you what he is going to
	41.39	said to Joseph, "God has **shown** you all this, so it is
Ex	9.16	But to **show** you my power I have let you live so
	13.21	a pillar of cloud to **show** them the way, and during the
	15.25	the Lord, and the Lord **showed** him a piece of wood, which
	25. 9	its furnishings according to the plan that I will **show** you.
	25.40	according to the plan that I **showed** you on the mountain.
	26.30	Tent according to the plan that I **showed** you on the mountain.
	27. 8	according to the plan that I **showed** you on the mountain.
	31.13	all time to come, to **show** that I, the Lord, have made
Lev	10. 6	or tear your clothes to **show** that you are in mourning.
	13.49	it is a spreading mildew and must be **shown** to the priest.
	19.24	dedicated as an offering to **show** your gratitude to me, the
	21. 5	cut gashes on his body to **show** that he is in mourning.
	21.10	uncombed or tear his clothes to **show** that he is in mourning.
	26.45	with their ancestors when I **showed** all the nations my power
Num	8. 4	according to the pattern that the Lord had **shown** Moses.
	13.26	they had seen and **showed** them the fruit they had brought.
	14.17	So now Lord, I pray, **show** us your power and do what
	16. 5	"Tomorrow morning the Lord will **show** us who belongs to him;
	17. 9	Moses took all the sticks and **showed** them to the Israelites.
	20.13	against the Lord and where he **showed** them that he was holy.
	33. 4	By doing this, the Lord **showed** that he was more powerful
Deut	1.33	To **show** you the way, he went in front of you in
	3.24	I know that you have **shown** me only the beginning of the
	4. 6	them faithfully, and this will **show** the people of other
	4.35	The Lord has **shown** you this, to prove to you that he
	5.24	said, 'The Lord our God **showed** us his greatness and his
	22.15	virgin, and they are to **show** it in court to the town
	34. 1	of Jericho, and there the Lord **showed** him the whole land:
Josh	3. 4	been here before, so they will **show** you the way to go.
	7. 6	till evening, with dust on their heads to **show** their sorrow.
Judg	1.24	leaving and said to him, **"Show** us how to get into the
	1.25	So he **showed** them, and the people of Ephraim and
	4.22	I'll **show** you the man you're looking for."
	13.23	he would not have **shown** us all this or told us such
Ruth	2.18	corn back into town and **showed** her mother-in-law how much
	4. 7	In this way the Israelites **showed** that the matter was settled.
1 Sam	2.34	the same day, this will **show** you that everything I have said
	4.12	To **show** his grief, he had torn his clothes and put earth
	17.18	and bring back something to **show** that you saw them and that
	24.18	Today you have **shown** how good you are to me, because you
2 Sam	1. 2	To **show** his grief, he had torn his clothes and put earth
1 Kgs	10. 9	He has **shown** how pleased he is with you by making you
	13.12	They **showed** him the road [13]and he told them to saddle his
2 Kgs	5. 8	man to me, and I'll **show** him that there is a prophet
	6. 6	The man **showed** him the place, and Elisha cut off a stick,
	8.13	"The Lord has **shown** me that you will be king of Syria,"
	11. 4	He **showed** them King Ahaziah's son Joash [5]and gave them the
	20.13	welcomed the messengers and **showed** them his wealth—
	20.13	or anywhere in his kingdom that he did not **show** them.
	20.15	There is nothing in the storerooms that I didn't **show** them."
1 Chr	17.19	to do this for me and to **show** me my future greatness.
2 Chr	9. 8	He has **shown** how pleased he is with you by making you
Neh	9.19	cloud or the fire that **showed** them the path by day and
Esth	5. 9	Mordecai did not rise or **show** any sign of respect as he
Job	19. 3	time you insult me and **show** no shame for the way you
	21.19	let him **show** that he does it because of their sins.
	24.21	widows and **showed** no kindness to childless women.
	34.32	Have you asked God to **show** you your faults, and have you
	36. 3	use what I know to **show** that God, my Creator, is just.
	36. 9	have done, [9]God **shows** them their sins and their pride.
	37. 7	he **shows** them what he can do.
	38.17	Has anyone ever **shown** you the gates that guard the dark
	38.20	Can you **show** them how far to go, or send them back
Ps	16.11	You will **show** me the path that leads to life;
	19. 1	How plainly it **shows** what he has done!
	26. 6	I wash my hands to **show** that I am innocent and march
	31.21	How wonderfully he **showed** his love for me when I was
	44. 3	of your presence, which **showed** that you loved them.
	48. 3	God has **shown** that there is safety with him inside the
	57. 5	**Show** your greatness in the sky, O God, and your glory over
	57.11	**Show** your greatness in the sky, O God, and your glory
	65. 6	in place by your strength, **showing** your mighty power.
	65. 9	You **show** your care for the land by sending rain;
	68.28	**Show** your power, O God, the power you have used on our
	77.14	you **showed** your might among the nations.
	80. 2	**Show** us your strength;
	86.17	**Show** me proof of your goodness, Lord;
	89.14	love and faithfulness are **shown** in all you do.
	92.15	This **shows** that the Lord is just, that there is no wrong
	99. 8	you **showed** them that you are a God who forgives, even
	106. 8	them, as he had promised, in order to **show** his great power.
	108. 5	**Show** your greatness in the sky, O God, and your glory over
	111. 6	He has **shown** his power to his people by giving them the
	119.41	**Show** me how much you love me, Lord, and save me
	138. 2	and faithfulness, because you have **shown** that your name and
	143. 8	**show** me the way I should go.
Prov	3. 6	in everything you do, and he will **show** you the right way.
	5. 2	properly, and your words will **show** that you have knowledge.
	14. 2	Be honest and you **show** that you have reverence for the Lord;
	14. 2	be dishonest and you **show** that you do not.
	14.29	you have a hot temper, you only **show** how stupid you are.
	17.17	Friends always **show** their love.
	18. 2	all he wants to do is to **show** how clever he is.
	18.22	it **shows** that the Lord is good to you.
	20.11	Even a child **shows** what he is by what he does;
	21.24	**Show** me a conceited person and I will show you someone
	22.29	**Show** me a man who does a good job,
	22.29	and I will **show** you a man who is better
	23.22	When your mother is old, **show** her your appreciation.
	23.29	**Show** me someone who drinks too much, who has to
	23.29	new drink, and I will **show** you someone miserable and sorry
	29. 2	**Show** me a righteous ruler
	29. 2	and I will **show** you a happy people.
	29. 2	**Show** me a wicked ruler
	29. 2	and I will **show** you a miserable people.
	30. 6	said, he will reprimand you and **show** that you are a liar."
	30.11	and do not **show** their appreciation for their mothers.
	31.28	Her children **show** their appreciation, and her husband praises
Ecc	1. 3	working, labouring, and what do you have to **show** for it?
	2.22	way through life, and what do you have to **show** for it?
	3.18	God is testing us, to **show** us that we are no better
Is	5.16	the Lord Almighty **shows** his greatness by doing what is right,
	11.12	raise a signal flag to **show** the nations that he is gathering
	26.11	**Show** them how much you love your people.
	30.27	Fire and smoke **show** his anger.
	33.10	I will **show** how powerful I am.
	33.21	The Lord will **show** us his glory.
	39. 2	Hezekiah welcomed the messengers and **showed** them his
	39. 2	or anywhere in his kingdom that he did not **show** them.
	39. 4	There is nothing in the storerooms that I didn't **show** them."
	42.13	he **shows** his power against his enemies.
	44.23	The Lord has **shown** his greatness by saving his people Israel.
	44.25	wise I refute and **show** that their wisdom is foolishness.
	49. 7	"Kings will see you released and will rise to **show** their respect;
	49.23	they will humbly **show** their respect for you.
	55. 4	of nations, and through him I **showed** them my power.
	60.14	oppressed you will come And bow low to **show** their respect.
	66. 5	and say, 'Let the Lord **show** his greatness and save you, so
	66.14	who obey me, and I **show** my anger against my enemies."
Jer	16. 6	one will gash himself or shave his head to **show** his grief.
	24. 1	The Lord **showed** me two baskets of figs placed in front of
	29.10	years are over, I will **show** my concern for you and keep
	36.24	who heard all this was afraid or **showed** any sign of sorrow.
	38.21	But the Lord has **shown** me in a vision what will happen
	42. 3	the Lord our God will **show** us the way we should go
	51.10	people shout, 'The Lord has **shown** that we are in the right.
Lam	1. 9	was easily seen, but she **showed** no concern for her fate.
	4.16	He **showed** no regard for our priests and leaders.
Ezek	1.28	This was the dazzling light that **shows** the presence of the Lord.
	5. 6	rebelled against my commands and **showed** that she was more
	7.27	This will **show** you that I am the Lord."
	8. 4	the dazzling light that **shows** the presence of Israel's God,
	8. 7	of the outer courtyard and **showed** me a hole in the wall.
	8.14	gate of the Temple and **showed** me women weeping over the
	11.25	and I told the exiles everything that the Lord had **shown** me.
	16.54	your disgrace will **show** your sisters how well-off they are.
	20.26	was to punish them and **show** them that I am the Lord.
	20.34	I will **show** you my power and my anger when I gather
	21.20	One will **show** the king the way to the Ammonite city of
	21.24	You **show** your sins in your every action.
	28.22	am the Lord, when I **show** how holy I am by punishing
	36.23	I will use you to **show** the nations that I am holy.
	38.16	my land in order to **show** the nations who I am,
	38.16	to **show** my holiness by what I do
	38.23	In this way I will **show** all the nations that I am

Ezek	39.21	nations see my glory and **show** them how I use my power
	39.27	In order to **show** the many nations that I am holy, I
	40. 4	close attention to everything I **show** you, because this is
	46.21	to the outer courtyard and **showed** me that in each of its
Dan	2.23	answered my prayer and **shown** us what to tell the king."
	2.29	who reveals mysteries, **showed** you what is going to happen.
	3.25	not tied up, and they **show** no sign of being hurt—and
	4. 2	wonders and miracles which the Supreme God has **shown** me.
	4. 3	"How great are the wonders God **shows** us!
	5.11	father was king, this man **showed** good sense, knowledge, and
	6. 3	Daniel soon **showed** that he could do better work than the
	8.19	feet, [19]and said, "I am **showing** you what the result of
	9. 5	do and have turned away from what you **showed** us was right.
	9.15	"O Lord our God, you **showed** your power by bringing
Joel	2.13	Let your broken heart **show** your sorrow;
	2.18	Then the Lord **showed** concern for his land;
Amos	7. 8	"I am using it to **show** that my people are like a
Jon	3. 5	the least, put on sackcloth to **show** that they had repented.
Mic	1. 8	To **show** my sorrow, I will walk about barefoot and naked.
	1.10	of Beth Leaphrah, **show** your despair by rolling in the dust!
	7.20	will **show** your faithfulness and constant love to your people,
Hab	2. 3	time is coming quickly, and what I **show** you will come true.
	2. 6	will taunt their conquerors and **show** their scorn for them.
Zeph	1.18	the day when the Lord **shows** his fury, not even all their
	2. 2	Lord comes upon you, before the day when he **shows** his fury.
	2. 3	escape punishment on the day when the Lord **shows** his anger.
Zech	1. 9	He answered, "I will **show** you what they mean.
	1.20	Then the Lord **showed** me four workmen with hammers.
	3. 1	In another vision the Lord **showed** me the High Priest
Mal	3.14	says or of trying to **show** the Lord Almighty that we are
Mt	3. 8	Do those things that will **show** that you have turned from
	3.11	baptize you with water to **show** that you have repented,
	4. 8	a very high mountain and **showed** him all the kingdoms of the
	6. 2	do not make a big **show** of it, as the hypocrites do
	11.19	God's wisdom, however, is **shown** to be true by its results."
	11.21	sprinkled ashes on themselves, to **show** that they had turned
	11.25	thank you because you have **shown** to the unlearned what you
	13.26	the ears of corn began to form, then the weeds **showed** up.
	16. 1	a miracle for them, to **show** that God approved of him.
	18.15	brother sins against you, go to him and **show** him his fault.
	21.32	the Baptist came to you **showing** you the right path to take,
	22.19	**Show** me the coin for paying the tax!"
	24. 3	"and what will happen to **show** that it is the time
Mk	8.11	to perform a miracle to **show** that God approved of him.
	12.40	of their homes, and then make a **show** of saying long prayers.
	13. 4	what will happen to **show** that the time has come
	14.15	Then he will **show** you a large upstairs room, prepared and furnished,
Lk	3. 8	Do those things that will **show** that you have turned from
	4. 5	Devil took him up and **showed** him in a second all the
	6.47	words and obeys them—I will **show** you what he is like.
	7.35	God's wisdom, however, is **shown** to be true by all who
	7.47	the great love she has **shown** proves that her many sins have
	7.47	But whoever has been forgiven little **shows** only a little love."
	10.13	sprinkled ashes on themselves, to **show** that they had turned
	10.21	thank you because you have **shown** to the unlearned what you
	11.16	to perform a miracle to **show** that God approved of him.
	12. 5	I will **show** you whom to fear:
	20.24	and said to them, [24]"**Show** me a silver coin.
	20.47	and then make a **show** of saying long prayers!
	21. 7	will happen in order to **show** that the time has come
	22.12	He will **show** you a large furnished room upstairs,
	24.40	He said this and **showed** them his hands and his feet.
Jn	2.18	miracle can you perform to **show** us that you have the right
	3.20	because he does not want his evil deeds to be **shown** up.
	3.21	that the light may **show** that what he did
	5.20	Father loves the Son and **shows** him all that he himself is
	5.20	He will **show** him even greater things to do than this,
	5.36	speak on my behalf and **show** that the Father has sent me.
	8.38	about what my Father has **shown** me, but you do what your
	14. 8	Philip said to him, "Lord, **show** us the Father;
	14. 9	Why, then, do you say, '**Show** us the Father'?
	14.13	so that the Father's glory will be **shown** through the Son.
	15. 8	My Father's glory is **shown** by your bearing much fruit;
	17. 4	I have **shown** your glory on earth;
	17.10	and my glory is **shown** through them.
	20.20	After saying this, he **showed** them his hands and his side.
Acts	1.24	the thoughts of everyone, so **show** us which of these two
	2.28	You have **shown** me the paths that lead to life,
	7. 3	and go to the land that I will **show** you.'
	7.44	make it, according to the pattern that Moses had been **shown.**
	9.16	And I myself will **show** him all that he must suffer
	9.39	crowded round him, crying and **showing** him all the shirts and
	10.28	But God has **shown** me that I must not consider any person
	15. 8	knows the thoughts of everyone, **showed** his approval of the
	15.14	just explained how God first **showed** his care for the
	19.31	a message begging him not to **show** himself in the theatre.
	20.35	I have **shown** you in all things that by working hard in
	26.16	and what I will **show** you in the future.
	26.20	and do the things that would **show** they had repented.
Rom	1. 4	his divine holiness, he was **shown** with great power to be the
	2.15	Their conduct **shows** that what the Law commands is
	2.15	Their consciences also **show** that this is true, since their
	3. 4	says, "You must be **shown** to be right when you speak;
	3. 5	wrong serves to **show** up more clearly God's doing right?
	3. 9	I have already **shown** that Jews and Gentiles alike are all
	3.25	In this way God **shows** that he himself is righteous
	4.11	circumcision was a sign to **show** that because of his faith
	5. 8	But God has **shown** us how much he loves us—
	7.13	commandment sin is **shown** to be even more terribly sinful.
	7.16	don't want to do, this **shows** that I agree that the Law
Rom	9.17	to use you to **show** my power
	9.22	He wanted to **show** his anger and to make his power known.
	12. 8	whoever **shows** kindness to others should do it cheerfully.
	15. 8	behalf of the Jews, to **show** that God is faithful,
1 Cor	1.20	God has **shown** that this world's wisdom is foolishness!
	3.13	the fire will test it and **show** its real quality.
	6. 7	among yourselves **shows** that you have failed completely.
	11.10	covering over her head to **show** that she is under her
	12. 7	The Spirit's presence is **shown** in some way in each person
	15.15	More than that, we are **shown** to be lying about God,
2 Cor	4. 7	clay pots, in order to **show** that the supreme power belongs
	6. 4	in everything we do we **show** that we are God's servants
	6. 6	patience, and kindness we have **shown** ourselves to be God's servants—
	6.13	**show** us the same feelings that we have for you.
	7.11	You have **shown** yourselves to be without fault in the whole matter.
	8. 8	But by **showing** how eager others are to help, I am trying
	8.19	Lord's glory, and in order to **show** that we want to help.
	8.24	**Show** your love to them, so that all the churches will be
	9. 5	and it will **show** that you give because you want
	9.14	because of the extraordinary grace God has **shown** you.
	11.30	I will boast about things that **show** how weak I am.
	12. 5	about myself, except the things that **show** how weak I am.
	13. 3	instead, he **shows** his power among you.
	13. 7	not in order to **show** that we are a success,
Gal	2.18	then I **show** myself to be someone who breaks
	3.19	was added in order to **show** what wrongdoing is,
	4. 6	To **show** that you are his sons, God sent the Spirit of
	4.17	Those other people **show** a deep interest in you, but
	5.19	It **shows** itself in immoral, filthy, and indecent actions;
	6.17	I have on my body **show** that I am the slave of
Eph	2. 7	of his grace in the love he **showed** us in Christ Jesus.
	4. 2	**Show** your love by being tolerant with one another.
Phil	2.16	of Christ, because it will **show** that all my effort and work
	4. 5	**Show** a gentle attitude towards everyone.
	4.10	once more had the chance of **showing** that you care for me.
	4.10	stopped caring for me—you just had no chance to **show** it.
1 Tim	1.16	order that Christ Jesus might **show** his full patience in
	3.16	appeared in human form, was **shown** to be right by the Spirit,
	5.21	to obey these instructions without **showing** any prejudice or
Tit	1. 9	true teaching and also to **show** the error of those who are
	2.10	Instead, they must **show** that they are always good and faithful,
	3. 2	and always to **show** a gentle attitude towards everyone.
Heb	2. 2	ancestors by the angels was **shown** to be true,
	4. 7	This is **shown** by the fact that God sets another day,
	6.10	did or the love you **showed** for him in the help you
	8. 5	according to the pattern you were **shown** on the mountain."
	12. 7	your suffering **shows** that God is treating you as his sons.
	12.27	The words "once more" plainly **show** that the created
Jas	2.18	My answer is, "**Show** me how anyone can have faith without actions.
	2.18	I will **show** you my faith by my actions."
	2.20	Do you want to be **shown** that faith without actions is useless?
2 Pet	2.22	What happened to them **shows** that the proverbs are true:
1 Jn	3.18	it must be true love, which **shows** itself in action.
	4. 9	And God **showed** his love for us by sending his only Son
Jude	13	of the sea, with their shameful deeds **showing** up like foam.
Rev	1. 1	this revelation in order to **show** his servants what must happen
	4. 1	and I will **show** you what must happen after this."
	12.10	Now God has **shown** his power as King!
	12.10	Now his Messiah has **shown** his authority!
	17. 1	said, "Come, and I will **show** you how the famous prostitute
	21. 9	said, "Come, and I will **show** you the Bride,
	21.10	He **showed** me Jerusalem, the Holy City, coming down out of
	22. 1	The angel also **showed** me the river of the water of life,
	22. 6	has sent his angel to **show** his servants what must happen
	22. 8	the angel who had **shown** me these things,

SHOW OFF

Esth	1.11	and the king wanted to **show off** her beauty to the officials
Acts	17.18	Some of them asked, "What is this ignorant **show-off** trying to say?"
Gal	6.12	ones who want to **show off** and boast about external matters.

SHOWER

Deut	32. 2	My words will fall like **showers** on young plants, like gentle
Job	36.28	the rain pour from the clouds in **showers** for all mankind.
Ps	65.10	you soften the soil with **showers** and cause the young plants
	72. 6	like rain on the fields, like **showers** falling on the land.
Jer	3. 3	rains were held back, and the spring **showers** did not come.
	14.22	the sky by itself cannot make **showers** fall.
Ezek	34.26	I will bless them with **showers** of rain when they need it.
Mic	5. 7	the Lord for many nations, like **showers** on growing plants.
Zech	10. 1	clouds and **showers,** making the fields green for everyone.

SHREWD

2 Sam	13. 3	had a friend, a very **shrewd** man named Jonadab, the son of
Prov	17. 2	A **shrewd** servant will gain authority over a master's
	21.22	A **shrewd** general can take a city defended by strong men,
Lk	16. 8	dishonest manager praised him for doing such a **shrewd** thing;
	16. 8	this world are much more **shrewd** in handling their affairs

SHRILL

2 Pet	3.10	heavens will disappear with a **shrill** noise,

SHRINE

2 Kgs 17.29 placed them in the **shrines** that the Israelites had built.
18.22 It was the Lord's **shrines** and altars that Hezekiah destroyed,
2 Chr 32.12 one who destroyed the Lord's **shrines** and altars and then
Is 15. 2 The people of Dibon climb the hill to weep at the **shrine.**
16.12 to their mountain **shrines** and to their temples to pray,
36. 7 It was the Lord's **shrines** and altars that Hezekiah destroyed
65. 7 burnt incense at pagan hill **shrines** and spoken evil of me.
Ezek 7. 7 more celebrations at the mountain **shrines,** only confusion.
18. 6 Israelites or eat the sacrifices offered at forbidden **shrines.**
18.11 He eats sacrifices offered at forbidden **shrines** and seduces
18.12 He goes to pagan **shrines,** worships disgusting idols,
18.15 Israelites or eat the sacrifices offered at forbidden **shrines.**
Hos 10. 8 The hilltop **shrines** of Aven, where the people of Israel

SHRINK

Num 5.21 your genital organs to **shrink** and your stomach to swell up.
5.22 cause it to swell up and your genital organs to **shrink."**
5.27 stomach will swell up and her genital organs will **shrink.**
Nah 3. 7 All who see you will **shrink** back.
Zeph 2.15 Everyone who passes by will **shrink** back in horror.
Mt 9.16 for the new patch will **shrink** and make an even bigger hole
Mk 2.21 because the new patch will **shrink** and tear off some of the

SHRIVEL

Is 5.24 as straw and dry grass **shrivel** and burn in the fire, your
Lam 4. 8 their skin, dry as wood, has **shrivelled** on their bones.

SHUDDER

Job 4.14 I trembled and **shuddered;**
18.20 all who hear of his fate **shudder** and tremble with fear.
Ezek 32.10 When I swing my sword, kings will **shudder** with fright.

SHUNEM

City in Issachar.

Josh 19.18 Its area included Jezreel, Chesulloth, **Shunem,**
1 Sam 28. 4 Philistine troops assembled and camped near the town of **Shunem;**
1 Kgs 1. 3 a beautiful girl, and in **Shunem** they found such a girl named
1.15 and Abishag, the girl from **Shunem,** was taking care of him.
2.17 to let me have Abishag, the girl from **Shunem,** as my wife."
2 Kgs 4. 8 One day Elisha went to **Shunem,** where a rich woman lived.
4. 8 every time he went to **Shunem** he would have his meals at
4.11 One day Elisha returned to **Shunem** and went up to his
4.25 servant Gehazi, "Look—there comes the woman from **Shunem!**
8. 1 the woman who lived in **Shunem,** whose son he had brought back

SHUT

Gen 7.16 Then the Lord **shut** the door behind Noah.
19.10 out, pulled Lot back into the house, and **shut** the door.
Num 12.14 So let her be **shut** out of the camp for a week,
12.15 Miriam was **shut** out of the camp for seven days, and the
Josh 2. 7 The king's men left the city, and then the gate was **shut.**
6. 1 gates of Jericho were kept **shut** and guarded to keep the
1 Sam 6.10 hitched them to the wagon, and **shut** the calves in the barn.
2 Kgs 6.32 Now, when he gets here, **shut** the door and don't let him
2 Chr 14. 7 walls and towers, and gates that can be **shut** and barred.
Neh 13.19 the city gates to be **shut** at the beginning of every Sabbath,
Ps 33. 7 he **shut** up the ocean depths in storerooms.
63.11 name will praise him, but the mouths of liars will be **shut.**
Prov 17.28 and intelligent if he stays quiet and keeps his mouth **shut.**
Is 22.22 he opens, no one will **shut,** and what he shuts, no one
24.22 He will **shut** them in prison until the time of their
26.20 Go into your houses, my people, and **shut** the door behind you.
Lam 3. 5 He has **shut** me in a prison of misery and anguish.
Ezek 3.24 said to me, "Go home and **shut** yourself up in the house.
46. 2 The gate must not be **shut** until evening.
Dan 6.22 God sent his angel to **shut** the mouths of the lions so
Jon 2. 6 mountains, into the land whose gates lock **shut** for ever.
Heb 11.33 They **shut** the mouths of lions, [34] put out fierce fires,
Rev 11. 6 They have authority to **shut** up the sky

SHUTTLE

Job 7. 6 My days pass by without hope, pass faster than a weaver's **shuttle.**

SIBBOLETH

see also **SHIBBOLETH.**

Judg 12. 6 But he would say **"Sibboleth,"** because he could not pronounce

Am **SICK** see **ILL**

SICK

[SEA-SICK]

Num 11.20 it comes out of your ears, until you are **sick** of it.
Deut 7.15 will protect you from all **sickness,** and he will not bring on
1 Kgs 8.37 disease or **sickness** among them, [38] listen to their prayers.
2 Chr 6.28 disease or **sickness** among them, [29] listen to their prayers.
36.17 on anyone, young or old, man or woman, **sick** or healthy.
Job 6. 7 for food like that, and everything I eat makes me **sick.**
9.21 I am **sick** of living.
33.19 a man by sending **sickness** and filling his body with pain.
33.20 The **sick** man loses his appetite, and even the finest
Ps 35.13 But when they were **sick,** I dressed in mourning;
41. 3 them when they are **sick** and will restore them to health.
Prov 1.31 what you deserve, and your own actions will make you **sick.**
18.14 sustain you when you are **sick,** but if you lose it, your
23.34 on the ocean, **sea-sick,** swinging high up in the rigging
Ecc 5.17 our lives in darkness and grief, worried, angry, and **sick.**
Is 1. 5 covered with wounds, and your heart and mind are **sick.**
10.18 in the same way that a fatal **sickness** destroys a man.
Jer 6. 7 **sickness** and wounds are all I see.
8.18 I am **sick** at heart.
14. 4 and the ground is dried up, the farmers are **sick** at heart;
15. 9 she is disgraced and **sick** at heart.
17. 9 it is too **sick** to be healed.
Lam 1.22 I groan in misery, and I am **sick** at heart."
5.17 We are **sick** at our very hearts and can hardly see
Ezek 5.12 your people will die from **sickness** and hunger in the city;
5.17 and will send **sickness,** violence, and war to kill you.
7.15 in the streets, and **sickness** and hunger in the houses.
7.15 anyone in the city will be a victim of **sickness** and hunger.
34. 4 healed those that are **sick,** bandaged those that are hurt,
34.16 bandage those that are hurt, and heal those that are **sick;**
34.21 You pushed the **sick** ones aside and butted them away from
Hos 5.13 "When Israel saw how **sick** she was and when Judah saw
Mal 1. 8 you bring a blind or **sick** or lame animal to sacrifice to
1.13 you bring a stolen animal or one that is lame or **sick.**
Mt 4.23 Kingdom, and healing people who had all kinds of disease and **sickness.**
4.24 all those who were **sick,** suffering from all kinds of diseases
8. 6 "Sir, my servant is **sick** in bed at home, unable to move
8.14 there he saw Peter's mother-in-law **sick** in bed with a fever.
8.16 and healed all who were **sick.**
8.17 "He himself took our **sickness** and carried away our diseases."
9.12 well do not need a doctor, but only those who are **sick.**
9.35 Kingdom, and healed people with every kind of disease and **sickness.**
10. 1 evil spirits and to heal every disease and every **sickness.**
10. 8 Heal the **sick,** bring the dead back to life,
14.35 So they sent for the **sick** people in all the surrounding
15.30 dumb, and many other **sick** people, whom they placed at Jesus'
25.36 I was **sick** and you took care of me, in prison and
25.39 did we ever see you **sick** or in prison, and visit you?'
25.43 I was **sick** and in prison but you would not take care
25.44 a stranger or naked or **sick** or in prison, and would not
Mk 1.30 Simon's mother-in-law was **sick** in bed with a fever,
1.32 brought to Jesus all the **sick** and those who had demons.
1.34 Jesus healed many who were **sick** with all kinds of diseases
2.17 well do not need a doctor, but only those who are **sick.**
6. 5 he placed his hands on a few **sick** people and healed them.
6.13 and rubbed olive-oil on many **sick** people and healed them.
6.55 they brought to him **sick** people lying on their mats.
16.18 will place their hands on **sick** people, who will get well."
Lk 4.38 Simon's mother-in-law was **sick** with a high fever,
4.40 who had friends who were **sick** with various diseases brought
5.17 power of the Lord was present for Jesus to heal the **sick.**
5.31 well do not need a doctor, but only those who are **sick.**
7. 2 the man was **sick** and about to die.
7.21 many people of their **sicknesses,** diseases, and evil spirits,
9. 2 and to heal the **sick,** [3] after saying to them, "Take nothing
10. 9 heal the **sick** in that town, and say
Jn 5. 3 A large crowd of **sick** people were lying in the porches—
5. 7 The **sick** man answered, "Sir, I have no one here to put
Acts 5.15 what the apostles were doing, **sick** people were carried out
28. 8 Publius' father was in bed, **sick** with fever and dysentery.
28. 9 all the other **sick** people on the island came
Jas 5.15 This prayer made in faith will heal the **sick** person;

SICKLE

Deut 23.25 your hands, but you must not cut any corn with a **sickle.**
1 Sam 13.20 to get their ploughs, hoes, axes, and **sickles** sharpened;
Mk 4.29 cutting it with his **sickle,** because harvest time has come.
Rev 14.14 of gold on his head and a sharp **sickle** in his hand.
14.15 on the cloud, "Use your **sickle** and reap the harvest,
14.16 on the cloud swung his **sickle** on the earth, and the earth's
14.17 of the temple in heaven, and he also had a sharp **sickle.**
14.18 angel who had the sharp **sickle,** "Use your sickle, and cut
14.19 So the angel swung his **sickle** on the earth, cut the

SIDE

[OTHER SIDE]

Gen 6.16 Build it with three decks and put a door in the **side.**
38.16 over to her at the **side** of the road and said, "All
49.17 be a snake at the **side** of the road, A poisonous snake
Ex 32.26 "Everyone who is on the Lord's **side** come over here!"
Num 33.55 and thorns in your **sides,** and they will fight against you.
Deut 30.13 Nor is it on the **other side** of the ocean.
Josh 10.14 The Lord fought on Israel's **side!**
Judg 3.16 He had it fastened on his right **side** under his clothes.
3.21 the sword from his right **side** and plunged it into the king's
4.21 the peg right through the **side** of his head and into the
5. 6 went through the land, and travellers used the **side** roads.
1 Sam 14.21 had been on the Philistine **side** and had gone with them to
14.21 the camp, changed **sides** again and joined Saul and Jonathan.
20.21 I tell him, 'Look, the arrows are on this **side** of you;
20.22 arrows are on the **other side** of you,' then leave, because
20.30 I know you are taking **sides** with David and are disgracing
23.26 his men were on one **side** of the hill,
23.26 from David and his men, who were on the **other side.**
26.13 crossed over to the **other side** of the valley to the top
28. 1 understand that you and your men are to fight on my **side."**

1 Sam 31. 7 the Israelites on the **other side** of the Valley of Jezreel
2 Sam 2.13 one group on one **side** of the pool
2.13 and the other group on the opposite **side.**
2.14 the young men from each **side** to fight an armed contest."
2.16 his sword into his opponent's **side,**
3.12 and I will help you win all Israel over to your **side."**
10. 4 David's messengers, shaved off one **side** of their beards, cut
15. 3 the law is on your **side,** but there is no representative of
16.18 I am on the **side** of the one chosen by the Lord,
18. 4 Then he stood by the **side** of the gate as his men
1 Kgs 1. 8 Rei, and David's bodyguard were not on Adonijah's **side.**
2.22 and Abiathar the priest and Joab are on his **side!"**
3.20 took my son from my **side** while I was asleep, and carried
6.27 They were placed **side by side** in the Most Holy Place, so
7. 4 In each of the two **side** walls there were three rows of
2 Kgs 2. 8 and he and Elisha crossed to the **other side** on dry ground.
2.14 again, and it divided, and he walked over to the **other side.**
6.11 one of you is on the **side** of the king of Israel?"
6.16 "We have more on our **side** than they have on theirs."
9.32 Jehu looked up and shouted, "Who is on my **side?"**
1 Chr 11.13 He fought on David's **side** against the Philistines at the
12.18 God is on your **side."**
12.19 Manasseh went over to David's **side** when he was marching out
12.20 Manasseh who went over to David's **side** when he was returning:
22.18 God has been with you and given you peace on all **sides.**
2 Chr 3.11 where they stood **side by side** facing the entrance.
14. 7 He has protected us and given us security on every **side."**
14.10 to fight him, and both **sides** took up their positions in the
15. 9 had come over to Asa's **side** from Ephraim, Manasseh, and
15.15 and he accepted them and gave them peace on every **side.**
19. 2 wicked and to take the **side** of those who hate the Lord?
19.11 and may the Lord be on the **side** of the right!"
20.30 ruled in peace, and God gave him security on every **side.**
32. 7 We have more power on our **side** than he has on his.
35.21 God is on my **side,** so don't oppose me, or he will
Neh 2. 6 The emperor, with the empress sitting at his **side,** approved
6.18 Judah were on his **side** because of his Jewish father-in-law,
Job 3.23 God keeps their future hidden and hems them in on every **side.**
11. 6 He would tell you there are many **sides** to wisdom;
16.13 arrows at me from every **side**— arrows that pierce and wound
16.19 someone in heaven to stand up for me and take my **side.**
18.12 disaster stands and waits at his **side.**
19.10 He batters me from every **side.**
23.11 the road he chooses, and never wander to either **side.**
29.16 to the poor and took the **side** of strangers in trouble.
32.21 I will not take **sides** in this debate;
34.19 He does not take the **side** of rulers nor favour the rich
Ps 3. 6 of the thousands of enemies who surround me on every **side.**
17. 7 at your **side** I am safe from my enemies.
56. 9 God is on my **side**— [10] the Lord, whose promises I praise.
60.12 With God on our **side** we will win;
88.17 they close in on me from every **side.**
94.16 Who took my **side** against the evildoers?
108.13 With God on our **side** we will win;
110. 5 The Lord is at your right **side;**
118.11 They were round me on every **side;**
121. 5 he is by your **side** to protect you.
124. 1 What if the Lord had not been on our **side?**
124. 2 had not been on our **side** when our enemies attacked us,
139. 5 You are all round me on every **side;**
Prov 28. 4 regard for the law, you are on the **side** of the wicked;
Ecc 4. 1 help them, because their oppressors had power on their **side.**
Is 7. 6 the people into joining their **side,** and then put Tabeel's
26.15 territory on every **side,** and this has brought you honour.
52.12 Lord your God will lead you and protect you on every **side.**
54. 3 You will extend your boundaries on all **sides;**
58. 8 my presence will protect you on every **side.**
59. 4 You go to court, but you haven't got justice on your **side.**
Jer 12. 9 people are like a bird attacked from all **sides** by hawks.
20.11 you, Lord, are on my **side,** strong and mighty, and those who
47. 3 their hands will hang limp at their **sides.**
49. 5 I will bring terror on you from every **side.**
49.32 short, and I will bring disaster on them from every **side.**
50.26 Attack it from every **side** and break open the places
51. 2 they will attack from every **side** and leave the land bare.
51.31 Babylonia that his city has been broken into from every **side.**
Lam 1.17 The Lord has called enemies against me from every **side;**
Ezek 4. 4 lie down on your left **side,** and I will place on you
4. 6 turn over on your right **side** and suffer for the guilt of
4. 8 you cannot turn from one **side** to the other until the siege
4. 9 eat during the 390 days you are lying on your left **side.**
16.24 evil, and then [24] by the **side** of every road you built
28.23 be attacked from every **side,** and your people will be killed.
32.21 who fought on the Egyptian **side** welcome the Egyptians to the
36. 9 I am on your **side,** and I will make sure that your
38.22 his army and on the many nations that are on his **side.**
42.17 measured the north side, the south side, and the west **side;**
Mt 4.15 to the sea, on the **other side** of the Jordan, Galilee, land
4.25 Jerusalem, Judaea, and the land on the **other side** of the Jordan.
8.18 ordered his disciples to go to the **other side** of the lake.
8.28 territory of Gadara on the **other side** of the lake, he was
8.32 whole herd rushed down the **side** of the cliff into the lake
14.22 go on ahead to the **other side** of the lake, while he
16. 5 disciples crossed over to the **other side** of the lake, they
19. 1 territory of Judaea on the **other side** of the River Jordan.
21.19 saw a fig-tree by the **side** of the road and went to
Mk 3. 8 the territory on the east **side** of the Jordan, and from the
4.35 "Let us go across to the **other side** of the lake."
5. 1 his disciples arrived on the **other side** of Lake Galilee, in
5.13 in all—rushed down the **side** of the cliff into the lake
5.21 Jesus went back across to the **other side** of the lake.
Mk 5.24 with Jesus that they were crowding him from every **side.**
6.45 him to Bethsaida, on the **other side** of the lake, while he
8.13 the boat, and started across to the **other side** of the lake.
16.19 taken up to heaven and sat at the right **side** of God.
Lk 8.22 them, "Let us go across to the **other side** of the lake."
8.33 whole herd rushed down the **side** of the cliff into the lake
8.40 When Jesus returned to the **other side** of the lake, the
8.42 As Jesus went along, the people were crowding him from every **side.**
9.47 child, stood him by his **side,** [48] and said to them,
10.31 he saw the man, he walked on by, on the **other side.**
10.32 at the man, and then walked on by, on the **other side.**
16.23 up and saw Abraham, far away, with Lazarus at his **side.**
17.24 lights it up from one **side** to the other, so will the
19.43 blockade you, and close in on you from every **side.**
Jn 1.18 God and is at the Father's **side,** he has made him known.
1.28 in Bethany on the east **side** of the River Jordan, where John
3.26 with you on the east **side** of the Jordan, the one you
6.22 which had stayed on the **other side** of the lake realized that
6.25 people found Jesus on the **other side** of the lake, they said
8.44 has never been on the **side** of truth, because there is no
13.25 disciple moved closer to Jesus' **side** and asked, "Who is it,
19.18 two other men, one on each **side,** with Jesus between them.
19.34 plunged his spear into Jesus' **side,** and at once blood and
20.20 After saying this, he showed them his hands and his **side.**
20.25 those scars and my hand in his **side,** I will not believe."
20.27 then stretch out your hand and put it in my **side.**
21. 6 net out on the right **side** of the boat, and you will
Acts 2.33 been raised to the right-hand **side** of God, his Father, and
5.31 raised him to his right-hand **side** as Leader and Saviour, to
7.55 God's glory and Jesus standing at the right-hand **side** of God.
7.56 and the Son of Man standing at the right-hand **side** of God!"
14.19 the crowd over to their **side,** stoned Paul and dragged him
27. 4 us, we sailed on the sheltered **side** of the island of Cyprus.
27. 7 we sailed down the sheltered **side** of the island of Crete,
Rom 8.34 and is at the right-hand **side** of God, pleading with him for
Eph 1.20 and seated him at his right **side** in the heavenly world.
Phil 2.25 worked and fought by my **side** and who has served as your
Col 3. 1 Christ sits on his throne at the right-hand **side** of God.
Heb 1. 3 in heaven at the right-hand **side** of God, the Supreme Power.
10.12 ever, and then he sat down at the right-hand **side** of God.
12. 2 he is now seated at the right-hand **side** of God's throne.
1 Pet 3.22 and is at the right-hand **side** of God, ruling over all angels
Rev 4. 6 throne on each of its **sides,** were four living creatures
5. 1 with writing on both **sides** and was sealed with seven seals.
21.13 There were three gates on each **side:**
22. 2 On each **side** of the river was the tree of life, which

SIDON (1)

Port on the Mediterranean coast, in n. Palestine.

Gen 10.19 Canaanite borders reached from **Sidon** southwards to Gerar
49.13 His territory will reach as far as **Sidon.**
Deut 3. 9 Hermon is called Sirion by the **Sidonians,**
Josh 11. 8 north as Misrephoth Maim and **Sidon,** and as far east as the
13. 4 Mearah (which belonged to the **Sidonians),** as far as Aphek,
13. 6 all the territory of the **Sidonians,** who live in the
19.28 Cabul, [28] Ebron, Rehob, Hammon, and Kanah, as far as **Sidon.**
Judg 1.31 in the cities of Acco, **Sidon,** Ahlab, Achzib, Helbah, Aphek,
3. 3 cities, all the Canaanites, the **Sidonians,** and the Hivites
10. 6 the gods of Syria, of **Sidon,** of Moab, of Ammon, and of
10.12 the Philistines, [12] the **Sidonians,** the Amalekites,
18. 7 saw how safely the people there were living, like the **Sidonians.**
18. 7 lived far away from the **Sidonians** and had no dealings with
18.27 was a long way from **Sidon,** and they had no dealings with
2 Sam 24. 6 they went to Dan, and from Dan they went west to **Sidon.**
1 Kgs 11. 1 Hittite women and women from Moab, Ammon, Edom, and **Sidon.**
11. 5 worshipped Astarte the goddess of **Sidon,** and Molech the
11.33 Astarte, the goddess of **Sidon;**
16.31 the daughter of King Ethbaal of **Sidon,** and worshipped Baal.
17. 9 "Now go to the town of Zarephath, near **Sidon,** and stay there.
2 Kgs 23.13 idols—Astarte the goddess of **Sidon,** Chemosh the god of Moab,
1 Chr 22. 4 the people of Tyre and **Sidon** to bring him a large number
Ezra 3. 7 of Tyre and **Sidon** in exchange for cedar-trees from Lebanon,
Is 23. 2 Wail, you merchants of **Sidon!**
23. 4 City of **Sidon,** you are disgraced!
23.12 City of **Sidon,** your happiness has ended, and your people
Jer 25.19 all the kings of Tyre and **Sidon;**
27. 3 Edom, Moab, Ammon, Tyre, and **Sidon** through their ambassadors
47. 4 to cut off from Tyre and **Sidon** all the help that remains.
Ezek 27. 8 Your oarsmen were from the cities of **Sidon** and Arvad.
28.21 The Lord said to me, [21] "Mortal man, denounce the city of **Sidon.**
28.22 I am your enemy, **Sidon;**
32.30 princes of the north are there, and so are the **Sidonians.**
Joel 3. 4 to do to me, Tyre, **Sidon,** and all the regions of Philistia?
Zech 9. 2 so do the cities of Tyre and **Sidon,** with all their skill.
Mt 11.21 been performed in Tyre and **Sidon,** the people there would
11.22 more mercy to the people of Tyre and **Sidon** than to you!
15.21 went off to the territory near the cities of Tyre and **Sidon.**
Mk 3. 8 Jordan, and from the region round the cities of Tyre and **Sidon.**
7.31 Tyre and went on through **Sidon** to Lake Galilee, going by way
Lk 4.26 to a widow living in Zarephath in the territory of **Sidon.**
6.17 Jerusalem and from the coastal cities of Tyre and **Sidon;**
10.13 been performed in Tyre and **Sidon,** the people there would
10.14 more mercy on Judgement Day to Tyre and **Sidon** than to you.
Acts 12.20 the people of Tyre and **Sidon,** so they went in a group
27. 3 The next day we arrived at **Sidon.**

SIEGE

Deut 20.19 its fruit-trees, even though the **siege** lasts a long time.
20.20 use them in the **siege** mounds until the city is captured.
28.54 become so desperate during the **siege** that he will eat some
1 Kgs 20. 1 chariots, he marched up, laid **siege** to Samaria, and launched
2 Kgs 6.24 army against Israel and laid **siege** to the city of Samaria.
6.25 As a result of the **siege** the food shortage in the city
17. 5 the third year of the **siege,** [6] which was the ninth year of
18.10 In the third year of the **siege,** Samaria fell;
19.32 near the city, and no **siege-mounds** will be built round it.
24.11 During the **siege** Nebuchadnezzar himself came to Jerusalem,
25. 1 camp outside the city, built **siege** walls round it, [2] and
25. 2 and kept it under **siege** until Zedekiah's eleventh year.
2 Chr 32.10 people the confidence to remain in Jerusalem under **siege.**
Job 19.12 they dig trenches and lay **siege** to my tent.
Is 1. 8 is left, a city under **siege**—as defenceless as a watchman's
21. 2 Army of Media, lay **siege** to the cities!
23.13 who put up **siege-towers,** tore down the fortifications of Tyre,
37.33 near the city, and no **siege-mounds** will be built round it.
Jer 10.17 People of Jerusalem, you are under **siege!**
13.19 The towns of southern Judah are under **siege;**
19. 9 The **siege** will be so terrible that the people inside the
32.24 "The Babylonians have built **siege** mounds round the city
33. 4 be torn down as a result of the **siege** and the attack.
52. 4 camp outside the city, built **siege** walls round it, [5] and
52. 5 and kept it under **siege** until Zedekiah's eleventh year.
Ezek 4. 2 Then, to represent a **siege,** put trenches, earthworks,
4. 3 It is under **siege,** and you are the one besieging it.
4. 7 "Fix your eyes on the **siege** of Jerusalem.
4. 8 turn from one side to the other until the **siege** is over.
5. 2 a third of it in the city when the **siege** is over.
24. 2 the king of Babylonia is beginning the **siege** of Jerusalem.
Dan 11.15 king of Syria will lay **siege** to a fortified city and capture
Nah 3.14 Draw water to prepare for a **siege,** and strengthen

SIEVE

Amos 9. 9 command and shake the people of Israel like corn in a **sieve.**

SIFT

2 Sam 4. 6 drowsy while she was **sifting** wheat and had fallen asleep,

SIGH

Ps 5. 1 Listen to my words, O Lord, and hear my **sighs.**
77. 3 When I think of God, I **sigh;**
2 Cor 5. 2 And now we **sigh,** so great is our desire that our home

SIGHT
[EYESIGHT, SHORT-SIGHTED]

Gen 6.11 was evil in God's **sight,** and violence had spread everywhere.
48.10 Jacob's **eyesight** was failing because of his age, and he
Ex 4.11 Who gives him **sight** or makes him blind?
10.28 He said to Moses, "Get out of my **sight!**
Num 15.15 You and they are alike in the Lord's **sight;**
20.27 up Mount Hor in the **sight** of the whole community, [28] and
25. 6 into his tent in the **sight** of Moses and the whole community,
Deut 4.25 is evil in the Lord's **sight,** and it will make him angry.
11. 6 In the **sight** of everyone the earth opened up and swallowed them,
34. 7 he was as strong as ever, and his **eyesight** was still good.
34.12 things that Moses did in the **sight** of all Israel.
Josh 10.10 The Lord made the Amorites panic at the **sight** of Israel's army.
1 Sam 2.17 extremely serious in the Lord's **sight,** because they treated
6.13 They were overjoyed at the **sight.**
9.17 When Samuel caught **sight** of Saul, the Lord said to him,
2 Sam 6.20 fool in the **sight** of the servant-girls of his officials!"
13.17 personal servant and said, "Get this woman out of my **sight!**
16.22 palace roof, and in the **sight** of everyone Absalom went in
1 Kgs 21.20 completely to doing what is wrong in the Lord's **sight.**
21.25 doing wrong in the Lord's **sight** as Ahab—all at the urging
22.43 him, he did what was right in the **sight** of the Lord;
2 Kgs 6.20 their **sight,** and they saw that they were inside Samaria.
17.17 what is wrong in the Lord's **sight,** and so aroused his anger.
17.18 them from his **sight,** leaving only the kingdom
17.20 enemies until at last he had banished them from his **sight.**
17.23 Lord banished them from his **sight,** as he had warned through
22.19 will make it a terrifying **sight,** a place whose name people
23.27 people of Judah from my **sight,** and I will reject Jerusalem,
24. 3 people of Judah from his **sight** because of all the sins that
24.20 Jerusalem and Judah that he banished them from his **sight.**
2 Chr 20.32 him, he did what was right in the **sight** of the Lord;
Job 4.17 anyone be righteous in the **sight** of God or be pure before
11. 4 you claim you are pure in the **sight** of God.
15.15 even they are not pure in his **sight.**
25. 4 Can anyone be righteous or pure in God's **sight?**
26. 6 no covering shields it from his **sight.**
33. 6 are the same in God's **sight,** both of us were formed from
35. 1 you are innocent in God's **sight,** [3] or to ask God, "How does
Ps 5. 5 You cannot stand the **sight** of proud men;
39. 5 In your **sight** my lifetime seems nothing.
107.18 they couldn't stand the **sight** of food and were close to death.
118.23 what a wonderful **sight** it is!
143. 2 no one is innocent in your **sight.**
146. 8 The Lord sets prisoners free [8] and gives **sight** to the blind.
Prov 23.33 Weird **sights** will appear before your eyes, and you will
Is 30.22 throw them away like filth, shouting, "Out of my **sight!"**
66.24 The **sight** of them will be disgusting to all mankind."
Jer 7.15 drive you out of my **sight** as I drove out your relatives,
10. 2 not be disturbed by unusual **sights** in the sky, even though
10.14 At the **sight** of this, men feel stupid and senseless;
14. 6 their **eyesight** fails them because they have no food.
15. 1 make them get out of my **sight.**
16.17 their sins do not escape my **sight.**
25. 9 leave them in ruins for ever, a terrible and shocking **sight.**
25.11 and will be a shocking **sight,** and the neighbouring nations
25.18 desert, a terrible and shocking **sight,** and so that people
42.18 You will be a horrifying **sight;**
44. 6 in ruins and became a horrifying **sight,** as they are today.
44.12 They will be a horrifying **sight;**
44.22 It has become a horrifying **sight,** and people use its name as
49.13 city of Bozrah will become a horrifying **sight** and a desert;
51.17 At the **sight** of this, men feel stupid and senseless;
51.37 It will be a horrible **sight;**
51.41 What a horrifying **sight** Babylon has become to the nations!
51.43 become a horrifying **sight** and are like a waterless desert,
52. 3 Jerusalem and Judah that he banished them from his **sight.**
Ezek 32.31 "The **sight** of all these who were killed in battle will
Hab 1.13 evil, and you cannot stand the **sight** of people doing wrong.
Mt 9.30 and their **sight** was restored.
20.33 "Sir," they answered, "we want you to give us our **sight!"**
21.42 what a wonderful **sight** it is!'
Mk 8.25 his **eyesight** returned, and he saw everything clearly.
12.11 what a wonderful **sight** it is!'"
Lk 1. 6 lived good lives in God's **sight** and obeyed fully all the
1.15 He will be a great man in the Lord's **sight.**
4.18 liberty to the captives and recovery of **sight** to the blind;
7.21 diseases, and evil spirits, and gave **sight** to many blind people.
12.21 up riches for themselves but are not rich in God's **sight."**
16.15 right in other people's **sight,** but God knows your hearts.
16.15 of great value by man are worth nothing in God's **sight.**
24.31 and they recognized him, but he disappeared from their **sight.**
Jn 9.15 Pharisees, then, asked the man again how he had received his **sight.**
9.32 ever heard of anyone giving **sight** to a person born blind.
10.21 How could a demon give **sight** to blind people?"
11.37 said, "He gave **sight** to the blind man, didn't he?
Acts 1. 9 as they watched him, and a cloud hid him from their **sight.**
4.19 which is right in God's **sight**—to obey you or to obey
8.21 because your heart is not right in God's **sight.**
Rom 3.20 is put right in God's **sight** by doing what the Law requires;
4. 2 would have something to boast about—but not in God's **sight.**
4.17 promise is good in the **sight** of God, in whom Abraham
1 Cor 3.19 world considers to be wisdom is nonsense in God's **sight.**
2 Cor 4. 2 we live in God's **sight** and try to commend ourselves
5. 7 For our life is a matter of faith, not of **sight.**
7.12 plain to you, in God's **sight,** how deep your devotion to us
8.21 right, not only in the **sight** of the Lord,
8.21 but also in the **sight** of man.
2 Tim 2.15 win full approval in God's **sight,** as a worker who is not
Heb 12.21 The **sight** was so terrifying that Moses said, "I am trembling
1 Pet 3. 4 quiet spirit, which is of the greatest value in God's **sight.**
2 Pet 1. 9 not have them is so **short-sighted** that he cannot see and has
3. 8 no difference in the Lord's **sight** between one day and a
3.14 pure and faultless in God's **sight** and to be at peace with
Rev 3. 2 have done is not yet perfect in the **sight** of my God.
12. 1 Then a great and mysterious **sight** appeared in the sky.
12. 3 Another mysterious **sight** appeared in the sky.
13.13 come down out of heaven to earth in the **sight** of everyone.
15. 1 Then I saw in the sky another mysterious **sight,** great and amazing.

SIGN (1)

Gen 9.12 As a **sign** of this everlasting covenant which I am making
9.13 It will be the **sign** of my covenant with the world.
9.17 That is the **sign** of the promise which I am making to
17.13 this will be a physical **sign** to show that my covenant with
Ex 12.13 the door-posts will be a **sign** to mark the houses in which
29. 6 tie on it the sacred **sign** of dedication engraved 'Dedicated
31.13 rest, because it is a **sign** between you and me for all
31.16 Israel are to keep this day as a **sign** of the covenant.
31.17 It is a permanent **sign** between the people of Israel and me,
39.30 ornament, the sacred **sign** of dedication, out of pure gold,
Lev 8. 9 the gold ornament, the sacred **sign** of dedication, just as
Num 6. 6 His hair is the **sign** of his dedication to God, and so
Josh 2.12 treated you, and give me some **sign** that I can trust you.
22.27 but instead, as a **sign** for our people and yours,
22.28 or for sacrifice, but as a **sign** for our people and yours.'
1 Sam 14.10 because that will be the **sign** that the Lord has given us
2 Sam 15.30 was barefoot and had his head covered as a **sign** of grief.
1 Kgs 20.33 watching for a good **sign,** and when Ahab said "brother,"
2 Kgs 4.31 child, but there was no sound or any other **sign** of life.
19.29 said to King Hezekiah, "This is a **sign** of what will happen.
20. 8 Hezekiah asked, "What is the **sign** to prove that the Lord
20. 9 Lord will give you a **sign** to prove that he will keep
2 Chr 32.24 prayed, and the Lord gave him a **sign** that he would recover.
Neh 9. 1 sackcloth and put dust on their heads as **signs** of grief.
Esth 5. 9 not rise or show any **sign** of respect as he passed, Haman
Ps 60. 8 throw my sandals on Edom, as a **sign** that I own it.
74. 4 they have placed their flags there as **signs** of victory.
108. 9 throw my sandals on Edom, as a **sign** that I own it.
Prov 24.26 An honest answer is a **sign** of true friendship.
Is 7.11 "Ask the Lord your God to give you a **sign.**
7.12 Ahaz answered, "I will not ask for a **sign.**
7.14 Well then, the Lord himself will give you a **sign:**
20. 3 This is a **sign** of what will happen to Egypt and Sudan.
37.30 said to King Hezekiah, "This is a **sign** of what will happen.
38. 7 Lord will give you a **sign** to prove that he will keep
38.22 Hezekiah asked, "What is the **sign** to prove that I will be

Is 55.13 This will be a **sign** that will last for ever, a reminder
65.20 die before that would be a **sign** that I had punished them.
Jer 31.21 Set up **signs** and mark the road;
36.24 who heard all this was afraid or showed any **sign** of sorrow.
Ezek 4. 3 This will be a **sign** to the nation of Israel.
12.11 you have done is a **sign** of what will happen to them
20.12 keeping of the Sabbath a **sign** of the agreement between us,
20.20 that it will be a **sign** of the covenant we made, and
24.17 Do not go bareheaded or barefoot as a **sign** of mourning.
24.24 Then I will be a **sign** to you;
24.27 way you will be a **sign** to the people, and they will
31.15 make the underground waters cover it as a **sign** of mourning.
Dan 3.25 up, and they show no **sign** of being hurt—and the fourth
Zech 3. 8 of his, you that are the **sign** of a good future:
Mt 16. 3 but you cannot interpret the **signs** concerning these times!
24.30 Then the **sign** of the Son of Man will appear in the
Lk 1.22 to say a word, he made **signs** to them with his hands.
1.62 Then they made **signs** to his father, asking him what name
2.34 He will be a **sign** from God which many people will speak
11.30 the prophet Jonah was a **sign** for the people of Nineveh,
11.30 will be a **sign** for the people of this day.
Acts 7. 8 Abraham the ceremony of circumcision as a **sign** of the covenant.
Rom 4.11 and his circumcision was a **sign** to show that because of his
Gal 2. 9 with Barnabas and me, as a **sign** that we were all partners.

SIGN (2)

1 Kgs 21. 8 Then she wrote some letters, **signed** them with Ahab's name,
Neh 10. 1 The first to **sign** was the governor, Nehemiah son of Hacaliah,
10. 1 and then Zedekiah **signed.**
10. 1 The following also **signed:**
Is 30. 1 I did not make, and **sign** treaties against my will, piling
Jer 32.10 I **signed** and sealed the deed, had it witnessed, and
32.12 of the witnesses who had **signed** the deed of purchase and of
32.44 will buy them, and the deeds will be **signed,** sealed, and
Dan 6. 8 Majesty issue this order and **sign** it, and it will be in
6. 9 And so King Darius **signed** the order.
6.10 When Daniel learnt that the order had been **signed,** he
6.12 They said, "Your Majesty, you **signed** an order that for the
Gal 3.15 agree on a matter and **sign** an agreement, no one can break
2 Thes 3.17 This is the way I **sign** every letter;

AV SIGN
see also **MIRACLE**

Ex 13. 9 This observance will be a **reminder,** like something tied on
Num 16.38 It will be a **warning** to the people of Israel."
26.10 they became a **warning** to the people.
Deut 6. 8 on your arms and wear them on your foreheads as a **reminder.**
11.18 on your arms and wear them on your foreheads as a **reminder.**
28.46 They will be the **evidence** of God's judgement on you and
Josh 4. 6 These stones will **remind** the people of what the Lord has done.
Judg 6.17 with me, give me some **proof** that you are really the Lord.
20.38 Israelite army and the men in hiding had arranged a **signal.**
Is 19.20 They will be **symbols** of the Lord Almighty's presence in Egypt.
Jer 6. 1 trumpet in Tekoa and build a **signal** fire in Beth Haccherem.
44.29 the Lord, will give you **proof** that I will punish you in
Ezek 12. 6 What you do will be a **warning** to the Israelites."
14. 8 I will make an **example** of him.
39.15 bone, they will put a **marker** beside it so that the
Mt 26.48 The traitor had given the crowd a **signal:**
Mk 8.12 No such **proof** will be given to these people!"
Lk 2.12 And this is what will **prove** it to you:
1 Cor 14.22 speaking in strange tongues is **proof** for unbelievers,
Rev 15. 1 Then I saw in the sky another mysterious **sight,** great and amazing.

SIGNAL

Num 10. 9 attacked you, sound the **signal** for battle on these trumpets.
31. 6 of the sacred objects and the trumpets for giving **signals.**
Judg 20.38 Israelite army and the men in hiding had arranged a **signal.**
20.40 Then the **signal** appeared;
2 Sam 2.28 blew the trumpet as a **signal** for his men to stop pursuing
20.22 blew the trumpet as a **signal** for his men to leave the
Is 5.26 The Lord gives a **signal** to call for a distant nation.
7.18 Lord will whistle as a **signal** for the Egyptians to come like
11.12 The Lord will raise a **signal** flag to show the nations
13. 2 raise your arm as the **signal** for them to attack the gates
18. 3 Look for a **signal** flag to be raised on the tops of
49.22 "I will **signal** to the nations, and they will bring your
62.10 Put up a **signal** so that the nations can know [11] That the
Jer 6. 1 trumpet in Tekoa and build a **signal** fire in Beth Haccherem.
50. 2 Give the **signal** and announce the news!
51.12 Give the **signal** to attack Babylon's walls.
51.27 "Give the **signal** to attack!
Mt 26.48 The traitor had given the crowd a **signal:**
Mk 14.44 The traitor had given the crowd a **signal:**

SIGNET RING

Jer 22.24 even if you were the **signet-ring** on my right hand, I would

SIGNPOST

Ezek 21.19 Put up a **signpost** where the roads fork.
21.21 of Babylonia stands by the **signpost** at the fork of the road.

SIHON
King of the Amorites, defeated by the Israelites before they crossed R. Jordan.

Num 21.21 of Israel sent messengers to the Amorite king **Sihon** to say:
21.23 But **Sihon** would not permit the people of Israel to pass
21.26 city of the Amorite king **Sihon,** who had fought against the
21.27 "Come to Heshbon, to King **Sihon's** city!
21.28 this city of Heshbon **Sihon's** army went forth like a fire;
21.34 him what you did to **Sihon,** the Amorite king who ruled at
32.33 all the territory of King **Sihon** of the Amorites and King Og
Deut 1. 4 the Lord had defeated King **Sihon** of the Amorites, who ruled
2.24 am placing in your power **Sihon,** the Amorite king of Heshbon,
2.26 desert of Kedemoth to King **Sihon** of Heshbon with the
2.30 "But King **Sihon** would not let us pass through his country.
2.31 'Look, I have made King **Sihon** and his land helpless before you;
2.32 **Sihon** came out with all his men to fight us near the
3. 2 him as you did to **Sihon** the Amorite king who ruled in
3. 6 we did in the towns that belonged to King **Sihon** of Heshbon.
3.21 the Lord your God did to those two kings, **Sihon** and Og;
4.45 that had belonged to King **Sihon** of the Amorites, who had
29. 7 came to this place, King **Sihon** of Heshbon and King Og of
31. 4 just as he defeated **Sihon** and Og, kings of the Amorites,
Josh 2.10 also heard how you killed **Sihon** and Og, the two Amorite
9.10 King **Sihon** of Heshbon and King Og of Bashan, who lived in
12. 2 One was **Sihon,** the Amorite king who ruled at Heshbon.
12. 5 Gilead, as far as the territory of King **Sihon** of Heshbon.
13.10 ruled by the Amorite king **Sihon,** who had ruled at Heshbon.
13.21 kingdom of the Amorite king **Sihon,** who had ruled at Heshbon.
13.21 All of them had ruled the land for King **Sihon.**
13.27 Zaphon, the rest of the kingdom of King **Sihon** of Heshbon.
Judg 11.19 Israelites sent messengers to **Sihon,** the Amorite king
11.20 But **Sihon** would not let Israel do it.
11.21 gave the Israelites victory over **Sihon** and his army.
1 Kgs 4.19 had been ruled by King **Sihon** of the Amorites and King Og
Neh 9.22 land of Heshbon, where **Sihon** ruled, and the land of Bashan,
Ps 135.11 **Sihon,** king of the Amorites, Og, king of Bashan, and all
136.19 **Sihon,** king of the Amorites;
Jer 48.45 Heshbon, the city that King **Sihon** once ruled, but it is in

SILAS
Paul's companion on his second missionary journey.

Acts 15.22 Judas, called Barsabbas, and **Silas,** [23] and they sent the following letter
15.27 send you, then, Judas and **Silas,** who will tell you in person
15.32 Judas and **Silas,** who were themselves prophets,
15.40 for Cyprus, [40] while Paul chose **Silas** and left, commended
16.19 gone, they seized Paul and **Silas** and dragged them to the
16.22 And the crowd joined in the attack against Paul and **Silas.**
16.22 clothes off Paul and **Silas** and ordered them to be whipped.
16.25 About midnight Paul and **Silas** were praying and singing hymns to God,
16.29 rushed in, and fell trembling at the feet of Paul and **Silas.**
16.34 Then he took Paul and **Silas** up into his house and gave
16.36 have sent an order for you and **Silas** to be released.
16.38 that Paul and **Silas** were Roman citizens, they were afraid.
16.40 Paul and **Silas** left the prison and went to Lydia's house.
17. 1 Paul and **Silas** travelled on through Amphipolis and
17. 4 Some of them were convinced and joined Paul and **Silas;**
17. 5 attempt to find Paul and **Silas** and bring them out to the
17.10 as night came, the believers sent Paul and **Silas** to Berea.
17.14 but both **Silas** and Timothy stayed in Berea.
17.15 with instructions from Paul that **Silas** and Timothy should
17.16 was waiting in Athens for **Silas** and Timothy, he was greatly
18. 5 When **Silas** and Timothy arrived from Macedonia, Paul gave
2 Cor 1.19 was preached among you by **Silas,** Timothy, and myself, is not
1 Thes 1. 1 From Paul, **Silas,** and Timothy— To the people of the church
2 Thes 1. 1 From Paul, **Silas,** and Timothy— To the people of the church
1 Pet 5.12 letter with the help of **Silas,** whom I regard as a faithful

SILENCE

Gen 24.21 man kept watching her in **silence,** to see if the Lord had
24.45 Before I had finished my **silent** prayer, Rebecca came
Lev 10. 3 But Aaron remained **silent.**
Num 13.30 Caleb **silenced** the people who were complaining against Moses,
1 Sam 1.13 She was praying **silently;**
2. 3 **silence** your proud words.
Neh 5. 8 The leaders were **silent** and could find nothing to say.
Job 3. 1 Finally Job broke the **silence** and cursed the day on which
4.10 like lions, but God **silences** them and breaks their teeth.
4.16 Then I heard a voice out of the **silence:**
5.16 He gives hope to the poor and **silences** the wicked.
12.20 He **silences** men who are trusted, and takes the wisdom of
13.19 If you do, I am ready to be **silent** and die.
16. 6 I say helps, and being **silent** does not calm my pain.
16.18 Don't let my call for justice be **silenced!**
21. 5 Isn't that enough to make you stare in shocked **silence?**
29.10 even the most important men kept **silent.**
29.21 I gave advice, people were **silent** and listened carefully to
32.16 Shall I go on waiting when they are **silent?**
Ps 4. 4 think deeply about this, when you lie in **silence** on your beds.
12. 3 **Silence** those flattering tongues, O Lord!
30.12 So I will not be **silent;**
31.17 may they go **silently** down to the world of the dead.
31.18 **Silence** those liars— all the proud and arrogant who
35.22 So don't be **silent,** Lord;
40.10 I have not been **silent** about your loyalty and constant love.
50. 3 Our God is coming, but not in **silence;**
76. 8 world was afraid and kept **silent,** [9] when you rose up to

Ps 83. 1 O God, do not keep **silent;**
94.17 me, I would have gone quickly to the land of **silence.**
107.42 this and are glad, but all the wicked are put to **silence.**
109. 1 don't remain **silent!**
115.17 the dead, by any who go down to the land of **silence.**
Ecc 3. 7 for mending, the time for **silence** and the time for talk.
10.20 Don't criticize the king, even **silently,**
Is 15. 1 in a single night, and **silence** covers the land of Moab.
25. 5 But you, Lord, have **silenced** our enemies;
25. 5 you **silence** the shouts of cruel men, as a cloud cools a
41. 1 "Be **silent** and listen to me, you distant lands!
42.14 "For a long time I kept **silent;**
47. 5 "Sit in **silence** and darkness;
57.11 stopped honouring me because I have kept **silent** for so long?
62. 1 I will not be **silent** until she is saved, And her victory
62. 6 They must never be **silent** day or night.
Jer 16. 9 I will **silence** the sounds of joy and gladness and the happy
25.10 I will **silence** their shouts of joy and gladness and the
47. 5 to the people of Gaza, and Ashkelon's people are **silent.**
48. 2 The town of Madmen will be **silenced;**
51.55 I am destroying Babylon and putting it to **silence.**
Lam 2.10 sit on the ground in **silence,** With dust on their heads and
3.28 When we suffer, we should sit alone in **silent** patience;
Ezek 26.13 all your songs, and I will **silence** the music of your harps.
27.32 can be compared to Tyre, To Tyre now **silent** in the sea?
Amos 8. 3 They will be thrown out in **silence."**
Hab 1.13 So why are you **silent** while they destroy people who are more
2.20 let everyone on earth be **silent** in his presence.
Zeph 1. 7 so be **silent** in his presence.
Zech 2.13 Be **silent,** everyone, in the presence of the Lord, for he
Mt 22.34 Pharisees heard that Jesus had **silenced** the Sadducees, they came together,
Lk 1.20 you will remain **silent** until the day my promise to you comes
Acts 15.12 The whole group was **silent** as they heard Barnabas and
19.33 for the people to be **silent,** and he tried to make a
21.40 and motioned with his hand for the people to be **silent.**
2 Cor 11.10 boast of mine will not be **silenced** anywhere in all Achaia.
1 Tim 2.11 Women should learn in **silence** and all humility.
1 Pet 2.15 For God wants you to **silence** the ignorant talk of
Rev 8. 1 the seventh seal, there was **silence** in heaven for about half

SILK

Ezek 16.10 of the best leather, a linen headband, and a **silk** cloak.
16.13 and you always wore clothes of embroidered linen and **silk.**
Rev 18.12 their goods of linen, purple cloth, **silk,** and scarlet cloth;

SILLY

Prov 22.15 Children just naturally do **silly,** careless things, but a
26. 4 If you answer a **silly** question,
26. 4 you are just as **silly** as the person who asked it.
26. 5 Give a **silly** answer to a silly question, and the one who
Ecc 10.13 He starts out with **silly** talk and ends up with pure madness.
Hos 7.11 Israel flits about like a **silly** pigeon;

SILVER

[PIECE OF SILVER]

Gen 13. 2 with sheep, goats, and cattle, as well as **silver** and gold.
20.16 your brother a thousand **pieces of silver** as proof to all who
23.15 only four hundred **pieces of silver**—what is that between us?
23.16 the people—four hundred **pieces of silver,** according to the
24.35 and goats, cattle, **silver,** gold, male and female slaves,
24.53 he brought out clothing and **silver** and gold jewellery, and
33.19 of Hamor father of Shechem for a hundred **pieces of silver.**
37.28 sold him for twenty **pieces of silver** to the Ishmaelites, who
44. 2 Put my **silver** cup in the top of the youngest brother's sack,
44. 5 Why did you steal my master's **silver** cup?
44. 8 Why then should we steal **silver** or gold from your master's
45.22 Benjamin three hundred **pieces of silver**
Ex 3.22 and will ask for clothing and for gold and **silver** jewellery.
11. 2 to ask their neighbours for gold and **silver** jewellery."
12.35 Egyptians for gold and **silver** jewellery and for clothing.
20.23 make for yourselves gods of **silver** or gold to be worshipped
21.32 of the slave thirty **pieces of silver,** and the bull shall be
25. 3 gold, **silver,** and bronze;
26.19 the south side [19] and forty **silver** bases to go under them,
26.21 the Tent [21] and forty **silver** bases, two under each frame.
26.25 with their sixteen **silver** bases, two under each frame.
26.32 with gold, fitted with hooks, and set in four **silver** bases.
27.10 in twenty bronze bases, with hooks and rods made of **silver.**
27.17 are to be connected with **silver** rods,
27.17 hooks are to be made of **silver** and their bases of bronze.
31. 4 for planning skilful designs and working them in gold, **silver,**
35. 5 do so is to bring an offering of gold, **silver,** or bronze;
35.24 who were able to contribute **silver** or bronze brought their
35.32 for planning skilful designs and working them in gold, **silver**
36.24 the south side [24] and forty **silver** bases to go under them,
36.26 the Tent [26] and forty **silver** bases, two under each frame.
36.30 frames and sixteen **silver** bases, two under each frame.
36.36 Then they made four **silver** bases to hold the posts.
38.10 in twenty bronze bases, with hooks and rods made of **silver.**
38.12 posts and ten bases and with hooks and rods made of **silver.**
38.17 the covering of the tops of the posts were made of **silver.**
38.17 the posts round the enclosure were connected with **silver** rods.
38.19 covering of their tops, and their rods were made of **silver.**
38.25 The **silver** from the census of the community weighed 3,430
38.27 Of the **silver,** 3,400 kilogrammes were used to make the
38.28 remaining 30 kilogrammes of **silver** Bezalel made the rods,
Lev 27. 3 50 **pieces of silver**

Lev 27. 3 30 **pieces of silver**
27. 3 20 **pieces of silver**
27. 3 10 **pieces of silver**
27. 3 5 **pieces of silver**
27. 3 3 **pieces of silver**
27. 3 15 **pieces of silver**
27. 3 10 **pieces of silver**
27.16 the rate of ten **pieces of silver** for every twenty kilogrammes
Num 3.47 five **pieces of silver,** according to the official standard,
3.50 and took [50] the 1,365 **pieces of silver** [51] and gave them to
7.12 one **silver** bowl weighing 1.5 kilogrammes
7.12 and one **silver** basin weighing 800 grammes,
7.84 twelve **silver** bowls and twelve silver basins weighing a
10. 2 "Make two trumpets of hammered **silver** to use for calling
18.16 five **pieces of silver,** according to the official standard.
22.18 Balak gave me all the **silver** and gold in his palace, I
24.13 you gave me all the **silver** and gold in your palace, I
31.22 not burn, such as gold, **silver,** bronze, iron, tin, or lead,
Deut 7.25 Do not desire the **silver** or gold that is on them, and
8.13 your cattle and sheep, your **silver** and gold, and all your
17.17 and he is not to make himself rich with **silver** and gold.
22.19 fine him a hundred **pieces of silver** and give the money to
22.29 bride price of fifty **pieces of silver,** and she is to become
29.17 You saw their disgusting idols made of wood, stone, **silver,**
Josh 6.19 Everything made of **silver,** gold, bronze, or iron is set
6.24 the things made of gold, **silver,** bronze, and iron, which
7.21 cloak, about two kilogrammes of **silver,** and a bar of gold
7.21 buried inside my tent, with the **silver** at the bottom."
7.22 really were buried there, with the **silver** at the bottom.
7.24 of Israel, seized Achan, the **silver,** the cloak, and the bar
22. 6 of livestock, **silver,** gold, bronze, iron, and many clothes.
24.32 the father of Shechem, for a hundred **pieces of silver.**
Judg 5.19 the kings of Canaan fought, but they took no **silver** away.
9. 4 They gave him seventy **pieces of silver** from the temple
16. 5 Each one of us will give you eleven hundred **pieces of silver."**
17. 2 stole those eleven hundred **pieces of silver** from you, you
17. 3 son, I myself am solemnly dedicating the **silver** to the Lord.
17. 3 It will be used to make a wooden idol covered with **silver.**
17. 3 So now I will give the **pieces of silver** back to you."
17. 4 two hundred of the **pieces of silver** and gave them to a
17. 4 idol, carving it from wood and covering it with the **silver.**
17.10 will give you ten **pieces of silver** a year, some clothes, and
18.14 of these houses there is a wooden idol covered with **silver?**
18.17 the wooden idol covered with **silver,** the other idols, and
1 Sam 9. 8 The servant answered, "I have a small **silver coin.**
2 Sam 8.10 Joram took David presents made of gold, **silver,** and bronze.
8.11 in worship, along with the **silver** and gold he took from the
18.11 would have given you ten **pieces of silver** and a belt."
18.12 gave me a thousand **pieces of silver,** I wouldn't lift a
21. 4 family can't be settled with **silver** or gold, nor do we want
24.24 the threshing-place and the oxen for fifty **pieces of silver.**
1 Kgs 7.51 David had dedicated to the Lord—the **silver,**
10.21 No **silver** was used, since it was not considered valuable in
10.22 years his fleet would return, bringing gold, **silver,** ivory,
10.25 him a gift—articles of **silver** and gold, robes, weapons,
10.27 During his reign **silver** was as common in Jerusalem as stone,
10.29 selling chariots for 600 **pieces of silver** each and horses
15.15 as the gold and **silver** objects that he himself dedicated.
15.18 King Asa took all the **silver** and gold that was left in
15.19 This **silver** and gold is a present for you.
16.24 Samaria for six thousand **pieces of silver** from a man named Shemer.
20. 3 you surrender to him your **silver** and gold, your women and
20. 5 hand over to me your **silver** and gold, your women and your
20. 7 my wives and children, my **silver** and gold, and I agreed."
20.39 life or else pay a fine of three thousand **pieces of silver.'**
2 Kgs 5. 5 thousand **pieces of silver,** six thousand pieces of gold,
5.22 give them three thousand **pieces of silver** and two changes of
5.23 "Please take six thousand **pieces of silver,"** Naaman replied.
5.23 on it, tied up the **silver** in two bags, gave them and
6.25 donkey's head cost eighty **pieces of silver,**
6.25 two hundred grammes of dove's dung cost five **pieces of silver.**
7. 1 or six kilogrammes of barley for one **piece of silver."**
7. 8 there, grabbed the **silver,** gold, and clothing they found,
7.16 kilogrammes of barley were sold for one **piece of silver.**
7.18 in Samaria for one **piece of silver,** [19] to which the officer
12.10 the High Priest would come, melt down the **silver,** and weigh
12.11 amount, they would hand the **silver** over to the men in charge
12.13 used to pay for making **silver** cups, bowls, trumpets, or
12.13 the lamps, or any other article of **silver** or of gold.
14.14 He took all the **silver** and gold he could find, all the
15.19 thousand kilogrammes of **silver** to gain his support
15.20 Israel by forcing each one to contribute fifty **pieces of silver.**
16. 8 Ahaz took the **silver** and gold from the Temple and the
18.14 kilogrammes of **silver** and a thousand
18.15 Hezekiah sent him all the **silver** in the Temple and in
20.13 his wealth—his **silver** and gold, his spices and perfumes,
23.33 Judah pay 3,400 kilogrammes of **silver** and thirty-four
25.15 was made of gold or **silver,** including the small bowls and
1 Chr 18.10 Joram brought David presents made of gold, **silver,** and
18.11 in worship, along with the **silver** and gold he took from the
19. 6 paid thirty-four thousand kilogrammes of **silver** to hire
22.14 over 34,000 metric tons of **silver** to be used in building it.
22.16 of every sort who can work [16] with gold, **silver,** bronze,
28.14 instructions as to how much **silver** and gold was to be used
28.16 lamp and lampstand, [16] for the **silver** tables, and for each
28.17 bowls, and jars, how much **silver** and gold in making dishes,
29. 2 materials for the Temple—gold, **silver,** bronze, iron, timber,
29. 3 have provided, I have given **silver** and gold from my personal
29. 4 forty metric tons of pure **silver** for decorating the walls of
29. 7 340 metric tons of **silver,** almost 620 metric tons of bronze,

2 Chr 1.15 During his reign **silver** and gold became as common in
1.17 chariots for six hundred **pieces of silver** each and horses
2. 7 in engraving, in working gold, **silver,** bronze, and iron, and
2.14 to make things out of gold, **silver,** bronze, iron, stone, and
5. 1 David had dedicated to the Lord—the **silver,**
9.14 of the Israelite districts also brought him **silver** and gold.
9.20 **Silver** was not considered valuable in Solomon's day.
9.21 years his fleet would return, bringing gold, **silver,** ivory,
9.24 brought Solomon gifts—articles of **silver** and gold, robes,
9.27 During his reign **silver** was as common in Jerusalem as stone,
15.18 as the gold and **silver** objects that he himself dedicated.
16. 2 So Asa took **silver** and gold from the treasuries of the
16. 3 This **silver** and gold is a present for you.
17.11 Jehoshaphat a large amount of **silver** and other gifts, and
21. 3 amounts of gold, **silver,** and other valuable possessions,
24.14 finished, the remaining gold and **silver** was given to the
25. 6 from Israel at a cost of about 3,400 kilogrammes of **silver.**
25. 9 "But what about all that **silver** I have already paid for them?"
25.24 loot all the gold and **silver** in the Temple, the temple
27. 5 3,400 kilogrammes of **silver,** 1,000 metric tons of wheat, and
32.27 storerooms built for his gold, **silver,** precious stones,
36. 3 Judah pay 3,400 kilogrammes of **silver** and 34 kilogrammes of
Ezra 1. 4 them with **silver** and gold, supplies and pack animals,
1. 6 **silver** utensils, gold, supplies, pack animals, other valuables,
1. 9 **silver** bowls for offerings 1,000
1. 9 small **silver** bowls 410
1.11 there were 5,400 gold and **silver** bowls and other articles
2.69 2,800 kilogrammes of **silver,** and 100 robes for priests.
5.14 He restored the gold and **silver** temple utensils which
6. 5 Also the gold and **silver** utensils which King
7.15 with you the gold and **silver** offerings which I and my
7.16 also to take all the **silver** and gold which you collect
7.18 You may use the **silver** and gold that is left over for
7.22 of 3,400 kilogrammes of **silver,** 10,000 kilogrammes of wheat,
8.25 Then I weighed out the **silver,** the gold, and the
8.26 **silver** - 22 metric tons 100 silver utensils - 70 kilogrammes
8.28 and so are all the **silver** and gold utensils brought to him
8.30 Levites took charge of the **silver,** the gold, and the utensils,
8.33 the Temple, weighed the **silver,** the gold, and the utensils,
Neh 5.15 people and had demanded forty **silver coins** a day for food
7.70 1,250 kilogrammes of **silver**
7.70 140 kilogrammes of **silver**
10.32 each contribute five grammes of **silver** to help pay the
Esth 1. 6 of fine purple linen to **silver** rings on marble columns.
1. 6 Couches made of gold and **silver** had been placed in the courtyard,
3. 9 more than 340,000 kilogrammes of **silver** into the royal
Job 3.15 gold and **silver,** [16]or sleeping like a still-born child.
22.25 be your gold, and let him be **silver,** piled high for you.
27.16 wicked may have too much **silver** to count and more clothes
27.17 wear the clothes, and some honest man will get the **silver.**
28. 1 There are mines where **silver** is dug;
28.15 It cannot be bought with **silver** or gold.
Ps 12. 6 as genuine as **silver** refined seven times in the furnace.
66.10 as **silver** is purified by fire so you have tested us.
68.13 figures of doves covered with **silver,** whose wings glittered
68.30 calves, until they all bow down and offer you their **silver.**
105.37 they carried **silver** and gold, and all of them were healthy
115. 4 Their gods are made of **silver** and gold, formed by human hands.
135.15 The gods of the nations are made of **silver** and gold;
Prov 2. 4 it as hard as you would for **silver** or some hidden treasure.
3.14 There is more profit in it than there is in **silver;**
8.10 Choose my instruction instead of **silver;**
8.19 better than the finest gold, better than the purest **silver.**
10.20 A good man's words are like pure **silver;**
16.16 better—to have wisdom and knowledge than gold and **silver.**
17. 3 Gold and **silver** are tested by fire, and a person's heart
25. 4 Take the impurities out of **silver** and the artist can
25.11 An idea well-expressed is like a design of gold, set in **silver.**
27.21 Fire tests gold and **silver;**
Ecc 2. 8 I also piled up **silver** and gold from the royal treasuries
12. 6 The **silver** chain will snap, and the golden lamp will fall
Song 1.11 will make for you a chain of gold with ornaments of **silver.**
3.10 Its posts are covered with **silver;**
8. 9 If she is a wall, we will build her a **silver** tower.
8.11 each one pays a thousand **silver coins.**
Is 1.22 Jerusalem, you were once like **silver,** but now you are worthless;
2. 7 Their land is full of **silver** and gold, and there is no
2.20 throw away the gold and **silver** idols they have made, and
7.23 each worth a thousand **pieces of silver,** will be overgrown
13.17 They care nothing for **silver** and are not tempted by gold.
30.22 idols plated with **silver** and your idols covered with gold,
31. 7 throw away the sinful idols you made out of **silver** and gold.
39. 2 his wealth—his **silver** and gold, his spices and perfumes,
40.19 metalworkers cover with gold and set in a base of **silver.**
40.20 The man who cannot afford **silver** or gold chooses wood
46. 6 they weigh out **silver** on the scales.
48.10 the fire of suffering, as **silver** is refined in a furnace.
60. 9 They bring with them **silver** and gold To honour the name of
60.17 you gold instead of bronze, **Silver** and bronze instead of
Jer 10. 4 of the woodcarver, [4]and decorated with **silver** and gold.
10. 9 Their idols are covered with **silver** from Spain and with
32. 9 the price came to seventeen **pieces of silver.**
52.19 They took away everything that was made of gold or **silver:**
Ezek 7.19 throw their gold and **silver** away in the streets like refuse,
7.19 because neither **silver** nor gold can save them
7.19 Gold and **silver** led them into sin.
16.13 had ornaments of gold and **silver,** and you always wore
16.17 You took the **silver** and gold jewellery that I had given you,
22.18 lead—left over after **silver** has been refined in a furnace.
22.20 way that the ore of **silver,** copper, iron, lead, and tin is
22.22 melted in Jerusalem just as **silver** is melted in a furnace,
Ezek 27.12 business in Spain and took **silver,** iron, tin, and lead in
28. 4 and skill made you rich with treasures of gold and **silver.**
38.13 Do you intend to get **silver** and gold, livestock and property,
Dan 2.32 its chest and arms were made of **silver;**
2.35 once the iron, clay, bronze, **silver,** and gold crumbled and
2.45 it struck the statue made of iron, bronze, clay, **silver,** and
5. 2 bring in the gold and **silver** cups and bowls which his father
5. 4 and praised gods made of gold, **silver,** bronze, iron, wood,
5.23 praised gods made of gold, **silver,** bronze, iron, wood, and
11. 8 and the articles of gold and **silver** dedicated to those gods.
11.38 He will offer gold, **silver,** jewels, and other rich gifts to
11.43 Egypt's hidden treasures of gold and **silver** and its other
Hos 2. 8 the olive-oil, and all the **silver** and gold that she used in
3. 2 So I paid fifteen **pieces of silver** and 150 kilogrammes of
8. 4 They took their **silver** and gold and made idols—for their own
9. 6 Their treasures of **silver** and the places where their homes
13. 2 images to worship—idols of **silver,** designed by human minds,
Joel 3. 5 You have taken my **silver** and gold and carried my rich
Nah 2. 9 Plunder the **silver!**
Hab 2.19 It may be covered with **silver** and gold, but there is no
Zeph 1.18 his fury, not even all their **silver** and gold will save them.
Hag 2. 8 All the **silver** and gold of the world is mine.
Zech 6.11 a crown out of the **silver** and gold they have given, and
9. 3 has piled up so much **silver** and gold that it is as
11.12 So they paid me thirty **pieces of silver** as my wages.
11.13 I took the thirty **pieces of silver**—the magnificent sum they
13. 9 survives and will purify them as **silver** is purified by fire.
14.14 the nations—gold, **silver,** and clothing in great abundance.
Mal 3. 3 He will come to judge like one who refines and purifies **silver.**
3. 3 As a metal-worker refines **silver** and gold, so the Lord's
Mt 10. 9 Do not carry any gold, **silver,** or copper money in your pockets;
20. 2 them the regular wage, a **silver coin** a day, and sent them
20. 9 begun to work at five o'clock were paid a **silver coin** each.
20.10 but they too were given a **silver coin** each.
20.13 you agreed to do a day's work for one **silver coin.**
26.15 They counted out thirty **silver coins** and gave them to him.
27. 3 and took back the thirty **silver coins** to the chief priests
27. 9 "They took the thirty **silver coins,** the amount the people
Mk 6.37 go and spend two hundred **silver coins** on bread in order to
12.15 Bring a **silver coin,** and let me see it."
14. 5 for more than three hundred **silver coins** and the money given
Lk 7.41 "One owed him five hundred **silver coins,** and the other owed
10.35 day he took out two **silver coins** and gave them to the
15. 8 a woman who has ten **silver coins** loses one of them—what
20.24 their trick and said to them, [24]"Show me a **silver coin.**
Jn 6. 7 more than two hundred **silver coins** to buy enough bread."
12. 5 perfume sold for three hundred **silver coins** and the money
Acts 17.29 an image of gold or **silver** or stone, shaped by the art
19.19 books, and the total came to fifty thousand **silver coins.**
19.24 A certain **silversmith** named Demetrius
19.24 made **silver** models of the temple
20.33 I have not wanted anyone's **silver** or gold or clothing.
1 Cor 3.12 Some will use gold or **silver** or precious stones in
2 Tim 2.20 some are made of **silver** and gold, others of wood and clay;
Jas 5. 3 Your gold and **silver** are covered with rust, and this rust
1 Pet 1.18 not something that can be destroyed, such as **silver** or gold;
Rev 9.20 the idols of gold, **silver,** bronze, stone, and wood, which cannot
18.12 no one buys their gold, **silver,** precious stones, and

SIMEON (1)

Jacob and Leah's son, the tribe descended from him and its territory in far s. of Palestine, not clearly distinguished from Judah.

Gen 29.33 so she named him **Simeon.**
34.25 two of Jacob's sons, **Simeon** and Levi, the brothers of Dinah,
34.30 Jacob said to **Simeon** and Levi, "You have brought trouble
35.23 Leah were Reuben (Jacob's eldest son), **Simeon,** Levi, Judah,
42.24 he came back, picked out **Simeon,** and had him tied up in
42.36 **Simeon** is gone;
43.23 Then he brought **Simeon** to them.
46.10 **Simeon** and his sons:
48. 5 and Manasseh are just as much my sons as Reuben and **Simeon.**
49. 5 **"Simeon** and Levi are brothers.
Ex 1. 2 with his family, were [2]Reuben, **Simeon,** Levi, Judah,
6.15 **Simeon** had six sons:
Num 10.19 command of the tribe of **Simeon,** [20]and Eliasaph son of
25.14 of Salu, the head of a family in the tribe of **Simeon.**
26.12 The tribe of **Simeon:**
Deut 27.12 **Simeon,** Levi, Judah, Issachar, Joseph, and Benjamin.
Josh 19. 1 assignment made was for the families of the tribe of **Simeon.**
19. 8 of the tribe of **Simeon** received as their possession.
19. 9 part of its territory was given to the tribe of **Simeon.**
21. 4 thirteen cities from the territories of Judah, **Simeon,**
21. 9 the territories of Judah and **Simeon** which were given [10]to
21.16 nine cities from the tribes of Judah and **Simeon.**
Judg 1. 3 said to the people of **Simeon,** "Go with us into the
1. 3 So the tribes of **Simeon** [4]and Judah went into battle together.
1.17 went with the people of **Simeon,** and together they defeated
1 Chr 2. 1 Reuben, **Simeon,** Levi, Judah, Issachar, Zebulun, [2]Dan,
4.24 **Simeon** had five sons:
4.27 children, and the tribe of **Simeon** did not grow as much as
4.28 the descendants of **Simeon** lived in the following towns:
4.42 other members of the tribe of **Simeon** went east to Edom.
6.65 territories of Judah, **Simeon,** and Benjamin, mentioned above,
2 Chr 15. 9 Manasseh, and **Simeon,** and were living in his kingdom,
34. 6 Manasseh, Ephraim, and **Simeon,** and as far north as Naphtali.
Ezek 48.23 Benjamin **Simeon** Issachar Zebulun Gad
48.30 those in the south wall, after **Simeon,** Issachar, and
Rev 7. 5 **Simeon,** Levi, Issachar, Zebulun, Joseph, and Benjamin.

also Num 1.5 Num 1.20 Num 2.10 Num 7.12 Num 13.3 Num 34.19 1 Chr 12.23 1 Chr 27.16

SIMEON (2)
An ancestor of Jesus.

Lk 3.30 the son of **Simeon,** the son of Judah,

SIMEON (3)
An old man who greeted the baby Jesus in the Temple.

Lk 2.25 there was a man named **Simeon** living in Jerusalem.
2.27 Led by the Spirit, **Simeon** went into the Temple.
2.28 **Simeon** took the child in his arms
2.33 and mother were amazed at the things **Simeon** said about him.
2.34 **Simeon** blessed them and said to Mary, his mother,

SIMEON (4)
Simeon the Black, a leader of the church in Antioch.

Acts 13. 1 Barnabas, **Simeon** (called the Black), Lucius (from Cyrene),

AV **SIMILITUDE**

Num 12. 8 he has even seen my **form!**
Deut 4.12 him speaking but did not see him in any **form** at all.
4.15 from the fire on Mount Sinai, you did not see any **form.**
4.16 yourselves an idol in any **form** at all—whether man or woman,
2 Chr 4. 3 The decorations were in the **shape** of bulls, which had been
Ps 106.20 glory of God for the **image** of an animal that eats grass.
Jas 3. 9 curse our fellow-man, who is created in the **likeness** of God.

SIMON (1) see **PETER**

SIMON (2)
Simon the Patriot, one of the twelve apostles.

Mt 10. 4 **Simon the Patriot,** and Judas Iscariot, who betrayed Jesus.
Mk 3.18 Thaddaeus, **Simon the Patriot,** [19] and Judas Iscariot,
Lk 6.15 and **Simon (who was called the Patriot),**
Acts 1.13 James son of Alphaeus, **Simon the Patriot,** and Judas son of James.

SIMON (3)
Jesus' brother.

Mt 13.55 aren't James, Joseph, **Simon,** and Judas his brothers?
Mk 6. 3 and the brother of James, Joseph, Judas, and **Simon?**

SIMON (4)
Simon of Cyrene.

Mt 27.32 a man from Cyrene named **Simon,** and the soldiers forced him
Mk 15.21 they met a man named **Simon,** who was coming into the city
15.21 **(Simon** was from Cyrene and was the father of Alexander and Rufus.)
Lk 23.26 a man from Cyrene named **Simon** who was coming into the city

SIMON (5)
Simon Iscariot, Judas' father.

Jn 6.71 He was talking about Judas, the son of **Simon Iscariot.**
13. 2 Judas, the son of **Simon Iscariot,** the thought of betraying Jesus.
13.26 dipped it, and gave it to Judas, the son of **Simon Iscariot.**

SIMON (6)
Simon of Bethany.

Mt 26. 6 Bethany at the house of **Simon,** a man who had suffered from
Mk 14. 3 Bethany at the house of **Simon,** a man who had suffered from

SIMON (7)
Simon the Pharisee.

Lk 7.40 said to him, **"Simon,** I have something to tell you."
7.43 "I suppose," answered **Simon,** "that it would be the one
7.44 said to **Simon,** "Do you see this woman?

SIMON (8)
Simon the tanner.

Acts 9.43 Joppa for many days with a tanner of leather named **Simon.**
10. 6 a tanner of leather named **Simon,** who lives by the sea."
10.32 guest in the home of **Simon** the tanner of leather,

SIMON (9)
Simon the magician.

Acts 8. 9 A man named **Simon** lived there, who for some time had
8.13 **Simon** himself also believed;
8.18 **Simon** saw that the Spirit had been given to the believers
8.24 **Simon** said to Peter and John, "Please pray to the Lord

SIMPLE

Lev 23.43 people of Israel live in **simple** shelters when he led them
Ecc 7.29 God made us plain and **simple,** but we have made ourselves

SIN (1)
see also **SIN-OFFERING**

Gen 4. 7 because you have done evil, **sin** is crouching at your door.
13.13 whose people were wicked and **sinned** against the Lord.
18.20 against Sodom and Gomorrah, and their **sin** is very great.
20. 6 so I kept you from **sinning** against me and did not let
39. 9 then could I do such an immoral thing and **sin** against God?"
Ex 9.27 for Moses and Aaron and said, "This time I have **sinned;**
9.34 When the king saw what had happened, he **sinned** again.
10.16 Aaron and said, "I have **sinned** against the Lord your God
10.17 Now forgive my **sin** this once and pray to the Lord your
20.20 make you keep on obeying him, so that you will not **sin."**
23.33 if you do, they will make you **sin** against me.
29.14 This is an offering to take away the **sins** of the priests.
29.36 offer a bull as a sacrifice, so that **sin** may be forgiven.
30.10 four projections the blood of the animal sacrificed for **sin.**
32. 7 whom you led out of Egypt, have **sinned** and rejected me.
32.21 you, that you have made them commit such a terrible **sin?"**
32.30 Moses said to the people, "You have committed a terrible **sin.**
32.30 perhaps I can obtain forgiveness for your **sin."**
32.31 Lord and said, "These people have committed a terrible **sin.**
32.32 Please forgive their **sin;**
32.33 "It is those who have **sinned** against me whose names I will
32.34 is coming when I will punish these people for their **sin."**
34. 7 for thousands of generations and forgive evil and **sin;**
34. 7 and fourth generation for the **sins** of their parents."
34. 9 forgive our evil and our **sin,** and accept us as your own
Lev 1. 4 it will be accepted as a sacrifice to take away his **sins.**
4. 2 of Israel that anyone who **sinned** and broke any of the Lord's
4. 3 is the High Priest who **sins** and so brings guilt on the
4. 3 any defects and sacrifice it to the Lord for his **sin.**
4.13 whole community of Israel that **sins** and becomes guilty of
4.14 then as soon as the **sin** becomes known, the community
4.20 sacrifice for the people's **sin,** and they will be forgiven.
4.21 it, just as he burns the bull offered for his own **sin.**
4.21 This is an offering to take away the **sin** of the community.
4.22 it is a ruler who **sins** and becomes guilty of breaking one
4.23 attention is called to the **sin,** he shall bring as his
4.24 This is an offering to take away **sin.**
4.26 offer the sacrifice for the **sin** of the ruler, and he will
4.27 of the common people who **sins** and becomes guilty of breaking
4.28 attention is called to the **sin,** he shall bring as his
4.31 the sacrifice for the man's **sin,** and he will be forgiven.
4.35 the sacrifice for the man's **sin,** and he will be forgiven.
5. 5 guilty, he must confess the **sin,**
5. 6 as the penalty for his **sin** he must bring to the Lord
5. 6 The priest shall offer the sacrifice for the man's **sin.**
5. 7 as the payment for his **sin** two doves or two pigeons, one
5. 9 This is an offering to take away **sin.**
5.10 the sacrifice for the man's **sin,** and he will be forgiven.
5.12 It is an offering to take away **sin.**
5.13 the sacrifice for the man's **sin,** and he will be forgiven.
5.15 If anyone **sins** unintentionally by failing to hand over
5.16 as a sacrifice for the man's **sin,** and he will be forgiven.
5.17 If anyone **sins** unintentionally by breaking any of the Lord's
5.18 for the **sin** which the man committed unintentionally,
5.19 repayment-offering for the **sin** he committed against the Lord.
6. 2 be made if any one **sins** against the Lord by refusing to
6. 4 When a man **sins** in any of these ways, he must repay
6. 7 the sacrifice for the man's **sin,** and he will be forgiven.
6.30 the ritual to take away **sin,** the animal must not be eaten;
8.34 what we have done today, in order to take away your **sin.**
9. 7 to take away your **sins** and the sins of the people.
9. 7 offering to take away the **sins** of the people, just as the
9.15 be offered for the people's **sins,** killed it, and offered it,
10.17 to you in order to take away the **sin** of the community.
16. 6 sacrifice to take away his own **sins** and those of his family.
16.10 to Azazel, in order to take away the **sins** of the people.
16.16 uncleanness of the people of Israel and from all their **sins.**
16.19 to purify it from the **sins** of the people of Israel and
16.21 over it all the evils, **sins,** and rebellions of the people of
16.22 goat will carry all their **sins** away with him into some
16.24 to remove his own **sins** and those of the people.
16.27 Holy Place to take away **sin,** shall be carried outside the
16.30 purify them from all their **sins,** so that they will be
16.34 a year to purify the people of Israel from all their **sins.**
17.11 be poured out on the altar to take away the people's **sins.**
17.11 Blood, which is life, takes away **sins.**
19.17 him, so that you will not commit a **sin** because of him.
19.22 to remove the man's **sin,** and God will forgive him.
23.26 is to be performed to take away the **sins** of the people.
23.28 it is the day for performing the ritual to take away **sin.**
26.39 away because of your own **sin** and the sin of your ancestors.
26.40 will confess their **sins** and the sins of their ancestors,
26.41 paid the penalty for their **sin** and rebellion, [42] I will
Num 5. 7 someone, [7] he must confess his **sin** and make full repayment,
9.13 He must suffer the consequences of his **sin.**
12.11 do not make us suffer this punishment for our foolish **sin.**
14.18 show great love and faithfulness and forgive **sin** and rebellion.
14.18 third and fourth generation for the **sins** of their parents.'
14.19 love, forgive, I pray, the **sin** of these people, just as you
14.34 suffer the consequences of your **sin** for forty years, one
14.40 We admit that we have **sinned."**
15.27 If an individual **sins** unintentionally, he is to offer a
15.28 to purify the man from his **sin,** and he will be forgiven.
15.29 everyone who unintentionally commits a **sin,** whether he is a
15.30 But any person who **sins** deliberately, whether he is a
16.22 When one man **sins,** do you get angry with the whole community?"
16.26 you will be wiped out with them for all their **sins."**
16.38 put to death for their **sin,** beat them into thin plates, and

Num	19. 9	This ritual is performed to remove **sin.**
	19.17	which was burnt to remove **sin** shall be taken and put in
	21. 7	to Moses and said, "We **sinned** when we spoke against the
	22.34	Balaam replied, "I have **sinned.**
	25.13	to me and brought about forgiveness for the people's **sin."**
	27. 3	he died because of his own **sin.**
	32.14	place, a new generation of **sinful** men ready to bring down
	32.23	I warn you that you will be **sinning** against the Lord.
	32.23	you will be punished for your **sin.**
Deut	1.41	"You replied, 'Moses, we have **sinned** against the Lord.
	4.16	that you do not **sin** by making for yourselves an idol
	4.25	do not **sin** by making for yourselves an idol
	9.16	you, and that you had **sinned** against him by making
	9.18	did this because you had **sinned** against the Lord and had
	9.21	I took that **sinful** thing that you had made—that metal
	9.27	to the stubbornness, wickedness, and **sin** of this people.
	17. 2	some man or woman has **sinned** against the Lord and broken his
	20.18	they will not make you **sin** against the Lord by teaching you
	22.26	girl, because she has not committed a **sin** worthy of death.
	23.21	to your vow, and it is a **sin** not to keep it.
	23.22	It is no **sin** not to make a vow to the Lord,
	24. 4	to commit such a terrible **sin** in the land that the Lord
	24.15	against you to the Lord, and you will be guilty of **sin.**
	32. 5	unworthy to be his people, a **sinful** and deceitful nation.
	32.43	on his enemies and forgives the **sins** of his people."
Josh	7.11	Israel has **sinned!**
	7.20	"I have **sinned** against the Lord, Israel's God, and this is
	22.17	Remember our **sin** at Peor, when the Lord punished his own
	22.17	Wasn't that **sin** enough?
	22.20	Achan was not the only one who died because of his **sin."**
	24.19	He is a holy God and will not forgive your **sins.**
Judg	2.11	Then the people of Israel **sinned** against the Lord and
	3. 7	**sinned** against him and worshipped the idols of Baal and Asherah.
	3.12	The people of Israel **sinned** against the Lord again.
	4. 1	After Ehud died, the people of Israel **sinned** against the Lord
	6. 1	again the people of Israel **sinned** against the Lord, so he
	10. 6	Once again the Israelites **sinned** against the Lord by
	10.10	Lord and said, "We have **sinned** against you, for we left you,
	10.15	But the people of Israel said to the Lord, "We have **sinned.**
	13. 1	The Israelites **sinned** against the Lord again, and he let
1 Sam	2.17	This **sin** of the sons of Eli was extremely serious in
	2.25	If a man **sins** against another man, God can defend him;
	2.25	but who can defend a man who **sins** against the Lord?"
	3.14	be able to remove the consequences of this terrible **sin."**
	6. 3	send with it a gift to him to pay for your **sin.**
	6. 8	are sending to him as a gift to pay for your **sins.**
	6.17	gift to pay for their **sins,** one each for the cities of
	7. 6	They said, "We have **sinned** against the Lord."
	12.10	and said, 'We have **sinned,** because we turned away from you,
	12.17	that you committed a great **sin** against the Lord when you
	12.19	that, besides all our other **sins,**
	12.19	we have **sinned** by asking for a king."
	12.23	Lord forbid that I should **sin** against him by no longer
	12.25	But if you continue to **sin,** you and your king will be
	14.33	told, "Look, the people are **sinning** against the Lord by
	14.34	they must not **sin** against the Lord by eating meat with blood
	14.38	"Come here and find out what **sin** was committed today.
	15.23	bad as witchcraft, and arrogance is as **sinful** as idolatry.
	15.24	"Yes, I have **sinned,"** Saul replied.
	15.25	I beg you, forgive my **sin** and go back with me, so
	15.30	"I have **sinned,"** Saul replied.
2 Sam	12.12	You **sinned** in secret, but I will make this happen in
	12.13	"I have **sinned** against the Lord," David said.
	19.20	know, sir, that I have **sinned,** and this is why I am
	24.10	the Lord, "I have committed a terrible **sin** in doing this!
1 Kgs	8.33	their enemies because they have **sinned** against you, and then
	8.34	Forgive the **sins** of your people, and bring them back to the
	8.35	rain because your people have **sinned** against you, and then
	8.36	Forgive the **sins** of the king and of the people of Israel.
	8.46	"When your people **sin** against you—and there is no one
	8.46	no one who does not **sin**—and in your anger you let
	8.47	to you, confessing how **sinful** and wicked they have been,
	8.50	Forgive all their **sins** and their rebellion against you,
	11. 6	He **sinned** against the Lord and was not true to him as
	11.39	Because of Solomon's **sin** I will punish the descendants of David,
	12.30	And so the people **sinned,** going to worship in Bethel and
	13.34	This **sin** on his part brought about the ruin and total
	14. 9	You have committed far greater **sins** than those who ruled before
	14.16	because Jeroboam sinned and led the people of Israel into **sin."**
	14.22	The people of Judah **sinned** against the Lord and did
	15. 3	He committed the same **sins** as his father and was not
	15.26	he sinned against the Lord and led Israel into **sin.**
	15.30	God of Israel, by the **sins** that he committed and that he
	15.34	he sinned against the Lord and led Israel into **sin.**
	16. 2	have sinned like Jeroboam and have led my people into **sin.**
	16. 2	Their **sins** have aroused my anger, [3]and so I will do away
	16. 7	because of the **sins** that Baasha committed against the Lord.
	16.13	because they led Israel into **sin,** Baasha and his son Elah
	16.19	This happened because of his **sins** against the Lord.
	16.19	the Lord by his own **sins** and by leading Israel into sin.
	16.25	Omri **sinned** against the Lord more than any of his predecessors.
	16.26	by his sins and by leading the people into **sin** and idolatry.
	16.30	He **sinned** against the Lord more than any of his predecessors.
	16.31	It was not enough for him to **sin** like King Jeroboam;
	17.18	to remind God of my **sins** and so cause my son's death?"
	21.22	you have stirred up my anger by leading Israel into **sin.'**
	21.26	He committed the most shameful **sins** by worshipping idols,
	22.52	He **sinned** against the Lord, following the wicked example
	22.52	Jezebel, and King Jeroboam, who had led Israel into **sin.**
2 Kgs	3. 2	He **sinned** against the Lord, but he was not as bad as
	3. 3	Nebat before him, he led Israel into **sin,** and would not stop.
2 Kgs	8.18	He **sinned** against the Lord, [19]but the Lord was not willing
	8.27	King Ahab by marriage, he **sinned** against the Lord, just as
	10.29	But he imitated the **sin** of King Jeroboam,
	10.29	who led Israel into the **sin** of worshipping the gold
	10.31	followed the example of Jeroboam, who led Israel into **sin.**
	12.16	and for the offerings for **sin** was not deposited in the box;
	13. 2	he sinned against the Lord and led Israel into **sin;**
	13. 6	did not give up the **sins** into which King Jeroboam had led
	13.11	He too **sinned** against the Lord and followed the evil
	13.11	evil example of King Jeroboam, who had led Israel into **sin.**
	14.24	He **sinned** against the Lord, following the wicked example
	14.24	King Jeroboam son of Nebat, who led Israel into **sin.**
	15. 9	He, like his predecessors, **sinned** against the Lord.
	15. 9	of King Jeroboam son of Nebat, who led Israel into **sin.**
	15.18	He **sinned** against the Lord, for until the day of his
	15.18	Nebat, who led Israel into **sin** till the day of his death.
	15.24	He **sinned** against the Lord, following the wicked example
	15.24	of King Jeroboam son of Nebat, who led Israel into **sin.**
	15.28	He **sinned** against the Lord, following the wicked example
	15.28	of King Jeroboam son of Nebat, who led Israel into **sin.**
	17. 2	He **sinned** against the Lord, but not as much as the kings
	17. 7	Samaria fell because the Israelites **sinned** against the Lord
	17.21	made them abandon the Lord and led them into terrible **sins.**
	17.22	continued to practise all the **sins** he had committed,
	21. 2	as his people advanced, Manasseh **sinned** against the Lord.
	21. 6	He **sinned** greatly against the Lord and stirred up his anger.
	21. 9	them to commit even greater **sins** than those committed by the
	21.11	with his idols he has led the people of Judah into **sin.**
	21.15	my people because they have **sinned** against me and have
	21.16	Judah into idolatry, causing them to **sin** against the Lord.
	21.17	that Manasseh did, including the **sins** he committed, is
	21.20	Like his father Manasseh, he **sinned** against the Lord;
	23.15	by King Jeroboam son of Nebat, who led Israel into **sin.**
	23.32	the example of his ancestors, he **sinned** against the Lord.
	23.37	example of his ancestors, Jehoiakim **sinned** against the Lord.
	24. 3	because of all the **sins** that King Manasseh had committed,
	24. 9	the example of his father, Jehoiachin **sinned** against the Lord.
	24.19	King Zedekiah **sinned** against the Lord, just as King Jehoiakim
1 Chr	6.49	and for the sacrifices by which God forgives Israel's **sins.**
	9. 1	Judah had been deported to Babylon as punishment for their **sins.**
	21. 8	to God, "I have committed a terrible **sin** in doing this!
	28.11	rooms, and for the Most Holy Place, where **sins** are forgiven.
2 Chr	6.24	their enemies because they have **sinned** against you and then
	6.25	Forgive the **sins** of your people and bring them back to the
	6.26	rain because your people have **sinned** against you and then
	6.27	in heaven and forgive the **sins** of your servants, the people
	6.36	"When your people **sin** against you—and there is no one
	6.36	no one who does not **sin**—and in your anger you let
	6.37	to you, confessing how **sinful** and wicked they have been,
	6.39	merciful to them and forgive all the **sins** of your people.
	7.14	forgive their **sins,** and make their land prosperous again.
	12. 6	leaders admitted that they had **sinned,** and they said, "What
	12. 7	"Because they admit their **sin,** I will not destroy them.
	19.10	that they do not become guilty of **sinning** against the Lord.
	21. 6	He **sinned** against the Lord, [7]but the Lord was not willing
	21.11	the people of Judah and Jerusalem to **sin** against the Lord.
	22. 4	He **sinned** against the Lord, because after his father's
	24.18	Their guilt for these **sins** brought the Lord's anger on Judah
	27. 2	his father he did not **sin** by burning incense in the Temple.
	27. 2	The people, however, went on **sinning.**
	28. 5	Because King Ahaz **sinned,** the Lord his God let the
	28.10	that you also have committed **sins** against the Lord your God?
	28.13	We have already **sinned** against the Lord and made him angry
	28.22	worst, that man Ahaz **sinned** against the Lord more than ever.
	29.21	offering to take away the **sins** of the royal family and of
	29.24	sacrifice to take away the **sin** of all the people, for the
	33. 2	as his people advanced, Manasseh **sinned** against the Lord.
	33. 6	He **sinned** greatly against the Lord and stirred up his anger.
	33. 9	Judah to commit even greater **sins** than those committed by
	33.19	and an account of the **sins** he committed before he
	33.22	Like his father Manasseh, he **sinned** against the Lord,
	33.23	he was even more **sinful** than his father had been.
	36. 5	He **sinned** against the Lord his God.
	36. 9	He too **sinned** against the Lord.
	36.12	He **sinned** against the Lord and did not listen humbly to
	36.14	and the people followed the **sinful** example of the nations
Ezra	6.17	goats as offerings for **sin,** one for each tribe of Israel.
	8.35	they also offered 12 goats to purify themselves from **sin.**
	9. 4	Israel had said about the **sins** of those who had returned
	9. 6	Our **sins** pile up, high above our heads;
	9. 7	ancestors until now, we, your people, have **sinned** greatly.
	9. 7	Because of our **sins** we, our kings, and our priests have
	9.13	us in punishment for our **sins** and wrongs, we know that you,
	10. 1	and confessing these **sins,** a large group of Israelites—men,
	10.11	Now then, confess your **sins** to the Lord, the God of your
	10.13	two days, because so many of us are involved in this **sin.**
	10.19	and they offered a ram as a sacrifice for their **sins.**
Neh	1. 6	I confess that we, the people of Israel, have **sinned.**
	1. 6	My ancestors and I have **sinned.**
	4. 5	do and don't forget their **sins,** for they have insulted us
	6.13	him to frighten me into **sinning,** so that they could ruin my
	9. 1	Israel assembled to fast in order to show sorrow for their **sins.**
	9. 1	and began to confess the **sins** that they and their ancestors
	9. 3	confessed their **sins** and worshipped the Lord their God.
	9.28	When peace returned, they **sinned** again, and again you
	9.33	you have been faithful, even though we have **sinned.**
	9.35	but they failed to turn from **sin** and serve you.
	9.37	goes to the kings that you put over us because we **sinned.**
	10.33	offerings to take away the **sins** of Israel, and anything else
	13.26	I said, "It was foreign women that made King Solomon **sin.**
	13.26	him king over all Israel, and yet he fell into this **sin.**

Job 1. 5 of them might have **sinned** by insulting God unintentionally.
1.22 that had happened, Job did not **sin** by blaming God.
7.20 Are you harmed by my **sin,** you jailer?
7.21 Can't you ever forgive my **sin?**
8. 4 Your children must have **sinned** against God, and so he
9.30 No soap can wash away my **sins.**
10. 6 you track down all my **sins** and hunt down every fault I
10.14 to see if I would **sin,** so that you could refuse to
10.15 As soon as I **sin,** I'm in trouble with you, but when
13.23 What are my **sins?**
14.16 step I take, but you will not keep track of my **sins.**
19.29 that brings God's wrath on **sin,** so that you will know there
20.27 Heaven reveals this man's **sin,** and the earth gives testimony
21.19 You claim God punishes a child for the **sins** of his father.
21.19 Let God punish the **sinners** themselves;
21.19 let him show that he does it because of their **sins.**
21.20 Let **sinners** bear their own punishment;
22. 5 No, it's because you have **sinned** so much;
24.19 heat and drought, so a **sinner** vanishes from the land of the
31. 7 hands are stained with **sin,** [8] then let my crops be destroyed,
31.28 Such a **sin** should be punished by death;
31.30 I never **sinned** by praying for their death.
31.33 try to hide their **sins,** but I have never concealed mine.
33. 9 I am innocent and free from **sin.**
33.17 to make them stop their **sinning** and to save them from
33.27 He will say in public, "I have **sinned.**
34. 6 I am fatally wounded, but I am **sinless."**
34. 8 He likes the company of evil men and goes about with **sinners.**
34.22 There is no darkness dark enough to hide a **sinner** from God.
34.26 He punishes **sinners** where all can see it, [27] because
34.31 Job, have you confessed your **sins** to God
34.31 and promised not to **sin** again?
34.37 To his **sins** he adds rebellion;
35. 3 God's sight, [3] or to ask God, "How does my **sin** affect you?
35. 3 What have I gained by not **sinning?"**
35. 6 If you **sin,** that does no harm to God.
35. 8 fellow-man who suffers from your **sins,** and the good you do
35.15 God does not punish, that he pays little attention to **sin.**
36. 6 He does not let **sinners** live on, and he always treats the
36. 9 have done, [9] God shows them their **sins** and their pride.
Ps 1. 1 not follow the example of **sinners** or join those who have no
1. 5 **Sinners** will be condemned by God and kept apart from God's
4. 4 Tremble with fear and stop **sinning;**
5.10 because of their many **sins** and their rebellion against you.
19.13 Keep me safe, also, from wilful **sins;**
19.13 Then I shall be perfect and free from the evil of **sin.**
25. 7 Forgive the **sins** and errors of my youth.
25. 8 and good, he teaches **sinners** the path they should follow.
25.11 Keep your promise, Lord, and forgive my **sins,** for they are many.
25.18 Consider my distress and suffering and forgive all my **sins.**
26. 9 Do not destroy me with the **sinners;**
32. 1 Happy are those whose **sins** are forgiven,
32. 3 I did not confess my **sins,** I was worn out from crying
32. 5 Then I confessed my **sins** to you;
32. 5 to confess them to you, and you forgave all my **sins.**
36. 1 **Sin** speaks to the wicked man deep in his heart;
36. 2 thinks that God will not discover his **sin** and condemn it.
37.38 has descendants, [38] but **sinners** are completely destroyed,
38. 3 my whole body is diseased because of my **sins.**
38. 4 I am drowning in the flood of my **sins;**
38.18 I confess my **sins;**
39. 1 what I do and will not let my tongue make me **sin;**
39. 8 Save me from all my **sins,** and don't let fools laugh at
39.11 You punish a man's **sins** by your rebukes, and like a moth
40. 6 whole on the altar or for sacrifices to take away **sins.**
40.12 My **sins** have caught up with me, and I can no longer
41. 4 I said, "I have **sinned** against you, Lord;
51. 1 Because of your great mercy wipe away my **sins!**
51. 2 Wash away all my evil and make me clean from my **sin!**
51. 3 I am always conscious of my **sins.**
51. 4 I have **sinned** against you—only against you— and done what
51. 5 from the time I was conceived, I have been **sinful.**
51. 7 Remove my **sin,** and I will be clean;
51. 9 Close your eyes to my **sins** and wipe out all my evil.
51.13 Then I will teach **sinners** your commands, and they will
58.10 The righteous will be glad when they see **sinners** punished;
59. 3 is not because of any **sin** or wrong I have done, [4] nor
59.12 **Sin** is on their lips;
59.12 all their words are **sinful;**
65. 3 People everywhere will come to you [3] on account of their **sins.**
66.18 If I had ignored my **sins,** the Lord would not have
68.21 of his enemies, of those who persist in their **sinful** ways.
69. 5 My **sins,** O God, are not hidden from you;
69.27 Keep a record of all their **sins;**
73.13 that I have kept myself pure and have not committed **sin?**
78.17 But they continued to **sin** against God, and in the desert
78.32 In spite of all this the people kept **sinning;**
78.38 He forgave their **sin** and did not destroy them.
79. 8 Do not punish us for the **sins** of our ancestors.
79. 9 rescue us and forgive our **sins** for the sake of your own
85. 2 have forgiven your people's **sins** and pardoned all their wrongs.
89.32 commandments, [32] then I will punish them for their **sins;**
90. 8 You place our **sins** before you,
90. 8 our secret **sins** where you can see them.
94.23 them for their wickedness and destroy them for their **sins;**
99. 8 God who forgives, even though you punished them for their **sins.**
103. 3 He forgives all my **sins** and heals all my diseases.
103.10 as we deserve or repay us according to our **sins** and wrongs.
103.12 from the west, so far does he remove our **sins** from us.
104.35 May **sinners** be destroyed from the earth;
106. 6 We have **sinned** as our ancestors did;
Ps 106.43 they chose to rebel against him and sank deeper into **sin.**
107.17 suffering because of their **sins** and because of their evil;
109.14 evil of his ancestors and never forgive his mother's **sins.**
109.15 the Lord always remember their **sins,** but may they themselves
119.11 law in my heart, so that I will not **sin** against you.
119.115 Go away from me, you **sinful** people.
130. 3 a record of our **sins,** who could escape being condemned?
130. 8 He will save his people Israel from all their **sins.**
Prov 1.10 When **sinners** tempt you, my son, don't give in.
2.13 live in the darkness of **sin,** [14] men who find pleasure in
2.22 from the land and pull **sinners** out of it like plants from
5.22 The **sins** of a wicked man are a trap.
5.22 He gets caught in the net of his own **sin.**
10.16 for doing good is life, but **sin** leads only to more sin.
10.19 The more you talk, the more likely you are to **sin.**
11.31 can be sure that wicked and **sinful** people will be punished.
13. 6 wickedness is the downfall of **sinners.**
13.21 Trouble follows **sinners** everywhere, but righteous people
13.22 but the wealth of **sinners** will go to righteous men.
14. 9 people don't care if they **sin,** but good people want to be
14.21 it is a **sin** to despise anyone.
14.34 **sin** is a disgrace to any nation.
16. 6 Be loyal and faithful, and God will forgive your **sin.**
17.19 To like **sin** is to like making trouble.
18. 3 **Sin** and shame go together.
20. 9 his conscience is clear, that he has got rid of his **sin?**
21. 4 by their conceit and arrogance, and this is **sinful.**
23.17 Don't be envious of **sinful** people;
24. 9 Any scheme a fool thinks up is **sinful.**
28. 2 When a nation **sins,** it will have one ruler after another.
28.13 will never succeed in life if you try to hide your **sins.**
29. 6 are trapped in their own **sins,** while honest people are happy
Ecc 2.26 please him, but he makes **sinners** work, earning and saving,
5. 6 own words lead you into **sin,** so that you have to tell
7.26 who pleases God can get away, but she will catch the **sinner.**
8.12 A **sinner** may commit a hundred crimes and still live.
9. 2 A good man is no better off than a **sinner;**
9.18 good than weapons, but one **sinner** can undo a lot of good.
Is 1. 4 You are doomed, you **sinful** nation, you corrupt and evil people!
1. 4 Your **sins** drag you down!
1.13 they are all corrupted by your **sins.**
1.18 You are stained red with **sin,** but I will wash you as
1.28 But he will crush everyone who **sins** and rebels against him;
3. 9 They **sin** as openly as the people of Sodom did.
5.18 You are unable to break free from your **sins.**
6. 5 sinful, and I live among a people whose every word is **sinful.**
6. 7 and now your guilt is gone, and your **sins** are forgiven."
13. 9 be made a wilderness, and every **sinner** will be destroyed.
13.11 on the earth and punish all wicked people for their **sins.**
14.21 The sons of this king will die because of their ancestors' **sins.**
24.20 The world is weighed down by its **sins;**
26.21 to punish the people of the earth for their **sins.**
27. 9 But Israel's **sins** will be forgiven only when the stones of
29.20 Every **sinner** will be destroyed.
30. 1 sign treaties against my will, piling one **sin** on another.
31. 6 "People of Israel, you have **sinned** against me and opposed me.
31. 7 you will throw away the **sinful** idols you made out of silver
33.14 The **sinful** people of Zion are trembling with fright.
33.24 again complain of being ill, and all **sins** will be forgiven.
35. 8 No **sinner** will ever travel that road;
38.17 You forgive all my **sins.**
40. 2 have suffered long enough and their **sins** are now forgiven.
40. 2 I have punished them in full for all their **sins."**
42.24 It was the Lord himself, against whom we **sinned!**
43.24 Instead you burdened me with your **sins;**
43.25 the God who forgives your **sins,** and I do this because of
43.25 I will not hold your **sins** against you.
43.27 Your earliest ancestor **sinned;**
43.27 your leaders **sinned** against me, [28] and your rulers profaned
44.22 I have swept your **sins** away like a cloud.
46. 8 "Remember this, you **sinners;**
48.22 "There is no safety for **sinners,"** says the Lord.
50. 1 No, you went away captive because of your **sins;**
53. 5 But because of our **sins** he was wounded, beaten because of
53. 8 He was put to death for the **sins** of our people.
53.12 took the place of many **sinners** and prayed that they might be
57. 3 Come here to be judged, you **sinners!**
57.17 with them because of their **sin** and greed, and so I punished
57.21 There is no safety for **sinners,"** says the Lord.
58. 1 Tell my people Israel about their **sins!**
59. 2 It is because of your **sins** that he doesn't hear you.
59. 2 It is your **sins** that separate you from God when you try
59.12 Our **sins** accuse us.
59.20 you and to save all of you that turn from your **sins.**
64. 5 You were angry with us, but we went on **sinning;**
64. 6 All of us have been **sinful;**
64. 6 Because of our **sins** we are like leaves that wither and are
64. 7 yourself from us and have abandoned us because of our **sins.**
64. 9 too angry with us or hold our **sins** against us for ever.
65. 7 repay them [7] for their **sins** and the sins of their ancestors.
Jer 1.16 I will punish my people because they have **sinned;**
2.13 and astonished, [13] for my people have committed two **sins:**
2.23 Look how you **sinned** in the valley;
2.35 Lord, will punish you because you deny that you have **sinned.**
3.21 pleading, because they have lived **sinful** lives and have
3.25 We and our ancestors have always **sinned** against the Lord
4.14 How long will you go on thinking **sinful** thoughts?
4.18 Your **sin** has caused this suffering;
5. 3 You were stubborn and would not turn from your **sins.**
5. 6 be torn apart because their **sins** are numerous and time after
5. 7 The Lord asked, "Why should I forgive the **sins** of my people?

Jer 5.25 Instead, your **sins** have kept these good things from you.
7.12 I did to it because of the **sins** of my people Israel.
7.13 You have committed all these **sins**, and even though I
8.14 us poison to drink, because we have **sinned** against him.
9. 5 their tongues to lie and will not give up their **sinning**.
11.10 have gone back to the **sins** of their ancestors, who refused
13.22 you have been raped—it is because your **sin** is so terrible.
14. 7 to me, 'Even though our **sins** accuse us, help us, Lord, as
14. 7 we have **sinned** against you.
14.10 they have done and punish them because of their **sins**."
14.20 We have **sinned** against you, Lord;
14.20 we confess our own **sins** and the sins of our ancestors.
15.13 them for the **sins** they have committed throughout the land.
16.10 are guilty of and what **sin** they have committed against the
16.17 their **sins** do not escape my sight.
16.18 them pay double for their **sin** and wickedness, because they
17. 1 "People of Judah, your **sin** is written with an iron pen;
17. 3 of all the **sins** you have committed throughout your land.
18.11 Tell them to stop living **sinful** lives—to change their ways
18.23 Do not forgive their evil or pardon their **sin**.
23.13 I have seen the **sin** of Samaria's prophets:
25.12 After that I will punish Babylonia and its king for their **sin**.
29.23 they are guilty of terrible **sins**—they have committed
30.14 has been harsh because your **sins** are many and your
30.15 you like this because your **sins** are many and your wickedness
31.19 ashamed and disgraced, because we **sinned** when we were young.'
31.30 and everyone will die because of his own **sin**."
31.34 I will forgive their **sins** and I will no longer remember
32.18 but you also punish people for the **sins** of their parents.
32.35 would do such a thing and make the people of Judah **sin**."
33. 8 will purify them from the **sins** that they have committed
33. 8 and I will forgive their **sins** and their rebellion.
36. 3 Then I will forgive their wickedness and their **sins**."
36.31 and your officials because of the **sins** all of you commit.
40. 3 your people **sinned** against the Lord and disobeyed him.
44.23 sacrifices to other gods and **sinned** against the Lord by not
50. 7 Their enemies say, 'They **sinned** against the Lord, and so
50.14 your arrows at Babylon, because it has **sinned** against me,
50.20 When that time comes, no **sin** will be found in Israel and
51. 5 Judah, even though they have **sinned** against me, the Holy One
51. 6 Do not be killed because of Babylonia's **sin**.
52. 2 King Zedekiah **sinned** against the Lord, just as King Jehoiakim
Lam 1. 5 The Lord has made her suffer for all her many **sins**;
1. 8 Jerusalem made herself filthy with terrible **sin**.
1.14 "He took note of all my **sins** and tied them all together;
1.20 My heart is broken in sorrow for my **sins**.
1.22 Punish them as you punished me for my **sins**.
2.14 Their preaching deceived you by never exposing your **sin**.
3.39 Why should we ever complain when we are punished for our **sin**?
3.42 heaven and pray, [42] "We have **sinned** and rebelled, and you,
4.13 it happened because her prophets **sinned** and her priests were
4.22 Zion has paid for her **sin**;
5. 7 Our ancestors **sinned**, but now they are gone,
5. 7 and we are suffering for their **sins**.
5.16 We **sinned**, and now we are doomed.
Ezek 3.18 he will die, still a **sinner**, and I will hold you responsible
3.19 and he doesn't stop **sinning**, he will die, still a sinner,
3.20 will die because of his **sins**—I will not remember the good
3.21 a good man not to **sin** and he listens to you
3.21 listens to you and doesn't **sin**, he will stay alive,
4.17 despair, and they will waste away because of their **sins**."
7.16 All of them will moan over their **sins**.
7.19 Gold and silver led them into **sin**.
9. 9 "The people of Israel and Judah are guilty of terrible **sins**.
14. 3 hearts to idols and are letting idols lead them into **sin**.
14. 4 lets them lead him into **sin** and who then comes to consult
14.11 Israelites from deserting me and defiling themselves by their **sins**.
14.13 he said, "if a country **sins** and is unfaithful to me, I
16.51 "Samaria did not **sin** half as much as you have.
16.52 Your **sins** are so much worse than those of your sisters that
18. 4 The person who **sins** is the one who will die.
18.14 He sees all the **sins** his father practised, but does not
18.17 because of his father's **sins**, but he will certainly live.
18.18 And so he died because of the **sins** he himself had committed.
18.19 'Why shouldn't the son suffer because of his father's **sins**?'
18.20 It is the one who **sins** who will die.
18.20 suffer because of his father's **sins**,
18.20 nor a father because of the **sins** of his son.
18.21 "If an evil man stops **sinning** and keeps my laws, if he
18.22 All his **sins** will be forgiven, and he will live, because
18.24 He will die because of his unfaithfulness and his **sins**.
18.27 When an evil man stops **sinning** and does what is right
18.28 he is doing and stops **sinning**, so he will certainly not die,
18.30 the evil you are doing, and don't let your **sin** destroy you.
18.32 "Turn away from your **sins** and live."
20.30 must you commit the same **sins** your fathers did and go
20.38 away from among you those who are rebellious and **sinful**.
21.23 to remind them of their **sins** and to warn them that they
21.24 Your **sins** are exposed.
21.24 You show your **sins** in your every action.
22.28 The prophets have hidden these **sins** like men covering a
23.49 you for your immorality and your **sin** of worshipping idols.
24.14 I will not ignore your **sins** or show pity or be merciful.
24.23 waste away because of your **sins**, and you will groan to one
28.16 buying and selling, and this led you to violence and **sin**.
33. 6 will come and kill those **sinners**, but I will hold the
33. 8 he will die, still a **sinner**, and I will hold you responsible
33. 9 and he doesn't stop **sinning**, he will die, still a sinner,
33.10 'We are burdened with our **sins** and the wrongs we have done.
33.11 am the living God, I do not enjoy seeing a **sinner** die.
33.11 I would rather see him stop **sinning** and live.
Ezek 33.12 that when a good man **sins**, the good he has done will
33.12 if a good man starts **sinning**, his life will not be spared.
33.13 is enough and begins to **sin**, I will not remember any of
33.13 He will die because of his **sins**.
33.14 die, but if he stops **sinning** and does what is right and
33.15 he stole—if he stops **sinning** and follows the laws that give
33.16 I will forgive the **sins** he has committed, and he will
33.19 an evil man gives up **sinning** and does what is right and
33.29 the people for their **sins** and make the country a waste,
35. 5 of her disaster, the time of final punishment for her **sins**.
36.31 with yourselves because of your **sins** and your iniquities.
36.33 you clean from all your **sins**, I will let you live in
37.23 disgusting idols any more or corrupt themselves with **sin**.
37.23 them from all the ways in which they **sin** and betray me.
39.23 exile because of the **sins** which they committed against me.
40.39 whole or to be sacrifices for **sin** or as repayment-offerings.
42.13 the sacrifices offered for **sin** or as repayment-offerings.
43.10 Make them ashamed of their **sinful** actions.
43.19 give them a young bull to offer as a sacrifice for **sin**.
43.21 offered as a sacrifice for **sin** and burn it at the specified
43.22 without any defects and offer it as a sacrifice for **sin**.
43.25 offer a goat, a bull, and a ram as sacrifices for **sin**.
44.12 way led the people into **sin**, I, the Sovereign Lord, solemnly
45. 9 Lord said, "You have **sinned** too long, you rulers of Israel!
45.13 fellowship-offerings, so that your **sins** will be forgiven.
45.17 to take away the **sins** of the people of Israel."
45.20 of anyone who **sins** unintentionally or through ignorance.
45.22 as a sacrifice for his **sins** and for those of all the
45.25 days the same sacrifice for **sin**, the same offerings to be
46.20 offered as sacrifices for **sin** or as repayment-offerings,
Dan 4.27 Stop **sinning**, do what is right, and be merciful to the poor.
8.12 People **sinned** there instead of offering the proper daily
8.13 How long will an awful **sin** replace the daily sacrifices?
9. 4 to the Lord my God and confessed the **sins** of my people.
9. 5 "We have **sinned**, we have been evil, we have done wrong.
9. 8 our ancestors have acted shamefully and **sinned** against you,
9.11 We **sinned** against you, and so you brought on us the curses
9.13 you by turning from our **sins** or by following your truth.
9.15 We have **sinned**;
9.16 people because of our **sins** and the evil our ancestors did.
9.20 went on praying, confessing my **sins** and the sins of my
9.24 freeing your people and your holy city from **sin** and evil.
9.24 **Sin** will be forgiven and eternal justice established, so
Hos 4. 7 there are, the more you **sin** against me, and so I will
4. 8 You grow rich from the **sins** of my people,
4. 8 and so you want them to **sin** more and more.
5. 5 Their **sins** make them stumble and fall, and the people of
5.15 have suffered enough for their **sins** and come looking for me.
7. 2 their **sins** surround them, and I cannot avoid seeing them."
8.11 of Israel build for removing **sin**,
8.11 the more places they have for **sinning**!
8.13 and now I will remember their **sin** and punish them for it;
9. 7 You people hate me so much because your **sin** is so great.
9. 9 God will remember their **sin** and punish them for it.
10. 2 people whose hearts are deceitful must now suffer for their **sins**.
10. 9 of Israel have not stopped **sinning** against me
10. 9 since the time of their **sin** at Gibeah.
10.10 I will attack this **sinful** people and punish them.
10.10 them, and they will be punished for their many **sins**.
13. 1 But the people **sinned** by worshipping Baal, and for this they
13. 2 They still keep on **sinning** by making metal images to
13.12 "Israel's **sin** and guilt are on record, and the records
14. 1 Your **sin** has made you stumble and fall.
14. 2 "Forgive all our **sins** and accept our prayer, and we will
14. 9 live by following them, but **sinners** stumble and fall because
Amos 1. 3 "The people of Damascus have **sinned** again and again, and
1. 6 "The people of Gaza have **sinned** again and again, and for
1. 9 "The people of Tyre have **sinned** again and again, and for
1.11 "The people of Edom have **sinned** again and again, and for
1.13 "The people of Ammon have **sinned** again and again, and for
2. 1 "The people of Moab have **sinned** again and again, and for
2. 4 "The people of Judah have **sinned** again and again, and for
2. 6 "The people of Israel have **sinned** again and again, and for
3. 2 That is what makes your **sins** so terrible, and that is why
3.14 people of Israel for their **sins**, I will destroy the altars
4. 4 go to the holy place in Bethel and **sin**, if you must!
4. 4 Go to Gilgal and **sin** with all your might!
5.12 I know how terrible your **sins** are and how many crimes
9. 8 Sovereign Lord, am watching this **sinful** kingdom of Israel,
9.10 The **sinners** among my people will be killed in war—all
Mic 1. 5 the people of Israel have **sinned** and rebelled against God.
1.13 You imitated the **sins** of Israel and so caused Jerusalem to sin.
2.10 Your **sins** have doomed this place to destruction.
3. 8 courage to tell the people of Israel what their **sins** are.
6. 7 Shall I offer him my first-born child to pay for my **sins**?
6.13 already begun your ruin and destruction because of your **sins**.
7. 9 We have **sinned** against the Lord, so now we must endure his
7.18 you forgive the **sins** of your people who have survived.
7.19 You will trample our **sins** underfoot and send them to the
Zeph 1.17 They have **sinned** against me, and now their blood will be
Zech 1. 4 telling them not to live evil, **sinful** lives any longer.
3. 4 "I have taken away your **sin** and will give you new clothes
3. 9 a single day I will take away the **sin** of this land.
5. 6 a basket, and it stands for the **sin** of the whole land."
13. 1 David and the people of Jerusalem from their **sin** and idolatry.
Mt 1.21 him Jesus—because he will save his people from their **sins**."
3. 2 "Turn away from your **sins**," he said, "because the
3. 6 They confessed their **sins**, and he baptized them in the Jordan.
3. 8 things that will show that you have turned from your **sins**.
4.17 "Turn away from your **sins**, because the Kingdom of heaven is
near!"

Mt 5.29 right eye causes you to **sin,** take it out and throw it
5.30 right hand causes you to **sin,** cut it off and throw it
9. 2 Your **sins** are forgiven."
9. 5 easier to say, 'Your **sins** are forgiven,' or to say,
9. 6 the Son of Man has authority on earth to forgive **sins."**
11.20 did not turn from their **sins,** so he reproached those towns.
11.21 on themselves, to show that they had turned from their **sins!**
12.31 people can be forgiven any **sin** and any evil thing they say;
12.41 because they turned from their **sins** when they heard Jonah preach;
13.41 those who cause people to **sin** and all others who do evil
18.15 "If your brother **sins** against you, go to him and show
18.21 if my brother keeps on **sinning** against me, how many times do
23.28 but inside you are full of hypocrisy and **sins.**
26.28 my blood poured out for many for the forgiveness of **sins.**
26.45 to be handed over to the power of **sinful** men.
27. 4 "I have **sinned** by betraying an innocent man to death!"
Mk 1. 4 "Turn away from your **sins** and be baptized,"
1. 4 he told the people, "and God will forgive your **sins."**
1. 5 They confessed their **sins,** and he baptized them in the River Jordan.
1.15 Turn away from your **sins** and believe the Good News!"
2. 5 Jesus said to the paralysed man, "My son, your **sins** are forgiven."
2. 7 God is the only one who can forgive **sins!"**
2. 9 to this paralysed man, 'Your **sins** are forgiven', or to say,
2.10 the Son of Man has authority on earth to forgive **sins."**
3.28 can be forgiven all their **sins** and all the evil things
3.29 Spirit will never be forgiven, because he has committed an eternal **sin."**
6.12 preached that people should turn away from their **sins.**
14.41 is now being handed over to the power of **sinful** men.
Lk 1.77 they will be saved by having their **sins** forgiven.
3. 3 preaching, "Turn away from your **sins** and be baptized,
3. 3 be baptized, and God will forgive your **sins."**
3. 8 things that will show that you have turned from your **sins.**
5. 8 I am a **sinful** man!"
5.20 he said to the man, "Your **sins** are forgiven, my friend."
5.21 God is the only one who can forgive **sins!"**
5.23 easier to say, 'Your **sins** are forgiven you,' or to say,
5.24 the Son of Man has authority on earth to forgive **sins."**
6.32 Even **sinners** love those who love them!
6.33 Even **sinners** do that!
6.34 Even **sinners** lend to sinners, to get back the same amount!
7.37 In that town was a woman who lived a **sinful** life.
7.39 he would know what kind of **sinful** life she lives!"
7.47 she has shown proves that her many **sins** have been forgiven.
7.48 Then Jesus said to the woman, "Your **sins** are forgiven."
7.49 to say to themselves, "Who is this, who even forgives **sins?"**
10.13 on themselves, to show that they had turned from their **sins!**
11. 4 Forgive us our **sins,** for we forgive everyone who does us wrong.
11.32 because they turned from their **sins** when they heard Jonah preach;
13. 2 that they were worse **sinners** than all the other Galileans?
13. 3 not turn from your **sins,** you will all die as they
13. 5 not turn from your **sins,** you will all die as they
15. 7 joy in heaven over one **sinner** who repents than over
15.10 the angels of God rejoice over one **sinner** who repents."
15.18 Father, I have **sinned** against God and against you.
15.21 'Father,' the son said, 'I have **sinned** against God and against you.
16.30 then they would turn from their **sins.'**
17. 1 that make people fall into **sin** are bound to happen,
17. 2 than for him to cause one of these little ones to **sin.**
17. 3 "If your brother **sins,** rebuke him, and if he repents,
17. 4 If he **sins** against you seven times in one day,
18.13 and said, 'God, have pity on me, a **sinner!'**
19. 7 gone as a guest to the home of a **sinner!"**
24. 7 must be handed over to **sinful** men, be crucified,
24.47 and the forgiveness of **sins** must be preached to all nations,
Jn 1.29 the Lamb of God, who takes away the **sin** of the world!
5.14 so stop **sinning** or something worse may happen to you."
8. 7 of you has committed no **sin** may throw the first stone
8.11 Go, but do not **sin** again."
8.21 you will look for me, but you will die in your **sins.**
8.24 is why I told you that you will die in your **sins.**
8.24 you will die in your **sins** if you do not believe
8.34 everyone who **sins** is a slave of sin.
8.46 Which one of you can prove that I am guilty of **sin?**
9. 2 asked him, "Teacher, whose **sin** caused him to be born blind?
9. 2 Was it his own or his parents' **sin?"**
9. 3 has nothing to do with his **sins** or his parents' sins.
9.16 a man who is a **sinner** perform such miracles as these?"
9.24 We know that this man who cured you is a **sinner."**
9.25 not know if he is a **sinner** or not," the man replied.
9.31 We know that God does not listen to **sinners;**
9.34 born and brought up in **sin**—and you are trying to teach
15.22 not have been guilty of **sin** if I had not come
15.22 as it is, they no longer have any excuse for their **sin.**
15.24 not have been guilty of **sin** if I had not done among
16. 8 that they are wrong about **sin** and about what is right
16. 9 They are wrong about **sin,** because they do not believe in me;
19.11 who handed me over to you is guilty of a worse **sin."**
20.23 If you forgive people's **sins,** they are forgiven;
Acts 2.23 and you killed him by letting **sinful** men crucify him.
2.38 must turn away from his **sins** and be baptized
2.38 name of Jesus Christ, so that your **sins** will be forgiven;
3.19 turn to God, so that he will forgive your **sins.**
5.31 Israel the opportunity to repent and have their **sins** forgiven.
7.60 Do not remember this **sin** against them!"
8.23 you are full of bitter envy and are a prisoner of **sin."**
10.43 will have his **sins** forgiven through the power of his
13.24 Israel that they should turn from their **sins** and be baptized.
Acts 13.38 the message about forgiveness of **sins** is preached to you;
13.38 set free from all the **sins** from which the Law of Moses
15. 9 he forgave their **sins** because they believed.
19. 4 "The baptism of John was for those who turned from their **sins;**
20.21 they should turn from their **sins** to God
22.16 baptized and have your **sins** washed away by praying to him.'
26.18 they will have their **sins** forgiven and receive their place
26.20 they must repent of their **sins** and turn to God
Rom 1.18 from heaven against all the **sin** and evil of the people
2.12 they **sin** and are lost apart from the Law.
2.12 they **sin** and are judged by the Law.
3. 7 Why should I still be condemned as a **sinner?**
3. 9 that Jews and Gentiles alike are all under the power of **sin.**
3.20 the Law does is to make man know that he has **sinned.**
3.23 everyone has **sinned** and is far away from God's saving presence.
3.25 the means by which people's **sins** are forgiven through their faith
3.25 In the past he was patient and overlooked people's **sins;**
3.25 he deals with their **sins,** in order to demonstrate his righteousness.
4. 7 "Happy are those whose wrongs are forgiven, whose **sins** are pardoned!
4. 8 Happy is the person whose **sins** the Lord will not keep
4.25 Because of our **sins** he was handed over to die,
5. 8 it was while we were still **sinners** that Christ died for us!
5.12 **Sin** came into the world through one man,
5.12 and his **sin** brought death with it.
5.12 spread to the whole human race because everyone has **sinned.**
5.13 There was **sin** in the world before the Law was given;
5.13 but where there is no law, no account is kept of **sins.**
5.14 over those who did not **sin** in the same way that Adam
5.15 because God's free gift is not like Adam's **sin.**
5.15 that many people died because of the **sin** of that one man.
5.16 is a difference between God's gift and the **sin** of one man.
5.16 After the one **sin,** came the judgement of "Guilty";
5.16 so many **sins,** comes the undeserved gift of "Not guilty!"
5.17 is true that through the **sin** of one man death began to
5.18 So then, as the one **sin** condemned all mankind,
5.19 as all people were made **sinners** as the result of the
5.20 but where **sin** increased, God's grace increased much more.
5.21 So then, just as **sin** ruled by means of death,
6. 1 continue to live in **sin** so that God's grace will increase?
6. 2 We have died to **sin**—how then can we go on living
6. 6 that the power of the **sinful** self might be destroyed,
6. 6 so that we should no longer be the slaves of **sin.**
6. 7 a person dies, he is set free from the power of **sin.**
6.10 And so, because he died, **sin** has no power over him;
6.11 as dead, so far as **sin** is concerned, but living in
6.12 **Sin** must no longer rule in your mortal bodies,
6.13 part of yourselves to **sin** to be used for wicked purposes.
6.14 **Sin** must not be your master;
6.15 Shall we **sin,** because we are not under law but under God's
6.16 master you obey—either of **sin,** which results in death, or of
6.17 time you were slaves to **sin,** you have obeyed with all your
6.18 You were set free from **sin** and became the slaves of righteousness.
6.20 When you were the slaves of **sin,** you were free from righteousness.
6.22 have been set free from **sin** and are the slaves of God.
6.23 For **sin** pays its wage—death;
7. 5 to our human nature, the **sinful** desires stirred up by the
7. 7 Shall we say, then, that the Law itself is **sinful?**
7. 7 But it was the Law that made me know what **sin** is.
7. 8 by means of that commandment **sin** found its chance to stir up
7. 8 Apart from law, **sin** is a dead thing.
7. 9 the commandment came, **sin** sprang to life, [10] and I died.
7.11 **Sin** found its chance, and by means of the commandment it
7.13 It was **sin** that did it;
7.13 by using what is good, **sin** brought death to me,
7.13 in order that its true nature as **sin** might be revealed.
7.13 sin is shown to be even more terribly **sinful.**
7.14 but I am a mortal man, sold as a slave to **sin.**
7.17 rather it is the **sin** that lives in me.
7.20 instead, it is the **sin** that lives in me.
7.23 prisoner to the law of **sin** which is at work in my
7.25 while my human nature serves the law of **sin.**
8. 2 Jesus, has set me free from the law of **sin** and death.
8. 3 He condemned **sin** in human nature by sending his own Son,
8. 3 with a nature like man's **sinful** nature, to do away with sin.
8.10 even though your bodies are going to die because of **sin.**
8.13 you put to death your **sinful** actions, you will live.
11.11 Because they **sinned,** salvation has come to the Gentiles,
11.12 The **sin** of the Jews brought rich blessings to the world,
11.27 make this covenant with them when I take away their **sins."**
13.14 attention to your **sinful** nature and satisfying its desires.
14.13 that would make your brother stumble or fall into **sin.**
14.20 eat anything that will cause someone else to fall into **sin.**
14.23 And anything that is not based on faith is **sin.**
1 Cor 5. 7 remove the old yeast of **sin** so that you will be entirely
5. 8 having the old yeast of **sin** and wickedness, but with the
6.11 But you have been purified from **sin;**
6.18 Any other **sin** a man commits does not affect his body;
6.18 is guilty of sexual immorality **sins** against his own body.
7.28 But if you do marry, you haven't committed a **sin;**
7.28 if an unmarried woman marries, she hasn't committed a **sin.**
7.36 There is no **sin** in this.
8. 9 action make those who are weak in the faith fall into **sin.**
8.12 this way you will be **sinning** against Christ
8.12 by **sinning** against your Christian brothers
8.13 if food makes my brother **sin,** I will never eat meat again,
8.13 so as not to make my brother fall into **sin.**
11.27 he is guilty of **sin** against the Lord's body and blood.
14.24 he will be convinced of his **sin** by what he hears.

1 Cor 15. 3 that Christ died for our **sins**, as written in the Scriptures;
15.17 faith is a delusion and you are still lost in your **sins.**
15.34 Come back to your right senses and stop your **sinful** ways.
15.56 its power to hurt from **sin,**
15.56 and **sin** gets its power from the Law.
2 Cor 5.19 keep an account of their **sins,** and he has given us the
5.21 Christ was without **sin,** but for our sake
5.21 God made him share our **sin** in order that in union with
11.29 when someone is led into **sin,** I am filled with distress.
12.21 shall weep over many who **sinned** in the past
12.21 things they have done—their lust and their sexual **sins.**
13. 2 those of you who have **sinned** in the past,
Gal 1. 4 Christ gave himself for our **sins,** in obedience to the will
2.15 Jews by birth and not "Gentile **sinners,"** as they are called.
2.17 we are found to be **sinners** as much as the Gentiles are
2.17 does this mean that Christ is serving the cause of **sin?**
3.22 says that the whole world is under the power of **sin;**
Eph 1. 7 we are set free, that is, our **sins** are forgiven.
2. 1 you were spiritually dead because of your disobedience and **sins.**
4.26 your anger lead you into **sin,** and do not stay angry all
Phil 2.15 children, who live in a world of corrupt and **sinful** people.
Col 1.14 by whom we are set free, that is, our **sins** are forgiven.
2.11 consists of being freed from the power of this **sinful** self.
2.13 spiritually dead because of your **sins** and because you were Gentiles
2.13 God forgave us all our **sins;**
1 Thes 2.16 to completion all the **sins** they have always committed.
2 Thes 2.12 truth, but have taken pleasure in **sin,** will be condemned.
1 Tim 1. 9 for the godless and **sinful,** for those who are not religious
1.15 Christ Jesus came into the world to save **sinners.**
1.16 with me, the worst of **sinners,** as an example for all those
5.20 publicly all those who commit **sins,** so that the rest may be
5.22 Take no part in the **sins** of others;
5.24 The **sins** of some people are plain to see,
5.24 and their **sins** go ahead of them to judgement;
5.24 but the **sins** of others are seen only later.
2 Tim 3. 6 by the guilt of their **sins** and driven by all kinds of
Tit 3.11 a person is corrupt, and his **sins** prove that he is wrong.
Heb 1. 3 After achieving forgiveness for the **sins** of mankind, he sat down
2.11 He purifies people from their **sins,**
2.17 service to God, so that the people's **sins** would be forgiven.
3.13 of you be deceived by **sin** and become stubborn,
3.17 With the people who **sinned,** who fell down dead in the desert.
4.15 was tempted in every way that we are, but did not **sin.**
5. 1 to offer sacrifices and offerings for **sins.**
5. 3 sacrifices not only for the **sins** of the people
5. 3 but also for his own **sins.**
7.26 he has no fault or **sin** in him;
7.26 been set apart from **sinners** and raised above the heavens.
7.27 every day for his own **sins** first
7.27 and then for the **sins** of the people.
8.12 I will forgive their **sins** and will no longer remember their wrongs."
9. 5 with their wings spread over the place where **sins** were forgiven.
9. 7 for the **sins** which the people have committed
9. 7 without knowing they were **sinning.**
9.22 is purified by blood, and **sins** are forgiven only if blood is
9.26 and for all, to remove **sin** through the sacrifice of himself.
9.28 was offered in sacrifice once to take away the **sins** of many.
9.28 time, not to deal with **sin,** but to save those who are
10. 2 really been purified from their **sins,**
10. 2 would not feel guilty of **sin** any more, and all sacrifices
10. 3 serve year after year to remind people of their **sins.**
10. 4 For the blood of bulls and goats can never take away **sins.**
10. 6 whole on the altar or with sacrifices to take away **sins.**
10. 8 burnt on the altar and the sacrifices to take away **sins."**
10.10 we are all purified from **sin** by the offering that he made
10.11 but these sacrifices can never take away **sins.**
10.12 however, offered one sacrifice for **sins,** an offering that is
10.14 has made perfect for ever those who are purified from **sin.**
10.17 "I will not remember their **sins** and evil deeds any longer."
10.18 an offering to take away **sins** is no longer needed.
10.26 sacrifice that will take away **sins**
10.26 if we purposely go on **sinning** after the truth has been made
10.29 the blood of God's covenant which purified him from **sin?**
11.25 God's people rather than to enjoy **sin** for a little while.
12. 1 the way, and of the **sin** which holds on to us
12. 3 how he put up with so much hatred from **sinners!**
12. 4 For in your struggle against **sin** you have not yet had to
13.11 the Most Holy Place to offer it as a sacrifice for **sins;**
13.12 in order to purify the people from **sin** with his own blood.
Jas 1.15 Then his evil desire conceives and gives birth to **sin;**
1.15 and **sin,** when it is full-grown, gives birth to death.
2. 9 you are guilty of **sin,** and the Law condemns you
3.14 jealous, bitter, and selfish, don't **sin** against the truth by boasting
4. 8 Wash your hands, you **sinners!**
4.17 do the good he knows he should do is guilty of **sin.**
5.15 and the **sins** he has committed will be forgiven.
5.16 So then, confess your **sins** to one another
5.20 whoever turns a **sinner** back from his wrong way
5.20 will save that **sinner's** soul from death
5.20 and bring about the forgiveness of many **sins.**
1 Pet 2.22 He committed no **sin,** and no one ever heard a lie come
2.24 Christ himself carried our **sins** in his body to the cross,
2.24 so that we might die to **sin** and live for righteousness.
3.18 For Christ died for **sins** once and for all,
3.18 good man on behalf of **sinners,** in order to lead you
4. 1 whoever suffers physically is no longer involved with **sin.**
4. 8 Above everything, love one another earnestly, because love covers over many **sins.**
4.18 what, then, will become of godless **sinners?"**
2 Pet 1. 9 has forgotten that he has been purified from his past **sins.**
2. 4 not spare the angels who **sinned,** but threw them into hell,
2.14 their appetite for **sin** is never satisfied.
2.16 would get for doing wrong [16]and was rebuked for his **sin.**
3. 9 but wants all to turn away from their **sins.**
1 Jn 1. 7 the blood of Jesus, his Son, purifies us from every **sin.**
1. 8 say that we have no **sin,** we deceive ourselves, and there is
1. 9 But if we confess our **sins** to God, he will keep his
1. 9 he will forgive us our **sins** and purify us from all our
1.10 say that we have not **sinned,** we make God out to be
2. 1 writing this to you, my children, so that you will not **sin;**
2. 1 but if anyone does **sin,** we have someone who pleads with the
2. 2 the means by which our **sins** are forgiven,
2. 2 and not our sins only, but also the **sins** of everyone.
2.10 there is nothing in him that will cause someone else to **sin.**
2.12 my children, because your **sins** are forgiven for the sake of
2.16 what the **sinful** self desires, what people see
3. 4 Whoever **sins** is guilty of breaking God's law,
3. 4 because **sin** is a breaking of the law.
3. 5 to take away sins, and that there is no **sin** in him.
3. 6 who lives in union with Christ does not continue to **sin;**
3. 6 whoever continues to **sin** has never seen him or known him.
3. 8 Whoever continues to **sin** belongs to the Devil,
3. 8 because the Devil has **sinned** from the very beginning.
3. 9 does not continue to **sin,** for God's very nature is in
3. 9 and because God is his Father, he cannot continue to **sin.**
4.10 his Son to be the means by which our **sins** are forgiven.
5.16 see your brother commit a **sin** that does not lead to death,
5.16 This applies to those whose **sins** do not lead to death.
5.16 But there is **sin** which leads to death, and I do not
5.17 All wrongdoing is **sin,**
5.17 but there is **sin** which does not lead to death.
5.18 child of God keeps on **sinning,** for the Son of God keeps
Jude 8 have visions which make them **sin** against their own bodies;
15 words that godless **sinners** have spoken against him!"
23 but hate their very clothes, stained by their **sinful** lusts.
Rev 1. 5 has freed us from our **sins** [6]and made us a kingdom
2. 5 Turn from your **sins** and do what you did at first.
2. 5 you don't turn from your **sins,** I will come to you and
2.14 the people of Israel into **sin** by persuading them to eat food
2.16 Now turn from your **sins!**
2.21 time to repent of her **sins,** but she does not want to
3. 3 obey it and turn from your **sins.**
3.19 Be in earnest, then, and turn from your **sins.**
16. 9 But they would not turn from their **sins** and praise his greatness.
18. 4 You must not take part in her **sins;**
18. 5 For her **sins** are piled up as high as heaven,

SIN-OFFERING

Lev 4.14 the community shall bring a young bull as a **sin-offering.**
4.20 with the bull for the **sin-offering,** and in this way he shall
4.32 brings a sheep as a **sin-offering,** it must be a female
5. 1 **Sin-offerings** are required in the following cases.
5. 7 one for a **sin-offering** and the other for a burnt-offering.
5. 8 priest, who will first offer the bird for the **sin-offering.**
5.11 he shall bring one kilogramme of flour as a **sin-offering.**
5.11 on it, because it is a **sin-offering,** not a grain-offering.
6.16 very holy, like the **sin-offerings** and the repayment-offerings.
6.25 Aaron and his sons the following regulations for **sin-offerings.**
6.25 The animal for a **sin-offering** shall be killed on the north
7. 7 applies to both the **sin-offering** and the repayment-offering:
7.37 **sin-offerings,**
8. 2 the young bull for the **sin-offering,** the two rams, and the
8.14 the young bull for the **sin-offering,** and Aaron and his sons
9. 2 bull for a **sin-offering** and the ram for a burnt-offering.
9. 3 a male goat for a **sin-offering,** a one-year-old calf, and a
9. 7 the altar and offer the **sin-offering** and the burnt-offering
9. 8 killed the young bull which was for his own **sin-offering.**
9.15 and offered it, as he had done with his own **sin-offering.**
10.16 about the goat for the **sin-offering** and learnt that it had
10.17 "Why didn't you eat the **sin-offering** in a sacred place?
10.19 had eaten the **sin-offering** today, would the Lord have approved?
10.19 The people presented their **sin-offering** to the Lord today,
12. 6 a burnt-offering and a pigeon or a dove for a **sin-offering.**
12. 8 and the other for a **sin-offering,** and the priest shall
14.13 for the **sin-offerings** and the burnt-offerings are killed.
14.13 because the repayment-offering, like the **sin-offering,**
14.19 the **sin-offering** and perform the ritual of purification.
14.22 one for the **sin-offering** and one for the burnt-offering.
14.31 doves or pigeons [31]as the **sin-offering** and the other as
15.15 of them as a **sin-offering** and the other as a burnt-offering.
15.30 of them as a **sin-offering** and the other as a burnt-offering,
16. 3 bull for a **sin-offering** and a ram for a burnt-offering."
16. 5 goats for a **sin-offering** and a ram for a burnt-offering.
16. 9 chosen by lot for the Lord and offer it as a **sin-offering.**
16.11 the bull as the **sin-offering** for himself and his family,
16.15 kill the goat for the **sin-offering** for the people, bring its
16.25 on the altar the fat of the animal for the **sin-offering.**
16.27 the goat used for the **sin-offering,** whose blood was brought
23.19 one male goat as a **sin-offering** and two one-year-old male
Num 6.11 one as a **sin-offering** and the other as a burnt-offering,
6.14 for a **sin-offering,** and a ram for a fellowship-offering.
6.16 the Lord and offer the **sin-offering** and the burnt-offering.
7.12 one goat for the **sin-offering;**
7.84 twelve goats for the **sin-offerings**
8. 8 and you are to take another bull for the **sin-offering.**
8.12 offered as a **sin-offering** and the other as a burnt-offering,
15.24 In addition, they are to offer a male goat as a **sin-offering.**
15.25 brought their **sin-offering** as a food-offering to the Lord.
15.27 he is to offer a one-year-old female goat as a **sin-offering.**

Num 18. 9 the **sin-offerings,** and the repayment offerings.
28.15 its wine-offering, offer one male goat as a **sin-offering.**
28.22 one male goat as a **sin-offering,** and in this way perform the
28.30 one male goat as a **sin-offering,** and in this way perform the
29. 5 one male goat as a **sin-offering,** and in this way perform the
29.11 one male goat as a **sin-offering,** in addition to the goat
29.16 Also offer one male goat as a **sin-offering.**
2 Chr 29.24 and **sin-offerings** to be made for all Israel.
Ezek 44.29 **sin-offerings** and the repayment-offerings will be the priests'
45.17 He is to provide the **sin-offerings,** the grain-offerings, the
45.19 of the blood of this **sin-offering** and put it on the
45.23 is also to sacrifice a male goat each day as a **sin-offering.**

SINAI

Mountain between Egypt and Palestine where Moses received the Law.

Ex 3. 1 across the desert and came to **Sinai,** the holy mountain.
16. 1 came to the desert of Sin, which is between Elim and **Sinai.**
17. 6 I will stand before you on a rock at Mount **Sinai.**
19. 1 after they had left Egypt they came to the desert of **Sinai.**
19. 1 at the foot of Mount **Sinai,** [3]and Moses went up the mountain
19.11 will come down on Mount **Sinai,** where all the people can see
19.18 The whole of Mount **Sinai** was covered with smoke, because
19.20 on the top of Mount **Sinai** and called Moses to the top
24.15 Moses went up Mount **Sinai,** and a cloud covered it.
31.18 speaking to Moses on Mount **Sinai,** he gave him the two stone
33. 6 So after they left Mount **Sinai,** the people of Israel no
34. 2 morning, and come up Mount **Sinai** to meet me there at the
34. 4 them up Mount **Sinai,** just as the Lord had commanded.
34.29 Moses went down from Mount **Sinai** carrying the Ten Commandments,
34.32 all the laws that the Lord had given him on Mount **Sinai.**
Lev 7.38 There on Mount **Sinai** in the desert, the Lord gave these
25. 1 spoke to Moses on Mount **Sinai** and commanded him [2]to give
26.46 Lord gave to Moses on Mount **Sinai** for the people of Israel.
27.34 Lord gave Moses on Mount **Sinai** for the people of Israel.
Num 1. 1 Moses there in the Tent of his presence in the **Sinai** Desert.
1.19 In the **Sinai** Desert, Moses registered the people.
3. 1 Moses at the time the Lord spoke to Moses on Mount **Sinai.**
3. 4 they offered unholy fire to the Lord in the **Sinai** Desert.
3.14 In the **Sinai** Desert the Lord commanded Moses [15]to
9. 1 spoke to Moses in the **Sinai** Desert in the first month of
9. 5 day of the first month they did so in the **Sinai** Desert.
10.12 Israelites started on their journey out of the **Sinai** Desert.
10.33 When the people left **Sinai,** the holy mountain, they
26.64 Aaron had listed in the first census in the **Sinai** Desert.
28. 6 was first offered at Mount **Sinai** as a food-offering, a smell
33.15 **Sinai** Desert, Kibroth Hattaavah (or "Graves of Craving"),
Deut 1. 2 days to travel from Mount **Sinai** to Kadesh Barnea by way of
1. 6 "When we were at Mount **Sinai,** the Lord our God said to
1. 9 we were still at Mount **Sinai,** I told you, 'The
1.19 We left Mount **Sinai** and went through that vast and fearful
4.10 Lord your God at Mount **Sinai,** when he said to me, 'Assemble
4.15 from the fire on Mount **Sinai,** you did not see any form.
5. 2 At Mount **Sinai** the Lord our God made a covenant, [3]not
9. 8 Even at Mount **Sinai** you made the Lord angry—angry enough
18.16 you were gathered at Mount **Sinai,** you begged not to hear the
29. 1 covenant which the Lord had made with them at Mount **Sinai.**
33. 2 The Lord came from Mount **Sinai;**
Judg 5. 5 quaked before the Lord of **Sinai,** before the Lord, the God of
1 Kgs 8. 9 had placed there at Mount **Sinai,** when the Lord made a
19. 8 strength to walk forty days to **Sinai,** the holy mountain.
2 Chr 5.10 had placed there at Mount **Sinai,** when the Lord made a
Neh 9.13 At Mount **Sinai** you came down from heaven;
Ps 68. 8 coming of the God of **Sinai,** the coming of the God of
68.17 chariots the Lord comes from **Sinai** into the holy place.
106.19 They made a gold bull-calf at **Sinai** and worshipped that idol;
Ezek 20.36 I condemned your fathers in the **Sinai** Desert,"
Mal 4. 4 I gave him at Mount **Sinai** for all the people of Israel
Acts 7.30 the flames of a burning bush in the desert near Mount **Sinai.**
7.38 spoke to him on Mount **Sinai,** and he received God's living
Gal 4.24 Hagar, and she represents the covenant made at Mount **Sinai.**
4.25 Hagar, who stands for Mount **Sinai** in Arabia, is a figure
Heb 12.18 you can feel, to Mount **Sinai** with its blazing fire, the

SINCERE

Josh 24.14 Joshua continued, "honour the Lord and serve him **sincerely** and faithfully.
Judg 9.16 "were you really honest and **sincere** when you made Abimelech king?
9.19 Gideon and his family was **sincere** and honest, then be happy
1 Kgs 8.48 that land they truly and **sincerely** repent, and pray to you
1 Chr 29.17 In honesty and **sincerity** I have willingly given all this
2 Chr 6.38 that land they truly and **sincerely** repent and pray to you as
11.16 of Israel people who **sincerely** wanted to worship the Lord,
Job 16.17 guilty of any violence, and my prayer to God is **sincere.**
33. 3 All my words are **sincere,** and I am speaking the truth.
Ps 15. 2 are true and **sincere,** [3]and who does not slander others.
41. 6 Those who come to see me are not **sincere;**
51. 6 **Sincerity** and truth are what you require;
78.36 nothing they said was **sincere.**
145.18 to those who call to him, who call to him with **sincerity.**
Jer 3.10 she was not **sincere.**
Hos 7.14 have not prayed to me **sincerely,** but instead they throw
Joel 2.12 now," says the Lord, "repent **sincerely** and return to me
Lk 20.20 men to pretend they were **sincere,** and they sent them to trap
Rom 12. 9 Love must be completely **sincere.**
2 Cor 1.12 God-given frankness and **sincerity,** by the power of God's grace,
2.17 we speak with **sincerity** in his presence,
Eph 6. 5 and do it with a **sincere** heart, as though you were serving
Phil 1.17 others do not proclaim Christ **sincerely,** but from a spirit
Col 3.22 but do it with a **sincere** heart because of your reverence
1 Tim 3. 8 Church helpers must also have a good character and be **sincere;**
2 Tim 1. 5 I remember the **sincere** faith you have,
Tit 2. 7 Be **sincere** and serious in your teaching.
Heb 10.22 near to God with a **sincere** heart and a sure faith,
1 Pet 1.22 have come to have a **sincere** love for your fellow-believers,

SINEWS

Job 10.11 my body with bones and **sinews** and covered the bones with
Ezek 37. 6 I will give you **sinews** and muscles, and cover you with skin.
37. 8 were covered with **sinews** and muscles, and then with skin.

SING

[SANG, SUNG]

Gen 31.27 your way with rejoicing and **singing** to the music of
Ex 15. 1 Then Moses and the Israelites **sang** this song to the Lord:
15. 1 "I will **sing** to the Lord, because he has won a glorious
15. 2 him, my father's God, and I will **sing** about his greatness.
15.21 Miriam **sang** for them:
15.21 "**Sing** to the Lord, because he has won a glorious victory;
32.18 it's the sound of **singing.**"
Num 21.17 At that time the people of Israel **sang** this song:
21.27 That is why the poets **sing,**
Deut 31.21 this song will still be **sung,** and it will stand as evidence
Judg 5. 1 On that day Deborah and Barak son of Abinoam **sang** this song:
5. 3 I will **sing,** I will play music to Israel's God, the Lord.
5.12 **Sing** a song!
15.16 So Samson **sang,**
16.23 They **sang,** "Our god has given us victory over our enemy Samson!"
16.24 When the people saw him, they **sang** praise to their god:
1 Sam 18. 6 They were **singing** joyful songs, dancing, and playing
18. 7 In their celebration the women **sang,** "Saul has killed thousands,
21.11 man about whom the women **sang,** as they danced, 'Saul has
29. 5 one about whom the women **sang,** as they danced, 'Saul has
2 Sam 1.17 David **sang** this lament for Saul and his son Jonathan,
3.33 David **sang** this lament for Abner:
6. 5 the Israelites were dancing and **singing** with all their might
19.35 I eat and drink, and I can't hear the voices of **singers.**
22. 1 Saul and his other enemies, David **sang** this song to the Lord:
22.50 I **sing** praises to you.
1 Chr 13. 8 They **sang** and played musical instruments—harps, drums,
15.16 to assign various Levites to **sing** and to play joyful music
15.17 From the clans of **singers** they chose the following
16. 4 in front of the Covenant Box, by **singing** and praising him.
16. 7 the responsibility for **singing** praises to the Lord.
16. 9 **Sing** praise to the Lord;
16.23 **Sing** to the Lord, all the world!
16.41 who were specifically chosen to **sing** praises to the Lord for
16.42 which were played when the songs of praise were **sung.**
25. 3 the music of harps, and **sang** praise and thanks to the Lord.
2 Chr 5.11 The **singers** were accompanied in perfect harmony by trumpets,
5.11 and other instruments, as they praised the Lord, **singing:**
7. 6 and **singing** the hymn, "His Love Is Eternal!"
8.14 the priests in **singing** hymns and in doing their work.
20.21 on sacred occasions and to march ahead of the army, **singing:**
20.22 When they began to **sing,** the Lord threw the invading
29.27 the offering began, the people **sang** praise to the Lord, and
29.28 joined in worship, and the **singing** and the rest of the music
29.30 nation told the Levites to **sing** to the Lord the songs of
29.30 So everyone **sang** with great joy as they knelt and worshipped God.
35.25 custom in Israel for the **singers,** both men and women, to use
Ezra 3.11 They **sang** the Lord's praises, repeating the refrain:
Neh 4.10 The people of Judah had a song they **sang:**
11.17 He led the temple choir in **singing** the prayer of thanksgiving.
12. 8 were in charge of the **singing** of hymns of thanksgiving:
12. 9 The following formed the choir that **sang** the responses:
12.28 The Levite families of **singers** gathered from the area
12.32 Hoshaiah marched behind the **singers,** followed by half
12.42 The **singers,** led by Jezrahiah,
12.42 **sang** at the top of their voices.
Job 38. 7 of that day the stars **sang** together, and the heavenly beings
Ps 5.11 they can always **sing** for joy.
7.17 Lord for his justice, I **sing** praises to the Lord, the Most
8. 2 it is **sung** by children and babies.
9. 2 I will **sing** with joy because of you.
9. 2 I will **sing** praise to you, Almighty God.
9.11 **Sing** praise to the Lord, who rules in Zion!
13. 6 I will **sing** to you, O Lord, because you have been good
18.49 I **sing** praises to you.
21.13 We will **sing** and praise your power.
26. 7 I **sing** a hymn of thanksgiving and tell of all your
27. 6 I will **sing,** I will praise the Lord.
30. 4 **Sing** praise to the Lord, all his faithful people!
30.12 I will **sing** praise to you.
32. 7 I **sing** aloud of your salvation, because you protect me.
33. 2 the Lord with harps, **sing** to him with stringed instruments.
33. 3 **Sing** a new song to him, play the harp with skill, and
40. 3 He taught me to **sing** a new song, a song of praise
42. 4 along, a happy crowd, **singing** and shouting praise to God.
43. 4 will play my harp and **sing** praise to you, O God, my
47. 6 **Sing** praise to God;
47. 6 **sing** praise to our king!
57. 7 I will **sing** and praise you!
59.16 But I will **sing** about your strength;
59.16 every morning I will **sing** aloud of your constant love.
61. 8 So I will always **sing** praises to you, as I offer you

Ps	63. 5	be satisfied, and I will **sing** glad songs of praise to you.
	63. 7	In the shadow of your wings I **sing** for joy.
	65.13	Everything shouts and **sings** for joy.
	66. 2	**Sing** to the glory of his name;
	66. 4	they **sing** praises to you, they sing praises to your name."
	67. 4	the nations be glad and **sing** for joy, because you judge the
	68. 4	**Sing** to God, sing praises to his name;
	68.25	The **singers** are in front, the musicians are behind, in
	68.32	**Sing** to God, kingdoms of the world, sing praise to the Lord,
	71.23	with my whole being I will **sing** because you have saved me.
	75. 9	speaking of the God of Jacob or **singing** praises to him.
	81. 1	**sing** praise to the God of Jacob!
	84. 2	With my whole being I **sing** for joy to the living God.
	84. 4	who live in your Temple, always **singing** praise to you.
	87. 7	They dance and **sing,** "In Zion is the source of all our
	89. 1	O Lord, I will always **sing** of your constant love;
	89. 5	The heavens **sing** of the wonderful things you do;
	89. 5	the holy ones **sing** of your faithfulness, Lord.
	89.12	Mount Tabor and Mount Hermon **sing** to you for joy.
	90.14	love, so that we may **sing** and be glad all our life.
	92. 1	to you, O Lord, to **sing** in your honour, O Most High
	92. 4	because of what you have done, I **sing** for joy.
	95. 1	Let us **sing** for joy to God, who protects us!
	95. 2	him with thanksgiving and **sing** joyful songs of praise.
	96. 1	**Sing** a new song to the Lord!
	96. 1	**Sing** to the Lord, all the world!
	96. 2	**Sing** to the Lord, and praise him!
	98. 1	**Sing** a new song to the Lord;
	98. 4	**Sing** for joy to the Lord, all the earth;
	98. 5	**Sing** praises to the Lord!
	98. 7	**sing,** earth, and all who live on you!
	98. 8	you hills, **sing** together with joy before the Lord,
	100. 1	**Sing** to the Lord, all the world!
	101. 1	about loyalty and justice, and I **sing** it to you, O Lord.
	104.12	In the trees near by, the birds make their nests and **sing.**
	104.33	I will **sing** to the Lord all my life;
	104.33	as long as I live I will **sing** praises to my God.
	105. 2	**Sing** praise to the Lord;
	105.43	his chosen people out, and they **sang** and shouted for joy.
	106.12	Then his people believed his promises and **sang** praises to him.
	108. 1	I will **sing** and praise you!
	119.172	I will **sing** about your law, because your commands are just.
	126. 2	How we laughed, how we **sang** for joy!
	126. 6	the seed will come back **singing** for joy, as they bring in
	132.16	all they do, and her people will **sing** and shout for joy.
	135. 3	**sing** praises to his name, because he is kind.
	137. 3	Those who captured us told us to **sing;**
	137. 3	**"Sing** us a song about Zion."
	137. 4	How can we **sing** a song to the Lord in a foreign
	137. 6	I never be able to **sing** again if I do not remember
	138. 1	I **sing** praise to you before the gods.
	138. 5	They will **sing** about what you have done and about your
	144. 9	I will **sing** you a new song, O God;
	144. 9	I will play the harp and **sing** to you.
	145. 7	tell about all your goodness and **sing** about your kindness.
	146. 2	I will **sing** to my God all my life.
	147. 1	It is good to **sing** praise to our God;
	147. 7	**Sing** hymns of praise to the Lord;
	149. 1	**Sing** a new song to the Lord;
	149. 5	rejoice in their triumph and **sing** joyfully all night long.
Prov	25.20	**Singing** to a person who is depressed is like taking off
Ecc	2. 8	Men and women **sang** to entertain me, and I had all the
	7. 5	reprimand you than to have stupid people **sing** your praises.
Song	2.12	This is the time for **singing;**
	6. 9	queens and concubines **sing** her praises.
Is	5. 1	Listen while I **sing** you this song, a song of my friend
	12. 1	A day is coming when people will **sing,**
	12. 4	A day is coming when people will **sing,**
	12. 5	**Sing** to the Lord because of the great things he has done.
	12. 6	Let everyone who lives in Zion shout and **sing!**
	14. 7	world enjoys rest and peace, and everyone **sings** for joy.
	16.10	No one shouts or **sings** in the vineyards.
	23.16	Play and **sing** your songs again to bring men back once more.
	24. 9	There is no more happy **singing** over wine;
	24.14	Those who survive will **sing** for joy.
	26. 1	coming when the people will **sing** this song in the land of
	26.19	sleeping in their graves will wake up and **sing** for joy.
	30.29	people, will be happy and **sing** as you do on the night
	35. 2	The desert will **sing** and shout for joy;
	35.10	reach Jerusalem with gladness, **singing** and shouting for joy.
	38.20	We will play harps and **sing** your praise,
	38.20	**Sing** praise in your Temple
	42.10	**Sing** a new song to the Lord;
	42.10	**sing** his praise, all the world!
	42.10	**Sing,** distant lands and all who live there!
	43.21	people I made for myself, and they will **sing** my praises!"
	49.13	**Sing,** heavens!
	51.11	Jerusalem with gladness, **singing** and shouting for joy.
	54. 1	a childless woman, but now you can **sing** and shout for joy.
	55.12	and hills will burst into **singing,** and the trees will shout
	65.14	They will **sing** for joy, but you will cry with a broken
Jer	7.29	**Sing** a funeral song on the hill-tops, because I, the Lord,
	9.17	mourners to come, for the women who **sing** funeral songs."
	9.18	"Tell them to hurry and **sing** a funeral song for us, until
	9.20	how to mourn, and your friends how to **sing** a funeral song.
	20.13	**Sing** to the Lord!
	30.19	The people who live there will **sing** praise;
	31. 7	**"Sing** with joy for Israel, the greatest of the nations.
	31. 7	**Sing** your song of praise, 'The Lord has saved his people;
	31.12	They will come and **sing** for joy on Mount Zion and be
	33.11	You will hear people **sing** as they bring thank-offerings
Lam	1. 4	The girls who **sang** there suffer, and the priests can only groan.
Ezek	19. 1	The Lord told me to **sing** this song of sorrow for two
	19.14	it has been **sung** again and again.
	26.17	They will **sing** this funeral song for you:
	27. 2	said to me, [2]"Mortal man, **sing** a funeral song for Tyre,
	32.16	women of the nations will **sing** it to mourn for Egypt and
	33.32	than an entertainer **singing** love songs or playing a harp.
Amos	5. 1	of Israel, to this funeral song which I **sing** over you:
Jon	2. 9	But I will **sing** praises to you;
Mic	2. 4	of disaster, and they will **sing** this song of despair about
Zeph	3.14	**Sing** and shout for joy, people of Israel!
	3.17	He will **sing** and be joyful over you, [18]as joyful as people
Zech	2.10	The Lord said, **"Sing** for joy, people of Jerusalem!
Mt	11.17	We **sang** funeral songs, but you wouldn't cry!'
	26.30	Then they **sang** a hymn and went out to the Mount
Mk	14.26	Then they **sang** a hymn and went out to the Mount
Lk	2.13	angels appeared with the angel, **singing** praises to God:
	2.20	The shepherds went back, **singing** praises to God
	7.32	We **sang** funeral songs, but you wouldn't cry!'
Acts	16.25	and Silas were praying and **singing** hymns to God,
Rom	15. 9	I will **sing** praises to you."
1 Cor	14.15	I will **sing** with my spirit,
	14.15	but I will **sing** also with my mind.
Eph	5.19	**sing** hymns and psalms to the Lord with praise in your hearts.
Col	3.16	**Sing** psalms, hymns, and sacred songs;
	3.16	**sing** to God with thanksgiving in your hearts.
Jas	5.13	He should **sing** praises.
Rev	4. 8	Day and night they never stop **singing:**
	4. 9	The four living creatures **sing** songs of glory and honour
	5. 9	They **sang** a new song:
	5.12	creatures, and the elders, [12]and **sang** in a loud voice:
	5.13	all living beings in the universe—and they were **singing:**
	14. 3	they were **singing** a new song, which only they could learn.
	15. 3	and **singing** the song of Moses,

SINGED

Dan	3.27	Their hair was not **singed,** their clothes were not burnt, and

SINGLE

Ex	25.36	lamp-stand are to be a **single** piece of pure hammered gold.
	37.22	the lamp-stand were a **single** piece of pure hammered gold.
Deut	12.11	The Lord will choose a **single** place where he is to be
Judg	3.28	they did not allow a **single** man to cross.
	9. 5	on the top of a **single** stone he killed his seventy brothers,
	9.18	men on a **single** stone—and just because Abimelech,
2 Sam	17.13	Not a **single** stone will be left there on top of the
2 Kgs	19.32	will not enter this city or shoot a **single** arrow against it.
Esth	3.13	that on a **single** day, the thirteenth day of Adar,
Job	4. 7	Name a **single** case where a righteous man met with disaster.
Ps	14. 3	Not one of them does what is right, not a **single** one.
	53. 3	Not one of them does what is right, not a **single** one.
Is	9.14	In a **single** day the Lord will punish Israel's leaders
	10.17	a flame, which in a **single** day will burn up everything, even
	15. 1	Kir are destroyed in a **single** night, and silence covers the
	22. 3	ran away and were captured before they shot a **single** arrow.
	37.33	will not enter this city or shoot a **single** arrow against it.
	47. 9	in a moment, in a **single** day, both of these things will
Jer	32.39	I will give them a **single** purpose in life:
Ezek	33.32	to all your words and don't obey a **single** one of them.
Hos	1.11	will choose for themselves a **single** leader, and once again
Zech	3. 9	placing in front of Joshua a **single** stone with seven facets.
	3. 9	on it, and in a **single** day I will take away the
	11. 8	me, and I got rid of them all in a **single** month.
Mt	5.36	because you cannot make a **single** hair white or black.
	24. 2	not a **single** stone here will be left in its place;
	27.14	Jesus refused to answer a **single** word,
Mk	13. 2	Not a **single** stone here will be left in its place;
Lk	19.44	not a **single** stone will they leave in its place,
	19.48	kept listening to him, not wanting to miss a **single** word.
	21. 6	will come when not a **single** stone here will be left
	21.18	But not a **single** hair from your heads will be lost.
Jn	12.24	remains no more than a **single** grain unless it is dropped
1 Cor	1. 7	not failed to receive a **single** blessing, as you wait for our
	7.11	she must remain **single** or else be reconciled
	12.12	Christ is like a **single** body, which has many parts;
Gal	3.16	meaning many people, but the **singular** "descendant," meaning one person only,
Heb	12.16	like Esau, who for a **single** meal sold his rights
Rev	21.21	each gate was made from a **single** pearl.

SINK
[SANK, SUNK]

Gen	42.28	Their hearts **sank,** and in fear they asked one another,
Ex	15. 5	they **sank** to the bottom like a stone.
	15.10	they **sank** like lead in the terrible water.
Judg	5.27	He **sank** to his knees, fell down and lay still
	5.27	At her feet he **sank** to his knees and fell;
Neh	9.11	drowned in deep water, as a stone **sinks** in the raging sea.
Job	29.22	My words **sank** in like drops of rain;
Ps	35.12	They pay me back evil for good, and I **sink** in despair.
	69. 2	I am **sinking** in deep mud, and there is no solid ground;
	69.14	Save me from **sinking** in the mud;
	69.15	don't let me drown in the depths or **sink** into the grave.
	106.43	they chose to rebel against him and **sank** deeper into sin.
	142. 6	Listen to my cry for help, for I am **sunk** in despair.
Is	2.16	He will **sink** even the largest and most beautiful ships.
	25.11	God will humiliate them, and their hands will **sink** helplessly.
Jer	38. 6	water in the well, only mud, and I **sank** down in it.

Jer 38.22 now that his feet have **sunk** in the mud, his friends have
51.64 happen to Babylonia—it will **sink** and never rise again,
Ezek 23.14 "She **sank** deeper and deeper in her immorality.
27.34 You have **sunk** to the ocean depths.
Hab 3. 6 the everlasting hills **sink** down, the hills where he walked
Mt 8.24 storm hit the lake, and the boat was in danger of **sinking.**
13.21 But it does not **sink** deep into them, and they don't last
14.30 he was afraid and started to **sink** down in the water.
Mk 4.17 But it does not **sink** deep into them, and they don't last
Lk 5. 7 boats so full of fish that the boats were about to **sink.**
8.13 But it does not **sink** deep into them;
Acts 27.40 the anchors and let them **sink** in the sea,

SIR

Gen 18. 3 touching the ground, [3]he said, **"Sirs,** please do not pass
19. 2 down before them [2]and said, **"Sirs,** I am here to serve you.
19.18 But Lot answered, "No, please don't make us do that, **sir.**
23. 6 They answered, [6]"Listen to us, **sir.**
23.11 in the hearing of everyone there, [11]"Listen, **sir;**
23.15 Ephron answered, [15]**"Sir,** land worth only four hundred
24.18 She said, "Drink, **sir,"** and quickly lowered her jar
31.35 not be angry with me, **sir,** but I am not able to
32. 5 I am sending you word, **sir,** in the hope of gaining your
33. 5 "These, **sir,** are the children whom God has been good
42.10 "No, **sir,"** they answered.
42.11 We are not spies, **sir,** we are honest men."
42.13 were twelve brothers in all, **sir,** sons of the same man in
43.20 in charge, [20]"If you please, **sir,** we came here once
44. 7 answered him, "What do you mean, **sir,** by talking like this?
44. 9 **Sir,** if any one of us is found to have it, he
44.16 "What can we say to you, **sir?"**
44.18 to Joseph and said, "Please, **sir,** allow me to speak with
44.19 **Sir,** you asked us, 'Have you got a father or another brother?'
44.21 **Sir,** you told us to bring him here, so that you could
44.30 "And now, **sir,"** Judah continued, "if I go back
44.33 And now, **sir,** I will stay here as your slave in place
47. 3 "We are shepherds, **sir,** just as our ancestors were," they
47.18 hide the fact from you, **sir,** that our money is all gone
47.25 have been good to us, **sir,** and we will be the king's
Num 11.28 young man, spoke up and said to Moses, "Stop them, **sir!"**
12.11 he said to Moses, "Please, **sir,** do not make us suffer
31.49 went to Moses [49]and reported, **"Sir,** we have counted the
32.25 of Gad and Reuben said, **"Sir,** we will do as you command.
32.31 of Gad and Reuben answered, **"Sir,** we will do as the Lord
Josh 5.14 on the ground in worship and said, "I am your servant, **sir.**
9. 9 from a very distant land, **sir,** because we have heard of the
9.24 They answered, "We did it, **sir,** because we learnt that
10. 6 "Do not abandon us, **sir!**
Judg 4.18 went out to meet Sisera and said to him, "Come in, **sir;**
6.13 him, "If I may ask, **sir,** why has all this happened to
Ruth 2.13 Ruth answered, "You are very kind to me, **sir.**
3. 9 "It's Ruth, **sir,"** she answered.
1 Sam 1.15 "No, I'm not drunk, **sir,"** she answered.
1.26 Hannah said to him, "Excuse me, **sir.**
3. 4 He answered, "Yes, **sir!"**
3.16 "Yes, **sir,"** answered Samuel.
12.19 they said to Samuel, "Please, **sir,** pray to the Lord your
16.16 So give us the order, **sir,** and we will look for a
19. 4 David to Saul and said, **"Sir,** don't do wrong to your
22.12 "At your service, **sir,"** he answered.
25.24 at David's feet, and said to him, "Please, **sir,** listen
25.25 I wasn't there when your servants arrived, **sir.**
25.27 Please, **sir,** accept this present I have brought you, and
25.28 Please forgive me, **sir,** for any wrong I have done.
25.31 to feel regret or remorse, **sir,** for having killed without
25.31 the Lord has blessed you, **sir,** please do not forget me."
26.18 And he added, "Why, **sir,** are you still pursuing me,
27. 5 There is no need, **sir,** for me to live with you in
28.21 she said to him, "Please, **sir,** I risked my life by doing
29. 8 David answered, "What have I done wrong, **sir?**
2 Sam 1. 7 I answered, 'Yes, **sir!'**
1.10 from his arm, and I have brought them to you, **sir."**
9. 2 "At your service, **sir,"** he answered.
9. 6 "Mephibosheth," and he answered, "At your service, **sir."**
9. 8 again and said, "I am no better than a dead dog, **sir!**
14. 5 "I am a poor widow, **sir,"** she answered.
14. 6 **Sir,** I had two sons, and one day they got into a
14. 7 And now, **sir,** all my relatives have turned against me and
14.17 to myself that your promise, **sir,** would make me safe,
15. 7 Absalom said to King David, **"Sir,** let me go to Hebron and
18.10 him and reported to Joab, **"Sir,** I saw Absalom hanging in an
18.29 Ahimaaz answered, **"Sir,** when your officer Joab sent me, I
18.32 happen to all your enemies, **sir,** and to all who rebel
19.20 I know, **sir,** that I have sinned, and this is why I
20.17 "Listen to me, **sir,"** she said.
1 Kgs 1.26 he did not invite me, **sir,** or Zadok the priest, or Benaiah,
18. 7 bowed low before him, and asked, "Is it really you, **sir?"**
2 Kgs 2.19 and said, "As you know, **sir,** this is a fine city, but
4. 1 went to Elisha and said, **"Sir,** my husband has died!
4.16 "Please, **sir,** don't lie to me.
4.28 The woman said to him, **"Sir,** did I ask you for a
5.13 up to him and said, **"Sir,** if the prophet had told you
5.15 so please, **sir,** accept a gift from me."
5.25 "Oh, nowhere, **sir,"** he answered.
6. 5 "What shall I do, **sir?"**
6.15 He went back to Elisha and exclaimed, "We are doomed, **sir!**
6.21 saw the Syrians, he asked Elisha, "Shall I kill them, **sir?**
8.12 "Why are you crying, **sir?"**
9. 5 He said, **"Sir,** I have a message for you."
9. 5 "To you, **sir,"** he replied.
2 Kgs 18.26 and Joah told the official, "Speak Aramaic to us, **sir.**
Is 21. 8 The sentry calls out, **"Sir,** I have been standing guard at
Dan 10.16 I said to him, **"Sir,** this vision makes me so weak that
10.19 felt even stronger and said, **"Sir,** tell me what you have to
12. 8 So I asked, "But, **sir,** how will it all end?"
Zech 1. 9 I asked him, **"Sir,** what do these horses mean?"
4. 4 Then I asked the angel, "What do these things stand for, **sir?"**
4. 5 "No, I don't, **sir,"** I replied.
4.13 "No, I don't, **sir,"** I answered.
6. 4 Then I asked the angel, **"Sir,** what do these chariots mean?"
Mt 8. 2 down before him, and said, **"Sir,** if you want to, you can
8. 6 **"Sir,** my servant is sick in bed at home, unable to move
8. 8 "Oh no, **sir,"** answered the officer.
8.21 who was a disciple, said, **"Sir,** first let me go back and
9.28 "Yes, **sir!"**
13.27 came to him and said, **'Sir,** it was good seed you sowed
15.22 "Have mercy on me, **sir!**
15.25 "Help me, **sir!"**
15.27 "That's true, **sir,"** she answered;
17.15 knelt before him, [15]and said, **"Sir,** have mercy on my son!
20.30 Take pity on us, **sir!"**
20.31 Take pity on us, **sir!"**
20.33 **"Sir,"** they answered, "we want you to give us our sight!"
21.30 'Yes, **sir,'** he answered, but he did not go.
25.11 **'Sir, sir!**
25.20 'You gave me five thousand coins, **sir,'** he said.
25.22 and said, 'You gave me two thousand coins, **sir.**
25.24 came in and said, **'Sir,** I know you are a hard
27.63 met with Pilate [63]and said, **"Sir,** we remember that while
Mk 7.28 **"Sir,"** she answered, "even the dogs under the table
Lk 5.12 himself down and begged him, **"Sir,** if you want to, you can
7. 6 the officer sent friends to tell him, **"Sir,** don't trouble yourself.
9.59 But that man said, **"Sir,** first let me go back and bury
9.61 Another man said, "I will follow you, **sir;**
13. 8 But the gardener answered, 'Leave it alone, **sir,** just one more year;
13.23 Someone asked him, **"Sir,** will just a few people be saved?"
13.25 knock on the door and say, 'Open the door for us, **sir!'**
14.22 has been carried out, **sir,** but there is room for more.'
18.41 **"Sir,"** he answered, "I want to see again."
19. 8 Zacchaeus stood up and said to the Lord, "Listen, **sir!**
19.16 first one came and said, **'Sir,** I have earned ten gold coins
19.18 second servant came and said, **'Sir,** I have earned five gold
19.20 "Another servant came and said, **'Sir,** here is your gold coin;
19.25 But they said to him, **'Sir,** he already has ten coins!'
Jn 4.11 **"Sir,"** the woman said, "you haven't got a bucket,
4.15 **"Sir,"** the woman said, "give me that water!
4.19 "I see you are a prophet, **sir,"** the woman said.
4.49 **"Sir,"** replied the official, "come with me before my child dies."
5. 7 The sick man answered, **"Sir,** I have no one here to put
6.34 **"Sir,"** they asked him, "give us this bread always."
8.11 "No one, **sir,"** she answered.
9.36 "Tell me who he is, **sir,** so that I can believe
12.21 Bethsaida in Galilee) and said, **"Sir,** we want to see Jesus."
20.15 "If you took him away, **sir,** tell me where
Acts 10. 4 stared at the angel in fear and said, "What is it, **sir?"**
16.30 led them out and asked, **"Sirs,** what must I do to be
Rev 7.14 "I don't know, **sir.**

SISERA (1)

Canaanite military leader defeated by Israel.

Judg 4. 2 The commander of his army was **Sisera,** who lived at
4. 7 I will bring **Sisera,** the commander of Jabin's army,
4. 9 because the Lord will hand **Sisera** over to a woman."
4.12 When **Sisera** learnt that Barak had gone up to Mount Tabor,
4.14 Today he has given you victory over **Sisera."**
4.15 the Lord threw **Sisera** into confusion
4.15 **Sisera** got down from his chariot and fled on foot.
4.16 Harosheth-of-the-Gentiles, and **Sisera's** whole army was killed.
4.17 **Sisera** ran away to the tent of Jael, the wife of Heber
4.18 Jael went out to meet **Sisera** and said to him, "Come in,
4.21 **Sisera** was so tired that he fell sound asleep.
4.22 When Barak came looking for **Sisera,** Jael went out
4.22 with her, and there was **Sisera** on the ground, dead, with the
5.20 as they moved across the sky, they fought against **Sisera.**
5.25 **Sisera** asked for water, but she gave him milk;
5.26 she struck **Sisera** and crushed his skull;
5.28 **Sisera's** mother looked out of the window;
5.30 every soldier, rich cloth for **Sisera,** embroidered pieces for
1 Sam 12. 9 the king of Moab and **Sisera,** commander of the army of the
Ps 83. 9 Midianites, and to **Sisera** and Jabin at the River Kishon.

SISTER

Gen 4.22 The **sister** of Tubal Cain was Naamah.
12.13 Tell them that you are my **sister;**
12.19 say that she was your **sister,** and let me take her as
19.31 daughter said to her **sister,** "Our father is getting old,
19.34 daughter said to her **sister,** "I slept with him last night;
20. 2 in Gerar, [2]he said that his wife Sarah was his **sister.**
20. 5 said that she was his **sister,** and she said the same thing.
20.12 She really is my **sister.**
24.30 and the bracelets on his **sister's** arms and had heard her say
24.60 "May you, **sister,** become the mother of millions!
25.20 Bethuel (an Aramean from Mesopotamia) and **sister** of Laban.
26. 7 there asked about his wife, he said that she was his **sister.**
26. 9 Why did you say she was your **sister?"**
28. 9 married his daughter Mahalath, who was the **sister** of Nebaioth.
30. 1 she became jealous of her **sister** and said to Jacob, "Give
30. 8 have fought a hard fight with my **sister,** but I have won";

Gen	34.13	Because Shechem had disgraced their **sister** Dinah,
	34.14	him, "We cannot let our **sister** marry a man who is not
	34.27	looted the town to take revenge for their **sister's** disgrace.
	34.31	"We cannot let our **sister** be treated like a common whore."
	36. 3	and Basemath, the daughter of Ishmael and **sister** of Nebaioth.
	36.22	(Lotan had a **sister** named Timna.)
	46.17	Imnah, Ishvah, Ishvi, Beriah, and their **sister** Serah.
Ex	2. 4	The baby's **sister** stood some distance away to see what
	2. 7	Then his **sister** asked her, "Shall I go and call a Hebrew
	6.20	Amram married his father's **sister** Jochebed,
	6.23	Elisheba, the daughter of Amminadab and **sister** of Nahshon;
	15.20	The prophet Miriam, Aaron's **sister,** took her tambourine,
Lev	18. 9	not have intercourse with your **sister** or your stepsister,
	18.11	she, too, is your **sister.**
	18.12	whether she is your father's **sister** or your mother's sister.
	18.18	Do not take your wife's **sister** as one of your wives, as
	20.17	If a man marries his **sister** or half-sister, they shall
	20.17	He has had intercourse with his **sister** and must suffer the
	21. 3	brother, [3]or unmarried **sister** living in his house.
Num	6. 6	not even that of his father, mother, brother, or **sister.**
Deut	27.22	anyone who has intercourse with his **sister** or half sister.'
Josh	2.13	and mother, my brothers and **sisters,** and all their families!
Judg	15. 2	But her younger **sister** is prettier, anyway.
2 Sam	13. 1	Absalom had a beautiful unmarried **sister** named Tamar.
	13. 4	in love with Tamar, the **sister** of my half-brother Absalom,"
	13. 5	to him, 'Please ask my **sister** Tamar to come and feed me.
	13.20	Please, **sister,** don't let it upset you so much.
	13.22	much for having raped his **sister** Tamar that he would no
	13.32	to do this from the time that Amnon raped his **sister** Tamar.
	17.25	daughter of Nahash and the **sister** of Joab's mother Zeruiah.)
1 Kgs	11.19	king gave his sister-in-law, the **sister** of Queen Tahpenes,
1 Chr	1.38	(Lotan had a **sister** named Timna.)
	2.21	old, he married Machir's daughter, the **sister** of Gilead.
	4.19	Hodiah married the **sister** of Naham.
	7.15	His **sister's** name was Maacah.
	7.18	Gilead's **sister** Hammolecheth had three sons:
2 Chr	28.11	These prisoners are your brothers and **sisters.**
Job	1. 4	and they always invited their three **sisters** to join them.
	17.14	worms that eat me I will call my mother and my **sisters.**
	42.11	All Job's brothers and **sisters** and former friends came
Prov	7. 4	Treat wisdom as your **sister,** and insight as your closest friend.
Song	8. 8	We have a young **sister,** and her breasts are still small.
Jer	3. 7	did not return, and her unfaithful **sister** Judah saw it all.
	3. 8	But Judah, Israel's unfaithful **sister,** was not afraid.
	3.10	Israel's unfaithful **sister,** only pretended to return to me;
Ezek	16.45	like your **sisters,** who hated their husbands and their children.
	16.45	You and your **sister** cities had a Hittite mother and an
	16.46	"Your elder **sister** is Samaria, in the north, with her villages.
	16.46	Your younger **sister,** with her villages, is Sodom, in the
	16.48	the Sovereign Lord says, "your **sister** Sodom and her
	16.51	Your corruption makes your **sisters** look innocent by comparison.
	16.52	those of your **sisters** that they look innocent beside you.
	16.52	bear your shame, because you make your **sisters** look pure."
	16.54	your disgrace will show your **sisters** how well-off they are.
	16.61	when you get your elder **sister** and your younger sister back.
	23. 2	"Mortal man," he said, "there were once two **sisters.**
	23.11	"Even though her **sister** Oholibah saw this, she was
	23.13	immoral, that the second **sister** was as bad as the first.
	23.18	was as disgusted with her as I had been with her **sister.**
	23.31	You followed in your **sister's** footsteps, and so I will
	23.32	"You will drink from your **sister's** cup;
	23.33	that cup of fear and ruin, your **sister** Samaria's cup.
	23.40	The two **sisters** would bathe and put on eye-shadow and jewellery.
	23.49	And you two **sisters**—I will punish you for your
	44.25	one of his children or a brother or an unmarried **sister.**
Mt	12.50	wants him to do is my brother, my **sister,** and my mother."
	13.56	Aren't all his **sisters** living here?
	19.29	left houses or brothers or **sisters** or father or mother or
Mk	3.32	your brothers and **sisters** are outside, and they want you."
	3.35	God wants him to do is my brother, my **sister,** my mother."
	6. 3	Aren't his **sisters** living here?"
	10.29	leaves home or brothers or **sisters** or mother or father or
	10.30	hundred times more houses, brothers, **sisters,** mothers,
Lk	10.39	She had a **sister** named Mary,
	10.40	don't you care that my **sister** has left me to do all
	14.26	children, his brothers and his **sisters,** and himself as well.
Jn	11. 1	Bethany was the town where Mary and her **sister** Martha lived.
	11. 3	The **sisters** sent Jesus a message:
	11. 5	Jesus loved Martha and her **sister** and Lazarus.
	11.28	she went back and called her **sister** Mary privately.
	11.39	Martha, the dead man's **sister,** answered, "There will be a bad smell,
	19.25	his mother's **sister,** Mary the wife of Clopas,
Acts	23.16	But the son of Paul's **sister** heard about the plot;
Rom	16. 1	I recommend to you our **sister** Phoebe,
	16.15	to Nereus and his **sister,**
Phil	4. 2	please, I beg you, try to agree as **sisters** in the Lord.
1 Tim	5. 2	mothers, and the younger women as **sisters,** with all purity.
Phlm	2	and our **sister** Apphia, and our fellow-soldier Archippus:
Jas	2.15	Suppose there are brothers or **sisters** who need clothes
1 Pet	5.13	Your **sister** church in Babylon, also chosen by God, sends you greetings,
2 Jn	13	The children of your dear **Sister** send you their greetings.

SISTER-IN-LAW

Ruth	1.15	said to her, "Ruth, your **sister-in-law** has gone back to her
1 Kgs	11.19	king gave his **sister-in-law,** the sister of Queen Tahpenes,

SIT
[SAT]

Gen	18. 1	As Abraham was **sitting** at the entrance of his tent during
	19. 1	to Sodom that evening, Lot was **sitting** at the city gate.
	21.16	under a bush [16]and **sat** down about a hundred metres away.
	21.16	While she was **sitting** there, she began to cry.
	23.10	Ephron himself was **sitting** with the other Hittites at
	27.19	Please **sit** up and eat some of the meat that I have
	27.31	He said, "Please, father, **sit** up and eat some of the meat
	31.34	and put them in a camel's saddlebag and was **sitting** on them.
	38.14	face with a veil, and **sat** down at the entrance to Enaim,
	48. 2	to see him, he gathered his strength and **sat** up in bed.
Ex	2.15	One day, when Moses was **sitting** by a well, seven daughters
	16. 3	There we could at least **sit** down and eat meat and as
	17.12	a stone for him to **sit** on, while they stood beside him
	32. 6	The people **sat** down to a feast, which turned into an orgy
Lev	15. 4	Any bed on which he **sits** or lies is unclean.
	15. 6	who touches his bed [6]or **sits** on anything
	15. 6	on anything the man has **sat** on must wash his clothes
	15. 9	or seat on which the man with the discharge **sits** is unclean.
	15.10	anything on which the man **sat** is unclean until evening.
	15.10	anything on which the man **sat** must wash his clothes
	15.20	Anything on which she **sits** or lies during her monthly
	15.21	anything on which she has **sat** must wash his clothes
	15.26	and anything on which she **sits** during this time is unclean.
Deut	22. 6	ground with the mother bird **sitting** either on the eggs or
Judg	3.20	Then, as the king was **sitting** there alone in his cool
	4. 5	She used to **sit** under a certain palm-tree between Ramah
	5.10	that ride on white donkeys, **sitting** on saddles, and you that
	6.11	the village of Ophrah and **sat** under the oak-tree that
	13. 9	came back to the woman while she was **sitting** in the fields.
	19. 6	So the two men **sat** down and ate and drank together.
	19.15	went into the city and **sat** down in the square, but no
	20.26	They **sat** there in the Lord's presence and did not eat until
	21. 2	Israel went to Bethel and **sat** there in the presence of God
Ruth	2.14	So she **sat** with the workers, and Boaz passed some roasted
	4. 1	to the meeting place at the town gate and **sat** down there.
	4. 1	Boaz called to him, "Come over here, my friend, and **sit** down."
	4. 1	So he went over and **sat** down.
	4. 2	leaders of the town and asked them to **sit** down there too.
	4. 4	want it, buy it in the presence of these men **sitting** here.
1 Sam	1. 9	Eli the priest was **sitting** in his place by the door.
	4.13	the Covenant Box, was **sitting** on a seat beside the road,
	19. 9	He was **sitting** in his house with his spear in his hand,
	20.25	came to the meal [25]and **sat** in his usual place
	20.25	Abner **sat** next to him, and Jonathan sat opposite him.
	22. 6	Saul was in Gibeah, **sitting** under a tamarisk-tree on a hill,
	28.23	gave in, got up from the ground, and **sat** on the bed.
2 Sam	2.13	the pool, where they all **sat** down, one group on one side
	7.18	Tent of the Lord's presence, **sat** down and prayed, "I am not
	18.24	David was **sitting** in the space between the inner and
	19. 8	the king got up, and went and **sat** near the city gate.
1 Kgs	1.35	Follow him back here when he comes to **sit** on my throne.
	2.19	Then he **sat** on his throne and had another one brought in
	2.19	on which she **sat** at his right.
	2.33	success to David's descendants who **sit** on his throne."
	13.14	the prophet from Judah and found him **sitting** under an oak.
	13.20	As they were **sitting** at the table, the word of the Lord
	19. 4	He stopped and **sat** down in the shade of a tree and
	22.10	in their royal robes, were **sitting** on their thrones at the
	22.19	I saw the Lord **sitting** on his throne in heaven, with all
2 Kgs	1. 9	The officer found him **sitting** on a hill and said to him,
	18.27	to the people who are **sitting** on the wall, who will have
1 Chr	17.16	Tent of the Lord's presence, **sat** down, and prayed, "I am
2 Chr	18. 9	in their royal robes, were **sitting** on their thrones at the
	18.18	I saw the Lord **sitting** on his throne in heaven, with all
Ezra	9. 3	tore my hair and my beard, and **sat** down crushed with grief.
	9. 4	I **sat** there grieving until the time for the evening
Neh	1. 4	When I heard all this, I **sat** down and wept.
	2. 6	The emperor, with the empress **sitting** at his side, approved
Esth	3.15	The king and Haman **sat** down and had a drink while the
	5.13	I see that Jew Mordecai **sitting** at the entrance of the palace."
	6.10	You will find him **sitting** at the entrance of the palace."
Job	2. 8	Job went and **sat** by the rubbish heap and took a piece
	2.13	Then they **sat** there on the ground with him for seven
	16.15	made of sackcloth, and I **sit** here in the dust defeated.
Ps	47. 8	God **sits** on his sacred throne;
	110. 1	to my lord, the king, "**Sit** here at my right until I
	122. 5	Here the kings of Israel **sat** to judge their people.
	137. 1	By the rivers of Babylon we **sat** down;
Prov	9.14	She **sits** at the door of her house or on a seat
	14.23	if you **sit** around talking you will be poor.
	20. 8	The king **sits** in judgement and knows evil when he sees it.
	23. 1	When you **sit** down to eat with an important man, keep in
Song	2. 3	I love to **sit** in its shadow, and its fruit is sweet
Is	3.26	will be like a woman **sitting** on the ground, stripped naked.
	6. 1	He was **sitting** on his throne, high and exalted, and his robe
	14.13	You thought you would **sit** like a king on that mountain in
	21. 5	rugs are spread for the guests to **sit** on.
	28. 8	The tables where they **sit** are all covered with vomit, and
	36.12	to the people who are **sitting** on the wall, who will have
	40.22	made by the one who **sits** on his throne above the earth
	42. 7	of the blind and set free those who **sit** in dark prisons.
	47. 1	down from your throne, and **sit** in the dust on the ground.
	47. 5	"**Sit** in silence and darkness;
	52. 2	Rise from the dust and **sit** on your throne!
Jer	8.14	"Why are we **sitting** still?"
	16. 8	Do not **sit** down with them to eat and drink.
	21.13	You, Jerusalem, are **sitting** high above the valleys, like
	32.12	purchase and of the men who were **sitting** in the courtyard.

Jer 36.15 **"Sit** down," they said, "and read the scroll to us."
36.22 winter and the king was **sitting** in his winter palace in
48.18 your place of honour and **sit** on the ground in the dust;
Lam 2.10 Jerusalem's old men **sit** on the ground in silence, With
3.28 When we suffer, we should **sit** alone in silent patience;
5.14 The old people no longer **sit** at the city gate, and the
Ezek 1.26 throne made of sapphire, and **sitting** on the throne was a
8. 1 of the exiles from Judah were **sitting** in my house with me.
20. 1 about the Lord's will, and they **sat** down in front of me.
23.41 They would **sit** on a beautiful couch, and in front of
26.16 their embroidered clothes and **sit** trembling on the ground.
28. 2 that like a god you **sit** on a throne, surrounded by the
Dan 7. 9 had been living for ever **sat** down on one of the thrones.
7.26 the heavenly court will **sit** in judgement, take away his power,
9. 3 fasting, wearing sackcloth, and **sitting** in ashes.
11.27 Then the two kings will **sit** down to eat at the same
Joel 3.12 I, the Lord, will **sit** to judge all the surrounding nations.
Jon 3. 6 took off his robe, put on sackcloth, and **sat** down in ashes.
4. 5 Jonah went out east of the city and **sat** down.
4. 5 a shelter for himself and **sat** in its shade, waiting to see
Zeph 1. 7 The day is near when the Lord will **sit** in judgement;
Zech 5. 7 the lid was raised, and there in the basket **sat** a woman!
8. 4 a stick when they walk, will be **sitting** in the city squares.
14. 1 The day when the Lord will **sit** in judgement is near.
Mt 5. 1 saw the crowds and went up a hill, where he **sat** down.
8.11 east and the west and **sit** down with Abraham, Isaac, and
9. 9 he saw a tax collector, named Matthew, **sitting** in his office.
11.16 They are like children **sitting** in the market-place.
13. 1 and went to the lake-side, where he **sat** down to teach.
13. 2 got into a boat and **sat** in it, while the crowd stood
13.48 they pull it to shore and **sit** down to divide the fish:
14.19 He ordered the people to **sit** down on the grass;
15.29 He climbed a hill and **sat** down.
15.35 So Jesus ordered the crowd to **sit** down on the ground.
19.28 when the Son of Man **sits** on his glorious throne
19.28 followers of mine will also **sit** on thrones, to rule the
20.21 two sons of mine will **sit** at your right and your left
20.23 right to choose who will **sit** at my right and my left.
20.30 Two blind men who were **sitting** by the road heard that
22.44 **Sit** here on my right until I put your enemies under your
23.22 is swearing by God's throne and by him who **sits** on it.
24. 3 As Jesus **sat** on the Mount of Olives,
25.31 angels with him, he will **sit** on his royal throne,
26.20 Jesus and the twelve disciples **sat** down to eat.
26.36 and he said to them, **"Sit** here while I go over there
26.55 Every day I **sat** down and taught in the Temple,
26.58 went into the courtyard and **sat** down with the guards
26.64 see the Son of Man **sitting** on the right of the Almighty
26.69 Peter was **sitting** outside in the courtyard
27.19 While Pilate was **sitting** in the judgement hall,
27.36 After that they **sat** there and watched him.
27.61 Mary Magdalene and the other Mary were **sitting** there, facing the tomb.
28. 2 came down from heaven, rolled the stone away, and **sat** on it.
Mk 2. 6 of the Law who were **sitting** there thought to themselves,
2.14 tax collector, Levi son of Alphaeus, **sitting** in his office.
3.32 A crowd was **sitting** round Jesus, and they said to him,
3.34 He looked at the people **sitting** round him and said,
4. 1 he got into a boat and **sat** in it.
4.36 Jesus was already **sitting,** and they took him with them.
5.15 He was **sitting** there, clothed and in his right mind;
6.39 people divide into groups and **sit** down on the green grass.
6.40 So the people **sat** down in rows, in groups of a hundred
8. 6 He ordered the crowd to **sit** down on the ground.
9.35 Jesus **sat** down, called the twelve disciples, and said to them,
10.37 They answered, "When you **sit** on your throne in your glorious Kingdom,
10.37 want you to let us **sit** with you, one at your right
10.40 right to choose who will **sit** at my right and my left.
10.46 named Bartimaeus son of Timaeus was **sitting** by the road.
12.36 **Sit** here on my right until I put your enemies under your
12.41 As Jesus **sat** near the temple treasury, he watched the people
13. 3 Jesus was **sitting** on the Mount of Olives, across from the Temple,
14.32 Gethsemane, and Jesus said to his disciples, **"Sit** here while I pray."
14.54 There he **sat** down with the guards, keeping himself warm
16. 5 they saw a young man **sitting** on the right, wearing a white
16.19 taken up to heaven and **sat** at the right side of God.
Lk 2.46 found him in the Temple, **sitting** with the Jewish teachers,
4.20 the scroll, gave it back to the attendant, and **sat** down.
5. 3 Jesus **sat** in the boat and taught the crowd.
5.17 teachers of the Law were **sitting** there who had come from
5.27 saw a tax collector named Levi, **sitting** in his office.
7.15 The dead man **sat** up and began to talk,
7.32 They are like children **sitting** in the market-place.
7.36 and Jesus went to his house and **sat** down to eat.
7.49 The others **sitting** at the table began to say to themselves,
8.35 the demons had gone out **sitting** at the feet of Jesus,
9.14 his disciples, "Make the people **sit** down in groups of about
10.13 would long ago have **sat** down, put on sackcloth,
10.39 a sister named Mary, who **sat** down at the feet of
11.37 so he went in and **sat** down to eat.
12.37 his coat, ask them to **sit** down, and will wait on them.
13.29 north and the south, and **sit** down at the feast in the
14. 8 to a wedding feast, do not **sit** down in the best place.
14. 9 would be embarrassed and have to **sit** in the lowest place.
14.10 you are invited, go and **sit** in the lowest place, so that
14.15 When one of the men **sitting** at table heard this, he said
14.15 happy are those who will **sit** down at the feast in the
14.28 to build a tower, he **sits** down first and works out what
14.31 twenty thousand men, he will **sit** down first and decide if he
Lk 16. 6 **'sit** down and write fifty.'
16.22 carried by the angels to **sit** beside Abraham at the feast in
18.35 near Jericho, there was a blind man **sitting** by the road,
20.42 **Sit** here on my right [43]until I put your enemies as a
22.27 is greater, the one who **sits** down to eat or the one
22.27 The one who **sits** down, of course.
22.30 my Kingdom, and you will **sit** on thrones to rule over the
22.55 and Peter joined those who were **sitting** round it.
22.56 of the servant-girls saw him **sitting** there at the fire,
24.30 He **sat** down to eat with them, took the bread, and said
Jn 2.14 and also the money-changers **sitting** at their tables.
4. 6 and Jesus, tired out by the journey, **sat** down by the well.
6. 3 Jesus went up a hill and **sat** down with his disciples.
6.10 "Make the people **sit** down," Jesus told them.
6.10 So all the people **sat** down;
6.11 and distributed it to the people who were **sitting** there.
8. 2 gathered round him, and he **sat** down and began to teach them.
9. 8 this, asked, "Isn't this the man who used to **sit** and beg?"
12. 2 one of those who were **sitting** at the table with Jesus.
13.23 the one whom Jesus loved, was **sitting** next to Jesus.
19.13 he took Jesus outside and **sat** down on the judge's seat
20.12 angels there dressed in white, **sitting** where the body of
Acts 2. 2 and it filled the whole house where they were **sitting.**
2.34 **Sit** here at my right [35]until I put your enemies as a
3.10 as the beggar who had **sat** at the Beautiful Gate,
6.15 All those **sitting** in the Council fixed their eyes on Stephen
8.31 invited Philip to climb up and **sit** in the carriage with him.
9.40 She opened her eyes, and when she saw Peter, she **sat** up.
12.21 put on his royal robes, **sat** on his throne,
13.14 on the Sabbath they went into the synagogue and **sat** down.
14. 9 He **sat** there and listened to Paul's words.
16.13 We **sat** down and talked to the women who gathered there.
20. 9 young man named Eutychus was **sitting** in the window,
23. 3 You **sit** there to judge me according to the Law, yet you
25. 6 On the next day he **sat** down in the court of judgement
25.17 the very next day I **sat** in the court and ordered the
1 Cor 5.11 Don't even **sit** down to eat with such a person.
10. 7 the scripture says, "The people **sat** down to a feast which
14.30 But if someone **sitting** in the meeting receives a message from God,
Col 3. 1 in heaven, where Christ **sits** on his throne at the right-hand
2 Thes 2. 4 will even go in and **sit** down in God's Temple and claim
Heb 1. 3 the sins of mankind, he **sat** down in heaven at the right-hand
1.13 **"Sit** here on my right until I put your enemies as a
8. 1 such a High Priest, who **sits** at the right of the throne
10.12 and then he **sat** down at the right-hand side
Jas 2. 3 man, "Stand over there, or **sit** here on the floor by my
Rev 3.21 will give the right to **sit** beside me on my throne, just
3.21 been victorious and now **sit** by my Father on his throne.
4. 2 There in heaven was a throne with someone **sitting** on it.
4. 9 thanks to the one who **sits** on the throne,
4.10 before the one who **sits** on the throne, and worship him
5. 1 in the right hand of the one who **sits** on the throne;
5. 7 from the right hand of the one who **sits** on the throne.
5.13 "To him who **sits** on the throne and to the Lamb,
6.16 eyes of the one who **sits** on the throne
7.10 comes from our God, who **sits** on the throne,
7.15 He who **sits** on the throne will protect them with his presence.
11.16 Then the twenty-four elders who **sit** on their thrones in
14.14 was a white cloud, and **sitting** on the cloud was what looked
14.15 to the one who was **sitting** on the cloud, "Use your sickle
14.16 Then the one who **sat** on the cloud swung his sickle
17. 3 There I saw a woman **sitting** on a red beast
17. 9 The seven heads are seven hills, on which the woman **sits.**
17.15 on which the prostitute is **sitting,** are nations, peoples,
18. 7 'Here I **sit,** a queen!
20. 4 saw thrones, and those who **sat** on them were given the power
20.11 saw a great white throne and the one who **sits** on it.
21. 5 Then the one who **sits** on the throne said,

SITE

Ezra 2.68 offerings to help rebuild the Temple on its old **site.**
3. 8 they came back to the **site** of the Temple in Jerusalem, they

SIVAN

Third month of the Hebrew calendar.

Esth 8. 9 the twenty-third day of the third month, the month of **Sivan.**

SIX

Gen 1.31 Evening passed and morning came—that was the **sixth** day.
30.19 Leah became pregnant again and bore Jacob a **sixth** son.
30.20 husband will accept me, because I have borne him **six** sons";
31.41 to win your two daughters—and **six** years for your flocks.
Ex 6.15 Simeon had **six** sons:
16. 5 On the **sixth** day they are to bring in twice as much
16.22 On the **sixth** day they gathered twice as much food, four
16.26 You must gather food for **six** days, but on the seventh day,
16.29 that is why on the **sixth** day I will always give you
20. 9 You have **six** days in which to do your work, [10]but the
20.11 In **six** days I, the Lord, made the earth, the sky, the
21. 2 you buy a Hebrew slave, he shall serve you for **six** years.
23.10 "For **six** years sow your field and gather in what it produces.
23.12 "Work **six** days a week, but do no work on the seventh
24.16 cloud covered the mountain for **six** days, and on the seventh
25.32 **Six** branches shall extend from its sides, three from each side.
25.33 Each of the **six** branches is to have three decorative
26. 9 them together in one set, and the other **six** in another set.
26. 9 Fold the **sixth** piece double over the front of the Tent.

Ex 26.22 Tent on the west, make **six** frames, [23]and two frames for
28.10 their birth, with six on one stone and **six** on the other.
30.23 "Take the finest spices—**six** kilogrammes of liquid myrrh,
30.24 sweet-smelling cane, [24]and **six** kilogrammes of cassia
31.15 You have **six** days in which to do your work, but the
31.17 made heaven and earth in **six** days, and on the seventh day
34.21 "You have **six** days in which to do your work, but do
35. 2 You have **six** days in which to do your work, but the
36.16 them together in one set and the other **six** in another set.
36.27 on the west, they made **six** frames [28]and two frames for the
37.18 **Six** branches extended from its sides, three from each side.
37.19 Each of the **six** branches had three decorative flowers
Lev 23. 3 You have **six** days in which to do your work, but remember
24. 6 the loaves in two rows, **six** in each row, on the table
25. 3 prune your vineyards, and gather your crops for **six** years.
25.21 bless the land in the **sixth** year so that it will produce
25.22 what you harvested during the **sixth** year, and you will have
Num 7. 3 **six** wagons and twelve oxen, a wagon for every two leaders
29.29 On the **sixth** day offer eight young bulls, two rams, and
35. 6 are to give the Levites **six** cities of refuge to which a
35.13 Choose **six** cities, [14]three east of the Jordan and
Deut 5.13 You have **six** days in which to do your work, [14]but the
15.12 are to release him after he has served you for **six** years.
15.18 he has served you for **six** years at half the cost of
16. 8 For the next **six** days you are to eat bread prepared
Josh 6. 3 are to march round the city once a day for **six** days.
6.14 They did this for **six** days.
15.59 **six** cities, along with the towns round them.
15.62 **six** cities, along with the towns round them.
19.32 The **sixth** assignment made was for the families of the
Judg 12. 7 Jephthah led Israel for **six** years.
2 Sam 3. 2 The following **six** sons, in the order of their birth, were
6.13 the Covenant Box had gone **six** steps, David made them stop
21.20 had six fingers on each hand and **six** toes on each foot.
1 Kgs 10.19 The throne had **six** steps leading up to it, with
11.15 his men remained in Edom **six** months, and during that time
16.23 The first **six** years he ruled in Tirzah, [24]and then he
2 Kgs 7. 1 of the best wheat or **six** kilogrammes of barley for one piece
7.16 of the best wheat or **six** kilogrammes of barley were sold for
7.18 of the best wheat or **six** kilogrammes of barley would be sold
11. 3 For **six** years Jehosheba took care of the boy and kept him
13.19 should have struck five or **six** times, and then you would
15. 8 king of Israel, and he ruled in Samaria for **six** months.
18.10 this was the **sixth** year of Hezekiah's reign, and the ninth
1 Chr 1.32 Abraham had a concubine named Keturah, who bore him **six** sons:
2.47 (A man named Jahdai had **six** sons:
3. 4 All **six** were born in Hebron during the seven and a half
4.27 Shimei had sixteen sons and **six** daughters, but his
7. 2 Tola had **six** sons:
8.38 Azel had **six** sons:
9.44 Azel had **six** sons:
15.11 Zadok and Abiathar and the **six** Levites, Uriel, Asaiah, Joel,
20. 6 with six fingers on each hand and **six** toes on each foot.
25. 3 The **six** sons of Jeduthun:
26. 6 Obed Edom's eldest son, Shemaiah, had **six** sons:
26.17 On the east, **six** guards were on duty each day, on the
27. 2 Shamhuth, a descendant of Izhar **Sixth** month:
2 Chr 9.18 **Six** steps led up to the throne, and there was a
21. 2 Jehoram son of King Jehoshaphat of Judah had **six** brothers:
22.12 For **six** years he remained there in hiding, while
23. 1 After waiting **six** years Jehoiada the priest decided that
Ezra 6.15 the month Adar in the **sixth** year of the reign of Darius
Neh 3.30 of Shelemiah and Hanun, the **sixth** son of Zalaph, built the
5.18 day I served one ox, **six** of the best sheep, and many
Esth 1. 4 For **six** whole months he made a show of the riches of
2.12 with oil of myrrh for **six** months
2.12 and with oil of balsam for **six** more.
Is 6. 2 flaming creatures were standing, each of which had **six** wings.
Jer 34.14 set free any Hebrew slave who had served them for **six** years.
Ezek 8. 1 the fifth day of the **sixth** month of the sixth year of
9. 2 At once **six** men came from the outer north gate of the
40.11 It was **six** and a half metres altogether, and the space
40.49 room, which was ten metres wide and **six** metres deep.
43.16 top of the altar was a square, **six** metres on each side.
46. 1 be kept closed during the **six** working days, but it is to
46. 4 sacrifices to be burnt whole, **six** lambs and one ram, all
46. 6 will offer a young bull, **six** lambs, and a ram, all without
Hag 1. 1 the first day of the **sixth** month, the Lord spoke through the
1.15 the twenty-fourth day of the **sixth** month of the second year
Mt 14.25 Between three and **six** o'clock in the morning Jesus came
17. 1 **Six** days later Jesus took with him Peter and the brothers
Mk 6.48 some time between three and **six** o'clock in the morning he
9. 2 **Six** days later Jesus took with him Peter, James, and John,
Lk 1.26 In the **sixth** month of Elizabeth's pregnancy God sent the
1.36 but she herself is now **six** months pregnant,
13.14 "There are **six** days in which we should work;
Jn 2. 6 and for this purpose **six** stone water jars were there,
6.19 had rowed about five or **six** kilometres when they saw Jesus
12. 1 **Six** days before the Passover, Jesus went to Bethany,
Acts 11.12 These **six** fellow-believers from Joppa accompanied me to Caesarea,
Jude 14 It was Enoch, the **sixth** direct descendant from Adam,
Rev 4. 8 the four living creatures had **six** wings,
6.12 And I saw the Lamb break open the **sixth** seal.
9.13 Then the **sixth** angel blew his trumpet.
9.14 The voice said to the **sixth** angel, "Release the four angels
16.12 Then the **sixth** angel poured out his bowl on the great
21.20 the fifth onyx, the **sixth** carnelian, the seventh yellow quartz,
also Num 7.12 1 Chr 24.7 1 Chr 25.9

SIZE

Ex 26. 2 Make each piece the same **size**, twelve metres long and two
26. 8 Make them all the same **size**, thirteen metres long and two
36. 9 Each piece was the same **size**, twelve metres long and two
36.15 made them all the same **size**, thirteen metres long and two
Num 26.53 "Divide the land among the tribes, according to their **size**.
35. 8 to be determined according to the **size** of its territory."
1 Kgs 6.24 Both were of the same **size** and shape.
7.37 they were all alike, having the same **size** and shape.
2 Kgs 10.32 the Lord began to reduce the **size** of Israel's territory.
1 Chr 26.13 Each family, regardless of **size**, drew lots to see which
Job 28.25 gave the wind its power And determined the **size** of the sea;
Is 28.27 instead he uses light sticks of the proper **size**.
Ezek 40.10 passage were all the same **size**, and the walls between them
40.28 and it was the same **size** as the gateways in the outer
40.29 walls were the same **size** as those in the other gateways.
40.32 the gateway, and it was the same **size** as the others.
40.35 He measured it, and it was the same **size** as the others.
Rev 18.21 picked up a stone the **size** of a large millstone and threw

SKILL

Gen 21.20 in the wilderness of Paran and became a **skilful** hunter.
25.27 up, and Esau became a **skilled** hunter, a man who loved the
Ex 28.11 Get a **skilful** jeweller to engrave on the two stones the
31. 3 I have given him understanding, **skill**, and ability for every
31. 4 planning **skilful** designs and working them in gold,
31. 6 ability to all the other **skilful** craftsmen, so that they can
35.10 "All the **skilled** workmen among you are to come and make
35.25 All the **skilled** women brought fine linen thread
35.31 his power and given him **skill**, ability, and understanding
35.32 for planning **skilful** designs and working them in gold,
35.35 He has given them **skill** in all kinds of work done by
35.35 are able to do all kinds of work and are **skilful** designers.
36. 1 whom the Lord has given **skill** and understanding, who know
36. 2 Oholiab, and all the other **skilled** men to whom the Lord had
36. 4 Then the **skilled** men who were doing the work went [5]and
36. 8 The most **skilled** men among those doing the work made the
39. 6 they were **skilfully** engraved with the names of the twelve
1 Kgs 7.13 living in the city of Tyre, who was **skilled** in bronze work.
7.14 was from Tyre, and had also been a **skilled** bronze craftsman;
2 Kgs 18.20 that words can take the place of military **skill** and might?
24.14 deported all the **skilled** workmen, including the blacksmiths,
24.16 and one thousand **skilled** workers, including the blacksmiths,
25.11 in the city, the remaining **skilled** workmen, and those who
1 Chr 4.14 Valley of Craftsmen, where all the people were **skilled** workmen.
15.22 Because of his **skill** in music Chenaniah was chosen to
27.32 Jonathan, King David's uncle, was a **skilful** adviser
28.21 Workmen with every kind of **skill** are eager to help you, and
2 Chr 2. 7 send me a man with **skill** in engraving, in working gold,
2. 8 I know how **skilful** your woodmen are, so send me cedar,
2.12 son, full of understanding and **skill**, who now plans to build
2.13 I am sending you a wise and **skilful** master craftsman
25. 5 ready for battle, **skilled** in using spears and shields.
30.22 praised the Levites for their **skill** in conducting the
34.12 (The Levites were all **skilful** musicians.)
Job 26.12 by his **skill** he destroyed the monster Rahab.
37.16 clouds float in the sky, the work of God's amazing **skill?**
Ps 33. 3 song to him, play the harp with **skill**, and shout for joy!
76. 5 all their strength and **skill** was useless.
78.72 of them with unselfish devotion and led them with **skill.**
107.27 staggered like drunken men— all their **skill** was useless.
Ecc 2.21 all your wisdom, knowledge, and **skill**, and then you have to
Song 3. 8 All of them are **skilful** with the sword;
Is 11. 2 him wisdom, and the knowledge and **skill** to rule his people.
19.10 weavers and **skilled** workmen will be broken and depressed.
36. 5 that words can take the place of military **skill** and might?
40.20 He finds a **skilful** craftsman to make an image that won't
45. 9 Does the pot complain that its maker has no **skill?**
66.19 and Lydia, with its **skilled** bowmen, and to Tubal and Greece.
Jer 10. 9 in violet and purple cloth woven by **skilled** weavers.
24. 1 leaders of Judah, the craftsmen, and the **skilled** workers.)
29. 2 and the **skilled** workmen had been taken into exile.
46. 9 and **skilled** bowmen from Lydia.' "
50. 9 They are **skilful** hunters, shooting arrows that never miss
52.15 in the city, the remaining **skilled** workmen, and those who
Ezek 27. 8 Your own **skilful** men were the sailors.
28. 4 Your wisdom and **skill** made you rich with treasures of gold
28. 7 beautiful things you have acquired by your **skill** and wisdom.
Dan 1.17 young men knowledge and **skill** in literature and philosophy.
1.17 he gave Daniel **skill** in interpreting visions and dreams.
5.12 is wise and **skilful** in interpreting dreams, solving riddles,
5.14 you and that you are **skilful** and have knowledge and wisdom.
Zech 9. 2 so do the cities of Tyre and Sidon, with all their **skill.**
Acts 17.29 or silver or stone, shaped by the art and **skill** of man.
1 Cor 1.20 or the **skilful** debaters of this world?
2. 4 message were not delivered with **skilful** words of human wisdom,

SKIM

Is 60. 8 What are these ships that **skim** along like clouds, Like

SKIN

[SMOOTH-SKINNED]
see also **WINESKIN**

Gen 3.21 made clothes out of animal **skins** for Adam and his wife, and
25.25 one was reddish, and his **skin** was like a hairy robe, so
27.11 know that Esau is a hairy man, but I have smooth **skin.**
27.16 She put the **skins** of the goats on his arms and on

Ex 25. 5 rams' **skin** dyed red;
26.14 more coverings, one of rams' **skin** dyed red and the other of
29.14 bull's flesh, its **skin,** and its intestines outside the camp.
35. 7 rams' **skin** dyed red;
35.23 rams' **skin** dyed red;
36.19 more coverings, one of rams' **skin** dyed red and the other of
39.34 the covering of rams' **skin** dyed red;
Lev 1. 6 Then he shall **skin** the animal and cut it up, [7]and the
4.11 But he shall take its **skin,** all its flesh, its head, its
7. 8 The **skin** of an animal offered as a burnt-offering belongs
8.17 of the bull, including its **skin,** flesh, and intestines, and
9.11 But he burnt the meat and the **skin** outside the camp.
13. 2 has a sore on his **skin** or a boil or an inflammation
13. 2 could develop into a dreaded **skin-disease,** he shall be
13. 3 be deeper than the surrounding **skin,**
13. 3 it is a dreaded **skin-disease,** and the priest shall
13. 4 to be deeper than the **skin** round it and the hairs have
13. 8 it is a dreaded **skin-disease.**
13. 9 If anyone has a dreaded **skin-disease,** he shall be brought
13.10 a white sore on his **skin** which turns the hairs white and
13.11 white and is full of pus, [11]it is a chronic **skin-disease.**
13.12 If the **skin-disease** spreads and covers the person
13.13 If his whole **skin** has turned white, he is ritually clean.
13.15 An open sore means a dreaded **skin-disease,**
13.20 be deeper than the surrounding **skin** and the hairs in it have
13.20 It is a dreaded **skin-disease** that has started in the boil.
13.21 deeper than the surrounding **skin,** but is light in colour,
13.25 appears deeper than the surrounding **skin,**
13.25 it is a dreaded **skin-disease** that has started in the burn,
13.26 deeper than the surrounding **skin,** but is light in colour,
13.27 spreading, it is a dreaded **skin-disease,** and the priest
13.28 and is light in colour, it is not a dreaded **skin-disease.**
13.30 be deeper than the surrounding **skin** and the hairs in it are
13.30 thin, it is a dreaded **skin-disease,** and he shall pronounce
13.31 be deeper than the surrounding **skin,** but there are still no
13.32 be deeper than the surrounding **skin,** [33]the person shall
13.34 the surrounding **skin,** he shall pronounce him ritually clean.
13.38 spots on the **skin,** [39]the priest shall examine that person.
13.39 it is only a blemish that has broken out on the **skin;**
13.42 sore appears on the bald spot, it is a dreaded **skin-disease.**
13.44 unclean, because of the dreaded **skin-disease** on his head.
13.45 who has a dreaded **skin-disease** must wear torn clothes,
14. 2 purification of a person cured of a dreaded **skin-disease.**
14. 7 to be purified from his **skin-disease,** and then he shall
14.32 man who has a dreaded **skin-disease** but who cannot afford the
14.54 These are the laws about dreaded **skin-diseases;**
16.27 **Skin,** meat, and intestines shall all be burnt.
21.20 no one with any eye or **skin disease;**
22. 4 Aaron who has a dreaded **skin-disease** or a discharge may eat
22.22 or that has a running sore or a **skin** eruption or scabs.
Num 5. 2 camp everyone with a dreaded **skin disease** or a bodily
6. 4 from a grapevine, not even the seeds or **skins** of grapes.
12.10 cloud left the Tent, Miriam's **skin** was suddenly covered with
19. 5 The whole animal, including **skin,** meat, blood, and intestines,
Deut 24. 8 are suffering from a dreaded **skin-disease,** be sure to do
2 Sam 3.29 has gonorrhoea or a dreaded **skin disease** or is fit only to
2 Kgs 1. 8 a cloak made of animal **skins,** tied with a leather belt,"
5. 1 a great soldier, but he suffered from a dreaded **skin-disease.**
5.27 left, he had the disease—his **skin** was as white as snow.
7. 3 a dreaded **skin-disease** were outside the gates of Samaria,
15. 5 struck Uzziah with a dreaded **skin-disease** that stayed with
2 Chr 26.19 a dreaded **skin-disease** broke out on his forehead.
35.11 had been killed, the Levites **skinned** them, and the priests
Job 10.11 and sinews and covered the bones with muscles and **skin.**
16. 8 I am **skin** and bones, and people take that as proof of
19.20 My **skin** hangs loose on my bones;
19.26 Even after my **skin** is eaten by disease, while still in
30.30 My **skin** has turned dark;
41.23 There is not a weak spot in his **skin;**
Ps 102. 5 I am nothing but **skin** and bones.
109.24 I am nothing but **skin** and bones.
Is 18. 2 nation, to your tall and **smooth-skinned** people, who are
18. 7 powerful nation, this tall and **smooth-skinned** people, who
Jer 13.23 the colour of his **skin,** or a leopard remove its spots?
Lam 4. 8 their **skin,** dry as wood, has shrivelled on their bones.
5.10 burn with fever, until our **skin** is as hot as an oven.
Ezek 16. 9 I rubbed olive-oil on your **skin.**
37. 6 I will give you sinews and muscles, and cover you with **skin.**
37. 8 were covered with sinews and muscles, and then with **skin.**
Mic 3. 2 You **skin** my people alive and tear the flesh off their bones.
3. 3 You strip off their **skin,** break their bones, and chop them
Mt 8. 2 man suffering from a dreaded **skin-disease** came to him, knelt down
9.17 into used wineskins, for the **skins** will burst,
9.17 the wine will pour out, and the **skins** will be ruined.
10. 8 heal those who suffer from dreaded **skin-diseases,** and drive out demons.
11. 5 those who suffer from dreaded **skin-diseases** are made clean,
26. 6 Simon, a man who had suffered from a dreaded **skin-disease.**
Mk 1.40 man suffering from a dreaded **skin-disease** came to Jesus, knelt down,
2.22 the wine will burst the **skins,**
2.22 and both the wine and the **skins** will be ruined.
14. 3 Simon, a man who had suffered from a dreaded **skin-disease.**
Lk 4.27 people suffering from a dreaded **skin-disease** who lived in Israel
5.12 there was a man who was suffering from a dreaded **skin-disease.**
5.37 new wine will burst the **skins,**
5.37 the wine will pour out, and the **skins** will be ruined.
7.22 those who suffer from dreaded **skin-diseases** are made clean,
17.12 he was met by ten men suffering from a dreaded **skin-disease.**
Heb 11.37 They went round clothed in **skins** of sheep or goats—poor,

SKIP

Ps 114. 4 The mountains **skipped** like goats;
114. 6 You mountains, why did you **skip** like goats?

SKIRT

Is 47. 2 Lift up your **skirts** to cross the streams!

SKULL

Judg 5.26 she struck Sisera and crushed his **skull;**
9.53 threw a millstone down on his head and fractured his **skull.**
1 Sam 17.49 the forehead and broke his **skull,** and Goliath fell face
2 Kgs 9.35 her found nothing except her **skull,** and the bones of her
Jer 2.16 Yes, the men of Memphis and Tahpanhes have cracked his **skull.**
Mt 27.33 called Golgotha, which means, "The Place of the **Skull.**"
Mk 15.22 called Golgotha, which means "The Place of the **Skull.**"
Lk 23.33 to the place called "The **Skull,**" they crucified Jesus there,
Jn 19.17 and came to "The Place of the **Skull,**" as it is called.

SKY

Gen 1. 8 He named the dome **"Sky."**
1. 9 "Let the water below the **sky** come together in one place, so
1.14 "Let lights appear in the **sky** to separate day from night
1.15 they will shine in the **sky** to give light to the earth"
1.17 placed the lights in the **sky** to shine on the earth, [18]to
7.11 all the floodgates of the **sky** were opened, [12]and rain fell
8. 2 beneath the earth and the floodgates of the **sky** were closed.
9.14 Whenever I cover the **sky** with clouds and the rainbow appears,
11. 4 a tower that reaches the **sky,** so that we can make a
15. 5 and said, "Look at the **sky** and try to count the stars;
22.17 there are stars in the **sky** or grains of sand along the
26. 4 there are stars in the **sky,** and I will give them all
Ex 9.22 "Raise your hand towards the **sky,** and hail will fall over
9.23 raised his stick towards the **sky,** and the Lord sent thunder
10.21 "Raise your hand towards the **sky,** and a darkness thick
10.22 raised his hand towards the **sky,** and there was total
16. 4 to make food rain down from the **sky** for all of you.
20.11 made the earth, the **sky,** the sea, and everything in them,
24.10 what looked like a pavement of sapphire, as blue as the **sky.**
32.13 there are stars in the **sky** and to give their descendants all
Deut 1.10 God has made you as numerous as the stars in the **sky.**
1.28 and that they live in cities with walls that reach the **sky.**
4.11 thick clouds of dark smoke and fire blazing up to the **sky.**
4.19 what you see in the **sky**—the sun, the moon, and the
9. 1 Their cities are large, with walls that reach the **sky.**
10.22 God has made you as numerous as the stars in the **sky.**
11.21 live there as long as there is a **sky** above the earth.
28.12 his rich storehouse in the **sky** and bless all your work, so
28.62 as the stars in the **sky,** only a few of you will
30.12 It is not up in the **sky.**
32. 1 "Earth and **sky,** hear my words, listen closely to what I say.
33.26 riding in splendour across the **sky,** riding through the
33.28 of corn and wine, where dew from the **sky** waters the ground.
Josh 8.20 of Ai looked back, they saw the smoke rising to the **sky.**
10.13 in the middle of the **sky** and did not go down for
Judg 5. 4 of Edom, the earth shook, and rain fell from the **sky.**
5.20 The stars fought from the **sky;**
5.20 as they moved across the **sky,** they fought against Sisera.
2 Sam 22. 8 the foundations of the **sky** rocked and quivered because God
22.10 He tore the **sky** apart and came down, with a dark cloud
22.14 the Lord thundered from the **sky,** and the voice of Almighty
1 Kgs 8.12 placed the sun in the **sky,** yet you have chosen to live
18.45 In a little while the **sky** was covered with dark clouds,
2 Kgs 19.15 You created the earth and the **sky.**
1 Chr 16.31 Be glad, earth and **sky!**
27.23 the people of Israel as numerous as the stars in the **sky.**
Neh 9. 6 you made the heavens and the stars of the **sky.**
9.23 there are stars in the **sky,** and let them conquer and live
Job 9. 9 hung the stars in the **sky**—the Great Bear, Orion, the
11. 8 The **sky** is no limit for God, but it lies beyond your
14.12 They will never wake up while the **sky** endures;
20. 6 grow great, towering to the **sky,** so great that his head
22.14 him from seeing, as he walks on the dome of the **sky.**
26. 7 God stretched out the northern **sky** and hung the earth in
26.11 that hold up the **sky,** they shake and tremble with fear.
26.13 his breath that made the **sky** clear, and his hand that killed
28.24 sees the ends of the earth, Sees everything under the **sky.**
35. 5 Look at the **sky!**
36.29 or how the thunder roars through the **sky,** where God dwells.
36.30 sends lightning through all the **sky,** but the depths of the
37. 3 sends the lightning across the **sky,** from one end of the
37.16 clouds float in the **sky,** the work of God's amazing skill?
37.18 help God stretch out the **sky** and make it as hard as
37.21 now the light in the **sky** is dazzling, too bright for us
37.21 and the **sky** has been swept clean by the wind.
38.33 the laws that govern the **skies,** and can you make them apply
Ps 8. 3 When I look at the **sky,** which you have made, at the
18. 9 He tore the **sky** apart and came down with a dark cloud
18.13 Then the Lord thundered from the **sky;**
19. 1 How clearly the **sky** reveals God's glory!
19. 4 God made a home in the **sky** for the sun;
19. 6 at one end of the **sky** and goes across to the other.
36. 5 your faithfulness extends to the **skies.**
57. 5 Show your greatness in the **sky,** O God, and your glory over
57.10 your faithfulness touches the **skies.**
57.11 Show your greatness in the **sky,** O God, and your glory
66.15 bulls and goats, and the smoke will go up to the **sky.**
68. 8 the earth shook, and the **sky** poured down rain, because of

Ps 68.33 the Lord, [33] to him who rides in the **sky,** the ancient sky.
68.34 his majesty is over Israel, his might is in the **skies.**
71.19 Your righteousness, God, reaches the **skies.**
77.17 thunder crashed from the **sky,** and lightning flashed
78.23 But he spoke to the **sky** above and commanded its doors to
89. 2 time, that your faithfulness is as permanent as the **sky.**
89.29 His dynasty will be as permanent as the **sky;**
89.37 permanent as the moon, that faithful witness in the **sky."**
96.11 Be glad, earth and **sky!**
103.11 As high as the **sky** is above the earth, so great is
104.13 From the **sky** you send rain on the hills, and the earth
108. 4 your faithfulness touches the **skies.**
108. 5 Show your greatness in the **sky,** O God, and your glory over
144. 5 O Lord, tear the **sky** apart and come down;
147. 8 He spreads clouds over the **sky;**
148. 4 Praise him, highest heavens, and the waters above the **sky.**
Prov 3.19 by his knowledge he set the **sky** in place.
8.27 there when he set the **sky** in place, when he stretched the
8.28 placed the clouds in the **sky,** when he opened the springs of
25. 3 like the heights of the **sky** or the depths of the ocean.
30.19 an eagle flying in the **sky,**
Is 1. 2 The Lord said, "Earth and **sky,** listen to what I am saying!
8.21 may look up to the **sky** [22] or stare at the ground, but
24. 4 both earth and **sky** decay.
24.18 will pour from the **sky,** and earth's foundations will shake.
34. 4 The **sky** will disappear like a scroll being rolled up, and
37.16 You created the earth and the **sky.**
40.12 the ocean by handfuls or measure the **sky** with his hands?
40.22 who sits on his throne above the earth and beyond the **sky;**
40.22 He stretched out the **sky** like a curtain, like a tent in
40.26 Look up at the **sky!**
45. 8 I will send victory from the **sky** like rain;
48.13 When I summon earth and **sky,** they come at once and present
50. 3 I can make the **sky** turn dark, as if it were in
55.10 the rain that come down from the **sky** to water the earth.
64. 1 Why don't you tear the **sky** apart and come down?
Jer 2.12 And so I command the **sky** to shake with horror, to be
4.23 at the **sky**—there was no light.
4.28 the **sky** will grow dark.
10. 2 sights in the **sky,** even though other nations are terrified.
10.11 who did not make the earth and the **sky** will be destroyed.
10.13 At his command the waters above the **sky** roar;
14.22 the **sky** by itself cannot make showers fall.
31.37 If one day the **sky** could be measured and the foundations
32.17 made the earth and the **sky** by your great power and might;
33.22 count the stars in the **sky** or the grains of sand on
33.25 night, and I have made the laws that control earth and **sky.**
51.16 At his command the waters above the **sky** roar;
51.48 on earth and in the **sky** will shout for joy when Babylonia
51.53 Babylon could climb to the **sky** and build a strong fortress
Lam 4.19 Swifter than eagles swooping from the **sky,** they chased us down.
Ezek 1. 1 The **sky** opened, and I saw a vision of God.
1. 4 from a huge cloud, and the **sky** round it was glowing.
32. 7 destroy you, I will cover the **sky** and blot out the stars.
Dan 4.11 bigger until it reached the **sky** and could be seen by
4.20 tall that it reached the **sky,** could be seen by everyone in
4.22 great that you reach the **sky,** and your power extends over
4.34 the king, "I looked up at the **sky,** and my sanity returned.
12. 3 The wise leaders will shine with all the brightness of the **sky.**
12. 7 raised both hands towards the **sky** and made a solemn promise
Joel 2.10 the **sky** trembles.
2.30 give warnings of that day in the **sky** and on the earth;
3.16 earth and **sky** tremble.
Amos 9. 6 heavens, and over the earth he puts the dome of the **sky.**
Nah 3.16 You produced more merchants than there are stars in the **sky!**
Hab 3.10 water poured down from the **skies.**
Zech 12. 1 Lord who spread out the **skies,** created the earth, and gave
Mt 16. 2 'We are going to have fine weather, because the **sky** is red.'
16. 3 'It is going to rain, because the **sky** is red and dark.'
16. 3 weather by looking at the **sky,** but you cannot interpret the
24.27 flashes across the whole **sky** from the east to the west.
24.30 the sign of the Son of Man will appear in the **sky;**
Lk 12.56 can look at the earth and the **sky** and predict the weather;
17.24 the lightning flashes across the **sky** and lights it up
21.11 will be strange and terrifying things coming from the **sky.**
Acts 1.10 their eyes fixed on the **sky** as he went away,
1.11 "Galileans, why are you standing there looking up at the **sky?**
2. 2 was a noise from the **sky** which sounded like a strong wind
2.19 will perform miracles in the **sky** above and wonders on the
9. 3 Damascus, suddenly a light from the **sky** flashed round him.
22. 6 a bright light from the **sky** flashed suddenly round me.
26.13 the sun, coming from the **sky** and shining round me
Phil 2.15 like stars lighting up the **sky,** [16] as you offer them the
Heb 11.12 there are stars in the **sky,** as many as the numberless grains
Jas 5.18 again he prayed, and the **sky** poured out its rain
Rev 6.14 The **sky** disappeared like a scroll being rolled up,
8.10 a torch, dropped from the **sky** and fell on a third of
11. 6 authority to shut up the **sky** so that there will be no
12. 1 Then a great and mysterious sight appeared in the **sky.**
12. 3 Another mysterious sight appeared in the **sky.**
12. 4 the stars out of the **sky** and threw them down
15. 1 Then I saw in the **sky** another mysterious sight, great and amazing.
16.21 fifty kilogrammes, fell from the **sky** on people, who cursed God

SLANDER

Job 5.21 God will rescue you from **slander;**
Ps 15. 3 are true and sincere, [3] and who does not **slander** others.
64. 4 they destroy good men with cowardly **slander.**
Is 29.21 God will destroy those who **slander** others, those who
Jer 9. 4 as deceitful as Jacob, and everyone **slanders** his friends.
Mt 15.19 to rob, lie, and **slander** others.
Mk 7.22 jealousy, **slander,** pride, and folly—[23] all these evil things
1 Cor 5.11 worships idols or is a **slanderer** or a drunkard or a thief.
6.10 are drunkards or who **slander** others or are thieves—
2 Tim 3. 3 they will be unkind, merciless, **slanderers,** violent, and
Tit 2. 3 They must not be **slanderers** or slaves to wine.

SLAP

1 Kgs 22.24 Zedekiah went up to Micaiah, **slapped** his face, and asked,
2 Chr 18.23 Zedekiah went up to Micaiah, **slapped** his face, and asked,
Job 16.10 they crowd round me and **slap** my face.
Mt 5.39 If anyone **slaps** you on the right cheek,
5.39 let him **slap** your left cheek too.
26.67 and those who **slapped** him [68] said, "Prophesy for us,
Mk 14.65 And the guards took him and **slapped** him.
Jn 18.22 one of the guards there **slapped** him and said, "How dare you
19. 3 And they went up and **slapped** him.
2 Cor 11.20 you or looks down on you or **slaps** you in the face.

SLASH

Jer 47. 6 How long will you go on **slashing?**
48.10 Curse the man who does not **slash** and kill!)

SLAUGHTER

Gen 34.27 After the **slaughter** Jacob's other sons looted the town
Num 22.40 town of Huzoth, [40] where Balak **slaughtered** cattle and sheep
Deut 3. 3 Og and his people in our power, and we **slaughtered** them all.
16. 2 one place of worship and **slaughter** there one of your sheep
16. 5 **"Slaughter** the Passover animals at the one place of
Josh 10.10 The Israelites **slaughtered** them at Gibeon and pursued them
10.20 and the men of Israel **slaughtered** them, although some
Judg 11.33 There was a great **slaughter,** and the Ammonites were defeated
1 Sam 4. 8 They are the gods who **slaughtered** the Egyptians in the desert!
4.10 There was a great **slaughter:**
6.19 the Lord had caused such a great **slaughter** among them.
11.11 By noon they had **slaughtered** them.
14.14 In that first **slaughter** Jonathan and the young man
14.32 enemy, took sheep and cattle, **slaughtered** them on the spot,
14.34 They are to **slaughter** them and eat them here;
14.34 they all brought their cattle and **slaughtered** them there.
22.21 He told him how Saul had **slaughtered** the priests of the Lord.
25.11 and the animals I have **slaughtered** for my shearers, and give
1 Kgs 3. 3 father David, but he also **slaughtered** animals and offered
11.24 had defeated Hadadezer and had **slaughtered** his Syrian allies.)
13. 2 He will **slaughter** on you the priests serving at the pagan
2 Kgs 3.24 Israelites kept up the pursuit, **slaughtering** the Moabites
8.12 their fortresses on fire, **slaughter** their finest young men,
2 Chr 18. 2 a large number of sheep and cattle **slaughtered** for a feast.
28. 9 now he has heard of the vicious way you **slaughtered** them.
Ezra 9. 7 been **slaughtered,** robbed, and carried away as prisoners.
Esth 3.13 They were to be **slaughtered** without mercy and their
7. 4 My people and I have been sold for **slaughter.**
8.11 **slaughter** them to the last man and take their possessions.
8.12 the day set for the **slaughter** of the Jews, the thirteenth of
9. 5 They attacked them with swords and **slaughtered** them.
9.18 a holiday, since they had **slaughtered** their enemies on the
Ps 37.14 poor and needy, to **slaughter** those who do what is right;
44.11 You allowed us to be **slaughtered** like sheep;
44.22 the time, that we are treated like sheep to be **slaughtered.**
Prov 7.22 on the way to be **slaughtered,** like a deer prancing into a
Is 14.21 Let the **slaughter** begin!
15. 9 there will be a bloody **slaughter** of everyone left in Moab.
34. 6 he will make this a great **slaughter** in the land of Edom.
53. 7 a lamb about to be **slaughtered,** like a sheep about to be
Jer 5.17 They will **slaughter** your flocks and your herds and destroy
7.32 Topheth or the Valley of Hinnom, but the Valley of **Slaughter.**
12. 3 guard them until it is time for them to be **slaughtered.**
19. 6 Instead, it will be known as the Valley of **Slaughter.**
25.34 come for you to be **slaughtered,** and you will be butchered
48.15 its finest young men have been **slaughtered.**
50.27 **Slaughter** them!
51.23 to **slaughter** shepherds and their flocks,
51.23 to **slaughter** ploughmen and their horses,
51.40 I will take them to be **slaughtered,** like lambs, goats,
Lam 2.21 You **slaughtered** them without mercy on the day of your anger.
Ezek 6. 8 escape the **slaughter** and be scattered among the nations,
21.14 It is a sword that kills, a sword that terrifies and **slaughters.**
26.15 be terrified at the screams of those who are **slaughtered.**
32.13 I will **slaughter** your cattle at every water-hole.
35. 5 let her people be **slaughtered** in the time of her disaster,
Zeph 1. 8 "On that day of **slaughter,"** says the Lord, "I will
Acts 7.42 not to me that you **slaughtered** and sacrificed animals for
8.32 that is taken to be **slaughtered,** like a lamb that makes no
Rom 8.36 we are treated like sheep that are going to be **slaughtered."**
Jas 5. 5 You have made yourselves fat for the day of **slaughter.**

SLAVE

[ENSLAVE]

Gen 9.25 He will be a **slave** to his brothers.
9.26 Canaan will be the **slave** of Shem.
9.27 Canaan will be the **slave** of Japheth."
12. 5 the wealth and all the **slaves** they had acquired in Haran,
12.16 gave him flocks of sheep and goats, cattle, donkeys, **slaves,**
15. 3 children, and one of my **slaves** will inherit my property."
15. 4 "This **slave** Eliezer will not inherit your property;
15.13 they will be **slaves** there and will be treated cruelly for

Gen	15.14	will punish the nation that **enslaves** them, and when they
	16. 1	But she had an Egyptian **slave-girl** named Hagar, [2]and so she
	16. 2	Why don't you sleep with my **slave-girl?**
	16. 6	"Very well, she is your **slave** and under your control;
	16. 8	to Shur [8]and said, "Hagar, **slave** of Sarai, where have you
	16. 9	He said, "Go back to her and be her **slave."**
	17.11	slaves born in your homes and **slaves** bought from foreigners.
	17.23	in his household, including the **slaves** born in his home and
	17.27	on the same day, [27]together with all Abraham's **slaves.**
	20.14	and at the same time he gave him sheep, cattle, and **slaves.**
	20.17	wife and his **slave-girls,** so that they could have children.
	21.10	said to Abraham, "Send this **slave-girl** and her son away.
	21.12	"Don't be worried about the boy and your **slave** Hagar.
	21.13	to the son of the **slave-girl,** so that they will become a
	24.35	and goats, cattle, silver, gold, male and female **slaves,**
	25.12	whom Hagar, the Egyptian **slave** of Sarah, bore to Abraham,
	27.37	over you, and I have made all his relatives his **slaves.**
	27.40	You will live by your sword, But be your brother's **slave.**
	29.24	(Laban gave his **slave-girl** Zilpah to his daughter Leah
	29.29	(Laban gave his **slave-girl** Bilhah to his daughter Rachel
	30. 3	She said, "Here is my **slave-girl** Bilhah;
	30. 9	she gave her **slave-girl** Zilpah to Jacob as his wife.
	30.18	given me my reward, because I gave my **slave** to my husband";
	30.43	He had many flocks, **slaves,** camels, and donkeys.
	31.33	the tent of the two **slave-women,** but he did not find his
	32. 5	I own cattle, donkeys, sheep, goats, and **slaves.**
	35.25	The sons of Rachel's **slave** Bilhah were Dan and Naphtali.
	35.26	The sons of Leah's **slave** Zilpah were Gad and Asher.
	39.17	"That Hebrew **slave** that you brought here came into my room
	41.12	was there with us, a **slave** of the captain of the guard.
	42.10	"We have come as your **slaves,** to buy food.
	43.18	attack us, take our donkeys, and make us his **slaves."**
	44. 9	put to death, and the rest of us will become your **slaves."**
	44.10	the cup will become my **slave,** and the rest of you can
	44.16	of us are now your **slaves** and not just the one with
	44.17	Only the one who had the cup will be my **slave.**
	44.33	I will stay here as your **slave** in place of the boy;
	46.18	of Jacob by Zilpah, the **slave-girl** whom Laban gave to his
	46.25	of Jacob by Bilhah, the **slave-girl** whom Laban gave to his
	47.19	We will be the king's **slaves,** and he will own our land.
	47.21	Joseph made **slaves** of the people from one end of Egypt
	47.25	been good to us, sir, and we will be the king's **slaves."**
	49.15	to carry the load And is forced to work as a **slave.**
	50.18	"Here we are before you as your **slaves,"** they said.
Ex	1.13	and made their lives miserable by forcing them into cruel **slavery.**
	2. 5	basket in the tall grass and sent a **slave-girl** to get it.
	2.23	Israelites were still groaning under their **slavery** and cried
	2.25	saw the **slavery** of the Israelites and was concerned for them.
	5. 4	Get those **slaves** back to work!
	6. 5	Egyptians have **enslaved,** and I have remembered my covenant.
	6. 6	you and set you free from your **slavery** to the Egyptians.
	6. 7	Lord your God when I set you free from **slavery** in Egypt.
	6. 9	their spirit had been broken by their cruel **slavery.**
	9.20	they brought their **slaves** and animals indoors for shelter.
	9.21	and left their **slaves** and animals out in the open.
	11. 5	the throne, to the son of the **slave-woman** who grinds corn.
	12.44	the Passover meal, [44]but any **slave** that you have bought
	13. 3	on which you left Egypt, the place where you were **slaves.**
	13.14	Lord brought us out of Egypt, the place where we were **slaves.**
	14. 5	Israelites escape, and we have lost them as our **slaves!"**
	14.12	us alone and let us go on being **slaves** of the Egyptians.
	14.12	would be better to be **slaves** there than to die here in
	15.16	have marched past— the people you set free from **slavery.**
	18.10	Praise the Lord, who saved his people from **slavery!**
	20. 2	God who brought you out of Egypt, where you were **slaves.**
	20.10	neither you, your children, your **slaves,** your animals, nor
	20.17	not desire his wife, his **slaves,** his cattle, his donkeys, or
	21. 2	If you buy a Hebrew **slave,** he shall serve you for six
	21. 3	unmarried when he became your **slave,** he is not to take a
	21. 3	married when he became your **slave,** he may take his wife with
	21. 5	But if the **slave** declares that he loves his master, his
	21. 6	Then he will be his **slave** for life.
	21. 7	sells his daughter as a **slave,**
	21. 7	she is not to be set free, as male **slaves** are.
	21. 9	a man buys a female **slave** to give to his son, he
	21.16	to keep him as a **slave,** is to be put to death.
	21.20	a stick and beats his **slave,** whether male or female,
	21.20	and the **slave** dies on the spot,
	21.21	But if the **slave** does not die for a day or two,
	21.26	hits his male or female **slave** in the eye so that he
	21.26	it, he is to free the **slave** as payment for the eye.
	21.27	tooth, he is to free the **slave** as payment for the tooth.
	21.32	kills a male or female **slave,** its owner shall pay
	21.32	the owner of the **slave** thirty pieces of silver,
	22. 2	shall be sold as a **slave** to pay for what he has
	23.12	seventh day, so that your **slaves** and the foreigners who work
Lev	19.20	"If a **slave-girl** is the recognized concubine of a man
	19.20	be punished but not put to death, since she is a **slave.**
	22.11	But a priest's **slaves,** bought with his own money or born
	25. 6	provide food for you, your **slaves,** your hired men, the
	25.10	who has been sold as a **slave** shall return to his family.
	25.39	slave, you shall not make him do the work of a **slave.**
	25.42	of Israel are the Lord's **slaves,** and he brought them out of
	25.42	they must not be sold into **slavery.**
	25.44	If you need **slaves,** you may buy them from the nations
	25.47	and sells himself as a **slave** to that foreigner or to a
	25.55	Israelite cannot be a permanent **slave,**
	25.55	because the people of Israel are the Lord's **slaves.**
	26.13	you out of Egypt so that you would no longer be **slaves.**
Deut	5. 6	Lord your God, who rescued you from Egypt, where you were **slaves.**
Deut	5.14	neither you, your children, your **slaves,** your animals, nor
	5.14	Your **slaves** must rest just as you do.
	5.15	Remember that you were **slaves** in Egypt, and that I, the
	5.21	his house, his land, his **slaves,** his cattle, his donkeys, or
	6.12	the Lord who rescued you from Egypt, where you were **slaves.**
	6.21	Then tell them, 'We were **slaves** of the king of Egypt,
	7. 8	might and set you free from **slavery** to the king of Egypt.
	8.14	Lord your God who rescued you from Egypt, where you were **slaves.**
	13. 5	the Lord, who rescued you from Egypt, where you were **slaves.**
	13.10	Lord your God, who rescued you from Egypt, where you were **slaves.**
	15.12	himself to you as a **slave,** you are to release him after
	15.15	Remember that you were **slaves** in Egypt and the Lord your
	15.16	"But your **slave** may not want to leave;
	15.17	he will then be your **slave** for life.
	15.17	Treat your female **slave** in the same way.
	15.18	Do not be resentful when you set a **slave** free;
	16.12	do not forget that you were **slaves** in Egypt.
	20.11	are all to become your **slaves** and do forced labour for you.
	21.14	with you, you cannot treat her as a **slave** and sell her.
	23.15	"If a **slave** runs away from his owner and comes to you
	24. 7	fellow-Israelite and makes him his **slave**
	24. 7	or sells him into **slavery** is to be put to death.
	24.18	Remember that you were **slaves** in Egypt and that the Lord
	24.22	Never forget that you were **slaves** in Egypt;
	26. 6	The Egyptians treated us harshly and forced us to work as **slaves.**
	28.32	will be given as **slaves** to foreigners while you look on.
	28.68	yourselves to your enemies as **slaves,** but no one will want
Josh	5. 9	I have removed from you the disgrace of being **slaves** in Egypt."
	6.23	all, family and **slaves,** to safety near the Israelite camp.
	9.23	Your people will always be **slaves,** cutting wood and carrying
	9.27	same time he made them **slaves,** to cut wood and carry water
	16.10	to this day, but they have been forced to work as **slaves.**
	24.17	fathers and us out of **slavery** in Egypt, and we saw the
Judg	6. 8	"I brought you out of **slavery** in Egypt.
1 Sam	2.27	Aaron and his family were **slaves** of the king of Egypt, I
	4. 9	become slaves to the Hebrews, just as they were our **slaves.**
	8.17	And you yourselves will become his **slaves.**
	17. 8	I am a Philistine, you **slaves** of Saul!
	17. 9	If he wins and kills me, we will be your **slaves;**
	17. 9	but if I win and kill him, you will be our **slaves.**
	25.10	The country is full of runaway **slaves** nowadays!
	30.13	"I am an Egyptian, the **slave** of an Amalekite," he
2 Sam	7.23	whom you rescued from **slavery** to make them your own people.
	18.21	he said to his Sudanese **slave,** "Go and tell the king what
	18.21	The **slave** bowed and ran off.
	18.23	through the Jordan Valley, and soon he passed the **slave.**
	18.31	Then the Sudanese **slave** arrived and said to the king,
	18.32	The **slave** answered, "I wish that what has happened to him
1 Kgs	2.39	later, however, two of Shimei's **slaves** ran away to the king
	2.40	donkey and went to King Achish in Gath, to find his **slaves.**
	9.20	descendants continue to be **slaves** down to the present time.
	9.22	Solomon did not make **slaves** of Israelites;
2 Kgs	4. 1	my two sons as **slaves** in payment for my husband's debt."
1 Chr	17.21	whom you rescued from **slavery** to make them your own people.
2 Chr	8. 7	descendants continue to be **slaves** down to the present time.
	28.10	make the men and women of Jerusalem and Judah your **slaves.**
	36.20	him and his descendants as **slaves** until the rise of the
Ezra	9. 8	some of us escape from **slavery** and live in safety in this
	9. 8	You have freed us from **slavery** and given us new life.
	9. 9	We were **slaves,** but you did not leave us in slavery.
	9. 9	We were slaves, but you did not leave us in **slavery.**
Neh	5. 5	But we have to make **slaves** of our children.
	5. 5	Some of our daughters have already been sold as **slaves.**
	9.17	they chose a leader to take them back to **slavery** in Egypt.
	9.36	And now we are **slaves** in the land that you gave us,
Esth	7. 4	serious than being sold into **slavery,** I would have kept
Job	3.19	the famous and the unknown, and **slaves** at last are free.
	6.27	even throw dice for orphan **slaves** and make yourselves rich
	7. 2	hard manual labour, [2]like a **slave** longing for cool shade;
	24. 9	Evil men make **slaves** of fatherless infants and take the
	27.18	web or like the hut of a **slave** guarding the fields.
Ps	74. 2	ago, whom you brought out of **slavery** to be your own tribe.
	105.17	man ahead of them, Joseph, who had been sold as a **slave.**
	129. 4	But the Lord, the righteous one, has freed me from **slavery."**
Prov	12.24	being lazy will make you a **slave.**
	19.10	live in luxury, and **slaves** should not rule over noblemen.
	22. 7	Poor people are the rich man's **slaves.**
	22. 7	Borrow money and you are the lender's **slave.**
	30.22	a **slave** who becomes a king,
Ecc	2. 7	I bought many **slaves,** and there were slaves born in my household.
	10. 7	slaves on horseback while noblemen go on foot like **slaves.**
Is	14. 2	Lord gave them, and there the nations will serve Israel as **slaves.**
	24. 2	and the people, **slaves** and masters, buyers and sellers,
	31. 8	run from battle, and their young men will be made **slaves.**
	45.14	be yours, and the tall men of Seba will be your **slaves;**
	47. 1	You are now a **slave!**
	50. 1	into captivity like a man who sells his children as **slaves?**
	52. 3	people, "When you became **slaves,** no money was paid for you;
Jer	2.14	"Israel is not a **slave;**
	2.14	he was not born into **slavery.**
	25.14	many nations and great kings will make **slaves** of them.' "
	30. 8	chains, and they will no longer be the **slaves** of foreigners.
	34. 9	to set free [9]their Hebrew **slaves,** both male and female,
	34. 9	so that no one would have a fellow-Israelite as a **slave.**
	34.10	agreed to free their **slaves** and never to enslave them again.
	34.11	took them back, and forced them to become **slaves** again.
	34.13	I rescued them from Egypt and set them free from **slavery.**
	34.14	to set free any Hebrew **slave** who had served them for six

Jer	34.16	of you took back the **slaves** whom you had set free
	34.16	as they desired, and you forced them into **slavery** again.
Lam	1. 1	The noblest of cities has fallen into **slavery.**
	1. 3	Judah's people are helpless **slaves,** forced away from home.
	5. 8	who are no better than **slaves,** and no one can save us
	5.13	Our young men are forced to grind corn like **slaves;**
Ezek	27.13	and traded your goods for **slaves** and for articles of bronze.
	34.27	from those who made them **slaves,** then they will know that I
Dan	10.17	I am like a **slave** standing before his master.
Hos	12.13	the people of Israel from **slavery** in Egypt and to take care
Joel	3. 3	and girls into **slavery** to pay for prostitutes and wine.
Amos	1. 6	whole nation and sold them as **slaves** to the people of Edom.
	2. 6	They sell into **slavery** honest men who cannot pay their debts,
	2. 7	with the same **slave-girl,** and so profane my holy name.
	8. 6	of a pair of sandals, and we'll buy him as a **slave."**
Mic	6. 4	I rescued you from **slavery;**
Nah	3. 4	she enchanted nations and **enslaved** them.
Mt	6.24	"No one can be a **slave** of two masters;
	8. 9	and I order my **slave,** 'Do this!'
	10.24	no **slave** is greater than his master.
	10.25	to become like his teacher, and a **slave** like his master.
	18.25	to be sold as a **slave,** with his wife and his children
	18.32	'You worthless **slave!'**
	20.27	first, he must be your **slave—**[28] like the Son of Man,
	21.34	the grapes, he sent his **slaves** to the tenants to receive his
	21.35	The tenants seized his **slaves,** beat one, killed another, and stoned another.
	21.36	Again the man sent other **slaves,** more than the first time,
	26.51	struck at the High Priest's **slave,** cutting off his ear.
Mk	10.44	wants to be first, he must be the **slave** of all.
	12. 2	he sent a **slave** to the tenants to receive
	12. 3	The tenants seized the **slave,** beat him, and sent him back
	12. 4	Then the owner sent another **slave;**
	12. 5	The owner sent another **slave,** and they killed him;
	14.47	struck at the High Priest's **slave,** cutting off his ear.
Lk	7. 8	and I order my **slave,** 'Do this!'
	15.29	worked for you like a **slave,** and I have never disobeyed
	16.13	"No servant can be the **slave** of two masters;
	20.10	he sent a **slave** to the tenants to receive from
	20.10	But the tenants beat the **slave** and sent him back
	20.11	So he sent another **slave;**
	20.12	Then he sent a third **slave;**
	22.50	struck the High Priest's **slave** and cut off his right ear.
Jn	8.33	Abraham," they answered, "and we have never been anybody's **slaves.**
	8.34	everyone who sins is a **slave** of sin.
	8.35	A **slave** does not belong to a family permanently, but a
	13.16	no **slave** is greater than his master,
	15.20	'No **slave** is greater than his master.'
	18.10	struck the High Priest's **slave,** cutting off his right ear.
	18.10	The name of the **slave** was Malchus.
	18.26	One of the High Priest's **slaves,** a relative of the man
Acts	7. 6	country, where they will be **slaves** and will be badly treated
	7. 9	their brother Joseph and sold him to be a **slave** in Egypt.
	16.16	we were met by a **slave-girl** who had an evil spirit that
Rom	6. 6	destroyed, so that we should no longer be the **slaves** of sin.
	6.16	when you surrender yourselves as **slaves** to obey someone,
	6.16	you are in fact the **slaves** of the master you obey—either
	6.17	at one time you were **slaves** to sin, you have obeyed with
	6.18	You were set free from sin and became the **slaves** of righteousness.
	6.19	you surrendered yourselves entirely as **slaves** to impurity
	6.19	entirely as **slaves** of righteousness for holy purposes.
	6.20	When you were the **slaves** of sin, you were free from righteousness.
	6.22	have been set free from sin and are the **slaves** of God.
	7.14	but I am a mortal man, sold as a **slave** to sin.
	8.15	you does not make you **slaves** and cause you to be afraid;
	8.21	be set free from its **slavery** to decay
1 Cor	6.12	but I am not going to let anything make me its **slave.**
	7.21	Were you a **slave** when God called you?
	7.22	For a **slave** who has been called by the Lord
	7.22	a free man who has been called by Christ is his **slave.**
	7.23	so do not become **slaves** of men.
	9.19	I am a free man, nobody's **slave;**
	9.19	but I make myself everybody's **slave** in order to win as many
	12.13	whether Jews or Gentiles, whether **slaves** or free, have been
Gal	2. 4	They wanted to make **slaves** of us, [5] but in order to keep
	3.28	between Jews and Gentiles, between **slaves** and free men,
	4. 1	is treated just like a **slave** while he is young,
	4. 3	same way, we too were **slaves** of the ruling spirits of the
	4. 7	So then, you are no longer a **slave** but a son.
	4. 8	God, and so you were **slaves** of beings who are not gods.
	4. 9	Why do you want to become their **slaves** all over again?
	4.22	two sons, one by a **slave-woman,** the other by a free woman.
	4.23	His son by the **slave-woman** was born in the usual way,
	4.24	whose children are born in **slavery** is Hagar, and she
	4.25	the present city of Jerusalem, in **slavery** with all its people.
	4.30	It says, "Send the **slave-woman** and her son away;
	4.30	for the son of the **slave-woman** will not have a part of
	4.31	are not the children of a **slave-woman** but of a free woman.
	5. 1	people, and do not allow yourselves to become **slaves** again.
	6.17	have on my body show that I am the **slave** of Jesus.
Eph	6. 5	**Slaves,** obey your human masters with fear and trembling;
	6. 6	with all your heart do what God wants, as **slaves** of Christ.
	6. 7	Do your work as **slaves** cheerfully, as though you served the Lord,
	6. 8	Lord will reward everyone, whether **slave** or free, for the
	6. 9	in the same way towards your **slaves** and stop using threats.
	6. 9	Remember that you and your **slaves** belong to the same Master
Col	2. 8	then, that no one **enslaves** you by means of the worthless
	3.11	circumcised and uncircumcised, barbarians, savages, **slaves,**
Col	3.22	**Slaves,** obey your human masters in all things, not only
	4. 1	Masters, be fair and just in the way you treat your **slaves.**
1 Tim	6. 1	Those who are **slaves** must consider their masters worthy of all respect,
	6. 2	**Slaves** belonging to Christian masters must not despise them,
Tit	2. 3	They must not be slanderers or **slaves** to wine.
	2. 9	**Slaves** are to submit to their masters and please them in
	3. 3	We were **slaves** to passions and pleasures of all kinds.
Phlm	16	he is not just a **slave,** but much more than a slave:
	16	to you, both as a **slave** and as a brother
Heb	2.15	set free those who were **slaves** all their lives because of
1 Pet	2.16	your freedom to cover up any evil, but live as God's **slaves.**
2 Pet	2.19	freedom while they themselves are **slaves** of destructive
	2.19	for a person is a **slave** of anything that has conquered him.
Rev	6.15	and all other men, **slave** and free, hid themselves in caves
	13.16	rich and poor, **slave** and free, to have a mark
	18.13	sheep, horses and carriages, **slaves,** and even human lives.
	19.18	the flesh of all people, **slave** and free, great and small!"

SLAVE-DRIVER

Ex	1.11	So the Egyptians put **slave-drivers** over them to crush
	3. 7	I have heard them cry out to be rescued from their **slave-drivers.**
	5. 6	the Egyptian **slave-drivers**
	5.10	The **slave-drivers** and the Israelite foremen went out and
	5.13	The **slave-drivers** kept trying to force them to make the
	5.14	The Egyptian **slave-drivers** beat the Israelite foremen,

SLAY
[SLAIN]

Ps	88. 5	I am like the **slain** lying in their graves, those you have
Jer	51.22	kill men and women, to **slay** old and young, to kill boys

SLEDGE HAMMER

Ps	74. 6	smashed all the wooden panels with their axes and **sledge-hammers.**

SLEEK

Gen	41. 2	when seven cows, fat and **sleek,** came up out of the river
	41.18	when seven cows, fat and **sleek,** came up out of the river

SLEEP
[SLEPT, SLEPT WITH]

Gen	2.21	man fall into a deep **sleep,** and while he was sleeping, he
	15.12	Abram fell into a deep **sleep,** and fear and terror came over
	16. 2	Why don't you **sleep with** my slave-girl?
	19.32	drunk, so that we can **sleep with** him and have children by
	19.34	daughter said to her sister, "I **slept with** him last night;
	19.34	let's make him drunk again tonight, and you **sleep with** him.
	26.10	my men might easily have **slept with** your wife, and you would
	28.11	He lay down to **sleep,** resting his head on a stone.
	30. 3	**sleep with** her, so that she can have a child for me.
	30.15	your son's mandrakes, you can **sleep with** Jacob tonight."
	30.16	said, "You are going to **sleep with** me tonight, because I
	31.40	I was not able to **sleep.**
	38. 8	Er's brother Onan, "Go and **sleep with** your brother's widow.
	49. 4	the most important, For you **slept with** my concubine And
Ex	22.27	What else can he **sleep** in?
Lev	26. 6	land, and you will **sleep** without being afraid of anyone.
Num	24. 9	When it is **sleeping,** no one dares wake it.
Deut	24.13	him each evening, so that he can have it to **sleep** in.
Judg	16.14	Delilah then lulled him to **sleep,** took his seven locks of hair,
	16.19	Delilah lulled Samson to **sleep** in her lap and then
Ruth	3. 7	He went to the pile of barley and lay down to **sleep.**
1 Sam	2.22	and that they were even **sleeping with** the women who worked
	3. 2	Eli, who was now almost blind, was **sleeping** in his own room;
	3. 3	Samuel was **sleeping** in the sanctuary, where the sacred
	9.26	up a bed for Saul on the roof, [26] and he **slept** there.
	26. 5	Saul and Abner son of Ner, commander of Saul's army, **slept.**
	26. 5	Saul **slept** inside the camp, and his men camped round him.
	26. 7	Saul's camp and found Saul **sleeping** in the centre of the
	26. 7	Abner and the troops were **sleeping** round him.
	26.12	because the Lord had sent a heavy **sleep** on them all.
2 Sam	3. 7	Saul accused Abner of **sleeping with** Saul's concubine Rizpah,
	11. 9	instead he **slept** at the palace gate with the king's guards.
	11.11	could I go home, eat and drink, and **sleep with** my wife?
	11.13	instead he **slept** on his blanket in the palace guardroom.
1 Kgs	18.27	Or maybe he's **sleeping,** and you've got to wake him up!"
	21.27	He refused food, **slept** in the sackcloth, and went about
Esth	6. 1	king could not get to **sleep,** so he ordered the official
Job	3.14	would be at rest now, [14] **sleeping** like the kings and rulers
	3.15	Then I would be **sleeping** like princes who filled their
	3.16	gold and silver, [16] or **sleeping** like a still-born child.
	4.13	Like a nightmare it disturbed my **sleep.**
	7. 4	When I lie down to **sleep,** the hours drag;
	14.12	they will never stir from their **sleep.**
	17.13	the dead, where I will lie down to **sleep** in the dark.
	24. 7	At night they **sleep** with nothing to cover them, nothing to
	31.10	cook another man's food and **sleep** in another man's bed.
	31.32	into my home and never let them **sleep** in the streets.
Ps	3. 5	I lie down and **sleep,** and all night long the Lord protects
	4. 8	When I lie down, I go to **sleep** in peace;
	76. 5	of all they had and now are sleeping the **sleep** of death;
	78.65	At last the Lord woke up as though from **sleep;**
	121. 4	The protector of Israel never dozes or **sleeps.**
	132. 4	I will not rest or **sleep,** [5] until I provide a place for
Prov	3.24	you go to bed, and you will **sleep** soundly through the night.

Prov 4.16 Wicked people cannot **sleep** unless they have done something wrong.
6. 4 Don't let yourself go to **sleep** or even stop to rest.
6.11 while he **sleeps,** poverty will attack him like an armed robber.
6.29 It is just as dangerous to **sleep with** another man's wife.
10. 5 it is a disgrace to **sleep** through the time of harvest.
19.15 **sleep** on, but you will go hungry.
20.13 If you spend your time **sleeping,** you will be poor.
23.21 you do is eat and **sleep,** you will soon be wearing rags.
24.33 Have a nap and **sleep** if you want to.
Ecc 4.11 it is cold, two can **sleep** together and stay warm,
5.12 to eat, but at least he can get a good night's **sleep.**
12. 4 but even the song of a bird will wake you from **sleep.**
Song 5. 2 While I **slept,** my heart was awake.
Is 5.27 They never doze or **sleep.**
26.19 All those **sleeping** in their graves will wake up and sing for
28.20 the proverb, who tries to **sleep** in a bed too short to
29.10 Lord has made you drowsy, ready to fall into a deep **sleep.**
38.15 My heart is bitter, and I cannot **sleep.**
56.10 How they love to **sleep!**
57. 8 large beds with your lovers, whom you pay to **sleep with** you.
Jer 31.26 people will say, 'I went to **sleep** and woke up refreshed.'
51.39 They will go to **sleep** and never wake up.
51.57 They will go to **sleep** and never wake up.
Ezek 16.15 your beauty and fame to **sleep with** everyone who came along.
16.33 and bribed them to come from everywhere to **sleep with** you.
22.10 Some of them **sleep with** their father's wife.
23. 8 she was a girl, men **slept with** her and treated her like
34.25 can live safely in the fields and **sleep** in the forests.
Dan 2. 1 he couldn't **sleep,** [2] so he sent for his fortune-tellers,
2.29 "While Your Majesty was **sleeping,** you dreamt about the future;
4.25 grass like an ox, and **sleep** in the open air, where the
5.21 grass like an ox, and **slept** in the open air with nothing
6.18 the palace and spent a **sleepless** night, without food or any
Amos 2. 8 every place of worship men **sleep** on clothing that they have
Zeph 2. 7 their flocks there and **sleep** in the houses of Ashkelon.
Zech 4. 1 me came again and roused me as if I had been **sleeping.**
Mt 9.24 The little girl is not dead—she is only **sleeping!"**
26.45 disciples and said, "Are you still **sleeping** and resting?
Mk 4.27 He **sleeps** at night, is up and about during the day, and
4.38 the back of the boat, **sleeping** with his head on a pillow.
5.39 The child is not dead—she is only **sleeping!"**
14.41 time, he said to them, "Are you still **sleeping** and resting?
Lk 8.52 the child is not dead—she is only **sleeping!"**
17.34 tell you, there will be two people **sleeping** in the same bed:
22.46 He said to them, "Why are you **sleeping?**
Jn 11.13 Lazarus had died, but they thought he meant natural **sleep.**
Acts 12. 6 out to the people, Peter was **sleeping** between two guards.
20. 9 Eutychus got **sleepier and sleepier,** until he finally went sound asleep
Rom 13.11 the time has come for you to wake up from your **sleep.**
1 Cor 5. 1 I am told that a man is **sleeping with** his stepmother!
15.20 guarantee that those who **sleep** in death will also be raised.
2 Cor 6. 5 we have been overworked and have gone without **sleep** or food.
11.27 often I have gone without **sleep;**
Eph 5.14 it is said, "Wake up, **sleeper,** and rise from death,
1 Thes 5. 6 So then, we should not be **sleeping** like the others;
5. 7 It is at night that people **sleep;**

SLEEVES

Gen 37. 3 He made a long robe with full **sleeves** for him.
37.23 brothers, they ripped off his long robe with full **sleeves.**
2 Sam 13.18 a long robe with full **sleeves,** the usual clothing for an

SLICED

2 Kgs 4.39 He brought them back and **sliced** them up into the stew,

SLIME

Ps 58. 8 May they be like snails that dissolve into **slime;**

Am **SLING** see **CATAPULT**

SLING

[SLUNG]

Judg 20.15 Every one of them could **sling** a stone at a strand of
1 Sam 17. 6 and he carried a bronze javelin **slung** over his shoulder.
17.49 his bag and took out a stone, which he **slung** at Goliath.
2 Kgs 3.25 Kir Heres was left, and the **slingers** surrounded it and attacked
1 Chr 12. 2 They could shoot arrows and **sling** stones either right-handed
2 Chr 26.14 coats of armour, bows and arrows, and stones for **slinging.**
Ezek 30.21 or put it in a **sling** so that it could heal

SLIP (1)

Gen 31.27 Why did you deceive me and **slip** away without telling me?
Ruth 3. 7 Ruth **slipped** over quietly, lifted the covers and lay down
2 Sam 4. 6 and had fallen asleep, so Rechab and Baanah **slipped** in.
2 Kgs 9.14 make sure that no one **slips** out of Ramoth
Jon 2. 7 When I felt my life **slipping** away, then, O Lord, I prayed
Jn 5.13 was a crowd in that place, and Jesus had **slipped** away.
10.39 tried to seize Jesus, but he **slipped** out of their hands.
Gal 2. 4 fellow-believers, these men **slipped** into our group as spies,
Jude 4 For some godless people have **slipped** in unnoticed among us,

SLIP (2)

Ps 35. 6 their path be dark and **slippery** while the angel of the Lord
73.18 You will put them in **slippery** places and make them fall
Is 19.14 and staggers like a drunken man **slipping** on his own vomit.
Jer 23.12 The paths they follow will be **slippery** and dark;

SLOPE

Num 21.15 the River Arnon, [15] and the **slope** of the valleys
Josh 10.40 hill-country, the eastern **slopes,** and the western foothills,
12. 8 and its foothills, the eastern **slopes,** and the dry country
13.20 Bethpeor, the **slopes** of Mount Pisgah, and Beth Jeshimoth.
18.12 and then went up the **slope** north of Jericho and westwards
18.13 border then went to the **slope** on the south side of Luz

SLOW

Gen 33.14 me, and I will follow **slowly,** going as fast as I can
Ex 4.10 I am a poor speaker, **slow** and hesitant."
Judg 5.28 "Why are his horses so **slow** to return?"
2 Kgs 4.24 as it can, and don't **slow** down, unless I tell you to."
Neh 9.17 you are gracious and loving, **slow** to be angry.
Ps 103. 8 Lord is merciful and loving, **slow** to become angry
145. 8 Lord is loving and merciful, **slow** to become angry
Prov 17.22 It is **slow** death to be gloomy all the time.
Is 19. 6 The channels of the river will stink as they **slowly** go dry.
Lam 2.12 though they were wounded, And **slowly** die
4. 9 who died later, who starved **slowly** to death, with no food
Hab 2. 3 It may seem **slow** in coming, but wait for it;
Lk 18. 7 Will he be **slow** to help them?
24.25 "How foolish you are, how **slow** you are to believe
Acts 27. 7 We sailed **slowly** for several days and with great
Heb 5.11 to explain to you, because you are so **slow** to understand.
Jas 1.19 quick to listen, but slow to speak and **slow** to become angry.
2 Pet 3. 9 The Lord is not **slow** to do what he has promised, as

SMALL

Gen 1.24 domestic and wild, large and **small"**—and it was done.
1.26 and all animals, domestic and wild, large and **small."**
7.14 domestic and wild, large and **small,** and every kind of bird.
19.20 see it is just a **small** place—and I will be safe."
19.22 Because Lot called it **small,** the town was named Zoar.
45.19 Egypt for their wives and **small** children and to bring their
46. 5 His sons put him, their **small** children, and their wives in
50. 8 Only their **small** children and their sheep, goats, and cattle
Ex 12. 4 If his family is too **small** to eat a whole animal, he
16.31 It was like a **small** white seed, and tasted like biscuits
18.22 but they themselves can decide all the **smaller** disputes.
18.26 to Moses but deciding the **smaller** disputes themselves.
Lev 11.23 But all other **small** things that have wings and also
11.41 not eat any of the **small** animals that move on the ground,
Num 11. 7 (Manna was like **small** seeds, whitish yellow in colour.
13.33 We felt as **small** as grasshoppers, and that is how we must
16. 9 Do you consider it a **small** matter that the God of Israel
22.18 the command of the Lord my God in even the **smallest** matter.
26.54 to a large tribe and a **small** one to a small tribe."
33.54 to a large clan and a **small** one to a small clan.
Deut 7. 7 you were the **smallest** nation on earth.
28.38 seed, but reap only a **small** harvest, because the locusts
Josh 17.15 hill-country of Ephraim is too **small** for you, then go into
1 Sam 9. 8 The servant answered, "I have a **small** silver coin.
9.21 the tribe of Benjamin, the **smallest** tribe in Israel, and my
13.21 the charge was one **small** coin for sharpening axes and
27. 5 are my friend, let me have a **small** town to live in.
2 Sam 21. 2 they were a **small** group of Amorites whom the Israelites had
1 Kgs 2.20 She said, "I have a **small** favour to ask of you;
8.64 the bronze altar was too **small** for all these offerings.
10.17 He also made three hundred **smaller** shields, overlaying
17.13 But first make a **small** loaf from what you have and bring
20.27 The Israelites looked like two **small** flocks of goats
2 Kgs 4. 2 "Nothing at all, except a **small** jar of olive-oil," she
4. 5 closed the door, took the **small** jar of olive-oil, and poured
4.10 Let's build a **small** room on the roof, put a bed, a
6. 1 complained to him, "The place where we live is too **small!**
16.10 priest an exact model of it, down to the **smallest** details.
17. 9 their towns, from the **smallest** village to the largest city.
18. 8 settlements, from the **smallest** village to the largest city,
25.15 gold or silver, including the **small** bowls and the pans used
2 Chr 7. 7 which he had made was too **small** for all these offerings.
9.16 beaten gold, [16] and three hundred **smaller** shields, each
24.24 The Syrian army was **small,** but the Lord let them defeat
Ezra 1. 9 **small** gold bowls 30
1. 9 **small** silver bowls 410
Esth 9.19 why Jews who live in **small** towns observe the fourteenth day
Job 8.12 first to wither, while still too **small** to be cut and used.
Ps 44.12 your own people for a **small** price as though they had little
49. 2 great and **small** alike, rich and poor together.
62. 9 great and **small** alike are worthless.
68.27 First comes Benjamin, the **smallest** tribe, then the
104.25 where countless creatures live, large and **small** alike.
115.13 everyone who honours him, the great and the **small** alike.
Prov 28.21 But some judges will do wrong to get even the **smallest** bribe.
30.24 four animals in the world that are **small,** but very, very
Song 8. 8 We have a young sister, and her breasts are still **small.**
Is 41.14 **"Small** and weak as you are, Israel, don't be afraid;
49.19 now it will be too **small** for those who are coming to
49.20 you, 'This land is too **small**— we need more room to
60.22 Even your **smallest** and humblest family Will become as
Jer 6.13 Everyone, great and **small,** tries to make money dishonestly;

Jer 8.10 Everyone, great and **small**, tries to make money dishonestly.
36.23 cut them off with a **small** knife and threw them into the
44.12 All of them, great and **small**, will die in Egypt, either in
52.19 the **small** bowls, the pans used for carrying live coals, the
Ezek 17.24 cut down the tall trees and make the **small** trees grow tall.
38.20 bird, every animal large and **small**, and every human being on
40.16 There were **small** openings in the outside walls of all
41. 5 the Temple, was a series of **small** rooms two metres wide.
46.21 four corners there was a **smaller** courtyard, twenty metres
47. 2 A **small** stream of water was flowing out at the south side
Dan 11.23 and stronger, even though he rules only a **small** nation.
Amos 6.11 command, houses large and **small** will be smashed to pieces.
7. 2 They are so **small** and weak!"
7. 5 They are so **small** and weak!"
Mic 5. 2 you are one of the **smallest** towns in Judah, but out of
Hag 1. 9 "You hoped for large harvests, but they turned out to be **small**.
Mt 5.18 the least point nor the **smallest** detail of the Law will be
13.32 It is the **smallest** of all seeds, but when it grows up,
15.34 "Seven loaves," they answered, "and a few **small** fish."
25.21 have been faithful in managing **small** amounts, so I will put
25.23 have been faithful in managing **small** amounts, so I will put
Mk 4.31 takes a mustard seed, the **smallest** seed in the world, and
8. 7 They also had a few **small** fish.
Lk 12.26 can't manage even such a **small** thing, why worry about the
16.10 Whoever is faithful in **small** matters will be faithful in large ones;
16.10 dishonest in **small** matters will be dishonest in large ones.
16.17 to disappear than for the **smallest** detail of the Law to be
19.17 Since you were faithful in **small** matters, I will put you in
Acts 26.22 here giving my witness to all, to **small** and great alike.
Rom 11. 5 there is a **small** number left of those whom God has chosen
11. 7 It was only the **small** group that God chose who found it;
1 Cor 6. 2 the world, aren't you capable of judging **small** matters?
2 Cor 4.17 And this **small** and temporary trouble we suffer will
9. 6 that the person who sows few seeds will have a **small** crop;
Jas 3. 4 be steered by a very **small** rudder, and it goes wherever the
3. 5 **small** as it is, it can boast about great things.
Rev 10. 2 He had a **small** scroll open in his hand.
11.18 all who have reverence for you, great and **small** alike.
13.16 beast forced all the people, **small** and great, rich and poor,
19. 5 people, both great and **small**, who have reverence for him!"
19.18 the flesh of all people, slave and free, great and **small**!"
20.12 I saw the dead, great and **small** alike, standing before the throne.

Am **SMART** see **CLEVER, INTELLIGENT, SENSIBLE**

SMASH

Num 24. 8 devour their enemies, Crush their bones, **smash** their arrows.
Deut 12. 3 Tear down their altars and **smash** their sacred stone pillars
2 Kgs 11.18 they **smashed** the altars and the idols, and killed Mattan,
23.12 he **smashed** the altars to bits and threw them into the valley
2 Chr 23.17 They **smashed** the altars and idols there and killed Mattan,
34. 4 Under his direction his men **smashed** the altars where Baal
34. 7 of the Northern Kingdom he **smashed** the altars and the
Ps 37.15 killed by their own swords, and their bows will be **smashed**.
74. 6 They **smashed** all the wooden panels with their axes
74.13 divided the sea and **smashed** the heads of the sea-monsters;
107.16 He breaks down doors of bronze and **smashes** iron bars.
137. 9 who takes your babies and **smashes** them against a rock.
Is 45. 2 I will break down bronze gates and **smash** their iron bars.
Jer 13.14 Then I will **smash** them like jars against one another,
Lam 2. 6 He **smashed** to pieces the Temple where we worshipped him;
2. 9 The gates lie buried in rubble, their bars **smashed** to pieces.
Ezek 6. 6 and their idols will be **smashed** to pieces, their
Dan 8. 7 was so angry that he **smashed** into him and broke the two
Hos 8. 6 The gold bull worshipped in Samaria will be **smashed** to pieces!
Amos 1. 5 I will **smash** the city gates of Damascus and remove the
6.11 command, houses large and small will be **smashed** to pieces.
Mic 1. 7 its precious idols will be **smashed** to pieces, everything
Mk 5. 4 time he broke the chains and **smashed** the irons on his feet.

SMELL

[SWEET-SMELLING]

Gen 27.27 up to kiss him, Isaac **smelt** his clothes—so he gave him
27.27 He said, "The pleasant **smell** of my son is like the smell
Ex 7.21 the river died, and it **smelt** so bad that the Egyptians could
16.20 was full of worms and **smelt** rotten, and Moses was angry with
25. 6 for the anointing oil and for the **sweet-smelling** incense;
30. 7 the lamps ready, he is to burn **sweet-smelling** incense on it.
30.23 liquid myrrh, three kilogrammes of **sweet-smelling** cinnamon,
30.23 three kilogrammes of **sweet-smelling** cane, [24] and six kilogrammes of cassia
31.11 the anointing oil, and the **sweet-smelling** incense for the Holy Place.
35. 8 for the anointing oil and for the **sweet-smelling** incense;
35.15 the **sweet-smelling** incense;
35.28 for the anointing oil, and for the **sweet-smelling** incense.
37.29 and the pure **sweet-smelling** incense, mixed like perfume.
39.38 the **sweet-smelling** incense;
40.27 the curtain, [27] and burnt the **sweet-smelling** incense, just
Lev 1. 9 The **smell** of this food-offering is pleasing to the Lord.
1.13 The **smell** of this food-offering is pleasing to the Lord.
1.17 The **smell** of this food-offering is pleasing to the Lord.
2. 2 The **smell** of this food-offering is pleasing to the Lord.
2. 9 The **smell** of this food-offering is pleasing to the Lord.
3. 5 The **smell** of this food-offering is pleasing to the Lord.
4.31 burn it on the altar so that the **smell** pleases the Lord.
6.15 The **smell** of this offering is pleasing to the Lord.
6.21 presented as a grain-offering, a **smell** pleasing to the Lord.
Lev 8.20 a food-offering, and the **smell** was pleasing to the Lord.
8.28 a food-offering, and the **smell** was pleasing to the Lord.
17. 6 the fat to produce a **smell** that is pleasing to the Lord.
23.13 The **smell** of this offering is pleasing to the Lord.
23.18 The **smell** of this offering is pleasing to the Lord.
Num 15. 3 the **smell** of these food-offerings is pleasing to the Lord.
15. 7 The **smell** of these sacrifices is pleasing to the Lord.
15.10 The **smell** of this sacrifice is pleasing to the Lord.
15.13 he presents a food-offering, a **smell** pleasing to the Lord.
15.14 basis, makes a food-offering, a **smell** that pleases the Lord,
15.24 bull as a burnt-offering, a **smell** that pleases the Lord,
18.17 burn their fat as a food-offering, a **smell** pleasing to me.
28. 6 Mount Sinai as a food-offering, a **smell** pleasing to the Lord.
28. 8 It also is a food-offering, a **smell** pleasing to the Lord.
28.13 are food-offerings, a **smell** pleasing to the Lord.
28.24 offer to the Lord a food-offering, a **smell** pleasing to him.
28.27 Offer a burnt-offering as a **smell** pleasing to the Lord:
29. 2 Present a burnt-offering to the Lord, a **smell** pleasing to him:
29. 6 These food-offerings are a **smell** pleasing to the Lord.
29. 8 Offer a burnt-offering to the Lord, a **smell** pleasing to him:
29.13 offer a food-offering to the Lord, a **smell** pleasing to him:
29.36 as a food-offering to the Lord, a **smell** pleasing to him:
Deut 4.28 wood and stone, gods that cannot see or hear, eat or **smell**.
Job 19.17 My wife can't stand the **smell** of my breath, and my own
39.25 they can **smell** a battle before they get near, and they
Ps 115. 6 They have ears, but cannot hear, and noses, but cannot **smell**.
Song 7.13 You can **smell** the scent of mandrakes, and all the
Is 1.13 I am disgusted with the **smell** of the incense you burn.
Dan 3.27 were not burnt, and there was no **smell** of smoke on them.
Jn 11.39 dead man's sister, answered, "There will be a bad **smell**,
12. 3 The sweet **smell** of the perfume filled the whole house.
1 Cor 12.17 And if it were only an ear, how could it **smell**?
2 Cor 2.15 For we are like a **sweet-smelling** incense offered by Christ to God,
Eph 5. 2 for us as a **sweet-smelling** offering and sacrifice that pleases God.
Phil 4.18 They are like a **sweet-smelling** offering to God, a sacrifice

SMILE

Gen 4. 7 If you had done the right thing, you would be **smiling**;
Job 9.27 If I **smile** and try to forget my pain, all my
10. 3 And then to **smile** on the schemes of wicked men?
29.24 I **smiled** on them when they had lost confidence;
Prov 15.13 When people are happy, they **smile**, but when they are sad,
15.30 **Smiling** faces make you happy, and good news makes you feel better.
Ecc 8. 1 Wisdom makes him **smile** and makes his frowns disappear.

SMIRK

Ps 35.19 hate me for no reason **smirk** with delight over my sorrow.

SMOKE

Gen 15.17 and it was dark, a **smoking** fire-pot and a flaming torch
19.28 smoke rising from the land, like **smoke** from a huge furnace.
Ex 19.18 Mount Sinai was covered with **smoke**, because the Lord had
19.18 The **smoke** went up like the smoke of a furnace, and all
20.18 saw the lightning and the **smoking** mountain, they trembled
Lev 16.13 on the fire, and the **smoke** of the incense will hide the
Deut 4.11 with thick clouds of dark **smoke** and fire blazing up to the
Josh 8.20 of Ai looked back, they saw the **smoke** rising to the sky.
Judg 20.38 saw a big cloud of **smoke** going up from the town, [39] the
20.40 a cloud of **smoke** began to go up from the town.
2 Sam 22. 9 **Smoke** poured out of his nostrils, a consuming flame and
Job 41.20 **Smoke** comes pouring out of his nose, like smoke from
Ps 18. 8 **Smoke** poured out of his nostrils, a consuming flame and
37.20 they will disappear like **smoke**.
66.15 bulls and goats, and the **smoke** will go up to the sky.
68. 2 As **smoke** is blown away, so he drives them off;
102. 3 My life is disappearing like **smoke**;
104.32 he touches the mountains, and they pour out **smoke**.
144. 5 touch the mountains, and they will pour out **smoke**.
Prov 10.26 irritating as vinegar on your teeth or **smoke** in your eyes.
Song 3. 6 like a column of **smoke**, fragrant with incense and myrrh,
Is 4. 5 cloud in the daytime and **smoke** and a bright flame at night.
6. 4 Temple shake, and the Temple itself was filled with **smoke**.
7. 4 no more dangerous than the **smoke** from two smouldering sticks.
9.18 It burns like a forest fire that sends up columns of **smoke**.
30.27 Fire and **smoke** show his anger.
34.10 burn day and night, and **smoke** will rise from it for ever.
51. 6 The heavens will disappear like **smoke**;
Ezek 8.11 an incense-burner, and **smoke** was rising from the incense.
Dan 3.27 were not burnt, and there was no smell of **smoke** on them.
Hos 13. 3 blows from the threshing-place, like **smoke** from a chimney.
Joel 2.30 there will be bloodshed, fire, and clouds of **smoke**.
Acts 2.19 There will be blood, fire, and thick **smoke**;
Jas 4.14 are like a puff of **smoke**, which appears for a moment and
Rev 8. 4 The **smoke** of the burning incense went up with the prayers
9. 2 smoke poured out of it, like the **smoke** from a large furnace;
9. 2 and the air were darkened by the **smoke** from the abyss.
9. 3 came down out of the **smoke** upon the earth, and they were
9.17 lions' heads, and from their mouths came out fire, **smoke**,
9.18 fire, the **smoke**, and the sulphur coming out of the horses'
14.11 The **smoke** of the fire that torments them goes up for
15. 8 The temple was filled with **smoke** from the glory and power
18. 9 when they see the **smoke** from the flames that consume her.
18.18 out as they saw the **smoke** from the flames that consumed her:
19. 3 The **smoke** from the flames that consume the great city goes

SMOOTH

Gen	27.11	know that Esau is a hairy man, but I have **smooth** skin.
1 Sam	17.40	and then picked up five **smooth** stones from the stream and
Ps	5. 9	words are flattering and **smooth,** but full of deadly deceit.
	55.21	His words were **smoother** than cream, but there was hatred
Prov	2.16	to seduce you with her **smooth** talk, [17] who is faithless to
	5. 3	honey and her kisses as **smooth** as olive-oil, [4] but when it
	7.21	him with her charms, and he gave in to her **smooth** talk.
	23.31	though it sparkles in the cup, and it goes down **smoothly.**
Song	4. 4	tower of David, round and **smooth,** with a necklace like a
	5.11	His face is bronzed and **smooth;**
	5.14	His body is like **smooth** ivory, with sapphires set in it.
Is	18. 2	nation, to your tall and **smooth-skinned** people, who are
	18. 7	powerful nation, this tall and **smooth-skinned** people, who
	26. 7	Lord, you make the path **smooth** for good men;
	40. 4	become a plain, and the rough country will be made **smooth.**
	41. 7	man who beats the idol **smooth** encourages the one who nails
	42.16	into light and make rough country **smooth** before them.
	57. 6	You take **smooth** stones from there and worship them as gods.
Jer	31. 9	of water, on a **smooth** road where they will not stumble.
Lk	3. 5	must be made straight, and the rough paths made **smooth.**

SMOTHER

1 Kgs	3.19	she accidentally rolled over on her baby and **smothered** it.
2 Kgs	8.15	took a blanket, soaked it in water, and **smothered** the king.

SMOULDER

Is	7. 4	no more dangerous than the smoke from two **smouldering** sticks.
Hos	7. 4	Their hatred **smoulders** like the fire in an oven, which is
	7. 6	All night their anger **smouldered,** and in the morning it

SNAIL

Ps	58. 8	May they be like **snails** that dissolve into slime;

SNAKE

Gen	3. 1	Now the **snake** was the most cunning animal that the Lord
	3. 1	The **snake** asked the woman, "Did God really tell you not to
	3. 4	The **snake** replied, "That's not true;
	3.13	She replied, "The **snake** tricked me into eating it."
	3.14	Lord God said to the **snake,** "You will be punished for this;
	49.17	Dan will be a **snake** at the side of the road,
	49.17	A poisonous **snake** beside the path,
Ex	4. 3	down, it turned into a **snake,** and he ran away from it.
	7. 9	in front of the king, and it will turn into a **snake."**
	7.10	of the king and his officers, and it turned into a **snake.**
	7.12	They threw down their sticks, and the sticks turned into **snakes.**
	7.15	that was turned into a **snake,** and wait for him on the
Num	21. 6	Then the Lord sent poisonous **snakes** among the people, and
	21. 7	Now pray to the Lord to take these **snakes** away."
	21. 8	Moses to make a metal **snake** and put it on a pole,
	21. 9	So Moses made a bronze **snake** and put it on a pole.
	21. 9	been bitten would look at the bronze **snake** and be healed.
Deut	8.15	desert where there were poisonous **snakes** and scorpions.
	32.24	animals to attack them, and poisonous **snakes** to bite them.
	32.33	grapes, [33] like wine made from the venom of **snakes.**
1 Kgs	1. 9	fattened calves at **Snake** Rock, near the spring of Enrogel.
2 Kgs	18. 4	broke in pieces the bronze **snake** that Moses had made, which
Job	20.16	it kills him like the bite of a deadly **snake.**
Ps	58. 4	They are full of poison like **snakes;**
	58. 5	hear the voice of the **snake-charmer,** or the chant of the
	91.13	trample down lions and **snakes,** fierce lions and poisonous snakes.
	140. 3	Their tongues are like deadly **snakes;**
Prov	23.32	will feel as if you had been bitten by a poisonous **snake.**
	30.19	a **snake** moving on a rock,
Ecc	10. 8	if you break through a wall, a **snake** bites you.
	10.11	Knowing how to charm a **snake** is of no use
	10.11	if you let the **snake** bite first.
Is	11. 8	baby will not be harmed if it plays near a poisonous **snake.**
	14.29	When one **snake** dies, a worse one comes in its place.
	14.29	A **snake's** egg hatches a flying dragon.
	30. 6	and where there are poisonous **snakes** and flying dragons.
	59. 5	you make are as deadly as the eggs of a poisonous **snake.**
	59. 5	Crush an egg, out comes a **snake!**
	65.25	straw, as cattle do, and **snakes** will no longer be dangerous.
Jer	8.17	snakes among you, poisonous **snakes** that cannot be charmed,
	46.22	Egypt runs away, hissing like a **snake,** as the enemy's army
Ezek	8.10	covered with drawings of **snakes** and other unclean animals,
Amos	5.19	his hand on the wall—only to be bitten by a **snake!**
Mic	7.17	They will crawl in the dust like **snakes;**
Mt	3. 7	he said to them, "You **snakes**—who told you that you could
	7.10	would you give him a **snake** when he asks for a fish?
	10.16	You must be as cautious as **snakes** and as gentle as doves.
	12.34	You **snakes**—how can you say good things when you are evil?
	23.33	You **snakes** and sons of snakes!
Mk	16.18	if they pick up **snakes** or drink any poison, they will
Lk	3. 7	"You **snakes!"**
	10.19	that you can walk on **snakes** and scorpions and overcome all
	11.11	are fathers give your son a **snake** when he asks for fish?
Jn	3.14	Moses lifted up the bronze **snake** on a pole in the desert,
Acts	28. 3	on the fire when a **snake** came out on account of the
	28. 4	The natives saw the **snake** hanging on Paul's hand and said
	28. 5	But Paul shook the **snake** off into the fire without being
Rom	3.13	dangerous threats, like **snake's** poison, from their lips;
1 Cor	10. 9	test, as some of them did—and they were killed by **snakes.**
2 Cor	11. 3	same way that Eve was deceived by the **snake's** clever lies.
Rev	9.19	Their tails are like **snakes** with heads, and they use them to

SNAP

Judg	16. 9	But he **snapped** the bowstrings just as thread breaks when
	16.12	But he **snapped** the ropes off his arms like thread.
Ecc	12. 6	The silver chain will **snap,** and the golden lamp will fall

SNARE

Job	18.10	On the ground a **snare** is hidden;
Ps	140. 5	they have laid their **snares** and along the path they have
	141. 9	they have set for me, from the **snares** of those evildoers.

SNARL

Ps	59. 6	come back in the evening, **snarling** like dogs as they go
	59.14	come back in the evening, **snarling** like dogs as they go

SNATCH

2 Sam	23.21	with his club, **snatched** the spear from the Egyptian's hand,
1 Chr	11.23	with a club, **snatched** the spear from the Egyptian's hand,
Ps	52. 5	he will take hold of you and **snatch** you from your home;
Prov	2.22	But God will **snatch** wicked men from the land and pull
Is	9.20	Everywhere in the country people **snatch** and eat any bit
Zech	3. 2	This man is like a stick **snatched** from the fire."
Mt	13.19	The Evil One comes and **snatches** away what was sown in them.
Jn	10.12	so the wolf **snatches** the sheep and scatters them.
	10.28	No one can **snatch** them away from me.
	10.29	and no one can **snatch** them away from the Father's care.
2 Cor	12. 2	who fourteen years ago was **snatched** up to the highest heaven
	12. 3	know that this man was **snatched** to Paradise (again, I do not
Jude	23	save others by **snatching** them out of the fire;
Rev	12. 5	But the child was **snatched** away and taken to God and his

SNEER

Job	16.10	People **sneer** at me;
	21. 3	to speak and then, when I am through, **sneer** if you like.
Ps	10. 5	he **sneers** at his enemies.
	44.16	with shame [16] from hearing the **sneers** and insults of my
Lam	2.16	They curl their lips and **sneer,** "We have destroyed it!
Ezek	5.14	you who passes by will **sneer** at you and keep his distance.
	22. 4	let the nations mock you and all the countries **sneer** at you.
	22. 5	countries far away **sneer** at you because of your lawlessness.
	34.29	The other nations will not **sneer** at them any more.
	36.15	to the nations mocking it or see the peoples **sneer** at it.
Lk	16.14	Pharisees heard all this, they **sneered** at Jesus, because they loved money.

SNEEZE

2 Kgs	4.35	The boy **sneezed** seven times, and then opened his eyes.
Job	41.18	Light flashes when he **sneezes,** and his eyes glow like

SNORT

Job	39.20	leap like locusts and frighten men with their **snorting?**
	39.25	At each blast of the trumpet they **snort;**
Jer	8.16	we hear the **snorting** of their horses.

SNOUT

Job	40.24	Or who can catch his **snout** in a trap?
	41. 2	put a rope through his **snout** or put a hook through his
Prov	11.22	good judgement is like a gold ring in a pig's **snout.**

SNOW

Ex	4. 6	out, it was diseased, covered with white spots, like **snow.**
Num	12.10	covered with a dreaded disease and turned as white as **snow.**
2 Sam	23.20	down into a pit on a **snowy** day and killed a lion.
2 Kgs	5.27	left, he had the disease—his skin was as white as **snow.**
1 Chr	11.22	down into a pit on a **snowy** day and killed a lion.
Job	6.16	The streams are choked with **snow** and ice, [17] but in the
	24.19	As **snow** vanishes in heat and drought, so a sinner
	37. 6	He commands **snow** to fall on the earth, and sends torrents
	38.22	visited the storerooms, where I keep the **snow** and the hail?
Ps	51. 7	wash me, and I will be whiter than **snow.**
	68.14	the kings on Mount Zalmon, he caused **snow** to fall there.
	147.16	He spreads **snow** like a blanket and scatters frost like dust.
	148. 8	**snow** and clouds, strong winds that obey his command.
Prov	26. 1	is out of place, like **snow** in summer or rain at harvest
	31.21	She doesn't worry when it **snows,** because her family has warm
Is	1.18	red with sin, but I will wash you as clean as **snow.**
	55.10	"My word is like the **snow** and the rain that come down
Jer	18.14	Are Lebanon's rocky heights ever without **snow?**
Lam	4. 7	and pure as **snow,** vigorous and strong, glowing with health.
Dan	7. 9	His clothes were white as **snow,** and his hair was like pure
Mt	28. 3	His appearance was like lightning, and his clothes were white as **snow.**
Rev	1.14	white as wool, or as **snow,** and his eyes blazed like fire;

SNUFF

1 Kgs	7.50	the cups, lamp **snuffers,** bowls, dishes for incense, and
2 Chr	4.22	the lamp **snuffers,** the bowls, the dishes for incense, the
Is	43.17	they fell, never to rise, **snuffed** out like the flame of a

SO-CALLED

Deut 32.21 me angry, jealous with their **so-called** gods, gods that are
32.21 So I will use a **so-called** nation to make them angry;
2 Chr 13. 9 consecrated as a priest of those **so-called** gods of yours.
Rom 10.19 "I will use a **so-called** nation to make my people jealous;
1 Cor 1.21 Instead, by means of the **so-called** "foolish" message we preach,
8. 5 Even if there are **so-called** "gods," whether in heaven or on earth,
8.10 matter sees you, who have **so-called** "knowledge," eating in
2 Cor 11. 5 bit inferior to those very special **so-called** "apostles"
2 Thes 2. 4 He will oppose every **so-called** god or object of worship

SOAK

Gen 4.11 It has **soaked** up your brother's blood as if it had opened
Lev 11.38 But if the seed is **soaking** in water and one of them
2 Kgs 8.15 day Hazael took a blanket, **soaked** it in water, and smothered
Ps 6. 6 my pillow is **soaked** with tears.
65.10 rain on the ploughed fields and **soak** them with water;
109.18 may his own curses **soak** into his body like water and into
Mt 27.48 at once, took a sponge, **soaked** it in cheap wine, put it
Mk 15.36 ran up with a sponge, **soaked** it in cheap wine, and put
Jn 19.29 so a sponge was **soaked** in the wine, put on a stalk

SOAP

Job 9.30 No **soap** can wash away my sins.
Jer 2.22 you washed with the strongest **soap,** I would still see the
Mal 3. 2 He will be like strong **soap,** like a fire that refines metal.

SOB

Gen 45. 2 He cried with such loud **sobs** that the Egyptians heard it,
Jer 48. 5 Hear the sound of their **sobs** along the road up to Luhith,
Ezek 24.17 Don't let your **sobbing** be heard.

SOBER

Gen 9.24 When Noah was **sober** again and learnt what his youngest
1 Sam 1.14 Stop your drinking and **sober** up!"
25.37 Then, after he had **sobered** up, she told him everything.
Acts 26.25 I am speaking the **sober** truth.
1 Thes 5. 6 we should be awake and **sober.**
5. 8 But we belong to the day, and we should be **sober.**
1 Tim 3. 2 he must have only one wife, be **sober,** self-controlled, and
3.11 they must be **sober** and honest in everything.
Tit 2. 2 Instruct the older men to be **sober,** sensible, and self-controlled;

SOCIETY

Acts 8.10 from all classes of **society,** paid close attention to him.
13.50 Gentile women of high **social standing** who worshipped God.
17.12 many Greek women of high **social standing** and many Greek men
1 Cor 1.26 few of you were wise or powerful or of high **social standing.**

SOCKETS

Song 5.15 His thighs are columns of alabaster set in **sockets** of gold.

SODOM

City near the Dead Sea destroyed by fire in Abraham's time.

Gen 10.19 eastwards to **Sodom,** Gomorrah, Admah, and Zeboiim near Lasha.
13.10 the Lord had destroyed the cities of **Sodom** and Gomorrah.)
13.12 the valley and camped near **Sodom,** [13] whose people were
14. 2 Bera of **Sodom,** Birsha of Gomorrah, Shinab of Admah,
14. 8 Then the kings of **Sodom,** Gomorrah, Admah, Zeboiim, and
14.10 and when the kings of **Sodom** and Gomorrah tried to run away
14.11 took everything in **Sodom** and Gomorrah, including the food,
14.12 Abram's nephew, was living in **Sodom,** so they took him and
14.17 other kings, the king of **Sodom** went out to meet him in
14.21 The king of **Sodom** said to Abram, "Keep the loot, but
18.16 they could look down at **Sodom,** and Abraham went with them to
18.20 "There are terrible accusations against **Sodom** and Gomorrah,
18.22 went on towards **Sodom,** but the Lord remained with Abraham.
18.26 find fifty innocent people in **Sodom,** I will spare the whole
19. 1 the two angels came to **Sodom** that evening, Lot was sitting
19. 4 guests went to bed, the men of **Sodom** surrounded the house.
19. 5 The men of **Sodom** wanted to have sex with them.
19.13 against these people and has sent us to destroy **Sodom."**
19.24 sulphur on the cities of **Sodom** and Gomorrah [25] and
19.28 He looked down at **Sodom** and Gomorrah and the whole
Deut 29.23 like the cities of **Sodom** and Gomorrah, of Admah and Zeboiim,
32.32 Their enemies, corrupt as **Sodom** and Gomorrah, are like
Is 1. 9 Jerusalem would have been totally destroyed, just as **Sodom**
1.10 rulers and your people are like those of **Sodom** and Gomorrah.
3. 9 They sin as openly as the people of **Sodom** did.
13.19 Lord, will overthrow Babylon as I did **Sodom** and Gomorrah!
Jer 23.14 they are all as bad as the people of **Sodom** and Gomorrah.
49.18 to Edom as happened to **Sodom** and Gomorrah, when they and the
50.40 to Babylon as happened to **Sodom** and Gomorrah, when I
Lam 4. 6 more than the inhabitants of **Sodom,** which met with a sudden
Ezek 16.46 Your younger sister, with her villages, is **Sodom,** in the
16.48 Sovereign Lord says, "your sister **Sodom** and her villages
16.53 will make them prosperous again—**Sodom** and her villages and
16.56 Didn't you joke about **Sodom** in those days when you were
Amos 4.11 "I destroyed some of you as I destroyed **Sodom** and Gomorrah.
Zeph 2. 9 Moab and Ammon are going to be destroyed like **Sodom** and Gomorrah.
Mt 10.15 mercy to the people of **Sodom** and Gomorrah than to the people
11.23 you had been performed in **Sodom,** it would still be in
11.24 Judgement Day God will show more mercy to **Sodom** than to you!"
Lk 10.12 Day God will show more mercy to **Sodom** than to that town!
17.29 On the day Lot left **Sodom,** fire and sulphur rained down
Rom 9.29 have become like **Sodom,** we would have been like Gomorrah."
2 Pet 2. 6 God condemned the cities of **Sodom** and Gomorrah, destroying them with fire,
Jude 7 Remember **Sodom** and Gomorrah, and the nearby towns, whose
Rev 11. 8 The symbolic name of that city is **Sodom,** or Egypt.

SOFT

1 Kgs 19.12 And after the fire, there was the **soft** whisper of a voice.
Job 41.27 is as flimsy as straw, and bronze as **soft** as rotten wood.
Ps 65.10 you **soften** the soil with showers and cause the young plants
Is 47. 1 city unconquered, but you are **soft** and delicate no longer!
Acts 27.13 A **soft** wind from the south began to blow, and the men

SOIL

Gen 2. 7 the Lord God took some **soil** from the ground and formed a
2.19 So he took some **soil** from the ground and formed all the
3.19 and sweat to make the **soil** produce anything,
3.19 until you go back to the **soil** from which you were formed.
3.19 You were made from **soil,** and you will become soil again."
3.23 made him cultivate the **soil** from which he had been formed.
4.11 are placed under a curse and can no longer farm the **soil.**
4.12 If you try to grow crops, the **soil** will not produce anything;
Num 13.20 Find out whether the **soil** is fertile and whether the
1 Sam 26.20 Don't let me be killed on foreign **soil,** away from the Lord.
Job 5. 6 does not grow in the **soil,** nor does trouble grow out of
14.19 wear down rocks, and heavy rain will wash away the **soil;**
29. 6 of milk, and my olive-trees grew in the rockiest **soil.**
39.14 on the ground for the heat in the **soil** to warm them.
Ps 65.10 you soften the **soil** with showers and cause the young plants
107.34 He made rich **soil** become a salty wilderness because of
Prov 8.26 the earth and its fields or even the first handful of **soil.**
Is 5. 2 He dug the **soil** and cleared it of stones;
28.25 Once he has prepared the **soil,** he sows the seeds of
34. 9 Edom will turn into tar, and the **soil** will turn into sulphur.
40.12 Can anyone hold the **soil** of the earth in a cup or
Mt 13. 5 Some of it fell on rocky ground, where there was little **soil.**
13. 5 The seeds soon sprouted, because the **soil** wasn't deep.
13. 8 But some seeds fell in good **soil,** and the plants produced corn;
13.23 seeds sown in the good **soil** stand for those who hear the
Mk 4. 5 Some of it fell on rocky ground, where there was little **soil.**
4. 5 The seeds soon sprouted, because the **soil** wasn't deep.
4. 8 some seeds fell in good **soil,** and the plants sprouted, grew,
4.20 But other people are like the seeds sown in good **soil.**
4.28 The **soil** itself makes the plants grow and bear fruit;
Lk 8. 6 sprouted, they dried up because the **soil** had no moisture.
8. 8 And some seeds fell in good **soil;**
8.15 seeds that fell in good **soil** stand for those who hear the
13. 7 Why should it go on using up the **soil?'**
14.35 It is no good for the **soil** or for the manure heap;
Heb 6. 7 God blesses the **soil** which drinks in the rain that often

SOLDERING

Is 41. 7 They say, 'The **soldering** is good'— and they fasten the idol

SOLDIER

[FELLOW-SOLDIER, FOOT-SOLDIERS]

Num 31.27 parts, one part for the **soldiers** and the other part for the
31.28 part that belongs to the **soldiers,** withhold as a tax for the
31.32 what was captured by the **soldiers,** in addition to what they
31.36 The half-share of the **soldiers** was 337,500 sheep and goats,
31.36 36,000 cattle for the **soldiers,** of which 72 were the tax for
31.36 30,500 donkeys for the **soldiers,** of which 61 were the tax
31.36 and 16,000 virgins for the **soldiers,** of which 32 were the
31.42 of the community was the same as that for the **soldiers:**
31.49 "Sir, we have counted the **soldiers** under our command and
Josh 1.14 will stay here, but your **soldiers,** armed for battle, will
5.13 and asked, "Are you one of our **soldiers,** or an enemy?"
6. 2 hands Jericho, with its king and all its brave **soldiers.**
6. 3 You and your **soldiers** are to march round the city once a
6. 4 seventh day you and your **soldiers** are to march round the
6.12 second time the priests and **soldiers** marched round the city
8. 1 to Joshua, "Take all the **soldiers** with you and go on up
8. 3 So Joshua got ready to go to Ai with all his **soldiers.**
8.10 in the morning Joshua got up and called the **soldiers** together.
8.11 The **soldiers** with him went towards the main entrance to
8.13 The **soldiers** were arranged for battle with the main camp
11. 4 They came with all their **soldiers**—an army with as many men
Judg 3.29 they killed about ten thousand of the best Moabite **soldiers;**
4. 7 will have his chariots and **soldiers,** but I will give you
5.23 come to help the Lord, come as **soldiers** to fight for him."
5.30 girl or two for every **soldier,** rich cloth for Sisera,
8.10 120,000 **soldiers** had been killed.
11. 1 Jephthah, a brave **soldier** from Gilead, was the son of
18.16 Meanwhile the six hundred **soldiers** from Dan, ready for battle,
20. 2 gathering of God's people, and there were 400,000 **foot-soldiers.**
20.15 They called out twenty-six thousand **soldiers** from their cities
20.17 The rest of the Israelite tribes gathered 400,000 trained **soldiers.**
20.20 and placed the **soldiers** in position facing the city.
20.21 over they had killed twenty-two thousand Israelite **soldiers.**
20.22 encouraged, and they placed their **soldiers** in the same
20.25 they killed eighteen thousand trained Israelite **soldiers.**
20.29 So the Israelites put some **soldiers** in hiding round Gibeah.
20.30 and placed their **soldiers** in battle position facing Gibeah,
20.44 Eighteen thousand of the best Benjaminite **soldiers** were killed.

Judg 20.46 Benjaminites were killed that day—all of them brave **soldiers.**
1 Sam 2. 4 bows of strong **soldiers** are broken, but the weak grow strong.
4.10 thirty thousand Israelite **soldiers** were killed.
8.11 "He will make **soldiers** of your sons;
13. 5 thousand horsemen, and as many **soldiers** as there are grains
13.15 of the people followed Saul as he went to join his **soldiers.**
13.17 The Philistine **soldiers** went out on raids from their
13.22 battle none of the Israelite **soldiers** except Saul and his
13.23 Philistines sent a group of **soldiers** to defend the pass
14.15 the raiders and the **soldiers** in the camp trembled with fear;
14.17 his men, "Count the **soldiers** and find out who is missing."
15. 4 were 200,000 **soldiers** from Israel and 10,000 from Judah.
16.18 brave and handsome man, a good **soldier,** and an able speaker.
17. 7 A **soldier** walked in front of him carrying his shield.
17.33 just a boy, and he has been a **soldier** all his life!"
17.46 the bodies of the Philistine **soldiers** to the birds and
18. 6 killing Goliath and as the **soldiers** were coming back home,
18.17 a brave and loyal **soldier,** and fight the Lord's battles."
24. 2 three thousand of the best **soldiers** in Israel and went
26. 2 three thousand of the best **soldiers** in Israel to the
2 Sam 1.19 The bravest of our **soldiers** have fallen!
1.25 "The brave **soldiers** have fallen, they were killed in battle.
1.27 "The brave **soldiers** have fallen, their weapons abandoned
2.21 "Run after one of the **soldiers** and take what he has."
4.12 gave the order, and his **soldiers** killed Rechab and Baanah
6. 1 David called together the best **soldiers** in Israel, a total
8. 4 hundred of his horsemen and twenty thousand of his **foot soldiers.**
10. 6 twenty thousand Syrian **soldiers** from Bethrehob and Zobah,
10. 9 chose the best of Israel's **soldiers** and put them in position
13.34 Just then the **soldier** on sentry duty saw a large crowd
15.18 The six hundred **soldiers** who had followed him from Gath also
17. 8 Your father is an experienced **soldier** and does not stay with
17.10 your father is a great **soldier** and that his men are hard
18.15 Then ten of Joab's **soldiers** closed in on Absalom and
19. 3 into the city quietly, like **soldiers** who are ashamed because
20. 7 bodyguard, and all the other **soldiers** left Jerusalem with
23. 8 These are the names of David's famous **soldiers:**
23.16 three famous **soldiers** forced their way through the Philistine
23.17 Those were the brave deeds of the three famous **soldiers.**
23.20 Benaiah son of Jehoiada, from Kabzeel, was another famous **soldier;**
23.24 There were thirty-seven famous **soldiers** in all.
1 Kgs 9.22 as his **soldiers,** officers, commanders, chariot captains,
12.21 together 180,000 of the best **soldiers** from the tribes of
20.11 that a real **soldier** does his boasting after a battle,
20.14 Lord says that the young **soldiers** under the command of the
20.15 the young **soldiers** who were under the district commanders,
20.17 The young **soldiers** advanced first.
20.17 to him that a group of **soldiers** was coming out of Samaria.
20.19 young **soldiers** led the attack, followed by the Israelite army,
20.39 in the battle when a **soldier** brought a captured enemy to me
22. 4 Jehoshaphat answered, "and so are my **soldiers** and my cavalry.
22.34 By chance, however, a Syrian **soldier** shot an arrow which
2 Kgs 5. 1 He was a great **soldier,** but he suffered from a dreaded
6.22 "Not even **soldiers** you had captured in combat would you put
8.21 out and escape, and his **soldiers** scattered to their homes.
14. 7 Amaziah killed ten thousand Edomite **soldiers** in Salt Valley;
14.12 Amaziah's army was defeated, and all his **soldiers** fled
19.24 that the feet of your **soldiers** tramped the River Nile dry.
19.32 No **soldiers** with shields will come near the city, and no
19.35 Lord went to the Assyrian camp and killed 185,000 **soldiers.**
25. 4 Babylonians were surrounding the city, all the **soldiers** escaped during the night.
25. 5 the plains near Jericho, and all his **soldiers** deserted him.
25.10 in Jerusalem, [10] and his **soldiers** tore down the city walls.
25.23 the Judaean officers and **soldiers** who had not surrendered
1 Chr 5.18 there were 44,760 **soldiers,** well-trained in the use of shields,
5.24 all outstanding **soldiers,** well-known leaders of their clans.
7. 2 of families of the clan of Tola and were famous **soldiers.**
7. 7 heads of families in the clan and were all famous **soldiers.**
7.11 heads of families in the clan and were all famous **soldiers.**
8.40 Ulam's sons were outstanding **soldiers** and archers.
11.10 This is the list of David's famous **soldiers.**
11.15 three of the thirty leading **soldiers** went to a rock where
11.18 three famous **soldiers** forced their way through the Philistine
11.19 These were the brave deeds of the three famous **soldiers.**
11.22 Benaiah son of Jehoiada from Kabzeel was a famous **soldier;**
11.26 These are the other outstanding **soldiers:**
11.26 his own group of thirty **soldiers)** Hanan son of Maacah
12. 1 reliable **soldiers,** [2] members of the tribe of Benjamin,
12. 3 These were the **soldiers:**
12. 3 Ishmaiah from Gibeon, a famous **soldier** and one of the
12. 8 names of the famous, experienced **soldiers** from the tribe of
12.19 Some **soldiers** from the tribe of Manasseh went over to
12.20 These are the **soldiers** from Manasseh who went over to
12.21 over his troops, because they were all outstanding **soldiers.**
12.23 was at Hebron, many trained **soldiers** joined his army to help
12.38 All these **soldiers,** ready for battle, went to Hebron,
18. 4 seven thousand horsemen, and twenty thousand **foot soldiers.**
19.10 chose the best of Israel's **soldiers** and put them in position
19.18 thousand Syrian chariot drivers and forty thousand **foot-soldiers.**
26.31 of Hebron's descendants, and outstanding **soldiers** belonging
28. 1 leading **soldiers,** and important men—gathered in Jerusalem.
28. 3 it, because I am a **soldier** and have shed too much blood.
29.24 All the officials and **soldiers,** and even all of David's
2 Chr 8. 9 but served as **soldiers,** officers, chariot commanders,
11. 1 eighty thousand of the best **soldiers** from the tribes of
12. 3 and more **soldiers** than could be counted, including Libyan,
13. 3 raised an army of 400,000 **soldiers,** and Jeroboam opposed him
13.17 defeat—half a million of Israel's best **soldiers** were killed.
17.14 the clans of Judah, and he had 300,000 **soldiers** under him.
2 Chr 17.15 rank was Jehohanan, with 280,000 **soldiers,** [16] and third was
17.17 Benjamin was Eliada, an outstanding **soldier,** in command of
17.19 in addition he stationed other **soldiers** in the other
18.33 By chance, however, a Syrian **soldier** shot an arrow which
25. 6 In addition, he hired 100,000 **soldiers** from Israel at a
25. 7 said to him, "Don't take these Israelite **soldiers** with you.
25.11 Edomite **soldiers**
25.13 Meanwhile the Israelite **soldiers** that Amaziah had not
25.22 Judaean army was defeated, and the **soldiers** fled to their homes.
26.13 Under them were 307,500 **soldiers** able to fight
28. 5 and kill 120,000 of the bravest Judaean **soldiers** in one day.
28. 7 An Israelite **soldier** named Zichri killed King Ahaz' son
32.21 that killed the **soldiers** and officers of the Assyrian army.
Neh 11.14 There were 128 members of this clan who were outstanding **soldiers.**
Job 16.14 he attacks like a **soldier** gone mad with hate.
Ps 33.16 a **soldier** does not triumph because of his strength.
76. 5 Their brave **soldiers** have been stripped of all they had
89.19 faithful servants, "I have given help to a famous **soldier;**
120. 4 With a **soldier's** sharp arrows, with red-hot charcoal!
127. 4 has when he is young are like arrows in a **soldier's** hand.
147.10 is not in strong horses, nor his delight in brave **soldiers;**
Song 3. 7 sixty **soldiers** form the bodyguard, the finest soldiers in Israel.
Is 3. 2 their heroes and their **soldiers,** their judges and their prophets,
5.29 The **soldiers** roar like lions that have killed an animal
13. 2 Shout to the **soldiers** and raise your arm as the signal for
13. 3 out his proud and confident **soldiers** to fight a holy war and
14.19 covered by the bodies of **soldiers** killed in battle, thrown
15. 4 Even the **soldiers** tremble;
18. 6 The corpses of their **soldiers** will be left exposed to the
22. 6 The **soldiers** from the land of Elam came riding on horseback,
22. 6 **Soldiers** from the land of Kir had their shields ready.
22. 7 **soldiers** on horseback stood in front of Jerusalem's gates.
30.17 one enemy soldier, and five **soldiers** will be enough to make
31. 1 on Egypt's vast military strength—horses, chariots, and **soldiers.**
37.25 that the feet of your **soldiers** tramped the River Nile dry.
37.33 No **soldiers** with shields will come near the city, and no
37.36 Lord went to the Assyrian camp and killed 185,000 **soldiers.**
49.24 Can you take away a **soldier's** loot?
49.25 The **soldier's** prisoners will be taken away, and the tyrant's
54.16 I also create the **soldier,** who uses the weapons to kill.
Jer 5.16 Their bowmen are mighty **soldiers** who kill without mercy.
14. 9 a man taken by surprise, like a **soldier** powerless to help?
21. 4 I will pile up your **soldiers'** weapons in the centre of the
22.25 give you to King Nebuchadnezzar of Babylonia and his **soldiers.**
26.21 When King Jehoiakim and his **soldiers** and officials heard
37.13 officer in charge of the **soldiers** on duty there, a man by
38. 4 he is making the **soldiers** in the city lose their courage,
39. 4 King Zedekiah and all his **soldiers** saw what was happening,
40. 7 Some of the Judaean officers and **soldiers** had not surrendered.
40.13 and the leaders of the **soldiers** who had not surrendered came
41. 3 at Mizpah and the Babylonian **soldiers** who happened to be there.
41.16 as prisoners from Mizpah after murdering Gedaliah—**soldiers,**
46. 5 Their **soldiers** are beaten back;
46. 6 the **soldiers** cannot escape.
46. 9 Send out the **soldiers:**
46.12 One **soldier** trips over another, and both of them fall to the
46.16 Your **soldiers** have stumbled and fallen;
46.21 Even her hired **soldiers** are helpless as calves.
46.23 their **soldiers** outnumber the locusts.
48.14 do you claim to be heroes, brave **soldiers** tested in war?
48.41 On that day Moab's **soldiers** will be as frightened as a woman
49.22 On that day Edom's **soldiers** will be as frightened as a woman
49.26 killed in the city streets, and all her **soldiers** destroyed.
50.27 Kill all their **soldiers!**
50.30 streets, and all its **soldiers** will be destroyed on that day.
50.36 Death to its **soldiers**— how terrified they are!
50.37 Death to its hired **soldiers**— how weak they are!
51. 3 Don't give its **soldiers** time to shoot their arrows or to
51.30 The Babylonian **soldiers** have stopped fighting and remain
51.32 The Babylonian **soldiers** have panicked.
51.56 its **soldiers** are captured, and their bows are broken.
51.57 its rulers drunk— men of wisdom, leaders, and **soldiers.**
52. 7 Babylonians were surrounding the city, all the **soldiers** escaped
52. 8 the plains near Jericho, and all his **soldiers** deserted him.
52.14 and his **soldiers** tore down the city walls.
Lam 1.15 "The Lord jeered at all my strongest **soldiers;**
Ezek 17.21 His best **soldiers** will be killed in battle, and the
23. 6 They were **soldiers** in uniforms of purple, noblemen
23.12 the Assyrian noblemen and officers—**soldiers** in bright
27.10 "**Soldiers** from Persia, Lydia, and Libya served in your army.
27.11 **Soldiers** from Arvad guarded your walls, and men from
27.27 and your merchants, Every **soldier** on board the ship—
29.18 He made his **soldiers** carry such heavy loads that their heads
30. 5 war will also kill the **soldiers** hired from Sudan, Lydia,
32.12 I will let **soldiers** from cruel nations draw their swords
32.22 "Assyria is there, with the graves of her **soldiers** all around.
32.23 All her **soldiers** fell in battle, and their graves surround
32.24 "Elam is there, with the graves of her **soldiers** all around.
32.25 battle, and the graves of her **soldiers** are all around her.
32.26 Tubal are there, with the graves of their **soldiers** all around.
32.29 They were powerful **soldiers,** but now they lie in the world
38. 4 riders, is enormous, and every **soldier** carries a shield and
38.15 a large, powerful army of **soldiers** from many nations, all of
39.18 to eat the bodies of **soldiers** and drink the blood of the
39.20 of horses and their riders and of **soldiers** and fighting men.
Dan 11.12 victory and of the many **soldiers** he has killed, but he will
11.15 The **soldiers** of Egypt will not continue to fight;
11.26 Many of his **soldiers** will be killed, and his army will be
11.31 Some of his **soldiers** will desecrate the Temple.
Hos 10.13 number of your **soldiers,** [14] war will come to your people,

Joel 2. 7 they climb the walls like **soldiers.**
3. 9 gather all your **soldiers** and march!
Amos 2. 2 while **soldiers** are shouting and trumpets are sounding.
2.14 will lose their strength, and **soldiers** will not be able to
2.16 even the bravest **soldiers** will drop their weapons and run."
5. 3 Israel sends out a thousand **soldiers,** but only a hundred return;
Obad 9 will be terrified, and every **soldier** in Edom will be killed.
Nah 2. 3 The enemy **soldiers** carry red shields and wear uniforms of red.
2.13 Your **soldiers** will be killed in war, and I will take away
3.13 Your **soldiers** are like women, and your country stands
Zeph 1.14 day, for even the bravest **soldiers** will cry out in despair!
1.16 of **soldiers** attacking fortified cities and high towers.
Zech 9.13 use Judah like a **soldier's** bow and Israel like the arrows.
10. 5 Judah will be victorious like **soldiers** who trample their
10. 7 Israel will be strong like **soldiers,** happy like men who have
Mt 8. 9 of superior officers, and I have **soldiers** under me.
22. 7 so he sent his **soldiers,** who killed those murderers and
27.27 Then Pilate's **soldiers** took Jesus into the governor's palace,
27.32 Cyrene named Simon, and the **soldiers** forced him to carry Jesus'
27.54 the army officer and the **soldiers** with him who were watching
28.11 their way, some of the **soldiers** guarding the tomb went back
28.12 sum of money to the **soldiers** [13]and said, "You are to say
Mk 15.16 The **soldiers** took Jesus inside to the courtyard of the
15.21 the country, and the **soldiers** forced him to carry Jesus'
Lk 3.14 Some **soldiers** also asked him, "What about us?
7. 8 of superior officers, and I have **soldiers** under me.
23.11 Herod and his **soldiers** mocked Jesus and treated him with contempt;
23.26 The **soldiers** led Jesus away, and as they were going,
23.36 The **soldiers** also mocked him:
Jn 18. 3 him a group of Roman **soldiers,** and some temple guards sent
18.12 Then the Roman **soldiers** with their commanding officer
19. 2 The **soldiers** made a crown out of thorny branches and put
19.23 After the **soldiers** had crucified Jesus, they took his
19.23 and divided them into four parts, one part for each **soldier.**
19.24 The **soldiers** said to one another, "Let's not tear it;
19.24 And this is what the **soldiers** did.
19.32 So the **soldiers** went and broke the legs of the first man
19.34 One of the **soldiers,** however, plunged his spear into Jesus'
Acts 10. 7 his house servants and a **soldier,** a religious man who was
12. 4 over to be guarded by four groups of four **soldiers** each.
21.32 some officers and **soldiers** and rushed down to the crowd.
21.32 When the people saw him with the **soldiers,** they stopped beating Paul.
21.35 with him, and then the **soldiers** had to carry him because the
21.37 As the **soldiers** were about to take Paul into the fort,
23.10 So he ordered his **soldiers** to go down into the group, get
23.23 said, "Get two hundred **soldiers** ready to go to Caesarea,
23.27 a Roman citizen, so I went with my **soldiers** and rescued him.
23.31 The **soldiers** carried out their orders.
23.32 The next day the **foot-soldiers** returned to the fort and
27.31 to the army officer and **soldiers,** "If the sailors don't
27.32 So the **soldiers** cut the ropes that held the boat and let
27.42 The **soldiers** made a plan to kill all the prisoners, in
28.16 Paul was allowed to live by himself with a **soldier** guarding him.
1 Cor 9. 7 What **soldier** ever has to pay his own expenses in the army?
2 Tim 2. 3 Take your part in suffering, as a loyal **soldier** of Christ Jesus.
2. 4 A **soldier** on active service wants to please his commanding
Phlm 2 and our sister Apphia, and our **fellow-soldier** Archippus:
Rev 19.18 flesh of kings, generals, and **soldiers,** the flesh of horses

SOLEMN

Gen 14.22 Abram answered, "I **solemnly** swear before the Lord,
24. 7 of my relatives, and he **solemnly** promised me that he would
26.28 we think that there should be a **solemn** agreement between us.
31.53 Isaac worshipped, Jacob **solemnly** vowed to keep this promise.
47.29 my thighs and make a **solemn** vow that you will not bury
50.11 Atad, they said, "What a **solemn** ceremony of mourning the
50.24 land to the land he **solemnly** promised to Abraham, Isaac, and
Ex 6. 8 to the land that I **solemnly** promised to give to Abraham,
13. 5 The Lord **solemnly** promised your ancestors to give you the
13.11 which he **solemnly** promised to you and your ancestors.
13.19 as Joseph had made the Israelites **solemnly** promise to do.
31.15 the seventh day is a **solemn** day of rest dedicated to me.
32.13 Remember the **solemn** promise you made to them to give them as
35. 2 is to be sacred, a **solemn** day of rest dedicated to me,
Deut 1.34 became angry, and so he **solemnly** declared, [35]'Not one of
4.21 was angry with me and **solemnly** declared that I would not
29.19 here today who hears these **solemn** demands and yet convinces
Josh 6.26 At that time Joshua issued a **solemn** warning:
9.15 of Israel gave their **solemn** promise to keep the treaty.
9.18 their leaders had made a **solemn** promise to them in the name
9.19 answered, "We have made our **solemn** promise to them in the
21.43 the land that he had **solemnly** promised their ancestors he
Judg 8.19 I **solemnly** swear that if you had not killed them, I would
11.35 I have made a **solemn** promise to the Lord, and I cannot
17. 3 son, I myself am **solemnly** dedicating the silver to the Lord.
21. 1 at Mizpah, they had made a **solemn** promise to the Lord:
21. 5 (They had taken a **solemn** oath that anyone who had not gone
21. 7 We have made a **solemn** promise to the Lord that we will
1 Sam 1.11 Hannah made a **solemn** promise:
3.14 So I **solemnly** declare to the family of Eli that no
12.22 The Lord has made a **solemn** promise, and he will not
14.24 day, because Saul, with a **solemn** oath, had given the order:
2 Sam 3.35 something, but he made a **solemn** promise, "May God strike me
1 Kgs 1.13 didn't you **solemnly** promise me that my son Solomon
1.17 Majesty, you made me a **solemn** promise in the name of the
2. 8 Jordan, I gave him my **solemn** promise in the name of the
2.23 Then Solomon made a **solemn** promise in the Lord's name,
Ezra 10. 3 Now we must make a **solemn** promise to our God that we
Neh 9.38 hereby make a **solemn** written agreement, and our leaders,
Job 31. 1 I have made a **solemn** promise never to look with lust at
Ps 95.11 I was angry and made a **solemn** promise:
106.26 So he gave them a **solemn** warning that he would make them
110. 4 The Lord made a **solemn** promise and will not take it back:
119.106 I will keep my **solemn** promise to obey your just instructions.
132.11 You made a **solemn** promise to David— a promise you will
Prov 30. 1 These are the **solemn** words of Agur son of Jakeh:
31. 1 These are the **solemn** words which King Lemuel's mother said
Is 19.21 They will make **solemn** promises to him and do what they promise.
45.23 I **solemnly** promise by all that I am:
62. 8 The Lord has made a **solemn** promise, And by his power he
Jer 11. 7 ancestors out of Egypt, I **solemnly** warned them to obey me,
44.24 your wives have made **solemn** promises to the Queen of Heaven.
Ezek 32. 2 he said, "give a **solemn** warning to the king of Egypt.
32.16 This **solemn** warning will become a funeral song.
36. 7 I, the Sovereign Lord, **solemnly** promise that the
44.12 Sovereign Lord, **solemnly** swear that they must be punished.
47.14 I **solemnly** promised your ancestors that I would give
Dan 12. 7 the sky and made a **solemn** promise in the name of the
Amos 6. 8 The Sovereign Lord Almighty has given this **solemn** warning:
Nah 1.15 your festivals and give God what you **solemnly** promised him.
Lk 1.73 With a **solemn** oath to our ancestor Abraham he
Acts 20.21 and Gentiles alike I gave **solemn** warning that they should
20.26 So I **solemnly** declare to you this very day:
23.14 said, "We have taken a **solemn** vow together not to eat a
1 Tim 5.21 of the holy angels I **solemnly** call upon you to obey these
2 Tim 2.14 this, and give them a **solemn** warning in God's presence not
4. 1 rule as King, I **solemnly** urge you [2]to preach the message,
Heb 3.11 I was angry and made a **solemn** promise:
3.18 When God made his **solemn** promise, "They will never
4. 3 just as he said, "I was angry and made a **solemn** promise:
7.21 "The Lord has made a **solemn** promise and will not take it
Rev 22.18 I, John, **solemnly** warn everyone who hears the prophetic

SOLID

Ex 15. 8 the deepest part of the sea became **solid.**
Deut 8.15 waterless land he made water flow out of **solid** rock for you.
2 Chr 24.13 the Temple to its original condition, as **solid** as ever.
Job 14.18 a time when mountains fall and **solid** cliffs are moved away.
37.10 of God freezes the waters, and turns them to **solid** ice.
Ps 69. 2 I am sinking in deep mud, and there is no **solid** ground;
114. 8 into pools of water and **solid** cliffs into flowing springs.
Is 28.16 it I am putting a **solid** cornerstone on which are written the
Jer 15.20 will make you like a **solid** bronze wall as far as they
Ezek 26. 8 earthworks, and make a **solid** wall of shields against you.
42. 7 building was **solid** for twenty-five metres, half its length;
Obad 3 Your capital is a fortress of **solid** rock;
Mt 27.60 own tomb, which he had just recently dug out of **solid** rock.
Mk 15.46 it in a tomb which had been dug out of **solid** rock.
Lk 23.53 had been dug out of **solid** rock and which had never been
1 Cor 3. 2 feed you with milk, not **solid** food, because you were not
1 Tim 6.19 a treasure which will be a **solid** foundation for the future.
2 Tim 2.19 But the **solid** foundation that God has laid cannot be shaken;
Heb 5.12 Instead of eating **solid** food, you still have to drink milk.
5.14 **Solid** food, on the other hand, is for adults, who

SOLOMON

David's son, who succeeded him as king of Israel and built the Temple.

2 Sam 5.1-16 **David becomes king of Israel and Judah**
12.24-25 **Solomon is born**
1 Kgs 1.5-10 **Adonijah claims the throne**
11-53 **Solomon is made king**
2.1-9 **David's last instructions to Solomon**
10-12 **The death of David**
13-25 **The death of Adonijah**
26-35 **Abiathar's banishment and Joab's death**
36-46 **The death of Shimei**
3.1-15 **Solomon prays for wisdom**
16-28 **Solomon judges a difficult case**
4.1-19 **Solomon's officials**
20-34 **Solomon's prosperous reign**
5.1-18 **Solomon prepares to build the Temple**
6.1-14 **Solomon builds the Temple**
6.15-38 **The interior furnishings of the Temple**
7.1-12 **Solomon's palace**
13-14 **Huram's task**
40-51 **Summary list of Temple furnishings**
8.1-13 **The Covenant Box is brought to the Temple**
14-21 **Solomon's address to the people**
22-53 **Solomon's prayer**
54-61 **The final prayer**
62-66 **The dedication of the Temple**
9.1-9 **God appears to Solomon again**
10-14 **Solomon's agreement with Hiram**
15-28 **Further achievements of Solomon**
10.1-13 **The visit of the queen of Sheba**
14-29 **King Solomon's wealth**
11.1-13 **Solomon turns away from God**
14-25 **Solomon's enemies**
26-40 **God's promise to Jeroboam**
41-43 **The death of Solomon**
1 Chr 3.1-9 **King David's children**
10-16 **The descendants of King Solomon**
6.1-15 **The family line of the high priests**
14.1-7 **David's activities in Jerusalem**
18.1-17 **David's military victories**

1 Chr 22.2–23.1 **Preparations for building the Temple**
28.1-21 **David's instructions for the Temple**
29.1-9 **Gifts for building the Temple**
10-25 **David praises God**
26-30 **Summary of David's reign**
2 Chr 1.1-12 **King Solomon prays for wisdom**
13-17 **King Solomon's power and wealth**
2.1-16 **Preparations for building the Temple**
2.17–3.14 **Construction of the Temple begins**
4.1–5.1 **Equipment for the Temple**
5.2-10 **The Covenant Box is brought to the Temple**
6.1-11 **Solomon's address to the people**
12-42 **Solomon's prayer**
7.1-10 **The dedication of the Temple**
11-22 **God appears to Solomon again**
8.1-18 **Solomon's achievements**
9.1-12 **The visit of the queen of Sheba**
13-28 **King Solomon's wealth**
29-31 **Summary of Solomon's reign**
1 Kgs 12. 2 Egypt to escape from King **Solomon,** heard this news, he
12. 4 said to him, [4]"Your father **Solomon** treated us harshly and
12. 6 older men who had served as his father **Solomon's** advisers.
14.21 **Solomon's** son Rehoboam was forty-one years old when he
14.26 in the palace, including the gold shields **Solomon** had made.
2 Kgs 21. 7 about which the Lord had said to David and his son **Solomon:**
23.13 the altars that King **Solomon** had built east of Jerusalem,
24.13 the gold utensils which King **Solomon** had made for use in the
25.16 The bronze objects that King **Solomon** had made for the
1 Chr 6.32 during the time before King **Solomon** built the Temple.
2 Chr 10. 2 Egypt to escape from King **Solomon,** heard this news,
10. 6 older men who had served as his father **Solomon's** advisers.
11.17 they supported Rehoboam son of **Solomon** and lived as they had
11.17 as they had under the rule of King David and King **Solomon.**
12. 9 including the gold shields that King **Solomon** had made.
13. 6 Jeroboam son of Nebat rebelled against **Solomon,** his king.
13. 7 will on Rehoboam son of **Solomon,** who was too young and
30.26 happened since the days of King **Solomon,** the son of David.
33. 7 place about which God had said to David and his son **Solomon:**
35. 3 Box in the Temple that King **Solomon,** the son of David,
35. 4 David and his son King **Solomon,** [5]and arrange yourselves so
Ezra 2.55 Clans of **Solomon's** servants who returned from exile:
2.58 the temple workmen and of **Solomon's** servants who returned
Neh 7.57 Clans of **Solomon's** servants who returned from exile:
7.60 the temple workmen and of **Solomon's** servants who returned
11. 3 workmen, and the descendants of **Solomon's** servants lived on
12.45 with the regulations made by King David and his son **Solomon.**
13.26 I said, "It was foreign women that made King **Solomon** sin.
Prov 1. 1 The proverbs of **Solomon,** son of David and king of Israel.
10. 1 These are **Solomon's** proverbs:
25. 1 Here are more of **Solomon's** proverbs, copied by men at the
Song 1. 1 The most beautiful of songs, by **Solomon.**
1. 5 Kedar, but beautiful as the curtains in **Solomon's** palace.
3. 7 **Solomon** is coming, carried on his throne;
3. 9 King **Solomon** is carried on a throne made of the finest wood.
3.11 Women of Zion, come and see King **Solomon.**
8.11 **Solomon** has a vineyard in a place called Baal Hamon.
8.12 **Solomon** is welcome to his thousand coins, and the
Jer 52.20 The bronze objects that King **Solomon** had made for the
Mt 1. 6 **Solomon** (his mother was the woman who had been Uriah's wife),
6.29 you that not even King **Solomon** with all his wealth had
12.42 from her country to listen to King **Solomon's** wise teaching;
12.42 I assure you that there is something here greater than **Solomon!**
Lk 11.31 from her country to listen to King **Solomon's** wise teaching;
11.31 and I tell you there is something here greater than **Solomon.**
12.27 you that not even King **Solomon** with all his wealth had
Acts 7.47 But it was **Solomon** who built him a house.

SOLOMON'S PORCH

Jn 10.23 Jesus was walking in **Solomon's Porch** in the Temple,
Acts 3.11 to Peter and John in **Solomon's Porch,** as it was called, the
5.12 All the believers met together in **Solomon's Porch.**

SOLVE

Judg 14.14 Three days later they had still not **solved** the riddle.
14.19 their fine clothes to the men who had **solved** the riddle.
Dan 5.12 dreams, **solving** riddles, and explaining mysteries;

SOMEONE

Mt 3. 3 about when he said, **"Someone** is shouting in the desert,
5.25 "If **someone** brings a lawsuit against you and takes you to court,
5.39 do not take revenge on **someone** who wrongs you.
5.40 And if **someone** takes you to court to sue you for your
5.42 When **someone** asks you for something, give it to him;
5.42 when **someone** wants to borrow something, lend it to him.
10.11 go in and look for **someone** who is willing to welcome you,
11. 3 John said was going to come, or should we expect **someone else?"**
12.12 our Law does allow us to help **someone** on the Sabbath."
23.16 You teach, 'If **someone** swears by the Temple, he isn't bound
23.18 You also teach, 'If **someone** swears by the altar, he
23.22 and when **someone** swears by heaven, he is swearing by
Mk 1. 3 **Someone** is shouting in the desert, 'Get the road ready for
11. 3 And if **someone** asks you why you are doing that, tell him
Lk 3. 4 **"Someone** is shouting in the desert:
3.16 baptize you with water, but **someone** is coming who is much
6.29 if **someone** takes your coat, let him have your shirt as well.
6.30 you for something, and when **someone** takes what is yours, do
7.19 John said was going to come, or should we expect **someone else?"**
Lk 7.20 was going to come, or if we should expect **someone else."**
8.20 **Someone** said to Jesus, "Your mother and brothers are
8.46 But Jesus said, **"Someone** touched me, for I knew it when
12.58 If **someone** brings a lawsuit against you and takes you to court,
13.23 **Someone** asked him, "Sir, will just a few people be saved?"
14. 8 "When **someone** invites you to a wedding feast, do not sit
14. 8 It could happen that **someone** more important than you has been invited,
16.12 faithful with what belongs to **someone else,** who will give
16.30 But if **someone** were to rise from death and go to them,
16.31 not be convinced even if **someone** were to rise from death.' "
19.31 If **someone** asks you why you are untying it, tell him
20.18 if that stone falls on **someone,** it will crush him to dust."
Jn 1.23 "I am 'the voice of **someone** shouting in the desert:
4.33 among themselves, "Could **somebody** have brought him food?"
5. 7 I am trying to get in, **somebody** else gets there first."
5.32 But there is **someone else** who testifies on my behalf,
5.43 **someone** comes with his own authority, you will receive him.
10. 5 They will not follow **someone else;**
16.30 you do not need **someone** to ask you questions.
21.18 stretch out your hands and **someone else** will bind you and
Acts 1.20 It is also written, 'May **someone else** take his place of service.'
1.21 "So then, **someone** must join us as a witness to
5.36 time ago, claiming to be **somebody** great, and about four
8. 9 He claimed that he was **someone** great, [10]and everyone in the city,
8.31 "How can I understand unless **someone** explains it to me?"
8.34 Of himself or of **someone else?"**
10.32 Send **someone** to Joppa for a man whose full name is Simon
11.13 who said to him, 'Send **someone** to Joppa for a man whose
13.11 walked about trying to find **someone** to lead him by the hand.
13.41 will not believe, even when **someone** explains it to you!' "
17.28 as **someone** has said, 'In him we live and move and exist.'
Rom 5. 7 a difficult thing for **someone** to die for a righteous person.
5. 7 It may even be that **someone** might dare to die for a
6.16 yourselves as slaves to obey **someone,** you are in fact the
7. 7 not desire what belongs to **someone else,"** I would not have
12.17 If **someone** has done you wrong, do not repay him with a
13. 9 not desire what belongs to **someone else"**—all these, and any
13.10 If you love **someone,** you will never do him wrong;
14. 4 Who are you to judge the servant of **someone else?**
14. 5 important than other days, while **someone else** thinks that
14.18 And when **someone** serves Christ in this way, he pleases
14.20 eat anything that will cause **someone else** to fall into sin.
15.20 so as not to build on a foundation laid by **someone else.**
1 Cor 6.12 **Someone** will say, "I am allowed to do anything."
6.13 **Someone else** will say, "Food is for the stomach, and
10.28 But if **someone** says to you, "This food was offered to idols,"
10.29 "Well, then," **someone** asks, "why should my freedom to
14. 5 strange tongues—unless there is **someone** present who can
14.27 If **someone** is going to speak in strange tongues, two or
14.27 one after the other, and **someone else** must explain what is
14.30 But if **someone** sitting in the meeting receives a message from God,
15. 8 me—even though I am like **someone** whose birth was abnormal.
15.35 **Someone** will ask, "How can the dead be raised to life?
2 Cor 2. 5 Now, if anyone has made **somebody** sad, he has not done it
2.10 When you forgive **someone** for what he has done, I forgive
10. 7 Is there **someone** there who reckons himself to belong to Christ?
10.10 **Someone** will say, "Paul's letters are severe and strong,
11.29 When **someone** is weak, then I feel weak too;
11.29 when **someone** is led into sin, I am filled with distress.
12.16 But **someone** will say that I was crafty, and trapped you with
Gal 2.18 down, then I show myself to be **someone** who breaks the Law.
6. 1 My brothers, if **someone** is caught in any kind of wrongdoing,
6. 3 If **someone** thinks he is somebody when really he is nobody,
6. 4 having to compare it with what **someone else** has done.
Col 3.13 whenever any of you has a complaint against **someone else.**
2 Thes 3.14 It may be that **someone** there will not obey the message
1 Tim 5.22 hurry to lay hands on **someone** to dedicate him to the Lord's
Heb 3. 4 of course, is built by **someone**—and God is the one who
5.12 teachers—yet you still need **someone** to teach you the first
6.16 he uses the name of **someone** greater than himself, and the
7.24 and his work as priest does not pass on to **someone else.**
Jas 2.14 what good is it for **someone** to say that he has faith
2.18 But **someone** will say, "One person has faith, another has actions."
1 Pet 5. 8 Devil, roams round like a roaring lion, looking for **someone** to devour.
1 Jn 2. 1 anyone does sin, we have **someone** who pleads with the Father
2. 4 If **someone** says that he knows him, but does not obey his
2.10 there is nothing in him that will cause **someone else** to sin.
4.20 If **someone** says he loves God, but hates his brother, he
2 Jn 10 So then, if **someone** comes to you who does not bring this
Rev 4. 2 There in heaven was a throne with **someone** sitting on it.

SOMETIMES

Rom 2.15 thoughts **sometimes** accuse them and sometimes defend them.
2 Cor 4. 8 **sometimes** in doubt, but never in despair;

SON

N.B. Genealogies have not been included.
see also **SON OF DAVID, SON OF GOD, SON OF MAN**

Gen 4. 1 She bore a **son** and said,
4. 1 "By the Lord's help I have acquired a **son."**
4. 2 Later she gave birth to another **son,** Abel.
4.17 Cain and his wife had a **son** and named him Enoch.
4.17 Then Cain built a city and named it after his **son.**
4.25 Adam and his wife had another **son.**
4.25 "God has given me a **son** to replace Abel, whom Cain killed."
4.26 Seth had a **son** whom he named Enosh.

Gen 5.32 was 500 years old, he had three **sons,** Shem, Ham, and
6. 9 He had three **sons,** Shem, Ham, and Japheth.
6.18 Go into the boat with your wife, your **sons,** and their wives.
7. 7 and his wife, and his **sons** and their wives, went into the
7.13 the boat with their three **sons,** Shem, Ham, and Japheth, and
8.16 out of the boat with your wife, your **sons,** and their wives.
8.18 out of the boat with his wife, his **sons,** and their wives.
9. 1 God blessed Noah and his **sons** and said, "Have many children,
9. 8 said to Noah and his **sons,** [9]"I am now making my covenant
9.18 The **sons** of Noah who went out of the boat were Shem,
9.19 These three **sons** of Noah were the ancestors of all the
9.24 and learnt what his youngest **son** had done to him, [25]he
10. 1 These three had **sons** after the flood.
10.32 nations of the earth were descended from the **sons** of Noah.
11.31 Terah took his **son** Abram, his grandson Lot,
15. 4 your own **son** will be your heir."
16.11 are going to have a **son,** and you will name him Ishmael,
16.12 But your **son** will live like a wild donkey;
16.15 Hagar bore Abram a **son,** and he named him Ishmael.
17.16 will bless her, and I will give you a **son** by her.
17.19 Sarah will bear you a **son** and you will name him Isaac.
17.21 keep my covenant with your **son** Isaac, who will be born to
17.23 obeyed God and circumcised his **son** Ishmael and all the other
17.25 he was circumcised, [25]and his **son** Ishmael was thirteen.
18.10 I will come back, and your wife Sarah will have a **son."**
18.14 months from now I will return, and Sarah will have a **son."**
18.19 that he may command his **sons** and his descendants to obey me
19.12 you have anyone else here—**sons,** daughters, sons-in-law, or
19.37 The elder daughter had a **son,** whom she named Moab.
19.38 The younger daughter also had a **son,** whom she named Benammi.
21. 2 became pregnant and bore a **son** to Abraham when he was old.
21. 7 Yet I have borne him a **son** in his old age."
21. 9 had borne to Abraham, was playing with Sarah's **son** Isaac.
21.10 said to Abraham, "Send this slave-girl and her **son** away.
21.10 The **son** of this woman must not get any part
21.10 of your wealth, which my **son** Isaac should inherit."
21.11 This troubled Abraham very much, because Ishmael was also his **son.**
21.13 give many children to the **son** of the slave-girl, so that
21.13 He too is your **son."**
22. 2 "Take your **son,"** God said, "your only son, Isaac, whom
22. 7 He answered, "Yes, my **son?"**
22. 9 He tied up his **son** and placed him on the altar, on
22.12 because you have not kept back your only **son** from me."
22.13 it and offered it as a burnt-offering instead of his **son.**
22.16 not keep back your only **son** from me, [17]I promise that I
24. 3 choose a wife for my **son** from the people here in Canaan.
24. 4 and get a wife for my **son** Isaac from among my relatives."
24. 5 Shall I send your **son** back to the land you came from?"
24. 6 "Make sure that you don't send my **son** back there!
24. 7 you, so that you can get a wife there for my **son.**
24. 8 But you must not under any circumstances take my **son** back there."
24.36 master's wife, bore him a **son** when she was old, and my
24.37 choose a wife for my **son** from the girls in the land
24.40 You will get for my **son** a wife from my own people,
24.44 one that you have chosen as the wife for my master's **son.'**
24.48 relative, where I found his daughter for my master's **son.**
24.51 wife of your master's **son,** as the Lord himself has said."
25. 6 he gave presents to the **sons** his other wives had borne him.
25. 6 Then he sent these **sons** to the land of the East,
25. 6 away from his **son** Isaac.
25. 9 His **sons** Isaac and Ishmael buried him in Machpelah Cave,
25.11 of Abraham, God blessed his **son** Isaac, who lived near "The
25.19 This is the story of Abraham's **son** Isaac.
25.24 time came for her to give birth, and she had twin **sons.**
25.31 to you if you give me your rights as the first-born **son."**
25.34 That was all Esau cared about his rights as the first-born **son.**
27. 1 sent for his elder son Esau and said to him, "My **son!"**
27. 8 Now, my **son,"** Rebecca continued, "listen to me and do
27.13 answered, "Let any curse against you fall on me, my **son;**
27.18 "Which of my **sons** are you?"
27.19 Jacob answered, "I am your elder **son** Esau;
27.20 Isaac said, "How did you find it so quickly, my **son?"**
27.26 his father said to him, "Come closer and kiss me, my **son."**
27.27 "The pleasant smell of my **son** is like the smell of a
27.32 "Your elder **son** Esau," he answered.
27.36 my rights as the first-born **son,** and now he has taken away
27.37 Now there is nothing that I can do for you, my **son!"**
27.43 Now, my **son,** do what I say.
27.45 Why should I lose both my **sons** on the same day?"
29.12 "I am your father's relative, the **son** of Rebecca."
29.32 Leah became pregnant and gave birth to a **son.**
29.33 She became pregnant again and gave birth to another **son.**
29.33 Lord has given me this **son** also, because he heard that I
29.34 Once again she became pregnant and gave birth to another **son.**
29.34 more tightly to me, because I have borne him three **sons";**
29.35 Then she became pregnant again and gave birth to another **son.**
30. 5 Bilhah became pregnant and bore Jacob a **son.**
30. 6 He has heard my prayer and has given me a **son";**
30. 7 Bilhah became pregnant again and bore Jacob a second **son.**
30.10 Then Zilpah bore Jacob a **son.**
30.12 Zilpah bore Jacob another **son,** [13]and Leah said,
30.14 said to Leah, "Please give me some of your **son's** mandrakes."
30.15 Now you are even trying to take away my **son's** mandrakes."
30.15 you will give me your **son's** mandrakes, you can sleep with
30.16 because I have paid for you with my **son's** mandrakes."
30.17 Leah's prayer, and she became pregnant and bore Jacob a fifth **son.**
30.18 so she named her **son** Issachar.
30.19 Leah became pregnant and bore Jacob a sixth **son.**

Gen 30.20 husband will accept me, because I have borne him six **sons";**
30.23 She became pregnant and gave birth to a **son.**
30.23 said, "God has taken away my disgrace by giving me a **son.**
30.24 May the Lord give me another **son";**
30.35 He put his **sons** in charge of them, [36]and then went away
31. 1 Jacob heard that Laban's **sons** were saying, "Jacob has
34. 5 been disgraced, but because his **sons** were out in the fields
34. 7 just as Jacob's **sons** were coming in from the fields.
34. 8 Hamor said to him, "My **son** Shechem has fallen in love
34.13 disgraced their sister Dinah, Jacob's **sons** answered Shechem
34.18 fair to Hamor and his **son** Shechem, [19]and the young man
34.20 Hamor and his **son** Shechem went to the meeting-place at
34.25 their circumcision, two of Jacob's **sons,** Simeon and Levi,
34.26 killed all the men, [26]including Hamor and his **son** Shechem.
34.27 After the slaughter Jacob's other **sons** looted the town
35. 5 When Jacob and his **sons** started to leave, great fear fell
35.18 her last, she named her **son** Benoni, but his father named him
35.22 Jacob had twelve **sons.**
35.23 The **sons** of Leah were Reuben (Jacob's eldest son),
35.23 Leah were Reuben (Jacob's eldest **son),** Simeon, Levi, Judah,
35.26 These **sons** were born in Mesopotamia.
35.29 and his **sons** Esau and Jacob buried him.
36. 5 All these **sons** were born to Esau in the land of Canaan.
36. 6 Esau took his wives, his **sons,** his daughters, and all the
37. 3 more than all his other **sons,** because he had been born to
37.32 Does it belong to your **son?"**
37.33 My **son** Joseph has been torn to pieces!"
37.34 He mourned for his **son** a long time.
37.35 All his **sons** and daughters came to comfort him, but he
37.35 down to the world of the dead still mourning for my **son."**
37.35 So he continued to mourn for his **son** Joseph.
38.11 house and remain a widow until my **son** Shelah grows up."
38.14 she well knew, Judah's youngest **son** Shelah had now grown up,
38.26 her—I should have given her to my **son** Shelah in marriage."
41.50 Before the years of famine came, Joseph had two **sons** by Asenath.
41.51 so he named his first **son** Manasseh.
41.52 so he named his second **son** Ephraim.
42. 1 in Egypt, he said to his **sons,** "Why don't you do something?
42. 5 The **sons** of Jacob came with others to buy corn, because
42.13 twelve brothers in all, sir, **sons** of the same man in the
42.32 We were twelve brothers in all, **sons** of the same father.
42.37 not bring Benjamin back to you, you can kill my two **sons.**
42.38 But Jacob said, "My **son** cannot go with you;
43. 2 Egypt, Jacob said to his **sons,** "Go back and buy a little
43.29 God bless you, my **son."**
44.27 us, 'You know that my wife Rachel bore me only two **sons.**
45. 9 father and tell him that this is what his **son** Joseph says:
45.21 Jacob's **sons** did as they were told.
45.28 "My **son** Joseph is still alive!"
46. 5 His **sons** put him, their small children, and their wives in
46. 7 his **sons,** his grandsons, his daughters, and his granddaughters.
46. 8 Egypt with him were his eldest **son** Reuben [9]and Reuben's sons:
46.12 (Judah's other **sons,** Er and Onan, had died in Canaan.)
46.23 Dan and his **son** Hushim.
46.26 went to Egypt was sixty-six, not including his **sons'** wives.
47.29 die, he called for his **son** Joseph and said to him, "Place
48. 1 So he took his two **sons,** Manasseh and Ephraim, and went to
48. 2 Jacob was told that his **son** Joseph had come to see him,
48. 5 Jacob continued, "Joseph, your two **sons,** who were born to
48. 5 and Manasseh are just as much my **sons** as Reuben and Simeon.
48. 6 If you have any more **sons,** they will not be considered mine;
48. 8 When Jacob saw Joseph's **sons,** he asked, "Who are these boys?"
48. 9 Joseph answered, "These are my **sons,** whom God has given
48.19 His father refused, saying, "I know, my **son,** I know.
49. 1 Jacob called for his **sons** and said, "Gather round, and I
49. 2 "Come together and listen, **sons** of Jacob.
49. 3 of my manhood, The proudest and strongest of all my **sons.**
49.28 said as he spoke a suitable word of farewell to each **son.**
49.29 Then Jacob commanded his **sons,** "Now that I am going to
49.33 instructions to his **sons,** he lay down again and died.
50.12 So Jacob's **sons** did as he had commanded them;
Ex 1. 1 The **sons** of Jacob who went to Egypt with him, each with
1. 5 His **son** Joseph was already in Egypt.
2. 2 a woman of his own tribe, [2]and she bore him a **son.**
2.10 him to the king's daughter, who adopted him as her own **son.**
2.22 his daughter Zipporah in marriage, [22]who bore him a **son.**
3.22 put these things on their **sons** and daughters and carry away
4.20 took his wife and his **sons,** put them on a donkey, and
4.22 him that I, the Lord, say, 'Israel is my first-born **son.**
4.23 told you to let my **son** go, so that he might worship
4.23 Now I am going to kill your first-born **son.' "**
4.25 off the foreskin of her **son,** and touched Moses' feet with
10. 9 We will take our **sons** and daughters, our sheep and goats,
11. 5 through Egypt, [5]and every first-born **son** in Egypt will die,
11. 5 from the king's **son,** who is heir to the throne,
11. 5 to the **son** of the slave-woman who grinds corn.
12.29 Lord killed all the first-born **sons** in Egypt,
12.29 from the king's **son,** who was heir to the throne,
12.29 to the **son** of the prisoner in the dungeon;
12.30 was not one home in which there was not a dead **son.**
13. 8 festival begins, explain to your **sons** that you do all this
13.14 In the future, when your **son** asks what this observance means,
13.15 male animal to the Lord, but buy back our first-born **sons.**
18. 3 so he had named one **son** Gershom.
18. 4 so he had named the other **son** Eliezer.
18. 5 Moses' wife and her two **sons** into the desert where Moses was
21. 4 wife and she bore him **sons** or daughters, the woman and her
21. 9 slave to give to his **son,** he is to treat her like
22.29 "Give me your first-born **sons.**
28. 9 the names of the twelve **sons** of Jacob, [10]in the order of
28.11 stones the names of the **sons** of Jacob, and mount the stones

Ex. 28.21 name of one of the **sons** of Jacob, to represent the tribes
29. 8 "Bring his **sons** and put shirts on them;
29.21 his **sons,** and their clothes will then be dedicated to me.
29.29 be handed on to his **sons** after his death, for them to
29.30 The **son** of Aaron who succeeds him as priest and who goes
32. 2 which your wives, your **sons,** and your daughters are wearing,
32.29 the Lord by killing your **sons** and brothers, so the Lord has
34.16 Your **sons** might marry those foreign women, who would
34.19 "Every first-born **son** and first-born male domestic animal
34.20 Buy back every first-born **son.**
39. 6 engraved with the names of the twelve **sons** of Jacob.
39.14 name of one of the **sons** of Jacob, in order to represent
40.14 Bring his **sons** and put the shirts on them.
Lev 9. 9 His **sons** brought him the blood, and he dipped his finger
9.12 His **sons** brought him the blood, and he threw it on all
9.18 His **sons** brought him the blood, and he threw it on all
10. 9 to Aaron, [9] "You and your **sons** are not to enter the Tent
10.13 belongs to you and your **sons** from the food offered to the
12. 2 woman gives birth to a **son,** she is ritually unclean, as she
12. 6 is completed, whether for a **son** or daughter, she shall bring
16. 1 the death of the two **sons** of Aaron who were killed when
21. 2 it is his mother, father, **son,** daughter, brother, [3] or
25.46 as an inheritance to your **sons,** whom they must serve as long
Num 3.12 as my own the eldest **son** of each Israelite family and the
3.12 instead of having the first-born **sons** of Israel as my own, I
3.40 "All of Israel's first-born **sons** belong to me.
3.45 of all the first-born Israelite **sons,** and dedicate the
3.46 the first-born Israelite **sons** outnumber the Levites by 273,
3.46 you must buy back the extra **sons.**
8.16 place of all the first-born **sons** of the Israelites, and they
8.17 as my own the eldest **son** of each Israelite family and the
18. 1 said to Aaron, "You, your **sons,** and the Levites must suffer
18. 1 but only you and your **sons** will suffer the consequences of
18. 2 help you while you and your **sons** are serving at the Tent.
18. 5 You and your **sons** alone must fulfil the responsibilities
18. 7 But you and your **sons** alone shall fulfil all the
18. 9 to me as a sacred offering belongs to you and your **sons.**
18.11 giving them to you, your **sons,** and your daughters for all
18.19 giving to you, to your **sons,** and to your daughters, for all
20.25 Take Aaron and his **son** Eleazar up Mount Hor, [26] and
21.35 the Israelites killed Og, his **sons,** and all his people,
26. 5 The tribe of Reuben (Reuben was the eldest **son** of Jacob):
26.28 who was the father of two **sons,** Manasseh and Ephraim.
26.33 Zelophehad son of Hepher had no **sons,** but only daughters;
27. 3 "Our father died in the wilderness without leaving any **sons.**
27. 4 Just because he had no **sons,** why should our father's name
27. 8 man dies without leaving a **son,** his daughter is to inherit
33. 4 who were burying the first-born **sons** that the Lord had killed.
Deut 1.31 way to this place, just as a father would carry his **son.'**
2.33 our power, and we killed him, his **sons,** and all his men.
13. 6 "Even your brother or your **son** or your daughter or the
21.15 and they both bear him **sons,** but the first son is not
21.16 to show partiality to the **son** of his favourite wife
21.16 by giving him the share that belongs to the first-born **son.**
21.17 his possessions to his first **son,**
21.17 even though he is not the **son** of his favourite wife.
21.17 man must acknowledge his first **son** and give him the share he
21.18 "Suppose a man has a **son** who is stubborn and rebellious,
21.18 a **son** who will not obey his parents,
21.20 to say to them, 'Our **son** is stubborn and rebellious and
25. 5 of them dies, leaving no **son,** then his widow is not to
25. 6 The first **son** that they have
25. 6 will be considered the **son** of the dead man, so that
28.32 Your **sons** and daughters will be given as slaves to
28.41 You will have **sons** and daughters, but you will lose them,
32.19 Lord saw this, he was angry and rejected his **sons** and daughters.
Josh 5. 7 The **sons** of these men had never been circumcised, and it
6.26 Whoever lays the foundation will lose his eldest **son;**
7.19 Joshua said to him, "My **son,** tell the truth here before
17. 3 son of Manasseh, did not have any **sons,** but only daughters.
24.33 of Ephraim which had been given to his **son** Phinehas.
Judg 6.11 His **son** Gideon was threshing some wheat secretly in a winepress,
6.30 said to Joash, "Bring your **son** out here, so that we can
8.18 like you—every one of them like the **son** of a king."
8.19 Gideon said, "They were my brothers, my own mother's **sons.**
8.20 he said to Jether, his eldest **son,** "Go ahead, kill them!"
8.23 Gideon answered, "I will not be your ruler, nor will my **son.**
8.30 He had seventy **sons,** because he had many wives.
8.31 she bore him a **son,** and he named him Abimelech.
9. 1 Gideon's **son** Abimelech went to the town of Shechem, where
9. 2 governed by all seventy of Gideon's **sons** or by just one man?
9. 5 single stone he killed his seventy brothers, Gideon's **sons.**
9. 5 But Jotham, Gideon's youngest **son,** hid and was not killed.
9.18 You killed his **sons**—seventy men on a single stone—and just
9.18 Abimelech, his **son** by his servant-girl, is your relative,
9.24 to murder Gideon's seventy **sons,** would pay for their crime.
9.28 The **son** of Gideon!
10. 4 He had thirty **sons** who rode thirty donkeys.
11. 1 a brave soldier from Gilead, was the **son** of a prostitute.
11. 2 His father Gilead [2] had other **sons** by his wife, and when
11. 2 you are the **son** of another woman."
12. 9 He had thirty **sons** and thirty daughters.
12. 9 thirty girls from outside the clan for his **sons** to marry.
12.14 He had forty **sons** and thirty grandsons,
13. 3 have children, but you will soon be pregnant and have a **son.**
13. 5 and after your **son** is born, you must never cut his hair,
13. 7 did tell me that I would become pregnant and have a **son.**
13.24 The woman gave birth to a **son** and named him Samson.
17. 2 His mother said, "May the Lord bless you, my **son!"**
17. 3 curse from falling on my **son,** I myself am solemnly
17. 5 and an ephod, and appointed one of his **sons** as his priest.
Judg 17.11 agreed to stay with Micah and became like a **son** to him.
Ruth 1. 1 wife Naomi and their two **sons** Mahlon and Chilion to live for
1. 3 left alone with her two **sons,** [4] who married Moabite girls,
1. 5 and Naomi was left all alone, without husband or **sons.**
1.11 Do you think I could have **sons** again for you to marry?
1.12 got married tonight and had **sons,** [13] would you wait until
4.13 The Lord blessed her, and she became pregnant and had a **son.**
4.15 loves you, and has done more for you than seven **sons.**
4.17 They told everyone, "A **son** has been born to Naomi!"
1 Sam 1. 8 Don't I mean more to you than ten **sons?"**
1.11 If you give me a **son,** I promise that I will dedicate
1.20 it was that she became pregnant and gave birth to a **son.**
2.12 The **sons** of Eli were scoundrels.
2.17 This sin of the **sons** of Eli was extremely serious in
2.21 bless Hannah, and she had three more **sons** and two daughters.
2.22 kept hearing about everything his **sons** were doing to the
2.24 Stop it, my **sons!**
2.29 Eli, do you honour your **sons** more than me by letting them
3. 6 But Eli answered, "My **son,** I didn't call you;
3.13 ever because his **sons** have spoken evil things against me.
4.16 Eli asked him, "What happened, my **son?"**
4.20 You have a **son!"**
7. 1 They consecrated his **son** Eleazar to be in charge of it.
8. 1 When Samuel grew old, he made his **sons** judges in Israel.
8. 2 The elder **son** was named Joel and the younger one Abijah;
8. 5 you are getting old and your **sons** don't follow your example.
8.11 "He will make soldiers of your **sons;**
8.12 Your **sons** will have to plough his fields, harvest his crops,
9. 2 He had a **son** named Saul, a handsome man in the prime
10. 2 you, and he keeps asking, 'What shall I do about my **son?'**
10.11 asked one another, "What has happened to the **son** of Kish?
12. 2 me, I am old and grey, and my **sons** are with you.
13. 2 sending one thousand with his **son** Jonathan to Gibeah, in the
13.16 Saul, his **son** Jonathan, and their men camped in Geba in
13.22 Israelite soldiers except Saul and his **son** Jonathan had swords
14.39 will be put to death, even if he is my **son** Jonathan."
14.42 Then Saul said, "Decide between my **son** Jonathan and me."
16. 1 Jesse, because I have chosen one of his **sons** to be king."
16. 5 also told Jesse and his **sons** to purify themselves, and he
16. 8 Then Jesse called his **son** Abinadab and brought him to Samuel.
16.10 In this way Jesse brought seven of his **sons** to Samuel.
16.11 Then he asked him, "Have you any more **sons?"**
16.18 the town of Bethlehem, has a **son** who is a good musician.
16.19 to say, "Send me your **son** David, the one who takes care
17.12 David was the **son** of Jesse, who was an Ephrathite from
17.12 Jesse had eight **sons,** and at the time Saul was king, he
17.13 His three eldest **sons** had gone with Saul to war.
17.14 David was the youngest **son,** and while the three eldest
17.55 the commander of his army, "Abner, whose **son** is he?"
17.58 Saul asked him, "Young man, whose **son** are you?"
17.58 "I am the **son** of your servant Jesse from Bethlehem,"
18. 1 After that, Saul's **son** Jonathan was deeply attracted to
19. 1 Saul told his **son** Jonathan and all his officials that he
22. 8 told me that my own **son** had made an alliance with David.
22. 8 a chance to kill me, and that my **son** has encouraged him!"
24.16 speaking, Saul said, "Is that really you, David my **son?"**
26.17 recognized David's voice and asked, "David, is that you, my **son?"**
26.21 Come back, David, my **son!**
26.25 Saul said to David, "God bless you, my **son!**
28.19 Tomorrow you and your **sons** will join me, and the Lord will
30. 3 that their wives, **sons,** and daughters had been carried away.
30.19 got back all his men's **sons** and daughters, and all the loot
31. 1 and the rest of them, including King Saul and his **sons,**
31. 6 that is how Saul, his three **sons,** and the young man died;
2 Sam 1. 4 Saul and his **son** Jonathan were also killed."
1.17 lament for Saul and his **son** Jonathan, [18] and ordered it to
2. 8 with Saul's **son** Ishbosheth across the Jordan to Mahanaim.
3. 2 The following six **sons,** in the order of their birth, were
3. 5 All of these **sons** were born in Hebron.
5.13 more concubines and wives, and had more **sons** and daughters.
7.12 will make one of your **sons** king and will keep his kingdom
7.14 I will be his father, and he will be my **son.**
7.14 does wrong, I will punish him as a father punishes his **son.**
8.10 So he sent his **son** Joram to greet King David and
9.10 You, your **sons,** and your servants will farm the land for
9.11 ate at the king's table, just like one of the king's **sons.**
9.12 Mephibosheth had a young **son** named Mica.
10. 1 King Nahash of Ammon died, and his **son** Hanun became king.
11.27 she became his wife and bore him a **son.**
12.24 with her, and she bore a **son,** whom David named Solomon.
13. 1 David's **son** Absalom had a beautiful unmarried sister
13. 4 Amnon, "You are the king's **son,** yet day after day I see
13.23 of Ephraim, and he invited all the king's **sons** to be there.
13.25 "No, my **son,"** the king answered.
13.30 "Absalom has killed all your **sons**—not one of them is left!"
13.32 said, "Your Majesty, they haven't killed all your **sons.**
13.33 So don't believe the news that all your **sons** are dead;
13.35 to David, "Those are your **sons** coming, just as I said they
13.37 David mourned a long time for his **son** Amnon;
13.39 Amnon's death, he was filled with longing for his **son** Absalom.
14. 6 Sir, I had two **sons,** and one day they got into a
14. 7 demanding that I hand my **son** over to them, so that they
14. 7 If they do this, I will be left without a **son.**
14. 7 leave my husband without a **son** to keep his name alive."
14.11 avenging the death of my **son**
14.11 will not commit a greater crime by killing my other **son."**
14.11 Lord," David replied, "that your **son** will not be harmed in
14.13 have not allowed your own **son** to return from exile, and so
14.16 is trying to kill my **son** and me and so remove us
15.27 to Zadok, "Look, take your **son** Ahimaaz and Abiathar's son
16. 8 given the kingdom to your **son** Absalom, and you are ruined,

2 Sam	16.11	to all his officials, "My own **son** is trying to kill me;
	16.19	After all, whom should I serve, if not my master's **son?**
	18.12	of silver, I wouldn't lift a finger against the king's **son.**
	18.18	King's Valley, because he had no **son** to keep his name alive.
	18.20	may do so, but not today, for the king's **son** is dead."
	18.22	"Why do you want to do it, my **son?"**
	18.33	As he went, he cried, "O my **son!**
	18.33	My **son** Absalom!
	18.33	Absalom, my **son!**
	18.33	If only I had died in your place, my **son!**
	18.33	Absalom, my **son!"**
	19. 2	because they heard that the king was mourning for his **son.**
	19. 4	The king covered his face and cried loudly, "O my **son!**
	19. 4	My **son** Absalom!
	19. 4	Absalom, my **son!"**
	19. 5	and the lives of your **sons** and daughters and of your wives
	19.17	also came with his fifteen **sons** and twenty servants, and
	19.37	Here is my **son** Chimham, who will serve you;
	21. 7	David spared Jonathan's **son** Mephibosheth, the grandson of Saul.
	21. 8	he also took the five **sons** of Saul's daughter Merab, whom
	21.12	of Saul and of his **son** Jonathan from the people of Jabesh
	23. 1	David **son** of Jesse was the man whom God made great, whom
	23.24	Bahurim Eliahba from Shaalbon The **sons** of Jashen Jonathan
1 Kgs	1. 5	the son of David and Haggith, was the eldest surviving **son.**
	1. 9	He invited the other **sons** of King David and the king's
	1.12	and the life of your **son** Solomon, I would advise you [13] to
	1.13	promise me that my **son** Solomon would succeed you as king?
	1.17	Lord your God that my **son** Solomon would be king after you.
	1.19	calves, and he invited your **sons,** and Abiathar the priest,
	1.19	army to the feast, but he did not invite your **son** Solomon.
	1.21	as you are dead my **son** Solomon and I will be treated
	1.25	He invited all your **sons,** Joab the commander of your army,
	1.30	God of Israel, that your **son** Solomon would succeed me as king."
	1.33	let my **son** Solomon ride my own mule, and escort him down
	2. 1	to die, he called his **son** Solomon and gave him his last
	2. 7	"But show kindness to the **sons** of Barzillai from Gilead
	3. 6	love by giving him a **son** who today rules in his place.
	3.20	during the night, took my **son** from my side while I was
	3.26	full of love for her **son,** said to the king, "Please, Your
	4. 3	Elihoreph and Ahijah, **sons** of Shisha
	4.31	Heman, Calcol, and Darda, the **sons** of Mahol, and his fame
	5. 5	promised my father David, 'Your **son,** whom I will make king
	5. 7	giving David such a wise **son** to succeed him as king of
	8.19	It is your **son,** your own son, who will build my temple.'
	11.12	do this in your lifetime, but during the reign of your **son.**
	11.20	queen in the palace, where he lived with the king's **sons.**
	11.35	away from Solomon's **son** and will give you ten tribes,
	11.36	but I will let Solomon's **son** keep one tribe, so that I
	13.11	His **sons** came and told him what the prophet from Judah had
	13.27	Then he said to his **sons,** "Saddle my donkey for me."
	13.30	grave, and he and his **sons** mourned over it, saying, "Oh my
	13.31	the prophet said to his **sons,** "When I die, bury me in
	14. 1	At that time King Jeroboam's **son** Abijah fell ill.
	14. 3	is going to happen to our **son,** and he will tell you."
	14. 5	wife was coming to ask him about her **son,** who was ill.
	14.12	As soon as you enter the town your **son** will die.
	15. 4	his God gave Abijah a **son** to rule after him in Jerusalem
	16.13	into sin, Baasha and his **son** Elah had aroused the anger of
	16.34	Nun, Hiel lost his eldest **son** Abiram when he laid the
	16.34	and his youngest **son** Segub when he built the gates.
	17.12	home and prepare what little I have for my **son** and me.
	17.13	to me, and then prepare the rest for you and your **son.**
	17.17	Some time later the widow's **son** fell ill;
	17.18	to remind God of my sins and so cause my **son's** death?"
	17.20	enough to take care of me, and now you kill her **son!"**
	17.23	to his mother and said to her, "Look, your **son** is alive!"
	18.31	twelve tribes named after the **sons** of Jacob, the man to whom
	21.29	it will be during his **son's** lifetime that I will bring
2 Kgs	1.17	Ahaziah had no **sons,** so his brother Joram succeeded him as
	3.27	So he took his eldest **son,** who was to succeed him as
	4. 1	to take away my two **sons** as slaves in payment for my
	4. 4	"Then you and your **sons** go into the house, close the door,
	4. 5	into her house with her **sons,** closed the door, took the
	4. 5	poured oil into the jars as her **sons** brought them to her.
	4. 6	"That was the last one," one of her **sons** answered.
	4. 7	enough money left over for you and your **sons** to live on."
	4.14	answered, "Well, she has no **son,** and her husband is an old
	4.16	time next year you will be holding a **son** in your arms."
	4.17	about that time the following year she gave birth to a **son.**
	4.26	is all right with her, her husband, and her **son."**
	4.28	woman said to him, "Sir, did I ask you for a **son?**
	4.36	When she came in, he said to her, "Here's your **son."**
	4.37	then she took her **son** and left.
	6.29	So we cooked my **son** and ate him.
	6.29	her that we would eat her **son,** but she had hidden him!"
	8. 1	who lived in Shunem, whose **son** he had brought back to life,
	8. 5	and here is her **son** whom Elisha brought back to life!"
	11. 1	mother Athaliah learnt of her **son's** murder, she gave orders
	13. 3	Hazael of Syria and his **son** Benhadad to defeat Israel time
	14. 9	'Give your daughter in marriage to my **son.'**
	14.21	Judah then crowned his sixteen-year-old **son** Uzziah as king.
	15. 5	of all duties, while his **son** Jotham governed the country.
	16. 3	He even sacrificed his own **son** as a burnt-offering to idols,
	17.17	They sacrificed their **sons** and daughters as burnt-offerings
	21. 6	He sacrificed his **son** as a burnt-offering.
	21. 7	about which the Lord had said to David and his **son** Solomon:
	23.10	no one could sacrifice his **son** or daughter as a
	24.12	mother, his **sons,** his officers, and the palace officials,
1 Chr	1.10	(Cush had a **son** named Nimrod, who became the world's
	1.29	the name of Ishmael's eldest **son),** Kedar, Adbeel, Mibsam,
	2. 3	His eldest **son,** Er, was so evil that the Lord killed him.
1 Chr	3.10	the line of King Solomon's descendants from father to **son:**
	5. 1	rights belonging to the first-born **son,** and those rights
	7.23	with his wife again, and she became pregnant and had a **son.**
	7.25	Ephraim also had a **son** named Rephah, whose descendants
	14. 3	David married more wives and had more **sons** and daughters.
	17.11	will make one of your **sons** king and will keep his kingdom
	17.13	I will be his father and he will be my **son.**
	18.10	So he sent his **son** Joram to greet King David and
	18.17	and King David's **sons** held high positions in his service.
	21.20	threshing-place Araunah and his four **sons** were threshing wheat,
	21.20	and when they saw the angel, the **sons** ran and hid.
	22. 5	thought, "The Temple that my **son** Solomon is to build must
	22. 6	He sent for his **son** Solomon and commanded him to build a
	22. 7	David said to him, "My **son,** I wanted to build a temple
	22. 9	said, 'You will have a **son** who will rule in peace, because
	22.10	He will be my **son,** and I will be his father.
	22.11	David continued, "Now, my **son,** may the Lord your God
	23. 1	David was very old, he made his **son** Solomon king of Israel.
	25. 5	prophet, these fourteen **sons** and also three daughters,
	25. 6	All his **sons** played cymbals and harps under their father's
	26.10	even though he was not the eldest **son),**
	27.32	Hachmoni were in charge of the education of the king's **sons.**
	28. 1	to the king and his **sons**—indeed all the palace officials,
	28. 5	He gave me many **sons,** and out of them all he chose
	28. 6	Lord said to me, 'Your **son** Solomon is the one who will
	28. 6	chosen him to be my **son,** and I will be his father.
	28. 9	to Solomon he said, "My **son,** I charge you to acknowledge
	28.20	David said to his **son** Solomon, "Be confident and determined.
	29. 1	"My **son** Solomon is the one whom God has chosen, but he
	29.19	Give my **son** Solomon a wholehearted desire to obey
	29.24	even all of David's other **sons** promised to be loyal to
	29.28	and respected, and his **son** Solomon succeeded him as king.
2 Chr	2.12	King David a wise **son,** full of understanding and skill,
	6. 9	It is your **son,** your own son, who will build my temple.'
	11.22	and he favoured her **son** Abijah over all his other children,
	11.23	wisely assigned responsibilities to his **sons,**
	21.17	the king's wives and sons except Ahaziah, his youngest **son.**
	22.10	mother Athaliah learnt of her **son's** murder, she gave orders
	23. 3	and there they made a covenant with Joash, the king's **son.**
	23. 3	Jehoiada said to them, "Here is the **son** of the late king!
	25.18	'Give your daughter in marriage to my **son.'**
	26.21	of all duties, while his **son** Jotham governed the country.
	28. 3	even sacrificed his own **sons** as burnt-offerings to idols,
	29.11	My **sons,** do not lose any time.
	32.21	some of his **sons** killed him with their swords.
	33. 6	sacrificed his **sons** in the Valley of Hinnom as burnt-offerings.
	33. 7	place about which God had said to David and his **son** Solomon:
	33.25	Judah killed Amon's assassins and made his **son** Josiah king.
	35. 4	by King David and his **son** King Solomon, [5] and arrange
Ezra	6.10	of Heaven and pray for his blessing on me and my **sons.**
Neh	10.36	The first **son** born to each of us we will take to
	12.45	with the regulations made by King David and his **son** Solomon.
Esth	5.11	rich he was, how many **sons** he had, how the king had
	9.25	for the Jews—he and his **sons** were hanged from the gallows.
Job	1.18	the home of your eldest **son,** [19] when a storm swept in from
	5. 4	Their **sons** can never find safety;
	14.21	His **sons** win honour, but he never knows it, nor is he
	20.10	and his **sons** will make good what he stole from the poor.
	27.14	They may have many **sons,** but all will be killed in war;
Ps	2. 7	'You are my **son;**
	45.16	will have many **sons** to succeed your ancestors as kings,
	78.51	He killed the first-born **sons** of all the families of Egypt.
	82. 6	'all of you are **sons** of the Most High.'
	89.27	I will make him my first-born **son,** the greatest of all kings.
	105.36	He killed the first-born **sons** of all the families of Egypt.
	106.37	They offered their own **sons** and daughters as sacrifices
	127. 4	The **sons** a man has when he is young are like arrows
	128. 3	and your **sons** will be like young olive-trees
	132.11	will make one of your **sons** king, and he will rule after
	132.12	If your **sons** are true to my covenant and to the commands
	132.12	their **sons,** also, will succeed you
	136.10	He killed the first-born **sons** of the Egyptians;
	144.12	May our **sons** in their youth be like plants that grow up
Prov	1. 8	Pay attention to what your father and mother tell you, my **son.**
	1.10	When sinners tempt you, my **son,** don't give in.
	1.15	Don't go with people like that, my **son.**
	2. 1	what I teach you, my **son,** and never forget what I tell
	3. 1	Don't forget what I teach you, my **son.**
	3.11	the Lord corrects you, my **son,** pay close attention and take
	3.12	loves, as a father corrects a **son** of whom he is proud.
	3.21	Hold on to your wisdom and insight, my **son.**
	4. 1	Listen to what your father teaches you, my **sons.**
	4. 3	boy, my parents' only **son,** [4] my father would teach me.
	4.10	Listen to me, my **son.**
	4.20	Pay attention to what I say, my **son.**
	5. 1	Pay attention, my **son,** and listen to my wisdom and insight.
	5. 7	Now listen to me, my **sons,** and never forget what I am
	5.20	Why should you give your love to another woman, my **son?**
	6. 1	promised to be responsible for someone else's debts, my **son?**
	6. 3	Well then, my **son,** you are in that man's power, but this
	6.20	your father tells you, my **son,** and never forget what your
	7. 1	Remember what I say, my **son,** and never forget what I tell
	7.24	Now then, my **sons,** listen to me.
	10. 1	A wise **son** makes his father proud of him;
	13. 1	A wise **son** pays attention when his father corrects him,
	13.24	If you don't punish your **son,** you don't love him.
	15.20	A wise **son** makes his father happy.
	17. 2	authority over a master's worthless **son** and receive a part
	17.21	and sorrow for a father whose **son** does foolish things.
	17.25	A foolish **son** brings grief to his father and bitter
	19.13	A stupid **son** can bring his father to ruin.

Prov 19.27 **Son,** when you stop learning, you will soon neglect what
23.15 **Son,** if you become wise, I will be very happy.
23.19 Listen, my **son,** be wise and give serious thought to the
23.24 You can take pride in a wise **son.**
23.26 Pay close attention, **son,** and let my life be your example.
24.13 **Son,** eat honey;
24.21 Have reverence for the Lord, my **son,** and honour the king.
27.11 Be wise, my **son,** and I will be happy;
29.17 Discipline your **son** and you can always be proud of him.
30. 4 Who is his **son?**
31. 2 "You are my own dear **son,** the answer to my prayers.
Ecc 1. 1 of the Philosopher, David's **son,** who was king in Jerusalem.
4. 8 He has no **son,** no brother, yet he is always working, never
12.12 My **son,** there is something else to watch out for.
Is 7. 3 said to Isaiah, "Take your **son** Shear Jashub, and go to meet
7. 6 their side, and then put Tabeel's **son** on the throne.
7.14 is pregnant will have a **son** and will name him 'Immanuel.'
8. 3 When our **son** was born, the Lord said to me, "Name him
9. 6 A **son** is given to us!
14.21 The **sons** of this king will die because of their ancestors'
23. 4 I never brought up **sons** or daughters."
56. 5 among my people longer than if you had **sons** and daughters.
60. 4 Your **sons** will come from far away;
60.14 The **sons** of those who oppressed you will come And bow
Jer 3.19 to accept you as my **son** and give you a delightful land,
3.24 us lose flocks and herds, **sons** and daughters—everything that
5.17 they will kill your **sons** and your daughters.
6.21 Fathers and **sons** will die, and so will friends and neighbours."
6.26 you would for an only **son,** because the one who comes to
7.31 they can sacrifice their **sons** and daughters in the fire.
14.16 them—including their wives, their **sons,** and their daughters.
20.15 You have a **son!"**
22.10 But weep bitterly for Joahaz, his **son;**
27. 7 and they will serve his **son** and his grandson until the time
31. 9 am like a father to Israel, and Ephraim is my eldest **son."**
31.20 "Israel, you are my dearest **son,** the child I love best.
32. 7 that Hanamel, my uncle Shallum's **son,** would come to me
32.35 to sacrifice their **sons** and daughters to the god Molech.
35. 3 all his brothers and **sons**—[4]and brought them to the Temple.
35. 8 wine, and neither do our wives, our **sons,** or our daughters.
48.46 have been destroyed, and their **sons** and daughters have been
Ezek 16.20 "Then you took the **sons** and the daughters you had borne
18.10 suppose this man has a **son** who robs and kills, who does
18.14 "Now suppose this second man has a **son.**
18.19 'Why shouldn't the **son** suffer because of his father's sins?'
18.19 The answer is that the **son** did what was right and good.
18.20 A **son** is not to suffer because of his father's sins,
18.20 nor a father because of the sins of his **son.**
20.26 offerings, and I let them sacrifice their first-born **sons.**
23.10 stripped her naked, seized her **sons** and daughters, and then
23.25 Yes, they will take your **sons** and daughters from you and
23.37 with idols and murder of the **sons** they bore me.
23.37 They sacrificed my **sons** to their idols.
24.25 And I will take away their **sons** and daughters.
46.16 owns to one of his **sons** as a present, it will belong
46.16 it will belong to that **son** as a part of his family
46.17 to him, and only he and his **sons** can own it permanently.
46.18 land he gives to his **sons** must be from the land that
Dan 5.22 "But you, his **son,** have not humbled yourself, even
11.10 "The **sons** of the king of Syria will prepare for war
Hos 1. 3 of their first child, a **son,** [4]the Lord said to Hosea,
1. 8 her daughter, she became pregnant again and had another **son.**
4. 6 I reject you and will not acknowledge your **sons** as my priests.
11. 1 I loved him and called him out of Egypt as my **son.**
Joel 2.28 your **sons** and daughters will proclaim my message;
3. 8 I will let your **sons** and daughters be sold to the people
Amos 2.11 I chose some of your **sons** to be prophets, and some of
8.10 and you will be like parents mourning for their only **son.**
Mic 5. 3 enemies until the woman who is to give birth has her **son.**
7. 6 In these times **sons** treat their fathers like fools,
Zeph 1. 8 the king's **sons,** and all who practise foreign customs.
Zech 12.10 mourn bitterly, like those who have lost their first-born **son.**
Mal 1. 6 says to the priests, "A **son** honours his father, and a
3.17 them, as a father is merciful to the **son** who serves him.
Mt 1.21 She will have a **son,** and you will name him Jesus—because
1.23 pregnant and have a **son,** and he will be called Immanuel"
1.25 sexual relations with her before she gave birth to her **son.**
4.21 saw two other brothers, James and John, the **sons of Zebedee.**
5.45 so that you may become the **sons** of your Father in heaven.
7. 9 who are fathers give your **son** a stone when he asks for
9. 2 they had, he said to the paralysed man, "Courage, my **son!**
10. 2 James and his brother John, the **sons of Zebedee;**
10. 3 James **son** of Alphaeus, and Thaddaeus;
10.35 I came to set **sons** against their fathers, daughters against their mothers,
10.37 whoever loves his **son** or daughter more than me is not fit
13.55 Isn't he the carpenter's **son?**
16.17 "Good for you, Simon **son** of John!"
17.15 Jesus, knelt before him, [15]and said, "Sir, have mercy on my **son!**
20.20 to Jesus with her two **sons,** bowed before him, and asked him
20.21 "Promise me that these two **sons** of mine will sit at your
20.22 "You don't know what you are asking for," Jesus answered the **sons.**
21.28 There was once a man who had two **sons.**
21.28 the elder one and said, **'Son,** go and work in the vineyard
21.30 the father went to the other **son** and said the same thing.
21.37 Last of all he sent his **son** to them.
21.37 'Surely they will respect my **son,'** he said.
21.38 when the tenants saw the **son,**
21.38 they said to themselves, 'This is the owner's **son.**
22. 2 there was a king who prepared a wedding feast for his **son.**
Mt 23.33 You snakes and **sons** of snakes!
23.35 to the murder of Zachariah **son** of Berachiah, whom you
26.37 He took with him Peter and the two **sons of Zebedee.**
Mk 1.19 saw two other brothers, James and John, the **sons of Zebedee.**
2. 5 Jesus said to the paralysed man, "My **son,** your sins are forgiven."
2.14 tax collector, Levi **son** of Alphaeus, sitting in his office.
3.17 his brother John, the **sons of Zebedee** (Jesus gave them the
3.18 Philip, Bartholomew, Matthew, Thomas, James **son** of Alphaeus, Thaddaeus, Simon the Patriot,
6. 3 Isn't he the carpenter, the **son** of Mary, and the brother
9.17 answered, "Teacher, I brought my **son** to you, because he has
10.35 Then James and John, the **sons of Zebedee,** came to Jesus.
10.46 a blind beggar named Bartimaeus **son** of Timaeus was sitting
12. 6 The only one left to send was the man's own dear **son.**
12. 6 Last of all, then, he sent his **son** to the tenants.
12. 6 'I am sure they will respect my **son,'** he said.
12. 7 But those tenants said to one another, 'This is the owner's **son.**
12. 8 So they seized the **son** and killed him and threw his body
Lk 1.13 your prayer, and your wife Elizabeth will bear you a **son.**
1.31 and give birth to a **son,** and you will name him Jesus.
1.57 Elizabeth to have her baby, and she gave birth to a **son.**
2. 7 gave birth to her first **son,** wrapped him in strips of cloth
2.48 mother said to him, "My **son,** why have you done this to
3. 2 word of God came to John **son** of Zechariah in the desert.
3.23 He was the **son,** so people thought, of Joseph, who was the
3.38 the son of Seth, the son of Adam, the **son** of God.
4.22 They said, "Isn't he the **son** of Joseph?"
5.10 of Simon's partners, James and John, the **sons of Zebedee.**
6.15 Bartholomew, [15]Matthew and Thomas, James **son** of Alphaeus,
6.16 the Patriot), [16]Judas **son** of James, and Judas Iscariot,
6.35 great reward, and you will be **sons** of the Most High God.
7.12 dead man was the only **son** of a woman who was a
9.38 I beg you, look at my **son**—my only son!
9.41 Then he said to the man, "Bring your **son** here."
11.11 who are fathers give your **son** a snake when he asks for
12.53 Fathers will be against their **sons,**
12.53 and **sons** against their fathers;
14. 5 one of you had a **son** or an ox that happened to
15.11 on to say, "There was once a man who had two **sons.**
15.12 So the man divided his property between his two **sons.**
15.13 a few days the younger **son** sold his part of the property
15.19 I am no longer fit to be called your **son;**
15.20 and he ran, threw his arms round his **son,** and kissed him.
15.21 'Father,' the **son** said, 'I have sinned against God and against you.
15.21 I am no longer fit to be called your **son.'**
15.24 For this **son** of mine was dead, but now he is alive;
15.25 "In the meantime the elder **son** was out in the field.
15.30 But this **son** of yours wasted all your property on prostitutes,
15.31 **'My son,'** the father answered, 'you are always here with me,
16.25 "But Abraham said, 'Remember, my **son,** that in your
20.13 I will send my own dear **son;**
20.14 saw him, they said to one another, 'This is the owner's **son.**
20.36 They are the **sons of God,** because they have risen from death.
Jn 1.42 said, "Your name is Simon **son** of John, but you will be
1.45 He is Jesus **son** of Joseph, from Nazareth."
4. 5 far from the field that Jacob had given to his **son** Joseph.
4.12 he and his **sons** and his flocks all drank from it.
4.46 A government official was there whose **son** was ill in Capernaum.
4.47 go to Capernaum and heal his **son,** who was about to die.
4.50 Jesus said to him, "Go, your **son** will live!"
4.52 time it was when his **son** got better, and they answered, "It
4.53 very hour when Jesus had told him, "Your **son** will live."
6.42 So they said, "This man is Jesus **son** of Joseph, isn't
6.71 He was talking about Judas, the **son** of Simon Iscariot.
7.22 ordered you to circumcise your **sons** (although it was not
8.35 to a family permanently, but a **son** belongs there for ever.
8.41 Father we have," they answered, "and we are his true **sons."**
9.19 called his parents [19]and asked them, "Is this your **son?**
9.20 know that he is our **son,** and we know that he was
13. 2 the heart of Judas, the **son** of Simon Iscariot, the thought
13.26 dipped it, and gave it to Judas, the **son** of Simon Iscariot.
19.26 so he said to his mother, "He is your **son."**
21. 2 Cana in Galilee), the **sons of Zebedee,** and two other
21.15 said to Simon Peter, "Simon **son** of John, do you love me
21.16 Jesus said to him, "Simon **son** of John, do you love me?"
21.17 time Jesus said, "Simon **son** of John, do you love me?"
Acts 1.13 Thomas, Bartholomew and Matthew, James **son** of Alphaeus,
1.13 Simon the Patriot, and Judas **son** of James.
2.17 Your **sons** and daughters will proclaim my message;
7. 8 Isaac circumcised his **son** Jacob,
7. 8 Jacob circumcised his twelve **sons,** the famous ancestors of our race.
7. 9 "Jacob's **sons** became jealous of their brother Joseph and
7.12 in Egypt, he sent his **sons,** our ancestors, on their first
7.15 Then Jacob went to Egypt, where he and his **sons** died.
7.21 daughter adopted him and brought him up as her own **son.**
7.29 There he had two **sons.**
13.10 at the magician [10]and said, "You **son** of the Devil!
13.21 king, God gave them Saul **son** of Kish from the tribe of
13.22 'I have found that David **son** of Jesse is the kind of
19.14 Seven brothers, who were the **sons** of a Jewish High Priest
20. 4 Sopater **son** of Pyrrhus, from Berea, went with him;
23. 6 I am a Pharisee, the **son** of Pharisees.
23.16 But the **son** of Paul's sister heard about the plot;
Rom 8.14 Those who are led by God's Spirit are God's **sons.**
8.19 waits with eager longing for God to reveal his **sons.**
8.23 God to make us his **sons** and set our whole being free.
9. 4 he made them his **sons** and revealed his glory to them;
9. 9 right time I will come back, and Sarah will have a **son."**
9.10 For Rebecca's two **sons** had the same father, our ancestor Isaac.
9.11 that the choice of one **son** might be completely the result of

Rom	9.26	there they will be called the **sons** of the living God.”
	16.13	and to his mother, who has always treated me like a **son.**
1 Cor	4.17	who is my own dear and faithful **son** in the Christian life.
2 Cor	6.18	shall be my **sons** and daughters, says the Lord Almighty.”
Gal	3.26	that all of you are God’s **sons** in union with Christ Jesus.
	4. 1	But now to continue—the **son** who will receive his father’s
	4. 4	He came as the **son** of a human mother and lived under
	4. 5	who were under the Law, so that we might become God’s **sons.**
	4. 6	show that you are his **sons,** God sent the Spirit of his
	4. 7	So then, you are no longer a slave but a **son.**
	4. 7	And since you are his **son,**
	4. 7	God will give you all that he has for his **sons.**
	4.22	says that Abraham had two **sons,** one by a slave-woman, the
	4.23	His **son** by the slave-woman was born in the usual way,
	4.23	but his **son** by the free woman was born
	4.29	At that time the **son** who was born in the usual way
	4.30	It says, “Send the slave-woman and her **son** away;
	4.30	for the **son** of the slave-woman will not have a part of
	4.30	father’s property along with the **son** of the free woman.”
Eph	1. 5	he would make us his **sons**—this was his pleasure and purpose.
Phil	2.22	he and I, like a **son** and his father, have worked together
1 Tim	1. 2	Jesus our hope— [2] To Timothy, my true **son** in the faith:
2 Tim	1. 2	have in union with Christ Jesus— [2] To Timothy, my dear **son:**
	2. 1	As for you, my **son,** be strong through the grace that is
Tit	1. 4	write to Titus, my true **son** in the faith that we have
Phlm	10	you on behalf of Onesimus, who is my own **son** in Christ;
Heb	2.10	suffering, in order to bring many **sons** to share his glory.
	11.17	that made Abraham offer his **son** Isaac as a sacrifice when
	11.17	yet he was ready to offer his only **son** as a sacrifice.
	11.21	Jacob bless each of the **sons** of Joseph just before he died.
	11.24	up, refuse to be called the **son** of the king’s daughter.
	11.28	Angel of Death would not kill the first-born **sons** of the Israelites.
	12. 5	the encouraging words which God speaks to you as his **sons?**
	12. 5	“My **son,** pay attention when the Lord corrects you, and do
	12. 6	he loves, and punishes everyone he accepts as a **son.”**
	12. 7	your suffering shows that God is treating you as his **sons.**
	12. 7	Was there ever a **son** who was not punished by his father?
	12. 8	not punished, as all his **sons** are,
	12. 8	it means you are not real **sons,** but bastards.
	12.16	who for a single meal sold his rights as the elder **son.**
	12.23	of God’s first-born **sons,** whose names are written in heaven.
Jas	2.21	his actions, when he offered his **son** Isaac on the altar.
1 Pet	5.13	chosen by God, sends you greetings, and so does my **son** Mark.
2 Pet	2.15	the path taken by Balaam **son** of Beor, who loved the money
Rev	12. 5	she gave birth to a **son,** who will rule over all nations
	21. 7	I will be his God, and he will be my **son.**

SON OF DAVID
[DAVID’S SON]

Mt	9.27	“Take pity on us, **Son of David!”**
	12.23	“Could he be the **Son of David?”**
	15.22	**“Son of David!”**
	20.30	Jesus was passing by, so they began to shout, **“Son of David!**
	20.31	But they shouted even more loudly, **“Son of David!**
	21. 9	those walking behind began to shout, “Praise to **David’s Son!**
	21.15	and the children shouting in the Temple, “Praise to **David’s Son!”**
Mk	10.47	**Son of David!**
	10.48	shouted even more loudly, **“Son of David,** take pity on me!”
Lk	18.38	**Son of David!**
	18.39	But he shouted even more loudly, **“Son of David!**

SON OF GOD
[GOD’S SON, HIS SON]

Mt	2.15	the prophet come true, “I called my **Son** out of Egypt.”
	3.17	heaven, “This is my own dear **Son,** with whom I am pleased.”
	4. 3	and said, “If you are **God’s Son,** order these stones to turn
	4. 6	to him, “If you are **God’s Son,** throw yourself down, for the
	8.29	they screamed, “What do you want with us, you **Son of God?**
	11.27	No one knows the **Son** except the Father, and no one
	11.27	knows the Father except the **Son**
	11.27	and those to whom the **Son** chooses to reveal him.
	14.33	“Truly you are the **Son of God!”**
	16.16	Peter answered, “You are the Messiah, the **Son of the living God.”**
	17. 5	“This is my own dear **Son,** with whom I am pleased—listen
	24.36	and hour will come—neither the angels in heaven nor the **Son;**
	26.63	tell us if you are the Messiah, the **Son of God.”**
	27.40	Save yourself if you are **God’s Son!**
	27.43	He trusts in God and claims to be **God’s Son.**
	27.54	were terrified and said, “He really was the **Son of God!”**
	28.19	name of the Father, the **Son,** and the Holy Spirit, [20] and
Mk	1. 1	This is the Good News about Jesus Christ, the **Son of God.**
	1.11	And a voice came from heaven, “You are my own dear **Son.**
	3.11	fall down before him and scream, “You are the **Son of God!”**
	5. 7	screamed in a loud voice, “Jesus, **Son of the Most High God!**
	9. 7	from the cloud, “This is my own dear **Son**—listen to him!”
	13.32	or hour will come—neither the angels in heaven, nor the **Son;**
	14.61	him, “Are you the Messiah, the **Son of the Blessed God?”**
	15.39	“This man was really the **Son of God!”**
Lk	1.32	great and will be called the **Son of the Most High God.**
	1.35	this reason the holy child will be called the **Son of God.**
	3.22	And a voice came from heaven, “You are my own dear **Son.**
	4. 3	to him, “If you are **God’s Son,** order this stone to turn
	4. 9	him, “If you are **God’s Son,** throw yourself down from here.
	4.41	out from many people, screaming, “You are the **Son of God!”**
	8.28	at his feet, and shouted, “Jesus, **Son of the Most High God!**
	9.35	the cloud, “This is my **Son,** whom I have chosen—listen to
	10.22	No one knows who the **Son** is except the Father,
	10.22	no one knows who the Father is except the **Son**
	10.22	and those to whom the **Son** chooses to reveal him.”
Lk	22.70	They all said, “Are you, then, the **Son of God?”**
Jn	1.14	the glory which he received as the Father’s only **Son.**
	1.18	The only **Son,** who is the same as God and is at
	1.34	John, “and I tell you that he is the **Son of God.”**
	1.49	“Teacher,” answered Nathanael, “you are the **Son of God!**
	3.16	that he gave his only **Son,** so that everyone who believes in
	3.17	For God did not send **his Son** into the world to be
	3.18	Whoever believes in the **Son** is not judged;
	3.18	been judged, because he has not believed in God’s only **Son.**
	3.35	The Father loves **his Son** and has put everything in his power.
	3.36	Whoever believes in the **Son** has eternal life;
	3.36	whoever disobeys the **Son** will not have life, but will remain
	5.19	the **Son** can do nothing on his own;
	5.19	What the Father does, the **Son** also does.
	5.20	For the Father loves the **Son** and shows him all that he
	5.21	in the same way the **Son** gives life to those he wants
	5.22	He has given **his Son** the full right to judge, [23] so that
	5.23	that all will honour the **Son** in the same way as they
	5.23	Whoever does not honour the **Son** does not honour the Father
	5.25	the voice of the **Son of God,** and those who hear it
	5.26	same way he has made **his Son** to be the source of
	5.27	And he has given the **Son** the right to judge, because he
	6.40	that all who see the **Son** and believe in him should have
	8.36	If the **Son** sets you free, then you will be really free.
	10.36	I blaspheme because I said that I am the **Son of God?**
	11. 4	be the means by which the **Son of God** will receive glory.”
	11.27	are the Messiah, the **Son of God,** who was to come into
	14.13	so that the Father’s glory will be shown through the **Son.**
	17. 1	Give glory to your **Son,**
	17. 1	so that the **Son** may give glory to you.
	19. 7	ought to die, because he claimed to be the **Son of God.”**
	20.31	is the Messiah, the **Son of God,** and that through your faith
Acts	9.20	and began to preach that Jesus was the **Son of God.**
	13.32	As it is written in the second Psalm, ‘You are my **Son;**
	20.28	he made his own through the sacrificial death of **his Son.**
Rom	1. 3	It is about **his Son,** our Lord Jesus Christ:
	1. 4	power to be the **Son of God** by being raised from death.
	1. 9	with all my heart by preaching the Good News about **his Son.**
	5.10	but he made us his friends through the death of **his Son.**
	8. 3	nature by sending his own **Son,** who came with a nature like
	8.29	set apart to become like **his Son,**
	8.29	so that the **Son** would be the first among many
	8.32	even keep back his own **Son,** but offered him for us all!
	8.32	He gave us **his Son**—will he not also freely give us
1 Cor	1. 9	called you to have fellowship with **his Son** Jesus Christ, our
	15.28	then he himself, the **Son,** will place himself under God,
2 Cor	1.19	For Jesus Christ, the **Son of God,** who was preached among
Gal	1.16	when he decided [16] to reveal **his Son** to me, so that I
	2.20	by faith in the **Son of God,** who loved me and gave
	4. 4	But when the right time finally came, God sent his own **Son.**
	4. 6	God sent the Spirit of **his Son** into our hearts, the Spirit
Eph	1. 6	grace, for the free gift he gave us in his dear **Son!**
	4.13	in our faith and in our knowledge of the **Son of God;**
Col	1.13	the kingdom of his dear **Son,** [14] by whom we are set free,
	1.15	He is the first-born **Son,** superior to all created things.
	1.18	He is the first-born **Son,** who was raised from death, in
	1.19	God’s own decision that the **Son** has in himself the full
	1.20	Through the **Son,** then, God decided to bring the whole
	1.20	God made peace through **his Son’s** sacrificial death on the cross
	1.22	of the physical death of **his Son,** God has made you his
1 Thes	1.10	God [10] and to wait for **his Son** to come from heaven—
	1.10	**his Son** Jesus, whom he raised
Heb	1. 2	in these last days he has spoken to us through **his Son.**
	1. 4	The **Son** was made greater than the angels, just as the name
	1. 5	God never said to any of his angels, “You are my **Son;**
	1. 5	“I will be his Father, and he will be my **Son.”**
	1. 6	about to send his first-born **Son** into the world, he said,
	1. 8	About the **Son,** however, God said:
	3. 6	But Christ is faithful as the **Son** in charge of God’s house.
	4.14	gone into the very presence of God—Jesus, the **Son of God.**
	5. 5	Instead, God said to him, “You are my **Son;**
	5. 8	even though he was **God’s Son,** he learnt through his sufferings
	6. 6	are again crucifying the **Son of God** and exposing him to
	7. 3	He is like the **Son of God;**
	7.28	than the Law, appoints the **Son,** who has been made perfect
	10.29	What, then, of the person who despises the **Son of God?**
2 Pet	1.17	saying, “This is my own dear **Son,** with whom I am pleased!”
1 Jn	1. 3	that we have with the Father and with **his Son** Jesus Christ.
	1. 5	that we have heard from **his Son** and announce is this:
	1. 7	the blood of Jesus, **his Son,** purifies us from every sin.
	2.22	the Enemy of Christ—he rejects both the Father and the **Son.**
	2.23	For whoever rejects the **Son** also rejects the Father;
	2.23	whoever accepts the **Son** has the Father also.
	2.24	you will always live in union with the **Son** and the Father.
	3. 8	The **Son of God** appeared for this very reason, to destroy
	3.23	is that we believe in **his Son** Jesus Christ and love one
	4. 9	us by sending his only **Son** into the world, so that we
	4.10	he loved us and sent **his Son** to be the means by
	4.14	others that the Father sent **his Son** to be the Saviour of
	4.15	that Jesus is the **Son of God,** he lives in union with
	5. 5	Only the person who believes that Jesus is the **Son of God.**
	5. 9	stronger, and he has given this testimony about **his Son.**
	5.10	whoever believes in the **Son of God** has this testimony in his
	5.10	because he has not believed what God has said about **his Son.**
	5.11	us eternal life, and this life has its source in **his Son.**
	5.12	Whoever has the **Son** has this life;
	5.12	whoever does not have the **Son of God** does not have life.
	5.13	you have eternal life—you that believe in the **Son of God.**
	5.18	on sinning, for the **Son of God** keeps him safe, and the
	5.20	We know that the **Son of God** has come and has given
	5.20	union with the true God—in union with **his Son** Jesus Christ.

2 Jn 3 and Jesus Christ, the Father's **Son,** give us grace, mercy,
9 does stay with the teaching has both the Father and the **Son.**
Rev 2.18 the message from the **Son of God,** whose eyes blaze like fire,

SON OF MAN

see also **MORTAL (Man)**

Mt 8.20 have nests, but the **Son of Man** has nowhere to lie down
9. 6 you, then, that the **Son of Man** has authority on earth to
10.23 in all the towns of Israel before the **Son of Man** comes.
11.19 When the **Son of Man** came, he ate and drank, and everyone
12. 8 for the **Son of Man** is Lord of the Sabbath."
12.32 Anyone who says something against the **Son of Man** can be forgiven;
12.40 fish, so will the **Son of Man** spend three days and nights
13.37 "The man who sowed the good seed is the **Son of Man;**
13.41 the **Son of Man** will send out his angels to gather up
16.13 his disciples, "Who do people say the **Son of Man** is?"
16.27 For the **Son of Man** is about to come in the glory
16.28 die until they have seen the **Son of Man** come as King."
17. 9 have seen until the **Son of Man** has been raised from death."
17.12 In the same way they will also ill-treat the **Son of Man."**
17.22 said to them, "The **Son of Man** is about to be handed
19.28 sure that when the **Son of Man** sits on his glorious throne
20.18 to Jerusalem, where the **Son of Man** will be handed over to
20.28 your slave—[28] like the **Son of Man,** who did not come to
24.27 For the **Son of Man** will come like the lightning which
24.30 the sign of the **Son of Man** will appear in the sky;
24.30 as they see the **Son of Man** coming on the clouds of
24.37 The coming of the **Son of Man** will be like what happened
24.39 That is how it will be when the **Son of Man** comes.
24.44 be ready, because the **Son of Man** will come at an hour
25.31 "When the **Son of Man** comes as King and all the angels
26. 2 Passover Festival, and the **Son of Man** will be handed over to
26.24 The **Son of Man** will die as the Scriptures say he will,
26.24 but how terrible for that man who betrays the **Son of Man!**
26.45 has come for the **Son of Man** to be handed over to
26.64 you will see the **Son of Man** sitting on the right of
Mk 2.10 you, then, that the **Son of Man** has authority on earth to
2.28 So the **Son of Man** is Lord even of the Sabbath."
8.31 "The **Son of Man** must suffer much and be rejected by the
8.38 wicked day, then the **Son of Man** will be ashamed of him
9. 9 you have seen, until the **Son of Man** has risen from death."
9.12 Scriptures say that the **Son of Man** will suffer much and be
9.31 "The **Son of Man** will be handed over to men who will
10.33 to Jerusalem where the **Son of Man** will be handed over to
10.45 For even the **Son of Man** did not come to be served;
13.26 Then the **Son of Man** will appear, coming in the clouds
14.21 The **Son of Man** will die as the Scriptures say he will;
14.21 but how terrible for that man who betrays the **Son of Man!**
14.41 Look, the **Son of Man** is now being handed over to the
14.62 will all see the **Son of Man** seated on the right of
Lk 5.24 you, then, that the **Son of Man** has authority on earth to
6. 5 And Jesus concluded, "The **Son of Man** is Lord of the Sabbath."
6.22 say that you are evil, all because of the **Son of Man!**
7.34 The **Son of Man** came, and he ate and drank, and you
9.22 said to them, "The **Son of Man** must suffer much and be
9.26 my teaching, then the **Son of Man** will be ashamed of him
9.44 The **Son of Man** is going to be handed over to the
9.58 have nests, but the **Son of Man** has nowhere to lie down
11.30 of Nineveh, so the **Son of Man** will be a sign for
12. 8 belongs to me, the **Son of Man** will do the same for
12. 9 rejects me publicly, the **Son of Man** will also reject him
12.10 who says a word against the **Son of Man** can be forgiven;
12.40 be ready, because the **Son of Man** will come at an hour
17.22 the days of the **Son of Man,** but you will not see
17.24 the other, so will the **Son of Man** be in his day.
17.26 so shall it be in the days of the **Son of Man.**
17.30 it will be on the day the **Son of Man** is revealed.
18. 8 But will the **Son of Man** find faith on earth when he
18.31 the prophets wrote about the **Son of Man** will come true.
19.10 The **Son of Man** came to seek and to save the lost."
21.27 Then the **Son of Man** will appear, coming in a cloud with
21.36 that will happen and to stand before the **Son of Man."**
22.22 The **Son of Man** will die as God has decided, but how
22.48 is it with a kiss that you betray the **Son of Man?"**
22.69 from now on the **Son of Man** will be seated on the
24. 7 'The **Son of Man** must be handed over to sinful men, be
Jn 1.51 God's angels going up and coming down on the **Son of Man."**
3.13 heaven except the **Son of Man,** who came down from heaven."
3.14 the same way the **Son of Man** must be lifted up, [15] so
5.27 Son the right to judge, because he is the **Son of Man.**
6.27 the food which the **Son of Man** will give you, because God,
6.53 the flesh of the **Son of Man** and drink his blood, you
6.62 you should see the **Son of Man** go back up to the
8.28 you lift up the **Son of Man,** you will know that 'I
9.35 man and asked him, "Do you believe in the **Son of Man?"**
12.23 has now come for the **Son of Man** to receive great glory.
12.34 can you say that the **Son of Man** must be lifted up?
12.34 Who is this **Son of Man?"**
13.31 left, Jesus said, "Now the **Son of Man's** glory is revealed;
13.32 the glory of the **Son of Man** in himself, and he will
Acts 7.56 heaven opened and the **Son of Man** standing at the right-hand

SON-IN-LAW

Gen 19.12 anyone else here—sons, daughters, **sons-in-law,** or any other
1 Sam 18.18 is my family that I should become the king's **son-in-law?"**
18.21 time Saul said to David, "You will be my **son-in-law."**
18.23 honour to become the king's **son-in-law,** too great for
18.26 was delighted with the thought of becoming the king's **son-in-law.**
1 Sam 18.27 them all out to him, so that he might become his **son-in-law.**
22.14 He is your own **son-in-law,** captain of your bodyguard, and

SONG

Ex 15. 1 Then Moses and the Israelites sang this **song** to the Lord:
Num 21.17 At that time the people of Israel sang this **song:**
21.17 will greet it with a **song**— [18] The well dug by princes
Deut 31.19 "Now, write down this **song.**
31.21 But this **song** will still be sung, and it will stand as
31.22 day Moses wrote down the **song** and taught it to the people
31.30 Then Moses recited the entire **song** while all the people
32.44 son of Nun recited this **song,** so that the people of Israel
Judg 5. 1 On that day Deborah and Barak son of Abinoam sang this **song:**
5.12 Sing a **song!**
1 Sam 18. 6 were singing joyful **songs,** dancing, and playing tambourines
2 Sam 22. 1 Saul and his other enemies, David sang this **song** to the Lord:
23. 1 and who was the composer of beautiful **songs** for Israel.
1 Kgs 4.32 He composed three thousand proverbs and more than a thousand **songs.**
1 Chr 16.42 which were played when the **songs** of praise were sung.
2 Chr 29.30 sing to the Lord the **songs** of praise that were written by
35.25 men and women, to use this **song** when they mourn for him.
35.25 The **song** is found in the collection of laments.
Neh 4.10 The people of Judah had a **song** they sang:
12.27 in celebrating the dedication with **songs** of thanksgiving and
12.46 musicians have led **songs** of praise and thanksgiving to God.
Ps 28. 7 I praise him with joyful **songs.**
33. 3 Sing a new **song** to him, play the harp with skill,
40. 3 to sing a new song, a **song** of praise to our God.
42. 8 that I may have a **song** at night, a prayer to the
45. 1 words fill my mind, as I compose this **song** for the king.
45.17 My **song** will keep your fame alive for ever,
47. 1 Praise God with loud **songs!**
47. 7 praise him with **songs!**
63. 5 be satisfied, and I will sing glad **songs** of praise to you.
66.17 I praised him with **songs.**
69.12 me in the streets, and drunkards make up **songs** about me.
69.30 I will praise God with a **song;**
89.15 people who worship you with **songs,** who live in the light of
95. 2 him with thanksgiving and sing joyful **songs** of praise.
96. 1 Sing a new **song** to the Lord!
98. 1 Sing a new **song** to the Lord;
98. 4 praise him with **songs** and shouts of joy!
100. 2 come before him with happy **songs!**
101. 1 My **song** is about loyalty and justice,
104.34 he be pleased with my **song,** for my gladness comes from him.
107.22 him with sacrifices, and with **songs** of joy must tell all
119.54 During my brief earthly life I compose **songs**
137. 3 "Sing us a **song** about Zion."
137. 4 How can we sing a **song** to the Lord in a foreign
144. 9 I will sing you a new **song,** O God;
149. 1 Sing a new **song** to the Lord;
Ecc 12. 4 it plays, but even the **song** of a bird will wake you
Song 1. 1 The most beautiful of **songs,** by Solomon.
2.12 the **song** of doves is heard in the fields.
Is 5. 1 sing you this song, a **song** of my friend and his vineyard:
23.15 are over, Tyre will be like the prostitute in the **song:**
23.16 Play and sing your **songs** again to bring men back once more.
24.16 the world we will hear **songs** in praise of Israel,
26. 1 when the people will sing this **song** in the land of Judah:
38. 9 recovered from his illness, he wrote this **song** of praise:
42.10 Sing a new **song** to the Lord;
49.13 Let the mountains burst into **song!**
51. 3 will be there, and **songs** of praise and thanks to me.
61. 3 instead of grief, A **song** of praise instead of sorrow.
Jer 7.29 Sing a funeral **song** on the hill-tops, because I, the Lord,
9.17 mourners to come, for the women who sing funeral **songs."**
9.18 hurry and sing a funeral **song** for us, until our eyes fill
9.20 how to mourn, and your friends how to sing a funeral **song.**
31. 7 Sing your **song** of praise, 'The Lord has saved his people;
48.36 like someone playing a funeral **song** on a flute, because
Ezek 19. 1 told me to sing this **song** of sorrow for two princes of
19.14 This is a **song** of sorrow;
26.13 an end to all your **songs,** and I will silence the music
26.17 They will sing this funeral **song** for you:
27. 2 "Mortal man, sing a funeral **song** for Tyre, [3] that city
27.32 They chant a funeral **song** for you:
32.16 This solemn warning will become a funeral **song.**
33.32 than an entertainer singing love **songs** or playing a harp.
Amos 5. 1 of Israel, to this funeral **song** which I sing over you:
5.23 Stop your noisy **songs;**
6. 5 You like to compose **songs,** as David did, and play them on
8. 3 On that day the **songs** in the palace will become cries of
8.10 funerals and change your glad **songs** into cries of grief.
Mic 2. 4 they will sing this **song** of despair about your experience:
Mt 11.17 We sang funeral **songs,** but you wouldn't cry!'
Lk 7.32 We sang funeral **songs,** but you wouldn't cry!'
Eph 5.19 another with the words of psalms, hymns, and sacred **songs;**
Col 3.16 Sing psalms, hymns, and sacred **songs;**
Rev 4. 9 The four living creatures sing **songs** of glory and honour
5. 9 They sang a new **song:**
14. 3 they were singing a new **song,** which only they could learn.
15. 3 singing the **song** of Moses, the servant of God,
15. 3 and the **song** of the Lamb:

SONS OF GOD see CHILD OF GOD

SONS OF ZEBEDEE see ZEBEDEE

SOON

Mt 12.26 it is already divided into groups and will **soon** fall apart!
13. 5 The seeds **soon** sprouted, because the soil wasn't deep.
13. 6 roots had not grown deep enough, the plants **soon** dried up.
Mk 4. 5 The seeds **soon** sprouted, because the soil wasn't deep.
4. 6 roots had not grown deep enough, the plants **soon** dried up.
Lk 9.31 way in which he would **soon** fulfil God's purpose by dying in
14.22 **Soon** the servant said, 'Your order has been carried out,
21.20 armies, then you will know that she will **soon** be destroyed.
Acts 25. 4 in Caesarea, and I myself will be going back there **soon.**
27.14 But **soon** a very strong wind—the one called
Rom 16.20 God, our source of peace, will **soon** crush Satan under your feet.
1 Cor 4.19 I will come to you **soon,** and then I will find out
Phil 2.19 to send Timothy to you **soon,** so that I may be encouraged
2.24 Lord that I myself will be able to come to you **soon.**
4. 5 The Lord is coming **soon.**
1 Tim 3.14 this letter to you, I hope to come and see you **soon.**
2 Tim 4. 9 Do your best to come to me **soon.**
Heb 8.13 anything that becomes old and worn out will **soon** disappear.
13.19 earnestly to pray that God will send me back to you **soon.**
13.23 If he comes **soon** enough, I will have him with me when
2 Pet 1.14 I know that I shall **soon** put off this mortal body, as
3.12 best to make it come **soon**—the Day when the heavens will
3 Jn 14 I hope to see you **soon,** and then we will talk personally.
Rev 1. 1 in order to show his servants what must happen very **soon.**
2.16 I will come to you **soon** and fight against those people with
3.11 I am coming **soon.**
11.14 The second horror is over, but the third horror will come **soon!**
12. 2 She was **soon** to give birth, and the pains and suffering of
22. 6 his angel to show his servants what must happen very **soon."**
22. 7 "I am coming **soon!**
22.12 "I am coming **soon!**
22.20 I am coming **soon!"**

SOOTHING

Ps 55.21 his words were as **soothing** as oil, but they cut like sharp

SORCERER

Job 3. 8 Tell the **sorcerers** to curse that day, those who know how
Is 57. 3 You are no better than **sorcerers,** adulterers, and prostitutes.
Dan 2. 2 sent for his fortune-tellers, magicians, **sorcerers,** and

SORE

Gen 34.25 when the men were still **sore** from their circumcision, two of
Ex 9. 9 that become open **sores** on the people and the animals."
9.10 boils that became open **sores** on the people and the animals.
Lev 13. 2 If anyone has a **sore** on his skin or a boil or
13. 3 The priest shall examine the **sore,** and if the hairs in it
13. 3 have turned white and the **sore** appears to be deeper than the
13. 4 But if the **sore** is white and does not appear to be
13. 5 if in his opinion the **sore** looks the same and has not
13. 6 seventh day, and if the **sore** has faded and has not spread,
13. 6 it is only a **sore.**
13. 7 But if the **sore** spreads after the priest has examined him
13.10 If there is a white **sore** on his skin which turns the
13.14 But from the moment an open **sore** appears, he is unclean.
13.15 and if he sees an open **sore,** he shall pronounce him unclean.
13.15 An open **sore** means a dreaded skin-disease,
13.16 But when the **sore** heals and becomes white again, the
13.17 If the **sore** has turned white, he is ritually clean, and the
13.29 or a woman has a **sore** on the head or the chin,
13.31 the priest examines him, the **sore** does not appear to be
13.32 The priest shall examine the **sore** again on the seventh day,
13.33 the person shall shave the head except the area round the **sore.**
13.34 priest shall again examine the **sore,** and if it has not
13.35 But if the **sore** spreads after he has been pronounced clean,
13.36 If the **sore** has spread, he need not look for yellowish hairs;
13.37 in the priest's opinion the **sore** has not spread and healthy
13.37 are growing in it, the **sore** has healed, and the priest shall
13.42 But if a reddish-white **sore** appears on the bald spot, it
13.43 **sore,** [44]the priest shall
14.55 **sores,** boils, or inflammations;
22.22 or that has a running **sore** or a skin eruption or scabs.
Deut 28.27 He will make your bodies break out with **sores.**
28.35 The Lord will cover your legs with incurable, painful **sores;**
Job 2. 7 Lord's presence and made **sores** break out all over Job's body.
2. 8 heap and took a piece of broken pottery to scrape his **sores.**
7. 5 pus runs out of my **sores.**
Ps 38. 5 Because I have been foolish, my **sores** stink and rot.
38.11 and neighbours will not come near me, because of my **sores;**
Is 1. 6 You are covered with bruises and **sores** and open wounds.
Jer 30.13 you, no remedy for your **sores,** no hope of healing for you.
Lk 16.20 man named Lazarus, covered with **sores,** who used to be
16.21 Even the dogs would come and lick his **sores.**
2 Tim 2.17 Such teaching is like an open **sore** that eats away the flesh.
Rev 16. 2 Terrible and painful **sores** appeared on those who had the
16.11 and they cursed the God of heaven for their pains and **sores.**

SORROW

Gen 37.29 that Joseph was not there, he tore his clothes in **sorrow.**
37.34 Jacob tore his clothes in **sorrow** and put on sackcloth.
42.38 an old man, and the **sorrow** you would cause me would kill
44.13 brothers tore their clothes in **sorrow,** loaded their donkeys,
44.29 something happens to him, the **sorrow** you would cause me
44.30 is so old that the **sorrow** we would cause him would kill
48. 7 To my great **sorrow** she died in the land of Canaan, not
Num 14. 6 tore their clothes in **sorrow** [7]and said to the people,
Josh 7. 6 till evening, with dust on their heads to show their **sorrow.**
Judg 11.35 he tore his clothes in **sorrow** and said, "Oh, my daughter!
2 Sam 1.11 David tore his clothes in **sorrow,** and all his men did
13.31 tore his clothes in **sorrow,** and threw himself to the ground.
1 Kgs 8.38 people Israel, out of heartfelt **sorrow,** stretch out their
2 Chr 6.29 people Israel, out of heartfelt **sorrow,** stretch out their
Neh 9. 1 Israel assembled to fast in order to show **sorrow** for their sins.
Ps 13. 2 How long will **sorrow** fill my heart day and night?
30.11 you have taken away my **sorrow** and surrounded me with joy.
31.10 I am exhausted by **sorrow,** and weeping has shortened my life.
35.19 hate me for no reason smirk with delight over my **sorrow.**
42. 6 He has sent waves of **sorrow** over my soul;
80. 5 You have given us **sorrow** to eat, a large cup of tears
90.10 yet all they bring us is trouble and **sorrow;**
119.28 I am overcome by **sorrow;**
Prov 14.13 When happiness is gone, **sorrow** is always there.
17.21 is nothing but sadness and **sorrow** for a father whose son
Ecc 3. 4 He sets the time for **sorrow** and the time for joy, the
7. 3 **Sorrow** is better than laughter;
Is 25. 7 suddenly remove the cloud of **sorrow** that has been hanging
35.10 be happy for ever, for ever free from **sorrow** and grief.
51.11 be happy for ever, for ever free from **sorrow** and grief.
61. 3 instead of grief, A song of praise instead of **sorrow.**
Jer 8.18 My **sorrow** cannot be healed;
14. 2 on the ground in **sorrow,** and Jerusalem cries out for help.
14.17 commanded me to tell the people about my **sorrow** and to say:
20.18 to have trouble and **sorrow,** to end my life in disgrace?
31.13 turn their mourning into joy, their **sorrow** into gladness.
36.24 who heard all this was afraid or showed any sign of **sorrow.**
42.10 The destruction I brought on you has caused me great **sorrow.**
45. 3 The Lord has added **sorrow** to my troubles.
47. 5 Great **sorrow** has come to the people of Gaza, and
Lam 1.20 My heart is broken in **sorrow** for my sins.
2. 5 He has brought on the people of Judah unending **sorrow.**
3.32 He may bring us **sorrow,** but his love for us is sure
Ezek 6.11 Cry in **sorrow** because of all the evil, disgusting things the
19. 1 me to sing this song of **sorrow** for two princes of Israel:
19.14 This is a song of **sorrow;**
21. 6 Groan in **sorrow** where everyone can watch you.
Joel 2.13 Let your broken heart show your **sorrow;**
Amos 5.16 "There will be wailing and cries of **sorrow** in the city streets.
Mic 1. 8 To show my **sorrow,** I will walk about barefoot and naked.
Nah 2. 7 her servants moan like doves and beat their breasts in **sorrow.**
Mt 26.38 he said to them, "The **sorrow** in my heart is so great
Mk 14.34 he said to them, "The **sorrow** in my heart is so great
Lk 2.35 And **sorrow,** like a sharp sword, will break your own heart."
23.48 they all went back home, beating their breasts in **sorrow.**
Rom 9. 2 say how great is my **sorrow,** how endless the pain in my
Phil 2.27 him but on me, too, and spared me an even greater **sorrow.**
2.28 again when you see him, and my own **sorrow** will disappear.
1 Tim 6.10 the faith and have broken their hearts with many **sorrows.**
Jas 4. 9 Be **sorrowful,** cry, and weep;

SORRY

Gen 6. 6 all the time, [6]he was **sorry** that he had ever made them
6. 7 the birds, because I am **sorry** that I made any of them."
Ex 2. 6 He was crying, and she felt **sorry** for him.
Judg 21. 6 The people of Israel felt **sorry** for their brothers the
21.15 The people felt **sorry** for the Benjaminites because the
Ruth 1.13 Lord has turned against me, and I feel very **sorry** for you."
1 Sam 15.11 Lord said to Samuel, [11]"I am **sorry** that I made Saul king;
15.35 The Lord was **sorry** that he had made Saul king of Israel.
24.10 kill you, but I felt **sorry** for you and said that I
2 Chr 21.20 Nobody was **sorry** when he died.
Job 30.25 with people in trouble and feel **sorry** for those in need?
Ps 106.46 He made all their oppressors feel **sorry** for them.
Prov 23.29 show you someone miserable and **sorry** for himself, always
Is 1.29 You will be **sorry** that you ever worshipped trees and
Jer 8. 6 Not one of you has been **sorry** for his wickedness;
Jon 1. 6 Maybe he will feel **sorry** for us and spare our lives."
4.10 and you didn't make it grow—yet you feel **sorry** for it!
Mal 3.14 the Lord Almighty that we are **sorry** for what we have done?
Mt 15.32 him and said, "I feel **sorry** for these people, because they
18.27 The king felt **sorry** for him, so he forgave him the debt
Mk 3. 5 the same time he felt **sorry** for them, because they were so
8. 2 him and said, [2]"I feel **sorry** for these people, because
2 Cor 7. 7 want to see me, how **sorry** you are, how ready you are
7. 8 of mine made you sad, I am not **sorry** I wrote it.
7. 8 I could have been **sorry** when I saw that it made you

SOUGHT see SEEK

SOUL

Deut 6. 5 your heart, with all your **soul,** and with all your strength.
Josh 22. 5 to him, and serve him with all your heart and **soul."**
23.14 knows in his heart and **soul** that the Lord your God has
1 Kgs 2. 4 obey his commands faithfully with all their heart and **soul.**
2 Kgs 23. 3 with all his heart and **soul,** and to put into practice the
1 Chr 22.19 Now serve the Lord your God with all your heart and **soul.**
2 Chr 15.12 the God of their ancestors, with all their heart and **soul.**
34.31 with all his heart and **soul,** and to put into practice the
Ps 42. 6 He has sent waves of sorrow over my **soul;**
57. 8 Wake up, my **soul!**
63. 1 worn-out, and waterless land, my **soul** is thirsty for you.
63. 5 My **soul** will feast and be satisfied, and I will sing glad
103. 1 Praise the Lord, my **soul!**
103. 2 Praise the Lord, my **soul,** and do not forget how kind he

Ps 103.22 Praise the Lord, my **soul!**
104. 1 Praise the Lord, my **soul!**
104.35 Praise the Lord, my **soul!**
108. 1 Wake up, my **soul!**
143. 6 like dry ground my **soul** is thirsty for you.
146. 1 Praise the Lord, my **soul!**
Prov 24.14 you may be sure that wisdom is good for the **soul.**
Lam 1.20 "Look, O Lord, at my agony, at the anguish of my **soul!**
2.11 my **soul** is in anguish.
Mt 10.28 afraid of those who kill the body but cannot kill the **soul;**
10.28 afraid of God, who can destroy both body and **soul** in hell.
22.37 all your heart, with all your **soul,** and with all your mind.'
Mk 12.30 your heart, with all your **soul,** with all your mind, and with
Lk 1.47 my **soul** is glad because of God my Saviour, [48]for he
10.27 all your heart, with all your **soul,** with all your strength,
2 Cor 7. 1 everything that makes body or **soul** unclean, and let us be
Phil 2. 2 sharing the same love, and being one in **soul** and mind.
1 Thes 5.23 keep your whole being—spirit, **soul,** and body—free from every
Heb 4.12 the way through, to where **soul** and spirit meet, to where
13.17 They watch over your **souls** without resting, since they must
Jas 5.20 way will save that sinner's **soul** from death and bring about
1 Pet 1. 9 receiving the salvation of your **souls,** which is the purpose
2.11 bodily passions, which are always at war against the **soul.**
2.25 back to follow the Shepherd and Keeper of your **souls.**
Rev 6. 9 saw underneath the altar the **souls** of those who had been
20. 4 I also saw the **souls** of those who had been executed because

AV SOUL

see also **HEART, LIFE**

Gen 2. 7 breath into his nostrils and the man began to **live.**
35.18 was dying, and as she **breathed** her last, she named her son
Lev 22.11 But a priest's **slaves,** bought with his own money or born
Num 11. 6 But now our **strength** is gone.
21. 4 lost their **patience** [5]and spoke against God and Moses.
Deut 11.18 "Remember these commands and **cherish** them.
1 Sam 1.15 I have been praying, pouring out my **troubles** to the Lord.
2 Kgs 4.27 Can't you see she's deeply **distressed?**
Job 3.20 Why let men go on living in **misery?**
14.22 pain of his own body and the grief of his own **mind.**
Ps 23. 3 He gives me new **strength.**
107.26 In such danger the men lost their **courage;**
Prov 19.16 Keep God's laws and you will **live** longer;
24.12 of your business, but God knows and judges your **motives.**
Jer 4.10 there would be peace, but a sword is at their **throats."**
Jon 2. 5 The water came over me and **choked** me;
Mk 12.33 his heart and with all his **mind** and with all his strength;
Heb 10.39 Instead, we have faith and are **saved.**
2 Pet 2. 8 day after day he suffered **agony** as he saw and heard their
3 Jn 2 be in good health—as I know you are well in **spirit.**
Rev 16. 3 a dead person, and every living **creature** in the sea died.

SOUND (1)

Gen 27.22 him and said, "Your voice **sounds** like Jacob's voice, but
Ex 19.19 The **sound** of the trumpet became louder and louder.
28.35 when he leaves it, the **sound** of the bells will be heard,
32.17 said to Moses, "I hear the **sound** of battle in the camp."
32.18 Moses said, "That doesn't **sound** like a shout of victory
32.18 it's the **sound** of singing."
Lev 23.23 rest, and come together for worship when the trumpets **sound.**
26.36 exile so terrified that the **sound** of a leaf blowing in the
Num 10. 3 When long blasts are **sounded** on both trumpets, the whole
10. 4 when only one trumpet is **sounded,** then only the leaders of
10. 5 When short blasts are **sounded,** the tribes camped on the
10. 6 When short blasts are **sounded** a second time, the tribes on
10. 6 short blasts are to be **sounded** to break camp,
10. 7 to call the community together, long blasts are to be **sounded.**
10. 9 enemy who has attacked you, **sound** the signal for battle on
Josh 6. 5 Then they are to **sound** one long note.
6. 8 All this time the trumpets were **sounding.**
6.12 All this time the trumpets were **sounding.**
6.16 the priests were about to **sound** the trumpets, Joshua ordered
1 Sam 1.13 her lips were moving, but she made no **sound.**
2 Sam 5.24 When you hear the **sound** of marching in the tree-tops,
6.15 to Jerusalem with shouts of joy and the **sound** of trumpets.
15.10 say, "When you hear the **sound** of trumpets, shout, 'Absalom
1 Kgs 18.29 but no answer came, not a **sound** was heard.
2 Kgs 4.31 child, but there was no **sound** or any other sign of life.
7. 6 made the Syrians hear what **sounded** like the advance of a
1 Chr 14.15 When you hear the **sound** of marching in the tree-tops,
15.28 with shouts of joy, the **sound** of trumpets, horns, and
16. 5 Asaph was to **sound** the cymbals, [6]and two priests, Benaiah
Neh 4.18 The man who was to **sound** the alarm on the bugle stayed
Job 9.20 and faithful, but my words **sound** guilty, and everything I
37. 4 voice is heard, the majestic **sound** of thunder, and all the
Ps 19. 3 No speech or words are used, no **sound** is heard;
51. 8 Let me hear the **sounds** of joy and gladness;
115. 7 they cannot make a **sound.**
Prov 26.25 They may **sound** fine, but don't believe him, because his
Song 1. 3 the **sound** of your name recalls it.
Is 6. 4 **sound** of their voices made the foundation of the Temple shake,
13. 4 the **sound** of a great crowd of people,
13. 4 the **sound** of nations and kingdoms gathering.
15. 8 Everywhere at Moab's borders the **sound** of crying is heard.
17.12 are in commotion with a **sound** like the roar of the sea,
18. 1 Sudan there is a land where the **sound** of wings is heard.
60.18 The **sounds** of violence will be heard no more;
66. 6 that **sound** in the Temple,
66. 6 is the **sound** of the Lord punishing his enemies!
Jer 6. 1 **Sound** the trumpet in Tekoa and build a signal fire in Beth
6.23 They **sound** like the roaring sea, as they ride their horses.
7.34 put an end to the **sounds** of joy and gladness
7.34 and to the happy **sounds** of wedding feasts.
9.10 The **sound** of livestock is no longer heard;
9.19 Listen to the **sound** of crying in Zion,
16. 9 I will silence the **sounds** of joy and gladness
16. 9 and the happy **sounds** of wedding feasts.
25.10 of joy and gladness and the happy **sounds** of wedding feasts.
25.31 will hear him, [31]and the **sound** will echo to the ends of
31.15 "A **sound** is heard in Ramah, the sound of bitter weeping.
33.11 of gladness and joy and the happy **sounds** of wedding feasts.
48. 5 Hear the **sound** of their sobs along the road up to Luhith,
50.42 They **sound** like the roaring sea, as they ride their horses.
51.54 "Listen to the **sound** of crying in Babylon, of mourning for
Ezek 1.24 it **sounded** like the roar of the sea, like the noise of
1.25 but there was still a **sound** coming from above the dome
7.14 The trumpet **sounds,** and everyone gets ready.
10. 5 It **sounded** like the voice of Almighty God.
23.42 The **sound** of a carefree crowd could be heard, a group of
33. 3 the enemy approaching, he **sounds** the alarm to warn everyone.
33. 6 enemy coming and does not **sound** the alarm, the enemy will
43. 2 God's voice **sounded** like the roar of the sea, and the earth
Dan 3. 5 You will hear the **sound** of the trumpets, followed by the
3. 7 soon as they heard the **sound** of the instruments, the people
3.15 soon as you hear the **sound** of the trumpets, oboes, lyres,
10. 6 polished bronze, and his voice **sounded** like the roar of a
Hos 5. 8 **Sound** the alarm in Ramah!
8. 1 The Lord says, **"Sound** the alarm!
Joel 2. 1 **sound** the alarm on Zion, God's sacred hill.
Amos 2. 2 while soldiers are shouting and trumpets are **sounding.**
3. 6 Does the war trumpet **sound** in a city without making the
Zeph 1.10 Lord, "you will hear the **sound** of crying at the Fish Gate
1.10 part of the city and a great crashing **sound** in the hills.
1.16 a day filled with the **sound** of war-trumpets and the
Zech 9.14 The Sovereign Lord will **sound** the trumpet;
Mt 2.18 "A **sound** is heard in Ramah, the sound of bitter weeping.
24.31 The great trumpet will **sound,** and he will send out his
Jn 3. 8 you hear the **sound** it makes, but you do not know where
Acts 2. 2 noise from the sky which **sounded** like a strong wind blowing,
8.32 a lamb that makes no **sound** when its wool is cut off,
17.20 things we hear you say **sound** strange to us, and we would
Rom 10.18 "The **sound** of their voice went out to all the world;
1 Cor 14. 7 is being played unless the notes are **sounded** distinctly?
14. 8 plays the bugle does not **sound** a clear call, who will
15.51 but when the last trumpet **sounds,** we shall all be changed in
15.51 For when the trumpet **sounds,** the dead will be raised, never
2 Cor 3. 1 Does this **sound** as if we were again boasting about ourselves?
11.23 I **sound** like a madman—but I am a better servant than
Gal 1.10 Does this **sound** as if I am trying to win man's approval?
1 Thes 4.16 command, the archangel's voice, the **sound** of God's trumpet,
Heb 12.19 storm, [19]the blast of a trumpet, and the **sound** of a voice.
Rev 1.10 loud voice, that **sounded** like a trumpet, speaking behind me.
1.15 polished, and his voice **sounded** like a roaring waterfall.
4. 1 And the voice that **sounded** like a trumpet, which I had heard
6. 1 living creatures say in a voice that **sounded** like thunder,
6. 6 I heard what **sounded** like a voice coming from among the
8.13 live on earth when the **sound** comes from the trumpets that
9. 9 like iron breastplates, and the **sound** made by their wings
10. 3 out in a loud voice that **sounded** like the roar of lions.
14. 2 a voice from heaven that **sounded** like a roaring waterfall,
14. 2 It **sounded** like the music made by musicians playing their harps.
18.22 and the **sound** of the millstone will be heard no more!
19. 1 After this I heard what **sounded** like the roar of a large
19. 5 came from the throne the **sound** of a voice, saying, "Praise
19. 6 Then I heard what **sounded** like a large crowd,
19. 6 like the **sound** of a roaring waterfall,

SOUND (2)

[SAFE AND SOUND]

Gen 43. 9 back to you **safe and sound,** I will always bear the blame.
44.17 rest of you may go back **safe and sound** to your father."
Judg 4.21 Sisera was so tired that he fell **sound asleep.**
8. 9 to come back **safe and sound,** and when I do, I will
1 Sam 26.12 woke up—they were all **sound asleep,** because the Lord had
2 Sam 4. 7 Ishbosheth's bedroom, where he was **sound asleep,** and killed him.
Neh 9.13 to your people and gave them good laws and **sound** teachings.
Ps 111.10 he gives **sound** judgement to all who obey his commands.
Prov 3.24 you go to bed, and you will sleep **soundly** through the night.
8.12 I have knowledge and **sound** judgement.
Jon 1. 5 gone below and was lying in the ship's hold, **sound asleep.**
Mt 6.22 If your eyes are **sound,** your whole body will be full of
Lk 9.32 Peter and his companions were **sound asleep,** but they
11.34 When your eyes are **sound,** your whole body is full of light;
15.27 the prize calf, because he got him back **safe and sound.'**
Acts 20. 9 sleepier, until he finally went **sound asleep** and fell from
1 Tim 1.10 or who do anything else contrary to **sound** doctrine.
2 Tim 4. 3 people will not listen to **sound** doctrine, but will follow
Tit 2. 1 But you must teach what agrees with **sound** doctrine.
2. 2 to be **sound** in their faith, love, and endurance.
2. 8 Use **sound** words that cannot be criticized, so that your

SOUP

Gen 25.29 Jacob was cooking some bean **soup,** Esau came in from hunting.
25.34 Then Jacob gave him some bread and some of the **soup.**

SOUR

Is 5. 2 He waited for the grapes to ripen, but every grape was **sour.**
5. 4 Then why did it produce **sour** grapes and not the good grapes

Jer 31.29 ate the sour grapes, But the children got the **sour** taste.'
31.30 Instead, whoever eats **sour** grapes will have his own
Ezek 18. 2 ate the sour grapes, But the children got the **sour** taste.'
Rev 10. 9 it will turn **sour** in your stomach, but in your mouth it
10.10 But after I swallowed it, it turned **sour** in my stomach.

SOURCE

Num 16.22 ground and said, "O, God, you are the **source** of all life.
27.16 Moses prayed, [16]"Lord God, **source** of all life,
Job 22.26 in God and find that he is the **source** of your joy.
28.11 They dig to the **sources** of rivers And bring to light
28.20 Where, then, is the **source** of wisdom?
38.19 the light comes from or what the **source** of darkness is?
Ps 36. 9 You are the **source** of all life, and because of your light
43. 4 you are the **source** of my happiness.
87. 7 and sing, "In Zion is the **source** of all our blessings."
119.92 law had not been the **source** of my joy, I would have
Prov 8.30 architect, I was his daily **source** of joy, always happy in
18. 4 person's words can be a **source** of wisdom, deep as the ocean,
Is 22.23 and he will be a **source** of honour to his whole family.
49. 5 he is the **source** of my strength.
Jer 33. 9 Jerusalem will be a **source** of joy, honour, and pride to me;
51.36 I will dry up the **source** of Babylonia's water and make its
Lam 4.20 They captured the **source** of our life, the king the Lord
Ezek 47.11 They will remain there as a **source** of salt.
Hos 14. 8 I am the **source** of all their blessings."
Jn 1. 4 The Word was the **source** of life, and this life brought
5.26 the Father is himself the **source** of life,
5.26 he has made his Son to be the **source** of life.
Rom 15. 5 And may God, the **source** of patience and encouragement, enable you
15.13 May God, the **source** of hope, fill you with all joy
15.33 May God, our **source** of peace, be with all of you.
16.20 And God, our **source** of peace, will soon crush Satan
Col 1.18 he is the **source** of the body's life.
2 Thes 3.16 Lord Himself, who is our **source** of peace, give you peace
1 Tim 6.10 the love of money is a **source** of all kinds of evil.
Heb 5. 9 he became the **source** of eternal salvation for all
1 Jn 5.11 eternal life, and this life has its **source** in his Son.

SOUTH

Gen 10.19 Canaanite borders reached from Sidon **southwards** to Gerar
12. 8 After that, he moved on **south** to the hill-country east of
12. 9 place to place, going towards the **southern** part of Canaan.
12.10 bad that Abram went farther **south** to Egypt, to live there
13. 1 out of Egypt to the **southern** part of Canaan with his wife
20. 1 moved from Mamre to the **southern** part of Canaan and lived
24.62 Who Sees Me" and was staying in the **southern** part of Canaan.
35. 8 Deborah died and was buried beneath the oak **south** of Bethel.
Ex 26.18 Make twenty frames for the **south** side [19]and forty
26.35 side of the Tent and the lamp-stand against the **south** side.
27. 9 On the **south** side the curtains are to be 44 metres long,
36.23 made twenty frames for the **south** side [24]and forty silver
38. 9 On the **south** side the curtains were 44 metres long,
40.24 in the Tent, on the **south** side, opposite the table, [25]and
Num 2.10 On the **south**, those under the banner of the
3.29 was to camp on the **south** side of the Tent, [30]with
10. 6 sounded a second time, the tribes on the **south** will move out.
13.17 north from here into the **southern** part of the land of Canaan
13.21 wilderness of Zin in the **south** all the way to Rehob, near
13.22 They went first into the **southern** part of the land and
13.29 Amalekites live in the **southern** part of the land;
21. 1 king of Arad in the **southern** part of Canaan heard that the
33.40 The king of Arad in **southern** Canaan heard that the
34. 3 The **southern** border will extend from the wilderness of Zin
34. 3 begin on the east at the **southern** end of the Dead Sea.
34. 4 Then it will turn **southwards** towards Akrabbim Pass
34. 4 and continue on through Zin as far **south** as Kadesh Barnea.
34.11 It will then go **south** to Harbel, east of Ain, and on
34.12 shore of Lake Galilee, [12]then **south** along the River Jordan
Deut 1. 7 to the **southern** region, and to the Mediterranean coast.
2.23 over all their land as far **south** as the city of Gaza.)
3.16 of the river was their **southern** boundary, and their northern
3.17 the Dead Sea in the **south** and to the foot of Mount
3.27 the north and to the **south**, to the east and to the
4.49 the River Jordan as far **south** as the Dead Sea and east
11.24 from the desert in the **south** to the Lebanon Mountains in the
33.23 Their land reaches to the **south** from Lake Galilee."
34. 3 the **southern** part of Judah;
Josh 1. 4 from the desert in the **south** to the Lebanon Mountains in the
10.10 keeping up the attack as far **south** as Azekah and Makkedah.
10.40 foothills, as well as those of the dry country in the **south.**
10.41 from Kadesh Barnea in the **south** to Gaza near the coast,
11. 2 the Jordan Valley **south** of Lake Galilee, in the foothills,
11.16 and foothills, both north and **south,** all the area of Goshen
11.16 and the dry country **south** of it,
11.17 from Mount Halak in the **south** near Edom, as far as Baalgad
11.17 the north, in the valley of Lebanon **south** of Mount Hermon.
12. 3 Jordan Valley from Lake Galilee **south** to Beth Jeshimoth
12. 7 the valley of Lebanon to Mount Halak in the **south** near Edom.
12. 8 the eastern slopes, and the dry country in the **south.**
13. 3 as well as all the territory of the Avvim to the **south.**
13. 5 Baalgad, which is **south** of Mount Hermon, to Hamath Pass.
15. 1 The land reached **south**
15. 1 to the **southernmost** point of the wilderness of Zin,
15. 2 This **southern** border ran from the south end of the Dead Sea,
15. 2 southern border ran from the **south** end of the Dead Sea,
15. 3 of the Dead Sea, [3]went **southwards** from the Akrabbim Pass
15. 3 It ran **south** of Kadesh Barnea, past Hezron and up to Addar,
Josh 15. 4 That was the **southern** border of Judah.
15. 7 which faces Adummim Pass on the **south** side of the valley.
15. 8 Valley of Hinnom on the **south** side of the hill where the
15.21 The cities farthest **south** that belonged to them, those
16. 1 The **southern** boundary of the land assigned to the
17. 7 The border then went **south** to include the people of Entappuah.
17. 9 The cities **south** of the stream belonged to Ephraim, even
17.10 Ephraim was to the **south,** and Manasseh was to the north,
18. 5 in its territory in the **south,** and Joseph in its territory
18.13 to the slope on the **south** side of Luz (also called Bethel),
18.13 to Ataroth Addar, on the mountain **south** of Lower Beth Horon.
18.14 went in another direction, turning **south** from the western
18.15 The **southern** border started on the edge of Kiriath
18.16 It then went **south** through the Valley of Hinnom,
18.16 **south** of the Jebusite ridge, towards Enrogel.
18.19 This was the **southern** border.
19. 8 cities as far as Baalath Beer (or Ramah), in the **south.**
19.34 Hukkok, touching Zebulun on the **south,** Asher on the west,
Judg 1. 9 in the foothills, and in the dry country to the **south.**
1.16 palm-trees, into the barren country **south** of Arad in Judah.
6. 4 and destroy the crops as far **south** as the area round Gaza.
11.22 from the Arnon in the **south** to the Jabbok in the north
20. 1 north to Beersheba in the **south,** as well as from the land
21.19 (Shiloh is north of Bethel, **south** of Lebonah, and east of
1 Sam 14. 5 facing Michmash, and the other was on the **south** side, facing
23.19 Hachilah, in the **southern** part of the Judaean wilderness.
23.24 valley in the **southern** part of the Judaean wilderness.
27.10 he had gone to the **southern** part of Judah or to the
30. 1 The Amalekites had raided **southern** Judah and attacked Ziklag.
30.14 of the Cherethites in the **southern** part of Judah and the
30.27 people in Ramah in the **southern** part of Judah, and to the
2 Sam 24. 5 crossed the Jordan and camped **south** of Aroer, the city in
24. 7 Then they went **south** to the fortified city of Tyre, on to
24. 7 and finally to Beersheba, in the **southern** part of Judah.
1 Kgs 4.12 near the town of Zarethan, **south** of the town of Jezreel, as
6. 8 the annexe was on the **south** side of the Temple, with stairs
7.21 the one on the **south** side was named Jachin, and the one
7.39 of the carts on the **south** side of the Temple, and the
7.49 Holy Place, five on the **south** side and five on the north;
8.65 Hamath Pass in the north and the Egyptian border in the **south.**
2 Kgs 10.33 of the Jordan, as far **south** as the town of Aroer on
14.25 Hamath Pass in the north to the Dead Sea in the **south.**
23.13 had built east of Jerusalem, **south** of the Mount of Olives,
1 Chr 9.24 facing in each direction, north, **south,** east, and west, and
13. 5 Egyptian border in the **south** to Hamath Pass in the north,
26.15 Obed Edom was allotted the **south** gate, and his sons were
26.17 duty each day, on the north, four, and on the **south,** four.
2 Chr 3.17 the one on the **south** side was named Jachin, and the one
4. 6 to be placed on the **south** side of the Temple and five
7. 8 Hamath Pass in the north and the Egyptian border in the **south.**
11.13 territory of Israel priests and Levites came **south** to Judah.
19. 4 people, from Beersheba in the **south** to the edge of the
28.18 the towns in the western foothills and in **southern** Judah.
30. 5 north to Beersheba in the **south,** to come together in
Neh 2.13 on the west and went **south** past Dragon's Fountain to the
11.30 territory between Beersheba in the **south** and the Valley of
Job 9. 9 Great Bear, Orion, the Pleiades, and the stars of the **south.**
23. 9 in the north and the **south,** but still I have not seen
37. 9 storm winds come from the **south,** and the biting cold from
37.17 suffer in the heat when the **south** wind oppresses the land.
39.26 you how to fly when it spreads its wings towards the **south?**
Ps 75. 6 east or from the west, from the north or from the **south;**
78.26 to blow, and by his power he stirred up the **south** wind;
89.12 You created the north and the **south;**
107. 3 countries, from east and west, from north and **south.**
Ecc 1. 6 The wind blows **south,** the wind blows north—round and round
Song 4.16 **South** Wind, blow on my garden;
Is 30. 6 This is God's message about the animals of the **southern** desert:
43. 6 to let them go and the **south** not to hold them back.
49.12 from the north and the west, and from Aswan in the **south."**
Jer 13.19 The towns of **southern** Judah are under siege;
17.26 the foothills, from the mountains, and from **southern** Judah.
32.44 the hill-country, in the foothills, and in **southern** Judah.
33.13 and in **southern** Judah, in the territory of Benjamin,
44. 1 and Memphis, and in the **southern** part of the country.
44.15 the Israelites who lived in **southern** Egypt—a large crowd in
Ezek 6.14 it a waste from the **southern** desert to the city of Riblah
10. 3 creatures were standing to the **south** of the Temple when he
16.46 Your younger sister, with her villages, is Sodom, in the **south.**
20.46 "Mortal man," he said, "look towards the **south.**
20.46 Speak against the **south** and prophesy against the forest of the south.
20.47 Tell the **southern** forest to hear what the Sovereign Lord
20.47 It will spread from **south** to north, and everyone will feel
21. 4 I will use my sword against everyone from north to **south.**
29.10 city of Aswan in the **south,** all the way to the Sudanese
29.14 I will let them live in **southern** Egypt, their original home.
30. 6 north to Aswan in the **south,** all Egypt's defenders will be
30.14 I will make **southern** Egypt desolate and set fire to the
40.24 man took me to the **south** side, and there we saw another
40.28 man took me through the **south** gateway into the inner courtyard.
40.44 one facing **south** beside the north gateway
40.44 and the other facing north beside the **south** gateway.
40.45 that the room which faced **south** was for the priests who
41. 8 side of the Temple, and one into those on the **south** side.
42. 9 At the **south** side of the Temple there was an identical
42.12 under the rooms on the **south** side of the building, at the
42.17 measured the north side, the **south** side, and the west side;
46. 9 are to leave by the **south** gate after they have worshipped,
46. 9 those who enter by the **south** gate are to leave by the
46.19 near the gate on the **south** side of the inner courtyard.

Ezek 47. 1 flowing down from under the **south** part of the temple
47. 1 past the **south** side of the altar.
47. 2 of water was flowing out at the **south** side of the gate.
47.18 "The eastern boundary runs **south** from a point between
47.19 "The **southern** boundary runs south-west from Tamar to
48. 1 Mediterranean Sea, in the following order from north to **south:**
48. 8 kilometres wide from north to **south,** and the same length
48.10 a half kilometres, and from north to **south,** five kilometres.
48.13 are to have a special area, **south** of that of the priests.
48.13 five kilometres from north to **south.**
48.18 the area immediately to the **south** of the holy area—five
48.21 Judah and on the **south** by the section belonging to Benjamin.
48.23 **South** of this special section, each of the
48.23 Mediterranean Sea, in the following order from north to **south:**
48.28 On the **south** side of the portion given to the tribe of
48.30 those in the **south** wall, after Simeon, Issachar, and
Dan 8. 4 with his horns to the west, the north, and the **south.**
8. 9 whose power extended towards the **south** and the east and
Amos 6.14 in the north to the brook of the Arabah in the **south."**
Obad 19 "People from **southern** Judah will occupy Edom;
20 who are in Sardis will capture the towns of **southern** Judah.
Mic 7.12 from Egypt in the **south,** from the region of the Euphrates,
Zech 6. 6 the dappled horses were going to the country in the **south.**
7. 7 also in the **southern** region and in the western foothills.
9.14 he will march in the storms from the **south.**
14. 4 Half the mountain will move northwards and half of it **southwards.**
14.10 in the north to Rimmon in the **south,** will be made level.
Lk 12.55 And when you feel the **south** wind blowing, you say that
13.29 from the north and the **south,** and sit down at the feast
Acts 8.26 Philip, "Get ready and go **south** to the road that goes from
21. 3 could see Cyprus, and then sailed **south** of it on to Syria.
27.13 A soft wind from the **south** began to blow, and the men
27.16 when we passed to the **south** of the little island of Cauda.
28.13 began to blow from the **south,** and in two days we came
Rev 21.13 the east, three on the **south,** three on the north, and three

SOUTH-EAST

1 Kgs 7.39 the tank he placed at the **south-east** corner.
2 Chr 4.10 The tank was placed near the **south-east** corner of the Temple.

SOUTH-WEST

1 Chr 4.33 surrounding villages, as far **south-west** as the town of Baalath.
Ezek 47.19 "The southern boundary runs **south-west** from Tamar to
48.28 of Gad, the boundary runs **south-west** from Tamar to the oasis
Acts 27.12 Phoenix is a harbour in Crete that faces **south-west** and north-west.

SOVEREIGN

Gen 15. 2 Abram answered, **"Sovereign Lord,** what good will your reward
15. 8 But Abram asked, **"Sovereign Lord,** how can I know that it
Deut 3.24 that time I earnestly prayed, [24] **'Sovereign Lord,** I know
9.26 And I prayed, **'Sovereign Lord,** don't destroy your own people,
Josh 7. 7 And Joshua said, **"Sovereign Lord!**
Judg 6.22 Lord's angel he had seen, and he said in terror, **"Sovereign Lord!**
16.28 Then Samson prayed, **"Sovereign Lord,** please remember me;
2 Sam 7.18 have already done for me, **Sovereign Lord,** nor is my family.
7.19 Yet now you are doing even more, **Sovereign Lord;**
7.19 And you let a man see this, **Sovereign Lord!**
7.22 How great you are, **Sovereign Lord!**
7.28 "And now, **Sovereign Lord,** you are God;
7.29 You, **Sovereign Lord,** have promised this, and your blessing
1 Kgs 8.52 **"Sovereign Lord,** may you always look with favour on
Ps 69. 6 shame on those who trust in you, **Sovereign Lord** Almighty!
71. 5 **Sovereign Lord,** I put my hope in you;
71.16 I will praise your power, **Sovereign Lord;**
73.28 to find protection with the **Sovereign Lord** and to proclaim
109.21 But my **Sovereign Lord,** help me as you have promised, and
140. 7 My **Sovereign Lord,** my strong defender, you have protected me
141. 8 But I keep trusting in you, my **Sovereign Lord.**
Is 3.15 I, the **Sovereign Lord** Almighty, have spoken."
10.23 country the **Sovereign Lord** Almighty will bring destruction,
10.24 The **Sovereign Lord** Almighty says to his people who live in Zion,
22. 5 Valley of Vision, and the **Sovereign Lord** Almighty has sent
22.12 **Sovereign Lord** Almighty was calling you then to weep and mourn,
22.14 The **Sovereign Lord** Almighty himself spoke to me and said,
22.14 I, the **Sovereign Lord** Almighty, have spoken."
22.15 The **Sovereign Lord** Almighty told me to go to Shebna, the
25. 8 The **Sovereign Lord** will destroy death for ever!
28.16 This, now, is what the **Sovereign Lord** says:
30.15 **Sovereign Lord,** the holy God of Israel, says to the people,
40.10 The **Sovereign Lord** is coming to rule with power,
48.16 (Now the **Sovereign Lord** has given me his power and sent me.)
49.22 The **Sovereign Lord** says to his people:
50. 4 The **Sovereign Lord** has taught me what to say, so that I
50. 7 cannot hurt me because the **Sovereign Lord** gives me help.
50. 9 The **Sovereign Lord** himself defends me— who, then, can
52. 3 The **Sovereign Lord** says to his people, "When you became slaves,
56. 8 The **Sovereign Lord,** who has brought his people Israel home
61. 1 The **Sovereign Lord** has filled me with his spirit.
61.11 sprout and grow, The **Sovereign Lord** will save his people,
65.15 I, the **Sovereign Lord,** will put you to death.
Jer 1. 6 I answered, **"Sovereign Lord,** I don't know how to speak;
2.19 I, the **Sovereign Lord** Almighty, have spoken."
2.20 The **Sovereign Lord** says,
4.10 Then I said, **"Sovereign Lord,** you have completely
7.20 And so I, the **Sovereign Lord,** will pour out my fierce
14.13 Then I said, **"Sovereign Lord,** you know that the
32.17 purchase to Baruch, I prayed, [17] **"Sovereign Lord,** you made
Jer 32.25 Yet, **Sovereign Lord,** you are the one who ordered me to
44.26 a vow by saying, 'I swear by the living **Sovereign Lord!'**
46.10 This is the day of the **Sovereign Lord** Almighty:
50.25 them out, because I, the **Sovereign Lord** Almighty, have work
50.31 pride, so I, the **Sovereign Lord** Almighty, am against you!
Ezek 2. 4 to tell them what I, the **Sovereign Lord,** am saying to them.
3.11 tell them what I, the **Sovereign Lord,** am saying to them,
3.27 speech, you will tell them what I, the **Sovereign Lord,** am
4.14 But I replied, "No, **Sovereign Lord!**
5. 5 The **Sovereign Lord** said, "Look at Jerusalem.
5. 7 Now listen, Jerusalem, to what I, the **Sovereign Lord,** am
5. 8 And so I, the **Sovereign Lord,** am telling you that I am
5.11 is the word of the **Sovereign Lord**—because you defiled my
6. 3 hear what I, the **Sovereign Lord,** am telling the mountains,
6.11 The **Sovereign Lord** said, "Wring your hands!
7. 2 "this is what I, the **Sovereign Lord,** am saying to the land
7. 5 This is what the **Sovereign Lord** is saying, "One disaster
8. 1 Suddenly the power of the **Sovereign Lord** came on me.
9. 8 on the ground and shouted, **"Sovereign Lord,** are you so
11. 7 "So this is what I, the **Sovereign Lord,** am saying to you.
11.13 downwards on the ground and shouted, "No, **Sovereign Lord!**
11.17 "So tell them what I, the **Sovereign Lord,** am saying.
11.21 The **Sovereign Lord** has spoken.
12.10 tell them what I, the **Sovereign Lord,** am saying to them.
12.19 is the message of the **Sovereign Lord** to the people of
12.23 them what I, the **Sovereign Lord,** have to say about that.
12.25 I have spoken," says the **Sovereign Lord.**
12.28 So tell them that I, the **Sovereign Lord,** am saying:
12.28 I, the **Sovereign Lord,** have spoken!"
13. 3 This is what the **Sovereign Lord** says:
13. 8 So the **Sovereign Lord** says to them, "Your words are false,
13. 9 Then you will know that I am the **Sovereign Lord.**
13.13 Now this is what the **Sovereign Lord** says:
13.16 The **Sovereign Lord** has spoken.
13.18 and tell them what the **Sovereign Lord** is saying to them:
13.20 Now this is what the **Sovereign Lord** says:
14. 4 and tell them what I, the **Sovereign Lord,** am saying to them:
14. 6 "Now then, tell the Israelites what I, the **Sovereign Lord,**
14.11 The **Sovereign Lord** has spoken.
14.14 The **Sovereign Lord** has spoken.
14.16 as surely as I, the **Sovereign Lord,** am the living God—they
14.18 as surely as I, the **Sovereign Lord,** am the living God—they
14.20 as surely as I, the **Sovereign Lord,** am the living God—they
14.21 This is what the **Sovereign Lord** is saying:
14.23 The **Sovereign Lord** has spoken.
15. 6 Now this is what the **Sovereign Lord** is saying, "Just as a
15. 8 The **Sovereign Lord** has spoken.
16. 3 Tell Jerusalem what the **Sovereign Lord** is saying to her:
16. 8 This is what the **Sovereign Lord** says.
16.14 This is what the **Sovereign Lord** says.
16.19 This is what the **Sovereign Lord** says.
16.23 The **Sovereign Lord** said, "You are doomed!
16.30 This is what the **Sovereign Lord** is saying:
16.36 This is what the **Sovereign Lord** says:
16.43 The **Sovereign Lord** has spoken.
16.48 am the living God," the **Sovereign Lord** says, "your sister
16.59 The **Sovereign Lord** says, "I will treat you as you deserve,
16.63 The **Sovereign Lord** has spoken.
17. 3 let them know what I, the **Sovereign Lord,** am saying to them:
17. 9 "So I, the **Sovereign Lord,** ask:
17.16 the living God," says the **Sovereign Lord,** "this king will
17.19 The **Sovereign Lord** says, "As surely as I am the living God,
17.22 This is what the **Sovereign Lord** says:
18. 3 the living God," says the **Sovereign Lord,** "you will not
18. 9 He is righteous, and he will live," says the **Sovereign Lord.**
18.23 asks the **Sovereign Lord.**
18.30 "Now I, the **Sovereign Lord,** am telling you Israelites
18.32 I do not want anyone to die," says the **Sovereign Lord.**
20. 3 these men and tell them that the **Sovereign Lord** is saying:
20. 3 I, the **Sovereign Lord,** have spoken.
20.27 Israelites what I, the **Sovereign Lord,** am saying to them.
20.30 Now tell the Israelites what I, the **Sovereign Lord,** am
20.31 As surely as I, the **Sovereign Lord,** am the living God, I
20.33 "As surely as I, the **Sovereign Lord,** am the living God,
20.36 your fathers in the Sinai Desert," says the **Sovereign Lord.**
20.39 The **Sovereign Lord** said, "And now, all you Israelites,
20.44 The **Sovereign Lord** has spoken.
20.47 Tell the southern forest to hear what the **Sovereign Lord**
20.49 But I protested, **"Sovereign Lord,** don't make me do it!
21. 7 The **Sovereign Lord** has spoken.
21.24 This then is what I, the **Sovereign Lord,** am saying:
21.26 I, the **Sovereign Lord,** have spoken.
21.28 Announce what I, the **Sovereign Lord,** am saying to the Ammonites,
22. 3 Tell the city what I, the **Sovereign Lord,** am saying:
22.12 The **Sovereign Lord** has spoken.
22.19 So now I, the **Sovereign Lord,** am telling them that they
22.28 speak the word of the **Sovereign Lord,** but I, the Lord, have
22.31 The **Sovereign Lord** has spoken.
23.22 this is what I, the **Sovereign Lord,** am saying to you.
23.28 This is what the **Sovereign Lord** says:
23.32 The **Sovereign Lord** says,
23.34 I, the **Sovereign Lord,** have spoken."
23.35 Now this is what the **Sovereign Lord** is saying:
23.46 This is what the **Sovereign Lord** says:
23.49 Then you will know that I am the **Sovereign Lord."**
24. 3 this parable that I, the **Sovereign Lord,** have for them:
24. 6 This is what the **Sovereign Lord** is saying:
24. 9 This is what the **Sovereign Lord** is saying:
24.14 I, the **Sovereign Lord,** have spoken.
24.14 The **Sovereign Lord** has spoken.

Ezek 24.24 happens, you will know that he is the **Sovereign Lord."**
25. 3 Tell them to listen to what I, the **Sovereign Lord,** am
25. 6 "This is what the **Sovereign Lord** is saying:
25. 8 The **Sovereign Lord** said, "Because Moab has said that
25.12 The **Sovereign Lord** said, "The people of Edom took cruel
25.14 The **Sovereign Lord** has spoken.
25.15 The **Sovereign Lord** said, "The Philistines have taken
26. 3 "Now then, this is what I, the **Sovereign Lord,** am saying:
26. 5 I, the **Sovereign Lord,** have spoken.
26. 7 The **Sovereign Lord** says, "I am going to bring the
26.14 I, the **Sovereign Lord,** have spoken."
26.15 The **Sovereign Lord** has this to say to the city of Tyre:
26.19 The **Sovereign Lord** says:
26.21 The **Sovereign Lord** has spoken.
27. 3 Tell her what the **Sovereign Lord** is saying:
28. 2 ruler of Tyre what I, the **Sovereign Lord,** am saying to him:
28. 6 "Now then, this is what I, the **Sovereign Lord,** am saying:
28.10 I, the **Sovereign Lord,** have given the command."
28.12 Tell him what I, the **Sovereign Lord,** am saying:
28.22 Tell the people there what I, the **Sovereign Lord,** say
28.24 And they will know that I am the **Sovereign Lord."**
28.25 The **Sovereign Lord** said, "I will bring back the people
29. 3 that this is what the **Sovereign Lord** is telling the king of
29. 8 Now then, I, the **Sovereign Lord,** am telling you that I
29.13 The **Sovereign Lord** says, "After forty years I will
29.16 Then Israel will know that I am the **Sovereign Lord."**
29.19 So now this is what I, the **Sovereign Lord,** am saying:
29.20 I, the **Sovereign Lord,** have spoken.
30. 2 he said, "prophesy and announce what I, the **Sovereign Lord,**
30. 6 I, the **Sovereign Lord,** have spoken.
30.10 The **Sovereign Lord** says, "I will use King
30.13 The **Sovereign Lord** says, "I will destroy the idols and
30.22 Now then, this is what I, the **Sovereign Lord,** say:
31.10 "Now then, I, the **Sovereign Lord,** will tell you what is
31.15 This is what the **Sovereign Lord** says:
31.18 I have spoken," says the **Sovereign Lord.**
32. 8 I, the **Sovereign Lord,** have spoken.
32.11 The **Sovereign Lord** says to the king of Egypt, "You will
32.14 I, the **Sovereign Lord,** have spoken.
32.16 I, the **Sovereign Lord,** have spoken."
32.31 the king of Egypt and his army," says the **Sovereign Lord.**
32.32 The **Sovereign Lord** has spoken.
33.11 as surely as I, the **Sovereign Lord,** am the living God, I
33.25 "Tell them what I, the **Sovereign Lord,** am saying:
33.27 "Tell them that I, the **Sovereign Lord,** warn them that
34. 2 them, and tell them what I, the **Sovereign Lord,** say to them:
34.10 I, the **Sovereign Lord,** declare that I am your enemy.
34.11 "I, the **Sovereign Lord,** tell you that I myself will
34.15 I, the **Sovereign Lord,** have spoken.
34.17 then, my flock, I, the **Sovereign Lord,** tell you that I will
34.20 "So now, I, the **Sovereign Lord,** tell you that I will
34.30 I, the **Sovereign Lord,** have spoken.
34.31 my people, and I am your God," says the **Sovereign Lord.**
35. 3 Tell the people what I, the **Sovereign Lord,** am saying:
35. 6 as surely as I, the **Sovereign Lord,** am the living God—death
35.11 as surely as I, the **Sovereign Lord,** am the living God, I
35.14 The **Sovereign Lord** says, "I will make you so desolate
36. 2 listen to the message which I, [2]the **Sovereign Lord,** have
36. 3 "Prophesy, then, and announce what I, the **Sovereign Lord,**
36. 4 listen to what I, the **Sovereign Lord,** say to you mountains
36. 5 "I, the **Sovereign Lord,** have spoken out in the heat of my
36. 6 and valleys what I, the **Sovereign Lord,** am saying in jealous
36. 7 I, the **Sovereign Lord,** solemnly promise that the
36.13 "I, the **Sovereign Lord,** say:
36.14 I, the **Sovereign Lord,** have spoken.
36.15 I, the **Sovereign Lord,** have spoken."
36.22 the Israelites the message that I, the **Sovereign Lord,** have
36.23 I, the **Sovereign Lord,** have spoken.
36.32 I, the **Sovereign Lord,** have spoken."
36.33 The **Sovereign Lord** says, "When I make you clean from
36.37 The **Sovereign Lord** says, "I will once again let the
37. 3 I replied, **"Sovereign Lord,** only you can answer that!"
37. 5 Tell them that I, the **Sovereign Lord,** am saying to them:
37. 9 Tell the wind that the **Sovereign Lord** commands it to come
37.12 tell them that I, the **Sovereign Lord,** am going to open their
37.19 tell them that I, the **Sovereign Lord,** am going to take
37.21 tell them that I, the **Sovereign Lord,** am going to take all
38. 3 him, [3]and tell him that I, the **Sovereign Lord,** am his
38.10 This is what the **Sovereign Lord** says to Gog:
38.14 So the **Sovereign Lord** sent me to tell Gog what he was
38.17 The **Sovereign Lord** has spoken.
38.18 The **Sovereign Lord** says, "On the day when Gog invades Israel,
38.21 I, the **Sovereign Lord,** have spoken.
39. 1 The **Sovereign Lord** said, "Mortal man, denounce Gog, the
39. 5 I, the **Sovereign Lord,** have spoken.
39. 8 The **Sovereign Lord** said, "The day I spoke about is
39.10 The **Sovereign Lord** has spoken.
39.13 I, the **Sovereign Lord,** have spoken.
39.17 The **Sovereign Lord** said to me, "Mortal man, call all
39.20 I, the **Sovereign Lord,** have spoken."
39.25 The **Sovereign Lord** said, "But now I will be merciful to
39.29 I, the **Sovereign Lord,** have spoken."
43.18 The **Sovereign Lord** said to me, "Mortal man, listen to
43.19 I, the **Sovereign Lord,** command this.
43.27 I, the **Sovereign Lord,** have spoken."
44. 6 of Israel that I, the **Sovereign Lord,** will no longer
44. 9 "I, the **Sovereign Lord,** declare that no uncircumcised
44.12 people into sin, I, the **Sovereign Lord,** solemnly swear that
44.15 The **Sovereign Lord** said, "Those priests belonging to
44.27 I, the **Sovereign Lord,** have spoken.
45. 9 The **Sovereign Lord** said, "You have sinned too long, you
Ezek 45. 9 I, the **Sovereign Lord,** am telling you this.
45.13 I, the **Sovereign Lord,** command it.
45.18 The **Sovereign Lord** said, "On the first day of the first
46. 1 The **Sovereign Lord** says, "The east gateway to the inner
46.16 The **Sovereign Lord** commands:
47.13 The **Sovereign Lord** said, "These are the boundaries of
47.23 I, the **Sovereign Lord,** have spoken."
48.29 The **Sovereign Lord** said, "That is the way the land is
Amos 3. 7 The **Sovereign Lord** never does anything without revealing
3. 8 When the **Sovereign Lord** speaks, who can avoid proclaiming
3.13 descendants of Jacob," says the **Sovereign Lord** Almighty.
4. 2 As the **Sovereign Lord** is holy, he has promised, "The days
4. 4 The **Sovereign Lord** says, "People of Israel, go to the
5. 3 The **Sovereign Lord** says, "A city in Israel sends out a
5.16 And so the **Sovereign Lord** Almighty says, "There will
6. 8 The **Sovereign Lord** Almighty has given this solemn warning:
7. 1 I had a vision from the **Sovereign Lord.**
7. 2 and then I said, **"Sovereign Lord,** forgive your people!
7. 4 I had another vision from the **Sovereign Lord.**
7. 5 Then I said, "Stop, **Sovereign Lord!**
8. 1 I had another vision from the **Sovereign Lord.**
8. 9 I, the **Sovereign Lord,** have spoken.
8.11 I, the **Sovereign Lord,** have spoken.
9. 5 The **Sovereign Lord** Almighty touches the earth, and it quakes;
9. 8 I, the **Sovereign Lord,** am watching this sinful kingdom
Obad 1 prophecy of Obadiah—what the **Sovereign Lord** said about the
Mic 1. 2 The **Sovereign Lord** will testify against you.
Hab 3.19 The **Sovereign Lord** gives me strength.
Zech 9.14 The **Sovereign Lord** will sound the trumpet;

SOW

Gen 26.12 Isaac **sowed** seed in that land, and that year he
26.12 times as much as he had **sown,** because the Lord blessed him.
47.19 corn to keep us alive and seed to **sow** in our fields."
47.23 Here is seed for you to **sow** in your fields.
Ex 23.10 "For six years **sow** your field and gather in what it produces.
Lev 11.37 on seed that is going to be **sown,** the seed remains clean.
25. 3 You shall **sow** your fields, prune your vineyards, and
25. 4 Do not **sow** your fields or prune your vineyards.
25. 5 grows by itself without being **sown,** and do not gather the
25.11 You shall not **sow** your fields or harvest the corn that
25.20 seventh year, when no fields are **sown** and no crops gathered.
25.22 When you **sow** your fields in the eighth year, you will
26. 5 will still be picking grapes when it is time to **sow** corn.
26.16 You will **sow** your seed, but it will do you no good,
27.16 of seed it takes to **sow** it, at the rate of ten
Deut 11.10 There, when you **sowed** seed, you had to work hard to irrigate
28.38 "You will **sow** plenty of seed, but reap only a small harvest,
Judg 6. 3 Whenever the Israelites **sowed** any seed, the Midianites
2 Kgs 19.29 you will be able to **sow** your corn and harvest it, and
Job 4. 8 people plough fields of evil and **sow** wickedness like seed;
Ps 107.37 They **sowed** the fields and planted grapevines and reaped
126. 5 those who wept as they **sowed** their seed, gather the harvest
Prov 22. 8 If you **sow** the seeds of injustice, disaster will spring up,
Ecc 11. 4 you will never **sow** anything and never harvest anything.
11. 6 Do your **sowing** in the morning and in the evening, too.
11. 6 well or whether one **sowing** will do better than the other.
Is 19. 7 wither, [7]and all the crops **sown** along the banks of the Nile
28.24 ploughing his fields and getting them ready for **sowing.**
28.25 has prepared the soil, he **sows** the seeds of herbs such as
28.25 He **sows** rows of wheat and barley,
28.25 and at the edges of his fields he **sows** other grain.
30.23 Whenever you **sow** your seeds, the Lord will send rain to
37.30 you will be able to **sow** your corn and harvest it, and
55.10 the crops grow and provide seed for **sowing** and food to eat.
62. 9 But you that **sowed** and harvested the corn Will eat the
Jer 2. 2 through the desert, through a land that had not been **sown.**
4. 3 do not **sow** your seeds among thorns.
12.13 My people **sowed** wheat, but gathered weeds;
50.16 Do not let seeds be **sown** in that country or let a
Ezek 36. 9 your land is ploughed again and that seeds are **sown** there.
Hos 8. 7 When they **sow** the wind, they will reap a storm!
Mic 6.15 You will **sow** corn, but not harvest the crop.
Hag 1. 6 You have **sown** much corn, but have harvested very little.
Zech 8.12 They will **sow** their crops in peace.
Mt 6.26 they do not **sow** seeds, gather a harvest and put it in
13. 3 "Once there was a man who went out to **sow** corn.
13.18 "Listen, then, and learn what the parable of the **sower** means.
13.19 The Evil One comes and snatches away what was **sown** in them.
13.23 And the seeds **sown** in the good soil stand for those who
13.24 A man **sowed** good seed in his field.
13.25 asleep, an enemy came and **sowed** weeds among the wheat and
13.27 and said, 'Sir, it was good seed you **sowed** in your field;
13.31 A man takes a mustard seed and **sows** it in his field.
13.37 Jesus answered, "The man who **sowed** the good seed is the
13.39 and the enemy who **sowed** the weeds is the Devil.
25.24 harvests where you did not **sow,** and you gather crops where
25.26 harvests where I did not **sow,** and gather crops where I did
Mk 4. 3 Once there was a man who went out to **sow** corn.
4.14 The **sower** sows God's message.
4.18 Other people are like the seeds **sown** among the thorn bushes.
4.20 But other people are like the seeds **sown** in good soil.
Lk 8. 5 "Once there was a man who went out to **sow** corn.
12.24 they don't **sow** seeds or gather a harvest;
13.19 A man takes a mustard seed and **sows** it in his field.
19.21 take what is not yours and reap what you did not **sow.'**
19.22 taking what is not mine and reaping what I have not **sown.**
Jn 4.36 so the man who **sows** and the man who reaps will be
4.37 The saying is true, 'One man **sows,** another man reaps.'
1 Cor 3. 6 I **sowed** the seed, Apollos watered the plant, but it was

1 Cor 3. 7 The one who **sows** and the one who waters really do not
3. 8 difference between the man who **sows** and the man who waters;
9.11 We have **sown** spiritual seed among you.
15.36 When you **sow** a seed in the ground, it does not sprout
15.37 And what you **sow** is a bare seed, perhaps a grain of
2 Cor 9. 6 Remember that the person who **sows** few seeds will have a
9. 6 the one who **sows** many seeds will have a large crop.
9.10 God, who supplies seed to **sow** and bread to eat, will also
Gal 6. 7 A person will reap exactly what he **sows.**
6. 8 If he **sows** in the field of his natural desires, from it
6. 8 if he **sows** in the field of the Spirit, from the Spirit

SPACE (1)

Gen 6.16 the boat and leave a **space** of 44 centimetres between the
32.16 of me, and leave a **space** between each herd and the one
Ex 3. 8 out of Egypt to a **spacious** land, one which is rich and
2 Sam 18.24 David was sitting in the **space** between the inner and
1 Kgs 7.36 and palm-trees, wherever there was **space** for them, with
Jer 22.14 "I will build myself a mansion with **spacious** rooms upstairs."
Ezek 40.11 half metres altogether, and the **space** between the open gates
41. 8 priests there was an open **space** ten metres across, along the
41.12 far end of the open **space** on the west side of the
41.13 the Temple, across the open **space** to the far side of the
41.14 the Temple, including the open **space** on either side, was
42. 3 one side it faced the **space** ten metres wide which was
45. 2 surrounded by an open **space** twenty-five metres wide.
48.17 on each side there will be an open **space** 125 metres across.

SPACE (2)

Job 26. 7 out the northern sky and hung the earth in empty **space.**
Mt 24.29 the powers in **space** will be driven from their courses.
Mk 13.25 the powers in **space** will be driven from their courses.
Lk 21.26 the powers in **space** will be driven from their courses.
Eph 2. 2 spiritual powers in **space,** the spirit who now controls

SPAIN

Country at the w. end of the Mediterranean Sea, called "Tarshish" in other translations.

Gen 10. 4 descendants of Javan were the people of Elishah, **Spain,**
1 Chr 1. 7 descendants of Javan were the people of Elishah, **Spain,**
Ps 72.10 The kings of **Spain** and of the islands will offer him gifts;
Is 23. 6 Try to escape to **Spain!**
23.10 Go and farm the land, you people in the colonies in **Spain!**
66.19 to **Spain,** Libya, and Lydia, with its skilled bowmen,
Jer 10. 9 are covered with silver from **Spain** and with gold from Uphaz,
Ezek 27.12 "You did business in **Spain** and took silver, iron, tin,
38.13 merchants from the towns of **Spain** will ask you, 'Have you
Jon 1. 3 to Joppa, where he found a ship about to go to **Spain.**
1. 3 the crew to sail to **Spain,** where he would be away from
4. 2 That's why I did my best to run away to **Spain!**
Rom 15.24 on my way to **Spain,** and be helped by you
15.28 I shall leave for **Spain** and visit you on my way

SPANKING

Prov 22.15 things, but a good **spanking** will teach them how to behave.
23.13 A good **spanking** won't kill him.

SPARE

Gen 18.24 Won't you **spare** it in order to save the fifty?
18.26 in Sodom, I will **spare** the whole city for their sake."
42.18 God-fearing man, and I will **spare** your lives on one condition.
Ex 4.25 And so the Lord **spared** Moses' life.
8.22 But I will **spare** the region of Goshen, where my people live,
12.27 He killed the Egyptians, but **spared** us.' "
Num 22.33 If it hadn't, I would have killed you and **spared** the donkey."
Deut 32.25 neither babies nor old men will be **spared.**
32.42 I will **spare** no one who fights against me;
Josh 6.17 Rahab and her household will be **spared,** because she hid our
6.25 But Joshua **spared** the lives of the prostitute Rahab and
10.30 They **spared** no one, but killed every person in it.
10.32 had done at Libnah, they **spared** no one, but killed every
10.40 He **spared** no one;
1 Sam 15. 9 But Saul and his men **spared** Agag's life and did not kill
24.21 Lord's name that you will **spare** my descendants, so that my
26.21 harm you again, because you have **spared** my life tonight.
26.24 Just as I have **spared** your life today, may the Lord do
2 Sam 21. 7 to each other, David **spared** Jonathan's son Mephibosheth,
1 Kgs 20.31 ropes round our necks, and maybe he will **spare** your life."
2 Kgs 1.13 **Spare** our lives!
7. 4 can do is kill us, but maybe they will **spare** our lives."
10.17 Jehu killed all of Ahab's relatives, not **sparing** even one.
1 Chr 21.17 my God, punish me and my family, and **spare** your people."
2 Chr 36.15 his people, because he wanted to **spare** them and the Temple.
Neh 13.22 for this also, and **spare** me because of your great love.
Esth 4.11 gold sceptre to someone, then that person's life is **spared.**
Job 21.30 and punishes, it is the wicked man who is always **spared.**
33.27 I have not done right, but God **spared** me.
Ps 26. 9 **spare** me from the fate of murderers— [10]men who do evil
34.22 those who go to him for protection will be **spared.**
51.14 **Spare** my life, O God, and save me, and I will gladly
78.50 not restrain his anger or **spare** their lives, but killed them
119.80 obey your commandments and be **spared** the shame of defeat.
Is 28.15 are certain that disaster will **spare** you when it comes,
66.19 "But I will **spare** some of them and send them to the
Jer 6.11 be taken away, and even the very old will not be **spared.**
17.18 Bring disgrace on those who persecute me, but **spare** me,
Jer 21. 7 He will not **spare** any of you or show mercy or pity
21.10 up my mind not to **spare** this city, but to destroy it.
38.17 officers, your life will be **spared,** and this city will not
38.17 Both you and your family will be **spared.**
38.20 all will go well with you, and your life will be **spared.**
41. 8 So he **spared** them.
50.20 I will forgive those people whose lives I have **spared.**
51. 3 Do not **spare** the young men!
Ezek 3.19 he will die, still a sinner, but your life will be **spared.**
3.21 he will stay alive, and your life will also be **spared."**
6.14 not **sparing** any place where the Israelites live.
7. 4 I will not **spare** you or show you any mercy.
7. 9 I will not **spare** you or show you any mercy.
8.18 I will not **spare** them or show them any mercy.
9. 5 **Spare** no one;
33. 9 will die, still a sinner, but your life will be **spared."**
33.12 if a good man starts sinning, his life will not be **spared.**
Dan 11.42 he invades all those countries, even Egypt will not be **spared.**
Joel 3.20 I will not **spare** the guilty.
Jon 1. 6 Maybe he will feel sorry for us and **spare** our lives."
Mk 12.44 the others put in what they had to **spare** of their riches;
Lk 21. 4 their gifts from what they had to **spare** of their riches;
Acts 20.29 will come among you, and they will not **spare** the flock.
27.24 his goodness to you has **spared** the lives of all those who
Rom 11.21 God did not **spare** the Jews, who are like natural branches;
11.21 do you think he will **spare** you?
1 Cor 7.28 But I would rather **spare** you the everyday troubles that
2 Cor 1.23 It was in order to **spare** you that I decided not to
Phil 2.27 him but on me, too, and **spared** me an even greater sorrow.
2 Pet 2. 4 God did not **spare** the angels who sinned, but threw them
2. 5 God did not **spare** the ancient world, but brought the flood

SPARK

Job 5. 7 trouble on himself, as surely as **sparks** fly up from a fire.
41.19 Flames blaze from his mouth, and streams of **sparks** fly out.
Is 1.31 set on fire by a **spark,** so powerful men will be destroyed

SPARKLE

1 Sam 16.12 He was a handsome, healthy young man, and his eyes **sparkled.**
2 Sam 23. 4 dawn, the sun that makes the grass **sparkle** after rain."
Prov 23.31 is rich red, though it **sparkles** in the cup, and it goes
Is 26.19 As the **sparkling** dew refreshes the earth, so the Lord will
Ezek 28.14 You lived on my holy mountain and walked among **sparkling** gems.
28.16 who guarded you drove you away from the **sparkling** gems.
Rev 22. 1 of the water of life, **sparkling** like crystal, and coming

SPARROW

Ps 84. 3 Even the **sparrows** have built a nest, and the swallows have
Mt 10.29 penny you can buy two **sparrows,** yet not one sparrow falls
10.31 you are worth much more than many **sparrows!**
Lk 12. 6 "Aren't five **sparrows** sold for two pennies?
12. 6 Yet not one **sparrow** is forgotten by God.
12. 7 you are worth much more than many **sparrows!**

SPATTERED

Lev 6.27 article of clothing is **spattered** with the animal's blood,
2 Kgs 9.33 her down, and her blood **spattered** the wall and the horses.

SPEAK

[SPOKE, SPOKE EVIL, SPOKEN, SPOKEN AGAINST]

Gen 10. 5 tribes and countries, each group **speaking** its own language.
10.20 tribes and countries, each group **speaking** its own language.
10.31 tribes and countries, each group **speaking** its own language.
11. 6 these are all one people and they **speak** one language;
15. 4 Then he heard the Lord **speaking** to him again:
16.13 called the Lord who had **spoken** to her "A God Who Sees."
17.22 When God finished **speaking** to Abraham, he left him.
18.27 Abraham **spoke** again:
18.27 "Please forgive my boldness in continuing to **speak** to you,
18.29 Abraham **spoke** again:
18.30 "Please don't be angry, Lord, but I must **speak** again.
18.31 "Please forgive my boldness in continuing to **speak** to you,
18.32 "Please don't be angry, Lord, and I will **speak** just once more.
18.33 After he had finished **speaking** with Abraham, the Lord went
21.17 heaven the angel of God **spoke** to Hagar, "What are you
22.16 own name—the Lord is **speaking**—that I will richly bless you.
24.33 Laban said, "Go on and **speak."**
31.11 The angel of God **spoke** to me in the dream and said,
34.20 at the city gate and **spoke** to their fellow-townsmen:
35.14 There, where God had **spoken** to him, Jacob set up a
37. 4 much that they would not **speak** to him in a friendly manner.
42.23 they had been **speaking** to him through an interpreter.
42.24 When he was able to **speak** again, he came back, picked out
42.30 "The governor of Egypt **spoke** harshly to us and accused
44.18 and said, "Please, sir, allow me to **speak** with you freely.
46. 2 God **spoke** to him in a vision at night and called, "Jacob,
49.28 their father said as he **spoke** a suitable word of farewell to
Ex 1.15 Then the king of Egypt **spoke** to Shiphrah and Puah, the
4. 6 Lord **spoke** to Moses again, "Put your hand inside your robe."
4.10 have never been a good **speaker,** and I haven't become one
4.10 and I haven't become one since you began to **speak** to me.
4.10 I am a poor **speaker,** slow and hesitant."
4.12 I will help you to **speak,** and I will tell you what
4.14 I know that he can **speak** well.
4.15 You can **speak** to him and tell him what to say.

Ex	4.15	help both of you to **speak,** and I will tell you both
	4.16	He will be your spokesman and **speak** to the people for you.
	5.23	went to the king to **speak** for you, he has treated them
	6. 2	God **spoke** to Moses and said, "I am the Lord.
	6.12	I am such a poor **speaker."**
	6.28	When the Lord **spoke** to Moses in the land of Egypt,
	6.30	But Moses answered, "You know that I am such a poor **speaker;**
	7. 1	and your brother Aaron will **speak** to him as your prophet.
	7. 7	At the time when they **spoke** to the king, Moses was eighty
	11. 2	Now **speak** to the people of Israel and tell all of them
	12. 1	The Lord **spoke** to Moses and Aaron in Egypt:
	16.10	As Aaron **spoke** to the whole community, they turned towards
	19. 9	the people will hear me **speaking** with you and will believe
	19.19	Moses **spoke,** and God answered him with thunder.
	20. 1	God **spoke,** and these were his words:
	20.19	They said to Moses, "If you **speak** to us, we will listen;
	20.19	we are afraid that if God **speaks** to us, we will die."
	20.22	have seen how I, the Lord, have **spoken** to you from heaven.
	22.28	"Do not **speak** evil of God, and do not curse a leader
	29.42	That is where I will meet my people and **speak** to you.
	31.18	When God had finished **speaking** to Moses on Mount Sinai,
	33. 9	the Tent, and the Lord would **speak** to Moses from the cloud.
	33.11	The Lord would **speak** with Moses face to face,
	33.11	just as a man **speaks** with a friend.
	34.29	face was shining because he had been **speaking** with the Lord;
	34.31	of the community went to him, and Moses **spoke** to them.
	34.33	When Moses had finished **speaking** to them, he covered his
	34.34	of the Lord's presence to **speak** to the Lord, he took the
	34.35	on until the next time he went to **speak** to the Lord.
Lev	10. 3	is what the Lord was **speaking** about when he said, 'All who
	16. 1	The Lord **spoke** to Moses after the death of the two sons
	19.16	on trial for his life, **speak** out if your testimony can help
	25. 1	The Lord **spoke** to Moses on Mount Sinai and commanded him
Num	1. 1	Israel left Egypt, the Lord **spoke** to Moses there in the Tent
	3. 1	Moses at the time the Lord **spoke** to Moses on Mount Sinai.
	5.19	make the woman agree to this oath **spoken** by the priest:
	7.89	Lord, he heard the Lord **speaking** to him from above the lid
	9. 1	The Lord **spoke** to Moses in the Sinai Desert in the first
	11.17	I will come down and **speak** with you there, and I will
	11.25	Then the Lord came down in the cloud and **spoke** to him.
	11.28	he was a young man, **spoke** up and said to Moses, "Stop
	12. 2	They said, "Has the Lord **spoken** only through Moses?
	12. 2	Hasn't he also **spoken** through us?"
	12. 6	myself to them in visions and **speak** to them in dreams.
	12. 7	It is different when I **speak** with my servant Moses;
	12. 8	So I **speak** to him face to face, clearly and not in
	12. 8	How dare you **speak** against my servant Moses?"
	14.28	I, the Lord, have **spoken.**
	14.35	I, the Lord, have **spoken.' "**
	16. 8	Moses continued to **speak** to Korah.
	16.31	soon as he had finished **speaking,** the ground under Dathan
	17. 6	So Moses **spoke** to the Israelites, and each of their
	20. 8	in front of them all **speak** to that rock over there, and
	21. 5	lost their patience [5]and **spoke** against God and Moses.
	21. 7	"We sinned when we **spoke** against the Lord and against you.
	21.14	That is why The Book of the Lord's Battles **speaks** of
	23. 7	'Come and **speak** for me,' he said.
	23. 8	God has not cursed, Or **speak** of doom when the Lord has
	23.19	He **speaks,** and it is done.
Deut	1. 1	are the words that Moses **spoke** to the people of Israel when
	4.12	Tell them how the Lord **spoke** to you from the fire, how
	4.12	fire, how you heard him **speaking** but did not see him in
	4.15	"When the Lord **spoke** to you from the fire on Mount Sinai,
	4.33	lived after hearing a god **speak** to them from a fire, as
	4.36	you see his holy fire, and he **spoke** to you from it.
	5. 4	mountain the Lord **spoke** to you face-to-face from the fire.
	5.22	When he **spoke** with a mighty voice from the fire and from
	5.24	and his glory when we heard him **speak** from the fire!
	5.24	man to continue to live, even though God has **spoken** to him.
	5.25	sure to die if we hear the Lord our God **speak** again.
	5.26	ever lived after hearing the living God **speak** from a fire?
	10. 4	he gave you when he **spoke** from the fire on the day
	18.16	not to hear the Lord **speak** again or to see his fiery
	18.19	He will **speak** in my name, and I will punish anyone who
	18.20	if any prophet dares to **speak** a message in my name when
	18.20	so must any prophet who **speaks** in the name of other gods.'
	18.22	If a prophet **speaks** in the name of the Lord and what
	18.22	That prophet has **spoken** on his own authority, and you are
	20. 9	When the officers have finished **speaking** to the army,
	25. 8	Then the town leaders are to summon him and **speak** to him.
	27.14	The Levites will **speak** these words in a loud voice:
	31. 1	Moses continued **speaking** to the people of Israel, [2]and
	31.23	Then the Lord **spoke** to Joshua son of Nun and said to
	33.16	the goodness of the Lord, Who **spoke** from the burning bush.
	34.10	the Lord **spoke** with him face to face.
Josh	1. 1	Lord's servant Moses, the Lord **spoke** to Moses' helper,
	10.12	Israel victory over the Amorites, Joshua **spoke** to the Lord.
	10.21	No one in the land dared even to **speak** against the Israelites.
	22.16	Gad, and East Manasseh, [16]and **speaking** for the whole
	23. 7	peoples left among you or **speak** the names of their gods or
	24.27	has heard all the words that the Lord has **spoken** to us.
Judg	6.39	let me **speak** just once more.
	9.27	where they ate and drank and **spoke** scornfully of Abimelech.
Ruth	2.13	made me feel better by **speaking** gently to me, even though I
1 Sam	3. 6	the Lord, because the Lord had never **spoken** to him before.
	3. 9	you again, say, **'Speak,** Lord, your servant is listening.' "
	3.10	Samuel answered, **"Speak;**
	3.13	ever because his sons have **spoken** evil things against me.
	3.21	where he had appeared to Samuel and had **spoken** to him.
	3.21	And when Samuel **spoke,** all Israel listened.
	14.19	As Saul was **speaking** to the priest, the confusion in the
1 Sam	16.18	brave and handsome man, a good soldier, and an able **speaker.**
	18.22	He ordered his officials to **speak** privately to David
	19. 3	where you are hiding, and I will **speak** to him about you.
	24.16	When David had finished **speaking,** Saul said,
2 Sam	2.27	"that if you had not **spoken,** my men would have kept on
	3.19	Abner **spoke** also to the people of the tribe of Benjamin
	3.27	as though he wanted to **speak** privately with him, and there
	12.18	was living, David wouldn't answer us when we **spoke** to him.
	13.13	Please, **speak** to the king, and I'm sure that he will give
	13.22	his sister Tamar that he would no longer even **speak** to him.
	14.15	reason I have come to **speak** to you is that the people
	14.15	to myself that I would **speak** to you in the hope that
	19.21	Abishai son of Zeruiah **spoke** up:
	20.16	I want to **speak** with him."
	23. 2	The spirit of the Lord **speaks** through me;
	23. 3	The God of Israel has **spoken;**
1 Kgs	1.22	She was still **speaking,** when Nathan arrived at the palace.
	1.42	Before he finished **speaking,** Jonathan, the son of the priest
	2.18	"I will **speak** to the king for you."
	2.19	went to the king to **speak** to him on behalf of Adonijah.
	3.15	up and realized that God had **spoken** to him in the dream.
	4.33	He **spoke** of trees and plants, from the Lebanon cedars to
	12.13	of the older men and **spoke** harshly to the people, [14]as the
	12.15	bring about what he had **spoken** to Jeroboam son of Nebat
	13. 3	Then you will know that the Lord has **spoken** through me."
	13.32	The words that he **spoke** at the Lord's command against
	14.11	I, the Lord, have **spoken.' "**
	16. 1	The Lord **spoke** to the prophet Jehu son of Hanani and gave
	17.24	a man of God and that the Lord really **speaks** through you!"
	19. 9	Suddenly the Lord **spoke** to him, "Elijah, what are you doing
	21.27	When Elijah finished **speaking,** Ahab tore his clothes,
	22.16	But Ahab replied, "When you **speak** to me in the name of
	22.24	"Since when did the Lord's spirit leave me and **speak** to you?"
	22.28	Micaiah exclaimed, "then the Lord has not **spoken** through me!"
2 Kgs	9. 5	Jehu asked, "Which one of us are you **speaking** to?"
	9.25	the Lord **spoke** these words against Ahab:
	9.36	Lord said would happen, when he **spoke** through his servant Elijah:
	18.26	Shebna, and Joah told the official, **"Speak** Aramaic to us,
	18.26	Don't **speak** Hebrew;
	19. 4	your God hear these insults and punish those who **spoke** them.
	19.33	I, the Lord, have **spoken.**
2 Chr	10.13	of the older men and **spoke** harshly to the people, [14]as the
	10.15	bring about what he had **spoken** to Jeroboam son of Nebat
	12. 7	the Lord saw this, he **spoke** again to Shemaiah and said to
	15. 8	that Azariah son of Oded had **spoken,** he was encouraged.
	18.15	But Ahab replied, "When you **speak** to me in the name of
	18.23	"Since when did the Lord's spirit leave me and **speak** to you?"
	18.27	Micaiah exclaimed, "then the Lord has not **spoken** through me!"
	24.27	sons of Joash, the prophecies **spoken** against him, and the
	29. 5	the east courtyard of the Temple [5]and **spoke** to them there.
	31. 9	The king **spoke** to the priests and the Levites about these gifts,
	33.18	messages of the prophets who **spoke** to him in the name of
	36.12	to the prophet Jeremiah, who **spoke** the word of the Lord.
Ezra	5. 1	son of Iddo, began to **speak** in the name of the God
	10.10	Ezra the priest stood up and **spoke** to them.
Neh	6.12	realized that God had not **spoken** to Shemaiah, but that
	9.13	you **spoke** to your people and gave them good laws and sound
	9.30	You inspired your prophets to **speak,** but your people were deaf,
	13.24	Half their children **spoke** the language of Ashdod or some
	13.24	other language and didn't know how to **speak** our language.
Esth	1.22	be the master of his home and **speak** with final authority.
	8. 3	Then Esther **spoke** to the king again, throwing herself at
Job	1.16	Before he had finished **speaking,** another servant came and said,
	1.17	Before he had finished **speaking,** another servant came and said,
	1.18	Before he had finished **speaking,** another servant came and said,
	4. 1	Job, will you be annoyed if I **speak?**
	7.11	I have to **speak.**
	9.16	then, if he lets me **speak,** I can't believe he would listen
	13.13	give me a chance to **speak,** and let the results be what
	13.22	**Speak** first, O God, and I will answer.
	13.22	Or let me **speak,** and you answer me.
	15. 6	you are condemned by every word you **speak.**
	15.11	We have **spoken** for him with calm, even words.
	21. 3	Give me a chance to **speak** and then, when I am through,
	23. 6	No, he would listen as I **spoke.**
	26. 4	Who inspired you to **speak** like this?
	29. 1	Job began **speaking** again.
	32. 4	one there, he had waited until everyone finished **speaking.**
	32. 6	could not answer Job, he was angry [6]and began to **speak.**
	32. 7	myself that you ought to **speak,** that you older men should
	32.11	listened patiently while you were **speaking** and waited while
	32.14	Job was **speaking** to you, not to me, but I would never
	32.18	I can hardly wait to **speak.**
	32.19	don't get a chance to **speak,** I will burst like a wineskin
	32.20	I have to **speak.**
	33. 3	All my words are sincere, and I am **speaking** the truth.
	33.14	Although God **speaks** again and again, no one pays
	33.15	At night when men are asleep, God **speaks** in dreams and visions.
	33.17	God **speaks** to make them stop their sinning and to save
	33.31	be quiet and let me **speak.**
	34.35	will say [35]that Job is **speaking** from ignorance and that
	37.20	I won't ask to **speak** with God;
	38. 1	Then out of the storm the Lord **spoke** to Job.
	40. 3	I **spoke** foolishly, Lord.
	40. 6	Then out of the storm the Lord **spoke** to Job once again.
	42. 4	me to listen while you **spoke** and to try to answer your
	42. 7	After the Lord had finished **speaking** to Job, he said to Eliphaz,
	42. 7	friends, because you did not **speak** the truth about me, as my
	42. 8	You did not **speak** the truth about me as he did."
Ps	10. 7	he is quick to **speak** hateful, evil words.
	17. 4	I **speak** no evil as others do;

Ps 17.10 they have no pity and **speak** proudly.
22.30 men will **speak** of the Lord to the coming generation.
31.18 and arrogant who **speak** with contempt about righteous men.
33. 6 his command, the sun, moon, and stars by his **spoken** word.
33. 9 When he **spoke,** the world was created;
34.13 Then hold back from **speaking** evil and from telling lies.
35.20 They do not **speak** in a friendly way;
36. 1 Sin **speaks** to the wicked man deep in his heart;
38.13 deaf man and cannot hear, like a dumb man and cannot **speak.**
40. 5 I could never **speak** of them all— their number is so
40.10 I have always **spoken** of your faithfulness and help.
45. 2 you are an eloquent **speaker.**
49. 3 I will **speak** words of wisdom.
50. 1 The Almighty God, the Lord, **speaks;**
50. 7 "Listen, my people, and I will **speak;**
50.19 "You are always ready to **speak** evil;
51.15 Help me to **speak,** Lord, and I will praise you.
62. 4 You **speak** words of blessing, but in your heart you curse him.
71.15 all day long I will **speak** of your salvation, though it is
71.24 I will **speak** of your righteousness all day long, because
73. 8 They laugh at other people and **speak** of evil things;
73. 9 They **speak** evil of God in heaven and give arrogant orders
75. 9 But I will never stop **speaking** of the God of Jacob or
77. 4 I am so worried that I cannot **speak.**
78.19 They **spoke** against God and said, "Can God supply food
78.23 But he **spoke** to the sky above and commanded its doors to
88.11 Is your constant love **spoken** of in the grave or your
99. 7 He **spoke** to them from the pillar of cloud;
106.33 made him so bitter that he **spoke** without stopping to think.
115. 5 They have mouths, but cannot **speak,** and eyes, but cannot see.
119.43 Enable me to **speak** the truth at all times, because my
120. 7 When I **speak** of peace, they are for war.
135.16 They have mouths, but cannot **speak,** and eyes, but cannot see.
139. 4 Even before I **speak,** you already know what I will say.
139.20 they **speak** evil things against your name.
145. 5 They will **speak** of your glory and majesty, and I will
145. 6 People will **speak** of your mighty deeds, and I will
145.11 They will **speak** of the glory of your royal power and
Prov 10.14 they can, but when fools **speak,** trouble is not far off.
10.31 Righteous people **speak** wisdom,
10.31 but the tongue that **speaks** evil will be stopped.
11.12 It is foolish to **speak** scornfully of others.
12.18 as deeply as any sword, but wisely **spoken** words can heal.
15. 2 When wise people **speak,** they make knowledge attractive,
16.10 The king **speaks** with divine authority;
16.13 wants to hear the truth and will favour those who **speak** it.
16.23 Intelligent people think before they **speak;**
17.20 Anyone who thinks and **speaks** evil can expect to find
18. 7 When a fool **speaks,** he is ruining himself;
18.17 The first man to **speak** in court always seems right until
18.23 When the poor man **speaks,** he has to beg politely, but
23.16 I will be proud when I hear you **speaking** words of wisdom.
23.33 eyes, and you will not be able to think or **speak** clearly.
29.20 a stupid fool than for someone who **speaks** without thinking.
31. 8 "Speak up for people who cannot **speak** for themselves.
31. 9 **Speak** for them and be a righteous judge.
31.26 She **speaks** with a gentle wisdom.
Ecc 5. 2 Think before you **speak,** and don't make any rash promises to God.
Song 2.10 My lover **speaks** to me.
4. 3 how lovely they are when you **speak.**
8.13 my companions are waiting to hear you **speak.**
Is 1.20 I, the Lord, have **spoken."**
2. 3 from Zion he **speaks** to his people."
3.15 I, the Sovereign Lord Almighty, have **spoken."**
8. 5 The Lord **spoke** to me again.
14.22 I, the Lord, have **spoken.**
14.23 I, the Lord Almighty, have **spoken."**
17. 3 I, the Lord Almighty, have **spoken."**
17. 6 I, the Lord God of Israel, have **spoken."**
19. 4 I, the Lord Almighty, have **spoken."**
19.18 the Hebrew language will be **spoken** in five Egyptian cities.
21.17 I, the Lord God of Israel, have **spoken."**
22.14 The Sovereign Lord Almighty himself **spoke** to me and said,
22.14 I, the Sovereign Lord Almighty, have **spoken."**
22.25 The Lord has **spoken.**
24. 3 The Lord has **spoken** and it will be done.
25. 8 The Lord himself has **spoken!**
28.11 then God will use foreigners **speaking** some strange-sounding
29. 4 like a ghost struggling to **speak** from under the ground, a
30. 1 The Lord has **spoken:**
30.27 He **speaks,** and his words burn like fire.
31. 9 The Lord has **spoken**—the Lord who is worshipped in Jerusalem
32. 6 A fool **speaks** foolishly and thinks up evil things to do.
33.19 foreigners who **speak** a language that you can't understand.
35. 6 and dance, and those who cannot **speak** will shout for joy.
36.11 and Joah said to the official, **"Speak** Aramaic to us.
36.11 Don't **speak** Hebrew;
37. 4 your God hear these insults and punish those who **spoke** them.
37.34 I, the Lord, have **spoken.**
40. 9 **Speak** out and do not be afraid.
41. 1 you will have your chance to **speak.**
45.13 The Lord Almighty has **spoken.**
45.19 I have not **spoken** in secret or kept my purpose hidden.
45.19 I am the Lord, and I **speak** the truth;
46.11 I have **spoken,** and it will be done.
48.15 I am the one who **spoke** and called him;
48.16 From the beginning I have **spoken** openly, and have always
52. 6 acknowledge that I am God and that I have **spoken** to you."
54.17 The Lord has **spoken.**
55.11 be the word that I **speak**— it will not fail to
58.14 I, the Lord, have **spoken."**
Is 62. 1 I will **speak** out to encourage Jerusalem;
65. 7 burnt incense at pagan hill shrines and **spoken** evil of me.
65.12 did not answer when I called you or listen when I **spoke.**
66. 4 no one answered when I called or listened when I **spoke.**
66. 9 The Lord has **spoken.**
Jer 1. 2 The Lord **spoke** to Jeremiah in the thirteenth year that
1. 3 king of Judah, [3]and he **spoke** to him again when Josiah's son
1. 3 After that, the Lord **spoke** to him many times, until the
1. 6 I answered, "Sovereign Lord, I don't know how to **speak;**
1. 8 I, the Lord, have **spoken!"**
1. 9 to me, "Listen, I am giving you the words you must **speak.**
1.13 Then the Lord **spoke** to me again.
1.18 I, the Lord, have **spoken."**
2. 3 I, the Lord, have **spoken."**
2. 8 prophets **spoke** in the name of Baal and worshipped useless idols.
2.19 I, the Sovereign Lord Almighty, have **spoken."**
3.10 I, the Lord, have **spoken."**
3.13 I, the Lord, have **spoken.**
3.20 I, the Lord, have **spoken."**
4.17 The Lord has **spoken.**
4.28 The Lord has **spoken** and will not change his mind.
5.11 I, the Lord, have **spoken."**
5.31 prophets **speak** nothing but lies;
6.10 would listen to me if I **spoke** to them and warned them?
6.15 I, the Lord, have **spoken."**
7.13 sins, and even though I **spoke** to you over and over again,
7.15 I, the Lord, have **spoken."**
7.27 "So, Jeremiah, you will **speak** all these words to my people,
8. 3 I, the Lord Almighty, have **spoken."**
8. 6 I listened carefully, but you did not **speak** the truth.
8.12 I, the Lord, have **spoken.**
9. 8 Everyone **speaks** friendly words to his neighbour, but is
9. 9 I, the Lord, have **spoken."**
9.24 I, the Lord, have **spoken."**
10. 5 they cannot **speak;**
10.18 The Lord has **spoken.**
12. 2 They always **speak** well of you, yet they do not really care
12. 6 Do not trust them, even though they **speak** friendly words."
12.17 I, the Lord, have **spoken."**
13. 3 Then the Lord **spoke** to me again, and said, [4]"Go to the
13. 8 Then the Lord **spoke** to me again.
13.15 People of Israel, the Lord has **spoken!**
14.14 did I give them any orders or **speak** one word to them.
14.15 did not send but who **speak** in my name and say war
15. 9 I, the Lord, have **spoken."**
15.16 You **spoke** to me, and I listened to every word.
15.21 I, the Lord, have **spoken."**
16. 1 Again the Lord **spoke** to me and said, [2]"Do not marry or
16.15 I, the Lord, have **spoken."**
18.20 I came to you and **spoke** on their behalf, so that you
20. 8 Whenever I **speak,** I have to cry out and shout, "Violence!
20. 9 the Lord and no longer **speak** in his name," then your
21. 2 "Please **speak** to the Lord for us, because King
21. 3 Then the Lord **spoke** to me, and I told the men who
21. 7 I, the Lord, have **spoken."**
21.10 I, the Lord, have **spoken."**
21.14 I, the Lord, have **spoken."**
22. 5 I, the Lord, have **spoken.**
22.17 The Lord has **spoken.**
22.21 The Lord **spoke** to you when you were prosperous,
22.30 I, the Lord, have **spoken."**
23. 4 I, the Lord, have **spoken."**
23.12 I, the Lord, have **spoken.**
23.13 they have **spoken** in the name of Baal and have led my
23.21 not give them any message, but still they **spoke** in my name.
23.25 those prophets have said who **speak** lies in my name and claim
23.31 also against those prophets who **speak** their own words and
23.32 I, the Lord, have **spoken."**
25. 3 very day, the Lord has **spoken** to me, and I have never
25. 9 I, the Lord, have **spoken.**
25.13 on the nations when I **spoke** through Jeremiah—all the
25.29 I, the Lord Almighty, have **spoken.**
25.31 The Lord has **spoken.' "**
26. 8 Lord had commanded me to **speak,** they seized me and shouted,
26.11 sentenced to death because he has **spoken** against our city.
26.16 and the prophets, "This man **spoke** to us in the name of
26.20 Shemaiah from Kiriath Jearim, who **spoke** in the name of the
27.11 I, the Lord, have **spoken."**
27.22 I, the Lord, have **spoken."**
28. 1 prophet from the town of Gibeon, **spoke** to me in the Temple.
28. 4 I, the Lord, have **spoken."**
28. 8 The prophets who **spoke** long ago, before my time and yours,
29. 9 I, the Lord Almighty, have **spoken.'**
29.14 I, the Lord, have **spoken.'**
29.21 the God of Israel, has **spoken** about Ahab son of Kolaiah and
29.23 The Lord has **spoken."**
29.27 Anathoth, who has been **speaking** as a prophet to the people?
29.31 not send him, but he **spoke** to you as if he were
29.31 I, the Lord, have **spoken."**
30. 3 I, the Lord, have **spoken."**
30.11 I, the Lord, have **spoken."**
30.17 I, the Lord, have **spoken."**
30.21 I, the Lord, have **spoken."**
31.14 I, the Lord, have **spoken."**
31.17 I, the Lord, have **spoken.**
31.34 I, the Lord, have **spoken."**
31.37 The Lord has **spoken.**
32. 1 The Lord **spoke** to me in the tenth year that Zedekiah was
32. 4 see him face to face and will **speak** to him in person.
32. 5 I, the Lord, have **spoken."**
32. 8 So I knew that the Lord had really **spoken** to me.

Jer 32.44 I, the Lord, have **spoken."**
33. 2 earth, who formed it and set it in place, **spoke** to me.
33.11 I, the Lord, have **spoken."**
33.13 I, the Lord, have **spoken."**
34. 1 The Lord **spoke** to me when King Nebuchadnezzar of Babylonia
34. 5 I, the Lord, have **spoken."**
34.22 I, the Lord, have **spoken."**
35.14 But I have kept on **speaking** to you, and you have not
35.17 would not listen when I **spoke** to you, and you would not
36. 2 from the time I first **spoke** to you, when Josiah was king,
39.18 I, the Lord, have **spoken."**
40. 1 The Lord **spoke** to me after Nebuzaradan, the commanding officer,
42. 7 Ten days later the Lord **spoke** to me;
42.12 I, the Lord, have **spoken.'**
44. 1 Lord **spoke** to me concerning all the Israelites living in Egypt,
45. 5 I, the Lord, have **spoken."**
46. 1 The Lord **spoke** to me about the nations, [2]beginning with Egypt.
46.13 Babylonia came to attack Egypt, the Lord **spoke** to me.
46.24 I, the Lord, have **spoken."**
46.26 I, the Lord, have **spoken."**
46.28 I, the Lord, have **spoken."**
47. 1 Egypt attacked Gaza, the Lord **spoke** to me about Philistia.
48. 8 I, the Lord, have **spoken.**
48.15 I am the king, the Lord Almighty, and I have **spoken.**
48.25 I, the Lord, have **spoken."**
48.35 I, the Lord, have **spoken.**
48.39 I, the Lord, have **spoken."**
48.43 The Lord has **spoken.**
49. 6 I, the Lord, have **spoken."**
49.13 I, the Lord, have **spoken."**
49.16 The Lord has **spoken."**
49.18 I, the Lord, have **spoken.**
49.27 I, the Lord Almighty, have **spoken."**
49.33 I, the Lord, have **spoken."**
49.34 of Judah, the Lord Almighty **spoke** to me about the country of
49.39 I, the Lord, have **spoken."**
50.10 I, the Lord, have **spoken."**
50.20 I, the Lord, have **spoken."**
50.21 I, the Lord, have **spoken.**
50.30 I, the Lord, have **spoken.**
50.40 I, the Lord, have **spoken.**
51.26 I, the Lord, have **spoken.**
51.33 I, the Lord Almighty, the God of Israel, have **spoken."**
51.40 I, the Lord, have **spoken."**
51.49 I, the Lord, have **spoken."**
51.53 I, the Lord, have **spoken."**
51.57 I, the king, have **spoken,** I am the Lord Almighty.
51.58 I, the Lord Almighty, have **spoken."**
Ezek 1. 3 Chebar, I heard the Lord **speak** to me and I felt his
2. 2 While the voice was **speaking,** God's spirit entered me and
3. 1 then go and **speak** to the people of Israel."
3. 5 you to a nation that **speaks** a difficult foreign language,
3. 6 that **spoke** difficult languages you didn't understand,
3.16 After the seven days had passed, the Lord **spoke** to me.
3.27 Then, when I **speak** to you again and give you back the
5.13 that I, the Lord, have **spoken** to you because I am outraged
5.17 I, the Lord, have **spoken."**
6. 1 The Lord **spoke** to me.
7. 1 The Lord **spoke** to me.
11.14 The Lord **spoke** to me.
11.21 The Sovereign Lord has **spoken.**
12. 1 The Lord **spoke** to me.
12. 8 The next morning the Lord **spoke** to me.
12.17 The Lord **spoke** to me.
12.21 The Lord **spoke** to me.
12.25 I, the Lord, will **speak** to them, and what I say will
12.25 I have **spoken,"** says the Sovereign Lord.
12.28 I, the Sovereign Lord, have **spoken!"**
13. 1 The Lord **spoke** to me.
13. 6 They claim that they are **speaking** my message, but I have not
13. 7 say that they are my words, but I haven't **spoken** to you!"
13.16 The Sovereign Lord has **spoken.**
14. 2 Then the Lord **spoke** to me.
14. 4 "Now **speak** to them and tell them what I, the Sovereign Lord,
14.11 The Sovereign Lord has **spoken.**
14.12 The Lord **spoke** to me.
14.14 The Sovereign Lord has **spoken.**
14.23 The Sovereign Lord has **spoken.**
15. 1 The Lord **spoke** to me.
15. 8 The Sovereign Lord has **spoken.**
16. 1 The Lord **spoke** to me again.
16.43 The Sovereign Lord has **spoken.**
16.58 The Lord has **spoken.**
16.63 The Sovereign Lord has **spoken.**
17. 1 The Lord **spoke** to me.
17.21 Then you will know that I, the Lord, have **spoken."**
17.24 I, the Lord, have **spoken.**
18. 1 The Lord **spoke** to me [2]and said, "What is this proverb
20. 2 Then the Lord **spoke** to me.
20. 3 "Mortal man," he said, **"speak** to these men and tell
20. 3 I, the Sovereign Lord, have **spoken.**
20.44 The Sovereign Lord has **spoken.**
20.45 The Lord **spoke** to me.
20.46 **Speak** against the south and prophesy against the forest
20.49 Everyone is already complaining that I always **speak** in riddles."
21. 1 The Lord **spoke** to me.
21. 7 The Sovereign Lord has **spoken.**
21.17 I, the Lord, have **spoken."**
21.18 The Lord **spoke** to me.
21.26 I, the Sovereign Lord, have **spoken.**

Ezek 21.32 The Lord has **spoken.**
22. 1 The Lord **spoke** to me.
22.12 The Sovereign Lord has **spoken.**
22.14 I, the Lord, have **spoken,** and I keep my word.
22.23 The Lord **spoke** to me again.
22.28 They claim to **speak** the word of the Sovereign Lord, but I,
22.28 Sovereign Lord, but I, the Lord, have not **spoken** to them.
22.31 The Sovereign Lord has **spoken.**
23. 1 The Lord **spoke** to me.
23.34 I, the Sovereign Lord, have **spoken."**
24. 1 of the ninth year of our exile, the Lord **spoke** to me.
24.14 I, the Sovereign Lord, have **spoken.**
24.14 The Sovereign Lord has **spoken.**
24.15 The Lord **spoke** to me.
24.20 said to them, "The Lord **spoke** to me and told me [21] to
25. 1 The Lord **spoke** to me.
25.14 The Sovereign Lord has **spoken.**
26. 1 of the eleventh year of our exile, the Lord **spoke** to me.
26. 5 I, the Sovereign Lord, have **spoken.**
26.14 I, the Sovereign Lord, have **spoken."**
26.21 The Sovereign Lord has **spoken.**
28. 1 The Lord **spoke** to me.
28.11 The Lord **spoke** to me again.
29. 1 of the tenth year of our exile, the Lord **spoke** to me.
29.17 the twenty-seventh year of our exile, the Lord **spoke** to me.
29.20 I, the Sovereign Lord, have **spoken.**
29.21 and let you, Ezekiel, **speak** out where everyone can hear you,
30. 1 The Lord **spoke** again.
30. 6 I, the Sovereign Lord, have **spoken.**
30.12 I, the Lord, have **spoken."**
30.20 of the eleventh year of our exile, the Lord **spoke** to me.
31. 1 of the eleventh year of our exile, the Lord **spoke** to me.
31.18 I have **spoken,"** says the Sovereign Lord.
32. 1 of the twelfth year of our exile, the Lord **spoke** to me.
32. 8 I, the Sovereign Lord, have **spoken.**
32.14 I, the Sovereign Lord, have **spoken.**
32.16 I, the Sovereign Lord, have **spoken."**
32.17 of the twelfth year of our exile, the Lord **spoke** to me.
32.32 The Sovereign Lord has **spoken.**
33. 1 The Lord **spoke** to me.
33.10 The Lord **spoke** to me.
33.23 The Lord **spoke** to me.
34. 1 The Lord **spoke** to me.
34.15 I, the Sovereign Lord, have **spoken.**
34.24 I have **spoken.**
34.30 I, the Sovereign Lord, have **spoken.**
35. 1 The Lord **spoke** to me.
36. 1 The Lord said, "Mortal man, **speak** to the mountains of Israel
36. 5 "I, the Sovereign Lord, have **spoken** out in the heat of my
36.14 I, the Sovereign Lord, have **spoken.**
36.15 I, the Sovereign Lord, have **spoken."**
36.16 The Lord **spoke** to me.
36.23 I, the Sovereign Lord, have **spoken.**
36.32 I, the Sovereign Lord, have **spoken."**
37. 7 While I was **speaking,** I heard a rattling noise, and the
37.14 I, the Lord, have **spoken."**
37.15 The Lord **spoke** to me again.
38. 1 The Lord **spoke** to me.
38.17 The Sovereign Lord has **spoken.**
38.21 I, the Sovereign Lord, have **spoken.**
39. 5 I, the Sovereign Lord, have **spoken.**
39. 8 Sovereign Lord said, "The day I **spoke** about is certain to come.
39.10 The Sovereign Lord has **spoken.**
39.13 I, the Sovereign Lord, have **spoken.**
39.20 I, the Sovereign Lord, have **spoken."**
39.29 I, the Sovereign Lord, have **spoken."**
43. 6 and I heard the Lord **speak** to me out of the Temple:
43.27 I, the Sovereign Lord, have **spoken."**
44.27 I, the Sovereign Lord, have **spoken.**
47.23 I, the Sovereign Lord, have **spoken."**
Dan 3.29 or language **speaks** disrespectfully of the God of Shadrach,
4.31 his mouth, a voice **spoke** from heaven, "King Nebuchadnezzar,
7.25 He will **speak** against the Supreme God and oppress God's people.
9. 6 servants the prophets, who **spoke** in your name to our kings,
Hos 1. 2 When the Lord first **spoke** to Israel through Hosea, he
2.13 The Lord has **spoken.**
2.17 I will never let her **speak** the name of Baal again.
11.11 I, the Lord, have **spoken."**
12. 4 Bethel God came to our ancestor Jacob and **spoke** with him.
12.10 "I **spoke** to the prophets and gave them many visions,
13. 1 when the tribe of Ephraim **spoke,** the other tribes of Israel
Joel 3. 8 I, the Lord, have **spoken.**
Amos 2.11 I, the Lord, have **spoken.**
2.12 and ordered the prophets not to **speak** my message.
2.16 The Lord has **spoken.**
3. 1 message which the Lord has **spoken** about you, the entire
3. 8 When the Sovereign Lord **speaks,** who can avoid proclaiming
5.10 challenges injustice and **speaks** the whole truth in court.
5.17 The Lord has **spoken.**
8. 9 I, the Sovereign Lord, have **spoken.**
8.11 I, the Sovereign Lord, have **spoken.**
9.15 The Lord your God has **spoken.**
Obad 18 I, the Lord, have **spoken.**
Jon 1. 1 One day, the Lord **spoke** to Jonah son of Amittai.
1. 2 "Go to Nineveh, that great city, and **speak** out against it;
3. 1 Once again the Lord **spoke** to Jonah.
Mic 1. 2 He **speaks** from his heavenly temple.
2. 7 Doesn't he **speak** kindly to those who do right?"
4. 2 from Zion he **speaks** to his people."
Zeph 1. 3 I, the Lord, have **spoken.**
3.20 The Lord has **spoken.**

Hag 1. 1 the sixth month, the Lord **spoke** through the prophet Haggai.
2. 1 same year, the Lord **spoke** again through the prophet Haggai.
2. 2 He told Haggai to **speak** to Zerubbabel, the governor of Judah,
2. 9 The Lord Almighty has **spoken.**
2.10 the Lord Almighty **spoke** again to the prophet Haggai.
2.23 The Lord Almighty has **spoken.**
Zech 1.19 the angel that had been **speaking** to me, "What do these
2. 3 the angel who had been **speaking** to me step forward, and
4. 1 The angel who had been **speaking** to me came again and
7.13 did not listen when I **spoke,** I did not answer when they
8. 9 the same words the prophets **spoke** at the time the foundation
8.16 **Speak** the truth to one another.
10.12 The Lord has **spoken.**
11.11 and they knew that the Lord was **speaking** through what I did.
13. 3 he claimed to speak the Lord's word, but **spoke** lies instead.
Mal 3.16 people who feared the Lord **spoke** to one another, and the
Mt 4. 4 on bread alone, but needs every word that God **speaks.'** "
5.47 And if you **speak** only to your friends, have you done
7.22 In your name we **spoke** God's message, by your name we drove
9. 3 Law said to themselves, "This man is **speaking** blasphemy!"
9.30 Jesus **spoke** sternly to them, "Don't tell this to anyone!"
10.20 For the words you will **speak** will not be yours;
10.20 come from the Spirit of your Father **speaking** through you.
11. 7 While John's disciples were leaving, Jesus **spoke** about him to the crowds:
11.13 the prophets and the Law of Moses **spoke** about the Kingdom;
12.34 For the mouth **speaks** what the heart is full of.
12.36 to give account of every useless word he has ever **spoken.**
12.38 Then some teachers of the Law and some Pharisees **spoke** up.
12.46 They stood outside, asking to **speak** with him.
12.47 are standing outside, and they want to **speak** with you."
13.35 said come true, "I will use parables when I **speak** to them;
14.27 Jesus **spoke** to them at once.
14.28 Then Peter **spoke** up.
15.15 Peter **spoke** up, "Explain this saying to us."
15.31 as they saw the dumb **speaking,** the crippled made whole, the
17. 4 So Peter **spoke** up and said to Jesus, "Lord, how good it
17.25 went into the house, Jesus **spoke** up first, "Simon, what is
19.27 Then Peter **spoke** up.
20.17 the twelve disciples aside and **spoke** to them privately, as
23. 1 Then Jesus **spoke** to the crowds and to his disciples.
24. 5 Many men, claiming to **speak** for me, will come and say, 'I
24.15 "You will see 'The Awful Horror' of which the prophet Daniel **spoke.**
26.25 Judas, the traitor, **spoke** up.
26.33 Peter **spoke** up and said to Jesus, "I will never leave you,
26.47 Jesus was still **speaking** when Judas, one of the twelve disciples,
26.55 Then Jesus **spoke** to the crowd, "Did you have to come
26.63 Again the High Priest **spoke** to him, "In the name of the
26.73 "After all, the way you **speak** gives you away!"
28. 5 The angel **spoke** to the women.
Mk 1.43 Then Jesus **spoke** sternly to him and sent him away at once,
3.23 So Jesus called them to him and **spoke** to them in parables:
4.34 He would not **speak** to them without using parables, but
6.50 Jesus **spoke** to them at once, "Courage!"
7.32 was deaf and could hardly **speak,** and they begged Jesus to
7.36 Then Jesus ordered the people not to **speak** of it to anyone;
7.36 but the more he ordered them not to, the more they **spoke.**
7.37 "He even causes the deaf to hear and the dumb to **speak!"**
9. 5 Peter **spoke** up and said to Jesus, "Teacher, how good it
10.28 Then Peter **spoke** up, "Look, we have left everything and followed you."
10.32 the twelve disciples aside and **spoke** of the things that were
12. 1 Then Jesus **spoke** to them in parables:
13. 6 Many men, claiming to **speak** for me, will come and say, 'I
13.11 For the words you **speak** will not be yours;
14.43 Jesus was still **speaking** when Judas, one of the twelve disciples,
14.48 Then Jesus **spoke** up and said to them, "Did you have to
15.12 Pilate **spoke** again to the crowd, "What, then, do you
16.17 they will **speak** in strange tongues;
Lk 1.19 God, who sent me to **speak** to you and tell you this
1.20 Because you have not believed, you will be unable to **speak;**
1.22 came out, he could not **speak** to them, and so they knew
1.64 Zechariah was able to **speak** again, and he started praising God.
1.67 Zechariah was filled with the Holy Spirit, and he **spoke** God's message:
2.34 which many people will **speak against** [35] and so reveal
2.38 gave thanks to God and **spoke** about the child to all who
4.22 with him and marvelled at the eloquent words that he **spoke.**
4.32 at the way he taught, because he **spoke** with authority.
4.38 sick with a high fever, and they **spoke** to Jesus about her.
4.41 and would not let them **speak,** because they knew that he was
5. 4 When he finished **speaking,** he said to Simon, "Push the
5.21 to themselves, "Who is this man who **speaks** such blasphemy!
6.26 "How terrible when all people **speak** well of you;
6.45 For the mouth **speaks** what the heart is full of.
7.24 had left, Jesus began to **speak** about him to the crowds:
7.40 Jesus **spoke** up and said to him, "Simon, I have
9.11 He welcomed them, **spoke** to them about the Kingdom of God,
9.34 While he was still **speaking,** a cloud appeared and
9.49 John **spoke** up, "Master, we saw a man driving out demons
11.27 had said this, a woman **spoke** up from the crowd and said
11.37 When Jesus finished **speaking,** a Pharisee invited him to eat with him;
13.14 on the Sabbath, so he **spoke** up and said to the people,
19.39 Then some of the Pharisees in the crowd **spoke** to Jesus.
20.37 about the burning bush he **speaks** of the Lord as 'the God
20.39 of the teachers of the Law **spoke** up, "A good answer,
21. 8 Many men, claiming to **speak** for me, will come and say, 'I
22. 4 So Judas went off and **spoke** with the chief priests and the
22.47 Jesus was still **speaking** when a crowd arrived, led by
Lk 22.60 At once, while he was still **speaking,** a cock crowed.
Jn 1.15 John **spoke** about him.
1.20 did not refuse to answer, but **spoke** out openly and clearly,
2.21 But the temple Jesus was **speaking** about was his body.
3.11 we **speak** of what we know and report what we have seen,
3.26 on the east side of the Jordan, the one you **spoke** about?
3.31 belongs to the earth and **speaks** about earthly matters, but
3.34 one whom God has sent **speaks** God's words, because God gives
5.33 sent your messengers, and he **spoke** on behalf of the truth.
5.36 gave me to do, these **speak** on my behalf and show that
5.39 And these very Scriptures **speak** about me!
6.63 The words I have **spoken** to you bring God's life-giving Spirit.
7.17 teach comes from God or whether I **speak** on my own authority.
7.18 A person who **speaks** on his own authority is trying to
8.12 Jesus **spoke** to the Pharisees again.
9.29 We know that God **spoke** to Moses;
10.25 The things I do by my Father's authority **speak** on my behalf;
12.28 Then a voice **spoke** from heaven, "I have brought glory to it,
12.29 was thunder, while others said, "An angel **spoke** to him!"
12.30 was not for my sake that this voice **spoke,** but for yours.
12.41 Isaiah said this because he saw Jesus' glory and **spoke** about him.
12.48 The words I have **spoken** will be his judge on the last
12.49 true, because I have not **spoken** on my own authority, but the
12.49 who sent me has commanded me what I must say and **speak.**
14.10 The words that I have **spoken** to you," Jesus said to his
15.22 guilty of sin if I had not come and **spoken** to them;
15.26 him to you from the Father, and he will **speak** about me.
15.27 And you, too, will **speak** about me, because you have been
16.13 He will not **speak** on his own authority,
16.13 but he will **speak** of what he hears,
16.25 of speech, but will **speak** to you plainly about the Father.
16.29 "Now you are **speaking** plainly, without using figures of speech.
18.16 other disciple went back out, **spoke** to the girl at the gate,
18.20 Jesus answered, "I have always **spoken** publicly to everyone;
18.26 relative of the man whose ear Peter had cut off, **spoke** up.
18.37 the world for this one purpose, to **speak** about the truth.
19.10 Pilate said to him, "You will not **speak** to me?
19.35 who saw this happen has **spoken** of it, so that you also
19.35 he said is true, and he knows that he **speaks** the truth.)
21.24 He is the disciple who **spoke** of these things, the one
Acts 1.15 a hundred and twenty in all, and Peter stood up to **speak.**
1.16 in which the Holy Spirit, **speaking** through David, made a
2. 4 in other languages, as the Spirit enabled them to **speak.**
2. 6 of them heard the believers **speaking** in his own language.
2. 8 all of us hear them **speaking** in our own native languages?
2.11 all of us hear them **speaking** in our own languages about the
2.14 apostles and in a loud voice began to **speak** to the crowd:
2.16 Instead, this is what the prophet Joel **spoke** about:
2.29 "My brothers, I must **speak** to you plainly about our
2.31 the future, and so he **spoke** about the resurrection of the
4. 1 Peter and John were still **speaking** to the people when some priests,
4.17 these men never again to **speak** to anyone in the name of
4.18 no condition were they to **speak** or to teach in the name
4.20 For we cannot stop **speaking** of what we ourselves have
4.25 of the Holy Spirit you **spoke** through our ancestor David,
4.29 us, your servants, to **speak** your message with all boldness.
5.13 to join them, even though the people **spoke** highly of them.
5.40 and ordered them never again to **speak** in the name of Jesus;
6.10 Stephen such wisdom that when he **spoke,** they could not refute him.
6.11 "We heard him **speaking against** Moses and against God!"
7.38 and with the angel who **spoke** to him on Mount Sinai, and
8.24 that none of these things you **spoke** of will happen to me."
8.35 Then Philip began to **speak;**
9.27 Lord on the road and that the Lord had **spoken** to him.
10.15 The voice **spoke** to him again, "Do not consider anything
10.34 Peter began to **speak:**
10.43 All the prophets **spoke** about him, saying that everyone
10.44 While Peter was still **speaking,** the Holy Spirit came
10.46 For they heard them **speaking** in strange tongues and praising God's greatness.
10.46 Peter **spoke** up:
11. 9 The voice **spoke** again from heaven, 'Do not consider
11.14 He will **speak** words to you by which you and all your
11.15 And when I began to **speak,** the Holy Spirit came down on
12.22 "It isn't a man **speaking,** but a god!"
13.15 "Brothers, we want you to **speak** to the people if you have
13.16 Paul stood up, motioned with his hand, and began to **speak:**
13.43 The apostles **spoke** to them and encouraged them to keep on
13.46 But Paul and Barnabas **spoke** out even more boldly:
13.46 that the word of God should be **spoken** first to you.
14. 1 went to the synagogue and **spoke** in such a way that a
14. 3 there for a long time, **speaking** boldly about the Lord, who
14.12 Zeus, and Paul the name Hermes, because he was the chief **speaker.**
15.13 When they had finished speaking, James **spoke** up:
15.32 Silas, who were themselves prophets, **spoke** a long time with them,
16. 2 All the believers in Lystra and Iconium **spoke** well of Timothy.
16.40 There they met the believers, **spoke** words of encouragement to them,
17.32 When they heard Paul **speak** about a raising from death,
17.32 others said, "We want to hear you **speak** about this again."
18. 9 be afraid, but keep on **speaking** and do not give up,
18.14 Paul was about to **speak** when Gallio said to the Jews,
18.24 He was an eloquent **speaker** and had a thorough knowledge of
18.26 He began to **speak** boldly in the synagogue.
19. 6 **spoke** in strange tongues and also proclaimed God's message.
19. 8 and during three months **spoke** boldly with the people,
20. 7 Paul **spoke** to the people and kept on speaking until midnight,

Acts 21.37 about to take Paul into the fort, he **spoke** to the commander:
21.37 "You **speak** Greek, do you?"
21.39 Please let me **speak** to the people."
21.40 When they were quiet, Paul **spoke** to them in Hebrew:
22. 2 When they heard him **speaking** to them in Hebrew, they
22. 9 not hear the voice of the one who was **speaking** to me.
22.14 Servant, and to hear him **speaking** with his own voice.
23. 5 scripture says, 'You must not **speak evil** of the ruler of
23. 9 Perhaps a spirit or an angel really did **speak** to him!"
24.10 then motioned to Paul to **speak,** and Paul said, "I know that
26. 1 Paul, "You have permission to **speak** on your own behalf."
26.25 I am **speaking** the sober truth.
26.26 I can **speak** to you with all boldness, because you know about
28.22 we know that everywhere people **speak against** this party to
28.25 "How well the Holy Spirit **spoke** through the prophet Isaiah
28.31 Lord Jesus Christ, **speaking** with all boldness and freedom.
Rom 1.30 They gossip [30] and **speak evil** of one another;
2.24 "Because of you Jews, the Gentiles **speak evil** of God."
3. 4 says, "You must be shown to be right when you **speak;**
4. 6 what David meant when he **spoke** of the happiness of the
4. 9 Does this happiness that David **spoke** of belong only to
9. 1 I am **speaking** the truth;
9.33 the "stumbling stone" [33] that the scripture **speaks** of:
11.13 I am **speaking** now to you Gentiles:
12. 6 If our gift is to **speak** God's message, we should do it
15.18 I will be bold and **speak** only about what Christ has done
1 Cor 2.13 So then, we do not **speak** in words taught by human wisdom,
10.15 I **speak** to you as sensible people;
12.10 to another, the gift of **speaking** God's message;
12.10 he gives the ability to **speak** in strange tongues,
12.28 others or to direct them or to **speak** in strange tongues.
12.30 to heal diseases or to **speak** in strange tongues or to
13. 1 I may be able to **speak** the languages of men and even
13. 8 gifts of **speaking** in strange tongues, but they will cease;
14. 2 The one who **speaks** in strange tongues
14. 2 does not **speak** to others but to God,
14. 2 He is **speaking** secret truths by the power of the Spirit.
14. 3 God's message **speaks** to people and gives them help,
14. 4 The one who **speaks** in strange tongues helps only himself,
14. 5 I would like all of you to **speak** in strange tongues;
14. 5 value than the one who **speaks** in strange tongues—unless
14. 6 use will I be to you if I **speak** in strange tongues?
14.11 not know the language being **spoken,** the person who uses it
14.13 The person who **speaks** in strange tongues, then, must
14.18 I thank God that I **speak** in strange tongues much more
14.19 I would rather **speak** five words that can be understood,
14.19 than **speak** thousands of words in strange tongues.
14.21 "By means of men **speaking** strange languages
14.21 I will **speak** to my people, says the Lord.
14.21 I will **speak** through lips of foreigners, but even then my
14.22 So then, the gift of **speaking** in strange tongues is
14.23 meets together and everyone starts **speaking** in strange
14.27 If someone is going to **speak** in strange tongues, two or
14.27 three at the most should **speak,** one after the other, and
14.28 then the one who **speaks** in strange tongues
14.28 be quiet and **speak** only to himself and to God.
14.29 are given God's message should **speak,** while the others are
14.30 a message from God, the one who is **speaking** should stop.
14.32 message should be under the **speaker's** control, [33] because
14.34 They are not allowed to **speak;**
14.35 It is a disgraceful thing for a woman to **speak** in church.
14.39 God's message, but do not forbid the **speaking** in strange tongues.
2 Cor 1.18 As surely as God **speaks** the truth, my promise to you was
2.17 God has sent us, we **speak** with sincerity in his presence, as
4.13 The scripture says, "I **spoke** because I believed."
4.13 In the same spirit of faith, we also **speak** because we believe.
5.20 Here we are, then, **speaking** for Christ, as though God
6. 8 We are treated as liars, yet we **speak** the truth;
6.11 We have **spoken** frankly to you;
6.13 I **speak** now as though you were my children:
7.14 We have always **spoken** the truth to you, and in the same
11. 6 Perhaps I am an amateur in **speaking,** but certainly not in knowledge;
12. 3 be put into words, things that human lips may not **speak.**
12.19 We **speak** as Christ would wish us to speak in the presence
13. 3 have all the proof you want that Christ **speaks** through me.
Eph 4.15 Instead, by **speaking** the truth in a spirit of love, we
5.19 **Speak** to one another with the words of psalms, hymns,
6.19 when I am ready to **speak,** so that I may speak boldly
6.20 I may be bold in **speaking** about the gospel as I should.
Col 4. 4 Pray, then, that I may **speak,** as I should, in such a
1 Thes 1. 9 All those people **speak** about how you received us when we
2. 4 Instead, we always **speak** as God wants us to, because he
1 Tim 1. 7 the matters about which they **speak** with so much confidence.
1.13 though in the past I **spoke evil** of him and persecuted and
1.18 with the words of prophecy **spoken** in the past about you.
3.13 standing and are able to **speak** boldly about their faith in
4.14 to you when the prophets **spoke** and the elders laid their
5.14 as to give our enemies no chance of **speaking evil** of us.
6. 1 so that no one will **speak evil** of the name of God
Tit 1.12 of their own prophets, who **spoke** the truth when he said,
2. 5 so that no one will **speak evil** of the message that comes
3. 2 Tell them not to **speak evil** of anyone, but to be peaceful
Heb 1. 1 In the past, God **spoke** to our ancestors many times and in
1. 2 in these last days he has **spoken** to us through his Son.
2. 5 over the new world to come—the world of which we **speak.**
3. 5 as a servant, and he **spoke** of the things that God would
3.18 I would have given them rest"—of whom was he **speaking?**
4. 1 us the promise that we may receive that rest he **spoke** about.
4. 5 This same matter is **spoken** of again:
4. 7 Many years later he **spoke** of it through David in the
Heb 4. 8 God had promised, God would not have **spoken** later about another day.
6. 9 But even if we **speak** like this, dear friends, we feel sure
7.14 Moses did not mention this tribe when he **spoke** of priests.
8.13 By **speaking** of a new covenant, God has made the first
11. 4 of his faith Abel still **speaks,** even though he is dead.
11.22 he was about to die, **speak** of the departure of the
11.32 enough time for me to **speak** of Gideon, Barak, Samson,
12. 5 the encouraging words which God **speaks** to you as his sons?
12.25 Be careful, then, and do not refuse to hear him who **speaks.**
12.25 then, if we turn away from the one who **speaks** from heaven!
13. 7 Remember your former leaders, who **spoke** God's message to you.
Jas 1.19 quick to listen, but slow to **speak** and slow to become angry.
2. 7 They are the ones who **speak evil** of that good name which
2.12 **Speak** and act as people who will be judged by the law
5.10 remember the prophets who **spoke** in the name of the Lord.
1 Pet 1.12 but for yours, as they **spoke** about those things which you
3.10 times, must keep from **speaking evil** and stop telling lies.
3.16 you are insulted, those who **speak evil** of your good conduct
2 Pet 1.21 Holy Spirit as they **spoke** the message that came from God.
2. 2 what they do, others will **speak evil** of the Way of truth.
2.16 His donkey **spoke** with a human voice and stopped the
3. 2 the words that were **spoken** long ago by the holy prophets,
1 Jn 1. 2 so we **speak** of it and tell you about the eternal life
4. 5 Those false prophets **speak** about matters of the world, and
2 Jn 6 This love I **speak** of means that we must live in obedience
3 Jn 6 They have **spoken** to the church here about your love.
12 Everyone **speaks** well of Demetrius;
12 truth itself **speaks** well of him.
Jude 15 words that godless sinners have **spoken against** him!"
Rev 1.10 loud voice, that sounded like a trumpet, **speaking** behind me.
4. 1 trumpet, which I had heard **speaking** to me before, said,
10. 4 As soon as they **spoke,** I was about to write.
10. 4 But I heard a voice **speak** from heaven, "Keep secret what
10. 8 that I had heard **speaking** from heaven spoke to me again,
13.11 two horns like a lamb's horns, and it **spoke** like a dragon.
16. 1 I heard a loud voice **speaking** from the temple to the seven
21. 3 I heard a loud voice **speaking** from the throne:
21.15 The angel who **spoke** to me had a gold measuring-rod to

SPEAR
[FISHING-SPEARS]

Num 25. 7 He took a **spear,** [8] followed the man and the woman
25. 8 into the tent, and drove the **spear** through both of them.
Josh 8.18 Then the Lord said to Joshua, "Point your **spear** at Ai;
8.25 Joshua kept his **spear** pointed at Ai and did not
Judg 5. 8 thousand men in Israel, did anyone carry shield or **spear?**
1 Sam 13.19 determined to keep the Hebrews from making swords and **spears.**
13.22 soldiers except Saul and his son Jonathan had swords or **spears.**
17. 7 His **spear** was as thick as the bar on a weaver's loom,
17.45 coming against me with sword, **spear,** and javelin, but I come
17.47 the Lord does not need swords or **spears** to save his people.
18.10 harp, as he did every day, and Saul was holding a **spear.**
18.11 Saul said to himself, and he threw the **spear** at him twice;
19. 9 in his house with his **spear** in his hand, and David was
19.10 spear, but David dodged, and the **spear** stuck in the wall.
20.33 At that, Saul threw his **spear** at Jonathan to kill him,
21. 8 Ahimelech, "Have you got a **spear** or a sword you can give
22. 6 on a hill, with his **spear** in his hand, and all his
26. 7 of the camp with his **spear** stuck in the ground near his
26. 8 let me plunge his own **spear** through him and pin him to
26.11 Let's take his **spear** and his water jar, and go."
26.12 So David took the **spear** and the water jar from just
26.16 Where is the king's **spear?**
26.22 David replied, "Here is your **spear,** Your Majesty.
2 Sam 1. 6 Saul was leaning on his **spear** and that the chariots and
2.23 a backward thrust of his **spear,** struck him through the belly
2.23 so that the **spear** came out at his back.
18.14 He took three **spears** and plunged them into Absalom's chest
21.16 who was carrying a bronze **spear** that weighed about three and
21.19 killed Goliath from Gath, whose **spear** had a shaft as thick
23. 7 You must use an iron tool or a **spear;**
23. 8 he fought with his **spear** against eight hundred men and
23.18 He fought with his **spear** against three hundred men
23.21 killed an Egyptian, a huge man who was armed with a **spear.**
23.21 snatched the **spear** from the Egyptian's hand,
2 Kgs 11.10 He gave the officers the **spears** and shields that had
1 Chr 11.11 He fought with his **spear** against three hundred men and
11.20 He fought with his **spear** against three hundred men
11.23 over two metres tall, who was armed with a gigantic **spear.**
11.23 snatched the **spear** from the Egyptian's hand,
12. 8 were experts with shields and **spears,** as fierce-looking as
12.23 6,800 well-equipped men, armed with shields and **spears;**
12.23 together with 37,000 men armed with shields and **spears;**
20. 5 of Goliath from Gath, whose **spear** had a shaft as thick as
2 Chr 11.12 food, olive-oil, and wine, [12] and also shields and **spears.**
14. 8 with shields and **spears,** and 280,000 men from Benjamin,
23. 9 Jehoiada gave the officers the **spears** and shields that had
25. 5 ready for battle, skilled in using **spears** and shields.
26.14 the army with shields, **spears,** helmets, coats of armour,
32. 5 He also had a large number of **spears** and shields made.
Neh 4.13 armed the people with swords, **spears,** and bows, and
4.16 guard, wearing coats of armour and armed with **spears,**
4.21 on the wall, while the other half stood guard with **spears.**
Job 41. 7 you fill his hide with **fishing-spears** or pierce his head
41.26 no **spear** or arrow or lance that can harm him.
41.29 is a piece of straw, and he laughs when men throw **spears.**
Ps 35. 3 Lift up your **spear** and your axe against those who pursue me.
46. 9 he breaks bows, destroys **spears,** and sets shields on fire.
57. 4 Their teeth are like **spears** and arrows;

Is 2. 4 They will hammer their swords into ploughs and their **spears** into pruning-knives.
Jer 46. 4 Sharpen your **spears!**
Ezek 39. 9 with the shields, bows, arrows, **spears,** and clubs, and will
Joel 3.10 ploughs into swords and your pruning-knives into **spears.**
Mic 4. 3 They will hammer their swords into ploughs and their **spears** into pruning-knives.
Nah 3. 3 Horsemen charge, swords flash, **spears** gleam!
Hab 3.11 the gleam of your shining **spear,** the sun and the moon stood
Jn 19.34 the soldiers, however, plunged his **spear** into Jesus' side,
Acts 23.23 seventy horsemen and two hundred **spearmen,** and be ready to

SPECIAL

Gen 2. 3 set it apart as a **special** day, because by that day he
Ex 29.24 and tell them to dedicate it to me as a **special** gift.
29.26 of this ram and dedicate it to me as a **special** gift.
29.27 dedicated to me as a **special** gift and set aside for the
Lev 7.14 of each kind of bread as a **special** contribution to the Lord;
7.29 part of it as a **special** gift to the Lord, [30] bringing it
7.30 its breast and present it as a **special** gift to the Lord.
7.32 shall be given as a **special** contribution [33] to the priest
7.34 of the animal is a **special** gift,
7.34 right hind leg is a **special** contribution that the Lord has
8.27 sons, and they presented it as a **special** gift to the Lord.
8.29 the breast and presented it as a **special** gift to the Lord.
9.21 right hind legs as the **special** gift to the Lord for the
10.14 the special gift and the **special** contribution to the Lord
14.12 shall present them as a **special** gift to the Lord for the
14.21 lamb as his repayment-offering, a **special** gift to the Lord
14.24 and present them as a **special** gift to the Lord for the
23.11 shall present it as a **special** offering to the Lord, so that
23.17 of bread and present them to the Lord as a **special** gift.
23.20 the two lambs as a **special** gift to the Lord for the
23.23 the seventh month observe a **special** day of rest, and come
23.32 observe this day as a **special** day of rest, during which
23.39 The first day shall be a **special** day of rest.
27. 2 Lord in fulfilment of a **special** vow, that person may be set
Num 5. 9 Also every **special** contribution which the Israelites offer
6. 2 or woman who makes a **special** vow to become a Nazirite and
6.20 the priest shall present them as a **special** gift to the Lord;
8.11 Levites to me as a **special** gift from the Israelites, so that
8.13 "Dedicate the Levites as a **special** gift to me, and put
8.21 and Aaron dedicated them as a **special** gift to the Lord.
15.19 is to be set aside as a **special** contribution to the Lord.
15.20 is to be presented as a **special** contribution to the Lord.
15.20 the same way as the **special** contribution you make from the
15.21 all time to come, this **special** gift is to be given to
18. 8 am giving you all the **special** contributions made to me that
18.11 "In addition, any other **special** contributions that the
18.18 the breast and the right hind leg of the **special** offering.
18.19 time to come, all the **special** contributions which the
18.24 the Israelites present to me as a **special** contribution.
18.26 present a tenth of it as a **special** contribution to the Lord.
18.27 This **special** contribution will be considered as the
18.28 you also will present the **special** contribution that belongs
18.28 You are to give this **special** contribution for the Lord to
31.29 to Eleazar the priest as a **special** contribution to the Lord.
31.41 Eleazar the tax as a **special** contribution to the Lord, as
Deut 7. 6 peoples on earth he chose you to be his own **special** people.
12.11 and your offerings, and those **special** gifts that you have
Judg 20.15 seven hundred **specially** chosen men who were left-handed.
20.34 Ten thousand men, **specially** chosen out of all Israel,
1 Sam 1.21 yearly sacrifice and the **special** sacrifice he had promised.
21. 5 how much more this time when we are on a **special** mission!"
2 Chr 30. 1 He took **special** care to send letters to the tribes of
Esth 2. 9 beginning her beauty treatment of massage and **special** diet.
2. 9 harem and assigned seven girls **specially** chosen from the
Jer 45. 5 Are you looking for **special** treatment for yourself?
Ezek 16.34 You are a **special** kind of prostitute.
48. 8 section of the land is to be set apart for **special** use.
48. 9 centre of this section, a **special** area twelve and a half
48.12 they are to have a **special** area next to the area belonging
48.13 also are to have a **special** area, south of that of the
48.15 The part of the **special** area that is left, twelve and a
48.23 South of this **special** section, each of the
Zech 2.12 again Judah will be the **special** possession of the Lord in
Rom 9.21 lump of clay, one for **special** occasions and the other for
1 Cor 7. 7 but each one has a **special** gift from God, one person this
12.23 very nice are treated with **special** modesty, [24] which the
2 Cor 8. 6 it and help you complete this **special** service of love.
11. 5 bit inferior to those very **special** so-called "apostles"
12.11 am in no way inferior to those very **special** "apostles" of
Gal 2. 9 leaders, recognized that God had given me this **special** task;
4.10 You pay **special** attention to certain days, months,
Eph 3. 7 of the gospel by God's **special** gift, which he gave me
4. 7 of us has received a **special** gift in proportion to what
Col 2.18 to be superior because of **special** visions and who insists on
2 Tim 2.20 some are for **special** occasions, others for ordinary use.
2.21 he will be used for **special** purposes, because he is
Tit 3. 8 I want you to give **special** emphasis to these matters, so
1 Pet 4.10 good of others the **special** gift he has received from God.

SPECK

Gen 13.16 be as easy to count all the **specks** of dust on earth!
28.14 will be as numerous as the **specks** of dust on the earth.
Mt 7. 3 do you look at the **speck** in your brother's eye, and pay
7. 4 'Please, let me take that **speck** out of your eye,' when you
7. 5 to see clearly to take the **speck** out of your brother's eye.
Lk 6.41 do you look at the **speck** in your brother's eye, but pay
Lk 6.42 brother, let me take that **speck** out of your eye,' yet cannot
6.42 to see clearly to take the **speck** out of your brother's eye.

SPECKLED

Gen 30.32 every black lamb and every spotted or **speckled** young goat.
30.33 have any goat that isn't **speckled** or spotted or any sheep
30.35 all the females that were **speckled** and spotted or which had
30.39 branches, they produced young that were streaked, **speckled,**
31. 8 Whenever Laban said, 'The **speckled** goats shall be your wages,'
31. 8 all the flocks produced **speckled** young.
31.10 goats that were mating were striped, spotted, and **speckled.**
31.12 male goats that are mating are striped, spotted, and **speckled.**

SPECTACLE

Lk 23.48 gathered there to watch the **spectacle** saw what happened,
1 Cor 4. 9 die in public as a **spectacle** for the whole world of angels
Col 2.15 he made a public **spectacle** of them by leading them as

SPEECH

Num 22.28 the donkey the power of **speech,** and it said to Balaam,
Job 8. 1 Are you finally through with your windy **speech?**
11. 3 That your mocking words will leave us **speechless?**
Ps 10. 7 His **speech** is filled with curses, lies, and threats;
19. 3 No **speech** or words are used, no sound is heard;
36. 3 His **speech** is wicked and full of lies;
55. 9 Confuse the **speech** of my enemies, O Lord!
Prov 22.11 and graciousness of **speech,** the king will be your friend.
Is 42. 2 or raise his voice or make loud **speeches** in the streets.
52.15 marvel at him, and kings will be **speechless** with amazement.
Ezek 3.27 you back the power of **speech,** you will tell them what I,
24.27 get back the power of **speech** which you had lost, and you
33.22 next morning, the Lord gave me back the power of **speech.**
Dan 10.15 When he said this, I stared at the ground, **speechless.**
Amos 7.10 His **speeches** will destroy the country.
Mt 12.19 not argue or shout, or make loud **speeches** in the streets.
Mk 7.35 was able to hear, his **speech** impediment was removed, and he
Acts 12.21 robes, sat on his throne, and made a **speech** to the people.
19.33 to be silent, and he tried to make a **speech** of defence.
Rom 3.14 their **speech** is filled with bitter curses.
16.18 By their fine words and flattering **speech** they deceive innocent people.
1 Cor 1. 5 rich in all things, including all **speech** and all knowledge.
13. 1 I have no love, my **speech** is no more than a noisy
13.11 I was a child, my **speech,** feelings, and thinking were all
2 Cor 8. 7 in faith, **speech,** and knowledge, in your eagerness to help
Col 4. 6 Your **speech** should always be pleasant and interesting, and
1 Tim 4.12 for the believers in your **speech,** your conduct, your love,

SPEED

Esth 8.14 the riders mounted royal horses and rode off at top **speed.**
Ezek 1.14 darted to and fro with the **speed** of lightning.
Hab 3.11 At the flash of your **speeding** arrows and the gleam of

SPELL

Deut 18.10 look for omens or use **spells** [11] or charms, and don't let
Is 47.12 Keep all your magic **spells** and charms;
Hos 4.17 The people of Israel are under the **spell** of idols.
Gal 3. 1 Who put a **spell** on you?

SPELT

Ezek 4. 9 "Now take some wheat, barley, beans, peas, millet, and **spelt.**

SPEND (1)

Gen 5.24 He **spent** his life in fellowship with God,
19. 2 "No, we will **spend the night** here in the city square."
24.23 in his house for my men and me to **spend the night?"**
24.54 the men with him ate and drank, and **spent the night** there.
31.54 After they had eaten, they **spent the night** on the mountain.
32.13 After **spending the night** there, Jacob chose from
32.21 the gifts on ahead of him and **spent that night** in camp.
40. 4 They **spent** a long time in prison, and the captain assigned
42.27 the place where they **spent the night,** one of them opened his
Ex 19.10 people and tell them to **spend** today and tomorrow purifying
Num 14.34 for each of the forty days you **spent** exploring the land.
22. 8 Balaam said to them, **"Spend the night** here, and tomorrow
Deut 2. 1 Lord had commanded, and we **spent** a long time wandering about
2. 3 told me [3] that we had **spent** enough time wandering about in
Josh 2. 1 city, they went to **spend the night** in the house of a
5. 4 the forty years the people **spent** crossing the desert, none
6.11 Then they came back to camp and **spent the night** there.
8. 9 Joshua **spent the night** in camp.
8.13 Joshua **spent the night** in the valley.
Judg 19. 4 The couple had their meals and **spent the nights** there.
19. 6 to him, "Please **spend the night** here and enjoy yourself."
19. 7 father urged him to stay, so he **spent another night** there.
19.10 did not want to **spend another night** there, so he and his
19.10 we stop and **spend the night** here in this Jebusite city?"
19.12 a little farther and **spend the night** at Gibeah or Ramah."
19.15 They turned off the road to go and **spend the night** there.
19.20 you don't have to **spend the night** in the square."
20. 4 to Gibeah in the territory of Benjamin to **spend the night.**
2 Sam 12.16 went into his room and **spent the night** lying on the floor.
17.16 to David not to **spend the night** at the river crossings in
1 Kgs 5.14 10,000 men, and each group **spent** one month in Lebanon and

1 Kgs 19. 9 There he went into a cave to **spend the night.**
1 Chr 12.39 They **spent** three days there with David, feasting on the
16.43 and David went home to **spend** some time with his family.
2 Chr 7. 9 They had **spent** seven days for the dedication of the altar
20.25 They **spent** three days gathering the loot, but there was so
Ezra 10. 6 son of Eliashib, and **spent the night** there grieving over the
Neh 13.20 kinds of goods **spent Friday night** outside the city walls.
Job 39. 9 Is he willing to **spend the night** in your stable?
Ps 77. 6 **I spend the night** in deep thought;
84.10 One day **spent** in your Temple is better than a thousand
Prov 20.13 If you **spend** your time sleeping, you will be poor.
Ecc 1. 3 You **spend** your life working, labouring, and what do you
2. 3 the best way people can **spend** their short lives on earth.
Song 7.11 out to the countryside and **spend the night** in the villages.
Is 5.11 start drinking, and you **spend** long evenings getting drunk.
10.29 They have crossed the pass and are **spending the night** at Geba!
Jer 5. 7 committed adultery and **spent** their time with prostitutes.
15.17 I did not **spend** my time with other people, laughing and
Dan 6.18 to the palace and **spent a sleepless night,** without food or
Mt 4. 2 After **spending** forty days and nights without food, Jesus was hungry.
12.40 the same way that Jonah **spent** three days and nights in the
12.40 will the Son of Man **spend** three days and nights in the
21.17 went out of the city to Bethany, where he **spent the night.**
Lk 1.21 and wondering why he was **spending** such a long time in the
2. 8 of the country who were **spending the night** in the fields,
6.12 a hill to pray and **spent the whole night** there praying to
8.27 not stay at home, but **spent** his time in the burial caves.
21.37 Jesus **spent** those days teaching in the Temple, and when evening came,
21.37 he would go out and **spend the night** on the Mount of
24.53 filled with great joy, [53]and **spent** all their time in the
Jn 1.39 saw where he lived, and **spent** the rest of that day with
3.22 of Judaea, where he **spent** some time with them and baptized.
4.43 After **spending** two days there, Jesus left and went to Galilee.
Acts 2.42 They **spent** their time in learning from the apostles,
9.36 She **spent** all her time doing good and helping the poor.
10.23 the men in and persuaded them to **spend the night** there.
12.19 After this, Herod left Judaea and **spent** some time in Caesarea.
15.33 After **spending** some time there, they were sent off in
15.35 Paul and Barnabas **spent** some time in Antioch, and
16.12 We **spent** several days there.
17.21 who lived there liked to **spend** all their time telling and
18.23 After **spending** some time there, he left and went through
19.22 helpers, to Macedonia, while he **spent** more time in the
20. 6 days later we joined them in Troas, where we **spent** a week.
20.18 them, "You know how I **spent** the whole time I was with
21.15 After **spending** some time there, we got our things ready
25. 6 Festus **spent** another eight or ten days with them and then
26. 4 They know how I have **spent** my whole life, at first in
27. 9 We **spent** a long time there, until it became dangerous to
27.12 The harbour was not a good one to **spend** the winter in;
27.12 Phoenix, if possible, in order to **spend** the winter there.
28.11 "The Twin Gods," which had **spent** the winter in the island.
1 Cor 7. 5 so for a while in order to **spend** your time in prayer;
16. 6 I shall probably **spend** some time with you, perhaps the whole winter,
16. 7 I hope to **spend** quite a long time with you, if the
2 Cor 11.25 shipwrecks, and once I **spent** twenty-four hours in the water.
Tit 3. 3 We **spent** our lives in malice and envy;
3.12 Nicopolis, because I have decided to **spend** the winter there.
3.14 Our people must learn to **spend** their time doing good, in
1 Pet 1.17 so then, **spend** the rest of your lives here on earth in
4. 3 You have **spent** enough time in the past doing what the
4. 3 Your lives were **spent** in indecency, lust, drunkenness, orgies, drinking parties,

SPEND (2)

Gen 31.15 us, and now he has **spent** all the money he was paid
47.15 in Egypt and Canaan was **spent,** the Egyptians came to Joseph
Ex 30.16 the people of Israel and **spend** it for the upkeep of the
Deut 14.26 **Spend** it on whatever you want—beef, lamb, wine, beer—and there,
Ezra 7.17 "You are to **spend** this money carefully and buy bulls,
Prov 11.24 Some people **spend** their money freely and still grow richer.
17.16 a fool no good to **spend** money on an education, because he
21.20 and luxury, but stupid people **spend** their money as fast as
29. 3 It is a foolish waste to **spend** money on prostitutes.
31. 3 Don't **spend** all your energy on sex and all your money on
Is 55. 2 Why **spend** money on what does not satisfy?
55. 2 Why **spend** your wages and still be hungry?
Mk 5.26 She had **spent** all her money, but instead of getting better
6.37 want us to go and **spend** two hundred silver coins on bread
Lk 8.43 she had **spent** all she had on doctors, but no one had
10.35 this way, I will pay you whatever else you **spend** on him.'"
15.14 He **spent** everything he had.
2 Cor 12.15 I will be glad to **spend** all I have, and myself as

SPEW

Jon 2.10 Lord ordered the fish to **spew** Jonah up on the beach, and

SPICE

Gen 37.25 Their camels were loaded with **spices** and resins.
43.11 a little resin, a little honey, **spices,** pistachio nuts, and
Ex 25. 6 **spices** for the anointing oil and for the sweet-smelling incense;
30.23 "Take the finest **spices**—six kilogrammes of liquid myrrh,
30.34 **spices**—stacte, onycha, galbanum, and pure frankincense.
35. 8 **spices** for the anointing oil and for the sweet-smelling incense;
Ex 35.28 and the breast-piece [28]and **spices** and oil for the lamps,
1 Kgs 10. 2 well as camels loaded with **spices,** jewels, and a large
10.10 of gold and a very large amount of **spices** and jewels.
10.10 The amount of **spices** she gave him was by far the greatest
10.25 gift—articles of silver and gold, robes, weapons, **spices,**
2 Kgs 20.13 his silver and gold, his **spices** and perfumes, and all his
1 Chr 9.29 and of the flour, wine, olive-oil, incense, and **spices.**
9.30 responsibility for mixing the **spices** belonged to the priests.
2 Chr 2. 4 by burning incense of fragrant **spices,** where we will present
9. 1 well as camels loaded with **spices,** jewels, and a large
9. 9 of gold and a very large amount of **spices** and jewels.
9. 9 have never been any other **spices** as fine as those that the
9.24 gifts—articles of silver and gold, robes, weapons, **spices,**
16.14 used **spices** and perfumed oils to prepare his body for burial,
32.27 stones, **spices,** shields, and other valuable objects.
Prov 9. 2 killed for a feast, mixed **spices** in the wine, and laid the
Song 4.10 your perfume more fragrant than any **spice.**
5. 1 I am gathering my **spices** and myrrh;
5.13 as lovely as a garden that is full of herbs and **spices.**
7. 2 A bowl is there, that never runs out of **spiced** wine.
8. 2 I would give you **spiced** wine, my pomegranate wine to drink.
8.14 like a young stag on the mountains where **spices** grow.
Is 39. 2 his silver and gold, his **spices** and perfumes, and all his
Jer 6.20 they bring me from Sheba, or the **spices** from a distant land?
Ezek 27.17 paid for your goods with wheat, honey, olive-oil, and **spices.**
27.18 They exchanged wrought iron and **spices** for your goods.
27.22 Sheba and Raamah exchanged jewels, gold, and the finest **spices.**
Mk 16. 1 of James, and Salome bought **spices** to go and anoint the body
Lk 23.56 home and prepared the **spices** and perfumes for the body.
24. 1 went to the tomb, carrying the **spices** they had prepared.
Jn 19.39 thirty kilogrammes of **spices,** a mixture of myrrh and aloes.
19.40 it in linen with the **spices** according to the Jewish custom
Rev 18.13 and cinnamon, **spice,** incense, myrrh, and frankincense;

SPIDER

Job 8.14 They trust a thread—a **spider's** web.
27.18 wicked build houses like a **spider's** web or like the hut of

SPIKE

Is 41.15 like a threshing-board, with **spikes** that are new and sharp.

SPILL

Gen 38. 9 widow, he let the semen **spill** on the ground, so that there
2 Sam 14.14 we are like water **spilt** on the ground, which can't be
20.10 him in the belly, and his entrails **spilt** out on the ground.
1 Kgs 13. 5 fell apart and the ashes **spilt** to the ground, as the prophet
Ps 22.14 My strength is gone, gone like water **spilt** on the ground.
Ezek 24. 7 but the blood was not **spilt** on the ground where the dust
24. 7 it was **spilt** on a bare rock.
Mk 4.37 and the waves began to **spill** over into the boat, so that
Acts 1.18 he burst open and all his bowels **spilt** out.

SPIN

Prov 31.19 She **spins** her own thread and weaves her own cloth.
Is 21. 4 My head is **spinning,** and I am trembling with fear.

SPIRAL

1 Kgs 7.29 the lions and bulls, there were **spiral** figures in relief.
7.30 the supports were decorated with **spiral** figures in relief.
7.36 there was space for them, with **spiral** figures all round.

SPIRIT (1) (GOD'S SPIRIT)

[GOD'S SPIRIT, HOLY SPIRIT, LORD'S SPIRIT]
see also **HELPER (2)**

Gen 41.38 better man than Joseph, a man who has **God's spirit** in him."
Num 11.17 will take some of the **spirit** I have given you and give
11.25 He took some of the **spirit** he had given to Moses and
11.25 When the **spirit** came on them, they began to shout like prophets,
11.26 There in the camp the **spirit** came on them, and they too
11.29 the Lord would give his **spirit** to all his people and make
24. 2 The **spirit of God** took control of him, [3]and he uttered this
Judg 3.10 The **spirit of the Lord** came upon him, and he became
6.34 The **spirit of the Lord** took control of Gideon, and he
11.29 Then the **spirit of the Lord** came upon Jephthah.
1 Sam 10. 6 Suddenly the **spirit of the Lord** will take control of you,
10.10 Suddenly the **spirit of God** took control of him, and he
11. 6 Saul heard this, the **spirit of God** took control of him, and
16.13 Immediately the **spirit of the Lord** took control of David and
16.14 The **Lord's spirit** left Saul, and an evil spirit sent by
19.20 Then the **spirit of God** took control of Saul's men, and they
19.23 was going there, the **spirit of God** took control of him also,
2 Sam 23. 2 The **spirit of the Lord** speaks through me;
1 Kgs 18.12 What if the **spirit of the Lord** carries you off to some
22.24 asked, "Since when did the **Lord's spirit** leave me and speak
2 Kgs 2.16 Maybe the **spirit of the Lord** has carried him away and left
1 Chr 12.18 **God's spirit** took control of one of them, Amasai,
2 Chr 15. 1 The **spirit of God** came upon Azariah son of Oded, [2]and he
18.23 asked, "Since when did the **Lord's spirit** leave me and speak
20.14 The **spirit of the Lord** came upon a Levite who was
24.20 Then the **spirit of God** took control of Zechariah son of
Job 32. 8 But it is the **spirit of Almighty God** that comes to men
33. 4 **God's spirit** made me and gave me life.
Ps 51.11 do not take your **holy spirit** away from me.
Is 11. 2 The **spirit of the Lord** will give him wisdom, and the
32.15 But once more God will send us his **spirit.**

Is 33.11 My **spirit** is like a fire that will destroy you.
42. 1 have filled him with my **spirit,** and he will bring justice to
44. 3 I will pour out my **spirit** on your children and my blessing
61. 1 The Sovereign Lord has filled me with his **spirit.**
63.10 but they rebelled against him and made his **holy spirit** sad.
63.11 Where is the Lord, who gave his **spirit** to Moses?
Ezek 2. 2 While the voice was speaking, **God's spirit** entered me
3.12 Then **God's spirit** lifted me up, and I heard behind me
3.14 great force, and as his **spirit** carried me off, I felt bitter
3.24 but **God's spirit** entered me and raised me
8. 3 Then in this vision **God's spirit** lifted me high in the air
11. 1 **God's spirit** lifted me up and took me to the east gate
11. 5 The **spirit of the Lord** took control of me, and the Lord
11.24 In the vision the **spirit of God** lifted me up and brought
36.27 I will put my **spirit** in you and I will see to
37. 1 of the Lord, and his **spirit** took me and set me down
39.29 I will pour out my **spirit** on the people of Israel and
43. 5 The **Lord's spirit** lifted me up and took me into the inner
Joel 2.28 "Afterwards I will pour out my **spirit** on everyone:
2.29 I will pour out my **spirit** even on servants, both men and
Mic 3. 8 Lord fills me with his **spirit** and power, and gives me a
Zech 4. 6 by military might or by your own strength, but by my **spirit.**
Mt 1.18 that she was going to have a baby by the **Holy Spirit.**
1.20 For it is by the **Holy Spirit** that she has conceived.
3.11 after me will baptize you with the **Holy Spirit** and fire.
3.16 and he saw the **Spirit of God** coming down like a dove
4. 1 Then the **Spirit** led Jesus into the desert to be tempted by
10.20 come from the **Spirit** of your Father speaking through you.
11.29 and learn from me, because I am gentle and humble in **spirit;**
12.18 I will send my **Spirit** upon him, and he will announce my
12.28 it is not Beelzebul, but **God's Spirit,** who gives me the
12.31 says evil things against the **Holy Spirit** will not be forgiven.
12.32 says something against the **Holy Spirit** will not be forgiven—now
22.43 Jesus asked, "did the **Spirit** inspire David to call him 'Lord'?
28.19 Father, the Son, and the **Holy Spirit,** [20] and teach them to
Mk 1. 8 with water, but he will baptize you with the **Holy Spirit."**
1.10 saw heaven opening and the **Spirit** coming down on him like a
1.12 At once the **Spirit** made him go into the desert,
3.29 says evil things against the **Holy Spirit** will never be forgiven,
12.36 The **Holy Spirit** inspired David to say:
13.11 they will come from the **Holy Spirit.**
Lk 1.15 will be filled with the **Holy Spirit,** [16] and he will bring
1.35 The angel answered, "The **Holy Spirit** will come on you,
1.41 Elizabeth was filled with the **Holy Spirit** [42] and said in a
1.67 was filled with the **Holy Spirit,** and he spoke God's message:
2.25 The **Holy Spirit** was with him [26] and had assured him that he
2.27 Led by the **Spirit,** Simeon went into the Temple.
3.16 He will baptize you with the **Holy Spirit** and fire.
3.22 heaven was opened, [22] and the **Holy Spirit** came down upon
4. 1 the Jordan full of the **Holy Spirit** and was led by the
4. 1 and was led by the **Spirit** into the desert, [2] where he was
4.14 to Galilee, and the power of the **Holy Spirit** was with him.
4.18 it is written, [18] "The **Spirit of the Lord** is upon me,
10.21 filled with joy by the **Holy Spirit** and said, "Father, Lord
11.13 Father in heaven give the **Holy Spirit** to those who ask him!"
12.10 says evil things against the **Holy Spirit** will not be forgiven.
12.12 For the **Holy Spirit** will teach you at that time what you
Jn 1.32 "I saw the **Spirit** come down like a dove from heaven and
1.33 me, 'You will see the **Spirit** come down and stay on a
1.33 he is the one who baptizes with the **Holy Spirit.'**
3. 5 Kingdom of God unless he is born of water and the **Spirit.**
3. 6 of human parents, but he is born spiritually of the **Spirit.**
3. 8 It is like that with everyone who is born of the **Spirit."**
3.34 God's words, because God gives him the fullness of his **Spirit.**
4.23 when by the power of **God's Spirit** people will worship the
4.24 God is **Spirit,** and only by the power of his Spirit can
6.63 What gives life is **God's Spirit;**
6.63 The words I have spoken to you bring God's life-giving **Spirit.**
7.39 Jesus said this about the **Spirit,** which those who
7.39 At that time the **Spirit** had not yet been given, because
14.17 He is the **Spirit** who reveals the truth about God.
14.26 The Helper, the **Holy Spirit,** whom the Father will send
15.26 "The Helper will come—the **Spirit,** who reveals the truth
16.13 When, however, the **Spirit** comes, who reveals the truth about God,
16.15 why I said that the **Spirit** will take what I give him
20.22 Then he breathed on them and said, "Receive the **Holy Spirit.**
Acts 1. 2 by the power of the **Holy Spirit** to the men he had
1. 5 in a few days you will be baptized with the **Holy Spirit."**
1. 8 But when the **Holy Spirit** comes upon you, you will be
1.16 come true in which the **Holy Spirit,** speaking through David,
2. 4 were all filled with the **Holy Spirit** and began to talk in
2. 4 in other languages, as the **Spirit** enabled them to speak.
2.17 I will pour out my **Spirit** on everyone.
2.18 I will pour out my **Spirit** in those days, and they will
2.33 has received from him the **Holy Spirit,** as he had promised.
2.38 and you will receive God's gift, the **Holy Spirit.**
4. 8 Peter, full of the **Holy Spirit,** answered them,
4.25 By means of the **Holy Spirit** you spoke through our ancestor David,
4.31 were all filled with the **Holy Spirit** and began to proclaim
5. 3 make you lie to the **Holy Spirit** by keeping part of the
5. 9 your husband decide to put the Lord's **Spirit** to the test?
5.32 these things—we and the **Holy Spirit,** who is God's gift to
6. 3 to be full of the **Holy Spirit** and wisdom, and we will
6. 5 full of faith and the **Holy Spirit,** and Philip, Prochorus, Nicanor,
6.10 But the **Spirit** gave Stephen such wisdom that when he spoke,
7.51 you too have always resisted the **Holy Spirit!**
7.55 But Stephen, full of the **Holy Spirit,** looked up to heaven
8.15 prayed for the believers that they might receive the **Holy Spirit.**
8.16 For the **Holy Spirit** had not yet come down on any of
Acts 8.17 John placed their hands on them, and they received the **Holy Spirit.**
8.18 Simon saw that the **Spirit** had been given to the
8.19 anyone I place my hands on will receive the **Holy Spirit."**
8.29 The **Holy Spirit** said to Philip, "Go over to that carriage
8.39 out of the water, the **Spirit of the Lord** took Philip away.
9.17 you might see again and be filled with the **Holy Spirit."**
9.31 Through the help of the **Holy Spirit** it was strengthened and
10.19 to understand what the vision meant, when the **Spirit** said,
10.38 and how God poured out on him the **Holy Spirit** and power.
10.44 Peter was still speaking, the **Holy Spirit** came down on all
10.45 poured out his gift of the **Holy Spirit** on the Gentiles also.
10.47 "These people have received the **Holy Spirit,** just as we also did.
11.12 The **Spirit** told me to go with them without hesitation.
11.15 I began to speak, the **Holy Spirit** came down on them just
11.16 with water, but you will be baptized with the **Holy Spirit.'**
11.24 good man, full of the **Holy Spirit** and faith, and many people
11.28 by the power of the **Spirit** predicted that a severe famine
13. 2 the Lord and fasting, the **Holy Spirit** said to them, "Set
13. 4 Having been sent by the **Holy Spirit,** Barnabas and Saul
13. 9 Then Saul—also known as Paul—was filled with the **Holy Spirit;**
13.52 The believers in Antioch were full of joy and the **Holy Spirit.**
15. 8 the Gentiles by giving the **Holy Spirit** to them, just as he
15.28 The **Holy Spirit** and we have agreed not to put any other
16. 6 and Galatia because the **Holy Spirit** did not let them preach
16. 7 of Bithynia, but the **Spirit** of Jesus did not allow them.
19. 2 "Did you receive the **Holy Spirit** when you became believers?"
19. 2 even heard that there is a **Holy Spirit,"** they answered.
19. 6 his hands on them, and the **Holy Spirit** came upon them;
20.22 in obedience to the **Holy Spirit** I am going to Jerusalem,
20.23 that in every city the **Holy Spirit** has warned me that prison
20.28 all the flock which the **Holy Spirit** has placed in your care.
21. 4 By the power of the **Spirit** they told Paul not to go
21.11 with it, and said, "This is what the **Holy Spirit** says:
28.25 "How well the **Holy Spirit** spoke through the prophet Isaiah
Rom 2.29 this is the work of **God's Spirit,** not of the written Law.
5. 5 hearts by means of the **Holy Spirit,** who is God's gift to
7. 6 of a written law, but in the new way of the **Spirit.**
8. 2 For the law of the **Spirit,** which brings us life in union
8. 4 according to the **Spirit,** and not according to human nature.
8. 5 Those who live as the **Spirit** tells them to,
8. 5 have their minds controlled by what the **Spirit** wants.
8. 6 to be controlled by the **Spirit** results in life and peace.
8. 9 instead, you live as the **Spirit** tells you to—
8. 9 if, in fact, **God's Spirit** lives in you.
8. 9 Whoever does not have the **Spirit** of Christ does not belong
8.10 Christ lives in you, the **Spirit** is life for you because you
8.11 If the **Spirit of God,** who raised Jesus from death, lives
8.11 to your mortal bodies by the presence of his **Spirit** in you.
8.13 but if by the **Spirit** you put to death your sinful actions,
8.14 Those who are led by **God's Spirit** are God's sons.
8.15 For the **Spirit** that God has given you does not make you
8.15 instead, the **Spirit** makes you God's children, and by the
8.15 God's children, and by the **Spirit's** power we cry out to God,
8.16 **God's Spirit** joins himself to our spirits to declare
8.23 we who have the **Spirit** as the first of God's gifts also
8.26 In the same way the **Spirit** also comes to help us, weak
8.26 the **Spirit** himself pleads with God for us in groans that
8.27 into our hearts, knows what the thought of the **Spirit** is;
8.27 because the **Spirit** pleads with God on behalf of his people
9. 1 My conscience, ruled by the **Holy Spirit,** also assures me
14.17 of the righteousness, peace, and joy which the **Holy Spirit** gives.
15.13 hope will continue to grow by the power of the **Holy Spirit.**
15.16 acceptable to God, dedicated to him by the **Holy Spirit.**
15.19 miracles and wonders, and by the power of the **Spirit of God.**
15.30 our Lord Jesus Christ and by the love that the **Spirit** gives:
1 Cor 2. 4 but with convincing proof of the power of **God's Spirit.**
2.10 us that God made known his secret by means of his **Spirit.**
2.10 The **Spirit** searches everything, even the hidden depths of God's purposes.
2.11 in the same way, only **God's Spirit** knows all about God.
2.12 instead, we have received the **Spirit** sent by God,
2.13 in words taught by the **Spirit,**
2.13 as we explain spiritual truths to those who have the **Spirit.**
2.14 Whoever does not have the **Spirit**
2.14 cannot receive the gifts that come from **God's Spirit.**
2.15 Whoever has the **Spirit,** however, is able to judge the
3. 1 talk to you as I talk to people who have the **Spirit;**
3.16 you are God's temple and that **God's Spirit** lives in you!
6.11 by the Lord Jesus Christ and by the **Spirit of our God.**
6.19 is the temple of the **Holy Spirit,** who lives in you and
7.40 is my opinion, and I think that I too have **God's Spirit.**
12. 1 Now, concerning what you wrote about the gifts from the **Holy Spirit.**
12. 3 one who is led by **God's Spirit** can say "A curse on
12. 3 "Jesus is Lord," unless he is guided by the **Holy Spirit.**
12. 4 kinds of spiritual gifts, but the same **Spirit** gives them.
12. 7 The **Spirit's** presence is shown in some way in each person
12. 8 The **Spirit** gives one person a message full of wisdom,
12. 8 person the same **Spirit** gives a message full of knowledge.
12. 9 One and the same **Spirit** gives faith to one person,
12.10 The **Spirit** gives one person the power to work miracles;
12.10 gifts that come from the **Spirit** and those that do not.
12.11 But it is one and the same **Spirit** who does all this;
12.13 one body by the same **Spirit,**
12.13 and we have all been given the one **Spirit** to drink.
14. 2 He is speaking secret truths by the power of the **Spirit.**
14.12 have the gifts of the **Spirit,** you must try above everything
15.45 but the last Adam is the life-giving **Spirit.**
2 Cor 1.22 who has given us the **Holy Spirit** in our hearts as the
3. 3 but with the **Spirit of the living God,** and not on stone

2 Cor	3. 6	which consists not of a written law but of the **Spirit.**
	3. 6	The written law brings death, but the **Spirit** gives life.
	3. 8	is the glory that belongs to the activity of the **Spirit!**
	3.17	Now, "the Lord" in this passage is the **Spirit;**
	3.17	where the **Spirit of the Lord** is present, there is freedom.
	3.18	the Lord, who is the **Spirit,** transforms us into his likeness
	5. 5	and he gave us his **Spirit** as the guarantee of all that
	6. 6	be God's servants—by the **Holy Spirit,** by our true love, [7] by
	11. 4	completely different from the **Spirit** and the gospel you received
	13.13	God, and the fellowship of the **Holy Spirit** be with you all.
Gal	3. 2	did you receive **God's Spirit** by doing what the Law requires
	3. 3	You began by **God's Spirit;**
	3. 5	Does God give you the **Spirit** and work miracles among you
	3.14	through faith we might receive the **Spirit** promised by God.
	4. 6	God sent the **Spirit** of his Son into our hearts,
	4. 6	the **Spirit** who cries out, "Father, my Father."
	4.29	way persecuted the one who was born because of **God's Spirit;**
	5. 5	for by the power of **God's Spirit** working through our faith.
	5.16	let the **Spirit** direct your lives, and you will not satisfy
	5.17	is opposed to what the **Spirit** wants,
	5.17	and what the **Spirit** wants is opposed to what our
	5.18	If the **Spirit** leads you, then you are not subject to the
	5.22	But the **Spirit** produces love, joy, peace, patience, kindness,
	5.25	The **Spirit** has given us life;
	6. 8	in the field of the **Spirit,**
	6. 8	from the **Spirit** he will gather the harvest
Eph	1.13	on you by giving you the **Holy Spirit** he had promised.
	1.14	The **Spirit** is the guarantee that we shall receive what
	1.17	Father, to give you the **Spirit,** who will make you wise and
	2.18	to come in the one **Spirit** into the presence of the Father.
	2.22	the others into a place where God lives through his **Spirit.**
	3. 5	it now by the **Spirit** to his holy apostles and prophets.
	3.16	give you power through his **Spirit** to be strong in your inner
	4. 3	preserve the unity which the **Spirit** gives by means of the
	4. 4	is one body and one **Spirit,** just as there is one hope
	4.30	And do not make God's **Holy Spirit** sad;
	4.30	for the **Spirit** is God's mark of ownership on you, a
	5.18	instead, be filled with the **Spirit.**
	6.17	the word of God as the sword which the **Spirit** gives you.
	6.18	Pray on every occasion, as the **Spirit** leads.
Phil	1.19	help which comes from the **Spirit** of Jesus Christ I shall be
	2. 1	You have fellowship with the **Spirit,** and you have kindness
	3. 3	God by means of his **Spirit** and rejoice in our life in
Col	1. 8	has told us of the love that the **Spirit** has given you.
	1. 9	with all the wisdom and understanding that his **Spirit** gives.
1 Thes	1. 5	also with power and the **Holy Spirit,** and with complete conviction
	1. 6	the message with the joy that comes from the **Holy Spirit.**
	4. 8	not rejecting man, but God, who gives you his **Holy Spirit.**
	5.19	Do not restrain the **Holy Spirit;**
2 Thes	2.13	to be saved by the **Spirit's** power to make you his holy
1 Tim	3.16	shown to be right by the **Spirit,** and was seen by angels.
	4. 1	The **Spirit** says clearly that some people will abandon the
2 Tim	1. 7	For the **Spirit** that God has given us does not make us
	1. 7	his **Spirit** fills us with power, love, and self-control.
	1.14	Through the power of the **Holy Spirit,** who lives in us,
Tit	3. 5	he saved us, through the **Holy Spirit,** who gives us new birth
	3. 6	God poured out the **Holy Spirit** abundantly on us through Jesus
Heb	2. 4	distributing the gifts of the **Holy Spirit** according to his will.
	3. 7	So then, as the **Holy Spirit** says, "If you hear God's
	6. 4	tasted heaven's gift and received their share of the **Holy Spirit;**
	9. 8	The **Holy Spirit** clearly teaches from all these arrangements
	9.14	Through the eternal **Spirit** he offered himself as a perfect
	10.15	And the **Holy Spirit** also gives us his witness.
	10.29	who insults the **Spirit** of grace?
1 Pet	1. 2	a holy people by his **Spirit,** to obey Jesus Christ and be
	1.11	the time to which Christ's **Spirit** in them was pointing, in
	1.12	Good News by the power of the **Holy Spirit** sent from heaven.
	4.14	the glorious Spirit, the **Spirit of God,** is resting on you.
2 Pet	1.21	under the control of the **Holy Spirit** as they spoke the
1 Jn	2.20	But you have had the **Holy Spirit** poured out on you by
	2.27	But as for you, Christ has poured out his **Spirit** on you.
	2.27	As long as his **Spirit** remains in you, you do not need
	2.27	For his **Spirit** teaches you about everything, and what he
	2.27	Obey the **Spirit's** teaching, then, and remain in union with Christ.
	3.24	And because of the **Spirit** that God has given us we know
	4. 1	who claim to have the **Spirit,** but test them
	4. 2	how you will be able to know whether it is **God's Spirit:**
	4. 2	came as a human being has the **Spirit** who comes from God.
	4. 3	denies this about Jesus does not have the **Spirit** from God.
	4. 4	the false prophets, because the **Spirit** who is in you
	4. 6	how we can tell the difference between the **Spirit** of truth
	4.13	lives in union with us, because he has given us his **Spirit.**
	5. 6	And the **Spirit** himself testifies that this is true,
	5. 6	because the **Spirit** is truth.
	5. 8	the **Spirit,** the water, and the blood;
Jude	19	by their natural desires, who do not have the **Spirit.**
	20	in the power of the **Holy Spirit,** [21] and keep yourselves in
Rev	1.10	On the Lord's day the **Spirit** took control of me, and I
	2. 7	listen to what the **Spirit** says to the churches!
	2.11	listen to what the **Spirit** says to the churches!
	2.17	listen to what the **Spirit** says to the churches!
	2.29	listen to what the **Spirit** says to the churches!
	3. 6	listen to what the **Spirit** says to the churches!
	3.13	listen to what the **Spirit** says to the churches!
	3.22	listen to what the **Spirit** says to the churches!"
	4. 2	At once the **Spirit** took control of me.
	14.13	answers the **Spirit.**
	17. 3	The **Spirit** took control of me,
	21.10	The **Spirit** took control of me,
	22. 6	Lord God, who gives his **Spirit** to the prophets, has sent his
	22.17	The **Spirit** and the Bride say, "Come!"

SPIRIT (2)

Ex	1.11	Egyptians put slave-drivers over them to crush their **spirits**
	6. 9	listen to him, because their **spirit** had been broken by their
Lev	19.31	go for advice to people who consult the **spirits** of the dead.
	20. 6	to people who consult the **spirits** of the dead, I will turn
	20.27	or woman who consults the **spirits** of the dead shall be
Deut	18.11	or charms, and don't let them consult the **spirits** of the dead.
1 Sam	16.14	spirit left Saul, and an **evil spirit** sent by the Lord
	16.15	him, "We know that an **evil spirit** sent by God is tormenting
	16.16	Then when the **evil spirit** comes on you, the man can play
	16.23	From then on, whenever the **evil spirit** sent by God came
	16.23	The **evil spirit** would leave, and Saul would feel better and
	18.10	The next day an **evil spirit** from God suddenly took
	19. 9	One day an **evil spirit** from the Lord took control of Saul.
	28. 8	"Consult the **spirits** for me and tell me what is going to
	28. 8	"Call up the **spirit** of the man I name."
	28.13	"I see a **spirit** coming up from the earth," she answered.
1 Kgs	22.21	until a **spirit** stepped forward, approached the Lord,
	22.22	The **spirit** replied, 'I will go and make all Ahab's prophets
2 Kgs	5.26	said, "Wasn't I there in **spirit** when the man got out of
1 Chr	10.13	find guidance by consulting the **spirits** of the dead
2 Chr	18.20	until a **spirit** stepped forward, approached the Lord,
	18.21	The **spirit** replied, 'I will go and make all Ahab's
	31.21	Law, he did in a **spirit** of complete loyalty and devotion to
Job	26. 5	The **spirits** of the dead tremble in the waters under the earth.
Ps	51.10	me, O God, and put a new and loyal **spirit** in me.
	51.17	My sacrifice is a humble **spirit,** O God;
Prov	15. 4	Kind words bring life, but cruel words crush your **spirit.**
Ecc	3.21	be sure that a man's **spirit** goes upwards
	3.21	while an animal's **spirit** goes down into the ground?
Is	8.19	ask for messages from the **spirits** and consult the dead on
	19. 3	consult mediums and ask the **spirits** of the dead for advice.
	65. 4	go to caves and tombs to consult the **spirits** of the dead.
Jer	27. 9	or by calling up the **spirits** of the dead or by magic.
	50.39	be haunted by demons and **evil spirits,** and by unclean birds.
Lam	3.20	I think of it constantly and my **spirit** is depressed.
	3.34	The Lord knows when our **spirits** are crushed in prison;
Dan	4. 8	The **spirit** of the holy gods is in him, so I told
	4. 9	fortune-tellers, I know that the **spirit** of the holy gods is
	4.18	but you can, because the **spirit** of the holy gods is in
	5.11	your kingdom who has the **spirit** of the holy gods in him.
	5.14	I have heard that the **spirit** of the holy gods is in
Zech	12.10	Jerusalem with the spirit of mercy and the **spirit** of prayer.
Mal	2.15	Didn't God make you one body and **spirit** with her?
Mt	8.16	Jesus drove out the **evil spirits** with a word and healed all
	10. 1	authority to drive out **evil spirits** and to heal every disease
	12.43	"When an **evil spirit** goes out of a person, it travels
	12.45	and brings along seven other **spirits** even worse than itself,
	26.41	The **spirit** is willing, but the flesh is weak."
Mk	1.23	then a man with an **evil spirit** in him came into the
	1.25	Jesus ordered the **spirit,** "Be quiet, and come out of the man!"
	1.26	The **evil spirit** shook the man hard, gave a loud scream,
	1.27	to give orders to the **evil spirits,** and they obey him!"
	3.11	whenever the people who had **evil spirits** in them saw him,
	3.12	Jesus sternly ordered the **evil spirits** not to tell anyone who
	3.30	some people were saying, "He has an **evil spirit** in him.")
	5. 2	This man had an **evil spirit** in him [3] and lived among the
	5. 8	because Jesus was saying, **"Evil spirit,** come out of this man!")
	5.10	Jesus not to send the **evil spirits** out of that region.
	5.12	So the **spirits** begged Jesus, "Send us to the pigs, and
	5.13	let them go, and the **evil spirits** went out of the man
	6. 7	gave them authority over the **evil spirits** [8] and ordered them,
	7.25	whose daughter had an **evil spirit** in her, heard about Jesus
	9.17	because he has an **evil spirit** in him and cannot talk.
	9.18	Whenever the **spirit** attacks him, it throws him to the ground,
	9.18	disciples to drive the **spirit** out, but they could not."
	9.20	As soon as the **spirit** saw Jesus, it threw the boy into
	9.22	"Many times the **evil spirit** has tried to kill him by
	9.25	in on them, so he gave a command to the **evil spirit.**
	9.25	"Deaf and dumb **spirit,"** he said, "I order you to come out
	9.26	The **spirit** screamed, threw the boy into a bad fit, and
	9.28	him privately, "Why couldn't we drive the **spirit** out?"
	14.38	The **spirit** is willing, but the flesh is weak."
Lk	1.80	The child grew and developed in body and **spirit.**
	4.33	a man who had the **spirit** of an evil demon in him;
	4.35	Jesus ordered the **spirit,** "Be quiet and come out of the man!"
	4.36	man gives orders to the **evil spirits,** and they come out!"
	6.18	who were troubled by **evil spirits** also came and were healed.
	7.21	sicknesses, diseases, and **evil spirits,** and gave sight to many
	8. 2	some women who had been healed of **evil spirits** and diseases:
	8.29	because Jesus had ordered the **evil spirit** to go out of him.
	9.39	A **spirit** attacks him with a sudden shout and throws him
	9.42	gave a command to the **evil spirit,** healed the boy, and gave
	10.20	But don't be glad because the **evil spirits** obey you;
	11.24	"When an **evil spirit** goes out of a person, it travels
	11.26	out and brings seven other **spirits** even worse than itself,
	13.11	A woman there had an **evil spirit** that had made her ill
	23.46	In your hands I place my **spirit!"**
Acts	5.16	bringing those who were ill or who had **evil spirits** in them;
	7.59	called out to the Lord, "Lord Jesus, receive my **spirit!"**
	8. 7	**Evil spirits** came out from many people with a loud cry,
	16.16	a slave-girl who had an **evil spirit** that enabled her to
	16.18	round and said to the **spirit,** "In the name of Jesus Christ
	16.18	The **spirit** went out of her that very moment.
	19.12	were driven away, and the **evil spirits** would go out of them.
	19.13	travelled round and drove out **evil spirits** also tried to use
	19.13	They said to the **evil spirits,** "I command you in the name
	19.15	But the **evil spirit** said to them, "I know Jesus, and I
	19.16	The man who had the **evil spirit** in him attacked them
	23. 8	not rise from death and that there are no angels or **spirits;**

Acts 23. 9 Perhaps a **spirit** or an angel really did speak to him!"
Rom 8.16 Spirit joins himself to our **spirits** to declare that we are
1 Cor 2.11 is only a person's own **spirit** within him that knows all
2.12 We have not received this world's **spirit;**
4.21 you with a whip, or in a **spirit** of love and gentleness?
5. 3 from you in body, still I am there with you in **spirit;**
5. 3 meet with you in my **spirit,** by the power of our Lord
5. 5 be destroyed, so that his **spirit** may be saved in the Day
7.34 because she wants to be dedicated both in body and **spirit;**
14.14 pray in this way, my **spirit** prays indeed, but my mind has
14.15 I will pray with my **spirit,** but I will pray also with
14.15 I will sing with my **spirit,** but I will sing also with
14.16 give thanks to God in **spirit** only, how can an ordinary
2 Cor 4.13 In the same **spirit** of faith, we also speak because we believe.
11. 4 and you accept a **spirit** and a gospel
Gal 4. 3 were slaves of the ruling **spirits** of the universe before we
4. 9 want to turn back to those weak and pitiful ruling **spirits?**
Eph 2. 2 spiritual powers in space, the **spirit** who now controls the
4.15 speaking the truth in a **spirit** of love, we must grow up
Phil 1.17 Christ sincerely, but from a **spirit** of selfish ambition;
Col 2. 5 I am with you in **spirit,** and I am glad as I
2. 8 men and from the ruling **spirits** of the universe, and not
2.20 Christ and are set free from the ruling **spirits** of the universe.
1 Thes 5.23 and keep your whole being—**spirit,** soul, and body—free from
1 Tim 4. 1 will obey lying **spirits** and follow the teachings of demons.
2 Tim 4.22 The Lord be with your **spirit.**
Heb 1.14 They are **spirits** who serve God and are sent by him to
4.12 through, to where soul and **spirit** meet, to where joints and
12.23 all mankind, and to the **spirits** of good people made perfect.
Jas 2.26 as the body without the **spirit** is dead, so also faith
4. 5 the scripture that says, "The **spirit** that God placed in us
1 Pet 3. 4 of a gentle and quiet **spirit,** which is of the greatest value
3.19 existence he went and preached to the imprisoned **spirits.**
3.20 These were the **spirits** of those who had not obeyed God
1 Jn 4. 1 to find out if the **spirit** they have comes from God.
4. 3 The **spirit** that he has is from the Enemy of Christ;
4. 4 is more powerful than the **spirit** in those who belong to the
4. 6 between the Spirit of truth and the **spirit** of error.
3 Jn 2 be in good health—as I know you are well in **spirit.**
Rev 1. 4 come, and from the seven **spirits** in front of his throne,
3. 1 one who has the seven **spirits** of God and the seven stars.
4. 5 torches were burning, which are the seven **spirits** of God.
5. 6 eyes, which are the seven **spirits** of God that have been sent
16.13 Then I saw three unclean **spirits** that looked like frogs.
16.14 They are the **spirits** of demons that perform miracles.
16.14 These three **spirits** go out to all the kings of the world,
16.16 Then the **spirits** brought the kings together in the place
18. 2 She is now haunted by demons and unclean **spirits;**

SPIRITUAL
[UNSPIRITUAL]

1 Chr 24. 5 there were temple officials and **spiritual** leaders among the
Mt 5. 3 "Happy are those who know they are **spiritually** poor;
Jn 3. 6 of human parents, but he is born **spiritually** of the Spirit.
Acts 3.20 If you do, [20] times of **spiritual** strength will come from the Lord,
Rom 1.11 in order to share a **spiritual** blessing with you to make you
4.11 And so Abraham is the **spiritual** father of all who believe in
4.16 For Abraham is the **spiritual** father of us all;
7.14 We know that the Law is **spiritual;**
11.12 to the world, and their **spiritual** poverty brought rich
11.17 and now you share the strong **spiritual** life of the Jews.
15.27 Since the Jews shared their **spiritual** blessings with the Gentiles,
1 Cor 2. 6 a message of wisdom to those who are **spiritually** mature.
2.13 the Spirit, as we explain **spiritual** truths to those who have
2.14 because their value can be judged only on a **spiritual** basis.
6.17 joins himself to the Lord becomes **spiritually** one with him.
9.11 We have sown **spiritual** seed among you.
10. 4 All ate the same spiritual bread [4] and drank the same **spiritual** drink.
10. 4 They drank from the **spiritual** rock that went with them;
12. 4 There are different kinds of **spiritual** gifts, but the same Spirit
14. 1 Set your hearts on **spiritual** gifts, especially the gift of
14.37 God's messenger or has a **spiritual** gift, he must realize
15.24 Christ will overcome all **spiritual** rulers, authorities, and
15.44 when raised, it will be a **spiritual** body.
15.44 a physical body, so there has to be a **spiritual** body.
15.46 It is not the **spiritual** that comes first,
15.46 but the physical, and then the **spiritual.**
2 Cor 4. 7 Yet we who have this **spiritual** treasure are like common clay pots,
4.16 decaying, yet our **spiritual** being is renewed day after day.
Gal 4. 3 of the universe before we reached **spiritual** maturity.
6. 1 those of you who are **spiritual** should set him right;
Eph 1. 3 by giving us every **spiritual** blessing in the heavenly world.
2. 1 In the past you were **spiritually** dead because of your
2. 2 the ruler of the **spiritual** powers in space, the spirit
2. 5 great, [5] that while we were **spiritually** dead in our
6.12 against the wicked **spiritual** forces in the heavenly world,
Phil 3.15 All of us who are **spiritually** mature should have this same attitude.
Col 1.16 including **spiritual** powers, lords, rulers, and authorities.
2.10 He is supreme over every **spiritual** ruler and authority.
2.13 You were at one time **spiritually** dead because of your
2.15 Christ freed himself from the power of the **spiritual** rulers and authorities;
1 Tim 1. 9 who are not religious or **spiritual,** for those who kill their
4. 6 Jesus, as you feed yourself **spiritually** on the words of
4. 8 some value, but **spiritual** exercise is valuable in every way,
4.14 Do not neglect the **spiritual** gift that is in you, which
Phlm 10 for while in prison I have become his **spiritual** father.
Heb 12. 9 then, should we submit to our **spiritual** Father and live!
12.16 no one become immoral or **unspiritual** like Esau, who for a
Jas 3.15 it belongs to the world, it is **unspiritual** and demonic.
1 Pet 2. 2 always thirsty for the pure **spiritual** milk, so that by
2. 5 be used in building the **spiritual** temple, where you will serve
2. 5 as holy priests to offer **spiritual** and acceptable sacrifices to God
3.18 but made alive **spiritually,** [19] and in his spiritual
3.19 alive spiritually, [19] and in his **spiritual** existence he
4. 6 them so that in their **spiritual** existence they may live as

Am **SPIT**
see also **SPEW**

SPIT
[SPAT]

Lev 15. 8 with the discharge **spits** on anyone who is ritually clean,
Num 12.14 answered, "If her father had **spat** in her face, she would
Deut 25. 9 off one of his sandals, **spit** in his face, and say, 'This
Job 7.19 Won't you look away long enough for me to swallow my **spittle?**
17. 6 they come and **spit** in my face.
30.10 too good for me, and even come and **spit** in my face.
Is 50. 6 pulled out the hairs of my beard and **spat** in my face.
Mt 26.67 Then they **spat** in his face and beat him;
27.30 They **spat** on him, and took the stick and hit him over
Mk 7.33 in the man's ears, **spat,** and touched the man's tongue.
8.23 After **spitting** on the man's eyes, Jesus placed his hands on
10.34 Gentiles, [34] who will mock him, **spit** on him, whip him, and
14.65 Some of them began to **spit** on Jesus, and they
15.19 the head with a stick, **spat** on him, fell on their knees,
Lk 18.32 Gentiles, who will mock him, insult him, and **spit** on him.
Jn 9. 6 Jesus spat on the ground and made some mud with the **spittle;**
Rev 3.16 nor cold, I am going to **spit** you out of my mouth!

SPITEFUL

Job 21.27 I know what **spiteful** thoughts you have.

SPLASH

Ezek 32. 2 but you are more like a crocodile **splashing** through a river.

SPLENDOUR

Ex 33.19 "I will make all my **splendour** pass before you and in your
Deut 33.26 like your God, riding in **splendour** across the sky, riding
1 Chr 22. 5 son Solomon is to build must be **splendid** and world-famous.
29.11 You are great and powerful, glorious, **splendid,** and
Esth 1. 4 of the imperial court with all its **splendour** and majesty.
Is 33.17 see a king ruling in **splendour** over a land that stretches in
35. 2 Everyone will see the Lord's **splendour,** see his greatness
52. 1 Holy city of God, clothe yourself with **splendour!**
63. 1 Who is this so **splendidly** dressed in red, marching along in
Jer 46.20 Egypt is like a **splendid** cow, attacked by a stinging fly
48. 2 the **splendour** of Moab is gone.
Lam 1. 6 The **splendour** of Jerusalem is a thing of the past.
1. 7 A lonely ruin now, Jerusalem recalls her ancient **splendour.**
2. 1 Its heavenly **splendour** he has turned into ruins.
Ezek 7.11 nothing of their wealth, their **splendour,** or their glory.
Dan 2.48 position, presented him with many **splendid** gifts, put him in
Hos 10. 5 They will wail when it is stripped of its golden **splendour.**
Hab 3. 3 His **splendour** covers the heavens;
Hag 2. 3 who can still remember how **splendid** the Temple used to be?
2. 9 new Temple will be more **splendid** than the old one, and there
Rev 18. 1 He had great authority, and his **splendour** brightened the whole earth.

SPLINTERS

Num 33.55 will be as troublesome as **splinters** in your eyes and thorns

SPLIT

Num 16.31 ground under Dathan and Abiram **split** open [32] and swallowed
1 Kgs 19.11 sent a furious wind that **split** the hills and shattered the
Ps 78.15 He **split** rocks open in the desert and gave them water
141. 7 Like wood that is **split** and chopped into bits, so their
Ecc 10. 9 If you **split** wood, you get hurt doing it.
Is 24.19 The earth will crack and shatter and **split** open.
48.21 he **split** the rock open, and water flowed out.
Ezek 37.22 be divided into two nations or **split** into two kingdoms.
Hab 3. 9 Your lightning **split** open the earth.
Zech 14. 4 Mount of Olives will be **split** in two from east to west
Mt 27.51 The earth shook, the rocks **split** apart, [52] the graves broke open,
Rev 16.19 The great city was **split** into three parts, and the

SPOIL

Ex 16.24 it did not **spoil** or get worms in it.
1 Pet 1. 4 in heaven, where they cannot decay or **spoil** or fade away.

SPOILS

Ezek 38.13 and property, and to march off with all those **spoils?'** "

SPOKES

1 Kgs 7.33 their axles, rims, **spokes,** and hubs were all of bronze.

SPOKESMAN

Ex 4.16 He will be your **spokesman** and speak to the people for you.

SPONGE

Mt 27.48 up at once, took a **sponge**, soaked it in cheap wine, put
Mk 15.36 them ran up with a **sponge,** soaked it in cheap wine, and
Jn 19.29 so a **sponge** was soaked in the wine, put on a stalk

SPORT

Gen 49. 6 For they killed men in anger And they crippled bulls for **sport.**

SPOT

Gen 30.32 every black lamb and every **spotted** or speckled young goat.
30.33 isn't speckled or **spotted** or any sheep that isn't black,
30.35 goats that had stripes or **spots** and all the females
30.35 that were speckled and **spotted** or which had white on them;
30.39 produced young that were streaked, speckled, and **spotted.**
31.10 that the male goats that were mating were striped, **spotted,**
31.12 'all the male goats that are mating are striped, **spotted,**
Ex 4. 6 his hand out, it was diseased, covered with white **spots,**
Lev 13.19 swelling or a reddish-white **spot** appears where the boil was,
13.20 examine him, and if the **spot** seems to be deeper than the
13.22 If the **spot** spreads, the priest shall pronounce him unclean;
13.25 If the hairs in the **spot** have turned white and it appears
13.28 But if the **spot** remains unchanged and does not spread
13.38 or a woman has white **spots** on the skin, [39]the priest shall
13.39 If the **spots** are dull white, it is only a blemish that
13.42 sore appears on the bald **spot,** it is a dreaded skin-disease.
13.58 the object and the **spot** disappears, he shall wash it again,
14.37 there are greenish or reddish **spots** that appear to be eating
2 Kgs 5.11 his God, wave his hand over the diseased **spot,** and cure me!
Jer 13.23 the colour of his skin, or a leopard remove its **spots?**
Eph 5.27 without **spot** or wrinkle or any other imperfection.
Jude 12 they are like dirty **spots** in your fellowship meals.

SPOUT

Prov 15. 2 knowledge attractive, but stupid people **spout** nonsense.

SPRANG see SPRING (3)

SPREAD

[OUTSPREAD, WIDE-SPREADING]

Gen 6. 1 When mankind had **spread** all over the world, and girls were
6.11 was evil in God's sight, and violence had **spread** everywhere.
8.17 so that they may reproduce and **spread** over all the earth."
10.18 different tribes of the Canaanites **spread** out, [19]until the
41.56 The famine grew worse and **spread** over the whole country,
Ex 1.12 in number and the further they **spread** through the land.
9. 9 They will **spread** out like fine dust over all the land of
9.16 you live so that my fame might **spread** over the whole world.
22. 6 in his field and it **spreads** through the weeds to another
23. 1 "Do not **spread** false rumours, and do not help a guilty
25.20 across the lid, and their **outspread** wings are to cover it.
37. 9 other across the lid, and their **outspread** wings covered it.
40.19 He **spread** out the covering over the Tent and put the
Lev 13. 5 the same and has not **spread,** he shall isolate him for
13. 6 and has not **spread,** he shall pronounce him ritually clean;
13. 7 But if the sore **spreads** after the priest has examined him
13. 8 again, and if it has **spread,** he shall pronounce him unclean;
13.12 If the skin-disease **spreads** and covers the person
13.22 If the spot **spreads,** the priest shall pronounce him unclean;
13.23 remains unchanged and does not **spread,** it is only the scar
13.27 day, and if it is **spreading,** it is a dreaded skin-disease,
13.28 unchanged and does not **spread** and is light in colour,
13.32 and if it has not **spread** and there are no yellowish hairs
13.34 and if it has not **spread** and does not seem to be
13.35 But if the sore **spreads** after he has been pronounced clean,
13.36 If the sore has **spread,** he need not look for yellowish hairs;
13.37 opinion the sore has not **spread** and healthy hairs are
13.49 greenish or reddish, it is a **spreading** mildew and must be
13.51 day, and if the mildew has **spread,** the object is unclean.
13.52 it, because it is a **spreading** mildew which must be destroyed
13.53 that the mildew has not **spread** on the object, [54]he shall
13.55 colour, even though it has not **spread,** it is still unclean;
13.57 the mildew reappears, it is **spreading** again, and the owner
14.34 regulations about houses affected by **spreading** mildew.
14.39 If the mildew has **spread,** [40]he shall order the stones on
14.44 If it has **spread,** the house is unclean.
19.16 Do not **spread** lies about anyone, and when someone is on
Num 4. 6 fine leather cover over it, **spread** a blue cloth on top, and
4. 7 They shall **spread** a blue cloth over the table for the
4. 8 They shall **spread** a red cloth over all this, put a fine
4.11 Next they shall **spread** a blue cloth over the gold altar,
4.13 ashes from the altar and **spread** a purple cloth over it.
11.32 They **spread** them out to dry all round the camp.
13.32 So they **spread** a false report among the Israelites about
22. 5 its people are **spreading** out everywhere and threatening to
22.11 who came from Egypt has **spread** out over the whole land.
Deut 32.11 catching them safely on its **spreading** wings, the Lord kept
Josh 6.27 with Joshua, and his fame **spread** through the whole country.
Judg 7.12 and the desert tribesmen were **spread** out in the valley like
8.25 They **spread** out a cloth, and everyone put on it the earrings
20.37 they **spread** out in the city and killed everyone there.
Ruth 3.15 said to her, "Take off your cloak and **spread** it out here."
1 Sam 4.13 The man **spread** the news throughout the town, and everyone
2 Sam 7.23 you did for them have **spread** your fame throughout the world.
17.19 man's wife took a covering, **spread** it over the opening of
18. 8 The fighting **spread** over the countryside, and more men
1 Kgs 4.31 his fame **spread** throughout all the neighbouring countries.
20.27 with the Syrians, who **spread** out over the countryside.
2 Kgs 9.13 At once Jehu's fellow-officers **spread** their cloaks at
1 Chr 4.39 families continued to grow, [39]they **spread** out westwards
14.17 David's fame **spread** everywhere, and the Lord made every
17.21 you did for them **spread** your fame throughout the world.
28.18 for the winged creatures that **spread** their wings over the
2 Chr 3.11 2.2 metres long, which were **spread** out so that they touched
26. 8 he became so powerful that his fame **spread** even to Egypt.
26.15 His fame **spread** everywhere, and he became very powerful
Neh 4.19 and leaders, "The work is **spread** out over such a distance
Job 6. 4 me with arrows, and their poison **spreads** through my body.
8.16 in the sun, like weeds that **spread** all through the garden.
9. 8 No one helped God **spread** out the heavens or trample the
18.13 A deadly disease **spreads** over his body and causes his
39.26 you how to fly when it **spreads** its wings towards the south?
Ps 15. 3 to his friends nor **spreads** rumours about his neighbours.
57. 6 My enemies have **spread** a net to catch me;
64. 4 They are quick to **spread** their shameless lies;
80. 9 its roots went deep, and it **spread** out over the whole land.
104. 2 You have **spread** out the heavens like a tent [3]and built your
147. 8 He **spreads** clouds over the sky;
147.16 He **spreads** snow like a blanket and scatters frost like dust.
Prov 1.17 It does no good to **spread** a net when the bird you
10.18 Anyone who **spreads** gossip is a fool.
15. 7 Knowledge is **spread** by people who are wise, not by fools.
16.28 Gossip is **spread** by wicked people;
Is 8. 8 His **outspread** wings protect the land.
16. 8 At one time the vines **spread** as far as the city of
21. 5 rugs are **spread** for the guests to sit on.
33.22 the sails cannot be **spread!**
48.13 made the earth's foundations and **spread** the heavens out.
58. 5 a blade of grass, and **spread** out sackcloth and ashes to lie
Jer 5.26 in wait like men who **spread** nets to catch birds, but they
6.28 They are all corrupt, going round and **spreading** gossip.
8. 2 They will be **spread** out before the sun, the moon, and the
23.15 because they have **spread** ungodliness throughout the land."
43.10 that you buried, and will **spread** the royal tent over them.
48.40 like an eagle with its **outspread** wings, [41]and the towns
49.22 Bozrah like an eagle swooping down with **outspread** wings.
51.46 Every year a different rumour **spreads**—rumours of violence in
Ezek 1. 9 wings of each creature were **spread** out so that the creatures
5. 4 From them fire will **spread** to the whole nation of Israel."
8.17 here and with **spreading** violence throughout the country.
10.16 Whenever they **spread** their wings to fly, the wheels still
10.19 They **spread** their wings and flew up from the earth while
12.13 But I will **spread** out my net and trap him in it.
17. 3 eagle with beautiful feathers and huge wings, **spread** wide.
17. 6 The plant sprouted and became a low, **wide-spreading** grapevine.
17.20 I will **spread** out a hunter's net and catch him in it.
19. 8 They **spread** their hunting nets and caught him in their trap.
20.47 It will **spread** from south to north, and everyone will feel
31. 9 I made it beautiful, with **spreading** branches.
32. 6 out your blood until it **spreads** over the mountains and fills
32. 9 will be troubled when I **spread** the news of your destruction
32.24 In life they **spread** terror, but now they lie dead and disgraced.
32.25 In life they **spread** terror, but now they lie dead and disgraced,
32.30 Their power once **spread** terror, but now they go down in
47.10 the sea, and they will **spread** out their nets there to dry.
Hos 4.13 they burn incense under tall, **spreading** trees, because the
5. 1 trap at Mizpah, a net **spread** on Mount Tabor, [2]a deep pit
7.12 But I will **spread** out a net and catch them like birds
Joel 2. 2 of locusts advances like darkness **spreading** over the mountains.
Nah 3.16 are gone, like locusts that **spread** their wings and fly away.
Hab 1. 7 They **spread** fear and terror, and in their pride they are a
Zech 12. 1 Lord, the Lord who **spread** out the skies, created the earth,
Mt 4.24 The news about him **spread** through the whole country of Syria,
9.26 The news about this **spread** all over that part of the country.
9.31 But they left and **spread** the news about Jesus all over
21. 8 A large crowd of people **spread** their cloaks on the road
21. 8 cut branches from the trees and **spread** them on the road.
24.12 Such will be the **spread** of evil that many people's love
28.15 so that is the report **spread** round by the Jews to this
Mk 1.28 so the news about Jesus **spread** quickly everywhere in the
1.45 But the man went away and began to **spread** the news everywhere.
2. 1 back to Capernaum, and the news **spread** that he was at home.
5.14 the pigs ran away and **spread** the news in the town and
6.14 King Herod heard about all this, because Jesus' reputation had **spread** everywhere.
10.22 the man heard this, gloom **spread** over his face, and he went
11. 8 Many people **spread** their cloaks on the road, while others
11. 8 cut branches in the fields and **spread** them on the road.
Lk 1.65 these things **spread** through all the hill-country of Judaea.
4.14 The news about him **spread** throughout all that territory.
4.25 years and a severe famine **spread** throughout the whole land.
4.37 And the report about Jesus **spread** everywhere in that region.
5.15 But the news about Jesus **spread** all the more widely, and
8.34 so they ran off and **spread** the news in the town and
15.14 Then a severe famine **spread** over that country, and he was
19.36 As he rode on, people **spread** their cloaks on the road.
Jn 21.23 So a report **spread** among the followers of Jesus that
Acts 2. 3 of fire which **spread** out and touched each person there.
4.17 this matter from **spreading** any further among the people,
5.28 You have **spread** your teaching all over Jerusalem, and you
6. 7 And so the word of God continued to **spread.**
9.42 The news about this **spread** all over Joppa, and many

Acts 12.24 Meanwhile the word of God continued to **spread** and grow.
13.49 The word of the Lord **spread** everywhere in that region.
19.20 the word of the Lord kept **spreading** and growing stronger.
19.29 The uproar **spread** throughout the whole city.
21.30 Confusion **spread** through the whole city, and the people all ran together,
Rom 5.12 As a result, death has **spread** to the whole human race
9.17 show my power and to **spread** my fame over the whole world."
2 Cor 2.14 about Christ **spread** everywhere like a sweet fragrance.
2.15 by Christ to God, which **spreads** among those who are being
Phil 4. 3 worked hard with me to **spread** the gospel, together with
Col 1. 6 bringing blessings and is **spreading** throughout the world,
2 Thes 3. 1 Lord's message may continue to **spread** rapidly and be received with honour,
1 Tim 4. 2 Such teachings are **spread** by deceitful liars, whose consciences are dead,
Heb 9. 5 God's presence, with their wings **spread** over the place where
Jas 3. 6 in our bodies and **spreading** evil through our whole being.
Rev 20. 9 They **spread** out over the earth and surrounded the camp of

SPRIG

Ex 12.22 Take a **sprig of hyssop**, dip it in the bowl containing
Lev 14. 4 a piece of cedar-wood, a red cord, and a **sprig of hyssop.**
14.49 birds, some cedar-wood, a red cord, and a **sprig of hyssop.**
Num 19. 6 take some cedar-wood, a **sprig of hyssop,** and a red cord and
19.18 is to take a **sprig of hyssop,** dip it in the water,
Heb 9.19 all the people, using a **sprig of hyssop** and some red wool.

SPRING (1)

Gen 16. 7 Lord met Hagar at a **spring** in the desert on the road
36.24 Anah who found the hot **springs** in the wilderness when he was
49.22 a wild donkey by a **spring,** A wild colt on a hillside.
Ex 15.27 where there were twelve **springs** and seventy palm-trees;
Lev 11.36 be broken, [36] but a **spring** or a cistern remains clean,
14. 5 to be killed over a clay bowl containing fresh **spring** water.
14.50 of the birds over a clay bowl containing fresh **spring** water.
15.13 clothes and bathe in fresh **spring** water, and he will be
Num 27.14 (Meribah is the **spring** at Kadesh in the wilderness of Zin.)
33. 9 were twelve **springs** of water and seventy palm-trees there.
Deut 8. 7 land that has rivers and **springs,** and underground streams
Josh 15. 7 then went on to the **springs** of Enshemesh, out to Enrogel,
15. 9 there it went to the **Springs** of Nephtoah and out to the
15.19 So Caleb gave her the upper and lower **springs.**
16. 1 a point east of the **springs** of Jericho, and went into the
18.15 edge of Kiriath Jearim and went to the **Springs** of Nephtoah.
Judg 1.15 So Caleb gave her the upper and lower **springs.**
7. 1 his men got up early and camped beside the **Spring** of Harod.
15.19 So the **spring** was named Hakkore;
1 Sam 29. 1 Israelites camped at the **spring** in the Valley of Jezreel.
2 Sam 17.17 Ahimaaz were waiting at the **spring** of Enrogel, on the
1 Kgs 1. 9 fattened calves at Snake Rock, near the **spring** of Enrogel.
1.33 escort him down to the **spring** of Gihon, [34] where Zadok and
1.38 King David's mule, and escorted him to the **spring** of Gihon.
1.45 Zadok and Nathan anointed him as king at the **spring** of Gihon.
18. 5 go and look at every **spring** and every river-bed in the land
2 Kgs 2.21 and he went to the **spring,** threw the salt in the water,
3.19 their fruit-trees, stop all their **springs,** and ruin all
3.25 also stopped up the **springs** and cut down the fruit-trees.
2 Chr 32. 3 and stopped up all the **springs,** so that no more water flowed
32.30 blocked the outlet for the **Spring** of Gihon and channelled
33.14 in the valley near the **spring** of Gihon north to the Fish
Job 38.16 Have you been to the **springs** in the depths of the sea?
38.27 Who waters the dry and thirsty land, so that grass **springs** up?
Ps 74.15 You made **springs** and fountains flow;
81. 7 I put you to the test at the **springs** of Meribah.
84. 6 the dry valley of Baca, it becomes a place of **springs;**
104.10 You make **springs** flow in the valleys, and rivers run
106.32 At the **springs** of Meribah the people made the Lord angry,
107.33 made rivers dry up completely and stopped **springs** from flowing.
107.35 into pools of water and dry land into flowing **springs.**
114. 8 into pools of water and solid cliffs into flowing **springs.**
Prov 8.24 before the oceans, when there were no **springs** of water.
8.28 sky, when he opened the **springs** of the ocean [29] and ordered
25.26 evil reminds you of a polluted **spring** or a poisoned well.
Song 4.12 is a secret garden, a walled garden, a private **spring;**
Is 35. 7 become a lake, and dry land will be filled with **springs.**
41.18 among barren hills and **springs** of water run in the valleys.
41.18 into pools of water and the dry land into flowing **springs.**
49.10 He will lead them to **springs** of water.
58.11 plenty of water, like a **spring** of water that never runs dry.
Jer 2.13 turned away from me, the **spring** of fresh water, and they
17.13 have abandoned you, the Lord, the **spring** of fresh water.
Ezek 47.10 From the **Springs** of Engedi all the way to
47.10 the **Springs** of Eneglaim, there will be fishermen
Hos 13.15 from the desert, and it will dry up their **springs** and wells.
Jn 4.14 will become in him a **spring** which will provide him with
Jas 3.11 No **spring** of water pours out sweet water and bitter
3.12 bear figs, nor can a salty **spring** produce sweet water.
2 Pet 2.17 These men are like dried-up **springs,** like clouds blown
Rev 7.17 and he will guide them to **springs** of life-giving water.
8.10 on a third of the rivers and on the **springs** of water.
11. 6 have authority also over the **springs** of water, to turn them
14. 7 Worship him who made heaven, earth, sea, and the **springs** of water!"
16. 4 on the rivers and the **springs** of water, and they turned into
21. 6 right to drink from the **spring** of the water of life without

SPRING (2)

Deut 11.14 the autumn and in the **spring,** so that there will be corn,
2 Sam 11. 1 The following **spring,** at the time of the year when kings
21. 9 It was late in the **spring,** at the beginning of the barley
1 Kgs 20.22 because the king of Syria will attack again next **spring."**
20.26 The following **spring** he called up his men and marched
1 Chr 20. 1 The following **spring,** at the time of the year when kings
2 Chr 36.10 When **spring** came, King Nebuchadnezzar took Jehoiachin
Job 29.23 everyone welcomed them just as farmers welcome rain in **spring.**
Prov 16.15 the clouds that bring rain in the **springtime**—life is there.
Jer 3. 3 rains were held back, and the **spring** showers did not come.
5.24 the autumn rains and the **spring** rains and give you the
Hos 6. 3 as surely as the **spring** rains that water the earth."
Joel 2.23 down the winter rain for you and the **spring** rain as before.
Zech 10. 1 Ask the Lord for rain in the **spring** of the year.
Jas 5. 7 He waits patiently for the autumn and **spring** rains.

SPRING (3)

[SPRANG]

Prov 22. 8 seeds of injustice, disaster will **spring** up, and your
Amos 3. 5 Does a trap **spring** unless something sets it off?
Rom 7. 9 the commandment came, sin **sprang** to life, [10] and I died.

SPRINKLE

Ex 29.21 of the anointing oil, and **sprinkle** it on Aaron and his
30.36 Tent of my presence, and **sprinkle** it in front of the
Lev 4. 6 finger in the blood and **sprinkle** it in front of the sacred
4.17 his finger in it, and **sprinkle** it in front of the curtain
5. 9 pulling off its head [9] and **sprinkle** some of its blood
8.11 some of the oil and **sprinkled** it seven times on the altar
8.30 was on the altar and **sprinkled** them on Aaron and his sons
14. 7 He shall **sprinkle** the blood seven times on the person who
14.16 right hand in it, and **sprinkle** some of it seven times there
14.27 finger of his right hand **sprinkle** some of it seven times
14.51 And he shall **sprinkle** the house seven times.
16.14 blood and with his finger **sprinkle** it on the front
16.14 of the lid and then **sprinkle** some of it seven times in
16.15 the Most Holy Place, and **sprinkle** it on the lid and then
16.19 With his finger he must **sprinkle** some of the blood on
Num 8. 7 **sprinkle** them with the water of purification and tell them
19. 4 blood and with his finger **sprinkle** it seven times in the
19.18 it in the water, and **sprinkle** the tent, everything in it,
19.18 is ritually clean is to **sprinkle** the water on the man who
19.19 clean is to **sprinkle** the water on the unclean person.
19.21 The person who **sprinkles** the water for purification must
2 Sam 13.19 She **sprinkled** ashes on her head, tore her robe, and with
2 Chr 29.22 and then the lambs, and **sprinkled** the blood of each
30.16 sacrifices to the priests, who **sprinkled** it on the altar.
35.11 skinned them, and the priests **sprinkled** the blood on the altar.
Job 18.15 in his tent— after sulphur is **sprinkled** to disinfect it!
Ezek 36.25 I will **sprinkle** clean water on you and make you clean
43.18 sacrifices on it and by **sprinkling** on it the blood of the
43.24 The priests will **sprinkle** salt on them and burn them as an
Mt 11.21 have put on sackcloth and **sprinkled** ashes on themselves, to
Lk 10.13 down, put on sackcloth, and **sprinkled** ashes on themselves,
Heb 9.13 of a burnt calf are **sprinkled** on the people who are ritually
9.19 mixed it with water, and **sprinkled** it on the book of the
9.21 the same way Moses also **sprinkled** the blood on the Covenant
11.28 order the blood to be **sprinkled** on the doors, so that the
12.24 new covenant, and to the **sprinkled** blood that promises much

SPROUT

Gen 2. 5 earth and no seeds had **sprouted,** because he had not sent any
41. 6 seven other ears of corn **sprouted,** thin and scorched by the
41.23 Then seven ears of corn **sprouted,** thin and scorched by
Num 17. 5 Then the stick of the man I have chosen will **sprout.**
17. 8 Aaron's stick, representing the tribe of Levi, had **sprouted.**
Job 8.16 Evil men **sprout** like weeds in the sun, like weeds that spread
14. 7 it can come back to life and **sprout.**
14. 9 the ground, [9] with water it will **sprout** like a young plant.
Ps 90. 5 We are like weeds that **sprout** in the morning, [6] that grow
Is 11. 1 but just as new branches **sprout** from a stump, so a new
17.11 But even if they **sprouted** and blossomed the very morning
61.11 As surely as seeds **sprout** and grow, The Sovereign Lord
Ezek 17. 6 The plant **sprouted** and became a low, wide-spreading grapevine.
17.22 the top of a tall cedar and break off a tender **sprout;**
Mt 13. 5 The seeds soon **sprouted,** because the soil wasn't deep.
Mk 4. 5 The seeds soon **sprouted,** because the soil wasn't deep.
4. 8 good soil, and the plants **sprouted,** grew, and produced corn:
4.27 day, and all the while the seeds are **sprouting** and growing.
Lk 8. 6 ground, and when the plants **sprouted,** they dried up because
1 Cor 15.36 in the ground, it does not **sprout** to life unless it dies.
Heb 9. 4 it, Aaron's stick that had **sprouted** leaves, and the two

SPY

Gen 42. 9 dreams he had dreamt about them and said, "You are **spies;**
42.11 We are not **spies,** sir, we are honest men."
42.14 "You are **spies.**
42.16 Otherwise, as sure as the king lives, you are **spies."**
42.30 harshly to us and accused us of **spying** against his country.
42.31 'We are not **spies,**' we answered, 'we are honest men.
42.34 Then I will know that you are not **spies,** but honest men;
Num 13. 2 tribes and send them as **spies** to explore the land of Canaan,
13.16 These are the **spies** Moses sent to explore the land.
13.25 land for forty days, the **spies** returned [26] to Moses, Aaron,
14. 6 of Jephunneh, two of the **spies,** tore their clothes in sorrow

Num 14.38 Of the twelve **spies** only Joshua and Caleb survived.
Deut 1.22 men ahead of us to **spy** out the land, so that they
Josh 2. 1 Then Joshua sent two **spies** from the camp at Acacia with
2. 2 had come that night to **spy** out the country, [3] so he sent
2. 3 men in your house have come to **spy** out the whole country!
2. 4 Rahab had taken the two **spies** up on the roof and hidden
2. 7 went looking for the Israelite **spies** as far as the place
2. 8 Before the **spies** settled down for the night, Rahab went up
2.22 The **spies** went into the hills and hid.
2.23 Then the two **spies** came down from the hills, crossed the river,
6.17 Rahab and her household will be spared, because she hid our **spies.**
6.22 men who had served as **spies,** "Go into the prostitute's
6.25 she had hidden the two **spies** that he had sent to Jericho.
14. 7 Moses sent me from Kadesh Barnea to **spy** out this land.
Judg 1.22 They sent **spies** to the city, [24] who saw a man leaving and
18.17 The five **spies** went straight on into the house and took
1 Sam 26. 4 look for him, [4] he sent **spies** and found out that Saul was
2 Sam 10. 3 has sent them here as **spies** to explore the city, so that
1 Chr 19. 3 has sent them here as **spies** to explore the land, so that
Ps 10. 8 He **spies** on his helpless victims;
Is 33.18 of foreign tax-collectors and **spies** will be only a memory.
Lk 20.21 These **spies** said to Jesus, "Teacher, we know that what
Gal 2. 4 slipped into our group as **spies,** in order to find out about
Heb 11.31 God, for she gave the Israelite **spies** a friendly welcome.
Jas 2.25 actions, by welcoming the Israelite **spies** and helping them

SQUARE

Gen 19. 2 "No, we will spend the night here in the city **square.**"
Ex 27. 1 It is to be **square,** 2.2 metres long and 2.2 metres wide,
28.16 It is to be **square** and folded double, 22 centimetres
30. 2 It is to be **square,** 45 centimetres long and 45 centimetres wide,
37.25 It was **square,** 45 centimetres long and 45 centimetres wide,
38. 1 It was **square,** 2.2 metres long and 2.2 metres wide, and it
39. 9 It was **square** and folded double, 22 centimetres long and
Num 35. 5 so that there is a **square** area measuring 900 metres on
Deut 2. 5 to give you so much as a **square metre** of their land.
13.16 people who live there and pile them up in the town **square.**
Judg 19.15 and sat down in the **square,** but no one offered to take
19.17 the traveller in the city **square** and asked him, "Where do
19.20 you don't have to spend the night in the **square.**"
2 Sam 21.12 stolen them from the public **square** in Beth Shan, where the
1 Kgs 7.28 They were made of **square** panels which were set in frames,
2 Chr 4. 1 made, which was nine metres **square** and four and a half
6.13 It was 2.2 metres **square** and 1.3 metres high.
32. 6 them to assemble in the open **square** at the city gate.
Ezra 10. 9 and Benjamin came to Jerusalem and assembled in the temple **square.**
Neh 8. 1 in Jerusalem, in the **square** just inside the Water Gate.
8. 3 There in the **square** by the gate he read the Law to
8.16 courtyard, and in the public **squares** by the Water Gate and
Esth 4. 6 Mordecai in the city **square** at the entrance of the palace.
6. 9 and lead him, mounted on the horse, through the city **square.**
6.11 led him through the city **square,** announcing to the people as
Is 15. 3 the city **squares** and on the house-tops people mourn and cry.
59.14 Truth stumbles in the public **square,** and honesty finds no place
Jer 48.38 and in all its public **squares** there is nothing but mourning,
Ezek 1. 9 the creatures formed a **square** with their wing tips touching.
40. 7 Each of the rooms was **square,** three metres on each side, and
40.12 (The rooms were three metres **square.**)
40.42 and their tops were seventy-five centimetres **square.**
40.47 man measured the inner courtyard, and it was fifty metres **square.**
41. 4 He measured the room itself, and it was ten metres **square.**
41.21 The door-posts of the Holy Place were **square.**
42.20 so that the wall enclosed a **square** 250 metres on each side.
43.16 top of the altar was a **square,** six metres on each side.
43.17 middle section was also a **square,** seven metres on each side,
45. 2 there is to be a **square** plot of land for the Temple,
48.16 and it will be a **square,** measuring 2,250 metres on each side.
48.20 set apart will be a **square** measuring twelve and a half
Nah 2. 4 the streets, rushing to and fro through the city **squares.**
Zech 8. 4 a stick when they walk, will be sitting in the city **squares.**
Acts 7. 5 his own, not even a **square metre** of ground, but God promised
16.19 Silas and dragged them to the authorities in the public **square.**
17.17 and also in the public **square** every day with the people who
Rev 21.16 The city was perfectly **square,** as wide as it was long.

SQUEEZE

Gen 40.11 I took the grapes and **squeezed** them into the cup and gave
Judg 6.38 early the next morning, he **squeezed** the wool and wrung
Rev 14.20 The grapes were **squeezed** out in the winepress outside the city,

SQUIRM

Ezek 16. 6 "Then I passed by and saw you **squirming** in your own blood.
16.22 you were naked, **squirming** in your own blood."

STAB

2 Sam 3.27 privately with him, and there he **stabbed** him in the belly.
20.10 his other hand, and Joab **stabbed** him in the belly, and his
Is 13.15 Anyone who is caught will be **stabbed** to death.
Jer 4.18 it has **stabbed** you through the heart.
Zech 12.10 at the one whom they **stabbed** to death, and they will mourn
13. 3 his own father and mother will **stab** him to death.

STABILITY

Is 33. 6 with justice and integrity [6] and give **stability** to the nation.

STABLE

Esth 8.10 by riders mounted on fast horses from the royal **stables.**
Job 39. 9 Is he willing to spend the night in your **stable?**

STACKED

Ex 22. 6 that has been cut and **stacked,** the one who started the fire

STACTE

Ex 30.34 spices—**stacte,** onycha, galbanum, and pure frankincense.

STAFF (1)

Ps 23. 4 Your shepherd's rod and **staff** protect me.

STAFF (2)

1 Kgs 10. 5 organization of his palace **staff** and the uniforms they wore,
2 Chr 9. 4 organization of his palace **staff** and the uniforms they wore,
26.11 under the supervision of Hananiah, a member of the king's **staff.**

STAG

Song 2. 9 My lover is like a gazelle, like a young **stag.**
2.17 like a gazelle, like a **stag** on the mountains of Bether.
8.14 like a young **stag** on the mountains where spices grow.

STAGGER

Job 12.25 they grope in the dark and **stagger** like drunkards.
Ps 60. 3 we **stagger** around as though we were drunk.
107.27 they stumbled and **staggered** like drunken men— all
Is 19.14 Egypt does everything wrong and **staggers** like a drunken man
24.20 The earth itself will **stagger** like a drunken man and
28. 7 Even the prophets and the priests are so drunk that they **stagger.**
29. 9 **Stagger** without drinking a drop!
51.17 you drank it down, and it made you **stagger.**
51.21 of Jerusalem, you that **stagger** as though you were drunk,
51.22 no longer have to drink the wine that makes you **stagger.**
Jer 25.16 drink from it, they will **stagger** and go out of their minds
Lam 3. 9 I **stagger** as I walk;
4.21 you too will **stagger** naked in shame.
5.13 boys go **staggering** under heavy loads of wood.
Hab 2.15 you made them **stagger** as though they were drunk.
2.16 You yourself will drink and **stagger.**
Zech 12. 2 nations round her will drink and **stagger** like drunken men.

STAGNANT

Lam 3. 6 He has forced me to live in the **stagnant** darkness of death.

STAIN

Job 31. 7 evil, if my hands are **stained** with sin, [8] then let my crops
Is 1.18 You are **stained** red with sin, but I will wash you as
1.18 Although your **stains** are deep red, you will be as white as
63. 3 in my anger, and their blood has **stained** all my clothing.
Jer 2.22 strongest soap, I would still see the **stain** of your guilt.
2.34 clothes are **stained** with the blood of the poor and innocent,
Lam 4.14 streets like blind men, so **stained** with blood that no one
Ezek 23.45 practise adultery and their hands are **stained** with blood."
Jude 23 but hate their very clothes, **stained** by their sinful lusts.

STAIRS

Gen 28.12 dreamt that he saw a **stairway** reaching from earth to heaven,
1 Kgs 6. 8 side of the Temple, with **stairs** leading up to the second and
2 Kgs 20. 9 prefer the shadow on the **stairway** to go forward ten steps or
20.11 go back ten steps on the **stairway** set up by King Ahaz.
2 Chr 9.11 used the wood to make **stairs** for the Temple and for his
Is 38. 8 On the **stairway** built by King Ahaz, the Lord will make the
Ezek 41. 7 of the rooms, two wide **stairways** were built, so that it was

STALK

Gen 41. 5 Seven ears of corn, full and ripe, were growing on one **stalk.**
41.22 ears of corn which were full and ripe, growing on one **stalk.**
Josh 2. 4 and hidden them under some **stalks** of flax that she had put
Mk 4.28 first the tender **stalk** appears, then the ear, and finally
Jn 19.29 the wine, put on a **stalk** of hyssop, and lifted up to

STALL

1 Kgs 4.23 ten **stall-fed** cattle, twenty pasture-fed cattle,
4.26 Solomon had forty thousand **stalls** for his
2 Chr 9.25 Solomon also had four thousand **stalls** for his chariots
Mal 4. 2 be as free and happy as calves let out of a **stall.**
Lk 13.15 or his donkey from the **stall** and take it out to give

STALLION

Song 1. 9 men as a mare excites the **stallions** of Pharaoh's chariots.
Jer 5. 8 They were like well-fed **stallions** wild with desire, each
13.27 after his neighbour's wife or like a **stallion** after a mare.
Ezek 23.20 men who had all the lustfulness of donkeys and **stallions.**"

STAMP (1)

Esth 3.10 was used to **stamp** proclamations and make them official,
3.12 issued in the name of King Xerxes and **stamped** with his ring.
8. 8 in the king's name and **stamped** with the royal seal cannot be
8. 8 write it in my name and **stamp** it with the royal seal."
8.10 of King Xerxes, and he **stamped** them with the royal seal.
Eph 1.13 and God put his **stamp of ownership** on you by giving you

STAMP (2)

Judg 5.22 Then the horses came galloping on, **stamping** the ground
Ezek 6.11 **Stamp** your feet!

Am **STAND**
see also **ENDURE**

STAND
[STOOD]
see also **STAND FOR**

Gen 2. 9 the middle of the garden **stood** the tree that gives life and
18. 2 of the day, [2]he looked up and saw three men **standing** there.
19.27 the place where he had **stood** in the presence of the Lord.
24.30 Abraham's servant, who was **standing** by his camels at the well,
24.31 Why are you **standing** out here?
28.13 And there was the Lord **standing** beside him.
31.35 sir, but I am not able to **stand** up in your presence;
37. 7 of wheat, when my sheaf got up and **stood** up straight.
41. 1 Egypt dreamt that he was **standing** by the River Nile, [2]when
41. 3 They came and **stood** by the other cows on the river-bank,
41.17 "I dreamt that I was **standing** on the bank of the Nile,
Ex 2. 4 The baby's sister **stood** some distance away to see what
3. 5 Take off your sandals, because you are **standing** on holy ground.
9.10 So they got some ashes and **stood** before the king;
14.13 **Stand** your ground, and you will see what the Lord will do
14.31 Lord had defeated the Egyptians, they **stood** in awe of the Lord;
15. 8 it **stood** up straight like a wall;
15.16 your strength, O Lord, and **stand** helpless with fear until
16. 9 whole community to come and **stand** before the Lord, because
17. 6 I will **stand** before you on a rock at Mount Sinai.
17. 9 I will **stand** on top of the hill holding the stick that
17.12 to sit on, while they **stood** beside him and held up his
18.14 this all alone, with people **standing** here from morning till
19.17 to meet God, and they **stood** at the foot of the mountain.
20.18 mountain, they trembled with fear and **stood** a long way off.
20.21 But the people continued to **stand** a long way off, and
21. 6 he is to make him **stand** against the door or the door-post
32.26 So he **stood** at the gate of the camp and shouted,
33. 8 out there, the people would **stand** at the door of their tents
33.21 is a place beside me where you can **stand** on a rock.
34. 5 came down in a cloud, **stood** with him there, and pronounced
Lev 16.16 to the Tent, because it **stands** in the middle of the camp,
Num 5.16 the woman forward and make her **stand** in front of the altar.
5.29 woman shall be made to **stand** in front of the altar, and
8. 9 Israel and make the Levites **stand** in front of the Tent of
11.10 the people complaining as they **stood** about in groups at the
11.16 Tent of my presence, and tell them to **stand** there beside you.
12. 5 in a pillar of cloud, **stood** at the entrance of the Tent,
16.18 and incense on it, and **stood** at the entrance of the Tent
16.19 the whole community, and they **stood** facing Moses and Aaron
16.21 said to Moses and Aaron, [21]**"Stand** back from these people,
16.26 He said to the people, **"Stand** away from the tents of
16.27 come out and were **standing** at the entrance of their tents,
16.43 Moses and Aaron went and **stood** in front of the Tent,
16.45 the Lord said to Moses, [45]**"Stand** back from these people,
16.48 and he was left **standing** between the living and the dead.
20. 6 away from the people and **stood** at the entrance of the Tent.
22.22 the angel of the Lord **stood** in the road to bar his
22.23 the donkey saw the angel **standing** there holding a sword, it
22.24 Then the angel **stood** where the road narrowed between two
22.26 he **stood** in a narrow place where there was no room at
22.31 Lord let Balaam see the angel **standing** there with his sword;
22.34 not know that you were **standing** in the road to oppose me;
23. 3 Then Balaam said to Balak, **"Stand** here by your burnt-offering,
23. 6 back and found Balak still **standing** by his burnt-offering,
23.15 Balaam said to Balak, **"Stand** here by your burnt-offering,
23.17 back and found Balak still **standing** by his burnt-offering,
27. 2 They went and **stood** before Moses, Eleazar the priest, the
27.19 Make him **stand** in front of Eleazar the priest and the
27.22 He made Joshua **stand** before Eleazar the priest and the whole
Deut 4.10 grandchildren [10]about the day you **stood** in the presence of
4.11 children how you went and **stood** at the foot of the mountain
5. 5 I **stood** between you and the Lord at that time to tell
9. 2 you have heard it said that no one can **stand** against them.
27.12 the following tribes are to **stand** on Mount Gerizim when the
27.13 And the following tribes will **stand** on Mount Ebal when
29.10 "Today you are **standing** in the presence of the Lord your God,
29.15 with all of us who **stand** here in his presence today and
29.18 man, woman, family, or tribe **standing** here today turns from
31.15 a pillar of cloud that **stood** by the door of the Tent.
Josh 3. 8 the river, they must wade in and **stand** near the bank."
3.17 carrying the Lord's Covenant Box **stood** on dry ground in the
4. 3 Jordan, from the very place where the priests were **standing.**
4. 9 where the priests carrying the Covenant Box had **stood.**
4.10 The priests **stood** in the middle of the Jordan until
5.13 he suddenly saw a man **standing** in front of him, holding a
5.15 you are **standing** on holy ground."
7.12 This is why the Israelites cannot **stand** against their enemies.
7.13 You cannot **stand** against your enemies until you get rid of
Josh 8.33 as the foreigners among them, **stood** on two sides of the
8.33 Half the people **stood** with their backs to Mount Gerizim and
10. 8 Not one of them will be able to **stand** against you."
10.12 "Sun, **stand** still over Gibeon;
10.13 The sun **stood** still and the moon did not move until the
10.13 The sun **stood** still in the middle of the sky and did
21.44 enemies had been able to **stand** against them, because the
22.29 the Lord our God that **stands** in front of the Tent of
23. 9 advanced and no one has ever been able to **stand** against you.
Judg 3.20 The king **stood** up.
4.20 Then he told her, **"Stand** at the door of the tent, and
5. 7 The towns of Israel **stood** abandoned, Deborah;
5. 7 they **stood** empty until you came, came like a mother for Israel.
6.24 (It is still **standing** at Ophrah, which belongs to the clan
6.31 those who confronted him, "Are you **standing** up for Baal?
6.31 Anyone who **stands** up for him will be killed before morning.
7.21 Every man **stood** in his place round the camp, and the
9. 7 about this, he went and **stood** on top of Mount Gerizim and
9.35 saw Gaal come out and **stand** at the city gate, they got
16.24 him entertain them and made him **stand** between the pillars.
18.16 from Dan, ready for battle, were **standing** at the gate.
20. 8 All the people **stood** up together and said, "None of us,
1 Sam 1.26 I am the woman you saw **standing** here, praying to the Lord.
3.10 The Lord came and **stood** there, and called as he had before,
6.20 Beth Shemesh said, "Who can **stand** before the Lord, this
12. 7 Now **stand** where you are, and I will accuse you before the
12.16 So then, **stand** where you are, and you will see the great
14.40 to them, "All of you **stand** over there,
14.40 and Jonathan and I will **stand** over here."
16. 6 said to himself, "This man **standing** here in the Lord's
17. 8 Goliath **stood** and shouted at the Israelites, "What are you
17.51 He ran to him, **stood** over him, took Goliath's sword out
19. 3 I will go and **stand** by my father in the field where
20.38 Don't just **stand** there!
22. 6 in his hand, and all his officers were **standing** round him.
22. 9 Doeg was **standing** there with Saul's officers, and he
22.17 to the guards **standing** near him, "Kill the Lord's priests!
2 Sam 2.23 to the place where he was lying stopped and **stood** there.
2.25 Abner again and took their **stand** on the top of a hill.
13.31 The king **stood** up, tore his clothes in sorrow, and threw
15. 2 up early and go and **stand** by the road at the city
15.18 All his officials **stood** next to him as the royal
18. 4 Then he **stood** by the side of the gate as his men
18.24 top of the wall and **stood** on the roof of the gateway;
18.30 **"Stand** over there," the king said;
18.30 and he went over and **stood** there.
20.11 One of Joab's men **stood** by Amasa's body and called out,
23.10 Israelites fell back, [10]but he **stood** his ground and fought
23.12 Philistines, [12]but Shammah **stood** his ground in the field,
1 Kgs 1.28 Bathsheba to come back in"—and she came and **stood** before him.
2.19 The king **stood** up to greet his mother and bowed to her.
3.15 he went to Jerusalem and **stood** in front of the Lord's
7.49 God, [49]the ten lamp-stands that **stood** in front of the Most
8. 8 could be seen by anyone **standing** directly in front of the
8.14 As the people **stood** there, King Solomon turned to face them,
8.22 the people Solomon went and **stood** in front of the altar,
8.54 praying to the Lord, he **stood** up in front of the altar,
13. 1 and arrived there as Jeroboam **stood** at the altar to offer
13.24 on the road, and the donkey and the lion **stood** beside it.
13.25 saw the body on the road, with the lion **standing** near by.
13.28 the road, with the donkey and the lion still **standing** by it.
19.11 "Go out and **stand** before me on top of the mountain,"
19.13 cloak and went out and **stood** at the entrance of the cave.
20.38 disguise himself, and went and **stood** by the road, waiting
22.19 throne in heaven, with all his angels **standing** beside him.
2 Kgs 2. 7 river, and the fifty prophets **stood** a short distance away.
2.13 him, and went back and **stood** on the bank of the Jordan.
4.15 She came and **stood** in the doorway, [16]and Elisha said to her,
9.13 the steps for Jehu to **stand** on, blew trumpets, and shouted,
9.30 eyeshadow, arranged her hair, and **stood** looking down at the
11.14 she saw the new king **standing** by the column at the entrance
13.21 Elisha's bones, the man came back to life and **stood** up.
18.28 Then the official **stood** up and shouted in Hebrew,
23. 3 He **stood** by the royal column and made a covenant with the
23.14 ground where they had **stood** he covered with human bones.
23.16 the festival as King Jeroboam was **standing** by the altar.
1 Chr 9.18 Formerly they had **stood** guard at the gates to the camps of
11.14 and his men made a **stand** in the middle of the field
21.15 The angel was **standing** by the threshing-place of Araunah, a
21.16 David saw the angel **standing** in mid air, holding his
28. 2 David **stood** before them and addressed them:
2 Chr 3.11 Most Holy Place, [11-13]where they **stood** side by side
5. 9 could be seen by anyone **standing** directly in front of the
5.11 The Levites **stood** near the east side of the altar with
6. 3 All the people of Israel were **standing** there.
6.12 the people Solomon went and **stood** in front of the altar and
7. 6 The priests **stood** in the places that were assigned to them,
7. 6 and facing them **stood** the Levites, praising the Lord
7. 6 The priests blew trumpets while all the people **stood.**
9.18 the throne, and the figure of a lion **stood** at each side.
15. 8 the altar of the Lord that **stood** in the temple courtyard.
18.18 throne in heaven, with all his angels **standing** beside him.
20. 5 King Jehoshaphat went and **stood** before them [6]and prayed aloud,
20. 9 then they could come and **stand** in front of this Temple where
20.13 their wives and children, were **standing** there at the Temple.
20.19 clans of Kohath and Korah **stood** up and with a loud shout
23.13 king at the temple entrance, **standing** by the column reserved
24.20 He **stood** where the people could see him and called out,
26.19 Uzziah was **standing** there in the Temple beside the
29.26 The priests also **stood** there with trumpets.
33.15 where the Temple **stood** and in other places in Jerusalem;

2 Chr 34.31 He **stood** by the royal column and made a covenant with
Ezra 3. 3 the land, they rebuilt the altar where it had **stood** before.
3.10 the Levites of the clan of Asaph **stood** there with cymbals.
5.15 and to rebuild the Temple where it had **stood** before.
6. 7 Jewish leaders rebuild the Temple of God where it **stood** before.
10.10 Ezra the priest **stood** up and spoke to them.
10.13 We can't **stand** here in the open like this.
Neh 4. 3 Tobiah was **standing** there beside him, and he added, "What
4.16 my men worked and half **stood** guard, wearing coats of armour
4.21 on the wall, while the other half **stood** guard with spears.
8. 4 Ezra was **standing** on a wooden platform that had been built
8. 4 The following men **stood** at his right:
8. 4 and the following **stood** at his left:
8. 5 As Ezra **stood** there on the platform high above the people,
8. 5 As soon as he opened the book, they all **stood** up.
8. 7 Then they rose and **stood** in their places, and the
9. 1 Then they **stood** and began to confess the sins that they and
9. 4 the Levites, and on it **stood** Jeshua, Bani, Kadmiel,
9. 5 **"Stand** up and praise the Lord your God;
Esth 5. 1 royal robes and went and **stood** in the inner courtyard of the
5. 2 king saw Queen Esther **standing** outside, she won his favour,
8. 4 sceptre to her, so she **stood** up and said, [5] "If it please
9. 2 were afraid of them, and no one could **stand** against them.
Job 1.20 Then Job **stood** up and tore his clothes in grief.
4. 4 stumbled, weak and tired, your words encouraged him to **stand.**
4.16 I could see something **standing** there;
5. 4 no one **stands** up to defend them in court.
8.15 If they grab for a thread, will it help them **stand?"**
9. 4 no man can **stand** up against him.
16.19 is someone in heaven to **stand** up for me and take my
17.10 all of them came and **stood** before me, I would not find
18.12 disaster **stands** and waits at his side.
22. 4 It is not because you **stand** in awe of God that he
25. 1 all must **stand** in awe of him;
29. 8 they saw me, and old men **stood** up to show me respect.
30.28 I **stand** up in public and plead for help.
32.16 They **stand** there with nothing more to say.
38. 3 **Stand** up now like a man and answer the questions I ask
38.14 makes the hills and valleys **stand** out like the folds of a
39.24 when the trumpet blows, they can't **stand** still.
40. 7 **Stand** up now like a man, and answer my questions.
40.10 If so, **stand** up in your honour and pride;
40.12 crush the wicked where they **stand.**
40.17 His tail **stands** up like a cedar, and the muscles in his
41.10 no one would dare to **stand** before him.
Ps 7. 6 **Stand** up against the fury of my enemies;
9.14 O Lord, [14] that I may **stand** before the people of Jerusalem
20. 8 will stumble and fall, but we will rise and **stand** firm.
45. 9 the right of your throne **stands** the queen, wearing ornaments
76. 7 No one can **stand** in your presence when you are angry.
77. 8 Does his promise no longer **stand?**
78.13 he made the waters **stand** like walls.
84.10 I would rather **stand** at the gate of the house of my
89. 7 and all of them **stand** in awe of you.
94.16 Who **stood** up for me against the wicked?
106.23 people, his chosen servant, Moses, **stood** up against God and
106.30 But Phinehas **stood** up and punished the guilty, and the
110. 7 by the road, and strengthened, he will **stand** victorious.
122. 2 And now we are here, **standing** inside the gates of Jerusalem!
130. 4 you forgive us, so that we should **stand** in awe of you.
135. 2 servants of the Lord, [2] who **stand** in the Lord's house, in
Prov 7.12 always walked the streets [12] or **stood** waiting at a corner,
8. 2 On the hilltops near the road and at the cross-roads she **stands.**
12. 3 but righteous people **stand** firm.
12.12 is to find evil things to do, but the righteous **stand** firm.
14.11 man's house will still be **standing** after an evil man's house
25. 6 When you **stand** before the king, don't try to impress him
Ecc 3.14 thing God does is to make us **stand** in awe of him.
5. 7 how much you talk, you must still **stand** in awe of God.
Song 2. 9 There he **stands** beside the wall.
5.12 brook, doves washed in milk and **standing** by the stream.
Is 2. 2 the mountain where the Temple **stands** will be the highest one
6. 2 Round him flaming creatures were **standing,** each of which had
22. 7 soldiers on horseback **stood** in front of Jerusalem's gates.
29.23 You will honour me and **stand** in awe of me.
36.13 Then the official **stood** up and shouted in Hebrew,
46. 7 in place, and there it **stands,** unable to move from where it
Jer 6.16 Lord said to his people, **"Stand** at the crossroads and look.
7. 1 He told me to **stand** there and announce what the Lord Almighty,
7.10 and then you come and **stand** in my presence, in my own
12. 5 If you can't even **stand** up in open country, how will you
14. 6 The wild donkeys **stand** on the hill-tops and pant for
15. 1 if Moses and Samuel were **standing** here pleading with me, I
17.12 is like a glorious throne, **standing** on a high mountain from
19.14 I went and **stood** in the court of the Temple and told
26. 2 the Lord said to me, **"Stand** in the court of the Temple
26.17 that, some of the elders **stood** up and said to the people
28. 5 all the people who were **standing** in the Temple, I said to
36.21 the king and all the officials who were **standing** round him.
44.15 all the women who were **standing** there, including the
46.18 the mountains and Mount Carmel **stands** high above the sea, so
46.21 They did not **stand** and fight;
48.19 You that live in Aroer, **stand** by the road and wait;
Ezek 1.23 There under the dome **stood** the creatures, each
2. 1 Then I heard a voice [1] saying, "Mortal man, **stand** up.
9. 2 They all came and **stood** by the bronze altar.
9. 6 with the leaders who were **standing** there at the Temple.
10. 3 The creatures were **standing** to the south of the Temple
10. 6 creatures, the man went in and **stood** by one of the wheels.
21.21 The king of Babylonia **stands** by the signpost at the fork
22.30 build a wall, who could **stand** in the places where the walls
Ezek 26. 5 dry their nets on it, there where it **stands** in the sea.
27. 3 for Tyre, [3] that city which **stands** at the edge of the sea
37.10 Breath entered the bodies, and they came to life and **stood** up.
40. 3 and a measuring-rod and was **standing** by a gateway.
41.22 "This is the table which **stands** in the presence of the Lord."
43. 6 The man **stood** beside me there, and I heard the Lord speak
46. 2 room by the gateway and **stand** beside the posts of the gate
Dan 2. 2 When they came and **stood** before the king, [3] he said to them,
2.31 in your vision you saw **standing** before you a giant statue,
3. 3 for the dedication and **stood** in front of the statue,
7. 4 The beast was lifted up and made to **stand** like a man.
7. 5 The second beast looked like a bear **standing** on its hind legs.
7.10 there to serve him, and millions of people **stood** before him.
7.16 up to one of those **standing** there and asked him to explain
8. 2 I was **standing** by the River Ulai, [3] and there beside the
8. 6 ram, which I had seen **standing** beside the river, and rushed
8.15 meant, when suddenly someone was **standing** in front of me.
8.17 Gabriel came and **stood** beside me, and I was so terrified
9.25 defences, and will **stand** for seven times sixty-two years,
10. 4 of the year, I was **standing** on the bank of the mighty
10.11 **Stand** up and listen carefully to what I am going to say.
10.11 When he had said this, I **stood** up, still trembling.
10.17 I am like a slave **standing** before his master.
11.16 He will **stand** in the Promised Land and have it completely in
11.45 between the sea and the mountain on which the Temple **stands.**
12. 5 Then I saw two men **standing** by a river, one on each
12. 6 asked the angel who was **standing** further upstream, "How
Hos 9. 6 places where their homes once **stood** will be overgrown with
Amos 5.21 I cannot **stand** them!
7. 7 In it I saw him **standing** beside a wall that had been
9. 1 I saw the Lord **standing** by the altar.
Obad 11 You **stood** aside on that day when enemies broke down their
14 You should not have **stood** at the cross-roads to catch
Mic 4. 1 the mountain where the Temple **stands** will be the highest one
Hab 3.11 of your shining spear, the sun and the moon **stood** still.
Zech 3. 1 High Priest Joshua **standing** before the angel of the Lord.
3. 1 And there beside Joshua **stood** Satan, ready to bring an
3. 3 Joshua was **standing** there, wearing filthy clothes.
3. 5 new clothes on him while the angel of the Lord **stood** there.
6.13 A priest will **stand** by his throne, and they will work
14. 4 At that time he will **stand** on the Mount of Olives, to
Mt 6. 5 They love to **stand** up and pray in the houses of worship
12.41 the people of Nineveh will **stand** up and accuse you, because
12.42 the Queen of Sheba will **stand** up and accuse you, because she
12.46 They **stood** outside, asking to speak with him.
12.47 your mother and brothers are **standing** outside, and they want
13. 2 boat and sat in it, while the crowd **stood** on the shore.
18. 2 called a child, made him **stand** in front of them, [3] and said,
20. 3 o'clock and saw some men **standing** there doing nothing, [4] so
20. 6 market-place and saw some other men still **standing** there.
24.15 It will be **standing** in the holy place."
26.62 The High Priest **stood** up and said to Jesus, "Have you
26.73 After a little while the men **standing** there came to Peter.
27.11 Jesus **stood** before the Roman governor, who questioned him.
27.47 Some of the people **standing** there heard him and said,
Mk 3.31 They **stood** outside the house and sent in a message, asking
4. 1 the water, and the crowd **stood** on the shore at the water's
4.39 Jesus **stood** up and commanded the wind, "Be quiet!"
9.27 by the hand and helped him to rise, and he **stood** up.
9.36 he took a child and made him **stand** in front of them.
11.25 And when you **stand** and pray, forgive anything you may
13. 9 you will **stand** before rulers and kings for my sake to tell
13.14 will see 'The Awful Horror' **standing** in the place where he
14.47 But one of those **standing** there drew his sword and
14.57 Then some men **stood** up and told this lie against Jesus:
14.60 The High Priest **stood** up in front of them all and
15.39 The army officer who was **standing** there in front of the
Lk 1.11 the Lord appeared to him, **standing** on the right of the altar
1.19 "I **stand** in the presence of God, who sent me to speak
4.16 He **stood** up to read the Scriptures [17] and was handed the
4.39 He went and **stood** at her bedside and ordered the fever
5. 1 One day Jesus was **standing** on the shore of Lake Gennesaret
6. 8 and said to the man, **"Stand** up and come here to the
6. 8 The man got up and **stood** there.
6.17 hill with the apostles, he **stood** on a level place with a
7.38 jar full of perfume [38] and **stood** behind Jesus, by his feet,
8.20 "Your mother and brothers are **standing** outside and want to see you."
9.32 saw Jesus' glory and the two men who were **standing** with him.
9.47 so he took a child, **stood** him by his side, [48] and said
11.31 the Queen of Sheba will **stand** up and accuse the people of
11.32 the people of Nineveh will **stand** up and accuse you, because
13.25 then when you **stand** outside and begin to knock on the door
17.12 They **stood** at a distance [13] and shouted, "Jesus!
18.11 "The Pharisee **stood** apart by himself and prayed, 'I
18.13 "But the tax collector **stood** at a distance and would
19. 8 Zacchaeus **stood** up and said to the Lord, "Listen, sir!
19.24 said to those who were **standing** there, 'Take the gold coin
21.19 **Stand firm,** and you will save yourselves.
21.28 these things begin to happen, **stand** up and raise your heads,
21.36 that will happen and to **stand** before the Son of Man."
23.35 The people **stood** there watching while the Jewish leaders jeered at him:
23.49 followed him from Galilee, **stood** at a distance to watch.
24. 4 They **stood** there puzzled about this,
24. 4 suddenly two men in bright shining clothes **stood** by them.
24.17 They **stood** still, with sad faces.
24.36 suddenly the Lord himself **stood** among them and said to them,
Jn 1.26 with water, but among you **stands** the one you do not know.
1.35 The next day John was **standing** there again with two of
3.29 but the bridegroom's friend, who **stands** by and listens, is

Jn 7.37 day of the festival Jesus **stood** up and said in a loud
8. 3 adultery, and they made her **stand** before them all.
8. 7 As they **stood** there asking him questions, he straightened
8. 9 Jesus was left alone, with the woman still **standing** there.
12.29 The crowd **standing** there heard the voice, and some of
18. 5 Judas, the traitor, was **standing** there with them.
18.18 fire and were **standing** round it, warming themselves.
18.18 So Peter went over and **stood** with them, warming himself.
18.25 Peter was still **standing** there keeping himself warm.
19.25 **Standing** close to Jesus' cross were his mother, his mother's sister,
19.26 Jesus saw his mother and the disciple he loved **standing** there;
20.11 Mary **stood** crying outside the tomb.
20.14 Then she turned round and saw Jesus **standing** there;
20.19 Then Jesus came and **stood** among them.
20.26 locked, but Jesus came and **stood** among them and said,
21. 4 the sun was rising, Jesus **stood** at the water's edge, but the
Acts 1.10 dressed in white suddenly **stood** beside them [11] and said,
1.11 "Galileans, why are you **standing** there looking up at the sky?
1.15 a hundred and twenty in all, and Peter **stood** up to speak.
2.14 Then Peter **stood** up with the other eleven apostles and
3. 8 he jumped up, **stood** on his feet, and started walking around.
4. 7 They made the apostles **stand** before them and asked them,
4.10 should know, that this man **stands** here before you completely
4.14 man who had been healed **standing** there with Peter and John.
5.20 said to them, [20] "Go and **stand** in the Temple, and tell the
5.27 the apostles in, made them **stand** before the Council, and the
5.34 highly respected by all the people, **stood** up in the Council.
7.33 off, for the place where you are **standing** is holy ground.
7.55 God's glory and Jesus **standing** at the right-hand side of God.
7.56 and the Son of Man **standing** at the right-hand side of God!"
9.18 He **stood** up and was baptized;
10.17 house was, and they were now **standing** in front of the gate.
10.26 **"Stand** up," he said;
10.30 in shining clothes **stood** in front of me [31] and said:
11.13 he had seen an angel **standing** in his house, who said to
11.28 One of them, named Agabus, **stood** up and by the power of
12. 7 an angel of the Lord **stood** there, and a light shone in
12.14 the door, and announced that Peter was **standing** outside.
13.16 Paul **stood** up, motioned with his hand, and began to speak:
14.10 and said in a loud voice, **"Stand** up straight on your feet!"
14.13 the god Zeus, whose temple **stood** just outside the town,
15. 5 the party of the Pharisees **stood** up and said, "The Gentiles
15. 7 After a long debate Peter **stood** up and said, "My
16. 9 which he saw a Macedonian **standing** and begging him, "Come
17.22 Paul **stood** up in front of the city council and said, "I
21.40 gave him permission, so Paul **stood** on the steps and motioned
22.13 He came to me, **stood** by me, and said, 'Brother Saul, see
22.25 Paul said to the officer **standing** there, "Is it lawful for
22.30 Then he took Paul and made him **stand** before them.
23. 2 Ananias ordered those who were **standing** close to Paul to
23. 9 the party of the Pharisees **stood** up and protested strongly:
23.11 That night the Lord **stood** by Paul and said, "Don't be afraid!
24.20 me guilty of when I **stood** before the Council—[21] except for
24.21 for the one thing I called out when I **stood** before them:
25. 7 who had come from Jerusalem **stood** round him and started
25.10 Paul said, "I am **standing** before the Emperor's own court of judgement,
25.18 His opponents **stood** up, but they did not accuse him of
26. 6 And now I **stand** here to be tried because of the hope
26.16 But get up and **stand** on your feet.
26.22 by God, and so I **stand** here giving my witness to all,
27.21 long time without food, Paul **stood** before them and said,
27.24 You must **stand** before the Emperor.
Rom 3. 7 God's glory by making his truth **stand** out more clearly?
14.10 All of us will **stand** before God to be judged by him.
16.25 is able to make you **stand firm** in your faith, according to
1 Cor 10.12 Whoever thinks he is **standing firm** had better be careful
15. 1 which you received, and on which your faith **stands firm.**
15.58 So then, my dear brothers, **stand firm** and steady.
16.13 Be alert, **stand firm** in the faith, be brave, be strong.
2 Cor 1.24 we know that you **stand firm** in the faith.
2. 9 out how well you had **stood** the test and whether you are
Gal 5. 1 **Stand,** then, as free people, and do not allow yourselves to
Eph 6.11 will be able to **stand** up against the Devil's evil tricks.
6.14 So **stand** ready, with truth as a belt tight round your waist,
Phil 1.27 will hear that you are **standing firm** with one common purpose
4. 1 brothers, is how you should **stand firm** in your life in the
Col 2. 5 firmness with which you **stand** together in your faith
4.12 asking God to make you **stand firm,** as mature and fully
1 Thes 3. 8 we really live if you **stand firm** in your life in union
2 Thes 2.15 So then, our brothers, **stand firm** and hold on to those
2 Tim 4.16 No one **stood** by me the first time I defended myself;
Heb 9. 8 not yet been opened as long as the outer Tent still **stands.**
Jas 2. 3 say to the poor man, **"Stand** over there, or sit here on
1 Pet 5.12 **Stand firm** in it.
Rev 3.20 I **stand** at the door and knock;
5. 6 Then I saw a Lamb **standing** in the centre of the throne,
5.11 They **stood** round the throne, the four living creatures, and the elders,
6.17 day of their anger is here, and who can **stand** against it?"
7. 1 this I saw four angels **standing** at the four corners of the
7. 9 nation, and language, and they **stood** in front of the throne
7.11 All the angels **stood** round the throne, the elders, and
7.15 That is why they **stand** before God's throne and serve him
8. 2 saw the seven angels who **stand** before God, and they were
8. 3 who had a gold incense-burner, came and **stood** at the altar.
8. 3 to offer it on the gold altar that **stands** before the throne.
8. 4 God's people from the hands of the angel **standing** before God.
9.13 from the four corners of the gold altar **standing** before God.
10. 5 the angel that I saw **standing** on the sea and on the
10. 8 the hand of the angel **standing** on the sea and on the
Rev 11. 4 and the two lamps that **stand** before the Lord of the earth.
11.11 breath came from God and entered them, and they **stood** up;
12. 4 He **stood** in front of the woman, in order to eat her
12.10 For the one who **stood** before our God and accused our
12.18 And the dragon **stood** on the sea-shore.
14. 1 Then I looked, and there was the Lamb **standing** on Mount Zion;
14. 3 The 144,000 people **stood** before the throne, the four living creatures
15. 2 They were **standing** by the sea of glass, holding harps that
15. 4 Who will not **stand** in awe of you, Lord?
18.10 They **stand** a long way off, because they are afraid of
18.15 business in that city, will **stand** a long way off, because
18.17 their living on the sea, **stood** a long way off, [18] and cried
19.17 Then I saw an angel **standing** on the sun.
20.12 I saw the dead, great and small alike, **standing** before the throne.
21.25 The gates of the city will **stand** open all day;

STAND FOR

Zech 1.19 He answered, "They **stand for** the world powers that have
4. 4 Then I asked the angel, "What do these things **stand for,**
5. 6 is a basket, and it **stands for** the sin of the whole
Mt 13.20 that fell on rocky ground **stand for** those who receive the
13.22 among thorn bushes **stand for** those who hear the message;
13.23 sown in the good soil **stand for** those who hear the message
Lk 8.12 The seeds that fell along the path **stand for** those who hear;
8.13 that fell on rocky ground **stand for** those who hear the
8.14 The seeds that fell among thorn bushes **stand for** those who hear;
8.15 that fell in good soil **stand for** those who hear the message
1 Cor 8. 4 we know that an idol **stands for** something that does not
Gal 4.25 Hagar, who **stands for** Mount Sinai in Arabia, is a figure
Rev 13.17 the beast's name or the number that **stands for** the name.
13.18 of the beast, because the number **stands for** a man's name.

STANDARD

Gen 23.16 according to the **standard** weights used by the merchants.
Ex 16.36 (The **standard** dry measure then in use equalled twenty litres.)
30.13 amount of money, weighed according to the official **standard.**
30.24 of cassia (all weighed according to the official **standard).**
38.24 thousand kilogrammes, weighed according to the official **standard.**
38.25 3,430 kilogrammes, weighed according to the official **standard.**
38.26 required amount, weighed according to the official **standard.**
Lev 5.15 Its value is to be determined according to the official **standard.**
5.18 Its value is to be determined according to the official **standard.**
6. 6 Its value is to be determined according to the official **standard.**
27. 3 sums of money, [3-7] according to the official **standard:**
27. 8 too poor to pay the **standard** price, he shall bring the
27.25 All prices shall be fixed according to the official **standard.**
27.27 be bought back at the **standard** price plus an additional
27.27 back, it may be sold to someone else at the **standard** price.
27.31 back, he must pay the **standard** price plus an additional
Num 3.47 silver, according to the official **standard,** [48] and give
7.12 800 grammes, by the official **standard,** both of them full of
18.16 five pieces of silver, according to the official **standard.**
Deut 3.11 almost two metres wide according to **standard** measurements.
2 Sam 14.26 two kilogrammes according to the royal **standard** of weights.
Ezek 45.11 The **standard** is the homer.
Jn 7.24 Stop judging by external **standards,** and judge by true standards."
Rom 2.11 For God judges everyone by the same **standard.**
12. 2 not conform yourselves to the **standards** of this world, but
1 Cor 3. 3 that you belong to this world, living by its **standards?**
3.18 is wise by this world's **standards,** he should become a fool,
4. 3 about being judged by you or by any human **standard;**
2 Cor 5.16 No longer, then, do we judge anyone by human **standards.**
5.16 Christ according to human **standards,** we no longer do so.
10.12 They make up their own **standards** to measure themselves by,
10.12 and they judge themselves by their own **standards!**
Eph 4. 1 that measures up to the **standard** God set when he called you.
6. 9 Master in heaven, who judges everyone by the same **standard.**
Col 3.25 he does, because God judges everyone by the same **standard.**
1 Pet 1.17 all people by the same **standard,** according to what each one
Rev 21.17 metres high, according to the **standard** unit of measure which

STANDING

[SOCIAL STANDING]

Acts 13.50 Gentile women of high **social standing** who worshipped God.
17.12 many Greek women of high **social standing** and many Greek men
1 Cor 1.26 few of you were wise or powerful or of high **social standing.**
6. 4 to be settled by people who have no **standing** in the church?
1 Tim 3.13 win for themselves a good **standing** and are able to speak

STANDSTILL

Ezra 4.24 and had remained at a **standstill** until the second year of

STAR

Gen 1.16 he also made the **stars.**
15. 5 and said, "Look at the sky and try to count the **stars;**
22.17 many descendants as there are **stars** in the sky or grains of
26. 4 many descendants as there are **stars** in the sky, and I will
37. 9 the sun, the moon, and eleven **stars** bowing down to me."
Ex 32.13 many descendants as there are **stars** in the sky and to give
Num 24.17 A king, like a bright **star,** will arise in that nation.
Deut 1.10 God has made you as numerous as the **stars** in the sky.
4.19 you see in the sky—the sun, the moon, and the **stars.**
10.22 God has made you as numerous as the **stars** in the sky.
17. 3 or the moon or the **stars,** contrary to the Lord's command.

Deut 28.62 become as numerous as the **stars** in the sky, only a few
Judg 5.20 The **stars** fought from the sky;
2 Kgs 17.16 Asherah, worshipped the **stars,** and served the god Baal.
21. 3 Manasseh also worshipped the **stars.**
21. 5 of the Temple he built altars for the worship of the **stars.**
23. 4 worship of Baal, of the goddess Asherah, and of the **stars.**
23. 5 to Baal, to the sun, the moon, the planets, and the **stars.**
1 Chr 27.23 the people of Israel as numerous as the **stars** in the sky.
2 Chr 33. 3 images of the goddess Asherah, and worshipped the **stars.**
33. 5 of the Temple he built altars for the worship of the **stars.**
Neh 4.21 day, from dawn until the **stars** came out at night, half of
9. 6 you made the heavens and the **stars** of the sky.
9.23 many children as there are **stars** in the sky, and let them
Job 3. 9 Keep the morning **star** from shining;
9. 7 the sun from rising, and the **stars** from shining at night.
9. 9 God hung the **stars** in the sky—
9. 9 Great Bear, Orion, the Pleiades, and the **stars** of the south.
22.12 and look down on the **stars,** even though they are high?
25. 5 his eyes even the moon is not bright, nor the **stars** pure.
38. 7 dawn of that day the **stars** sang together, and the heavenly
38.32 Can you guide the **stars** season by season and direct the
Ps 8. 3 at the moon and the **stars,** which you set in their places
33. 6 his command, the sun, moon, and **stars** by his spoken word.
136. 9 the moon and the **stars** to rule over the night;
147. 4 decided the number of the **stars** and calls each one by name.
148. 3 praise him, shining **stars.**
Ecc 12. 2 sun, the moon, and the **stars** will grow dim for you, and
Is 13.10 Every **star** and every constellation will stop shining,
14.12 "King of Babylonia, bright morning **star,** you have fallen
14.13 to heaven and to place your throne above the highest **stars.**
34. 4 The sun, moon, and **stars** will crumble to dust.
34. 4 being rolled up, and the **stars** will fall like leaves
40.26 Who created the **stars** you see?
45.12 I control the sun, the moon, and the **stars.**
47.13 those people who study the **stars,** who map out the zones of
Jer 8. 2 sun, the moon, and the **stars,** which these people have loved
19.13 has been burnt to the **stars** and where wine has been poured
31.35 light by day, the moon and the **stars** to shine at night.
33.22 it is to count the **stars** in the sky or the grains
Ezek 32. 7 destroy you, I will cover the sky and blot out the **stars.**
Dan 8.10 the army of heaven, the **stars** themselves, and it threw some
12. 3 to do what is right will shine like the **stars** for ever."
Joel 2.10 sun and the moon grow dark, and the **stars** no longer shine.
3.15 sun and the moon grow dark, and the **stars** no longer shine.
Amos 5. 8 The Lord made the **stars,** the Pleiades and Orion.
5.26 god, and of Kaiwan, your **star** god, you will have to carry
Obad 4 seems to be among the **stars,** yet I will pull you down.
Nah 3.16 You produced more merchants than there are **stars** in the sky!
Zeph 1. 5 on the roof and worships the sun, the moon, and the **stars.**
Mt 2. 1 some men who studied the **stars** came from the east to
2. 2 We saw his **star** when it came up in the east, and
2. 7 found out from them the exact time the **star** had appeared.
2. 9 way they saw the same **star** they had seen in the east.
2.16 the visitors about the time when the **star** had appeared.
24.29 will no longer shine, the **stars** will fall from heaven, and
Mk 13.25 will no longer shine, [25] the **stars** will fall from heaven,
Lk 21.25 things happening to the sun, the moon, and the **stars.**
Acts 7.42 them over to worship the **stars** of heaven, as it is written
7.43 Molech that you carried, and the image of Rephan, your **star** god;
27.20 see the sun or the **stars,** and the wind kept on blowing
Rom 4.18 says, "Your descendants will be as many as the **stars."**
1 Cor 15.41 the moon another beauty, and the **stars** a different beauty;
15.41 and even among **stars** there are different kinds of beauty.
Phil 2.15 must shine among them like **stars** lighting up the sky, [16] as
Heb 11.12 many descendants as there are **stars** in the sky, as many as
2 Pet 1.19 and the light of the morning **star** shines in your hearts.
Jude 13 They are like wandering **stars,** for whom God has reserved a
Rev 1.16 He held seven **stars** in his right hand, and a sharp
1.20 secret meaning of the seven **stars** that you see in my right
1.20 the seven **stars** are the angels of the seven churches, and
2. 1 one who holds the seven **stars** in his right hand and who
2.26 I will also give them the morning **star.**
3. 1 one who has the seven spirits of God and the seven **stars.**
6.13 The **stars** fell down to the earth, like unripe figs
8.10 A large **star,** burning like a torch, dropped from the sky and
8.11 (The name of the **star** is "Bitterness.")
8.12 and a third of the **stars,** so that their light lost a
9. 1 I saw a **star** which had fallen down to the earth, and
9. 2 The **star** opened the abyss, and smoke poured out of it,
12. 1 under her feet and a crown of twelve **stars** on her head.
12. 4 dragged a third of the **stars** out of the sky and threw
22.16 I am the bright morning **star."**

STARE

Num 24. 4 With **staring** eyes I see in a trance A vision from Almighty
24.16 With **staring** eyes I see in a trance A vision from Almighty
1 Sam 4.13 was sitting on a seat beside the road, **staring.**
2 Kgs 8.11 Then Elisha **stared** at him with a horrified look on his
2 Chr 26.20 Azariah and the other priests **stared** at the king's forehead
Esth 7. 6 Haman **stared** at the king and queen in terror.
Job 4.16 I **stared,** but couldn't tell what it was.
21. 5 Isn't that enough to make you **stare** in shocked silence?
Ps 22.17 My enemies look at me and **stare.**
Is 8.22 up to the sky [22] or **stare** at the ground, but they will
14.16 "The dead will **stare** and gape at you.
Dan 7. 8 While I was **staring** at the horns, I saw a little horn
10.15 When he said this, I **stared** at the ground, speechless.
Nah 3. 6 People will **stare** at you in horror.
Acts 3.12 are you surprised at this, and why do you **stare** at us?
10. 4 He **stared** at the angel in fear and said, "What is it,

START

Gen 7.24 The water did not **start** going down for a hundred and
8. 1 he caused a wind to blow, and the water **started** going down.
12. 4 was seventy-five years old, he **started** out from Haran, as
12. 5 in Haran, and they **started** out for the land of Canaan.
22. 3 They **started** out for the place that God had told him about.
22. 6 carried a knife and live coals for **starting** the fire.
24.61 to go with Abraham's servant, and they all **started** out.
28.10 Jacob left Beersheba and **started** towards Haran.
31.21 He crossed the River Euphrates and **started** for the hill-country
33.16 So that day Esau **started** on his way back to Edom.
35. 5 When Jacob and his sons **started** to leave, great fear fell
Ex 17.11 when he put his arms down, the Amalekites **started** winning.
22. 6 "If a man **starts** a fire in his field and it spreads
22. 6 and stacked, the one who **started** the fire is to pay for
36. 2 were willing to help, and Moses told them to **start** working.
Lev 13.20 It is a dreaded skin-disease that has **started** in the boil.
13.25 a dreaded skin-disease that has **started** in the burn, and the
Num 10.12 presence lifted, [12] and the Israelites **started** on their
10.14 by the tribe of Judah **started** out first, company by company,
10.17 of Gershon and Merari, who carried it, would **start** out.
10.18 the tribe of Reuben would **start** out, company by company,
10.21 clan of Kohath would **start** out, carrying the sacred objects.
10.22 the tribe of Ephraim would **start** out, company by company,
10.25 of all the divisions, would **start** out, company by company,
10.29 Midianite, "We are about to **start** out for the place which
10.35 Whenever the Covenant Box **started** out, Moses would say,
14.40 the next morning they **started** out to invade the hill-country,
Deut 2. 5 you, [5] but you must not **start** a war with them, because I
2. 9 Moab, the descendants of Lot, or **start** a war against them.
2.19 Don't trouble them or **start** a war against them, because I am
2.24 Lord said to us, 'Now, **start** out and cross the River Arnon.
20. 2 Before you **start** fighting, a priest is to come forward and
Josh 2. 4 were going, but if you **start** after them quickly, you can
6. 7 he ordered his men to **start** marching round the city, with an
6. 8 had ordered, an advance guard **started** out ahead of the
9.12 left home with it and **started** out to meet you, it was
9.17 So the people of Israel **started** out and three days later
10. 7 army, including the best troops, **started** out from Gilgal.
16. 1 descendants of Joseph **started** from the Jordan near Jericho,
18.15 The southern border **started** on the edge of Kiriath
22. 9 the land of Canaan and **started** out for their own land, the
Judg 16.22 But his hair **started** growing again.
18.21 They turned round and **started** off, with their children,
19. 8 of the fifth day he **started** to leave, but the girl's father
19. 9 and the servant once more **started** to leave, the father said,
19.10 so he and his concubine **started** on their way, with their
19.22 town surrounded the house and **started** beating on the door.
19.28 put her body across the donkey and **started** on his way home.
20.19 So the Israelites **started** out the next morning and made
Ruth 1. 7 They **started** out together to go back to Judah, but on the
1. 9 But they **started** crying [10] and said to her, "No!
1.14 Again they **started** crying.
1 Sam 6. 8 **Start** the wagon on its way and let it go by itself.
6.12 The cows **started** off on the road to Beth Shemesh and
7. 7 Mizpah, the five Philistine kings **started** out with their men
9. 5 thinking about the donkeys and **start** worrying about us."
9.12 who are invited won't **start** eating until he gets there,
11. 4 they told the news, the people **started** crying in despair.
17.41 The Philistine **started** walking towards David, with his
17.48 Goliath **started** walking towards David again, and David
19.22 Then he himself **started** out for Ramah.
24. 7 Saul got up, left the cave, and **started** on his way.
24.16 And he **started** crying.
29. 8 me since the day I **started** serving you, why shouldn't I go
29.11 So David and his men **started** out early the following
30. 4 David and his men **started** crying and did not stop until
30. 9 and his six hundred men **started** out, and when they arrived
31.12 to Saul, [12] the bravest men **started** out and marched all
2 Sam 2.19 deer, [19] **started** chasing Abner, running straight for him.
2.24 But Joab and Abishai **started** out after Abner, and at
5. 9 built the city round it, **starting** at the place where land
13.36 **started** crying, and David and his officials also wept bitterly.
16. 6 Shimei **started** throwing stones at David and his officials,
17.22 So David and his men **started** crossing the Jordan, and by
19. 9 All over the country they **started** quarrelling among themselves.
20.21 of Ephraim, **started** a rebellion against King David.
1 Kgs 15.17 Baasha invaded Judah and **started** to fortify Ramah in
17.22 the child **started** breathing again and revived.
18. 2 So Elijah **started** out.
18.27 At noon Elijah **started** making fun of them:
18.45 Ahab got into his chariot and **started** back to Jezreel.
20.29 On the seventh day they **started** fighting, and the Israelites
2 Kgs 4. 4 house, close the door, and **start** pouring oil into the jars.
4.30 So the two of them **started** back together.
4.34 out over the boy, the boy's body **started** to get warm.
5. 7 It's plain that he is trying to **start** a quarrel with me!"
9.22 witchcraft and idolatry that your mother Jezebel **started?"**
10.15 Jehu **started** out again, and on his way he was met by
1 Chr 11. 8 He rebuilt the city, **starting** at the place where land was
11.13 a barley-field when the Israelites **started** to run away,
14.13 Philistines returned to the valley and **started** plundering it
22.19 **Start** building the Temple, so that you can place in it the
28.20 **Start** the work and don't let anything stop you.
2 Chr 16. 1 of Israel invaded Judah and **started** to fortify Ramah in
20.20 As they were **starting** out, Jehoshaphat addressed them
31. 7 The gifts **started** arriving in the third month and
31.10 "Since the people **started** bringing their gifts to the Temple,
Ezra 3. 6 the people had not yet **started** to rebuild the Temple, they
3.10 When the men **started** to lay the foundation of the Temple,

Ezra 3.11 the work on the foundation of the Temple had been **started.**
Neh 2.18 They responded, "Let's **start** rebuilding!"
2.18 And they got ready to **start** the work.
2.20 We are his servants, and we are going to **start** building.
13.12 the people of Israel again **started** bringing to the temple
Job 11.12 Stupid men will **start** being wise when wild donkeys are born tame.
41.21 His breath **starts** fires burning;
Ps 19. 6 It **starts** at one end of the sky and goes across to
81. 2 **Start** the music and beat the tambourines;
118.27 With branches in your hands, **start** the festival and march
Prov 17.14 The **start** of an argument is like the first break in a
17.24 at wise action, but a fool **starts** off in many directions.
18. 6 When some fool **starts** an argument, he is asking for a beating.
20. 3 Any fool can **start** arguments;
26.27 People who **start** landslides get crushed.
Ecc 1. 5 going wearily back to where it must **start** all over again.
1. 7 to where the rivers began, and **starts** all over again.
2.12 So I **started** thinking about what it meant to be wise or
10.13 He **starts** out with silly talk and ends up with pure madness.
Song 7.12 vines to see whether they've **started** to grow, whether the
Is 5.11 early in the morning to **start** drinking, and you spend long
Jer 37.12 So I **started** to leave Jerusalem and go to the territory
41.10 Ishmael took them prisoner and **started** off in the direction
Ezek 3.20 "If a truly good man **starts** doing evil and I put him
9. 6 **Start** here at my Temple."
12. 3 just as a refugee would, and **start** out before nightfall.
18.24 man stops doing good and **starts** doing all the evil,
18.26 man stops doing good and **starts** doing evil and then dies, he
20.47 I am **starting** a fire, and it will burn up every tree
21.19 Both of them are to **start** in the same country.
33.12 and if a good man **starts** sinning, his life will not be
33.13 good man, but if he **starts** thinking that his past goodness
33.18 man stops doing good and **starts** doing evil, he will die for
38.10 "When that time comes, you will **start** thinking up an evil plan.
39. 6 I will **start** a fire in the land of Magog and along
Dan 3. 5 As soon as the music **starts,** you are to bow down and
3.10 as soon as the music **starts,** everyone is to bow down and
Amos 3. 3 Do two men **start** travelling together without arranging to meet?
7. 1 hay had been cut and the grass was **starting** to grow again.
7. 4 ocean under the earth, and **started** to burn up the land.
8. 5 When will the Sabbath end, so that we can **start** selling again?
Jon 3. 4 Jonah **started** through the city, and after walking a whole day,
Hag 2.15 Before you **started** to rebuild the Temple, [16] you would go
Mt 3. 1 John the Baptist came to the desert of Judaea and **started** preaching.
6.31 "So do not **start** worrying:
9.27 and as he walked along, two blind men **started** following him.
9.33 out, the man **started** talking, and everyone was amazed.
14.29 out of the boat and **started** walking on the water to Jesus.
14.30 wind, he was afraid and **started** to sink down in the water.
16. 7 They **started** discussing among themselves, "He says this
18.28 He grabbed him and **started** choking him.
20. 8 and pay them their wages, **starting** with those who were hired
20.11 They took their money and **started** grumbling against the employer.
21.25 They **started** to argue among themselves, "What shall we say?
23.32 Go on, then, and finish what your ancestors **started!**
24.32 green and tender and it **starts** putting out leaves, you know
27.23 Then they **started** shouting at the top of their voices:
Mk 1.27 all so amazed that they **started** saying to one another,
2.13 A crowd came to him, and he **started** teaching them.
4.29 corn is ripe, the man **starts** cutting it with his sickle,
5.24 Then Jesus **started** off with him.
5.42 She got up at once and **started** walking around.
6.32 So they **started** out in a boat by themselves for a lonely
8.11 Some Pharisees came to Jesus and **started** to argue with him.
8.13 back into the boat, and **started** across to the other side of
8.16 They **started** discussing among themselves:
9.10 but among themselves they **started** discussing the matter,
10.17 As Jesus was **starting** on his way again, a man ran up,
11.31 They **started** to argue among themselves:
13.28 green and tender and it **starts** putting out leaves, you know
14.11 So Judas **started** looking for a good chance to hand Jesus
Lk 1.64 Zechariah was able to speak again, and he **started** praising God.
2.43 the festival was over, they **started** back home, but the boy
2.44 a whole day and then **started** looking for him among their
3. 8 And don't **start** saying among yourselves that Abraham is your ancestor.
4.42 The people **started** looking for him, and when they found him,
8.22 So they **started** out.
9.62 said to him, "Anyone who **starts** to plough and then keeps
15. 2 the teachers of the Law **started** grumbling, "This man
15.20 So he got up and **started** back to his father.
19. 7 the people who saw it **started** grumbling, "This man has gone
19.40 keep quiet, the stones themselves will **start** shouting."
20. 5 They **started** to argue among themselves, "What shall we say?
22. 6 Judas agreed to it and **started** looking for a good chance
23. 5 "With his teaching he is **starting** a riot among the people
Jn 4.33 So the disciples **started** asking among themselves,
5. 9 he picked up his mat and **started** walking.
6.41 The people **started** grumbling about him, because he said,
6.52 This **started** an angry argument among them.
7.22 Moses but your ancestors who **started** it), and so you
Acts 3. 8 he jumped up, stood on his feet, and **started** walking around.
4.15 Council room, and then they **started** discussing among themselves.
5.21 and at dawn they entered the Temple and **started** teaching.
6. 9 Jews from the provinces of Cilicia and Asia **started** arguing with Stephen.
8.35 **starting** from this passage of scripture, he told him the
13.50 They **started** a persecution against Paul and Barnabas and
Acts 14.10 The man jumped up and **started** walking around.
14.11 Paul had done, they **started** shouting in their own Lycaonian language,
15. 1 from Judaea to Antioch and **started** teaching the believers,
17.13 came there and **started** exciting and stirring up the mob.
19.28 and **started** shouting, "Great is Artemis of Ephesus!"
21.38 fellow who some time ago **started** a revolution and led four
22.22 but then they **started** shouting at the top of their voices,
23. 7 this, the Pharisees and Sadducees **started** to quarrel, and
24. 5 he **starts** riots among the Jews all over the world and is
25. 7 Jerusalem stood round him and **started** making many serious charges against him,
28. 2 It had **started** to rain and was cold, so they lit a
1 Cor 14.23 church meets together and everyone **starts** speaking in
Gal 2.13 The other Jewish brothers also **started** acting like cowards along with Peter;
2.18 If I **start** to rebuild the system of Law that I tore
Eph 4.28 rob must stop robbing and **start** working, in order to earn an
2 Tim 1.17 he arrived in Rome, he **started** looking for me until he found
Tit 3.13 lawyer and Apollos to get **started** on their travels, and see
1 Pet 4.17 If it **starts** with us, how will it end with those who

STARTLE

Neh 2. 2 I was **startled** [3] and answered, "May Your Majesty live for ever!
Is 29.14 So I will **startle** them with one unexpected blow after another.

Am **STARVATION**
see also **FAMINE**

STARVE

Gen 25.30 He was hungry [30] and said to Jacob, "I'm **starving;**
41.36 In this way the people will not **starve."**
42. 2 go there and buy some to keep us from **starving** to death."
42.19 and take back to your **starving** families the corn that you
42.33 rest will take corn for your **starving** families and leave.
43. 8 Then none of us will **starve** to death.
45.11 I do not want you, your family, and your livestock to **starve.'"**
Ex 16. 3 us out into this desert to **starve** us all to death."
Deut 28.51 your livestock and your crops, and you will **starve** to death.
1 Kgs 17.12 will be our last meal, and then we will **starve** to death."
2 Kgs 7. 4 into the city, because we would **starve** to death in there;
Neh 5. 3 and houses to get enough corn to keep us from **starving."**
Job 31.39 the farmers that grew it **starve**— [40] then instead of wheat
Ecc 4. 5 a fool to fold his hands and let himself **starve** to death.
Is 5.13 Your leaders will **starve** to death, and the common people
29. 8 Jerusalem will be like a **starving** man who dreams he is
51.19 land has been devastated by war, and your people have **starved.**
Jer 11.22 their children will die of **starvation.**
14.12 I will kill them in war and by **starvation** and disease."
14.13 will be no war or **starvation,** because you have promised,
14.15 name and say war and **starvation** will not strike this land—
14.15 I will kill them in war and by **starvation.**
14.18 when I go into the towns, I see people **starving** to death.
15. 2 are doomed to die of **starvation**— that's where they will go!
16. 4 in war or die of **starvation,** and their bodies will be food
18.21 But now, Lord, let their children **starve** to death;
21. 9 the city will be killed in war or by **starvation** or disease.
24.10 I will bring war, **starvation,** and disease on them until
27. 8 punish that nation by war, **starvation,** and disease until I
27.13 you and your people die in war or of **starvation** or disease?
28. 8 and yours, predicted that war, **starvation,** and disease would
29.17 says, 'I am bringing war, **starvation,** and disease on them,
29.18 will pursue them with war, **starvation,** and disease, and all
32.24 **starvation,** and disease will make the city fall into their hands.
32.36 people are saying that war, **starvation,** and disease will
34.17 the freedom to die by war, disease, and **starvation.**
38. 2 in the city will die in war or of **starvation** or disease.
38. 9 is sure to die of **starvation,** since there is no more food
42.17 in Egypt will die either in war or of **starvation** or disease.
42.22 die in war or of **starvation** or disease in the land where
44.12 small, will die in Egypt, either in war or of **starvation.**
44.13 in Egypt, just as I punished Jerusalem—with war, **starvation,**
44.18 and our people have died in war and of **starvation."**
Lam 2.19 Children **starving** to death on every street corner!
4. 5 who once ate the finest foods die **starving** in the streets;
4. 9 those who died later, who **starved** slowly to death, with no
Ezek 5.16 I will cut off your supply of food and let you **starve.**
6.12 those who survive will **starve** to death.
36.12 own land, and it will never again let your children **starve.**
Lk 15.17 more than they can eat, and here I am about to **starve!**

STATE (1)

2 Sam 8. 3 king of the Syrian **state** of Zobah, Hadadezer son of Rehob,
1 Chr 18. 3 King Hadadezer of the Syrian **state** of Zobah, near the
19. 6 Mesopotamia and from the Syrian **states** of Maacah and Zobah.
19.16 brought troops from the Syrian **states** on the east side of
Rom 13. 1 Everyone must obey the **state authorities,** because no

STATE (2)

Judg 11.11 Jephthah **stated** his terms at Mizpah in the presence of the Lord.
Neh 11.23 There were royal regulations **stating** how the clans
Job 13. 6 Listen while I **state** my case.
13.15 I am going to **state** my case to him.
13.18 I am ready to **state** my case, because I know I am
23. 4 I would **state** my case before him and present all the
Is 3.13 The Lord is ready to **state** his case;

Jer 2. 9 so I, the Lord, will **state** my case against my people again.
2 Pet 2.18 They make proud and stupid **statements,** and use immoral

STATELY

Ps 144.12 May our daughters be like **stately** pillars which adorn the

STATESMEN

Prov 8.16 governs with my help, **statesmen** and noblemen alike.
Is 3. 2 and their **statesmen,** [3] their military and civilian leaders,

STATIONED

1 Kgs 10.26 Jerusalem and the rest he **stationed** in various other cities.
2 Kgs 3.21 the youngest, were called out and **stationed** at the border.
10.24 He had **stationed** eighty men outside the temple
11.11 in the Temple, [11] and he **stationed** the men with drawn
1 Chr 9.18 of their clans had been **stationed** at the eastern entrance to
26.17 Four guards were **stationed** at the storerooms daily,
2 Chr 1.14 and the rest he **stationed** in various other cities.
8. 6 and the cities where his horses and chariots were **stationed.**
9.25 Jerusalem and the rest he **stationed** in various other cities.
11.23 responsibilities to his sons, and **stationed** them throughout
17. 2 He **stationed** troops in the fortified cities of Judah, in
17.13 In Jerusalem he **stationed** outstanding officers,
17.19 Jerusalem, and in addition he **stationed** other soldiers in
23. 5 and the rest will be **stationed** at the Foundation Gate.
23.10 He **stationed** the men with drawn swords all round the
29.25 he **stationed** Levites in the Temple, with harps and cymbals,
33.14 He also **stationed** an army officer in command of a unit of
Neh 4.13 and bows, and **stationed** them by clans behind the wall,
13.19 I **stationed** some of my men at the gates to make sure

STATUE

Lev 26. 1 make idols or set up **statues,** stone pillars, or carved
1 Sam 5. 2 temple of their god Dagon, and set it up beside his **statue.**
5. 3 of Ashdod saw that the **statue** of Dagon had fallen face
5. 4 morning they saw that the **statue** had again fallen down in
Dan 2.31 standing before you a giant **statue,** bright and shining, and
2.34 the iron and clay feet of the **statue,** and shattered them.
2.45 and how it struck the **statue** made of iron, bronze, clay,
3. 1 King Nebuchadnezzar had a gold **statue** made, twenty-seven
3. 2 of the **statue** which King Nebuchadnezzar had set up.
3. 3 stood in front of the **statue,** [4] a herald announced in a loud
3. 5 worship the gold **statue** that King Nebuchadnezzar has set up.
3. 7 the gold **statue** which King Nebuchadnezzar had set up.
3.10 down and worship the gold **statue,** [11] and that anyone who
3.12 worship your god or bow down to the **statue** you set up."
3.14 and to bow down to the gold **statue** I have set up?
3.15 all the other instruments, bow down and worship the **statue.**
3.18 not bow down to the gold **statue** that you have set up."

STATURE

Eph 4.13 reaching to the very height of Christ's full **stature.**

STATUS

Mt 22.16 think, because you pay no attention to a man's **status.**
Mk 12.14 no attention to a man's **status,** but teach the truth about
Lk 20.21 no attention to a man's **status,** but teach the truth about

AV STATUTE

Lev 3.17 this is a **rule** to be kept for ever by all Israelites
Num 19.21 You are to observe this **rule** for all time to come.
27.11 to observe this as a **legal** requirement, just as I, the Lord,
35.29 These **rules** apply to you and your descendants
Josh 24.25 and there at Shechem he gave them **laws** and rules to follow.
1 Sam 30.25 David made this a **rule,** and it has been followed in
Ps 81. 4 This is the **law** in Israel, an order from the God of
Dan 6. 7 Your Majesty should issue an **order** and enforce it strictly.
6.15 the Medes and Persians no **order** which the king issues can be

STAY

Gen 13. 6 the two of them to **stay** together, because they had too many
13.12 Abram **stayed** in the land of Canaan, and Lot settled
19. 2 You can wash your feet and **stay** the night.
19. 5 "Where are the men who came to **stay** with you tonight?
19.30 Because Lot was afraid to **stay** in Zoar, he and his two
22. 5 Then he said to the servants, **"Stay** here with the donkey.
24.25 at our house, and there is a place for you to **stay."**
24.55 mother said, "Let the girl **stay** with us a week or ten
24.56 But he said, "Don't make us **stay.**
24.62 Who Sees Me" and was **staying** in the southern part of Canaan.
25.27 outdoor life, but Jacob was a quiet man who **stayed** at home.
26. 2 **stay** in this land, where I tell you to stay.
26.17 camp in the Valley of Gerar, where he **stayed** for some time.
27.44 brother Laban in Haran, [44] and **stay** with him for a while,
29.14 Jacob **stayed** there a whole month.
29.19 **stay** here with me."
32. 4 Esau that I have been **staying** with Laban and that I have
32.24 sent across all that he owned, [24] but he **stayed** behind,
34.10 Then you may **stay** here in our country with us;
36. 7 had too much livestock and could no longer **stay** together.
38. 1 his brothers and went to **stay** with a man named Hirah, who
39.20 where the king's prisoners were kept, and there he **stayed.**
42.19 honest, one of you will **stay** in the prison where you have
Gen 42.33 One of you will **stay** with me;
42.34 brother back to you, and you can **stay** here and trade.' "
44.33 And now, sir, I will **stay** here as your slave in place
50. 8 sheep, goats, and cattle **stayed** in the region of Goshen.
Ex 9.28 you don't have to **stay** here any longer."
10.24 But your sheep, goats, and cattle must **stay** here."
16.29 Everyone is to **stay** where he is on the seventh day and
21.18 who was hit has to **stay** in bed, but later is able
22.30 Let the first-born male **stay** with its mother for seven days,
24.18 There he **stayed** for forty days and nights.
32. 1 from the mountain but was **staying** there a long time, they
33. 9 cloud would come down and **stay** at the door of the Tent,
33.11 who was his helper, Joshua son of Nun, **stayed** in the Tent.
33.20 one can see me and **stay** alive, [21] but here is a place
34.28 Moses **stayed** there with the Lord forty days and nights,
40.37 As long as the cloud **stayed** there, they did not move
Lev 8.35 You must **stay** at the entrance of the Tent day and night
22.10 eat them—not even someone **staying** with a priest or hired by
25.40 He shall **stay** with you as a hired man and serve you
Num 9.18 cloud stayed over the Tent, they **stayed** in the same camp.
9.19 When the cloud **stayed** over the Tent for a long time,
11.26 leaders, Eldad and Medad, had **stayed** in the camp and had not
20.17 We will **stay** on the main road until we are out of
20.19 of Israel said, "We will **stay** on the main road, and if
21.22 we will **stay** on the main road until we are out of
22. 8 So the Moabite leaders **stayed** with Balaam.
22. 9 and asked, "Who are these men that are **staying** with you?"
22.19 But please **stay** the night, as the others did, so that I
31.19 touched a corpse must **stay** outside the camp for seven days.
32. 6 replied, "Do you want to **stay** here while your
Deut 1. 6 God said to us, 'You have **stayed** long enough at this mountain.
1.46 "So then, after we had **stayed** at Kadesh for a long time,
5.31 But you, Moses, **stay** here with me, and I will give you
9. 9 I **stayed** there forty days and nights and did not eat or
10.10 "I **stayed** on the mountain forty days and nights, as I
15.16 he may love you and your family and be content to **stay.**
21.13 She is to **stay** in your home and mourn for her parents
23.10 the night, he is to go outside the camp and **stay** there.
24. 5 year, so that he can **stay** at home and make his wife
Josh 1.14 and your livestock will **stay** here, but your soldiers,
3. 4 **stay** about a kilometre behind it."
5. 8 was completed, the whole nation **stayed** in the camp until the
7. 7 Why didn't we just **stay** on the other side of the Jordan?
7.12 I will not **stay** with you any longer unless you destroy the
10.19 Place some guards there, [19] but don't **stay** there yourselves.
10.26 them on five trees, where their bodies **stayed** until evening.
18. 5 Judah will **stay** in its territory in the south, and Joseph in
20. 4 him a place to live in, so that he can **stay** there.
20. 6 He may **stay** in the city until he has received a public
Judg 5.16 Why did they **stay** behind with the sheep?
5.17 The tribe of Gad **stayed** east of the Jordan, and the
5.17 The tribe of Asher **stayed** by the sea-coast;
6.18 He said, "I will **stay** until you come back."
7. 3 go back home, and we will **stay** here at Mount Gilead.' "
7. 3 So twenty-two thousand went back, but ten thousand **stayed.**
11.17 So the Israelites **stayed** at Kadesh.
13.15 angel said, "If I do **stay,** I will not eat your food.
14.11 they sent thirty young men to **stay** with him.
15. 8 Then he went and **stayed** in the cave in the cliff at
16. 3 But Samson **stayed** in bed only until midnight.
17.10 Micah said, **"Stay** with me.
17.11 The young Levite agreed to **stay** with Micah and became
18. 2 the hill-country of Ephraim, they **stayed** at Micah's house.
18. 9 Don't **stay** here doing nothing;
18.17 the ephod, while the priest **stayed** at the gate with the six
19. 2 father's house in Bethlehem, and **stayed** there four months.
19. 4 The father insisted that he **stay,**
19. 4 and so he **stayed** for three days.
19. 7 father urged him to **stay,** so he spent another night there.
19. 9 you might as well **stay** all night.
19. 9 **stay** here and have a good time.
20.47 to the Rock of Rimmon, and they **stayed** there four months.
Ruth 1. 8 she said to them, "Go back home and **stay** with your mothers.
2. 9 watch them to see where they are reaping and **stay** with them.
3.13 **Stay** here the rest of the night, and in the morning we
3.13 Now lie down and **stay** here till morning."
4. 5 so that the field will **stay** in the dead man's family."
1 Sam 1.22 the house of the Lord, where he will **stay** all his life."
1.23 **stay** at home until you have weaned him.
1.23 So Hannah **stayed** at home and nursed her child.
2.11 Ramah, but the boy Samuel **stayed** in Shiloh and served the
3.15 Samuel **stayed** in bed until morning;
5. 7 We can't let the Covenant Box **stay** here any longer."
7. 2 Covenant Box of the Lord **stayed** in Kiriath Jearim a long time,
9.27 servant left, and Samuel continued, **"Stay** here a minute,
14. 9 them to come to us, then we will **stay** where we are.
16.22 Let him **stay** here in my service."
17.14 while the three eldest brothers **stayed** with Saul, [15] David
19. 2 hide in some secret place and **stay** there.
19.18 Then he and Samuel went to Naioth and **stayed** there.
22. 3 father and mother come and **stay** with you until I find out
22. 4 king of Moab, and they **stayed** there as long as David was
22. 5 Then the prophet Gad came to David and said, "Don't **stay** here;
22.23 **Stay** with me and don't be afraid.
23.14 David **stayed** in hiding in the hill-country, in the wilderness
23.18 David **stayed** at Horesh, and Jonathan went home.
23.25 to a rocky hill in the wilderness of Maon and **stayed** there.
23.29 went to the region of Engedi, where he **stayed** in hiding.
30. 9 arrived at the brook of Besor, some of them **stayed** there.
30.10 men were too tired to cross the brook and so **stayed** behind.
30.21 go with him and had **stayed** behind at the brook of Besor.

1 Sam 30.24 whoever **stays** behind with the supplies gets the same share
2 Sam 1. 1 over the Amalekites and **stayed** in Ziklag for two days.
6.11 It **stayed** there three months, and the Lord blessed Obed
10. 5 sent word that they should **stay** in Jericho and not return
11. 1 But David himself **stayed** in Jerusalem.
11.12 So David said, "Then **stay** here the rest of the day,
11.12 So Uriah **stayed** in Jerusalem that day and the next.
13.37 Geshur, Talmai son of Ammihud, and **stayed** there three years.
14.32 It would have been better for me to have **stayed** there.' "
15.19 Go back and **stay** with the new king.
15.25 me come back to see it and the place where it **stays.**
15.29 took the Covenant Box back into Jerusalem and **stayed** there.
16. 3 "He is **staying** in Jerusalem," Ziba answered, "because he
16.18 I will **stay** with you.
17. 8 experienced soldier and does not **stay** with his men at night.
18. 3 will be better if you **stay** here in the city and send
19.32 the king with food while he was **staying** at Mahanaim.
21.10 the corpses were, and she **stayed** there from the beginning of
1 Kgs 1. 2 find a young woman to **stay** with you and take care of
11.40 King Shishak of Egypt and **stayed** there until Solomon's death.
17. 5 Lord's command, and went and **stayed** by the brook of Cherith.
17. 9 "Now go to the town of Zarephath, near Sidon, and **stay** there.
17.19 the room where he was **staying,** and laid him on the bed.
20.29 Syrians and the Israelites **stayed** in their camps,
2 Kgs 2. 2 and on the way Elijah said to Elisha, "Now **stay** here;
2. 4 Then Elijah said to Elisha, "Now **stay** here;
2. 6 Then Elijah said to Elisha, "Now **stay** here;
4.10 lamp in it, and he can **stay** there whenever he visits us."
7. 4 but if we **stay** here, we'll die also.
11. 8 Joash with drawn swords and **stay** with him wherever he goes.
14.10 Be satisfied with your fame and **stay** at home.
15. 5 with a dreaded skin-disease that **stayed** with him the rest of
1 Chr 11.15 a rock where David was **staying** near the cave of Adullam,
13.14 It **stayed** there three months, and the Lord blessed Obed
19. 5 sent word for them to **stay** in Jericho and not return until
20. 1 King David, however, **stayed** in Jerusalem.
28.20 abandon you, but he will **stay** with you until you finish the
2 Chr 6.41 of your power, enter the Temple and **stay** here for ever.
23. 6 people must obey the Lord's instructions and **stay** outside.
23. 7 drawn, and are to **stay** with the king wherever he goes.
25.19 defeated the Edomites, but I advise you to **stay** at home.
Ezra 6. 6 "**Stay** away from the Temple [7] and do not interfere with its
10.14 Let our officials **stay** in Jerusalem and take charge
Neh 4.18 who was to sound the alarm on the bugle **stayed** with me.
4.22 all their helpers had to **stay** in Jerusalem at night, so that
Esth 7. 7 him for this, so he **stayed** behind to beg Queen Esther for
Job 2. 4 "A man will give up everything in order to **stay** alive.
21.23 Some men **stay** healthy till the day they die;
31.34 kept quiet or **stayed** indoors because I feared their scorn.
Ps 22.11 Do not **stay** away from me!
22.19 O Lord, don't **stay** away from me!
37.24 they fall, they will not **stay** down, because the Lord will
38.21 do not **stay** away, my God!
49.11 there they **stay** for all time, though they once had lands
68.13 (Why did some of you **stay** among the sheep pens on the
71.12 Don't **stay** so far away, O God;
73.23 Yet I always **stay** close to you, and you hold me by
103. 5 good things, so that I **stay** young and strong like an eagle.
106.25 They **stayed** in their tents and grumbled and would not
132. 8 Covenant Box, the symbol of your power, and **stay** here for ever.
Prov 1.15 **Stay** away from them.
5. 6 She does not **stay** on the road to life;
8.34 happy— the man who **stays** at my door every day, waiting
14. 7 **Stay** away from foolish people;
14.16 Wise people are careful to **stay** out of trouble, but
14.29 If you **stay** calm, you are wise, but if you have a
16.19 better to be humble and **stay** poor than to be one of
17.27 People who **stay** calm have real insight.
17.28 and intelligent if he **stays** quiet and keeps his mouth shut.
20. 3 the honourable thing is to **stay** out of them.
20.19 **Stay** away from people who talk too much.
21.23 If you want to **stay** out of trouble, be careful what you
22. 5 If you love your life, **stay** away from the traps that catch
22.13 The lazy man **stays** at home;
28.12 celebrates, but when bad men rule, people **stay** in hiding.
28.28 People **stay** in hiding when bad men come to power.
Ecc 1. 4 come and generations go, but the world **stays** just the same.
4.11 two can sleep together and **stay** warm, but how can you keep
5.12 A rich man, however, has so much that he **stays** awake worrying.
8. 3 don't **stay** in such a dangerous place.
8.16 I realized that you could **stay** awake night and day [17] and
Song 4. 6 I will **stay** on the hill of myrrh, the hill of incense,
Is 7. 4 him to keep alert, to **stay** calm, and not to be frightened
16. 4 Let us **stay** in your land.
Jer 9. 2 I had a place to **stay** in the desert where I could
14. 8 in our land, like a traveller who **stays** for only one night?
15.17 obedience to your orders I **stayed** by myself and was filled
17. 8 when hot weather comes, because its leaves **stay** green;
21. 9 Anyone who **stays** in the city will be killed in war or
24. 8 people of Jerusalem who have **stayed** in this land or moved to
27.11 then I will let it **stay** on in its own land, to
37.21 I **stayed** there, and each day I was given a loaf of
38. 2 the Lord had said, "Whoever **stays** on in the city will die
39.14 And so I **stayed** there among the people.
40. 5 You may **stay** with him and live among the people, or you
40. 6 I went to **stay** with Gedaliah in Mizpah and lived among the
40.10 I myself will **stay** in Mizpah and be your representative
40.11 had allowed some Israelites to **stay** on in Judah and that he
47. 6 Go back to your scabbard, **stay** there and rest!'
Lam 5. 6 To get food enough to **stay** alive, we went begging to Egypt
Ezek 3.15 and for seven days I **stayed** there, overcome by what I had
Ezek 3.21 and doesn't sin, he will **stay** alive, and your life will also
4. 4 For 390 days you will **stay** there and suffer because of their
26.20 I will make you **stay** in that underground world among eternal
37.26 put my Temple in their land, where it will **stay** for ever.
44. 2 me, "This gate will **stay** closed and will never be opened.
Mic 7.18 You do not **stay** angry for ever, but you take pleasure in
Nah 3.17 a swarm of locusts that **stay** in the walls on a cold
Mt 2.13 and escape to Egypt, and **stay** there until I tell you to
2.15 the night for Egypt, [15] where he **stayed** until Herod died.
4.13 He did not **stay** in Nazareth, but went to live in Capernaum,
5.26 There you will **stay,** I tell you, until you pay the last
6.25 you need in order to **stay** alive, or about clothes for your
10.11 willing to welcome you, and **stay** with him until you leave
17.17 How long must I **stay** with you?
24.43 be sure that he would **stay** awake and not let the thief
26.38 **Stay** here and keep watch with me."
Mk 1.13 where he **stayed** forty days, being tempted by Satan.
1.45 Instead, he **stayed** out in lonely places, and people came to
6.10 said, "Wherever you are welcomed, **stay** in the same house
7.24 anyone to know he was there, but he could not **stay** hidden.
9.19 How long must I **stay** with you?
14.34 **Stay** here and keep watch."
14.37 Weren't you able to **stay** awake even for one hour?"
Lk 1.56 Mary **stayed** about three months with Elizabeth and then went back home.
2. 7 manger—there was no room for them to **stay** in the inn.
2.43 started back home, but the boy Jesus **stayed** in Jerusalem.
8.27 without clothes and would not **stay** at home, but spent his
9. 4 Wherever you are welcomed, **stay** in the same house until
9.41 How long must I **stay** with you?
10. 7 **Stay** in that same house, eating and drinking whatever they offer you,
12.22 the food you need to **stay** alive or about the clothes you
12.59 There you will **stay,** I tell you, until you pay the last
19. 5 Zacchaeus, "Hurry down, Zacchaeus, because I must **stay** in your house today."
22.28 "You have **stayed** with me all through my trials;
24.29 but they held him back, saying, "**Stay** with us;
24.29 So he went in to **stay** with them.
Jn 1.32 Spirit come down like a dove from heaven and **stay** on him.
1.33 'You will see the Spirit come down and **stay** on a man;
2.12 disciples went to Capernaum and **stayed** there a few days.
4.40 they begged him to **stay** with them,
4.40 and Jesus **stayed** there two days.
6.22 day the crowd which had **stayed** on the other side of the
7. 9 He said this, and then **stayed** on in Galilee.
10.40 place where John had been baptizing, and he **stayed** there.
11. 6 that Lazarus was ill, he **stayed** where he was for two more
11.20 she went out to meet him, but Mary **stayed** in the house.
11.54 a town named Ephraim, where he **stayed** with the disciples.
14.16 give you another Helper, who will **stay** with you for ever.
18.16 High Priest's house, [16] while Peter **stayed** outside by the gate.
19.22 Pilate answered, "What I have written **stays** written."
19.31 not want the bodies to **stay** on the crosses on the Sabbath,
Acts 1.13 the city and went up to the room where they were **staying:**
7.45 And it **stayed** there until the time of David.
8.13 and after being baptized, he **stayed** close to Philip and was
8.29 Philip, "Go over to that carriage and **stay** close to it."
9.19 Saul **stayed** for a few days with the believers in Damascus.
9.28 And so Saul **stayed** with them and went all over Jerusalem,
9.43 Peter **stayed** on in Joppa for many days with a tanner of
10.48 Then they asked him to **stay** with them for a few days.
11.11 me from Caesarea arrived at the house where I was **staying.**
14. 3 The apostles **stayed** there for a long time, speaking boldly
14.28 And they **stayed** a long time there with the believers.
15.38 him, because he had not **stayed** with them to the end of
16.15 she invited us, "Come and **stay** in my house if you have
17.14 but both Silas and Timothy **stayed** in Berea.
18. 3 went to see them, [3] and **stayed** and worked with them, because
18.11 So Paul **stayed** there for a year and a half, teaching the
18.18 Paul **stayed** on with the believers in Corinth for many days,
18.20 The people asked him to **stay** longer, but he would not consent.
20. 3 Then he came to Achaia, [3] where he **stayed** three months.
21. 4 There we found some believers and **stayed** with them a week.
21. 7 we greeted the believers and **stayed** with them for a day.
21. 8 There we **stayed** at the house of Philip the evangelist, one
21.16 man we were going to **stay** with —Mnason, from Cyprus, who
27.31 soldiers, "If the sailors don't **stay** on board, you have no
28.12 in the city of Syracuse and **stayed** there for three days.
28.14 some believers there who asked us to **stay** with them a week.
28.23 of them came that day to the place where Paul was **staying.**
1 Cor 7.26 think it is better for a man to **stay** as he is.
7.40 She will be happier, however, if she **stays** as she is.
16. 8 I will **stay** here in Ephesus until the day of Pentecost.
2 Cor 1. 8 and so heavy that we gave up all hope of **staying** alive.
10.13 it will **stay** within the limits of the work which God has
Gal 1.18 information from Peter, and I **stayed** with him for two weeks.
Eph 4.26 anger lead you into sin, and do not **stay** angry all day.
Phil 1.25 am sure of this, and so I know that I will **stay.**
1.25 I will **stay** on with you all, to add to your progress
1 Thes 3. 1 So we decided to **stay** on alone in Athens [2] while we sent
1 Tim 1. 3 I want you to **stay** in Ephesus, just as I urged you
2 Tim 4.17 But the Lord **stayed** with me and gave me strength, so
4.20 Erastus **stayed** in Corinth, and I left Trophimus in Miletus,
Jas 4.13 certain city, where we will **stay** a year and go into business
1 Jn 2.19 belonged to our fellowship, they would have **stayed** with us.
2 Jn 9 Anyone who does not **stay** with the teaching of Christ, but
9 Whoever does **stay** with the teaching has both the Father and
Jude 6 the angels who did not **stay** within the limits of their
Rev 12. 8 his angels were not allowed to **stay** in heaven any longer.
16.15 Happy is he who **stays** awake and guards his clothes, so that

AV **STEADFAST**
see also **FAITHFUL, FIRM**

Job 11.15 Then face the world again, **firm** and courageous.
Ps 78. 8 trust in God was never **firm** and who did not remain faithful
78.37 they were not **faithful** to their covenant with him.
Dan 6.26 "He is a living God, and he will **rule** for ever.
1 Cor 7.37 forced to do so, has **firmly** made up his mind not to
15.58 So then, my dear brothers, stand **firm** and steady.
2 Cor 1. 7 So our hope in you is never **shaken;**
Col 2. 5 as I see the resolute **firmness** with which you stand together
Heb 2. 2 angels was shown to be **true,** and anyone who did not follow
3.14 with Christ if we hold **firmly** to the end the confidence we
6.19 It is **safe** and sure, and goes through the curtain of the
1 Pet 5. 9 Be **firm** in your faith and resist him, because you know
2 Pet 3.17 errors of lawless people and fall from your **safe** position.

STEADY

Gen 49.24 But his bow remains **steady,** And his arms are made strong
Ex 17.12 up his arms, holding them **steady** until the sun went down.
2 Chr 21.19 almost two years it grew **steadily** worse until finally the
Ezra 5. 8 is being done with great care and is moving ahead **steadily.**
Ezek 7.26 will follow another, and a **steady** stream of bad news will
1 Cor 15.58 So then, my dear brothers, stand firm and **steady.**

STEAL
[STOLE, STOLEN]

Gen 30.33 that isn't black, you will know that it has been **stolen."**
31.19 and during his absence Rachel **stole** the household gods that
31.30 get back home, but why did you **steal** my household gods?"
31.32 Jacob did not know that Rachel had **stolen** Laban's gods.
31.39 make good anything that was **stolen** during the day or during
44. 5 Why did you **steal** my master's silver cup?
44. 8 Why then should we **steal** silver or gold from your master's
Ex 20.15 "Do not **steal.**
22. 1 "If a man **steals** a cow or a sheep and kills it
22. 2 He must pay for what he **stole.**
22. 2 be sold as a slave to pay for what he has **stolen.**
22. 2 If the **stolen** animal, whether a cow, a donkey, or a sheep,
22. 7 for him and they are **stolen** from his house, the thief, if
22. 8 an oath that he has not **stolen** the other man's property.
22.11 take an oath that he has not **stolen** the other man's animal.
22.11 If the animal was not **stolen,** the owner shall accept the loss,
22.12 but if the animal was **stolen,** the man must repay the owner.
Lev 6. 2 as a deposit or by **stealing** something from him or by
19.11 "Do not **steal** or cheat or lie.
Deut 5.19 " 'Do not **steal.**
Josh 7.11 They **stole** them, lied about it, and put them with their own
Judg 17. 2 to his mother, "When someone **stole** those eleven hundred
1 Sam 23. 1 town of Keilah and were **stealing** the newly-harvested corn.
25. 7 that belonged to them was **stolen** all the time they were at
25.15 them in the fields, nothing that belonged to us was **stolen.**
25.21 that belonged to him was **stolen,** and this is how he pays
2 Sam 21.12 (They had **stolen** them from the public square in Beth Shan,
1 Chr 7.21 killed when they tried to **steal** the livestock belonging to
Job 1.15 Suddenly the Sabeans attacked and **stole** them all.
20.10 and his sons will make good what he **stole** from the poor.
20.15 The wicked man vomits up the wealth he **stole;**
24. 2 they **steal** sheep and put them with their own flocks.
24.14 and goes out to kill the poor, and at night he **steals.**
31.38 If I have **stolen** the land I farm and taken it from
Ps 69. 4 They made me give back things I did not **steal.**
80.12 Now anyone passing by can **steal** its grapes;
89.41 All who pass by **steal** his belongings;
Prov 1.14 Come and join us, and we'll all share what we **steal."**
6.30 don't despise a thief if he **steals** food when he is hungry;
9.17 To the foolish man she says, [17]**"Stolen** water is sweeter.
9.17 **Stolen** bread tastes better."
28.24 thinks it isn't wrong to **steal** from his parents is no better
30. 9 I am poor, I might **steal** and bring disgrace on my God.
Song 4. 9 and the necklace you are wearing have **stolen** my heart.
Is 10. 6 sent them to loot and **steal** and trample on the people like
Jer 7. 9 You **steal,** murder, commit adultery, tell lies under oath,
51.44 the god of Babylonia, and make him give up his **stolen** goods;
Ezek 33.15 or gives back what he **stole**—if he stops sinning and follows
Hos 4. 2 they lie, murder, **steal,** and commit adultery.
5.10 of Judah have invaded Israel and **stolen** land from her.
7. 1 they break into houses and **steal;**
Mic 2. 8 there you are, waiting to **steal** the coats off their backs.
Zeph 1. 9 worship like pagans and who **steal** and kill in order to fill
Mal 1.13 to me you bring a **stolen** animal or one that is lame
Mt 6.19 moths and rust destroy, and robbers break in and **steal.**
6.20 rust cannot destroy, and robbers cannot break in and **steal.**
19.18 do not **steal;**
27.64 be able to go and **steal** the body, and then tell the
28.13 during the night and **stole** his body while you were asleep.
Mk 10.19 do not **steal;**
Lk 11.22 the owner was depending on and divides up what he **stole.**
18.20 do not **steal;**
Jn 10.10 The thief comes only in order to **steal,** kill, and
Rom 2.21 You preach, "Do not **steal"**—but do you yourself steal?
13. 9 do not **steal;**
1 Cor 6.10 or homosexual perverts [10]or who **steal** or are greedy or are
Tit 2.10 They must not answer them back [10]or **steal** from them.
Rev 9.21 their magic, their sexual immorality, or their **stealing.**

STEER

Acts 27.40 same time they untied the ropes that held the **steering** oars.
Jas 3. 4 strong winds, it can be **steered** by a very small rudder, and

STEM

Ezek 19.14 The **stem** of the vine caught fire;

STENCH

2 Cor 2.16 those who are being lost, it is a deadly **stench** that kills;

STEP
[DOORSTEPS]

Ex 20.26 not build an altar for me with **steps** leading up to it;
20.26 you do, you will expose yourselves as you go up the **steps.**
Lev 9.22 over the people and blessed them, and then **stepped** down.
Num 12. 5 The two of them **stepped** forward, [6]and the Lord said, "Now
Josh 3.14 As soon as the priests **stepped** into the river, [16]the water
1 Sam 5. 5 all his worshippers in Ashdod **step** over that place and do
20. 3 the living Lord that I am only a **step** away from death!"
2 Sam 6.13 Covenant Box had gone six **steps,** David made them stop while
1 Kgs 10.19 The throne had six **steps** leading up to it, with
10.19 lion at each end of every **step,** a total of twelve lions.
22.21 until a spirit **stepped** forward, approached the Lord,
2 Kgs 9.13 at the top of the **steps** for Jehu to stand on, blew
20. 9 stairway to go forward ten **steps** or go back ten steps?"
20.10 "It's easy to make the shadow go forward ten **steps!**
20.10 Make it go back ten **steps."**
20.11 the shadow go back ten **steps** on the stairway set up by
2 Chr 9.18 Six **steps** led up to the throne, and there was a
9.19 figures of lions were on the **steps,**
9.19 one at either end of each **step.**
18.20 until a spirit **stepped** forward, approached the Lord,
Neh 3.15 garden, as far as the **steps** leading down from David's City.
12.37 Gate they went up the **steps** that led to David's City, past
Job 9.33 there is no one to **step** between us— no one to
13.27 you watch every **step** I take, and even examine my footprints.
14.16 Then you will watch every **step** I take, but you will not
18. 7 His **steps** were firm, but now he stumbles;
18.11 it follows him at every **step.**
23.10 Yet God knows every **step** I take;
29. 8 place among them, [8]young men **stepped** aside as soon as they
31. 4 he sees every **step** I take.
34.21 He watches every **step** men take.
Prov 4.27 Don't go one **step** off the right way.
14.15 sensible people watch their **step.**
Is 3.16 They take dainty little **steps,** and the bracelets
28.13 Then you will stumble with every **step** you take.
38. 8 King Ahaz, the Lord will make the shadow go back ten **steps."**
38. 8 And the shadow moved back ten **steps.**
Ezek 40. 6 He went up the **steps,** and at the top he measured the
40.22 Here seven **steps** led up to it, and the entrance room
40.26 Seven **steps** led up to it, and its entrance room was also
40.31 Eight **steps** led up to this gate.
40.34 Eight **steps** led up to this gate.
40.37 Eight **steps** led up to this gate.
40.49 **Steps** led up to the entrance room, which was ten metres
43.17 The **steps** going up the altar were on the east side.
Zeph 2.14 Crows will caw on the **doorsteps.**
Zech 2. 3 had been speaking to me **step** forward, and another angel came
Mt 10.38 cross and follow in my **steps** is not fit to be my
26.60 Finally two men **stepped** up [61]and said, "This man said, 'I
Lk 1.79 of death, to guide our **steps** into the path of peace."
8. 5 the path, where it was **stepped** on, and the birds ate it
8.27 As Jesus **stepped** ashore, he was met by a man from the
12. 1 together, so that they were **stepping** on each other, Jesus
23.10 the teachers of the Law **stepped** forward and made strong
Jn 18. 4 happen to him, so he **stepped** forward and asked them, "Who
21. 9 When they **stepped** ashore, they saw a charcoal fire there
Acts 21.35 got as far as the **steps** with him, and then the soldiers
21.40 so Paul stood on the **steps** and motioned with his hand for
1 Pet 2.21 left you an example, so that you would follow in his **steps.**

STEPHEN
First Christian martyr, and one of the seven helpers in the Jerusalem church.

Acts 6. 5 apostles' proposal, so they chose **Stephen,** a man full of
6. 8 **Stephen,** a man richly blessed by God and full of power,
6. 9 Jews from the provinces of Cilicia and Asia started arguing with **Stephen.**
6.10 But the Spirit gave **Stephen** such wisdom that when he spoke,
6.12 They seized **Stephen** and took him before the Council.
6.15 Council fixed their eyes on **Stephen** and saw that his face
7. 1 The High Priest asked **Stephen,** "Is this true?"
7. 2 **Stephen** answered, "Brothers and fathers, listen to me!
7.51 **Stephen** went on to say.
7.54 of the Council listened to **Stephen,** they became furious and
7.55 But **Stephen,** full of the Holy Spirit, looked up to
7.59 They kept on stoning **Stephen** as he called out to the Lord,
8. 2 Some devout men buried **Stephen,** mourning for him with loud cries.
11.19 persecution which took place when **Stephen** was killed went as
22.20 And when your witness **Stephen** was put to death, I myself

STEPMOTHER

1 Cor 5. 1 I am told that a man is sleeping with his **stepmother!**

STEPSISTER

Lev	18. 9	with your sister or your **stepsister,** whether or not she was

STERILE

Deut	7.14	None of you nor any of your livestock will be **sterile.**

STERNLY

Gen	43. 3	said to him, "The man **sternly** warned us that we would not
Mt	9.30	Jesus spoke **sternly** to them, "Don't tell this to anyone!"
Mk	1.43	Then Jesus spoke **sternly** to him and sent him away at once,
	3.12	Jesus **sternly** ordered the evil spirits not to tell

STEW

2 Kgs	4.38	a big pot on the fire and make some **stew** for them.
	4.39	sliced them up into the **stew,** not knowing what they were.
	4.40	The **stew** was poured out for the men to eat, but as
	4.41	the pot, and said, "Pour out some more **stew** for them."

STEWARD

Gen	40. 1	the king of Egypt's wine **steward** and his chief baker
	40. 5	there in prison the wine **steward** and the chief baker each
	40. 9	So the wine **steward** said, "In my dream there was a
	40.13	his cup as you did before when you were his wine **steward.**
	40.16	interpretation of the wine **steward's** dream was favourable,
	40.20	he released his wine **steward** and his chief baker and brought
	40.21	He restored the wine **steward** to his former position,
	40.23	But the wine **steward** never gave Joseph another
	41. 9	Then the wine **steward** said to the king, "I must confess
Neh	1.11	In those days I was the emperor's wine **steward.**

STICK (1)

[WALKING-STICK]

Gen	32.10	Jordan with nothing but a **walking-stick,** and now I have come
	38.18	"Your seal with its cord and the **stick** you are carrying."
	38.25	whose they are—this seal with its cord and this **stick."**
Ex	4. 2	"A **stick,"** he answered.
	4. 4	Moses bent down and caught it, and it became a **stick** again.
	4.17	Take this **stick** with you;
	4.20	them for Egypt, carrying the **stick** that God had told him to
	7. 9	tell Aaron to take his **stick** and throw it down in front
	7.10	Aaron threw his **stick** down in front of the king and his
	7.12	They threw down their **sticks,** and the sticks turned into snakes.
	7.12	But Aaron's **stick** swallowed theirs.
	7.15	Take with you the **stick** that was turned into a snake, and
	7.17	of the river with this **stick,** and the water will be turned
	7.19	"Tell Aaron to take his **stick** and hold it out over all
	7.20	his officers, Aaron raised his **stick** and struck the surface
	8. 5	Aaron to hold out his **stick** over the rivers, the canals, and
	8.16	strike the ground with his **stick,** and all over the land of
	8.17	struck the ground with his **stick,** and all the dust in Egypt
	9.23	So Moses raised his **stick** towards the sky, and the Lord
	10.13	So Moses raised his **stick,** and the Lord caused a wind
	12.11	with your sandals on your feet and your **stick** in your hand.
	14.16	Lift up your **stick** and hold it out over the sea.
	17. 5	Take along the **stick** with which you struck the Nile.
	17. 9	of the hill holding the **stick** that God told me to carry."
	21.18	with the help of a **stick,** the man who hit him is
	21.20	"If a man takes a **stick** and beats his slave, whether
Num	17. 2	Israel to give you twelve **sticks,** one from the leader of
	17. 2	each man's name on his **stick**
	17. 3	and then write Aaron's name on the **stick** representing Levi.
	17. 3	There will be one **stick** for each tribal leader.
	17. 5	Then the **stick** of the man I have chosen will sprout.
	17. 6	their leaders gave him a **stick,** one for each tribe,
	17. 6	twelve in all, and Aaron's **stick** was put with them.
	17. 7	Moses then put all the **sticks** in the Tent in front of
	17. 8	he saw that Aaron's **stick,** representing the tribe of Levi,
	17. 9	Moses took all the **sticks** and showed them to the Israelites.
	17. 9	what had happened, and each leader took his own **stick** back.
	17.10	said to Moses, "Put Aaron's **stick** back in front of the
	20. 8	said to Moses, [8]"Take the **stick** that is in front of the
	20. 9	Moses went and got the **stick,** as the Lord had commanded.
	20.11	Then Moses raised the **stick** and struck the rock twice with it,
	21.18	people, Dug with a royal sceptre And with their **sticks."**
	22.27	lost his temper and began to beat the donkey with his **stick.**
Deut	23.13	Carry a **stick** as part of your equipment, so that when
Judg	6.21	and the bread with the end of the **stick** he was holding.
1 Sam	14.27	he reached out with the **stick** he was carrying, dipped it in
	14.43	"I ate a little honey with the **stick** I was holding.
	17.40	He took his shepherd's **stick** and then picked up five
	17.43	He said to David, "What's that **stick** for?
2 Kgs	4.29	Take my **stick** and go.
	4.29	Go straight to the house and hold my **stick** over the boy."
	4.31	on ahead and held Elisha's **stick** over the child, but there
	6. 6	and Elisha cut off a **stick,** threw it in the water, and
	18.21	using a reed as a **walking-stick**—it would break and jab your
Ecc	12.11	are like the sharp **sticks** that shepherds use to guide sheep,
Is	7. 4	no more dangerous than the smoke from two smouldering **sticks.**
	28.27	instead he uses light **sticks** of the proper size.
	36. 6	using a reed as a **walking-stick**—it would break and jab your
Ezek	29. 6	Egyptians for support, but you were no better than a weak **stick.**
	37.16	he said, "take a wooden **stick** and write on it the words,
	37.16	Then take another **stick** and write on it the words, 'The
	37.17	Then hold the two **sticks** end to end in your hand
	37.17	so that they look like one **stick.**
Ezek	37.19	am going to take the **stick** representing Israel and put it
	37.19	two I will make one **stick** and hold it in my hand.
	37.20	in your hand the two **sticks** and let the people see them.
Hos	4.12	A **stick** tells them what they want to know!
Amos	4.11	who survived were like a burning **stick** saved from a fire.
Zech	3. 2	This man is like a **stick** snatched from the fire."
	8. 4	old that they use a **stick** when they walk, will be sitting
	11. 7	I took two **sticks:**
	11.10	Then I took the **stick** called "Favour" and broke it, to
	11.14	Then I broke the second **stick,** the one called "Unity,"
Mt	10.10	for the journey or an extra shirt or shoes or a **stick.**
	27.29	it on his head, and put a **stick** in his right hand;
	27.30	on him, and took the **stick** and hit him over the head.
	27.48	on the end of a **stick,** and tried to make him drink
Mk	6. 8	on your journey except a **stick**—no bread, no beggar's bag, no
	15.19	over the head with a **stick,** spat on him, fell on their
	15.36	in cheap wine, and put it on the end of a **stick.**
Lk	9. 3	no **stick,** no beggar's bag, no food, no money, not even an
Acts	26.14	hitting back, like an ox kicking against its owner's **stick.'**
	28. 3	gathered up a bundle of **sticks** and was putting them on the
Heb	9. 4	the manna in it, Aaron's **stick** that had sprouted leaves, and
	11.21	He leaned on the top of his **walking-stick** and worshipped God.
Rev	11. 1	I was then given a **stick** that looked like a measuring-rod,

STICK (2)

[STUCK]

Ex	14.25	wheels of their chariots get **stuck,** so that they moved with
Ps	22.15	as dust, and my tongue **sticks** to the roof of my mouth.
Ezek	29. 4	jaw and make the fish in your river **stick** fast to you.
	29. 4	up out of the Nile, with all the fish **sticking** to you.
Lk	10.11	dust from your town that **sticks** to our feet we wipe off
Acts	27.41	part of the ship got **stuck** and could not move, while the

STICK (3)

[STUCK]

Judg	3.22	king's belly, and it **stuck** out behind, between his legs.
1 Sam	2.14	he would **stick** the fork into the cooking-pot,
	19.10	spear, but David dodged, and the spear **stuck** in the wall.
	26. 7	the camp with his spear **stuck** in the ground near his head.
2 Chr	33.11	They captured Manasseh, **stuck** hooks in him, put him in chains,
Job	20.25	An arrow **sticks** through his body;
Ps	22. 7	they **stick** out their tongues and shake their heads.

STIFF

2 Sam	23.10	until his hand was so **stiff** that he could not let go
Mk	9.18	at the mouth, grits his teeth, and becomes **stiff** all over.

AV **STIFFNECKED** see **STUBBORN**

STILL

Josh	10.12	"Sun, stand **still** over Gibeon;
	10.13	The sun stood **still** and the moon did not move until the
	10.13	The sun stood **still** in the middle of the sky and did
Judg	5.27	sank to his knees, fell down and lay **still** at her feet.
Job	39.24	when the trumpet blows, they can't stand **still.**
Ps	83. 1	do not be **still,** do not be quiet!
Jer	8.14	"Why are we sitting **still?"**
Hab	3.11	of your shining spear, the sun and the moon stood **still.**
Mk	4.39	and he said to the waves, "Be **still!"**
Lk	24.17	They stood **still,** with sad faces.

STILL-BORN

see also **BORN**

Job	3.16	gold and silver, [16]or sleeping like a **still-born** child.

STING

Jer	46.20	a splendid cow, attacked by a **stinging** fly from the north.
Rev	9. 5	the torture is like the pain caused by a scorpion's **sting.**
	9.10	They have tails and **stings** like those of a scorpion, and

STINGY

Prov	23. 6	at the table of a **stingy** man or be greedy for the

STINK

[STANK]

Ex	7.18	die, and the river will **stink** so much that the Egyptians
	8.14	them up in great heaps, until the land **stank** with them.
Ps	38. 5	Because I have been foolish, my sores **stink** and rot.
Ecc	10. 1	a whole bottle of perfume **stink,** and a little stupidity can
Is	3.24	Instead of using perfumes, they will **stink;**
	19. 6	The channels of the river will **stink** as they slowly go dry.
	34. 3	will not be buried, but will lie there rotting and **stinking;**
Joel	2.20	Their dead bodies will **stink.**
Amos	4.10	your nostrils with the **stink** of dead bodies in your camps.

STIR

1 Kgs	21.22	of Ahijah, because you have **stirred up** my anger by leading
2 Kgs	14.10	Why **stir up** trouble that will only bring disaster on you and
	21. 6	He sinned greatly against the Lord and **stirred up** his anger.
	21.15	sinned against me and have **stirred up** my anger from the time
	22.17	other gods, and so have **stirred up** my anger by all they

2 Chr 25.19 Why **stir up** trouble that will only bring disaster on you and
33. 6 He sinned greatly against the Lord and **stirred up** his anger.
34.25 other gods, and so have **stirred up** my anger by all they
Job 14.12 they will never **stir** from their sleep.
Ps 78.26 to blow, and by his power he **stirred up** the south wind;
106.29 They **stirred up** the Lord's anger by their actions, and a
107.25 and a mighty wind began to blow and **stirred up** the waves.
140. 2 They are always plotting evil, always **stirring up** quarrels.
Prov 2.12 you away from people who **stir up** trouble by what they say
6.14 in their perverted minds, **stirring up** trouble everywhere.
6.16 and a man who **stirs up**
10.12 Hate **stirs up** trouble, but love overlooks all offences.
15. 1 A gentle answer quietens anger, but a harsh one **stirs it up.**
16.28 they **stir up** trouble and break up friendships.
17.11 to wicked people who are always **stirring up** trouble.
30.33 If you **stir up** anger, you get into trouble.
Is 9.11 The Lord has **stirred up** their enemies to attack them.
13.17 The Lord says, "I am **stirring up** the Medes to attack Babylon.
14. 9 ghosts of those who were powerful on earth are **stirring** about.
19. 2 The Lord says, "I will **stir up** civil war in Egypt and
45.13 I myself have **stirred** Cyrus to action to fulfil my
51.15 I **stir up** the sea and make its waves roar.
Jer 31.35 He **stirs up** the sea and makes it roar;
43. 3 Baruch son of Neriah has **stirred you up** against us, so
50. 9 I am going to **stir up** a group of strong nations in
51.11 The Lord has **stirred up** the kings of Media, because he
Ezek 16.40 "They will **stir up** a crowd to stone you, and they will
Hos 7. 4 an oven, which is not **stirred** by the baker until the dough
Mt 9.23 funeral and the people all **stirred up,** [24] he said, "Get
Mk 15.11 But the chief priests **stirred up** the crowd to ask,
Jn 5. 7 to put me in the pool when the water is **stirred up;**
6.18 By then a strong wind was blowing and **stirring up** the water.
Acts 6.12 In this way they **stirred up** the people, the elders, and
13.50 But the Jews **stirred up** the leading men of the city and
14. 2 Jews who would not believe **stirred up** the Gentiles and
17.13 came there and started exciting and **stirring up** the mob.
21.27 They **stirred up** the whole crowd and seized Paul.
24.12 nor did they find me **stirring up** the people, either in the
Rom 7. 5 human nature, the sinful desires **stirred up** by the Law were
7. 8 sin found its chance to **stir up** all kinds of selfish desires
2 Cor 8.20 are taking care not to **stir up** any complaints about the way
9. 2 Your eagerness has **stirred up** most of them.
2 Pet 1.13 only right for me to **stir up** your memory of these matters

STOIC

Those who followed the teachings of the Greek philosopher Zeno (died 265 B.C.), who taught that happiness is to be found in being free from pleasure and pain.

Acts 17.18 Certain Epicurean and **Stoic** teachers also debated with him.

STOMACH

Num 5.21 your genital organs to shrink and your **stomach** to swell up.
5.22 May this water enter your **stomach** and cause it to swell
5.27 **stomach** will swell up and her genital organs will shrink.
Deut 18. 3 are to be given the shoulder, the jaw, and the **stomach.**
Job 20.14 But in his **stomach** the food turns bitter, as bitter as
20.15 God takes it back, even out of his **stomach.**
Jer 30. 6 man with his hands on his **stomach** like a woman in labour?
Ezek 3. 3 fill your **stomach** with it."
7.19 They cannot use it to satisfy their desires or fill their **stomachs.**
Mt 15.17 person's mouth goes into his **stomach** and then goes on out of his
Mk 7.19 his heart but into his **stomach** and then goes on out of
1 Cor 6.13 "Food is for the **stomach,** and the stomach is for food."
Rev 10. 9 will turn sour in your **stomach,** but in your mouth it will
10.10 But after I swallowed it, it turned sour in my **stomach.**

STONE (1)

[STUMBLING STONE]

Gen 28.11 He lay down to sleep, resting his head on a **stone.**
28.18 early next morning, took the **stone** that was under his head,
28.22 This memorial **stone** which I have set up will be the
29. 2 from this well, which had a large **stone** over the opening.
29. 3 the shepherds would roll the **stone** back and water them.
29. 3 Then they would put the **stone** back in place.
29. 8 all the flocks are here and the **stone** has been rolled back;
29.10 to the well, rolled the **stone** back, and watered the sheep.
31.13 Bethel, where you dedicated a **stone** as a memorial by pouring
31.44 us make a pile of **stones** to remind us of our agreement."
31.45 So Jacob took a **stone** and set it up as a memorial.
31.51 I have piled up between us, and here is the memorial **stone.**
31.52 Both this pile and this memorial **stone** are reminders.
31.52 go beyond it or beyond this memorial **stone** to attack me.
35.14 Jacob set up a memorial **stone** and consecrated it by pouring
35.20 Jacob set up a memorial **stone** there, and it still marks
Ex 4.25 his wife, took a sharp **stone,** cut off the foreskin of her
7.19 will be blood, even in the wooden tubs and **stone** jars."
8.26 them where they can see us, they will **stone** us to death.
15. 5 they sank to the bottom like a **stone.**
17. 4 They are almost ready to **stone** me."
17.12 Aaron and Hur brought a **stone** for him to sit on, while
19.13 he must either be **stoned** or shot with arrows, without
20.25 you make an altar of **stone** for me, do not build it
20.25 out of cut **stones,** because when you use
20.25 a chisel on **stones,** you make them unfit for my
21.18 man hits another with a **stone** or with his fist, but does
21.28 death, it is to be **stoned,** and its flesh shall not be
21.29 death, it is to be **stoned,** and its owner is to be
21.32 pieces of silver, and the bull shall be **stoned** to death.
Ex 24. 4 mountain and set up twelve **stones,** one for each of the
Lev 14.40 spread, [40] he shall order the **stones** on which the mildew is
14.42 Then other **stones** are to be used to replace the stones
14.43 in the house after the **stones** have been removed and the
14.45 be torn down, and its **stones,** its wood, and all its plaster
16. 8 draw lots, using two **stones,** one marked "for the Lord"
20. 2 god Molech shall be **stoned** to death by the whole community.
20.27 consults the spirits of the dead shall be **stoned** to death;
24.14 and then the whole community shall **stone** him to death.
24.16 shall be **stoned** to death by the whole community.
24.23 they took the man outside the camp and **stoned** him to death.
26. 1 set up statues, stone pillars, or carved **stones** to worship.
Num 14.10 whole community was threatening to **stone** them to death, but
15.35 whole community is to **stone** him to death outside the camp."
15.36 him outside the camp and **stoned** him to death, as the Lord
22.24 between two vineyards and had a **stone** wall on each side.
32.16 "First, allow us to build **stone** enclosures here for our
33.52 Destroy all their **stone** and metal idols and all their places
35.16 a weapon of iron or **stone** or wood to kill someone, he
35.23 looking, a man throws a **stone** that kills someone whom he did
Deut 3.11 His coffin, made of **stone,** was four metres long and almost
4.28 hands, gods of wood and **stone,** gods that cannot see or hear,
13. 9 to stone him, and then let everyone else **stone** him too.
13.10 **Stone** him to death!
17. 5 then take that person outside the town and **stone** him to death.
17. 7 are to throw the first **stones,**
17. 7 and then the rest of the people are to **stone** that person;
21.21 of the city are to **stone** him to death, and so you
22.21 where the men of her city are to **stone** her to death.
22.24 are to take them outside the town and **stone** them to death.
27. 2 to set up some large **stones,** cover them with plaster, [3] and
27. 4 the Jordan, set up these **stones** on Mount Ebal, as I am
27. 5 an altar there made of **stones** that have had no iron tools
27. 6 build for the Lord your God must be made of uncut **stones.**
27. 8 On the **stones** covered with plaster write clearly every
27.15 who makes an idol of **stone,** wood, or metal and secretly
28.36 there you will serve gods made of wood and **stone.**
28.64 gods made of wood and **stone,** gods that neither you nor your
29.17 You saw their disgusting idols made of wood, **stone,**
32.13 their olive-trees flourished in **stony** ground.
Josh 4. 3 command them to take twelve **stones** out of the middle of the
4. 3 Tell them to carry these **stones** with them and to put them
4. 5 one of you take a **stone** on your shoulder, one for each
4. 6 These **stones** will remind the people of what the Lord has done.
4. 6 your children ask what these **stones** mean to you, [7] you will
4. 7 These **stones** will always remind the people of Israel of what
4. 8 they took twelve **stones** from the middle of the Jordan,
4. 9 Joshua also set up twelve **stones** in the middle of the Jordan,
4. 9 (Those **stones** are still there.)
4.20 There Joshua set up the twelve **stones** taken from the Jordan.
4.21 children ask you what these **stones** mean, [22] you will tell
7.25 All the people then **stoned** Achan to death;
7.25 they also **stoned** and burnt his family and possessions.
7.26 put a huge pile of **stones** over him, which is there to
8.29 it with a huge pile of **stones,** which is still there today.
8.31 "an altar made of **stones** which have not been cut with iron
8.32 on, Joshua made on the **stones** a copy of the Law which
10.18 He said, "Roll some big **stones** in front of the entrance
10.27 Large **stones** were placed at the entrance to the cave, and
15. 6 it went up to the **Stone** of Bohan (Bohan was a son
18.17 then went down to the **Stone** of Bohan (Bohan was a son
24.26 Then he took a large **stone** and set it up under the
24.27 He said to all the people, "This **stone** will be our witness.
Judg 3.19 back at the carved **stones** near Gilgal, went back to Eglon,
3.26 He went past the carved **stones** and escaped to Seirah.
9. 5 the top of a single **stone** he killed his seventy brothers,
9.18 seventy men on a single **stone**—and just because Abimelech,
20.15 of them could sling a **stone** at a strand of hair and
1 Sam 7.12 Then Samuel took a **stone,** set it up between Mizpah and Shen,
14.33 "Roll a big **stone** over here to me."
14.41 Lord, God of Israel, answer me by the sacred **stones.**
17.40 then picked up five smooth **stones** from the stream and put
17.49 his bag and took out a **stone,** which he slung at Goliath.
17.50 David defeated and killed Goliath with a catapult and a **stone!**
20.19 the other time, and hide behind the pile of **stones** there.
20.41 from behind the pile of **stones,** fell on his knees and bowed
25.29 throw them away, as a man hurls **stones** with his catapult.
30. 6 their children, and they were threatening to **stone** him;
2 Sam 16. 6 Shimei started throwing **stones** at David and his officials,
16.13 he was cursing and throwing **stones** and earth at them as he
17.13 Not a single **stone** will be left there on top of the
18.17 in the forest, and covered it with a huge pile of **stones.**
1 Kgs 5.15 hill-country quarrying **stone,** with 70,000 men to carry it,
5.17 quarried fine large **stones** for the foundation of the Temple.
5.18 city of Byblos prepared the **stones** and the timber to build
6. 7 The **stones** with which the Temple was built had been
6.18 with cedar, so that the **stones** of the walls could not be
6.36 one layer of cedar beams for every three layers of **stone.**
7. 9 were made of fine **stones** from the foundations to the eaves.
7. 9 The **stones** were prepared at the quarry and cut to measure,
7.10 were made of large **stones** prepared at the quarry,
7.11 of them were other **stones,** cut to measure, and cedar beams.
7.12 layer of cedar beams for every three layers of cut **stones.**
10.27 as common in Jerusalem as **stone,** and cedar was as plentiful
12.18 to go to the Israelites, but they **stoned** him to death.
15.22 carry away from Ramah the **stones** and timber that Baasha had
18.31 He took twelve **stones,** one for each of the twelve tribes
18.32 With these **stones** he rebuilt the altar for the worship
18.38 sacrifice, the wood, and the **stones,** scorched the earth and
21.10 Then take him out of the city and **stone** him to death."
21.13 and so he was taken outside the city and **stoned** to death.

2 Kgs 3.19 all their fertile fields by covering them with **stones."**
3.25 every Israelite would throw a **stone** on it until finally all
12.12 the masons, and the **stone-cutters,**
12.12 buy the timber and the **stones** used in the repairs, and pay
16.17 twelve bronze bulls, and placed it on a **stone** foundation.
19.18 at all, only images of wood and **stone** made by human hands.
22. 6 and buy the timber and the **stones** used in the repairs.
23.15 down the altar, broke its **stones** into pieces, and pounded
1 Chr 12. 2 They could shoot arrows and sling **stones** either right-handed
22. 2 Some of them prepared **stone** blocks for building the Temple.
22.14 I also have wood and **stone** ready, but you must get more.
22.15 men to work in the **stone** quarries, and there are masons and
2 Chr 1.15 as common in Jerusalem as **stone,** and cedar was as plentiful
2. 2 materials, and eighty thousand men to work quarrying **stone.**
2.14 to make things out of gold, silver, bronze, iron, **stone,** and
2.18 materials and 80,000 to cut **stones** in the mountains, and
9.27 as common in Jerusalem as **stone,** and cedar was as plentiful
10.18 to go to the Israelites, but they **stoned** him to death.
14. 3 worship, broke down the sacred **stone** columns, and cut down
16. 6 them to carry off the **stones** and timber that Baasha had been
24.21 orders the people **stoned** Zechariah in the temple courtyard.
26.14 coats of armour, bows and arrows, and **stones** for slinging.
26.15 arrows and for throwing large **stones** from the towers and
34.11 the builders to buy the **stones** and the timber used to repair
Ezra 5. 8 is being rebuilt with large **stone** blocks and with wooden
6. 4 one layer of wood on top of every three layers of **stone.**
Neh 9.11 drowned in deep water, as a **stone** sinks in the raging sea.
Job 6.12 Am I made of **stone?**
8.17 Their roots wrap round the **stones** and hold fast to every rock.
19.24 chisel carve my words in **stone** and write them so that they
24. 2 Men move boundary **stones** to get more land;
28. 2 iron out of the ground And melt copper out of the **stones.**
28. 6 The **stones** of the earth contain sapphires, And its dust
38.30 which turn the waters to **stone** and freeze the face of
41.15 of rows of shields, fastened together and hard as **stone.**
41.24 His **stony** heart is without fear, as unyielding and hard
Ps 91.12 hands to keep you from hurting your feet on the **stones.**
118.22 The **stone** which the builders rejected as worthless
Prov 24.31 The **stone** wall round them had fallen down.
26. 8 stupid makes as much sense as tying a **stone** in a catapult.
27. 3 The weight of **stone** and sand is nothing compared to the
Ecc 10. 9 If you work in a **stone** quarry,
10. 9 you get hurt by **stones.**
Is 5. 2 He dug the soil and cleared it of **stones;**
8.14 awesome holiness I am like a **stone** that people stumble over;
9.10 fallen down, but we will replace them with **stone** buildings.
22. 9 some of them down to get **stones** to repair the city walls.
27. 9 be forgiven only when the **stones** of pagan altars are ground
37.19 at all, only images of wood and **stone** made by human hands.
57. 6 You take smooth **stones** from there and worship them as gods.
60.17 bronze instead of iron and wood, And iron instead of **stone.**
62.10 clear it of **stones!**
Jer 3. 9 and she committed adultery by worshipping **stones** and trees.
43. 9 to me, [9] "Get some large **stones** and bury them in the mortar
43.10 put his throne over these **stones** that you buried, and will
43.13 He will destroy the sacred **stone** monuments at Heliopolis
51.26 None of the **stones** from your ruins will ever be used
51.63 then tie it to a **stone** and throw it into the River
Lam 3. 9 **stone** walls block me wherever I turn.
3.53 me alive into a pit and closed the opening with a **stone.**
4. 1 the **stones** of the Temple lie scattered in the streets.
Ezek 11.19 away their stubborn heart of **stone** and will give them an
13.10 up a wall of loose **stones,** and then the prophets have come
13.14 to shatter it, and to leave the foundation **stones** bare.
16.40 stir up a crowd to **stone** you, and they will cut you
23.47 Let the mob **stone** them and attack them with swords, kill
26.12 They will take the **stones** and wood and all the rubble, and
36.26 your stubborn heart of **stone** and give you an obedient heart.
40.17 paved with **stones,** [18] which extended round the courtyard.
40.42 prepare the offerings to be burnt whole, were of cut **stone.**
46.23 Each one had a **stone** wall round it, with fireplaces
Dan 2.34 looking at it, a great **stone** broke loose from a cliff
2.35 But the **stone** grew to be a mountain that covered the whole
2.45 You saw how a **stone** broke loose from a cliff without
5. 4 praised gods made of gold, silver, bronze, iron, wood, and **stone.**
5.23 silver, bronze, iron, wood, and **stone**—gods that cannot see
6.17 A **stone** was put over the mouth of the pit, and the
6.17 of his noblemen on the **stone,** so that no one could rescue
Hos 12.11 there will become piles of **stone** in the open fields."
Amos 5.11 not live in the fine **stone** houses you build or drink wine
Hab 2.11 Even the **stones** of the walls cry out against you, and
2.19 or to a block of **stone,** "Get up!"
Zech 3. 9 placing in front of Joshua a single **stone** with seven facets.
4. 7 as you put the last **stone** in place, the people will shout,
12. 3 make Jerusalem like a heavy **stone**—any nation that tries to
Mt 3. 9 God can take these **stones** and make descendants for Abraham!
4. 3 "If you are God's Son, order these **stones** to turn into bread."
4. 6 so that not even your feet will be hurt on the **stones.' "**
7. 9 are fathers give your son a **stone** when he asks for bread?
21.35 The tenants seized his slaves, beat one, killed another, and **stoned** another.
21.42 'The **stone** which the builders rejected as worthless turned
23.37 You kill the prophets and **stone** the messengers God has sent you!
24. 2 not a single **stone** here will be left in its place;
27.60 Then he rolled a large **stone** across the entrance to the tomb
27.66 putting a seal on the **stone** and leaving the guard on watch.
28. 2 came down from heaven, rolled the **stone** away, and sat on it.
Mk 5. 5 the hills, screaming and cutting himself with **stones.**
12.10 'The **stone** which the builders rejected as worthless turned
13. 1 What wonderful **stones** and buildings!"
13. 2 Not a single **stone** here will be left in its place;
Mk 15.46 Then he rolled a large **stone** across the entrance to the tomb.
16. 3 "Who will roll away the **stone** for us from the entrance to
16. 3 (It was a very large **stone.)**
16. 3 up and saw that the **stone** had already been rolled back.
Lk 3. 8 God can take these **stones** and make descendants for Abraham!
4. 3 "If you are God's Son, order this **stone** to turn into bread."
4.11 so that not even your feet will be hurt on the **stones.' "**
13.34 You kill the prophets, you **stone** the messengers God has sent you!
19.40 keep quiet, the **stones** themselves will start shouting."
19.44 not a single **stone** will they leave in its place, because you
20. 6 this whole crowd here will **stone** us, because they are
20.17 'The **stone** which the builders rejected as worthless turned
20.18 Everyone who falls on that **stone** will be cut to pieces;
20.18 and if that **stone** falls on someone, it will crush him to
21. 5 it looked with its fine **stones** and the gifts offered to God.
21. 6 come when not a single **stone** here will be left in its
22.41 the distance of a **stone's throw** and knelt down and prayed.
24. 2 They found the **stone** rolled away from the entrance to the tomb,
Jn 2. 6 and for this purpose six **stone** water jars were there, each
8. 5 Law Moses commanded that such a woman must be **stoned** to death.
8. 7 you has committed no sin may throw the first **stone** at her."
8.59 Then they picked up **stones** to throw at him, but Jesus
10.31 Then the people again picked up **stones** to throw at him.
10.32 for which one of these do you want to **stone** me?"
10.33 "We do not want to **stone** you because of any good deeds,
11. 8 "just a short time ago the people there wanted to **stone** you;
11.38 tomb, which was a cave with a **stone** placed at the entrance.
11.39 "Take the **stone** away!"
11.41 They took the **stone** away.
20. 1 tomb and saw that the **stone** had been taken away from the
Acts 4.11 whom the scripture says, 'The **stone** that you the builders
5.26 because they were afraid that the people might **stone** them.
7.58 him at once, [58] threw him out of the city, and **stoned** him.
7.59 They kept on **stoning** Stephen as he called out to the Lord,
14. 5 leaders, decided to ill-treat the apostles and **stone** them.
14.19 crowd over to their side, **stoned** Paul and dragged him out of
17.29 of gold or silver or **stone,** shaped by the art and skill
19.35 Artemis and of the sacred **stone** that fell down from heaven.
Rom 9.31 so they stumbled over the **"stumbling stone"**
9.33 I place in Zion a **stone** that will make people stumble, a
2 Cor 3. 3 living God, and not on **stone** tablets but on human hearts.
3. 7 was carved in letters on **stone** tablets, and God's glory
11.25 and once I was **stoned.**
Heb 9. 4 sprouted leaves, and the two **stone** tablets with the
11.37 They were **stoned,** they were sawn in two, they were
12.20 animal touches the mountain, it must be **stoned** to death."
1 Pet 2. 4 to the Lord, the living **stone** rejected by man as worthless
2. 5 Come as living **stones,** and let yourselves be used in
2. 6 says, "I chose a valuable **stone,** which I am placing as the
2. 7 This **stone** is of great value for you that believe;
2. 7 "The **stone** which the builders rejected as worthless turned
2. 8 says, "This is the **stone** that will make people stumble,
Rev 2.17 each of them a white **stone** on which is written a new
9.20 of gold, silver, bronze, **stone,** and wood, which cannot see,
18.21 mighty angel picked up a **stone** the size of a large millstone

STONE (2)

[PRECIOUS STONE]

Gen 2.12 gold is found there and also rare perfume and **precious stones.)**
Ex 28. 9 Take two carnelian **stones** and engrave on them the names of
28.10 their birth, with six on one **stone** and six on the other.
28.11 to engrave on the two **stones** the names of
28.11 the sons of Jacob, and mount the **stones** in gold settings.
28.17 Mount four rows of **precious stones** on it;
28.21 Each of these twelve **stones** is to have engraved on it
39.10 They mounted four rows of **precious stones** on it:
39.14 Each of the twelve **stones** had engraved on it the name of
1 Chr 29. 2 iron, timber, **precious stones** and gems, stones for mosaics,
29. 8 Those who had **precious stones** gave them to the temple treasury,
2 Chr 3. 6 the Temple with beautiful **precious stones** and with gold
32.27 **precious stones,** spices, shields, and other valuable objects.
Job 28.10 As they tunnel through the rocks, They discover **precious stones.**
Is 54.11 you, I will rebuild your foundations with **precious stones.**
54.12 with rubies, your gates with **stones** that glow like fire, and
Ezek 1.16 one shone like a **precious stone,** and each had another wheel
10. 9 The wheels shone like **precious stones,** and each one had
1 Cor 3.12 or silver or **precious stones** in building on the foundation;
Rev 4. 3 His face gleamed like such **precious stones** as jasper and carnelian,
17. 4 scarlet, and covered with gold ornaments, **precious stones,**
18.12 no one buys their gold, silver, **precious stones,** and
18.16 and cover herself with gold ornaments, **precious stones,**
21.11 The city shone like a **precious stone,** like a jasper, clear
21.19 city wall were adorned with all kinds of **precious stones.**

STONE OF HELP

1 Sam 7.12 helped us all the way"—and he named it **"Stone of Help."**

STONE PAVEMENT

Jn 19.13 the judge's seat in the place called "The **Stone Pavement."**

STONE PILLAR see PILLAR

STONE TABLETS see TABLET

STONEMASON
see also **MASON**

2 Sam 5.11 logs and with carpenters and **stone-masons** to build a palace.
1 Chr 14. 1 logs and with **stone-masons** and carpenters to build a palace.
2 Chr 24.12 the Temple, and they hired **stonemasons,** carpenters, and
Ezra 3. 7 to pay the **stonemasons** and the carpenters and gave food,

STOOL

Mt 21.12 the money-changers and the **stools** of those who sold pigeons,
Mk 11.15 the money-changers and the **stools** of those who sold pigeons,

STOP

Gen 2. 2 day God finished what he had been doing and **stopped** working.
2. 3 that day he had completed his creation and **stopped** working.
8. 2 The rain **stopped,** [3]and the water gradually went down for a
11. 8 them all over the earth, and they **stopped** building the city.
18. 3 he said, "Sirs, please do not pass by my home without **stopping;**
18.11 and Sarah had **stopped** having her monthly periods.
19.17 Don't look back and don't **stop** in the valley.
26.18 which the Philistines had **stopped** up after Abraham's death.
29.35 Then she **stopped** having children.
30. 9 Leah realized that she had **stopped** having children, she gave
41.49 so much corn that Joseph **stopped** measuring it—it was like
Ex 5. 5 And now you want to **stop** working!"
5. 7 **"Stop** giving the people straw for making bricks.
9.29 The thunder will **stop,** and there will be no more hail, so
9.33 The thunder, the hail, and the rain all **stopped.**
31.17 and on the seventh day I **stopped** working and rested."
32.10 Now, don't try to **stop** me.
32.12 **Stop** being angry;
Lev 15. 3 whether the penis runs with it or is **stopped** up by it.
15.28 After her flow **stops,** she must wait seven days, and then
Num 10.36 And whenever it **stopped,** he would say, "Return, Lord,
11.28 a young man, spoke up and said to Moses, **"Stop** them,
14.14 plainly seen when your cloud **stops** over us, and that you go
16.48 This **stopped** the plague, and he was left standing
16.50 When the plague had **stopped,** Aaron returned to Moses at
17. 5 way I will put a **stop** to the constant complaining of these
17.10 Israelites that they will die unless their complaining **stops."**
25. 8 that was destroying Israel was **stopped,** [9]but it had already
Deut 7.24 No one will be able to **stop** you;
9.14 Don't try to **stop** me.
10.16 from now on be obedient to the Lord and **stop** being stubborn.
11.25 he has promised, and no one will be able to **stop** you.
28.59 diseases and horrible epidemics that can never be **stopped.**
Josh 3.13 the water, the Jordan will **stop** flowing, and the water
3.16 into the river, [16]the water **stopped** flowing and piled up,
4. 7 the water of the Jordan **stopped** flowing when the Lord's
5.12 The manna **stopped** falling then, and the Israelites no longer
10.12 Moon, **stop** over Aijalon Valley."
22.25 might make our descendants **stop** worshipping the Lord.
22.29 rebel against the Lord or **stop** following him now by building
Judg 2.12 They **stopped** worshipping the Lord, the God of their ancestors,
2.13 They **stopped** worshipping the Lord and served the Baals
2.17 Lord's commands, but this new generation soon **stopped** doing so.
9. 9 you, I would have to **stop** producing my oil, which is used
9.11 you, I would have to **stop** producing my good sweet fruit.'
9.13 you, I would have to **stop** producing my wine, that makes gods
10. 6 They abandoned the Lord and **stopped** worshipping him.
15. 7 I swear that I won't **stop** until I pay you back!"
17. 3 mother, and she said, "To **stop** the curse from falling on my
19.10 his master, "Why don't we **stop** and spend the night here in
19.12 said, "We're not going to **stop** in a city where the people
19.25 abused her all night long and didn't **stop** until morning.
20.43 the enemy trapped, and without **stopping** they pursued them as
Ruth 2. 7 morning and has just now **stopped** to rest for a while under
2.15 the bundles are lying, and don't say anything to **stop** her.
1 Sam 1.14 and said to her, **"Stop** making a drunken show of yourself!
1.14 **Stop** your drinking and sober up!"
2. 3 **Stop** your loud boasting;
2.24 **Stop** it, my sons!
3.13 Eli knew they were doing this, but he did not **stop** them.
6. 5 Perhaps he will **stop** punishing you, your gods, and your
6.14 in Beth Shemesh, and it **stopped** there near a large rock.
9. 5 home, or my father might **stop** thinking about the donkeys and
14.46 After that, Saul **stopped** pursuing the Philistines, and
15.16 **"Stop,"** Samuel ordered, "and I will tell you what
23.28 Saul **stopped** pursuing David and went to fight the Philistines.
30. 4 and did not **stop** until they were completely exhausted.
2 Sam 2.21 **"Stop** chasing me!"
2.22 Once more Abner said to him, **"Stop** chasing me!
2.23 to the place where he was lying **stopped** and stood there.
2.26 will it be before you order your men to **stop** chasing us?"
2.28 as a signal for his men to **stop** pursuing the Israelites;
2.28 and so the fighting **stopped.**
6.13 six steps, David made them **stop** while he offered the Lord a
15.17 men were leaving the city, they **stopped** at the last house.
18.16 trumpet to be blown to **stop** the fighting, and his troops
20.12 man saw that everybody was **stopping,** so he dragged the body
22.38 I do not **stop** until I destroy them.
24.16 people and said to the angel who was killing them, **"Stop!**
24.21 an altar for the Lord, in order to **stop** the epidemic."
24.25 Lord answered his prayer, and the epidemic in Israel was **stopped.**
1 Kgs 9. 6 if you or your descendants **stop** following me, if you disobey
15.21 happened, he **stopped** fortifying Ramah and went to Tirzah.
18.44 his chariot and go back home before the rain **stops** him."
19. 4 He **stopped** and sat down in the shade of a tree and
19.11 The wind **stopped** blowing, and then there was an earthquake—
1 Kgs 19.20 I'm not **stopping** you!"
22.33 was not the king of Israel, and they **stopped** their attack.
2 Kgs 2. 7 Elijah and Elisha **stopped** by the river, and the fifty prophets
3. 3 Nebat before him, he led Israel into sin, and would not **stop.**
3.19 cut down all their fruit-trees, **stop** all their springs, and
3.25 also **stopped** up the springs and cut down the fruit-trees.
4. 6 And the olive-oil **stopped** flowing.
4.29 Don't **stop** to greet anyone you meet, and if anyone greets you,
5. 9 and chariot, and **stopped** at the entrance to Elisha's house.
6.23 From then on the Syrians **stopped** raiding the land of Israel.
13.18 The king struck the ground three times, and then **stopped.**
17. 4 his help, and **stopped** paying the annual tribute to Assyria.
18.14 **stop** your attack, and I will pay whatever you demand."
18.30 you, and that he will **stop** our Assyrian army from capturing
23.29 King Josiah tried to **stop** the Egyptian army at Megiddo and
1 Chr 21.15 but he changed his mind and said to the angel, **"Stop!**
21.22 I can build an altar to the Lord, to **stop** the epidemic.
28.20 Start the work and don't let anything **stop** you.
2 Chr 16. 5 he **stopped** fortifying Ramah and abandoned the work.
18.32 he was not the king of Israel, so they **stopped** pursuing him.
24.18 So the people **stopped** worshipping in the Temple of the Lord,
25.16 **Stop** talking, or I'll have you killed!"
25.16 The prophet **stopped,** but not before saying, "Now I know
32. 3 number of people out and **stopped** up all the springs, so that
35.20 Josiah tried to **stop** him, [21]but Neco sent Josiah this message:
Ezra 4.13 are completed, the people will **stop** paying taxes, and your
4.21 that those men are to **stop** rebuilding the city until I give
4.23 Jerusalem and forced the Jews to **stop** rebuilding the city.
4.24 on the Temple had been **stopped** and had remained at a
Neh 6. 3 going to let the work **stop** just to go and see you."
6. 9 They were trying to frighten us into **stopping** work.
Esth 8. 3 him to do something to **stop** the evil plot that Haman, the
9.18 thirteenth and fourteenth and then **stopped** on the fifteenth.
Job 3.17 In the grave wicked men **stop** their evil, and tired
3.24 Instead of eating, I mourn, and I can never **stop** groaning.
6.29 **Stop** being unjust.
9.12 He takes what he wants, and no one can **stop** him;
9.34 **Stop** punishing me, God!
11.10 you and brings you to trial, who is there to **stop** him?
13.21 **stop** punishing me, and don't crush me with terror.
14.11 Like rivers that **stop** running, and lakes that go dry,
18. 1 If you **stopped** to listen, we could talk to you.
22.21 make peace with God and **stop** treating him like an enemy;
23.13 one can oppose him or **stop** him from doing what he wants
29. 9 The leaders of the people would **stop** talking;
30.13 and there is no one to **stop** them.
30.17 the pain that gnaws me never **stops.**
33.17 God speaks to make them **stop** their sinning and to save
34.27 see it, [27]because they have **stopped** following him and
34.32 you your faults, and have you agreed to **stop** doing evil?
37. 7 He brings the work of men to a **stop;**
38.11 Here your powerful waves must **stop."**
Ps 4. 4 Tremble with fear and **stop** sinning;
7. 9 **Stop** the wickedness of evil men and reward those who are good.
8. 2 you **stop** anyone who opposes you.
12. 4 We will say what we wish, and no one can **stop** us."
18.37 I do not **stop** until I destroy them.
34. 1 I will never **stop** praising him.
38.12 they never **stop** plotting against me.
40. 9 You know that I will never **stop** telling it.
40.11 Lord, I know you will never **stop** being merciful to me.
44.20 If we had **stopped** worshipping our God and prayed to a
46. 9 He **stops** wars all over the world;
46.10 **"Stop** fighting," he says, "and know that I am God,
58. 4 they **stop** up their ears like a deaf cobra, [5]which does
75. 5 I tell them to **stop** their boasting."
75. 9 But I will never **stop** speaking of the God of Jacob or
77. 8 Has he **stopped** loving us?
82. 2 "You must **stop** judging unjustly;
85. 3 **stopped** being angry with them and held back your furious rage.
85. 4 back, O God our saviour, and **stop** being displeased with us!
89.33 But I will not **stop** loving David or fail to keep my
106.30 stood up and punished the guilty, and the plague was **stopped.**
106.33 made him so bitter that he spoke without **stopping** to think.
107.33 made rivers dry up completely and **stopped** springs from flowing.
114. 3 the River Jordan **stopped** flowing.
114. 5 And you, O Jordan, why did you **stop** flowing?
116. 8 he **stopped** my tears and kept me from defeat.
Prov 6. 4 Don't let yourself go to sleep or even **stop** to rest.
10.31 wisdom, but the tongue that speaks evil will be **stopped.**
17.14 **stop** it before it goes any further.
19.27 Son, when you **stop** learning, you will soon neglect what
26.20 without gossip, quarrelling **stops.**
27.16 Have you ever tried to **stop** the wind or ever tried to
28.17 Don't try to **stop** him.
30.32 foolish enough to be arrogant and plan evil, **stop** and think!
Song 2.11 the rains have **stopped;**
Is 1.16 **Stop** all this evil that I see you doing.
1.16 Yes, **stop** doing evil [17]and learn to do right.
1.31 deeds, and no one will be able to **stop** the destruction.
13.10 star and every constellation will **stop** shining, the sun will
14. 6 never **stopped** persecuting the nations they had conquered.
14.27 stretched out his arm to punish, and no one can **stop** him.
30.11 Get out of our way and **stop** blocking our path.
36.15 you and that he will **stop** our Assyrian army from capturing
47. 3 I will take vengeance, and no one will **stop** me."
47.11 will come upon you, and none of your magic can **stop** it.
50. 6 I did not **stop** them when they insulted me, when they
57.11 Have you **stopped** honouring me because I have kept silent for
57.20 whose waves never **stop** rolling in, bringing filth and muck.
59.15 little honesty that anyone who **stops** doing evil finds

Jer	7. 4	**Stop** believing those deceitful words, 'We are safe!
	7. 5	way you are living and **stop** doing the things you are doing.
	7. 6	**Stop** taking advantage of aliens, orphans, and widows.
	7. 6	**Stop** killing innocent people in this land.
	7. 6	**Stop** worshipping other gods, for that will destroy you.
	13.14	No pity, compassion, or mercy will **stop** me from killing them."
	14.17	and night, may I never **stop** weeping, for my people are
	15. 5	Who will **stop** long enough to ask how you are?
	15. 7	I killed your children because you did not **stop** your evil ways.
	18.11	Tell them to **stop** living sinful lives—to change their ways
	18.18	bring charges against him, and **stop** listening to what he says."
	23.14	to do wrong, so that no one **stops** doing what is evil.
	29.28	He must be **stopped** because he told the people in
	30. 6	Now **stop** and think!
	31.16	**Stop** your crying and wipe away your tears.
	32.40	I will never **stop** doing good things for them, and I will
	34.21	Babylonian army, which has **stopped** its attack against you.
	37.13	Shelemiah and grandson of Hananiah, **stopped** me and said,
	38. 5	I can't **stop** you."
	41.17	On the way, they **stopped** at Chimham, near Bethlehem.
	42.11	**Stop** being afraid of the king of Babylonia.
	44.18	ever since we **stopped** sacrificing to the Queen of Heaven
	44.18	and **stopped** pouring out wine-offerings to her,
	48.33	I have made the wine **stop** flowing from the winepresses;
	48.35	I will **stop** the people of Moab from making
	51.30	The Babylonian soldiers have **stopped** fighting and remain
Ezek	1.21	time the creatures moved or **stopped** or rose in the air, the
	1.24	When they **stopped** flying, they folded their wings, [25] but
	3.19	evil man and he doesn't **stop** sinning, he will die, still a
	10.17	When the creatures **stopped,** the wheels stopped;
	16.41	I will make you **stop** being a prostitute
	16.41	and make you **stop** giving gifts to your lovers.
	18.21	"If an evil man **stops** sinning and keeps my laws, if he
	18.24	"But if a righteous man **stops** doing good and starts
	18.26	When a righteous man **stops** doing good and starts doing
	18.27	When an evil man **stops** sinning and does what is right
	18.28	what he is doing and **stops** sinning, so he will certainly not
	20.39	have to obey me and **stop** dishonouring my holy name by
	23.27	I will put a **stop** to your lust and to the obscenities
	23.48	land I will put a **stop** to immorality, as a warning to
	26.16	at your fate that they will not be able to **stop** trembling.
	33. 9	evil man and he doesn't **stop** sinning, he will die, still a
	33.11	I would rather see him **stop** sinning and live.
	33.11	Israel, **stop** the evil you are doing.
	33.12	If an evil man **stops** doing evil, he won't be punished, and
	33.14	to die, but if he **stops** sinning and does what is right
	33.15	what he stole—if he **stops** sinning and follows the laws that
	33.18	When a righteous man **stops** doing good and starts doing evil,
	43. 9	Now they must **stop** worshipping other gods and remove the
	45. 9	**Stop** your violence and oppression.
	47.12	will never wither, and they will never **stop** bearing fruit.
Dan	4.27	**Stop** sinning, do what is right, and be merciful to the poor.
	8. 4	No animal could **stop** him or escape his power.
	8.11	**stopped** the daily sacrifices offered to him,
	10.16	"Sir, this vision makes me so weak that I can't **stop** trembling.
	11.31	They will **stop** the daily sacrifices and set up The Awful Horror.
	12.11	time the daily sacrifices are **stopped,** that is, from the
Hos	2. 2	Plead with her to **stop** her adultery and prostitution.
	9. 1	People of Israel, **stop** celebrating your festivals like pagans.
	10. 9	people of Israel have not **stopped** sinning against me since
Joel	2. 8	They swarm through defences, and nothing can **stop** them.
Amos	5.23	**Stop** your noisy songs;
	7. 5	Then I said, **"Stop,** Sovereign Lord!
	7.16	You tell me to **stop** prophesying, to stop raving against the
Jon	1.11	asked him, "What should we do to you to **stop** the storm?"
	3. 9	perhaps he will **stop** being angry, and we will not die!"
Nah	2. 8	**"Stop!**
Hab	1.10	No fortress can **stop** them—they pile up earth against it and
	3. 6	When he **stops,** the earth shakes;
Zech	1. 8	He had **stopped** among some myrtle-trees in a valley, and
Mal	2. 6	but they also helped many others to **stop** doing evil.
Mt	2. 9	ahead of them until it **stopped** over the place where the
	8.26	winds and the waves to **stop,** and there was a great calm.
	13.15	are dull, and they have **stopped** up their ears and have
	19.14	to me and do not **stop** them, because the Kingdom of heaven
	20.32	Jesus **stopped** and called them.
Mk	5.29	She touched his cloak, and her bleeding **stopped** at once;
	9.38	and we told him to **stop,** because he doesn't belong to our
	9.39	"Do not try to **stop** him," Jesus told them, "because
	10.14	to me, and do not **stop** them, because the Kingdom of God
	10.49	Jesus **stopped** and said, "Call him."
Lk	7.14	and touched the coffin, and the men carrying it **stopped.**
	7.45	kiss, but she has not **stopped** kissing my feet since I came.
	8.44	the edge of his cloak, and her bleeding **stopped** at once.
	9.36	When the voice **stopped,** there was Jesus all alone.
	9.49	and we told him to **stop,** because he doesn't belong to our
	9.50	"Do not try to **stop** him," Jesus said to him and to
	10. 4	don't **stop** to greet anyone on the road.
	11.52	not go in, and you **stop** those who are trying to go
	18.16	to me and do not **stop** them, because the Kingdom of God
	18.40	So Jesus **stopped** and ordered the blind man to be brought
	23.44	twelve o'clock when the sun **stopped** shining and darkness
Jn	2.16	**Stop** making my Father's house a market-place!"
	5.14	so **stop** sinning or something worse may happen to you."
	6.43	Jesus answered, **"Stop** grumbling among yourselves.
	7.24	**Stop** judging by external standards, and judge by true standards."
	20.27	**Stop** your doubting, and believe!"
Acts	4.20	For we cannot **stop** speaking of what we ourselves have
	8.38	official ordered the carriage to **stop,** and both Philip and
	9. 7	were travelling with Saul had **stopped,** not saying a word;
	10.47	Can anyone, then, **stop** them from being baptized with water?"
Acts	11. 5	by its four corners from heaven, and it **stopped** next to me.
	11.17	who was I, then, to try to **stop** God!"
	11.18	When they heard this, they **stopped** their criticism and praised God,
	21.32	When the people saw him with the soldiers, they **stopped** beating Paul.
	27.43	wanted to save Paul, so he **stopped** them from doing this.
	28.27	are dull, and they have **stopped** up their ears and closed
Rom	3.19	the Law, in order to **stop** all human excuses and bring the
	13.12	Let us **stop** doing the things that belong to the dark, and
	13.14	the Lord Jesus Christ, and **stop** paying attention to your
	14.13	So then, let us **stop** judging one another.
1 Cor	14.30	a message from God, the one who is speaking should **stop.**
	15.34	Come back to your right senses and **stop** your sinful ways.
Gal	5. 7	Who made you **stop** obeying the truth?
Eph	1.16	God's people, [16] I have not **stopped** giving thanks to God for you.
	4.28	who used to rob must **stop** robbing and start working, in
	6. 9	in the same way towards your slaves and **stop** using threats.
Phil	4.10	don't mean that you had **stopped** caring for me—you just had
Col	2.19	way of thinking [19] and has **stopped** holding on to Christ,
1 Thes	2.16	They even tried to **stop** us from preaching to the
1 Tim	1. 3	teaching false doctrines, and you must order them to **stop.**
	1.20	this will teach them to **stop** their blasphemy.
Tit	1.11	It is necessary to **stop** their talk, because they are
Heb	10. 2	feel guilty of sin any more, and all sacrifices would **stop.**
1 Pet	3.10	times, must keep from speaking evil and **stop** telling lies.
2 Pet	2.16	with a human voice and **stopped** the prophet's insane action.
3 Jn	10	when they come, and even **stops** those who want to receive
Rev	4. 8	Day and night they never **stop** singing:
	9.20	They did not **stop** worshipping demons, nor the idols of gold,

STORE

Gen	41.35	and give them authority to **store** up corn in the cities and
	41.48	all of which Joseph collected and **stored** in the cities.
	41.48	In each city he **stored** the food from the fields around it.
	41.56	opened all the **storehouses** and sold corn to the Egyptians.
Deut	14.28	the tithe of all your crops and **store** it in your towns.
	28.12	in season from his rich **storehouse** in the sky and bless all
1 Kgs	7. 2	over **store-rooms,** which were supported by the pillars.
	7.51	he placed in the temple **storerooms** all the things that his
2 Kgs	20.13	There was nothing in his **storerooms** or anywhere in his
	20.15	There is nothing in the **storerooms** that I didn't show them."
	20.17	everything that your ancestors have **stored** up to this day,
1 Chr	26.15	gate, and his sons were allotted to guard the **storerooms.**
	26.17	Four guards were stationed at the **storerooms** daily, two at each storeroom.
	26.20	treasury and the **storerooms** for gifts dedicated to God.
	26.22	Zetham and Joel, had charge of the temple treasury and **storerooms.**
	27.25	Royal **storerooms:**
	27.25	Local **storerooms:**
	28.11	buildings, for the **storerooms** and all the other rooms,
	28.12	around them, and for the **storerooms** for the temple equipment
2 Chr	5. 1	he placed in the temple **storerooms** all the things that his
	8. 4	the cities in Hamath that were centres for **storing** supplies.
	8. 6	all the cities where he **stored** supplies, and the cities
	8.15	and the Levites concerning the **storehouses** and other matters
	16. 4	and all the cities of Naphtali where supplies were **stored.**
	17.13	and cities, [13] where supplies were **stored** in huge amounts.
	31.11	the king's orders they prepared **storerooms** in the Temple
	32.27	He had **storerooms** built for his gold, silver, precious stones,
	32.28	In addition, he had **storehouses** built for his corn,
	34.14	being taken out of the **storeroom,** Hilkiah found the book of
Neh	10.38	to take to the temple **storerooms** one tenth of all the tithes
	10.39	wine, and olive-oil to the **storerooms** where the utensils for
	12.25	of guarding the **storerooms** by the gates to the Temple:
	12.44	put in charge of the **storerooms** where contributions for the
	13. 4	in charge of the temple **storerooms,** had for a long time been
	13. 5	was intended only for **storing** offerings of corn and incense,
	13.12	bringing to the temple **storerooms** their tithes of corn,
	13.13	I put the following men in charge of the **storerooms:**
Job	30.23	me off to my death, to the fate in **store** for everyone.
	38.22	Have you ever visited the **storerooms,** where I keep the
Ps	17.14	Punish them with the sufferings you have **stored** up for them;
	33. 7	he shut up the ocean depths in **storerooms.**
	135. 7	the storms, and he brings out the wind from his **storeroom.**
Prov	3.10	will have too much wine to be able to **store** it all.
	6. 8	or ruler, [8] but they **store** up their food during the summer,
	30.25	they are weak, but they **store** up their food in the summer.
Is	10.13	between nations and took the supplies they had **stored.**
	10.22	Destruction is in **store** for the people, and it is fully deserved.
	15. 9	God has something even worse in **store** for the people there.
	22. 9	In order to **store** water, [11] you built a reservoir inside
	23.18	She will not **store** it away, but those who worship the Lord
	39. 2	There was nothing in his **storerooms** or anywhere in his
	39. 4	There is nothing in the **storerooms** that I didn't show them."
	39. 6	everything that your ancestors have **stored** up to this day,
Jer	10.13	flash in the rain and sends the wind from his **storeroom.**
	38.11	the men to the palace **storeroom** and got some worn-out
	40.10	But you can gather and **store** up wine, fruit, and olive-oil,
	50.25	place where my weapons are **stored,** and in my anger I have
	50.26	side and break open the places where its grain is **stored!**
	51.16	flash in the rain and sends the wind from his **storeroom.**
Dan	1. 2	and put the captured treasures in the temple **storerooms.**
Hos	13.12	guilt are on record, and the records are safely **stored** away.
Joel	1.17	is no grain to be **stored,** and so the empty granaries are
Mt	6.19	"Do not **store** up riches for yourselves here on earth,
	6.20	Instead, **store** up riches for yourselves in heaven, where
	13.52	a house who takes new and old things out of his **storeroom."**
Lk	12.18	bigger ones, where I will **store** my corn and all my other

Lk 12.24 they don't have **store-rooms** or barns;
1 Tim 6.19 In this way they will **store** up for themselves a treasure

STOREY
[THREE-STORIED]

1 Kgs 6. 5 back of the Temple, a **three-storied** annexe was built,
6. 5 each **storey** 2.2 metres high.
6. 6 Each room in the lowest **storey** was 2.2 metres wide,
6. 6 in the middle **storey** 2.7 metres wide,
6. 6 and in the top **storey** 3.1 metres wide.
6. 8 The entrance to the lowest **storey** of the annexe was on
6. 8 with stairs leading up to the second and third **storeys.**
6.10 The **three-storied** annexe,
6.10 each **storey** 2.2 metres high,
Ezek 41. 6 These rooms were in three **storeys,** with thirty rooms on each
41. 7 to go from the lower **storey**
41. 7 to the middle and the upper **storeys.**
Acts 20. 9 sound asleep and fell from the third **storey** to the ground.

STORK

Lev 11.13 seagulls, **storks,** herons, pelicans, cormorants;
Deut 14.12 sea-gulls, **storks,** herons, pelicans, cormorants;
Job 39.13 But no ostrich can fly like a **stork.**
Ps 104.17 the **storks** nest in the fir-trees.
Jer 8. 7 Even **storks** know when it is time to return;
Zech 5. 9 flying towards me with powerful wings like those of a **stork.**

STORM
[DUSTSTORMS, HAILSTORM, SANDSTORMS, THUNDERSTORM]

Ex 9.18 I will cause a heavy **hailstorm,** such as Egypt has never
9.24 The Lord sent [24]a heavy **hailstorm,** with lightning flashing
9.24 It was the worst **storm** that Egypt had ever known in all
Deut 28.24 the Lord will send down **duststorms**
28.24 and **sandstorms** until you are destroyed.
Job 1.19 your eldest son, [19]when a **storm** swept in from the desert.
4. 9 Like a **storm,** God destroys them in his anger.
9.17 He sends **storms** to batter and bruise me without any
21.18 straw in the wind, or like dust carried away in a **storm?**
30.22 you toss me about in a raging **storm.**
36.33 Thunder announces the approaching **storm,** and the cattle know
37. 1 The **storm** makes my heart beat wildly.
37. 9 The **storm** winds come from the south, and the biting cold
38. 1 Then out of the **storm** the Lord spoke to Job.
38.25 the pouring rain and cleared the way for the **thunderstorm?**
40. 6 Then out of the **storm** the Lord spoke to Job once again.
Ps 48. 7 to bear a child, [7]like ships tossing in a furious **storm.**
50. 3 fire is in front of him, a furious **storm** is round him.
55. 8 find myself a shelter from the raging wind and the **storm.**
57. 1 wings I find protection until the raging **storms** are over.
81. 7 From my hiding-place in the **storm,** I answered you.
83.15 chase them away with your **storm** and terrify them with
107.29 He calmed the raging **storm,** and the waves became quiet.
135. 7 He brings **storm** clouds from the ends of the earth;
135. 7 he makes lightning for the **storms,** and he brings out the
Prov 1.27 comes on you like a **storm,** bringing fierce winds of trouble,
3.25 sudden disasters, such as come on the wicked like a **storm.**
10.25 **Storms** come, and the wicked are blown away, but honest
Is 4. 6 it a place of safety, sheltered from the rain and **storm.**
24.20 like a drunken man and sway like a hut in a **storm.**
25. 4 give them shelter from **storms** and shade from the burning heat.
25. 4 attack like a winter **storm,** [5]like drought in a dry land.
28. 2 who will come like a **hailstorm,** like a torrent of rain, like
28.17 **Hailstorms** will sweep away all the lies you depend on, and
29. 6 the Lord Almighty will rescue you with violent **thunderstorms**
32. 2 a shelter from the wind and a place to hide from **storms.**
41.16 carry them off, and they will be scattered by the **storm.**
66.15 on the wings of a **storm** to punish those he is angry
Jer 23.19 His anger is a **storm,** a furious wind that will rage over
25.32 after another, and a great **storm** is gathering at the far
30.23 The Lord's anger is a **storm,** a furious wind that
Ezek 1. 4 I looked up and saw a **storm** coming from the north.
1. 5 At the centre of the **storm,** I saw what looked like four
26.11 Their horsemen will **storm** through your streets, killing
38. 9 him will attack like a **storm** and cover the land like a
38.16 attack my people Israel like a **storm** moving across the land.
Hos 8. 7 When they sow the wind, they will reap a **storm!**
Amos 1.14 the day of battle, and the fighting will rage like a **storm.**
Jon 1. 4 on the sea, and the **storm** was so violent that the ship
1.11 The **storm** was getting worse all the time, so the sailors
1.11 asked him, "What should we do to you to stop the **storm?"**
1.12 it is my fault that you are caught in this violent **storm."**
1.13 But the **storm** was getting worse and worse, and they got nowhere.
Nah 1. 3 Where the Lord walks, **storms** arise;
Hab 3. 8 the **storm** cloud was your chariot, as you brought victory
3.14 when it came like a **storm** to scatter us, gloating like those
Zech 7.14 Like a **storm** I swept them away to live in foreign countries.
9.14 he will march in the **storms** from the south.
Mt 8.24 Suddenly a fierce **storm** hit the lake, and the boat was
Lk 8.24 up and gave an order to the wind and the **stormy** water;
Acts 27.18 The violent **storm** continued, so on the next day they
27.27 were being driven about in the Mediterranean by the **storm.**
Heb 12.18 and the gloom, the **storm,** [19]the blast of a trumpet,
2 Pet 2.17 like dried-up springs, like clouds blown along by a **storm;**

STORY

Gen 6. 9 This is the **story** of Noah.
24.28 The girl ran to her mother's house and told the whole **story.**
Gen 25.19 This is the **story** of Abraham's son Isaac.
37. 2 had lived, [2]and this is the **story** of Jacob's family.
39.17 Then she told him the same **story:**
Josh 9. 9 Then they told him this **story:**
1 Kgs 1.14 with King David, I will come in and confirm your **story."**
11.27 This is the **story** of the revolt.
2 Kgs 8. 6 king's question, she confirmed Gehazi's **story,** and so the
2 Chr 24.27 Book of Kings contains the **stories** of the sons of Joash, the
Esth 10. 2 as well as the whole **story** of how he promoted Mordecai to
Mic 2. 4 comes, people will use your **story** as an example of disaster,
Mt 8.33 where they told the whole **story** and what had happened to the
Mk 14.56 Many witnesses told lies against Jesus, but their **stories** did not agree.
14.59 Not even they, however, could make their **stories** agree.
2 Pet 1.16 have not depended on made-up **stories** in making known to you
2. 3 will make a profit out of telling you made-up **stories.**

STOVE

Lev 11.35 a clay **stove** or oven shall be broken, [36]but a spring or

STRAGGLING

Deut 25.18 and exhausted, and killed all who were **straggling** behind.

STRAIGHT

Gen 37. 7 of wheat, when my sheaf got up and stood up **straight.**
Ex 15. 8 it stood up **straight** like a wall;
2 Sam 14.20 But he did it in order to **straighten** out this whole matter.
Ps 107. 7 He led them by a **straight** road to a city where they
Ecc 1.15 You can't **straighten** out what is crooked;
7.13 How can anyone **straighten** out what God has made crooked?
Is 45.13 I will **straighten** every road that he travels.
Ezek 1. 7 Their legs were **straight,** and they had hoofs like those of
Mt 3. 3 make a **straight** path for him to travel!' "
Mk 1. 3 make a **straight** path for him to travel!' "
Lk 3. 4 make a **straight** path for him to travel!
3. 5 must be made **straight,** and the rough paths made smooth.
13.11 she was bent over and could not **straighten** up at all.
13.13 and at once she **straightened** herself up and praised God.
Jn 1.23 Make a **straight** path for the Lord to travel!' "
8. 7 he **straightened** himself up and said to them,
8.10 He **straightened** himself up and said to her, "Where are they?
Acts 14.10 and said in a loud voice, "Stand up **straight** on your feet!"
16.11 ship from Troas and sailed **straight** across to Samothrace,
21. 1 After sailing **straight** across, we came to Cos;
1 Cor 9.26 That is why I run **straight** for the finishing-line;
Gal 2.14 they were not walking a **straight** path in line with the truth
Phil 3.14 So I run **straight** towards the goal in order to win the
Heb 12.13 Keep walking on **straight** paths, so that the lame foot
2 Pet 2.15 They have left the **straight** path and have lost their way;

STRAIGHT STREET

Acts 9.11 "Get ready and go to **Straight Street,**

STRAIN (1)

Mt 23.24 You **strain** a fly out of your drink, but swallow a camel!

STRAIN (2)

Deut 28.32 Every day you will **strain** your eyes, looking in vain for
Ps 69. 3 I have **strained** my eyes, looking for your help.
Mk 6.48 saw that his disciples were **straining** at the oars,

STRAND

Judg 20.15 could sling a stone at a **strand** of hair and never miss.

STRANGE

Ex 3. 3 "This is **strange,"** he thought.
18. 3 (Moses had said, "I have been a foreigner in a **strange** land";
Ps 139.14 all you do is **strange** and wonderful.
Is 28.11 some **strange-sounding** language to teach you a lesson.
28.21 do what he intends to do—**strange** as his actions may seem.
Hos 8.12 for the people, but they reject them as **strange** and foreign.
Mk 16.17 they will speak in **strange tongues;**
Lk 21.11 will be **strange** and terrifying things coming from the sky.
21.25 "There will be **strange** things happening to the sun,
Jn 9.30 The man answered, "What a **strange** thing that is!
Acts 10.46 For they heard them speaking in **strange tongues** and praising God's greatness.
17.20 we hear you say sound **strange** to us, and we would like
19. 6 spoke in **strange tongues** and also proclaimed God's message.
1 Cor 12.10 the ability to speak in **strange tongues,** and to another he
12.28 others or to direct them or to speak in **strange tongues.**
12.30 diseases or to speak in **strange tongues** or to explain what
13. 8 gifts of speaking in **strange tongues,** but they will cease;
14. 2 The one who speaks in **strange tongues** does not speak to
14. 4 The one who speaks in **strange tongues** helps only himself,
14. 5 I would like all of you to speak in **strange tongues;**
14. 5 the one who speaks in **strange tongues**—unless there is
14. 6 use will I be to you if I speak in **strange tongues?**
14. 9 about if your message given in **strange tongues** is not clear?
14.13 The person who speaks in **strange tongues,** then, must
14.18 God that I speak in **strange tongues** much more than any of
14.19 others, than speak thousands of words in **strange tongues.**
14.21 "By means of men speaking **strange** languages I will speak to

1 Cor 14.22 of speaking in **strange tongues** is proof for unbelievers,
14.23 and everyone starts speaking in **strange tongues**—and if some
14.26 God, another a message in **strange tongues**, and still another
14.27 is going to speak in **strange tongues**, two or three at the
14.28 the one who speaks in **strange tongues** must be quiet and
14.39 God's message, but do not forbid the speaking in **strange tongues.**
Heb 13. 9 not let all kinds of **strange** teachings lead you from the

STRANGER

Gen 15.13 him, "Your descendants will be **strangers** in a foreign land;
1 Chr 16.19 God's people were few in number, **strangers** in the land
29.15 life like exiles and **strangers**, as our ancestors did.
Job 19.13 I am a **stranger** to those who knew me;
19.15 my servant-girls treat me like a **stranger** and a foreigner.
19.27 him with my own eyes, and he will not be a **stranger.**
29.16 to the poor and took the side of **strangers** in trouble.
31.31 who work for me know that I have always welcomed **strangers.**
Ps 35.15 **strangers** beat me and kept striking me.
69. 8 I am like a **stranger** to my brothers, like a foreigner to
94. 6 and orphans, and murder the **strangers** who live in our land.
105.12 God's people were few in number, **strangers** in the land
109.11 property, and may **strangers** get everything he worked for.
146. 9 He protects the **strangers** who live in our land;
Prov 5.10 Yes, **strangers** will take all your wealth, and what you
5.17 Your children should grow up to help you, not **strangers.**
11.15 If you promise to pay a **stranger's** debt, you will regret it.
20.16 to be responsible for a **stranger's** debts ought to have his
27. 2 Let other people praise you—even **strangers;**
27.13 to be responsible for a **stranger's** debts deserves to have
Ecc 6. 2 Some **stranger** will enjoy it instead.
10. 3 will be evident even to **strangers** he meets along the way;
Jer 5.19 land, so they will serve **strangers** in a land that is not
14. 8 Why are you like a **stranger** in our land, like a traveller
35. 7 we might remain in this land where we live like **strangers.**
Lam 5. 2 Our property is in the hands of **strangers;**
Ezek 16.32 adultery with **strangers** instead of loving her husband.
Obad 11 were as bad as those **strangers** who carried off Jerusalem's
Mt 25.35 I was a **stranger** and you received me in your homes,
25.38 we ever see you a **stranger** and welcome you in our homes,
25.43 I was a **stranger** but you would not welcome me in your
25.44 hungry or thirsty or a **stranger** or naked or sick or in
Rom 12.13 needy fellow-Christians, and open your homes to **strangers.**
Eph 2.19 So then, you Gentiles are not foreigners or **strangers** any longer;
1 Tim 3. 2 he must welcome **strangers** in his home;
5.10 up her children well, received **strangers** in her home,
Heb 13. 2 Remember to welcome **strangers** in your homes.
1 Pet 2.11 to you, my friends, as **strangers** and refugees in this world!
3 Jn 5 do for your fellow-Christians, even when they are **strangers.**

STRANGLED

Job 7.15 I would rather be **strangled** than live in this miserable body.
Acts 15.20 not to eat any animal that has been **strangled,** or any blood.
15.29 eat no animal that has been **strangled;**
21.25 any animal that has been **strangled,** and that they must keep

STRAP
[SHOULDER-STRAPS]

Gen 14.23 keep anything of yours, not even a thread or a sandal **strap.**
Ex 28. 7 Two **shoulder-straps,** by which it can be fastened, are to
28.12 Put them on the **shoulder-straps** of the ephod to
28.25 attach them in front to the **shoulder-straps** of the ephod.
28.27 the front of the two **shoulder-straps** of the ephod near the
39. 4 They made two **shoulder-straps** for the ephod and attached
39. 7 They put them on the **shoulder-straps** of the ephod to
39.18 attached them in front to the **shoulder-straps** of the ephod.
39.20 the front of the two **shoulder straps** of the ephod, near the
1 Sam 17.39 David **strapped** Saul's sword over the armour and tried to walk,
Neh 4.18 everyone who was building kept a sword **strapped** to his waist.
Is 5.27 not a sandal **strap** is broken.
Jer 27. 2 a yoke out of leather **straps** and wooden crossbars and to put
Mt 23. 5 Look at the **straps with scripture verses on them** which they

STRAW

Gen 24.25 "There is plenty of **straw** and fodder at our house, and
24.32 Laban unloaded the camels and gave them **straw** and fodder.
Ex 5. 7 "Stop giving the people **straw** for making bricks.
5.10 has said that he will not supply you with any more **straw.**
5.12 So the people went all over Egypt looking for **straw.**
5.13 every day as they had made when they were given **straw.**
5.16 We are given no **straw,** but we are still ordered to make
5.18 will not be given any **straw,** but you must still make the
15. 7 your anger blazes out and burns them up like **straw.**
Judg 19.19 though we have fodder and **straw** for our donkeys, as well as
1 Kgs 4.28 his share of barley and **straw,** where it was needed, for the
Job 13.25 you are attacking a piece of dry **straw.**
21.18 and blow them away like **straw** in the wind, or like dust
41.27 iron is as flimsy as **straw,** and bronze as soft as rotten
41.28 rocks thrown at him are like bits of **straw.**
41.29 club is a piece of **straw,** and he laughs when men throw
Ps 1. 4 they are like **straw** that the wind blows away.
35. 5 May they be like **straw** blown by the wind as the angel
83.13 them like dust, O God, like **straw** blown away by the wind.
Is 1.31 Just as **straw** is set on fire by a spark, so powerful
5.24 So now, just as **straw** and dry grass shrivel and burn in
11. 7 Lions will eat **straw** as cattle do.
17.13 away like dust on a hillside, like **straw** in a whirlwind.
25.10 Moab will be trampled down, just as **straw** is trampled in manure.
Is 29. 5 dust, and their terrifying armies will fly away like **straw.**
40.24 Lord sends a wind, they dry up and blow away like **straw.**
41. 2 His arrows scatter them like **straw** before the wind.
47.14 will be like bits of **straw,** and a fire will burn them
65.25 lions will eat **straw,** as cattle do, and snakes will no
Jer 13.24 Lord will scatter you like **straw** that is blown away by the
15. 7 town in the land I threw you to the wind like **straw.**
23.28 What good is **straw** compared with wheat?
51. 2 to destroy Babylonia like a wind that blows **straw** away.
Nah 1.10 Like tangled thorns and dry **straw,** you drunkards will be burnt up!
Mal 4. 1 coming when all proud and evil people will burn like **straw.**
1 Cor 3.12 others will use wood or grass or **straw.**

STRAY

Ex 22. 5 or a vineyard and they **stray** away and eat up the crops
Ps 17. 5 always walked in your way and have never **strayed** from it.
Is 63.17 Why do you let us **stray** from your ways?

STREAKED

Gen 30.39 of the branches, they produced young that were **streaked,**
30.40 of the **streaked** and black animals of Laban's flock.

STREAM

Gen 2.10 A **stream** flowed in Eden and watered the garden;
Num 20.11 with it, and a great **stream** of water gushed out, and all
Deut 8. 7 rivers and springs, and underground **streams** gushing out into
9.21 the dust into the **stream** that flowed down the mountain.
21. 4 to a spot near a **stream** that never runs dry and where
Josh 13. 3 (The land from the **stream** of Shihor, at the Egyptian border,
15. 4 to Azmon, and followed the **stream** on the border of Egypt to
15.47 and villages, reaching to the **stream** on the border of Egypt
16. 8 west from Tappuah to the **stream** of Kanah and ended at the
17. 9 The border then went down to the **stream** of Kanah.
17. 9 The cities south of the **stream** belonged to Ephraim, even
17. 9 north side of the **stream** and ended at the Mediterranean Sea.
19.11 Mareal, touching Dabbesheth and the **stream** east of Jokneam.
Judg 5.19 Taanach, by the **stream** of Megiddo, the kings came and fought;
7.24 the River Jordan and the **streams** as far as Bethbarah, to
7.24 held the River Jordan and the **streams** as far as Bethbarah.
1 Sam 17.40 five smooth stones from the **stream** and put them in his bag.
1 Kgs 14.15 Israel, and she will shake like a reed shaking in a **stream.**
2 Kgs 3.16 'Dig ditches all over this dry **stream** bed.
3.17 any rain or wind, this **stream** bed will be filled with water,
Job 6.15 friends, you deceive me like **streams** that go dry when no
6.16 The **streams** are choked with snow and ice, [17] but in the
6.17 heat they disappear, and the **stream** beds lie bare and dry.
6.20 Sheba and Tema search, [20] but their hope dies beside dry **streams.**
6.21 You are like those **streams** to me, you see my fate and
20.17 of olive-oil or **streams** that flow with milk and honey.
22.24 dump your finest gold in the dry **stream** bed.
36.12 ignorance and cross the **stream** into the world of the dead.
40.22 the willows by the **stream** give him shelter in their shade.
41.19 Flames blaze from his mouth, and **streams** of sparks fly out.
Ps 1. 3 trees that grow beside a **stream,** that bear fruit at the
42. 1 a deer longs for a **stream** of cool water, so I long
65. 9 You fill the **streams** with water;
78.16 He caused a **stream** to come out of the rock and made
110. 7 will drink from the **stream** by the road, and strengthened,
Prov 18. 4 of wisdom, deep as the ocean, fresh as a flowing **stream.**
21. 1 a king as easily as he directs the course of a **stream.**
Song 4.15 Fountains water the garden, **streams** of flowing water,
5.12 brook, doves washed in milk and standing by the **stream.**
Is 2. 2 Many nations will come **streaming** to it, [3] and their people
11.15 Euphrates, leaving only seven tiny **streams,** so that anyone
30.25 and their people are killed, **streams** of water will flow from
30.33 Lord will breathe out a **stream** of flame to set it on
32. 2 They will be like **streams** flowing in a desert, like the
33.21 live beside broad rivers and **streams,** but hostile ships will
35. 6 **Streams** of water will flow through the desert;
43.19 through the wilderness and give you **streams** of water there.
44. 3 the thirsty land and make **streams** flow on the dry ground.
44. 4 grass, like willows by **streams** of running water.
47. 2 Lift up your skirts to cross the **streams!**
48.18 have flowed for you like a **stream** that never goes dry!
57. 5 as sacrifices in the rocky caves near the bed of a **stream.**
Jer 15.18 disappoint me like a **stream** that goes dry in the summer?"
17. 8 a tree growing near a **stream** and sending out roots to the
18.14 Do its cool mountain **streams** ever run dry?
31. 9 I will guide them to **streams** of water, on a smooth road
Lam 3.49 pour out in a ceaseless **stream** [50] Until the Lord looks down
Ezek 7.26 another, and a steady **stream** of bad news will pour in.
19.10 Your mother was like a grapevine planted near a **stream.**
31. 4 tree was growing And sent **streams** to all the trees of the
31. 7 Its roots reached down to the deep-flowing **streams.**
31.15 hold back the rivers and not let the many **streams** flow out.
32. 6 until it spreads over the mountains and fills the **streams.**
34.13 to the mountains and the **streams** of Israel and will feed
47. 2 A small **stream** of water was flowing out at the south side
47. 3 to the east and told me to wade through the **stream** there.
47. 5 metres more, and there the **stream** was so deep I could not
47. 9 Wherever the **stream** flows, there will be all kinds of
47. 9 The **stream** will make the water of the Dead Sea fresh, and
47.12 On each bank of the **stream** all kinds of trees will grow
47.12 they are watered by the **stream** that flows from the Temple.
Dan 7.10 blazing with fire, [10] and a **stream** of fire was pouring out
Joel 1.20 animals cry out to you because the **streams** have become dry.
3.18 there will be plenty of water for all the **streams** of Judah.
3.18 A **stream** will flow from the Temple of the Lord, and it

Amos 5.24 let justice flow like a **stream,** and righteousness like a
Mic 4. 1 Many nations will come **streaming** to it, [2]and their people
6. 7 I bring him thousands of sheep or endless **streams** of olive-oil?
Jn 7.38 says, 'Whoever believes in me, **streams** of life-giving water

STREET

Deut 32.25 War will bring death in the **streets;**
1 Sam 9.26 got up, and he and Samuel went out to the **street** together.
2 Sam 1.20 Do not announce it in Gath or in the **streets** of Ashkelon.
22.43 I trample on them like mud in the **streets.**
2 Kgs 9.30 looking down at the **street** from a window in the palace.
21.16 that the **streets** of Jerusalem were flowing with blood;
Esth 8.15 Then the **streets** of Susa rang with cheers and joyful shouts.
Job 31.32 into my home and never let them sleep in the **streets.**
Ps 18.42 I trample on them like mud in the **streets.**
31.11 when they see me in the **street,** they run away.
55.11 the **streets** are full of oppression and fraud.
69.12 talk about me in the **streets,** and drunkards make up songs
144.14 May there be no cries of distress in our **streets.**
Prov 1.20 is calling out in the **streets** and market-places, [21]calling
7. 8 He was walking along the **street** near the corner where a
7.11 always walked the **streets** [12]or stood waiting at a corner,
7.12 sometimes in the **streets,** sometimes in the market-place.
26.17 is like going down the **street** and grabbing a dog by the
Ecc 12. 4 Your ears will be deaf to the noise of the **street.**
12. 5 place, and then there will be mourning in the **streets.**
Song 3. 2 wandering through the city, through its **streets** and alleys.
8. 1 I met you in the **street,** I could kiss you and no
Is 5.25 of those who die will be left in the **streets** like rubbish.
10. 6 steal and trample on the people like dirt in the **streets."**
15. 3 The people in the **streets** are dressed in sackcloth;
24.11 People shout in the **streets** because there is no more wine.
42. 2 or raise his voice or make loud speeches in the **streets.**
51.20 At the corner of every **street** your people collapse
51.23 you lie down in the **streets** and trampled on you as if
Jer 5. 1 People of Jerusalem, run through your **streets!**
6.11 on the children in the **streets** and on the gatherings of the
7.17 in the cities of Judah and in the **streets** of Jerusalem?
7.34 of Judah and in the **streets** of Jerusalem I will put an
9.21 down the children in the **streets** and the young men in the
11. 6 "Go to the cities of Judah and to the **streets** of Jerusalem.
11.13 that disgusting god Baal as there are **streets** in the city.
14.16 be thrown out into the **streets** of Jerusalem, and there will
33.10 the towns of Judah and the **streets** of Jerusalem are empty;
44. 6 of Judah and on the **streets** of Jerusalem, and I set them
44. 9 of Judah and in the **streets** of Jerusalem by your ancestors,
44.17 do in the towns of Judah and in the **streets** of Jerusalem.
44.21 of Judah and in the **streets** of Jerusalem—do you think that
49.26 killed in the city **streets,** and all her soldiers destroyed.
50.30 be killed in the city **streets,** and all its soldiers will be
51. 4 They will be wounded and die in the **streets** of their cities.
Lam 1.19 leaders died in the city **streets,** Looking for food to keep
1.20 There is murder in the **streets;**
2.11 Children and babies are fainting in the **streets** of the city.
2.12 They fall in the **streets** as though they were wounded, And
2.19 Children starving to death on every **street** corner!
2.21 alike lie dead in the **streets,** Young men and women, killed
4. 1 the stones of the Temple lie scattered in the **streets.**
4. 5 who once ate the finest foods die starving in the **streets;**
4. 8 Now they lie unknown in the **streets,** their faces blackened
4.14 Her leaders wandered through the **streets** like blind men,
4.18 we could not even walk in the **streets.**
Ezek 7.15 There is fighting in the **streets,** and sickness and
7.19 and silver away in the **streets** like refuse, because neither
11. 6 here in the city that the **streets** are full of corpses.
16.31 On every **street** you built places to worship idols
26.11 through your **streets,** killing your people
28.23 send diseases on you and make blood flow in your **streets.**
Dan 9.25 Jerusalem will be rebuilt with **streets** and strong defences,
Hos 7. 1 they rob people in the **streets.**
Amos 5.16 "There will be wailing and cries of sorrow in the city **streets.**
7.17 become a prostitute on the **streets,** and your children will
Mic 7.10 We will see them defeated, trampled down like mud in the **streets.**
Nah 2. 4 Chariots dash wildly through the **streets,** rushing to and
3.10 At every **street** corner their children were beaten to death.
Zeph 3. 6 the **streets** are empty—no one is left.
Zech 8. 5 And the **streets** will again be full of boys and girls playing.
10. 5 who trample their enemies into the mud of the **streets.**
Mt 6. 2 hypocrites do in the houses of worship and on the **streets.**
6. 5 of worship and on the **street** corners, so that everyone will
12.19 not argue or shout, or make loud speeches in the **streets.**
22. 9 Now go to the main **streets** and invite to the feast as
22.10 servants went out into the **streets** and gathered all the
Mk 11. 4 a colt out in the **street,** tied to the door of a
Lk 10.10 welcomed, go out in the **streets** and say, [11]'Even the dust
14.21 servant, 'Hurry out to the **streets** and alleys of the town,
Acts 5.15 were carried out into the **streets** and placed on beds and
9.11 ready and go to Straight **Street,** and at the house of Judas
12.10 They walked down a **street,** and suddenly the angel left Peter.
17. 5 of the worthless loafers from the **streets** and formed a mob.
Rev 11. 8 bodies will lie in the **street** of the great city, where their
21.21 The **street** of the city was of pure gold, transparent as glass.
22. 2 the Lamb [2]and flowing down the middle of the city's **street.**

STRENGTH

Gen 18. 5 it will give you **strength** to continue your journey.
31. 6 that I have worked for your father with all my **strength.**
48. 2 to see him, he gathered his **strength** and sat up in bed.
49. 3 my first-born, you are my **strength** And the first child of my
Ex 15.13 by your **strength** you guided them to your sacred land.
15.16 They see your **strength,** O Lord, and stand helpless with fear
Num 11. 6 But now our **strength** is gone.
Deut 1.38 **strengthen** the determination of your helper, Joshua son of Nun.
3.28 **Strengthen** his determination, because he will lead the
4.34 Before your very eyes he used his great power and **strength;**
5.15 Lord your God, rescued you by my great power and **strength.**
6. 5 your heart, with all your soul, and with all your **strength.**
7.19 and the great power and **strength** by which the Lord your God
8.17 have made yourselves wealthy by your own power and **strength.**
9.26 and brought out of Egypt by your great **strength** and power.
26. 8 By his great power and **strength** he rescued us from Egypt.
32.36 rescue his people when he sees that their **strength** is gone.
33.17 Joseph has the **strength** of a bull, The horns of a wild
Judg 5.21 I shall march, march on, with **strength!**
6.14 "Go with all your great **strength** and rescue Israel
13.25 the Lord's power began to **strengthen** him while he was
16. 9 So they still did not know the secret of his **strength.**
16.17 cut, I would lose my **strength** and be as weak as anybody
16.19 Then she began to torment him, for he had lost his **strength.**
16.28 please, God, give me my **strength** just once more, so that
1 Sam 2. 9 a man does not triumph by his own **strength.**
30.12 After he had eaten, his **strength** returned;
2 Sam 15.12 gained **strength,** and Absalom's followers grew in number.
22.30 You give me **strength** to attack my enemies and power to
22.40 give me **strength** for the battle and victory over my enemies.
1 Kgs 19. 8 food gave him enough **strength** to walk forty days to Sinai,
2 Kgs 9.24 bow, and with all his **strength** shot an arrow that struck
15.19 support in **strengthening** Menahem's power over the country.
17.36 who brought you out of Egypt with great power and **strength;**
23.25 his heart, mind, and **strength,** obeying all the Law of Moses;
1 Chr 29.12 you rule everything by your **strength** and power;
2 Chr 11.17 This **strengthened** the kingdom of Judah, and for three
16. 9 the whole world, to give **strength** to those whose hearts are
17. 1 Asa as king and **strengthened** his position against Israel.
26. 9 Uzziah **strengthened** the fortifications of Jerusalem by
30.21 Levites and the priests praised the Lord with all their **strength.**
32. 5 king **strengthened** the city's defences by repairing the wall,
Neh 1.10 You rescued them by your great power and **strength.**
Job 4. 3 You have taught many people and given **strength** to feeble hands.
6.11 What **strength** have I got to keep on living?
6.13 I have no **strength** left to save myself;
10.10 You gave my father **strength** to beget me;
12. 6 live in peace, though their only god is their own **strength.**
12.21 those in power and puts an end to the **strength** of rulers.
16. 5 **strengthen** you with advice and keep talking to comfort you.
21.16 they succeed by their own **strength,** but their way of
23. 6 Would God use all his **strength** against me?
24.22 God, in his **strength,** destroys the mighty;
26.12 It is his **strength** that conquered the sea;
29.20 Everyone was always praising me, and my **strength** never failed
36.19 all your **strength** can't help you now.
39.11 you rely on his great **strength** and expect him to do your
39.21 they rush into battle with all their **strength.**
40.16 like a cow, [16]but what **strength** there is in his body, and
Ps 6. 2 Give me **strength;**
10.10 brute **strength** has defeated them.
13. 3 Restore my **strength;**
18.29 You give me **strength** to attack my enemies and power to
18.39 give me **strength** for the battle and victory over my enemies.
19. 7 it gives new **strength.**
21. 1 The king is glad, O Lord, because you gave him **strength;**
21.13 We praise you, Lord, for your great **strength!**
22.14 My **strength** is gone, gone like water spilt on the ground.
23. 3 He gives me new **strength.**
29.11 Lord gives **strength** to his people and blesses them with peace.
32. 4 my **strength** was completely drained, as moisture is dried
33.16 a soldier does not triumph because of his **strength.**
33.17 their great **strength** cannot save.
37.17 Lord will take away the **strength** of the wicked, but protect
38.10 My heart is pounding, my **strength** is gone, and my eyes
44. 3 power and your **strength,** by the assurance of your presence,
45. 4 Your **strength** will win you great victories!
46. 1 God is our shelter and **strength,** always ready to help in
59. 9 I have confidence in your **strength;**
59.11 Scatter them by your **strength** and defeat them, O Lord,
59.16 But I will sing about your **strength;**
65. 6 in place by your **strength,**
68.35 He gives **strength** and power to his people.
71.20 and suffering on me, but you will restore my **strength;**
73.26 mind and my body may grow weak, but God is my **strength;**
74.13 With your mighty **strength** you divided the sea and
76. 5 all their **strength** and skill was useless.
80. 2 Show us your **strength;**
84. 5 How happy are those whose **strength** comes from you, who are
86.16 **strengthen** me and save me, because I serve you, just as my
88. 4 all my **strength** is gone.
89.10 with your mighty **strength** you defeated your enemies.
89.13 How great is your **strength!**
89.21 My **strength** will always be with him, my power will make
93. 1 He is clothed with majesty and **strength.**
98. 1 By his own power and holy **strength** he has won the victory.
104.15 to make him cheerful, and bread to give him **strength.**
110. 7 stream by the road, and **strengthened,** he will stand victorious.
119.28 **strengthen** me, as you have promised.
119.116 Give me **strength,** as you promised, and I shall live;
138. 3 with your **strength** you strengthened me.
150. 1 Praise his **strength** in heaven!
Prov 20.29 We admire the **strength** of youth and respect the grey
24. 5 yes, knowledge is more important than **strength.**
Ecc 9.16 that wisdom is better than **strength,** but no one thinks of a

Song 2. 5 Restore my **strength** with raisins and refresh me with apples!
Is 12. 2 The Lord gives me power and **strength;**
31. 1 They are relying on Egypt's vast military **strength**—horses,
35. 3 Give **strength** to hands that are tired and to knees that
40.29 He **strengthens** those who are weak and tired.
40.31 in the Lord for help will find their **strength** renewed.
41.13 I **strengthen** you and say, 'Do not be afraid;
42. 1 is my servant, whom I **strengthen**— the one I have chosen,
45. 5 I will give you the **strength** you need, although you do not
45.24 that only through me are victory and **strength** to be found;
49. 4 I have used up my **strength,** but have accomplished nothing."
49. 5 he is the source of my **strength.**
50. 4 taught me what to say, so that I can **strengthen** the weary.
51.12 "I am the one who **strengthens** you.
54. 2 lengthen its ropes and **strengthen** the pegs!
57.10 idols give you **strength,** and so you never grow weak.
63. 1 dressed in red, marching along in power and **strength?"**
Jer 1.18 But today I am giving you the **strength** to resist them;
9.23 strong men of their **strength,** nor rich men of their wealth.
16.19 Lord, you are the one who protects me and gives me **strength;**
17. 5 and puts his trust in man, in the **strength** of mortal man.
27. 5 "By my great power and **strength** I created the world,
46.18 sea, so will be the **strength** of the one who attacks you.
48. 7 "Moab, you trusted in your **strength** and your wealth, but
49. 4 Your **strength** is failing.
51.12 **Strengthen** the guard!
Lam 1. 6 are weak from hunger, Whose **strength** is almost gone as they
2. 3 In his fury he shattered the **strength** of Israel;
Ezek 17. 9 It will not take much **strength** or a mighty nation to pull
22. 6 Israel's leaders trust in their own **strength** and commit murder.
22.14 any courage left or have **strength** enough to lift your hand
24.21 You are proud of the **strength** of the Temple.
30.18 and put an end to the **strength** they were so proud of.
30.25 Yes, I will weaken him and **strengthen** the king of Babylonia.
Dan 2.23 You have given me wisdom and **strength;**
2.41 will have something of the **strength** of iron, because there
8. 7 The ram had no **strength** to resist.
10. 8 I had no **strength** left, and my face was so changed that
10.17 I have no **strength** or breath left in me."
11.15 even the best of them will not have enough **strength.**
Hos 7. 9 reliance on foreigners has robbed them of their **strength.**
Amos 2.14 strong men will lose their **strength,** and soldiers will not
Mic 5. 4 rule his people with the **strength** that comes from the Lord
7.16 see this and be frustrated in spite of all their **strength.**
Nah 2.10 knees tremble, **strength** is gone;
3.14 prepare for a siege, and **strengthen** your fortresses!
Hab 3.19 The Sovereign Lord gives me **strength.**
Zech 4. 6 by military might or by your own **strength,** but by my spirit.
12. 5 'The Lord God Almighty gives **strength** to his people who live
Mk 12.30 your soul, with all your mind, and with all your **strength.'**
12.33 his heart and with all his mind and with all his **strength;**
Lk 10.27 your soul, with all your **strength,** and with all your mind';
21.36 that you will have the **strength** to go safely through all
22.32 And when you turn back to me, you must **strengthen** your brothers."
22.43 An angel from heaven appeared to him and **strengthened** him.
Acts 3.16 the power of his name that gave **strength** to this lame man.
3.20 times of spiritual **strength** will come from the Lord,
9.19 and after he had eaten, his **strength** came back.
9.31 the Holy Spirit it was **strengthened** and grew in numbers,
14.22 They **strengthened** the believers and encouraged them to remain
15.32 spoke a long time with them, giving them courage and **strength.**
15.41 He went through Syria and Cilicia, **strengthening** the churches.
18.23 region of Galatia and Phrygia, **strengthening** all the believers.
Rom 14.19 things that bring peace and that help to **strengthen** one another.
1 Cor 1.25 seems to be God's weakness is stronger than human **strength.**
10.13 he will give you the **strength** to endure it, and so provide
2 Cor 1. 6 helped and given the **strength** to endure with patience the same
Eph 1.19 the same as the mighty **strength** [20] which he used when he
6.10 Finally, build up your **strength** in union with the Lord
Phil 4.13 I have the **strength** to face all conditions by the power
Col 1.11 strong with all the **strength** which comes from his glorious power,
1.29 and struggle, using the mighty **strength** which Christ supplies
1 Thes 3. 2 We sent him to **strengthen** you and help your faith, [3] so that
3.13 In this way he will **strengthen** you, and you will be
2 Thes 2.17 encourage you and **strengthen** you to always do and say
3. 3 is faithful, and he will **strengthen** you and keep you safe
1 Tim 1.12 Christ Jesus our Lord, who has given me **strength** for my work.
2 Tim 1. 8 the Good News, as God gives you the **strength** to do it.
4.17 with me and gave me **strength,** so that I was able to
Heb 12.12 Lift up your tired hands, then, and **strengthen** your trembling knees!
13. 9 is good to receive inner **strength** from God's grace, and not
1 Pet 4. 1 you too must **strengthen** yourselves with the same way of
4.11 serves must serve with the **strength** that God gives him, so
5.10 and give you firmness, **strength,** and a sure foundation.
Rev 3. 2 So wake up, and **strengthen** what you still have before it
5.12 power, wealth, wisdom, and **strength,** honour, glory, and praise!"
14.10 he has poured at full **strength** into the cup of his anger!

STRETCH
[OUTSTRETCHED]

Gen 49. 9 and returning to his den, **Stretching out** and lying down.
49.14 a donkey That lies **stretched out** between its saddlebags.
Ex 15.12 You **stretched out** your right hand, and the earth swallowed
1 Sam 28.20 Saul fell down and lay **stretched out** on the ground,
1 Kgs 6.27 so that two of their **outstretched** wings touched each other
8. 7 Their **outstretched** wings covered the box and the poles it
8.38 Israel, out of heartfelt sorrow, **stretch out** their hands in
17.21 Then Elijah **stretched** himself out on the boy three times
2 Kgs 4.34 As he lay **stretched out** over the boy, the boy's body started
4.35 and then went back and again **stretched** himself over the boy.
1 Chr 5. 9 east as the desert that **stretches** all the way to the River
13. 9 the oxen stumbled, and Uzzah **stretched out** his hand and took
2 Chr 3.11 either side of the room, **stretching** across the full width of
5. 8 Their **outstretched** wings covered the Box and the carrying-poles.
6.29 Israel, out of heartfelt sorrow, **stretch out** their hands in
Ezra 9. 5 I knelt in prayer and **stretched out** my hands to the Lord
Job 26. 7 God **stretched out** the northern sky and hung the earth in
37.18 Can you help God **stretch out** the sky and make it as
38. 5 Who **stretched** the measuring-line over it?
Prov 8.27 in place, when he **stretched** the horizon across the ocean,
Is 5.25 his people and has **stretched out** his hand to punish them.
5.25 ended, but his hand will still be **stretched out** to punish.
9.12 his hand is still **stretched out** to punish.
9.17 ended, but his hand will still be **stretched out** to punish.
9.21 his hand is still **stretched out** to punish.
10. 4 his hand will still be **stretched out** to punish.
10.10 I **stretched out** my hand to punish those kingdoms
14.26 world, and my arm is **stretched out** to punish the nations."
14.27 he has **stretched out** his arm to punish, and no one can
19.16 the Lord Almighty has **stretched out** his hand to punish them.
23.11 The Lord has **stretched out** his hand over the sea and
25.11 They will **stretch out** their hands as if they were trying
28.20 a bed too short to **stretch out** on, with a blanket too
33.17 in splendour over a land that **stretches** in all directions.
40.22 He **stretched out** the sky like a curtain, like a tent in
42. 5 God created the heavens and **stretched** them out;
44.24 I alone **stretched out** the heavens;
45.12 By my power I **stretched out** the heavens;
51.13 Lord who made you, who **stretched out** the heavens and laid
51.16 I **stretched out** the heavens and laid the earth's foundations;
Jer 1. 9 Then the Lord **stretched out** his hand, touched my lips, and
4.31 Jerusalem gasping for breath, **stretching out** her hand and saying,
10.12 by his wisdom he created the world and **stretched out** the heavens.
15. 6 So I **stretched out** my hand and crushed you because I was
51.15 by his wisdom he created the world and **stretched out** the heavens.
Lam 1.17 "I **stretch out** my hands, but no one will help me.
Ezek 1.23 dome stood the creatures, each **stretching out** two wings
2. 9 I saw a hand **stretched out** towards me, and it was holding
6.14 Yes, I will **stretch out** my hand and destroy their country.
8. 3 He **stretched out** what seemed to be a hand and seized me
14.13 unfaithful to me, I will **stretch out** my hand and destroy its
Dan 10.16 who looked like a man, **stretched out** his hand and touched my
Amos 6. 4 will be for you that **stretch out** on your luxurious couches,
Mt 8. 3 Jesus **stretched out** his hand and touched him.
12.13 the man with the paralysed hand, **"Stretch out** your hand."
12.13 He **stretched it out,** and it became well again, just like
Mk 1.41 filled with pity, and **stretched out** his hand and touched him.
3. 5 Then he said to the man, **"Stretch out** your hand."
3. 5 He **stretched it out,** and it became well again.
Lk 1.51 He has **stretched out** his mighty arm and scattered the proud
5.13 Jesus **stretched out** his hand and touched him.
6.10 then he said to the man, **"Stretch out** your hand."
11.46 but you yourselves will not **stretch out** a finger to help
Jn 20.27 then **stretch out** your hand and put it in my side.
21.18 you are old, you will **stretch out** your hands and someone
Acts 4.30 **Stretch out** your hand to heal, and grant that wonders
26. 1 Paul **stretched out** his hand and defended himself as follows:

STRICT

1 Sam 8. 9 to them, but give them **strict** warnings and explain how their
2 Kgs 22. 2 ancestor King David, **strictly** obeying all the laws of God.
2 Chr 34. 2 ancestor King David, **strictly** obeying all the laws of God.
Dan 3.22 because the king had given **strict** orders for the furnace to
6. 7 Your Majesty should issue an order and enforce it **strictly.**
6.12 The king replied, "Yes, a **strict** order, a law of the Medes
Mk 5.43 But Jesus gave them **strict** orders not to tell anyone,
Lk 9.21 Then Jesus gave them **strict** orders not to tell this to anyone.
Acts 5.28 "We gave you **strict** orders not to teach in the name of
22. 3 I received **strict** instruction in the Law of our ancestors
26. 5 a member of the **strictest** party of our religion, the Pharisees.
1 Cor 9.25 in training submits to **strict** discipline, in order to be crowned
Jas 3. 1 we teachers will be judged with greater **strictness** than others.

STRIKE
[STRUCK]

Gen 4.23 I have killed a young man because he **struck** me.
19.11 Then they **struck** all the men outside with blindness, so
32.25 not winning the struggle, he **struck** Jacob on the hip, and it
32.32 because it was on this muscle that Jacob was **struck.**
49.17 snake beside the path, That **strikes** at the horse's heel, So
Ex 7.17 Look, I am going to **strike** the surface of the river with
7.20 Aaron raised his stick and **struck** the surface of the river,
7.25 Seven days passed after the Lord **struck** the river.
8.16 to Moses, "Tell Aaron to **strike** the ground with his stick,
8.17 So Aaron **struck** the ground with his stick, and all the
9.15 raised my hand to **strike** you and your people with disease,
9.23 Lord sent thunder and hail, and lightning **struck** the ground.
9.25 All over Egypt the hail **struck** down everything in the open,
17. 5 Take along the stick with which you **struck** the Nile.
17. 6 **Strike** the rock, and water will come out of it for the
Num 1.53 near and cause my anger to **strike** the community of Israel."
8.19 from the disaster that would **strike** them if they came too
14.36 And so the Lord **struck** them with a disease, and they died.
20.11 Moses raised the stick and **struck** the rock twice with it,
24.17 He will **strike** the leaders of Moab And beat down all the

Num	35.21	something at him [21] or by **striking** him with his fist, he is
Deut	28.22	The Lord will **strike** you with infectious diseases,
	28.28	he will **strike** you with blindness and confusion.
	32.25	terrors will **strike** in the homes.
Judg	5.26	she **struck** Sisera and crushed his skull;
	11.33	He **struck** at them from Aroer to the area round Minnith,
1 Sam	14.44	said to him, "May God **strike** me dead if you are not
	20.13	harm you, may the Lord **strike** me dead if I don't let
	25.22	May God **strike** me dead if I don't kill every last one
	25.38	Some ten days later the Lord **struck** Nabal and he died.
	26. 8	ground with just one blow—I won't have to **strike** twice!"
2 Sam	1.15	The man **struck** the Amalekite and mortally wounded him,
	1.22	Saul was merciless, **striking** down the mighty, killing the enemy.
	2.23	backward thrust of his spear, **struck** him through the belly
	3. 9	Now may God **strike** me dead if I don't make this come
	3.35	a solemn promise, "May God **strike** me dead if I eat anything
	19.13	May God **strike** me dead if I don't!"
	20.10	He died immediately, and Joab did not have to **strike** again.
	22.39	I **strike** them down, and they cannot rise;
1 Kgs	2.23	the Lord's name, "May God **strike** me dead if I don't make
	19. 2	"May the gods **strike** me dead if by this time tomorrow I
	20.10	May the gods **strike** me dead if I don't!"
	22.34	soldier shot an arrow which **struck** King Ahab between the
2 Kgs	2. 8	off his cloak, rolled it up, and **struck** the water with it;
	2.14	He **struck** the water with Elijah's cloak, and said,
	2.14	Then he **struck** the water again, and it divided, and he
	6.18	Elisha prayed, "O Lord, **strike** these men blind!"
	6.18	The Lord answered his prayer and **struck** them blind.
	6.31	He exclaimed, "May God **strike** me dead if Elisha is not
	9.24	strength shot an arrow that **struck** Joram in the back and
	13.18	to take the other arrows and **strike** the ground with them.
	13.18	The king **struck** the ground three times, and then stopped.
	13.19	the king, "You should have **struck** five or six times, and
	15. 5	The Lord **struck** Uzziah with a dreaded skin-disease that
2 Chr	13.20	Finally the Lord **struck** him down, and he died.
	18.33	soldier shot an arrow which **struck** King Ahab between the
	20. 9	that if any disaster **struck** them to punish them—a war,
	35.23	During the battle King Josiah was **struck** by Egyptian arrows.
Job	1.16	servant came and said, "Lightning **struck** the sheep and the
	19.21	The hand of God has **struck** me down.
	27.20	Terror will **strike** like a sudden flood;
	34.20	God **strikes** men down and they perish;
Ps	18.38	I **strike** them down, and they cannot rise;
	35. 6	and slippery while the angel of the Lord **strikes** them down!
	35.15	strangers beat me and kept **striking** me.
	38. 2	you have **struck** me down.
	69.23	**Strike** them with blindness!
	78.20	It is true that he **struck** the rock, and water flowed out
	91. 6	day [6] or the plagues that **strike** in the dark or the evils
	91.10	and so no disaster will **strike** you, no violence will
Prov	1.26	will mock you when terror **strikes**—[27] when it comes on you
	6.15	Because of this, disaster will **strike** them without warning,
	28.22	rich that they do not know when poverty is about to **strike.**
Song	5. 7	they **struck** me and bruised me;
Is	28.19	It will **strike** you again and again, morning after morning.
	30.32	As the Lord **strikes** them again and again, his people
	34. 5	heaven, and now it will **strike** Edom, those people whom he
	41. 2	His sword **strikes** them down as if they were dust.
Jer	5. 3	He **struck** you, but you paid no attention;
	14.15	war and starvation will not **strike** this land—I will kill
	15. 8	I suddenly **struck** them with anguish and terror.
	22.23	pitiful you'll be when pains **strike** you, pains like those of
	33. 5	whom I am going to **strike** down in my anger and fury.
	46.15	The Lord has **struck** him down!'
Ezek	17.10	Won't it wither when the east wind **strikes** it?
	21.14	Clap your hands, and the sword will **strike** again and again.
Dan	2.34	cliff without anyone touching it, **struck** the iron and clay
	2.45	touching it and how it **struck** the statue made of iron,
Amos	3. 6	Does disaster **strike** a city unless the Lord sends it?
	9. 1	**"Strike** the tops of the temple columns so hard that the
Hab	3.13	You **struck** down the leader of the wicked and completely
Zech	2. 8	Anyone who **strikes** you strikes what is most precious to me."
	10.11	trouble, I, the Lord, will **strike** the waves, and the depths
	14. 5	ancestors did when the earthquake **struck** in the time of King
	14.18	Shelters, then they will be **struck** by the same disease that
Mt	26.51	Jesus drew his sword and **struck** at the High Priest's slave,
Mk	14.47	there drew his sword and **struck** at the High Priest's slave,
Lk	22.50	And one of them **struck** the High Priest's slave and cut
Jn	18.10	a sword, drew it and **struck** the High Priest's slave, cutting
Acts	12.23	the angel of the Lord **struck** Herod down, because he did not
	23. 2	who were standing close to Paul to **strike** him on the mouth.
	23. 3	"God will certainly **strike** you—you whitewashed wall!
	23. 3	yet you break the Law by ordering them to **strike** me!"
Rev	8.12	third of the sun was **struck,** and a third of the moon,
	11. 6	they have authority also to **strike** the earth with every kind
	18. 8	one day she will be **struck** with plagues— disease,

STRINGED

Ps	33. 2	the Lord with harps, sing to him with **stringed** instruments.
	92. 3	night, [3] with the music of **stringed** instruments and with

STRIP (1)

Gen	30.37	almond, and plane trees and **stripped** off some of the bark so
Judg	14.19	where he killed thirty men, **stripped** them, and gave their
1 Sam	31. 9	They cut off Saul's head, **stripped** off his armour, and
2 Sam	23.10	to where Eleazar was and **stripped** the armour from the dead.
2 Kgs	18.16	he also **stripped** the gold from the temple doors and the
1 Chr	10. 9	They cut off Saul's head, **stripped** off his armour, and
Ps	29. 9	voice shakes the oaks and **strips** the leaves from the trees
Ps	76. 5	Their brave soldiers have been **stripped** of all they had
Is	3.26	will be like a woman sitting on the ground, **stripped** naked.
	32.11	**Strip** off your clothes and tie rags round your waist.
	45. 1	he sends him to **strip** kings of their power;
	47. 2	**Strip** off your fine clothes!
Jer	5.10	I will tell them to **strip** away the branches, because those
	6. 9	to me, "Israel will be **stripped** clean like a vineyard from
	13.26	The Lord himself will **strip** off your clothes and expose
	49.10	But I have **stripped** Esau's descendants completely
Ezek	12.19	Their land will be **stripped** bare, because everyone who lives
	16.36	"You **stripped** off your clothes and, like a prostitute, you
	16.37	circle, and then I will **strip** off your clothes and let them
	23.10	They **stripped** her naked, seized her sons and daughters,
	23.29	for and leave you **stripped** naked, exposed like a prostitute.
Dan	4.14	**strip** off its leaves and scatter its fruit.
Hos	2. 3	she does not, I will **strip** her as naked as she was
	2.10	I will **strip** her naked in front of her lovers, and no
	10. 5	They will wail when it is **stripped** of its golden splendour.
Joel	1. 7	They have **stripped** off the bark, till the branches are white.
Mic	3. 3	You **strip** off their skin, break their bones, and chop them
Nah	3. 5	I will **strip** you naked and let the nations see you, see
Zeph	2.14	The cedar-wood of her buildings will be **stripped** away.
Mt	27.28	They **stripped** off his clothes and put a scarlet robe on him.
Lk	10.30	robbers attacked him, **stripped** him, and beat him up, leaving

STRIP (2)

Ex	39. 3	and cut them into thin **strips** to be worked into the fine
Lk	2. 7	son, wrapped him in **strips of cloth** and laid him in a
	2.12	a baby wrapped in **strips of cloth** and lying in a manger."

STRIPE

Gen	30.35	the male goats that had **stripes** or spots and all the females
	30.37	of the bark so that the branches had white **stripes** on them.
	31. 8	striped goats shall be your wages,' all the flocks produced **striped** young.
	31.10	that the male goats that were mating were **striped,** spotted,
	31.12	'all the male goats that are mating are **striped,** spotted,

STRIVE

Ps	34.14	**strive** for peace with all your heart.
1 Cor	14. 1	It is love, then, that you should **strive** for.
2 Cor	13.11	**Strive** for perfection;
Phil	3.12	I keep **striving** to win the prize for which Christ Jesus has
1 Tim	6.11	**Strive** for righteousness, godliness, faith, love, endurance,
2 Tim	2.22	the passions of youth, and **strive** for righteousness, faith, love,
1 Pet	3.11	he must **strive** for peace with all his heart.

STROKE

1 Sam	25.37	He suffered a **stroke** and was completely paralysed.

STRONG

Gen	25.23	One will be **stronger** than the other;
	49. 3	of my manhood, The proudest and **strongest** of all my sons.
	49.24	And his arms are made **strong** By the power of the Mighty
Ex	1. 7	so numerous and **strong** that Egypt was filled with them.
	1. 9	Israelites are so numerous and **strong** that they are a threat
	1.20	And the Israelites continued to increase and become **strong.**
	10.19	east wind into a very **strong** west wind, which picked up the
	14.21	and the Lord drove the sea back with a **strong** east wind.
	15. 2	The Lord is my **strong** defender;
Num	11. 4	They had a **strong** craving for meat, and even the Israelites
	13.18	it is, how many people live there, and how **strong** they are.
	13.30	we are **strong** enough to conquer it."
	13.31	Caleb said, "No, we are not **strong** enough to attack them;
	21.24	because the Ammonite border was **strongly** defended.
Deut	1.28	that the people there are **stronger** and taller than we are,
	2.36	No town had walls too **strong** for us.
	9. 2	The people themselves are tall and **strong;**
	10.15	for your ancestors was so **strong** that he chose you instead
	33.11	Lord, help their tribe to grow **strong;**
	34. 7	he was as **strong** as ever, and his eyesight was still good.
Josh	14.11	old [11] and I'm just as **strong** today as I was when Moses
	14.11	I am still **strong** enough for war or for anything else.
	17.13	Even when the Israelites became **stronger,** they did not
	17.18	they do have iron chariots and are a **strong** people."
Judg	1.28	When the Israelites became **stronger,** they forced the
	3.12	this the Lord made King Eglon of Moab **stronger** than Israel.
	6. 2	The Midianites were **stronger** than Israel, and the people
	9.51	There was a **strong** tower there, and every man and woman
	14. 6	of the Lord made Samson **strong,** and he tore the lion apart
	14.14	Out of the **strong** came something sweet."
	14.18	What could be **stronger** than a lion?"
	14.19	of the Lord made him **strong,** and he went down to Ashkelon,
	15.14	of the Lord made him **strong,** and he broke the ropes round
	16. 5	you why he is so **strong** and how we can overpower him,
	16. 6	Delilah said to Samson, "Please tell me what makes you so **strong.**
	16.15	and you still haven't told me what makes you so **strong."**
	18.26	saw that they were too **strong** for him, so he turned and
1 Sam	2. 4	The bows of **strong** soldiers are broken, but the weak grow strong.
	13. 6	Then they launched a **strong** attack against the Israelites,
	14.52	found a man who was **strong** or brave, he would enlist him
	28.22	You must eat so that you will be **strong** enough to travel."
2 Sam	1.23	swifter than eagles, **stronger** than lions.
	2. 7	Be **strong** and brave!
	3. 1	As David became **stronger and stronger,** his opponents became weaker

2 Sam 5.10 He grew **stronger** all the time, because the Lord God
7.12 make one of your sons king and will keep his kingdom **strong.**
10.12 Be **strong** and courageous!
11.16 sent Uriah to a place where he knew the enemy was **strong.**
11.23 He said, "Our enemies were **stronger** than we were and
11.25 Tell him to launch a **stronger** attack on the city and capture
13.14 and since he was **stronger** than she was, he overpowered her
22. 2 he is my **strong** fortress.
22.18 all those who hate me— they were too **strong** for me.
22.33 This God is my **strong** refuge;
22.35 trains me for battle, so that I can use the **strongest** bow.
22.47 Proclaim the greatness of the **strong** God who saves me!
1 Kgs 20. 3 and gold, your women and the **strongest** of your children."
2 Kgs 2.16 and said, "There are fifty of us here, all **strong** men.
1 Chr 5. 2 Judah, however, that became the **strongest** and provided a
11. 9 David grew **stronger and stronger,**
11.10 as the Lord had promised, and they kept his kingdom **strong.**
17.11 make one of your sons king and will keep his kingdom **strong.**
19.13 Be **strong** and courageous!
29.12 and you are able to make anyone great and **strong.**
29.18 keep such devotion for ever **strong** in your people's hearts
2 Chr 11.11 He had them **strongly** fortified and appointed a commander
15. 7 But you must be **strong** and not be discouraged.
25. 8 that they will make you **stronger** in battle, but it is God
26.16 But when King Uzziah became **strong,** he grew arrogant,
26.17 priest, accompanied by eighty **strong** and courageous priests,
Neh 6. 9 I prayed, "But now, God, make me **strong!"**
8.10 The joy that the Lord gives you will make you **strong."**
Job 12.16 God is **strong** and always victorious;
12.23 He makes nations **strong** and great, but then he defeats
33.25 His body will grow young and **strong** again;
36. 5 How **strong** God is!
39. 4 In the wilds their young grow **strong;**
39.19 made horses so **strong** and gave them their flowing manes?
40. 9 Are you as **strong** as I am?
40.17 up like a cedar, and the muscles in his legs are **strong.**
40.18 His bones are as **strong** as bronze, and his legs are like
41.12 Leviathan's legs and describe how great and **strong** he is.
41.25 When he rises up, even the **strongest** are frightened;
Ps 18. 2 he is my **strong** fortress.
18.17 all those who hate me— they were too **strong** for me.
18.32 is the God who makes me **strong,** who makes my pathway safe.
18.34 trains me for battle, so that I can use the **strongest** bow.
24. 8 He is the Lord, **strong** and mighty, the Lord, victorious in battle.
31.24 Be **strong,** be courageous, all you that hope in the Lord.
35.10 You protect the weak from the **strong,** the poor from the oppressor."
38.19 My enemies are healthy and **strong;**
61. 3 for you are my protector, my **strong** defence against my enemies.
62. 3 attack a man who is no **stronger** than a broken-down fence?
62. 7 he is my **strong** protector;
69. 4 they are **strong** and want to kill me.
71. 3 Be my secure shelter and a **strong** fortress to protect me;
71. 7 example to many, because you have been my **strong** defender.
73. 4 they are **strong** and healthy.
75. 8 cup in his hand, filled with the **strong** wine of his anger.
78.31 with them and killed their **strongest** men, the best young men
78.65 he was like a **strong** man excited by wine.
80.15 that you planted, this young vine you made grow so **strong!**
80.17 the people you have chosen, the nation you made so **strong.**
83. 8 joined them as a **strong** ally of the Ammonites and Moabites,
84. 7 They grow **stronger** as they go;
85. 6 Make us **strong** again, and we, your people, will praise you.
87. 5 belong there and that the Almighty will make her **strong.**
89.21 strength will always be with him, my power will make him **strong.**
90.10 years is all we have— eighty years, if we are **strong;**
92.10 You have made me as **strong** as a wild ox;
92.14 bear fruit in old age and are always green and **strong.**
103. 5 good things, so that I stay young and **strong** like an eagle.
103.20 Praise the Lord, you **strong** and mighty angels,
105.24 to his people and made them **stronger** than their enemies.
105.37 silver and gold, and all of them were healthy and **strong.**
112. 7 his faith is **strong,** and he trusts in the Lord.
117. 2 His love for us is **strong** and his faithfulness is eternal.
118.14 The Lord makes me powerful and **strong;**
136.12 with his **strong** hand, his powerful arm;
140. 7 my **strong** defender, you have protected me in battle.
142. 6 they are too **strong** for me.
144.12 our sons in their youth be like plants that grow up **strong.**
147.10 His pleasure is not in **strong** horses, nor his delight in
147.13 He keeps your gates **strong;**
148. 8 snow and clouds, **strong** winds that obey his command.
148.14 He made his nation **strong,** so that all his people praise
Prov 8.14 I have understanding, and I am **strong.**
16.12 justice is what makes a government **strong.**
18.10 The Lord is like a **strong** tower, where the righteous can
18.11 wealth protects them like high, **strong** walls round a city.
18.19 will protect you like a **strong** city wall, but if you quarrel
21.22 take a city defended by **strong** men, and destroy the walls
24. 5 Being wise is better than being **strong;**
25.15 down the **strongest** resistance and can even convince rulers.
28. 2 But a nation will be **strong** and endure when it has intelligent,
29. 4 justice, the nation will be **strong,** but when he is only
30.26 they are not **strong** either, but they make their homes among
30.30 lions, **strongest** of all animals and afraid of none;
31.17 She is a hard worker, **strong** and industrious.
31.25 She is **strong** and respected and not afraid of the future.
Ecc 6.10 a man cannot argue with someone who is **stronger** than he.
12. 3 will tremble, and your legs, now **strong,** will grow weak.
Song 5.10 My lover is handsome and **strong;**
8. 6 passion is as **strong** as death itself.

Is 3.25 city, yes, even the **strongest** men, will be killed in war.
7. 8 Because Syria is no **stronger** than Damascus, its capital city,
7. 8 and Damascus is no **stronger** than King Rezin.
7. 9 Israel is no **stronger** than Samaria, its capital city,
7. 9 and Samaria is no **stronger** than King Pekah.
10.13 I am **strong** and wise and clever.
18. 2 divided by rivers, to your **strong** and powerful nation, to
18. 7 land divided by rivers, this **strong** and powerful nation,
26. 1 Our city is **strong!**
26. 5 he destroyed the **strong** city they lived in, and sent its
28. 2 The Lord has someone **strong** and powerful ready to attack them,
28.16 "I am placing in Zion a foundation that is firm and **strong.**
30.15 Then you will be **strong** and secure."
31. 3 When the Lord acts, the **strong** nation will crumble, and the
33.16 will be as secure as if you were in a **strong** fortress.
35. 4 Tell everyone who is discouraged, "Be **strong** and don't be afraid!
41.10 I will make you **strong** and help you;
44.12 His **strong** arm swings a hammer to pound the metal into shape.
52. 1 Jerusalem, be **strong** and great again!
54.14 Justice and right will make you **strong.**
58.11 I will keep you **strong** and well.
59.17 will clothe himself with the **strong** desire to set things
59.19 He will come like a rushing river, like a **strong** wind.
63. 5 But my anger made me **strong,** and I won the victory myself.
66.14 it will make you **strong** and healthy.
Jer 2.22 if you washed with the **strongest** soap, I would still see the
4.12 comes at the Lord's command will be much **stronger** than that!
5.15 It is a **strong** and ancient nation, a nation whose language
9.23 boast of their wisdom, nor **strong** men of their strength, nor
20. 7 You are **stronger** than I am, and you have overpowered me.
20.11 Lord, are on my side, **strong** and mighty, and those who
50. 9 stir up a group of **strong** nations in the north and make
50.34 will rescue them is **strong**—his name is the Lord Almighty.
51.53 the sky and build a **strong** fortress there, I would still
Lam 1.15 "The Lord jeered at all my **strongest** soldiers;
3.32 bring us sorrow, but his love for us is sure and **strong.**
4. 7 and pure as snow, vigorous and **strong,** glowing with health.
Ezek 7.24 Your **strongest** men will lose their confidence when I let the
13.11 will fall on it, and a **strong** wind will blow against it.
13.13 anger I will send a **strong** wind, pouring rain, and
16. 7 You grew **strong** and tall and became a young woman.
19.11 Its branches were **strong,** and grew to be royal sceptres.
19.14 The branches will never again be **strong,**
20.33 will rule over you with a **strong** hand, with all my power.
24.25 take away from them the **strong** Temple that was their pride
29.21 make the people of Israel **strong** and let you, Ezekiel, speak
30.21 it could heal and be **strong** enough to hold a sword again.
30.24 of the king of Babylonia **strong** and put my sword in his
34.16 those that are fat and **strong** I will destroy, because I am
34.20 I will judge between you **strong** sheep and the weak sheep.
Dan 1.15 up, they looked healthier and **stronger** than all those who
2.40 be a fourth empire, as **strong** as iron, which shatters and
2.42 part of the empire will be **strong** and part of it weak.
3.20 And he commanded the **strongest** men in his army to tie
4.22 "Your Majesty, you are the tree, tall and **strong.**
8.10 It grew **strong** enough to attack the army of heaven, the
8.22 and which will not be as **strong** as the first kingdom.
8.24 He will grow **strong**—but not by his own power.
9.25 be rebuilt with streets and **strong** defences, and will stand
10.18 Once more he took hold of me, and I felt **stronger.**
10.19 said this, I felt even **stronger** and said, "Sir, tell me
11. 5 "The king of Egypt will be **strong.**
11. 5 however, will be even **stronger** and rule a greater kingdom.
11.23 he will grow **stronger and stronger,** even though he rules
Hos 7.15 them up and made them **strong,** they plotted against me.
11. 8 My love for you is too **strong.**
Amos 2. 9 men who were as tall as cedar-trees and as **strong** as oaks.
2.14 **strong** men will lose their strength, and soldiers will not
6.13 You boast, "We were **strong** enough to take Karnaim."
Jon 1. 4 But the Lord sent a **strong** wind on the sea, and the
Mic 4.13 I will make you as **strong** as a bull with iron horns
5. 5 defences, we will send our **strongest** leaders to fight them.
Nah 1.12 "Even though the Assyrians are **strong** and numerous, they
Hab 1.12 Babylonians and made them **strong** so that they can punish us.
Zech 9.17 The young people will grow **strong** on its corn and wine.
10. 6 "I will make the people of Judah **strong;**
10. 7 people of Israel will be **strong** like soldiers, happy like
10.12 I will make my people **strong;**
12. 8 the weakest among them will become as **strong** as David was.
Mal 3. 2 He will be like **strong** soap, like a fire that refines metal.
Mt 12.29 one can break into a **strong** man's house and take
12.29 away his belongings unless he first ties up the **strong** man;
14.30 But when he noticed the **strong** wind, he was afraid and
Mk 3.27 one can break into a **strong** man's house and take
3.27 away his belongings unless he first ties up the **strong** man;
4.37 Suddenly a **strong** wind blew up, and the waves began to
5. 4 He was too **strong** for anyone to control him.
14.31 Peter answered even more **strongly,** "I will never say that,
Lk 1.15 He must not drink any wine or **strong** drink.
1.17 of the Lord, **strong** and mighty like the prophet Elijah.
2.40 The child grew and became **strong;**
8.23 Suddenly a **strong** wind blew down on the lake, and the boat
11.21 "When a **strong** man, with all his weapons ready, guards
11.22 But when a **stronger** man attacks him and defeats him,
14.31 and decide if he is **strong** enough to face that other king.
16. 3 I am not **strong** enough to dig ditches, and I am ashamed
22.59 hour later another man insisted **strongly,** "There isn't any doubt
23. 5 But they insisted even more **strongly,** "With his teaching he is
23.10 stepped forward and made **strong** accusations against Jesus.
Jn 6.18 By then a **strong** wind was blowing and stirring up the water.
Acts 2. 2 sky which sounded like a **strong** wind blowing, and it filled

Acts 3. 7 At once the man's feet and ankles became **strong;**
4.21 Council warned them even more **strongly** and then set them free.
15.16 I will rebuild its ruins and make it **strong** again.
16. 5 So the churches were made **stronger** in the faith and grew
18.28 For with his **strong** arguments he defeated the Jews
19.20 the word of the Lord kept spreading and growing **stronger.**
23. 9 the party of the Pharisees stood up and protested **strongly:**
27.14 But soon a very **strong** wind—the one called "North-easter"—
Rom 1.11 to share a spiritual blessing with you to make you **strong.**
11.17 and now you share the **strong** spiritual life of the Jews.
15. 1 We who are **strong** in the faith ought to help the weak
1 Cor 1.25 what seems to be God's weakness is **stronger** than human strength.
4.10 We are weak, but you are **strong!**
7.36 if his passions are too **strong** and he feels that they ought
10.22 Do we think that we are **stronger** than he?
15.43 when raised, it will be beautiful and **strong.**
16.13 Be alert, stand firm in the faith, be brave, be **strong.**
2 Cor 3. 7 was fading, it was so **strong** that the people of Israel could
7.15 his love for you grows **stronger,** as he remembers how all of
10.10 "Paul's letters are severe and **strong,** but when he is with
12.10 For when I am weak, then I am **strong.**
13. 9 We are glad when we are weak but you are **strong.**
Eph 3.16 through his Spirit to be **strong** in your inner selves,
Phil 2. 1 Your life in Christ makes you **strong,** and his love comforts you.
Col 1.11 May you be made **strong** with all the strength which
2. 7 lives on him, and become **stronger** in your faith, as you were
1 Thes 4. 6 you this before, and we **strongly** warned you that the Lord
2 Tim 2. 1 for you, my son, be **strong** through the grace that is ours
Heb 11.34 They were weak, but became **strong;**
Jas 3. 4 is and driven by such **strong** winds, it can be steered by
4. 2 you **strongly** desire things, but you cannot get them,
4. 6 But the grace that God gives is even **stronger.**
2 Pet 2.11 who are so much **stronger** and mightier than these false teachers,
1 Jn 2.14 I am writing to you, young men, because you are **strong;**
5. 9 God's testimony is much **stronger,** and he has given this testimony
Rev 6.13 figs falling from the tree when a **strong** wind shakes it.
14. 8 drink her wine—the **strong** wine of her immoral lust!"
18. 3 have drunk her wine—the **strong** wine of her immoral lust.
18. 6 with a drink twice as **strong** as the drink she prepared for

STRONGHOLD

Judg 9.46 in the **stronghold** of the temple of Baal-of-the-Covenant.
9.49 Abimelech and piled the wood up against the **stronghold.**
Amos 5. 9 He brings destruction on the mighty and their **strongholds.**
2 Cor 10. 4 but God's powerful weapons, which we use to destroy **strongholds.**

STRUGGLE

Gen 25.22 were born, they **struggled** against each other in her womb.
32.25 he was not winning the **struggle,** he struck Jacob on the hip,
32.28 You have **struggled** with God and with men, and you have won;
Prov 15.15 is a constant **struggle,** but happy people always enjoy life.
Is 19. 2 fight each other, and rival kings will **struggle** for power.
29. 4 be like a ghost **struggling** to speak from under the ground,
Hos 12. 3 Their ancestor Jacob **struggled** with his twin brother Esau
Col 1.29 this done I toil and **struggle,** using the mighty strength
1 Tim 4.10 We **struggle** and work hard, because we have placed our
Heb 10.32 you suffered many things, yet were not defeated by the **struggle.**
12. 4 For in your **struggle** against sin you have not yet had to

STRUTTING

Prov 30.31 goats, **strutting** cocks, and kings in front of their people.

STUBBLE

Obad 18 they will destroy the people of Esau as fire burns **stubble.**

STUBBORN

Ex 4.21 I will make the king **stubborn,** and he will not let the
7. 3 I will make the king **stubborn,** and he will not listen to
7.13 The king, however, remained **stubborn**
7.14 Moses, "The king is very **stubborn** and refuses to let the
7.22 means of their magic, and the king was as **stubborn** as ever.
8.15 frogs were dead, he became **stubborn** again and, just as the
8.19 But the king was **stubborn** and, just as the Lord had said,
8.32 this time the king became **stubborn,** and again he would not
9. 7 But he was **stubborn** and would not let the people go.
9.12 the Lord made the king **stubborn** and, just as the Lord had
9.34 and his officials remained as **stubborn** as ever [35] and, just
10. 1 made him and his officials **stubborn,** in order that I may
10.20 the Lord made the king **stubborn,** and he did not let the
10.27 The Lord made the king **stubborn,** and he would not let
11.10 but the Lord made him **stubborn,** and he would not let the
13.15 the king of Egypt was **stubborn** and refused to let us go,
14. 4 I will make him **stubborn,** and he will pursue you, and my
14. 8 The Lord made the king **stubborn,** and he pursued the Israelites,
14.17 will make the Egyptians so **stubborn** that they will go in
32. 9 I know how **stubborn** these people are.
33. 3 myself, because you are a **stubborn** people, and I might
33. 5 commanded Moses to say to them, "You are a **stubborn** people.
34. 9 These people are **stubborn,** but forgive our evil and our sin,
Lev 26.19 I will break your **stubborn** pride;
Deut 2.30 your God had made him **stubborn** and rebellious, so that we
9. 6 No, you are a **stubborn** people.
9.13 Lord also said to me, 'I know how **stubborn** these people are.
9.27 to the **stubbornness,** wickedness, and sin of this people.
10.16 from now on be obedient to the Lord and stop being **stubborn.**
Deut 21.18 has a son who is **stubborn** and rebellious, a son who will
21.20 to them, 'Our son is **stubborn** and rebellious and refuses to
29.19 be well with him, even if he **stubbornly** goes his own way.
31.27 I know how **stubborn** and rebellious they are.
32.20 those **stubborn,** unfaithful people.
1 Sam 6. 6 Why should you be **stubborn,** as the king of Egypt and the
2 Kgs 17.14 they were **stubborn** like their ancestors, who had not trusted
2 Chr 30. 8 Do not be **stubborn** as they were, but obey the Lord.
36.13 He **stubbornly** refused to repent and return to the Lord, the
Neh 9.16 grew proud and **stubborn** and refused to obey your commands.
9.29 Obstinate and **stubborn,** they refused to obey.
Job 15.26 he **stubbornly** holds up his shield and rushes to fight against God.
Ps 81.12 I let them go their **stubborn** ways and do whatever they wanted.
95. 8 "Don't be **stubborn,** as your ancestors were at Meribah, as
Prov 28.14 If you are **stubborn,** you will be ruined.
29. 1 If you get more **stubborn** every time you are corrected, one
Is 46.12 "Listen to me, you **stubborn** people who think that
48. 4 you would prove to be **stubborn,** as rigid as iron and
57.17 But they were **stubborn** and kept on going their own way.
63.17 do you make us so **stubborn** that we turn away from you?
65. 2 to welcome my people, who **stubbornly** do what is wrong and go
Jer 3.17 no longer do what their **stubborn** and evil hearts tell them.
5. 3 You were **stubborn** and would not turn from your sins.
5.23 You are **stubborn** and rebellious;
6.10 They are **stubborn** and refuse to listen to your message;
6.28 They are all **stubborn** rebels, hard as bronze and iron.
7.24 Instead, they did whatever their **stubborn** and evil hearts
7.26 became more **stubborn** and rebellious than your ancestors.
9.14 Instead, they have been **stubborn** and have worshipped the
11. 8 everyone continued to be as **stubborn** and evil as ever.
13.10 They have been as **stubborn** and wicked as ever, and have
16.12 All of you are **stubborn** and evil, and you do not obey
17.23 Instead, they became **stubborn;**
18.12 will all be just as **stubborn** and evil as we want to
19.15 I would, because you are **stubborn** and will not listen to
23.17 who is **stubborn** that disaster will never touch him."
Ezek 2. 4 They are **stubborn** and do not respect me, so I am sending
3. 7 All of them are **stubborn** and defiant.
3. 8 I will make you as **stubborn** and as tough as they are.
11.19 I will take away their **stubborn** heart of stone and will give
16.50 They were proud and **stubborn** and did the things that I hate,
36.26 I will take away your **stubborn** heart of stone and give you
Dan 5.20 But because he became proud, **stubborn,** and cruel, he was
8.23 there will be a **stubborn,** vicious, and deceitful king.
Hos 4.16 The people of Israel are as **stubborn** as mules.
8. 9 **Stubborn** as wild donkeys, the people of Israel go their own way.
Zech 7.11 "But my people **stubbornly** refused to listen.
Mk 3. 5 sorry for them, because they were so **stubborn** and wrong.
16.14 and because they were too **stubborn** to believe those who had
Acts 7.51 "How **stubborn** you are!"
19. 9 But some of them were **stubborn** and would not believe, and
Rom 2. 5 you have a hard and **stubborn** heart, and so you are making
9.18 anyone he wishes, and he makes **stubborn** anyone he wishes.
11.25 It is that the **stubbornness** of the people of Israel is not
Eph 4.18 life that God gives, for they are completely ignorant and **stubborn.**
Heb 3. 8 voice today, [8] do not be **stubborn,** as your ancestors were when
3.13 deceived by sin and become **stubborn,** you must help one another
3.15 voice today, do not be **stubborn,** as your ancestors were when
4. 7 "If you hear God's voice today, do not be **stubborn.**"

STUCK see STICK (2), STICK (3)

STUDY

Ex 13. 9 to continue to recite and **study** the Law of the Lord, because
Josh 1. 8 **Study** it day and night, and make sure that you obey
Ezra 7.10 had devoted his life to **studying** the Law of the Lord, to
Neh 8.13 the Levites, went to Ezra to **study** the teachings of the Law.
Job 5.27 Job, we have learnt this by long **study.**
Ps 1. 2 the Law of the Lord, and they **study** it day and night.
119.15 I **study** your instructions;
119.23 meet and plot against me, but I will **study** your teachings.
Prov 22.17 **Study** their teachings, [18] and you will be glad if you
Ecc 1.13 that I would examine and **study** all the things that are done
7.25 But I devoted myself to knowledge and **study;**
12. 9 He **studied** proverbs and honestly tested their truth.
12.12 the writing of books, and too much **study** will wear you out.
Is 47.13 you— those people who **study** the stars, who map out the
Ezek 43.10 of Israel about the Temple, and let them **study** its plan.
Dan 9. 2 of his reign, I was **studying** the sacred books and thinking
Mt 2. 1 afterwards, some men who **studied** the stars came from the east
Lk 1. 3 Excellency, because I have carefully **studied** all these matters
Jn 5.39 You **study** the Scriptures, because you think that in them
7.52 **Study** the Scriptures and you will learn that no prophet ever
Acts 17.11 and every day they **studied** the Scriptures to see if what
22. 3 but brought up here in Jerusalem as a **student** of Gamaliel.

STUFF

Deut 32.15 they were fat and **stuffed** with food.
Prov 23.20 who drink too much wine or **stuff** themselves with food.

STUMBLE

Lev 19.14 of a blind man so as to make him **stumble** over it.
26.37 You will **stumble** over one another when no one is chasing you,
2 Sam 6. 6 threshing-place of Nacon, the oxen **stumbled,** and Uzzah
1 Chr 13. 9 threshing-place of Chidon, the oxen **stumbled,** and Uzzah
Job 4. 4 When someone **stumbled,** weak and tired, your words encouraged him

Job 18. 7 His steps were firm, but now he **stumbles;**
Ps 20. 8 Such people will **stumble** and fall, but we will rise and
27. 2 men attack me and try to kill me, they **stumble** and fall.
107.27 they **stumbled** and staggered like drunken men— all
Prov 3.23 You can go safely on your way and never even **stumble.**
4.12 if you walk wisely, and you will not **stumble** when you run.
4.19 They fall, but cannot see what they have **stumbled** over.
24.17 enemy meets disaster, and don't rejoice when he **stumbles.**
Is 5.27 none of them **stumbles.**
8.14 awesome holiness I am like a stone that people **stumble** over;
8.15 Many will **stumble;**
28. 7 so much wine and liquor that they **stumble** in confusion.
28.13 Then you will **stumble** with every step you take.
59.10 We **stumble** at noon, as if it were night, as if we
59.14 Truth **stumbles** in the public square,
63.12 they were as sure-footed as wild horses, and never **stumbled.**
Jer 6.21 And so I will make these people **stumble** and fall.
13.16 he brings darkness, and you **stumble** on the mountains;
18.15 They have **stumbled** in the way they should go, they no longer
23.12 I will make them **stumble** and fall.
31. 9 of water, on a smooth road where they will not **stumble.**
46. 6 In the north, by the Euphrates, they **stumble** and fall.
46.16 Your soldiers have **stumbled** and fallen;
50.32 Your proud nation will **stumble** and fall, and no one will
Ezek 21.15 It makes my people lose courage and **stumble.**
Hos 5. 5 Their sins make them **stumble** and fall, and the people of
14. 1 Your sin has made you **stumble** and fall.
14. 9 but sinners **stumble** and fall because they ignore them.
Nah 2. 5 they **stumble** as they press forward.
3. 3 high, dead bodies without number— men **stumble** over them!
Hab 3.16 My body goes limp, and my feet **stumble** beneath me.
Jn 11. 9 in broad daylight does not **stumble,** for he sees the light of
11.10 during the night he **stumbles,** because he has no light."
Rom 9.32 so they stumbled over the **"stumbling stone"**
9.33 stone that will make people **stumble,** a rock that will make
11.11 When the Jews **stumbled,** did they fall to their ruin?
14.13 that would make your brother **stumble** or fall into sin.
1 Pet 2. 8 stone that will make people **stumble,** the rock that will make
2. 8 They **stumbled** because they did not believe in the word;

AV STUMBLINGBLOCK

Is 57.14 Remove every **obstacle** from their path!
Ezek 3.20 I put him in a **dangerous** situation, he will die if you
Rom 11. 9 may they **fall,** may they be punished!
1 Cor 1.23 Christ, a message that is **offensive** to the Jews and nonsense
8. 9 action make those who are weak in the faith **fall** into sin.

AV STUMBLINGSTONE see STUMBLE

STUMP

Job 14. 8 roots grow old, and its **stump** dies in the ground, [9]with
Is 6.13 he will be like the **stump** of an oak-tree that has been
6.13 (The **stump** represents a new beginning for God's people.)
11. 1 new branches sprout from a **stump,** so a new king will arise
Dan 4.15 But leave the **stump** in the ground with a band of iron
4.23 tree down and destroy it, but leave the **stump** in the ground.
4.26 The angel ordered the **stump** to be left in the ground.

STUNNED

Gen 45.26 Jacob was **stunned** and could not believe them.
1 Sam 3.11 terrible that everyone who hears about it will be **stunned.**
2 Kgs 19.26 they were frightened and **stunned.**
21.12 everyone who hears about it will be **stunned.**
Job 4. 5 to be in trouble, and you are too **stunned** to face it.
21. 6 has happened to me, I am **stunned,** and I tremble and shake.
Is 37.27 they were frightened and **stunned.**
Jer 19. 3 this place that everyone who hears about it will be **stunned.**

STUNTED

Lev 22.23 offer an animal that is **stunted** or not perfectly formed, but

STUPID

Job 11.12 **Stupid** men will start being wise when wild donkeys are born tame.
18. 3 What makes you think we are as **stupid** as cattle?
Ps 32. 9 Don't be **stupid** like a horse or a mule, which must be
49.10 that even wise men die, as well as foolish and **stupid** men.
73.22 my feelings were hurt, [22]I was as **stupid** as an animal;
82. 5 How **stupid!**
92. 6 a **stupid** man cannot understand:
94. 8 My people, how can you be such **stupid** fools?
Prov 1. 7 **Stupid** people have no respect for wisdom and refuse to learn.
1.32 **Stupid** people are destroyed by their own lack of concern.
3.35 gain an honourable reputation, but **stupid** men will only add
5.23 His utter **stupidity** will send him to his grave.
9.13 **Stupidity** is like a loud, ignorant, shameless woman.
10.13 **stupid** people need to be punished.
10.21 many people, but you can kill yourself with **stupidity.**
12. 1 It is **stupid** to hate being corrected.
12. 8 if you are **stupid,** people will look down on you.
12.11 to eat, but it is **stupid** to waste time on useless projects.
12.15 **Stupid** people always think they are right.
12.23 they know, but **stupid** people advertise their ignorance.
13.16 they act, but **stupid** people advertise their ignorance.
13.19 **Stupid** people refuse to turn away from evil.
Prov 13.20 If you make friends with **stupid** people, you will be ruined.
14. 8 Why is a **stupid** person foolish?
14.16 stay out of trouble, but **stupid** people are careless and act
14.29 you have a hot temper, you only show how **stupid** you are.
15. 2 knowledge attractive, but **stupid** people spout nonsense.
15.14 **stupid** people are satisfied with ignorance.
15.21 **Stupid** people are happy with their foolishness, but the
16.22 but trying to educate **stupid** people is a waste of time.
17.12 her cubs than to meet some fool busy with a **stupid** project.
18.13 If you don't you are being **stupid** and insulting.
19. 3 by their own **stupid** actions and then blame the Lord.
19.13 A **stupid** son can bring his father to ruin.
20. 1 It's **stupid** to get drunk.
20.16 Anyone **stupid** enough to promise to be responsible for a
21.20 in wealth and luxury, but **stupid** people spend their money as
24. 7 Wise sayings are too deep for a **stupid** person to understand.
24.30 through the fields and vineyards of a lazy, **stupid** man.
26. 8 Praising someone who is **stupid** makes as much sense as
26.11 A fool doing some **stupid** thing a second time is like a
26.12 The most **stupid** fool is better off than someone who
27. 3 nothing compared to the trouble that **stupidity** can cause.
27.13 **stupid** enough to promise to be responsible for a stranger's debts
29.11 **Stupid** people express their anger openly, but sensible
29.20 is more hope for a **stupid** fool than for someone who speaks
Ecc 7. 5 reprimand you than to have **stupid** people sing your praises.
7.25 and to learn how wicked and foolish **stupidity** is.
10. 1 and a little **stupidity** can cancel out the greatest wisdom.
10. 3 His **stupidity** will be evident even to strangers he meets
10. 6 **Stupid** people are given positions of authority while rich men are ignored.
10.15 Only someone too **stupid** to find his way home would wear
Is 19.11 Egypt's wisest men give **stupid** advice!
29. 9 Go ahead and be **stupid!**
32. 7 A **stupid** person is evil and does evil things;
44.18 Such people are too **stupid** to know what they are doing.
Jer 4.22 The Lord says, "My people are **stupid;**
5.21 Pay attention, you foolish and **stupid** people, who have
10. 8 All of them are **stupid** and foolish.
10.14 At the sight of this, men feel **stupid** and senseless;
10.21 I answered, "Our leaders are **stupid;**
51.17 At the sight of this, men feel **stupid** and senseless;
2 Cor 10.12 How **stupid** they are!
2 Tim 3. 9 get very far, because everyone will see how **stupid** they are.
Tit 3. 9 But avoid **stupid** arguments, long lists of ancestors, quarrels,
2 Pet 2.18 They make proud and **stupid** statements, and use immoral bodily

STUPOR

Nah 3.11 Nineveh, you too will fall into a drunken **stupor!**

SUB-CLAN

Num 4. 2 Levite clan of Kohath by **sub-clans** and families, [3]and to
4.22 Levite clan of Gershon by **sub-clans** and families, [23]and to
4.29 Levite clan of Merari by **sub-clans** and families, [30]and to
4.34 They did this by **sub-clans** and families and registered all
26.58 Their descendants included the **subclans** of Libni,

SUBDUE

2 Sam 22.48 he **subdues** the nations under me [49]and saves me from my foes.
Ps 18.47 he **subdues** the nations under me [48]and saves me from my foes.
144. 2 He **subdues** the nations under me.
Zech 1.11 found that the whole world lies helpless and **subdued."**

AV SUBDUE
see also **DEFEAT**

Num 32.22 the Lord defeats them [22]and takes **possession** of the land.
32.29 help you are able to **conquer** the land, then give them the
Deut 20.20 use them in the siege mounds until the city is **captured.**
Josh 18. 1 After they had **conquered** the land, the entire community of
Judg 4.23 That day God gave the Israelites **victory** over Jabin,
2 Sam 8.11 from the nations he had **conquered**—[12]Edom, Moab, Ammon,
22.40 You give me strength for the battle and **victory** over my enemies.
1 Chr 22.18 He let me **conquer** all the people who used to live in
Ps 18.39 You give me strength for the battle and **victory** over my enemies.
1 Cor 15.28 have been placed under Christ's **rule,** then he himself, the Son,
Heb 11.33 Through faith they fought whole countries and **won.**

SUBJECT (1)

Gen 3.16 desire for your husband, yet you will be **subject** to him."
Ex 21.22 husband demands, **subject** to the approval of the judges.
Judg 3.14 The Israelites were **subject** to Eglon for eighteen years.
2 Sam 3.28 "The Lord knows that my **subjects** and I are completely
8. 2 So the Moabites became his **subjects** and paid taxes to him.
8. 6 and they became his **subjects** and paid taxes to him.
8.14 throughout Edom, and the people there became his **subjects.**
10.19 When the kings who were **subject** to Hadadezer realized
10.19 they made peace with them and became their **subjects.**
22.44 people I did not know have now become my **subjects.**
1 Kgs 4.21 They paid him taxes and were **subject** to him all his life.
4.24 west of the Euphrates were **subject** to him, and he was at
12. 4 make life easier for us, we will be your loyal **subjects."**
1 Chr 18. 2 Moabites, who became his **subjects** and paid taxes to him.
18. 6 and they became his **subjects** and paid taxes to him.
18.13 Edom, and the people there became King David's **subjects.**
19.19 When the kings who were **subject** to Hadadezer realized
19.19 Israel, they made peace with David and became his **subjects.**
22.18 land, and they are now **subject** to you and to the Lord.

2 Chr 10. 4 make life easier for us, we will be your loyal **subjects."**
21.19 His **subjects** did not light a bonfire in mourning for him as
Ps 18.43 people I did not know have now become my **subjects.**
106.42 by their enemies and were in complete **subjection** to them.
Jer 34. 1 nations and races that were **subject** to him, were attacking
1 Cor 9.20 though I myself am not **subject** to the Law of Moses,
Gal 4.21 ask those of you who want to be **subject** to the Law:
5.18 the Spirit leads you, then you are not **subject** to the Law.

SUBJECT (2)

Ps 131. 1 with great matters or with **subjects** too difficult for me.
Rom 15.15 quite bold about certain **subjects** of which I have reminded you.
2 Pet 3.16 he says in all his letters when he writes on the **subject.**

AV SUBJECT
see also **OBEY**

Gen 16. 9 He said, "Go back to her and be her **slave."**
2 Sam 22.45 Foreigners **bow** before me;
Ps 18.44 Foreigners **bow** before me;
66. 3 is so great that your enemies **bow down** in fear before you.
68.30 until they all **bow down** and offer you their silver.
Rom 8.20 creation was **condemned** to lose its purpose, not of its own
1 Cor 14.32 should be under the speaker's **control,** [33]because God does not
16.16 beg you, my brothers, [16]to **follow** the leadership of such
Eph 5.24 And so wives must **submit** completely to their husbands
Heb 2. 5 not placed the angels as **rulers** over the new world to come
2. 8 glory and honour, [8]and made him **ruler** over all things."
2. 8 It says that God made man **"ruler** over all things";
2.15 set free those who were **slaves** all their lives because of
1 Pet 2.18 You servants must **submit** to your masters and show them complete
3.22 the right-hand side of God, **ruling** over all angels and heavenly
5. 5 you must put on the apron of humility, to **serve** one another;

AV SUBJECTION

Jer 34.11 took them back, and forced them to become **slaves** again.
34.16 as they desired, and you forced them into **slavery** again.
1 Cor 9.27 and bring it under complete **control,** to keep myself from being
2 Cor 9.13 glory to God for your **loyalty** to the gospel of Christ,
1 Tim 2.11 Women should learn in silence and all **humility.**
3. 4 family well and make his children **obey** him with all respect.
Heb 12. 9 then, should we **submit** to our spiritual Father and live!
1 Pet 3. 1 same way you wives must **submit** to your husbands, so that if
3. 5 make themselves beautiful by **submitting** to their husbands.

SUBMIT

Ex 10. 3 says 'How much longer will you refuse to **submit** to me?
2 Kgs 18. 7 against the emperor of Assyria and refused to **submit** to him.
24. 1 for three years Jehoiakim was forced to **submit** to his rule;
2 Chr 12.12 Because he **submitted** to the Lord, the Lord's anger did
Ps 32. 9 be controlled with a bit and bridle to make it **submit."**
Jer 27. 8 nation or kingdom will not **submit** to his rule, then I will
27. 9 They all tell you not to **submit** to the king of Babylonia.
27.11 But if any nation **submits** to the king of Babylonia and
27.12 King Zedekiah of Judah, **"Submit** to the king of Babylonia.
27.13 to any nation that does not **submit** to the king of Babylonia.
27.17 **Submit** to the king of Babylonia and you will live!
Lam 3.29 We should bow in **submission,** for there may still be hope.
5.11 in every Judaean village our daughters have been forced to **submit.**
Rom 10. 3 and so they did not **submit** themselves to God's way of
1 Cor 9.25 Every athlete in training **submits** to strict discipline,
Gal 6.13 they can boast that you **submitted** to this physical ceremony.
Eph 5.21 **Submit** yourselves to one another because of your reverence for Christ.
5.22 Wives, **submit** to your husbands as to the Lord.
5.24 And so wives must **submit** completely to their husbands
5.24 just as the church **submits** itself to Christ.
Col 3.18 Wives, **submit** to your husbands, for that is what you
Tit 2. 5 to be good housewives who **submit** to their husbands, so that
2. 9 Slaves are to **submit** to their masters and please them in
3. 1 Remind your people to **submit** to rulers and authorities,
Heb 12. 9 then, should we **submit** to our spiritual Father and live!
Jas 1.21 **Submit** to God and accept the word that he plants in your
4. 7 So then, **submit** to God.
1 Pet 2.13 For the sake of the Lord **submit** to every human authority:
2.18 You servants must **submit** to your masters and show them complete
3. 1 same way you wives must **submit** to your husbands, so that if
3. 5 make themselves beautiful by **submitting** to their husbands.
5. 5 the same way you younger men must **submit** to the older men.

SUBSTANCE

Mt 27.34 There they offered Jesus wine mixed with a bitter **substance;**

AV SUBSTANCE
see also **BEING**

Gen 12. 5 nephew Lot, and all the **wealth** and all the slaves they had
13. 6 of them to stay together, because they had too many **animals.**
15.14 that foreign land, they will take great **wealth** with them.
34.23 Won't all their livestock and everything else they **own** be ours?
36. 6 his livestock and all the **possessions** he had acquired in the
1 Chr 28. 1 clans, the supervisors of the **property** and livestock that
2 Chr 31. 3 From his own **flocks** and herds he provided animals for the
32.29 cattle and so much other **wealth** that he built many cities.
2 Chr 35. 7 from his own herds and **flocks** thirty thousand sheep, lambs,
Ezra 8.21 and protect us and our children and all our **possessions.**
10. 8 within three days, all his **property** would be confiscated,
Job 1. 3 and **owned** seven thousand sheep, three thousand camels,
15.29 nothing he **owns** will last.
22.20 All that the wicked **own** is destroyed, and fire burns up
Ps 105.21 him in charge of his **government** and made him ruler over all
Prov 1.13 We'll find all kinds of **riches** and fill our houses with loot!
3. 9 an offering from the best of all that your land **produces.**
28. 8 If you get **rich** by charging interest and taking advantage
29. 3 It is a foolish waste to spend **money** on prostitutes.
Hos 12. 8 'We've made a **fortune.**
Obad 13 and to seize their **riches** on the day of their disaster.
Lk 8. 3 used their own **resources** to help Jesus and his disciples.
15.13 far away, where he wasted his **money** in reckless living.
Heb 11. 1 have faith is to be **sure** of the things we hope for,

SUBSTITUTE

Lev 27.10 who made the vow may not **substitute** another animal for it.
27.33 animals are chosen, and he may not make any **substitutions.**
27.33 If he does **substitute** one animal for another, then both

SUCCEED (1)

Gen 24.12 my master Abraham, give me **success** today and keep your
24.21 her in silence, to see if the Lord had given him **success.**
24.40 obeyed, will send his angel with you and give you **success.**
24.42 master Abraham, please give me **success** in what I am doing.
24.56 The Lord has made my journey a **success;**
39. 2 The Lord was with Joseph and made him **successful.**
39. 3 Joseph and had made him **successful** in everything he did.
39.23 Lord was with Joseph and made him **succeed** in everything he did.
Num 14.41 You will not **succeed!**
Deut 29. 9 so that you will be **successful** in everything you do.
Josh 1. 7 neglect any part of it and you will **succeed** wherever you go.
1. 8 Then you will be prosperous and **successful.**
15.16 in marriage to the man who **succeeds** in capturing Kiriath Sepher."
Judg 1.12 in marriage to the man who **succeeds** in capturing Kiriath Sepher."
18. 5 ask God if we are going to be **successful** on our journey."
1 Sam 18. 5 David was **successful** in all the missions on which Saul sent him,
18.14 men in battle [14]and was **successful** in all he did, because
18.15 Saul noticed David's **success** and became even more afraid of him.
18.16 loved David because he was such a **successful** leader.
18.30 David was more **successful** than any of Saul's other officers.
26.25 You will **succeed** in everything you do!"
1 Kgs 2.33 the Lord will always give **success** to David's descendants who
22.13 the other prophets have prophesied **success** for the king, and
22.21 You will **succeed.' "**
2 Kgs 18. 7 Lord was with him, and he was **successful** in everything he did.
1 Chr 12.18 **Success** to you and those who help you!
22.11 promise to make you **successful** in building a temple for him.
22.13 the Lord gave to Moses for Israel, you will be **successful.**
29.23 He was a **successful** king, and the whole nation of Israel
2 Chr 7.11 Temple and the palace, **successfully** completing all his plans
8.16 Lord's Temple to its completion, all the work had been **successful.**
18.12 the other prophets have prophesied **success** for the king, and
18.21 You will **succeed.' "**
20.20 Believe what his prophets tell you, and you will **succeed."**
31.21 He was **successful,** because everything he did for the
32.30 Hezekiah **succeeded** in everything he did, [31]and even when
Ezra 9.12 to help them prosper or **succeed** if we wanted to enjoy the
Neh 1.11 Give me **success** today and make the emperor merciful to me."
2.20 I answered, "The God of Heaven will give us **success.**
Job 5.12 men in their own schemes, so that nothing they do **succeeds;**
10.16 If I have any **success** at all, you hunt me down like
20.22 At the height of his **success** all the weight of misery
21.16 They claim they **succeed** by their own strength, but their
22.28 You will **succeed** in all you do, and light will shine on
Ps 1. 3 They **succeed** in everything they do.
10. 5 A wicked man **succeeds** in everything.
20. 4 give you what you desire and make all your plans **succeed.**
21.11 plans, and plot against him, but they will not **succeed.**
35.27 He is pleased with the **success** of his servant."
37. 7 those who prosper or those who **succeed** in their evil plans.
49.18 is praised because he is **successful,** [19]he will join all
89.22 His enemies will never **succeed** against him;
90.17 Give us **success** in all we do!
118.25 Give us **success,** O Lord!
119.87 They have almost **succeeded** in killing me, but I have not
140. 8 don't let their plots **succeed.**
140.11 May those who accuse others falsely not **succeed;**
Prov 2. 5 to fear the Lord and you will **succeed** in learning about God.
8.18 I have riches and honour to give, prosperity and **success.**
15.22 Get all the advice you can, and you will **succeed;**
16. 3 plans, and you will be **successful** in carrying them out.
16.20 Pay attention to what you are taught, and you will be **successful;**
20.18 Get good advice and you will **succeed;**
28.13 You will never **succeed** in life if you try to hide your
Ecc 4. 4 I have also learnt why people work so hard to **succeed:**
7.18 If you have reverence for God, you will be **successful** anyway.
Is 8.10 But they will never **succeed.**
28.29 The plans God makes are wise, and they always **succeed!**
48.15 I led him out and gave him **success.**
52.13 "My servant will **succeed** in his task;
53.10 live a long life, and through him my purpose will **succeed.**
65.23 work they do will be **successful,** and their children will not
Jer 12. 1 Why do dishonest men **succeed?**
15.15 not be so patient with them that they **succeed** in killing me.

Jer 20.11 They will be disgraced for ever, because they cannot **succeed.**
22.30 to lose his children, to be a man who will never **succeed.**
32. 5 Even if he fights the Babylonians, he will not be **successful.**
Lam 1. 5 Her enemies **succeeded;**
Ezek 17.15 Will he **succeed?**
Dan 8.12 The horn was **successful** in everything it did.
8.24 He will cause terrible destruction and be **successful**
8.25 Because he is cunning, he will **succeed** in his deceitful ways.
11.17 but his plan will not **succeed.**
11.25 king of Egypt will be deceived and will not be **successful.**
Zech 4. 6 "You will **succeed,** not by military might or by your own strength,
Mt 23.15 and when you **succeed,** you make him twice as deserving of
Lk 23.23 Jesus should be crucified, and finally their shouting **succeeded.**
Jn 12.19 to one another, "You see, we are not **succeeding** at all!
Acts 19.26 at all, and he has **succeeded** in convincing many people,
Rom 14. 4 his own Master who will decide whether he **succeeds** or fails.
14. 4 will succeed, because the Lord is able to make him **succeed.**
2 Cor 13. 7 show that we are a **success,** but so that you may do
Phil 3.12 that I have already **succeeded** or have already become perfect.
Jas 1. 3 know that when your faith **succeeds** in facing such trials,
1.12 under trials, because when he **succeeds** in passing such a test,

SUCCEED (2)

Ex 29.30 The son of Aaron who **succeeds** him as priest and who goes
Lev 16.32 properly ordained and consecrated to **succeed** his father, is
Num 27.19 and there before them all proclaim him as your **successor.**
27.23 hands on Joshua's head and proclaimed him as his **successor.**
Deut 10. 6 and was buried, and his son Eleazar **succeeded** him as priest.
34. 9 wisdom, because Moses had appointed him to be his **successor.**
1 Kgs 1.13 promise me that my son Solomon would **succeed** you as king?
1.20 to you to tell them who is to **succeed** you as king.
1.24 "Your Majesty, have you announced that Adonijah would **succeed** you
1.27 even tell your officials who is to **succeed** you as king?"
1.30 God of Israel, that your son Solomon would **succeed** me as king."
1.35 He will **succeed** me as king, because he is the one I
1.48 made one of my descendants **succeed** me as king, and has let
2.12 Solomon **succeeded** his father David as king, and his
3. 7 God, you have let me **succeed** my father as king, even though
5. 1 he heard that Solomon had **succeeded** his father David as king
5. 7 such a wise son to **succeed** him as king of that great
8.20 I have **succeeded** my father as king of Israel, and I have
11.43 David's City, and his son Rehoboam **succeeded** him as king.
14.20 and was buried, and his son Nadab **succeeded** him as king.
14.31 in David's City, and his son Abijah **succeeded** him as king.
15. 8 in David's City, and his son Asa **succeeded** him as king.
15.24 and his son Jehoshaphat **succeeded** him as king.
15.28 And so Baasha **succeeded** Nadab as king of Israel.
16. 6 buried in Tirzah, and his son Elah **succeeded** him as king.
16.10 Zimri entered the house, assassinated Elah, and **succeeded** him
16.28 buried in Samaria, and his son Ahab **succeeded** him as king.
19.16 Elisha son of Shaphat from Abel Meholah to **succeed** you as prophet.
22.40 At his death his son Ahaziah **succeeded** him as king.
22.50 in David's City, and his son Jehoram **succeeded** him as king.
2 Kgs 1.17 sons, so his brother Joram **succeeded** him as king in the
2. 9 power that will make me your **successor,"** Elisha answered.
3.27 eldest son, who was to **succeed** him as king, and offered him
8.15 And Hazael **succeeded** Benhadad as king of Syria.
8.24 in David's City, and his son Ahaziah **succeeded** him as king.
10.35 in Samaria, and his son Jehoahaz **succeeded** him as king.
12.20 in David's City, and his son Amaziah **succeeded** him as king.
13. 9 in Samaria, and his son Jehoash **succeeded** him as king.
13.13 in Samaria, and his son Jeroboam II **succeeded** him as king.
14.16 in Samaria, and his son Jeroboam II **succeeded** him as king.
14.29 royal tombs, and his son Zechariah **succeeded** him as king.
15. 7 in David's City, and his son Jotham **succeeded** him as king.
15.10 King Zechariah, assassinated him at Ibleam, and **succeeded** him
15.14 assassinated Shallum, and **succeeded** him as king.
15.22 and was buried, and his son Pekahiah **succeeded** him as king.
15.25 inner fortress in Samaria, and **succeeded** him as king.
15.30 assassinated him, and **succeeded** him as king.
15.38 and his son Ahaz **succeeded** him as king.
16.20 and his son Hezekiah **succeeded** him as king.
19.37 Another of his sons, Esarhaddon, **succeeded** him as emperor.
20.21 Hezekiah died, and his son Manasseh **succeeded** him as king.
21.18 and his son Amon **succeeded** him as king.
21.26 and his son Josiah **succeeded** him as king.
23.34 Eliakim king of Judah as **successor** to Josiah, and changed
24. 6 Jehoiakim died, and his son Jehoiachin **succeeded** him as king.
1 Chr 27. 2 (his son Amizzabad **succeeded** him as commander of this group)
27. 2 Asahel, brother of Joab (his son Zebadiah **succeeded** him)
28. 8 you may hand it on to **succeeding** generations for ever."
29.23 So Solomon **succeeded** his father David on the throne
29.28 and respected, and his son Solomon **succeeded** him as king.
2 Chr 1. 8 father David, and now you have let me **succeed** him as king.
6.10 I have **succeeded** my father as king of Israel, and I have
9.31 David's City, and his son Rehoboam **succeeded** him as king.
11.14 Jeroboam of Israel and his **successors** would not let them
11.22 children, choosing him as the one to **succeed** him as king.
12.16 in David's City and his son Abijah **succeeded** him as king.
14. 1 His son Asa **succeeded** him as king, and under Asa the land
17. 1 Jehoshaphat **succeeded** his father Asa as king and
21. 1 in David's City and his son Jehoram **succeeded** him as king.
21. 3 because Jehoram was the eldest, Jehoshaphat made him his **successor.**
21.13 as Ahab and his **successors** led Israel into unfaithfulness.
22. 1 of Jerusalem made Ahaziah king as his father's **successor.**
24.27 His son Amaziah **succeeded** him as king.
26. 1 chose Amaziah's sixteen-year-old son Uzziah to **succeed** his father
2 Chr 26.23 His son Jotham **succeeded** him as king.
27. 9 in David's City and his son Ahaz **succeeded** him as king.
28.27 His son Hezekiah **succeeded** him as king.
32.33 His son Manasseh **succeeded** him as king.
33.20 at the palace, and his son Amon **succeeded** him as king.
36. 8 His son Jehoiachin **succeeded** him as king.
Ps 45.16 will have many sons to **succeed** your ancestors as kings, and
132.12 their sons, also, will **succeed** you for all time as kings."
Ecc 2.18 to leave it to my **successor,** [19] and he might be wise, or
Is 9. 7 will rule as King David's **successor,** basing his power on
19.11 that they are **successors** to the ancient scholars and kings?
37.38 Another of his sons, Esarhaddon, **succeeded** him as emperor.
Jer 22.11 Josiah's son Joahaz, who **succeeded** his father as king of Judah,
22.30 descendants who will rule in Judah as David's **successors.**
Mt 2.22 Joseph heard that Archelaus had **succeeded** his father Herod
Acts 24.27 After two years had passed, Porcius Festus **succeeded** Felix as governor.

SUDAN

Country s. of Egypt, called "Ethiopia" or "Cush" in other translations.

2 Sam 18.21 Then he said to his **Sudanese** slave, "Go and tell the
18.31 Then the **Sudanese** slave arrived and said to the king,
2 Kgs 19. 9 led by King Tirhakah of **Sudan,** was coming to attack them.
2 Chr 12. 3 be counted, including Libyan, Sukkite, and **Sudanese** troops.
14. 9 A **Sudanese** named Zerah invaded Judah with an army of a
14.12 The Lord defeated the **Sudanese** army when Asa and the
14.13 So many of the **Sudanese** were killed that the army was unable
16. 8 Didn't the **Sudanese** and the Libyans have large armies with
21.16 Arabs lived near where some **Sudanese** had settled along the coast.
Esth 1. 1 Xerxes ruled over 127 provinces, all the way from India to **Sudan.**
8. 9 and officials of all the 127 provinces from India to **Sudan.**
Ps 68.31 the **Sudanese** will raise their hands in prayer to God.
87. 4 of Jerusalem the people of Philistia, Tyre, and **Sudan."**
Is 11.11 in the lands of Pathros, **Sudan,** Elam, Babylonia, and Hamath,
18. 1 Beyond the rivers of **Sudan** there is a land where the sound
18. 5 the enemy will destroy the **Sudanese** as easily as a knife
20. 3 This is a sign of what will happen to Egypt and **Sudan.**
20. 5 have put their trust in **Sudan** and have boasted about Egypt
37. 9 led by King Tirhakah of **Sudan,** was coming to attack them.
43. 3 I will give up **Sudan** and Seba.
45.14 "The wealth of Egypt and **Sudan** will be yours, and the tall
Jer 38. 7 Ebedmelech the **Sudanese,** a eunuch who worked in the royal palace,
39.16 to tell Ebedmelech the **Sudanese** that the Lord Almighty,
46. 9 men from **Sudan** and Libya, carrying shields,
Ezek 29.10 of Aswan in the south, all the way to the **Sudanese** border.
30. 4 There will be war in Egypt And great distress in **Sudan.**
30. 5 kill the soldiers hired from **Sudan,** Lydia, Libya, Arabia,
30. 9 unsuspecting people of **Sudan,** and they will be terrified.
38. 5 Men from Persia, **Sudan,** and Libya are with him, and all
Dan 11.43 He will conquer Libya and **Sudan.**
Amos 9. 7 as much of the people of **Sudan** as I do of you.
Nah 3. 9 She ruled **Sudan** and Egypt, there was no limit to her power;
Zeph 2.12 The Lord will also put the people of **Sudan** to death.
3.10 Even from distant **Sudan** my scattered people will bring offerings

SUDDEN

Gen 15.17 fire-pot and a flaming torch **suddenly** appeared and passed
19.24 **Suddenly** the Lord rained burning sulphur on the cities
29. 2 **Suddenly** he came upon a well out in the fields with three
37.25 While they were eating, they **suddenly** saw a group of
43.18 They will **suddenly** attack us, take our donkeys, and make us
43.30 Then Joseph left **suddenly,** because his heart was full of
Ex 2. 5 **Suddenly** she noticed the basket in the tall grass and sent a
12.39 driven out of Egypt so **suddenly** that they did not have time
16.10 turned towards the desert, and **suddenly** the dazzling light
Lev 9.24 **Suddenly** the Lord sent a fire, and it consumed the
10. 2 **Suddenly** the Lord sent fire, and it burnt them to death
Num 6. 9 is right beside someone who **suddenly** dies, he must wait
11.31 **Suddenly** the Lord sent a wind that brought quails from the sea,
12. 4 **Suddenly** the Lord said to Moses, Aaron, and Miriam, "I
12.10 the Tent, Miriam's skin was **suddenly** covered with a dreaded
14.10 stone them to death, but **suddenly** the people saw the
16.19 **Suddenly** the dazzling light of the Lord's presence appeared
Josh 5.13 Joshua was near Jericho, he **suddenly** saw a man standing in
Judg 9.33 morning at sunrise and make a **sudden** attack on the city.
14. 6 **Suddenly** the power of the Lord made Samson strong, and he
14.19 **Suddenly** the power of the Lord made him strong, and he
15.14 **Suddenly** the power of the Lord made him strong, and he broke
19.22 themselves when all of a **sudden** some sexual perverts from
20.33 Baaltamar, the men surrounding Gibeah **suddenly** rushed out of
Ruth 3. 8 the night he woke up **suddenly,** turned over, and was
1 Sam 4.19 were dead, she **suddenly** went into labour and gave birth.
6.13 wheat in the valley, when **suddenly** they looked up and saw
10. 6 **Suddenly** the spirit of the Lord will take control of you,
10.10 **Suddenly** the spirit of God took control of him, and he
18.10 an evil spirit from God **suddenly** took control of Saul, and
25.20 bend on a hillside when **suddenly** she met David and his men
2 Sam 16. 1 of the hill, he was **suddenly** met by Ziba, the servant of
18. 9 **Suddenly** Absalom met some of David's men.
1 Kgs 8.10 leaving the Temple, it was **suddenly** filled with a cloud
13. 5 The altar **suddenly** fell apart and the ashes spilt to the ground,
18. 7 As Obadiah was on his way, he **suddenly** met Elijah.
19. 5 **Suddenly** an angel touched him and said, "Wake up and eat."
19. 9 **Suddenly** the Lord spoke to him, "Elijah, what are you doing here?"
2 Kgs 2.11 then **suddenly** a chariot of fire pulled by horses of fire

2 Kgs 4.19 **Suddenly** he cried out to his father, "My head hurts!
6. 5 was cutting down a tree, **suddenly** his iron axe-head fell in
8.11 **Suddenly** Elisha burst into tears.
2 Chr 5.11 leaving the Temple, it was **suddenly** filled with a cloud
Job 1.15 **Suddenly** the Sabeans attacked and stole them all.
5. 3 secure, but I called down a **sudden** curse on their homes.
9.23 When an innocent man **suddenly** dies, God laughs.
22.10 pitfalls all round you, and **suddenly** you are full of fear.
27.20 Terror will strike like a **sudden** flood;
34.20 A man may **suddenly** die at night.
Ps 2.12 anger will be quickly aroused, and you will **suddenly** die.
6.10 in **sudden** confusion they will be driven away.
64. 7 But God shoots his arrows at them, and **suddenly** they are wounded.
78.33 days like a breath and their lives with **sudden** disaster.
91. 5 any dangers at night or **sudden** attacks during the day [6] or
Prov 3.25 not have to worry about **sudden** disasters, such as come on
5.14 And **suddenly** I found myself publicly disgraced."
7.22 **Suddenly** he was going with her like an ox on the way
28.18 If you are dishonest, you will **suddenly** fall.
Ecc 9. 3 minds are full of evil and madness, and **suddenly** they die.
9.12 Like birds **suddenly** caught in a trap, like fish caught in a
Is 21. 5 **Suddenly** the command rings out:
21. 9 **Suddenly,** here they come!
25. 7 Here he will **suddenly** remove the cloud of sorrow that has
29. 5 **Suddenly** and unexpectedly [6] the Lord Almighty will rescue
30.13 **suddenly** you will collapse.
47.11 Ruin will come on you **suddenly**— ruin you never dreamt of!
48. 3 then **suddenly** I made it happen.
66. 7 is like a woman who **suddenly** gives birth to a child, without
Jer 4.20 **Suddenly** our tents are destroyed;
6.26 the one who comes to destroy you will **suddenly** attack.
15. 8 I **suddenly** struck them with anguish and terror.
49.19 and make the Edomites run away **suddenly** from their country.
50.44 and make the Babylonians run away **suddenly** from their city.
51. 8 Babylonia has **suddenly** fallen and is destroyed!
Lam 4. 6 which met with a **sudden** downfall at the hands of God.
Ezek 8. 1 **Suddenly** the power of the Sovereign Lord came on me.
Dan 3.24 **Suddenly** Nebuchadnezzar leapt to his feet in amazement.
5. 5 **Suddenly** a human hand appeared and began writing on the
8. 2 In the vision I **suddenly** found myself in the walled city
8.15 what the vision meant, when **suddenly** someone was standing in
Zeph 1.18 will put an end—a **sudden** end—to everyone who lives on
Mal 3. 1 Lord you are looking for will **suddenly** come to his Temple.
Mt 8.24 **Suddenly** a fierce storm hit the lake, and the boat was
28. 2 **Suddenly** there was a violent earthquake;
28. 9 **Suddenly** Jesus met them and said, "Peace be with you."
Mk 4.37 **Suddenly** a strong wind blew up, and the waves began to
13.36 If he comes **suddenly,** he must not find you asleep.
Lk 2.13 **Suddenly** a great army of heaven's angels appeared with the angel,
8.23 **Suddenly** a strong wind blew down on the lake, and the boat
9.30 **Suddenly** two men were there talking with him.
9.39 spirit attacks him with a **sudden** shout and throws him into a
21.34 life, or that Day may **suddenly** catch you [35] like a trap.
24. 4 about this, when **suddenly** two men in bright shining clothes
24.36 were telling them this, **suddenly** the Lord himself stood among them
Acts 1.10 two men dressed in white **suddenly** stood beside them [11] and said,
2. 2 **Suddenly** there was a noise from the sky which sounded like
9. 3 near the city of Damascus, **suddenly** a light from the sky
10.30 **Suddenly** a man dressed in shining clothes stood in front of
12. 7 **Suddenly** an angel of the Lord stood there, and a light
12.10 They walked down a street, and **suddenly** the angel left Peter.
16.26 **Suddenly** there was a violent earthquake, which shook the prison
22. 6 midday a bright light from the sky flashed **suddenly** round me.
28. 6 were waiting for him to swell up or **suddenly** fall down dead.
1 Thes 5. 3 "Everything is quiet and safe," then **suddenly** destruction will hit
5. 3 It will come as **suddenly** as the pains that come upon a
2 Pet 2. 1 and so they will bring upon themselves **sudden** destruction.

SUE

Mt 5.40 takes you to court to **sue** you for your shirt, let him

SUFFER

Gen 31.40 Many times I **suffered** from the heat during the day and
41.51 me forget all my **sufferings** and all my father's family";
42.21 another, "Yes, now we are **suffering** the consequences of
42.36 I am the one who **suffers!"**
Ex 3. 7 I know all about their **sufferings,** [8] and so I have come down
Lev 5. 1 he has seen or heard, he must **suffer** the consequences.
7.18 unclean, and whoever eats it will **suffer** the consequences.
17.16 If he does not, he must **suffer** the consequences.
20.17 had intercourse with his sister and must **suffer** the consequences.
20.19 aunt, both of them must **suffer** the consequences for incest.
24.15 anyone who curses God must **suffer** the consequences [16] and
Num 5.31 but the woman, if guilty, must **suffer** the consequences.
9.13 He must **suffer** the consequences of his sin.
12.11 do not make us **suffer** this punishment for our foolish sin.
14.33 for forty years, **suffering** for your unfaithfulness,
14.34 You will **suffer** the consequences of your sin for forty years,
18. 1 sons, and the Levites must **suffer** the consequences of any
18. 1 you and your sons will **suffer** the consequences of service in
20.14 we have **suffered,** [15] how our ancestors went to Egypt,
30.15 annuls the vow, he must **suffer** the consequences for the
Deut 16. 3 be called the bread of **suffering**—so that as long as you
16. 3 the day you came out of Egypt, that place of **suffering.**
24. 8 "When you are **suffering** from a dreaded skin-disease, be
26. 7 He heard us and saw our **suffering,** hardship, and misery.
Deut 28.34 Your **sufferings** will make you lose your mind.
29.22 will see the disasters and **sufferings** that the Lord has
Josh 22.17 We are still **suffering** because of that.
Judg 2.18 because they groaned under their **suffering** and oppression.
9.57 men of Shechem **suffer** for their wickedness, just as Jotham,
1 Sam 9.16 I have seen the **suffering** of my people and have heard their
25.37 He **suffered** a stroke and was completely paralysed.
2 Sam 19. 7 be the worst disaster you have **suffered** in all your life."
1 Kgs 2. 5 for what he did, and I **suffer** the consequences.
2 Kgs 5. 1 a great soldier, but he **suffered** from a dreaded skin-disease.
7. 3 Four men who were **suffering** from a dreaded skin-disease
14.26 The Lord saw the terrible **suffering** of the Israelites;
19. 3 "Today is a day of **suffering;**
2 Chr 21.15 You yourself will **suffer** a painful disease of the
32.25 Lord had done for him, and Judah and Jerusalem **suffered** for it.
33.12 In his **suffering** he became humble, turned to the Lord his God,
Neh 9. 9 "You saw how our ancestors **suffered** in Egypt;
9.32 Assyrian kings oppressed us, even till now, how much we have **suffered!**
9.32 prophets, our ancestors, and all our people have **suffered.**
9.32 Remember how much we have **suffered!**
Esth 9.25 with the result that Haman **suffered** the fate he had planned
Job 2.10 In spite of everything he **suffered,** Job said nothing against God.
2.11 how much Job had been **suffering,** they decided to go and
2.13 saying a word, because they saw how much he was **suffering.**
9.27 to forget my pain, all my **suffering** comes back to haunt me;
17. 5 his friends for money, and his children **suffer** for it.
21.13 They live out their lives in peace and quietly die without **suffering.**
30.16 there is no relief for my **suffering.**
30.27 I have had day after day of **suffering.**
31.29 been glad when my enemies **suffered,** or pleased when they met
35. 8 It is your fellow-man who **suffers** from your sins, and the
36. 8 are bound in chains, **suffering** for what they have done,
36.15 But God teaches men through **suffering** and uses distress
36.21 your **suffering** was sent to keep you from it.
37.17 No, you can only **suffer** in the heat when the south wind
Ps 9.12 God remembers those who **suffer;**
9.13 See the **sufferings** my enemies cause me!
10.12 Remember those who are **suffering!**
10.14 of trouble and **suffering** and are always ready to help.
17.14 Punish them with the **sufferings** you have stored up for them;
22.24 He does not neglect the poor or ignore their **suffering;**
25.18 Consider my distress and **suffering** and forgive all my sins.
31. 7 You see my **suffering;**
32.10 The wicked will have to **suffer,** but those who trust in
34.19 The good man **suffers** many troubles, but the Lord saves
35.26 May those who gloat over my **suffering** be completely defeated
37.19 They will not **suffer** when times are bad;
39. 2 my **suffering** only grew worse, [3] and I was overcome with anxiety.
39. 9 word, for you are the one who made me **suffer** like this.
42. 9 Why must I go on **suffering** from the cruelty of my enemies?"
43. 2 Why must I go on **suffering** from the cruelty of my enemies?
44.24 Don't forget our **suffering** and trouble!
60. 3 You have made your people **suffer** greatly;
69.26 they talk about the **sufferings** of those you have wounded.
71.20 You have sent troubles and **suffering** on me, but you will
73. 4 They do not **suffer** pain;
73. 5 They do not **suffer** as other people do;
73.14 O God, you have made me **suffer** all day long;
88. 9 my eyes are weak from **suffering.**
88.15 Ever since I was young, I have **suffered** and been near death;
89.32 I will make them **suffer** for their wrongs.
107.10 in gloom and darkness, prisoners **suffering** in chains,
107.17 Some were fools, **suffering** because of their sins and
107.39 humiliated by cruel oppression and **suffering,** [40] he showed
119.50 Even in my **suffering** I was comforted because your
119.92 the source of my joy, I would have died from my **sufferings.**
119.107 My **sufferings,** Lord, are terrible indeed;
119.153 Look at my **suffering,** and save me, because I have not
Prov 6.29 Whoever does it will **suffer.**
9.12 and if you reject it, you are the one who will **suffer.**
21.18 on themselves the **suffering** they try to cause good people.
30.10 You will be cursed and **suffer** for it.
Ecc 2.15 I thought to myself, "I will **suffer** the same fate as fools.
8. 9 some men have power and others have to **suffer** under them.
Is 14. 3 relief from their pain and **suffering,** and from the hard work
14.32 Zion and that his **suffering** people will find safety there.
16. 7 The people of Moab will weep because of the troubles they **suffer.**
21. 2 God will put an end to the **suffering** which Babylon has caused.
25. 8 the disgrace his people have **suffered** throughout the world.
26.11 Lord, put them to shame and let them **suffer;**
26.11 let them **suffer** the punishment you have prepared.
37. 3 "Today is a day of **suffering;**
40. 2 Tell them they have **suffered** long enough and their sins are
40.27 Lord doesn't know your troubles or care if you **suffer** injustice?
42.25 feel the force of his anger and **suffer** the violence of war.
44.11 trial—they will be terrified and will **suffer** disgrace.
45.24 but all who hate me will **suffer** disgrace.
47. 8 would never be a widow or **suffer** the loss of your children.
48.10 you in the fire of **suffering,** as silver is refined in a
48.21 through a hot, dry desert, they did not **suffer** from thirst.
49.13 he will have pity on his **suffering** people.
50.11 you will **suffer** a miserable fate.
51.21 You **suffering** people of Jerusalem, you that stagger as
53. 3 he endured **suffering** and pain.
53. 4 "But he endured the **suffering** that should have been ours,
53. 4 we thought that his **suffering** was punishment sent by God.
53. 5 healed by the punishment he **suffered,** made whole by the
53.10 "It was my will that he should **suffer;**
53.11 After a life of **suffering,** he will again have joy;
53.11 he will know that he did not **suffer** in vain.

Is 54.11 “O Jerusalem, you **suffering,** helpless city,
58. 5 When you fast, you make yourselves **suffer;**
59.17 and to punish and avenge the wrongs that people **suffer.**
63. 9 And so he saved them [9] from all their **suffering.**
64.12 to do nothing and make us **suffer** more than we can endure?
66. 8 Zion will not have to **suffer** long, before the nation is born.
Jer 2. 3 I sent **suffering** and disaster on everyone who hurt you.
4.18 Your sin has caused this **suffering;**
15. 8 young men in their prime and made their mothers **suffer.**
15.18 Why do I keep on **suffering?**
51.35 “May Babylonia be held responsible for what we have **suffered!”**
Lam 1. 4 The girls who sang there **suffer,** and the priests can only groan.
1. 5 The Lord has made her **suffer** for all her many sins;
1.21 make my enemies **suffer** as I do.
2.13 No one has ever **suffered** like this.
3.15 Bitter **suffering** is all he has given me for food and drink.
3.28 When we **suffer,** we should sit alone in silent patience;
5. 7 but now they are gone, and we are **suffering** for their sins.
Ezek 4. 4 390 days you will stay there and **suffer** because of their guilt.
4. 6 on your right side and **suffer** for the guilt of Judah for
16.58 You must **suffer** for the obscene, disgusting things you have done.”
18.19 ‘Why shouldn't the son **suffer** because of his father's sins?’
18.20 A son is not to **suffer** because of his father's sins,
18.20 and an evil man will **suffer** for the evil he does.
23.35 me, you will **suffer** for your lust and your prostitution.”
Dan 9.18 we are in and the **suffering** of the city that bears your
12. 2 enjoy eternal life, and some will **suffer** eternal disgrace.
Hos 4. 9 You will **suffer** the same punishment as the people!
5.11 Israel is **suffering** oppression;
5.15 my people until they have **suffered** enough for their sins and
5.15 Perhaps in their **suffering** they will try to find me.”
10. 2 The people whose hearts are deceitful must now **suffer**
Joel 1.18 the flocks of sheep also **suffer.**
Obad 13 people to gloat over their **suffering** and to seize their
Mic 1. 9 be healed, and Judah is about to **suffer** in the same way;
4. 6 the people I punished, those who have **suffered** in exile.
4. 9 Why are you **suffering** like a woman in labour?
Nah 1.12 My people, I made you **suffer,** but I will not do it
Zech 1. 6 but they disregarded them and **suffered** the consequences.
1.15 those nations made the **sufferings** of my people worse.
9. 5 The city of Gaza will see it and **suffer** great pain.
9. 8 I have seen how my people have **suffered.”**
9.12 you twice over with blessing for all you have **suffered.**
Mt 4.24 all those who were sick, **suffering** from all kinds of diseases
8. 2 Then a man **suffering** from a dreaded skin-disease came to him,
8. 6 in bed at home, unable to move and **suffering** terribly.”
9.20 A woman who had **suffered** from severe bleeding for twelve years
10. 8 heal those who **suffer** from dreaded skin-diseases, and drive out
11. 5 those who **suffer** from dreaded skin-diseases are made clean,
11.12 the Kingdom of heaven has **suffered** violent attacks,
16.21 must go to Jerusalem and **suffer** much from the elders, the
20.22 you drink the cup of **suffering** that I am about to drink?”
26. 6 Simon, a man who had **suffered** from a dreaded skin-disease.
26.39 Father, if it is possible, take this cup of **suffering** from me!
26.42 Father, if this cup of **suffering** cannot be taken away unless
27.19 in a dream last night I **suffered** much on account of him.”
Mk 1.40 A man **suffering** from a dreaded skin-disease came to Jesus,
5.25 a woman who had **suffered** terribly from severe bleeding for twelve
8.31 “The Son of Man must **suffer** much and be rejected by the
9.12 say that the Son of Man will **suffer** much and be rejected?
10.38 Can you drink the cup of **suffering** that I must drink?
14. 3 Simon, a man who had **suffered** from a dreaded skin-disease.
14.35 he might not have to go through that time of **suffering.**
14.36 Take this cup of **suffering** away from me.
Lk 4.27 And there were many people **suffering** from a dreaded skin-disease
5.12 there was a man who was **suffering** from a dreaded skin-disease.
7.22 those who **suffer** from dreaded skin-diseases are made clean,
8.43 a woman who had **suffered** from severe bleeding for twelve years;
9.22 “The Son of Man must **suffer** much and be rejected by the
17.12 he was met by ten men **suffering** from a dreaded skin-disease.
17.25 But first he must **suffer** much and be rejected by the
22.15 so much to eat this Passover meal with you before I **suffer!**
22.42 “if you will, take this cup of **suffering** away from me.
24.26 necessary for the Messiah to **suffer** these things and then to
24.46 Messiah must **suffer** and must rise from death three days later,
Jn 12.27 I came—so that I might go through this hour of **suffering.**
12.33 this he indicated the kind of death he was going to **suffer.)**
16.21 birth, she is sad because her hour of **suffering** has come;
16.21 is born, she forgets her **suffering,** because she is happy
16.33 The world will make you **suffer.**
18.11 drink the cup of **suffering** which my Father has given me?”
Acts 3.18 ago through all the prophets that his Messiah had to **suffer;**
5.41 considered them worthy to **suffer** disgrace for the sake of Jesus.
7.11 a famine all over Egypt and Canaan, which caused much **suffering.**
7.34 I have seen the cruel **suffering** of my people in Egypt.
8. 1 the church in Jerusalem began to **suffer** cruel persecution.
9.16 myself will show him all that he must **suffer** for my sake.”
17. 3 them that the Messiah had to **suffer** and rise from death.
26.23 that the Messiah must **suffer** and be the first one to
Rom 2. 9 There will be **suffering** and pain for all those who do what
8.17 we share Christ's **suffering,** we will also share his glory.
8.18 I consider that what we **suffer** at this present time
1 Cor 12.26 one part of the body **suffers,** all the other parts suffer
2 Cor 1. 5 a share in Christ's many **sufferings,** so also through Christ
1. 6 If we **suffer,** it is for your help and salvation;
1. 6 to endure with patience the same **sufferings** that we also endure.
1. 7 as you share in our **sufferings,** you also share in the help
4.17 small and temporary trouble we **suffer** will bring us a tremendous
Eph 2. 3 we, like everyone else, were destined to **suffer** God's anger.
3.13 then, not to be discouraged because I am **suffering** for you;
Phil 1.29 not only by believing in him, but also by **suffering** for him.
3.10 to share in his **sufferings** and become like him in his
Col 1.24 I am happy about my **sufferings** for you,
1.24 by means of my physical **sufferings** I am helping to complete
1.24 what still remains of Christ's **sufferings** on behalf of his body,
1 Thes 1. 6 and even though you **suffered** much, you received the message
2.14 You **suffered** the same persecutions from your own countrymen
2.14 that they **suffered** from the Jews, [15] who killed the
3. 7 all our trouble and **suffering** we have been encouraged about you,
5. 9 did not choose us to **suffer** his anger, but to possess
2 Thes 1. 4 through all the persecutions and **sufferings** you are experiencing.
1. 5 become worthy of his Kingdom, for which you are **suffering.**
1. 6 he will bring **suffering** on those who make you suffer,
1. 7 will give relief to you who **suffer** and to us as well.
1. 9 They will **suffer** the punishment of eternal destruction,
2 Tim 1. 8 Instead, take your part in **suffering** for the Good News, as
1.12 News, [12] and it is for this reason that I **suffer** these things.
2. 3 Take your part in **suffering,** as a loyal soldier of Christ Jesus.
2. 9 preach the Good News, I **suffer** and I am even chained like
3.11 my love, my endurance, [11] my persecutions, and my **sufferings.**
4. 5 **suffering,** do the work of a preacher of the Good News,
Heb 2. 9 with glory and honour because of the death he **suffered.**
2.10 make Jesus perfect through **suffering,** in order to bring many sons
2.18 those who are tempted, because he himself was tempted and **suffered.**
5. 8 God's Son, he learnt through his **sufferings** to be obedient.
9.26 he would have had to **suffer** many times ever since the
10.32 had shone on you, you **suffered** many things, yet were not
10.34 You shared the **sufferings** of prisoners, and when all your
11.25 He preferred to **suffer** with God's people rather than to
11.26 He reckoned that to **suffer** scorn for the Messiah was
12. 7 Endure what you **suffer** as being a father's punishment;
12. 7 your **suffering** shows that God is treating you as his sons.
13. 3 Remember those who are **suffering,** as though you were suffering
Jas 1.27 orphans and widows in their **suffering** and to keep oneself from
5.10 Take them as examples of patient endurance under **suffering.**
1 Pet 1. 6 for a while because of the many kinds of trials you **suffer.**
1.11 in predicting the **sufferings** that Christ would have to endure
2.19 endure the pain of undeserved **suffering** because you are conscious
2.20 But if you endure **suffering** even when you have done right,
2.21 called you, for Christ himself **suffered** for you and left you
2.23 when he **suffered,** he did not threaten, but placed his hopes
3.14 But even if you should **suffer** for doing what is right,
3.17 For it is better to **suffer** for doing good, if this
4. 1 Since Christ **suffered** physically, you too must strengthen
4. 1 whoever **suffers** physically is no longer involved with sin.
4.12 the painful test you are **suffering,** as though something unusual
4.13 that you are sharing Christ's **sufferings,** so that you may be
4.15 If any of you **suffers,** it must not be because he is
4.16 However, if you **suffer** because you are a Christian, don't be
4.19 So then, those who **suffer** because it is God's will for them,
5. 1 am a witness of Christ's **sufferings,** and I will share in the
5. 9 all the world are going through the same kind of **sufferings.**
5.10 But after you have **suffered** for a little while, the God
2 Pet 2. 8 and day after day he **suffered** agony as he saw and heard
2.13 will be paid with suffering for the **suffering** they have caused.
Jude 7 they **suffer** the punishment of eternal fire as a plain
Rev 1. 9 in patiently enduring the **suffering** that comes to those who belong
2. 3 You are patient, you have **suffered** for my sake, and you
2.10 Don't be afraid of anything you are about to **suffer.**
2.22 and those who committed adultery with her will **suffer** terribly.
11.10 because those two prophets brought much **suffering** upon mankind.
12. 2 and the pains and **suffering** of childbirth made her cry out.
18. 7 Give her as much **suffering** and grief as the glory and
18.10 off, because they are afraid of sharing in her **suffering.**
18.15 off, because they are afraid of sharing in her **suffering.**

SUFFICIENT

Num 35.30 is not **sufficient** to support an accusation of murder.

SUGGEST

Gen 30.31 to take care of your flocks if you agree to this **suggestion:**
30.34 We will do as you **suggest.”**
34.19 time in doing what was **suggested,** because he was in love
Josh 9.21 This was what the leaders **suggested.**
2 Kgs 6.28 other day this woman here **suggested** that we eat my child,
1 Chr 13. 4 The people were pleased with the **suggestion** and agreed to it.
2 Chr 2.14 of engraving and can follow any design **suggested** to him.
Ezra 4.14 this happen, and so we **suggest** [15] that you order a search
Neh 6. 2 Geshem sent me a message, **suggesting** that I meet with them
6. 7 hear about this, so I **suggest** that you and I meet to
Esth 1.21 liked this idea, and the king did what Memucan **suggested.**
2. 2 who were close to him **suggested,** “Why don't you make a
5.14 wife and all his friends **suggested,** “Why don't you have a
6.10 Do everything for him that you have **suggested.**
Mt 14. 8 At her mother's **suggestion** she asked him, “Give me here
Gal 2. 6 those leaders, I say, made no new **suggestions** to me.

SUICIDE

Prov 20. 2 making him angry is **suicide.**

Am **SUIT** see **PLEASE**

SUIT

Gen 2.18 I will make a **suitable** companion to help him."
2.20 but not one of them was a **suitable** companion to help him.
49.28 said as he spoke a **suitable** word of farewell to each son.
Num 32. 1 When they saw how **suitable** the land of Jazer and Gilead was
Eph 2. 3 desires, doing whatever **suited** the wishes of our own bodies

SUKKOTH (1)

City e. of R. Jordan.

Gen 33.17 But Jacob went to **Sukkoth,** where he built a house for
33.17 That is why the place was named **Sukkoth.**
Josh 13.27 it included Beth Haram, Bethnimrah, **Sukkoth,** and Zaphon, the
Judg 8. 5 When they arrived at **Sukkoth,** he said to the men of the
8. 6 But the leaders of **Sukkoth** said, "Why should we give your
8. 8 men of Penuel gave the same answer as the men of **Sukkoth.**
8.14 he captured a young man from **Sukkoth** and questioned him.
8.14 Gideon the names of the seventy-seven leading men of **Sukkoth.**
8.15 went to the men of **Sukkoth** and said, "Remember when you
8.16 the desert and used them to punish the leaders of **Sukkoth.**
Ps 60. 6 Shechem and distribute the Valley of **Sukkoth** to my people.
108. 7 Shechem and distribute the Valley of **Sukkoth** to my people.

SULPHUR

In the Bible this refers to a chemical which burns with great heat and produces an unpleasant smell.

Gen 19.24 Suddenly the Lord rained burning **sulphur** on the cities
Deut 29.23 The fields will be a barren waste, covered with **sulphur** and salt;
Job 18.15 in his tent— after **sulphur** is sprinkled to disinfect it!
Ps 11. 6 He sends down flaming coals and burning **sulphur** on the wicked;
Is 34. 9 Edom will turn into tar, and the soil will turn into **sulphur.**
Ezek 38.22 hail, together with fire and **sulphur,** will pour down on him
Lk 17.29 Lot left Sodom, fire and **sulphur** rained down from heaven
Rev 9.17 breastplates red as fire, blue as sapphire, and yellow as **sulphur.**
9.17 and from their mouths came out fire, smoke, and **sulphur.**
9.18 fire, the smoke, and the **sulphur** coming out of the horses'
14.10 be tormented in fire and **sulphur** before the holy angels
19.20 thrown alive into the lake of fire that burns with **sulphur.**
20.10 the lake of fire and **sulphur,** where the beast and the false
21. 8 burning with fire and **sulphur,** which is the second death."

SUM (1)

Ex 22.17 must pay the father a **sum** of money equal to the bride-price
Lev 25.27 man who bought it a **sum** that will make up for the
27. 2 the payment of the following **sums** of money,
2 Chr 24.11 And so they collected a large **sum** of money.
Zech 11.13 pieces of silver—the magnificent **sum** they thought I was
Mt 28.12 they gave a large **sum** of money to the soldiers [13]and said,
Acts 7.16 had bought from the clan of Hamor for a **sum** of money.

SUM (2)

Rom 13. 9 and any others besides, are **summed up** in the one command,
Gal 5.14 For the whole Law is **summed up** in one commandment:

SUMMER

Gen 8.22 be cold and heat, **summer** and winter, day and night."
Ps 32. 4 drained, as moisture is dried up by the **summer** heat.
74.17 you made **summer** and winter.
Prov 6. 8 up their food during the **summer,** getting ready for winter.
11.28 but the righteous will prosper like the leaves of **summer.**
26. 1 out of place, like snow in **summer** or rain at harvest time.
30.25 they are weak, but they store up their food in the **summer.**
Is 18. 6 In **summer** the birds will feed on them, and in winter, the
Jer 8.20 The people cry out, "The **summer** is gone, the harvest is over,
15.18 disappoint me like a stream that goes dry in the **summer?"**
48.32 But now your **summer** fruits and your grapes have been destroyed.
Dan 2.35 and became like the dust on a threshing-place in **summer.**
Amos 3.15 I will destroy winter houses and **summer** houses.
Mt 24.32 it starts putting out leaves, you know that **summer** is near.
Mk 13.28 it starts putting out leaves, you know that **summer** is near.
Lk 21.30 their leaves beginning to appear, you know that **summer** is near.

SUMMON

Ex 28. 1 **"Summon** your brother Aaron and his sons, Nadab, Abihu,
Lev 5. 1 If someone is officially **summoned** to give evidence in court
Num 22. 5 King Balak [5]sent messengers to **summon** Balaam son of Beor,
Deut 25. 8 Then the town leaders are to **summon** him and speak to him.
2 Sam 21. 3 So David **summoned** the people of Gibeon and said to them,
1 Kgs 8. 1 Then King Solomon **summoned** all the leaders of the tribes
18.20 So Ahab **summoned** all the Israelites and the prophets of
2 Kgs 23. 1 King Josiah **summoned** all the leaders of Judah and Jerusalem,
1 Chr 15. 3 So David **summoned** all the people of Israel to Jerusalem in
2 Chr 5. 2 Then King Solomon **summoned** all the leaders of the tribes
15. 9 Asa **summoned** all of them and the people of Judah and Benjamin.
25.11 Amaziah **summoned** up his courage and led his army to the
34.29 King Josiah **summoned** all the leaders of Judah and Jerusalem,
Esth 4.11 sees the king without being **summoned,** that person must die.
Is 43. 8 **"Summon** my people to court.
43. 9 **Summon** the nations to come to the trial.
48.13 When I **summon** earth and sky, they come at once and present
55. 5 Now you will **summon** foreign nations;
Nah 2. 5 The officers are **summoned;**

SUN

Gen 1.16 the two larger lights, the **sun** to rule over the day and
15.12 When the **sun** was going down, Abram fell into a deep sleep,
15.17 When the **sun** had set and it was dark, a smoking fire-pot
19.23 The **sun** was rising when Lot reached Zoar.
32.31 The **sun** rose as Jacob was leaving Peniel, and he was
37. 9 in which I saw the **sun,** the moon, and eleven stars bowing
Ex 16.21 and when the **sun** grew hot, what was left on the ground
17.12 up his arms, holding them steady until the **sun** went down.
22.26 back to him before the **sun** sets, [27]because it is the only
Lev 22. 7 After the **sun** sets he is clean, and then he may eat
Deut 4.19 you see in the sky—the **sun,** the moon, and the stars.
17. 3 serving other gods or the **sun** or the moon or the stars,
33. 2 he rose like the **sun** over Edom and shone on his people
33.14 their land be blessed with **sun-ripened** fruit, Rich with the
Josh 10.12 **"Sun,** stand still over Gibeon;
10.13 The **sun** stood still and the moon did not move until the
10.13 The **sun** stood still in the middle of the sky and did
Judg 5.31 O Lord, but may your friends shine like the rising **sun!**
2 Sam 23. 4 to God, [4]is like the **sun** shining on a cloudless dawn,
23. 4 the **sun** that makes the grass sparkle
1 Kgs 8.12 "You, Lord, have placed the **sun** in the sky, yet you have
2 Kgs 3.22 up the following morning, the **sun** was shining on the water,
23. 5 sacrifices to Baal, to the **sun,** the moon, the planets, and
23.11 to the worship of the **sun,** and he burnt the chariots used
Job 3. 5 cover it with clouds, and blot out the **sun.**
8.16 sprout like weeds in the **sun,** like weeds that spread all
9. 7 He can keep the **sun** from rising, and the stars from
11.17 life will be brighter than **sunshine** at noon, and life's
30.28 I go about in gloom, without any **sunshine;**
31.26 I have never worshipped the **sun** in its brightness or the
38.24 to the place where the **sun** comes up, or the place from
39.23 The weapons which their riders carry rattle and flash in the **sun.**
41.18 when he sneezes, and his eyes glow like the rising **sun.**
Ps 19. 4 God made a home in the sky for the **sun;**
33. 6 heavens by his command, the **sun,** moon, and stars by his
37. 6 he will make your righteousness shine like the noonday **sun.**
57. 8 I will wake up the **sun.**
72. 5 you as long as the **sun** shines, as long as the moon
72.17 may his fame last as long as the **sun.**
74.16 you set the **sun** and the moon in their places;
89.36 I will watch over his kingdom as long as the **sun** shines.
104.19 the **sun** knows the time to set.
104.22 When the **sun** rises, they go back and lie down in their
108. 2 I will wake up the **sun.**
121. 6 The **sun** will not hurt you during the day, nor the moon
136. 7 He made the **sun** and the moon;
136. 8 the **sun** to rule over the day;
148. 3 Praise him, **sun** and moon;
Ecc 1. 5 The **sun** still rises, and it still goes down, going wearily
12. 2 when the light of the **sun,** the moon, and the stars will
Song 1. 6 on me because of my colour, because the **sun** has tanned me.
1. 7 Where will they rest from the noonday **sun?**
6.10 beautiful and bright, as dazzling as the **sun** or the moon.
Is 13.10 will stop shining, the **sun** will be dark when it rises,
18. 4 time, as serenely as the **sun** shines in the heat of the
19.18 One of the cities will be called, "City of the **Sun."**
24.23 will grow dark, and the **sun** will no longer shine, for the
30.26 be as bright as the **sun,**
30.26 and the **sun** will be seven times brighter
34. 4 The **sun,** moon, and stars will crumble to dust.
45.12 I control the **sun,** the moon, and the stars.
49.10 **Sun** and desert heat will not hurt them, for they will be
58. 8 on you like the morning **sun,** and your wounds will be quickly
60. 1 Arise, Jerusalem, and shine like the **sun;**
60.19 "No longer will the **sun** be your light by day Or the
60.20 be your eternal light, More lasting than the **sun** and moon.
Jer 8. 2 be spread out before the **sun,** the moon, and the stars, which
31.35 The Lord provides the **sun** for light by day, the moon and
36.30 will be exposed to the **sun** during the day and to the
Ezek 8.16 bowing low towards the east, worshipping the rising **sun.**
32. 7 The **sun** will hide behind the clouds, and the moon will give
Joel 2.10 The **sun** and the moon grow dark, and the stars no longer
2.31 The **sun** will be darkened, and the moon will turn red as
3.15 The **sun** and the moon grow dark, and the stars no longer
Amos 8. 9 when I will make the **sun** go down at noon and the
Jon 4. 8 After the **sun** had risen, God sent a hot east wind, and
4. 8 faint from the heat of the **sun** beating down on his head.
Mic 3. 6 the **sun** is going down on you.
Nah 3.17 But when the **sun** comes out, they fly away, and no one
Hab 3.11 of your shining spear, the **sun** and the moon stood still.
Zeph 1. 5 on the roof and worships the **sun,** the moon, and the stars.
Mal 4. 2 rise on you like the **sun**
4. 2 and bring healing like the **sun's** rays.
Mt 5.45 For he makes his **sun** to shine on bad and good people
13. 6 But when the **sun** came up, it burnt the young plants;
13.43 God's people will shine like the **sun** in their Father's Kingdom.
16. 2 But Jesus answered, "When the **sun** is setting, you say,
17. 2 shining like the **sun,** and his clothes were dazzling white.
20.12 day's work in the hot **sun**—yet you paid them the same
24.29 trouble of those days, the **sun** will grow dark, the moon will
Mk 1.32 After the **sun** had set and evening had come people
4. 6 Then, when the **sun** came up, it burnt the young plants;
13.24 that time of trouble the **sun** will grow dark, the moon will
Lk 9.12 When the **sun** was beginning to set, the twelve disciples
21.25 be strange things happening to the **sun,** the moon, and the
23.44 about twelve o'clock when the **sun** stopped shining and darkness
Jn 21. 4 As the **sun** was rising, Jesus stood at the water's edge,
Acts 2.20 the **sun** will be darkened, and the moon will turn red
26.13 light much brighter than the **sun,** coming from the sky and

Acts	27.20	we could not see the **sun** or the stars, and the wind
1 Cor	15.41	The **sun** has its own beauty, the moon another beauty,
Jas	1.11	The **sun** rises with its blazing heat and burns the plant;
Rev	1.16	His face was as bright as the midday **sun.**
	6.12	earthquake, and the **sun** became black like coarse black cloth,
	7.16	neither **sun** nor any scorching heat will burn them,
	8.12	A third of the **sun** was struck, and a third of the
	9. 2	the **sunlight** and the air were darkened by the smoke from the
	10. 1	his face was like the **sun,** and his legs were like pillars
	12. 1	woman, whose dress was the **sun** and who had the moon under
	16. 8	out his bowl on the **sun,** and it was allowed to burn
	19.17	Then I saw an angel standing on the **sun.**
	21.23	has no need of the **sun** or the moon to shine on
	22. 5	will not need lamps or **sunlight,** because the Lord God will

SUNDAY

Mt	28. 1	After the Sabbath, as **Sunday** morning was dawning, Mary
Mk	16. 2	Very early on **Sunday** morning, at sunrise, they went to the tomb.
	16. 9	from death early on **Sunday,** he appeared first to Mary Magdalene,
Lk	24. 1	Very early on **Sunday** morning the women went to the tomb,
Jn	20. 1	Early on **Sunday** morning, while it was still dark, Mary Magdalene
	20.19	It was late that **Sunday** evening, and the disciples were gathered
1 Cor	16. 2	Every **Sunday** each of you must put aside some money,

SUNRISE

Judg	9.33	Get up tomorrow morning at **sunrise** and make a sudden
Neh	7. 3	the morning until well after **sunrise** and to have them closed
Ps	5. 3	at **sunrise** I offer my prayer and wait for your answer.
	119.147	Before **sunrise** I call to you for help;
Prov	4.18	righteous travel is like the **sunrise,** getting brighter and
Lam	3.23	continue, [23] Fresh as the morning, as sure as the **sunrise.**
Mk	13.35	in the evening or at midnight or before dawn or at **sunrise.**
	16. 2	Very early on Sunday morning, at **sunrise,** they went to the tomb.
Acts	20.11	talking with them for a long time, even until **sunrise,** Paul

SUNSET
[SET]

Gen	15.17	When the sun had **set** and it was dark, a smoking fire-pot
	28.11	At **sunset** he came to a holy place and camped there.
Ex	22.26	to him before the sun **sets,** [27] because it is the only
Lev	22. 7	After the sun **sets** he is clean, and then he may eat
	23. 5	honour the Lord, begins at **sunset** on the fourteenth day of
	23.32	From **sunset** on the ninth day of the month
	23.32	to **sunset** on the tenth observe this day
Num	9. 2	of this month, beginning at **sunset,** the people of Israel are
	19.19	water over himself, becomes ritually clean at **sunset.**
Deut	16. 5	Do it at **sunset,** the time of day when you left Egypt.
	23.11	to wash himself, and at **sunset** he may come back into camp.
	24.15	Each day before **sunset** pay him for that day's work;
Josh	2. 4	They left at **sunset** before the city gate was closed.
	8.29	At **sunset** Joshua gave orders for the body to be removed, and
	10.27	At **sunset** Joshua gave orders, and their bodies were
Judg	19.14	It was **sunset** when they came to Gibeah in the territory of
2 Sam	2.24	out after Abner, and at **sunset** they came to the hill of
1 Kgs	22.36	Near **sunset** the order went out through the Israelite ranks:
2 Chr	18.34	At **sunset** he died.
Neh	7. 3	closed and barred before the guards went off duty at **sunset.**
Ps	104.19	the sun knows the time to **set.**
Dan	6.14	He kept trying until **sunset.**
Mt	16. 2	answered, "When the sun is **setting,** you say, 'We are going
Mk	1.32	After the sun had **set** and evening had come, people
Lk	4.40	After **sunset** all who had friends who were sick with various
	9.12	the sun was beginning to **set,** the twelve disciples came to

SUPERIOR

Is	3. 5	and worthless people will not respect their **superiors.**
Dan	11.36	is greater than any god, **superior** even to the Supreme God.
Mt	8. 9	man under the authority of **superior** officers, and I have soldiers
Lk	7. 8	under the authority of **superior** officers, and I have soldiers
1 Cor	4. 7	Who made you **superior** to others?
Eph	1.21	he has a title **superior** to all titles of authority in this
Col	1.15	He is the first-born Son, **superior** to all created things.
	2.18	anyone who claims to be **superior** because of special visions
Heb	8. 6	priestly work which is **superior** to theirs, just as the covenant

SUPERNATURAL

Is	31. 3	Their horses are not **supernatural.**

SUPERVISE

1 Kgs	5.16	3,300 foremen in charge of them to **supervise** their work.
1 Chr	9.20	had **supervised** them at one time.
	28. 1	leaders of the clans, the **supervisors** of the property and
2 Chr	2. 2	men responsible for **supervising** the work.
	2.18	the mountains, and appointed 3,600 **supervisors** to make sure
	26.11	Jeiel and Maaseiah under the **supervision** of Hananiah, a
	34.12	They were **supervised** by four Levites:
	34.13	materials and **supervising** the workmen on various jobs,
	34.17	Temple and handed it over to the workmen and their **supervisors."**
Neh	3. 5	do the manual labour assigned to them by the **supervisors.**
	11.21	called Ophel and worked under the **supervision** of Ziha and Gishpa.
	11.22	The **supervisor** of the Levites who lived in Jerusalem was Uzzi,
Dan	6. 2	Daniel and two others to **supervise** the governors and to look
	6. 3	do better work than the other **supervisors** or the governors.
	6. 4	Then the other **supervisors** and the governors tried to find
	6. 7	**supervisors,** the governors, the lieutenant-governors,

SUPPER
[LORD'S SUPPER]

2 Sam	11.13	David invited him to **supper** and made him drunk.
Lk	17. 8	say to him, 'Get my **supper** ready, then put on your apron
	22.20	them the cup after the **supper,** saying, "This cup is God's
Jn	13. 2	Jesus and his disciples were at **supper.**
1 Cor	10.16	we use in the **Lord's Supper** and for which we give thanks
	11.20	as a group, it is not the **Lord's Supper** that you eat.
	11.25	the same way, after the **supper** he took the cup and said,
	11.33	gather together to eat the **Lord's Supper,** wait for one another.

AV SUPPLICATION
see also **PRAY(ER)**

1 Sam	13.12	in Gilgal, and I have not tried to win the Lord's **favour.'**
Esth	4. 8	ask her to go and **plead** with the king and beg him
Job	8. 5	But turn now and **plead** with Almighty God;
	9.15	all I can do is **beg** for mercy from God my judge.
Ps	30. 8	I **begged** for your help:
	55. 1	don't turn away from my **plea!**
	142. 1	I **plead** with him.
Is	45.14	bow down to you and **confess,** 'God is with you—he alone
Jer	37.20	And now, Your Majesty, I **beg** you to listen to me and
	38.26	Just tell them you were **begging** me not to send you back
	42. 9	you sent me with your **request** has said, [10] 'If you are
Hos	12. 4	He wept and **asked for** a blessing.

SUPPLY

Gen	41.36	food will be a reserve **supply** for the country during the
	47.17	That year he **supplied** them with food in exchange for all
Ex	1.11	Pithom and Rameses to serve as **supply** centres for the king.
	5.10	has said that he will not **supply** you with any more straw.
Lev	26.26	will cut off your food **supply,** so that ten women will need
Judg	7. 8	the three hundred, who kept all the **supplies** and trumpets.
1 Sam	10.22	The Lord answered, "Saul is over there, hiding behind the **supplies."**
	17.22	officer in charge of the **supplies,** ran to the battle line,
	21. 3	Now, then, what **supplies** have you got?
	25.13	of his men, leaving two hundred behind with the **supplies.**
	30.24	whoever stays behind with the **supplies** gets the same share
2 Sam	12.27	"I have attacked Rabbah and have captured its water **supply.**
	19.32	was very rich and had **supplied** the king with food while he
1 Kgs	4.22	The **supplies** Solomon needed each day were five thousand
	4.27	the month assigned to him, **supplied** the food King Solomon
	4.27	they always **supplied** everything needed.
	4.28	Each governor also **supplied** his share of barley and straw,
	5. 9	part, I would like you to **supply** the food for my men."
	5.10	So Hiram **supplied** Solomon with all the cedar and pine
	9.19	Judah, [19] the cities where his **supplies** were kept, the
	10.29	They **supplied** the Hittite and Syrian kings with horses
	17. 4	The brook will **supply** you with water to drink, and I have
	18.13	two groups of fifty, and **supplied** them with food and water?
1 Chr	9.26	for the rooms in the Temple and for the **supplies** kept there.
	22. 3	He **supplied** a large amount of iron for making nails and
	22.14	Besides that, there is an unlimited **supply** of bronze and iron.
2 Chr	1.17	They **supplied** the Hittite and Syrian kings with horses
	8. 4	the cities in Hamath that were centres for storing **supplies.**
	8. 6	the cities where he stored **supplies,** and the cities where
	11.11	in each one he placed **supplies** of food, olive-oil, and wine,
	16. 4	all the cities of Naphtali where **supplies** were stored.
	17.13	and cities, [13] where **supplies** were stored in huge amounts.
	20.25	many cattle, **supplies,** clothing, and other valuable objects.
	26.14	Uzziah **supplied** the army with shields, spears, helmets,
	32. 3	decided to cut off the **supply** of water outside the city in
Ezra	1. 4	them with silver and gold, **supplies** and pack animals, as
	1. 6	utensils, gold, **supplies,** pack animals, other valuables,
Neh	2. 8	royal forests, instructing him to **supply** me with timber for
	5.18	and every ten days I provided a fresh **supply** of wine.
	13.13	in distributing the **supplies** to their fellow-workers.
Ps	57. 2	to God, the Most High, to God, who **supplies** my every need.
	78.19	against God and said, "Can God **supply** food in the desert?
	145.19	He **supplies** the needs of those who honour him;
Is	10.13	between nations and took the **supplies** they had stored.
	10.28	They left their **supplies** at Michmash!
Ezek	4.16	I am going to cut off the **supply** of bread for Jerusalem.
	5.16	I will cut off your **supply** of food and let you starve.
	14.13	I will stretch out my hand and destroy its **supply** of food.
	23.24	bringing a large army with chariots and **supply** wagons.
Amos	4. 1	and demand that your husbands keep you **supplied** with liquor!
Acts	12.20	their country got its food **supplies** from the king's country.
	17.25	need anything that we can **supply** by working for him, since
2 Cor	9.10	And God, who **supplies** seed to sow and bread to eat,
	9.10	will also **supply** you with all the seed
Phil	4.19	wealth through Christ Jesus, my God will **supply** all your needs.
Col	1.29	the mighty strength which Christ **supplies** and which is at
1 Thes	3.10	see you personally and **supply** what is needed in your faith.

SUPPORT

Gen	36. 7	where he and Jacob were living was not able to **support** them;
Ex	27.10	to be 44 metres long, [10] **supported** by twenty bronze posts
	27.16	It is to be **supported** by four posts in four bases.
	38.10	curtains were 44 metres long, [10] **supported** by twenty bronze
	38.19	It was **supported** by four posts in four bronze bases.
Lev	25.35	you becomes poor and cannot **support** himself, you must
Num	35.30	is not sufficient to **support** an accusation of murder.

Deut 33.27 his eternal arms are your **support.**
2 Sam 3. 1 The fighting between the forces **supporting** Saul's family and those supporting
7.15 I will not withdraw my **support** from him as I did from
19. 6 You oppose those who love you and **support** those who hate you!
1 Kgs 1. 7 Abiathar the priest, and they agreed to **support** his cause.
2.28 (He had **supported** Adonijah, but not Absalom.)
7. 2 over store-rooms, which were **supported** by the pillars.
7. 6 It had a covered porch, **supported** by columns.
7.30 At the four corners were bronze **supports** for a basin;
7.30 the **supports** were decorated with spiral figures in relief.
7.34 There were four **supports** at the bottom corners of each cart,
7.35 its **supports** and the panels were of one piece with the cart.
7.36 The **supports** and panels were decorated with figures of winged creatures,
7.40 The twelve bulls **supporting** the tank
18.19 prophets of the goddess Asherah who are **supported** by Queen Jezebel."
20. 1 gathered all his troops, and **supported** by thirty-two other
2 Kgs 10.15 Will you **support** me?"
15.19 of silver to gain his **support** in strengthening Menahem's
1 Chr 17.13 I will not withdraw my **support** from him as I did from
2 Chr 4.11 The twelve bulls **supporting** the tank
11.17 and for three years they **supported** Rehoboam son of Solomon
24. 6 the people to pay for **support** of the Tent of the Lord's
Ezra 6.22 to them, so that he **supported** them in their work of
8.36 Euphrates, who then gave their **support** to the people and the
10.15 Tikvah, who had the **support** of Meshullam and of Shabbethai,
Neh 4.16 our leaders gave their full **support** to the people [17] who
12.47 gave daily gifts for the **support** of the temple musicians and
Job 9. 6 he rocks the pillars that **support** the earth.
17. 3 There is no one else to **support** what I say.
38. 6 What holds up the pillars that **support** the earth?
Ps 94.15 in the courts, and all righteous people will **support** it.
Jer 26.24 But because I had the **support** of Ahikam son of Shaphan,
34. 1 of Babylonia and his army, **supported** by troops from all the
52.20 the twelve bulls that **supported** it—were too heavy to weigh.
Ezek 29. 6 relied on you Egyptians for **support,** but you were no better
42. 6 on terraces and were not **supported** by columns like the other
Dan 11.32 the king will win the **support** of those who have already
Mal 2. 2 will put a curse on the things you receive for your **support.**
Rom 11.18 you don't **support** the roots—the roots support you.
2 Thes 3. 8 We did not accept anyone's **support** without paying for it.
3. 9 this, not because we have no right to demand our **support;**
1 Tim 3.15 of the living God, the pillar and **support** of the truth.

SUPREME

Deut 10.17 The Lord your God is **supreme** over all gods and over all
1 Chr 29.11 earth is yours, and you are king, **supreme** ruler over all.
2 Chr 9.26 He was **supreme** ruler of all the kings in the territory
Ps 46.10 I am God, supreme among the nations, **supreme** over the world."
47. 9 he rules **supreme.**
83.18 you alone are the Lord, **supreme** ruler over all the earth.
92. 8 destroyed, [8] because you, Lord, are **supreme** for ever.
93. 4 The Lord rules **supreme** in heaven, greater than the roar of
99. 2 he is **supreme** over all the nations.
138. 2 have shown that your name and your commands are **supreme.**
150. 2 Praise his **supreme** greatness.
Dan 3.26 Servants of the **Supreme** God!
4. 2 wonders and miracles which the **Supreme** God has shown me.
4.17 people everywhere know that the **Supreme** God has power over
4.24 and this is what the **Supreme** God has declared will happen to
4.25 will admit that the **Supreme** God controls all human kingdoms,
4.32 you will acknowledge that the **Supreme** God has power over
4.34 I praised the **Supreme** God and gave honour and glory to the
5.18 "The **Supreme** God made your father Nebuchadnezzar a
5.21 Finally he admitted that the **Supreme** God controls all human
7.18 And the people of the **Supreme** God will receive royal
7.22 judgement in favour of the people of the **Supreme** God.
7.25 He will speak against the **Supreme** God and oppress God's people.
7.27 on earth will be given to the people of the **Supreme** God.
11.36 is greater than any god, superior even to the **Supreme** God.
1 Cor 11. 3 to understand that Christ is **supreme** over every man,
11. 3 the husband is **supreme** over his wife,
11. 3 and God is **supreme** over Christ.
2 Cor 4. 7 order to show that the **supreme** power belongs to God, not to
Eph 1.22 and gave him to the church as **supreme** Lord over all things.
Col 2.10 He is **supreme** over every spiritual ruler and authority.
Heb 1. 3 in heaven at the right-hand side of God, the **Supreme** Power.
1 Pet 2.13 Emperor, who is the **supreme** authority, [14] and to the governors,
2 Pet 1.17 came to him from the **Supreme** Glory, saying, "This is my own

SUR GATE

2 Kgs 11. 6 to stand guard at the **Sur Gate,** and the other third are

SURE

Gen 24. 6 "Make **sure** that you don't send my son back there!
42.16 Otherwise, as **sure** as the king lives, you are spies."
45. 7 way and to make **sure** that you and your descendants survive.
46.34 what your occupation is, [34] be **sure** to tell him that you
Ex 4.21 going back to Egypt, be **sure** to perform before the king all
Num 13.20 And be **sure** to bring back some of the fruit that grows
14.21 But I promise that as **surely** as I live
14.21 and as **surely** as my presence fills the earth,
14.28 'I swear that as **surely** as I live, I will do to
18.32 But be **sure** not to profane the sacred gifts of the
Deut 5. 1 Learn them and be **sure** that you obey them.
5.25 We are **sure** to die if we hear the Lord our God
5.32 "People of Israel, be **sure** that you do everything that
6.17 Be **sure** that you obey all the laws that he has given
8.14 other possessions have increased, [14] make **sure** that you do
9. 6 You can be **sure** that the Lord is not giving you this
10.18 He makes **sure** that orphans and widows are treated fairly;
11.32 it and settle there, [32] be **sure** to obey all the laws that
12.19 Be **sure,** also, not to neglect the Levites, as long as
12.30 Lord destroys those nations, make **sure** that you don't follow
16.12 Be **sure** that you obey these commands;
17.15 Make **sure** that the man you choose to be king is the
22. 8 build a new house, be **sure** to put a railing round the
23.23 but if you make one voluntarily, be **sure** that you keep it.
24. 8 from a dreaded skin-disease, be **sure** to do exactly what the
25.19 who live around you, be **sure** to kill all the Amalekites, so
29.18 Make **sure** that no man, woman, family, or tribe standing
29.19 Make **sure** that there is no one here today who hears
32.40 As **surely** as I am the living God, I raise my hand
32.46 the people, [46] he said, "Make **sure** you obey all these
Josh 1. 7 and make **sure** that you obey the whole Law that my servant
1. 8 Be **sure** that the book of the Law is always read in
1. 8 day and night, and make **sure** that you obey everything
2.24 and then said, "We are **sure** that the Lord has given us
3.10 As you advance, he will **surely** drive out the Canaanites,
22. 5 Make **sure** you obey the law that Moses commanded you:
23.13 with them, [13] you may be **sure** that the Lord your God will
Judg 13.13 answered, "Your wife must be **sure** to do everything that I
13.22 to his wife, "We are **sure** to die, because we have seen
Ruth 2. 2 I am **sure** to find someone who will let me work with
3. 4 Be **sure** to notice where he lies down, and after he falls
1 Sam 16. 6 in the Lord's presence is **surely** the one he has chosen."
20.23 other, the Lord will make **sure** that we will keep it for
20.42 The Lord will make **sure** that you and I, and your descendants
22.22 that day, I knew that he would be **sure** to tell Saul.
23.20 our territory, and we will make **sure** that you catch him."
23.22 Go and make **sure** once more;
23.23 where he hides, and be **sure** to bring back a report to
24.20 Now I am **sure** that you will be king of Israel and
2 Sam 7.13 and I will make **sure** that his dynasty continues for ever.
8.15 over all Israel and made **sure** that his people were always
13.13 to the king, and I'm **sure** that he will give me to
23. 5 that will be my victory, and God will **surely** bring it about.
1 Kgs 11.38 Israel and will make **sure** that your descendants rule after you,
13.32 of worship in the towns of Samaria will **surely** come true."
2 Kgs 4. 9 to her husband, "I am **sure** that this man who comes here
7. 9 wait until morning to tell it, we are **sure** to be punished.
9.14 you are with me, make **sure** that no one slips out of
10.23 to the people there, "Make **sure** that only worshippers of
1 Chr 15.26 and seven sheep, to make **sure** that God would help the
17.12 and I will make **sure** that his dynasty continues for ever.
18.14 over all Israel and made **sure** that his people were always
2 Chr 2.18 appointed 3,600 supervisors to make **sure** the work was done.
Ezra 7.23 his Temple, and so make **sure** that he is never angry with
Neh 13.19 at the gates to make **sure** that nothing was brought into the
13.22 the gates to make **sure** that the Sabbath was kept holy.
Job 5. 7 brings trouble on himself, as **surely** as sparks fly up from a
38.21 I am **sure** you can, because you're so old and were there
Ps 50.23 that honours me, and I will **surely** save all who obey me."
68.21 God will **surely** break the heads of his enemies, of those
85. 9 **Surely** he is ready to save those who honour him, and his
Prov 11.21 You can be **sure** that evil men will be punished, but
11.31 earth, so you can be **sure** that wicked and sinful people will
17.27 Someone who is **sure** of himself does not talk all the time.
19.29 A conceited fool is **sure** to get a beating.
21.29 Righteous people are **sure** of themselves;
24.14 your tongue, [14] you may be **sure** that wisdom is good for the
24.27 are ready, and you are **sure** that you can earn a living.
25.23 Gossip brings anger just as **surely** as the north wind brings rain.
Ecc 3.21 How can anyone be **sure** that a man's spirit goes upwards
Is 47.10 "You felt **sure** of yourself in your evil;
48.19 and I would have made **sure** they were never destroyed."
49.18 As **surely** as I am the living God, you will be proud
52.11 Make **sure** you leave Babylonia,
61.11 As **surely** as seeds sprout and grow, The Sovereign Lord
Jer 3. 7 after she had done all this, she would **surely** return to me.
5. 3 **Surely** the Lord looks for faithfulness.
22.24 King Jehoiakim of Judah, "As **surely** as I am the living God,
26.15 But be **sure** of this:
33.26 And just as **surely** as I have done this, so I will
37.20 If you do, I will **surely** die there."
38. 9 the well, where he is **sure** to die of starvation, since there
51.61 you get to Babylon, be **sure** to read aloud to the people
Lam 2. 8 He measured them off to make **sure** of total destruction.
3.23 continue, [23] Fresh as the morning, as **sure** as the sunrise.
3.32 bring us sorrow, but his love for us is **sure** and strong.
Ezek 14.16 three men lived there—as **surely** as I, the Sovereign Lord, am
14.18 three men lived there—as **surely** as I, the Sovereign Lord, am
14.20 and Job lived there—as **surely** as I, the Sovereign Lord, am
16.48 "As **sure** as I am the living God," the Sovereign Lord says,
17.14 rising again and to make **sure** that the treaty would be kept.
17.16 "As **surely** as I am the living God," says the Sovereign Lord,
17.19 The Sovereign Lord says, "As **surely** as I am the living God,
18. 3 "As **surely** as I am the living God," says the Sovereign Lord,
20. 3 As **surely** as I am the living God, I will not let
20.31 As **surely** as I, the Sovereign Lord, am the living God, I
20.33 "As **surely** as I, the Sovereign Lord, am the living God,
33.11 Tell them that as **surely** as I, the Sovereign Lord, am
33.27 Lord, warn them that as **surely** as I am the living God,
34. 8 As **surely** as I am the living God, you had better listen
35. 6 So then—as **surely** as I, the Sovereign Lord, am the living
35.11 So then, as **surely** as I, the Sovereign Lord, am the
36. 9 side, and I will make **sure** that your land is ploughed again

Ezek 39. 7 I will make **sure** that my people Israel know my holy name,
Dan 3.18 doesn't, Your Majesty may be **sure** that we will not worship
Hos 5. 9 People of Israel, this will **surely** happen!
6. 1 He has hurt us, but he will be **sure** to heal us;
6. 3 will come to us as **surely** as the day dawns,
6. 3 as **surely** as the spring rains that water
Zeph 2. 9 As **surely** as I am the living Lord, the God of Israel,
Mal 2.15 So make **sure** that none of you breaks his promise to his
2.16 Make **sure** that you do not break your promise to be faithful
Mt 6.30 Won't he be all the more **sure** to clothe you?
10.42 You can be **sure** that whoever gives even a drink of cold
11.24 You can be **sure** that on the Judgement Day God will show
12.36 "You can be **sure** that on Judgement Day everyone will
19.28 to them, "You can be **sure** that when the Son of Man
24.15 be **sure** to understand what this means!)
24.43 would come, you can be **sure** that he would stay awake
Mk 12. 6 'I am **sure** they will respect my son,' he said.
13.14 be **sure** to understand what this means!)
Lk 4.23 said to them, "I am **sure** that you will quote this proverb
12.28 Won't he be all the more **sure** to clothe you?
12.39 And you can be **sure** that if the owner of a house
18. 9 parable to people who were **sure** of their own goodness
Acts 2.36 are to know for **sure** that this Jesus, whom you crucified,
13.34 you the sacred and **sure** blessings that I promised to David.'
21.22 They are **sure** to hear that you have arrived.
26.26 I am **sure** that you have taken notice of every one of
Rom 2.19 you are **sure** that you are a guide for the blind,
4.21 He was absolutely **sure** that God would be able to do what
15.14 I myself feel **sure** that you are full of goodness, that you
1 Cor 1.17 wisdom, in order to make **sure** that Christ's death on the
7.16 How can you be **sure,** Christian wife, that you will not
7.16 Or how can you be **sure,** Christian husband, that you will not
16.10 Timothy comes your way, be **sure** to make him feel welcome
2 Cor 1.15 I was so **sure** of all this that I made plans at
1.21 makes us, together with you, **sure** of our life in union with
7. 4 I am so **sure** of you;
8.24 all the churches will be **sure** of it and know that we
9. 4 not to speak of your shame—for feeling so **sure** of you!
10. 2 for I am **sure** I can deal harshly with those who say
Eph 5. 5 You may be **sure** that no one who is immoral, indecent,
Phil 1. 6 And so I am **sure** that God, who began this good work
1.22 worthwhile work, then I am not **sure** which I should choose.
1.25 I am **sure** of this, and so I know that I will
Col 1.23 on a firm and **sure** foundation, and must not allow yourselves
4.16 you read this letter, make **sure** that it is read also in
4.17 And say to Archippus, "Be **sure** to finish the task you
2 Thes 3. 4 in you, and we are **sure** that you are doing and will
2 Tim 1. 5 I am **sure** that you have it also.
1.12 have trusted, and I am **sure** that he is able to keep
Phlm 21 I am **sure,** as I write this, that you will do what
Heb 6. 9 if we speak like this, dear friends, we feel **sure** about you.
6.19 It is safe and **sure,** and goes through the curtain of the
8. 5 God said to him, "Be **sure** to make everything according to
10.22 a sincere heart and a **sure** faith, with hearts that have been
11. 1 have faith is to be **sure** of the things we hope for,
13.18 We are **sure** we have a clear conscience, because we want to
Jas 1. 4 Make **sure** that your endurance carries you all the way
1 Pet 5.10 and give you firmness, strength, and a **sure** foundation.
1 Jn 2. 3 we obey God's commands, then we are **sure** that we know him.
2. 5 is how we can be **sure** that we are in union with
2.24 Be **sure,** then, to keep in your hearts the message you
4.13 We are **sure** that we live in union with God and that
5.14 God's presence, because we are **sure** that he hears us if we

SURE-FOOTED

2 Sam 22.34 He makes me **sure-footed** as a deer;
Ps 18.33 He makes me **sure-footed** as a deer;
Is 63.12 they were as **sure-footed** as wild horses, and never stumbled.
Hab 3.19 He makes me **sure-footed** as a deer, and keeps me safe on

SURFACE

Gen 2. 6 come up from beneath the **surface** and water the ground.
7.18 The water became deeper, and the boat drifted on the **surface.**
Ex 7.17 am going to strike the **surface** of the river with this stick,
7.20 his stick and struck the **surface** of the river, and all the
16.14 was something thin and flaky on the **surface** of the desert.
Is 24. 1 He will twist the earth's **surface** and scatter its people.
Dan 7. 2 from all directions and lashing the **surface** of the ocean.

SURPLUS

2 Chr 31.10 there has been enough to eat and a large **surplus** besides.

SURPRISE

Josh 8. 2 Prepare to attack the city by **surprise** from the rear."
10. 9 Gilgal to Gibeon, and they made a **surprise** attack on the Amorites.
11. 7 Joshua and all his men attacked them by **surprise** at Merom Brook.
Judg 8.11 of Nobah and Jogbehah, and attacked the army by **surprise.**
14. 8 had killed, and he was **surprised** to find a swarm of bees
Ruth 3. 8 suddenly, turned over, and was **surprised** to find a woman
2 Sam 16.11 so why should you be **surprised** at this Benjaminite?
Job 6. 3 sands of the sea, so my wild words should not **surprise** you.
Prov 12.20 are in for a rude **surprise,** but those who work for good
Ecc 5. 8 Don't be **surprised** when you see that the government
Jer 14. 9 a man taken by **surprise,** like a soldier powerless to help?
Lam 4.19 they took us by **surprise** in the desert.
Mt 8.10 Jesus heard this, he was **surprised** and said to the people
27.14 with the result that the Governor was greatly **surprised.**
Mk 6. 6 He was greatly **surprised,** because the people did not have faith.
9.15 saw Jesus, they were greatly **surprised,** and ran to him
15.44 Pilate was **surprised** to hear that Jesus was already dead.
Lk 1.63 How **surprised** they all were!
7. 9 Jesus was **surprised** when he heard this;
11.38 The Pharisee was **surprised** when he noticed that Jesus had not
24.22 Some of the women of our group **surprised** us;
Jn 3. 7 Do not be **surprised** because I tell you that you must all
4.27 and they were greatly **surprised** to find him talking with
5.28 Do not be **surprised** at this;
7.15 The Jewish authorities were greatly **surprised** and said,
7.21 "I performed one miracle, and you were all **surprised.**
Acts 3.10 they were all **surprised** and amazed at what had happened
3.12 "Fellow-Israelites, why are you **surprised** at this, and why do you
Gal 1. 6 I am **surprised** at you!
1 Thes 5. 4 and the Day should not take you by **surprise** like a thief.
1 Pet 4. 4 And now the heathen are **surprised** when you do not join
4.12 dear friends, do not be **surprised** at the painful test you
1 Jn 3.13 So do not be **surprised,** my brothers, if the people of

SURRENDER

Lev 26.25 you, and you will be forced to **surrender** to your enemies.
Deut 20.10 attack a city, first give its people a chance to **surrender.**
20.11 they open the gates and **surrender,** they are all to become
20.12 that city will not **surrender,** but choose to fight, surround
1 Sam 11. 3 If no one will help us, then we will **surrender** to you."
11.10 to Nahash, "Tomorrow we will **surrender** to you, and you can
1 Kgs 20. 3 "King Benhadad demands that [3] you **surrender** to him your silver
2 Kgs 15.16 surrounding territory, because the city did not **surrender** to him.
17. 3 Hoshea **surrendered** to Shalmaneser and paid him tribute every year.
18.31 Assyria commands you to come out of the city and **surrender.**
24.12 and the palace officials, **surrendered** to the Babylonians.
25.23 and soldiers who had not **surrendered** heard about this, they
Is 36. 2 force to demand that King Hezekiah should **surrender.**
36.16 Assyria commands you to come out of the city and **surrender.**
Jer 21. 9 But whoever goes out and **surrenders** to the Babylonians, who
27.14 listen to the prophets who tell you not to **surrender** to him.
38. 2 But whoever goes out and **surrenders** to the Babylonians will
38.17 "If you **surrender** to the king of Babylonia's officers,
38.18 But if you do not **surrender,** then this city will be
38.21 me in a vision what will happen if you refuse to **surrender.**
40. 7 Some of the Judaean officers and soldiers had not **surrendered.**
40. 9 need for you to be afraid to **surrender** to the Babylonians.
40.13 the soldiers who had not **surrendered** came to Gedaliah at
50.15 Now Babylon has **surrendered.**
Rom 6.13 Nor must you **surrender** any part of yourselves to sin
6.13 from death to life, and **surrender** your whole being to him
6.16 know that when you **surrender** yourselves as slaves to obey someone,
6.19 At one time you **surrendered** yourselves entirely as slaves
6.19 must now **surrender** yourselves entirely as slaves of righteousness

SURROUND

Gen 19. 4 guests went to bed, the men of Sodom **surrounded** the house.
Ex 38.20 Tent and for the **surrounding** enclosure were made of bronze.
38.31 the bases for the **surrounding** enclosure and for the entrance
38.31 all the pegs for the Tent and the **surrounding** enclosure.
40. 8 Put up the **surrounding** enclosure and hang the curtain
Lev 13. 3 than the **surrounding** skin, it is a dreaded skin-disease,
13.20 to be deeper than the **surrounding** skin and the hairs in it
13.21 deeper than the **surrounding** skin, but is light in colour,
13.25 it appears deeper than the **surrounding** skin, it is a dreaded
13.26 deeper than the **surrounding** skin, but is light in colour,
13.30 to be deeper than the **surrounding** skin and the hairs in it
13.31 to be deeper than the **surrounding** skin, but there are still
13.32 to be deeper than the **surrounding** skin, [33] the person shall
13.34 to be deeper than the **surrounding** skin, he shall pronounce
Num 21.25 Heshbon and all the **surrounding** towns, and settled in them.
21.32 Israelites captured it and its **surrounding** towns and drove
Deut 1. 7 Amorites and to all the **surrounding** regions—to the Jordan Valley,
20.12 surrender, but choose to fight, **surround** it with your army.
Josh 7. 9 They will **surround** us and kill every one of us!
8.22 of Ai found themselves completely **surrounded** by Israelites,
10. 5 Eglon, joined forces, **surrounded** Gibeon, and attacked it.
10.31 on from Libnah to Lachish, **surrounded** it and attacked it.
10.34 on from Lachish to Eglon, **surrounded** it and attacked it.
17.11 and Ibleam, along with their **surrounding** towns, as well as
17.11 Endor, Taanach, Megiddo, and their **surrounding** towns.
17.16 in Beth Shan and its **surrounding** towns and those who live in
21.11 of Judah, along with the pasture land **surrounding** it.
Judg 1.18 Ashkelon, or Ekron, with their **surrounding** territories.
9.50 Abimelech went to Thebez, **surrounded** that city, and captured it.
16. 2 Samson was there, so they **surrounded** the place and waited
19.22 sexual perverts from the town **surrounded** the house and
20. 5 Gibeah came to attack me and **surrounded** the house at night.
20.33 regrouped at Baaltamar, the men **surrounding** Gibeah suddenly
1 Sam 5. 6 and the people in the **surrounding** territory by causing them
2 Sam 16. 6 though David was **surrounded** by his men and his bodyguard.
22.12 thick clouds, full of water, **surrounded** him;
2 Kgs 3.25 Kir Heres was left, and the slingers **surrounded** it and attacked it.
6.14 They reached the town at night and **surrounded** it.
6.15 Syrian troops with their horses and chariots **surrounding** the town.
8.21 chariots for Zair, where the Edomite army **surrounded** them.
11.14 He was **surrounded** by the officers and the trumpeters, and
15.16 Tappuah, its inhabitants, and the **surrounding** territory,

2 Kgs 17.15 followed the customs of the **surrounding** nations, disobeying
18. 8 largest city, including Gaza and its **surrounding** territory.
25. 4 Although the Babylonians were **surrounding** the city, all the
1 Chr 4.33 Tochen, and Ashan, [33] and the **surrounding** villages, as far
6.70 of Aner and Bileam with the **surrounding** pasture lands.
6.71 the following towns, with the **surrounding** pasture lands:
6.77 the following towns with the **surrounding** pasture lands:
8.12 the cities of Ono and Lod and the **surrounding** villages.
16.27 Glory and majesty **surround** him, power and joy fill his Temple.
18. 1 their control the city of Gath and its **surrounding** villages.
29.30 to him, to Israel, and to the **surrounding** kingdoms.
2 Chr 13.14 The Judaeans looked round and saw that they were **surrounded.**
17.10 The Lord made all the **surrounding** kingdoms afraid to go
21. 9 There the Edomite army **surrounded** them, but during the night
23.13 column reserved for kings and **surrounded** by the army
Neh 5.17 all the people who came to me from the **surrounding** nations.
6.16 When our enemies in the **surrounding** nations heard this,
Job 29. 5 was with me then, and I was **surrounded** by all my children.
Ps 3. 6 of the thousands of enemies who **surround** me on every side.
17. 9 Deadly enemies **surround** me;
18.11 thick clouds, full of water, **surrounded** him.
22.12 Many enemies **surround** me like bulls;
27. 3 Even if a whole army **surrounds** me, I will not be afraid;
30.11 you have taken away my sorrow and **surrounded** me with joy.
31.21 showed his love for me when I was **surrounded** and attacked!
40.12 I am **surrounded** by many troubles— too many to count!
49. 5 of danger when I am **surrounded** by enemies, [6] by evil men who
55.10 and riots in the city, [10] **surrounding** it day and night,
57. 4 I am **surrounded** by enemies, who are like man-eating lions.
79. 4 The **surrounding** nations insult us;
80. 6 You let the **surrounding** nations fight over our land;
88.17 All day long they **surround** me like a flood;
96. 6 Glory and majesty **surround** him;
97. 2 Clouds and darkness **surround** him;
125. 2 As the mountains **surround** Jerusalem,
125. 2 so the Lord **surrounds** his people now and for ever.
138. 7 When I am **surrounded** by troubles, you keep me safe.
Prov 5.19 let her **surround** you with her love.
Ecc 9.14 He **surrounded** it and prepared to break through the walls.
Song 7. 2 A sheaf of wheat is there, **surrounded** by lilies.
Is 29. 3 God will attack the city, **surround** it, and besiege it.
Jer 4.17 Judah [17] and will **surround** Jerusalem like men guarding a field,
19. 9 The enemy will **surround** the city and try to kill its people.
48.39 It is in ruins, and all the **surrounding** nations jeer at it.
50.14 "Bowmen, line up for battle against Babylon and **surround** it.
50.29 **Surround** the city and don't let anyone escape.
52. 7 Although the Babylonians were **surrounding** the city, all the
Lam 1. 3 to call their own— **Surrounded** by enemies, with no way to
Ezek 23.22 make them angry with you and bring them to **surround** you.
23.24 Protected by shields and helmets, they will **surround** you.
28. 2 like a god you sit on a throne, **surrounded** by the seas.
28.24 Lord said, "None of the **surrounding** nations that treated
32.23 her soldiers fell in battle, and their graves **surround** her tomb.
36. 4 were plundered and mocked by all the **surrounding** nations.
36. 5 the **surrounding** nations, and especially against Edom.
36. 7 solemnly promise that the **surrounding** nations will be humiliated.
43.12 All the area **surrounding** it on the top of the mountain is
45. 2 metres along each side, entirely **surrounded** by an open space
Dan 1. 1 Babylonia attacked Jerusalem and **surrounded** the city.
2.22 hidden in darkness, and he himself is **surrounded** by light.
7.13 He was approaching me, **surrounded** by clouds, and he went to
Hos 7. 2 their sins **surround** them, and I cannot avoid seeing them."
11.12 "The people of Israel have **surrounded** me with lies and deceit,
Joel 3.11 Hurry and come, all you **surrounding** nations,
3.12 There I, the Lord, will sit to judge all the **surrounding** nations.
Amos 3. 9 "Gather together in the hills **surrounding** Samaria and see
3.11 And so an enemy will **surround** their land, destroy their defences,
Obad 16 But all the **surrounding** nations will drink a still more
Zech 3.10 and security, **surrounded** by your vineyards and fig-trees."
12. 6 of ripe corn—they will destroy all the **surrounding** nations.
Mt 14.35 in all the **surrounding country** and brought them to Jesus.
Lk 7.17 Jesus went out through all the country and the **surrounding territory.**
19.43 come when your enemies will **surround** you with barricades,
21.20 "When you see Jerusalem **surrounded** by armies, then you will know
Acts 14. 6 Lystra and Derbe in Lycaonia and to the **surrounding territory.**
Rev 4. 6 **Surrounding** the throne on each of its sides, were four living
5. 6 the centre of the throne, **surrounded** by the four living creatures
20. 9 out over the earth and **surrounded** the camp of God's people

SURVIVE

Gen 45. 7 way and to make sure that you and your descendants **survive.**
Ex 10.12 that grows, everything that has **survived** the hail."
Lev 26.39 The few of you who **survive** in the land of your enemies
Num 14.38 Of the twelve spies only Joshua and Caleb **survived.**
21.35 leaving no **survivors,** and then they occupied his land.
24.19 Israel will trample them down And wipe out the last **survivors."**
Deut 2.34 We left no **survivors.**
4.27 among other nations, where only a few of you will **survive.**
28.62 a few of you will **survive,** because you did not obey the
Judg 21.17 the tribe of Benjamin to **survive,** [18] but we cannot allow
1 Sam 2.36 Any of your descendants who **survive** will have to go to
4. 3 When the **survivors** came back to camp, the leaders of Israel said,
11.11 The **survivors** scattered, each man running off by himself.
2 Sam 17.12 Neither he nor any of his men will **survive.**
1 Kgs 1. 5 the son of David and Haggith, was the eldest **surviving** son.
15.29 not one **survived.**
20.30 The **survivors** fled into the city of Aphek, where the
2 Kgs 19. 4 So pray to God for those of our people who **survive."**
2 Kgs 19.30 Those in Judah who **survive** will flourish like plants
19.31 on Mount Zion who will **survive,** because the Lord is
21.14 will abandon the people who **survive,** and will hand them over
1 Chr 4.43 There they killed the **surviving** Amalekites, and they
2 Chr 12. 7 But when Shishak attacks, they will barely **survive.**
30. 6 "People of Israel, You have **survived** the Assyrian conquest
36.20 He took all the **survivors** to Babylonia, where they
Ezra 9.13 us less than we deserve and have allowed us to **survive.**
9.14 that you will destroy us completely and let no one **survive.**
9.15 God of Israel, you are just, but you have let us **survive.**
Neh 1. 3 me that those who had **survived** and were back in the homeland
Job 18.19 He has no descendants, no **survivors.**
27.15 Those who **survive** will die from disease, and even their
Ps 21.10 None of their descendants will **survive;**
76.10 those who **survive** the wars will keep your festivals.
Prov 10.30 have security, but the wicked will not **survive** in the land.
Is 1. 9 people **survive,** Jerusalem would have been totally destroyed,
4. 2 the people of Israel who **survive** will take delight and pride
4. 3 whom God has chosen for **survival,** will be called holy.
7. 8 years it will be too shattered to **survive** as a nation.
7.22 Yes, the few **survivors** left in the land will have milk and
10.20 people of Israel who have **survived** will no longer rely on
11.16 his people Israel who have **survived** there, just as there was
13.12 Those who **survive** will be scarcer than gold.
14.20 None of your evil family will **survive.**
14.22 I will leave nothing—no children, no **survivors** at all.
16.14 people, only a few will **survive,** and they will be weak."
17. 3 Those Syrians who **survive** will be in disgrace like the
17. 6 Only a few people will **survive,** and Israel will be like an
20. 6 How will we ever **survive?'** "
24.14 Those who **survive** will sing for joy.
28. 5 like a glorious crown of flowers for his people who **survive.**
33.14 Can any of us **survive** a fire like that?"
33.15 You can **survive** if you say and do what is right.
37. 4 So pray to God for those of our people who **survive."**
37.31 Those in Judah who **survive** will flourish like plants
37.32 on Mount Zion who will **survive,** because the Lord Almighty is
45.20 of the nations, all who **survive** the fall of the empire;
49. 6 people of Israel who have **survived,** but I will also make you
Jer 8. 3 of this evil nation who **survive,** who live in the places
11.23 and when that time comes, none of them will **survive."**
21. 7 officials, and the people who **survive** the war, the famine,
30. 7 a time of distress for my people, but they will **survive."**
42. 2 Pray for all of us who have **survived.**
42.17 Not one of them will **survive,** not one will escape the
44.14 left and have come to Egypt to live will escape or **survive.**
44.28 Then the **survivors** will know whose words have come true,
Ezek 6. 7 killed everywhere, and those who **survive** will acknowledge
6.12 those who **survive** will starve to death.
7.13 Those who are evil cannot **survive.**
12.16 let a few of them **survive** the war, the famine, and the
14.22 If anyone does **survive** and save his children, look at
17.21 and the **survivors** will be scattered in every direction.
36.36 neighbouring nations that have **survived** will know that I,
Joel 2.11 Who will **survive** it?
2.32 those whom I choose will **survive.'**
Amos 3.12 so only a few will **survive** of Samaria's people, who now
4.11 Those of you who **survived** were like a burning stick saved
7. 2 How can they **survive?**
7. 5 How can your people **survive?**
Obad 18 No descendant of Esau will **survive.**
Mic 5. 7 The people of Israel who **survive** will be like refreshing
7.18 you forgive the sins of your people who have **survived.**
Nah 1. 6 When he is angry, who can **survive?**
1. 6 Who can **survive** his terrible fury?
Hab 2. 4 who are evil will not **survive,** but those who are righteous
2. 8 but now those who have **survived** will plunder you because of
Zeph 1. 3 I will destroy all mankind, and no **survivors** will be left.
2. 7 The people of Judah who **survive** will occupy your land.
2. 9 Those of my people who **survive** will plunder them and take
3.13 The people of Israel who **survive** will do no wrong to anyone,
Zech 8.11 But now I am treating the **survivors** of this nation differently.
8.12 all these blessings to the people of my nation who **survive.**
9. 7 All the **survivors** will become part of my people and be like
10. 9 They and their children will **survive** and return home together.
13. 9 will test the third that **survives** and will purify them as
14.16 Then all the **survivors** from the nations that have
Mal 3. 2 Who will be able to **survive** when he appears?
Mt 24.22 had he not done so, nobody would **survive.**
Mk 13.20 if he had not, nobody would **survive.**
Acts 27.34 you need it in order to **survive.**
1 Cor 3.14 built on the foundation **survives** the fire, the builder will receive

SUSA

Capital of the Persian empire.

Ezra 4. 9 from Erech, Babylon, and **Susa** in the land of Elam,
Neh 1. 1 of Persia, I, Nehemiah, was in **Susa,** the capital city.
Esth 1. 1 capital city of **Susa,** King Xerxes ruled over 127 provinces,
1. 5 the men in the capital city of **Susa,** rich and poor alike.
2. 3 young girls to your harem here in **Susa,** the capital city.
2. 5 There in **Susa** lived a Jew named Mordecai son of Jair;
2. 8 girls were being brought to **Susa,** Esther was among them.
3.15 in the capital city of **Susa,** and runners carried the news to
3.15 while the city of **Susa** was being thrown into confusion.
4. 8 been issued in **Susa,** ordering the destruction of the Jews.
4.16 "Go and gather all the Jews in **Susa** together;
8.14 The decree was also made public in **Susa,** the capital city.
8.15 Then the streets of **Susa** rang with cheers and joyful shouts.
9. 6 In **Susa,** the capital city itself, the Jews killed five hundred men.
9.11 number of people killed in **Susa** was reported to the king.

Esth 9.12 said to Queen Esther, "In **Susa** alone the Jews have killed
9.13 Majesty, let the Jews in **Susa** do again tomorrow what they
9.14 this to be done, and the proclamation was issued in **Susa.**
9.15 of Adar the Jews of **Susa** got together again and killed three
9.18 The Jews of **Susa,** however, made the fifteenth a holiday,
Dan 8. 2 myself in the walled city of **Susa** in the province of Elam.

SUSPECT

Gen 34.25 the city without arousing **suspicion,** and killed all the men,
Num 5.12 a man becomes **suspicious** that his wife is unfaithful
5.12 happen that a husband becomes **suspicious** of his wife,
5.15 is an offering from a **suspicious** husband,
5.29 and becomes **suspicious** that his wife has committed adultery.
Judg 18.10 you will find that the people don't **suspect** a thing.
1 Sam 18. 9 so he was jealous and **suspicious** of David from that day on.
Acts 27.27 the sailors **suspected** that we were getting close to land.
1 Tim 6. 4 disputes, insults, evil **suspicions,** [5]and constant arguments

SUSPENSE

Jn 10.24 and asked, "How long are you going to keep us in **suspense?**

SUSTAIN

Deut 8. 3 depend on bread alone to **sustain** him, but on everything that
Prov 18.14 Your will to live can **sustain** you when you are sick, but
Heb 1. 3 of God's own being, **sustaining** the universe with his powerful word.

SWALLOW (1)

Gen 41. 7 wind, [7]and the thin ears of corn **swallowed** the full ones.
41.24 wind, [24]and the thin ears of corn **swallowed** the full ones.
Ex 7.12 But Aaron's stick **swallowed** theirs.
15.12 stretched out your right hand, and the earth **swallowed** our enemies.
Lev 26.38 You will die in exile, **swallowed** up by the land of your
Num 16.30 the earth opens up and **swallows** them with all they own, so
16.32 Abiram split open [32]and **swallowed** them and their families,
16.34 The earth might **swallow** us too!"
26.10 The ground opened and **swallowed** them, and they died with
Deut 11. 6 opened up and **swallowed** them, along with their families,
Job 7.19 Won't you look away long enough for me to **swallow** my spittle?
20.16 What the evil man **swallows** is like poison;
Ps 106.17 the earth opened up and **swallowed** Dathan and buried Abiram
124. 3 us, [3]then they would have **swallowed** us alive in their
Prov 18. 8 Gossip is so tasty—how we love to **swallow** it!
26.22 How we love to **swallow** it!
Is 5.30 The light is **swallowed** by darkness.
Jer 51.34 like a monster he **swallowed** it.
Jon 1.17 Lord's command a large fish **swallowed** Jonah, and he was
Mt 23.24 You strain a fly out of your drink, but **swallow** a camel!
Heb 11.29 the Egyptians tried to do it, the water **swallowed** them up.
Rev 10.10 But after I **swallowed** it, it turned sour in my stomach.
12.16 it opened its mouth and **swallowed** the water that had come

SWALLOW (2)

Ps 84. 3 have built a nest, and the **swallows** have their own home;
Jer 8. 7 **swallows,** and thrushes know when it is time to migrate.

SWAMP

Job 8.11 they are never found outside a **swamp.**
40.21 the thorn-bushes, and hides among the reeds in the **swamp.**

SWARM

Ex 8.24 The Lord sent great **swarms** of flies into the king's
10.14 They came in **swarms** and settled over the whole country.
10.14 It was the largest **swarm** of locusts that had ever been seen
Deut 1.44 in those hills came out against you like a **swarm** of bees.
Judg 7.12 in the valley like a **swarm** of locusts, and they had as
14. 8 was surprised to find a **swarm** of bees and some honey inside
1 Kgs 8.37 destroyed by scorching winds or **swarms** of locusts,
2 Chr 6.28 destroyed by scorching winds or **swarms** of locusts,
Ps 105.31 flies and gnats **swarmed** throughout the whole country.
118.12 They **swarmed** round me like bees, but they burnt out as
Is 7.19 They will **swarm** in the rugged valleys and in the caves
Jer 51.14 to attack Babylonia like a **swarm** of locusts, and they will
51.27 Bring up the horses like a **swarm** of locusts.
Joel 1. 4 **Swarm after swarm** of locusts settled on the crops;
1. 4 what one **swarm** left, the next swarm devoured.
2. 8 They **swarm** through defences, and nothing can stop them.
2.25 lost in the years when **swarms** of locusts ate your crops.
Amos 7. 1 I saw him create a **swarm** of locusts just after the king's
Nah 3.17 Your officials are like a **swarm** of locusts that stay in
Hab 1.14 like fish or like a **swarm** of insects that have no ruler

SWAY

Is 24.20 like a drunken man and **sway** like a hut in a storm.

SWEAR
[SWORE, SWORN]

Gen 14.22 "I solemnly **swear** before the Lord, the Most High God,
42.15 I **swear** by the name of the king that you will never
44. 7 We **swear** that we have done no such thing.
Ex 10.10 The king said, "I **swear** by the Lord that I will never
Lev 6. 3 that has been lost and **swearing** that he did not find it.
Num 14.28 'I **swear** that as surely as I live, I will do to
14.35 I **swear** that I will do this to you wicked people who
32.11 'I **swear** that because they did not remain loyal to me,
Josh 2.12 Now **swear** by him that you will treat my family as kindly
5. 4 Just as he had **sworn,** they were not allowed to see the
Judg 8.19 I solemnly **swear** that if you had not killed them, I would
15. 7 I **swear** that I won't stop until I pay you back!"
Ruth 3.13 if not, then I **swear** by the living Lord that I will
1 Sam 18. 3 Jonathan **swore** eternal friendship with David because of
20. 3 I **swear** to you by the living Lord that I am only
20.21 I **swear** by the living Lord that you will be in no
25.26 And now I **swear** to you by the living Lord that your
25.34 But I **swear** by the living God of Israel that if you
26.16 I **swear** by the living Lord that all of you deserve to
29. 6 and said to him, "I **swear** by the living God of Israel
2 Sam 2.27 "I **swear** by the living God," Joab answered, "that if
11.11 By all that's sacred, I **swear** that I could never do such
12. 5 rich man and said, "I **swear** by the living Lord that the
12.11 I **swear** to you that I will cause someone from your own
14.19 She answered, "I **swear** by all that is sacred, Your
15.21 Ittai answered, "Your Majesty, I **swear** to you in the Lord's
19. 7 I **swear** by the Lord's name that if you don't, not one
1 Kgs 1.51 I want King Solomon to **swear** to me that he will not
2.24 I **swear** by the living Lord that Adonijah will die this very
17.12 living Lord your God I **swear** that I haven't got any bread.
18.10 living Lord, your God, I **swear** that the king has made a
18.10 require that ruler to **swear** that you could not be found.
2 Kgs 2. 2 But Elisha answered, "I **swear** by my loyalty to the living
2. 4 But Elisha answered, "I **swear** by my loyalty to the living
2. 6 But Elisha answered, "I **swear** by my loyalty to the living
3.14 Lord, whom I serve, I **swear** that I would have nothing to
4.30 woman said to Elisha, "I **swear** by my loyalty to the living
5.16 Lord, whom I serve, I **swear** that I will not accept a
2 Chr 36.13 who had forced him to **swear** in God's name that he would
Neh 5.12 priests and made the leaders **swear** in front of them to keep
Job 27. 1 I **swear** by the living Almighty God, who refuses me
31. 5 I **swear** I have never acted wickedly and never tried to
31.35 I **swear** that every word is true.
Song 2. 7 **swear** by the swift deer and the gazelles that you will not
3. 5 **swear** by the swift deer and the gazelles that you will not
Is 14.24 The Lord Almighty has **sworn** an oath:
48. 1 You **swear** by the name of the Lord and claim to worship
65.16 Whoever takes an oath will **swear** by the name of the Faithful
Jer 4. 2 hate, [2]it will be right for you to **swear** by my name.
12.16 of my people and will **swear,** 'As the Lord lives'—as they
12.16 once taught my people to **swear** by Baal—then they will also
16.14 when people will no longer **swear** by me as the living God
16.15 Instead, they will **swear** by me as the living God who
22. 5 obey my commands, then I **swear** to you that this palace will
23. 7 "when people will no longer **swear** by me as the living God
23. 8 Instead, they will **swear** by me as the living God who
38.16 promised me in secret, "I **swear** by the living God, the God
44.26 a vow by saying, 'I **swear** by the living Sovereign Lord!'
49.13 I myself have **sworn** that the city of Bozrah will become
51.14 The Lord Almighty has **sworn** by his own life that he will
Ezek 17.13 made a treaty with him, and made him **swear** to be loyal.
17.19 for breaking the treaty which he **swore** in my name to keep.
44.12 Sovereign Lord, solemnly **swear** that they must be punished.
Amos 8. 7 the God of Israel, has **sworn,** "I will never forget their
8.14 Those who **swear** by the idols of Samaria, who say, 'By
Zeph 1. 5 those who worship me and **swear** loyalty to me, but then take
2. 9 the God of Israel, I **swear** that Moab and Ammon are going
Mt 5.34 Do not **swear** by heaven, for it is God's throne;
5.36 Do not even **swear** by your head, because you cannot make
14. 7 that he promised her, "I **swear** that I will give you
23.16 You teach, 'If someone **swears** by the Temple, he isn't bound
23.16 but if he **swears** by the gold in the Temple, he is
23.18 You also teach, 'If someone **swears** by the altar, he
23.18 but if he **swears** by the gift on the altar, he is
23.20 So then, when a person **swears** by the altar,
23.20 he is **swearing** by it and by all the
23.21 and when he **swears** by the Temple,
23.21 he is **swearing** by it and by God,
23.22 and when someone **swears** by heaven,
23.22 he is **swearing** by God's throne and by him
26.72 it and answered, "I **swear** that I don't know that man!"
26.74 Then Peter said, "I **swear** that I am telling the truth!
Mk 6.23 he said to her, "I **swear** that I will give you anything
14.71 Then Peter said, "I **swear** that I am telling the truth!
Jas 5.12 Do not **swear** by heaven or by earth or by anything else.

SWEAT

Gen 3.19 to work hard and **sweat** to make the soil produce anything,
Lk 22.44 his **sweat** was like drops of blood falling to the ground.

SWEEP
[SWEPT]

Judg 5.21 A flood in the Kishon **swept** them away— the onrushing
1 Kgs 14.10 they will be **swept** away like dung.
Job 1.19 your eldest son, [19]when a storm **swept** in from the desert.
24.18 The wicked man is **swept** away by floods, and the land he
27.21 the east wind will **sweep** them from their homes;
37.21 and the sky has been **swept** clean by the wind.
Is 8. 8 They will **sweep** through Judah in a flood, rising shoulder
14.23 I will **sweep** Babylon with a broom that will sweep everything away.
21. 1 Like a whirlwind **sweeping** across the desert, disaster will
28.17 Hailstorms will **sweep** away all the lies you depend on, and

Is 28.18 When disaster **sweeps** down, you will be overcome.
30.28 It **sweeps** nations to destruction and puts an end to their
44.22 I have **swept** your sins away like a cloud.
Ezek 26. 4 Then I will **sweep** away all the dust and leave only a
26.17 Her ships have been **swept** from the seas.
Dan 11.10 One of them will **sweep** on like a flood and attack an
11.22 even God's High Priest, will be **swept** away and wiped out.
Hos 11. 6 War will **sweep** through their cities and break down the city gates.
Amos 5. 6 do not go, he will **sweep** down like fire on the people
Hab 1.11 Then they **sweep** on like the wind and are gone, these men
Zech 7.14 Like a storm I **swept** them away to live in foreign countries.
Mt 24.39 was happening until the flood came and **swept** them all away.
Lk 15. 8 She lights a lamp, **sweeps** her house, and looks carefully
Gal 2.13 and even Barnabas was **swept** along by their cowardly action.

SWEET

Ex 25. 6 for the anointing oil and for the **sweet-smelling** incense;
30. 7 the lamps ready, he is to burn **sweet-smelling** incense on it.
30.23 liquid myrrh, three kilogrammes of **sweet-smelling** cinnamon,
30.23 three kilogrammes of **sweet-smelling** cane, [24]and six kilogrammes of cassia
30.34 of each of the following **sweet** spices—stacte, onycha,
31.11 the anointing oil, and the **sweet-smelling** incense for the Holy Place.
35. 8 for the anointing oil and for the **sweet-smelling** incense;
35.15 the **sweet-smelling** incense;
35.28 for the anointing oil, and for the **sweet-smelling** incense.
37.29 and the pure **sweet-smelling** incense, mixed like perfume.
39.38 the **sweet-smelling** incense;
40.27 the curtain, [27]and burnt the **sweet-smelling** incense, just
Judg 9.11 you, I would have to stop producing my good **sweet** fruit.'
14.14 Out of the strong came something **sweet."**
14.18 "What could be **sweeter** than honey?
Ps 19.10 they are **sweeter** than the purest honey.
119.103 How **sweet** is the taste of your instructions—
119.103 **sweeter** even than honey!
Prov 5. 3 man's wife may be as **sweet** as honey and her kisses as
9.17 To the foolish man she says, [17]"Stolen water is **sweeter.**
16.24 Kind words are like honey—**sweet** to the taste and good
24.13 honey from the comb is **sweet** on your tongue, [14]you may be
27. 7 but when you are hungry, even bitter food tastes **sweet.**
Song 2. 3 sit in its shadow, and its fruit is **sweet** to my taste.
5.16 His mouth is **sweet** to kiss;
Is 5.20 You make what is bitter **sweet,**
5.20 and what is **sweet** you make bitter.
Ezek 3. 3 I ate it, and it tasted as **sweet** as honey.
Amos 9.13 The mountains will drip with **sweet** wine, and the hills will
Jn 12. 3 The **sweet** smell of the perfume filled the whole house.
2 Cor 2.14 knowledge about Christ spread everywhere like a **sweet** fragrance.
2.15 For we are like a **sweet-smelling** incense offered by Christ to God,
Eph 5. 2 for us as a **sweet-smelling** offering and sacrifice that pleases God.
Phil 4.18 They are like a **sweet-smelling** offering to God, a sacrifice
Jas 3.11 spring of water pours out **sweet** water and bitter water from
3.12 cannot bear figs, nor can a salty spring produce **sweet** water.
Rev 10. 9 your stomach, but in your mouth it will be **sweet** as honey."
10.10 and ate it, and it tasted **sweet** as honey in my mouth.

SWEETHEART

Song 4. 9 look in your eyes, my **sweetheart** and bride, and the necklace
4.10 Your love delights me, my **sweetheart** and bride.
4.12 My **sweetheart,** my bride, is a secret garden, a walled garden,
5. 1 I have entered my garden, my **sweetheart,** my bride.
5. 2 Let me come in, my darling, my **sweetheart,** my dove.

SWELL
[SWOLLEN]

Lev 13.19 and if afterwards a white **swelling** or a reddish-white spot
Num 5.21 your genital organs to shrink and your stomach to **swell** up.
5.22 stomach and cause it to **swell** up and your genital organs to
5.27 stomach will **swell** up and her genital organs will shrink.
Deut 8. 4 clothes have not worn out, nor have your feet **swollen** up.
28.22 strike you with infectious diseases, with **swelling** and fever;
Neh 9.21 never wore out, and their feet were not **swollen** with pain.
Job 16.16 red, and my eyes are **swollen** and circled with shadows,
Ps 6. 7 my eyes are so **swollen** from the weeping caused by my enemies.
Lk 14. 2 whose legs and arms were **swollen** came to Jesus, [3]and Jesus
Acts 28. 6 were waiting for him to **swell** up or suddenly fall down dead.
1 Tim 3. 6 so that he will not **swell** up with pride and be condemned,
6. 4 teaching of our religion [4]is **swollen** with pride and knows nothing.
2 Tim 3. 4 they will be treacherous, reckless, and **swollen** with pride;

SWIFT

2 Sam 1.23 **swifter** than eagles, stronger than lions.
22.11 He flew **swiftly** on his winged creature;
Job 9.26 My life passes like the **swiftest** boat, as fast as an
Ps 18.10 He flew **swiftly** on a winged creature;
Song 2. 7 swear by the **swift** deer and the gazelles that you will not
3. 5 swear by the **swift** deer and the gazelles that you will not
Is 5.26 And here they come, **swiftly,** quickly!
18. 2 Go back home, **swift** messengers!
19. 1 The Lord is coming to Egypt, riding **swiftly** on a cloud.
Lam 4.19 **Swifter** than eagles swooping from the sky, they chased us down.
Hos 11.11 will come from Egypt, as **swiftly** as birds, and from Assyria,

SWIM

Is 25.11 if they were trying to **swim,** but God will humiliate them,
Ezek 47. 5 It was too deep to cross except by **swimming.**
Acts 27.42 prisoners, in order to keep them from **swimming** ashore and escaping.
27.43 men who could swim to jump overboard first and **swim** ashore;

SWING
[SWUNG]

Prov 23.34 out on the ocean, sea-sick, **swinging** high up in the rigging
26.14 He gets no farther than a door **swinging** on its hinges.
Is 44.12 His strong arm **swings** a hammer to pound the metal into shape.
Ezek 32.10 When I **swing** my sword, kings will shudder with fright.
41.24 They were double doors that **swung** open in the middle.
Rev 14.16 who sat on the cloud **swung** his sickle on the earth,
14.19 So the angel **swung** his sickle on the earth, cut the

SWIRLING

Is 43.16 a road through the sea, a path through the **swirling** waters.

SWOLLEN see SWELL

SWOOP

Deut 28.49 They will **swoop** down on you like an eagle.
Job 9.26 boat, as fast as an eagle **swooping** down on a rabbit.
Is 46.11 he will **swoop** down like a hawk and accomplish what I have
Jer 48.40 promised that a nation will **swoop** down on Moab like an eagle
49.22 Bozrah like an eagle **swooping** down with outspread wings.
Lam 4.19 Swifter than eagles **swooping** from the sky, they chased us down.
Hos 8. 1 Enemies are **swooping** down on my land like eagles!
Hab 1. 8 They come **swooping** down like eagles attacking their prey.

SWORD

Gen 3.24 and a flaming **sword** which turned in all directions.
27.40 You will live by your **sword,** But be your brother's slave.
34.25 brothers of Dinah, took their **swords,** went into the city
48.22 which I took from the Amorites with my **sword** and my bow."
Ex 15. 9 I will draw my **sword** and take all they have.'
32.27 you to put on his **sword** and go through the camp from
Num 22.23 angel standing there holding a **sword,** it left the road and
22.29 If I had a **sword,** I would kill you."
22.31 Lord let Balaam see the angel standing there with his **sword;**
Deut 32.41 I will sharpen my flashing **sword** and see that justice is done.
32.42 with their blood, and my **sword** will kill all who oppose me.
33.29 is your shield and your **sword,** to defend you and give you
Josh 5.13 saw a man standing in front of him, holding a **sword.**
6.21 With their **swords** they killed everyone in the city, men
24.12 Your **swords** and bows had nothing to do with it.
Judg 3.16 Ehud had made himself a double-edged **sword**
3.21 left hand Ehud took the **sword** from his right side and
3.22 The whole **sword** went in, handle and all, and the fat
7.14 His friend replied, "It's the **sword** of the Israelite,
7.20 right, and shouted, "A **sword** for the Lord and for Gideon!"
7.22 Lord made the enemy troops attack each other with their **swords.**
8.20 But the boy did not draw his **sword.**
9.54 his weapons and ordered, "Draw your **sword** and kill me.
1 Sam 13.19 Philistines were determined to keep the Hebrews from making **swords**
13.22 soldiers except Saul and his son Jonathan had **swords** or spears.
15.33 Samuel said, "As your **sword** has made many mothers childless,
17.39 David strapped Saul's **sword** over the armour and tried to walk,
17.45 are coming against me with **sword,** spear, and javelin, but I
17.47 the Lord does not need **swords** or spears to save his people.
17.50 And so, without a **sword,** David defeated and killed
17.51 stood over him, took Goliath's **sword** out of its sheath, and
18. 4 David, together with his armour and also his **sword,** bow, and
21. 8 "Have you got a spear or a **sword** you can give me?
21. 8 I didn't have time to get my **sword** or any other weapon."
21. 9 Ahimelech answered, "I have the **sword** of Goliath the Philistine,
21. 9 "There is not a better **sword** anywhere!"
22.10 David some food and the **sword** of Goliath the Philistine."
22.13 give him some food and a **sword,** and consult God for him?
25.13 "Buckle on your **swords!"**
25.13 David also buckled on his **sword** and left with about four
31. 4 carrying his weapons, "Draw your **sword** and kill me, so that
31. 4 So Saul took his own **sword** and threw himself on it.
31. 5 he too threw himself on his own **sword** and died with Saul.
2 Sam 1.22 Jonathan's bow was deadly, the **sword** of Saul was merciless,
2.16 the head and plunged his **sword** into his opponent's side, so
2.16 And so that place in Gibeon is called "Field of **Swords."**
20. 8 dressed for battle, with a **sword** in its sheath fastened to
20. 8 As he came forward, the **sword** fell out.
20.10 not on guard against the **sword** that Joab was holding in his
21.16 who was wearing a new **sword,** thought he could kill David.
23.10 was so stiff that he could not let go of his **sword.**
1 Kgs 3.24 He sent for a **sword,** and when it was brought, [25]he
2 Kgs 3.26 battle, he took seven hundred **swordsmen** with him and tried
10.25 They went in with drawn **swords,** killed them all, and dragged
11. 8 guard King Joash with drawn **swords** and stay with him
11.11 stationed the men with drawn **swords** all round the front of
19.37 Sharezer, killed him with their **swords,** and then escaped to
1 Chr 5.18 44,760 soldiers, well-trained in the use of shields, **swords,**
10. 4 carrying his weapons, "Draw your **sword** and kill me, to keep
10. 4 So Saul took his own **sword** and threw himself on it.
10. 5 was dead, so he too threw himself on his **sword** and died.

1 Chr 21.12 Lord attacks you with his **sword** and sends an epidemic on
21.16 in mid air, holding his **sword** in his hand, ready to destroy
21.27 told the angel to put his **sword** away, and the angel obeyed.
21.30 because he was afraid of the **sword** of the Lord's angel.
2 Chr 23. 7 round the king, with their **swords** drawn, and are to stay
23.10 stationed the men with drawn **swords** all round the front of
32.21 of his god, some of his sons killed him with their **swords.**
Neh 4.13 I armed the people with **swords,** spears, and bows, and
4.18 and everyone who was building kept a **sword** strapped to his waist.
Esth 9. 5 They attacked them with **swords** and slaughtered them.
Job 15.22 from darkness, for somewhere a **sword** is waiting to kill him,
19.29 now, be afraid of the **sword**—
19.29 the **sword** that brings God's wrath on sin,
20.24 to escape from an iron **sword,** a bronze bow will shoot him
39.22 know the meaning of fear, and no **sword** can turn them back.
41.26 There is no **sword** that can wound him;
Ps 7.12 If they do not change their ways, God will sharpen his **sword.**
17.13 Save me from the wicked by your **sword;**
22.20 Save me from the **sword;**
37.14 The wicked draw their **swords** and bend their bows to kill
37.15 killed by their own **swords,** and their bows will be smashed.
44. 3 Your people did not conquer the land with their **swords;**
44. 6 not trust in my bow or in my **sword** to save me;
45. 3 Buckle on your **sword,** mighty king;
55.21 were as soothing as oil, but they cut like sharp **swords.**
57. 4 their tongues are like sharp **swords.**
59. 7 Their tongues are like **swords** in their mouths, yet they
64. 3 sharpen their tongues like **swords** and aim cruel words like arrows.
76. 3 enemy, their shields and **swords,** yes, all their weapons.
149. 6 praise God, with their sharp **swords** in their hands [7]to
Prov 12.18 as deeply as any **sword,** but wisely spoken words can heal.
25.18 is as deadly as a **sword,** a club, or a sharp arrow.
Song 3. 8 All of them are skilful with the **sword;**
3. 8 is armed with a **sword,** on guard against a night attack.
Is 2. 4 They will hammer their **swords** into ploughs
21.15 fleeing to escape from **swords** that are ready to kill them,
27. 1 and deadly **sword** to punish Leviathan, that wriggling,
34. 5 The Lord has prepared his **sword** in heaven, and now it will
34. 6 His **sword** will be covered with their blood and fat, like
37.38 Sharezer, killed him with their **swords** and then escaped to
41. 2 His **sword** strikes them down as if they were dust.
49. 2 He made my words as sharp as a **sword.**
66.16 By fire and **sword** he will punish all the people of the
Jer 4.10 there would be peace, but a **sword** is at their throats."
6.23 They have taken up their bows and **swords;**
20. 4 you will see them all killed by the **swords** of their enemies.
41. 2 men with him pulled out their **swords** and killed Gedaliah.
46.10 His **sword** will eat them until it is full, and drink their
46.16 Let's go home to our people and escape the enemy's **sword!'**
47. 6 You cry out, **'Sword** of the Lord!
50.42 They have taken their bows and **swords;**
Lam 2.21 the streets, Young men and women, killed by enemy **swords.**
Ezek 5. 1 "Mortal man, take a sharp **sword** and use it to shave off
5. 2 chop it up with your **sword** as you move about outside the
5. 2 third to the winds, and I will pursue it with my **sword.**
5.12 a third will be cut down by **swords** outside the city;
5.12 the last third to the winds and pursue them with a **sword.**
6. 3 I will send a **sword** to destroy the places where people
11. 8 Are you afraid of **swords?**
11. 8 I will bring men with **swords** to attack you.
16.40 you, and they will cut you to pieces with their **swords.**
21. 3 I will draw my **sword** and kill all of you, good and
21. 4 I will use my **sword** against everyone from north to south.
21. 5 the Lord, have drawn my **sword** and that I will not put
21. 9 A **sword,** a sword is sharpened and polished.
21.11 The **sword** is being polished, to make it ready for use.
21.12 this **sword** is meant for my people and for all the leaders
21.14 Clap your hands, and the **sword** will strike again and again.
21.14 It is a **sword** that kills, a sword that terrifies and slaughters.
21.15 threatening their city with a **sword** that flashes like
21.16 Cut to the right and the left, you sharp **sword!**
21.19 by which the king of Babylonia can come with his **sword.**
21.28 'A **sword** is ready to destroy;
21.29 The **sword** is going to fall on your necks.
21.30 'Put up the **sword!**
23.10 her sons and daughters, and then killed her with a **sword.**
23.47 them and attack them with **swords,** kill their children, and
26. 6 plunder Tyre, [6]and with their **swords** they will kill those
26.11 through your streets, killing your people with their **swords.**
29. 8 men to attack you with **swords,** and they will kill your
30.11 They will attack Egypt with **swords,** and the land will be
30.21 it could heal and be strong enough to hold a **sword** again.
30.22 one already broken—and the **sword** will fall from his hand.
30.24 the king of Babylonia strong and put my **sword** in his hands.
30.25 When I give him my **sword** and he points it towards Egypt,
32.10 When I swing my **sword,** kings will shudder with fright.
32.11 Egypt, "You will face the **sword** of the king of Babylonia.
32.12 cruel nations draw their **swords** and kill all your people.
32.20 A **sword** is ready to kill them all.
32.27 world of the dead, their **swords** placed under their heads and
33.26 You rely on your **swords.**
38. 4 every soldier carries a shield and is armed with a **sword.**
38.21 His men will turn their **swords** against one another.
Hos 1. 7 do it by war—with **swords** or bows and arrows or with
2.18 war from the land, all **swords** and bows, and will let my
Joel 3.10 ploughs into **swords** and your pruning-knives into spears.
Mic 4. 3 They will hammer their **swords** into ploughs
Nah 3. 3 Horsemen charge, **swords** flash, spears gleam!
Hab 1.17 they going to use their **swords** for ever and keep on
Zech 9.13 men of Zion like a **sword,** to fight the men of Greece."
Zech 13. 7 Lord Almighty says, "Wake up, **sword,** and attack the
Mt 10.34 No, I did not come to bring peace, but a **sword.**
26.47 a large crowd armed with **swords** and clubs and sent by the
26.51 were with Jesus drew his **sword** and struck at the High
26.52 "Put your **sword** back in its place," Jesus said to him.
26.52 "All who take the **sword** will die by the sword.
26.55 you have to come with **swords** and clubs to capture me,
Mk 14.43 was a crowd armed with **swords** and clubs, and sent by the
14.47 standing there drew his **sword** and struck at the High Priest's
14.48 you have to come with **swords** and clubs to capture me,
Lk 2.35 And sorrow, like a sharp **sword,** will break your own heart."
21.24 will be killed by the **sword,** and others will be taken
22.36 and whoever has no **sword** must sell his coat and buy one.
22.38 Here are two **swords,** Lord!"
22.49 was going to happen, they asked, "Shall we use our **swords,**
22.52 you have to come with **swords** and clubs, as though I were
Jn 18.10 Simon Peter, who had a **sword,** drew it and struck the
18.11 Jesus said to Peter, "Put your **sword** back in its place!
Acts 12. 2 had James, the brother of John, put to death by the **sword.**
16.27 so he pulled out his **sword** and was about to kill himself.
Eph 6.17 the word of God as the **sword** which the Spirit gives you.
Heb 4.12 God is alive and active, sharper than any double-edged **sword.**
11.34 put out fierce fires, escaped being killed by the **sword.**
11.37 they were sawn in two, they were killed by the **sword.**
Rev 1.16 hand, and a sharp two-edged **sword** came out of his mouth.
2.12 the message from the one who has the sharp two-edged **sword.**
2.16 those people with the **sword** that comes out of my mouth.
6. 4 He was given a large **sword.**
13.10 be killed by the sword will surely be killed by the **sword.**
13.14 the beast that had been wounded by the **sword** and yet lived.
19.15 his mouth came a sharp **sword,** with which he will defeat the
19.21 armies were killed by the **sword** that comes out of the mouth

SYCOMORE

1 Kgs 10.27 as plentiful as ordinary **sycomore** in the foothills of Judah.
1 Chr 27.25 Olives and **sycomore-trees** (in the western foothills):
2 Chr 1.15 Jerusalem as stone, and cedar was as plentiful as ordinary **sycomore.**
9.27 as plentiful as ordinary **sycomore** in the foothills of Judah.
Is 9.10 The beams of **sycomore** wood have been cut down, but we will
Lk 19. 4 the crowd and climbed a **sycomore tree** to see Jesus, who was

SYMBOL

Ex 34.13 pillars, and cut down the **symbols** of their goddess Asherah.
Deut 7. 5 in pieces, cut down the **symbols** of their goddess Asherah,
12. 3 Burn their **symbols** of the goddess Asherah
16.21 do not put beside it a wooden **symbol** of the goddess Asherah.
Judg 6.25 Baal, and cut down the **symbol** of the goddess Asherah, which
6.26 for firewood the **symbol** of Asherah you have cut down."
6.28 altar to Baal and the **symbol** of Asherah had been cut down,
6.30 to Baal and cut down the **symbol** of Asherah beside it."
1 Kgs 14.23 put up stone pillars and **symbols** of Asherah to worship on
2 Kgs 21. 7 He placed the **symbol** of the goddess Asherah in the Temple,
23. 6 removed from the Temple the **symbol** of the goddess Asherah,
23.14 to pieces, cut down the **symbols** of the goddess Asherah, and
2 Chr 6.41 with the Covenant Box, the **symbol** of your power, enter the
14. 3 columns, and cut down the **symbols** of the goddess Asherah.
17. 6 of worship and the **symbols** of the goddess Asherah in Judah.
19. 3 You have removed all the **symbols** of the goddess Asherah
31. 1 stone pillars, cut down the **symbols** of the goddess Asherah,
33.19 places of worship and the **symbols** of the goddess Asherah
34. 3 pagan places of worship, the **symbols** of the goddess Asherah,
34. 7 smashed the altars and the **symbols** of Asherah, ground the
Ps 74. 9 All our sacred **symbols** are gone;
78.61 the Covenant Box, the **symbol** of his power and glory.
132. 8 with the Covenant Box, the **symbol** of your power, and stay
Is 11.10 the royal line of David will be a **symbol** to the nations.
17. 8 trust in their own handiwork—**symbols** of the goddess Asherah
19.20 They will be **symbols** of the Lord Almighty's presence in Egypt.
27. 9 incense-altars or **symbols** of the goddess Asherah are left.
Jer 9.25 circumcised, but have not kept the covenant it **symbolizes.**
17. 2 at the altars and the **symbols** that have been set up for
1 Pet 3.21 water, [21] which was a **symbol** pointing to baptism, which now saves
Rev 11. 8 The **symbolic** name of that city is Sodom, or Egypt.

SYMPATHY

2 Sam 10. 2 So David sent messengers to express his **sympathy.**
10. 3 that David has sent these men to express **sympathy** to you?
1 Chr 19. 2 So David sent messengers to express his **sympathy.**
19. 3 that David has sent these men to express **sympathy** to you?
Job 42.11 They expressed their **sympathy** and comforted him for all the
Ps 69.20 I had hoped for **sympathy,** but there was none;
Is 51.19 There is no one to show you **sympathy.**
Jer 16. 7 No one will show **sympathy,** not even for someone who has lost
Dan 1. 9 and God made Ashpenaz **sympathetic** to Daniel.
Nah 3. 7 Who has any **sympathy** for her?
Heb 4.15 High Priest is not one who cannot feel **sympathy** for our weaknesses.

SYNAGOGUE

Mt 4.23 over Galilee, teaching in the **synagogues,** preaching the Good News
9.35 He taught in the **synagogues,** preached the Good News
10.17 take you to court, and they will whip you in the **synagogues.**
12. 9 place and went to a **synagogue,** [10] where there was a man who
13.54 He taught in the **synagogue,** and those who heard him were amazed.

Mt 23. 6 places at feasts and the reserved seats in the **synagogues;**
23.34 and whip others in the **synagogues** and chase them from town
Mk 1.21 next Sabbath Jesus went to the **synagogue** and began to teach.
1.23 came into the **synagogue** and screamed, [24] "What do you want
1.29 James and John, left the **synagogue** and went straight to the
1.39 over Galilee, preaching in the **synagogues** and driving out demons.
3. 1 Jesus went back to the **synagogue,** where there was a man who
3. 6 So the Pharisees left the **synagogue** and met at once with
5.22 official of the local **synagogue,** arrived, and when he saw Jesus,
6. 2 On the Sabbath he began to teach in the **synagogue.**
12.39 reserved seats in the **synagogues** and the best places at feasts.
13. 9 You will be beaten in the **synagogues;**
Lk 4.15 He taught in the **synagogues** and was praised by everyone.
4.16 up, and on the Sabbath he went as usual to the **synagogue.**
4.20 All the people in the **synagogue** had their eyes fixed on him,
4.28 When the people in the **synagogue** heard this, they were filled
4.33 In the **synagogue** was a man who had the spirit of an
4.38 Jesus left the **synagogue** and went to Simon's house.
4.44 So he preached in the **synagogues** throughout the country.
6. 6 On another Sabbath Jesus went into a **synagogue** and taught.
7. 5 He loves our people and he himself built a **synagogue** for us."
8.41 he was an official in the local **synagogue.**
11.43 reserved seats in the **synagogues** and to be greeted with respect
12.11 to be tried in the **synagogues** or before governors or rulers,
13.10 One Sabbath Jesus was teaching in a **synagogue.**
13.14 The official of the **synagogue** was angry that Jesus had
20.46 reserved seats in the **synagogues** and the best places at feasts;
21.12 handed over to be tried in **synagogues** and be put in prison;
Jn 6.59 Jesus said this as he taught in the **synagogue** in Capernaum.
9.22 that Jesus was the Messiah would be expelled from the **synagogue.**
9.34 And they expelled him from the **synagogue.**
12.42 it openly, so as not to be expelled from the **synagogue.**
16. 2 will be expelled from the **synagogues,** and the time will come
18.20 teaching was done in the **synagogues** and in the Temple, where
Acts 6. 9 who were members of the **synagogue** of the Freedmen (as it was
9. 2 letters of introduction to the **synagogues** in Damascus, so that if
9.20 He went straight to the **synagogues** and began to preach
13. 5 at Salamis, they preached the word of God in the **synagogues.**
13.14 on the Sabbath they went into the **synagogue** and sat down.
13.15 the prophets, the officials of the **synagogue** sent them a message:
13.42 and Barnabas were leaving the **synagogue,** the people invited them
14. 1 and Barnabas went to the **synagogue** and spoke in such a way
15.21 very long time in the **synagogues** every Sabbath, and his
17. 1 Apollonia and came to Thessalonica, where there was a **synagogue.**
17. 2 According to his usual habit Paul went to the **synagogue.**
17.10 When they arrived, they went to the **synagogue.**
17.17 he held discussions in the **synagogue** with the Jews and with
18. 4 He held discussions in the **synagogue** every Sabbath,
18. 7 his house was next to the **synagogue.**
18. 8 was the leader of the **synagogue,** believed in the Lord, together
18.17 Sosthenes, the leader of the **synagogue,** and beat him in front
18.19 He went into the **synagogue** and held discussions with the Jews.
18.26 He began to speak boldly in the **synagogue.**
19. 8 Paul went into the **synagogue** and during three months spoke boldly
22.19 that I went to the **synagogues** and arrested and beat those
24.12 either in the **synagogues** or anywhere else in the city.
26.11 had them punished in the **synagogues** and tried to make them

SYRIA

[KING OF SYRIA]
Kingdom n. of Israel, centred on Damascus.

Num 23. 7 Moab has brought me From **Syria,** from the eastern mountains.
Judg 10. 6 well as the gods of **Syria,** of Sidon, of Moab, of Ammon,
2 Sam 8. 3 defeated the king of the **Syrian** state of Zobah, Hadadezer
8. 5 When the **Syrians** of Damascus sent an army to help King Hadadezer,
10. 6 twenty thousand **Syrian** soldiers from Bethrehob and Zobah,
10. 8 while the others, both the **Syrians** and the men from Tob and
10. 9 Israel's soldiers and put them in position facing the **Syrians.**
10.11 "If you see that the **Syrians** are defeating me, come and
10.13 Joab and his men advanced to attack, and the **Syrians** fled.
10.14 When the Ammonites saw the **Syrians** running away, they
10.15 The **Syrians** realized that they had been defeated by the Israelites,
10.16 King Hadadezer sent for the **Syrians** who were on the east
10.17 Helam, where the **Syrians** took up their position facing him.
10.18 and the Israelites drove the **Syrian** army back.
10.18 hundred **Syrian** chariot drivers and forty thousand horsemen,
10.19 And the **Syrians** were afraid to help the Ammonites any more.
15. 8 was living in Geshur in **Syria,** I promised the Lord that if
1 Kgs 10.29 They supplied the Hittite and **Syrian** kings with horses
11.24 David had defeated Hadadezer and had slaughtered his **Syrian** allies.)
11.24 and lived in Damascus, where his men made him **king of Syria.**
15.18 Damascus, to King Benhadad of **Syria,** the son of Tabrimmon
19.15 then enter the city and anoint Hazael as **king of Syria;**
20. 1 King Benhadad of **Syria** gathered all his troops, and
20.20 The **Syrians** fled, with the Israelites in hot pursuit, but
20.21 and chariots, and inflicted a severe defeat on the **Syrians.**
20.22 the **king of Syria** will attack again next spring."
20.27 marched out and camped in two groups facing the **Syrians.**
20.27 with the **Syrians,** who spread out over the countryside.
20.28 'Because the **Syrians** say that I am a god of the hills
20.29 the **Syrians** and the Israelites stayed in their camps,
20.29 and the Israelites killed a hundred thousand **Syrians.**
22. 1 was peace between Israel and **Syria** for the next two years,
22. 3 to get back Ramoth in Gilead from the **king of Syria?**
1 Kgs 22.11 'With these you will fight the **Syrians** and totally defeat them.' "
22.31 The **king of Syria** had ordered his thirty-two chariot
22.34 By chance, however, a **Syrian** soldier shot an arrow which
22.35 King Ahab remained propped up in his chariot, facing the **Syrians.**
2 Kgs 3.26 escape to the **king of Syria,** but he failed.
5. 1 Naaman, the commander of the **Syrian** army, was highly respected
5. 1 esteemed by the **king of Syria,** because through Naaman
5. 1 through Naaman the Lord had given victory to the **Syrian** forces.
5. 2 their raids against Israel, the **Syrians** had carried off a
5. 7 "How can the **king of Syria** expect me to cure this
5.18 to the temple of Rimmon, the god of **Syria,** and worship him.
5.20 He should have accepted what that **Syrian** offered him.
6. 8 The **king of Syria** was at war with Israel.
6. 9 place, because the **Syrians** were waiting in ambush there.
6.11 The **Syrian king** became greatly upset over this;
6.15 and saw the **Syrian** troops with their horses and chariots
6.18 When the **Syrians** attacked, Elisha prayed, "O Lord, strike
6.21 king of Israel saw the **Syrians,** he asked Elisha, "Shall I
6.23 eaten and drunk, he sent them back to the **king of Syria.**
6.23 From then on the **Syrians** stopped raiding the land of Israel.
6.24 time later King Benhadad of **Syria** led his entire army
7. 4 So let's go to the **Syrian** camp;
7. 5 they went to the **Syrian** camp, but when they reached it,
7. 6 The Lord had made the **Syrians** hear what sounded like the
7. 6 horses and chariots, and the **Syrians** thought that the king
7. 7 So that evening the **Syrians** had fled for their lives,
7.10 So they left the **Syrian** camp, went back to Samaria and
7.10 "We went to the **Syrian** camp and didn't see or hear anybody;
7.10 untied, and the tents are just as the **Syrians** left them."
7.12 officials, "I'll tell you what the **Syrians** are planning!
7.14 to go and find out what had happened to the **Syrian** army.
7.15 and equipment that the **Syrians** had abandoned as they fled.
7.16 The people of Samaria rushed out and looted the **Syrian** camp.
8. 7 to Damascus at a time when King Benhadad of **Syria** was ill.
8.13 shown me that you will be **king of Syria,"** Elisha replied.
8.15 And Hazael succeeded Benhadad as **king of Syria.**
8.28 King Joram of Israel in a war against King Hazael of **Syria.**
9.14 in the battle at Ramoth against King Hazael of **Syria.**
10.32 King Hazael of **Syria** conquered all the Israelite territory
12.17 that time King Hazael of **Syria** attacked the city of Gath and
13. 3 he allowed King Hazael of **Syria** and his son Benhadad to
13. 4 how harshly the **king of Syria** was oppressing the Israelites,
13. 5 who freed them from the **Syrians,** and so the Israelites lived
13. 7 because the **king of Syria** had destroyed the rest,
13.17 the king opened the window that faced towards **Syria.**
13.17 the Lord's arrow, with which he will win victory over **Syria.**
13.17 You will fight the **Syrians** in Aphek until you defeat them."
13.19 then you would have won complete victory over the **Syrians;**
13.22 King Hazael of **Syria** oppressed the Israelites
13.24 death of King Hazael of **Syria** his son Benhadad became king.
15.37 first sent King Rezin of **Syria** and King Pekah of Israel to
16. 5 King Rezin of **Syria** and King Pekah of Israel attacked
16. 7 me from the kings of **Syria** and of Israel, who are attacking
24. 2 sent armed bands of Babylonians, **Syrians,** Moabites, and
1 Chr 18. 3 attacked King Hadadezer of the **Syrian** state of Zobah, near
18. 5 When the **Syrians** of Damascus sent an army to help King Hadadezer,
19. 6 Upper Mesopotamia and from the **Syrian** states of Maacah and Zobah.
19.10 Israel's soldiers and put them in position facing the **Syrians.**
19.12 "If you see that the **Syrians** are defeating me, come and
19.14 Joab and his men advanced to attack, and the **Syrians** fled.
19.15 When the Ammonites saw the **Syrians** running away, they fled
19.16 The **Syrians** realized that they had been defeated
19.16 they brought troops from the **Syrian** states on the east side
19.17 the Jordan, and put them in position facing the **Syrians.**
19.18 and the Israelites drove the **Syrian** army back.
19.18 **Syrian** chariot drivers
19.18 They also killed the **Syrian** commander, Shobach.
19.19 The **Syrians** were never again willing to help the Ammonites.
2 Chr 1.17 They supplied the Hittite and **Syrian** kings with horses
16. 2 to Damascus, to King Benhadad of **Syria,** with this message:
16. 7 you relied on the **king of Syria**
18.10 'With these you will fight the **Syrians** and totally defeat them.' "
18.30 The **king of Syria** had ordered his chariot commanders
18.33 By chance, however, a **Syrian** soldier shot an arrow which
18.34 King Ahab remained propped up in his chariot, facing the **Syrians.**
22. 5 King Joram of Israel in a war against King Hazael of **Syria.**
24.23 that year, the **Syrian** army attacked Judah and Jerusalem,
24.24 The **Syrian** army was small, but the Lord let them defeat
28. 5 his God let the **king of Syria** defeat him
28.23 sacrifices to the gods of the **Syrians,** who had defeated him.
28.23 He said, "The **Syrian** gods helped the kings of Syria, so if
Is 7. 1 **king of Syria,** and Pekah son of Remaliah, king of Israel,
7. 2 Judah that the armies of **Syria** were already in the territory
7. 4 of King Rezin and his **Syrians** and of King Pekah is no
7. 5 **Syria,** together with Israel and its king, has made a plot.
7. 8 Because **Syria** is no stronger than Damascus, its capital city,
9.12 **Syria** on the east and Philistia on the west have opened
17. 2 The cities of **Syria** will be deserted for ever.
17. 3 Those **Syrians** who survive will be in disgrace like the
Jer 35.11 Jerusalem to get away from the Babylonian and **Syrian** armies.
Ezek 27.16 The people of **Syria** bought your merchandise
Dan 11. 6 an alliance with the **king of Syria** and give him his daughter
11. 7 the army of the **king of Syria,** enter their fortress,
11. 9 the **king of Syria** will invade Egypt,
11.10 "The sons of the **king of Syria** will prepare for war
11.11 to war against the **king of Syria** and capture his huge army.
11.13 "The **king of Syria** will go back and gather a larger
11.15 So the **king of Syria** will lay siege to a fortified city

Dan 11.16 The **Syrian** invader will do with them as he pleases,
11.17 "The **king of Syria** will plan an expedition,
11.18 he will turn the arrogance of **Syria's king** back on him.
11.21 "The next **king of Syria** will be an evil man
11.28 The **king of Syria** will return home with all the loot
11.36 "The **king of Syria** will do as he pleases.
11.40 "When the **king of Syria's** final hour has almost come,
11.40 attack him, and the **king of Syria** will fight back
Amos 1. 5 The people of **Syria** will be taken away as prisoners to the
9. 7 Philistines from Crete and the **Syrians** from Kir, just as I
Zech 9. 1 of Israel, but also the capital of **Syria** belong to the Lord.
Mt 4.24 through the whole country of **Syria,** so that people brought
Mk 7.26 was a Gentile, born in the region of Phoenicia in **Syria.**
Lk 2. 2 this first census took place, Quirinius was the governor of **Syria.**
4.27 not one of them was healed, but only Naaman the **Syrian."**
Acts 15.23 brothers of Gentile birth who live in Antioch, **Syria,** and Cilicia.
15.41 He went through **Syria** and Cilicia, strengthening the churches.
18.18 them and sailed off with Priscilla and Aquila for **Syria.**
20. 3 getting ready to go to **Syria** when he discovered that the
21. 3 could see Cyprus, and then sailed south of it on to **Syria.**
Gal 1.21 Afterwards I went to places in **Syria** and Cilicia.

SYSTEM

Esth 1.22 in the language and the **system** of writing of that province,
3.12 translated into every language and **system** of writing used in
8. 9 in its own language and **system** of writing
8. 9 and to the Jews in their language and **system** of writing.
2 Cor 3. 9 The **system** which brings condemnation was glorious;
Gal 2.18 I start to rebuild the **system** of Law that I tore down,

AV **TABERNACLE** see **TENT (2)**

AV **TABERNACLES, FEAST OF** see **SHELTERS**

TABLE

Gen 43.32 Joseph was served at one **table** and his brothers at another.
43.33 brothers had been seated at **table,** facing Joseph, in the
43.34 served to them from Joseph's **table,** and Benjamin was served
Ex 25.23 "Make a **table** out of acacia-wood,
25.27 the poles for carrying the **table** are to be placed near the
25.30 The **table** is to be placed in front of the Covenant Box,
25.30 and on the **table** there is always to be the
26.35 Most Holy Place put the **table** against the north side
30.27 the Covenant Box, [27] the **table** and all its equipment,
31. 8 furnishings of the Tent, [8] the **table** and its equipment, the
35.13 the **table,** its poles, and all its equipment;
37.10 He made the **table** out of acacia-wood, 88 centimetres long,
37.14 the poles for carrying the **table** were placed near the rim.
37.16 He made the dishes of pure gold for the **table:**
39.36 the **table** and all its equipment, and the bread offered to God;
40. 4 Bring in the **table** and place the equipment on it.
40.22 He put the **table** in the Tent, on the north side outside
40.24 the south side, opposite the **table,** [25] and there in the
Lev 24. 6 in each row, on the **table** covered with pure gold, which is
Num 3.31 for the Covenant Box, the **table,** the lamp-stand, the altars,
4. 7 a blue cloth over the **table** for the bread offered to the
4. 7 There shall always be bread on the **table.**
Judg 1. 7 and big toes cut off have picked up scraps under my **table.**
1 Sam 9.22 at the head of the **table** where the guests, about thirty in
20. 6 that I am not at **table,** tell him that I begged your
20.29 That is why he isn't in his place at your **table."**
20.34 Jonathan got up from the **table** in a rage and ate nothing
21. 6 removed from the sacred **table** and replaced by fresh bread.
2 Sam 9. 7 Saul, and you will always be welcome at my **table."**
9.10 But Mephibosheth himself will always be a guest at my **table."**
9.11 Mephibosheth ate at the king's **table,** just like one of the
9.13 in Jerusalem, eating all his meals at the king's **table.**
19.28 Majesty, but you gave me the right to eat at your **table.**
1 Kgs 7.48 the altar, the **table** for the bread offered to God, [49] the
10. 5 served at his **table,** the living quarters for his officials,
13.20 they were sitting at the **table,** the word of the Lord came
2 Kgs 4.10 roof, put a bed, a **table,** a chair, and a lamp in
25.29 to dine at the king's **table** for the rest of his life.
1 Chr 28.16 for the silver **tables,** and for each gold table
2 Chr 4. 7 and ten **tables,** and placed them in the main
4. 7 of the Temple, five lampstands and five **tables** on each side.
4.19 the altar and the **tables** for the bread offered to God;
9. 4 served at his **table,** the living-quarters for his officials,
13.11 offerings of bread on a **table** that is ritually clean, and
29.18 altar for burnt-offerings, the **table** for the sacred bread,
Neh 5.17 I regularly fed at my **table** a hundred and fifty of the
Job 36.16 your **table** was piled high with food.
Ps 128. 3 your sons will be like young olive-trees round your **table.**
Prov 9. 2 for a feast, mixed spices in the wine, and laid the **table.**
23. 6 Don't eat at the **table** of a stingy man or be greedy
Is 28. 8 The **tables** where they sit are all covered with vomit, and
Jer 52.33 to dine at the king's **table** for the rest of his life.
Ezek 23.41 them they would have a **table** covered with good things,
39.20 At my **table** they will eat all they can hold of horses
40.39 entrance room there were four **tables,** two on each side
40.39 It was on these **tables** that they killed the animals to be
40.40 room there were four similar **tables,** two on either side of
40.41 Altogether there were eight **tables** on which the animals
40.42 The four **tables** in the annexe, used to prepare the offerings
40.42 used in killing the sacrificial animals was kept on these **tables.**
40.43 Ledges seventy-five millimetres wide ran round the edge of the **tables.**
Ezek 40.43 meat to be offered in sacrifice was placed on the **tables.**
41.22 to me, "This is the **table** which stands in the presence of
Dan 11.27 to eat at the same **table,** but their motives will be evil,
Mt 9.10 came and joined Jesus and his disciples at the **table.**
15.27 eat the leftovers that fall from their masters' **table."**
21.12 He overturned the **tables** of the money-changers and the stools
Mk 2.15 and many of them joined him and his disciples at the **table.**
7.28 "even the dogs under the **table** eat the children's leftovers!"
11.15 He overturned the **tables** of the money-changers and the stools
14.18 While they were at the **table** eating, Jesus said, "I
Lk 7.49 The others sitting at the **table** began to say to themselves,
14.15 of the men sitting at **table** heard this, he said to Jesus,
16.21 eat the bits of food that fell from the rich man's **table.**
22.14 came, Jesus took his place at the **table** with the apostles.
22.21 The one who betrays me is here at the **table** with me!
22.30 eat and drink at my **table** in my Kingdom, and you will
Jn 2.14 pigeons, and also the money-changers sitting at their **tables.**
2.15 he overturned the **tables** of the money-changers and scattered
12. 2 was one of those who were sitting at the **table** with Jesus.
13. 4 So he rose from the **table,** took off his outer garment,
13.12 garment back on and returned to his place at the **table.**
13.28 of the others at the **table** understood why Jesus said this to
1 Cor 10.21 eat at the Lord's table and also at the **table** of demons.
Heb 9. 2 the lampstand and the **table** with the bread offered to God.

TABLET

Ex 24.12 will give you two stone **tablets** which contain all the laws
25.16 the box the two stone **tablets** that I will give you, on
25.21 Put the two stone **tablets** inside the box and put the lid
26.33 put the Covenant Box containing the two stone **tablets.**
31.18 the two stone **tablets** on which God himself had written
32.15 carrying the two stone **tablets** with the commandments
32.16 God himself had made the **tablets** and had engraved the
32.19 he threw down the **tablets** he was carrying and broke them.
34. 1 to Moses, "Cut two stone **tablets** like the first ones,
34. 1 the words that were on the first **tablets,** which you broke.
34. 4 Moses cut two more stone **tablets,** and early the next morning
34.28 He wrote on the **tablets** the words of the covenant—the Ten
38.21 presence, where the two stone **tablets** were kept on which the
39.35 the Covenant Box containing the stone **tablets,** its
40.20 he took the two stone **tablets** and put them in the Covenant
Deut 4.13 the Ten Commandments, which he wrote on two stone **tablets.**
5.22 he wrote them on two stone **tablets** and gave them to me.
9. 9 mountain to receive the stone **tablets** on which was written
9.10 gave me the two stone **tablets** on which he had written with
9.11 gave me the two stone **tablets** on which he had written the
9.15 the two stone **tablets** on which the covenant was written.
9.17 you I threw the stone **tablets** down and broke them to pieces.
10. 1 to me, 'Cut two stone **tablets** like the first ones and make
10. 2 I will write on those **tablets**
10. 2 what I wrote on the **tablets** that you broke,
10. 3 acacia-wood and cut two stone **tablets** like the first ones
10. 4 the Lord wrote on those **tablets** the same words that he had
10. 4 The Lord gave me the **tablets,** [5] and I turned and went down
1 Kgs 8. 9 Box except the two stone **tablets** which Moses had placed
8.21 Covenant Box containing the stone **tablets** of the covenant
2 Chr 5.10 Box except the two stone **tablets** which Moses had placed
6.11 Box, which contains the stone **tablets** of the covenant which
Hab 2. 2 "Write down clearly on clay **tablets** what I reveal to you,
Lk 1.63 Zechariah asked for a writing **tablet** and wrote, "His name is John."
2 Cor 3. 3 living God, and not on stone **tablets** but on human hearts.
3. 7 carved in letters on stone **tablets,** and God's glory appeared
Heb 9. 4 and the two stone **tablets** with the commandments written on them.

TAIL

Ex 4. 4 said to Moses, "Bend down and pick it up by the **tail."**
29.22 fat, the fat **tail,** the fat covering the internal organs,
Lev 3. 9 the fat, the entire fat **tail** cut off near the backbone, all
7. 3 the fat **tail,** the fat covering the internal organs, [4] the
8.25 took the fat, the fat **tail,** all the fat covering the
Judg 15. 4 by two, he tied their **tails** together and put torches in the
Job 40.17 His **tail** stands up like a cedar, and the muscles in his
Is 9.14 he will cut them off, head and **tail.**
9.15 are the head—and the **tail** is the prophets whose teachings
Rev 9.10 They have **tails** and stings like those of a scorpion,
9.10 and it is with their **tails** that they have the power to
9.19 of the horses is in their mouths and also in their **tails.**
9.19 Their **tails** are like snakes with heads, and they use them to
12. 4 With his **tail** he dragged a third of the stars out

TAKE

see also **TAKE AWAY (SIN), TAKE OFF, TAKE UP**

Gen 2. 7 Then the Lord God **took** some soil from the ground and
2.19 So he **took** some soil from the ground and formed all the
2.21 while he was sleeping, he **took** out one of the man's ribs
2.23 my own kind— Bone **taken** from my bone, and flesh from
2.23 'Woman' is her name because she was **taken** out of man."
3. 6 So she **took** some of the fruit and ate it.
3.22 must not be allowed to **take** fruit from the tree that gives
4.15 If anyone kills you, seven lives will be **taken** in revenge."
4.24 If seven lives are **taken** to pay for killing Cain,
4.24 Seventy-seven will be **taken** if anyone kills me."
5.24 God, and then he disappeared, because God **took** him away.
6. 2 girls were beautiful, so they **took** the ones they liked.
6.19 **Take** into the boat with you a male and a female of
6.21 **Take** along all kinds of food for you and for them."

Gen 7. 2 **Take** with you seven pairs of each kind of ritually clean animal,
7. 3 **Take** also seven pairs of each kind of bird.
8. 9 back to the boat, and Noah reached out and **took** it in.
8.17 **Take** all the birds and animals out with you, so that
8.20 he **took** one of each kind of ritually clean animal and bird,
9. 5 If anyone **takes** human life, he will be punished.
9. 5 I will punish with death any animal that **takes** a human life.
9.23 Then Shem and Japheth **took** a robe and held it behind
11.31 Terah **took** his son Abram, his grandson Lot, who was the
12. 5 Abram **took** his wife Sarai, his nephew Lot, and all the
12.15 so she was **taken** to his palace.
12.17 But because the king had **taken** Sarai, the Lord sent
12.19 she was your sister, and let me **take** her as my wife?
12.19 **take** her and get out!"
12.20 to his men, so they **took** Abram and put him out of
14.11 The four kings **took** everything in Sodom and Gomorrah,
14.12 living in Sodom, so they **took** him and all his possessions.
14.16 of Damascus, [16]and recovered the loot that had been **taken.**
14.24 I will **take** nothing for myself.
14.24 But let my allies, Aner, Eshcol, and Mamre, **take** their share."
15. 5 The Lord **took** him outside and said, "Look at the sky and
15.14 that foreign land, they will **take** great wealth with them.
18. 6 and said to Sarah, "Quick, **take** a sack of your best flour,
18. 8 He **took** some cream, some milk, and the meat, and set the
19.15 **"Take** your wife and your two daughters and get out, so that
19.16 so the men **took** him, his wife, and his two daughters by
20. 3 "You are going to die, because you have **taken** this woman;
22. 2 **"Take** your son," God said, "your only son, Isaac, whom
22. 3 loaded his donkey, and **took** Isaac and two servants with him.
24. 8 But you must not under any circumstances **take** my son back there."
24.10 in charge of Abraham's property, **took** ten of his master's
24.22 she had finished, the man **took** an expensive gold ring and
24.51 **take** her and go.
24.65 So she **took** her scarf and covered her face.
27. 3 **Take** your bow and arrows, go out into the country, and
27.10 You can **take** it to him to eat, and he will give
27.15 she **took** Esau's best clothes, which she kept in the house,
27.31 He also cooked some tasty food and **took** it to his father.
27.35 He has **taken** away your blessing."
27.36 He **took** my rights as the first-born son,
27.36 and now he has **taken** away my blessing.
28. 4 blessed Abraham, and may you **take** possession of this land,
28.18 got up early next morning, **took** the stone that was under his
29. 7 why don't you water them and **take** them back to pasture?"
29.23 night, instead of Rachel, he **took** Leah to Jacob, and Jacob
30.15 "Isn't it enough that you have **taken** away my husband?
30.15 Now you are even trying to **take** away my son's mandrakes."
30.23 She said, "God has **taken** away my disgrace by giving me a
30.32 all your flocks today and **take** every black lamb and every
31. 1 "Jacob has **taken** everything that belonged to our father.
31. 9 God has **taken** flocks away from your father and given them
31.16 this wealth which God has **taken** from our father belongs to
31.21 He **took** everything he owned and left in a hurry.
31.23 He **took** his men with him and pursued Jacob for seven
31.31 I thought that you might **take** your daughters away from me.
31.32 for anything that belongs to you and **take** what is yours."
31.34 Rachel had **taken** the household gods and put them in a
31.39 I didn't **take** it to you to show that it was not
31.45 So Jacob **took** a stone and set it up as a memorial.
32.22 night Jacob got up, **took** his two wives, his two concubines,
34. 2 chief of that region, saw her, he **took** her and raped her.
34.17 our terms and be circumcised, we will **take** her and leave."
34.25 Levi, the brothers of Dinah, **took** their swords, went into
34.26 Then they **took** Dinah from Shechem's house and left.
34.28 They **took** the flocks, the cattle, the donkeys, and
34.29 They **took** everything of value, captured all the women
36. 6 Then Esau **took** his wives, his sons, his daughters, and all
37.24 Then they **took** him and threw him into the well, which
37.28 pieces of silver to the Ishmaelites, who **took** him to Egypt.
37.32 They **took** the robe to their father and said, "We found this.
38.20 sent his friend Hirah to **take** the goat and get back from
38.24 Judah ordered, **"Take** her out and burn her to death."
38.25 As she was being **taken** out, she sent word to her father-in-law:
39. 1 Now the Ishmaelites had **taken** Joseph to Egypt and sold him
40.11 so I **took** the grapes and squeezed them into the cup and
41.34 also appoint other officials and **take** a fifth of the crops
42.19 of you may go and **take** back to your starving families the
42.33 rest will **take** corn for your starving families and leave.
42.36 and now you want to **take** away Benjamin.
43.11 it has to be, then **take** the best products of the land
43.12 **Take** with you also twice as much money,
43.12 because you must **take** back the money that was returned
43.13 **Take** your brother and return at once.
43.15 So the brothers **took** the gifts and twice as much money,
43.16 in charge of his house, **"Take** these men to my house.
43.17 he was commanded and **took** the brothers to Joseph's house.
43.18 They will suddenly attack us, **take** our donkeys, and make us
43.24 The servant **took** the brothers into the house.
43.26 When Joseph got home, they **took** the gifts into the house
44.10 only the one who has **taken** the cup will become my slave,
44.29 If you **take** this one from me now and something happens
45. 2 Egyptians heard it, and the news was **taken** to the king's palace.
45.19 Tell them also to **take** wagons with them from Egypt for
45.27 which Joseph had sent to **take** him to Egypt, he recovered
46. 6 They **took** their livestock and the possessions they had
46. 6 Jacob **took** all his descendants with him:
47. 1 So Joseph **took** five of his brothers and went to the king.
47.14 Joseph collected all the money and **took** it to the palace.
48. 1 So he **took** his two sons, Manasseh and Ephraim, and went to
48.12 Then Joseph **took** them from Jacob's lap and bowed down

Gen 48.17 so he **took** his father's hand to move it from Ephraim's head
48.21 be with you and will **take** you back to the land of
48.22 that fertile region which I **took** from the Amorites with my
50. 4 king's officials, "Please **take** this message to the king:
50.25 leads you to that land, you will **take** my body with you."

Ex 1.22 **"Take** every new-born Hebrew boy and throw him into the Nile,
2. 3 hide him any longer, she **took** a basket made of reeds and
2. 9 The princess told the woman, **"Take** this baby and nurse
2. 9 So she **took** the baby and nursed him.
2.10 child was old enough, she **took** him to the king's daughter,
3.17 being treated cruelly, and will **take** them to a rich and
4. 6 and when he **took** his hand out, it was diseased, covered with
4. 7 did so, and when he **took** it out this time, it was
4. 9 listen to what you say, **take** some water from the Nile and
4.17 **Take** this stick with you;
4.20 So Moses **took** his wife and his sons, put them on a
4.20 Egypt, carrying the stick that God had told him to **take.**
4.25 Then Zipporah, his wife, **took** a sharp stone, cut
7. 9 a miracle, tell Aaron to **take** his stick and throw it down
7.15 **Take** with you the stick that was turned into a snake, and
7.19 to Moses, "Tell Aaron to **take** his stick and hold it out
8. 8 "Pray to the Lord to **take** away these frogs, and I will
8.12 prayed to the Lord to **take** away the frogs which he had
9. 8 said to Moses and Aaron, **"Take** a few handfuls of ashes from
10. 9 We will **take** our sons and daughters, our sheep and goats,
10.10 Lord that I will never let you **take** your women and children!
10.17 Lord your God to **take** away this fatal punishment from me."
10.26 No, we will **take** our animals with us;
11. 8 they will beg me to **take** all my people and go away.
12. 7 The people are to **take** some of the blood and put it
12.22 **Take** a sprig of hyssop, dip it in the bowl containing
12.32 **Take** your sheep, goats, and cattle, and leave.
12.46 it must not be **taken** outside.
13.17 people go, God did not **take** them by the road that goes
13.19 Moses **took** the body of Joseph with him, as Joseph had
15. 9 I will divide their wealth and **take** all I want;
15. 9 I will draw my sword and **take** all they have.'
15.20 The prophet Miriam, Aaron's sister, **took** her tambourine,
16.33 Moses said to Aaron, **"Take** a jar, put two litres of
17. 5 The Lord said to Moses, **"Take** some of the leaders of
17. 5 **Take** along the stick with which you struck the Nile.
21. 3 slave, he is not to **take** a wife with him when he
21. 3 when he became your slave, he may **take** his wife with him.
21. 6 then his master shall **take** him to the place of worship.
21.20 "If a man **takes** a stick and beats his slave, whether
21.33 "If a man **takes** the cover off a pit or if he
22. 9 the property shall be **taken** to the place of worship.
22.26 If you **take** someone's cloak as a pledge that he will pay
23. 4 enemy's cow or donkey running loose, **take** it back to him.
23.23 go ahead of you and **take** you into the land of the
23.25 you with food and water and **take** away all your illnesses.
23.30 there are enough of you to **take** possession of the land.
24. 6 Moses **took** half the blood of the animals and put it in
24. 7 Then he **took** the book of the covenant, in which the Lord's
24. 8 Then Moses **took** the blood in the bowls and threw it on
25.15 to be left in the rings and must not be **taken** out.
28. 9 **Take** two carnelian stones and engrave on them the names of
29. 1 **Take** one young bull and two rams without any defects.
29. 7 Then **take** the anointing oil, pour it on his head, and
29.12 **Take** some of the bull's blood and with your finger put
29.13 Next, **take** all the fat which covers the internal organs,
29.15 **"Take** one of the rams and tell Aaron and his sons to
29.16 Kill it, and **take** its blood and throw it against all
29.19 **"Take** the other ram—the ram used for dedication—and
29.20 Kill it, and **take** some of its blood and put it on
29.21 **Take** some of the blood that is on the altar and some
29.23 which has been offered to me, **take** one loaf of each kind:
29.25 Then **take** it from them and burn it on the altar, on
29.26 **"Take** the breast of this ram and dedicate it to me as
29.31 **"Take** the meat of the ram used for the ordination of
30.23 The Lord said to Moses, [23]**"Take** the finest spices—six
30.34 The Lord said to Moses, **"Take** an equal part of each of
30.36 it into a fine powder, **take** it into the Tent of my
32. 4 **took** the earrings, melted them, poured the gold into a mould,
32.20 He **took** the bull-calf which they had made, melted it,
33. 7 set up camp, Moses would **take** the sacred Tent and put it
33.23 Then I will **take** my hand away, and you will see my
40.20 Then he **took** the two stone tablets and put them in the

Lev 2. 2 The officiating priest shall **take** a handful of the flour and
2. 3 very holy, since it is **taken** from the food offered to the
2. 8 present it to the priest, who will **take** it to the altar.
2. 9 The priest will **take** part of it as a token that it
2.10 very holy, since it is **taken** from the food offered to the
4. 4 Then the High Priest shall **take** some of the bull's blood and
4. 8 From this bull he shall **take** all the fat, the fat on
4.10 The priest shall **take** this fat and burn it on the altar
4.11 But he shall **take** its skin, all its flesh, its head, its
4.16 The High Priest shall **take** some of the bull's blood into
4.19 Then he shall **take** all its fat and burn it on the
4.21 Then he shall **take** the bull outside the camp and burn it,
5.12 to the priest, who will **take** a handful of it as a
6.11 shall change his clothes and **take** the ashes outside the camp
6.15 Then he shall **take** a handful of the flour and oil, and
7.14 belongs to the priest who **takes** the blood of the animal and
7.34 contribution that the Lord has **taken** from the people of
8. 2 The Lord said to Moses, [2]**"Take** Aaron and his sons to the
8.10 Then Moses **took** the anointing oil and put it on the Tent
8.11 He **took** some of the oil and sprinkled it seven times on
8.15 Moses killed it and **took** some of the blood, and with his
8.16 Moses **took** all the fat on the internal organs, the best
8.17 He **took** the rest of the bull, including its skin, flesh,

Lev 8.23 Moses killed it and **took** some of the blood and put it
8.25 He **took** the fat, the fat tail, all the fat covering the
8.26 Then he **took** one loaf of bread from the basket of
8.28 Then Moses **took** the food from them and burnt it on the
8.29 Then Moses **took** the breast and presented it as a special
8.30 Moses **took** some of the anointing oil and some of the
8.31 to Aaron and his sons, "**Take** the meat to the entrance of
9. 2 He said to Aaron, "**Take** a young bull and a ram without
9. 3 the people of Israel to **take** a male goat for a sin-offering,
9.15 He **took** the goat that was to be offered for the people's
9.17 He presented the grain-offering and **took** a handful of
10. 1 sons Nadab and Abihu, each **took** his fire-pan, put live coals
10.12 "**Take** the grain-offering that is left over
14. 3 priest, [3]and the priest shall **take** him outside the camp and
14. 6 He shall **take** the other bird and dip it, together with the
14.11 The priest shall **take** the man and these offerings to the
14.12 Then the priest shall **take** one of the male lambs and
14.14 The priest shall **take** some of the blood of the lamb and
14.15 The priest shall **take** some of the olive-oil and pour it
14.17 He shall **take** some of the oil that is in the palm
14.24 The priest shall **take** the lamb and the olive-oil and
14.25 shall kill the lamb and **take** some of the blood and put
14.49 purify the house, he shall **take** two birds, some cedar-wood,
14.51 Then he shall **take** the cedar-wood, the hyssop, the red
15.14 the eighth day he shall **take** two doves or two pigeons to
15.29 the eighth day she shall **take** two doves or two pigeons to
16. 7 Then he shall **take** the two goats to the entrance of the
16.12 and his family, [12]he shall **take** a fire-pan full of burning
16.14 He shall **take** some of the bull's blood and with his
16.18 He must **take** some of the bull's blood and some of the
18. 3 people in the land of Canaan, where I am now **taking** you.
18.18 Do not **take** your wife's sister as one of your wives, as
22.26 born, it must not be **taken** from its mother for seven days,
23. 9 you harvest your corn, **take** the first sheaf to the priest.
23.40 On that day **take** some of the best fruit from your trees,
23.40 **take** palm branches
24. 5 **Take** twelve kilogrammes of flour and bake twelve loaves of bread.
24.10 he cursed God, so they **took** him to Moses, [12]put him under
24.14 The Lord said to Moses, [14]"**Take** that man out of the camp.
24.23 the people of Israel, they **took** the man outside the camp and
27.11 to the Lord, the man shall **take** the animal to the priest.
Num 1.51 your camp, the Levites shall **take** the Tent down and set it
3.49 Moses obeyed and **took** [50]the 1,365 pieces of silver
4. 5 sons shall enter the Tent, **take** down the curtain in front of
4. 9 They shall **take** a blue cloth and cover the lampstand, with
4.12 They shall **take** all the utensils used in the Holy Place,
5.15 In either case the man shall **take** his wife to the priest.
5.15 He shall also **take** the required offering of one kilogramme
5.17 into a clay bowl and **take** some of the earth that is
5.25 bitter pain, [25]the priest shall **take** the offering of flour
5.26 Then he shall **take** a handful of it as a token offering.
6.19 is boiled, the priest shall **take** it and put it, together
8. 8 Then they are to **take** a young bull and the required
8. 8 and you are to **take** another bull for the sin-offering.
8.18 I am now **taking** the Levites instead of all the
10.17 Then the Tent would be **taken** down, and the clans of
11.17 you there, and I will **take** some of the spirit I have
11.25 He **took** some of the spirit he had given to Moses and
13.30 Moses, and said, "We should attack now and **take** the land;
14. 3 Why is the Lord **taking** us into that land?
14. 8 pleased with us, he will **take** us there and give us that
15.33 He was **taken** to Moses, Aaron, and the whole community,
15.36 So the whole community **took** him outside the camp and
16. 6 you and your followers **take** firepans,
16. 6 live coals and incense on them, and **take** them to the altar.
16.15 I have not even **taken** one of their donkeys."
16.17 Each of you will **take** his firepan, put incense on it,
16.18 So every man **took** his firepan, put live coals and
16.38 So **take** the firepans of these men who were put to death
16.39 So Eleazar the priest **took** the firepans and had them
16.46 and Moses said to Aaron, "**Take** your firepan, put live
16.47 Aaron obeyed, **took** his firepan and ran into the middle
17. 4 **Take** them to the Tent of my presence and put them in
17. 9 Moses **took** all the sticks and showed them to the Israelites.
17. 9 what had happened, and each leader **took** his own stick back.
19. 3 It is to be **taken** outside the camp and killed in his
19. 4 Then Eleazar is to **take** some of its blood and with his
19. 6 Then he is to **take** some cedar-wood, a sprig of hyssop, and
19.17 to remove sin shall be **taken** and put in a pot, and
19.18 is ritually clean is to **take** a sprig of hyssop, dip it
20. 8 The Lord said to Moses, [8]"**Take** the stick that is in
20.25 **Take** Aaron and his son Eleazar up Mount Hor, [26]and
21. 7 Now pray to the Lord to **take** these snakes away."
21.33 Then the Israelites turned and **took** the road to Bashan,
22. 7 the Moabite and Midianite leaders **took** with them the payment
22.41 Next morning Balak **took** Balaam up to Bamoth Baal, from
23.14 He **took** him to the field of Zophim on the top of
23.27 said, "Come with me, and I will **take** you to another place.
23.28 So he **took** Balaam to the top of Mount Peor overlooking
24.22 But you Kenites will be destroyed When Assyria **takes** you captive."
25. 4 and said to Moses, "**Take** all the leaders of Israel and,
25. 6 One of the Israelites **took** a Midianite woman into his tent
25. 7 He **took** a spear, [8]followed the man and the woman into the
27.18 The Lord said to Moses, "**Take** Joshua son of Nun, a
31. 9 women and children, **took** their cattle and their flocks,
31.11 They **took** all the loot that they had captured, including
31.27 Divide what was **taken** into two equal parts, one part for
31.30 the rest of the people, **take** one out of every fifty
31.47 From this share Moses **took** one out of every fifty
Num 31.50 rings, earrings, and necklaces that each of us has **taken.**
31.53 Those who were not officers kept the loot they had **taken.**
31.54 So Moses and Eleazar **took** the gold to the Tent, so that
32.14 And now you have **taken** your fathers' place, a new
32.18 all the other Israelites have **taken** possession of the land
32.19 We will not **take** possession of any property among them
32.22 the Lord defeats them [22]and **takes** possession of the land.
34.18 **Take** also one leader from each tribe to help them divide it."
Deut 1.15 So I **took** the wise and experienced leaders you chose
1.22 us the best route to **take** and what kind of cities are
2.21 that the Ammonites **took** over their land and settled there.
2.22 so that the Edomites **took** over their land and settled there,
2.23 the original inhabitants, and had **taken** over all their land
2.30 defeat him and **take** his territory, which we still occupy.
2.31 **take** his land and occupy it.'
2.35 We **took** the livestock and plundered the towns.
3. 4 all his towns—there was not one that we did not **take.**
3. 7 We **took** the livestock and plundered the towns.
3. 8 "At that time we **took** from those two Amorite kings the
3.10 We **took** all the territory of King Og of Bashan:
3.12 "When we **took** possession of the land, I assigned to
3.14 from the tribe of Manasseh, **took** the entire region of Argob,
4. 2 to what I command you, and do not **take** anything away.
4.34 ever dared to go and **take** a people from another nation and
6.18 You will be able to **take** possession of the fertile land that
7.25 gold that is on them, and do not **take** it for yourselves.
9. 5 what is right that the Lord is letting you **take** their land.
9.21 I **took** that sinful thing that you had made—that metal
9.23 with orders to go and **take** possession of the land that he
9.28 that you were unable to **take** your people into the land that
9.28 They will say that you **took** your people out into the desert
10. 3 tablets like the first ones and **took** them up the mountain.
10.11 you, so that you could **take** possession of the land that he
11.31 When you **take** it and settle there, [32]be sure to obey all
12. 2 the land that you are **taking,** destroy all the places where
12.26 **Take** to the one place of worship your offerings and the
12.32 do not add anything to it or **take** anything from it.
14.25 Sell your produce and **take** the money with you to the one
15.17 Then **take** him to the door of your house and there pierce
17. 5 has happened in Israel, [5]then **take** that person outside the
17.14 "After you have **taken** possession of the land that the
19. 1 you and after you have **taken** their cities and houses and
20.14 You may, however, **take** for yourselves the women, the
21. 4 They are to **take** it down to a spot near a stream
21.10 victory in battle and you **take** prisoners, [11]you may see
21.12 **Take** her to your home, where she will shave her head,
21.19 His parents are to **take** him before the leaders of the
22. 1 **take** it back to him.
22. 2 you don't know who owns it, then **take** it home with you.
22. 6 or with her young, you are not to **take** the mother bird.
22. 7 You may **take** the young birds, but you must let the mother
22.15 the girl's parents are to **take** the blood-stained wedding
22.18 Then the town leaders are to **take** the husband and beat him.
22.21 virgin, [21]then they are to **take** her out to the entrance of
22.24 You are to **take** them outside the town and stone them to
24. 6 something, you are not to **take** as security his millstones
24. 6 This would **take** away the family's means of preparing food to
24.17 and do not **take** a widow's garment as security for a loan.
26. 2 you harvest and you must **take** it with you to the one
26. 4 "The priest will **take** the basket from you and place it
26. 5 a wandering Aramean, who **took** his family to Egypt to live.
26.14 I have not **taken** any of it out of my house when
28.33 A foreign nation will **take** all the crops that you have
28.36 "The Lord will **take** you and your king away to a
28.41 them, because they will be **taken** away as prisoners of war.
29. 8 But we defeated them, [8]**took** their land, and divided it
30. 5 so that you may again **take** possession of the land where
31.20 I will **take** them into this rich and fertile land, as I
31.21 Even now, before I **take** them into the land that I promised
31.26 of the Lord's Covenant Box, [26]"**Take** this book of God's
33.21 They **took** the best of the land for themselves;
Josh 2. 4 (Now Rahab had **taken** the two spies up on the roof and
2.14 said to her, "May God **take** our lives if we don't do
3. 6 he told the priests to **take** the Covenant Box and go with
4. 3 tribe, [3]and command them to **take** twelve stones out of the
4. 5 Each one of you **take** a stone on your shoulder, one for
4. 8 Lord had commanded Joshua, they **took** twelve stones from the
4.20 There Joshua set up the twelve stones **taken** from the Jordan.
6. 6 priests and said to them, "**Take** the Covenant Box, and seven
6.11 this group of men to **take** the Lord's Covenant Box round the
6.18 But you are not to **take** anything that is to be destroyed;
6.23 They **took** them all, family and slaves, to safety near the
6.24 and iron, which they **took** and put in the Lord's treasury.
7. 1 command to Israel not to **take** from Jericho anything that was
7.11 They have **taken** some of the things condemned to destruction.
7.12 unless you destroy the things you were ordered not to **take!**
7.21 I wanted them so much that I **took** them.
7.23 them out of the tent, **took** them to Joshua and all the
7.24 and they **took** them to Trouble Valley.
8. 1 The Lord said to Joshua, "**Take** all the soldiers with you
8. 8 After you have **taken** the city, set it on fire, just as
8.12 He **took** about five thousand men and put them in hiding
8.21 saw that the others had **taken** the city and that it was
8.23 He was captured and **taken** to Joshua.
9. 5 The bread they **took** with them was dry and mouldy.
10.24 Lachish, and Eglon were brought out [24]and **taken** to Joshua.
10.27 orders, and their bodies were **taken** down and thrown into the
10.41 Joshua's campaign **took** him from Kadesh Barnea in the
11.14 The people of Israel **took** all the valuables and
13. 1 are very old, but there is still much land to be **taken:**
17.18 you will clear it and **take** possession of it from one end

Josh	18. 3	before you go in and **take** the land that the Lord, the
	21.43	When they had **taken** possession of it, they settled down there.
	22. 6	with your fellow-tribesmen what you **took** from your enemies."
	22. 9	of Gilead, which they had **taken** as the Lord had commanded
	24. 3	Then I **took** Abraham, your ancestor, from the land beyond
	24. 8	You **took** their land, and I destroyed them as you advanced.
	24.26	Then he **took** a large stone and set it up under the
Judg	1. 7	He was **taken** to Jerusalem, where he died.
	1.18	of Judah, and they **took** possession of the hill-country.
	2. 1	said to the Israelites, "I **took** you out of Egypt and
	2. 6	and each man went to **take** possession of his own share of
	3.17	Then he **took** the gifts to Eglon, who was a very fat
	3.21	With his left hand Ehud **took** the sword from his right
	3.25	did not open the door, they **took** the key and opened it.
	4. 6	'**Take** ten thousand men from the tribes of Naphtali and
	4.21	Then Jael **took** a hammer and a tent-peg, went up to him
	5.19	the kings of Canaan fought, but they **took** no silver away.
	5.26	She **took** a tent peg in one hand, a workman's hammer in
	6. 4	They would **take** all the sheep, cattle, and donkeys, and
	6.25	night the Lord told Gideon, "**Take** your father's bull and
	6.26	Then **take** the second bull and burn it whole as an offering,
	6.27	So Gideon **took** ten of his servants and did what the Lord
	7. 4	**Take** them down to the water, and I will separate them for
	7. 5	Gideon **took** the men down to the water, and the Lord said
	8.16	He then **took** thorns and briars from the desert and used
	8.21	So Gideon killed them and **took** the ornaments that were on
	8.24	Every one of you give me the earrings you **took.**"
	8.25	and everyone put on it the earrings that he had **taken.**
	9.43	into the fields, [43] so he **took** his men, divided them into
	9.48	There he **took** an axe, cut a branch off a tree, and
	11. 9	said to them, "If you **take** me back home to fight the
	11.13	came out of Egypt, they **took** away my land from the River
	11.15	is not true that Israel **took** away the land of Moab or
	11.21	So the Israelites **took** possession of all the territory of
	11.24	Are you going to try to **take** it back?
	11.26	Why haven't you **taken** them back in all this time?
	11.35	a solemn promise to the Lord, and I cannot **take** it back!"
	13.19	So Manoah **took** a young goat and some grain, and offered
	14. 9	tell them that he had **taken** the honey from the dead body
	15. 1	his wife during the wheat harvest and **took** her a young goat.
	15.10	They answered, "We came to **take** Samson prisoner and to
	16.14	then lulled him to sleep, **took** his seven locks of hair, and
	16.21	They **took** him to Gaza, chained him with bronze chains, and
	16.31	They **took** him back and buried him between Zorah and Eshtaol
	17. 2	I am the one who **took** it."
	17. 4	She **took** two hundred of the pieces of silver and gave them
	18. 9	Go on in and **take** it over!
	18.17	into the house and **took** the wooden idol covered with silver,
	18.18	went into Micah's house and **took** the sacred objects, the
	18.20	priest very happy, so he **took** the sacred objects and went
	18.24	You **take** my priest and the gods that I made, and walk
	18.27	the men from Dan had **taken** the priest and the things that
	18.30	their priests until the people were **taken** away into exile.
	19. 1	He **took** a girl from Bethlehem in Judah to be his concubine,
	19. 3	He **took** his servant and two donkeys with him.
	19.15	square, but no one offered to **take** them home for the night.
	19.21	So he **took** them home with him and fed their donkeys.
	19.25	So the Levite **took** his concubine and put her outside with them.
	19.29	He **took** his concubine's body, cut it into twelve pieces, and
	20. 6	I **took** her body, cut it in pieces, and sent one piece
	21.21	Each of you **take** a wife by force from among the girls
	21.21	and **take** her back to the territory
	21.22	them, because we did not **take** them from you in battle to
Ruth	2.18	She **took** the corn back into town and showed her
	4.13	So Boaz **took** Ruth home as his wife.
	4.16	Naomi **took** the child, held him close, and took care of him.
1 Sam	1.22	child is weaned, I will **take** him to the house of the
	1.24	she took him to Shiloh, **taking** along a three-year-old bull,
	1.24	She **took** Samuel, young as he was, to the house of the
	1.25	After they had killed the bull, they **took** the child to Eli.
	2.15	even before the fat was **taken** off and burnt, the priest's
	2.16	then **take** what you want," the priest's servant would say,
	2.16	If you don't, I will have to **take** it by force!"
	2.19	make a little robe and **take** it to him when she accompanied
	5. 2	to their city of Ashdod, [2] **took** it into the temple of their
	5. 8	"**Take** it over to Gath," they answered;
	5. 8	so they **took** it to Gath, another Philistine city.
	6. 8	**Take** the Lord's Covenant Box, put it on the wagon, and
	6.10	they **took** two cows and hitched them to the wagon, and shut
	7. 1	the Lord's Covenant Box and **took** it to the house of a
	7.12	Then Samuel **took** a stone, set it up between Mizpah and Shen,
	8.14	He will **take** your best fields, vineyards, and olive-groves,
	8.15	He will **take** a tenth of your corn and of your grapes
	8.16	He will **take** your servants and your best cattle and donkeys,
	8.17	He will **take** a tenth of your flocks.
	9. 3	so he said to Saul, "**Take** one of the servants with you
	10. 1	Then Samuel **took** a jar of olive-oil and poured it on
	11. 7	He **took** two oxen, cut them in pieces, and sent messengers
	12. 3	Have I **taken** anybody's cow or anybody's donkey?
	12. 3	any of these things, I will pay back what I have **taken.**"
	12. 4	you have not **taken** anything from anyone."
	14.30	had eaten the food they **took** when they defeated the enemy.
	14.32	had captured from the enemy, **took** sheep and cattle,
	15.15	Saul answered, "My men **took** them from the Amalekites.
	16. 2	The Lord answered, "**Take** a calf with you and say that you
	16.13	Samuel **took** the olive-oil and anointed David
	16.13	the spirit of the Lord **took** control of David and was with
	17.17	day Jesse said to David, "**Take** ten kilogrammes of this
	17.18	And **take** these ten cheeses to the commanding officer.
	17.20	in charge of the sheep, **took** the food, and went as Jesse
	17.40	He **took** his shepherd's stick and then picked up five
1 Sam	17.49	hand into his bag and **took** out a stone, which he slung
	17.51	him, stood over him, **took** Goliath's sword out of its sheath,
	17.54	picked up Goliath's head and **took** it to Jerusalem, but he
	17.57	returned to camp after killing Goliath, Abner **took** him to Saul.
	18.27	He **took** their foreskins to the king and counted them all out
	19. 7	then he **took** him to Saul, and David served the king as
	19.13	Then she **took** the household idol, laid it on the bed,
	20. 8	Why **take** me to your father to be killed?"
	20.35	He **took** a young boy with him [36] and said to him, "Run
	20.40	the boy and told him to **take** them back to the town.
	21. 9	If you want it, **take** it—it's the only weapon here."
	23. 5	they killed many of them and **took** their livestock.
	23. 6	and joined David in Keilah, he **took** the ephod with him.
	24. 2	Saul **took** three thousand of the best soldiers in Israel
	25.11	I'm not going to **take** my bread and water, and the
	25.40	her, "David sent us to **take** you to him to be his
	26.11	Let's **take** his spear and his water jar, and go."
	26.12	So David **took** the spear and the water jar from just
	27. 9	the men and women and **taking** the sheep, cattle, donkeys,
	28.17	he has **taken** the kingdom away from you and given it to
	28.24	Then she **took** some flour, prepared it, and baked some bread
	30. 2	anyone, but had **taken** everyone with them when they left.
	30. 5	Even David's two wives, Ahinoam and Abigail, had been **taken** away.
	30.18	the Amalekites had **taken,** including his two wives;
	30.19	and daughters, and all the loot the Amalekites had **taken.**
	30.22	They can **take** their wives and children and go away."
	30.26	for you from the loot we **took** from the Lord's enemies."
	31. 4	So Saul **took** his own sword and threw himself on it.
	31.12	They **took** down the bodies of Saul and his sons from the
	31.13	Then they **took** the bones and buried them under the
2 Sam	1.10	Then I **took** the crown from his head and the bracelet from
	2. 2	So David went to Hebron, **taking** with him his two wives:
	2. 3	He also **took** his men and their families, and they settled
	2.21	"Run after one of the soldiers and **take** what he has."
	2.32	Joab and his men **took** Asahel's body and buried it in the
	3. 9	promised David that he would **take** the kingdom away from Saul
	3.15	So Ishbosheth **took** her away from her husband Paltiel
	3.27	Abner arrived in Hebron, Joab **took** him aside at the gate, as
	4. 7	they cut off his head, **took** it with them, and walked all
	4.12	They **took** Ishbosheth's head and buried it in Abner's tomb
	5.13	Hebron to Jerusalem, David **took** more concubines and wives,
	6. 3	They **took** it from Abinadab's home on the hill and placed
	6. 9	and said, "How can I **take** the Covenant Box with me now?"
	6.10	So he decided not to **take** it with him to Jerusalem;
	6.10	turned off the road and **took** it to the house of Obed
	6.12	Box from Obed's house to **take** it to Jerusalem with a great
	6.15	he and all the Israelites **took** the Covenant Box up to
	7. 8	Almighty, say to him, 'I **took** you from looking after sheep
	8. 7	carried by Hadadezer's officials and **took** them to Jerusalem.
	8. 8	also **took** a great quantity of bronze from Betah and Berothai,
	8.10	Joram **took** David presents made of gold, silver, and bronze.
	8.11	the silver and gold he **took** from the nations he had
	8.12	as well as part of the loot he had **taken** from Hadadezer.
	12. 4	instead, he **took** the poor man's lamb and cooked a meal for
	12. 6	thing, he must pay back four times as much as he **took.**"
	12. 9	you let the Ammonites kill him, and then you **took** his wife!
	12.10	because you have disobeyed me and have **taken** Uriah's wife.
	12.11	will see it when I **take** your wives from you and give
	12.28	rest of your forces, attack the city and **take** it yourself.
	12.30	the Ammonite god Molech David **took** a gold crown which
	12.30	David **took** the jewel and put it in his own crown.
	12.30	He also **took** a large amount of loot from the city [31] and
	13. 8	She **took** some dough, prepared it, and made some cakes there
	13.10	She **took** the cakes and went over to him.
	15. 8	Lord that if he would **take** me back to Jerusalem, I would
	15.20	Go back and **take** your fellow-countrymen with you—and may the
	15.25	the king said to Zadok, "**Take** the Covenant Box back to the
	15.27	to say to Zadok, "Look, **take** your son Ahimaaz and
	15.29	So Zadok and Abiathar **took** the Covenant Box back into
	16. 8	You **took** Saul's kingdom, and now the Lord is punishing you
	17.19	The man's wife **took** a covering, spread it over the
	18.14	He **took** three spears and plunged them into Absalom's chest
	18.17	They **took** Absalom's body, threw it into a deep pit in
	18.20	"No," Joab said, "today you will not **take** any good news.
	18.22	please let me **take** the news also."
	19.37	**take** him with you, Your Majesty, and do for him as you
	19.38	The king answered, "I will **take** him with me and do for
	19.41	they had the right to **take** you away and escort you, your
	20. 3	his palace in Jerusalem, he **took** the ten concubines he had
	20. 6	**Take** my men and go after him, or else he may occupy
	21. 8	However, he **took** Armoni and Mephibosheth, the two sons
	21. 8	he also **took** the five sons of Saul's daughter Merab, whom
	21.13	David **took** the bones of Saul and Jonathan and also
	24.13	over, and tell me what answer to **take** back to the Lord."
	24.22	"**Take** it, Your Majesty," Araunah said, "and offer to
1 Kgs	1.33	in, [33] he said to them, "**Take** my court officials with you;
	1.39	Zadok **took** the container of olive-oil which he had
	3.20	got up during the night, **took** my son from my side while
	8. 1	Jerusalem in order to **take** the Lord's Covenant Box from Zion,
	8.46	their enemies defeat them and **take** them as prisoners to some
	9.20	had not killed when they **took** possession of their land.
	11.11	I promise that I will **take** the kingdom away from you and
	11.13	And I will not **take** the whole kingdom away from him;
	11.31	and said to Jeroboam, "**Take** ten pieces for yourself,
	11.31	'I am going to **take** the kingdom away from Solomon,
	11.34	But I will not **take** the whole kingdom away from Solomon,
	11.35	I will **take** the kingdom away from Solomon's son and will
	13.18	an angel told me to **take** you home with me and offer
	14. 3	**Take** him ten loaves of bread, some cakes, and a jar of
	14. 8	I **took** the kingdom away from David's descendants and gave

1 Kgs 14.26 He **took** away all the treasures in the Temple and in the
15.18 So King Asa **took** all the silver and gold that was left
17.12 to gather some firewood to **take** back home and prepare what
17.19 He **took** the boy from her arms, carried him upstairs to the
17.23 Elijah **took** the boy back downstairs to his mother and
18. 4 killing the Lord's prophets, Obadiah **took** a hundred of them,
18.23 let the prophets of Baal **take** one, kill it, cut it in
18.25 so many of you, you **take** a bull and prepare it first.
18.26 They **took** the bull that was brought to them, prepared
18.31 He **took** twelve stones, one for each of the twelve tribes
19. 3 he **took** his servant and went to Beersheba in Judah.
19. 4 "**Take** away my life;
20. 6 officials, and to **take** everything they consider valuable.
20.18 He ordered, "**Take** them alive, no matter whether they
20.34 you the towns my father **took** from your father, and you may
21.10 Then **take** him out of the city and stone him to death."
21.13 king, and so he was **taken** outside the city and stoned to
21.15 Now go and **take** possession of the vineyard which he refused
21.16 At once Ahab went to the vineyard to **take** possession of it.
21.18 him in Naboth's vineyard, about to **take** possession of it.
21.19 'After murdering the man, are you **taking** over his property as well?'
22.26 his officers, "Arrest Micaiah and **take** him to Amon, the
22.37 His body was **taken** to Samaria and buried.
2 Kgs 2. 1 came for the Lord to **take** Elijah up to heaven in a
2. 3 Lord is going to **take** your master away from you today?"
2. 5 Lord is going to **take** your master away from you today?"
2. 9 you want me to do for you before I am **taken** away."
2.10 if you see me as I am being **taken** away from you;
3. 8 What route shall we **take** for the attack?"
3.26 was losing the battle, he **took** seven hundred swordsmen with
3.27 So he **took** his eldest son, who was to succeed him as
4. 1 money to has come to **take** away my two sons as slaves
4. 5 her sons, closed the door, **took** the small jar of olive-oil,
4.29 **Take** my stick and go.
4.37 then she **took** her son and left.
5. 5 "Go to the king of Israel and **take** this letter to him."
5. 5 So Naaman set out, **taking** thirty thousand pieces of silver,
5. 6 The letter that he **took** read:
5.17 two mule-loads of earth to **take** home with me, because from
5.23 "Please **take** six thousand pieces of silver," Naaman replied.
5.24 hill where Elisha lived, Gehazi **took** the two bags and
6. 7 "**Take** it out," he ordered, and the man bent down and
7.12 and then they will **take** us alive and capture the city."
8. 8 Hazael, one of his officials, "**Take** a gift to the prophet,
8.15 the following day Hazael **took** a blanket, soaked it in water,
9. 1 **Take** this jar of olive-oil with you, [2]and when you get
9. 2 **Take** him to a private room away from his companions, [3]pour
9.26 So **take** Joram's body," Jehu ordered his aide, "and throw
9.28 His officials **took** his body back to Jerusalem in a
9.34 Only then did he say, "**Take** that damned woman and bury her;
10.14 Jehu ordered his men, "**Take** them alive!"
11. 2 She **took** him and his nurse into a bedroom in the Temple
11.15 "**Take** her out between the rows of guards, and kill anyone
11.16 They seized her, **took** her to the palace, and there at
12. 9 Then Jehoiada **took** a box, made a hole in the lid, and
12.18 Joash of Judah **took** all the offerings that his predecessors
13.18 Elisha told the king to **take** the other arrows and strike the
13.25 the cities that had been **taken** by Benhadad during the reign
14.13 Jehoash **took** Amaziah prisoner, advanced on Jerusalem,
14.14 He **took** all the silver and gold he could find, all the
14.14 He also **took** hostages with him.
15.29 and Naphtali, and **took** the people to Assyria as prisoners.
16. 8 Ahaz **took** the silver and gold from the Temple and the
16. 9 killed King Rezin, and **took** the people to Kir as prisoners.
16.17 he also **took** the bronze tank from the backs of the twelve
17. 6 captured Samaria, **took** the Israelites to Assyria as prisoners,
17.23 the people of Israel were **taken** into exile to Assyria, where
17.24 emperor of Assyria **took** people from the cities of Babylon,
17.24 They **took** possession of these cities and lived there.
18.11 The Assyrian emperor **took** the Israelites to Assyria as
19.14 King Hezekiah **took** the letter from the messengers and read it.
19.28 bit in your mouth, and **take** you back by the same road
20.18 own direct descendants will be **taken** away and made eunuchs
22. 9 "Your servants have **taken** the money that was in the Temple
23. 4 of the Kidron, and then had the ashes **taken** to Bethel.
23. 6 symbol of the goddess Asherah, **took** it out of the city to
23.16 he had the bones **taken** out of them and burnt on the
23.30 body in a chariot and **took** it back to Jerusalem, where he
23.33 when King Neco of Egypt **took** him prisoner in Riblah, in the
23.34 Joahaz was **taken** to Egypt by King Neco, and there he died.
24.12 year of Nebuchadnezzar's reign he **took** Jehoiachin prisoner
24.15 Nebuchadnezzar **took** Jehoiachin to Babylon as a prisoner,
25. 6 Zedekiah was **taken** to King Nebuchadnezzar, who was in the
25. 7 put out, placed him in chains, and **took** him to Babylon.
25.11 Then Nebuzaradan **took** away to Babylonia the people who
25.13 large bronze tank, and they **took** all the bronze to Babylon.
25.14 They also **took** away the shovels and the ash containers
25.15 They **took** away everything that was made of gold or silver,
25.18 addition, Nebuzaradan, the commanding officer, **took** away as
25.19 From the city he **took** the officer who had been in
25.20 Nebuzaradan **took** them to the king of Babylonia, who was
25.22 of all those who had not been **taken** away to Babylonia.
25.27 year after Jehoiachin had been **taken** away as prisoner.
1 Chr 3.17 King Jehoiachin, who was **taken** prisoner by the Babylonians.
5.21 and 2,000 donkeys, and **took** 100,000 prisoners of war.
7.28 The territory which they **took** and settled in included
10. 4 So Saul **took** his own sword and threw himself on it.
10.12 the bodies of Saul and his sons and **took** them to Jabesh.
13.12 and said, "How can I **take** the Covenant Box with me now?"
13.13 So David did not **take** it with him to Jerusalem.
1 Chr 16. 1 They **took** the Covenant Box to the tent which David had
17. 7 Almighty, say to him, 'I **took** you from looking after sheep
18. 1 He **took** out of their control the city of Gath and its
18. 7 carried by Hadadezer's officials and **took** them to Jerusalem.
18. 8 He also **took** a great quantity of bronze from Tibhath and Kun,
18.11 silver and gold he **took** from the nations he conquered—Edom,
20. 2 was a jewel, which David **took** and put in his own crown.
20. 2 He also **took** a large amount of loot from the city.
20. 3 He **took** the people of the city and put them to work
21.23 "**Take** it, Your Majesty," Araunah said, "and do whatever you wish.
26.27 They **took** some of the loot they captured in battle and
28. 4 it was his pleasure to **take** me and make me king over
2 Chr 2.16 From there you can **take** them to Jerusalem."
5. 2 in order to **take** the Lord's Covenant Box from Zion,
6.36 their enemies defeat them and **take** them as prisoners to some
8. 7 had not killed when they **took** possession of the land.
12. 9 Shishak came to Jerusalem and **took** the treasures from the
12. 9 **took** everything, including the gold shields that King Solomon
14.13 Lord and his army, and the army **took** large amounts of loot.
16. 2 So Asa **took** silver and gold from the treasuries of the
17. 9 They **took** the book of the Law of the Lord and went
18.25 his officers, "Arrest Micaiah and **take** him to Amon, the
19. 7 God does not tolerate fraud or partiality or the **taking** of bribes."
20.25 his troops moved in to **take** the loot, and they found many
20.25 but there was so much that they could not **take** everything.
22. 9 They **took** him to Jehu and put him to death.
22.11 one of Ahaziah's sons, Joash, **took** him away from the other
23.14 the army officers and said, "**Take** her out between the rows
23.15 They seized her, **took** her to the palace, and there at
24.11 Every day the Levites would **take** the box to the royal
24.11 the High Priest's representative would **take** the money out
24.23 killed all the leaders, and **took** large amounts of loot back
25. 7 said to him, "Don't **take** these Israelite soldiers with you.
25.12 They **took** the prisoners to the top of the cliff at the
25.23 Jehoash captured Amaziah and **took** him to Jerusalem.
25.24 He **took** back to Samaria as loot all the gold and silver
25.24 He also **took** hostages with him.
28. 5 of Syria defeat him and **take** a large number of Judaeans back
28. 8 and children as prisoners and **took** them back to Samaria,
28.15 prisoners were **taken** back to Judaean territory at Jericho,
28.21 So Ahaz **took** the gold from the Temple, the palace, and
28.24 In addition, he **took** all the temple equipment and broke
29. 9 our wives and children have been **taken** away as prisoners.
29.16 From there the Levites **took** it all outside the city to the
29.19 the equipment which King Ahaz **took** away during those years
29.21 to purify the Temple, they **took** seven bulls, seven sheep,
29.23 Finally they **took** the goats to the king and to the other
30. 9 Lord, then those who have **taken** your relatives away as
30.14 They **took** all the altars that had been used in Jerusalem
33.11 hooks in him, put him in chains, and **took** him to Babylon.
33.15 **took** all these things outside the city and threw them away.
34.14 While the money was being **taken** out of the storeroom,
34.16 He gave Shaphan the book, [16]and Shaphan **took** it to the king.
34.17 We have **taken** the money that was kept in the Temple and
35.23 He ordered his servants, "**Take** me away;
35.24 chariot which he had there, and **took** him to Jerusalem.
36. 3 King Neco of Egypt **took** him prisoner and made Judah pay
36. 4 Joahaz was **taken** to Egypt by Neco.
36. 6 captured Jehoiakim, and **took** him to Babylonia in chains.
36.10 Nebuchadnezzar **took** Jehoiachin to Babylonia as a prisoner,
36.18 king and his officials, and **took** everything back to Babylon.
36.20 He **took** all the survivors to Babylonia, where they
Ezra 1. 7 cups that King Nebuchadnezzar had **taken** from the Temple in
1.11 and other articles which Sheshbazzar **took** with him when he
2. 1 since King Nebuchadnezzar had **taken** them there as prisoners.
5.12 and the people were **taken** into exile in Babylonia.
5.14 temple utensils which Nebuchadnezzar had **taken** from the
5.15 The emperor told him to **take** them and return them to the
7.15 You are to **take** with you the gold and silver offerings
7.16 You are also to **take** all the silver and gold which you
8.30 and the utensils, to **take** them to the Temple in Jerusalem.
8.36 They also **took** the document the emperor had given them
Neh 2. 1 when Emperor Artaxerxes was dining, I **took** the wine to him.
2.12 got up and went out, **taking** a few of my companions with
2.12 The only animal we **took** was the donkey that I rode on.
4. 4 have, and let them be **taken** as prisoners to a foreign land.
4.10 There's so much rubble to **take** away.
5. 5 our fields and vineyards have been **taken** away from us."
5.13 "God will **take** away your houses and everything you own, and
7. 6 since King Nebuchadnezzar had **taken** them there as prisoners.
9.17 they chose a leader to **take** them back to slavery in Egypt.
9.19 You did not **take** away the cloud or the fire that showed
10.35 We will **take** to the Temple each year an offering of the
10.36 each of us we will **take** to the priests in the Temple
10.37 We will **take** to the priests in the Temple the dough made
10.37 We will **take** to the Levites, who collect tithes in our
10.38 Temple the Levites are to **take** to the temple storerooms one
10.39 and the Levites are to **take** the contributions of corn, wine,
13.15 things on their donkeys and **taking** them into Jerusalem;
Esth 2. 4 Then **take** the girl you like best and make her queen in
2. 6 When King Nebuchadnezzar of Babylon **took** King Jehoiachin
2.12 After that, each girl would be **taken** in turn to King Xerxes.
2.14 next morning she would be **taken** to another harem and put in
3.13 **took** this proclamation to every province of the empire.
3.13 without mercy and their belongings were to be **taken.**
4. 8 Mordecai asked him to **take** it to Esther, explain the
4.10 and Esther gave him this message to **take** back to Mordecai:
6.14 arrived in a hurry to **take** Haman to Esther's banquet.
8. 2 on it (which he had **taken** back from Haman) and gave it
8.11 slaughter them to the last man and **take** their possessions.
Job 1.11 But now suppose you **take** away everything he has—he will

Job 1.17 of Chaldean raiders attacked us, **took** away the camels, and
1.21 The Lord gave, and now he has **taken** away.
2. 8 by the rubbish heap and **took** a piece of broken pottery to
4.21 All that he has is **taken** away;
9.12 He **takes** what he wants, and no one can stop him;
9.19 Should I **take** him to court?
12.17 He **takes** away the wisdom of rulers and makes leaders act
12.20 men who are trusted, and **takes** the wisdom of old men away.
13.27 you watch every step I **take,** and even examine my footprints.
14.16 will watch every step I **take,** but you will not keep track
16.12 living in peace, but God **took** me by the throat and battered
19. 9 He has **taken** away all my wealth and destroyed my reputation.
20.15 God **takes** it back, even out of his stomach.
22. 6 the money he owed, you **took** away his clothes and left him
22. 8 your power and your position to **take** over the whole land.
23.10 Yet God knows every step I **take;**
24. 3 They **take** donkeys that belong to orphans, and keep a
24. 9 slaves of fatherless infants and **take** the poor man's
30.23 I know you are **taking** me off to my death, to the
31. 4 he sees every step I **take.**
31.38 the land I farm and **taken** it from its rightful owners—
34.14 If God **took** back the breath of life, [15] then everyone
34.21 He watches every step men **take.**
36.27 It is God who **takes** water from the earth and turns it
42. 8 Now **take** seven bulls and seven rams to Job and offer them
Ps 7.13 he **takes** up his deadly weapons and aims his burning arrows.
26.10 do evil all the time and are always ready to **take** bribes.
30.11 you have **taken** away my sorrow and surrounded me with joy.
35. 2 **Take** your shield and armour and come to my rescue.
37.17 because the Lord will **take** away the strength of the wicked,
44.10 our enemies, and they **took** for themselves what was ours.
49.17 he cannot **take** it with him when he dies;
51.11 do not **take** your holy spirit away from me.
60. 9 Who, O God, will **take** me into the fortified city?
61. 2 **Take** me to a safe refuge, [3] for you are my protector, my
68.18 He goes up to the heights, **taking** many captives with him;
78.13 He divided the sea and **took** them through it;
78.70 he **took** him from the pastures, [71] where he looked after
81. 6 voice saying, [6] "I **took** the burdens off your backs;
83.12 Zalmunna, [12] who said, "We will **take** for our own the land
89.34 my covenant with him or **take** back even one promise I made
89.44 You have **taken** away his royal sceptre and hurled his
102.24 O God, do not **take** me away now before I grow old.
104.29 when you **take** away your breath, they die and go back to
105.16 Lord sent famine to their country and **took** away all their food.
105.44 other peoples and let them **take** over their fields, [45] so
108.10 Who, O God, will **take** me into the fortified city?
109. 8 may another man **take** his job!
109.11 May his creditors **take** away all his property, and may
110. 4 The Lord made a solemn promise and will not **take** it back:
132.11 solemn promise to David— a promise you will not **take** back:
137. 9 done to us— [9] who **takes** your babies and smashes them against
146. 9 he helps widows and orphans, but **takes** the wicked to their ruin.
Prov 5. 5 She will **take** you down to the world of the dead;
5.10 Yes, strangers will **take** all your wealth, and what you
7.20 He **took** plenty of money with him and won't be back for
11.30 Righteousness gives life, but violence **takes** it away.
15.27 Don't **take** bribes and you will live longer.
18.16 **Take** him a gift and it will be easy.
20.24 can anyone understand the direction his own life is **taking?**
21.22 A shrewd general can **take** a city defended by strong men,
22.27 should be unable to pay, they will **take** away even your bed.
23.10 Never move an old boundary-mark or **take** over land owned by orphans.
24.15 scheme to rob an honest man or to **take** away his home.
25. 4 **Take** the impurities out of silver and the artist can
25. 7 better to be asked to **take** a higher position than to be
29.21 on, some day he will **take** over everything you own.
Ecc 3.14 You can't add anything to it or **take** anything away from it.
5.15 of all our work there is nothing we can **take** with us.
7. 7 If you **take** a bribe, you ruin your character.
Song 1. 4 **Take** me with you, and we'll run away;
1. 4 be my king and **take** me to your room.
3. 4 let him go until I **took** him to my mother's house, to
8. 2 I would **take** you to my mother's house, where you could
Is 1. 7 While you look on, foreigners **take** over your land and bring
3. 1 Almighty Lord, is about to **take** away from Jerusalem and
3. 1 He is going to **take** away their food and their water, [2] their
3.14 your houses are full of what you have **taken** from the poor.
3.16 They **take** dainty little steps,
3.18 coming when the Lord will **take** away from the women of
3.19 He will **take** away their veils [20] and their hats;
5. 5 I will **take** away the hedge round it, break down the wall
5.29 carrying it off where no one can **take** it away from them.
6. 6 burning coal that he had **taken** from the altar with a pair
7. 3 The Lord said to Isaiah, "**Take** your son Shear Jashub, and
8. 1 The Lord said to me, "**Take** a large piece of writing
10. 2 That is how you **take** the property that belongs to widows and
10.13 between nations and **took** the supplies they had stored.
18. 2 **Take** a message back to your land divided by rivers, to your
23.16 **Take** your harp, go round the town, you poor forgotten whore!
25. 8 tears from everyone's eyes and **take** away the disgrace his
27. 8 He **took** them away with a cruel wind from the east.
28.13 Then you will stumble with every step you **take.**
28.13 You will be wounded, trapped, and **taken** prisoner.
29.11 If you **take** it to someone who knows how to read and
30.22 You will **take** your idols plated with silver and your
33. 4 Their belongings are pounced upon and **taken** as loot.
34.11 Owls and ravens will **take** over the land.
37.14 Hezekiah **took** the letter from the messengers and read it.
37.29 in your mouth and will **take** you back by the road on
Is 38.12 Like a tent that is **taken** down, Like cloth that is cut
39. 7 own direct descendants will be **taken** away and made eunuchs
44.12 The metalworker **takes** a piece of metal and works with it
49.24 Can you **take** away a soldier's loot?
49.25 The soldier's prisoners will be **taken** away, and the tyrant's
51.18 you, no one among your people to **take** you by the hand.
51.22 you and says, "I am **taking** away the cup that I gave
52. 4 however, **took** you away by force and paid nothing for you.
54. 7 with deep love I will **take** you back.
57. 6 You **take** smooth stones from there and worship them as gods.
62. 5 Like a young man **taking** a virgin as his bride, He who
Jer 1. 3 of that year the people of Jerusalem were **taken** into exile.
3. 1 becomes another man's wife, he cannot **take** her back again.
3.14 I will **take** one of you from each town and two from
6.11 Husbands and wives will be **taken** away, and even the very old
6.23 They have **taken** up their bows and swords;
6.29 my people, because those who are evil are not **taken** away.
8. 1 who lived in Jerusalem, will be **taken** out of their graves.
8.13 I have allowed outsiders to **take** over the land."
11.19 was like a trusting lamb **taken** out to be killed, and I
12.14 I will **take** those wicked people away from their countries
12.15 But after I have **taken** them away, I will have mercy on
13.17 because the Lord's people have been **taken** away as captives.
13.19 All the people of Judah have been **taken** away into exile."
15. 2 Others are doomed to be **taken** away as prisoners— that's
15.19 "If you return, I will **take** you back, and you will be
17. 3 I will make your enemies **take** away your wealth and your
18. 4 turned out imperfect, he would **take** the clay and make it
19. 1 He also told me to **take** some of the elders of the
20. 4 he will **take** some away as prisoners to his country and put
20. 6 family will also be captured and **taken** off to Babylonia.
22.10 they are **taking** him away, never to return, never again to
22.12 the country where they have **taken** him, and he will never
22.22 by the wind, your allies **taken** as prisoners of war, your
22.28 and his children have been **taken** into exile to a land they
23.30 am against those prophets who **take** each other's words and
24. 1 King Nebuchadnezzar of Babylonia had **taken** away Jehoiakim's son,
24. 5 that the people who were **taken** away to Babylonia are like
25.15 **Take** it to all the nations to whom I send you, and
25.17 So I **took** the cup from the Lord's hand, gave it to
25.28 And if they refuse to **take** the cup from your hand and
25.33 mourn for them, and they will not be **taken** away and buried.
27.10 and will cause you to be **taken** far away from your country.
27.18 Temple and in the royal palace to be **taken** to Babylonia."
27.19 King Nebuchadnezzar **took** away to Babylonia the king of Judah,
27.22 They will be **taken** to Babylonia and will remain there
28. 3 temple treasures that King Nebuchadnezzar **took** to Babylonia.
28. 6 and all the people who were **taken** away as prisoners.
29. 1 the others whom Nebuchadnezzar had **taken** away as prisoners
29. 2 and the skilled workmen had been **taken** into exile.
29. 4 whom he allowed Nebuchadnezzar to **take** away as prisoners
29.16 relatives who were not **taken** away as prisoners with you.
29.22 When the people who were **taken** away as prisoners from
30. 3 I gave their ancestors, and they will **take** possession of it again.
30.16 and all your enemies will be **taken** away as prisoners.
31. 4 Once again you will **take** up your tambourines and dance joyfully.
31.32 with their ancestors when I **took** them by the hand and led
32. 5 Zedekiah will be **taken** to Babylonia, and he will remain
32.11 Then I **took** both copies of the deed of purchase—the
32.14 Israel, has ordered you to **take** these deeds, both the sealed
32.23 came into this land and **took** possession of it, they did not
33.12 once again be pastures where shepherds can **take** their sheep.
34.11 they changed their minds, **took** them back, and forced them to
34.16 All of you **took** back the slaves whom you had set free
35. 3 So I **took** the entire Rechabite clan—Jaazaniah (the son of
35. 4 I **took** them into the room of the disciples of the prophet
36.21 He **took** it from the room of Elishama and read it to
36.28 the Lord told me [28] to **take** another scroll and write on it
36.32 I **took** another scroll and gave it to my secretary Baruch,
37.12 the territory of Benjamin to **take** possession of my share of
37.14 Instead, he arrested me and **took** me to the officials.
38. 6 So they **took** me and let me down by ropes into Prince
38.10 the king ordered Ebedmelech to **take** with him three men and
38.23 women and children will be **taken** out to the Babylonians, and
38.23 You will be **taken** prisoner by the king of Babylonia, and
39. 5 Then they **took** him to King Nebuchadnezzar, who was in the
39. 7 out and had him placed in chains to be **taken** to Babylonia.
39. 9 Nebuzaradan, the commanding officer, **took** away as prisoners
40. 1 I had been **taken** there in chains, along with all the other
40. 1 who were being **taken** away as prisoners to Babylonia.
40. 2 The commanding officer **took** me aside and said, "The Lord
40. 5 present and some food to **take** with me, and let me go
40. 7 those who had not been **taken** away to Babylonia—the poorest
41. 5 They were **taking** corn and incense to offer in the Temple.
41.10 Ishmael **took** them prisoner and started off in the direction
41.16 the people whom Ishmael had **taken** away as prisoners from
43. 3 us and can either kill us or **take** us away to Babylonia."
43. 5 and all the army officers **took** everybody left in Judah away
43. 6 They **took** everyone whom Nebuzaradan the commanding officer
43.11 those doomed to be **taken** away as prisoners
43.11 will be **taken** away as prisoners,
46.19 Get ready to be **taken** prisoner, you people of Egypt!
46.25 I am going to **take** the king of Egypt and all who
48.11 "Moab has always lived secure and has never been **taken** into exile.
48.33 Happiness and joy have been **taken** away from the fertile
48.46 their sons and daughters have been **taken** away as prisoners.
49. 1 the people who worship Molech **take** the territory of the
49. 2 Then Israel will **take** its land back from those who took it
49. 3 Your god Molech will be **taken** into exile, together with his

Jer 49. 9 when robbers come at night, they **take** only what they want.
49.29 **Take** their camels and tell the people, 'Terror is all round you!'
49.32 "**Take** their camels and all their livestock!
50.10 and those who loot it will **take** everything they want.
50.25 in my anger I have **taken** them out, because I, the Sovereign
50.42 They have **taken** their bows and swords;
51.34 He **took** what he wanted and threw the rest away.
51.40 I will **take** them to be slaughtered, like lambs, goats,
51.51 completely helpless because foreigners have **taken** over the
52. 9 Zedekiah was **taken** to King Nebuchadnezzar, who was in the
52.11 put out and had him placed in chains and **taken** to Babylon.
52.15 Then Nebuzaradan **took** away to Babylonia the people who
52.17 large bronze tank, and they **took** all the bronze to Babylon.
52.18 They also **took** away the shovels and the ash containers
52.19 They **took** away everything that was made of gold or silver:
52.24 Nebuzaradan, the commanding officer, **took** away as prisoners
52.25 From the city he **took** the officer who had been in
52.26 Nebuzaradan **took** them to the king of Babylonia, who was
52.28 of the people that Nebuchadnezzar **took** away as prisoners:
52.30 and in his twenty-third year, 745—**taken** away by Nebuzaradan.
52.30 In all, 4,600 people were **taken** away.
52.31 year after Jehoiachin had been **taken** away as a prisoner.
Lam 1. 5 Her children have been captured and **taken** away.
1.18 My young men and women have been **taken** away captive.
5.12 Our leaders have been **taken** and hanged;
Ezek 1. 2 fifth year since King Jehoiachin had been **taken** into exile.)
4. 3 **Take** an iron pan and set it up like a wall between
4. 9 "Now **take** some wheat, barley, beans, peas, millet, and
5. 1 The Lord said, "Mortal man, **take** a sharp sword and use it
5. 2 **Take** another third and chop it up with your sword as you
5. 4 Then **take** a few of them out again, throw them in the
7.21 "and law-breakers will **take** all their wealth and defile it.
8. 3 spirit lifted me high in the air and **took** me to Jerusalem.
8. 3 He **took** me to the inner entrance of the north gate of
8. 7 He **took** me to the entrance of the outer courtyard and
8.14 So he **took** me to the north gate of the Temple and
8.16 So he **took** me to the inner courtyard of the Temple.
10. 6 man wearing linen clothes to **take** some fire from between the
10. 7 The man **took** the coals and left.
11. 1 spirit lifted me up and **took** me to the east gate of
11. 9 I will **take** you out of the city and hand you over
11.19 I will **take** away their stubborn heart of stone and will give
12. 5 the wall of your house and **take** your pack out through it.
12.13 Then I will **take** him to the city of Babylon, where he
14.19 and in my anger **take** many lives, killing people and animals,
15. 6 "Just as a vine is **taken** from the forest and burnt,
15. 6 so I will **take** the people who live in Jerusalem
16. 9 "Then I **took** water and washed the blood off you.
16.17 You **took** the silver and gold jewellery that I had given you,
16.18 You **took** the embroidered clothes I gave you and put them
16.20 "Then you **took** the sons and the daughters you had borne
16.21 be unfaithful to me, [21] without **taking** my children and
16.27 to punish you and to **take** away your share of my blessing.
16.39 They will **take** away your clothes and jewels and leave you
17. 5 Then he **took** a young plant from the land of Israel and
17.12 Babylonia came to Jerusalem and **took** the king and his
17.13 He **took** one of the king's family, made a treaty with him,
17.13 He **took** important men as hostages [14] to keep the nation
17.20 I will **take** him to Babylonia and punish him there, because
17.22 "I will **take** the top of a tall cedar and break off
19. 9 him in a cage and **took** him to the king of Babylonia.
20. 6 then that I promised to **take** them out of Egypt and lead
20.15 desert that I would not **take** them to the land I had
20.38 I will **take** away from among you those who are rebellious
20.38 I will **take** them out of the lands where they are living
22.25 They kill the people, **take** all the money and property they
23.25 Yes, they will **take** your sons and daughters from you and
23.26 They will tear off your clothes and **take** your jewels.
23.29 they hate you, they will **take** away everything you have
24. 6 after piece of meat is **taken** out, and not one is left.
24.16 blow I am going to **take** away the person you love most.
24.25 "Now, mortal man, I will **take** away from them the strong
24.25 And I will **take** away their sons and daughters.
26.12 They will **take** the stones and wood and all the rubble, and
27. 6 They **took** oak-trees from Bashan to make oars;
27.12 did business in Spain and **took** silver, iron, tin, and lead
30.17 die in the war, and the other people will be **taken** prisoner.
30.18 and the people of all her cities will be **taken** prisoner.
33.15 he returns the security he **took** for a loan or gives back
34.10 I will **take** my sheep away from you and never again let
34.13 I will **take** them out of foreign countries, gather them together,
36. 5 they captured my land and **took** possession of its pastures.
36.24 I will **take** you from every nation and country and bring
36.26 I will **take** away your stubborn heart of stone and give you
37. 1 the Lord, and his spirit **took** me and set me down in
37.12 I am going to **take** them out and bring them back to
37.16 "Mortal man," he said, "**take** a wooden stick and write
37.16 Then **take** another stick and write on it the words, 'The
37.19 Sovereign Lord, am going to **take** the stick representing
37.21 Sovereign Lord, am going to **take** all my people out of the
40. 1 year after we had been **taken** into exile and the fourteenth
40. 2 In a vision God **took** me to the land of Israel and
40. 3 He **took** me closer, and I saw a man who shone like
40. 5 The man **took** his measuring-rod, which was three metres long,
40.17 The man **took** me through the gateway into the courtyard.
40.24 Next, the man **took** me to the south side, and there we
40.28 man **took** me through the south gateway into the inner courtyard.
40.32 man **took** me through the east gateway into the inner courtyard.
40.35 Then the man **took** me to the north gateway.
40.48 Then he **took** me into the entrance room of the Temple.
41. 1 Next, the man **took** me into the central room, the Holy Place.
Ezek 42. 1 Then the man **took** me into the outer courtyard and led me
42.15 inside the temple area, he **took** me out through the east gate
42.16 He **took** the measuring-rod and measured the east side,
43. 1 The man **took** me to the gate that faces east, [2] and there
43. 5 spirit lifted me up and **took** me into the inner courtyard,
43.20 You are to **take** some of its blood and put it on
43.21 You are to **take** the bull that is offered as a sacrifice
43.22 next day you are to **take** a male goat without any defects
43.23 you have finished doing that, **take** a young bull and a young
44. 4 Then the man **took** me through the north gate to the front
44.11 me in the Temple by **taking** charge of the gates and by
45.16 people of the land must **take** these offerings to the ruling
45.19 The priest will **take** some of the blood of this
46.18 The ruling prince must not **take** any of the people's
46.18 will not oppress any of my people by **taking** their land."
46.19 Then the man **took** me to the entrance of the rooms facing
47. 2 The man then **took** me out of the temple area by way
47. 6 Then the man **took** me back to the bank of the river,
Dan 1. 2 He **took** some prisoners back with him to the temple of his
1.18 the king, Ashpenaz **took** all the young men to Nebuchadnezzar.
2.24 **Take** me to the king, and I will tell him what his
2.25 At once Arioch **took** Daniel into King Nebuchadnezzar's
3.22 flames burnt up the guards who **took** the men to the furnace.
4.31 Your royal power is now **taken** away from you.
5.23 and brought in the cups and bowls **taken** from his Temple.
7.12 other beasts had their power **taken** away, but they were
7.26 court will sit in judgement, **take** away his power, and
11.43 He will **take** away Egypt's hidden treasures of gold and
Hos 2. 9 at harvest time I will **take** back my gifts of corn
2. 9 and wine, and will **take** away the wool and the linen
2.14 So I am going to **take** her into the desert again;
3. 1 gods and like to **take** offerings of raisins to idols."
5. 6 They **take** their sheep and cattle to offer as sacrifices to
8. 4 They **took** their silver and gold and made idols—for their own
9. 4 none of it will be **taken** as an offering to the Lord's
9.12 bring up children, I would **take** them away and not leave one
11. 3 I **took** my people up in my arms, but they did not
13.11 given you kings, and in my fury I have **taken** them away.
13.15 It will **take** away everything of value.
Joel 3. 5 You have **taken** my silver and gold and carried my rich
3. 6 You have **taken** the people of Judah and Jerusalem far from
Amos 1. 5 people of Syria will be **taken** away as prisoners to the land
2. 8 on clothing that they have **taken** from the poor as security
2. 8 wine which they have **taken** from those who owe them money.
3.10 "These people fill their mansions with things **taken** by crime
4.10 I killed your young men in battle and **took** your horses away.
5.12 You persecute good men, **take** bribes, and prevent the poor
5.27 carry those images [27] when I **take** you into exile in a land
6.10 charge of the funeral, will **take** the body out of the house.
6.13 You boast, "We were strong enough to **take** Karnaim."
7.11 Israel will be **taken** away from their land into exile.' "
7.15 But the Lord **took** me from my work as a shepherd and
7.17 of Israel will certainly be **taken** away from their own land
9. 4 If they are **taken** away into captivity by their enemies, I
Obad 5 "When thieves come at night, they **take** only what they want.
19 the people of Benjamin will **take** Gilead.
Jon 1.14 pray, don't punish us with death for **taking** this man's life!
Mic 1.16 your children will be **taken** away from you into exile.
2. 2 when they want houses, they **take** them.
2. 4 The Lord has **taken** our land away
2. 4 And given it to those who **took** us captive."
5.10 "At that time I will **take** away your horses and destroy your
Nah 2. 7 The queen is **taken** captive;
2.13 in war, and I will **take** away everything
2.13 that you **took** from others.
Hab 2. 6 They will say, "You **take** what isn't yours, but you are doomed!
2. 9 family rich with what you **took** by violence, and have tried
Zeph 1.12 "At that time I will **take** a lamp and search Jerusalem.
2. 9 people who survive will plunder them and **take** their land."
3.18 "I have ended the threat of doom and **taken** away your disgrace.
Hag 2.12 Suppose someone **takes** a piece of consecrated meat from a
2.23 On that day I will **take** you, Zerubbabel my servant, and
Zech 3. 4 said to his heavenly attendants, "**Take** away the filthy
5. 3 everyone who tells lies under oath will also be **taken** away.
5.10 I asked the angel, "Where are they **taking** it?"
6.10 He said, "**Take** the gifts given by the exiles Heldai,
8. 7 lands where they have been **taken**, [8] and will bring them back
9. 4 But the Lord will **take** away everything she has.
9.10 from Israel and **take** the horses from Jerusalem;
11. 7 I **took** two sticks:
11.10 Then I **took** the stick called "Favour" and broke it, to
11.13 So I **took** the thirty pieces of silver—the magnificent sum
13. 2 be a prophet and will **take** away the desire to worship idols.
14. 2 The city will be **taken**, the houses looted, and the women raped.
14. 2 the rest of them will not be **taken** away from the city.
14.14 They will **take** as loot the wealth of all the nations—gold,
Mal 2. 3 you sacrifice—and you will be **taken** out to the dunghill.
Mt 1. 6 the people of Israel were **taken** into exile in Babylon,
1.20 David, do not be afraid to **take** Mary to be your wife.
2.13 So get up, **take** the child and his mother and escape to
2.14 Joseph got up, **took** the child and his mother, and left
2.20 Egypt [20] and said, "Get up, **take** the child and his mother,
2.21 So Joseph got up, **took** the child and his mother, and
3. 9 tell you that God can **take** these stones and make descendants
4. 5 Then the Devil **took** Jesus to Jerusalem, the Holy City, set
4. 8 Then the Devil **took** Jesus to a very high mountain and
5.25 a lawsuit against you and **takes** you to court, settle the
5.29 eye causes you to sin, **take** it out and throw it away!
5.40 And if someone **takes** you to court to sue you for your
7. 4 brother, 'Please, let me **take** that speck out of your eye,'
7. 5 First **take** the log out of your own eye, and then you

Mt 7. 5 able to see clearly to **take** the speck out of your brother's
8.17 come true, "He himself **took** our sickness and carried away our
9.15 when the bridegroom will be **taken** away from them, and then
10.13 if they do not welcome you, then **take** back your greeting.
10.17 who will arrest you and **take** you to court, and they will
10.38 Whoever does not **take up** his cross and follow in my
11.29 **Take** my yoke and put it on you, and learn from me,
12.29 a strong man's house and **take** away his belongings unless he
13.12 who has nothing will have **taken** away from him even the
13.31 A man **takes** a mustard seed and sows it in his field.
13.33 A woman **takes** some yeast and mixes it with forty litres of
13.52 owner of a house who **takes** new and old things out of
14.11 dish and given to the girl, who **took** it to her mother.
14.19 then he **took** the five loaves and the two fish, looked up
14.20 Then the disciples **took** up twelve baskets full of what was
15.26 "It isn't right to **take** the children's food and throw it
15.36 Then he **took** the seven loaves and the fish, gave thanks
15.37 the disciples **took** up seven baskets full of pieces left over.
16. 5 the other side of the lake, they forgot to **take** any bread.
16.22 Peter **took** him aside and began to rebuke him.
17. 1 Six days later Jesus **took** with him Peter and the brothers
17.27 **Take** it and pay them our taxes."
18. 9 makes you lose your faith, **take** it out and throw it away!
18.16 will not listen to you, **take** one or two other persons with
20.11 **took** their money and started grumbling against the employer.
20.14 Now **take** your pay and go home.
20.17 to Jerusalem, he **took** the twelve disciples aside and spoke
21.32 you the right path to **take,** and you would not believe him;
21.43 Kingdom of God will be **taken** away from you and given to
24.40 one will be **taken** away, the other will be left behind.
24.41 one will be **taken** away, the other will be left behind.
25. 1 there were ten girls who **took** their oil lamps and went out
25. 3 The foolish ones **took** their lamps but did not take any
25. 3 their lamps but did not **take** any extra oil with them,
25. 4 while the wise ones **took** containers full of oil for their
25.28 Now, **take** the money away from him and give it to the
25.29 even the little that he has will be **taken** away from him.
26.26 While they were eating, Jesus **took** a piece of bread,
26.26 **"Take** and eat it," he said;
26.27 Then he **took** a cup, gave thanks to God, and gave it
26.37 He **took** with him Peter and the two sons of Zebedee.
26.39 Father, if it is possible, **take** this cup of suffering from me!
26.42 cup of suffering cannot be **taken** away unless I drink it,
26.52 "All who **take** the sword will die by the sword.
26.57 Those who had arrested Jesus **took** him to the house of Caiaphas,
27. 3 been condemned, he repented and **took** back the thirty silver coins
27. 9 "They **took** the thirty silver coins, the amount the people of
27.24 riot might break out, he **took** some water, washed his hands
27.27 Then Pilate's soldiers **took** Jesus into the governor's palace,
27.30 They spat on him, and **took** the stick and hit him over
27.48 them ran up at once, **took** a sponge, soaked it in cheap
27.59 So Joseph **took** it, wrapped it in a new linen sheet,
27.65 **"Take** a guard," Pilate told them;
28.15 The guards **took** the money and did what they were told to
Mk 1.31 He went to her, **took** her by the hand, and helped her
2.20 when the bridegroom will be **taken** away from them, and then
3.27 a strong man's house and **take** away his belongings unless he
4.15 as they hear the message, Satan comes and **takes** it away.
4.25 who has nothing will have **taken** away from him even the
4.31 A man **takes** a mustard seed, the smallest seed in the world,
4.36 Jesus was already sitting, and they **took** him with them.
5.40 he put them all out, **took** the child's father and mother and
5.41 He **took** her by the hand and said to her, "Talitha,
6. 8 spirits [8] and ordered them, "Don't **take** anything with you
6.29 this, they came and **took** away his body, and buried it.
6.41 Then Jesus **took** the five loaves and the two fish, looked
6.43 the disciples **took** up twelve baskets full of what was left
6.56 towns, or farms, people would **take** those who were ill to the
7.27 It isn't right to **take** the children's food and throw it to
8. 6 Then he **took** the seven loaves, gave thanks to God, broke
8. 8 the disciples **took** up seven baskets full of pieces left over.
8.19 How many baskets full of leftover pieces did you **take up?"**
8.20 Jesus, "how many baskets full of leftover pieces did you **take up?"**
8.23 Jesus **took** the blind man by the hand and led him out
8.32 So Peter **took** him aside and began to rebuke him.
9. 2 Six days later Jesus **took** with him Peter, James, and John,
9.27 But Jesus **took** the boy by the hand and helped him to
9.36 Then he **took** a child and made him stand in front of
9.47 And if your eye makes you lose your faith, **take** it out!
10.16 Then he **took** the children in his arms, placed his hands
10.32 Once again Jesus **took** the twelve disciples aside and spoke of
13. 9 You will be arrested and **taken** to court.
13.11 when you are arrested and **taken** to court, do not worry
13.15 going down into the house to get anything to **take** with him.
14.22 While they were eating, Jesus **took** a piece of bread,
14.22 **"Take** it," he said, "this is my body."
14.23 Then he **took** a cup, gave thanks to God, and handed it
14.33 He **took** Peter, James, and John with him.
14.36 **Take** this cup of suffering away from me.
14.44 Arrest him and **take** him away under guard."
14.53 Then Jesus was **taken** to the High Priest's house, where
14.65 And the guards **took** him and slapped him.
15.16 soldiers **took** Jesus inside to the courtyard of the governor's
15.22 They **took** Jesus to a place called Golgotha, which means
15.46 Joseph bought a linen sheet, **took** the body down, wrapped it
Lk 1.25 "He has **taken** away my public disgrace!"
2. 1 Augustus ordered a census to be **taken** throughout the Roman Empire.
2.22 So they **took** the child to Jerusalem to present him to the
2.28 what the Law required, [28] Simeon **took** the child in his arms
Lk 3. 8 tell you that God can **take** these stones and make descendants
3.14 He said to them, "Don't **take** money from anyone by force or
4. 5 Then the Devil **took** him up and showed him in a second
4. 9 Then the Devil **took** him to Jerusalem and set him on the
4.29 out of the town, and **took** him to the top of the
5.18 bed, and they tried to **take** him into the house and put
5.19 the crowd, however, they could find no way to **take** him in.
5.25 in front of them all, **took** the bed he had been lying
5.35 when the bridegroom will be **taken** away from them, and then
6. 4 into the house of God, **took** the bread offered to God, ate
6.29 if someone **takes** your coat, let him have your shirt as well.
6.30 for something, and when someone **takes** what is yours, do not
6.42 'Please, brother, let me **take** that speck out of your eye,'
6.42 First **take** the log out of your own eye, and then you
6.42 able to see clearly to **take** the speck out of your brother's
8.12 but the Devil comes and **takes** the message away from their
8.18 whoever has nothing will have **taken** away from him even the
8.54 But Jesus **took** her by the hand and called out, "Get up,
9. 3 after saying to them, **"Take** nothing with you for the journey:
9.10 He **took** them with him, and they went off by themselves to
9.16 had done so, [16] Jesus **took** the five loaves and two fish,
9.17 had enough, and the disciples **took** up twelve baskets of what
9.23 me, he must forget self, **take up** his cross every day,
9.28 said these things, Jesus **took** Peter, John, and James with him
9.47 they were thinking, so he **took** a child, stood him by his
10. 4 Don't **take** a purse or a beggar's bag or shoes;
10. 6 if not, **take** back your greeting of peace.
10.34 on his own animal and **took** him to an inn, where he
10.35 The next day he **took** out two silver coins and gave them
10.42 the right thing, and it will not be **taken** away from her."
12.58 a lawsuit against you and **takes** you to court, do your best
13.15 donkey from the stall and **take** it out to give it water
13.19 A man **takes** a mustard seed and sows it in his field.
13.21 A woman **takes** some yeast and mixes it with forty litres of
14. 4 Jesus **took** the man, healed him, and sent him away.
15.15 sent him out to his farm to **take** care of the pigs.
17.34 one will be **taken** away, the other will be left behind.
17.35 one will be **taken** away, the other will be left behind."
18.31 Jesus **took** the twelve disciples aside and said to them,
19.21 You **take** what is not yours and reap what you did not
19.22 I am a hard man, **taking** what is not mine and reaping
19.24 those who were standing there, **'Take** the gold coin away from
19.26 even the little that he has will be **taken** away from him.
19.35 needs it," they answered, [35] and they **took** the colt to Jesus.
21.24 and others will be **taken** as prisoners to all countries;
22.17 Then Jesus **took** a cup, gave thanks to God,
22.17 and said, **"Take** this and share it among yourselves.
22.19 Then he **took** a piece of bread, gave thanks to God, broke
22.36 Jesus said, "whoever has a purse or a bag must **take** it;
22.42 he said, "if you will, **take** this cup of suffering away from
22.54 They arrested Jesus and **took** him away into the house of
23. 1 whole group rose up and **took** Jesus before Pilate, [2] where they
23.53 Then he **took** the body down, wrapped it in a linen sheet,
24.30 to eat with them, **took** the bread, and said the blessing;
24.43 of cooked fish, [43] which he **took** and ate in their presence.
Jn 1.22 "We have to **take** an answer back to those who sent us.
1.42 Then he **took** Simon to Jesus.
2. 8 draw some water out and **take** it to the man in charge
2. 8 They **took** him the water, [9] which now had turned into wine,
2.16 the men who sold the pigeons, **"Take** them out of here!
6.11 Jesus **took** the bread, gave thanks to God, and distributed it
6.21 they willingly **took** him into the boat, and immediately the boat
9.13 Then they **took** to the Pharisees the man who had been blind.
10.18 No one **takes** my life away from me.
10.18 give it up, and I have the right to **take** it back.
11.39 **"Take** the stone away!"
11.41 They **took** the stone away.
12. 3 Then Mary **took** half a litre of a very expensive perfume
12.13 So they **took** branches of palm-trees and went out to meet him,
13.26 So he **took** a piece of bread, dipped it, and gave it
13.27 As soon as Judas **took** the bread, Satan entered him.
14. 3 I will come back and **take** you to myself, so that you
16.14 me glory, because he will **take** what I say and tell it
16.15 said that the Spirit will **take** what I give him and tell
16.22 the kind of gladness that no one can **take** away from you.
17.15 do not ask you to **take** them out of the world,
18. 3 Judas went to the garden, **taking** with him a group of Roman
18.13 arrested Jesus, bound him, [13] and **took** him first to Annas.
18.28 the morning Jesus was **taken** from Caiaphas' house to the governor's
18.31 to them, "Then you yourselves **take** him and try him
19. 1 Then Pilate **took** Jesus and had him whipped.
19. 6 Pilate said to them, "You **take** him, then, and crucify him.
19.13 Pilate heard these words, he **took** Jesus outside and sat down
19.23 had crucified Jesus, they **took** his clothes and divided them into
19.23 They also **took** the robe, which was made of one piece of
19.27 From that time the disciple **took** her to live in his home.
19.31 crucified, and to **take** the bodies down from the crosses.
19.38 the town of Arimathea, asked Pilate if he could **take** Jesus'
19.38 he could have the body, so Joseph went and **took** it away.
19.39 went with Joseph, **taking** with him about thirty kilogrammes
19.40 The two men **took** Jesus' body and wrapped it in linen
20. 1 saw that the stone had been **taken** away from the entrance.
20. 2 and told them, "They have **taken** the Lord from the tomb,
20.13 She answered, "They have **taken** my Lord away, and I do not
20.15 said to him, "If you **took** him away, sir, tell me where
21.13 So Jesus went over, **took** the bread, and gave it to them;
21.18 else will bind you and **take** you where you don't want to
Acts 1.11 This Jesus, who was **taken** from you into heaven, will come
1.20 It is also written, 'May someone else **take** his place of service.'
3. 7 Then he **took** him by his right hand and helped him up.

Acts 5.34 ordered the apostles to be **taken** out for a while, [35] and
6.12 They seized Stephen and **took** him before the Council.
7.16 Their bodies were **taken** to Shechem, where they were
8.32 "Like a sheep that is **taken** to be slaughtered, like a lamb
8.39 out of the water, the Spirit of the Lord **took** Philip away.
9. 8 So they **took** him by the hand and led him into Damascus.
9.21 arresting those people and **taking** them back to the chief priests?"
9.25 one night Saul's followers **took** him and let him down through
9.27 Then Barnabas came to his help and **took** him to the apostles.
9.30 found out about this, they **took** Saul to Caesarea and sent
9.39 When he arrived, he was **taken** to the room upstairs, where
10.16 times, and then the thing was **taken** back up into heaven.
11.26 When he found him, he **took** him to Antioch, and for a
12.25 mission and returned from Jerusalem, **taking** John Mark with them.
13.29 Scriptures say about him, they **took** him down from the cross
15.14 care for the Gentiles by **taking** from among them a people to
15.37 Barnabas wanted to **take** John Mark with them, [38] but
15.38 think it was right to **take** him, because he had not stayed
15.39 Barnabas **took** Mark and sailed off for Cyprus,
16. 3 Paul wanted to **take** Timothy along with him, so he circumcised him.
16.33 of the night the jailer **took** them and washed their wounds;
16.34 Then he **took** Paul and Silas up into his house and gave
17.15 The men who were **taking** Paul went with him as far
17.19 So they **took** Paul, brought him before the city council,
18.12 the Jews got together, seized Paul, and **took** him into court.
18.18 he had his head shaved because of a vow he had **taken.**
18.26 and Aquila heard him, they **took** him home with them and
19. 9 So Paul left them and **took** the believers with him,
19.12 aprons he had used were **taken** to those who were ill,
20.12 They **took** the young man home alive and were greatly comforted.
20.13 off to Assos, where we were going to **take** Paul aboard.
20.14 met us in Assos, we **took** him aboard and went on to
21.11 He came to us, **took** Paul's belt, tied up his own feet
21.16 also went with us and **took** us to the house of the
21.23 There are four men here who have **taken** a vow.
21.26 So Paul **took** the men and the next day performed the
21.29 and they thought that Paul had **taken** him into the Temple.)
21.32 the commander **took** some officers and soldiers and rushed down
21.34 so he ordered his men to **take** Paul up into the fort.
21.37 the soldiers were about to **take** Paul into the fort, he spoke
22.11 light, and so my companions **took** me by the hand and led
22.24 commander ordered his men to **take** Paul into the fort,
22.30 Then he **took** Paul and made him stand before them.
23.10 get Paul away from them, and **take** him into the fort.
23.14 elders and said, "We have **taken** a solemn vow together not
23.17 and said to him, **"Take** this young man to the commander;
23.18 The officer **took** him, led him to the commander, and said,
23.19 The commander **took** him by the hand, led him off by himself,
23.20 to ask you tomorrow to **take** Paul down to the Council,
23.21 They have **taken** a vow not to eat or drink until they
23.28 were accusing him of, so I **took** him down to their Council.
23.31 They got Paul and **took** him that night as far as Antipatris.
23.33 **took** him to Caesarea, delivered the letter to the governor,
24. 4 I do not want to **take up** too much of your time,
24.17 years, I went there to **take** some money to my own people
27.22 But now I beg you, **take** heart!
27.25 So **take** heart, men!
27.35 After saying this, Paul **took** some bread, gave thanks to God
Rom 7.24 will rescue me from this body that is **taking** me to death?
13.12 the dark, and let us **take up** weapons for fighting in the
13.14 But **take up** the weapons of the Lord Jesus Christ, and
1 Cor 6. 4 are you going to **take** them to be settled by people
6.15 Shall I **take** a part of Christ's body and make it part
9. 5 Lord's brothers and Peter, by **taking** a Christian wife with
11.23 the night he was betrayed, **took** a piece of bread, [24] gave
11.25 after the supper he **took** the cup and said, "This cup
16. 3 have approved, and send them to **take** your gift to Jerusalem.
2 Cor 4.14 us up with Jesus and **take** us, together with you, into his
10. 5 we **take** every thought captive and make it obey Christ.
12. 8 to the Lord about this and asked him to **take** it away.
Gal 2. 1 I went back to Jerusalem with Barnabas, **taking** Titus along with me.
4.15 say that you would have **taken** out your own eyes, if you
Eph 3. 8 gave me this privilege of **taking** to the Gentiles the Good
4. 8 up to the very heights, he **took** many captives with him;
Phil 2. 7 gave up all he had, and **took** the nature of a servant.
1 Thes 4.14 we believe that God will **take** back with Jesus those who have
2 Thes 2. 7 the one who holds it back is **taken** out of the way.
1 Tim 5.22 **Take** no part in the sins of others;
5.23 not drink water only, but **take** a little wine to help your
6. 7 What can we **take** out of the world?
2 Tim 1. 8 Instead, **take** your part in suffering for the Good News, as
2. 2 **Take** the teachings that you heard me proclaim in the
2. 3 **Take** your part in suffering, as a loyal soldier of Christ Jesus.
4.18 from all evil and **take** me safely into his heavenly Kingdom.
Heb 5. 5 same way, Christ did not **take** upon himself the honour of
7. 2 and Abraham gave him a tenth of all he had **taken.**
7.21 Lord has made a solemn promise and will not **take** it back:
8. 9 ancestors on the day I **took** them by the hand and led
9. 7 He **takes** with him blood which he offers to God on behalf
9.12 Holy Place, he did not **take** the blood of goats and bulls
9.12 he **took** his own blood and obtained eternal salvation for us.
9.19 Then he **took** the blood of bulls and goats, mixed it with
11.36 and others were put in chains and **taken** off to prison.
2 Pet 2.15 they have followed the path **taken** by Balaam son of Beor,
Jude 11 They have followed the way that Cain **took.**
Rev 2. 5 I will come to you and **take** your lamp-stand from its place.
5. 7 The Lamb went and **took** the scroll from the right hand of
5. 9 "You are worthy to **take** the scroll and to break open its

Rev 8. 5 Then the angel **took** the incense-burner, filled it with fire
10. 8 me again, saying, "Go and **take** the open scroll which is in
10. 9 He said to me, **"Take** it and eat it;
10.10 I **took** the little scroll from his hand and ate it,
11.17 thank you that you have **taken** your great power and have
12. 5 the child was snatched away and **taken** to God and his throne;
17.16 they will **take** away everything she has and leave her naked;
19.20 The beast was **taken** prisoner, together with the false prophet
22.19 And if anyone **takes** anything away from the prophetic words
22.19 of this book, God will **take** away from him his share of

TAKE ADVANTAGE see ADVANTAGE

TAKE AWAY (SIN)

Ex 29.14 This is an offering to **take away** the sins of the priests.
Lev 1. 4 it will be accepted as a sacrifice to **take away** his sins.
4.21 This is an offering to **take away** the sin of the community.
4.24 This is an offering to **take away** sin.
5. 9 This is an offering to **take away** sin.
5.12 It is an offering to **take away** sin.
6.30 used in the ritual to **take away** sin, the animal must not
8.34 what we have done today, in order to **take away** your sin.
9. 7 sin-offering and the burnt-offering to **take away** your sins
9. 7 Present this offering to **take away** the sins of the people,
10.17 to you in order to **take away** the sin of the community.
12. 7 and perform the ritual to **take away** her impurity, and she
12. 8 shall perform the ritual to **take away** her impurity, and she
16. 6 bull as a sacrifice to **take away** his own sins and those
16.10 to Azazel, in order to **take away** the sins of the people.
16.27 the Most Holy Place to **take away** sin, shall be carried
17.11 be poured out on the altar to **take away** the people's sins.
17.11 Blood, which is life, **takes away** sins.
23.26 is to be performed to **take away** the sins of the people.
23.28 it is the day for performing the ritual to **take away** sin.
2 Chr 29.21 As an offering to **take away** the sins of the royal family
29.24 altar as a sacrifice to **take away** the sin of all the
Neh 10.33 offerings, the offerings to **take away** the sins of Israel,
Ps 40. 6 whole on the altar or for sacrifices to **take away** sins.
Ezek 45.17 whole, and the fellowship-offerings, to **take away** the sins
Zech 3. 4 said to Joshua, "I have **taken away** your sin and will give
3. 9 a single day I will **take away** the sin of this land.
Jn 1.29 the Lamb of God, who **takes away** the sin of the world!
Rom 11.27 make this covenant with them when I **take away** their sins."
Heb 9.13 and this purifies them by **taking away** their ritual impurity.
9.28 was offered in sacrifice once to **take away** the sins of many.
10. 4 For the blood of bulls and goats can never **take away** sins.
10. 6 whole on the altar or with sacrifices to **take away** sins.
10. 8 burnt on the altar and the sacrifices to **take away** sins."
10.11 but these sacrifices can never **take away** sins.
10.18 an offering to **take away** sins is no longer needed.
10.26 longer any sacrifice that will **take away** sins if we
1 Jn 3. 5 Christ appeared in order to **take away** sins, and that there

TAKE CARE see CARE

TAKE OFF

Gen 9.21 the wine, he became drunk, **took off** his clothes, and lay
38.19 Tamar went home, **took off** her veil, and put her widow's
Ex 3. 5 **Take off** your sandals, because you are standing on holy ground.
32. 2 Aaron said to them, **"Take off** the gold earrings which your wives,
32. 3 So all the people **took off** their gold earrings and brought
32.24 those who had any **took them off** and gave them to me.
33. 5 Now **take off** your jewellery, and I will decide what to do
34.34 Lord's presence to speak to the Lord, he **took the veil off.**
Lev 16.23 shall go into the Tent, **take off** the priestly garments that
Deut 25. 9 presence of the town leaders, **take off** one of his sandals,
Josh 5.15 of the Lord's army told him, **"Take your sandals off;**
Ruth 3.15 Boaz said to her, **"Take off** your cloak and spread it
4. 7 custom for the seller to **take off** his sandal and give it
4. 8 Boaz, "You buy it," he **took off** his sandal and gave it
1 Sam 17.39 So he **took it all off.**
18. 4 He **took off** the robe he was wearing and gave it to
19.24 He **took off** his clothes and danced and shouted in Samuel's
1 Kgs 11.30 Ahijah **took off** the new robe he was wearing, tore it
19.19 Elijah **took off** his cloak and put it on Elisha.
21.27 Ahab tore his clothes, **took them off,** and put on sackcloth.
2 Kgs 2. 8 Then Elijah **took off** his cloak, rolled it up, and struck
Neh 4.23 I didn't **take off** my clothes even at night, neither did
5.13 Then I **took off** the sash I was wearing round my waist
Esth 3.10 The king **took off** his ring, which was used to stamp
8. 2 The king **took off** his ring with his seal on it (which
Prov 25.20 who is depressed is like **taking off** his clothes on a cold
Is 20. 2 Isaiah son of Amoz to **take off** his sandals and the sackcloth
57. 8 you **take off** your clothes and climb into your large beds
Jer 28.10 Then Hananiah **took the yoke off** my neck, broke it in pieces,
40. 4 Now, I am **taking the chains off** your wrists and setting
Ezek 21.26 **Take off** your crown and your turban.
26.16 They will **take off** their robes and their embroidered clothes
44.19 people are, they must first **take off** the clothes they wore
Jon 3. 6 got up from his throne, **took off** his robe, put on sackcloth,
Mt 27.31 finished mocking him, they **took the robe off** and put his own
Mk 15.20 had finished mocking him, they **took off** the purple robe and
Lk 12.37 I tell you, he will **take off** his coat, ask them to
Jn 13. 4 he rose from the table, **took off** his outer garment, and tied
21. 7 him (for he had **taken his clothes off)** and jumped into the
Acts 7.33 Lord said to him, **'Take your sandals off,** for the place
13.25 I am not good enough to **take his sandals off** his feet.'

Acts 22.30 day he had Paul's chains **taken off** and ordered the chief
Col 3. 9 one another, for you have **taken off** the old self with its

TAKE PLACE see PLACE (2)

TAKE UP

2 Kgs 2.11 them, and Elijah was **taken up** to heaven by a whirlwind.
Mk 16.19 talked with them, he was **taken up** to heaven and sat at
Lk 9.51 near when Jesus would be **taken up** to heaven, he made up
24.51 them, he departed from them and was **taken up** into heaven.
Acts 1. 2 began his work [2]until the day he was **taken up** to heaven.
1. 2 Before he was **taken up,** he gave instructions by the power of
1. 9 After saying this, he was **taken up** to heaven as they
1.21 until the day Jesus was **taken up** from us to heaven."
1 Tim 3.16 in throughout the world, and was **taken up** to heaven.
Heb 11. 5 Instead, he was **taken up** to God,
11. 5 and nobody could find him, because God had **taken him up.**
11. 5 says that before Enoch was **taken up,** he had pleased God.

TALENT

1 Chr 26. 6 the last two were especially **talented.**

AV TALENT see COIN

TALITHA KOUM

Mk 5.41 and said to her, **"Talitha, koum,"** which means, "Little girl,

TALK

Gen 27. 5 While Isaac was **talking** to Esau, Rebecca was listening.
29. 9 While Jacob was still **talking** to them, Rachel arrived
34. 6 father Hamor went out to **talk** with Jacob, [7]just as Jacob's
44. 7 They answered him, "What do you mean, sir, by **talking** like this?
45.15 After that, his brothers began to **talk** with him.
49. 6 not join in their secret **talks,** Nor will I take part in
Num 7.89 went into the Tent to **talk** with the Lord, he heard the
Deut 11.19 **Talk** about them when you are at home and when you are
Josh 22.33 They no longer **talked** about going to war to devastate the
Judg 9. 3 His mother's relatives **talked** to the men of Shechem about
9.38 Then Zebul said to him, "Where is all your big **talk** now?
13.11 and asked, "Are you the man who was **talking** to my wife?"
14. 7 Then he went and **talked** to the girl, and he liked her.
1 Sam 2.24 is an awful thing the people of the Lord are **talking** about!
9.21 Why, then, do you **talk** like this to me?"
17.23 As he was **talking** to them, Goliath came forward and
17.28 Eliab, David's eldest brother, heard David **talking** to the men.
2 Sam 19.43 we were the first to **talk** about bringing the king back!"
1 Kgs 1. 7 He **talked** with Joab (whose mother was Zeruiah) and with
1.14 "Then, while you are still **talking** with King David, I will
4.33 he **talked** about animals, birds, reptiles, and fish.
2 Kgs 2. 3 "But let's not **talk** about it."
2. 5 "But let's not **talk** about it."
2.11 They kept **talking** as they walked on;
8. 4 She found the king **talking** with Gehazi, Elisha's servant;
18.27 No, I am also **talking** to the people who are sitting on
2 Chr 25.16 Stop **talking,** or I'll have you killed!"
32.19 They **talked** about the God of Jerusalem in the same way
32.19 that they **talked** about the gods of the other
Neh 6. 7 I suggest that you and I meet to **talk** the situation over."
6.19 People would **talk** in front of me about all the good
Esth 6.14 While they were still **talking,** the palace eunuchs
Job 2.10 Job answered, "You are **talking** nonsense!
6.25 Honest words are convincing, but you are **talking** nonsense.
6.26 You think I am **talking** nothing but wind;
9.35 I am going to **talk** because I know my own heart.
11. 1 Does **talking** so much put a man in the right?
15. 3 No wise man would **talk** as you do or defend himself with
16. 3 Are you going to keep on **talking** for ever?
16. 5 I could strengthen you with advice and keep **talking** to comfort you.
18. 1 If you stopped to listen, we could **talk** to you.
21.29 Haven't you **talked** with people who travel?
27.12 so why do you **talk** such nonsense?
29. 9 The leaders of the people would stop **talking;**
34.36 you will see that he **talks** like an evil man.
35.16 It is useless for you to go on **talking;**
42. 3 I **talked** about things I did not understand, about marvels
Ps 3. 2 They **talk** about me and say, "God will not help him."
50.16 Why should you **talk** about my covenant?
55.14 We had intimate **talks** with each other and worshipped
69.12 They **talk** about me in the streets, and drunkards make up
69.26 they **talk** about the sufferings of those you have wounded.
71.10 they **talk** and plot against me.
Prov 2.16 seduce you with her smooth **talk,** [17]who is faithless to her
7.21 him with her charms, and he gave in to her smooth **talk.**
10. 8 People who **talk** foolishly will come to ruin.
10.13 Intelligent people **talk** sense,
10.19 The more you **talk,** the more likely you are to sin.
11. 9 can be ruined by the **talk** of godless people, but the wisdom
13. 3 A careless **talker** destroys himself.
14. 3 A fool's pride makes him **talk** too much;
14.23 if you sit around **talking** you will be poor.
17.27 Someone who is sure of himself does not **talk** all the time.
20. 6 Everyone **talks** about how loyal and faithful he is, but
20.15 you know what you are **talking** about, you have something more
20.19 Stay away from people who **talk** too much.
Prov 23. 9 Don't try to **talk** sense to a fool;
26.23 Insincere **talk** that hides what you are really thinking
26.28 Insincere **talk** brings nothing but ruin.
29.19 You cannot correct a servant just by **talking** to him.
Ecc 3. 7 for mending, the time for silence and the time for **talk.**
5. 3 dreams, and the more you **talk,** the more likely you are to
5. 7 do, or how much you **talk,** you must still stand in awe
10.13 He starts out with silly **talk** and ends up with pure madness.
10.14 A fool **talks** on and on.
Is 8.10 **Talk** as much as you like!
30.10 They say, "Don't **talk** to us about what's right.
36.12 No, I am also **talking** to the people who are sitting on
58.13 by not travelling, working, or **talking** idly on that day,
Jer 3.16 that land, people will no longer **talk** about my Covenant Box.
5. 5 I will go to the people in power, and **talk** with them.
7.28 No longer is it even **talked** about.
14.14 The visions they **talk** about have not come from me;
15.19 If instead of **talking** nonsense you proclaim a worthwhile message,
34. 3 will see him face to face and **talk** to him in person;
35. 2 "Go to the members of the Rechabite clan and **talk** to them.
38. 4 By **talking** like this he is making the soldiers in the city
38.25 officials hear that I have **talked** with you, they will come
Lam 3.62 All day long they **talk** about me and make their plans.
Ezek 2. 1 I want to **talk** to you."
3.22 I will **talk** to you there."
11.15 who live in Jerusalem are **talking** about you and your
24.18 Early in the day I was **talking** with the people.
24.27 of speech which you had lost, and you will **talk** with him.
33.30 "Mortal man, your people are **talking** about you when they
35.13 I have heard the wild, boastful way you have **talked** against me."
38.17 are the one I was **talking** about long ago, when I announced
Dan 1.19 The king **talked** with them all, and Daniel, Hananiah,
8.18 While he was **talking,** I fell to the ground unconscious.
10.17 How can I **talk** to you?
Hos 7.16 Because their leaders **talk** arrogantly, they will die
Hab 2.18 for its maker to trust it—a god that can't even **talk!**
Mal 2.17 You have tired the Lord out with your **talk.**
Mt 3. 3 the prophet Isaiah was **talking** about when he said, "Someone is
9.32 Jesus a man who could not **talk** because he had a demon.
9.33 was driven out, the man started **talking,** and everyone was amazed.
12.22 who was blind and could not **talk** because he had a demon.
12.22 healed the man, so that he was able to **talk** and see.
12.46 Jesus was still **talking** to the people when his mother
13.10 "Why do you use parables when you **talk** to the people?"
13.13 reason I use parables in **talking** to them is that they look,
16.11 don't understand that I was not **talking** to you about bread?
17. 3 Then the three disciples saw Moses and Elijah **talking** with Jesus.
17. 5 While he was **talking,** a shining cloud came over them,
17.13 understood that he was **talking** to them about John the Baptist.
21.45 and knew that he was **talking** about them, [46]so they tried
22. 1 Jesus again used parables in **talking** to the people.
26.70 don't know what you are **talking** about," he answered,
Mk 1.45 Indeed, he **talked** so much that Jesus could not go into a
2. 7 thought to themselves, [7]"How does he dare to **talk** like this?
7.35 impediment was removed, and he began to **talk** without any trouble.
9. 4 Then the three disciples saw Elijah and Moses **talking** with Jesus.
9.17 because he has an evil spirit in him and cannot **talk.**
14.68 don't understand what you are **talking** about," he answered,
14.71 I do not know the man you are **talking** about!"
16.19 After the Lord Jesus had **talked** with them, he was taken
Lk 7.15 sat up and began to **talk,** and Jesus gave him back to
9.30 Suddenly two men were there **talking** with him.
9.31 appeared in heavenly glory and **talked** with Jesus about the
11.14 Jesus was driving out a demon that could not **talk;**
11.14 and when the demon went out, the man began to **talk.**
18.34 them, and they did not know what Jesus was **talking** about.
21. 5 Some of the disciples were **talking** about the Temple,
22.60 But Peter answered, "Man, I don't know what you are **talking** about!"
24.14 from Jerusalem, [14]and they were **talking** to each other about
24.15 As they **talked** and discussed, Jesus himself drew near and walked
24.17 to them, "What are you **talking** about to each other, as you
24.32 burning in us when he **talked** to us on the road
Jn 1.15 is the one I was **talking** about when I said, 'He comes
1.30 is the one I was **talking** about when I said, 'A man
4.26 Jesus answered, "I am he, I who am **talking** with you."
4.27 they were greatly surprised to find him **talking** with a woman.
4.27 or asked him, "Why are you **talking** with her?"
6.71 He was **talking** about Judas, the son of Simon Iscariot.
7.13 But no one **talked** about him openly, because they were
7.26 He is **talking** in public, and they say nothing against him!
7.46 The guards answered, "Nobody has ever **talked** like this man!"
8.27 not understand that Jesus was **talking** to them about the Father.
8.38 I **talk** about what my Father has shown me, but you do
9.37 and he is the one who is **talking** with you now."
10.21 were saying, "A man with a demon could not **talk** like this!
12.42 the Pharisees they did not **talk** about it openly, so as not
13.18 "I am not **talking** about all of you;
13.24 to him and said, "Ask him whom he is **talking** about."
14.30 I cannot **talk** with you much longer, because the ruler of
16.18 We don't know what he is **talking** about!"
18.22 said, "How dare you **talk** like that to the High Priest!"
Acts 1. 3 They saw him, and he **talked** with them about the Kingdom of
2. 4 Holy Spirit and began to **talk** in other languages, as the
2. 7 "These people who are **talking** like this are Galileans!
6.13 they said, "is always **talking** against our sacred Temple and the
9.29 He also **talked** and disputed with the Greek-speaking Jews,
10.27 Peter kept on **talking** to Cornelius as he went into the house,

Acts 16.13 We sat down and **talked** to the women who gathered there.
17.18 Others answered, "He seems to be **talking** about foreign gods."
17.19 know what this new teaching is that you are **talking** about.
20. 9 and as Paul kept on **talking,** Eutychus got sleepier and sleepier,
20.11 After **talking** with them for a long time, even until sunrise,
24.24 listened to him as he **talked** about faith in Christ Jesus.
24.26 this reason he would often send for him and **talk** with him.
28.20 That is why I asked to see you and **talk** with you.
1 Cor 3. 1 talk to you as I **talk** to people who have the Spirit;
3. 1 I had to **talk** to you as though you belonged to this
14. 9 anyone understand what you are **talking** about if your message
2 Cor 11.17 in this matter of boasting I am really **talking** like a fool.
11.21 boast about something—I am **talking** like a fool—I will be
12. 1 But I will now **talk** about visions and revelations given me
Eph 5.12 really too shameful even to **talk** about the things they do in
Col 3. 8 No insults or obscene **talk** must ever come from your lips.
1 Thes 2. 5 come to you with flattering **talk,** nor did we use words to
1 Tim 5.13 to be gossips and busybodies, **talking** of things they should not.
6.20 Avoid the profane **talk** and foolish arguments of what some people
Tit 1.11 to stop their **talk,** because they are upsetting whole families
1 Pet 2.15 you to silence the ignorant **talk** of foolish people by the
1 Jn 3.18 My children, our love should not be just words and **talk;**
2 Jn 12 hope to visit you and **talk** with you personally, so that we
3 Jn 14 I hope to see you soon, and then we will **talk** personally.
Rev 1.12 round to see who was **talking** to me, and I saw seven
13.15 so that the image could **talk** and put to death all those

Am **TALK ABOUT**
see also **PLAN**

TALL

Ex 2. 3 then placed it in the **tall** grass at the edge of the
2. 5 noticed the basket in the **tall** grass and sent a slave-girl
36.21 Each frame was four metres **tall** and sixty-six centimetres wide,
Num 13.32 Everyone we saw was very **tall,** [33] and we even saw giants there,
Deut 1.28 people there are stronger and **taller** than we are, and that
2.10 They were as **tall** as the Anakim, another race of giants.
2.21 They were as **tall** as the Anakim.
9. 2 The people themselves are **tall** and strong;
1 Sam 9. 2 Saul was a head **taller** than anyone else in Israel and more
10.23 they could see that he was a head **taller** than anyone else.
16. 7 to him, "Pay no attention to how **tall** and handsome he is.
17. 4 He was nearly three metres **tall** [5] and wore bronze armour
1 Kgs 6.23 and placed in the Most Holy Place, each one 4.4 metres **tall.**
7.15 each one 8 metres **tall** and 5.3 metres in circumference,
7.16 capitals, each one 2.2 metres **tall,** to be placed on top of
7.19 shaped like lilies, 1.8 metres **tall,** [20] and were placed on
2 Kgs 19.23 there you cut down the **tallest** cedars and the finest
1 Chr 11.23 huge man over two metres **tall,** who was armed with a gigantic
2 Chr 3.15 fifteen and a half metres **tall,** and placed them in front of
3.15 Each one had a capital 2.2 metres **tall.**
Esth 5.14 "Why don't you have a gallows built, twenty-two metres **tall?**
7. 9 And it's twenty-two metres **tall!"**
Is 2.13 He will destroy the **tall** cedars of Lebanon and all the
18. 2 and powerful nation, to your **tall** and smooth-skinned people,
18. 7 and powerful nation, this **tall** and smooth-skinned people,
37.24 cut down the **tallest** cedars and the finest cypress-trees,
45.14 will be yours, and the **tall** men of Seba will be your
Ezek 16. 7 You grew strong and **tall** and became a young woman.
17.22 take the top of a **tall** cedar and break off a tender
17.24 I cut down the **tall** trees
17.24 and make the small trees grow **tall.**
19.11 The vine grew **tall** enough to reach the clouds;
19.11 everyone saw how leafy and **tall** it was.
31. 3 A tree so **tall** it reaches the clouds.
31. 5 Because it was well-watered, It grew **taller** than other trees.
31. 7 How beautiful the tree was— So **tall,** with such long branches.
31.10 As it grew **taller** it grew proud;
31.14 it is, will grow as **tall** as that again or push its
31.18 Not even the trees in Eden were so **tall** and impressive.
Dan 4.20 The tree, so **tall** that it reached the sky, could be seen
4.22 "Your Majesty, you are the tree, **tall** and strong.
Hos 4.13 hills they burn incense under **tall,** spreading trees, because
Amos 2. 9 Amorites, men who were as **tall** as cedar-trees and as strong

TAMAR (1)
David's daughter.

2 Sam 13. 1 David's son Absalom had a beautiful unmarried sister named **Tamar.**
13. 4 "I'm in love with **Tamar,** the sister of my half-brother Absalom,"
13. 5 to him, 'Please ask my sister **Tamar** to come and feed me.
13. 6 said to him, "Please let **Tamar** come and make a few cakes
13. 7 So David sent word to **Tamar** in the palace:
13.18 **Tamar** was wearing a long robe with full sleeves,
13.20 So **Tamar** lived in Absalom's house, sad and lonely.
13.22 for having raped his sister **Tamar** that he would no longer
13.32 to do this from the time that Amnon raped his sister **Tamar.**
1 Chr 3. 9 He also had a daughter, **Tamar.**

TAMARISK-TREE

Gen 21.33 Then Abraham planted a **tamarisk-tree** in Beersheba
1 Sam 22. 6 in Gibeah, sitting under a **tamarisk-tree** on a hill, with his
31.13 and buried them under the **tamarisk-tree** in the town, and

TAMBOURINE

Gen 31.27 rejoicing and singing to the music of **tambourines** and harps.
Ex 15.20 Aaron's sister, took her **tambourine,**
15.20 and all the women followed her, playing **tambourines** and dancing.
Judg 11.34 coming out to meet him, dancing and playing the **tambourine.**
1 Sam 18. 6 singing joyful songs, dancing, and playing **tambourines** and lyres.
Ps 68.25 in between are the girls beating the **tambourines.**
81. 2 Start the music and beat the **tambourines;**
Is 5.12 At your feasts you have harps and **tambourines** and flutes—and wine.
Jer 31. 4 Once again you will take up your **tambourines** and dance joyfully.

TAME
[UNTAMED]

Job 11.12 Stupid men will start being wise when wild donkeys are born **tame.**
39. 7 noisy cities, and no one can **tame** them and make them work.
Ps 148.10 all animals, **tame** and wild, reptiles and birds.
Jer 31.18 'Lord, we were like an **untamed** animal, but you taught us to
Jas 3. 7 Man is able to **tame** and has tamed all other creatures—wild
3. 8 But no one has ever been able to **tame** the tongue.

TAMPER

Amos 8. 5 overcharge, use false measures, and **tamper** with the scales

TANGLE

Nah 1.10 Like **tangled** thorns and dry straw, you drunkards will be burnt up!

TANK

1 Kgs 7.23 Huram made a round **tank** of bronze, 2.2 metres deep,
7.24 of the rim of the **tank** were two rows of bronze gourds,
7.24 been cast all in one piece with the rest of the **tank.**
7.25 The **tank** rested on the backs of twelve bronze bulls that
7.26 The sides of the **tank** were 75 millimetres thick.
7.26 The **tank** held about forty thousand litres.
7.39 the **tank** he placed at the south-east corner.
7.40 The **tank**
7.40 The twelve bulls supporting the **tank**
2 Kgs 16.17 he also took the bronze **tank** from the backs of the twelve
25.13 together with the large bronze **tank,** and they took all the
25.16 the carts, and the large **tank**—were too heavy to weigh.
1 Chr 18. 8 this bronze to make the **tank,** the columns, and the bronze
2 Chr 4. 2 He also made a round **tank** of bronze, 2.2 metres deep,
4. 3 of the rim of the **tank** were two rows of decorations, one
4. 3 been cast all in one piece with the rest of the **tank.**
4. 4 The **tank** rested on the backs of twelve bronze bulls that
4. 5 The sides of the **tank** were 75 millimetres thick.
4. 5 The **tank** held about sixty thousand litres.
4. 6 The water in the large **tank** was for the priests to use
4.10 The **tank** was placed near the south-east corner of the Temple.
4.11 The **tank**
4.11 The twelve bulls supporting the **tank**
Jer 27.19 left the columns, the bronze **tank,** the carts, and some of
52.17 together with the large bronze **tank,** and they took all the
52.20 columns, the carts, the large **tank,** and the twelve bulls

TANNED

Song 1. 6 on me because of my colour, because the sun has **tanned** me.

TANNER

Acts 9.43 Joppa for many days with a **tanner** of leather named Simon.
10. 6 in the home of a **tanner** of leather named Simon, who lives
10.32 the home of Simon the **tanner** of leather, who lives by the

TAPE MEASURE

Ezek 40. 3 He was holding a linen **tape-measure** and a measuring-rod and

TAR

Gen 6.14 make rooms in it and cover it with **tar** inside and out.
11. 3 they had bricks to build with and **tar** to hold them together.
14.10 The valley was full of **tar** pits, and when the kings of
Ex 2. 3 made of reeds and covered it with **tar** to make it watertight.
Is 34. 9 of Edom will turn into **tar,** and the soil will turn into
34. 9 The whole country will burn like **tar.**

AV **TARES** see **WEEDS**

TARGET

1 Sam 20.20 then shoot three arrows at it, as though it were a **target.**
Job 7.20 Why use me for your **target-practice?**
16.12 God uses me for **target-practice** [13] and shoots arrows at me
Lam 3.12 He drew his bow and made me the **target** for his arrows.

TASK

Num 4.19 and assign each man his **task** and tell him what to carry.
4.26 They shall perform all the **tasks** required for these things.
4.49 responsibility for his **task** of serving or carrying.
Is 49. 6 "I have a greater **task** for you, my servant.
52.13 "My servant will succeed in his **task;**
Rom 15.28 When I have finished this **task** and have handed over to

1 Cor 9.17 matter of duty, because God has entrusted me with this **task.**
2 Cor 2.16 Who, then, is capable of such a **task?**
5.18 and gave us the **task** of making others his friends also.
Gal 2. 7 God had given me the **task** of preaching the gospel to the
2. 7 he had given Peter the **task** of preaching the gospel to the
2. 9 leaders, recognized that God had given me this special **task;**
Col 1.25 by God, who gave me this **task** to perform for your good.
1.25 It is the **task** of fully proclaiming his message,
4.17 "Be sure to finish the **task** you were given in the Lord's

TASSEL

Num 15.38 "Make **tassels** on the corners of your garments
15.38 and put a blue cord on each **tassel.**
15.39 The **tassels** will serve as reminders, and each time you
15.40 The **tassels** will remind you to keep all my commands, and
Deut 22.12 "Sew **tassels** on the four corners of your clothes.
Mt 23. 5 Notice also how long are the **tassels on their cloaks!**

TASTE

Gen 27. 4 Cook me some of that **tasty** food that I like, and bring
27.17 She handed him the **tasty** food, together with the bread
27.31 He also cooked some **tasty** food and took it to his father.
Ex 16.31 small white seed, and **tasted** like biscuits made with honey.
Num 11. 8 It **tasted** like bread baked with olive-oil.)
2 Sam 19.35 I can't **taste** what I eat and drink, and I can't hear
2 Kgs 4.40 but as soon as they **tasted** it they exclaimed to Elisha,
Job 6. 6 But who can eat **tasteless,** unsalted food?
12.11 tongue enjoys **tasting** food, your ears enjoy hearing words.
20.12 Evil **tastes** so good to him that he keeps some in
30. 4 and ate them, even the **tasteless** roots of the broom-tree!
34. 3 know good food when you **taste** it, but not wise words when
Ps 119.103 How sweet is the **taste** of your instructions— sweeter
Prov 9.17 Stolen bread **tastes** better."
16.24 are like honey—sweet to the **taste** and good for your health.
18. 8 Gossip is so **tasty**—how we love to swallow it!
19.28 Wicked people love the **taste** of evil.
26.22 Gossip is so **tasty!**
27. 7 but when you are hungry, even bitter food **tastes** sweet.
Song 2. 3 sit in its shadow, and its fruit is sweet to my **taste.**
4.11 The **taste** of honey is on your lips, my darling;
Is 24. 9 no one enjoys its **taste** any more.
Jer 31.29 ate the sour grapes, But the children got the sour **taste.'**
48.11 has never been ruined, and it **tastes** as good as ever.
Ezek 3. 3 I ate it, and it **tasted** as sweet as honey.
18. 2 ate the sour grapes, But the children got the sour **taste.'**
Mic 7. 1 All the grapes and all the **tasty** figs have been picked.
Mt 27.34 but after **tasting** it, he would not drink it.
Lk 14.24 none of those men who were invited will **taste** my dinner!' "
Jn 2. 9 water, [9] which now had turned into wine, and he **tasted** it.
Col 2.21 "Don't **taste** that," "Don't touch the other"?
Heb 6. 4 they **tasted** heaven's gift and received their share of the Holy
Rev 10.10 and ate it, and it **tasted** sweet as honey in my mouth.

TATTOO

Lev 19.28 or trim your beard [28] or **tattoo** yourselves or cut gashes in

TAUNT

Is 51. 7 Do not be afraid when people **taunt** and insult you;
Mic 7.10 disgraced—the same enemies who **taunted** us by asking, "Where
Hab 2. 6 The conquered people will **taunt** their conquerors and show
Zeph 2. 8 Moab and Ammon insulting and **taunting** my people, and

TAX
[TEMPLE-TAX]

Ex 30.16 This **tax** will be the payment for their lives, and I will
Num 31.28 the soldiers, withhold as a **tax** for the Lord one out of
31.36 sheep and goats, of which 675 were the **tax** for the Lord;
31.36 for the soldiers, of which 72 were the **tax** for the Lord;
31.36 for the soldiers, of which 61 were the **tax** for the Lord;
31.36 for the soldiers, of which 32 were the **tax** for the Lord.
31.41 So Moses gave Eleazar the **tax** as a special contribution
1 Sam 17.25 and will not require his father's family to pay **taxes."**
2 Sam 8. 2 So the Moabites became his subjects and paid **taxes** to him.
8. 6 and they became his subjects and paid **taxes** to him.
1 Kgs 4.21 They paid him **taxes** and were subject to him all his life.
10.15 gold [15] in addition to the **taxes** paid by merchants, the
2 Kgs 23.35 King Jehoiakim collected a **tax** from the people in
1 Chr 18. 2 Moabites, who became his subjects and paid **taxes** to him.
18. 6 and they became his subjects and paid **taxes** to him.
2 Chr 9.14 in addition to the **taxes** paid by the traders and merchants.
24. 6 from Judah and Jerusalem the **tax** which Moses, the servant of
24. 9 bring to the Lord the **tax** which Moses, God's servant, had
24.10 leaders, and they brought their **tax** money and filled the box
Ezra 4.13 stop paying **taxes,** and your royal revenues will decrease.
4.20 province of West Euphrates, collecting **taxes** and revenue.
6. 8 the royal funds received from **taxes** in West Euphrates, so
7.24 are forbidden to collect any **taxes** from the priests,
Neh 5. 4 money to pay the royal **tax** on our fields and vineyards.
Dan 11.20 to oppress the people with **taxes** in order to increase the
Mt 17.24 the collectors of the **temple-tax** came to Peter
17.24 and asked, "Does your teacher pay the **temple-tax?"**
17.25 Who pays duties or **taxes** to the kings of this world?
17.27 will find a coin worth enough for my **temple-tax** and yours.
17.27 Take it and pay them our **taxes."**
22.17 against our Law to pay **taxes** to the Roman Emperor, or not?"
22.19 Show me the coin for paying the **tax!"**
Mk 12.14 is it against our Law to pay **taxes** to the Roman Emperor?
Lk 20.22 Law for us to pay **taxes** to the Roman Emperor, or not?"
23. 2 telling them not to pay **taxes** to the Emperor and claiming
Rom 13. 6 is also why you pay **taxes,** because the authorities are working
13. 7 your personal and property **taxes,** and show respect and honour

TAX COLLECTOR

Is 33.18 Your old fears of foreign **tax-collectors** and spies will
Mt 5.46 Even the **tax collectors** do that!
9. 9 walked along, he saw a **tax collector,** named Matthew, sitting
9.10 meal in Matthew's house, many **tax collectors** and other outcasts
10. 3 Thomas and Matthew, the **tax collector;**
11.19 a drinker, a friend of **tax collectors** and other outcasts!'
18.17 treat him as though he were a pagan or a **tax collector.**
21.31 the **tax collectors** and the prostitutes are going into the Kingdom
21.32 but the **tax collectors** and the prostitutes believed him.
Mk 2.14 walked along, he saw a **tax collector,** Levi son of Alphaeus,
2.15 A large number of **tax collectors** and other outcasts
2.16 these outcasts and **tax collectors,** so they asked his disciples,
Lk 3.12 Some **tax collectors** came to be baptized, and they asked him,
5.27 went out and saw a **tax collector** named Levi, sitting in his
5.29 was a large number of **tax collectors** and other people.
5.30 "Why do you eat and drink with **tax collectors** and other outcasts?"
7.29 and especially the **tax collectors** were the ones who had obeyed
7.34 a drinker, a friend of **tax collectors** and other outcasts!'
15. 1 One day when many **tax collectors** and other outcasts came
18.10 one was a Pharisee, the other a **tax collector.**
18.11 thank you that I am not like that **tax collector** over there.
18.13 "But the **tax collector** stood at a distance and would
18.14 tell you," said Jesus, "the **tax collector,** and not the Pharisee,
19. 2 There was a chief **tax collector** there named Zacchaeus, who

TEACH
[TAUGHT]

Ex 18.20 You should **teach** them God's commands and explain to them
35.34 tribe of Dan, the ability to **teach** their crafts to others.
Lev 10.11 You must **teach** the people of Israel all the laws which I
Deut 1. 5 Moab that Moses began to explain God's laws and **teachings.**
4. 1 the laws that I am **teaching** you, and you will live and
4. 5 "I have **taught** you all the laws, as the Lord my God
4. 8 has laws so just as those that I have **taught** you today.
4.10 and so that they will **teach** their children to do the same.'
4.14 The Lord told me to **teach** you all the laws that you
4.44 Moses gave God's laws and **teachings** to the people of Israel.
5.31 **Teach** them to the people, so that they will obey them in
6. 1 the laws that the Lord your God commanded me to **teach** you.
6. 7 **Teach** them to your children.
7.11 So now, obey what you have been **taught;**
8. 3 He did this to **teach** you that man must not depend on
11.19 **Teach** them to your children.
17.18 book of God's laws and **teachings** made from the original copy
19. 9 love the Lord your God and live according to his **teachings.)**
20.18 sin against the Lord by **teaching** you to do all the
27. 3 plaster, [3] and write on them all these laws and **teachings.**
27.26 anyone who does not obey all of God's laws and **teachings.'**
28.58 not obey faithfully all God's **teachings** that are written in
28.61 book of God's laws and **teachings,** and you will be destroyed.
29. 6 your needs in order to **teach** you that he is your God.
29.21 that is written in this book of the Lord's **teachings.**
30.10 all his laws that are written in this book of his **teachings.**
31.12 the Lord your God and to obey his **teachings** faithfully.
31.19 **Teach** it to the people of Israel, so that it will stand
31.22 wrote down the song and **taught** it to the people of Israel.
31.29 will become wicked and reject what I have **taught** them.
32. 2 My **teaching** will fall like drops of rain and form on the
32.11 Like an eagle **teaching** its young to fly, catching them
32.45 Moses had finished giving God's **teachings** to the people,
32.46 so that they may faithfully obey all God's **teachings.**
32.47 These **teachings** are not empty words;
33.10 They will **teach** your people to obey your Law;
Judg 3. 2 in order to **teach** each generation of Israelites about war,
1 Sam 12.23 Instead, I will **teach** you what is good and right for you
2 Sam 1.18 and ordered it to be **taught** to the people of Judah.
7.21 you have done all these great things in order to **teach** me.
1 Kgs 8.36 **Teach** them to do what is right.
2 Kgs 4.38 While he was **teaching** a group of prophets, he told his
17.27 live there, in order to **teach** the people the law of the
17.28 lived in Bethel, where he **taught** the people how to worship
22.13 all the people of Judah about the **teachings** of this book.
2 Chr 6.27 the people of Israel, and **teach** them to do what is right.
14. 4 God of their ancestors, and to obey his **teachings** and commands.
15. 3 true God, without priests to **teach** them, and without a law.
17. 7 out the following officials to **teach** in the cities of Judah:
17. 9 through all the towns of Judah, **teaching** it to the people.
34.21 Find out about the **teachings** of this book.
Ezra 7.10 to practising it, and to **teaching** all its laws and
7.25 You must **teach** that Law to anyone who does not know it.
Neh 8.13 the Levites, went to Ezra to study the **teachings** of the Law.
9.13 to your people and gave them good laws and sound **teachings.**
9.14 You **taught** them to keep your Sabbaths holy, and through
9.29 warned them to obey your **teachings,** but in pride they
Job 4. 3 You have **taught** many people and given strength to feeble hands.
6.24 All right, **teach** me;
8.10 But let the ancient wise men **teach** you;
12. 7 Even birds and animals have much they could **teach** you;
15.18 Wise men have **taught** me truths which they learnt from their fathers,
21.22 Can a man **teach** God, who judges even those in high places?

Job 22.22 Accept the **teaching** he gives;
27.11 Let me **teach** you how great is God's power, and explain
33.33 listen to me, and I will **teach** you how to be wise.
36.15 But God **teaches** men through suffering and uses distress
37.19 **Teach** us what to say to God;
Ps 25. 4 **Teach** me your ways, O Lord;
25. 5 **Teach** me to live according to your truth, for you are my
25. 8 and good, he **teaches** sinners the path they should follow.
25. 9 the humble in the right way and **teaches** them his will.
27.11 **Teach** me, Lord, what you want me to do, and lead me
32. 8 The Lord says, "I will **teach** you the way you should go;
34.11 listen to me, and I will **teach** you to honour the Lord.
40. 3 He **taught** me to sing a new song, a song of praise
40. 8 I keep your **teaching** in my heart."
51.13 Then I will **teach** sinners your commands, and they will
71.17 You have **taught** me ever since I was young, and I still
72. 1 **Teach** the king to judge with your righteousness, O God;
78. 1 Listen, my people, to my **teaching**, and pay attention to
78. 5 He instructed our ancestors to **teach** his laws to their children,
86.11 **Teach** me, Lord, what you want me to do, and I will
86.11 **teach** me to serve you with complete devotion.
90.12 **Teach** us how short our life is, so that we may become
94.12 person you instruct, the one to whom you **teach** your law!
119.12 **teach** me your ways.
119.15 I examine your **teachings.**
119.17 your servant, so that I may live and obey your **teachings.**
119.23 meet and plot against me, but I will study your **teachings.**
119.26 **teach** me your ways.
119.27 your laws, and I will meditate on your wonderful **teachings.**
119.29 the wrong way, and in your goodness **teach** me your law.
119.33 **Teach** me, Lord, the meaning of your laws, and I will
119.45 in perfect freedom, because I try to obey your **teachings.**
119.64 **teach** me your commandments.
119.68 **Teach** me your commands.
119.108 Accept my prayer of thanks, O Lord, and **teach** me your commands.
119.124 Treat me according to your constant love, and **teach** me your commands.
119.125 give me understanding, so that I may know your **teachings.**
119.129 Your **teachings** are wonderful;
119.130 The explanation of your **teachings** gives light and
119.135 Bless me with your presence and **teach** me your laws.
119.141 I am unimportant and despised, but I do not neglect your **teachings.**
119.167 I obey your **teachings;**
119.171 I will always praise you, because you **teach** me your laws.
143.10 **teach** me to do your will.
Prov 1. 3 They can **teach** you how to live intelligently and how to be
1. 4 person clever and **teach** young men how to be resourceful.
1. 9 Their **teaching** will improve your character as a handsome
2. 1 Learn what I **teach** you, my son, and never forget what I
3. 1 Don't forget what I **teach** you, my son.
3. 2 My **teaching** will give you a long and prosperous life.
4. 1 Listen to what your father **teaches** you, my sons.
4. 2 What I am **teaching** you is good, so remember it all.
4. 4 boy, my parents' only son, [4] my father would **teach** me.
4.11 I have **taught** you wisdom and the right way to live.
6.20 you, my son, and never forget what your mother **taught** you.
6.22 Their **teaching** will lead you when you travel, protect you at night,
6.23 their correction can **teach** you how to live.
7. 2 as careful to follow my **teaching** as you are to protect your
7. 3 Keep my **teaching** with you all the time;
8.33 Listen to what you are **taught.**
13.14 The **teachings** of the wise are a fountain of life;
14. 7 they have nothing to **teach** you.
15. 5 It is foolish to ignore what your father **taught** you;
16.20 Pay attention to what you are **taught,** and you will be successful;
21.11 One who is wise will learn from what he is **taught.**
22. 6 **Teach** a child how he should live, and he will remember it
22.15 things, but a good spanking will **teach** them how to behave.
22.17 Listen, and I will **teach** you what wise men have said.
22.17 Study their **teachings,** [18] and you will be glad if you
22.21 advice, [21] and will **teach** you what the truth really is.
28.26 Be safe, and follow the **teachings** of wiser people.
Ecc 12. 9 Philosopher was wise, he kept on **teaching** the people what he knew.
Song 8. 2 you to my mother's house, where you could **teach** me love.
Is 1.10 Pay attention to what our God is **teaching** you.
2. 3 He will **teach** us what he wants us to do;
2. 3 For the Lord's **teaching** comes from Jerusalem;
5.24 what the Lord Almighty, Israel's holy God, has **taught**
8.20 to answer them, "Listen to what the Lord is **teaching** you!
9.15 head—and the tail is the prophets whose **teachings** are lies!
28. 9 They say, "Who does that man think he's **teaching?**
28.10 He is trying to **teach** us letter by letter, line by line,
28.11 some strange-sounding language to **teach** you a lesson.
28.13 the Lord is going to **teach** you letter by letter, line by
28.26 He knows how to do his work, because God has **taught** him.
29.24 those who are always grumbling will be glad to be **taught."**
30. 9 lying, always refusing to listen to the Lord's **teachings.**
30.20 himself will be there to **teach** you, and you will not have
40.13 Who can **teach** him or give him advice?
42. 4 Distant lands eagerly wait for his **teaching."**
42.21 he exalted his laws and **teachings,** and he wanted his people
42.24 he wanted us to live or obey the **teachings** he gave us.
48.17 the one who wants to **teach** you for your own good and
50. 4 The Sovereign Lord has **taught** me what to say, so that I
50. 4 makes me eager to hear what he is going to **teach** me.
51. 4 I give my **teaching** to the nations;
51. 7 what is right, who have my **teaching** fixed in your hearts.
51.16 I have given you my **teaching,** and I protect you with my
Is 54.13 "I myself will **teach** your people, and give them prosperity
59.21 you my power and my **teachings** to be yours for ever, and
59.21 are to obey me and **teach** your children and your descendants
Jer 6.19 they have rejected my **teaching** and have not obeyed my words.
9. 5 they have **taught** their tongues to lie and will not give up
9.13 my people have abandoned the **teaching** that I gave them.
9.14 the idols of Baal as their fathers **taught** them to do.
9.20 **Teach** your daughters how to mourn, and your friends how to
12.16 Lord lives'—as they once **taught** my people to swear by Baal
16.11 They abandoned me and did not obey my **teachings.**
26. 4 obey me by following the **teaching** that I gave you, [5] and by
31.18 we were like an untamed animal, but you **taught** us to obey.
31.34 will have to **teach** his fellow-countryman to know the Lord,
32.23 not obey your commands or live according to your **teaching;**
32.33 and though I kept on **teaching** them, they would not listen
Lam 2. 9 The Law is no longer **taught,** and the prophets have no
Ezek 7.26 priests will have nothing to **teach** the people, and the
19. 3 She reared a cub and **taught** him to hunt;
20.11 gave them my commands and **taught** them my laws, which bring
22.26 They do not **teach** the difference between clean and unclean things,
44.23 "The priests are to **teach** my people the difference
Dan 1. 4 to **teach** them to read and write the Babylonian language.
12. 3 And those who have **taught** many people to do what is right
Hos 4. 6 me and have rejected my **teaching,** and so I reject you and
8. 1 I made with them and have rebelled against my **teaching.**
8.12 I write down countless **teachings** for the people, but
11. 3 Yet I was the one who **taught** Israel to walk.
Amos 2. 4 They have despised my **teachings** and have not kept my commands.
Mic 4. 2 For he will **teach** us what he wants us to do;
4. 2 For the Lord's **teaching** comes from Jerusalem;
Zeph 3. 7 that they would never forget the lesson I **taught** them.
Zech 7.12 would not listen to the **teaching** which I sent through the
Mal 2. 6 They **taught** what was right, not what was wrong.
2. 7 is the duty of priests to **teach** the true knowledge of God.
2. 8 Your **teaching** has led many to do wrong.
2. 9 my will, and when you **teach** my people, you do not treat
4. 4 "Remember the **teachings** of my servant Moses, the laws and
Mt 4.19 "Come with me, and I will **teach** you to catch men."
4.23 Jesus went all over Galilee, **teaching** in the synagogues,
5. 2 His disciples gathered round him, [2] and he began to **teach** them:
5.17 with the Law of Moses and the **teachings** of the prophets.
5.17 to do away with them, but to make their **teachings** come true.
5.19 important of the commandments and **teaches** others to do the same,
5.19 whoever obeys the Law and **teaches** others to do the same,
7.12 of the Law of Moses and of the **teachings** of the prophets.
7.28 these things, the crowd was amazed at the way he **taught.**
7.29 instead, he **taught** with authority.
9.35 He **taught** in the synagogues, preached the Good News
11. 1 place and went off to **teach** and preach in the towns near
12.42 from her country to listen to King Solomon's wise **teaching;**
13. 1 house and went to the lake-side, where he sat down to **teach.**
13.54 He **taught** in the synagogue, and those who heard him were amazed.
15. 2 your disciples disobey the **teaching** handed down by our ancestors?
15. 3 "And why do you disobey God's command and follow your own **teaching?**
15. 5 But you **teach** that if a person has something he could use
15. 6 God's command, in order to follow your own **teaching.**
15. 9 worship me, because they **teach** man-made rules as though they were
16.12 in bread but from the **teaching** of the Pharisees and Sadducees.
19. 8 to divorce your wives because you are so hard to **teach.**
19.11 Jesus answered, "This **teaching** does not apply to everyone,
19.12 Let him who can accept this **teaching** do so."
21.23 and as he **taught,** the chief priests and the elders came to
22.16 You **teach** the truth about God's will for man, without worrying
22.33 When the crowds heard this, they were amazed at his **teaching.**
22.40 Law of Moses and the **teachings** of the prophets depend on
23.16 You **teach,** 'If someone swears by the Temple, he isn't bound
23.18 You also **teach,** 'If someone swears by the altar, he
23.23 to obey the really important **teachings** of the Law, such as
24.32 "Let the fig-tree **teach** you a lesson.
26. 1 When Jesus had finished **teaching** all these things, he said
26.55 day I sat down and **taught** in the Temple, and you did
28.20 the Holy Spirit, [20] and **teach** them to obey everything I have
Mk 1.17 "Come with me, and I will **teach** you to catch men."
1.21 next Sabbath Jesus went to the synagogue and began to **teach.**
1.22 amazed at the way he **taught,** for he wasn't like the teachers
1.22 instead, he **taught** with authority.
1.27 Is it some kind of new **teaching?**
2.13 A crowd came to him, and he started **teaching** them.
4. 1 Again Jesus began to **teach** beside Lake Galilee.
4. 2 He used parables to **teach** them many things, saying to them:
6. 2 On the Sabbath he began to **teach** in the synagogue.
6. 6 Then Jesus went to the villages round there, **teaching** the people.
6.30 met with Jesus, and told him all they had done and **taught.**
6.34 So he began to **teach** them many things.
7. 3 the Jews, follow the **teaching** they received from their ancestors:
7. 5 disciples do not follow the **teaching** handed down by our ancestors,
7. 7 to worship me, because they **teach** man-made rules as though
7. 8 "You put aside God's command and obey the **teachings** of men."
7. 9 of rejecting God's law in order to uphold your own **teaching.**
7.11 But you **teach** that if a person has something he could
7.13 In this way the **teaching** you pass on to others cancels
8.31 Then Jesus began to **teach** his disciples:
8.38 of me and of my **teaching** in this godless and wicked day,

Mk 9.31 to know where he was, [31]because he was **teaching** his disciples:
9.32 did not understand what this **teaching** meant, and they were afraid
10. 1 to him again, and he **taught** them, as he always did.
10. 5 wrote this law for you because you are so hard to **teach.**
11.17 He then **taught** the people:
11.18 of him, because the whole crowd was amazed at his **teaching.**
12.14 to a man's status, but **teach** the truth about God's will for
12.35 As Jesus was **teaching** in the Temple, he asked the question,
12.38 As he **taught** them, he said, "Watch out for the teachers
13.28 "Let the fig-tree **teach** you a lesson.
14.49 day I was with you **teaching** in the Temple, and you did
Lk 1. 4 know the full truth about everything which you have been **taught.**
4.15 He **taught** in the synagogues and was praised by everyone.
4.31 town in Galilee, where he **taught** the people on the Sabbath.
4.32 at the way he **taught,** because he spoke with authority.
5. 3 Jesus sat in the boat and **taught** the crowd.
5.17 One day when Jesus was **teaching,** some Pharisees and teachers
6. 6 On another Sabbath Jesus went into a synagogue and **taught.**
9.26 of me and of my **teaching,** then the Son of Man will
10.39 down at the feet of the Lord and listened to his **teaching.**
11. 1 "Lord, **teach** us to pray, just as John **taught** his disciples."
11.31 from her country to listen to King Solomon's wise **teaching;**
12.12 For the Holy Spirit will **teach** you at that time what you
13.10 One Sabbath Jesus was **teaching** in a synagogue.
13.22 went through towns and villages, **teaching** the people and making
13.26 you **taught** in our town!'
18. 1 his disciples a parable to **teach** them that they should
19.47 Every day Jesus **taught** in the Temple.
20. 1 Jesus was in the Temple **teaching** the people and preaching
20.21 Jesus, "Teacher, we know that what you say and **teach** is right.
20.21 to a man's status, but **teach** the truth about God's will for
21.37 Jesus spent those days **teaching** in the Temple, and when evening
23. 5 even more strongly, "With his **teaching** he is starting a riot
Jn 6.45 The prophets wrote, 'Everyone will be **taught** by God.'
6.59 Jesus said this as he **taught** in the synagogue in Capernaum.
6.60 followers heard this and said, "This **teaching** is too hard.
7.14 half over when Jesus went to the Temple and began **teaching.**
7.16 Jesus answered, "What I **teach** is not my own teaching,
7.17 will know whether what I **teach** comes from God or whether I
7.28 As Jesus **taught** in the Temple, he said in a loud voice,
7.35 Greek cities where our people live, and **teach** the Greeks?
8. 2 gathered round him, and he sat down and began to **teach** them.
8.20 said all this as he **taught** in the Temple, in the room
8.31 him, "If you obey my **teaching,** you are really my disciples;
8.37 trying to kill me, because you will not accept my **teaching.**
8.51 whoever obeys my **teaching** will never die."
8.52 yet you say that whoever obeys your **teaching** will never die.
9.34 and brought up in sin—and you are trying to **teach** us?"
14.23 Jesus answered him, "Whoever loves me will obey my **teaching.**
14.24 Whoever does not love me does not obey my **teaching.**
14.24 And the **teaching** you have heard is not mine, but comes from
14.26 send in my name, will **teach** you everything and make you
15. 3 been made clean already by the **teaching** I have given you.
15.20 if they obeyed my **teaching,** they will obey yours too.
18.19 questioned Jesus about his disciples and about his **teaching.**
18.20 my **teaching** was done in the synagogues and in the Temple,
Acts 1. 1 things that Jesus did and **taught** from the time he began his
4. 2 the two apostles were **teaching** the people that Jesus had risen
4.18 were they to speak or to **teach** in the name of Jesus.
5.21 and at dawn they entered the Temple and started **teaching.**
5.25 you put in prison are in the Temple **teaching** the people!"
5.28 you strict orders not to **teach** in the name of this man,"
5.28 You have spread your **teaching** all over Jerusalem, and you
5.42 people's homes they continued to **teach** and preach the Good
7.22 He was **taught** all the wisdom of the Egyptians and became
11.26 met with the people of the church and **taught** a large group.
13.12 for he was greatly amazed at the **teaching** about the Lord.
14.22 through many troubles to enter the Kingdom of God," they **taught.**
15. 1 Judaea to Antioch and started **teaching** the believers,
15.35 together with many others they **taught** and preached the word
16.21 They are **teaching** customs that are against our law;
17.19 know what this new **teaching** is that you are talking about.
18.11 a year and a half, **teaching** the people the word of God.
18.25 he proclaimed and **taught** correctly the facts about Jesus.
20.20 you as I preached and **taught** in public and in your homes.
20.31 tears, day and night, I **taught** every one of you for three
21.21 told that you have been **teaching** all the Jews who live in
21.28 who goes everywhere **teaching** everyone against the people of Israel,
28.31 the Kingdom of God and **taught** about the Lord Jesus Christ,
Rom 2.21 You **teach** others—why don't you teach yourself?
6.17 your heart the truths found in the **teaching** you received.
12. 7 if it is to **teach,** we should teach;
15. 4 the Scriptures was written to **teach** us, in order that we
15.14 all knowledge, and that you are able to **teach** one another.
16.17 people's faith and go against the **teaching** which you have received.
1 Cor 2. 4 over with fear, [4]and my **teaching** and message were not delivered
2.13 do not speak in words **taught** by human wisdom,
2.13 but in words **taught** by the Spirit, as we explain
4.17 Christ Jesus and which I **teach** in all the churches everywhere.
7.17 This is the rule I **teach** in all the churches.
11. 2 remember me and follow the **teachings** that I have handed on
11.14 Why, nature itself **teaches** you that long hair on a man
11.23 received from the Lord the **teaching** that I passed on to you:
14. 6 God or some knowledge or some inspired message, or some **teaching.**
14.19 in order to **teach** others, than speak thousands of words
14.26 has a hymn, another a **teaching,** another a revelation from God,
Gal 1.12 receive it from any man, nor did anyone **teach** it to me.
Gal 6. 6 The man who is being **taught** the Christian message should share
Eph 4.14 every shifting wind of the **teaching** of deceitful men,
4.21 as his followers you were **taught** the truth that is in Jesus.
Col 1.28 possible wisdom we warn and **teach** them in order to bring
2. 7 and become stronger in your faith, as you were **taught.**
2. 8 wisdom, which comes from the **teachings** handed down by men
2.22 they are only man-made rules and **teachings.**
3.16 **Teach** and instruct each other with all wisdom.
1 Thes 4. 8 whoever rejects this **teaching** is not rejecting man, but God,
4. 9 You yourselves have been **taught** by God how you should love
4.15 What we are **teaching** you now is the Lord's teaching:
2 Thes 2.15 to those truths which we **taught** you, both in our preaching
1 Tim 1. 3 Some people there are **teaching** false doctrines, and you must
1.11 That **teaching** is found in the gospel that was entrusted
1.20 this will **teach** them to stop their blasphemy.
2.12 do not allow them to **teach** or to have authority over men;
3. 2 he must be able to **teach;**
4. 1 will obey lying spirits and follow the **teachings** of demons.
4. 2 Such **teachings** are spread by deceitful liars, whose consciences
4. 3 Such people **teach** that it is wrong to marry and to eat
4. 6 of faith and of the true **teaching** which you have followed.
4.11 Give them these instructions and these **teachings.**
4.13 the public reading of the Scriptures and to preaching and **teaching.**
4.16 Watch yourself and watch your **teaching.**
5.17 especially those who work hard at preaching and **teaching.**
6. 1 will speak evil of the name of God and of our **teaching.**
6. 2 You must **teach** and preach these things.
6. 3 Whoever **teaches** a different doctrine and does not agree
6. 3 Jesus Christ and with the **teaching** of our religion [4]is swollen
2 Tim 1.13 the true words that I **taught** you, as the example for you
2. 2 Take the **teachings** that you heard me proclaim in the
2. 2 to reliable people, who will be able to **teach** others also.
2. 8 descendant of David, as is **taught** in the Good News I preach.
2.15 work, one who correctly **teaches** the message of God's truth.
2.17 Such **teaching** is like an open sore that eats away the flesh.
2.17 Two men who have **taught** such things are Hymenaeus and Philetus.
3.10 But you have followed my **teaching,** my conduct, and my purpose
3.14 continue in the truths that you were **taught** and firmly believe.
3.16 God and is useful for **teaching** the truth, rebuking error,
4. 2 convince, reproach, and encourage, as you **teach** with all patience.
Tit 1. 1 lead them to the truth **taught** by our religion, [2]which is
1. 9 encourage others with the true **teaching** and also to show the
1.11 are upsetting whole families by **teaching** what they should not,
2. 1 But you must **teach** what agrees with sound doctrine.
2. 3 They must **teach** what is good, [4]in order to train the
2. 7 Be sincere and serious in your **teaching.**
2.10 to bring credit to the **teaching** about God our Saviour in all
2.15 **Teach** these things and use your full authority as you encourage
Heb 5.12 you still need someone to **teach** you the first lessons of
6. 1 go forward, then, to mature **teaching** and leave behind us the
6. 2 of the **teaching** about baptisms and the laying on of hands;
8.11 of them will have to **teach** his fellow-citizen or say to his
9. 8 The Holy Spirit clearly **teaches** from all these arrangements
13. 9 all kinds of strange **teachings** lead you from the right way.
1 Jn 2.27 Spirit remains in you, you do not need anyone to **teach** you.
2.27 For his Spirit **teaches** you about everything,
2.27 and what he **teaches** is true, not false.
2.27 Obey the Spirit's **teaching,** then, and remain in union with Christ.
2 Jn 9 not stay with the **teaching** of Christ, but goes beyond it,
9 Whoever does stay with the **teaching** has both the Father and
10 who does not bring this **teaching,** do not welcome him in your
Rev 2.14 among you who follow the **teaching** of Balaam, who taught Balak
2.15 have people among you who follow the **teaching** of the Nicolaitans.
2.20 By her **teaching** she misleads my servants into practising sexual
2.24 of you in Thyatira have not followed this evil **teaching;**
3. 3 Remember, then, what you were **taught** and what you heard;
3. 8 you have followed my **teaching** and have been faithful to me.

TEACHER

see also **TEACHER OF THE LAW**

2 Chr 35. 3 instructions to the Levites, the **teachers** of Israel, who
Ezra 8.16 and Meshullam, and for two **teachers,** Joiarib and Elnathan.
Job 36.22 he is the greatest **teacher** of all.
Ps 94.10 He is the **teacher** of all men—hasn't he any knowledge?
119.99 all my **teachers,** because I meditate on your instructions.
119.102 not neglected your instructions, for you yourself are my **teacher.**
Prov 5.13 I wouldn't listen to my **teachers.**
23.12 Pay attention to your **teacher** and learn all you can.
Mt 8.19 **"Teacher,"** he said, "I am ready to go with you wherever
9.11 asked his disciples, "Why does your **teacher** eat with such people?"
10.24 "No pupil is greater than his **teacher;**
10.25 to become like his **teacher,** and a slave like his master.
12.38 **"Teacher,"** they said, "we want to see you perform a miracle."
17.24 came to Peter and asked, "Does your **teacher** pay the temple-tax?"
19.16 **"Teacher,"** he asked, "what good thing must I do to receive
22.16 **"Teacher,"** they said, "we know that you tell the truth.
22.24 **"Teacher,"** they said, "Moses said that if a man who
22.36 **"Teacher,"** he asked, "which is the greatest commandment in the Law?"
23. 7 with respect in the market-places and to be called **'Teacher.'**
23. 8 You must not be called **'Teacher'**, because you are all
23. 8 brothers of one another and have only one **Teacher.**
23.34 you that I will send you prophets and wise men and **teachers;**
26.18 'The **Teacher** says, My hour has come;
26.25 "Surely, **Teacher,** you don't mean me?"
26.49 Jesus and said, "Peace be with you, **Teacher,"** and kissed him.
Mk 4.38 woke him up and said, **"Teacher,** don't you care that we are

Mk 5.35 Why bother the **Teacher** any longer?"
9. 5 up and said to Jesus, **"Teacher,** how good it is that we
9.17 in the crowd answered, **"Teacher,** I brought my son to you,
9.38 John said to him, **"Teacher,** we saw a man who was
10.17 and asked him, "Good **Teacher,** what must I do to receive
10.20 **"Teacher,"** the man said, "ever since I was young, I
10.35 **"Teacher,"** they said, "there is something we want you to
10.51 **"Teacher,"** the blind man answered, "I want to see again."
11.21 said to Jesus, "Look, **Teacher,** the fig-tree you cursed has died!"
12.14 came to him and said, **"Teacher,** we know that you tell the
12.19 to Jesus and said, [19]**"Teacher,** Moses wrote this law for us:
12.32 The teacher of the Law said to Jesus, "Well done, **Teacher!**
13. 1 leaving the Temple, one of his disciples said, "Look, **Teacher!**
14.14 'The **Teacher** says, Where is the room where my disciples and
14.45 as Judas arrived, he went up to Jesus and said, **"Teacher!"**
Lk 2.46 Temple, sitting with the Jewish **teachers,** listening to them
3.12 and they asked him, **"Teacher,** what are we to do?"
6.40 No pupil is greater than his **teacher;**
6.40 when he has completed his training, will be like his **teacher.**
7.40 "Yes, **Teacher,"** he said, "tell me."
8.49 "don't bother the **Teacher** any longer."
9.38 A man shouted from the crowd, **"Teacher!**
10.25 **"Teacher,"** he asked, "what must I do to receive eternal life?"
11.45 the Law said to him, **"Teacher,** when you say this, you
12.13 the crowd said to Jesus, **"Teacher,** tell my brother to divide
18.18 leader asked Jesus, "Good **Teacher,** what must I do to receive
19.39 **"Teacher,"** they said, "command your disciples to be quiet!"
20.21 These spies said to Jesus, **"Teacher,** we know that what
20.28 to Jesus and said, [28]**"Teacher,** Moses wrote this law for us:
20.39 teachers of the Law spoke up, "A good answer, **Teacher!"**
21. 7 **"Teacher,"** they asked, "when will this be?
22.11 'The **Teacher** says to you, Where is the room where my
Jn 1.38 (This word means **"Teacher.")**
1.49 **"Teacher,"** answered Nathanael, "you are the Son of God!
3. 2 "Rabbi, we know that you are a **teacher** sent by God.
3.10 "You are a great **teacher** in Israel, and you don't know
3.26 went to John and said, **"Teacher,** you remember the man who
4.31 disciples were begging Jesus, **"Teacher,** have something to eat!"
6.25 lake, they said to him, **"Teacher,** when did you get here?"
8. 4 **"Teacher,"** they said to Jesus, "this woman was caught
9. 2 His disciples asked him, **"Teacher,** whose sin caused him
11. 8 **"Teacher,"** the disciples answered, "just a short time ago the
11.16 us all go with the **Teacher,** so that we may die with
11.28 "The **Teacher** is here," she told her, "and is asking for you."
13.13 "You call me **Teacher** and Lord, and it is right that you
13.14 I, your Lord and **Teacher,** have just washed your feet.
20.16 (This means **"Teacher.")**
Acts 13. 1 In the church at Antioch there were some prophets and **teachers:**
17.18 Certain Epicurean and Stoic **teachers** also debated with him.
Rom 2.20 an instructor for the foolish, and a **teacher** for the ignorant.
1 Cor 12.28 in the second place prophets, and in the third place **teachers;**
12.29 They are not all apostles or prophets or **teachers.**
Gal 6. 6 should share all the good things he has with his **teacher.**
Eph 4.11 others to be evangelists, others to be pastors and **teachers.**
1 Tim 2. 7 sent as an apostle and **teacher** to proclaim the Gentiles, to proclaim
2 Tim 1.11 me as an apostle and **teacher** to proclaim the Good News,
2.24 a good and patient **teacher,** [25] who is gentle as he corrects
3.14 You know who your **teachers** were, [15] and you remember that ever
4. 3 themselves more and more **teachers** who will tell them what they
Heb 5.12 time for you to be **teachers**—yet you still need someone to
Jas 3. 1 My brothers, not many of you should become **teachers.**
3. 1 As you know, we **teachers** will be judged with greater strictness
2 Pet 2. 1 and in the same way false **teachers** will appear among you.
2. 3 In their greed these false **teachers** will make a profit out
2.10 These false **teachers** are bold and arrogant, and show no respect
2.11 and mightier than these false **teachers,** do not accuse them with

TEACHER OF THE LAW

Men who in New Testament times taught and explained the teachings of the Old Testament, especially the first five books.

Mt 2. 4 chief priests and the **teachers of the Law** and asked them,
5.20 more faithful than the **teachers of the Law** and the Pharisees
7.29 He wasn't like the **teachers of the Law;**
8.19 A **teacher of the Law** came to him.
9. 3 Then some **teachers of the Law** said to themselves, "This
12.38 Then some **teachers of the Law** and some Pharisees spoke up.
13.52 means, then, that every **teacher of the Law** who becomes a
15. 1 Then some Pharisees and **teachers of the Law** came from Jerusalem
16.21 the elders, the chief priests, and the **teachers of the Law.**
17.10 Jesus, "Why do the **teachers of the Law** say that Elijah has
20.18 over to the chief priests and the **teachers of the Law.**
21.15 chief priests and the **teachers of the Law** became angry when
22.35 one of them, a **teacher of the Law,** tried to trap him
23. 2 "The **teachers of the Law** and the Pharisees are the authorized
23.13 "How terrible for you, **teachers of the Law** and Pharisees!
23.15 "How terrible for you, **teachers of the Law** and Pharisees!
23.23 "How terrible for you, **teachers of the Law** and Pharisees!
23.25 "How terrible for you, **teachers of the Law** and Pharisees!
23.27 "How terrible for you, **teachers of the Law** and Pharisees!
23.29 "How terrible for you, **teachers of the Law** and Pharisees!
26.57 High Priest, where the **teachers of the Law** and the elders
27.41 chief priests and the **teachers of the Law** and the elders
Mk 1.22 way he taught, for he wasn't like the **teachers of the Law;**
2. 6 Some **teachers of the Law** who were sitting there thought
2.16 Some **teachers of the Law,** who were Pharisees, saw that Jesus
3.22 Some **teachers of the Law** who had come from Jerusalem
7. 1 Pharisees and **teachers of the Law** who had come from Jerusalem
7. 5 the Pharisees and the **teachers of the Law** asked Jesus,
Mk 8.31 the elders, the chief priests, and the **teachers of the Law.**
9.11 Jesus, "Why do the **teachers of the Law** say that Elijah has
9.14 round them and some **teachers of the Law** arguing with them.
10.33 over to the chief priests and the **teachers of the Law.**
11.18 chief priests and the **teachers of the Law** heard of this,
11.27 the chief priests, the **teachers of the Law,** and the elders
12.28 A **teacher of the Law** was there who heard the discussion.
12.32 The **teacher of the Law** said to Jesus, "Well done,
12.35 question, "How can the **teachers of the Law** say that the
12.38 "Watch out for the **teachers of the Law,** who like to walk
14. 1 chief priests and the **teachers of the Law** were looking for a
14.43 the chief priests, the **teachers of the Law,** and the elders.
14.53 the elders, and the **teachers of the Law** were gathering.
15. 1 the elders, the **teachers of the Law,** and the whole Council,
15.31 chief priests and the **teachers of the Law** jeered at Jesus,
Lk 5.17 teaching, some Pharisees and **teachers of the Law** were sitting
5.21 The **teachers of the Law** and the Pharisees began to say
5.30 Some Pharisees and some **teachers of the Law** who belonged to
6. 7 Some **teachers of the Law** and some Pharisees wanted a
7.30 Pharisees and the **teachers of the Law** rejected God's purpose for
9.22 the elders, the chief priests, and the **teachers of the Law.**
10.25 A **teacher of the Law** came up and tried to trap Jesus.
10.29 But the **teacher of the Law** wanted to justify himself, so
10.37 The **teacher of the Law** answered, "The one who was kind
11.45 One of the **teachers of the Law** said to him, "Teacher,
11.46 Jesus answered, "How terrible also for you **teachers of the Law!**
11.52 "How terrible for you **teachers of the Law!**
11.53 left that place, the **teachers of the Law** and the Pharisees
14. 3 and Jesus asked the **teachers of the Law** and the Pharisees,
15. 2 the Pharisees and the **teachers of the Law** started grumbling,
19.47 The chief priests, the **teachers of the Law,** and the leaders
20. 1 chief priests and the **teachers of the Law,** together with the
20.19 The **teachers of the Law** and the chief priests tried to
20.39 Some of the **teachers of the Law** spoke up, "A good answer,
20.46 your guard against the **teachers of the Law,** who like to walk
22. 2 chief priests and the **teachers of the Law** were afraid of the
22.66 chief priests, and the **teachers of the Law** met together,
23.10 chief priests and the **teachers of the Law** stepped forward
Jn 8. 3 The **teachers of the Law** and the Pharisees brought in a
Acts 4. 5 the elders, and the **teachers of the Law** gathered in Jerusalem.
5.34 Gamaliel, who was a **teacher of the Law** and was highly
6.12 up the people, the elders, and the **teachers of the Law.**
23. 9 and some of the **teachers of the Law** who belonged to the
1 Tim 1. 7 They want to be **teachers of God's law,** but they do not

TEAM

1 Kgs 19.19 Elijah left and found Elisha ploughing with a **team** of oxen;
19.19 there were eleven **teams** ahead of him, and he was ploughing
19.21 Then Elisha went to his **team** of oxen, killed them, and

TEAR (1)

[TORE, TORN]

Gen 37.29 that Joseph was not there, he **tore** his clothes in sorrow.
37.33 My son Joseph has been **torn** to pieces!"
37.34 Jacob **tore** his clothes in sorrow and put on sackcloth.
44.13 brothers **tore** their clothes in sorrow, loaded their donkeys,
44.28 He must have been **torn** to pieces by wild animals, because I
Ex 28.32 be reinforced with a woven binding to keep it from **tearing.**
34.13 Instead, **tear** down their altars, destroy their sacred pillars,
39.23 was reinforced with a woven binding to keep it from **tearing.**
Lev 1.17 tear its body open, without **tearing** the wings off, and then
10. 6 leave your hair uncombed or **tear** your clothes to show that
13.45 must wear **torn** clothes, leave his hair uncombed,
13.56 mildew has faded, he shall **tear** it out of the clothing or
14.45 It must be **torn** down, and its stones, its wood, and all
21.10 leave his hair uncombed or **tear** his clothes to show that he
22.24 testicles have been crushed, cut, bruised, or **torn** off.
26.30 of worship on the hills, **tear** down your incense-altars, and
Num 14. 6 Jephunneh, two of the spies, **tore** their clothes in sorrow
23.24 doesn't rest until it has **torn** and devoured, Until it has
Deut 7. 5 So then, **tear** down their altars, break their sacred stone
12. 3 **Tear** down their altars and smash their sacred stone pillars
33.20 waits like a lion To **tear** off an arm or a scalp.
Josh 7. 6 and the leaders of Israel **tore** their clothes in grief, threw
9.13 They are **torn.**
Judg 2. 2 You must **tear** down their altars.'
6.25 bull seven years old, **tear** down your father's altar to Baal,
6.30 He **tore** down the altar to Baal and cut down the symbol
6.31 It is his altar that was **torn** down."
6.32 it is his altar that was **torn** down."
8. 9 and sound, and when I do, I will **tear** your tower down!"
8.17 He also **tore** down the tower at Penuel and killed the men
9.45 the city, killed its people, **tore** it down, and covered the
11.35 When he saw her, he **tore** his clothes in sorrow and said,
14. 6 made Samson strong, and he **tore** the lion apart with his bare
1 Sam 4.12 show his grief, he had **torn** his clothes and put earth on
15.27 to leave, but Saul caught hold of his cloak, and it **tore.**
15.28 to him, "The Lord has **torn** the kingdom of Israel away from
2 Sam 1. 2 show his grief, he had **torn** his clothes and put earth on
1.11 David **tore** his clothes in sorrow, and all his men did
3.31 Joab and his men to **tear** their clothes, wear sackcloth, and
13.19 sprinkled ashes on her head, **tore** her robe, and with her
13.31 The king stood up, **tore** his clothes in sorrow, and threw
13.31 The servants who were there with him **tore** their clothes also.
15.32 met him with his clothes **torn** and with earth on his head.
22.10 He **tore** the sky apart and came down, with a dark cloud
1 Kgs 11.30 new robe he was wearing, **tore** it into twelve pieces, [31] and
18.30 repairing the altar of the Lord which had been **torn** down.
19.10 broken their covenant with you, **torn** down your altars, and

1 Kgs 19.14 broken their covenant with you, **torn** down your altars, and
20.41 The prophet **tore** the cloth from his face, and at once
21.27 When Elijah finished speaking, Ahab **tore** his clothes,
2 Kgs 2.12 In grief, Elisha **tore** his cloak in two.
2.24 out of the woods and **tore** forty-two of the boys to pieces.
5. 7 read the letter, he **tore** his clothes in dismay and exclaimed,
6.30 Hearing this, the king **tore** his clothes in dismay, and
11.14 Athaliah **tore** her clothes in distress and shouted,
11.18 the people went to the temple of Baal and **tore** it down;
14. 4 He did not **tear** down the pagan places of worship, and the
14.13 prisoner, advanced on Jerusalem, and **tore** down the city wall
18.37 Then Eliakim, Shebna, and Joah **tore** their clothes in grief,
19. 1 Hezekiah heard their report, he **tore** his clothes in grief,
22.11 the book being read, he **tore** his clothes in dismay, [12]and
22.19 yourself before me, **tearing** your clothes and weeping,
23. 8 He also **tore** down the altars dedicated to the goat-demons
23.12 King Ahaz' quarters, King Josiah **tore** down, along with the
23.15 Josiah also **tore** down the place of worship in Bethel
23.19 city of Israel King Josiah **tore** down all the pagan places of
25.10 in Jerusalem, [10]and his soldiers **tore** down the city walls.
2 Chr 23.13 She **tore** her clothes in distress and shouted, "Treason!
23.17 they all went to the temple of Baal and **tore** it down.
25.23 There he **tore** down the city wall from Ephraim Gate to the
26. 6 He **tore** down the walls of the cities of Gath, Jamnia, and
34. 4 Baal was worshipped and **tore** down the incense-altars near them.
34.19 the book being read, he **tore** his clothes in dismay [20]and
34.27 yourself before me, **tearing** your clothes and weeping,
Ezra 6.11 wooden beam is to be **torn** out of his house, sharpened at
9. 3 tore my clothes in despair, **tore** my hair and my beard, and
9. 5 grieving, and still wearing my **torn** clothes, I knelt in
Esth 4. 1 of all that had been done, he **tore** his clothes in anguish.
Job 1.20 Then Job stood up and **tore** his clothes in grief.
2.12 began to weep and wail, **tearing** their clothes in grief and
12.14 When God **tears** down, who can rebuild, and who can free
16. 9 In anger God **tears** me limb from limb;
18.14 He is **torn** from the tent where he lived secure, and is
28. 5 But underneath the same earth All is **torn** up and crushed.
30.27 I am **torn** apart by worry and pain;
31.22 may they be **torn** from my shoulders.
41.13 No one can **tear** off his outer coat or pierce the armour
41.30 they **tear** up the muddy ground like a threshing-sledge.
Ps 7. 2 one can save me, and there they will **tear** me to pieces.
17.12 like lions, waiting for me, wanting to **tear** me to pieces.
18. 9 He **tore** the sky apart and came down with a dark cloud
22.13 They open their mouths like lions, roaring and **tearing** at me.
22.16 they **tear** at my hands and feet.
89.40 You have **torn** down the walls of his city and left his
137. 7 Remember how they kept saying, **"Tear** it down to the ground!"
144. 5 O Lord, **tear** the sky apart and come down;
Ecc 3. 3 the time for **tearing** down and the time for building.
3. 7 away, [7]the time for **tearing** and the time for mending,
Song 5. 7 the guards at the city wall **tore** off my cape.
Is 22. 9 the houses in Jerusalem and **tore** some of them down to get
23.13 who put up siege-towers, **tore** down the fortifications of Tyre,
32.19 will fall on the forests, and the city will be **torn** down.)
36.22 Then Eliakim, Shebna, and Joah **tore** their clothes in
37. 1 Hezekiah heard their report, he **tore** his clothes in grief,
64. 1 Why don't you **tear** the sky apart and come down?
Jer 4.20 their curtains are **torn** to pieces.
5. 6 wolves from the desert will **tear** them to pieces, and
5. 6 go out, they will be **torn** apart because their sins are
9.19 our homes have been **torn** down."
13.22 why your clothes have been **torn** off and you have been raped
24. 6 I will build them up and not **tear** them down;
31.40 The city will never again be **torn** down or destroyed."
33. 4 palace of Judah will be **torn** down as a result of the
39. 8 houses of the people and **tore** down the walls of Jerusalem.
41. 5 They had shaved off their beards, **torn** their clothes,
42.10 land, then I will build you up and not **tear** you down;
45. 4 "But I, the Lord, am **tearing** down what I have built and
48. 1 is captured, its mighty fortress **torn** down, and its people
50.15 Its walls have been broken through and **torn** down.
52.14 and his soldiers **tore** down the city walls.
Lam 2. 2 every village in Judah And **tore** down the forts that defended
2. 7 He allowed the enemy to **tear** down its walls.
3.11 chased me off the road, **tore** me to pieces, and left me.
Ezek 6. 4 The altars will be **torn** down and the incense-altars broken.
16.39 their power, and they will **tear** down the places where you
22.27 are like wolves **tearing** apart the animals they have killed.
23.26 They will **tear** off your clothes and take your jewels.
23.34 drain it dry, and with its broken pieces **tear** your breast.
26. 4 They will destroy your city walls and **tear** down your towers.
26. 9 battering-rams and **tear** down your towers with iron bars.
36.35 the cities which were **torn** down, looted, and left in ruins,
Dan 2. 5 you can't, I'll have you **torn** limb from limb and make your
3.29 Abednego, he is to be **torn** limb from limb, and his house
7. 4 While I was watching, the wings were **torn** off.
7. 8 It **tore** out three of the horns that were already there.
Hos 5.14 I myself will **tear** them to pieces and then leave them.
13. 8 bear that has lost her cubs, and I will **tear** you open.
13. 8 on the spot, and will **tear** you to pieces like a wild
Joel 2.13 **tearing** your clothes is not enough."
Mic 3. 2 You skin my people alive and **tear** the flesh off their bones.
5. 8 sheep, pounces on them, and **tears** them to pieces—and there
5.11 the cities in your land and **tear** down all your defences.
Nah 2.12 lion killed his prey and **tore** it to pieces for his mate
2.12 he filled his den with **torn** flesh.
Zech 11.16 the meat of the fattest sheep and **tears** off their hoofs.
Mal 1. 4 Lord will reply, "Let them rebuild—I will **tear** them down again.
Mt 26.61 said, 'I am able to **tear** down God's Temple and three days
26.65 the High Priest **tore** his clothes and said, "Blasphemy!
Mt 27.40 "You were going to **tear** down the Temple and build it up
27.51 hanging in the Temple was **torn** in two from top to bottom.
Mk 2.21 new patch will shrink and **tear** off some of the old cloth,
14.58 heard him say, 'I will **tear** down this Temple which men have
14.63 The High Priest **tore** his robes and said, "We don't need
15.29 You were going to **tear** down the Temple and build it up
15.38 hanging in the Temple was **torn** in two, from top to bottom.
Lk 5.36 "No one **tears** a piece off a new coat to patch up
5.36 he does, he will have **torn** the new coat, and the piece
12.18 'I will **tear** down my barns and build bigger ones, where I
23.45 and the curtain hanging in the Temple was **torn** in two.
Jn 2.19 Jesus answered, **"Tear** down this Temple, and in three days
19.24 The soldiers said to one another, "Let's not **tear** it;
21.11 even though there were so many, still the net did not **tear.**
Acts 6.14 this Jesus of Nazareth will **tear** down the Temple and change
14.14 were about to do, they **tore** their clothes and ran into the
16.22 the officials **tore** the clothes off Paul and Silas and ordered
19.16 from his house, wounded and with their clothes **torn** off.
23.10 the commander was afraid that Paul would be **torn** to pieces.
Rom 11. 3 "Lord, they have killed your prophets and **torn** down your altars;
2 Cor 5. 1 body here on earth—is **torn** down, God will have a house
10. 8 given us—authority to build you up, not to **tear** you down.
13.10 given me—authority to build you up, not to **tear** you down.
Gal 2.18 system of Law that I **tore** down, then I show myself to

TEAR (2)

Judg 14.16 wife went to him in **tears** and said, "You don't love me!
2 Kgs 8.11 Suddenly Elisha burst into **tears.**
20. 5 ancestor David, have heard your prayer and seen your **tears.**
Job 16.20 my eyes pour out **tears** to God.
Ps 6. 6 my pillow is soaked with **tears.**
30. 5 **Tears** may flow in the night, but joy comes in the morning.
42. 3 Day and night I cry, and **tears** are my only food;
56. 8 you have kept a record of my **tears.**
80. 5 given us sorrow to eat, a large cup of **tears** to drink.
102. 9 ashes are my food, and my **tears** are mixed with my drink.
116. 8 he stopped my **tears** and kept me from defeat.
119.136 My **tears** pour down like a river, because people do not
Is 16. 9 My **tears** fall for Heshbon and Elealeh, because there is no
25. 8 He will wipe away the **tears** from everyone's eyes and take
38. 5 ancestor David, have heard your prayer and seen your **tears;**
Jer 6.26 Mourn with bitter **tears** as you would for an only son,
9. 1 my eyes a fountain of **tears,** so that I could cry day
9.18 until our eyes fill with **tears,** and our eyelids are wet from
13.17 will cry bitterly, and my **tears** will flow because the Lord's
14.17 "May my eyes flow with **tears** day and night, may I never
31.16 Stop your crying and wipe away your **tears.**
Lam 1. 2 **tears** run down her cheeks.
1.16 "That is why my eyes are overflowing with **tears.**
2.18 Let your **tears** flow like rivers night and day;
3.48 flow with rivers of **tears** at the destruction of my people.
3.49 "My **tears** will pour out in a ceaseless stream [50]Until
5.17 can hardly see through our **tears,** [18]because Mount Zion.
Ezek 24.16 You are not to complain or cry or shed any **tears.**
Mal 2.13 drown the Lord's altar with **tears,** weeping and wailing
Lk 7.38 Jesus, by his feet, crying and wetting his feet with her **tears.**
7.44 washed my feet with her **tears** and dried them with her hair.
Acts 20.19 With all humility and many **tears** I did my work as the
20.31 and remember that with many **tears,** day and night, I taught
2 Cor 2. 4 with a greatly troubled and distressed heart and with many **tears;**
Phil 3.18 you this many times before, and now I repeat it with **tears:**
2 Tim 1. 4 I remember your **tears,** and I want to see you very much,
Heb 5. 7 requests with loud cries and **tears** to God, who could save
12.17 what he had done, even though in **tears** he looked for it.
Rev 7.17 And God will wipe away every **tear** from their eyes."
21. 4 He will wipe away all **tears** from their eyes.

TEBETH

Tenth month of the Hebrew calendar.

Esth 2.16 tenth month, the month of **Tebeth,** Esther was brought to King

TEKOA

City in Judah, Amos's home.

2 Sam 14. 2 much, [2]so he sent for a clever woman who lived in **Tekoa.**
23.24 Ira son of Ikkesh from **Tekoa** Abiezer from Anathoth Mebunnai
1 Chr 2.24 They had a son named Ashhur, who founded the town of **Tekoa.**
4. 5 founded the town of **Tekoa,** had two wives, Helah and Naarah.
11.26 Ira son of Ikkesh from **Tekoa**
27. 2 Ira son of Ikkesh from **Tekoa**
2 Chr 11. 6 Bethlehem, Etam, **Tekoa,** [7]Bethzur, Soco, Adullam, [8]Gath,
20.20 morning the people went out to the wild country near **Tekoa.**
Neh 3. 5 The men of **Tekoa** built the next section, but the leading
3.27 The men of **Tekoa** built the next section, their second one,
Jer 6. 1 Sound the trumpet in **Tekoa** and build a signal fire in Beth
Amos 1. 1 are the words of Amos, a shepherd from the town of **Tekoa.**

TELL

[TOLD]

Gen 1.22 He blessed them all and **told** the creatures that live in
1.22 fill the sea, and he **told** the birds to increase in number.
3. 1 the woman, "Did God really **tell** you not to eat fruit from
3. 3 God **told** us not to eat the fruit of that tree or
3.11 "Who **told** you that you were naked?"
3.11 "Did you eat the fruit that I **told** you not to eat?"
3.17 wife and ate the fruit which I **told** you not to eat.
9.22 his father was naked, he went out and **told** his two brothers.
12. 4 started out from Haran, as the Lord had **told** him to do;

Gen 12.13 **Tell** them that you are my sister;
12.15 officials saw her and **told** the king how beautiful she was;
12.18 Why didn't you **tell** me that she was your wife?
16.13 "Have I really seen God and lived to **tell** about it?"
19. 9 Who are you to **tell** us what to do?
20. 8 called all his officials and **told** them what had happened,
20.13 are to me by **telling** everyone that I am your brother.' "
21.12 Do whatever Sarah **tells** you, because it is through Isaac
21.26 You didn't **tell** me about it, and this is the first I
22. 3 They started out for the place that God had **told** him about.
22. 9 the place which God had **told** him about, Abraham built an
24.23 He said, "Please **tell** me who your father is.
24.28 The girl ran to her mother's house and **told** the whole story.
24.30 arms and had heard her say what the man had **told** her.
24.49 towards my master and treat him fairly, please **tell** me;
24.66 The servant **told** Isaac everything he had done.
26. 2 stay in this land, where I **tell** you to stay.
26.32 day Isaac's servants came and **told** him about the well which
27.19 I have done as you **told** me.
29.12 He **told** her, "I am your father's relative,
29.12 She ran to **tell** her father;
29.13 When Jacob **told** Laban everything that had happened,
31.16 Do whatever God has **told** you."
31.22 Three days later Laban was **told** that Jacob had fled.
31.27 Why did you deceive me and slip away without **telling** me?
31.27 If you had **told** me, I would have sent you on your
31.46 He **told** his men to gather some rocks and pile them up.
32. 9 You **told** me, Lord, to go back to my land and to
32.29 Jacob said, "Now **tell** me your name."
34.12 **Tell** me what presents you want, and set the payment for
37. 5 a dream, and when he **told** his brothers about it, they hated
37.10 He also **told** the dream to his father, and his father
37.14 then come back and **tell** me."
37.16 "Can you **tell** me where they are?"
38.13 Someone **told** Tamar that her father-in-law was going to
39.17 Then she **told** him the same story:
40. 8 "**Tell** me your dreams."
41. 8 He **told** them his dreams, but no one could explain them to
41.12 We **told** him our dreams, and he interpreted them for us.
41.15 I have been **told** that you can interpret dreams."
41.24 I **told** the dreams to the magicians, but none of them could
41.25 God has **told** you what he is going to do.
41.28 It is just as I **told** you—God has shown you what
41.55 ordered them to go to Joseph and do what he **told** them.
42.22 Reuben said, "I **told** you not to harm the boy, but you
42.29 father Jacob in Canaan, they **told** him all that had happened
43. 5 not go, because the man **told** us we would not be admitted
43. 6 me so much trouble by **telling** the man that you had another
43. 7 we know that he would **tell** us to bring our brother with
43.25 noon, because they had been **told** that they were to eat with
43.27 health and then said, "You **told** me about your old
43.29 "So this is your youngest brother, the one you **told** me about.
44. 2 He did as he was **told**.
44.21 Sir, you **told** us to bring him here, so that you could
44.24 went back to our father, we **told** him what you had said.
44.25 Then he **told** us to return and buy a little food.
44.32 I **told** him that if I did not bring the boy back
45. 1 else was with him when Joseph **told** his brothers who he was.
45. 9 back to my father and **tell** him that this is what his
45.13 **Tell** my father how powerful I am here in Egypt
45.13 and **tell** him about everything that you have
45.17 He said to Joseph, "**Tell** your brothers to load their
45.19 **Tell** them also to take wagons with them from Egypt for
45.21 Jacob's sons did as they were **told**.
45.26 they **told** him.
45.27 But when they **told** him all that Joseph had said to them,
46.31 family, "I must go and **tell** the king that my brothers and
46.32 I will **tell** him that you are shepherds and take care of
46.34 occupation is, [34] be sure to **tell** him that you have taken
48. 1 Some time later Joseph was **told** that his father was ill.
48. 2 When Jacob was **told** that his son Joseph had come to see
49. 1 "Gather round, and I will **tell** you what will happen to you
50.17 "Before our father died, [17] he **told** us to ask you, 'Please
Ex 2. 9 The princess **told** the woman, "Take this baby and nurse
3.13 So what can I **tell** them?"
3.15 **Tell** the Israelites that I, the Lord, the God of their ancestors,
3.16 leaders of Israel together and **tell** them that I, the Lord,
3.16 **Tell** them that I have come to them and have seen what
4.12 help you to speak, and I will **tell** you what to say."
4.15 You can speak to him and **tell** him what to say.
4.15 you to speak, and I will **tell** you both what to do.
4.16 Then you will be like God, **telling** him what to say.
4.20 Egypt, carrying the stick that God had **told** him to take.
4.22 Then you must **tell** him that I, the Lord, say, 'Israel is
4.23 I **told** you to let my son go, so that he might
4.28 Then Moses **told** Aaron everything that the Lord had said
4.28 when he **told** him to return to Egypt;
4.28 he also **told** him about the miracles which the Lord had
4.30 Aaron **told** them everything that the Lord had said to Moses,
5.19 in trouble when they were **told** that they had to make the
6. 6 So **tell** the Israelites that I say to them, 'I am the
6. 9 Moses **told** this to the Israelites, but they would not
6.11 said to Moses, [11] "Go and **tell** the king of Egypt that he
6.13 "**Tell** the Israelites and the king of Egypt that I have
6.27 They were the men who **told** the king of Egypt to free
6.29 **Tell** the king of Egypt everything I tell you."
7. 2 **Tell** Aaron everything I command you,
7. 2 and he will **tell** the king to let the Israelites
7. 9 yourselves by performing a miracle, **tell** Aaron to take his
7.16 the Hebrews, sent me to **tell** you to let his people go,
7.19 The Lord said to Moses, "**Tell** Aaron to take his stick
Ex 8. 1 "Go to the king and **tell** him that the Lord says, 'Let
8. 5 The Lord said to Moses, "**Tell** Aaron to hold out his stick
8.16 The Lord said to Moses, "**Tell** Aaron to strike the
8.20 goes to the river, and **tell** him that the Lord says, 'Let
9. 1 "Go to the king and **tell** him that the Lord, the God
9. 7 what had happened and was **told** that none of the animals of
9.13 meet with the king and **tell** him that the Lord, the God
10. 2 you may be able to **tell** your children and grandchildren how
11. 2 the people of Israel and **tell** all of them to ask their
14. 2 the Lord said to Moses, [2] "**Tell** the Israelites to turn back
14. 4 The Israelites did as they were **told**.
14. 5 the king of Egypt was **told** that the people had escaped, he
14.12 Didn't we **tell** you before we left that this would happen?
14.12 We **told** you to leave us alone and let us go on
14.15 **Tell** the people to move forward.
16. 9 Moses said to Aaron, "**Tell** the whole community to come
16.12 **Tell** them that at twilight they will have meat to eat, and
16.22 of the community came and **told** Moses about it, [23] and he
17. 9 of the hill holding the stick that God **told** me to carry."
17.14 **Tell** Joshua that I will completely destroy the Amalekites."
18. 8 Moses **told** Jethro everything that the Lord had done to the
18. 8 He also **told** him about the hardships the people had faced on
18.16 them is right, and I **tell** them God's commands and laws."
19. 3 him from the mountain and **told** him to say to the Israelites,
19. 7 of the people together and **told** them everything that the
19. 9 Moses **told** the Lord what the people had answered, [10] and
19.10 "Go to the people and **tell** them to spend today and tomorrow
19.12 people must not cross, and **tell** them not to go up the
19.14 came down the mountain and **told** the people to get ready for
19.25 down to the people and **told** them what the Lord had said.
24. 3 Moses went and **told** the people all the Lord's commands and
25. 2 The Lord said to Moses, [2] "**Tell** the Israelites to make an
28. 3 I have given ability, and **tell** them to make Aaron's clothes,
28. 4 **Tell** them to make a breast-piece, an ephod, a robe, an
29. 4 Tent of my presence, and **tell** them to take a ritual bath.
29.10 Tent of my presence and **tell** Aaron and his sons to put
29.15 one of the rams and **tell** Aaron and his sons to put
29.19 ram used for dedication—and **tell** Aaron and his sons to put
29.24 Aaron and his sons and **tell** them to dedicate it to me
32.34 Now go, lead the people to the place I **told** you about.
33.12 is true that you have **told** me to lead these people to
33.12 land, but you did not **tell** me whom you would send with
33.13 Now if you are, **tell** me your plans, so that I may
34.34 he came out, he would **tell** the people of Israel everything
36. 2 were willing to help, and Moses **told** them to start working.
40.12 entrance of the Tent, and **tell** them to take a ritual bath.
Lev 4. 2 The Lord commanded Moses [2] to **tell** the people of Israel
7.38 Moses on the day he **told** the people of Israel to make
8. 6 and his sons forward and **told** them to take a ritual bath.
9. 3 Then **tell** the people of Israel to take a male goat for
14.34 his house, then he must go and **tell** the priest about it.
15.31 The Lord **told** Moses to warn the people of Israel about
16. 2 He said, "**Tell** your brother Aaron that only at the proper
17.12 is why the Lord has **told** the people of Israel that neither
17.14 is why the Lord has **told** the people of Israel that they
18. 1 The Lord **told** Moses [2] to say to the people of Israel, "I
19. 1 The Lord **told** Moses [2] to say to the community of Israel,
20. 1 The Lord **told** Moses [2] to say to the people of Israel,
24. 1 The Lord **told** Moses [2] to give the following orders to the
24.12 waited for the Lord to **tell** them what to do with him.
24.15 Then **tell** the people of Israel that anyone who curses
Num 4. 1 The Lord **told** Moses [2] to take a census of the Levite clan
4.19 and assign each man his task and **tell** him what to carry.
4.21 The Lord **told** Moses [22] to take a census of the Levite
4.29 The Lord **told** Moses to take a census of the Levite clan
6.23 The Lord commanded Moses [23] to **tell** Aaron and his sons
7.11 the Lord said to Moses, "**Tell** them that each day for a
8. 2 The Lord said to Moses, [2] "**Tell** Aaron that when he puts
8. 7 the water of purification and **tell** them to shave their whole
9. 4 So Moses **told** the people to observe the Passover, [5] and on
9. 9 The Lord **told** Moses [10] to say to the people of Israel,
11.16 Tent of my presence, and **tell** them to stand there beside you.
11.18 Now **tell** the people, 'Purify yourselves for tomorrow;
11.24 So Moses went out and **told** the people what the Lord had
11.27 young man ran out to **tell** Moses what Eldad and Medad were
14.14 to your people, [14] they will **tell** it to the people who live
14.39 When Moses **told** the Israelites what the Lord had said,
14.40 ready to go to the place which the Lord **told** us about.
16.24 The Lord said to Moses, [24] "**Tell** the people to move
16.37 the Lord said to Moses, [37] "**Tell** Eleazar son of Aaron the
17. 2 The Lord said to Moses, [2] "**Tell** the people of Israel to
18.24 That is why I **told** them that they would have no permanent
21. 8 Then the Lord **told** Moses to make a metal snake and put
22. 8 tomorrow I will report to you whatever the Lord **tells** me."
22.10 Moab has sent them to **tell** me [11] that a people who came
22.14 they returned to Balak and **told** him that Balaam had refused
22.19 whether or not the Lord has something else to **tell** me."
22.20 them, get ready to go, but do only what I **tell** you."
22.35 with these men, but say only what I **tell** you to say."
22.38 I can say only what God **tells** me to say."
23. 2 Balak did as he was **told**, and he and Balaam offered a
23. 3 I will **tell** you whatever he reveals to me."
23. 5 The Lord **told** Balaam what to say and sent him back to
23.12 answered, "I can say only what the Lord **tells** me to say."
23.16 The Lord met Balaam, **told** him what to say, and sent him
23.26 Balaam answered, "Didn't I **tell** you
23.26 that I had to do everything that the Lord **told** me?"
23.30 Balak did as he was **told**, and offered a bull and a
24.12 Balaam answered, "I **told** the messengers you sent to me
24.13 I will say only what the Lord **tells** me to say."
25.12 So **tell** him that I am making a covenant with him that

Num 27. 8 **Tell** the people of Israel that whenever a man dies without
29.40 So Moses **told** the people of Israel everything that the
35. 2 the Lord said to Moses, [2]"**Tell** the Israelites that from
35. 9 The Lord **told** Moses [10] to say to the people of Israel:
Deut 1. 3 they had left Egypt, Moses **told** the people
1. 3 everything the Lord had commanded him to **tell** them.
1. 9 still at Mount Sinai, I **told** you, 'The responsibility for
1.22 land, so that they can **tell** us the best route to take
1.28 The men we sent **tell** us that the people there are stronger
1.43 I **told** you what the Lord had said, but you paid no
2. 2 "Then the Lord **told** me [3] that we had spent enough time
2. 4 He **told** me to give you the following instructions:
2.13 we crossed the River Zered as the Lord **told** us to do.
4. 5 all the laws, as the Lord my God **told** me to do.
4. 9 **Tell** your children and your grandchildren [10] about the day
4.11 "**Tell** your children how you went and stood at the foot
4.12 **Tell** them how the Lord spoke to you from the fire, how
4.13 He **told** you what you must do to keep the covenant he
4.14 The Lord **told** me to teach you all the laws that you
5. 5 Lord at that time to **tell** you what he said, because you
5.27 Then return and **tell** us what he said to you.
5.30 Go and **tell** them to return to their tents.
6.21 Then **tell** them, 'We were slaves of the king of Egypt,
7.17 "Do not **tell** yourselves that these peoples outnumber
10.11 Then he **told** me to go and lead you, so that you
12.21 you may eat the meat at home, as I have **told** you.
13. 5 dreams or prophet that **tells** you to rebel against the Lord,
17.10 their decision, and you are to do exactly as they **tell** you.
18.18 I will **tell** him what to say,
18.18 and he will **tell** the people everything I command.
18.21 may wonder how you can **tell** when a prophet's message does
19. 8 enlarges your territory, as he **told** your ancestors he would,
24. 8 be sure to do exactly what the levitical priests **tell** you;
31. 2 besides this, the Lord has **told** me that I will not cross
31. 5 and you are to treat them exactly as I have **told** you.
31.28 officials before me, so that I can **tell** them these things;
32. 3 of the Lord, and his people will **tell** of his greatness.
32. 7 ask your fathers to **tell** you what happened,
32. 7 ask the old men to **tell** of the past.
33.27 enemies as you advanced, and **told** you to destroy them all.
Josh 1. 3 As I **told** Moses, I have given you and all my people
1.13 how Moses, the Lord's servant, **told** you that the Lord your
1.16 will do everything you have **told** us and will go wherever you
2.14 If you do not **tell** anyone what we have been doing, we
2.20 However, if you **tell** anyone what we have been doing,
2.23 They **told** him everything that had happened, [24] and then said,
3. 6 Then he **told** the priests to take the Covenant Box and go
3. 8 **Tell** the priests carrying the Covenant Box that when they
4. 3 **Tell** them to carry these stones with them and to put them
4. 7 mean to you, [7] you will **tell** them that the water of the
4.10 done that the Lord ordered Joshua to **tell** the people to do.
4.12 the rest of the people, as Moses had **told** them to do.
4.15 Then the Lord **told** Joshua [16] to command the priests
4.22 these stones mean, [22] you will **tell** them about the time
4.23 **Tell** them that the Lord your God dried up the water of
5. 2 Then the Lord **told** Joshua, "Make some knives out of flint
5.15 of the Lord's army **told** him, "Take your sandals off;
5.15 And Joshua did as he was **told.**
6.11 So he **told** this group of men to take the Lord's Covenant
6.22 Joshua then **told** the two men who had served as spies,
7.13 **Tell** them to be ready tomorrow, because I, the Lord God of
7.14 So **tell** them that in the morning they will be brought forward,
7.19 said to him, "My son, **tell** the truth here before the Lord,
7.19 **Tell** me now what you have done.
8.18 Joshua did as he was **told,** [19] and as soon as he lifted
8.27 and goods captured in the city, as the Lord had **told** Joshua.
9. 9 Then they **told** him this story:
9.11 that live in our land **told** us to get some food ready
9.11 We were **told** to put ourselves at your service and ask you
9.22 did you deceive us and **tell** us that you were from far
10.17 Someone found them, and Joshua was **told** where they were hiding.
13.14 As the Lord had **told** Moses, they were to receive as their
13.33 He **told** them that their possession was to be a share of
14.12 We **told** you then that the race of giants called the Anakim
20. 1 Then the Lord **told** Joshua [2] to say to the people of Israel,
20. 2 cities of refuge that I commanded Moses to **tell** you about.
22.11 The rest of the people of Israel were **told,** "Listen!
Judg 2. 2 But you have not done what I **told** you.
2. 3 So I **tell** you now that I will not drive these people
3.18 given him the gifts, he **told** the men who had carried them
4.20 Then he **told** her, "Stand at the door of the tent, and
5.10 **Tell** of it, you that ride on white donkeys, sitting on saddles,
5.11 crowds round the wells are **telling** of the Lord's victories,
5.29 ladies answered her, and she **told** herself over and over,
6.10 I **told** you that I am the Lord your God and that
6.13 wonderful things that our fathers **told** us the Lord used to
6.25 That night the Lord **told** Gideon, "Take your father's
6.27 ten of his servants and did what the Lord had **told** him.
7. 4 If I **tell** you a man should go with you, he will
7. 4 If I **tell** you a man should not go with you, he
7. 7 **Tell** everyone else to go home."
7.13 Gideon arrived, he heard a man **telling** a friend about a dream.
7.17 He **told** them, "When I get to the edge of the camp,
9. 1 his mother's relatives lived, and **told** them [2] to ask the men
9.25 Abimelech was **told** about this.
9.47 Abimelech was **told** that they had gathered there, [48] so
9.48 He **told** his men to be quick and do the same thing.
11.38 He **told** her to go and sent her away for two months.
12. 6 If he said, "No," [6] they would **tell** him to say "Shibboleth."
13. 6 him where he came from, and he didn't **tell** me his name.
13. 7 But he did **tell** me that I would become pregnant and have
Judg 13. 7 He **told** me not to drink any wine or beer, or eat
13. 8 come back to us and **tell** us what we must do with
13.13 wife must be sure to do everything that I have **told** her.
13.14 She must do everything that I have **told** her."
13.17 Manoah replied, "**Tell** us your name, so that we can
13.23 not have shown us all this or **told** us such things now."
14. 6 But he did not **tell** his parents what he had done.
14. 9 it, but Samson did not **tell** them that he had taken the
14.12 fine clothes that you can't **tell** me its meaning before the
14.12 "**Tell** us your riddle," they said.
14.15 "Trick your husband into **telling** us what the riddle means.
14.16 my friends a riddle and didn't **tell** me what it means!"
14.16 He said, "Look, I haven't even **told** my father and mother.
14.16 Why should I **tell** you?"
14.17 on the seventh day he **told** her what the riddle meant, for
14.17 Then she **told** the Philistines.
15. 7 Samson **told** them, "So this is how you act!
16. 5 and said, "Trick Samson into **telling** you why he is so
16. 6 Delilah said to Samson, "Please **tell** me what makes you so strong.
16.10 Please **tell** me how someone could tie you up."
16.13 **Tell** me how someone could tie you up."
16.15 and you still haven't **told** me what makes you so strong."
20. 3 The Israelites asked, "**Tell** us, how was this crime committed?"
20.39 They **told** themselves, "Yes, we've beaten them just as we did
Ruth 2.19 So Ruth **told** Naomi that she had been working in a field
2.21 said, "Best of all, he **told** me to keep picking up corn
3. 4 He will **tell** you what to do."
3. 6 and did just what her mother-in-law had **told** her.
3.16 Ruth **told** her everything that Boaz had done for her.
3.17 She added, "He **told** me I must not come back to you
4.17 They **told** everyone, "A son has been born to Naomi!"
1 Sam 1.22 She **told** her husband, "As soon as the child is weaned, I
2.23 Everybody **tells** me about the evil you are doing.
3.13 I have already **told** him that I am going to punish his
3.15 He was afraid to **tell** Eli about the vision.
3.17 "What did the Lord **tell** you?"
3.17 you severely if you don't **tell** me everything he said."
3.18 So Samuel **told** him everything;
4.14 The man hurried to Eli to **tell** him the news.
6.10 They did what they were **told:**
8.10 Samuel **told** the people who were asking him for a king
8.21 to everything they said and then went and **told** the Lord.
8.22 Then Samuel **told** all the men of Israel to go back home.
9. 6 him, and maybe he can **tell** us where we can find the
9. 8 that, and then he will **tell** us where we can find them."
9.17 Lord said to him, "This is the man I **told** you about.
9.18 the gate, and asked, "**Tell** me, where does the seer live?"
9.23 of meat I gave you, which I **told** you to set aside."
9.27 town, Samuel said to Saul, "**Tell** the servant to go on ahead
9.27 here a minute, and I will **tell** you what God has said."
10. 2 They will **tell** you that the donkeys you were looking for
10. 8 there seven days until I come and **tell** you what to do."
10. 9 And everything Samuel had **told** him happened that day.
10.15 "And what did he **tell** you?"
10.16 "He **told** us that the animals had been found," Saul
10.16 answered—but he did not **tell** his uncle what Samuel had said
11. 4 Saul lived, and when they **told** the news, the people started
11. 5 They **told** him what the messengers from Jabesh had reported.
11. 9 to the messengers from Jabesh, "**Tell** your people that
13. 4 All the Israelites were **told** that Saul had killed the
14. 1 But Jonathan did not **tell** his father Saul, [2] who was camping
14. 9 If they **tell** us to wait for them to come to us,
14.10 But if they **tell** us to go to them, then we will,
14.12 We have something to **tell** you!"
14.33 Saul was **told,** "Look, the people are sinning against
14.34 "Go among the people and **tell** them all to bring their
15.16 Samuel ordered, "and I will **tell** you what the Lord said to
15.16 "**Tell** me," Saul said.
15.18 He **told** you to fight until you had killed them all.
15.20 "I went out as he **told** me to, brought back King Agag,
16. 3 Jesse to the sacrifice, and I will **tell** you what to do.
16. 3 You will anoint as king the man I **tell** you to."
16. 4 Samuel did what the Lord **told** him to do and went to
16. 5 He also **told** Jesse and his sons to purify themselves, and he
16.11 "**Tell** him to come here," Samuel said.
17.20 sheep, took the food, and went as Jesse had **told** him to.
17.27 They **told** him what would be done for the man who killed
17.31 what David had said, and they **told** Saul, who sent for him.
18.22 speak privately to David and **tell** him, "The king is pleased
18.23 So they **told** David this, and he answered, "It's a
18.24 The officials **told** Saul what David had said, [25] and
18.25 Saul what David had said, [25] and Saul ordered them to **tell** David:
19. 1 Saul **told** his son Jonathan and all his officials that he
19. 7 So Jonathan called David and **told** him everything;
19.14 men came to get David, Michal **told** them that he was ill.
19.18 to Samuel in Ramah and **told** him everything that Saul had
19.19 Saul was **told** that David was in Naioth in Ramah, [20] so
19.22 Samuel and David were and was **told** that they were at Naioth.
20. 2 My father **tells** me everything he does, important or not, and
20. 6 I am not at table, **tell** him that I begged your permission
20. 9 father was determined to harm you, wouldn't I **tell** you?"
20.21 Then I will **tell** my servant to go and find them.
20.21 And if I **tell** him, 'Look, the arrows are on this side
20.22 But if I **tell** him, 'The arrows are on the other side
20.40 weapons to the boy and **told** him to take them back to
21. 2 "He **told** me not to let anyone know what he sent me
21. 2 for my men, I have **told** them to meet me at a
22. 6 He was **told** that David and his men had been found, [7] and
22. 8 Not one of you **told** me that my own son had made
22. 8 is concerned about me or **tells** me that David, one of my
22.17 with David and did not **tell** me that he had run away,

1 Sam 22.21 He **told** him how Saul had slaughtered the priests of the Lord.
22.22 that day, I knew that he would be sure to **tell** Saul.
23. 7 Saul was **told** that David had gone to Keilah, and he said,
24. 1 fighting the Philistines, he was **told** that David was in the
24. 4 The Lord has **told** you that he would put your enemy in
24.10 Some of my men **told** me to kill you, but I felt
25. 8 Just ask them, and they will **tell** you.
25.12 men went back to him and **told** him what Nabal had said.
25.36 so she did not **tell** him anything until the next morning.
25.37 Then, after he had sobered up, she **told** him everything.
26. 1 to Saul at Gibeah and **told** him that David was hiding on
27.10 and David would **tell** him that he had gone to the southern
28. 8 the spirits for me and **tell** me what is going to happen,"
28.10 that you will not be punished for doing this," he **told**
28.15 have called you, for you to **tell** me what I must do."
28.17 The Lord has done to you what he **told** you through me:
31. 9 with them throughout Philistia to **tell** the good news to
2 Sam 1. 4 **"Tell** me what happened," David said.
1. 8 who I was, and I **told** him that I was an Amalekite.
3.19 then went to Hebron to **tell** David what the people of
3.21 Abner **told** David, "I will go now and win all Israel
3.23 his men arrived, he was **told** that Abner had come to King
4.10 to me at Ziklag and **told** me of Saul's death thought he
5.17 The Philistines were **told** that David had been made king
7. 5 said to Nathan, [5] "Go and **tell** my servant David that I say
7. 8 "So **tell** my servant David that I, the Lord Almighty, say
7.17 Nathan **told** David everything that God had revealed to him.
7.27 me, your servant, and have **told** me that you will make my
9. 2 Saul's family named Ziba, and he was **told** to go to David.
11. 5 she was pregnant and sent a message to David to **tell** him.
11.18 sent a report to David **telling** him about the battle, [19] and
11.19 "After you have **told** the king all about the battle,
11.21 the king asks you this, **tell** him, 'Your officer Uriah was
11.22 messenger went to David and **told** him what Joab had commanded
11.25 messenger, "Encourage Joab and **tell** him not to be upset,
11.25 since you never can **tell** who will die in battle.
11.25 **Tell** him to launch a stronger attack on the city and capture
12.18 and David's officials were afraid to **tell** him the news.
12.18 How can we **tell** him that his child is dead?
13.20 He is your half-brother, so don't **tell** anyone about it."
13.30 While they were on their way home, David was **told:**
13.32 You could **tell** by looking at Absalom that he had made up
14. 3 the king and say to him what I **tell** you to say."
14. 3 Then Joab **told** her what to say.
14.18 ask you a question, and you must **tell** me the whole truth."
14.19 indeed your officer Joab who **told** me what to do and what
14.33 Joab went to King David and **told** him what Absalom had said.
15. 2 And after the man had **told** him what tribe he was from,
15.31 David was **told** that Ahithophel had joined Absalom's rebellion,
15.34 returning to the city and **telling** Absalom that you will now
15.35 **tell** them everything you hear in the king's palace.
16.10 curses me because the Lord **told** him to, who has the right
16.11 The Lord **told** him to curse;
17. 6 If not, you **tell** us what to do."
17.15 Then Hushai **told** the priests Zadok and Abiathar what
17.17 would regularly go and **tell** them what was happening,
17.17 and then they would go and **tell** King David.
17.18 one day a boy happened to see them, and he **told** Absalom;
17.21 They **told** him what Ahithophel had planned against him and said,
18.21 Sudanese slave, "Go and **tell** the king what you have seen."
18.25 He called down and **told** the king, and the king said,
18.29 I saw a great commotion, but I couldn't **tell** what it was."
19. 1 Joab was **told** that King David was weeping and mourning
19.13 David also **told** them to say to Amasa, "You are my relative.
19.26 I **told** my servant to saddle my donkey so that I could
20.16 **Tell** Joab to come here;
24.11 Gad, David's prophet, "Go and **tell** David that I am giving
24.13 up, [13] Gad went to him, **told** him what the Lord had said,
24.13 Now think it over, and **tell** me what answer to take back
24.19 David obeyed the Lord's command and went as Gad had **told** him.
1 Kgs 1.20 are looking to you to **tell** them who is to succeed you
1.23 The king was **told** that the prophet was there, and Nathan
1.27 all this and not even **tell** your officials who is to succeed
1.51 King Solomon was **told** that Adonijah was afraid of him
2. 4 promise he made when he **told** me that my descendants would
2.30 went back to the king and **told** him what Joab had said.
8.25 to my father when you **told** him that there would always be
8.53 your own people, as you **told** them through your servant Moses
9. 5 your father David when I **told** him that Israel would always
10. 7 wisdom and wealth are much greater than what I was **told.**
12.10 They replied, "This is what you should **tell** them:
12.11 **Tell** them, 'My father placed heavy burdens on you;
12.22 But God **told** the prophet Shemaiah [23] to give this
13.11 His sons came and **told** him what the prophet from Judah had
13.13 him the road [13] and he **told** them to saddle his donkey for
13.18 the Lord's command an angel **told** me to take you home with
14. 3 is going to happen to our son, and he will **tell** you."
14. 5 The Lord had **told** him that Jeroboam's wife was coming to
14. 5 And the Lord **told** Ahijah what to say.
14. 7 Go and **tell** Jeroboam that this is what the Lord, the God
17. 1 Israel, whom I serve, I **tell** you that there will be no
17.15 and did as Elijah had **told** her, and all of them had
18. 8 "Go and **tell** your master the king that I am here."
18.11 you want me to go and **tell** him that you are here?
18.12 Then, when I **tell** Ahab that you are here, and he can't
18.14 order me to go and **tell** the king that you are here?
18.16 went to King Ahab and **told** him, and Ahab set off to
18.43 Seven times in all Elijah **told** him to go and look.
18.44 "Go to King Ahab and **tell** him to get into his chariot
19. 1 King Ahab **told** his wife Jezebel everything that Elijah had

1 Kgs 20. 4 **"Tell** my lord, King Benhadad, that I agree;
20. 9 Ahab replied to Benhadad's messengers, **"Tell** my lord the
20.11 King Ahab answered, **"Tell** King Benhadad that a real
21. 6 one for it, but he **told** me that I couldn't have it!"
21.19 **Tell** him that I, the Lord, say to him, 'After murdering
21.19 **Tell** him that this is what I say:
22. 9 in a court official and **told** him to go and fetch Micaiah
22.14 Lord I promise that I will say what he **tells** me to!"
22.16 speak to me in the name of the Lord, **tell** the truth!
22.16 How many times do I have to **tell** you that?"
22.18 said to Jehoshaphat, "Didn't I **tell** you that he never
22.21 replied, 'I will go and make all Ahab's prophets **tell** lies.'
22.27 **Tell** them to throw him in prison and to put him on
2 Kgs 1. 4 **Tell** the king that the Lord says, 'You will not recover
1 6 met by a man who **told** us to come back
1. 6 and **tell** you that the Lord says
2. 9 There, Elijah said to Elisha, **"Tell** me what you want me
2.18 and he said to them, "Didn't I **tell** you not to go?"
4. 2 **"Tell** me, what have you got at home?"
4. 3 and borrow as many empty jars as you can," Elisha **told** her.
4.12 He **told** his servant Gehazi to go and call the woman.
4.15 **"Tell** her to come here," Elisha ordered.
4.24 as it can, and don't slow down, unless I **tell** you to."
4.26 She **told** Gehazi that everything was all right, [27] but when
4.27 And the Lord has not **told** me a thing about it."
4.28 Didn't I **tell** you not to raise my hopes?"
4.36 Elisha called Gehazi and **told** him to call the boy's mother.
4.38 a group of prophets, he **told** his servant to put a big
4.42 Elisha **told** his servant to feed the group of prophets
5. 4 went to the king and **told** him what the girl had said.
5.10 sent a servant out to **tell** him to go and wash himself
5.13 "Sir, if the prophet had **told** you to do something difficult,
5.22 my master sent me to **tell** you that just now two members
6.12 The prophet Elisha **tells** the king of Israel what you say
6.13 When he was **told** that Elisha was in Dothan, [14] he sent a
6.29 The next day I **told** her that we would eat her son,
7. 9 we wait until morning to **tell** it, we are sure to be
7. 9 Let's go at once and **tell** the king's officers!"
7.12 officials, "I'll **tell** you what the Syrians are planning!
7.18 Elisha had **told** the king that by that time the following
8. 1 Now Elisha had **told** the woman who lived in Shunem, whose
8. 5 While Gehazi was **telling** the king how Elisha had brought a
8. 6 king called an official and **told** him to give back to her
8. 7 When the king was **told** that Elisha was there, [8] he said to
8.10 but go to him and **tell** him that he will recover."
8.14 **told** me that you would certainly get well," Hazael answered.
9.12 **"Tell** us what he said!"
9.12 "He **told** me that the Lord proclaims:
10. 8 When Jehu was **told** that the heads of Ahab's descendants
10.17 This is what the Lord had **told** Elijah would happen.
11. 4 of the palace guards, and **told** them to come to the Temple,
13.16 Jehoash got them, [16] and Elisha **told** him to get ready to shoot.
13.18 Then Elisha **told** the king to take the other arrows and
17.26 The emperor of Assyria was **told** that the people he had
18.19 One of the Assyrian officials **told** them that the emperor
18.22 went on, "Or will you **tell** me that you are relying on
18.22 that Hezekiah destroyed, when he **told** the people of Judah
18.25 The Lord himself **told** me to attack it and destroy it."
18.26 Eliakim, Shebna, and Joah **told** the official, "Speak Aramaic
18.28 "Listen to what the emperor of Assyria is **telling** you!
18.36 people kept quiet, just as King Hezekiah had **told** them to;
19. 3 This is the message which he **told** them to give Isaiah:
19. 6 "The Lord **tells** you not to let the Assyrians frighten you
19.10 you are trusting in has **told** you that you will not fall
19.20 Then Isaiah sent a message **telling** King Hezekiah that
20. 1 said to him, "The Lord **tells** you that you are to put
20. 4 of the palace the Lord **told** him [5] to go back to Hezekiah,
20. 7 Then Isaiah **told** the king's attendants to put on his boil
22. 5 **Tell** him to give the money to the men who are in
22. 8 order to Hilkiah, and Hilkiah **told** him that he had found the
22.15 what had happened, [15] and she **told** them to go back to the
1 Chr 10. 9 with them throughout Philistia to **tell** the good news to
11. 5 The Jebusites **told** David he would never get inside the city,
13. 2 Levites in their towns, and **tell** them to assemble here with us.
16. 8 **tell** the nations what he has done.
16. 9 **tell** the wonderful things he has done.
16.31 **Tell** the nations that the Lord is king.
17. 4 said to Nathan, [4] "Go and **tell** my servant David that I say
17. 7 "So **tell** my servant David that I, the Lord Almighty, say
17.15 Nathan **told** David everything that God had revealed to him.
17.25 me, your servant, and have **told** me that you will make my
21.10 Gad, David's prophet, [10] "Go and **tell** David that I am
21.11 Gad went to David, **told** him what the Lord had said, and
21.18 The angel of the Lord **told** Gad to command David to go
21.19 obeyed the Lord's command and went, as Gad had **told** him to.
21.27 The Lord **told** the angel to put his sword away, and the
22. 8 But the Lord **told** me that I had killed too many people
29.30 The records **tell** how he ruled, how powerful he was, and
2 Chr 6.16 to my father when you **told** him that there would always be
7.18 your father David when I **told** him that Israel would always
9. 6 did not believe what they **told** me until I came and saw
10.10 They replied, "This is what you should **tell** them:
10.11 **Tell** them, 'My father placed heavy burdens on you;
11. 2 But the Lord **told** the prophet Shemaiah [3] to give this
18. 8 in a court official and **told** him to go and fetch Micaiah
18.13 the living Lord, I will say what my God **tells** me to!"
18.15 speak to me in the name of the Lord, **tell** the truth!
18.15 How many times do I have to **tell** you that?"
18.17 Ahab said to Jehoshaphat, "I **told** you that he never
18.21 replied, 'I will go and make all Ahab's prophets **tell** lies.'
18.26 **Tell** them to throw him in prison and to put him on

2 Chr 20.20 Believe what his prophets **tell** you, and you will succeed."
24. 5 He **told** them to act promptly, but the Levites delayed, [6]so
25.10 Amaziah sent the hired troops away and **told** them to go home.
29.21 The king **told** the priests, who were descendants of Aaron, to
29.30 the leaders of the nation **told** the Levites to sing to the
31. 4 In addition, the king **told** the people of Jerusalem to
32.11 Hezekiah **tells** you that the Lord your God will save you
32.12 shrines and altars and then **told** the people of Judah and
34.23 what had happened, [23]and she **told** them to go back to the
35.21 but to fight my enemies, and God has **told** me to hurry.
Ezra 2.63 The Jewish governor **told** them that they could not eat
5. 9 leaders of the people to **tell** us who had given them
5.15 The emperor **told** him to take them and return them to the
6. 9 the priests in Jerusalem whatever they **tell** you they need:
8.22 our journey, because I had **told** him that our God blesses
9. 1 people of Israel came and **told** me that the people, the
9.11 They **told** us that the land we were going to occupy was
9.12 They **told** us that we were never to intermarry with those
Neh 1. 3 They **told** me that those who had survived and were back in
1. 3 They also **told** me that the walls of Jerusalem were still
1. 8 Remember now what you **told** Moses:
2. 6 would be gone and when I would return, and I **told** him.
2.12 three days [12]I did not **tell** anyone what God had inspired
2.18 And I **told** them how God had been with me and helped
4.19 I **told** the people and their officials and leaders, "The
4.22 During this time I **told** the men in charge that they and
5. 7 people and **told** them, "You are oppressing your brothers!"
6. 6 "Geshem **tells** me that a rumour is going round among the
6.19 deeds Tobiah had done and would **tell** him everything I said.
7. 3 I **told** them not to have the gates of Jerusalem opened in
7. 3 I also **told** them to appoint guards from among the people who
7.65 The Jewish governor **told** them that they could not eat
8. 9 who were explaining the Law **told** all the people, "This day
8.11 about calming the people and **telling** them not to be sad on
9.15 You **told** them to take control of the land which you had
9.20 In your goodness you **told** them what they should do;
9.26 who warned them, who **told** them to turn back to you.
Esth 1.12 But when the servants **told** Queen Vashti of the king's command,
1.18 queen's behaviour they will be **telling** their husbands about
2.20 Mordecai had **told** her not to tell anyone, and she obeyed him
2.22 Mordecai learnt about it and **told** Queen Esther,
2.22 who then **told** the king what Mordecai had found
3. 4 So they **told** Haman about this, wondering if he would tolerate
3. 8 So Haman **told** the king, "There is a certain race of
3.11 The king **told** him, "The people and their money are yours;
4. 4 servant-girls and eunuchs **told** her what Mordecai was doing,
4. 5 servant by the king, and **told** him to go to Mordecai and
4. 7 Mordecai **told** him everything that had happened to him and
4.17 left and did everything that Esther had **told** him to do.
5. 3 **"Tell** me what you want, and you shall have it—even if
5. 6 wine the king asked her, **"Tell** me what you want, and you
5. 8 At that time I will **tell** you what I want."
6.13 He **told** his wife and all his friends everything that had
7. 2 **Tell** me and you shall have it.
8. 1 Esther **told** the king that Mordecai was related to her, and
9.12 **Tell** me what else you want, and you shall have it."
9.21 far, throughout the Persian Empire, [21]**telling** them to
9.22 They were **told** to observe these days with feasts and parties,
Job 1.15 I am the only one who escaped to **tell** you."
1.16 I am the only one who escaped to **tell** you."
1.17 I am the only one who escaped to **tell** you."
1.19 I am the only one who escaped to **tell** you."
3. 8 **Tell** the sorcerers to curse that day, those who know how
4.16 I stared, but couldn't **tell** what it was.
6.24 **tell** me my faults.
6.30 I am lying— you think I can't **tell** right from wrong.
10. 2 **Tell** me!
11. 6 He would **tell** you there are many sides to wisdom;
14.21 he never knows it, nor is he **told** when they are disgraced.
21.14 The wicked **tell** God to leave them alone;
27. 4 never say anything evil, my tongue will never **tell** a lie.
31.37 I would **tell** God everything I have done, and hold my
32. 6 are old, so I was afraid to **tell** you what I think.
32. 7 I **told** myself that you ought to speak, that you older men
32.10 let me **tell** you what I think.
32.17 will give my own answer now and **tell** you what I think.
33.12 But I **tell** you, Job, you are wrong.
34.33 **tell** us now what you think.
36.23 No one can **tell** God what to do or accuse him of
38. 4 If you know so much, **tell** me about it.
38.11 I **told** it, "So far and no farther!
38.36 Who **tells** the ibis when the Nile will flood,
38.36 or who **tells** the cock that rain will fall?
41.12 Let me **tell** you about Leviathan's legs and describe how
42. 4 You **told** me to listen while you spoke and to try to
42. 5 knew only what others had **told** me, but now I have seen
42. 9 did what the Lord had **told** them to do, and the Lord
Ps 9. 1 I will **tell** of all the wonderful things you have done.
9.11 **Tell** every nation what he has done!
9.14 the people of Jerusalem and **tell** them all the things for
22.22 I will **tell** my people what you have done;
22.31 People not yet born will be **told:**
26. 7 hymn of thanksgiving and **tell** of all your wonderful deeds.
39. 4 **Tell** me how soon my life will end."
40. 9 all your people, Lord, I **told** the good news that you save
40. 9 You know that I will never stop **telling** it.
41. 6 bad news about me and then go out and **tell** it everywhere.
44. 1 God— our ancestors have **told** us about it, about the great
48.13 the fortresses, so that you may **tell** the next generation:
50.19 you never hesitate to **tell** lies.
58. 3 they **tell** lies from the day they are born.
Ps 62. 8 **Tell** him all your troubles, for he is our refuge.
64. 9 think about what God has done and **tell** about his deeds.
66.16 honour God, and I will **tell** you what he has done for
69. 4 My enemies **tell** lies against me;
71.15 I will **tell** of your goodness;
71.17 since I was young, and I still **tell** of your wonderful acts.
75. 1 how great you are and **tell** of the wonderful things you have
75. 4 I **tell** the wicked not to be arrogant;
75. 5 I **tell** them to stop their boasting."
78. 3 we have heard and known, things that our fathers **told** us.
78. 4 we will **tell** the next generation about the Lord's power
78. 6 might learn them and in turn should **tell** their children.
90. 3 You **tell** man to return to what he was;
105. 1 **tell** the nations what he has done.
105. 2 **tell** of the wonderful things he has done.
106. 2 Who can **tell** all the great things he has done?
107.22 and with songs of joy must **tell** all that he has done.
109. 2 They **tell** lies about me [3]and they say evil things about me,
119. 4 given us your laws and **told** us to obey them faithfully.
129. 1 Israel, **tell** us how your enemies have persecuted you ever
137. 3 Those who captured us **told** us to sing;
137. 3 they **told** us to entertain them:
142. 2 I **tell** him all my troubles.
144. 8 power of foreigners, [8]who never **tell** the truth and lie even
144.11 power of foreigners, who never **tell** the truth and lie even
145. 7 They will **tell** about all your goodness
145.11 of your royal power and **tell** of your might, [12]so that
Prov 1. 8 Pay attention to what your father and mother **tell** you, my
2. 1 you, my son, and never forget what I **tell** you to do.
3. 1 Always remember what I **tell** you to do.
3.28 Never **tell** your neighbour to wait until tomorrow if you
4. 4 Do as I **tell** you, and you will live.
4.10 Take seriously what I am **telling** you, and you will live a
6.20 Do what your father **tells** you, my son, and never forget
7. 1 say, my son, and never forget what I **tell** you to do.
8. 6 all I **tell** you is right.
9. 9 Whatever you **tell** a righteous man will add to his knowledge.
12. 1 Anyone who loves knowledge wants to be **told** when he is wrong.
12.17 When you **tell** the truth, justice is done, but lies lead
17. 7 Respected people do not **tell** lies, and fools have nothing
19. 5 If you **tell** lies in court, you will be punished—there will
20.11 you can **tell** if he is honest and good.
22.19 that is why I am going to **tell** them to you now.
25. 7 higher position than to be **told** to give your place to
31. 2 What shall I **tell** you?
31.15 for her family and to **tell** her servant-girls what to do.
Ecc 1.14 done in this world, and I **tell** you, it is all useless.
1.16 I **told** myself, "I have become a great man, far wiser
3.17 I **told** myself, "God is going to judge the righteous and
5. 6 so that you have to **tell** God's priest that you didn't mean
8. 7 is going to happen, and there is no one to **tell** us.
10.14 next, and no one can **tell** us what will happen after we
10.20 A bird might carry the message and **tell** them what you said.
Song 1. 7 **Tell** me, my love, Where will you lead your flock to graze?
5. 8 find my lover, you will **tell** him I am weak from passion.
6. 1 **Tell** us which way your lover went, so that we can help
Is 6. 9 So he **told** me to go and give the people this message:
7. 4 **Tell** him to keep alert, to stay calm, and not to be
8.19 But people will **tell** you to ask for messages from
8.20 listen to mediums—what they **tell** you will do you no good."
12. 4 **Tell** all the nations what he has done!
12. 4 **Tell** them how great he is!
14.32 We will **tell** them that the Lord has established Zion and
16. 3 They say to the people of Judah, **"Tell** us what to do.
19.11 How dare they **tell** the king that they are successors to the
19.12 Perhaps they can **tell** you what plans the Lord Almighty has
20. 2 years earlier the Lord had **told** Isaiah son of Amoz to take
21. 6 and post a sentry, and **tell** him to report what he sees.
21.11 **Tell** me how soon it will end."
22.15 The Sovereign Lord Almighty **told** me to go to Shebna, the
24.14 Those in the west will **tell** how great the Lord is, [15]and
28.23 pay attention to what I am **telling** you.
29.21 of criminals, and those who **tell** lies to keep honest men
30. 8 God **told** me to write down in a book what the people
30.10 They **tell** the prophets to keep quiet.
30.10 **Tell** us what we want to hear.
30.12 "You ignore what I **tell** you and rely on violence and deceit.
35. 4 **Tell** everyone who is discouraged, "Be strong and don't be afraid!
36. 4 The Assyrian official **told** them that the emperor wanted to
36. 7 went on, "Or will you **tell** me that you are relying on
36. 7 that Hezekiah destroyed when he **told** the people of Judah and
36.10 The Lord himself **told** me to attack it and destroy it."
36.13 "Listen to what the emperor of Assyria is **telling** you.
36.21 people kept quiet, just as King Hezekiah had **told** them to;
37. 3 This is the message which he **told** them to give to Isaiah:
37. 6 "The Lord **tells** you not to let the Assyrians frighten you
37.10 you are trusting in has **told** you that you will not fall
37.21 Then Isaiah sent a message **telling** King Hezekiah that in
38. 1 said to him, "The Lord **tells** you that you are to put
38. 6 Isaiah **told** the king to put a paste made of figs on
38.19 Fathers **tell** their children how faithful you are.
39. 5 Isaiah then **told** the king, "The Lord Almighty says that
40. 2 **Tell** them they have suffered long enough and their sins are
40. 9 **Tell** the towns of Judah that their God is coming!
40.13 Can anyone **tell** the Lord what to do?
40.21 Were you not **told** long ago?
41.22 court the events of the past, and **tell** us what they mean.
41.23 **Tell** us what the future holds— then we will know that
41.27 I, the Lord, was the first to **tell** Zion the news;
42. 9 Now I will **tell** you of new things even before they begin
43. 6 I will **tell** the north to let them go and the south

Is	44.26	I **tell** Jerusalem that people will live there again, and the
	45.11	about my children or to **tell** me what I ought to do!
	47.13	zones of the heavens and **tell** you from month to month what
	48. 6	Now I will **tell** you of new things to come, events that
	56. 9	The Lord has **told** the foreign nations to come like wild
	57.11	afraid, so that you **tell** me lies and forget me completely?
	58. 1	**Tell** my people Israel about their sins!
	60. 6	People will **tell** the good news of what the Lord has done!
	62.11	**"Tell** the people of Jerusalem That the Lord is coming to
	63. 7	I will **tell** of the Lord's unfailing love;
	65.13	And so I **tell** you that those who worship and obey me
Jer	1. 7	I send you to, and **tell** them everything I command you to
	1.17	go and **tell** them everything I command you to say.
	2. 1	The Lord **told** me [2]to proclaim this message to everyone
	3.11	Then the Lord **told** me that, even though Israel had
	3.12	He **told** me to go and say to Israel, "Unfaithful Israel,
	3.17	no longer do what their stubborn and evil hearts **tell** them.
	4. 5	**Tell** the people of Judah and Jerusalem to run to the
	4.11	people of Jerusalem will be **told** that a scorching wind is
	4.16	warn the nations and to **tell** Jerusalem that enemies are
	5.10	I will **tell** them to strip away the branches, because those
	5.19	I did all these things, **tell** them, Jeremiah, that just as
	5.20	The Lord says, **"Tell** the descendants of Jacob,
	5.20	**tell** the people of Judah:
	6.10	they laugh at what you **tell** me to say.
	7. 1	He **told** me to stand there and announce what the Lord Almighty,
	7. 9	You steal, murder, commit adultery, **tell** lies under oath,
	7.23	And I **told** them to live as I had commanded them, so
	7.24	their stubborn and evil hearts **told** them to do, and they
	7.28	You will **tell** them that their nation does not obey me,
	8. 4	The Lord **told** me to say to his people, "When someone
	9. 3	They are always ready to **tell** lies;
	9. 8	they always **tell** lies.
	9.12	To whom have you explained it so that he can **tell** others?"
	9.13	They have not obeyed me or done what I **told** them.
	9.18	**"Tell** them to hurry and sing a funeral song for us, until
	9.22	This is what the Lord has **told** me to say."
	10.11	(You people must **tell** them that the gods who did not
	11. 2	**Tell** the people of Judah and of Jerusalem [3]that I, the Lord
	11. 4	I **told** them to obey me and to do everything that I
	11. 4	I **told** them that if they obeyed, they would be my people
	11. 6	Proclaim my message there and **tell** the people to listen to
	11.21	wanted me killed, and they **told** me that they would kill me
	13. 1	The Lord **told** me to go and buy myself some linen shorts
	13. 1	but he **told** me not to put them in water.
	13. 6	Some time later the Lord **told** me to go back to the
	13.12	God said to me, "Jeremiah, **tell** the people of Israel that
	13.13	Then **tell** them that I, the Lord, am going to fill the
	13.18	The Lord said to me, **"Tell** the king and his mother to
	14.13	know that the prophets are **telling** the people that there
	14.15	I, the Lord, **tell** you what I am going to do to
	14.17	The Lord commanded me to **tell** the people about my sorrow
	15. 2	ask you where they should go, **tell** them that I have said:
	16. 3	I will **tell** you what is going to happen to the children
	16.10	"When you **tell** them all this, they will ask you why I
	16.11	Then **tell** them that the Lord has said, 'Your ancestors
	17.20	**Tell** the kings and all the people of Judah and everyone
	17.21	**Tell** them that if they love their lives, they must not
	17.24	**"Tell** these people that they must obey all my commands.
	18.11	Now then, **tell** the people of Judah and of Jerusalem that
	18.11	**Tell** them to stop living sinful lives—to change their ways
	19. 1	The Lord **told** me to go and buy a clay jar.
	19. 1	He also **told** me to take some of the elders of the
	19. 3	The Lord **told** me to say, "Kings of Judah and people of
	19.10	Then the Lord **told** me to break the jar in front of
	19.11	gone with me [11]and to **tell** them that the Lord Almighty had
	19.14	court of the Temple and **told** all the people [15]that the
	21. 3	spoke to me, and I **told** the men who had been sent
	21. 4	been sent to me [4]to **tell** Zedekiah that the Lord, the God
	21. 8	Then the Lord **told** me to say to the people, "Listen!
	21.11	The Lord **told** me to give this message to the royal
	22. 1	The Lord **told** me to go to the palace of the king
	22. 1	descendant of David, and there **tell** the king, his officials,
	23.14	they commit adultery and **tell** lies;
	23.16	They **tell** you what they have imagined and not what I have
	23.17	And they **tell** everyone who is stubborn that disaster will
	23.27	that the dreams they **tell** will make my people forget me,
	23.32	am against the prophets who **tell** their dreams that are full
	23.32	They **tell** these dreams and lead my people astray with their
	23.33	you are to **tell** him, 'You are a burden to the Lord,
	23.38	words 'the Lord's burden,' then **tell** them that [39]I will
	25. 3	me, and I have never failed to **tell** you what he said.
	25. 5	They **told** you to turn from your wicked way of life and
	25. 6	They **told** you not to worship and serve other gods and not
	25.27	the Lord said to me, **"Tell** the people that I, the Lord
	25.28	and drink from it, then **tell** them that the Lord Almighty has
	25.30	You must **tell** these people,
	26. 4	The Lord **told** me to say to the people, "I, the Lord,
	26.18	the prophet Micah of Moresheth **told** all the people that the
	27. 1	king of Judah, the Lord **told** me [2]to make myself a yoke
	27. 3	Then the Lord **told** me to send a message to the kings
	27. 4	Almighty, the God of Israel, **told** me to command them
	27. 4	to **tell** their kings that the Lord
	27. 9	They all **tell** you not to submit to the king of Babylonia.
	27.14	listen to the prophets who **tell** you not to surrender to him.
	27.16	Then I **told** the priests and the people that the Lord had
	28. 1	and of the people he **told** me [2]that the Lord Almighty, the
	28.12	time after this the Lord **told** me [13]to go and say to
	28.15	Then I **told** Hananiah this, and added, "Listen,
	28.16	will die because you have **told** the people to rebel against
	29.28	must be stopped because he **told** the people in Babylonia that
Jer	29.30	me, [30]and then the Lord **told** me [31-32]to send to all
	29.31	do for my people, because he **told** them to rebel against me.
	30. 2	book everything that I have **told** you, [3]because the time is
	32. 6	The Lord **told** me [7]that Hanamel, my uncle Shallum's son,
	33. 3	I will **tell** you wonderful and marvellous things that you
	34. 2	Lord, the God of Israel, **told** me to go and say to
	34.13	Lord, [13]the God of Israel, **told** me to say to the people:
	34.13	I **told** them that [14]every seven years they were to set free
	35. 6	ancestor Jonadab son of Rechab **told** us that neither we nor
	35. 7	He also **told** us not to build houses or farm the land,
	35.12	Almighty, the God of Israel, **told** me to go and say to
	35.15	the prophets, and they have **told** you to give up your evil
	35.18	Then I **told** the Rechabite clan that the Lord Almighty,
	36. 2	it everything that I have **told** you about Israel and Judah
	36. 2	Write everything that I have **told** you from the time I first
	36. 8	words in the Temple exactly as I had **told** him to do.
	36.13	Micaiah **told** them everything that he had heard Baruch
	36.14	and great-grandson of Cushi) to **tell** Baruch to bring the
	36.17	Then they asked him, **"Tell** us, now, how did you come to
	36.27	dictated to Baruch, the Lord **told** me [28]to take another
	36.29	The Lord **told** me to say to the king, "You have burnt
	37. 6	Lord, the God of Israel, **told** me [7]to say to Zedekiah, "The
	37.19	happened to your prophets who **told** you that the king of
	38. 1	Malchiah heard that I was **telling** the people that [2]the Lord
	38. 3	I was also **telling** them that the Lord had said, "I am
	38.12	He **told** me to put the rags under my arms, so that
	38.14	a question, and I want you to **tell** me the whole truth."
	38.15	I answered, "If I **tell** you the truth, you will put me
	38.17	Then I **told** Zedekiah that the Lord Almighty,
	38.25	promise not to put you to death if you **tell** them everything.
	38.26	Just **tell** them you were begging me not to send you back
	38.27	I told them exactly what the king had **told** me to say.
	39.15	the palace courtyard, the Lord **told** me [16]to tell
	39.16	the Lord told me [16]to **tell** Ebedmelech the Sudanese that
	42. 4	as you have asked, and whatever he says, I will **tell** you.
	42.19	I continued, "The Lord has **told** you people who are left in
	42.21	And now I have **told** you, but you are disobeying
	42.21	everything that the Lord our God sent me to **tell** you.
	43. 1	I finished **telling** the people
	43. 1	everything that the Lord their God had sent me to **tell** them.
	43. 2	did not send you to **tell** us not to go and live
	43.10	Then **tell** them that I, the Lord Almighty, the God of Israel,
	44. 4	my servants the prophets, who **told** you not to do this
	44.16	listen to what you have **told** us in the name of the
	44.24	I **told** all the people, especially the women, what the Lord
	45. 1	Then I **told** him [2]that the Lord, the God of Israel, had
	49. 7	Can their advisers no longer **tell** them what to do?
	49.14	has sent a messenger to **tell** the nations to assemble their
	49.29	Take their camels and **tell** the people, 'Terror is all round you!'
	50. 2	**"Tell** the news to the nations!
	50.28	come to Jerusalem, and they **tell** how the Lord our God took
	50.29	**"Tell** the bowmen to attack Babylon.
	51.10	Let's go and **tell** the people in Jerusalem what the Lord our
	51.27	**Tell** the kingdoms of Ararat, Minni, and Ashkenaz to attack.
	51.31	Messenger after messenger runs to **tell** the king of
	51.61	I **told** Seraiah, "When you get to Babylon, be sure to
Lam	2.14	Your prophets had nothing to **tell** you but lies;
	3.57	You answered me and **told** me not to be afraid.
Ezek	2. 4	I am sending you to **tell** them what I, the Sovereign Lord,
	2. 7	You will **tell** them whatever I tell you to say, whether
	2. 8	"Mortal man, listen to what I **tell** you.
	3. 4	of Israel and say to them whatever I **tell** you to say.
	3.10	pay close attention and remember everything I **tell** you.
	3.11	who are in exile and **tell** them what I, the Sovereign Lord,
	3.27	of speech, you will **tell** them what I, the Sovereign Lord,
	5. 8	I, the Sovereign Lord, am **telling** you that I am your enemy.
	6. 3	**Tell** the mountains of Israel to hear the word of the Lord
	6. 3	I, the Sovereign Lord, am **telling** the mountains, the hills,
	11. 5	of me, and the Lord **told** me to give the people this
	11.16	"Now **tell** your fellow-exiles what I am saying.
	11.17	"So **tell** them what I, the Sovereign Lord, am saying.
	11.25	the vision faded, [25]and I **told** the exiles everything that
	12. 7	I did what the Lord **told** me to do.
	12.10	what you're doing, [10]**tell** them what I, the Sovereign Lord,
	12.11	**Tell** them that what you have done is a sign of what
	12.19	**Tell** the whole nation that this is the message of the
	12.23	Now **tell** them what I, the Sovereign Lord, have to say
	12.23	**Tell** them instead:
	12.28	So **tell** them that I, the Sovereign Lord, am saying:
	13. 2	**Tell** them to listen to the word of the Lord."
	13. 7	I **tell** them:
	13.11	**Tell** the prophets that their wall is going to fall down.
	13.15	Then I will **tell** you that the wall is gone and so
	13.18	Denounce them [18]and **tell** them what the Sovereign Lord is
	13.19	So you **tell** lies to my people, and they believe you."
	14. 4	"Now speak to them and **tell** them what I, the Sovereign Lord,
	14. 6	"Now then, **tell** the Israelites what I, the Sovereign Lord,
	16. 3	**Tell** Jerusalem what the Sovereign Lord is saying to her:
	17. 2	"Mortal man," he said, **"tell** the Israelites a parable
	17.12	**Tell** them that the king of Babylonia came to Jerusalem and
	18.30	I, the Sovereign Lord, am **telling** you Israelites that I will
	19. 1	The Lord **told** me to sing this song of sorrow for two
	20. 3	"speak to these men and **tell** them that the Sovereign Lord
	20. 5	**Tell** them what I am saying.
	20. 5	I revealed myself to them in Egypt and **told** them:
	20. 7	I **told** them to throw away the disgusting idols they loved
	20.27	mortal man, **tell** the Israelites what I, the Sovereign Lord,
	20.30	Now **tell** the Israelites what I, the Sovereign Lord, am
	20.47	**Tell** the southern forest to hear what the Sovereign Lord is saying:
	21. 7	you why you are groaning, **tell** them it is because of the
	21. 9	**Tell** the people what I, the Lord, am saying:

Ezek 21.22 It **tells** him to go and set up battering-rams, to shout the
22. 3 **Tell** the city what I, the Sovereign Lord, am saying:
22. 9 Some of your people **tell** lies about others in order to
22.19 I, the Sovereign Lord, am **telling** them that they are just as
22.24 "**tell** the Israelites that their land is unholy,
24. 3 **Tell** my rebellious people this parable that I, the Sovereign Lord,
24.18 died, and the next day I did as I had been **told.**
24.20 Lord spoke to me and **told** me [21] to give you Israelites this
24.26 who escapes the destruction will come and **tell** you about it.
25. 3 **Tell** them to listen to what I, the Sovereign Lord, am
27. 3 **Tell** her what the Sovereign Lord is saying:
28. 2 "Mortal man," he said, "**tell** the ruler of Tyre what I,
28.12 **Tell** him what I, the Sovereign Lord, am saying:
28.22 **Tell** the people there what I, the Sovereign Lord, say about them:
29. 2 **Tell** him how he and all the land of Egypt will be
29. 3 is what the Sovereign Lord is **telling** the king of Egypt:
29. 8 I, the Sovereign Lord, am **telling** you that I will get men
31.10 I, the Sovereign Lord, will **tell** you what is going to happen
33. 2 "Mortal man," he said, "**tell** your people what happens
33.11 **Tell** them that as surely as I, the Sovereign Lord, am
33.12 "Now, mortal man, **tell** the Israelites that when a good man sins,
33.21 from Jerusalem came and **told** me that the city had fallen.
33.25 "**Tell** them what I, the Sovereign Lord, am saying:
33.27 "**Tell** them that I, the Sovereign Lord, warn them that
33.31 to say, but they don't do what you **tell** them to do.
34. 2 Prophesy to them, and **tell** them what I, the Sovereign Lord,
34. 7 "Now, you shepherds, listen to what I, the Lord, am **telling** you.
34.11 "I, the Sovereign Lord, **tell** you that I myself will
34.17 flock, I, the Sovereign Lord, **tell** you that I will judge
34.20 now, I, the Sovereign Lord, **tell** you that I will judge
35. 3 **Tell** the people what I, the Sovereign Lord, am saying:
36. 1 the mountains of Israel and **tell** them to listen to the
36. 6 **tell** the mountains, hills, brooks, and valleys
37. 4 **Tell** these dry bones to listen to the word of the Lord.
37. 5 **Tell** them that I, the Sovereign Lord, am saying to them:
37. 7 So I prophesied as I had been **told.**
37. 9 **Tell** the wind that the Sovereign Lord commands it to come
37.10 So I prophesied as I had been **told.**
37.12 my people Israel and **tell** them that I, the Sovereign Lord,
37.18 your people ask you to **tell** them what this means,
37.19 **tell** them that I, the Sovereign Lord,
37.21 Then **tell** them that I, the Sovereign Lord, am going to
38. 3 Denounce him, [3] and **tell** him that I, the Sovereign Lord, am
38. 7 **Tell** him to get ready and have all his troops ready at
38.14 Sovereign Lord sent me to **tell** Gog what he was saying to
39. 1 of Meshech and Tubal, and **tell** him that I am his enemy.
40. 4 You are to **tell** the people of Israel everything you see."
40.45 The man **told** me that the room which faced south was for
43.10 the Lord continued, "Mortal man, **tell** the people of Israel
43.18 Lord said to me, "Mortal man, listen to what I **tell** you.
44. 5 I am going to **tell** you the rules and regulations for the
44. 6 "**Tell** those rebellious people of Israel that I, the Sovereign Lord,
45. 9 I, the Sovereign Lord, am **telling** you this.
46.24 The man **told** me, "These are the kitchens where the
47. 3 downstream to the east and **told** me to wade through the
Dan 2. 4 **Tell** us your dream, and we will explain it to you."
2. 5 must tell me the dream and then **tell** me what it means.
2. 6 But if you can **tell** me both the dream and its meaning,
2. 6 Now then, **tell** me what the dream was and what it means."
2. 7 "If Your Majesty will only **tell** us what the dream was, we
2. 9 of you the same punishment if you don't **tell** me the dream.
2. 9 **Tell** me what the dream was, and then
2. 9 I will know that you can also **tell** me what it means."
2.10 of the earth who can **tell** Your Majesty what you want to
2.15 So Arioch **told** Daniel what had happened.
2.16 time, so that he could **tell** the king what the dream meant.
2.17 Then Daniel went home and **told** his friends Hananiah,
2.18 He **told** them to pray to the God of heaven for mercy
2.23 answered my prayer and shown us what to **tell** the king."
2.24 to the king, and I will **tell** him what his dream means."
2.25 into King Nebuchadnezzar's presence and **told** the king, "I
2.25 the Jewish exiles, who can **tell** Your Majesty the meaning of
2.26 also called Belteshazzar), "Can you **tell** me what I dreamt
2.27 fortune-teller, or astrologer who can **tell** you that.
2.28 Now I will **tell** you the dream, the vision you had while
2.36 Now I will **tell** Your Majesty what it means.
2.45 The great God is **telling** Your Majesty what will happen in
2.45 I have **told** you exactly what you dreamt, and have given you
4. 6 to me so that they could **tell** me what the dream meant.
4. 7 were brought in, and I **told** them my dream, but they could
4. 8 gods is in him, so I **told** him what I had dreamt.
4. 9 **Tell** me what it means.
4.18 "Now, Belteshazzar, **tell** me what it means.
4.18 of my royal advisers could **tell** me, but you can, because the
5. 7 can read this writing and **tell** me what it means will be
5. 8 them could read the writing or **tell** the king what it meant.
5.12 Belteshazzar, and he will **tell** you what all this means."
5.15 to read this writing and **tell** me what it means, but they
5.16 can read this writing and **tell** me what it means, you will
5.17 Your Majesty what has been written and **tell** you what it means.
7.16 So he **told** me the meaning.
9. 2 according to what the Lord had **told** the prophet Jeremiah.
9.10 Lord our God, when you **told** us to live according to the
9.23 loves you, and so I have come to **tell** you the answer.
10.19 even stronger and said, "Sir, **tell** me what you have to say.
11. 2 And what I am now going to **tell** you is true."
Hos 3. 3 I **told** her that for a long time she would have to
4.12 A stick **tells** them what they want to know!
Joel 1. 3 **Tell** your children about it;
1. 3 they will **tell** their children,
1. 3 who in turn will **tell** the next generation.
Amos 7.16 You **tell** me to stop prophesying, to stop raving against the
Jon 1. 8 "Now then, **tell** us!
1.10 Jonah went on to **tell** them that he was running away from
Mic 1.10 Don't **tell** our enemies in Gath about our defeat;
3. 8 justice and the courage to **tell** the people of Israel what
6. 8 No, the Lord has **told** us what is good.
7. 3 The influential man **tells** them what he wants, and so they
Hab 2. 1 see what the Lord will **tell** me to say and what answer
Zeph 3.13 do no wrong to anyone, **tell** no lies, nor try to deceive.
Hag 1.12 in Babylonia, did what the Lord their God **told** them to do.
2. 2 He **told** Haggai to speak to Zerubbabel, the governor of Judah,
Zech 1. 2 The Lord Almighty **told** Zechariah to say to the people,
1. 4 gave them my message, **telling** them not to live evil,
1.14 comforting words, [14] and the angel **told** me to proclaim what
1.17 The angel also **told** me to proclaim:
2. 4 to the other, "Run and **tell** that young man with the
3. 6 Then the angel **told** Joshua that [7] the Lord Almighty had said:
4. 6 angel **told** me to give Zerubbabel this message from the Lord:
6.12 **Tell** him that the Lord Almighty says, 'The man who is
7. 5 He said, "**Tell** the people of the land and the priests
9.12 I **tell** you now, I will repay you twice over with blessing
13. 3 own father and mother will **tell** him that he must be put
13. 9 I will **tell** them that they are my people, and they will
Mal 1. 1 that the Lord gave Malachi to **tell** the people of Israel.
1. 7 I will **tell** you—by showing contempt for my altar.
Mt 1.24 Mary, as the angel of the Lord had **told** him to do.
2.13 escape to Egypt, and stay there until I **tell** you to leave."
3. 7 to them, "You snakes—who **told** you that you could escape
3. 9 I **tell** you that God can take these stones and make
5.20 I **tell** you, then, that you will be able to enter the
5.21 have heard that people were **told** in the past, 'Do not commit
5.22 But now I **tell** you:
5.26 There you will stay, I **tell** you, until you pay the last
5.28 But now I **tell** you:
5.32 But now I **tell** you:
5.33 also heard that people were **told** in the past, 'Do not break
5.34 But now I **tell** you:
5.39 But now I **tell** you:
5.44 But now I **tell** you:
6.25 "This is why I **tell** you not to be worried about the
6.29 But I **tell** you that not even King Solomon with all his
8. 4 Don't **tell** anyone, but go straight to the priest and let him
8.10 the people following him, "I **tell** you, I have never found
8.32 "Go," Jesus **told** them;
8.33 into the town, where they **told** the whole story and what had
9.30 Jesus spoke sternly to them, "Don't **tell** this to anyone!"
10.18 before rulers and kings, to **tell** the Good News to them
10.27 What I am **telling** you in the dark you must repeat in
11. 3 "**Tell** us," they asked Jesus, "are you the one John said
11. 4 Jesus answered, "Go back and **tell** John what you are hearing
11. 9 **Tell** me, what did you go out to see?
12. 6 I **tell** you that there is something here greater than the Temple.
12.16 ill [16] and gave them orders not to **tell** others about him.
12.31 And so I **tell** you that people can be forgiven any sin
12.41 I **tell** you that there is something here greater than Jonah!
13. 3 He used parables to **tell** them many things.
13.24 Jesus **told** them another parable:
13.30 Then I will **tell** the harvest workers to pull up the weeds
13.31 Jesus **told** them another parable:
13.33 Jesus **told** them still another parable:
13.34 Jesus used parables to **tell** all these things to the crowds;
13.35 I will **tell** them things unknown since the creation of the world."
13.36 came to him and said, "**Tell** us what the parable about the
14. 2 Baptist, who has come back to life," he **told** his officials.
14. 4 time John the Baptist had **told** Herod, "It isn't right for
14.12 then they went and **told** Jesus.
16.18 And so I **tell** you, Peter:
16.20 his disciples not to **tell** anyone that he was the Messiah.
17. 9 Jesus ordered them, "Don't **tell** anyone about this vision you have
17.12 But I **tell** you that Elijah has already come and people
18.10 Their angels in heaven, I **tell** you, are always in the
18.13 When he finds it, I **tell** you, he feels far happier over
18.17 not listen to them, then **tell** the whole thing to the church.
18.18 "And so I **tell** all of you:
18.19 "And I **tell** you more:
18.31 very upset and went to the king and **told** him everything.
19. 9 I **tell** you, then, that any man who divorces his wife,
20. 4 there doing nothing, [4] so he **told** them, 'You also go and
20. 7 then, you also go and work in the vineyard,' he **told** them.
20. 8 evening came, the owner **told** his foreman, 'Call the workers
20.18 "Listen," he **told** them, "we are going up to Jerusalem,
20.23 drink from my cup," Jesus **told** them, "but I do not have
20.31 The crowd scolded them and **told** them to be quiet.
21. 3 And if anyone says anything, **tell** him, 'The Master needs them';
21. 5 "**Tell** the city of Zion, Look, your king is coming to you!
21. 6 the disciples went and did what Jesus had **told** them to do:
21.24 me an answer, I will **tell** you what right I have to
21.27 to them, "Neither will I **tell** you, then, by what right I
21.31 So Jesus said to them, "I **tell** you:
21.43 "And so I **tell** you," added Jesus, "the Kingdom of God
22. 3 He sent his servants to **tell** the invited guests to come to
22.13 Then the king **told** the servants, 'Tie him up hand and foot,
22.16 "Teacher," they said, "we know that you **tell the truth.**
22.17 **Tell** us, then, what do you think?
22.31 haven't you ever read what God has **told** you?
23. 3 So you must obey and follow everything they **tell** you to do;
23.34 And so I **tell** you that I will send you prophets
23.36 I **tell** you indeed:
23.39 From now on, I **tell** you, you will never see me again
24. 2 I **tell** you this:
24. 3 "**Tell** us when all this will be," they asked, "and what

Mt 24.25 I have **told** you this before the time comes.
24.26 "Or, if people should **tell** you, 'Look, he is out in the
24.47 Indeed, I **tell** you, the master will put that servant in
24.48 a bad servant, he will **tell** himself that his master will not
25.40 The King will reply, 'I **tell** you, whenever you did this
25.45 The King will reply, 'I **tell** you, whenever you refused
26.13 what she has done will be **told** in memory of her."
26.18 certain man in the city," he said to them, "and **tell** him:
26.19 did as Jesus had **told** them and prepared the Passover meal.
26.21 the meal Jesus said, "I **tell** you, one of you will betray
26.29 I **tell** you, I will never again drink this wine until the
26.34 Jesus said to Peter, "I **tell** you that before the cock
26.63 **tell** us if you are the Messiah, the Son of God."
26.64 But I **tell** all of you:
26.74 Then Peter said, "I swear that I am **telling the truth!**
26.75 a cock crowed, [75]and Peter remembered what Jesus had **told** him:
27.64 steal the body, and then **tell** the people that he was raised
27.65 "Take a guard," Pilate **told** them;
28. 7 Go quickly now, and **tell** his disciples, 'He has been
28. 7 Remember what I have **told** you."
28. 8 and yet filled with joy, and ran to **tell** his disciples.
28.10 "Go and **tell** my brothers to go to Galilee, and there they
28.11 back to the city and **told** the chief priests everything that
28.15 guards took the money and did what they were **told** to do.
28.16 to the hill in Galilee where Jesus had **told** them to go.
Mk 1. 4 and be baptized," he **told** the people, "and God will forgive
1.30 fever, and as soon as Jesus arrived, he was **told** about her.
1.44 after saying to him, "Listen, don't **tell** anyone about this.
2.11 to the paralysed man, [11]"I **tell** you, get up, pick up your
3. 9 was so large that Jesus **told** his disciples to get a boat
3.12 ordered the evil spirits not to **tell** anyone who he was.
3.14 "I have chosen you to be with me," he **told** them.
4.33 he **told** them as much as they could understand.
5.16 Those who had seen it **told** the people what had happened to
5.19 Instead, he **told** him, "Go back home to your family
5.19 and **tell** them how much the Lord has
5.20 through the Ten Towns, **telling** what Jesus had done for him.
5.33 with fear, knelt at his feet, and **told him the whole truth.**
5.35 came from Jairus' house and **told** him, "Your daughter has died.
5.36 to what they said, but **told** him, "Don't be afraid, only believe."
5.41 "Talitha, koum," which means, "Little girl, I **tell** you to get up!"
5.43 them strict orders not to **tell** anyone, and he said, "Give
6.18 John the Baptist kept **telling** Herod, "It isn't right for you
6.30 and met with Jesus, and **told** him all they had done and
6.38 When they found out, they **told** him, "Five loaves and also
6.39 Jesus then **told** his disciples to make all the people divide
8. 7 gave thanks for these and **told** the disciples to distribute them
8.12 No, I **tell** you!
8.27 the way he asked them, **"Tell** me, who do people say I
8.30 Then Jesus ordered them, "Do not **tell** anyone about me."
8.34 to come with me," he **told** them, "he must forget self,
9. 1 went on to say, "I **tell** you, there are some here who
9. 9 Jesus ordered them, "Don't **tell** anyone what you have seen,
9.13 I **tell** you, however, that Elijah has already come and
9.38 in your name, and we **told** him to stop, because he doesn't
9.39 to stop him," Jesus **told** them, "because no one who performs
10. 2 **"Tell** us," they asked, "does our Law allow a man to
10.29 said to them, "and I **tell** you that anyone who leaves home
10.33 "Listen," he **told** them, "we are going up to Jerusalem
10.48 Many of the people scolded him and **told** him to be quiet.
10.52 "Go," Jesus **told** him, "your faith has made you well."
11. 3 why you are doing that, **tell** him that the Master needs it
11. 6 answered just as Jesus had **told** them, and the men let them
11.23 I assure you that whoever **tells** this hill to get up
11.24 For this reason I **tell** you:
11.29 me an answer, I will **tell** you what right I have to
11.30 **Tell** me, where did John's right to baptize come from:
11.33 to them, "Neither will I **tell** you, then, by what right I
12.12 because they knew that he had **told** this parable against them.
12.14 we know that you **tell the truth,** without worrying about what
12.14 **Tell** us, is it against our Law to pay taxes to the
12.34 answer was, and so he **told** him, "You are not far from
12.43 and said to them, "I **tell** you that this poor widow put
13. 4 **"Tell** us when this will be," they said,
13. 4 "and **tell** us what will happen to show
13. 9 rulers and kings for my sake to **tell** them the Good News.
13.23 I have **told** you everything before the time comes.
13.34 work to do and after **telling** the doorkeeper to keep watch.
14. 9 what she has done will be **told** in memory of her."
14.16 to the city, and found everything just as Jesus had **told** them;
14.18 table eating, Jesus said, "I **tell** you that one of you will
14.25 I **tell** you, I will never again drink this wine until the
14.30 Jesus said to Peter, "I **tell** you that before the cock
14.71 Then Peter said, "I swear that I am **telling the truth!**
15.45 the officer's report, Pilate **told** Joseph he could have the body.
16. 7 there you will see him, just as he **told** you.' "
16. 9 and gave them a brief account of all they had been **told.**
16.10 She went and **told** his companions.
16.13 They returned and **told** the others, but they would not believe
Lk 1. 2 wrote what we have been **told** by those who saw these things
1.19 sent me to speak to you and **tell** you this good news.
1.77 his road for him, [77]to **tell** his people that they will be
2.15 this thing that has happened, which the Lord has **told** us."
2.17 the shepherds saw him, they **told** them what the angel had
2.20 it had been just as the angel had **told** them.
3. 7 "Who **told** you that you could escape from the punishment God
3. 8 I **tell** you that God can take these stones and make
3.13 "Don't collect more than is legal," he **told** them.
4. 6 all this power and all this wealth," the Devil **told** him.
4.23 You will also **tell** me to do here in my home town
4.24 I **tell** you this," Jesus added, "a prophet is never welcomed
Lk 5.14 Jesus ordered him, "Don't **tell** anyone, but go straight to the
5.24 to the paralysed man, "I **tell** you, get up, pick up your
5.36 Jesus also **told** them this parable:
6.27 "But I **tell** you who hear me:
6.39 And Jesus **told** them this parable:
6.46 call me, 'Lord, Lord,' and yet don't do what I **tell** you?
7. 6 the officer sent friends to **tell** him, "Sir, don't trouble yourself.
7. 9 the crowd following him, "I **tell** you, I have never found
7.14 Get up, I **tell** you!"
7.18 John's disciples **told** him about all these things, he called two
7.22 John's messengers, "Go back and **tell** John what you have seen
7.26 **Tell** me, what did you go out to see?
7.28 I **tell** you," Jesus added, "John is greater than any
7.40 and said to him, "Simon, I have something to **tell** you."
7.40 "Yes, Teacher," he said, **"tell** me."
7.47 I **tell** you, then, the great love she has shown proves
8. 4 and when a great crowd gathered, Jesus **told** this parable:
8.36 Those who had seen it **told** the people how the man had
8.39 "Go back home and **tell** what God has done for you."
8.39 went through the town, **telling** what Jesus had done for him.
8.47 in front of everybody, she **told** him why she had touched him
8.49 "Your daughter has died," he **told** Jairus;
8.56 but Jesus commanded them not to **tell** anyone what had happened.
9.10 The apostles came back and **told** Jesus everything they had done.
9.21 Then Jesus gave them strict orders not to **tell** this to anyone.
9.36 quiet about all this, and **told** no one at that time anything
9.44 disciples, [44]"Don't forget what I am about to **tell** you!
9.49 in your name, and we **told** him to stop, because he doesn't
10.24 I **tell** you that many prophets and kings wanted to see
10.35 'Take care of him,' he **told** the innkeeper, 'and when I come
10.40 **Tell** her to come and help me!"
11. 8 I **tell** you that even if he will not get up
11.31 and I **tell** you there is something here greater than Solomon.
11.51 Yes, I **tell** you, the people of this time will be punished
12. 4 "I **tell** you, my friends, do not be afraid of those who
12.13 said to Jesus, "Teacher, **tell** my brother to divide with me
12.16 Then Jesus **told** them this parable:
12.18 This is what I will do,' he **told** himself;
12.22 the disciples, "And so I **tell** you not to worry about the
12.27 But I **tell** you that not even King Solomon with all his
12.37 I **tell** you, he will take off his coat, ask them to
12.44 Indeed, I **tell** you, the master will put that servant in
12.59 There you will stay, I **tell** you, until you pay the last
13. 1 people were there who **told** Jesus about the Galileans whom Pilate
13. 3 And I **tell** you that if you do not turn from your
13. 5 And I **tell** you that if you do not turn from your
13. 6 Then Jesus **told** them this parable:
13.32 Jesus answered them, "Go and **tell** that fox:
14. 7 the best places, so he **told** this parable to all of them:
14.17 sent his servant to **tell** his guests, 'Come, everything is ready!'
14.18 The first one **told** the servant, 'I have bought a field and
14.21 "The servant went back and **told** all this to his master.
14.24 I **tell** you all that none of those men who were invited
15. 3 So Jesus **told** them this parable:
15. 7 In the same way, I **tell** you, there will be more joy
15.10 In the same way, I **tell** you, the angels of God rejoice
16. 1 The rich man was **told** that the manager was wasting his
16. 6 'Here is your account,' the manager **told** him;
16. 7 'Here is your account,' the manager **told** him;
16. 9 And Jesus went on to say, "And so I **tell** you:
16.16 Kingdom of God is being **told,** and everyone forces his way in.
17. 7 from the field, do you **tell** him to hurry and eat his
17.10 done all you have been **told** to do, say, 'We are ordinary
17.34 On that night, I **tell** you, there will be two people
18. 1 Then Jesus **told** his disciples a parable to teach them that
18. 8 I **tell** you, he will judge in their favour and do it
18. 9 Jesus also **told** this parable to people who were sure of
18.14 I **tell** you," said Jesus, "the tax collector,
18.37 "Jesus of Nazareth is passing by," they **told** him.
18.39 The people in front scolded him and **told** him to be quiet.
19.11 were listening to this, Jesus continued and **told** them a parable.
19.13 each a gold coin and **told** them, 'See what you can earn
19.26 'I **tell** you,' he replied, 'that to every person who has something,
19.31 why you are untying it, **tell** him that the Master needs it.'
19.32 their way and found everything just as Jesus had **told** them.
19.40 Jesus answered, "I **tell** you that if they keep quiet,
20. 2 came [2]and said to him, **"Tell** us, what right have you to
20. 3 **Tell** me, [4]did John's right to baptize come from God or from
20. 8 to them, "Neither will I **tell** you, then, by what right I
20. 9 Then Jesus **told** the people this parable:
20.19 because they knew that he had **told** this parable against them;
20.22 **Tell** us, is it against our Law for us to pay taxes
21. 3 He said, "I **tell** you that this poor widow put in more
21.13 This will be your chance to **tell** the Good News.
21.29 Then Jesus **told** them this parable:
22.13 just as Jesus had **told** them, and they prepared the Passover
22.16 For I **tell** you, I will never eat it until it is
22.18 I **tell** you that from now on I will not drink this
22.34 "I **tell** you, Peter," Jesus said, "the cock will not
22.37 For I **tell** you that the scripture which says, 'He shared
22.67 **"Tell** us," they said, "are you the Messiah?"
22.67 He answered, "If I **tell** you, you will not believe me;
23. 2 this man misleading our people, **telling** them not to pay
24. 9 returned from the tomb, and **told** all these things to the
24.10 the other women with them **told** these things to the apostles.
24.23 seen a vision of angels who **told** them that he is alive.
24.36 While the two were **telling** them this, suddenly the Lord himself
24.44 are the very things I **told** you about while I was still
Jn 1. 7 named John, [7]who came to **tell** people about the light, so
1. 8 he came to **tell** about the light.
1.22 "Then **tell** us who you are," they said.

Jn 1.34 said John, "and I **tell** you that he is the Son
1.41 his brother Simon and **told** him, "We have found the Messiah."
1.45 Philip found Nathanael and **told** him, "We have found the one
1.50 you believe just because I **told** you I saw you when you
1.51 And he said to them, "I am **telling you the truth:**
2. 4 "You must not **tell** me what to do," Jesus replied.
2. 5 Jesus' mother then told the servants, "Do whatever he **tells** you."
2. 8 the brim, [8]and then he **told** them, "Now draw some water out
2.25 no need for anyone to **tell** him about them, because he
3. 3 Jesus answered, "I am **telling you the truth:**
3. 5 "I am **telling you the truth,"** replied Jesus.
3. 7 not be surprised because I **tell** you that you must all be
3.11 I am **telling you the truth:**
3.12 not believe me when I **tell** you about the things of this
3.12 me, then, when I **tell** you about the things of heaven?
3.32 He **tells** what he has seen and heard, yet no one accepts
4.16 "Go and call your husband," Jesus **told** her, "and come back."
4.18 You have **told me the truth."**
4.25 Messiah will come, and when he comes, he will **tell** us everything."
4.29 and see the man who **told** me everything I have ever done.
4.35 But I **tell** you, take a good look at the fields;
4.39 woman had said, "He **told** me everything I have ever done."
4.53 very hour when Jesus had **told** him, "Your son will live."
5.10 so the Jewish authorities **told** the man who had been healed,
5.11 man who made me well **told** me to pick up my mat
5.12 asked him, "Who is the man who **told** you to do this?"
5.15 Then the man left and **told** the Jewish authorities that
5.19 So Jesus answered them, "I am **telling you the truth:**
5.24 "I am **telling you the truth:**
5.25 I am **telling you the truth:**
5.30 I judge only as God **tells** me, so my judgement is right,
6.10 "Make the people sit down," Jesus **told** them.
6.20 "Don't be afraid," Jesus **told** them, "it is I!"
6.26 Jesus answered, "I am **telling you the truth:**
6.32 "I am **telling you the truth,"** Jesus said.
6.35 "I am the bread of life," Jesus **told** them.
6.36 Now, I **told** you that you have seen me but will not
6.47 I am **telling you the truth:**
6.53 Jesus said to them, "I am **telling you the truth:**
6.61 Without being **told,** Jesus knew that they were grumbling about
6.65 is the very reason I **told** you that no one can come
7. 7 hates me, because I keep **telling** it that its ways are bad.
8.24 That is why I **told** you that you will die in your
8.25 Jesus answered, "What I have **told** you from the very beginning.
8.26 however, is truthful, and I **tell** the world only what I have
8.34 Jesus said to them, "I am **telling you the truth:**
8.38 has shown me, but you do what your father has **told** you."
8.40 ever done is to **tell you the truth** I heard from God,
8.45 But I **tell the truth,** and that is why you do not
8.46 If I **tell the truth,** then why do you not believe me?
8.51 I am **telling you the truth:**
8.58 "I am **telling you the truth,"** Jesus replied.
9.11 it on my eyes, and **told** me to go to Siloam and
9.15 He **told** them, "He put some mud on my eyes;
9.24 to him, "Promise before God that you will **tell the truth!**
9.27 have already **told** you," he answered, "and you would not listen.
9.36 The man answered, **"Tell** me who he is, sir, so that I
10. 1 Jesus said, "I am **telling you the truth:**
10. 6 Jesus **told** them this parable, but they did not understand what
10. 7 So Jesus said again, "I am **telling you the truth:**
10.24 **Tell us the plain truth:**
10.25 answered, "I have already **told** you, but you would not believe
11.14 Jesus **told** them plainly, "Lazarus is dead, [15]but for your sake
11.23 "Your brother will rise to life," Jesus **told** her.
11.28 "The Teacher is here," she **told** her, "and is asking for you."
11.40 said to her, "Didn't I **tell** you that you would see God's
11.44 "Untie him," Jesus **told** them, "and let him go."
11.46 returned to the Pharisees and **told** them what Jesus had done.
12.22 Philip went and **told** Andrew,
12.22 and the two of them went and **told** Jesus.
12.24 I am **telling you the truth:**
12.34 The crowd answered, "Our Law **tells** us that the Messiah
12.38 "Lord, who believed the message we **told?**
12.50 I say, then, is what the Father has **told** me to say."
13.16 I am **telling you the truth:**
13.19 I **tell** you this now before it happens, so that when it
13.20 I am **telling you the truth:**
13.21 deeply troubled and declared openly, "I am **telling you the truth:**
13.29 disciples thought that Jesus had **told** him to go and buy what
13.33 but I **tell** you now what I told the Jewish authorities,
13.38 I am **telling you the truth:**
14. 1 "Do not be worried and upset," Jesus **told** them.
14. 2 I would not **tell** you this if it were not so.
14.12 I am **telling you the truth:**
14.25 "I have **told** you this while I am still with you.
14.26 everything and make you remember all that I have **told** you.
14.29 I have **told** you this now before it all happens, so that
15.11 "I have **told** you this so that my joy may be in
15.15 friends, because I have **told** you everything I have heard from
15.20 Remember what I **told** you:
16. 1 "I have **told** you this, so that you will not give up
16. 4 But I have **told** you this, so that when the time comes
16. 4 them to do these things, you will remember that I **told** you.
16. 4 "I did not **tell** you these things at the beginning, for I
16. 6 And now that I have **told** you, your hearts are full of
16. 7 But I am **telling you the truth:**
16.12 "I have much more to **tell** you, but now it would be
16.13 of what he hears, and will **tell** you of things to come.
16.14 because he will take what I say and **tell** it to you.
16.15 Spirit will take what I give him and **tell** it to you.
16.17 He **tells** us that in a little while we will not see

Jn 16.20 I am **telling you the truth:**
16.23 I am **telling you the truth:**
16.25 "I have used figures of speech to **tell** you these things.
16.33 I have **told** you this so that you will have peace by
18. 8 "I have already **told** you that I am he," Jesus said.
18.21 Ask them what I **told** them—they know what I said."
18.23 "If I have said anything wrong, **tell** everyone here what it was.
18.34 question come from you or have others **told** you about me?"
19.38 Pilate **told** him he could have the body, so Joseph went
20. 2 whom Jesus loved, and **told** them, "They have taken the Lord
20.15 you took him away, sir, **tell** me where you have put him,
20.17 hold on to me," Jesus **told** her, "because I have not yet
20.17 go to my brothers and **tell** them that I am returning
20.18 Mary Magdalene went and **told** the disciples that she had seen
20.18 seen the Lord and related to them what he had **told** her.
20.25 So the other disciples **told** him, "We have seen the Lord!"
21. 3 "We will come with you," they **told** him.
21.18 I am **telling you the truth:**

Acts 1. 4 wait for the gift I **told** you about, the gift my Father
2.14 Jerusalem, listen to me and let me **tell** you what this means.
3.22 You are to obey everything that he **tells** you to do.
4.15 So they **told** them to leave the Council room, and then
4.18 called them back in and **told** them that on no condition were
4.23 returned to their group and **told** them what the chief priests
5. 8 Peter asked her, **"Tell** me, was this the full amount you
5.20 stand in the Temple, and **tell** the people all about this new
5.38 so in this case, I **tell** you, do not take any action
7.14 message to his father Jacob, **telling** him and the whole family,
7.44 been made as God had **told** Moses to make it, according to
8.33 one will be able to **tell** about his descendants, because his
8.34 The official asked Philip, **"Tell** me, of whom is the prophet
8.35 passage of scripture, he **told** him the Good News about Jesus.
9. 6 into the city, where you will be **told** what you must do."
9.13 "Lord, many people have **told** me about this man and about
9.24 made plans to kill Saul, [24]but he was **told** of their plan.
9.27 He also **told** them how boldly Saul had preached in the name
10. 8 He **told** them what had happened and sent them off to Joppa.
10.22 An angel of God **told** him to invite you to his house,
11.12 The Spirit **told** me to go with them without hesitation.
11.13 He **told** us how he had seen an angel standing in his
11.19 Phoenicia, Cyprus, and Antioch, **telling** the message to Jews only.
11.20 the message to Gentiles also, **telling** them the Good News
12.15 they **told** her.
12.17 **"Tell** this to James and the rest of the believers," he
13.42 back the next Sabbath and **tell** them more about these things.
14.27 of the church together and **told** them about all that God had
15. 4 the elders, to whom they **told** all that God had done through
15. 5 Gentiles must be circumcised and **told** to obey the Law of Moses."
15.20 we should write a letter **telling** them not to eat any food
15.27 Judas and Silas, who will **tell** you in person the same things
16. 4 and elders in Jerusalem, and **told** them to obey those rules.
16.16 She earned a lot of money for her owners by **telling** fortunes.
16.36 So the jailer **told** Paul, "The officials have sent an order
17.21 all their time **telling** and hearing the latest new thing.)
18.21 Instead, he **told** them as he left, "If it is the will
19. 4 and he **told** the people of Israel to believe in the one
20.13 He had **told** us to do this, because he was going there
21. 4 power of the Spirit they **told** Paul not to go to Jerusalem.
21.21 They have been **told** that you have been teaching all the
21.21 abandon the Law of Moses, **telling** them not to circumcise
21.24 things that they have been **told** about you, but that you
21.25 have sent them a letter **telling** them we decided that they
22. 5 and the whole Council can prove that I am **telling the truth.**
22.10 and there you will be **told** everything that God has
22.15 a witness for him to **tell** everyone what you have seen
22.24 into the fort, and he **told** them to whip him in order
22.27 to Paul and asked him, **"Tell me,** are you a Roman citizen?"
23.16 so he went to the fort and **told** Paul.
23.17 he has something to **tell** him."
23.19 by himself, and asked him, "What have you got to **tell** me?"
23.22 The commander said, "Don't **tell** anyone that you have reported
23.30 I have **told** his accusers to make their charges against him
24.20 Or let these men here **tell** what crime they found me
24.22 the commander arrives," he **told** them, "I will decide your case."
25.16 But I **told** them that we Romans are not in the habit
26.16 You are to **tell** others what you have seen of me today
27.25 trust in God that it will be just as I was **told.**

Rom 8. 5 as their human nature **tells** them to, have their minds controlled
8. 5 who live as the Spirit **tells** them to, have their minds
8. 9 But you do not live as your human nature **tells** you to;
8. 9 you live as the Spirit **tells** you to—if, in fact, God's
9.26 very place where they were **told,** 'You are not my people,'
15. 8 For I **tell** you that Christ's life of service was on behalf
15.21 says, "Those who were not **told** about him will see, and

1 Cor 1.11 from Chloe's family have **told** me quite plainly, my brothers,
1.17 He sent me to **tell** the Good News,
1.17 and to **tell** it without using the language of
5. 1 I am **told** that a man is sleeping with his stepmother!
5. 9 that I wrote you I **told** you not to associate with immoral
7. 6 I **tell** you this not as an order, but simply
10.28 sake of the one who **told** you and for conscience' sake—
11.18 first place, I have been **told** that there are opposing groups
12.10 the ability to **tell** the difference between gifts that come
16. 1 You must do what I **told** the churches in Galatia to do.

2 Cor 5.19 us the message which **tells** how he makes them his friends.
7. 7 He **told** us how much you want to see me, how sorry
12. 6 would not be a fool, because I would be **telling the truth.**

Gal 1.11 Let me **tell** you, my brothers, that the gospel I preach
1.13 You have been **told** how I used to live when I was
3. 2 **Tell** me this one thing:
4.16 Have I now become your enemy by **telling you the truth?**

Gal 5. 2 I, Paul, **tell** you that if you allow yourselves to be circumcised,
Eph 3. 5 past times mankind was not **told** this secret, but God has
4.25 Everyone must **tell the truth** to his fellow-believer,
6.22 sending him to you—to **tell** you how all of us are
Phil 1. 8 witness that I am **telling the truth** when I say that my
3.18 I have **told** you this many times before, and now I repeat
Col 1. 8 He has **told** us of the love that the Spirit has given
2. 1 Let me **tell** you how hard I have worked for you
2. 4 I **tell** you, then, do not let anyone deceive you with false
4. 8 to cheer you up by **telling** you how all of us are
4. 9 They will **tell** you everything that is happening here.
1 Thes 2. 2 God gave us courage to **tell** you the Good News that comes
3. 4 were still with you, we **told** you beforehand that we were
3. 6 He has **told** us that you always think well of us
4. 6 We have **told** you this before, and we strongly warned you
4.11 and to earn your own living, just as we **told** you before.
2 Thes 1.10 because you have believed the message that we **told** you.
2. 5 I **told** you all this while I was with you.
3. 4 you are doing and will continue to do what we **tell** you.
1 Tim 1. 4 **Tell** them to give up those legends and those long lists of
2. 7 I am **telling the truth!**
4. 7 keep away from those godless legends, which are not worth **telling.**
2 Tim 4. 3 and more teachers who will **tell** them what they are itching
Tit 3. 2 **Tell** them not to speak evil of anyone, but to be peaceful
Heb 2.12 says to God, "I will **tell** my brothers what you have done;
2 Pet 1.14 this mortal body, as our Lord Jesus Christ plainly **told** me.
2. 3 will make a profit out of **telling** you made-up stories.
1 Jn 1. 2 we speak of it and **tell** you about the eternal life which
2.18 You were **told** that the Enemy of Christ would come;
4.14 And we have seen and **tell** others that the Father sent
2 Jn 12 I have so much to **tell** you, but I would rather not
3 Jn 3 some Christian brothers arrived and **told** me how faithful you are
10 the terrible things he says about us and the lies he **tells!**
13 I have so much to **tell** you, but I do not want
Jude 17 my friends, what you were **told** in the past by the apostles
Rev 1. 2 angel to him, [2]and John has **told** all that he has seen.
6.11 robe, and they were **told** to rest a little while longer,
7. 4 And I was **told** that the number of those who were marked
9. 4 They were **told** not to harm the grass or the trees or
9.16 I was **told** the number of the mounted troops:
10.11 Then I was **told,** "Once again you must proclaim God's message
11. 1 like a measuring-rod, and was **told,** "Go and measure the temple
13.14 The beast **told** them to build an image in honour of the
17. 7 "I will **tell** you the secret meaning of the woman and of
18. 7 For she keeps **telling** herself:

TELL LIES see LIE(2)

TEMPER

[BAD-TEMPERED, QUICK-TEMPERED]

Gen 31.36 Then Jacob lost his **temper.**
Num 22.27 Balaam lost his **temper** and began to beat the donkey with his
1 Sam 25. 2 beautiful and intelligent, but he was a mean, **bad-tempered** man.
Prov 14.17 People with a hot **temper** do foolish things;
14.29 if you have a hot **temper,** you only show how stupid you
15.18 Hot **tempers** cause arguments, but patience brings peace.
19.11 If you are sensible, you will control your **temper.**
19.19 If someone has a hot **temper,** let him take the consequences.
22.24 Don't make friends with people who have hot, violent **tempers.**
29.22 People with quick **tempers** cause a lot of quarrelling and trouble.
Ecc 7. 9 Keep your **temper** under control;
Dan 3.19 Then Nebuchadnezzar lost his **temper,** and his face
2 Cor 12.20 quarrelling and jealousy, hot **tempers** and selfishness, insults
Tit 1. 7 must not be arrogant or **quick-tempered,** or a drunkard or violent

TEMPESTS

Is 29. 6 He will send **tempests** and raging fire;

TEMPLE (1) (OF GOD)

see also **TEMPLE GUARD, TEMPLE TREASURY**

Ex 15.17 for your home, the **Temple** that you yourself have built.
2 Sam 7. 5 not the one to build a **temple** for me to live in.
7. 6 Israel from Egypt until now, I have never lived in a **temple;**
7. 7 why they had not built me a **temple** made of cedar.'
7.13 the one to build a **temple** for me, and I will make
22. 7 In his **temple** he heard my voice;
1 Kgs 3. 1 his palace, the **Temple,** and the wall round Jerusalem.
3. 2 A **temple** had not yet been built for the Lord, and so
5. 3 he could not build a **temple** for the worship of the Lord
5. 5 I will make king after you, will build a **temple** for me.'
5. 5 now decided to build that **temple** for the worship of the Lord
5.17 quarried fine large stones for the foundation of the **Temple.**
5.18 Byblos prepared the stones and the timber to build the **Temple.**
8.16 of Israel in which a **temple** should be built where I would
8.17 David planned to build a **temple** for the worship of the Lord
8.18 in wanting to build a **temple** for me, [19]but you will never
8.19 It is your son, your own son, who will build my **temple.'**
8.20 and I have built the **Temple** for the worship of the Lord
8.21 provided a place in the **Temple** for the Covenant Box
8.27 you, so how can this **Temple** that I have built be large
8.29 Watch over this **Temple** day and night, this place where
8.29 Hear me when I face this **Temple** and pray.
8.31 to your altar in this **Temple** to take an oath that he
8.33 come to this **Temple,** humbly praying to you for forgiveness,
8.35 they repent and face this **Temple,** humbly praying to you,
8.38 hands in prayer towards this **Temple,** [39]hear their prayer.
1 Kgs 8.41 you and to pray at this **Temple,** [43]listen to his prayer.
8.43 they will know that this **Temple** I have built is the place
8.44 you have chosen and this **Temple** which I have built for you,
8.48 you have chosen, and this **Temple** which I have built for you,
8.63 And so the king and all the people dedicated the **Temple.**
8.64 area in front of the **Temple,** and then he offered there the
8.65 There at the **Temple,** Solomon and all the people of
9. 1 Solomon had finished building the **Temple** and the palace and
9. 3 I consecrate this **Temple** which you have built as the place
9. 7 I will also abandon this **Temple** which I have consecrated as
9. 8 This **Temple** will become a pile of ruins, and everyone who
9. 8 'Why did the Lord do this to this land and this **Temple?'**
9.10 It took Solomon twenty years to build the **Temple** and his palace.
9.15 forced labour to build the **Temple** and the palace, to fill in
9.25 And so he finished building the **Temple.**
10. 5 him at feasts, and the sacrifices he offered in the **Temple.**
10.12 to build railings in the **Temple** and the palace, and also to
12.26 to the Lord in the **Temple** there, they will transfer their
14.26 all the treasures in the **Temple** and in the palace, including
14.28 the king went to the **Temple,** the guards carried the shields,
15.15 He placed in the **Temple** all the objects his father had
15.18 that was left in the **Temple** and the palace, and sent it
2 Kgs 11. 2 into a bedroom in the **Temple** and hid him from Athaliah, so
11. 3 him hidden in the **Temple,** while Athaliah ruled as queen.
11. 4 them to come to the **Temple,** where he made them agree under
11. 7 to stand guard at the **Temple** to protect the king.
11.10 had been kept in the **Temple,** [11]and he stationed the men
11.11 all round the front of the **Temple,** to protect the king.
11.13 so she hurried to the **Temple,** where the crowd had gathered.
11.14 the column at the entrance of the **Temple,** as was the custom.
11.15 want Athaliah killed in the **temple** area, so he ordered the
11.18 guards on duty at the **Temple,** [19]and then he, the officers,
11.19 escorted the king from the **Temple** to the palace, followed by
12. 4 with the sacrifices in the **Temple,** both the dues paid for
12. 5 the money was to be used to repair the **Temple,** as needed.
12. 6 the priests still had not made any repairs to the **Temple.**
12. 7 and asked them, "Why aren't you repairing the **Temple?**
12. 8 this and also agreed not to make the repairs in the **Temple.**
12. 9 by the altar, on the right side as one enters the **Temple.**
12.11 the work in the **Temple,** and these would pay the carpenters,
12.18 in the treasuries of the **Temple** and the palace, and sent
14.14 find, all the **temple** equipment and all the palace treasures,
15.35 It was Jotham who built the North Gate of the **Temple.**
16. 8 silver and gold from the **Temple** and the palace treasury and
16.14 the new altar and the **Temple,** so Ahaz moved it to the
16.17 bronze carts used in the **Temple** and removed the basins that
16.18 Ahaz also removed from the **Temple** the platform for the royal
16.18 and closed up the king's private entrance to the **Temple.**
18.15 him all the silver in the **Temple** and in the palace treasury;
18.16 stripped the gold from the **temple** doors and the gold with
19. 1 grief, put on sackcloth, and went to the **Temple** of the Lord.
19.14 Then he went to the **Temple,** placed the letter there in the
20. 5 heal you, and in three days you will go to the **Temple.**
20. 8 three days later I will be able to go to the **Temple?"**
21. 4 built pagan altars in the **Temple,** the place that the Lord
21. 5 the two courtyards of the **Temple** he built altars for the
21. 7 the goddess Asherah in the **Temple,** the place about which the
21. 7 "Here in Jerusalem, in this **Temple,** is the place that I
22. 3 grandson of Meshullam, to the **Temple** with the order:
22. 4 the entrance to the **Temple** have collected from the people.
22. 5 the men who are in charge of the repairs in the **Temple.**
22. 8 that he had found the book of the Law in the **Temple.**
22. 9 money that was in the **Temple** and have handed it over to
22.14 grandson of Harhas, was in charge of the **temple** robes.)
23. 2 together they went to the **Temple,** accompanied by the priests
23. 2 book of the covenant which had been found in the **Temple.**
23. 4 at the entrance to the **Temple**
23. 4 to bring out of the **Temple** all the objects used in the
23. 6 He removed from the **Temple** the symbol of the goddess Asherah,
23. 7 He destroyed the living-quarters in the **Temple** occupied by the temple prostitutes.
23. 9 allowed to serve in the **Temple,** but they could eat the
23.11 (These were kept in the **temple** courtyard, near the gate and
23.12 put up by King Manasseh in the two courtyards of the **Temple;**
23.24 Hilkiah had found in the **Temple,** King Josiah removed from
23.27 city I chose, and the **Temple,** the place I said was where
24.13 to Babylon all the treasures in the **Temple** and the palace.
24.13 utensils which King Solomon had made for use in the **Temple.**
25. 9 He burnt down the **Temple,** the palace, and the houses of
25.13 were in the **Temple,** together with the large bronze tank,
25.14 all the other bronze articles used in the **temple** service.
25.16 Solomon had made for the **Temple**—the two columns, the carts,
25.18 in rank, and the three other important **temple** officials.
1 Chr 6.10 served in the **Temple** which King Solomon built in Jerusalem),
6.32 Lord's presence during the time before King Solomon built the **Temple.**
9. 2 Israelite laymen, priests, Levites, and **temple** workmen.
9.10 (the chief official in the **Temple**), whose ancestors included
9.13 They were experts in all the work carried on in the **Temple.**
9.23 their descendants continued to guard the gates to the **Temple.**
9.26 for the rooms in the **Temple** and for the supplies kept there.
9.27 They lived near the **Temple,** because it was their duty to
9.32 preparing the sacred bread for the **Temple** every Sabbath.
9.33 Some Levite families were responsible for the **temple** music.
9.33 lived in some of the **temple** buildings and were free from
16.27 Glory and majesty surround him, power and joy fill his **Temple.**
16.29 bring an offering and come into his **Temple.**
17. 4 not the one to build a **temple** for me to live in.
17. 5 Israel from Egypt until now, I have never lived in a **temple;**
17. 6 why they had not built me a **temple** made of cedar.'
17.12 the one to build a **temple** for me, and I will make

1 Chr 18. 8 tank, the columns, and the bronze utensils for the **Temple.)**
22. 1 said, "This is where the **Temple** of the Lord God will be.
22. 2 Some of them prepared stone blocks for building the **Temple.**
22. 5 David thought, "The **Temple** that my son Solomon is to
22. 6 commanded him to build a **temple** for the Lord, the God of
22. 7 I wanted to build a **temple** to honour the Lord my God.
22. 8 have caused, he would not let me build a **temple** for him.
22.10 He will build a **temple** for me.
22.11 promise to make you successful in building a **temple** for him.
22.14 As for the **Temple,** by my efforts I have accumulated more
22.19 Start building the **Temple,** so that you can place in it the
23. 4 administer the work of the **Temple,** six thousand to keep
23.24 or older, had a share in the work of the Lord's **Temple.**
23.28 descended from Aaron with the **temple** worship, to take care
23.29 to weigh and measure the **temple** offerings;
23.32 Lord's presence and the **Temple,** and of assisting their relatives,
23.32 the priests descended from Aaron, in the **temple** worship.
24. 5 Since there were **temple** officials and spiritual leaders
24.19 assignments for going to the **Temple** and performing the
25. 6 their father's direction, to accompany the **temple** worship.
26.12 duties in the **Temple,** just as the other Levites were.
26.20 were in charge of the **temple** treasury and the storerooms for
26.22 Zetham and Joel, had charge of the **temple** treasury and storerooms.
26.24 the chief official responsible for the **temple** treasury.
26.27 captured in battle and dedicated it for use in the **Temple.**
26.28 dedicated for use in the **Temple,** including the gifts brought
29.16 this wealth to build a **temple** to honour your holy name, but
29.19 command and to build the **Temple** for which I have made these
2 Chr 2. 1 Solomon decided to build a **temple** where the Lord would be worshipped,
2. 4 I am building a **temple** to honour the Lord my God.
2. 5 intend to build a great **temple,** because our God is greater
2. 6 one can really build a **temple** for God, because even all the
2. 6 then can I build a **temple** that would be anything more than
2. 9 quantities of timber, because this **temple** I intend to build
2.12 now plans to build a **temple** for the Lord and a palace
5.11 the priests were leaving the **Temple,** it was suddenly filled
6. 2 I have built a majestic **temple** for you, a place for you
6. 5 the place to build a **temple** where I would be worshipped, and
6. 7 David planned to build a **temple** for the worship of the Lord
6. 8 in wanting to build a **temple** for me, [9] but you will never
6. 9 It is your son, your own son, who will build my **temple.'**
6.10 and I have built a **temple** for the worship of the Lord
6.11 I have placed in the **Temple** the Covenant Box, which
6.18 you, so how can this **Temple** that I have built be large
6.20 Watch over this **Temple** day and night.
6.20 be worshipped, so hear me when I face this **Temple** and pray.
6.22 to your altar in this **Temple** to take an oath that he
6.24 come to this **Temple,** humbly praying to you for forgiveness,
6.26 they repent and face this **Temple,** humbly praying to you,
6.29 hands in prayer towards this **Temple,** [30] hear their prayer.
6.32 he comes to pray at this **Temple,** [33] listen to his prayer.
6.33 they will know that this **Temple** I have built is where you
6.34 you have chosen and this **Temple** which I have built for you,
6.38 you have chosen, and this **Temple** which I have built for you,
6.41 of your power, enter the **Temple** and stay here for ever.
7. 1 the dazzling light of the Lord's presence filled the **Temple.**
7. 2 Because the **Temple** was full of the dazzling light, the
7. 3 and the light fill the **Temple,** they fell face downwards on
7. 5 And so he and all the people dedicated the **Temple.**
7. 7 area in front of the **Temple,** and then offered there the
7.11 King Solomon had finished the **Temple** and the palace,
7.12 prayer, and I accept this **Temple** as the place where
7.15 I will watch over this **Temple** and be ready to hear all
7.20 and I will abandon this **Temple** that I have consecrated as
7.21 "The **Temple** is now greatly honoured, but then everyone
7.21 'Why did the Lord do this to this land and this **Temple?'**
8. 1 It took Solomon twenty years to build the **Temple** and his palace.
8.12 on the altar which he had built in front of the **Temple.**
8.16 the foundation of the Lord's **Temple** to its completion, all
9. 4 him at feasts, and the sacrifices he offered in the **Temple.**
9.11 to make stairs for the **Temple** and for his palace, and to
12. 9 took the treasures from the **Temple** and from the palace.
12.11 the king went to the **Temple,** the guards carried the shields
15. 8 the altar of the Lord that stood in the **temple** courtyard.
15.18 He placed in the **Temple** all the objects his father
16. 2 from the treasuries of the **Temple** and the palace and sent it
20. 5 of Jerusalem gathered in the new courtyard of the **Temple.**
20. 8 here and have built a **temple** to honour you, knowing [9] that
20. 9 and stand in front of this **Temple** where you are worshipped.
20.13 their wives and children, were standing there at the **Temple.**
20.28 city, they marched to the **Temple,** to the music of harps and
22.11 and hid him and a nurse in a bedroom at the **Temple.**
23. 3 They all gathered in the **Temple,** and there they made a
23. 4 of them will guard the **temple** gates, [5] another third will
23. 5 All the people will assemble in the **temple** courtyard.
23. 6 one is to enter the **temple** buildings except the priests and
23. 7 Anyone who tries to enter the **Temple** is to be killed."
23. 9 had belonged to King David and had been kept in the **Temple.**
23.10 all round the front of the **Temple,** to protect the king.
23.12 so she hurried to the **Temple,** where the crowd had gathered.
23.13 the new king at the **temple** entrance, standing by the column
23.13 and blowing trumpets, and the **temple** musicians with their
23.14 want Athaliah killed in the **temple** area, so he called out
23.18 the priests and Levites in charge of the work of the **Temple.**
23.19 guards on duty at the **temple** gates to keep out anyone who
23.20 that brought the king from the **Temple** to the palace.
24. 4 king for a while, Joash decided to have the **Temple** repaired.
24. 5 enough money to make the annual repairs on the **Temple.**
24. 7 corrupt woman, had damaged the **Temple** and had used many of
2 Chr 24. 8 a box for contributions and to place it at the **temple** gate.
24.12 charge of repairing the **Temple,** and they hired stonemasons,
24.13 and they restored the **Temple** to its original condition,
24.14 it to have bowls and other utensils made for the **Temple.**
24.14 Jehoiada was alive, sacrifices were offered regularly at the **Temple.**
24.16 done for the people of Israel, for God, and for the **Temple.**
24.18 people stopped worshipping in the **Temple** of the Lord, the
24.21 orders the people stoned Zechariah in the **temple** courtyard.
24.27 against him, and the record of how he rebuilt the **Temple.**
25.24 gold and silver in the **Temple,**
25.24 the **temple** equipment guarded by the descendants of
26.16 God by going into the **Temple** to burn incense on the altar
26.19 was standing there in the **Temple** beside the incense altar
26.20 forehead in horror, and then forced him to leave the **Temple.**
26.21 Unable to enter the **Temple** again, he lived in his own house,
27. 2 his father he did not sin by burning incense in the **Temple.**
27. 3 the North Gate of the **Temple** and did extensive work on the
28.21 took the gold from the **Temple,** the palace, and the homes of
28.24 he took all the **temple** equipment and broke it in pieces.
28.24 He closed the **Temple** and set up altars in every part of
30. 1 them to come to the **Temple** in Jerusalem to celebrate the
30. 8 Come to the **Temple** in Jerusalem, which the Lord your God has
30.15 and now they could sacrifice burnt-offerings in the **Temple.**
30.16 took their places in the **Temple** according to the
31. 2 fellowship-offerings, taking part in the **temple** worship, and
31. 2 giving praise and thanks in the various parts of the **Temple.**
31.10 bringing their gifts to the **Temple,** there has been enough to
31.11 they prepared storerooms in the **Temple** area [12] and put all
31.14 the East Gate of the **Temple,** was in charge of receiving the
31.16 in the **Temple** in accordance with their positions.
31.21 he did for the **Temple** or in observance of the Law,
33. 4 built pagan altars in the **Temple,** the place that the Lord
33. 5 the two courtyards of the **Temple** he built altars for the
33. 7 placed an image in the **Temple,** the place about which God had
33. 7 "Here in Jerusalem, in this **Temple,** is the place that I
33.15 He removed from the **Temple** the foreign gods and the
33.15 on the hill where the **Temple** stood and in other places in
34. 8 purified the land and the **Temple** by ending pagan worship,
34. 8 Josiah sent three men to repair the **Temple** of the Lord God:
34. 9 guards had collected in the **Temple** was handed over to
34.10 men in charge of the **temple** repairs, and they gave it to
34.15 "I have found the book of the Law here in the **Temple."**
34.17 that was kept in the **Temple** and handed it over to the
34.22 grandson of Harhas, was in charge of the **temple** robes.)
34.30 together they went to the **Temple,** accompanied by the priests
34.30 book of the covenant, which had been found in the **Temple.**
35. 2 were to perform in the **Temple** and encouraged them to do them
35. 3 sacred Covenant Box in the **Temple** that King Solomon, the son
35. 4 Take your places in the **Temple** by clans, according to the
35. 8 officials in charge of the **Temple**—Hilkiah, the High Priest,
35.15 The guards at the **temple** gates did not need to leave their
35.20 done all this for the **Temple,** King Neco of Egypt led an
36. 7 of the treasures of the **Temple** and put them in his palace
36.10 Babylonia as a prisoner, and carried off the treasures of the **Temple.**
36.14 and so they defiled the **Temple,** which the Lord himself had
36.15 his people, because he wanted to spare them and the **Temple.**
36.17 The king killed the young men of Judah, even in the **Temple.**
36.18 king of Babylonia looted the **Temple,**
36.18 the **temple** treasury, and the wealth of the
36.19 He burnt down the **Temple** and the city, with all its
36.23 of building a **temple** for him in Jerusalem in Judah.
Ezra 1. 2 of building a **temple** for him in Jerusalem in Judah.
1. 3 to Jerusalem and rebuild the **Temple** of the Lord, the God of
1. 4 offerings to present in the **Temple** of God in Jerusalem."
1. 5 got ready to go and rebuild the Lord's **Temple** in Jerusalem.
1. 6 animals, other valuables, and offerings for the **Temple.**
1. 7 Nebuchadnezzar had taken from the **Temple** in Jerusalem
2.40 **Temple** musicians (descendants of Asaph) - 128
2.43 Clans of **temple** workmen who returned from exile:
2.58 number of descendants of the **temple** workmen and of Solomon's
2.68 exiles arrived at the Lord's **Temple** in Jerusalem, some of
2.68 offerings to help rebuild the **Temple** on its old site.
2.70 and the **temple** workmen settled in nearby towns;
3. 6 yet started to rebuild the **Temple,** they began on the first
3. 8 to the site of the **Temple** in Jerusalem, they began work.
3. 8 were put in charge of the work of rebuilding the **Temple.**
3. 9 joined together in taking charge of the rebuilding of the **Temple.**
3.10 lay the foundation of the **Temple,** the priests in their robes
3.11 the work on the foundation of the **Temple** had been started.
3.12 clans had seen the first **Temple,** and as they watched the
3.12 foundation of this **Temple** being laid, they cried and wailed.
4. 1 from exile were rebuilding the **Temple** of the Lord, the God
4. 2 clans and said, "Let us join you in building the **Temple.**
4. 3 need your help to build a **temple** for the Lord our God.
4.24 Work on the **Temple** had been stopped and had remained at
5. 2 they began to rebuild the **Temple** in Jerusalem, and the two
5. 3 "Who gave you orders to build this **Temple** and equip it?"
5. 4 names of all the men who were helping to build the **Temple.**
5. 8 Judah and found that the **Temple** of the great God is being
5. 9 given them authority to rebuild the **Temple** and to equip it.
5.11 and we are rebuilding the **Temple** which was originally built
5.12 The **Temple** was destroyed, and the people were taken into
5.13 Babylonia, Cyrus issued orders for the **Temple** to be rebuilt.
5.14 restored the gold and silver **temple** utensils which
5.14 Nebuchadnezzar had taken from the **Temple** in Jerusalem and
5.15 and return them to the **Temple** in Jerusalem,
5.15 and to rebuild the **Temple** where it had stood before.
5.16 until the present, but the **Temple** is still not finished.'
5.17 Cyrus gave orders for this **Temple** in Jerusalem to be rebuilt,

Ezra 6. 3 the emperor commanded that the **Temple** in Jerusalem be
6. 3 The **Temple** is to be twenty-seven metres high
6. 5 brought to Babylon from the **Temple** in Jerusalem are to be
6. 5 returned to their proper place in the Jerusalem **Temple.**"
6. 6 "Stay away from the **Temple** [7]and do not interfere
6. 7 Jewish leaders rebuild the **Temple** of God where it stood before.
6.12 defies this command and tries to destroy the **Temple** there.
6.14 with the building of the **Temple,** encouraged by the prophets
6.14 They completed the **Temple** as they had been commanded by the
6.15 They finished the **Temple** on the third day of the month
6.16 who had returned from exile—joyfully dedicated the **Temple.**
6.18 and the Levites for the **temple** services in Jerusalem,
6.22 their work of rebuilding the **Temple** of the God of Israel.
7. 6 Israelites which included priests, Levites, **temple** musicians,
7.15 to give to the God of Israel, whose **Temple** is in Jerusalem.
7.16 priests give for the **Temple** of their God in Jerusalem.
7.17 wine and offer them on the altar of the **Temple** in Jerusalem.
7.19 that have been given to you for use in the **temple** services.
7.20 which you need for the **Temple,** you may get from the royal
7.23 of Heaven requires for his **Temple,** and so make sure that he
7.24 guards, workmen, or anyone else connected with this **Temple.**
7.27 to honour in this way the **Temple** of the Lord in Jerusalem.
8.17 him and his associates, the **temple** workmen,
8.17 to send us people to serve God in the **Temple.**
8.20 In addition there were 220 **temple** workmen whose
8.25 to be used in the **Temple,** and I gave it to the
8.29 Guard them carefully until you reach the **Temple.**
8.30 and the utensils, to take them to the **Temple** in Jerusalem.
8.33 day we went to the **Temple,** weighed the silver, the gold, and
8.36 gave their support to the people and the **temple** worship.
9. 9 living and to rebuild your **Temple,** which was in ruins, and
10. 1 in front of the **Temple,** weeping and confessing these sins,
10. 6 from in front of the **Temple** into the living-quarters of
10. 9 came to Jerusalem and assembled in the **temple** square.
Neh 2. 8 the fort that guards the **Temple,** for the city walls, and for
3.25 east near the Water Gate and the tower guarding the **Temple.**
3.25 of the city called Ophel, where the **temple** workmen lived.)
3.27 the large tower guarding the **Temple** as far as the wall near
3.31 the building used by the **temple** workmen and the merchants,
6.10 the Holy Place of the **Temple** and lock the doors, because
6.11 I would try to save my life by hiding in the **Temple?**
7.43 **Temple** musicians (descendants of Asaph) – 148
7.46 Clans of **temple** workmen who returned from exile:
7.60 number of descendants of the **temple** workmen and of Solomon's
7.70 contributed to help pay the cost of restoring the **Temple:**
7.73 of the ordinary people, the **temple** workmen—all the people of
8.16 in their yards, in the **temple** courtyard, and in the public
10.28 the temple guards, the **temple** musicians, the temple workmen,
10.32 grammes of silver to help pay the expenses of the **Temple.**
10.33 We will provide for the **temple** worship the following:
10.33 and anything else needed for the **Temple.**
10.35 We will take to the **Temple** each year an offering of the
10.36 to the priests in the **Temple** and there, as required by the
10.37 to the priests in the **Temple** the dough made from the first
10.38 and for use in the **Temple** the Levites
10.38 are to take to the **temple** storerooms one tenth of all the
10.39 where the utensils for the **Temple** are kept and where the
10.39 and the members of the **temple** choir have their quarters.
11. 3 the priests, the Levites, the **temple** workmen, and the
11.12 In all, 822 members of this clan served in the **Temple.**
11.16 prominent Levites in charge of the work outside the **Temple.**
11.17 He led the **temple** choir in singing the prayer of thanksgiving.
11.21 The **temple** workmen lived in the part of Jerusalem called
11.22 that was responsible for the music in the **temple** services.
11.23 should take turns in leading the **temple** music each day.
12.25 of guarding the storerooms by the gates to the **Temple:**
12.39 We ended our march near the gate to the **Temple.**
12.40 that were giving thanks to God reached the **temple** area.
12.44 storerooms where contributions for the **Temple** were kept,
12.45 The **temple** musicians and the temple guards also performed
12.47 the support of the **temple** musicians and the temple guards.
13. 4 was in charge of the **temple** storerooms, had for a long time
13. 5 equipment used in the **Temple,** the offerings for the priests,
13. 5 Levites, to the **temple** musicians, and to the temple guards.
13. 7 Eliashib had allowed Tobiah to use a room in the **Temple.**
13. 9 purified and for the **temple** equipment, grain-offerings,
13.10 I also learnt that the **temple** musicians and other
13.11 I reprimanded the officials for letting the **Temple** be neglected.
13.11 and musicians back to the **Temple** and put them to work again.
13.12 bringing to the **temple** storerooms their tithes of corn,
13.14 things that I have done for your **Temple** and its worship.
Ps 5. 7 can worship in your holy **Temple** and bow down to you in
11. 4 The Lord is in his holy **temple;**
15. 1 Lord, who may enter your **Temple?**
18. 6 In his **temple** he heard my voice;
20. 2 send you help from his **Temple** and give you aid from Mount
24. 3 Who may enter his holy **Temple?**
27. 5 keep me safe in his **Temple** and make me secure on a
27. 6 With shouts of joy I will offer sacrifices in his **Temple;**
28. 2 for help, when I lift my hands towards your holy **Temple.**
29. 9 while everyone in his **Temple** shouts, "Glory to God!"
43. 3 Zion, your sacred hill, and to your **Temple,** where you live.
48. 9 Inside your **Temple,** O God, we think of your constant love.
55.14 with each other and worshipped together in the **Temple.**
65. 4 things of your house, the blessings of your sacred **Temple.**
68. 5 his sacred **Temple,** cares for orphans and protects widows.
68.29 on our behalf [29]from your **Temple** in Jerusalem, where kings
69. 9 My devotion to your **Temple** burns in me like a fire;
73.17 was too difficult for me [17]until I went into your **Temple.**
74. 3 our enemies have destroyed everything in the **Temple.**
74. 4 Your enemies have shouted in triumph in your **Temple;**
Ps 74. 7 They wrecked your **Temple** and set it on fire;
78.69 There he built his **Temple** like his home in heaven;
79. 1 They have desecrated your holy **Temple** and left Jerusalem in ruins.
84. 1 How I love your **Temple,** Lord Almighty!
84. 2 I long to be in the Lord's **Temple.**
84. 4 who live in your **Temple,** always singing praise to you.
84.10 One day spent in your **Temple** is better than a thousand
92.13 Lord, that flourish in the **Temple** of our God, [14]that still
93. 5 are eternal, Lord, and your **Temple** is holy indeed, for ever
96. 6 power and beauty fill his **Temple.**
96. 8 bring an offering and come into his **Temple.**
100. 4 Enter the **temple** gates with thanksgiving,
116.18 in the sanctuary of your **Temple** in Jerusalem, I will give
118.19 Open to me the gates of the **Temple;**
118.26 From the **Temple** of the Lord we bless you.
132. 8 Come to the **Temple,** Lord, with the Covenant Box, the
134. 1 all his servants, all who serve in his **Temple** at night.
134. 2 Raise your hands in prayer in the **Temple,** and praise the Lord!
135. 2 who stand in the Lord's house, in the **Temple** of our God.
138. 2 I face your holy **Temple,** bow down, and praise your name
150. 1 Praise God in his **Temple!**
Ecc 5. 1 Be careful about going to the **Temple.**
Is 1.12 Who asked you to do all this tramping about in my **Temple?**
2. 2 come the mountain where the **Temple** stands will be the
2. 3 up the hill of the Lord, to the **Temple** of Israel's God.
6. 1 high and exalted, and his robe filled the whole **Temple.**
6. 4 made the foundation of the **Temple** shake,
6. 4 and the **Temple** itself was filled with smoke.
30.29 on their way to the **Temple** of the Lord, the defender of
37. 1 grief, put on sackcloth, and went to the **Temple** of the Lord.
37.14 Then he went to the **Temple,** placed the letter there in the
38.20 your praise, Sing praise in your **Temple** as long as we live.
38.22 to prove that I will be able to go to the **Temple?"**
44.28 Jerusalem to be rebuilt and the **Temple** foundations to be laid.' "
52.11 leave Babylonia, all you that carry the **temple** equipment!
56. 5 will be remembered in my **Temple** and among my people longer
56. 7 My **Temple** will be called a house of prayer for the people
57.13 will live in the land and will worship me in my **Temple."**
60. 7 The Lord will make his **Temple** more glorious than ever.
60.13 To make my **Temple** beautiful, To make my city glorious.
62. 9 grapes Will drink the wine in the courts of my **Temple."**
64.11 a deserted ruin, [11]and our **Temple,** the sacred and
66. 6 city, that sound in the **Temple,** is the sound of the Lord
66.20 bring grain-offerings to the **Temple** in ritually clean containers.
Jer 7. 1 to the gate of the **Temple** where the people of Judah went
7. 4 This is the Lord's **Temple,**
7. 4 this is the Lord's **Temple,** this is the Lord's Temple!'
7.10 in my presence, in my own **Temple,** and say, 'We are safe!'
7.11 Do you think that my **Temple** is a hiding place for robbers?
7.14 I will do to this **Temple** of mine, in which you trust.
7.20 Sovereign Lord, will pour out my fierce anger on this **Temple.**
7.30 their idols, which I hate, in my **Temple** and have defiled it.
11.15 What right have they to be in my **Temple?**
17.12 Our **Temple** is like a glorious throne, standing on a high
17.26 They will bring to my **Temple** burnt-offerings and sacrifices,
19.14 in the court of the **Temple** and told all the people [15]that
20. 1 chief officer of the **Temple,** heard me proclaim these things,
20. 2 placed in chains near the upper Benjamin Gate in the **Temple.**
23.11 I have caught them doing evil in the **Temple** itself.
24. 1 showed me two baskets of figs placed in front of the **Temple.**
26. 2 in the court of the **Temple** and proclaim all I have commanded
26. 6 I will do to this **Temple** what I did to Shiloh, and
26. 7 saying these things in the **Temple,** [8]and as soon as I had
26. 9 the Lord's name that this **Temple** will become like Shiloh and
26.10 the royal palace to the **Temple** and took their places at the
26.12 you heard me say against this **Temple** and against this city.
26.18 a pile of ruins, and the **Temple** hill will become a forest.'
27.16 prophets who say that the **temple** treasures will soon be
27.18 treasures that remain in the **Temple** and in the royal palace
27.19 tank, the carts, and some of the other **temple** treasures.)
27.21 that are left in the **Temple** and in the royal palace in
28. 1 prophet from the town of Gibeon, spoke to me in the **Temple.**
28. 3 to this place all the **temple** treasures that King
28. 5 people who were standing in the **Temple,** I said to Hananiah:
28. 6 back from Babylonia all the **temple** treasures and all the
29.26 Jehoiada, and you are now the chief officer in the **Temple.**
32.34 their disgusting idols in the **Temple** built for my worship,
33.11 You will hear people sing as they bring thank-offerings to my **Temple;**
34.15 in my presence, in the **Temple** where I am worshipped.
35. 2 one of the rooms in the **Temple** and offer them some wine."
35. 4 all his brothers and sons—[4]and brought them to the **Temple.**
35. 4 an important official in the **Temple,** and near the rooms of
36. 5 "I am no longer allowed to go into the **Temple.**
36. 8 the Lord's words in the **Temple** exactly as I had told him
36.10 He did this in the **Temple,** from the room of Gemariah son
36.10 court near the entrance of the New Gate of the **Temple.**
38.14 the third entrance to the **Temple,** and he said, "I am going
41. 5 They were taking corn and incense to offer in the **Temple.**
50.28 God took revenge for what the Babylonians had done to his **Temple.)**
51.11 how he will take revenge for the destruction of his **Temple.**
51.51 foreigners have taken over the holy places in the **Temple.'**
52.13 He burnt down the **Temple,** the palace, and the houses of
52.17 were in the **Temple,** together with the large bronze tank,
52.18 all the other bronze articles used in the **temple** service.
52.20 Solomon had made for the **Temple**—the two columns, the carts,
52.24 in rank, and the three other important **temple** officials.
Lam 1. 4 No one comes to the **Temple** now to worship on the holy
1.10 She saw them enter the **Temple** itself, Where the Lord had

Lam 2. 1 On the day of his anger he abandoned even his **Temple.**
2. 6 He smashed to pieces the **Temple** where we worshipped him;
2. 7 The Lord rejected his altar and deserted his holy **Temple;**
2.20 Priests and prophets are being killed in the **Temple** itself!
4. 1 the stones of the **Temple** lie scattered in the streets.
Ezek 5.11 Lord—because you defiled my **Temple** with all the evil,
7.22 not interfere when my treasured **Temple** is profaned, when
8. 3 the north gate of the **Temple,** where there was an idol that
8.14 the north gate of the **Temple** and showed me women weeping
8.16 So he took me to the inner courtyard of the **Temple.**
8.17 do them here in the **Temple** itself and make me even more
9. 2 outer north gate of the **Temple,** each one carrying a weapon.
9. 3 where it had been, and moved to the entrance of the **Temple.**
9. 6 Start here at my **Temple."**
9. 6 with the leaders who were standing there at the **Temple.**
9. 7 God said to them, "Defile the **Temple.**
10. 3 to the south of the **Temple** when he went in, and a
10. 4 from the creatures and moved to the entrance of the **Temple.**
10. 4 Then the cloud filled the **Temple,** and the courtyard was
10.18 left the entrance of the **Temple** and moved to a place above
10.19 the east gate of the **Temple,** and the dazzling light was over
11. 1 me up and took me to the east gate of the **Temple.**
23.38 They profaned my **Temple** and broke the Sabbath,
23.39 to idols, they came to my **Temple** and profaned it!
24.21 You are proud of the strength of the **Temple.**
24.25 from them the strong **Temple** that was their pride and joy,
25. 3 were delighted to see my **Temple** profaned, to see the land of
37.26 their population, and put my **Temple** in their land, where it
37.28 When I place my **Temple** there to be among them for ever,
Dan 1. 2 King Jehoiakim and seize some of the **temple** treasures.
5. 2 Nebuchadnezzar had carried off from the **Temple** in Jerusalem.
5.23 and brought in the cups and bowls taken from his **Temple.**
8.11 daily sacrifices offered to him, and desecrated the **Temple.**
8.13 will the army of heaven and the **Temple** be trampled on?"
8.14 Then the **Temple** will be restored."
9.17 Restore your **Temple,** which has been destroyed;
9.20 pleading with the Lord my God to restore his holy **Temple.**
9.24 will come true, and the holy **Temple** will be rededicated.
9.26 The city and the **Temple** will be destroyed by the invading
9.27 the highest point of the **Temple** and will remain there until
11.31 Some of his soldiers will desecrate the **Temple.**
11.45 between the sea and the mountain on which the **Temple** stands.
Hos 9. 4 of it will be taken as an offering to the Lord's **Temple.**
9. 8 Even in God's **Temple** the people are the prophet's enemies.
Joel 1. 9 There is no corn or wine to offer in the **Temple;**
1.13 Go into the **Temple** and mourn all night!
1.14 people of Judah into the **Temple** of the Lord your God and
1.16 There is no joy in the **Temple** of our God.
2.17 altar and the entrance of the **Temple,** must weep and pray:
3.18 stream will flow from the **Temple** of the Lord, and it will
Amos 9. 1 "Strike the tops of the **temple** columns so hard that the
Jon 2. 4 your presence and would never see your holy **Temple** again.
2. 7 I prayed to you, and in your holy **Temple** you heard me.
Mic 1. 2 He speaks from his heavenly **temple.**
3.12 a pile of ruins, and the **Temple** hill will become a forest.
4. 1 come the mountain where the **Temple** stands will be the
4. 2 up the hill of the Lord, to the **Temple** of Israel's God.
Hab 2.20 The Lord is in his holy **Temple;**
Hag 1. 2 say that this is not the right time to rebuild the **Temple."**
1. 4 living in well-built houses while my **Temple** lies in ruins?
1. 8 Now go up into the hills, get timber, and rebuild the **Temple;**
1. 9 Because my **Temple** lies in ruins while every one of you is
1.14 The Lord inspired everyone to work on the **Temple:**
1.14 They began working on the **Temple** of the Lord Almighty,
2. 3 who can still remember how splendid the **Temple** used to be?
2. 7 be brought here, and the **Temple** will be filled with wealth.
2. 9 The new **Temple** will be more splendid than the old one, and
2.15 you started to rebuild the **Temple,** [16]you would go to a
2.18 day that the foundation of the **Temple** has been completed.
Zech 1.16 My **Temple** will be restored, and the city will be rebuilt."
3. 7 be in charge of my **Temple** and its courts, and I will
4. 7 You will rebuild the **Temple,** and as you put the last stone
4. 9 foundation of the **Temple,** and he will finish the building.
4.10 Zerubbabel continuing to build the **Temple,** and they will be glad."
6.12 The Branch will flourish where he is and rebuild the Lord's
Temple.
6.14 a memorial in the Lord's **Temple** in honour of Heldai,
6.15 away will come and help to rebuild the **Temple** of the Lord.
7. 2 and their men to the **Temple** of the Lord Almighty to pray
7. 3 of the destruction of the **Temple,** by fasting in the fifth
8. 9 time the foundation was being laid for rebuilding my **Temple.**
11.13 The Lord said to me, "Put them in the **temple** treasury."
11.13 thought I was worth—and put them in the **temple** treasury.
14.20 The cooking-pots in the **Temple** will be as sacred as the
14.21 longer be any merchant in the **Temple** of the Lord Almighty.
Mal 1.10 of you would close the **temple** doors so as to prevent you
2.11 They have defiled the **Temple** which the Lord loves.
3. 1 Lord you are looking for will suddenly come to his **Temple.**
3.10 of your tithes to the **Temple,** so that there will be plenty
Mt 4. 5 the highest point of the **Temple,** [6]and said to him, "If you
12. 5 Sabbath the priests in the **Temple** actually break the Sabbath law,
12. 6 I tell you that there is something here greater than the **Temple.**
17.24 Capernaum, the collectors of the **temple-tax** came to Peter
17.24 and asked, "Does your teacher pay the **temple-tax?"**
17.27 will find a coin worth enough for my **temple-tax** and yours.
21.12 Jesus went into the **Temple** and drove out all those who
21.13 Scriptures that God said, 'My **Temple** will be called a house
21.14 the crippled came to him in the **Temple,** and he healed them.
21.15 and the children shouting in the **Temple,** "Praise to David's Son!"
21.23 Jesus came back to the **Temple;**
23.16 'If someone swears by the **Temple,** he isn't bound by his vow;

Mt 23.16 if he swears by the gold in the **Temple,** he is bound.'
23.17 important, the gold or the **Temple** which makes the gold holy?
23.21 when he swears by the **Temple,** he is swearing by it
23.35 whom you murdered between the **Temple** and the altar.
23.38 And so your **Temple** will be abandoned and empty.
24. 1 was going away from the **Temple** when his disciples came to
26.55 down and taught in the **Temple,** and you did not arrest me.
26.61 able to tear down God's **Temple** and three days later build it
27. 5 Judas threw the coins down in the **Temple** and left;
27. 6 it is against our Law to put it in the **temple** treasury."
27.40 going to tear down the **Temple** and build it up again in
27.51 the curtain hanging in the **Temple** was torn in two from top
Mk 11.11 Jesus entered Jerusalem, went into the **Temple,** and looked round
11.15 Jerusalem, Jesus went to the **Temple** and began to drive out
11.16 would not let anyone carry anything through the **temple**
courtyards.
11.17 Scriptures that God said, 'My **Temple** will be called a house
11.27 Jesus was walking in the **Temple,** the chief priests, the teachers
12.35 Jesus was teaching in the **Temple,** he asked the question,
12.41 As Jesus sat near the **temple** treasury, he watched the people
13. 1 As Jesus was leaving the **Temple,** one of his disciples said,
13. 3 of Olives, across from the **Temple,** when Peter, James, John,
14.49 with you teaching in the **Temple,** and you did not arrest me.
14.58 'I will tear down this **Temple** which men have made, and after
15.29 going to tear down the **Temple** and build it up again in
15.38 The curtain hanging in the **Temple** was torn in two, from
Lk 1. 8 as a priest in the **Temple,** taking his turn in the daily
1. 9 So he went into the **Temple** of the Lord, [10]while the crowd
1.21 why he was spending such a long time in the **Temple.**
1.22 so they knew that he had seen a vision in the **Temple.**
1.23 of service in the **Temple** was over, Zechariah went back home.
2.27 Led by the Spirit, Simeon went into the **Temple.**
2.27 the child Jesus into the **Temple** to do for him what the
2.36 She never left the **Temple;**
2.46 they found him in the **Temple,** sitting with the Jewish teachers,
4. 9 the highest point of the **Temple,** and said to him, "If you
13.35 And so your **Temple** will be abandoned.
18.10 there were two men who went up to the **Temple** to pray:
19.45 Then Jesus went into the **Temple** and began to drive out
19.46 Scriptures that God said, 'My **Temple** will be called a house
19.47 Every day Jesus taught in the **Temple.**
20. 1 when Jesus was in the **Temple** teaching the people and preaching
21. 1 dropping their gifts in the **temple** treasury, [2]and he also saw
21. 5 disciples were talking about the **Temple,** how beautiful it looked
21.37 those days teaching in the **Temple,** and when evening came, he
21.38 morning all the people went to the **Temple** to listen to him.
22.53 was with you in the **Temple** every day, and you did not
23.45 and the curtain hanging in the **Temple** was torn in two.
24.53 and spent all their time in the **Temple** giving thanks to God.
Jn 2.14 There in the **Temple** he found men selling cattle, sheep,
2.15 animals out of the **Temple,** both the sheep and the cattle;
2.19 Jesus answered, "Tear down this **Temple,** and in three days
2.20 "It has taken forty-six years to build this **Temple!"**
2.21 But the **temple** Jesus was speaking about was his body.
5.14 Jesus found him in the **Temple** and said, "Listen, you are
7.14 half over when Jesus went to the **Temple** and began teaching.
7.28 As Jesus taught in the **Temple,** he said in a loud voice,
8. 2 Early the next morning he went back to the **Temple.**
8.20 as he taught in the **Temple,** in the room where the offering
8.59 to throw at him, but Jesus hid himself and left the **Temple.**
10.22 Festival of the Dedication of the **Temple** was being celebrated in
Jerusalem.
10.23 in Solomon's Porch in the **Temple,** [24]when the people gathered
11.48 authorities will take action and destroy our **Temple** and our
nation!"
11.56 as they gathered in the **Temple,** they asked one another,
18.20 synagogues and in the **Temple,** where all the people come
together.
Acts 2.46 as a group in the **Temple,** and they had their meals together
3. 1 John went to the **Temple** at three o'clock in the afternoon,
3. 2 for money from the people who were going into the **Temple.**
3. 8 Then he went into the **Temple** with them, walking and jumping
5.20 "Go and stand in the **Temple,** and tell the people all
5.21 obeyed, and at dawn they entered the **Temple** and started
teaching.
5.25 you put in prison are in the **Temple** teaching the people!"
5.42 And every day in the **Temple** and in people's homes they
6.13 "is always talking against our sacred **Temple** and the Law of
Moses.
6.14 Nazareth will tear down the **Temple** and change all the customs
21.26 Then he went into the **Temple** and gave notice of how many
21.27 some Jews from the province of Asia saw Paul in the **Temple.**
21.28 the people of Israel, the Law of Moses, and this **Temple.**
21.28 brought some Gentiles into the **Temple** and defiled this holy
place!"
21.29 and they thought that Paul had taken him into the **Temple.)**
21.30 together, seized Paul, and dragged him out of the **Temple.**
21.30 At once the **Temple** doors were closed.
22.17 I was praying in the **Temple,** I had a vision, [18]in which
24. 6 He also tried to defile the **Temple,** and we arrested him.
24.12 arguing with anyone in the **Temple,** nor did they find me
24.18 they found me in the **Temple** after I had completed the
25. 8 Jews or against the **Temple** or against the Roman Emperor."
26.21 while I was in the **Temple,** and they tried to kill me.
1 Cor 3.16 know that you are God's **temple** and that God's Spirit lives
3.17 So if anyone destroys God's **temple,** God will destroy him.
3.17 For God's **temple** is holy, and you yourselves are his temple.
6.19 that your body is the **temple** of the Holy Spirit, who lives
9.13 men who work in the **Temple** get their food from the Temple
2 Cor 6.16 How can God's **temple** come to terms with pagan idols?
6.16 For we are the **temple** of the living God!

Eph 2.21 makes it grow into a sacred **temple** dedicated to the Lord.
2 Thes 2. 4 in and sit down in God's **Temple** and claim to be God.
Heb 6.19 the curtain of the heavenly **temple** into the inner sanctuary.
1 Pet 2. 5 used in building the spiritual **temple,** where you will serve
Rev 3.12 victorious a pillar in the **temple** of my God, and he will
7.15 God's throne and serve him day and night in his **temple.**
11. 1 told, "Go and measure the **temple** of God and the altar,
11. 1 and count those who are worshipping in the **temple.**
11.19 God's **temple** in heaven was opened, and the Covenant Box
14.15 angel came out from the **temple** and cried out in a loud
14.17 angel come out of the **temple** in heaven, and he also had
15. 5 After this I saw the **temple** in heaven open, with the Tent
15. 6 plagues came out of the **temple,** dressed in clean shining linen
15. 8 The **temple** was filled with smoke from the glory and power
15. 8 one could go into the **temple** until the seven plagues brought
16. 1 a loud voice speaking from the **temple** to the seven angels:
16.17 came from the throne in the **temple,** saying, "It is done!"
21.22 I did not see a **temple** in the city,
21.22 because its **temple** is the Lord God Almighty and

TEMPLE (2) (OF OTHER GODS)

Judg 9. 4 pieces of silver from the **temple** of Baal-of-the-Covenant,
9.27 They went into the **temple** of their god, where they ate and
9.46 in the stronghold of the **temple** of Baal-of-the-Covenant.
1 Sam 5. 2 Ashdod, [2]took it into the **temple** of their god Dagon, and
31.10 put his weapons in the **temple** of the goddess Astarte, and
1 Kgs 16.32 He built a **temple** to Baal in Samaria,
16.32 made an altar for him, and put it in the **temple.**
2 Kgs 5.18 accompany my king to the **temple** of Rimmon, the god of Syria,
10.21 They all went into the **temple** of Baal, filling it from one
10.23 Jehu himself went into the **temple** with Jonadab son of Rechab
10.24 He had stationed eighty men outside the **temple**
10.25 the inner sanctuary of the **temple,** [26]brought out the
10.27 the sacred pillar and the **temple,**
10.27 and turned the **temple** into a latrine—which it still
11.18 the people went to the **temple** of Baal and tore it down;
19.37 he was worshipping in the **temple** of his god Nisroch, two of
1 Chr 10.10 weapons in one of their **temples**
10.10 and hung his head in the **temple** of their god Dagon.
2 Chr 23.17 they all went to the **temple** of Baal and tore it down.
32.21 when he was in the **temple** of his god, some of his
Ezra 1. 7 and had put in the **temple** of his gods.
5.14 in Jerusalem and had placed in the **temple** in Babylon.
Is 16.12 mountain shrines and to their **temples** to pray, but it will
37.38 he was worshipping in the **temple** of his god Nisroch, two of
Jer 43.12 will set fire to the **temples** of Egypt's gods,
43.13 Egypt and will burn down the **temples** of the Egyptian gods."
Dan 1. 2 back with him to the **temple** of his gods in Babylon,
1. 2 and put the captured treasures in the **temple** storerooms.
Joel 3. 5 and gold and carried my rich treasures into your **temples.**
Amos 2. 8 In the **temple** of their God they drink wine which they have
7.13 This is the king's place of worship, the national **temple."**
Nah 1.14 destroy the idols that are in the **temples** of their gods.
Zech 5.11 "To Babylonia, where they will build a **temple** for it.
5.11 When the **temple** is finished, the basket will be placed there
Acts 14.13 of the god Zeus, whose **temple** stood just outside the town,
17.24 Lord of heaven and earth and does not live in man-made **temples.**
19.24 made silver models of the **temple** of the goddess Artemis, and
19.27 also the danger that the **temple** of the great goddess Artemis
19.35 is the keeper of the **temple** of the great Artemis and of
19.37 though they have not robbed **temples** or said evil things
Rom 2.22 You detest idols—but do you rob **temples?**
1 Cor 8.10 who have so-called "knowledge," eating in the **temple** of an idol;

TEMPLE GUARD

1 Chr 9.17 The following **temple guards** lived in Jerusalem:
15.17 Azaziah, and the **temple guards,** Obed Edom and Jeiel.
26. 1 of work for the Levites who served as **temple guards.**
26.11 thirteen members of Hosah's family who were **temple guards.**
26.12 The **temple guards** were divided into groups,
2 Chr 8.14 He also organized the **temple guards** in sections for
Ezra 2.40 **Temple guards** (descendants of Shallum, Ater, Talmon, Akkub,
2.70 the musicians, the **temple guards,** and the temple workmen
7. 6 which included priests, Levites, temple musicians, **temple guards,**
10.24 **Temple guards:**
Neh 7. 1 put in place, and the **temple guards,** the members of the
7.43 **Temple guards**
7.73 The priests, the Levites, the **temple guards,** the
10.28 Levites, the **temple guards,** the temple musicians, the temple
10.39 who are on duty, the **temple guards,** and the members of the
11.19 **Temple guards:**
12.25 The following **temple guards** were in charge of guarding
12.45 The temple musicians and the **temple guards** also performed
12.47 the support of the temple musicians and the **temple guards.**
13. 5 Levites, to the temple musicians, and to the **temple guards.**
Lk 22. 4 and the officers of the **temple guard** about how he could
22.52 and the officers of the **temple guard** and the elders who had
Jn 18. 3 Roman soldiers, and some **temple guards** sent by the chief priests
19. 6 the chief priests and the **temple guards** saw him, they shouted,
Acts 4. 1 officer in charge of the **temple guards,** and some Sadducees arrived.
5.24 officer in charge of the **temple guards** heard this, they wondered

TEMPLE PROSTITUTE see PROSTITUTE

TEMPLE TREASURY

Mt 27. 6 it is against our Law to put it in the **temple treasury."**
Mk 12.41 As Jesus sat near the **temple treasury,** he watched the people
Lk 21. 1 dropping their gifts in the **temple treasury,** [2]and he also saw

TEMPLE-TAX see TAX

TEMPORARY

Ex 12.45 No **temporary** resident or hired worker may eat it.
Num 15.14 among you, whether on a **temporary** or a permanent basis,
35.15 for foreigners who are **temporary** or permanent residents.
Neh 8.14 live in **temporary** shelters during the Festival of Shelters.
1 Cor 13. 8 There are inspired messages, but they are **temporary;**
2 Cor 4.17 And this small and **temporary** trouble we suffer will

TEMPT

Ex 34.15 them, and you will be **tempted** to eat the food they offer
Deut 4.19 Do not be **tempted** to worship and serve what you see in
Prov 1.10 When sinners **tempt** you, my son, don't give in.
6.25 Don't be **tempted** by their beauty;
7.21 So she **tempted** him with her charms, and he gave in to
23.31 Don't let wine **tempt** you, even though it is rich red,
Is 13.17 They care nothing for silver and are not **tempted** by gold.
Mt 4. 1 Spirit led Jesus into the desert to be **tempted** by the Devil.
26.41 Keep watch and pray that you will not fall into **temptation.**
Mk 1.13 the desert, [13]where he stayed forty days, being **tempted** by Satan.
14.38 "Keep watch, and pray that you will not fall into **temptation.**
Lk 4. 2 desert, [2]where he was **tempted** by the Devil for forty days.
4.13 When the Devil finished **tempting** Jesus in every way, he
22.40 to them, "Pray that you will not fall into **temptation."**
22.46 Get up and pray that you will not fall into **temptation."**
1 Cor 7. 5 in to Satan's **temptation** because of your lack of self-control.
Gal 6. 1 an eye on yourselves, so that you will not be **tempted,** too.
1 Thes 3. 5 be that the Devil had **tempted** you and all our work had
1 Tim 6. 9 to get rich fall into **temptation** and are caught in the trap
Heb 2.18 can help those who are **tempted,** because he himself was tempted
4.15 a High Priest who was **tempted** in every way that we are,
Jas 1.13 If a person is **tempted** by such trials,
1.13 he must not say, "This **temptation** comes from God."
1.13 God cannot be tempted by evil, and he himself **tempts** no one.
1.14 But a person is **tempted** when he is drawn away and

AV TEMPTATION see TEST(ing)

AV TEMPTER see DEVIL

TEN
[ONE-TENTH]
see also **TITHE**

Gen 8. 5 the first day of the **tenth** month the tops of the mountains
14.20 And Abram gave Melchizedek a **tenth** of all the loot he had
16. 3 (This happened after Abram had lived in Canaan for **ten** years.)
18.32 What if only **ten** are found?"
18.32 He said, "I will not destroy it if there are **ten."**
24.10 charge of Abraham's property, took **ten** of his master's
24.55 with us a week or **ten** days, and then she may go."
28.22 and I will give you a **tenth** of everything you give me."
31. 7 Yet he has cheated me and changed my wages **ten** times.
31.41 And even then, you changed my wages **ten** times.
32.13 their young, forty cows and **ten** bulls,
32.13 twenty female donkeys and **ten** males.
42. 3 So Joseph's **ten** half-brothers went to buy corn in Egypt,
45.23 He sent his father **ten** donkeys loaded with the best
45.23 Egyptian goods and **ten** donkeys loaded with corn, bread,
Ex 12. 3 On the **tenth** day of this month each man must choose either
18.21 leaders of thousands, hundreds, fifties, and **tens.**
18.25 leaders of thousands, hundreds, fifties, and **tens.**
26. 1 of my presence, out of **ten** pieces of fine linen woven with
27.12 to be curtains 22 metres long, with **ten** posts and ten bases.
34.28 the tablets the words of the covenant—the **Ten** Commandments.
34.29 from Mount Sinai carrying the **Ten** Commandments, his face was
36. 8 They made it out of **ten** pieces of fine linen woven with
38.12 curtains 22 metres long, with **ten** posts and ten bases and
38.21 were kept on which the **Ten** Commandments were written.
40. 3 the Covenant Box containing the **Ten** Commandments and put the
Lev 16.29 On the **tenth** day of the seventh month the Israelites and the
23.26 The **tenth** day of the seventh month is the day when
23.32 month to sunset on the **tenth** observe this day as a special
25. 9 Then, on the **tenth** day of the seventh month, the Day of
26.26 your food supply, so that **ten** women will need only one oven
27. 3 **10** pieces of silver
27. 3 **10** pieces of silver
27.16 it, at the rate of **ten** pieces of silver for every twenty
27.30 **One-tenth** of all the produce of the land, whether grain or fruit,
27.32 One out of every **ten** domestic animals belongs to the Lord.
27.32 When the animals are counted, every **tenth** one belongs to the Lord.
Num 11.19 two days, or five, or **ten,** or even twenty days, [20]but for
18.26 possession, you must present a **tenth** of it as a special
29. 7 Gather for worship on the **tenth** day of the seventh month;
29.23 On the fourth day offer **ten** young bulls, two rams, and
Deut 1.15 some for a hundred, some for fifty, and some for **ten.**
4.13 you—you must obey the **Ten** Commandments, which he wrote on
10. 4 written the first time, the **Ten** Commandments that he gave

Deut 14.22 "Set aside a tithe—a **tenth** of all that your fields
23. 2 a person, even in the **tenth** generation, may be included
23. 3 their descendants, even in the **tenth** generation—may be
26.12 year give the tithe—a **tenth** of your crops—to the Levites,
Josh 4.19 crossed the Jordan on the **tenth** day of the first month and
15.57 **ten** cities, along with the towns round them.
17. 5 That is why Manasseh received **ten** shares in addition to
21. 5 Kohath was assigned **ten** cities from the territories of Ephraim,
21.26 the clan of Kohath received **ten** cities in all, with their
22.14 **Ten** leading men went with Phinehas, one from each of the
22.30 Phinehas the priest and the **ten** leading men of the
Judg 6.19 a young goat and used **ten** kilogrammes of flour to make bread
6.27 So Gideon took **ten** of his servants and did what the Lord
12.11 After Ibzan, Elon from Zebulun led Israel for **ten** years.
17.10 and I will give you **ten** pieces of silver a year, some
20.10 One **tenth** of the men in Israel will provide food for the
Ruth 1. 4 About **ten** years later [5]Mahlon and Chilion also died, and
2.17 had beaten it out, she found she had nearly **ten** kilogrammes.
4. 2 Then Boaz got **ten** of the leaders of the town and asked
1 Sam 1. 8 Don't I mean more to you than **ten** sons?"
1.24 along a three-year-old bull, **ten** kilogrammes of flour,
8.15 He will take a **tenth** of your corn and of your grapes
8.17 He will take a **tenth** of your flocks.
17.17 Jesse said to David, "Take **ten** kilogrammes of this roasted
17.17 grain and these **ten** loaves of bread, and hurry
17.18 And take these **ten** cheeses to the commanding officer.
25. 5 about it, [5]so he sent **ten** young men with orders to go
25.38 Some **ten** days later the Lord struck Nabal and he died.
2 Sam 15.16 family and officials, except for **ten** concubines, whom he
18.11 would have given you **ten** pieces of silver and a belt."
18.15 Then **ten** of Joab's soldiers closed in on Absalom and
19.43 The Israelites replied, "We have **ten** times as many
20. 3 in Jerusalem, he took the **ten** concubines he had left to take
1 Kgs 4.23 **ten** stall-fed cattle, twenty pasture-fed cattle,
7.27 Huram also made **ten** bronze carts;
7.38 Huram also made **ten** basins, one for each cart.
7.40 The **ten** carts The ten basins
7.49 bread offered to God, [49]the **ten** lamp-stands that stood in
11.31 and said to Jeroboam, "Take **ten** pieces for yourself,
11.31 kingdom away from Solomon, and I will give you **ten** tribes.
11.35 son and will give you **ten** tribes, [36]but I will let
14. 3 Take him **ten** loaves of bread, some cakes, and a jar of
2 Kgs 5. 5 thousand pieces of gold, and **ten** changes of fine clothes.
13. 7 forces left except fifty horsemen, **ten** chariots, and ten
15.17 king of Israel, and he ruled in Samaria for **ten** years.
20. 9 stairway to go forward **ten** steps or go back **ten** steps?"
20.10 "It's easy to make the shadow go forward **ten** steps!
20.10 Make it go back **ten** steps."
20.11 made the shadow go back **ten** steps on the stairway set up
25. 1 and attacked Jerusalem on the **tenth** day of the tenth month
25.25 to Mizpah with **ten** men, attacked Gedaliah and killed him.
1 Chr 6.61 **Ten** towns in the territory of West Manasseh were
27. 2 **Tenth** month:
2 Chr 4. 6 They also made **ten** basins, five to be placed on the south
4. 7 They made **ten** gold lampstands according to the usual pattern,
4. 7 and **ten** tables,
4.11 The **ten** carts The ten basins
14. 1 as king, and under Asa the land enjoyed peace for **ten** years.
31.13 **Ten** Levites were assigned to work under them:
36. 9 and he ruled in Jerusalem for three months and **ten** days.
Ezra 8.24 I chose Sherebiah, Hashabiah, and **ten** others.
10.16 first day of the **tenth** month they began their investigation,
Neh 5.18 and many chickens, and every **ten** days I provided a fresh
10.38 temple storerooms one **tenth** of all the tithes they collect.
11. 1 one family out of every **ten** to go and live
Esth 2.16 year as king, in the **tenth** month, the month of Tebeth,
9. 7 Among them were the **ten** sons of Haman
9.12 Jews have killed five hundred men, including Haman's **ten** sons.
9.13 order the bodies of Haman's **ten** sons to be hung from the
9.14 The bodies of Haman's **ten** sons were publicly displayed.
Ecc 7.19 more for a person than **ten** rulers can do for a city.
Is 5.10 The grapevines growing on **ten** hectares of land will
6.13 if one person out of **ten** remains in the land, he too
38. 8 the Lord will make the shadow go back **ten** steps."
38. 8 And the shadow moved back **ten** steps.
Jer 32. 1 spoke to me in the **tenth** year that Zedekiah was king of
39. 1 In the **tenth** month of the ninth year that Zedekiah was
41. 1 chief officers, went to Mizpah with **ten** men to see Gedaliah.
41. 2 meal together, [2]Ishmael and the **ten** men with him pulled out
41. 8 But there were **ten** men in the group who said to Ishmael,
42. 7 **Ten** days later the Lord spoke to me;
52. 4 and attacked Jerusalem on the **tenth** day of the tenth month
52.12 On the **tenth** day of the fifth month of the nineteenth
Ezek 20. 1 It was the **tenth** day of the fifth month of the seventh
24. 1 On the **tenth** day of the tenth month of the ninth year
29. 1 the tenth month of the **tenth** year of our exile, the Lord
33.21 the fifth day of the **tenth** month of the twelfth year of
40. 1 It was the **tenth** day of the new year, which was the
40.14 He measured that room and found it was **ten** metres wide.
40.49 room, which was **ten** metres wide and six metres deep.
41. 2 it was twenty metres long, and **ten** metres wide.
41. 4 He measured the room itself, and it was **ten** metres square.
41. 8 there was an open space **ten** metres across, along the sides
42. 3 side it faced the space **ten** metres wide which was alongside
45. 1 be twelve and a half kilometres long by **ten** kilometres wide.
45.11 1 homer = **10** ephahs = 10 baths
45.13 **10** baths = 1 homer = 1 kor.)
48. 9 and a half kilometres by **ten** kilometres is to be dedicated
Dan 1.12 "Test us for **ten** days," he said.
1.14 He agreed to let them try it for **ten** days.
1.20 he raised, these four knew **ten** times more than any
Dan 7. 7 Unlike the other beasts, it had **ten** horns.
7.20 wanted to know about the **ten** horns on its head and the
7.24 The **ten** horns are ten kings who will rule that empire.
Amos 5. 3 another city sends out a hundred, but only **ten** come back."
6. 9 If there are **ten** men left in a family, they will die.
Zech 8.19 the fourth, fifth, seventh, and **tenth** months will become
8.23 In those days **ten** foreigners will come to one Jew and say,
Mt 20.24 When the other **ten** disciples heard about this, they became
23.23 You give to God a **tenth** even of the seasoning herbs,
25. 1 Once there were **ten** girls who took their oil lamps and went
25. 7 The **ten** girls woke up and trimmed their lamps.
Mk 10.41 When the other **ten** disciples heard about it, they became angry
Lk 11.42 You give God a **tenth** of the seasoning herbs, such as mint
15. 8 suppose a woman who has **ten** silver coins loses one of them
17.12 he was met by **ten** men suffering from a dreaded skin-disease.
17.17 Jesus said, "There were **ten** men who were healed;
18.12 a week, and I give you a **tenth** of all my income.'
19.13 he left, he called his **ten** servants and gave them each a
19.16 said, 'Sir, I have earned **ten** gold coins with the one you
19.17 in small matters, I will put you in charge of **ten** cities.'
19.24 from him and give it to the servant who has **ten** coins.'
19.25 But they said to him, 'Sir, he already has **ten** coins!'
Acts 25. 6 Festus spent another eight or **ten** days with them and then
Heb 7. 2 him, [2]and Abraham gave him a **tenth** of all he had taken.
7. 4 famous ancestor, gave him a **tenth** of all he got in the
7. 5 the Law to collect a **tenth** from the people of Israel,
7. 6 Levi, but he collected a **tenth** from Abraham and blessed him,
7. 8 case of the priests the **tenth** is collected by men who die;
7. 8 as for Melchizedek the **tenth** was collected by one who lives,
7. 9 when Abraham paid the **tenth**,
7. 9 Levi (whose descendants collect the **tenth**) also paid it.
Rev 2.10 thrown into prison, and your troubles will last **ten** days.
11.13 a **tenth** of the city was destroyed, and seven thousand people
12. 3 dragon with seven heads and **ten** horns and a crown on each
13. 1 It had **ten** horns and seven heads;
17. 3 the beast had seven heads and **ten** horns.
17. 7 that carries her, the beast with seven heads and **ten** horns.
17.12 ten horns you saw are **ten** kings who have not yet begun
17.13 These **ten** all have the same purpose, and they give their
17.16 The **ten** horns you saw, and the beast, will hate the prostitute;
21.20 the ninth topaz, the **tenth** chalcedony, the eleventh turquoise,
also Num 7.12 1 Chr 24.7 1 Chr 25.9

TEN TOWNS

Mt 4.25 him from Galilee and the **Ten Towns**, from Jerusalem, Judaea,
Mk 5.20 and went all through the **Ten Towns**, telling what Jesus had
7.31 Lake Galilee, going by way of the territory of the **Ten Towns**.

TENANT

Mt 21.33 he let out the vineyard to **tenants** and went on a journey.
21.34 sent his slaves to the **tenants** to receive his share of the
21.35 The **tenants** seized his slaves, beat one, killed another,
21.36 the first time, and the **tenants** treated them the same way.
21.38 But when the **tenants** saw the son, they said to themselves,
21.40 of the vineyard comes, what will he do to those **tenants?"**
21.41 the vineyard out to other **tenants**, who will give him his
Mk 12. 1 let out the vineyard to **tenants** and left home on a journey.
12. 2 sent a slave to the **tenants** to receive from them his share
12. 3 The **tenants** seized the slave, beat him, and sent him back
12. 4 **tenants** beat him over the head and treated him shamefully.
12. 6 Last of all, then, he sent his son to the **tenants**.
12. 7 But those **tenants** said to one another, 'This is the owner's son.
12. 9 kill those men and hand the vineyard over to other **tenants**.
Lk 20. 9 vineyard, let it out to **tenants**, and then left home for a
20.10 sent a slave to the **tenants** to receive from them his share
20.10 But the **tenants** beat the slave and sent him back without a
20.11 but the **tenants** beat him also, treated him shamefully,
20.12 the **tenants** wounded him, too, and threw him out.
20.14 But when the **tenants** saw him, they said to one another,
20.15 "What, then, will the owner of the vineyard do to the **tenants?"**
20.16 those men, and hand the vineyard over to other **tenants."**

TEND

2 Kgs 12.13 bowls, trumpets, or tools for **tending** the lamps, or any
25.14 altar, the tools used in **tending** the lamps, the bowls used
Is 61. 5 of your flocks And farm your land and **tend** your vineyards.
62. 9 You that **tended** and gathered the grapes Will drink the wine
Jer 52.18 altar, the tools used in **tending** the lamps, the bowls used
Ezek 34. 2 You take care of yourselves, but never **tend** the sheep.
34. 3 But you never **tend** the sheep.

TENDER

Gen 18. 7 out a calf that was **tender** and fat, and gave it to
43.30 his heart was full of **tender** feelings for his brother.
Deut 32. 2 showers on young plants, like gentle rain on **tender** grass.
Ezek 17.22 the top of a tall cedar and break off a **tender** sprout;
Mt 24.32 branches become green and **tender** and it starts putting out leaves,
Mk 4.28 first the **tender** stalk appears, then the ear, and finally
13.28 branches become green and **tender** and it starts putting out leaves,
Lk 1.78 Our God is merciful and **tender**.
Eph 4.32 Instead, be kind and **tender-hearted** to one another, and forgive

TENT (1)

Gen 4.20 the ancestor of those who raise livestock and live in **tents**.
9.21 drunk, took off his clothes, and lay naked in his **tent**.
9.23 They walked backwards into the **tent** and covered their father,

Gen	18. 1	at the entrance of his **tent** during the hottest part of the
	18. 6	Abraham hurried into the **tent** and said to Sarah, "Quick,
	18. 9	"She is there in the **tent,**" he answered.
	18.10	Sarah was behind him, at the door of the **tent,** listening.
	24.67	Isaac brought Rebecca into the **tent** that his mother Sarah
	31.33	Laban went and searched Jacob's **tent;**
	31.33	into Leah's tent, and the **tent** of the two slave-women, but
	31.33	Then he went into Rachel's **tent.**
	31.34	Laban searched through the whole **tent,** but did not find them.
Ex	18. 7	They asked about each other's health and then went into Moses'
		tent.
	33. 8	at the door of their **tents** and watch Moses until he entered
Lev	14. 8	the camp, but he must live outside his **tent** for seven days.
Num	11.10	they stood about in groups at the entrances of their **tents.**
	16.24	people to move away from the **tents** of Korah, Dathan, and
	16.26	people, "Stand away from the **tents** of these wicked men and
	16.27	So they moved away from the **tents** of Korah, Dathan, and
	16.27	the entrance of their **tents,** with their wives and children.
	19.14	If someone dies in a **tent,** anyone who is in the tent
	19.15	jar and pot in the **tent** that has no lid on it
	19.18	the water, and sprinkle the **tent,** everything in it, and the
	24. 5	The **tents** of Israel are beautiful, [6] Like long rows of
	25. 6	a Midianite woman into his **tent** in the sight of Moses and
	25. 8	and the woman into the **tent,** and drove the spear through
Deut	5.30	Go and tell them to return to their **tents.**
	11. 6	families, their **tents,** and all their servants and animals.
Josh	7.21	buried inside my **tent,** with the silver at the bottom."
	7.22	men, who ran to the **tent** and found that the condemned things
	7.23	brought them out of the **tent,** took them to Joshua and all
	7.24	donkeys, and sheep, his **tent,** and everything else he owned;
Judg	4.11	Kenite had set up his **tent** close to Kedesh near the oak-tree
	4.17	Sisera ran away to the **tent** of Jael, the wife of Heber
	4.18	come into my **tent.**
	4.20	at the door of the **tent,** and if anyone comes and asks
	5.24	the Kenite— the most fortunate of women who live in **tents.**
	6. 5	They would come with their livestock and **tents,**
	7.13	loaf of barley bread rolled into our camp and hit a **tent.**
	7.13	The **tent** collapsed and lay flat on the ground."
	20. 8	whether he lives in a **tent** or in a house, will go
1 Sam	17.54	Jerusalem, but he kept Goliath's weapons in his own **tent.**
2 Sam	16.22	So they set up a **tent** for Absalom on the palace roof,
1 Kgs	20.12	his allies, the other rulers, were drinking in their **tents.**
	20.16	Benhadad and his thirty-two allies were getting drunk in their
		tents.
2 Kgs	7. 7	for their lives, abandoning their **tents,** horses, and
	7. 8	camp, they went into a **tent,** ate and drank what was there,
	7. 8	they returned, entered another **tent,** and did the same thing.
	7.10	not been untied, and the **tents** are just as the Syrians left
1 Chr	4.41	to Gerar and destroyed the **tents** and huts of the people who
	17. 5	I have always lived in **tents** and moved from place to place.
Job	5.24	Then you will live at peace in your **tent;**
	18. 6	The lamp in his **tent** will be darkened.
	18.14	He is torn from the **tent** where he lived secure, and is
	18.15	anyone may live in his **tent**— after sulphur is sprinkled to
	19.12	they dig trenches and lay siege to my **tent.**
Ps	69.25	may no one be left alive in their **tents.**
	78.28	they fell in the middle of the camp all round the **tents.**
	104. 2	out the heavens like a **tent** [3] and built your home on the
	106.25	They stayed in their **tents** and grumbled and would not
	118.15	to the glad shouts of victory in the **tents** of God's people:
Song	1. 5	beautiful, dark as the desert **tents** of Kedar, but beautiful
	1. 8	find pasture for your goats near the **tents** of the shepherds.
Is	13.20	Arab will ever pitch his **tent** there, and no shepherd will
	33.20	It will be like a **tent** that is never moved, whose pegs
	38.12	off and ended, Like a **tent** that is taken down, Like cloth
	40.22	the sky like a curtain, like a **tent** in which to live.
	54. 2	Make the **tent** you live in larger;
Jer	4.20	Suddenly our **tents** are destroyed;
	6. 3	They will pitch their **tents** round the city, and each one
	10.20	Our **tents** are ruined;
	10.20	there is no one left to put up our **tents** again;
	35. 7	us always to live in **tents,** so that we might remain in
	35. 9	for homes—we live in **tents**—and we own no vineyards, fields,
	37.10	are left, lying in their **tents,** those men would still get up
	43.10	that you buried, and will spread the royal **tent** over them.
	49.29	Seize their **tents** and their flocks,
	49.29	their tent curtains and everything in their **tents.**
Dan	11.45	set up his huge royal **tents** between the sea and the mountain
Hos	12. 9	will make you live in **tents** again, as you did when I
Mt	17. 4	wish, I will make three **tents** here, one for you, one for
Mk	9. 5	We will make three **tents,** one for you, one for Moses,
Lk	9.33	We will make three **tents,** one for you, one for Moses,
Acts	7.43	It was the **tent** of the god Molech that you carried,
	18. 3	he earned his living by making **tents,** just as they did.
2 Cor	5. 1	we know that when this **tent** we live in—our body here
	5. 4	we live in this earthly **tent,** we groan with a feeling of
Heb	8. 2	that is, in the real **tent** which was put up by the
	11. 9	He lived in **tents,** as did Isaac and Jacob, who received the

TENT (2) (OF THE LORD'S PRESENCE)

The large tent described in detail in Exodus 26, where the Israelites worshipped God until Solomon built the Temple. It is also called the Tabernacle or Tent of Meeting.

Ex	25. 8	people must make a sacred **tent** for me, so that I may
	26. 1	the interior of the sacred **Tent,** the Tent of my presence,
	26. 7	"Make a cover for the **Tent** out of eleven pieces of cloth
	26. 9	Fold the sixth piece double over the front of the **Tent.**
	26.12	Hang the extra half-piece over the back of the **Tent.**
	26.13	is to hang over the sides of the **Tent** to cover it.
	26.15	"Make upright frames for the **Tent** out of acacia-wood.
Ex	26.20	the north side of the **Tent** [21] and forty silver bases, two
	26.22	For the back of the **Tent** on the west, make six frames,
	26.26	on one side of the **Tent,** [27] five for the frames on the
	26.28	is to extend from one end of the **Tent** to the other.
	26.30	Set up the **Tent** according to the plan that I showed you
	26.33	in the roof of the **Tent,** and behind the curtain put the
	26.35	the north side of the **Tent** and the lamp-stand against the
	26.36	"For the entrance of the **Tent** make a curtain of fine
	27. 9	"For the **Tent** of my presence make an enclosure out of
	27.19	that is used in the **Tent**
	27.19	all the pegs for the **Tent** and for the enclosure
	27.21	the lamp in the **Tent** of my presence outside the curtain
	28.43	when they go into the **Tent** of my presence or approach the
	29. 4	to the entrance of the **Tent** of my presence, and tell them
	29.10	to the front of the **Tent** of my presence and tell Aaron
	29.11	bull there in my holy presence at the entrance of the **Tent.**
	29.30	and who goes into the **Tent** of my presence to serve in
	29.32	At the entrance of the **Tent** of my presence they are to
	29.42	in my presence at the entrance of the **Tent** of my presence.
	29.44	I will make the **Tent** and the altar holy, and I will
	30.16	and spend it for the upkeep of the **Tent** of my presence.
	30.18	Place it between the **Tent** and the altar, and put water in
	30.20	before they go into the **Tent** or approach the altar to
	30.26	Use it to anoint the **Tent** of my presence, the Covenant Box,
	30.36	powder, take it into the **Tent** of my presence, and sprinkle
	31. 7	the **Tent** of my presence, the Covenant Box and its lid, all
	31. 7	the furnishings of the **Tent,** [8] the table and its equipment,
	33. 7	Moses would take the sacred **Tent** and put it up some distance
	33. 7	It was called the **Tent** of the Lord's presence, and anyone
	33. 9	at the door of the **Tent,** and the Lord would speak to
	33.10	of cloud at the door of the **Tent,** they would bow down.
	33.11	who was his helper, Joshua son of Nun, stayed in the **Tent.**
	34.34	Whenever Moses went into the **Tent** of the Lord's presence
	35.11	the **Tent,** its covering and its outer covering, its hooks
	35.15	the curtain for the entrance of the **Tent;**
	35.18	the pegs and ropes for the **Tent** and the enclosure;
	35.21	to the Lord for making the **Tent** of the Lord's presence.
	36. 1	needed to build the sacred **Tent,** are to make everything just
	36. 3	the Israelites had brought for constructing the sacred **Tent.**
	36. 6	was to make any further contribution for the sacred **Tent;**
	36. 8	those doing the work made the **Tent** of the Lord's presence.
	36.14	made a cover for the **Tent** out of eleven pieces of cloth
	36.20	They made upright frames of acacia-wood for the **Tent.**
	36.25	the north side of the **Tent** [26] and forty silver bases, two
	36.27	For the back of the **Tent,** on the west, they made six
	36.31	on one side of the **Tent,** [32] five for the frames on the
	36.33	the frames, extended from one end of the **Tent** to the other.
	36.37	For the entrance of the **Tent** they made a curtain of fine
	38. 8	served at the entrance of the **Tent** of the Lord's presence.
	38. 9	For the **Tent** of the Lord's presence he made the enclosure
	38.20	All the pegs for the **Tent** and for the surrounding
	38.21	the metals used in the **Tent** of the Lord's presence, where
	38.24	the Lord for the sacred **Tent** weighed a thousand kilogrammes,
	38.27	hundred bases for the sacred **Tent** and for the curtain, 34
	38.30	for the entrance of the **Tent** of the Lord's presence, the
	38.31	all the pegs for the **Tent** and the surrounding enclosure.
	39.32	All the work on the **Tent** of the Lord's presence was
	39.33	They brought to Moses the **Tent** and all its equipment,
	39.38	the curtain for the entrance of the **Tent;**
	39.40	the pegs for the **Tent;**
	39.40	all the equipment to be used in the **Tent;**
	40. 2	of the first month set up the **Tent** of the Lord's presence.
	40. 5	Covenant Box and hang the curtain at the entrance of the **Tent.**
	40. 6	Put in front of the **Tent** the altar for burning offerings.
	40. 7	Put the wash-basin between the **Tent** and the altar and fill
	40. 9	"Then dedicate the **Tent** and all its equipment by
	40.12	to the entrance of the **Tent,** and tell them to take a
	40.17	after they left Egypt, the **Tent** of the Lord's presence was
	40.19	out the covering over the **Tent** and put the outer covering
	40.21	he put the box in the **Tent** and hung up the curtain.
	40.22	put the table in the **Tent,** on the north side outside the
	40.24	put the lamp-stand in the **Tent,** on the south side, opposite
	40.26	the gold altar in the **Tent,** in front of the curtain, [27] and
	40.28	at the entrance of the **Tent,** [29] and there in front of the
	40.30	put the wash-basin between the **Tent** and the altar and filled
	40.32	whenever they went into the **Tent** or to the altar, just
	40.33	up the enclosure round the **Tent** and the altar and hung the
	40.34	Then the cloud covered the **Tent** and the dazzling light
	40.35	Because of this, Moses could not go into the **Tent.**
	40.36	to another place only when the cloud lifted from the **Tent.**
	40.38	the Lord's presence over the **Tent** during the day and a fire
Lev	1. 1	called to Moses from the **Tent** of the Lord's presence and
	1. 3	at the entrance of the **Tent** of the Lord's presence so that
	1. 5	sides of the altar which is at the entrance of the **Tent.**
	3. 2	kill it at the entrance of the **Tent** of the Lord's presence.
	3. 8	hand on its head and kill it in front of the **Tent.**
	3.13	hand on its head and kill it in front of the **Tent.**
	4. 4	to the entrance of the **Tent,** put his hand on its head,
	4. 5	take some of the bull's blood and carry it into the **Tent.**
	4. 7	projections at the corners of the incense-altar in the **Tent.**
	4. 7	burning sacrifices, which is at the entrance of the **Tent.**
	4.14	They shall bring it to the **Tent** of the Lord's presence;
	4.16	the bull's blood into the **Tent,** [17] dip his finger in it,
	4.18	of the incense-altar inside the **Tent** and pour out the rest
	4.18	burning sacrifices, which is at the entrance of the **Tent.**
	6.16	place, the courtyard of the **Tent** of the Lord's presence.
	6.26	place, the courtyard of the **Tent** of the Lord's presence.
	6.30	blood is brought into the **Tent** and used in the ritual to
	8. 2	to the entrance of the **Tent** of my presence and bring the
	8.10	and put it on the **Tent** of the Lord's presence and everything
	8.31	to the entrance of the **Tent** of the Lord's presence, boil it,

Lev 8.33 leave the entrance of the **Tent** for seven days, until your
8.35 at the entrance of the **Tent** day and night for seven days,
9. 5 the front of the **Tent** everything that Moses had commanded,
9.23 and Aaron went into the **Tent** of the Lord's presence, and
10. 4 away from the sacred **Tent** and put them outside the camp."
10. 7 leave the entrance of the **Tent** or you will die, because you
10. 9 are not to enter the **Tent** of my presence after drinking wine
10.18 not brought into the sacred **tent,** you should have eaten the
12. 4 holy or enter the sacred **Tent** until the time of her
12. 6 at the entrance of the **Tent** of the Lord's presence a
14.11 to the entrance of the **Tent** of the Lord's presence.
14.23 shall bring them to the priest at the entrance of the **Tent.**
15.14 to the entrance of the **Tent** of the Lord's presence and give
15.29 priest at the entrance of the **Tent** of the Lord's presence.
15.31 they would not defile the **Tent** of his presence, which was in
16. 7 goats to the entrance of the **Tent** of the Lord's presence.
16.16 must do this to the **Tent,** because it stands in the middle
16.17 until he comes out, there must be no one in the **Tent.**
16.20 Place, the rest of the **Tent** of the Lord's presence, and the
16.23 Aaron shall go into the **Tent,** take off the priestly garments
16.33 Place, the rest of the **Tent** of the Lord's presence, the
17. 3 at the entrance of the **Tent** of the Lord's presence has
17. 5 entrance of the **Tent** and kill them as fellowship-offerings.
17. 6 at the entrance of the **Tent** and burn the fat to produce
17. 9 at the entrance of the **Tent** shall no longer be considered
19.21 of the **Tent** of my presence as his repayment-offering,
20. 3 makes my sacred **Tent** unclean and disgraces my holy name,
21.11 he to defile my sacred **Tent** by leaving it and entering a
24. 2 for the lamps in the **Tent,** so that a light may be
26.11 among you in my sacred **tent,** and I will never turn away
Num 1. 1 to Moses there in the **Tent** of his presence in the Sinai
1.50 Levites in charge of the **Tent** of my presence and all its
1.51 the Levites shall take the **Tent** down and set it up again
1.51 Anyone else who comes near the **Tent** shall be put to death.
1.53 Levites shall camp round the **Tent** to guard it, so that no
2. 2 The camp is to be set up all round the **Tent.**
2.17 and the last two the Levites are to march carrying the **Tent.**
3. 7 the work required for the **Tent** of my presence and perform
3. 8 all the equipment of the **Tent** and perform the duties for the
3.23 on the west behind the **Tent,** [24] with Eliasaph son of Lael
3.25 They were responsible for the **Tent,**
3.26 court which is round the **Tent** and the altar, and the curtain
3.29 the south side of the **Tent,** [30] with Elizaphan son of Uzziel
3.35 the north side of the **Tent,** with Zuriel son of Abihail as
3.36 for the frames for the **Tent,** its bars, posts, bases, and all
3.38 sons were to camp in front of the **Tent** on the east.
4. 3 were qualified to work in the **Tent** of the Lord's presence.
4. 5 his sons shall enter the **Tent,** take down the curtain in
4.15 of the clan of Kohath whenever the **Tent** is moved.
4.16 be responsible for the whole **Tent** and for the oil for the
4.16 and everything else in the **Tent** that has been consecrated to
4.20 if the Kohathites enter the **Tent** and see the priests
4.23 were qualified to work in the **Tent** of the Lord's presence.
4.25 the **Tent,** its inner cover, its outer cover, the fine
4.26 court that is round the **Tent** and the altar, the curtains for
4.28 These are the responsibilities of the Gershon clan in the **Tent;**
4.30 were qualified to work in the **Tent** of the Lord's presence.
4.31 posts, and bases of the **Tent,** [32] and the posts, bases,
4.32 of the court round the **Tent,** with all the fittings used in
4.33 of the Merari clan in their service in the **Tent:**
4.34 qualified to work in the **Tent** of the Lord's presence,
5.17 on the floor of the **Tent** of the Lord's presence and put
6.10 priest at the entrance of the **Tent** of the Lord's presence.
6.13 to the entrance of the **Tent** [14] and present to the Lord
6.18 At the entrance of the **Tent** the Nazirite shall shave off
7. 1 Moses finished setting up the **Tent** of the Lord's presence,
7. 1 he anointed and dedicated the **Tent** and all its equipment,
7. 5 gifts for use in the work to be done for the **Tent;**
7.89 When Moses went into the **Tent** to talk with the Lord, he
8. 9 make the Levites stand in front of the **Tent** of my presence.
8.15 the Levites, they will be qualified to work in the **Tent.**
8.19 Israelites, to work in the **Tent** for the people of Israel and
8.22 qualified to work in the **Tent** under Aaron and his sons.
8.24 perform his duties in the **Tent** of my presence, [25] and at
8.26 performing their duties in the **Tent,** but he must not perform
9.15 On the day the **Tent** of the Lord's presence was set up,
9.18 cloud stayed over the **Tent,** they stayed in the same camp.
9.19 the cloud stayed over the **Tent** for a long time, they obeyed
9.20 Sometimes the cloud remained over the **Tent** for only a few days;
9.22 as the cloud remained over the **Tent,** they did not move on;
10. 3 gather round you at the entrance to the **Tent** of my presence.
10.11 the cloud over the **Tent** of the Lord's presence lifted,
10.17 Then the **Tent** would be taken down, and the clans of
10.21 arrived at the next camp, the **Tent** had been set up again.
11.16 them to me at the **Tent** of my presence, and tell them
11.24 He assembled seventy of the leaders and placed them round the **Tent.**
11.26 stayed in the camp and had not gone out to the **Tent.**
12. 4 three of you to come out to the **Tent** of my presence."
12. 5 cloud, stood at the entrance of the **Tent,** and called out,
12.10 and the cloud left the **Tent,** Miriam's skin was suddenly
14.10 dazzling light of the Lord's presence appear over the **tent.**
16. 9 your service in the Lord's **Tent,** and minister to the
16.16 250 followers must come to the **Tent** of the Lord's presence;
16.18 and stood at the entrance of the **Tent** with Moses and Aaron.
16.19 stood facing Moses and Aaron at the entrance of the **Tent.**
16.42 Aaron, they turned towards the **Tent** and saw that the cloud
16.43 stood in front of the **Tent,** [44] and the Lord said to Moses,
16.50 Aaron returned to Moses at the entrance of the **Tent.**
17. 4 Take them to the **Tent** of my presence and put them in
17. 7 all the sticks in the **Tent** in front of the Lord's Covenant
Num 17. 8 when Moses went into the **Tent,** he saw that Aaron's stick,
17.13 who even comes near the **Tent** must die, then we are all
18. 1 any guilt connected with serving in the **Tent** of my presence;
18. 2 help you while you and your sons are serving at the **Tent.**
18. 3 and their responsibilities for the **Tent,** but they must not
18. 4 all the service in the **Tent,** but no unqualified person may
18. 6 me, so that they can carry out their duties in the **Tent.**
18.21 for their service in taking care of the **Tent** of my presence.
18.22 must no longer approach the **Tent** and in this way bring on
18.23 will take care of the **Tent** and bear the full responsibility
18.31 because it is your wages for your service in the **Tent.**
19. 4 finger sprinkle it seven times in the direction of the **Tent.**
19.13 He defiles the Lord's **Tent,** and he will no longer be
19.20 He defiles the Lord's **Tent** and will no longer be considered
20. 3 front of the Lord's **Tent** along with our fellow-Israelites.
20. 6 away from the people and stood at the entrance of the **Tent.**
25. 6 mourning at the entrance of the **Tent** of the Lord's presence.
27. 2 at the entrance of the **Tent** of the Lord's presence and said,
31.30 them to the Levites who are in charge of the Lord's **Tent."**
31.47 them to the Levites who were in charge of the Lord's **Tent.**
31.54 took the gold to the **Tent,** so that the Lord would protect
Deut 31.14 and bring him to the **Tent,** so that I may give him
31.14 and Joshua went to the **Tent,** [15] and the Lord appeared to
31.15 a pillar of cloud that stood by the door of the **Tent.**
Josh 18. 1 at Shiloh and set up the **Tent** of the Lord's presence.
19.51 Shiloh, at the entrance of the **Tent** of the Lord's presence.
22.19 in, come over into the Lord's land, where his **Tent** is.
22.27 the Lord before his sacred **Tent** with our offerings to be
22.29 our God that stands in front of the **Tent** of his presence."
Judg 18.31 all the time that the **Tent** where God was worshipped remained
1 Sam 2.22 worked at the entrance to the **Tent** of the Lord's presence.
2 Sam 6.17 in its place in the **Tent** that David had set up for
7. 2 built of cedar, but God's Covenant Box is kept in a **tent!"**
7. 6 I have travelled round living in a **tent.**
7.18 King David went into the **Tent** of the Lord's presence, sat
1 Kgs 1.39 he had brought from the **Tent** of the Lord's presence, and
1.50 of Solomon, went to the **Tent** of the Lord's presence and took
2.28 So he fled to the **Tent** of the Lord's presence and took
2.29 Joab had fled to the **Tent** and was by the altar, Solomon
2.30 He went to the **Tent** of the Lord's presence and said to
2.34 So Benaiah went to the **Tent** of the Lord's presence and
8. 4 the priests also moved the **Tent** of the Lord's presence and
1 Chr 6.32 turns of duty at the **Tent** of the Lord's presence during the
9.19 guarding the entrance to the **Tent** of the Lord's presence,
9.21 a guard at the entrance to the **Tent** of the Lord's presence.
15. 1 place for God's Covenant Box and put up a **tent** for it.
16. 1 the Covenant Box to the **tent** which David had prepared for it
17. 1 of cedar, but the Lord's Covenant Box is kept in a **tent!"**
17.16 King David went into the **Tent** of the Lord's presence, sat
21.29 The **Tent** of the Lord's presence which Moses had made in
23.26 the Levites to carry the **Tent** of the Lord's presence and all
23.32 of taking care of the **Tent** of the Lord's presence and the
2 Chr 1. 3 that was where the **Tent** of the Lord's presence was located,
1. 4 in Jerusalem, kept in a **tent** which King David had set up
1. 5 also in Gibeon in front of the **Tent** of the Lord's presence.
1. 6 In front of the **Tent** the king worshipped the Lord by
1.13 at Gibeon, where the **Tent** of the Lord's presence was,
5. 5 the Levites also moved the **Tent** of the Lord's presence and
24. 6 to pay for support of the **Tent** of the Lord's presence?"
Ps 78.60 He abandoned his **tent** in Shiloh, the home where he had
Acts 7.44 "Our ancestors had the **Tent** of God's presence with them
7.45 our ancestors who received the **tent** from their fathers carried it
Heb 8. 5 about to build the Covenant **Tent,** God said to him, "Be sure
9. 2 A **Tent** was put up, the outer one, which was called the
9. 3 Behind the second curtain was the **Tent** called the Most Holy Place.
9. 6 go into the outer **Tent** every day to perform their duties,
9. 7 Priest goes into the inner **Tent,** and he does so only once
9. 8 not yet been opened as long as the outer **Tent** still stands.
9.11 The **tent** in which he serves is greater and more perfect;
9.11 it is not a man-made **tent,** that is, it is not a
9.12 When Christ went through the **tent** and entered once and
9.21 the blood on the Covenant **Tent** and over all the things used
Rev 15. 5 in heaven open, with the **Tent** of God's presence in it.

TENT-PEG

Judg 4.21 took a hammer and a **tent-peg,** went up to him quietly, and
4.22 Sisera on the ground, dead, with the **tent-peg** through his head.
5.26 She took a **tent peg** in one hand, a workman's hammer in

TERMS

Gen 34.17 you will not accept our **terms** and be circumcised, we will
34.18 These **terms** seemed fair to Hamor and his son Shechem,
Deut 29. 1 These are the **terms** of the covenant that the Lord
29. 9 Obey faithfully all the **terms** of this covenant, so that
Judg 11.11 Jephthah stated his **terms** at Mizpah in the presence of the Lord.
1 Kgs 20.34 Ahab replied, "On these **terms,** then, I will set you free."
Neh 13. 4 had for a long time been on good **terms** with Tobiah.
Jer 11. 2 The Lord said to me, [2] "Listen to the **terms** of the covenant.
11. 3 on everyone who does not obey the **terms** of this covenant.
11. 6 people to listen to the **terms** of the covenant and to obey
34.18 But they broke the covenant and did not keep its **terms.**
Lk 14.32 other king, to ask for **terms** of peace while he is still
2 Cor 6.16 How can God's temple come to **terms** with pagan idols?

TERRACE

Ezek 41. 8 saw that there was a **terrace** two and a half metres wide
41. 8 Between the **terrace** and the buildings used by the priests
42. 6 all three levels were on **terraces** and were not supported by

TERRIBLE

Gen 4.10 Then the Lord said, "Why have you done this **terrible** thing?
12.17 taken Sarai, the Lord sent **terrible** diseases on him and on
18.20 "There are **terrible** accusations against Sodom and Gomorrah,
19.13 The Lord has heard the **terrible** accusations against these
41.31 because the famine which follows will be so **terrible.**
Ex 6. 6 my mighty arm to bring **terrible** punishment upon them, and I
9. 3 punish you by sending a **terrible** disease on all your
15.10 they sank like lead in the **terrible** water.
32.21 you, that you have made them commit such a **terrible** sin?"
32.30 Moses said to the people, "You have committed a **terrible** sin.
32.31 Lord and said, "These people have committed a **terrible** sin.
Lev 10.19 but still these **terrible** things have happened to me."
Num 21.29 How **terrible** for you, people of Moab!
Deut 5.25 That **terrible** fire will destroy us.
7.19 Remember the **terrible** plagues that you saw with your own eyes,
24. 4 not to commit such a **terrible** sin in the land that the
29. 3 You saw the **terrible** plagues, the miracles, and the great
31.17 Many **terrible** disasters will come upon them, and then they
31.21 covenant, [21] and many **terrible** disasters will come on them.
32.24 they will die from **terrible** diseases.
Josh 7.15 owns, for he has brought **terrible** shame on Israel and has
1 Sam 3.11 of Israel that is so **terrible** that everyone who hears about
3.14 be able to remove the consequences of this **terrible** sin."
4.17 it was a **terrible** defeat for us!
6. 9 God of the Israelites who has sent this **terrible** disaster on us.
14.29 Jonathan answered, "What a **terrible** thing my father
26.21 I have done a **terrible** thing!"
2 Sam 18. 7 a **terrible** defeat, with twenty thousand men killed that day.
24.10 the Lord, "I have committed a **terrible** sin in doing this!
1 Kgs 17.20 God, why have you done such a **terrible** thing to this widow?
2 Kgs 14.26 The Lord saw the **terrible** suffering of the Israelites;
17.21 Jeroboam made them abandon the Lord and led them into **terrible** sins.
1 Chr 21. 8 to God, "I have committed a **terrible** sin in doing this!
Ps 14. 1 They are all corrupt, and they have done **terrible** things;
53. 1 They are all corrupt, and they have done **terrible** things;
88.16 your **terrible** attacks destroy me.
106.15 asked for, but also sent a **terrible** disease among them.
106.29 their actions, and a **terrible** disease broke out among them.
119.107 My sufferings, Lord, are **terrible** indeed;
Ecc 5.13 Here is a **terrible** thing that I have seen in this world:
Is 14.30 But he will send a **terrible** famine on you Philistines, and
Jer 5.30 A **terrible** and shocking thing has happened in the land:
13.22 you have been raped—it is because your sin is so **terrible.**
15. 3 have decided that four **terrible** things will happen to them:
16. 4 They will die of **terrible** diseases, and no one will mourn
18.13 The people of Israel have done a **terrible** thing!
19. 8 I will bring such **terrible** destruction on this city that
19. 9 The siege will be so **terrible** that the people inside the
21. 6 people and animals alike will die of a **terrible** disease.
22.18 his death or say, 'How **terrible,** my friend, how terrible!'
23. 1 How **terrible** will be the Lord's judgement on those rulers
25. 9 leave them in ruins for ever, a **terrible** and shocking sight.
25.18 would become a desert, a **terrible** and shocking sight, and so
26.19 Now we are about to bring a **terrible** disaster on ourselves."
29.23 because they are guilty of **terrible** sins—they have committed
30. 7 A **terrible** day is coming;
36. 7 Lord has threatened this people with his **terrible** anger and fury."
44. 4 who told you not to do this **terrible** thing that I hate.
49.17 on Edom will be so **terrible** that everyone who passes by will
Lam 1. 8 Jerusalem made herself filthy with **terrible** sin.
1. 9 Her downfall was **terrible;**
Ezek 9. 9 "The people of Israel and Judah are guilty of **terrible** sins.
Dan 8.24 He will cause **terrible** destruction
Hos 9.12 When I abandon these people, **terrible** things will happen to them."
10.15 of Bethel, because of the **terrible** evil that you have done.
Joel 2.11 How **terrible** is the day of the Lord!
2.31 blood before the great and **terrible** day of the Lord comes.
Amos 3. 2 what makes your sins so **terrible,** and that is why I must
5.12 I know how **terrible** your sins are and how many crimes
5.18 How **terrible** it will be for you who long for the day
6. 1 How **terrible** it will be for you that have such an easy
6. 4 How **terrible** it will be for you that stretch out on your
Mic 2. 1 How **terrible** it will be for those who lie awake and plan
Nah 1. 6 Who can survive his **terrible** fury?
Zech 14.12 The Lord will bring a **terrible** disease on all the
14.15 A **terrible** disease will also fall on the horses, the
Mal 3.13 "You have said **terrible** things about me," says the
4. 5 "But before the great and **terrible** day of the Lord comes,
Mt 6.23 the light in you is darkness, how **terribly** dark it will be!
7.27 And what a **terrible** fall that was!"
8. 6 in bed at home, unable to move and suffering **terribly."**
11.21 "How **terrible** it will be for you, Chorazin!
11.21 How **terrible** for you too, Bethsaida!
15.22 My daughter has a demon and is in a **terrible** condition."
17.15 an epileptic and has such **terrible** fits that he often falls
18. 7 How **terrible** for the world that there are things that make
18. 7 always happen—but how **terrible** for the one who causes them!
23.13 "How **terrible** for you, teachers of the Law and Pharisees!
23.15 "How **terrible** for you, teachers of the Law and Pharisees!
23.16 "How **terrible** for you, blind guides!
23.23 "How **terrible** for you, teachers of the Law and Pharisees!
Mt 23.25 "How **terrible** for you, teachers of the Law and Pharisees!
23.27 "How **terrible** for you, teachers of the Law and Pharisees!
23.29 "How **terrible** for you, teachers of the Law and Pharisees!
24.19 How **terrible** it will be in those days for women who are
24.21 time will be far more **terrible** than any there has ever been,
26.24 say he will, but how **terrible** for that man who betrays the
Mk 4.41 But they were **terribly** afraid and said to one another,
5.25 a woman who had suffered **terribly** from severe bleeding for twelve
13.17 How **terrible** it will be in those days for women who are
14.21 but how **terrible** for that man who betrays the Son of Man!
Lk 2. 9 They were **terribly** afraid, [10] but the angel said to them,
2.48 Your father and I have been **terribly** worried trying to find you."
6.24 "But how **terrible** for you who are rich now;
6.25 "How **terrible** for you who are full now;
6.25 "How **terrible** for you who laugh now;
6.26 "How **terrible** when all people speak well of you;
6.49 house it fell at once—and what a **terrible** crash that was!"
8.37 asked Jesus to go away, because they were **terribly** afraid.
10.13 "How **terrible** it will be for you, Chorazin!
10.13 How **terrible** for you too, Bethsaida!
11.42 "How **terrible** for you Pharisees!
11.43 "How **terrible** for you Pharisees!
11.44 How **terrible** for you!
11.46 Jesus answered, "How **terrible** also for you teachers of the Law!
11.47 How **terrible** for you!
11.52 "How **terrible** for you teachers of the Law!
17. 1 bound to happen, but how **terrible** for the one who makes them
21.11 There will be **terrible** earthquakes, famines, and plagues
21.23 How **terrible** it will be in those days for women who are
21.23 **Terrible** distress will come upon this land, and God's punishment
22.22 God has decided, but how **terrible** for that man who betrays him!"
Acts 9.13 man and about all the **terrible** things he has done to your
Rom 7.13 commandment sin is shown to be even more **terribly** sinful.
1 Cor 5. 1 sexual immorality among you so **terrible** that not even the heathen
5. 3 passed judgement on the man who has done this **terrible** thing.
9.16 And how **terrible** it would be for me if I did not
2 Cor 1.10 From such **terrible** dangers of death he saved us, and
2 Tim 3.11 Antioch, Iconium, and Lystra, the **terrible** persecutions I endured!
3 Jn 10 the **terrible** things he says about us and the lies he tells!
Jude 11 How **terrible** for them!
15 performed and for all the **terrible** words that godless sinners
Rev 2.22 she and those who committed adultery with her will suffer **terribly.**
6.17 The **terrible** day of their anger is here, and who can
7.14 "These are the people who have come safely through the **terrible** persecution.
12.12 But how **terrible** for the earth and the sea!
16. 2 **Terrible** and painful sores appeared on those who had the
16.18 rumblings and peals of thunder, and a **terrible** earthquake.
16.21 the plague of hail, because it was such a **terrible** plague.
18.10 They say, "How **terrible!**
18.16 They will cry and mourn, [16] and say, "How **terrible!**
18.19 their heads, they cried and mourned, saying, "How **terrible!**

TERRIFY

Gen 20. 8 and told them what had happened, and they were **terrified.**
28.17 He was afraid and said, "What a **terrifying** place this is!
45. 3 this, they were so **terrified** that they could not answer.
Ex 3.20 and will punish Egypt by doing **terrifying** things there.
7. 3 to you, no matter how many **terrifying** things I do in Egypt.
14.10 marching against them, they were **terrified** and cried out to
15.15 The leaders of Edom are **terrified;**
Lev 26.17 you will be so **terrified** that you will run when no one
26.36 who are in exile so **terrified** that the sound of a leaf
Num 22. 3 Israelites there were, [3] he and all his people became **terrified.**
Deut 4.34 and wonders, and caused **terrifying** things to happen.
6.22 him work miracles and do **terrifying** things to the Egyptians
8.15 you through that vast and **terrifying** desert where there were
26. 8 and caused **terrifying** things to happen.
28.25 people on earth will be **terrified** when they see what happens
34.12 to do the great and **terrifying** things that Moses did in the
Josh 2. 9 Everyone in the country is **terrified** of you.
2.24 All the people there are **terrified** of us."
9.24 We did it because we were **terrified** of you;
1 Sam 5. 6 Lord punished the people of Ashdod severely and **terrified** them.
14.15 All the Philistines in the countryside were **terrified;**
17.11 When Saul and his men heard this, they were **terrified.**
28. 5 the Philistine army, he was **terrified,** [6] and so he asked the
28.20 out on the ground, **terrified** by what Samuel had said.
28.21 and saw that he was **terrified,** so she said to him, "Please,
31. 4 But the young man was too **terrified** to do it.
2 Kgs 3.27 The Israelites were **terrified** and so they drew back from the
10. 4 The rulers of Samaria were **terrified.**
22.19 I will make it a **terrifying** sight, a place whose name people
1 Chr 10. 4 But the young man was too **terrified** to do it.
2 Chr 14.14 Gerar, because the people there were **terrified** of the Lord.
20.29 Israel's enemies was **terrified,** [30] so Jehoshaphat ruled in peace,
Neh 4.14 Remember how great and **terrifying** the Lord is, and fight for
9.32 How **terrifying,** how powerful!
Job 7.14 But you—you **terrify** me with dreams;
41.14 his jaws, ringed with those **terrifying** teeth?
41.22 His neck is so powerful that all who meet him are **terrified.**
Ps 2. 5 Then he warns them in anger and **terrifies** them with his fury.
14. 5 But then they will be **terrified,** for God is with those who
46. 6 Nations are **terrified,** kingdoms are shaken;
53. 5 But then they will be **terrified,** as they have never been before,
55. 3 I am **terrified** by the threats of my enemies, crushed by
55. 4 I am **terrified,** and the terrors of death crush me.

Ps 76.12 he humbles proud princes and **terrifies** great kings.
83.15 with your storm and **terrify** them with your fierce winds.
83.17 May they be defeated and **terrified** for ever;
90. 7 we are **terrified** by your fury.
Is 7. 2 all his people were so **terrified** that they trembled like
7. 6 to invade Judah, **terrify** the people into joining their side,
7.16 lands of those two kings who **terrify** you will be deserted.
8.22 nothing but trouble and darkness, **terrifying** darkness into
10.29 the town of Ramah are **terrified,** and the people in King
13. 8 They will all be **terrified** and overcome with pain, like
14.31 Be **terrified,** all of you!
19.17 people of Egypt will be **terrified** of Judah every time they
21. 1 the desert, disaster will come from a **terrifying** land.
29. 5 dust, and their **terrifying** armies will fly away like straw.
30.31 The Assyrians will be **terrified** when they hear the
41.10 I am your God—let nothing **terrify** you!
44.11 trial—they will be **terrified** and will suffer disgrace.
64. 3 you came and did **terrifying** things that we did not expect;
Jer 10. 2 sights in the sky, even though other nations are **terrified.**
17.18 Fill them with terror, but do not **terrify** me.
23. 4 no longer be afraid or **terrified,** and I will not punish them
24. 9 on them that all the nations of the world will be **terrified.**
29.18 will be shocked and **terrified** at what has happened to them.
30.10 people of Israel, do not be **terrified.**
32.21 of miracles and wonders that **terrified** our enemies, you used
46.27 do not be afraid, people of Israel, do not be **terrified.**
49.17 terrible that everyone who passes by will be shocked and **terrified.**
50.36 Death to its soldiers— how **terrified** they are!
50.38 Babylonia is a land of **terrifying** idols, that have made
51.37 one will live there, and all who see it will be **terrified.**
Ezek 5.15 punish you, all the nations around you will be **terrified.**
19. 7 The people of the land were **terrified** every time he roared.
21.14 It is a sword that kills, a sword that **terrifies** and slaughters.
26.15 along the coast will be **terrified** at the screams of those
26.16 They will be so **terrified** at your fate that they will not
26.17 ruled the seas And **terrified** all who lived on the coast.
26.21 I will make you a **terrifying** example, and that will be
27.35 their kings are **terrified,** and fear is written on their faces.
27.36 all over the world are **terrified,** afraid that they will
28.14 I put a **terrifying** angel there to guard you.
28.19 come to know you are **terrified,** afraid that they will share
30. 9 unsuspecting people of Sudan, and they will be **terrified.**
30.13 one to rule over Egypt, and I will **terrify** all the people.
32.23 Yet once they **terrified** the land of the living.
32.26 Yet once they **terrified** the living.
32.27 These heroes were once powerful enough to **terrify** the living.
34.28 They will live in safety, and no one will **terrify** them.
38.21 I will **terrify** Gog with all sorts of calamities.
Dan 2.31 giant statue, bright and shining, and **terrifying** to look at.
4. 5 dream and saw **terrifying** visions while I was asleep.
7. 7 It was powerful, horrible, **terrifying.**
7.19 any of the others—the **terrifying** beast which crushed its
7.20 It was more **terrifying** than any of the others.
8.17 me, and I was so **terrified** that I fell to the ground.
10. 7 not see anything, but they were **terrified** and ran and hid.
Joel 2. 6 As they approach, everyone is **terrified;**
Obad 9 men of Teman will be **terrified,** and every soldier in Edom
Jon 1. 5 The sailors were **terrified** and cried out for help, each
1.10 The sailors were **terrified,** and said to him, "That was an
Hab 1. 9 conquest, and everyone is **terrified** as they approach.
2.17 now animals will **terrify** you.
Zeph 2.11 The Lord will **terrify** them.
Zech 1.21 answered, "They have come to **terrify** and overthrow the
12. 4 At that time I will **terrify** all their horses and make all
Mt 14.26 When they saw him walking on the water, they were **terrified.**
17. 6 they were so **terrified** that they threw themselves face downwards
27.54 else that happened, they were **terrified** and said, "He really
Mk 6.50 They were all **terrified** when they saw him.
16. 8 So they went out and ran from the tomb, distressed and **terrified.**
Lk 21.11 will be strange and **terrifying** things coming from the sky.
24.37 They were **terrified,** thinking that they were seeing a ghost.
Jn 6.19 on the water, coming near the boat, and they were **terrified.**
Acts 5. 5 and all who heard about it were **terrified.**
5.11 church and all the others who heard of this were **terrified.**
Heb 10.31 It is a **terrifying** thing to fall into the hands of the
12.21 The sight was so **terrifying** that Moses said, "I am trembling
Rev 11.11 and all who saw them were **terrified.**
11.13 rest of the people were **terrified** and praised the greatness

TERRITORY

Gen 25.18 of Ishmael lived in the **territory** between Havilah and Shur,
26. 3 to give all this **territory** to you and to your descendants.
26. 4 stars in the sky, and I will give them all this **territory.**
28.14 They will extend their **territory** in all directions, and
49.13 His **territory** will reach as far as Sidon.
Ex 34.24 before you and extended your **territory,** no one will try to
Num 20.16 we are at Kadesh, a town at the border of your **territory.**
20.17 stay on the main road until we are out of your **territory."**
20.21 the Israelites pass through their **territory,** the Israelites
21. 4 Gulf of Aqaba, in order to go round the **territory** of Edom.
21.11 ruins of Abarim in the wilderness east of Moabite **territory.**
21.13 River Arnon, in the wilderness which extends into Amorite **territory.**
21.20 to the valley in the **territory** of the Moabites, below the
21.22 stay on the main road until we are out of your **territory."**
21.23 permit the people of Israel to pass through his **territory.**
21.31 of Israel settled in the **territory** of the Amorites, [32]and
32.33 tribe of Manasseh all the **territory** of King Sihon of the
33.41 Abarim in the **territory** of Moab, Dibon Gad, Almon Diblathaim,
34. 2 you, the borders of your **territory** will be as follows.
Num 35. 8 to be determined according to the size of its **territory."**
Deut 1. 5 of the Jordan in the **territory** of Moab that Moses began to
2. 4 of Edom, the **territory** of your distant relatives,
2.18 are to pass through the **territory** of Moab by way of Ar.
2.20 (This **territory** is also known as the land of the Rephaim,
2.29 live in Ar, allowed us to pass through their **territory.'**
2.30 defeat him and take his **territory,** which we still occupy.
2.37 did not go near the **territory** of the Ammonites or to the
3. 2 going to give him, his men, and all his **territory** to you.
3.10 We took all the **territory** of King Og of Bashan:
3.12 of Reuben and Gad the **territory** north of the town of Aroer
3.16 Gad I assigned the **territory** from Gilead to the River Arnon.
3.17 On the west their **territory** extended to the River Jordan,
4.43 tribe of Gad there was Ramoth, in the **territory** of Gilead;
4.43 of Manasseh there was Golan, in the **territory** of Bashan.
4.45 This was in the **territory** that had belonged to King Sihon of
11.24 Your **territory** will extend from the desert in the south to
11.30 the River Jordan in the **territory** of the Canaanites who live
12. 5 Out of the **territory** of all your tribes the Lord will
12.14 the Lord will choose in the **territory** of one of your tribes.
12.20 Lord your God enlarges your **territory,** as he has promised,
19. 2 settled there, [2-3]divide the **territory** into three parts,
19. 8 Lord your God enlarges your **territory,** as he told your
29.16 was like to travel through the **territory** of other nations.
33.20 "Praise God, who made their **territory** large.
34. 1 the **territory** of Gilead as far north as the town of Dan;
34. 2 the entire **territory** of Naphtali;
34. 2 the **territories** of Ephraim and Manasseh;
34. 2 the **territory** of Judah as far west as the Mediterranean Sea;
Josh 10.42 kings and their **territory** in one campaign because the Lord,
11.17 The **territory** extended from Mount Halak in the south near Edom,
11.17 with the kings of this **territory** for a long time, but he
12. 5 Gilead, as far as the **territory** of King Sihon of Heshbon.
12. 7 all the kings in the **territory** west of the Jordan, from
13. 2 all the **territory** of Philistia and Geshur,
13. 3 as well as all the **territory** of the Avvim to the south.
13. 6 This includes all the **territory** of the Sidonians, who live
13. 9 Their **territory** extended to Aroer
13.16 Their **territory** extended to Aroer
13.25 Their **territory** included Jazer and all the cities of Gilead,
13.30 Their **territory** extended to Mahanaim and included all of
14. 2 Lord had commanded Moses, the **territories** of the nine and a
14. 3 However, Moses gave the Levites no portion of the **territory.**
15.13 commanded Joshua, part of the **territory** of Judah was given
16. 5 This was the **territory** of the Ephraimite families:
17. 7 The **territory** of Manasseh reached from Asher to Michmethath,
17. 9 Ephraim, even though they were in the **territory** of Manasseh.
17.11 Within the **territories** of Issachar and Asher, Manasseh
18. 4 country to map out the **territory** that they would like to
18. 5 Judah will stay in its **territory** in the south,
18. 5 and Joseph in its **territory** in the north.
18.11 The **territory** belonging to the families of the tribe of
19. 1 Its **territory** extended into the land assigned to the tribe
19. 9 was needed, part of its **territory** was given to the tribe of
19.46 Mejarkon, and Rakkon, as well as the **territory** round Joppa.
20. 8 of Jericho, they chose Bezer in the **territory** of Reuben;
20. 8 Ramoth in Gilead, in the **territory** of Gad;
20. 8 and Golan in Bashan, in the **territory** of Manasseh.
21. 3 certain cities and pasture lands out of their own **territories.**
21. 4 were assigned thirteen cities from the **territories** of Judah,
21. 5 from the **territories** of Ephraim, Dan, and West Manasseh.
21. 6 assigned thirteen cities from the **territories** of Issachar,
21. 7 were assigned twelve cities from the **territories** of Reuben,
21. 9 of the cities from the **territories** of Judah and Simeon which
21.17 From the **territory** of Benjamin they were given four cities:
21.20 Kohath were assigned some cities from the **territory** of Ephraim.
21.23 From the **territory** of Dan they were given four cities:
21.25 From the **territory** of West Manasseh they were given two cities:
21.27 received from the **territory** of East Manasseh two cities:
21.28 From the **territory** of Issachar they received four cities:
21.30 From the **territory** of Asher they received four cities:
21.32 From the **territory** of Naphtali they received three cities:
21.34 Merari, received from the **territory** of Zebulun four cities:
21.36 From the **territory** of Reuben they received four cities:
Judg 1. 3 "Go with us into the **territory** assigned to us, and we will
1. 3 Then we will go with you into the **territory** assigned to you."
1.18 Ashkelon, or Ekron, with their surrounding **territories.**
6.35 He sent messengers throughout the **territory** of both
11.21 took possession of all the **territory** of the Amorites who
11.22 They occupied all the Amorite **territory** from the Arnon
12.12 died and was buried at Aijalon in the **territory** of Zebulun.
12.15 buried at Pirathon in the **territory** of Ephraim in the
18. 1 of Dan was looking for **territory** to claim and occupy because
19.14 came to Gibeah in the **territory** of the tribe of Benjamin.
20. 4 to Gibeah in the **territory** of Benjamin to spend the night.
20.12 sent messengers all through the **territory** of the tribe of
21.21 and take her back to the **territory** of Benjamin with you.
21.23 their own **territory,** rebuilt their towns, and lived there.
1 Sam 5. 6 the surrounding **territory** by causing them to have tumours.
7.13 Lord prevented them from invading Israel's **territory**
7.14 to Israel, and so Israel got back all its **territory.**
9. 4 Then they went through the **territory** of Benjamin, but still
10. 2 near Rachel's tomb at Zelzah in the **territory** of Benjamin.
11. 1 town of Jabesh in the **territory** of Gilead and besieged it.
13. 2 Jonathan to Gibeah, in the **territory** of the tribe of Benjamin.
13. 7 crossed the River Jordan into the **territories** of Gad and Gilead.
13.15 They went from Gilgal to Gibeah in the **territory** of Benjamin.
13.16 and their men camped in Geba in the **territory** of Benjamin;
13.17 went towards Ophrah in the **territory** of Shual, [18]another
14.16 watch at Gibeah in the **territory** of Benjamin saw the

1 Sam	14.46	the Philistines, and they went back to their own **territory.**
	23.19	"David is hiding in our **territory** at Horesh on Mount Hachilah,
	23.20	so come to our **territory,** and we will make sure that you
	27.10	of Judah or to the **territory** of the clan of Jerahmeel
	27.10	or to the **territory** where the Kenites lived.
	30.14	We had raided the **territory** of the Cherethites in the
	30.14	part of Judah and the **territory** of the clan of Caleb,
2 Sam	2. 9	made Ishbosheth king of the **territories** of Gilead, Asher,
	8. 3	his control over the **territory** by the upper Euphrates.
	8. 6	up military camps in their **territory,** and they became his
	20.14	Sheba passed through the **territory** of all the tribes of
	21.14	Kish, in Zela in the **territory** of Benjamin, doing all that
	24. 5	city in the middle of the valley, in the **territory** of Gad.
	24. 6	and on to Gilead and to Kadesh, in Hittite **territory.**
1 Kgs	4.10	and Socoh and all the **territory** of Hepher
	4.15	the **territory** of Naphtali
	4.17	the **territory** of Issachar
	4.18	the **territory** of Benjamin
	11.28	the forced labour in the **territory** of the tribes of Manasseh
	11.37	and you will rule over all the **territory** that you want.
	12.17	only of the people who lived in the **territory** of Judah.
	14.21	had chosen from all the **territory** of Israel as the place
	15.19	that he will have to pull his troops out of my **territory."**
	15.20	area near Lake Galilee, and the whole **territory** of Naphtali.
	15.22	Asa fortified Mizpah and Geba, a city in the **territory** of Benjamin.
2 Kgs	9.10	body will be eaten by dogs in the **territory** of Jezreel.'"
	9.36	'Dogs will eat Jezebel's body in the **territory** of Jezreel.
	10.32	the Lord began to reduce the size of Israel's **territory.**
	10.32	Syria conquered all the Israelite **territory** [33] east of the Jordan,
	10.33	Arnon—this included the **territories** of Gilead and Bashan,
	14.25	He reconquered all the **territory** that had belonged to Israel,
	15.16	its inhabitants, and the surrounding **territory,** because the
	15.29	Kedesh, and Hazor, and the **territories** of Gilead, Galilee,
	18. 8	largest city, including Gaza and its surrounding **territory.**
	21. 7	chosen out of all the **territory** of the twelve tribes of
	24. 7	controlled all the **territory** that had belonged to Egypt,
	25.21	was in the city of Riblah [21] in the **territory** of Hamath.
1 Chr	2.22	Jair ruled twenty-three cities in the **territory** of Gilead.
	5. 8	in Aroer and in the **territory** from there north to Nebo and
	5.16	They lived in the **territory** of Bashan and Gilead, in the
	5.22	And they went on living in that **territory** until the exile.
	5.23	East Manasseh settled in the **territory** of Bashan as far
	6.54	This is the **territory** assigned to the descendants of
	6.55	This included Hebron in the **territory** of Judah and the
	6.60	In the **territory** of Benjamin they were assigned the
	6.61	Ten towns in the **territory** of West Manasseh were
	6.62	assigned thirteen towns in the **territories** of Issachar,
	6.63	way, twelve towns in the **territories** of Reuben, Gad, and
	6.65	(The towns in the **territories** of Judah, Simeon, and Benjamin,
	6.66	assigned towns and pasture lands in the **territory** of Ephraim:
	6.70	In the **territory** of West Manasseh they were assigned the
	6.71	In the **territory** of East Manasseh:
	6.72	In the **territory** of Issachar:
	6.74	In the **territory** of Asher:
	6.76	In the **territory** of Naphtali:
	6.77	In the **territory** of Zebulun:
	6.78	In the **territory** of Reuben, east of the River Jordan beyond Jericho:
	6.80	In the **territory** of Gad:
	7.28	The **territory** which they took and settled in included
	9.14	Elkanah, who lived in the **territory** that belonged to the
	13. 6	to Kiriath Jearim, in the **territory** of Judah, to fetch the
	18. 3	near the **territory** of Hamath, because Hadadezer was trying
	18. 3	to gain control of the **territory** by the upper Euphrates.
	18. 6	up military camps in their **territory,** and they became his
	26.31	were found living at Jazer in the **territory** of Gilead.
	26.32	River Jordan—the **territories** of Reuben, Gad, and East Manasseh.
	27. 2	Abiezer from Anathoth in the **territory** of the tribe of Benjamin
	27. 2	Benaiah from Pirathon in the **territory** of the tribe of Ephraim
2 Chr	8. 3	He captured the **territory** of Hamath and Zobah [4] and
	8. 6	in Lebanon, and throughout the **territory** that he ruled over.
	9.26	all the kings in the **territory** from the River Euphrates to
	10.17	only of the people who lived in the **territory** of Judah.
	11.13	From all the **territory** of Israel priests and Levites
	12.13	had chosen from all the **territory** of Israel as the place
	16. 3	that he will have to pull his troops out of my **territory."**
	17. 2	cities which Asa had captured in the **territory** of Ephraim.
	28.15	to Judaean **territory** at Jericho, the city of palm-trees.
	30.10	to every city in the **territory** of the tribes of Ephraim and
	31. 1	the rest of Judah, and the **territories** of Benjamin, Ephraim,
	33. 7	chosen out of all the **territory** of the twelve tribes of
	34. 7	Throughout the **territory** of the Northern Kingdom he
	34.33	were in the **territory** belonging to the people of Israel,
Ezra	4.12	came here from your other **territories** have settled in
	10. 9	the men living in the **territory** of Judah and Benjamin came
Neh	11.30	of Judah lived in the **territory** between Beersheba in the
	11.36	that had lived in the **territory** of Judah were assigned to
Is	7. 2	Syria were already in the **territory** of Israel, he and all
	26.15	our nation grow, enlarging its **territory** on every side, and
Jer	1. 1	of the town of Anathoth in the **territory** of Benjamin.
	17.26	come from the **territory** of Benjamin, from the foothills,
	32. 7	field at Anathoth in the **territory** of Benjamin, because I
	32.44	will take place in the **territory** of Benjamin, in the
	33.13	in southern Judah, in the **territory** of Benjamin, in the
	37.12	Jerusalem and go to the **territory** of Benjamin to take
	39. 5	city of Riblah in the **territory** of Hamath, and there
	41.10	and started off in the direction of the **territory** of Ammon.
	49. 1	who worship Molech take the **territory** of the tribe of Gad
	50.19	crops that grow in the **territories** of Ephraim and Gilead.
	52. 9	city of Riblah in the **territory** of Hamath, and there
	52.27	was in the city of Riblah [27] in the **territory** of Hamath.
Ezek	47.16	(they are located between the **territory** of the kingdom of
	47.18	point between the **territory** of Damascus and that of Hauran,
Amos	1.13	In their wars for more **territory** they even ripped open
	6. 2	Was their **territory** larger than yours?
Obad	19	Israelites will possess the **territory** of Ephraim and Samaria;
Mic	5. 6	save us from the Assyrians when they invade our **territory.**
	7.11	At that time your **territory** will be enlarged.
Mt	4.13	by Lake Galilee, in the **territory** of Zebulun and Naphtali.
	8.28	When Jesus came to the **territory** of Gadara on the other
	8.34	when they saw him, they begged him to leave their **territory.**
	10. 5	"Do not go to any Gentile **territory** or any Samaritan towns.
	15.21	and went off to the **territory** near the cities of Tyre
	15.39	got into a boat, and went to the **territory** of Magadan.
	16.13	Jesus went to the **territory** near the town of Caesarea Philippi,
	19. 1	Galilee and went to the **territory** of Judaea on the other
Mk	3. 8	territory of Idumea, from the **territory** on the east side of
	5. 1	the other side of Lake Galilee, in the **territory** of Gerasa.
	5.17	So they asked Jesus to leave their **territory.**
	7.24	left and went away to the **territory** near the city of Tyre.
	7.31	Lake Galilee, going by way of the **territory** of the Ten Towns.
Lk	3. 1	Philip was ruler of the **territory** of Iturea and Trachonitis;
	3. 3	John went throughout the whole **territory** of the River Jordan,
	4.14	The news about him spread throughout all that **territory.**
	4.26	to a widow living in Zarephath in the **territory** of Sidon.
	7.17	went out through all the country and the surrounding **territory.**
	8.26	sailed on over to the **territory** of Gerasa, which is across
	8.37	all the people from that **territory** asked Jesus to go away,
Acts	14. 6	Lystra and Derbe in Lycaonia and to the surrounding **territory.**
	14.24	After going through the **territory** of Pisidia, they came to Pamphylia.

TERROR

Gen	15.12	fell into a deep sleep, and fear and **terror** came over him.
Ex	15.14	the Philistines are seized with **terror.**
	15.16	**Terror** and dread fall upon them.
Deut	28.66	you will be filled with **terror,** and you will live in
	32.25	**terrors** will strike in the homes.
Judg	6.22	angel he had seen, and he said in **terror,** "Sovereign Lord!
1 Sam	17.24	When the Israelites saw Goliath, they ran away in **terror.**
Esth	7. 6	Haman stared at the king and queen in **terror.**
Job	6. 4	God has lined up his **terrors** against me.
	9.34	Keep your **terrors** away!
	13.11	reprimand you, [11] and his power will fill you with **terror.**
	13.21	stop punishing me, and don't crush me with **terror.**
	15.21	Voices of **terror** will scream in his ears, and robbers
	18.11	All round him **terror** is waiting;
	20.25	its shiny point drips with his blood, and **terror** grips his heart.
	21. 9	they never have to live in **terror.**
	24.17	the light of day, but darkness holds no **terror** for them.
	27.20	**Terror** will strike like a sudden flood;
	30.15	I am overcome with **terror;**
Ps	10.18	their favour, so that mortal men may cause **terror** no more.
	31.13	**terror** is all round me.
	55. 4	I am terrified, and the **terrors** of death crush me.
Prov	1.26	I will mock you when **terror** strikes—[27] when it comes on you
Is	17.14	In the evening they cause **terror,** but by morning they are gone.
	19.16	They will tremble in **terror** when they see that the Lord
	21. 3	vision has filled me with **terror** and pain, pain like that of
	21. 4	evening to come, but it has brought me nothing but **terror.**
	24.17	There are **terrors,** pits, and traps waiting for you.
	24.18	tries to escape from the **terror** will fall into a pit, and
	28.19	Each new message from God will bring new **terror!**
	31. 9	emperor will run away in **terror,** and the officers will be so
	54.14	You will be safe from oppression and **terror.**
Jer	6.25	because our enemies are armed and **terror** is all round us."
	8.15	**terror** came instead.
	14.19	we hoped for healing, but **terror** came instead.
	15. 8	I suddenly struck them with anguish and **terror.**
	17.17	Do not be a **terror** to me;
	17.18	Fill them with **terror,** but do not terrify me.
	18.22	make them cry out in **terror.**
	20. 3	The name he has given you is **'Terror** Everywhere.'
	20. 4	going to make you a **terror** to yourself and to your friends,
	20.10	I hear everybody whispering, **"Terror** is everywhere!
	26.21	so he fled in **terror** and escaped to Egypt.
	30. 5	"I heard a cry of **terror,** a cry of fear and not
	46. 5	"They are turning back in **terror.**
	48.43	**Terror,** pits, and traps are waiting for the people of Moab.
	48.44	Whoever tries to escape the **terror** will fall into the pits,
	49. 5	I will bring **terror** on you from every side.
	49.24	The people of Damascus are weak and have fled in **terror.**
	49.29	Take their camels and tell the people, **'Terror** is all round you!'
Lam	2.22	to hold a carnival of **terror** all round me, And no one
Ezek	30. 2	A day of **terror** is coming!
	32.24	In life they spread **terror,** but now they lie dead and disgraced.
	32.25	In life they spread **terror,** but now they lie dead and disgraced,
	32.30	Their power once spread **terror,** but now they go down in
Joel	1.15	What **terror** that day will bring!
Nah	2. 6	the palace is filled with **terror.**
Hab	1. 7	They spread fear and **terror,** and in their pride they are a

TERRORIZE

Ezek	23.46	"Bring a mob to **terrorize** them and rob them.
	32.32	made the king of Egypt **terrorize** the living, but he and all
Acts	21.38	and led four thousand armed **terrorists** out into the desert?"

TEST
[TO THE TEST]

Gen 22. 1 Some time later God **tested** Abraham;
42.15 This is how you will be **tested:**
42.16 under guard until the truth of what you say can be **tested.**
Ex 15.25 gave them laws to live by, and there he also **tested** them.
16. 4 In this way I can **test** them to find out if they
17. 2 Why are you putting the Lord **to the test?"**
17. 7 put the Lord **to the test** when they asked, "Is the Lord
20.20 God has only come to **test** you and make you keep on
Deut 6.16 the Lord your God **to the test,** as you did at Massah.
8. 2 forty years, sending hardships to **test** you, so that he might
8.16 sent hardships on you to **test** you, so that in the end
13. 3 God is using him to **test** you, to see if you love
33. 8 You put them **to the test** at Massah And proved them true
Judg 3. 1 nations in the land to **test** the Israelites who had not been
3. 4 They were to be a **test** for Israel, to find out whether
6.39 Please let me make one more **test** with the wool.
1 Kgs 10. 1 travelled to Jerusalem to **test** him with difficult questions.
1 Chr 29.17 I know that you **test** everyone's heart and are pleased
2 Chr 9. 1 travelled to Jerusalem to **test** him with difficult questions.
32.31 Hezekiah go his own way only in order to **test** his character.
Job 7.18 You inspect him every morning and **test** him every minute.
23.10 if he **tests** me, he will find me pure.
28.27 then he saw wisdom and **tested** its worth— He gave it
Ps 26. 2 Examine me and **test** me, Lord;
66.10 You have put us **to the test,** God;
66.10 as silver is purified by fire so you have **tested** us.
78.18 put God **to the test** by demanding the food they wanted.
78.41 they put God **to the test** and brought pain to the Holy
78.56 But they rebelled against Almighty God and put him **to the test.**
81. 7 I put you **to the test** at the springs of Meribah.
95. 9 they put me **to the test** and tried me, although they had
106.14 filled with craving in the desert and put God **to the test;**
139.23 **test** me, and discover my thoughts.
Prov 17. 3 Gold and silver are **tested** by fire,
17. 3 and a person's heart is **tested** by the Lord.
27.21 Fire **tests** gold and silver;
27.21 a person's reputation can also be **tested.**
Ecc 3.18 I concluded that God is **testing** us, to show us that we
7.23 I used my wisdom to **test** all of this.
12. 9 He studied proverbs and honestly **tested** their truth.
Is 7.12 I refuse to put the Lord **to the test."**
48.10 I have **tested** you in the fire of suffering, as silver is
Jer 6.27 Jeremiah, **test** my people, as you would test metal, and
9. 7 will refine my people like metal and put them **to the test.**
11.20 you **test** people's thoughts and feelings.
17.10 I, the Lord, search the minds and **test** the hearts of men.
20.12 But, Almighty Lord, you **test** men justly;
48.14 do you claim to be heroes, brave soldiers **tested** in war?
Ezek 21.13 I am **testing** my people, and if they refuse to repent,
Dan 1.12 **"Test** us for ten days," he said.
Zech 13. 9 And I will **test** the third that survives and will purify
13. 9 I will **test** them as gold is tested.
Mal 3.10 Put me **to the test** and you will see that I will
3.15 not only prosper, but they **test** God's patience with their
Mt 4. 7 also says, 'Do not put the Lord your God **to the test.' "**
6.13 not bring us to hard **testing,** but keep us safe from the
Lk 4.12 says, 'Do not put the Lord your God **to the test.' "**
8.13 a while but when the time of **testing** comes, they fall away.
11. 4 And do not bring us to hard **testing.' "**
22.31 Satan has received permission to **test** all of you, to separate
Jn 6. 6 (He said this to **test** Philip;
Acts 5. 9 your husband decide to put the Lord's Spirit **to the test?**
15.10 want to put God **to the test** by laying a load on
1 Cor 3.13 the fire will **test** it and show its real quality.
10. 9 not put the Lord **to the test,** as some of them did
10.13 Every **test** that you have experienced is the kind that normally
10.13 not allow you to be **tested** beyond your power to remain firm;
10.13 time you are put **to the test,** he will give you the
2 Cor 2. 9 well you had stood the **test** and whether you are always ready
8. 2 They have been severely **tested** by the troubles they went through;
8.22 we have **tested** him many times and found him always very
13. 5 Put yourselves **to the test** and judge yourselves, to find out
1 Thes 2. 4 try to please men, but to please God, who **tests** our motives.
5.21 Put all things **to the test:**
1 Tim 3.10 They should be **tested** first,
3.10 and then, if they pass the **test,** they are to serve.
Heb 3. 8 that day in the desert when they put him **to the test.**
3. 9 There they put me **to the test** and tried me, says God,
11.17 son Isaac as a sacrifice when God put Abraham **to the test.**
Jas 1.12 succeeds in passing such a **test,** he will receive as his
1 Pet 1. 7 Even gold, which can be destroyed, is **tested** by fire;
1. 7 than gold, must also be **tested,** so that it may endure.
4.12 be surprised at the painful **test** you are suffering,
1 Jn 4. 1 to have the Spirit, but **test** them to find out if the
Rev 2. 2 men and that you have **tested** those who say they are apostles
2.10 Devil will put you **to the test** by having some of you
3.10 is coming upon the world to **test** all the people on earth.

AV TESTAMENT see COVENANT, WILL

TESTICLES

Lev 22.24 the Lord any animal whose **testicles** have been crushed, cut,

TESTIFY

Lev 24.14 on the man's head to **testify** that he is guilty, and then
Deut 17. 6 to death only if two or more witnesses **testify** against him;
Ps 15. 5 and cannot be bribed to **testify** against the innocent.
35.11 Evil men **testify** against me and accuse me of crimes I
50. 7 I will **testify** against you, Israel.
Is 43. 9 they are right, to **testify** to the truth of their words.
Mic 1. 2 The Sovereign Lord will **testify** against you.
Mal 3. 5 to judge, and I will **testify** at once against those who
Jn 5.31 "If I **testify** on my own behalf, what I say is not
5.32 there is someone else who **testifies** on my behalf, and I know
5.37 And the Father, who sent me, also **testifies** on my behalf.
8.13 Pharisees said to him, "Now you are **testifying** on your own behalf;
8.14 answered, "even though I do **testify** on my own behalf, what
8.18 I **testify** on my own behalf,
8.18 and the Father who sent me also **testifies** on my behalf."
Acts 10.42 to the people and to **testify** that he is the one whom
18. 5 time to preaching the message, **testifying** to the Jews that Jesus
26. 5 if they are willing to **testify,** that from the very first I
Col 4.13 I can personally **testify** to his hard work for you and
1 Jn 5. 6 And the Spirit himself **testifies** that this is true,

AV TESTIFY
see also **WARN**

Num 35.30 the **evidence** of one witness is not sufficient to support an
Deut 19.16 to harm another by falsely **accusing** him of a crime,
19.18 man has made a false **accusation** against his fellow-Israelite,
31.21 still be sung, and it will stand as **evidence** against them.
Ruth 1.21 Naomi when the Lord Almighty has **condemned** me and sent me trouble?"
2 Sam 1.16 You **condemned** yourself when you admitted that you killed the
Job 15. 6 you are **condemned** by every word you speak.
Is 59.12 Our sins **accuse** us.
Jer 14. 7 'Even though our sins **accuse** us, help us, Lord,
Hos 5. 5 The arrogance of the people of Israel **cries** out against them.
7.10 The arrogance of the people of Israel **cries** out against them.
Mic 6. 3 **Answer** me.
Jn 2.25 no need for anyone to **tell** him about them, because he
3.11 of what we know and **report** what we have seen, yet none
3.32 He **tells** what he has seen and heard, yet no one accepts
5.39 And these very Scriptures **speak** about me!
7. 7 hates me, because I keep **telling** it that its ways are bad.
13.21 he was deeply troubled and **declared** openly, "I am telling you
15.26 him to you from the Father, and he will **speak** about me.
21.24 He is the disciple who **spoke** of these things, the one
Acts 2.40 with many other words he **urged** them, saying, "Save yourselves
8.25 they had given their **testimony** and proclaimed the Lord's message,
20.24 to do, which is to **declare** the Good News about the grace
23.11 You have given your **witness** for me here in Jerusalem,
28.23 From morning till night he **explained** to them his message
1 Tim 2. 6 That was the **proof** at the right time that God wants everyone
Heb 11. 4 because God himself **approved** of his gifts.
1 Pet 1.11 was pointing, in **predicting** the sufferings that Christ would have
5.12 encourage you and give my **testimony** that this is the true
1 Jn 4.14 And we have seen and **tell** others that the Father sent
5. 9 and he has given this **testimony** about his Son.
3 Jn 3 some Christian brothers arrived and **told** me how faithful you are
Rev 22.16 have sent my angel to **announce** these things to you
22.20 He who gives his **testimony** to all this says, "Yes

TESTIMONY

Lev 19.16 for his life, speak out if your **testimony** can help him.
Job 20.27 and the earth gives **testimony** against him.
Prov 21.28 The **testimony** of a liar is not believed, but the word of
Zech 8.17 Do not give false **testimony** under oath.
Mal 3. 5 against those who give false **testimony,** those who cheat
Mt 18.16 may be upheld by the **testimony** of two or more witnesses,'
Jn 1.32 And John gave this **testimony:**
Acts 8.25 they had given their **testimony** and proclaimed the Lord's message,
1 Tim 1.10 who lie and give false **testimony** or who do anything else
1 Pet 5.12 encourage you and give my **testimony** that this is the true
1 Jn 5. 8 and all three give the same **testimony.**
5. 9 We believe man's **testimony;**
5. 9 but God's **testimony** is much stronger,
5. 9 and he has given this **testimony** about his Son.
5.10 in the Son of God has this **testimony** in his own heart;
5.11 The **testimony** is this:
3 Jn 12 And we add our **testimony,** and you know that what we say
Rev 22.20 He who gives his **testimony** to all this says, "Yes

AV TESTIMONY
for Tabernacle of the Testimony see also **(TENT) (2)**

Ex 16.34 it in front of the **Covenant Box,** so that it could be
25.16 the box the two stone **tablets** that I will give you, on
25.21 Put the two stone **tablets** inside the box and put the lid
26.33 put the **Covenant Box** containing the two stone tablets.
26.34 Put the lid on the **Covenant Box.**
27.21 outside the curtain which is in front of the **Covenant Box.**
30. 6 the curtain which hangs in front of the **Covenant Box.**
30.26 Tent of my presence, the **Covenant Box,** [27] the table and all
30.36 my presence, and sprinkle it in front of the **Covenant Box.**
31. 7 Tent of my presence, the **Covenant Box** and its lid, all the
31.18 tablets on which God himself had written the **commandments.**
32.15 stone tablets with the **commandments** written on both sides.
34.29 Mount Sinai carrying the Ten **Commandments,** his face was

Ex 38.21 presence, where the two stone **tablets** were kept on which the
39.35 the **Covenant Box** containing the stone tablets, its
40. 3 Covenant Box containing the Ten **Commandments** and put the
40. 5 incense in front of the **Covenant Box** and hang the curtain at
40.20 he took the two stone **tablets** and put them in the Covenant
40.21 way he screened off the **Covenant Box,** just as the Lord had
Lev 16.13 hide the lid of the **Covenant Box** so that he will not
24. 3 curtain in front of the **Covenant Box,** which is in the Most
Num 1.50 Levites in charge of the **Tent** of my presence and all its
1.53 Levites shall camp round the **Tent** to guard it, so that no
4. 5 curtain in front of the **Covenant Box,** and cover the Box with
7.89 lid on the **Covenant Box,** between the two winged creatures.
9.15 On the day the **Tent** of the Lord's presence was set up,
10.11 the cloud over the **Tent** of the Lord's presence lifted,
17. 4 put them in front of the **Covenant Box,** where I meet you.
17.10 "Put Aaron's stick back in front of the **Covenant Box.**
Deut 4.45 opposite the town of Bethpeor, that he gave them these **laws.**
6.17 sure that you obey all the **laws** that he has given you.
6.20 did the Lord our God command us to obey all these **laws?'**
Josh 4.16 command the priests carrying the **Covenant Box** to come up out
Ruth 4. 7 In this way the Israelites showed that the matter was **settled.**
1 Kgs 2. 3 Obey all his laws and **commands,** as written in the Law of
2 Kgs 11.12 head, and gave him a copy of the **laws** governing kingship.
17.15 with their ancestors, and they disregarded his **warnings.**
23. 3 to keep his laws and **commands** with all his heart and soul,
1 Chr 29.19 to obey everything that you **command** and to build the Temple
2 Chr 23.11 head, and gave him a copy of the **laws** governing kingship.
34.31 to keep his laws and **commands** with all his heart and soul,
Neh 9.34 They did not listen to your commands and **warnings.**
Ps 19. 7 The **law** of the Lord is perfect;
25.10 he leads all who keep his covenant and obey his **commands.**
78. 5 of Israel and **commandments** to the descendants of Jacob.
78.56 They did not obey his **commandments,** [57] but were rebellious
93. 5 Your **laws** are eternal, Lord, and your Temple is holy indeed,
99. 7 they obeyed the **laws** and commands that he gave them.
119. 2 are those who follow his **commands,** who obey him with all
119.14 I delight in following your **commands** more than in having great wealth.
119.22 their insults and scorn, because I have kept your **laws.**
119.24 Your **instructions** give me pleasure;
119.31 I have followed your **instructions,** Lord;
119.36 me the desire to obey your **laws** rather than to get rich.
119.46 I will announce your **commands** to kings and I will not be
119.59 considered my conduct, and I promise to follow your **instructions.**
119.88 love be good to me, so that I may obey your **laws.**
119.95 are waiting to kill me, but I will meditate on your **laws.**
119.99 than all my teachers, because I meditate on your **instructions.**
119.111 Your **commandments** are my eternal possession;
119.119 all the wicked like rubbish, and so I love your **instructions.**
119.125 give me understanding, so that I may know your **teachings.**
119.129 Your **teachings** are wonderful;
119.138 The **rules** that you have given are completely fair and right.
119.144 Your **instructions** are always just;
119.146 save me, and I will keep your **laws.**
119.152 Long ago I learnt about your **instructions;**
119.157 and oppressors, but I do not fail to obey your **laws.**
119.167 I obey your **teachings;**
119.168 I obey your commands and your **instructions;**
122. 4 to give thanks to the Lord according to his **command.**
132.12 my covenant and to the **commands** I give them, their sons,
Is 8.16 to guard and preserve the **messages** that God has given me.
8.20 to answer them, "Listen to what the Lord is **teaching** you!
Jer 44.23 sinned against the Lord by not obeying all his **commands."**
Mt 8. 4 then in order to **prove** to everyone that you are cured, offer
10.18 before rulers and kings, to **tell** the Good News to them
Mk 1.44 then in order to **prove** to everyone that you are cured, offer
6.11 That will be a **warning** to them!"
13. 9 rulers and kings for my sake to **tell** them the Good News.
Lk 5.14 then to **prove** to everyone that you are cured, offer the
9. 5 and shake the dust off your feet as a **warning** to them."
21.13 This will be your chance to **tell** the Good News.
Jn 3.32 what he has seen and heard, yet no one accepts his **message.**
3.33 whoever accepts his **message** confirms by this that God is truthful.
5.34 It is not that I must have a man's **witness;**
8.17 Law that when two **witnesses** agree, what they say is true.
Acts 14. 3 about the Lord, who **proved** that their message about his grace
22.18 because the people here will not accept your **witness** about me.'
1 Cor 1. 6 The **message** about Christ has become so firmly established in
2. 1 brothers, to preach God's secret **truth,** I did not use big
2 Cor 1.12 are proud that our conscience **assures** us that our lives in
2 Thes 1.10 because you have believed the **message** that we told you.
2 Tim 1. 8 Do not be ashamed, then, of **witnessing** for our Lord;
Heb 3. 5 as a servant, and he **spoke** of the things that God would
Rev 1. 2 concerning the message from God and the truth **revealed** by Jesus
1. 9 I had proclaimed God's word and the truth that Jesus **revealed.**
6. 9 proclaimed God's word and had been faithful in their **witnessing.**
11. 7 they finish **proclaiming their message,** the beast that comes up out
12.11 blood of the Lamb and by the truth which they **proclaimed;**
12.17 and are faithful to the truth **revealed** by Jesus.
19.10 all those who hold to the truth that Jesus **revealed.**
19.10 For the truth that Jesus **revealed** is what inspires the prophets.

TEXT

Ezra 4.11 This is the **text** of the letter:

THANK

Gen 18. 5 They replied, **"Thank** you;
47.31 Joseph made the vow, and Jacob gave **thanks** there on his bed.
Lev 22.29 you offer a sacrifice of **thanksgiving** to the Lord, follow
Deut 8.10 eat, and you will give **thanks** to the Lord your God for
1 Sam 25.33 **Thank** God for your good sense and for what you have done
1 Chr 16. 8 Give **thanks** to the Lord, proclaim his greatness;
16.34 Give **thanks** to the Lord, because he is good;
16.35 so that we may be **thankful** and praise your holy name."
25. 3 the music of harps, and sang praise and **thanks** to the Lord.
29.13 God, we give you **thanks,** and we praise your glorious name.
2 Chr 29.31 bring sacrifices as offerings of **thanksgiving** to the Lord."
31. 2 worship, and giving praise and **thanks** in the various parts
Neh 11.17 He led the temple choir in singing the prayer of **thanksgiving.**
12. 8 The following were in charge of the singing of hymns of **thanksgiving:**
12.24 praised God responsively and gave **thanks** to him, in
12.27 the dedication with songs of **thanksgiving** and with the music
12.31 large groups to march round the city, giving **thanks** to God.
12.38 group of those who gave **thanks** went to the left along the
12.40 that were giving **thanks** to God reached the temple area.
12.46 musicians have led songs of praise and **thanksgiving** to God.
Ps 7.17 I **thank** the Lord for his justice, I sing praises to the
16. 9 And so I am **thankful** and glad, and I feel completely secure,
26. 7 I sing a hymn of **thanksgiving** and tell of all your
30. 4 Remember what the Holy One has done, and give him **thanks!**
30.12 Lord, you are my God, I will give you **thanks** for ever.
33. 2 Give **thanks** to the Lord with harps, sing to him with
34. 1 I will always **thank** the Lord;
35.18 Then I will **thank** you in the assembly of your people;
40.16 May all who are **thankful** for your salvation always say,
44. 8 We will always praise you and give **thanks** to you for ever.
50.14 Let the giving of **thanks** be your sacrifice to God, and
50.23 Giving **thanks** is the sacrifice that honours me, and I
52. 9 I will always **thank** you, God, for what you have done;
54. 6 I will give you **thanks** because you are good.
56.12 give you my offering of **thanksgiving,** [13] because you have
57. 9 I will **thank** you, O Lord, among the nations.
63. 4 I will give you **thanks** as long as I live;
69.30 I will proclaim his greatness by giving him **thanks.**
70. 4 May all who are **thankful** for your salvation always say,
75. 1 We give **thanks** to you, O God, we give thanks to you!
79.13 sheep of your flock, will **thank** you for ever and praise you
92. 1 good it is to give **thanks** to you, O Lord, to sing
95. 2 him with **thanksgiving** and sing joyful songs of praise.
97.12 Remember what the holy God has done, and give **thanks** to him.
100. 4 Enter the temple gates with **thanksgiving,**
100. 4 Give **thanks** to him and praise him.
105. 1 Give **thanks** to the Lord, proclaim his greatness;
106. 1 Give **thanks** to the Lord, because he is good;
106.47 so that we may be **thankful** and praise your holy name.
107. 1 "Give **thanks** to the Lord, because he is good;
107. 8 They must **thank** the Lord for his constant love, for the
107.15 They must **thank** the Lord for his constant love, for the
107.21 They must **thank** the Lord for his constant love, for the
107.22 They must **thank** him with sacrifices, and with songs of
107.31 They must **thank** the Lord for his constant love, for the
108. 3 I will **thank** you, O Lord, among the nations.
109.30 I will give loud **thanks** to the Lord;
111. 1 all my heart I will **thank** the Lord in the assembly of
115.18 we, the living, will give **thanks** to him now and for ever.
116.13 a wine-offering to the Lord, to **thank** him for saving me.
116.17 you a sacrifice of **thanksgiving** and offer my prayer to you.
118. 1 Give **thanks** to the Lord, because he is good, and his love
118.19 I will go in and give **thanks** to the Lord!
118.28 You are my God, and I give you **thanks;**
118.29 Give **thanks** to the Lord, because he is good, and his
119.108 Accept my prayer of **thanks,** O Lord, and teach me your commands.
119.164 Seven times each day I **thank** you for your righteous judgements.
122. 4 tribes of Israel, to give **thanks** to the Lord according to
124. 6 Let us **thank** the Lord, who has not let our enemies destroy
136. 1 Give **thanks** to the Lord, because he is good;
136. 2 Give **thanks** to the greatest of all gods;
136. 3 Give **thanks** to the mightiest of all lords;
136.26 Give **thanks** to the God of heaven;
138. 1 I **thank** you, Lord, with all my heart;
145. 1 I will **thank** you for ever and ever.
145. 2 Every day I will **thank** you;
145.10 will praise you, and all your people will give you **thanks.**
Is 12. 4 "Give **thanks** to the Lord!
51. 3 will be there, and songs of praise and **thanks** to me.
Jer 33.11 'Give **thanks** to the Lord Almighty, because he is good and
Amos 4. 5 and offer your bread in **thanksgiving** to God, and boast about
Mt 11.25 I **thank** you because you have shown to the unlearned what you
14.19 the two fish, looked up to heaven, and gave **thanks** to God.
15.36 loaves and the fish, gave **thanks** to God, broke them, and
26.26 bread, gave a prayer of **thanks,** broke it, and gave it to
26.27 he took a cup, gave **thanks** to God, and gave it to
Mk 6.41 the two fish, looked up to heaven, and gave **thanks** to God.
8. 6 took the seven loaves, gave **thanks** to God, broke them, and
8. 7 Jesus gave **thanks** for these and told the disciples to distribute
14.22 bread, gave a prayer of **thanks,** broke it, and gave it to
14.23 he took a cup, gave **thanks** to God, and handed it to
Lk 2.28 Simeon took the child in his arms and gave **thanks** to God:
2.38 hour she arrived and gave **thanks** to God and spoke about the
9.16 fish, looked up to heaven, **thanked** God for them, broke them,
10.21 I **thank** you because you have shown to the unlearned what you
17. 9 The servant does not deserve **thanks** for obeying orders,
17.16 He threw himself to the ground at Jesus' feet and **thanked** him.

Lk 17.18 the only one who came back to give **thanks** to God?"
18.11 by himself and prayed, 'I **thank** you, God, that I am not
18.11 I **thank** you that I am not like that tax collector over
18.43 able to see, and he followed Jesus, giving **thanks** to God.
19.37 of his disciples began to **thank** God and praise him in loud
22.17 Jesus took a cup, gave **thanks** to God, and said, "Take this
22.19 a piece of bread, gave **thanks** to God, broke it, and gave
24.53 and spent all their time in the Temple giving **thanks** to God.
Jn 6.11 Jesus took the bread, gave **thanks** to God, and
6.23 crowd had eaten the bread after the Lord had given **thanks.**
11.41 looked up and said, "I **thank** you, Father, that you listen
Acts 27.35 Paul took some bread, gave **thanks** to God before them all,
28.15 When Paul saw them, he **thanked** God and was greatly encouraged.
Rom 1. 8 First, I **thank** my God through Jesus Christ for all of you,
1.21 him the honour that belongs to him, nor do they **thank** him.
6.17 But **thanks** be to God!
7.25 **Thanks** be to God, who does this through our Lord Jesus Christ!
14. 6 of the Lord, because he gives **thanks** to God for the food.
14. 6 so in honour of the Lord, and he gives **thanks** to God.
1 Cor 1. 4 I always give **thanks** to my God for you because of the
1.14 I **thank** God that I did not baptize any of you except
10.16 in the Lord's Supper and for which we give **thanks** to God:
10.30 If I **thank** God for my food, why should anyone criticize
10.30 criticize me about food for which I give **thanks?"**
11.24 a piece of bread, [24] gave **thanks** to God, broke it, and
14.16 When you give **thanks** to God in spirit only, how can an
14.16 part in the meeting say "Amen" to your prayer of **thanksgiving?**
14.17 Even if your prayer of **thanks** to God is quite good, the
14.18 I **thank** God that I speak in strange tongues much more
15.57 But **thanks** be to God who gives us the victory through
2 Cor 1. 3 Let us give **thanks** to the God and Father of our Lord
1.11 many will raise their voices to him in **thanksgiving** for us.
2.14 But **thanks** be to God!
4.15 offer to the glory of God more prayers of **thanksgiving.**
8.16 How we **thank** God for making Titus as eager as we are
9.11 times, so that many will **thank** God for your gifts which they
9.15 Let us **thank** God for his priceless gift!
Eph 1. 3 Let us give **thanks** to the God and Father of our Lord
1.16 God's people, [16] I have not stopped giving **thanks** to God for you.
5. 4 Rather you should give **thanks** to God.
5.20 Lord Jesus Christ, always give **thanks** for everything to God the Father.
Phil 1. 3 I **thank** my God for you every time I think of you;
4. 6 God for what you need, always asking him with a **thankful** heart.
Col 1. 3 We always give **thanks** to God, the Father of our Lord Jesus
1.11 And with joy give **thanks** to the Father, who has made you
2. 7 And be filled with **thanksgiving.**
3.15 And be **thankful.**
3.16 sing to God with **thanksgiving** in your hearts.
3.17 Lord Jesus, as you give **thanks** through him to God the Father.
4. 2 in prayer, and keep alert as you pray, giving **thanks** to God.
1 Thes 1. 2 We always **thank** God for you all and always mention you in
2.13 And there is another reason why we always give **thanks** to God.
3. 9 Now we can give **thanks** to our God for you.
3. 9 We **thank** him for the joy we have in his presence because
5.18 pray at all times, [18] be **thankful** in all circumstances.
2 Thes 1. 3 Our brothers, we must **thank** God at all times for you.
2.13 We must **thank** God at all times for you, brothers, you
1 Tim 1.12 I give **thanks** to Christ Jesus our Lord, who has given me
1.12 I **thank** him for considering me worthy and appointing me to
2. 1 prayers, requests, and **thanksgivings** be offered to God for all
4. 3 after a prayer of **thanks,** by those who are believers
4. 4 received with a prayer of **thanks,** [5] because the word of God
2 Tim 1. 3 I give **thanks** to God, whom I serve with a clear conscience,
1. 3 I **thank** him as I remember you always in my prayers night
Phlm 4 time I pray, I mention you and give **thanks** to my God.
Heb 12.28 Let us be **thankful,** then, because we receive a kingdom
Jas 3. 9 We use it to give **thanks** to our Lord and Father
3.10 Words of **thanksgiving** and cursing pour out from the same mouth.
1 Pet 1. 3 Let us give **thanks** to the God and Father of our Lord
4.16 ashamed of it, but **thank** God that you bear Christ's name.
Rev 4. 9 of glory and honour and **thanks** to the one who sits on
7.12 Praise, glory, wisdom, **thanksgiving,** honour, power, and might
11.17 We **thank** you that you have taken your great power and have

THANK-OFFERING

Lev 7.12 this offering as a **thank-offering** to God, he shall present,
Jer 17.26 grain-offerings and incense, as well as **thank-offerings.**
33.11 people sing as they bring **thank-offerings** to my Temple;

THANKSGIVING-OFFERING

2 Chr 33.16 he sacrificed fellowship-offerings and **thanksgiving-offerings**

THEATRE

Acts 19.29 travelling with Paul, and rushed with them to the **theatre.**
19.31 a message begging him not to show himself in the **theatre.**

THESSALONICA

Capital of the Roman province of Macedonia.

Acts 17. 1 Apollonia and came to **Thessalonica,** where there was a synagogue.
17.11 people there were more open-minded than the people in **Thessalonica.**
17.13 But when the Jews in **Thessalonica** heard that Paul had preached
20. 4 so did Aristarchus and Secundus, from **Thessalonica;**
27. 2 Aristarchus, a Macedonian from **Thessalonica,** was with us.
Phil 4.16 once when I needed help in **Thessalonica,** you sent it to me.
1 Thes 1. 1 people of the church in **Thessalonica,** who belong to God the
2. 2 insulted in Philippi before we came to you in **Thessalonica.**
2 Thes 1. 1 people of the church in **Thessalonica,** who belong to God our
2 Tim 4.10 this present world and has deserted me, going off to **Thessalonica.**

THICK

Ex 10.21 the sky, and a darkness **thick** enough to be felt will cover
19. 9 come to you in a **thick** cloud, so that the people will
19.16 and lightning, a **thick** cloud appeared on the mountain,
Lev 2. 4 It may be **thick** loaves made of flour mixed with olive-oil or
7.12 either **thick** loaves made of flour mixed with olive-oil or
Num 6.15 **thick** loaves made of flour mixed with olive-oil and biscuits
6.19 put it, together with one **thick** loaf of bread and one
Deut 4.11 mountain which was covered with **thick** clouds of dark smoke
5.22 the fire and from the **thick** clouds, he gave these
Judg 6. 5 with their livestock and tents, as **thick** as locusts.
1 Sam 17. 7 His spear was as **thick** as the bar on a weaver's loom,
2 Sam 14.26 His hair was very **thick,** and he had to cut it once
21.19 spear had a shaft as **thick** as the bar on a weaver's
22.12 **thick** clouds, full of water, surrounded him;
1 Kgs 7.26 The sides of the tank were 75 millimetres **thick.**
12.10 'My little finger is **thicker** than my father's waist!'
1 Chr 20. 5 spear had a shaft as **thick** as the bar on a weaver's
2 Chr 4. 5 The sides of the tank were 75 millimetres **thick.**
10.10 'My little finger is **thicker** than my father's waist.'
Job 3. 5 Make it a day of gloom and **thick** darkness;
22.14 You think the **thick** clouds keep him from seeing, as he
Ps 18.11 **thick** clouds, full of water, surrounded him.
Jer 46.23 men cutting down trees [23] and destroying a **thick** forest.
49.19 lion coming out of the **thick** woods along the Jordan up to
50.44 lion coming out of the **thick** woods along the Jordan up to
52.21 They were hollow, and the metal was 75 millimetres **thick.**
Lam 3.44 a cloud of fury too **thick** for our prayers to get through.
Ezek 17. 7 "There was another giant eagle with huge wings and **thick** plumage.
31. 5 Its branches grew **thick** and long.
40. 5 It was three metres high and three metres **thick.**
40. 7 and the walls between them were two and a half metres **thick.**
40. 8 Temple, and at its far end the walls were one metre **thick.**
40.10 and the walls between them were all of the same **thickness.)**
40.12 low wall fifty centimetres high and fifty centimetres **thick.**
40.48 wide, with walls one and a half metres **thick** on either side.
41. 2 wide, with walls two and a half metres **thick** on either side.
41. 3 with walls on either side three and a half metres **thick.**
41. 5 The man measured the **thickness** of the inner wall of the
41. 7 seemed to have the same **thickness** all the way to the top.
41. 8 outside wall of these rooms was two and a half metres **thick;**
41.12 its walls were two and a half metres **thick** all round.
Acts 2.19 There will be blood, fire, and **thick** smoke;

THIEF

Ex 22. 2 "If a **thief** is caught breaking into a house at night and
22. 7 stolen from his house, the **thief,** if he is found, shall
22. 8 But if the **thief** is not found, the man who was keeping
Judg 17. 2 pieces of silver from you, you put a curse on the **thief.**
Job 12. 6 But **thieves** and godless men live in peace, though their
24.16 At night **thieves** break into houses, but by day they hide
30. 5 them away with shouts, as if they were shouting at **thieves.**
Ps 50.18 become the friend of every **thief** you see and you associate
Prov 6.30 People don't despise a **thief** if he steals food when he
28.24 to steal from his parents is no better than a common **thief.**
29.24 A **thief's** partner is his own worst enemy.
Is 1.23 Your leaders are rebels and friends of **thieves;**
Jer 2.26 Lord says, "Just as a **thief** is disgraced when caught, so
Joel 2. 9 up the houses and go in through the windows like **thieves.**
Obad 5 "When **thieves** come at night, they take only what they want.
Zech 5. 3 it says that every **thief** will be removed from the land;
5. 4 enter the house of every **thief** and the house of everyone who
Mt 21.13 But you are making it a hideout for **thieves!"**
24.43 knew the time when the **thief** would come, you can be sure
24.43 would stay awake and not let the **thief** break into his house.
Mk 11.17 But you have turned it into a hideout for **thieves!"**
Lk 12.33 will never decrease, because no **thief** can get to them, and
12.39 knew the time when the **thief** would come,
12.39 he would not let the **thief** break into his house.
19.46 But you have turned it into a hideout for **thieves!"**
Jn 10. 1 but climbs in some other way, is a **thief** and a robber.
10. 8 who came before me are **thieves** and robbers, but the sheep
10.10 The **thief** comes only in order to steal, kill, and
12. 6 because he cared about the poor, but because he was a **thief.**
1 Cor 5.10 are immoral or greedy or are **thieves** or who worship idols.
5.11 worships idols or is a slanderer or a drunkard or a **thief.**
6.10 slander others or are **thieves**—none of these will possess God's
1 Thes 5. 2 Day of the Lord will come as a **thief** comes at night.
5. 4 and the Day should not take you by surprise like a **thief.**
1 Pet 4.15 is a murderer or a **thief** or a criminal or a meddler
2 Pet 3.10 But the Day of the Lord will come like a **thief.**
Rev 3. 3 come upon you like a **thief,** and you will not even know
16.15 I am coming like a **thief!**

THIGH

Gen 24. 2 he had, "Place your hand between my **thighs** and make a vow.
24. 9 put his hand between the **thighs** of Abraham, his master, and
47.29 "Place your hand between my **thighs** and make a solemn vow
Ex 28.42 from the waist to the **thighs,** so that they will not expose
29.22 the two kidneys with the fat on them, and the right **thigh.**
29.27 ordained, the breast and the **thigh** of the ram being used for

Ex 29.28 fellowship-offerings, the breast and the **thigh** of the animal
Song 5.15 His **thighs** are columns of alabaster set in sockets of gold.
7. 1 The curve of your **thighs** is like the work of an artist.
Rev 19.16 On his robe and on his **thigh** was written the name:

THIN

Gen 41. 3 they were **thin** and bony.
41. 4 on the river-bank, [4]and the **thin** cows ate up the fat cows.
41. 6 ears of corn sprouted, **thin** and scorched by the desert wind,
41. 7 the desert wind, [7]and the **thin** ears of corn swallowed the
41.19 Then seven other cows came up which were **thin** and bony.
41.20 The **thin** cows ate up the fat ones, [21]but no one would
41.23 ears of corn sprouted, **thin** and scorched by the desert wind,
41.24 the desert wind, [24]and the **thin** ears of corn swallowed the
41.27 The seven **thin** cows which came up later
41.27 and the seven **thin** ears of corn scorched
Ex 16.14 dew evaporated, there was something **thin** and flaky on the
39. 3 gold and cut them into **thin** strips to be worked into the
Lev 13.30 in it are yellowish and **thin**, it is a dreaded skin-disease,
Num 16.38 their sin, beat them into **thin** plates, and make a covering
16.39 and had them beaten into **thin** plates to make a covering for
1 Kgs 6. 6 wall on each floor was **thinner** than on the floor below so
Job 17. 7 my arms and legs are as **thin** as shadows.
Is 38.14 My voice was **thin** and weak, And I moaned like a dove.
Ezek 41. 6 wall on each floor was **thinner** than on the floor below, so

THINK
[THOUGHT, THOUGHTS]

Gen 3. 6 be to eat, and she **thought** how wonderful it would be to
6. 5 was and how evil their **thoughts** were all the time, [6]he was
8.21 know that from the time he is young his **thoughts** are evil.
17.17 began to laugh when he **thought**, "Can a man have a child
19.14 But they **thought** he was joking.
20.11 Abraham answered, "I **thought** that there would be no one
26. 9 He answered, "I **thought** I would be killed if I said she
26.28 is with you, and we **think** that there should be a solemn
27.41 He **thought**, "The time to mourn my father's death is near;
31.31 "I was afraid, because I **thought** that you might take your
32. 8 He **thought**, "If Esau comes and attacks the first group,
32.20 Jacob was **thinking**, "I will win him over with the gifts,
33.13 are weak, and I must **think** of the sheep and livestock with
37. 8 "Do you **think** you are going to be a king and rule
37.10 Do you **think** that your mother, your brothers, and I are
37.11 him, but his father kept **thinking** about the whole matter.
38.15 When Judah saw her, he **thought** that she was a prostitute,
40.23 never gave Joseph another **thought**—he forgot all about him.
43.18 house, they were afraid and **thought**, "We are being brought
Ex 3. 3 "This is strange," he **thought**.
13.17 God **thought**, "I do not want the people to change their
14. 3 The king will **think** that the Israelites are wandering
Num 22.34 but now if you **think** it is wrong for me to go
22.37 Did you **think** I wasn't able to reward you enough?"
Deut 1.41 you got ready to fight, **thinking** it would be easy to invade
8.17 So then, you must never **think** that you have made
15. 9 Do not let such an evil **thought** enter your mind.
17.20 This will keep him from **thinking** that he is better than
31.21 I promised to give them, I know what they are **thinking**."
32. 7 "**Think** of the past, of the time long ago;
Josh 8. 6 They will **think** that we are running away from them, as we
9.25 do with us what you **think** is right."
Judg 3.24 were locked, but they only **thought** that the king was inside,
3.25 waited as long as they **thought** they should, but when he
7. 2 They might **think** that they had won by themselves, and so
11.25 Do you **think** you are any better than Balak son of Zippor,
15. 2 said to Samson, "I really **thought** that you hated her, so I
16. 2 **thinking** to themselves, "We'll wait until daybreak,
16.20 He woke up and **thought**, "I'll get loose and go free, as
18.14 What do you **think** we should do?"
21.19 Then they **thought**, "The yearly festival of the Lord at
Ruth 1.11 Do you **think** I could have sons again for you to marry?
1.12 Even if I **thought** there was still hope, and so got married
4. 4 Elimelech, [4]and I **think** you ought to know about it.
1 Sam 1.13 So Eli **thought** that she was drunk, [14]and said to her,
1.16 Don't **think** I am a worthless woman.
1.18 "May you always **think** kindly of me," she replied.
1.23 Elkanah answered, "All right, do whatever you **think** best;
9. 5 or my father might stop **thinking** about the donkeys and start
10.12 "How about these other prophets—who do you **think** their fathers are?"
13.12 So I **thought**, 'The Philistines are going to attack me
14.30 Just **think** how many more Philistines they would have killed!"
14.36 "Do whatever you **think** best," they answered.
14.40 "Do whatever you **think** best," they answered.
15.32 with fear, **thinking** to himself, "What a bitter thing
17.43 Do you **think** I'm a dog?"
18.17 **thinking** that in this way the Philistines would kill David,
18.26 David was delighted with the **thought** of becoming the king's son-in-law.
20. 9 "Don't even **think** such a thing!"
20.26 day, because he **thought**, "Something has happened to him,
22. 7 Do you **think** that David will give fields and vineyards to
24.11 you that I have no **thought** of rebelling against you or of
25.17 Please **think** this over and decide what to do.
25.21 David had been **thinking**, "Why did I ever protect that
2 Sam 3. 8 "Do you **think** that I would betray Saul?
3. 8 Do you really **think** I'm serving Judah?"
4.10 told me of Saul's death **thought** he was bringing good news.
5. 6 The Jebusites, who lived there, **thought** that David would not
6.22 You may **think** I am nothing,
2 Sam 6.22 but those girls will **think** highly of me!"
10. 3 to the king, "Do you **think** that it is in your father's
12.22 I **thought** that the Lord might be merciful to me and not
14.16 I **thought** you would listen to me and save me from the
18. 4 "I will do whatever you **think** best," the king answered.
19.19 Don't hold it against me or **think** about it any more.
19.37 with you, Your Majesty, and do for him as you **think** best."
19.41 brothers, the men of Judah, **think** they had the right to take
21. 4 "What, then, do you **think** I should do for you?"
21.16 who was wearing a new sword, **thought** he could kill David.
24.13 Now **think** it over, and tell me what answer to take back
1 Kgs 8.39 You alone know the **thoughts** of the human heart.
10. 2 she asked him all the questions that she could **think** of.
12.28 After **thinking** it over, he made two bull-calves of gold
22.32 saw King Jehoshaphat, they all **thought** that he was the king
2 Kgs 1. 3 Is it because you **think** there is no god in Israel?
1. 6 Is it because you **think** there is no god in Israel?
4.43 but he answered, "Do you **think** this is enough for a
5. 7 Does he **think** that I am God, with the power of life
5.11 in a rage, saying, "I **thought** that he would at least come
7. 6 and chariots, and the Syrians **thought** that the king of
7.12 They **think** that we will leave the city to find food, and
10. 5 do whatever you **think** best."
10.15 Jehu greeted him and said, "You and I **think** alike.
18.20 He demanded, "Do you **think** that words can take the
18.20 Who do you **think** will help you rebel against Assyria?
18.25 Do you **think** I have attacked your country and destroyed
18.27 He replied, "Do you **think** you and the king are the
18.30 Don't **think** that the Lord will save you, and that he will
18.32 Hezekiah fool you into **thinking** that the Lord will rescue you.
18.35 Then what makes you **think** the Lord can save Jerusalem?"
19.11 Do you **think** that you can escape?
19.22 Whom do you **think** you have been insulting and ridiculing?
1 Chr 19. 3 to the king, "Do you **think** that it is in your father's
22. 5 David **thought**, "The Temple that my son Solomon is to
28. 9 He knows all our **thoughts** and desires.
2 Chr 6.30 You alone know the **thoughts** of the human heart.
9. 1 she asked him all the questions that she could **think** of.
18.31 saw King Jehoshaphat, they all **thought** that he was the king
19. 2 said to him, "Do you **think** it is right to help those
25. 8 You may **think** that they will make you stronger in battle,
32.14 Then what makes you **think** that your god can save you?
Neh 2.19 laughed at us and said, "What do you **think** you're doing?
4. 2 "What do these miserable Jews **think** they're doing?
4. 2 Do they **think** that by offering sacrifices they can finish
4.11 Our enemies **thought** we would not see them or know what
6.11 Do you **think** I would try to save my life by hiding
6.12 When I **thought** it over, I realized that God had not
Esth 2. 1 had cooled down, he kept **thinking** about what Vashti had done
2. 4 The king **thought** this was good advice, so he followed it.
5.14 Haman **thought** this was a good idea, so he had the gallows
6. 6 Haman **thought** to himself, "Now who could the king want to
Job 1. 5 always did this because he **thought** that one of them might
4. 7 **Think** back now.
4.19 Do you **think** he will trust a creature of clay, a thing
6.26 You **think** I am talking nothing but wind;
6.30 But you **think** I am lying—
6.30 you **think** I can't tell right from wrong.
7.12 Do you **think** I am a sea-monster?
11. 3 Job, do you **think** we can't answer you?
13. 5 Say nothing, and someone may **think** you are wise!
13. 7 Do you **think** your lies will benefit God?
13. 9 Do you **think** you can fool God as you fool men?
15. 7 Do you **think** you were the first man born?
15.21 in his ears, and robbers attack when he **thinks** he is safe.
18. 3 What makes you **think** we are as stupid as cattle?
19. 5 You **think** you are better than I am, and regard my troubles
21. 6 When I **think** of what has happened to me, I am stunned,
21.15 They **think** there is no need to serve God nor any
21.16 own strength, but their way of **thinking** I can't accept.
21.27 I know what spiteful **thoughts** you have.
22.14 You **think** the thick clouds keep him from seeing, as he
22.18 prosperous— I can't understand the **thoughts** of the wicked.
26. 4 Who do you **think** will hear all your words?
30.10 they **think** they are too good for me, and even come and
32. 6 are old, so I was afraid to tell you what I **think**.
32.10 let me tell you what I **think**.
32.17 will give my own answer now and tell you what I **think**.
34.17 Do you **think** that he hates justice?
34.33 tell us now what you **think**.
34.36 **Think** through everything that Job says;
35.15 You **think** that God does not punish, that he pays little
Ps 4. 4 **think** deeply about this, when you lie in silence on your beds.
7. 9 You are a righteous God and judge our **thoughts** and desires.
7.14 See how wicked people **think** up evil;
8. 4 in their places— [4]what is man, that you **think** of him;
10. 4 in his pride he **thinks** that God doesn't matter.
19.14 May my words and my **thoughts** be acceptable to you, O
24. 4 pure in act and in **thought**, who do not worship idols or
26. 2 judge my desires and **thoughts**.
31.22 I was afraid and **thought** that he had driven me out of
33.15 He forms all their **thoughts** and knows everything they do.
36. 2 Because he **thinks** so highly of himself,
36. 2 he **thinks** that God will not discover
39. 3 The more I **thought**, the more troubled I became;
42. 6 my heart is breaking, and so I turn my **thoughts** to him.
44.21 surely have discovered it, because you know our secret **thoughts**.
48. 9 Inside your Temple, O God, we **think** of your constant love.
49. 3 My **thoughts** will be clear;
50.21 I have said nothing, so you **thought** that I was like you.
58. 2 You **think** only of the evil you can do, and commit crimes

Ps 59. 7 in their mouths, yet they **think** that no one hears them.
60. 8 Did the Philistines **think** they would shout in triumph over me?"
63. 6 all night long I **think** of you, [7]because you have always
64. 9 they will **think** about what God has done and tell about his
73.16 I tried to **think** this problem through, but it was too
73.21 When my **thoughts** were bitter and my feelings were hurt,
77. 3 When I **think** of God, I sigh;
77. 5 I **think** of days gone by and remember years of long ago.
77. 6 I spend the night in deep **thought;**
77.12 I will **think** about all that you have done;
92. 5 How deep are your **thoughts!**
94.11 The Lord knows what they **think;**
106.33 They made him so bitter that he spoke without stopping to **think.**
107.43 May those who are wise **think** about these things;
109.16 That man never **thought** of being kind;
119.55 the night I remember you, Lord, and I **think** about your law.
119.97 I **think** about it all day long.
137. 6 you, if I do not **think** of you as my greatest joy!
139. 2 from far away you understand all my **thoughts.**
139.17 O God, how difficult I find your **thoughts;**
139.23 test me, and discover my **thoughts.**
143. 5 I **think** about all that you have done, I bring to mind
Prov 3. 5 Never rely on what you **think** you know.
3. 7 Never let yourself **think** that you are wiser than you are;
4.23 Be careful how you **think;**
4.23 your life is shaped by your **thoughts.**
6.16 a mind that **thinks** up wicked plans,
12.15 Stupid people always **think** they are right.
13.16 Sensible people always **think** before they act, but stupid
14. 8 Because he only **thinks** he knows.
14.12 What you **think** is the right road may lead to death.
14.33 Wisdom is in every **thought** of an intelligent man;
15.11 how then can a man hide his **thoughts** from God?
15.26 The Lord hates evil **thoughts,**
15.28 Good people **think** before they answer.
16. 2 You may **think** everything you do is right, but the Lord
16.23 Intelligent people **think** before they speak;
16.25 What you **think** is the right road may lead to death.
16.30 they have **thought** of something evil.
17. 8 Some people **think** a bribe works like magic;
17.20 Anyone who **thinks** and speaks evil can expect to find
17.28 even a fool may be **thought** wise and intelligent if he stays
20. 5 A person's **thoughts** are like water in a deep well, but
20.25 **Think** carefully before you promise an offering to God.
21. 2 You may **think** that everything you do is right, but
21.26 all he does is **think** about what he would like to have.
21.28 the word of someone who **thinks** matters through is accepted.
23. 7 What he **thinks** is what he really is.
23.19 son, be wise and give serious **thought** to the way you live.
23.33 eyes, and you will not be able to **think** or speak clearly.
24. 2 Causing trouble is all they ever **think** about;
24. 9 Any scheme a fool **thinks** up is sinful.
24.32 I looked at this, **thought** about it, and learned a lesson
25. 3 You never know what a king is **thinking;**
25. 3 his **thoughts** are beyond us, like the heights of the sky or
26. 5 asked it will realize that he's not as clever as he **thinks.**
26.12 better off than someone who **thinks** he is wise when he is
26.16 A lazy man will **think** he is more intelligent than seven
26.23 hides what you are really **thinking** is like a fine glaze on
27. 5 openly than to let him **think** you don't care for him at
28.11 Rich people always **think** they are wise, but a poor
28.24 Anyone who **thinks** it isn't wrong to steal from his
29.20 a stupid fool than for someone who speaks without **thinking.**
29.25 be concerned with what others **think** of you, but if you trust
30.12 There are people who **think** they are pure when they are
30.13 There are people who **think** they are so good—
30.13 oh, how good they **think** they are!
30.32 foolish enough to be arrogant and plan evil, stop and **think!**
Ecc 2. 3 I **thought** that this might be the best way people can spend
2.11 Then I **thought** about all that I had done and how hard
2.12 So I started **thinking** about what it meant to be wise or
2.15 I **thought** to myself, "I will suffer the same fate as fools.
4.15 I **thought** about all the people who live in this world,
5. 2 **Think** before you speak, and don't make any rash promises to God.
7. 4 Someone who is always **thinking** about happiness is a fool.
7. 4 A wise person **thinks** about death.
7.13 **Think** about what God has done.
8. 9 saw all this when I **thought** about the things that are done
9. 1 I **thought** long and hard about all this and saw that God
9.10 will be no action, no **thought,** no knowledge, no wisdom in
9.15 But no one **thought** about him.
9.16 than strength, but no one **thinks** of a poor man as wise
Is 1.11 He says, "Do you **think** I want all these sacrifices you
5.21 You **think** you are wise, so very clever.
14.13 You **thought** you would sit like a king on that mountain in
22.16 household, and say to him, [16]"Who do you **think** you are?
28. 9 They say, "Who does that man **think** he's teaching?
29.15 their schemes in secret and **think** no one will see them or
30.16 You **think** your horses are fast enough, but those who pursue
32. 5 No one will **think** that a fool is honourable or say that
32. 6 A fool speaks foolishly and **thinks** up evil things to do.
36. 5 He demanded, "Do you **think** that words can take the place
36. 5 Who do you **think** will help you rebel against Assyria?
36.10 Do you **think** I have attacked your country and destroyed
36.12 He replied, "Do you **think** you and the king are the only
36.15 Don't **think** that the Lord will save you and that he will
36.18 Hezekiah fool you into **thinking** that the Lord will rescue you.
36.20 Then what makes you **think** the Lord can save Jerusalem?"
37.11 Do you **think** that you can escape?
37.23 Whom do you **think** you have been insulting and ridiculing?
38.10 I **thought** that in the prime of life I was going to
Is 38.11 I **thought** that in this world of the living I would never
38.12 I **thought** that God was ending my life.
38.13 I **thought** that God was ending my life.
40.28 No one understands his **thoughts.**
46.12 me, you stubborn people who **think** that victory is far away.
47. 7 You **thought** you would always be a queen, and did not take
47. 7 take these things to heart or **think** how it all would end.
47. 8 lover of pleasure, you that **think** you are safe and secure.
47. 8 You **thought** that you would never be a widow or suffer the
47.10 you **thought** that no one could see you.
50. 1 "Do you **think** I sent my people away like a man who
50. 1 Do you **think** I sold you into captivity like a man who
51. 1 **Think** of the rock from which you came, the quarry from which
51. 2 **Think** of your ancestor, Abraham, and of Sarah, from whom
53. 4 All the while we **thought** that his suffering was punishment
55. 7 leave their way of life and change their way of **thinking.**
55. 8 "My **thoughts,"** says the Lord, "are not like yours, and
55. 9 the earth, so high are my ways and **thoughts** above yours.
56. 3 should never **think** that because he cannot have children,
57. 6 Do you **think** I am pleased with all this?
57.10 You **think** your obscene idols give you strength, and so you
57.12 You **think** that what you do is right, but I will expose
58. 4 Do you **think** this kind of fasting will make me listen to
58. 5 Do you **think** I will be pleased with that?
59. 1 Don't **think** that the Lord is too weak to save you or
59.13 Our **thoughts** are false;
66. 9 Do not **think** that I will bring my people to the point
66.18 I know their **thoughts** and their deeds.
Jer 2.18 What do you **think** you will gain by going to Egypt to
2.18 What do you **think** you will gain by going to Assyria to
3. 7 I **thought** that after she had done all this, she would
3.16 They will no longer **think** about it or remember it;
4.14 How long will you go on thinking sinful **thoughts?**
5. 4 Then I **thought,** "These are only the poor and ignorant.
5.24 You never **thought** to honour me, even though I send the
7.11 Do you **think** that my Temple is a hiding place for robbers?
9.17 **"Think** about what is happening!
10.19 And we **thought** this was something we could endure!
11.15 Do they **think** they can prevent disaster by making promises
11.20 you test people's **thoughts** and feelings.
13.21 you say when people you **thought** were your friends conquer
23.18 "None of these prophets has ever known the Lord's secret **thoughts.**
23.22 they had known my secret **thoughts,** then they could have
23.27 They **think** that the dreams they tell will make my people
25.29 Do they **think** they will go unpunished?
26.14 Do with me whatever you **think** is fair and right.
30. 6 Now stop and **think!**
31.20 Whenever I mention your name, I **think** of you with love.
37. 9 not to deceive yourselves into **thinking** that the Babylonians
40. 5 the people, or you may go anywhere you **think** you should."
44.21 streets of Jerusalem—do you **think** that the Lord did not know
48.29 conceited the people are, how much they **think** of themselves.
49.12 cup of punishment, do you **think** that you will go unpunished?
49.16 No one fears you as much as you **think** they do.
51.50 you are far from home, **think** about me, your Lord, and
Lam 2.14 They made you **think** you did not need to repent.
3.19 The **thought** of my pain, my homelessness, is bitter poison;
3.20 I **think** of it constantly and my spirit is depressed.
3.54 Water began to close over me, and I **thought** death was near.
Ezek 12.27 me, [27]"Mortal man, the Israelites **think** that your visions
14. 3 Do they **think** I will give them an answer?
18.23 Do you **think** I enjoy seeing an evil man die?"
18.25 Do you **think** my way of doing things isn't right?
18.29 You **think** my way isn't right, do you?
22.14 Do you **think** you will have any courage left or have
23.27 look at any more idols or **think** about Egypt any more."
28. 3 You **think** you are wiser than Danel, that no secret can be
28. 6 Because you **think** you are as wise as a god, [7]I will
32.19 "Do you **think** you are more beautiful than anyone else?
33.13 man, but if he starts **thinking** that his past goodness is
33.25 What makes you **think** that the land belongs to you?
33.26 What makes you **think** that the land is yours?
38.10 "When that time comes, you will start **thinking** up an evil plan.
Dan 2. 8 At that, the king exclaimed, "Just as I **thought!**
2.30 dream and understand the **thoughts** that have come to you.
3.15 Do you **think** there is any god who can save you?"
4.13 "While I was **thinking** about the vision, I saw coming
9. 2 studying the sacred books and **thinking** about the seventy
11.37 every god, because he will **think** he is greater than any of
Hos 9. 1 Baal and have loved the corn you **thought** he paid you with!
11. 6 my people because they do what they themselves **think** best.
Amos 4.13 He makes his **thoughts** known to man;
9. 7 says, "People of Israel, I **think** as much of the people of
Jon 2. 4 I **thought** I had been banished from your presence and would
Mic 2. 7 Do you **think** the people of Israel are under a curse?
2. 8 Men return from battle, **thinking** they are safe at home, but
Zeph 2.15 is so proud of its own power and **thinks** it is safe.
2.15 Its people **think** that their city is the greatest in the world.
3. 7 I **thought** that then my people would have reverence for me
Zech 11.13 silver—the magnificent sum they **thought** I was worth—and put
Mal 1. 8 to me, do you **think** there's nothing wrong with that?
1.13 Do you **think** I will accept that from you?
2.17 By saying, "The Lord Almighty **thinks** all evildoers are good;
Mt 1.20 While he was **thinking** about this, an angel of the Lord
3. 9 And don't **think** you can escape punishment by saying that Abraham
5.17 "Do not **think** that I have come to do away with the
6. 7 as the pagans do, who **think** that their gods will hear them
9. 4 Jesus perceived what they were **thinking,** so he said,
9. 4 "Why are you **thinking** such evil things?

Mt	10.34	"Do not **think** that I have come to bring peace to the
	12.25	Jesus knew what they were **thinking,** so he said to them,
	16.23	my way, because these **thoughts** of yours don't come from God,
	18.12	"What do you **think** a man does who has a hundred sheep
	20.10	be hired came to be paid, they **thought** they would get more;
	21.28	"Now, what do you **think?**
	22.16	without worrying about what people **think,** because you pay
	22.17	Tell us, then, what do you **think?**
	22.42	Jesus asked them, [42]"What do you **think** about the Messiah?
	26.66	What do you **think?"**
Mk	2. 6	Law who were sitting there **thought** to themselves, [7]"How does he
	2. 8	Jesus knew what they were **thinking,**
	2. 8	so he said to them, "Why do you **think** such things?
	6.49	they **thought,** and screamed.
	8.33	"Your **thoughts** don't come from God but from man!"
	12.14	you tell the truth, without worrying about what people **think.**
Lk	1. 3	matters from their beginning, I **thought** it would be good to
	1.17	disobedient people back to the way of **thinking** of the righteous;
	1.66	Everyone who heard of it **thought** about it and asked,
	2.19	Mary remembered all these things and **thought** deeply about them.
	2.35	people will speak against [35]and so reveal their secret **thoughts.**
	2.44	they **thought** that he was with the group, so they
	3.23	was the son, so people **thought,** of Joseph, who was the son
	5.22	Jesus knew their **thoughts**
	5.22	and said to them, "Why do you **think** such things?
	5.34	Jesus answered, "Do you **think** you can make the guests
	6. 8	But Jesus knew their **thoughts** and said to the man, "Stand
	8.18	have taken away from him even the little he **thinks** he has."
	9.47	Jesus knew what they were **thinking,** so he took a child,
	11.17	Jesus knew what they were **thinking,** so he said to them,
	12.17	He began to **think** to himself, 'I haven't anywhere to
	13. 2	in that way, do you **think** it proves that they were worse
	21.29	**"Think** of the fig-tree and all the other trees.
	22.24	to which one of them should be **thought** of as the greatest.
	24.11	But the apostles **thought** that what the women said was nonsense,
	24.37	They were terrified, **thinking** that they were seeing a ghost.
Jn	5.39	study the Scriptures, because you **think** that in them you
	5.45	Do not **think,** however, that I am the one who will accuse
	8.53	Who do you **think** you are?"
	11.13	Lazarus had died, but they **thought** he meant natural sleep.
	11.31	They **thought** that she was going to the grave to weep there.
	11.56	in the Temple, they asked one another, "What do you **think?**
	13. 2	the son of Simon Iscariot, the **thought** of betraying Jesus.
	13.29	bag, some of the disciples **thought** that Jesus had told him
	16. 2	anyone who kills you will **think** that by doing this he is
	18.11	Do you **think** that I will not drink the cup of suffering
	18.35	Pilate replied, "Do you **think** I am a Jew?
	20.15	She **thought** he was the gardener, so she said to him, "If
Acts	1.24	"Lord, you know the **thoughts** of everyone, so show us which
	3.12	Do you **think** that it was by means of our own power
	7.25	(He **thought** that his own people would understand that God was
	8.20	money go to hell, for **thinking** that you can buy God's gift
	8.22	that he will forgive you for **thinking** such a thing as this.
	12. 9	he **thought** he was seeing a vision.
	13.25	mission, he said to the people, 'Who do you **think** I am?
	14.19	and dragged him out of the town, **thinking** that he was dead.
	15. 8	And God, who knows the **thoughts** of everyone, showed his approval
	15.38	them, [38]but Paul did not **think** it was right to take him,
	16.13	to the river-side, where we **thought** there would be a place
	16.27	the prison doors open, he **thought** that the prisoners had escaped;
	21.29	in the city, and they **thought** that Paul had taken him into
	25.18	him of any of the evil crimes that I **thought** they would.
	26. 9	"I myself **thought** that I should do everything I could against
	26.28	this short time do you **think** you will make me a Christian?"
	27.13	to blow, and the men **thought** that they could carry out their
Rom	1.21	Instead, their **thoughts** have become complete nonsense,
	1.30	they **think** of more ways to do evil;
	2. 3	Do you **think** you will escape God's judgement?
	2.15	since their **thoughts** sometimes accuse them and sometimes defend
	2.16	God through Jesus Christ will judge the secret **thoughts** of all.
	4.19	did not weaken when he **thought** of his body, which was
	6.11	same way you are to **think** of yourselves as dead, so far
	8.27	into our hearts, knows what the **thought** of the Spirit is;
	11.21	do you **think** he will spare you?
	11.25	know, for it will keep you from **thinking** how wise you are.
	12. 3	Do not **think** of yourself more highly than you should.
	12. 3	Instead, be modest in your **thinking,** and judge yourself according
	12.16	Do not **think** of yourselves as wise.
	14. 5	One person **thinks** that a certain day is more important
	14. 5	days, while someone else **thinks** that all days are the same.
	14. 6	Whoever **thinks** highly of a certain day does so in honour
1 Cor	1.10	Be completely united, with only one **thought** and one purpose.
	1.28	despises, and **thinks** is nothing,
	1.28	in order to destroy what the world **thinks** is important.
	2. 9	heard, what no one ever **thought** could happen, is the very
	3.18	If anyone among you **thinks** that he is wise by this world's
	3.20	"The Lord knows that the **thoughts** of the wise are worthless."
	4. 1	You should **think** of us as Christ's servants, who have been
	4.18	become proud because you have **thought** that I would not be
	7.26	Considering the present distress, I **think** it is better
	7.40	is my opinion, and I **think** that I too have God's Spirit.
	8. 2	Whoever **thinks** he knows something really doesn't know as he ought
	8. 7	eat such food they still **think** of it as food that belongs
	10.12	Whoever **thinks** he is standing firm had better be careful
	10.22	Do we **think** that we are stronger than he?
	10.33	all that I do, not **thinking** of my own good, but of
	12.23	and those parts that we **think** aren't worth very much are
1 Cor	13.11	my speech, feelings, and **thinking** were all those of a child;
	14.20	Do not be like children in your **thinking,** my brothers;
	14.20	far as evil is concerned, but be grown-up in your **thinking.**
	14.25	he hears, [25]his secret **thoughts** will be brought into the open,
2 Cor	9. 5	So I **thought** it was necessary to urge these brothers to go
	10. 5	we take every **thought** captive and make it obey Christ.
	10. 7	let him **think** again about himself, because we belong to Christ
	10.18	it is when the Lord **thinks** well of a person that
	10.18	is really approved, and not when he **thinks** well of himself.
	11. 5	I do not **think** that I am the least bit inferior to
	11.16	no one should **think** that I am a fool.
	12.19	Perhaps you **think** that all along we have been trying to
Gal	6. 3	If someone **thinks** he is somebody when really he is nobody,
Eph	3.20	much more than we can ever ask for, or even **think** of:
	4.17	live like the heathen, whose **thoughts** are worthless
Phil	1. 3	I thank my God for you every time I **think** of you;
	1.17	they **think** that they will make more trouble for me while I
	2. 2	happy by having the same **thoughts,** sharing the same love,
	2. 6	God, but he did not **think** that by force he should try
	2.25	have **thought** it necessary to send you our brother Epaphroditus,
	3. 4	If anyone **thinks** he can trust in external ceremonies, I have
	3.13	brothers, I really do not **think** that I have already won it;
	3.19	be ashamed of, and they **think** only of things that belong to
Col	1.21	his enemies because of the evil things you did and **thought.**
	2.18	by his human way of **thinking** [19]and has stopped holding on
1 Thes	2.17	little while—not in our **thoughts,** of course, but only in
	3. 6	told us that you always **think** well of us and that you
2 Thes	2. 2	so easily confused in your **thinking** or upset by the claim
	2. 2	Perhaps it is **thought** that we said this while prophesying or
1 Tim	6. 5	They **think** that religion is a way to become rich.
2 Tim	2. 7	**Think** about what I am saying, because the Lord will enable
Phlm	17	So, if you **think** of me as your partner, welcome him back
Heb	2. 6	"What is man, O God, that you should **think** of him;
	3. 1	**Think** of Jesus, whom God sent to be the High Priest of
	4.12	It judges the desires and **thoughts** of man's heart.
	10.29	Just **think** how much worse is the punishment he will deserve!
	11.15	They did not keep **thinking** about the country they had left;
	12. 2	was waiting for him, he **thought** nothing of the disgrace of
	12. 3	**Think** of what he went through;
	13. 7	**Think** back on how they lived and died, and imitate their faith.
Jas	1. 7	all he does, must not **think** that he will receive anything
	1.26	Does anyone **think** he is religious?
	3. 4	Or **think** of a ship:
	3. 5	Just **think** how large a forest can be set on fire by
	4. 5	Don't **think** that there is no truth in the scripture that says,
	4.12	Who do you **think** you are, to judge your fellow-man?
1 Pet	4. 1	strengthen yourselves with the same way of **thinking** that he had;
2 Pet	1.13	I **think** it only right for me to stir up your memory
	3. 1	have tried to arouse pure **thoughts** in your minds by
	3. 9	is not slow to do what he has promised, as some **think.**
Rev	2. 5	**Think** how far you have fallen!
	2.23	that I am the one who knows everyone's **thoughts** and wishes.

Am **THINK UP** see **PLAN**

THIRD

[ONE-THIRD, TWO-THIRDS]

Gen	1.13	Evening passed and morning came—that was the **third** day.
	2.14	The **third** river is the Tigris, which flows east of Assyria,
	22. 4	On the **third** day Abraham saw the place in the distance.
	32.19	order to the second, the **third,** and to all the others who
	42.18	On the **third** day Joseph said to them, "I am a
Ex	19. 1	the first day of the **third** month after they had left Egypt
	19.16	On the morning of the **third** day there was thunder and lightning,
	20. 5	their descendants down to the **third** and fourth generation.
	28.19	in the **third** row, a turquoise, an agate, and an amethyst;
	34. 7	children and grandchildren to the **third** and fourth
	39.12	in the **third** row, a turquoise, an agate, and an amethyst;
Lev	7.17	Any meat that still remains on the **third** day must be burnt.
	7.18	it is eaten on the **third** day, God will not accept the
	14.10	mixed with olive-oil, and a **third** of a litre of olive-oil.
	14.12	lambs and together with the **one-third** of a litre of oil he
	14.21	for a grain-offering and a **third** of a litre of olive-oil.
	19. 6	Any meat left on the **third** day must be burnt, [7]because it
Num	2.18	The division of Ephraim shall march **third.**
	14.18	children and grandchildren to the **third** and fourth
	19.12	for purification on the **third** day and on the seventh day,
	19.12	purify himself on both the **third** and the seventh day, he
	19.19	On the **third** day and on the seventh the person who is
	29.20	On the **third** day offer eleven young bulls, two rams, and
	31.19	On the **third** day and on the seventh day purify yourselves
Deut	5. 9	their descendants down to the **third** and fourth generation.
	14.28	At the end of every **third** year bring the tithe of all
	23. 8	From the **third** generation onward their descendants may be
	26.12	"Every **third** year give the tithe—a tenth of your
Josh	19.10	The **third** assignment made was for the families of the
Judg	20.30	Then for the **third** successive day they marched against
1 Sam	3. 8	The Lord called Samuel a **third** time;
	10. 3	loaves of bread, and the **third** one will have a leather bag
	17.13	was Eliab, the next was Abinadab, and the **third** was Shammah.
	19.21	He sent messengers the **third** time, and the same thing
2 Sam	23.11	The **third** of the famous three was Shammah son of Agee,
1 Kgs	6. 8	with stairs leading up to the second and **third** storeys.
	15.28	This happened during the **third** year of the reign of King
	15.33	In the **third** year of the reign of King Asa of Judah,
	18. 1	After some time, in the **third** year of the drought, the
	22. 2	two years, [2]but in the **third** year King Jehoshaphat of Judah
2 Kgs	11. 5	duty on the Sabbath, one **third** of you are to guard the
	11. 6	another **third** are to stand guard at the Sur Gate,

2 Kgs 11. 6 and the other **third** are to stand guard at the
17. 5 In the **third** year of the siege, [6]which was the ninth year
18. 1 In the **third** year of the reign of Hoshea son of Elah
18.10 In the **third** year of the siege, Samaria fell;
1 Chr 2.51 and his **third** son Hareph founded Bethgader.
6.44 of the clan of Merari was the leader of the **third** choir.
23.19 Kohath's **third** son, Hebron, had four sons:
27. 2 **Third** month:
2 Chr 15.10 assembled in Jerusalem in the **third** month of the fifteenth
17. 7 In the **third** year of his reign he sent out the following
17.16 280,000 soldiers, [16]and **third** was Amasiah son of Zichri,
23. 4 duty on the Sabbath, one **third** of them will guard the temple
23. 5 temple gates, [5]another **third** will guard the royal palace,
31. 7 gifts started arriving in the **third** month and continued to
Ezra 6.15 finished the Temple on the **third** day of the month Adar in
Esth 1. 3 In the **third** year of his reign he gave a banquet for
5. 1 On the **third** day of her fast Esther put on her royal
8. 9 the twenty-third day of the **third** month, the month of Sivan.
Jer 38.14 brought to him at the **third** entrance to the Temple, and he
Ezek 5. 2 Burn a **third** of it in the city when the siege is
5. 2 Take another **third** and chop it up with your sword as you
5. 2 Scatter the remaining **third** to the winds, and I will pursue
5.12 A **third** of your people will die from sickness and hunger
5.12 a **third** will be cut down by swords outside the city;
5.12 I will scatter the last **third** to the winds and pursue them
10.14 second a human face, the **third** the face of a lion, and
31. 1 the first day of the **third** month of the eleventh year of
Dan 1. 1 In the **third** year that Jehoiakim was king of Judah, King
2.39 yours, and after that a **third**, an empire of bronze, which
5. 7 round his neck, and be the **third** in power in the kingdom."
5.16 your neck, and be the **third** in power in the kingdom."
5.29 And he made him the **third** in power in the kingdom.
8. 1 In the **third** year that Belshazzar was king, I saw a second
10. 1 (In the **third** year that Cyrus was emperor of Persia, a
Amos 4. 4 after morning, and bring your tithes every **third** day.
Zech 6. 3 second by black horses, [3]the **third** by white horses, and the
13. 8 and throughout the land **two-thirds** of the people will die.
13. 9 And I will test the **third** that survives and will purify
Mt 22.26 the second brother, to the **third**, and finally to all seven.
26.44 went away, and prayed the **third** time, saying the same words.
27.64 carefully guarded until the **third** day, so that his disciples will
Mk 12.21 happened to the **third** brother, [22]and then to the rest:
14.41 When he came back the **third** time, he said to them, "Are
Lk 2.46 On the **third** day they found him in the Temple, sitting
13.32 and tomorrow, and on the **third** day I shall finish my work.'
20.12 Then he sent a **third** slave;
20.31 Then the second one married the woman, [31]and then the **third.**
23.22 Pilate said to them the **third** time, "But what crime has
24.21 Besides all that, this is now the **third** day since it happened.
Jn 21.14 This, then, was the **third** time Jesus appeared to the disciples
21.17 A **third** time Jesus said, "Simon son of John, do you
21.17 because Jesus asked him the **third** time, "Do you love me?"
Acts 20. 9 sound asleep and fell from the **third** storey to the ground.
1 Cor 12.28 in the second place prophets, and in the **third** place teachers;
2 Cor 12.14 This is now the **third** time that I am ready to come
13. 1 This is now the **third** time that I am coming to visit
Rev 4. 7 the **third** had a face like a man's face;
6. 5 Then the Lamb broke open the **third** seal;
6. 5 and I heard the **third** living creature say, "Come!"
8. 7 A **third** of the earth was burnt up,
8. 7 a **third** of the trees, and every blade
8. 8 A **third** of the sea was turned into blood,
8. 9 a **third** of the living creatures
8. 9 in the sea died, and a **third** of the ships were destroyed.
8.10 Then the **third** angel blew his trumpet.
8.10 sky and fell on a **third** of the rivers and on the
8.11 A **third** of the water turned bitter, and many people died
8.12 A **third** of the sun was struck,
8.12 and a **third** of the moon,
8.12 and a **third** of the stars,
8.12 so that their light lost a **third** of its brightness;
8.12 was no light during a **third** of the day
8.12 and a **third** of the night.
9.15 they had been kept ready to kill a **third** of all mankind.
9.18 A **third** of mankind was killed by those three plagues:
11.14 The second horror is over, but the **third** horror will come soon!
12. 4 his tail he dragged a **third** of the stars out of the
14. 9 A **third** angel followed the first two, saying in a loud voice,
16. 4 Then the **third** angel poured out his bowl on the rivers and
21.19 jasper, the second sapphire, the **third** agate, the fourth emerald,

THIRST

Ex 17. 3 the people were very **thirsty** and continued to complain to Moses.
17. 3 To kill us and our children and our livestock with **thirst?"**
Deut 28.48 You will be hungry, **thirsty,** and naked—in need of everything.
Judg 4.19 I'm **thirsty."**
15.18 Then Samson became very **thirsty,** so he called to the
15.18 now going to die of **thirst** and be captured by these heathen
Ruth 2. 9 And whenever you are **thirsty,** go and drink from the water
2 Sam 17.28 men would be hungry, **thirsty,** and tired in the wilderness.
2 Chr 32.11 is deceiving you and will let you die of hunger and **thirst.**
Neh 9.15 from heaven, and water from a rock when they were **thirsty.**
Job 5. 5 among thorns— and **thirsty** people will envy his wealth.
24.11 oil, and grapes for wine, but they themselves are **thirsty.**
38.27 Who waters the dry and **thirsty** land, so that grass springs up?
Ps 42. 2 I **thirst** for you, the living God;
63. 1 worn-out, and waterless land, my soul is **thirsty** for you.
69.21 when I was **thirsty,** they offered me vinegar.
104.11 there the wild donkeys quench their **thirst.**
107. 5 They were hungry and **thirsty** and had given up all hope.
Ps 107. 9 He satisfies those who are **thirsty** and fills the hungry
143. 6 like dry ground my soul is **thirsty** for you.
Prov 25.21 if he is **thirsty,** give him a drink.
25.25 like a drink of cold water when you are dry and **thirsty.**
Is 5.13 starve to death, and the common people will die of **thirst.**
12. 3 water brings joy to the **thirsty,** so God's people rejoice
21.14 give water to the **thirsty** people who come to you.
29. 8 like a man dying of **thirst** who dreams he is drinking and
32. 6 feeds the hungry or gives **thirsty** people anything to drink.
41.17 their throats are dry with **thirst,** then I, the Lord, will
44. 3 will give water to the **thirsty** land and make streams flow on
44.12 As he works, he gets hungry, **thirsty,** and tired.
48.21 through a hot, dry desert, they did not suffer from **thirst.**
49.10 they will never be hungry or **thirsty.**
55. 1 "Come, everyone who is **thirsty**— here is water!
65.13 plenty to eat and drink, but you will be hungry and **thirsty.**
Lam 2.12 Hungry and **thirsty,** they cry to their mothers;
4. 4 They let their babies die of hunger and **thirst;**
Hos 2. 3 like a dry and barren land, and she will die of **thirst.**
Amos 4. 8 Weak with **thirst,** the people of several cities went to a
8.11 they will be **thirsty,** but not for water.
8.11 They will hunger and **thirst** for a message from the Lord.
8.13 even healthy young men and women will collapse from **thirst.**
Mt 25.35 hungry and you fed me, **thirsty** and you gave me a drink;
25.37 you hungry and feed you, or **thirsty** and give you a drink?
25.42 you would not feed me, **thirsty** but you would not give me
25.44 ever see you hungry or **thirsty** or a stranger or naked or
Jn 4.13 drinks this water will be **thirsty** again, [14]but whoever drinks
4.14 the water that I will give him will never be **thirsty** again.
4.15 Then I will never be **thirsty** again, nor will I have to
6.35 he who believes in me will never be **thirsty.**
7.37 voice, "Whoever is **thirsty** should come to me and drink.
19.28 to make the scripture come true, he said, "I am **thirsty."**
Rom 12.20 if he is **thirsty,** give him a drink;
1 Cor 4.11 To this very moment we go hungry and **thirsty;**
2 Cor 11.27 I have been hungry and **thirsty;**
1 Pet 2. 2 like new-born babies, always **thirsty** for the pure spiritual milk,
Rev 7.16 Never again will they hunger or **thirst;**
21. 6 To anyone who is **thirsty** I will give the right to drink
22.17 Come, whoever is **thirsty;**

THIS WORLD see WORLD

THISTLE

Job 31.40 then instead of wheat and barley, may weeds and **thistles** grow.
Is 9.18 burns like a fire that destroys thorn-bushes and **thistles.**
10.17 day will burn up everything, even the thorns and **thistles.**
34.13 Thorns and **thistles** will grow up in all the palaces and

THOMAS

One of the twelve apostles, known as "the Twin".

Mt 10. 3 **Thomas** and Matthew, the tax collector;
Mk 3.18 Philip, Bartholomew, Matthew, **Thomas,** James son of Alphaeus,
Lk 6.15 Bartholomew, [15]Matthew and **Thomas,** James son of Alphaeus,
Jn 11.16 **Thomas** (called the Twin) said to his fellow-disciples, "Let us
14. 5 **Thomas** said to him, "Lord, we do not know where you are
20.24 One of the twelve disciples, **Thomas** (called the Twin),
20.25 **Thomas** said to them, "Unless I see the scars of the nails
20.26 disciples were together again indoors, and **Thomas** was with them.
20.27 Then he said to **Thomas,** "Put your finger here, and look
20.28 **Thomas** answered him, "My Lord and my God!"
21. 2 Simon Peter, **Thomas** (called the Twin), Nathanael (the one from
Acts 1.13 James and Andrew, Philip and **Thomas,** Bartholomew and Matthew,

THORN

Gen 3.18 It will produce weeds and **thorns,** and you will have to
Num 33.55 splinters in your eyes and **thorns** in your sides, and they
Josh 23.13 painful as a whip on your back or **thorns** in your eyes.
Judg 8. 7 I will beat you with **thorns** and briars from the desert!"
8.16 He then took **thorns** and briars from the desert and used
9.14 trees said to the **thorn-bush,** 'You come and be our king.'
9.15 The **thorn-bush** answered, 'If you really want to make me your king,
9.15 will blaze out of my **thorny** branches and burn up the cedars
2 Sam 23. 6 But godless men are like **thorns** that are thrown away;
2 Kgs 14. 9 "Once a **thorn bush** on the Lebanon Mountains sent a message
2 Chr 25.18 "Once, a **thorn bush** in the Lebanon Mountains sent a message
Job 5. 5 even the grain growing among **thorns**— and thirsty people will
40.21 He lies down under the **thorn-bushes,** and hides among the
40.22 The **thorn-bushes** and the willows by the stream give him
Ps 118.12 bees, but they burnt out as quickly as a fire among **thorns;**
Prov 24.31 They were full of **thorn bushes** and overgrown with weeds.
26. 9 a drunk man trying to pick a **thorn** out of his hand.
Ecc 7. 6 When a fool laughs, it is like **thorns** crackling in a fire.
Song 2. 2 Like a lily among **thorns** is my darling among women.
Is 5. 6 instead I will let briars and **thorns** cover it.
7.19 and they will cover every **thorn-bush** and every pasture.
7.23 will be overgrown with **thorn-bushes** and briars.
7.24 the whole country will be full of briars and **thorn-bushes.**
7.25 will be so overgrown with **thorns** that no one will go there.
9.18 burns like a fire that destroys **thorn-bushes** and thistles.
10.17 day will burn up everything, even the **thorns** and thistles.
27. 4 If only there were **thorns** and briars to fight against, then
32.13 vineyards have been destroyed, [13]and **thorn-bushes** and
33.12 like rocks burnt to make lime, like **thorns** burnt to ashes.
34.13 **Thorns** and thistles will grow up in all the palaces and

Is 55.13 myrtle-trees will come up in place of **thorns.**
Jer 4. 3 do not sow your seeds among **thorns.**
Ezek 28.24 will ever again be like **thorns** and briars to hurt Israel.
Hos 2. 6 to fence her in with **thorn-bushes** and build a wall to block
9. 6 once stood will be overgrown with weeds and **thorn-bushes.**
10. 8 **Thorns** and weeds will grow up over their altars.
Nah 1.10 Like tangled **thorns** and dry straw, you drunkards will be burnt up!
Mt 7.16 **Thorn bushes** do not bear grapes, and briars do not bear figs.
13. 7 of the seed fell among **thorn bushes,** which grew up and
13.22 The seeds that fell among **thorn bushes** stand for those
27.29 made a crown out of **thorny branches** and placed it on his
Mk 4. 7 of the seed fell among **thorn bushes,** which grew up and
4.18 Other people are like the seeds sown among the **thorn bushes.**
15.17 made a crown out of **thorny branches,** and put it on his
Lk 6.44 do not pick figs from **thorn bushes** or gather grapes from
8. 7 of the seed fell among **thorn bushes,** which grew up with the
8.14 The seeds that fell among **thorn bushes** stand for those who hear;
Jn 19. 2 made a crown out of **thorny branches** and put it on his
19. 5 Jesus came out, wearing the crown of **thorns** and the purple robe.
Heb 6. 8 But if it grows **thorns** and weeds, it is worth nothing;

THOROUGH

Deut 13.14 If you hear such a rumour, investigate it **thoroughly;**
17. 4 If you hear such a report, then investigate it **thoroughly.**
19.18 The judges will investigate the case **thoroughly;**
1 Sam 19. 8 David attacked them and defeated them so **thoroughly** that they fled.
2 Kgs 12.15 charge of the work were **thoroughly** honest, so there was no
22. 7 charge of the work are **thoroughly** honest, so there is no
2 Chr 34.12 The men who did the work were **thoroughly** honest.
Ezra 7. 6 was a scholar with a **thorough** knowledge of the Law which the
7.11 and scholar, who had a **thorough** knowledge of the laws and

THOUGHT see THINK

THOUGHTLESS

Prov 12.18 **Thoughtless** words can wound as deeply as any sword, but

THOUSAND

Gen 20.16 am giving your brother a **thousand** pieces of silver as proof
Ex 18.21 leaders of **thousands,** hundreds, fifties, and tens.
18.25 He appointed them as leaders of **thousands,** hundreds,
20. 6 I show my love to **thousands** of generations of those who love
34. 7 I keep my promise for **thousands** of generations and forgive
38.24 the sacred Tent weighed a **thousand** kilogrammes, weighed
Num 10.36 "Return, Lord, to the **thousands** of families of Israel."
11.32 no one gathered less than a **thousand** kilogrammes.
31. 4 From each tribe of Israel send a **thousand** men to war."
31. 5 So a **thousand** men were chosen from each tribe, a total of
Deut 1.11 you increase a **thousand** times more and make you prosperous,
1.15 Some were responsible for a **thousand** people, some for a hundred,
5.10 I show my love to **thousands** of generations of those who love
7. 9 his constant love to a **thousand** generations of those who
32.30 Why were a **thousand** defeated by one, and ten thousand by
33.17 His horns are Manasseh's **thousands** And Ephraim's ten thousands.
Josh 23.10 of you can make a **thousand** men run away, because the Lord
Judg 9.49 the people of the fort died—about a **thousand** men and women.
15.15 down and picked it up, and killed a **thousand** men with it.
15.16 "With the jaw-bone of a donkey I killed a **thousand** men;
1 Sam 8.12 officers in charge of a **thousand** men, and others in charge
13. 2 Bethel and sending one **thousand** with his son Jonathan to Gibeah,
18. 7 "Saul has killed **thousands,** but David tens of thousands."
18. 8 "For David they claim tens of thousands, but only **thousands** for me.
18.13 sent him away and put him in command of a **thousand** men.
21.11 they danced, 'Saul has killed **thousands,** but David has
25. 2 the owner of three thousand sheep and one **thousand** goats.
29. 2 out with their units of a hundred and of a **thousand** men;
29. 5 they danced, 'Saul has killed **thousands,** but David has
2 Sam 10. 6 men from Tob, and the king of Maacah with a **thousand** men.
18. 1 them into units of a **thousand** and of a hundred, and placed
18. 4 men marched out in units of a **thousand** and of a hundred.
18.12 if you gave me a **thousand** pieces of silver, I wouldn't lift
19.17 He had with him a **thousand** men from the tribe of Benjamin.
1 Kgs 4.32 composed three thousand proverbs and more than a **thousand** songs.
2 Kgs 18.14 and a **thousand** kilogrammes of gold.
24.16 and one **thousand** skilled workers, including the blacksmiths,
1 Chr 12.14 officers in command of a **thousand** men, and others were
12.20 In Manasseh they had all commanded units of a **thousand** men.
12.23 **1,000** leaders, together with 37,000 men armed with shields and spears;
13. 1 command of units of a **thousand** men and units of a hundred
18. 4 David captured a **thousand** of his chariots,
29.21 a thousand bulls, a **thousand** rams, and a thousand lambs,
2 Chr 1. 2 charge of units of a **thousand** men and of a hundred men,
1. 6 he had a **thousand** animals killed and burnt whole on it.
25. 5 command of units of a **thousand** men and units of a hundred
27. 5 1,000 metric tons of wheat, and **1,000** metric tons of barley.
30.24 King Hezekiah contributed a **thousand** bulls
30.24 gave them another **thousand** bulls and ten thousand sheep.
Ezra 1. 9 silver bowls for offerings **1,000**
1. 9 other utensils **1,000**
Job 1. 3 sheep, three thousand camels, one **thousand** head of cattle,
9. 3 He can ask a **thousand** questions that no one could ever answer.
21.33 **thousands** join the funeral procession,
Job 33.23 aid— one of God's **thousands** of angels, who remind men of
42.12 two thousand head of cattle, and one **thousand** donkeys.
Ps 3. 6 am not afraid of the **thousands** of enemies who surround me on
50.10 the forest are mine and the cattle on **thousands** of hills.
68.17 With his many **thousands** of mighty chariots the Lord
84.10 in your Temple is better than a **thousand** anywhere else;
90. 4 A **thousand** years to you are like one day;
91. 7 A **thousand** may fall dead beside you, ten thousand all round you,
105. 8 covenant for ever, his promises for a **thousand** generations.
Ecc 7.28 found one man in a **thousand** that I could respect, but not
Song 4. 4 with a necklace like a **thousand** shields hung round it.
8.11 each one pays a **thousand** silver coins.
8.12 Solomon is welcome to his **thousand** coins, and the
Is 7.23 each with a **thousand** vines
7.23 and each worth a **thousand** pieces of silver,
30.17 A **thousand** of you will run away when you see one enemy
Jer 32.18 have shown constant love to **thousands,** but you also punish
Dan 5. 1 King Belshazzar invited a **thousand** noblemen to a great banquet,
7.10 There were many **thousands** of people there to serve him, and
Joel 3.14 **Thousands** and thousands are in the Valley of Judgement.
Amos 5. 3 Israel sends out a **thousand** soldiers, but only a hundred return;
Mic 6. 7 pleased if I bring him **thousands** of sheep or endless streams
Mt 25.15 he gave two thousand, and to another he gave one **thousand.**
25.18 servant who had received one **thousand** coins went off, dug a
25.24 servant who had received one **thousand** coins came in and said,
Lk 12. 1 **thousands** of people crowded together, so that they were stepping
16. 7 'A **thousand** sacks of wheat,' he answered.
Acts 21.20 you can see how many **thousands** of Jews have become believers,
1 Cor 14.19 to teach others, than speak **thousands** of words in strange tongues.
Heb 12.22 living God, the heavenly Jerusalem, with its **thousands** of angels.
2 Pet 3. 8 in the Lord's sight between one day and a **thousand** years;
Jude 14 Lord will come with many **thousands** of his holy angels
Rev 5.11 I looked, and I heard angels, **thousands** and millions of them!
20. 2 the Devil, or Satan—and chained him up for a **thousand** years.
20. 3 deceive the nations any more until the **thousand** years were over.
20. 4 to life and ruled as kings with Christ for a **thousand** years.
20. 5 did not come to life until the **thousand** years were over.)
20. 6 Christ, and they will rule with him for a **thousand** years.
20. 7 After the **thousand** years are over, Satan will be let loose

THREAD

Gen 14.23 keep anything of yours, not even a **thread** or a sandal strap.
38.28 caught it, tied a red **thread** round it, and said, "This one
38.30 was born with the red **thread** on his arm, and he was
Ex 28. 5 blue, purple, and red wool, gold **thread,** and fine linen.
28. 6 gold **thread,** and fine linen, decorated with embroidery.
35.25 skilled women brought fine linen **thread**
35.25 and **thread** of blue, purple, and red wool,
35.26 They also made **thread** of goats' hair.
39. 2 and gold **thread.**
Judg 15.14 ropes round his arms and hands as if they were burnt **thread.**
16. 9 the bowstrings just as **thread** breaks when fire touches it.
16.12 But he snapped the ropes off his arms like **thread.**
Job 8.14 They trust a **thread**—a spider's web.
8.15 If they grab for a **thread,** will it help them stand?"
Ps 45.13 Her gown is made of gold **thread.**
Prov 31.19 She spins her own **thread** and weaves her own cloth.
Jer 51.13 but its time is up, and its **thread** of life is cut.

THREAT

Gen 31.24 to him, "Be careful not to **threaten** Jacob in any way."
31.29 of your father warned me not to **threaten** you in any way.
Ex 1. 9 are so numerous and strong that they are a **threat** to us.
32.14 did not bring on his people the disaster he had **threatened.**
Num 14.10 The whole community was **threatening** to stone them to death,
22. 5 out everywhere and **threatening** to take over our land.
Deut 7.22 of wild animals would increase and be a **threat** to you.
Josh 23.15 that he made to you, so he will carry out every **threat.**
Judg 8.28 Midian was defeated by the Israelites and was no longer a **threat.**
1 Sam 3.12 will carry out all my **threats** against Eli's family, from
14.27 Jonathan had not heard his father **threaten** the people with a curse;
14.28 with hunger, but your father **threatened** us and said, 'A
30. 6 their children, and they were **threatening** to stone him;
2 Sam 14.10 The king replied, "If anyone **threatens** you, bring him to me,
14.15 you is that the people **threatened** me, and so I said to
2 Kgs 22.19 heard how I **threatened** to punish Jerusalem and its people.
2 Chr 34.27 heard how I **threatened** to punish Jerusalem and its people.
Job 26.11 When he **threatens** the pillars that hold up the sky, they
Ps 10. 7 His speech is filled with curses, lies, and **threats;**
27.12 me to my enemies, who attack me with lies and **threats.**
38.12 me, and those who want to hurt me **threaten** to ruin me;
55. 3 I am terrified by the **threats** of my enemies, crushed by
59. 7 Listen to their insults and **threats.**
76. 6 When you **threatened** them, O God of Jacob, the horses and
140. 9 make their **threats** against me fall back on them.
Prov 12. 6 the words of the righteous rescue those who are **threatened.**
13. 8 money to save his life, but no one **threatens** a poor man.
22.23 case for them and **threaten** the life
22.23 of anyone who **threatens** theirs.
Is 31. 2 He carries out his **threats** to punish evil men and those who
Jer 11.17 but now I **threaten** them with disaster.
17.15 to me, "Where are those **threats** the Lord made against us?
25.13 all the disasters that I **threatened** to bring on the nations
36. 7 ways, because the Lord has **threatened** this people with his
36.31 bring on all of you the disaster that I have **threatened."**
40. 2 "The Lord your God **threatened** this land with destruction,
Lam 2.17 The Lord has finally done what he **threatened** to do:
Ezek 6.10 I am the Lord and that my warnings were not empty **threats."**

Ezek 21.15 I am **threatening** their city with a sword that flashes like
39.26 land, with no one to **threaten** them, they will be able to
Mic 3. 5 to those who pay them, but **threaten** war for those who don't.
Zeph 3.18 "I have ended the **threat** of doom and taken away your disgrace.
Zech 11.16 does not help the sheep that are **threatened** by destruction;
14.11 live there in safety, no longer **threatened** by destruction.
Acts 4.29 Lord, take notice of the **threats** they have made, and allow
9. 1 Saul kept up his violent **threats** of murder against the followers
Rom 3.13 and dangerous **threats**, like snake's poison, from their lips;
Eph 6. 9 in the same way towards your slaves and stop using **threats**.
1 Pet 2.23 suffered, he did not **threaten**, but placed his hopes in God,

THREE
see also **THIRD**

Gen 5.32 was 500 years old, he had **three** sons, Shem, Ham, and
6. 9 He had **three** sons, Shem, Ham, and Japheth.
6.16 Build it with **three** decks and put a door in the side.
7.13 into the boat with their **three** sons, Shem, Ham, and Japheth,
9.19 These **three** sons of Noah were the ancestors of all the
10. 1 These **three** had sons after the flood.
10.10 Babylon, Erech, and Accad, all **three** of them in Babylonia.
14.10 but the other **three** kings escaped to the mountains.
15. 9 a ram, each of them **three** years old, and a dove and
18. 2 of the day, [2]he looked up and saw **three** men standing there.
29. 2 out in the fields with **three** flocks of sheep lying round it.
29.34 more tightly to me, because I have borne him **three** sons";
30.36 with this flock as far as he could travel in **three** days.
31.22 **Three** days later Laban was told that Jacob had fled.
34.25 **Three** days later, when the men were still sore
36.14 the daughter of Anah son of Zibeon, bore him **three** sons:
38.24 About **three** months later someone said to Judah, "Your
40.10 a grapevine in front of me [10]with **three** branches on it.
40.12 the **three** branches are three days.
40.13 In **three** days the king will release you, pardon you, and
40.16 I was carrying **three** bread-baskets on my head.
40.18 the **three** baskets are three days.
40.19 In **three** days the king will release you—and have your
40.20 On his birthday **three** days later the king gave a banquet
42.17 Then he put them in prison for **three** days.
Ex 2. 2 what a fine baby he was, she hid him for **three** months.
3.18 allow us to travel for **three** days into the desert to offer
5. 3 Allow us to travel for **three** days into the desert to offer
6.16 Levi had **three** sons:
6.21 Izhar had **three** sons:
6.22 Uzziel also had **three** sons:
6.24 Korah had **three** sons:
8.27 We must travel **three** days into the desert to offer
10.22 there was total darkness throughout Egypt for **three** days.
15.22 For **three** days they walked through the desert, but found no water.
23.14 "Celebrate **three** festivals a year to honour me.
23.17 Every year at these **three** festivals all your men must
25.32 Six branches shall extend from its sides, **three** from each side.
25.33 six branches is to have **three** decorative flowers shaped like
25.35 to be one bud below each of the **three** pairs of branches.
27.14 be 6.6 metres of curtains, with **three** posts and three bases.
30.23 **three** kilogrammes of sweet-smelling cinnamon,
30.23 **three** kilogrammes of sweet-smelling cane,
34.23 "**Three** times a year all your men must come to worship me,
34.24 try to conquer your country during the **three** festivals.
37.18 Six branches extended from its sides, **three** from each side.
37.19 of the six branches had **three** decorative flowers shaped like
37.21 There was one bud below each of the **three** pairs of branches.
38.14 6.6 metres of curtains, with **three** posts and three bases.
Lev 14.10 defects, **three** kilogrammes of flour mixed with olive-oil,
19.23 the fruit ritually unclean for the first **three** years.
20.14 woman and her mother, all **three** shall be burnt to death
Num 3.17 Levi had **three** sons:
4.34 took a census of the **three** Levite clans, Kohath, Gershon,
6.14 present to the Lord **three** animals without any defects:
10.33 Sinai, the holy mountain, they travelled for **three** days.
12. 4 and Miriam, "I want the **three** of you to come out to
15. 9 a fellowship-offering, [9]a grain-offering of **three**
16. 1 He was joined by **three** members of the tribe of Reuben—Dathan
22.28 Why have you beaten me these **three** times?"
22.32 "Why have you beaten your donkey **three** times like this?
22.33 But your donkey saw me and turned aside **three** times.
24.10 to curse my enemies, but **three** times now you have blessed
28.12 with each bull, **three** kilogrammes of flour;
28.20 **three** kilogrammes with each bull, two kilogrammes with the ram,
28.28 **three** kilogrammes with each bull, two kilogrammes with the ram,
29. 3 **three** kilogrammes of flour with the bull,
29. 9 **three** kilogrammes of flour with the bull,
29.14 **three** kilogrammes of flour with each bull,
33. 8 after a **three** days' march they camped at Marah.
35.14 Choose six cities, [14]**three** east of the Jordan
35.14 and **three** in the land of Canaan.
Deut 4.41 Then Moses set aside **three** cities east of the River
16.16 come to worship the Lord **three** times a year at the one
19. 2 there, [2-3]divide the territory into **three** parts, each
19. 5 he can run to one of those **three** cities and be safe.
19. 7 This is why I order you to set aside **three** cities.
19. 9 he has promised, [9]then you are to select **three** more cities.
Josh 1.11 some food ready, because in **three** days you are going to
2.16 Hide there for **three** days until they come back.
2.22 all over the countryside for **three** days, but they did not
3. 2 **Three** days later the leaders went through the camp [3]and
9.16 **Three** days after the treaty had been made, the
Josh 9.17 of Israel started out and **three** days later arrived at the
18. 4 Let me have **three** men from each tribe.
21.32 From the territory of Naphtali they received **three** cities:
Judg 1.20 drove out of the city the **three** clans descended from Anak.
7.16 his three hundred men into **three** groups and gave each man a
9.22 Abimelech ruled Israel for **three** years.
9.43 men, divided them into **three** groups, and hid in the fields,
14.14 **Three** days later they had still not solved the riddle.
16.15 made a fool of me **three** times, and you still haven't told
19. 4 insisted that he stay, and so he stayed for **three** days.
1 Sam 1.24 along a **three-year-old** bull, ten kilogrammes of flour,
2.21 bless Hannah, and she had **three** more sons and two daughters.
9.20 that were lost **three** days ago, don't worry about them;
10. 3 Tabor, where you will meet **three** men on their way to offer
10. 3 of them will be leading **three** young goats,
10. 3 another one will be carrying **three** loaves of bread,
11.11 Saul divided his men into **three** groups, and at dawn they
13.17 soldiers went out on raids from their camp in **three** groups:
17. 4 He was nearly **three** metres tall [5]and wore bronze armour
17.13 His **three** eldest sons had gone with Saul to war.
17.14 son, and while the **three** eldest brothers stayed with Saul,
20.20 I will then shoot **three** arrows at it, as though it were
20.41 his knees and bowed with his face to the ground **three** times.
30.12 had not had anything to eat or drink for **three** full days.
30.13 "My master left me behind **three** days ago because I was ill.
31. 2 up with them and killed **three** of Saul's sons, Jonathan,
31. 6 that is how Saul, his **three** sons, and the young man died;
31. 8 the bodies of Saul and his **three** sons lying on Mount Gilboa.
2 Sam 2.18 The **three** sons of Zeruiah were there:
6.11 It stayed there **three** months, and the Lord blessed Obed
8. 2 ground and put two out of every **three** of them to death.
13.37 Geshur, Talmai son of Ammihud, and stayed there **three** years.
14.27 Absalom had **three** sons and one daughter named Tamar, a
18. 2 he sent them out in **three** groups, with Joab and Joab's
18.14 He took **three** spears and plunged them into Absalom's chest
21. 1 there was a severe famine which lasted for **three** full years.
21.16 bronze spear that weighed about **three** and a half kilogrammes
23. 8 Josheb Basshebeth from Tachemon, who was the leader of "The **Three"**;
23. 9 The second of the famous **three** was Eleazar son of Dodo, of
23.11 The third of the famous **three** was Shammah son of Agee,
23.13 the beginning of harvest time **three** of "The Thirty" went
23.16 The **three** famous soldiers forced their way through the Philistine camp,
23.17 Those were the brave deeds of the **three** famous soldiers.
23.19 their leader, but he was not as famous as "The **Three."**
23.23 among them, but was not as famous as "The **Three."**
24.11 "Go and tell David that I am giving him **three** choices.
24.13 **Three** years of famine in your land
24.13 or **three** months of running away
24.13 or **three** days of an epidemic
1 Kgs 2.39 **Three** years later, however, two of Shimei's slaves ran
5.14 He divided them into **three** groups of 10,000 men, and each
6.36 one layer of cedar beams for every **three** layers of stone.
7. 2 It had **three** rows of cedar pillars, fifteen in each row,
7. 4 each of the two side walls there were **three** rows of windows.
7. 5 had rectangular frames, and the **three** rows of windows in
7.10 the quarry, some of them **three** and a half metres long and
7.12 layer of cedar beams for every **three** layers of cut stones.
7.25 bulls that faced outwards, **three** facing in each direction.
9.25 **Three** times a year Solomon offered burnt-offerings and
10.22 Every **three** years his fleet would return, bringing gold,
12. 5 "Come back in **three** days and I will give you my answer,"
12.12 **Three** days later Jeroboam and all the people returned
15. 2 king of Judah, [2]and he ruled for **three** years in Jerusalem.
17. 1 rain for the next two or **three** years until I say so."
17.21 himself out on the boy **three** times and prayed, "O Lord my
2 Kgs 2.17 high and low for Elijah for **three** days, but didn't find him.
3.10 "The Lord has put the **three** of us at the mercy of
3.12 So the **three** kings went to Elisha.
3.13 Lord who has put us **three** kings at the mercy of the
3.21 Moabites heard that the **three** kings had come to attack them,
3.23 "The **three** enemy armies must have fought and killed each other!
7. 1 able to buy in Samaria **three** kilogrammes of the best wheat
7.16 as the Lord had said, **three** kilogrammes of the best wheat or
7.18 that time the following day **three** kilogrammes of the best
9.32 Two or **three** palace officials looked down at him from a window,
13.18 The king struck the ground **three** times, and then stopped.
13.19 but now you will defeat them only **three** times."
13.25 Jehoash of Israel defeated Benhadad **three** times and
18.17 it was commanded by his **three** highest officials.
18.18 sent for King Hezekiah, and **three** of his officials went out
20. 5 will heal you, and in **three** days you will go to the
20. 8 will heal me and that **three** days later I will be able
23.31 king of Judah, and he ruled in Jerusalem for **three** months.
24. 1 Babylonia invaded Judah, and for **three** years Jehoiakim was
24. 8 king of Judah, and he ruled in Jerusalem for **three** months.
25.18 in rank, and the **three** other important temple officials.
1 Chr 1. 4 Noah had **three** sons:
2. 3 By his wife Bathshua, a Canaanite, he had **three** sons:
2. 9 Hezron had **three** sons:
2.16 Jesse's daughter Zeruiah had **three** sons:
2.18 She had **three** sons:
2.26 Ram had **three** sons:
2.46 a concubine named Ephah, and by her he had **three** more sons:
3.23 Neariah had **three** sons:
4. 3 Hur had **three** sons:
4. 3 Etam had **three** sons:
4. 7 Ashhur and Helah had **three** sons:
4.12 Mehir was the father of Eshton, [12]who had **three** sons:
4.15 Caleb son of Jephunneh had **three** sons:

1 Chr 4.17 a woman from the tribe of Judah, and they had **three** sons:
6. 1 Levi had **three** sons:
6.16 Levi had **three** sons:
7. 6 Benjamin had **three** sons:
7.18 Gilead's sister Hammolecheth had **three** sons:
7.32 Heber had **three** sons:
7.33 Japhlet also had **three** sons:
7.34 His brother Shomer had **three** sons:
8.12 Elpaal had **three** sons:
8.36 the father of Jehoaddah, who was the father of **three** sons:
8.39 Azel's brother Eshek had **three** sons:
9.42 was the father of Jarah, who was the father of **three** sons:
10. 2 up with them and killed **three** of Saul's sons, Jonathan,
10. 6 So Saul and his **three** sons all died together and none of
11.11 Jashobeam of the clan of Hachmon, the leader of "The **Three.**"
11.12 Next among the famous **"Three"** was Eleazar son of Dodo,
11.15 One day **three** of the thirty leading soldiers went to a
11.18 The **three** famous soldiers forced their way through
11.19 These were the brave deeds of the **three** famous soldiers.
11.21 their leader, but he was not as famous as "The **Three.**"
11.25 among "The Thirty," but not as famous as "The **Three.**"
12.39 They spent **three** days there with David, feasting on the
13.14 It stayed there **three** months, and the Lord blessed Obed
20. 8 These **three,** who were killed by David and his men, were
21.10 "Go and tell David that I am giving him **three** choices.
21.12 **Three** years of famine?
21.12 Or **three** months of running away from the armies of your enemies?
21.12 Or **three** days during which the Lord attacks you
23. 6 David divided the Levites into **three** groups,
23. 8 Ladan had **three** sons:
23. 9 (Shimei had **three** sons:
23.23 Merari's second son, Mushi, had **three** sons:
24.27 Jaaziah had **three** sons:
24.30 Mushi had **three** sons:
25. 5 fourteen sons and also **three** daughters, as he had promised,
29.29 recorded in the records of the **three** prophets, Samuel,
2 Chr 4. 4 bulls that faced outwards, **three** facing in each direction.
8.13 New Moon Festivals, and the **three** annual festivals—the
9.16 each covered with about **three** kilogrammes of beaten gold.
9.21 Every **three** years his fleet would return, bringing gold,
10. 5 Rehoboam replied, "Give me **three** days to consider the matter.
10.12 **Three** days later Jeroboam and all the people returned
11.17 kingdom of Judah, and for **three** years they supported
11.19 They had **three** sons, Jeush, Shemariah, and Zaham.
13. 2 king of Judah, [2]and he ruled for **three** years in Jerusalem.
20.25 They spent **three** days gathering the loot, but there was so
27. 5 to pay him the following tribute each year for **three** years:
34. 8 pagan worship, King Josiah sent **three** men to repair the
34.10 then handed over to the **three** men in charge of the temple
36. 2 king of Judah, and he ruled in Jerusalem for **three** months.
36. 9 and he ruled in Jerusalem for **three** months and ten days.
Ezra 6. 4 one layer of wood on top of every **three** layers of stone.
8.15 runs to the town of Ahava, and we camped there **three** days.
8.32 When we reached Jerusalem, we rested for **three** days.
10. 8 anyone failed to come within **three** days, all his property
10. 9 Within the **three** days, on the twentieth day of the ninth month,
10.17 investigation, [17]and within the next **three** months they
Neh 2.11 on to Jerusalem, and for **three** days [12]I did not tell
9. 3 For about **three** hours the Law of the Lord their God was
9. 3 and for the next **three** hours they confessed their sins
Esth 4.16 Don't eat or drink anything for **three** days and nights.
Job 1. 2 He had seven sons and **three** daughters,
1. 4 and they always invited their **three** sisters to join them.
1.17 and said, **"Three** bands of Chaldean raiders attacked us,
2.11 **Three** of Job's friends were Eliphaz, from the city of Teman,
32. 1 of his own innocence, the **three** men gave up trying to answer
32. 3 He was also angry with Job's **three** friends.
32. 5 When he saw that the **three** men could not answer Job, he
42.10 Job had prayed for his **three** friends, the Lord made him
42.13 He was the father of seven sons and **three** daughters.
Ecc 4.12 A rope made of **three** cords is hard to break.
Is 16.14 "In exactly **three** years Moab's great wealth will disappear.
17. 6 been picked except two or **three** at the very top, or a
19.24 Egypt and Assyria, and these **three** nations will be a
20. 2 **Three** years earlier the Lord had told Isaiah son of Amoz
20. 3 Isaiah has been going about naked and barefoot for **three** years.
36. 3 **Three** Judaeans came out to meet him:
Jer 36.23 soon as Jehudi finished reading **three** or four columns, the
38.10 Ebedmelech to take with him **three** men and to pull me out
52.24 in rank, and the **three** other important temple officials.
Ezek 5. 1 Then weigh the hair on scales and divide it into **three** parts.
14.14 Even if those **three** men, Noah, Danel, and Job, were living there,
14.16 it, [16]and even if those **three** men lived there—as surely as
14.18 alike, [18]and even if those **three** men lived there—as surely
40. 5 which was **three** metres long, and measured the wall.
40. 5 It was **three** metres high and three metres thick.
40. 6 it was **three** metres deep.
40. 7 was a passage, which had **three** guardrooms on each side.
40. 7 of the rooms was square, **three** metres on each side, and the
40. 7 guardrooms there was a passage **three** metres long that led to
40.12 (The rooms were **three** metres square.)
40.21 The **three** guardrooms on each side of the passage, the
41. 1 it was **three** metres deep [2]and five metres wide, with walls
41. 3 was one metre deep and **three** metres wide,
41. 3 with walls on either side **three** and a half metres thick.
41. 5 inner wall of the temple building, and it was **three** metres.
41. 6 These rooms were in **three** storeys, with thirty rooms on each floor.
41. 8 it was **three** metres above the ground and it was level with
42. 3 It was built on **three** levels, each one set further back than
Ezek 42. 6 The rooms at all **three** levels were on terraces and were
45.24 and a half litres of corn and **three** litres of olive-oil.
46. 5 grain-offering he is to bring **three** litres of olive-oil.
46. 7 **Three** litres of olive-oil are to be offered
46.11 **Three** litres of olive-oil are to be offered
48.30 measures 2,250 metres and has **three** gates in it, each named
Dan 1. 5 After **three** years of this training they were to appear
1.11 Ashpenaz had placed in charge of him and his **three** friends.
1.18 At the end of **three** years set by the king, Ashpenaz took
3. 1 twenty-seven metres high and nearly **three** metres wide, and
3.13 a rage and ordered the **three** men to be brought before him.
3.20 his army to tie the **three** men up and throw them into
3.24 officials, "Didn't we tie up **three** men and throw them into
3.27 gathered to look at the **three** men, who had not been harmed
6.10 at the open windows and prayed to God **three** times a day.
6.13 He prays regularly **three** times a day."
7. 5 It was holding **three** ribs between its teeth, and a voice
7. 8 It tore out **three** of the horns that were already there.
7.20 had come up afterwards and had made **three** of the horns fall.
7.24 from the earlier ones and will overthrow **three** kings.
7.25 people will be under his power for **three** and a half years.
10. 2 At that time, I was mourning for **three** weeks.
10. 3 any wine, or comb my hair until the **three** weeks were past.
11. 2 The angel said, **"Three** more kings will rule over Persia,
12. 7 I heard him say, "It will be **three** and a half years.
Hos 6. 2 In two or **three** days he will revive us, and we will
Jon 1.17 and he was inside the fish for **three** days and nights.
3. 3 city so large that it took **three** days to walk through it.
Zech 11. 8 I lost patience with **three** other shepherds, who hated me,
Mt 12.40 same way that Jonah spent **three** days and nights in the big
12.40 the Son of Man spend **three** days and nights in the depths
14.25 Between **three** and six o'clock in the morning Jesus came to
15.32 have been with me for **three** days and now have nothing to
16.21 be put to death, but **three** days later I will be raised
17. 3 the **three** disciples saw Moses and Elijah talking with Jesus.
17. 4 you wish, I will make **three** tents here, one for you,
17.23 but **three** days later he will be raised to life."
18.20 For where two or **three** come together in my name, I am
20. 5 o'clock and again at **three** o'clock he did the same thing.
20.19 but **three** days later he will be raised to life."
26.34 crows tonight, you will say **three** times that you do not know
26.40 Then he returned to the **three** disciples and found them asleep;
26.40 "How is it that you **three** were not able to keep watch
26.61 down God's Temple and **three** days later build it up again.' "
26.75 cock crows, you will say **three** times that you do not know
27.40 tear down the Temple and build it up again in **three** days!
27.45 country was covered with darkness, which lasted for **three** hours.
27.46 At about **three** o'clock Jesus cried out with a loud shout,
27.63 alive he said, 'I will be raised to life **three** days later.'
Mk 5.40 father and mother and his **three** disciples, and went into the
6.48 so some time between **three** and six o'clock in the morning he
8. 2 have been with me for **three** days and now have nothing to
8.31 be put to death, but **three** days later he will rise to
9. 4 the **three** disciples saw Elijah and Moses talking with Jesus.
9. 5 We will make **three** tents, one for you, one for Moses,
9.31 **Three** days later, however, he will rise to life."
10.34 but **three** days later he will rise to life."
14.30 twice tonight, you will say **three** times that you do not know
14.37 Then he returned and found the **three** disciples asleep.
14.58 men have made, and after **three** days I will build one that
14.72 crows twice, you will say **three** times that you do not know
15.29 tear down the Temple and build it up again in **three** days!
15.33 country was covered with darkness, which lasted for **three** hours.
15.34 At **three** o'clock Jesus cried out with a loud shout,
Lk 1.56 Mary stayed about **three** months with Elizabeth and then went
4.25 there was no rain for **three** and a half years and a
9.22 be put to death, but **three** days later he will be raised
9.33 We will make **three** tents, one for you, one for Moses,
9.37 day Jesus and the **three** disciples went down from the hill,
10.36 which one of these **three** acted like a neighbour towards the
11. 5 say to him, 'Friend, let me borrow **three** loaves of bread.
12.52 will be divided, **three** against two and two against three.
13. 7 to his gardener, 'Look, for **three** years I have been coming
18.33 and kill him, but **three** days later he will rise to
22.34 tonight until you have said **three** times that you do not know
22.61 crows tonight, you will say **three** times that you do not know
23.44 and darkness covered the whole country until **three** o'clock;
24. 7 men, be crucified, and **three** days later rise to life.' "
24.46 and must rise from death **three** days later, [47]and in his
Jn 2.19 down this Temple, and in **three** days I will build it again."
2.20 "Are you going to build it again in **three** days?"
11.18 Bethany was less than **three** kilometres from Jerusalem,
13.38 cock crows you will say **three** times that you do not know
Acts 3. 1 went to the Temple at **three** o'clock in the afternoon, the
5. 7 About **three** hours later his wife, not knowing what had happened,
7.20 cared for at home for **three** months, [21]and when he was put
9. 9 For **three** days he was not able to see, and during that
10. 3 It was about **three** o'clock one afternoon when he had a vision,
10.16 This happened **three** times, and then the thing was taken back
10.19 **Three** men are here looking for you.
10.30 "It was about this time **three** days ago that I was praying
10.30 I was praying in my house at **three** o'clock in the afternoon.
10.40 God raised him from death **three** days later and caused him to
11.10 happened **three** times, and finally the whole thing was drawn back
11.11 At that very moment **three** men who had been sent to me
17. 2 There during **three** Sabbaths he held discussions with the people,
19. 8 synagogue and during **three** months spoke boldly with the people,
20. 3 Then he came to Achaia, [3]where he stayed **three** months.
20.31 day and night, I taught every one of you for **three** years.
23. 8 but the Pharisees believe in all **three.)**
25. 1 **Three** days after Festus arrived in the province, he went from

Acts 28. 7 He welcomed us kindly and for **three** days we were his guests.
28.11 After **three** months we sailed away on a ship from Alexandria,
28.12 in the city of Syracuse and stayed there for **three** days.
28.17 After **three** days Paul called the local Jewish leaders to
1 Cor 13.13 Meanwhile these **three** remain:
14.27 in strange tongues, two or **three** at the most should speak,
14.29 Two or **three** who are given God's message should speak,
15. 4 he was raised to life **three** days later, as written in the
2 Cor 11.25 **three** times I was whipped by the Romans;
11.25 have been in **three** shipwrecks, and once I spent twenty-four hours
12. 8 **Three** times I prayed to the Lord about this and asked him
Gal 1.18 It was **three** years later that I went to Jerusalem to
Col 4.11 These **three** are the only Jewish believers who work with me
Heb 11.23 of Moses hide him for **three** months after he was born.
Jas 5.17 no rain fell on the land for **three** and a half years.
1 Jn 5. 7 There are **three** witnesses:
5. 8 and all **three** give the same testimony.
Rev 6. 6 for a day's wages, and **three** litres of barley for a day's
8.13 comes from the trumpets that the other **three** angels must blow!"
9.18 A third of mankind was killed by those **three** plagues:
11. 9 look at their bodies for **three** and a half days and will
11.11 After **three** and a half days a life-giving breath came
12.14 be taken care of for **three** and a half years, safe from
16.13 Then I saw **three** unclean spirits that looked like frogs.
16.14 These **three** spirits go out to all the kings of the world,
16.19 great city was split into **three** parts, and the cities of all
21.13 There were **three** gates on each side:
21.13 **three** on the east, three on the south,
21.13 three on the north, and **three** on the west.
also Lev 27.3 Num 7.12 1 Chr 24.7 1 Chr 25.9

THREE INNS

Acts 28.15 the towns of Market of Appius and **Three Inns** to meet us.

THREE STORIED

see also **STOREY**

1 Kgs 6. 5 back of the Temple, a **three-storied** annexe was built, each
6.10 The **three-storied** annexe, each storey 2.2 metres high,

THREE-PRONGED

1 Sam 2.13 the priest's servant would come with a **three-pronged** fork.

Am THRESH

see also **SEPARATE**

THRESH

Gen 50.10 When they came to the **threshing-place** at Atad east of the Jordan,
Num 15.20 the special contribution you make from the corn you **thresh.**
Deut 16.13 "After you have **threshed** all your corn and pressed all your grapes,
25. 4 not muzzle an ox when you are using it to **thresh** corn.
Judg 6.11 His son Gideon was **threshing** some wheat secretly in a winepress,
6.37 putting some wool on the ground where we **thresh** the wheat.
Ruth 3. 2 This evening he will be **threshing** the barley.
3. 3 Then go where he is **threshing,** but don't let him know you
3. 6 So Ruth went to the **threshing-place** and did just what her
2 Sam 6. 6 As they came to the **threshing-place** of Nacon, the oxen stumbled,
24.16 The angel was by the **threshing-place** of Araunah,
24.18 him, "Go up to Araunah's **threshing-place** and build an altar
24.21 David answered, "To buy your **threshing-place** and build an
24.22 are their yokes and the **threshing-boards** to use as fuel."
24.24 And he bought the **threshing-place** and the oxen for fifty
1 Kgs 22.10 thrones at the **threshing-place** just outside the gate of Samaria,
1 Chr 13. 9 As they came to the **threshing-place** of Chidon, the oxen stumbled,
21.15 The angel was standing by the **threshing-place** of Araunah,
21.18 and build an altar to the Lord at Araunah's **threshing-place.**
21.20 at the **threshing-place** Araunah
21.20 and his four sons were **threshing** wheat,
21.21 David approaching, he left the **threshing-place** and bowed low,
21.22 to him, "Sell me your **threshing-place,** so that I can build
21.23 altar, and here are the **threshing-boards** to use as fuel, and
21.25 And he paid Araunah six hundred gold coins for the **threshing-place.**
21.28 sacrifices on the altar at Araunah's **threshing-place.**
2 Chr 3. 1 which Araunah the Jebusite had used as a **threshing-place.**
18. 9 thrones at the **threshing-place** just outside the gate of Samaria,
Job 39.12 harvest and gather the grain from your **threshing-place?**
41.30 they tear up the muddy ground like a **threshing-sledge.**
Is 21.10 people Israel, you have been **threshed** like wheat, but now I
28.28 not ruin the wheat by **threshing** it endlessly, and he knows
28.28 and he knows how to **thresh** it by driving a cart over
41.15 will make you like a **threshing-board,** with spikes that are
41.15 You will **thresh** mountains and destroy them;
Jer 50.11 about like a cow **threshing** corn or like a neighing horse,
51.33 them down and trample them like corn on a **threshing-place.**
Dan 2.35 and became like the dust on a **threshing-place** in summer.
Hos 10.11 a well-trained young cow, ready and willing to **thresh** grain.
13. 3 blows from the **threshing-place,** like smoke from a chimney.
Joel 2.24 The **threshing-places** will be full of corn;
Mic 4.12 in the same way that corn is brought in to be **threshed.**
Mt 3.12 his winnowing shovel with him to **thresh** out all the grain.
Lk 3.17 winnowing shovel with him, to **thresh** out all the grain and
1 Cor 9. 9 not muzzle an ox when you are using it to **thresh** corn."
1 Tim 5.18 you are using it to **thresh** corn" and "A worker should be

THRESHOLD

2 Chr 3. 7 to overlay the temple walls, the rafters, the **thresholds,**
Ezek 43. 8 The kings built the **thresholds** and door-posts of their palace
43. 8 right against the **thresholds** and door-posts of my Temple,

THRILL

Song 5. 4 hand to the door, and I was **thrilled** that he was near.

THRIVE

Is 44. 4 They will **thrive** like well-watered grass,

THROAT

1 Sam 17.35 me, I grab it by the **throat** and beat it to death.
Job 16.12 God took me by the **throat** and battered me and crushed me.
Ps 22.15 My **throat** is as dry as dust, and my tongue sticks to
69. 3 am worn out from calling for help, and my **throat** is aching.
Is 29. 8 who dreams he is drinking and wakes with a dry **throat.**
41.17 look for water, when their **throats** are dry with thirst, then
Jer 2.25 feet out, or let your **throat** become dry from chasing after
4.10 there would be peace, but a sword is at their **throats."**

THRONE

[DETHRONES, ENTHRONE]

Ex 11. 5 who is heir to the **throne,** to the son of the slave-woman
12.29 who was heir to the **throne,** to the son of the prisoner
1 Sam 4. 4 who is **enthroned** above the winged creatures.
2 Sam 6. 2 Lord Almighty, who is **enthroned** above the winged creatures.
1 Kgs 1.35 Follow him back here when he comes to sit on my **throne.**
2.19 Then he sat on his **throne** and had another one brought in
2.22 "You might as well ask me to give him the **throne** too.
2.24 Lord has firmly established me on the **throne** of my father David;
2.33 success to David's descendants who sit on his **throne."**
7. 7 The **Throne** Room, also called the Hall of Judgement, where
10.18 He also had a large **throne** made.
10.19 The **throne** had six steps leading up to it,
10.19 At the back of the **throne** was the figure of a bull's
10.19 No **throne** like this had ever existed in any other kingdom.
22.10 robes, were sitting on their **thrones** at the threshing-place
22.19 the Lord sitting on his **throne** in heaven, with all his
2 Kgs 11.19 entered by the Guard Gate and took his place on the **throne.**
16.18 the platform for the royal **throne** and closed up the king's
19.15 the God of Israel, **enthroned** above the winged creatures,
1 Chr 13. 6 the name of the Lord **enthroned** above the winged creatures.
29.23 father David on the **throne** which the Lord had established.
2 Chr 9.17 The king also had a large **throne** made.
9.18 steps led up to the **throne,** and there was a footstool
9.18 on each side of the **throne,** and the figure of a lion
9.19 No **throne** like this had ever existed in any other kingdom.
18. 9 robes, were sitting on their **thrones** at the threshing-place
18.18 the Lord sitting on his **throne** in heaven, with all his
23.20 the main gate, and the king took his place on the **throne.**
Esth 1. 1 From his royal **throne** in Persia's capital city of Susa,
5. 1 the inner courtyard of the palace, facing the **throne** room.
5. 1 The king was inside, seated on the royal **throne,**
Job 12.18 He **dethrones** kings and makes them prisoners;
Ps 2. 4 From his **throne** in heaven the Lord laughs and mocks their
9. 7 he has set up his **throne** for judgement.
11. 4 he has his **throne** in heaven.
22. 3 But you are **enthroned** as the Holy One, the one whom Israel
45. 9 on the right of your **throne** stands the queen, wearing
47. 5 God goes up to his **throne.**
47. 8 God sits on his sacred **throne;**
80. 1 Seated on your **throne** above the winged creatures, ²reveal
89.19 I have given the **throne** to one I chose from the people.
89.44 away his royal sceptre and hurled his **throne** to the ground.
93. 2 Your **throne,** O Lord, has been firm from the beginning, and
99. 1 He is **enthroned** above the winged creatures and the earth shakes.
99. 5 worship before his **throne!**
103.19 The Lord placed his **throne** in heaven;
132. 7 let us worship before his **throne."**
Ecc 4.13 go from prison to the **throne,** but if in his old age
Song 3. 7 Solomon is coming, carried on his **throne;**
3. 9 King Solomon is carried on a **throne** made of the finest wood.
Is 6. 1 He was sitting on his **throne,** high and exalted, and his robe
7. 6 their side, and then put Tabeel's son on the **throne.**
8.18 The Lord Almighty, whose **throne** is on Mount Zion, has sent
14. 9 The ghosts of kings are rising from their **thrones.**
14.13 to heaven and to place your **throne** above the highest stars.
37.16 "Almighty Lord, God of Israel, **enthroned** above the winged creatures,
40.22 one who sits on his **throne** above the earth and beyond the
47. 1 "Babylon, come down from your **throne,** and sit in the dust
52. 2 Rise from the dust and sit on your **throne!**
66. 1 Lord says, "Heaven is my **throne,** and the earth is my footstool.
Jer 1.15 kings will set up their **thrones** at the gates of Jerusalem
3.17 Jerusalem will be called 'The **Throne** of the Lord,' and all
13.18 to come down from their **thrones,** because their beautiful
14.21 do not bring disgrace on Jerusalem, the place of your glorious **throne.**
17.12 Temple is like a glorious **throne,** standing on a high
30. 9 and a descendant of David, whom I will **enthrone** as king.
43.10 he will put his **throne** over these stones that you buried,
49.38 destroy their kings and leaders, and set up my **throne** there.
Ezek 1.26 something that looked like a **throne** made of sapphire,
1.26 and sitting on the **throne** was a figure that looked like
10. 1 was something that seemed to be a **throne** made of sapphire.

Ezek 17.16 made with the king of Babylonia, who put him on the **throne.**
26.16 of the seafaring nations will come down from their **thrones.**
28. 2 like a god you sit on a **throne,** surrounded by the seas.
43. 7 "Mortal man, here is my **throne.**
Dan 5.20 removed from his royal **throne** and lost his place of honour.
7. 9 While I was looking, **thrones** were put in place.
7. 9 had been living for ever sat down on one of the **thrones.**
7. 9 His **throne,** mounted on fiery wheels, was blazing with fire,
Jon 3. 6 he got up from his **throne,** took off his robe, put on
Zech 6.13 priest will stand by his **throne,** and they will work together
Mt 5.34 Do not swear by heaven, for it is God's **throne;**
19.28 Man sits on his glorious **throne** in the New Age, then you
19.28 mine will also sit on **thrones,** to rule the twelve tribes of
23.22 he is swearing by God's **throne** and by him who sits on
25.31 will sit on his royal **throne,** [32]and the people of all the
Mk 10.37 "When you sit on your **throne** in your glorious Kingdom, we
Lk 1.52 brought down mighty kings from their **thrones,** and lifted up
22.30 and you will sit on **thrones** to rule over the twelve tribes
Acts 7.49 prophet says, [49]'Heaven is my **throne,** says the Lord,
12.21 royal robes, sat on his **throne,** and made a speech to the
Col 3. 1 Christ sits on his **throne** at the right-hand side of God.
Heb 4.16 and approach God's **throne,** where there is grace.
8. 1 at the right of the **throne** of the Divine Majesty in heaven.
12. 2 he is now seated at the right-hand side of God's **throne.**
Rev 1. 4 spirits in front of his **throne,** [5]and from Jesus Christ,
2.13 I know where you live, there where Satan has his **throne.**
3.21 sit beside me on my **throne,** just as I have been victorious
3.21 and now sit by my Father on his **throne.**
4. 2 There in heaven was a **throne** with someone sitting on it.
4. 3 and all round the **throne** there was a rainbow the colour
4. 4 In a circle round the **throne** were twenty-four other thrones,
4. 5 From the **throne** came flashes of lightning, rumblings, and peals
4. 5 In front of the **throne** seven lighted torches were burning,
4. 6 Also in front of the **throne** there was what looked like a
4. 6 Surrounding the **throne** on each of its sides, were four living
4. 9 one who sits on the **throne,** who lives for ever and ever.
4.10 one who sits on the **throne,** and worship him who lives for
4.10 down in front of the **throne** and say, [11]"Our Lord and God!
5. 1 in the right hand of the one who sits on the **throne;**
5. 6 the centre of the **throne,** surrounded by the four living creatures
5. 7 from the right hand of the one who sits on the **throne.**
5.11 They stood round the **throne,** the four living creatures, and the
5.13 him who sits on the **throne** and to the Lamb, be praise
6.16 one who sits on the **throne** and from the anger of the
7. 9 stood in front of the **throne** and of the Lamb, dressed in
7.10 from our God, who sits on the **throne,** and from the Lamb!"
7.11 angels stood round the **throne,** the elders, and the four living
7.11 face downwards in front of the **throne** and worshipped God,
7.15 why they stand before God's **throne** and serve him day and
7.15 He who sits on the **throne** will protect them with his presence.
7.17 in the centre of the **throne,** will be their shepherd, and he
8. 3 to offer it on the gold altar that stands before the **throne.**
11.16 elders who sit on their **thrones** in front of God threw
12. 5 the child was snatched away and taken to God and his **throne.**
13. 2 the beast his own power, his **throne,** and his vast authority.
14. 3 The 144,000 people stood before the **throne,** the four living creatures, and
16.10 fifth angel poured out his bowl on the **throne** of the beast.
16.17 loud voice came from the **throne** in the temple, saying, "It
19. 4 fell down and worshipped God, who was seated on the **throne.**
19. 5 Then there came from the **throne** the sound of a voice,
20. 4 Then I saw **thrones,** and those who sat on them were given
20.11 I saw a great white **throne** and the one who sits on
20.12 I saw the dead, great and small alike, standing before the **throne.**
21. 3 I heard a loud voice speaking from the **throne:**
21. 5 one who sits on the **throne** said, "And now I make all
22. 1 crystal, and coming from the **throne** of God and of the Lamb
22. 3 The **throne** of God and of the Lamb will be in the

THROW

[THREW]

Gen 32.25 struck Jacob on the hip, and it was **thrown** out of joint.
33. 4 Esau ran to meet him, **threw** his arms round him, and kissed
37.20 now, let's kill him and **throw** his body into one of the
37.22 "Just **throw** him into this well in the wilderness, but
37.24 Then they took him and **threw** him into the well, which
45.14 He **threw** his arms round his brother Benjamin and began to cry;
46.29 When they met, Joseph **threw** his arms round his father's neck
49.17 horse's heel, So that the rider is **thrown** off backwards.
50. 1 Joseph **threw** himself on his father, crying and kissing his face.
Ex 1.22 every new-born Hebrew boy and **throw** him into the Nile, but
4. 3 The Lord said, "**Throw** it on the ground."
4. 3 When Moses **threw** it down, it turned into a snake, and he
7. 9 to take his stick and **throw** it down in front of the
7.10 Aaron **threw** his stick down in front of the king and his
7.12 They **threw** down their sticks, and the sticks turned into snakes.
9. 8 Moses shall **throw** them into the air in front of the king.
9.10 Moses **threw** them into the air, and they produced boils that
14.24 and cloud at the Egyptian army and **threw** them into a panic.
14.27 escape from the water, but the Lord **threw** them into the sea.
15. 1 he has **thrown** the horses and their riders into the sea.
15. 4 "He **threw** Egypt's army and its chariots into the sea;
15.21 he has **thrown** the horses and their riders into the sea."
15.25 showed him a piece of wood, which he **threw** into the water;
23.28 I will **throw** your enemies into a panic;
24. 6 and the other half he **threw** against the altar.
24. 8 took the blood in the bowls and **threw** it on the people.
29.16 and take its blood and **throw** it against all four sides of
29.20 **Throw** the rest of the blood against all four sides of the
32.19 foot of the mountain, he **threw** down the tablets he was
Ex 32.24 I **threw** the ornaments into the fire and out came this bull-calf!"
Lev 1. 5 to the Lord and then **throw** it against all four sides of
1.11 altar, and the priests shall **throw** its blood on all four
1.16 crop and its contents and **throw** them away on the east side
3. 2 The Aaronite priests shall **throw** the blood against all four
3. 8 The priests shall **throw** its blood against all four sides of
3.13 The priests shall **throw** its blood against all four sides of
7. 2 its blood is to be **thrown** against all four sides of the
7.14 the blood of the animal and **throws** it against the altar.
8.19 Moses killed it and **threw** the blood on all four sides of
8.24 Moses then **threw** the rest of the blood on all four sides
9.12 him the blood, and he **threw** it on all four sides of
9.18 him the blood, and he **threw** it on all four sides of
14.40 found to be removed and **thrown** into some unclean place
17. 6 The priest shall **throw** the blood against the sides of the
26.10 then you will have to **throw** away what is left of the
26.30 tear down your incense-altars, and **throw** your dead bodies on
Num 16. 4 When Moses heard this, he **threw** himself on the ground and prayed.
18.17 **Throw** their blood against the altar and burn their fat as a
19. 6 of hyssop, and a red cord and **throw** them into the fire.
19.13 the water for purification has not been **thrown** over him.
19.20 the water for purification has not been **thrown** over him.
22.31 and Balaam **threw** himself face downwards on the ground.
35.20 pushing him down or by **throwing** something at him [21]or by
35.22 whether by pushing him down or by **throwing** something at him.
35.23 that, without looking, a man **throws** a stone that kills
Deut 9.17 in front of you I **threw** the stone tablets down and broke
9.21 had made—that metal bull-calf—and **threw** it into the fire.
9.21 ground it to dust, and **threw** the dust into the stream that
17. 7 The witnesses are to **throw** the first stones, and then the
29.28 them from their land and **threw** them into a foreign land, and
Josh 5.14 Joshua **threw** himself on the ground in worship and said, "I
7. 6 tore their clothes in grief, **threw** themselves to the ground
8.29 be removed, and it was **thrown** down at the entrance to the
10.27 bodies were taken down and **thrown** into the same cave where
24.12 As you advanced, I **threw** them into panic in order to
Judg 4.15 with his army, the Lord **threw** Sisera into confusion together
9.53 But a woman **threw** a millstone down on his head and
13.20 and his wife **threw** themselves face downwards on the ground.
15.17 After that, he **threw** the jaw-bone away.
20.41 round, and the Benjaminites were **thrown** into a panic because
1 Sam 18.11 Saul said to himself, and he **threw** the spear at him twice;
20.33 At that, Saul **threw** his spear at Jonathan to kill him,
25.23 David, she quickly dismounted and **threw** herself on the
25.29 your enemies, however, he will **throw** them away, as a man
31. 4 So Saul took his own sword and **threw** himself on it.
31. 5 was dead, so he too **threw** himself on his own sword and
2 Sam 11.21 at Thebez, where a woman **threw** a millstone down from the
13.17 **Throw** her out and lock the door!"
13.31 tore his clothes in sorrow, and **threw** himself to the ground.
14.22 Joab **threw** himself to the ground in front of David in respect,
16. 6 Shimei started **throwing** stones at David and his officials,
16.13 he was cursing and **throwing** stones and earth at them as he
18.17 They took Absalom's body, **threw** it into a deep pit in
18.28 a greeting to the king, **threw** himself down to the ground
19.18 getting ready to cross, Shimei **threw** himself down in front
20.12 from the road into the field and **threw** a blanket over it.
20.21 "We will **throw** his head over the wall to you," she said.
20.22 cut off Sheba's head and **threw** it over the wall to Joab.
23. 6 But godless men are like thorns that are **thrown** away;
24.20 He **threw** himself on the ground in front of David [21]and asked,
1 Kgs 18.39 saw this, they **threw** themselves on the ground and exclaimed,
22.27 Tell them to **throw** him in prison and to put him on
2 Kgs 2.21 he went to the spring, **threw** the salt in the water, and
3.25 fertile field, every Israelite would **throw** a stone on it
4.41 Elisha asked for some meal, **threw** it into the pot, and
6. 6 Elisha cut off a stick, **threw** it in the water, and made
9.25 Bidkar, "Get his body and **throw** it in the field that
9.26 Jehu ordered his aide, "and **throw** it in the field that
9.33 a window, [33]and Jehu said to them, "**Throw** her down!"
9.33 They **threw** her down, and her blood spattered the wall and
13.21 was seen, and the people **threw** the corpse into Elisha's tomb
23.12 the altars to bits and **threw** them into the valley of the
1 Chr 10. 4 So Saul took his own sword and **threw** himself on it.
10. 5 was dead, so he too **threw** himself on his sword and died.
2 Chr 18.26 Tell them to **throw** him in prison and to put him on
20.22 to sing, the Lord **threw** the invading armies into a panic.
25.12 the city of Sela and **threw** them off, so that they were
26.15 for shooting arrows and for **throwing** large stones from the
30.14 sacrifices and burning incense and **threw** them into the
33.15 took all these things outside the city and **threw** them away.
Neh 13. 8 I was furious and **threw** out all Tobiah's belongings.
Esth 3.15 while the city of Susa was being **thrown** into confusion.
7. 8 He had just **thrown** himself down on Esther's couch to beg
8. 3 to the king again, **throwing** herself at his feet and crying.
Job 1.20 He shaved his head and **threw** himself face downwards on the ground.
2.12 their clothes in grief and **throwing** dust into the air and on
6.27 You would even **throw** dice for orphan slaves and make
9.31 God **throws** me into a pit of filth, and even my clothes
22.24 **Throw** away your gold;
30.19 He **throws** me down in the mud;
41.28 rocks **thrown** at him are like bits of straw.
41.29 is a piece of straw, and he laughs when men **throw** spears.
Ps 2. 3 "let us **throw** off their control."
31.12 I am like something **thrown** away.
60. 8 my wash-basin and I will **throw** my sandals on Edom, as a
72. 9 his enemies will **throw** themselves to the ground.
88. 6 You have **thrown** me into the depths of the tomb, into the
89.39 covenant with your servant and **thrown** his crown in the mud.

Ps 102. 9 You picked me up and **threw** me away.
108. 9 my wash-basin and I will **throw** my sandals on Edom, as a
140.10 may they be **thrown** into a pit and never get out.
141. 6 When their rulers are **thrown** down from rocky cliffs, the
Prov 7.13 She **threw** her arms round the young man, kissed him,
29. 8 no regard for others can **throw** whole cities into turmoil.
Ecc 3. 6 saving and the time for **throwing** away, [7] the time for
Is 2.20 that day comes, they will **throw** away the gold and silver
14.12 nations, but now you have been **thrown** to the ground.
14.19 you have no tomb, and your corpse is **thrown** out to rot.
14.19 killed in battle, **thrown** with them into a rocky pit,
22.17 important, but the Lord will pick you up and **throw** you away.
22.18 up like a ball and **throw** you into a much larger country.
30.22 covered with gold, and will **throw** them away like filth,
31. 7 when all of you will **throw** away the sinful idols you made
Jer 7.29 cut off your hair and **throw** it away.
10.18 The Lord is going to **throw** you out of this land;
14.16 Their bodies will be **thrown** out into the streets of Jerusalem,
15. 7 town in the land I **threw** you to the wind like straw.
16.13 So then, I will **throw** you out of this land into a
18.23 **Throw** them down in defeat and deal with them while you are
22. 7 its beautiful cedar pillars, and **throw** them into the fire.
22.19 be dragged away and **thrown** outside Jerusalem's gates."
22.28 a broken jar that is **thrown** away and that no one wants?
23.39 certainly pick them up and **throw** them far away from me, both
26.23 killed and his body **thrown** into the public burial-ground.)
31.40 are buried and refuse is **thrown**, and all the fields above
36.23 them off with a small knife and **threw** them into the fire.
36.30 Your corpse will be **thrown** out where it will be exposed to
41. 7 and his men killed them and **threw** their bodies in a well.
41. 9 The well into which Ishmael **threw** the bodies of the men he
51.34 He took what he wanted and **threw** the rest away.
51.58 of mighty Babylon will be **thrown** to the ground, and its
51.63 it to a stone and **throw** it into the River Euphrates, [64] and
Lam 3.53 They **threw** me alive into a pit and closed the opening
Ezek 5. 4 few of them out again, **throw** them in the fire, and let
7.19 They will **throw** their gold and silver away in the
9. 8 I **threw** myself face downwards on the ground
11. 7 will not be here—I will **throw** you out of the city!
11.13 I **threw** myself face downwards on the ground and shouted,
16. 5 You were **thrown** out in an open field.
19.12 pulled it up by the roots and **threw** it to the ground.
20. 7 I told them to **throw** away the disgusting idols they loved
20. 8 They did not **throw** away their disgusting idols or give up
21.22 the gates, to **throw** up earthworks, and to dig trenches.
26.11 Your mighty pillars will be **thrown** to the ground.
27.30 all mourn bitterly for you, **Throwing** dust on their heads and
29. 5 I will **throw** you and all those fish into the desert.
32. 4 I will **throw** you out on the ground and bring all the
43. 3 Then I **threw** myself face downwards on the ground.
44. 4 I **threw** myself face downwards on the ground, [5] and the Lord
Dan 3. 6 worship will immediately be **thrown** into a blazing furnace."
3.11 down and worship it is to be **thrown** into a blazing furnace.
3.15 not, you will immediately be **thrown** into a blazing furnace.
3.20 the three men up and **throw** them into the blazing furnace.
3.21 caps, and all—and **threw** them into the blazing furnace.
3.24 tie up three men and **throw** them into the blazing furnace?"
6. 7 this order is to be **thrown** into a pit filled with lions.
6.12 except you, would be **thrown** into a pit filled with lions."
6.16 arrested and he was **thrown** into the pit filled with lions.
6.24 accused Daniel, and they were **thrown**, together with their
7.11 and its body was **thrown** into the flames and destroyed.
8. 7 He was **thrown** to the ground and trampled on, and there was
8.10 the stars themselves, and it **threw** some of them to the
8.12 sacrifices, and true religion was **thrown** to the ground.
Hos 7.14 me sincerely, but instead they **throw** themselves down and
Joel 3. 3 They **threw** dice to decide who would get the captives.
Amos 4. 3 dragged to the nearest break in the wall and **thrown** out."
8. 3 They will be **thrown** out in silence."
Jon 1. 5 order to lessen the danger, they **threw** the cargo overboard.
1.12 Jonah answered, "**Throw** me into the sea, and it will calm down.
1.15 they picked Jonah up and **threw** him into the sea, and it
2. 3 You **threw** me down into the depths, to the very bottom of
Zech 9. 4 He will **throw** her wealth into the sea, and the city will
Mt 3.10 bear good fruit will be cut down and **thrown** in the fire.
4. 6 "If you are God's Son, **throw** yourself down, for the scripture
5.13 worthless, so it is **thrown** out and people trample on it.
5.29 eye causes you to sin, take it out and **throw** it away!
5.29 of your body than to have your whole body **thrown** into hell.
5.30 hand causes you to sin, cut it off and **throw** it away!
7. 6 Do not **throw** your pearls in front of pigs—they will only
7.19 not bear good fruit is cut down and **thrown** in the fire.
8.12 in the Kingdom will be **thrown** out into the darkness, where
11.23 You will be **thrown** down to hell!
13.42 evil things, [42] and they will **throw** them into the fiery furnace,
13.47 Some fishermen **throw** their net out in the lake and catch all
13.48 go into their buckets, the worthless ones are **thrown** away.
13.50 among the good [50] and will **throw** them into the fiery furnace,
15.26 to take the children's food and **throw** it to the dogs."
17. 6 that they **threw** themselves face downwards on the ground.
18. 8 makes you lose your faith, cut it off and **throw** it away!
18. 8 hands and both feet and be **thrown** into the eternal fire.
18. 9 makes you lose your faith, take it out and **throw** it away!
18. 9 to keep both eyes and be **thrown** into the fire of hell.
18.30 instead, he had him **thrown** into jail until he should pay the
21. 7 the donkey and the colt, **threw** their cloaks over them, and
21.10 Jesus entered Jerusalem, the whole city was **thrown** into an uproar.
21.21 this hill, 'Get up and **throw** yourself in the sea,' and it
21.39 So they seized him, **threw** him out of the vineyard, and
22.13 him up hand and foot, and **throw** him outside in the dark.
Mt 24. 2 every one of them will be **thrown** down."
25.30 As for this useless servant—**throw** him outside in the darkness;
26.39 farther on, **threw** himself face downwards on the ground,
27. 5 Judas **threw** the coins down in the Temple and left;
27.35 and then divided his clothes among them by **throwing** dice.
Mk 5.22 when he saw Jesus, he **threw** himself down at his feet
7.27 to take the children's food and **throw** it to the dogs."
9.18 the spirit attacks him, it **throws** him to the ground, and he
9.20 the spirit saw Jesus, it **threw** the boy into a fit,
9.22 tried to kill him by **throwing** him in the fire and into
9.26 The spirit screamed, **threw** the boy into a bad fit, and
9.42 millstone tied round his neck and be **thrown** into the sea.
9.45 a foot than to keep both feet and be **thrown** into hell.
9.47 one eye than to keep both eyes and be **thrown** into hell.
10.50 He **threw** off his cloak, jumped up, and came to Jesus.
11. 7 brought the colt to Jesus, **threw** their cloaks over the animal,
11.23 hill to get up and **throw** itself in the sea and does
12. 8 son and killed him and **threw** his body out of the vineyard.
13. 2 every one of them will be **thrown** down."
14.35 went a little farther on, **threw** himself on the ground, and
15.24 his clothes among themselves, **throwing** dice to see who would get
Lk 3. 9 bear good fruit will be cut down and **thrown** in the fire."
4. 9 him, "If you are God's Son, **throw** yourself down from here.
4.29 They meant to **throw** him over the cliff, [30] but he walked
4.35 The demon **threw** the man down in front of them and went
5.12 When he saw Jesus, he **threw** himself down and begged him,
8.28 he gave a loud cry, **threw** himself down at his feet,
8.41 He **threw** himself down at Jesus' feet and begged him to go
8.47 so she came trembling and **threw** herself at Jesus' feet.
9.39 with a sudden shout and **throws** him into a fit, so that
9.42 demon knocked him to the ground and **threw** him into a fit.
10.15 You will be **thrown** down to hell!"
12. 5 God, who, after killing, has the authority to **throw** into hell.
13.28 prophets in the Kingdom of God, while you are **thrown** out!
14.35 it is **thrown** away.
15.20 with pity, and he ran, **threw** his arms round his son,
17. 2 his neck and he were **thrown** into the sea than for him
17.16 He **threw** himself to the ground at Jesus' feet and thanked him.
19.35 Then they **threw** their cloaks over the animal and helped
20.12 the tenants wounded him, too, and **threw** him out.
20.15 So they **threw** him out of the vineyard and killed him.
21. 6 every one will be **thrown** down."
22.41 the distance of a stone's **throw** and knelt down and prayed.
23.34 They divided his clothes among themselves by **throwing** dice.
Jn 8. 7 you has committed no sin may **throw** the first stone at her."
8.59 they picked up stones to **throw** at him, but Jesus hid himself
10.31 Then the people again picked up stones to **throw** at him.
15. 6 not remain in me is **thrown** out like a branch and dries
15. 6 branches are gathered up and **thrown** into the fire, where
19.24 let's **throw** dice to see who will get it."
21. 6 He said to them, "**Throw** your net out on the right side
21. 6 So they **threw** the net out and could not pull it back
Acts 7.58 rushed at him at once, [58] **threw** him out of the city,
8. 3 believers, both men and women, and **threw** them into jail.
13.50 against Paul and Barnabas and **threw** them out of their region.
16.23 a severe beating, they were **thrown** into jail, and the jailer
16.24 receiving this order, the jailer **threw** them into the inner cell
16.37 Then they **threw** us in prison.
17. 8 With these words they **threw** the crowd and the city authorities
20.10 But Paul went down and **threw** himself on him and hugged him.
22. 4 I arrested men and women and **threw** them into prison.
22.23 screaming, waving their clothes, and **throwing** dust up in the air.
27.18 day they began to **throw** some of the ship's cargo overboard,
27.19 following day they **threw** part of the ship's equipment overboard.
27.38 lightened the ship by **throwing** all the wheat into the sea.
Phil 3. 8 For his sake I have **thrown** everything away;
2 Pet 2. 4 the angels who sinned, but **threw** them into hell, where they
Rev 2.10 by having some of you **thrown** into prison, and your troubles
2.22 And so I will **throw** her on to a bed where she
4.10 They **throw** their crowns down in front of the throne and say,
7.11 Then they **threw** themselves face downwards in front of the throne
8. 5 with fire from the altar, and **threw** it on the earth.
8. 8 looked like a huge mountain on fire was **thrown** into the sea.
11.16 front of God **threw** themselves face downwards and worshipped God,
12. 4 stars out of the sky and **threw** them down to the earth.
12. 9 huge dragon was **thrown** out—that ancient serpent, called the Devil,
12. 9 He was **thrown** down to earth, and all his angels with him.
12.10 our brothers day and night has been **thrown** out of heaven.
12.13 realized that he had been **thrown** down to the earth, he began
14.19 grapes from the vine, and **threw** them into the winepress of
18.19 They **threw** dust on their heads, they cried and mourned,
18.21 of a large millstone and **threw** it into the sea, saying,
18.21 city Babylon will be violently **thrown** down and will never be
19.20 the false prophet were both **thrown** alive into the lake of
20. 3 The angel **threw** him into the abyss, locked it, and sealed
20.10 Devil, who deceived them, was **thrown** into the lake of fire
20.10 where the beast and the false prophet had already been **thrown**;
20.14 the world of the dead were **thrown** into the lake of fire.
20.15 of the living was **thrown** into the lake of fire.

THRUSH

Jer 8. 7 swallows, and **thrushes** know when it is time to migrate.

THRUST

2 Sam 2.23 with a backward **thrust** of his spear, struck him through

THUMB

Ex 29.20 and his sons, on the **thumbs** of their right hands and on
Lev 8.23 Aaron's right ear, on the **thumb** of his right hand, and on
8.24 their right ears, on the **thumbs** of their right hands, and on
14.14 the right ear, on the **thumb** of the right hand, and on
14.17 the right ear, on the **thumb** of the right hand, and on
14.25 man's right ear, on the **thumb** of his right hand, and on
14.28 man's right ear, on the **thumb** of his right hand, and on
Judg 1. 6 chased him, caught him, and cut off his **thumbs** and big toes.
1. 7 said, "Seventy kings with their **thumbs** and big toes cut off

THUMMIM

Urim and Thummim were two small objects used by Israelite priests to find out God's will.

Ex 28.30 Put the Urim and **Thummim** in the breast-piece, so that
Lev 8. 8 the breast-piece on him and put the Urim and **Thummim** in it.
Num 27.21 who will learn my will by using the Urim and **Thummim.**
Deut 33. 8 will by the Urim and **Thummim** Through your faithful servants,
1 Sam 14.41 it belongs to your people Israel, answer by the **Thummim."**
28. 6 dreams or by the use of Urim and **Thummim** or by prophets.
Ezra 2.63 there was a priest who could use the Urim and **Thummim.**
Neh 7.65 there was a priest who could use the Urim and **Thummim.**

THUNDER

[MEN OF THUNDER]

Ex 9.23 sky, and the Lord sent **thunder** and hail, and lightning
9.28 We have had enough of this **thunder** and hail!
9.29 The **thunder** will stop, and there will be no more hail, so
9.33 The **thunder,** the hail, and the rain all stopped.
19.16 the third day there was **thunder** and lightning, a thick cloud
19.19 Moses spoke, and God answered him with **thunder.**
20.18 When the people heard the **thunder** and the trumpet blast
1 Sam 2.10 he will **thunder** against them from heaven.
7.10 but just then the Lord **thundered** from heaven against them.
12.17 But I will pray, and the Lord will send **thunder** and rain.
12.18 prayed, and on that same day the Lord sent **thunder** and rain.
2 Sam 22.14 Then the Lord **thundered** from the sky, and the voice of
Job 28.26 And the path that the **thunderclouds** travel;
36.29 clouds move or how the **thunder** roars through the sky, where
36.33 **Thunder** announces the approaching storm,
37. 2 the voice of God, to the **thunder** that comes from his mouth.
37. 4 heard, the majestic sound of **thunder,** and all the while the
38.25 the pouring rain and cleared the way for the **thunderstorm?**
40. 9 Can your voice **thunder** as loud as mine?
Ps 18.13 Then the Lord **thundered** from the sky;
29. 3 the glorious God **thunders,** and his voice echoes over the ocean.
42. 6 like a flood, like waterfalls **thundering** down to the Jordan
46. 6 God **thunders,** and the earth dissolves.
77.17 **thunder** crashed from the sky, and lightning flashed
77.18 The crash of your **thunder** rolled out, and flashes of
Is 29. 6 the Lord Almighty will rescue you with violent **thunderstorms**
Jer 11.16 now, with a roar like **thunder** I will set its leaves on
25.30 Lord will roar from heaven and **thunder** from the heights of heaven.
Joel 2.11 The Lord **thunders** commands to his army.
3.16 his voice **thunders** from Jerusalem;
Amos 1. 2 his voice **thunders** from Jerusalem.
Mk 3.17 (Jesus gave them the name Boanerges, which means **"Men of Thunder");**
Jn 12.29 of them said it was **thunder,** while others said, "An angel
Rev 4. 5 throne came flashes of lightning, rumblings, and peals of **thunder.**
6. 1 creatures say in a voice that sounded like **thunder,** "Come!"
8. 5 were rumblings and peals of **thunder,** flashes of lightning,
10. 3 After he had called out, the seven **thunders** answered with a roar.
10. 4 from heaven, "Keep secret what the seven **thunders** have said;
11.19 rumblings and peals of **thunder,** an earthquake, and heavy hail.
14. 2 like a roaring waterfall, like a loud peal of **thunder.**
16.18 rumblings and peals of **thunder,** and a terrible earthquake.
19. 6 sound of a roaring waterfall, like loud peals of **thunder.**

TIDE

Lk 21.25 despair, afraid of the roar of the sea and the raging **tides.**

TIDY

Mt 12.44 it goes back and finds the house empty, clean, and all **tidy.**
Lk 11.25 So it goes back and finds the house clean and **tidy.**

TIE

[TYING]

Gen 22. 9 He **tied** up his son and placed him on the altar, on
37. 7 were all in the field **tying** up sheaves of wheat, when my
38.28 the midwife caught it, **tied** a red thread round it, and said,
42.24 picked out Simeon, and had him **tied** up in front of them.
49.11 He **ties** his young donkey to a grapevine, To the very
Ex 13. 9 be a reminder, like something **tied** on your hand or on your
13.16 be a reminder, like something **tied** on our hands or on our
28.28 **Tie** the rings of the breast-piece to the rings of the
28.37 **Tie** it to the front of the turban with a blue cord.
29. 6 the turban on him and **tie** on it the sacred sign of
29. 9 put sashes round their waists and **tie** caps on their heads.
39.21 Lord had commanded Moses, they **tied** the rings of the
39.31 They **tied** it to the front of the turban with a blue
Lev 8.13 sashes round their waists, and **tied** caps on their heads,
Deut 6. 8 **Tie** them on your arms and wear them on your foreheads as
11.18 **Tie** them on your arms and wear them on your foreheads as
Josh 2.18 When we invade your land, **tie** this red cord to the window
2.21 When they had gone, she **tied** the red cord to the window.
Judg 15. 4 Two by two, he **tied** their tails together and put torches in
15.12 "We have come here to **tie** you up, so that we can
15.13 "we are only going to **tie** you up and hand you over
15.13 So they **tied** him up with two new ropes and brought him
16. 5 how we can overpower him, **tie** him up, and make him helpless.
16. 6 If someone wanted to **tie** you up and make you helpless, how
16. 7 Samson answered, "If they **tie** me up with seven new
16. 8 bowstrings that were not dried out, and she **tied** Samson up.
16.10 Please tell me how someone could **tie** you up."
16.11 He answered, "If they **tie** me with new ropes that have
16.12 So Delilah got some new ropes and **tied** him up.
16.13 Tell me how someone could **tie** you up."
2 Sam 3.34 His hands were not **tied,** And his feet were not bound;
1 Kgs 5. 9 to the sea, and will **tie** them together in rafts to float
2 Kgs 1. 8 of animal skins, **tied** with a leather belt," they answered.
5.23 He insisted on it, **tied** up the silver in two bags, gave
Esth 1. 6 blue and white cotton curtains, **tied** by cords of fine purple
Job 38.31 Can you **tie** the Pleiades together or loosen the bonds
41. 1 Leviathan with a fish-hook or **tie** his tongue down with a rope?
41. 5 Will you **tie** him up like a pet bird, like something to
Prov 3. 3 **Tie** them round your neck;
26. 8 stupid makes as much sense as **tying** a stone in a catapult.
Is 32.11 Strip off your clothes and **tie** rags round your waist.
Jer 51.63 book to the people, then **tie** it to a stone and throw
Lam 1.14 "He took note of all my sins and **tied** them all together;
Ezek 3.25 You will be **tied** with ropes, mortal man, and you will
4. 8 I will **tie** you up so that you cannot turn from one
Dan 3.20 men in his army to **tie** the three men up and throw
3.21 So they **tied** them up, fully dressed—shirts, robes, caps,
3.23 Shadrach, Meshach, and Abednego, still **tied** up, fell into
3.24 asked his officials, "Didn't we **tie** up three men and throw
3.25 "They are not **tied** up, and they show no sign of being
Mt 12.29 away his belongings unless he first **ties** up the strong man;
13.30 pull up the weeds first, **tie** them in bundles and burn them,
18. 6 to have a large millstone **tied** round his neck and be drowned
21. 2 you will find a donkey **tied** up with her colt beside her.
22.13 the king told the servants, '**Tie** him up hand and foot,
23. 4 They **tie** on to people's backs loads that are heavy and
Mk 3.27 away his belongings unless he first **ties** up the strong man;
6.53 and came to land at Gennesaret, where they **tied** up the boat.
9.42 to have a large millstone **tied** round his neck and be thrown
11. 2 you will find a colt **tied** up that has never been ridden.
11. 4 colt out in the street, **tied** to the door of a house.
Lk 17. 2 if a large millstone were **tied** round his neck and he were
19.30 you will find a colt **tied** up that has never been ridden.
Jn 13. 4 off his outer garment, and **tied** a towel round his waist.
Acts 12. 6 He was **tied** with two chains, and there were guards on duty
21.11 to us, took Paul's belt, **tied** up his own feet and hands
21.11 of this belt will be **tied** up in this way by the
21.13 ready not only to be **tied** up in Jerusalem but even to
22.25 But when they had **tied** him up to be whipped, Paul said
27.28 a line with a weight **tied** to it and found that the
Rev 15. 6 clean shining linen and with gold belts **tied** around their chests.

TIGHT

Gen 25.26 one was born holding on **tightly** to the heel of Esau, so
29.34 husband will be bound more **tightly** to me, because I have
Judg 16.13 a loom, and make it **tight** with a peg, I'll be as
16.14 She made it **tight** with a peg and shouted, "Samson!
1 Kgs 18.46 he fastened his clothes **tight** round his waist and ran ahead
Job 41.16 Each one is joined so **tight** to the next, not even a
Jer 13.11 Just as shorts fit **tightly** round the waist, so I
13.11 all the people of Israel and Judah to hold **tightly** to me.
Mt 26.50 Then they came up, arrested Jesus, and held him **tight.**
Mk 14.46 So they arrested Jesus and held him **tight.**
Acts 5.23 we found it locked up **tight** and all the guards on watch
16.23 into jail, and the jailer was ordered to lock them up **tight.**
27.17 it aboard and then fastened some ropes **tight** round the ship.
Eph 6.14 with truth as a belt **tight** round your waist, with righteousness
Heb 12. 1 holds on to us so **tightly,** and let us run with determination

TIGLATH PILESER

Emperor of Assyria who attacked Israel and took some of its territory.

2 Kgs 15.19 **Tiglath Pileser,** the emperor of Assyria, invaded Israel,
15.20 So **Tiglath Pileser** went back to his own country.
15.29 Pekah was king that **Tiglath Pileser,** the emperor of Assyria,
16. 7 Ahaz sent men to **Tiglath Pileser,** the emperor of Assyria,
16. 9 **Tiglath Pileser,** in answer to Ahaz' plea, marched out with
16.10 to Damascus to meet Emperor **Tiglath Pileser,** he saw the
1 Chr 5. 4 The Assyrian emperor, **Tiglath Pileser,** captured Beerah, a leader of the tribe,
5.26 Emperor Pul of Assyria (also known as **Tiglath Pileser)** invade their country.
2 Chr 28.16 so King Ahaz asked **Tiglath Pileser,** the emperor of Assyria,

TILE

Lk 5.19 made an opening in the **tiles,** and let him down on his

TILT

Job 38.37 to count the clouds and **tilt** them over to pour out the

TIMBER

Gen 6.14 Build a boat for yourself out of good **timber;**
1 Kgs 5.18 Byblos prepared the stones and the **timber** to build the Temple.
15.22 from Ramah the stones and **timber** that Baasha had been using
2 Kgs 12.12 and the stone-cutters, buy the **timber** and the stones used in
22. 6 the masons, and buy the **timber** and the stones used in the
1 Chr 29. 2 Temple—gold, silver, bronze, iron, **timber,** precious stones and
2 Chr 2. 9 in preparing large quantities of **timber,** because this
16. 6 carry off the stones and **timber** that Baasha had been using
34.11 buy the stones and the **timber** used to repair the buildings
Neh 2. 8 him to supply me with **timber** for the gates of the fort
Ezek 27. 5 fir-trees from Mount Hermon for **timber** And a cedar from
Hag 1. 8 Now go up into the hills, get **timber,** and rebuild the Temple;

TIME

[AT ALL TIMES, FOR A LONG TIME, FOR ALL TIME]

Gen 1.14 night and to show the **time** when days, years, and religious
6. 9 had no faults and was the only good man of his **time.**
8.21 I know that from the **time** he is young his thoughts are
8.22 there will be a time for planting and a **time** for harvest.
10.25 named Peleg, because during his **time** the people of the world
17.21 who will be born to Sarah about this **time** next year."
21. 2 boy was born at the **time** God had said he would be
22.15 Abraham from heaven a second **time,** [16]"I make a vow by my
24.11 It was late afternoon, the **time** when women came out to get
25.24 The **time** came for her to give birth, and she had twin
26.12 year he harvested a hundred **times** as much as he had sown,
27.36 Esau said, "This is the second **time** that he has cheated me.
27.41 He thought, "The **time** to mourn my father's death is near;
29. 7 broad daylight and not yet **time** to bring the flocks in, why
29.20 could have Rachel, and the **time** seemed like only a few days
29.21 Then Jacob said to Laban, "The **time** is up;
30.30 Now it is **time** for me to look out for my own
31. 7 Yet he has cheated me and changed my wages ten **times.**
31.41 And even then, you changed my wages ten **times.**
33. 3 down to the ground seven **times** as he approached his brother.
34.19 the young man lost no **time** in doing what was suggested,
35. 3 who helped me in the **time** of my trouble and who has
35.16 some distance from Ephrath, the **time** came for Rachel to have
38. 1 About that **time** Judah left his brothers and went to stay
38.12 When he had finished the **time** of mourning, he and his friend
38.27 When the **time** came for her to give birth, it was
41.31 The **time** of plenty will be entirely forgotten, because
43.34 and Benjamin was served five **times** as much as the rest of
47.24 At the **time** of harvest you must give one-fifth to the king.
47.29 When the **time** drew near for him to die, he called for
50. 3 It took forty days, the normal **time** for embalming.
50. 4 When the **time** of mourning was over, Joseph said to the
Ex 1. 6 In the course of **time** Joseph, his brothers, and all the
4. 7 he took it out this **time,** it was healthy, just like the
5. 9 so that they won't have **time** to listen to a pack of
8. 9 Just set the **time** when I am to pray for you, your
8.32 But even this **time** the king became stubborn, and again
9. 5 have set tomorrow as the **time** when I will do this.' "
9.14 This **time** I will punish not only your officials and your people,
9.18 This **time** tomorrow I will cause a heavy hailstorm, such
9.27 for Moses and Aaron and said, "This **time** I have sinned;
12.14 Celebrate it **for all time** to come."
12.17 **For all time** to come you must celebrate this day as a
12.39 that they did not have **time** to get their food ready or
12.42 dedicated to the Lord **for all time** to come as a night
13.10 Celebrate this festival at the appointed **time** each year.
21.18 to pay for his lost **time** and take care of him until
29.38 "Every day **for all time** to come, sacrifice on the altar
29.42 **For all time** to come, this burnt-offering is to be offered
30. 8 is to continue without interruption **for all time** to come.
30.10 This is to be done every year **for all time** to come.
30.31 is to be used in my service **for all time** to come.
31.13 between you and me **for all time** to come, to show that
32.34 will guide you, but the **time** is coming when I will punish
34.21 the seventh day, not even during ploughing **time** or harvest.
34.23 "Three **times** a year all your men must come to worship me,
34.35 back on until the next **time** he went to speak to the
40.15 This anointing will make them priests **for all time** to come."
Lev 4. 6 and sprinkle it in front of the sacred curtain seven **times.**
4.17 in it, and sprinkle it in front of the curtain seven **times.**
6.18 **For all time** to come any of the male descendants of
6.22 **For all time** to come this offering is to be made by
7.34 of Israel must give to the priests **for all time** to come.
7.36 that the people of Israel must obey **for all time** to come.
8.11 oil and sprinkled it seven **times** on the altar and its
14. 7 shall sprinkle the blood seven **times** on the person who is to
14.16 some of it seven **times** there in the Lord's presence.
14.27 some of it seven **times** there in the Lord's presence.
14.51 And he shall sprinkle the house seven **times.**
16. 2 that only at the proper **time** is he to go behind the
16.14 some of it seven **times** in front of the Covenant Box.
16.17 From the **time** Aaron enters the Most Holy Place to
16.19 he must sprinkle some of the blood on the altar seven **times.**
16.29 following regulations are to be observed **for all time** to come.
16.31 These regulations are to be observed **for all time** to come.
16.34 These regulations are to be observed **for all time** to come.
17. 7 of Israel must keep this regulation **for all time** to come.
21.17 This applies **for all time** to come.
22. 3 This applies **for all time** to come.
23. 4 Proclaim the following festivals at the appointed **times.**
23.14 be observed by all your descendants **for all time** to come.
23.21 to observe this regulation **for all time** to come, no matter
23.41 is to be kept by your descendants **for all time** to come.
Lev 24. 3 This regulation is to be observed **for all time** to come.
24. 8 Every Sabbath, **for all time** to come, the bread must be
25. 8 Count seven **times** seven years, a total of forty-nine years.
25.50 count the years from the **time** he sold himself until the next
26. 4 you rain at the right **time,** so that the land will produce
26. 5 harvesting corn when it is **time** to pick grapes, and you will
26. 5 will still be picking grapes when it is **time** to sow corn.
26.18 do not obey me, I will increase your punishment seven **times.**
26.21 obey me, I will again increase your punishment seven **times.**
26.24 turn on you and punish you seven **times** harder than before.
26.28 again make your punishment seven **times** worse than before.
Num 3. 1 Aaron and Moses at the **time** the Lord spoke to Moses on
6. 5 the vow for the full **time** that he is dedicated to the
6.12 hair [12]and rededicate to the Lord his **time** as a Nazirite.
6.12 The previous period of **time** doesn't count, because his
9.13 he did not present the offering to me at the appointed **time.**
10. 6 blasts are sounded a second **time,** the tribes on the south
10. 8 "The following rule is to be observed **for all time** to come.
15.15 **For all time** to come, the same rules are binding on you
15.21 **For all time** to come, this special gift is to be given
15.38 You are to do this **for all time** to come.
18.11 to you, your sons, and your daughters **for all time** to come.
18.19 and to your daughters, **for all time** to come, all the special
19. 4 finger sprinkle it seven **times** in the direction of the Tent.
19.10 This regulation is valid **for all time** to come, both for the
19.21 You are to observe this rule **for all time** to come.
22.27 This **time,** when the donkey saw the angel, it lay down.
22.28 Why have you beaten me these three **times?"**
22.32 "Why have you beaten your donkey three **times** like this?
22.33 But your donkey saw me and turned aside three **times.**
22.37 "Why didn't you come when I sent for you the first **time?**
24.10 enemies, but three **times** now you have blessed them instead.
25.12 a covenant with him that is valid **for all time** to come.
28. 2 to God at the appointed **times** the required food-offerings
Deut 1.11 you increase a thousand **times** more and make you prosperous,
4.32 "Search the past, the **time** before you were born, all
4.32 the way back to the **time** when God created man on the
6.20 "In **time** to come your children will ask you, 'Why did
10. 4 he had written the first **time,** the Ten Commandments that he
10.10 the mountain forty days and nights, as I did the first **time.**
12. 8 "When that **time** comes, you must not do as you have been
16. 5 Do it at sunset, the **time** of day when you left Egypt.
16.16 to worship the Lord three **times** a year at the one place
24.21 grapes once, do not go back over the vines a second **time;**
31.29 And in **time** to come they will meet with disaster, because
32. 7 "Think of the past, of the **time** long ago;
32.34 he waits for the right **time** to punish them.
32.35 the **time** will come when they will fall;
Josh 5.11 next day was the first **time** they ate food grown in Canaan:
6. 4 the city seven **times** while the priests blow the trumpets.
6.12 morning, and for the second **time** the priests and soldiers
6.15 at daybreak and marched seven **times** round the city in the
6.15 was the only day that they marched round it seven **times.**
6.16 The seventh **time** round, when the priests were about to
8. 2 and its king, but this **time** you may keep its goods and
8. 5 we will turn and run, just as we did the first **time.**
8.33 to do this when the **time** came for them to receive the
11. 6 By this **time** tomorrow I will have killed all of them for
23.14 "Now my **time** has come to die.
Judg 2.15 Every **time** they went into battle, the Lord was against them,
6.39 This **time** let the wool be dry, and the ground be wet."
15. 3 Samson said, "This **time** I'm not going to be responsible
16.15 a fool of me three **times,** and you still haven't told me
16.17 dedicated to God as a Nazirite from the **time** I was born.
20.24 They marched against the army of Benjamin a second **time.**
20.25 And for the second **time** the Benjaminites came out of Gibeah,
20.25 and this **time** they killed eighteen thousand trained Israelite
1 Sam 1. 4 Each **time** Elkanah offered his sacrifice, he would give one
1.21 The **time** came again for Elkanah and his family to go to
1.22 But this **time** Hannah did not go.
2.30 family and your clan would serve me as priests **for all time.**
2.31 Listen, the **time** is coming when I will kill all the
3. 8 The Lord called Samuel a third **time;**
4.19 pregnant, and it was almost **time** for her baby to be born.
5. 4 This **time** its head and both its arms were broken off and
8.18 When that **time** comes, you will complain bitterly
9.16 to Samuel, [16]"Tomorrow about this **time** I will send you a
9.24 for you to eat at this **time** with the people I invited."
14.19 Saul said to him, "There's no **time** to consult the Lord!"
17.30 the same question, and every **time** he asked, he got the same
18.11 but David dodged each **time.**
18.19 But when the **time** came for Merab to be given to David,
18.21 So for the second **time** Saul said to David, "You will be
18.22 now is a good **time** for you to marry his daughter."
19.21 He sent messengers the third **time,** and the same thing
20. 6 to Bethlehem, since it's the **time** for the annual sacrifice
20.12 At this **time** tomorrow and on the following day I will
20.41 his knees and bowed with his face to the ground three **times.**
21. 5 how much more this **time** when we are on a special mission!"
21. 8 hurry that I didn't have **time** to get my sword or any
22.15 Yes, I consulted God for him, and it wasn't the first **time.**
26.10 kill Saul, either when his **time** comes to die a natural death
27.10 would ask him, "Where did you go on a raid this **time?"**
2 Sam 5. 6 The **time** came when King David and his men set out to
7. 6 From the **time** I rescued the people of Israel from Egypt
7.25 now, Lord God, fulfil **for all time** the promise you made
7.26 And you will preserve my dynasty **for all time.**
11. 1 The following spring, at the **time** of the year when kings
11.27 When the **time** of mourning was over, David sent for her
12. 6 thing, he must pay back four **times** as much as he took."
17. 7 "The advice Ahithophel gave you this **time** is no good.

2 Sam 18.14 “I'm not going to waste any more **time** with you,” Joab
19.24 washed his clothes from the **time** the king left Jerusalem
19.43 Israelites replied, “We have ten **times** as many claims on
20. 5 he did not get back by the **time** the king had set.
24. 3 of Israel a hundred **times** more numerous than they are now,
24.15 lasted from that morning until the **time** that he had chosen.
1 Kgs 2. 2 “My **time** to die has come.
8.16 when he said, [16]‘From the **time** I brought my people out of
8.59 Lord our God remember **at all times** this prayer and these
9. 3 I will watch over it and protect it **for all time.**
9.20 descendants continue to be slaves down to the present **time.**
9.25 Three **times** a year Solomon offered burnt-offerings and
11. 4 from God, [4]and by the **time** he was old they had led
11.39 I will punish the descendants of David, but not **for all time.’ ”**
12.19 Ever since that **time** the people of the northern kingdom
14.28 Every **time** the king went to the Temple, the guards
17.21 out on the boy three **times** and prayed, “O Lord my God,
18.43 Seven **times** in all Elijah told him to go and look.
18.44 The seventh **time** he returned and said, “I saw a little
19. 2 me dead if by this **time** tomorrow I don't do the same
19. 7 woke him up a second **time,** saying, “Get up and eat, or
20. 6 They will be there about this **time** tomorrow.”
20.25 Israelites in the plains, and this **time** we will defeat them.”
2 Kgs 2. 1 The **time** came for the Lord to take Elijah up to heaven
3.20 The next morning, at the **time** of the regular morning sacrifice,
4.16 said to her, “By this **time** next year you will be holding
4.17 had said, at about that **time** the following year she gave
4.20 held him in her lap until noon, at which **time** he died.
4.29 meet, and if anyone greets you, don't take **time** to answer.
4.35 The boy sneezed seven **times,** and then opened his eyes.
5.10 go and wash himself seven **times** in the River Jordan, and he
5.14 dipped himself in it seven **times,** as Elisha had instructed,
5.26 This is no **time** to accept money and clothes,
7. 1 By this **time** tomorrow you will be able to buy in Samaria
7.18 the king that by that **time** the following day three
10. 6 King Ahab's descendants to me at Jezreel by this **time** tomorrow.”
13.18 The king struck the ground three **times,** and then stopped.
13.19 have struck five or six **times,** and then you would have won
13.19 but now you will defeat them only three **times.”**
13.25 of Israel defeated Benhadad three **times** and recaptured the
18. 5 had another king like him, either before or after his **time.**
20.17 Lord Almighty says that [17]a **time** is coming when everything
21.15 up my anger from the **time** their ancestors came out of Egypt
1 Chr 1.19 named Peleg, because during his **time** the people of the world
9.20 had supervised them at one **time.**
9.25 to take turns at guard duty for seven days at a **time.**
9.28 them out and checked them back in every **time** they were used.
12.15 month of one year, the **time** when the River Jordan overflowed
12.23 knew what Israel should do and the best **time** to do it);
15.13 to carry it the first **time,** the Lord our God punished us
17. 5 From the **time** I rescued the people of Israel from Egypt
17.23 now, O Lord, fulfil **for all time** the promise you made about
17.24 And you will preserve my dynasty **for all time.**
20. 1 The following spring, at the **time** of the year when kings
21. 3 of Israel a hundred **times** more numerous than they are now!
23.31 the number of Levites assigned to do this work each **time.**
23.31 Levites were assigned the duty of worshipping the Lord **for all time.**
29.22 For a second **time** they proclaimed Solomon king.
2 Chr 5. 3 They all assembled at the **time** of the Festival of Shelters.
6. 5 said to him, [5]‘From the **time** I brought my people out of
7.16 I will watch over it and protect it **for all time.**
8. 7 descendants continue to be slaves down to the present **time.**
12.11 Every **time** the king went to the Temple, the guards
23. 1 Jehoiada the priest decided that it was **time** to take action.
29.11 My sons, do not lose any **time.**
30. 1 Passover Festival at the proper **time,** in the first month,
31. 4 they could give all their **time** to the requirements of the
Ezra 9. 4 sat there grieving until the **time** for the evening sacrifice
9. 5 When the **time** came for the evening sacrifice, I got up
10.14 wife come at a set **time,** together with the leaders and the
Neh 6. 4 me the same message four **times,**
6. 4 and each **time** I sent them the same reply.
8.17 This was the first **time** it had been done since the days
13.31 be brought at the proper **times,** and for the people to bring
Esth 2. 9 He lost no **time** in beginning her beauty treatment of massage
2.15 The **time** came for Esther to go to the king.
4.14 you keep quiet at a **time** like this, help will come from
4.14 maybe it was for a **time** like this that you were made
7. 2 king and Haman went to eat with Esther [2]for a second **time.**
9.19 as a joyous holiday, a **time** for feasting and giving gifts of
9.22 had been turned from a **time** of grief and despair
9.22 into a **time** of joy and happiness.
9.27 Jew, that at the proper **time** each year these two days would
9.28 and observe the days of Purim **for all time** to come.
9.31 of Purim at the proper **time,** just as they had adopted rules
9.31 rules for the observance of fasts and **times** of mourning.
Job 10.20 Let me enjoy the **time** I have left.
12. 4 but there was a **time** when God answered my prayers.
14.13 your anger is over, and then set a **time** to remember me.
14.14 for better times, wait till this **time** of trouble is ended.
14.18 There comes a **time** when mountains fall and solid cliffs
15.32 Before his **time** is up he will wither, wither like a
22.16 Even before their **time** had come, they were washed away
24. 1 Why doesn't God set a **time** for judging, a day of justice
27.19 One last **time** they will lie down rich, and when they
34.23 not need to set a **time** for men to go and be
36.20 Don't wish for night to come, the **time** when nations will perish.
38.23 I keep them ready for **times** of trouble, for days of
39. 2 Do you know the **time** for their birth?
Ps 1. 3 bear fruit at the right **time,** and whose leaves do not dry

Ps 9. 9 for the oppressed, a place of safety in **times** of trouble.
12. 6 they are as genuine as silver refined seven **times** in the furnace.
25.15 the Lord for help **at all times,** and he rescues me from
27. 5 In **times** of trouble he will shelter me;
32. 6 all your loyal people should pray to you in **times** of need;
33.19 he keeps them alive in **times** of famine.
37.26 **At all times** he gives freely and lends to others, and
37.39 The Lord saves righteous men and protects them in **times** of trouble.
45.17 for ever, and everyone will praise you **for all time** to come.
46. 1 and strength, always ready to help in **times** of trouble.
48.14 he will lead us **for all time** to come.”
49.11 there they stay **for all time,** though they once had lands
51. 5 from the **time** I was conceived, I have been sinful.
55.15 May my enemies die before their **time;**
59.16 been a refuge for me, a shelter in my **time** of trouble.
62. 8 Trust in God **at all times,** my people.
69.13 answer me, God, at a **time** you choose.
72.15 may prayers be said for him **at all times;**
75. 2 “I have set a **time** for judgement,” says God, “and I
77. 2 In **times** of trouble I pray to the Lord;
78.69 he made it firm like the earth itself, secure **for all time.**
79.12 the other nations back seven **times** for all the insults they
79.13 thank you for ever and praise you **for all time** to come.
86. 7 I call to you in **times** of trouble, because you answer my
89. 2 your love will last **for all time,** that your faithfulness is
89.45 made him old before his **time** and covered him with disgrace.
93. 2 firm from the beginning, and you existed before **time** began.
102.13 the **time** has come to have mercy on her;
102.13 this is the right **time.**
104.19 the sun knows the **time** to set.
106.31 his favour ever since and will be **for all time** to come.
111. 8 They last **for all time;**
116. 2 He listens to me every **time** I call to him.
119.20 I want to know your judgements **at all times.**
119.33 meaning of your laws, and I will obey them **at all times.**
119.43 to speak the truth **at all times,** because my hope is in
119.126 Lord, it is **time** for you to act, because people are
119.164 Seven **times** each day I thank you for your righteous judgements.
132.12 their sons, also, will succeed you **for all time** as kings.”
146.10 Your God, O Zion, will reign **for all time.**
Prov 6.31 he must pay back seven **times** more—he must give up everything
10.27 The wicked die before their **time.**
12.11 to eat, but it is stupid to waste **time** on useless projects.
16.22 but trying to educate stupid people is a waste of **time.**
17.10 than a fool learns from being beaten a hundred **times.**
20. 4 his fields at the right **time** will have nothing to harvest.
24. 2 **time** they open their mouth someone is going to be hurt.
26.11 some stupid thing a second **time** is like a dog going back
28.19 People who waste **time** will always be poor.
29. 1 you get more stubborn every **time** you are corrected, one day
Ecc 3. 1 Everything that happens in this world happens at the **time** God chooses.
3. 2 He sets the **time** for birth and the time for death,
3. 2 time for planting and the **time** for pulling up,
3. 3 time for killing and the **time** for healing,
3. 3 the time for tearing down and the **time** for building.
3. 4 He sets the **time** for sorrow and the time for joy,
3. 4 time for mourning and the **time** for dancing,
3. 5 the **time** for making love
3. 5 and the **time** for not making love,
3. 5 the time for kissing and the **time** for not kissing.
3. 6 He sets the **time** for finding and the time for losing,
3. 6 time for saving and the **time** for throwing away,
3. 7 time for tearing and the **time** for mending,
3. 7 the time for silence and the **time** for talk.
3. 8 He sets the **time** for love and the time for hate,
3. 8 the time for war and the **time** for peace.
3.11 He has set the right **time** for everything.
3.17 thing, every action, will happen at its own set **time.”**
5.13 up their money for a **time** when they may need it, [14]and
8. 6 There is a right **time** and a right way to do everything,
9.12 You never know when your **time** is coming.
10.17 who eat at the proper **time,** who control themselves and don't
Song 1. 6 I had no **time** to care for myself.
2.12 This is the **time** for singing;
Is 3. 6 A **time** will come when the members of a clan will choose
3. 6 to wear, so be our leader in this **time** of trouble.”
4. 1 When that **time** comes, seven women will grab hold of one
4. 2 The **time** is coming when the Lord will make every plant and
7.16 Even before that **time** comes, the lands of those two
7.18 “When that **time** comes, the Lord will whistle as a
7.20 “When that **time** comes, the Lord will hire a barber from
7.21 “When that **time** comes, even if a farmer has been able
7.23 “When that **time** comes, the fine vineyards, each with a
9. 1 be no way for them to escape from this **time** of trouble.
9. 7 power on right and justice, from now until the end of **time.**
10.20 A **time** is coming when the people of Israel who have
10.27 When that **time** comes, I will free you from the power of
13.22 Babylon's **time** has come!
18. 7 A **time** is coming when the Lord Almighty will receive
19.16 A **time** is coming when the people of Egypt will be as
19.18 When that **time** comes, the Hebrew language will be spoken
19.19 When that **time** comes, there will be an altar to the Lord
19.23 When that **time** comes, there will be a highway between
19.24 When that **time** comes, Israel will rank with Egypt and Assyria,
20. 6 When that **time** comes, the people who live along the coast
22. 5 This is a **time** of panic, defeat, and confusion in the
23.15 A **time** is coming when Tyre will be forgotten for seventy years,
24.21 A **time** is coming when the Lord will punish the powers
24.22 them in prison until the **time** of their punishment comes.

Is	25. 4	have fled to you and have been safe in **times** of trouble.
	30.20	make you go through hard **times,** but he himself will be there
	30.26	the sun will be seven **times** brighter than usual, like the
	30.32	again, his people will keep **time** with the music of drums and
	31. 7	A **time** is coming when all of you will throw away the
	32.10	be satisfied now, but this **time** next year you will be in
	33. 2	Protect us day by day and save us in **times** of trouble.
	34. 8	This is the **time** when the Lord will rescue Zion and take
	39. 6	Lord Almighty says that [6]a **time** is coming when everything
	42.14	But now the **time** to act has come;
	44. 2	from the **time** you were born, I have helped you.
	44. 7	would happen from the very beginning to the end of **time?**
	46. 3	I have cared for you from the **time** you were born.
	49. 8	"When the **time** comes to save you, I will show you favour
	51. 5	the **time** of my victory is near.
	51. 8	my victory will endure **for all time."**
	52. 6	In **time** to come you will acknowledge that I am God and
	52.12	This **time** you will not have to leave in a hurry;
	59.21	and your descendants to obey me **for all time** to come."
	60.22	When the right **time** comes, I will make this happen quickly.
	61. 2	me to proclaim That the **time** has come When the Lord will
	63. 4	I decided that the **time** to save my people had come;
	63. 4	it was **time** to punish their enemies.
	65.23	I will bless them and their descendants **for all time** to come.
Jer	3.17	When that **time** comes, Jerusalem will be called 'The
	4.11	The **time** is coming when the people of Jerusalem will be
	6. 9	So you must rescue everyone you can while there is still **time."**
	7.32	And so, the **time** will come when it will no longer be
	8. 7	Even storks know when it is **time** to return;
	8. 7	swallows, and thrushes know when it is **time** to migrate.
	8.15	hoped for peace and a **time** of healing, but it was no
	9.25	The Lord says, "The **time** is coming when I will
	11.23	I have set a **time** for bringing disaster on the people of
	11.23	and when that **time** comes, none of them will survive."
	12. 3	guard them until it is **time** for them to be slaughtered.
	16.14	The Lord says, "The **time** is coming when people will no
	16.19	you help me in **times** of trouble.
	17.16	I did not wish a **time** of trouble for them.
	19. 6	So then, the **time** will come when this place will no longer
	23. 5	The Lord says, "The **time** is coming when I will choose as
	23. 7	"The **time** is coming," says the Lord, "when people will
	23.12	the **time** of their punishment is coming.
	25.34	The **time** has come for you to be slaughtered, and you will
	27. 7	and his grandson until the **time** comes for his own nation to
	28. 8	long ago, before my **time** and yours, predicted that war,
	30. 3	have told you, [3]because the **time** is coming when I will
	30. 7	compare with it— a **time** of distress for my people, but
	31. 1	The Lord says, "The **time** is coming when I will be the
	31. 6	Yes, the **time** is coming when watchmen will call out on the
	31.27	the Lord, say that the **time** is coming when I will fill
	31.29	When that **time** comes, people will no longer say,
	31.31	The Lord says, "The **time** is coming when I will make a
	31.38	"The **time** is coming," says the Lord, "when all
	32.39	to honour me **for all time,** for their own good and the
	33.14	The Lord said, "The **time** is coming when I will fulfil
	33.20	the night, so that they always come at their proper **times;**
	36. 2	have told you from the **time** I first spoke to you, when
	46.21	The day of their doom had arrived, the **time** of their destruction.
	47. 4	The **time** has come to destroy Philistia, to cut off from
	48.12	"So now, the **time** is coming when I will send people to
	48.44	because the Lord has set the **time** for Moab's destruction.
	49. 2	But the **time** is coming when I will make the people of
	49. 8	destroy Esau's descendants, because the **time** has come for me
	50. 4	The Lord says, "When that **time** comes, the people of both
	50.20	When that **time** comes, no sin will be found in Israel and
	50.27	The **time** has come for them to be punished!"
	50.31	The **time** has come for me to punish you.
	50.39	Never again will people live there, not **for all time** to come.
	51. 3	Don't give its soldiers **time** to shoot their arrows or to
	51.13	and rich treasures, but its **time** is up, and its thread of
	51.47	And so the **time** is coming when I will deal with
	51.52	then, I say that the **time** is coming when I will deal
Lam	5.19	are king for ever, and will rule to the end of **time.**
Ezek	7. 7	The **time** is near when there will be no more celebrations at
	7.12	The **time** is coming.
	12.22	'**Time** goes by, and predictions come to nothing'?
	12.23	The **time** has come, and the predictions are coming true!
	16. 8	again, I saw that the **time** had come for you to fall
	19. 7	The people of the land were terrified every **time** he roared.
	21. 7	The **time** has come;
	22. 3	defiled yourself by worshipping idols, your **time** is coming.
	22. 4	you made, and so your day is coming, your **time** is up!
	24.14	The **time** has come for me to act.
	35. 5	people be slaughtered in the **time** of her disaster,
	35. 5	the **time** of final punishment for her sins.
	38.10	"When that **time** comes, you will start thinking up an evil plan.
	38.16	When the **time** comes, I will send you to invade my land
Dan	1.15	When the **time** was up, they looked healthier and stronger
	1.20	raised, these four knew ten **times** more than any
	2. 8	You are trying to gain **time,** because you see that I have
	2.16	obtained royal permission for more **time,** so that he could
	2.21	He controls the **times** and the seasons;
	3.19	his men to heat the furnace seven **times** hotter than usual.
	4. 3	he will rule **for all time.**
	4.34	will rule for ever, and his kingdom will last **for all time.**
	6.10	at the open windows and prayed to God three **times** a day.
	6.13	He prays regularly three **times** a day."
	7.22	The **time** had arrived for God's people to receive royal power.
	8.19	The vision refers to the **time** of the end.
	9.21	It was the **time** for the evening sacrifice to be offered.
	9.24	years is the length of **time** God has set for freeing your
Dan	9.25	From the **time** the command is given to rebuild Jerusalem,
	9.25	times sixty-two years, but this will be a **time** of troubles.
	9.26	at the end of that **time** God's chosen leader will be killed
	9.27	years, and when half this **time** is past, he will put an
	11.13	When the proper **time** comes, he will return with a large,
	11.24	plans to attack fortresses, but his **time** will soon run out.
	11.27	what they want, because the **time** for it has not yet come.
	11.29	Egypt again, but this **time** things will turn out differently.
	11.35	continue until the end comes, the **time** that God has set.
	12. 1	Then there will be a **time** of troubles, the worst since
	12. 1	When that **time** comes, all the people of your nation whose
	12.11	"From the **time** the daily sacrifices are stopped,
	12.11	that is, from the **time** of The Awful Horror,
	12.13	you will rise to receive your reward at the end of **time."**
Hos	1. 5	I will at that **time** destroy Israel's military power."
	1. 6	Gomer had a second child—this **time** it was a girl.
	3. 5	But the **time** will come when the people of Israel will once
	6.11	Judah, I have set a **time** to punish you also for what
	9. 5	And when the **time** comes for the appointed festivals in
	9. 7	The **time** for punishment has come, the time when people will
	10.12	It is **time** for you to turn to me, your Lord, and
Amos	8. 9	The **time** is coming when I will make the sun go down
	8.11	"The **time** is coming when I will send famine on the land.
Mic	2. 4	When that **time** comes, people will use your story as an
	2. 5	So then, when the **time** comes for the land to be given
	3. 4	The **time** is coming when you will cry out to the Lord,
	4. 6	"The **time** is coming," says the Lord, "when I will
	7.11	People of Jerusalem, the **time** to rebuild the city walls is coming.
Nah	1. 7	he protects his people in **times** of trouble;
Hab	2. 3	writing, because it is not yet **time** for it to come true.
	2. 3	But the **time** is coming quickly, and what I show you will
	3.16	will quietly wait for the **time** to come when God will punish
Zeph	3.16	The **time** is coming when they will say to Jerusalem, "Do
	3.19	The **time** is coming!
	3.20	The **time** is coming!
Hag	1. 2	say that this is not the right **time** to rebuild the Temple."
Zech	5. 1	I looked again, and this **time** I saw a scroll flying
	6. 1	This **time** I saw four chariots coming out from between two
	8.20	The Lord Almighty says, "The **time** is coming when people
	11.15	again act the part of a shepherd, this **time** a worthless one.
	12. 3	But when that **time** comes, I will make Jerusalem like a
	13. 1	"When that **time** comes," says the Lord Almighty,
	13. 4	When that **time** comes, no prophet will be proud of his visions,
	14. 6	When that **time** comes, there will no longer be cold or frost,
	14.21	When that **time** comes, there will no longer be any merchant
Mt	2. 7	found out from them the exact **time** the star had appeared.
	2.16	from the visitors about the **time** when the star had appeared.
	5.25	with him while there is **time,** before you get to court.
	8.29	Have you come to punish us before the right **time?"**
	10.19	when the **time** comes, you will be given what you will say.
	16. 3	but you cannot interpret the signs concerning these **times!**
	21.34	When the **time** came to gather the grapes, he sent his
	21.41	will give him his share of the harvest at the right **time."**
	24. 3	show that it is the **time** for your coming and the end
	24.10	Many will give up their faith at that **time;**
	24.17	house must not take the **time** to go down and get his
	24.21	For the trouble at that **time** will be far more terrible
	24.25	I have told you this before the **time** comes.
	24.33	you will know that the **time** is near, ready to begin.
	24.43	of a house knew the **time** when the thief would come,
	24.45	other servants to give them their food at the proper **time.**
	24.48	will not come back **for a long time,** [49]and he will begin
	24.50	does not expect him and at a **time** he does not know.
	25. 1	"At that **time** the Kingdom of heaven will be like this.
	25.14	"At that **time** the Kingdom of heaven will be like this.
	25.19	"After a **long time** the master of those servants came back
Mk	1.15	"The right **time** has come," he said, "and the Kingdom
	3.20	gathered that Jesus and his disciples had no **time** to eat.
	4.29	starts cutting it with his sickle, because harvest **time** has come.
	6.31	that Jesus and his disciples didn't even have **time** to eat.
	6.48	so some **time** between three and six o'clock in the morning he
	11.13	only leaves, because it was not the right **time** for figs.
	12. 2	When the **time** came to gather the grapes, he sent a slave
	13. 4	happen to show that the **time** has come for all these things
	13.11	when the **time** comes, say whatever is then given to you.
	13.19	very beginning when God created the world until the present **time.**
	13.23	I have told you everything before the **time** comes.
	13.24	"In the days after that **time** of trouble the sun will
	13.29	you will know that the **time** is near, ready to begin.
	13.33	be alert, for you do not know when the **time** will come.
	14.35	he might not have to go through that **time** of suffering.
	15.44	officer and asked him if Jesus had been dead a **long time.**
Lk	1.20	believed my message, which will come true at the right **time.**
	1.21	why he was spending such a **long time** in the Temple.
	4.19	oppressed [19]and announce that the **time** has come when the
	8.13	a while but when the **time** of testing comes, they fall away.
	8.27	**For a long time** this man had gone without clothes and would
	11.50	So the people of this **time** will be punished for the
	11.51	the people of this **time** will be punished for them all!
	12.39	of a house knew the **time** when the thief would come,
	12.42	other servants their share of the food at the proper **time.**
	12.45	his master is taking a **long time** to come back and if
	12.46	does not expect him and at a **time** he does not know.
	12.56	why, then, don't you know the meaning of this present **time?**
	13.35	not see me until the **time** comes when you say, 'God bless
	14.17	When it was **time** for the feast, he sent his servant to
	17.22	said to the disciples, "The **time** will come when you will
	18. 4	**For a long time** the judge refused to act, but at last
	19.43	**time** will come when your enemies will surround you with barricades,
	19.44	you did not recognize the **time** when God came to save you!"

Lk 20. 9 it out to tenants, and then left home **for a long time.**
20.10 When the **time** came to gather the grapes, he sent a slave
21. 6 "All this you see—the **time** will come when not a single
21. 7 order to show that the **time** has come for it to take
21. 8 and, 'The **time** has come!'
23. 8 him and had been wanting to see him **for a long time.**
24.53 and spent all their **time** in the Temple giving thanks to
Jn 2. 4 "My **time** has not yet come."
4.21 "Believe me, woman, the **time** will come when people will not
4.23 But the **time** is coming and is already here, when by the
4.52 He asked them what **time** it was when his son got better,
5. 6 knew that the man had been ill for such a **long time;**
5.25 the **time** is coming—the time has already come—when the dead
5.28 the **time** is coming when all the dead will hear his voice
6. 4 The **time** for the Passover Festival was near.
7. 2 **time** for the Festival of Shelters was near, [3]so Jesus' brothers
7. 6 said to them, "The right **time** for me has not yet come.
7. 6 Any **time** is right for you.
7. 8 this festival, because the right **time** has not come for me."
8.56 Abraham rejoiced that he was to see the **time** of my coming;
11.55 **time** for the Passover Festival was near, and many people went
12.31 Now is the **time** for this world to be judged;
14. 9 Jesus answered, **"For a long time** I have been with you all;
16. 2 from the synagogues, and the **time** will come when anyone who
16. 4 so that when the **time** comes for them to do these
16.25 But the **time** will come when I will not use figures of
16.32 The **time** is coming, and is already here, when all of you
Acts 1. 7 Jesus said to them, "The **times** and occasions are set by
2.25 said about him, 'I saw the Lord before me **at all times;**
3.20 **times** of spiritual strength will come from the Lord,
8.11 because for such a **long time** he had astonished them with
10.30 said, "It was about this **time** three days ago that I was
14. 3 The apostles stayed there **for a long time,** speaking boldly
14.17 he gives you rain from heaven and crops at the right **times;**
14.28 And they stayed a **long time** there with the believers.
15. 7 brothers, you know that a **long time** ago God chose me from
15.21 read for a very **long time** in the synagogues every Sabbath,
15.32 prophets, spoke a **long time** with them, giving them courage
17.26 fixed beforehand the exact **times** and the limits of the places
17.30 God has overlooked the **times** when people did not know him,
20.11 After talking with them **for a long time,** even until sunrise,
20.19 Lord's servant during the hard **times** that came to me because
20.30 The **time** will come when some men from your own group
24. 3 welcome this everywhere and **at all times,** and we are deeply
26.29 a short time or a **long time,"** Paul answered, "my prayer to
27. 9 We spent a **long time** there, until it became dangerous to
27.21 the men had gone a **long time** without food, Paul stood before
28. 6 But after waiting **for a long time** and not seeing anything
Rom 3.25 but in the present **time** he deals with their sins, in order
5. 6 Christ died for the wicked at the **time** that God chose.
8.18 we suffer at this present **time** cannot be compared at all
8.22 up to the present **time** all of creation groans with pain,
8.36 "For your sake we are in danger of death **at all times;**
9. 9 "At the right **time** I will come back, and Sarah will have
11.10 and make them bend under their troubles **at all times."**
12.12 be patient in your troubles, and pray **at all times.**
13.11 because you know that the **time** has come for you to wake
1 Cor 4. 5 should not pass judgement on anyone before the right **time** comes.
7.29 there is not much **time** left, and from now on married men
10.11 For we live at a **time** when the end is about to
15.23 then, at the **time** of his coming, those who belong to him.
16. 6 shall probably spend some **time** with you, perhaps the whole winter,
16. 7 hope to spend quite a **long time** with you, if the Lord
16.12 is not completely convinced that he should go at this **time.**
2 Cor 4.10 **At all times** we carry in our mortal bodies the death of
6. 2 "When the **time** came for me to show you favour I heard
9.11 enough to be generous **at all times,** so that many will thank
11. 6 made this clear to you **at all times** and in all conditions.
Gal 4. 2 and manage his affairs until the **time** set by his father.
4. 4 But when the right **time** finally came, God sent his own Son.
6. 9 do not give up, the **time** will come when we will reap
Eph 1.10 God will complete when the **time** is right, is to bring all
2. 7 did this to demonstrate **for all time** to come the
3. 5 In past **times** mankind was not told this secret, but God
3.10 order that at the present **time,** by means of the church,
3.21 church and in Christ Jesus **for all time,** for ever and ever!
6. 3 and you may live a **long time** in the land."
6.16 **At all times** carry faith as a shield;
Phil 1.20 my duty, but that **at all times,** and especially just now,
1 Thes 4.17 who are living at that **time** will be gathered up along with
5. 1 to you, brothers, about the **times** and occasions when these things
5.15 wrong for wrong, but **at all times** make it your aim to
5.17 pray **at all times,** [18]be thankful in all circumstances.
2 Thes 1. 3 Our brothers, we must thank God **at all times** for you.
2. 6 At the proper **time,** then, the Wicked One will appear.
2.13 We must thank God **at all times** for you, brothers,
3.16 give you peace **at all times** and in every way.
1 Tim 2. 6 the proof at the right **time** that God wants everyone to be
4. 1 clearly that some people will abandon the faith in later **times;**
4.13 Until I come, give your **time** and effort to the public
6.15 brought about at the right **time** by God, the blessed and only
2 Tim 1. 9 before the beginning of **time,** [10]but now it has been revealed
3. 1 Remember that there will be difficult **times** in the last days.
4. 2 proclaiming it (whether the **time** is right or not), to convince,
4. 3 The **time** will come when people will not listen to sound doctrine,
4. 6 the **time** is here for me to leave this life.
Tit 1. 2 life before the beginning of **time,**
1. 3 and at the right **time** he revealed it in his message.
3. 8 be concerned with giving their **time** to doing good deeds,
3.14 must learn to spend their **time** doing good, in order to
Phlm 15 short time so that you might have him back **for all time.**
Heb 4. 3 work had been finished from the **time** he created the world.
5.12 There has been enough **time** for you to be teachers—yet
9. 5 But now is not the **time** to explain everything in detail.
9. 9 This is an illustration which points to the present **time.**
9.26 now when all ages of **time** are nearing the end, he has
11. 2 by their faith that people of ancient **times** won God's approval.
11.32 There isn't enough **time** for me to speak of Gideon, Barak,
12.11 seems to us at the **time** something to make us sad, not
13.18 because we want to do the right thing **at all times.**
1 Pet 1. 5 salvation which is ready to be revealed at the end of **time.**
1.11 to find out when the **time** would be and how it would
1.11 This was the **time** to which Christ's Spirit in them was pointing,
3.10 and wishes to see good **times,** must keep from speaking evil
3.15 Be ready **at all times** to answer anyone who asks you to
4.17 The **time** has come for judgement to begin, and God's own
5. 6 so that he will lift you up in his own good **time.**
2 Pet 1.15 you to remember these matters **at all times** after my death.
2. 3 **For a long time** now their Judge has been ready, and their
Rev 1. 3 For the **time** is near when all these things will happen.
2.21 I have given her **time** to repent of her sins, but she
3. 3 and you will not even know the **time** when I will come.
3.10 keep you safe from the **time** of trouble which is coming upon
11.18 filled with rage, because the **time** for your anger has come,
11.18 the **time** for the dead to be judged.
11.18 The **time** has come to reward your servants, the prophets, and
11.18 The **time** has come to destroy those who destroy the earth!"
12.12 because he knows that he has only a little **time** left."
14. 7 For the **time** has come for him to judge mankind.
14.15 "Use your sickle and reap the harvest, because the **time** has come;
19. 7 For the **time** has come for the wedding of the Lamb,
22.10 book a secret, because the **time** is near when all this will

TIMID

Is 19.16 coming when the people of Egypt will be as **timid** as women.
2 Cor 11.21 ashamed to admit that we were too **timid** to do those things!
1 Thes 5.14 warn the idle, encourage the **timid,** help the weak, be patient
2 Tim 1. 7 the Spirit that God has given us does not make us **timid;**

TIMOTHY

Paul's companion on his journeys who had a Gentile father and a Jewish mother.

Acts 16. 1 to Derbe and Lystra, where a Christian named **Timothy** lived.
16. 2 All the believers in Lystra and Iconium spoke well of **Timothy.**
16. 3 Paul wanted to take **Timothy** along with him, so he circumcised
16. 3 who lived in those places knew that **Timothy's** father was Greek.
17.14 but both Silas and **Timothy** stayed in Berea.
17.15 from Paul that Silas and **Timothy** should join him as soon as
17.16 in Athens for Silas and **Timothy,** he was greatly upset when
18. 5 Silas and **Timothy** arrived from Macedonia, Paul gave his whole
19.22 he sent **Timothy** and Erastus, two of his helpers, to Macedonia,
20. 4 and **Timothy.**
Rom 16.21 **Timothy,** my fellow-worker, sends you his greetings;
1 Cor 4.17 I am sending to you **Timothy,** who is my own dear
16.10 If **Timothy** comes your way, be sure to make him feel
2 Cor 1. 1 and from our brother **Timothy**— To the church of God
1.19 preached among you by Silas, **Timothy,** and myself, is not one
Phil 1. 1 From Paul and **Timothy,** servants of Christ Jesus— To all
2.19 will be able to send **Timothy** to you soon, so that I
Col 1. 1 and from our brother **Timothy**— [2]To God's people in Colossae,
1 Thes 1. 1 From Paul, Silas, and **Timothy**— To the people of the church
3. 2 in Athens [2]while we sent **Timothy,** our brother who works
3. 5 That is why I had to send **Timothy.**
3. 6 Now **Timothy** has come back, and he has brought us the
2 Thes 1. 1 From Paul, Silas, and **Timothy**— To the people of the church
1 Tim 1. 2 Jesus our hope— [2]To **Timothy,** my true son in the faith:
1.18 **Timothy,** my child, I entrust to you this command, which
6.20 **Timothy,** keep safe what has been entrusted to your care.
2 Tim 1. 2 have in union with Christ Jesus— [2]To **Timothy,** my dear son:
Phlm 1 and from our brother **Timothy**— To our friend and fellow-worker
Heb 13.23 to know that our brother **Timothy** has been let out of prison.

TIN

Num 31.22 as gold, silver, bronze, iron, **tin,** or lead, is to be
Ezek 22.18 like the waste metal—copper, **tin,** iron, and lead—left over
22.20 copper, iron, lead, and **tin** is put in a refining furnace.
27.12 Spain and took silver, iron, **tin,** and lead in payment for

TINY

Is 11.15 the Euphrates, leaving only seven **tiny** streams, so that
40.22 the people below look as **tiny** as ants.
Jas 3. 5 large a forest can be set on fire by a **tiny** flame!

TIP (1)

Esth 5. 2 She then came up and touched the **tip** of it.
Ezek 1. 9 the creatures formed a square with their wing **tips** touching.
1.11 so that they touched the **tips** of the wings of the creatures

TIP (2)

Jer 1.13 in the north, and it is about to **tip** over this way."

TIRED

Gen 27.46 to Isaac, "I am sick and **tired** of Esau's foreign wives.
Ex 17.12 When Moses' arms grew **tired,** Aaron and Hur brought a

Deut	25.18	the rear when you were **tired** and exhausted, and killed all
Judg	4.21	Sisera was so **tired** that he fell sound asleep.
	16.16	He got so sick and **tired** of her nagging him about it
1 Sam	30.10	two hundred men were too **tired** to cross the brook and so
2 Sam	16. 2	for them to drink when they get **tired** in the wilderness."
	17. 2	I will attack him while he is **tired** and discouraged.
	17.28	men would be hungry, thirsty, and **tired** in the wilderness.
	21.15	During one of the battles David grew **tired.**
Job	3.17	men stop their evil, and **tired** workmen find rest at last.
	4. 4	When someone stumbled, weak and **tired,** your words encouraged him
	7.16	I am **tired** of living.
	10. 1	I am **tired** of living.
	22. 7	water to those who were **tired,** and refused to feed those who
Ps	31. 9	my eyes are **tired** from so much crying;
	119.82	My eyes are **tired** from watching for what you promised,
	119.123	My eyes are **tired** from watching for your saving help,
Prov	25.17	he may get **tired** of you and come to hate you.
Is	1.11	I am **tired** of the blood of bulls and sheep and goats.
	1.14	they are a burden that I am **tired** of bearing.
	5.27	None of them grows **tired;**
	35. 3	strength to hands that are **tired** and to knees that tremble
	38.14	My eyes grew **tired** from looking to heaven.
	40.28	He never grows **tired** or weary.
	40.29	He strengthens those who are weak and **tired.**
	43.22	"But you were **tired** of me, Israel;
	44.12	As he works, he gets hungry, thirsty, and **tired.**
	46. 1	loaded on donkeys, a burden for the backs of **tired** animals.
Jer	12. 5	"Jeremiah, if you get **tired** racing against men, how can you
	15. 6	crushed you because I was **tired** of controlling my anger.
Lam	5. 5	donkeys or camels, we are **tired,** but are allowed no rest.
Ezek	23.22	You are **tired** of those lovers, but I will make them angry
Mal	1.13	You say, 'How **tired** we are of all this!'
	2.17	You have **tired** the Lord out with your talk.
	2.17	But you ask, "How have we **tired** him?"
Mt	11.28	all of you who are **tired** from carrying heavy loads, and I
Jn	4. 6	well was there, and Jesus, **tired** out by the journey, sat
Gal	6. 9	So let us not become **tired** of doing good;
2 Thes	3.13	But you, brothers, must not get **tired** of doing good.
Heb	12.12	Lift up your **tired** hands, then, and strengthen your trembling knees!

TIRZAH (1)

City in the n. kingdom (Israel), Jeroboam's capital.

Josh	12.24	(on the coast), Goiim (in Galilee), [24]and **Tirzah**—thirty-one kings in all.
1 Kgs	14.17	Jeroboam's wife went back to **Tirzah.**
	15.21	happened, he stopped fortifying Ramah and went to **Tirzah.**
	15.33	of all Israel, and he ruled in **Tirzah** for twenty-four years,
	16. 6	died and was buried in **Tirzah,** and his son Elah succeeded
	16. 8	became king of Israel, and he ruled in **Tirzah** for two years.
	16. 9	One day in **Tirzah,** Elah was getting drunk in the home of
	16.15	Asa of Judah, Zimri ruled in **Tirzah** over Israel for seven days.
	16.17	Omri and his troops left Gibbethon and went and besieged **Tirzah.**
	16.23	six years he ruled in **Tirzah,** [24]and then he bought the
2 Kgs	15.14	of Gadi went from **Tirzah** to Samaria, assassinated Shallum,
	15.16	was on his way from **Tirzah,** he completely destroyed the city
Song	6. 4	the city of **Tirzah,** as breathtaking as these great cities.

TITHE

A tenth part of a person's crops or income, given to God.
see also **TEN**

Num	18.21	given to the Levites every **tithe** that the people of Israel
	18.24	them as their possession the **tithe** which the Israelites
	18.26	receive from the Israelites the **tithe** that the Lord gives
	18.28	Lord from all the **tithes** which you receive from the Israelites.
Deut	12. 6	and your other sacrifices, your **tithes** and your offerings,
	12.11	and your other sacrifices, your **tithes** and your offerings,
	12.17	the **tithes** of your corn, your wine, or your olive-oil,
	14.22	"Set aside a **tithe**—a tenth of all that your fields
	14.23	in his presence eat the **tithes** of your corn, wine, and
	14.24	you to carry there the **tithe** of the produce that the Lord
	14.28	every third year bring the **tithe** of all your crops and store
	26.12	"Every third year give the **tithe**—a tenth of your
	26.13	the Lord, 'None of the sacred **tithe** is left in my house;
	26.13	or forgotten any of your commands concerning the **tithe.**
	26.14	I have done everything you commanded concerning the **tithe.**
2 Chr	31. 5	and they also brought the **tithes** of everything they had.
	31. 6	cities of Judah brought **tithes** of their cattle and sheep,
	31.12	and put all the gifts and **tithes** in them for safe-keeping.
Neh	10.37	to the Levites, who collect **tithes** in our farming villages,
	10.37	the **tithes** from the crops that grow on
	10.38	be with the Levites when **tithes** are collected, and for use
	10.38	temple storerooms one tenth of all the **tithes** they collect.
	12.44	Temple were kept, including the **tithes** and the first corn
	13. 5	for the priests, and the **tithes** of corn, wine, and olive-oil
	13.12	bringing to the temple storerooms their **tithes** of corn,
Amos	4. 4	after morning, and bring your **tithes** every third day.
Mal	3. 8	In the matter of **tithes** and offerings.
	3.10	the full amount of your **tithes** to the Temple, so that there

TITLE

Lk	22.25	and the rulers claim the **title** 'Friends of the People.'
Eph	1.21	a title superior to all **titles** of authority in this world

TITUS

Paul's companion and a missionary to Crete.

2 Cor	2.13	I was deeply worried, because I could not find our brother **Titus.**
	7. 6	encourages the downhearted, encouraged us with the coming of **Titus.**
	7.13	how happy **Titus** made us with his happiness over the way in
	7.14	the same way the boast we made to **Titus** has proved true.
	8. 6	So we urged **Titus,** who began this work, to continue it
	8.16	we thank God for making **Titus** as eager as we are
	8.23	As for **Titus,** he is my partner and works with me
	12.18	I begged **Titus** to go, and I sent the other Christian
	12.18	Would you say that **Titus** took advantage of you?
Gal	2. 1	went back to Jerusalem with Barnabas, taking **Titus** along with me.
	2. 3	My companion **Titus,** even though he is Greek, was not
2 Tim	4.10	Crescens went to Galatia, and **Titus** to Dalmatia.
Tit	1. 4	I write to **Titus,** my true son in the faith

TO AND FRO

Ex	9.24	a heavy hailstorm, with lightning flashing **to and fro.**
Esth	2.11	day Mordecai would walk **to and fro** in front of the courtyard
Is	16. 2	Arnon and move aimlessly **to and fro,** like birds driven from
	19.23	two countries will travel **to and fro** between them, and the
Jer	4.24	were shaking, and the hills were rocking **to and fro.**
Ezek	1.14	The creatures themselves darted **to and fro**
Nah	2. 4	the streets, rushing **to and fro** through the city squares.

TOBIAH (1)

One of Nehemiah's chief opponents.

Neh	2.10	town of Beth Horon, and **Tobiah,** an official in the province
	2.19	When Sanballat, **Tobiah,** and an Arab named Geshem heard
	4. 3	**Tobiah** was standing there beside him, and he added, "What
	4. 7	Sanballat, **Tobiah,** and the people of Arabia, Ammon, and
	6. 1	Sanballat, **Tobiah,** Geshem, and the rest of our enemies
	6.12	spoken to Shemaiah, but that **Tobiah** and Sanballat had bribed
	6.14	I prayed, "God, remember what **Tobiah** and Sanballat have
	6.17	the Jewish leaders had been in correspondence with **Tobiah.**
	6.19	about all the good deeds **Tobiah** had done and would tell him
	13. 4	had for a long time been on good terms with **Tobiah.**
	13. 5	He allowed **Tobiah** to use a large room that was intended
	13. 7	find that Eliashib had allowed **Tobiah** to use a room
	13. 8	I was furious and threw out all **Tobiah's** belongings.

TODAY

Gen	22.14	even **today** people say, "On the Lord's mountain he provides."
	24.12	master Abraham, give me success **today** and keep your promise
	24.42	I came to the well **today,** I prayed, 'Lord, God of my
	30.32	go through all your flocks **today** and take every black lamb
	32.32	Even **today** the descendants of Israel do not eat the
	40. 7	He asked them, "Why do you look so worried **today?"**
	41. 9	to the king, "I must confess **today** that I have done wrong.
	47.26	This law still remains in force **today.**
	50.20	of many people who are alive **today** because of what happened.
Ex	2.18	he asked, "Why have you come back so early **today?"**
	14.13	you will see what the Lord will do to save you **today;**
	16.23	Bake **today** what you want to bake and boil what you want
	16.25	said, "Eat this today, because **today** is the Sabbath, a day
	19.10	spend **today** and tomorrow purifying themselves for worship.
	32.29	Moses said to the Levites, **"Today** you have consecrated
	34.11	Obey the laws that I am giving you **today.**
Lev	8.34	do what we have done **today,** in order to take away your
	9. 4	They must do this because the Lord will appear to them **today."**
	10.19	"If I had eaten the sin-offering **today,** would the Lord have
	10.19	to the Lord **today,** and they brought their burnt-offering,
Deut	2.18	the Lord said to us, [18]**'Today** you are to pass through
	2.25	From **today** on I will make people everywhere afraid of you.
	4. 4	were faithful to the Lord your God are still alive **today.**
	4. 8	has laws so just as those that I have taught you **today.**
	4.20	you out to make you his own people, as you are **today.**
	4.26	as witnesses against you **today** that, if you disobey me,
	4.39	So remember **today** and never forget:
	4.40	that I have given you **today,** and all will go well with
	5. 1	Israel, listen to all the laws that I am giving you **today.**
	5. 3	with our fathers, but with all of us who are living **today.**
	5.24	**Today** we have seen that it is possible for a man to
	6. 6	Never forget these commands that I am giving you **today.**
	7.11	obey all the laws that I have given you **today.**
	8. 1	that I have given you **today,** so that you may live, increase
	8.11	to obey any of his laws that I am giving you **today.**
	8.18	because he is still faithful **today** to the covenant that he
	8.19	then I warn you **today** that you will certainly be destroyed.
	9. 1	**Today** you are about to cross the River Jordan and occupy the
	10.13	I am giving them to you **today** for your benefit.
	11. 2	Remember **today** what you have learned about the Lord
	11. 8	"Obey all the laws that I have given you **today.**
	11.13	"So then, obey the commands that I have given you **today;**
	11.26	**"Today** I am giving you the choice between a blessing
	11.27	commands of the Lord your God that I am giving you **today;**
	11.32	sure to obey all the laws that I am giving you **today.**
	13.18	that I have given you **today,** and do what he requires.
	15. 5	and carefully observe everything that I command you **today.**
	19. 9	everything that I command you **today** and if you love the Lord
	20. 3	**Today** you are going into battle.
	26.16	**"Today** the Lord your God commands you to obey all his laws;
	26.17	**Today** you have acknowledged the Lord as your God;
	26.18	**Today** the Lord has accepted you as his own people, as he
	27. 1	"Obey all the instructions that I am giving you **today.**

Deut 27. 4 as I am instructing you **today,** and cover them with plaster.
27. 9 **Today** you have become the people of the Lord your God;
27.10 him and keep all his laws that I am giving you **today."**
28. 1 that I am giving you **today,** he will make you greater than
28.13 obey faithfully all his commands that I am giving you **today.**
28.15 that I am giving you **today,** all these evil things will
29.10 **"Today** you are standing in the presence of the Lord
29.12 You are here **today** to enter into this covenant that the
29.15 stand here in his presence **today** and also with our
29.18 family, or tribe standing here **today** turns from the Lord our
29.19 there is no one here **today** who hears these solemn demands
29.28 threw them into a foreign land, and there they are **today.'**
30. 2 that I am giving you **today,** [3]then the Lord your God will
30. 8 him and keep all his commands that I am giving you **today.**
30.11 that I am giving you **today** is not too difficult or beyond
30.15 **"Today** I am giving you a choice between good and evil,
30.16 God, which I give you **today,** if you love him, obey him,
32.46 you obey all these commands that I have given you **today.**
Josh 3. 7 to Joshua, "What I do **today** will make all the people of
5. 9 The Lord said to Joshua, **"Today** I have removed from you
8.28 It is still like that **today.**
8.29 it with a huge pile of stones, which is still there **today.**
14.11 and I'm just as strong **today** as I was when Moses sent
22.18 you rebel against the Lord **today,** he will be angry with
24.15 willing to serve him, decide **today** whom you will serve, the
Judg 4.14 **Today** he has given you victory over Sisera."
9.18 But **today** you turned against my father's family.
9.19 then, if what you did **today** to Gideon and his family was
10.15 Do whatever you like, but please, save us **today."**
11.27 He will decide **today** between the Israelites and the Ammonites."
21. 6 brothers the Benjaminites and said, **"Today** Israel has lost
Ruth 3.18 Boaz will not rest **today** until he settles the matter."
4. 9 there, "You are all witnesses **today** that I have bought from
4.10 You are witnesses to this **today."**
4.14 He has given you a grandson **today** to take care of you.
1 Sam 4. 3 "Why did the Lord let the Philistines defeat us **today?**
4.16 from the battle and have run all the way here **today."**
5. 5 (That is why even **today** the priests of Dagon and all his
9.12 He arrived in town **today** because the people are going to
9.19 Both of you are to eat with me **today.**
10. 2 When you leave me **today,** you will meet two men near
10.19 your troubles and difficulties, but **today** you have rejected
11.13 will be put to death **today,** for this is the day the
12. 5 he has chosen are witnesses **today** that you have found me to
14.24 anyone who eats any food **today** before I take revenge on my
14.28 said, 'A curse be on anyone who eats any food **today.' "**
14.30 better it would have been **today** if our people had eaten the
14.38 "Come here and find out what sin was committed **today.**
14.41 God of Israel, "Lord, why have you not answered me **today?**
14.45 What he did **today** was done with God's help."
15.28 of Israel away from you **today** and given it to someone who
20.27 "Why didn't David come to the meal either yesterday or **today?"**
24.18 **Today** you have shown how good you are to me, because you
24.19 The Lord bless you for what you have done to me **today!**
25.32 Lord, the God of Israel, who sent you **today** to meet me!
25.33 for what you have done **today** in keeping me from the crime
26.23 **Today** he put you in my power, but I did not harm
26.24 I have spared your life **today,** may the Lord do the same
2 Sam 3. 8 yet **today** you find fault with me about a woman!
3.39 though I am the king chosen by God, I feel weak **today.**
4. 8 **Today** the Lord has allowed Your Majesty to take revenge on
6.20 "The king of Israel made a big name for himself **today!"**
18.20 "No," Joab said, **"today** you will not take any good news.
18.20 may do so, but not **today,** for the king's son is dead."
18.31 **Today** the Lord has given you victory over all who rebelled
19. 5 house and said to him, **"Today** you have humiliated your
19. 6 happy if Absalom were alive **today** and all of us were dead.
19.20 the northern tribes to come and meet Your Majesty **today."**
19.22 Israel now, and no Israelite will be put to death **today."**
1 Kgs 1.30 from all my troubles, [30]that **today** I will keep the promise
1.48 God of Israel, who has **today** made one of my descendants
3. 6 love by giving him a son who **today** rules in his place.
5. 7 he said, "Praise the Lord **today** for giving David such a
8. 8 (The poles are still there **today.)**
8.24 **today** every word has been fulfilled.
8.28 to my prayer, and grant the requests I make to you **today.**
8.61 God, obeying all his laws and commands, as you do **today."**
18.15 I promise that I will present myself to the king **today."**
20.13 give you victory over it **today,** and you will know that I
2 Kgs 2. 3 Lord is going to take your master away from you **today?"**
2. 5 Lord is going to take your master away from you **today?"**
4.23 "Why do you have to go **today?"**
10.27 turned the temple into a latrine—which it still is **today.**
19. 3 **"Today** is a day of suffering;
2 Chr 5. 9 (The poles are still there **today.)**
6.15 **today** every word has been fulfilled.
Ezra 9. 7 We have been totally disgraced, as we still are **today.**
Neh 1.11 Give me success **today** and make the emperor merciful to me."
4.10 How can we build the wall **today?"**
8.10 **Today** is holy to our Lord, so don't be sad.
9.10 You won then the fame you still have **today.**
Esth 9.13 Susa do again tomorrow what they were allowed to do **today.**
Ps 2. 7 **today** I have become your father.
95. 7 Listen **today** to what he says:
Prov 7.14 said, [14]"I made my offerings **today** and have the meat from
Is 10.32 **Today** the enemy are in the town of Nob, and there they
37. 3 **"Today** is a day of suffering;
56.12 Tomorrow will be even better than **today!" "**
Jer 1.10 **Today** I give you authority over nations and kingdoms to
1.18 But **today** I am giving you the strength to resist them;
44. 6 in ruins and became a horrifying sight, as they are **today.**
Jer 46.10 **today** he will take revenge;
46.10 **today** he will punish his enemies.
46.10 **Today** the Almighty sacrifices his victims in the north,
Ezek 20.31 Even **today** you offer the same gifts and defile
24. 2 man," he said, "write down **today's** date, because this is
Hag 2.18 **Today** is the twenty-fourth day of the ninth month, the
Mt 6.11 Give us **today** the food we need.
6.30 grass that is here **today** and gone tomorrow, burnt up in
11.23 performed in Sodom, it would still be in existence **today!**
21.28 one and said, 'Son, go and work in the vineyard **today.'**
Lk 4.21 scripture has come true **today,** as you heard it being read."
5.26 praised God, saying, "What marvellous things we have seen **today!"**
11.31 and accuse the people of **today,** because she travelled all
12.28 grass that is here **today** and gone tomorrow, burnt up in
13.32 out demons and performing cures **today** and tomorrow, and on the
13.33 I must be on my way **today,** tomorrow, and the next day;
19. 5 "Hurry down, Zacchaeus, because I must stay in your house **today."**
19. 9 has come to this house **today,** for this man, also, is
19.42 saying, "If you only knew **today** what is needed for peace!
23.43 "I promise you that **today** you will be in Paradise with
Acts 4. 9 if we are being questioned **today** about the good deed done
13.32 **today** I have become your Father.'
13.41 For what I am doing **today** is something that you will not
19.40 For after what has happened **today,** there is the danger that
22. 3 dedicated to God as are all of you who are here **today.**
24.21 am being tried by you **today** for believing that the dead will
26. 2 I consider myself fortunate that **today** I am to defend myself
26.16 you have seen of me **today** and what I will show you
26.29 who are listening to me **today** might become what I am—except,
2 Cor 3.15 Even **today,** whenever they read the Law of Moses, the veil
6. 2 **today** is the day to be saved!
Heb 1. 5 **today** I have become your Father."
3. 7 "If you hear God's voice **today,** [8]do not be stubborn, as
3.13 long as the word **"Today"** in the scripture applies to us.
3.15 "If you hear God's voice **today,** do not be stubborn, as
4. 7 fact that God sets another day, which is called **"Today."**
4. 7 "If you hear God's voice **today,** do not be stubborn."
5. 5 **today** I have become your Father."
13. 8 Jesus Christ is the same yesterday, **today,** and for ever.
Jas 4.13 to me, you that say, **"Today** or tomorrow we will travel to

TOE

Ex 29.20 their right hands and on the big **toes** of their right feet.
Lev 8.23 his right hand, and on the big **toe** of his right foot.
8.24 their right hands, and on the big **toes** of their right feet.
14.14 hand, and on the big **toe** of the right foot of the
14.17 hand, and on the big **toe** of the right foot of the
14.25 his right hand, and on the big **toe** of his right foot.
14.28 his right hand, and on the big **toe** of his right foot.
Judg 1. 6 chased him, caught him, and cut off his thumbs and big **toes.**
1. 7 with their thumbs and big **toes** cut off have picked up scraps
2 Sam 21.20 had six fingers on each hand and six **toes** on each foot.
1 Chr 20. 6 with six fingers on each hand and six **toes** on each foot.
Dan 2.41 that the feet and the **toes** were partly clay and partly iron.
2.42 The **toes**—partly iron and partly clay—mean that part of

TOGETHER

Gen 1. 9 water below the sky come **together** in one place, so that the
1.10 and the water which had come **together** he named "Sea."
3. 7 so they sewed fig leaves **together** and covered themselves.
11. 3 they had bricks to build with and tar to hold them **together.**
13. 6 of them to stay **together,** because they had too many animals.
14.14 had been captured, he called **together** all the fighting men
22. 6 As they walked along **together,** [7]Isaac said, "Father!"
22. 8 And the two of them walked on **together.**
22.19 and they went **together** to Beersheba, where Abraham settled.
29. 3 Whenever all the flocks came **together** there, the shepherds
34.30 if they all band **together** against me and attack me, our
36. 7 had too much livestock and could no longer stay **together.**
49. 2 "Come **together** and listen, sons of Jacob.
Ex 3.16 gather the leaders of Israel **together** and tell them that I,
4.29 went to Egypt and gathered all the Israelite leaders **together.**
19. 7 the leaders of the people **together** and told them everything
19. 8 Then all the people answered **together,** "We will do
24. 3 and all the people answered **together,** "We will do
24.11 they saw God, and then they ate and drank **together.**
26. 3 Sew five of them **together** in one set, and do the same
26. 9 Sew five of them **together** in one set, and the other six
26.17 matching projections, so that the frames can be joined **together.**
35. 1 Moses called **together** the whole community of the people of
36.10 They sewed five of them **together** in one set and did the
36.16 They sewed five of them **together** in one set and the
36.22 matching projections, so that the frames could be joined **together.**
Lev 8. 3 Then call the whole community **together** there."
23.23 rest, and come **together** for worship when the trumpets sound.
23.26 **together** for worship, and present a food-offering
23.35 first of these days come **together** for worship and do none of
23.36 On the eighth day come **together** again for worship and
23.37 Lord by gathering **together** for worship
Num 1.18 men Moses and Aaron [18]called **together** the whole community
10. 2 use for calling the people **together** and for breaking camp.
10. 7 call the community **together,** long blasts are to be sounded.
14.35 to you wicked people who have gathered **together** against me.
21.16 "Bring the people **together,** and I will give them water."
26. 3 and Eleazar obeyed, and called **together** all the men of that
Deut 5. 1 Moses called **together** all the people of Israel and said
13.16 Bring **together** all the possessions of the people who

Deut 19. 5 men go into the forest **together** to cut wood and if, as
22.10 "Do not hitch an ox and a donkey **together** for ploughing.
22.11 "Do not wear cloth made by weaving wool and linen **together.**
29. 2 Moses called **together** all the people of Israel and said
30. 4 your God will gather you **together** and bring you back, [5]so
31.12 Call **together** all the men, women, and children, and the
33. 5 Israel when their tribes and leaders were gathered **together.**
33.21 and laws When the leaders of Israel were gathered **together."**
Josh 2.18 and all your father's family **together** in your house.
8.10 in the morning Joshua got up and called the soldiers **together.**
8.16 the city had been called **together** to go after them, and as
9. 2 They all came **together** and joined forces to fight against
11. 5 kings joined forces and came **together** and set up camp at
22. 1 Then Joshua called **together** the people of the tribes of Reuben,
22.12 this, the whole community came **together** at Shiloh to go to
24. 1 Joshua gathered all the tribes of Israel **together** at Shechem.
Judg 1. 3 assigned to us, and we will fight the Canaanites **together.**
1. 4 So the tribes of Simeon [4]and Judah went into battle **together.**
1.17 the people of Simeon, and **together** they defeated the
7.24 men of Ephraim were called **together,** and they held the River
9. 6 of Shechem and Bethmillo got **together** and went to the sacred
9. 8 time the trees got **together** to choose a king for themselves.
10.17 The men of Israel came **together** and camped at Mizpah in Gilead.
11.20 He brought his whole army **together,** made camp at Jahaz, and
12. 4 all the men of Gilead **together,** fought the men of Ephraim
15. 4 he tied their tails **together** and put torches in the knots.
16.23 The Philistine kings met **together** to celebrate and
19. 6 So the two men sat down and ate and drank **together.**
19. 8 So the two men ate **together.**
20. 8 All the people stood up **together** and said, "None of us,
Ruth 1. 7 They started out **together** to go back to Judah, but on the
1 Sam 5. 8 they sent messengers and called **together** all five of the
8. 4 the leaders of Israel met **together,** went to Samuel in Ramah,
9.26 got up, and he and Samuel went out to the street **together.**
10.17 Samuel called the people **together** for a religious
11. 7 and all of them, without exception, came out **together.**
15. 4 Saul called his forces **together** and inspected them at Telem:
25. 1 Samuel died, and all the Israelites came **together** and mourned
29. 1 Philistines brought all their troops **together** at Aphek,
2 Sam 1.23 **together** in life, together in death;
2.16 so that all twenty-four of them fell down dead **together.**
6. 1 Once more David called **together** the best soldiers in Israel,
10.15 by the Israelites, so they called all their troops **together.**
15.23 his men, and **together** they went out towards the wilderness.
17.11 you bring all the Israelites **together** from one end of the
18. 1 David brought all his men **together,** divided them into units
20. 4 "Call the men of Judah **together** and be back here with them
21. 9 before the Lord—and all seven of them died **together.**
1 Kgs 5. 9 sea, and will tie them **together** in rafts to float them down
12. 3 and then they all went **together** to Rehoboam and said to him,
12.21 arrived in Jerusalem, he called **together** 180,000 of the best
21. 9 of fasting, call the people **together,** and give Naboth the
21.12 of fasting, called the people **together,** and gave Naboth the
2 Kgs 4.30 So the two of them started back **together.**
6. 4 he agreed, [4]and they set out **together.**
9.25 and I were riding **together** behind King Joram's father
10.16 And they rode on **together** to Samaria.
10.18 called the people of Samaria **together** and said, "King Ahab
10.19 Call **together** all the prophets of Baal, all his worshippers,
23. 2 Judah and Jerusalem, [2]and **together** they went to the Temple,
1 Chr 10. 6 his three sons all died **together** and none of his descendants
16.35 gather us **together;**
23. 2 King David brought **together** all the Israelite leaders and
29.16 our God, we have brought **together** all this wealth to build a
2 Chr 2.16 cedars you need, bind them **together** in rafts, and float them
10. 3 him, and they all went **together** to Rehoboam and said to him,
11. 1 arrived in Jerusalem, he called **together** a hundred and
13. 7 Later he gathered **together** a group of worthless scoundrels,
29.20 men of the city, and **together** they went to the Temple.
30. 5 in the south, to come **together** in Jerusalem and celebrate
34.30 Judah and Jerusalem, [30]and **together** they went to the Temple,
Ezra 3. 9 (the clan of Hodaviah) joined **together** in taking charge of
Neh 4. 8 So they all plotted **together** to come and attack Jerusalem
6.10 I must go and hide **together** in the Holy Place of the
Esth 4.16 "Go and gather all the Jews in Susa **together;**
9.15 the Jews of Susa got **together** again and killed three hundred
Job 30. 7 howled like animals and huddled **together** under the bushes.
38. 7 that day the stars sang **together,** and the heavenly beings
38.31 Can you tie the Pleiades **together** or loosen the bonds
41.15 of rows of shields, fastened **together** and hard as stone.
41.17 all are fastened so firmly **together** that nothing can ever
Ps 2. 2 kings revolt, their rulers plot **together** against the Lord
7. 7 you demand, [7]so bring **together** all the peoples round you,
34. 3 let us praise his name **together!**
48. 4 The kings gathered **together** and came to attack Mount Zion.
49. 2 great and small alike, rich and poor **together.**
55.14 with each other and worshipped **together** in the Temple.
98. 8 you hills, sing **together** with joy before the Lord,
102.22 when nations and kingdoms come **together** and worship the Lord.
133. 1 how pleasant, for God's people to live **together** in harmony!
139.13 you put me **together** in my mother's womb.
139.15 being formed, carefully put **together** in my mother's womb,
Prov 1.21 at the city gates and wherever people come **together:**
18. 3 Sin and shame go **together.**
Ecc 4. 9 than one, because **together** they can work more effectively.
4.11 is cold, two can sleep **together** and stay warm, but how can
Song 1. 4 We will be happy **together,** drink deep, and lose ourselves in love.
Is 8. 9 Gather **together** in fear, you nations!
9.21 Ephraim attack each other, and **together** they attack Judah.
11. 6 Wolves and sheep will live **together** in peace, and leopards
11. 6 and lion cubs will feed **together,** and little children will
Is 11. 7 Cows and bears will eat **together,** and their calves and
11.12 nations that he is gathering **together** again the scattered
11.14 **Together** they will attack the Philistines on the west
19.23 fro between them, and the two nations will worship **together.**
24.22 God will crowd kings **together** like prisoners in a pit.
34.16 he himself will bring them **together.**
40.11 he will gather the lambs **together** and carry them in his arms;
41. 1 Let us come **together** to decide who is right.
41. 7 the idol smooth encourages the one who nails it **together.**
45.20 "Come **together,** people of the nations, all who survive the
50. 8 Let us go to court **together!**
52. 8 who guard the city are shouting, shouting **together** for joy!
65.25 Wolves and lambs will eat **together;**
66.18 When they come **together,** they will see what my power can do
Jer 3.18 will join with Judah, and **together** they will come from exile
19.11 like this broken clay jar that cannot be put **together** again.
41. 1 were all eating a meal **together,** [2]Ishmael and the ten men
42. 8 so I called **together** Johanan, all the army leaders who
49. 5 there will be no one to bring your troops **together** again.
Lam 1.14 "He took note of all my sins and tied them all **together;**
2. 8 The towers and walls now lie in ruins **together.**
Ezek 3.13 wings of the creatures beating **together** in the air, and the
4. 9 Mix them all **together** and make bread.
10.11 They all moved **together** in the direction they wanted to go,
16.37 bring all your former lovers **together**—the ones you liked and
20.34 anger when I gather you **together** and bring you back from all
20.41 been scattered and gather you **together,** I will accept the
22.19 I will bring them all **together** in Jerusalem [20]in the same
34.12 sheep that were scattered and are brought **together** again.
34.13 of foreign countries, gather them **together,** and bring them
37. 7 I heard a rattling noise, and the bones began to join **together.**
37.21 they have gone, gather them **together,** and bring them back to
38. 8 the people were brought back **together** from many nations and
Dan 3. 2 come **together**—the princes, governors,
5. 1 noblemen to a great banquet, and they drank wine **together.**
6.12 all of them went **together** to the king to accuse Daniel.
Hos 8.10 But now I am going to gather them **together** and punish them.
10.10 Nations will join **together** against them, and they will be
Joel 2.16 Gather the people **together;**
Amos 3. 3 Do two men start travelling **together** without arranging to meet?
3. 9 "Gather **together** in the hills surrounding Samaria and see
Mic 2.12 "But I will gather you **together,** all you people of
2.12 I will bring you **together** like sheep returning to the fold.
4. 6 Lord, "when I will gather **together** the people I punished,
4.12 that they have been gathered **together** to be punished in the
7. 3 man tells them what he wants, and so they scheme **together.**
Zech 6.13 throne, and they will work **together** in peace and harmony.'
10. 8 "I will call my people and gather them **together.**
10. 9 They and their children will survive and return home **together.**
14. 2 will bring all the nations **together** to make war on Jerusalem.
Mal 4. 6 He will bring fathers and children **together** again;
Mt 13.30 Let the wheat and the weeds both grow **together** until harvest.
17.22 the disciples all came **together** in Galilee, Jesus said to them,
18.20 where two or three come **together** in my name, I am there
19. 6 Man must not separate, then, what God has joined **together."**
22.34 silenced the Sadducees, they came **together,** [35]and one of them,
Mk 10. 9 Man must not separate, then, what God has joined **together."**
Lk 1.17 He will bring fathers and children **together** again;
15. 6 calls his friends and neighbours **together** and says to them,
15. 9 calls her friends and neighbours **together,** and says to them,
17.35 Two women will be grinding corn **together:**
Jn 4.36 man who sows and the man who reaps will be glad **together.**
11.52 but also to bring **together** into one body all the scattered
18.20 synagogues and in the Temple, where all the people come **together.**
20.26 the disciples were **together** again indoors, and Thomas was with
21. 2 of Zebedee, and two other disciples of Jesus were all **together.**
Acts 1. 4 And when they came **together,** he gave them this order:
2.44 All the believers continued **together** in close fellowship
2.46 they had their meals **together** in their homes, eating with glad
4.24 believers heard it, they all joined **together** in prayer to God:
19.34 Jew, they all shouted **together** the same thing for two hours:
23.13 There were more than forty who planned this **together.**
23.14 have taken a solemn vow **together** not to eat a thing until
Rom 15. 6 so that all of you **together** may praise with one voice the
1 Cor 3. 9 For we are partners working **together** for God, and you are
5. 3 As you meet **together,** and I meet with you in my spirit,
11.20 When you meet **together** as a group, it is not the Lord's
12.24 himself has put the body **together** in such a way as to
2 Cor 6.14 Do not try to work **together** as equals with unbelievers,
6.14 How can light and darkness live **together?**
7. 3 to us that we are always **together,** whether we live or die.
Eph 1.10 to bring all creation **together,** everything in heaven and on earth,
2.21 who holds the whole building **together** and makes it grow into
2.22 you too are being built **together** with all the others into a
4. 3 Spirit gives by means of the peace that binds you **together.**
4.13 so we shall all come **together** to that oneness in our faith
4.16 parts of the body fit **together,** and
4.16 the whole body is held **together** by every joint
4.25 we are all members **together** in the body of Christ.
Phil 1.27 you are fighting **together** for the faith of the gospel.
2.22 his father, have worked **together** for the sake of the gospel.
Col 2. 2 courage and may be drawn **together** in love, and so have the
2. 5 firmness with which you stand **together** in your faith in Christ.
2.19 body is nourished and held **together** by its joints and ligaments,
3.14 add love, which binds all things **together** in perfect unity.
1 Tim 2. 5 who brings God and mankind **together,** the man Christ Jesus,
Heb 4.12 soul and spirit meet, to where joints and marrow come **together.**
Jas 2.22 His faith and his actions worked **together;**
Rev 17.17 out his purpose by acting **together** and giving the beast their
20. 8 Satan will bring them all **together** for battle, as many as

TOIL

2 Cor 11.27 There has been work and **toil;**
Col 1.29 To get this done I **toil** and struggle, using the mighty
1 Thes 2. 9 Surely you remember, our brothers, how we worked and **toiled!**
2 Thes 3. 8 Instead, we worked and **toiled;**

TOKEN

Lev 2. 2 on the altar as a **token** that it has all been offered
2. 9 part of it as a **token** that it has all been offered
2.16 is to serve as a **token,** and also all the incense, as
5.12 handful of it as a **token** that it has all been offered
6.15 on the altar as a **token** that all of it has been
24. 7 on each row, as a **token** food-offering to the Lord to take
Num 5.26 handful of it as a **token** offering and burn it on the

TOLERATE

Ex 20. 5 because I am the Lord your God and I **tolerate** no rivals.
34.14 any other god, because I, the Lord, **tolerate** no rivals.
Num 25.11 He refused to **tolerate** the worship of any god but me, and
25.13 priests, because he did not **tolerate** any rivals to me and
Deut 4.24 he **tolerates** no rivals.
5. 9 for I am the Lord your God and I **tolerate** no rivals.
6.15 Lord your God, who is present with you, **tolerates** no rivals.
Josh 24.19 He will **tolerate** no rivals, [20]and if you leave him to
2 Chr 19. 7 Lord our God does not **tolerate** fraud or partiality or the
Esth 3. 4 wondering if he would **tolerate** Mordecai's conduct.
3. 8 so it is not in your best interests to **tolerate** them.
Ps 101. 3 a pure life in my house, [3]and will never **tolerate** evil.
101. 5 I will not **tolerate** a man who is proud and arrogant.
Prov 6.16 There are seven things that the Lord hates and cannot **tolerate:**
16.12 Kings cannot **tolerate** evil, because justice is what makes
30.21 There are four things that the earth itself cannot **tolerate:**
Ezek 44. 6 Sovereign Lord, will no longer **tolerate** the disgusting
Nah 1. 2 The Lord God **tolerates** no rivals;
Rom 2. 4 perhaps you despise his great kindness, **tolerance,** and patience.
2 Cor 11. 1 I wish you would **tolerate** me, even when I am a bit
11. 4 For you gladly **tolerate** anyone who comes to you and
11.19 You yourselves are so wise, and so you gladly **tolerate** fools!
11.20 You **tolerate** anyone who orders you about or takes advantage
Eph 4. 2 Show your love by being **tolerant** with one another.
Col 3.13 Be **tolerant** with one another and forgive one another whenever
Rev 2. 2 I know that you cannot **tolerate** evil men and that you have
2.20 you **tolerate** that woman Jezebel, who calls herself a messenger

TOMB

Gen 50. 5 would bury him in the **tomb** which he had prepared in the
Judg 8.32 and was buried in the **tomb** of his father Joash, at Ophrah,
16.31 between Zorah and Eshtaol in the **tomb** of his father Manoah.
1 Sam 10. 2 meet two men near Rachel's **tomb** at Zelzah in the territory
2 Sam 2.32 Asahel's body and buried it in the family **tomb** at Bethlehem.
4.12 and buried it in Abner's **tomb** there at Hebron.
1 Kgs 14.31 was buried in the royal **tombs** in David's City, and his son
15.24 was buried in the royal **tombs** in David's City, and his son
22.50 was buried in the royal **tombs** in David's City, and his son
2 Kgs 8.24 was buried in the royal **tombs** in David's City, and his son
9.28 chariot and buried him in the royal **tombs** in David's City.
12.20 was buried in the royal **tombs** in David's City, and his son
13.13 was buried in the royal **tombs** in Samaria, and his son
13.21 the people threw the corpse into Elisha's **tomb** and ran off.
14.16 was buried in the royal **tombs** in Samaria, and his son
14.20 a horse and was buried in the royal **tombs** in David's City.
14.29 was buried in the royal **tombs,** and his son Zechariah
15.38 was buried in the royal **tombs** in David's City, and his son
16.20 was buried in the royal **tombs** in David's City, and his son
21.26 Amon was buried in the **tomb** in the garden of Uzza, and
23.16 Then Josiah looked round and saw some **tombs** there on the hill;
23.16 looked round and saw the **tomb** of the prophet who had made
23.17 "Whose **tomb** is that?"
23.17 Bethel answered, "It is the **tomb** of the prophet who came
23.30 back to Jerusalem, where he was buried in the royal **tombs.**
2 Chr 12.16 was buried in the royal **tombs** in David's City and his son
14. 1 Abijah died and was buried in the royal **tombs** in David's City.
16.14 was buried in the rock **tomb** which he had carved out for
21. 1 was buried in the royal **tombs** in David's City and his son
21.20 They buried him in David's City, but not in the royal **tombs.**
24.16 buried him in the royal **tombs** in David's City in recognition
24.25 He was buried in David's City, but not in the royal **tombs.**
25.28 and he was buried in the royal **tombs** in David's City.
26.23 because of his disease he was not buried in the royal **tombs.**
28.27 and was buried in Jerusalem, but not in the royal **tombs.**
32.33 died and was buried in the upper section of the royal **tombs.**
35.24 There he died and was buried in the royal **tombs.**
Neh 3.16 as far as David's **tomb,** the pool, and the barracks.
Job 21.32 to his well-guarded **tomb,** [33]thousands join the funeral
Ps 88. 6 the depths of the **tomb,** into the darkest and deepest pit.
Is 14.18 lie in their magnificent **tombs,** [19]but you have no tomb,
22.16 have you to carve a **tomb** for yourself out of the rocky
65. 4 they go to caves and **tombs** to consult the spirits of the
Jer 48. 9 Set up a **tombstone** for Moab;
Ezek 32.23 her soldiers fell in battle, and their graves surround her **tomb.**
Mt 23.27 You are like whitewashed **tombs,** which look fine on the outside
23.29 You make fine **tombs** for the prophets and decorate the monuments
27.60 placed it in his own **tomb,** which he had just recently dug
27.60 a large stone across the entrance to the **tomb** and went away.
27.61 Magdalene and the other Mary were sitting there, facing the **tomb.**
27.64 Give orders, then, for his **tomb** to be carefully guarded until
Mt 27.65 "go and make the **tomb** as secure as you can."
27.66 they left and made the **tomb** secure by putting a seal on
28. 1 Mary Magdalene and the other Mary went to look at the **tomb.**
28. 8 So they left the **tomb** in a hurry, afraid and yet filled
28.11 of the soldiers guarding the **tomb** went back to the city
Mk 5. 3 man had an evil spirit in him [3]and lived among the **tombs.**
5. 5 he wandered among the **tombs** and through the hills, screaming and
15.46 and placed it in a **tomb** which had been dug out of
15.46 Then he rolled a large stone across the entrance to the **tomb.**
16. 2 Very early on Sunday morning, at sunrise, they went to the **tomb.**
16. 3 roll away the stone for us from the entrance to the **tomb?"**
16. 5 So they entered the **tomb,** where they saw a young man
16. 8 they went out and ran from the **tomb,** distressed and terrified.
Lk 11.47 make fine **tombs** for the prophets—the very prophets your ancestors
11.48 they murdered the prophets, and you build their **tombs.**
23.53 and placed it in a **tomb** which had been dug out of
23.55 with Joseph and saw the **tomb** and how Jesus' body was placed
24. 1 went to the **tomb,** carrying the spices they had prepared.
24. 2 away from the entrance to the **tomb,** [3]so they went in;
24. 9 returned from the **tomb,** and told all these things to
24.12 But Peter got up and ran to the **tomb;**
24.22 went at dawn to the **tomb,** [23]but could not find his body.
24.24 our group went to the **tomb** and found it exactly as the
Jn 11.38 Jesus went to the **tomb,** which was a cave with a
19.41 there was a new **tomb** where no one had ever been
19.42 Sabbath and because the **tomb** was close by, they placed Jesus'
20. 1 Mary Magdalene went to the **tomb** and saw that the stone had
20. 2 taken the Lord from the **tomb,** and we don't know where they
20. 3 Then Peter and the other disciple went to the **tomb.**
20. 4 other disciple ran faster than Peter and reached the **tomb** first.
20. 6 Behind him came Simon Peter, and he went straight into the **tomb.**
20. 8 the other disciple, who had reached the **tomb** first, also
20.11 Mary stood crying outside the **tomb.**
20.11 and looked in the **tomb** [12]and saw two angels there dressed
Acts 13.29 took him down from the cross and placed him in a **tomb.**

TOMORROW

Ex 8.10 The king answered, "Pray for me **tomorrow."**
8.20 Lord said to Moses, "Early **tomorrow** morning go and meet the
8.23 This miracle will take place **tomorrow.'"**
8.29 pray to the Lord that **tomorrow** the flies will leave you,
9. 5 I, the Lord, have set **tomorrow** as the time when I will
9.13 then said to Moses, "Early **tomorrow** morning meet with the
9.18 This time **tomorrow** I will cause a heavy hailstorm, such
10. 4 then I will bring locusts into your country **tomorrow.**
16.19 to them, "No one is to keep any of it for **tomorrow."**
16.23 "The Lord has commanded that **tomorrow** is a holy day of rest,
16.23 Whatever is left should be put aside and kept for **tomorrow."**
17. 9 "Pick out some men to go and fight the Amalekites **tomorrow.**
19.10 spend today and **tomorrow** purifying themselves for worship.
19.11 must wash their clothes [11]and be ready the day after **tomorrow.**
19.15 ready by the day after **tomorrow** and don't have sexual
32. 5 the gold bull and announced, **"Tomorrow** there will be a
34. 2 Be ready **tomorrow** morning, and come up Mount Sinai to meet
Num 11.18 Now tell the people, 'Purify yourselves for **tomorrow;**
14.25 Turn back **tomorrow** and go into the wilderness in the
16. 5 to Korah and his followers, **"Tomorrow** morning the Lord will
16. 6 **Tomorrow** morning you and your followers take firepans,
16.16 Moses said to Korah, **"Tomorrow** you and your 250
22. 8 "Spend the night here, and **tomorrow** I will report to you
Josh 3. 5 the people, "Purify yourselves, because **tomorrow** the Lord
7.13 Tell them to be ready **tomorrow,** because I, the Lord God of
11. 6 By this time **tomorrow** I will have killed all of them for
22.18 Lord today, he will be angry with everyone in Israel **tomorrow.**
Judg 9.33 Get up **tomorrow** morning at sunrise and make a sudden
19. 9 **Tomorrow** you can get up early for your journey and go home."
20.27 **Tomorrow** I will give you victory over them."
1 Sam 9.16 Lord had said to Samuel, [16]**"Tomorrow** about this time I
9.19 **Tomorrow** morning I will answer all your questions and send
11. 9 your people that before noon **tomorrow** they will be rescued."
11.10 and said to Nahash, **"Tomorrow** we will surrender to you,
19. 2 Please be careful **tomorrow** morning;
19.11 "If you don't get away tonight, **tomorrow** you will be dead."
20. 5 **"Tomorrow** is the New Moon Festival," David replied,
20. 5 in the fields until the evening of the day after **tomorrow.**
20.12 At this time **tomorrow** and on the following day I will
20.18 said to him, "Since **tomorrow** is the New Moon Festival,
20.19 The day after **tomorrow** your absence will be noticed even more;
28.19 **Tomorrow** you and your sons will join me, and the Lord will
29.10 So then, David, **tomorrow** morning all of you who left
2 Sam 2.27 men would have kept on chasing you until **tomorrow** morning."
11.12 here the rest of the day, and **tomorrow** I'll send you back."
19. 7 don't, not one of them will be with you by **tomorrow** morning.
20. 4 and be back here with them by the day after **tomorrow."**
1 Kgs 19. 2 dead if by this time **tomorrow** I don't do the same thing
20. 6 They will be there about this time **tomorrow."**
2 Kgs 7. 1 By this time **tomorrow** you will be able to buy in Samaria
10. 6 King Ahab's descendants to me at Jezreel by this time **tomorrow."**
2 Chr 20.16 Attack them **tomorrow** as they come up the pass at Ziz.
Esth 5. 8 Haman to be my guests **tomorrow** at another banquet that I
5.12 one but the king and me, and we are invited back **tomorrow.**
5.14 **Tomorrow** morning you can ask the king to have Mordecai
9.13 Jews in Susa do again **tomorrow** what they were allowed to do
Prov 3.28 neighbour to wait until **tomorrow** if you can help him now.
27. 1 Never boast about **tomorrow.**
Is 22.13 **Tomorrow** we'll be dead."
56.12 **Tomorrow** will be even better than today!'"
Mt 6.30 that is here today and gone **tomorrow,** burnt up in the oven.

Mt 6.34 So do not worry about **tomorrow;**
Lk 12.28 that is here today and gone **tomorrow,** burnt up in the oven.
13.32 and performing cures today and **tomorrow,** and on the third
13.33 I must be on my way today, **tomorrow,** and the next day;
Acts 23.20 have agreed to ask you **tomorrow** to take Paul down to the
25.22 "You will hear him **tomorrow,"** Festus answered.
1 Cor 15.32 goes, "Let us eat and drink, for **tomorrow** we will die."
Jas 4.13 you that say, "Today or **tomorrow** we will travel to a
4.14 You don't even know what your life **tomorrow** will be!

TON

1 Kgs 5.11 1 Chr 22.14 1 Chr 22.14 1 Chr 29.4 1 Chr 29.4 1 Chr 29.7 1 Chr 29.7 1 Chr 29.7 1 Chr 29.7 2 Chr 2.10 2 Chr 2.10 2 Chr 3.8 2 Chr 27.5 Ezra 8.26

TONGS

Ex 25.38 Make its **tongs** and trays of pure gold.
37.23 lamp-stand, and he made its **tongs** and trays of pure gold.
Num 4. 9 its lamps, **tongs,** trays, and all the olive-oil containers.
1 Kgs 7.49 the flowers, lamps, and **tongs;**
2 Chr 4.21 the flower decorations, the lamps, and the **tongs;**
Is 6. 6 that he had taken from the altar with a pair of **tongs.**

TONGUE
[STRANGE TONGUES]

Judg 7. 5 up the water with his **tongue** like a dog, from everyone who
Job 12.11 But just as your **tongue** enjoys tasting food, your ears
27. 4 never say anything evil, my **tongue** will never tell a lie.
41. 1 Leviathan with a fish-hook or tie his **tongue** down with a rope?
Ps 12. 3 Silence those flattering **tongues,** O Lord!
22. 7 they stick out their **tongues** and shake their heads.
22.15 dry as dust, and my **tongue** sticks to the roof of my
39. 1 what I do and will not let my **tongue** make me sin;
45. 1 pen of a good writer my **tongue** is ready with a poem.
52. 2 your **tongue** is like a sharp razor.
57. 4 their **tongues** are like sharp swords.
59. 7 Their **tongues** are like swords in their mouths, yet they
64. 3 They sharpen their **tongues** like swords and aim cruel words
140. 3 Their **tongues** are like deadly snakes;
Prov 6.16 a lying **tongue,**
10.31 wisdom, but the **tongue** that speaks evil will be stopped.
24.13 comb is sweet on your **tongue,** [14]you may be sure that
Song 4.11 your **tongue** is milk and honey for me.
Jer 9. 5 they have taught their **tongues** to lie and will not give up
9. 8 Their **tongues** are like deadly arrows;
Ezek 3.26 I will paralyse your **tongue** so that you won't be able to
Zech 14.12 their eyes and their **tongues** will rot away.
Mk 7.33 in the man's ears, spat, and touched the man's **tongue.**
16.17 they will speak in **strange tongues;**
Lk 16.24 some water and cool my **tongue,** because I am in great pain
Acts 10.46 For they heard them speaking in **strange tongues** and praising God's greatness.
19. 6 spoke in **strange tongues** and also proclaimed God's message.
1 Cor 12.10 the ability to speak in **strange tongues,** and to another he
12.28 others or to direct them or to speak in **strange tongues.**
12.30 diseases or to speak in **strange tongues** or to explain what
13. 8 gifts of speaking in **strange tongues,** but they will cease;
14. 2 The one who speaks in **strange tongues** does not speak to
14. 4 The one who speaks in **strange tongues** helps only himself,
14. 5 I would like all of you to speak in **strange tongues;**
14. 5 the one who speaks in **strange tongues**—unless there is
14. 6 use will I be to you if I speak in **strange tongues?**
14. 9 about if your message given in **strange tongues** is not clear?
14.13 The person who speaks in **strange tongues,** then, must
14.18 God that I speak in **strange tongues** much more than any of
14.19 others, than speak thousands of words in **strange tongues.**
14.22 of speaking in **strange tongues** is proof for unbelievers,
14.23 and everyone starts speaking in **strange tongues**—and if some
14.26 God, another a message in **strange tongues,** and still another
14.27 is going to speak in **strange tongues,** two or three at the
14.28 the one who speaks in **strange tongues** must be quiet and
14.39 God's message, but do not forbid the speaking in **strange tongues.**
Jas 1.26 he does not control his **tongue,** his religion is worthless
3. 5 So it is with the **tongue:**
3. 6 And the **tongue** is like a fire.
3. 8 But no one has ever been able to tame the **tongue.**
Rev 16.10 and people bit their **tongues** because of their pain, [11]and they

TONIGHT

Gen 19. 5 "Where are the men who came to stay with you **tonight?**
19.34 let's make him drunk again **tonight,** and you sleep with him.
30.15 your son's mandrakes, you can sleep with Jacob **tonight."**
30.16 going to sleep with me **tonight,** because I have paid for you
Josh 4. 3 with them and to put them down where you camp **tonight."**
Ruth 1.12 have, and so got married **tonight** and had sons, [13]would you
1 Sam 19.11 "If you don't get away **tonight,** tomorrow you will be dead."
26. 8 to David, "God has put your enemy in your power **tonight.**
26.21 harm you again, because you have spared my life **tonight.**
2 Sam 17. 1 twelve thousand men, and **tonight** I will set out after David.
Esth 5. 4 Haman to be my guests **tonight** at a banquet I am preparing
Mt 26.34 before the cock crows **tonight,** you will say three times that
Mk 14.30 before the cock will not crow twice **tonight,** you will say three times
Lk 22.34 "the cock will not crow **tonight** until you have said three
22.61 "Before the cock crows **tonight,** you will say three times that
Acts 23.23 spearmen, and be ready to leave by nine o'clock **tonight.**

TOOL

Gen 4.22 Cain, who made all kinds of **tools** out of bronze and iron.
Deut 27. 5 that have had no iron **tools** used on them, [6]because any
Josh 8.31 made of stones which have not been cut with iron **tools."**
2 Sam 23. 7 You must use an iron **tool** or a spear;
1 Kgs 6. 7 or any other iron **tools** as the Temple was being built.
2 Kgs 12.13 cups, bowls, trumpets, or **tools** for tending the lamps,
25.14 in cleaning the altar, the **tools** used in tending the lamps,
Is 44.13 carves it out with his **tools,** and makes it in the form
Jer 10. 3 it is carved by the **tools** of the woodcarver, [4]and
52.18 in cleaning the altar, the **tools** used in tending the lamps,

TOOTH
[TEETH]

Gen 49.12 from drinking wine, His **teeth** white from drinking milk.
Ex 21.24 for life, [24]eye for eye, **tooth for tooth,** hand for hand,
21.27 If he knocks out a **tooth,**
21.27 he is to free the slave as payment for the **tooth.**
Lev 24.20 knocks out a tooth, one of his **teeth** shall be knocked out.
Deut 19.21 eye for an eye, a **tooth for a tooth,** a hand for
Job 4.10 like lions, but God silences them and breaks their **teeth.**
41.14 Who can make him open his jaws, ringed with those terrifying **teeth?**
Ps 57. 4 Their **teeth** are like spears and arrows;
58. 6 Break the **teeth** of these fierce lions, O God.
Prov 10.26 irritating as vinegar on your **teeth** or smoke in your eyes.
25.19 to chew with a loose **tooth** or walk with a crippled foot.
Ecc 12. 3 Your **teeth** will be too few to chew your food, and your
Song 4. 2 Your **teeth** are as white as sheep that have just been shorn
6. 6 Your **teeth** are as white as a flock of sheep that have
7. 9 flow straight to my lover, flowing over his lips and **teeth.**
Jer 31.30 eats sour grapes will have his own **teeth** set on edge;
Lam 3.16 my face in the ground and broke my **teeth** on the gravel.
Dan 7. 5 three ribs between its **teeth,** and a voice said to it,
7. 7 With its huge iron **teeth** it crushed its victims, and then it
7.19 its bronze claws and iron **teeth** and then trampled on them.
Joel 1. 6 their **teeth** are as sharp as those of a lion.
Mt 5.38 said, 'An eye for an eye, and a **tooth for a tooth.'**
8.12 the darkness, where they will cry and grind their **teeth."**
13.42 fiery furnace, where they will cry and grind their **teeth.**
13.50 fiery furnace, where they will cry and grind their **teeth.**
22.13 There he will cry and grind his **teeth.' "**
24.51 There he will cry and grind his **teeth.**
25.30 there he will cry and grind his **teeth.'**
Mk 9.18 at the mouth, grits his **teeth,** and becomes stiff all over.
Lk 13.28 will cry and grind your **teeth** when you see Abraham, Isaac,
Acts 7.54 they became furious and ground their **teeth** at him in anger.
Rev 9. 8 Their hair was like women's hair, their teeth were like lions' **teeth.**

TOP

Gen 7.20 it was about seven metres above the **tops** of the mountains.
8. 5 day of the tenth month the **tops** of the mountains appeared.
22. 9 son and placed him on the altar, on **top** of the wood.
40.17 In the **top** basket there were all kinds of pastries for
42.27 his donkey and found his money at the **top** of the sack.
43.12 back the money that was returned in the **top** of your sacks.
43.21 found his money in the **top** of his sack—every bit of
44. 1 carry, and put each man's money in the **top** of his sack.
44. 2 my silver cup in the **top** of the youngest brother's sack,
44. 8 of Canaan the money we found in the **top** of our sacks.
Ex 17. 9 I will stand on **top** of the hill holding the stick that
17.10 Moses, Aaron, and Hur went up to the **top** of the hill.
19.20 Lord came down on the **top** of Mount Sinai
19.20 and called Moses to the **top** of the mountain.
24.16 the light looked like a fire burning on **top** of the mountain.
25.21 tablets inside the box and put the lid on **top** of it.
26.24 joined at the bottom and connected all the way to the **top.**
27. 2 Make projections at the **top** of the four corners.
29.17 legs, and put them on **top** of the head and the other
29.25 it on the altar, on **top** of the burnt-offering, as a
30. 3 Cover its **top,** all four sides, and its projections
34. 2 and come up Mount Sinai to meet me there at the **top.**
36.29 joined at the bottom and connected all the way to the **top.**
36.38 with hooks, covered their **tops** and their rods with gold,
37.26 He covered its **top,** all four sides, and its projections
38. 2 made the projections at the **top** of the four corners, so that
38.17 and the covering of the **tops** of the posts were made of
38.19 hooks, the covering of their **tops,** and their rods were made
38.28 the hooks for the posts, and the covering for their **tops.**
Lev 8.26 and he put them on **top** of the fat and the right
8.28 it on the altar, on **top** of the burnt-offering, as an
9.14 them on the altar on **top** of the rest of the burnt-offering.
9.20 bull and the ram [20]on **top** of the breasts of the animals
Num 4. 6 a blue cloth on **top,** and then insert the carrying-poles.
4.25 the fine leather cover on **top** of it, the curtain for the
8. 4 From **top** to bottom the lamp-stand was made of hammered gold,
20.28 There on the **top** of the mountain Aaron died, and Moses and
21.20 of the Moabites, below the **top** of Mount Pisgah, looking out
23. 3 he went alone to the **top** of a hill, [4]and God met
23.14 him to the field of Zophim on the **top** of Mount Pisgah.
23.28 took Balaam to the **top** of Mount Peor overlooking the desert.
Deut 34. 1 to Mount Nebo, to the **top** of Mount Pisgah east of Jericho,
Josh 15. 8 then proceeded up to the **top** of the hill on the west
Judg 6.26 altar to the Lord your God on **top** of this mound.
9. 5 Ophrah, and there on the **top** of a single stone he killed
9. 7 he went and stood on **top** of Mount Gerizim and shouted out
16. 3 them all the way to the **top** of the hill overlooking Hebron.
1 Sam 26.13 of the valley to the **top** of the hill, a safe distance

2 Sam 2.25 Abner again and took their stand on the **top** of a hill.
15.32 When David reached the **top** of the hill, where there was
16. 1 gone a little beyond the **top** of the hill, he was suddenly
17.13 a single stone will be left there on **top** of the hill."
18.24 watchman went up to the **top** of the wall and stood on
1 Kgs 6. 6 2.7 metres wide, and in the **top** storey 3.1 metres wide.
6.31 the **top** of the doorway was a pointed arch.
7.11 On **top** of them were other stones, cut to measure, and
7.16 one 2.2 metres tall, to be placed on **top** of the columns.
7.17 The **top** of each column was decorated with a design of
7.22 The lily-shaped bronze capitals were on **top** of the columns.
7.31 There was a circular frame on **top** for the basin.
7.31 upwards 45 centimetres from the **top** of the cart and 18
7.35 There was a 22 centimetre band round the **top** of each cart;
7.40 The two bowl-shaped capitals on **top** of the columns
18.42 eat, Elijah climbed to the **top** of Mount Carmel, where he
19.11 and stand before me on **top** of the mountain," the Lord said
2 Kgs 9.13 spread their cloaks at the **top** of the steps for Jehu to
25.17 metres high, with a bronze capital on **top,** 1.3 metres high.
2 Chr 3.16 The **tops** of the columns were decorated with a design of
4.11 The two bowl-shaped capitals on **top** of the columns The
25.12 took the prisoners to the **top** of the cliff at the city
Ezra 6. 4 one layer of wood on **top** of every three layers of stone.
Neh 3.31 Gate, near the room on **top** of the north-east corner of the
12.31 the leaders of Judah on **top** of the wall and put them
12.31 went to the right on **top** of the wall towards the Rubbish
12.38 to the left along the **top** of the wall, and I followed
12.42 The singers, led by Jezrahiah, sang at the **top** of their voices.
Esth 8.14 the riders mounted royal horses and rode off at **top** speed.
Job 30.14 holes in my defences and come crashing down on **top** of me;
Song 4. 8 Come down from the **top** of Mount Amana, from Mount Senir and
Is 13. 2 On the **top** of a barren hill raise the battle flag!
14.14 you would climb to the **tops** of the clouds and be like
17. 6 or three at the very **top,** or a few that are left
18. 3 a signal flag to be raised on the **tops** of the mountains!
30.17 your army except a lonely flagstaff on the **top** of a hill!
42.11 city of Sela shout for joy from the **tops** of the mountains!
Jer 49.16 You live on the rocky cliffs, high on **top** of the mountain;
52.21 On **top** of each column was a bronze capital 2.2 metres high,
Ezek 6.13 every high hill, on the **top** of every mountain, under every
17. 3 Mountains and broke off the **top** of a cedar-tree, [4] which he
17.22 "I will take the **top** of a tall cedar and break off
31.14 that again or push its **top** through the clouds and reach such
40. 6 went up the steps, and at the **top** he measured the entrance;
40.42 and their **tops** were seventy-five centimetres square.
41. 7 seemed to have the same thickness all the way to the **top.**
42. 7 At the **top** level there were rooms in the entire length of
43.12 area surrounding it on the **top** of the mountain is sacred and
43.14 of the altar, from the **top** of the base, was one metre
43.15 This **top** section, on which the sacrifices were burnt,
43.15 on the four corners were higher than the rest of the **top.**
43.16 The **top** of the altar was a square, six metres on each
43.20 on the projections on the **top** corners of the altar, and on
Joel 2. 5 As they leap on the **tops** of the mountains, they rattle
Amos 9. 1 "Strike the **tops** of the temple columns so hard that the
9. 3 If they hide on the **top** of Mount Carmel, I will search
Mic 1. 3 he will come down and walk on the **tops** of the mountains.
Zech 4. 2 "At the **top** is a bowl for the oil.
Mt 27.51 hanging in the Temple was torn in two from **top** to bottom.
Mk 15.38 hanging in the Temple was torn in two, from **top** to bottom.
Lk 4.29 and took him to the **top** of the hill on which their
Heb 11.21 He leaned on the **top** of his walking-stick and worshipped God.
Rev 21.10 the angel carried me to the **top** of a very high mountain.

TOPAZ

A semi-precious stone, usually yellow in colour.

Ex 28.17 in the first row mount a ruby, a **topaz,** and a garnet;
39.10 the first row they mounted a ruby, a **topaz,** and a garnet;
Job 28.19 The finest **topaz** and the purest gold Cannot compare with
Ezek 28.13 **topaz,** beryl, carnelian, and jasper;
Rev 21.20 the eighth beryl, the ninth **topaz,** the tenth chalcedony,

TORCH

Gen 15.17 smoking fire-pot and a flaming **torch** suddenly appeared and
Judg 7.16 each man a trumpet and a jar with a **torch** inside it.
7.20 They all held the **torches** in their left hands, the trumpets
15. 4 he tied their tails together and put **torches** in the knots.
15. 5 he set fire to the **torches** and turned the foxes loose in
Is 62. 1 is saved, And her victory shines like a **torch** in the night.
Ezek 1.13 that looked like a blazing **torch,** constantly moving.
Nah 2. 4 They flash like **torches** and dart about like lightning.
Jn 18. 3 they were armed and carried lanterns and **torches.**
Rev 4. 5 of the throne seven lighted **torches** were burning, which are the
8.10 large star, burning like a **torch,** dropped from the sky and

TORMENT

Judg 16.19 Then she began to **torment** him, for he had lost his strength.
1 Sam 1. 6 Peninnah, her rival, would **torment** and humiliate her,
16.14 Saul, and an evil spirit sent by the Lord **tormented** him.
16.15 "We know that an evil spirit sent by God is **tormenting** you.
Job 15.20 oppresses others will be in **torment** as long as he lives.
16. 1 the comfort you give is only **torment.**
19. 1 Why do you keep **tormenting** me with words?
19.22 Haven't you **tormented** me enough?
19.28 because you said, [28] "How can we **torment** him?"
Ps 78.45 sent flies among them, that **tormented** them, and frogs that
Rev 14.10 who do this will be **tormented** in fire and sulphur before the
14.11 smoke of the fire that **torments** them goes up for ever and
20.10 and they will be **tormented** day and night for ever and ever.

TORRENT

Job 37. 6 to fall on the earth, and sends **torrents** of drenching rain.
Ps 78.20 that he struck the rock, and water flowed out in a **torrent;**
124. 5 covered us, [5] the raging **torrent** would have drowned us."
Is 24.18 **Torrents** of rain will pour from the sky, and earth's
28. 2 like a hailstorm, like a **torrent** of rain, like a rushing,
30.30 will be flames, cloudbursts, hailstones, and **torrents** of rain.
Ezek 38.22 **Torrents** of rain and hail, together with fire and sulphur,

TORTURE

Jer 38.19 I may be handed over to them and **tortured."**
Lam 2.20 Look at those you are **torturing!**
Heb 11.35 to accept freedom, died under **torture** in order to be raised
Rev 9. 5 to kill these people, but only to **torture** them for five months.
9. 5 The pain caused by the **torture** is like the pain caused by

TOSS

Job 7. 4 I **toss** all night and long for dawn.
30.22 you **toss** me about in a raging storm.
Ps 48. 7 like ships **tossing** in a furious storm.
Prov 23.34 sea-sick, swinging high up in the rigging of a **tossing** ship.
Is 41.16 You will **toss** them in the air;
Jer 5.22 The sea may **toss,** but it cannot go beyond it;
Mt 14.24 far out in the lake, **tossed about** by the waves, because the

TOTAL

Acts 19.19 books, and the **total** came to fifty thousand silver coins.
27.37 There was a **total** of 276 of us on board.

TOUCH

Gen 3. 3 not to eat the fruit of that tree or even **touch** it;
17. 3 bowed down with his face **touching** the ground, and God said,
17.17 bowed down with his face **touching** the ground, but he began
18. 2 Bowing down with his face **touching** the ground, [3] he said,
20. 6 you from sinning against me and did not let you **touch** her.
27.12 Perhaps my father will **touch** me and find out that I am
27.21 said to Jacob, "Please come closer so that I can **touch** you.
50.21 So he reassured them with kind words that **touched** their hearts.
Ex 4.25 off the foreskin of her son, and **touched** Moses' feet with
19.13 be stoned or shot with arrows, without anyone **touching** him.
29.37 and anyone or anything that **touches** it will be harmed by the
30.29 and anyone or anything that **touches** them will be harmed by
Lev 5. 2 If someone unintentionally **touches** anything ritually unclean,
5. 3 **touches** anything of human origin that is unclean,
6.18 Anyone else who **touches** a food-offering will be harmed by
6.27 Anyone or anything that **touches** the flesh of the animal
7.21 offering after he has **touched** anything ritually unclean,
11. 8 Do not eat these animals or even **touch** their dead bodies;
11.11 You must not eat them or even **touch** their dead bodies.
11.24 Whoever **touches** the dead bodies of the following
11.31 Whoever **touches** them or their dead bodies will be unclean
11.36 anything else that **touches** their dead bodies is unclean.
11.39 dies, anyone who **touches** it will be unclean until evening.
12. 4 she must not **touch** anything that is holy or enter the sacred
15. 5 Anyone who **touches** his bed [6] or sits on anything the man
15. 7 Anyone who **touches** the man with the discharge must wash
15.10 Anyone who **touches** anything on which the man sat is
15.11 man who has a discharge **touches** someone without first having
15.12 clay pot that the man **touches** must be broken,
15.12 and any wooden bowl that he **touches** must be washed.
15.19 Anyone who **touches** her is unclean until evening.
15.21 Anyone who **touches** her bed or anything on which
15.27 Anyone who **touches** them is unclean and must wash his
22. 4 priest is unclean if he **touches** anything which is unclean
22. 5 of semen [5] or if he has **touched** an unclean animal or person.
Num 4.15 clan of Kohath must not **touch** the sacred objects, or they
9. 6 ritually unclean because they had **touched** a corpse, and they
9. 7 are unclean because we have **touched** a corpse, but why should
9.10 your descendants are unclean from **touching** a corpse or are
16.26 wicked men and don't **touch** anything that belongs to them.
19.11 Whoever **touches** a corpse is ritually unclean for seven days.
19.13 Whoever **touches** a corpse and does not purify himself
19.16 If someone **touches** a person who has been killed or has
19.16 of doors or if someone **touches** a human bone or a grave,
19.18 on the man who had **touched** the human bone or the dead
19.21 **touches** the water remains ritually unclean until evening.
19.22 Whatever an unclean person **touches** is unclean, and
19.22 anyone else who **touches** it remains unclean until evening.
31.19 have killed anyone or have **touched** a corpse must stay
Deut 14. 8 eat any of these animals or even **touch** their dead bodies.
Josh 19.11 border went west to Mareal, **touching** Dabbesheth and the
19.22 The border also **touched** Tabor, Shahazumah, and Beth Shemesh,
19.26 On the west it **touched** Carmel and Shihor Libnath.
19.27 the border went to Bethdagon, **touching** Zebulun and the
19.34 Tabor, from there to Hukkok, **touching** Zebulun on the south,
Judg 6.21 Lord's angel reached out and **touched** the meat and the bread
16. 9 the bowstrings just as thread breaks when fire **touches** it.
16.26 by the hand, "Let me **touch** the pillars that hold up the
Ruth 2.10 down with her face **touching** the ground, and said to Boaz,
1 Sam 10.26 Some powerful men, whose hearts God had **touched,** went with
2 Sam 23. 6 no one can **touch** them with bare hands.
1 Kgs 1.52 is loyal, not even a hair on his head will be **touched;**
6.27 two of their outstretched wings **touched** each other in the

1 Kgs 6.27 of the room, and the other two wings **touched** the walls.
19. 5 Suddenly an angel **touched** him and said, "Wake up and eat."
2 Kgs 4.37 She fell at Elisha's feet, with her face **touching** the ground;
1 Chr 13.10 became angry with Uzzah and killed him for **touching** the box.
16.22 do not **touch** my prophets."
21.16 sackcloth—bowed low, with their faces **touching** the ground.
21.21 and bowed low, with his face **touching** the ground.
2 Chr 3.11 spread out so that they **touched** each other in the centre of
20.18 bowed low, with his face **touching** the ground, and all the
Esth 5. 2 She then came up and **touched** the tip of it.
Job 4.15 A light breeze **touched** my face, and my hair bristled
41. 8 **Touch** him once and you'll never try it again;
Ps 57.10 your faithfulness **touches** the skies.
104.32 he **touches** the mountains, and they pour out smoke.
105.15 do not **touch** my prophets."
108. 4 your faithfulness **touches** the skies.
144. 5 **touch** the mountains, and they will pour out smoke.
Is 6. 7 He **touched** my lips with the burning coal and said,
6. 7 "This has **touched** your lips, and now your guilt
41. 3 safely on, so fast that he hardly **touches** the ground!
51.13 Their fury can no longer **touch** you.
52.11 **Touch** no forbidden thing;
65. 5 we are too holy for you to **touch!**"
Jer 1. 9 Lord stretched out his hand, **touched** my lips, and said to me,
23.17 who is stubborn that disaster will never **touch** him."
Lam 4.14 men, so stained with blood that no one would **touch** them.
4.15 Don't **touch** me!"
Ezek 1. 9 the creatures formed a square with their wing tips **touching.**
1.11 were raised so that they **touched** the tips of the wings of
1.15 creatures, I saw four wheels **touching** the ground, one beside
9. 6 But don't **touch** anyone who has the mark on his forehead.
44.25 to become ritually unclean by **touching** a corpse, unless it
Dan 2.34 from a cliff without anyone **touching** it, struck the iron and
2.45 from a cliff without anyone **touching** it and how it struck
8. 5 west, moving so fast that his feet didn't **touch** the ground.
10.16 like a man, stretched out his hand and **touched** my lips.
Amos 9. 5 The Sovereign Lord Almighty **touches** the earth, and it quakes;
Hag 2.12 he then lets his robe **touch** any bread, cooked food, wine,
2.13 "Suppose a man is defiled because he has **touched** a dead body.
2.13 If he then **touches** any of these foods, will that make them
Mt 8. 3 Jesus stretched out his hand and **touched** him.
8.15 He **touched** her hand;
9.20 came up behind Jesus and **touched** the edge of his cloak.
9.21 to herself, "If I only **touch** his cloak, I will get well."
9.29 Then Jesus **touched** their eyes and said, "Let it happen, then,
14.36 those who were ill at least **touch** the edge of his cloak;
14.36 and all who **touched** it were made well.
17. 7 Jesus came to them and **touched** them.
20.34 Jesus had pity on them and **touched** their eyes;
Mk 1.41 with pity, and stretched out his hand and **touched** him.
3.10 ill kept pushing their way to him in order to **touch** him.
5.28 to herself, "If I just **touch** his clothes, I will get well."
5.29 She **touched** his cloak, and her bleeding stopped at once;
5.30 turned round in the crowd and asked, "Who **touched** my clothes?"
5.31 why do you ask who **touched** you?"
6.56 him to let them at least **touch** the edge of his cloak;
6.56 and all who **touched** it were made well.
7.33 fingers in the man's ears, spat, and **touched** the man's tongue.
8.22 brought a blind man to Jesus and begged him to **touch** him.
Lk 5.13 Jesus stretched out his hand and **touched** him.
6.19 All the people tried to **touch** him, for power was going
7.14 Then he walked over and **touched** the coffin, and the men
7.39 he would know who this woman is who is **touching** him;
8.44 the crowd behind Jesus and **touched** the edge of his cloak,
8.45 Jesus asked, "Who **touched** me?"
8.46 But Jesus said, "Someone **touched** me, for I knew it when
8.47 told him why she had **touched** him and how she had been
22.51 He **touched** the man's ear and healed him.
Jn 11.33 his heart was **touched,** and he was deeply moved.
Acts 2. 3 tongues of fire which spread out and **touched** each person there.
Col 2.21 "Don't taste that," "Don't **touch** the other"?
Heb 12.20 said, "If even an animal **touches** the mountain, it must be
1 Jn 1. 1 yes, we have seen it, and our hands have **touched** it.

TOUGH

Ezek 3. 8 I will make you as stubborn and as **tough** as they are.

TOWEL

Jn 13. 4 off his outer garment, and tied a **towel** round his waist.
13. 5 disciples' feet and dry them with the **towel** round his waist.

TOWER

[SIEGE-TOWERS, WATCH-TOWER]

Gen 11. 4 build a city with a **tower** that reaches the sky, so that
11. 5 see the city and the **tower** which those men had built, [6]and
35.21 up his camp on the other side of the **tower** of Eder.
Judg 8. 9 and sound, and when I do, I will tear your **tower** down!"
8.17 He also tore down the **tower** at Penuel and killed the men
9.51 There was a strong **tower** there, and every man and woman
9.52 Abimelech came to attack the **tower,**
9.52 he went up to the door to set the **tower** on fire.
2 Kgs 9.17 guard on duty in the **watch-tower** at Jezreel saw Jehu and his
9.18 The guard on the **watch-tower** reported that the messenger
2 Chr 14. 7 cities by building walls and **towers,** and gates that can be
20.24 the Judaean army reached a **tower** that was in the desert,
26. 9 of Jerusalem by building **towers** at the Corner Gate,
26.10 He also built fortified **towers** in the open country and
26.15 large stones from the **towers** and corners of the city wall.
2 Chr 27. 4 built cities, and in the forests he built forts and **towers.**
32. 5 by repairing the wall, building **towers** on it, and building
Neh 3. 1 wall as far as the **Tower** of the Hundred
3. 1 and the **Tower** of Hananel.
3.11 Moab built both the next section and the **Tower** of the Ovens.
3.25 of the wall and the **tower** of the upper palace near the
3.25 east near the Water Gate and the **tower** guarding the Temple.
3.27 a point opposite the large **tower** guarding the Temple as far
12.38 We marched past the **Tower** of the Ovens to the Broad Wall,
12.39 Gate, the Fish Gate, the **Tower** of Hananel,
12.39 and the **Tower** of the Hundred, to the Sheep
Job 20. 6 He may grow great, **towering** to the sky, so great that his
Ps 36. 6 Your righteousness is **towering** like the mountains;
37.35 he **towered** over everyone like a cedar of Lebanon;
48.12 People of God, walk round Zion and count the **towers;**
Prov 18.10 Lord is like a strong **tower,** where the righteous can go and
Song 4. 4 Your neck is like the **tower** of David, round and smooth,
5.15 like the Lebanon Mountains with their **towering** cedars.
7. 4 Your neck is like a **tower** of ivory.
7. 4 is as lovely as the **tower** of Lebanon that stands guard at
8. 9 If she is a wall, we will build her a silver **tower.**
8.10 I am a wall, and my breasts are its **towers.**
Is 2. 2 be the highest one of all, **towering** above all the hills.
2.15 every high **tower,** and the walls of every fortress.
5. 2 He built a **tower** to guard them, dug a pit for treading
13.22 The **towers** and palaces will echo with the cries of
23.13 who put up **siege-towers,** tore down the fortifications of Tyre,
54.12 I will build your **towers** with rubies, your gates with
Jer 31.38 as my city, from Hananel **Tower** west to the Corner Gate.
46.18 As Mount Tabor **towers** above the mountains and Mount Carmel
51.58 be thrown to the ground, and its **towering** gates burnt down.
Lam 2. 8 The **towers** and walls now lie in ruins together.
Ezek 26. 4 They will destroy your city walls and tear down your **towers.**
26. 9 battering-rams and tear down your **towers** with iron bars.
27.11 Arvad guarded your walls, and men from Gamad guarded your **towers.**
Mic 4. 1 be the highest one of all, **towering** above all the hills.
Hab 2. 1 I will climb my **watch-tower** and wait to see what the Lord
Zeph 1.16 of soldiers attacking fortified cities and high **towers.**
3. 6 their cities and left their walls and **towers** in ruins.
Zech 14.10 Jerusalem will **tower** above the land round it;
14.10 and from the **Tower** of Hananel to the royal winepresses.
Mt 21.33 dug a hole for the winepress, and built a **watch-tower.**
Mk 12. 1 dug a hole for the winepress, and built a **watch-tower.**
Lk 13. 4 in Siloam who were killed when the **tower** fell on them?
14.28 is planning to build a **tower,** he sits down first and works
14.29 not be able to finish the **tower** after laying the foundation;

TOWN

[TEN TOWNS]
see also **TOWN CLERK**

Gen 19.20 Do you see that little **town?**
19.21 I won't destroy that **town.**
19.22 Because Lot called it small, the **town** was named Zoar.
28.19 (The **town** there was once known as Luz.)
34.27 Jacob's other sons looted the **town** to take revenge for their
35. 5 people of the nearby **towns,** and they did not pursue them.
38.14 at the entrance to Enaim, a **town** on the road to Timnah.
Num 13.19 the people live in open **towns** or in fortified cities.
20.16 we are at Kadesh, a **town** at the border of your territory.
21.25 Heshbon and all the surrounding **towns,** and settled in them.
21.32 captured it and its surrounding **towns** and drove out the
32. 3 the Israelites to occupy—the **towns** of Ataroth, Dibon, Jazer,
32.16 here for our sheep and fortified **towns** for our dependants.
32.17 live here in the fortified **towns,** safe from the people of
32.24 So build your **towns** and the enclosures for your sheep,
32.26 cattle and sheep will remain here in the **towns** of Gilead.
32.33 of Bashan, including the **towns** and the country round them.
32.34 Gad rebuilt the fortified **towns** of Dibon, Ataroth, Aroer,
32.38 They gave new names to the **towns** they rebuilt.
Deut 1. 1 on one side and the **towns** of Tophel, Laban, Hazeroth, and
1. 4 Og of Bashan, who ruled in the **towns** of Ashtaroth and Edrei.
2. 8 road that goes from the **towns** of Elath and Eziongeber to the
2.34 and destroyed every **town,** and put everyone to death,
2.35 We took the livestock and plundered the **towns.**
2.36 let us capture all the **towns** from Aroer, on the edge of
2.36 No **town** had walls too strong for us.
2.37 River Jabbok or to the **towns** of the hill-country or to any
3. 4 time we captured all his **towns**—there was not one that we
3. 4 In all we captured sixty **towns**—the whole region of Argob,
3. 5 All these **towns** were fortified with high walls, gates, and
3. 6 We destroyed all the **towns** and put to death all the men,
3. 6 as we did in the **towns** that belonged to King Sihon of
3. 7 We took the livestock and plundered the **towns.**
3.10 of Bashan, as far east as the **towns** of Salecah and Edrei."
3.12 and part of the hill-country of Gilead, along with its **towns.**
3.19 will remain behind in the **towns** that I have assigned to you.
12.12 your servants, and the Levites who live in your **towns;**
12.18 Levites who live in your **towns,** are to eat these offerings
13.12 you are living in the **towns** that the Lord your God gives
13.13 misled the people of their **town** to worship gods that you
13.15 all the people in that **town** and all their livestock too.
13.15 Destroy that **town** completely.
13.16 people who live there and pile them up in the **town** square.
13.16 Then burn the **town** and everything in it as an offering to
14.27 "Do not neglect the Levites who live in your **towns;**
14.28 the tithe of all your crops and store it in your **towns.**
14.29 the foreigners, orphans, and widows who live in your **towns.**
15. 7 "If in any of the **towns** in the land that the Lord
16.11 foreigners, orphans, and widows who live in your **towns.**

Deut	16.14	foreigners, orphans, and widows who live in your **towns.**
	16.18	and other officials in every **town** that the Lord your God
	17. 2	that in one of your **towns** some man or woman has sinned
	17. 5	then take that person outside the **town** and stone him to death.
	18. 6	to may come from any **town** in Israel to the one place
	19.12	the leaders of his own **town** are to send for him and
	21. 2	place where the body was found to each of the nearby **towns.**
	21. 3	Then the leaders of the **town** nearest to where the body was
	21. 6	all the leaders from the **town** nearest the place where the
	21.19	before the leaders of the **town** where he lives and make him
	22.15	and they are to show it in court to the **town** leaders.
	22.18	Then the **town** leaders are to take the husband and beat him.
	22.23	man is caught in a **town** having intercourse with a girl who
	22.24	are to take them outside the **town** and stone them to death.
	22.24	although she was in a **town,** where she could have been heard.
	23.16	live in any of your **towns** that he chooses, and you are
	24.14	fellow-Israelite or a foreigner living in one of your **towns.**
	25. 7	is to go before the **town** leaders and say, ‘My husband's
	25. 8	Then the **town** leaders are to summon him and speak to him.
	25. 9	in the presence of the **town** leaders, take off one of his
	28. 3	"The Lord will bless your **towns** and your fields.
	28.16	"The Lord will curse your **towns** and your fields.
	28.52	They will attack every **town** in the land that the Lord
	28.53	your enemies are besieging your **towns,** you will become so
	28.56	When the enemy besieges her **town,** she will become so
	31.12	foreigners who live in your **towns,** so that everyone may hear
	33.25	May his **towns** be protected with iron gates, And may he
Josh	10.37	everyone else in the city as well as in the nearby **towns.**
	10.39	He captured it, with its king and all the nearby **towns.**
	13.23	These were the cities and **towns** given to the families of the
	13.28	These were the cities and **towns** given to the families of
	15.32	twenty-nine cities in all, along with the **towns** round them.
	15.36	fourteen cities, along with the **towns** round them.
	15.41	sixteen cities, along with the **towns** round them.
	15.44	nine cities, along with the **towns** round them.
	15.45	There was Ekron with its **towns** and villages, [46]and all
	15.46	and all the cities and **towns** near Ashdod, from Ekron to
	15.47	Ashdod and Gaza, with their **towns** and villages, reaching to
	15.51	eleven cities, along with the **towns** round them.
	15.54	nine cities, along with the **towns** round them.
	15.57	ten cities, along with the **towns** round them.
	15.59	six cities, along with the **towns** round them.
	15.60	two cities, along with the **towns** round them.
	15.62	six cities, along with the **towns** round them.
	16. 9	their possession, [9]along with some **towns** and villages that
	17.11	Ibleam, along with their surrounding **towns,** as well as Dor
	17.11	Endor, Taanach, Megiddo, and their surrounding **towns.**
	17.16	Beth Shan and its surrounding **towns** and those who live in
	18. 9	divided it into seven parts, making a list of the **towns.**
	18.24	twelve cities, along with the **towns** round them.
	18.28	fourteen cities, along with the **towns** round them.
	19. 6	thirteen cities, along with the **towns** round them.
	19. 7	four cities, along with the **towns** round them.
	19. 8	This included all the **towns** round these cities as far as
	19.15	twelve cities, along with the **towns** round them.
	19.16	These cities and their **towns** were in the land which the
	19.22	It included sixteen cities along with the **towns** round them.
	19.23	These cities and their **towns** were in the land which the
	19.30	twenty-two cities, along with the **towns** round them.
	19.31	These cities and their **towns** were in the land which the
	19.38	nineteen cities, along with the **towns** round them.
	19.39	These cities and their **towns** were in the land which the
	19.48	These cities and their **towns** were in the land which the
	20. 6	back home to his own **town,** from which he had run away."
	21.12	city, as well as its **towns,** had already been given to Caleb
	24.33	was buried at Gibeah, the **town** in the hill-country of
Judg	1.27	Beth Shan, Taanach, Dor, Ibleam, Megiddo, and the nearby **towns;**
	5. 7	The **towns** of Israel stood abandoned, Deborah;
	6.27	and the people of the **town** to do it by day, so
	6.28	When the people of the **town** got up early the next morning,
	8. 5	to the men of the **town,** "Please give my men some loaves
	8.27	idol from the gold and put it in his home **town,** Ophrah.
	8.32	father Joash, at Ophrah, the **town** of the clan of Abiezer.
	11.26	Heshbon and Aroer, and the **towns** round them, and all the
	12. 7	Then he died and was buried in his home **town** in Gilead.
	18. 2	and sent them from the **towns** of Zorah and Eshtaol with
	18.27	went and attacked Laish, that **town** of peaceful, quiet people
	18.27	They killed the inhabitants and burnt the **town.**
	18.27	The men from Dan rebuilt the **town** and settled down there.
	19.22	some sexual perverts from the **town** surrounded the house and
	20.11	in Israel assembled with one purpose—to attack the **town.**
	20.38	smoke going up from the **town,** [39]the Israelites out on the
	20.40	a cloud of smoke began to go up from the **town.**
	20.48	They burnt every **town** in the area.
	21.23	their own territory, rebuilt their **towns,** and lived there.
Ruth	1.19	When they arrived, the whole **town** got excited, and the women
	2.18	took the corn back into **town** and showed her mother-in-law
	3.11	as everyone in **town** knows, you are a fine woman.
	3.15	Then she returned to the **town** with it.
	4. 1	to the meeting place at the **town** gate and sat down there.
	4. 2	of the leaders of the **town** and asked them to sit down
	4.10	family line will continue among his people and in his **town.**
1 Sam	4.13	news throughout the **town,** and everyone cried out in fear.
	6.18	both the fortified **towns** and the villages without walls.
	9. 6	In this **town** there is a holy man who is highly respected
	9. 9	So they went to the **town** where the holy man lived.
	9. 9	up the hill to the **town,** they met some girls who were
	9. 9	They asked the girls, "Is the seer in **town?"**
	9.12	As soon as you go into the **town,** you will find him.
	9.12	He arrived in **town** today because the people are going to
	9.14	servant went on to the **town,** and as they were going in,
1 Sam	9.25	place of worship to the **town,** they made up a bed for
	9.27	at the edge of the **town,** Samuel said to Saul, "Tell the
	10. 5	At the entrance to the **town** you will meet a group of
	17. 1	The Philistines gathered for battle in Socoh, a **town** in Judah;
	18. 6	back home, women from every **town** in Israel came out to meet
	20.29	celebrating the sacrificial feast in **town,** and my brother
	20.40	the boy and told him to take them back to the **town.**
	20.42	Then David left, and Jonathan went back to the **town.**
	23. 5	And that was how David saved the **town.**
	23. 7	himself by going into a walled **town** with fortified gates."
	27. 5	are my friend, let me have a small **town** to live in.
	29. 4	to him, "Send that fellow back to the **town** you gave him.
	30. 1	They had burnt down the **town** [2]and captured all the women;
	30. 3	arrived, they found that the **town** had been burnt down and
	30.27	to the people in the **towns** of Jattir, [28]Aroer, Siphmoth,
	30.30	in the **towns** of Hormah, Borashan, Athach, [31]and Hebron.
	31. 7	sons had been killed, they abandoned their **towns** and fled.
	31.13	the tamarisk-tree in the **town,** and fasted for seven days.
2 Sam	2. 1	I go and take control of one of the **towns** of Judah?"
	2. 3	their families, and they settled in the **towns** round Hebron.
	12. 1	and said, "There were two men who lived in the same **town;**
	12.31	the same to the people of all the other **towns** of Ammon.
	20. 6	he may occupy some fortified **towns** and escape from us."
	21. 6	Lord at Gibeah, the **town** of Saul, the Lord's chosen king."
1 Kgs	4.13	Argob in Bashan, sixty large **towns** in all, fortified with
	9.11	King Solomon gave Hiram twenty **towns** in the region of Galilee.
	9.13	"So these, my brother, are the **towns** you have given me!"
	13.32	of worship in the **towns** of Samaria will surely come true."
	14.12	As soon as you enter the **town** your son will die.
	15.23	his brave deeds and the **towns** he fortified, are all recorded
	16.24	the hill, built a **town** there, and named it Samaria,
	17.10	to the gate of the **town,** he saw a widow gathering firewood.
	20.34	restore to you the **towns** my father took from your father,
2 Kgs	2.23	some boys came out of a **town** and made fun of him.
	6.14	They reached the **town** at night and surrounded it.
	6.15	Syrian troops with their horses and chariots surrounding the **town.**
	6.19	this is not the **town** you are looking for.
	17. 9	of worship in all their **towns,** from the smallest village to
1 Chr	2.23	Geshur and Aram conquered sixty **towns** there, including
	2.23	the villages of Jair and Kenath, and the **towns** near by.
	2.49	and Shevah, who founded the **towns** of Machbenah and Gibea.
	4.23	of the king and lived in the **towns** of Netaim and Gederah.
	4.28	the descendants of Simeon lived in the following **towns:**
	5.16	Bashan and Gilead, in the **towns** there and all over the
	6.57	The following **towns** were assigned to Aaron's descendants:
	6.57	of refuge, Jattir, and the **towns** of Libnah, Eshtemoa, Hilen,
	6.60	were assigned the following **towns** with their pasture lands:
	6.60	made a total of thirteen **towns** for all their families to
	6.61	Ten **towns** in the territory of West Manasseh were
	6.62	were assigned thirteen **towns** in the territories of Issachar,
	6.63	In the same way, twelve **towns** in the territories of Reuben,
	6.64	people of Israel assigned **towns** for the Levites to live in,
	6.64	together with the pasture lands round the **towns.**
	6.65	(The **towns** in the territories of Judah, Simeon, and Benjamin, mentioned above,
	6.66	clan of Kohath were assigned **towns** and pasture lands in the
	6.70	Manasseh they were assigned the **towns** of Aner and Bileam
	6.71	Gershon were assigned the following **towns,**
	6.77	Merari were assigned the following **towns**
	7.24	She built the **towns** of Upper and Lower Beth Horon, and Uzzen
	7.28	in included Bethel and the **towns** round it, as far east as
	7.28	Naaran and as far west as Gezer and the **towns** round it.
	7.28	the cities of Shechem and Ayyah, and the **towns** round them.
	7.29	Beth Shan, Taanach, Megiddo, and Dor, and the **towns** round them.
	10. 7	his sons had died, they abandoned their **towns** and ran off.
	13. 2	priests and Levites in their **towns,** and tell them to
	20. 3	the same to the people of all the other **towns** of Ammon.
2 Chr	17. 9	and went through all the **towns** of Judah, teaching it to the
	28.18	the Philistines were raiding the **towns** in the western
	28.25	In every city and **town** in Judah, he built pagan places
Ezra	2.21	whose ancestors had lived in the following **towns** also returned:
	2.59	Nekoda who returned from the **towns** of Tel Melah, Tel Harsha,
	2.70	guards, and the temple workmen settled in nearby **towns;**
	2.70	settled in the **towns** where their ancestors had lived.
	3. 1	month the people of Israel were all settled in their **towns.**
Neh	3. 5	the leading men of the **town** refused to do the manual labour
	7.26	whose ancestors had lived in the following **towns** also returned:
	7.61	Nekoda who returned from the **towns** of Tel Melah, Tel Harsha,
	7.73	people of Israel—settled in the **towns** and cities of Judah.
	8. 1	month the people of Israel were all settled in their **towns.**
	8.15	them all through Jerusalem and the other cities and **towns:**
	11. 1	while the rest were to live in the other cities and **towns.**
	11. 3	In the other **towns** and cities the people of Israel, the
	11. 3	Solomon's servants lived on their own property in their own **towns.**
	11.20	their own property in the other cities and **towns** of Judah.
	11.25	Many of the people lived in **towns** near their farms.
	11.30	in Zanoah, in Adullam, and in the villages near these **towns.**
	12.28	Jerusalem and from the **towns** round Netophah,
Esth	9.19	Jews who live in small **towns** observe the fourteenth day of
Ps	69.35	He will save Jerusalem and rebuild the **towns** of Judah.
Prov	9. 3	to call out from the highest place in the **town:**
	9.14	the highest part of the **town,** [15]and calls out to people
Ecc	9.14	There was a little **town** without many people in it.
	9.15	was poor, but so clever that he could have saved the **town.**
Is	10.29	and the people in King Saul's **town** of Gibeah have run away.
	15. 8	It is heard at the **towns** of Eglaim and Beerelim.
	23.16	Take your harp, go round the **town,** you poor forgotten whore!
	34.13	all the palaces and walled **towns,** and jackals and owls will
	40. 9	Tell the **towns** of Judah that their God is coming!
	42.11	Let the desert and its **towns** praise God;
Jer	2.15	a desert, and his **towns** lie in ruins, completely abandoned.

Jer 3.14 one of you from each **town** and two from each clan, and
4.29 Every **town** will be left empty, and no one will live in
5. 6 to pieces, and leopards will prowl through their **towns.**
13.19 The **towns** of southern Judah are under siege;
14.18 when I go into the **towns,** I see people starving to death.
15. 7 In every **town** in the land I threw you to the wind
17.26 People will come from the **towns** of Judah and from the
19.15 city and on every nearby **town** all the punishment that I said
25.18 Jerusalem and all the **towns** of Judah, together with its
26. 2 people who come from the **towns** of Judah to worship there.
31.21 Come back, people of Israel, come home to the **towns** you left.
31.23 once again say in the land of Judah and in its **towns,**
31.24 Judah and in all its **towns,** and there will be farmers, and
32.44 villages round Jerusalem, in the **towns** of Judah,
32.44 and in the **towns** in the hill-country, in the foothills,
33.10 the **towns** of Judah and the streets of Jerusalem are empty;
33.13 In the **towns** of the hill-country, in the foothills, and
33.13 round Jerusalem, and in the **towns** of Judah, shepherds will
34. 1 to him, were attacking Jerusalem and its nearby **towns.**
34.22 I will make the **towns** of Judah like a desert where no
36. 6 the people of Judah who have come in from their **towns.**
36. 9 Jerusalem and by all who came there from the **towns** of Judah.
40. 5 king of Babylonia has made governor of the **towns** of Judah.
44. 6 anger and fury on the **towns** of Judah and on the streets
44. 9 have been done in the **towns** of Judah and in the streets
44.17 used to do in the **towns** of Judah and in the streets
44.21 the land offered in the **towns** of Judah and in the streets
46.14 "Proclaim it in the **towns** of Egypt, in Migdol, Memphis,
48. 1 "Pity the people of Nebo— their **town** is destroyed!
48. 8 Not a **town** will escape the destruction;
48. 9 Its **towns** will be left in ruins, and no one will live
48.28 "You people who live in Moab, leave your **towns!**
48.41 wings, [41] and the **towns** and fortresses will be captured.
49.18 and Gomorrah, when they and the near-by **towns** were destroyed.
50.40 Sodom and Gomorrah, when I destroyed them and the near-by **towns.**
51.43 The **towns** have become a horrifying sight and are like a
Ezek 19. 7 He wrecked forts, he ruined **towns.**
26. 6 they will kill those who live in her **towns** on the mainland.
26. 8 Those who live in the **towns** on the mainland will be killed
38.11 peace and security in unwalled **towns** that have no defences.
38.13 and the merchants from the **towns** of Spain will ask you,
39.16 (There will be a **town** near by named after the army.)
45. 5 There will be **towns** there for them to live in.
Obad 20 who are in Sardis will capture the **towns** of southern Judah.
Mic 1.15 you over to an enemy, who is going to capture your **town.**
5. 2 are one of the smallest **towns** in Judah, but out of you
Zech 7. 7 living not only in the **towns** round the city but also in
Mal 1. 4 the Edomites, say, "Our **towns** have been destroyed,
Mt 2. 1 Jesus was born in the **town** of Bethlehem in Judaea, during
2. 5 "In the **town** of Bethlehem in Judaea," they answered.
2.23 of Galilee [23] and made his home in a **town** named Nazareth.
4.13 to live in Capernaum, a **town** by Lake Galilee, in the
4.25 him from Galilee and the **Ten Towns,** from Jerusalem, Judaea,
8.33 away and went into the **town,** where they told the whole story
8.34 So everyone from the **town** went out to meet Jesus;
9. 1 the lake to his own **town,** [2] where some people brought to him
9.35 Jesus went round visiting all the **towns** and villages.
10. 5 "Do not go to any Gentile territory or any Samaritan **towns.**
10.11 "When you come to a **town** or village, go in and look
10.14 And if some home or **town** will not welcome you or listen
10.15 of Sodom and Gomorrah than to the people of that **town!**
10.23 When they persecute you in one **town,** run away to another one.
10.23 your work in all the **towns** of Israel before the Son of
11. 1 and went off to teach and preach in the **towns** near there.
11.20 The people in the **towns** where Jesus had performed most
11.20 did not turn from their sins, so he reproached those **towns.**
12.25 any **town** or family that divides itself into groups which fight
13.54 he left that place [54] and went back to his home **town.**
13.57 respected everywhere except in his home **town** and by his own
14.13 about it, so they left their **towns** and followed him by land.
16.13 the territory near the **town** of Caesarea Philippi, where he asked
23.34 others in the synagogues and chase them from town to **town.**
Mk 1.21 his disciples came to the **town** of Capernaum, and on the next
1.33 All the people of the **town** gathered in front of the house.
1.35 He went out of the **town** to a lonely place, where he
1.45 talked so much that Jesus could not go into a **town** publicly.
5.14 and spread the news in the **town** and among the farms.
5.20 and went all through the **Ten Towns,** telling what Jesus had
6. 1 and went back to his home **town,** followed by his disciples.
6. 4 except in his own home **town** and by his relatives and his
6.11 If you come to a **town** where people do not welcome you
6.33 they went from all the **towns** and ran ahead by land
6.56 everywhere Jesus went, to villages, **towns,** or farms, people would
7.31 Lake Galilee, going by way of the territory of the **Ten Towns.**
11. 1 approached Jerusalem, near the **towns** of Bethphage and Bethany,
Lk 1.26 God sent the angel Gabriel to a **town** in Galilee named Nazareth.
1.39 and hurried off to a **town** in the hill-country of Judaea.
2. 3 Everyone, then, went to register himself, each to his own **town.**
2. 4 Joseph went from the **town** of Nazareth in Galilee
2. 4 to the **town** of Bethlehem in Judaea, the birthplace
2.11 This very day in David's **town** your Saviour was
2.39 Lord, they returned to their home **town** of Nazareth in Galilee.
4.23 do here in my home **town** the same things you heard were
4.24 Jesus added, "a prophet is never welcomed in his home **town.**
4.29 dragged Jesus out of the **town,** and took him
4.29 to the top of the hill on which their **town** was built.
4.31 Jesus went to Capernaum, a **town** in Galilee, where he taught
4.42 At daybreak Jesus left the **town** and went off to a lonely
4.43 Kingdom of God in other **towns** also, because that is what God
Lk 5.12 Once Jesus was in a **town** where there was a man who
5.17 who had come from every **town** in Galilee and Judaea and from
7.11 Jesus went to a **town** called Nain, accompanied by his disciples
7.12 the gate of the **town,** a funeral procession was coming out.
7.12 a widow, and a large crowd from the **town** was with her.
7.37 In that **town** was a woman who lived a sinful life.
8. 1 Jesus travelled through **towns** and villages, preaching the Good
8. 4 People kept coming to Jesus from one **town** after another;
8.27 met by a man from the **town** who had demons in him.
8.34 and spread the news in the **town** and among the farms.
8.39 The man went through the **town,** telling what Jesus had done
9. 4 welcomed, stay in the same house until you leave that **town;**
9. 5 don't welcome you, leave that **town** and shake the dust off
9.10 and they went off by themselves to a **town** called Bethsaida.
10. 1 ahead of him to every **town** and place where he himself was
10. 8 Whenever you go into a **town** and are made welcome, eat what
10. 9 heal the sick in that **town,** and say to the people there,
10.10 whenever you go into a **town** and are not welcomed, go out
10.11 'Even the dust from your **town** that sticks to our feet
10.12 Day God will show more mercy to Sodom than to that **town!**
13.22 Jesus went through **towns** and villages, teaching the people
13.26 you taught in our **town!'**
14.21 streets and alleys of the **town,** and bring back the poor,
18. 2 "In a certain **town** there was a judge who neither feared
18. 3 a widow in that same **town** who kept coming to him
23.50 was a man named Joseph from Arimathea, a **town** in Judaea.
Jn 1.44 (Philip was from Bethsaida, the **town** where Andrew and Peter
2. 1 later there was a wedding in the **town** of Cana in Galilee.
4. 5 Samaria he came to a **town** named Sychar, which was not far
4. 8 (His disciples had gone into **town** to buy food.)
4.28 went back to the **town,** and said to the people there,
4.30 So they left the **town** and went to Jesus.
4.39 the Samaritans in that **town** believed in Jesus because the woman
7.42 and will be born in Bethlehem, the **town** where David lived."
11. 1 Bethany was the **town** where Mary and her sister Martha lived.
11.54 near the desert, to a **town** named Ephraim, where he stayed
19.38 Joseph, who was from the **town** of Arimathea, asked Pilate if
Acts 5.16 people came in from the **towns** around Jerusalem, bringing those
8.40 and on the way he preached the Good News in every **town.**
13.44 Sabbath nearly everyone in the **town** came to hear the word of
14.13 temple stood just outside the **town,** brought bulls and flowers to
14.19 and dragged him out of the **town,** thinking that he was dead.
14.20 gathered round him, he got up and went back into the **town.**
15.21 synagogues every Sabbath, and his words are preached in every **town."**
15.36 visit our brothers in every **town** where we preached the word
16. 4 As they went through the **towns,** they delivered to the believers
27. 7 and with great difficulty finally arrived off the **town** of Cnidus.
27. 8 place called Safe Harbours, not far from the **town** of Lasea.
28.13 south, and in two days we came to the **town** of Puteoli.
28.15 came as far as the **towns** of Market of Appius and Three
Tit 1. 5 that still needed doing and appoint church elders in every **town.**
Jude 7 and Gomorrah, and the nearby **towns,** whose people acted as those

TOWN CLERK

Acts 19.35 At last the **town clerk** was able to calm the crowd.

TRACE

Gen 36.20 were divided into tribes which **traced** their ancestry to the
Num 26.29 and the following clans **traced** their ancestry to Gilead:
26.36 The clan of Eran **traced** its descent from Shuthelah.
26.40 The clans of Ard and Naaman **traced** their descent from Bela.
26.45 clans of Heber and Malchiel **traced** their descent from Beriah.
1 Chr 5.14 son of Huri, whose ancestors were **traced** back as follows:
Ezra 7. 1 He **traced** his ancestors back to Aaron, the High Priest, as
Dan 2.35 The wind carried it all away, leaving not a **trace.**
Zeph 1. 4 I will destroy the last **trace** of the worship of Baal there,

TRACK

Job 10. 6 Then why do you **track** down all my sins and hunt down
14.16 step I take, but you will not keep **track** of my sins.
Ps 107. 4 Some wandered in the **trackless** desert and could not find
107.40 their oppressors and made them wander in **trackless** deserts.
Lam 4.19 They **tracked** us down in the hills;

Am **TRADE**
see also **EXCHANGE**

TRADE

Gen 34.10 live anywhere you wish, **trade** freely, and own property."
37.28 agreed, [28] and when some Midianite **traders** came by, the
42.34 brother back to you, and you can stay here and **trade.'"**
Deut 33.18 Zebulun be prosperous in their **trade** on the sea, And may
2 Sam 5.11 King Hiram of Tyre sent a **trade** mission to David;
1 Kgs 10.15 by merchants, the profits from **trade,** and tribute paid by
1 Chr 14. 1 King Hiram of Tyre sent a **trade** mission to David;
2 Chr 9.14 in addition to the taxes paid by the **traders** and merchants.
Ecc 11. 1 Invest your money in foreign **trade,** and one of these days
Song 3. 6 with incense and myrrh, the incense sold by the **traders?**
Is 23.17 go back to her old **trade,** and she will hire herself out
Ezek 27.13 Greece, Tubal, and Meshech and **traded** your goods for slaves
27.15 The people of Rhodes **traded** with you;
27.23 the cities of Asshur and Chilmad—they all **traded** with you.
Rev 18.22 No workman in any **trade** will ever be found in you again;

TRADITION

1 Chr 4.22 (These **traditions** are very old.)
Neh 2.20 in Jerusalem, and you have no share in its **traditions."**
Is 29.13 rules and **traditions,** which they have simply memorized.
Gal 1.14 and was much more devoted to the **traditions** of our ancestors.

AV TRADITION

Mt 15. 2 your disciples disobey the **teaching** handed down by our ancestors?
15. 3 "And why do you disobey God's command and follow your own **teaching?**
15. 6 God's command, in order to follow your own **teaching.**
Mk 7. 3 the Jews, follow the **teaching** they received from their ancestors:
7. 5 disciples do not follow the **teaching** handed down by our ancestors,
7. 8 "You put aside God's command and obey the **teachings** of men."
7. 9 of rejecting God's law in order to uphold your own **teaching.**
7.13 In this way the **teaching** you pass on to others cancels
Col 2. 8 wisdom, which comes from the **teachings** handed down by men
2 Thes 3. 6 and who do not follow the **instructions** that we gave them.
1 Pet 1.18 the worthless manner of life **handed down** by your ancestors.

TRAFFIC

1 Kgs 15.17 in order to cut off all **traffic** in and out of Judah.
2 Chr 16. 1 in order to cut off all **traffic** in and out of Judah.

TRAIN
[WELL-TRAINED]

Judg 20.17 the Israelite tribes gathered 400,000 **trained** soldiers.
20.25 they killed eighteen thousand **trained** Israelite soldiers.
2 Sam 22.35 He **trains** me for battle, so that I can use the strongest
1 Chr 5.18 44,760 soldiers, **well-trained** in the use of shields,
12.23 David was at Hebron, many **trained** soldiers joined his army
12.23 7,100 **well-trained** men;
12.23 men ready to fight, **trained** to use all kinds of weapons;
12.23 28,600 **trained** men;
12.23 120,000 men **trained** to use all kinds of weapons.
25. 7 and their fellow-Levites were **trained** musicians.
2 Chr 14. 8 All of them were brave, **well-trained** men.
Ps 18.34 He **trains** me for battle, so that I can use the strongest
144. 1 He **trains** me for battle and prepares me for war.
Ezek 27. 9 The ship's carpenters Were **well-trained** men from Byblos.
Dan 1. 4 to be handsome, intelligent, **well-trained,** quick to learn,
1. 5 After three years of this **training** they were to appear
Hos 10.11 "Israel was once like a **well-trained** young cow, ready
Mt 21.16 'You have **trained** children and babies to offer perfect praise.' "
Lk 6.40 when he has completed his **training,** will be like his teacher.
Jn 7.15 this man know so much when he has never had any **training?"**
1 Cor 9.25 Every athlete in **training** submits to strict discipline,
1 Tim 4. 7 Keep yourself in **training** for a godly life.
Tit 2. 4 is good, [4] in order to **train** the younger women to love their
2 Pet 2.14 Their hearts are **trained** to be greedy.

TRAITOR

1 Sam 14.33 "You are **traitors!"**
1 Kgs 1.21 dead my son Solomon and I will be treated as **traitors."**
Ps 59. 5 show no mercy to evil **traitors!**
119.158 When I look at those **traitors,** I am filled with disgust,
Is 24.16 **Traitors** continue to betray, and their treachery grows worse
Jer 9. 2 They are all unfaithful, a mob of **traitors.**
Mt 26.25 Judas, the **traitor,** spoke up.
26.48 The **traitor** had given the crowd a signal:
27. 3 When Judas, the **traitor,** learnt that Jesus had been condemned,
Mk 14.44 The **traitor** had given the crowd a signal:
Lk 6.16 Judas son of James, and Judas Iscariot, who became the **traitor.**
Jn 18. 2 Judas, the **traitor,** knew where it was, because many times Jesus
18. 5 Judas, the **traitor,** was standing there with them.
Rev 21. 8 But cowards, **traitors,** perverts, murderers, the immoral,

TRAMP

2 Kgs 19.24 that the feet of your soldiers **tramped** the River Nile dry.
Is 1.12 Who asked you to do all this **tramping** about in my Temple?
37.25 that the feet of your soldiers **tramped** the River Nile dry.

TRAMPLE

Num 24.19 The nation of Israel will **trample** them down And wipe out
Deut 33.29 come begging for mercy, and you will **trample** them down.
2 Sam 22.43 I **trample** on them like mud in the streets.
2 Kgs 7.17 The officer was **trampled** to death there by the people and died,
7.20 happened to him—he died, **trampled** to death by the people at
13. 7 Syria had destroyed the rest, **trampling** them down like dust.
14. 9 A wild animal passed by and **trampled** the bush down.
2 Chr 25.18 A wild animal passed by and **trampled** the bush down.
Job 9. 8 God spread out the heavens or **trample** the sea-monster's back.
Ps 18.42 I **trample** on them like mud in the streets.
66.12 You let our enemies **trample** over us;
80.13 wild pigs **trample** it down, and wild animals feed on it.
91.13 You will **trample** down lions and snakes, fierce lions
Is 5. 5 it, and let wild animals eat it and **trample** it down.
10. 6 to loot and steal and **trample** on the people like dirt in
10.13 Like a bull I have **trampled** on the people who live there.
14.19 thrown with them into a rocky pit, and **trampled** down.
14.25 in my land of Israel and **trample** upon them on my mountains.
16.10 No one **tramples** grapes to make wine;
Is 25.10 people of Moab will be **trampled** down,
25.10 just as straw is **trampled** in manure.
26. 6 oppressed walk over it now and **trample** it under their feet.
28. 3 The pride of those drunken leaders will be **trampled** underfoot.
41.25 He **tramples** on rulers as if they were mud, like a potter
41.25 rulers as if they were mud, like a potter **trampling** clay.
51.23 down in the streets and **trampled** on you as if you were
63. 2 red, like that of a man who **tramples** grapes to make wine?"
63. 3 The Lord answers, "I have **trampled** the nations like grapes,
63. 3 I **trampled** them in my anger, and their blood has stained all
63. 6 In my anger I **trampled** whole nations and shattered them.
63.18 they **trampled** down your sanctuary.
Jer 12.10 they have **trampled** down my fields;
51.33 them down and **trample** them like corn on a threshing-place.
Ezek 34.18 you even **trample** down what you don't eat!
34.19 to eat the grass you **trample** down and drink the water you
Dan 7. 7 teeth it crushed its victims, and then it **trampled** on them.
7.19 its bronze claws and iron teeth and then **trampled** on them.
7.23 It will crush the whole earth and **trample** it down.
8. 7 thrown to the ground and **trampled** on, and there was no one
8.10 it threw some of them to the ground and **trampled** on them.
8.13 will the army of heaven and the Temple be **trampled** on?"
Amos 2. 7 They **trample** down the weak and helpless and push the poor
8. 4 Listen to this, you that **trample** on the needy and try to
Mic 7.10 see them defeated, **trampled** down like mud in the streets.
7.19 You will **trample** our sins underfoot and send them to the
Nah 3.14 **Trample** the clay to make bricks, and get the brick moulds ready!
Hab 3.12 in fury you **trampled** the nations.
3.15 **trampled** the sea with your horses, and the mighty waters foamed.
Zech 10. 5 be victorious like soldiers who **trample** their enemies into
Mt 5.13 worthless, so it is thrown out and people **trample** on it.
7. 6 pearls in front of pigs—they will only **trample** them underfoot.
Lk 21.24 the heathen will **trample** over Jerusalem until their time is up.
Rev 11. 2 to the heathen, who will **trample** on the Holy City for
19.15 of iron, and he will **trample** out the wine in the winepress

TRANCE

Num 24. 4 staring eyes I see in a **trance** A vision from Almighty God.
24.16 staring eyes I see in a **trance** A vision from Almighty God.

TRANSFER

Lev 16.21 people of Israel, and so **transfer** them to the goat's head.
1 Kgs 12.26 they will **transfer** their allegiance to King Rehoboam
Ezek 48.14 it may be sold or exchanged or **transferred** to anyone else.

TRANSFORM

Rom 12. 2 but let God **transform** you inwardly by a complete change
2 Cor 3.18 Lord, who is the Spirit, **transforms** us into his likeness in
5. 4 over us, so that what is mortal will be **transformed** by life.

AV TRANSGRESS
see also **SIN**

Ex 23.21 for I have sent him, and he will not pardon such **rebellion.**
Lev 16.21 all the evils, sins, and **rebellions** of the people of Israel,
Num 14.18 I show great love and faithfulness and forgive sin and **rebellion.**
14.41 But Moses said, "Then why are you **disobeying** the Lord now?
Deut 17. 2 sinned against the Lord and **broken** his covenant [3] by
26.13 I have not **disobeyed** or forgotten any of your commands
Josh 7.11 They have **broken** the agreement with me that I ordered them
7.15 brought terrible shame on Israel and has **broken** my covenant."
22.22 we rebelled and did not **keep** faith with the Lord,
23.16 If you do not **keep** the covenant
Judg 2.20 and say, "This nation has **broken** the covenant that I
1 Sam 2.24 is an awful thing the people of the Lord are **talking** about!
14.33 "You are **traitors!"**
15.24 "I **disobeyed** the Lord's command and your instructions.
24.11 I have no thought of **rebelling** against you or of harming you.
1 Kgs 8.50 all their sins and their **rebellion** against you, and make
2 Kgs 18.12 the Lord their God, but **broke** the covenant he had made with
1 Chr 5.25 But the people were **unfaithful** to the God of their
10.13 Saul died because he was **unfaithful** to the Lord.
2 Chr 12. 2 their **disloyalty** to the Lord was punished.
24.20 God asks why you have **disobeyed** his commands
26.16 He **defied** the Lord his God by going into the Temple
28.19 of his people and had **defied** the Lord, the Lord brought
29.19 during those years he was **unfaithful** to God, and we have
36.14 and the people **followed** the sinful example of the nations
Ezra 10. 6 night there grieving over the **unfaithfulness** of the exiles.
10.10 He said, "You have been **faithless** and have brought guilt on
10.13 two days, because so many of us are **involved** in this sin.
Neh 1. 8 you people of Israel are **unfaithful** to me, I will scatter
13.27 your example and **disobey** our God by marrying foreign women?"
Esth 3. 3 asked him why he was **disobeying** the king's command;
Job 8. 4 against God, and so he punished them as they **deserved.**
13.23 What **crimes** am I charged with?
33. 9 I have done nothing **wrong.**
35. 6 If you do **wrong** many times, does that affect him?
Ps 17. 4 I speak no **evil** as others do;
25. 3 in you, but to those who are quick to **rebel** against you.
25. 7 Forgive the sins and **errors** of my youth.
51. 3 I recognize my **faults;**
59. 3 because of any sin or **wrong** I have done, [4] nor because of
59. 5 show no mercy to evil **traitors!**
119.158 When I look at those **traitors,** I am filled with disgust,
Prov 11. 3 People who can't be **trusted** are destroyed by their own dishonesty.
11. 6 someone who can't be **trusted** is trapped by his own greed.

Prov	12.13	is trapped by his own **words,** but an honest man gets himself
	13. 2	but those who are **deceitful** are hungry for violence.
	13.15	but those who can't be **trusted** are on the road to ruin.
	17. 9	want people to like you, forgive them when they **wrong** you.
	19.11	When someone **wrongs** you, it is a great virtue to ignore it.
	21.18	The **wicked** bring on themselves the suffering they try to
	22.12	that truth is kept safe by disproving the words of **liars.**
	23.28	for you like robbers and cause many men to be **unfaithful.**
	28.21	But some judges will do **wrong** to get even the smallest bribe.
	28.24	Anyone who thinks it isn't **wrong** to steal from his
	29.16	When evil men are in power, **crime** increases.
	29.22	People with quick tempers cause a lot of quarrelling and **trouble.**
Is	24. 5	have defiled the earth by **breaking** God's laws and by
	48. 8	be trusted, that you have always been known as a **rebel.**
	50. 1	you were sent away because of your **crimes.**
	53.12	He willingly gave his life and shared the fate of **evil** men.
	57. 4	Who are you **liars** jeering at?
	59.12	"Lord, our **crimes** against you are many.
	59.13	We have **rebelled** against you, rejected you, and refused
	66.24	see the dead bodies of those who have **rebelled** against me.
Jer	2. 8	The rulers **rebelled** against me;
	2.29	Why have you **rebelled** against me?
	3.13	are guilty and that you have **rebelled** against the Lord, your
	33. 8	me, and I will forgive their sins and their **rebellion.**
	34.18	But they **broke** the covenant and did not keep its terms.
Ezek	2. 3	They have rebelled and **turned** against me and are still rebels,
	18.30	Turn away from all the **evil** you are doing, and don't let
	18.31	Give up all the **evil** you have been doing, and get
	20.38	away from among you those who are **rebellious** and sinful.
	21.24	Everyone knows how **guilty** you are.
	39.24	and their **wickedness,** and I turned away from them."
Dan	8.23	and they have become so **wicked** that they must be punished,
	9.11	All Israel **broke** your laws and refused to listen to what
	9.24	freeing your people and your holy city from sin and **evil.**
Hos	6. 7	the land at Adam, they **broke** the covenant I had made with
	7.13	They have left me and **rebelled** against me.
	8. 1	My people have **broken** the covenant I made with them and have
Mic	1. 5	the people of Israel have sinned and **rebelled** against God.
	1. 5	Who is to blame for Israel's **rebellion?**
Hab	2. 5	Wealth is **deceitful.**
Zeph	3.11	no longer need to be ashamed that you **rebelled** against me.
Mt	15. 2	that your disciples **disobey** the teaching handed down by our
	15. 3	"And why do you **disobey** God's command and follow your own
Lk	15.29	you like a slave, and I have never **disobeyed** your orders.
	22.37	'He shared the fate of **criminals,**' must come true about me,
Rom	2.27	by the Gentiles because you **break** the Law, even though you
	4.15	where there is no law, there is no **disobeying** of the law.
	5.14	the same way that Adam did when he **disobeyed** God's command.
Gal	2.18	then I show myself to be someone who **breaks** the Law.
	3.19	in order to show what **wrongdoing** is, and it was meant to
1 Tim	2.14	it was the woman who was deceived and **broke** God's law.
Heb	2. 2	and anyone who **did not follow** it or obey it received the
	9.15	sets people free from the **wrongs** they did while the first
Jas	2. 9	guilty of sin, and the Law condemns you as a **law-breaker.**
	2.11	you have become a **law-breaker** if you commit murder.
1 Jn	3. 4	Whoever sins is guilty of **breaking** God's law,
	3. 4	because sin is a **breaking** of the law.

TRANSLATE

Ezra	4. 7	was written in Aramaic and was to be **translated** when read.
	4.18	"The letter which you sent has been **translated** and read to me.
Neh	8. 8	They gave an oral **translation** of God's Law and explained
Esth	3.12	dictated a proclamation to be **translated** into every language

TRANSPARENT

Rev	21.21	The street of the city was of pure gold, **transparent** as glass.

TRANSPORT

2 Chr	2. 2	seventy thousand men to work **transporting** materials, and
	2.18	assigned 70,000 of them to **transport** materials and 80,000 to
	34.13	Levites were in charge of **transporting** materials and

TRAP

Ex	23.33	you worship their gods, it will be a fatal **trap** for you."
	34.12	you are going, because this could be a fatal **trap** for you.
Josh	23.13	dangerous for you as a **trap** or a pit and as painful
Judg	2. 3	and you will be **trapped** by the worship of their gods."
	8.27	It was a **trap** for Gideon and his family.
	20.43	The Israelites had the enemy **trapped,** and without
1 Sam	18.21	I will use her to **trap** him, and he will be killed
	23. 7	David has **trapped** himself by going into a walled town with
	28. 9	Why, then, are you trying to **trap** me and get me killed?"
2 Sam	22. 6	death was round me, and the grave set its **trap** for me.
Job	5.12	of cunning men, and **traps** wise men in their own schemes,
	18. 9	a **trap** catches his heels and holds him.
	18.10	a **trap** has been set in his path.
	19. 6	He has set a **trap** to catch me.
	40.24	Or who can catch his snout in a **trap?**
Ps	7.15	in the **traps** they set for others, they themselves get caught.
	9.15	they have been caught in their own **trap.**
	9.16	judgements, and the wicked are **trapped** by their own deeds.
	10. 2	catch them in the **traps** they have made.
	10. 9	he catches them in his **trap** and drags them away.
	18. 5	death was round me, and the grave set its **trap** for me.
	31. 4	Keep me safe from the **trap** that has been set for me;
	35. 7	any reason they laid a **trap** for me and dug a deep
	35. 8	be caught in their own **trap** and fall to their destruction!
Ps	38.12	want to kill me lay **traps** for me, and those who want
	64. 5	they plan where to place their **traps.**
	66.11	let us fall into a **trap** and placed heavy burdens on our
	94.13	days of trouble until a pit is dug to **trap** the wicked.
	119.61	The wicked have laid a **trap** for me, but I do not
	119.85	who do not obey your law, have dug pits to **trap** me.
	119.110	Wicked men lay a **trap** for me, but I have not disobeyed
	124. 7	We have escaped like a bird from a hunter's **trap;**
	124. 7	the **trap** is broken, and we are free!
	140. 5	Proud men have set a **trap** for me;
	140. 5	snares and along the path they have set **traps** to catch me.
	141. 9	Protect me from the **traps** they have set for me, from the
	141.10	wicked fall into their own **traps** while I go by unharmed.
	142. 3	path where I walk, my enemies have hidden a **trap** for me.
Prov	1.18	like that are setting a **trap** for themselves,
	1.18	a **trap** in which they will die.
	3.26	He will not let you fall into a **trap.**
	5.22	The sins of a wicked man are a **trap.**
	6. 2	been caught by your own words, **trapped** by your own promises?
	6. 5	Get out of the **trap** like a bird or a deer escaping
	6.25	don't be **trapped** by their flirting eyes.
	7.22	a deer prancing into a **trap** [23] where an arrow would pierce
	11. 6	someone who can't be trusted is **trapped** by his own greed.
	12.13	A wicked man is **trapped** by his own words, but an honest
	18. 7	he gets caught in the **trap** of his own words.
	22. 5	life, stay away from the **traps** that catch the wicked along
	22.14	Adultery is a **trap**—it catches those with whom the Lord
	23.27	Prostitutes and immoral women are a deadly **trap.**
	26.27	People who set **traps** for others get caught themselves.
	28.10	person into doing evil, you will fall into your own **trap.**
	29. 5	If you flatter your friends, you set a **trap** for yourself.
	29. 6	Evil people are **trapped** in their own sins, while honest
Ecc	7.26	offers you will catch you like a **trap** or like a net;
	9.12	birds suddenly caught in a **trap,** like fish caught in a net,
	9.12	we are **trapped** at some evil moment
Is	8.14	I am like a **trap** that will catch the people of the
	8.15	They will be caught in a **trap."**
	24.17	There are terrors, pits, and **traps** waiting for you.
	24.18	anyone who escapes from the pit will be caught in a **trap.**
	28.13	You will be wounded, **trapped,** and taken prisoner.
Jer	5.26	to catch birds, but they have set their **traps** to catch men.
	8. 9	they are confused and **trapped.**
	9. 8	to his neighbour, but is really setting a **trap** for him.
	18.22	for me to fall in and have set **traps** to catch me.
	48.43	Terror, pits, and **traps** are waiting for the people of Moab.
	48.44	will be caught in the **traps,** because the Lord has set the
	50.24	have been caught in the **trap** I set for you, even though
Lam	1.13	He set a **trap** for me and brought me to the ground.
	3.52	"I was **trapped** like a bird by enemies who had no cause
Ezek	12.13	But I will spread out my net and **trap** him in it.
	19. 4	The nations heard about him and **trapped** him in a pit.
	19. 8	They spread their hunting nets and caught him in their **trap.**
Hos	5. 1	You have become a **trap** at Mizpah, a net spread on Mount
	9. 8	Yet wherever I go, you try to **trap** me like a bird.
Amos	3. 5	get caught in a trap if the **trap** has not been baited?
	3. 5	Does a **trap** spring unless something sets it off?
Obad	7	Those friends who ate with you have laid a **trap** for you;
Mt	16. 1	came to Jesus wanted to **trap** him, so they asked him to
	19. 3	to him and tried to **trap** him by asking, "Does our Law
	22.15	Pharisees went off and made a plan to **trap** Jesus with questions.
	22.18	Why are you trying to **trap** me?
	22.35	a teacher of the Law, tried to **trap** him with a question.
Mk	8.11	They wanted to **trap** him, so they asked him to perform
	10. 2	Some Pharisees came to him and tried to **trap** him.
	12.13	Herod's party were sent to Jesus to **trap** him with questions.
	12.15	their trick and answered, "Why are you trying to **trap** me?
Lk	10.25	A teacher of the Law came up and tried to **trap** Jesus.
	11.16	Others wanted to **trap** Jesus, so they asked him to perform
	11.54	many things, [54] trying to lay **traps** for him and catch him
	20.20	and they sent them to **trap** Jesus with questions, so that
	21.35	life, or that Day may suddenly catch you [35] like a **trap.**
Jn	8. 6	They said this to **trap** Jesus, so that they could accuse him.
Rom	11. 9	David says, "May they be caught and **trapped** at their feasts;
1 Cor	3.19	As the scripture says, "God **traps** the wise in their cleverness";
2 Cor	11.20	takes advantage of you or **traps** you or looks down on you
	12.16	will say that I was crafty, and **trapped** you with lies.
1 Tim	3. 7	he will not be disgraced and fall into the Devil's **trap.**
	6. 9	are caught in the **trap** of many foolish and harmful desires,
2 Tim	2.26	senses and escape from the **trap** of the Devil, who had caught
Jas	1.14	when he is drawn away and **trapped** by his own evil desire.
2 Pet	2.14	They lead weak people into a **trap.**
	2.18	use immoral bodily lusts to **trap** those who are just

AV **TRAVAIL**

see also **BEAR (3), LABOUR**

Ex	18. 8	also told him about the **hardships** the people had faced on
Num	20.14	You know the **hardships** we have suffered, [15] how our
Job	15.20	oppresses others will be in **torment** as long as he lives.
Ps	7.14	See how wicked people **think** up evil;
Ecc	1.13	God has laid a miserable **fate** upon us.
	2.23	everything you do brings nothing but worry and **heartache.**
	2.26	him, but he makes sinners **work,** earning and saving, so that
	3.10	I know the heavy **burdens** that God has laid on us.
	4. 4	I have also learnt why people **work** so hard to succeed:
	4. 6	of mind, than to be **busy** all the time with both hands,
	5.14	it all in some unlucky **deal** and end up with nothing left
Is	53.11	After a life of **suffering,** he will again have joy;
	66. 8	Zion will not have to **suffer** long, before the nation is born.
Lam	3. 5	He has shut me in a prison of misery and **anguish.**
1 Thes	2. 9	Surely you remember, our brothers, how we worked and **toiled!**

1 Thes	5. 3	come as suddenly as the **pains** that come upon a woman in
2 Thes	3. 8	Instead, we worked and **toiled;**

TRAVEL

Gen	12. 6	they arrived in Canaan, [6]Abram **travelled** through the land
	30.36	with this flock as far as he could **travel** in three days.
	34.21	let them live in the land with us and **travel** freely.
	37.25	saw a group of Ishmaelites **travelling** from Gilead to Egypt.
	41.45	He left the king's court and **travelled** all over the land.
Ex	3.18	Now allow us to **travel** for three days into the desert to
	5. 3	Allow us to **travel** for three days into the desert to offer
	8.27	We must **travel** three days into the desert to offer
	12.11	are to be dressed for **travel,** with your sandals on your feet
	13.21	to give them light, so that they could **travel** night and day.
	23.20	to protect you as you **travel** and to bring you to the
Num	10.33	Sinai, the holy mountain, they **travelled** for three days.
	11. 4	There were some foreigners **travelling** with the Israelites.
Deut	1. 2	(It takes eleven days to **travel** from Mount Sinai to Kadesh
	29.16	was like to **travel** through the territory of other nations.
Judg	5. 6	went through the land, and **travellers** used the side roads.
	17. 8	While he was **travelling,** he came to Micah's house in the
	18.22	They had **travelled** a good distance from the house when
	19.17	The old man noticed the **traveller** in the city square and
1 Sam	28.22	You must eat so that you will be strong enough to **travel."**
2 Sam	7. 6	I have **travelled** round living in a tent.
	7. 7	In all my **travelling** with the people of Israel I never
	22.11	he **travelled** on the wings of the wind.
	24. 8	to Jerusalem, having **travelled** through the whole country.
1 Kgs	10. 1	of Solomon's fame, and she **travelled** to Jerusalem to test
	11.18	Then they **travelled** to Egypt and went to the king, who gave
	11.29	One day, as Jeroboam was **travelling** from Jerusalem,
1 Chr	17. 6	In all my **travelling** with the people of Israel I never
	21. 4	Joab went out, **travelled** through the whole country of Israel,
2 Chr	9. 1	King Solomon's fame, and she **travelled** to Jerusalem to test
	19. 4	lived in Jerusalem, he **travelled** regularly among the people,
	23. 2	They **travelled** to all the cities of Judah and brought back
Ezra	8.31	us from enemy attacks and from ambush as we **travelled.**
Neh	2. 7	instructing them to let me **travel** to Judah.
Job	21.29	Haven't you talked with people who **travel?**
	28. 4	Or human feet ever **travel,** Men dig the shafts of mines.
	28. 8	No lion or other fierce beast Ever **travels** those lonely roads.
	28.26	would fall, And the path that the thunderclouds **travel;**
	31.32	I invited **travellers** into my home and never let them
Ps	18.10	he **travelled** on the wings of the wind.
Prov	2.18	you go to her house, you are **travelling** the road to death.
	4.18	The road the righteous **travel** is like the sunrise,
	6.22	will lead you when you **travel,** protect you at night, and
	16.17	Those who are good **travel** a road that avoids evil;
Is	19.23	of those two countries will **travel** to and fro between them,
	26. 7	the road they **travel** is level.
	30. 6	"The ambassadors **travel** through dangerous country, where
	33. 8	The highways are so dangerous that no one **travels** on them.
	34.10	age after age, and no one will ever **travel** through it again.
	35. 8	No sinner will ever **travel** that road;
	35. 9	Those whom the Lord has rescued will **travel** home by that road.
	42.16	"I will lead my blind people by roads they have never **travelled.**
	45.13	I will straighten every road that he **travels.**
	49.11	the mountains and prepare a road for my people to **travel.**
	58.13	and honour it by not **travelling,** working, or talking idly on
Jer	2. 6	land where no one lives and no one will even **travel.**
	9.10	they have dried up, and no one **travels** through them.
	9.12	and dry as a desert, so that no one **travels** through it?
	14. 8	in our land, like a **traveller** who stays for only one night?
	51.43	like a waterless desert, where no one lives or even **travels.**
Ezek	14.15	dangerous that no one could **travel** through it, [16]and even
	33.28	so wild that no one will be able to **travel** through them.
	35. 7	of Edom a waste and kill everyone who **travels** through it.
	39.14	men will be chosen to **travel** through the land in order to
Amos	3. 3	Do two men start **travelling** together without arranging to meet?
Mt	3. 3	make a straight path for him to **travel!" "**
	7.13	leads to it is easy, and there are many who **travel** it.
	8.28	and were so fierce that no one dared **travel** on that road.
	12.42	accuse you, because she **travelled** all the way from her country
	12.43	out of a person, it **travels** over dry country looking for
Mk	1. 3	make a straight path for him to **travel!" "**
	1.39	So he **travelled** all over Galilee, preaching in the synagogues
Lk	2.44	with the group, so they **travelled** a whole day and then
	3. 4	make a straight path for him to **travel!**
	8. 1	Some time later Jesus **travelled** through towns and villages,
	9. 6	The disciples left and **travelled** through all the villages,
	10.33	But a Samaritan who was **travelling** that way came upon the man,
	11.24	out of a person, it **travels** over dry country looking for
	11.31	of today, because she **travelled** all the way from her country
Jn	1.23	Make a straight path for the Lord to **travel!" "**
	7. 1	After this, Jesus **travelled** in Galilee;
	7. 1	did not want to **travel** in Judaea, because the Jewish authorities
	11.54	So Jesus did not **travel** openly in Judaea, but left and
Acts	1.21	time that the Lord Jesus **travelled** about with us, beginning from
	8.36	As they **travelled** down the road, they came to a place
	9. 7	The men who were **travelling** with Saul had stopped, not
	9.32	Peter **travelled** everywhere, and on one occasion he went to
	13.31	appeared to those who had **travelled** with him from Galilee to
	16. 1	Paul **travelled** on to Derbe and Lystra, where a Christian named
	16. 6	They **travelled** through the region of Phrygia and Galatia
	16. 8	So they **travelled** right on through Mysia and went to Troas.
	17. 1	Paul and Silas **travelled** on through Amphipolis and Apollonia
	19. 1	Paul **travelled** through the interior of the province
	19.13	Jews who **travelled** round and drove out evil spirits also tried
	19.21	made up his mind to **travel** through Macedonia and Achaia and
	19.29	two Macedonians who were **travelling** with Paul, and rushed with
Acts	22. 6	"As I was **travelling** and coming near Damascus, about midday
	26.13	the sky and shining round me and the men **travelling** with me.
Rom	15.19	And so, in **travelling** all the way from Jerusalem to Illyricum,
1 Cor	9. 5	and Peter, by taking a Christian wife with me on my **travels?**
2 Cor	8.19	appointed by the churches to **travel** with us as we carry out
	11.26	In my many **travels** I have been in danger from floods and
Tit	3.13	to get started on their **travels,** and see to it that they
Jas	4.13	"Today or tomorrow we will **travel** to a certain city, where

TRAVELLERS' VALLEY

Ezek	39.11	in Israel, in **Travellers' Valley,** east of the Dead Sea.

TRAY

Ex	25.38	Make its tongs and **trays** of pure gold.
	37.23	lamp-stand, and he made its tongs and **trays** of pure gold.
Num	4. 9	its lamps, tongs, **trays,** and all the olive-oil containers.

TREACHERY

Is	24.16	continue to betray, and their **treachery** grows worse and worse.
	33. 1	themselves will become victims of robbery and **treachery.**
Hos	7. 4	They are all **treacherous** and disloyal.
	12. 1	**Treachery** and acts of violence increase among them.
Hab	1.13	But how can you stand these **treacherous,** evil men?
Zeph	3. 4	The prophets are irresponsible and **treacherous;**
2 Tim	3. 4	they will be **treacherous,** reckless, and swollen with pride;

TREAD

Is	5. 2	a tower to guard them, dug a pit for **treading** the grapes.
Jer	25.30	he will shout like a man **treading** grapes.

TREASON

2 Kgs	9.23	"It's **treason,** Ahaziah!"
	11.14	Athaliah tore her clothes in distress and shouted, **"Treason!**
	11.14	**Treason!"**
2 Chr	23.13	She tore her clothes in distress and shouted, **"Treason!**
	23.13	**Treason!"**

TREASURE

Deut	33. 4	Law that Moses gave us, our nation's most **treasured** possession.
1 Sam	25.29	God will keep you safe, as a man guards a precious **treasure.**
1 Kgs	14.26	He took away all the **treasures** in the Temple and in the
2 Kgs	14.14	all the palace **treasures,** and carried them back to Samaria.
	24.13	to Babylon all the **treasures** in the Temple and the palace.
2 Chr	1.11	of asking for wealth or **treasure** or fame or the death of
	1.12	will give you more wealth, **treasure,** and fame than any king
	12. 9	to Jerusalem and took the **treasures** from the Temple and from
	25.24	by the descendants of Obed Edom, and the palace **treasures.**
	36. 7	carried off some of the **treasures** of the Temple and put them
	36.10	as a prisoner, and carried off the **treasures** of the Temple.
Job	3.21	they prefer a grave to any **treasure.**
Ps	119.162	your promises— as happy as someone who finds rich **treasure.**
Prov	2. 4	it as hard as you would for silver or some hidden **treasure.**
	8.21	wealth to those who love me, filling their houses with **treasures.**
Is	2. 7	of silver and gold, and there is no end to their **treasures.**
	33. 6	Their greatest **treasure** is their reverence for the Lord.
	45. 3	I will give you **treasures** from dark, secret places;
Jer	15.13	carry away the wealth and **treasures** of my people, in order
	17. 3	away your wealth and your **treasures** because of all the sins
	20. 5	and property, even the **treasures** of the kings of Judah,
	27.16	who say that the temple **treasures** will soon be brought back
	27.18	Almighty, not to allow the **treasures** that remain in the
	27.19	tank, the carts, and some of the other temple **treasures.)**
	27.21	of Israel, say about the **treasures** that are left in the
	28. 3	temple **treasures** that King Nebuchadnezzar took to Babylonia.
	28. 6	from Babylonia all the temple **treasures** and all the people
	50.37	Destroy its **treasures;**
	51.13	has many rivers and rich **treasures,** but its time is up, and
Lam	1.10	Her enemies robbed her of all her **treasures.**
	1.11	exchange their **treasures** for food to keep themselves alive.
Ezek	7.22	will not interfere when my **treasured** Temple is profaned,
	28. 4	and skill made you rich with **treasures** of gold and silver.
Dan	1. 2	King Jehoiakim and seize some of the temple **treasures.**
	1. 2	and put the captured **treasures** in the temple storerooms.
	11.43	will take away Egypt's hidden **treasures** of gold and silver
Hos	9. 6	Their **treasures** of silver and the places where their homes
Joel	3. 5	and gold and carried my rich **treasures** into your temples.
Obad	6	Descendants of Esau, your **treasures** have been looted.
Mic	6.10	In the houses of evil men are **treasures** which they got
Nah	2. 9	The city is full of **treasure!**
Hag	2. 7	all the nations, and their **treasures** will be brought here,
Mt	12.35	brings good things out of his **treasure** of good things;
	12.35	person brings bad things out of his **treasure** of bad things.
	13.44	A man happens to find a **treasure** hidden in a field.
Lk	2.51	His mother **treasured** all these things in her heart.
	6.45	brings good out of the **treasure** of good things in his heart;
	6.45	a bad person brings bad out of his **treasure** of bad things.
2 Cor	4. 7	we who have this spiritual **treasure** are like common clay pots,
Col	2. 3	key that opens all the hidden **treasures** of God's wisdom and
1 Tim	6.19	store up for themselves a **treasure** which will be a
Heb	11.26	far more than all the **treasures** of Egypt, for he kept his

TREASURER

Dan	3. 2	governors, lieutenant-governors, commissioners, **treasurers,**
Rom	16.23	Erastus, the city **treasurer,** and our brother Quartus send you

TREASURY

Josh 6.19 It is to be put in the Lord's **treasury."**
6.24 and iron, which they took and put in the Lord's **treasury.**
2 Kgs 12.18 all the gold in the **treasuries** of the Temple and the palace,
16. 8 the Temple and the palace **treasury** and sent it as a present
18.15 him all the silver in the Temple and in the palace **treasury;**
1 Chr 26.20 in charge of the temple **treasury** and the storerooms for
26.22 had charge of the temple **treasury** and storerooms.
26.24 Moses' son Gershom, was the chief official responsible for the temple **treasury.**
29. 8 gave them to the temple **treasury,** which was administered by
2 Chr 16. 2 silver and gold from the **treasuries** of the Temple and the
36.18 looted the Temple, the temple **treasury,** and the wealth of
Ezra 1. 8 Mithredath, chief of the royal **treasury,** who made an
6. 4 All expenses are to be paid by the royal **treasury.**
7.20 need for the Temple, you may get from the royal **treasury.**
7.21 "I command all the **treasury** officials in the province
Esth 3. 9 the royal **treasury** for the administration of the empire."
4. 7 to put into the royal **treasury** if all the Jews were killed.
Ecc 2. 8 and gold from the royal **treasuries** of the lands I ruled.
Zech 11.13 The Lord said to me, "Put them in the temple **treasury."**
11.13 thought I was worth—and put them in the temple **treasury.**
Mt 27. 6 it is against our Law to put it in the temple **treasury."**
Mk 12.41 Jesus sat near the temple **treasury,** he watched the people as
Lk 21. 1 their gifts in the temple **treasury,** [2]and he also saw a very
Acts 8.27 official in charge of the **treasury** of the queen of Ethiopia,

TREAT

Gen 12.13 because of you they will let me live and **treat** me well."
12.16 Because of her the king **treated** Abram well and gave him
15.13 there and will be **treated** cruelly for four hundred years.
16. 6 Then Sarai **treated** Hagar so cruelly that she ran away.
19. 9 Out of our way, or we will **treat** you worse than them."
24.49 towards my master and **treat** him fairly,
31.15 He **treats** us like foreigners.
34.31 "We cannot let our sister be **treated** like a common whore."
Ex 3. 7 "I have seen how cruelly my people are being **treated** in Egypt;
3.17 Egypt, where they are being **treated** cruelly, and will take
4.31 were being **treated** cruelly, they bowed down and worshipped.
5.23 to the king to speak for you, he has **treated** them cruelly.
12.48 He is then to be **treated** like a native-born Israelite and
18.11 the Egyptians **treated** the Israelites with such contempt."
21. 8 sell her to foreigners, because he has **treated** her unfairly.
21. 9 give to his son, he is to **treat** her like a daughter.
30.32 It is holy, and you must **treat** it as holy.
30.36 **Treat** this incense as completely holy.
30.37 **Treat** it as a holy thing dedicated to me.
Lev 19. 8 it will be guilty of **treating** as ordinary what is dedicated
19.34 **Treat** them as you would a fellow-Israelite, and love
22. 2 on my holy name, so **treat** with respect the sacred offerings
25.31 houses in unwalled villages are to be **treated** like fields;
25.43 Do not **treat** them harshly, but obey your God.
25.46 But you must not **treat** any of your fellow-Israelites harshly.
25.53 His master must not **treat** him harshly.
Num 11.11 he said to the Lord, "Why have you **treated** me so badly?
11.15 If you are going to **treat** me like this, take pity on
15.30 a foreigner, is guilty of **treating** the Lord with contempt,
22.30 Have I ever **treated** you like this before?"
Deut 10.18 He makes sure that orphans and widows are **treated** fairly;
15.17 **Treat** your female slave in the same way.
21.14 intercourse with you, you cannot **treat** her as a slave and
23.16 that he chooses, and you are not to **treat** him harshly.
26. 6 Egyptians **treated** us harshly and forced us to work as slaves.
28.33 receive nothing but constant oppression and harsh **treatment.**
31. 5 them, and you are to **treat** them exactly as I have told
32. 6 you should **treat** the Lord, you foolish, senseless people?
Josh 2.12 by him that you will **treat** my family
2.12 as kindly as I have **treated** you, and give me some sign
2.14 when the Lord gives us this land, we will **treat** you well."
Judg 8. 1 Why did you **treat** us like this?"
9.16 you respect Gideon's memory and **treat** his family properly,
9.38 These are the men you were **treating** so scornfully.
15.10 to take Samson prisoner and to **treat** him as he treated us."
1 Sam 2.14 who came to Shiloh to offer sacrifices were **treated** like this.
2.17 the Lord's sight, because they **treated** the offerings to the
2.30 me, and I will **treat** with contempt those who despise me."
8. 9 warnings and explain how their kings will **treat** them."
8.11 "This is how your king will **treat** you," Samuel explained.
2 Sam 2. 6 I too will **treat** you well because of what you have done.
8.15 sure that his people were always **treated** fairly and justly.
1 Kgs 1.21 dead my son Solomon and I will be **treated** as traitors."
8.50 you, and make their enemies **treat** them with kindness.
9. 7 everywhere will ridicule Israel and **treat** her with contempt.
12. 4 to him, [4]"Your father Solomon **treated** us harshly and
2 Kgs 9. 9 I will **treat** his family as I did the families of King
25.28 Evilmerodach **treated** him kindly, and gave him a position
1 Chr 17.17 you, Lord God, are already **treating** me like a great man.
18.14 sure that his people were always **treated** fairly and justly.
2 Chr 7.20 everywhere will ridicule it and **treat** it with contempt.
16.10 time that Asa began **treating** some of the people cruelly.
Esth 1.20 every woman will **treat** her husband with proper respect,
2. 3 of your women, and let them be given a beauty **treatment.**
2. 9 beginning her beauty **treatment** of massage and special diet.
2.12 The regular beauty **treatment** for the women lasted a
Job 13.24 Why do you **treat** me like an enemy?
19.11 he **treats** me like his worst enemy.
19.15 my servant-girls **treat** me like a stranger and a foreigner.
22.21 make peace with God and stop **treating** him like an enemy;
30.10 They **treat** me with disgust;
Job 30.21 You are **treating** me cruelly;
31.13 complained against me, I would listen and **treat** him fairly.
33.10 God finds excuses for attacking me and **treats** me like an enemy.
34.11 people for what they do and **treats** them as they deserve.
36. 6 live on, and he always **treats** the poor with justice.
Ps 31.11 enemies, and especially my neighbours, **treat** me with contempt;
44.22 the time, that we are **treated** like sheep to be slaughtered.
105.25 Egyptians hate his people and **treat** his servants with deceit.
119.119 You **treat** all the wicked like rubbish, and so I love
119.124 **Treat** me according to your constant love, and teach me
123. 3 we have been **treated** with so much contempt.
Prov 2. 8 He protects those who **treat** others fairly, and guards
7. 4 **Treat** wisdom as your sister, and insight as your closest friend.
12. 5 Honest people will **treat** you fairly;
21.21 others will respect you and **treat** you fairly.
Is 47. 6 I **treated** them as no longer mine:
47. 6 even the aged you **treated** harshly.
53. 7 "He was **treated** harshly, but endured it humbly;
58.13 The Lord says, "If you **treat** the Sabbath as sacred and
63.19 You **treat** us as though you had never been our ruler, as
66.12 by its mother, carried in her arms, and **treated** with love.
Jer 7. 5 Be fair in your **treatment** of one another.
17.10 I **treat** each one according to the way he lives, according to
24. 5 like these good figs, and I will **treat** them with kindness.
24. 8 Egypt—I, the Lord, will **treat** them all like these figs that
29.22 will say, 'May the Lord **treat** you like Zedekiah and Ahab,
42.18 people will **treat** you with scorn and use your name as a
44. 8 every nation on earth will **treat** you with scorn and use your
44.12 people will **treat** them with scorn and use their name as a
45. 5 Are you looking for special **treatment** for yourself?
48.27 You **treated** them as though they had been caught with a gang
50.15 revenge on them, and **treat** them as they have treated others.
50.29 all it has done, and **treat** it as it has treated others,
51.56 God who punishes evil, and I will **treat** Babylon as it deserves.
52.32 Evilmerodach **treated** him kindly and gave him a position
Lam 1.17 They **treat** me like some filthy thing.
4. 2 us as gold, but now they are **treated** like common clay pots.
Ezek 16.43 You have forgotten how I **treated** you when you were young,
16.59 Sovereign Lord says, "I will **treat** you as you deserve,
23. 8 girl, men slept with her and **treated** her like a prostitute.
28.24 of the surrounding nations that **treated** Israel with scorn
28.26 punish all their neighbours who **treated** them with scorn, and
34. 4 Instead, you **treated** them cruelly.
47.22 They are to be **treated** like full Israelite citizens and are
Hos 11. 8 you as I did Admah, or **treat** you as I did Zeboiim?
Amos 1. 3 They **treated** the people of Gilead with savage cruelty.
Mic 6.16 People everywhere will **treat** you with contempt."
7. 6 In these times sons **treat** their fathers like fools,
Nah 3. 6 I will **treat** you with contempt and cover you with filth.
Hab 1.10 They **treat** kings with contempt and laugh at high officials.
1.14 How can you **treat** people like fish or like a swarm of
Zech 8.11 now I am **treating** the survivors of this nation differently.
Mal 2. 9 you teach my people, you do not **treat** everyone alike."
Mt 17.12 did not recognize him, but **treated** him just as they pleased.
18.17 not listen to the church, **treat** him as though he were a
18.35 my Father in heaven will **treat** every one of you unless you
21.36 the first time, and the tenants **treated** them the same way.
Mk 5.26 even though she had been **treated** by many doctors.
9.13 already come and that people **treated** him just as they pleased,
12. 4 tenants beat him over the head and **treated** him shamefully.
12. 5 they **treated** many others the same way, beating some and killing
Lk 15.19 **treat** me as one of your hired workers.'
20.11 tenants beat him also, **treated** him shamefully, and sent him back
23.11 and his soldiers mocked Jesus and **treated** him with contempt;
Acts 7. 6 be slaves and will be badly **treated** for four hundred years.
7.23 he decided to find out how his fellow-Israelites were being **treated.**
10.34 that it is true that God **treats** everyone on the same basis.
Rom 8.36 we are **treated** like sheep that are going to be slaughtered."
16.13 and to his mother, who has always **treated** me like a son.
1 Cor 12.23 very much are the ones which we **treat** with greater care;
12.23 don't look very nice are **treated** with special modesty,
2 Cor 6. 8 We are **treated** as liars, yet we speak the truth;
8.13 In this way both are **treated** equally.
12.13 How were you **treated** any worse than the other churches,
Gal 4. 1 receive his father's property is **treated** just like a slave while
Eph 6. 4 Parents, do not **treat** your children in such a way as to
Col 2.23 and false humility, and severe **treatment** of the body;
4. 1 Masters, be fair and just in the way you **treat** your slaves.
1 Thes 2.11 You know that we **treated** each one of you
2.11 just as a father **treats** his own children.
5.13 **Treat** them with the greatest respect and love because of the
2 Thes 3.15 But do not **treat** him as an enemy;
1 Tim 5. 1 **Treat** the younger men as your brothers, [2]the older women as
Heb 10.29 who **treats** as a cheap thing the blood of God's covenant
10.33 were ready to join those who were being **treated** in this way.
12. 7 your suffering shows that God is **treating** you as his sons.
Jas 2. 1 you must never **treat** people in different ways according to
2. 9 But if you **treat** people according to their outward
1 Pet 3. 7 **Treat** them with respect, because they also will receive, together with you,
Rev 18. 6 **Treat** her exactly as she has treated you;

TREATY

Ex 34.12 Do not make any **treaties** with the people of the country
34.15 Do not make any **treaties** with the people of the country,
Josh 9. 6 We want you to make a **treaty** with us."
9. 7 men of Israel said, "Why should we make a **treaty** with you?
9.11 at your service and ask you to make a **treaty** with us.
9.15 Joshua made a **treaty** of friendship with the people of
9.15 of Israel gave their solemn promise to keep the **treaty.**

Josh 9.16 Three days after the **treaty** had been made, the
1 Sam 11. 1 said to Nahash, "Make a **treaty** with us, and we will accept
11. 2 answered, "I will make a **treaty** with you on one condition:
1 Kgs 5.12 Hiram and Solomon, and they made a **treaty** with each other.
20.34 He made a **treaty** with him and let him go.
Is 28.15 that you have made a **treaty** with death and reached an
28.18 The **treaty** you have made with death will be abolished,
30. 1 did not make, and sign **treaties** against my will, piling one
33. 8 **Treaties** are broken and agreements are violated.
Ezek 17.13 the king's family, made a **treaty** with him, and made him
17.14 rising again and to make sure that the **treaty** would be kept.
17.15 He cannot break the **treaty** and go unpunished!
17.16 broke his oath and the **treaty** he had made with the king
17.18 He broke his oath and the **treaty** he had made.
17.19 punish him for breaking the **treaty** which he swore in my name
21.23 won't believe this, because of the **treaties** they have made.
Dan 11.23 By making **treaties,** he will deceive other nations, and
Hos 10. 4 utter empty words and make false promises and useless **treaties.**
12. 1 They make **treaties** with Assyria and do business with Egypt."
Amos 1. 9 and did not keep the **treaty** of friendship they had made.

TREE

[FRUIT TREE]

Gen 2. 9 kinds of beautiful **trees** grow there and produce good fruit.
2. 9 of the garden stood the **tree** that gives life
2. 9 and the **tree** that gives knowledge of what is
2.16 eat the fruit of any **tree** in the garden,
2.17 except the **tree** that gives knowledge of what is
2.17 You must not eat the fruit of that **tree;**
3. 1 tell you not to eat fruit from any **tree** in the garden?"
3. 2 the fruit of any **tree** in the garden," the woman answered,
3. 3 "except the **tree** in the middle of it.
3. 3 not to eat the fruit of that **tree** or even touch it;
3. 6 woman saw how beautiful the **tree** was and how good its fruit
3. 8 in the garden, and they hid from him among the **trees.**
3.22 to take fruit from the **tree** that gives life, eat it, and
3.24 to keep anyone from coming near the **tree** that gives life.
12. 6 he came to the sacred **tree** of Moreh, the holy place at
13.18 and settled near the sacred **trees** of Mamre at Hebron, and
14.13 living near the sacred **trees** belonging to Mamre the Amorite.
18. 1 The Lord appeared to Abraham at the sacred **trees** of Mamre.
18. 4 you can rest here beneath this **tree.**
18. 8 There under the **tree** he served them himself, and they ate.
23.17 in it, and all the **trees** in the field up to the
30.37 of poplar, almond, and plane **trees** and stripped off some of
Ex 9.25 down all the plants in the fields and broke all the **trees.**
10. 5 that the hail did not destroy, even the **trees** that are left.
10.15 the hail had left, including all the fruit on the **trees.**
10.15 thing was left on any **tree** or plant in all the land
Lev 19.23 plant any kind of **fruit tree,** consider the fruit ritually unclean
19.25 If you do all this, your **trees** will bear more fruit.
23.40 the best fruit from your **trees,** take palm branches
23.40 and the branches of leafy **trees,** and begin a religious
26. 4 the land will produce crops and the **trees** will bear fruit.
26.20 will not produce crops and the **trees** will not bear fruit.
Deut 11.30 not far from the sacred **trees** of Moreh near the town of
12. 2 gods on high mountains, on hills, and under green **trees.**
19. 5 them is chopping down a **tree,** the head of the axe comes
20.19 do not cut down its **fruit-trees,** even though the siege lasts
20.19 Eat the fruit, but do not destroy the **trees;**
20.19 the **trees** are not your enemies.
20.20 may cut down the other **trees** and use them in the siege
22. 6 a bird's nest in a **tree** or on the ground with the
28.42 All your **trees** and crops will be devoured by insects.
Josh 8.29 king of Ai from a **tree** and left his body there until
10.26 them on five **trees,** where their bodies stayed until evening.
24.13 plant, and olives from **trees** that you did not plant.'"
Judg 9. 8 Once upon a time the **trees** got together to choose a king
9.10 Then the **trees** said to the fig-tree, 'You come and be
9.12 So the **trees** then said to the grapevine, 'You come and
9.14 So then all the **trees** said to the thorn-bush, 'You come
9.48 cut a branch off a **tree,** and put it on his shoulder.
9.49 So every man cut off a branch of a **tree;**
1 Sam 10. 3 you come to the sacred **tree** at Tabor, where you will meet
2 Sam 5.24 sound of marching in the **tree-tops,** then attack because I
1 Kgs 4.33 He spoke of **trees** and plants, from the Lebanon cedars to
5. 6 don't know how to cut down **trees** as well as yours do."
14.23 of Asherah to worship on the hills and under shady **trees.**
19. 4 down in the shade of a **tree** and wished he would die.
19. 5 He lay down under the **tree** and fell asleep.
2 Kgs 3.19 will cut down all their **fruit-trees,** stop all their springs,
3.25 also stopped up the springs and cut down the **fruit-trees.**
6. 2 Jordan and cut down some **trees,** so that we can build a
6. 5 them was cutting down a **tree,** suddenly his iron axe-head
16. 4 and under every shady **tree,** Ahaz offered sacrifices
17.10 hills and under every shady **tree** they put up stone pillars
18.31 and figs from your own **trees,** and to drink water from your
1 Chr 14.15 sound of marching in the **tree-tops,** then attack, because I
16.33 The **trees** in the woods will shout for joy when the Lord
2 Chr 28. 4 and under every shady **tree** Ahaz offered sacrifices
Neh 8.15 olives, myrtles, palms, and other **trees** to make shelters
9.25 cisterns already dug, olive-trees, **fruit-trees,** and vineyards.
10.35 we harvest and of the first fruit that ripens on our **trees.**
Job 14. 7 There is hope for a **tree** that has been cut down;
15.30 He will be like a **tree** whose branches are burnt by fire,
24.20 he is eaten by worms and destroyed like a fallen **tree.**
29.19 I was like a **tree** whose roots always have water and
Ps 1. 3 They are like **trees** that grow beside a stream, that bear
29. 9 leaves from the **trees** while everyone in his Temple shouts,
74. 5 They looked like woodmen cutting down **trees** with their axes.
Ps 92.13 They are like **trees** planted in the house of the Lord,
96.12 The **trees** in the woods will shout for joy [13] when the Lord
104.12 In the **trees** near by, the birds make their nests and sing.
104.16 get plenty of rain— the Lord's own **trees,** which he planted.
105.33 their grapevines and fig-trees and broke down all the **trees.**
148. 9 Praise him, hills and mountains, **fruit-trees** and forests;
Ecc 2. 5 gardens and orchards, with all kinds of **fruit-trees** in them;
11. 3 matter in which direction a **tree** falls, it will lie where it
Song 2. 3 Like an apple-tree among the **trees** of the forest, so is my
Is 1.29 that you ever worshipped **trees** and planted sacred gardens.
4. 2 will make every plant and **tree** in the land grow large and
7. 2 that they trembled like **trees** shaking in the wind.
10.19 There will be so few **trees** left that even a child will
10.33 will bring them crashing down like branches cut off a **tree.**
10.34 will cut them down as **trees** in the heart of the forest
10.34 down with an axe, as even the finest **trees** of Lebanon fall!
11. 1 line of David is like a **tree** that has been cut down;
16. 3 Protect us like a **tree** that casts a cool shadow in the
24.13 have been beaten off every **tree** and the last grapes picked
27. 6 will take root like a **tree,** and they will blossom and bud.
27.11 The branches of the **trees** are withered and broken, and
33. 9 Bashan and on Mount Carmel the leaves are falling from the **trees.**
36.16 and figs from your own **trees,** and to drink water from your
40.16 to our God, and its **trees** are too few to kindle the
42.15 the hills and mountains and dry up the grass and **trees.**
44.15 man uses part of a **tree** for fuel and part of it
44.23 Shout for joy, mountains, and every **tree** of the forest!
55.12 will burst into singing, and the **trees** will shout for joy.
57. 5 gods by having sex under those sacred **trees** of yours.
61. 3 They will be like **trees** That the Lord himself has planted.
65.21 Like **trees,** my people will live long lives.
Jer 2.20 and under every green **tree** you worshipped fertility gods.
2.27 you that say that a **tree** is your father and that a
3. 6 and under every green **tree** she has acted like a prostitute.
3. 9 and she committed adultery by worshipping stones and **trees.**
3.13 Confess that under every green **tree** you have given your love
6. 6 these kings to cut down **trees** and build mounds in order to
7.20 and animals alike, and even on the **trees** and the crops.
10. 3 A **tree** is cut down in the forest;
11.19 "Let's chop down the **tree** while it is still healthy;
17. 2 goddess Asherah by every green **tree,** on the hill-tops [3] and
17. 8 He is like a **tree** growing near a stream and sending out
46.22 men cutting down **trees** [23] and destroying a thick forest.
Ezek 6.13 every mountain, under every green **tree** and every large oak,
15. 2 "Mortal man," he said, "how does a vine compare with a **tree?**
15. 2 branch of a grapevine compared with the **trees** of the forest?
17.24 All the **trees** in the land will know that I am the
17.24 cut down the tall trees and make the small **trees** grow tall.
17.24 up the green trees and make the dry **trees** become green.
20.28 the high hills and green **trees,** they offered sacrifices at
20.32 who live in other countries and worship **trees** and rocks.
20.47 it will burn up every **tree** in you, whether green or dry.
31. 3 A **tree** so tall it reaches the clouds.
31. 4 watered the place where the **tree** was growing
31. 4 And sent streams to all the **trees** of the forest.
31. 5 Because it was well-watered, It grew taller than other **trees.**
31. 7 How beautiful the **tree** was— So tall, with such long branches.
31. 8 No **tree** in God's own garden was so beautiful.
31. 9 was the envy of every **tree** in Eden, the garden of God.
31.10 going to happen to that **tree** that grew until it reached the
31.11 He will give that **tree** what it deserves for its wickedness.
31.13 and perch on the fallen **tree,** and the wild animals will walk
31.14 so from now on, no **tree,** no matter how well-watered it is,
31.15 "On the day when the **tree** goes to the world of the
31.15 Because the **tree** has died, I will bring darkness over the
31.15 Lebanon Mountains and make all the **trees** of the forest wither.
31.16 All the **trees** of Eden
31.16 and all the choice, well-watered **trees** of Lebanon who have
31.18 "The **tree** is the king of Egypt and all his people.
31.18 Not even the **trees** in Eden were so tall and impressive.
31.18 But now, like the **trees** of Eden, it will go down to
34.27 The **trees** will bear fruit, the fields will produce crops,
36. 8 the mountains of Israel the **trees** will again grow leaves and
36.30 increase the yield of your **fruit-trees** and your fields, so that
39.10 the fields or cut down **trees** in the forest, because they
41.19 face that was turned towards the **tree** on the other side.
45.13 1/100th of the yield of your **trees**
47. 7 there I saw that there were very many **trees** on each bank.
47.12 of the stream all kinds of **trees** will grow to provide food.
47.12 The **trees** will provide food, and their leaves will be used
Dan 4.10 a vision of a huge **tree** in the middle of the earth.
4.14 a loud voice, 'Cut the **tree** down and chop off its branches;
4.20 The **tree,** so tall that it reached the sky, could be seen
4.22 "Your Majesty, you are the **tree,** tall and strong.
4.23 heaven and said, 'Cut the **tree** down and destroy it, but
Hos 4.13 tall, spreading **trees,** because the shade
14. 5 they will be firmly rooted like the **trees** of Lebanon.
14. 8 Like an evergreen **tree** I will shelter them;
Joel 1.12 all the **fruit-trees** have wilted and died.
1.19 Lord, because the pastures and **trees** are dried up, as though
2.22 the **trees** bear their fruit, and there are plenty of figs
Mic 7. 1 no fruit left on the **trees** and no grapes on the vines.
Nah 3.12 shake the **trees,** and the fruit falls right into your mouth!
Zech 11. 2 those glorious **trees** have been destroyed!
Mt 3.10 The axe is ready to cut down the **trees** at the roots;
3.10 every **tree** that does not bear good fruit will be cut down
7.17 **tree** bears good fruit, but a poor **tree** bears bad fruit.
7.18 A healthy **tree** cannot bear bad fruit,
7.18 and a poor **tree** cannot bear good fruit.
7.19 And any **tree** that does not bear good fruit is cut down
12.33 "To have good fruit you must have a healthy **tree;**

Mt 12.33 if you have a poor **tree,** you will have bad fruit.
12.33 A **tree** is known by the kind of fruit it bears.
13.32 It becomes a **tree,** so that birds come and make their nests
21. 8 cut branches from the **trees** and spread them on the road.
21.19 So he said to the **tree,** "You will never again bear fruit!"
Mk 8.24 "Yes, I can see people, but they look like **trees** walking about."
Lk 3. 9 The axe is ready to cut down the **trees** at the roots;
3. 9 every **tree** that does not bear good fruit will be cut down
6.43 "A healthy **tree** does not bear bad fruit,
6.43 nor does a poor **tree** bear good fruit.
6.44 Every **tree** is known by the fruit it bears;
13. 9 Then if the **tree** bears figs next year, so much the better;
13.19 plant grows and becomes a **tree,** and the birds make their
17. 6 could say to this mulberry **tree,** 'Pull yourself up by the
19. 4 and climbed a sycomore **tree** to see Jesus, who was going
21.29 "Think of the fig-tree and all the other **trees.**
Rom 11.16 if the roots of a **tree** are offered to God, the branches
11.24 The Jews are like this cultivated **tree;**
11.24 God to join these broken-off branches to their own **tree** again.
Gal 3.13 "Anyone who is hanged on a **tree** is under God's curse."
Jude 12 They are like **trees** that bear no fruit, even in autumn,
12 **trees** that have been pulled up
Rev 2. 7 eat the fruit of the **tree** of life that grows in the
6.13 figs falling from the **tree** when a strong wind shakes it.
7. 1 should blow on the earth or the sea or against any **tree.**
7. 3 earth, the sea, or the **trees,** until we mark the servants of
8. 7 a third of the **trees,** and every blade of green grass.
9. 4 not to harm the grass or the **trees** or any other plant;
22. 2 of the river was the **tree** of life, which bears fruit twelve
22.14 eat the fruit from the **tree** of life and to go through
22.19 of the fruit of the **tree** of life and of the Holy

TREMBLE

Gen 27.33 Isaac began to **tremble** and shake all over, and he asked,
Ex 15.14 The nations have heard, and they **tremble** with fear;
15.15 Moab's mighty men are **trembling;**
19.16 All the people in the camp **trembled** with fear.
19.18 smoke of a furnace, and all the people **trembled** violently.
20.18 and the smoking mountain, they **trembled** with fear and stood
Deut 2.25 Everyone will **tremble** with fear at the mention of your name.'
1 Sam 13. 7 at Gilgal, and the people with him were **trembling** with fear.
14.15 the raiders and the soldiers in the camp **trembled** with fear;
15.32 Agag came to him, **trembling** with fear, thinking to himself,
16. 4 where the city leaders came **trembling** to meet him and asked,
21. 1 Ahimelech came out **trembling** to meet him and asked, "Why
2 Sam 22. 8 Then the earth **trembled** and shook;
22.46 lose their courage and come **trembling** from their fortresses.
1 Chr 16.30 **tremble** before him, all the earth!
Ezra 10. 9 and the importance of the meeting everyone was **trembling.**
Job 4.14 I **trembled** and shuddered;
18.20 all who hear of his fate shudder and **tremble** with fear.
21. 6 has happened to me, I am stunned, and I **tremble** and shake.
23.15 I **tremble** with fear before him.
26. 5 The spirits of the dead **tremble** in the waters under the earth.
26.11 that hold up the sky, they shake and **tremble** with fear.
39.24 **Trembling** with excitement, the horses race ahead;
Ps 2.11 **tremble** [12] and bow down to him;
4. 4 **Tremble** with fear and stop sinning;
18. 7 Then the earth **trembled** and shook;
18.45 lose their courage and come **trembling** from their fortresses.
55. 5 I am gripped by fear and **trembling;**
60. 2 You have made the land **tremble,** and you have cut it open;
75. 3 every living creature **tremble** and the earth itself be shaken,
77.16 O God, they were afraid, and the depths of the sea **trembled.**
77.18 the earth **trembled** and shook.
96. 9 **tremble** before him, all the earth!
97. 4 the earth sees it and **trembles.**
99. 1 and the people **tremble.**
104.32 He looks at the earth, and it **trembles;**
114. 7 **Tremble,** earth, at the Lord's coming, at the presence of
Ecc 12. 3 that have protected you, will **tremble,** and your legs, now
Song 6.12 I am **trembling;**
Is 7. 2 that they **trembled** like trees shaking in the wind.
8. 6 of Shiloah, and **tremble** before King Rezin and King Pekah,
13.13 I will make the heavens **tremble,** and the earth will be
14.16 'Is this the man who shook the earth and made kingdoms **tremble?**
15. 4 Even the soldiers **tremble;**
19. 1 The Egyptian idols **tremble** before him, and the people of
19.16 They will **tremble** in terror when they see that the Lord
21. 4 My head is spinning, and I am **trembling** with fear.
32.11 but now, **tremble** with fear!
33.14 The sinful people of Zion are **trembling** with fright.
35. 3 that are tired and to knees that **tremble** with weakness.
41. 5 they are frightened and **tremble** with fear.
60. 5 You will **tremble** with excitement.
64. 2 They would **tremble** like water boiling over a hot fire.
64. 2 your enemies, and make the nations **tremble** at your presence!
Jer 5.22 Why don't you **tremble** before me?
8.16 The whole land **trembles** when their horses neigh.
10.10 When you are angry, the world **trembles;**
23. 9 My heart is crushed, and I am **trembling.**
33. 9 the world will fear and **tremble** when they hear about the
51.29 The earth **trembles** and shakes because the Lord is
Ezek 7.18 They will put on sackcloth and they will **tremble** all over.
12.18 "Mortal man," he said, **"tremble** when you eat, and
12.19 They will **tremble** when they eat and shake with fear when
21. 7 limp, their courage will fail, and their knees will **tremble.**
26.16 their embroidered clothes and sit **trembling** on the ground.
26.16 at your fate that they will not be able to stop **trembling.**
26.18 has fallen, The islands are **trembling,** And their people are
Ezek 32.10 all of them will **tremble** in fear for their own lives."
38.20 on the face of the earth will **tremble** for fear of me.
Dan 5.19 races, and languages were afraid of him and **trembled.**
10.10 I was still **trembling.**
10.11 When he had said this, I stood up, still **trembling.**
10.16 "Sir, this vision makes me so weak that I can't stop **trembling.**
Joel 2. 1 **Tremble,** people of Judah!
2.10 the sky **trembles.**
3.16 earth and sky **tremble.**
Mic 7.17 they will come from their fortresses, **trembling** and afraid.
Nah 1. 5 the world and all its people **tremble.**
2.10 knees **tremble,** strength is gone;
Hab 2. 7 Enemies will come and make you **tremble.**
3. 6 at his glance the nations **tremble.**
3. 7 people of Cushan afraid and the people of Midian **tremble.**
3.10 When the mountains saw you, they **trembled;**
3.16 I hear all this, and I **tremble;**
Mt 28. 4 were so afraid that they **trembled** and became like dead men.
Mk 5.33 so she came, **trembling** with fear, knelt at his feet,
Lk 8.47 so she came **trembling** and threw herself at Jesus' feet.
Acts 7.32 Moses **trembled** with fear and dared not look.
16.29 light, rushed in, and fell **trembling** at the feet of Paul and
1 Cor 2. 3 I was weak and **trembled** all over with fear, [4] and my
2 Cor 7.15 obey his instructions, how you welcomed him with fear and **trembling.**
Eph 6. 5 Slaves, obey your human masters with fear and **trembling;**
Phil 2.12 on working with fear and **trembling** to complete your salvation,
Heb 12.12 up your tired hands, then, and strengthen your **trembling** knees!
12.21 was so terrifying that Moses said, "I am **trembling** and afraid!"
Jas 2.19 The demons also believe—and **tremble** with fear.

TREMENDOUS

1 Chr 29. 1 work to be done is **tremendous,** because this is not a palace
Acts 12.18 morning came, there was a **tremendous** confusion among the guards—
2 Cor 4.17 suffer will bring us a **tremendous** and eternal glory, much greater

TRENCH

1 Kgs 18.32 He dug a **trench** round it, large enough to hold almost
18.35 The water ran down round the altar and filled the **trench.**
18.38 scorched the earth and dried up the water in the **trench.**
Job 19.12 they dig **trenches** and lay siege to my tent.
Ezek 4. 2 to represent a siege, put **trenches,** earthworks, camps, and
17.17 Babylonians build earthworks and dig **trenches** in order to kill
21.22 the gates, to throw up earthworks, and to dig **trenches.**
26. 8 The enemy will dig **trenches,** build earthworks, and make a

AV TRESPASS
see also **SIN**

Gen 31.36 "What **crime** have I committed?"
50.17 ask you, 'Please forgive the **crime** your brothers committed
50.17 Now please forgive us the **wrong** that we, the servants of
Ex 22. 9 "In every case of a **dispute** about property,
Lev 5. 6 the sin, [6] and as the **penalty** for his sin he must bring
5.15 he shall bring as his **repayment-offering** to the Lord a male
6. 4 the day he is found **guilty,** he must repay the owner in
22.16 this would bring **guilt** and punishment on such a person.
26.40 ancestors, who resisted me and **rebelled** against me, [41] and
Num 5. 6 the Lord and commits a **wrong** against someone, [7] he must
5. 7 an additional twenty per cent, to the person he has **wronged.**
5. 8 no near relative to whom **payment** can be made, it shall be
5.12 suspicious that his wife is **unfaithful** to him and has defiled herself
5.27 If she has committed **adultery,** the water will cause bitter pain;
31.16 and at Peor led the people to be **unfaithful** to the Lord.
Deut 32.51 because both of you were **unfaithful** to me in the
Josh 7. 1 A man named Achan **disobeyed** that order,
22.16 "Why have you done this **evil** thing against the God of Israel?
22.20 how Achan son of Zerah **refused** to obey the command about the
22.31 You have not **rebelled** against him, and so you have saved the
1 Sam 6. 3 course, send with it a **gift** to him to pay for your
6. 4 "What **gift** shall we send him?"
25.28 Please forgive me, sir, for any **wrong** I have done.
1 Kgs 8.31 a person is accused of **wronging** another and is brought to
1 Chr 21. 3 do you want to do this and make the whole nation **guilty?"**
2 Chr 19.10 that they do not become **guilty** of sinning against the Lord.
19.10 But if you do your duty, you will not be **guilty.**
24.18 Their **guilt** for these sins brought the Lord's anger on Judah
26.18 You have **offended** the Lord God, and you no longer have his
28.13 Now you want to do something that will increase our **guilt."**
29. 6 Our ancestors were **unfaithful** to the Lord our God and did
30. 7 fellow-Israelites who were **unfaithful** to the Lord their God.
33.19 committed before he repented—the **evil** he did, the pagan
Ezra 9. 2 The leaders and officials were the chief **offenders.**
9.13 punishment for our sins and **wrongs,** we know that you, our
9.15 We confess our **guilt** to you;
10. 2 said to Ezra, "We have **broken** faith with God by marrying
10.10 and have brought **guilt** on Israel by marrying foreign women.
Ezek 14.13 a country sins and is **unfaithful** to me, I will stretch out
15. 8 They have been **unfaithful** to me, and so I will make the
17.20 Babylonia and punish him there, because he was **unfaithful** to me.
18.24 starts doing all the **evil,** disgusting things that evil men do,
18.24 He will die because of his **unfaithfulness** and his sins.
20.27 This is another way their fathers insulted me by their **unfaithfulness.**
39.26 to forget how they were disgraced for having **betrayed** me.
Dan 9. 7 countries near and far because they were **unfaithful** to you.
Mt 6.14 "If you forgive others the **wrongs** they have done to you,

Mt 6.15 then your Father will not forgive the **wrongs** you have done.
Mk 11.25 Father in heaven will forgive the **wrongs** you have done."
Eph 2. 1 you were spiritually dead because of your **disobedience** and sins.

AV **TRESPASS OFFERING** see **REPAYMENT-OFFERING**

TRIAL see **TRY (2)**

TRIBE

see also **TRIBESMEN, ASHER, BENJAMIN, DAN, EPHRAIM, GAD, ISSACHAR, JUDAH, MANASSEH, NAPHTALI, REUBEN, SIMEON, ZEBULUN**

Gen 10. 5 Japheth, living in their different **tribes** and countries,
10.18 The different **tribes** of the Canaanites spread out, [19]until
10.20 Ham, living in their different **tribes** and countries, each
10.31 Shem, living in their different **tribes** and countries, each
25.16 were the ancestors of twelve **tribes,** and their names were
36.15 These are the **tribes** descended from Esau.
36.15 Esau's first son Eliphaz was the ancestor of the following **tribes:**
36.17 Esau's son Reuel was the ancestor of the following **tribes:**
36.18 The following **tribes** were descended from Esau
36.19 All these **tribes** were descended from Esau.
36.20 of Edom were divided into **tribes** which traced their ancestry
36.29 These are the Horite **tribes** in the land of Edom:
36.40 Esau was the ancestor of the following Edomite **tribes:**
36.40 area where each of these **tribes** lived
36.40 was known by the name of the **tribe.**
49.16 They will be like the other **tribes** of Israel.
49.28 These are the twelve **tribes** of Israel, and this is what
Ex 2. 1 time a man from the **tribe** of Levi married
2. 1 a woman of his own **tribe,** [2]and she bore him a son.
6.25 heads of the families and the clans of the **tribe** of Levi.
6.26 the Lord said, "Lead the **tribes** of Israel out of Egypt."
7. 3 on Egypt and lead the **tribes** of my people out of the
12.17 was on this day that I brought your **tribes** out of Egypt.
12.41 all the **tribes** of the Lord's people left Egypt.
12.51 On that day the Lord brought the Israelite **tribes** out of Egypt.
24. 4 twelve stones, one for each of the twelve **tribes** of Israel.
28.12 of the ephod to represent the twelve **tribes** of Israel.
28.21 one of the sons of Jacob, to represent the **tribes** of Israel.
28.29 with the names of the **tribes** of Israel, so that I, the
31. 2 grandson of Hur, from the **tribe** of Judah, [3]and I have
31. 6 son of Ahisamach, from the **tribe** of Dan, to work with him.
35.30 son of Uri and grandson of Hur, from the **tribe** of Judah.
35.34 son of Ahisamach, from the **tribe** of Dan, the ability to
38.22 grandson of Hur, from the **tribe** of Judah, made everything
38.23 son of Ahisamach, from the **tribe** of Dan, was an engraver, a
39. 7 ephod to represent the twelve **tribes** of Israel, just as the
39.14 of Jacob, in order to represent the twelve **tribes** of Israel.
Lev 24.10 Shelomith, the daughter of Dibri from the **tribe** of Dan.
Num 1. 4 Ask one clan chief from each **tribe** to help you."
1. 5 the men, leaders within their **tribes,** who were chosen from
1.20 beginning with the **tribe** of Reuben, Jacob's eldest son.
1.47 not registered with the other **tribes,** [48]because the Lord
1.49 fit for military service, do not include the **tribe** of Levi.
3. 6 to Moses, [6]"Bring forward the **tribe** of Levi and appoint
7. 2 who were leaders in the **tribes** of Israel, the same men who
10. 5 short blasts are sounded, the **tribes** camped on the east will
10. 6 a second time, the **tribes** on the south will move out.
10.14 the division led by the **tribe** of Judah started out first,
10.15 was in command of the **tribe** of Issachar,
10.16 Eliab son of Helon was in command of the **tribe** of Zebulun.
10.18 the division led by the **tribe** of Reuben would start out,
10.19 was in command of the **tribe** of Simeon,
10.20 Eliasaph son of Deuel was in command of the **tribe** of Gad.
10.22 the division led by the **tribe** of Ephraim would start out,
10.23 was in command of the **tribe** of Manasseh,
10.24 Abidan son of Gideoni was in command of the **tribe** of Benjamin.
10.25 the division led by the **tribe** of Dan, serving as the
10.26 was in command of the **tribe** of Asher,
10.27 Ahira son of Enan was in command of the **tribe** of Naphtali.
13. 2 from each of the twelve **tribes** and send them as spies to
16. 1 by three members of the **tribe** of Reuben—Dathan and Abiram,
17. 2 give you twelve sticks, one from the leader of each **tribe.**
17. 3 There will be one stick for each **tribal** leader.
17. 6 a stick, one for each **tribe,** twelve in all, and Aaron's
17. 8 he saw that Aaron's stick, representing the **tribe** of Levi,
18. 2 Bring in your relatives, the **tribe** of Levi, to work with
20.14 "This message is from your kinsmen, the **tribes** of Israel.
24. 2 desert [2]and saw the people of Israel camped **tribe** by tribe.
25. 5 kill every man in your **tribe** who has become a worshipper of
25.14 of Salu, the head of a family in the **tribe** of Simeon.
26. 5 The **tribe** of Reuben (Reuben was the eldest son of Jacob):
26.12 The **tribe** of Simeon:
26.15 The **tribe** of Gad:
26.19 The **tribe** of Judah:
26.23 The **tribe** of Issachar:
26.26 The **tribe** of Zebulun:
26.28 The **tribes** of Joseph, who was the father of two sons,
26.29 The **tribe** of Manasseh:
26.35 The **tribe** of Ephraim:
26.38 The **tribe** of Benjamin:
26.42 The **tribe** of Dan:
26.44 The **tribe** of Asher:
26.48 The **tribe** of Naphtali:
26.53 "Divide the land among the **tribes,** according to their size.
26.54 large share to a large **tribe**
26.54 and a small one to a small **tribe."**
Num 26.57 The **tribe** of Levi consisted of the clans of Gershon,
30. 1 instructions to the leaders of the **tribes** of Israel.
31. 4 From each **tribe** of Israel send a thousand men to war."
31. 5 men were chosen from each **tribe,** a total of twelve thousand
32. 1 The **tribes** of Reuben and Gad had a lot of livestock.
32.33 So Moses assigned to the **tribes** of Gad and Reuben and to
32.33 Reuben and to half the **tribe** of Manasseh all the territory
32.34 The **tribe** of Gad rebuilt the fortified towns of Dibon,
32.37 The **tribe** of Reuben rebuilt Heshbon, Elealeh,
32.41 Jair, of the **tribe** of Manasseh, attacked and captured
33. 1 they left Egypt in their **tribes** under the leadership of
33.54 the land among the various **tribes** and clans by drawing lots,
34.13 that the Lord has assigned to the nine and a half **tribes.**
34.14 The **tribes** of Reuben and Gad and the eastern half of
34.18 Take also one leader from each **tribe** to help them divide it."
35. 8 of Levite cities in each **tribe** is to be determined according
36. 3 they marry men of another **tribe,** their property
36. 3 will then belong to that **tribe,** and the total allotted to us
36. 4 be permanently added to the **tribe** into which they marry
36. 4 and will be lost to our **tribe."**
36. 5 He said, "What the **tribe** of Manasseh says is right, [6]and
36. 6 to marry anyone they wish but only within their own **tribe.**
36. 7 The property of every Israelite will remain attached to his **tribe.**
36. 8 inherits property in an Israelite **tribe**
36. 8 must marry a man belonging to that **tribe.**
36. 9 and the property will not pass from one **tribe** to another.
36. 9 Each **tribe** will continue to possess its own property."
36.12 within the clans of the **tribe** of Manasseh son of Joseph,
36.12 and their property remained in their father's **tribe.**
Deut 1.13 and experienced men from each **tribe,** and I will put them in
1.15 leaders you chose from your **tribes,** and I placed them in
1.15 I also appointed other officials throughout the **tribes.**
1.23 thing to do, so I selected twelve men, one from each **tribe.**
3.12 land, I assigned to the **tribes** of Reuben and Gad the
3.13 To half the **tribe** of Manasseh I assigned the rest of
3.14 Jair, from the **tribe** of Manasseh, took the entire region
3.15 Gilead to the clan of Machir of the **tribe** of Manasseh.
3.16 And to the **tribes** of Reuben and Gad I assigned the
3.18 Jordan ahead of the other **tribes** of Israel, to help them to
4.43 For the **tribe** of Reuben there was the city of Bezer, on
4.43 for the **tribe** of Gad there was Ramoth, in the territory of
4.43 and for the **tribe** of Manasseh there was Golan, in the
5.23 and the chiefs of your **tribes** came to me [24]and said, 'The
10. 8 appointed the men of the **tribe** of Levi to be in charge
10. 9 That is why the **tribe** of Levi received no land as the
10. 9 the tribe of Levi received no land as the other **tribes** did;
11. 6 Dathan and Abiram, the sons of Eliab of the **tribe** of Reuben.
12. 5 the territory of all your **tribes** the Lord will choose the
12.14 the Lord will choose in the territory of one of your **tribes.**
18. 1 "The priestly **tribe** of Levi is not to receive any share
18. 2 They are to own no land, as the other **tribes** do;
18. 5 Lord chose from all your **tribes** the tribe of Levi to serve
27.12 crossed the Jordan, the following **tribes** are to stand on
27.13 And the following **tribes** will stand on Mount Ebal when
29. 8 tribes of Reuben and Gad, and half the **tribe** of Manasseh.
29.18 no man, woman, family, or **tribe** standing here today turns
29.21 of him before all the **tribes** of Israel and will bring
31.28 Assemble all your **tribal** leaders and officials before me,
33. 5 Israel when their **tribes** and leaders were gathered together.
33. 6 Moses said about the **tribe** of Reuben:
33. 7 About the **tribe** of Judah he said:
33. 7 Unite them again with the other **tribes.**
33. 8 About the **tribe** of Levi he said:
33.11 Lord, help their **tribe** to grow strong;
33.12 About the **tribe** of Benjamin he said:
33.12 "This is the **tribe** the Lord loves and protects;
33.13 About the **tribe** of Joseph he said:
33.16 these blessings come to the **tribe** of Joseph, Because he was
33.18 About the **tribes** of Zebulun and Issachar he said:
33.20 About the **tribe** of Gad he said:
33.22 About the **tribe** of Dan he said:
33.23 About the **tribe** of Naphtali he said:
33.24 About the **tribe** of Asher he said:
33.24 "Asher is blessed more than the other **tribes.**
Josh 1.12 Joshua said to the **tribes** of Reuben and Gad and to half
1.12 Gad and to half the **tribe** of Manasseh, [13]"Remember how Moses,
1.15 given safety to all the **tribes** of Israel, then you may come
3.12 Now choose twelve men, one from each of the **tribes** of Israel.
4. 2 twelve men, one from each **tribe,** [3]and command them to take
4. 5 on your shoulder, one for each of the **tribes** of Israel.
4. 8 one for each of the **tribes** of Israel, carried them to the
4.12 The men of the **tribes** of Reuben and Gad
4.12 and of half the **tribe** of Manasseh, ready for battle, crossed
7. 1 to the clan of Zerah, a part of the **tribe** of Judah.)
7.14 in the morning they will be brought forward, **tribe by tribe.**
7.14 The **tribe** that I pick out will then come forward, clan by
7.16 Joshua brought Israel forward, **tribe by tribe,**
7.16 and the **tribe** of Judah was picked out.
7.17 He brought the **tribe** of Judah forward, clan by clan, and
11.23 their own and divided it into portions, one for each **tribe.**
12. 6 gave their land to the **tribes** of Reuben and Gad
12. 6 and to half the **tribe** of Manasseh, to be their possession.
12. 7 divided this land among the **tribes** and gave it to them as
13. 7 land among the other nine **tribes** and half of the tribe of
13. 8 The **tribes** of Reuben and Gad
13. 8 the other half of the **tribe** of Manasseh had already received
13.14 Moses had given no land to the **tribe** of Levi.
13.15 to the families of the **tribe** of Reuben as their possession.
13.23 The Jordan was the western border of the **tribe** of Reuben.
13.23 to the families of the **tribe** of Reuben as their possession.
13.24 to the families of the **tribe** of Gad as their possession.

Josh 13.28 to the families of the **tribe** of Gad as their possession.
13.29 families of half the **tribe** of Manasseh as their possession.
13.33 But Moses did not assign any land to the **tribe** of Levi.
14. 1 of the Israelite **tribes** divided it among the population.
14. 2 the nine and a half **tribes** west of the Jordan were
14. 3 east of the Jordan to the other two and a half **tribes.**
14. 3 (The descendants of Joseph were divided into two **tribes:**
14. 6 day some people from the **tribe** of Judah came to Joshua at
15. 1 The families of the **tribe** of Judah received a part of the
15.13 given to Caleb son of Jephunneh, from the **tribe** of Judah.
15.20 families of the **tribe** of Judah received as their possession.
16. 4 descendants of Joseph, the **tribes** of Ephraim and West Manasseh,
16. 8 to the families of the **tribe** of Ephraim as their possession,
17.17 Joshua said to the **tribes** of Ephraim and West Manasseh,
18. 2 There were still seven **tribes** of the people of Israel who
18. 4 Let me have three men from each **tribe.**
18. 7 And of course, the **tribes** of Gad, Reuben, and East Manasseh
18.10 assigned each of the remaining **tribes** of Israel a certain
18.11 to the families of the **tribe** of Benjamin was the first to
18.11 Their land lay between the **tribes** of Judah and Joseph.
18.14 (or Kiriath Jearim), which belongs to the **tribe** of Judah.
18.20 of the **tribe** of Benjamin received as their possession.
18.21 to the families of the **tribe** of Benjamin were Jericho, Beth
18.28 of the **tribe** of Benjamin received as their possession.
19. 1 assignment made was for the families of the **tribe** of Simeon.
19. 1 extended into the land assigned to the **tribe** of Judah.
19. 8 of the **tribe** of Simeon received as their possession.
19. 9 part of its territory was given to the **tribe** of Simeon.
19.10 made was for the families of the **tribe** of Zebulun.
19.16 of the **tribe** of Zebulun received as their possession.
19.17 made was for the families of the **tribe** of Issachar.
19.23 of the **tribe** of Issachar received as their possession.
19.24 assignment made was for the families of the **tribe** of Asher.
19.31 of the **tribe** of Asher received as their possession.
19.32 made was for the families of the **tribe** of Naphtali.
19.39 of the **tribe** of Naphtali received as their possession.
19.40 assignment made was for the families of the **tribe** of Dan.
19.48 families of the **tribe** of Dan received as their possession.
19.51 of the families of the **tribes** of Israel assigned these parts
21. 1 to the heads of the families of all the **tribes** of Israel.
21.16 nine cities from the **tribes** of Judah and Simeon.
21.38 From the **tribe** of Gad they received four cities:
22. 1 the people of the **tribes** of Reuben, Gad, and East Manasseh.
22. 6 to one half of the **tribe** of Manasseh, but to the other
22. 6 given land west of the Jordan, along with the other **tribes.**
22. 9 So the people of the **tribes** of Reuben, Gad, and East
22.10 When the **tribes** of Reuben, Gad, and East Manasseh arrived
22.11 The people of the **tribes** of Reuben, Gad, and East Manasseh
22.12 together at Shiloh to go to war against the eastern **tribes.**
22.13 to the people of the **tribes** of Reuben, Gad, and East
22.14 from each of the western **tribes** and each one the head of
22.21 people of the **tribes** of Reuben, Gad, and East Manasseh
22.21 answered the heads of the families of the western **tribes:**
22.30 of families of the western **tribes,** heard what the people of
22.30 the **tribes** of Reuben, Gad, and East Manasseh
23. 4 as the possession of your **tribes** the land of the nations
24. 1 Joshua gathered all the **tribes** of Israel together at Shechem.
Judg 1. 1 the Lord, "Which of our **tribes** should be the first to go
1. 2 The Lord answered, "The **tribe** of Judah will go first.
1. 3 So the **tribes** of Simeon [4] and Judah went into battle together.
1.21 But the people of the **tribe** of Benjamin did not drive
1.22 The **tribes** of Ephraim and Manasseh went to attack
1.27 The **tribe** of Manasseh did not drive out the people
1.29 The **tribe** of Ephraim did not drive out the Canaanites
1.30 The **tribe** of Zebulun did not drive out the people
1.31 The **tribe** of Asher did not drive out the people living
1.33 The **tribe** of Naphtali did not drive out the people
1.34 forced the people of the **tribe** of Dan into the hill-country
1.35 and Mount Heres, but the **tribes** of Ephraim and Manasseh kept
3.15 man, who was the son of Gera, from the **tribe** of Benjamin.
4. 6 ten thousand men from the **tribes** of Naphtali and Zebulun and
4.10 Barak called the **tribes** of Zebulun and Naphtali to Kedesh,
5.14 into the valley, behind the **tribe** of Benjamin and its people.
5.15 But the **tribe** of Reuben was divided;
5.16 Yes, the **tribe** of Reuben was divided;
5.17 The **tribe** of Gad stayed east of the Jordan,
5.17 and the **tribe** of Dan remained by the ships.
5.17 The **tribe** of Asher stayed by the sea-coast;
6. 3 with the Amalekites and the desert **tribes** and attack them.
6.15 is the weakest in the **tribe** of Manasseh, and I am the
6.33 and the desert **tribes** assembled, crossed the River Jordan,
6.35 He sent messengers to the **tribes** of Asher, Zebulun, and
7.23 Then men from the **tribes** of Naphtali, Asher, and both
10. 1 He was from the **tribe** of Issachar and lived at Shamir in
10. 9 crossed the Jordan to fight the **tribes** of Judah, Benjamin,
10.18 the leaders of the Israelite **tribes** asked one another, "Who
13. 2 He was a member of the **tribe** of Dan.
18. 1 In those days the **tribe** of Dan was looking for territory to
18. 1 received any land of their own among the **tribes** of Israel.
18. 2 all the families in the **tribe** and sent them from the towns
18.11 hundred men from the **tribe** of Dan left Zorah and Eshtaol,
18.19 priest for a whole Israelite **tribe** than for the family of
18.30 as a priest for the **tribe** of Dan, and his descendants served
19.14 came to Gibeah in the territory of the **tribe** of Benjamin.
19.16 (The other people there were from the **tribe** of Benjamin.)
19.29 and sent one piece to each of the twelve **tribes** of Israel.
20. 2 The leaders of all the **tribes** of Israel were present at
20. 6 and sent one piece to each of the twelve **tribes** of Israel.
20.12 The Israelite **tribes** sent messengers
20.12 through the territory of the **tribe** of Benjamin to say,
20.17 rest of the Israelite **tribes** gathered 400,000 trained soldiers.
Judg 20.18 God, "Which **tribe** should attack the Benjaminites first?"
20.18 The Lord answered, "The **tribe** of Judah."
21. 3 Why is the **tribe** of Benjamin about to disappear from Israel?"
21. 5 group out of all the **tribes** of Israel that did not go
21. 6 Benjaminites and said, "Today Israel has lost one of its **tribes.**
21. 8 some group out of the **tribes** of Israel that had not gone
21.15 the Lord had broken the unity of the **tribes** of Israel.
21.16 said, "There are no more women in the **tribe** of Benjamin.
21.17 Israel must not lose one of its twelve **tribes.**
21.17 find a way for the **tribe** of Benjamin to survive, [18] but we
21.24 went back to his own **tribe** and family and to his own
1 Sam 1. 1 man named Elkanah, from the **tribe** of Ephraim, who lived in
2.28 From all the **tribes** of Israel I chose his family to be
4.12 A man from the **tribe** of Benjamin ran all the way from
9. 1 and influential man named Kish, from the **tribe** of Benjamin;
9.16 time I will send you a man from the **tribe** of Benjamin;
9.21 answered, "I belong to the **tribe** of Benjamin,
9.21 the smallest **tribe** in Israel,
9.21 and my family is the least important one in the **tribe.**
10.19 yourselves before the Lord by **tribes** and by clans.' "
10.20 Then Samuel made each **tribe** come forward,
10.20 and the Lord picked the **tribe** of Benjamin.
10.21 made the families of the **tribe** of Benjamin come forward, and
13. 2 Jonathan to Gibeah, in the territory of the **tribe** of Benjamin.
15.17 no importance, you are the leader of the **tribes** of Israel.
2 Sam 2.10 But the **tribe** of Judah was loyal to David, [11] and he ruled
2.15 men, representing Ishbosheth and the **tribe** of Benjamin,
2.25 The men from the **tribe** of Benjamin gathered round Abner
2.31 had killed 360 of Abner's men from the **tribe** of Benjamin.
3.19 to the people of the **tribe** of Benjamin and then went to
4. 2 sons of Rimmon, from Beeroth in the **tribe** of Benjamin.
5. 1 Then all the **tribes** of Israel came to David at Hebron and
15. 2 had told him what **tribe** he was from, [3] Absalom would say,
15.10 sent messengers to all the **tribes** of Israel to say, "When
19.17 He had with him a thousand men from the **tribe** of Benjamin.
19.20 first one from the northern **tribes** to come and meet Your
20. 1 named Sheba son of Bikri, of the **tribe** of Benjamin.
20.14 the territory of all the **tribes** of Israel and came to the
24. 2 your officers through all the **tribes** of Israel from one end
1 Kgs 7.14 his mother was from the **tribe** of Naphtali.
8. 1 all the leaders of the **tribes** and clans of Israel to come
11.13 I will leave him one **tribe** for the sake of my servant
11.28 in the territory of the **tribes** of Manasseh and Ephraim.
11.31 kingdom away from Solomon, and I will give you ten **tribes.**
11.32 Solomon will keep one **tribe,** for the sake of my servant
11.35 and will give you ten **tribes,** [36] but I will let Solomon's
11.36 let Solomon's son keep one **tribe,** so that I will always have
12. 3 The people of the northern **tribes** sent for him, and then
12.20 Only the **tribe** of Judah remained loyal to David's descendants.
12.21 of the best soldiers from the **tribes** of Judah and Benjamin.
12.21 and restore his control over the northern **tribes** of Israel.
12.23 and to all the people of the **tribes** of Judah and Benjamin:
12.31 priests from families who were not of the **tribe** of Levi.
15.27 son of Ahijah, of the **tribe** of Issachar, plotted against
18.31 for each of the twelve **tribes** named after the sons of Jacob,
2 Kgs 10.33 Gilead and Bashan, where the **tribes** of Gad, Reuben, and East
21. 7 the territory of the twelve **tribes** of Israel as the place
1 Chr 1.29 The sons of Ishmael became the heads of twelve **tribes:**
1.36 Eliphaz became the ancestor of the following **tribes:**
1.37 became the ancestor of the **tribes** of Nahath, Zerah, Shammah,
1.51 The people of Edom were divided into the following **tribes:**
2.10 (a prominent man of the **tribe** of Judah), [11] Salmon, Boaz,
4.17 married a woman from the **tribe** of Judah, and they had three
4.27 had fewer children, and the **tribe** of Simeon did not grow
4.27 as much as the **tribe** of Judah did.
4.42 other members of the **tribe** of Simeon went east to Edom.
5. 2 It was the **tribe** of Judah, however, that became
5. 2 the strongest and provided a ruler for all the **tribes.)**
5. 4 captured Beerah, a leader of the **tribe,** and deported him.
5. 7 list the following clan leaders in the **tribe** of Reuben:
5.10 time of King Saul the **tribe** of Reuben attacked the Hagrites,
5.11 The **tribe** of Gad lived to the north of Reuben in the
5.13 members of the **tribe** belonged to the following seven clans:
5.18 In the **tribes** of Reuben, Gad, and East Manasseh there
5.19 went to war against the Hagrite **tribes** of Jetur, Naphish,
5.26 He deported the **tribes** of Reuben, Gad, and East Manasseh and
7. 5 all the families of the **tribe** of Issachar listed 87,000 men
7.12 Shuppim and Huppim also belonged to this **tribe.**
8.40 All those named above were members of the **tribe** of Benjamin.
9. 3 People from the **tribes** of Judah, Benjamin, Ephraim, and
9. 4 690 families of the **tribe** of Judah who lived in Jerusalem.
9. 7 following members of the **tribe** of Benjamin lived in Jerusalem:
9. 9 There were 956 families of this **tribe** living there.
11.26 (a leading member of the **tribe** of Reuben, with his own group
12. 2 members of the **tribe** of Benjamin, to which Saul belonged.
12. 8 famous, experienced soldiers from the **tribe** of Gad who
12.14 of these men from the **tribe** of Gad were senior officers in
12.16 group of men from the **tribes** of Benjamin and Judah went out
12.19 Some soldiers from the **tribe** of Manasseh went over to
12.23 Benjamin (Saul's own **tribe):**
12.23 **Tribes** east of the Jordan—Reuben, Gad, and East Manasseh:
12.40 far away as the northern **tribes** of Issachar, Zebulun, and
21. 6 did not take any census of the **tribes** of Levi and Benjamin.
27. 2 clan of Perez, a part of the **tribe** of Judah)
27. 2 clan of Zerah, a part of the **tribe** of Judah)
27. 2 Anathoth in the territory of the **tribe** of Benjamin
27. 2 Pirathon in the territory of the **tribe** of Ephraim
27.16 This is the list of the administrators of the **tribes** of Israel:
28. 1 all the officials of the **tribes,** the officials who
28. 4 He chose the **tribe** of Judah to provide leadership, and out
29. 6 the officials of the **tribes,** the commanders of the army,

2 Chr 2.14 was a member of the **tribe** of Dan and his father was
5. 2 all the leaders of the **tribes** and clans of Israel to
10. 3 The people of the northern **tribes** sent for him, and they
11. 1 of the best soldiers from the **tribes** of Benjamin and Judah.
11. 1 and restore his control over the northern **tribes** of Israel.
11. 3 and to all the people of the **tribes** of Judah and Benjamin:
11.16 From all the **tribes** of Israel people who sincerely
25. 5 all the men of the **tribes** of Judah and Benjamin into army
30. 1 to send letters to the **tribes** of Ephraim and Manasseh,
30.10 in the territory of the **tribes** of Ephraim and Manasseh, and
30.10 as far north as the **tribe** of Zebulun, but people laughed at
30.11 there were some from the **tribes** of Asher, Manasseh, and
30.18 who had come from the **tribes** of Ephraim, Manasseh, Issachar,
33. 7 the territory of the twelve **tribes** of Israel as the place
Ezra 1. 5 of the clans of the **tribes** of Judah and Benjamin, the
6.17 goats as offerings for sin, one for each **tribe** of Israel.
Neh 11. 4 Members of the **tribe** of Judah:
11. 7 Members of the **tribe** of Benjamin:
11.24 clan of Zerah and the **tribe** of Judah, represented the people
11.25 Those who were of the **tribe** of Judah lived in Kiriath Arba,
11.31 The people of the **tribe** of Benjamin lived in Geba,
Esth 2. 5 he was from the **tribe** of Benjamin and was a descendant of
Ps 68.27 First comes Benjamin, the smallest **tribe**, then the
74. 2 ago, whom you brought out of slavery to be your own **tribe**.
78.55 divided their land among the **tribes** of Israel and gave their
78.67 he did not select the **tribe** of Ephraim.
78.68 Instead he chose the **tribe** of Judah and Mount Zion,
80. 2 creatures, [2]reveal yourself to the **tribes** of Ephraim,
122. 4 This is where the **tribes** come, the tribes of Israel, to
Is 9. 1 land of the **tribes** of Zebulun and Naphtali was once disgraced,
21.16 year the greatness of the **tribes** of Kedar will be at an
65. 9 Israelites who belong to the **tribe** of Judah, and their
Jer 2. 4 Lord's message, you descendants of Jacob, you **tribes** of Israel.
25.19 all the kings of the desert **tribes**;
31. 1 the God of all the **tribes** of Israel, and they will be
33.18 always be priests from the **tribe** of Levi to serve me and
33.21 with the priests from the **tribe** of Levi that they would
33.22 number of priests from the **tribe** of Levi, so that it will
49. 1 Molech take the territory of the **tribe** of Gad and settle there?
49.28 the Lord said about the **tribe** of Kedar and the districts
49.28 the people of Kedar and destroy that **tribe** of eastern people!
Ezek 25. 4 I will let the **tribes** from the eastern desert conquer you.
25.10 I will let the **tribes** of the eastern desert conquer Moab,
40.46 the only members of the **tribe** of Levi who are permitted to
43.19 Those priests belonging to the **tribe** of Levi who are
44.15 "Those priests belonging to the **tribe** of Levi who are
45. 1 is divided to give each **tribe** a share, one part is to
45. 7 length of one of the areas allotted to the **tribes** of Israel.
45. 8 let the rest of the country belong to the **tribes** of Israel.
47.13 be divided among the twelve **tribes**,
47.13 with the **tribe** of Joseph receiving two sections.
47.21 "Divide this land among your **tribes**;
47.22 lots for shares of the land along with the **tribes** of Israel.
47.23 share with the people of the **tribe** among whom he is living.
48. 1 Each **tribe** is to receive one section of land extending from
48. 8 from east to west as the sections given to the **tribes**.
48.11 doing wrong, as the other members of the **tribe** of Levi did.
48.19 the city, no matter which **tribe** he comes from, may farm that
48.23 section, each of the remaining **tribes** is to receive one
48.28 the portion given to the **tribe** of Gad, the boundary runs
48.29 into sections for the **tribes** of Israel to possess."
48.30 has three gates in it, each named after one of the **tribes**.
Dan 1. 6 and Azariah, all of whom were from the **tribe** of Judah.
Hos 13. 1 tribe of Ephraim spoke, the other **tribes** of Israel were afraid;
Zech 9. 1 Not only the **tribes** of Israel, but also the capital of Syria
9. 7 my people and be like a clan in the **tribe** of Judah.
Mt 19.28 also sit on thrones, to rule the twelve **tribes** of Israel.
Lk 2.36 widow named Anna, daughter of Phanuel of the **tribe** of Asher.
22.30 sit on thrones to rule over the twelve **tribes** of Israel.
Acts 13.21 son of Kish from the **tribe** of Benjamin, to be their king
26. 7 thing that the twelve **tribes** of our people hope to receive,
Rom 11. 1 a descendant of Abraham, a member of the **tribe** of Benjamin.
Phil 3. 5 an Israelite by birth, of the **tribe** of Benjamin, a pure-blooded
Heb 7.13 said, belonged to a different **tribe**,
7.13 and no member of his **tribe** ever served as a priest.
7.14 known that he was born a member of the **tribe** of Judah;
7.14 Moses did not mention this **tribe** when he spoke of priests.
Rev 5. 5 The Lion from Judah's **tribe**, the great descendant of David,
5. 9 you bought for God people from every **tribe**, language, nation,
7. 4 They were from the twelve **tribes** of Israel,
7. 5 twelve thousand from each **tribe**:
7. 9 were from every race, **tribe**, nation, and language, and they stood
11. 9 People from all nations, **tribes**, languages, and races will look
13. 7 and it was given authority over every **tribe**, nation, language,
14. 6 peoples of the earth, to every race, **tribe**, language, and nation.
21.12 the names of the twelve **tribes** of the people of Israel.

TRIBESMEN
[FELLOW-TRIBESMEN]

Josh 22. 6 Share with your **fellow-tribesmen** what you took from your enemies."
Judg 7.12 the Amalekites, and the desert **tribesmen** were spread out in
8.10 Of the whole army of desert **tribesmen**, only about 15,000

AV **TRIBULATION** see **PERSECUTE, SUFFER, TROUBLE**

TRIBUTE

Gen 49.10 Nations will bring him **tribute** And bow in obedience before him.
1 Kgs 10.15 the profits from trade, and **tribute** paid by the Arabian
2 Kgs 3. 4 every year he gave as **tribute** to the king of Israel 100,000
17. 3 surrendered to Shalmaneser and paid him **tribute** every year.
17. 4 his help, and stopped paying the annual **tribute** to Assyria.
23.33 of silver and thirty-four kilogrammes of gold as **tribute**.
23.35 needed to pay the **tribute** demanded by the king of Egypt.
2 Chr 26. 8 The Ammonites paid **tribute** to Uzziah, and he became so
27. 5 Ammonites to pay him the following **tribute** each year
36. 3 of silver and 34 kilogrammes of gold as **tribute**.
Hos 10. 6 be carried off to Assyria as **tribute** to the great emperor.

Am **TRICK** see **MISLEAD**

TRICK

Gen 3.13 She replied, "The snake **tricked** me into eating it."
29.25 Why have you **tricked** me?"
Judg 14.15 they said to Samson's wife, "**Trick** your husband into
16. 5 went to her and said, "**Trick** Samson into telling you why he
1 Sam 19.17 asked Michal, "Why have you **tricked** me like this and let my
28.12 she screamed and said to Saul, "Why have you **tricked** me?
2 Kgs 10.19 (This was a **trick** on the part of Jehu by which he
Neh 6. 2 This was a **trick** of theirs to try to harm me.
Prov 23. 3 he may be trying to **trick** you.
28.10 If you **trick** an honest person into doing evil, you will
Jer 20.10 "Perhaps he can be **tricked**," they say;
Dan 11.21 but he will come unexpectedly and seize power by **trickery**.
Mt 2.16 the visitors from the east had **tricked** him, he was furious.
Mk 12.15 But Jesus saw through their **trick** and answered,
Lk 20.23 But Jesus saw through their **trick** and said to them,
Acts 7.19 He **tricked** our ancestors and was cruel to them, forcing them
13.10 of all kinds of evil **tricks**, and you always keep trying to
Eph 4.14 men, who lead others into error by the **tricks** they invent.
6.11 will be able to stand up against the Devil's evil **tricks**.
1 Thes 2. 3 on error or impure motives, nor do we try to **trick** anyone.

Am **TRIM** see **PRUNE**

TRIM

Lev 19.27 sides of your head or **trim** your beard [28]or tattoo
21. 5 part of his head or **trim** his beard or cut gashes on
2 Sam 19.24 had not washed his feet, **trimmed** his beard, or washed his
1 Kgs 7. 9 measure, with their inner and outer sides **trimmed** with saws.
Mt 25. 7 The ten girls woke up and **trimmed** their lamps.

Am **TRIP**
see also **JOURNEY**

TRIP (1)

Jer 46.12 One soldier **trips** over another, and both of them fall to the

TRIP (2)

1 Cor 16.11 help him to continue his **trip** in peace, so that he will

TRIUMPH

Ex 14. 8 he pursued the Israelites, who were leaving **triumphantly**.
15. 7 In majestic **triumph** you overthrow your foes;
1 Sam 2. 9 a man does not **triumph** by his own strength.
2 Chr 20.27 troops back to Jerusalem in **triumph**, because the Lord had
Esth 9. 1 But instead, the Jews **triumphed** over them.
Job 17. 4 don't let them **triumph** over me now.
Ps 13. 2 How long will my enemies **triumph** over me?
20. 5 victory and celebrate your **triumph** by praising our God.
24.10 The **triumphant** Lord—he is the great king!
27. 6 So I will **triumph** over my enemies around me.
33.16 a soldier does not **triumph** because of his strength.
41.11 They will not **triumph** over me, and I will know that you
49.14 The righteous will **triumph** over them, as their bodies
60. 6 sanctuary God has said, "In **triumph** I will divide Shechem
60. 8 Did the Philistines think they would shout in **triumph** over me?"
68.24 O God, your march of **triumph** is seen by all, the
74. 4 Your enemies have shouted in **triumph** in your Temple;
89.17 in your love you make us **triumphant**.
108. 7 sanctuary God has said, "In **triumph** I will divide Shechem
108. 9 I will shout in **triumph** over the Philistines."
149. 5 God's people rejoice in their **triumph** and sing joyfully
Is 41. 2 from the east, and makes him **triumphant** wherever he goes?
46.13 My **triumph** will not be delayed.
Jer 19. 7 I will let their enemies **triumph** over them and kill them in
Zech 9. 9 He comes **triumphant** and victorious, but humble and riding on
Mt 12.20 until he causes justice to **triumph**, [21]and in him all peoples
Jas 2.13 but mercy **triumphs** over judgement.

TROOPS

Josh 8. 3 thirty thousand of his best **troops** and sent them out at
10. 7 army, including the best **troops**, started out from Gilgal.
Judg 7.22 Lord made the enemy **troops** attack each other with their swords.
1 Sam 13.15 Saul inspected his **troops**, about six hundred men.
23. 8 So Saul called his **troops** to war, to march against Keilah
26. 7 Abner and the **troops** were sleeping round him.

1 Sam 26.14 away, [14]and shouted to Saul's **troops** and to Abner,
28. 1 the Philistines gathered their **troops** to fight Israel,
28. 4 Philistine **troops** assembled and camped near the town of Shunem;
29. 1 The Philistines brought all their **troops** together at Aphek,
2 Sam 10. 9 Joab saw that the enemy **troops** would attack him in front
10.10 placed the rest of his **troops** under the command of his
10.15 by the Israelites, so they called all their **troops** together.
10.17 he gathered the Israelite **troops**, crossed the River Jordan,
11. 7 him if Joab and the **troops** were well, and how the fighting
11.17 enemy **troops** came out of the city and fought Joab's forces;
18. 5 all the **troops** heard David give this command to his officers.
18.16 and his **troops** came back from pursuing the Israelites.
19. 2 into sadness for all David's **troops** that day, because they
1 Kgs 15.19 that he will have to pull his **troops** out of my territory."
16.15 The Israelite **troops** were besieging the city of Gibbethon
16.17 Omri and his **troops** left Gibbethon and went and besieged Tirzah.
20. 1 of Syria gathered all his **troops**, and supported by
2 Kgs 3. 6 At once King Joram left Samaria and gathered all his **troops**.
6.15 house, and saw the Syrian **troops** with their horses and
25.19 been in command of the **troops**, five of the king's personal
1 Chr 12. 8 of Gad who joined David's **troops** when he was at the desert
12.21 as officers over his **troops**, because they were all outstanding
19.10 Joab saw that the enemy **troops** would attack him in
19.11 placed the rest of his **troops** under the command of his
19.16 the Israelites, so they brought **troops** from the Syrian
19.17 it, he gathered the Israelite **troops**, crossed the Jordan,
2 Chr 12. 3 be counted, including Libyan, Sukkite, and Sudanese **troops**.
13.13 had sent some of his **troops** to ambush the Judaean army from
14.13 and Asa and his **troops** pursued them as far as Gerar.
16. 3 that he will have to pull his **troops** out of my territory."
17. 2 He stationed **troops** in the fortified cities of Judah, in
17.14 was the commander of the **troops** from the clans of Judah, and
17.17 commander of the **troops** from the clans of Benjamin was Eliada,
20.25 Jehoshaphat and his **troops** moved in to take the loot,
20.27 Jehoshaphat led his **troops** back to Jerusalem in triumph,
25. 5 They were picked **troops**, ready for battle, skilled in using
25.10 So Amaziah sent the hired **troops** away and told them to
33.14 command of a unit of **troops** in each of the fortified cities
Ezra 8.22 ask the emperor for a **troop** of cavalry to guard us from
Neh 2. 9 some army officers and a **troop** of horsemen with me, and I
4. 2 his companions and the Samaritan **troops** he said, "What do
Job 29.25 as a king leads his **troops**, and gave them comfort in their
Is 13. 4 The Lord of Armies is preparing his **troops** for battle.
Jer 34. 1 and his army, supported by **troops** from all the nations and
49. 5 there will be no one to bring your **troops** together again.
52.25 been in command of the **troops**, seven of the king's personal
Ezek 38. 4 hooks in his jaws, and drag him and all his **troops** away.
38. 7 to get ready and have all his **troops** ready at his command.
Joel 2.11 The **troops** that obey him are many and mighty.
Mt 5.41 if one of the occupation **troops** forces you to carry his pack
Acts 21.31 the commander of the Roman **troops** that all Jerusalem was rioting.
Rev 9.16 I was told the number of the mounted **troops**:

TROUBLE

Gen 3.16 woman, "I will increase your **trouble** in pregnancy and your
21.11 **troubled** Abraham very much, because Ishmael was also his son.
21.17 angel of God spoke to Hagar, "What are you **troubled** about,
29.32 "The Lord has seen my **trouble**, and now my husband will love
31.42 But God has seen my **trouble** and the work I have done,
34.30 Jacob said to Simeon and Levi, "You have brought **trouble** on me;
35. 3 in the time of my **trouble** and who has been with me
41.52 "God has given me children in the land of my **trouble**";
42.21 we saw the great **trouble** he was in when he begged for
42.21 That is why we are in this **trouble** now."
43. 6 you cause me so much **trouble** by telling the man that you
Ex 5.19 realized that they were in **trouble** when they were told that
10. 7 to him, "How long is this man going to give us **trouble**?
Num 11. 1 The people began to complain to the Lord about their **troubles**.
23.21 that Israel's future Will bring her no misfortune or **trouble**.
33.55 are left will be as **troublesome** as splinters in your eyes
Deut 2. 9 Lord said to me, 'Don't **trouble** the people of Moab, the
2.19 Don't **trouble** them or start a war against them, because I am
4.30 When you are in **trouble** and all those things happen to you,
28.20 you disaster, confusion, and **trouble** in everything you do,
Josh 6.18 will bring **trouble** and destruction on the Israelite camp.
7.24 and they took them to **Trouble** Valley.
7.25 And Joshua said, "Why have you brought such **trouble** on us?
7.25 The Lord will now bring **trouble** on you!"
7.26 That is why that place is still called **Trouble** Valley.
15. 7 a son of Reuben), [7]from **Trouble** Valley up to Debir, and
24. 5 I sent Moses and Aaron, and I brought great **trouble** on Egypt.
Judg 10.14 Let them rescue you when you get into **trouble**."
10.16 and he became **troubled** over Israel's distress.
11. 7 Why come to me now that you're in **trouble**?"
Ruth 1.21 when the Lord Almighty has condemned me and sent me **trouble**?"
1 Sam 1.11 See my **trouble** and remember me!
1.15 I have been praying, pouring out my **troubles** to the Lord.
2.32 You will be **troubled** and look with envy on all the
10.19 rescues you from all your **troubles** and difficulties, but
24. 5 then David's conscience began to **trouble** him, [6]and he said
26.24 Lord do the same to me and free me from all **troubles**!"
28.15 Saul answered, "I am in great **trouble**!
30. 6 David was now in great **trouble**, because his men were all
2 Sam 12.11 cause someone from your own family to bring **trouble** on you.
13.25 "It would be too much **trouble** for you if we all went."
14.10 bring him to me, and he will never **trouble** you again."
19.22 Are you going to give me **trouble**?
20. 6 to Abishai, "Sheba will give us more **trouble** than Absalom.
2 Sam 22. 7 In my **trouble** I called to the Lord;
22.19 When I was in **trouble**, they attacked me, but the Lord
24. 1 Israel once more, and he made David bring **trouble** on them.
24.10 census, his conscience began to **trouble** him, and he said to
1 Kgs 1.29 rescued me from all my **troubles**, [30]that today I will keep
2.26 with my father David, and you shared in all his **troubles**."
18.17 "So there you are—the worst **troublemaker** in Israel!"
18.18 "I'm not the **troublemaker**," Elijah answered.
2 Kgs 4.13 in return for all the **trouble** she has had in providing for
6.28 What's your **trouble**?"
6.33 said, "It's the Lord who has brought this **trouble** on us!
14.10 Why stir up **trouble** that will only bring disaster on you and
1 Chr 7.23 because of the **trouble** that had come to their family.
21. 1 Satan wanted to bring **trouble** on the people of Israel, so
2 Chr 15. 4 But when **trouble** came, they turned to the Lord, the God of
15. 5 because there was **trouble** and disorder in every land.
15. 6 city, because God was bringing **trouble** and distress on them.
20. 9 pray to you in their **trouble**, and you would hear them and
25.19 Why stir up **trouble** that will only bring disaster on you and
28.19 and had defied the Lord, the Lord brought **troubles** on Judah.
28.20 instead of helping Ahaz, opposed him and caused him **trouble**.
28.22 When his **troubles** were at their worst, that man Ahaz
Ezra 4.15 ancient times it has given **trouble** to kings and to rulers of
4.19 and that it has been full of rebels and **troublemakers**.
Neh 2.17 said to them, "See what **trouble** we are in because Jerusalem
9.27 In their **trouble** they called to you for help, and you
Job 2.10 How can we complain when he sends us **trouble**?"
3.10 letting me be born, for exposing me to **trouble** and grief.
3.26 I have no peace, no rest, and my **troubles** never end.
4. 5 your turn to be in **trouble**, and you are too stunned to
5. 6 grow in the soil, nor does **trouble** grow out of the ground.
5. 7 Man brings **trouble** on himself, as surely as sparks fly up
6. 1 If my **troubles** and griefs were weighed on scales,
6.14 In **trouble** like this I need loyal friends— whether I've
10.15 as I sin, I'm in **trouble** with you, but when I do
11.16 Then all your **troubles** will fade from your memory, like
12. 5 You have no **troubles**, and yet you make fun of me;
14. 1 All lead the same short, **troubled** life.
14.14 for better times, wait till this time of **trouble** is ended.
15.35 These are the men who plan **trouble** and do evil;
19. 5 than I am, and regard my **troubles** as proof of my guilt.
21.10 Yes, all their cattle breed and give birth without **trouble**.
27. 9 When **trouble** comes, will God hear their cries?
29.16 to the poor and took the side of strangers in **trouble**.
30.25 I weep with people in **trouble** and feel sorry for those in
30.26 hoped for happiness and light, but **trouble** and darkness came
36.16 God brought you out of **trouble**, and let you enjoy security;
38.23 ready for times of **trouble**, for days of battle and war.
42.11 him for all the **troubles** the Lord had brought on him.
Ps 4. 1 When I was in **trouble**, you helped me.
6. 3 I am completely exhausted [3]and my whole being is deeply **troubled**.
7.14 they plan **trouble** and practise deception.
9. 9 for the oppressed, a place of safety in times of **trouble**.
10. 1 Why do you hide yourself when we are in **trouble**?
10. 6 I will never be in **trouble**."
10.14 you take notice of **trouble** and suffering and are always
13. 2 How long must I endure **trouble**?
16. 4 Those who rush to other gods bring many **troubles** on themselves.
18. 6 In my **trouble** I called to the Lord;
18.18 When I was in **trouble**, they attacked me, but the Lord
20. 1 May the Lord answer you when you are in **trouble**!
22.11 **Trouble** is near, and there is no one to help.
25.17 Relieve me of my worries and save me from all my **troubles**.
25.22 From all their **troubles**, O God, save your people Israel!
27. 5 In times of **trouble** he will shelter me;
31. 7 you know my **trouble**.
31. 9 Be merciful to me, Lord, for I am in **trouble**;
31.10 I am weak from all my **troubles**;
32. 6 when a great flood of **trouble** comes rushing in, it will
32. 7 you will save me from **trouble**.
34. 6 he saves them from all their **troubles**.
34.17 he rescues them from all their **troubles**.
34.19 The good man suffers many **troubles**, but the Lord saves
35.15 But when I was in **trouble**, they were all glad and
37. 8 it only leads to **trouble**.
37.39 Lord saves righteous men and protects them in times of **trouble**.
38. 8 my heart is **troubled**, and I groan with pain.
39. 3 The more I thought, the more **troubled** I became;
40.12 I am surrounded by many **troubles**— too many to count!
40.14 happy because of my **troubles** be turned back and disgraced.
41. 1 the Lord will help them when they are in **trouble**.
42. 5 Why am I so **troubled**?
42.11 Why am I so **troubled**?
43. 5 Why am I so **troubled**?
44.24 Don't forget our suffering and **trouble**!
46. 1 and strength, always ready to help in times of **trouble**.
50.15 Call to me when **trouble** comes;
54. 7 rescued me from all my **troubles**, and I have seen my enemies
55. 3 They bring **trouble** on me;
55.10 surrounding it day and night, filling it with crime and **trouble**.
55.22 Leave your **troubles** with the Lord, and he will defend you;
56. 5 My enemies make **trouble** for me all day long;
56. 8 You know how **troubled** I am;
59.16 been a refuge for me, a shelter in my time of **trouble**.
62. 8 Tell him all your **troubles**, for he is our refuge.
64. 1 I am in **trouble**, God—listen to my prayer!
66.14 give you what I said I would when I was in **trouble**.
69.17 I am in great **trouble**—answer me now!
70. 2 happy because of my **troubles** be turned back and disgraced.
71.20 You have sent **troubles** and suffering on me, but you will

Ps 73. 5 they do not have the **troubles** that others have.
77. 2 In times of **trouble** I pray to the Lord;
81. 7 When you were in **trouble,** you called to me, and I saved
86. 7 to you in times of **trouble,** because you answer my prayers.
88. 3 So many **troubles** have fallen on me that I am close to
90.10 yet all they bring us is **trouble** and sorrow;
91.15 when they are in **trouble,** I will be with them.
94.13 him rest from days of **trouble** until a pit is dug to
102. 2 When I am in **trouble,** don't turn away from me!
106.32 the Lord angry, and Moses was in **trouble** on their account.
107. 6 Then in their **trouble** they called to the Lord, and he
107.13 Then in their **trouble** they called to the Lord, and he
107.19 Then in their **trouble** they called to the Lord, and he
107.28 Then in their **trouble** they called to the Lord, and he
119.143 I am filled with **trouble** and anxiety, but your
120. 1 When I was in **trouble,** I called to the Lord, and he
138. 7 When I am surrounded by **troubles,** you keep me safe.
142. 2 I tell him all my **troubles.**
143.11 in your goodness save me from my **troubles!**
145.14 He helps those who are in **trouble;**
Prov 1.26 So when you get into **trouble,** I will laugh at you.
1.27 storm, bringing fierce winds of **trouble,** and you are in pain
2.12 from people who stir up **trouble** by what they say—[13]men who
6.14 in their perverted minds, stirring up **trouble** everywhere.
6.16 **trouble** among friends.
10.10 holds back the truth causes **trouble,** but one who openly
10.12 Hate stirs up **trouble,** but love overlooks all offences.
10.14 they can, but when fools speak, **trouble** is not far off.
11. 8 The righteous are protected from **trouble;**
11.27 if you are looking for **trouble,** that is what you will get.
11.29 The man who brings **trouble** on his family will have
12.13 own words, but an honest man gets himself out of **trouble.**
12.21 righteous people, but the wicked have nothing but **trouble.**
13.10 Arrogance causes nothing but **trouble.**
13.13 If you refuse good advice, you are asking for **trouble;**
13.17 Unreliable messengers cause **trouble,**
13.21 **Trouble** follows sinners everywhere, but righteous people
14.16 careful to stay out of **trouble,** but stupid people are
15.16 poor and fear the Lord than to be rich and in **trouble.**
15.19 but if you are honest, you will have no **trouble.**
15.27 a profit dishonestly, you will get your family into **trouble.**
15.28 Evil people have a quick reply, but it causes **trouble.**
16.28 they stir up **trouble** and break up friendships.
17. 1 mind than to have a banquet in a house full of **trouble.**
17.11 to wicked people who are always stirring up **trouble.**
17.17 What are brothers for if not to share **trouble?**
17.19 To like sin is to like making **trouble.**
17.19 If you brag all the time, you are asking for **trouble.**
19. 2 impatience will get you into **trouble.**
19.19 you get him out of **trouble** once, you will have to do
21.23 you want to stay out of **trouble,** be careful what you say.
22. 3 Sensible people will see **trouble** coming and avoid it, but
23.29 for himself, always causing **trouble**
24. 2 Causing **trouble** is all they ever think about;
24. 8 planning evil, you will earn a reputation as a **troublemaker.**
26. 6 you are asking for **trouble.**
26.21 the fire burning, and **troublemakers** keep arguments alive.
27. 3 nothing compared to the **trouble** that stupidity can cause.
27. 9 you feel happier, but **trouble** shatters your peace of mind.
27.10 If you are in **trouble,** don't ask your brother for help;
27.12 Sensible people will see **trouble** coming and avoid it,
28.25 Selfishness only causes **trouble.**
29.22 People with quick tempers cause a lot of quarrelling and **trouble.**
30.33 If you stir up anger, you get into **trouble.**
Ecc 2.17 because everything in it had brought me nothing but **trouble.**
7.14 well for you, be glad, and when **trouble** comes, just remember:
7.14 God sends both happiness and **trouble;**
9. 9 it, because that is all you will get for all your **trouble.**
10.16 A country is in **trouble** when its king is a youth and
Is 1.24 on you, my enemies, and you will cause me no more **trouble.**
3. 6 to wear, so be our leader in this time of **trouble."**
7.17 whole royal family, days of **trouble** worse than any that have
8.22 they will see nothing but **trouble** and darkness, terrifying
9. 1 be no way for them to escape from this time of **trouble.**
16. 7 people of Moab will weep because of the **troubles** they suffer.
17.11 There would be only **trouble** and incurable pain.
25. 4 have fled to you and have been safe in times of **trouble.**
29.22 Israel, who rescued Abraham from **trouble,** says, "My people,
33. 2 Protect us day by day and save us in times of **trouble.**
38.14 Lord, rescue me from all this **trouble.**
40.27 Lord doesn't know your **troubles** or care if you suffer
43. 2 your **troubles** will not overwhelm you.
65.10 in the west and in the Valley of **Trouble** in the east.
65.16 The **troubles** of the past will be gone and forgotten."
Jer 2.24 No male that wants her has to **trouble** himself;
2.27 But when you are in **trouble,** you ask me to come and
2.28 When you are in **trouble,** let them save you—if they can!
6. 8 People of Jerusalem, let these **troubles** be a warning to you,
11.14 When they are in **trouble** and call to me for help, I
15.11 behalf of my enemies when they were in **trouble** and distress.
16.19 you help me in times of **trouble.**
17.16 I did not wish a time of **trouble** for them.
17.17 you are my place of safety when **trouble** comes.
20.18 Was it only to have **trouble** and sorrow, to end my life
44.17 had plenty of food, we were prosperous, and had no **troubles.**
45. 3 The Lord has added sorrow to my **troubles.**
49.23 are worried and **troubled** because they have heard bad news.
50.34 to the earth, but **trouble** to the people of Babylonia."
Ezek 5. 7 you have caused more **trouble** than the nations around you.
9. 4 everyone who is distressed and **troubled** because of all the
29.18 the king nor his army got anything for all their **trouble.**
Ezek 30. 3 Lord will act, A day of clouds and **trouble** for the nations.
32. 9 "Many nations will be **troubled** when I spread the news of
Dan 9.18 at us, and see the **trouble** we are in and the suffering
9.25 times sixty-two years, but this will be a time of **troubles.**
12. 1 will be a time of **troubles,** the worst since nations first
Hos 2.15 vineyards she had and make **Trouble** Valley a door of hope.
Mic 2. 3 going to find yourselves in **trouble,** and then you will not
Nah 1. 7 he protects his people in times of **trouble;**
Hab 1. 3 Why do you make me see such **trouble?**
Zeph 1.15 of fury, a day of **trouble** and distress, a day of ruin
Zech 10. 2 They are in **trouble** because they have no leader.
10.11 pass through their sea of **trouble,** I, the Lord, will strike
Mt 6.34 There is no need to add to the **troubles** each day brings.
13.21 So when **trouble** or persecution comes because of the message,
24. 6 but do not be **troubled.**
24.21 For the **trouble** at that time will be far more terrible
24.29 "Soon after the **trouble** of those days, the sun will grow dark,
Mk 4.17 So when **trouble** or persecution comes because of the message,
5.29 feeling inside herself that she was healed of her **trouble.**
5.34 Go in peace, and be healed of your **trouble."**
7.35 impediment was removed, and he began to talk without any **trouble.**
13. 7 And don't be **troubled** when you hear the noise of battles
13.19 For the **trouble** of those days will be far worse than any
13.24 days after that time of **trouble** the sun will grow dark,
Lk 1.29 Mary was deeply **troubled** by the angel's message,
6.18 who were **troubled** by evil spirits also came and were healed.
7. 6 officer sent friends to tell him, "Sir, don't **trouble** yourself.
10.41 You are worried and **troubled** over so many things,
18. 5 yet because of all the **trouble** this widow is giving me, I
Jn 12.27 "Now my heart is **troubled**—and what shall I say?
13.21 he was deeply **troubled** and declared openly, "I am telling
Acts 2.25 he is near me, and I will not be **troubled.**
2.37 heard this, they were deeply **troubled** and said to Peter and
7.10 God was with him [10]and brought him safely through all his **troubles.**
14.22 "We must pass through many **troubles** to enter the Kingdom of God,"
15.19 "that we should not **trouble** the Gentiles who are turning to
15.24 went from our group have **troubled** and upset you by what they
16.20 "These men are Jews, and they are causing **trouble** in our city.
17. 6 and shouted, "These men have caused **trouble** everywhere!
19.23 time that there was serious **trouble** in Ephesus because of
20.23 Holy Spirit has warned me that prison and **troubles** wait for me.
Rom 5. 3 We also boast of our **troubles,** because we know that
5. 3 **trouble** produces endurance, [4]endurance brings God's approval,
8.35 Can **trouble** do it, or hardship or persecution or hunger
11.10 and make them bend under their **troubles** at all times."
12.12 joyful, be patient in your **troubles,** and pray at all times.
1 Cor 7.28 would rather spare you the everyday **troubles** that married people
10.32 way as to cause no **trouble** either to Jews or Gentiles or
2 Cor 1. 4 helps us in all our **troubles,** so that we are able to
1. 4 who have all kinds of **troubles,** using the same help that we
1. 8 remind you, brothers, of the **trouble** we had in the province
2. 4 to you with a greatly **troubled** and distressed heart and with
4. 8 We are often **troubled,** but not crushed;
4.17 And this small and temporary **trouble** we suffer will bring us
4.17 a tremendous and eternal glory, much greater than the **trouble.**
6. 4 that we are God's servants by patiently enduring **troubles,**
7. 4 In all our **troubles** I am still full of courage;
7. 5 There were **troubles** everywhere, quarrels with others, fears in
8. 2 have been severely tested by the **troubles** they went through;
Gal 5.11 preaching about the cross of Christ would cause no **trouble.**
6.17 one give me any more **trouble,** because the scars I have on
Phil 1.17 that they will make more **trouble** for me while I am in
4.14 it was very good of you to help me in my **troubles.**
1 Thes 2. 9 we would not be any **trouble** to you as we preached to
3. 7 So, in all our **trouble** and suffering we have been encouraged
1 Tim 5.10 helped people in **trouble,** and devoted herself to doing good.
Heb 12.15 plant that grows up and causes many **troubles** with its poison.
Jas 5.13 Is anyone among you in **trouble?**
Rev 2. 9 I know your **troubles;**
2.10 thrown into prison, and your **troubles** will last ten days.
3.10 safe from the time of **trouble** which is coming upon the world

AV TROUBLE

Judg 11.35 Why must it be you that causes me **pain?**
1 Chr 22.14 for the Temple, by my **efforts** I have accumulated more than
2 Chr 32.18 in order to frighten and **discourage** the people of Jerusalem
Job 15.24 **disaster,** like a powerful king, is waiting to attack him.
Ps 3. 1 I have so many **enemies,** Lord, so many who turn against me!
9.13 See the **sufferings** my enemies cause me!
60.11 Help us against the **enemy;**
78.33 days like a breath and their lives with sudden **disaster.**
78.49 He caused them great **distress** by pouring out his anger
107.26 In such **danger** the men lost their courage;
116. 3 the **horrors** of the grave closed in on me;
Prov 25.19 an unreliable person in a **crisis** is like trying to chew with
Is 1.14 they are a **burden** that I am tired of bearing.
17.14 In the evening they cause **terror,** but by morning they are gone.
26.16 You punished your people, Lord, and in **anguish** they prayed
30. 6 "The ambassadors travel through **dangerous** country, where
46. 7 prays to it, it cannot answer or save him from **disaster.**
65.23 and their children will not meet with **disaster.**
Jer 8.15 **terror** came instead.
11.12 will not be able to save them when this **destruction** comes.
14. 8 you are the one who saves us from **disaster.**
14.19 we hoped for healing, but **terror** came instead.
30. 7 it— a time of **distress** for my people, but they will

Lam	1.21	My enemies are glad that you brought **disaster** on me.
Ezek	32.13	will be no people or cattle to **muddy** the water any more.
Dan	4.19	Belteshazzar, was so **alarmed** that he could not say anything.
	5.10	Please do not be so **disturbed** and look so pale.
	11.44	east and the north will **frighten** him, and he will fight
Mt	26.10	so he said to them, "Why are you **bothering** this woman?
Mk	14. 6	Why are you **bothering** her?
Lk	11. 7	suppose your friend should answer from inside, 'Don't **bother** me!
Acts	20.10	"Don't **worry,**" he said, "he is still alive!"
Gal	1. 7	are some people who are **upsetting** you and trying to change
	5.12	that the people who are **upsetting** you would go all the way;
2 Thes	1. 6	he will bring **suffering** on those who make you suffer,

TROUBLE VALLEY

[VALLEY OF TROUBLE]

Josh	7.24	and they took them to **Trouble Valley.**
	7.26	That is why that place is still called **Trouble Valley.**
	15. 7	a son of Reuben), [7] from **Trouble Valley** up to Debir, and
Is	65.10	in the west and in the **Valley of Trouble** in the east.
Hos	2.15	vineyards she had and make **Trouble Valley** a door of hope.

TROUGH

[DRINKING-TROUGH]

Gen	24.20	her jar into the animals' **drinking-trough** and ran to the well
	30.38	these branches in front of the flocks at their **drinking-troughs.**
	30.41	front of them at the **drinking-troughs,** so that they would breed
Ex	2.15	and fill the **troughs** for their father's sheep and goats.

TROUSERS

Ezek	44.18	are to wear linen turbans and linen **trousers,** but no belt.

TRUE

[TRULY]

Gen	3. 4	The snake replied, "That's not **true;**
	18.21	or not the accusations which I have heard are **true."**
Ex	33.12	to the Lord, "It is **true** that you have told me to
Deut	13. 2	if what he promises comes **true,** [3] do not pay any attention
	13.14	and if it is **true** that this evil thing did happen, [15] then
	17. 4	If it is **true** that this evil thing has happened in Israel,
	18.22	he says does not come **true,** then it is not the Lord's
	22.20	"But if the charge is **true** and there is no proof that
	25.15	Use **true** and honest weights and measures, so that you
	32. 4	Your God is faithful and **true;**
	33. 8	at Massah And proved them **true** at the waters of Meribah.
Josh	7.20	"It's **true,"** Achan answered.
	9.24	learnt that it was really **true** that the Lord your God had
Judg	11.15	"It is not **true** that Israel took away the land of Moab
	13.12	Manoah asked, "When your words come **true,** what must the boy do?
	13.17	so that we can honour you when your words come **true."**
Ruth	3.12	It is **true** that I am a close relative and am responsible
1 Sam	1.23	And may the Lord make your promise come **true."**
	2.34	will show you that everything I have said will come **true.**
	3.19	Lord was with him and made everything that Samuel said come **true.**
	9. 6	is highly respected because everything he says comes **true.**
	20. 2	It isn't **true!"**
2 Sam	3. 9	may God strike me dead if I don't make this come **true!"**
1 Kgs	2.27	Shiloh about the priest Eli and his descendants come **true.**
	8.26	of Israel, let everything come **true** that you promised to my
	8.48	If in that land they **truly** and sincerely repent, and
	10. 6	heard in my own country about you and your wisdom is **true!**
	11. 6	the Lord and was not **true** to him as his father David
	13.32	of worship in the towns of Samaria will surely come **true."**
2 Kgs	3.12	"He is a **true** prophet," King Jehoshaphat said.
	10.10	the Lord said about the descendants of Ahab will come **true.**
2 Chr	6.17	of Israel, let everything come **true** that you promised to
	6.38	If in that land they **truly** and sincerely repent and pray
	9. 5	heard in my own country about you and your wisdom is **true!**
	15. 3	Israel lived without the **true** God, without priests to teach
	36.22	Lord made what he had said through the prophet Jeremiah come **true.**
Ezra	1. 1	Lord made what he had said through the prophet Jeremiah come **true.**
Neh	6. 8	"Nothing of what you are saying is **true.**
Esth	2.23	discovered that the report was **true,** so both men were hanged
Job	3.25	Everything I fear and dread comes **true.**
	5.27	It is **true,** so now accept it.
	11. 4	You claim that what you say is **true;**
	24.25	Can anyone prove that my words are not **true?**
	26.14	Who can know how **truly** great God is?
	28.13	No one knows its **true** value.
	31.35	I swear that every word is **true.**
	36. 4	you see before you a **truly** wise man.
Ps	5.11	because of you they are **truly** happy.
	15. 2	is right, whose words are **true** and sincere, [3] and who does
	33. 4	of the Lord are **true** and all his works are dependable.
	78.20	It is **true** that he struck the rock, and water flowed out
	103.18	generations [18] of those who are **true** to his covenant and
	105.19	round his neck, [19] until what he had predicted came **true.**
	119.142	righteousness will last for ever, and your law is always **true.**
	132.12	If your sons are **true** to my covenant and to the commands
	141. 6	cliffs, the people will admit that my words were **true.**
	144.15	Happy is the nation of whom this is **true;**
Prov	4.24	Never say anything that isn't **true.**
	8. 8	Everything I say is **true;**
	13.12	heart is crushed, but a wish come **true** fills you with joy.
Prov	24.26	An honest answer is a sign of **true** friendship.
Is	10.20	They will **truly** put their trust in the Lord, Israel's holy God.
	42. 9	The things I predicted have now come **true.**
	44.26	my plans, I make those plans and predictions come **true.**
	45.23	My promise is **true,** and it will not be changed.
	48.16	I have spoken openly, and have always made my words come **true."**
Jer	1.12	said, "and I am watching to see that my words come **true."**
	10.10	But you, Lord, are the **true** God, you are the living God
	15.11	may all their curses come **true** if I have not served you
	28. 6	will make your prophecy come **true** and will bring back from
	28. 9	prophet whom the Lord has **truly** sent
	28. 9	when that prophet's predictions come **true."**
	32.24	You can see that all you have said has come **true.**
	40.16	What you are saying about Ishmael is not **true!"**
	42. 5	"May the Lord be a **true** and faithful witness against us if
	44.28	will know whose words have come **true,** mine or theirs.
	44.29	that my promise to bring destruction on you will come **true.**
Ezek	3.20	"If a **truly** good man starts doing evil and I put him
	12.23	The time has come, and the predictions are coming **true!**
	13. 6	Yet they expect their words to come **true!**
	18. 5	"Suppose there is a **truly** good man, righteous and honest.
	33.33	when all your words come **true**—and they will come true—then
	36.13	It is **true** that people call the land a man-eater, and they
Dan	2.45	what you dreamt, and have given you its **true** meaning."
	3.14	Meshach, and Abednego, is it **true** that you refuse to worship
	4.33	The words came **true** immediately.
	8.12	sacrifices, and **true** religion was thrown to the ground.
	8.26	sacrifices which has been explained to you will come **true.**
	8.26	because it will be a long time before it does come **true."**
	9. 7	This is **true** of all of us who live in Judaea and
	9.24	and the prophecy will come **true,** and the holy Temple will be
	10. 1	The message was **true** but extremely hard to understand.
	11. 2	And what I am now going to tell you is **true."**
Hos	2.19	I will be **true** and faithful;
Amos	2.11	Isn't this **true,** people of Israel?
Hab	2. 3	writing, because it is not yet time for it to come **true.**
	2. 3	time is coming quickly, and what I show you will come **true.**
Mal	2. 7	is the duty of priests to teach the **true** knowledge of God.
	2.15	It was that you should have children who are **truly** God's people.
Mt	1.22	said through the prophet come **true,** [23] "A virgin will become
	2.15	said through the prophet come **true,** "I called my Son out of
	2.17	In this way what the prophet Jeremiah had said came **true:**
	2.23	And so what the prophets had said came **true:**
	4.14	prophet Isaiah had said come **true,** [15] "Land of Zebulun and land
	5.17	to do away with them, but to make their teachings come **true.**
	8.17	prophet Isaiah had said come **true,** "He himself took our sickness
	11.19	God's wisdom, however, is shown to be **true** by its results."
	12.17	what God had said through the prophet Isaiah come **true:**
	13.35	the prophet had said come **true,** "I will use parables when I
	14.33	**"Truly** you are the Son of God!"
	15.27	"That's **true,** sir," she answered;
	21. 4	in order to make what the prophet had said come **true:**
	26.54	how could the Scriptures come **true** which say that this is
	26.56	make what the prophets wrote in the Scriptures come **true."**
	27. 9	Then what the prophet Jeremiah had said came **true:**
Mk	12.32	It is **true,** as you say, that only the Lord is God
	14.49	But the Scriptures must come **true."**
	16.20	proved that their preaching was **true** by the miracles that were
Lk	1.20	believed my message, which will come **true** at the right time.
	1.20	remain silent until the day my promise to you comes **true."**
	1.45	to believe that the Lord's message to you will come **true!"**
	4.21	passage of scripture has come **true** today, as you heard it
	4.25	it is **true** that there were many widows in Israel during the
	5.10	The same was **true** of Simon's partners, James and John,
	7.35	wisdom, however, is shown to be **true** by all who accept it."
	12.15	because a person's **true** life is not made up of the things
	16.11	handling worldly wealth, how can you be trusted with **true** wealth?
	18.31	the prophets wrote about the Son of Man will come **true.**
	21.22	Days of Punishment,' to make all that the Scriptures say come **true.**
	22.37	fate of criminals,' must come **true** about me,
	22.37	because what was written about me is coming **true."**
	24.44	writings of the prophets, and the Psalms had to come **true."**
Jn	3.21	But whoever does what is **true** comes to the light in
	4.23	he really is, offering him the **true** worship that he wants.
	4.37	The saying is **true,** 'One man sows, another man reaps.'
	5.32	and I know that what he says about me is **true.**
	7.24	Stop judging by external standards, and judge by **true** standards."
	8.14	what I say is **true,** because I know where I came
	8.16	so, my judgement would be **true,** because I am not alone in
	8.17	Law that when two witnesses agree, what they say is **true.**
	8.41	Father we have," they answered, "and we are his **true** sons."
	10.35	We know that what the scripture says is **true** for ever;
	10.41	they said, "but everything he said about this man was **true."**
	12.38	so that what the prophet Isaiah had said might come **true:**
	12.49	This is **true,** because I have not spoken on my own authority,
	13.18	But the scripture must come **true** that says, 'The man who
	15.25	happen so that what is written in their Law may come **true:**
	17. 3	means knowing you, the only **true** God, and knowing Jesus Christ,
	17. 8	they know that it is **true** that I came from you,
	17.12	was bound to be lost—so that the scripture might come **true.**
	17.19	in order that they, too, may be **truly** dedicated to you.
	18. 9	(He said this so that what he had said might come **true:**
	18.32	the words of Jesus come **true,** the words he used when he
	19.24	This happened in order to make the scripture come **true:**
	19.28	to make the scripture come **true,** he said, "I am thirsty."
	19.35	What he said is **true,**
	19.36	This was done to make the scripture come **true:**
	21.24	and we know that what he said is **true.**
Acts	1.16	"the scripture had to come **true** in which the Holy Spirit,

Acts 3.18 and he made it come **true** in this way.
7. 1 The High Priest asked Stephen, "Is this **true?"**
10.34 now realize that it is **true** that God treats everyone on the
11.23 all to be faithful and **true** to the Lord with all their
12.11 to him, and said, "Now I know that it is really **true!**
12.15 But she insisted that it was **true.**
13.27 Yet they made the prophets' words come **true** by condemning Jesus.
14. 3 message about his grace was **true** by giving them the power to
14.22 the believers and encouraged them to remain **true** to the faith.
16.15 you have decided that I am a **true** believer in the Lord."
17.11 the Scriptures to see if what Paul said was really **true.**
24. 9 Jews joined in the accusation and said that all this was **true.**
Rom 1. 9 that what I say is **true**—the God whom I serve with
1.28 to keep in mind the **true** knowledge about God, he has given
2.15 show that this is **true,** since their thoughts sometimes accuse
2.28 After all, who is a real Jew, **truly** circumcised?
3. 4 God must be **true,** even though every man is a liar.
5.15 It is **true** that many people died because of the sin of
5.17 It is **true** that through the sin of one man death began
7.13 in order that its **true** nature as sin might be revealed.
9. 4 they have the **true** worship;
9. 8 a result of God's promise are regarded as the **true** descendants.
9.22 And the same is **true** of what God has done.
10. 2 but their devotion is not based on **true** knowledge.
10.18 Is it **true** that they did not hear the message?
11.20 That is **true.**
12. 1 This is the **true** worship that you should offer.
15. 8 promises to their ancestors come **true,** [9]and to enable even the
1 Cor 8. 1 It is **true,** of course, that "all of us have knowledge,"
10.23 That is **true,** but not everything is good.
11.18 and this I believe is partly **true.**
14.25 and worship God, confessing, **"Truly** God is here among you!"
15.13 If that is **true,** it means that Christ was not raised;
15.15 but if it is **true** that the dead are not raised
15.29 If it is **true,** as some claim, that the dead are not
15.54 been changed into the immortal, then the scripture will come **true:**
2 Cor 6. 6 Holy Spirit, by our **true** love, [7]by our message of truth,
7.14 the same way the boast we made to Titus has proved **true.**
10. 3 It is **true** that we live in the world, but we do
11.13 Those men are not **true** apostles—they are false apostles,
Gal 1.20 What I write is **true.**
4.18 purpose is good—this is **true** always, and not merely when I
5.11 If that were **true,** then my preaching about the cross of
Eph 1.13 when you heard the **true** message, the Good News that brought
3.15 every family in heaven and on earth receives its **true** name.
4.24 reveals itself in the **true** life that is upright and holy.
5.13 out to the light, then their **true** nature is clearly revealed;
Phil 1. 9 and more, together with **true** knowledge and perfect judgement,
1.11 will be filled with the **truly** good qualities which only Jesus
3. 3 who have received the **true** circumcision, for we worship God by
4. 8 that are **true,** noble, right, pure, lovely, and honourable.
Col 1. 5 When the **true** message, the Good News, first came to you,
2. 2 the full wealth of assurance which **true** understanding brings.
1 Thes 1. 9 to God, to serve the **true** and living God [10]and to wait
1 Tim 1. 2 Jesus our hope— [2]To Timothy, my **true** son in the faith:
1.15 This is a **true** saying, to be completely accepted and believed:
3. 1 This is a **true** saying:
4. 6 of faith and of the **true** teaching which you have followed.
4. 9 This is a **true** saying, to be completely accepted and believed.
6. 3 does not agree with the **true** words of our Lord Jesus Christ
6.19 they will be able to win the life which is **true** life.
2 Tim 1.13 Hold firmly to the **true** words that I taught you,
2.11 This is a **true** saying:
Tit 1. 4 I write to Titus, my **true** son in the faith that we
1. 9 to encourage others with the **true** teaching and also to show
3. 8 This is a **true** saying.
Heb 2. 2 angels was shown to be **true,** and anyone who did not follow
2. 3 and those who heard him proved to us that it is **true.**
6.11 the end, so that the things you hope for will come **true.**
9.14 Since this is **true,** how much more is accomplished by the
Jas 2.23 And the scripture came **true** that said, "Abraham believed God,
1 Pet 3. 4 beauty should consist of your **true** inner self, the ageless beauty
5.12 and give my testimony that this is the **true** grace of God.
2 Pet 1. 3 we need to live a **truly** religious life through our knowledge
2.22 What happened to them shows that the proverbs are **true:**
1 Jn 2.27 about everything, and what he teaches is **true,** not false.
3.18 it must be **true** love, which shows itself in action.
5. 6 Spirit himself testifies that this is **true,**
5.15 since we know this is **true,** we know also that he gives
5.20 has given us understanding, so that we know the **true** God.
5.20 live in union with the **true** God—in union with his Son
5.20 This is the **true** God, and this is eternal life.
2 Jn 1 To the dear Lady and to her children, whom I **truly** love.
3 Jn 1 From the Elder— To my dear Gaius, whom I **truly** love.
12 add our testimony, and you know that what we say is **true.**
Rev 2.13 You are **true** to me, and you did not abandon your faith
3. 7 "This is the message from the one who is holy and **true.**
3.14 the Amen, the faithful and **true** witness, who is the origin
6.10 They shouted in a loud voice, "Almighty Lord, holy and **true!**
15. 3 King of the nations, how right and **true** are your ways!
16. 7 **True** and just indeed are your judgements!"
17.17 the beast their power to rule until God's words come **true.**
19. 2 **True** and just are his judgements!
19. 9 And the angel added, "These are the **true** words of God."
19.11 Its rider is called Faithful and **True;**
21. 5 "Write this, because these words are **true** and can be trusted."
22. 6 angel said to me, "These words are **true** and can be trusted.

TRULY see **TRUE**

TRUMPET
[WAR TRUMPET]

Ex 19.13 But when the **trumpet** is blown, then the people are to go
19.16 on the mountain, and a very loud **trumpet** blast was heard.
19.19 The sound of the **trumpet** became louder and louder.
20.18 heard the thunder and the **trumpet** blast and saw the
Lev 23.23 rest, and come together for worship when the **trumpets** sound.
25. 9 send a man to blow a **trumpet** throughout the whole land.
Num 10. 2 said to Moses, [2]"Make two **trumpets** of hammered silver to
10. 3 blasts are sounded on both **trumpets,** the whole community is
10. 4 But when only one **trumpet** is sounded, then only the
10. 8 The **trumpets** are to be blown by Aaron's sons, the
10. 9 attacked you, sound the signal for battle on these **trumpets.**
10.10 you are to blow the **trumpets** when you present your
29. 1 On that day **trumpets** are to be blown.
31. 6 of the sacred objects and the **trumpets** for giving signals.
Josh 6. 4 Seven priests, each carrying a **trumpet,** are to go in front
6. 4 the city seven times while the priests blow the **trumpets.**
6. 6 and seven of you go in front of it, carrying **trumpets."**
6. 8 started out ahead of the priests who were blowing **trumpets;**
6. 8 All this time the **trumpets** were sounding.
6.12 next, the seven priests blowing the seven **trumpets;**
6.12 All this time the **trumpets** were sounding.
6.16 to sound the **trumpets,** Joshua ordered his men to shout,
6.20 So the priests blew the **trumpets.**
Judg 3.27 of Ephraim, he blew a **trumpet** to call the men of Israel
6.34 Gideon, and he blew a **trumpet** to call the men of the
7. 8 the three hundred, who kept all the supplies and **trumpets.**
7.16 and gave each man a **trumpet** and a jar with a torch
7.18 group and I blow our **trumpets,** then you blow yours all round
7.19 Then they blew the **trumpets** and broke the jars they were holding,
7.20 in their left hands, the **trumpets** in their right, and
7.22 Gideon's men were blowing their **trumpets,** the Lord made the
1 Sam 13. 3 Hebrews to war by blowing a **trumpet** throughout the whole country.
2 Sam 2.28 Then Joab blew the **trumpet** as a signal for his men to
6.15 to Jerusalem with shouts of joy and the sound of **trumpets.**
15.10 you hear the sound of **trumpets,** shout, 'Absalom has become
18.16 Joab ordered the **trumpet** to be blown to stop the fighting,
20. 1 He blew the **trumpet** and called out, "Down with David!
20.22 He blew the **trumpet** as a signal for his men to leave
1 Kgs 1.34 Then blow the **trumpet** and shout, 'Long live King Solomon!'
1.39 They blew the **trumpet,** and all the people shouted, "Long
1.41 And when Joab heard the **trumpet,** he asked, "What's the
2 Kgs 9.13 Jehu to stand on, blew **trumpets,** and shouted, "Jehu is king!"
11.14 by the officers and the **trumpeters,**
11.14 and the people were all shouting joyfully and blowing **trumpets.**
12.13 cups, bowls, **trumpets,** or tools for tending the lamps,
1 Chr 13. 8 played musical instruments—harps, drums, cymbals, and **trumpets.**
15.23 were chosen to blow **trumpets** in front of the Covenant Box.
15.28 of joy, the sound of **trumpets,** horns, and cymbals, and the
16. 6 and Jahaziel, were to blow **trumpets** regularly in front of
16.42 also had charge of the **trumpets** and cymbals and the other
2 Chr 5.11 them were a hundred and twenty priests playing **trumpets.**
5.11 perfect harmony by **trumpets,** cymbals,
7. 6 The priests blew **trumpets** while all the people stood.
13.12 his priests are here with **trumpets,** ready to blow them and
13.14 to the Lord for help, and the priests blew the **trumpets.**
15.14 keep the covenant, and then they shouted and blew **trumpets.**
20.28 marched to the Temple, to the music of harps and **trumpets.**
23.13 and surrounded by the army officers and the **trumpeters.**
23.13 were shouting joyfully and blowing **trumpets,** and the temple
29.26 The priests also stood there with **trumpets.**
29.27 began to play the **trumpets** and all the other instruments.
Ezra 3.10 robes took their places with **trumpets** in their hands, and
Neh 12.33 The following priests, blowing **trumpets,** marched
12.41 my group included the following priests, blowing **trumpets:**
Job 39.24 when the **trumpet** blows, they can't stand still.
39.25 At each blast of the **trumpet** they snort;
Ps 47. 5 of joy and the blast of **trumpets,** as the Lord goes up.
81. 3 Blow the **trumpet** for the festival, when the moon is new
98. 6 Blow **trumpets** and horns, and shout for joy to the Lord,
150. 3 Praise him with **trumpets.**
Is 27.13 When that day comes, a **trumpet** will be blown to call
Jer 4. 5 Blow the **trumpet** throughout the land!
4.19 I hear the **trumpets** and the shouts of battle.
4.21 I see the battle raging and hear the blasts of **trumpets?**
6. 1 Sound the **trumpet** in Tekoa and build a signal fire in Beth
6.17 Lord appointed watchmen to listen for the **trumpet's** warning.
51.27 Blow the **trumpet** so that the nations can hear!
Ezek 7.14 The **trumpet** sounds, and everyone gets ready.
Dan 3. 5 the sound of the **trumpets,** followed by the playing of oboes,
3.15 hear the sound of the **trumpets,** oboes, lyres, zithers,
Hos 5. 8 Blow the **war trumpets** in Gibeah!
Joel 2. 1 Blow the **trumpet;**
2.15 Blow the **trumpet** on Mount Zion;
Amos 2. 2 while soldiers are shouting and **trumpets** are sounding.
3. 6 Does the **war trumpet** sound in a city without making the
Zeph 1.16 filled with the sound of **war-trumpets** and the battle-cry of
Zech 9.14 The Sovereign Lord will sound the **trumpet;**
Mt 24.31 The great **trumpet** will sound, and he will send out his
1 Cor 15.51 but when the last **trumpet** sounds, we shall all be changed
15.51 For when the **trumpet** sounds, the dead will be raised, never
1 Thes 4.16 voice, the sound of God's **trumpet,** and the Lord himself will
Heb 12.19 storm, [19]the blast of a **trumpet,** and the sound of a voice.
Rev 1.10 a loud voice, that sounded like a **trumpet,** speaking behind me.
4. 1 voice that sounded like a **trumpet,** which I had heard

Rev 8. 2 angels who stand before God, and they were given seven **trumpets.**
8. 6 the seven angels with the seven **trumpets** prepared to blow them.
8. 7 The first angel blew his **trumpet.**
8. 8 Then the second angel blew his **trumpet.**
8.10 Then the third angel blew his **trumpet.**
8.12 Then the fourth angel blew his **trumpet.**
8.13 sound comes from the **trumpets** that the other three angels must
9. 1 Then the fifth angel blew his **trumpet.**
9.13 Then the sixth angel blew his **trumpet.**
10. 7 the seventh angel blows his **trumpet,** then God will accomplish his
11.15 the seventh angel blew his **trumpet,** and there were loud voices
18.22 of the flute and the **trumpet,** will never be heard in you

TRUST

Gen 15. 6 Abram put his **trust** in the Lord, and because of this the
Ex 18.21 God-fearing men who can be **trusted** and who cannot be bribed.
Num 14.11 longer will they refuse to **trust** in me, even though I have
Deut 1.32 said, you still would not **trust** the Lord, [33]even though he
9.23 you did not **trust** him or obey him.
28.52 and the high, fortified walls in which you **trust** will fall.
32.37 Lord will ask his people, 'Where are those mighty gods you **trusted?**
Josh 2.12 treated you, and give me some sign that I can **trust** you.
1 Sam 27.12 But Achish **trusted** David and said to himself, "He is
2 Sam 15.32 a place of worship, his **trusted** friend Hushai the Archite
16.16 When Hushai, David's **trusted** friend, met Absalom, he
2 Kgs 17.14 their ancestors, who had not **trusted** in the Lord their God.
18. 5 Hezekiah **trusted** in the Lord, the God of Israel;
19.10 him, "The god you are **trusting** in has told you that you
1 Chr 5.20 They put their **trust** in God and prayed to him for help,
2 Chr 20.20 Put your **trust** in the Lord your God, and you will stand
Ezra 8.22 our God blesses everyone who **trusts** him, but that he is
Neh 13.13 I knew I could **trust** these men to be honest in distributing
Job 4.18 God does not **trust** his heavenly servants;
4.19 Do you think he will **trust** a creature of clay, a thing
8.14 They **trust** a thread—a spider's web.
12.20 He silences men who are **trusted,** and takes the wisdom of
15.15 Why, God does not **trust** even his angels;
15.31 he is foolish enough to **trust** in evil, then evil will be
22.26 Then you will always **trust** in God and find that he is
31.24 I have never **trusted** in riches [25]or taken pride in my wealth.
Ps 4. 5 right sacrifices to the Lord, and put your **trust** in him.
5. 9 What my enemies say can never be **trusted;**
9.10 Those who know you, Lord, will **trust** you;
11. 1 I **trust** in the Lord for safety.
12. 6 The promises of the Lord can be **trusted;**
16. 1 I **trust** in you for safety.
19. 7 commands of the Lord are **trustworthy,** giving wisdom to those
20. 7 Some **trust** in their war-chariots and others in their horses,
20. 7 but we **trust** in the power of the Lord
21. 7 The king **trusts** in the Lord Almighty;
22. 4 Our ancestors put their **trust** in you;
22. 4 they **trusted** you, and you saved them.
22. 5 they **trusted** you and were not disappointed.
25. 2 in you, my God, I **trust.**
25. 3 not come to those who **trust** in you, but to those who
25. 5 I always **trust** in you.
25.21 May my goodness and honesty preserve me, because I **trust** in you.
26. 1 O Lord, because I do what is right and **trust** you completely.
27. 3 even if enemies attack me, I will still **trust** God.
27.14 **Trust** in the Lord.
27.14 **Trust** in the Lord.
28. 7 I **trust** in him.
31. 6 You hate those who worship false gods, but I **trust** in you.
31.14 But my **trust** is in you, O Lord;
31.19 good you are, how securely you protect those who **trust** you.
32.10 to suffer, but those who **trust** in the Lord are protected by
33.18 those who obey him, those who **trust** in his constant love.
33.21 we **trust** in his holy name.
37. 3 **Trust** in the Lord and do good;
37. 5 **trust** in him, and he will help you;
37. 9 Those who **trust** in the Lord will possess the land, but the
38.15 But I **trust** in you, O Lord;
40. 3 will take warning and will put their **trust** in the Lord.
40. 4 Happy are those who **trust** the Lord, who do not turn to
41. 9 best friend, the one I **trusted** most, the one who shared my
44. 6 I do not **trust** in my bow or in my sword to
49. 6 enemies, [6]by evil men who **trust** in their riches and boast
49.13 what happens to those who **trust** in themselves, the fate of
52. 7 on God for safety, but **trusted** instead in his great wealth
52. 8 I **trust** in his constant love for ever and ever.
55.23 As for me, I will **trust** in you.
56. 3 I am afraid, O Lord Almighty, I put my **trust** in you.
56. 4 I **trust** in God and am not afraid;
56.11 In him I **trust,** and I will not be afraid.
62. 8 **Trust** in God at all times, my people.
62.10 Don't put your **trust** in violence;
65. 5 over the world and across the distant seas **trust** in you.
69. 6 shame on those who **trust** in you, Sovereign Lord Almighty!
71. 5 I have **trusted** in you since I was young.
78. 7 they also would put their **trust** in God and not forget what
78. 8 rebellious and disobedient people, whose **trust** in God was
78.32 in spite of his miracles they did not **trust** him.
84.12 Lord Almighty, how happy are those who **trust** in you!
86. 2 save me, for I am your servant and I **trust** in you.
91. 2 in you I **trust."**
112. 7 his faith is strong, and he **trusts** in the Lord.
115. 8 who made them and who **trust** in them become like the idols
115. 9 **Trust** in the Lord, you people of Israel.
Ps 115.10 **Trust** in the Lord, you priests of God.
115.11 **Trust** in the Lord, all you that worship him.
116.11 even when I was afraid and said, "No one can be **trusted."**
118. 8 It is better to **trust** in the Lord than to depend on
118. 9 It is better to **trust** in the Lord than to depend on
119.42 answer those who insult me because I **trust** in your word.
119.66 Give me wisdom and knowledge, because I **trust** in your commands.
119.74 be glad when they see me, because I **trust** in your promise.
119.81 I place my **trust** in your word.
119.86 Your commandments are all **trustworthy;**
125. 1 Those who **trust** in the Lord are like Mount Zion, which can
130. 5 wait eagerly for the Lord's help, and in his word I **trust.**
130. 7 Israel, **trust** in the Lord, because his love is constant
131. 3 Israel, **trust** in the Lord now and for ever!
135.18 who made them and who **trust** in them become like the idols
141. 8 But I keep **trusting** in you, my Sovereign Lord.
143. 8 morning of your constant love, for I put my **trust** in you.
144. 2 my shelter and saviour, in whom I **trust** for safety.
146. 3 Don't put your **trust** in human leaders;
147.11 who honour him, in those who **trust** in his constant love.
Prov 2.15 senseless evil, [15]unreliable men who cannot be **trusted.**
3. 5 **Trust** in the Lord with all your heart.
3.29 he lives beside you, **trusting** you.
11. 3 People who can't be **trusted** are destroyed by their own dishonesty.
11. 6 someone who can't be **trusted** is trapped by his own greed.
11.13 No one who gossips can be **trusted** with a secret,
11.13 but you can put confidence in someone who is **trustworthy.**
13.15 but those who can't be **trusted** are on the road to ruin.
13.17 cause trouble, but those who can be **trusted** bring peace.
14.22 You will earn the **trust** and respect of others if you
16.20 **trust** in the Lord and you will be happy.
20.22 **Trust** the Lord and he will make it right.
22.19 I want you to put your **trust** in the Lord;
28.25 You are much better off to **trust** the Lord.
29.25 think of you, but if you **trust** the Lord, you are safe.
Is 8.17 from his people, but I **trust** him and place my hope in
10.20 They will truly put their **trust** in the Lord, Israel's holy God.
12. 2 I will **trust** him and not be afraid.
17. 8 with their own hands, or **trust** in their own
20. 5 Those who have put their **trust** in Sudan and have boasted
25. 9 We have put our **trust** in him, and he has rescued us.
25. 9 We have put our **trust** in him, and now we are happy
26. 3 who keep their purpose firm and put their **trust** in you.
26. 4 **Trust** in the Lord for ever;
30. 2 Egypt to protect them, so they put their **trust** in Egypt's king.
30. 5 will regret that they ever **trusted** that unreliable nation, a
30.15 says to the people, "Come back and quietly **trust** in me.
30.18 Happy are those who put their **trust** in the Lord.
37.10 him, "The god you are **trusting** in has told you that you
38.18 The dead cannot **trust** in your faithfulness.
40.31 But those who **trust** in the Lord for help will find their
42.17 All who **trust** in idols, who call images their gods, will
48. 8 knew that you couldn't be **trusted,** that you have always been
49. 4 Yet I can **trust** the Lord to defend my cause;
50.10 may be dark indeed, but **trust** in the Lord, rely on your
57.13 But those who **trust** in me will live in the land and
Jer 2.37 I, the Lord, have rejected those you **trust;**
5.17 cities in which you **trust** will be destroyed by their army.
7. 8 "Look, you put your **trust** in deceitful words.
7.14 I will do to this Temple of mine, in which you **trust.**
9. 4 guard against his friend, and no one can **trust** his brother;
11.19 I was like a **trusting** lamb taken out to be killed, and
12. 6 Do not **trust** them, even though they speak friendly words."
13.25 you have forgotten him and have **trusted** in false gods.
17. 5 from me and puts his **trust** in man, in the strength of
17. 7 "But I will bless the person who puts his **trust** in me.
39.18 escape with your life because you have put your **trust** in me.
46.25 and all who put their **trust** in him, [26]and hand them over
48. 7 "Moab, you **trusted** in your strength and your wealth, but
48.13 Israelites were disillusioned with Bethel, a god in whom they **trusted.**
49. 4 Why do you **trust** in your power and say that no one
50. 7 Their ancestors **trusted** in the Lord, and they themselves
Lam 3.25 is good to everyone who **trusts** in him, [26]So it is best
4.20 the one we had **trusted** to protect us from every invader.
Ezek 22. 6 Israel's leaders **trust** in their own strength and commit murder.
Dan 3.28 his angel and rescued these men who serve and **trust** him.
6.23 that he had not been hurt at all, for he **trusted** God.
Hos 10.13 "Because you **trusted** in your chariots and in the large
12. 6 So now, descendants of Jacob, **trust** in your God and return
Mic 7. 5 Don't believe your neighbour or **trust** your friend.
Hab 2.18 do for its maker to **trust** it—a god that can't even
Zeph 3. 2 It has not put its **trust** in the Lord or asked for
Mt 27.43 He **trusts** in God and claims to be God's Son.
Lk 16.11 handling worldly wealth, how can you be **trusted** with true wealth?
Jn 2.24 But Jesus did not **trust** himself to them, because he knew
Acts 14.23 them to the Lord, in whom they had put their **trust.**
27.25 For I **trust** in God that it will be just as I
Rom 3. 2 In the first place, God **trusted** his message to the Jews.
1 Cor 1. 9 God is to be **trusted,** the God who called you to have
7.25 opinion as one who by the Lord's mercy is worthy of **trust.**
2 Cor 13. 6 I **trust** you will know that we are not failures.
Phil 2.24 And I **trust** in the Lord that I myself will be able
3. 3 We do not put any **trust** in external ceremonies.
3. 4 I could, of course, put my **trust** in such things.
3. 4 If anyone thinks he can **trust** in external ceremonies, I have
2 Tim 1.12 I know whom I have **trusted,** and I am sure that he
Tit 1. 9 message which can be **trusted** and which agrees with the doctrine.
Heb 2.13 He also says, "I will put my **trust** in God."

Heb 10.23 we profess, because we can **trust** God to keep his promise.
11.11 He **trusted** God to keep his promise.
1 Pet 4.19 should by their good actions **trust** themselves completely to their
Rev 21. 5 "Write this, because these words are true and can be **trusted."**
22. 6 angel said to me, "These words are true and can be **trusted.**

TRUTH
[BOOK OF TRUTH]

Gen 42.16 kept under guard until the **truth** of what you say can be
42.20 you have been telling the **truth,** and I will not put you
Num 5.15 a suspicious husband, made to bring the **truth** to light.
Josh 7.19 him, "My son, tell the **truth** here before the Lord, the God
Judg 16.10 been making a fool of me and not telling me the **truth.**
16.13 still making a fool of me and not telling me the **truth.**
16.17 nagging him about it [17]that he finally told her the **truth.**
16.18 he had told her the **truth,** she sent a message to the
16.18 He has told me the **truth."**
2 Sam 14.18 ask you a question, and you must tell me the whole **truth."**
1 Kgs 22.16 speak to me in the name of the Lord, tell the **truth!**
2 Chr 18.15 speak to me in the name of the Lord, tell the **truth!**
Job 8. 8 consider the **truths** our fathers learnt.
15.18 Wise men have taught me **truths** which they learnt
33. 3 All my words are sincere, and I am speaking the **truth.**
42. 7 you did not speak the **truth** about me, as my servant Job
42. 8 You did not speak the **truth** about me as he did."
Ps 25. 5 to live according to your **truth,** for you are my God, who
43. 3 Send your light and your **truth;**
45. 4 in majesty to victory for the defence of **truth** and justice!
51. 6 Sincerity and **truth** are what you require;
52. 3 You love evil more than good and falsehood more than **truth.**
111. 8 they were given in **truth** and righteousness.
119.18 eyes, so that I may see the wonderful **truths** in your law.
119.43 Enable me to speak the **truth** at all times, because my
119.160 heart of your law is **truth,** and all your righteous
144. 8 who never tell the **truth** and lie even under oath.
144.11 who never tell the **truth** and lie even under oath.
Prov 8. 7 What I say is the **truth;**
10.10 Someone who holds back the **truth** causes trouble, but one
12.17 When you tell the **truth,** justice is done, but lies lead
12.19 A lie has a short life, but **truth** lives on for ever.
14. 5 reliable witness always tells the **truth,** but an unreliable
14.25 A witness saves lives when he tells the **truth;**
16.13 king wants to hear the **truth** and will favour those who speak
22.12 Lord sees to it that **truth** is kept safe by disproving the
22.21 advice, [21]and will teach you what the **truth** really is.
23.23 **Truth,** wisdom, learning, and good sense—these are
29.24 punished if he tells the **truth** in court, and God will curse
Ecc 12. 9 He studied proverbs and honestly tested their **truth.**
Is 43. 9 they are right, to testify to the **truth** of their words.
44.18 They close their eyes and their minds to the **truth.**
45.19 I am the Lord, and I speak the **truth;**
58. 3 Lord says to them, "The **truth** is that at the same time
59.14 **Truth** stumbles in the public square, and honesty finds no place
Jer 8. 6 I listened carefully, but you did not speak the **truth.**
9. 3 dishonesty instead of **truth** rules the land.
9. 5 They all mislead their friends, and no one tells the **truth;**
38.14 a question, and I want you to tell me the whole **truth."**
38.15 "If I tell you the **truth,** you will put me to death,
Dan 9.13 you by turning from our sins or by following your **truth.**
10.20 to reveal to you what is written in the **Book of Truth.**
Amos 5.10 challenges injustice and speaks the whole **truth** in court.
Zech 8.16 Speak the **truth** to one another.
8.19 You must love **truth** and peace."
Mt 16.17 "For this **truth** did not come to you from any human being,
22.16 "Teacher," they said, "we know that you tell the **truth.**
22.16 You teach the **truth** about God's will for man, without worrying
26.74 Then Peter said, "I swear that I am telling the **truth!**
Mk 5.33 with fear, knelt at his feet, and told him the whole **truth.**
12.14 we know that you tell the **truth,** without worrying about what
12.14 man's status, but teach the **truth** about God's will for man.
14.71 Then Peter said, "I swear that I am telling the **truth!**
Lk 1. 4 you will know the full **truth** about everything which you have
20.21 man's status, but teach the **truth** about God's will for man.
Jn 1.14 a human being and, full of grace and **truth,** lived among us.
1.17 Law through Moses, but grace and **truth** came through Jesus Christ.
1.51 And he said to them, "I am telling you the **truth:**
3. 3 Jesus answered, "I am telling you the **truth:**
3. 5 "I am telling you the **truth,"** replied Jesus.
3.11 I am telling you the **truth:**
3.33 whoever accepts his message confirms by this that God is **truthful.**
4.18 You have told me the **truth."**
5.19 So Jesus answered them, "I am telling you the **truth:**
5.24 "I am telling you the **truth:**
5.25 I am telling you the **truth:**
5.33 sent your messengers, and he spoke on behalf of the **truth.**
6.26 Jesus answered, "I am telling you the **truth:**
6.32 "I am telling you the **truth,"** Jesus said.
6.47 I am telling you the **truth:**
6.53 Jesus said to them, "I am telling you the **truth:**
7.28 He who sent me, however, is **truthful.**
8.26 who sent me, however, is **truthful,** and I tell the world only
8.32 you will know the truth, and the **truth** will set you free."
8.34 Jesus said to them, "I am telling you the **truth:**
8.40 is to tell you the **truth** I heard from God, yet you
8.44 on the side of truth, because there is no **truth** in him.
8.45 But I tell the **truth,** and that is why you do not
8.46 If I tell the **truth,** then why do you not believe me?
8.51 I am telling you the **truth:**
8.58 "I am telling you the **truth,"** Jesus replied.
Jn 9.24 to him, "Promise before God that you will tell the **truth!**
10. 1 Jesus said, "I am telling you the **truth:**
10. 7 So Jesus said again, "I am telling you the **truth:**
10.24 Tell us the plain **truth:**
12.24 I am telling you the **truth:**
13.16 I am telling you the **truth:**
13.17 Now that you know this **truth,** how happy you will be if
13.20 I am telling you the **truth:**
13.21 deeply troubled and declared openly, "I am telling you the **truth:**
13.38 I am telling you the **truth:**
14. 6 Jesus answered him, "I am the way, the **truth,** and the
14.12 I am telling you the **truth:**
14.17 He is the Spirit who reveals the **truth** about God.
15.26 the Spirit, who reveals the **truth** about God and who comes
16. 7 But I am telling you the **truth:**
16.13 Spirit comes, who reveals the **truth** about God,
16.13 he will lead you into all the **truth.**
16.20 I am telling you the **truth:**
16.23 I am telling you the **truth:**
17.17 Dedicate them to yourself by means of the **truth;**
17.17 your word is **truth.**
18.37 the world for this one purpose, to speak about the **truth.**
18.37 Whoever belongs to the **truth** listens to me."
18.38 "And what is **truth?"**
19.35 and he knows that he speaks the **truth.)**
21.18 I am telling you the **truth:**
Acts 13.10 you always keep trying to turn the Lord's **truths** into lies!
21.24 know that there is no **truth** in any of the things that
22. 5 and the whole Council can prove that I am telling the **truth.**
25.11 But if there is no **truth** in the charges they bring against
26.25 I am speaking the sober **truth.**
Rom 1.18 people whose evil ways prevent the **truth** from being known.
1.25 They exchange the **truth** about God for a lie;
2.20 the Law you have the full content of knowledge and of **truth.**
3. 7 serves God's glory by making his **truth** stand out more clearly?
6.17 your heart the **truths** found in the teaching you received.
9. 1 I am speaking the **truth;**
11.25 There is a secret **truth,** my brothers, which I want you
16.25 the revelation of the secret **truth** which was hidden for long
16.26 Now, however, that **truth** has been brought out into the open
1 Cor 2. 1 brothers, to preach God's secret **truth,** I did not use big
2.13 as we explain spiritual **truths** to those who have the Spirit.
4. 1 servants, who have been put in charge of God's secret **truths.**
5. 8 the bread that has no yeast, the bread of purity and **truth.**
8. 7 But not everyone knows this **truth.**
12. 1 I want you to know the **truth** about them, my brothers.
13. 6 love is not happy with evil, but is happy with the **truth.**
14. 2 He is speaking secret **truths** by the power of the Spirit.
15.20 But the **truth** is that Christ has been raised from death,
15.51 Listen to this secret **truth:**
2 Cor 1.18 surely as God speaks the **truth,** my promise to you was not
4. 2 In the full light of **truth** we live in God's sight and
6. 7 love, [7]by our message of **truth,** and by the power of God.
6. 8 We are treated as liars, yet we speak the **truth;**
7.14 We have always spoken the **truth** to you, and in the same
11.10 By Christ's **truth** in me, I promise that this boast of
12. 6 would not be a fool, because I would be telling the **truth.**
13. 8 we cannot do a thing against the **truth,** but only for it.
Gal 2. 5 in order to keep the **truth** of the gospel safe for you,
2.14 path in line with the **truth** of the gospel, I said to
4.16 Have I now become your enemy by telling you the **truth?**
5. 7 Who made you stop obeying the **truth?**
Eph 4.15 Instead, by speaking the **truth** in a spirit of love, we
4.21 as his followers you were taught the **truth** that is in Jesus.
4.25 Everyone must tell the **truth** to his fellow-believer,
5. 9 a rich harvest of every kind of goodness, righteousness, and **truth.**
5.32 There is a deep secret **truth** revealed in this scripture,
6.14 So stand ready, with **truth** as a belt tight round your waist,
Phil 1. 8 witness that I am telling the **truth** when I say that my
1 Thes 1. 5 and the Holy Spirit, and with complete conviction of its **truth.**
4.13 want you to know the **truth** about those who have died,
2 Thes 2.10 did not welcome and love the **truth** so as to be saved.
2.12 have not believed the **truth,** but have taken pleasure in sin,
2.13 make you his holy people and by your faith in the **truth.**
2.15 and hold on to those **truths** which we taught you, both in
1 Tim 2. 4 wants everyone to be saved and to come to know the **truth.**
2. 7 of the Gentiles, to proclaim the message of faith and **truth.**
2. 7 I am telling the **truth!**
3. 9 should hold to the revealed **truth** of the faith with a clear
3.15 of the living God, the pillar and support of the **truth.**
4. 3 by those who are believers and have come to know the **truth.**
6. 5 minds do not function and who no longer have the **truth.**
2 Tim 2.15 work, one who correctly teaches the message of God's **truth.**
2.18 have left the way of **truth** and are upsetting the faith of
2.25 them the opportunity to repent and come to know the **truth.**
3. 7 trying to learn but who can never come to know the **truth.**
3. 8 are opposed to the **truth**—people whose minds do not function
3.14 for you, continue in the **truths** that you were taught and
3.16 is useful for teaching the **truth,** rebuking error, correcting
4. 4 away from listening to the **truth** and give their attention to
Tit 1. 1 to lead them to the **truth** taught by our religion, [2]which is
1.12 own prophets, who spoke the **truth** when he said, "Cretans are
1.14 commandments which come from people who have rejected the **truth.**
Heb 2. 1 the more firmly to the **truths** we have heard, so that we
10.26 go on sinning after the **truth** has been made known to us.
Jas 1.18 being through the word of **truth,** so that we should have
3.14 don't sin against the **truth** by boasting of your wisdom.
4. 5 think that there is no **truth** in the scripture that says,
5.19 wanders away from the **truth** and another one brings him back
1 Pet 1.22 by your obedience to the **truth** you have purified yourselves

2 Pet 1.12 them and are firmly grounded in the **truth** you have received.
2. 2 what they do, others will speak evil of the Way of **truth.**
1 Jn 1. 8 no sin, we deceive ourselves, and there is no **truth** in us.
2. 4 a person is a liar and there is no **truth** in him.
2. 8 you is new, because its **truth** is seen in Christ and also
2.20 on you by Christ, and so all of you know the **truth.**
2.21 writing to you, then, not because you do not know the **truth;**
2.21 and you also know that no lie ever comes from the **truth.**
3.19 then, is how we will know that we belong to the **truth;**
4. 6 difference between the Spirit of **truth** and the spirit of error.
5. 6 because the Spirit is **truth.**
2 Jn 1 but all who know the **truth** love you,
2 because the **truth** remains in us and will be
3 may they be ours in **truth** and love.
4 children live in the **truth,** just as the Father commanded us.
3 Jn 3 faithful you are to the **truth**—
3 just as you always live in the **truth.**
4 me happier than to hear that my children live in the **truth.**
8 people, so that we may share in their work for the **truth.**
12 **truth** itself speaks well of him.
Rev 1. 2 the message from God and the **truth** revealed by Jesus Christ.
1. 9 I had proclaimed God's word and the **truth** that Jesus revealed.
12.11 blood of the Lamb and by the **truth** which they proclaimed;
12.17 commandments and are faithful to the **truth** revealed by Jesus.
19.10 brothers, all those who hold to the **truth** that Jesus revealed.
19.10 For the **truth** that Jesus revealed is what inspires the prophets.
20. 4 because they had proclaimed the **truth** that Jesus revealed

TRY (1)

Gen 4.12 If you **try** to grow crops, the soil will not produce anything;
14.10 of Sodom and Gomorrah **tried** to run away from the battle,
15. 5 and said, "Look at the sky and **try** to count the stars;
19.15 At dawn the angels **tried** to make Lot hurry.
30.15 Now you are even **trying** to take away my son's mandrakes."
34. 3 he fell in love with her and **tried** to win her affection.
37.21 Reuben heard them and **tried** to save Joseph.
38.23 I did **try** to pay her, but you couldn't find her."
39.14 came into my room and **tried** to rape me, but I screamed
Ex 2.15 about what had happened, he **tried** to have Moses killed, but
4.24 way to Egypt, the Lord met Moses and **tried** to kill him.
5.13 The slave-drivers kept **trying** to force them to make the
8.18 The magicians **tried** to use their magic to make gnats appear,
14.27 The Egyptians **tried** to escape from the water, but the Lord
32.10 Now, don't **try** to stop me.
34.24 your territory, no one will **try** to conquer your country
Lev 20.16 If a woman **tries** to have sexual relations with an animal,
Num 3.10 anyone else who **tries** to do so shall be put to death."
3.38 Anyone else who **tried** to do so was to be put to
16.10 honour—and now you are **trying** to get the priesthood too!
16.14 as our possession, and now you are **trying** to deceive us.
20.18 If you **try,** we will march out and attack you."
32. 7 How dare you **try** to discourage the people of Israel from
Deut 9.14 Don't **try** to stop me.
12.30 Don't **try** to find out how they worship their gods, so that
13. 5 man is evil and is **trying** to lead you away from the
13.10 He **tried** to lead you away from the Lord your God, who
15. 2 he must not **try** to collect the money;
19.16 If one man **tries** to harm another by falsely accusing him
20.19 "When you are **trying** to capture a city, do not cut
25.11 and the wife of one **tries** to help her husband by grabbing
28.68 There you will **try** to sell yourselves to your enemies as slaves,
Josh 6.26 "Anyone who **tries** to rebuild the city of Jericho will be
7.19 Don't **try** to hide it from me."
Judg 11.24 Are you going to **try** to take it back?
12. 5 Ephraimite who was **trying** to escape asked permission to cross,
19. 3 to go after her and **try** to persuade her to return to
1 Sam 13.12 in Gilgal, and I have not **tried** to win the Lord's favour.'
17.39 sword over the armour and **tried** to walk, but he couldn't,
19. 2 so he said to him, "My father is **trying** to kill you.
19.10 Saul **tried** to pin David to the wall with his spear, but
21.13 and acted like a madman when they **tried** to restrain him;
23.14 Saul was always **trying** to find him, but God did not hand
24. 9 listen to people who say that I am **trying** to harm you?
24.14 Look at what the king of Israel is **trying** to kill!
25.29 anyone should attack you and **try** to kill you, the Lord your
26.11 Lord forbid that I should **try** to harm the one whom the
27. 4 David had fled to Gath, he gave up **trying** to find him.
28. 9 Why, then, are you **trying** to trap me and get me killed?"
2 Sam 3.35 All day long the people **tried** to get David to eat something,
4. 8 the son of your enemy Saul, who **tried** to kill you.
12.17 officials went to him and **tried** to make him get up, but
14.16 from the one who is **trying** to kill my son and me
16.11 to all his officials, "My own son is **trying** to kill me;
19.10 So why doesn't somebody **try** to bring King David back?"
20.19 Why are you **trying** to destroy it?
21. 2 to protect, but Saul had **tried** to destroy them because of
1 Kgs 11.40 And so Solomon **tried** to kill Jeroboam, but he escaped
19.10 am the only one left—and they are **trying** to kill me!"
19.14 am the only one left—and they are **trying** to kill me."
2 Kgs 3.26 hundred swordsmen with him and **tried** to force his way
5. 7 It's plain that he is **trying** to start a quarrel with me!"
11.15 rows of guards, and kill anyone who **tries** to rescue her."
20. 3 and that I have always **tried** to do what you wanted me
23.29 King Josiah **tried** to stop the Egyptian army at Megiddo and
1 Chr 7.21 who were killed when they **tried** to steal the livestock
10.13 he **tried** to find guidance by consulting the spirits of the
12.17 even though I have not **tried** to hurt you, the God of
18. 3 because Hadadezer was **trying** to gain control of the territory
2 Chr 10. 7 kind to these people and **try** to please them by giving a
12.14 was evil, because he did not **try** to find the Lord's will.
2 Chr 18. 2 He **tried** to persuade Jehoshaphat to join him in attacking
19. 3 and you have **tried** to follow God's will."
23. 7 Anyone who **tries** to enter the Temple is to be killed."
23.14 rows of guards, and kill anyone who **tries** to rescue her."
35.20 Josiah **tried** to stop him, [21] but Neco sent Josiah this
Ezra 4. 4 been living in the land **tried** to discourage and frighten the
6.12 defies this command and **tries** to destroy the Temple there.
Neh 5.12 We'll give the property back and not **try** to collect the debts."
6. 2 This was a trick of theirs to **try** to harm me.
6. 9 They were **trying** to frighten us into stopping work.
6.11 Do you think I would **try** to save my life by hiding
6.14 Nodiah and all the other prophets who **tried** to frighten me."
6.19 And he kept sending me letters to **try** to frighten me.
13.21 If you **try** this again, I'll use force against you."
Esth 9. 2 organized themselves to attack anyone who **tried** to harm them.
Job 7.13 I lie down and **try** to rest;
9.19 Should I **try** force?
9.19 **Try** force on God?
9.27 If I smile and **try** to forget my pain, all my
13. 8 Are you **trying** to defend him?
13.20 agree to them, and I will not **try** to hide from you;
13.25 Are you **trying** to frighten me?
15. 5 you are **trying** to hide behind clever words.
20.24 When he **tries** to escape from an iron sword, a bronze bow
21.33 You **try** to comfort me with nonsense!
27.22 on them without pity while they **try** their best to escape.
30.13 They cut off my escape and **try** to destroy me;
31. 5 I have never acted wickedly and never **tried** to deceive others.
31.33 Other men **try** to hide their sins, but I have never
32. 1 own innocence, the three men gave up **trying** to answer him.
34. 9 that it never does any good to **try** to follow God's will.
40. 3 I will not **try** to say anything else.
40. 8 Are you **trying** to prove that I am unjust— to put
41. 8 Touch him once and you'll never **try** it again;
42. 4 listen while you spoke and to **try** to answer your questions.
Ps 27. 2 evil men attack me and **try** to kill me, they stumble and
35. 4 May those who **try** to kill me be defeated and disgraced!
37.32 A wicked man watches a good man and **tries** to kill him;
38.20 evil for good are against me because I **try** to do right.
40.14 May those who **try** to kill me be completely defeated
45.12 rich people will **try** to win your favour.
54. 3 cruel men are **trying** to kill me— men who do not
63. 9 Those who are **trying** to kill me will go down into the
70. 2 May those who **try** to kill me be defeated and confused.
71.13 May those who **try** to hurt me be shamed and disgraced.
71.24 day long, because those who **tried** to harm me have been
73.16 I **tried** to think this problem through, but it was too
86.14 gang of cruel men is **trying** to kill me— people who
119.10 With all my heart I **try** to serve you;
119.45 in perfect freedom, because I **try** to obey your teachings.
119.94 I have **tried** to obey your commands.
Prov 2. 2 Listen to what is wise and **try** to understand it.
2.16 resist any immoral woman who **tries** to seduce you with her
15.27 If you **try** to make a profit dishonestly, you will get
16.14 A wise man will **try** to keep the king happy;
16.22 life to the wise, but **trying** to educate stupid people is a
19. 6 Everyone **tries** to gain the favour of important people;
19. 7 No matter how hard he **tries,** he cannot win any.
20. 6 faithful he is, but just **try** to find someone who really is!
21.18 on themselves the suffering they **try** to cause good people.
23. 3 he may be **trying** to trick you.
23. 4 Be wise enough not to wear yourself out **trying** to get rich.
23. 9 Don't **try** to talk sense to a fool;
24. 1 of evil people, and don't **try** to make friends with them.
25. 6 stand before the king, don't **try** to impress him and pretend
25.19 in a crisis is like **trying** to chew with a loose tooth
25.27 bad for you, and so is **trying** to win too much praise.
26. 9 you of a drunk man **trying** to pick a thorn out of
27.16 Have you ever **tried** to stop the wind
27.16 or ever **tried** to hold a handful of oil?
28.13 will never succeed in life if you **try** to hide your sins.
28.17 Don't **try** to stop him.
Ecc 4. 6 all the time with both hands, **trying** to catch the wind.
5.16 We labour, **trying** to catch the wind, and what do we get?
8.16 Whenever I **tried** to become wise and learn what goes on
8.17 However hard you **try,** you will never find out.
12.10 The Philosopher **tried** to find comforting words, but the
Song 8. 7 But if anyone **tried** to buy love with his wealth, contempt is
Is 2.10 holes in the ground to **try** to escape from the Lord's anger
2.19 holes in the ground to **try** to escape from the Lord's anger
2.21 in the rocky hills to **try** to escape from his anger and
15. 7 Valley of Willows, **trying** to escape with all their possessions.
22. 4 Don't **try** to comfort me.
23. 6 **Try** to escape to Spain!
24.18 Anyone who **tries** to escape from the terror will fall
25.11 hands as if they were **trying** to swim, but God will humiliate
28.10 He is **trying** to teach us letter by letter, line by line,
28.20 man in the proverb, who **tries** to sleep in a bed too
29.15 Those who **try** to hide their plans from the Lord are doomed!
33. 7 ambassadors who **tried** to bring about peace are crying bitterly.
38. 3 and that I have always **tried** to do what you wanted me
52.12 you will not be **trying** to escape.
59. 2 sins that separate you from God when you **try** to worship him
65. 1 ready for them to find me, but they did not even **try.**
Jer 5. 1 who does what is right and **tries** to be faithful to God?
6.13 Everyone, great and small, **tries** to make money dishonestly;
8.10 Everyone, great and small, **tries** to make money dishonestly.
19. 9 The enemy will surround the city and **try** to kill its people.
20. 9 I **try** my best to hold it in, but can no longer
26.19 Hezekiah honoured the Lord and **tried** to win his favour.
26.21 what Uriah had said, the king **tried** to have him killed.

Jer	38. 4	He is not **trying** to help the people;
	39. 4	saw what was happening, they **tried** to escape from the city
	48.44	Whoever **tries** to escape the terror will fall into the pits,
	48.45	Helpless refugees **try** to find protection in Heshbon, the
	51. 9	Foreigners living there said, 'We **tried** to help Babylonia,
Ezek	24.13	Although I **tried** to purify you, you remained defiled.
	34. 6	earth, and no one looked for them or **tried** to find them.
	34. 8	My shepherds did not **try** to find the sheep.
Dan	1.14	He agreed to let them **try** it for ten days.
	2. 8	You are **trying** to gain time, because you see that I have
	2.43	empire will **try** to unite their families by intermarriage,
	3.16	answered, "Your Majesty, we will not **try** to defend ourselves.
	6. 4	other supervisors and the governors **tried** to find something
	6.14	He kept **trying** until sunset.
	7.25	He will **try** to change their religious laws and festivals,
	8.15	I was **trying** to understand what the vision meant, when
	9.13	our God, we have not **tried** to please you by turning from
	11.30	back in a rage and **try** to destroy the religion of God's
	12. 4	their efforts **trying** to understand what is happening."
Hos	5.15	Perhaps in their suffering they will **try** to find me."
	6. 3	Let us **try** to know the Lord.
	9. 8	Yet wherever I go, you **try** to trap me like a bird.
Joel	3. 4	"What are you **trying** to do to me, Tyre, Sidon, and all
	3. 4	Are you **trying** to pay me back for something?
Amos	5. 5	Do not **try** to find me at Bethel—Bethel will come to
	8. 4	trample on the needy and **try** to destroy the poor of the
Obad	14	stood at the cross-roads to catch those **trying** to escape.
Jon	1.13	Instead, the sailors **tried** to get the ship to shore,
Nah	3.11	You too will **try** to escape from your enemies.
Hab	2. 9	took by violence, and have **tried** to make your own home safe
Zeph	3.13	do no wrong to anyone, tell no lies, nor **try** to deceive.
Hag	1.11	on men and animals, on everything you **try** to grow."
	2.17	hail to ruin everything you **tried** to grow, but still you did
Zech	12. 3	heavy stone—any nation that **tries** to lift it will be hurt.
	12. 9	I will destroy every nation that **tries** to attack Jerusalem.
Mal	1. 8	**Try** giving an animal like that to the governor!
	1. 9	Now, you priests, **try** asking God to be good to us.
	3.14	what he says or of **trying** to show the Lord Almighty that
Mt	2.20	Israel, because those who **tried** to kill the child are dead."
	3.14	But John **tried** to make him change his mind.
	10.39	Whoever **tries** to gain his own life will lose it;
	11.12	heaven has suffered violent attacks, and violent men **try** to seize
	19. 3	Pharisees came to him and **tried** to trap him by asking,
	21.46	he was talking about them, [46]so they **tried** to arrest him.
	22.18	Why are you **trying** to trap me?
	22.35	a teacher of the Law, **tried** to trap him with a question.
	23.13	nor do you allow in those who are **trying** to enter!
	26.59	priests and the whole Council **tried** to find some false evidence
	27.48	the end of a stick, and **tried** to make him drink it.
Mk	9.22	times the evil spirit has **tried** to kill him by throwing him
	9.39	"Do not **try** to stop him," Jesus told them, "because
	10. 2	Some Pharisees came to him and **tried** to trap him.
	12.12	The Jewish leaders **tried** to arrest Jesus, because they knew
	12.15	their trick and answered, "Why are you **trying** to trap me?
	14.51	They **tried** to arrest him, [52]but he ran away naked, leaving
	14.55	and the whole Council **tried** to find some evidence against Jesus
	15.23	There they **tried** to give him wine mixed with a drug
Lk	2.48	Your father and I have been terribly worried **trying** to find you."
	4.42	when they found him, they **tried** to keep him from leaving.
	5.18	on a bed, and they **tried** to take him into the house
	6.19	All the people **tried** to touch him, for power was going
	9. 9	And he kept **trying** to see Jesus.
	9.50	"Do not **try** to stop him," Jesus said to him and to
	10.25	A teacher of the Law came up and **tried** to trap Jesus.
	11.52	go in, and you stop those who are **trying** to go in!"
	11.54	him questions about many things, [54]**trying** to lay traps for him
	13.24	because many people will surely **try** to go in but will not
	17.33	Whoever **tries** to save his own life will lose it;
	19. 3	He was **trying** to see who Jesus was, but he was
	20.19	Law and the chief priests **tried** to arrest Jesus on the spot,
	22. 2	people, and so they were **trying** to find a way of putting
	22.53	the Temple every day, and you did not **try** to arrest me.
Jn	5. 7	I am **trying** to get in, somebody else gets there first."
	5.30	right, because I am not **trying** to do what I want, but
	5.44	another, but you do not **try** to win praise from the one
	7.18	on his own authority is **trying** to gain glory for himself.
	7.19	Why are you **trying** to kill me?"
	7.20	"Who is **trying** to kill you?"
	7.25	said, "Isn't this the man the authorities are **trying** to kill?
	7.30	Then they **tried** to seize him, but no one laid a hand
	8.37	Yet you are **trying** to kill me, because you will not accept
	8.40	truth I heard from God, yet you are **trying** to kill me.
	9.34	and brought up in sin—and you are **trying** to teach us?"
	10.33	are only a man, but you are **trying** to make yourself God!"
	10.39	Once more they **tried** to seize Jesus, but he slipped out
	19.12	When Pilate heard this, he **tried** to find a way to set
Acts	7.26	two Israelites fighting, and he **tried** to make peace between them.
	8. 3	But Saul **tried** to destroy the church;
	9.26	Saul went to Jerusalem and **tried** to join the disciples.
	9.29	disputed with the Greek-speaking Jews, but they **tried** to kill him.
	10.19	Peter was still **trying** to understand what the vision meant,
	11.17	who was I, then, to **try** to stop God!"
	13. 8	his name in Greek), who **tried** to turn the governor away from
	13.10	and you always keep **trying** to turn the Lord's truths into
	13.11	and he walked about **trying** to find someone to lead him
	16. 7	the border of Mysia, they **tried** to go into the province of
	17.18	of them asked, "What is this ignorant show-off **trying** to say?"
	18. 4	synagogue every Sabbath, **trying** to convince both Jews and Greeks.
	18.13	man," they said, "is **trying** to persuade people to worship God
	19. 8	holding discussions with them and **trying** to convince them about
Acts	19.13	drove out evil spirits also **tried** to use the name of the
	19.33	to be silent, and he **tried** to make a speech of defence.
	21.31	The mob was **trying** to kill Paul, when a report was sent
	24. 6	He also **tried** to defile the Temple, and we arrested him.
	26.11	in the synagogues and **tried** to make them deny their faith.
	26.21	while I was in the Temple, and they **tried** to kill me.
	27.12	putting out to sea and **trying** to reach Phoenix, if possible,
	27.15	the wind, we gave up **trying** and let it be carried along
	27.30	Then the sailors **tried** to escape from the ship;
	28.23	Kingdom of God, and he **tried** to convince them about Jesus by
Rom	2. 4	God is kind, because he is **trying** to lead you to repent.
	9.30	Gentiles, who were not **trying** to put themselves right with God,
	10. 3	and instead, they have **tried** to set up their own way;
	11. 3	am the only one left, and they are **trying** to kill me."
	12.17	**Try** to do what everyone considers to be good.
1 Cor	7.18	God's call, he should not **try** to remove the marks of circumcision;
	7.27	Then don't **try** to get rid of her.
	7.32	the Lord's work, because he is **trying** to please the Lord.
	7.35	I am not **trying** to put restrictions on you.
	10.33	I **try** to please everyone in all that I do, not thinking
	14.12	of the Spirit, you must **try** above everything else to make
2 Cor	1.24	We are not **trying** to dictate to you what you must believe;
	4. 2	in God's sight and **try** to commend ourselves to everyone's good
	5.11	means to fear the Lord, and so we **try** to persuade others.
	5.12	We are not **trying** again to recommend ourselves to you;
	5.12	rather, we are **trying** to give you a good reason to be
	6. 3	with our work, so we **try** not to put obstacles in anyone's
	6.14	Do not **try** to work together as equals with unbelievers,
	7. 2	have ruined no one, nor **tried** to take advantage of anyone.
	8. 8	are to help, I am **trying** to find out how real your
	8.13	I am not **trying** to relieve others by putting a
	10. 9	to appear that I am **trying** to frighten you with my letters.
	12.19	all along we have been **trying** to defend ourselves before you.
Gal	1. 7	are upsetting you and **trying** to change the gospel of Christ.
	1.10	Does this sound as if I am **trying** to win man's approval?
	1.10	Am I **trying** to be popular with men?
	1.10	If I were still **trying** to do so, I would not be
	1.23	is now preaching the faith that he once **tried** to destroy!"
	2.14	How, then, can you **try** to force Gentiles to live like Jews?"
	2.17	If, then, as we **try** to be put right with God by
	5. 4	Those of you who **try** to be put right with God by
	6.12	The people who are **trying** to force you to be circumcised
Eph	5. 1	you are God's dear children, you must **try** to be like him.
	5.10	**Try** to learn what pleases the Lord.
	5.17	Don't be fools, then, but **try** to find out what the Lord
Phil	2. 6	think that by force he should **try** to become equal with God.
	4. 2	Syntyche, please, I beg you, **try** to agree as sisters in the
1 Thes	2. 3	on error or impure motives, nor do we **try** to trick anyone.
	2. 4	We do not **try** to please men, but to please God,
	2. 6	We did not **try** to get praise from anyone, either from you
	2.16	They even **tried** to stop us from preaching to the Gentiles
	2.17	we missed you and how hard we **tried** to see you again!
	2.18	I myself **tried** to go back more than once, but Satan would
2 Tim	3. 7	women who are always **trying** to learn but who can never
Heb	11.29	the Egyptians **tried** to do it, the water swallowed them up.
	12.14	**Try** to be at peace with everyone,
	12.14	and **try** to live a holy life, because
1 Pet	1.11	They **tried** to find out when the time would be and how
	5. 3	Do not **try** to rule over those who have been put in
2 Pet	1.10	So then, my brothers, **try** even harder to make God's call
	3. 1	In both letters I have **tried** to arouse pure thoughts in your
1 Jn	2.26	this to you about those who are **trying** to deceive you.
3 Jn	10	want to receive them and **tries** to drive them out of the
Rev	11. 5	If anyone **tries** to harm them, fire comes out of their
	11. 5	and in this way, whoever **tries** to harm them will be killed.

TRY (2)

[TRIAL]

Ex	23. 3	Do not show partiality to a poor man at his **trial.**
Lev	19.16	and when someone is on **trial** for his life, speak out if
Num	14.22	but they have **tried** my patience over and over again
	35.12	is not to be put to death without a public **trial.**
Deut	21.19	leaders of the town where he lives and make him stand **trial.**
Josh	20. 6	he has received a public **trial** and until the death of the
	20. 9	not be killed unless he had first received a public **trial.**
2 Chr	19.10	to conduct themselves during the **trial,** so that they do not
Job	11.10	you and brings you to **trial,** who is there to stop him?
	14. 3	look at me, God, or put me on **trial** and judge me?
	22. 4	awe of God that he reprimands you and brings you to **trial.**
Ps	37.33	enemy's power or let him be condemned when he is on **trial.**
	95. 9	me to the test and **tried** me, although they had seen what
	109. 6	Choose some corrupt judge to **try** my enemy, and let one of
	109. 7	May he be **tried** and found guilty;
	143. 2	Don't put me, your servant, on **trial;**
Prov	23.29	too much, who has to **try** out some new drink, and I
Is	43. 2	the hard **trials** that come will not hurt you.
	43. 9	Summon the nations to come to the **trial.**
	44.11	Let them come and stand **trial**—they will be terrified and
	45.20	present yourselves for the **trial!**
Jer	22.16	gave the poor a fair **trial,** and all went well with him.
	25.31	will bring all people to **trial** and put the wicked to death.
Mt	5.21	anyone who does will be brought to **trial.'**
	5.22	brother will be brought to **trial,** whoever calls his brother
	10.18	you will be brought to **trial** before rulers and kings, to
	10.19	When they bring you to **trial,** do not worry about what
Lk	12.11	they bring you to be **tried** in the synagogues or before
	14.19	pairs of oxen and am on my way to **try** them out;
	21.12	be handed over to be **tried** in synagogues and be put in
	22.28	"You have stayed with me all through my **trials;**
Jn	18.31	yourselves take him and **try** him according to your own law."

Acts	12. 4	Herod planned to put him on **trial** in public after Passover.
	22.25	a Roman citizen who hasn't even been **tried** for any crime?"
	23. 6	I am on **trial** here because of the hope I have that
	24.21	'I am being **tried** by you today for believing that the dead
	25. 9	Jerusalem and be **tried** on these charges before me there?"
	25.10	the Emperor's own court of judgement, where I should be **tried.**
	25.20	to go to Jerusalem and be **tried** there on these charges.
	26. 6	I stand here to be **tried** because of the hope I have
Rom	3. 4	you must win your case when you are being **tried."**
Gal	4.14	physical condition was a great **trial** to you, you did not
Heb	3. 9	me to the test and **tried** me, says God, although they had
Jas	1. 2	fortunate when all kinds of **trials** come your way, [3] for you
	1. 3	faith succeeds in facing such **trials,** the result is the ability
	1.12	who remains faithful under **trials,** because when he succeeds in
	1.13	is tempted by such **trials,** he must not say, "This temptation
1 Pet	1. 6	for a while because of the many kinds of **trials** you suffer.
2 Pet	2. 9	rescue godly people from their **trials** and how to keep the

TUB

Ex	7.19	will be blood, even in the wooden **tubs** and stone jars."

TUMBLE

Is	25.12	high walls and bring them **tumbling** down into the dust.

TUMOURS

1 Sam	5. 6	the surrounding territory by causing them to have **tumours.**
	5. 9	He punished them with **tumours** which developed in all the
	5.12	who did not die developed **tumours** and the people cried out
	6. 4	answered, "Five gold models of **tumours** and five gold mice,
	6. 5	make these models of the **tumours** and of the mice that are
	6.11	containing the gold models of the mice and of the **tumours.**
	6.17	Philistines sent the five gold **tumours** to the Lord as a gift

TUNE

1 Cor	14. 7	how will anyone know the **tune** that is being played unless

TUNNEL

2 Sam	5. 8	the water **tunnel** and attack those poor blind cripples."
2 Kgs	20.20	a reservoir and dug a **tunnel** to bring water into the city,
2 Chr	32.30	water to flow through a **tunnel** to a point inside the walls
Job	28.10	As they **tunnel** through the rocks, They discover precious stones.

TURBAN

Ex	28. 4	an ephod, a robe, an embroidered shirt, a **turban,** and a
	28.37	Tie it to the front of the **turban** with a blue cord.
	28.39	fine linen and make a **turban** of fine linen and also a
	29. 6	Put the **turban** on him and tie on it the sacred sign
	39.28	his sons, [28] and the **turban,** the caps, the linen shorts,
	39.31	to the front of the **turban** with a blue cord, just as
Lev	8. 9	He placed the **turban** on his head, and on the front of
	16. 4	the linen robe and shorts, the belt, and the **turban.**
Prov	1. 9	a handsome **turban** or a necklace improves your appearance.
Ezek	21.26	Take off your crown and your **turban.**
	23.14	sashes round their waists and fancy **turbans** on their heads.
	44.18	are to wear linen **turbans** and linen trousers, but no belt.
Zech	3. 5	commanded the attendants to put a clean **turban** on Joshua's head.

TURMOIL

Prov	29. 8	with no regard for others can throw whole cities into **turmoil.**

TURN

Gen	3.24	and a flaming sword which **turned** in all directions.
	4. 8	in the fields, Cain **turned** on his brother and killed him.
	9.23	their father, keeping their faces **turned** away so as not to
	14. 7	Then they **turned** round and came back to Kadesh (then known
	19.26	Lot's wife looked back and was **turned** into a pillar of salt.
	41.13	Things **turned** out just as he said:
	49.19	by a band of robbers, But he will **turn** and pursue them.
	50.20	evil against me, but God **turned** it into good, in order to
Ex	4. 3	Moses threw it down, it **turned** into a snake, and he ran
	4. 9	The water will **turn** into blood."
	5.22	Then Moses **turned** to the Lord again and said, "Lord,
	7. 9	in front of the king, and it will **turn** into a snake."
	7.10	of the king and his officers, and it **turned** into a snake.
	7.12	They threw down their sticks, and the sticks **turned** into snakes.
	7.15	you the stick that was **turned** into a snake, and wait for
	7.17	with this stick, and the water will be **turned** into blood.
	7.20	the river, and all the water in it was **turned** into blood.
	7.23	Instead, he **turned** and went back to his palace without
	8.17	the dust in Egypt was **turned** into gnats, which covered the
	10. 6	Then Moses **turned** and left.
	14. 2	Moses, [2] "Tell the Israelites to **turn** back and camp in
	14.21	It blew all night and **turned** the sea into dry land.
	16.10	to the whole community, they **turned** towards the desert, and
	23.27	and I will make all your enemies **turn** and run from you.
	32. 6	down to a feast, which **turned** into an orgy of drinking and
Lev	13. 3	the hairs in it have **turned** white and the sore appears to
	13. 4	and the hairs have not **turned** white, the priest shall
	13.10	sore on his skin which **turns** the hairs white and is full
	13.13	If his whole skin has **turned** white, he is ritually clean.
	13.17	If the sore has **turned** white, he is ritually clean, and the
	13.20	in it have **turned** white, he shall pronounce him unclean.
	13.21	hairs in it have not **turned** white and that it is not
Lev	13.25	hairs in the spot have **turned** white and it appears deeper
	13.26	hairs in it have not **turned** white and it is not deeper
	17.10	in it, the Lord will **turn** against him and no longer consider
	19.29	if you do, you will **turn to** other gods and the land
	20. 3	my holy name, I will **turn** against him and will no longer
	20. 5	to death, [5] I myself will **turn** against the man and his whole
	20. 6	of the dead, I will **turn** against him and will no longer
	26.11	in my sacred tent, and I will never **turn** away from you.
	26.17	I will **turn** against you, so that you will be defeated,
	26.24	defy me, [24] then I will **turn** on you and punish you seven
	26.28	in my anger I will **turn** on you and again make your
	26.31	In utter disgust [31] I will **turn** your cities into ruins,
	26.41	against me, [41] and made me **turn** against them and send them
Num	12.10	covered with a dreaded disease and **turned** as white as snow.
	14.25	**Turn** back tomorrow and go into the wilderness in the
	15.39	then you will not **turn away** from me and follow your own
	16.42	to Moses and Aaron, they **turned** towards the Tent and saw
	20.21	the Israelites **turned** and went another way.
	21.33	Then the Israelites **turned** and took the road to Bashan,
	22.23	a sword, it left the road and **turned** into the fields.
	22.33	But your donkey saw me and **turned** aside three times.
	24. 1	He **turned** towards the desert [2] and saw the people of Israel
	24.24	Assyria and Eber, But they, in **turn,** will perish for ever."
	33. 7	From there they **turned** back to Pi Hahiroth, east of Baal Zephon,
	34. 4	Then it will **turn** southwards towards Akrabbim Pass and
	34. 4	Then it will **turn** north-west to Hazar Addar and on to Azmon,
	34. 5	to Azmon, [5] where it will **turn** towards the valley at the
Deut	1.40	But as for you people, **turn** round and go back into the
	2. 1	a long time, [1] we finally **turned** and went into the desert,
	2. 8	and we **turned** north-east towards Moab.
	4.30	you, then you will finally **turn to** the Lord and obey him.
	8.19	the Lord your God or **turn to** other gods to worship and
	9.12	They have already **turned away** from what I commanded them to do,
	9.15	"So I **turned** and went down the mountain, carrying the
	10. 5	me the tablets, [5] and I **turned** and went down the mountain.
	11.28	you disobey these commands and **turn away** to worship other
	13.17	and then the Lord will **turn** from his fierce anger and show
	17.17	wives, because this would make him **turn away** from the Lord;
	23. 5	he **turned** the curse into a blessing, because he loved you.
	23.14	indecent that would cause the Lord to **turn** his back on you.
	29.18	or tribe standing here today **turns from** the Lord our God to
	30. 2	you and your descendants will **turn back** to the Lord and with
	30. 7	He will **turn** all these curses against your enemies, who
	30.10	You will have to **turn to** him with all your heart.
	31.20	But they will **turn away** and worship other gods.
Josh	8. 5	out against us, we will **turn** and run, just as we did
	8.20	towards the barren country now **turned** round to attack them.
	8.21	it was on fire, they **turned** round and began killing the men
	10.38	Then Joshua and his army **turned** back to Debir and attacked it.
	11.10	Joshua then **turned** back, captured Hazor and killed its king.
	15. 3	Hezron and up to Addar, **turned** towards Karka, [4] went on to Azmon,
	15. 7	up to Debir, and then **turned** north towards Gilgal, which
	15. 9	There it **turned** towards Baalah (or Kiriath Jearim),
	15.11	north of Ekron, **turned** towards Shikkeron, past Mount Baalah,
	18.14	then went in another direction, **turning** south from the
	18.17	It then **turned** north to Enshemesh and then on to Geliloth,
	19.13	to Gath Hepher and Ethkazin, **turning** in the direction of
	19.14	On the north the border **turned** towards Hannathon, ending
	19.27	As it **turned** east, the border went to Bethdagon,
	19.29	The border then **turned** to Ramah,
	19.29	then it **turned** to Hosah and ended at the Mediterranean Sea.
	19.34	There the border **turned** west to Aznoth Tabor,
	24.20	serve foreign gods, he will **turn** against you and punish you.
Judg	3.19	But Ehud himself **turned** back at the carved stones near Gilgal,
	9.18	But today you **turned** against my father's family.
	11. 8	said to Jephthah, "We are **turning** to you now because we
	15. 5	fire to the torches and **turned** the foxes loose in the
	18.21	They **turned** round and started off, with their children,
	18.23	The men from Dan **turned** round and asked Micah,
	18.26	were too strong for him, so he **turned** and went back home.
	19.15	They **turned** off the road to go and spend the night there.
	20.39	the Israelites out on the battlefield were to **turn** round.
	20.41	Then the Israelites **turned** round, and the Benjaminites
	20.45	The others **turned** and ran towards the open country to
	20.48	The Israelites **turned** back against the rest of the
Ruth	1.13	The Lord has **turned** against me, and I feel very sorry for
	3. 8	night he woke up suddenly, **turned** over, and was surprised to
	3.18	"Now be patient, Ruth, until you see how this all **turns** out.
1 Sam	6.12	and headed straight towards it, without **turning** off the road.
	7. 3	"If you are going to **turn to** the Lord with all your
	8. 8	out of Egypt, they have **turned away** from me and worshipped
	10. 9	When Saul **turned** to leave Samuel, God gave Saul a new nature.
	12.10	'We have sinned, because we **turned away** from you, Lord, and
	12.20	an evil thing, do not **turn away** from the Lord, but serve
	15.11	he has **turned away** from me and disobeyed my commands."
	15.27	Then Samuel **turned** to leave, but Saul caught hold of his cloak,
	17.30	He **turned** to another man and asked him the same question,
	17.35	if the lion or bear **turns** on me, I grab it by
	22.13	Now he has **turned** against me and is waiting for a chance
	24. 8	Saul **turned** round, and David bowed down to the ground in
	26.19	is the Lord who has **turned** you against me, an offering to
	29. 4	he might **turn** against us during the fighting.
2 Sam	1. 7	Then he **turned** round, saw me, and called to me.
	6.10	instead, he **turned** off the road and took it to the house
	10.14	Then Joab **turned** back from fighting the Ammonites and went
	14. 7	sir, all my relatives have **turned** against me and are
	15.31	"Please, Lord, **turn** Ahithophel's advice into nonsense!"
	16.20	Absalom **turned** to Ahithophel and said, "Now that we are here,
	18. 3	if the rest of us **turn** and run, or even if half

2 Sam 19. 2 the joy of victory was **turned** into sadness for all David's
22.22 I have not **turned away** from my God.
1 Kgs 8.14 people stood there, King Solomon **turned** to face them, and he
8.33 you, and then when they **turn to** you and come to this
11. 3 They made him **turn away** from God, [4]and by the time he
11. 9 Solomon did not obey the Lord, but **turned away** from him.
11.14 Hadad, of the royal family of Edom, to **turn** against Solomon.
11.23 God also caused Rezon son of Eliada to **turn** against Solomon.
11.26 man who **turned** against King Solomon was one of his officials,
13.33 of Israel still did not **turn from** his evil ways, but
22.32 he was the king of Israel, and they **turned** to attack him.
22.34 "**Turn** round and pull out of the battle!"
2 Kgs 2.24 Elisha **turned** round, glared at them, and cursed them in
4.29 Elisha **turned** to Gehazi and said, "Hurry!
9.23 Joram cried out, as he **turned** his chariot round and fled.
10.27 pillar and the temple, and **turned** the temple into a
19.25 you the power to **turn** fortified cities into piles of rubble.
20. 2 Hezekiah **turned** his face to the wall and prayed:
21.13 clean as a plate that has been wiped and **turned** upside down.
1 Chr 6.32 They took regular **turns** of duty at the Tent of the
9.25 and who had to take **turns** at guard duty for seven days
24. 6 of Eleazar and of Ithamar took **turns** in drawing lots.
28. 9 but if you **turn away** from him, he will abandon you for
2 Chr 6. 3 The king **turned** to face them and asked God's blessing on them.
6.24 you and then when they **turn to** you and come to this
7.14 to me and repent and **turn away** from the evil they have
15. 2 you find him, but if you **turn away**, he will abandon you.
15. 4 But when trouble came, they **turned to** the Lord, the God of
16.12 even then he did not **turn to** the Lord for help, but
18.31 he was the king of Israel, and they **turned** to attack him.
18.31 Lord God rescued him and **turned** the attack away from him.
18.33 "**Turn** round and pull out of the battle!"
20.23 it, and then they **turned** on each other in savage fighting.
20.33 people still did not **turn wholeheartedly to** the worship of
26. 9 Corner Gate, at the Valley Gate, and where the wall **turned.**
29. 6 They abandoned him and **turned** their backs on the place where
33.12 his suffering he became humble, **turned to** the Lord his God,
33.23 his father, he did not become humble and **turn to** the Lord;
Ezra 8.22 displeased with and punishes anyone who **turns away** from him.
10.14 In this way God's anger over this situation will be **turned** away."
Neh 1. 9 But then if you **turn back** to me and do what I
3.19 of the armoury, as far as the place where the wall **turns;**
9.26 they **turned** their backs on your Law.
9.26 who warned them, who told them to **turn back** to you.
9.35 but they failed to **turn from** sin and serve you.
11.23 how the clans should take **turns** in leading the temple music
13. 2 curse Israel, but our God **turned** the curse into a blessing.
Esth 1.14 Those he most often **turned** to for advice were Carshena,
2.12 After that, each girl would be taken in **turn** to King Xerxes.
2.15 When her **turn** came, she wore just what Hegai, the eunuch in
9.22 a month that had been **turned** from a time of grief and
Job 1. 4 used to take it in **turns** to give a feast, to which
3. 4 **Turn** that day into darkness, God.
4. 5 Now it's your **turn** to be in trouble, and you are too
5. 1 Is there any angel to whom you can **turn?**
5. 8 I were you, I would **turn to** God and present my case
6.13 there is nowhere I can **turn** for help.
8. 5 But **turn** now and plead with Almighty God;
12.15 floods come when he **turns** water loose.
19.19 those I loved most have **turned** against me.
20.11 to be young and vigorous, but soon it will **turn** to dust.
20.14 in his stomach the food **turns** bitter, as bitter as any
28.28 To understand, you must **turn from** evil."
29.12 I gave help to orphans who had nowhere to **turn.**
30.11 and helpless, they **turn** against me with all their fury.
30.30 My skin has **turned** dark;
31. 7 If I have **turned from** the right path or let myself be
34.15 then everyone living would die and **turn** into dust again.
35.10 But they don't **turn to** God, their Creator, who gives
35.11 They don't **turn to** God, who makes us wise, wiser than
36.10 He makes them listen to his warning to **turn away** from evil.
36.21 Be careful not to **turn to** evil;
36.27 takes water from the earth and **turns** it into drops of rain.
37.10 of God freezes the waters, and **turns** them to solid ice.
38.30 ice and the frost, [30]which **turn** the waters to stone and
39. 5 Who **turned** them loose and let them roam?
39.22 know the meaning of fear, and no sword can **turn** them back.
41.32 a shining path behind him and **turns** the sea to white foam.
Ps 3. 1 I have so many enemies, Lord, so many who **turn** against me!
9. 3 My enemies **turn** back when you appear;
17. 6 so **turn** to me and listen to my words.
17.11 round me now, wherever I **turn,** watching for a chance to pull
18.21 I have not **turned away** from my God.
21.12 will shoot his arrows at them and make them **turn** and run.
22.24 he does not **turn** away from them, but answers when they
22.27 From every part of the world they will **turn to** him;
25.16 **Turn** to me, Lord, and be merciful to me, because I am
27. 9 don't **turn** your servant away.
34.14 **Turn away** from evil and do good;
35. 4 May those who plot against me be **turned** back and confused!
37.27 **Turn away** from evil and do good, and your descendants
40. 4 who do not **turn to** idols or join those who
40.14 happy because of my troubles be **turned** back and disgraced.
41. 9 most, the one who shared my food, has **turned** against me.
42. 6 my heart is breaking, and so I **turn** my thoughts to him.
49. 4 I will **turn** my attention to proverbs and explain their
51.13 sinners your commands, and they will **turn back** to you.
53. 3 But they have all **turned away;**
55. 1 don't **turn** away from my plea!
56. 9 The day I call to you, my enemies will be **turned** back.
60. 1 you have been angry with us—but now **turn** back to us.
Ps 69.16 in your great compassion **turn** to me!
70. 2 happy because of my troubles be **turned** back and disgraced.
73.10 so that even God's people **turn** to them and eagerly
78. 6 might learn them and in **turn** should tell their children.
78.34 Whenever he killed some of them, the rest would **turn to** him;
78.44 He **turned** the rivers into blood, and the Egyptians had
79. 6 **Turn** your anger on the nations that do not worship you, on
80.14 **Turn** to us, Almighty God!
80.18 We will never **turn away** from you again;
86.16 **Turn** to me and have mercy on me;
88.14 Why do you **turn** away from me?
101. 3 I hate the actions of those who **turn away** from God;
102. 2 When I am in trouble, don't **turn** away from me!
104.29 When you **turn** away, they are afraid;
105.29 He **turned** their rivers into blood and killed all their fish.
118.22 the builders rejected as worthless **turned** out to be the most
119.132 **Turn** to me and have mercy on me as you do on
131. 1 I have given up my pride and **turned** away from my arrogance.
139.11 the light round me to **turn** into night, [12]but even darkness
Prov 4.26 what you do, and whatever you do will **turn** out right.
13.19 Stupid people refuse to **turn away** from evil.
19.26 ill-treat his father or **turn** his mother away from his home.
26.14 The lazy man **turns** over in bed.
Ecc 12. 5 Your hair will **turn** white;
Song 6. 5 **Turn** your eyes away from me;
Is 1. 4 the holy God of Israel, and have **turned** your backs on him.
3.12 misleading you, so that you do not know which way to **turn.**
3.24 their beauty will be **turned** to shame!
5.20 You **turn** darkness into light and light into darkness.
5.28 as flint, and their chariot-wheels **turn** like a whirlwind.
6.10 If they did, they might **turn to** me and be healed."
14.17 man who destroyed cities and **turned** the world into a desert?
14.23 I will **turn** Babylon into a marsh, and owls will live there.
17. 7 that day comes, people will **turn** for help to their Creator,
19. 2 and **turn** brother against brother
19.22 They will **turn to** him, and he will hear their prayers and
25. 2 You have **turned** cities into ruins
29.14 Those who are wise will **turn** out to be fools, and all
29.16 They **turn** everything upside down.
34. 9 The rivers of Edom will **turn** into tar,
34. 9 and the soil will **turn** into sulphur.
37.26 you the power to **turn** fortified cities into piles of rubble.
38. 2 Hezekiah **turned** his face to the wall and prayed:
38.17 My bitterness will **turn** into peace.
41.18 I will **turn** the desert into pools of water and the dry
42.15 I will **turn** the river valleys into deserts and dry up the
42.16 I will **turn** their darkness into light and make rough country
43.14 gates, and the shouts of her people will **turn** into crying.
45.22 "**Turn to** me now and be saved, people all over the world!
47. 2 **Turn** the millstone!
50. 2 sea with a command and **turn** rivers into a desert, so that
50. 3 I can make the sky **turn** dark, as if it were in
50. 5 and I have not rebelled or **turned away** from him.
54. 8 I **turned** away angry for only a moment, but I will show
55. 6 **Turn to** the Lord and pray to him, now that he is
55. 7 Let them **turn to** the Lord, our God;
58.10 the darkness around you will **turn** to the brightness of noon.
59.13 We have oppressed others and **turned away** from you.
59.20 you and to save all of you that **turn from** your sins.
63.17 do you make us so stubborn that we **turn away** from you?
64. 7 No one **turns to** you in prayer;
Jer 2. 5 What made them **turn away** from me?
2.13 they have **turned away** from me, the spring of fresh water,
2.19 will punish you, and your **turning from** me will condemn you.
2.25 I can't **turn** back.
2.27 This will happen because you **turned away** from me
2.27 instead of **turning to** me.
2.36 cheapened yourself by **turning to** the gods of other nations.
2.37 You will **turn** away from Egypt, hanging your head in shame.
3. 6 She has **turned away** from me, and on every high hill and
3. 8 her away because she had **turned from** me and had become a
3.11 that, even though Israel had **turned away** from him, she had
3.19 you to call me father, and never again **turn away** from me.
3.22 Return, all of you who have **turned away** from the Lord;
4. 1 of Israel, if you want to turn, then **turn back** to me.
4. 8 fierce anger of the Lord has not **turned** away from Judah.
4.28 He has made his decision and will not **turn** back.
5. 3 You were stubborn and would not **turn from** your sins.
5. 6 are numerous and time after time they have **turned from** God.
5.19 Jeremiah, that just as they **turned away** from me and served
5.23 you have **turned** aside and left me.
6. 8 I will **turn** your city into a desert, a place where no
8. 4 If someone misses the road, doesn't he **turn** back?
8. 5 my people, do you **turn away** from me
8. 5 without ever **turning back?**
10.22 its army will **turn** the cities of Judah into a desert, a
10.25 **Turn** your anger on the nations that do not worship you
12. 8 My chosen people have **turned** against me;
12.10 they have **turned** my lovely land into a desert.
13.16 before he **turns** into deep darkness the light you hoped for.
14. 7 We have **turned away** from you many times;
15. 6 you have **turned** your backs on me.
15. 9 Her daylight has **turned** to darkness;
16.11 Lord has said, 'Your ancestors **turned away** from me and
17. 5 will condemn the person who **turns away** from me and puts his
18. 4 Whenever a piece of pottery **turned** out imperfect, he would
18. 8 kingdom, [8]but then that nation **turns from** its evil, I will
18.17 I will **turn** my back on them;
23.27 me, just as their fathers forgot me and **turned** to Baal.
25. 5 They told you to **turn from** your wicked way of life and
25.38 Lord's fierce anger have **turned** the country into a desert.

Jer 27.22 Babylonia and will remain there until I **turn** my attention to them.
31.13 I will comfort them and **turn** their mourning into joy, their
31.19 We **turned away** from you, but soon we wanted to return.
32.33 They **turned** their backs on me;
32.40 all their heart, so that they will never **turn away** from me.
33. 5 I have **turned** away from this city because of the evil things
36. 3 to bring on them, they will **turn from** their evil ways.
36. 7 pray to the Lord and **turn from** their evil ways, because the
36.16 he had read it, they **turned** to one another in alarm, and
41.14 with him, they were glad, [14]and **turned** and ran to them.
44.11 God of Israel, will **turn** against you and destroy all Judah.
46. 5 "They are **turning** back in terror.
46.21 all of them **turned** and ran.
47. 3 Fathers will not **turn** back for their children;
49. 8 People of Dedan, **turn** and run!
Lam 2. 1 Its heavenly splendour he has **turned** into ruins.
3. 9 stone walls block me wherever I **turn.**
3.40 Let us examine our ways and **turn back** to the Lord.
4.11 The Lord **turned** loose the full force of his fury;
Ezek 1. 9 they moved as a group without **turning** their bodies.
1.12 could go wherever they wished, without having to **turn.**
2. 3 They have rebelled and **turned** against me and are still rebels,
4. 6 When you finish that, **turn** over on your right side and
4. 8 up so that you cannot **turn** from one side to the other
8.16 They had **turned** their backs to the sanctuary and were bowing
10.11 they could go in any direction without **turning.**
10.11 direction they wanted to go, without having to **turn** round.
14. 5 All those idols have **turned** the Israelites away from me,
14. 6 **Turn back** and leave your disgusting idols.
14. 7 Israelite community **turns away** from me and worships idols,
17. 7 its roots towards him and **turned** its leaves towards him, in
18.30 **Turn away** from all the evil you are doing, and don't let
18.32 **"Turn away** from your sins and live."
21.16 Cut wherever you **turn.**
21.31 feel my anger when I **turn** it loose on you like a
22.31 So I will **turn** my anger loose on them, and like a
23.35 "Because you forgot me and **turned** your back on me, you will
25. 5 I will **turn** the city of Rabbah into a place to keep
38. 4 I will **turn** him round, put hooks in his jaws, and drag
38.21 His men will **turn** their swords against one another.
39. 2 I will **turn** him in a new direction and lead him out
39.23 I **turned** away from them and let their enemies defeat them
39.24 and their wickedness, and I **turned** away from them."
39.29 on the people of Israel and never again **turn** away from them.
41.19 a human face that was **turned** towards the palm-tree on one side,
41.19 a lion's face that was **turned** towards the tree on the other
44.15 when the rest of the people of Israel **turned away** from me.
Dan 3.19 his temper, and his face **turned** red with anger at Shadrach,
5. 6 He **turned** pale and was so frightened that his knees began
7.28 was so frightened that I **turned** pale, and I kept everything
9. 5 us to do and have **turned away** from what you showed us
9.13 tried to please you by **turning from** our sins or by following
11.18 he will **turn** the arrogance of Syria's king back on him.
11.29 Egypt again, but this time things will **turn** out differently.
11.30 "Then he will **turn** back in a rage and try to destroy
Hos 2.12 I will **turn** her vineyards and orchards into a wilderness;
3. 1 of Israel, even though they **turn to** other gods and like to
3. 5 of Israel will once again **turn to** the Lord their God, and
4. 7 against me, and so I will **turn** your honour into disgrace.
4.10 no children, because you have **turned away** from me to follow
7.16 They keep on **turning away** from me to a god that is
9. 1 You have **turned away** from your God and have been unfaithful
10.12 is time for you to **turn to** me, your Lord, and I
11. 2 more I called to him, the more he **turned away** from me.
11. 7 They insist on **turning away** from me.
14. 3 show mercy to those who have no one else to **turn** to."
Joel 1. 3 their children, who in **turn** will tell the next generation.
2. 6 every face **turns** pale.
2.31 darkened, and the moon will **turn** red as blood before the
Amos 1. 2 The pastures dry up, and the grass on Mount Carmel **turns** brown."
5. 8 He **turns** darkness into daylight, and day into night.
6.12 Yet you have **turned** justice into poison, and right into wrong.
8.10 I will **turn** your festivals into funerals and change your
Mic 3. 9 of Israel, you that hate justice and **turn** right into wrong.
7.17 They will **turn** in fear to the Lord our God.
Nah 1. 4 of Bashan wither, Mount Carmel **turns** brown, and the flowers
1. 7 he takes care of those who **turn to** him.
2. 8 the cry rings out— but no one **turns** back.
Hab 2.16 You in **turn** will be covered with shame instead of honour.
2.16 of punishment, and your honour will be **turned** to disgrace.
Zeph 1. 6 destroy those who have **turned** back and no longer follow me,
2. 3 **Turn to** the Lord, all you humble people of the land, who
3.19 I will **turn** their shame to honour, and all the world will
Hag 1. 9 "You hoped for large harvests, but they **turned** out to be small.
Zech 8.10 I **turned** people against one another.
Mal 1.13 and you **turn** up your nose at me.
2. 8 "But now you priests have **turned away** from the right path.
2. 9 So I, in **turn,** will make the people of Israel despise you
3. 7 your ancestors before you, have **turned away** from my laws and
3. 7 **Turn back** to me, and I will turn to you.
3. 7 But you ask, 'What must we do to **turn back** to you?'
Mt 3. 2 **"Turn away from your sins,"** he said, "because the Kingdom of
3. 8 things that will show that you have **turned from your sins.**
4. 3 "If you are God's Son, order these stones to **turn** into bread."
4.17 **"Turn away from your sins,** because the Kingdom of heaven is near!"
7. 6 what is holy to dogs—they will only **turn** and attack you.
9.22 Jesus **turned round** and saw her, and said, "Courage, my
10.21 children will **turn** against their parents and have them put
11.20 his miracles did not **turn from their sins,** so he reproached
11.21 on themselves, to show that they had **turned from their sins!**
12.41 because they **turned from their sins** when they heard Jonah
13.15 understand, and they would **turn to me,** says God, and I would
16.23 Jesus **turned** around and said to Peter, "Get away from me,
21.42 rejected as worthless **turned** out to be the most important
Mk 1. 4 **"Turn away from your sins** and be baptized," he told the people,
1.15 **Turn away from your sins** and believe the Good News!"
4.12 did, they would **turn to God,** and he would forgive them.' "
5.30 out of him, so he **turned round** in the crowd and asked,
6.12 and preached that people should **turn away from their sins.**
8.33 Jesus **turned round,** looked at his disciples, and rebuked Peter.
11.17 But you have **turned** it into a hideout for thieves!"
12.10 rejected as worthless **turned** out to be the most important
13.12 Children will **turn** against their parents and have them put
Lk 1. 8 priest in the Temple, taking his **turn** in the daily service.
1.17 he will **turn** disobedient people back to the way of thinking
3. 3 Jordan, preaching, **"Turn away from your sins** and be baptized,
3. 8 things that will show that you have **turned from your sins.**
4. 3 "If you are God's Son, order this stone to **turn** into bread."
7. 9 he **turned round** and said to the crowd following him, "I
7.44 Then he **turned** to the woman and said to Simon, "Do you
9.55 Jesus **turned** and rebuked them.
10.13 on themselves, to show that they had **turned from their sins!**
10.23 Then Jesus **turned** to the disciples and said to them privately,
11.32 because they **turned from their sins** when they heard Jonah
13. 3 if you do not **turn from your sins,** you will all die
13. 5 if you do not **turn from your sins,** you will all die
14.25 along with Jesus, he **turned** and said to them, [26]"Whoever comes
16.30 death and go to them, then they would **turn from their sins.'**
19.46 But you have **turned** it into a hideout for thieves!"
20.17 rejected as worthless **turned** out to be the most important
22.32 And when you **turn back to me,** you must strengthen your brothers."
22.61 The Lord **turned round** and looked straight at Peter,
23.28 Jesus **turned** to them and said, "Women of Jerusalem!
Jn 1.38 Jesus **turned,** saw them following him, and asked, "What are
2. 9 water, [9]which now had **turned** into wine, and he tasted it.
4.46 to Cana in Galilee, where he had **turned** the water into wine.
6.37 I will never **turn away** anyone who comes to me, [38]because I
6.66 many of Jesus' followers **turned back** and would not go with
12.40 and they would not **turn to me,** says God, for me to
13.18 that says, 'The man who shared my food **turned** against me.'
16.20 you will be sad, but your sadness will **turn** into gladness.
20.14 Then she **turned round** and saw Jesus standing there;
20.16 She **turned** towards him and said in Hebrew, "Rabboni!"
21.20 Peter **turned round** and saw behind him that other disciple,
Acts 2.20 darkened, and the moon will **turn** red as blood, before the
2.38 of you must **turn away from his sins** and be baptized in
3.14 Pilate to do you the favour of **turning** loose a murderer.
3.19 Repent, then, and **turn to God,** so that he will forgive
3.26 by making every one of you **turn away from his wicked ways."**
4.11 you the builders despised **turned** out to be the most important
7.42 So God **turned away** from them and gave them over to
9.35 in Lydda and Sharon saw him, and they **turned to the Lord.**
9.40 then he **turned** to the body and said, "Tabitha, get up!"
11.21 a great number of people believed and **turned to the Lord.**
13. 8 Greek), who tried to **turn** the governor away from the faith.
13.10 you always keep trying to **turn** the Lord's truths into lies!
13.24 Israel that they should **turn from their sins** and be baptized.
14. 2 stirred up the Gentiles and **turned** them against the believers.
14.15 the Good News, to **turn you away** from these worthless things
15. 3 and Samaria, they reported how the Gentiles had **turned to God;**
15.19 "that we should not trouble the Gentiles who are **turning to God.**
15.38 mission, but had **turned back** and left them in Pamphylia.
16.18 became so upset that he **turned round** and said to the spirit,
17.30 all of them everywhere to **turn away from their evil** ways.
19. 4 "The baptism of John was for those who **turned from their sins;**
20.21 warning that they should **turn from their sins** to God and
26.18 to open their eyes and **turn** them from the darkness to the
26.20 of their sins and **turn to God** and do the things that
28.27 understand, and they would **turn to me,** says God, and I would
Rom 3.12 All have **turned away** from God;
1 Cor 9.15 Nobody is going to **turn** my rightful boast into empty words!
10. 7 down to a feast which **turned** into an orgy of drinking and
2 Cor 3.16 "His veil was removed when he **turned to the Lord."**
9. 3 you in this matter may not **turn** out to be empty words.
Gal 4. 9 it that you want to **turn back** to those weak and pitiful
Phil 2.23 as I know how things are going to **turn** out for me.
1 Thes 1. 9 and how you **turned away from idols** to God, to serve
3. 3 that none of you should **turn back** because of these persecutions.
1 Tim 1. 6 Some people have **turned away** from these and have lost
5.11 want to marry, they **turn away** from Christ, [12]and so become
5.15 For some widows have already **turned away** to follow Satan.
2 Tim 2.19 he belongs to the Lord must **turn away from wrongdoing."**
4. 4 They will **turn away** from listening to the truth and give
Heb 3.12 and unbelieving that he will **turn away** from the living God.
6. 1 lay again the foundation of **turning away** from useless works and
10.38 but if any of them **turns** back, I will not be pleased
10.39 We are not people who **turn back** and are lost.
11.27 As though he saw the invisible God, he refused to **turn back.**
12.15 Guard against **turning back** from the grace of God.
12.17 but he was **turned away,** because he could not find any way
12.25 we escape, then, if we **turn away** from the one who speaks
Jas 1.17 heavenly lights, who does not change or cause darkness by **turning.**
5.20 whoever **turns** a sinner back from his wrong way will save
1 Pet 2. 7 rejected as worthless **turned** out to be the most important
3.11 He must **turn away from evil** and do good;
2 Pet 2.21 to know it and then **turn away** from the sacred command that
3. 9 be destroyed, but wants all to **turn away from their sins.**
Rev 1.12 I **turned round** to see who was talking to me, and I
2. 5 **Turn from your sins** and do what you did at first.

Rev 2. 5 If you don't **turn from your sins,** I will come to you
2.16 Now **turn from your sins!**
2.21 her sins, but she does not want to **turn from her immorality.**
3. 3 obey it and **turn from your sins.**
3.19 Be in earnest, then, and **turn from your sins.**
6.12 black cloth, and the moon **turned** completely red like blood.
8. 8 third of the sea was **turned** into blood, [9]a third of the
8.11 A third of the water **turned** bitter, and many people
8.11 died from drinking the water, because it had **turned** bitter.
9.20 by these plagues, did not **turn away** from what they
10. 9 it will **turn** sour in your stomach, but in your mouth it
10.10 But after I swallowed it, it **turned** sour in my stomach.
11. 6 also over the springs of water, to **turn** them into blood;
16. 4 rivers and the springs of water, and they **turned** into blood.
16. 9 But they would not **turn from their sins** and praise his greatness.
16.11 But they did not **turn from their evil** ways.

Am **TURN OVER** see **HAND (over)**

TURQUOISE
A semi-precious stone, blue or bluish green in colour.
Ex 28.19 in the third row, a **turquoise,** an agate, and an amethyst;
39.12 in the third row, a **turquoise,** an agate, and an amethyst;
Esth 1. 6 red feldspar, shining mother-of-pearl, and blue **turquoise.**
Rev 21.20 tenth chalcedony, the eleventh **turquoise,** the twelfth amethyst.

TWELVE
Gen 14. 4 the control of Chedorlaomer for **twelve** years, but in the
17.20 will be the father of **twelve** princes, and I will make a
25.16 They were the ancestors of **twelve** tribes, and their
35.22 Jacob had **twelve** sons.
42.13 They said, "We were **twelve** brothers in all, sir, sons
42.32 We were **twelve** brothers in all, sons of the same father.
49.28 These are the **twelve** tribes of Israel, and this is what
Ex 15.27 where there were **twelve** springs and seventy palm-trees;
24. 4 the mountain and set up **twelve** stones,
24. 4 one for each of the **twelve** tribes of Israel.
26. 2 piece the same size, **twelve** metres long and two metres wide.
28. 9 them the names of the **twelve** sons of Jacob, [10]in the order
28.12 of the ephod to represent the **twelve** tribes of Israel.
28.21 Each of these **twelve** stones is to have engraved on it
36. 9 was the same size, **twelve** metres long and two metres wide.
39. 6 engraved with the names of the **twelve** sons of Jacob.
39. 7 the ephod to represent the **twelve** tribes of Israel, just as
39.14 Each of the **twelve** stones had engraved on it the name of
39.14 of Jacob, in order to represent the **twelve** tribes of Israel.
Lev 24. 5 Take **twelve** kilogrammes of flour and bake twelve loaves of bread.
Num 1.17 With the help of these **twelve** men Moses and Aaron
7. 3 six wagons and **twelve** oxen, a wagon for every two leaders
7.11 day for a period of **twelve** days one of the leaders is
7.84 the offerings brought by the **twelve** leaders for the dedication
7.84 **twelve** silver bowls and twelve silver basins
7.84 **twelve** gold dishes weighing a total of 1.32 kilogrammes,
7.84 **twelve** bulls, twelve rams, and twelve one-year-old lambs,
7.84 **twelve** goats for the sin-offerings
13. 2 leaders from each of the **twelve** tribes and send them as
14.38 Of the **twelve** spies only Joshua and Caleb survived.
17. 2 of Israel to give you **twelve** sticks, one from the leader of
17. 6 stick, one for each tribe, **twelve** in all, and Aaron's stick
29.17 On the second day offer **twelve** young bulls, two rams,
33. 9 they camped, because there were **twelve** springs of water and
Deut 1.23 thing to do, so I selected **twelve** men, one from each tribe.
Josh 3.12 Now choose **twelve** men, one from each of the tribes of Israel.
4. 2 Lord said to Joshua, [2]"Choose **twelve** men, one from each tribe,
4. 3 and command them to take **twelve** stones out of the middle
4. 4 Then Joshua called the **twelve** men he had chosen, [5]and
4. 8 had commanded Joshua, they took **twelve** stones from the
4. 9 Joshua also set up **twelve** stones in the middle of the Jordan,
4.20 There Joshua set up the **twelve** stones taken from the Jordan.
18.24 **twelve** cities, along with the towns round them.
19.15 **twelve** cities, along with the towns round them.
21. 7 Merari were assigned **twelve** cities from the territories of Reuben,
21.40 So the clan of Merari was assigned a total of **twelve** cities.
Judg 19.29 concubine's body, cut it into **twelve** pieces,
19.29 and sent one piece to each of the **twelve** tribes of Israel.
20. 6 and sent one piece to each of the **twelve** tribes of Israel.
21.17 Israel must not lose one of its **twelve** tribes.
2 Sam 2.15 So **twelve** men, representing Ishbosheth and the tribe of Benjamin,
2.15 fought **twelve** of David's men.
1 Kgs 4. 7 Solomon appointed **twelve** men as district governors in Israel.
4. 8 are the names of these **twelve** officers and the districts
4.19 Besides these **twelve,** there was one governor
4.27 His **twelve** governors, each one in the month assigned to him,
7.25 on the backs of **twelve** bronze bulls that faced outwards,
7.40 The **twelve** bulls supporting the tank
10.19 lion at each end of every step, a total of **twelve** lions.
11.30 tore it into **twelve** pieces, [31]and said to Jeroboam,
16.23 Omri became king of Israel, and he ruled for **twelve** years.
18.31 He took **twelve** stones, one for each of the twelve tribes
2 Kgs 3. 1 king of Israel, and he ruled in Samaria for **twelve** years.
8.25 In the **twelfth** year of the reign of Joram son of Ahab
16.17 from the backs of the **twelve** bronze bulls, and placed it on
17. 1 In the **twelfth** year of the reign of King Ahaz of Judah,
21. 1 Manasseh was **twelve** years old when he became king of Judah,
21. 7 all the territory of the **twelve** tribes of Israel as the
25.27 the twenty-seventh day of the **twelfth** month of the

1 Chr 1.29 The sons of Ishmael became the heads of **twelve** tribes:
2. 1 Jacob had **twelve** sons:
6.63 In the same way, **twelve** towns in the territories of Reuben,
25. 9 families into twenty-four groups of **twelve,** with a leader in
27. 2 **Twelfth** month:
2 Chr 4. 4 on the backs of **twelve bronze bulls that faced outwards,**
4.11 The **twelve bulls supporting the tank**
9.19 **Twelve** figures of lions were on the steps, one at either
33. 1 Manasseh was **twelve** years old when he became king of Judah,
33. 7 all the territory of the **twelve** tribes of Israel as the
Ezra 6.17 lambs as sacrifices, and **twelve** goats as offerings for sin,
8.31 It was on the **twelfth** day of the first month that we
8.35 They offered **12** bulls for all Israel, 96 rams, and 77 lambs;
8.35 they also offered **12** goats to purify themselves from sin.
Neh 5.14 During all the **twelve** years that I was governor of the
Esth 3. 7 In the **twelfth** year of King Xerxes' rule, in the first month,
3. 7 The thirteenth day of the **twelfth** month, the month of Adar,
8.12 of the Jews, the thirteenth of Adar, the **twelfth** month.
Jer 52.20 the large tank, and the **twelve** bulls that supported it—were
52.31 the twenty-fifth day of the **twelfth** month of the
Ezek 29. 1 On the **twelfth** day of the tenth month of the tenth year
32. 1 the twelfth month of the **twelfth** year of our exile, the Lord
32.17 the first month of the **twelfth** year of our exile, the Lord
33.21 the tenth month of the **twelfth** year of our exile, a man
40.13 the passage from it, and it was **twelve** and a half metres.
40.21 twenty-five metres and the width **twelve** and a half metres.
40.25 twenty-five metres, and the width **twelve** and a half metres.
40.29 twenty-five metres and the width **twelve** and a half metres.
40.33 twenty-five metres and the width **twelve** and a half metres.
40.36 twenty-five metres and its width **twelve** and a half metres.
45. 1 It is to be **twelve** and a half kilometres long by ten
45. 3 of this area, a section **twelve** and a half kilometres by five
45. 6 the holy area, another section, **twelve** and a half kilometres
47.13 to be divided among the **twelve** tribes, with the tribe of
48. 8 It is to be **twelve** and a half kilometres wide from north
48. 9 this section, a special area **twelve** and a half kilometres by
48.10 their portion is to measure **twelve** and a half kilometres,
48.13 It too is to be **twelve** and a half kilometres from east
48.15 special area that is left, **twelve** and a half kilometres by
48.20 will be a square measuring **twelve** and a half kilometres on
48.30 There are **twelve** entrances to the city of Jerusalem.
Dan 4.29 Only **twelve** months later, while he was walking about on
Mt 9.20 suffered from severe bleeding for **twelve** years came up behind
10. 1 Jesus called his **twelve** disciples together and gave them
10. 2 These are the names of the **twelve** apostles:
10. 5 These **twelve** men were sent out by Jesus with the following
11. 1 these instructions to his **twelve** disciples, he left that place
14.20 Then the disciples took up **twelve** baskets full of what was
19.28 the New Age, then you **twelve** followers of mine
19.28 also sit on thrones, to rule the **twelve** tribes of Israel.
20. 5 Then at **twelve** o'clock and again at three o'clock he did the
20.17 to Jerusalem, he took the **twelve** disciples aside and spoke to
26.14 one of the **twelve** disciples—the one named Judas Iscariot—went
26.20 was evening, Jesus and the **twelve** disciples sat down to eat.
26.47 still speaking when Judas, one of the **twelve** disciples, arrived.
26.53 at once he would send me more than **twelve** armies of angels?
Mk 3.14 They came to him, [14]and he chose **twelve,** whom he named apostles.
3.16 These are the **twelve** he chose:
4.10 came to him with the **twelve** disciples and asked him to
5.25 from severe bleeding for **twelve** years, [26]even though she had
5.42 (She was **twelve** years old.)
6. 7 He called the **twelve** disciples together and sent them out
6.43 the disciples took up **twelve** baskets full of what was left
8.19 **"Twelve,"** they answered.
9.35 Jesus sat down, called the **twelve** disciples, and said to them,
10.32 Once again Jesus took the **twelve** disciples aside and spoke
11.11 the day, he went out to Bethany with the **twelve** disciples.
14.10 Iscariot, one of the **twelve** disciples, went off to the chief
14.17 When it was evening, Jesus came with the **twelve** disciples.
14.20 will be one of you **twelve,** one who dips his bread in
14.43 still speaking when Judas, one of the **twelve** disciples, arrived.
Lk 2.42 When Jesus was **twelve** years old, they went to the festival
6.13 to him and chose **twelve** of them, whom he named apostles:
8. 1 The **twelve** disciples went with him, [2]and so did some women
8.42 his only daughter, who was **twelve** years old, was dying.
8.43 a woman who had suffered from severe bleeding for **twelve** years;
9. 1 Jesus called the **twelve** disciples together and gave them power
9.12 beginning to set, the **twelve** disciples came to him and said,
9.17 the disciples took up **twelve** baskets of what was left over.
18.31 Jesus took the **twelve** disciples aside and said to them, "Listen!
22. 3 Judas, called Iscariot, who was one of the **twelve** disciples.
22.30 sit on thrones to rule over the **twelve** tribes of Israel.
22.47 a crowd arrived, led by Judas, one of the **twelve** disciples.
23.44 It was about **twelve** o'clock when the sun stopped shining
Jn 6.13 them all up and filled **twelve** baskets with the pieces left
6.67 he asked the **twelve** disciples, "And you—would you also like
6.70 Jesus replied, "I chose the **twelve** of you, didn't I?
6.71 was one of the **twelve** disciples, was going to betray him.
11. 9 Jesus said, "A day has **twelve** hours, hasn't it?
20.24 One of the **twelve** disciples, Thomas (called the Twin), was not
Acts 6. 2 the **twelve** apostles called the whole group of believers together
7. 8 Jacob circumcised his **twelve** sons, the famous ancestors of our
19. 7 They were about **twelve** men in all.
24.11 it was no more than **twelve** days ago that I went to
26. 7 the very thing that the **twelve** tribes of our people hope
1 Cor 15. 5 that he appeared to Peter and then to all **twelve** apostles.
Rev 7. 4 They were from the **twelve** tribes of Israel,
12. 1 under her feet and a crown of **twelve** stars on her head.
21.12 a great, high wall with **twelve** gates
21.12 and with **twelve** angels in charge of the gates.

Rev 21.12 the names of the **twelve** tribes of the people of Israel.
21.14 city's wall was built on **twelve** foundation-stones, on which
21.14 were written the names of the **twelve** apostles of the Lamb.
21.20 tenth chalcedony, the eleventh turquoise, the **twelfth** amethyst.
21.21 The twelve gates were **twelve** pearls;
22. 2 which bears fruit **twelve** times a year, once each month;
also Num 7.12 1 Chr 24.7 1 Chr 25.9

TWICE

Gen 43.10 so long, we could have been there and back **twice** by now."
43.12 Take with you also **twice** as much money, because you must
43.15 brothers took the gifts and **twice** as much money, and set out
Ex 16. 5 they are to bring in **twice** as much as usual and prepare
16.22 the sixth day they gathered **twice** as much food, four litres
Num 20.11 stick and struck the rock **twice** with it, and a great stream
1 Sam 18.11 Saul said to himself, and he threw the spear at him **twice;**
26. 8 ground with just one blow—I won't have to strike **twice!"**
2 Sam 12. 8 had not been enough, I would have given you **twice** as much.
1 Kgs 11. 9 Israel, had appeared to Solomon **twice** and had commanded him
Neh 13.20 Once or **twice** merchants who sold all kinds of goods
Job 42.10 prosperous again and gave him **twice** as much as he had had
Zech 9.12 now, I will repay you **twice** over with blessing for all you
Mt 23.15 you succeed, you make him **twice** as deserving of going to
Mk 14.30 before the cock crows **twice** tonight, you will say three times
14.72 "Before the cock crows **twice,** you will say three times that
2 Cor 1.15 to visit you, in order that you might be blessed **twice.**
Rev 18. 6 her cup with a drink **twice** as strong as the drink she

TWILIGHT

Ex 16.12 Tell them that at **twilight** they will have meat to eat, and
Job 24.15 The adulterer waits for **twilight** to come;

TWIN

Gen 25.22 She was going to have **twins,** and before they were born,
25.24 time came for her to give birth, and she had **twin** sons.
38.27 birth, it was discovered that she was going to have **twins.**
Song 4. 5 Your breasts are like gazelles, **twin** deer feeding among lilies.
7. 3 Your breasts are like **twin** deer, like two gazelles.
Hos 12. 3 ancestor Jacob struggled with his **twin** brother Esau while
Jn 11.16 Thomas (called the **Twin**) said to his fellow-disciples,
20.24 Thomas (called the **Twin**), was not with them when Jesus
21. 2 Simon Peter, Thomas (called the **Twin**), Nathanael (the one from

TWIN GODS

Acts 28.11 ship from Alexandria, called "The **Twin Gods,"** which had spent

TWIST

Ex 28.14 two chains of pure gold **twisted** like cords, and attach them
28.22 For the breast-piece make chains of pure gold, **twisted** like cords.
39.15 they made chains of pure gold, **twisted** like cords.
Job 8. 3 God never **twists** justice;
14.20 his face is **twisted** in death.
30.18 seizes me by my collar and **twists** my clothes out of shape.
Is 24. 1 He will **twist** the earth's surface and scatter its people.
27. 1 to punish Leviathan, that wriggling, **twisting** dragon, and to
Amos 5. 7 You are doomed, you that **twist** justice and cheat people
Mic 4.10 **Twist** and groan, people of Jerusalem, like a woman giving birth,
Zeph 3. 4 defile what is sacred, and **twist** the law of God to their

TWO

Gen 1. 6 and to keep it in **two** separate places"—and it was done.
1.16 So God made the **two** larger lights, the sun to rule over
4.19 Lamech had **two** wives, Adah and Zillah.
9.22 his father was naked, he went out and told his **two** brothers.
10.25 Eber had **two** sons:
11.10 **Two** years after the flood, when Shem was 100 years old, he
13. 6 enough pasture land for the **two** of them to stay together,
13.11 That is how the **two** men parted.
15.10 half, and placed the halves opposite each other in **two** rows;
18.22 Then the **two** men left and went on towards Sodom, but the
19. 1 When the **two** angels came to Sodom that evening, Lot was
19. 8 Look, I have **two** daughters who are still virgins.
19.10 But the **two** men inside reached out, pulled Lot back into
19.12 The **two** men said to Lot, "If you have anyone else here
19.15 "Take your wife and your **two** daughters and get out, so that
19.16 him, his wife, and his **two** daughters by the hand and led
19.30 in Zoar, he and his **two** daughters moved up into the hills
21.27 cattle to Abimelech, and the **two** of them made an agreement.
21.31 because it was there that the **two** of them made a vow.
22. 3 loaded his donkey, and took Isaac and **two** servants with him.
22. 8 And the **two** of them walked on together.
24.22 in her nose and put **two** large gold bracelets on her arms.
25.23 **"Two** nations are within you;
25.23 You will give birth to **two** rival peoples.
26.34 forty years old, he married **two** Hittite girls, Judith the
27. 9 the flock and pick out **two** fat young goats, so that I
29.16 Laban had **two** daughters;
31.33 and the tent of the **two** slave-women, but he did not find
31.41 I worked to win your **two** daughters—and six years for your
32. 7 He divided into **two** groups the people who were with him, and
32.10 and now I have come back with these **two** groups.
32.22 Jacob got up, took his **two** wives, his two concubines, and
33. 1 the children among Leah, Rachel, and the **two** concubines.
34.25 their circumcision, **two** of Jacob's sons, Simeon and Levi,
36.24 Zibeon had **two** sons, Aiah and Anah.

Gen 40. 2 He was angry with these **two** officials [3]and put them in
41. 1 After **two** years had passed, the king of Egypt dreamt that
41.25 Joseph said to the king, "The **two** dreams mean the same thing;
41.50 Before the years of famine came, Joseph had **two** sons by Asenath.
42.37 not bring Benjamin back to you, you can kill my **two** sons.
44.27 us, 'You know that my wife Rachel bore me only **two** sons.
46.19 Jacob's wife Rachel bore him **two** sons:
46.20 In Egypt Joseph had **two** sons, Manasseh and Ephraim, by
46.27 **Two** sons were born to Joseph in Egypt, bringing to
48. 1 So he took his **two** sons, Manasseh and Ephraim, and went to
48. 5 Jacob continued, "Joseph, your **two** sons, who were born to
Ex 1.15 Shiphrah and Puah, the **two** midwives who helped the Hebrew women.
2.13 The next day he went back and saw **two** Hebrew men fighting.
4. 9 If in spite of these **two** miracles they still will not
6.17 Gershon had **two** sons:
6.19 Merari had **two** sons:
16.16 of it as he needs, **two** litres for each member of his
16.29 sixth day I will always give you enough food for **two** days.
16.33 Aaron, "Take a jar, put **two** litres of manna in it, and
18. 3 who had been left behind, [3]and Gershom and Eliezer, her **two**
18. 5 with Moses' wife and her **two** sons into the desert where
18.16 When **two** people have a dispute, they come to me, and I
21.21 die for a day or **two,** the master is not to be
21.35 kills another man's bull, the **two** men shall sell the live
22. 2 is found alive in his possession, he shall pay **two** for one.
22. 9 any other lost object, the **two** men claiming the property
24.12 here, I will give you **two** stone tablets which contain all
25.12 attach them to its four legs, with **two** rings on each side.
25.16 put in the box the **two** stone tablets that I will give
25.18 Make **two** winged creatures of hammered gold, [19]one for
25.21 Put the **two** stone tablets inside the box and put the lid
25.22 above the lid between the **two** winged creatures I will give
26. 2 piece the same size, twelve metres long and **two** metres wide.
26. 6 gold hooks with which to join the **two** sets into one piece.
26. 8 all the same size, thirteen metres long and **two** metres wide.
26.11 the loops to join the **two** sets so as to form one
26.14 "Make **two** more coverings, one of rams' skin dyed red
26.17 and 66 centimetres wide, [17]with **two** matching projections,
26.19 two bases under each frame to hold its **two** projections.
26.21 the Tent [21]and forty silver bases, **two** under each frame.
26.23 west, make six frames, [23]and **two** frames for the corners.
26.24 The **two** frames that form the two corners are to be made
26.25 with their sixteen silver bases, **two** under each frame.
26.33 put the Covenant Box containing the **two** stone tablets.
28. 7 **Two** shoulder-straps, by which it can be fastened, are to
28. 9 Take **two** carnelian stones and engrave on them the names of
28.11 jeweller to engrave on the **two** stones the names of the sons
28.13 Make **two** gold settings [14]and two chains of pure gold
28.14 Make two gold settings [14]and **two** chains of pure gold
28.23 Make **two** gold rings and attach them to the upper corners
28.24 and fasten the **two** gold cords to the two rings.
28.25 Fasten the other **two** ends of the cords to the two settings,
28.26 Then make **two** rings of gold and attach them to the lower
28.27 Make **two** more gold rings and attach them to the lower
28.27 of the front of the **two** shoulder-straps of the ephod near
29. 1 Take one young bull and **two** rams without any defects.
29. 3 them to me when you sacrifice the bull and the **two** rams.
29.13 of the liver, and the **two** kidneys with the fat on them
29.22 part of the liver, the **two** kidneys with the fat on them,
29.38 time to come, sacrifice on the altar **two** one-year-old lambs.
30. 4 Make **two** gold carrying-rings for it and attach them
30. 4 the border on **two** sides to hold the poles with
31.18 Sinai, he gave him the **two** stone tablets on which God
32.15 down the mountain, carrying the **two** stone tablets with the
34. 1 Lord said to Moses, "Cut **two** stone tablets like the first ones,
34. 4 So Moses cut **two** more stone tablets, and early the next
36. 9 was the same size, twelve metres long and **two** metres wide.
36.13 gold hooks, with which to join the **two** sets into one piece.
36.15 all the same size, thirteen metres long and **two** metres wide.
36.18 bronze hooks to join the **two** sets, so as to form one
36.19 They made **two** more coverings, one of rams' skin dyed red
36.22 centimetres wide, [22]with **two** matching projections,
36.24 two bases under each frame to hold its **two** projections.
36.26 the Tent [26]and forty silver bases, **two** under each frame.
36.28 they made six frames [28]and **two** frames for the corners.
36.29 The **two** frames that formed the two corners were made in this
36.30 frames and sixteen silver bases, **two** under each frame.
37. 3 attached them to its four feet, with **two** rings on each side.
37. 7 He made **two** winged creatures of hammered gold, [8]one for
37.27 He made **two** gold carrying-rings for it and attached them
37.27 below the border on the **two** sides, to hold the poles with
38.21 the Lord's presence, where the **two** stone tablets were kept
39. 4 They made **two** shoulder-straps for the ephod and attached
39.16 They made **two** gold settings and two gold rings
39.16 and attached the **two** rings to the upper corners of
39.17 They fastened the **two** gold cords to the two rings
39.18 and fastened the other **two** ends of the cords
39.18 to the **two** settings and in this way attached
39.19 They made **two** rings of gold and attached them to the
39.20 They made **two** more gold rings and attached them to the
39.20 of the front of the **two** shoulder straps of the ephod, near
40.20 Then he took the **two** stone tablets and put them in the
Lev 5. 7 the payment for his sin **two** doves or two pigeons, one for
5.11 If a man cannot afford **two** doves or two pigeons, he
8. 2 bull for the sin-offering, the **two** rams, and the basket of
10.12 to Aaron and his **two** remaining sons, Eleazar and Ithamar,
12. 8 a lamb, she shall bring **two** doves or two pigeons, one for
14. 4 the priest shall order **two** ritually clean birds to be brought,
14.10 eighth day he shall bring **two** male lambs and one female lamb
14.22 He shall also bring **two** doves or two pigeons, one for

Lev	14.49	the house, he shall take **two** birds, some cedar-wood, a red
	15.14	eighth day he shall take **two** doves or two pigeons to the
	15.29	eighth day she shall take **two** doves or two pigeons to the
	16. 1	after the death of the **two** sons of Aaron who were killed
	16. 5	of Israel shall give Aaron **two** male goats for a sin-offering
	16. 7	Then he shall take the **two** goats to the entrance of the
	16. 8	draw lots, using **two** stones, one marked "for the Lord"
	16.12	coals from the altar and **two** handfuls of fine incense and
	19.19	Do not plant **two** kinds of seed in the same field.
	19.19	Do not wear clothes made of **two** kinds of material.
	23.13	With it you shall present **two** kilogrammes of flour mixed
	23.17	Each family is to bring **two** loaves of bread and present
	23.17	loaf shall be made of **two** kilogrammes of flour baked with
	23.18	one-year-old lambs, one bull, and **two** rams, none of which
	23.19	and **two** one-year-old male lambs as a fellowship-offering.
	23.20	present the bread with the **two** lambs as a special gift to
	24. 6	Put the loaves in **two** rows, six in each row, on the
	25.21	year so that it will produce enough food for **two** years.
Num	2.17	Then, between the first **two** divisions and the last two
	3.17	Gershon had **two** sons:
	3.17	and Merari had **two** sons:
	6.10	eighth day he shall bring **two** doves or two pigeons to the
	7. 3	oxen, a wagon for every **two** leaders and an ox for each
	7. 7	He gave **two** wagons and four oxen to the Gershonites, [8]and
	7.12	and **two** bulls, five rams, five goats, and five one-year-old
	7.89	lid on the Covenant Box, between the **two** winged creatures.
	8.12	shall then put their hands on the heads of the **two** bulls;
	9.22	Whether it was **two** days, a month, a year, or longer, as
	10. 2	Lord said to Moses, [2]"Make **two** trumpets of hammered silver
	11.19	not just for one or **two** days, or five, or ten, or
	11.26	**Two** of the seventy leaders, Eldad and Medad, had stayed
	12. 5	The **two** of them stepped forward, [6]and the Lord said, "Now
	13.23	so heavy that it took **two** men to carry it on a
	14. 6	and Caleb son of Jephunneh, **two** of the spies, tore their
	15. 6	When a ram is offered, **two** kilogrammes of flour mixed with
	15. 9	kilogrammes of flour mixed with **two** litres of olive-oil is
	15.10	is to be presented, [10]together with **two** litres of wine.
	16.45	The **two** of them bowed down with their faces to the ground,
	20.24	going to die, because the **two** of you rebelled against my
	22.22	his donkey, accompanied by his **two** servants, the angel of
	22.24	where the road narrowed between **two** vineyards and had a
	26.19	(**Two** of Judah's sons, Er and Onan, had died in the land
	26.28	who was the father of **two** sons, Manasseh and Ephraim.
	26.59	She bore Amram **two** sons, Aaron and Moses, and a daughter,
	28. 3	**two** one-year-old male lambs without any defects.
	28. 9	On the Sabbath day offer **two** one-year-old male lambs
	28. 9	**two** kilogrammes of flour mixed with olive-oil
	28.11	**two** young bulls, one ram, seven one-year-old male lambs, all
	28.12	with the ram, **two** kilogrammes;
	28.14	The proper wine-offering is **two** litres of wine with each bull,
	28.19	**two** young bulls, one ram, and seven one-year-old male lambs,
	28.20	kilogrammes with each bull, **two** kilogrammes with the ram,
	28.27	**two** young bulls, one ram, and seven one-year-old male lambs,
	28.28	kilogrammes with each bull, **two** kilogrammes with the ram,
	29. 3	of flour with the bull, **two** kilogrammes with the ram, [4]and
	29. 9	of flour with the bull, **two** kilogrammes with the ram,
	29.13	young bulls, **two** rams, and fourteen one-year-old male lambs,
	29.14	of flour with each bull, **two** kilogrammes with each ram,
	29.17	young bulls, **two** rams, and fourteen one-year-old male lambs,
	29.20	young bulls, **two** rams, and fourteen one-year-old male lambs,
	29.23	young bulls, **two** rams, and fourteen one-year-old male lambs,
	29.26	young bulls, **two** rams, and fourteen one-year-old male lambs,
	29.29	young bulls, **two** rams, and fourteen one-year-old male lambs,
	29.32	young bulls, **two** rams, and fourteen one-year-old male lambs,
	31.27	Divide what was taken into **two** equal parts, one part for
	35.30	put to death only on the evidence of **two** or more witnesses;
Deut	3. 8	time we took from those **two** Amorite kings the land east of
	3.11	almost **two** metres wide according to standard measurements.
	3.21	the Lord your God did to those **two** kings, Sihon and Og;
	4.13	the Ten Commandments, which he wrote on **two** stone tablets.
	5.22	Then he wrote them on **two** stone tablets and gave them to
	9.10	the Lord gave me the **two** stone tablets on which he had
	9.11	the Lord gave me the **two** stone tablets on which he had
	9.15	down the mountain, carrying the **two** stone tablets on which
	10. 1	Lord said to me, 'Cut **two** stone tablets like the first ones
	10. 3	box of acacia-wood and cut **two** stone tablets like the first
	11.30	(These **two** mountains are west of the River Jordan in the
	17. 6	to death only if **two** or more witnesses testify against him;
	19. 5	For example, if **two** men go into the forest together to cut
	19.15	at least **two** witnesses are necessary to prove that a man is
	21.15	"Suppose a man has **two** wives and they both bear him sons,
	25. 1	"Suppose **two** Israelites go to court to settle a dispute,
	25. 5	"If **two** brothers live on the same property and one of
	25.11	"If **two** men are having a fight and the wife of one
	32.30	a thousand defeated by one, and ten thousand by only **two?**
Josh	2. 1	Then Joshua sent **two** spies from the camp at Acacia with
	2. 4	(Now Rahab had taken the **two** spies up on the roof and
	2.10	Sihon and Og, the **two** Amorite kings east of the Jordan.
	2.23	Then the **two** spies came down from the hills,
	6.22	Joshua then told the **two** men who had served as spies,
	6.25	because she had hidden the **two** spies that he had sent to
	7. 3	Send only about **two** or three thousand men.
	7.21	beautiful Babylonian cloak, about **two** kilogrammes of silver,
	8.33	among them, stood on **two** sides of the Lord's Covenant Box,
	9.10	what he did to the **two** Amorite kings east of the Jordan:
	12. 1	They defeated **two** kings.
	12. 6	These **two** kings were defeated by Moses and the people of Israel.
	14. 3	east of the Jordan to the other **two** and a half tribes.
	14. 3	(The descendants of Joseph were divided into **two** tribes:
	15.60	**two** cities, along with the towns round them.
	21.25	From the territory of West Manasseh they were given **two** cities:
Josh	21.27	received from the territory of East Manasseh **two** cities:
	24.12	them into panic in order to drive out the **two** Amorite kings.
Judg	5.30	and divide, a girl or **two** for every soldier, rich cloth for
	7.20	were holding, [20]and the other **two** groups did the same.
	7.25	They captured the **two** Midianite chiefs, Oreb and Zeeb;
	8. 3	power of God you killed the **two** Midianite chiefs, Oreb and
	8.12	The **two** Midianite kings, Zebah and Zalmunna, ran away,
	9.44	the city gate, the other **two** companies attacked the people
	11.37	Leave me alone for **two** months, so that I can go with
	11.38	He told her to go and sent her away for **two** months.
	11.39	After **two** months she came back to her father.
	14.15	You **two** invited us so that you could rob us, didn't you?"
	15. 4	**Two** by two, he tied their tails together and put torches in
	15.13	they tied him up with **two** new ropes and brought him back
	16.28	get even with the Philistines for putting out my **two** eyes."
	16.29	Samson took hold of the **two** middle pillars holding up the building.
	19. 3	He took his servant and **two** donkeys with him.
	19. 6	So the **two** men sat down and ate and drank together.
	19. 8	So the **two** men ate together.
	19.10	way, with their servant and **two** donkeys with pack saddles.
Ruth	1. 1	his wife Naomi and their **two** sons Mahlon and Chilion to live
	1. 3	left alone with her **two** sons, [4]who married Moabite girls,
1 Sam	1. 2	Elkanah had **two** wives, Hannah and Peninnah.
	1. 3	where Hophni and Phinehas, the **two** sons of Eli, were priests
	2.21	bless Hannah, and she had three more sons and **two** daughters.
	2.34	When your **two** sons Hophni and Phinehas both die on the
	4. 4	And Eli's **two** sons, Hophni and Phinehas, came along with the
	6. 7	prepare a new wagon and **two** cows that have never been yoked;
	6.10	they took **two** cows and hitched them to the wagon, and shut
	10. 2	me today, you will meet **two** men near Rachel's tomb at Zelzah
	10. 4	greet you and offer you **two** of the loaves, which you are
	11. 7	He took **two** oxen, cut them in pieces, and sent messengers
	13.21	ox-goads, and **two** coins for sharpening ploughs or hoes.)
	14. 4	the Philistine camp, there were **two** large jagged rocks, one
	23.18	The **two** of them made a sacred promise of friendship to
	25.18	two hundred loaves of bread, **two** leather bags full of wine,
	26. 6	was Zeruiah), "Which of you **two** will go to Saul's camp with
	27. 3	David had his **two** wives with him, Ahinoam from Jezreel, and
	28. 8	after dark he went with **two** of his men to see the
	30. 1	**Two** days later David and his men arrived back at Ziklag.
	30. 5	Even David's **two** wives, Ahinoam and Abigail, had been taken away.
	30.12	and water, [12]some dried figs, and **two** bunches of raisins.
	30.18	the Amalekites had taken, including his **two** wives;
2 Sam	1. 1	over the Amalekites and stayed in Ziklag for **two** days.
	2. 2	So David went to Hebron, taking with him his **two** wives:
	2.10	he was made king of Israel, and he ruled for **two** years.
	4. 2	Ishbosheth had **two** officers who were leaders of raiding parties,
	8. 2	on the ground and put **two** out of every three of them
	12. 1	him and said, "There were **two** men who lived in the same
	13.23	**Two** years later Absalom was having his sheep sheared at Baal Hazor,
	14. 6	Sir, I had **two** sons, and one day they got into a
	14.26	It would weigh more than **two** kilogrammes according to the
	14.28	Absalom lived **two** years in Jerusalem without seeing the king.
	21. 8	took Armoni and Mephibosheth, the **two** sons that Rizpah the
	23.20	brave deeds, including killing **two** great Moabite warriors.
1 Kgs	2. 5	to me by killing the **two** commanders of Israel's armies,
	2.32	Joab killed **two** innocent men who were better men than he:
	2.39	Three years later, however, **two** of Shimei's slaves ran
	3.16	**two** prostitutes came and presented themselves before King Solomon.
	3.18	**Two** days after my child was born she also gave birth to
	3.18	Only the **two** of us were there in the house—no one
	3.25	"Cut the living child in **two** and give each woman half of
	3.26	go ahead and cut it in **two."**
	5.14	group spent one month in Lebanon and **two** months back home.
	6.23	**Two** winged creatures were made of olive wood and placed
	6.24	Each had **two** wings, each wing 2.2 metres long, so that the
	6.27	Most Holy Place, so that **two** of their outstretched wings
	6.27	of the room, and the other **two** wings touched the walls.
	6.28	The **two** winged creatures were covered with gold.
	6.34	There were **two** folding doors made of pine [35]and
	7. 4	In each of the **two** side walls there were three rows of
	7.15	Huram cast **two** bronze columns, each one 8 metres tall
	7.16	He also made **two** bronze capitals, each one 2.2 metres tall,
	7.18	interwoven chains, [18]and **two** rows of bronze pomegranates.
	7.20	There were two hundred pomegranates in **two** rows round each capital.
	7.21	Huram placed these **two** bronze columns in front of the
	7.24	rim of the tank were **two** rows of bronze gourds, which had
	7.40	The **two** columns The two bowl-shaped capitals on top of the
	7.40	four hundred bronze pomegranates, in **two** rows of a hundred each
	8. 9	the Covenant Box except the **two** stone tablets which Moses
	10.17	each one of them with almost **two** kilogrammes of gold.
	10.19	and beside each of the **two** arms was the figure of a
	12.28	thinking it over, he made **two** bull-calves of gold and said
	15.25	son Nadab became king of Israel, and he ruled for **two** years.
	16. 8	became king of Israel, and he ruled in Tirzah for **two** years.
	17. 1	or rain for the next **two** or three years until I say
	18. 4	hid them in caves in **two** groups of fifty, and provided them
	18.13	of them in caves, in **two** groups of fifty, and supplied them
	18.23	Bring **two** bulls;
	20.27	marched out and camped in **two** groups facing the Syrians.
	20.27	The Israelites looked like **two** small flocks of goats
	21.13	The **two** scoundrels publicly accused him of cursing God
	22. 1	and Syria for the next **two** years, [2]but in the third year
	22.10	The **two** kings, dressed in their royal robes, were
	22.51	king of Israel, and he ruled in Samaria for **two** years.
2 Kgs	1.14	The **two** other officers and their men were killed by fire

2 Kgs 2.12 In grief, Elisha tore his cloak in **two.**
2.24 Then **two** she-bears came out of the woods and tore forty-two
4. 1 come to take away my **two** sons as slaves in payment for
4.30 So the **two** of them started back together.
5.17 gift, then let me have **two** mule-loads of earth to take home
5.22 tell you that just now **two** members of the group of prophets
5.22 pieces of silver and **two** changes of fine clothes."
5.23 tied up the silver in **two** bags,
5.23 gave them and **two** changes of fine clothes
5.23 to **two** of his servants, and sent them
5.24 Elisha lived, Gehazi took the **two** bags and carried them into
7.14 the king sent them in **two** chariots with instructions to go
9. 6 Then the **two** of them went indoors, and the young prophet
9.32 **Two** or three palace officials looked down at him from a window,
10. 8 to be piled up in **two** heaps at the city gate and
11. 7 The **two** groups that go off duty on the Sabbath are to
12.20 officials plotted against him, and **two** of them, Jozacar son
15.23 king of Israel, and he ruled in Samaria for **two** years.
17.16 Lord their God and made **two** metal bull-calves to worship;
19.37 his god Nisroch, **two** of his sons, Adrammelech and Sharezer,
21. 5 In the **two** courtyards of the Temple he built altars for
21.19 king of Judah, and he ruled in Jerusalem for **two** years.
23.12 put up by King Manasseh in the **two** courtyards of the Temple;
25. 4 through the gateway connecting the **two** walls, and fled in
25.16 made for the Temple—the **two** columns, the carts, and the
25.17 The **two** columns were identical:

1 Chr 1.19 Eber had **two** sons;
1.28 Abraham had **two** sons, Isaac and Ishmael.
1.32 Jokshan had **two** sons:
1.34 Abraham's son Isaac had **two** sons, Esau and Jacob.
1.38 Zibeon, who had **two** sons, Aiah and Anah.
2. 4 By his daughter-in-law Tamar, Judah had **two** more sons,
2. 5 Perez had **two** sons, Hezron and Hamul.
2.16 He also had **two** daughters, Zeruiah and Abigail.
2.28 Onam had **two** sons, Shammai and Jada,
2.28 and Shammai also had **two** sons, Nadab and Abishur.
2.29 woman named Abihail, and they had **two** sons, Ahban and Molid.
2.30 Abishur's brother Nadab had **two** sons, Seled and Appaim,
2.32 the brother of Shammai, had **two** sons, Jether and Jonathan,
2.33 Jonathan had **two** sons, Peleth and Zaza.
2.48 Maacah, who bore him **two** sons, Sheber and Tirhanah.
2.49 Later she had **two** more sons:
2.54 of the Zorites, who were one of the **two** clans in Manahath.
3.16 Jehoiakim had **two** sons:
3.19 Pedaiah had **two** sons, Zerubbabel and Shimei.
3.19 Zerubbabel was the father of **two** sons, Meshullam and Hananiah,
3.21 Hananiah had **two** sons, Pelatiah and Jeshaiah.
4. 5 founded the town of Tekoa, had **two** wives, Helah and Naarah.
4.13 Kenaz had **two** sons, Othniel and Seraiah.
4.13 Othniel also had **two** sons, Hathath and Meonothai.
4.17 had a daughter, Miriam, and **two** sons, Shammai and Ishbah.
4.20 Ishi had **two** sons:
6. 3 Amram had **two** sons, Aaron and Moses, and one daughter,
6.25 Elkanah had **two** sons, Amasai and Ahimoth.
6.28 Samuel had **two** sons:
7.14 By his Aramean concubine, Manasseh had **two** sons,
7.16 Machir's wife, gave birth to **two** sons, whom they named
7.16 Peresh had **two** sons, Ulam and Rakem, [17]and Ulam had a son
7.21 Ephraim had **two** other sons besides Shuthelah:
7.31 Beriah had **two** sons, Heber and Malchiel.
8. 8 Shaharaim divorced **two** wives, Hushim and Baara.
8.11 He also had **two** sons by Hushim:
11.22 brave deeds, including killing **two** great Moabite warriors.
11.23 Egyptian, a huge man over **two** metres tall, who was armed
16. 6 sound the cymbals, [6]and **two** priests, Benaiah and Jahaziel,
23. 7 Gershon had **two** sons:
23.15 Moses had **two** sons, Gershom and Eliezer.
23.20 Kohath's fourth son, Uzziel, had **two** sons, Micah and Isshiah.
23.21 Merari had **two** sons, Mahli and Mushi.
23.21 Mahli also had **two** sons, Eleazar and Kish,
24.28 Mahli had **two** sons, Eleazar and Kish.
26. 6 the last **two** were especially talented.
26.17 stationed at the storerooms daily, **two** at each storeroom.
26.18 were four guards by the road and **two** at the pavilion itself.
26.22 Ladan's **two** other sons, Zetham and Joel, had charge of

2 Chr 3.10 his workmen to make **two** winged creatures out of metal,
3.11 Each had **two** wings, each wing 2.2 metres long, which were
3.15 The king made **two** columns, each one fifteen and a half
4. 3 rim of the tank were **two** rows of decorations, one above the
4.11 The **two** columns The two bowl-shaped capitals on top of the
4.11 hundred bronze pomegranates arranged in **two** rows round the
5.10 the Covenant Box except the **two** stone tablets which Moses
16.13 **Two** years later he died [14]and was buried in the rock
17. 8 They were accompanied by nine Levites and **two** priests.
18. 9 The **two** kings, dressed in their royal robes, were sitting
21.19 For almost **two** years it grew steadily worse until
24. 3 Jehoiada chose **two** wives for King Joash, and they bore him
24.25 and when the enemy withdrew, **two** of his officials plotted
33. 5 In the **two** courtyards of the Temple he built altars for
33.21 king of Judah, and he ruled in Jerusalem for **two** years.

Ezra 5. 1 At that time **two** prophets, Haggai and Zechariah son of Iddo,
5. 2 the Temple in Jerusalem, and the **two** prophets helped them.
8.16 and Meshullam, and for **two** teachers, Joiarib and Elnathan.
8.33 Eleazar son of Phinehas and **two** Levites, Jozabad son of
10.13 be done in one or **two** days, because so many of us

Neh 7. 2 I put **two** men in charge of governing the city of Jerusalem:
12.24 **Two** groups at a time praised God responsively and gave
12.31 put them in charge of **two** large groups to march round the

Esth 1. 7 served in gold cups, no **two** of them alike, and the king
2.21 the palace, Bigthana and Teresh, **two** of the palace eunuchs
6. 2 by Bigthana and Teresh, the **two** palace eunuchs who had
9.27 proper time each year these **two** days would be regularly

Job 13.20 Let me ask for **two** things;
42. 7 angry with you and your **two** friends, because you did not

Prov 7.20 plenty of money with him and won't be back for **two** weeks."
18.18 If **two** powerful men are opposing each other in court,
30. 7 ask you, God, to let me have **two** things before I die:
30.15 A leech has **two** daughters, and both are named "Give me!"

Ecc 4. 9 **Two** are better off than one, because together they can
4.11 If it is cold, **two** can sleep together and stay warm, but
4.12 **Two** men can resist an attack that would defeat one man alone.

Song 7. 3 Your breasts are like twin deer, like **two** gazelles.

Is 6. 2 creature covered its face with **two** wings,
6. 2 and its body with two, and used the other **two** for flying.
7. 4 no more dangerous than the smoke from **two** smouldering sticks.
7.16 comes, the lands of those **two** kings who terrify you will be
7.21 only one young cow and **two** goats, [22]they will give so much
8. 2 Get **two** reliable men, the priest Uriah and Zechariah
17. 6 olives have been picked except **two** or three at the very top,
19.23 The people of those **two** countries will travel to and fro
19.23 between them, and the **two** nations will worship together.
20. 4 naked the prisoners he captures from those **two** countries.
21. 7 sees men coming on horseback, **two** by two, and men riding on
21. 9 Men on horseback, **two** by two.
29. 1 Let another year or **two** come and go, with its feasts and
37.38 his god Nisroch, **two** of his sons, Adrammelech and Sharezer,

Jer 2.13 and astonished, [13]for my people have committed **two** sins:
3.14 you from each town and **two** from each clan, and I will
24. 1 The Lord showed me **two** baskets of figs placed in front of
28. 3 Within **two** years I will bring back to this place all the
28.11 and he will do this within **two** years."
33.24 I have rejected Israel and Judah, the **two** families that I chose?
34.18 the two halves of a bull that they had cut in **two.**
39. 4 through the gateway connecting the **two** walls, and escaped in
52. 7 through the gateway connecting the **two** walls, and fled in
52.20 for the Temple—the **two** columns, the carts, the large tank,
52.21 The **two** columns were identical:

Ezek 1. 9 **Two** wings of each creature were spread out so that the
1.11 **Two** wings of each creature were raised so that they
1.11 and their other **two** wings were folded against their bodies.
1.23 the creatures, each stretching out **two** wings towards the ones
1.23 next to it and covering its body with the other **two** wings.
4.11 have a limited amount of water to drink, **two** cups a day.
11. 1 Azzur and Pelatiah son of Benaiah, **two** leaders of the nation.
19. 1 me to sing this song of sorrow for **two** princes of Israel:
21.19 man," he said, "mark out **two** roads by which the king of
23. 2 "Mortal man," he said, "there were once **two** sisters.
23.40 The **two** sisters would bathe and put on eye-shadow and jewellery.
23.49 And you **two** sisters—I will punish you for your
35.10 "You said that the **two** nations, Judah and Israel,
37.17 Then hold the **two** sticks end to end in your hand so
37.19 Out of the **two** I will make one stick and hold it
37.20 "Hold in your hand the **two** sticks and let the people
37.22 be divided into **two** nations or split into two kingdoms.
40. 7 and the walls between them were **two** and a half metres thick.
40.19 distance between the **two** gateways, and it was fifty metres.
40.23 between these **two** gateways, and it was fifty metres.
40.39 room there were four tables, **two** on each side of the room.
40.40 there were four similar tables, **two** on either side of the
40.44 There were **two** rooms opening on the inner courtyard, one
40.48 it was **two** and a half metres deep and seven metres wide,
40.49 There were **two** columns, one on each side of the entrance.
41. 2 five metres wide, with walls **two** and a half metres thick on
41. 5 the Temple, was a series of small rooms **two** metres wide.
41. 7 the outside of the rooms, **two** wide stairways were built, so
41. 8 outside wall of these rooms was **two** and a half metres thick;
41. 8 that there was a terrace **two** and a half metres wide all
41.12 its walls were **two** and a half metres thick all round.
41.18 Each creature had **two** faces:
42. 9 Below these **two** rooms at the east end of the building,
43.14 edge fifty centimetres all round, and was **two** metres high.
43.15 which the sacrifices were burnt, was also **two** metres high.
45. 6 a half kilometres long and **two** and a half kilometres wide,
46.14 Also an offering of **two** kilogrammes of flour is to be
47.13 tribes, with the tribe of Joseph receiving **two** sections.
48.15 and a half kilometres by **two** and a half kilometres, is not
48.18 holy area—five kilometres by **two** and a half kilometres on
48.18 east and five kilometres by **two** and a half kilometres on the

Dan 6. 2 addition, he chose Daniel and **two** others to supervise the
8. 3 saw a ram that had **two** long horns, one of which was
8. 7 so angry that he smashed into him and broke the **two** horns.
8.20 ram you saw that had **two** horns represents the kingdoms of
11.27 Then the **two** kings will sit down to eat at the same
12. 5 Then I saw **two** men standing by a river, one on each

Hos 6. 2 In **two** or three days he will revive us, and we will
12. 3 twin brother Esau while the **two** of them were still in their

Amos 1. 1 **Two** years before the earthquake, when Uzziah was king of
3. 3 Do **two** men start travelling together without arranging to meet?
3.12 "As a shepherd recovers only **two** legs or an ear of a

Zech 4. 3 There are **two** olive-trees beside the lamp-stand, one on
4.11 asked him, "What do the **two** olive-trees on either side of
4.12 is the meaning of the **two** olive branches
4.12 beside the **two** gold pipes from which the olive-oil
4.14 he said, "These are the **two** men whom God has chosen and
5. 9 I looked up and saw **two** women flying towards me with
6. 1 I saw four chariots coming out from between **two** bronze mountains.
11. 7 I took **two** sticks:
14. 4 Olives will be split in **two** from east to west by a
14. 5 You will escape through this valley that divides the mountain in **two.**

Mt 2.16 and its neighbourhood who were **two** years old and younger—

Mt 4.18 of Lake Galilee, he saw **two** brothers who were fishermen, Simon
4.21 He went on and saw **two** other brothers, James and John,
5.41 to carry his pack one kilometre, carry it **two** kilometres.
6.24 "No one can be a slave of **two** masters;
8.28 lake, he was met by **two** men who came out of the
9.27 and as he walked along, **two** blind men started following him.
9.28 Jesus had gone indoors, the **two** blind men came to him,
10.29 a penny you can buy **two** sparrows, yet not one sparrow falls
14.17 "All we have here are five loaves and **two** fish,"
14.19 the five loaves and the **two** fish, looked up to heaven, and
18.16 to you, take one or **two** other persons with you, so that
18.16 upheld by the testimony of **two** or more witnesses,' as the
18.19 **two** of you on earth agree about anything you pray for,
18.20 For where **two** or three come together in my name, I am
19. 5 and unite with his wife, and the **two** will become one.'
19. 6 So they are no longer **two,** but one.
20.20 came to Jesus with her **two** sons, bowed before him, and asked
20.21 answered, "Promise me that these **two** sons of mine will sit
20.24 heard about this, they became angry with the **two** brothers.
20.30 **Two** blind men who were sitting by the road heard that
21. 1 There Jesus sent **two** of the disciples on ahead
21.28 There was once a man who had **two** sons.
21.31 Which one of the **two** did what his father wanted?"
22.40 the teachings of the prophets depend on these **two** commandments."
24.40 At that time **two** men will be working in a field:
24.41 **Two** women will be at a mill grinding meal:
25.32 he will divide them into **two** groups, just as a shepherd
26. 2 said to his disciples, [2]"In **two** days, as you know, it will
26.37 He took with him Peter and the **two** sons of Zebedee.
26.60 Finally **two** men stepped up [61]and said, "This man said, 'I
27.21 crowd, "Which one of these **two** do you want me to set
27.38 Then they crucified **two** bandits with Jesus, one on his right
27.51 hanging in the Temple was torn in **two** from top to bottom.

Mk 1.16 Lake Galilee, he saw **two** fishermen, Simon and his brother Andrew,
1.19 little farther on and saw **two** other brothers, James and John,
6. 7 the twelve disciples together and sent them out **two** by two.
6.38 found out, they told him, "Five loaves and also **two** fish."
6.41 the five loaves and the **two** fish, looked up to heaven, and
6.41 He also divided the **two** fish among them all.
10. 8 and unite with his wife, [8]and the **two** will become one.'
10. 8 So they are no longer **two,** but one.
11. 1 Jesus sent **two** of his disciples on ahead
12.31 There is no other commandment more important than these **two."**
12.33 more important to obey these **two** commandments than to offer
12.42 came along and dropped in **two** little copper coins, worth about
14. 1 It was now **two** days before the Festival of Passover
14.13 Then Jesus sent **two** of them with these instructions:
15.27 They also crucified **two** bandits with Jesus, one on his right
15.32 And the **two** who were crucified with Jesus insulted him also.
15.38 hanging in the Temple was torn in **two,** from top to bottom.
16.12 in a different manner to **two** of them while they were on

Lk 2.24 a pair of doves or **two** young pigeons, as required by the
3.11 He answered, "Whoever has **two** shirts must give one to
5. 2 He saw **two** boats pulled up on the beach;
7.18 all these things, he called **two** of them [19]and sent them to
7.41 "There were **two** men who owed money to a money-lender,"
9.13 They answered, "All we have are five loaves and **two** fish.
9.16 took the five loaves and **two** fish, looked up to heaven,
9.30 Suddenly **two** men were there talking with him.
9.32 saw Jesus' glory and the **two** men who were standing with him.
10. 1 sent them out two by **two,** to go ahead of him
10.35 next day he took out **two** silver coins and gave them to
12. 6 "Aren't five sparrows sold for **two** pennies?
12.14 right to judge or to divide the property between you **two?"**
12.52 will be divided, three against **two** and two against three.
15.11 on to say, "There was once a man who had **two** sons.
15.12 So the man divided his property between his **two** sons.
16.13 "No servant can be the slave of **two** masters;
17.34 tell you, there will be **two** people sleeping in the same bed:
17.35 **Two** women will be grinding corn together:
18.10 "Once there were **two** men who went up to the Temple to
18.12 I fast **two** days a week, and I give you a tenth
19.29 he sent **two** disciples ahead [30]with these instructions:
21. 2 saw a very poor widow dropping in **two** little copper coins.
22.38 Here are **two** swords, Lord!"
23.32 **Two** other men, both of them criminals, were also led out
23.33 crucified Jesus there, and the **two** criminals, one on his right
23.45 and the curtain hanging in the Temple was torn in **two.**
24. 4 when suddenly **two** men in bright shining clothes stood
24.13 On that same day **two** of Jesus' followers were going to a
24.35 The **two** then explained to them what had happened on the road,
24.36 the **two** were telling them this, suddenly the Lord himself stood

Jn 1.35 standing there again with **two** of his disciples, [36]when he saw
1.37 The **two** disciples heard him say this and went with Jesus.
2. 1 **Two** days later there was a wedding in the town of Cana
4.40 him to stay with them, and Jesus stayed there **two** days.
4.43 After spending **two** days there, Jesus left and went to Galilee.
6. 9 boy here who has five loaves of barley bread and **two** fish.
8.17 in your Law that when **two** witnesses agree, what they say is
11. 6 Lazarus was ill, he stayed where he was for **two** more days.
12.22 and told Andrew, and the **two** of them went and told Jesus.
19.18 and they also crucified **two** other men, one on each side,
19.40 The **two** men took Jesus' body and wrapped it in linen
20. 4 The **two** of them were running, but the other disciple ran
20.12 the tomb [12]and saw **two** angels there dressed in white, sitting
21. 2 the sons of Zebedee, and **two** other disciples of Jesus were

Acts 1.10 as he went away, when **two** men dressed in white suddenly
1.23 So they proposed **two** men:
1.24 show us which of these **two** you have chosen [25]to serve as
1.26 lots to choose between the **two** men, and the one chosen was
4. 2 were annoyed because the **two** apostles were teaching the people
7.26 The next day he saw **two** Israelites fighting, and he
7.29 There he had **two** sons.
9.38 was in Lydda, they sent **two** men to him with the message,
10. 7 went away, and Cornelius called **two** of his house servants
11.26 for a whole year the **two** met with the people of the
12. 6 him out to the people, Peter was sleeping between **two** guards.
12. 6 He was tied with **two** chains, and there were guards on duty
15.22 They chose **two** men who were highly respected by the believers,
19.10 This went on for **two** years, so that all the people who
19.22 he sent Timothy and Erastus, **two** of his helpers, to Macedonia,
19.29 seized Gaius and Aristarchus, **two** Macedonians who were travelling
19.34 Jew, they all shouted together the same thing for **two** hours:
21.33 Paul, arrested him, and ordered him to be bound with **two** chains.
23.23 Then the commander called **two** of his officers and said,
24.27 **two** years had passed, Porcius Festus succeeded Felix as governor.
28.13 from the south, and in **two** days we came to the town
28.30 For **two** years Paul lived in a place he rented for himself,

Rom 5.15 But the **two** are not the same, because God's free gift is
9.10 For Rebecca's **two** sons had the same father, our ancestor Isaac.
9.21 he wishes, and to make **two** pots from the same lump of

1 Cor 4. 6 Apollos and me, using the **two** of us as an example,
6.16 The scripture says quite plainly, "The **two** will become one body."
7.34 and so he is pulled in **two** directions.
14.27 to speak in strange tongues, **two** or three at the most should
14.29 **Two** or three who are given God's message should speak,

2 Cor 13. 1 upheld by the evidence of **two** or more witnesses"—

Gal 1.18 information from Peter, and I stayed with him for **two** weeks.
3.15 when **two** people agree on a matter and sign an agreement,
4.22 It says that Abraham had **two** sons, one by a slave-woman,
4.24 the **two** women represent two covenants.
5.17 These **two** are enemies, and this means that you cannot do

Eph 2.15 to create out of the **two** races one new people in union
5.31 and unite with his wife, and the **two** will become one."

Phil 1.23 I am pulled in **two** directions.

1 Tim 5.19 an elder unless it is brought by **two** or more witnesses.

2 Tim 2.17 **Two** men who have taught such things are Hymenaeus and Philetus.

Tit 3.10 Give at least **two** warnings to the person who causes divisions,

Heb 6.18 There are these **two** things, then, that cannot change
9. 4 and the **two** stone tablets with the commandments written
10.28 when judged guilty on the evidence of **two** or more witnesses.
11.37 they were sawn in **two,** they were killed by the sword.

2 Pet 3. 8 to him the **two** are the same.

Rev 9.12 after this there are still **two** more horrors to come.
11. 3 I will send my **two** witnesses dressed in sackcloth, and they
11. 4 The **two** witnesses are the two olive-trees and
11. 4 the **two** lamps that stand before the Lord
11.10 the earth will be happy because of the death of these **two.**
11.10 because those **two** prophets brought much suffering upon mankind.
11.12 Then the **two** prophets heard a loud voice say to them
12.14 She was given the **two** wings of a large eagle in order
13.11 It had **two** horns like a lamb's horns, and it spoke like
14. 9 third angel followed the first **two,** saying in a loud voice,
14.20 a flood three hundred kilometres long and nearly **two** metres deep.

also Ex 38.18 Num 7.12 1 Chr 24.7 1 Chr 25.9 Ezra 8.26

TWO THIRDS

Zech 13. 8 and throughout the land **two-thirds** of the people will die.

TWO-EDGED

see also **DOUBLE-EDGED**

Rev 1.16 hand, and a sharp **two-edged** sword came out of his mouth.
2.12 the message from the one who has the sharp **two-edged** sword.

TYPE

1 Chr 25. 1 with the **type** of service that each group performed:

TYRANT

Job 6.23 on my behalf [23]or to save me from some enemy or **tyrant?**

Ps 37.35 I once knew a wicked man who was a **tyrant;**

Prov 28.16 A ruler without good sense will be a cruel **tyrant.**

Is 19. 4 the Egyptians over to a **tyrant,** to a cruel king who will
49.24 Can you rescue the prisoners of a **tyrant?**
49.25 will be taken away, and the **tyrant's** loot will be seized.

Zech 9. 8 I will not allow **tyrants** to oppress my people any more.

TYRE

Important sea-port on the e. Mediterranean coast of Palestine.

Josh 19.29 The border then turned to Ramah, reaching the fortified city of **Tyre;**

2 Sam 5.11 King Hiram of **Tyre** sent a trade mission to David;
24. 7 to the fortified city of **Tyre,** on to all the cities of

1 Kgs 5. 1 King Hiram of **Tyre** had always been a friend of David's,
7.13 living in the city of **Tyre,** who was skilled in bronze work.
7.14 no longer living, was from **Tyre,** and had also been a skilled
9.11 King Hiram of **Tyre** had provided him with all the cedar

1 Chr 14. 1 King Hiram of **Tyre** sent a trade mission to David;
22. 4 arranged for the people of **Tyre** and Sidon to bring him a

2 Chr 2. 3 Solomon sent a message to King Hiram of **Tyre:**
2.14 the tribe of Dan and his father was a native of **Tyre.**

Ezra 3. 7 sent to the cities of **Tyre** and Sidon in exchange for

Neh 13.16 men from the city of **Tyre** were living in Jerusalem, and they

Ps 45.12 The people of **Tyre** will bring you gifts;
83. 7 the people of Gebal, Ammon, and Amalek, and of Philistia and **Tyre.**
87. 4 the inhabitants of Jerusalem the people of Philistia, **Tyre,**
Is 23. 1 This is a message about **Tyre.**
23. 1 Your home port of **Tyre** has been destroyed;
23. 5 and dismayed when they learn that **Tyre** has been destroyed.
23. 7 Can this be the joyful city of **Tyre,** founded so long ago?
23. 8 to bring all this on **Tyre,** that imperial city, whose
23.13 not the Assyrians, who let the wild animals overrun **Tyre.**
23.13 the fortifications of **Tyre,** and left the city in ruins.
23.15 A time is coming when **Tyre** will be forgotten for seventy years,
23.15 When those years are over, **Tyre** will be like the prostitute
23.17 over, the Lord will let **Tyre** go back to her old trade,
Jer 25.19 all the kings of **Tyre** and Sidon;
27. 3 kings of Edom, Moab, Ammon, **Tyre,** and Sidon through their
47. 4 Philistia, to cut off from **Tyre** and Sidon all the help that
Ezek 26. 2 is what the people in the city of **Tyre** are cheering about.
26. 3 I am your enemy, city of **Tyre.**
26. 5 The nations will plunder **Tyre,** [6]and with their swords they
26. 6 Then **Tyre** will know that I am the Lord."
26. 7 king of all—King Nebuchadnezzar of Babylonia—to attack **Tyre.**
26.15 The Sovereign Lord has this to say to the city of **Tyre:**
27. 2 sing a funeral song for **Tyre,** [3]that city which stands at
27. 3 **Tyre,** you boasted of your perfect beauty.
27.32 can be compared to Tyre, To **Tyre** now silent in the sea?
28. 2 said, "tell the ruler of **Tyre** what I, the Sovereign Lord,
28.12 "grieve for the fate that is waiting for the king of **Tyre.**
29.18 "King Nebuchadnezzar of Babylonia launched an attack on **Tyre.**
Joel 3. 4 trying to do to me, **Tyre,** Sidon, and all the regions of
Amos 1. 9 Lord says, "The people of **Tyre** have sinned again and again,
1.10 upon the city walls of **Tyre** and burn down its fortresses."
Zech 9. 2 so do the cities of **Tyre** and Sidon, with all their skill.
9. 3 **Tyre** has built fortifications for herself and has piled up
Mt 11.21 had been performed in **Tyre** and Sidon, the people there would
11.22 more mercy to the people of **Tyre** and Sidon than to you!
15.21 went off to the territory near the cities of **Tyre** and Sidon.
Mk 3. 8 Jordan, and from the region round the cities of **Tyre** and Sidon.
7.24 left and went away to the territory near the city of **Tyre.**
7.31 then left the neighbourhood of **Tyre** and went on through
Lk 6.17 Jerusalem and from the coastal cities of **Tyre** and Sidon;
10.13 had been performed in **Tyre** and Sidon, the people there would
10.14 more mercy on Judgement Day to **Tyre** and Sidon than to you.
Acts 12.20 angry with the people of **Tyre** and Sidon, so they went in
21. 3 We went ashore at **Tyre,** where the ship was going to unload
21. 7 our voyage, sailing from **Tyre** to Ptolemais, where we greeted the

UGLY

1 Cor 15.43 When buried, it is **ugly** and weak;

UMBILICAL CORD

Ezek 16. 4 born, no one cut your **umbilical cord** or washed you or rubbed

UN-

Where not listed below, see under main part of word. e.g. for "unnecessary" see NECESSARY

UNAUTHORIZED

Lev 22.16 offerings [16]by letting any **unauthorized** person eat them;

UNBELIEVER

Mt 17.17 Jesus answered, "How **unbelieving** and wrong you people are!
Mk 9.19 Jesus said to them, "How **unbelieving** you people are!
Lk 9.41 Jesus answered, "How **unbelieving** and wrong you people are!
Rom 11.23 if the Jews abandon their **unbelief,** they will be put back in
15.31 be kept safe from the **unbelievers** in Judaea and that my
1 Cor 6. 6 to court against another and lets **unbelievers** judge the case!
7.12 a wife who is an **unbeliever** and she agrees to go on
7.13 a man who is an **unbeliever** and he agrees to go on
7.14 the **unbelieving** husband is made acceptable to God by being united
7.14 to his wife, and the **unbelieving** wife is made acceptable to
10.27 If an **unbeliever** invites you to a meal and you decide to
14.22 strange tongues is proof for **unbelievers,** not for believers,
14.22 message is proof for believers, not for **unbelievers.**
14.23 if some ordinary people or **unbelievers** come in, won't they say
14.24 proclaiming God's message when some **unbeliever** or ordinary person
2 Cor 6.14 to work together as equals with **unbelievers,** for it cannot be
6.15 What does a believer have in common with an **unbeliever?**
1 Tim 5. 8 he has denied the faith and is worse than an **unbeliever.**
Tit 1.15 who are defiled and **unbelieving,** for their minds and consciences
Heb 3.12 a heart so evil and **unbelieving** that he will turn away from
3 Jn 7 the service of Christ without accepting any help from **unbelievers.**

UNBREAKABLE
see also **BREAK**

Num 18.19 This is an **unbreakable** covenant that I have made with you
2 Chr 13. 5 God of Israel, made an **unbreakable** covenant with David,

UNBROKEN
see also **BREAK**

1 Sam 20.16 may our promise to each other still be **unbroken.**

UNCERTAIN see CERTAIN (1)

UNCIRCUMCISED see CIRCUMCISE

UNCLE

Gen 28. 2 one of the girls there, one of your **uncle** Laban's daughters.
29.10 Jacob saw Rachel with his **uncle** Laban's flock, he went to
Lev 10. 4 the sons of Uzziel, Aaron's **uncle,** and said to them, "Come
18.14 Do not have intercourse with your **uncle's** wife;
20.20 intercourse with his **uncle's** wife, he disgraces his uncle,
25.49 of his brothers [49]or his **uncle** or his cousin or another of
Num 27.11 he has no brothers or **uncles,** then his nearest relative is
1 Sam 10.14 Saul's **uncle** saw him and the servant, and he asked them,
10.15 Saul's **uncle** asked.
10.16 he did not tell his **uncle** what Samuel had said about his
14.50 commander was his cousin Abner, the son of his **uncle** Ner.
2 Kgs 24.17 Nebuchadnezzar made Jehoiachin's **uncle** Mattaniah king
1 Chr 27.32 Jonathan, King David's **uncle,** was a skilful adviser and a scholar.
2 Chr 36.10 Nebuchadnezzar made Jehoiachin's **uncle** Zedekiah king of Judah
Jer 32. 7 told me [7]that Hanamel, my **uncle** Shallum's son, would come

UNCLEAN

Gen 7. 2 animal, but only one pair of each kind of **unclean** animal.
7. 8 ritually clean or **unclean,** [9]went into the boat with Noah,
Lev 5. 2 touches anything ritually **unclean,** such as a dead animal,
5. 2 he is **unclean** and guilty as soon as he
5. 3 of human origin that is **unclean,** whatever it may be, he is
7.18 credit but will be considered **unclean,** and whoever eats it
7.19 with anything ritually **unclean,** it must not be eaten,
7.21 he has touched anything ritually **unclean,** whether from a man
10.10 use, between what is ritually clean and what is **unclean.**
11. 4 They must be considered **unclean;**
11. 7 They must be considered **unclean;**
11. 8 they are **unclean.**
11.11 Such creatures must be considered **unclean.**
11.20 All winged insects are **unclean,** [21]except those that hop.
11.23 that have wings and also crawl must be considered **unclean.**
11.24 bodies of the following animals will be **unclean** until evening:
11.24 wash his clothes, but he will still be **unclean** until evening.
11.29 Moles, rats, mice, and lizards must be considered **unclean.**
11.31 touches them or their dead bodies will be **unclean** until evening.
11.32 And if their dead bodies fall on anything, it will be **unclean.**
11.32 dipped in water, but it will remain **unclean** until evening.
11.33 is in it shall be **unclean,** and you must break the pot.
11.34 and anything drinkable in such a pot is **unclean.**
11.35 Anything on which the dead bodies fall is **unclean;**
11.36 anything else that touches their dead bodies is **unclean.**
11.38 water and one of them falls on it, the seed is **unclean.**
11.39 dies, anyone who touches it will be **unclean** until evening.
11.40 his clothes, but he will still be **unclean** until evening;
11.40 his clothes, but he will still be **unclean** until evening.
11.43 Do not make yourselves **unclean** by eating any of these.
11.47 what is ritually clean and **unclean,** between animals that may
12. 2 a son, she is ritually **unclean,** as she is during her monthly
12. 5 a daughter, she is ritually **unclean,** as she is during her
13. 3 and the priest shall pronounce the person **unclean.**
13. 8 again, and if it has spread, he shall pronounce him **unclean;**
13.11 The priest shall pronounce him **unclean;**
13.11 is no need to isolate him, because he is obviously **unclean.**
13.14 But from the moment an open sore appears, he is **unclean.**
13.15 and if he sees an open sore, he shall pronounce him **unclean.**
13.15 An open sore means a dreaded skin-disease, and the person is **unclean.**
13.20 in it have turned white, he shall pronounce him **unclean.**
13.22 If the spot spreads, the priest shall pronounce him **unclean;**
13.25 in the burn, and the priest shall pronounce him **unclean.**
13.27 skin-disease, and the priest shall pronounce him **unclean.**
13.30 skin-disease, and he shall pronounce the person **unclean.**
13.36 the person is obviously **unclean.**
13.40 or the front of his head, this does not make him **unclean.**
13.44 the priest shall pronounce him **unclean,** because of the
13.45 lower part of his face, and call out, **"Unclean,** unclean!"
13.46 He remains **unclean** as long as he has the disease, and he
13.51 day, and if the mildew has spread, the object is **unclean.**
13.55 colour, even though it has not spread, it is still **unclean;**
13.59 is made as to whether it is ritually clean or **unclean.**
14.36 otherwise everything in the house will be declared **unclean.**
14.40 removed and thrown into some **unclean** place outside the city.
14.41 and the plaster dumped in an **unclean** place outside the city.
14.44 If it has spread, the house is **unclean.**
14.45 plaster must be carried out of the city to an **unclean** place.
14.46 house while it is locked up will be **unclean** until evening.
14.57 laws determine when something is **unclean** and when it is clean.
15. 2 his penis, the discharge is **unclean,** [3]whether the penis
15. 4 Any bed on which he sits or lies is **unclean.**
15. 6 and have a bath, and he remains **unclean** until evening.
15. 7 and have a bath, and he remains **unclean** until evening.
15. 8 and have a bath, and he remains **unclean** until evening.
15. 9 or seat on which the man with the discharge sits is **unclean.**
15.10 anything on which the man sat is **unclean** until evening.
15.10 and have a bath, and he remains **unclean** until evening.
15.11 and have a bath, and he remains **unclean** until evening.
15.16 bathe his whole body, and he remains **unclean** until evening.
15.17 falls must be washed, and it remains **unclean** until evening.
15.18 must have a bath, and they remain **unclean** until evening.
15.19 has her monthly period, she remains **unclean** for seven days.
15.19 Anyone who touches her is **unclean** until evening.

Lev	15.20	which she sits or lies during her monthly period is **unclean.**
	15.21	and have a bath, and he remains **unclean** until evening.
	15.24	by her impurity and remains **unclean** for seven days,
	15.24	and any bed on which he lies is **unclean.**
	15.25	period, she remains **unclean** as long as the flow continues,
	15.26	and anything on which she sits during this time is **unclean.**
	15.27	Anyone who touches them is **unclean** and must wash his clothes
	15.27	he remains **unclean** until evening.
	15.31	people of Israel about their **uncleanness,** so that they would
	15.33	sexual intercourse with a woman who is ritually **unclean.**
	16.16	Most Holy Place from the **uncleanness** of the people of Israel
	16.16	stands in the middle of the camp, which is ritually **unclean.**
	18.19	during her monthly period, because she is ritually **unclean.**
	18.20	that would make you ritually **unclean.**
	18.23	that perversion makes you ritually **unclean.**
	18.24	Do not make yourselves **unclean** by any of these acts, for
	18.24	how the pagans made themselves **unclean,** those pagans who
	18.25	Their actions made the land **unclean,** and so the Lord is
	18.26	things and made the land **unclean,** but you must not do them.
	18.30	do not make yourselves **unclean** by doing any of these things.
	19. 7	because it is ritually **unclean,** and if anyone eats it,
	19.23	the fruit ritually **unclean** for the first three years.
	19.31	If you do, you will be ritually **unclean.**
	20. 3	and makes my sacred Tent **unclean** and disgraces my holy name,
	20.18	they have broken the regulations about ritual **uncleanness.**
	20.21	He has done a ritually **unclean** thing and has disgraced his brother.
	20.25	Do not eat **unclean** animals or birds.
	20.25	I have declared them **unclean,** and eating them would make you unclean.
	21. 1	is to make himself ritually **unclean** by taking part in the
	21. 4	He shall not make himself **unclean** at the death of those
	21.11	not to make himself ritually **unclean** nor is he to defile my
	21.15	his children, who ought to be holy, will be ritually **unclean.**
	22. 3	descendants, while he is ritually **unclean,** comes near the
	22. 4	Any priest is **unclean** if he touches anything which is unclean
	22. 5	of semen [5] or if he has touched an **unclean** animal or person.
	22. 6	Any priest who becomes **unclean** remains unclean until evening,
	22. 8	it will make him **unclean.**
	27.11	the vow concerns a ritually **unclean** animal, which is not
	27.27	but the first-born of an **unclean** animal may be bought
Num	5. 2	and everyone who is **unclean** by contact with a corpse.
	5. 3	Send all these ritually **unclean** people out, so that they
	9. 6	who were ritually **unclean** because they had touched a corpse,
	9. 7	"We are **unclean** because we have touched a corpse,
	9.10	you or your descendants are **unclean** from touching a corpse
	18.15	for every first-born animal that is ritually **unclean.**
	19. 7	but he remains ritually **unclean** until evening.
	19. 8	over himself, but he also remains **unclean** until evening.
	19. 9	to use in preparing the water for removing ritual **uncleanness.**
	19.10	must wash his clothes, but he remains **unclean** until evening.
	19.11	Whoever touches a corpse is ritually **unclean** for seven days.
	19.13	does not purify himself remains **unclean,** because the water
	19.14	or who enters it becomes ritually **unclean** for seven days.
	19.15	in the tent that has no lid on it also becomes **unclean.**
	19.16	a human bone or a grave, he becomes **unclean** for seven days.
	19.17	To remove the **uncleanness,** some ashes from the red cow
	19.19	clean is to sprinkle the water on the **unclean** person.
	19.20	Anyone who has become ritually **unclean** and
	19.20	does not purify himself remains **unclean,** because the water
	19.21	touches the water remains ritually **unclean** until evening.
	19.22	Whatever an **unclean** person touches is unclean,
	19.22	and anyone else who touches it remains **unclean** until evening.
Deut	12.15	you, whether ritually clean or **unclean,** may eat them, just
	12.22	Anyone, ritually clean or **unclean,** may eat that meat,
	14. 3	"Do not eat anything that the Lord has declared **unclean.**
	14. 7	They must be considered **unclean;**
	14. 8	They must be considered **unclean;**
	14.10	it must be considered **unclean.**
	14.19	"All winged insects are **unclean;**
	15.22	you, whether ritually clean or **unclean,** may eat them, just
	23. 9	are to avoid anything that would make you ritually **unclean.**
	23.10	If a man becomes **unclean** because he has had a wet dream
	26.14	any of it out of my house when I was ritually **unclean;**
2 Chr	23.19	temple gates to keep out anyone who was ritually **unclean.**
	26.21	King Uzziah was ritually **unclean** because of his disease.
	29.16	the temple courtyard everything that was ritually **unclean.**
Job	14. 4	Nothing clean can ever come from anything as **unclean** as man.
Jer	19.13	to other gods—they will all be as **unclean** as Topheth."
	50.39	be haunted by demons and evil spirits, and by **unclean** birds.
Lam	1. 9	Her **uncleanness** was easily seen, but she showed no concern
Ezek	4.14	I have never eaten any food considered **unclean."**
	8.10	drawings of snakes and other **unclean** animals, and of the
	20. 7	not to make themselves **unclean** with the false gods of Egypt,
	22.26	clean and **unclean** things, and they ignore the Sabbath.
	36.17	behaviour as being as ritually **unclean** as a woman is during
	39.24	they deserved for their **uncleanness** and their wickedness,
	44.25	is not to become ritually **unclean** by touching a corpse,
Dan	1. 8	to let himself become ritually **unclean** by eating the food
Mt	15.11	goes into a person's mouth that makes him ritually **unclean;**
	15.11	rather, what comes out of it makes him **unclean."**
	15.18	and these are the things that make a person ritually **unclean.**
	15.20	These are the things that make a person **unclean.**
	15.20	as they say you should—this doesn't make a person **unclean."**
Mk	7. 2	hands that were ritually **unclean**—that is, they had not washed
	7. 5	by our ancestors, but instead eat with ritually **unclean** hands?"
	7.15	person from the outside which can make him ritually **unclean.**
	7.15	it is what comes out of a person that makes him **unclean."**
	7.18	outside can really make him **unclean,** [19] because it does not go
	7.20	"It is what comes out of a person that makes him **unclean.**
	7.23	things come from inside a person and make him **unclean."**
Acts	10.14	I have never eaten anything ritually **unclean** or defiled."
	10.15	"Do not consider anything **unclean** that God has declared clean."
	10.28	that I must not consider any person ritually **unclean** or defiled.
	11. 8	No ritually **unclean** or defiled food has ever entered my mouth.'
	11. 9	'Do not consider anything **unclean** that God has declared clean.'
	15.20	any food that is ritually **unclean** because it has been
Rom	14.14	Jesus makes me certain that no food is of itself ritually **unclean;**
	14.14	believes that some food is **unclean,**
	14.14	then it becomes **unclean** for him.
2 Cor	6.17	nothing to do with what is **unclean,** and I will accept you.
	7. 1	that makes body or soul **unclean,** and let us be completely
Heb	9.13	people who are ritually **unclean,** and this purifies them by taking
Rev	16.13	Then I saw three **unclean spirits** that looked like frogs.
	18. 2	She is now haunted by demons and **unclean spirits;**

UNCOMBED see COMB (1)

UNCONDITIONAL

Lev	27.28	buy back what he has **unconditionally** dedicated to the Lord,
	27.29	who has been **unconditionally** dedicated may be bought back;
Num	18.14	**unconditionally** dedicated to me belongs to you.
	21. 2	conquer these people, we will **unconditionally** dedicate them

UNCONSCIOUS

Dan	8.18	While he was talking, I fell to the ground **unconscious.**
	10. 9	I fell to the ground **unconscious** and lay there face downwards.

UNCONTROLLABLE see CONTROL

UNCOOKED

Lev	7.10	But all **uncooked** grain-offerings, whether mixed with oil or dry,

UNCOVER

Gen	44.16	God has **uncovered** our guilt.
2 Sam	22.16	foundations of the earth were **uncovered** when the Lord
Esth	6. 2	account of how Mordecai had **uncovered** a plot to assassinate
Ps	18.15	of the earth were **uncovered,** when you rebuked your enemies,
Jer	49.10	Esau's descendants completely and **uncovered** their hiding places,
Mt	10.26	now covered up will be **uncovered,** and every secret will be
Mk	4.22	into the open, and whatever is covered up will be **uncovered.**
Lk	12. 2	is covered up will be **uncovered,** and every secret will be
2 Cor	3.18	then, reflect the glory of the Lord with **uncovered** faces;

UNCUT

Deut	27. 6	build for the Lord your God must be made of **uncut** stones.

UNDERFOOT

Is	28. 3	The pride of those drunken leaders will be trampled **underfoot.**
Mic	7.19	You will trample our sins **underfoot** and send them to the
Mt	7. 6	in front of pigs—they will only trample them **underfoot.**

UNDERGROUND

Deut	8. 7	has rivers and springs, and **underground** streams gushing out
Jer	37.16	I was put in an **underground** cell and kept there a long
Ezek	26.20	make you stay in that **underground** world among eternal ruins,
	31. 4	water to make it grow, And **underground** rivers to feed it.
	31.15	dead, I will make the **underground** waters cover it as a sign

UNDERNEATH

1 Kgs	7.29	on the frames, above and **underneath** the lions and bulls,
Job	28. 5	out of the earth, But **underneath** the same earth All is torn
Rev	6. 9	I saw **underneath** the altar the souls of those who had been

UNDERPRIVILEGED
see also **PRIVILEGE**

Ezek	16.49	they did not take care of the poor and the **underprivileged.**

UNDERSTAND

Gen	3. 7	were given **understanding** and realized that they were naked;
	11. 7	language so that they will not **understand** one another."
	28. 8	Esau then **understood** that his father Isaac did not approve
	42.23	Joseph **understood** what they said, but they did not know it,
Ex	31. 3	I have given him **understanding,** skill, and ability for every
	35.31	ability, and **understanding** for every kind of artistic work,
	36. 1	Lord has given skill and **understanding,** who know how to make
Deut	1.13	Choose some wise, **understanding,** and experienced men
	4. 6	say, 'What wisdom and **understanding** this great nation has!'
	29. 4	day he has not let you **understand** what you have experienced.
	32.29	they cannot **understand** what happened.
1 Sam	28. 1	to David, "Of course you **understand** that you and your men
2 Sam	3.37	all the people in Israel **understood** that the king had no
	12.21	"We don't **understand** this," his officials said to him.
1 Kgs	3.12	give you more wisdom and **understanding** than anyone has ever
2 Kgs	18.26	We **understand** it.
	20.19	King Hezekiah **understood** this to mean that there would
2 Chr	2.12	a wise son, full of **understanding** and skill, who now plans
Neh	8. 2	women, and the children who were old enough to **understand.**
	8. 8	God's Law and explained it so that the people could **understand** it.
	8.12	others, because they **understood** what had been read to them.

Neh 10.28 our children old enough to **understand,** [29] do hereby join
Job 5. 9 We cannot **understand** the great things he does, and to his
9.10 We cannot **understand** the great things he does, and to
13. 1 I **understand** it all;
22.18 prosperous— I can't **understand** the thoughts of the wicked.
24.13 they don't **understand** it or go where it leads.
28.12 Where can we learn to **understand?**
28.20 Where can we learn to **understand?**
28.28 To **understand,** you must turn from evil."
34.10 Listen to me, you men who **understand!**
36. 5 there is nothing he doesn't **understand.**
37. 5 amazing things happen, wonderful things that we can't **understand.**
42. 3 about things I did not **understand,** about marvels too great
Ps 10. 5 He cannot **understand** God's judgements;
19. 8 of the Lord are just and give **understanding** to the mind.
71.15 of your salvation, though it is more than I can **understand.**
73.17 Then I **understood** what will happen to the wicked.
73.22 I did not **understand** you.
92. 6 a stupid man cannot **understand:**
106. 7 Our ancestors in Egypt did not **understand** God's wonderful acts;
111. 2 All who are delighted with them want to **understand** them.
119.27 Help me to **understand** your laws, and I will meditate on
119.32 your commands, because you will give me more **understanding.**
119.70 These men have no **understanding,** but I find pleasure in your law.
119.73 give me **understanding,** so that I may learn your laws.
119.99 I **understand** more than all my teachers, because I
119.125 give me **understanding,** so that I may know your teachings.
119.144 give me **understanding,** and I shall live.
119.169 Give me **understanding,** as you have promised.
139. 2 from far away you **understand** all my thoughts.
139. 6 it is beyond my **understanding.**
145. 3 his greatness is beyond **understanding.**
Prov 1. 2 and good advice, and **understand** sayings with deep meaning.
1. 6 educated, [6] so that they can **understand** the hidden meanings
2. 2 Listen to what is wise and try to **understand** it.
2. 6 from him come knowledge and **understanding.**
2.11 Your insight and **understanding** will protect you
3.13 Happy is the man who becomes wise—who gains **understanding.**
4. 1 Pay attention, and you will have **understanding.**
4.22 They will give life and health to anyone who **understands** them.
8.14 I have **understanding,** and I am strong.
9.10 If you know the Holy One, you have **understanding.**
16.21 A wise, mature person is known for his **understanding.**
18. 2 A fool does not care whether he **understands** a thing or not;
20.24 can anyone **understand** the direction his own life is taking?
24. 3 Homes are built on the foundation of wisdom and **understanding.**
24. 7 Wise sayings are too deep for a stupid person to **understand.**
28. 5 is, but those who worship the Lord **understand** it well.
29. 7 the poor, but wicked people cannot **understand** such things.
29.19 He may **understand** you, but he will pay no attention.
30.18 There are four things that are too mysterious for me to **understand:**
Ecc 3.11 us the satisfaction of fully **understanding** what he does.
7. 3 may sadden your face, but it sharpens your **understanding.**
7.24 It is too deep for us, too hard to **understand.**
8.17 day [17] and never be able to **understand** what God is doing.
11. 5 and you can no more **understand** what he does
11. 5 than you **understand** how new life begins
Is 1. 3 They don't **understand** at all."
5.12 But you don't **understand** what the Lord is doing, [13] and so
6. 9 "No matter how much you listen, you will not **understand.**
6.10 eyes blind, so that they cannot see or hear or **understand.**
27.11 Because the people have **understood** nothing, God their
28. 7 are too drunk to **understand** the visions that God sends,
29.24 Foolish people will learn to **understand,** and those who
32. 4 will act with **understanding** and will say what they mean.
33.19 foreigners who speak a language that you can't **understand.**
36.11 We **understand** it.
39. 8 King Hezekiah **understood** this to mean that there would be
40.14 in order to know and **understand** and to learn how things
40.28 No one **understands** his thoughts.
41.20 They will come to **understand** that Israel's holy God has made
43.10 and believe in me and **understand** that I am the only God.
50. 5 The Lord has given me **understanding,** and I have not
52.15 They will see and **understand** something they had never known."
56.11 These leaders have no **understanding.**
57. 1 Good people die, and no one **understands** or even cares.
Jer 3.15 me, and they will rule you with wisdom and **understanding.**
4.22 they have no **understanding.**
9.12 Who is wise enough to **understand** this?
9.24 he knows and **understands** me, because my love is constant,
15.15 Then I said, "Lord, you **understand.**
17. 9 "Who can **understand** the human heart?
23.18 them has ever heard or **understood** his message, or ever
23.20 In days to come his people will **understand** this clearly."
30.23 In days to come his people will **understand** this clearly.
Ezek 3. 6 languages you didn't **understand,** they would listen to you.
Dan 2.21 it is he who gives wisdom and **understanding.**
2.30 meaning of your dream and **understand** the thoughts that have
4. 9 holy gods is in you, and that you **understand** all mysteries.
8.15 I was trying to **understand** what the vision meant, when
8.17 He said to me, "Mortal man, **understand** the meaning.
8.27 I was puzzled by the vision and could not **understand** it.
9.22 "Daniel, I have come here to help you **understand** the prophecy.
9.25 Note this and **understand** it:
10. 1 The message was true but extremely hard to **understand.**
10.12 decided to humble yourself in order to gain **understanding.**
10.14 have come to make you **understand** what will happen to your
12. 4 their efforts trying to **understand** what is happening."
12. 8 I heard what he said, but I did not **understand** it.
Dan 12.10 are wicked will not **understand** but will go on being wicked;
12.10 only those who are wise will **understand.**
Hos 14. 9 May those who are wise **understand** what is written here,
Mt 13.13 do not see, and they listen, but do not hear or **understand.**
13.14 'This people will listen and listen, but not **understand;**
13.15 their minds would **understand,** and they would turn to me,
13.19 the Kingdom but do not **understand** it are like the seeds that
13.23 soil stand for those who hear the message and **understand** it:
13.51 "Do you **understand** these things?"
15.10 the crowd to him and said to them, "Listen and **understand!**
15.17 Don't you **understand?**
16. 9 Don't you **understand** yet?
16.11 is it that you don't **understand** that I was not talking to
16.12 the disciples **understood** that he was not warning them to guard
17.13 the disciples **understood** that he was talking to them about John
24.15 be sure to **understand** what this means!)
Mk 4.12 they may listen and listen, yet not **understand.**
4.13 Then Jesus asked them, "Don't you **understand** this parable?
4.13 How, then, will you ever **understand** any parable?
4.33 he told them as much as they could **understand.**
6.52 they had not **understood** the real meaning of the feeding
7.14 said to them, "Listen to me, all of you, and **understand.**
7.18 "Don't you **understand?**
8.17 Don't you know or **understand** yet?
8.21 "And you still don't **understand?"**
9.32 But they did not **understand** what this teaching meant,
13.14 be sure to **understand** what this means!)
14.68 I don't **understand** what you are talking about," he answered,
Lk 2.50 But they did not **understand** his answer.
8.10 they may look but not see, and listen but not **understand.**
9.45 so that they could not **understand** it, and they were afraid
18.34 But the disciples did not **understand** any of these things;
24.45 he opened their minds to **understand** the Scriptures,
Jn 6.26 and had all you wanted, not because you **understood** my miracles.
8.27 They did not **understand** that Jesus was talking to them about
8.43 Why do you not **understand** what I say?
10. 6 this parable, but they did not **understand** what he meant.
12.16 His disciples did not **understand** this at the time;
12.40 and their minds would not **understand,** and they would not
13. 7 answered him, "You do not **understand** now what I am doing,
13. 7 but you will **understand** later."
13.12 "Do you **understand** what I have just done to you?"
13.28 others at the table **understood** why Jesus said this to him.
20. 9 (They still did not **understand** the scripture which said that he
Acts 7.25 that his own people would **understand** that God was going to
7.25 use him to set them free, but they did not **understand.)**
8.30 He asked him, "Do you **understand** what you are reading?"
8.31 official replied, "How can I **understand** unless someone explains
10.19 Peter was still trying to **understand** what the vision meant,
13.27 the Saviour, nor did they **understand** the words of the prophets
28.26 You will listen and listen, but not **understand;**
28.27 their minds would **understand,** and they would turn to me,
Rom 7. 1 you will **understand** what I am about to say, my brothers,
7.15 I do not **understand** what I do;
10.19 Did the people of Israel not **understand?**
11.33 Who can **understand** his ways?
15.21 will see, and those who have not heard will **understand."**
1 Cor 1.19 of the wise and set aside the **understanding** of the scholars."
2.14 Such a person really does not **understand** them;
11. 3 But I want you to **understand** that Christ is supreme over
13. 2 I may have all knowledge and **understand** all secrets;
14. 2 speak to others but to God, because no one **understands** him.
14. 9 how will anyone **understand** what you are talking about if
14.19 five words that can be **understood,** in order to teach others,
2 Cor 1.13 We write to you only what you can read and **understand.**
1.13 But even though you now **understand** us only in part, I hope
1.13 that you will come to **understand** us completely, so that in
10.11 Such a person must **understand** that there is no difference
Gal 4.24 These things can be **understood** as a figure:
Eph 3. 4 you can learn about my **understanding** of the secret of Christ.)
3.18 may have the power to **understand** how broad and long, how
5.32 in this scripture, which I **understand** as applying to Christ and
Phil 4. 7 which is far beyond human **understanding,** will keep your hearts
Col 1. 9 with all the wisdom and **understanding** that his Spirit gives.
2. 2 the full wealth of assurance which true **understanding** brings.
2 Thes 3. 5 lead you into a greater **understanding** of God's love and the
1 Tim 1. 7 law, but they do not **understand** their own words or the
2 Tim 2. 7 because the Lord will enable you to **understand** it all.
Phlm 6 will bring about a deeper **understanding** of every blessing which
Heb 5.11 to explain to you, because you are so slow to **understand.**
11. 3 is by faith that we **understand** that the universe was created
Jas 3.13 Is there anyone among you who is wise and **understanding?**
1 Pet 1.12 These are things which even the angels would like to **understand.**
3. 7 wives with the proper **understanding** that they are the weaker sex.
2 Pet 2.12 they attack with insults anything they do not **understand.**
3. 3 First of all, you must **understand** that in these last days
1 Jn 5.20 come and has given us **understanding,** so that we know the
Jude 10 these people attack with insults anything they do not **understand;**
Rev 17. 9 "This calls for wisdom and **understanding.**

UNDIVIDED

1 Chr 28. 9 and to serve him with an **undivided** heart and a willing mind.

UNDO

Ecc 9.18 good than weapons, but one sinner can **undo** a lot of good.
Is 52. 2 **Undo** the chains that bind you, captive people of Zion!

UNDRESSED see DRESS

UNDYING

Eph 6.24 all those who love our Lord Jesus Christ with **undying** love.

UNENDING

Lam 2. 5 He has brought on the people of Judah **unending** sorrow.

UNFAILING

Ps 30. 9 Can they proclaim your **unfailing** goodness?
Is 63. 7 I will tell of the Lord's **unfailing** love;
Lam 3.22 The Lord's **unfailing** love and mercy still continue,
2 Thes 2.16 in his grace gave us **unfailing** courage and a firm hope,

UNFAITHFUL

Ex 34.16 would lead them to be **unfaithful** to me and to worship their
Lev 17. 7 Israel must no longer be **unfaithful** to the Lord by killing
20. 5 join him in being **unfaithful** to me and worshipping Molech.
Num 5. 6 When anyone is **unfaithful** to the Lord and commits a wrong
5.12 suspicious that his wife is **unfaithful** to him and has
5.12 of his wife, even though she has not been **unfaithful.**
14.33 forty years, suffering for your **unfaithfulness,** until the
31.16 and at Peor led the people to be **unfaithful** to the Lord.
Deut 31.16 death the people will become **unfaithful** to me and break the
32. 5 But you are **unfaithful,** unworthy to be his people, a
32.20 see what happens to them, those stubborn, **unfaithful** people.
32.51 because both of you were **unfaithful** to me in the
Judg 2.17 Israel was **unfaithful** to the Lord and worshipped other gods.
8.33 Israel were again **unfaithful** to God and worshipped the Baals.
1 Chr 5.25 But the people were **unfaithful** to the God of their
10.13 Saul died because he was **unfaithful** to the Lord.
2 Chr 21.13 Judah and Jerusalem into being **unfaithful** to God, just as
21.13 as Ahab and his successors led Israel into **unfaithfulness.**
29. 6 Our ancestors were **unfaithful** to the Lord our God and did
29.19 during those years he was **unfaithful** to God, and we have
30. 7 fellow-Israelites who were **unfaithful** to the Lord their God.
Ezra 10. 6 night there grieving over the **unfaithfulness** of the exiles.
Neh 1. 8 you people of Israel are **unfaithful** to me, I will scatter
Ps 73.27 you will destroy those who are **unfaithful** to you.
106.39 impure by their actions and were **unfaithful** to God.
Prov 23.28 for you like robbers and cause many men to be **unfaithful.**
30.20 This is how an **unfaithful** wife acts:
Is 54. 4 You will forget your **unfaithfulness** as a young wife, and
Jer 3. 6 to me, "Have you seen what Israel, that **unfaithful** woman,
3. 7 did not return, and her **unfaithful** sister Judah saw it all.
3. 8 But Judah, Israel's **unfaithful** sister, was not afraid.
3.10 after all this, Judah, Israel's **unfaithful** sister, only
3.11 from him, she had proved to be better than **unfaithful** Judah.
3.12 go and say to Israel, **"Unfaithful** Israel, come back to me.
3.14 **"Unfaithful** people, come back;
3.20 But like an **unfaithful** wife, you have not been faithful to me.
9. 2 They are all **unfaithful,** a mob of traitors.
23.10 The land is full of people **unfaithful** to the Lord;
49. 4 Why do you **unfaithful** people boast?
Ezek 5.13 spoken to you because I am outraged at your **unfaithfulness.**
14.13 a country sins and is **unfaithful** to me, I will stretch out
15. 8 They have been **unfaithful** to me, and so I will make the
16.20 it bad enough to be **unfaithful** to me, [21] without taking my
17.20 Babylonia and punish him there, because he was **unfaithful** to me.
18.24 He will die because of his **unfaithfulness** and his sins.
20.27 This is another way their fathers insulted me by their **unfaithfulness.**
Dan 9. 7 countries near and far because they were **unfaithful** to you.
Hos 1. 2 your wife will be **unfaithful,** and your children will be just
1. 2 In the same way, my people have left me and become **unfaithful."**
4.15 you people of Israel are **unfaithful** to me, may Judah not be
5. 3 She has been **unfaithful,** and her people are unfit to worship me."
5. 7 They have been **unfaithful** to the Lord;
9. 1 turned away from your God and have been **unfaithful** to him.
Mt 5.32 any cause other than her **unfaithfulness,** then he is guilty of
19. 9 any cause other than her **unfaithfulness** commits adultery if he
Jas 4. 4 **Unfaithful** people!

UNFIT see FIT (1)

AV UNFRUITFUL

1 Cor 14.14 my spirit prays indeed, but my mind has no **part** in it.
Eph 5.11 nothing to do with the **worthless** things that people do,
Tit 3.14 they should not live **useless** lives.
2 Pet 1. 8 make you active and **effective** in your knowledge of our Lord

UNGODLY

Ps 43. 1 O God, declare me innocent, and defend my cause against the **ungodly;**
Jer 23.15 because they have spread **ungodliness** throughout the land."
Ezek 31.18 of the dead and join the **ungodly** and those killed in battle.
32.19 to the world of the dead and lie there among the **ungodly.**
32.21 'The **ungodly** who were killed in battle have come down here,
Tit 2.12 instructs us to give up **ungodly** living and worldly passions,

AV UNGODLY
see also **GODLESS**

2 Sam 22. 5 the waves of **destruction** rolled over me.
2 Chr 19. 2 to help those who are **wicked** and to take the side of
Job 16.11 God has handed me over to **evil** men.
34.18 God condemns kings and rulers when they are **worthless**
Ps 1. 1 who reject the advice of **evil** men, who do not follow the
1. 4 But **evil** men are not like this at all;
1. 5 **Sinners** will be condemned by God and kept apart from God's
1. 6 by the Lord, but the **evil** are on the way to their
18. 4 the waves of **destruction** rolled over me.
73.12 That is what the **wicked** are like.
Prov 16.27 **Evil** people look for ways to harm others;
Rom 1.18 from heaven against all the **sin** and evil of the people
4. 5 the God who declares the **guilty** to be innocent, it is his
5. 6 Christ died for the **wicked** at the time that God chose.
11.26 from Zion and remove all **wickedness** from the descendants of Jacob.
2 Tim 2.16 foolish discussions, which only drive people further away **from God.**

UNHOLY

Lev 16. 1 were killed when they offered **unholy** fire to the Lord.
Num 3. 4 were killed when they offered **unholy** fire to the Lord in the
26.61 Nadab and Abihu died when they offered **unholy** fire to the Lord.
Neh 13.17 You're making the Sabbath **unholy.**
Ezek 21.25 "You wicked, **unholy** ruler of Israel, your day, the day
22.24 Israelites that their land is **unholy,** and so I am punishing

UNIFORM

1 Kgs 10. 5 his palace staff and the **uniforms** they wore,
2 Chr 9. 4 his palace staff and the **uniforms** they wore,
Ezek 23. 6 They were soldiers in **uniforms** of purple,
23.12 and officers—soldiers in bright **uniforms—**
38. 4 army, with its horses and **uniformed** riders, is enormous, and
Nah 2. 3 The enemy soldiers carry red shields and wear **uniforms** of red.

UNINTENTIONAL

Lev 5. 2 If someone **unintentionally** touches anything ritually unclean,
5. 3 **unintentionally** touches anything of human origin that is unclean,
5.15 If anyone sins **unintentionally** by failing to hand over
5.17 sins **unintentionally** by breaking any of the Lord's commands,
5.18 the man committed **unintentionally,** and he will be forgiven.
Num 15.22 But suppose someone **unintentionally** fails to keep some
15.25 forgiven, because the mistake was **unintentional** and they
15.27 If an individual sins **unintentionally,** he is to offer a
15.29 applies to everyone who **unintentionally** commits a sin,
Job 1. 5 of them might have sinned by insulting God **unintentionally.**
Ezek 45.20 of anyone who sins **unintentionally** or through ignorance.

UNINVITED

Jer 30.21 me when I invite him, for who would dare come **uninvited?**

UNION

Rom 6. 3 when we were baptized into **union with** Christ Jesus,
6. 3 we were baptized into **union with** his death.
6.23 gift is eternal life in **union with** Christ Jesus our Lord.
8. 1 now for those who live in **union with** Christ Jesus.
8. 2 which brings us life in **union with** Christ Jesus, has set me
12. 5 we are one body in **union with** Christ, and we are all
14.14 My **union with** the Lord Jesus makes me certain that no
15.17 In **union with** Christ Jesus, then, I can be proud of my
1 Cor 1. 2 who belong to him in **union with** Christ Jesus, together with
1. 5 For in **union with** Christ you have become rich in all things,
1.30 God has brought you into **union with** Christ Jesus, and God
4.10 but you are wise in **union with** Christ!
4.15 For in your life in **union with** Christ Jesus I have become
4.17 in the new life in **union with** Christ Jesus and which I
9. 2 Because of your life in **union with** the Lord you yourselves
15.22 people die because of their **union with** Adam, in the same way
15.22 will be raised to life because of their **union with** Christ.
15.31 in our life in **union with** Christ Jesus our Lord, makes
2 Cor 1.21 together with you, sure of our life in **union with** Christ;
2.14 For in **union with** Christ we are always led by God as
5.21 sin in order that in **union with** him we might share the
13. 4 In **union with** him we also are weak;
Gal 2. 4 about the freedom we have through our **union with** Christ Jesus.
2.17 right with God by our **union with** Christ, we are found to
3.26 that all of you are God's sons in **union with** Christ Jesus.
3.27 were baptized into **union with** Christ, and now you are clothed,
3.28 you are all one in **union with** Christ Jesus.
5. 6 when we are in **union with** Christ Jesus, neither circumcision nor
5.10 Our life in **union with** the Lord makes me confident that you
Eph 1. 1 who are faithful in their life in **union with** Christ Jesus:
1. 3 For in our **union with** Christ he has blessed us by giving
1. 4 to be his through our **union with** Christ, so that we would
1.11 be his own people in **union with** Christ because of his own
2. 6 In our **union with** Christ Jesus he raised us up with him
2.10 we are, and in our **union with** Christ Jesus he has created
2.13 But now, in **union with** Christ Jesus, you who used to be
2.15 one new people in **union with** himself, in this way making
2.22 In **union with** him you too are being built together with
3.12 In **union with** Christ and through our faith in him we
6.10 build up your strength in **union with** the Lord and by means
Phil 1. 1 Philippi who are in **union with** Christ Jesus, including the church

Phil 1.26 be proud of me in your life in **union with** Christ Jesus.
3. 1 conclusion, my brothers, be joyful in your **union with** the Lord.
3. 3 Spirit and rejoice in our life in **union with** Christ Jesus.
4. 4 May you always be joyful in your **union with** the Lord.
4. 7 keep your hearts and minds safe in **union with** Christ Jesus.
4.10 In my life in **union with** the Lord it is a great
Col 1. 2 in Colossae, who are our faithful brothers in **union with** Christ:
1.17 before all things, and in **union with** him all things have
1.28 into God's presence as a mature individual in **union with** Christ.
2. 6 have accepted Christ Jesus as Lord, live in **union with** him.
2.10 and you have been given full life in **union with** him.
2.11 In **union with** Christ you were circumcised, not with the
1 Thes 3. 8 if you stand firm in your life in **union with** the Lord.
5.18 God wants from you in your life in **union with** Christ Jesus.
1 Tim 1.14 faith and love which are ours in **union with** Christ Jesus.
2 Tim 1. 1 life which we have in **union with** Christ Jesus— [2]To Timothy,
1.13 the faith and love that are ours in **union with** Christ Jesus.
2. 1 through the grace that is ours in **union with** Christ Jesus.
3.12 a godly life in **union with** Christ Jesus will be persecuted;
Phlm 6 blessing which we have in our life in **union with** Christ.
1 Pet 5.10 share his eternal glory in **union with** Christ, will himself
1 Jn 2. 5 how we can be sure that we are in **union with** God:
2. 6 says that he remains in **union with** God should live just as
2.24 you will always live in **union with** the Son and the Father.
2.27 Obey the Spirit's teaching, then, and remain in **union with** Christ.
2.28 Yes, my children, remain in **union with** him, so that when
3. 6 So everyone who lives in **union with** Christ does not
3.24 obeys God's commands lives in **union with** God
3.24 and God lives in **union with** him.
3.24 has given us we know that God lives in **union with** us.
4.12 one another, God lives in **union with** us, and his love is
4.13 sure that we live in **union with** God
4.13 and that he lives in **union with** us,
4.15 he lives in **union with** God
4.15 and God lives in **union with** him.
4.16 lives in love lives in **union with** God
4.16 and God lives in **union with** him.
5.20 We live in **union with** the true God—
5.20 in **union with** his Son Jesus Christ.

UNIT

Deut 20. 9 to the army, leaders are to be chosen for each **unit.**
1 Sam 29. 2 kings marched out with their **units** of a hundred and of a
2 Sam 18. 1 men together, divided them into **units** of a thousand and of a
18. 4 his men marched out in **units** of a thousand and of a
1 Chr 12.20 In Manasseh they had all commanded **units** of a thousand men.
13. 1 the officers in command of **units** of a thousand men
13. 1 and **units** of a hundred men.
2 Chr 1. 2 the officers in charge of **units** of a thousand men and of
25. 5 Judah and Benjamin into army **units,** according to the clans
25. 5 placed officers in command of **units** of a thousand men
25. 5 and **units** of a hundred men.
33.14 officer in command of a **unit** of troops in each of the
Ezek 43.13 the altar, using the same **unit** of measurement as in
Rev 21.17 according to the standard **unit** of measure which he was using.

UNITE
[REUNITED]

Gen 2.24 father and mother and is **united** with his wife, and they
Deut 33. 7 **Unite** them again with the other tribes.
Judg 21.15 the Lord had broken the **unity** of the tribes of Israel.
1 Chr 12.38 of the people of Israel were **united** in the same purpose.
2 Chr 30.12 at work in Judah and **united** the people in their
Ezek 37.22 I will **unite** them into one nation in the land, on the
37.24 They will all be **united** under one ruler and will obey my
Dan 2.43 empire will try to **unite** their families by intermarriage,
Hos 1.11 The people of Judah and the people of Israel will be **reunited.**
Mic 5. 3 who are in exile will be **reunited** with their own people.
Zech 11. 7 one I called "Favour," and the other **"Unity."**
11.14 second stick, the one called **"Unity,"**
11.14 and the **unity** of Judah and Israel was shattered.
Mt 19. 5 his father and mother and **unite** with his wife, and the two
Mk 10. 7 his father and mother and **unite** with his wife, [8]and the two
Jn 15. 4 Remain united to me, and I will remain **united** to you.
16.33 this so that you will have peace by being **united** to me.
1 Cor 1.10 Be completely **united,** with only one thought and one purpose.
7.14 acceptable to God by being **united** to his wife,
7.14 made acceptable to God by being **united** to her Christian husband.
Eph 2.16 means of the cross he **united** both races into one body and
4. 3 to preserve the **unity** which the Spirit gives
5.31 his father and mother and **unite** with his wife, and the two
Phil 3. 9 that I may gain Christ [9]and be completely **united** with him.
Col 3.14 love, which binds all things together in perfect **unity.**

UNIVERSE

Gen 1. 1 God created the **universe,** [2]the earth was formless and desolate.
2. 1 And so the whole **universe** was completed.
2. 4 And that is how the **universe** was created.
2. 4 the Lord God made the **universe,** [5]there were no plants on
Is 66. 2 I myself created the whole **universe!**
Gal 4. 3 the ruling spirits of the **universe** before we reached spiritual
Eph 4.10 beyond the heavens, to fill the whole **universe** with his presence.
Col 1.16 God created the whole **universe** through him and for him.
1.20 then, God decided to bring the whole **universe** back to himself.
2. 8 the ruling spirits of the **universe,** and not from Christ.
2.20 Christ and are set free from the ruling spirits of the **universe.**
Heb 1. 2 through whom God created the **universe,** the one whom God has
1. 3 God's own being, sustaining the **universe** with his powerful word.
Heb 11. 3 that we understand that the **universe** was created by God's word,
Rev 5.13 living beings in the **universe**—and they were singing:

UNJUST

Deut 16.19 They are not to be **unjust** or show partiality in their judgements;
Job 6.29 Stop being **unjust.**
34.12 he is never **unjust** to anyone.
40. 8 to prove that I am **unjust**— to put me in the
Ps 82. 2 "You must stop judging **unjustly;**
119.161 Powerful men attack me **unjustly,** but I respect your law.
Prov 13.23 for the poor, but **unjust** men keep them from being farmed.
24.11 Don't hesitate to rescue someone who is about to be executed **unjustly.**
Is 10. 1 You make **unjust** laws that oppress my people.
59. 8 Everything you do is **unjust.**
Dan 9.26 of that time God's chosen leader will be killed **unjustly.**
Rom 9.14 Shall we say, then, that God is **unjust?**

AV UNJUST

Ps 43. 1 deliver me from lying and **evil** men!
Prov 11. 7 When a **wicked** man dies, his hope dies with him.
28. 8 and taking **advantage** of people, your wealth will go
29.27 The righteous hate the **wicked,**
Is 26.10 kind to wicked men, they never learn to do what is **right.**
26.10 Even here in a land of righteous people they still do **wrong;**
Zeph 3. 5 And yet the **unrighteous** people there keep on doing wrong and
Mt 5.45 rain to those who do good and to those who do **evil.**
Lk 16. 8 the master of this **dishonest** manager praised him for doing such
16.10 whoever is **dishonest** in small matters
16.10 will be **dishonest** in large ones.
18. 6 the Lord continued, "Listen to what that **corrupt** judge said.
18.11 am not greedy, **dishonest,** or an adulterer, like everybody else.
Acts 24.15 all people, both the good and the **bad,** will rise from death.
1 Cor 6. 1 how dare he go before **heathen** judges instead of letting God's
1 Pet 3.18 good man on behalf of **sinners,** in order to lead you
2 Pet 2. 9 and how to keep the **wicked** under punishment for the Day of
Rev 22.11 Whoever is **evil** must go on doing evil, and whoever is

UNKIND

2 Tim 3. 3 they will be **unkind,** merciless, slanderers, violent, and

UNKNOWN

1 Kgs 18.12 carries you off to some **unknown** place as soon as I leave?
Job 3.19 the famous and the **unknown,** and slaves at last are free.
Ps 81. 5 I hear an **unknown** voice saying, [6]"I took the burdens off
Is 19.15 Egypt, rich or poor, important or **unknown,** can offer help.
Lam 4. 8 Now they lie **unknown** in the streets,
Mt 13.35 I will tell them things **unknown** since the creation of the world."
Acts 17.23 I found an altar on which is written, 'To an **Unknown** God'.
2 Cor 6. 9 as **unknown,** yet we are known by all;

UNLEAVENED
[WITHOUT YEAST]

The Israelite festival of Unleavened Bread lasted seven days after Passover; it also celebrated the deliverance of the ancient Hebrews from Egypt. The name came from the practice of not using leaven (yeast) in making bread during that week. It was held from the 15th to the 22nd day of the month Nisan (about the first week of April).
see also **LEAVEN, YEAST**

Ex 12. 8 eaten with bitter herbs and with bread made **without yeast.**
12.15 not eat any bread made with yeast—eat only **unleavened** bread.
12.34 baking-pans with **unleavened** dough, wrapped them in clothing,
12.39 They baked **unleavened** bread from the dough that they had
13. 6 seven days you must eat **unleavened** bread and on the seventh
23.15 Egypt, celebrate the Festival of **Unleavened Bread** in the way
34.18 "Keep the Festival of **Unleavened Bread.**
34.18 I have commanded you, eat **unleavened** bread for seven days in
Lev 2. 4 is bread baked in an oven, it must be made **without yeast.**
2. 5 to be made of flour mixed with olive-oil but **without yeast.**
6.16 be made into bread baked **without yeast** and eaten in a holy
7.12 to be sacrificed, an offering of bread made **without yeast:**
7.13 In addition, he shall offer loaves of bread baked **without yeast.**
8. 2 the two rams, and the basket of **unleavened** bread.
8.26 from the basket of **unleavened** bread dedicated to the Lord,
10.12 offered to the Lord, make **unleavened** bread with it and eat
23. 6 fifteenth day the Festival of **Unleavened Bread** begins, and
Num 6.15 He shall also offer a basket of bread made **without yeast:**
9.11 Celebrate it with **unleavened** bread and bitter herbs.
28.17 which only bread prepared **without yeast** is to be eaten.
Deut 16. 3 are to eat bread prepared **without yeast,** as you did when you
16. 8 are to eat bread prepared **without yeast,** and on the seventh
Josh 5.11 roasted grain and bread made **without yeast.**
1 Sam 28.24 some flour, prepared it, and baked some bread **without yeast.**
2 Kgs 23. 9 eat the **unleavened** bread provided for their fellow-priests.
1 Chr 23.29 the wafers made **without yeast,** the baked offerings,
2 Chr 8.13 Festival of **Unleavened Bread,** the Harvest Festival,
30.13 to celebrate the Festival of **Unleavened Bread.**
30.21 celebrated the Festival of **Unleavened Bread** with great joy, and day
35.17 the Passover and the Festival of **Unleavened Bread.**
Ezra 6.22 they joyfully celebrated the Festival of **Unleavened Bread.**
Ezek 45.21 For seven days everyone will eat bread made **without yeast.**
Mt 26.17 of the Festival of **Unleavened Bread** the disciples came to Jesus
Mk 14. 1 now two days before the Festival of Passover and **Unleavened Bread.**

Mk 14.12 day of the Festival of **Unleavened Bread,** the day the lambs
Lk 22. 1 the Festival of **Unleavened Bread,** which is called the Passover.
22. 7 came during the Festival of **Unleavened Bread** when the lambs for
Acts 12. 3 (This happened during the time of the Festival of **Unleavened Bread.)**
20. 6 Philippi after the Festival of **Unleavened Bread,** and five days

UNLIMITED

1 Chr 22.14 Besides that, there is an **unlimited** supply of bronze and iron.

UNLOAD

Gen 24.32 into the house, and Laban **unloaded** the camels and gave them
Acts 21. 3 at Tyre, where the ship was going to **unload** its cargo.

UNLOVED

Hos 1. 6 said to Hosea, "Name her **'Unloved,'** because I will no
2.23 to those who were called **"Unloved,"** and to those who were

UNMAKES

Dan 2.21 he makes and **unmakes** kings;

UNMARKED see MARK (1)

UNMARRIED

Ex 21. 3 If he was **unmarried** when he became your slave, he is not
Lev 21. 3 brother, [3]or **unmarried** sister living in his house.
Num 30. 6 If an **unmarried** woman makes a vow,
30.16 concerning vows made by an **unmarried** woman living in her
Judg 11.38 because she was going to die **unmarried** and childless.
2 Sam 13. 1 David's son Absalom had a beautiful **unmarried** sister named Tamar.
13.18 the usual clothing for an **unmarried** princess in those days.
Is 4. 1 we won't have to endure the shame of being **unmarried."**
Ezek 44.25 one of his children or a brother or an **unmarried** sister.
Acts 21. 9 He had four **unmarried** daughters who proclaimed God's message.
1 Cor 7. 8 Now, to the **unmarried** and to the widows I say that it
7.25 Now, concerning what you wrote about **unmarried** people:
7.27 Are you **unmarried?**
7.28 if an **unmarried** woman marries, she hasn't committed a sin.
7.32 An **unmarried** man concerns himself with the Lord's work,
7.34 **unmarried** woman or a virgin concerns herself with the Lord's work,

UNMOVED

Is 64.12 Lord, are you **unmoved** by all this?

UNNATURAL

Rom 1.26 pervert the natural use of their sex by **unnatural** acts.

UNNOTICED

Job 4.20 in the morning, but die **unnoticed** before evening comes.
Jude 4 godless people have slipped in **unnoticed** among us, persons who

UNPLOUGHED

Jer 4. 3 of Judah and Jerusalem, "Plough up your **unploughed** fields;

AV UNPROFITABLE

Job 15. 3 as you do or defend himself with such **meaningless** words.
Mt 25.30 As for this **useless** servant—throw him outside in the darkness;
Lk 17.10 you have been told to do, say, 'We are **ordinary** servants;
Rom 3.12 they have all gone **wrong;**
Tit 3. 9 They are **useless** and worthless.
Phlm 11 time he was of no **use** to you, but now he is
Heb 13.17 it with sadness, and that would be of no **help** to you.

UNREASONABLE

Acts 25.27 it seems **unreasonable** to me to send a prisoner without clearly

UNRELIABLE see RELY

UNRESTRAINED

Rev 18. 3 businessmen of the world grew rich from her **unrestrained** lust."

AV UNRIGHTEOUS
see also **WRONG**

Ex 23. 1 and do not help a guilty man by giving **false** evidence.
Lev 19.15 "Be **honest** and just when you make decisions in legal
19.35 "Do not **cheat** anyone by using false measures of length,
Deut 25.16 The Lord hates people who **cheat.**
Ps 71. 4 me from wicked men, from the power of cruel and **evil** men.
Is 10. 1 You make **unjust** laws that oppress my people.
55. 7 Let the **wicked** leave their way of life and change their
Jer 22.13 builds his house by **injustice** and enlarges it by dishonesty;
Lk 16. 9 make friends for yourselves with **worldly** wealth,
16.11 not been faithful in handling **worldly** wealth, how can you be
Jn 7.18 who sent him is honest, and there is nothing **false** in him.
Rom 1.18 against all the sin and **evil** of the people
1.18 whose **evil** ways prevent the truth from being
1.29 They are filled with all kinds of **wickedness,** evil, greed,
3. 5 But what if our doing **wrong** serves to show up more clearly
3. 5 Can we say that God does **wrong** when he punishes us?
6.13 part of yourselves to sin to be used for **wicked** purposes.
9.14 Shall we say, then, that God is **unjust?**
1 Cor 6. 9 Surely you know that the **wicked** will not possess God's Kingdom.
2 Thes 2.10 and use every kind of **wicked** deceit on those who will perish.
2.12 truth, but have taken pleasure in **sin,** will be condemned.
Heb 6.10 God is not **unfair.**
8.12 I will forgive their **sins** and will no longer remember their wrongs."
2 Pet 2.13 will be paid with suffering for the **suffering** they have caused.

UNROLLED

Ezek 2.10 The hand **unrolled** the scroll, and I saw that there was
Lk 4.17 He **unrolled** the scroll and found the place where it is written,

UNSALTED see SALT (1)

AV UNSEARCHABLE

Job 5. 9 We cannot **understand** the great things he does, and to his
Ps 145. 3 his greatness is beyond **understanding.**
Rom 11.33 Who can **explain** his decisions?
Eph 3. 8 the Good News about the **infinite** riches of Christ,

UNSEEN

Mt 6. 6 close the door, and pray to your Father, who is **unseen.**
6.18 that you are fasting—only your Father, who is **unseen,** will
2 Cor 4.18 not on things that are seen, but on things that are **unseen.**
Col 1.16 the seen and the **unseen** things, including spiritual powers,

AV UNSPEAKABLE

2 Cor 9.15 Let us thank God for his **priceless** gift!
12. 3 which cannot be put into **words,** things that human lips may
1 Pet 1. 8 great and glorious joy which **words** cannot express, [9]because

UNSTABLE

2 Pet 3.16 his letters which ignorant and **unstable** people explain falsely,

UNSUSPECTING

Ezek 30. 9 in ships to arouse the **unsuspecting** people of Sudan, and

UNTHINKING

Prov 21.11 his punishment, even an **unthinking** person learns a lesson.
22. 3 and avoid it, but an **unthinking** person will walk right into
27.12 and avoid it, but an **unthinking** person will walk right into

UNTIE

1 Kgs 5. 9 There my men will **untie** them, and your men will take charge
2 Kgs 7.10 and donkeys have not been **untied,** and the tents are just as
Mt 21. 2 **Untie** them and bring them to me.
Mk 1. 7 am not good enough even to bend down and **untie** his sandals.
11. 2 **Untie** it and bring it here.
11. 4 As they were **untying** it, [5]some of the bystanders asked them,
11. 5 "What are you doing, **untying** that colt?"
Lk 3.16 I am not good enough even to **untie** his sandals.
13.15 Any one of you would **untie** his ox or his donkey from
19.30 **Untie** it and bring it here.
19.31 asks you why you are **untying** it, tell him that the Master
19.33 As they were **untying** the colt, its owners said to them,
19.33 "Why are you **untying** it?"
Jn 1.27 but I am not good enough even to **untie** his sandals."
11.44 **"Untie** him," Jesus told them, "and let him go."
Acts 27.40 at the same time they **untied** the ropes that held the

UNTRUE

Rom 3. 7 But what if my **untruth** serves God's glory by making his
2 Pet 2. 1 bring in destructive, **untrue** doctrines, and will deny the Master

UNUSED

Prov 13.23 **Unused** fields could yield plenty of food for the poor,

UNUSUAL

1 Kgs 4.29 God gave Solomon **unusual** wisdom and insight, and
2 Chr 32.31 came to inquire about the **unusual** event that had happened in
Jer 10. 2 do not be disturbed by **unusual** sights in the sky, even
Dan 5.12 He has **unusual** ability and is wise and skilful in interpreting
Mt 13.46 he finds one that is **unusually** fine, he goes and sells
Acts 19.11 God was performing **unusual** miracles through Paul.
28. 6 not seeing anything **unusual** happening to him, they changed their
1 Pet 4.12 are suffering, as though something **unusual** were happening to you.

UNWALLED see WALL

UNWILLING

1 Pet 5. 2 of it willingly, as God wants you to, and not **unwillingly.**

UNYIELDING

Job 41.23 it is as hard and **unyielding** as iron.
41.24 is without fear, as **unyielding** and hard as a millstone.
Is 48. 4 to be stubborn, as rigid as iron and **unyielding** as bronze.

UPHOLD

[UPHELD]

Mt 18.16 that 'every accusation may be **upheld** by the testimony of two
Mk 7. 9 of rejecting God's law in order to **uphold** your own teaching.
Rom 3.31 instead, we **uphold** the Law.
2 Cor 13. 1 "Any accusation must be **upheld** by the evidence of two or

UPKEEP

Ex 30.16 and spend it for the **upkeep** of the Tent of my presence.

UPLIFTED

see also **LIFT**

1 Kgs 8.54 the altar, where he had been kneeling with **uplifted** hands.
Ps 141. 2 my prayer as incense, my **uplifted** hands as an evening sacrifice.

UPPER

Ex 28.23 and attach them to the **upper** corners of the breast-piece,
39.16 the two rings to the **upper** corners of the breast-piece.
Num 21.28 of Ar in Moab And devoured the hills of the **upper** Arnon.
Josh 15.19 So Caleb gave her the **upper** and lower springs.
16. 5 from Ataroth Addar eastwards to **Upper** Beth Horon, [6]and from
Judg 1.15 So Caleb gave her the **upper** and lower springs.
2 Sam 8. 3 his control over the territory by the **upper** Euphrates.
2 Kgs 18.17 work, by the ditch that brings water from the **upper** pond.
1 Chr 7.24 She built the towns of **Upper** and Lower Beth Horon, and Uzzen
18. 3 to gain control of the territory by the **upper** Euphrates.
19. 6 hire chariots and charioteers from **Upper** Mesopotamia and
26.16 the west gate and the Shallecheth Gate on the **upper** road.
2 Chr 3. 9 the walls of the **upper** rooms were also covered with gold.
8. 5 **Upper** Beth Horon and Lower Beth Horon (fortified cities with
32.33 died and was buried in the **upper** section of the royal tombs.
Neh 3.25 and the tower of the **upper** palace near the court of the
Is 7. 3 the end of the ditch that brings water from the **upper** pool.
36. 2 work, by the ditch that brings water from the **upper** pond.
Jer 20. 2 placed in chains near the **upper** Benjamin Gate in the Temple.
36.10 His room was in the **upper** court near the entrance of the
Ezek 41. 7 from the lower storey to the middle and the **upper** storeys.
42. 5 The rooms at the **upper** level of the building were narrower
2 Cor 2.11 in order to keep Satan from getting the **upper** hand of us;

UPRIGHT

Ex 26.15 "Make **upright** frames for the Tent out of acacia-wood.
36.20 They made **upright** frames of acacia-wood for the Tent.
Eph 4.24 reveals itself in the true life that is **upright** and holy.
Tit 1. 8 He must be self-controlled, **upright,** holy, and disciplined.
2.12 to live self-controlled, **upright,** and godly lives in this world,

AV UPRIGHT

see also **GOOD, HONEST, RIGHT (1), RIGHTEOUS**

Lev 26.13 you down and I let you walk with your head held **high."**
1 Sam 29. 6 the living God of Israel that you have been **loyal** to me;
2 Sam 22.24 He knows that I am **faultless,** that I have kept myself
22.26 to you, and completely good to those who are **perfect.**
1 Chr 29.17 test everyone's heart and are pleased with people of **integrity.**
2 Chr 29.34 (The Levites were more **faithful** in keeping ritually clean
Job 1. 1 the land of Uz, who worshipped God and was **faithful** to him.
1. 1 He was a good man, careful not to do anything **evil.**
1. 8 is no one on earth as **faithful** and good as he is.
2. 3 is no one on earth as faithful and **good** as he is.
4. 6 You worshipped God, and your life was **blameless;**
33. 3 All my words are **sincere,** and I am speaking the truth.
33.23 of God's thousands of angels, who remind men of their **duty.**
Ps 7.10 he saves those who **obey** him.
9. 8 he judges the nations with **justice.**
15. 2 A person who **obeys** God in everything and always does what
18.23 He knows that I am **faultless,** that I have kept myself
18.25 completely good to those who are **perfect.**
19.13 Then I shall be **perfect** and free from the evil of sin.
32.11 You that **obey** him, shout for joy!
33. 1 praise him, all you that **obey** him.
37.18 takes care of those who **obey** him, and the land will be
58. 1 Do you judge all men **fairly?**
75. 2 judgement," says God, "and I will judge with **fairness.**
92.15 shows that the Lord is **just,** that there is no wrong
119. 7 righteous judgements, I will praise you with a **pure** heart.
119.137 You are righteous, Lord, and your laws are **just.**
125. 4 to those who are good, to those who **obey** your commands.
143.10 Be good to me, and guide me on a **safe** path.
Prov 13. 6 Righteousness protects the **innocent;**
28.10 The **innocent** will be well rewarded.
Ecc 7.29 God made us **plain** and simple, but we have made ourselves
Is 26. 7 Lord, you make the path **smooth** for good men;
Amos 5.10 challenges injustice and speaks the whole **truth** in court.
Mic 7. 2 an honest person left in the land, no one **loyal** to God.
Gal 2.14 they were not walking a **straight** path in line with the truth

UPROAR

1 Kgs 1.45 city, shouting for joy, and the people are now in an **uproar.**
Ps 65. 7 you calm the **uproar** of the peoples.
Is 22. 2 The whole city is in an **uproar,** filled with noise and excitement.
Mt 21.10 Jesus entered Jerusalem, the whole city was thrown into an **uproar.**
Acts 17. 5 the whole city in an **uproar** and attacked the home of
17. 8 they threw the crowd and the city authorities into an **uproar.**
19.29 The **uproar** spread throughout the whole city.
19.32 Meanwhile the whole meeting was in an **uproar:**
19.40 no excuse for all this **uproar,** and we would not be able
20. 1 After the **uproar** died down, Paul called together the believers

UPROOT

Deut 28.63 You will be **uprooted** from the land that you are about to
29.28 in his great anger he **uprooted** them from their land and
1 Kgs 14.15 He will **uproot** the people of Israel from this good land
Job 19.10 He **uproots** my hope and leaves me to wither and die.
Jer 1.10 over nations and kingdoms to **uproot** and to pull down, to
12.14 from their countries like an **uprooted** plant, and I will
12.17 not obey, then I will completely **uproot** it and destroy it.
18. 7 that I am going to **uproot,** break down, or destroy any nation
31.28 as I took care to **uproot,** to pull down, to overthrow, to

UPSET

Gen 40. 6 came to them in the morning, he saw that they were **upset.**
45. 5 Now do not be **upset** or blame yourselves because you sold
48.17 Joseph was **upset** when he saw that his father had put his
1 Sam 1. 7 of the Lord, Peninnah would **upset** Hannah so much that she
2 Sam 11.25 tell him not to be **upset,** since you never can tell who
13.20 Please, sister, don't let it **upset** you so much.
2 Kgs 5. 8 "Why are you so **upset?**
6.11 The Syrian king became greatly **upset** over this;
Job 5.12 He **upsets** the plans of cunning men, and traps wise
20. 1 Job, you **upset** me.
Ps 49.16 Don't be **upset** when a man becomes rich, when his wealth
Dan 6.14 king heard this, he was **upset** and did his best to find
Mt 2. 3 about this, he was very **upset,** and so was everyone else in
18.31 had happened, they were very **upset** and went to the king and
26.22 The disciples were very **upset** and began to ask him, one
Mk 14.19 The disciples were **upset** and began to ask him, one after
Lk 10.40 Martha was **upset** over all the work she had to do,
12.29 don't be all **upset,** always concerned about what you will eat
Jn 14. 1 "Do not be worried and **upset,"** Jesus told them.
14.27 Do not be worried and **upset;**
Acts 15.24 our group have troubled and **upset** you by what they said;
16.18 until Paul became so **upset** that he turned round and said
17.16 and Timothy, he was greatly **upset** when he noticed how full
Rom 16.17 those who cause divisions and **upset** people's faith and go against
Gal 1. 7 are some people who are **upsetting** you and trying to change
5.10 that the man who is **upsetting** you, whoever he is, will be
5.12 that the people who are **upsetting** you would go all the way;
Phil 2.26 you all and is very **upset** because you had heard that he
2 Thes 2. 2 confused in your thinking or **upset** by the claim that the Day
2 Tim 2.18 way of truth and are **upsetting** the faith of some believers
Tit 1.11 their talk, because they are **upsetting** whole families by teaching

UPSIDE DOWN

2 Kgs 21.13 clean as a plate that has been wiped and turned **upside down.**
Is 29.16 They turn everything **upside down.**

UPSTAIRS

1 Kgs 17.19 from her arms, carried him **upstairs** to the room where he was
Jer 22.14 "I will build myself a mansion with spacious rooms **upstairs."**
Dan 6.10 In an **upstairs** room of his house there were windows that
Mk 14.15 will show you a large **upstairs** room, prepared and furnished,
Lk 22.12 a large furnished room **upstairs,** where you will get everything
Acts 9.37 Her body was washed and laid in a room **upstairs.**
9.39 taken to the room **upstairs,** where all the widows crowded round
20. 8 lamps were burning in the **upstairs** room where we were meeting.
20.11 Then he went back **upstairs,** broke bread, and ate.

UPSTREAM

Josh 3.16 piled up, far **upstream** at Adam, the city beside Zarethan.
Dan 12. 6 angel who was standing further **upstream,** "How long will it

UPWARD

1 Kgs 7.31 It projected **upwards** 45 centimetres from the top of the cart
Prov 15.24 walk the road that leads **upwards** to life, not the road that
Ecc 3.21 that a man's spirit goes **upwards** while an animal's spirit
Ezek 17. 6 The branches grew **upward** towards the eagle, and the roots grew deep.

URGE

Gen 19. 3 He kept on **urging** them, and finally they went with him to
33.11 Jacob kept on **urging** him until he accepted.
Ex 12.33 The Egyptians **urged** the people to hurry and leave the country;
Josh 15.18 On the wedding day Othniel **urged** her to ask her father
Judg 1.14 On the wedding day Othniel **urged** her to ask her father
19. 7 to go, but the father **urged** him to stay, so he spent
1 Sam 28.23 But his officers also **urged** him to eat.
1 Kgs 21.25 Lord's sight as Ahab—all at the **urging** of his wife Jezebel.
2 Kgs 6. 3 One of them **urged** him to go with them;

Esth 3. 4 day after day they **urged** him to give in, but he would
Jer 17.16 But, Lord, I never **urged** you to bring disaster on them;
Lk 3.18 Good News to the people and **urged** them to change their ways.
Acts 2.40 with many other words he **urged** them, saying, "Save yourselves
11.23 people, he was glad and **urged** them all to be faithful and
18.27 writing to the believers in Achaia, **urging** them to welcome him.
Rom 15.30 I **urge** you, brothers, by our Lord Jesus Christ and by
16.17 I **urge** you, my brothers:
2 Cor 8. 6 So we **urged** Titus, who began this work, to continue it and
9. 5 thought it was necessary to **urge** these brothers to go to you
Eph 4. 1 I **urge** you, then—I who am a prisoner because I serve
Phil 2. 2 I **urge** you, then, to make me completely happy by having
1 Thes 2.12 comforted you, and we kept **urging** you to live the kind of
4. 1 And now we beg and **urge** you in the name of the
5.14 We **urge** you, our brothers, to warn the idle, encourage
5.27 I **urge** you by the authority of the Lord to read this
1 Tim 1. 3 in Ephesus, just as I **urged** you when I was on my
2. 1 First of all, then, I **urge** that petitions, prayers, requests,
2 Tim 4. 1 rule as King, I solemnly **urge** you [2] to preach the message,
Tit 2. 6 In the same way **urge** the young men to be self-controlled.

URIAH (1)

Hittite soldier, Bathsheba's husband, whose death was arranged by David.

2 Sam 11. 3 the daughter of Eliam and the wife of **Uriah** the Hittite.
11. 6 "Send me **Uriah** the Hittite."
11. 7 When **Uriah** arrived, David asked him if Joab and the troops
11. 8 Then he said to **Uriah,** "Go home and rest a while."
11. 8 **Uriah** left, and David sent a present to his home.
11. 9 But **Uriah** did not go home;
11.10 When David heard that **Uriah** had not gone home, he asked
11.11 **Uriah** answered, "The men of Israel and Judah are away
11.12 So **Uriah** stayed in Jerusalem that day and the next.
11.13 But again that night **Uriah** did not go home;
11.14 morning David wrote a letter to Joab and sent it by **Uriah.**
11.15 "Put **Uriah** in the front line, where the fighting is heaviest,
11.16 besieging the city, he sent **Uriah** to a place where he knew
11.17 some of David's officers were killed, and so was **Uriah.**
11.21 this, tell him, 'Your officer **Uriah** was also killed.' "
11.24 your officer **Uriah** was also killed."
12. 9 You had **Uriah** killed in battle;
12.10 because you have disobeyed me and have taken **Uriah's** wife.
12.15 Lord caused the child that **Uriah's** wife had borne to David
23.24 Joab's armour bearer Ira and Gareb from Jattir **Uriah** the Hittite.
1 Kgs 15. 5 of his commands, except in the case of **Uriah** the Hittite.
1 Chr 11.26 Ira and Gareb from Jattir **Uriah** the Hittite Zabad son of
Mt 1. 6 the woman who had been **Uriah's** wife),

URIM

see also **THUMMIM**

Ex 28.30 Put the **Urim** and Thummim in the breast-piece, so that
Lev 8. 8 the breast-piece on him and put the **Urim** and Thummim in it.
Num 27.21 who will learn my will by using the **Urim** and Thummim.
Deut 33. 8 will by the **Urim** and Thummim Through your faithful servants,
1 Sam 14.41 If the guilt is Jonathan's or mine, answer by the **Urim;**
28. 6 dreams or by the use of **Urim** and Thummim or by prophets.
Ezra 2.63 there was a priest who could use the **Urim** and Thummim.
Neh 7.65 there was a priest who could use the **Urim** and Thummim.

URINE

2 Kgs 18.27 their excrement and drink their **urine,** just as you will."
Is 36.12 their excrement and drink their **urine,** just as you will."

USE

Gen 4.26 that people began **using** the Lord's holy name in worship.
11. 1 whole world had only one language and **used** the same words.
14.24 I will accept only what my men have **used.**
23.16 according to the standard weights **used** by the merchants.
44. 5 is the one he drinks from, the one he **uses** for divination.
47.24 You can **use** the rest for seed and for food for yourselves
48.20 "The Israelites will **use** your names when they pronounce blessings.
49. 5 They **use** their weapons to commit violence.
Ex 3.20 But I will **use** my power and will punish Egypt by doing
8. 7 But the magicians **used** magic, and they too made frogs come
8.18 The magicians tried to **use** their magic to make gnats appear,
8.26 If we **use** these animals and offend the Egyptians by
13.14 you will answer him, 'By **using** great power the Lord brought
16.36 (The standard dry measure then in **use** equalled twenty litres.)
20. 7 "Do not **use** my name for evil purposes, for I, the Lord
20.25 use a chisel on stones, you make them unfit for my **use.**
21.26 so that he loses the **use** of it, he is to free
25.29 cups, jars, and bowls to be **used** for the wine-offerings.
25.39 **Use** thirty-five kilogrammes of pure gold to make the
27.19 All the equipment that is **used** in the Tent and all the
28. 5 The craftsmen are to **use** blue, purple, and red wool, gold
28.15 for the High Priest to **use** in determining God's will.
29. 2 **Use** the best wheat flour, but no yeast, and make some
29.19 the other ram—the ram **used** for dedication—and tell Aaron and
29.27 thigh of the ram being **used** for the ordination are to be
29.31 the meat of the ram **used** for the ordination of Aaron and
29.33 They shall eat what was **used** in the ritual of
30.19 and his sons are to **use** the water to wash their hands
30.26 **Use** it to anoint the Tent of my presence, the Covenant Box,
30.31 anointing oil is to be **used** in my service for all time
30.32 men, and you must not **use** the same formula to make any
30.33 makes any like it or **uses** any of it on anyone who
Ex 30.35 **Use** them to make incense, mixed like perfume.
30.37 Do not **use** the same formula to make any incense like it
30.38 makes any like it for **use** as perfume, he will no longer
31.10 Aaron and his sons to **use** when they serve as priests,
35.21 They brought everything needed for **use** in worship and for
35.24 had acacia-wood which could be **used** for any of the work
37.16 the jars, and the bowls to be **used** for the wine-offering.
37.24 He **used** 35 kilogrammes of pure gold to make the
38.21 the amounts of the metals **used** in the Tent of the Lord's
38.27 the silver, 3,400 kilogrammes were **used** to make the hundred
39.40 all the equipment to be **used** in the Tent;
Lev 2.11 you must never **use** yeast or honey in food offered to the
3. 6 a sheep or goat is **used** as a fellowship-offering, it may be
4. 7 the base of the altar **used** for burning sacrifices, which is
4.10 burn it on the altar **used** for the burnt-offerings, just as
4.18 the base of the altar **used** for burning sacrifices, which is
6.28 if a metal pot is **used,** it must be scrubbed and rinsed
6.30 brought into the Tent and **used** in the ritual to take away
7.24 not be eaten, but it may be **used** for any other purpose.
7.26 Israelites live, they must never **use** the blood of birds or
10.10 and what is for general **use,** between what is ritually clean
11.32 cloth, leather, or sacking, no matter what it is **used** for.
14.42 other stones are to be **used** to replace the stones that were
14.42 removed, and new plaster will be **used** to cover the walls.
16. 8 There he shall draw lots, **using** two stones, one marked
16.27 The bull and the goat **used** for the sin-offering, whose
18.21 of your children to be **used** in the worship of the god
19.35 "Do not cheat anyone by **using** false measures of length,
19.36 **Use** honest scales, honest weights, and honest measures.
20. 2 of his children to be **used** in the worship of the god
25.23 you are like foreigners who are allowed to make **use** of it.
Num 3.31 altars, the utensils the priests **use** in the Holy Place, and
4.12 shall take all the utensils **used** in the Holy Place, wrap
4.14 on it all the equipment **used** in the service at the altar:
4.26 and all the fittings **used** in setting up these objects.
4.32 the Tent, with all the fittings **used** in setting them up.
5. 8 in addition to the ram **used** to perform the ritual of
6.23 Aaron and his sons to **use** the following words in blessing
7. 5 Moses, [5] "Accept these gifts for **use** in the work to be done
10. 2 trumpets of hammered silver to **use** for calling the people
19. 9 for the Israelite community to **use** in preparing the water
23.23 witchcraft, That can be **used** against the nation of Israel.
27.21 who will learn my will by **using** the Urim and Thummim.
35.16 "If, however, a man **uses** a weapon of iron or
Deut 4.34 Before your very eyes he **used** his great power and strength;
5.11 " 'Do not **use** my name for evil purposes, for I, the
12.16 But you must not **use** their blood as food;
12.24 Do not **use** the blood for food;
13. 3 The Lord your God is **using** him to test you, to see
15.19 don't **use** any of these cattle for work and don't shear any
15.23 But do not **use** their blood for food;
18.10 or look for omens or **use** spells [11] or charms, and don't let
20.14 You may **use** everything that belongs to your enemies.
20.20 down the other trees and **use** them in the siege mounds until
21. 3 to select a young cow that has never been **used** for work.
22. 9 do, you are forbidden to **use** either the grapes or the
24. 6 take as security his millstones **used** for grinding his corn.
25. 4 not muzzle an ox when you are **using** it to thresh corn.
25.13 "Do not cheat when you **use** weights and measures.
25.15 **Use** true and honest weights and measures, so that you
27. 5 have had no iron tools **used** on them, [6] because any altar you
32.21 So I will **use** a so-called nation to make them angry;
32.23 them endless disasters and **use** all my arrows against them.
Josh 22.23 on or to **use** for grain-offerings or fellowship-offerings,
23. 7 names of their gods or **use** those names in taking vows or
Judg 2.22 I will **use** them to find out whether or not these
5. 6 went through the land, and travellers **used** the side roads.
6.13 fathers told us the Lord **used** to do—how he brought them
6.19 cooked a young goat and **used** ten kilogrammes of flour to
6.26 it whole as an offering, **using** for firewood the symbol of
6.36 "You say that you have decided to **use** me to rescue Israel.
6.37 will know that you are going to **use** me to rescue Israel."
8.16 briars from the desert and **used** them to punish the leaders
9. 9 producing my oil, which is **used** to honour gods and men.'
16.11 ropes that have never been **used,** I'll be as weak as anybody
17. 3 It will be **used** to make a wooden idol covered with silver.
1 Sam 17.39 but he couldn't, because he wasn't **used** to wearing them.
17.39 "I'm not **used** to it."
18.21 I will **use** her to trap him, and he will be killed
28. 6 by dreams or by the **use** of Urim and Thummim or by
2 Sam 3.18 Lord has said, 'I will **use** my servant David to rescue my
8.11 King David dedicated them for **use** in worship, along with
21.10 Rizpah, the daughter of Aiah, **used** sackcloth to make a
22.35 trains me for battle, so that I can **use** the strongest bow.
23. 7 You must **use** an iron tool or a spear;
24.22 are their yokes and the threshing-boards to **use** as fuel."
1 Kgs 7.50 for incense, and the pans **used** for carrying live coals;
9.15 Solomon **used** forced labour to build the Temple and the palace,
9.15 He also **used** it to rebuild the cities of Hazor, Megiddo, and
9.17 **Using** his forced labour, Solomon also rebuilt Lower Beth Horon,
9.20 For his forced labour Solomon **used** the descendants
10.12 Solomon **used** the wood to build railings in the Temple
10.21 No silver was **used,** since it was not considered valuable in
15.22 stones and timber that Baasha had been **using** to fortify it.
19.21 them, and cooked the meat, **using** the yoke as fuel for the
21. 2 palace, and I want to **use** the land for a vegetable garden.
2 Kgs 7. 4 It's no **use** going into the city, because we would starve
12. 5 the money was to be **used** to repair the Temple, as needed.
12.12 the timber and the stones **used** in the repairs, and pay all
12.13 the money, however, was **used** to pay for making silver cups,
12.14 It was all **used** to pay the workmen and to buy the

2 Kgs	12.14	the workmen and to buy the materials **used** in the repairs.
	16.15	"**Use** this large altar of mine for the morning
	16.15	But keep the bronze altar for me to **use** for divination."
	16.17	took apart the bronze carts **used** in the Temple and removed
	18.21	but that would be like **using** a reed as a walking-stick—it
	22. 6	and buy the timber and the stones **used** in the repairs.
	22.19	sight, a place whose name people will **use** as a curse.
	23. 4	the Temple all the objects **used** in the worship of Baal, of
	23. 7	there that women wove robes **used** in the worship of Asherah.)
	23.11	of the sun, and he burnt the chariots **used** in this worship.
	24.13	utensils which King Solomon had made for **use** in the Temple.
	25.14	shovels and the ash containers **used** in cleaning the altar,
	25.14	the tools **used** in tending the lamps,
	25.14	the bowls **used** for catching the blood
	25.14	the bowls **used** for burning incense,
	25.14	all the other bronze articles **used** in the temple service.
	25.15	the small bowls and the pans **used** for carrying live coals.
1 Chr	5.18	were 44,760 soldiers, well-trained in the **use** of shields,
	9.28	Other Levites were responsible for the utensils **used** in worship.
	9.28	them out and checked them back in every time they were **used.**
	12.23	men ready to fight, trained to **use** all kinds of weapons;
	12.23	120,000 men trained to **use** all kinds of weapons.
	14.11	He said, "God has **used** me to break through the enemy army
	15. 1	For his own **use,** David built houses in David's City.
	18. 8	(Solomon later **used** this bronze to make the tank, the
	18.11	King David dedicated them for **use** in worship, along with
	21.12	an epidemic on your land, **using** his angel to bring death
	21.23	here are the threshing-boards to **use** as fuel, and wheat to
	22.14	over 34,000 metric tons of silver to be **used** in building it.
	22.19	Lord and all the other sacred objects **used** in worshipping him."
	23. 5	thousand to praise the Lord, **using** the musical instruments
	23.26	Tent of the Lord's presence and all the equipment **used** in worship."
	23.29	offered to God, the flour **used** in offerings, the wafers made
	26.27	captured in battle and dedicated it for **use** in the Temple.
	26.28	that had been dedicated for **use** in the Temple, including the
	28.14	and gold was to be **used** for making the utensils, [15] for
	28.17	pure gold was to be **used** in making forks, bowls, and jars,
2 Chr	3. 1	which Araunah the Jebusite had **used** as a threshing-place.
	3. 7	He **used** the gold to overlay the temple walls, the rafters,
	3. 8	metric tons of gold were **used** to cover the walls of the
	3. 9	570 grammes of gold were **used** for making nails, and the
	4. 6	They were to be **used** to rinse the parts of the animals
	4. 6	in the large tank was for the priests to **use** for washing.
	4.11	King Solomon had commanded, for **use** in the Temple of the Lord.
	4.18	that no one determined the total weight of the bronze **used.**
	4.22	for incense, and the pans **used** for carrying live coals.
	8. 9	Israelites were not **used** in forced labour, but served as soldiers,
	9.11	Solomon **used** the wood to make stairs for the Temple and
	16. 6	timber that Baasha had been **using** at Ramah, and they used
	16. 6	using at Ramah, and they **used** them to fortify the cities of
	16.14	They **used** spices and perfumed oils to prepare his body for burial,
	22. 7	God **used** this visit to Joram to bring about Ahaziah's downfall.
	24. 7	damaged the Temple and had **used** many of the sacred objects
	24.14	the king and Jehoiada, who **used** it to have bowls and other
	25. 5	ready for battle, skilled in **using** spears and shields.
	29.26	instruments like those that King David had **used.**
	30.14	the altars that had been **used** in Jerusalem for offering
	34.11	the stones and the timber **used** to repair the buildings that
	35. 7	For the **use** of the people at the Passover, King Josiah
	35. 8	for the people, the priests, and the Levites to **use.**
	35.25	both men and women, to **use** this song when they mourn for
Ezra	2.63	there was a priest who could **use** the Urim and Thummim.
	7.18	You may **use** the silver and gold that is left over for
	7.19	that have been given to you for **use** in the temple services.
	7.25	"You, Ezra, **using** the wisdom which your God has given you,
	8.25	Israel had given to be **used** in the Temple, and I gave
Neh	3.31	as far as the building **used** by the temple workmen and the
	7.65	there was a priest who could **use** the Urim and Thummim.
	10.38	tithes are collected, and for **use** in the Temple the Levites
	13. 5	He allowed Tobiah to **use** a large room that was intended
	13. 5	corn and incense, the equipment **used** in the Temple, the
	13. 7	Eliashib had allowed Tobiah to **use** a room in the Temple.
	13.21	I warned them, "It's no **use** waiting out there for
	13.21	If you try this again, I'll **use** force against you."
	13.31	I arranged for the wood **used** for burning the offerings
Esth	3.10	off his ring, which was **used** to stamp proclamations and make
	3.12	language and system of writing **used** in the empire and to be
Job	7.20	Why **use** me for your target-practice?
	8.12	first to wither, while still too small to be cut and **used.**
	16.12	God **uses** me for target-practice [13] and shoots arrows at me
	17. 6	And now people **use** this proverb against me;
	22. 1	man, even the wisest, who could ever be of **use** to God?
	22. 8	You **used** your power and your position to take over the
	23. 6	Would God **use** all his strength against me?
	36. 3	I will **use** what I know to show that God, my Creator,
	36.15	God teaches men through suffering and **uses** distress to open their eyes.
Ps	1. 1	example of sinners or join those who have no **use** for God.
	18.34	trains me for battle, so that I can **use** the strongest bow.
	19. 3	No speech or words are **used,** no sound is heard;
	54. 5	May God **use** their own evil to punish my enemies.
	60. 8	But I will **use** Moab as my wash-basin and I will throw
	68.28	God, the power you have **used** on our behalf [29] from your
	78. 2	I am going to **use** wise sayings and explain mysteries from
	102. 8	those who mock me **use** my name in cursing.
	104. 3	You **use** the clouds as your chariot and ride on the wings
	104. 4	You **use** the winds as your messengers and flashes of
	104.14	and plants for man to **use,** so that he can grow his
	108. 9	But I will **use** Moab as my wash-basin and I will throw
Prov	1.29	You have never had any **use** for knowledge and have always
Prov	3.34	He has no **use** for conceited people, but shows favour to
	11. 1	The Lord hates people who **use** dishonest scales.
	13. 8	A rich man has to **use** his money to save his life,
	19. 7	Even the brothers of a poor man have no **use** for him;
	20.10	The Lord hates people who **use** dishonest weights and measures.
	20.23	The Lord hates people who **use** dishonest scales and weights.
	26. 7	A fool can **use** a proverb
	26. 7	about as well as a crippled man can **use** his legs.
Ecc	2.11	It was like chasing the wind—of no **use** at all.
	5. 4	He has no **use** for a fool.
	7.23	I **used** my wisdom to test all of this.
	10.10	you don't sharpen it, you have to work harder to **use** it.
	10.11	a snake is of no **use** if you let the snake bite
	12.11	the sharp sticks that shepherds **use** to guide sheep, and
Is	3. 3	everyone who **uses** magic to control events.
	3.24	Instead of **using** perfumes, they will stink;
	6. 2	and its body with two, and **used** the other two for flying.
	10. 5	I **use** Assyria like a club to punish those with whom I
	10.15	an axe claim to be greater than the man who **uses** it?
	11.11	the Lord will once again **use** his power and bring back home
	23.18	who worship the Lord will **use** her money to buy the food
	27. 1	that day the Lord will **use** his powerful and deadly sword to
	28.11	God will **use** foreigners speaking some strange-sounding language
	28.27	He never **uses** a heavy club to beat out dill seeds or
	28.27	instead he **uses** light sticks of the proper size.
	33.15	Don't **use** your power to cheat the poor and don't accept bribes.
	36. 6	but that would be like **using** a reed as a walking-stick—it
	44.14	might cut down cedars to **use,** or choose oak or cypress wood
	44.15	A man **uses** part of a tree for fuel and part of
	47. 9	of all the magic you **use,** you will lose your husband and
	47.12	you have **used** them since you were young.
	49. 2	He made me like an arrow, sharp and ready for **use.**
	49. 4	I have **used** up my strength, but have accomplished nothing."
	51. 9	**Use** your power and save us;
	51. 9	**use** it as you did in ancient times.
	52.10	The Lord will **use** his holy power;
	54.16	I also create the soldier, who **uses** the weapons to kill.
	59.16	So he will **use** his own power to rescue them and to
	65.15	My chosen people will **use** your name as a curse.
	65.21	in them themselves—they will not be **used** by someone else.
Jer	8.15	for peace and a time of healing, but it was no **use;**
	23.34	prophet or a priest even **uses** the words 'the Lord's burden,'
	23.36	So they must no longer **use** the words 'the Lord's burden,'
	23.38	disobey my command and **use** the words 'the Lord's burden,'
	24. 9	about them, ridicule them, and **use** their name as a curse
	25.18	and so that people would **use** their name as a curse—as
	26. 6	nations of the world will **use** the name of this city as
	29.18	People will mock them and **use** their name as a curse.
	32.21	that terrified our enemies, you **used** your power and might to
	42.18	will treat you with scorn and **use** your name as a curse.
	44. 8	will treat you with scorn and **use** your name as a curse?
	44.12	will treat them with scorn and **use** their name as a curse.
	44.22	a horrifying sight, and people **use** its name as a curse
	44.26	I let any of you **use** my name to make a vow
	49.13	people will jeer at it and **use** its name as a curse.
	50.29	Send out everyone who knows how to **use** the bow and arrow.
	51.20	I **used** you to crush nations and kingdoms, [21] to shatter
	51.26	stones from your ruins will ever be **used** again for building.
	52.18	shovels and the ash containers **used** in cleaning the altar,
	52.18	the tools **used** in tending the lamps,
	52.18	the bowls **used** for catching the blood
	52.18	the bowls **used** for burning incense,
	52.18	all the other bronze articles **used** in the temple service.
	52.19	the small bowls, the pans **used** for carrying live coals,
	52.19	lampstands, the bowls **used** for incense,
	52.19	and the bowls **used** for pouring out offerings of wine.
Ezek	4.15	I will let you **use** cow dung instead, and you can bake
	5. 1	take a sharp sword and **use** it to shave off your beard
	7.19	They cannot **use** it to satisfy their desires or fill their stomachs.
	7.20	jewels, but they **used** them to make disgusting idols.
	13.18	death over my people and to **use** it for your own benefit.
	13.20	hate the wristbands that you **use** in your attempt to control
	15. 3	Can you **use** it to make anything?
	16.16	You **used** some of your clothes to decorate your places of worship,
	16.17	that I had given you, **used** it to make male images, and
	16.26	with you, and you **used** your prostitution to make me angry.
	16.44	The Lord said, "People will **use** this proverb about you,
	21. 4	I will **use** my sword against everyone from north to south.
	21.11	The sword is being polished, to make it ready for **use.**
	22.18	to me, [18] "Mortal man, the Israelites are of no **use** to me.
	23.17	They **used** her and defiled her so much that finally she
	23.43	to myself that they were **using** as a prostitute a woman worn
	24. 5	**Use** the meat of the finest sheep;
	27. 5	They **used** fir-trees from Mount Hermon for timber And a
	30.10	Sovereign Lord says, "I will **use** King Nebuchadnezzar of
	36.23	I will **use** you to show the nations that I am holy.
	39.21	and show them how I **use** my power to carry out my
	40.42	four tables in the annexe, **used** to prepare the offerings to
	40.42	All the equipment **used** in killing the sacrificial animals
	41. 8	the terrace and the buildings **used** by the priests there was
	43.13	the measurements of the altar, **using** the same unit of
	43.26	are to consecrate the altar and make it ready for **use.**
	44. 2	human being is allowed to **use** it, because I, the Lord God
	45.10	"Everyone must **use** honest weights and measures:
	47.12	food, and their leaves will be **used** for healing people."
	48. 8	section of the land is to be set apart for special **use.**
	48.15	is not holy, but is for the general **use** of the people.
	48.15	They may live there and **use** the land.
	48.18	the west—is to be **used** as farm land by the people
Dan	8.25	but he will be destroyed without the **use** of any human power.
	11.17	"The king of Syria will plan an expedition, **using** his whole army.

Dan 11.39 fortresses, he will **use** people who worship a foreign god.
11.40 with all his power, **using** chariots, horses, and many ships.
Hos 2. 8 the silver and gold that she **used** in the worship of Baal.
3. 4 pillars, without idols or images to **use** for divination.
9. 4 It will be **used** only to satisfy their hunger;
Amos 6. 6 wine by the bowlful and **use** the finest perfumes, but you do
7. 8 Then he said, "I am **using** it to show that my people
8. 5 Then we can overcharge, **use** false measures, and tamper with
Mic 2. 4 that time comes, people will **use** your story as an example of
5.12 charms you **use** and leave you without any fortune-tellers.
6.10 They **use** false measures, a thing that I hate.
6.11 How can I forgive men who **use** false scales and weights?
6.15 will press oil from olives, but never be able to **use** it.
Hab 1.17 Are they going to **use** their swords for ever and keep on
2.18 What's the **use** of an idol?
3. 9 You got ready to **use** your bow, ready to shoot your arrows.
Zeph 2.13 The Lord will **use** his power to destroy Assyria.
Zech 8. 4 women, so old that they **use** a stick when they walk, will
9.10 the bows **used** in battle will be destroyed.
9.13 I will **use** Judah like a soldier's bow and Israel like
9.13 I will **use** the men of Zion like a sword, to fight
14.21 will be set apart for **use** in the worship of the Lord
14.21 people who offer sacrifices will **use** them for boiling the
Mal 3.14 What's the **use** of doing what he says or of trying to
Mt 5.34 do not **use** any vow when you make a promise.
6. 7 "When you pray, do not **use** a lot of meaningless words,
9.17 pour new wine into **used** wineskins, for the skins will burst,
12.37 Your words will be **used** to judge you—to declare you
13. 3 He **used** parables to tell them many things.
13.10 asked him, "Why do you **use** parables when you talk to the
13.13 The reason I **use** parables in talking to them is that
13.34 Jesus **used** parables to tell all these things to the crowds;
13.34 he would not say a thing to them without **using** a parable.
13.35 come true, "I will **use** parables when I speak to them;
15. 5 has something he could **use** to help his father or mother,
15. 9 It is no **use** for them to worship me, because they teach
16.12 guard themselves from the yeast **used** in bread but from the
22. 1 Jesus again **used** parables in talking to the people.
27. 7 about it, they **used** the money to buy Potter's Field,
27.10 to pay for him, [10]and **used** the money to buy the potter's
27.24 saw that it was no **use** to go on, but that
Mk 2.21 "No one **uses** a piece of new cloth to patch up
2.22 pour new wine into **used** wineskins, because the wine will burst
4. 2 He **used** parables to teach them many things, saying to them:
4.24 The same rules you **use** to judge others
4.24 will be **used** by God to judge you—
4.30 "What parable shall we **use** to explain it?
4.33 preached his message to the people, **using** many other parables
4.34 not speak to them without **using** parables, but when he was
7. 7 It is no **use** for them to worship me, because they teach
7.11 has something he could **use** to help his father or mother,
14. 4 to one another, "What was the **use** of wasting the perfume?
Lk 5.37 pour new wine into **used** wineskins, because the new wine will
6.38 The measure you **use** for others
6.38 is the one that God will **use** for you."
8. 3 and many other women who **used** their own resources to help
9.62 keeps looking back is of no **use** to the Kingdom of God."
13. 7 Why should it go on **using** up the soil?'
19.22 I will **use** your own words to condemn you!
22.49 going to happen, they asked, "Shall we **use** our swords, Lord?"
23.53 been dug out of solid rock and which had never been **used.**
Jn 4. 9 (Jews will not **use** the same cups and bowls that Samaritans use.)
6.63 man's power is of no **use** at all.
16.25 "I have **used** figures of speech to tell you these things.
16.25 come when I will not **use** figures of speech, but will speak
16.29 "Now you are speaking plainly, without **using** figures of speech.
18.32 come true, the words he **used** when he indicated the kind of
Acts 4. 7 What power have you got or whose name did you **use?"**
5.26 They did not **use** force, however, because they were afraid that
7.25 that God was going to **use** him to set them free,
8.26 (This road is not **used** nowadays.)
19.12 handkerchiefs and aprons he had **used** were taken to those who
19.13 evil spirits also tried to **use** the name of the Lord Jesus
Rom 1.26 pervert the natural **use** of their sex by unnatural acts.
6.13 part of yourselves to sin to be **used** for wicked purposes.
6.13 your whole being to him to be **used** for righteous purposes.
6.19 (I **use** everyday language because of the weakness of your
7.13 by **using** what is good, sin brought death to me, in order
9.17 you king in order to **use** you to show my power and
9.21 pots has the right to **use** the clay as he wishes,
9.21 one for special occasions and the other for ordinary **use.**
10.19 "I will **use** a so-called nation to make my people jealous;
12. 6 So we are to **use** our different gifts in accordance with
15.27 the Gentiles ought to **use** their material blessings to help the
1 Cor 1.17 and to tell it without **using** the language of human wisdom,
2. 1 God's secret truth, I did not **use** big words and great learning.
3.10 **Using** the gift that God gave me, I did the work of
3.12 Some will **use** gold or silver or precious stones in building
3.12 others will **use** wood or grass or straw.
4. 6 this to Apollos and me, **using** the two of us as
6.13 body is not to be **used** for sexual immorality, but to serve
6.20 So **use** your bodies for God's glory.
7.21 if you have a chance to become a free man, **use** it.
8. 7 Some people have been so **used** to idols that to this day
9. 7 What shepherd does not **use** the milk from his own sheep?
9. 9 not muzzle an ox when you are **using** it to thresh corn."
9.12 But we haven't made **use** of this right.
9.15 But I haven't made **use** of any of these rights,
10.16 The cup we **use** in the Lord's Supper and for which we
13.11 I am a man, I have no more **use** for childish ways.
14. 6 to you, my brothers, what **use** will I be to you if
1 Cor 14.11 being spoken, the person who **uses** it will be a foreigner to
14.12 everything else to make greater **use** of those which help to
2 Cor 1. 4 have all kinds of troubles, **using** the same help that we
2.14 God **uses** us to make the knowledge about Christ spread everywhere
7. 9 That sadness was **used** by God, and so we caused you no
7.10 For the sadness that is **used** by God brings a change of
10. 4 The weapons we **use** in our fight are not the world's
10. 4 but God's powerful weapons, which we **use** to destroy strongholds.
13.10 deal harshly with you in **using** the authority that the Lord
Gal 3.15 My brothers, I am going to **use** an everyday example:
3.16 scripture does not **use** the plural "descendants," meaning many
5. 2 it means that Christ is of no **use** to you at all.
Eph 1.20 strength [20] which he **used** when he raised Christ from death
4.29 Do not **use** harmful words, but only helpful words,
5. 4 it fitting for you to **use** language which is obscene, profane,
5.16 Make good **use** of every opportunity you have,
6. 9 in the same way towards your slaves and stop **using** threats.
Phil 3.21 like his own glorious body, **using** that power by which he is
Col 1.29 and struggle, **using** the mighty strength which Christ supplies
2.22 these refer to things which become useless once they are **used;**
4. 5 are not believers, making good **use** of every opportunity you have.
1 Thes 2. 5 flattering talk, nor did we **use** words to cover up greed—
2 Thes 2.10 miracles and wonders, [10]and **use** every kind of wicked deceit
1 Tim 1. 8 Law is good if it is used as it should be **used.**
1.18 **Use** those words as weapons in order to fight well,
5.18 an ox when you are **using** it to thresh corn" and
2 Tim 2.20 some are for special occasions, others for ordinary **use.**
2.21 he will be **used** for special purposes, because he is
2.21 useful to his Master, ready to be **used** for every good deed.
Tit 2. 8 **Use** sound words that cannot be criticized, so that your enemies
2.15 Teach these things and **use** your full authority as you
Phlm 11 time he was of no **use** to you, but now he is
Heb 6.13 one greater than himself, he **used** his own name when he made
6.16 person makes a vow, he **uses** the name of someone greater than
9.18 first covenant came into effect only with the **use** of blood.
9.19 and all the people, **using** a sprig of hyssop and some
9.21 the Covenant Tent and over all the things **used** in worship.
Jas 3. 9 We **use** it to give thanks to our Lord and Father
4. 3 you ask for things to **use** for your own pleasures.
5.12 my brothers, do not **use** an oath when you make a
1 Pet 2. 5 and let yourselves be **used** in building the spiritual temple,
2.16 do not, however, **use** your freedom to cover up any evil,
3. 3 You should not **use** outward aids to make yourselves beautiful,
4.10 of God's different gifts, must **use** for the good of others
2 Pet 2.18 and stupid statements, and **use** immoral bodily lusts to trap those
3.15 Paul wrote to you, **using** the wisdom that God gave him.
Rev 9.19 like snakes with heads, and they **use** them to hurt people.
13.12 It **used** the vast authority of the first beast in its presence.
14.15 sitting on the cloud, **"Use** your sickle and reap the harvest,
14.18 who had the sharp sickle, **"Use** your sickle, and cut the
21.17 according to the standard unit of measure which he was **using.**

USEFUL

Rom 7. 4 in order that we might be **useful** in the service of God.
2 Tim 2.21 because he is dedicated and **useful** to his Master, ready to
3.16 inspired by God and is **useful** for teaching the truth,
Tit 3. 8 to doing good deeds, which are good and **useful** for everyone.
Phlm 11 but now he is **useful** both to you and to me.
Heb 6. 7 which grows plants that are **useful** to those for whom it is

USELESS

1 Sam 15. 9 they destroyed only what was **useless** or worthless.
2 Sam 1.27 "The brave soldiers have fallen, their weapons abandoned and **useless."**
Job 13.12 Your proverbs are as **useless** as ashes;
35.13 It is **useless** for them to cry out;
35.16 It is **useless** for you to go on talking;
Ps 2. 1 Why do people make their **useless** plots?
33.17 War-horses are **useless** for victory;
76. 5 all their strength and skill was **useless.**
89.43 You have made his weapons **useless** and let him be
107.27 staggered like drunken men— all their skill was **useless.**
119.83 I am as **useless** as a discarded wineskin;
119.118 their deceitful schemes are **useless.**
127. 1 not build the house, the work of the builders is **useless;**
127. 1 the city, it is **useless** for the sentries to stand guard.
127. 2 It is **useless** to work so hard for a living, getting up
Prov 12.11 to eat, but it is stupid to waste time on **useless** projects.
Ecc 1. 2 It is **useless, useless,** said the Philosopher.
1. 2 Life is **useless,** all useless.
1.14 done in this world, and I tell you, it is all **useless.**
2. 1 But I found that this is **useless,** too.
2.17 It had all been **useless;**
2.19 It is all **useless.**
2.21 It is **useless,** and it isn't right!
2.23 It is all **useless.**
2.26 It is all **useless.**
4. 4 But it is **useless.**
4. 7 I have noticed something else in life that is **useless.**
4. 8 This is **useless,** too—and a miserable way to live.
4.16 It is **useless.**
5. 7 much you dream, how much **useless** work you do, or how much
5.10 It is **useless.**
6. 2 It is **useless,** and it's all wrong.
6. 9 It is **useless;**
6.11 longer you argue, the more **useless** it is, and you are no
6.12 a man in this short, **useless** life of his—a life that
7.15 My life has been **useless,** but in it I have seen everything.

Ecc 8.10 It is **useless.**
8.14 I say it is **useless.**
9. 9 long as you live the **useless** life that God has given you
9. 9 Enjoy every **useless** day of it, because that is all you will
12. 8 **Useless, useless,** said the Philosopher.
12. 8 It is all **useless.**
Is 1.13 It's **useless** to bring your offerings.
8.10 But it is all **useless,** because God is with us.
19. 8 their hooks and their nets will be **useless.**
29.14 to be fools, and all their cleverness will be **useless."**
30. 7 The help that Egypt gives is **useless.**
33.11 You make worthless plans and everything you do is **useless.**
33.22 All the rigging on those ships is **useless;**
41.29 All these gods are **useless;**
44. 9 worthless, and the gods they prize so highly are **useless.**
59. 5 you no good—they are as **useless** as clothing made of cobwebs!
Jer 2. 8 the prophets spoke in the name of Baal and worshipped **useless** idols.
6.29 It is **useless** to go on refining my people, because those who
8.19 idols and by bowing down to your **useless** foreign gods?"
16.19 "Our ancestors had nothing but false gods, nothing but **useless** idols.
46.11 All your medicine has proved **useless;**
Ezek 13. 4 Israel, your prophets are as **useless** as foxes living among
15. 5 It was **useless** even before it was burnt.
15. 5 has burnt it and charred it, it is even more **useless."**
22.19 Lord, am telling them that they are just as **useless** as that.
Hos 8. 8 like any other nation and is as **useless** as a broken pot.
10. 4 They utter empty words and make false promises and **useless** treaties.
12. 1 Israel do from morning to night is **useless** and destructive.
Hab 1. 4 The law is weak and **useless,** and justice is never done.
2.13 conquered wore themselves out in **useless** labour, and all
Zech 10. 2 the comfort they give is **useless.**
Mal 1.10 as to prevent you from lighting **useless** fires on my altar.
3.14 You have said, 'It's **useless** to serve God.
Mt 12.36 to give account of every **useless** word he has ever spoken.
25.30 As for this **useless** servant—throw him outside in the darkness;
Acts 4.25 why did people make their **useless** plots?
1 Cor 15.58 that nothing you do in the Lord's service is ever **useless.**
Col 2.22 these refer to things which become **useless** once they are used;
Tit 3. 9 They are **useless** and worthless.
3.14 they should not live **useless** lives.
Heb 6. 1 of turning away from **useless** works and believing in God;
7.18 rule, then, is set aside, because it was weak and **useless.**
9.14 will purify our consciences from **useless** rituals,
Jas 2.20 Do you want to be shown that faith without actions is **useless?**

USUAL

Mk 15. 8 to ask Pilate for the **usual** favour, [9]he asked them, "Do
Lk 2.42 Jesus was twelve years old, they went to the festival as **usual.**
4.16 and on the Sabbath he went as **usual** to the synagogue.
22.39 and went, as he **usually** did, to the Mount of Olives;
Acts 17. 2 According to his **usual** habit Paul went to the synagogue.
Rom 9. 8 the children born in the **usual** way are not the children of
Gal 4.23 slave-woman was born in the **usual** way, but his son by the
4.29 who was born in the **usual** way persecuted the one who was

UTENSIL

Num 3.31 the lamp-stand, the altars, the **utensils** the priests use in
4.12 They shall take all the **utensils** used in the Holy Place,
1 Kgs 10.21 of gold, and all the **utensils** in the Hall of the Forest
2 Kgs 24.13 broke up all the gold **utensils** which King Solomon had made
1 Chr 9.28 Other Levites were responsible for the **utensils** used in worship.
18. 8 tank, the columns, and the bronze **utensils** for the Temple.)
28.13 of the Temple, and to take care of all the temple **utensils.**
28.14 for making the **utensils,** [15]for each lamp and lampstand,
2 Chr 9.20 of gold, and all the **utensils** in the Hall of the Forest
24.14 it to have bowls and other **utensils** made for the Temple.
Ezra 1. 6 **utensils,** gold, supplies, pack animals, other valuables,
1. 9 other **utensils** 1,000
5.14 the gold and silver temple **utensils** which Nebuchadnezzar had
5.14 Cyrus handed these **utensils** over to a man named Sheshbazzar,
6. 5 Also the gold and silver **utensils** which King
7.19 God in Jerusalem all the **utensils** that have been given to
8.25 silver, the gold, and the **utensils** which the emperor, his
8.26 100 silver **utensils** - 70 kilogrammes
8.28 and gold **utensils** brought to him as freewill offerings.
8.30 silver, the gold, and the **utensils,** to take them to the
8.33 silver, the gold, and the **utensils,** and handed them over to
Neh 10.39 to the storerooms where the **utensils** for the Temple are kept

UTTER

Num 23. 7 Balaam **uttered** this prophecy:
23.18 and Balaam **uttered** this prophecy:
24. 3 of God took control of him, [3]and he **uttered** this prophecy:
24.15 Then he **uttered** this prophecy:
24.20 Balaam saw the Amalekites and **uttered** this prophecy:
24.21 In his vision he saw the Kenites, and **uttered** this prophecy:
24.23 Balaam **uttered** this prophecy:
Hos 10. 4 They **utter** empty words and make false promises and useless treaties.

UZZIAH (1)

King of Judah who reigned for a long time.

2 Kgs 14.21 crowned his sixteen-year-old son **Uzziah** as king.
14.22 **Uzziah** reconquered and rebuilt Elath after his father's death.
2 Kgs 15. 1 King Jeroboam II of Israel, **Uzziah** son of Amaziah became
15. 5 The Lord struck **Uzziah** with a dreaded skin-disease that
15. 6 Everything else that **Uzziah** did is recorded in The
15. 7 **Uzziah** died and was buried in the royal burial ground in
15. 8 of the reign of King **Uzziah** of Judah, Zechariah son of
15.13 of the reign of King **Uzziah** of Judah, Shallum son of Jabesh
15.17 of the reign of King **Uzziah** of Judah, Menahem son of Gadi
15.23 of the reign of King **Uzziah** of Judah, Pekahiah son of
15.27 of the reign of King **Uzziah** of Judah, Pekah son of Remaliah
15.30 reign of Jotham son of **Uzziah** as king of Judah, Hoshea son
15.32 of Israel, Jotham son of **Uzziah** became king of Judah [33]at
15.34 the example of his father **Uzziah,** Jotham did what was
1 Chr 3.12 Jehoram, Ahaziah, Joash, [12]Amaziah, **Uzziah,**
2 Chr 26. 1 Amaziah's sixteen-year-old son **Uzziah** to succeed his father
26. 2 Amaziah that **Uzziah** recaptured Elath and rebuilt the city.)
26. 3 **Uzziah** became king at the age of sixteen, and he ruled in
26. 6 **Uzziah** went to war against the Philistines.
26. 8 The Ammonites paid tribute to **Uzziah,** and he became so
26. 9 **Uzziah** strengthened the fortifications of Jerusalem by
26.14 **Uzziah** supplied the army with shields, spears, helmets,
26.16 But when King **Uzziah** became strong, he grew arrogant,
26.18 They said, **"Uzziah!**
26.19 **Uzziah** was standing there in the Temple beside the
26.21 rest of his life King **Uzziah** was ritually unclean because of
26.22 all the other things that King **Uzziah** did during his reign.
26.23 **Uzziah** died and was buried in the royal burial-ground,
Is 1. 1 Amoz during the time when **Uzziah,** Jotham, Ahaz, and Hezekiah
6. 1 In the year that King **Uzziah** died, I saw the Lord.
7. 1 son of Jotham and grandson of **Uzziah,** ruled Judah, war broke
Hos 1. 1 Beeri during the time that **Uzziah,** Jotham, Ahaz, and
Amos 1. 1 years before the earthquake, when **Uzziah** was king of Judah
Zech 14. 5 the earthquake struck in the time of King **Uzziah** of Judah.
Mt 1. 6 Asa, Jehoshaphat, Jehoram, **Uzziah,** Jotham, Ahaz, Hezekiah,

UZZIEL (1)

Kohath's son.

Ex 6.18 Amram, Izhar, Hebron, and **Uzziel.**
6.22 **Uzziel** also had three sons:
Lev 10. 4 the sons of **Uzziel,** Aaron's uncle, and said to them,
Num 3.17 Amram, Izhar, Hebron, and **Uzziel;**
3.27 Kohath was composed of the families of Amram, Izhar, Hebron, and **Uzziel.**
3.30 Tent, [30]with Elizaphan son of **Uzziel** as chief of the clan.
1 Chr 6. 2 Amram, Izhar, Hebron, and **Uzziel.**
6.18 Kohath was the father of Amram, Izhar, Hebron, and **Uzziel;**
15.10 and from the clan of **Uzziel,** Amminadab, in charge of 112.
23.12 Amram, Izhar, Hebron, and **Uzziel.**
23.20 Kohath's fourth son, **Uzziel,** had two sons, Micah and Isshiah.
24.24 Shamir, a descendant of **Uzziel** through Micah;
24.25 Zechariah, a descendant of **Uzziel** through Isshiah, Micah's brother;
26.23 to the descendants of Amram, Izhar, Hebron, and **Uzziel.**

VAIN

Deut 28.32 your eyes, looking in **vain** for your children to return.
Is 53.11 he will know that he did not suffer in **vain.**

AV VAIN

see also **USELESS, WORTHLESS**

Ex 5. 9 that they won't have time to listen to a pack of **lies."**
Deut 32.47 These teachings are not **empty** words;
1 Sam 12.21 Don't go after **false gods;**
12.21 they cannot help you or save you, for they are not **real.**
2 Sam 6.20 exposed himself like a **fool** in the sight of the servant-girls
Job 11.12 **Stupid** men will start being wise when wild donkeys are born tame.
15. 1 **Empty** words, Job!
27.12 so why do you talk such **nonsense?**
Ps 39. 6 All he does is for **nothing;**
Prov 31.30 Charm is **deceptive** and beauty disappears,
Jer 4.14 How long will you go on thinking **sinful** thoughts?
23.16 they are filling you with **false** hopes.
Lam 2.14 Your prophets had nothing to tell you but **lies;**
Mt 6. 7 not use a lot of **meaningless** words, as the pagans do,
Rom 1.21 thoughts have become complete **nonsense,** and their empty minds
1 Cor 15.14 we have nothing to preach and you have **nothing** to believe.
15.17 then your faith is a **delusion** and you are still lost in
Eph 5. 6 Do not let anyone deceive you with **foolish** words;
1 Tim 1. 6 from these and have lost their way in **foolish** discussions.
6.20 Avoid the profane talk and **foolish** arguments of what some
2 Tim 2.16 Keep away from profane and **foolish** discussions, which
Tit 1.10 from Judaism, who rebel and deceive others with their **nonsense.**
Jas 2.20 You **fool!**

AV VAIN GLORY

Gal 5.26 **proud** or irritate one another or be jealous of one another.
Phil 2. 3 a cheap desire to **boast,** but be humble towards one another,

VALID

Num 19.10 This regulation is **valid** for all time to come, both for the
25.12 a covenant with him that is **valid** for all time to come.

VALLEY

Gen 13.10 saw that the whole Jordan **Valley,** all the way to Zoar had
13.11 Lot chose the whole Jordan **Valley** for himself and moved away

Gen	13.12	among the cities in the **valley** and camped near Sodom,
	14. 3	and joined forces in the **Valley** of Siddim, which is now the
	14. 8	armies for battle in the **Valley** of Siddim and fought
	14.10	The **valley** was full of tar pits, and when the kings of
	14.17	him in the Valley of Shaveh (also called the King's **Valley**).
	19.17	Don't look back and don't stop in the **valley**.
	19.25	destroyed them and the whole **valley**, along with all the
	19.28	and Gomorrah and the whole **valley** and saw smoke rising from
	19.29	destroyed the cities of the **valley** where Lot was living, he
	26.17	up his camp in the **Valley** of Gerar, where he stayed for
	26.19	Isaac's servants dug a well in the **valley** and found water.
	37.14	his father sent him on his way from the **Valley** of Hebron.
Num	13.23	They came to the **Valley** of Eshcol, and there they cut
	13.24	(That place was named the **Valley** of Eshcol because of
	14.25	possess the land [25] in whose **valleys** the Amalekites and the
	21.12	Then they camped in the **Valley** of Zered.
	21.14	the town of Waheb in the area of Suphah, and the **valleys**;
	21.15	and the slope of the **valleys** that extend to the town of
	21.20	and from Bamoth to the **valley** in the territory of the Moabites,
	25. 1	Israelites were camped in the **Valley** of Acacia, the men
	32. 9	went as far as the **Valley** of Eshcol and saw the land,
	33.41	between Beth Jeshimoth and the **Valley** of Acacia.
	34. 5	it will turn towards the **valley** at the border of Egypt and
Deut	1. 1	They were in the Jordan **Valley** near Suph, between the town
	1. 7	the Jordan **Valley**, to the hill-country and the lowlands,
	1.24	hill-country as far as the **Valley** of Eshcol and explored it.
	2.36	on the edge of the **valley** of the Arnon, and the city
	2.36	in the middle of that **valley**, all the way to Gilead.
	3.29	"So we remained in the **valley** opposite the town of Bethpeor."
	4.45	Egypt and were in the **valley** east of the River Jordan,
	8. 7	underground streams gushing out into the **valleys** and hills;
	11.11	is a land of mountains and **valleys**, a land watered by rain.
	11.30	territory of the Canaanites who live in the Jordan **Valley**.
	34. 6	Lord buried him in a **valley** in Moab, opposite the town of
Josh	7.24	and they took them to Trouble **Valley**.
	7.26	That is why that place is still called Trouble **Valley**.
	8.11	on the north side, with a **valley** between themselves and Ai.
	8.13	Joshua spent the night in the **valley**.
	8.14	went out towards the Jordan **Valley** to fight the Israelites
	10.12	Moon, stop over Aijalon **Valley**."
	11. 2	the orth, in the Jordan **Valley** south of Lake Galilee, in
	11. 8	Maim and Sidon, and as far east as the **valley** of Mizpah.
	11.16	the dry country south of it, as well as the Jordan **Valley**.
	11.17	the north, in the **valley** of Lebanon south of Mount Hermon.
	12. 1	the Jordan, from the Arnon Valley up the Jordan Valley and
	12. 2	(on the edge of the **valley** of the Arnon) and the city
	12. 2	in the middle of that **valley**, as far as the River Jabbok,
	12. 3	it included the Jordan **Valley** from Lake Galilee south to
	12. 7	Jordan, from Baalgad in the **valley** of Lebanon to Mount Halak
	12. 8	the Jordan **Valley** and its foothills, the eastern slopes,
	13. 9	the edge of the Arnon **Valley**) and the city
	13. 9	in the middle of that **valley** and included all the plateau
	13.16	the edge of the Arnon **Valley**) and the city
	13.16	in the middle of that **valley** and included all the plateau
	13.19	in the **valley**, [20] Bethpeor, the slopes of Mount Pisgah,
	13.27	In the Jordan **Valley** it included Beth Haram, Bethnimrah,
	15. 6	and went north of the ridge overlooking the Jordan **Valley**.
	15. 7	son of Reuben), [7] from Trouble **Valley** up to Debir, and then
	15. 7	which faces Adummim Pass on the south side of the **valley**.
	15. 8	Enrogel, [8] and up through the **Valley** of Hinnom on the south
	15. 8	the west side of the **Valley** of Hinnom,
	15. 8	at the northern end of the **Valley** of Rephaim.
	17.16	towns and those who live in the **Valley** of Jezreel."
	18.16	the mountain that overlooks the **Valley** of Hinnom,
	18.16	at the north end of the **Valley** of Rephaim.
	18.16	then went south through the **Valley** of Hinnom, south of the
	18.18	and passed north of the ridge overlooking the Jordan **Valley**.
	18.18	then went down into the **valley**, [19] passing north of the
	19.14	turned towards Hannathon, ending at the **Valley** of Iphtahel.
	19.27	Bethdagon, touching Zebulun and the **Valley** of Iphtahel on
Judg	5.14	came from Ephraim into the **valley**, behind the tribe of
	5.15	Issachar came and Barak too, and they followed him into the **valley**.
	6.33	the River Jordan, and camped in the **Valley** of Jezreel.
	7. 1	Midianite camp was in the **valley** to the north of them by
	7. 8	The Midianite camp was below them in the **valley**.
	7.12	were spread out in the **valley** like a swarm of locusts, and
	16. 4	a woman named Delilah, who lived in the **Valley** of Sorek.
	18.27	quiet people which was in the same **valley** as Bethrehob.
1 Sam	6.13	were harvesting wheat in the **valley**, when suddenly they
	13.18	border overlooking the **Valley** of Zeboim and the wilderness.
	17. 2	assembled and camped in the **Valley** of Elah, where they got
	17. 3	and the Israelites on another, with a **valley** between them.
	17.19	Israelites are in the **Valley** of Elah fighting the Philistines."
	21. 9	Goliath the Philistine, whom you killed in the **Valley** of Elah;
	23.24	of Maon, in a desolate **valley** in the southern part of the
	26.13	the other side of the **valley** to the top of the hill,
	29. 1	Israelites camped at the spring in the **Valley** of Jezreel.
	31. 7	the other side of the **Valley** of Jezreel and east of the
2 Sam	2.29	Abner and his men marched through the Jordan **Valley**
	4. 7	with them, and walked all night through the Jordan **Valley**.
	5.18	The Philistines arrived at the **Valley** of Rephaim and occupied it.
	5.22	went back to the **Valley** of Rephaim and occupied it again.
	8.13	killing eighteen thousand Edomites in the **Valley** of Salt.
	17.13	bring ropes and just pull the city into the **valley** below.
	18.18	monument for himself in King's **Valley**, because he had no son
	18.23	through the Jordan **Valley**, and soon he passed the slave.
	23.13	a band of Philistines was camping in the **Valley** of Rephaim.
	23.24	from Pirathon Hiddai from the **valleys** near Gaash Abialbon
	24. 5	city in the middle of the **valley**, in the territory of Gad.
1 Kgs	7.46	foundry between Sukkoth and Zarethan, in the Jordan **Valley**.
1 Kgs	15.13	down the idol and burnt it in the **valley** of the Kidron.
2 Kgs	2.16	him away and left him on some mountain or in some **valley**."
	14. 7	Amaziah killed ten thousand Edomite soldiers in Salt **Valley**;
	23. 4	outside the city near the **valley** of the Kidron, and then had
	23. 6	of the city to the **valley** of the Kidron, burnt it, pounded
	23.10	place of worship in the **Valley** of Hinnom, so that no one
	23.12	altars to bits and threw them into the **valley** of the Kidron.
	25. 4	two walls, and fled in the direction of the Jordan **Valley**.
1 Chr	4.14	Joab, the founder of the **Valley** of Craftsmen, where all the
	4.39	eastern side of the **valley** in which that city is located.
	10. 7	Israelites who lived in the **Valley** of Jezreel heard that the
	11.15	a band of Philistines was camping in the **Valley** of Rephaim.
	11.26	from Pirathon Hurai from the **valleys** near Gaash Abiel from
	12.15	people who lived in the **valleys** both east and west of the
	14. 9	The Philistines arrived at the **Valley** of Rephaim
	14.13	Soon the Philistines returned to the **valley**
	18.12	defeated the Edomites in the **Valley** of Salt and killed
	27.25	Cattle in the **valleys**: Shaphat son of Adlai
2 Chr	4.17	foundry between Sukkoth and Zeredah in the Jordan **Valley**.
	14.10	up their positions in the **Valley** of Zephathah near Mareshah.
	15.16	it up, and burnt the pieces in the **valley** of the Kidron.
	20.16	at the end of the **valley** that leads to the wild country
	20.26	day they assembled in the **Valley** of Beracah and praised the
	20.26	That is why the **valley** is called "Beracah."
	25.11	up his courage and led his army to the **Valley** of Salt.
	28. 3	made, [3] burnt incense in the **Valley** of Hinnom, and even
	29.16	took it all outside the city to the **valley** of the Kidron.
	30.14	incense and threw them into the **valley** of the Kidron.
	33. 6	He sacrificed his sons in the **Valley** of Hinnom as burnt-offerings.
	33.14	from a point in the **valley** near the spring of Gihon north
Neh	2.15	I went down into the **valley** of the Kidron and rode along,
	11.30	Beersheba in the south and the **Valley** of Hinnom in the north.
	11.35	Lod, and Ono, and in the **Valley** of Craftsmen.
Job	38.14	Daylight makes the hills and **valleys** stand out like the
	39.21	They eagerly paw the ground in the **valley**;
Ps	60. 6	Shechem and distribute the **Valley** of Sukkoth to my people.
	65.13	the **valleys** are full of wheat.
	84. 6	they pass through the dry **valley** of Baca, it becomes a place
	104. 8	the mountains and into the **valleys**, to the place you had
	104.10	flow in the **valleys**, and rivers run between the hills.
	108. 7	Shechem and distribute the **Valley** of Sukkoth to my people.
Song	2. 1	only a wild flower in Sharon, a lily in a mountain **valley**.
	6.11	the young plants in the **valley**, to see the new leaves on
Is	7.19	will swarm in the rugged **valleys** and in the caves in the
	15. 7	The people go across the **Valley** of Willows, trying to
	17. 5	as a field in the **valley** of Rephaim when it has been
	22. 1	This is a message about the **Valley** of Vision.
	22. 5	defeat, and confusion in the **Valley** of Vision, and the
	22. 7	The fertile **valleys** of Judah were filled with chariots;
	28.21	Mount Perazim and in the **valley** of Gibeon, in order to do
	33. 9	the fertile **valley** of Sharon is like a desert,
	40. 4	Fill every **valley**;
	41.18	among barren hills and springs of water run in the **valleys**.
	42.15	I will turn the river **valleys** into deserts and dry up the
	63.14	are led into a fertile **valley**, so the Lord gave his people
	65.10	in the west and in the **Valley** of Trouble in the east.
Jer	2.23	Look how you sinned in the **valley**;
	7.31	In the **Valley** of Hinnom they have built an altar called Topheth,
	7.32	Topheth or the Valley of Hinnom, but the **Valley** of Slaughter.
	19. 2	and to go through Potsherd Gate out to the **Valley** of Hinnom.
	19. 6	will no longer be called Topheth or the **Valley** of Hinnom.
	19. 6	Instead, it will be known as the **Valley** of Slaughter.
	21.13	are sitting high above the **valleys**, like a rock rising above
	31.40	The entire **valley**, where the dead are buried and refuse is thrown,
	32.35	altars to Baal in the **Valley** of Hinnom, to sacrifice their
	39. 4	walls, and escaped in the direction of the Jordan **Valley**.
	48. 8	both **valley** and plain will be ruined.
	52. 7	two walls, and fled in the direction of the Jordan **Valley**.
Ezek	3.22	him say to me, "Get up and go out into the **valley**.
	3.23	I went out into the **valley**, and there I saw the glory
	6. 3	the mountains, the hills, the gorges, and the **valleys**:
	7.16	escape to the mountains like doves frightened from the **valleys**.
	31.12	will fall on every mountain and **valley** in the country.
	32. 5	I will cover mountains and **valleys** with your rotting corpse.
	34.14	the mountain meadows and the **valleys** and in all the green
	35. 8	who are killed in battle will cover the hills and **valleys**.
	36. 4	hills, to you brooks and **valleys**, to you places that were
	36. 6	hills, brooks, and **valleys** what I, the Sovereign Lord,
	37. 1	set me down in a **valley** where the ground was covered with
	37. 2	led me all round the **valley**, and I could see that there
	39.11	in Israel, in Travellers' **Valley**, east of the Dead Sea.
	39.11	and the valley will be called 'The **Valley** of Gog's Army.'
	39.15	can come and bury it in the **Valley** of Gog's Army.
	47. 8	east and down into the Jordan **Valley** and to the Dead Sea.
Hos	1. 5	And in the **Valley** of Jezreel I will at that time destroy
	2.15	vineyards she had and make Trouble **Valley** a door of hope.
Joel	3. 2	all the nations and bring them to the **Valley** of Judgement.
	3.11	all you surrounding nations, and gather in the **valley**.' "
	3.12	"The nations must get ready and come to the **Valley** of Judgement.
	3.14	Thousands and thousands are in the **Valley** of Judgement.
	3.18	Temple of the Lord, and it will water the **Valley** of Acacia.
Amos	1. 5	remove the inhabitants of the **Valley** of Aven and the ruler
Mic	1. 4	pour down into the **valleys** like water pouring down a hill.
	1. 6	the city down into the **valley**, and will lay bare the city's
Zech	1. 8	among some myrtle-trees in a **valley**, and behind him were
	14. 4	be split in two from east to west by a large **valley**.
	14. 5	escape through this **valley** that divides the mountain in two.
Lk	3. 5	Every **valley** must be filled up, every hill and mountain levelled

VALLEY GATE

2 Chr 26. 9 Corner Gate, at the **Valley Gate,** and where the wall turned.
Neh 2.13 left the city through the **Valley Gate** on the west and went
2.15 come and went back into the city through the **Valley Gate.**
3.13 inhabitants of the city of Zanoah rebuilt the **Valley Gate.**

VALUABLES

Ex 22. 7 another man's money or other **valuables** for him and they are
22. 8 man who was keeping the **valuables** is to be brought to the
Josh 11.14 of Israel took all the **valuables** and livestock from these
Ezra 1. 6 animals, other **valuables,** and offerings for the Temple.

VALUE

Gen 34.29 They took everything of **value,** captured all the women and children,
Lev 5.15 Its **value** is to be determined according to the official standard.
5.18 Its **value** is to be determined according to the official standard.
6. 6 Its **value** is to be determined according to the official standard.
22.14 priest its full **value** plus an additional twenty per cent.
27.18 priest shall estimate the cash **value** according to the number
27.23 the priest shall estimate its **value** according to the
1 Kgs 10.21 used, since it was not considered **valuable** in Solomon's day.
20. 6 officials, and to take everything they consider **valuable.**
2 Kgs 8. 6 that was hers, including the **value** of all the crops that her
2 Chr 9.20 Silver was not considered **valuable** in Solomon's day.
20.25 many cattle, supplies, clothing, and other **valuable** objects.
21. 3 of gold, silver, and other **valuable** possessions, and placed
32.27 stones, spices, shields, and other **valuable** objects.
Ezra 8.26 2 fine bronze bowls, equal in **value** to gold bowls
Job 28.13 No one knows its true **value.**
28.16 The finest gold and jewels Cannot equal its **value.**
28.18 The **value** of wisdom is more Than coral or crystal or rubies.
28.19 the purest gold Cannot compare with the **value** of wisdom.
Ps 44.12 people for a small price as though they had little **value.**
Prov 3.15 Wisdom is more **valuable** than jewels;
20.15 you have something more **valuable** than gold or jewels.
23.23 are worth paying for, but too **valuable** for you to sell.
24. 4 the rooms are furnished with **valuable,** beautiful things.
25.12 willing to listen is more **valuable** than gold rings or
31.18 She knows the **value** of everything she makes, and works
Is 58.13 if you **value** my holy day and honour it by not travelling,
Hos 13.15 It will take away everything of **value.**
Lk 16.15 that are considered of great **value** by man are worth nothing
Rom 2.25 If you obey the Law, your circumcision is of **value;**
3. 1 Or is there any **value** in being circumcised?
1 Cor 2.14 nonsense to him, because their **value** can be judged only on
2.15 is able to judge the **value** of everything, but no one is
14. 5 God's message is of greater **value** than the one who speaks in
Phil 3. 8 what is so much more **valuable,** the knowledge of Christ Jesus
Col 2.23 they have no real **value** in controlling physical passions.
1 Tim 4. 8 Physical exercise has some **value,**
4. 8 but spiritual exercise is **valuable** in every way,
1 Pet 2. 4 rejected by man as worthless but chosen by God as **valuable.**
2. 6 scripture says, "I chose a **valuable** stone, which I am placing
2. 7 This stone is of great **value** for you that believe;
3. 4 quiet spirit, which is of the greatest **value** in God's sight.

VANISH

Num 16.33 The earth closed over them, and they **vanished.**
Job 8.22 who hate you, and the homes of the wicked will **vanish.**
15.29 Even his shadow will **vanish,** [30] and he will not escape
20. 8 He will **vanish** like a dream, like a vision at night, and
24.19 As snow **vanishes** in heat and drought,
24.19 so a sinner **vanishes** from the land of the living.
Ps 10.16 Those who worship other gods will **vanish** from his land.
37.20 the enemies of the Lord will **vanish** like wild flowers;
102.26 You will discard them like clothes, and they will **vanish.**
109.23 Like an evening shadow I am about to **vanish;**
Is 29. 7 weapons and equipment—everything—will **vanish** like a dream,
50. 9 they will **vanish** like moth-eaten cloth.
51. 8 they will **vanish** like moth-eaten clothing!
Ezek 27.34 all who worked for you Have **vanished** with you in the sea.'
Hos 6. 4 it is like dew, that **vanishes** early in the day.
13. 3 morning mist, like the dew that **vanishes** early in the day.
Obad 16 they will drink it all and **vanish** away.
1 Cor 14. 9 Your words will **vanish** in the air!
2 Pet 3.10 and the earth with everything in it will **vanish.**
Rev 16.20 All the islands disappeared, all the mountains **vanished.**
21. 1 first heaven and the first earth disappeared, and the sea **vanished.**

AV **VANITY**

see also **USELESS**

2 Kgs 17.15 They worshipped **worthless** idols and became worthless themselves,
Job 7. 3 Month after month I have **nothing** to live for;
7.16 My life makes no **sense.**
15.31 If he is **foolish** enough to trust in evil, then evil will
15.35 their hearts are always full of **deceit.**
31. 5 I have never acted wickedly and never tried to **deceive** others.
Ps 4. 2 will you love what is **worthless** and go after what is false?
10. 7 His speech is filled with curses, **lies,** and threats;
12. 2 All of them **lie** to one another;
24. 4 in thought, who do not worship **idols** or make false promises.
39. 5 In your sight my lifetime seems **nothing.**
39.11 Indeed a man is no more than a puff of **wind!**
41. 6 Those who come to see me are not **sincere;**
62. 9 great and small alike are **worthless.**
78.33 days like a **breath** and their lives with sudden disaster.
94.11 he knows how **senseless** their reasoning is.
119.37 Keep me from paying attention to what is **worthless;**
144. 4 He is like a puff of **wind;**
144. 8 who never tell the **truth** and lie even under oath.
144.11 who never tell the **truth** and lie even under oath.
Prov 21. 6 The riches you get by **dishonesty** soon disappear,
22. 8 sow the seeds of injustice, **disaster** will spring up,
Ecc 2.11 worked doing it, and I realized that it didn't **mean** a thing.
2.15 **"Nothing,"** I answered, "not a thing."
3.19 off than an animal, because life has no **meaning** for either.
7. 6 It doesn't **mean** a thing.
8.14 But this is **nonsense.**
11. 8 There is **nothing** at all to look forward to.
Is 40.17 The nations are **nothing** at all to him.
40.23 He brings down powerful rulers and reduces them to **nothing.**
57.13 A puff of **wind** will carry them off!
58. 9 to every gesture of contempt, and to every **evil** word;
Jer 2. 5 They worshipped **worthless** idols and became worthless themselves.
10.15 They are **worthless** and should be despised;
16.19 "Our ancestors had nothing but **false gods,**
18.15 they burn incense to **idols.**
51.18 They are **worthless** and should be despised;
Ezek 13. 6 Their visions are **false,** and their predictions are lies.
13. 8 to them, "Your words are **false,** and your visions are lies.
13. 9 who have **false** visions and make misleading predictions.
13.23 So now your **false** visions and misleading predictions are over.
21.29 visions that you see are **false,** and the predictions you make
22.28 They see **false** visions and make false predictions.
Hos 12.11 Yet **idols** are worshipped in Gilead, and those who worship
Zech 10. 2 but the answers they get are **lies** and nonsense.
Rom 8.20 was condemned to lose its **purpose,** not of its own will,
Eph 4.17 the heathen, whose thoughts are **worthless** [18] and whose minds
2 Pet 2.18 They make proud and **stupid** statements, and use immoral bodily

VARIOUS

Num 33.54 Divide the land among the **various** tribes and clans by drawing lots,
Josh 21.33 The **various** families of the clan of Gershon received a
1 Kgs 3. 3 animals and offered them as sacrifices on **various** altars.
9.23 labour working on Solomon's **various** building projects.
10.26 Jerusalem and the rest he stationed in **various** other cities.
1 Chr 15.16 of the Levites to assign **various** Levites to sing and to play
2 Chr 1.14 and the rest he stationed in **various** other cities.
8.10 the forced labour working on the **various** building projects.
9.25 Jerusalem and the rest he stationed in **various** other cities.
31. 2 giving praise and thanks in the **various** parts of the Temple.
34.13 and supervising the workmen on **various** jobs, and others kept
Neh 12.44 from the farms near the **various** cities the contributions for
Lk 4.40 friends who were sick with **various** diseases brought them to Jesus;
Heb 9.10 to do only with food, drink, and **various** purification ceremonies.

VASE

Job 28.17 is worth more than gold, Than a gold **vase** or finest glass.

VASHTI

King Xerxes's queen, who was succeeded by Esther.

Esth 1. 9 inside the royal palace Queen **Vashti** was giving a banquet
1.11 He ordered them to bring in Queen **Vashti,** wearing her royal crown.
1.12 when the servants told Queen **Vashti** of the king's command,
1.15 sent my servants to Queen **Vashti** with a command, and she
1.16 "Queen **Vashti** has insulted not only the king but also his
1.17 say, 'King Xerxes commanded Queen **Vashti** to come to him, and
1.19 issue a royal proclamation that **Vashti** may never again
2. 1 he kept thinking about what **Vashti** had done and about his
2. 4 girl you like best and make her queen in **Vashti's** place."
2.17 crown on her head and made her queen in place of **Vashti.**

VAST

Gen 7.11 all the outlets of the **vast** body of water beneath the earth
Deut 1.19 Sinai and went through that **vast** and fearful desert on the
2. 7 taken care of you as you wandered through this **vast** desert.
8.15 He led you through that **vast** and terrifying desert where
2 Chr 2. 6 because even all the **vastness** of heaven cannot contain him.
Is 31. 1 They are relying on Egypt's **vast** military strength—horses,
Rev 13. 2 the beast his own power, his throne, and his **vast** authority.
13.12 It used the **vast** authority of the first beast in its presence.

VAT

Hag 2.16 a hundred litres of wine from a **vat,** but find only forty.

VEAL

Amos 6. 4 out on your luxurious couches, feasting on **veal** and lamb!

VEGETABLES

1 Kgs 21. 2 palace, and I want to use the land for a **vegetable** garden.
Prov 15.17 Better to eat **vegetables** with people you love than to
Dan 1.12 "Give us **vegetables** to eat and water to drink.
1.16 to eat **vegetables** instead of what the king provided.
Rom 14. 2 the person who is weak in the faith eats only **vegetables.**

Rom 14. 3 the one who eats only **vegetables** is not to pass judgement on
14.10 You then, who eat only **vegetables**—why do you pass

VEIL

Gen 38.14 covered her face with a **veil**, and sat down at the entrance
38.19 went home, took off her **veil**, and put her widow's clothes
Ex 34.33 finished speaking to them, he covered his face with a **veil**.
34.34 Lord's presence to speak to the Lord, he took the **veil** off.
34.35 Then he would put the **veil** back on until the next time
Song 4. 1 How your eyes shine with love behind your **veil**.
4. 3 Your cheeks glow behind your **veil**.
6. 7 Your cheeks glow behind your **veil**.
Is 3.19 He will take away their **veils** [20] and their hats;
3.23 and the scarves and long **veils** they wear on their heads.
47. 2 Off with your **veil**!
2 Cor 3.13 who had to put a **veil** over his face so that the
3.14 are covered with the same **veil** as they read the books of
3.14 The **veil** is removed only when a person is joined to Christ.
3.15 read the Law of Moses, the **veil** still covers their minds.
3.16 "His **veil** was removed when he turned to the Lord."

VENGEANCE

Is 34. 8 Lord will rescue Zion and take **vengeance** on her enemies.
47. 3 I will take **vengeance**, and no one will stop me."

VENOM

Deut 32.33 grapes, [33] like wine made from the **venom** of snakes.

VERDICT

Deut 17.11 Accept their **verdict** and follow their instructions in every detail.

VERSES

Mt 23. 5 at the straps with scripture **verses** on them which they wear

AV VESSEL

Deut 23.24 you want, but you must not carry any away in a **container**.
2 Kgs 4. 6 they had filled all the **jars**, she asked if there were any
Ps 2. 9 you will shatter them in pieces like a clay **pot**.' "
Is 66.20 bring grain-offerings to the Temple in ritually clean **containers**.
Jer 22.28 Jehoiachin become like a broken **jar** that is thrown away and
48.11 left to settle undisturbed and never poured from **jar to jar**.
48.38 because I have broken Moab like a **jar** that no one wants.
51.34 He emptied the city like a **jar**;
Hos 8. 8 like any other nation and is as useless as a broken **pot**.
Lk 8.16 and covers it with a **bowl** or puts it under a bed.
Rom 9.21 and to make two **pots** from the same lump of clay,
1 Pet 3. 7 with the proper understanding that they are the weaker **sex**.

VETERAN

Song 3. 8 they are battle-hardened **veterans**.

VICE

Rom 1.29 are filled with all kinds of wickedness, evil, greed, and **vice**;
Eph 4.19 they give themselves over to **vice** and do all sorts of

VICIOUS

Gen 49.27 "Benjamin is like a **vicious** wolf.
2 Chr 28. 9 now he has heard of the **vicious** way you slaughtered them.
Dan 8.23 there will be a stubborn, **vicious**, and deceitful king.

VICTIM

Gen 49. 9 like a lion, Killing his **victim** and returning to his den,
Job 18. 7 he falls—a **victim** of his own advice.
29.17 I destroyed the power of cruel men and rescued their **victims**.
Ps 10. 8 He spies on his helpless **victims**;
10.10 The helpless **victims** lie crushed;
Prov 9.18 Her **victims** do not know that the people die who go to
Is 5. 7 do what was right, but their **victims** cried out for justice.
33. 1 themselves will become **victims** of robbery and treachery.
59.15 who stops doing evil finds himself the **victim** of crime."
Jer 3. 2 the roadside, as an Arab waits for **victims** in the desert.
46.10 Today the Almighty sacrifices his **victims** in the north,
Ezek 7.15 anyone in the city will be a **victim** of sickness and hunger.
Dan 7. 7 teeth it crushed its **victims**, and then it trampled on them.
7.19 terrifying beast which crushed its **victims** with its bronze
Amos 3. 4 a lion roar in the forest unless he has found a **victim**?

VICTORY

Gen 14.17 Abram came back from his **victory** over Chedorlaomer
14.20 Most High God, who gave you **victory** over your enemies, be
Ex 14. 4 will pursue you, and my **victory** over the king and his army
14.17 will gain honour by my **victory** over the king, his army, his
15. 1 sing to the Lord, because he has won a glorious **victory**;
15.21 "Sing to the Lord, because he has won a glorious **victory**;
17.14 "Write an account of this **victory**, so that it will be remembered.
32.18 doesn't sound like a shout of **victory** or a cry of defeat;
33.14 said, "I will go with you, and I will give you **victory**."
Lev 26. 7 You will be **victorious** over your enemies;
Num 21.34 I will give you **victory** over him, all his people, and his
24.18 And make their land his property, While Israel continues **victorious**.
Deut 20. 4 your God is going with you, and he will give you **victory**.'
21.10 Lord your God gives you **victory** in battle and you take prisoners,
23.14 to protect you and to give you **victory** over your enemies.
28.25 "The Lord will give your enemies **victory** over you.
31. 5 The Lord will give you **victory** over them, and you are to
33.29 shield and your sword, to defend you and give you **victory**.
Josh 8. 1 I will give you **victory** over the king of Ai;
9. 1 The **victories** of Israel became known to all the kings west
10. 8 I have already given you the **victory**.
10.12 gave the men of Israel **victory** over the Amorites, Joshua
10.19 The Lord your God has given you **victory** over them."
10.30 Lord also gave the Israelites **victory** over this city and its king.
10.32 The Lord gave the Israelites **victory** over Lachish on the
11. 1 When the news of Israel's **victories** reached King Jabin of Hazor,
11. 8 The Lord gave the Israelites **victory** over them;
21.44 Lord gave the Israelites the **victory** over all their enemies.
24. 8 They fought you, but I gave you **victory** over them.
24.11 But I gave you **victory** over them all.
Judg 1. 4 The Lord gave them **victory** over the Canaanites and the Perizzites,
2.23 he did not give Joshua **victory** over them, nor did he drive
3.10 and the Lord gave him **victory** over the king of Mesopotamia.
3.28 The Lord has given you **victory** over your enemies, the Moabites."
4. 7 and soldiers, but I will give you **victory** over him.' "
4. 9 get any credit for the **victory**, because the Lord will hand
4.14 Today he has given you **victory** over Sisera."
4.23 That day God gave the Israelites **victory** over Jabin,
5.11 of the Lord's **victories**, the victories of Israel's people!
7. 2 too many for me to give them **victory** over the Midianites.
7. 7 rescue you and give you **victory** over the Midianites with the
7. 9 I am giving you **victory** over it.
7.14 God has given him **victory** over Midian and our whole army!"
7.15 The Lord is giving you **victory** over the Midianite army!"
11. 9 Ammonites and the Lord gives me **victory**, I will be your ruler."
11.21 gave the Israelites **victory** over Sihon and his army.
11.30 "If you give me **victory** over the Ammonites, [31] I will burn
11.31 my house to meet me, when I come back from the **victory**.
11.32 river to fight the Ammonites, and the Lord gave him **victory**.
12. 3 to fight them, and the Lord gave me **victory** over them.
15.18 to the Lord and said, "You gave me this great **victory**;
16.23 They sang, "Our god has given us **victory** over our enemy Samson!"
16.24 "Our god has given us **victory** over our enemy, who
20.27 Tomorrow I will give you **victory** over them."
20.35 The Lord gave Israel **victory** over the army of Benjamin.
1 Sam 2.10 to his king, he will make his chosen king **victorious**."
14. 6 him from giving us the **victory**, no matter how few of us
14.10 be the sign that the Lord has given us **victory** over them."
14.12 The Lord has given Israel **victory** over them."
14.37 Will you give us **victory**?"
14.39 living Lord, who gives Israel **victory**, that the guilty one
14.45 who won this great **victory** for Israel, be put to death?
14.47 Wherever he fought he was **victorious**.
17.47 He is **victorious** in battle, and he will put all of you
19. 5 killed Goliath, and the Lord won a great **victory** for Israel.
23. 4 because I will give you **victory** over the Philistines."
30.23 He kept us safe and gave us **victory** over the raiders.
2 Sam 1. 1 David came back from his **victory** over the Amalekites and
5.19 Will you give me the **victory**?"
5.19 "I will give you the **victory**!"
8. 6 The Lord made David **victorious** everywhere.
8.10 and congratulate him on his **victory** over Hadadezer, against
8.14 The Lord made David **victorious** everywhere.
18.28 God, who has given you **victory** over the men who rebelled
18.31 Lord has given you **victory** over all who rebelled against you!"
19. 2 And so the joy of **victory** was turned into sadness for all
19.24 time the king left Jerusalem until he returned **victorious**.
22.40 You give me strength for the battle and **victory** over my enemies.
22.48 He gives me **victory** over my enemies;
22.49 O Lord, you give me **victory** over my enemies and protect me
22.51 God gives great **victories** to his king;
23. 5 that will be my **victory**, and God will surely bring it about.
23.10 The Lord won a great **victory** that day.
23.12 The Lord won a great **victory** that day.
1 Kgs 5. 3 God until the Lord had given him **victory** over all his enemies.
8.45 Hear them in heaven, and give them **victory**.
20.13 I will give you **victory** over it today, and you will know
20.28 plains, I will give you **victory** over their huge army, and
22. 6 "The Lord will give you **victory**."
22.12 "The Lord will give you **victory**."
22.15 The Lord will give you **victory**."
2 Kgs 3.18 he will also give you **victory** over the Moabites.
5. 1 Naaman the Lord had given **victory** to the Syrian forces.
13.17 the Lord's arrow, with which he will win **victory** over Syria.
13.19 then you would have won complete **victory** over the Syrians;
1 Chr 5.20 and made them **victorious** over the Hagrites and their allies.
11.14 The Lord gave him a great **victory**.
14.10 Will you give me the **victory**?"
14.10 I will give you the **victory**!"
18. 6 The Lord made David **victorious** everywhere.
18.10 and congratulate him for his **victory** over Hadadezer, against
18.13 The Lord made David **victorious** everywhere.
2 Chr 6.35 Hear them in heaven and give them **victory**.
13.18 the people of Judah were **victorious** over Israel, because
16. 8 you relied on the Lord, he gave you **victory** over them.
18. 5 "God will give you **victory**."
18.11 "The Lord will give you **victory**."
18.14 The Lord will give you **victory**."
20.17 you will see the Lord give you **victory**.

2 Chr	25. 8	has the power to give **victory** or defeat, and he will let
Esth	8.16	Jews there was joy and relief, happiness and a sense of **victory.**
Job	12.16	God is strong and always **victorious;**
	40.14	to praise you and admit that you won the **victory** yourself.
Ps	3. 3	you give me **victory** and restore my courage.
	3. 8	**Victory** comes from the Lord— may he bless his people.
	14. 7	How I pray that **victory** will come to Israel from Zion.
	18.39	You give me strength for the battle and **victory** over my enemies.
	18.47	He gives me **victory** over my enemies;
	18.48	O Lord, you give me **victory** over my enemies and protect me
	18.50	God gives great **victories** to his king;
	20. 5	shout for joy over your **victory** and celebrate your triumph
	20. 6	Now I know that the Lord gives **victory** to his chosen king;
	20. 6	his holy heaven and by his power gives him great **victories.**
	20. 9	Give **victory** to the king, O Lord;
	21. 1	he rejoices because you made him **victorious.**
	24. 8	He is the Lord, strong and mighty, the Lord, **victorious** in battle.
	33.17	War-horses are useless for **victory;**
	44. 4	you give **victory** to your people, [5]and by your power we
	45. 4	Ride on in majesty to **victory** for the defence of truth and
	45. 4	Your strength will win you great **victories!**
	47. 3	He gave us **victory** over the peoples;
	53. 6	How I pray that **victory** will come to Israel from Zion.
	63.11	Because God gives him **victory,** the king will rejoice.
	65. 5	answer us by giving us **victory** and you do wonderful things
	74. 4	they have placed their flags there as signs of **victory.**
	89.17	You give us great **victories;**
	89.24	I will make him always **victorious.**
	89.42	You have given the **victory** to his enemies;
	98. 1	By his own power and holy strength he has won the **victory.**
	98. 2	The Lord announced his **victory;**
	98. 3	All people everywhere have seen the **victory** of our God.
	110. 7	by the road, and strengthened, he will stand **victorious.**
	118.15	to the glad shouts of **victory** in the tents of God's people:
	118.16	His power has brought us **victory**— his mighty power in battle!"
	118.21	because you heard me, because you have given me **victory.**
	118.24	This is the day of the Lord's **victory;**
	140. 9	Don't let my enemies be **victorious;**
	144.10	You give **victory** to kings and rescue your servant David.
	149. 4	he honours the humble with **victory.**
	149. 9	This is the **victory** of God's people.
Prov	21.31	ready for battle, but it is the Lord who gives **victory.**
Is	26.18	We have won no **victory** for our land;
	41. 2	Who gives him **victory** over kings and nations?
	45. 8	I will send **victory** from the sky like rain;
	45.17	Israel is saved by the Lord, and her **victory** lasts for ever;
	45.24	that only through me are **victory** and strength to be found;
	46.12	me, you stubborn people who think that **victory** is far away.
	46.13	am bringing the day of **victory** near— it is not far
	48.18	**Victory** would have come to you like the waves that roll on
	51. 5	the time of my **victory** is near.
	51. 6	my **victory** will be final.
	51. 8	my **victory** will endure for all time."
	52. 7	He announces **victory** and says to Zion, "Your God is king!"
	54.17	I will defend my servants and give them **victory."**
	59.16	use his own power to rescue them and to win the **victory.**
	61.10	God has clothed her with salvation and **victory.**
	62. 1	she is saved, And her **victory** shines like a torch in the
	62. 2	Jerusalem, the nations will see you **victorious!**
	63. 1	"It is the Lord, powerful to save, coming to announce his **victory."**
	63. 5	But my anger made me strong, and I won the **victory** myself.
Jer	43.12	Babylonia will pick the land of Egypt clean and then leave **victorious.**
	51.14	Babylonia like a swarm of locusts, and they will shout with **victory.**
Lam	2. 7	They shouted in **victory** where once we had worshipped in joy.
	2.17	He gave our enemies **victory,** gave them joy at our downfall.
Ezek	39.13	they will be honoured for this on the day of my **victory.**
Dan	11.12	will be proud of his **victory** and of the many soldiers he
	11.12	he has killed, but he will not continue to be **victorious.**
Obad	21	The **victorious** men of Jerusalem will attack Edom and rule over it.
Nah	1.15	He is on his way to announce the **victory!**
Hab	3. 8	was your chariot, as you brought **victory** to your people.
Zeph	3.17	his power gives you **victory.**
Zech	9. 9	He comes triumphant and **victorious,** but humble and riding on
	10. 5	people of Judah will be **victorious** like soldiers who trample
	10. 7	Their descendants will remember this **victory** and be glad
	12. 7	"I, the Lord, will give **victory** to the armies of Judah first,
Rom	8.37	we have complete **victory** through him who loved us!
1 Cor	15.54	**victory** is complete!"
	15.55	"Where, Death, is your **victory?**
	15.57	God who gives us the **victory** through our Lord Jesus Christ!
2 Cor	2.14	always led by God as prisoners in Christ's **victory procession.**
Phil	1.28	you will win, because it is God who gives you the **victory.**
Col	2.15	by leading them as captives in his **victory procession.**
1 Thes	2.19	reason for boasting of our **victory** in the presence of our
2 Tim	4. 8	is waiting for me the **victory** prize of being put right with
1 Jn	5. 4	And we win the **victory** over the world by means of our
Rev	2. 7	"To those who win the **victory** I will give the right
	2.10	and I will give you life as your prize of **victory.**
	2.11	"Those who win the **victory** will not be hurt by the second
	2.17	"To those who win the **victory** I will give some of the
	2.26	To those who win the **victory,** who continue to the end
	3. 5	Those who win the **victory** will be clothed like this in white,
	3.11	so that no one will rob you of your **victory** prize.
	3.12	will make him who is **victorious** a pillar in the temple of
	3.21	To those who win the **victory** I will give the right
	3.21	just as I have been **victorious** and now sit by my Father
	5. 5	has won the **victory,** and he can break the seven
	12.11	Our brothers won the **victory** over him by the blood of
Rev	15. 2	those who had won the **victory** over the beast and its image
	21. 7	Whoever wins the **victory** will receive this from me:

VIEW

Rom	15. 5	the same point of **view** among yourselves by following the example
1 Cor	1.26	From the human point of **view** few of you were wise
Gal	5.10	will not take a different **view** and that the man who is

VIGOROUS

Job	20.11	used to be young and **vigorous,** but soon it will turn to
Lam	4. 7	and pure as snow, **vigorous** and strong, glowing with health.

VILLAGE

Gen	25.16	their names were given to their **villages** and camping-places.
Lev	25.31	But houses in unwalled **villages** are to be treated like fields;
Num	32.41	captured some **villages** and named them "Villages of Jair."
	32.42	captured Kenath and its **villages,** and he renamed it Nobah,
Deut	3. 5	the gates, and there were also many **villages** without walls.
	3.14	He named the **villages** after himself,
	3.14	and they are still known as the **villages** of Jair.)
Josh	13.30	as well as all sixty of the **villages** of Jair in Bashan.
	15.45	Ekron with its towns and **villages,** [46]and all the cities
	15.47	Gaza, with their towns and **villages,** reaching to the stream
	16. 9	along with some towns and **villages** that were within the
Judg	6.11	Lord's angel came to the **village** of Ophrah and sat under the
	10. 4	land of Gilead, which are still called the **villages** of Jair.
1 Sam	6.18	both the fortified towns and the **villages** without walls.
1 Kgs	4.13	Ramoth in Gilead, and the **villages** in Gilead belonging to
2 Kgs	17. 9	their towns, from the smallest **village** to the largest city.
	18. 8	settlements, from the smallest **village** to the largest city,
1 Chr	2.23	towns there, including the **villages** of Jair and Kenath,
	4.33	and Ashan, [33]and the surrounding **villages,** as far
	6.56	The fields and **villages,** however, that belonged to the
	8.12	the cities of Ono and Lod and the surrounding **villages.**
	9.22	They were registered according to the **villages** where they lived.
	9.25	relatives, who lived in the **villages** and who had to take
	18. 1	their control the city of Gath and its surrounding **villages.**
2 Chr	13.19	and Ephron, and the **villages** near each of these cities.
	28.18	Gimzo with their **villages,** and settled there permanently.
Neh	6. 2	with them in one of the **villages** in the Plain of Ono.
	10.37	collect tithes in our farming **villages,** the tithes from the
	11.25	and Jekabzeel, and in the **villages** near these cities.
	11.27	and Hazarshual, and in Beersheba and the **villages** around it.
	11.28	Ziklag, in Meconah and its **villages,** [29]in Enrimmon, in
	11.30	in Zanoah, in Adullam, and in the **villages** near these towns.
	11.30	and on the farms near by, and in Azekah and its **villages.**
	11.31	Ai, Bethel and the nearby **villages,** [32]Anathoth, Nob,
Ps	10. 8	He hides himself in the **villages,** waiting to murder innocent people.
Song	7.11	out to the countryside and spend the night in the **villages.**
Jer	17.26	the towns of Judah and from the **villages** round Jerusalem;
	32.44	territory of Benjamin, in the **villages** round Jerusalem, in
	33.13	territory of Benjamin, in the **villages** round Jerusalem, and
	40.10	fruit, and olive-oil, and live in the **villages** you occupy."
	49. 2	will be left in ruins and its **villages** burnt to the ground.
	49.13	All the near-by **villages** will be in ruins for ever.
Lam	2. 2	Lord destroyed without mercy every **village** in Judah And tore
	5.11	in every Judaean **village** our daughters have been forced to submit.
Ezek	16.46	"Your elder sister is Samaria, in the north, with her **villages.**
	16.46	Your younger sister, with her **villages,** is Sodom,
	16.48	"your sister Sodom and her **villages**
	16.48	never did the evil that you and your **villages** have done.
	16.53	again—Sodom and her **villages** and Samaria and her villages.
	16.55	again, and you and your **villages** will also be restored.
Mt	9.35	Jesus went round visiting all the towns and **villages.**
	10.11	come to a town or **village,** go in and look for someone
	14.15	let them go to the **villages** to buy food for themselves."
	21. 2	"Go to the **village** there ahead of you, and at once
Mk	1.38	Jesus answered, "We must go on to the other **villages** round here.
	6. 6	Then Jesus went to the **villages** round there, teaching the people.
	6.36	to the nearby farms and **villages** in order to buy themselves
	6.56	everywhere Jesus went, to **villages,** towns, or farms, people would
	8.23	blind man by the hand and led him out of the **village.**
	8.26	him home with the order, "Don't go back into the **village."**
	8.27	Jesus and his disciples went away to the **villages** near Caesarea Philippi.
	11. 2	"Go to the **village** there ahead of you.
Lk	8. 1	Jesus travelled through towns and **villages,** preaching the Good
	9. 6	and travelled through all the **villages,** preaching the Good News
	9.12	they can go to the **villages** and farms round here and find
	9.52	who went into a **village** in Samaria to get everything ready
	9.56	Then Jesus and his disciples went on to another **village.**
	10.38	he came to a **village** where a woman named Martha welcomed
	13.22	Jesus went through towns and **villages,** teaching the people
	17.12	He was going into a **village** when he was met by ten
	19.30	"Go to the **village** there ahead of you;
	24.13	were going to a **village** named Emmaus, about eleven kilometres
	24.28	As they came near the **village** to which they were going,
Jn	11.30	not yet arrived in the **village,** but was still in the place
Acts	8.25	they preached the Good News in many **villages** of Samaria.

VINE
[GRAPEVINE]

Gen	40. 9	my dream there was a **grapevine** in front of me
	49.11	his young donkey to a **grapevine,**

Gen 49.11 To the very best of the **vines.**
Lev 25. 5 sown, and do not gather the grapes from your unpruned **vines;**
Num 6. 4 anything that comes from a **grapevine,** not even the seeds or
Deut 22. 9 "Do not plant any crop in the same field as your **grapevines;**
24.21 grapes once, do not go back over the **vines** a second time;
28.39 or drink wine from them, because worms will eat the **vines.**
32.32 like **vines** that bear bitter and poisonous grapes,
Josh 24.13 there and eating grapes from **vines** that you did not plant,
Judg 9.12 then said to the **grapevine,** 'You come and be our king.'
9.13 But the **vine** answered, 'In order to govern you, I would
13.14 She must not eat anything that comes from the **grapevine;**
1 Kgs 4.25 each family with its own **grapevines** and fig-trees.
2 Kgs 4.39 He found a wild **vine,** and picked as many gourds as he
18.31 grapes from your own **vines,** and figs from your own trees,
19.29 your corn and harvest it, and plant **vines** and eat grapes.
Job 15.33 He will be like a **vine** that loses its unripe grapes;
Ps 78.47 killed their **grapevines** with hail and their fig-trees with frost.
80. 8 You brought a **grapevine** out of Egypt;
80.15 Come and save this **grapevine** that you planted,
80.15 this young **vine** you made grow so strong!
105.33 he destroyed their **grapevines** and fig-trees
107.37 They sowed the fields and planted **grapevines** and reaped
128. 3 will be like a fruitful **vine** in your home, and your sons
Song 2.13 the air is fragrant with blossoming **vines.**
6.11 on the **vines** and the blossoms on the pomegranate-trees.
7.12 early and look at the **vines** to see whether they've started
Is 5. 2 he planted the finest **vines.**
5. 6 I will not prune the **vines** or hoe the ground;
5. 7 the people of Judah are the **vines** he planted.
5.10 The **grapevines** growing on ten hectares of land will
7.23 vineyards, each with a thousand **vines** and each worth a
16. 8 At one time the **vines** spread as far as the city of
16. 9 Now I weep for Sibmah's **vines** as I weep for Jazer.
18. 5 the Sudanese as easily as a knife cuts branches from a **vine.**
24. 7 The **grapevines** wither, and wine is becoming scarce.
24.13 off every tree and the last grapes picked from the **vines.**
34. 4 will fall like leaves dropping from a **vine** or a fig-tree.
36.16 eat grapes from your own **vines** and figs from your own trees,
37.30 your corn and harvest it, and plant **vines** and eat grapes.
Jer 2.21 I planted you like a choice **vine** from the very best seed.
2.21 You are like a rotten, worthless **vine.**
5.17 flocks and your herds and destroy your **vines** and fig-trees.
8.13 but they are like a **vine** with no grapes, like a fig-tree
48.32 Sibmah, you are like a **vine** whose branches reach across the
49. 9 leave a few on the **vines,** and when robbers come at night,
Ezek 15. 2 "Mortal man," he said, "how does a **vine** compare with a tree?
15. 2 is a branch of a **grapevine** compared with the trees of the
15. 6 is saying, "Just as a **vine** is taken from the forest and
17. 6 The plant sprouted and became a low, wide-spreading **grapevine.**
17. 6 The **vine** was covered with branches and leaves.
17. 7 And now the **vine** sent its roots towards him and turned its
17. 8 But the **vine** had already been planted in a fertile,
17. 8 grow leaves and bear grapes and be a magnificent **vine.**
17. 9 Will this **vine** live and grow?
19.10 Your mother was like a **grapevine** planted near a stream.
19.10 of water, the **vine** was covered with leaves and fruit.
19.11 The **vine** grew tall enough to reach the clouds;
19.14 The stem of the **vine** caught fire;
Hos 2.12 I will destroy her **grapevines** and her fig-trees, which
10. 1 of Israel were like a **grapevine** that was full of grapes.
Joel 1. 7 They have destroyed our **grapevines** and chewed up our fig-trees.
1.12 The **grapevines** and fig-trees have withered;
Mic 1. 6 ruins in the open country, a place for planting **grapevines.**
7. 1 no fruit left on the trees and no grapes on the **vines.**
Hab 3.17 no grapes grow on the **vines,** even though the olive-crop
Hag 2.19 no corn left, and the **grapevines,** fig-trees, pomegranates,
Zech 8.12 Their **vines** will bear grapes, the earth will produce crops,
Mal 3.11 your crops, and your **grapevines** will be loaded with grapes.
Jn 15. 1 "I am the real **vine,** and my Father is the gardener.
15. 4 it can do so only if it remains in the **vine.**
15. 5 "I am the **vine,** and you are the branches.
Jas 3.12 a **grapevine** cannot bear figs, nor can a salty spring produce
Rev 14.19 cut the grapes from the **vine,** and threw them into the

VINEGAR

Ps 69.21 when I was thirsty, they offered me **vinegar.**
Prov 10.26 will be as irritating as **vinegar** on your teeth or smoke in

VINEYARD

Gen 9.20 who was a farmer, was the first man to plant a **vineyard.**
Ex 22. 5 in a field or a **vineyard** and they stray away and eat
22. 5 the loss with the crops from his own fields or **vineyards.**
23.11 Do the same with your **vineyards** and your olive-trees.
23.16 when you gather the fruit from your **vineyards** and orchards.
Lev 19.10 not go back through your **vineyard** to gather the grapes that
25. 3 sow your fields, prune your **vineyards,** and gather your crops
25. 4 Do not sow your fields or prune your **vineyards.**
25.11 by itself or gather the grapes in your unpruned **vineyards.**
Num 16.14 or given us fields and **vineyards** as our possession, and now
20.17 go into your fields or **vineyards,** and we will not drink from
21.22 go into your fields or **vineyards,** and we will not drink
22.24 the road narrowed between two **vineyards** and had a stone wall
Deut 6.11 you did not dig, and **vineyards** and olive orchards that you
20. 6 who has just planted a **vineyard,** but has not yet had the
23.24 a path in someone else's **vineyard,** you may eat all the
28.30 You will plant a **vineyard**—but never eat its grapes.
28.39 You will plant **vineyards** and take care of them, but you
Judg 9.27 all went out into their **vineyards** and picked the grapes,
14. 5 they were going through the **vineyards** there, he heard a
Judg 21.20 Benjaminites, "Go and hide in the **vineyards** [21]and watch.
21.21 to dance during the festival, you come out of the **vineyards.**
1 Sam 8.14 will take your best fields, **vineyards,** and olive-groves, and
22. 7 David will give fields and **vineyards** to all of you, and make
1 Kgs 21. 1 in Jezreel there was a **vineyard** owned by a man named Naboth.
21. 2 One day Ahab said to Naboth, "Let me have your **vineyard;**
21. 2 will give you a better **vineyard** for it, or, if you prefer,
21. 3 "I inherited this **vineyard** from my ancestors," Naboth replied.
21. 6 I offered to buy his **vineyard,** or, if he preferred, to give
21. 7 I will get you Naboth's **vineyard!"**
21.15 and take possession of the **vineyard** which he refused to sell
21.16 At once Ahab went to the **vineyard** to take possession of it.
21.18 him in Naboth's **vineyard,** about to take possession of it.
2 Kgs 5.26 and clothes, olive-groves and **vineyards,** sheep and cattle,
18.32 your own, where there are **vineyards** to give wine and there
25.12 property, and put them to work in the **vineyards** and fields.
1 Chr 27.25 **Vineyards:** Shimei from Ramah
2 Chr 26.10 encouraged the people to plant **vineyards** in the hill-country
Neh 5. 3 to mortgage our fields and **vineyards** and houses to get
5. 4 money to pay the royal tax on our fields and **vineyards.**
5. 5 our fields and **vineyards** have been taken away from us."
5.11 And give them back their fields, **vineyards,** olive-groves,
9.25 already dug, olive-trees, fruit-trees, and **vineyards.**
Job 24. 6 don't own, and gather grapes in wicked men's **vineyards.**
24.18 he no longer goes to work in his **vineyards.**
Prov 24.30 I walked through the fields and **vineyards** of a lazy,
31.16 it, and with money she has earned she plants a **vineyard.**
Ecc 2. 4 I built myself houses and planted **vineyards.**
Song 1. 6 were angry with me and made me work in the **vineyard.**
1.14 the wild flowers that bloom in the **vineyards** at Engedi.
2.15 the little foxes, before they ruin our **vineyard** in bloom.
8.11 Solomon has a **vineyard** in a place called Baal Hamon.
8.12 I have a **vineyard** of my own!
Is 1. 8 a watchman's hut in a **vineyard** or a shed in a cucumber
3.14 "You have plundered **vineyards,** and your houses are full of
5. 1 sing you this song, a song of my friend and his **vineyard:**
5. 1 My friend had a **vineyard** on a very fertile hill.
5. 3 in Jerusalem and Judah, judge between my **vineyard** and me.
5. 5 "This is what I am going to do to my **vineyard;**
5. 7 Israel is the **vineyard** of the Lord Almighty;
7.23 time comes, the fine **vineyards,** each with a thousand vines
16. 8 Heshbon and the **vineyards** of Sibmah are destroyed—those vineyards
16.10 No one shouts or sings in the **vineyards.**
27. 2 will say of his pleasant **vineyard,** [3]"I watch over it and
27. 4 I am no longer angry with the **vineyard.**
32.12 the fertile fields and the **vineyards** have been destroyed,
36.17 your own, where there are **vineyards** to give wine and there
61. 5 of your flocks And farm your land and tend your **vineyards.**
65.21 They will plant **vineyards** and enjoy the wine—it will not be
Jer 5.10 my people's **vineyards,** but not to destroy them completely.
6. 9 be stripped clean like a **vineyard** from which every grape has
12.10 Many foreign rulers have destroyed my **vineyard;**
31. 5 Once again you will plant **vineyards** on the hills of Samaria,
31. 5 those who plant them will eat what the **vineyards** produce.
32.15 said that houses, fields, and **vineyards** will again be bought
35. 7 or farm the land, and not to plant **vineyards** or buy them.
35. 9 we live in tents—and we own no **vineyards,** fields, or corn.
39.10 owned no property, and he gave them **vineyards** and fields.
52.16 and he put them to work in the **vineyards** and fields.
Ezek 28.26 They will build houses and plant **vineyards.**
Hos 2.12 I will turn her **vineyards** and orchards into a wilderness;
2.15 give back to her the **vineyards** she had and make Trouble
14. 7 They will grow corn and be fruitful like a **vineyard.**
Joel 1.11 that take care of the **vineyards,** because the wheat, the
3.18 mountains will be covered with **vineyards,** and cattle will be
Amos 4. 9 your gardens and **vineyards,** your fig-trees and olive-trees.
5.11 build or drink wine from the beautiful **vineyards** you plant.
5.17 There will be wailing in all the **vineyards.**
9.14 they will plant **vineyards** and drink the wine;
Mic 4. 4 in peace among his own **vineyards** and fig-trees, and no one
Zeph 1.13 or drink wine from the **vineyards** they are planting."
Hag 1.11 land—on its hills, cornfields, **vineyards,** and olive
Zech 3.10 and security, surrounded by your **vineyards** and fig-trees."
Mt 20. 1 in the morning to hire some men to work in his **vineyard.**
20. 2 silver coin a day, and sent them to work in his **vineyard.**
20. 4 go and work in the **vineyard,** and I will pay you
20. 7 then, you also go and work in the **vineyard,'** he told them.
21.28 one and said, 'Son, go and work in the **vineyard** today.'
21.33 a landowner who planted a **vineyard,** put a fence around it,
21.33 Then he let out the **vineyard** to tenants and went on a
21.39 seized him, threw him out of the **vineyard,** and killed him.
21.40 when the owner of the **vineyard** comes, what will he do to
21.41 they answered, "and let the **vineyard** out to other tenants,
Mk 12. 1 a man who planted a **vineyard,** put a fence round it,
12. 1 Then he let out the **vineyard** to tenants and left home on
12. 8 son and killed him and threw his body out of the **vineyard.**
12. 9 "What, then, will the owner of the **vineyard** do?"
12. 9 kill those men and hand the **vineyard** over to other tenants.
Lk 13. 6 was once a man who had a fig-tree growing in his **vineyard.**
20. 9 a man who planted a **vineyard,** let it out to tenants,
20.13 Then the owner of the **vineyard** said, 'What shall I do?
20.15 So they threw him out of the **vineyard** and killed him.
20.15 "What, then, will the owner of the **vineyard** do to the tenants?"
20.16 those men, and hand the **vineyard** over to other tenants."
1 Cor 9. 7 What farmer does not eat the grapes from his own **vineyard?**
Rev 6. 6 But do not damage the olive-trees and the **vineyards!"**
14.18 cut the grapes from the **vineyard** of the earth, because the

VIOLATE

2 Chr 19. 8 judges in cases involving a **violation** of the Law of the Lord
19.10 of homicide or any other **violation** of a law or commandment,
28.19 King Ahaz of Judah had **violated** the rights of his people and
Is 24. 5 breaking God's laws and by **violating** the covenant he made to
33. 8 Treaties are broken and agreements are **violated.**
Dan 6. 7 Anyone who **violates** this order is to be thrown into a pit

VIOLENT

Gen 6.11 was evil in God's sight, and **violence** had spread everywhere.
6.13 because the world is full of their **violent** deeds.
49. 5 They use their weapons to commit **violence.**
Ex 19.18 smoke of a furnace, and all the people trembled **violently.**
Deut 21. 5 they are to decide every legal case involving **violence.**
Judg 4. 3 people of Israel with cruelty and **violence** for twenty years.
1 Sam 2.33 and all your other descendants will die a **violent** death.
2 Sam 3.39 These sons of Zeruiah are too **violent** for me.
7.10 they have been attacked by **violent** people, but this will not
12.10 your descendants will die a **violent** death because you have
19.43 men of Judah were more **violent** in making their claims than
22. 3 he protects me and saves me from **violence.**
22.49 me victory over my enemies and protect me from **violent** men.
1 Chr 17. 9 they have been attacked by **violent** people, but this will not
Job 5.22 You will laugh at **violence** and hunger and not be afraid
16.17 am not guilty of any **violence,** and my prayer to God is
19. 7 I protest against his **violence,** but no one is listening;
27.13 This is how Almighty God punishes wicked, **violent** men.
38.15 for the wicked and restrains them from deeds of **violence.**
Ps 5. 6 You destroy all liars and despise **violent,** deceitful men.
7. 3 friend or without cause done **violence** to my enemy— if I
7.16 by their own evil and are hurt by their own **violence.**
17. 4 I have obeyed your command and have not followed paths of **violence.**
18.48 me victory over my enemies and protect me from **violent** men.
46. 3 roar and rage, and the hills are shaken by the **violence.**
55. 9 I see **violence** and riots in the city, [10] surrounding it day
58. 2 evil you can do, and commit crimes of **violence** in the land.
62.10 Don't put your trust in **violence;**
72.14 He rescues them from oppression and **violence;**
73. 6 they wear pride like a necklace and **violence** like a robe;
74.20 There is **violence** in every dark corner of the land.
78.64 Priests died by **violence,**
91.10 will strike you, no **violence** will come near your home.
139.19 How I wish **violent** men would leave me alone!
140. 1 keep me safe from **violent** men.
140. 4 keep me safe from **violent** men who plot my downfall.
140.11 may evil overtake **violent** men and destroy them.
Prov 1.19 is what happens to anyone who lives by **violence.**
3.31 Don't be jealous of **violent** people or decide to act as
4.17 Wickedness and **violence** are like food and drink to them.
10. 6 A wicked man's words hide a **violent** nature.
10.11 of life, but a wicked man's words hide a **violent** nature.
11.30 Righteousness gives life, but **violence** takes it away.
13. 2 say, but those who are deceitful are hungry for **violence.**
16.29 **Violent** people deceive their friends and lead them to disaster.
21. 7 The wicked are doomed by their own **violence;**
22.24 Don't make friends with people who have hot, **violent** tempers.
Is 10. 7 But the Assyrian emperor has his own **violent** plans in mind.
29. 6 the Lord Almighty will rescue you with **violent** thunderstorms
30.12 "You ignore what I tell you and rely on **violence** and deceit.
42.25 feel the force of his anger and suffer the **violence** of war.
58. 4 Your fasting makes you **violent,** and you quarrel and fight.
59. 3 You are guilty of lying, **violence,** and murder.
60.18 The sounds of **violence** will be heard no more;
65.12 your fate to die a **violent** death, because you did not answer
Jer 6. 7 I hear **violence** and destruction in the city;
9. 5 They do one **violent** thing after another, and one deceitful
15.21 I will rescue you from the power of wicked and **violent** men.
20. 8 Whenever I speak, I have to cry out and shout, **"Violence!**
22.17 you kill the innocent and **violently** oppress your people.
48. 3 The people of Horonaim cry out, **'Violence!**
51.35 "May Babylonia be held responsible for the **violence** done to us!"
51.46 different rumour spreads—rumours of **violence** in the land and
Ezek 5.17 and will send sickness, **violence,** and war to kill you.
7.10 **Violence** is flourishing.
7.11 **Violence** produces more wickedness.
7.23 land is full of murders and the cities are full of **violence.**
8.17 here and with spreading **violence** throughout the country.
28.16 buying and selling, and this led you to **violence** and sin.
45. 9 Stop your **violence** and oppression.
Dan 11.14 And some **violent** men from your nation, Daniel, will rebel
Hos 7.16 will die a **violent** death, and the Egyptians will laugh."
12. 1 Treachery and acts of **violence** increase among them.
Amos 3.10 fill their mansions with things taken by crime and **violence.**
Jon 1. 4 and the storm was so **violent** that the ship was in danger
1.12 it is my fault that you are caught in this **violent** storm."
Mic 4.13 the wealth they got by **violence** you will present to me, the
Hab 1. 2 help before you listen, before you save us from **violence?**
1. 3 Destruction and **violence** are all round me, and there is
1. 9 "Their armies advance in **violent** conquest, and everyone
2. 8 committed and because of your **violence** against the people of
2. 9 with what you took by **violence,** and have tried to make your
2.17 committed and because of your **violence** against the people of
Zech 8.17 I hate lying, injustice, and **violence."**
Mt 11.12 Kingdom of heaven has suffered **violent** attacks,
11.12 and **violent** men try to seize it.
23.25 inside is full of what you have obtained by **violence** and
28. 2 Suddenly there was a **violent** earthquake;
Lk 11.39 but inside you are full of **violence** and evil.
Acts 9. 1 Saul kept up his **violent** threats of murder against the followers
16.26 there was a **violent** earthquake, which shook the prison
19.16 them with such **violence** that he overpowered them all.
23.10 The argument became so **violent** that the commander was afraid
27.18 The **violent** storm continued, so on the next day they
27.41 was being broken to pieces by the **violence** of the waves.
1 Tim 3. 3 not be a drunkard or a **violent** man, but gentle and peaceful;
2 Tim 3. 3 they will be unkind, merciless, slanderers, **violent,** and
4.15 because he was **violently** opposed to our message.
Tit 1. 7 or quick-tempered, or a drunkard or **violent** or greedy for money.
Rev 6.12 There was a **violent** earthquake, and the sun became black
11.13 At that very moment there was a **violent** earthquake;
18.21 great city Babylon will be **violently** thrown down and will never

VIOLET

Jer 10. 9 in **violet** and purple cloth woven by skilled weavers.

AV **VIPER** see **SNAKE**

VIRGIN

Gen 19. 8 Look, I have two daughters who are still **virgins.**
24.16 She was a very beautiful young girl and still a **virgin.**
Ex 22.16 "If a man seduces a **virgin** who is not engaged, he must
22.17 a sum of money equal to the bride-price for a **virgin.**
Lev 21. 7 or a woman who is not a **virgin** or who is divorced;
21.13 He shall marry a **virgin,** [14] not a widow or a divorced
21.14 He shall marry only a **virgin** from his own clan.
Num 31.18 yourselves all the girls and all the women who are **virgins.**
31.32 61,000 donkeys, and 32,000 **virgins.**
31.36 and 16,000 **virgins** for the soldiers, of which 32 were the
31.42 30,500 donkeys, and 16,000 **virgins.**
Deut 22.14 accusing her of not being a **virgin** when they got married.
22.15 proves the girl was a **virgin,** and they are to show it
22.17 her, saying that she was not a **virgin** when he married her.
22.17 But here is the proof that my daughter was a **virgin;**
22.20 that the girl was a **virgin,** [21] then they are to take her
Judg 11.37 in the mountains and grieve that I must die a **virgin."**
11.39 what he had promised the Lord, and she died still a **virgin.**
19.24 Here is his concubine and my own daughter, who is a **virgin.**
21.11 all the males, and also every woman who is not a **virgin."**
21.12 they found four hundred young **virgins,** so they brought them
2 Sam 13. 2 as a **virgin,** she was kept from meeting men.
Esth 2. 2 "Why don't you make a search to find some beautiful young **virgins?**
Is 47. 1 You were once like a **virgin,** a city unconquered, but you are
62. 5 a young man taking a **virgin** as his bride, He who formed
Ezek 23. 3 in Egypt, they lost their **virginity** and became prostitutes.
23. 8 as a prostitute in Egypt, where she lost her **virginity.**
23.21 men played with your breasts and you lost your **virginity.)**
44.22 only an Israelite **virgin** or the widow of another priest.
Amos 5. 2 **Virgin** Israel has fallen, Never to rise again!
Mt 1.23 the prophet come true, [23] "A **virgin** will become pregnant
Lk 1.34 Mary said to the angel, "I am a **virgin.**
1 Cor 7.34 unmarried woman or a **virgin** concerns herself with the Lord's work,
2 Cor 11. 2 you are like a pure **virgin** whom I have promised in marriage
Rev 14. 4 they are **virgins.**

AV **VIRGIN**
see also **GIRL**

VIRTUE

Prov 11.16 is respected, but a woman without **virtue** is a disgrace.
19.11 When someone wrongs you, it is a great **virtue** to ignore it.

VISIBLE

Col 1.15 Christ is the **visible** likeness of the invisible God.
1 Jn 1. 2 When this life became **visible,** we saw it;

VISION

Gen 15. 1 After this, Abram had a **vision** and heard the Lord say to
46. 2 spoke to him in a **vision** at night and called, "Jacob,
Num 12. 6 myself to them in **visions** and speak to them in dreams.
24. 4 staring eyes I see in a trance A **vision** from Almighty God.
24.16 staring eyes I see in a trance A **vision** from Almighty God.
24.20 Then in his **vision** Balaam saw the Amalekites
24.21 In his **vision** he saw the Kenites, and uttered this prophecy:
1 Sam 3. 1 from the Lord, and **visions** from him were quite rare.
3.15 He was afraid to tell Eli about the **vision.**
2 Chr 9.29 of Shiloh, and in The **Visions** of Iddo the Prophet, which
32.32 Lord are recorded in The **Vision** of the Prophet Isaiah Son of
Job 7.14 you send me **visions** and nightmares [15] until I would
20. 8 like a dream, like a **vision** at night, and never be seen
33.15 At night when men are asleep, God speaks in dreams and **visions.**
Ps 89.19 In a **vision** long ago you said to your faithful servants,
Is 21. 2 I have seen a **vision** of cruel events, a vision of betrayal
21. 3 saw and heard in the **vision** has filled me with terror and
21. 5 In the **vision** a banquet is ready;
22. 1 This is a message about the Valley of **Vision.**
22. 5 confusion in the Valley of **Vision,** and the Sovereign Lord
28. 7 too drunk to understand the **visions** that God sends, and the
29.11 The meaning of every prophetic **vision** will be hidden from you;
Jer 14.14 The **visions** they talk about have not come from me;
38.21 has shown me in a **vision** what will happen if you refuse

Lam 2. 9 taught, and the prophets have no **visions** from the Lord.
Ezek 1. 1 The sky opened, and I saw a **vision** of God.
8. 2 I looked up and saw a **vision** of a fiery human form.
8. 3 Then in this **vision** God's spirit lifted me high in the air
10.13 were the same as those I had seen in my first **vision.**
11.24 In the **vision** the spirit of God lifted me up and brought
11.24 Then the **vision** faded, [25] and I told the exiles everything
12.24 there will be no more false **visions** or misleading prophecies.
12.27 the Israelites think that your **visions** and prophecies are
13. 3 They provide their own inspiration and invent their own **visions.**
13. 6 Their **visions** are false, and their predictions are lies.
13. 7 Those **visions** you see are false, and the predictions you
13. 8 to them, "Your words are false, and your **visions** are lies.
13. 9 who have false **visions** and make misleading predictions.
13.23 So now your false **visions** and misleading predictions are over.
21.29 The **visions** that you see are false, and the predictions
22.28 They see false **visions** and make false predictions.
40. 2 In a **vision** God took me to the land of Israel and
43. 3 This **vision** was like the one I had seen when God came
Dan 1.17 he gave Daniel skill in interpreting **visions** and dreams.
2.19 revealed to Daniel in a **vision,** and he praised the God of
2.28 you the dream, the **vision** you had while you were asleep.
2.31 "Your Majesty, in your **vision** you saw standing before
4. 5 dream and saw terrifying **visions** while I was asleep.
4.10 was asleep, I had a **vision** of a huge tree in the
4.13 I was thinking about the **vision,** I saw coming down from
7. 1 Babylonia, I had a dream and saw a **vision** in the night.
7.13 During this **vision** in the night, I saw what looked like
7.15 The **visions** I saw alarmed me, and I was deeply disturbed.
8. 1 third year that Belshazzar was king, I saw a second **vision.**
8. 2 In the **vision** I suddenly found myself in the walled city
8.13 "How long will these things that were seen in the **vision** continue?
8.15 trying to understand what the **vision** meant, when suddenly
8.17 The **vision** has to do with the end of the world."
8.19 The **vision** refers to the time of the end.
8.26 This **vision** about the evening and morning sacrifices
8.27 I was puzzled by the **vision** and could not understand it.
9.21 had seen in the earlier **vision,** came flying down to where I
9.23 Now pay attention while I explain the **vision.**
9.24 so that the **vision** and the prophecy will come true,
10. 1 It was explained to him in a **vision.)**
10. 7 I was the only one who saw the **vision.**
10. 8 I was left there alone, watching this amazing **vision.**
10.14 This is a **vision** about the future."
10.16 said to him, "Sir, this **vision** makes me so weak that I
11.14 will rebel because of a **vision** they have seen, but they will
Hos 12.10 prophets and gave them many **visions,** and through the
Joel 2.28 men will have dreams, and your young men will see **visions.**
Amos 7. 1 I had a **vision** from the Sovereign Lord.
7. 2 In my **vision** I saw the locusts eat up every green thing
7. 4 I had another **vision** from the Sovereign Lord.
7. 7 I had another **vision** from the Lord.
8. 1 I had another **vision** from the Sovereign Lord.
Mic 3. 6 will have no more prophetic **visions,** and you will not be
Nah 1. 1 Nineveh, the account of a **vision** seen by Nahum, who was from
Zech 1. 7 Shebat), the Lord gave me a message in a **vision** at night.
1.18 In another **vision** I saw four ox horns.
2. 1 In another **vision** I saw a man with a measuring-line in his
3. 1 In another **vision** the Lord showed me the High Priest
6. 1 I had another **vision.**
13. 4 will be proud of his **visions,** or act like a prophet, or
Mt 17. 9 "Don't tell anyone about this **vision** you have seen until
Lk 1.22 so they knew that he had seen a **vision** in the Temple.
24.23 saying they had seen a **vision** of angels who told them that
Acts 2.17 your young men will see **visions,** and your old men will
9.10 He had a **vision,** in which the Lord said to him, "Ananias!"
9.12 is praying, [12] and in a **vision** he has seen a man named
10. 3 afternoon when he had a **vision,** in which he clearly saw
10.10 while the food was being prepared, he had a **vision.**
10.17 about the meaning of this **vision,** the men sent by Cornelius
10.19 trying to understand what the **vision** meant, when the Spirit said,
11. 5 I was praying in the city of Joppa, I had a **vision.**
12. 9 he thought he was seeing a **vision.**
16. 9 That night Paul had a **vision** in which he saw a Macedonian
16.10 soon as Paul had this **vision,** we got ready to leave for
18. 9 One night Paul had a **vision** in which the Lord said to
22.17 the Temple, I had a **vision,** [18] in which I saw the Lord,
26.19 King Agrippa, I did not disobey the **vision** I had from heaven.
2 Cor 12. 1 I will now talk about **visions** and revelations given me by
12. 2 happened or whether he had a **vision**—only God knows).
12. 3 or whether it was a **vision**—only God knows),
Col 2.18 be superior because of special **visions** and who insists on false
Jude 8 these people have **visions** which make them sin against their
Rev 4. 1 this point I had another **vision** and saw an open door in
9.17 And in my **vision** I saw the horses and their riders:

VISIT

Gen 34. 1 Jacob and Leah, went to **visit** some of the Canaanite women.
Ex 2.11 up, he went out to **visit** his people, the Hebrews, and he
Judg 15. 1 time later Samson went to **visit** his wife during the wheat
1 Sam 16. 4 trembling to meet him and asked, "Is this a peaceful **visit,**
2 Sam 12. 4 One day a **visitor** arrived at the rich man's home.
1 Kgs 2.13 "Is this a friendly **visit?"**
2 Kgs 4.10 lamp in it, and he can stay there whenever he **visits** us."
6.32 Elisha was at home with some elders who were **visiting** him.
8.29 from his wounds, and Ahaziah went there to **visit** him.
9.16 not recovered, and King Ahaziah of Judah was there, **visiting**
13.14 as he lay dying King Jehoash of Israel went to **visit** him.
2 Chr 18. 2 later Jehoshaphat went to the city of Samaria to **visit** Ahab.
22. 6 from his wounds, and Ahaziah went there to **visit** him.
2 Chr 22. 7 God used this **visit** to Joram to bring about Ahaziah's downfall.
22. 8 Ahaziah's nephews that had accompanied Ahaziah on his **visit.**
Neh 6.10 this time I went to **visit** Shemaiah, the son of Delaiah and
Job 38.22 Have you ever **visited** the storerooms, where I keep the
42.11 and former friends came to **visit** him and feasted with him in
Prov 2.19 No one who **visits** her ever comes back.
25.17 Don't **visit** your neighbour too often;
Ezek 24.21 look at it and to **visit** it, but the Lord is going
24.25 pride and joy, which they liked to look at and to **visit.**
Mt 2. 7 So Herod called the **visitors** from the east to a secret
2.16 Herod realized that the **visitors** from the east had tricked him,
2.16 he had learned from the **visitors** about the time when the
9.35 Jesus went round **visiting** all the towns and villages.
25.36 and you took care of me, in prison and you **visited** me.'
25.39 did we ever see you sick or in prison, and **visit** you?'
Lk 1.43 thing happen to me, that my Lord's mother comes to **visit** me?
24.18 "Are you the only **visitor** in Jerusalem who doesn't know the
Jn 11.45 people who had come to **visit** Mary saw what Jesus did,
Acts 7.12 he sent his sons, our ancestors, on their first **visit** there.
7.13 On the second **visit** Joseph made himself known to his brothers,
9.32 occasion he went to **visit** God's people who lived in Lydda.
10.28 not allowed by his religion to **visit** or associate with Gentiles.
15.36 "Let us go back and **visit** our brothers in every town where
25.13 Bernice came to Caesarea to pay a **visit** of welcome to Festus.
Rom 1.10 may at last make it possible for me to **visit** you now.
1.13 times I have planned to **visit** you, but something has always
15.24 to go there, after I have enjoyed **visiting** you for a while.
15.28 I shall leave for Spain and **visit** you on my way there.
15.32 if it is God's will, and enjoy a refreshing **visit** to you.
1 Cor 4.18 you have thought that I would not be coming to **visit** you.
16.12 have often encouraged him to **visit** you with the other brothers,
2 Cor 1.15 made plans at first to **visit** you, in order that you might
1.16 For I planned to **visit** you on my way to Macedonia
12.14 am ready to come to **visit** you—and I will not make
13. 1 is now the third time that I am coming to **visit** you.
13. 2 it before during my second **visit** to you, but I will say
1 Thes 1. 9 you received us when we **visited** you, and how you turned away
2. 1 you yourselves know that our **visit** to you was not a failure.
2 Jn 12 instead, I hope to **visit** you and talk with you personally,

VOICE

Gen 4.10 out to me from the ground, like a **voice** calling for revenge.
27.22 felt him and said, "Your **voice** sounds like Jacob's voice,
Deut 4.36 He let you hear his **voice** from heaven so that he could
5.22 he spoke with a mighty **voice** from the fire and from the
5.23 fire and you heard the **voice** from the darkness, your leaders
27.14 The Levites will speak these words in a loud **voice:**
1 Sam 26.17 Saul recognized David's **voice** and asked, "David, is
2 Sam 19.35 I eat and drink, and I can't hear the **voices** of singers.
22. 7 In his temple he heard my **voice;**
22.14 from the sky, and the **voice** of Almighty God was heard.
1 Kgs 8.55 In a loud **voice** he asked God's blessings on all the
19.12 And after the fire, there was the soft whisper of a **voice.**
19.13 A **voice** said to him, "Elijah, what are you doing here?"
2 Chr 15.14 In a loud **voice** they took an oath in the Lord's name
Neh 12.42 The singers, led by Jezrahiah, sang at the top of their **voices.**
Job 4.16 Then I heard a **voice** out of the silence:
12. 1 Yes, you are the **voice** of the people.
15.21 **Voices** of terror will scream in his ears, and robbers
30.29 My **voice** is as sad and lonely as the cries of a
37. 2 all of you, to the **voice** of God, to the thunder that
37. 4 Then the roar of his **voice** is heard, the majestic sound of
40. 9 Can your **voice** thunder as loud as mine?
Ps 5. 3 you hear my **voice** in the morning;
18. 6 In his temple he heard my **voice;**
18.13 and the **voice** of the Most High was heard.
29. 3 The **voice** of the Lord is heard on the seas;
29. 3 the glorious God thunders, and his **voice** echoes over the ocean.
29. 4 The **voice** of the Lord is heard in all its might and
29. 5 The **voice** of the Lord breaks the cedars, even the cedars
29. 7 The **voice** of the Lord makes the lightning flash.
29. 8 His **voice** makes the desert shake;
29. 9 The Lord's **voice** shakes the oaks and strips the leaves
55.17 and groans go up to him, and he will hear my **voice.**
58. 5 which does not hear the **voice** of the snake-charmer, or the
81. 5 I hear an unknown **voice** saying, [6] "I took the burdens off
93. 3 The ocean depths raise their **voice,** O Lord;
93. 3 they raise their **voice** and roar.
Song 2. 8 I hear my lover's **voice.**
2.14 Let me see your lovely face and hear your enchanting **voice.**
5. 6 How I wanted to hear his **voice!**
8.13 Let me hear your **voice** from the garden, my love;
Is 6. 4 The sound of their **voices** made the foundation of the Temple shake,
29. 4 under the ground, a muffled **voice** coming from the dust.
30.21 left, you will hear his **voice** behind you saying, "Here is
30.30 let everyone hear his majestic **voice** and feel the force of
30.31 when they hear the Lord's **voice** and feel the force of his
38.14 My **voice** was thin and weak, And I moaned like a dove.
40. 3 A **voice** cries out, "Prepare in the wilderness a road for
40. 6 A **voice** cries out, "Proclaim a message!"
40. 9 Call out with a loud **voice,** Zion;
42. 2 not shout or raise his **voice** or make loud speeches in the
Ezek 1.24 the noise of a huge army, like the **voice** of Almighty God.
1.28 Then I heard a **voice** [1] saying, "Mortal man, stand up.
2. 2 While the **voice** was speaking, God's spirit entered me and
2. 2 and I heard the **voice** continue, [3] "Mortal man, I am sending
3.12 the loud roar of a **voice** that said, "Praise the glory of
10. 5 It sounded like the **voice** of Almighty God.
43. 2 God's **voice** sounded like the roar of the sea, and the earth

Dan 3. 4 herald announced in a loud **voice,** "People of all nations,
4.14 He proclaimed in a loud **voice,** 'Cut the tree down and
4.31 his mouth, a **voice** spoke from heaven, "King Nebuchadnezzar,
7. 5 between its teeth, and a **voice** said to it, "Go on, eat
8.16 I heard a **voice** call out over the River Ulai, "Gabriel,
10. 6 like polished bronze, and his **voice** sounded like the roar of
10. 9 When I heard his **voice,** I fell to the ground unconscious
Joel 3.16 his **voice** thunders from Jerusalem;
Amos 1. 2 his **voice** thunders from Jerusalem.
6.10 A **voice** will answer, "No!"
Mt 3.17 Then a **voice** said from heaven, "This is my own dear Son,
17. 5 came over them, and a **voice** from the cloud said, "This is
17. 6 When the disciples heard the **voice,** they were so terrified that
27.23 Then they started shouting at the top of their **voices:**
Mk 1.11 And a **voice** came from heaven, "You are my own dear Son.
5. 7 and screamed in a loud **voice,** "Jesus, Son of the Most
9. 7 with its shadow, and a **voice** came from the cloud, "This is
Lk 1.42 and said in a loud **voice,** "You are the most blessed of
3.22 And a **voice** came from heaven, "You are my own dear Son.
4.33 he screamed out in a loud **voice,** [34] "Ah!
9.35 A **voice** said from the cloud, "This is my Son, whom I
9.36 When the **voice** stopped, there was Jesus all alone.
17.15 he was healed, he came back, praising God in a loud **voice.**
19.37 and praise him in loud **voices** for all the great things that
23.23 at the top of their **voices** that Jesus should be crucified,
23.46 Jesus cried out in a loud **voice,** "Father!
Jn 1.23 "I am 'the **voice** of someone shouting in the desert:
3.29 and listens, is glad when he hears the bridegroom's **voice.**
5.25 the dead will hear the **voice** of the Son of God,
5.28 dead will hear his **voice** [29] and come out of their graves:
5.37 You have never heard his **voice** or seen his face,
7.28 he said in a loud **voice,** "Do you really know me
7.37 and said in a loud **voice,** "Whoever is thirsty should come
10. 3 the sheep hear his **voice** as he calls his own sheep
10. 4 and the sheep follow him, because they know his **voice.**
10. 5 from such a person, because they do not know his **voice."**
10.16 they will listen to my **voice,** and they will become one flock
10.27 My sheep listen to my **voice;**
11.43 said this, he called out in a loud **voice,** "Lazarus, come
12.28 Then a **voice** spoke from heaven, "I have brought glory to it,
12.29 crowd standing there heard the **voice,** and some of them said
12.30 was not for my sake that this **voice** spoke, but for yours.
12.44 Jesus said in a loud **voice,** "Whoever believes in me believes
Acts 2.14 apostles and in a loud **voice** began to speak to the crowd:
7.31 But he heard the Lord's **voice:**
7.60 He knelt down and cried out in a loud **voice,** "Lord!
9. 4 to the ground and heard a **voice** saying to him, "Saul, Saul!
9. 5 "I am Jesus, whom you persecute," the **voice** said.
9. 7 they heard the **voice** but could not see anyone.
10.13 A **voice** said to him, "Get up, Peter;
10.15 **voice** spoke to him again, "Do not consider anything unclean
11. 7 Then I heard a **voice** saying to me, 'Get up, Peter;
11. 9 **voice** spoke again from heaven, 'Do not consider anything unclean
12.14 She recognized Peter's **voice** and was so happy that she ran
14.10 and said in a loud **voice,** "Stand up straight on your feet!"
16.28 Paul shouted at the top of his **voice,** "Don't harm yourself!
22. 7 to the ground and heard a **voice** saying to me, 'Saul, Saul!
22. 9 but did not hear the **voice** of the one who was speaking
22.14 Servant, and to hear him speaking with his own **voice.**
22.22 started shouting at the top of their **voices,** "Away with him!
26.14 and I heard a **voice** say to me in Hebrew, 'Saul,
Rom 10.18 their **voice** went out to all the world;
15. 6 together may praise with one **voice** the God and Father of our
2 Cor 1.11 many will raise their **voices** to him in thanksgiving for us.
1 Thes 4.16 command, the archangel's **voice,** the sound of God's trumpet,
Heb 3. 7 says, "If you hear God's **voice** today, [8] do not be stubborn,
3.15 "If you hear God's **voice** today, do not be stubborn, as
3.16 Who were the people who heard God's **voice** and rebelled
4. 7 "If you hear God's **voice** today, do not be stubborn."
12.19 the blast of a trumpet, and the sound of a **voice.**
12.19 When the people heard the **voice,** they begged not to hear
12.26 His **voice** shook the earth at that time, but now he has
2 Pet 1.17 God the Father, when the **voice** came to him from the Supreme
1.18 We ourselves heard this **voice** coming from heaven,
2.16 donkey spoke with a human **voice** and stopped the prophet's insane
Rev 1.10 and I heard a loud **voice,** that sounded like a trumpet,
1.15 and his **voice** sounded like a roaring waterfall.
3.20 if anyone hears my **voice** and opens the door, I will come
4. 1 And the **voice** that sounded like a trumpet, which I had heard
5. 2 who announced in a loud **voice,** "Who is worthy to break the
5.12 living creatures, and the elders, [12] and sang in a loud **voice:**
6. 1 creatures say in a **voice** that sounded like thunder, "Come!"
6. 6 heard what sounded like a **voice** coming from among the four
6.10 They shouted in a loud **voice,** "Almighty Lord, holy and
7. 2 called out in a loud **voice** to the four angels to whom
7.10 They called out in a loud **voice:**
8.13 flying high in the air say in a loud **voice,** "O horror!
9.13 I heard a **voice** coming from the four corners of the gold
9.14 The **voice** said to the sixth angel, "Release the four angels
10. 3 called out in a loud **voice** that sounded like the roar of
10. 4 But I heard a **voice** speak from heaven, "Keep secret what
10. 8 Then the **voice** that I had heard speaking from heaven spoke
11.12 two prophets heard a loud **voice** say to them from heaven,
11.15 and there were loud **voices** in heaven, saying, "The power to
12.10 I heard a loud **voice** in heaven saying, "Now God's salvation
14. 2 And I heard a **voice** from heaven that sounded like a
14. 7 He said in a loud **voice,** "Honour God and praise his greatness!
14. 9 saying in a loud **voice,** "Whoever worships the beast and its
14.13 Then I heard a **voice** from heaven saying, "Write this:
14.15 cried out in a loud **voice** to the one who was sitting
14.18 He shouted in a loud **voice** to the angel who had the
16. 1 Then I heard a loud **voice** speaking from the temple to the
16. 7 Then I heard a **voice** from the altar saying, "Lord God Almighty!
16.17 A loud **voice** came from the throne in the temple, saying,
18. 2 He cried out in a loud **voice:**
18. 4 I heard another **voice** from heaven, saying, "Come out, my people!
18.22 of harps and of human **voices,** of players of the flute
18.23 no more will the **voices** of brides and grooms be heard in
19. 5 the sound of a **voice,** saying, "Praise our God, all his
19.17 He shouted in a loud **voice** to all the birds flying in
21. 3 I heard a loud **voice** speaking from the throne:

VOLUNTARY

Deut 23.23 but if you make one **voluntarily,** be sure that you keep it.
2 Chr 29.31 and some of them also **voluntarily** brought animals to be
Ezra 3. 5 all the offerings that were given to the Lord **voluntarily.**
Ezek 46.12 prince wants to make a **voluntary** offering to the Lord,

VOLUNTEER

Judg 5. 2 the people gladly **volunteered.**
5. 9 of Israel, with the people who gladly **volunteered.**
1 Chr 29. 6 administrators of the royal property **volunteered** to give
2 Chr 17.16 (Amasiah had **volunteered** to serve the Lord.)
Neh 11. 2 people praised anyone else who **volunteered** to live in Jerusalem.
Ps 110. 3 On the day you fight your enemies, your people will **volunteer.**

VOMIT

Job 20.15 The wicked man **vomits** up the wealth he stole;
Prov 23. 8 You will **vomit** up what you have eaten, and all your
25.16 too much may make you **vomit.**
26.11 a second time is like a dog going back to its **vomit.**
Is 19.14 and staggers like a drunken man slipping on his own **vomit.**
28. 8 sit are all covered with **vomit,** and not a clean spot is
Jer 25.27 until they are drunk and **vomit,** until they fall down and
48.26 Moab will roll in its own **vomit,** and people will laugh.
2 Pet 2.22 back to what it has **vomited"** and "A pig that has been

VOTE

Mk 14.64 They all **voted** against him:
Acts 26.10 they were sentenced to death, I also **voted** against them.

VOW

Gen 21.23 So make a **vow** here in the presence of God that you
21.31 because it was there that the two of them made a **vow.**
22.16 second time, [16] "I make a **vow** by my own name—the Lord
24. 2 he had, "Place your hand between my thighs and make a **vow.**
24. 3 want you to make a **vow** in the name of the Lord,
24. 9 his master, and made a **vow** to do what Abraham had asked.
24.37 My master made me promise with a **vow** to obey his command.
24.41 is only one way for you to be free from your **vow:**
25.33 Jacob answered, "First make a **vow** that you will give me
25.33 Esau made the **vow** and gave his rights to Jacob.
26.31 morning each man made his promise and sealed it with a **vow.**
26.33 He named the well **"Vow."**
28.20 Then Jacob made a **vow** to the Lord:
31.13 pouring olive-oil on it and where you made a **vow** to me.
31.53 Isaac worshipped, Jacob solemnly **vowed** to keep this promise.
47.29 thighs and make a solemn **vow** that you will not bury me
47.31 Jacob said, "Make a **vow** that you will."
47.31 Joseph made the **vow,** and Jacob gave thanks there on his bed.
50.25 Then Joseph asked his people to make a **vow.**
Lev 5. 4 If someone makes a careless **vow,** no matter what it is about,
7.16 in fulfilment of a **vow** or as his own freewill offering,
22.18 whether in fulfilment of a **vow** or as a freewill offering,
22.21 whether in fulfilment of a **vow** or as a freewill offering,
22.23 formed, but it is not acceptable in fulfilment of a **vow.**
23.38 your offerings in fulfilment of **vows,** and your freewill
27. 2 in fulfilment of a special **vow,** that person may be set free
27. 8 the man who made the **vow** is too poor to pay the
27. 9 If the **vow** concerns an animal that is acceptable as an
27.10 the man who made the **vow** may not substitute another animal
27.11 But if the **vow** concerns a ritually unclean animal, which
Num 6. 2 woman who makes a special **vow** to become a Nazirite and
6. 5 he is under the Nazirite **vow,** he must not cut his hair
6. 5 He is bound by the **vow** for the full time that he
6.13 When a Nazirite completes his **vow,** he shall perform the ritual.
6.21 an offering beyond what his **vow** requires him to give, he
15. 3 sacrifice in fulfilment of a **vow** or as a freewill offering
15. 8 in fulfilment of a **vow** or as a fellowship-offering,
21. 2 Then the Israelites made a **vow** to the Lord:
29.39 you give in fulfilment of a **vow** or as freewill offerings.
30. 2 When a man makes a **vow** to give something to the Lord
30. 3 her father's house makes a **vow** to give something to the Lord
30. 4 must do everything that she **vowed** or promised unless her
30. 5 forbids her to fulfil the **vow** when he hears about it, she
30. 6 woman makes a **vow,** whether deliberately or carelessly,
30. 7 must do everything that she **vowed** or promised unless her
30. 8 forbids her to fulfil the **vow** when he hears about it, she
30. 9 divorced woman must keep every **vow** she makes and every
30.10 woman makes a **vow** or promises to abstain from something,
30.11 must do everything that she **vowed** or promised unless her
30.12 forbids her to fulfil the **vow** when he hears about it, she
30.12 because her husband prevented her from keeping her **vow.**
30.13 affirm or to annul any **vow** or promise that she has made.
30.14 after he hears of the **vow,** he has raised no objection,

Num 30.14 she must do everything that she has **vowed** or promised.
30.14 He has affirmed the **vow** by not objecting on the day he
30.15 if he later annuls the **vow**, he must suffer the consequences
30.15 for the failure to fulfil the **vow**.
30.16 the Lord gave Moses concerning **vows** made by an unmarried
Deut 23.18 the house of the Lord your God in fulfilment of a **vow**.
23.21 "When you make a **vow** to the Lord your God, do not
23.21 will hold you to your **vow**, and it is a sin not
23.22 sin not to make a **vow** to the Lord, [23] but if you
32.40 raise my hand and I **vow** [41] that I will sharpen my flashing
Josh 23. 7 use those names in taking **vows** or worship those gods or bow
1 Sam 19. 6 Jonathan said and made a **vow** in the Lord's name that he
28.10 Then Saul made a sacred **vow**.
2 Sam 4. 9 answered them, "I make a **vow** by the living Lord, who has
Job 22.27 he will answer you, and you will keep the **vows** you made.
Ps 132. 2 Lord, what he promised, the **vow** he made to you, the Mighty
Prov 2.17 who is faithless to her own husband and forgets her sacred **vows**.
Is 45.23 come and kneel before me and **vow** to be loyal to me.
Jer 44.24 Carry out your **vows**!
44.26 But now listen to the **vow** that I, the Lord, have made
44.26 my name to make a **vow** by saying, 'I swear by the
Ezek 20.23 I **vowed** that I would scatter them all over the world.
Mt 5.33 but do what you have **vowed** to the Lord to do.'
5.34 do not use any **vow** when you make a promise.
23.16 'If someone swears by the Temple, he isn't bound by his **vow**;
23.18 'If someone swears by the altar, he isn't bound by his **vow**;
Mk 6.23 With many **vows** he said to her, "I swear that I will
6.26 refuse her because of the **vows** he had made in front of
Acts 2.30 God had made a **vow** that he would make one of David's
18.18 he had his head shaved because of a **vow** he had taken.
21.23 There are four men here who have taken a **vow**.
23.12 They took a **vow** that they would not eat or drink anything
23.14 "We have taken a solemn **vow** together not to eat a thing
23.21 They have taken a **vow** not to eat or drink until they
Heb 6.13 to Abraham, he made a **vow** to do what he had promised.
6.13 he used his own name when he made his **vow**.
6.16 When a person makes a **vow**, he uses the name of
6.16 someone greater than himself, and the **vow** settles all arguments.
6.17 so he added his **vow** to the promise.
7.20 In addition, there is also God's **vow**.
7.20 There was no such **vow** when the others were made priests.
7.21 priest by means of a **vow** when God said to him,
7.28 God's promise made with the **vow**, which came later than the Law,
Rev 10. 6 to heaven [6] and took a **vow** in the name of God,

VOYAGE

Acts 21. 7 We continued our **voyage**, sailing from Tyre to Ptolemais,
27. 9 became dangerous to continue the **voyage**, for by now the Day
27.10 "Men, I see that our **voyage** from here on will be dangerous;
28.10 we sailed, they put on board what we needed for the **voyage**.

VULGAR

Eph 5. 4 for you to use language which is obscene, profane, or **vulgar**.

VULTURE

Gen 15.11 **Vultures** came down on the bodies, but Abram drove them off.
Lev 11.13 buzzards, **vultures**, crows;
Deut 14.12 buzzards, **vultures**, crows;
1 Kgs 14.11 any who die in the open country will be eaten by **vultures**.
16. 4 who die in the open country will be eaten by **vultures**."
21.24 who die in the open country will be eaten by **vultures**."
Job 15.23 kill him, [23] and **vultures** are waiting to eat his corpse.
28. 7 roads to the mines, And no **vulture** ever flies over them.
Ps 79. 2 of your people for the **vultures**, the bodies of your servants
Prov 30.17 ought to be eaten by **vultures** or have his eyes picked out
Is 34.15 **Vultures** will gather there, one after another.
Mic 1.16 Make yourselves as bald as **vultures**, because your children
Mt 24.28 "Wherever there is a dead body, the **vultures** will gather.
Lk 17.37 "Wherever there is a dead body, the **vultures** will gather."

WADE

Josh 3. 8 the river, they must **wade** in and stand near the bank."
Ps 58.10 they will **wade** through the blood of the wicked.
68.23 ocean, [23] so that you may **wade** in their blood, and your
Ezek 47. 3 to the east and told me to **wade** through the stream there.
47. 5 there the stream was so deep I could not **wade** through it.

WAFER

1 Chr 23.29 the **wafers** made without yeast, the baked offerings,

WAGE

Gen 30.28 Name your **wages**, and I will pay them."
30.31 Jacob answered, "I don't want any **wages**.
30.32 That is all the **wages** I want.
30.33 to check up on my **wages**, if I have any goat that
31. 7 Yet he has cheated me and changed my **wages** ten times.
31. 8 speckled goats shall be your **wages**,'
31. 8 striped goats shall be your **wages**,'
31.41 And even then, you changed my **wages** ten times.
Lev 19.13 Do not hold back the **wages** of someone you have hired, not
25.50 release on the basis of the **wages** paid to a hired man.
Num 18.31 because it is your **wages** for your service in the Tent.
Is 55. 2 Why spend your **wages** and still be hungry?
Jer 22.13 countrymen work for nothing and does not pay their **wages**.
Zech 11.12 I said to them, "If you are willing, give me my **wages**.
Zech 11.12 So they paid me thirty pieces of silver as my **wages**.
Mal 3. 5 cheat employees out of their **wages**, and those who take
Mt 20. 2 to pay them the regular **wage**, a silver coin a day,
20. 4 work in the vineyard, and I will pay you a fair **wage**.'
20. 8 and pay them their **wages**, starting with those who were hired
Rom 4. 4 who works is paid his **wages**, but they are not regarded as
6.23 For sin pays its **wage**—death;
Jas 5. 4 You have not paid any **wages** to the men who work in
Rev 6. 6 of wheat for a day's **wages**,
6. 6 and three litres of barley for a day's **wages**.

WAGON

Gen 45.19 Tell them also to take **wagons** with them from Egypt for
45.21 Joseph gave them **wagons**, as the king had ordered, and food
45.27 and when he saw the **wagons** which Joseph had sent to take
46. 5 and their wives in the **wagons** which the king of Egypt had
Num 7. 3 six **wagons** and twelve oxen, a wagon for every two leaders
7. 3 wagons and twelve oxen, a **wagon** for every two leaders and an
7. 6 So Moses gave the **wagons** and the oxen to the Levites.
7. 7 He gave two **wagons** and four oxen to the Gershonites,
7. 8 and four **wagons** and eight oxen to the Merarites.
7. 9 But Moses gave no **wagons** or oxen to the Kohathites,
1 Sam 6. 7 So prepare a new **wagon** and two cows that have never been
6. 7 hitch them to the **wagon** and drive their calves back to the
6. 8 Box, put it on the **wagon**, and place in a box beside
6. 8 Start the **wagon** on its way and let it go by itself.
6.10 and hitched them to the **wagon**, and shut the calves in the
6.11 the Covenant Box in the **wagon**, together with the box
6.14 The **wagon** came to a field belonging to a man named Joshua,
6.14 people chopped up the wooden **wagon** and killed the cows and
Is 66.20 camels, and in chariots and **wagons**, just as Israelites bring
Ezek 23.24 bringing a large army with chariots and supply **wagons**.
26.10 noise of their horses pulling **wagons** and chariots will shake

WAIL

Ezra 3.12 foundation of this Temple being laid, they cried and **wailed**.
Esth 4. 1 and walked through the city, **wailing** loudly and bitterly,
4. 3 They fasted, wept and **wailed**, and most of them put on
Job 2.12 they began to weep and **wail**, tearing their clothes in grief
Is 15. 2 The people of Moab **wail** in grief over the cities of Nebo
23. 2 **Wail**, you merchants of Sidon!
29. 2 There will be weeping and **wailing**, and the whole city will
Jer 4. 8 on sackcloth, and weep and **wail** because the fierce anger of
Ezek 2.10 of grief were written there, and **wails** and groans.
Hos 7.14 they throw themselves down and **wail** as the heathen do.
10. 5 They will **wail** when it is stripped of its golden splendour.
Amos 5.16 Almighty says, "There will be **wailing** and cries of sorrow
5.17 There will be **wailing** in all the vineyards.
Mic 1. 8 I will howl like a jackal and **wail** like an ostrich.
Zeph 1.10 You will hear **wailing** in the newer part of the city and
1.11 **Wail** and cry when you hear this, you that live in the
Zech 11. 2 Weep and **wail**, cypress-trees— the cedars have fallen;
11. 2 Weep and **wail**, oaks of Bashan— the dense forest has been
Mal 2.13 altar with tears, weeping and **wailing** because he no longer
Mk 5.38 Jesus saw the confusion and heard all the loud crying and **wailing**.
Lk 23.27 them were some women who were weeping and **wailing** for him.
Jas 5. 1 Weep and **wail** over the miseries that are coming upon you!

WAIST

Ex 28.42 for them, reaching from the **waist** to the thighs, so that
29. 9 put sashes round their **waists** and tie caps on their heads.
Lev 8. 7 shirt and the robe on Aaron and the sash round his **waist**.
8. 7 it by putting its finely woven belt round his **waist**.
8.13 put sashes round their **waists**, and tied caps on their heads,
2 Sam 6.14 a linen cloth round his **waist**, danced with all his might to
1 Kgs 12.10 'My little finger is thicker than my father's **waist!**'
18.46 his clothes tight round his **waist** and ran ahead of Ahab all
20.31 with sackcloth round our **waists** and ropes round our necks,
20.32 sackcloth round their **waists** and ropes round their necks,
2 Chr 10.10 'My little finger is thicker than my father's **waist**.'
Neh 4.18 and everyone who was building kept a sword strapped to his **waist**.
5.13 the sash I was wearing round my **waist** and shook it out.
Is 3.20 magic charms they wear on their arms and at their **waists**;
32.11 Strip off your clothes and tie rags round your **waist**.
Jer 13.11 shorts fit tightly round the **waist**, so I intended all the
Ezek 8. 2 From the **waist** down his body looked like fire,
8. 2 and from the **waist** up he was shining
23.14 sashes round their **waists** and fancy turbans on their heads.
47. 4 hundred metres further down, the water was up to my **waist**.
Dan 2.32 its **waist** and hips of bronze;
Mt 3. 4 a leather belt round his **waist**, and his food was locusts and
Mk 1. 6 a leather belt round his **waist**, and his food was locusts and
Jn 13. 4 off his outer garment, and tied a towel round his **waist**.
13. 5 disciples' feet and dry them with the towel round his **waist**.
Eph 6.14 a belt tight round your **waist**, with righteousness as your breastplate,

WAIT (1)

[AWAITS]

Gen 8.10 He **waited** another seven days and sent out the dove again.
8.12 Then he **waited** another seven days and sent out the dove
29.27 **Wait** until the week's marriage celebrations are over,
43.10 If we had not **waited** so long, we could have been there
49.18 "I **wait** for your deliverance, Lord.
Ex 5.20 they met Moses and Aaron, who were **waiting** for them.
7.15 turned into a snake, and **wait** for him on the bank of
24.14 Moses said to the leaders, "**Wait** here in the camp for

Lev 15.13 of his discharge, he must **wait** seven days and then wash his
15.28 her flow stops, she must **wait** seven days, and then she will
17.15 clothes, have a bath, and **wait** until evening before he is
24.12 put him under guard, and **waited** for the Lord to tell
Num 6. 9 who suddenly dies, he must **wait** seven days and then shave
9. 8 "**Wait** until I receive instructions from the Lord."
Deut 24.11 **wait** outside and let him bring it to you himself.
32.34 he **waits** for the right time to punish them.
33.20 Gad **waits** like a lion To tear off an arm or a
Josh 3. 1 to the Jordan, where they camped while **waiting** to cross it.
8. 9 to their hiding place and **waited** there, west of Ai, between
18. 3 long are you going to **wait** before you go in and take
Judg 3.25 They **waited** as long as they thought they should, but
3.26 Ehud got away while they were **waiting.**
9.43 them into three groups, and hid in the fields, **waiting.**
16. 2 they surrounded the place and **waited** for him all night long
16. 2 night, thinking to themselves, "We'll **wait** until daybreak,
16. 9 She had some men **waiting** in another room, so she shouted,
16.12 The men were **waiting** in another room.
19. 8 **Wait** until later in the day."
Ruth 1.13 and had sons, [13]would you **wait** until they had grown up?
1 Sam 9. 6 The servant answered, "**Wait!**
10. 8 **Wait** there seven days until I come and tell you what to
13. 8 He **waited** seven days for Samuel, as Samuel had instructed
14. 9 If they tell us to **wait** for them to come to us,
15. 5 the city of Amalek and **waited** in ambush in a dry river-bed.
22.13 turned against me and is **waiting** for a chance to kill me!"
25. 9 Then they **waited** there, [10]and Nabal finally answered,
2 Sam 15.28 Meanwhile, I will **wait** at the river crossings in the
17.17 Zadok's son Ahimaaz were **waiting** at the spring of Enrogel,
1 Kgs 20.38 and stood by the road, **waiting** for the king of Israel to
2 Kgs 2.18 returned to Elisha, who had **waited** at Jericho, and he said
6. 9 place, because the Syrians were **waiting** in ambush there.
6.33 Why should I **wait** any longer for him to do something?"
7. 3 said to one another, "Why should we **wait** here until we die?
7. 9 If we **wait** until morning to tell it, we are sure to
2 Chr 20.17 Just take up your positions and **wait;**
23. 1 After **waiting** six years Jehoiada the priest decided that
Neh 13.21 them, "It's no use **waiting** out there for morning to come.
Esth 6. 5 So the servants answered, "Haman is here, **waiting** to see you."
Job 3.21 They **wait** for death, but it never comes;
7. 2 like a worker **waiting** for his pay.
14.14 will wait for better times, **wait** till this time of trouble
15.22 for somewhere a sword is **waiting** to kill him,
15.23 and vultures are **waiting** to eat his corpse.
15.24 disaster, like a powerful king, is **waiting** to attack him.
18.11 All round him terror is **waiting;**
18.12 disaster stands and **waits** at his side.
24.15 The adulterer **waits** for twilight to come;
31. 9 my neighbour's wife, and **waited,** hidden, outside her door,
32. 4 one there, he had **waited** until everyone finished speaking.
32.11 speaking and **waited** while you searched for wise phrases.
32.16 Shall I go on **waiting** when they are silent?
32.18 I can hardly **wait** to speak.
35.14 but **wait** patiently—your case is before him.
38.40 they hide in their caves, or lie in **wait** in their dens?
39.27 Does an eagle **wait** for your command to build its nest
Ps 5. 3 at sunrise I offer my prayer and **wait** for your answer.
6. 3 How long, O Lord, will you **wait** to help me?
10. 8 hides himself in the villages, **waiting** to murder innocent people.
10. 9 he **waits** in his hiding place like a lion.
10. 9 He lies in **wait** for the poor;
17.12 They are like lions, **waiting** for me, wanting to tear me
37. 7 Be patient and **wait** for the Lord to act;
40. 1 I **waited** patiently for the Lord's help;
59. 3 They are **waiting** to kill me;
62. 1 I **wait** patiently for God to save me;
106.13 what he had done and acted without **waiting** for his advice.
119.81 I am worn out, Lord, **waiting** for you to save me;
119.84 How much longer must I **wait?**
119.95 Wicked men are **waiting** to kill me, but I will meditate
119.166 I **wait** for you to save me, Lord, and I do what
130. 5 I **wait** eagerly for the Lord's help, and in his word I
130. 6 I **wait** for the Lord
130. 6 more eagerly than watchmen **wait** for the dawn—
130. 6 than watchmen **wait** for the dawn.
Prov 1.16 They can't **wait** to do something bad.
3.28 Never tell your neighbour to **wait** until tomorrow if you
7.12 walked the streets [12]or stood **waiting** at a corner,
8.34 at my door every day, **waiting** at the entrance to my home.
11.26 a man who hoards grain, **waiting** for a higher price, but they
21.16 Death is **waiting** for anyone who wanders away from good sense.
23.28 They **wait** for you like robbers and cause many men to be
Ecc 2.14 I also know that the same fate is **waiting** for us all.
3.19 After all, the same fate **awaits** man and animal alike.
7. 2 always remind themselves that death is **waiting** for us all.
11. 4 If you **wait** until the wind and the weather are just right,
Song 8.13 my companions are **waiting** to hear you speak.
Is 5. 2 He **waited** for the grapes to ripen, but every grape was sour.
16. 2 They **wait** on the banks of the River Arnon and move
24.17 There are terrors, pits, and traps **waiting** for you.
30.18 And yet the Lord is **waiting** to be merciful to you.
42. 4 Distant lands eagerly **wait** for his teaching."
44.14 might plant a laurel-tree and **wait** for the rain to make it
49.23 no one who **waits** for my help will be disappointed."
51. 5 Distant lands **wait** for me to come;
51. 5 they **wait** with hope for me to save them.
59. 7 planning something evil, and you can hardly **wait** to do it.
Jer 3. 2 You **waited** for lovers along the roadside,
3. 2 as an Arab **waits** for victims in the desert.
5.26 they lie in **wait** like men who spread nets to catch birds,
Jer 20.10 Even my close friends **wait** for my downfall.
48.19 You that live in Aroer, stand by the road and **wait;**
48.43 Terror, pits, and traps are **waiting** for the people of Moab.
51.50 Don't **wait!**
Lam 2.16 This is the day we have **waited** for!"
3.10 He **waited** for me like a bear;
3.26 to wait in patience—to **wait** for him to save us—
4.17 We kept **waiting** for help from a nation that had none to
Ezek 19. 5 She **waited** until she saw all hope was gone.
28.12 "grieve for the fate that is **waiting** for the king of Tyre.
44.26 become clean again, he must **wait** seven days [27]and then go
Hos 3. 3 she would have to **wait** for me without being a prostitute
3. 3 and during this time I would **wait** for her.
6. 9 like a gang of robbers who **wait** in ambush for a man.
12. 6 Be loyal and just, and **wait** patiently for your God to act.
13. 7 Like a leopard I will lie in **wait** along your path.
Amos 8. 5 to yourselves, "We can hardly **wait** for the holy days to be
Jon 4. 5 and sat in its shade, **waiting** to see what would happen to
Mic 1.12 The people of Maroth **wait** anxiously for relief, because
2. 8 home, but there you are, **waiting** to steal the coats off
7. 2 Everyone is **waiting** for a chance to commit murder.
7. 7 I will **wait** confidently for God, who will save me.
Hab 2. 1 will climb my watch-tower and **wait** to see what the Lord will
2. 3 It may seem slow in coming, but **wait** for it;
3.16 I will quietly **wait** for the time to come when God will
Zeph 3. 8 "Just **wait,**" the Lord says.
3. 8 "**Wait** for the day when I rise to accuse the nations.
Mt 27.49 But the others said, "**Wait,** let us see if Elijah is
Mk 15.36 Then he held it up to Jesus' lips and said, "**Wait!**
15.42 of the Council, who was **waiting** for the coming of the
Lk 1.21 the people were **waiting** for Zechariah and wondering why he
2.25 God-fearing man and was **waiting** for Israel to be saved.
2.38 to all who were **waiting** for God to set Jerusalem free.
8.40 people welcomed him, because they had all been **waiting** for him.
12.36 like servants who are **waiting** for their master to come back
21.26 faint from fear as they **wait** for what is coming over the
23.50 and honourable man, who was **waiting** for the coming of the
24.49 But you must **wait** in the city until the power from above
Acts 1. 4 "Do not leave Jerusalem, but **wait** for the gift I told you
10.24 in Caesarea, where Cornelius was **waiting** for him,
10.33 in the presence of God, **waiting** to hear anything that the
13.25 I am not the one you are **waiting** for.
17.16 While Paul was **waiting** in Athens for Silas and Timothy,
20. 5 They went ahead and **waited** for us in Troas.
20.23 Holy Spirit has warned me that prison and troubles **wait** for me.
22.16 And now, why **wait** any longer?
23.21 more than forty men who will be hiding and **waiting** for him.
23.21 are now ready to do it and are **waiting** for your decision."
27.33 "You have been **waiting** for fourteen days now, and all this
28. 6 They were **waiting** for him to swell up or suddenly fall
28. 6 But after **waiting** for a long time and not seeing anything
Rom 8.19 All of creation **waits** with eager longing for God to reveal
8.23 groan within ourselves, as we **wait** for God to make us his
8.25 for what we do not see, we **wait** for it with patience.
1 Cor 1. 7 a single blessing, as you **wait** for our Lord Jesus Christ to
4. 5 Final judgement must **wait** until the Lord comes;
11.33 gather together to eat the Lord's Supper, **wait** for one another.
Gal 5. 5 and this is what we **wait** for by the power of God's
Phil 3.20 and we eagerly **wait** for our Saviour, the Lord Jesus
1 Thes 1.10 and living God [10]and to **wait** for his Son to come from
2 Tim 4. 8 And now there is **waiting** for me the victory prize of being
4. 8 but to all those who **wait** with love for him to appear.
Tit 2.13 in this world, [13]as we **wait** for the blessed Day we hope
Heb 9.28 but to save those who are **waiting** for him.
10.13 There he now **waits** until God puts his enemies as a
10.27 that is left is to **wait** in fear for the coming Judgement
11.10 For Abraham was **waiting** for the city which God has designed
12. 2 of the joy that was **waiting** for him, he thought nothing of
Jas 5. 7 a farmer is as he **waits** for his land to produce precious
5. 7 He **waits** patiently for the autumn and spring rains.
1 Pet 3.20 not obeyed God when he **waited** patiently during the days that
2 Pet 2. 4 are kept chained in darkness, **waiting** for the Day of Judgement.
3.12 dedicated to God, [12]as you **wait** for the Day of God and
3.13 But we **wait** for what God has promised:
3.14 so, my friends, as you **wait** for that Day, do your best
Jude 21 love of God, as you **wait** for our Lord Jesus Christ in

WAIT (2)

1 Kgs 1. 4 She was very beautiful, and **waited on** the king and took
10. 5 they wore, the servants who **waited on** him at feasts, and the
2 Chr 9. 4 clothing of the servants who **waited on** him at feasts, and
Mt 8.15 left her, and she got up and began to **wait on** him.
Mk 1.31 The fever left her, and she began to **wait on** them.
Lk 4.39 and she got up at once and began to **wait on** them.
12.37 his coat, ask them to sit down, and will **wait on** them.
17. 8 put on your apron and **wait on** me while I eat

WAKE

[WOKE]

Gen 28.16 Jacob **woke** up and said, "The Lord is here!
41. 4 Then the king **woke** up.
41. 7 The king **woke** up and realized that he had been dreaming.
41.21 Then I **woke** up.
Num 24. 9 When it is sleeping, no one dares **wake** it.
Judg 16.14 But he **woke** up and pulled his hair loose from the loom.
16.20 He **woke** up and thought, "I'll get loose and go free, as
19. 5 of the fourth day they **woke** up early and got ready to
Ruth 3. 8 During the night he **woke** up suddenly, turned over, and was
1 Sam 26.12 had happened or even **woke** up—they were all sound asleep,

1 Sam	26.14	"Who is that shouting and **waking** up the king?"
1 Kgs	3.15	Solomon **woke** up and realized that God had spoken to him
	3.21	The next morning, when I **woke** up and was going to feed
	18.27	Or maybe he's sleeping, and you've got to **wake** him up!"
	19. 5	Suddenly an angel touched him and said, "**Wake** up and eat."
	19. 7	The Lord's angel returned and **woke** him up a second time,
2 Kgs	4.31	back to meet Elisha and said, "The boy didn't **wake** up."
Job	14.12	They will never **wake** up while the sky endures;
	27.19	down rich, and when they **wake** up, they will find their
Ps	44.23	**Wake** up, Lord!
	57. 8	**Wake** up, my soul!
	57. 8	**Wake** up, my harp and lyre!
	57. 8	I will **wake** up the sun.
	59. 5	**Wake** up and punish the heathen;
	78.65	At last the Lord **woke** up as though from sleep;
	108. 1	**Wake** up, my soul!
	108. 2	**Wake** up, my harp and lyre!
	108. 2	I will **wake** up the sun.
	119.62	middle of the night I **wake** up to praise you for your
Prov	23.35	Why can't I **wake** up?
	27.14	well curse your friend as **wake** him up early in the morning
Ecc	12. 4	but even the song of a bird will **wake** you from sleep.
Song	4.16	**Wake** up, North Wind.
	8. 5	Under the apple-tree I **woke** you, in the place where you were
Is	26.19	sleeping in their graves will **wake** up and sing for joy.
	29. 8	dreams he is eating and **wakes** up hungry, or like a man
	29. 8	who dreams he is drinking and **wakes** with a dry throat.
	51. 9	**Wake** up, Lord, and help us!
	51.17	Jerusalem, **wake** up!
Jer	31.26	people will say, 'I went to sleep and **woke** up refreshed.'
	51.39	They will go to sleep and never **wake** up.
	51.57	They will go to sleep and never **wake** up.
Joel	1. 5	**Wake** up and weep, you drunkards;
Hab	2.19	You say to a piece of wood, "**Wake** up!"
Zech	13. 7	The Lord Almighty says, "**Wake** up, sword, and attack the
Mt	1.24	So when Joseph **woke** up, he married Mary, as the angel
	8.25	The disciples went to him and **woke** him up.
	25. 7	The ten girls **woke** up and trimmed their lamps.
Mk	4.38	The disciples **woke** him up and said, "Teacher, don't you care
Lk	8.24	disciples went to Jesus and **woke** him up, saying, "Master, Master!
	9.32	were sound asleep, but they **woke** up and saw Jesus' glory
Jn	11.11	Lazarus has fallen asleep, but I will go and **wake** him up."
Acts	12. 7	angel shook Peter by the shoulder, **woke** him up, and said,
	16.27	The jailer **woke** up, and when he saw the prison doors open,
Rom	13.11	the time has come for you to **wake** up from your sleep.
Eph	5.14	is why it is said, "**Wake** up, sleeper, and rise from death,
Rev	3. 2	So **wake** up, and strengthen what you still have before it
	3. 3	If you do not **wake** up, I will come upon you like

WALK

Gen	3. 8	they heard the Lord God **walking** in the garden, and they hid
	9.23	They **walked** backwards into the tent and covered their father,
	22. 6	As they **walked** along together, [7] Isaac said, "Father!"
	22. 8	And the two of them **walked** on together.
	24.63	early evening to take a **walk** in the fields and saw camels
	24.65	"Who is that man **walking** towards us in the field?"
Ex	2. 5	river to bathe, while her servants **walked** along the bank.
	14.16	Israelites will be able to **walk** through the sea on dry ground.
	14.29	But the Israelites **walked** through the sea on dry ground,
	15.19	The Israelites **walked** through the sea on dry ground.
	15.22	For three days they **walked** through the desert, but found no water.
	21.18	able to get up and **walk** outside with the help of a
	23. 5	don't just **walk** off.
Lev	11.42	ground, [42] whether they crawl, or **walk** on four legs, or
	26.13	you down and I let you **walk** with your head held high."
Deut	23.24	"When you **walk** along a path in someone else's vineyard,
	23.25	When you **walk** along a path in someone else's cornfield,
	28.56	she has never had to **walk** anywhere, will behave in the same
Josh	3.17	While the people **walked** across on dry ground, the
	14. 9	receive as our possession the land which I **walked** over.
Judg	5.10	sitting on saddles, and you that must **walk** wherever you go.
	14. 9	honey out into his hands and ate it as he **walked** along.
	18.24	take my priest and the gods that I made, and **walk** off!
Ruth	2. 3	out to the fields and **walked** behind the workers, picking up
1 Sam	5. 5	in Ashdod step over that place and do not **walk** on it.)
	17. 7	A soldier **walked** in front of him carrying his shield.
	17.39	the armour and tried to **walk**, but he couldn't, because he
	17.41	The Philistine started **walking** towards David,
	17.41	with his shield-bearer **walking** in front of him.
	17.48	Goliath started **walking** towards David again, and David
2 Sam	3.31	And at the funeral King David himself **walked** behind the coffin.
	4. 7	with them, and **walked** all night through the Jordan Valley.
	6. 4	were guiding the cart, [4] with Ahio **walking** in front.
	11. 2	As he **walked** about up there, he saw a woman having a
	16.13	Shimei kept up with them, **walking** on the hillside;
1 Kgs	19. 4	Elijah **walked** a whole day into the wilderness.
	19. 8	gave him enough strength to **walk** forty days to Sinai, the
2 Kgs	2.11	They kept talking as they **walked** on;
	2.14	again, and it divided, and he **walked** over to the other side.
	4.35	Elisha got up, **walked** about the room, and then went back
	6.26	The king of Israel was **walking** by on the city wall when
2 Chr	28.15	who were too weak to **walk** were put on donkeys, and all
Esth	2.11	Every day Mordecai would **walk** to and fro in front of the
	4. 1	his head with ashes, and **walked** through the city, wailing
Job	1. 7	Satan answered, "I have been **walking** here and there,
	2. 2	Satan answered, "I have been **walking** here and there,
	16.22	years are passing now, and I **walk** the road of no return.
	18. 8	He **walks** into a net, and his feet are caught;
	22.14	him from seeing, as he **walks** on the dome of the sky.
Job	22.15	Are you determined to **walk** in the paths that evil men
	29. 3	me then and gave me light as I **walked** through the darkness.
	38.16	Have you **walked** on the floor of the ocean?
Ps	17. 5	I have always **walked** in your way and have never strayed
	42. 4	and led them as they **walked** along, a happy crowd, singing
	48.12	People of God, **walk** round Zion and count the towers;
	56.13	And so I **walk** in the presence of God, in the light
	74. 3	**Walk** over these total ruins;
	77.19	You **walked** through the waves;
	115. 7	They have hands, but cannot feel, and feet, but cannot **walk;**
	116. 9	And so I **walk** in the presence of the Lord in the
	119. 3	they **walk** in the Lord's ways.
	142. 3	In the path where I **walk,** my enemies have hidden a trap
Prov	4.12	in your way if you **walk** wisely, and you will not stumble
	4.27	Avoid evil and **walk** straight ahead.
	5. 5	the road she **walks** is the road to death.
	6.28	Can you **walk** on hot coals without burning your feet?
	7. 8	He was **walking** along the street near the corner where a
	7.11	and shameless woman who always **walked** the streets [12] or
	8.20	I **walk** the way of righteousness;
	15.24	Wise people **walk** the road that leads upwards to life,
	21. 8	Guilty people **walk** a crooked path;
	22. 3	but an unthinking person will **walk** right into it and regret
	24.30	I **walked** through the fields and vineyards of a lazy,
	25.19	to chew with a loose tooth or **walk** with a crippled foot.
	27.12	but an unthinking person will **walk** right into it and regret
	30.29	There are four things that are impressive to watch as they **walk:**
Ecc	12. 5	You will be afraid of high places, and **walking** will be dangerous.
Is	2. 3	we will **walk** in the paths he has chosen.
	2. 5	descendants of Jacob, let us **walk** in the light which the
	3.16	They **walk** along with their noses in the air.
	9. 2	The people who **walked** in darkness have seen a great light.
	11.15	tiny streams, so that anyone will be able to **walk** across.
	20. 4	Young and old, they will **walk** barefoot and naked, with their
	26. 6	Those who were oppressed **walk** over it now and trample it
	30.29	as happy as those who **walk** to the music of flutes on
	40.31	they will **walk** and not grow weak.
	50.10	his servant, the path you **walk** may be dark indeed, but trust
	59. 8	path, and no one who **walks** that path will ever be safe.
	59. 9	We hope for light to **walk** by, but there is only darkness,
Jer	6.16	**Walk** on it, and you will live in peace."
	6.25	go to the countryside or **walk** on the roads, because our
	10. 5	they have to be carried because they cannot **walk.**
	18.15	they **walk** on unmarked paths.
	34.18	a covenant with me by **walking** between the two halves of a
Lam	3. 9	I stagger as I **walk;**
	4.18	we could not even **walk** in the streets.
Ezek	28.14	You lived on my holy mountain and **walked** among sparkling gems.
	29.11	No human being or animal will **walk** through it.
	31.13	tree, and the wild animals will **walk** over its branches.
	36.34	Everyone who used to **walk** by your fields saw how
Dan	3.25	"Then why do I see four men **walking** about in the fire?"
	4.29	months later, while he was **walking** about on the roof of his
Hos	11. 3	Yet I was the one who taught Israel to **walk.**
Amos	4.13	He **walks** on the heights of the earth.
Jon	3. 3	city so large that it took three days to **walk** through it.
	3. 4	through the city, and after **walking** a whole day, he
Mic	1. 3	he will come down and **walk** on the tops of the mountains.
	1. 8	To show my sorrow, I will **walk** about barefoot and naked.
	2. 3	in trouble, and then you will not **walk** so proudly any more.
	4. 2	we will **walk** in the paths he has chosen.
Nah	1. 3	Where the Lord **walks,** storms arise;
Hab	3. 6	sink down, the hills where he **walked** in ancient times.
Zech	8. 4	use a stick when they **walk,** will be sitting in the city
Mt	4.18	As Jesus **walked** along the shore of Lake Galilee, he saw
	9. 5	say, 'Your sins are forgiven,' or to say, 'Get up and **walk'?**
	9. 9	and as he **walked** along, he saw a tax collector,
	9.27	and as he **walked** along, two blind men started following
	11. 5	the lame can **walk,** those who suffer from dreaded skin-diseases
	12. 1	Jesus was **walking** through some cornfields on the Sabbath.
	14.25	morning Jesus came to the disciples, **walking** on the water.
	14.26	When they saw him **walking** on the water, they were terrified.
	14.29	out of the boat and started **walking** on the water to Jesus.
	15.31	the crippled made whole, the lame **walking,** and the blind seeing;
	20.17	disciples aside and spoke to them privately, as they **walked** along.
	21. 9	The crowds **walking** in front of Jesus
	21. 9	and those **walking** behind began to shout, "Praise to
Mk	1.16	As Jesus **walked** along the shore of Lake Galilee, he saw
	2. 9	forgiven', or to say, 'Get up, pick up your mat, and **walk'?**
	2.14	As he **walked** along, he saw a tax collector, Levi
	2.23	Jesus was **walking** through some cornfields on the Sabbath.
	2.23	As his disciples **walked** along with him, they began to pick
	5.42	She got up at once and started **walking** around.
	6.48	in the morning he came to them, **walking** on the water.
	6.49	to pass them by, [49] but they saw him **walking** on the water.
	8.24	"Yes, I can see people, but they look like trees **walking** about."
	11.20	Early next morning, as they **walked** along the road, they saw
	11.27	Jesus was **walking** in the Temple, the chief priests, the teachers
	12.38	the Law, who like to **walk** around in their long robes and
Lk	4.30	over the cliff, [30] but he **walked** through the middle of the
	5.23	'Your sins are forgiven you,' or to say, 'Get up and **walk'?**
	6. 1	Jesus was **walking** through some cornfields on the Sabbath.
	7.14	he **walked** over and touched the coffin, and the men carrying
	7.22	the lame can **walk,** those who suffer from dreaded skin-diseases
	10.19	so that you can **walk** on snakes and scorpions and overcome
	10.31	he saw the man, he **walked** on by, on the other side.
	10.32	at the man, and then **walked** on by, on the other side.
	11.44	You are like unmarked graves which people **walk** on without knowing
	20.46	the Law, who like to **walk** about in their long robes and

Lk 24.15 Jesus himself drew near and **walked** along with them;
24.17 "What are you talking about to each other, as you **walk** along?"
Jn 1.36 with two of his disciples, [36] when he saw Jesus **walking** by.
5. 8 Jesus said to him, "Get up, pick up your mat, and **walk."**
5. 9 he picked up his mat and started **walking.**
5.11 made me well told me to pick up my mat and **walk."**
6.19 when they saw Jesus **walking** on the water, coming near the
8.12 have the light of life and will never **walk** in darkness."
9. 1 As Jesus was **walking** along, he saw a man who had been
10.23 Jesus was **walking** in Solomon's Porch in the Temple,
11. 9 So whoever **walks** in broad daylight does not stumble, for he
11.10 But if he **walks** during the night he stumbles, because he
12.35 for the one who **walks** in the dark does not know where
Acts 3. 6 I order you to get up and **walk!"**
3. 8 he jumped up, stood on his feet, and started **walking** around.
3. 8 into the Temple with them, **walking** and jumping and praising God.
3. 9 The people there saw him **walking** and praising God,
3.12 of our own power or godliness that we made this man **walk?**
12.10 They **walked** down a street, and suddenly the angel left Peter.
13.11 cover his eyes, and he **walked** about trying to find someone
14. 8 had been lame from birth and had never been able to **walk.**
14.10 The man jumped up and started **walking** around.
17.23 For as I **walked** through your city and looked at the
Gal 2.14 saw that they were not **walking** a straight path in line with
Phil 2. 8 He was humble and **walked** the path of obedience all the way
Heb 12.13 Keep **walking** on straight paths, so that the lame foot
1 Jn 2.11 he **walks** in it and does not know where he is going,
Rev 2. 1 right hand and who **walks** among the seven gold lamp-stands.
3. 4 You will **walk** with me, clothed in white, because you are
9.20 silver, bronze, stone, and wood, which cannot see, hear, or **walk.**
16.15 so that he will not **walk** around naked and be ashamed
21.24 peoples of the world will **walk** by its light, and the kings

WALKING STICK

Gen 32.10 Jordan with nothing but a **walking-stick,** and now I have come
2 Kgs 18.21 using a reed as a **walking-stick**—it would break and jab your
Is 36. 6 using a reed as a **walking-stick**—it would break and jab your
Heb 11.21 He leaned on the top of his **walking-stick** and worshipped God.

WALL

[UNWALLED]

Ex 14.22 the sea on dry ground, with **walls** of water on both sides.
14.29 the sea on dry ground, with **walls** of water on both sides.
15. 8 it stood up straight like a **wall;**
Lev 14.37 to be eating into the **wall,** [38] he shall leave the house and
14.41 must have all the interior **walls** scraped and the plaster
14.42 removed, and new plaster will be used to cover the **walls.**
25.29 sells a house in a **walled** city, he has the right to
25.31 But houses in **unwalled** villages are to be treated like fields;
Num 22.24 between two vineyards and had a stone **wall** on each side.
22.25 over against the **wall** and crushed Balaam's foot against it.
35. 4 outwards from the city **walls** 450 metres in each direction,
Deut 1.28 and that they live in cities with **walls** that reach the sky.
2.36 No town had **walls** too strong for us.
3. 5 towns were fortified with high **walls,** gates, and bars to
3. 5 the gates, and there were also many villages without **walls.**
9. 1 Their cities are large, with **walls** that reach the sky.
28.52 and the high, fortified **walls** in which you trust will fall.
Josh 2.15 house built into the city **wall,** so she let the men down
6. 5 are to give a loud shout, and the city **walls** will collapse.
6.20 heard it, they gave a loud shout, and the **walls** collapsed.
10.20 to find safety inside their city **walls** and were not killed.
14.12 giants called the Anakim were there in large **walled** cities.
1 Sam 6.18 both the fortified towns and the villages without **walls.**
18.11 "I'll pin him to the **wall,"** Saul said to himself, and
19.10 to pin David to the **wall** with his spear,
19.10 but David dodged, and the spear stuck in the **wall.**
20.25 to the meal [25] and sat in his usual place by the **wall.**
23. 7 himself by going into a **walled** town with fortified gates."
31.10 nailed his body to the **wall** of the city of Beth Shan.
31.12 and his sons from the **wall,** brought them back to Jabesh, and
2 Sam 11.20 Didn't you realize that they would shoot arrows from the **walls?**
11.21 a woman threw a millstone down from the **wall** and killed him.
11.21 Why, then, did you go so near the **wall?'**
11.24 arrows at us from the **wall,** and some of Your Majesty's
18.24 to the top of the **wall** and stood on the roof of
20.15 of earth against the outer **wall**
20.15 also began to dig under the **wall** to make it fall down.
20.16 a wise woman in the city who shouted from the **wall,**
20.21 "We will throw his head over the **wall** to you," she said.
20.22 cut off Sheba's head and threw it over the **wall** to Joab.
1 Kgs 3. 1 his palace, the Temple, and the **wall** round Jerusalem.
4.13 towns in all, fortified with **walls** and with bronze bars on
4.33 from the Lebanon cedars to the hyssop that grows on **walls;**
6. 4 The **walls** of the Temple had openings in them, narrower on
6. 5 Against the outside **walls,** on the sides and the back of
6. 6 The temple **wall** on each floor was thinner than on the floor
6. 6 rooms could rest on the **wall** without having their beams
6.10 was built against the outside **walls** of the Temple, and was
6.15 The inside **walls** were covered with cedar panels from
6.18 cedar, so that the stones of the **walls** could not be seen.
6.27 of the room, and the other two wings touched the **walls.**
6.29 The **walls** of the main room and of the inner room were
6.36 of the Temple, enclosed with **walls** which had one layer of
7. 4 each of the two side **walls** there were three rows of windows.
7. 5 three rows of windows in each **wall** faced the opposite rows.
7.12 room of the Temple had **walls** with one layer of cedar beams
9.15 the east side of the city, and to build the city **wall.**
1 Kgs 11.27 on the east side of Jerusalem and repairing the city **walls.**
20.30 where the city **walls** fell on twenty-seven thousand of them.
21. 4 lay down on his bed, facing the **wall,** and would not eat.
2 Kgs 3.27 offered him on the city **wall** as a sacrifice to the god
6.26 walking by on the city **wall** when a woman cried out, "Help
6.30 who were close to the **wall** could see that he was wearing
9.33 her down, and her blood spattered the **wall** and the horses.
14.13 and tore down the city **wall** from Ephraim Gate to the Corner
18.26 all the people on the **wall** are listening."
18.27 who are sitting on the **wall,** who will have to eat their
20. 2 Hezekiah turned his face to the **wall** and prayed:
25. 1 outside the city, built siege **walls** round it, [2] and kept it
25. 4 nothing left to eat, [4] the city **walls** were broken through.
25. 4 the gateway connecting the two **walls,** and fled in the
25.10 in Jerusalem, [10] and his soldiers tore down the city **walls.**
1 Chr 29. 4 pure silver for decorating the **walls** of the Temple [5] and for
2 Chr 3. 7 to overlay the temple **walls,** the rafters, the thresholds,
3. 7 On the **walls** the workmen carved designs of winged creatures.
3. 8 gold were used to cover the **walls** of the Most Holy Place;
3. 9 for making nails, and the **walls** of the upper rooms were also
3.11 the room and reached the **wall** on either side of the room,
14. 7 fortify the cities by building **walls** and towers, and gates
25.23 he tore down the city **wall** from Ephraim Gate to the Corner
26. 6 He tore down the **walls** of the cities of Gath, Jamnia, and
26. 9 Corner Gate, at the Valley Gate, and where the **wall** turned.
26.15 large stones from the towers and corners of the city **wall.**
27. 3 extensive work on the city **wall** in the area of Jerusalem
32. 1 orders for his army to break their way through the **walls.**
32. 5 the wall, building towers on it, and building an outer **wall.**
32.18 who were on the city **wall,** so that it would be easier
32.30 through a tunnel to a point inside the **walls** of Jerusalem.
33.14 the height of the outer **wall** on the east side of David's
36.19 its palaces and its wealth, and broke down the city **wall.**
Ezra 4.12 They have begun to rebuild the **walls** and will soon finish them.
4.13 city is rebuilt and its **walls** are completed, the people will
4.16 city is rebuilt and its **walls** are completed, Your Majesty
5. 8 large stone blocks and with wooden beams set in the **wall.**
6. 4 The **walls** are to be built with one layer of wood on
Neh 1. 3 also told me that the **walls** of Jerusalem were still broken
2. 8 the Temple, for the city **walls,** and for the house I was
2.13 went, I inspected the broken **walls** of the city and the gates
2.15 valley of the Kidron and rode along, looking at the **wall.**
2.17 Let's rebuild the city **walls** and put an end to our disgrace."
3. 1 This is how the city **wall** was rebuilt.
3. 1 They dedicated the **wall** as far as the Tower of the Hundred
3. 8 of perfumes, built the next section, as far as Broad **Wall.**
3.13 the gate, and repaired the **wall** for 440 metres, as far as
3.15 of Shelah he built the **wall** next to the royal garden, as
3.17 The following Levites rebuilt the next several sections of the **wall:**
3.19 of the armoury, as far as the place where the **wall** turns;
3.22 The following priests rebuilt the next several sections of the **wall:**
3.24 section, from Azariah's house to the corner of the **wall;**
3.25 at the corner of the **wall** and the tower of the upper
3.27 tower guarding the Temple as far as the **wall** near Ophel.
3.31 near the room on top of the north-east corner of the **wall.**
4. 1 Jews had begun rebuilding the **wall,** he was furious and began
4. 3 and he added, "What kind of **wall** could they ever build?
4. 6 we went on rebuilding the **wall,** and soon it was half its
4. 7 making progress in rebuilding the **wall** of Jerusalem
4. 7 that the gaps in the **wall** were being closed,
4.10 How can we build the **wall** today?"
4.13 by clans behind the **wall,** wherever it was still unfinished.
4.15 Then all of us went back to rebuilding the **wall.**
4.17 full support to the people [17] who were rebuilding the **wall.**
4.19 that we are widely separated from one another on the **wall.**
4.21 of us worked on the **wall,** while the other half stood guard
5.16 into rebuilding the **wall** and did not acquire any property.
6. 1 we had finished building the **wall** and that there were no
6. 6 to revolt and that this is why you are rebuilding the **wall.**
6.15 days of work the entire **wall** was finished on the
7. 1 And now the **wall** had been rebuilt, the gates had all been
12.27 When the city **wall** of Jerusalem was dedicated, the
12.30 for themselves, the people, the gates, and the city **wall.**
12.31 Judah on top of the **wall** and put them in charge of
12.31 to the right on top of the **wall** towards the Rubbish Gate.
12.37 palace, and back to the **wall** at the Water Gate, on the
12.38 along the top of the **wall,** and I followed with half the
12.38 the Ovens to the Broad **Wall,** [39] and from there we went past
13.20 kinds of goods spent Friday night outside the city **walls.**
Ps 48.13 take notice of the **walls** and examine the fortresses,
51.18 rebuild the **walls** of Jerusalem.
78.13 he made the waters stand like **walls.**
89.40 You have torn down the **walls** of his city and left his
122. 7 May there be peace inside your **walls** and safety in your palaces."
Prov 18.11 wealth protects them like high, strong **walls** round a city.
18.19 you like a strong city **wall,** but if you quarrel with him,
21.22 by strong men, and destroy the **walls** they relied on.
24.31 The stone **wall** round them had fallen down.
25.28 are as helpless as a city without **walls,** open to attack.
Ecc 9.14 He surrounded it and prepared to break through the **walls.**
10. 8 if you break through a **wall,** a snake bites you.
Song 2. 9 There he stands beside the **wall.**
4.12 is a secret garden, a **walled** garden, a private spring;
5. 7 the guards at the city **wall** tore off my cape.
8. 9 If she is a **wall,** we will build her a silver tower.
8.10 I am a **wall,** and my breasts are its towers.
Is 2.15 every high tower, and the **walls** of every fortress.
5. 5 round it, break down the **wall** that protects it, and let wild
22. 5 The **walls** of our city have been battered down, and cries for
22. 9 You found the places where the **walls** of Jerusalem needed repair.
22. 9 some of them down to get stones to repair the city **walls.**

Is 25.12 of Moab with their high **walls** and bring them tumbling down
26. 1 God himself defends its **walls!**
26. 5 they lived in, and sent its **walls** crashing into the dust.
30.13 You are like a high **wall** with a crack running down it;
34.13 in all the palaces and **walled** towns, and jackals and owls
36.11 all the people on the **wall** are listening."
36.12 who are sitting on the **wall,** who will have to eat their
38. 2 Hezekiah turned his face to the **wall** and prayed:
54.12 that glow like fire, and the **wall** around you with jewels.
58.12 who rebuilt the **walls,** who restored the ruined houses."
60.10 "Foreigners will rebuild your **walls,** And their kings will serve you.
60.18 I will protect and defend you like a **wall;**
62. 6 On your **walls,** Jerusalem, I have placed sentries;
Jer 1.15 of Jerusalem and round its **walls,** and also round the other
1.18 be like a fortified city, an iron pillar, and a bronze **wall.**
15.20 you like a solid bronze **wall** as far as they are concerned.
39. 2 the city **walls** were broken through.
39. 4 the gateway connecting the two **walls,** and escaped in the
39. 8 houses of the people and tore down the **walls** of Jerusalem.
49.27 I will set the **walls** of Damascus on fire and will burn
50.15 Its **walls** have been broken through and torn down.
51.12 Give the signal to attack Babylon's **walls.**
51.44 "Babylon's **walls** have fallen.
51.58 The **walls** of mighty Babylon will be thrown to the ground,
52. 4 outside the city, built siege **walls** round it, [5] and kept it
52. 7 nothing left to eat, [7] the city **walls** were broken through.
52. 7 the gateway connecting the two **walls,** and fled in the
52.14 and his soldiers tore down the city **walls.**
Lam 2. 7 He allowed the enemy to tear down its **walls.**
2. 8 The Lord was determined that the **walls** of Zion should fall;
2. 8 The towers and **walls** now lie in ruins together.
2.18 O Jerusalem, let your very **walls** cry out to the Lord!
3. 9 stone **walls** block me wherever I turn.
Ezek 4. 3 and set it up like a **wall** between you and the city.
8. 7 of the outer courtyard and showed me a hole in the **wall.**
8. 8 He said, "Mortal man, break through the **wall** here."
8.10 The **walls** were covered with drawings of snakes
12. 5 break a hole through the **wall** of your house and take your
12. 7 dug a hole in the **wall** with my hands and went out.
12.12 escape through a hole that they dig for him in the **wall.**
13. 5 guard the places where the **walls** have crumbled,
13. 5 nor do they rebuild the **walls,** and so Israel cannot be
13.10 people have put up a **wall** of loose stones, and then the
13.11 Tell the prophets that their **wall** is going to fall down.
13.12 The **wall** will collapse, and everyone will ask you what
13.13 wind, pouring rain, and hailstones to destroy the **wall.**
13.14 intend to break down the **wall** they whitewashed, to shatter
13.15 "The **wall** and those who covered it with whitewash will
13.15 will tell you that the **wall** is gone and so are those
22.28 hidden these sins like men covering a **wall** with whitewash.
22.30 someone who could build a **wall,** who could stand
22.30 in the places where the **walls** have crumbled
23.14 Babylonian officials carved into the **wall** and painted bright red,
26. 4 They will destroy your city **walls** and tear down your towers.
26. 8 earthworks, and make a solid **wall** of shields against you.
26. 9 They will pound in your **walls** with battering-rams and tear
26.10 and chariots will shake your **walls** as they pass through the
26.12 They will pull down your **walls** and shatter your luxurious houses.
27.11 Soldiers from Arvad guarded your **walls,** and men from
27.11 They hung their shields on your **walls.**
30.16 The **walls** of Thebes will be broken down, and the city will
33.30 they meet by the city **walls** or in the doorways of their
38.11 peace and security in **unwalled** towns that have no defences.
38.20 cliffs will crumble, and every **wall** will collapse.
40. 5 I saw was the Temple, and there was a **wall** round it.
40. 5 which was three metres long, and measured the **wall.**
40. 7 on each side, and the **walls** between them were two and a
40. 8 Temple, and at its far end the **walls** were one metre thick.
40.10 the same size, and the **walls** between them were all of the
40.12 guardrooms there was a low **wall** fifty centimetres high and
40.13 the distance from the back **wall** of one room
40.13 to the back **wall** of the room across the passage
40.15 the gateway from the outside **wall** of the gate to the far
40.16 small openings in the outside **walls** of all the rooms
40.16 and also in the inner **walls** between the rooms.
40.16 There were palm-trees carved on the inner **walls**
40.17 rooms built against the outer **wall,** and in front of them
40.21 side of the passage, the **walls** between them, and the
40.24 He measured its inner **walls** and its entrance room, and they
40.26 There were palm-trees carved on the inner **walls**
40.28 it was the same size as the gateways in the outer **wall.**
40.29 entrance room, and its inner **walls** were the same size as
40.31 and palm-trees were carved on the **walls** along the passage.
40.33 entrance room, and its inner **walls** measured the same as
40.34 Palm-trees were carved on the **walls** along the passage.
40.36 had guardrooms, decorated inner **walls,** an entrance room,
40.37 Palm-trees were carved on the **walls** along the passage.
40.48 and seven metres wide, with **walls** one and a half metres
41. 2 and five metres wide, with **walls** two and a half metres
41. 3 and three metres wide, with **walls** on either side three and a
41. 5 the thickness of the inner **wall** of the temple building, and
41. 5 Against this **wall,** all round the Temple, was a series of
41. 6 The Temple's outer **wall** on each floor was thinner than on
41. 6 rooms could rest on the **wall** without being anchored into it.
41. 7 And so the temple **walls,** when seen from the outside,
41. 7 Against the Temple's outer **wall,** on the outside of the rooms,
41. 8 The outside **wall** of these rooms was two and a half
41. 8 level with the foundation of the rooms by the temple **walls.**
41.12 its **walls** were two and a half metres thick all round.
41.17 The inside **walls** of the Temple, up as high as above the
41.19 like this all round the **wall,** [20] from the floor to above
Ezek 41.25 doors of the Holy Place, just as there were on the **walls.**
41.26 were windows, and the **walls** were decorated with palm-trees.
42. 7 the lower level the outer **wall** of the building was solid for
42. 9 of the building, where the **wall** of the courtyard began,
42.12 side of the building, at the east end where the **wall** began.
42.20 250 metres, [20] so that the **wall** enclosed a square 250
42.20 The **wall** served to separate what was holy from what was not.
43. 8 of my Temple, so that there was only a **wall** between us.
46.23 stone wall round it, with fireplaces built against the **wall.**
48.30 Each of the four **walls** measures 2,250 metres and has three
48.30 The gates in the north **wall** are named after Reuben, Judah,
48.30 those in the east **wall,** after Joseph, Benjamin, and Dan;
48.30 those in the south **wall,** after Simeon, Issachar, and
48.30 and those in the west **wall** are named after Gad, Asher, and
48.35 The total length of the **wall** on all four sides of the
Dan 5. 5 began writing on the plaster **wall** of the palace, where the
8. 2 suddenly found myself in the **walled** city of Susa in the
Hos 2. 6 her in with thorn-bushes and build a **wall** to block her way.
Joel 2. 7 they climb the **walls** like soldiers.
2. 9 they run over the **walls;**
Amos 1. 7 send fire upon the city **walls** of Gaza and burn down its
1.10 send fire upon the city **walls** of Tyre and burn down its
1.14 send fire upon the city **walls** of Rabbah and burn down its
4. 3 dragged to the nearest break in the **wall** and thrown out."
5.19 puts his hand on the **wall**—only to be bitten by a
7. 7 saw him standing beside a **wall** that had been built with the
7. 8 that my people are like a **wall** that is out of line.
9.11 I will repair its **walls** and restore it.
Mic 7.11 the time to rebuild the city **walls** is coming.
Nah 2. 5 The attackers rush to the **wall** and set up the shield for
3. 8 river to protect her like a **wall**—the Nile was her defence.
3.17 swarm of locusts that stay in the **walls** on a cold day.
Hab 2.11 Even the stones of the **walls** cry out against you, and
Zeph 3. 6 their cities and left their **walls** and towers in ruins.
Zech 2. 4 in Jerusalem that it will be too big to have **walls.**
2. 5 he himself will be a **wall** of fire round the city to
Lk 19.44 will completely destroy you and the people within your **walls;**
Acts 9.25 through an opening in the **wall,** lowering him in a basket.
23. 3 said to him, "God will certainly strike you—you whitewashed **wall!**
2 Cor 11.33 basket through an opening in the **wall** and escaped from him.
Eph 2.14 he broke down the **wall** that separated them and kept them
Heb 11.30 was faith that made the **walls** of Jericho fall down after the
Rev 21.12 It had a great, high **wall** with twelve gates and with
21.14 The city's **wall** was built on twelve foundation-stones,
21.15 measuring-rod to measure the city, its gates, and its **wall.**
21.17 The angel also measured the **wall,** and it was sixty metres high,
21.18 The **wall** was made of jasper, and the city itself was
21.19 foundation-stones of the city **wall** were adorned with all kinds of

WANDER

Gen 4.12 you will be a homeless **wanderer** on the earth."
4.14 I will be a homeless **wanderer** on the earth, and anyone who
11. 2 As they **wandered** about in the East, they came to a plain
21.14 She left and **wandered** about in the wilderness of Beersheba.
37.15 arrived at Shechem [15] and was **wandering** about in the
47. 9 Jacob answered, "My life of **wandering** has lasted a
47. 9 unlike the long years of my ancestors in their **wanderings."**
Ex 14. 3 think that the Israelites are **wandering** about in the country
40.38 During all their **wanderings** they could see the cloud of
Num 14.33 Your children will **wander** in the wilderness for forty years,
32.13 the people and made them **wander** in the wilderness for forty
Deut 2. 1 a long time **wandering** about in the hill-country of Edom.
2. 3 we had spent enough time **wandering** about in those hills and
2. 7 taken care of you as you **wandered** through this vast desert.
26. 5 'My ancestor was a **wandering** Aramean, who took his family to
32.10 "He found them **wandering** through the desert,
Judg 11.37 go with my friends to **wander** in the mountains and grieve
1 Sam 9. 3 belonging to Kish had **wandered** off, so he said to Saul,
2 Sam 15.20 short time, so why should I make you **wander** round with me?
1 Chr 16.20 They **wandered** from country to country,
Job 6.18 they **wander** and die in the desert.
12.24 He makes their leaders foolish and lets them **wander** confused
23.11 the road he chooses, and never **wander** to either side.
38.41 feeds the ravens when they **wander** about hungry, when their
Ps 105.13 They **wandered** from country to country,
107. 4 Some **wandered** in the trackless desert and could not find
107.40 their oppressors and made them **wander** in trackless deserts.
119.176 I **wander** about like a lost sheep;
Prov 5. 6 but **wanders** off, and does not realize what is happening.
7.25 don't go **wandering** after her.
21.16 Death is waiting for anyone who **wanders** away from good sense.
Song 3. 2 I went **wandering** through the city,
Is 8.21 The people will **wander** through the land, discouraged and hungry.
13.20 No **wandering** Arab will ever pitch his tent there, and no
30.21 If you **wander** off the road to the right or the left,
Jer 50. 6 They have **wandered** like sheep from one mountain to another,
Lam 4.14 Her leaders **wandered** through the streets like blind men,
4.15 So they **wandered** from nation to nation, welcomed by no one.
Ezek 34. 4 hurt, brought back those that **wandered** off, or looked for
34. 6 So my sheep **wandered** over the high hills and the mountains.
34.16 back those that **wander** off, bandage those that are hurt,
Hos 9.17 They will become **wanderers** among the nations.
Amos 8.12 People will **wander** from the Dead Sea to the
Zech 10. 2 So the people **wander** about like lost sheep.
Mk 5. 5 Day and night he **wandered** among the tombs and through the hills,
1 Cor 4.11 we **wander** from place to place;
1 Tim 6.10 that they have **wandered** away from the faith and have
Heb 11.38 **wandered** like refugees in the deserts and hills, living in caves

Jas 5.19 brothers, if one of you **wanders** away from the truth and
Jude 13 They are like **wandering** stars, for whom God has reserved a

WANDERING

Gen 4.16 in a land called **"Wandering,"** which is east of Eden.

WANT

Gen 4. 7 It **wants** to rule you, but you must overcome it."
11. 6 Soon they will be able to do anything they **want!**
13. 9 Choose any part of the land you **want.**
16. 6 do whatever you **want** with her."
19. 5 The men of Sodom **wanted** to have sex with them.
19. 8 out to you, and you can do whatever you **want** with them.
24. 3 I **want** you to make a vow in the name of the
24.19 water for your camels and let them have all they **want."**
24.58 Rebecca and asked, "Do you **want** to go with this man?"
26.28 We **want** you to promise [29] that you will not harm us, just
29.15 How much pay do you **want?"**
30.31 Jacob answered, "I don't **want** any wages.
30.32 That is all the wages I **want.**
32.29 But he answered, "Why do you **want** to know my name?"
33.15 no need for that for I only **want** to gain your favour."
34. 4 said to his father, "I **want** you to get this girl for
34.11 "Do me this favour, and I will give you whatever you **want.**
34.12 Tell me what presents you **want,** and set the payment for
37.13 Jacob said to Joseph, "I **want** you to go to Shechem,
38.23 We don't **want** people to laugh at us.
42.36 said to them, "Do you **want** to make me lose all my
42.36 and now you **want** to take away Benjamin.
45.11 and I do not **want** you, your family, and your livestock to
47.30 I **want** to be buried where my fathers are;
Ex 4.19 to Egypt, for all those who **wanted** to kill you are dead."
5. 5 And now you **want** to stop working!"
5.17 "You are lazy and don't **want** to work, and that is why
10.11 may go and worship the Lord if that is what you **want."**
12.48 has settled among you and **wants** to celebrate Passover to
13.13 If you do not **want** to buy back the donkey, break its
13.17 God thought, "I do not **want** the people to change their
15. 9 I will divide their wealth and take all I **want;**
16. 3 down and eat meat and as much other food as we **wanted.**
16. 8 as much bread as you **want** in the morning, because he has
16.12 and in the morning they will have all the bread they **want.**
16.23 Bake today what you **want** to bake
16.23 and boil what you **want** to boil.
21. 5 his children and does not **want** to be set free, [6] then his
33. 7 Lord's presence, and anyone who **wanted** to consult the Lord
35.22 All who **wanted** to, both men and women, brought decorative pins,
35.29 the people of Israel who **wanted** to brought their offering to
Lev 25.19 you will have all you **want** to eat and will live in
26. 5 will have all that you **want** to eat, and you will live
Num 9.10 on a journey, but still **want** to keep the Passover, [11] you
9.14 a foreigner living among you **wants** to keep the Passover, he
11. 5 to eat all the fish we **wanted,** and it cost us nothing.
12. 4 Moses, Aaron, and Miriam, "I **want** the three of you to come
20.19 we will pay for it—all we **want** is to pass through."
21.27 We **want** to see it rebuilt and restored.
22. 5 "I **want** you to know that a whole nation has come from
22.11 He **wants** me to curse them for him, so that he can
24. 1 Balaam knew that the Lord **wanted** him to bless the people of
32. 6 Moses replied, "Do you **want** to stay here while your
Deut 2.28 All we **want** to do is to pass through your country, [29] until
4.10 I **want** them to hear what I have to say, so that
6.11 and you have all you **want** to eat, [12] make certain that you
7. 8 the Lord loved you and **wanted** to keep the promise that he
8.10 You will have all you **want** to eat, and you will give
8.12 When you have all you **want** to eat and have built good
11.15 You will have all the food you **want.**
14.26 Spend it on whatever you **want**—beef, lamb, wine, beer—
15.16 "But your slave may not **want** to leave;
18. 6 "Any Levite who **wants** to may come from any town in
21.11 them a beautiful woman that you like and **want** to marry.
21.14 Later, if you no longer **want** her, you are to let her
22.13 man marries a girl and later he decides he doesn't **want** her.
22.16 to this man in marriage, and now he doesn't **want** her.
23.24 eat all the grapes you **want,** but you must not carry any
24. 1 later decides that he doesn't **want** her, because he finds
24. 3 also decides that he doesn't **want** her, so he also writes out
25. 7 dead man's brother does not **want** to marry her, she is to
28.68 your enemies as slaves, but no one will **want** to buy you."
31.20 have all the food they **want,** and they will live comfortably.
Josh 5.14 What do you **want** me to do?"
7.21 I **wanted** them so much that I took them.
9. 6 We **want** you to make a treaty with us."
15.18 down from her donkey, and Caleb asked her what she **wanted.**
15.19 She answered, "I **want** some pools of water.
22.22 knows why we did this, and we **want** you to know too!
Judg 1.14 down from her donkey, and Caleb asked her what she **wanted.**
1.15 She answered, "I **want** some pools of water.
9.15 answered, 'If you really **want** to make me your king,
9.54 I don't **want** it said that a woman killed me."
11. 8 to you now because we **want** you to go with us and
13.15 But if you **want** to prepare it, burn it as an offering
13.18 The angel asked, "Why do you **want** to know my name?
13.23 answered, "If the Lord had **wanted** to kill us, he would not
14. 2 I **want** to marry her."
14. 3 father, "She is the one I **want** you to get for me.
15. 1 said to her father, "I **want** to go to my wife's room."
16. 6 If someone **wanted** to tie you up and make you helpless, how
16.26 I **want** to lean on them."
Judg 18.10 has everything a person could **want,** and God has given it to
18.25 say anything else unless you **want** these men to get angry and
19.10 But the man did not **want** to spend another night there,
19.22 We **want** to have sex with him!"
19.24 Do with them whatever you **want.**
Ruth 1.11 "Why do you **want** to come with me?
3.14 seen, because Boaz did not **want** anyone to know that she had
4. 3 come back from Moab, she **wants** to sell the field that
4. 4 Now then, if you **want** it, buy it in the presence of
4. 4 But if you don't **want** it, say so, because the right to
1 Sam 2.16 then take what you **want,"** the priest's servant would say,
2.35 will be faithful to me and do everything I **want** him to.
8.19 We **want** a king, [20] so that we will be like other nations,
8.22 The Lord answered, "Do what they **want** and give them a king."
9. 9 seer, and so whenever someone **wanted** to ask God a question,
9.20 But who is it that the people of Israel **want** so much?
12.12 king and said to me, 'We **want** a king to rule us.'
13.14 the kind of man he **wants** and make him ruler of his
14. 7 The young man answered, "Whatever you **want** to do, I'm with you."
15.24 I was afraid of my men and did what they **wanted.**
18.25 "All the king **wants** from you as payment for the bride is
19. 5 Why, then, do you now **want** to do wrong to an innocent
20. 1 I done to your father to make him **want** to kill me?"
20. 4 Jonathan said, "I'll do anything you **want."**
21. 9 If you **want** it, take it—it's the only weapon here."
22.23 Saul **wants** to kill both you and me, but you will be
23.20 We know, Your Majesty, how much you **want** to capture him;
24. 4 your power and you could do to him whatever you **wanted** to."
25. 7 shearing your sheep, and he **wants** you to know that your
25.26 your enemies and all who **want** to harm you will be punished
25.35 I will do what you **want."**
2 Sam 3.17 "For a long time you have **wanted** David to be your king.
3.21 will get what you have **wanted** and will rule over the whole
3.27 the gate, as though he **wanted** to speak privately with him,
12. 4 The rich man didn't **want** to kill one of his own animals
12.28 I don't **want** to get the credit for capturing it."
13. 5 I **want** her to prepare the food here where I can see
14. 5 "What do you **want?"**
14.21 king said to Joab, "I have decided to do what you **want.**
14.24 "I don't **want** to see him," the king said.
14.32 I **wanted** you to go to the king and ask him from
14.32 And Absalom went on, "I **want** you to arrange for me to
15. 2 with a dispute that he **wanted** the king to settle, Absalom
15.14 must get away at once if we **want** to escape from Absalom!
17. 3 You **want** to kill only one man;
18.22 "Why do you **want** to do it, my son?"
18.23 "Whatever happens," Ahimaaz said again, "I **want** to go."
19.18 the royal party across and to do whatever the king **wanted.**
19.38 will take him with me and do for him whatever you **want.**
20.16 I **want** to speak with him."
20.19 Do you **want** to ruin what belongs to the Lord?"
21. 3 I **want** to make up for the wrong that was done to
21. 4 silver or gold, nor do we **want** to kill any Israelite."
21. 5 They answered, "Saul **wanted** to destroy us and leave none
21.17 hope of Israel, and we don't **want** to lose you," they said.
24. 2 I **want** to know how many there are."
24. 3 But why does Your Majesty **want** to do this?"
24.14 But I don't **want** to be punished by men.
1 Kgs 1.12 If you **want** to save your life and the life of your
1.16 low before the king, and he asked, "What do you **want?"**
1.51 and had said, "First, I **want** King Solomon to swear to me
5.10 and pine logs that he **wanted,** [11] and Solomon provided Hiram
8.18 him, 'You were right in **wanting** to build a temple for me,
8.58 will always live as he **wants** us to live, and keep all
9. 1 palace and everything else he **wanted** to build, [2] the Lord
9.11 and pine and with all the gold he **wanted** for this work.
9.19 and everything else he **wanted** to build in Jerusalem,
10.24 king, [24] and the whole world **wanted** to come and listen to
11.22 Is that why you **want** to go back home?"
11.37 and you will rule over all the territory that you **want.**
12. 7 They replied, "If you **want** to serve this people well,
13.33 He ordained as priest anyone who **wanted** to be one.
16.21 some of them **wanted** to make Tibni son of Ginath king, and
18. 9 have I done that you **want** to put me in danger of
18.11 And now you **want** me to go and tell him that you
20. 7 country and said, "You see that this man **wants** to ruin us.
21. 2 to my palace, and I **want** to use the land for a
2 Kgs 2. 9 Elisha, "Tell me what you **want** me to do for you before
5. 6 I **want** you to cure him of his disease."
8. 4 the king **wanted** to know about Elisha's miracles.
9.11 What did that crazy fellow **want** with you?"
9.11 "You know what he **wanted,"** Jehu answered.
9.18 said to him, "The king **wants** to know if you come as
10.30 "You have done to Ahab's descendants everything I **wanted** you to do.
11.15 Jehoiada did not **want** Athaliah killed in the temple area,
18.19 told them that the emperor **wanted** to know what made King
20. 3 that I have always tried to do what you **wanted** me to."
1 Chr 21. 1 Satan **wanted** to bring trouble on the people of Israel, so
21. 2 I **want** to know how many there are."
21. 3 Why do you **want** to do this and make the whole nation
21.13 But I don't **want** to be punished by men.
22. 7 to him, "My son, I **wanted** to build a temple to honour
28. 2 I **wanted** to build a permanent home for the Covenant Box, the
2 Chr 6. 8 him, 'You were right in **wanting** to build a temple for me,
9. 8 loves his people Israel and **wants** to preserve them for ever,
11.16 of Israel people who sincerely **wanted** to worship the Lord,
23.14 Jehoiada did not **want** Athaliah killed in the temple area,
28.13 Now you **want** to do something that will increase our guilt."
36.15 his people, because he **wanted** to spare them and the Temple.

Ezra	4.12	"We **want** Your Majesty to know that the Jews who came
	4.14	Your Majesty, we do not **want** to see this happen, and so
	9.12	prosper or succeed if we **wanted** to enjoy the land and pass
Neh	1.11	prayers of all your other servants who **want** to honour you.
	2. 4	The emperor asked, "What is it that you **want?"**
	9.25	They ate all they **wanted** and grew fat;
Esth	1. 8	servants that everyone could have as much as he **wanted.**
	1.11	beautiful woman, and the king **wanted** to show off her beauty
	2.13	the harem to the palace, she could wear whatever she **wanted.**
	5. 3	"Tell me what you **want,** and you shall have it—even if
	5. 6	asked her, "Tell me what you **want,** and you shall have it.
	5. 8	At that time I will tell you what I **want."**
	6. 6	to himself, "Now who could the king **want** to honour so much?
	7. 2	king asked her again, "Now, Queen Esther, what do you **want?**
	9. 5	So the Jews could do what they **wanted** with their enemies.
	9.12	What do you **want** now?
	9.12	Tell me what else you **want,** and you shall have it."
Job	9.12	He takes what he **wants,** and no one can stop him;
	13. 3	I **want** to argue my case with him.
	16.21	I **want** someone to plead with God for me, as a man
	20.23	Let him eat all he **wants!**
	21.14	they don't **want** to know his will for their lives.
	23. 5	I **want** to know what he would say and how he would
	23.13	oppose him or stop him from doing what he **wants** to do.
	32.10	So now I **want** you to listen to me;
	34.33	what God does, can you expect him to do what you **want?**
	42. 2	that you can do everything you **want.**
Ps	5. 9	they only **want** to destroy.
	12. 4	mouths that say, '"With our words we get what we **want.**
	17.12	like lions, waiting for me, **wanting** to tear me to pieces.
	17.14	save me from those who in this life have all they **want.**
	22.26	The poor will eat as much as they **want;**
	27. 4	one thing only do I **want:**
	27.11	Teach me, Lord, what you **want** me to do, and lead me
	34.12	Do you **want** long life and happiness?
	35.25	That's just what we **wanted!"**
	35.27	May those who **want** to see me acquitted shout for joy and
	38.12	Those who **want** to kill me lay traps for me,
	38.12	and those who **want** to hurt me threaten to ruin
	40. 6	You do not **want** sacrifices and offerings;
	41. 5	They **want** me to die and be forgotten.
	51.16	You do not **want** sacrifices, or I would offer them;
	62. 4	You only **want** to bring him down from his place of honour;
	68.23	blood, and your dogs may lap up as much as they **want."**
	69. 4	they are strong and **want** to kill me.
	71.10	My enemies **want** to kill me;
	73.25	Since I have you, what else could I **want** on earth?
	74. 8	They **wanted** to crush us completely;
	78.18	put God to the test by demanding the food they **wanted.**
	78.25	ate the food of angels, and God gave them all they **wanted.**
	78.29	God gave them what they **wanted.**
	81.12	I let them go their stubborn ways and do whatever they **wanted.**
	84. 2	How I **want** to be there!
	86.11	Teach me, Lord, what you **want** me to do, and I will
	107.30	the calm, and he brought them safe to the port they **wanted.**
	111. 2	All who are delighted with them **want** to understand them.
	119.20	I **want** to know your judgements at all times.
	119.40	I **want** to obey your commands;
	119.57	You are all I **want, O** Lord;
	119.101	avoided all evil conduct, because I **want** to obey your word.
	132.13	he **wants** to make it his home:
	132.14	this is where I **want** to rule.
	140. 8	Lord, don't give the wicked what they **want;**
	141. 4	Keep me from **wanting** to do wrong and from joining evil men
	142. 5	you are all I **want** in this life.
Prov	1.17	when the bird you **want** to catch is watching,
	1.22	How long do you **want** to be foolish?
	1.30	You have never **wanted** my advice or paid any attention
	3.15	nothing you could **want** can compare with it.
	7.15	I **wanted** to find you, and here you are!
	8.11	nothing you **want** can compare with me.
	10. 3	but he will keep the wicked from getting what they **want.**
	10.24	The righteous get what they **want,** but the wicked will
	11.23	What good people **want** always results in good;
	11.23	when the wicked get what they **want,** everyone is angry.
	12. 1	Anyone who loves knowledge **wants** to be told when he is wrong.
	12. 5	the wicked only **want** to deceive you.
	12.12	All that wicked people **want** is to find evil things to do,
	13. 4	much a lazy person may **want** something, he will never get it.
	13. 4	A hard worker will get everything he **wants.**
	13.19	How good it is to get what you **want!**
	14. 9	care if they sin, but good people **want** to be forgiven.
	14.21	If you **want** to be happy, be kind to the poor;
	14.27	Do you **want** to avoid death?
	15.14	Intelligent people **want** to learn, but stupid people are satisfied with ignorance.
	16.11	The Lord **wants** weights and measures to be honest and
	16.13	A king **wants** to hear the truth and will favour those who
	16.26	him work harder, because he **wants** to satisfy his hunger.
	17. 9	If you **want** people to like you, forgive them when they
	18. 2	all he **wants** to do is to show how clever he is.
	18.16	Do you **want** to meet an important person?
	19.15	Be lazy if you **want** to;
	21.23	If you **want** to stay out of trouble, be careful what you
	22.19	I **want** you to put your trust in the Lord;
	24.33	Have a nap and sleep if you **want** to.
	26.28	You have to hate someone to **want** to hurt him with lies.
	29.21	give your servant everything he **wants** from childhood on,
	29.26	Everybody **wants** the good will of the ruler, but only
	30.22	a fool who has all he **wants** to eat,
Ecc	2. 8	entertain me, and I had all the women a man could **want.**
Ecc	2.10	Anything I **wanted,** I got.
	5.10	you long to be rich, you will never get all you **want.**
	6. 2	and property, yes, everything he **wants,** but then will not
	6. 9	what you have than to be always **wanting** something else.
	11. 9	Do what you **want** to do, and follow your heart's desire.
Song	5. 6	How I **wanted** to hear his voice!
	6.13	Why do you **want** to watch me as I dance between the
Is	1. 5	Do you **want** to be punished even more?
	1.11	says, "Do you think I **want** all these sacrifices you keep
	2. 3	He will teach us what he **wants** us to do;
	16. 4	Protect us from those who **want** to destroy us."
	21.12	If you **want** to ask again, come back and ask."
	27. 5	the enemies of my people **want** my protection, let them make
	30. 2	They **want** Egypt to protect them, so they put their trust in
	30.10	Tell us what we **want** to hear.
	30.11	We don't **want** to hear about your holy God of Israel."
	36. 4	told them that the emperor **wanted** to know what made King
	38. 3	that I have always tried to do what you **wanted** me to."
	42.21	and teachings, and he **wanted** his people to honour them.
	42.24	would not live as he **wanted** us to live or obey the
	44.28	you will do what I **want** you to do:
	48.14	he will do what I **want** him to do.
	48.17	your God, the one who **wants** to teach you for your own
	51. 1	"Listen to me, you that **want** to be saved, you that come
	58. 2	They say they **want** me to give them just laws and that
	58. 6	"The kind of fasting I **want** is this:
	64. 5	what is right, those who remember how you **want** them to live.
Jer	2.24	No male that **wants** her has to trouble himself;
	3. 1	have had many lovers, and now you **want** to return to me!
	3.19	"Israel, I **wanted** to accept you as my son and give you
	3.19	I **wanted** you to call me father, and never again turn away
	4. 1	"People of Israel, if you **want** to turn, then turn back to
	4.30	Your lovers have rejected you and **want** to kill you.
	5. 4	what their God requires, what the Lord **wants** them to do.
	5. 5	what their God requires, what the Lord **wants** them to do."
	6. 3	round the city, and each one will camp wherever he **wants.**
	8.13	"I **wanted** to gather my people, as a man gathers his harvest;
	9.24	If anyone **wants** to boast, he should boast that he knows
	11.21	The men of Anathoth **wanted** me killed, and they told me
	18.12	all be just as stubborn and evil as we **want** to be.' "
	21. 7	King Nebuchadnezzar and by your enemies, who **want** to kill you.
	22.25	to people you are afraid of, people who **want** to kill you.
	22.28	a broken jar that is thrown away and that no one **wants?**
	29.22	Jerusalem to Babylonia **want** to bring a curse on someone,
	31.19	We turned away from you, but soon we **wanted** to return.
	34.20	over to their enemies, who **want** to kill them, and their
	34.21	of Judah and his officials to those who **want** to kill them.
	36. 6	But I **want** you to go there the next time the people
	38. 4	he only **wants** to hurt them."
	38.14	you a question, and I **want** you to tell me the whole
	38.16	or hand you over to the men who **want** to kill you."
	39.12	Do not harm him, but do for him whatever he **wants."**
	40. 4	If you **want** to go to Babylonia with me, you may do
	40. 4	But if you don't **want** to go, you don't have to.
	42.22	or disease in the land where you **want** to go and live."
	44. 7	Do you **want** to bring destruction on men and women, children
	44.30	Egypt to his enemies who **want** to kill him, just as I
	44.30	Babylonia, who was his enemy and **wanted** to kill him."
	46.26	them over to those who **want** to kill them, to King
	48.38	because I have broken Moab like a jar that no one **wants.**
	49. 9	when robbers come at night, they take only what they **want.**
	49.37	of Elam afraid of their enemies, who **want** to kill them.
	50.10	and those who loot it will take everything they **want.**
	50.19	they will eat all they **want** of the crops that grow in
	51.34	He took what he **wanted** and threw the rest away.
Ezek	2. 1	I **want** to talk to you."
	10.11	together in the direction they **wanted** to go, without having
	13.18	You **want** to possess the power of life and death over my
	18.31	Why do you Israelites **want** to die?
	18.32	I do not **want** anyone to die," says the Sovereign Lord.
	20.32	up your minds that you **want** to be like the other nations,
	23. 9	her over to her Assyrian lovers whom she **wanted** so much.
	23.21	(Oholibah, you **wanted** to repeat the immorality you were
	33.11	Why do you **want** to die?
	36.32	Israel, I **want** you to know that I am not doing all
	36.32	I **want** you to feel the shame and disgrace of what you
	42.14	been in the Temple and **want** to go to the outer courtyard,
	46. 5	with each lamb he is to bring whatever he **wants** to give.
	46. 7	the offering is to be whatever the prince **wants** to give.
	46.11	and whatever the worshipper **wants** to give with each lamb.
	46.12	"When the ruling prince **wants** to make a voluntary
Dan	2. 3	I **want** to know what it means."
	2.10	the earth who can tell Your Majesty what you **want** to know.
	5.19	If he **wanted** to kill someone, he did;
	5.19	if he **wanted** to keep someone alive, he did.
	5.19	He honoured or disgraced anyone he **wanted** to.
	7.19	Then I **wanted** to know more about the fourth beast,
	7.20	And I **wanted** to know about the ten horns on its head
	11. 3	He will rule over a huge empire and do whatever he **wants.**
	11.27	will not get what they **want,** because the time for it has
Hos	4. 8	my people, and so you **want** them to sin more and more.
	4.12	A stick tells them what they **want** to know!
	6. 5	What I **want** from you is plain and clear:
	6. 6	I **want** your constant love, not your animal sacrifices.
	7. 1	"Whenever I **want** to heal my people Israel and make them
	7.13	I **wanted** to save them, but their worship of me was false.
Amos	5.23	I do not **want** to listen to your harps.
Obad	5	"When thieves come at night, they take only what they **want.**
Mic	2. 2	When they **want** fields, they seize them;
	2. 2	when they **want** houses, they take them.
	2.11	"These people **want** the kind of prophet who goes about

Mic 4. 2 For he will teach us what he **wants** us to do;
7. 3 man tells them what he **wants,** and so they scheme together.
Nah 3. 7 Who will **want** to comfort her?' "
Zech 8.23 one Jew and say, 'We **want** to share in your destiny, because
Mt 1.19 was right, but he did not **want** to disgrace Mary publicly;
5.28 looks at a woman and **wants** to possess her is guilty of
5.42 when someone **wants** to borrow something, lend it to him.
7.12 "Do for others what you **want** them to do for you:
7.21 those who do what my Father in heaven **wants** them to do.
8. 2 and said, "Sir, if you **want** to, you can make me clean."
8. 3 "I do **want** to," he answered.
8.29 they screamed, "What do you **want** with us, you Son of God?
9.13 'It is kindness that I **want,** not animal sacrifices.'
11.23 Did you **want** to lift yourself up to heaven?
11.26 Yes, Father, this was how you **wanted** it to happen.
12. 7 'It is kindness that I **want,** not animal sacrifices.'
12.10 Some people were there who **wanted** to accuse Jesus of doing wrong,
12.38 "Teacher," they said, "we **want** to see you perform a miracle."
12.47 brothers are standing outside, and they **want** to speak with you."
12.50 what my Father in heaven **wants** him to do is my brother,
13.17 and many of God's people **wanted** very much to see what you
13.28 'Do you **want** us to go and pull up the weeds?'
14. 5 Herod **wanted** to kill him, but he was afraid of the Jewish
15.28 What you **want** will be done for you."
15.32 I don't **want** to send them away without feeding them,
16. 1 Sadducees who came to Jesus **wanted** to trap him, so they
16.24 to his disciples, "If anyone **wants** to come with me, he must
16.25 For whoever **wants** to save his own life will lose it;
17.27 But we don't **want** to offend these people.
18.14 Father in heaven does not **want** any of these little ones to
19.17 Keep the commandments if you **want** to enter life."
19.21 said to him, "If you **want** to be perfect, go and sell
20.14 I **want** to give this man who was hired last as much
20.21 "What do you **want?"**
20.26 If one of you **wants** to be great, he must be
20.27 and if one of you **wants** to be first, he must be
20.32 "What do you **want** me to do for you?"
20.33 "Sir," they answered, "we **want** you to give us our sight!"
21.29 'I don't **want** to,' he answered, but later he changed his
21.31 Which one of the two did what his father **wanted?"**
22. 3 to come to the feast, but they did not **want** to come.
23.37 How many times have I **wanted** to put my arms round all
26.17 asked him, "Where do you **want** us to get the Passover meal
26.39 Yet not what I want, but what you **want."**
26.48 "The man I kiss is the one you **want.**
27.17 "Which one do you **want** me to set free for you?
27.21 of these two do you **want** me to set free for you?"
27.43 Well, then, let us see if God **wants** to save him now!"
Mk 1.24 and screamed, [24] "What do you **want** with us, Jesus of Nazareth?
1.40 "If you **want** to," he said, "you can make me clean."
1.41 "I do **want** to," he answered.
3. 2 Some people were there who **wanted** to accuse Jesus of doing wrong;
3.13 went up a hill and called to himself the men he **wanted.**
3.32 and your brothers and sisters are outside, and they **want** you."
3.35 Whoever does what God **wants** him to do is my brother,
5. 7 What do you **want** with me?
6.19 a grudge against John and **wanted** to kill him, but she could
6.22 I will give you anything you **want."**
6.25 the king and demanded, "I **want** you to give me here and
6.37 They asked, "Do you **want** us to go and spend two hundred
7.24 a house and did not **want** anyone to know he was there,
8.11 They **wanted** to trap him, so they asked him to perform
8.34 "If anyone **wants** to come with me," he told them, "he must
8.35 For whoever **wants** to save his own life will lose it;
9.30 Jesus did not **want** anyone to know where he was,
9.35 and said to them, "Whoever **wants** to be first must place
10.35 they said, "there is something we **want** you to do for us."
10.37 in your glorious Kingdom, we **want** you to let us sit with
10.43 If one of you **wants** to be great, he must be
10.44 and if one of you **wants** to be first, he must be
10.51 "What do you **want** me to do for you?"
10.51 "Teacher," the blind man answered, "I **want** to see again."
14. 7 with you, and any time you **want** to, you can help them.
14.12 asked him, "Where do you **want** us to go and get the
14.36 Yet not what I **want,** but what you want."
14.44 "The man I kiss is the one you **want.**
15. 9 he asked them, "Do you **want** me to set free for you
15.12 "What, then, do you **want** me to do with the one
15.15 Pilate **wanted** to please the crowd, so he set Barabbas free
Lk 4.34 What do you **want** with us, Jesus of Nazareth?
5.12 begged him, "Sir, if you **want** to, you can make me clean!"
5.13 "I do **want** to," he answered.
5.39 And no one **wants** new wine after drinking old wine.
6. 7 the Law and some Pharisees **wanted** a reason to accuse Jesus
6.31 Do for others just what you **want** them to do for you.
8.20 mother and brothers are standing outside and **want** to see you."
8.28 What do you **want** with me?
9.13 Do you **want** us to go and buy food for this whole
9.23 to them all, "If anyone **wants** to come with me, he must
9.24 For whoever **wants** to save his own life will lose it,
9.54 they said, "Lord, do you **want** us to call fire down from
10.15 Did you **want** to lift yourself up to heaven?
10.21 Yes, Father, this was how you **wanted** it to happen.
10.24 that many prophets and kings **wanted** to see what you see,
10.29 the teacher of the Law **wanted** to justify himself, so he
11.16 Others **wanted** to trap Jesus, so they asked him to perform
12.47 who knows what his master **wants** him to do, but does not
12.48 not know what his master **wants,** and yet does something for
13.31 and go somewhere else, because Herod **wants** to kill you."

Lk 13.34 How many times have I **wanted** to put my arms round all
16.26 so that those who **want** to cross over from here to
18.41 Jesus asked him, [41] "What do you **want** me to do for you?"
18.41 "Sir," he answered, "I **want** to see again."
19.14 to say, 'We don't **want** this man to be our king.'
19.27 of mine who did not **want** me to be their king,
19.47 the leaders of the people **wanted** to kill him, [48] but they
19.48 kept listening to him, not **wanting** to miss a single word.
22. 9 "Where do you **want** us to get it ready?"
22.15 said to them, "I have **wanted** so much to eat this Passover
23. 8 about him and had been **wanting** for a long
23.20 Pilate **wanted** to set Jesus free, so he appealed to the
23.25 set free the man they **wanted,** the one who had been put
Jn 3.20 because he does not **want** his evil deeds to be shown
4.23 he really is, offering him the true worship that he **wants.**
4.27 But none of them said to her, "What do you **want?"**
5. 6 so he asked him, "Do you **want** to get well?"
5.21 the same way the Son gives life to those he **wants** to.
5.30 trying to do what I **want,**
5.30 but only what he who sent me **wants.**
6.11 with the fish, and they all had as much as they **wanted.**
6.26 bread and had all you **wanted,** not because you understood
6.28 we do in order to do what God **wants** us to do?"
6.29 Jesus answered, "What God **wants** you to do is to believe
6.40 For what my Father **wants** is that all who see the Son
6.61 he said to them, "Does this make you **want** to give up?
7. 1 did not **want** to travel in Judaea, because the Jewish authorities
7. 1 because the Jewish authorities there were **wanting** to kill him.
7. 4 hides what he is doing if he **wants** to be well known.
7.17 willing to do what God **wants** will know whether what I teach
7.18 But he who **wants** glory for the one who sent him is
7.44 Some **wanted** to seize him, but no one laid a hand on
8.44 father, the Devil, and you **want** to follow your father's desires.
9.27 Why do you **want** to hear it again?
9.31 people who respect him and do what he **wants** them to do.
10.32 for which one of these do you **want** to stone me?"
10.33 They replied, "We do not **want** to stone you because of
10.37 I am not doing the things my Father **wants** me to do.
11. 8 "just a short time ago the people there **wanted** to stone you;
12.21 and said, "Sir, we **want** to see Jesus."
12.26 Whoever **wants** to serve me must follow me, so that my
16.19 Jesus knew that they **wanted** to question him, so he said
17.24 them to me, and I **want** them to be with me where
18.28 for they **wanted** to keep themselves ritually clean,
18.39 Do you **want** me to set free for you the King of
18.40 We **want** Barabbas!"
19.15 Pilate asked them, "Do you **want** me to crucify your king?"
19.31 Friday, and they did not **want** the bodies to stay on the
21.18 young, you used to get ready and go anywhere you **wanted** to;
21.18 will bind you and take you where you don't **want** to go."
21.22 Jesus answered him, "If I **want** him to live until I come,
21.23 he said, "If I **want** him to live until I come,
Acts 5.28 all over Jerusalem, and you **want** to make us responsible for
5.33 were so furious that they **wanted** to have the apostles put to
7.28 'Do you **want** to kill me, just as you killed that
10.10 He became hungry and **wanted** something to eat;
13. 7 Saul before him because he **wanted** to hear the word of God.
13.15 "Brothers, we **want** you to speak to the people if you have
13.22 a man who will do all I **want** him to do.'
13.38 **want** you to know, my fellow-Israelites, that it is through Jesus
14.13 and the crowds **wanted** to offer sacrifice to the apostles.
15.10 then, why do you now **want** to put God to the test
15.37 Barnabas **wanted** to take John Mark with them,
16. 3 Paul **wanted** to take Timothy along with him, so he circumcised
16.37 And now they **want** to send us away secretly.
17.32 but others said, "We **want** to hear you speak about this
19.30 Paul himself **wanted** to go before the crowd, but the believers
19.39 is something more that you **want,** it will have to be settled
20.24 I only **want** to complete my mission and finish the work that
20.33 I have not **wanted** anyone's silver or gold or clothing.
21.23 This is what we **want** you to do.
22.30 The commander **wanted** to find out for certain what the Jews
23.15 pretending that you **want** to get more accurate information about
23.20 pretending that the Council **wants** to get more accurate information
23.28 I **wanted** to know what they were accusing him of,
24. 4 I do not **want** to take up too much of your time,
24.27 Felix **wanted** to gain favour with the Jews so he left Paul
25. 9 But Festus **wanted** to gain favour with the Jews, so he
27.43 But the army officer **wanted** to save Paul, so he stopped
28.18 After questioning me, the Romans **wanted** to release me,
Rom 1.11 For I **want** very much to see you, in order to share
1.13 I **want** to win converts among you also, as I have among
2.18 you know what God **wants** you to do, and you have learnt
7.16 do is what I don't **want** to do, this shows that I
7.19 I don't do the good I **want** to do;
7.19 instead, I do the evil that I do not **want** to do.
7.20 I do what I don't **want** to do, this means that I
7.21 when I **want** to do what is good, what is evil is
8. 5 have their minds controlled by what human nature **wants.**
8. 5 have their minds controlled by what the Spirit **wants.**
8.12 it is not to live as our human nature **wants** us to.
9.16 depends, not on what man **wants** or does, but only on God's
9.22 He **wanted** to show his anger and to make his power known.
9.23 And he also **wanted** to reveal his abundant glory,
11.25 truth, my brothers, which I **want** you to know, for it will
15.23 and since I have been **wanting** for so many years to come
16.19 I **want** you to be wise about what is good, but innocent
1 Cor 1.22 Jews **want** miracles for proof, and Greeks look for wisdom.
1.31 the scripture says, "Whoever **wants** to boast must boast of what
4.14 to you, not because I **want** to make you feel ashamed,

1 Cor 7.33 with worldly matters, because he **wants** to please his wife;
7.34 the Lord's work, because she **wants** to be dedicated both in
7.34 with worldly matters, because she **wants** to please her husband.
7.35 I am saying this because I **want** to help you.
7.35 Instead, I **want** you to do what is right and proper,
7.36 to marry, then they should get married, as he **wants** to.
10. 1 **want** you to remember, my brothers, what happened to our ancestors
10.20 And I do not **want** you to be partners with demons.
10.22 Or do we **want** to make the Lord jealous?
11. 3 But I **want** you to understand that Christ is supreme over
11.16 But if anyone **wants** to argue about it, all I have to
12. 1 I **want** you to know the truth about them, my brothers.
12. 3 I **want** you to know that no one who is led by
12.18 different part in the body just as he **wanted** it to be.
14.33 because God does not **want** us to be in disorder
14.35 If they **want** to find out about something, they should ask
15. 1 And now I **want** to remind you, my brothers, of the Good
16. 7 I **want** to see you more than just briefly in passing;
2 Cor 1. 8 We **want** to remind you, brothers, of the trouble we had in
2. 3 I did not **want** to come to you and be
2. 5 because I do not **want** to be too hard on him.)
2. 9 you that letter because I **wanted** to find out how well you
5. 4 it is not that we **want** to get rid of our earthly
5. 4 earthly body, but that we **want** to have the heavenly one
5. 9 than anything else, however, we **want** to please him, whether in
6. 3 We do not **want** anyone to find fault with our work,
7. 7 told us how much you **want** to see me, how sorry you
8. 1 brothers, we **want** you to know what God's grace has accomplished
8. 7 And so we **want** you to be generous also in this service
8.19 Lord's glory, and in order to show that we **want** to help.
9. 5 that you give because you **want** to, not because you have to.
10. 9 I do not **want** it to appear that I am trying to
10.17 scripture says, "Whoever **wants** to boast must boast about what
12. 6 If I **wanted** to boast, I would not be a fool, because
12. 6 because I do not **want** anyone to have a higher opinion
12.14 It is you I **want**, not your money.
13. 2 I **want** to say to those of you who have sinned in
13. 3 have all the proof you **want** that Christ speaks through me.
Gal 1.10 What I **want** is God's approval!
2. 2 I did not **want** my work in the past or in the
2. 4 was not forced to be circumcised, [4]although some **wanted** it done.
2. 4 They **wanted** to make slaves of us, [5]but in order to keep
3. 3 do you now **want** to finish by your own power?
4. 9 how is it that you **want** to turn back to those weak
4. 9 Why do you **want** to become their slaves all over again?
4.17 All they **want** is to separate you from me, so that you
4.21 ask those of you who **want** to be subject to the Law:
5.17 For what our human nature **wants** is
5.17 opposed to what the Spirit **wants,**
5.17 the Spirit wants is opposed to what our human nature **wants.**
5.17 and this means that you cannot do what you **want** to do.
6.12 circumcised are the ones who **want** to show off and boast
6.13 they **want** you to be circumcised so that they can boast that
Eph 5.17 but try to find out what the Lord **wants** you to do.
6. 6 they are watching you, because you **want** to gain their approval;
6. 6 with all your heart do what God **wants,** as slaves of Christ.
Phil 1.12 I **want** you to know, my brothers, that the things that
1.23 I **want** very much to leave this life and be with Christ,
3.10 All I **want** is to know Christ and to experience the power
4. 3 too, my faithful partner, I **want** you to help these women;
4.17 It is not that I just **want** to receive gifts;
4.17 rather, I **want** to see profit added to your account.
Col 1.10 to live as the Lord **wants** and will always do what pleases
2.19 joints and ligaments, and it grows as God **wants** it to grow.
3.22 they are watching you because you **want** to gain their approval;
1 Thes 2. 4 we always speak as God **wants** us to, because he has judged
2.18 We **wanted** to return to you.
3. 6 and that you **want** to see us
3. 6 just as much as we **want** to see you.
4. 3 God **wants** you to be holy and completely free from sexual immorality.
4.13 Our brothers, we **want** you to know the truth about those
5.18 This is what God **wants** from you in your life in union
1 Tim 1. 3 I **want** you to stay in Ephesus, just as I urged you
1. 7 They **want** to be teachers of God's law, but they do not
2. 4 pleases God our Saviour, [4]who **wants** everyone to be saved
2. 6 the right time that God **wants** everyone to be saved,
2. 8 In every church service I **want** the men to pray, men who
2. 9 I also **want** the women to be modest and sensible about
5.11 when their desires make them **want** to marry, they turn away
6. 9 But those who **want** to get rich fall into temptation
2 Tim 1. 4 remember your tears, and I **want** to see you very much,
2. 4 soldier on active service **wants** to please his commanding officer
3.12 Everyone who **wants** to live a godly life in union with
Tit 3. 8 I **want** you to give special emphasis to these matters,
Phlm 14 However, I do not **want** to force you to help me;
Heb 6.12 We do not **want** you to become lazy, but to be like
6.17 receive what he promised, God **wanted** to make it very clear
10. 5 "You do not **want** sacrifices and offerings, but you have prepared
10. 8 he said, "You neither **want** nor are you pleased with sacrifices
10.10 Jesus Christ did what God **wanted** him to do,
12.17 you know, he **wanted** to receive his father's blessing;
13.18 a clear conscience, because we **want** to do the right thing
13.23 I **want** you to know that our brother Timothy has been let
Jas 2.20 Do you **want** to be shown that faith without actions is useless?
3. 3 and we are able to make it go where we **want.**
3. 4 small rudder, and it goes wherever the pilot **wants** it to go.
4. 2 You **want** things, but you cannot have them, so you are
4. 2 do not have what you **want** because you do not ask God
Jas 4. 4 Whoever **wants** to be the world's friend makes himself God's enemy.
1 Pet 2.15 God **wants** you to silence the ignorant talk of foolish people
3.10 the scripture says, "Whoever **wants** to enjoy life and wishes to
5. 2 of it willingly, as God **wants** you to, and not unwillingly.
5.12 I **want** to encourage you and give my testimony that this is
2 Pet 2.14 They **want** to look at nothing but immoral women;
3. 2 I **want** you to remember the words that were spoken long ago
3. 9 because he does not **want** anyone to be destroyed,
3. 9 but **wants** all to turn away from their
1 Jn 2.16 what people see and **want,** and everything in this world that
3 Jn 10 and even stops those who **want** to receive them and tries to
13 but I do not **want** to do it with pen and
Jude 5 you know all this, I **want** to remind you of how the
Rev 2.21 but she does not **want** to turn from her immorality.
2.26 end to do what I **want,** I will give the same authority
9. 6 they will **want** to die, but death will flee from them.
22.17 accept the water of life as a gift, whoever **wants** it.

WAR

Gen 14. 2 and Tidal of Goiim, [2]went to **war** against five other kings:
31.26 me and carry off my daughters like women captured in **war?**
Ex 1.10 In case of **war** they might join our enemies in order to
5. 3 don't do so, he will kill us with disease or by **war."**
14. 6 The king got his **war chariot** and his army ready.
22.24 for help, [24]and I will be angry and kill you in **war.**
Lev 26. 6 animals in the land, and there will be no more **war** there.
26.25 I will bring **war** on you to punish you for breaking our
26.33 I will bring **war** on you and scatter you in foreign lands.
Num 10. 9 When you are at **war** in your land, defending yourselves
31. 3 the people, "Get ready for **war,** so that you can attack
31. 4 From each tribe of Israel send a thousand men to **war."**
31. 6 Moses sent them to **war** under the command of Phinehas son
31.14 of battalions and companies, who had returned from the **war.**
32. 6 "Do you want to stay here while your fellow-Israelites go to **war?**
Deut 2. 5 you must not start a **war** with them, because I am not
2. 9 Moab, the descendants of Lot, or start a **war** against them.
2.19 trouble them or start a **war** against them, because I am not
4.34 he brought plagues and **war,** worked miracles and wonders, and
23. 9 in camp in time of **war,** you are to avoid anything that
28.41 them, because they will be taken away as prisoners of **war.**
32.25 **War** will bring death in the streets;
Josh 4.13 forty thousand men ready for **war** crossed over to the plain
11.17 Joshua was at **war** with the kings of this territory for a
11.23 So the people rested from **war.**
14.11 I am still strong enough for **war** or for anything else.
22.12 together at Shiloh to go to **war** against the eastern tribes.
22.33 longer talked about going to **war** to devastate the land where
Judg 3. 1 the Israelites who had not been through the **wars** in Canaan.
3. 2 each generation of Israelites about **war,** especially those
3.10 Othniel went to **war,** and the Lord gave him victory over the
5. 8 Then there was **war** in the land when the Israelites chose
11. 4 time later that the Ammonites went to **war** against Israel.
11.25 Did he ever go to **war** against us?
11.27 You are doing wrong by making **war** on me.
21.13 were at the Rock of Rimmon and offered to end the **war.**
1 Sam 4. 1 Philistines gathered to go to **war** against Israel, so the
8.11 them will serve in his **war chariots,** others in his cavalry,
8.20 and to lead us out to **war** and to fight our battles."
13. 3 to call the Hebrews to **war** by blowing a trumpet throughout
13. 5 had thirty thousand **war chariots,** six thousand horsemen,
17.13 His three eldest sons had gone with Saul to **war.**
17.20 Israelites were going out to their battle line, shouting the **war-cry.**
19. 8 **War** with the Philistines broke out again.
23. 8 Saul called his troops to **war,** to march against Keilah and
28.15 The Philistines are at **war** with me, and God has abandoned me.
2 Sam 11. 1 when kings usually go to **war,** David sent out Joab with his
11.11 Judah are away at the **war,** and the Covenant Box is with
21.15 There was another **war** between the Philistines and Israel,
1 Kgs 2. 5 peace in revenge for deaths they had caused in time of **war.**
5. 3 that because of the constant **wars** my father David had to
12.21 He intended to go to **war** and restore his control over the
14.19 that King Jeroboam did, the **wars** he fought and how he ruled,
14.30 Rehoboam and Jeroboam were constantly at **war** with each other.
15. 6 The **war** which had begun between Rehoboam and Jeroboam
15.16 of Israel were constantly at **war** with each other as long as
15.32 of Israel were constantly at **war** with each other as long as
2 Kgs 3. 7 will you join me in **war** against him?"
6. 8 The king of Syria was at **war** with Israel.
8.28 King Joram of Israel in a **war** against King Hazael of Syria.
13.12 his bravery in the **war** against King Amaziah of Judah,
14.15 his bravery in the **war** against King Amaziah of Judah,
17. 3 Emperor Shalmaneser of Assyria made **war** against him;
1 Chr 5.19 They went to **war** against the Hagrite tribes of Jetur,
5.21 and took 100,000 prisoners of **war.**
5.22 They killed many of the enemy, because the **war** was God's will.
20. 1 when kings usually go to **war,** Joab led out the army and
20. 4 Later on, **war** broke out again with the Philistines at Gezer.
22. 8 that I had killed too many people and fought too many **wars.**
2 Chr 11. 1 He intended to go to **war** and restore his control over the
12.15 Rehoboam and Jeroboam were constantly at **war** with each other.
13. 2 **War** broke out between Abijah and Jeroboam.
14. 6 years there was no **war,** because the Lord gave him peace.
15.19 There was no more **war** until the thirty-fifth year of his reign.
16. 9 foolishly, and so from now on you will always be at **war."**
17.10 kingdoms afraid to go to **war** against King Jehoshaphat.
20. 9 them to punish them—a **war,** an epidemic, or a famine—then
21.16 The Lord incited them to go to **war** against Jehoram.
22. 5 King Joram of Israel in a **war** against King Hazael of Syria.
26. 6 Uzziah went to **war** against the Philistines.

2 Chr 27. 7 events of Jotham's reign, his **wars,** and his policies, are
35.21 "This **war** I am fighting does not concern you, King of
Job 5.20 he will keep you alive, and in **war** protect you from death.
15.28 had fled, but **war** will destroy those cities and houses.
27.14 They may have many sons, but all will be killed in **war;**
38.23 ready for times of trouble, for days of battle and **war.**
Ps 20. 7 Some trust in their **war-chariots** and others in their horses,
33.17 **War-horses** are useless for victory;
46. 9 He stops **wars** all over the world;
68.30 Scatter those people who love to make **war!**
76.10 those who survive the **wars** will keep your festivals.
78.63 Young men were killed in **war,** and young women had no one
120. 7 When I speak of peace, they are for **war.**
144. 1 He trains me for battle and prepares me for **war.**
Ecc 3. 8 time for hate, the time for **war** and the time for peace.
Is 2. 4 Nations will never again go to **war,** never prepare for battle
3.25 city, yes, even the strongest men, will be killed in **war.**
7. 1 son of Jotham and grandson of Uzziah, ruled Judah, **war** broke
13. 3 soldiers to fight a holy **war** and punish those he is angry
19. 2 "I will stir up civil **war** in Egypt and turn brother against
21.15 bows that are ready to shoot, from all the dangers of **war.**
22. 2 Your men who died in this **war** did not die fighting.
31. 8 Assyria will be destroyed in **war,** but not by human power.
42.13 He gives a **war-cry,** a battle-shout;
42.25 feel the force of his anger and suffer the violence of **war.**
51.19 your land has been devastated by **war,**
Jer 4.13 His **war-chariots** are like a whirlwind, and his horses are
5.12 we won't have **war** or famine."
6.22 a mighty nation far away is preparing for **war.**
11.22 Their young men will be killed in **war;**
12.12 I have sent **war** to destroy the entire land;
14.12 I will kill them in **war** and by starvation and disease."
14.13 will be no **war** or starvation, because you have promised,
14.15 in my name and say **war** and starvation will not strike
14.15 this land—I will kill them in **war** and by starvation.
14.18 into the fields, I see the bodies of men killed in **war;**
15. 2 are doomed to die in **war**— that's where they will go!
15. 3 they will be killed in **war,**
16. 4 They will be killed in **war** or die of starvation, and their
18.21 let them be killed in **war.**
21. 7 the people who survive the **war,** the famine, and the
21. 9 the city will be killed in **war** or by starvation or disease.
22.22 allies taken as prisoners of **war,** your city disgraced and
24.10 I will bring **war,** starvation, and disease on them until
25.16 their minds because of the **war** I am sending against them."
25.27 get up, because of the **war** that I am sending against them.
25.29 I am going to send **war** on all the people on earth.
25.38 The horrors of **war** and the Lord's fierce anger have turned
27. 8 will punish that nation by **war,** starvation, and disease
27.13 you and your people die in **war** or of starvation or disease?
28. 8 time and yours, predicted that **war,** starvation, and disease
29.17 'I am bringing **war,** starvation, and disease on them,
29.18 I will pursue them with **war,** starvation, and disease,
32.24 **War,** starvation, and disease will make the city fall into their hands.
32.36 the people are saying that **war,** starvation, and disease will
34.17 the freedom to die by **war,** disease, and starvation.
38. 2 in the city will die in **war** or of starvation or disease.
42.13 Egypt, where we won't face **war** any more or hear the call
42.16 in Egypt, [16]then the **war** that you fear will overtake you,
42.17 in Egypt will die either in **war** or of starvation or disease.
42.22 you will die in **war** or of starvation or disease in the
43.11 those doomed to be killed in **war** will be killed in war.
44.12 small, will die in Egypt, either in **war** or of starvation.
44.13 in Egypt, just as I punished Jerusalem—with **war,** starvation,
44.18 and our people have died in **war** and of starvation."
44.27 you will die, either in **war** or of disease, until not one
46.14 all you have will be destroyed in **war!**
48.14 do you claim to be heroes, brave soldiers tested in **war?**
48.45 and the mountain heights of the **war-loving** people of Moab.
50.15 Raise the **war cry** all round the city!
50.41 many kings are preparing for **war.**
51.20 "Babylonia, you are my hammer, my weapon of **war.**
51.27 Prepare the nations for **war** against Babylonia!
51.28 Prepare the nations for **war** against Babylonia.
Lam 4. 9 Those who died in the **war** were better off than those who
Ezek 5.17 and will send sickness, violence, and **war** to kill you.
6.11 They are going to die in **war,** by famine, and by disease.
6.12 those near by will be killed in **war;**
7.14 no one goes off to **war,** for God's anger will fall on
12.16 few of them survive the **war,** the famine, and the diseases,
13. 5 Israel cannot be defended when **war** comes on the day of the
14.17 "Or I might bring **war** on that country and send
14.21 four worst punishments on Jerusalem—**war,** famine, wild
24.21 families who are left in Jerusalem will be killed in **war.**
27.14 You sold your goods for draught-horses, **war-horses,** and mules
30. 4 There will be **war** in Egypt And great distress in Sudan.
30. 5 "That **war** will also kill the soldiers hired from Sudan,
30.17 Bubastis will die in the **war,** and the other people will be
33. 2 "tell your people what happens when I bring **war** to a land.
38. 8 from many nations and have lived without fear of **war.**
Dan 7.21 that horn made **war** on God's people and conquered them.
9.26 bringing the **war** and destruction which God has prepared.
11.10 king of Syria will prepare for **war** and gather a large army.
11.11 of Egypt will go to **war** against the king of Syria and
11.24 his followers the goods and property he has captured in **war.**
Hos 1. 7 will not do it by **war**—with swords or bows and arrows
2.18 also remove all weapons of **war** from the land, all swords and
5. 8 Blow the **war trumpets** in Gibeah!
5. 8 Raise the **war-cry** at Bethaven!
10. 9 So at Gibeah **war** will catch up with them.
Hos 10.14 number of your soldiers, [14]**war** will come to your people,
11. 6 **War** will sweep through their cities and break down the city gates.
13.16 Her people will die in **war;**
14. 3 Assyria can never save us, and **war-horses** cannot protect us.
Joel 2. 4 they run like **war-horses.**
3. 9 'Prepare for **war;**
Amos 1.13 In their **wars** for more territory they even ripped open
3. 6 Does the **war trumpet** sound in a city without making the
7.17 on the streets, and your children will be killed in **war.**
9. 1 I will kill the rest of the people in **war.**
9.10 people will be killed in **war**—all those who say, 'God will
Obad 15 Let us go to **war** against Edom!"
Mic 3. 5 to those who pay them, but threaten **war** for those who don't.
4. 3 Nations will never again go to **war,** never prepare for battle again.
6.14 anything you do save I will destroy in **war.**
Nah 2.13 soldiers will be killed in **war,** and I will take away
Zeph 1.16 filled with the sound of **war-trumpets** and the battle-cry of
Zech 9.10 "I will remove the **war-chariots** from Israel and take the horses
10. 3 They will be my powerful **war-horses.**
11.17 **War** will totally destroy his power.
14. 2 Lord will bring all the nations together to make **war** on Jerusalem.
14.12 disease on all the nations that make **war** on Jerusalem.
Lk 21. 9 Don't be afraid when you hear of **wars** and revolutions;
1 Pet 2.11 bodily passions, which are always at **war** against the soul.
Rev 6. 4 given the power to bring **war** on the earth, so that men
6. 8 to kill by means of **war,** famine, disease, and wild animals.
12. 7 Then **war** broke out in heaven.

WARES

Ezek 27.16 fine linen, coral, and rubies in payment for your **wares.**

WARM

Ex 22.27 because it is the only covering he has to keep him **warm.**
Josh 9.12 with it and started out to meet you, it was still **warm.**
Judg 19. 3 and when her father saw him, he gave him a **warm** welcome.
1 Sam 30.21 his men, and David went up to them and greeted them **warmly.**
1 Kgs 1. 1 servants covered him with blankets, he could not keep **warm.**
1. 2 She will lie close to you and keep you **warm."**
2 Kgs 4.34 out over the boy, the boy's body started to get **warm.**
Job 39.14 on the ground for the heat in the soil to **warm** them.
Prov 31.21 because her family has **warm** clothing.
Ecc 4.11 and stay warm, but how can you keep **warm** by yourself?
Is 18. 4 the dew forms in the **warm** nights of harvest time, as
44.15 one part he builds a fire to **warm** himself and bake bread;
44.16 He warms himself and says, "How nice and **warm!**
47.14 too hot for them, not a cosy fire to **warm** themselves by.
Hag 1. 6 You have clothing, but not enough to keep you **warm.**
Mk 14.54 sat down with the guards, keeping himself **warm** by the fire.
14.67 When she saw Peter **warming** himself, she looked straight at him
Jn 18.18 a charcoal fire and were standing round it, **warming** themselves.
18.18 So Peter went over and stood with them, **warming** himself.
18.25 Peter was still standing there keeping himself **warm.**
Acts 21.17 When we arrived in Jerusalem, the believers welcomed us **warmly.**
Rom 12.10 Love one another **warmly** as Christian brothers, and be eager
1 Cor 16.19 church that meets in their house send **warm** Christian greetings.
Jas 2.16 Keep **warm** and eat well!"

WARN

Gen 4.15 a mark on Cain to **warn** anyone who met him not to
20. 7 not give her back, I **warn** you that you are going to
26.11 Abimelech **warned** all the people:
31.29 the God of your father **warned** me not to threaten you in
43. 3 to him, "The man sternly **warned** us that we would not be
Ex 8.21 I **warn** you that if you refuse, I will punish you by
9.21 no attention to the Lord's **warning** and left their slaves and
19.21 to him, "Go down and **warn** the people not to cross the
21.29 and its owner had been **warned,** but did not keep it penned
Lev 15.31 The Lord told Moses to **warn** the people of Israel about
Num 16.38 It will be a **warning** to the people of Israel."
16.40 This was a **warning** to the Israelites that no one who was
17.10 to be kept as a **warning** to the rebel Israelites that they
24.14 before I go, I am **warning** you what the people of Israel
26.10 they became a **warning** to the people.
32.23 not keep your promise, I **warn** you that you will be sinning
Deut 1.42 the Lord said to me, **'Warn** them not to attack, for I
8.19 If you do, then I **warn** you today that you will certainly
30.18 gods, [18]you will be destroyed—I **warn** you here and now.
Josh 6.26 At that time Joshua issued a solemn **warning:**
1 Sam 8. 9 them, but give them strict **warnings** and explain how their
11. 7 the pieces throughout the land of Israel with this **warning:**
15. 6 He sent a **warning** to the Kenites, a people whose ancestors
19.11 David's wife, **warned** him, "If you don't get away tonight,
1 Kgs 2.42 And I **warned** you that if you ever did, you would certainly
2 Kgs 6. 9 to the king of Israel, **warning** him not to go near that
6.10 So the king of Israel **warned** the men who lived in that
9.14 slips out of Ramoth to go and **warn** the people in Jezreel."
17.13 sent his messengers and prophets to **warn** Israel and Judah:
17.15 with their ancestors, and they disregarded his **warnings.**
17.23 his sight, as he had **warned** through his servants the
18.29 He **warns** you not to let Hezekiah deceive you.
1 Chr 16.21 to protect them, he **warned** the kings:
2 Chr 20.37 from the town of Mareshah, **warned** Jehoshaphat, "Because you
24.19 The Lord sent prophets to **warn** them to return to him,
33.10 the Lord **warned** Manasseh and his people, they refused to listen.
36.15 continued to send prophets to **warn** his people, because he
Neh 4.12 among our enemies came to **warn** us of the plans our enemies
6.12 Tobiah and Sanballat had bribed him to give me this **warning.**

Neh 9.26 They killed the prophets who **warned** them, who told them to
9.29 You **warned** them to obey your teachings, but in pride
9.30 Year after year you patiently **warned** them.
9.34 They did not listen to your commands and **warnings.**
13.15 I **warned** them not to sell anything on the Sabbath.
13.21 I **warned** them, "It's no use waiting out there for
Esth 4.13 Mordecai received Esther's message, [13] he sent her this **warning:**
Job 9. 5 Without **warning** he moves mountains and in anger he destroys them.
33.16 to what he says, and they are frightened at his **warnings.**
36.10 He makes them listen to his **warning** to turn away from evil.
Ps 2. 5 Then he **warns** them in anger and terrifies them with his fury.
2.10 Now listen to this **warning,** you kings;
16. 7 he guides me, and in the night my conscience **warns** me.
40. 3 who see this will take **warning** and will put their trust in
60. 4 You have **warned** those who show you reverence, so that they
81. 8 Listen, my people, to my **warning;**
105.14 to protect them, he **warned** the kings:
106.26 he gave them a solemn **warning** that he would make them die
Prov 3.11 you, my son, pay close attention and take it as a **warning.**
6.15 them without **warning,** and they will be fatally wounded.
25.12 A **warning** given by an experienced person to someone
Is 8.11 his great power the Lord **warned** me not to follow the path
28.22 Don't laugh at the **warning** I am giving you!
36.14 He **warns** you not to let Hezekiah deceive you.
56.10 "All the leaders, who are supposed to **warn** my people, are
Jer 4.16 They have come to **warn** the nations and to tell Jerusalem
6. 8 let these troubles be a **warning** to you, or else I will
6.10 would listen to me if I spoke to them and **warned** them?
6.17 the Lord appointed watchmen to listen for the trumpet's **warning.**
11. 7 out of Egypt, I solemnly **warned** them to obey me, and I
11. 7 me, and I have kept on **warning** the people until this day.
11.11 So now, I, the Lord, **warn** them that I am going to
18.22 Send a mob to plunder their homes without **warning;**
26.15 it is the Lord who sent me to give you this **warning."**
29. 8 Lord, the God of Israel, **warn** you not to let yourselves be
35.15 They **warned** you not to worship and serve other gods, so that
36.31 paid any attention to my **warnings,** and so I will bring on
37. 9 I, the Lord, **warn** you not to deceive yourselves into
42.19 And so I **warn** you now [20] that you are making a fatal
49.30 of Hazor, I, the Lord, **warn** you to run far away and
Lam 2.17 He has destroyed us without mercy, as he **warned** us long ago.
Ezek 3.17 You will pass on to them the **warnings** I give you.
3.18 die but you do not **warn** him to change his ways so
3.19 If you do **warn** an evil man and he doesn't stop sinning,
3.20 a dangerous situation, he will die if you do not **warn** him.
3.21 If you do **warn** a good man not to sin and he
3.26 so that you won't be able to **warn** these rebellious people.
6.10 I am the Lord and that my **warnings** were not empty threats."
12. 6 What you do will be a **warning** to the Israelites."
12.25 rebels, I will do what I have **warned** you I would do.
20.18 Instead, I **warned** the young people among them:
20.33 am the living God, I **warn** you that in my anger I
20.39 But I **warn** you that after this you will have to obey
21. 2 **Warn** the land of Israel [3] that I, the Lord, am saying:
21.10 my people have disregarded every **warning** and punishment.
21.23 of their sins and to **warn** them that they will be captured.
23.48 stop to immorality, as a **warning** to every woman not to
28.17 to the ground and left you as a **warning** to other kings.
32. 2 he said, "give a solemn **warning** to the king of Egypt.
32.16 This solemn **warning** will become a funeral song.
33. 3 the enemy approaching, he sounds the alarm to **warn** everyone.
33. 5 his own fault, because he paid no attention to the **warning.**
33. 7 You must pass on to them the **warnings** I give you.
33. 8 die but you do not **warn** him to change his ways so
33. 9 If you do **warn** an evil man and he doesn't stop sinning,
33.14 I may **warn** an evil man that he is going to die,
33.27 that I, the Sovereign Lord, **warn** them that as surely as I
Dan 8.25 He will be proud of himself and destroy many people without **warning.**
11.24 invade a wealthy province without **warning** and will do things
Hos 9. 8 God has sent me as a prophet to **warn** his people Israel.
12.10 visions, and through the prophets I gave my people **warnings.**
Joel 2.30 "I will give **warnings** of that day in the sky and on
Amos 3.13 Listen now, and **warn** the descendants of Jacob," says
6. 8 The Sovereign Lord Almighty has given this solemn **warning:**
Mic 7. 4 punish the people, as he **warned** them through their watchmen,
Zech 1. 6 gave your ancestors commands and **warnings,** but they disregarded
Mt 2.12 another road, since God had **warned** them in a dream not to
16.12 understood that he was not **warning** them to guard themselves from
Mk 6.11 That will be a **warning** to them!"
8.15 "Take care," Jesus **warned** them, "and be on your guard
Lk 9. 5 and shake the dust off your feet as a **warning** to them."
16.28 Let him go and **warn** them so that they, at least, will
16.29 said, 'Your brothers have Moses and the prophets to **warn** them;
Acts 4.17 among the people, let us **warn** these men never again to speak
4.21 the Council **warned** them even more strongly and then set them
20.21 Gentiles alike I gave solemn **warning** that they should turn from
20.23 the Holy Spirit has **warned** me that prison and troubles wait
1 Cor 10. 6 an example for us, to **warn** us not to desire evil things,
10.11 for others, and they were written down as a **warning** for us.
Gal 5. 3 Once more I **warn** any man who allows himself to be
5.21 I **warn** you now as I have before:
Eph 4.17 In the Lord's name, then, I **warn** you:
Col 1.28 With all possible wisdom we **warn** and teach them in order to
1 Thes 4. 6 and we strongly **warned** you that the Lord will punish
5.14 urge you, our brothers, to **warn** the idle, encourage the timid,
2 Thes 3.12 we command these people and **warn** them to lead orderly lives
3.15 instead, **warn** him as a brother.
2 Tim 2.14 and give them a solemn **warning** in God's presence not to
Tit 3.10 Give at least two **warnings** to the person who causes divisions,
Heb 11. 7 that made Noah hear God's **warnings** about things in the future
Jude 7 the punishment of eternal fire as a plain **warning** to all.
Rev 22.18 I, John, solemnly **warn** everyone who hears the prophetic words

WARRIOR

Ex 15. 3 The Lord is a **warrior;**
2 Sam 23.20 brave deeds, including killing two great Moabite **warriors.**
1 Chr 11.22 brave deeds, including killing two great Moabite **warriors.**
Is 42.13 The Lord goes out to fight like a **warrior;**
Joel 2. 7 They attack like **warriors;**
3. 9 call your **warriors;**

WASH

Gen 18. 4 Let me bring some water for you to **wash** your feet;
19. 2 You can **wash** your feet and stay the night.
24.32 water for Abraham's servant and his men to **wash** their feet.
43.24 water so that they could **wash** their feet, and he fed their
43.31 After he had **washed** his face, he came out,
49.11 He **washes** his clothes in blood-red wine.
Ex 19.10 They must **wash** their clothes [11] and be ready
19.14 So they **washed** their clothes, [15] and Moses said to them,
29.17 **wash** its internal organs and its hind legs, and put them on
30.19 to use the water to **wash** their hands and feet [20] before
30.21 They must **wash** their hands and feet, so that they will
30.28 with all its equipment, and the **wash-basin** with its base.
31. 9 and all its equipment, the **wash-basin** and its base, [10] the
35.16 the **wash-basin** and its base;
39.39 the **wash-basin** and its base;
40. 7 Put the **wash-basin** between the Tent and the altar and fill
40.11 Also dedicate the **wash-basin** and its base in the same way.
40.30 He put the **wash-basin** between the Tent and the altar and
40.31 Moses, Aaron, and his sons **washed** their hands and their
Lev 1. 9 The man must **wash** the internal organs and the hind legs,
1.13 The man must **wash** the internal organs and the hind legs,
6.27 with the animal's blood, it must be **washed** in a holy place.
8.20 cut the ram in pieces, **washed** the internal organs and the
9.14 Then he **washed** the internal organs and the hind legs and
11.24 carries their dead bodies must **wash** his clothes, but he will
11.40 of the animal, he must **wash** his clothes, but he will still
11.40 carries the dead body must **wash** his clothes, but he will
13. 6 The person shall **wash** his clothes and be ritually clean.
13.34 The person shall **wash** his clothes, and he will be clean.
13.54 shall order it to be **washed** and put away for another seven
13.58 If he **washes** the object and the spot disappears,
13.58 he shall **wash** it again,
14. 8 The person shall **wash** his clothes, shave off all his hair,
14. 9 he shall **wash** his clothes and have a bath, and then he
14.47 who lies down or eats in the house must **wash** his clothes.
15. 6 man has sat on must **wash** his clothes and have a bath,
15. 7 with the discharge must **wash** his clothes and have a bath,
15. 8 clean, that person must **wash** his clothes and have a bath,
15.10 which the man sat must **wash** his clothes and have a bath,
15.11 touches someone without first having **washed** his hands,
15.11 that person must **wash** his clothes and have a bath,
15.12 broken, and any wooden bowl that he touches must be **washed.**
15.13 wait seven days and then **wash** his clothes and bathe in fresh
15.17 falls must be **washed,** and it remains unclean until evening.
15.21 which she has sat must **wash** his clothes and have a bath,
15.27 them is unclean and must **wash** his clothes and have a bath;
16.26 the desert to Azazel must **wash** his clothes and have a bath
16.28 one who burns them must **wash** his clothes and have a bath
17.15 killed by wild animals must **wash** his clothes, have a bath,
Num 5.23 write this curse down and **wash** the writing off into the bowl
8. 7 them to shave their whole bodies and to **wash** their clothes.
8.21 The Levites purified themselves and **washed** their clothes,
19. 7 After that, he is to **wash** his clothes and pour water over
19. 8 burnt the cow must also **wash** his clothes and pour water over
19.10 who collected the ashes must **wash** his clothes, but he
19.19 purify the man, who, after **washing** his clothes and pouring
19.21 the water for purification must also **wash** his clothes;
31.24 On the seventh day you must **wash** your clothes;
Deut 21. 6 man was found are to **wash** their hands over the cow
23.11 Towards evening he is to **wash** himself, and at sunset he
Judg 19.21 His guests **washed** their feet and had a meal.
Ruth 3. 3 So **wash** yourself, put on some perfume, and get dressed in
1 Sam 25.41 "I am his servant, ready to **wash** the feet of his servants."
2 Sam 19.24 He had not **washed** his feet, trimmed his beard, or washed his
1 Kgs 22.38 up his blood and prostitutes **washed** themselves, as the Lord
2 Kgs 5.10 tell him to go and **wash** himself seven times in the River
5.12 I could have **washed** in them and been cured!"
5.13 Now why can't you just **wash** yourself, as he said, and be
2 Chr 4. 6 in the large tank was for the priests to use for **washing.**
Job 9.30 No soap can **wash** away my sins.
14.19 wear down rocks, and heavy rain will **wash** away the soil;
22.16 their time had come, they were **washed** away by a flood.
Ps 26. 6 Lord, I **wash** my hands to show that I am innocent and
51. 2 **Wash** away all my evil and make me clean from my sin!
51. 7 **wash** me, and I will be whiter than snow.
60. 8 will use Moab as my **wash-basin** and I will throw my sandals
108. 9 will use Moab as my **wash-basin** and I will throw my sandals
Song 4. 2 are as white as sheep that have just been shorn and **washed.**
5. 3 I have **washed** my feet;
5.12 doves **washed** in milk
6. 6 as white as a flock of sheep that have just been **washed.**
Is 1.16 **Wash** yourselves clean.
1.18 red with sin, but I will **wash** you as clean as snow.
4. 4 and purify the nation and **wash** away the guilt of Jerusalem

Jer 2.22 Even if you **washed** with the strongest soap,
4.14 Jerusalem, **wash** the evil from your heart,
Ezek 16. 4 cut your umbilical cord or **washed** you or rubbed you with
16. 9 "Then I took water and **washed** the blood off you.
40.38 the courtyard, and there they **washed** the carcasses
Mt 6.17 When you go without food, **wash** your face and comb your hair,
15. 2 They don't **wash** their hands in the proper way before they eat!"
15.20 But to eat without **washing** your hands as they say you should
27.24 he took some water, **washed** his hands
Mk 7. 2 that is, they had not **washed** them in the way the Pharisees
7. 3 do not eat unless they **wash** their hands in the proper way;
7. 4 that comes from the market unless they **wash** it first.
7. 4 as the proper way to **wash** cups, pots, copper bowls,
9. 3 shining white—whiter than anyone in the world could **wash** them.
Lk 5. 2 the fishermen had left them and were **washing** the nets.
7.44 but she has **washed** my feet with her tears
11.38 surprised when he noticed that Jesus had not **washed** before eating.
Jn 2. 6 Jews have rules about ritual **washing,** and for this purpose
3.25 began arguing with a Jew about the matter of ritual **washing.**
9. 7 and said, "Go and **wash** your face in the Pool
9. 7 So the man went, **washed** his face, and came back seeing.
9.11 and told me to go to Siloam and **wash** my face.
9.11 So I went, and as soon as I **washed,** I could see."
9.15 I **washed** my face, and now I can see."
13. 5 a basin and began to **wash** the disciples' feet and dry them
13. 6 who said to him, "Are you going to **wash** my feet, Lord?"
13. 8 Peter declared, "Never at any time will you **wash** my feet!"
13. 8 "If I do not **wash** your feet," Jesus answered, "you will
13. 9 Simon Peter answered, "Lord, do not **wash** only my feet,
13. 9 **Wash** my hands and head, too!"
13.10 and does not have to **wash** himself, except for his feet.
13.12 After Jesus had **washed** their feet, he put his outer garment
13.14 I, your Lord and Teacher, have just **washed** your feet.
13.14 You, then, should **wash** one another's feet.
Acts 9.37 Her body was **washed** and laid in a room upstairs.
16.33 of the night the jailer took them and **washed** their wounds;
22.16 baptized and have your sins **washed** away by praying to him.'
Eph 5.26 after making it clean by **washing** it in water,
Tit 3. 5 Spirit, who gives us new birth and new life by **washing** us.
Heb 10.22 from a guilty conscience and with bodies **washed** with clean water.
Jas 4. 8 **Wash** your hands, you sinners!
1 Pet 3.21 It is not the **washing** away of bodily dirt, but the promise
2 Pet 2.22 "A pig that has been **washed** goes back to roll in the
Rev 7.14 They have **washed** their robes and made them white
22.14 Happy are those who **wash** their robes clean

Am **WASHBOWL** see **WASH-BASIN**

WASTE

Lev 26.16 that will make you blind and cause your life to **waste** away.
26.39 land of your enemies will **waste** away because of your own sin
Deut 21.20 he **wastes** money and is a drunkard.'
29.23 The fields will be a barren **waste,** covered with sulphur and salt;
2 Sam 18.14 "I'm not going to **waste** any more time with you," Joab
Job 33.21 His body **wastes** away to nothing;
39.16 not hers, and is unconcerned that her efforts were **wasted.**
Ps 31.10 even my bones are **wasting** away.
Prov 12.11 to eat, but it is stupid to **waste** time on useless projects.
16.22 but trying to educate stupid people is a **waste** of time.
23. 8 what you have eaten, and all your flattery will be **wasted.**
28.19 People who **waste** time will always be poor.
29. 3 It is a foolish **waste** to spend money on prostitutes.
Is 6.11 are uninhabited—until the land itself is a desolate **waste.**
24.16 I am **wasting** away!
32.15 The **waste** land will become fertile,
34.10 The land will lie **waste** age after age, and no one will
34.11 will make it a barren **waste** again, as it was before the
45.18 not make it a desolate **waste,** but a place for people to
45.19 the people of Israel to look for me in a desolate **waste.**
49. 8 you settle once again in your land that is now laid **waste.**
Jer 4.23 I looked at the earth—it was a barren **waste;**
6.29 furnace burns fiercely, but the **waste** metals do not melt and
Ezek 4.17 despair, and they will **waste** away because of their sins."
6.14 I will make it a **waste** from the southern desert to the
22.18 They are like the **waste** metal—copper, tin, iron, and
24.23 You will **waste** away because of your sins, and you will groan
25.13 I will make it a **waste,** from the city of Teman to
29. 9 Egypt will become an empty **waste.**
29.10 all of Egypt an empty **waste,** from the city of Migdol in
32.15 I make Egypt a desolate **waste** and destroy all who live there,
33.10 We are **wasting** away.
33.28 make the country a desolate **waste,** and the power they were
33.29 and make the country a **waste,** then they will know that I
35. 3 I will make you a desolate **waste.**
35. 7 the hill-country of Edom a **waste** and kill everyone who
36.36 I, the Lord, rebuild ruined cities and replant **waste** fields.
Dan 12. 4 Meanwhile, many people will **waste** their efforts trying to
Joel 3.19 desert, and Edom a ruined **waste,** because they attacked the
Mt 20. 6 'Why are you **wasting** the whole day here doing nothing?'
26. 8 "Why all this **waste?"**
Mk 14. 4 to one another, "What was the use of **wasting** the perfume?
Lk 15.13 far away, where he **wasted** his money in reckless living.
15.30 But this son of yours **wasted** all your property on prostitutes,
16. 1 told that the manager was **wasting** his master's money,
Jn 6.12 let us not **waste** any."
1 Cor 9.26 why I am like a boxer who does not **waste** his punches.
2 Cor 6. 1 you who have received God's grace not to let it be **wasted.**
Phil 2.16 will show that all my effort and work have not been **wasted.**
1 Tim 5.13 They also learn to **waste** their time in going round from

Am **WASTELAND** see **WASTE, WILDERNESS**

WATCH

Gen 24.21 The man kept **watching** her in silence, to see if the Lord
31.50 I don't know about it, remember that God is **watching** us.
Ex 2.12 saw that no one was **watching,** he killed the Egyptian and hid
12.42 night when the Lord kept **watch** to bring them out of Egypt;
12.42 as a night when the Israelites must keep **watch.**
33. 8 the door of their tents and **watch** Moses until he entered it.
Num 23. 9 I can **watch** them from the hills.
Deut 6.24 we do, he will always **watch** over our nation and keep it
11.12 care of this land and **watches** over it throughout the year.
Judg 7.17 the edge of the camp, **watch** me, and do what I do.
16.27 men and women on the roof, **watching** Samson entertain them.
21.21 Benjaminites, "Go and hide in the vineyards [21] and **watch.**
Ruth 2. 9 **watch** them to see where they are reaping and stay with them.
1 Sam 1.12 to the Lord for a long time, and Eli **watched** her lips.
6. 9 Then **watch** it go;
6.16 The five Philistine kings **watched** them do this and then
14.16 Saul's men on **watch** at Gibeah in the territory of
17.28 You just came to **watch** the fighting!"
19.11 Saul sent some men to **watch** David's house and kill him the
2 Sam 18.24 The **watchman** went up to the top of the wall and stood
18.26 Then the **watchman** saw another man running alone, and he
18.27 The **watchman** said, "I can see that the first man runs
1 Kgs 8.29 **Watch** over this Temple day and night, this place where
9. 3 I will **watch** over it and protect it for all time.
20.33 Benhadad's officials were **watching** for a good sign, and
2 Kgs 9.17 guard on duty in the **watch-tower** at Jezreel saw Jehu and his
9.18 The guard on the **watch-tower** reported that the messenger
2 Chr 6.20 **Watch** over this Temple day and night.
7.15 I will **watch** over this Temple and be ready to hear all
7.16 I will **watch** over it and protect it for all time.
16. 9 The Lord keeps close **watch** over the whole world, to give
Ezra 3.12 first Temple, and as they **watched** the foundation of this
5. 5 But God was **watching** over the Jewish leaders, and the
Job 10.14 You were **watching** to see if I would sin, so that you
13.27 you **watch** every step I take, and even examine my footprints.
14.16 Then you will **watch** every step I take, but you will not
17. 2 I **watch** how bitterly everyone mocks me.
21. 8 and grandchildren, and live to **watch** them all grow up.
29. 2 could once again be as it was when God **watched** over me.
33.11 he **watches** every move I make."
34.21 He **watches** every step men take.
36.25 but we can only **watch** from a distance.
39. 1 Have you **watched** wild deer give birth?
39.29 From there it **watches** near and far for something to kill
Ps 11. 4 He **watches** people everywhere and knows what they are doing.
17.11 me now, wherever I turn, **watching** for a chance to pull me
33.18 The Lord **watches** over those who obey him, those who
34.15 The Lord **watches** over the righteous and listens to their cries;
37.32 A wicked man **watches** a good man and tries to kill him;
56. 6 They gather in hiding-places and **watch** everything I do,
78.12 While their ancestors **watched,** God performed miracles in
89.36 have descendants, and I will **watch** over his kingdom as long
119.82 My eyes are tired from **watching** for what you promised,
119.123 My eyes are tired from **watching** for your saving help,
130. 6 watchmen wait for the dawn— than **watchmen** wait for the dawn.
Prov 1.17 you want to catch is **watching,** [18] but men like that are
5.21 Wherever you go, he is **watching.**
14.15 sensible people **watch** their step.
15. 3 he is **watching** us, whether we do good or evil.
16.17 so **watch** where you are going—it may save your life.
16.30 **Watch** out for people who grin and wink at you;
24.12 He keeps **watch** on you;
27. 6 But when an enemy puts his arm round your shoulder—**watch** out!
30.29 There are four things that are impressive to **watch** as they walk:
Ecc 12.12 My son, there is something else to **watch** out for.
Song 3. 3 The **watchmen** patrolling the city saw me.
5. 7 The **watchmen** patrolling the city found me;
6.13 Let us **watch** you as you dance.
6.13 Why do you want to **watch** me as I dance
Is 1. 8 siege—as defenceless as a **watchman's** hut in a vineyard or a
27. 3 vineyard, [3] "I **watch** over it and water it continually.
43.19 **Watch** for the new thing I am going to do.
56.10 They are like **watchdogs** that don't bark—they only lie about
Jer 1.12 Lord said, "and I am **watching** to see that my words come
6.17 the Lord appointed **watchmen** to listen for the trumpet's warning.
8.17 **"Watch** out!"
11.20 so let me **watch** you take revenge on these people."
24. 6 I will **watch** over them and bring them back to this land.
31. 6 the time is coming when **watchmen** will call out on the hills
Lam 4.18 The enemy was **watching** for us;
Ezek 3.17 said, "I am making you a **watchman** for the nation of Israel.
10. 2 I **watched** him go.
10.19 earth while I was **watching,** and the wheels went with them.
12. 4 you, and then let them **watch** you leave in the evening as
12. 5 While they are **watching,** break a hole through the wall of
12. 6 Let them **watch** you putting your pack on your shoulder and
12. 7 While everyone **watched,** I put the pack on my shoulder and left.
21. 6 Groan in sorrow where everyone can **watch** you.
33. 2 of that country choose one of their number to be a **watchman.**
33. 6 If, however, the **watchman** sees the enemy coming and does
33. 6 but I will hold the **watchman** responsible for their death.
33. 7 man, I am making you a **watchman** for the nation of Israel.

Ezek 37. 8 While I **watched,** the bones were covered with sinews and muscles,
40. 4 He said to me, **"Watch,** mortal man.
Dan 4.13 I saw coming down from heaven an angel, alert and **watchful.**
4.17 This is the decision of the alert and **watchful** angels.
4.23 While Your Majesty was **watching,** an angel came down from
7. 4 While I was **watching,** the wings were torn off.
7. 6 While I was **watching,** another beast appeared.
7. 7 As I was **watching,** a fourth beast appeared.
7.11 As I **watched,** the fourth beast was killed, and its body was
8. 4 I **watched** the ram butting with his horns to the west, the
8. 7 I **watched** him attack the ram.
10. 8 I was left there alone, **watching** this amazing vision.
Amos 9. 8 I, the Sovereign Lord, am **watching** this sinful kingdom of Israel,
Mic 4. 8 where God, like a shepherd, **watches** over his people, will
7. 4 punish the people, as he warned them through their **watchmen,**
7. 7 But I will **watch** for the Lord;
Hab 1. 5 said to his people, "Keep **watching** the nations round you,
2. 1 I will climb my **watch-tower** and wait to see what the Lord
Zech 5. 7 As I **watched,** the lid was raised, and there in the basket
11.11 and sold the sheep were **watching** me, and they knew that the
12. 4 I will **watch** over the people of Judah, but I will make
Mt 10.17 **Watch** out, for there will be men who will arrest you
21.33 dug a hole for the winepress, and built a **watch-tower.**
26.38 Stay here and keep **watch** with me."
26.40 were not able to keep **watch** with me even for one hour?
26.41 Keep **watch** and pray that you will not fall into temptation.
27.36 After that they sat there and **watched** him.
27.54 soldiers with him who were **watching** Jesus saw the earthquake
27.66 putting a seal on the stone and leaving the guard on **watch.**
Mk 2.12 While they all **watched,** the man got up, picked up his mat,
3. 2 so they **watched** him closely to see whether he would heal the
12. 1 dug a hole for the winepress, and built a **watch-tower.**
12.38 he taught them, he said, **"Watch** out for the teachers of the
12.41 the temple treasury, he **watched** the people as they dropped in
13.33 Be on **watch,** be alert, for you do not know when the
13.34 work to do and after telling the doorkeeper to keep **watch.**
13.37 **Watch!"**
14.34 Stay here and keep **watch."**
14.38 he said to them, "Keep **watch,** and pray that you will not
15.47 the mother of Joseph were **watching** and saw where the body of
Lk 6. 7 of doing wrong, so they **watched** him closely to see if he
12.15 to say to them all, **"Watch** out and guard yourselves from
14. 1 and people were **watching** Jesus closely.
17. 3 So **watch** what you do!
23.35 people stood there **watching** while the Jewish leaders jeered
23.48 who had gathered there to **watch** the spectacle saw what happened,
23.49 followed him from Galilee, stood at a distance to **watch.**
Acts 1. 9 up to heaven as they **watched** him, and a cloud hid him
5.23 locked up tight and all the guards on **watch** at the gates;
9.24 Day and night they **watched** the city gates in order to kill
20.28 So keep **watch** over yourselves and over all the flock which
20.31 **Watch,** then, and remember that with many tears, day and night,
Rom 16.17 **watch** out for those who cause divisions and upset people's faith
Gal 5.15 then **watch** out, or you will completely destroy
Eph 6. 6 not only when they are **watching** you, because you want to
Phil 3. 2 **Watch** out for those who do evil things, those dogs, those
Col 3.22 not only when they are **watching** you because you want to gain
1 Tim 4.16 **Watch** yourself and watch your teaching.
Heb 13.17 They **watch** over your souls without resting, since they must give
1 Pet 3.12 the Lord **watches** over the righteous and listens to their prayers;
5. 8 Be alert, be on the **watch!**
Rev 11.12 As their enemies **watched,** they went up into heaven in a cloud.

WATER

[WELL-WATERED]
see also **WATER GATE, WATERTIGHT**

Gen 1. 2 darkness, and the power of God was moving over the **water.**
1. 6 a dome to divide the **water** and to keep it in two
1. 6 and it separated the water under it from the **water** above it.
1. 9 Then God commanded, "Let the **water** below the sky come
1.10 the land "Earth," and the **water** which had come together he
1.20 Then God commanded, "Let the **water** be filled with many
1.21 of creatures that live in the **water,** and all kinds of birds.
1.22 creatures that live in the **water** to reproduce, and to fill
2. 6 water would come up from beneath the surface and **water** the ground.
2.10 A stream flowed in Eden and **watered** the garden;
7.11 of the vast body of **water** beneath the earth burst open, all
7.17 for forty days, and the **water** became deep enough for the
7.18 The **water** became deeper, and the boat drifted on the surface.
7.24 The **water** did not start going down for a hundred and
8. 1 he caused a wind to blow, and the **water** started going down.
8. 2 The outlets of the **water** beneath the earth and the
8. 3 The rain stopped, [3] and the **water** gradually went down for a
8. 5 The **water** kept going down, and on the first day of the
8. 7 but kept flying around until the **water** was completely gone.
8. 8 dove to see if the **water** had gone down,
8. 9 but since the **water** still covered all the land,
8.11 So Noah knew that the **water** had gone down.
8.13 on the first day of the first month, the **water** was gone.
13.10 to Zoar, had plenty of **water,** like the Garden of the Lord
18. 4 Let me bring some **water** for you to wash your feet;
21.14 Abraham gave Hagar some food and a leather bag full of **water.**
21.15 When the **water** was all gone, she left the child under a
21.19 filled the leather bag with **water** and gave some to the boy.
24.11 late afternoon, the time when women came out to get **water.**
24.13 the young women of the city will be coming to get **water.**
24.14 and I will also bring **water** for your camels,' may she be
Gen 24.15 praying, Rebecca arrived with a **water-jar** on her shoulder.
24.17 said, "Please give me a drink of **water** from your jar."
24.19 said, "I will also bring **water** for your camels and let them
24.20 to get more water, until she had **watered** all his camels.
24.32 Then he brought **water** for Abraham's servant and his men to
24.43 woman comes out to get **water,** I will ask her
24.43 to give me a drink of **water** from her jar.
24.44 and also offers to bring **water** for my camels, may she be
24.45 prayer, Rebecca came with a **water-jar** on her shoulder
24.45 and went down to the well to get **water.**
24.46 and said, 'Drink, and I will also **water** your camels.'
24.46 So I drank, and she **watered** the camels.
26.19 Isaac's servants dug a well in the valley and found **water.**
26.20 with Isaac's shepherds and said, "This **water** belongs to us."
26.32 They said, "We have found **water."**
29. 2 The flocks were **watered** from this well, which had a large
29. 3 the shepherds would roll the stone back and **water** them.
29. 7 flocks in, why don't you **water** them and take them back to
29. 8 then we will **water** the flocks."
29.10 to the well, rolled the stone back, and **watered** the sheep.
43.24 He gave them **water** so that they could wash their feet, and
49.25 from above And of deep **waters** from beneath the ground,
Ex 2.10 pulled him out of the **water,** and so I name him Moses."
2.15 of Midian, came to draw **water** and fill the troughs for their
2.17 Then Moses went to their rescue and **watered** their animals
2.19 "and he even drew **water** for us and watered our animals."
4. 9 what you say, take some **water** from the Nile and pour it
4. 9 The **water** will turn into blood."
7.17 with this stick, and the **water** will be turned into blood.
7.19 The **water** will become blood, and all over the land there
7.20 the river, and all the **water** in it was turned into blood.
7.24 water, because they were not able to drink **water** from the river.
8. 6 it out over all the **water,** and the frogs came out and
14.16 The **water** will divide, and the Israelites will be able to
14.21 The **water** was divided, [22] and the Israelites went through
14.22 the sea on dry ground, with walls of **water** on both sides.
14.26 over the sea, and the **water** will come back over the
14.27 sea, and at daybreak the **water** returned to its normal level.
14.27 tried to escape from the **water,** but the Lord threw them into
14.28 The **water** returned and covered the chariots, the
14.29 the sea on dry ground, with walls of **water** on both sides.
15. 8 You blew on the sea and the **water** piled up high;
15.10 they sank like lead in the terrible **water.**
15.19 sea, the Lord brought the **water** back, and it covered them.
15.22 For three days they walked through the desert, but found no **water.**
15.23 place called Marah, but the **water** there was so bitter that
15.25 showed him a piece of wood, which he threw into the **water;**
15.25 and the **water** became fit to drink.
15.27 there they camped by the **water.**
17. 1 camp at Rephidim, but there was no **water** there to drink.
17. 2 They complained to Moses and said, "Give us **water** to drink."
17. 6 Strike the rock, and **water** will come out of it for the
20. 4 in heaven or on earth or in the **water** under the earth.
23.25 you with food and **water** and take away all your illnesses.
30.18 it between the Tent and the altar, and put **water** in it.
30.19 sons are to use the **water** to wash their hands and feet
32.20 it, ground it into fine powder, and mixed it with **water.**
40. 7 between the Tent and the altar and fill it with **water.**
40.30 between the Tent and the altar and filled it with **water.**
Lev 6.28 pot is used, it must be scrubbed and rinsed with **water.**
8.20 and the hind legs with **water,** and burnt the head, the fat,
11.10 but anything living in the **water** that does not have fins
11.12 anything that lives in the **water** and does not have fins and
11.32 It shall be dipped in **water,** but it will remain unclean
11.34 be eaten, but on which **water** from such a pot has been
11.38 the seed is soaking in **water** and one of them falls on
11.46 everything that lives in the **water,** and everything that
14. 5 to be killed over a clay bowl containing fresh spring **water.**
14.50 of the birds over a clay bowl containing fresh spring **water.**
14.51 blood of the bird that was killed and in the fresh **water.**
14.52 blood, the fresh **water,** the live bird, the cedar-wood,
15.13 bathe in fresh spring **water,** and he will be ritually clean.
Num 5.17 He shall pour some holy **water** into a clay bowl and take
5.17 Lord's presence and put it in the **water** to make it bitter.
5.18 the bowl containing the bitter **water** that brings a curse.
5.19 you will not be harmed by the curse that this **water** brings.
5.22 May this **water** enter your stomach and cause it to swell
5.23 down and wash the writing off into the bowl of bitter **water.**
5.24 makes the woman drink the **water,** which may then cause her
5.26 Finally, he shall make the woman drink the **water.**
5.27 If she has committed adultery, the **water** will cause bitter pain;
8. 7 sprinkle them with the **water** of purification and tell them
19. 7 wash his clothes and pour **water** over himself, and then he
19. 8 wash his clothes and pour **water** over himself, but he also
19. 9 to use in preparing the **water** for removing ritual uncleanness.
19.12 must purify himself with the **water** for purification on the
19.13 himself remains unclean, because the **water** for purification
19.17 shall be taken and put in a pot, and fresh **water** added.
19.18 hyssop, dip it in the **water,** and sprinkle the tent,
19.18 clean is to sprinkle the **water** on the man who had touched
19.19 clean is to sprinkle the **water** on the unclean person.
19.19 washing his clothes and pouring **water** over himself,
19.20 himself remains unclean, because the **water** for purification
19.21 The person who sprinkles the **water** for purification must
19.21 touches the **water** remains ritually unclean until evening.
20. 2 There was no **water** where they camped, so the people
20. 5 There is not even any **water** to drink!"
20. 8 to that rock over there, and **water** will gush out of it.
20. 8 this way you will bring **water** out of the rock for the
20.10 Do we have to get **water** out of this rock for you?"

Num 20.11 and a great stream of **water** gushed out, and all the people
20.19 animals drink any of your **water,** we will pay for it—all
21. 5 to die in this desert, where there is no food or **water?**
21.16 "Bring the people together, and I will give them **water."**
21.17 "Wells, produce your **water;**
21.22 or vineyards, and we will not drink **water** from your wells;
24. 6 Like aloes planted by the Lord Or cedars beside the **water.**
24. 7 abundant rainfall And plant their seed in **well-watered** fields.
31.22 Everything else is to be purified by the **water** for purification.
33. 9 were twelve springs of **water** and seventy palm-trees there.
33.14 Next was Rephidim, where there was no **water** for them to drink.
Deut 2. 6 You may buy food and **water** from them.'
2.28 will pay for the food we eat and the **water** we drink.
5. 8 in heaven or on earth or in the **water** under the earth.
8.15 In that dry and **waterless** land
8.15 he made **water** flow out of solid rock
10. 7 to Gudgodah and then on to Jotbathah, a **well-watered** place.
11.11 is a land of mountains and valleys, a land **watered** by rain.
12.16 you must pour it out on the ground like **water.**
12.24 instead pour it out on the ground like **water.**
14.10 but anything living in the **water** that does not have fins
15.23 instead, you must pour it out on the ground like **water.**
23. 4 provide you with food and **water** when you were on your way
29.11 who live among you and cut wood and carry **water** for you.
32.51 When you were at the **waters** of Meribah, near the town of
33. 8 at Massah And proved them true at the **waters** of Meribah.
33.13 their land with rain And with **water** from under the earth.
33.28 of corn and wine, where dew from the sky **waters** the ground.
Josh 3.13 put their feet in the **water,** the Jordan will stop flowing,
3.13 and the **water** coming downstream will pile up
3.16 into the river, [16] the **water** stopped flowing and piled up,
4. 7 will tell them that the **water** of the Jordan stopped flowing
4.23 your God dried up the **water** of the Jordan for you until
9.21 but they will have to cut wood and carry **water** for us."
9.23 wood and carrying **water** for the sanctuary of my God."
9.27 to cut wood and carry **water** for the people of Israel and
15.19 She answered, "I want some pools of **water.**
Judg 1.15 She answered, "I want some pools of **water.**
4.19 He said to her, "Please give me a drink of **water;**
5. 4 Yes, **water** poured down from the clouds.
5.25 Sisera asked for **water,** but she gave him milk;
6.38 wrung enough dew out of it to fill a bowl with **water.**
7. 4 Take them down to the **water,** and I will separate them for
7. 5 the men down to the **water,** and the Lord said to him,
7. 5 everyone who laps up the **water** with his tongue like a dog,
7. 6 men who scooped up **water** in their hands and lapped it;
7. 7 Midianites with the three hundred men who lapped the **water.**
15.19 in the ground there at Lehi, and **water** came out of it.
Ruth 2. 9 go and drink from the **water jars** that they have filled."
1 Sam 7. 6 They drew some **water** and poured it out as an offering to
9. 9 town, they met some girls who were coming out to draw **water.**
25.11 to take my bread and **water,** and the animals I have
26.11 Let's take his spear and his **water jar,** and go."
26.12 the spear and the **water jar** from just beside Saul's head,
26.16 Where is the **water jar** that was beside his head?"
30.11 gave him some food and **water,** [12] some dried figs, and two
2 Sam 5. 8 Then go up through the **water** tunnel and attack those poor
12.27 "I have attacked Rabbah and have captured its **water** supply.
14.14 we are like **water** spilt on the ground, which can't be
22.12 thick clouds, full of **water,** surrounded him;
22.17 he pulled me out of the deep **waters.**
23.15 bring me a drink of **water** from the well by the gate
23.16 the Philistine camp, drew some **water** from the well, and
1 Kgs 17. 4 brook will supply you with **water** to drink, and I have
17. 6 He drank **water** from the brook, and ravens brought him
17.10 "Please bring me a drink of **water,"** he said to her.
18. 4 two groups of fifty, and provided them with food and **water.)**
18.13 two groups of fifty, and supplied them with food and **water?**
18.32 it, large enough to hold almost fourteen litres of **water.**
18.33 said, "Fill four jars with **water** and pour it on the
18.35 The **water** ran down round the altar and filled the trench.
18.38 scorched the earth and dried up the **water** in the trench.
19. 6 a loaf of bread and a jar of **water** near his head.
22.27 and to put him on bread and **water** until I return safely."
2 Kgs 2. 8 off his cloak, rolled it up, and struck the **water** with it;
2. 8 the **water** divided, and he and Elisha crossed to the other
2.14 He struck the **water** with Elijah's cloak, and said,
2.14 Then he struck the **water** again, and it divided, and he
2.19 fine city, but the **water** is bad and causes miscarriages."
2.21 threw the salt in the **water,** and said, "This is what the
2.21 'I make this **water** pure, and it will not cause any more
2.22 And that **water** has been pure ever since, just as Elisha
3. 9 days, they ran out of **water,** and there was none left for
3.17 bed will be filled with **water,** and you, your livestock, and
3.20 of the regular morning sacrifice, **water** came flowing from
3.22 sun was shining on the **water,** making it look as red as
6. 5 down a tree, suddenly his iron axe-head fell in the **water.**
6. 6 a stick, threw it in the **water,** and made the axe-head float.
8.15 Hazael took a blanket, soaked it in **water,** and smothered the king.
18.17 work, by the ditch that brings **water** from the upper pond.
18.31 own trees, and to drink **water** from your own wells—[32] until
19.24 you dug wells and drank **water** in foreign lands and that the
20.20 dug a tunnel to bring **water** into the city, are all recorded
1 Chr 11.17 bring me a drink of **water** from the well by the gate
11.18 the Philistine camp, drew some **water** from the well, and
2 Chr 4. 6 The **water** in the large tank was for the priests to use
18.26 and to put him on bread and **water** until I return safely."
32. 3 cut off the supply of **water** outside the city in order to
32. 3 Assyrians from having any **water** when they got near Jerusalem.
32. 3 all the springs, so that no more **water** flowed out of them.
32.30 of Gihon and channelled the **water** to flow through a tunnel
Neh 9.11 pursued them drowned in deep **water,** as a stone sinks in the
9.15 them bread from heaven, and **water** from a rock when they were
9.20 you fed them with manna and gave them **water** to drink.
13. 2 did not give food and **water** to the Israelites on their way
Job 5.10 He sends rain on the land and he **waters** the fields.
6.18 Caravans get lost looking for **water;**
8.11 "Reeds can't grow where there is no **water;**
8.12 If the **water** dries up, they are the first to wither,
12.15 floods come when he turns **water** loose.
14. 9 dies in the ground, [9] with **water** it will sprout like a young
14.19 **Water** will wear down rocks, and heavy rain will wash
15.16 And man drinks evil as if it were **water;**
22. 7 You refused **water** to those who were tired, and refused to
26. 5 The spirits of the dead tremble in the **waters** under the earth.
26. 8 who fills the clouds with **water** and keeps them from bursting
29.19 tree whose roots always have **water** and whose branches are
36.27 It is God who takes **water** from the earth and turns it
37.10 of God freezes the **waters,** and turns them to solid ice.
37.13 God sends rain to **water** the earth;
38.27 Who **waters** the dry and thirsty land, so that grass springs up?
38.30 the frost, [30] which turn the **waters** to stone and freeze the
41.31 up the sea like boiling **water** and makes it bubble like a
Ps 18.11 thick clouds, full of **water,** surrounded him.
18.16 he pulled me out of the deep **waters.**
22.14 My strength is gone, gone like **water** spilt on the ground.
23. 2 of green grass and leads me to quiet pools of fresh **water.**
24. 2 built it on the deep **waters** beneath the earth and laid its
29.10 The Lord rules over the deep **waters;**
42. 1 for a stream of cool **water,** so I long for you, O
58. 7 May they disappear like **water** draining away;
63. 1 like a dry, worn-out, and **waterless** land, my soul is
65. 9 You fill the streams with **water;**
65.10 rain on the ploughed fields and soak them with **water;**
69. 1 The **water** is up to my neck;
69. 2 I am out in deep **water,** and the waves are about to
69.14 keep me safe from my enemies, safe from the deep **water.**
77.16 When the **waters** saw you, O God, they were afraid, and
78.13 he made the **waters** stand like walls.
78.15 open in the desert and gave them **water** from the depths.
78.16 come out of the rock and made **water** flow like a river.
78.20 that he struck the rock, and **water** flowed out in a torrent;
78.44 rivers into blood, and the Egyptians had no **water** to drink.
79. 3 They shed your people's blood like **water;**
79. 3 blood flowed like **water** all through Jerusalem,
104. 3 like a tent [3] and built your home on the **waters** above.
104. 6 over it like a robe, and the **water** covered the mountains.
104. 7 When you rebuked the **waters,** they fled;
104.11 They provide **water** for the wild animals;
105.41 He opened a rock, and **water** gushed out, flowing through
106.11 But the **water** drowned their enemies;
107.35 into pools of **water** and dry land into flowing springs.
109.18 soak into his body like **water** and into his bones like oil!
114. 8 into pools of **water** and solid cliffs into flowing springs.
124. 4 have carried us away, the **water** would have covered us, [5] the
126. 4 just as the rain brings **water** back to dry river-beds.
136. 6 he built the earth on the deep **waters;**
144. 7 from above, pull me out of the deep **water,** and rescue me;
147.18 he sends the wind, and the **water** flows.
148. 4 Praise him, highest heavens, and the **waters** above the sky.
Prov 8.24 before the oceans, when there were no springs of **water.**
8.29 the ocean [29] and ordered the **waters** of the sea to rise no
9.17 To the foolish man she says, [17] "Stolen **water** is sweeter.
19.13 A nagging wife is like **water** going drip-drip-drip.
20. 5 A person's thoughts are like **water** in a deep well, but
25.13 who sends him, like cold **water** in the heat of harvest time.
25.25 like a drink of cold **water** when you are dry and thirsty.
27.15 A nagging wife is like **water** going drip-drip-drip on a rainy day.
27.19 you see reflected in the **water** and it is your own self
30. 4 Or wrapped up **water** in a piece of cloth?
Ecc 1. 7 The **water** returns to where the rivers began, and starts all
12. 6 at the well will break, and the **water jar** will be shattered.
Song 4.15 Fountains **water** the garden, streams of flowing water,
8. 7 **Water** cannot put it out;
Is 1.22 you were like good wine, but now you are only **water.**
1.30 wither like a dying oak, like a garden that no one **waters.**
3. 1 food and their **water,** [2] their heroes and their soldiers,
7. 3 the end of the ditch that brings **water** from the upper pool.
8. 6 have rejected the quiet **waters** from the brook of Shiloah,
8. 7 will advance like the flood **waters** of the River Euphrates,
11. 9 of knowledge of the Lord as the seas are full of **water.**
12. 3 As fresh **water** brings joy to the thirsty, so God's people
19. 5 The **water** will be low in the Nile, and the river will
21.14 barren country of Arabia, [14] give **water** to the thirsty
22. 9 In order to store **water,** [11] you built a reservoir inside
22.11 the city to hold the **water** flowing down from the old pool.
27. 3 vineyard, [3] "I watch over it and **water** it continually.
30.14 pick up hot coals with, or to scoop **water** from a cistern."
30.25 people are killed, streams of **water** will flow from every
32.20 will be with plenty of **water** for the crops and safe pasture
33.16 You will have food to eat and **water** to drink.
35. 6 Streams of **water** will flow through the desert;
36. 2 work, by the ditch that brings **water** from the upper pond.
36.16 own trees, and to drink **water** from your own wells—[17] until
37.25 you dug wells and drank **water** in foreign lands, and that the
40.15 Lord the nations are nothing, no more than a drop of **water;**
41.17 in their need look for **water,** when their throats are dry
41.18 among barren hills and springs of **water** run in the valleys.
41.18 the desert into pools of **water** and the dry land into flowing
42.15 river valleys into deserts and dry up the pools of **water.**
43. 2 When you pass through deep **waters,** I will be with you;
43.16 a road through the sea, a path through the swirling **waters.**

Is 43.19 through the wilderness and give you streams of **water** there.
43.20 flow in the desert to give **water** to my chosen people.
44. 3 "I will give **water** to the thirsty land and make streams
44. 4 They will thrive like **well-watered** grass,
44. 4 like willows by streams of running **water.**
48.21 He made **water** come from a rock for them;
48.21 he split the rock open, and **water** flowed out.
49.10 He will lead them to springs of **water.**
50. 2 desert, so that the fish in them die for lack of **water.**
51.10 made a path through the **water,** so that those you were saving
55. 1 "Come, everyone who is thirsty— here is **water!**
55.10 the rain that come down from the sky to **water** the earth.
58.11 plenty of water, like a spring of **water** that never runs dry.
63.12 things through Moses, dividing the **waters** of the sea and
63.12 the deep **water,** to win everlasting fame for himself?"
64. 2 They would tremble like **water** boiling over a hot fire.
Jer 2.13 me, the spring of fresh **water,** and they have dug cisterns,
2.13 cracked cisterns that can hold no **water** at all.
2.18 will gain by going to Egypt to drink **water** from the Nile?
2.18 gain by going to Assyria to drink **water** from the Euphrates?
6. 7 As a well keeps its **water** fresh, so Jerusalem keeps its
9. 1 head were a well of **water,** and my eyes a fountain of
10.13 At his command the **waters** above the sky roar;
13. 1 but he told me not to put them in **water.**
14. 3 The rich people send their servants for **water;**
14. 3 they go to the cisterns, but find no **water;**
17. 8 growing near a stream and sending out roots to the **water.**
17.13 have abandoned you, the Lord, the spring of fresh **water.**
31. 9 guide them to streams of **water,** on a smooth road where they
31.12 They will be like a **well-watered** garden;
38. 6 There was no **water** in the well, only mud, and I sank
47. 2 **Waters** are rising in the north and will rush like a river
50.12 it will become a dry and **waterless** desert.
51.16 At his command the **waters** above the sky roar;
51.36 the source of Babylonia's **water** and make its rivers go dry.
51.43 sight and are like a **waterless** desert, where no one lives or
Lam 3.54 **Water** began to close over me, and I thought death was near.
5. 4 We must pay for the **water** we drink;
Ezek 4.11 have a limited amount of **water** to drink, two cups a day.
4.16 they measure out the food they eat and the **water** they drink.
4.17 They will run out of bread and **water;**
16. 9 "Then I took **water** and washed the blood off you.
17. 5 fertile field, where there was always **water** to make it grow.
17. 7 he would give it more **water** than there was in the garden
17. 8 been planted in a fertile, **well-watered** field so that it
19.10 Because there was plenty of **water,** the vine was covered with
19.13 it is planted in the desert, in a dry and **waterless** land.
24. 3 Set the pot on the fire and fill it up with **water.**
24. 5 Let the **water** boil;
26.19 I will cover you with the **water** of the ocean depths.
28. 8 They will kill you and send you to a **watery** grave.
31. 4 There was **water** to make it grow, And underground rivers to
31. 4 They **watered** the place where the tree was growing And sent
31. 5 Because it was **well-watered,** It grew taller than other trees.
31.14 no tree, no matter how **well-watered** it is, will grow as tall
31.15 I will make the underground **waters** cover it as a sign of
31.16 Eden and all the choice, **well-watered** trees of Lebanon who
32. 2 You muddy the **water** with your feet and pollute the rivers.
32.13 I will slaughter your cattle at every **water-hole.**
32.13 will be no people or cattle to muddy the **water** any more.
32.14 I will let your **waters** settle and become clear and let
34.18 You drink the clear **water** and muddy what you don't drink!
34.19 the grass you trample down and drink the **water** you muddy.
36.25 I will sprinkle clean **water** on you and make you clean
47. 1 **Water** was coming out from under the entrance and flowing east,
47. 2 A small stream of **water** was flowing out at the south side
47. 3 The **water** came only to my ankles.
47. 4 five hundred metres, and the **water** came up to my knees.
47. 4 hundred metres further down, the **water** was up to my waist.
47. 8 He said to me, "This **water** flows through the land to the
47. 8 it replaces the salt **water** of that sea with fresh water.
47. 9 The stream will make the **water** of the Dead Sea fresh, and
47.11 But the **water** in the marshes and ponds along the shore
47.12 every month, because they are **watered** by the stream that
Dan 1.12 "Give us vegetables to eat and **water** to drink.
11.40 He will invade many countries, like the **waters** of a flood.
Hos 2. 4 me food and **water,** wool and linen, olive-oil and wine."
6. 3 as surely as the spring rains that **water** the earth."
10. 7 king will be carried off, like a chip of wood on **water.**
Joel 3.18 there will be plenty of **water** for all the streams of Judah.
3.18 Temple of the Lord, and it will **water** the Valley of Acacia.
Amos 4. 8 where they hoped to find **water,** but there was not enough to
5. 8 He calls for the **waters** of the sea and pours them out
8.11 they will be thirsty, but not for **water.**
9. 6 He calls for the **waters** of the sea and pours them out
Jon 2. 3 of the sea, where the **waters** were all round me, and all
2. 5 The **water** came over me and choked me;
Mic 1. 4 pour down into the valleys like **water** pouring down a hill.
Nah 2. 8 Like **water** from a broken dam the people rush from Nineveh!
3.14 Draw **water** to prepare for a siege, and strengthen your fortresses!
Hab 2.14 of the Lord's glory as the seas are full of **water.**
3.10 **water** poured down from the skies.
3.10 The **waters** under the earth roared, and their waves rose high.
3.15 You trampled the sea with your horses, and the mighty **waters** foamed.
Zeph 1.17 will be poured out like **water,** and their dead bodies will
2.13 the city of Nineveh a deserted ruin, a **waterless** desert.
Zech 9.11 set your people free— free from the **waterless** pit of exile.
14. 8 When that day comes, fresh **water** will flow from Jerusalem,
Mt 3.11 I baptize you with **water** to show that you have repented,
3.16 soon as Jesus was baptized, he came up out of the **water.**

Mt 10.42 even a drink of cold **water** to one of the least of
14.25 morning Jesus came to the disciples, walking on the **water.**
14.26 When they saw him walking on the **water,** they were terrified.
14.28 really you, order me to come out on the **water** to you."
14.29 out of the boat and started walking on the **water** to Jesus.
14.30 he was afraid and started to sink down in the **water.**
17.15 terrible fits that he often falls in the fire or into **water.**
27.24 he took some **water,** washed his hands in front of
Mk 1. 8 I baptize you with **water,** but he will baptize you with the
1.10 came up out of the **water,** he saw heaven opening and the
4. 1 boat was out in the **water,**
4. 1 and the crowd stood on the shore at the **water's** edge.
4.37 into the boat, so that it was about to fill with **water.**
6.48 in the morning he came to them, walking on the **water.**
6.49 to pass them by, [49] but they saw him walking on the **water.**
9.22 to kill him by throwing him in the fire and into **water.**
9.41 gives you a drink of **water** because you belong to me will
14.13 and a man carrying a jar of **water** will meet you.
Lk 3.16 "I baptize you with **water,** but someone is coming who is
5. 4 out further to the deep **water,** and you and your partners let
7.44 and you gave me no **water** for my feet, but she has
8.23 boat began to fill with **water,** so that they were all in
8.24 and gave an order to the wind and the stormy **water;**
13.15 and take it out to give it **water** on the Sabbath.
16.24 dip his finger in some **water** and cool my tongue, because I
22.10 the city, a man carrying a jar of **water** will meet you.
Jn 1.26 John answered, "I baptize with **water,** but among you stands
1.31 but I came baptizing with **water** in order to make him known
1.33 sent me to baptize with **water,** had said to me, 'You will
2. 6 for this purpose six stone **water jars** were there, each one
2. 7 Jesus said to the servants, "Fill these jars with **water."**
2. 8 told them, "Now draw some **water** out and take it to the
2. 8 They took him the **water,** [9] which now had turned into wine,
2. 9 (but, of course, the servants who had drawn out the **water** knew);
3. 5 Kingdom of God unless he is born of **water** and the Spirit.
3.23 from Salim, because there was plenty of **water** in that place.
4. 7 woman came to draw some **water,**
4. 7 and Jesus said to her, "Give me a drink of **water."**
4.10 you would ask him, and he would give you life-giving **water."**
4.11 Where would you get that life-giving **water?**
4.13 "Whoever drinks this **water** will be thirsty again,
4.14 but whoever drinks the **water** that I will give him will
4.14 The **water** that I will give him will become in him a
4.14 provide him with life-giving **water** and give him eternal life."
4.15 "Sir," the woman said, "give me that **water!**
4.15 thirsty again, nor will I have to come here to draw **water."**
4.28 Then the woman left her **water jar,** went back to the town,
4.46 to Cana in Galilee, where he had turned the **water** into wine.
5. 7 to put me in the pool when the **water** is stirred up;
6.18 By then a strong wind was blowing and stirring up the **water.**
6.19 saw Jesus walking on the **water,** coming near the boat, and
7.38 streams of life-giving **water** will pour out from his heart.' "
13. 5 Then he poured some **water** into a basin and began to wash
19.34 into Jesus' side, and at once blood and **water** poured out.
21. 4 Jesus stood at the **water's** edge, but the disciples did not
21. 7 (for he had taken his clothes off) and jumped into the **water.**
Acts 1. 5 John baptized with **water,** but in a few days you will be
8.36 was some water, and the official said, "Here is some **water.**
8.38 the official went down into the **water,** and Philip baptized him.
8.39 came up out of the **water,** the Spirit of the Lord took
10.47 Can anyone, then, stop them from being baptized with **water?"**
11.16 'John baptized with **water,** but you will be baptized with the
27.28 tied to it and found that the **water** was forty metres deep;
27.30 lowered the boat into the **water** and pretended that they were
1 Cor 3. 6 I sowed the seed, Apollos **watered** the plant, but it was
3. 7 one who sows and the one who **waters** really do not matter.
3. 8 difference between the man who sows and the man who **waters;**
2 Cor 11.25 three shipwrecks, and once I spent twenty-four hours in the **water.**
Eph 5.26 clean by washing it in **water,** [27] in order to present the
1 Tim 5.23 Do not drink **water** only, but take a little wine to help
Heb 9.19 and goats, mixed it with **water,** and sprinkled it on the book
10.22 from a guilty conscience and with bodies washed with clean **water.**
11.29 the Egyptians tried to do it, the **water** swallowed them up.
Jas 3.11 No spring of **water** pours out sweet water and bitter water
1 Pet 3.20 were saved by the **water,** [21] which was a symbol pointing to
2 Pet 3. 5 earth was formed out of **water** and by water,
3. 6 and it was also by **water,** the water of the flood, that
1 Jn 5. 6 one who came with the **water** of his baptism and the blood
5. 6 came not only with the **water,**
5. 6 but with both the **water** and the blood.
5. 8 the Spirit, the **water,** and the blood;
Rev 7.17 shepherd, and he will guide them to springs of life-giving **water.**
8.10 on a third of the rivers and on the springs of **water.**
8.11 A third of the **water** turned bitter, and many people died
8.11 died from drinking the **water,** because it had turned bitter.
11. 6 also over the springs of **water,** to turn them into blood;
12.15 poured out a flood of **water** after the woman, so that it
12.16 its mouth and swallowed the **water** that had come from the
14. 7 Worship him who made heaven, earth, sea, and the springs of **water!"**
16. 3 The **water** became like the blood of a dead person,
16. 4 rivers and the springs of **water,** and they turned into blood.
16. 5 angel in charge of the **waters** say, "The judgements you have
17.15 also said to me, "The **waters** you saw, on which the
21. 6 from the spring of the **water** of life without paying for it.
22. 1 the river of the **water** of life, sparkling like crystal,
22.17 accept the **water** of life as a gift, whoever wants it.

WATER GATE

Neh 3.25 on the east near the **Water Gate** and the tower guarding the
8. 1 in Jerusalem, in the square just inside the **Water Gate.**
8.16 public squares by the **Water Gate** and by the Ephraim Gate.
12.37 to the wall at the **Water Gate,** on the east side of

WATER-MELON

Num 11. 5 Remember the cucumbers, the **water-melons,** the leeks, the

WATERFALL

Ps 42. 6 me like a flood, like **waterfalls** thundering down to the
Rev 1.15 and his voice sounded like a roaring **waterfall.**
14. 2 sounded like a roaring **waterfall,** like a loud peal of thunder.
19. 6 sound of a roaring **waterfall,** like loud peals of thunder.

WATERTIGHT

Ex 2. 3 made of reeds and covered it with tar to make it **watertight.**

WAVE (1)

2 Sam 22. 5 The **waves** of death were all round me;
22. 5 the **waves** of destruction rolled over me.
Job 38.11 Here your powerful **waves** must stop."
Ps 18. 4 the **waves** of destruction rolled over me.
42. 6 He has sent **waves** of sorrow over my soul;
65. 7 calm the roar of the seas and the noise of the **waves;**
69. 2 out in deep water, and the **waves** are about to drown me.
77.19 You walked through the **waves;**
88. 7 anger lies heavy on me, and I am crushed beneath its **waves.**
89. 9 you calm its angry **waves.**
93. 4 roar of the ocean, more powerful than the **waves** of the sea.
107.25 and a mighty wind began to blow and stirred up the **waves.**
107.29 He calmed the raging storm, and the **waves** became quiet.
Is 17.12 like the roar of the sea, like the crashing of huge **waves.**
17.13 The nations advance like rushing **waves,** but God
48.18 have come to you like the **waves** that roll on the shore.
51.15 I stir up the sea and make its **waves** roar.
57.20 like the restless sea, whose **waves** never stop rolling in,
Jer 5.22 the **waves** may roar, but they cannot break through.
51.42 The sea has rolled over Babylon and covered it with roaring **waves.**
51.55 The armies rush in like roaring **waves** and attack with noisy shouts.
Ezek 26. 3 attack you, and they will come like the **waves** of the sea.
Jon 2. 3 all round me, and all your mighty **waves** rolled over me.
Hab 3.10 The waters under the earth roared, and their **waves** rose high.
Zech 10.11 the Lord, will strike the **waves,** and the depths of the Nile
Mt 8.26 ordered the winds and the **waves** to stop, and there was a
8.27 "Even the winds and the **waves** obey him!"
14.24 lake, tossed about by the **waves,** because the wind was blowing
Mk 4.37 wind blew up, and the **waves** began to spill over into the
4.39 and he said to the **waves,** "Be still!"
4.41 Even the wind and the **waves** obey him!"
Lk 8.25 He gives orders to the winds and **waves,** and they obey him!"
Acts 27.41 was being broken to pieces by the violence of the **waves.**
Eph 4.14 children, carried by the **waves** and blown about by every shifting
Jas 1. 6 Whoever doubts is like a **wave** in the sea that is driven
Jude 13 They are like wild **waves** of the sea, with their shameful

WAVE (2)
[WAVING]

2 Kgs 5.11 to the Lord his God, **wave** his hand over the diseased spot,
Acts 22.23 They were screaming, **waving** their clothes, and throwing dust

AV **WAVE-OFFERING** see **(special) GIFT**

WAVY

Song 5.11 his hair is **wavy,** black as a raven.

WAX

Ps 22.14 my heart is like melted **wax.**
68. 2 as **wax** melts in front of the fire, so do the wicked
97. 5 The hills melt like **wax** before the Lord, before the Lord
Mic 1. 4 Then the mountains will melt under him like **wax** in a fire;

WAY (1)
see also **HIGHWAY**

Gen 13. 9 You go one **way,** and I'll go the other."
18.16 Sodom, and Abraham went with them to send them on their **way.**
19. 2 the morning you can get up early and go on your **way."**
19. 9 But they said, "Get out of our **way,** you foreigner!
19. 9 Out of our **way,** or we will treat you worse than them."
24.41 There is only one **way** for you to be free from your
25.18 and Shur, to the east of Egypt on the **way** to Assyria.
29. 1 Jacob continued on his **way** and went towards the land of
31.27 have sent you on your **way** with rejoicing and singing to the
32. 1 As Jacob went on his **way,** some angels met him.
32. 6 brother Esau, and he is already on his **way** to meet you.
33.16 So that day Esau started on his **way** back to Edom.
37.14 his father sent him on his **way** from the Valley of Hebron.
38.29 the midwife said, "So this is how you break your **way** out!"
41.43 guard of honour went ahead of him and cried out, "Make **way!**
41.43 Make **way!"**
42.38 Something might happen to him on the **way.**
43.21 set up camp on the **way** home, we opened our sacks, and
44. 3 the brothers were sent on their **way** with their donkeys.
45.24 they left, he said to them, "Don't quarrel on the **way."**
48.18 He said to his father, "Not that **way,** father.
Ex 4.24 a camping place on the **way** to Egypt, the Lord met Moses
13.17 up the coast to Philistia, although it was the shortest **way.**
13.18 led them in a roundabout **way** through the desert towards the
13.21 cloud to show them the **way,** and during the night he went
18. 8 people had faced on the **way** and how the Lord had saved
20.18 mountain, they trembled with fear and stood a long **way** off.
20.21 continued to stand a long **way** off, and only Moses went near
32. 8 They have already left the **way** that I commanded them to follow;
33. 3 a stubborn people, and I might destroy you on the **way."**
Num 20.21 the Israelites turned and went another **way.**
21. 1 the Israelites were coming by **way** of Atharim, he attacked
21. 4 But on the **way** the people lost their patience [5] and spoke
22.22 angel of the Lord stood in the road to bar his **way.**
22.32 have come to bar your **way,** because you should not be making
24.25 got ready and went back home, and Balak went on his **way.**
Deut 1. 2 Mount Sinai to Kadesh Barnea by **way** of the hill-country of Edom.)
1.19 desert on the **way** to the hill-country of the Amorites.
1.33 To show you the **way,** he went in front of you in
2.18 are to pass through the territory of Moab by **way** of Ar.
22. 2 its owner lives a long **way** off or if you don't know
23. 4 when you were on your **way** out of Egypt, and they hired
28.29 blind man, and you will not be able to find your **way.**
Josh 2.16 After that you can go on your **way."**
3. 4 been here before, so they will show you the **way** to go.
7. 5 killed about thirty-six of them on the **way** down the hill.
18. 8 The men went on their **way** to map out the land after
19.13 turning in the direction of Neah on the **way** to Rimmon.
19.27 Valley of Iphtahel on the **way** north to Bethemek and Neiel.
Judg 2. 6 people of Israel on their **way,** and each man went to take
8.13 returning from the battle by **way** of Heres Pass, [14] he
9.25 and they robbed everyone who passed their **way.**
14. 8 On the **way** he left the road to look at the lion
18.27 because Laish was a long **way** from Sidon, and they had no
19.10 his concubine started on their **way,** with their servant and
19.14 So they went past Jebus and continued on their **way.**
19.18 now we are on our **way** home deep in the hill-country of
19.27 door to go on his **way,** he found his concubine lying in
19.28 put her body across the donkey and started on his **way** home.
Ruth 1. 7 to Judah, but on the **way** [8] she said to them, "Go back
1 Sam 6. 8 Start the wagon on its **way** and let it go by itself.
7.11 Philistines almost as far as Bethcar, killing them along the **way.**
7.12 has helped us all the **way"**—and he named it "Stone of
9.14 coming out towards them on his **way** to the place of worship.
9.19 I will answer all your questions and send you on your **way.**
9.26 the roof, "Get up, and I will send you on your **way."**
10. 3 meet three men on their **way** to offer a sacrifice to God
13.15 Samuel left Gilgal and went on his **way.**
24. 7 Saul got up, left the cave, and started on his **way.**
26.25 So David went on his **way,** and Saul returned home.
30.10 David continued on his **way** with four hundred men;
2 Sam 3.21 gave Abner a guarantee of safety and sent him on his **way.**
8. 3 as Hadadezer was on his **way** to restore his control over the
13.30 While they were on their **way** home, David was told:
19.15 On his **way** back the king was met at the River Jordan
19.36 I will go just a little **way** with you beyond the Jordan.
23.16 soldiers forced their **way** through the Philistine camp,
1 Kgs 1.49 and they all got up and left, each going his own **way.**
13. 9 a thing, and not to return home the same **way** I came."
13.10 not go back the same **way** he had come, but by another
13.12 "Which **way** did he go when he left?"
13.17 a thing, and not to return home the same **way** I came."
13.24 On the **way,** a lion met him and killed him.
18. 7 As Obadiah was on his **way,** he suddenly met Elijah.
2 Kgs 2. 2 from Gilgal, [2] and on the **way** Elijah said to Elisha, "Now
2.23 to Bethel, and on the **way** some boys came out of a
3. 8 "We will go the long **way,** through the wilderness of Edom,"
3.26 and tried to force his **way** through the enemy lines and
10.12 On the **way,** at a place called "Shepherds' Camp," [13] he
10.15 out again, and on his **way** he was met by Jonadab son
15.16 As Menahem was on his **way** from Tirzah, he completely
25. 4 They left by **way** of the royal garden, went through the
1 Chr 11.18 soldiers forced their **way** through the Philistine camp,
2 Chr 32. 1 orders for his army to break their **way** through the walls.
Neh 2.15 Then I returned the **way** I had come and went back into
9.12 in day-time, and at night you lighted their **way** with fire.
9.29 your laws, although keeping your Law is the **way** to life.
13. 2 food and water to the Israelites on their **way** out of Egypt.
Job 2.12 they were still a long **way** off they saw Job, but did
19. 8 God has blocked the **way,** and I can't get through;
28.23 God alone knows the **way,** Knows the place where wisdom is found,
38.25 the pouring rain and cleared the **way** for the thunderstorm?
Ps 1. 6 the Lord, but the evil are on the **way** to their doom.
5. 8 make your **way** plain for me to follow.
17. 5 always walked in your **way** and have never strayed from it.
25. 9 the humble in the right **way** and teaches them his will.
30. 3 I was on my **way** to the depths below, but you restored
32. 8 The Lord says, "I will teach you the **way** you should go;
37.23 guides a man in the **way** he should go and protects those
68. 4 prepare a **way** for him who rides on the clouds.
107. 4 and could not find their **way** to a city to live in.
119.29 me from going the wrong **way,** and in your goodness teach me
139.24 is any evil in me and guide me in the everlasting **way.**
143. 8 show me the **way** I should go.
Prov 3. 6 in everything you do, and he will show you the right **way.**

Prov	3.23	You can go safely on your **way** and never even stumble.
	4.12	Nothing will stand in your **way** if you walk wisely, and
	4.15	Refuse it and go on your **way.**
	4.27	Don't go one step off the right **way.**
	7.22	like an ox on the **way** to be slaughtered, like a deer
	7.27	house, you are on the **way** to the world of the dead.
	8.20	I walk the **way** of righteousness;
	9. 6	Follow the **way** of knowledge."
	18.12	arrogant people are on the **way** to ruin.
	22. 5	away from the traps that catch the wicked along the **way.**
	30.19	a ship finding its **way** over the sea,
Ecc	2.22	You work and worry your **way** through life, and what do
	8. 8	we cannot cheat our **way** out.
	8.10	their graves, but on the **way** back from the cemetery people
	10. 3	will be evident even to strangers he meets along the **way;**
	10.15	too stupid to find his **way** home would wear himself out with
Song	6. 1	Tell us which **way** your lover went, so that we can help
Is	3.12	misleading you, so that you do not know which **way** to turn.
	9. 1	There will be no **way** for them to escape from this time
	30.11	Get out of our **way** and stop blocking our path.
	30.29	music of flutes on their **way** to the Temple of the Lord,
	35. 9	no fierce animals will pass that **way.**
	40. 3	Clear the **way** in the desert for our God!
	45. 2	"I myself will prepare your **way,** levelling mountains and hills.
	48.17	your own good and direct you in the **way** you should go.
	53. 6	like sheep that were lost, each of us going his own **way.**
Jer	2.17	the Lord your God, while I was leading you along the **way.**
	4. 6	Point the **way** to Zion!
	18.15	They have stumbled in the **way** they should go, they no longer
	21. 8	way that leads to life and the **way** that leads to death.
	25.35	There will be no **way** for you to escape.
	31.21	find again the **way** by which you left.
	37. 7	Egyptian army is on its **way** to help you, but it will
	39. 4	They left by **way** of the royal garden, went through the
	40. 5	food to take with me, and let me go on my **way.**
	41.17	On the **way,** they stopped at Chimham, near Bethlehem.
	42. 3	God will show us the **way** we should go and what we
	48. 5	Luhith, the cries of distress on the **way** down to Horonaim.
	50. 5	They will ask the **way** to Zion and then go in that
	52. 7	They left by **way** of the royal garden, went through the
Ezek	21.20	will show the king the **way** to the Ammonite city of Rabbah,
	21.20	and the other the **way** to Judah, to the fortified city,
	21.21	To discover which **way** to go, he shakes the arrows;
	46. 8	gateway and go out by the same **way** as he went in.
	46. 9	go out by the same **way** as he entered, but must leave
	47. 2	of the temple area by **way** of the north gate and led
Hos	2. 6	her in with thorn-bushes and build a wall to block her **way.**
Amos	9. 2	Even if they dig their **way** down to the world of the
Mic	2.13	God will open the **way** for them and lead them out of
	6. 5	things that happened on the **way** from the camp at Acacia to
Nah	1.15	He is on his **way** to announce the victory!
Mal	3. 1	"I will send my messenger to prepare the **way** for me.
Mt	7.14	life is narrow and the **way** that leads to it is hard,
	11.10	send my messenger ahead of you to open the **way** for you.'
	16.23	are an obstacle in my **way,** because these thoughts of yours
Mk	1. 2	send my messenger ahead of you to clear the **way** for you.'
	3.10	were ill kept pushing their **way** to him in order to touch
	7.31	to Lake Galilee, going by **way** of the territory of the Ten
	8. 3	as they go, because some of them have come a long **way."**
Lk	5. 1	while the people pushed their **way** up to him to listen to
	7.27	send my messenger ahead of you to open the **way** for you.'
	10.33	Samaritan who was travelling that **way** came upon the man,
	10.35	when I come back this **way,** I will pay you whatever else
	14.32	for terms of peace while he is still a long **way** off.
	15.20	"He was still a long **way** from home when his father saw
	15.25	On his **way** back, when he came close to the house,
	16.16	Kingdom of God is being told, and everyone forces his **way** in.
	19. 4	sycomore tree to see Jesus, who was going to pass that **way.**
Jn	12.35	Continue on your **way** while you have the light, so that the
	14. 4	You know the **way** that leads to the place where I am
	14. 5	so how can we know the **way** to get there?"
	14. 6	Jesus answered him, "I am the **way,** the truth, and the
Acts	8.39	not see him again, but continued on his **way,** full of joy.
	14.16	In the past he allowed all people to go their own **way.**
	14.27	and how he had opened the **way** for the Gentiles to believe.
1 Cor	9.12	put any obstacle in the **way** of the Good News about Christ.
	10.13	strength to endure it, and so provide you with a **way** out.
	16.10	If Timothy comes your **way,** be sure to make him feel
2 Cor	2.12	found that the Lord had opened the **way** for the work there.
	6. 3	our work, so we try not to put obstacles in anyone's **way.**
Eph	2. 2	At that time you followed the world's evil **way;**
Phil	1.27	important thing is that your **way** of life should be as the
Col	4.10	already received instructions to welcome Mark if he comes your **way.)**
1 Thes	3.11	our Lord Jesus prepare the **way** for us to come to you!
2 Thes	2. 7	the one who holds it back is taken out of the **way.**
1 Tim	1. 6	away from these and have lost their **way** in foolish discussions.
	6.21	and as a result they have lost the **way** of faith.
2 Tim	2.18	They have left the **way** of truth and are upsetting the
Heb	9. 8	all these arrangements that the **way** into the Most Holy Place
	10.20	opened for us a new **way,** a living way, through the curtain
	11.13	promised, but from a long **way** off they saw them and welcomed
	12. 1	everything that gets in the **way,** and of the sin which holds
	13. 9	all kinds of strange teachings lead you from the right **way.**
Jas	1. 2	kinds of trials come your **way,** [3]for you know that when your
	5.20	sinner back from his wrong **way** will save that sinner's soul
1 Pet	2.25	sheep that had lost their **way,** but now you have been brought
2 Pet	2.15	They have left the straight path and have lost their **way;**
	2.21	never to have known the **way** of righteousness than to know it
Jude	11	They have followed the **way** that Cain took.
	16	and flatter others in order to get their own **way.**
Rev	16.12	dried up, to provide a **way** for the kings who come from
	18.10	They stand a long **way** off, because they are afraid of
	18.15	city, will stand a long **way** off, because they are afraid of
	18.17	the sea, stood a long **way** off, [18]and cried out as they

WAY (2)

Acts	9. 2	there any followers of the **Way of the Lord,** he would be
	18.25	had been instructed in the **Way of the Lord,** and with great
	18.26	them and explained to him more correctly the **Way of God.**
	19. 9	whole group they said evil things about the **Way of the Lord.**
	19.23	serious trouble in Ephesus because of the **Way of the Lord.**
	22. 4	I persecuted to the death the people who followed this **Way.**
	24.14	our ancestors by following that **Way** which they say is false.
	24.22	well informed about the **Way,** brought the hearing to a close.
2 Pet	2. 2	what they do, others will speak evil of the **Way** of truth.

WAY (3)

Deut	32. 4	Lord is your mighty defender, perfect and just in all his **ways;**
Judg	2.19	to return to the old **ways** and behave worse than the previous
	2.19	other gods, and refused to give up their own evil **ways.**
	2.22	Israelites will follow my **ways,** as their ancestors did."
1 Kgs	13.33	not turn from his evil **ways,** but continued to choose priests
2 Kgs	8.18	of Ahab he followed the evil **ways** of the kings of Israel.
	13. 2	he never gave up his evil **ways.**
	17.13	"Abandon your evil **ways** and obey my commands, which are
Ezra	6.21	had given up the pagan **ways** of the other people who were
Ps	7.12	If they do not change their **ways,** God will sharpen his sword.
	25. 4	Teach me your **ways,** O Lord;
	68.21	of his enemies, of those who persist in their sinful **ways.**
	81.12	I let them go their stubborn **ways** and do whatever they wanted.
	85. 8	own people, if we do not go back to our foolish **ways.**
	106.35	but they intermarried with them and adopted their pagan **ways.**
	119. 3	they walk in the Lord's **ways.**
	119.12	teach me your **ways.**
	119.26	teach me your **ways.**
	119.128	I hate all wrong **ways.**
	125. 5	punish the wicked, punish also those who abandon your **ways.**
Prov	8.13	I hate pride and arrogance, evil **ways** and false words.
	15. 9	The Lord hates the **ways** of evil people, but loves those
	20.30	Sometimes it takes a painful experience to make us change our **ways.**
Is	55. 8	"are not like yours, and my **ways** are different from yours.
	55. 9	the earth, so high are my **ways** and thoughts above yours.
	58. 2	that they are eager to know my **ways** and obey my laws.
	63.17	Why do you let us stray from your **ways?**
	66. 3	They take pleasure in disgusting **ways** of worship.
Jer	10. 2	"Do not follow the **ways** of other nations;
	15. 7	I killed your children because you did not stop your evil **ways.**
	18.11	lives—to change their **ways** and the things they are doing.
	18.15	the way they should go, they no longer follow the old **ways;**
	26. 3	Perhaps the people will listen and give up their evil **ways.**
	35.15	to give up your evil **ways** and to do what is right.
	36. 3	to bring on them, they will turn from their evil **ways.**
	36. 7	and turn from their evil **ways,** because the Lord has
Lam	3.40	Let us examine our **ways** and turn back to the Lord.
Ezek	3.18	warn him to change his **ways** so that he can save his
	33. 8	warn him to change his **ways** so that he can save his
	33.31	Loving words are on their lips, but they continue their greedy **ways.**
Dan	8.25	Because he is cunning, he will succeed in his deceitful **ways.**
Hos	14. 9	The Lord's **ways** are right,
Lk	3.18	Good News to the people and urged them to change their **ways.**
Jn	7. 7	hates me, because I keep telling it that its **ways** are bad.
Acts	3.26	by making every one of you turn away from his wicked **ways."**
	17.30	all of them everywhere to turn away from their evil **ways.**
Rom	1.18	people whose evil **ways** prevent the truth from being known.
	11.33	Who can understand his **ways?**
1 Cor	13.11	I am a man, I have no more use for childish **ways.**
	15.34	Come back to your right senses and stop your sinful **ways.**
2 Cor	7. 9	you sad, but because your sadness made you change your **ways.**
2 Pet	2. 2	Even so, many will follow their immoral **ways;**
	2.13	in your meals, all the while enjoying their deceitful **ways!**
Jude	4	order to excuse their immoral **ways,** and who reject Jesus Christ,
Rev	15. 3	King of the nations, how right and true are your **ways!**
	16.11	But they did not turn from their evil **ways.**
	18. 5	up as high as heaven, and God remembers her wicked **ways.**

WEAK

Gen	30.42	he did not put the branches in front of the **weak** animals.
	30.42	Soon Laban had all the **weak** animals, and Jacob all the
	33.13	know that the children are **weak,** and I must think of the
	42. 9	you have come to find out where our country is **weak."**
	42.12	You have come to find out where our country is **weak."**
	47.13	and the people of Egypt and Canaan became **weak** with hunger.
Deut	32.31	that their own gods are **weak,** not mighty like Israel's God.
Judg	6.15	My clan is the **weakest** in the tribe of Manasseh, and I
	16. 7	that are not dried out, I'll be as **weak** as anybody else."
	16.11	have never been used, I'll be as **weak** as anybody else."
	16.13	it tight with a peg, I'll be as **weak** as anybody else."
	16.17	I would lose my strength and be as **weak** as anybody else."
1 Sam	2. 4	The bows of strong soldiers are broken, but the **weak** grow strong.
	14.24	The Israelites were **weak** with hunger that day, because
	14.28	men said, "We are all **weak** with hunger, but your father
	14.31	time the Israelites were very **weak** with hunger, [32]and so
	28.20	He was **weak,** because he had not eaten anything all day and
	30.21	men who had been too **weak** to go with him and had
2 Sam	3. 1	his opponents became **weaker and weaker.**
	3.39	though I am the king chosen by God, I feel **weak** today.

2 Kgs	19. 3	is ready to give birth, but is too **weak** to do it.
2 Chr	14.11	Lord, you can help a **weak** army as easily as a powerful
	28.15	Those who were too **weak** to walk were put on donkeys, and
Neh	4.10	"We grow **weak** carrying burdens;
Job	4. 4	When someone stumbled, **weak** and tired, your words encouraged him
	14. 1	We are all born **weak** and helpless.
	26. 1	help you are to me— poor, **weak** man that I am!
	30. 2	bunch of worn-out men, too **weak** to do any work for me.
	30.11	Because God has made me **weak** and helpless, they turn
	41.23	There is not a **weak** spot in his skin;
Ps	25.16	Lord, and be merciful to me, because I am lonely and **weak.**
	31.10	I am **weak** from all my troubles;
	35.10	You protect the **weak** from the strong, the poor from the oppressor."
	40.17	I am **weak** and poor, O Lord, but you have not forgotten
	69.23	Make their backs always **weak!**
	70. 5	I am **weak** and poor;
	72.13	He has pity on the **weak** and poor;
	73.26	mind and my body may grow **weak,** but God is my strength;
	86. 1	to me, Lord, and answer me, for I am helpless and **weak.**
	88. 9	my eyes are **weak** from suffering.
	102.23	The Lord has made me **weak** while I am still young;
	109.24	My knees are **weak** from lack of food;
Prov	24.10	If you are **weak** in a crisis, you are weak indeed.
	30.25	they are **weak,** but they store up their food in the summer.
Ecc	12. 3	will tremble, and your legs, now strong, will grow **weak.**
Song	2. 5	I am **weak** from passion.
	5. 8	find my lover, you will tell him I am **weak** from passion.
Is	14.10	call out to him, 'Now you are as **weak** as we are!
	16.14	people, only a few will survive, and they will be **weak."**
	24. 4	the whole world grows **weak;**
	31. 3	will crumble, and the **weak** nation it helped will fall.
	35. 3	that are tired and to knees that tremble with **weakness.**
	37. 3	is ready to give birth, but is too **weak** to do it.
	38.14	My voice was thin and **weak,** And I moaned like a dove.
	40.29	He strengthens those who are **weak** and tired.
	40.30	Even those who are young grow **weak;**
	40.31	they will walk and not grow **weak.**
	41.14	"Small and **weak** as you are, Israel, don't be afraid;
	41.29	do nothing at all— these idols are **weak** and powerless."
	50. 2	Am I too **weak** to save them?
	51.20	At the corner of every street your people collapse from **weakness;**
	57.10	idols give you strength, and so you never grow **weak.**
	59. 1	that the Lord is too **weak** to save you or too deaf
Jer	31.25	weary and will satisfy with food everyone who is **weak** from hunger.
	49.15	is going to make you **weak,** and no one will respect you.
	49.24	The people of Damascus are **weak** and have fled in terror.
	50.37	Death to its hired soldiers— how **weak** they are!
Lam	1. 6	are like deer that are **weak** from hunger, Whose strength is
	1.14	them round my neck, and I grew **weak** beneath the weight.
Ezek	7.17	Everyone's hands will be **weak,** and their knees will shake.
	29. 6	Egyptians for support, but you were no better than a **weak** stick.
	29.14	There they will be a **weak** kingdom, [15] the weakest kingdom of all,
	29.15	be a weak kingdom, [15] the **weakest** kingdom of all, and they
	30.25	Yes, I will **weaken** him and strengthen the king of Babylonia.
	34. 4	not taken care of the **weak** ones, healed those that are sick,
	34.20	I will judge between you strong sheep and the **weak** sheep.
Dan	2.42	part of the empire will be strong and part of it **weak.**
	10.16	"Sir, this vision makes me so **weak** that I can't stop trembling.
Joel	3.10	Even the **weak** must fight.
Amos	2. 7	They trample down the **weak** and helpless and push the poor
	4. 1	of Bashan, who ill-treat the **weak,** oppress the poor, and
	4. 8	**Weak** with thirst, the people of several cities went to a
	7. 2	They are so small and **weak!"**
	7. 5	They are so small and **weak!"**
Obad	2	The Lord says to Edom, "I will make you **weak;**
Hab	1. 4	The law is **weak** and useless, and justice is never done.
Zech	12. 8	in Jerusalem, and even the **weakest** among them will become as
Mt	26.41	The spirit is willing, but the flesh is **weak."**
Mk	14.38	The spirit is willing, but the flesh is **weak."**
Acts	20.35	way we must help the **weak,** remembering the words that the
Rom	4.19	but his faith did not **weaken** when he thought of his body,
	6.19	everyday language because of the **weakness** of your natural selves.)
	8. 3	the Law could not do, because human nature was **weak,** God
	8.26	way the Spirit also comes to help us, **weak** as we are.
	14. 1	Welcome the person who is **weak** in faith, but do not argue
	14. 2	the person who is **weak** in the faith eats only vegetables.
	15. 1	in the faith ought to help the **weak** to carry their burdens.
1 Cor	1.25	what seems to be God's **weakness** is stronger than human strength.
	1.27	the world considers **weak** in order to shame the powerful.
	2. 3	came to you, I was **weak** and trembled all over with fear,
	4.10	We are **weak,** but you are strong!
	8. 7	their conscience is **weak,** and they feel they are defiled by
	8. 9	action make those who are **weak** in the faith fall into sin.
	8.10	a person whose conscience is **weak** in this matter sees you,
	8.11	And so this **weak** person, your brother for whom Christ died,
	8.12	your Christian brothers and wounding their **weak** conscience.
	9.22	Among the **weak** in faith I become weak like one of them,
	11.30	why many of you are **weak** and ill, and several have died.
	12.22	do without the parts of the body that seem to be **weaker;**
	15.43	When buried, it is ugly and **weak;**
2 Cor	10.10	with us in person, he is **weak,** and his words are nothing!"
	11.29	When someone is **weak,** then I feel weak too;
	11.30	boast, I will boast about things that show how **weak** I am.
	12. 5	about myself, except the things that show how **weak** I am.
	12. 9	all you need, for my power is greatest when you are **weak."**
	12. 9	to be proud of my **weaknesses,** in order to feel the
2 Cor	12.10	I am content with **weaknesses,** insults, hardships,
	12.10	For when I am **weak,** then I am strong.
	13. 3	When he deals with you, he is not **weak;**
	13. 4	even though it was in **weakness** that he was put to death
	13. 4	In union with him we also are **weak;**
	13. 9	We are glad when we are **weak** but you are strong.
Gal	4. 9	want to turn back to those **weak** and pitiful ruling spirits?
Phil	3.21	He will change our **weak** mortal bodies and make them like
1 Thes	5.14	encourage the timid, help the **weak,** be patient with everyone.
2 Tim	3. 6	and gain control over **weak** women who are burdened by the
Heb	4.15	High Priest is not one who cannot feel sympathy for our **weaknesses.**
	5. 2	Since he himself is **weak** in many ways, he is able to
	5. 3	because he is himself **weak,** he must offer sacrifices not only
	7.18	rule, then, is set aside, because it was **weak** and useless.
	11.34	They were **weak,** but became strong;
1 Pet	3. 7	wives with the proper understanding that they are the **weaker** sex.
2 Pet	2.14	They lead **weak** people into a trap.

WEALTH

Gen	12. 5	nephew Lot, and all the **wealth** and all the slaves they had
	15.14	that foreign land, they will take great **wealth** with them.
	21.10	part of your **wealth,** which my son Isaac should inherit."
	30.43	In this way Jacob became very **wealthy.**
	31. 1	All his **wealth** has come from what our father owned."
	31.16	All this **wealth** which God has taken from our father
Ex	3.22	and daughters and carry away the **wealth** of the Egyptians."
	12.36	the Israelites carried away the **wealth** of the Egyptians.
	15. 9	I will divide their **wealth** and take all I want;
Num	31. 9	their flocks, plundered all their **wealth,** [10] and burnt all
Deut	8.17	have made yourselves **wealthy** by your own power and strength.
	33.18	on the sea, And may Issachar's **wealth** increase at home.
	33.19	They get their **wealth** from the sea And from the sand along
1 Sam	9. 1	There was a **wealthy** and influential man named Kish, from
1 Kgs	3.13	your life you will have **wealth** and honour, more than that of
	10. 7	wisdom and **wealth** are much greater than what I was told.
	13. 8	you gave me half your **wealth,** I would not go with you
2 Kgs	20.13	messengers and showed them his **wealth**—his silver and gold,
	23.35	people in proportion to their **wealth,** in order to raise the
1 Chr	29.12	All riches and **wealth** come from you;
	29.16	have brought together all this **wealth** to build a temple to
	29.28	at a ripe old age, **wealthy** and respected, and his son
2 Chr	1.11	Instead of asking for **wealth** or treasure or fame or the
	1.12	I will give you more **wealth,** treasure, and fame than any
	17. 5	him gifts, so that he became **wealthy** and highly honoured.
	32.27	King Hezekiah became very **wealthy,** and everyone held him in honour.
	32.29	cattle and so much other **wealth** that he built many cities.
	36.18	treasury, and the **wealth** of the king and his officials,
	36.19	its palaces and its **wealth,** and broke down the city wall.
Neh	9.25	fertile land, houses full of **wealth,** cisterns already dug,
Job	5. 5	among thorns— and thirsty people will envy his **wealth.**
	8. 7	All the **wealth** you lost will be nothing compared with what
	19. 9	He has taken away all my **wealth** and destroyed my reputation.
	20.15	The wicked man vomits up the **wealth** he stole;
	20.18	no chance to enjoy his **wealth,** [19] because he oppressed and
	20.28	All his **wealth** will be destroyed in the flood of God's anger.
	27.19	and when they wake up, they will find their **wealth** gone.
	31.25	I have never trusted in riches [25] or taken pride in my **wealth.**
Ps	37.16	is worth more than the **wealth** of all the wicked, [17] because
	39. 6	he gathers **wealth,** but doesn't know who will get it.
	49. 6	who trust in their riches and boast of their great **wealth.**
	49.13	who are satisfied with their **wealth**— [14] they are doomed to
	49.16	a man becomes rich, when his **wealth** grows even greater;
	49.17	his **wealth** will not go with him to the grave.
	52. 7	trusted instead in his great **wealth** and looked for security
	112. 3	His family will be **wealthy** and rich, and he will be
	119.14	I delight in following your commands more than in having great **wealth.**
Prov	3.16	Wisdom offers you long life, as well as **wealth** and honour.
	5.10	strangers will take all your **wealth,** and what you have
	8.21	paths of justice, [21] giving **wealth** to those who love me,
	10. 2	**Wealth** that you get by dishonesty will do you no good, but
	10.15	**Wealth** protects the rich;
	10.22	It is the Lord's blessing that makes you **wealthy.**
	11.28	Those who depend on their **wealth** will fall like the
	13.11	easily you get your **wealth,** the sooner you will lose it.
	13.22	A good man will have **wealth** to leave to his grandchildren,
	13.22	but the **wealth** of sinners will go to righteous
	14.24	Wise people are rewarded with **wealth,** but fools are
	15. 6	Righteous men keep their **wealth,** but wicked men lose
	18.11	however, imagine that their **wealth** protects them like high,
	20.21	more easily you get your **wealth,** the less good it will do
	21.17	luxuries, wine, and rich food will never make you **wealthy.**
	21.20	Wise people live in **wealth** and luxury, but stupid people
	22. 1	good reputation and great **wealth,** choose a good reputation.
	27.24	carefully as you can, [24] because **wealth** is not permanent.
	28. 8	taking advantage of people, your **wealth** will go to someone
Ecc	4. 8	is always working, never satisfied with the **wealth** he has.
	5.19	If God gives a man **wealth** and property and lets him
	6. 2	God will give someone **wealth,** honour, and property,
Song	8. 7	to buy love with his **wealth,** contempt is all he would get.
Is	8. 4	'Mummy' and 'Daddy,' all the **wealth** of Damascus and all the
	9. 3	harvest their corn or when they divide captured **wealth.**
	10. 3	Where will you hide your **wealth?**
	10.14	and I gathered their **wealth** as easily as gathering eggs.
	16.14	"In exactly three years Moab's great **wealth** will disappear.
	17. 4	come to an end, and its **wealth** will be replaced by poverty.
	33.22	We will seize all the **wealth** of enemy armies, and there will
	39. 2	messengers and showed them his **wealth**—his silver and gold,

Is 45.14 “The **wealth** of Egypt and Sudan will be yours, and the tall
60. 5 The **wealth** of the nations will be brought to you;
60.11 So that the kings of the nations May bring you their **wealth.**
61. 6 You will enjoy the **wealth** of the nations And be proud that
61. 7 live in your own land, And your **wealth** will be doubled;
66.12 the **wealth** of the nations will flow to you like a river
Jer 9.23 strong men of their strength, nor rich men of their **wealth.**
15.13 enemies to carry away the **wealth** and treasures of my people,
17. 3 your enemies take away your **wealth** and your treasures
20. 5 their enemies plunder all the **wealth** of this city and seize
48. 7 in your strength and your **wealth,** but now even you will be
Ezek 7.11 nothing of their **wealth,** their splendour, or their glory.
7.20 That is why the Lord has made their **wealth** repulsive to them.
7.21 “and law-breakers will take all their **wealth** and defile it.
22.29 The **wealthy** cheat and rob.
26.12 Your enemies will help themselves to your **wealth** and merchandise.
27.27 All your **wealth** of merchandise, All the sailors in your crew,
27.33 Kings were made rich By the **wealth** of your goods.
28. 5 How proud you are of your **wealth!**
29.19 and carry off all the **wealth** of Egypt as his army's pay.
30.10 King Nebuchadnezzar of Babylonia to put an end to Egypt's **wealth.**
30.15 I will destroy the **wealth** of Thebes.
Dan 11. 2 height of his power and **wealth** he will challenge the kingdom
11.20 with taxes in order to increase the **wealth** of his kingdom.
11.24 He will invade a **wealthy** province without warning and
Obad 11 off Jerusalem's **wealth** and divided it among themselves.
Mic 4.13 crush many nations, and the **wealth** they got by violence you
Nah 3. 1 murderous city, full of **wealth** to be looted and plundered!
Hab 2. 5 **Wealth** is deceitful.
Zeph 1.13 Their **wealth** will be looted and their houses destroyed.
Hag 2. 7 be brought here, and the Temple will be filled with **wealth.**
Zech 9. 4 He will throw her **wealth** into the sea, and the city will
14.14 will take as loot the **wealth** of all the nations—gold,
Mt 6.29 King Solomon with all his **wealth** had clothes as beautiful as
Lk 4. 6 all this power and all this **wealth,**” the Devil told him.
12.27 King Solomon with all his **wealth** had clothes as beautiful as
16. 9 for yourselves with worldly **wealth,** so that when it gives out,
16.11 been faithful in handling worldly **wealth,**
16.11 how can you be trusted with true **wealth?**
Eph 3.16 I ask God from the **wealth** of his glory to give you
Phil 4.19 with all his abundant **wealth** through Christ Jesus, my God will
Col 2. 2 the full **wealth** of assurance which true understanding brings.
Rev 5.12 is worthy to receive power, **wealth,** wisdom, and strength, honour,
18.14 have disappeared, and all your **wealth** and glamour are gone,
18.17 And in one hour she has lost all this **wealth!**”
18.19 who have ships sailing the seas became rich on her **wealth!**
21.24 and the kings of the earth will bring their **wealth** into it.
21.26 The greatness and the **wealth** of the nations will be brought

WEANED

Gen 21. 8 on the day that he was **weaned,** Abraham gave a great feast.
1 Sam 1.22 soon as the child is **weaned,** I will take him to the
1.23 stay at home until you have **weaned** him.
1.24 After she had **weaned** him, she took him to Shiloh,
Is 28. 9 It's only good for babies that have just been **weaned!**
Hos 1. 8 After Gomer had **weaned** her daughter, she became pregnant

WEAPON

Gen 49. 5 They use their **weapons** to commit violence.
Num 35.16 however, a man uses a **weapon** of iron or stone or wood
Judg 9.54 man who was carrying his **weapons** and ordered, “Draw your
1 Sam 8.12 and make his **weapons** and the equipment for his chariots.
14. 1 young man who carried his **weapons,** “Let's go across to the
14.17 Jonathan and the young man who carried his **weapons** were missing.
16.21 very much and chose him as the man to carry his **weapons.**
17.54 Jerusalem, but he kept Goliath's **weapons** in his own tent.
20.40 Jonathan gave his **weapons** to the boy and told him to
21. 8 I didn't have time to get my sword or any other **weapon.**”
21. 9 If you want it, take it—it's the only **weapon** here.”
31. 4 man carrying his **weapons,** “Draw your sword and kill me,
31.10 Then they put his **weapons** in the temple of the goddess Astarte,
2 Sam 1.27 “The brave soldiers have fallen, their **weapons** abandoned
1 Kgs 10.25 gift—articles of silver and gold, robes, **weapons,** spices,
2 Kgs 10. 2 disposal chariots, horses, **weapons,** and fortified cities.
1 Chr 10. 4 man carrying his **weapons,** “Draw your sword and kill me,
10.10 They put his **weapons** in one of their temples and hung
12.23 men ready to fight, trained to use all kinds of **weapons;**
12.23 120,000 men trained to use all kinds of **weapons.**
2 Chr 9.24 gifts—articles of silver and gold, robes, **weapons,** spices,
Neh 4.17 one hand and kept a **weapon** in the other, [18] and everyone
4.23 And we all kept our **weapons** to hand.
Job 39.23 The **weapons** which their riders carry rattle and flash in the sun.
Ps 7.13 he takes up his deadly **weapons** and aims his burning arrows.
76. 3 enemy, their shields and swords, yes, all their **weapons.**
89.43 You have made his **weapons** useless and let him be
Prov 26.18 only joking is like a madman playing with a deadly **weapon.**
Ecc 9.18 Wisdom does more good than **weapons,** but one sinner can
Is 22. 8 When that happened, you brought **weapons** out of the arsenal.
29. 7 of God's altar, all their **weapons** and
54.16 “I create the blacksmith, who builds a fire and forges **weapons.**
54.16 I also create the soldier, who uses the **weapons** to kill.
54.17 But no **weapon** will be able to hurt you;
Jer 21. 4 pile up your soldiers' **weapons** in the centre of the city.
50.25 opened the place where my **weapons** are stored, and in my
51.20 “Babylonia, you are my hammer, my **weapon** of war.
Ezek 9. 1 Bring your **weapons** with you.”
9. 2 outer north gate of the Temple, each one carrying a **weapon.**
14.17 that country and send destructive **weapons** to wipe out people
39. 9 Israel will go out and collect the abandoned **weapons** for firewood.
39.10 because they will have the abandoned **weapons** to burn.
Hos 2.18 I will also remove all **weapons** of war from the land, all
Amos 2.16 even the bravest soldiers will drop their **weapons** and run.”
Lk 11.21 strong man, with all his **weapons** ready, guards his own house,
11.22 he carries away all the **weapons** the owner was depending on
Rom 13.12 dark, and let us take up **weapons** for fighting in the light.
13.14 But take up the **weapons** of the Lord Jesus Christ, and
2 Cor 6. 7 We have righteousness as our **weapon,** both to attack and to
10. 4 **weapons** we use in our fight are not the world's weapons
10. 4 but God's powerful **weapons,** which we use to destroy strongholds.
1 Tim 1.18 Use those words as **weapons** in order to fight well,

WEAR (1)

[WORE]

Gen 35. 4 that they had and also the ear-rings that they were **wearing.**
38.14 clothes she had been **wearing,** covered her face with a veil,
Ex 28.29 the Holy Place, he will **wear** this breast-piece engraved with
28.30 such times he must always **wear** this breast-piece, so that he
28.35 Aaron is to **wear** this robe when he serves as priest.
28.38 Aaron is to **wear** it on his forehead, so that I, the
28.43 and his sons must always **wear** them when they go into the
29.29 after his death, for them to **wear** when they are ordained.
29.30 in the Holy Place is to **wear** these garments for seven days.
32. 2 and your daughters are **wearing,** and bring them to me.”
33. 4 they began to mourn and did not **wear** jewellery any more.
33. 6 Mount Sinai, the people of Israel no longer **wore** jewellery.
35.19 garments the priests are to **wear** when they serve in the Holy
39. 1 which the priests were to **wear** when they served in the Holy
39.41 garments the priests were to **wear** in the Holy Place—the
Lev 6.10 Then the priest, **wearing** his linen robe and linen shorts,
13.45 must **wear** torn clothes, leave his hair uncombed,
19.19 Do not **wear** clothes made of two kinds of material.
21.10 and has been consecrated to **wear** the priestly garments, so
Deut 6. 8 them on your arms and **wear** them on your foreheads as a
11.18 them on your arms and **wear** them on your foreheads as a
22. 5 “Women are not to **wear** men's clothing,
22. 5 and men are not to **wear** women's clothing;
22.11 “Do not **wear** cloth made by weaving wool and linen together.
Judg 8.24 (The Midianites, like other desert people, **wore** gold earrings.)
8.26 that the kings of Midian **wore,** nor the collars that were
1 Sam 2.18 Samuel continued to serve the Lord, **wearing** a sacred linen apron.
2.28 to burn the incense, and to **wear** the ephod to consult me.
17. 5 nearly three metres tall [5] and **wore** bronze armour that
17.38 He gave his own armour to David for him to **wear:**
17.39 but he couldn't, because he wasn't used to **wearing** them.
18. 4 off the robe he was **wearing** and gave it to David, together
28.14 “He is **wearing** a cloak.”
2 Sam 3.31 to tear their clothes, **wear** sackcloth, and mourn for Abner.
6.14 David, **wearing** only a linen cloth round his waist,
13.18 Tamar was **wearing** a long robe with full sleeves, the usual
21.16 half kilogrammes and who was **wearing** a new sword, thought he
1 Kgs 10. 5 staff and the uniforms they **wore,** the servants who waited on
11.30 the new robe he was **wearing,** tore it into twelve pieces,
22.30 I will disguise myself, but you **wear** your royal garments.”
2 Kgs 1. 8 “He was **wearing** a cloak made of animal skins, tied with
6.30 could see that he was **wearing** sackcloth under his clothes.
19. 2 They also were **wearing** sackcloth.
1 Chr 15.27 David was **wearing** a robe made of the finest linen, and
15.27 David also **wore** a linen ephod.
21.16 people—all of whom were **wearing** sackcloth—bowed low, with
2 Chr 5.11 and the members of their clans—were **wearing** linen clothing.
9. 4 staff and the uniforms they **wore,** the clothing of the
18.29 I will disguise myself, but you **wear** your royal garments.”
20.21 put on the robes they **wore** on sacred occasions and to march
28.15 them clothes and sandals to **wear,** gave them enough to eat
Ezra 9. 5 had been grieving, and still **wearing** my torn clothes, I
Neh 4.16 worked and half stood guard, **wearing** coats of armour and
5.13 off the sash I was **wearing** round my waist and shook it
9. 1 They **wore** sackcloth and put dust on their heads as signs of
Esth 1.11 He ordered them to bring in Queen Vashti, **wearing** her royal crown.
2.13 the harem to the palace, she could **wear** whatever she wanted.
2.15 When her turn came, she **wore** just what Hegai,
2.15 the eunuch in charge of the harem, advised her to **wear.**
4. 2 go in because no one **wearing** sackcloth was allowed inside.
6. 7 to be brought for this man—robes that you yourself **wear.**
8.15 Mordecai left the palace, **wearing** royal robes of blue and white,
Job 16.15 I mourn and **wear** clothes made of sackcloth, and I sit
22. 6 you took away his clothes and left him nothing to **wear.**
27.17 but some good man will **wear** the clothes, and some honest
31.36 could see them, [36] I would **wear** them proudly on my shoulder
41.13 can tear off his outer coat or pierce the armour he **wears.**
Ps 45. 9 throne stands the queen, **wearing** ornaments of finest gold.
73. 6 And so they **wear** pride like a necklace and violence like a
109.29 may they **wear** their shame like a robe.
Prov 23.21 you do is eat and sleep, you will soon be **wearing** rags.
31.22 She makes bedspreads and **wears** clothes of fine purple linen.
Song 3.11 He is **wearing** the crown that his mother placed on his head
4. 9 and the necklace you are **wearing** have stolen my heart.
5.14 His hands are well-formed, and he **wears** rings set with gems.
Is 3. 6 at least have something to **wear,** so be our leader in this
3.18 the ornaments they **wear** on their ankles, on their heads,
3.20 magic charms they **wear** on their arms and at their waists;
3.21 the rings they **wear** on their fingers and in their noses;
3.23 and the scarves and long veils they **wear** on their heads.
3.24 instead of fine belts, they will **wear** coarse ropes;
20. 2 Amoz to take off his sandals and the sackcloth he was **wearing.**

Is 22.12 to weep and mourn, to shave your heads and **wear** sackcloth.
37. 2 They also were **wearing** sackcloth.
58. 7 those who have nothing to **wear,** and do not refuse to help
59.17 He will **wear** justice like a coat of armour and saving
Jer 48.37 gashes on their hands, and everyone is **wearing** sackcloth.
Ezek 9.11 the man **wearing** linen clothes returned and reported to the Lord,
10. 2 God said to the man **wearing** linen clothes, "Go between
10. 6 the Lord commanded the man **wearing** linen clothes to take
13.18 magic scarves for everyone to **wear** on their heads, so that
16.12 you a nose-ring and earrings and a beautiful crown to **wear.**
16.13 and you always **wore** clothes of embroidered linen and silk.
28.13 in Eden, the garden of God, and **wore** gems of every kind:
34. 3 You drink the milk, **wear** clothes made from the wool, and
42.14 rooms the holy clothing they **wore** while serving the Lord.
44.17 They must not **wear** anything made of wool when they are on
44.18 perspire, they are to **wear** linen turbans and linen trousers,
44.19 take off the clothes they **wore** on duty in the Temple and
Dan 5. 7 in robes of royal purple, **wear** a gold chain of honour round
5.16 in robes of royal purple, **wear** a gold chain of honour round
9. 3 pleading with him, fasting, **wearing** sackcloth,
10. 5 and saw someone who was **wearing** linen clothes and a belt of
12. 1 The angel **wearing** linen clothes said, "At that time the
Amos 8.10 you shave your heads and **wear** sackcloth, and you will be
Jon 3. 8 All persons and animals must **wear** sackcloth.
Nah 2. 3 The enemy soldiers carry red shields and **wear** uniforms of red.
Zech 3. 3 Joshua was standing there, **wearing** filthy clothes.
3. 4 "Take away the filthy clothes this man is **wearing."**
3. 4 away your sin and will give you new clothes to **wear."**
13. 4 act like a prophet, or **wear** a prophet's coarse garment in
Mt 3. 4 he **wore** a leather belt round his waist, and his food was
22.11 guests and saw a man who was not **wearing** wedding clothes.
23. 5 verses on them which they **wear** on their foreheads and arms,
Mk 1. 6 John **wore** clothes made of camel's hair, with a leather
6. 9 **Wear** sandals, but don't carry an extra shirt."
16. 5 man sitting on the right, **wearing** a white robe—and they were
Jn 19. 5 So Jesus came out, **wearing** the crown of thorns and the
1 Cor 15.49 Just as we **wear** the likeness of the man made of earth,
15.49 so we will **wear** the likeness of the Man from
1 Thes 5. 8 We must **wear** faith and love as a breastplate, and our hope
Jas 2. 2 Suppose a rich man **wearing** a gold ring and fine clothes
1 Pet 3. 3 hair, or the jewellery you put on, or the dresses you **wear.**
Rev 1.13 looked like a human being, **wearing** a robe that reached to
4. 4 twenty-four elders dressed in white and **wearing** crowns of gold.
19. 8 She has been given clean shining linen to **wear."**
19.12 a flame of fire, and he **wore** many crowns on his head.
19.13 The robe he **wore** was covered with blood.

WEAR (2)
[WORE OUT, WORN-OUT]

Gen 18.12 that I am old and **worn out,** can I still enjoy sex?
Ex 18.18 You will **wear yourself out** and these people as well.
18.23 commands, you will not **wear yourself out,** and all these
Deut 8. 4 years your clothes have not **worn out,** nor have your feet
29. 5 the desert, and your clothes and sandals never **wore out.**
Josh 9. 4 their donkeys with **worn-out** sacks and patched-up wineskins.
9. 5 put on ragged clothes and **worn-out** sandals that had been mended.
9.13 Our clothes and sandals are **worn out** from the long journey."
2 Sam 16.14 and all his men were **worn out** when they reached the Jordan,
Neh 9.21 their clothing never **wore out,** and their feet were not
Job 14.19 Water will **wear down** rocks, and heavy rain will wash
16. 7 You have **worn me out,** God;
30. 2 They were a bunch of **worn-out** men, too weak to do any
36.14 while they are still young, **worn out** by a life of disgrace.
Ps 6. 2 I am **worn out,** O Lord;
6. 6 I am **worn out** with grief;
31. 9 I am completely **worn out.**
32. 3 confess my sins, I was **worn out** from crying all day long.
38. 8 I am **worn out** and utterly crushed;
55. 2 I am **worn out** by my worries.
63. 1 like a dry, **worn-out,** and waterless land, my soul is
68. 9 caused abundant rain to fall and restored your **worn-out** land;
69. 3 I am **worn out** from calling for help, and my throat is
88.15 I am **worn out** from the burden of your punishments.
102.26 they will all **wear out** like clothes.
107.12 They were **worn out** from hard work;
119.81 I am **worn out,** Lord, waiting for you to save me;
Prov 23. 4 Be wise enough not to **wear yourself out** trying to get rich.
Ecc 10.15 to find his way home would **wear himself out** with work.
12.12 the writing of books, and too much study will **wear you out.**
Is 7.13 bad enough for you to **wear out** the patience of men—
7.13 must you **wear out** God's patience too?
16.12 The people of Moab **wear themselves out** going to their
43.23 demanding offerings or **wear you out** by asking for incense.
43.24 you **wore me out** with the wrongs you committed.
51. 6 the earth will **wear out** like old clothing, and all its
57.10 You **wear yourselves out** looking for other gods, but you
Jer 2.25 Israel, don't **wear your feet out,** or let your throat
38.11 palace storeroom and got some **worn-out** clothing which he let
45. 3 I am **worn out** from groaning, and I can't find any rest!'
Lam 2.11 My eyes are **worn out** with weeping;
2.18 **Wear yourself out** with weeping and grief!
Ezek 23.43 were using as a prostitute a woman **worn out** by adultery.
Hab 2.13 The nations you conquered **wore themselves out** in useless labour,
Lk 12.33 for yourselves purses that don't **wear out,** and save your riches
18. 5 I don't, she will keep on coming and finally **wear me out!'"**
22.45 disciples and found them asleep, **worn out** by their grief.
1 Cor 4.12 we **wear ourselves out** with hard work.
Heb 1.11 they will all **wear out** like clothes.
8.13 anything that becomes old and **worn out** will soon disappear.

WEARY

Ecc 1. 5 it still goes down, going **wearily** back to where it must
1. 8 Everything leads to **weariness**—a weariness too great for words.
Is 40.28 He never grows tired or **weary.**
40.31 they will run and not get **weary;**
50. 4 taught me what to say, so that I can strengthen the **weary.**
Jer 31.25 will refresh those who are **weary** and will satisfy with food

WEATHER

Ezra 10. 9 hard, and because of the **weather** and the importance of the
Ecc 11. 4 until the wind and the **weather** are just right, you will
Jer 17. 8 when hot **weather** comes, because its leaves stay green;
Mt 16. 2 'We are going to have fine **weather,** because the sky is red.'
16. 3 You can predict the **weather** by looking at the sky, but you
Lk 12.56 can look at the earth and the sky and predict the **weather;**

WEAVE
[INTERWOVEN, LINEN-WEAVERS, WOVE, WOVEN]

Ex 26. 1 ten pieces of fine linen **woven** with blue, purple, and red
26.31 a curtain of fine linen **woven** with blue, purple, and red
26.36 a curtain of fine linen **woven** with blue, purple, and red
27.16 long made of fine linen **woven** with blue, purple, and red
28. 8 A finely **woven** belt made of the same materials is to be
28.27 of the ephod near the seam and above the finely **woven** belt.
28.32 be reinforced with a **woven** binding to keep it from tearing.
28.39 **"Weave** Aaron's shirt of fine linen and make a turban of
35.35 done by engravers, designers, and **weavers** of fine linen;
36. 8 ten pieces of fine linen **woven** with blue, purple, and red
36.35 a curtain of fine linen, **woven** with blue, purple, and red
36.37 a curtain of fine linen **woven** with blue, purple, and red
38.18 was made of fine linen **woven** with blue, purple, and red wool
38.23 a designer, and a **weaver** of fine linen and of blue,
39. 5 The finely **woven** belt, made of the same materials, was
39.20 of the ephod, near the seam and above the finely **woven** belt.
39.23 was reinforced with a **woven** binding to keep it from tearing.
Lev 8. 7 it by putting its finely **woven** belt round his waist.
Deut 22.11 "Do not wear cloth made by **weaving** wool and linen together.
Judg 16.13 He answered, "If you **weave** my seven locks of hair into a
16.14 took his seven locks of hair, and **wove** them into the loom.
1 Sam 17. 7 as the bar on a **weaver's** loom, and its iron head weighed
2 Sam 21.19 had a shaft as thick as the bar on a **weaver's** loom.
1 Kgs 7.17 decorated with a design of **interwoven** chains,
7.40 The design of **interwoven** chains on each capital
2 Kgs 23. 7 (It was there that women **wove** robes used in the worship of
1 Chr 4.21 clan of **linen-weavers,** who lived in the town of Beth Ashbea;
20. 5 had a shaft as thick as the bar on a **weaver's** loom.
2 Chr 3.16 decorated with a design of **interwoven** chains and one hundred
4.11 The design of **interwoven** chains on each capital
Job 7. 6 My days pass by without hope, pass faster than a **weaver's** shuttle.
Prov 31.19 She spins her own thread and **weaves** her own cloth.
Song 3.10 purple cloth, lovingly **woven** by the women of Jerusalem.
Is 19.10 **weavers** and skilled workmen will be broken and depressed.
Jer 10. 9 in violet and purple cloth **woven** by skilled weavers.
10. 9 in violet and purple cloth woven by skilled **weavers.**
Jn 19.23 made of one piece of **woven** cloth without any seams in it.

WEB

Job 8.14 They trust a thread—a spider's **web.**
8.15 If they lean on a **web,** will it hold them up?
27.18 build houses like a spider's **web** or like the hut of a

WEDDING

Gen 29.22 So Laban gave a **wedding-feast** and invited everyone.
Deut 22.15 are to take the blood-stained **wedding** sheet that proves the
22.17 look at the bloodstains on the **wedding** sheet!'
Josh 15.18 On the **wedding** day Othniel urged her to ask her father
Judg 1.14 On the **wedding** day Othniel urged her to ask her father
14.12 before the seven days of the **wedding feast** are over."
14.20 to the man that had been his best man at the **wedding.**
1 Sam 18.26 the day set for the **wedding,** [27] David and his men went and
1 Kgs 9.16 he gave it as a **wedding** present to his daughter when she
Song 3.11 on his head on his **wedding** day, the day of his
Is 61.10 She is like a bride dressed for her **wedding.**
Jer 2.32 Does a young woman forget her jewellery, or a bride her **wedding-dress?**
7.34 joy and gladness and to the happy sounds of **wedding feasts.**
16. 9 of joy and gladness and the happy sounds of **wedding feasts.**
25.10 of joy and gladness and the happy sounds of **wedding feasts.**
33.11 of gladness and joy and the happy sounds of **wedding feasts.**
Mt 9.15 expect the guests at a **wedding party** to be sad as long
11.17 the other, [17] 'We played **wedding** music for you, but you wouldn't
22. 2 there was a king who prepared a **wedding feast** for his son.
22. 4 Come to the **wedding feast!'**
22. 8 and said to them, 'My **wedding feast** is ready, but the people
22.10 and the **wedding** hall was filled with people.
22.11 guests and saw a man who was not wearing **wedding** clothes.
22.12 'Friend, how did you get in here without **wedding** clothes?'
25.10 in with him to the **wedding feast,** and the door was closed.
Mk 2.19 you expect the guests at a **wedding party** to go without food?
Lk 5.34 make the guests at a **wedding party** go without food as long
7.32 the other, 'We played **wedding** music for you, but you wouldn't
12.36 waiting for their master to come back from a **wedding feast.**
14. 8 someone invites you to a **wedding feast,** do not sit down in

Jn 2. 1 days later there was a **wedding** in the town of Cana
2. 2 and Jesus and his disciples had also been invited to the **wedding.**
Rev 19. 7 time has come for the **wedding** of the Lamb, and his bride
19. 9 those who have been invited to the **wedding-feast** of the Lamb."

WEDLOCK

Deut 23. 2 "No one born out of **wedlock** or any descendant of such a

WEED

Gen 3.18 It will produce **weeds** and thorns, and you will have to
Ex 22. 6 and it spreads through the **weeds** to another man's field and
Deut 29.23 nothing will be planted, and not even **weeds** will grow there.
2 Kgs 19.26 grass in a field or **weeds** growing on a roof when the
Job 8.16 Evil men sprout like **weeds** in the sun,
8.16 like **weeds** that spread all through the garden.
24.24 then he withers like a **weed,** like an ear of corn that
31.40 then instead of wheat and barley, may **weeds** and thistles grow.
41.20 out of his nose, like smoke from **weeds** burning under a pot.
Ps 58. 7 may they be crushed like **weeds** on a path.
58. 9 Before they know it, they are cut down like **weeds;**
90. 5 We are like **weeds** that sprout in the morning, [6] that grow
92. 7 the wicked may grow like **weeds,** those who do wrong may prosper;
Prov 24.31 They were full of thorn bushes and overgrown with **weeds.**
Is 5. 6 I will let it be overgrown with **weeds.**
37.27 grass in a field or **weeds** growing on a roof when the
Jer 12.13 My people sowed wheat, but gathered **weeds;**
Hos 9. 6 once stood will be overgrown with **weeds** and thorn-bushes.
10. 4 injustice, growing like poisonous **weeds** in a ploughed field.
10. 8 Thorns and **weeds** will grow up over their altars.
13.15 Even though Israel flourishes like **weeds,** I will send a
Mic 7. 4 the best and most honest of them are as worthless as **weeds.**
Zeph 2. 9 of salt pits and everlasting ruin, overgrown with **weeds.**
Mt 13.25 an enemy came and sowed **weeds** among the wheat and went away.
13.26 the ears of corn began to form, then the **weeds** showed up.
13.27 where did the **weeds** come from?'
13.28 'Do you want us to go and pull up the **weeds?'**
13.29 'because as you gather the **weeds** you might pull up some of
13.30 Let the wheat and the **weeds** both grow together until harvest.
13.30 workers to pull up the **weeds** first, tie them in bundles
13.36 "Tell us what the parable about the **weeds** in the field means."
13.38 the **weeds** are the people who belong to the Evil One;
13.39 and the enemy who sowed the **weeds** is the Devil.
13.40 Just as the **weeds** are gathered up and burnt in the fire,
Heb 6. 8 But if it grows thorns and **weeds,** it is worth nothing;

WEEK

Gen 24.55 girl stay with us a **week** or ten days, and then she
29.27 Wait until the **week's** marriage celebrations are over,
29.28 and when the **week** of marriage celebrations was over,
Ex 23.12 "Work six days a **week,** but do no work on the seventh
Lev 23.15 Count seven full **weeks** from the day after the Sabbath on
Num 12.14 of the camp for a **week,** and after that she can be
Deut 16. 9 "Count seven **weeks** from the time that you begin to
2 Sam 12.18 A **week** later the child died, and David's officials were
Esth 1. 5 It lasted a whole **week** and was held in the gardens of
Prov 7.20 plenty of money with him and won't be back for two **weeks."**
Ezek 43.27 When the **week** is over, the priests are to begin offering
Dan 10. 2 At that time, I was mourning for three **weeks.**
10. 3 any wine, or comb my hair until the three **weeks** were past.
Lk 1.59 When the baby was a **week** old, they came to circumcise him,
2.21 A **week** later, when the time came for the baby to be
9.28 About a **week** after he had said these things, Jesus took Peter,
18.12 I fast two days a **week,** and I give you a tenth
Jn 20.26 A **week** later the disciples were together again indoors,
Acts 7. 8 So Abraham circumcised Isaac a **week** after he was born;
20. 6 days later we joined them in Troas, where we spent a **week.**
21. 4 There we found some believers and stayed with them a **week.**
28.14 some believers there who asked us to stay with them a **week.**
Gal 1.18 information from Peter, and I stayed with him for two **weeks.**
Phil 3. 5 I was circumcised when I was a **week** old.

WEEP
[WEPT]

Gen 35. 8 So it was named "Oak of **Weeping."**
45.15 Then, still **weeping,** he embraced each of his brothers
2 Sam 3.32 at Hebron, and the king **wept** aloud at the grave,
3.34 And the people **wept** for him again.
12.21 the child was alive, you **wept** for him and would not eat;
12.22 David answered, "I did fast and **weep** while he was still alive.
13.36 crying, and David and his officials also **wept** bitterly.
15.30 David went on up the Mount of Olives **weeping;**
15.30 All who followed him covered their heads and **wept** also.
18.33 He went up to the room over the gateway and **wept.**
19. 1 Joab was told that King David was **weeping** and mourning for Absalom.
2 Kgs 13.14 he exclaimed as he **wept.**
22.19 me, tearing your clothes and **weeping,** when you heard how I
2 Chr 34.27 me, tearing your clothes and **weeping,** when you heard how I
Ezra 10. 1 in front of the Temple, **weeping** and confessing these sins,
10. 1 Israelites—men, women, and children—gathered round him, **weeping** bitterly.
Neh 1. 4 When I heard all this, I sat down and **wept.**
Esth 4. 3 They fasted, **wept** and wailed, and most of them put on
Job 2.12 they did, they began to **weep** and wail, tearing their clothes
30.25 Didn't I **weep** with people in trouble and feel sorry for
30.31 I heard joyful music, now I hear only mourning and **weeping.**
Ps 6. 6 every night my bed is damp from my **weeping;**
6. 7 my eyes are so swollen from the **weeping** caused by my enemies.
6. 8 The Lord hears my **weeping;**
31.10 I am exhausted by sorrow, and **weeping** has shortened my life.
39.12 come to my aid when I **weep.**
126. 5 Let those who **wept** as they sowed their seed, gather the
126. 6 Those who **wept** as they went out carrying the seed will
137. 1 there we **wept** when we remembered Zion.
Ecc 4. 1 The oppressed were **weeping,** and no one would help them.
Is 15. 2 The people of Dibon climb the hill to **weep** at the shrine.
15. 5 Some climb the road to Luhith, **weeping** as they go;
16. 7 The people of Moab will **weep** because of the troubles they suffer.
16. 7 They will all **weep** when they remember the fine food
16. 9 Now I **weep** for Sibmah's vines as I weep for Jazer.
22. 4 Now leave me alone to **weep** bitterly over all those of my
22.12 was calling you then to **weep** and mourn, to shave your heads
29. 2 There will be **weeping** and wailing, and the whole city will
30.19 You people who live in Jerusalem will not **weep** any more.
32.13 **Weep** for all the houses where people were happy and for the
65.19 There will be no **weeping** there, no calling for help.
Jer 4. 8 So put on sackcloth, and **weep** and wail because the fierce
9.10 mourn for the mountains and **weep** for the pastures, because
14.17 night, may I never stop **weeping,** for my people are deeply
22.10 People of Judah, do not **weep** for King Josiah;
22.10 But **weep** bitterly for Joahaz, his son;
22.18 No one will **weep** for him or cry, 'My lord!
31. 9 My people will return **weeping,** praying as I lead them back.
31.15 "A sound is heard in Ramah, the sound of bitter **weeping.**
41. 6 Ishmael went out from Mizpah to meet them, **weeping** as he went.
48.20 'Moab has fallen,' they will answer, '**weep** for it;
48.31 And so I will **weep** for everyone in Moab and for the
50. 4 both Israel and Judah will come **weeping,** looking for me,
Lam 2.11 My eyes are worn out with **weeping;**
2.18 Wear yourself out with **weeping** and grief!
Ezek 8.14 Temple and showed me women **weeping** over the death of the god
27.31 Their hearts are bitter as they **weep.**
Hos 10. 5 They and the priests who serve the idol will **weep** over it.
12. 4 He **wept** and asked for a blessing.
Joel 1. 5 Wake up and **weep,** you drunkards;
1.13 Put on sackcloth and **weep,** you priests who serve at the altar!
2.12 return to me with fasting and **weeping** and mourning.
2.17 altar and the entrance of the Temple, must **weep** and pray:
Mic 1.10 don't let them see you **weeping.**
Zech 11. 2 **Weep** and wail, cypress-trees— the cedars have fallen;
11. 2 **Weep** and wail, oaks of Bashan— the dense forest has been
Mal 2.13 the Lord's altar with tears, **weeping** and wailing because he
Mt 2.18 "A sound is heard in Ramah, the sound of bitter **weeping.**
24.30 the peoples of earth will **weep** as they see the Son of
26.75 He went out and **wept** bitterly.
Lk 6.21 "Happy are you who **weep** now;
6.25 you will mourn and **weep!**
19.41 when he saw it, he **wept** over it, [42] saying, "If you only
22.62 Peter went out and **wept** bitterly.
23.27 them were some women who were **weeping** and wailing for him.
Jn 11.31 They thought that she was going to the grave to **weep** there.
11.33 Jesus saw her **weeping,** and he saw how
11.33 the people who were with her were **weeping** also;
11.35 Jesus **wept.**
16.20 you will cry and **weep,** but the world will be glad;
Rom 12.15 Be happy with those who are happy, **weep** with those who weep.
1 Cor 7.30 those who **weep,** as though they were not sad;
2 Cor 12.21 your presence, and I shall **weep** over many who sinned in the
Jas 4. 9 Be sorrowful, cry, and **weep;**
5. 1 **Weep** and wail over the miseries that are coming upon you!
Rev 18. 9 and lust will cry and **weep** over the city when they see

WEIGH

Gen 23.16 Abraham agreed and **weighed** out the amount that Ephron
23.16 according to the standard **weights** used by the merchants.
Ex 30.13 amount of money, **weighed** according to the official standard.
30.24 cassia (all **weighed** according to the official standard).
38.24 Tent weighed a thousand kilogrammes, **weighed** according to the official standard.
38.25 weighed 3,430 kilogrammes, **weighed** according to the official standard.
38.26 required amount, **weighed** according to the official standard.
Lev 19.35 not cheat anyone by using false measures of length, **weight,**
19.36 Use honest scales, honest **weights,** and honest measures.
Num 7.12 one silver bowl **weighing** 1.5 kilogrammes
7.12 silver basin **weighing** 800 grammes, by the official standard,
7.12 one gold dish **weighing** 110 grammes, full of incense;
7.84 twelve silver basins **weighing** a total of 27.6 kilogrammes
7.84 twelve gold dishes **weighing** a total of 1.32 kilogrammes,
31.52 **weighed** nearly two hundred kilogrammes.
Deut 25.13 "Do not cheat when you use **weights** and measures.
25.15 Use true and honest **weights** and measures, so that you
Josh 7.21 silver, and a bar of gold **weighing** over half a kilogramme.
Judg 8.26 that Gideon received **weighed** nearly twenty kilogrammes,
1 Sam 17. 5 and wore bronze armour that **weighed** about fifty-seven
17. 7 loom, and its iron head **weighed** about seven kilogrammes.
2 Sam 12.30 took a gold crown which **weighed** about thirty-five
14.26 It would **weigh** more than two kilogrammes
14.26 according to the royal standard of **weights.**
21.16 carrying a bronze spear that **weighed** about three and a half
1 Kgs 7.47 not have these bronze objects **weighed,** because there were
7.47 too many of them, and so their **weight** was never determined.
2 Kgs 12.10 the High Priest would come, melt down the silver, and **weigh**
25.16 the carts, and the large tank—were too heavy to **weigh.**
1 Chr 20. 2 had a gold crown which **weighed** about thirty-four kilogrammes.

1 Chr 22. 3 wooden gates, and so much bronze that no one could **weigh** it.
23.29 to **weigh** and measure the temple offerings;
2 Chr 4.18 that no one determined the total **weight** of the bronze used.
Ezra 8.25 Then I **weighed** out the silver, the gold, and the
8.29 There in the priests' room **weigh** them and hand them over to
8.33 we went to the Temple, **weighed** the silver, the gold, and the
8.34 Everything was counted and **weighed**, and a complete
Job 6. 1 and griefs were **weighed** on scales, [3]they would weigh
6. 3 weighed on scales, [3]they would **weigh** more than the sands of
20.22 of his success all the **weight** of misery will crush him.
26. 8 with water and keeps them from bursting with the **weight**.
31. 6 Let God **weigh** me on honest scales, and he will see how
Ps 62. 9 Put them on the scales, and they **weigh** nothing;
Prov 11. 1 He is happy with honest **weights**.
16.11 The Lord wants **weights** and measures to be honest and
20.10 The Lord hates people who use dishonest **weights** and measures.
20.23 The Lord hates people who use dishonest scales and **weights**.
27. 3 The **weight** of stone and sand is nothing compared to the
Is 24.20 The world is **weighed** down by its sins;
40.12 earth in a cup or **weigh** the mountains and hills on scales?
46. 6 they **weigh** out silver on the scales.
Jer 32. 9 the field from Hanamel and **weighed** out the money to him;
32.10 deed, had it witnessed, and **weighed** out the money on scales.
52.20 the twelve bulls that supported it—were too heavy to **weigh**.
Lam 1.14 them round my neck, and I grew weak beneath the **weight**.
Ezek 5. 1 Then **weigh** the hair on scales and divide it into three parts.
45.10 "Everyone must use honest **weights** and measures:
45.12 "Your **weights** are to be as follows:
Dan 5.25 'Number, number, **weight**, divisions.'
5.27 **weight**, you have been weighed on the scales and found to
Mic 6.11 How can I forgive men who use false scales and **weights**?
Acts 27.28 dropped a line with a **weight** tied to it and found that
Rev 16.21 Huge hailstones, each **weighing** as much as fifty kilogrammes,

WEIRD

Prov 23.33 **Weird** sights will appear before your eyes,

WELCOME

Judg 19. 3 and when her father saw him, he gave him a warm **welcome**.
19.20 The old man said, "You are **welcome** in my home!
1 Sam 13.10 out to meet him and **welcome** him, [11]but Samuel said, "What
2 Sam 9. 7 Saul, and you will always be **welcome** at my table."
14.33 The king **welcomed** him with a kiss.
2 Kgs 20.13 Hezekiah **welcomed** the messengers and showed them his
1 Chr 12.17 you are coming as friends to help me, you are **welcome** here.
12.18 David **welcomed** them and made them officers in his army.
Job 2.10 When God sends us something good, we **welcome** it.
29.23 everyone **welcomed** them just as farmers welcome rain in spring.
29.23 everyone welcomed them just as farmers **welcome** rain in spring.
31.31 who work for me know that I have always **welcomed** strangers.
Ps 23. 5 you **welcome** me as an honoured guest and fill my cup to
Prov 19.12 the roar of a lion, but his favour is like **welcome** rain.
Song 8.12 Solomon is **welcome** to his thousand coins, and the
Is 14. 9 the dead is getting ready to **welcome** the king of Babylonia.
39. 2 Hezekiah **welcomed** the messengers and showed them his
64. 5 You **welcome** those who find joy in doing what is right,
65. 2 have always been ready to **welcome** my people, who stubbornly
Lam 4.15 So they wandered from nation to nation, **welcomed** by no one.
Ezek 32.21 fought on the Egyptian side **welcome** the Egyptians to the
Dan 4.36 My officials and my noblemen **welcomed** me, and I was given
Mt 10.11 someone who is willing to **welcome** you, and stay with him
10.13 the people in that house **welcome** you, let your greeting of
10.13 if they do not **welcome** you, then take back your greeting.
10.14 home or town will not **welcome** you or listen to you, then
10.40 "Whoever welcomes you **welcomes** me;
10.40 and whoever **welcomes** me welcomes the one who sent me.
10.41 Whoever **welcomes** God's messenger because he is God's messenger,
10.41 And whoever **welcomes** a good man because he is good, will
18. 5 welcomes in my name one such child as this, **welcomes** me.
25.38 see you a stranger and **welcome** you in our homes, or naked
25.43 stranger but you would not **welcome** me in your homes, naked
Mk 6.10 said, "Wherever you are **welcomed**, stay in the same house until
6.11 town where people do not **welcome** you or will not listen to
9.37 "Whoever welcomes in my name one of these children, **welcomes** me;
9.37 and whoever **welcomes** me, welcomes not only me but also the
Lk 4.24 Jesus added, "a prophet is never **welcomed** in his home town.
7.45 You did not **welcome** me with a kiss, but she has not
8.40 of the lake, the people **welcomed** him, because they had all
9. 4 Wherever you are **welcomed**, stay in the same house until you
9. 5 people don't **welcome** you, leave that town and shake the dust
9.11 He **welcomed** them, spoke to them about the Kingdom of God,
9.48 "Whoever welcomes this child in my name, **welcomes** me;
9.48 and whoever **welcomes** me, also welcomes the one who sent me.
10. 8 a town and are made **welcome**, eat what is set before you,
10.10 a town and are not **welcomed**, go out in the streets and
10.38 village where a woman named Martha **welcomed** him in her home.
15. 2 "This man **welcomes** outcasts and even eats with them!"
16. 4 I shall have friends who will **welcome** me in their homes.'
16. 9 when it gives out, you will be **welcomed** in the eternal home.
19. 6 Zacchaeus hurried down and **welcomed** him with great joy.
Jn 4.45 in Galilee, the people there **welcomed** him, because they had gone
Acts 15. 4 in Jerusalem, they were **welcomed** by the church, the apostles,
18.27 writing to the believers in Achaia, urging them to **welcome** him.
21.17 When we arrived in Jerusalem, the believers **welcomed** us warmly.
24. 3 We **welcome** this everywhere and at all times, and we are
Acts 25.13 Bernice came to Caesarea to pay a visit of **welcome** to Festus.
28. 2 was cold, so they lit a fire and made us all **welcome**.
28. 7 He **welcomed** us kindly and for three days we were his guests.
28.30 for himself, and there he **welcomed** all who came to see him.
Rom 10.21 I held out my hands to **welcome** a disobedient and rebellious people."
14. 1 **Welcome** the person who is weak in faith, but do not argue
1 Cor 16.10 sure to make him feel **welcome** among you, because he is
2 Cor 7.15 how you **welcomed** him with fear and trembling.
8.17 Not only did he **welcome** our request;
Col 4.10 received instructions to **welcome** Mark if he comes your way.)
1 Thes 3. 6 has brought us the **welcome** news about your faith and love.
2 Thes 2.10 perish because they did not **welcome** and love the truth so as
1 Tim 3. 2 he must **welcome** strangers in his home;
Phlm 17 your partner, welcome him back just as you would **welcome** me.
Heb 11.13 they saw them and **welcomed** them, and admitted openly that they
11.31 for she gave the Israelite spies a friendly **welcome**.
13. 2 Remember to **welcome** strangers in your homes.
13. 2 There were some who did that and **welcomed** angels without knowing
Jas 2.25 through her actions, by **welcoming** the Israelite spies and helping
2 Jn 10 not bring this teaching, do not **welcome** him in your homes;

WELL (1)

Gen 29. 6 "Is he **well**?"
29. 6 "He is **well**," they answered.
43.27 Is he still alive and **well**?"
43.28 "Your humble servant, our father, is still alive and **well**."
Ex 21.18 his lost time and take care of him until he gets **well**.
1 Sam 17.18 something to show that you saw them and that they are **well**.
2 Sam 11. 7 Joab and the troops were **well**, and how the fighting was going.
12.16 David prayed to God that the child would get **well**.
2 Kgs 1.16 were no god in Israel to consult—you will not get **well**;
8. 8 to find out whether or not I am going to get **well**."
8.14 "He told me that you would certainly get **well**," Hazael answered.
20. 7 his boil a paste made of figs, and he would get **well**.
Prov 1.12 They may be alive and **well** when we find them, but
Is 38. 6 paste made of figs on his boil, and he would get **well**.
58.11 I will keep you strong and **well**.
Jer 17.14 Lord, heal me and I will be completely **well**;
30.17 I will make you **well** again;
Mt 8. 7 "I will go and make him **well**," Jesus said.
8. 8 Just give the order, and my servant will get **well**.
9.12 and answered, "People who are **well** do not need a doctor,
9.21 to herself, "If I only touch his cloak, I will get **well**."
9.22 Your faith has made you **well**."
9.22 At that very moment the woman became **well**.
12.13 it out, and it became **well** again, just like the other one.
14.36 and all who touched it were made **well**.
Mk 2.17 and answered, "People who are **well** do not need a doctor,
3. 5 He stretched it out, and it became **well** again.
5.23 your hands on her, so that she will get **well** and live!"
5.28 herself, "If I just touch his clothes, I will get **well**."
5.34 Jesus said to her, "My daughter, your faith has made you **well**.
6.56 and all who touched it were made **well**.
10.52 "Go," Jesus told him, "your faith has made you **well**."
16.18 will place their hands on sick people, who will get **well**."
Lk 5.31 answered them, "People who are **well** do not need a doctor,
6.10 He did so, and his hand became **well** again.
7. 7 Just give the order, and my servant will get **well**.
7.10 went back to the officer's house and found his servant **well**.
8.48 Jesus said to her, "My daughter, your faith has made you **well**.
8.50 only believe, and she will be **well**."
17.19 your faith has made you **well**."
18.42 Your faith has made you **well**."
Jn 5. 6 so he asked him, "Do you want to get **well**?"
5. 9 Immediately the man got **well**;
5.11 "The man who made me **well** told me to pick up my
5.14 him in the Temple and said, "Listen, you are **well** now;
7.23 with me because I made a man completely **well** on the Sabbath?
11.12 disciples answered, "If he is asleep, Lord, he will get **well**."
Acts 3.16 in Jesus that has made him **well**, as you can all see.
4.10 here before you completely **well** through the power of the name
9.34 "Aeneas," Peter said to him, "Jesus Christ makes you **well**.
3 Jn 2 be in good health—as I know you are **well** in spirit.

WELL (2)

Gen 16.14 why people call the **well** between Kadesh and Bered
16.14 "The **Well** of the Living One Who Sees Me."
21.19 Then God opened her eyes, and she saw a **well**.
21.25 complained to Abimelech about a **well** which the servants of
21.30 this, you admit that I am the one who dug this **well**."
24.11 he made the camels kneel down at the **well** outside the city.
24.13 Here I am at the **well** where the young women of the
24.16 She went down to the **well**, filled her jar, and came back.
24.20 drinking-trough and ran to the **well** to get more water, until
24.29 ran outside to go to the **well** where Abraham's servant was.
24.30 his camels at the **well**, [31]and said, "Come home with me.
24.42 "When I came to the **well** today, I prayed, 'Lord, God of
24.43 Here I am at the **well**.
24.45 on her shoulder and went down to the **well** to get water.
24.62 into the wilderness of "The **Well** of the Living One Who Sees
25.11 Isaac, who lived near "The **Well** of the Living One Who Sees
26.15 they filled in all the **wells** which the servants of his
26.18 He dug once again the **wells** which had been dug during
26.18 Isaac gave the **wells** the same names that his father had
26.19 Isaac's servants dug a **well** in the valley and found water.
26.20 So Isaac named the **well** "Quarrel."
26.21 Isaac's servants dug another **well**, and there was a

Gen 26.22 He moved away from there and dug another **well.**
26.25 set up his camp there, and his servants dug another **well.**
26.32 came and told him about the **well** which they had dug.
26.33 He named the **well** "Vow."
29. 2 Suddenly he came upon a **well** out in the fields with three
29. 2 flocks were watered from this **well,** which had a large stone
29.10 flock, he went to the **well,** rolled the stone back, and
37.20 kill him and throw his body into one of the dry **wells.**
37.22 "Just throw him into this **well** in the wilderness, but
37.24 they took him and threw him into the **well,** which was dry.
37.28 pulled Joseph out of the **well** and sold him for twenty pieces
37.29 Reuben came back to the **well** and found that Joseph was not
Ex 2.15 Moses was sitting by a **well,** seven daughters of Jethro, the
Num 20.17 fields or vineyards, and we will not drink from your **wells.**
21.17 **"Wells,** produce your water;
21.18 The **well** dug by princes And by leaders
21.22 or vineyards, and we will not drink water from your **wells;**
Deut 6.11 them, and there will be **wells** that you did not dig, and
10. 6 Israelites set out from the **wells** that belonged to the
Judg 5.11 crowds round the **wells** are telling of the Lord's victories,
1 Sam 13. 6 caves and holes or among the rocks or in pits and **wells;**
19.22 he came to the large **well** in Secu, he asked where Samuel
2 Sam 3.26 get Abner, and they brought him back from the **well** of Sirah;
17.18 He had a **well** near his house, and they got down into
17.19 over the opening of the **well** and scattered grain over it, so
17.21 came up out of the **well** and went and reported to King
23.15 a drink of water from the **well** by the gate at Bethlehem!"
23.16 drew some water from the **well,** and brought it back to David.
2 Kgs 18.31 drink water from your own **wells**—[32] until the emperor
19.24 You boasted that you dug **wells** and drank water in
1 Chr 11.17 a drink of water from the **well** by the gate in Bethlehem!"
11.18 drew some water from the **well,** and brought it back to David.
Prov 20. 5 like water in a deep **well,** but someone with insight can draw
25.26 evil reminds you of a polluted spring or a poisoned **well.**
Ecc 12. 6 the rope at the **well** will break, and the water jar will
Is 36.16 drink water from your own **wells**—[17] until the emperor
37.25 You boasted that you dug **wells** and drank water in foreign lands,
Jer 6. 7 As a **well** keeps its water fresh, so Jerusalem keeps its
9. 1 wish my head were a **well** of water, and my eyes a
38. 6 Prince Malchiah's **well,** which was in the palace courtyard.
38. 6 was no water in the **well,** only mud, and I sank down
38. 7 the royal palace, heard that they had put me in the **well.**
38. 9 have put Jeremiah in the **well,** where he is sure to die
38.10 men and to pull me out of the **well** before I died.
38.13 I did this, [13] and they pulled me up out of the **well.**
41. 7 and his men killed them and threw their bodies in a **well.**
41. 9 The **well** into which Ishmael threw the bodies of the men he
41. 9 Ishmael filled the **well** with the bodies.
Hos 13.15 from the desert, and it will dry up their springs and **wells.**
Lk 14. 5 happened to fall in a **well** on a Sabbath, would you not
Jn 4. 6 Jacob's **well** was there,
4. 6 Jesus, tired out by the journey, sat down by the **well.**
4.11 said, "you haven't got a bucket, and the **well** is deep.
4.12 It was our ancestor Jacob who gave us this **well;**

WELL (3)

Gen 12.13 because of you they will let me live and treat me **well."**
12.16 her the king treated Abram **well** and gave him flocks of sheep
30.26 You know how **well** I have served you."
32. 9 my relatives, and you would make everything go **well** for me.
32.12 promised to make everything go **well** for me and to give me
40.14 me when everything is going **well** for you, and please be kind
Deut 4.40 today, and all will go **well** with you and your descendants.
5.16 so that all may go **well** with you and so that you
5.29 so that everything would go **well** with them and their
5.33 so that everything will go **well** with you and so that you
6. 3 Then all will go **well** with you, and you will become a
6.18 says is right and good, and all will go **well** with you.
12.25 pleased, and all will go **well** for you and your descendants.
12.28 you, and all will go **well** for you and your descendants for
19.13 Israel of this murderer, so that all will go **well** with you.
29.19 himself that all will be **well** with him, even if he
Josh 2.14 when the Lord gives us this land, we will treat you **well."**
Judg 17.13 I know that the Lord will make things go **well** for me."
1 Sam 12.14 All will go **well** with you if you honour the Lord your
2 Sam 2. 6 I too will treat you **well** because of what you have done.
2 Kgs 25.24 the king of Babylonia, and all will go **well** with you."
2 Chr 12.12 not completely destroy him, and things went **well** for Judah.
35. 2 perform in the Temple and encouraged them to do them **well.**
Ezra 7.14 in order to see how **well** the Law of your God, which
Ps 73. 3 the proud when I saw that things go **well** for the wicked.
Prov 4.13 Your education is your life—guard it **well.**
27. 6 A friend means **well,** even when he hurts you.
28. 5 is, but those who worship the Lord understand it **well.**
Ecc 7.14 When things are going **well** for you, be glad, and when
8.13 be all right, [13] but it will not go **well** for the wicked.
11. 6 whether it will all grow **well** or whether one sowing will do
Is 3.10 Righteous men will be happy, and things will go **well** for them.
41. 7 The carpenter says to the goldsmith, **'Well** done!'
Jer 6.14 'All is **well,'** they say, when all is not well.
7.23 I had commanded them, so that things would go **well** for them.
8.11 'All is **well,'** they say, when all is not well.
12. 2 They always speak **well** of you, yet they do not really care
15.11 I have not served you **well,** if I have not pleaded with
22.16 gave the poor a fair trial, and all went **well** with him.
23.17 have said, they keep saying that all will go **well** with them.
38.20 then all will go **well** with you, and your life will be
40. 9 serve the king of Babylonia, and all will go **well** with you.
42. 6 All will go **well** with us if we obey him."
Ezek 13.10 "The prophets mislead my people by saying that all is **well.**
13.10 All is certainly not **well!**
13.16 Jerusalem that all was **well,** when all was not well!"
Mt 25.21 **'Well** done, you good and faithful servant!'
25.23 **'Well** done, you good and faithful servant!'
Mk 7.37 "How **well** he does everything!"
12.32 The teacher of the Law said to Jesus, **"Well** done,
Lk 6.26 "How terrible when all people speak **well** of you;
6.48 house but could not shake it, because it was **well** built.
19.17 **'Well** done,' he said;
Acts 15.29 You will do **well** if you take care not to do these
16. 2 All the believers in Lystra and Iconium spoke **well** of Timothy.
28.25 "How **well** the Holy Spirit spoke through the prophet Isaiah to
1 Cor 7. 1 A man does **well** not to marry.
7.37 what to do—then he does **well** not to marry the girl.
7.38 the man who marries does **well,** but the one who doesn't marry
2 Cor 2. 9 wanted to find out how **well** you had stood the test
10.18 is when the Lord thinks **well** of a person that he is
10.18 is really approved, and not when he thinks **well** of himself.
Gal 5. 7 You were doing so **well!**
Eph 6. 3 "so that all may go **well** with you, and you may live
1 Thes 3. 6 that you always think **well** of us and that you want
1 Tim 1.18 weapons in order to fight **well,** [19] and keep your faith
3. 4 to manage his own family **well** and make his children obey him
3.12 wife, and be able to manage his children and family **well.**
3.13 helpers who do their work **well** win for themselves a good
5.10 who brought up her children **well,** received strangers in her home,
Jas 2. 3 show more respect to the **well-dressed** man and say to him,
2.16 Keep warm and eat **well!"**
2 Pet 1.19 You will do **well** to pay attention to it, because it is
3 Jn 2 pray that everything may go **well** with you and that you may
12 Everyone speaks **well** of Demetrius;
12 truth itself speaks **well** of him.

WELL OF THE LIVING ONE WHO SEES ME

Gen 16.14 Kadesh and Bered "The **Well of the Living One Who Sees Me."**
24.62 the wilderness of "The **Well of the Living One Who Sees Me"**
25.11 who lived near "The **Well of the Living One Who Sees Me."**

WELL-

Where not listed below, see under main part of word. e.g. for "well-built" see BUILD

WELL-BEING

Mal 2. 5 I promised them life and **well-being,** and this is what I gave

WELL-KNOWN

Num 16. 1 by 250 other Israelites, **well-known** leaders chosen by the community.
1 Chr 5.24 outstanding soldiers, **well-known** leaders of their clans.
Esth 9. 4 It was **well known** throughout the empire that Mordecai was
Prov 31.23 Her husband is **well known,** one of the leading citizens.
Mt 27.16 there was a **well-known** prisoner named Jesus Barabbas.
Jn 7. 4 hides what he is doing if he wants to be **well known.**
18.15 That other disciple was **well known** to the High Priest, so he
Rom 16. 7 are **well known** among the apostles, and they became Christians
Heb 7.14 It is **well known** that he was born a member of the

WELL-OFF

Ecc 4.13 advice, he is not as **well off** as a young man who
Ezek 16.54 your disgrace will show your sisters how **well-off** they are.
Rev 3.17 You say, 'I am rich and **well off;**

WELLS

Num 21.16 on to a place called **Wells,** where the Lord said to Moses,

WEST

Gen 12. 8 his camp between Bethel on the **west** and Ai on the east.
Ex 10.19 wind into a very strong **west** wind, which picked up the
26.22 of the Tent on the **west,** make six frames, [23] and two frames
26.27 and five for the frames on the **west** end, at the back.
27.12 On the **west** side there are to be curtains 22 metres long,
36.27 of the Tent, on the **west,** they made six frames [28] and two
36.32 and five for the frames on the **west** end, at the back.
38.12 On the **west** side there were curtains 22 metres long,
Num 2.18 On the **west,** those under the banner of the
3.23 was to camp on the **west** behind the Tent, [24] with Eliasaph
34. 6 "The **western** border will be the Mediterranean Sea.
Deut 3.17 On the **west** their territory extended to the River Jordan,
3.20 the Lord is giving them **west** of the Jordan and until the
3.27 north and to the south, to the east and to the **west.**
11.24 River Euphrates in the east to the Mediterranean Sea in the **west.**
11.30 (These two mountains are **west** of the River Jordan in the
11.30 They are towards the **west,** not far from the sacred trees of
34. 2 the territory of Judah as far **west** as the Mediterranean Sea;
Josh 1. 4 the Hittite country, to the Mediterranean Sea in the **west.**
1.15 they have occupied the land **west** of the Jordan that the Lord
5. 1 All the Amorite kings **west** of the Jordan and all the
8. 9 place and waited there, **west** of Ai, between Ai and Bethel.
8.12 and put them in hiding **west** of the city, between Ai and
8.13 of the city and the rest of the men to the **west.**
9. 1 known to all the kings **west** of the Jordan—in the hills,
10.40 the eastern slopes, and the **western** foothills, as well as
12. 7 the kings in the territory **west** of the Jordan, from Baalgad

Josh 12. 8 portion included the hill-country, the **western** foothills,
13.23 The Jordan was the **western** border of the tribe of Reuben.
13.27 Their **western** border was the River Jordan as far north as
14. 1 how the land of Canaan **west** of the Jordan was divided among
14. 2 nine and a half tribes **west** of the Jordan were determined by
15. 8 of the hill on the **west** side of the Valley of Hinnom,
15.10 Kiriath Jearim), [10]where it circled **west** of Baalah towards
15.12 the Mediterranean Sea, [12]which formed the **western** border.
16. 3 It then went **west** to the area of the Japhletites, as far
16. 8 The border went **west** from Tappuah to the stream of Kanah
17. 1 A part of the land **west** of the Jordan was assigned to
17. 2 Land **west** of the Jordan was assigned to the rest of the
17.10 north, with the Mediterranean Sea as their **western** border.
18.12 slope north of Jericho and **westwards** through the
18.14 direction, turning south from the **western** side of this
18.14 This was the **western** border.
19.11 From there the border went **west** to Mareal, touching
19.26 On the **west** it touched Carmel and Shihor Libnath.
19.34 There the border turned **west** to Aznoth Tabor,
19.34 the south, Asher on the **west**, and the Jordan on the east.
20. 7 So, on the **west** side of the Jordan they set aside Kedesh
22. 6 half Joshua had given land **west** of the Jordan, along with
22.10 at Geliloth, still on the **west** side of the Jordan, they
22.14 one from each of the **western** tribes and each one the head
22.21 answered the heads of the families of the **western** tribes:
22.30 heads of families of the **western** tribes, heard what the
23. 4 River Jordan in the east to the Mediterranean Sea in the **west**.
Judg 11.22 from the desert on the east to the Jordan on the **west**.
18.12 They went up and made camp **west** of Kiriath Jearim in Judah.
2 Sam 24. 6 they went to Dan, and from Dan they went **west** to Sidon.
1 Kgs 4.24 ruled over all the land **west** of the River Euphrates, from
4.24 Tiphsah on the Euphrates as far **west** as the city of Gaza.
4.24 All the kings **west** of the Euphrates were subject to him, and
1 Chr 4.39 to grow, [39]they spread out **westwards** almost to Gerar and
7.28 as Naaran and as far **west** as Gezer and the towns round
9.24 north, south, east, and **west**, and each had a chief guard.
12.15 who lived in the valleys both east and **west** of the river.
26.16 and Hosah were allotted the **west** gate and the Shallecheth
26.18 Near the **western** pavilion there were four guards by the
26.30 and civil matters in Israel **west** of the River Jordan.
27.25 Olives and sycomore-trees (in the **western** foothills):
2 Chr 26.10 herds of livestock in the **western** foothills and plains.
28.18 the towns in the **western** foothills and in southern Judah.
Neh 2.13 the Valley Gate on the **west** and went south past Dragon's
Job 18.20 From east to **west**, all who hear of his fate shudder and
23. 8 I have not found him when I searched in the **west**.
Ps 50. 1 he calls to the whole earth from east to **west**.
75. 6 the east or from the **west**, from the north or from the
103.12 the east is from the **west**, so far does he remove our
107. 3 countries, from east and **west**, from north and south.
113. 3 From the east to the **west** praise the name of the Lord!
139. 9 the farthest place in the **west**, [10]you would be there to
Is 9.12 east and Philistia on the **west** have opened their mouths to
11.14 attack the Philistines on the **west** and plunder the people
16. 8 eastwards into the desert, and **westwards** to the other side
24.14 Those in the **west** will tell how great the Lord is, [15]and
43. 5 east and the farthest **west**, I will bring your people home.
49.12 from the north and the **west**, and from Aswan in the south."
59.19 From east to **west** everyone will fear him and his great power.
65.10 Plain of Sharon in the **west** and in the Valley of Trouble
Jer 2.10 Go **west** to the island of Cyprus, and send someone
31.38 as my city, from Hananel Tower **west** to the Corner Gate.
31.39 continue from there on the **west** to the hill of Gareb and
Ezek 40.47 The Temple was on the **west** side, and in front of it
41.12 the open space on the **west** side of the Temple there was
41.13 building to the **west**, the distance was also fifty metres.
41.15 building to the **west**, including its corridors on both sides,
42. 1 not far from the building at the **west** end of the Temple.
42. 9 not far from the building at the **west** end of the Temple.
42.17 measured the north side, the south side, and the **west** side;
45. 7 From the **western** boundary of the holy area
45. 7 it will extend **west** to the Mediterranean Sea;
46.19 out a place on the **west** side of the rooms [20]and said,
47.18 land of Israel on the **west** and Gilead on the east, as
47.20 "The **western** boundary is formed by the Mediterranean
47.20 and runs north to a point **west** of Hamath Pass.
48. 1 the eastern boundary **westwards** to the Mediterranean Sea,
48. 8 same length from east to **west** as the sections given to the
48.10 From east to **west** their portion is to measure twelve and a
48.13 half kilometres from east to **west**, by five kilometres from
48.18 a half kilometres on the **west**—is to be used as farm
48.21 the east and to the **west** of this area which contains the
48.21 the eastern boundary and **westwards** to the Mediterranean Sea,
48.23 the eastern boundary **westwards** to the Mediterranean Sea,
48.30 and those in the **west** wall are named after Gad, Asher, and
Dan 8. 4 butting with his horns to the **west**, the north, and the
8. 5 came rushing out of the **west**, moving so fast that his feet
Hos 11.10 They will hurry to me from the **west**.
Obad 19 those from the **western** foothills will capture Philistia;
Zech 6. 6 horses were going to the **west**, and the dappled horses were
7. 7 also in the southern region and in the **western** foothills.
8. 8 bring them back from east and **west** to live in Jerusalem.
14. 4 be split in two from east to **west** by a large valley.
Mt 8.11 from the east and the **west** and sit down with Abraham, Isaac,
24.27 flashes across the whole sky from the east to the **west**.
Mk 16.10 from the east to the **west** the sacred and ever-living message
Lk 12.54 cloud coming up in the **west**, at once you say that it
13.29 from the east and the **west**, from the north and the south,
Rev 21.13 on the south, three on the north, and three on the **west**.

WEST EUPHRATES see EUPHRATES (2)

WEST MANASSEH see MANASSEH (1)

WET

Deut 23.10 because he has had a **wet dream** during the night, he is
Judg 6.39 This time let the wool be dry, and the ground be **wet**."
6.40 morning the wool was dry, but the ground was **wet** with dew.
Job 29.19 always have water and whose branches are **wet** with dew.
Song 5. 2 My head is **wet** with dew, and my hair is damp from
5.13 His lips are like lilies, **wet** with liquid myrrh.
Jer 9.18 fill with tears, and our eyelids are **wet** from crying."
Zech 14. 8 the year round, in the dry season as well as the **wet**.
Lk 7.38 Jesus, by his feet, crying and **wetting** his feet with her tears.

WET-NURSE

see also **NURSE**

Ex 2. 7 I go and call a Hebrew woman to act as a **wet-nurse**?"

Am

WHEAT

see also **CORN**

WHEAT

Gen 30.14 During the **wheat-harvest** Reuben went into the fields
37. 7 field tying up sheaves of **wheat**, when my sheaf got up and
Ex 9.32 But none of the **wheat** was ruined, because it ripens later.
29. 2 Use the best **wheat** flour, but no yeast, and make some
29.40 offer one kilogramme of fine **wheat** flour mixed with one
34.22 the first crop of your **wheat**, and keep the Festival of
Deut 8. 8 a land that produces **wheat** and barley, grapes, figs,
32.14 goats, and cattle, the finest **wheat**, and the choicest wine.
Judg 6.11 son Gideon was threshing some **wheat** secretly in a winepress,
6.37 putting some wool on the ground where we thresh the **wheat**.
15. 1 visit his wife during the **wheat** harvest and took her a young
Ruth 2.23 corn until all the barley and **wheat** had been harvested.
1 Sam 6.13 of Beth Shemesh were harvesting **wheat** in the valley, when
2 Sam 4. 6 drowsy while she was sifting **wheat** and had fallen asleep, so
17.28 **wheat**, barley, meal, roasted grain, beans, peas, honey,
1 Kgs 5.11 two thousand metric tons of **wheat** and four hundred thousand
2 Kgs 6.27 Have I got any **wheat** or wine?
7. 1 three kilogrammes of the best **wheat** or six kilogrammes of
7.16 three kilogrammes of the best **wheat** or six kilogrammes of
7.18 three kilogrammes of the best **wheat** or six kilogrammes of
1 Chr 21.20 four sons were threshing **wheat**, and when they saw the angel,
21.23 to use as fuel, and **wheat** to give as an offering.
2 Chr 2.10 metric tons of **wheat**, two thousand metric tons of barley,
2.15 So now send us the **wheat**, barley, wine, and olive-oil
27. 5 1,000 metric tons of **wheat**, and 1,000 metric tons of barley.
Ezra 6. 9 offerings to the God of Heaven, or **wheat**, salt, wine, or
7.22 silver, 10,000 kilogrammes of **wheat**, 2,000 litres of wine,
Job 5.26 Like **wheat** that ripens till harvest time, you will live
24.10 they must go hungry while harvesting **wheat**.
31.40 starve— [40]then instead of **wheat** and barley, may weeds and
Ps 65.13 the valleys are full of **wheat**.
81.16 with the finest **wheat** and satisfy you with wild honey."
147.14 He keeps your borders safe and satisfies you with the finest **wheat**.
Song 7. 2 A sheaf of **wheat** is there, surrounded by lilies.
Is 21.10 you have been threshed like **wheat**, but now I have announced
27.12 by one, like someone separating the **wheat** from the chaff.
28.25 He sows rows of **wheat** and barley, and at the edges of
28.28 He does not ruin the **wheat** by threshing it endlessly,
Jer 12.13 My people sowed **wheat**, but gathered weeds;
23.28 What good is straw compared with **wheat**?
41. 8 We have **wheat**, barley, olive-oil, and honey hidden in the fields."
Ezek 4. 9 "Now take some **wheat**, barley, beans, peas, millet, and
27.17 and Israel paid for your goods with **wheat**, honey, olive-oil,
45.13 **Wheat**: 1/60th of your harvest
Joel 1.11 of the vineyards, because the **wheat**, the barley, yes all the
Amos 8. 6 We can sell worthless **wheat** at a high price.
Mt 3.12 He will gather his **wheat** into his barn, but he will burn
13.25 an enemy came and sowed weeds among the **wheat** and went away.
13.29 weeds you might pull up some of the **wheat** along with them.
13.30 Let the **wheat** and the weeds both grow together until harvest.
13.30 then to gather in the **wheat** and put it in my barn.' "
Lk 3.17 thresh out all the grain and gather the **wheat** into his barn;
16. 7 'A thousand sacks of **wheat**,' he answered.
22.31 the bad, as a farmer separates the **wheat** from the chaff.
Jn 12.24 a grain of **wheat** remains no more than a single grain unless
Acts 27.38 lightened the ship by throwing all the **wheat** into the sea.
1 Cor 15.37 seed, perhaps a grain of **wheat** or some other grain,
Rev 6. 6 which said, "A litre of **wheat** for a day's wages, and three
18.13 wine and oil, flour and **wheat**, cattle and sheep, horses

WHEEL

[CHARIOT-WHEELS]

Ex 14.25 He made the **wheels** of their chariots get stuck, so that
1 Kgs 7.30 Each cart had four bronze **wheels** with bronze axles.
7.32 The **wheels** were 66 centimetres high;
7.33 The **wheels** were like chariot wheels;
7.33 The wheels were like **chariot wheels;**
Is 5.28 as flint, and their **chariot-wheels** turn like a whirlwind.
Jer 18. 3 So I went there and saw the potter working at his **wheel**.
47. 3 of horses, the clatter of chariots, the rumble of **wheels**.

Ezek 1.15 four creatures, I saw four **wheels** touching the ground, one
1.16 All four **wheels** were alike;
1.16 and each had another **wheel** intersecting it at right angles,
1.17 right angles, [17] so that the **wheels** could move in any of
1.18 The rims of the **wheels** were covered with eyes.
1.19 Whenever the creatures moved, the **wheels** moved with them,
1.19 if the creatures rose up from the earth, so did the **wheels.**
1.20 and the **wheels** did exactly what the creatures did,
1.21 or rose in the air, the **wheels** did exactly the same.
3.13 air, and the noise of the **wheels,** as loud as an earthquake.
10. 2 linen clothes, "Go between the **wheels** under the creatures
10. 6 fire from between the **wheels** that were under the creatures,
10. 6 the man went in and stood by one of the **wheels.**
10. 9 there were four **wheels,** all alike, one beside each creature.
10. 9 The **wheels** shone like precious stones,
10. 9 one had another **wheel** which intersected it
10.12 backs, hands, wings, and **wheels** were covered with eyes.
10.13 These **wheels** were the same as those I had seen in my
10.16 rose in the air [16] and moved, the **wheels** went with them.
10.16 spread their wings to fly, the **wheels** still went with them.
10.17 When the creatures stopped, the **wheels** stopped;
10.17 when the creatures flew, the **wheels** went with them, because
10.19 earth while I was watching, and the **wheels** went with them.
11.22 The living creatures began to fly, and the **wheels** went with them.
Dan 7. 9 His throne, mounted on fiery **wheels,** was blazing with fire,
Nah 3. 2 the whip, the rattle of **wheels,** the gallop of horses, the

WHILE
[LITTLE WHILE]

Mt 26.73 After a **little while** the men standing there came to Peter.
Mk 14.70 A **little while** later the bystanders accused Peter again,
Lk 22.58 After a **little while** a man noticed Peter and said, "You
Jn 7.33 shall be with you a **little while** longer, and then I shall
14.19 In a **little while** the world will see me no more,
16.16 "In a **little while** you will not see me any more,
16.16 and then a **little while** later you will see me."
16.17 tells us that in a **little while** we will not see him,
16.17 and then a **little while** later we will see him;
16.18 What does this 'a **little while'** mean?
16.19 them, "I said, 'In a **little while** you will not see me,
16.19 and then a **little while** later you will see me.'
1 Thes 2.17 separated from you for a **little while**—not in our thoughts,
Heb 2. 7 You made him for a **little while** lower than the angels;
2. 9 see Jesus, who for a **little while** was made lower than the
10.37 the scripture says, "Just a **little while** longer, and he who
11.25 God's people rather than to enjoy sin for a **little while.**
1 Pet 5.10 you have suffered for a **little while,** the God of all grace,
Rev 6.11 were told to rest a **little while** longer, until the complete
17.10 when he comes, he must rule only a **little while.**
20. 3 After that he must be let loose for a **little while.**

WHINING

Num 11.13 They keep **whining** and asking for meat.
11.18 The Lord has heard you **whining** and saying that you wished

WHIP
[HORSEWHIP]

Deut 25. 2 is to make him lie face downwards and have him **whipped.**
Josh 23.13 and as painful as a **whip** on your back or thorns in
1 Kgs 12.11 He beat you with a **whip;**
12.11 I'll flog you with a **horsewhip!'** "
12.14 He beat you with a **whip;**
12.14 I'll flog you with a **horsewhip!"**
2 Chr 10.11 He beat you with a **whip;**
10.11 I'll flog you with a **horsewhip!'** "
10.14 He beat you with a **whip;**
10.14 I'll flog you with a **horsewhip!"**
Prov 26. 3 You have to **whip** a horse, you have to bridle a donkey,
Is 10.26 will beat them with my **whip** as I beat the people of
Nah 3. 2 The crack of the **whip,** the rattle of wheels, the gallop of
Mt 10.17 take you to court, and they will **whip** you in the synagogues.
20.19 the Gentiles, who will mock him, **whip** him, and crucify him;
23.34 crucify others, and **whip** others in the synagogues and chase
27.26 and after he had Jesus **whipped,** he handed him over to be
Mk 10.34 who will mock him, spit on him, **whip** him, and kill him;
15.15 Then he had Jesus **whipped** and handed him over to be crucified.
Lk 12.47 ready and do it, will be punished with a heavy **whipping.**
12.48 he deserves a whipping, will be punished with a light **whipping.**
18.33 They will **whip** him and kill him, but three days later he
23.16 So I will have him **whipped** and let him go."
23.22 I will have him **whipped** and set him free."
Jn 2.15 So he made a **whip** from cords and drove all the animals
19. 1 Then Pilate took Jesus and had him **whipped.**
Acts 5.40 the apostles in, had them **whipped,** and ordered them never again
16.22 clothes off Paul and Silas and ordered them to be **whipped.**
16.37 of any crime, yet they **whipped** us in public—and we are
22.24 and he told them to **whip** him in order to find out
22.25 tied him up to be **whipped,** Paul said to the officer standing
22.25 it lawful for you to **whip** a Roman citizen who hasn't even
1 Cor 4.21 come to you with a **whip,** or in a spirit of love
2 Cor 11.23 more times, I have been **whipped** much more, and I have been
11.25 three times I was **whipped** by the Romans;
Heb 11.36 Some were mocked and **whipped,** and others were put in chains

WHIRLWIND
see also **WIND (1)**

2 Kgs 2. 1 for the Lord to take Elijah up to heaven in a **whirlwind.**
2.11 them, and Elijah was taken up to heaven by a **whirlwind.**
Is 5.28 as flint, and their chariot-wheels turn like a **whirlwind.**
17.13 away like dust on a hillside, like straw in a **whirlwind.**
21. 1 Like a **whirlwind** sweeping across the desert, disaster will
Jer 4.13 His war-chariots are like a **whirlwind,** and his horses are

WHISPER

2 Sam 12.19 When David noticed them **whispering** to each other, he
1 Kgs 19.12 And after the fire, there was the soft **whisper** of a voice.
Job 26.14 hints of his power, only the **whispers** that we have heard.
Ps 31.13 I hear many enemies **whispering;**
41. 7 All who hate me **whisper** to each other about me, they
90. 9 it fades away like a **whisper.**
101. 5 rid of anyone who **whispers** evil things about someone else;
Jer 20.10 I hear everybody **whispering,** "Terror is everywhere!
Lk 12. 3 and whatever you have **whispered** in private in a closed room
Jn 7.12 There was much **whispering** about him in the crowd.
7.32 Pharisees heard the crowd **whispering** these things about Jesus,

WHISTLE

Is 5.26 He **whistles** for them to come from the ends of the earth.
7.18 time comes, the Lord will **whistle** as a signal for the

WHITE
[REDDISH-WHITE]

Gen 30.35 that were speckled and spotted or which had **white** on them;
30.37 of the bark so that the branches had **white** stripes on them.
49.12 from drinking wine, His teeth **white** from drinking milk.
Ex 4. 6 his hand out, it was diseased, covered with **white** spots,
16.31 It was like a small **white** seed, and tasted like biscuits
Lev 13. 3 hairs in it have turned **white** and the sore appears to be
13. 4 But if the sore is **white** and does not appear to be
13. 4 the hairs have not turned **white,** the priest shall isolate
13.10 If there is a **white** sore on his skin
13.10 which turns the hairs **white** and is full of pus,
13.13 If his whole skin has turned **white,** he is ritually clean.
13.16 the sore heals and becomes **white** again, the person shall go
13.17 If the sore has turned **white,** he is ritually clean, and the
13.19 healed [19] and if afterwards a **white** swelling
13.19 or a **reddish-white** spot appears where the boil was,
13.20 in it have turned **white,** he shall pronounce him unclean.
13.21 in it have not turned **white** and that it is not deeper
13.24 if the raw flesh becomes **white** or reddish-white, [25] the
13.25 in the spot have turned **white** and it appears deeper than the
13.26 in it have not turned **white** and it is not deeper than
13.38 man or a woman has **white** spots on the skin, [39] the priest
13.39 If the spots are dull **white,** it is only a blemish that
13.42 But if a **reddish-white** sore appears on the bald spot, it
13.43 and if there is a **reddish-white** sore, [44] the priest shall
Num 11. 7 (Manna was like small seeds, **whitish** yellow in colour.
12.10 covered with a dreaded disease and turned as **white** as snow.
Judg 5.10 it, you that ride on **white** donkeys, sitting on saddles, and
2 Kgs 5.27 left, he had the disease—his skin was as **white** as snow.
Esth 1. 6 was decorated with blue and **white** cotton curtains, tied by
1. 6 which was paved with **white** marble,
8.15 royal robes of blue and **white,** a cloak of fine purple linen,
Job 6. 6 What flavour is there in the **white** of an egg?
41.32 a shining path behind him and turns the sea to **white** foam.
Ps 51. 7 wash me, and I will be **whiter** than snow.
Ecc 12. 5 Your hair will turn **white;**
Song 4. 2 Your teeth are as **white** as sheep that have just been shorn
6. 6 Your teeth are as **white** as a flock of sheep that have
Is 1.18 your stains are deep red, you will be as **white** as wool.
Dan 7. 9 His clothes were **white** as snow, and his hair was like pure
Joel 1. 7 They have stripped off the bark, till the branches are **white.**
Zech 1. 8 and behind him were other horses—red, dappled, and **white.**
6. 3 black horses, [3] the third by **white** horses, and the fourth by
6. 6 north to Babylonia, the **white** horses were going to the west,
Mt 5.36 head, because you cannot make a single hair **white** or black.
17. 2 shining like the sun, and his clothes were dazzling **white.**
28. 3 appearance was like lightning, and his clothes were **white** as snow.
Mk 9. 3 his clothes became shining white—**whiter** than anyone in the world
16. 5 on the right, wearing a **white** robe—and they were alarmed.
Lk 9.29 his face changed its appearance, and his clothes became dazzling **white.**
Jn 20.12 two angels there dressed in **white,** sitting where the body of
Acts 1.10 when two men dressed in **white** suddenly stood beside them
Rev 1.14 His hair was **white** as wool, or as snow, and his eyes
2.17 give each of them a **white** stone on which is written
3. 4 walk with me, clothed in **white,** because you are worthy to do
3. 5 be clothed like this in **white,** and I will not remove their
3.18 Buy also **white** clothing to dress yourself and cover up your
4. 4 twenty-four elders dressed in **white** and wearing crowns of gold.
6. 2 I looked, and there was a **white** horse.
6.11 of them was given a **white** robe, and they were told to
7. 9 of the Lamb, dressed in **white** robes and holding palm branches
7.13 are these people dressed in **white** robes, and where do they
7.14 their robes and made them **white** with the blood of the Lamb.
14.14 looked, and there was a **white** cloud, and sitting on the
19.11 Then I saw heaven open, and there was a **white** horse.
19.14 riding on white horses and dressed in clean **white** linen.
20.11 Then I saw a great **white** throne and the one who sits

WHITEWASH

Ezek 13.10 then the prophets have come and covered it with **whitewash.**
13.12 and everyone will ask you what good the **whitewash** did."
13.14 break down the wall they **whitewashed,** to shatter it, and to
13.15 those who covered it with **whitewash** will feel the force of
13.15 and so are those who **whitewashed** it— [16] those prophets who
22.28 hidden these sins like men covering a wall with **whitewash.**
Mt 23.27 You are like **whitewashed** tombs, which look fine on the outside
Acts 23. 3 "God will certainly strike you—you **whitewashed** wall!

WHO

Mt 16.15 **"Who** do you say I am?"
Mk 8.29 **"Who** do you say I am?"
Lk 9.20 **"Who** do you say I am?"
Jn 1.19 priests and Levites to John, to ask him, **"Who are you?"**
1.21 **"Who are you,** then?"
6.14 "Surely this is the Prophet **who was to come** into the world!"
8.25 **"Who are you?"**
11.27 Messiah, the Son of God, **who was to come** into the world."
21.12 None of the disciples dared ask him, **"Who are you?"**
Acts 9. 5 **"Who are you,** Lord?"
19.15 but you—**who are you?"**
22. 8 **'Who are you,** Lord?'
26.15 **'Who are you,** Lord?'
Rom 5.14 Adam was a figure of the one **who was to come.**
9.20 But **who are you,** my friend, to answer God back?
14. 4 **Who are you** to judge the servant of someone else?
Rev 1. 4 is, who was, and **who is to come,** and from the seven
1. 8 Lord God Almighty, **who is, who was, and who is to come.**
4. 8 Lord God Almighty, **who was, who is, and who is to come."**

WHOLE

Gen 8.20 and bird, and burnt them **whole** as a sacrifice on the altar.
Ex 12. 9 boiled, but eat it roasted **whole,** including the head, the
18.12 an offering to be burnt **whole** and other sacrifices to be
27. 2 with the altar, and the **whole** is to be covered with bronze.
Lev 1.17 tearing the wings off, and then burn it **whole** on the altar.
Judg 6.26 second bull and burn it **whole** as an offering, using for
20.26 sacrifices and burnt some sacrifices **whole**—all in the
21. 4 fellowship sacrifices and burnt some sacrifices **whole.**
1 Sam 7. 9 young lamb and burnt it **whole** as a sacrifice to the Lord.
1 Kgs 8.64 there the sacrifices burnt **whole,** the grain-offerings,
1 Chr 16.40 they were to burn sacrifices **whole** on the altar in
29.21 and a thousand lambs, which they burnt **whole** on the altar.
2 Chr 1. 6 he had a thousand animals killed and burnt **whole** on it.
7. 7 there the sacrifices burnt **whole,** the grain-offerings,
13.11 they offer him incense and animal sacrifices burnt **whole.**
29.35 the sacrifices that were burnt **whole,** the priests were
35.14 animals that were burnt **whole** and the fat of the sacrifices.
Ezra 3. 5 regular sacrifices to be burnt **whole** and those to be offered
Ps 40. 6 not ask for animals burnt **whole** on the altar or for
Ezek 40.38 carcasses of the animals to be burnt **whole** as sacrifices.
40.39 sacrifices, either to be burnt **whole** or to be sacrifices for
40.42 prepare the offerings to be burnt **whole,** were of cut stone.
45.13 to be burnt **whole,** and animals for fellowship-offerings,
45.17 the animals to be burnt **whole,** the grain-offerings, and the
45.17 offerings to be burnt **whole,** and the fellowship-offerings,
45.23 and seven rams without any defects and burn them **whole.**
45.25 same offerings to be burnt **whole,** and the same offerings of
46. 2 his sacrifices **whole** and offer his fellowship-offerings.
46. 4 as sacrifices to be burnt **whole,** six lambs and one ram, all
46.12 an offering to be burnt **whole** or a fellowship-offering, the
46.13 defects is to be burnt **whole** as an offering to the Lord.
Mt 3. 5 from Jerusalem, from the **whole** province of Judaea, and from all
4.24 about him spread through the **whole** country of Syria, so that
5.14 "You are like light for the **whole** world.
5.29 of your body than to have your **whole** body thrown into hell.
5.30 of your limbs than for your **whole** body to go to hell.
6.22 your eyes are sound, your **whole** body will be full of light;
8.32 The **whole** herd rushed down the side of the cliff into the
8.33 town, where they told the **whole** story and what had happened
13.33 litres of flour until the **whole** batch of dough rises."
14. 6 the daughter of Herodias danced in front of the **whole** group.
15.31 dumb speaking, the crippled made **whole,** the lame walking,
16.26 gain anything if he wins the **whole** world but loses his life?
18.17 not listen to them, then tell the **whole** thing to the church.
18.32 'I forgave you the **whole** amount you owed me, just because
18.34 to be punished until he should pay back the **whole** amount."
20. 6 'Why are you wasting the **whole** day here doing nothing?'
20.12 we put up with a **whole** day's work in the hot sun
21.10 Jesus entered Jerusalem, the **whole** city was thrown into an uproar.
22.40 The **whole** Law of Moses and the teachings of the prophets
23.15 You sail the seas and cross **whole** countries to win one convert;
24.27 lightning which flashes across the **whole** sky from the east
26.59 chief priests and the **whole** Council tried to find some false
27.25 **whole** crowd answered, "Let the responsibility for his death fall
27.27 the governor's palace, and the **whole** company gathered round him.
27.45 At noon the **whole** country was covered with darkness,
Mk 5.13 The **whole** herd—about two thousand pigs in all—rushed down
5.33 with fear, knelt at his feet, and told him the **whole** truth.
6.55 So they ran throughout the **whole** region;
8.36 gain anything if he wins the **whole** world but loses his life?
11.18 of him, because the **whole** crowd was amazed at his teaching.
14.55 chief priests and the **whole** Council tried to find some evidence
15. 1 of the Law, and the **whole** Council, and made their plans.
15.33 At noon the **whole** country was covered with darkness,
Mk 16.15 to them, "Go throughout the **whole** world and preach the
Lk 2.44 so they travelled a **whole** day and then started looking for
3. 3 So John went throughout the **whole** territory of the River Jordan,
4.25 and a severe famine spread throughout the **whole** land.
6.12 hill to pray and spent the **whole** night there praying to God.
8.33 The **whole** herd rushed down the side of the cliff into the
9.13 you want us to go and buy food for this **whole** crowd?"
9.25 anything if he wins the **whole** world but is himself lost
11.34 When your eyes are sound, your **whole** body is full of light;
11.34 your eyes are no good, your **whole** body will be in darkness.
11.36 If your **whole** body is full of light, with no part of
13.21 litres of flour until the **whole** batch of dough rises."
20. 6 we say 'From man,' this **whole** crowd here will stone us,
21.25 On earth **whole** countries will be in despair, afraid of the
21.26 what is coming over the **whole** earth, for the powers in space
23. 1 The **whole** group rose up and took Jesus before Pilate,
23.18 The **whole** crowd cried out, "Kill him!
23.44 and darkness covered the **whole** country until three o'clock;
Jn 7. 4 doing these things, let the **whole** world know about you!"
11.50 for the people, instead of having the **whole** nation destroyed?"
12. 3 The sweet smell of the perfume filled the **whole** house.
12.19 Look, the **whole** world is following him!"
21.25 I suppose that the **whole** world could not hold the books
Acts 1.21 in our group during the **whole** time that the Lord Jesus
2. 2 wind blowing, and it filled the **whole** house where they were
5.11 The **whole** church and all the others who heard of this
6. 2 the twelve apostles called the **whole** group of believers together
6. 5 The **whole** group was pleased with the apostles' proposal,
7.14 Jacob, telling him and the **whole** family, seventy-five people
10. 2 he and his **whole** family worshipped God.
11.10 three times, and finally the **whole** thing was drawn back up
11.26 to Antioch, and for a **whole** year the two met with the
15.12 **whole** group was silent as they heard Barnabas and Paul report
15.22 the elders, together with the **whole** church, decided to choose
15.30 Antioch, where they gathered the **whole** group of believers
17. 5 They set the **whole** city in an uproar and attacked the home
17.26 races of mankind and made them live throughout the **whole** earth.
17.31 he will judge the **whole** world with justice by means of
18. 5 Paul gave his **whole** time to preaching the message, testifying
19. 9 not believe, and before the **whole** group they said evil things
19.26 here in Ephesus and in nearly the **whole** province of Asia.
19.29 The uproar spread throughout the **whole** city.
19.32 Meanwhile the **whole** meeting was in an uproar:
20.18 know how I spent the **whole** time I was with you,
20.27 held back from announcing to you the **whole** purpose of God.
21.27 They stirred up the **whole** crowd and seized Paul.
21.30 Confusion spread through the **whole** city, and the people
22. 5 The High Priest and the **whole** Council can prove that I am
22.30 and ordered the chief priests and the **whole** Council to meet.
26. 4 how I have spent my **whole** life, at first in my own
Rom 1. 8 of you, because the **whole** world is hearing about your faith.
3.19 all human excuses and bring the **whole** world under God's judgement.
5.12 spread to the **whole** human race because everyone has sinned.
6.13 to life, and surrender your **whole** being to him to be used
8.23 God to make us his sons and set our **whole** being free.
9.17 show my power and to spread my fame over the **whole** world."
11.16 bread is given to God, then the **whole** loaf is his also;
13.10 to love, then, is to obey the **whole** Law.
1 Cor 4. 9 as a spectacle for the **whole** world of angels and of mankind.
5. 6 "A little bit of yeast makes the **whole** batch of dough rise."
12.17 If the **whole** body were just an eye, how could it hear?
14. 4 but the one who proclaims God's message helps the **whole** church.
14. 5 what he says, so that the **whole** church may be helped.
14.23 the **whole** church meets together and everyone starts speaking in
16. 6 time with you, perhaps the **whole** winter, and then you can
2 Cor 7.11 You have shown yourselves to be without fault in the **whole** matter.
Gal 3.22 the scripture says that the **whole** world is under the power
5. 3 to be circumcised that he is obliged to obey the **whole** Law.
5. 9 little yeast to make the **whole** batch of dough rise," as
5.14 For the **whole** Law is summed up in one commandment:
Eph 2.21 the one who holds the **whole** building together and makes it
4.10 beyond the heavens, to fill the **whole** universe with his presence.
4.16 body fit together, and the **whole** body is held together by
4.16 works as it should, the **whole** body grows and builds itself
Phil 1.13 As a result, the **whole** palace guard and all the others
1.20 courage, so that with my **whole** being I shall bring honour to
Col 1.16 God created the **whole** universe through him and for him.
1.20 then, God decided to bring the **whole** universe back to himself.
2.19 Under Christ's control the **whole** body is nourished and held
1 Thes 5.23 every way and keep your **whole** being—spirit, soul, and
2 Tim 4. 5 Good News, and perform your **whole** duty as a servant of God.
Tit 1.11 because they are upsetting **whole** families by teaching what they
Heb 8. 1 The **whole** point of what we are saying is that we have
10. 6 not pleased with animals burnt **whole** on the altar or with
11.33 Through faith they fought **whole** countries and won.
Jas 1. 1 Greetings to all God's people scattered over the **whole** world.
3. 2 he is perfect and is also able to control his **whole** being.
3. 6 in our bodies and spreading evil through our **whole** being.
1 Jn 5.19 to God even though the **whole** world is under the rule of
Rev 5. 6 spirits of God that have been sent throughout the **whole** earth.
12. 9 called the Devil, or Satan, that deceived the **whole** world.
13. 3 The **whole** earth was amazed and followed the beast.
18. 1 had great authority, and his splendour brightened the **whole** earth.
20. 8 nations scattered over the **whole** world, that is, Gog and Magog.

AV **WHOLE** see **HEAL, WELL**

WHOLEHEARTED

1 Kgs 8.23 your love when they live in **whole-hearted** obedience to you.
1 Chr 29.19 Give my son Solomon a **wholehearted** desire to obey
2 Chr 6.14 your love when they live in **wholehearted** obedience to you.
20.33 people still did not turn **wholeheartedly** to the worship of

WHORE

Gen 34.31 "We cannot let our sister be treated like a common **whore."**
38.24 Tamar has been acting like a **whore,** and now she is pregnant."
Is 1.21 The city that once was faithful is behaving like a **whore!**
23.16 Take your harp, go round the town, you poor forgotten **whore!**
Ezek 16.35 Now then, Jerusalem, you **whore!**
23. 7 She was the **whore** for all the Assyrian officers, and her
23.18 She exposed herself publicly and let everyone know she was a **whore.**
Nah 3. 4 Nineveh the **whore** is being punished.

WICK

Zech 4. 2 are seven lamps, each one with places for seven **wicks.**

WICKED

Gen 6. 5 When the Lord saw how **wicked** everyone on earth was and how
13.13 whose people were **wicked** and sinned against the Lord.
15.16 Amorites until they become so **wicked** that they must be punished."
19. 7 to them, "Friends, I beg you, don't do such a **wicked** thing!
Num 14.27 "How much longer are these **wicked** people going to complain
14.35 will do this to you **wicked** people who have gathered together
16.26 from the tents of these **wicked** men and don't touch anything
Deut 9. 4 to drive these people out for you because they are **wicked.**
9. 5 them out because they are **wicked** and because he intends to
9.27 to the stubbornness, **wickedness,** and sin of this people.
31.29 death the people will become **wicked** and reject what I have
Judg 9.57 of Shechem suffer for their **wickedness,** just as Jotham,
1 Sam 2. 9 his faithful people, but the **wicked** disappear in darkness;
15.18 out with orders to destroy those **wicked** people of Amalek.
2 Sam 22.27 to those who are pure, but hostile to those who are **wicked.**
1 Kgs 8.47 you, confessing how sinful and **wicked** they have been, hear
22.52 the Lord, following the **wicked** example of his father Ahab,
2 Kgs 14.24 against the Lord, following the **wicked** example of his
15. 9 He followed the **wicked** example of King Jeroboam son of Nebat,
15.18 his death he followed the **wicked** example of King Jeroboam
15.24 against the Lord, following the **wicked** example of King
15.28 against the Lord, following the **wicked** example of King
17.11 Lord's anger with all their **wicked** deeds [12]and disobeyed
2 Chr 6.37 how sinful and **wicked** they have been, hear their prayers,
19. 2 to help those who are **wicked** and to take the side of
20.35 with King Ahaziah of Israel, who did many **wicked** things.
21. 6 He followed the **wicked** example of King Ahab and the other
Ezra 9.14 commandments again and intermarry with these **wicked** people?
Neh 1. 7 We have acted **wickedly** against you and have not done what
Job 3.17 In the grave **wicked** men stop their evil, and tired
4. 8 people plough fields of evil and sow **wickedness** like seed;
4. 8 now they harvest **wickedness** and evil.
4.10 The **wicked** roar and growl like lions, but God silences
5.16 He gives hope to the poor and silences the **wicked.**
8.22 who hate you, and the homes of the **wicked** will vanish.
9.24 God gave the world to the **wicked.**
10. 3 And then to smile on the schemes of **wicked** men?
11.20 But the **wicked** will look round in despair and find that
13.16 will save me, since no **wicked** man would dare to face God.
15. 5 Your **wickedness** is evident by what you say;
15.20 A **wicked** man who oppresses others will be in torment as
18. 5 The **wicked** man's light will still be put out;
20. 5 placed on earth, [5]no **wicked** man has been happy for long.
20.15 The **wicked** man vomits up the wealth he stole;
20.29 This is the fate of **wicked** men, the fate that God
21.14 The **wicked** tell God to leave them alone;
21.17 Was a **wicked** man's light ever put out?
21.17 Did God ever punish the **wicked** in anger [18]and blow them
21.30 and punishes, it is the **wicked** man who is always spared.
21.31 no one to accuse a **wicked** man or pay him back for
22.18 prosperous— I can't understand the thoughts of the **wicked.**
22.19 and innocent men laugh when they see the **wicked** punished.
22.20 All that the **wicked** own is destroyed, and fire burns up
24. 6 don't own, and gather grapes in **wicked** men's vineyards.
24.18 The **wicked** man is swept away by floods, and the land he
24.22 God acts—and the **wicked** man dies.
24.24 For a while the **wicked** man prospers, but then he withers
27. 7 fight against me be punished like **wicked,** unrighteous men.
27.13 This is how Almighty God punishes **wicked,** violent men.
27.16 The **wicked** may have too much silver to count and more
27.18 The **wicked** build houses like a spider's web or like the
31. 5 I have never acted **wickedly** and never tried to deceive others.
31.11 Such **wickedness** should be punished by death.
34.18 God condemns kings and rulers when they are worthless or **wicked.**
38.13 the earth and shake the **wicked** from their hiding places?
38.15 is too bright for the **wicked** and restrains them from deeds
40.12 crush the **wicked** where they stand.
Ps 5. 5 you hate all **wicked** people.
7. 9 Stop the **wickedness** of evil men and reward those who are good.
7.11 God is a righteous judge and always condemns the **wicked.**
7.14 See how **wicked** people think up evil;
9. 5 You have condemned the heathen and destroyed the **wicked;**
9.16 judgements, and the **wicked** are trapped by their own deeds.
9.17 the destiny of all the **wicked,** of all those who reject God.
Ps 10. 2 The **wicked** are proud and persecute the poor;
10. 3 The **wicked** man is proud of his evil desires;
10. 4 A **wicked** man does not care about the Lord;
10. 5 A **wicked** man succeeds in everything.
10.11 The **wicked** man says to himself, "God doesn't care!
10.12 O Lord, punish those **wicked** men!
10.13 How can a **wicked** man despise God and say to himself,
10.15 Break the power of **wicked** and evil men;
11. 2 to the mountains, [2]because the **wicked** have drawn their bows
11. 5 He examines the good and the **wicked** alike;
11. 6 He sends down flaming coals and burning sulphur on the **wicked;**
12. 7 **Wicked** men are everywhere, and everyone praises what is evil.
17. 9 the shadow of your wings [9]from the attacks of the **wicked.**
17.13 Save me from the **wicked** by your sword;
18.26 to those who are pure, but hostile to those who are **wicked.**
26. 5 I hate the company of evil men and avoid the **wicked.**
28. 3 not condemn me with the **wicked,** with those who do evil—
31.17 May the **wicked** be disgraced;
32.10 The **wicked** will have to suffer, but those who trust in
34.21 Evil will kill the **wicked;**
36. 1 Sin speaks to the **wicked** man deep in his heart;
36. 3 His speech is **wicked** and full of lies;
36.11 let proud men attack me or **wicked** men make me run away.
37. 1 Don't be worried on account of the **wicked;**
37. 9 Lord will possess the land, but the **wicked** will be driven out.
37.10 Soon the **wicked** will disappear;
37.12 The **wicked** man plots against the good man and glares at
37.13 But the Lord laughs at **wicked** men, because he knows they
37.14 The **wicked** draw their swords and bend their bows to kill
37.16 the wealth of all the **wicked,** [17]because the Lord will take
37.17 the strength of the **wicked,** but protect those who are good.
37.20 But the **wicked** will die;
37.21 The **wicked** man borrows and never pays back, but the good
37.28 ever, but the descendants of the **wicked** will be driven out.
37.32 A **wicked** man watches a good man and tries to kill him;
37.34 you the land, and you will see the **wicked** driven out.
37.35 I once knew a **wicked** man who was a tyrant;
37.40 he saves them from the **wicked,** because they go to him for
50.16 But God says to the **wicked,** "Why should you recite my commandments?
52. 7 his great wealth and looked for security in being **wicked."**
55. 3 of my enemies, crushed by the oppression of the **wicked.**
58.10 they will wade through the blood of the **wicked.**
64. 2 me from the plots of the **wicked,** from mobs of evil men.
68. 2 of the fire, so do the **wicked** perish in God's presence.
71. 4 My God, rescue me from **wicked** men, from the power of cruel
73. 3 the proud when I saw that things go well for the **wicked.**
73. 7 out evil, and their minds are busy with **wicked** schemes.
73.12 That is what the **wicked** are like.
73.17 Then I understood what will happen to the **wicked.**
75. 4 I tell the **wicked** not to be arrogant;
75. 8 He pours it out, and all the **wicked** drink it;
75.10 break the power of the **wicked,** but the power of the
82. 2 you must no longer be partial to the **wicked!**
84.10 house of my God than live in the homes of the **wicked.**
89.22 the **wicked** will not defeat him.
91. 8 You will look and see how the **wicked** are punished.
92. 7 the **wicked** may grow like weeds, those who do wrong may prosper;
92. 9 your enemies will die, and all the **wicked** will be defeated.
92.11 the defeat of my enemies and heard the cries of the **wicked.**
94. 3 How much longer will the **wicked** be glad?
94.13 days of trouble until a pit is dug to trap the **wicked.**
94.16 Who stood up for me against the **wicked?**
94.23 them for their **wickedness** and destroy them for their sins;
97.10 he rescues them from the power of the **wicked.**
101. 8 Day after day I will destroy the **wicked** in our land;
104.35 may the **wicked** be no more.
106. 6 we have been **wicked** and evil.
106.18 fire came down on their followers and burnt up those **wicked** people.
107.34 because of the **wickedness** of those who lived there.
107.42 this and are glad, but all the **wicked** are put to silence.
109. 2 **Wicked** men and liars have attacked me.
112.10 The **wicked** see this and are angry;
119.53 When I see the **wicked** breaking your law, I am filled
119.61 The **wicked** have laid a trap for me, but I do not
119.95 **Wicked** men are waiting to kill me, but I will meditate
119.110 **Wicked** men lay a trap for me, but I have not disobeyed
119.119 You treat all the **wicked** like rubbish, and so I love
119.155 The **wicked** will not be saved, for they do not obey
125. 3 The **wicked** will not always rule over the land of the righteous;
125. 5 But when you punish the **wicked,** punish also those who
139.19 O God, how I wish you would kill the **wicked!**
139.20 They say **wicked** things about you;
140. 4 Protect me, Lord, from the power of the **wicked;**
140. 8 Lord, don't give the **wicked** what they want;
141. 4 to do wrong and from joining evil men in their **wickedness.**
141.10 May the **wicked** fall into their own traps while I go by
145.20 He protects everyone who loves him, but he will destroy the **wicked.**
146. 9 he helps widows and orphans, but takes the **wicked** to their ruin.
147. 6 He raises the humble, but crushes the **wicked** to the ground.
Prov 2.22 But God will snatch **wicked** men from the land and pull
3.25 sudden disasters, such as come on the **wicked** like a storm.
3.33 curse on the homes of **wicked** men, but blesses the homes of
4.14 Do not follow the example of the **wicked.**
4.16 **Wicked** people cannot sleep unless they have done something wrong.
4.17 **Wickedness** and violence are like food and drink to them.
4.19 The road of the **wicked,** however, is dark as night.

Prov 5.22 The sins of a **wicked** man are a trap.
6.12 Worthless, **wicked** people go around telling lies.
6.16 a mind that thinks up **wicked** plans,
10. 3 but he will keep the **wicked** from getting what they want.
10. 6 A **wicked** man's words hide a violent nature.
10. 7 as a blessing, but the **wicked** will soon be forgotten.
10.11 of life, but a **wicked** man's words hide a violent nature.
10.20 a **wicked** man's ideas are worthless.
10.24 they want, but the **wicked** will get what they fear most.
10.25 Storms come, and the **wicked** are blown away, but honest
10.27 The **wicked** die before their time.
10.28 lead to joy, but **wicked** people can look forward to nothing.
10.30 have security, but the **wicked** will not survive in the land.
10.32 to say, but the **wicked** are always saying things that hurt.
11. 5 life easier, but a **wicked** man will cause his own downfall.
11. 7 When a **wicked** man dies, his hope dies with him.
11. 8 it comes to the **wicked** instead.
11.10 fortune, and there are joyful shouts when **wicked** men die.
11.11 a city is brought to ruin by the words of the **wicked.**
11.18 **Wicked** people do not really gain anything, but if you do
11.23 when the **wicked** get what they want, everyone is angry.
11.31 can be sure that **wicked** and sinful people will be punished.
12. 3 **Wickedness** does not give security, but righteous people stand firm.
12. 5 the **wicked** only want to deceive you.
12. 6 The words of **wicked** men are murderous, but the words of
12. 7 **Wicked** men meet their downfall and leave no descendants,
12.10 care of his animals, but **wicked** men are cruel to theirs.
12.12 All that **wicked** people want is to find evil things to do,
12.13 A **wicked** man is trapped by his own words, but an honest
12.21 righteous people, but the **wicked** have nothing but trouble.
12.26 his friend, but the path of the **wicked** leads them astray.
12.28 **wickedness** is the road to death.
13. 5 the words of **wicked** people are shameful and disgraceful.
13. 6 **wickedness** is the downfall of sinners.
13. 9 the **wicked** are like a lamp flickering out.
13.25 The righteous have enough to eat, but the **wicked** are always hungry.
14.32 **Wicked** people bring about their own downfall by their evil deeds,
15. 6 men keep their wealth, but **wicked** men lose theirs when hard
15. 8 pray, but hates the sacrifices that **wicked** men bring him.
16. 4 and the destiny of the **wicked** is destruction.
16.28 Gossip is spread by **wicked** people;
17.11 like a cruel messenger to **wicked** people who are always
17.15 the innocent or letting the **wicked** go—both are hateful to
19.28 **Wicked** people love the taste of evil.
21. 4 **Wicked** people are controlled by their conceit and arrogance,
21. 7 The **wicked** are doomed by their own violence;
21.10 **Wicked** people are always hungry for evil;
21.12 in the homes of the **wicked,**
21.12 and he will bring the **wicked** down to ruin.
21.18 The **wicked** bring on themselves the suffering they try to
21.27 The Lord hates it when **wicked** men offer him sacrifices,
21.29 the **wicked** have to pretend as best they can.
22. 5 away from the traps that catch the **wicked** along the way.
24.15 Don't be like the **wicked** who scheme to rob an honest man
24.16 but disaster destroys the **wicked.**
24.20 A **wicked** person has no future—nothing to look forward to.
28. 1 The **wicked** run when no one is chasing them, but an honest
28. 4 regard for the law, you are on the side of the **wicked;**
28.15 Poor people are helpless against a **wicked** ruler;
29. 2 Show me a **wicked** ruler and I will show you a miserable
29. 7 the poor, but **wicked** people cannot understand such things.
29.27 The righteous hate the **wicked,**
29.27 and the **wicked** hate the righteous.
Ecc 3.16 in this world you find **wickedness** where justice and right
7.17 But don't be too **wicked** or too foolish, either—why die
7.25 and to learn how **wicked** and foolish stupidity is.
8.10 Yes, I have seen **wicked** men buried and in their graves,
8.13 be all right, [13] but it will not go well for the **wicked.**
8.14 get the punishment of the **wicked,**
8.14 and **wicked** men get the reward of the
9. 2 to the righteous and the **wicked,** to the good and the bad,
Is 9.17 are godless and **wicked** and everything they say is evil.
9.18 The **wickedness** of the people burns like a fire that
13.11 on the earth and punish all **wicked** people for their sins.
26.10 though you are kind to **wicked** men, they never learn to do
55. 7 Let the **wicked** leave their way of life and change their
Jer 8. 6 Not one of you has been sorry for his **wickedness;**
12. 1 Why are **wicked** men so prosperous?
12. 4 because of the **wickedness** of our people, people who say,
12.14 I will take those **wicked** people away from their countries
13.10 have been as stubborn and **wicked** as ever, and have
14.16 I will make them pay for their **wickedness."**
15.21 I will rescue you from the power of **wicked** and violent men.
16.18 double for their sin and **wickedness,** because they have
23.10 they live **wicked** lives and misuse their power.
23.19 over the heads of the **wicked,** [20] and it will not end until
23.22 up the evil lives they live and the **wicked** things they do.
25. 5 you to turn from your **wicked** way of life and from the
25.31 will bring all people to trial and put the **wicked** to death.
26. 3 I plan to bring on them for all their **wicked** deeds."
30.14 because your sins are many and your **wickedness** is great.
30.15 because your sins are many and your **wickedness** is great.
30.23 a furious wind that will rage over the heads of the **wicked.**
36. 3 Then I will forgive their **wickedness** and their sins."
44. 9 Have you forgotten all the **wicked** things that have been
44.22 Lord could no longer endure your **wicked** and evil practices.
50.20 found in Israel and no **wickedness** in Judah, because I will
Lam 1.22 "Condemn them for all their **wickedness;**
Ezek 5. 6 showed that she was more **wicked** than the other nations, more
Ezek 7.11 Violence produces more **wickedness.**
20.44 I do not deal with you as your **wicked,** evil actions deserve."
21.25 "You **wicked,** unholy ruler of Israel, your day, the day
21.29 You are **wicked** and evil, and your day is coming, the day
31.11 He will give that tree what it deserves for its **wickedness.**
39.24 and their **wickedness,** and I turned away from them."
Dan 8.23 and they have become so **wicked** that they must be punished,
12.10 Those who are **wicked** will not understand
12.10 but will go on being **wicked;**
Hos 7. 1 all I can see is their **wickedness** and the evil they do.
Joel 3.13 They are very **wicked;**
Jon 1. 2 I am aware how **wicked** its people are."
3. 8 God and must give up his **wicked** behaviour and his evil actions.
3.10 he saw that they had given up their **wicked** behaviour.
Mic 7.13 a desert because of the **wickedness** of those who live on it.
Nah 1.11 a man full of **wicked** schemes, who plotted against the Lord.
1.15 The **wicked** will never invade your land again.
Hab 3.13 of the **wicked**
Zeph 1. 3 I will bring about the downfall of the **wicked.**
Zech 5. 8 The angel said, "This woman represents **wickedness."**
Mal 3.18 the righteous and to the **wicked,** to the person who serves me
4. 3 act, you will overcome the **wicked,** and they will be like
Mt 7.23 Get away from me, you **wicked** people!'
Mk 8.38 teaching in this godless and **wicked** day, then the Son of Man
Lk 6.35 For he is good to the ungrateful and the **wicked.**
13.27 Get away from me, all you **wicked** people!'
Acts 2.40 "Save yourselves from the punishment coming on this **wicked** people!"
3.26 by making every one of you turn away from his **wicked** ways."
Rom 1.29 They are filled with all kinds of **wickedness,** evil, greed,
3.13 **wicked** lies roll off their tongues, and dangerous threats,
5. 6 Christ died for the **wicked** at the time that God chose.
6.13 part of yourselves to sin to be used for **wicked** purposes.
6.19 as slaves to impurity and wickedness for **wicked** purposes.
11.26 from Zion and remove all **wickedness** from the descendants of Jacob.
1 Cor 5. 8 old yeast of sin and **wickedness,** but with the bread that has
6. 9 Surely you know that the **wicked** will not possess God's Kingdom.
Eph 6.12 but against the **wicked** spiritual forces in the heavenly world,
2 Thes 2. 3 Rebellion takes place and the **Wicked One** appears, who is destined
2. 6 At the proper time, then, the **Wicked One** will appear.
2. 7 The Mysterious **Wickedness** is already at work, but what is
2. 8 Then the **Wicked One** will be revealed, but when the Lord
2. 9 The **Wicked One** will come with the power of Satan and
2.10 and use every kind of **wicked** deceit on those who will perish.
3. 2 Pray also that God will rescue us from **wicked** and evil people;
Tit 1.12 "Cretans are always liars, **wicked** beasts, and lazy gluttons."
2.14 to rescue us from all **wickedness** and to make us a pure
Jas 1.21 So get rid of every filthy habit and all **wicked** conduct.
2 Pet 2. 9 and how to keep the **wicked** under punishment for the Day of
2.22 unless they repent of the **wicked** things they did with her.
Rev 18. 5 up as high as heaven, and God remembers her **wicked** ways.

WIDE
[WIDTH]

Gen 6.15 Make it 133 metres long, 22 metres **wide,** and 13 metres high.
Ex 25.10 66 centimetres **wide,** and 66 centimetres high.
25.17 of pure gold, 110 centimetres long and 66 centimetres **wide.**
25.23 44 centimetres **wide,** and 66 centimetres high.
25.25 Make a rim 75 millimetres **wide** round it and a gold
26. 2 piece the same size, twelve metres long and two metres **wide.**
26. 8 all the same size, thirteen metres long and two metres **wide.**
26.16 and 66 centimetres **wide,** [17] with two matching projections,
27. 1 metres long and 2.2 metres **wide,** and it is to be 1.3
27.13 the entrance is, the enclosure is also to be 22 metres **wide.**
27.18 to be 44 metres long, 22 metres **wide,** and 2.2 metres high.
28.16 folded double, 22 centimetres long and 22 centimetres **wide.**
30. 2 centimetres long and 45 centimetres **wide,** and it is to be 90
36. 9 was the same size, twelve metres long and two metres **wide.**
36.15 all the same size, thirteen metres long and two metres **wide.**
36.21 centimetres **wide,** [22] with two matching projections,
37. 1 110 centimetres long, 66 centimetres **wide,**
37. 6 of pure gold, 110 centimetres long and 66 centimetres **wide.**
37.10 88 centimetres long, 44 centimetres **wide,**
37.12 made a rim 75 millimetres **wide** round it and put a gold
37.25 and 45 centimetres **wide,** and it was 90 centimetres high.
38. 1 metres long and 2.2 metres **wide,** and it was 1.3 metres high.
38.13 the entrance was, the enclosure was also 22 metres **wide.**
39. 9 folded double, 22 centimetres long and 22 centimetres **wide.**
Num 24. 7 than Agag, And his rule shall be extended far and **wide.**
Deut 3.11 almost two metres **wide** according to standard measurements.
Josh 8.17 and the city was left **wide** open, with no one to defend
1 Kgs 6. 2 it was 27 metres long, 9 metres **wide,** and 13.5 metres high.
6. 3 deep and 9 metres **wide,** as wide as the sanctuary itself.
6. 6 lowest storey was 2.2 metres **wide,**
6. 6 the middle storey 2.7 metres **wide,**
6. 6 and in the top storey 3.1 metres **wide.**
6.20 nine metres long, nine metres **wide,** and nine metres high,
7. 2 22 metres **wide,** and 13.5 metres high.
7. 6 The Hall of Columns was 22 metres long and 13.5 metres **wide.**
7.27 was 1.8 metres long, 1.8 metres **wide,** and 1.3 metres high.
2 Chr 3. 3 twenty-seven metres long and nine metres **wide.**
3. 4 entrance room was the full **width** of the Temple, nine metres,
3. 8 metres long and nine metres **wide,**
3. 8 which was the full **width** of the Temple.
3.11 room, stretching across the full **width** of about nine metres.
Ezra 3.13 made was so loud that it could be heard far and **wide.**
6. 3 The Temple is to be twenty-seven metres high and twenty-seven metres **wide.**

Neh 4.19 a distance that we are **widely** separated from one another on
12.43 and the noise they all made could be heard far and **wide.**
Job 11. 9 God's greatness is broader than the earth, **wider** than the sea.
36. 3 My knowledge is **wide;**
Ps 24. 7 Fling **wide** the gates, open the ancient doors, and the
24. 9 Fling **wide** the gates, open the ancient doors, and the
104.25 the ocean, large and **wide,** where countless creatures live,
Is 5.14 the dead is hungry for them, and it opens its mouth **wide.**
30.33 It is deep and **wide,** and piled high with wood.
57. 9 you send messengers far and **wide,** even to the world of the
Ezek 17. 3 eagle with beautiful feathers and huge wings, spread **wide.**
17. 6 The plant sprouted and became a low, **wide-spreading** grapevine.
40.11 Next, the man measured the **width** of the passage in the gateway.
40.14 He measured that room and found it was ten metres **wide.**
40.21 twenty-five metres and the **width** twelve and a half metres.
40.25 twenty-five metres, and the **width** twelve and a half metres.
40.29 twenty-five metres and the **width** twelve and a half metres.
40.33 twenty-five metres and the **width** twelve and a half metres.
40.36 twenty-five metres and its **width** twelve and a half metres.
40.43 Ledges seventy-five millimetres **wide**
40.48 metres deep and seven metres **wide,** with walls one and a half
40.49 room, which was ten metres **wide** and six metres deep.
41. 2 metres deep [2]and five metres **wide,** with walls two and a
41. 2 it was twenty metres long, and ten metres **wide.**
41. 3 metre deep and three metres **wide,** with walls on either side
41. 5 the Temple, was a series of small rooms two metres **wide.**
41. 7 outside of the rooms, two **wide** stairways were built, so that
41. 8 a terrace two and a half metres **wide** all round the Temple;
41.12 forty-five metres long and thirty-five metres **wide;**
41.22 It was one and a half metres high and one metre **wide.**
42. 2 This building was fifty metres long and twenty-five metres **wide.**
42. 3 the space ten metres **wide** which was alongside the Temple,
42. 4 was a passage five metres **wide** and fifty metres long, with
43.13 centimetres deep and fifty centimetres **wide,** with a rim at
43.17 (The gutter was fifty centimetres **wide.)**
45. 1 be twelve and a half kilometres long by ten kilometres **wide.**
45. 2 surrounded by an open space twenty-five metres **wide.**
45. 6 two and a half kilometres **wide,** is to be set aside for
46.21 courtyard, twenty metres long and fifteen metres **wide.**
48. 8 twelve and a half kilometres **wide** from north to south, and
Dan 3. 1 high and nearly three metres **wide,** and he had it set up
Zech 2. 2 he answered, "to see how long and how **wide** it is."
5. 2 it is nine metres long and four and a half metres **wide."**
Mt 7.13 the gate to hell is **wide** and the road that leads to
Lk 5.15 Jesus spread all the more **widely,** and crowds of people came
2 Cor 6.11 we have opened our hearts **wide.**
6.13 Open your hearts **wide!**
2 Pet 2. 3 Judge has been ready, and their Destroyer has been **wide** awake!
Rev 21.16 The city was perfectly square, as **wide** as it was long.
21.16 2,400 kilometres long and was as **wide** and as high as it

WIDOW

Gen 38. 8 Er's brother Onan, "Go and sleep with your brother's **widow.**
38. 9 had intercourse with his brother's **widow,** he let the semen
38.11 house and remain a **widow** until my son Shelah grows up."
38.14 So she changed from the **widow's** clothes she had been wearing,
38.19 took off her veil, and put her **widow's** clothes back on.
Ex 22.22 Do not ill-treat any **widow** or orphan.
22.24 Your wives will become **widows,** and your children will be fatherless.
Lev 21.14 marry a virgin, [14]not a **widow** or a divorced woman or a
22.13 But a **widowed** or divorced daughter who has no children
Num 30. 9 A **widow** or a divorced woman must keep every vow she makes
Deut 10.18 He makes sure that orphans and **widows** are treated fairly;
14.29 the foreigners, orphans, and **widows** who live in your towns.
16.11 foreigners, orphans, and **widows** who live in your towns.
16.14 foreigners, orphans, and **widows** who live in your towns.
24.17 and do not take a **widow's** garment as security for a loan.
24.19 for the foreigners, orphans, and **widows,** so that the Lord
24.20 they are for the foreigners, orphans, and **widows.**
24.21 that are left are for the foreigners, orphans, and **widows.**
25. 5 leaving no son, then his **widow** is not to be married to
25. 9 to marry her, [9]his brother's **widow** is to go up to him
26.12 foreigners, the orphans, and the **widows,** so that in every
26.13 the orphans, and the **widows,** as you commanded me to do.
27.19 deprives foreigners, orphans, and **widows** of their rights.'
Ruth 4. 5 also buying Ruth, the Moabite **widow,** so that the field will
4.10 In addition, Ruth the Moabite, Mahlon's **widow,** becomes my wife.
1 Sam 27. 3 with him, Ahinoam from Jezreel, and Abigail, Nabal's **widow,**
2 Sam 2. 2 Jezreel, and Abigail, Nabal's **widow,** who was from Carmel.
3. 3 Chileab, whose mother was Abigail, Nabal's **widow,** from
14. 5 "I am a poor **widow,** sir," she answered.
20. 3 confined for the rest of their lives, living like **widows.**
1 Kgs 11.26 His mother was a **widow** named Zeruah.
17. 9 I have commanded a **widow** who lives there to feed you."
17.10 to the gate of the town, he saw a **widow** gathering firewood.
17.15 The **widow** went and did as Elijah had told her, and all
17.17 Some time later the **widow's** son fell ill;
17.20 God, why have you done such a terrible thing to this **widow?**
2 Kgs 4. 1 The **widow** of a member of a group of prophets went to
1 Chr 2.24 After Hezron died, his son Caleb married Ephrath, his father's **widow.**
Job 22. 9 not only refused to help **widows,** but you also robbed and
24. 3 to orphans, and keep a **widow's** ox till she pays her debts.
24.21 That happens because he ill-treated **widows** and showed no
27.15 disease, and even their **widows** will not mourn their death.
29.13 misery praised me, and I helped **widows** find security.
31.16 never have I let **widows** live in despair [17]or let orphans
Ps 68. 5 his sacred Temple, cares for orphans and protects **widows.**
78.64 and their **widows** were not allowed to mourn.
Ps 94. 6 They kill **widows** and orphans, and murder the strangers who
109. 9 May his children become orphans, and his wife a **widow!**
146. 9 he helps **widows** and orphans, but takes the wicked to their ruin.
Prov 15.25 of arrogant men, but he will protect a **widow's** property.
Is 1.17 oppressed, give orphans their rights, and defend **widows."**
1.23 orphans in court or listen when **widows** present their case.
9.17 pity to any of the **widows** and orphans, because all the
10. 2 you take the property that belongs to **widows** and orphans.
47. 8 you would never be a **widow** or suffer the loss of your
54. 4 as a young wife, and your desperate loneliness as a **widow.**
Jer 7. 6 Stop taking advantage of aliens, orphans, and **widows.**
15. 8 There are more **widows** in your land than grains of sand by
22. 3 Do not ill-treat or oppress foreigners, orphans, or **widows;**
49.11 Your **widows** can depend on me.
Lam 1. 1 Once honoured by the world, she is now like a **widow;**
5. 3 been killed by the enemy, and now our mothers are **widows.**
Ezek 22. 7 You cheat foreigners and take advantage of **widows** and orphans.
22.25 they can get, and by their murders leave many **widows.**
44.22 only an Israelite virgin or the **widow** of another priest.
Zech 7.10 Do not oppress **widows,** orphans, foreigners who live among you,
Mal 3. 5 those who take advantage of **widows,** orphans, and
Mt 22.24 his brother must marry the **widow** so that they can have
22.25 having children, so he left his **widow** to his brother.
Mk 12.19 man's brother must marry the **widow** so that they can have
12.40 They take advantage of **widows** and rob them of their homes,
12.42 then a poor **widow** came along and dropped in two little
12.43 tell you that this poor **widow** put more in the offering box
Lk 2.36 a very old prophetess, a **widow** named Anna, daughter of Phanuel
4.25 true that there were many **widows** in Israel during the time
4.26 but only to a **widow** living in Zarephath in the territory
7.12 a woman who was a **widow,** and a large crowd from the
18. 3 And there was a **widow** in that same town who kept coming
18. 5 of all the trouble this **widow** is giving me, I will see
20.28 man's brother must marry the **widow** so that they can have
20.47 who take advantage of **widows** and rob them of their homes,
21. 2 saw a very poor **widow** dropping in two little copper coins.
21. 3 tell you that this poor **widow** put in more than all the
Acts 6. 1 Greek-speaking Jews claimed that their **widows** were being neglected
9.39 room upstairs, where all the **widows** crowded round him, crying
9.41 believers, including the **widows,** and presented her alive to them.
1 Cor 7. 8 the unmarried and to the **widows** I say that it would be
1 Tim 5. 3 Show respect for **widows** who really are all alone.
5. 4 But if a **widow** has children or grandchildren, they should learn
5. 5 A **widow** who is all alone, with no one to take care
5. 6 But a **widow** who gives herself to pleasure has already died,
5. 9 Do not add any **widow** to the list
5. 9 to the list of **widows** unless she is over sixty years
5.11 But do not include younger **widows** in the list;
5.14 would prefer that the younger **widows** get married, have children,
5.15 For some **widows** have already turned away to follow Satan.
5.16 if any Christian woman has **widows** in her family, she must
5.16 that it may take care of the **widows** who are all alone.
Jas 1.27 take care of orphans and **widows** in their suffering and to
Rev 18. 7 I am no **widow,** I will never know grief!'

WIDTH see WIDE

WIFE

[HOUSEWIVES, THE DESERTED WIFE]

Gen 2.24 mother and is united with his **wife,** and they become one.
3.17 man, "You listened to your **wife** and ate the fruit which I
3.20 Adam named his **wife** Eve, because she was the mother of
3.21 of animal skins for Adam and his **wife,** and he clothed them.
4. 1 Then Adam had intercourse with his **wife,** and she became pregnant.
4.17 Cain and his **wife** had a son and named him Enoch.
4.19 Lamech had two **wives,** Adah and Zillah.
4.23 Lamech said to his **wives,**
4.25 Adam and his **wife** had another son.
6.18 Go into the boat with your **wife,** your sons, and their wives.
7. 7 He and his **wife,** and his sons and their wives, went into
7.13 same day Noah and his **wife** went into the boat
7.13 their three sons, Shem, Ham, and Japheth, and their **wives.**
8.16 out of the boat with your **wife,** your sons, and their wives.
8.18 out of the boat with his **wife,** his sons, and their wives.
11.31 and his daughter-in-law Sarai, Abram's **wife,** and with them
12. 5 Abram took his **wife** Sarai, his nephew Lot, and all the
12.11 he said to his **wife** Sarai, "You are a beautiful woman.
12.12 assume that you are my **wife,** and so they will kill me
12.14 Egypt, the Egyptians did see that his **wife** was beautiful.
12.18 Why didn't you tell me that she was your **wife?**
12.19 she was your sister, and let me take her as my **wife?**
12.19 Here is your **wife;**
12.20 country, together with his **wife** and everything he owned.
13. 1 part of Canaan with his **wife** and everything he owned, and
16. 1 Abram's **wife** Sarai had not borne him any children.
17.15 God said to Abraham, "You must no longer call your **wife** Sarai;
17.19 Your **wife** Sarah will bear you a son and you will name
18. 9 Then they asked him, "Where is your **wife** Sarah?"
18.10 I will come back, and your **wife** Sarah will have a son."
19.15 "Take your **wife** and your two daughters and get out, so that
19.16 the men took him, his **wife,** and his two daughters by the
19.26 But Lot's **wife** looked back and was turned into a pillar
20. 2 in Gerar, [2]he said that his **wife** Sarah was his sister.
20.11 for God and that they would kill me to get my **wife.**
20.17 had happened to Sarah, Abraham's **wife,** the Lord had made it
20.17 He also healed his **wife** and his slave-girls, so that they
21.21 His mother found an Egyptian **wife** for him.

Gen 23. 3 left the place where his **wife's** body was lying, went to the
23. 4 sell me some land, so that I can bury my **wife."**
23. 6 bury your **wife** in the best grave that we have.
23. 8 to let me bury my **wife** here, please ask Ephron son of
23.11 will give it to you, so that you can bury your **wife."**
23.13 Accept my payment, and I will bury my **wife** there."
23.15 Bury your **wife** in it."
23.19 Then Abraham buried his **wife** Sarah in that cave in the
24. 3 you will not choose a **wife** for my son from the people
24. 4 was born and get a **wife** for my son Isaac from among
24. 7 you, so that you can get a **wife** there for my son.
24.15 was the son of Abraham's brother Nahor and his **wife** Milcah.
24.36 Sarah, my master's **wife,** bore him a son when she was old,
24.37 said, 'Do not choose a **wife** for my son from the girls
24.38 people, to my relatives, and choose a **wife** for him.'
24.40 get for my son a **wife** from my own people, from my
24.44 one that you have chosen as the **wife** for my master's son.'
24.51 Let her become the **wife** of your master's son, as the Lord
24.67 that his mother Sarah had lived in, and she became his **wife.**
25. 1 Abraham married another **wife,** whose name was Keturah.
25. 6 he gave presents to the sons his other **wives** had borne him.
25.10 both Abraham and his **wife** Sarah were buried there.
26. 7 men there asked about his **wife,** he said that she was his
26. 7 admit that she was his **wife,** because he was afraid that the
26. 9 Abimelech sent for Isaac and said, "So she is your **wife!**
26. 9 thought I would be killed if I said she was my **wife."**
26.10 easily have slept with your **wife,** and you would have been
26.11 who ill-treats this man or his **wife** will be put to death."
27.46 to Isaac, "I am sick and tired of Esau's foreign **wives.**
28. 6 Jacob and sent him away to Mesopotamia to find a **wife.**
29.28 was over, Laban gave him his daughter Rachel as his **wife.**
30. 9 she gave her slave-girl Zilpah to Jacob as his **wife.**
30.26 Give me my **wives** and children that I have earned by
31.17 put his children and his **wives** on the camels, and drove all
32.22 got up, took his two **wives,** his two concubines, and his
34. 4 "I want you to get this girl for me as my **wife."**
36. 6 Then Esau took his **wives,** his sons, his daughters, and all
36.10 Esau's **wife** Adah bore him one son, Eliphaz, and
36.10 And by another **wife,** Timna, he had one more son, Amalek.
36.10 Esau's **wife** Basemath bore him one son, Reuel,
36.14 Esau's **wife** Oholibamah, the daughter of Anah son of Zibeon,
36.16 These were all descendants of Esau's **wife** Adah.
36.17 These were all descendants of Esau's **wife** Basemath.
36.18 from Esau by his **wife** Oholibamah, the daughter of Anah:
36.31 Hadad from Pau (his **wife** was Mehetabel, the daughter of Matred
38. 6 his first son Er, Judah got a **wife** whose name was Tamar.
38.12 After some time Judah's **wife** died.
39. 7 after a while his master's **wife** began to desire Joseph and
41.45 and he gave him a **wife,** Asenath, the daughter of Potiphera,
44.27 us, 'You know that my **wife** Rachel bore me only two sons.
45.19 them from Egypt for their **wives** and small children and to
46. 5 their small children, and their **wives** in the wagons which
46.19 Jacob's **wife** Rachel bore him two sons:
46.26 who went to Egypt was sixty-six, not including his sons' **wives.**
49.31 That is where they buried Abraham and his **wife** Sarah;
49.31 that is where they buried Isaac and his **wife** Rebecca;
Ex 4.20 So Moses took his **wife** and his sons, put them on a
4.25 Then Zipporah, his **wife,** took a sharp stone, cut
18. 2 with him Moses' **wife** Zipporah, who had been left behind,
18. 5 Jethro came with Moses' **wife** and her two sons into the
20.17 do not desire his **wife,** his slaves, his cattle, his donkeys,
21. 3 he is not to take a **wife** with him when he leaves;
21. 3 when he became your slave, he may take his **wife** with him.
21. 4 his master gave him a **wife** and she bore him sons or
21. 5 he loves his master, his **wife,** and his children and does not
21. 8 intends to make her his **wife,** but he doesn't like her, then
21.10 a man takes a second **wife,** he must continue
21.10 to give his first **wife** the same amount of food and
22.24 Your **wives** will become widows,
32. 2 the gold earrings which your **wives,** your sons, and your
Lev 18. 8 father by having intercourse with any of his other **wives.**
18.14 Do not have intercourse with your uncle's **wife;**
18.16 intercourse with your daughter-in-law [16] or with your brother's **wife.**
18.18 Do not take your **wife's** sister as one of your wives,
18.18 as long as your **wife** is living.
18.20 Do not have intercourse with another man's **wife;**
20.10 man commits adultery with the **wife** of a fellow-Israelite,
20.11 with one of his father's **wives** disgraces his father, and
20.20 intercourse with his uncle's **wife,** he disgraces his uncle,
20.21 If a man marries his brother's **wife,** they will die childless.
Num 5.12 man becomes suspicious that his **wife** is unfaithful to him
5.12 not be certain, for his **wife** may have kept it secret—there
5.12 husband becomes suspicious of his **wife,** even though she has
5.15 In either case the man shall take his **wife** to the priest.
5.29 and becomes suspicious that his **wife** has committed adultery.
14. 3 in battle, and our **wives** and children will be captured.
16.27 the entrance of their tents, with their **wives** and children.
32.26 Our **wives** and children and our cattle and sheep will
Deut 3.19 Only your **wives,** children, and livestock—I know you have
5.21 " 'Do not desire another man's **wife;**
13. 6 or your daughter or the **wife** you love or your closest friend
17.17 is not to have many **wives,** because this would make him turn
21.15 "Suppose a man has two **wives** and they both bear him sons,
21.15 but the first son is not the child of his favourite **wife.**
21.16 the son of his favourite **wife** by giving him the share that
21.17 son, even though he is not the son of his favourite **wife.**
22.19 will continue to be his **wife,** and he can never divorce her
22.22 having intercourse with another man's **wife,** both of them are
22.29 she is to become his **wife,** because he forced her to have
22.30 by having intercourse with any of his father's **wives.**

Deut 24. 5 so that he can stay at home and make his **wife** happy.
25.11 having a fight and the **wife** of one tries to help her
27.20 by having intercourse with any of his father's **wives.'**
28.54 his brother or to the **wife** he loves or to any of
Josh 1.14 Your **wives,** your children, and your livestock will stay here,
Judg 4. 4 Now Deborah, the **wife** of Lappidoth, was a prophet, and
4.17 the tent of Jael, the **wife** of Heber the Kenite, because King
5.24 of women is Jael, the **wife** of Heber the Kenite— the
8.30 He had seventy sons, because he had many **wives.**
11. 2 had other sons by his **wife,** and when they grew up, they
13. 2 His **wife** had never been able to have children.
13.11 Manoah got up and followed his **wife.**
13.11 and asked, "Are you the man who was talking to my **wife?"**
13.13 The Lord's angel answered, "Your **wife** must be sure to
13.20 the altar, Manoah and his **wife** saw the Lord's angel
13.20 and he and his **wife** threw themselves face downwards on the
13.22 Manoah said to his **wife,** "We are sure to die, because
13.23 But his **wife** answered, "If the Lord had wanted to kill us,
14. 3 you have to go to those heathen Philistines to get a **wife?**
14.15 day they said to Samson's **wife,** "Trick your husband into
14.16 So Samson's **wife** went to him in tears and said, "You
14.20 what had happened, [20] and his **wife** was given to the man
15. 1 Samson went to visit his **wife** during the wheat harvest and
15. 1 said to her father, "I want to go to my **wife's** room."
15. 6 Timnah, had given Samson's **wife** to a friend of Samson's.
21. 7 shall we do to provide **wives** for the men of Benjamin who
21.16 shall we do to provide **wives** for the men who are left?
21.21 Each of you take a **wife** by force from among the girls
21.22 did not take them from you in battle to be our **wives.**
21.23 each of them chose a **wife** from the girls who were dancing
Ruth 1. 1 in Judah, went with his **wife** Naomi and their two sons Mahlon
4.10 In addition, Ruth the Moabite, Mahlon's widow, becomes my **wife.**
4.11 May the Lord make your **wife** become like Rachel and Leah, who
4.13 So Boaz took Ruth home as his **wife.**
1 Sam 1. 2 Elkanah had two **wives,** Hannah and Peninnah.
1.19 Elkanah had intercourse with his **wife** Hannah, and the Lord
2. 5 The childless **wife** has borne seven children, but the mother
2.20 would bless Elkanah and his **wife,** and say to Elkanah, "May
4.19 Eli's daughter-in-law, the **wife** of Phinehas, was
14.50 His **wife** was Ahinoam, the daughter of Ahimaaz;
18.17 her to you as your **wife** on condition that you serve me
19.11 David's **wife,** warned him, "If you don't get away tonight,
25. 2 His **wife** Abigail was beautiful and intelligent, but he was a mean,
25.14 One of Nabal's servants said to Nabal's **wife** Abigail,
25.40 "David sent us to take you to him to be his **wife."**
25.42 maids, she went with David's servants and became his **wife.**
25.43 Ahinoam from Jezreel, and now Abigail also became his **wife.**
25.44 Michal, who had been David's **wife,** to Palti son of Laish,
27. 3 David had his two **wives** with him, Ahinoam from Jezreel, and
30. 3 burnt down and that their **wives,** sons, and daughters had
30. 5 Even David's two **wives,** Ahinoam and Abigail, had been taken away.
30.18 the Amalekites had taken, including his two **wives;**
30.22 They can take their **wives** and children and go away."
2 Sam 2. 2 So David went to Hebron, taking with him his two **wives:**
3.14 to Ishbosheth to say, "Give me back my **wife** Michal.
5.13 David took more concubines and **wives,**
11. 3 the daughter of Eliam and the **wife** of Uriah the Hittite.
11.11 could I go home, eat and drink, and sleep with my **wife?**
11.27 she became his **wife** and bore him a son.
12. 8 I gave you his kingdom and his **wives;**
12. 9 you let the Ammonites kill him, and then you took his **wife!**
12.10 because you have disobeyed me and have taken Uriah's **wife.**
12.11 it when I take your **wives** from you and give them to
12.15 caused the child that Uriah's **wife** had borne to David to
12.24 Then David comforted his **wife** Bathsheba.
17.19 The man's **wife** took a covering, spread it over the
19. 5 of your sons and daughters and of your **wives** and concubines.
1 Kgs 2.17 to let me have Abishag, the girl from Shunem, as my **wife."**
2.21 She answered, "Let your brother Adonijah have Abishag as his **wife."**
7. 8 kind of house for his **wife,** the daughter of the king of
9.24 of the city, after his **wife,** the daughter of the king of
10. 8 How fortunate are your **wives!**
11. 8 worship where all his foreign **wives** could burn incense and
14. 2 Jeroboam said to his **wife,** "Disguise yourself so that no
14. 5 had told him that Jeroboam's **wife** was coming to ask him
14. 5 When Jeroboam's **wife** arrived, she pretended to be someone else.
14. 6 I know you are Jeroboam's **wife.**
14.12 Ahijah went on to say to Jeroboam's **wife,** "Now go back home.
14.17 Jeroboam's **wife** went back to Tirzah.
19. 1 King Ahab told his **wife** Jezebel everything that Elijah had
20. 7 message demanding my **wives** and children, my silver and gold,
21. 5 His **wife** Jezebel went to him and asked, "Why are you so
21.25 Lord's sight as Ahab—all at the urging of his **wife** Jezebel.
2 Kgs 5. 2 Israelite girl, who became a servant of Naaman's **wife.**
8.18 His **wife** was Ahab's daughter, and like the family of
24.15 together with Jehoiachin's mother, his **wives,** his officials,
1 Chr 1.43 Hadad from Pau (his **wife** was Mehetabel, the daughter of Matred
2. 3 By his **wife** Bathshua, a Canaanite, he had three sons:
2.26 Jerahmeel had another **wife,** a woman named Atarah, and they
2.50 Hur was the eldest son of Caleb and his **wife** Ephrath.
3. 5 His **wife** Bathsheba, daughter of Ammiel, bore him four sons:
4. 3 son of his father Caleb's **wife** Ephrath, and his descendants
4. 5 founded the town of Tekoa, had two **wives,** Helah and Naarah.
7. 4 They had so many **wives** and children that their descendants
7.15 Machir found a **wife** for Huppim and one for Shuppim.
7.16 Maacah, Machir's **wife,** gave birth to two sons, whom
7.23 he had intercourse with his **wife** again, and she became
8. 8 Shaharaim divorced two **wives,** Hushim and Baara.
8.29 His **wife** was named Maacah, [30] and his eldest son, Abdon.

1 Chr 9.35 His **wife** was named Maacah.
14. 3 David married more **wives** and had more sons and daughters.
2 Chr 8.11 Solomon moved his **wife,** the daughter of the king of Egypt,
11.21 In all, Rehoboam had eighteen **wives** and sixty concubines,
11.21 Of all his **wives** and concubines he loved Maacah best,
11.23 and also secured many **wives** for them.
13.21 He had fourteen **wives** and fathered twenty-two sons and sixteen daughters.
20.13 men of Judah, with their **wives** and children, were standing
21.14 children, and your **wives,** and will destroy your possessions.
21.17 as prisoners all the king's **wives** and sons except Ahaziah,
24. 3 Jehoiada chose two **wives** for King Joash, and they bore him
29. 9 killed in battle, and our **wives** and children have been taken
31.18 together with their **wives,** children, and other dependants,
Ezra 10.11 living in our land and get rid of your foreign **wives."**
10.14 anyone who has a foreign **wife** come at a set time, together
10.17 they investigated all the cases of men with foreign **wives.**
10.18 This is the list of the men who had foreign **wives:**
10.19 They promised to divorce their **wives,** and they offered a
10.44 All these men had foreign **wives.**
Neh 4.14 your children, your **wives,** and your homes."
10.28 land, we, together with our **wives** and all our children old
Esth 1.18 When the **wives** of the royal officials of Persia and
1.18 **Wives** everywhere will have no respect for their husbands,
1.18 and husbands will be angry with their **wives.**
5.10 friends to his house and asked his **wife** Zeresh to join them.
5.14 So his **wife** and all his friends suggested, "Why don't
6.13 He told his **wife** and all his friends everything that had
Job 2. 9 His **wife** said to him, "You are still as faithful as ever,
19.17 My **wife** can't stand the smell of my breath, and my own
31. 9 my neighbour's **wife,** and waited, hidden, outside her door,
31.10 her door, [10]then let my **wife** cook another man's food and
Ps 109. 9 May his children become orphans, and his **wife** a widow!
113. 9 He honours the childless **wife** in her home;
128. 3 Your **wife** will be like a fruitful vine in your home, and
Prov 5. 3 The lips of another man's **wife** may be as sweet as honey
5.15 Be faithful to your own **wife** and give your love to her
5.18 So be happy with your **wife** and find your joy with the
5.20 Why should you prefer the charms of another man's **wife?**
6.24 bad women, from the seductive words of other men's **wives.**
6.29 It is just as dangerous to sleep with another man's **wife.**
7. 5 from other men's **wives,** from women with seductive words.
12. 4 A good **wife** is her husband's pride and joy;
12. 4 but a **wife** who brings shame on her husband is like a
18.22 Find a **wife** and you find a good thing;
19.13 A nagging **wife** is like water going drip-drip-drip.
19.14 parents, but only the Lord can give him a sensible **wife.**
21. 9 live on the roof than share the house with a nagging **wife.**
21.19 out in the desert than with a nagging, complaining **wife.**
25.24 live on the roof than share the house with a nagging **wife.**
27.15 A nagging **wife** is like water going drip-drip-drip on a rainy day.
30.20 This is how an unfaithful **wife** acts:
31.10 How hard it is to find a capable **wife!**
31.29 says, "Many women are good **wives,** but you are the best of
Is 8. 3 Some time later my **wife** became pregnant.
13.16 houses will be looted, and their **wives** will be raped."
50. 1 I sent my people away like a man who divorces his **wife?**
54. 4 your unfaithfulness as a young **wife,** and your desperate
54. 6 you are like a young **wife,** deserted by her husband and
62. 4 "Forsaken," Or your land be called **"The Deserted Wife."**
Jer 3. 1 "If a man divorces his **wife,** and she leaves him
3. 1 and becomes another man's **wife,** he cannot take her back again.
3.20 But like an unfaithful **wife,** you have not been faithful to me.
5. 8 wild with desire, each lusting for his neighbour's **wife.**
6.11 Husbands and **wives** will be taken away, and even the very old
6.12 given to others, and so will their fields and their **wives.**
8.10 their fields to new owners and their **wives** to other men.
13.27 man lusting after his neighbour's **wife** or like a stallion
14.16 them—including their **wives,** their sons, and their daughters.
35. 8 wine, and neither do our **wives,** our sons, or our daughters.
44. 9 kings of Judah and their **wives,** and by you and your wives?
44.15 who knew that their **wives** offered sacrifices to other gods,
44.24 "Both you and your **wives** have made solemn promises to the
Lam 5.11 Our **wives** have been raped on Mount Zion itself;
Ezek 18. 6 He doesn't seduce another man's **wife** or have intercourse
18.11 offered at forbidden shrines and seduces other men's **wives.**
18.15 He doesn't seduce another man's **wife** [16]or oppress anyone
22.10 Some of them sleep with their father's **wife.**
24.18 That evening my **wife** died, and the next day I did as
Dan 5. 2 that he, his noblemen, his **wives,** and his concubines could
5.23 You, your noblemen, your **wives,** and your concubines drank
6.24 were thrown, together with their **wives** and their children,
Hos 1. 2 your **wife** will be unfaithful, and your children will be just
2. 2 she is no longer a **wife** to me, and I am no
2.19 Israel, I will make you my **wife;**
12.12 in order to get a **wife,** he worked for another man and
Amos 7.17 Lord says to you, 'Your **wife** will become a prostitute on the
Mic 7. 5 Be careful what you say even to your **wife.**
Mal 2.14 your promise to the **wife** you married when you were young.
2.15 make sure that none of you breaks his promise to his **wife.**
2.16 when one of you does such a cruel thing to his **wife.**
2.16 do not break your promise to be faithful to your **wife."**
Mt 1. 6 woman who had been Uriah's **wife),** Rehoboam, Abijah, Asa,
1.20 do not be afraid to take Mary to be your **wife.**
5.31 'Anyone who divorces his **wife** must give her a written notice
5.32 if a man divorces his **wife,** for any cause other than her
14. 3 He had done this because of Herodias, his brother Philip's **wife.**
18.25 as a slave, with his **wife** and his children and all that
19. 3 a man to divorce his **wife** for whatever reason he wishes?"
19. 5 and unite with his **wife,** and the two will become one.'
19. 7 a man to hand his **wife** a divorce notice and send her
Mt 19. 8 you permission to divorce your **wives** because you are so hard
19. 9 any man who divorces his **wife,** for any cause other than her
19.10 between a man and his **wife,** it is better not to marry."
20.20 Then the **wife** of Zebedee came to Jesus with her two sons,
22.28 day when the dead rise to life, whose **wife** will she be?
27.19 sitting in the judgement hall, his **wife** sent him a message:
27.56 Mary the mother of James and Joseph, and the **wife** of Zebedee.
Mk 6.17 married, even though she was the **wife** of his brother Philip.
6.18 "It isn't right for you to be married to your brother's **wife!"**
10. 2 asked, "does our Law allow a man to divorce his **wife?"**
10. 4 a man to write a divorce notice and send his **wife** away."
10. 7 and unite with his **wife,** [8]and the two will become one.'
10.11 "A man who divorces his **wife** and marries another woman
10.11 commits adultery against his **wife.**
12.19 man dies and leaves a **wife** but no children, that man's
12.23 to life on the day of resurrection, whose **wife** will she be?
Lk 1. 5 His **wife's** name was Elizabeth;
1.13 your prayer, and your **wife** Elizabeth will bear you a son.
1.18 I am an old man, and my **wife** is old also."
1.24 Some time later his **wife** Elizabeth became pregnant
3.19 had married Herodias, his brother's **wife,** and had done many other
14.26 father and his mother, his **wife** and his children, his brothers
16.18 man who divorces his **wife** and marries another woman commits
17.32 Remember Lot's **wife!**
18.29 anyone who leaves home or **wife** or brothers or parents or
20.28 man dies and leaves a **wife** but no children, that man's
20.33 day when the dead rise to life, whose **wife** will she be?
Jn 19.25 his mother's sister, Mary the **wife** of Clopas, and Mary Magdalene.
Acts 5. 1 named Ananias, who with his **wife** Sapphira sold some property
5. 2 But with his **wife's** agreement he kept part of the money
5. 7 About three hours later his **wife,** not knowing what had happened,
18. 2 come from Italy with his **wife** Priscilla, for the Emperor Claudius
21. 5 of them, together with their **wives** and children, went with
24.24 some days Felix came with his **wife** Drusilla, who was Jewish.
1 Cor 7. 2 man should have his own **wife,** and every woman should have
7. 3 fulfil her duty as a **wife,** and each should satisfy the
7. 4 A **wife** is not the master of her own body,
7. 4 is not the master of his own body, but his **wife** is.
7.10 a **wife** must not leave her husband;
7.11 and a husband must not divorce his **wife.**
7.12 a Christian man has a **wife** who is an unbeliever and she
7.14 by being united to his **wife,**
7.14 and the unbelieving **wife** is made acceptable to God
7.15 the Christian partner, whether husband or **wife,** is free to act.
7.16 can you be sure, Christian **wife,** that you will not save your
7.16 sure, Christian husband, that you will not save your **wife?**
7.27 Have you got a **wife?**
7.27 Then don't look for a **wife.**
7.33 with worldly matters, because he wants to please his **wife;**
9. 5 and Peter, by taking a Christian **wife** with me on my travels?
11. 3 is supreme over his **wife,** and God is supreme over Christ.
Eph 5.22 **Wives,** submit to your husbands as to the Lord.
5.23 husband has authority over his **wife** just as Christ has authority
5.24 And so **wives** must submit completely to their husbands just as
5.25 Husbands, love your **wives** just as Christ loved the church
5.28 Men ought to love their **wives** just as they love their
5.28 A man who loves his **wife** loves himself.
5.31 and unite with his **wife,** and the two will become one."
5.33 every husband must love his **wife** as himself,
5.33 and every **wife** must respect her husband.
Col 3.18 **Wives,** submit to your husbands, for that is what you
3.19 Husbands, love your **wives** and do not be harsh with them.
1 Thes 4. 4 how to live with his **wife** in a holy and honourable way,
1 Tim 3. 2 must have only one **wife,** be sober, self-controlled, and orderly;
3.11 Their **wives** also must be of good character and must not gossip;
3.12 helper must have only one **wife,** and be able to manage his
Tit 1. 6 he must have only one **wife,** and his children must be
2. 5 pure, and to be good **housewives** who submit to their husbands,
Heb 13. 4 and husbands and **wives** must be faithful to each other.
1 Pet 3. 1 In the same way you **wives** must submit to your husbands,
3. 7 husbands must live with your **wives** with the proper understanding
Rev 21. 9 and I will show you the Bride, the **wife** of the Lamb."

WILD

Gen 1.24 domestic and **wild,** large and small"—and it was done.
1.26 and all animals, domestic and **wild,** large and small."
1.28 in charge of the fish, the birds, and all the **wild** animals.
1.30 but for all the **wild** animals and for all the birds I
3.18 weeds and thorns, and you will have to eat **wild** plants.
7.14 kind of animal, domestic and **wild,** large and small, and
16.12 But your son will live like a **wild** donkey;
31.39 a sheep was killed by **wild** animals, I always bore the loss
37.20 We can say that a **wild** animal killed him.
37.33 Some **wild** animal has killed him.
44.28 been torn to pieces by **wild** animals, because I have not seen
49.22 "Joseph is like a **wild** donkey by a spring,
49.22 A **wild** colt on a hillside.
Ex 22.13 If it was killed by **wild** animals, the man is to bring
22.13 he need not pay for what has been killed by **wild** animals.
22.31 the meat of any animal that has been killed by **wild** animals;
23.11 grows there, and the **wild** animals can have what is left.
23.29 would become deserted, and the **wild** animals would be too
Lev 7.24 has been killed by a **wild** animal must not be eaten, but
17.15 or has been killed by **wild** animals must wash his clothes,
22. 8 has died a natural death or has been killed by **wild** animals;
25. 7 your domestic animals, and the **wild** animals in your fields.
Num 23.22 He fights for them like a **wild** ox.
24. 8 He fights for them like a **wild** ox.

Deut 7.22 you did, the number of **wild** animals would increase and be a
14. 5 cattle, sheep, goats, [5]deer, **wild** sheep, wild goats, or
28.26 When you die, birds and **wild** animals will come and eat
32.13 They found **wild** honey among the rocks;
32.24 I will send **wild** animals to attack them, and poisonous
33.17 has the strength of a bull, The horns of a **wild** ox.
1 Sam 26.20 Why should he hunt me down like a **wild** bird?"
2 Sam 2.18 run as fast as a **wild** deer, [19]started chasing Abner,
21.10 and at night she would protect them from **wild** animals.
2 Kgs 4.39 He found a **wild** vine, and picked as many gourds as he
14. 9 A **wild** animal passed by and trampled the bush down.
19.29 next you will have only **wild** grain to eat, but the following
2 Chr 20.16 of the valley that leads to the **wild** country near Jeruel.
20.20 morning the people went out to the **wild** country near Tekoa.
25.18 A **wild** animal passed by and trampled the bush down.
Job 5.22 at violence and hunger and not be afraid of **wild** animals.
5.23 **wild** animals will never attack you.
6. 3 sands of the sea, so my **wild** words should not surprise you.
11.12 Stupid men will start being wise when **wild** donkeys are born tame.
24. 5 So the poor, like **wild** donkeys, search for food in the dry
30. 3 would gnaw dry roots— at night, in **wild,** desolate places.
30. 7 Out in the **wilds** they howled like animals and huddled
37. 1 The storm makes my heart beat **wildly.**
37. 8 The **wild** animals go to their dens.
39. 1 Have you watched **wild** deer give birth?
39. 4 In the **wilds** their young grow strong;
39. 5 Who gave the **wild** donkeys their freedom?
39. 9 Will a **wild** ox work for you?
39.15 that a foot may crush them or a **wild** animal break them.
40.20 Grass to feed him grows on the hills where **wild** beasts play.
41.34 he is king of all **wild** beasts.
Ps 8. 7 sheep and cattle, and the **wild** animals too;
22.21 I am helpless before these **wild** bulls.
37.20 the enemies of the Lord will vanish like **wild** flowers;
44.19 Yet you left us helpless among **wild** animals;
50.11 All the **wild** birds are mine and all living things in the
68.30 Rebuke Egypt, that **wild** animal in the reeds;
79. 2 the bodies of your servants for **wild** animals to eat.
80.13 **wild** pigs trample it down, and wild animals feed on it.
81.16 with the finest wheat and satisfy you with **wild** honey."
92.10 You have made me as strong as a **wild** ox;
102. 6 I am like a **wild** bird in the desert, like an owl
103.15 We grow and flourish like a **wild** flower;
104.11 They provide water for the **wild** animals;
104.11 there the **wild** donkeys quench their thirst.
104.18 The **wild** goats live in the high mountains, and the
104.20 night, and in the darkness all the **wild** animals come out.
148.10 all animals, tame and **wild,** reptiles and birds.
Prov 30.17 by vultures or have his eyes picked out by **wild** ravens.
Song 1.14 My lover is like the **wild** flowers that bloom in the
2. 1 I am only a **wild** flower in Sharon, a lily in a
Is 5. 5 that protects it, and let **wild** animals eat it and trample it
13.21 **wild** goats will prance through the ruins.
18. 6 will be left exposed to the birds and the **wild** animals.
23.13 not the Assyrians, who let the **wild** animals overrun Tyre.
32.14 **Wild** donkeys will roam there, and sheep will find pasture there.
34. 7 The people will fall like **wild** oxen and young bulls, and
34.14 **Wild** animals will roam there, and demons will call to each other.
37.30 next you will have only **wild** grain to eat, but the following
40. 6 they last no longer than **wild** flowers.
43.20 Even the **wild** animals will honour me;
56. 9 nations to come like **wild** animals and devour his people.
63.12 they were as sure-footed as **wild** horses, and never stumbled.
Jer 2.23 You are like a **wild** camel on heat, running about loose,
4.19 My heart is beating **wildly!**
5. 8 They were like well-fed stallions **wild** with desire, each
7.33 food for the birds and **wild** animals, and there will be no
9.10 birds and **wild** animals have fled and gone."
12. 9 Call the **wild** animals to come and join in the feast!
14. 6 The **wild** donkeys stand on the hill-tops and pant for
15. 3 birds will eat them, and **wild** animals will devour what is
16. 4 bodies will be food for the birds and the **wild** animals.
19. 7 their corpses to the birds and the **wild** animals as food.
27. 6 Babylonia, and I have made even the **wild** animals serve him.
28.14 he will make even the **wild** animals serve Nebuchadnezzar."
34.20 and their corpses will be eaten by birds and **wild** animals.
48. 6 'Run like a **wild** desert donkey!'
51.37 That country will become a pile of ruins where **wild** animals live.
Lam 5.18 lonely and deserted, and **wild** jackals prowl through its ruins.
Ezek 4.14 that died a natural death or was killed by **wild** animals.
5.17 I will send hunger and **wild** animals to kill your children,
14.15 "Or I might send **wild** animals to kill the people,
14.21 punishments on Jerusalem—war, famine, **wild** animals, and
23.11 Oholibah saw this, she was **wilder** and more of a prostitute
31. 6 The **wild** animals bore their young in its shelter;
31.13 tree, and the **wild** animals will walk over its branches.
33.27 Those living in the country will be eaten by **wild** animals.
33.28 of Israel will be so **wild** that no one will be able
34. 5 they were scattered, and **wild** animals killed and ate them.
34. 8 sheep have been attacked by **wild** animals that killed and ate
34.28 them any more, and the **wild** animals will not kill and eat
35.13 I have heard the **wild,** boastful way you have talked against me."
36.34 fields saw how overgrown and **wild** they were, but I will let
39. 4 let their bodies be food for all the birds and **wild** animals.
Dan 4.12 **Wild** animals rested in its shade, birds built nests in its branches,
4.21 **Wild** animals rested under it, and birds made their nests in
4.25 away from human society and will live with **wild** animals.
4.32 from human society, live with **wild** animals, and eat grass
5.21 He lived with **wild** donkeys, ate grass like an ox, and slept
Hos 2.12 **wild** animals will destroy them.
2.18 a covenant with all the **wild** animals and birds, so that they

Hos 8. 9 Stubborn as **wild** donkeys, the people of Israel go their own way.
13. 8 the spot, and will tear you to pieces like a **wild** animal.
Joel 1.20 Even the **wild** animals cry out to you because the streams
Nah 2. 4 Chariots dash **wildly** through the streets, rushing to and fro
Zeph 2.15 place it will become, a place where **wild** animals will rest!
Mt 3. 4 round his waist, and his food was locusts and **wild** honey.
6.28 Look how the **wild** flowers grow:
6.30 is God who clothes the **wild** grass—grass that is here today
7.15 outside, but on the inside they are really like **wild** wolves.
Mk 1. 6 round his waist, and his food was locusts and **wild** honey.
1.13 **Wild** animals were there also, but angels came and helped him.
Lk 12.27 Look how the **wild** flowers grow:
12.28 is God who clothes the **wild** grass—grass that is here today
Acts 10.12 In it were all kinds of animals, reptiles, and **wild** birds.
11. 6 and saw domesticated and **wild** animals, reptiles, and wild birds.
21.35 the soldiers had to carry him because the mob was so **wild.**
Rom 11.17 and a branch of a **wild** olive-tree has been joined to it.
11.17 You Gentiles are like that **wild** olive-tree, and now you share
11.24 like the branch of a **wild** olive-tree that is broken off
1 Cor 15.32 have, as it were, fought **"wild** beasts" here in Ephesus simply
2 Cor 11.26 the cities, dangers in the **wilds,** dangers on the high seas,
Gal 5.15 if you act like **wild** animals, hurting and harming each other,
Tit 1. 6 and not have the reputation of being **wild** or disobedient.
Jas 1.10 the rich will pass away like the flower of a **wild** plant.
3. 7 has tamed all other creatures—**wild** animals and birds, reptiles
1 Pet 1.24 are like grass, and all their glory is like **wild** flowers.
4. 4 join them in the same **wild** and reckless living, and so they
2 Pet 2.12 men act by instinct, like **wild** animals born to be captured
2.12 They will be destroyed like **wild** animals,
Jude 10 they know by instinct, like **wild** animals, are the very things
13 They are like **wild** waves of the sea, with their shameful
Rev 6. 8 to kill by means of war, famine, disease, and **wild** animals.

WILD GOAT ROCKS

1 Sam 24. 2 went looking for David and his men east of **Wild Goat Rocks.**

WILDERNESS

Gen 21.14 She left and wandered about in the **wilderness** of Beersheba.
21.20 in the **wilderness** of Paran and became a skilful hunter.
24.62 Isaac had come into the **wilderness** of "The Well of the
36.24 the hot springs in the **wilderness** when he was taking care of
37.22 him into this well in the **wilderness,** but don't hurt him."
Num 10.12 The cloud came to rest in the **wilderness** of Paran.
10.31 we can camp in the **wilderness,** and you can be our guide.
12.16 left Hazeroth and set up camp in the **wilderness** of Paran.
13. 3 Moses obeyed and from the **wilderness** of Paran he sent out leaders,
13.21 explored the land from the **wilderness** of Zin in the south
13.26 community of Israel at Kadesh in the **wilderness** of Paran.
14. 2 been better to die in Egypt or even here in the **wilderness!**
14.16 killed your people in the **wilderness** because you were not
14.22 in Egypt and in the **wilderness,** but they have tried my
14.25 tomorrow and go into the **wilderness** in the direction of the
14.29 your corpses will be scattered across this **wilderness.**
14.32 You will die here in this **wilderness.**
14.33 children will wander in the **wilderness** for forty years,
14.35 Here in the **wilderness** every one of you will die.
15.32 Israelites were still in the **wilderness,** a man was found
16.13 the fertile land of Egypt to kill us here in the **wilderness?**
20. 1 Israel came to the **wilderness** of Zin and camped at Kadesh.
20. 4 Why have you brought us out into this **wilderness?**
21.11 ruins of Abarim in the **wilderness** east of Moabite territory.
21.13 in the **wilderness** which extends into Amorite territory.
21.18 They moved from the **wilderness** to Mattanah, [19]and from
21.23 out to Jahaz in the **wilderness** and attacked the Israelites.
26.65 them would die in the **wilderness,** and except for Caleb son
27. 3 "Our father died in the **wilderness** without leaving any sons.
27.14 of you rebelled against my command in the **wilderness** of Zin.
27.14 (Meribah is the spring at Kadesh in the **wilderness** of Zin.)
32.13 made them wander in the **wilderness** for forty years until
32.15 all these people in the **wilderness,** and you will be
33.15 Abronah, Eziongeber, the **wilderness** of Zin (that is,
34. 3 border will extend from the **wilderness** of Zin along the
Deut 1. 1 Israel when they were in the **wilderness** east of the River Jordan.
32.10 wandering through the desert, a desolate, wind-swept **wilderness.**
32.51 town of Kadesh in the **wilderness** of Zin, you dishonoured me
Josh 15. 1 the southernmost point of the **wilderness** of Zin, at the
1 Sam 13.18 border overlooking the Valley of Zeboim and the **wilderness.**
17.28 care of those sheep of yours out there in the **wilderness?**
23.14 hiding in the hill-country, in the **wilderness** near Ziph.
23.15 David was at Horesh, in the **wilderness** near Ziph.
23.19 Mount Hachilah, in the southern part of the Judaean **wilderness.**
23.24 his men were in the **wilderness** of Maon, in a desolate valley
23.24 in the southern part of the Judaean **wilderness.**
23.25 to a rocky hill in the **wilderness** of Maon and stayed there.
24. 1 he was told that David was in the **wilderness** near Engedi.
25. 1 After this, David went to the **wilderness** of Paran.
25. 4 David, who was in the **wilderness,** heard about it, [5]so he
25.14 from the **wilderness** with greetings for our master,
25.21 I ever protect that fellow's property out here in the **wilderness?**
26. 1 on Mount Hachilah at the edge of the Judaean **wilderness.**
26. 2 in Israel to the **wilderness** of Ziph to look for David,
26. 3 David was still in the **wilderness,** and when he learnt that
2 Sam 2.24 the east of Giah on the road to the **wilderness** of Gibeon.
15.23 his men, and together they went out towards the **wilderness.**
15.28 crossings in the **wilderness** until I receive news from you."
16. 2 for them to drink when they get tired in the **wilderness."**
17.16 the river crossings in the **wilderness,** but to cross the
17.28 men would be hungry, thirsty, and tired in the **wilderness.**

1 Kgs	9.18	Horon, [18] Baalath, Tamar in the **wilderness** of Judah,
	19. 4	Elijah walked a whole day into the **wilderness.**
	19.15	Lord said, "Return to the **wilderness** near Damascus, then
2 Kgs	3. 8	will go the long way, through the **wilderness** of Edom,"
1 Chr	21.29	Moses had made in the **wilderness,** and the altar on which
2 Chr	1. 3	which Moses, the Lord's servant, had made in the **wilderness.**
	24. 9	Moses, God's servant, had first collected in the **wilderness.**
Job	24. 5	like wild donkeys, search for food in the dry **wilderness;**
Ps	55. 7	I would fly far away and live in the **wilderness.**
	107.34	rich soil become a salty **wilderness** because of the
Is	13. 9	will be made a **wilderness,** and every sinner will be destroyed.
	27.10	It is deserted like an empty **wilderness.**
	35. 1	The desert will rejoice, and flowers will bloom in the **wilderness.**
	40. 3	cries out, "Prepare in the **wilderness** a road for the Lord!
	43.19	make a road through the **wilderness** and give you streams of
Jer	2. 6	I rescued them from Egypt and led them through the **wilderness:**
	4.27	whole earth will become a **wilderness,** but that he will not
	12.11	They have made it a **wilderness;**
	17. 6	which grows in the dry **wilderness,** on salty ground where
Ezek	12.20	will be destroyed, and the country will be made a **wilderness.**
	14.16	their own lives, and the land would become a **wilderness.**
	15. 8	to me, and so I will make the country a **wilderness."**
	36.35	land, which was once a **wilderness,** has become like the
Hos	2.12	I will turn her vineyards and orchards into a **wilderness;**
Mic	7.14	apart in the **wilderness,** there is fertile land around them.

AV WILDERNESS

Lev	16.22	all their sins away with him into some **uninhabited** land.
Ps	106. 9	he led his people across on **dry** land.
	107.35	deserts into pools of water and **dry** land into flowing springs.
Jer	22. 6	but I will make it a **desolate** place where no one lives.
Ezek	6.14	I will make it a **waste** from the southern desert to the
	34.25	can live safely in the **fields** and sleep in the forests.
Hos	2. 3	will make her like a **dry** and barren land, and she will
Joel	3.19	desert, and Edom a ruined **waste,** because they attacked the
Lk	15. 4	other ninety-nine sheep in the **pasture** and goes looking for
2 Cor	11.26	the cities, dangers in the **wilds,** dangers on the high seas,

WILFUL

Ps	19.13	Keep me safe, also, from **wilful** sins;

WILL (1)

[FREE WILL, GOD'S WILL, GOOD WILL, LORD'S WILL]

Ex	18.15	do this because the people come to me to learn **God's will.**
	28.15	for the High Priest to use in determining **God's will.**
	28.30	so that he can determine my **will** for the people of Israel.
Num	27.21	who will learn my **will** by using the Urim and Thummim.
Deut	33. 8	"You, Lord, reveal your **will** by the Urim and Thummim
Josh	22. 5	Lord your God, do his **will,** obey his commandments, be
2 Sam	7.21	It was your **will** and purpose to do this;
	10.12	And may the **Lord's will** be done!"
1 Kgs	2.15	and my brother became king, because it was the **Lord's will.**
	12.15	It was the **will of the Lord** to bring about what he
	12.24	What has happened is my **will."**
1 Chr	5.22	They killed many of the enemy, because the war was **God's will.**
	13. 2	and if it is the **will of the Lord** our God, let
	17.19	It was your **will** and purpose to do this for me and
	19.13	And may the **Lord's will** be done."
2 Chr	10.15	It was the **will of the Lord God** to bring about what
	11. 4	What has happened is my **will."**
	12.14	was evil, because he did not try to find the **Lord's will.**
	13. 7	and they forced their **will** on Rehoboam son of Solomon,
	14. 4	of Judah to do the **will of the Lord,** the God of
	14. 7	land because we have done the **will of the Lord** our God.
	19. 3	and you have tried to follow **God's will."**
	25.20	It was **God's will** for Amaziah to be defeated, because he had
	30.12	their determination to obey his **will** by following the
Ezra	5.17	and then inform us what your **will** is in this matter."
	7.18	desire, in accordance with the **will of your God.**
Job	21.14	they don't want to know his **will** for their lives.
	23.12	I follow his **will,** not my own desires.
	34. 9	that it never does any good to try to follow **God's will.**
	37.12	Lightning flashes from the clouds, [12] as they move at **God's will.**
Ps	5. 8	Lead me to do your **will;**
	25. 9	the humble in the right way and teaches them his **will.**
	40. 8	How I love to do your **will,** my God!
	67. 2	kindness, [2] so that the whole world may know your **will;**
	103.21	you heavenly powers, you servants of his, who do his **will!**
	143.10	teach me to do your **will.**
Prov	16.33	to learn **God's will,** but God himself determines the answer.
	18.14	Your **will** to live can sustain you when you are sick, but
	19.21	kinds of things, but the **Lord's will** is going to be done.
	29.26	Everybody wants the **good will** of the ruler, but only
Is	11. 2	He will know the **Lord's will** and have reverence for him,
	26. 8	We follow your **will** and put our hope in you;
	30. 1	sign treaties against my **will,** piling one sin on another.
	52. 4	in Egypt as foreigners, you did so of your own free **will;**
	53. 2	It was the **will of the Lord** that his servant should grow
	53.10	"It was my **will** that he should suffer;
Jer	29.23	This was against the **Lord's will;**
Lam	3.37	The **will of the Lord** alone is always carried out.
Ezek	14. 1	of the Israelites came to consult me about the **Lord's will.**
	20. 1	consult me about the **Lord's will,** and they sat down in front
	20. 3	You have come to ask my **will,** have you?
	20.31	And then you Israelites still come to ask what my **will** is!
	29.15	will not be able to bend any other nation to their **will.**
Dan	4.35	No one can oppose his **will** or question what he does.
Mal	2. 7	to them to learn my **will,** because they are the messengers of
Mal	2. 9	you do not obey my **will,** and when you teach my people,
Mt	6.10	may your **will** be done on earth as it is in heaven.
	22.16	teach the truth about **God's will** for man, without worrying
	26.42	cannot be taken away unless I drink it, your **will** be done."
Mk	12.14	man's status, but teach the truth about **God's will** for man.
Lk	2.32	A light to reveal your **will** to the Gentiles and bring
	20.21	man's status, but teach the truth about **God's will** for man.
	22.42	Not my **will,** however, but your will be done."
Jn	4.34	them, "is to obey the **will** of the one who sent me
	6.38	to do not my own **will**
	6.38	but the **will** of him who sent me.
	6.39	And it is the **will** of him who sent me that I
	10.18	I give it up of my own **free will.**
Acts	2.47	praising God, and enjoying the **good will** of all the people.
	4.28	you by your power and **will** had already decided would happen.
	18.21	"If it is the **will of God,** I will come back
	22.14	chosen you to know his **will,** to see his righteous Servant,
Rom	1.10	that God in his **good will** may at last make it possible
	8.20	purpose, not of its own **will,**
	8.20	but because God **willed** it to be so.
	8.27	God on behalf of his people and in accordance with his **will.**
	9.19	Who can resist **God's will?"**
	12. 2	be able to know the **will of God**—what is good and
	15.32	joy, if it is **God's will,** and enjoy a refreshing visit to
1 Cor	1. 1	who was called by the **will of God** to be an apostle
	7.37	and if he has his **will** under complete control and has
2 Cor	1. 1	of Christ Jesus by **God's will,** and from our brother Timothy—
	8. 3	Of their own **free will** [4] they begged us and pleaded for the
	8. 5	and then, by **God's will** they gave themselves to us as well.
	8.17	that of his own **free will** he decided to go to you.
Gal	1. 4	our sins, in obedience to the **will of our God** and Father.
Eph	1. 1	From Paul, who by **God's will** is an apostle of Christ Jesus
Phil	2. 7	of his own **free will** he gave up all he had,
	2.19	If it is the **Lord's will,** I hope that I will be
Col	1. 1	From Paul, who by **God's will** is an apostle of Christ Jesus,
	1. 9	the knowledge of his **will,** with all the wisdom and understanding
	4.12	fully convinced Christians, in complete obedience to **God's will.**
1 Thes	3. 3	know that such persecutions are part of **God's will** for us.
2 Tim	1. 1	of Christ Jesus by **God's will,** sent to proclaim the promised
	2.26	the Devil, who had caught them and made them obey his **will.**
Phlm	14	I would like you to do it of your own **free will.**
Heb	2. 4	the gifts of the Holy Spirit according to his **will.**
	10. 7	I am, to do your **will,** O God, just as it is
	10. 9	Then he said, "Here I am, O God, to do your **will."**
	10.36	in order to do the **will of God** and receive what he
	13.20	in order to do his **will,** and may he, through Jesus Christ,
Jas	1.18	By his own **will** he brought us into being through the
1 Pet	2. 8	such was **God's will** for them.
	2.19	pain of undeserved suffering because you are conscious of his **will.**
	3.17	good, if this should be **God's will,** than for doing evil.
	4. 2	earthly lives controlled by **God's will** and not by human desires.
	4.19	suffer because it is **God's will** for them, should by their
1 Jn	5.14	if we ask him for anything that is according to his **will.**
Rev	17.17	placed in their hearts the **will** to carry out his purpose by

WILL (2)

Heb	9.16	In the case of a **will** it is necessary to prove that
	9.17	it has died, [17] for a **will** means nothing while the person

WILLING

Gen	23. 8	and said, "If you are **willing** to let me bury my wife
	24. 8	If the girl is not **willing** to come with you, you will
	43. 4	If you are **willing** to send our brother with us, we will
	43. 5	If you are not **willing,** we will not go, because the man
Ex	36. 2	given ability and who were **willing** to help, and Moses told
Num	23.27	Perhaps God will be **willing** to let you curse them for me
Josh	24.15	If you are not **willing** to serve him, decide today whom
2 Kgs	8.19	but the Lord was not **willing** to destroy Judah, because
1 Chr	19.19	The Syrians were never again **willing** to help the Ammonites.
	28. 9	and to serve him with an undivided heart and a **willing** mind.
	29. 5	Now who else is **willing** to give a generous offering to the
	29. 9	The people had given **willingly** to the Lord, and they were
	29.17	and sincerity I have **willingly** given all this to you,
2 Chr	21. 7	but the Lord was not **willing** to destroy the dynasty of David,
	30.11	Manasseh, and Zebulun who were **willing** to come to Jerusalem.
Ezra	7.27	He has made the emperor **willing** to honour in this way the
Neh	2. 5	pleased with me and is **willing** to grant my request, let me
Job	39. 9	Is he **willing** to spend the night in your stable?
Ps	51.12	comes from your salvation, and make me **willing** to obey you.
	130. 7	his love is constant and he is always **willing** to save.
Prov	1.25	my advice and have not been **willing** to let me correct you.
	19.20	listen to advice and are **willing** to learn, one day you will
	25.12	an experienced person to someone **willing** to listen is more
Is	53.12	He **willingly** gave his life and shared the fate of evil men.
Jer	42.10	has said, [10] 'If you are **willing** to go on living in this
Ezek	3. 7	But none of the people of Israel will be **willing** to listen;
Hos	10.11	a well-trained young cow, ready and **willing** to thresh grain.
Zech	11.12	I said to them, "If you are **willing,** give me my wages.
Mt	10.11	look for someone who is **willing** to welcome you, and stay
	11.14	if you are **willing** to believe their message, John is Elijah,
	23. 4	to carry, yet they aren't **willing** even to lift a finger to
	26.41	The spirit is **willing,** but the flesh is weak."
Mk	14.38	The spirit is **willing,** but the flesh is weak."
Jn	3.11	have seen, yet none of you is **willing** to accept our message.
	5.35	and shining, and you were **willing** for a while to enjoy his
	5.40	Yet you are not **willing** to come to me in order to
	6.21	they **willingly** took him into the boat, and immediately the boat
	7.17	Whoever is **willing** to do what God wants will know whether
	9.18	authorities, however, were not **willing** to believe that he had

Jn 10.11 am the good shepherd, who is **willing** to die for the sheep.
10.14 And I am **willing** to die for them.
10.17 loves me because I am **willing** to give up my life,
Acts 25. 9 asked Paul, "Would you be **willing** to go to Jerusalem and be
25.20 Paul if he would be **willing** to go to Jerusalem and be
26. 5 always known, if they are **willing** to testify, that from the
1 Cor 4.19 If the Lord is **willing,** however, I will come to you soon,
2 Cor 8.10 first, not only to act, but also to be **willing** to act.
9. 2 I know that you are **willing** to help, and I have boasted
Phil 2.13 in you to make you **willing** and able to obey his own
Jas 4.15 "If the Lord is **willing,** we will live and do this or
1 Pet 5. 2 to take care of it **willingly,** as God wants you to,
Rev 12.11 and they were **willing** to give up their lives and die.

WILLOW
[VALLEY OF WILLOWS]

Job 40.22 The thorn-bushes and the **willows** by the stream give him
Ps 137. 2 On the **willows** near by we hung up our harps.
Is 15. 7 go across the **Valley of Willows,** trying to escape with all
44. 4 like well-watered grass, like **willows** by streams of running water.

WILT

Joel 1.12 all the fruit-trees have **wilted** and died.

WIN
[WON]

Gen 30. 8 have fought a hard fight with my sister, but I have **won";**
31.41 fourteen years I worked to **win** your two daughters—and six
32.20 Jacob was thinking, "I will **win** him over with the gifts,
32.25 saw that he was not **winning** the struggle, he struck Jacob on
32.28 You have struggled with God and with men, and you have **won;**
34. 3 he fell in love with her and tried to **win** her affection.
Ex 15. 1 sing to the Lord, because he has **won** a glorious victory;
15.21 "Sing to the Lord, because he has **won** a glorious victory;
17.11 up his arms, the Israelites **won,**
17.11 when he put his arms down, the Amalekites started **winning.**
Judg 7. 2 might think that they had **won** by themselves, and so give me
1 Sam 13.12 in Gilgal, and I have not tried to **win** the Lord's favour.'
14.45 "Will Jonathan, who **won** this great victory for Israel,
17. 9 If he **wins** and kills me, we will be your slaves;
17. 9 but if I **win** and kill him, you will be our slaves.
19. 5 killed Goliath, and the Lord **won** a great victory for Israel.
29. 4 is there for him to **win** back his master's favour than by
2 Sam 3.12 and I will help you **win** all Israel over to your side."
3.21 "I will go now and **win** all Israel over to Your Majesty.
15. 6 came to the king for justice, and so he **won** their loyalty.
19.14 David's words **won** the complete loyalty of all the men of Judah,
23.10 The Lord **won** a great victory that day.
23.12 The Lord **won** a great victory that day.
1 Kgs 11.19 Hadad **won** the friendship of the king, and the king gave
11.38 live by my laws, and **win** my approval by doing what I
16.22 In the end, those in favour of Omri **won;**
22.12 "March against Ramoth and you will **win,"** they said.
22.15 "Of course you'll **win.**
2 Kgs 13.17 the Lord's arrow, with which he will **win** victory over Syria.
13.19 then you would have **won** complete victory over the Syrians;
2 Chr 13.12 You can't **win!"**
18.11 "March against Ramoth and you will **win,"** they said.
18.14 "Of course you'll **win.**
Ezra 7.28 By God's grace I have **won** the favour of the emperor, of
Neh 9.10 You **won** then the fame you still have today.
Esth 2. 9 Hegai liked Esther, and she **won** his favour.
2.17 than any of the others she **won** his favour and affection.
5. 2 Queen Esther standing outside, she **won** his favour, and he
Job 9. 1 But how can a man **win** his case against God?
14.21 His sons **win** honour, but he never knows it, nor is he
31.21 an orphan, knowing I could **win** in court, [22]then may my
40.14 to praise you and admit that you **won** the victory yourself.
Ps 33.16 A king does not **win** because of his powerful army;
44. 3 they did not **win** it by their own power;
45. 4 Your strength will **win** you great victories!
45.12 rich people will try to **win** your favour.
60.12 With God on our side we will **win;**
98. 1 By his own power and holy strength he has **won** the victory.
108.13 With God on our side we will **win;**
Prov 7.25 Do not let such a woman **win** your heart;
13.15 Intelligence **wins** respect, but those who can't be
16.32 It is better to **win** control over yourself than over whole cities.
19. 7 No matter how hard he tries, he cannot **win** any.
24. 6 more good advice you get, the more likely you are to **win.**
25.27 bad for you, and so is trying to **win** too much praise.
Ecc 9.11 fast runners do not always **win** the race,
9.11 and the brave do not always **win** the battle.
Is 26.18 We have **won** no victory for our land;
59. 4 You depend on lies to **win** your case.
59.16 use his own power to rescue them and to **win** the victory.
63. 5 But my anger made me strong, and I **won** the victory myself.
63.12 the deep water, to **win** everlasting fame for himself?"
Jer 26.19 Hezekiah honoured the Lord and tried to **win** his favour.
Lam 1. 9 Her enemies have **won,** and she cries to the Lord for mercy.
Ezek 14. 5 me, but by my answer I hope to **win** back their loyalty.
16.19 you offered it as a sacrifice to **win** the favour of idols."
27.10 They are the men who **won** glory for you.
Dan 11.32 By deceit the king will **win** the support of those who
Hos 2.14 there I will **win** her back with words of love.
12. 4 he fought against God—[4]he fought against an angel and **won.**
Mt 16.26 person gain anything if he **wins** the whole world but loses
18.15 If he listens to you, you have **won** your brother back.
Mt 23.15 You sail the seas and cross whole countries to **win** one convert;
Mk 8.36 person gain anything if he **wins** the whole world but loses
Lk 9.25 person gain anything if he **wins** the whole world but is
Jn 4. 1 heard that Jesus was **winning** and baptizing more disciples
5.44 you do not try to **win** praise from the one who alone
Acts 7.46 He **won** God's favour and asked God to allow him to
14.19 they **won** the crowd over to their side, stoned Paul and
14.21 Barnabas preached the Good News in Derbe and **won** many disciples.
Rom 1.13 I want to **win** converts among you also, as I have among
3. 4 you must **win** your case when you are being tried."
1 Cor 9.19 everybody's slave in order to **win** as many people as possible.
9.20 the Jews, I live like a Jew in order to **win** them;
9.20 were when working with those who are, in order to **win** them.
9.21 a Gentile, outside the Jewish Law, in order to **win** Gentiles.
9.22 I become weak like one of them, in order to **win** them.
9.24 part in a race, but only one of them **wins** the prize.
9.24 Run, then, in such a way as to **win** the prize.
Gal 1.10 Does this sound as if I am trying to **win** man's approval?
Phil 1.28 and that you will **win,** because it is God who gives
3.12 I keep striving to **win** the prize
3.12 for which Christ Jesus has already **won** me to himself.
3.13 brothers, I really do not think that I have already **won** it;
3.14 the goal in order to **win** the prize, which is God's call
1 Thes 4.12 In this way you will **win** the respect of those who are
1 Tim 3.13 who do their work well **win** for themselves a good standing
6.12 in the race of faith, and **win** eternal life for yourself;
6.19 they will be able to **win** the life which is true life.
2 Tim 2. 5 runs in a race cannot **win** the prize unless he obeys the
2.15 Do your best to **win** full approval in God's sight,
Heb 11. 2 faith that people of ancient times **won** God's approval.
11. 4 Through his faith he **won** God's approval as a righteous man,
11.33 Through faith they fought whole countries and **won.**
11.39 What a record all of these have **won** by their faith!
1 Pet 3. 1 believe God's word, your conduct will **win** them over to believe.
1 Jn 5. 4 And we **win** the victory over the world by means of our
Rev 2. 7 "To those who **win** the victory I will give the right to
2.11 "Those who **win** the victory will not be hurt by the second
2.17 "To those who **win** the victory I will give some of the
2.26 To those who **win** the victory, who continue to the
3. 5 Those who **win** the victory will be clothed like this in white,
3.21 To those who **win** the victory I will give the right to
5. 5 great descendant of David, has **won** the victory, and he can
12.11 Our brothers **won** the victory over him by the blood of
15. 2 also saw those who had **won** the victory over the beast and
21. 7 Whoever **wins** the victory will receive this from me:

WIND (1)
[WHIRLWIND]

Gen 8. 1 he caused a **wind** to blow, and the water started going down.
41. 6 and scorched by the desert **wind,** [7]and the thin ears of corn
41.23 and scorched by the desert **wind,** [24]and the thin ears of
41.27 corn scorched by the desert **wind** are seven years of famine.
Ex 10.13 and the Lord caused a **wind** from the east to blow on
10.19 the Lord changed the east **wind** into a very strong west wind,
14.21 and the Lord drove the sea back with a strong east **wind.**
Lev 26.36 sound of a leaf blowing in the **wind** will make you run.
Num 11.31 Suddenly the Lord sent a **wind** that brought quails from the sea,
Deut 28.22 will send drought and scorching **winds** to destroy your crops.
32.10 wandering through the desert, a desolate, **wind-swept** wilderness.
2 Sam 22.11 he travelled on the wings of the **wind.**
1 Kgs 8.37 crops are destroyed by scorching **winds** or swarms of locusts,
18.45 covered with dark clouds, the **wind** began to blow, and heavy
19.11 by and sent a furious **wind** that split the hills
19.11 and shattered the rocks—but the Lord was not in the **wind.**
19.11 The **wind** stopped blowing, and then there was an earthquake—
2 Kgs 2. 1 for the Lord to take Elijah up to heaven in a **whirlwind.**
2.11 them, and Elijah was taken up to heaven by a **whirlwind.**
3.17 not see any rain or **wind,** this stream bed will be filled
19.26 weeds growing on a roof when the hot east **wind** blasts them.
2 Chr 6.28 crops are destroyed by scorching **winds** or swarms of locusts,
Job 6.26 You think I am talking nothing but **wind;**
8. 1 Are you finally through with your **windy** speech?
15.30 burnt by fire, whose blossoms are blown away by the **wind.**
21.18 away like straw in the **wind,** or like dust carried away in
27.20 a **wind** in the night will blow them away;
27.21 the east **wind** will sweep them from their homes;
27.23 The **wind** howls at them as they run, frightening them
28.25 When God gave the **wind** its power And determined the size
30.15 gone like a puff of **wind,** and my prosperity like a cloud.
30.22 You let the **wind** blow me away;
37. 9 The storm **winds** come from the south, and the biting cold
37.17 suffer in the heat when the south **wind** oppresses the land.
37.21 and the sky has been swept clean by the **wind.**
38.24 sun comes up, or the place from which the east **wind** blows?
Ps 1. 4 they are like straw that the **wind** blows away.
11. 6 he punishes them with scorching **winds.**
18.10 he travelled on the wings of the **wind.**
18.42 so that they become like dust which the **wind** blows away.
35. 5 like straw blown by the **wind** as the angel of the Lord
39. 5 no more than a puff of **wind,** [6]no more than a shadow.
39.11 Indeed a man is no more than a puff of **wind!**
55. 8 find myself a shelter from the raging **wind** and the storm.
78.26 He also caused the east **wind** to blow,
78.26 and by his power he stirred up the south **wind;**
78.39 only mortal beings, like a **wind** that blows by and is gone.
83.13 them like dust, O God, like straw blown away by the **wind.**
83.15 with your storm and terrify them with your fierce **winds.**
103.16 then the **wind** blows on it, and it is gone— no
104. 3 clouds as your chariot and ride on the wings of the **wind.**

Ps 104. 4 You use the **winds** as your messengers and flashes of
107.25 He commanded, and a mighty **wind** began to blow and
135. 7 the storms, and he brings out the **wind** from his storeroom.
144. 4 He is like a puff of **wind;**
147.18 he sends the **wind,** and the water flows.
148. 8 snow and clouds, strong **winds** that obey his command.
Prov 1.27 like a storm, bringing fierce **winds** of trouble, and you are
25.14 never give are like clouds and **wind** that bring no rain.
25.23 Gossip brings anger just as surely as the north **wind** brings rain.
27.16 ever tried to stop the **wind** or ever tried to hold a
30. 4 Who has ever caught the **wind** in his hand?
Ecc 1. 6 The **wind** blows south, the wind blows north—round and round
1.14 It is like chasing the **wind.**
1.17 I found out that I might as well be chasing the **wind.**
2.11 It was like chasing the **wind**—of no use at all.
2.17 I had been chasing the **wind.**
2.26 It is like chasing the **wind.**
4. 4 It is like chasing the **wind.**
4. 6 all the time with both hands, trying to catch the **wind.**
4.16 It is like chasing the **wind.**
5.16 We labour, trying to catch the **wind,** and what do we get?
6. 9 it is like chasing the **wind.**
11. 4 If you wait until the **wind** and the weather are just right,
Song 4.16 Wake up, North **Wind.**
4.16 South **Wind,** blow on my garden;
Is 5.28 as flint, and their chariot-wheels turn like a **whirlwind.**
7. 2 that they trembled like trees shaking in the **wind.**
11.15 he will bring a hot **wind** to dry up the Euphrates, leaving
17.13 away like dust on a hillside, like straw in a **whirlwind.**
21. 1 Like a **whirlwind** sweeping across the desert, disaster will
27. 8 He took them away with a cruel **wind** from the east.
30.28 He sends the **wind** in front of him like a flood that
32. 2 like a shelter from the **wind** and a place to hide from
37.27 weeds growing on a roof when the hot east **wind** blasts them.
40. 7 fade, when the Lord sends the **wind** blowing over them.
40.24 When the Lord sends a **wind,** they dry up and blow away
41. 2 His arrows scatter them like straw before the **wind.**
41.16 the **wind** will carry them off, and they will be scattered
57.13 A puff of **wind** will carry them off!
59.19 He will come like a rushing river, like a strong **wind.**
64. 6 are like leaves that wither and are blown away by the **wind.**
Jer 4.11 be told that a scorching **wind** is blowing in from the desert
4.11 will not be a gentle **wind** that only blows away the chaff
4.12 blows away the chaff—[12] the **wind** that comes at the Lord's
4.13 His war-chariots are like a **whirlwind,** and his horses are
10.13 flash in the rain and sends the **wind** from his storeroom.
13.24 you like straw that is blown away by the desert **wind.**
15. 7 town in the land I threw you to the **wind** like straw.
18.17 before their enemies, like dust blown by the east **wind.**
22.22 be blown away by the **wind,** your allies taken as prisoners of
23.19 is a storm, a furious **wind** that will rage over the heads
30.23 is a storm, a furious **wind** that will rage over the heads
49.36 I will make **winds** blow against Elam from all directions,
51. 1 "I am bringing a destructive **wind** against Babylonia and its people.
51. 2 to destroy Babylonia like a **wind** that blows straw away.
51.16 flash in the rain and sends the **wind** from his storeroom.
Ezek 5. 2 the remaining third to the **winds,** and I will pursue it with
5.12 the last third to the **winds** and pursue them with a sword.
13.11 will fall on it, and a strong **wind** will blow against it.
13.13 I will send a strong **wind,** pouring rain, and hailstones to
17.10 Won't it wither when the east **wind** strikes it?
19.12 The east **wind** dried up its fruit.
27.26 you out to sea, An east **wind** wrecked you far from land.
37. 9 God said to me, "Mortal man, prophesy to the **wind.**
37. 9 Tell the **wind** that the Sovereign Lord commands it to come
Dan 2.35 The **wind** carried it all away, leaving not a trace.
7. 2 **Winds** were blowing from all directions and lashing the
Hos 4.19 carried away as by the **wind,** and they will be ashamed of
8. 7 When they sow the **wind,** they will reap a storm!
13. 3 be like chaff which the **wind** blows from the threshing-place,
13.15 will send a hot east **wind** from the desert, and it will
Amos 4. 9 "I sent a scorching **wind** to dry up your crops.
4.13 God is the one who made the mountains and created the **winds.**
Jon 1. 4 the Lord sent a strong **wind** on the sea, and the storm
4. 8 God sent a hot east **wind,** and Jonah was about to faint
Hab 1.11 they sweep on like the **wind** and are gone, these men whose
Zeph 2. 2 like chaff blown by the **wind,** before the burning anger of
Hag 2.17 I sent scorching **winds** and hail to ruin everything you
Zech 6. 5 He answered, "These are the four **winds;**
Mt 7.25 the rivers overflowed, and the **wind** blew hard against that house.
7.27 the rivers overflowed, the **wind** blew hard against that house,
8.26 got up and ordered the **winds** and the waves to stop,
8.27 "Even the **winds** and the waves obey him!"
11. 7 A blade of grass bending in the **wind?**
14.24 by the waves, because the **wind** was blowing against it.
14.30 when he noticed the strong **wind,** he was afraid and started
14.32 They both got into the boat, and the **wind** died down.
Mk 4.37 Suddenly a strong **wind** blew up, and the waves began to
4.39 Jesus stood up and commanded the **wind,** "Be quiet!"
4.39 The **wind** died down, and there was a great calm.
4.41 Even the **wind** and the waves obey him!"
6.48 straining at the oars, because they were rowing against the **wind;**
6.51 he got into the boat with them, and the **wind** died down.
Lk 7.24 A blade of grass bending in the **wind?**
8.23 Suddenly a strong **wind** blew down on the lake, and the boat
8.24 and gave an order to the **wind** and the stormy water;
8.25 He gives orders to the **winds** and waves, and they obey him!"
12.55 when you feel the south **wind** blowing, you say that it is
Jn 3. 8 The **wind** blows wherever it wishes;
6.18 By then a strong **wind** was blowing and stirring up the water.
Acts 2. 2 which sounded like a strong **wind** blowing, and it filled the
27. 4 and because the **winds** were blowing against us, we sailed
27. 7 The **wind** would not let us go any further in that direction,
27.13 A soft **wind** from the south began to blow, and the men
27.14 soon a very strong **wind**—the one called "North-easter"—blew down
27.15 the ship headed into the **wind,** we gave up trying
27.15 and let it be carried along by the **wind.**
27.17 lowered the sail and let the ship be carried by the **wind.**
27.20 sun or the stars, and the **wind** kept on blowing very hard.
27.40 the ship so that the **wind** would blow the ship forward,
28.13 The next day a **wind** began to blow from the south,
Eph 4.14 by every shifting **wind** of the teaching of deceitful men,
Heb 1. 7 "God makes his angels **winds,** and his servants flames of fire."
Jas 1. 6 in the sea that is driven and blown about by the **wind.**
3. 4 and driven by such strong **winds,** it can be steered by a
Jude 12 like clouds carried along by the **wind,** but bringing no rain.
Rev 6.13 figs falling from the tree when a strong **wind** shakes it.
7. 1 holding back the four **winds** so that no wind should blow

WIND (2)

Lk 3. 5 The **winding** roads must be made straight, and the rough paths

WINDBAGS

Jer 5.13 prophets are nothing but **windbags** and that they have no message

WINDOW

Gen 8. 6 After forty days Noah opened a **window** [7] and sent out a raven.
26. 8 Abimelech looked down from his **window** and saw Isaac and
Josh 2.15 so she let the men down from the **window** by a rope.
2.18 tie this red cord to the **window** you let us down from.
2.21 When they had gone, she tied the red cord to the **window.**
Judg 5.28 Sisera's mother looked out of the **window;**
1 Sam 19.12 let him down from a **window,** and he ran away and escaped.
2 Sam 6.16 daughter, looked out of the **window** and saw King David
1 Kgs 7. 4 each of the two side walls there were three rows of **windows.**
7. 5 The doorways and the **windows** had rectangular frames,
7. 5 and the three rows of **windows** in each wall faced the
2 Kgs 9.30 looking down at the street from a **window** in the palace.
9.32 down at him from a **window,** [33] and Jehu said to them,
13.17 the king opened the **window** that faced towards Syria.
1 Chr 15.29 daughter, looked out of the **window** and saw King David
Prov 7. 6 was looking out of the **window** of my house, [7] and I saw
Song 2. 9 He looks in through the **window** and glances through the lattice.
Jer 9.21 Death has come in through our **windows** and entered our palaces;
22.14 So he puts **windows** in his house, panels it with cedar, and
Ezek 40.22 The entrance room, the **windows,** and the carved
40.25 There were **windows** in the rooms of this gateway just as
40.29 There were also **windows** in the rooms of this gateway.
40.33 There were **windows** all round, and in the entrance room also.
40.36 inner walls, an entrance room, and **windows** all round.
41.16 were all panelled with wood from the floor to the **windows.**
41.16 These **windows** could be covered.
41.26 of this room there were **windows,** and the walls were
Dan 6.10 his house there were **windows** that faced towards Jerusalem.
6.10 knelt down at the open **windows** and prayed to God three times
Joel 2. 9 up the houses and go in through the **windows** like thieves.
Zeph 2.14 Owls will live among its ruins and hoot from the **windows.**
Mal 3.10 that I will open the **windows** of heaven and pour out on
Acts 20. 9 Eutychus was sitting in the **window,** and as Paul kept on talking,

Am **WINDSTORM** see **STORM, TEMPEST**

WINE

see also **WINE-OFFERING**

Gen 9.21 he drank some of the **wine,** he became drunk, took off his
14.18 High God, brought bread and **wine** to Abram, [19] blessed him,
19.33 That night they gave him **wine** to drink, and the elder
27.25 it to him, and he also brought him some **wine** to drink.
27.28 May he give you plenty of corn and **wine!**
27.37 I have given him corn and **wine.**
35.14 and consecrated it by pouring **wine** and olive-oil on it.
40. 1 later the king of Egypt's **wine** steward and his chief baker
40. 5 night there in prison the **wine** steward and the chief baker
40. 9 So the **wine** steward said, "In my dream there was a
40.13 his cup as you did before when you were his **wine** steward.
40.16 interpretation of the **wine** steward's dream was favourable,
40.20 he released his **wine** steward and his chief baker and brought
40.21 He restored the **wine** steward to his former position,
40.23 But the **wine** steward never gave Joseph another
41. 9 Then the **wine** steward said to the king, "I must confess
49.11 He washes his clothes in blood-red **wine.**
49.12 eyes are bloodshot from drinking **wine,**
Ex 22.29 offerings from your corn, your **wine,** and your olive-oil when
29.40 Pour out one litre of **wine** as an offering.
29.41 amounts of flour, olive-oil, and **wine** as in the morning.
Lev 10. 9 enter the Tent of my presence after drinking **wine** or beer;
23.13 shall also present with it an offering of one litre of **wine.**
Num 6. 3 himself to the Lord [3] shall abstain from **wine** and beer.
6.15 and in addition the required offerings of corn and **wine.**
6.17 he shall also present the offerings of corn and **wine.**
6.20 After that, the Nazirite may drink **wine.**
15. 4 as a grain-offering, together with a litre of **wine.**
15. 7 together with one and a half litres of **wine.**
15.10 is to be presented, [10] together with two litres of **wine.**
18.12 olive-oil, **wine,** and corn.

Num	18.27	offering which the farmer makes of new corn and new **wine.**
	28. 7	the first lamb, pour out at the altar one litre of **wine.**
	28.14	wine-offering is two litres of **wine** with each bull, one and
Deut	7.13	bless your fields, so that you will have corn, **wine,** and
	11.14	that there will be corn, **wine,** and olive-oil for you,
	12.17	tithes of your corn, your **wine,** or your olive-oil, nor the
	14.23	the tithes of your corn, **wine,** and olive-oil, and the
	14.26	whatever you want—beef, lamb, **wine,** beer—and there, in the
	15.14	what the Lord has blessed you with—sheep, corn, and **wine.**
	18. 4	to receive the first share of the corn, **wine,** olive-oil, and
	20. 6	if he is killed in battle, someone else will enjoy the **wine.**
	28.39	gather their grapes or drink **wine** from them, because worms
	28.51	They will not leave you any corn, **wine,** olive-oil,
	29. 6	have bread to eat or **wine** or beer to drink, but the
	32.14	goats, and cattle, the finest wheat, and the choicest **wine.**
	32.33	grapes, [33]like **wine** made from the venom of snakes.
	32.38	the fat of your sacrifices and offered them **wine** to drink.
	33.28	land full of corn and **wine,** where dew from the sky waters
Judg	9.13	to stop producing my **wine,** that makes gods and men happy.'
	9.27	picked the grapes, made **wine** from them, and held a festival.
	13. 4	care not to drink any **wine** or beer, or eat any forbidden
	13. 7	me not to drink any **wine** or beer, or eat any forbidden
	13.14	she must not drink any **wine** or beer, or eat any forbidden
	19.19	as well as bread and **wine** for my concubine and me and
1 Sam	1.24	ten kilogrammes of flour, and a leather bag full of **wine.**
	10. 3	and the third one will have a leather bag full of **wine.**
	16.20	a donkey loaded with bread, and a leather bag full of **wine.**
	25.18	two leather bags full of **wine,** five roasted sheep, seventeen
2 Sam	16. 1	bunches of fresh fruit, and a leather bag full of **wine.**
	16. 2	men to eat, and the **wine** is for them to drink when
2 Kgs	6.27	Have I got any wheat or **wine?**
	18.32	there are vineyards to give **wine** and there is corn for
1 Chr	9.29	other sacred equipment, and of the flour, **wine,** olive-oil,
	12.40	mules, and oxen loaded with food—flour, figs, raisins, **wine,**
	27.25	**Wine** cellars:
	29.21	They also brought the offerings of **wine.**
2 Chr	2.10	four hundred thousand litres of **wine,** and four hundred
	2.15	us the wheat, barley, **wine,** and olive-oil that you promised.
	11.11	food, olive-oil, and **wine,** [12]and also shields and spears.
	29.35	out the **wine** that was presented with the burnt-offerings.
	31. 5	finest corn, **wine,** olive-oil, honey, and other farm produce,
	32.28	In addition, he had storehouses built for his corn, **wine,**
Ezra	6. 9	offerings to the God of Heaven, or wheat, salt, **wine,** or
	7.17	bulls, rams, lambs, corn, and **wine** and offer them on the
	7.22	of wheat, 2,000 litres of **wine,** 2,000 litres of olive-oil,
Neh	1.11	In those days I was the emperor's **wine** steward.
	2. 1	when Emperor Artaxerxes was dining, I took the **wine** to him.
	5.11	the debts they owe you—money or corn or **wine** or olive-oil.
	5.15	and had demanded forty silver coins a day for food and **wine.**
	5.18	and every ten days I provided a fresh supply of **wine.**
	8.10	Share your food and **wine** with those who haven't enough.
	10.37	other offerings of **wine,** olive-oil, and all kinds of fruit.
	10.39	take the contributions of corn, **wine,** and olive-oil to the
	13. 5	tithes of corn, **wine,** and olive-oil given to the Levites,
	13.12	to the temple storerooms their tithes of corn, **wine,**
	13.15	Others were loading corn, **wine,** grapes, figs, and other
Esth	1. 7	them alike, and the king was generous with the royal **wine.**
	5. 6	Over the **wine** the king asked her, "Tell me what you want,
	7. 2	Over the **wine** the king asked her again, "Now, Queen Esther,
Job	24.11	oil, and grapes for **wine,** but they themselves are thirsty.
	32.19	to speak, I will burst like a wineskin full of new **wine.**
Ps	4. 7	more than they will ever have with all their corn and **wine.**
	75. 8	cup in his hand, filled with the strong **wine** of his anger.
	78.65	he was like a strong man excited by **wine.**
	104.15	grow his crops [15]and produce **wine** to make him happy,
Prov	3.10	you will have too much **wine** to be able to store it
	9. 2	for a feast, mixed spices in the **wine,** and laid the table.
	9. 5	"Come, eat my food and drink the **wine** that I have mixed.
	21.17	luxuries, **wine,** and rich food will never make you wealthy.
	23.20	who drink too much **wine** or stuff themselves with food.
	23.31	Don't let **wine** tempt you, even though it is rich red,
	31. 4	Kings should not drink **wine** or have a craving for alcohol.
Ecc	2. 3	decided to cheer myself up with **wine** and have a good time.
	9. 7	drink your **wine** and be cheerful.
	10.19	Feasting makes you happy and **wine** cheers you up, but you
Song	1. 2	your love is better than **wine.**
	4.10	Your love is better than **wine;**
	5. 1	I am drinking my **wine** and milk.
	7. 2	A bowl is there, that never runs out of spiced **wine.**
	7. 9	fragrance of apples, [9]and your mouth like the finest **wine.**
	7. 9	Then let the **wine** flow straight to my lover, flowing over
	8. 2	I would give you spiced **wine,** my pomegranate wine to drink.
Is	1.22	you were like good **wine,** but now you are only water.
	5.10	ten hectares of land will yield only eight litres of **wine.**
	5.12	At your feasts you have harps and tambourines and flutes—and **wine.**
	5.22	Heroes of the **wine** bottle!
	16. 8	are destroyed—those vineyards whose **wine** used to make the
	16.10	No one tramples grapes to make **wine;**
	22.13	You killed sheep and cattle to eat, and you drank **wine.**
	24. 7	The grapevines wither, and **wine** is becoming scarce.
	24. 9	There is no more happy singing over **wine;**
	24.11	People shout in the streets because there is no more **wine.**
	25. 6	the world—a banquet of the richest food and the finest **wine.**
	28. 7	They have drunk so much **wine** and liquor that they stumble in
	29. 9	Get drunk without any **wine!**
	36.17	there are vineyards to give **wine** and there is corn for
	51.22	no longer have to drink the **wine** that makes you stagger.
	55. 1	Buy **wine** and milk— it will cost you nothing!
	56.12	'Let's get some **wine,'** these drunkards say, 'and drink
	57. 6	You pour out **wine** as offerings to them
Is	62. 8	enemies, And foreigners will no longer drink your **wine.**
	62. 9	grapes Will drink the **wine** in the courts of my Temple."
	63. 2	red, like that of a man who tramples grapes to make **wine?"**
	65. 8	instead, they make **wine** with them.
	65.21	plant vineyards and enjoy the **wine**—it will not be drunk by
Jer	13.12	of Israel that every wine-jar should be filled with **wine.**
	13.12	that they know every wine-jar should be filled with **wine.**
	13.13	fill the people in this land with **wine** until they are drunk:
	19.13	to the stars and where **wine** has been poured out as an
	23. 9	man who is drunk, a man who has had too much **wine.**
	25.15	said to me, "Here is a **wine** cup filled with my anger.
	31.12	gifts of corn and **wine** and olive-oil, gifts of sheep and
	35. 2	one of the rooms in the Temple and offer them some **wine."**
	35. 5	cups and bowls full of **wine** before the Rechabites,
	35. 5	and I said to them, "Have some **wine."**
	35. 6	But they answered, "We do not drink **wine.**
	35. 6	neither we nor our descendants were ever to drink any **wine.**
	35. 8	We ourselves never drink **wine,** and neither do our wives, our
	35.14	his command not to drink **wine,** and to this very day none
	40.10	can gather and store up **wine,** fruit, and olive-oil, and live
	40.12	and there they gathered in large amounts of **wine** and fruit.
	48.11	Moab is like **wine** left to settle undisturbed and never
	48.12	coming when I will send people to pour Moab out like **wine.**
	48.12	They will empty its **wine-jars** and break them in pieces.
	48.33	I have made the **wine** stop flowing from the winepresses;
	48.33	there is no one to make the **wine** and shout for joy.
	51. 7	The nations drank its **wine** and went out of their minds.
	52.19	and the bowls used for pouring out offerings of **wine.**
Ezek	20.28	they burnt and by the **wine** they brought as offerings.
	27.18	paying for them with **wine** from Helbon and wool from Sahar.
	44.21	Priests must not drink any **wine** before going into the inner
Dan	1. 5	given the same food and **wine** as the members of the royal
	1. 8	the food and drinking the **wine** of the royal court, so he
	5. 1	noblemen to a great banquet, and they drank **wine** together.
	5. 3	in, and they all drank **wine** out of them [4]and praised gods
	5.23	wives, and your concubines drank **wine** out of them and
	10. 3	or any meat, drink any **wine,** or comb my hair until the
Hos	2. 4	me food and water, wool and linen, olive-oil and **wine."**
	2. 8	gave her the corn, the **wine,** the olive-oil, and all the
	2. 9	my gifts of corn and **wine,** and will take away the wool
	4.11	The Lord says, **"Wine,** both old and new, is robbing my
	4.18	After drinking much **wine,** they delight in their prostitution,
	7. 5	made the king and his officials drunk and foolish with **wine.**
	7.14	When they pray for corn and **wine,** they gash themselves like pagans.
	9. 2	have enough corn and olive-oil, and there will be no **wine.**
	9. 4	able to make offerings of **wine** to the Lord, or bring their
	14. 7	They will be as famous as the **wine** of Lebanon.
Joel	1. 5	cry, you **wine-drinkers;**
	1. 5	the grapes for making new **wine** have been destroyed.
	1. 9	There is no corn or **wine** to offer in the Temple;
	1.13	There is no corn or **wine** to offer your God.
	2.14	Then you can offer him corn and **wine.**
	2.19	to give you corn and **wine** and olive-oil, and you will be
	2.24	the pits beside the presses will overflow with **wine** and olive-oil.
	3. 3	and girls into slavery to pay for prostitutes and **wine.**
	3.13	are crushed in a full winepress until the **wine** runs over."
Amos	2. 8	of their God they drink **wine** which they have taken from
	2.12	you made the Nazirites drink **wine,** and ordered the prophets
	5.11	build or drink **wine** from the beautiful vineyards you plant.
	6. 6	You drink **wine** by the bowlful and use the finest perfumes,
	9.13	and grapes will grow faster than the **wine** can be made.
	9.13	mountains will drip with sweet **wine,** and the hills will flow
	9.14	they will plant vineyards and drink the **wine;**
Mic	2.11	says, 'I prophesy that **wine** and liquor will flow for you.'
	6.15	You will make **wine,** but never drink it.
Zeph	1.13	or drink **wine** from the vineyards they are planting."
Hag	1. 6	You have **wine** to drink, but not enough to get drunk on!
	2.12	touch any bread, cooked food, **wine,** olive-oil, or any kind
	2.16	draw a hundred litres of **wine** from a vat, but find only
Zech	9.17	The young people will grow strong on its corn and **wine.**
	10. 7	like soldiers, happy like men who have been drinking **wine.**
	12. 2	He says, [2]"I will make Jerusalem like a cup of **wine;**
Mt	9.17	Nor does anyone pour new **wine** into used wineskins, for
	9.17	the skins will burst, the **wine** will pour out, and the skins
	9.17	Instead, new **wine** is poured into fresh wineskins, and both will
	11.18	he fasted and drank no **wine,** and everyone said, 'He has a
	26.29	will never again drink this **wine** until the day
	26.29	I drink the new **wine** with you in my Father's Kingdom."
	27.34	There they offered Jesus **wine** mixed with a bitter substance;
	27.48	sponge, soaked it in cheap **wine,** put it on the end of
Mk	2.22	Nor does anyone pour new **wine** into used wineskins,
	2.22	because the **wine** will burst the skins,
	2.22	and both the **wine** and the skins will be ruined.
	2.22	Instead, new **wine** must be poured into fresh wineskins."
	14.25	will never again drink this **wine** until the day
	14.25	I drink the new **wine** in the Kingdom of God."
	15.23	they tried to give him **wine** mixed with a drug called myrrh,
	15.36	sponge, soaked it in cheap **wine,** and put it on the end
Lk	1.15	He must not drink any **wine** or strong drink.
	5.37	Nor does anyone pour new **wine** into used wineskins,
	5.37	because the new **wine** will burst the skins,
	5.37	the **wine** will pour out, and the skins
	5.38	Instead, new **wine** must be poured into fresh wineskins!
	5.39	And no one wants new **wine** after drinking old wine.
	7.33	he fasted and drank no **wine,** and you said, 'He has a
	10.34	to him, poured oil and **wine** on his wounds and bandaged them;
	22.18	I will not drink this **wine** until the Kingdom of God comes."
	23.36	and offered him cheap **wine,** [37]and said, "Save yourself if you
Jn	2. 3	When the **wine** had given out,
	2. 3	Jesus' mother said to him, "They have no **wine** left."

Jn 2. 9 water, [9] which now had turned into **wine,** and he tasted it.
2. 9 did not know where this **wine** had come from (but, of course,
2.10 "Everyone else serves the best **wine** first, and after
2.10 have had plenty to drink, he serves the ordinary **wine.**
2.10 But you have kept the best **wine** until now!"
4.46 to Cana in Galilee, where he had turned the water into **wine.**
19.29 A bowl was there, full of cheap **wine;**
19.29 sponge was soaked in the **wine,** put on a stalk of hyssop,
19.30 Jesus drank the **wine** and said, "It is finished!"
Rom 14.21 keep from eating meat, drinking **wine,** or doing anything else that
Eph 5.18 Do not get drunk with **wine,** which will only ruin you;
1 Tim 3. 8 they must not drink too much **wine** or be greedy for money;
5.23 but take a little **wine** to help your digestion, since you
Tit 2. 3 They must not be slanderers or slaves to **wine.**
Rev 14. 8 made all peoples drink her **wine**—
14. 8 the strong **wine** of her immoral lust!"
14.10 will himself drink God's **wine,** the wine of his fury, which
16.19 and made her drink the **wine** from his cup—
16.19 the **wine** of his furious anger.
17. 2 the world became drunk from drinking the **wine** of her immorality."
18. 3 have drunk her wine—the strong **wine** of her immoral lust.
18.13 **wine** and oil, flour and wheat, cattle and sheep,
19.15 he will trample out the **wine** in the winepress of the furious

Am **WINE-DRINKER** see **DRINKER**

WINE-OFFERING

Ex 25.29 Make plates, cups, jars, and bowls to be used for the **wine-offerings.**
30. 9 grain-offering, and do not pour out any **wine-offering** on it.
37.16 the jars, and the bowls to be used for the **wine-offering.**
Lev 23.18 Lord, together with a grain-offering and a **wine-offering.**
23.37 sacrifices, and **wine-offerings,** as required day by day.
Num 4. 7 the offering bowls, and the jars for the **wine-offering.**
15.24 the Lord, with the proper grain-offering and **wine-offering.**
28. 7 As the **wine-offering** with the first lamb, pour out at the
28. 8 as the morning offering, together with its **wine-offering.**
28. 9 with olive-oil as a grain-offering, and the **wine-offering.**
28.10 Sabbath in addition to the daily offering with its **wine-offering.**
28.14 The proper **wine-offering** is two litres of wine with each bull,
28.15 the daily burnt-offering with its **wine-offering,** offer one
28.24 Offer this in addition to the daily burnt-offering and **wine-offering.**
28.31 Offer these and the **wine-offering** in addition to the
29. 6 burnt-offering with its grain-offering and **wine-offering.**
29.11 burnt-offering with its grain-offering and **wine-offering.**
29.15 and one kilogramme with each lamb, with the required **wine-offerings.**
29.16 burnt-offering with its grain-offering and **wine-offering.**
29.39 the burnt-offerings, grain-offerings, **wine-offerings,**
2 Kgs 16.13 on it, and poured a **wine-offering** and the blood of a
16.15 king and the people, and for the people's **wine-offerings.**
Ps 116.13 I will bring a **wine-offering** to the Lord, to thank him
Jer 7.18 They also pour out **wine-offerings** to other gods, in order to
32.29 and by pouring out **wine-offerings** to other gods.
44.17 and we will pour out **wine-offerings** to her,
44.18 and stopped pouring out **wine-offerings** to her,
44.19 and poured out **wine-offerings** to her,
44.24 and pour out **wine-offerings** to her,
Ezek 45.17 and the **wine-offerings** for the whole nation of Israel

WINEPRESS

Judg 6.11 some wheat secretly in a **winepress,** so that the Midianites
7.25 killed Oreb at Oreb Rock, and Zeeb at the **Winepress** of Zeeb.
Jer 48.33 I have made the wine stop flowing from the **winepresses;**
Lam 1.15 He crushed my people like grapes in a **winepress.**
Joel 3.13 are crushed in a full **winepress** until the wine runs over."
Zech 14.10 and from the Tower of Hananel to the royal **winepresses.**
Mt 21.33 it, dug a hole for the **winepress,** and built a watch-tower.
Mk 12. 1 it, dug a hole for the **winepress,** and built a watch-tower.
Rev 14.19 and threw them into the **winepress** of God's furious anger.
14.20 were squeezed out in the **winepress** outside the city, and
14.20 blood came out of the **winepress** in a flood three hundred
19.15 out the wine in the **winepress** of the furious anger of the

WINESKIN
[SKINS]

Josh 9. 4 their donkeys with worn-out sacks and patched-up **wineskins.**
9.13 When we filled these **wineskins,** they were new, but look!
Job 32.19 to speak, I will burst like a **wineskin** full of new wine.
Ps 119.83 I am as useless as a discarded **wineskin;**
Mt 9.17 pour new wine into used **wineskins,** for the skins will burst,
9.17 the wine will pour out, and the **skins** will be ruined.
9.17 wine is poured into fresh **wineskins,** and both will keep in
Mk 2.22 pour new wine into used **wineskins,**
2.22 the wine will burst the **skins,**
2.22 and both the wine and the **skins** will be ruined.
2.22 Instead, new wine must be poured into fresh **wineskins."**
Lk 5.37 pour new wine into used **wineskins,**
5.37 new wine will burst the **skins,**
5.37 the wine will pour out, and the **skins** will be ruined.
5.38 Instead, new wine must be poured into fresh **wineskins!**

WING

Ex 19. 4 carries her young on her **wings,** and brought you here to me.
25.18 Make two **winged** creatures of hammered gold, [19] one for
25.20 The **winged** creatures are to face each other across the lid,
25.20 and their outspread **wings** are to cover it.
25.22 the lid between the two **winged** creatures I will give you all
26. 1 Embroider them with figures of **winged** creatures.
26.31 Embroider it with figures of **winged** creatures.
36. 8 red wool and embroidered with figures of **winged** creatures.
36.35 wool and embroidered it with figures of **winged** creatures.
37. 7 He made two **winged** creatures of hammered gold, [8] one for
37. 9 The **winged** creatures faced each other across the lid,
37. 9 and their outspread **wings** covered it.
Lev 1.17 shall take hold of its **wings** and tear its body open,
1.17 without tearing the **wings** off, and then burn it whole
11.20 All **winged** insects are unclean, [21] except those that hop.
11.23 other small things that have **wings** and also crawl must be
Num 7.89 lid on the Covenant Box, between the two **winged** creatures.
Deut 14.19 "All **winged** insects are unclean;
32.11 on its spreading **wings,** the Lord kept Israel from falling.
1 Sam 4. 4 who is enthroned above the **winged** creatures.
2 Sam 6. 2 Lord Almighty, who is enthroned above the **winged** creatures.
22.11 He flew swiftly on his **winged** creature;
22.11 he travelled on the **wings** of the wind.
1 Kgs 6.23 Two **winged** creatures were made of olive wood and placed
6.24 Each had two wings, each **wing** 2.2 metres long,
6.24 the distance from one **wing-tip** to the other was 4.4 metres.
6.27 that two of their outstretched **wings** touched each other in
6.27 of the room, and the other two **wings** touched the walls.
6.28 The two **winged** creatures were covered with gold.
6.29 were all decorated with carved figures of **winged** creatures,
6.32 were decorated with carved figures of **winged** creatures,
6.32 the **winged** creatures, and the palm-trees were covered with gold.
6.35 decorated with carved figures of **winged** creatures,
7.29 figures of lions, bulls, and **winged** creatures on the panels;
7.36 with figures of **winged** creatures, lions, and palm-trees,
8. 6 put it in the Most Holy Place, beneath the **winged** creatures.
8. 7 Their outstretched **wings** covered the box and the poles it
2 Kgs 19.15 enthroned above the **winged** creatures, you alone are God,
1 Chr 13. 6 the name of the Lord enthroned above the **winged** creatures.
28.18 the chariot for the **winged** creatures
28.18 that spread their **wings** over the Lord's Covenant Box.
2 Chr 3. 7 On the walls the workmen carved designs of **winged** creatures.
3.10 his workmen to make two **winged** creatures out of metal, cover
3.11 Each had two wings, each **wing** 2.2 metres long,
3.14 red, with designs of the **winged** creatures worked into it.
5. 7 put it in the Most Holy Place, beneath the **winged** creatures.
5. 8 Their outstretched **wings** covered the Box and the carrying-poles.
Job 39.13 How fast the **wings** of an ostrich beat!
39.26 you how to fly when it spreads its **wings** towards the south?
Ps 17. 8 the shadow of your **wings** [9] from the attacks of the wicked.
18.10 He flew swiftly on a **winged** creature;
18.10 he travelled on the **wings** of the wind.
36. 7 We find protection under the shadow of your **wings.**
55. 6 I wish I had **wings,** like a dove.
57. 1 In the shadow of your **wings** I find protection until the
61. 4 let me find safety under your **wings.**
63. 7 In the shadow of your **wings** I sing for joy.
68.13 doves covered with silver, whose **wings** glittered with fine gold.
80. 1 on your throne above the **winged** creatures, [2] reveal yourself
91. 4 He will cover you with his **wings;**
99. 1 He is enthroned above the **winged** creatures and the earth shakes.
104. 3 clouds as your chariot and ride on the **wings** of the wind.
Prov 23. 5 as if it had grown **wings** and flown away like an eagle.
Is 6. 2 flaming creatures were standing, each of which had six **wings.**
6. 2 covered its face with two **wings,** and its body with two, and
8. 8 His outspread **wings** protect the land.
10.14 Not a **wing** fluttered to scare me off;
18. 1 Sudan there is a land where the sound of **wings** is heard.
37.16 enthroned above the **winged** creatures, you alone are God,
40.31 They will rise on **wings** like eagles;
66.15 He will ride on the **wings** of a storm to punish those
Jer 48.40 an eagle with its outspread **wings,** [41] and the towns and
49.22 Bozrah like an eagle swooping down with outspread **wings.**
Ezek 1. 6 form, [6] but each of them had four faces and four **wings.**
1. 8 four faces and four **wings,**
1. 8 they each had four human hands, one under each **wing.**
1. 9 Two **wings** of each creature were spread out
1. 9 the creatures formed a square with their **wing** tips touching.
1.11 Two **wings** of each creature were raised so that they
1.11 touched the tips of the **wings** of the creatures next to it,
1.11 and their other two **wings** were folded against their bodies.
1.23 creatures, each stretching out two **wings** towards the ones
1.23 next to it and covering its body with the other two **wings.**
1.24 I heard the noise their **wings** made in flight;
1.24 stopped flying, they folded their **wings,** [25] but there was
3.13 I heard the **wings** of the creatures beating together in the air,
9. 3 Israel rose up from the **winged** creatures, where it had been,
10. 5 noise made by the creatures' **wings** was heard even in the
10. 8 had what looked like a human hand under each of its **wings.**
10.12 backs, hands, **wings,** and wheels were covered with eyes.
10.16 Whenever they spread their **wings** to fly, the wheels still
10.19 They spread their **wings** and flew up from the earth while
10.21 had four faces, four **wings,**
10.21 and what looked like a human hand under each **wing.**
17. 3 was a giant eagle with beautiful feathers and huge **wings,**
17. 7 "There was another giant eagle with huge **wings** and thick plumage.
41.18 with carvings [18] of palm-trees and **winged** creatures.
41.25 There were palm-trees and **winged** creatures carved on the
Dan 7. 4 first one looked like a lion, but had **wings** like an eagle.
7. 4 While I was watching, the **wings** were torn off.
7. 6 its back there were four **wings,** like the wings of a bird,
Nah 3.16 are gone, like locusts that spread their **wings** and fly away.

Zech 5. 9 flying towards me with powerful **wings** like those of a stork.
Mt 23.37 her chicks under her **wings,** but you would not let me!
Lk 13.34 her chicks under her **wings,** but you would not let me!
Heb 9. 5 Above the Box were the **winged** creatures representing
9. 5 God's presence, with their **wings** spread over the place where sins
Rev 4. 8 living creatures had six **wings,** and they were covered with eyes,
9. 9 the sound made by their **wings** was like the noise of many
12.14 She was given the two **wings** of a large eagle in order

WINK

Prov 6.13 They **wink** and make gestures to deceive you, [14]all the
16.30 Watch out for people who grin and **wink** at you;

WINNOWING SHOVEL

see also **SHOVEL**

Mt 3.12 He has his **winnowing shovel** with him to thresh out all
Lk 3.17 He has his **winnowing shovel** with him, to thresh out all

WINTER

Gen 8.22 be cold and heat, summer and **winter,** day and night."
Ps 74.17 you made summer and **winter.**
Prov 6. 8 up their food during the summer, getting ready for **winter.**
Song 2.11 The **winter** is over;
Is 18. 6 the birds will feed on them, and in **winter,** the animals."
25. 4 Cruel men attack like a **winter** storm, [5]like drought in a
Jer 36.22 It was **winter** and the king was sitting
36.22 in his **winter** palace in front of the fire.
Joel 2.23 he has poured down the **winter** rain for you and the spring
Amos 3.15 I will destroy **winter** houses and summer houses.
Mt 24.20 not have to run away during the **winter** or on a Sabbath!
Mk 13.18 Pray to God that these things will not happen in the **winter!**
Jn 10.22 It was **winter,** and the Festival of the Dedication of the
Acts 27.12 The harbour was not a good one to spend the **winter** in;
27.12 Phoenix, if possible, in order to spend the **winter** there.
28.11 "The Twin Gods," which had spent the **winter** in the island.
1 Cor 16. 6 with you, perhaps the whole **winter,** and then you can help me
2 Tim 4.21 Do your best to come before **winter.**
Tit 3.12 in Nicopolis, because I have decided to spend the **winter** there.

WIPE

Gen 6. 7 that he said, "I will **wipe out** these people I have created,
Ex 12.22 containing the animal's blood, and **wipe** the blood on the
Num 16.26 you will be **wiped out** with them for all their sins."
24.19 Israel will trample them down And **wipe out** the last survivors."
Deut 11. 4 saw how the Lord completely **wiped out** the Egyptian army,
2 Sam 4.11 for murdering him and will **wipe** you off the face of the
2 Kgs 10.28 That was how Jehu **wiped out** the worship of Baal in Israel.
21.13 I will **wipe** Jerusalem clean of its people,
21.13 clean as a plate that has been **wiped** and turned upside down.
Esth 9.24 he had planned to **wipe them out.**
Job 14.17 you will **wipe out** all the wrongs I have done.
Ps 37.38 completely destroyed, and their descendants are **wiped out.**
51. 1 Because of your great mercy **wipe** away my sins!
51. 9 Close your eyes to my sins and **wipe out** all my evil.
Is 10.13 I **wiped out** the boundaries between nations and took the
25. 8 He will **wipe** away the tears from everyone's eyes and take
Jer 31.16 Stop your crying and **wipe** away your tears.
49.37 Elam and send armies against them until I have **wiped them out.**
Lam 3.66 Hunt them down and **wipe** them off the earth!"
Ezek 14.17 destructive weapons to **wipe out** people and animals alike,
25.16 that I will attack the Philistines and **wipe them out.**
Dan 11.22 even God's High Priest, will be swept away and **wiped out.**
11.26 his soldiers will be killed, and his army will be **wiped out.**
Obad 5 But your enemies have **wiped you out** completely.
8 I will destroy their clever men and **wipe out** all their wisdom.
Nah 3.15 You will be **wiped out** like crops eaten up by locusts.
Zeph 3. 6 The Lord says, "I have **wiped out** whole nations;
Lk 10.11 your town that sticks to our feet we **wipe** off against you.
Jn 11. 2 the perfume on the Lord's feet and **wiped** them with her hair;
12. 3 poured it on Jesus' feet, and **wiped** them with her hair.
Rev 7.17 And God will **wipe** away every tear from their eyes."
21. 4 He will **wipe** away all tears from their eyes.

WISDOM

Gen 41.33 should choose some man with **wisdom** and insight and put him
41.39 that you have greater **wisdom** and insight than anyone else.
Deut 4. 6 say, 'What **wisdom** and understanding this great nation has!'
32.28 they have no **wisdom** at all.
34. 9 of Nun was filled with **wisdom,** because Moses had appointed
1 Kgs 3. 9 So give me the **wisdom** I need to rule your people with
3.11 you have asked for the **wisdom** to rule justly, instead of
3.12 I will give you more **wisdom** and understanding than anyone
3.28 God had given him the **wisdom** to settle disputes fairly.
4.29 God gave Solomon unusual **wisdom** and insight, and
4.34 the world heard of his **wisdom** and sent people to listen to
5.12 The Lord kept his promise and gave Solomon **wisdom.**
10. 4 queen of Sheba heard Solomon's **wisdom** and saw the palace he
10. 6 heard in my own country about you and your **wisdom** is true!
10. 7 **wisdom** and wealth are much greater than what I was told.
10.24 to come and listen to the **wisdom** that God had given him.
11.41 did, his career and his **wisdom,** are all recorded in The
1 Chr 22.12 God give you insight and **wisdom** so that you may govern
2 Chr 1.10 counted, [10]so give me the **wisdom** and knowledge I need to
1.11 yourself, you have asked for **wisdom** and knowledge so that
1.12 I will give you **wisdom** and knowledge.
9. 3 queen of Sheba heard Solomon's **wisdom** and saw the palace he
2 Chr 9. 5 heard in my own country about you and your **wisdom** is true!
9. 6 I had not heard of even half your **wisdom.**
9.23 consulted him, to hear the **wisdom** that God had given him.
Ezra 7.25 "You, Ezra, using the **wisdom** which your God has given you,
Job 4.21 he dies, still lacking **wisdom."**
8. 8 Look for a moment at ancient **wisdom;**
11. 6 He would tell you there are many sides to **wisdom;**
12. 1 When you die, **wisdom** will die with you.
12. 8 ask the creatures of earth and sea for their **wisdom.**
12.12 Old men have **wisdom,** but God has wisdom and power.
12.17 He takes away the **wisdom** of rulers and makes leaders act
12.20 men who are trusted, and takes the **wisdom** of old men away.
15. 8 Does human **wisdom** belong to you alone?
15.10 We learnt our **wisdom** from grey-haired men— men born
28.12 But where can **wisdom** be found?
28.13 **Wisdom** is not to be found among men;
28.14 of the oceans and seas Say that **wisdom** is not found there.
28.18 The value of **wisdom** is more Than coral or crystal or rubies.
28.19 the purest gold Cannot compare with the value of **wisdom.**
28.20 Where, then, is the source of **wisdom?**
28.23 way, Knows the place where **wisdom** is found, [24]Because he
28.27 It was then he saw **wisdom** and tested its worth— He
32. 7 to speak, that you older men should share your **wisdom.**
32. 8 of Almighty God that comes to men and gives them **wisdom.**
32.13 How can you claim you have discovered **wisdom?**
38. 2 Who are you to question my **wisdom** with your ignorant,
39.17 was I who made her foolish and did not give her **wisdom.**
42. 3 how I dare question your **wisdom** when I am so very ignorant.
Ps 19. 7 Lord are trustworthy, giving **wisdom** to those who lack it.
49. 3 I will speak words of **wisdom.**
51. 6 fill my mind with your **wisdom.**
119.66 Give me **wisdom** and knowledge, because I trust in your commands.
119.100 I have greater **wisdom** than old men, because I obey your commands.
119.104 I gain **wisdom** from your laws, and so I hate all bad
119.130 teachings gives light and brings **wisdom** to the ignorant.
136. 5 By his **wisdom** he made the heavens;
147. 5 his **wisdom** cannot be measured.
Prov 1. 2 will help you to recognize **wisdom** and good advice, and
1. 7 Stupid people have no respect for **wisdom** and refuse to learn.
1.20 **Wisdom** is calling out in the streets and market-places,
1.28 Then you will call for **wisdom,** but I will not answer.
1.32 Inexperienced people die because they reject **wisdom.**
2. 6 It is the Lord who gives **wisdom;**
3.15 **Wisdom** is more valuable than jewels;
3.16 **Wisdom** offers you long life, as well as wealth and honour.
3.17 **Wisdom** can make your life pleasant and lead you safely through it.
3.18 **wisdom** will give them life.
3.19 The Lord created the earth by his **wisdom;**
3.20 His **wisdom** caused the rivers to flow and the clouds to
3.21 Hold on to your **wisdom** and insight, my son.
4. 5 Get **wisdom** and insight!
4. 6 Do not abandon **wisdom,** and she will protect you;
4. 7 Getting **wisdom** is the most important thing you can do.
4. 8 Love **wisdom,** and she will make you great.
4.11 I have taught you **wisdom** and the right way to live.
5. 1 Pay attention, my son, and listen to my **wisdom** and insight.
7. 4 Treat **wisdom** as your sister, and insight as your closest friend.
8. 1 **Wisdom** is calling out.
8.11 "I am **Wisdom,** I am better than jewels;
8.12 I am **Wisdom,** and I have insight;
9. 1 **Wisdom** has built her house and made seven pillars for it.
9.11 **Wisdom** will add years to your life.
9.12 will profit if you have **wisdom,** and if you reject it, you
10.23 Intelligent people take pleasure in **wisdom.**
10.31 Righteous people speak **wisdom,** but the tongue that
11. 9 people, but the **wisdom** of the righteous can save you.
14. 1 Homes are made by the **wisdom** of women, but are destroyed
14.33 **Wisdom** is in every thought of an intelligent man;
14.33 fools know nothing about **wisdom.**
16.16 better—to have **wisdom** and knowledge than gold and silver.
16.22 **Wisdom** is a fountain of life to the wise, but trying to
18. 4 can be a source of **wisdom,** deep as the ocean, fresh as
21.30 Human **wisdom,** brilliance, insight—they are of no help if
23.16 I will be proud when I hear you speaking words of **wisdom.**
23.23 Truth, **wisdom,** learning, and good sense—these are worth paying for,
24. 3 Homes are built on the foundation of **wisdom** and understanding.
24.14 you may be sure that **wisdom** is good for the soul.
24.14 Get **wisdom** and you have a bright future.
29. 3 If you appreciate **wisdom,** your father will be proud of you.
30. 3 I have never learned any **wisdom,** and I know nothing at all
31.26 She speaks with a gentle **wisdom.**
Ecc 1.16 I know what **wisdom** and knowledge really are."
1.17 between knowledge and foolishness, **wisdom** and madness.
2. 3 on by my desire for **wisdom,** I decided to cheer myself up
2. 9 had ever lived in Jerusalem, and my **wisdom** never failed me.
2.13 Oh, I know, **"Wisdom** is better than foolishness, just as
2.19 have worked for, everything my **wisdom** has earned for me in
2.21 for something with all your **wisdom,** knowledge, and skill,
2.26 God gives **wisdom,** knowledge, and happiness to those who please him,
7.12 **Wisdom** keeps you safe—this is the advantage of knowledge.
7.19 **Wisdom** does more for a person than ten rulers can do for
7.23 I used my **wisdom** to test all of this.
7.25 I was determined to find **wisdom** and the answers to my questions,
8. 1 **Wisdom** makes him smile and makes his frowns disappear.
9.10 no thought, no knowledge, no **wisdom** in the world of the dead
9.13 saw, a good example of how **wisdom** is regarded in this world.

Ecc 9.16 I have always said that **wisdom** is better than strength,
9.18 **Wisdom** does more good than weapons, but one sinner can
10. 1 and a little stupidity can cancel out the greatest **wisdom.**
Is 11. 2 the Lord will give him **wisdom,** and the knowledge and skill
28.29 All this **wisdom** comes from the Lord Almighty.
33. 6 He always protects his people and gives them **wisdom** and knowledge.
44.25 wise I refute and show that their **wisdom** is foolishness.
47.10 Your **wisdom** and knowledge led you astray, and you said to yourself,
Jer 3.15 me, and they will rule you with **wisdom** and understanding.
8. 9 what **wisdom** have they got now?
9.23 not boast of their **wisdom,** nor strong men of their strength,
10.12 by his **wisdom** he created the world and stretched out the heavens.
49. 7 Has all their **wisdom** disappeared?
50.35 Death to its people, to its rulers, to its men of **wisdom.**
51.15 by his **wisdom** he created the world and stretched out the heavens.
51.57 will make its rulers drunk— men of **wisdom,** leaders, and
Ezek 28. 4 Your **wisdom** and skill made you rich with treasures of gold
28. 7 beautiful things you have acquired by your skill and **wisdom.**
Dan 2.21 it is he who gives **wisdom** and understanding.
2.23 You have given me **wisdom** and strength;
5.11 sense, knowledge, and **wisdom** like the wisdom of the gods.
5.14 you and that you are skilful and have knowledge and **wisdom.**
11.33 Wise leaders of the people will share their **wisdom**
Obad 8 I will destroy their clever men and wipe out all their **wisdom.**
Mt 11.19 God's **wisdom,** however, is shown to be true by its results."
13.54 "Where did he get such **wisdom?"**
Mk 6. 2 "What **wisdom** is this that has been given him?
Lk 2.40 he was full of **wisdom,** and God's blessings were upon him.
2.52 in body and in **wisdom,** gaining favour with God and men.
7.35 God's **wisdom,** however, is shown to be true by all who
11.49 For this reason the **Wisdom** of God said, 'I will send
21.15 give you such words and **wisdom** that none of your enemies
Acts 6. 3 of the Holy Spirit and **wisdom,** and we will put them in
6.10 Spirit gave Stephen such **wisdom** that when he spoke, they could
7.10 a pleasing manner and **wisdom,** and the king made Joseph governor
7.22 He was taught all the **wisdom** of the Egyptians and became
Rom 11.33 How deep are his **wisdom** and knowledge!
1 Cor 1.17 using the language of human **wisdom,** in order to make sure
1.19 says, "I will destroy the **wisdom** of the wise and set aside
1.20 God has shown that this world's **wisdom** is foolishness!
1.21 For God in his **wisdom** made it impossible
1.21 for people to know him by means of their own **wisdom.**
1.22 Jews want miracles for proof, and Greeks look for **wisdom.**
1.24 Christ, who is the power of God and the **wisdom** of God.
1.25 foolishness is wiser than human **wisdom,** and what seems to be
1.30 with Christ Jesus, and God has made Christ to be our **wisdom.**
2. 4 with skilful words of human **wisdom,** but with convincing proof of
2. 5 then, does not rest on human **wisdom** but on God's power.
2. 6 proclaim a message of **wisdom** to those who are spiritually mature.
2. 6 But it is not the **wisdom** that belongs to this world or
2. 7 wisdom I proclaim is God's secret **wisdom,** which is hidden
2. 8 None of the rulers of this world knew this **wisdom.**
2.13 in words taught by human **wisdom,** but in words taught by the
3.19 world considers to be **wisdom** is nonsense in God's sight.
12. 8 person a message full of **wisdom,** while to another person the
2 Cor 1.12 by the power of God's grace, and not by human **wisdom.**
Eph 1. 8 In all his **wisdom** and insight [9] God did what he had purposed,
3.10 world might learn of his **wisdom** in all its different forms.
Col 1. 9 with all the **wisdom** and understanding that his Spirit gives.
1.28 With all possible **wisdom** we warn and teach them in order to
2. 3 opens all the hidden treasures of God's **wisdom** and knowledge.
2. 8 worthless deceit of human **wisdom,** which comes from the teachings
2.23 to be based on **wisdom** in their forced worship of angels,
3.16 Teach and instruct each other with all **wisdom.**
2 Tim 3.15 able to give you the **wisdom** that leads to salvation through
Jas 1. 5 if any of you lacks **wisdom,** he should pray to God,
3.13 good life, by his good deeds performed with humility and **wisdom.**
3.14 don't sin against the truth by boasting of your **wisdom.**
3.15 Such **wisdom** does not come down from heaven;
3.17 But the **wisdom** from above is pure first of all;
2 Pet 3.15 Paul wrote to you, using the **wisdom** that God gave him.
Rev 5.12 worthy to receive power, wealth, **wisdom,** and strength, honour,
7.12 **wisdom,** thanksgiving, honour, power, and might belong to our God
13.18 This calls for **wisdom.**
17. 9 "This calls for **wisdom** and understanding.

WISE
[ALL-WISE]

Gen 3. 6 and she thought how wonderful it would be to become **wise.**
41. 8 so he sent for all the magicians and **wise** men of Egypt.
Ex 7.11 the king called for his **wise** men and magicians, and by their
Deut 1.13 Choose some **wise,** understanding, and experienced men
1.15 So I took the **wise** and experienced leaders you chose
4. 6 this will show the people of other nations how **wise** you are.
16.19 blind the eyes even of **wise** and honest men, and cause them
18.17 So the Lord said to me, 'They have made a **wise** request.
Judg 5.29 Her **wisest** ladies answered her, and she told herself
2 Sam 14.20 Your Majesty is as **wise** as the angel of God and knows
20.16 There was a **wise** woman in the city who shouted from the
1 Kgs 4.30 Solomon was wiser than the **wise** men of the East
4.30 or the **wise** men of Egypt.
4.31 He was the **wisest** of all men:
4.31 **wiser** than Ethan the Ezrahite, and Heman, Calcol, and Darda,
5. 7 for giving David such a **wise** son to succeed him as king
1 Kgs 10. 8 your presence and are privileged to hear your **wise** sayings!
10.23 King Solomon was richer and **wiser** than any other king,
2 Chr 2.12 King David a **wise** son, full of understanding and skill,
2.13 I am sending you a **wise** and skilful master craftsman named Huram.
9. 6 You are even **wiser** than people say.
9. 7 your presence and are privileged to hear your **wise** sayings!
9.22 King Solomon was richer and **wiser** than any other king
11.23 Rehoboam **wisely** assigned responsibilities to his sons,
Esth 6.13 Then she and those **wise** friends of his said to him, "You
Job 5.12 of cunning men, and traps **wise** men in their own schemes, so
8.10 But let the ancient **wise** men teach you;
9. 4 God is so **wise** and powerful;
11.12 Stupid men will start being **wise** when wild donkeys are born tame.
13. 5 Say nothing, and someone may think you are **wise!**
15. 3 No **wise** man would talk as you do or defend himself with
15.18 **Wise** men have taught me truths which they learnt from their fathers,
16. 4 I could shake my head **wisely** and drown you with a flood
17.10 stood before me, I would not find even one of them **wise.**
22. 1 there any man, even the **wisest,** who could ever be of use
28.28 said to men, "To be **wise,** you must have reverence for the
32. 9 growing old that makes men **wise** or helps them to know what
32.11 speaking and waited while you searched for **wise** phrases.
33.33 listen to me, and I will teach you how to be **wise.**
34. 1 You men are so **wise,** so clever;
34. 3 when you taste it, but not **wise** words when you hear them.
34.16 Now listen to me, if you are **wise.**
34.34 any **wise** man who hears me will say [35] that Job is
35.11 to God, who makes us **wise,** wiser than any animal or bird.
36. 4 you see before you a truly **wise** man.
37.24 of him, and that he ignores those who claim to be **wise.**
38.37 Who is **wise** enough to count the clouds and tilt them
Ps 14. 2 see if there are any who are **wise,** any who worship him.
36. 3 he no longer does what is **wise** and good.
37.30 A good man's words are **wise,** and he is always fair.
49.10 Anyone can see that even **wise** men die, as well as
53. 2 see if there are any who are **wise,** any who worship him.
78. 2 I am going to use **wise** sayings and explain mysteries from
90.12 us how short our life is, so that we may become **wise.**
104.24 How **wisely** you made them all!
107.43 May those who are **wise** think about these things;
111.10 The way to become **wise** is to honour the Lord;
119.98 with me all the time and makes me **wiser** than my enemies.
Prov 1. 5 add to the knowledge of **wise** men and give guidance to the
1. 6 meanings of proverbs and the problems that **wise** men raise.
2. 2 Listen to what is **wise** and try to understand it.
2.10 You will become **wise,** and your knowledge will give you pleasure.
3. 7 Never let yourself think that you are **wiser** than you are;
3.13 Happy is the man who becomes **wise**—who gains understanding.
3.18 Those who become **wise** are happy;
3.35 **Wise** men will gain an honourable reputation, but stupid
4.12 your way if you walk **wisely,** and you will not stumble when
8.33 Be **wise;**
9. 8 But if you correct a **wise** man, he will respect you.
9. 9 Anything you say to a **wise** man will make him wiser.
9.10 To be **wise** you must first have reverence for the Lord.
10. 1 A **wise** son makes his father proud of him;
10.14 The **wise** get all the knowledge they can, but when fools speak,
10.19 If you are **wise,** you will keep quiet.
11. 2 It is **wiser** to be modest.
11.29 Foolish men will always be servants to the **wise.**
12.15 **Wise** people listen to advice.
12.18 as deeply as any sword, but **wisely** spoken words can heal.
13. 1 A **wise** son pays attention when his father corrects him,
13.10 It is **wiser** to ask for advice.
13.14 The teachings of the **wise** are a fountain of life;
13.20 Keep company with the **wise** and you will become wise.
14. 3 a **wise** man's words protect him.
14. 6 Conceited people can never become **wise,**
14. 8 Why is a clever person **wise?**
14.16 **Wise** people are careful to stay out of trouble, but
14.17 **wiser** people remain calm.
14.24 **Wise** people are rewarded with wealth, but fools are
14.29 you stay calm, you are **wise,** but if you have a hot
15. 2 When **wise** people speak, they make knowledge attractive,
15. 5 it is **wise** to accept his correction.
15. 7 Knowledge is spread by people who are **wise,** not by fools.
15.12 they never ask for advice from those who are **wiser.**
15.20 A **wise** son makes his father happy.
15.21 with their foolishness, but the **wise** will do what is right.
15.24 **Wise** people walk the road that leads upwards to life,
15.31 If you pay attention when you are corrected, you are **wise.**
15.32 If you accept correction, you will become **wiser.**
16.14 A **wise** man will try to keep the king happy;
16.21 A **wise,** mature person is known for his understanding.
16.22 fountain of life to the **wise,** but trying to educate stupid
17.24 An intelligent person aims at **wise** action, but a fool
17.28 a fool may be thought **wise** and intelligent if he stays quiet
19.20 advice and are willing to learn, one day you will be **wise.**
19.25 If you are **wise,** you will learn when you are corrected.
20.26 A **wise** king will find out who is doing wrong, and will
21.11 One who is **wise** will learn from what he is taught.
21.20 **Wise** people live in wealth and luxury, but stupid people
22.17 Listen, and I will teach you what **wise** men have said.
23. 4 Be **wise** enough not to wear yourself out trying to get rich.
23.15 Son, if you become **wise,** I will be very happy.
23.19 Listen, my son, be **wise** and give serious thought to the
23.24 You can take pride in a **wise** son.
24. 5 Being **wise** is better than being strong;
24. 7 **Wise** sayings are too deep for a stupid person to understand.

Prov	24.23	**Wise** men have also said these things:
	26. 9	A fool quoting a **wise** saying reminds you of a drunk man
	26.12	off than someone who thinks he is **wise** when he is not.
	27.11	Be **wise**, my son, and I will be happy;
	28.11	people always think they are **wise**, but a poor person who has
	28.26	Be safe, and follow the teachings of **wiser** people.
	29. 8	Those who are **wise** keep things calm.
Ecc	1.16	become a great man, far **wiser** than anyone who ruled
	1.18	The **wiser** you are, the more worries you have;
	2.12	about what it meant to be **wise** or reckless or foolish.
	2.14	**Wise** men can see where they are going, and fools cannot."
	2.15	So what have I gained from being so **wise?"**
	2.16	No one remembers **wise** men, and no one remembers fools.
	2.16	We must all die—**wise** and foolish alike.
	2.19	successor, [19] and he might be **wise**, or he might be
	6. 8	How is a **wise** man better off than a fool?
	7. 4	A **wise** person thinks about death.
	7. 5	It is better to have **wise** people reprimand you than to
	7. 7	When a **wise** man cheats someone, he is acting like a fool.
	7.11	Everyone who lives ought to be **wise**;
	7.16	So don't be too good or too **wise**—why kill yourself?
	7.23	I was determined to be **wise**, but it was beyond me.
	8. 1	Only a **wise** man knows what things really mean.
	8. 5	you are safe, and a **wise** man knows how and when to
	8.16	Whenever I tried to become **wise** and learn what goes on
	8.17	**Wise** men may claim to know, but they don't.
	9. 1	God controls the actions of **wise** and righteous men, even
	9.11	**Wise** men do not always earn a living, intelligent men do not
	9.16	of a poor man as **wise** or pays any attention to what
	9.17	the quiet words of a **wise** man than to the shouts of
	10. 2	It is natural for a **wise** man to do the right thing
	10.12	What a **wise** man says brings him honour, but a fool is
	12. 9	But because the Philosopher was **wise**, he kept on teaching
	12.11	The sayings of **wise** men are like the sharp sticks that
Is	5.21	You think you are **wise**, so very clever.
	10.13	I am strong and **wise** and clever.
	19.11	Egypt's **wisest** men give stupid advice!
	28.29	The plans God makes are **wise**, and they always succeed!
	29.14	Those who are **wise** will turn out to be fools, and all
	44.25	The words of the **wise** I refute and show that their wisdom
Jer	8. 8	you say that you are **wise**, and that you know my laws?
	8. 9	Your **wise** men are put to shame;
	9.12	Who is **wise** enough to understand this?
	9.23	"**Wise** men should not boast of their wisdom, nor strong men
	10. 7	like you among all the **wise** men of the nations or among
	18.18	be priests to instruct us, **wise** men to give us counsel, and
	23. 5	That king will rule **wisely** and do what is right and just
	32.19	You make **wise** plans and do mighty things;
Ezek	28. 3	You think you are **wiser** than Danel, that no secret can be
	28. 6	you think you are as **wise** as a god, [7] I will bring
	28.12	How **wise** and handsome you were!
Dan	2.20	"God is **wise** and powerful!
	2.30	me, not because I am **wiser** than anyone else, but so that
	5.12	ability and is **wise** and skilful in interpreting dreams,
	11.33	**Wise** leaders of the people will share their wisdom with many others.
	11.35	Some of those **wise** leaders will be killed, but as a
	12. 3	The **wise** leaders will shine with all the brightness of the sky.
	12.10	only those who are **wise** will understand.
Hos	14. 9	May those who are **wise** understand what is written here,
Mic	6. 9	It is **wise** to fear the Lord.
Mt	7.24	obeys them is like a **wise** man who built his house on
	11.25	unlearned what you have hidden from the **wise** and learned.
	12.42	from her country to listen to King Solomon's **wise** teaching;
	23.34	that I will send you prophets and **wise** men and teachers;
	24.45	"Who, then, is a faithful and **wise** servant?
	25. 2	Five of them were foolish, and the other five were **wise**.
	25. 4	oil with them, [4] while the **wise** ones took containers full of
	25. 8	foolish ones said to the **wise** ones, 'Let us have some of
	25. 9	'No, indeed,' the **wise** ones answered, 'there is not enough for
Mk	12.34	Jesus noticed how **wise** his answer was, and so he told him,
Lk	10.21	unlearned what you have hidden from the **wise** and learned.
	11.31	from her country to listen to King Solomon's **wise** teaching;
	12.42	Lord answered, "Who, then, is the faithful and **wise** servant?
Acts	24. 2	Your **wise** leadership has brought us a long period of peace,
Rom	1.22	They say they are **wise**, but they are fools;
	3.11	is righteous, [11] no one who is **wise** or who worships God.
	11.25	for it will keep you from thinking how **wise** you are.
	12.16	Do not think of yourselves as **wise**.
	16.19	I want you to be **wise** about what is good, but innocent
	16.27	only God, who alone is **all-wise**, be glory through Jesus Christ
1 Cor	1.19	destroy the wisdom of the **wise** and set aside the
	1.20	So then, where does that leave the **wise?**
	1.25	God's foolishness is **wiser** than human wisdom, and what seems
	1.26	few of you were **wise** or powerful or of high social
	1.27	in order to shame the **wise**, and he chose what the world
	3.18	thinks that he is **wise** by this world's standards,
	3.18	he should become a fool, in order to be really **wise**.
	3.19	As the scripture says, "God traps the **wise** in their cleverness";
	3.20	"The Lord knows that the thoughts of the **wise** are worthless."
	4.10	but you are **wise** in union with Christ!
	6. 5	there is at least one **wise** person in your fellowship who can
2 Cor	11.19	You yourselves are so **wise**, and so you gladly tolerate fools!
Eph	1.17	Spirit, who will make you **wise** and reveal God to you,
	5.15	Don't live like ignorant people, but like **wise** people.
Col	4. 5	Be **wise** in the way you act towards those who are not
Jas	3.13	Is there anyone among you who is **wise** and understanding?

WISH

Gen	34.10	live anywhere you **wish**, trade freely, and own property."
	34.12	and set the payment for the bride as high as you **wish**;
Ex	16. 3	and said to them, "We **wish** that the Lord had killed us
	25. 2	Receive whatever offerings any man **wishes** to give.
	35. 5	Everyone who **wishes** to do so is to bring an offering of
	35.21	Israel left, [21] and everyone who **wished** to do so brought an
Lev	27.13	If the man **wishes** to buy it back, he must pay the
	27.15	one who dedicated the house **wishes** to buy it back, he must
	27.19	man who dedicated the field **wishes** to buy it back, he must
	27.31	If a man **wishes** to buy any of it back, he must
Num	11.18	whining and saying that you **wished** you had some meat and
	11.29	I **wish** that the Lord would give his spirit to all his
	15.39	turn away from me and follow your own **wishes** and desires.
	36. 6	to marry anyone they **wish** but only within their own tribe.
Deut	12.20	as he has promised, you may eat meat whenever you **wish**.
	12.21	far away, then, whenever you **wish**, you may kill any of the
	28.67	Every morning you will **wish** for evening;
	28.67	every evening you will **wish** for morning.
Judg	9.29	I **wish** I were leading this people!
1 Sam	11.10	to you, and you can do with us whatever you **wish**."
	25. 6	my friend, with his best **wishes** for you, your family, and
2 Sam	15. 4	And he would add, "How I **wish** I were a judge!
	15.26	with me—well, then, let him do to me what he **wishes**."
	18.32	The slave answered, "I **wish** that what has happened to him
	23.15	homesick and said, "How I **wish** someone would bring me a
	24.22	Araunah said, "and offer to the Lord whatever you **wish**.
1 Kgs	19. 4	down in the shade of a tree and **wished** he would die.
2 Kgs	5. 3	said to her mistress, "I **wish** that my master could go to
1 Chr	11.17	homesick and said, "How I **wish** someone would bring me a
	21.23	"Take it, Your Majesty," Araunah said, "and do whatever you **wish**.
Esth	6. 6	said to him, "There is someone I **wish** very much to honour.
	6. 9	'See how the king rewards a man he **wishes** to honour!' "
	6.11	"See how the king rewards a man he **wishes** to honour!"
	7. 3	grant my humble request, my **wish** is that I may live and
	8. 8	You may, however, write to the Jews whatever you **wish**;
	9.30	It **wished** the Jews peace and security [31] and directed them
Job	3.11	I **wish** I had died in my mother's womb or died the
	11. 5	How I **wish** God would answer you!
	14.13	I **wish** you would hide me in the world of the dead;
	19.23	How I **wish** that someone would remember my words and
	23. 3	How I **wish** I knew where to find him, and knew how
	36.20	Don't **wish** for night to come, the time when nations will perish.
Ps	12. 4	We will say what we **wish**, and no one can stop us."
	31. 8	you have given me freedom to go where I **wish**.
	55. 6	I **wish** I had wings, like a dove.
	81. 8	Israel, how I **wish** you would listen to me!
	81.13	How I **wish** my people would listen to me;
	81.13	how I **wish** they would obey me!
	115. 3	he does whatever he **wishes**.
	135. 6	He does whatever he **wishes** in heaven and on earth, in the
	139.19	O God, how I **wish** you would kill the wicked!
	139.19	How I **wish** violent men would leave me alone!
Prov	13.12	heart is crushed, but a **wish** come true fills you with joy.
Song	8. 1	I **wish** that you were my brother, that my mother had nursed
Jer	9. 1	I **wish** my head were a well of water, and my eyes
	9. 2	I **wish** I had a place to stay in the desert where
	17.16	I did not **wish** a time of trouble for them.
	38. 5	"Very well, then, do what you **wish** with him;
	40. 4	country to choose from, and you may go wherever you **wish**."
Ezek	1.12	could go wherever they **wished**, without having to turn.
	1.20	The creatures went wherever they **wished**, and the wheels
	13.22	lies you discourage good people, whom I do not **wish** to hurt.
Dan	4.19	Belteshazzar replied, "Your Majesty, I **wish** that the dream
Jon	4. 8	So he **wished** he were dead.
Mal	1.10	The Lord Almighty says, "I **wish** one of you would close
Mt	14. 9	of all his guests he gave orders that her **wish** be granted.
	17. 4	If you **wish**, I will make three tents here, one for you,
	19. 3	a man to divorce his wife for whatever reason he **wishes?"**
	20.15	have the right to do as I **wish** with my own money?
Lk	12.49	the earth on fire, and how I **wish** it were already kindled!
	15.16	He **wished** he could fill himself with the bean pods the
	17.22	will come when you will **wish** you could see one of the
	23.25	and he handed Jesus over for them to do as they **wished**.
Jn	3. 8	The wind blows wherever it **wishes**;
	15. 7	you will ask for anything you **wish**, and you shall have it.
Acts	7.39	they pushed him aside and **wished** that they could go back to
	15.29	With our best **wishes**."
Rom	9. 3	For their sake I could **wish** that I myself were under God's
	9.15	he said to Moses, "I will have mercy on anyone I **wish**;
	9.15	I will take pity on anyone I **wish**."
	9.18	has mercy on anyone he **wishes**,
	9.18	and he makes stubborn anyone he **wishes**.
	9.21	use the clay as he **wishes**, and to make two pots from
	10. 1	My brothers, how I **wish** with all my heart that my own
1 Cor	4. 8	Well, I **wish** you really were kings, so that we could be
	7.15	who is not a believer **wishes** to leave the Christian partner,
	7.39	married to any man she **wishes**, but only if he is a
	12.11	as he **wishes**, he gives a different gift to each person.
	15.38	God provides that seed with the body he **wishes**;
2 Cor	11. 1	I **wish** you would tolerate me, even when I am a bit
	12.19	We speak as Christ would **wish** us to speak in the presence
Gal	4.20	How I **wish** I were with you now, so that I could
	5.12	I **wish** that the people who are upsetting you would go
Eph	2. 3	doing whatever suited the **wishes** of our own bodies and minds.
Col	4.15	Give our best **wishes** to the brothers in Laodicea and to
1 Pet	3.10	wants to enjoy life and **wishes** to see good times, must keep
2 Jn	11	anyone who **wishes** him peace becomes his partner in the evil
Rev	2.23	that I am the one who knows everyone's thoughts and **wishes**.

Rev 3.15 How I **wish** you were either one or the other!
11. 6 the earth with every kind of plague as often as they **wish.**

WIT

Is 44.19 maker of idols hasn't the **wit** or the sense to say, "Some

WITCHCRAFT

Num 23.23 is no magic charm, no **witchcraft,** That can be used against
1 Sam 15.23 him is as bad as **witchcraft,** and arrogance is as sinful as
2 Kgs 9.22 we still have all the **witchcraft** and idolatry that your
Gal 5.20 in worship of idols and **witchcraft.**

WITHDRAW

2 Sam 7.15 But I will not **withdraw** my support from him as I did
20.21 Hand over this one man, and I will **withdraw** from the city."
2 Kgs 19.36 Then the Assyrian emperor Sennacherib **withdrew**
1 Chr 17.13 I will not **withdraw** my support from him as I did from
2 Chr 24.25 wounded, and when the enemy **withdrew,** two of his officials
Is 37.37 Then the Assyrian emperor Sennacherib **withdrew**

WITHER

Job 8.12 they are the first to **wither,** while still too small to be
14. 2 We grow and **wither** as quickly as flowers;
15.32 time is up he will **wither,** wither like a branch and never
18.16 His roots and branches are **withered** and dry.
19.10 He uproots my hope and leaves me to **wither** and die.
24.24 man prospers, but then he **withers** like a weed, like an ear
Ps 37. 2 they will die like plants that **wither.**
Is 1.30 You will **wither** like a dying oak, like a garden that no
15. 6 the grass beside it has **withered,** and nothing green is left.
19. 6 Reeds and rushes will **wither,** [7] and all the crops sown along
24. 4 The earth dries up and **withers;**
24. 7 The grapevines **wither,** and wine is becoming scarce.
27.11 branches of the trees are **withered** and broken, and women
33. 9 The forests of Lebanon have **withered,** the fertile valley of
40. 7 Grass **withers** and flowers fade, when the Lord sends the
40. 8 Yes, grass **withers** and flowers fade, but the word of our
64. 6 we are like leaves that **wither** and are blown away by the
Jer 8.13 even the leaves have **withered.**
12. 4 our land be dry, and the grass in every field be **withered?**
Ezek 17. 9 the grapes, and break off the branches and let them **wither?**
17.10 Won't it **wither** when the east wind strikes it?
17.10 Won't it **wither** there where it is growing?"
17.24 I **wither** up the green trees and make the dry trees become
31.15 Lebanon Mountains and make all the trees of the forest **wither.**
47.12 Their leaves will never **wither,** and they will never stop bearing
Joel 1.10 the grapes are dried up, and the olive-trees are **withered.**
1.12 The grapevines and fig-trees have **withered;**
Nah 1. 4 The fields of Bashan **wither,** Mount Carmel turns brown, and
Zech 11.17 His arm will **wither,** and his right eye will go blind."
1 Pet 1.24 The grass **withers,** and the flowers fall, [25] but the word of

WITHHOLD

Num 31.28 that belongs to the soldiers, **withhold** as a tax for the Lord
Job 12.15 Drought comes when God **withholds** rain;

WITHIN

Lk 1.41 Elizabeth heard Mary's greeting, the baby moved **within** her.
1.44 I heard your greeting, the baby **within** me jumped with gladness.
17.21 because the Kingdom of God is **within** you."
19.44 will completely destroy you and the people **within** your walls;
Rom 8.23 of God's gifts also groan **within** ourselves, as we wait for
1 Cor 2.11 a person's own spirit **within** him that knows all about him;
2 Cor 10.13 it will stay **within** the limits of the work which God has
10.14 since you are **within** those limits, we were not going beyond
10.15 work among you, always **within** the limits that God has set.
Jas 4. 1 desires for pleasure, which are constantly fighting **within** you.
Jude 6 who did not stay **within** the limits of their proper authority,

WITHOUT

Mt 10. 8 You have received **without paying,** so give without being paid.
Mk 12. 3 the slave, beat him, and sent him back **without a thing.**
Lk 15.14 spread over that country, and he was left **without a thing.**
20.10 tenants beat the slave and sent him back **without a thing.**
20.11 treated him shamefully, and sent him back **without a thing.**
1 Cor 9.18 of preaching the Good News **without charging** for it,
2 Cor 7.11 You have shown yourselves to be **without fault** in the whole matter.
Eph 1. 4 Christ, so that we would be holy and **without fault** before him.
Phil 3. 6 by obeying the commands of the Law, I was **without fault.**
1 Thes 2.10 conduct towards you who believe was pure, right, and **without fault.**
2 Thes 3. 8 We did not accept anyone's support **without paying** for it.
1 Tim 3. 2 A church leader must be **without fault;**
Rev 21. 6 from the spring of the water of life **without paying** for it.

WITHOUT YEAST see UNLEAVENED

WITNESS

Gen 31.32 Here, with our men as **witnesses,** look for anything that
Ex 22.10 and if there was no **witness,** [11] the man must go to the
Num 5.12 it secret—there was no **witness,** and she was not caught in
Num 35.30 put to death only on the evidence of two or more **witnesses;**
35.30 the evidence of one **witness** is not sufficient to support an
Deut 4.26 call heaven and earth as **witnesses** against you today that,
17. 6 to death only if two or more **witnesses** testify against him;
17. 6 not to be put to death if there is only one **witness.**
17. 7 The **witnesses** are to throw the first stones, and then the
19.15 "One **witness** is not enough to convict a man of a crime;
19.15 at least two **witnesses** are necessary to prove that a man is
30.19 and I call heaven and earth to **witness** the choice you make.
31.26 that it will remain there as a **witness** against his people.
31.28 I will call heaven and earth to be my **witnesses** against them.
Josh 22.34 said, "This altar is a **witness** to all of us that the
22.34 And so they named it **"Witness."**
24.22 them, "You are your own **witnesses** to the fact that you have
24.22 "Yes," they said, "we are **witnesses."**
24.27 He said to all the people, "This stone will be our **witness.**
24.27 So it will be a **witness** against you, to keep you from
Judg 11.10 The Lord is our **witness."**
Ruth 4. 9 others there, "You are all **witnesses** today that I have
4.10 You are **witnesses** to this today."
4.11 The leaders and the others said, "Yes, we are **witnesses.**
1 Sam 6.18 Lord's Covenant Box, is still there as a **witness** to what happened.
12. 5 king he has chosen are **witnesses** today that you have found
12. 5 "Yes, the Lord is our **witness,"** they answered.
20.12 said to David, "May the Lord God of Israel be our **witness!**
1 Chr 24. 6 families and of the Levite families, were all **witnesses.**
24.31 families of the priests and of the Levites were **witnesses.**
Job 10.17 You always have some **witness** against me;
Ps 50. 4 heaven and earth as **witnesses** to see him judge his people.
89.37 permanent as the moon, that faithful **witness** in the sky."
Prov 6.16 a **witness** who tells one lie after
14. 5 A reliable **witness** always tells the truth, but an
14.25 A **witness** saves lives when he tells the truth;
19.28 There is no justice where a **witness** is determined to hurt someone.
25. 8 If another **witness** later proves you wrong, what will you do then?
Is 8. 2 Uriah and Zechariah son of Jeberechiah, to serve as **witnesses."**
43. 9 gods bring in their **witnesses** to prove that they are right,
43.10 "People of Israel, you are my **witnesses;**
43.12 you are my **witnesses.**
44. 8 I have predicted all that would happen, and you are my **witnesses.**
Jer 29.23 what they have done, and he is a **witness** against them.
32.10 sealed the deed, had it **witnessed,** and weighed out the money
32.12 of Hanamel and of the **witnesses** who had signed the deed of
32.25 field in the presence of **witnesses,** even though the city is
32.44 them, and the deeds will be signed, sealed, and **witnessed.**
42. 5 be a true and faithful **witness** against us if we do not
Mt 18.16 the testimony of two or more **witnesses,'** as the scripture says.
24.14 preached through all the world for a **witness** to all mankind;
26.65 We don't need any more **witnesses!**
Mk 14.56 Many **witnesses** told lies against Jesus, but their stories
14.63 Priest tore his robes and said, "We don't need any more **witnesses!**
Lk 22.71 And they said, "We don't need any **witnesses!**
24.48 You are **witnesses** of these things.
Jn 3.28 You yourselves are my **witnesses** that I said, 'I am not
5.34 It is not that I must have a man's **witness;**
5.36 But I have a **witness** on my behalf
5.36 which is even greater than the **witness** that John gave:
8.17 Law that when two **witnesses** agree, what they say is true.
Acts 1. 8 and you will be **witnesses** for me in Jerusalem, in all
1.21 must join us as a **witness** to the resurrection of the Lord
2.32 Jesus from death, and we are all **witnesses** to this fact.
3.15 but God raised him from death—and we are **witnesses** to this.
4.33 the apostles gave **witness** to the resurrection of the Lord
5.32 We are **witnesses** to these things—we and the Holy Spirit,
7.58 The **witnesses** left their cloaks in the care of a young man
10.39 We are **witnesses** of everything that he did in the land
10.41 but only to the **witnesses** that God had already chosen,
13.31 They are now **witnesses** for him to the people of Israel.
22.15 For you will be a **witness** for him to tell everyone what
22.18 because the people here will not accept your **witness** about me.'
22.20 And when your **witness** Stephen was put to death, I myself
23.11 You have given your **witness** for me here in Jerusalem,
26.22 I stand here giving my **witness** to all, to small and great
Rom 1. 9 God is my **witness** that what I say is true—
3.21 the Law of Moses and the prophets gave their **witness** to it.
2 Cor 1.23 I call God as my **witness**—he knows my heart!
13. 1 evidence of two or more **witnesses"**—as the scripture says.
Phil 1. 8 God is my **witness** that I am telling the truth when I
1 Thes 2. 5 did we use words to cover up greed—God is our **witness!**
2.10 You are our **witnesses,** and so is God, that our conduct
1 Tim 5.19 an elder unless it is brought by two or more **witnesses.**
6.12 when you firmly professed your faith before many **witnesses.**
2 Tim 1. 8 Do not be ashamed, then, of **witnessing** for our Lord;
2. 2 presence of many **witnesses,** and entrust them to reliable people,
Heb 2. 4 same time God added his **witness** to theirs by performing all
10.15 And the Holy Spirit also gives us his **witness.**
10.28 when judged guilty on the evidence of two or more **witnesses.**
12. 1 As for us, we have this large crowd of **witnesses** round us.
Jas 5. 3 this rust will be a **witness** against you and will eat up
1 Pet 5. 1 I am a **witness** of Christ's sufferings, and I will share in
1 Jn 5. 7 There are three **witnesses:**
Rev 1. 5 Jesus Christ, the faithful **witness,** the first to be raised from
2.13 Antipas, my faithful **witness,** was killed there where Satan lives.
3.14 Amen, the faithful and true **witness,** who is the origin of
6. 9 proclaimed God's word and had been faithful in their **witnessing.**
11. 3 I will send my two **witnesses** dressed in sackcloth, and they
11. 4 The two **witnesses** are the two olive-trees and the two

WIZARD

Dan 2. 2 his fortune-tellers, magicians, sorcerers, and **wizards** to
2.10 a demand of his fortune-tellers, magicians, and **wizards.**
2.27 "Your Majesty, there is no **wizard,** magician, fortune-teller,
4. 7 magicians, **wizards,** and astrologers were brought in,
5. 7 He shouted for someone to bring in the magicians, **wizards,**
5.11 chief of the fortune-tellers, magicians, **wizards,** and astrologers.

WOLF

Gen 49.27 "Benjamin is like a vicious **wolf.**
Ps 63.10 They will be killed in battle, and their bodies eaten by **wolves.**
Is 11. 6 **Wolves** and sheep will live together in peace, and leopards
65.25 **Wolves** and lambs will eat together;
Jer 5. 6 **wolves** from the desert will tear them to pieces, and
Lam 4. 3 Even a mother **wolf** will nurse her cubs, but my people are
Ezek 22.27 The government officials are like **wolves** tearing apart
Hab 1. 8 "Their horses are faster than leopards, fiercer than hungry **wolves.**
Zeph 3. 3 its judges are like hungry **wolves,** too greedy to leave a
Mt 7.15 outside, but on the inside they are really like wild **wolves.**
10.16 am sending you out just like sheep to a pack of **wolves.**
Lk 10. 3 I am sending you like lambs among **wolves.**
Jn 10.12 own the sheep, sees a **wolf** coming, he leaves the sheep and
10.12 so the **wolf** snatches the sheep and scatters them.
Acts 20.29 that after I leave, fierce **wolves** will come among you, and

WOMAN

[MEN AND WOMEN, SLAVE-WOMAN]

Gen 2.22 He formed a **woman** out of the rib and brought her to
2.23 **'Woman'** is her name because she was taken out of man."
2.25 The man and the **woman** were both naked, but they were not
3. 1 The snake asked the **woman,** "Did God really tell you not to
3. 2 tree in the garden," the **woman** answered, [3] "except the
3. 6 The **woman** saw how beautiful the tree was and how good its
3.12 The man answered, "The **woman** you put here with me gave
3.13 The Lord God asked the **woman,** "Why did you do this?"
3.15 I will make you and the **woman** hate each other;
3.16 And he said to the **woman,** "I will increase your trouble
6. 4 were descendants of human **women** and the heavenly beings.
12.11 he said to his wife Sarai, "You are a beautiful **woman.**
14.16 together with the **women** and the other prisoners.
20. 3 "You are going to die, because you have taken this **woman;**
20. 7 But now, give the **woman** back to her husband.
20.17 for any **woman** in Abimelech's palace to have children.
21.10 The son of this **woman** must not get any part of your
24.11 late afternoon, the time when **women** came out to get water.
24.13 the well where the young **women** of the city will be coming
24.43 When a young **woman** comes out to get water, I will ask
24.61 Then Rebecca and her young **women** got ready and mounted
28. 6 Isaac blessed him, he commanded him not to marry a Canaanite **woman.**
28. 8 that his father Isaac did not approve of Canaanite **women.**
30.13 Now **women** will call me happy";
31.26 me and carry off my daughters like **women** captured in war?
31.33 the tent of the two **slave-women,** but he did not find his
31.50 or if you marry other **women,** even though I don't know about
32.11 attack us and destroy us all, even the **women** and children.
33. 5 looked round and saw the **women** and the children, he asked,
34. 1 Jacob and Leah, went to visit some of the Canaanite **women.**
34.29 of value, captured all the **women** and children, and carried
36. 2 Esau married Canaanite **women:**
38.20 and get back from the **woman** the articles he had pledged, but
46.10 Jachin, Zohar, and Shaul, the son of a Canaanite **woman.**
Ex 1.15 Shiphrah and Puah, the two midwives who helped the Hebrew **women.**
1.16 "When you help the Hebrew **women** give birth," he said to them,
1.19 They answered, "The Hebrew **women** are not like Egyptian women;
2. 1 tribe of Levi married a **woman** of his own tribe, [2] and she
2. 7 I go and call a Hebrew **woman** to act as a wet-nurse?"
2. 9 The princess told the **woman,** "Take this baby and nurse
3.22 Every Israelite **woman** will go to her Egyptian neighbours
3.22 and to any Egyptian **woman** living in her house
6.15 Jachin, Zohar, and Shaul, the son of a Canaanite **woman;**
10.10 Lord that I will never let you take your **women** and children!
10.24 even your **women** and children may go with you.
11. 5 the throne, to the son of the **slave-woman** who grinds corn.
12.37 about six hundred thousand men, not counting **women** and children.
15.20 all the **women** followed her, playing tambourines and dancing.
21. 4 him sons or daughters, the **woman** and her children belong to
21.22 and hurt a pregnant **woman** so that she loses her child,
21.22 be fined whatever amount the **woman's** husband demands,
21.23 But if the **woman** herself is injured, the punishment
22.18 "Put to death any **woman** who practises magic.
23.26 In your land no **woman** will have a miscarriage or be
34.16 sons might marry those foreign **women,** who would lead them to
35.22 wanted to, both men and **women,** brought decorative pins,
35.25 All the skilled **women** brought fine linen thread
38. 8 the mirrors belonging to the **women** who served at the
Lev 12. 2 For seven days after a **woman** gives birth to a son, she
12. 5 For fourteen days after a **woman** gives birth to a daughter,
12. 7 This, then, is what a **woman** must do after giving birth.
12. 8 If the **woman** cannot afford a lamb, she shall bring two
13.29 When a man or a **woman** has a sore on the head
13.38 When a man or a **woman** has white spots on the skin,
15.18 both the man and the **woman** must have a bath, and they
15.19 When a **woman** has her monthly period, she remains unclean
Lev 15.25 If a **woman** has a flow of blood for several days outside
15.33 an emission of semen, [33] a **woman** during her monthly period,
15.33 sexual intercourse with a **woman** who is ritually unclean.
18.17 granddaughter of a **woman** with whom you have had intercourse;
18.19 not have intercourse with a **woman** during her monthly period,
18.23 No man or **woman** is to have sexual relations with an animal;
20.10 both he and the **woman** shall be put to death.
20.11 father, and both he and the **woman** shall be put to death.
20.14 If a man marries a **woman** and her mother, all three shall
20.16 If a **woman** tries to have sexual relations with an animal,
20.18 man has intercourse with a **woman** during her monthly period,
20.20 his uncle, and he and the **woman** will pay the penalty;
20.27 "Any man or **woman** who consults the spirits of the dead
21. 7 priest shall not marry a **woman** who has been a prostitute
21. 7 or a **woman** who is not a virgin
21.14 or a divorced woman or a **woman** who has been a prostitute.
26.26 food supply, so that ten **women** will need only one oven to
Num 5.16 The priest shall bring the **woman** forward and make her
5.18 Then he shall loosen the **woman's** hair and put the
5.19 the priest shall make the **woman** agree to this oath spoken by
5.22 The **woman** shall respond, "I agree;
5.24 Before he makes the **woman** drink the water, which may
5.25 of flour out of the **woman's** hands, hold it out in dedication
5.26 Finally, he shall make the **woman** drink the water.
5.29 The **woman** shall be made to stand in front of the altar,
5.31 but the **woman,** if guilty, must suffer the consequences.
6. 2 Any man or **woman** who makes a special vow to become a
12. 1 Moses had married a Cushite **woman,** and Miriam and Aaron
21.29 And the **women** became captives of the Amorite king.
25. 1 sexual intercourse with the Moabite **women** who were there.
25. 2 These **women** invited them to sacrificial feasts, where the
25. 6 the Israelites took a Midianite **woman** into his tent in the
25. 8 followed the man and the **woman** into the tent, and drove
25.14 was killed with the Midianite **woman** was Zimri son of Salu,
25.15 The **woman's** name was Cozbi.
30. 3 When a young **woman** still living in her father's house
30. 6 If an unmarried **woman** makes a vow,
30. 9 A widow or a divorced **woman** must keep every vow she makes
30.10 If a married **woman** makes a vow or promises to abstain
30.16 vows made by an unmarried **woman** living in her father's house
30.16 or by a married **woman.**
31. 9 of Israel captured the Midianite **women** and children, took
31.15 He asked them, "Why have you kept all the **women** alive?
31.16 Remember that it was the **women** who followed Balaam's
31.17 boy and kill every **woman** who has had sexual intercourse,
31.18 yourselves all the girls and all the **women** who are virgins.
31.19 day purify yourselves and the **women** you have captured.
36. 8 Every **woman** who inherits property in an Israelite tribe
Deut 2.34 destroyed every town, and put everyone to death, men, **women,**
3. 6 to death all the men, **women,** and children, just as we did
4.16 man or **woman,** [17] animal or bird, [18] reptile or fish.
15.12 "If a fellow-Israelite, man or **woman,** sells himself to
17. 2 your towns some man or **woman** has sinned against the Lord and
20. 7 someone else will marry the **woman** he is engaged to.'
20.14 however, take for yourselves the **women,** the children, the
21.11 see among them a beautiful **woman** that you like and want to
22. 5 **"Women** are not to wear men's clothing,
22. 5 and men are not to wear **women's** clothing;
23.17 "No Israelite, man or **woman,** is to become a temple prostitute.
24. 1 "Suppose a man marries a **woman** and later decides that he
28.56 Even the most refined **woman** of noble birth, so
29.11 leaders and officials, your men, [11] **women,** and children,
29.18 Make sure that no man, **woman,** family, or tribe standing
31.12 Call together all the men, **women,** and children, and the
32.25 Young men and young **women** will die;
Josh 6.21 they killed everyone in the city, men and **women,** young and
8.25 of Ai was killed that day—twelve thousand men and **women.**
8.35 the whole gathering, which included **women** and children, as
Judg 4. 9 because the Lord will hand Sisera over to a **woman."**
5.24 The most fortunate of **women** is Jael, the wife of Heber
5.24 the Kenite— the most fortunate of **women** who live in tents.
9.49 the people of the fort died—about a thousand men and **women.**
9.51 and every man and **woman** in the city, including the leaders,
9.53 But a **woman** threw a millstone down on his head and
9.54 I don't want it said that a **woman** killed me."
11. 2 you are the son of another **woman."**
11.40 in Israel [40] that the young **women** would go away for four
13. 6 Then the **woman** went and said to her husband, "A man of
13. 9 angel came back to the **woman** while she was sitting in the
13.24 The **woman** gave birth to a son and named him Samson.
15. 6 Philistines went and burnt the **woman** to death and burnt down
16. 4 fell in love with a **woman** named Delilah, who lived in the
16.27 The building was crowded with men and **women.**
16.27 about three thousand men and **women** on the roof, watching
19.26 At dawn the **woman** came and fell down at the door of
20.48 them all—men, **women,** and children, and animals as well.
21.10 "Go and kill everyone in Jabesh, including the **women** and children.
21.11 all the males, and also every **woman** who is not a virgin."
21.16 said, "There are no more **women** in the tribe of Benjamin.
Ruth 1.19 and the **women** there exclaimed, "Is this really Naomi?"
2. 5 Boaz asked the man in charge, "Who is that young **woman?"**
2. 8 Work with the **women** here;
2.22 be better for you to work with the **women** in Boaz' field.
3. 2 that this man Boaz, whose **women** you have been working with,
3. 8 over, and was surprised to find a **woman** lying at his feet.
3.11 as everyone in town knows, you are a fine **woman.**
4.12 give you by this young **woman** make your family like the
4.14 The **women** said to Naomi, "Praise the Lord!
4.17 The **women** of the neighbourhood named the boy Obed.
1 Sam 1.16 Don't think I am a worthless **woman.**

1 Sam 1.26 I am the **woman** you saw standing here, praying to the Lord.
2.20 you other children by this **woman** to take the place of the
2.22 were even sleeping with the **women** who worked at the entrance
4.20 As she was dying, the **women** helping her said to her,
15. 3 kill all the men, **women,** children, and babies;
18. 6 soldiers were coming back home, **women** from every town in
18. 7 In their celebration the **women** sang, "Saul has killed thousands,
21.11 the man about whom the **women** sang, as they danced, 'Saul has
22.19 men and **women,** children and babies, cattle, donkeys, and
27. 9 killing all the men and **women** and taking the sheep,
27.11 would kill everyone, men and **women,** so that no one could go
28. 7 his officials, "Find me a **woman** who is a medium, and I
28. 8 dark he went with two of his men to see the **woman.**
28. 9 The **woman** answered, "Surely you know what King Saul has done,
28.11 the **woman** asked.
28.12 When the **woman** saw Samuel, she screamed and said to Saul,
28.21 The **woman** went over to him and saw that he was terrified,
28.24 The **woman** quickly killed a calf which she had been fattening.
29. 5 the one about whom the **women** sang, as they danced, 'Saul has
30. 2 They had burnt down the town [2]and captured all the **women;**
2 Sam 1.20 Do not make the **women** of Philistia glad;
1.24 **"Women** of Israel, mourn for Saul!
1.26 was your love for me, better even than the love of **women.**
3. 8 yet today you find fault with me about a **woman!**
3.29 fit only to do a **woman's** work or is killed in battle
4. 6 The **woman** at the door had become drowsy while she was
6.19 He gave each man and **woman** in Israel a loaf of bread,
11. 2 he walked about up there, he saw a **woman** having a bath.
11.21 was at Thebez, where a **woman** threw a millstone down from the
13.17 personal servant and said, "Get this **woman** out of my sight!
14. 2 much, [2]so he sent for a clever **woman** who lived in Tekoa.
14. 2 Act like a **woman** who has been in mourning for a long
14. 4 The **woman** went to the king, bowed down to the ground in
14.12 Your Majesty, let me say just one more thing," the **woman** said.
14.27 sons and one daughter named Tamar, a very beautiful **woman.**
17.20 and asked the **woman,** "Where are Ahimaaz and Jonathan?"
20.16 There was a wise **woman** in the city who shouted from the
1 Kgs 1. 2 let us find a young **woman** to stay with you and take
3.17 them said, "Your Majesty, this **woman** and I live in the same
3.22 But the other **woman** said, "No!
3.22 The first **woman** answered, "No!
3.25 the living child in two and give each **woman** half of it."
3.26 But the other **woman** said, "Don't give it to either of us;
3.27 Give it to the first **woman**—she is its real mother."
11. 1 Solomon loved many foreign **women.**
11. 1 he married Hittite women and **women** from Moab, Ammon, Edom,
14.24 all, there were men and **women** who served as prostitutes at
20. 3 and gold, your **women** and the strongest of your children."
20. 5 to me your silver and gold, your **women** and your children.
2 Kgs 4. 5 So the **woman** went into her house with her sons, closed
4. 8 One day Elisha went to Shunem, where a rich **woman** lived.
4.12 He told his servant Gehazi to go and call the **woman.**
4.25 servant Gehazi, "Look—there comes the **woman** from Shunem!
4.28 The **woman** said to him, "Sir, did I ask you for a
4.30 The **woman** said to Elisha, "I swear by my loyalty to
6.26 wall when a **woman** cried out, "Help me, Your Majesty!"
6.28 answered, "The other day this **woman** here suggested that we
8. 1 Now Elisha had told the **woman** who lived in Shunem, whose
8. 5 person back to life, the **woman** made her appeal to the king.
8. 5 "Your Majesty, here is the **woman** and here is her son whom
8.12 children to death, and rip open their pregnant **women."**
9.34 Only then did he say, "Take that damned **woman** and bury her;
15.16 He even ripped open the bellies of all the pregnant **women.**
19. 3 We are like a **woman** who is ready to give birth, but
22.14 Asaiah went to consult a **woman** named Huldah, a prophet who
23. 7 (It was there that **women** wove robes used in the worship of
1 Chr 2.26 Jerahmeel had another wife, a **woman** named Atarah, and they
2.29 Abishur married a **woman** named Abihail, and they had two sons,
4.17 Mered also married a **woman** from the tribe of Judah, and they
4.22 married Moabite **women** and then settled in Bethlehem.
16. 3 He gave each man and **woman** in Israel a loaf of bread,
2 Chr 6.18 can you, O God, really live on earth among men and **women?**
24. 7 followers of Athaliah, that corrupt **woman,** had damaged the
24.26 the son of an Ammonite **woman** named Shimeath,
24.26 and Jehozabad, the son of a Moabite **woman** named Shimrith).
28. 8 the Israelite army captured 200,000 **women** and children as
28.10 make the men and **women** of Jerusalem and Judah your slaves.
34.22 others went to consult a **woman** named Huldah, a prophet who
35.25 the singers, both men and **women,** to use this song when they
36.17 on anyone, young or old, man or **woman,** sick or healthy.
Ezra 2.61 of Barzillai had married a **woman** from the clan of Barzillai
9. 2 Jewish men were marrying foreign **women,** and so God's holy
10. 1 of Israelites—men, **women,** and children—gathered round him,
10. 2 with God by marrying foreign **women,** but even so there is
10. 3 God that we will send these **women** and their children away.
10.10 and have brought guilt on Israel by marrying foreign **women.**
Neh 5. 1 men and **women,** began to complain against their fellow-Jews.
6.14 Remember that **woman** Nodiah and all the other prophets who
7.63 of Barzillai had married a **woman** from the clan of Barzillai
8. 2 the people had gathered—men, **women,** and the children who
12.43 The **women** and the children joined in the celebration, and
13.23 of the Jewish men had married **women** from Ashdod, Ammon, and
13.26 I said, "It was foreign **women** that made King Solomon sin.
13.27 example and disobey our God by marrying foreign **women?"**
Esth 1. 9 palace Queen Vashti was giving a banquet for the **women.**
1.11 The queen was a beautiful **woman,** and the king wanted to show
1.17 Every **woman** in the empire will begin to look down on her
1.19 Then give her place as queen to some better **woman.**
1.20 over this huge empire, every **woman** will treat her husband
2. 3 is in charge of your **women,** and let them be given a
Esth 2.12 regular beauty treatment for the **women** lasted a
3.13 Jews—young and old, **women** and children—were to be killed.
4.11 "If anyone, man or **woman,** goes to the inner courtyard
8.11 men, their children or their **women,** the Jews could fight
Job 24.21 widows and showed no kindness to childless **women.**
42.15 There were no other **women** in the whole world as
Ps 48. 6 fear and anguish, like a **woman** about to bear a child, [7]like
68.11 The Lord gave the command, and many **women** carried the news:
68.12 The **women** at home divided what was captured:
78.63 were killed in war, and young **women** had no one to marry.
Prov 2.16 able to resist any immoral **woman** who tries to seduce you
5. 8 Keep away from such a **woman!**
5.16 Children that you have by other **women** will do you no good.
5.20 Why should you give your love to another **woman,** my son?
6.24 keep you away from bad **women,** from the seductive words of
7. 5 from other men's wives, from **women** with seductive words.
7. 8 the street near the corner where a certain **woman** lived.
7.11 was a bold and shameless **woman** who always walked the streets
7.25 Do not let such a **woman** win your heart;
9.13 Stupidity is like a loud, ignorant, shameless **woman.**
11.16 is respected, but a **woman** without virtue is a disgrace.
11.22 Beauty in a **woman** without good judgement is like a gold
14. 1 by the wisdom of **women,** but are destroyed by foolishness.
23.27 Prostitutes and immoral **women** are a deadly trap.
30.16 a **woman** without children,
30.19 and a man and a **woman** falling in
30.23 a hateful **woman** who gets married,
31. 3 spend all your energy on sex and all your money on **women;**
31.29 He says, "Many **women** are good wives, but you are the
31.30 and beauty disappears, but a **woman** who honours the Lord
Ecc 2. 8 Men and **women** sang to entertain me,
2. 8 and I had all the **women** a man could want.
7.26 I found something more bitter than death—**woman.**
7.28 man in a thousand that I could respect, but not one **woman.**
9. 9 Enjoy life with the **woman** you love, as long as you live
11. 5 how new life begins in the womb of a pregnant **woman.**
Song 1. 1 The **Woman**
1. 3 No **woman** could help loving you.
1. 4 No wonder all **women** love you!
1. 5 **Women** of Jerusalem, I am dark but beautiful, dark as the
1. 8 Don't you know the place, loveliest of **women?**
2. 2 Like a lily among thorns is my darling among **women.**
2. 7 Promise me, **women** of Jerusalem;
3. 5 Promise me, **women** of Jerusalem;
3.10 purple cloth, lovingly woven by the **women** of Jerusalem.
3.11 **Women** of Zion, come and see King Solomon.
5. 8 Promise me, **women** of Jerusalem, that if you find my lover,
5. 9 Most beautiful of **women,** is your lover different
5.16 This is what my lover is like, **women** of Jerusalem.
6. 1 Most beautiful of **women,** where has your lover gone?
6. 8 sixty queens, eighty concubines, young **women** without number!
6. 9 All **women** look at her and praise her;
8. 4 **women** of Jerusalem, that you will not interrupt our love.
8. 7 The **Woman's** Brothers
Is 3.16 The Lord said, "Look how proud the **women** of Jerusalem are!
3.18 will take away from the **women** of Jerusalem everything they
3.26 will be like a **woman** sitting on the ground, stripped naked.
4. 1 When that time comes, seven **women** will grab hold of one
7.14 a young **woman** who is pregnant will have a son and will
13. 8 and overcome with pain, like the pain of a **woman** in labour.
19.16 coming when the people of Egypt will be as timid as **women.**
21. 3 with terror and pain, pain like that of a **woman** in labour.
26.17 us cry out, as a **woman** in labour cries out in pain.
27.11 are withered and broken, and **women** gather them for firewood.
32. 9 You **women** who live an easy life, free from worries, listen
37. 3 We are like a **woman** who is ready to give birth, but
42.14 I cry out like a **woman** in labour.
49.15 "Can a **woman** forget her own baby and not love the child
54. 1 have been like a childless **woman,** but now you can sing and
54. 1 more children than a **woman** whose husband never left her!
66. 7 holy city is like a **woman** who suddenly gives birth to a
Jer 2.32 Does a young **woman** forget her jewellery,
2.33 Even the worst of **women** can learn from you.
3. 6 to me, "Have you seen what Israel, that unfaithful **woman,**
4.31 heard a cry, like a **woman** in labour,
4.31 a scream like a **woman** bearing her first child.
6.24 we are seized by anguish and pain like a **woman** in labour.
7.18 men build fires, and the **women** mix dough to bake cakes for
9.17 mourners to come, for the **women** who sing funeral songs."
9.20 "Listen to the Lord, you **women,** and pay attention to his words.
13.21 You will be in pain like a **woman** giving birth.
18.21 Let the **women** lose their husbands and children;
22.23 pains strike you, pains like those of a **woman** in labour.
30. 6 man with his hands on his stomach like a **woman** in labour?
31. 8 with them, pregnant **women** and those about to give birth.
31.22 and different, as different as a **woman** protecting a man."
38.22 it I saw all the **women** left in Judah's royal palace being
38.23 Then I added, "All your **women** and children will be
41.16 from Mizpah after murdering Gedaliah—soldiers, **women,**
43. 6 the men, the **women,** the children, and the king's daughters.
44. 7 bring destruction on men and **women,** children and babies, so
44.15 other gods, and all the **women** who were standing there,
44.19 And the **women** added, "When we baked cakes shaped like
44.20 all the men and the **women** who had answered me in this
44.24 the people, especially the **women,** what the Lord Almighty,
48.41 Moab's soldiers will be as frightened as a **woman** in labour.
49. 3 **Women** of Rabbah, go into mourning!
49.22 Edom's soldiers will be as frightened as a **woman** in labour."
49.24 They are in pain and misery like a **woman** in labour.
50.43 He is seized by anguish, by pain like a **woman** in labour.
51.22 drivers, [22]to kill men and **women,** to slay old and young,

Jer 51.30 They have lost their courage and have become like **women.**
Lam 1.18 My young men and **women** have been taken away captive.
2.20 **Women** are eating the bodies of the children they loved!
2.21 the streets, Young men and **women,** killed by enemy swords.
3.51 when I see what has happened to the **women** of the city.
Ezek 8.14 the Temple and showed me **women** weeping over the death of the
9. 6 Kill the old men, young men, young **women,** mothers, and
13.17 mortal man, look at the **women** among your people who make up
13.18 "You **women** are doomed!
16. 7 You grew strong and tall and became a young **woman.**
16.32 You are like a **woman** who commits adultery with strangers
16.41 houses down and let crowds of **women** see your punishment.
18. 6 wife or have intercourse with a **woman** during her period.
22.10 Some force **women** to have intercourse with them during their period.
23.10 **Women** everywhere gossiped about her fate.
23.42 They put bracelets on the **women's** arms and beautiful crowns
23.43 were using as a prostitute a **woman** worn out by adultery.
23.44 They went back to Oholah and Oholibah, those immoral **women.**
23.48 as a warning to every **woman** not to commit adultery as they
32.16 The **women** of the nations will sing it to mourn for Egypt
36.17 ritually unclean as a **woman** is during her monthly period.
44.22 No priest may marry a divorced **woman;**
Dan 11.37 god his ancestors served, and also the god that **women** love.
Hos 1. 3 So Hosea married a **woman** named Gomer, the daughter of Diblaim.
3. 1 show your love for a **woman** who is committing adultery with a
4.12 Like a **woman** who becomes a prostitute, they have given
9.11 to them, no more **women** pregnant, no more children conceived.
9.14 Make their **women** barren!
13.16 to the ground, and pregnant **women** will be ripped open."
Joel 2.29 pour out my spirit even on servants, both men and **women.**
Amos 1.13 territory they even ripped open pregnant **women** in Gilead.
4. 1 Listen to this, you **women** of Samaria, who grow fat like
8.13 even healthy young men and **women** will collapse from thirst.
Mic 2. 9 You drive the **women** of my people out of the homes they
4. 9 Why are you suffering like a **woman** in labour?
4.10 people of Jerusalem, like a **woman** giving birth, for now you
5. 3 to their enemies until the **woman** who is to give birth has
7. 6 mothers, and young **women** quarrel with their mothers-in-law;
Nah 3.13 Your soldiers are like **women,** and your country stands
Zech 5. 7 the lid was raised, and there in the basket sat a **woman!**
5. 8 The angel said, "This **woman** represents wickedness."
5. 9 looked up and saw two **women** flying towards me with powerful
8. [illegible] Once again old men and **women,** so old that they use a
12.12 men of each family will mourn separately from the **women.**
14. 2 The city will be taken, the houses looted, and the **women** raped.
Mal 2.11 Men have married **women** who worship foreign gods.
Mt 1. 6 Solomon (his mother was the **woman** who had been Uriah's wife),
5.28 anyone who looks at a **woman** and wants to possess her is
9.20 A **woman** who had suffered from severe bleeding for twelve years
9.22 At that very moment the **woman** became well.
13.33 A **woman** takes some yeast and mixes it with forty litres of
14.21 about five thousand, not counting the **women** and children.
15.22 A Canaanite **woman** who lived in that region came to him.
15.25 At this the **woman** came and fell at his feet.
15.28 So Jesus answered her, "You are a **woman** of great faith!
15.38 ate was four thousand, not counting the **women** and children.
19. 9 commits adultery if he marries some other **woman."**
22.27 Last of all, the **woman** died.
24.19 be in those days for **women** who are pregnant and for mothers
24.38 people ate and drank, **men and women** married, up to the very
24.41 Two **women** will be at a mill grinding meal:
26. 7 While Jesus was eating, a **woman** came to him with an
26.10 so he said to them, "Why are you bothering this **woman?**
27.55 There were many **women** there, looking on from a distance,
28. 5 The angel spoke to the **women.**
28.11 While the **women** went on their way, some of the soldiers
Mk 5.25 was a **woman** who had suffered terribly from severe bleeding for
5.33 The **woman** realized what had happened to her, so she came,
7.25 A **woman,** whose daughter had an evil spirit in her, heard
7.26 The **woman** was a Gentile, born in the region of Phoenicia
10.11 divorces his wife and marries another **woman** commits adultery
10.12 In the same way, a **woman** who divorces her husband and
12.21 the second one married the **woman,** and he also died without
12.22 seven brothers married the **woman** and died without having children.
12.22 Last of all, the **woman** died.
13.17 be in those days for **women** who are pregnant and for mothers
14. 3 While Jesus was eating, a **woman** came in with an alabaster
15.40 Some **women** were there, looking on from a distance.
15.41 Many other **women** who had come to Jerusalem with him were
16. 9 The **women** went to Peter and his friends and gave them a
Lk 1.42 the most blessed of all **women,** and blessed is the child you
7.12 the only son of a **woman** who was a widow,
7.37 In that town was a **woman** who lived a sinful life.
7.39 he would know who this **woman** is who is touching him;
7.44 Then he turned to the **woman** and said to Simon,
7.44 "Do you see this **woman?**
7.48 Then Jesus said to the **woman,** "Your sins are forgiven."
7.50 But Jesus said to the **woman,** "Your faith has saved you;
8. 2 him, [2] and so did some **women** who had been healed of evil
8. 3 and Susanna, and many other **women** who used their own
8.43 Among them was a **woman** who had suffered from severe bleeding
8.47 The **woman** saw that she had been found out, so she came
10.38 to a village where a **woman** named Martha welcomed him in her
11.27 Jesus had said this, a **woman** spoke up from the crowd
11.27 "How happy is the **woman** who bore you and nursed you!"
12.45 both the men and the **women,** and eats and drinks and gets
13.11 A **woman** there had an evil spirit that had made her ill
Lk 13.12 out to her, **"Woman,** you are free from your illness!"
13.21 A **woman** takes some yeast and mixes it with forty litres of
15. 8 "Or suppose a **woman** who has ten silver coins loses one
16.18 who divorces his wife and marries another **woman** commits adultery;
16.18 and the man who marries a divorced **woman** commits adultery.
17.27 eating and drinking, and **men and women** married, up to the
17.35 Two **women** will be grinding corn together:
20.30 Then the second one married the **woman,** [31] and then the third.
20.32 Last of all, the **woman** died.
20.34 Jesus answered them, "The **men and women** of this age marry,
20.35 but the **men and women** who are worthy to rise
21.23 be in those days for **women** who are pregnant and for mothers
22.57 But Peter denied it, **"Woman,** I don't even know him!"
23.27 them were some **women** who were weeping and wailing for him.
23.28 Jesus turned to them and said, **"Women** of Jerusalem!
23.29 say, 'How lucky are the **women** who never had children, who
23.49 Jesus personally, including the **women** who had followed him from Galilee,
23.55 The **women** who had followed Jesus from Galilee went with
24. 1 early on Sunday morning the **women** went to the tomb, carrying
24. 5 Full of fear, the **women** bowed down to the ground, as the
24. 8 Then the **women** remembered his words, [9] returned from the tomb,
24.10 The **women** were Mary Magdalene, Joanna, and Mary the mother of James;
24.10 they and the other **women** with them told these things to the
24.11 apostles thought that what the **women** said was nonsense, and
24.22 Some of the **women** of our group surprised us;
24.24 found it exactly as the **women** had said, but they did not
Jn 4. 7 A Samaritan **woman** came to draw some water, and Jesus said
4. 9 The **woman** answered, "You are a Jew, and I am a Samaritan
4.11 "Sir," the **woman** said, "you haven't got a bucket, and
4.15 "Sir," the **woman** said, "give me that water!
4.19 "I see you are a prophet, sir," the **woman** said.
4.21 said to her, "Believe me, **woman,** the time will come when
4.25 The **woman** said to him, "I know that the Messiah will come,
4.27 were greatly surprised to find him talking with a **woman.**
4.28 Then the **woman** left her water jar, went back to the town,
4.39 believed in Jesus because the **woman** had said, "He told me
4.42 and they said to the **woman,** "We believe now, not
8. 3 Pharisees brought in a **woman** who had been caught committing adultery,
8. 4 they said to Jesus, "this **woman** was caught in the very act
8. 5 Law Moses commanded that such a **woman** must be stoned to death.
8. 9 Jesus was left alone, with the **woman** still standing there.
16.21 When a **woman** is about to give birth, she is sad because
20.13 **"Woman,** why are you crying?"
20.15 **"Woman,** why are you crying?"
Acts 1.14 a group, together with the **women** and with Mary the mother of
2.18 on my servants, both **men and women,** I will pour out my
5.14 group—a crowd of **men and women** who believed in the Lord.
8. 3 believers, both **men and women,** and threw them into jail.
8.12 God and about Jesus Christ, they were baptized, both **men and women.**
9. 2 to arrest them, both **men and women,** and bring them back to
9.36 In Joppa there was a **woman** named Tabitha, who was a believer.
13.50 the city and the Gentile **women** of high social standing who
16.13 We sat down and talked to the **women** who gathered there.
16.14 She was a **woman** who worshipped God, and the Lord opened her
17. 4 did many of the leading **women** and a large group of Greeks
17.12 and many Greek **women** of high social standing and many Greek
17.34 was also a **woman** named Damaris, and some other people.
22. 4 I arrested **men and women** and threw them into prison.
Rom 1.26 Even the **women** pervert the natural use of their sex by
1.27 up natural sexual relations with **women** and burn with passion
7. 2 A married **woman,** for example, is bound by the law to her
7. 3 she is legally a free **woman** and does not commit adultery if
1 Cor 7. 2 his own wife, and every **woman** should have her own husband.
7. 3 as a husband, and a **woman** should fulfil her duty as a
7.13 And if a Christian **woman** is married to a man who is
7.28 if an unmarried **woman** marries, she hasn't committed a sin.
7.34 An unmarried **woman** or a virgin concerns herself with the Lord's work,
7.34 but a married **woman** concerns herself with worldly matters,
7.39 A married **woman** is not free as long as her husband lives;
11. 5 And any **woman** who prays or proclaims God's message in
11. 5 between her and a **woman** whose head has been shaved.
11. 6 If the **woman** does not cover her head, she might as well
11. 6 a shameful thing for a **woman** to shave her head or cut
11. 7 But **woman** reflects the glory of man;
11. 8 for man was not created from **woman,** but woman from man.
11. 9 Nor was man created for **woman's** sake,
11. 9 but **woman** was created for man's sake.
11.10 of the angels, then, a **woman** should have a covering over her
11.11 woman is not independent of man, nor is man independent of **woman.**
11.12 For as **woman** was made from man,
11.12 in the same way man is born of **woman;**
11.13 it is proper for a **woman** to pray to God in public
11.15 a disgrace, [15] but on a **woman** it is a thing of beauty.
14.34 God's people, [34] the **women** should keep quiet in the meetings.
14.35 It is a disgraceful thing for a **woman** to speak in church.
Gal 3.28 and Gentiles, between slaves and free men, between **men and women;**
4.22 two sons, one by a **slave-woman,** the other by a free woman.
4.23 His son by the **slave-woman** was born in the usual way,
4.23 his son by the free **woman** was born as a result of
4.24 the two **women** represent two covenants.
4.27 For the scripture says, "Be happy, you childless **woman!**

Gal 4.27 For the **woman** who was deserted will have more children
4.27 than the **woman** whose husband never left her."
4.30 It says, "Send the **slave-woman** and her son away;
4.30 for the son of the **slave-woman** will not have a part of
4.30 father's property along with the son of the free **woman."**
4.31 are not the children of a **slave-woman** but of a free woman.
Phil 4. 3 too, my faithful partner, I want you to help these **women;**
1 Thes 5. 3 pains that come upon a **woman** in labour, and people will not
1 Tim 2. 9 I also want the **women** to be modest and sensible about
2.10 deeds, as is proper for **women** who claim to be religious.
2.11 **Women** should learn in silence and all humility.
2.14 it was the **woman** who was deceived and broke God's law.
2.15 But a **woman** will be saved through having children, if
5. 2 the older **women** as mothers,
5. 2 and the younger **women** as sisters, with all purity.
5.10 a **woman** who brought up her children well, received strangers
5.16 But if any Christian **woman** has widows in her family, she
2 Tim 3. 6 and gain control over weak **women** who are burdened by the
3. 7 by all kinds of desires, [7] **women** who are always trying to
Tit 2. 3 older women to behave as **women** should who live a holy life.
2. 4 train the younger **women** to love their husbands and children,
Heb 11.35 Through faith **women** received their dead relatives raised back to life.
1 Pet 3. 5 For the devout **women** of the past who placed their hope in
2 Pet 2.14 They want to look at nothing but immoral **women;**
Rev 2.20 that **woman** Jezebel, who calls herself a messenger of God.
9. 8 Their hair was like **women's** hair, their teeth were like lions'
12. 1 There was a **woman,** whose dress was the sun and who had
12. 4 stood in front of the **woman,** in order to eat her child
12. 6 The **woman** fled to the desert, to a place God had prepared
12.13 he began to pursue the **woman** who had given birth to the
12.15 flood of water after the **woman,** so that it would carry her
12.16 But the earth helped the **woman;**
12.17 dragon was furious with the **woman** and went off to fight
14. 4 themselves pure by not having sexual relations with **women;**
17. 3 There I saw a **woman** sitting on a red beast that had
17. 4 The **woman** was dressed in purple and scarlet, and covered
17. 6 And I saw that the **woman** was drunk with the blood of
17. 7 the secret meaning of the **woman** and of the beast that
17. 9 The seven heads are seven hills, on which the **woman** sits.
17.18 "The **woman** you saw is the great city that rules over

WOMB

Gen 25.22 were born, they struggled against each other in her **womb.**
Job 3.11 had died in my mother's **womb** or died the moment I was
10.10 you made me grow in my mother's **womb.**
10.19 To go from the **womb** straight to the grave would have
38. 8 back the sea when it burst from the **womb** of the earth?
Ps 139.13 you put me together in my mother's **womb.**
139.15 put together in my mother's **womb,** when I was growing there
Ecc 11. 5 how new life begins in the **womb** of a pregnant woman.
Jer 20.17 Then my mother's **womb** would have been my grave.
Hos 12. 3 Esau while the two of them were still in their mother's **womb;**
13.13 about to be born, who refuses to come out of the **womb.**
Jn 3. 4 cannot enter his mother's **womb** and be born a second time!"

WONDER (1)

Gen 3. 6 and she thought how **wonderful** it would be to become wise.
Ex 15.11 Who is like you, **wonderful** in holiness?
Deut 3.24 of the great and **wonderful** things you are going to do.
4.34 and **wonders,** and caused terrifying things to happen.
7.19 own eyes, the miracles and **wonders,** and the great power and
13. 1 promise a miracle or a **wonder,** [2] in order to lead you to
26. 8 He worked miracles and **wonders,** and caused terrifying things
28.58 you do not honour the **wonderful** and awesome name of the Lord
29. 3 the miracles, and the great **wonders** that the Lord performed.
34.11 has ever done miracles and **wonders** like those that the Lord
Judg 6.13 What about all the **wonderful** things that our fathers told us
13.18 It is a name of **wonder."**
13.19 them on the rock altar to the Lord who works **wonders.**
2 Sam 1.23 "Saul and Jonathan, so **wonderful** and dear;
1.26 How **wonderful** was your love for me, better even than the
7.23 The great and **wonderful** things you did for them have spread
7.28 promises, and you have made this **wonderful** promise to me.
1 Chr 16. 9 tell the **wonderful** things he has done.
17.21 The great and **wonderful** things you did for them spread your
17.26 are God, and you have made this **wonderful** promise to me.
Esth 10. 2 All the great and **wonderful** things he did, as well as the
Job 37. 5 At God's command amazing things happen, **wonderful** things
37.14 consider the **wonderful** things God does.
Ps 9. 1 I will tell of all the **wonderful** things you have done.
16. 6 How **wonderful** are your gifts to me;
17. 7 Reveal your **wonderful** love and save me;
26. 7 hymn of thanksgiving and tell of all your **wonderful** deeds.
31.19 How **wonderful** are the good things you keep for those who
31.21 How **wonderfully** he showed his love for me when I was
40. 5 You have made many **wonderful** plans for us.
65. 5 giving us victory and you do **wonderful** things to save us.
66. 3 Say to God, "How **wonderful** are the things you do!
66. 5 Come and see what God has done, his **wonderful** acts among men.
71.17 since I was young, and I still tell of your **wonderful** acts.
72.18 He alone does these **wonderful** things.
73.28 But as for me, how **wonderful** to be near God, to find
75. 1 you are and tell of the **wonderful** things you have done.
77.11 I will recall the **wonders** you did in the past.
78. 4 and his great deeds and the **wonderful** things he has done.
86.10 You are mighty and do **wonderful** things;
87. 3 Listen, city of God, to the **wonderful** things he says about you:
89. 5 The heavens sing of the **wonderful** things you do;
Ps 98. 1 he has done **wonderful** things!
105. 2 tell of the **wonderful** things he has done.
106. 7 Our ancestors in Egypt did not understand God's **wonderful** acts;
106.22 What **wonderful** things he did there!
107. 8 constant love, for the **wonderful** things he did for them.
107.15 constant love, for the **wonderful** things he did for them.
107.21 constant love, for the **wonderful** things he did for them.
107.24 saw what the Lord can do, his **wonderful** acts on the seas.
107.31 constant love, for the **wonderful** things he did for them.
111. 2 How **wonderful** are the things the Lord does!
111. 4 The Lord does not let us forget his **wonderful** actions;
118.23 what a **wonderful** sight it is!
119.18 eyes, so that I may see the **wonderful** truths in your law.
119.27 your laws, and I will meditate on your **wonderful** teachings.
119.39 how **wonderful** are your judgements!
119.129 Your teachings are **wonderful;**
133. 1 How **wonderful** it is, how pleasant, for God's people to
135. 9 There he performed miracles and **wonders** to punish the king
139.14 all you do is strange and **wonderful.**
145. 5 and majesty, and I will meditate on your **wonderful** deeds.
Song 5. 9 What is there so **wonderful** about him that we should give you
7. 1 What a **wonderful** girl you are!
Is 9. 6 He will be called, **"Wonderful** Counsellor," "Mighty God,"
52. 7 How **wonderful** it is to see a messenger coming across the mountains,
Jer 28. 6 **"Wonderful!**
32.20 ago, you performed miracles and **wonders** in Egypt, and you
32.21 By means of miracles and **wonders** that terrified our enemies,
33. 3 I will tell you **wonderful** and marvellous things that you
Dan 4. 2 to my account of the **wonders** and miracles which the Supreme
4. 3 "How great are the **wonders** God shows us!
6.27 he performs **wonders** and miracles in heaven and on earth.
Joel 2.26 the Lord your God, who has done **wonderful** things for you.
Mt 21.15 angry when they saw the **wonderful** things he was doing and
21.42 what a **wonderful** sight it is!'
24.24 will perform great miracles and **wonders** in order to deceive
Mk 12.11 what a **wonderful** sight it is!'"
13. 1 What **wonderful** stones and buildings!"
13.22 They will perform miracles and **wonders** in order to deceive
Lk 1.58 neighbours and relatives heard how **wonderfully** good the Lord
13.17 people rejoiced over all the **wonderful** things that he did.
24.41 could not believe, they were so full of joy and **wonder;**
Jn 4.48 "None of you will ever believe unless you see miracles and **wonders."**
Acts 2. 7 In amazement and **wonder** they exclaimed, "These people who
2.19 miracles in the sky above and **wonders** on the earth below.
2.22 the miracles and **wonders** which God performed through him.
2.43 Many miracles and **wonders** were being done through the apostles,
4.30 to heal, and grant that **wonders** and miracles may be
5.12 Many miracles and **wonders** were being performed among the
6. 8 performed great miracles and **wonders** among the people.
7.36 of Egypt, performing miracles and **wonders** in Egypt and at
8.13 the great **wonders** and miracles that were being performed.
14. 3 by giving them the power to perform miracles and **wonders.**
15.12 report all the miracles and **wonders** that God had performed
Rom 10.15 As the scripture says, "How **wonderful** is the coming of
15.19 the power of miracles and **wonders,** and by the power of the
2 Cor 12. 7 pride because of the many **wonderful** things I saw, I was
12.12 The many miracles and **wonders** that prove that I am an
Eph 1.18 how rich are the **wonderful** blessings he promises his people,
2 Thes 2. 9 kinds of false miracles and **wonders,** [10] and use every kind
Heb 2. 4 all kinds of miracles and **wonders** and by distributing the
1 Pet 2. 9 people, chosen to proclaim the **wonderful** acts of God, who
Rev 15. 3 "Lord God Almighty, how great and **wonderful** are your deeds!

WONDER (2)

Deut 18.21 "You may **wonder** how you can tell when a prophet's
Esth 3. 4 **wondering** if he would tolerate Mordecai's conduct.
Job 20. 7 Those who used to know him will **wonder** where he has gone.
Dan 8. 5 While I was **wondering** what this meant, a goat came rushing
Lk 1.21 were waiting for Zechariah and **wondering** why he was spending
1.29 the angel's message, and she **wondered** what his words meant.
3.15 rise, and they began to **wonder** whether John perhaps might be
Acts 5.24 heard this, they **wondered** what had happened to the apostles.
10.17 While Peter was **wondering** about the meaning of this vision,

WOOD

[FIRE-WOOD]

Gen 22. 3 Abraham cut some **wood** for the sacrifice, loaded his donkey,
22. 6 Abraham made Isaac carry the **wood** for the sacrifice, and
22. 7 have the coals and the **wood,** but where is the lamb for
22. 9 about, Abraham built an altar and arranged the **wood** on it.
22. 9 son and placed him on the altar, on top of the **wood.**
Ex 7.19 will be blood, even in the **wooden** tubs and stone jars."
15.25 showed him a piece of **wood,** which he threw into the water;
31. 5 for carving **wood;**
35.33 for carving **wood;**
Lev 1. 7 the priests shall arrange **fire-wood** on the altar and light it.
4.12 poured out, and there he shall burn it on a **wood** fire.
6.12 priest shall put **firewood** on it, arrange the burnt-offering
11.32 applies to any article of **wood,** cloth, leather, or sacking,
14.45 down, and its stones, its **wood,** and all its plaster must be
15.12 must be broken, and any **wooden** bowl that he touches must be
Num 13.20 whether the soil is fertile and whether the land is **wooded.**
15.32 wilderness, a man was found gathering **firewood** on the Sabbath.
31.20 and everything made of leather, goats' hair, or **wood."**
35.16 of iron or stone or **wood** to kill someone, he is guilty
Deut 4.28 by human hands, gods of **wood** and stone, gods that cannot see

Deut	10. 1	the first ones and make a **wooden** box to put them in.
	16.21	do not put beside it a **wooden** symbol of the goddess Asherah.
	19. 5	the forest together to cut **wood** and if, as one of them
	27.15	an idol of stone, **wood**, or metal and secretly worships it;
	28.36	there you will serve gods made of **wood** and stone.
	28.64	will serve gods made of **wood** and stone, gods that neither
	29.11	who live among you and cut **wood** and carry water for you.
	29.17	You saw their disgusting idols made of **wood**, stone,
Josh	9.21	but they will have to cut **wood** and carry water for us."
	9.23	will always be slaves, cutting **wood** and carrying water for
	9.27	made them slaves, to cut **wood** and carry water for the people
Judg	6.26	as an offering, using for **firewood** the symbol of Asherah you
	9.49	Abimelech and piled the **wood** up against the stronghold.
	17. 3	It will be used to make a **wooden** idol covered with silver.
	17. 4	idol, carving it from **wood** and covering it with the silver.
	18.14	of these houses there is a **wooden** idol covered with silver?
	18.17	the house and took the **wooden** idol covered with silver, the
1 Sam	6.14	The people chopped up the **wooden** wagon and killed the cows
	14.25	They all came into a **wooded** area and found honey everywhere.
	14.26	The **woods** were full of honey, but no one ate any of
1 Kgs	6.23	creatures were made of olive **wood** and placed in the Most
	6.31	double door made of olive **wood** was set in place at the
	6.33	main room a rectangular door-frame of olive **wood** was made.
	10.11	from there a large amount of juniper **wood** and jewels.
	10.12	Solomon used the **wood** to build railings in the Temple
	10.12	It was the finest juniper **wood** ever imported into Israel;
	17.10	to the gate of the town, he saw a widow gathering **firewood**.
	17.12	came here to gather some **firewood** to take back home
	18.23	pieces, and put it on the **wood**—but don't light the fire.
	18.25	Pray to your god, but don't set fire to the **wood**."
	18.33	Then he placed the **wood** on the altar,
	18.33	cut the bull in pieces, and laid it on the **wood**.
	18.33	jars with water and pour it on the offering and the **wood**."
	18.38	burnt up the sacrifice, the **wood**, and the stones, scorched
2 Kgs	2.24	she-bears came out of the **woods** and tore forty-two of the
	19.18	at all, only images of **wood** and stone made by human hands.
1 Chr	16.33	The trees in the **woods** will shout for joy when the Lord
	22. 3	nails and clamps for the **wooden** gates, and so much bronze
	22.14	I also have **wood** and stone ready, but you must get more.
2 Chr	2. 8	I know how skilful your **woodmen** are, so send me cedar,
	2.14	things out of gold, silver, bronze, iron, stone, and **wood**.
	9.10	gold from Ophir also brought juniper **wood** and jewels.
	9.11	Solomon used the **wood** to make stairs for the Temple and
Ezra	5. 8	large stone blocks and with **wooden** beams set in the wall.
	6. 4	built with one layer of **wood** on top of every three layers
	6.11	anyone disobeys this order, a **wooden** beam is to be torn out
Neh	8. 4	Ezra was standing on a **wooden** platform that had been built
	10.34	which clans are to provide **wood** to burn the sacrifices
	13.31	I arranged for the **wood** used for burning the offerings
Job	13.28	As a result, I crumble like rotten **wood**, like a moth-eaten coat.
	41.27	is as flimsy as straw, and bronze as soft as rotten **wood**.
Ps	74. 5	They looked like **woodmen** cutting down trees with their axes.
	74. 6	They smashed all the **wooden** panels with their axes
	96.12	The trees in the **woods** will shout for joy [13]when the Lord
	141. 7	Like **wood** that is split and chopped into bits, so their
Prov	26.20	Without **wood**, a fire goes out;
	26.21	Charcoal keeps the embers glowing, **wood** keeps the fire burning,
Ecc	10. 9	If you split **wood**, you get hurt doing it.
Song	3. 9	King Solomon is carried on a throne made of the finest **wood**.
Is	9.10	The beams of sycomore **wood** have been cut down, but we will
	27.11	are withered and broken, and women gather them for **firewood**.
	30.33	It is deep and wide, and piled high with **wood**.
	37.19	at all, only images of **wood** and stone made by human hands.
	40.20	afford silver or gold chooses **wood** that will not rot.
	44.13	The carpenter measures the **wood**.
	44.14	to use, or choose oak or cypress **wood** from the forest.
	44.16	With some of the **wood** he makes a fire;
	44.17	The rest of the **wood** he makes into an idol, and then
	44.19	or the sense to say, "Some of the **wood** I burnt up.
	44.19	And the rest of the **wood** I made into an idol.
	44.19	Here I am bowing down to a block of **wood**!"
	45.20	parade with their idols of **wood** and pray to gods that cannot
	60.13	"The **wood** of the pine, the juniper, and the cypress,
	60.13	The finest **wood** from the forests of Lebanon,
	60.17	bronze instead of iron and **wood**, And iron instead of stone.
Jer	5.13	The people will be like **wood**, and the fire will burn them
	7.18	The children gather **firewood**, the men build fires,
	10. 3	of the **woodcarver**, [4]and decorated with silver and gold.
	10. 8	What can they learn from **wooden** idols?
	27. 2	out of leather straps and **wooden** crossbars and to put it on
	28.13	be able to break a **wooden** yoke, but he will replace it
	49.19	coming out of the thick **woods** along the Jordan up to the
	50.44	coming out of the thick **woods** along the Jordan up to the
Lam	4. 8	their skin, dry as **wood**, has shrivelled on their bones.
	5. 4	we must buy the **wood** we need for fuel.
	5.13	boys go staggering under heavy loads of **wood**.
Ezek	24. 5	pile the **wood** under the pot.
	24. 9	I myself will pile up the **firewood**.
	24.10	Bring more **wood**!
	26.12	will take the stones and **wood** and all the rubble, and dump
	37.16	man," he said, "take a **wooden** stick and write on it the
	39. 9	will go out and collect the abandoned weapons for **firewood**.
	39.10	will not have to gather **firewood** in the fields or cut down
	41.16	were all panelled with **wood** from the floor to the windows.
	41.22	there was something that looked like [22]a **wooden** altar.
	41.22	Its corner-posts, its base, and its sides were all made of **wood**.
	41.25	And there was a **wooden** covering over the outside of the
Dan	5. 4	and praised gods made of gold, silver, bronze, iron, **wood**,
	5.23	of gold, silver, bronze, iron, **wood**, and stone—gods that
Hos	4.12	They ask for revelations from a piece of **wood**!
	10. 7	king will be carried off, like a chip of **wood** on water.
Hab	2.19	You say to a piece of **wood**, "Wake up!"
Lk	23.31	these are done when the **wood** is green, what will happen when
Acts	16.24	cell and fastened their feet between heavy blocks of **wood**.
1 Cor	3.12	others will use **wood** or grass or straw.
2 Tim	2.20	some are made of silver and gold, others of **wood** and clay;
Rev	9.20	gold, silver, bronze, stone, and **wood**, which cannot see,
	18.12	all kinds of rare **woods** and all kinds of objects
	18.12	made of ivory and of expensive **wood**, of bronze, iron, and

Am **WOODWORKER** see **WOODCARVER**

WOOL

Ex	25. 4	blue, purple, and red **wool**;
	26. 1	pieces of fine linen woven with blue, purple, and red **wool**.
	26.31	curtain of fine linen woven with blue, purple, and red **wool**.
	26.36	blue, purple, and red **wool** and decorated with embroidery.
	27.16	blue, purple, and red **wool**, and decorated with embroidery.
	28. 5	blue, purple, and red **wool**, gold thread, and fine linen.
	28. 6	of blue, purple, and red **wool**, gold thread, and fine linen,
	28.31	goes under the ephod is to be made entirely of blue **wool**.
	28.33	of blue, purple, and red **wool**, alternating with gold bells.
	35. 6	blue, purple, and red **wool**;
	35.23	blue, purple, or red **wool**;
	35.25	thread of blue, purple, and red **wool**, which they had made.
	35.35	blue, purple, and red **wool**;
	36. 8	with blue, purple, and red **wool** and embroidered with figures
	36.35	with blue, purple, and red **wool** and embroidered it with
	36.37	blue, purple, and red **wool** and decorated with embroidery.
	38.18	blue, purple, and red **wool** and decorated with embroidery.
	38.23	a weaver of fine linen and of blue, purple, and red **wool**.
	39. 1	the blue, purple, and red **wool** they made the magnificent
	39. 2	blue, purple, and red **wool**;
	39. 3	into the fine linen and into the blue, purple, and red **wool**.
	39.22	that goes under the ephod was made entirely of blue **wool**.
	39.24	purple, and red **wool**, alternating with bells of pure gold,
	39.29	of blue, purple, and red **wool**, decorated with embroidery, as
Lev	13.47	is mildew on clothing, whether **wool** or linen,
	13.48	on any piece of linen or **wool** cloth or on leather or
	13.59	on clothing, whether it is **wool** or linen,
	13.59	or on linen or **wool** cloth
Deut	18. 4	the first share of the corn, wine, olive-oil, and **wool**.
	22.11	"Do not wear cloth made by weaving **wool** and linen together.
Judg	6.37	Well, I am putting some **wool** on the ground where we
	6.37	is dew only on the **wool** but not on the ground, then
	6.38	next morning, he squeezed the **wool** and wrung enough dew out
	6.39	Please let me make one more test with the **wool**.
	6.39	This time let the **wool** be dry, and the ground be wet."
	6.40	The next morning the **wool** was dry, but the ground was wet
2 Kgs	3. 4	of Israel 100,000 lambs, and the **wool** from 100,000 sheep.
Job	31.20	give him clothing made of **wool** that had come from my own
Prov	27.26	can make clothes from the **wool** of your sheep and buy land
	31.13	She keeps herself busy making **wool** and linen cloth.
Is	1.18	your stains are deep red, you will be as white as **wool**.
Ezek	27.18	paying for them with wine from Helbon and **wool** from Sahar.
	34. 3	wear clothes made from the **wool**, and kill and eat the finest
	44.17	not wear anything made of **wool** when they are on duty in
Dan	7. 9	clothes were white as snow, and his hair was like pure **wool**.
Hos	2. 4	me food and water, **wool** and linen, olive-oil and wine."
	2. 9	and will take away the **wool** and the linen I gave her
Acts	8.32	makes no sound when its **wool** is cut off, he did not
Heb	9.19	all the people, using a sprig of hyssop and some red **wool**.
Rev	1.14	His hair was white as **wool**, or as snow, and his eyes

WORD (1)

[GOD'S WORD, LORD'S WORD]

Gen	9.11	With these **words** I make my covenant with you:
	11. 1	whole world had only one language and used the same **words**.
	24.60	And they gave Rebecca their blessing in these **words**:
	31. 4	So Jacob sent **word** to Rachel and Leah to meet him in
	32. 5	I am sending you **word**, sir, in the hope of gaining your
	38.25	As she was being taken out, she sent **word** to her father-in-law:
	44. 6	When the servant caught up with them, he repeated these **words**.
	49.28	said as he spoke a suitable **word** of farewell to each son.
	50.21	So he reassured them with kind **words** that touched their hearts.
Ex	18. 6	He had sent **word** to Moses that they were coming, [7]so
	20. 1	God spoke, and these were his **words**:
	34. 1	will write on them the **words** that were on the first tablets,
	34.27	said to Moses, "Write these **words** down,
	34.27	on the basis of these **words** that I am making a covenant
	34.28	the tablets the **words** of the covenant—the Ten Commandments.
Num	6.23	use the following **words** in blessing the people of Israel:
	24. 3	Balaam son of Beor, The **words** of the man who can see
	24.15	Balaam son of Beor, The **words** of the man who can see
Deut	1. 1	In this book are the **words** that Moses spoke to the people
	10. 4	on those tablets the same **words** that he had written the
	26. 5	Then, in the Lord's presence you will recite these **words**:
	27. 8	with plaster write clearly every **word** of God's laws."
	27.14	The Levites will speak these **words** in a loud voice:
	32. 1	"Earth and sky, hear my **words**, listen closely to what I say.
	32. 2	My **words** will fall like showers on young plants, like gentle
	32.47	These teachings are not empty **words**;
Josh	2. 3	night to spy out the country, [3]so he sent **word** to Rahab:
	6.10	to shout, not to say a **word** until he gave the order.
	10. 6	The men of Gibeon sent **word** to Joshua at the camp in
	11. 1	Jabin of Hazor, he sent **word** to King Jobab of Madon, to
	11. 3	He also sent **word** to the Canaanites on both sides of the
	22. 6	Joshua sent them home with his blessing and with these **words**:
	24. 9	He sent **word** to Balaam son of Beor and asked him to

Josh	24.27	It has heard all the **words** that the Lord has spoken to
Judg	13.12	Then Manoah asked, “When your **words** come true, what
	13.17	so that we can honour you when your **words** come true.”
	15.12	“Give me your **word** that you won't kill me yourselves.”
	18.19	Don't say a **word.**
	21.13	Then the whole assembly sent **word** to the Benjaminites
1 Sam	2. 3	silence your proud **words.**
	20.12	If his attitude towards you is good, I will send you **word.**
	21.12	Their **words** made a deep impression on David, and he
2 Sam	3.11	was so afraid of Abner that he could not say a **word.**
	10. 5	what had happened, he sent **word** that they should stay in
	13. 7	So David sent **word** to Tamar in the palace:
	16.23	days was accepted as though it were the very **word of God;**
	19.14	David's **words** won the complete loyalty of all the men of Judah,
	19.14	and they sent him **word** to return with all his officials.
	19.23	Shimei, “I give you my **word** that you will not be put
	22.31	This God—how perfect are his deeds, how dependable his **words!**
	23. 1	These are David's last **words:**
1 Kgs	8.24	today every **word** has been fulfilled.
	13.20	at the table, the **word of the Lord** came to the old
	13.32	The **words** that he spoke at the Lord's command against
	18.21	But the people didn't say a **word.**
	20. 5	“I sent you **word** that you were to hand over to me
	20.42	then said to the king, “This is the **word of the Lord:**
2 Kgs	3. 7	He sent **word** to King Jehoshaphat of Judah:
	4.13	or the army commander and put in a good **word** for her.”
	5. 8	Elisha heard what had happened, he sent **word** to the king:
	6. 9	But Elisha sent **word** to the king of Israel, warning him
	9.25	the Lord spoke these **words** against Ahab:
	10.21	and Jehu sent **word** throughout all the land of Israel.
	18.20	demanded, “Do you think that **words** can take the place of
	18.36	they did not say a **word.**
	19. 9	**Word** reached the Assyrians that the Egyptian army, led by
	25.24	them, “I give you my **word** that there is no need for
1 Chr	19. 5	what had happened, he sent **word** for them to stay in Jericho
2 Chr	6.15	today every **word** has been fulfilled.
	20.20	Jehoshaphat addressed them with these **words:**
	24. 9	They sent **word** throughout Jerusalem and Judah for everyone
	30. 1	month, and the king sent **word** to all the people of Israel
	32. 8	The people were encouraged by these **words** of their king.
	34.21	have not obeyed the **word of the Lord** and have not done
	36.12	to the prophet Jeremiah, who spoke the **word of the Lord.**
	36.16	ignoring his **words** and laughing at his prophets,
Job	2.13	and nights without saying a **word,** because they saw how much
	4. 4	When someone stumbled, weak and tired, your **words** encouraged him
	6. 3	sands of the sea, so my wild **words** should not surprise you.
	6.25	Honest **words** are convincing, but you are talking nonsense.
	6.26	then why do you answer my **words** of despair?
	9.14	So how can I find **words** to answer God?
	9.20	innocent and faithful, but my **words** sound guilty, and
	11. 3	That your mocking **words** will leave us speechless?
	12.11	tongue enjoys tasting food, your ears enjoy hearing **words.**
	13.17	Now listen to my **words** of explanation.
	15. 1	Empty **words,** Job!
	15. 1	Empty **words!**
	15. 3	as you do or defend himself with such meaningless **words.**
	15. 5	you are trying to hide behind clever **words.**
	15. 6	you are condemned by every **word** you speak.
	15.11	We have spoken for him with calm, even **words.**
	16. 1	I have heard **words** like that before;
	16. 3	Do you always have to have the last **word?**
	16. 4	shake my head wisely and drown you with a flood of **words.**
	17. 3	Accept my **word.**
	19. 1	Why do you keep tormenting me with **words?**
	19.23	someone would remember my **words** and record them in a book!
	19.24	with a chisel carve my **words** in stone and write them so
	22.22	keep his **words** in your heart.
	24.25	Can anyone prove that my **words** are not true?
	26. 4	Who do you think will hear all your **words?**
	29.22	My **words** sank in like drops of rain;
	31.35	I swear that every **word** is true.
	31.40	The **words** of Job are ended.
	32.15	**Words** have failed them, Job;
	32.18	I can't hold back the **words.**
	33. 3	All my **words** are sincere, and I am speaking the truth.
	34. 3	when you taste it, but not wise **words** when you hear them.
	38. 2	Who are you to question my wisdom with your ignorant, empty **words?**
Ps	5. 1	Listen to my **words,** O Lord, and hear my sighs.
	5. 9	Their **words** are flattering and smooth, but full of deadly deceit.
	10. 7	he is quick to speak hateful, evil **words.**
	12. 4	mouths that say, [4]“With our **words** we get what we want.
	15. 2	does what is right, whose **words** are true and sincere, [3]and
	17. 6	so turn to me and listen to my **words.**
	18.30	How dependable his **words!**
	19. 3	No speech or **words** are used, no sound is heard;
	19.14	May my **words** and my thoughts be acceptable to you, O
	28. 3	do evil— men whose **words** are friendly, but who have hatred
	33. 4	The **words of the Lord** are true and all his works are
	33. 6	his command, the sun, moon, and stars by his spoken **word.**
	37.30	A good man's **words** are wise, and he is always fair.
	39. 2	I kept quiet, not saying a **word,** not even about anything good!
	39. 9	I will not say a **word,** for you are the one who
	45. 1	Beautiful **words** fill my mind, as I compose this song for
	49. 3	I will speak **words** of wisdom.
	52. 4	You love to hurt people with your **words,** you liar!
	54. 2	listen to my **words!**
	55.21	His **words** were smoother than cream, but there was hatred
	55.21	his **words** were as soothing as oil, but they cut like sharp
	59.12	all their **words** are sinful;
Ps	62. 4	You speak **words** of blessing, but in your heart you curse him.
	64. 3	sharpen their tongues like swords and aim cruel **words** like arrows.
	64. 8	He will destroy them because of those **words;**
	78.36	But their **words** were all lies;
	105.19	The **word of the Lord** proved him right.
	107. 2	Repeat these **words** in praise to the Lord, all you whom he
	119.42	answer those who insult me because I trust in your **word.**
	119.67	me, I used to go wrong, but now I obey your **word.**
	119.81	I place my trust in your **word.**
	119.89	Your **word,** O Lord, will last for ever;
	119.101	avoided all evil conduct, because I want to obey your **word.**
	119.105	Your **word** is a lamp to guide me and a light for
	130. 5	wait eagerly for the Lord's help, and in his **word** I trust.
	140. 3	their **words** are like a cobra's poison.
	141. 6	cliffs, the people will admit that my **words** were true.
Prov	4.20	Listen to my **words.**
	4.24	Have nothing to do with lies and misleading **words.**
	5. 2	properly, and your **words** will show that you have knowledge.
	6. 2	been caught by your own **words,** trapped by your own promises?
	6.21	Keep their **words** with you always, locked in your heart.
	6.24	bad women, from the seductive **words** of other men's wives.
	7. 5	from other men's wives, from women with seductive **words.**
	8. 6	Listen to my excellent **words;**
	8.13	I hate pride and arrogance, evil ways and false **words.**
	10. 6	A wicked man's **words** hide a violent nature.
	10.11	A good man's **words** are a fountain of life,
	10.11	but a wicked man's **words** hide a violent nature.
	10.20	A good man's **words** are like pure silver;
	10.21	A good man's **words** will benefit many people, but you can
	11.11	a city is brought to ruin by the **words** of the wicked.
	12. 6	The **words** of wicked men are murderous,
	12. 6	but the **words** of the righteous rescue
	12.13	is trapped by his own **words,** but an honest man gets himself
	12.18	Thoughtless **words** can wound as deeply as any sword,
	12.18	but wisely spoken **words** can heal.
	12.22	Lord hates liars, but is pleased with those who keep their **word.**
	12.25	can rob you of happiness, but kind **words** will cheer you up.
	13. 5	people hate lies, but the **words** of wicked people are
	14. 3	a wise man's **words** protect him.
	15. 4	Kind **words** bring life, but cruel words crush your spirit.
	15.23	it is to find just the right **word** for the right occasion!
	15.26	The Lord hates evil thoughts, but he is pleased with friendly **words.**
	16. 1	We may make our plans, but God has the last **word.**
	16.21	The more pleasant his **words,** the more persuasive he is.
	16.24	Kind **words** are like honey—sweet to the taste and good
	16.27	even their **words** burn with evil.
	18. 4	A person's **words** can be a source of wisdom, deep as the
	18. 7	he gets caught in the trap of his own **words.**
	18.21	so you must accept the consequences of your **words.**
	21.28	is not believed, but the **word** of someone who thinks matters
	22.12	that truth is kept safe by disproving the **words** of liars.
	23.16	I will be proud when I hear you speaking **words** of wisdom.
	26.24	A hypocrite hides his hate behind flattering **words.**
	30. 1	These are the solemn **words** of Agur son of Jakeh:
	31. 1	These are the solemn **words** which King Lemuel's mother said to him:
Ecc	1. 1	These are the **words** of the Philosopher, David's son, who
	1. 8	Everything leads to weariness—a weariness too great for **words.**
	5. 6	Don't let your own **words** lead you into sin, so that you
	9.17	to listen to the quiet **words** of a wise man than to
	10.12	brings him honour, but a fool is destroyed by his own **words.**
	12.10	Philosopher tried to find comforting **words,**
	12.10	but the **words** he wrote were honest.
Is	6. 5	I am doomed because every **word** that passes my lips is sinful,
	6. 5	and I live among a people whose every **word** is sinful.
	7. 2	When **word** reached the king of Judah that the armies of
	28.16	on which are written the **words,** ‘Faith that is firm is also
	29.13	to worship me, but their **words** are meaningless, and their
	30.27	He speaks, and his **words** burn like fire.
	36. 5	demanded, “Do you think that **words** can take the place of
	36.21	they did not say a **word.**
	37. 9	**Word** reached the Assyrians that the Egyptian army, led by
	40. 8	flowers fade, but the **word of our God** endures for ever.”
	41.26	None of you said a **word** about it;
	43. 9	they are right, to testify to the truth of their **words.**
	44.25	The **words** of the wise I refute and show that their wisdom
	44.27	With a **word** of command I dry up the ocean.
	48. 1	God of Israel— but you don't mean a **word** you say.
	48. 8	this at all, why no **word** of it ever came to your
	48.16	I have spoken openly, and have always made my **words** come true.”
	49. 2	He made my **words** as sharp as a sword.
	50.10	the Lord and obey the **words** of his servant, the path you
	53. 7	he never said a **word.**
	53. 7	like a sheep about to be sheared, he never said a **word.**
	55.10	“My **word** is like the snow and the rain that come down
	55.11	So also will be the **word** that I speak— it will
	58. 9	to every gesture of contempt, and to every evil **word;**
	59.13	our **words** are lies.
Jer	1. 9	to me, “Listen, I am giving you the **words** you must speak.
	1.12	said, “and I am watching to see that my **words** come true.”
	5.13	things, I will make my **words** like a fire in your mouth.
	6.19	they have rejected my teaching and have not obeyed my **words.**
	7. 4	Stop believing those deceitful **words,** ‘We are safe!
	7. 8	“Look, you put your trust in deceitful **words.**
	7.27	you will speak all these **words** to my people, but they will
	8. 9	They have rejected my **words;**
	9. 8	Everyone speaks friendly **words** to his neighbour, but is
	9.20	“Listen to the Lord, you women, and pay attention to his **words.**
	12. 6	Do not trust them, even though they speak friendly **words.”**

Jer 14.14 did I give them any orders or speak one **word** to them.
15.16 You spoke to me, and I listened to every **word.**
15.16 God Almighty, and so your **words** filled my heart with joy and
23. 9 Lord, because of his holy **words,** I am like a man who
23.30 who take each other's **words** and proclaim them as my message.
23.31 who speak their own **words** and claim they came from me.
23.34 a priest even uses the **words** 'the Lord's burden,' I will
23.36 must no longer use the **words** 'the Lord's burden,' because if
23.36 The people have perverted the **words** of their God, the living God,
23.38 my command and use the **words** 'the Lord's burden,' then tell
26. 5 by paying attention to the **words** of my servants, the
31.10 listen to me, and proclaim my **words** on the far-off shores.
36. 8 So Baruch read the **Lord's words** in the Temple exactly as I
36.18 Baruch answered, "Jeremiah dictated every **word** of it to me,
40. 9 them, "I give you my **word** that there is no need for
44.28 will know whose **words** have come true, mine or theirs.
51.64 The **words** of Jeremiah end here.
Ezek 5.11 God—this is the **word of the Sovereign Lord**—because you
6. 3 Israel to hear the **word of the Lord**—to hear what I,
13. 2 Tell them to listen to the **word of the Lord."**
13. 6 Yet they expect their **words** to come true!
13. 7 say that they are my **words,** but I haven't spoken to you!"
13. 8 Lord says to them, "Your **words** are false, and your visions
22.14 I, the Lord, have spoken, and I keep my **word.**
22.28 claim to speak the **word of the Sovereign Lord,** but I, the
30. 2 You are to shout these **words:**
33.30 'Let's go and hear what **word** has come from the Lord now.'
33.31 Loving **words** are on their lips, but they continue their greedy ways.
33.32 They listen to all your **words** and don't obey a single one
33.33 But when all your **words** come true—and they will come
37. 4 Tell these dry bones to listen to the **word of the Lord.**
37.16 stick and write on it the **words,** 'The kingdom of Judah.'
37.16 stick and write on it the **words,** 'The kingdom of Israel.'
Dan 2.14 Choosing his **words** carefully, [15]he asked Arioch why the
4.31 Before the **words** were out of his mouth, a voice spoke
4.33 The **words** came true immediately.
5.24 That is why God has sent the hand to write these **words.**
12. 9 go now, Daniel, because these **words** are to be kept secret
Hos 2.14 there I will win her back with **words** of love.
10. 4 They utter empty **words** and make false promises
Amos 1. 1 These are the **words** of Amos, a shepherd from the town of
Zech 1.13 answered the angel with comforting **words,** [14]and the angel
8. 9 are now hearing the same **words** the prophets spoke at the
13. 3 he claimed to speak the **Lord's word,** but spoke lies instead.
14.20 will be inscribed with the **words** "Dedicated to the Lord."
Mt 4. 4 on bread alone, but needs every **word** that God speaks.' "
6. 7 use a lot of meaningless **words,** as the pagans do, who think
7.24 then, anyone who hears these **words** of mine and obeys them is
7.26 "But anyone who hears these **words** of mine and does not
8.16 the evil spirits with a **word** and healed all who were sick.
10.20 For the **words** you will speak will not be yours;
12.36 to give account of every useless **word** he has ever spoken.
12.37 Your **words** will be used to judge you—to declare you
15. 8 God, honour me with their **words,** but their heart is really
15.23 But Jesus did not say a **word** to her.
24.35 earth will pass away, but my **words** will never pass away.
26.44 went away, and prayed the third time, saying the same **words.**
27.14 refused to answer a single **word,** with the result that the
Mk 7. 6 God, honour me with their **words,** but their heart is really
7.13 teaching you pass on to others cancels out the **word of God.**
10.24 were shocked at these **words,** but Jesus went on to say,
13.11 For the **words** you speak will not be yours;
13.31 earth will pass away, but my **words** will never pass away.
14.39 He went away once more and prayed, saying the same **words.**
14.61 But Jesus kept quiet and would not say a **word.**
15. 5 Again Jesus refused to say a **word,** and Pilate was amazed.
Lk 1.22 Unable to say a **word,** he made signs to them with his
1.29 the angel's message, and she wondered what his **words** meant.
3. 2 At that time the **word of God** came to John son of
4.22 with him and marvelled at the eloquent **words** that he spoke.
4.36 and said to one another, "What kind of **words** are these?
5. 1 their way up to him to listen to the **word of God.**
6.47 me and listens to my **words** and obeys them—I will show
6.49 But anyone who hears my **words** and does not obey them is
8.11 the seed is the **word of God.**
8.21 brothers are those who hear the **word of God** and obey it."
11.28 happy are those who hear the **word of God** and obey it!"
12.10 "Anyone who says a **word** against the Son of Man can be
18.34 the meaning of the **words** was hidden from them, and they did
19.22 I will use your own **words** to condemn you!
19.48 kept listening to him, not wanting to miss a single **word.**
21.15 I will give you such **words** and wisdom that none of your
21.33 earth will pass away, but my **words** will never pass away.
23.38 Above him were written these **words:**
24. 8 Then the women remembered his **words,** [9]returned from the tomb,
Jn 1.38 (This **word** means "Teacher.")
1.41 (This **word** means "Christ.")
3.34 whom God has sent speaks **God's words,** because God gives him
4.50 The man believed Jesus' **words** and went.
5.24 whoever hears my **words** and believes in him who sent me has
6.63 The **words** I have spoken to you bring God's life-giving Spirit.
6.68 You have the **words** that give eternal life.
8.47 He who comes from God listens to **God's words.**
8.55 But I do know him, and I obey his **word.**
10.19 Again there was a division among the people because of these **words.**
12.48 The **words** I have spoken will be his judge on the last
14.10 The **words** that I have spoken to you," Jesus said to his
15. 7 remain in me and my **words** remain in you, then you will

Jn 17. 6 They have obeyed your **word,** [7]and now they know that
17.17 your **word** is truth.
18.32 in order to make the **words** of Jesus come true,
18.32 the **words** he used when he indicated the
19.13 When Pilate heard these **words,** he took Jesus outside and
Acts 2.22 "Listen to these **words,** fellow-Israelites!
2.26 I am filled with gladness, and my **words** are full of joy.
2.40 them and with many other **words** he urged them, saying, "Save
6. 2 the preaching of **God's word** in order to handle finances.
6. 7 And so the **word of God** continued to spread.
7.22 of the Egyptians and became a great man in **words** and deeds.
8.14 Samaria had received the **word of God,** so they sent Peter and
8.32 when its wool is cut off, he did not say a **word.**
9. 7 were travelling with Saul had stopped, not saying a **word;**
11. 1 Judaea heard that the Gentiles also had received the **word of God.**
11.14 He will speak **words** to you by which you and all your
12.24 Meanwhile the **word of God** continued to spread and grow.
13. 5 at Salamis, they preached the **word of God** in the synagogues.
13. 7 Saul before him because he wanted to hear the **word of God.**
13.27 nor did they understand the **words** of the prophets that are
13.27 Yet they made the prophets' **words** come true by condemning Jesus.
13.44 everyone in the town came to hear the **word of the Lord.**
13.46 was necessary that the **word of God** should be spoken first to
13.49 The **word of the Lord** spread everywhere in that region.
14. 9 He sat there and listened to Paul's **words.**
14.18 Even with these **words** the apostles could hardly keep the
15.15 The **words** of the prophets agree completely with this.
15.21 every Sabbath, and his **words** are preached in every town."
15.35 many others they taught and preached the **word of the Lord.**
15.36 where we preached the **word of the Lord,** and let us find
16.32 Then they preached the **word of the Lord** to him and to
16.38 The police officers reported these **words** to the Roman officials;
16.40 met the believers, spoke **words** of encouragement to them,
17. 8 With these **words** they threw the crowd and the city
17.13 Paul had preached the **word of God** in Berea also, they came
18.11 a year and a half, teaching the people the **word of God.**
18.15 it is an argument about **words** and names and your own law,
19.10 Asia, both Jews and Gentiles, heard the **word of the Lord.**
19.20 this powerful way the **word of the Lord** kept spreading and
19.28 As the crowd heard these **words,** they became furious and started shouting,
20. 1 and with **words** of encouragement said goodbye to them.
20.35 remembering the **words** that the Lord Jesus himself said,
23.15 you and the Council send **word** to the Roman commander to
28.24 were convinced by his **words,** but others would not believe.
Rom 3.13 Their **words** are full of deadly deceit;
4.23 The **words** "he was accepted as righteous" were not
8.26 pleads with God for us in groans that **words** cannot express.
9. 9 For God's promise was made in these **words:**
10.18 their **words** reached the ends of the earth."
15.18 done this by means of **words** and deeds, [19]by the power of
16.18 By their fine **words** and flattering speech they deceive innocent people.
1 Cor 2. 1 God's secret truth, I did not use big **words** and great learning.
2. 4 were not delivered with skilful **words** of human wisdom, but
2.13 we do not speak in **words** taught by human wisdom,
2.13 but in **words** taught by the Spirit,
4.13 when we are insulted, we answer with kind **words.**
4.20 Kingdom of God is not a matter of **words** but of power.
9.15 Nobody is going to turn my rightful boast into empty **words!**
14. 9 Your **words** will vanish in the air!
14.19 I would rather speak five **words** that can be understood,
14.19 than speak thousands of **words** in strange tongues.
14.36 Or could it be that the **word of God** came from you?
15.27 clear, of course, that the **words** "all things" do not
2 Cor 4. 2 not act with deceit, nor do we falsify the **word of God.**
9. 3 you in this matter may not turn out to be empty **words.**
10.10 with us in person, he is weak, and his **words** are nothing!"
12. 3 which cannot be put into **words,** things that human lips may
Eph 4.29 Do not use harmful **words,** but only helpful words, the
5. 6 Do not let anyone deceive you with foolish **words;**
5.19 another with the **words** of psalms, hymns, and sacred songs;
5.26 church to God by his **word,** after making it clean by washing
6.17 a helmet, and the **word of God** as the sword which the
Phil 4. 9 received from me, both from my **words** and from my actions.
1 Thes 1. 5 News to you, not with **words** only, but also with power and
2. 5 talk, nor did we use **words** to cover up greed—God is
4.18 So then, encourage one another with these **words.**
1 Tim 1. 7 do not understand their own **words** or the matters about which
1.18 is in accordance with the **words** of prophecy spoken in the
1.18 Use those **words** as weapons in order to fight well, [19]and
4. 5 of thanks, [5]because the **word of God** and the prayer make it
4. 6 feed yourself spiritually on the **words** of faith and of the
6. 3 not agree with the true **words** of our Lord Jesus Christ and
6. 4 argue and quarrel about **words,** and this brings on jealousy,
2 Tim 1.13 Hold firmly to the true **words** that I taught you, as the
2. 9 But the **word of God** is not in chains, [10]and so I
2.14 a solemn warning in God's presence not to fight over **words.**
2.19 and on it are written these **words:**
Tit 2. 8 Use sound **words** that cannot be criticized, so that your
Heb 1. 3 God's own being, sustaining the universe with his powerful **word.**
3.13 day, as long as the **word** "Today" in the scripture applies
4.12 The **word of God** is alive and active, sharper than any
6. 5 they knew from experience that **God's word** is good, and
11. 3 the universe was created by **God's word,** so that what can be
12. 5 Have you forgotten the encouraging **words** which God speaks
12.19 begged not to hear another **word,** [20]because they could not
12.27 The **words** "once more" plainly show that the created
Jas 1.18 us into being through the **word** of truth, so that we should
1.21 to God and accept the **word** that he plants in your hearts,

Jas 1.22 Do not deceive yourselves by just listening to his **word;**
1.23 Whoever listens to the **word** but does not put it into
3.10 **Words** of thanksgiving and cursing pour out from the same mouth.
1 Pet 1. 8 great and glorious joy which **words** cannot express, [9]because
1.23 the living and eternal **word of God** you have been born again
1.25 fall, [25]but the **word of the Lord** remains for ever."
1.25 This **word** is the Good News that was proclaimed to you.
2. 8 They stumbled because they did not believe in the **word;**
3. 1 of them do not believe **God's word,** your conduct will win
3. 1 for you to say a **word,** [2]because they will see how pure
2 Pet 3. 2 want you to remember the **words** that were spoken long ago by
1 Jn 1. 6 darkness, we are lying both in our **words** and in our actions.
1.10 out to be a liar, and his **word** is not in us.
2. 5 But whoever obeys his **word** is the one whose love for God
2.14 the **word of God** lives in you, and you have defeated the
3.18 My children, our love should not be just **words** and talk;
Jude 9 Devil with insulting **words,** but said, "The Lord rebuke you!"
15 and for all the terrible **words** that godless sinners have
Rev 1. 3 those who listen to the **words** of this prophetic message and
1. 9 Patmos because I had proclaimed **God's word** and the truth that
6. 9 because they had proclaimed **God's word** and had been faithful
17.17 the beast their power to rule until **God's words** come true.
19. 9 And the angel added, "These are the true **words of God."**
20. 4 the truth that Jesus revealed and the **word of God.**
21. 5 "Write this, because these **words** are true and can be trusted."
22. 6 angel said to me, "These **words** are true and can be trusted.
22. 7 Happy are those who obey the prophetic **words** in this book!"
22. 9 prophets and of all those who obey the **words** in this book.
22.10 "Do not keep the prophetic **words** of this book a secret,
22.15 idols and those who are liars both in **words** and deeds.
22.18 John, solemnly warn everyone who hears the prophetic **words** of this book:
22.19 anything away from the prophetic **words** of this book, God

WORD (2)

Jn 1. 1 Before the world was created, the **Word** already existed;
1. 2 From the very beginning the **Word** was with God.
1. 4 The **Word** was the source of life, and this life brought
1.10 The **Word** was in the world, and though God made the world
1.14 The **Word** became a human being and, full of grace and truth,
1 Jn 1. 1 to you about the **Word of life,** which has existed from the
Rev 19.13 His name is "The **Word of God."**

WORK

[HARD-WORKING, OVERWORKED]

Gen 2. 2 day God finished what he had been doing and stopped **working.**
2. 3 that day he had completed his creation and stopped **working.**
3.17 You will have to **work** hard all your life to make it
3.19 You will have to **work** hard and sweat to make the soil
5.29 this child will bring us relief from all our hard **work";**
29.15 said to Jacob, "You shouldn't **work** for me for nothing just
29.18 so he said, "I will **work** seven years for you, if you
29.20 Jacob **worked** seven years so that he could have Rachel,
29.25 I **worked** to get Rachel.
29.27 you Rachel, if you will **work** for me another seven years."
29.30 Then he **worked** for Laban another seven years.
30.26 that I have earned by **working** for you, and I will leave.
30.29 "You know how I have **worked** for you and how your flocks
31. 6 both know that I have **worked** for your father with all my
31.41 For fourteen years I **worked** to win your two daughters—and
31.42 seen my trouble and the **work** I have done, and last night
39.11 the house to do his **work,** none of the house servants was
49.15 to carry the load And is forced to **work** as a slave.
Ex 1.13 made them **work** on their building projects and in their fields,
5. 4 "What do you mean by making the people neglect their **work?**
5. 4 Get those slaves back to **work!**
5. 5 And now you want to stop **working!"**
5. 8 They haven't enough **work** to do, and that is why they keep
5. 9 Make these men **work** harder and keep them busy, so that
5.14 Israelite foremen, whom they had put in charge of the **work.**
5.17 lazy and don't want to **work,** and that is why you ask
5.18 Now get back to **work!**
8.22 will know that I, the Lord, am at **work** in this land.
12.16 No **work** is to be done on those days, but you may
15.11 Who can **work** miracles and mighty acts like yours?
16.30 So the people did no **work** on the seventh day.
20. 9 in which to do your **work,** [10]but the seventh day is a
20.10 day no one is to **work**—neither you, your children, your
23.12 **"Work** six days a week, but do no work on the seventh
23.12 slaves and the foreigners who **work** for you and even your
31. 3 every kind of artistic **work**—[4]for planning skilful designs
31. 4 and **working** them in gold, silver, and bronze;
31. 5 and for every other kind of artistic **work.**
31. 6 son of Ahisamach, from the tribe of Dan, to **work** with him.
31.14 does not keep it, but **works** on that day, is to be
31.15 in which to do your **work,** but the seventh day is a
31.15 Whoever does any **work** on that day is to be put to
31.17 and on the seventh day I stopped **working** and rested."
34.21 in which to do your **work,**
34.21 but do not **work** on the seventh day, not even
35. 2 in which to do your **work,** but the seventh day is to
35. 2 Anyone who does any **work** on that day is to be put
35.24 which could be used for any of the **work** brought it.
35.29 to the Lord for the **work** which he had commanded Moses to
35.31 every kind of artistic **work,** [32]for planning skilful designs
35.32 and **working** them in gold, silver and bronze;
35.33 and for every other kind of artistic **work.**
35.35 skill in all kinds of **work** done by engravers, designers, and
35.35 are able to do all kinds of **work** and are skilful designers.

Ex 36. 2 were willing to help, and Moses told them to start **working.**
36. 4 men who were doing the **work** went [5]and reported to Moses,
36. 5 than is needed for the **work** which the Lord commanded to be
36. 7 been brought was more than enough to finish all the **work.**
36. 8 men among those doing the **work** made the Tent of the Lord's
38.21 made by the Levites who **worked** under the direction of
39. 3 into thin strips to be **worked** into the fine linen and into
39.32 All the **work** on the Tent of the Lord's presence was
39.42 Israelites had done all the **work** just as the Lord had
40.33 So he finished all the **work.**
Lev 16.29 living among them must fast and must not do any **work.**
16.31 day, one on which they fast and do no **work** at all.
23. 3 in which to do your **work,** but remember that the seventh day,
23. 3 On that day do not **work,** but gather for worship.
23. 7 you shall gather for worship and do none of your daily **work.**
23. 8 for worship, but you shall do none of your daily **work.**
23.21 that day do none of your daily **work,** but gather for worship.
23.25 a food-offering to the Lord and do none of your daily **work.**
23.28 Do no **work** on that day, because it is the day for
23.30 And if anyone does any **work** on that day, the Lord
23.35 come together for worship and do none of your daily **work.**
23.36 It is a day for worship, and you shall do no **work.**
25.39 slave, you shall not make him do the **work** of a slave.
26.20 All your hard **work** will do you no good, because your
Num 1. 5 tribes, who were chosen from the community for this **work:**
3. 7 They shall do the **work** required for the Tent of my
4. 3 fifty who were qualified to **work** in the Tent of the Lord's
4.23 fifty who were qualified to **work** in the Tent of the Lord's
4.30 fifty who were qualified to **work** in the Tent of the Lord's
4.34 fifty who were qualified to **work** in the Tent of the Lord's
7. 5 gifts for use in the **work** to be done for the Tent;
7. 5 them to the Levites according to the **work** they have to do."
7. 8 All their **work** was to be done under the direction of Ithamar
8.11 gift from the Israelites, so that they may do my **work.**
8.15 the Levites, they will be qualified to **work** in the Tent.
8.19 gift from the Israelites, to **work** in the Tent for the people
8.22 the Levites were qualified to **work** in the Tent under Aaron
11.32 and all the next day, the people **worked** catching quails;
18. 2 the tribe of Levi, to **work** with you and help you while
18. 4 They are to **work** with you and fulfil their
18. 4 in the Tent, but no unqualified person may **work** with you.
19. 2 has never been put to **work,** [3]and they will give it to
28.18 are to gather for worship, and no **work** is to be done.
28.25 Meet for worship on the seventh day and do no **work.**
28.26 are to gather for worship, and no **work** is to be done.
29. 1 are to gather for worship, and no **work** is to be done.
29. 7 eat no food and do no **work.**
29.12 in honour of the Lord for seven days and do no **work.**
29.35 On the eighth day gather for worship and do no **work.**
Deut 4.34 he brought plagues and war, **worked** miracles and wonders, and
5.13 in which to do your **work,** [14]but the seventh day is a
5.14 day no one is to **work**—neither you, your children, your
6. 7 you are away, when you are resting and when you are **working.**
6.22 own eyes we saw him **work** miracles and do terrifying things
11.10 you sowed seed, you had to **work** hard to irrigate the fields;
11.19 you are away, when you are resting and when you are **working.**
12. 7 eat and enjoy the good things that you have **worked** for.
15.19 any of these cattle for **work** and don't shear any of these
16. 8 worship the Lord your God, and do no **work** on that day.
16.15 Be joyful, because the Lord has blessed your harvest and your **work.**
21. 3 to select a young cow that has never been used for **work.**
24.15 Each day before sunset pay him for that day's **work;**
26. 6 Egyptians treated us harshly and forced us to **work** as slaves.
26. 8 He **worked** miracles and wonders, and caused terrifying things
28. 8 your God will bless your **work** and fill your barns with corn.
28.12 sky and bless all your **work,** so that you will lend to
28.33 the crops that you have **worked** so hard to grow, while you
Josh 9.27 have continued to do this **work** in the place where the Lord
16.10 to this day, but they have been forced to **work** as slaves.
17.13 the Canaanites, but they did force them to **work** for them.
Judg 1.28 they forced the Canaanites to **work** for them, but still they
1.30 to live there with them and were forced to **work** for them.
1.33 the local Canaanites, but forced them to **work** for them.
1.35 them under their rule and forced them to **work** for them.
13. 5 He will begin the **work** of rescuing Israel from the Philistines."
13.19 them on the rock altar to the Lord who **works** wonders.
16.21 chains, and put him to **work** grinding at the mill in the
19.16 came by at the end of a day's **work** in the fields.
Ruth 2. 2 am sure to find someone who will let me **work** with him."
2. 7 She has been **working** since early morning and has just now
2. 8 **Work** with the women here;
2.19 Whose field have you been **working** in?
2.19 Naomi that she had been **working** in a field belonging to a
2.22 be better for you to **work** with the women in Boaz' field.
2.23 So Ruth **worked** with them and gathered corn until all the
3. 2 whose women you have been **working** with, is our relative.
1 Sam 2.22 sleeping with the women who **worked** at the entrance to the
8.13 make perfumes for him and **work** as his cooks and his bakers.
8.16 your best cattle and donkeys, and make them **work** for him.
2 Sam 3.29 only to do a woman's **work** or is killed in battle or
12.31 and put its people to **work** with saws, iron hoes,
12.31 and iron axes, and forced them to **work** at making bricks.
1 Kgs 5. 6 My men will **work** with them, and I will pay your men
5.16 3,300 foremen in charge of them to supervise their **work.**
6. 1 month, the month of Ziv, Solomon began **work** on the Temple.
7.13 living in the city of Tyre, who was skilled in bronze **work.**
7.14 King Solomon's invitation to be in charge of all the bronze **work.**
7.22 And so the **work** on the columns was completed.
7.40 completed all his **work** for King Solomon for the Lord's Temple.
7.51 King Solomon finished all the **work** on the Temple, he placed

1 Kgs	9.11	and pine and with all the gold he wanted for this **work.**
	9.23	forced labour **working** on Solomon's various building projects.
	11.28	Solomon noticed how hard he **worked,** he put him in charge of
2 Kgs	6. 4	When they arrived at the Jordan, they began to **work.**
	12.11	men in charge of the **work** in the Temple, and these would
	12.15	men in charge of the **work** were thoroughly honest, so there
	18.17	the road where the clothmakers **work,** by the ditch that
	22. 7	men in charge of the **work** are thoroughly honest, so there is
	25.12	property, and put them to **work** in the vineyards and fields.
1 Chr	9.13	They were experts in all the **work** carried on in the Temple.
	20. 3	city and put them to **work** with saws, iron hoes, and axes.
	22. 2	the land of Israel to assemble, and he put them to **work.**
	22.15	There are men to **work** in the stone quarries, and there are
	22.15	of every sort who can **work** [16] with gold, silver, bronze,
	22.16	Now begin the **work,** and may the Lord be with you."
	23. 4	twenty-four thousand to administer the **work** of the Temple,
	23.24	or older, had a share in the **work** of the Lord's Temple.
	23.31	the number of Levites assigned to do this **work** each time.
	26. 1	These are the assignments of **work** for the Levites who
	26. 8	a total of sixty-two highly qualified men for this **work.**
	27. 1	their officials who administered the **work** of the kingdom.
	28. 1	the officials who administered the **work** of the kingdom, the
	28.13	their duties, to do the **work** of the Temple, and to take
	28.20	Start the **work** and don't let anything stop you.
	28.20	you until you finish the **work** to be done on his Temple.
	29. 1	The **work** to be done is tremendous, because this is not a
	29. 7	to give [7] the following for the **work** on the Temple:
2 Chr	2. 2	put seventy thousand men to **work** transporting materials,
	2. 2	and eighty thousand men to **work** quarrying stone.
	2. 2	six hundred men responsible for supervising the **work.**
	2. 7	with skill in engraving, in **working** gold, silver, bronze,
	2. 7	He will **work** with the craftsmen of Judah and Jerusalem whom
	2.14	He can **work** with blue, purple, and red cloth, and with linen.
	2.14	Let him **work** with your craftsmen
	2.14	and with those who **worked** for your father, King David.
	2.18	appointed 3,600 supervisors to make sure the **work** was done.
	3. 5	which were **worked** designs of palm-trees and chain patterns.
	3.14	red, with designs of the winged creatures **worked** into it.
	5. 1	King Solomon finished all the **work** on the Temple, he placed
	8.10	the forced labour **working** on the various building projects.
	8.14	David, he organized the daily **work** of the priests and of the
	8.14	the priests in singing hymns and in doing their **work.**
	8.16	Temple to its completion, all the **work** had been successful.
	15. 7	The **work** that you do will be rewarded."
	16. 5	he stopped fortifying Ramah and abandoned the **work.**
	23.18	the priests and Levites in charge of the **work** of the Temple.
	24.13	All the workmen **worked** hard, and they restored the
	27. 3	the Temple and did extensive **work** on the city wall in the
	29.17	The **work** was begun on the first day of the first month,
	29.17	Then they **worked** for the next eight days, until the
	29.34	the Levites helped them until the **work** was finished.
	30.12	God was also at **work** in Judah and united the people in
	31.13	Ten Levites were assigned to **work** under them:
	31.17	years of age or older were assigned theirs by **work** groups.
	34.12	The men who did the **work** were thoroughly honest.
Ezra	2.69	as they could for this **work,** and the total came to 500
	3. 8	to the site of the Temple in Jerusalem, they began **work.**
	3. 8	exiles who had come back to Jerusalem, joined in the **work.**
	3. 8	were put in charge of the **work** of rebuilding the Temple.
	3.11	praising the Lord, because the **work** on the foundation of the
	4. 5	also bribed Persian government officials to **work** against them.
	4.24	**Work** on the Temple had been stopped and had remained at
	5. 8	The **work** is being done with great care and is moving ahead
	5.10	that we could inform you who the leaders of this **work** are.
	6. 8	in West Euphrates, so that the **work** is not interrupted.
	6.22	he supported them in their **work** of rebuilding the Temple of
Neh	2.10	that someone had come to **work** for the good of the people
	2.16	or anyone else who would be taking part in the **work.**
	2.18	And they got ready to start the **work.**
	3.12	(His daughters helped with the **work.)**
	4. 2	by offering sacrifices they can finish the **work** in one day?
	4. 6	its full height, because the people were eager to **work.**
	4.11	already upon us, killing us and putting an end to our **work.**
	4.16	then on half my men **worked** and half stood guard, wearing
	4.17	those who carried building materials **worked** with one hand
	4.19	their officials and leaders, "The **work** is spread out over
	4.21	at night, half of us **worked** on the wall, while the other
	4.22	guard the city at night as well as **work** in the daytime.
	5.10	and so have my companions and the men who **work** for me.
	5.16	Everyone who **worked** for me joined in the rebuilding.
	6. 3	them, "I am doing important **work** and can't go down there.
	6. 3	not going to let the **work** stop just to go and see
	6. 9	They were trying to frighten us into stopping **work.**
	6.15	After fifty-two days of **work** the entire wall was
	6.16	everyone knew that the **work** had been done with God's help.
	7. 1	choir, and the other Levites had been assigned their **work.**
	9.10	You **worked** amazing miracles against the king, against
	11.16	prominent Levites in charge of the **work** outside the Temple.
	11.21	of Jerusalem called Ophel and **worked** under the supervision
	13.11	and musicians back to the Temple and put them to **work** again.
Esth	10. 3	He **worked** for the good of his people and for the security
Job	10.16	to hurt me you even **work** miracles.
	20.18	He will have to give up all he has **worked** for;
	23. 9	God has been at **work** in the north and the south, but
	24.18	he no longer goes to **work** in his vineyards.
	28. 4	There they **work** in loneliness, Clinging to ropes in the pits.
	30. 2	bunch of worn-out men, too weak to do any **work** for me.
	31.31	All the men who **work** for me know that I have always
	37. 7	He brings the **work** of men to a stop;
	37.16	clouds float in the sky, the **work** of God's amazing skill?
	39. 7	noisy cities, and no one can tame them and make them **work.**
Job	39. 9	Will a wild ox **work** for you?
	39.11	on his great strength and expect him to do your heavy **work?**
Ps	33. 4	words of the Lord are true and all his **works** are dependable.
	77.14	You are the God who **works** miracles;
	104.23	people go out to do their **work**
	104.23	and keep **working** until evening.
	107.12	They were worn out from hard **work;**
	109.11	property, and may strangers get everything he **worked** for.
	127. 1	not build the house, the **work** of the builders is useless;
	127. 2	It is useless to **work** so hard for a living, getting up
	128. 2	Your **work** will provide for your needs;
	138. 8	Complete the **work** that you have begun.
	139. 3	You see me, whether I am **working** or resting;
Prov	5.10	and what you have **worked** for will belong to someone else.
	8.22	created me first of all, the first of his **works,** long ago.
	10. 4	lazy will make you poor, but hard **work** will make you rich.
	10.10	but one who openly criticizes **works** for peace.
	10.22	Hard **work** can make you no richer.
	12. 9	to be an ordinary man **working** for a living than to play
	12.11	A **hard-working** farmer has plenty to eat, but it is
	12.20	surprise, but those who **work** for good will find happiness.
	12.24	Hard **work** will give you power;
	12.27	are after, but if you **work** hard, you will get a fortune.
	14.22	earn the trust and respect of others if you **work** for good;
	14.22	if you **work** for evil, you are making a mistake.
	14.23	**Work** and you will earn a living;
	16.26	A labourer's appetite makes him **work** harder, because he
	17. 8	Some people think a bribe **works** like magic;
	21.25	A lazy man who refuses to **work** is only killing himself;
	28.19	A **hard-working** farmer has plenty to eat.
	31.18	of everything she makes, and **works** late into the night.
Ecc	1. 3	You spend your life **working,** labouring, and what do you
	2.10	proud of everything I had **worked** for, and all this was my
	2.11	and how hard I had **worked** doing it, and I realized that
	2.18	Nothing that I had **worked** for and earned meant a thing
	2.19	will own everything I have **worked** for, everything my wisdom
	2.20	So I came to regret that I had **worked** so hard.
	2.21	You **work** for something with all your wisdom, knowledge,
	2.21	leave it all to someone who hasn't had to **work** for it.
	2.22	You **work** and worry your way through life, and what do
	2.26	him, but he makes sinners **work,** earning and saving, so that
	3. 9	What do we gain from all our **work?**
	3.13	us should eat and drink and enjoy what we have **worked** for.
	3.22	thing we can do is to enjoy what we have **worked** for.
	4. 4	I have also learnt why people **work** so hard to succeed:
	4. 8	brother, yet he is always **working,** never satisfied with the
	4. 8	For whom is he **working** so hard and denying himself any pleasure?
	4. 9	than one, because together they can **work** more effectively.
	5. 6	Why let him destroy what you have **worked** for?
	5. 7	you dream, how much useless **work** you do, or how much you
	5.12	A **working** man may or may not have enough to eat, but
	5.15	In spite of all our **work** there is nothing we can take
	5.18	and enjoy what he has **worked** for during the short life that
	5.19	he should be grateful and enjoy what he has **worked** for.
	6. 7	A man does all his **work** just to get something to eat,
	9.10	**Work** hard at whatever you do, because there will be no action,
	10. 9	If you **work** in a stone quarry, you get hurt by stones.
	10.10	you don't sharpen it, you have to **work** harder to use it.
	10.15	to find his way home would wear himself out with **work.**
Song	1. 6	were angry with me and made me **work** in the vineyard.
	7. 1	The curve of your thighs is like the **work** of an artist.
Is	3.10	They will be able to enjoy what they have **worked** for.
	7. 3	road where the cloth makers **work,** at the end of the ditch
	14. 3	suffering, and from the hard **work** they were forced to do.
	22.25	the peg that was firmly fastened will **work** loose and fall.
	28.21	He will complete his **work,** his mysterious work.
	28.26	He knows how to do his **work,** because God has taught him.
	36. 2	the road where the clothmakers **work,** by the ditch that
	44.12	takes a piece of metal and **works** with it over a fire.
	44.12	As he **works,** he gets hungry, thirsty, and tired.
	49. 4	I said, "I have **worked,** but how hopeless it is!
	58.13	it by not travelling, **working,** or talking idly on that day,
	65.21	They will fully enjoy the things that they have **worked** for.
	65.23	The **work** they do will be successful, and their children
Jer	3.24	that our ancestors have **worked** for since ancient times.
	10. 9	Spain and with gold from Uphaz, all the **work** of artists;
	12.13	they have **worked** hard, but got nothing for it.
	14.18	and priests carry on their **work,** but they don't know what
	17.22	They must not **work** on the Sabbath;
	17.24	as a sacred day and must not do any **work** at all.
	18. 3	So I went there and saw the potter **working** at his wheel.
	22.13	who makes his countrymen **work** for nothing and does not pay
	25.29	I will begin my **work** of destruction in my own city.
	29. 7	**Work** for the good of the cities where I have made you
	38. 7	the Sudanese, a eunuch who **worked** in the royal palace, heard
	47. 7	how can it rest, when I have given it **work** to do?
	48.10	man who does not do the Lord's **work** with all his heart!
	50.25	the Sovereign Lord Almighty, have **work** to do in Babylonia.
	51.58	The **work** of the nations is all for nothing;
	52.16	and he put them to **work** in the vineyards and fields.
Ezek	9. 7	Get to **work!"**
	23.29	everything you have **worked** for and leave you stripped naked,
	27.34	Your goods and all who **worked** for you Have vanished with you
	29.20	for his services, because his army was **working** for me.
	44.11	of the gates and by performing the **work** of the Temple.
	44.14	assigning to them the menial **work** that is to be done in
	45. 5	possession of the Levites, who do the **work** in the Temple.
	46. 1	kept closed during the six **working** days, but it is to be
Dan	6. 3	that he could do better **work** than the other supervisors or
	8.27	and went back to the **work** that the king had assigned to

Hos 10.11 on her beautiful neck and to harness her for harder **work.**
12.12 to get a wife, he **worked** for another man and took care
Amos 7.15 Lord took me from my **work** as a shepherd and ordered me
Mic 7.15 **Work** miracles for us, Lord, as you did in the days when
Hag 1. 6 And the **working** man cannot earn enough to live on.
1. 9 while every one of you is busy **working** on his own house.
1.14 The Lord inspired everyone to **work** on the Temple:
1.14 They began **working** on the Temple of the Lord Almighty, their
2. 4 Do the **work,** for I am with you.
Zech 6.13 throne, and they will **work** together in peace and harmony.'
13. 7 "Wake up, sword, and attack the shepherd who **works** for me!
Mt 5. 9 "Happy are those who **work** for peace;
6.28 they do not **work** or make clothes for themselves.
10.23 you will not finish your **work** in all the towns of Israel
20. 1 in the morning to hire some men to **work** in his vineyard.
20. 2 silver coin a day, and sent them to **work** in his vineyard.
20. 4 them, 'You also go and **work** in the vineyard, and I will
20. 7 then, you also go and **work** in the vineyard,' he told them.
20. 9 men who had begun to **work** at five o'clock were paid a
20.12 men who were hired last **worked** only one hour,' they said,
20.12 up with a whole day's **work** in the hot sun—yet you
20.13 all, you agreed to do a day's **work** for one silver coin.
21.28 one and said, 'Son, go and **work** in the vineyard today.'
24.40 At that time two men will be **working** in a field:
Mk 13.34 to each one his own **work** to do and after telling the
16.20 preached everywhere, and the Lord **worked** with them and
Lk 1. 8 day Zechariah was doing his **work** as a priest in the Temple,
3.23 When Jesus began his **work,** he was about thirty years old.
5. 5 "Master," Simon answered, "we **worked** hard all night long and caught nothing.
10.40 was upset over all the **work** she had to do, so she
10.40 my sister has left me to do all the **work** by myself?
12.27 they don't **work** or make clothes for themselves.
13.14 to the people, "There are six days in which we should **work;**
13.32 and tomorrow, and on the third day I shall finish my **work.'**
14.28 he sits down first and **works** out what it will cost, to
15.15 So he went to **work** for one of the citizens of that
15.29 all these years I have **worked** for you like a slave, and
Jn 3.19 This is how the judgement **works:**
4.34 sent me and to finish the **work** he gave me to do.
4.38 to reap a harvest in a field where you did not **work;**
4.38 others **worked** there,
4.38 and you profit from their **work."**
5.17 "My Father is always **working,**
5.17 and I too must **work."**
6.27 Do not **work** for food that goes bad;
6.27 instead, **work** for the food that lasts for eternal life.
9. 3 blind so that God's power might be seen at **work** in him.
9. 4 we must keep on doing the **work** of him who sent me;
9. 4 night is coming when no one can **work.**
14.10 The Father, who remains in me, does his own **work.**
17. 4 I have finished the **work** you gave me to do.
Acts 1. 1 the time he began his **work** [2] until the day he was taken
1.17 for he had been chosen to have a part in our **work."**
6. 4 give our full time to prayer and the **work** of preaching."
8.21 part or share in our **work,** because your heart is not right
10. 4 pleased with your prayers and **works** of charity, and is ready
10.31 your prayer and has taken notice of your **works** of charity.
13. 2 and Saul, to do the **work** to which I have called them."
13. 5 They had John Mark with them to help in the **work.**
13.24 Before Jesus began his **work,** John preached to all the
14.26 care of God's grace for the **work** they had now completed.
17.25 that we can supply by **working** for him, since it is he
18. 3 see them, [3] and stayed and **worked** with them, because he
19.25 all together with others whose **work** was like theirs and said
19.25 "Men, you know that our prosperity comes from this **work.**
20.19 many tears I did my **work** as the Lord's servant during the
20.24 my mission and finish the **work** that the Lord Jesus gave me
20.34 yourselves know that I have **worked** with these hands of mine
20.35 in all things that by **working** hard in this way we must
21.19 that God had done among the Gentiles through his **work.**
Rom 2.29 circumcised, and this is the **work** of God's Spirit, not of
4. 4 A person who **works** is paid his wages, but they are not
7. 5 by the Law were at **work** in our bodies, and all we
7.21 So I find that this law is at **work:**
7.23 see a different law at **work** in my body—a law that
7.23 to the law of sin which is at **work** in my body.
8.28 that in all things God **works** for good with those who love
11.13 an apostle to the Gentiles, I will take pride in my **work.**
12. 8 whoever has authority should **work** hard;
12.11 **Work** hard and do not be lazy.
13. 4 because he is God's servant **working** for your own good.
13. 6 taxes, because the authorities are **working** for God when they
15.16 of being a servant of Christ Jesus to **work** for the Gentiles.
15.23 that I have finished my **work** in these regions and since I
16. 6 Greetings to Mary, who has **worked** so hard for you.
16.12 to Tryphaena and Tryphosa, who **work** in the Lord's service,
16.12 dear friend Persis, who has done so much **work** for the Lord.
1 Cor 3. 5 one of us does the **work** which the Lord gave him to
3. 8 God will reward each one according to the **work** he has done.
3. 9 For we are partners **working** together for God, and you are
3.10 gave me, I did the **work** of an expert builder and laid
3.13 the quality of each person's **work** will be seen when the Day
3.13 For on that Day fire will reveal everyone's **work;**
3.15 But if anyone's **work** is burnt up, then he will lose it;
4.12 we wear ourselves out with hard **work.**
7.32 concerns himself with the Lord's **work,** because he is trying
7.34 concerns herself with the Lord's **work,** because she wants to
9. 1 And aren't you the result of my **work** for the Lord?
9. 4 I the right to be given food and drink for my **work?**
9. 6 and I the only ones who have to **work** for our living?
1 Cor 9.10 who reaps should do their **work** in the hope of getting a
9.13 know that the men who **work** in the Temple get their food
9.17 If I did my **work** as a matter of free choice, then
9.18 it, without claiming my rights in my **work** for the gospel.
9.20 While **working** with the Jews, I live like a Jew in order
9.20 as though I were when **working** with those who are, in order
9.21 In the same way, when **working** with Gentiles, I live like
12.10 The Spirit gives one person the power to **work** miracles;
12.29 everyone has the power to **work** miracles [30] or to heal
15.10 On the contrary, I have **worked** harder than any of the other
15.10 not really my own doing, but God's grace **working** with me.
15.58 Keep busy always in your **work** for the Lord, since you know
16. 9 and worthwhile **work,** even though there are many opponents.
16.10 among you, because he is **working** for the Lord, just as I
16.14 Do all your **work** in love.
16.16 these, and of anyone else who **works** and serves with them.
2 Cor 1.24 Instead, we are **working** with you for your own happiness.
2.12 found that the Lord had opened the way for the **work** there.
3. 5 allows us to claim that we are capable of doing this **work.**
4. 1 mercy has given us this **work** to do, and so we are
4.12 means that death is at **work** in us,
4.12 but life is at **work** in you.
6. 1 In our **work** together with God, then, we beg you who have
6. 3 to find fault with our **work,** so we try not to put
6. 5 we have been **overworked** and have gone without sleep or food.
6.14 Do not try to **work** together as equals with unbelievers,
8. 6 urged Titus, who began this **work,** to continue it and help
8.18 in all the churches for his **work** in preaching the gospel.
8.23 Titus, he is my partner and **works** with me to help you;
10.13 within the limits of the **work** which God has set for us,
10.13 and this includes our **work** among you.
10.15 do not boast about the **work** that others have done beyond the
10.15 to do a much greater **work** among you, always within the
10.16 to boast about **work** already done in another man's field.
11. 8 While I was **working** among you, I was paid by other churches.
11.12 boasting and saying that they **work** in the same way that we
11.13 apostles, who lie about their **work** and disguise themselves
11.23 I have **worked** much harder, I have been in prison more times,
11.27 There has been **work** and toil;
Gal 2. 2 I did not want my **work** in the past or in the
2. 9 that Barnabas and I would **work** among the Gentiles and they
3. 5 give you the Spirit and **work** miracles among you because you
4.11 it be that all my **work** for you has been for nothing?
5. 5 for by the power of God's Spirit **working** through our faith.
5. 6 what matters is faith that **works** through love.
Eph 1.19 how very great is his power at **work** in us who believe.
1.19 This power **working** in us is the same as the mighty strength
3. 2 his grace has given me this **work** to do for your good.
3. 7 gift, which he gave me through the **working** of his power.
3.20 by means of his power **working** in us is able to do
4. 6 who is Lord of all, **works** through all, and is in all.
4.12 all God's people for the **work** of Christian service, in order
4.16 So when each separate part **works** as it should, the whole
4.28 must stop robbing and start **working,** in order to earn an
6. 7 Do your **work** as slaves cheerfully, as though you served the Lord,
6. 8 everyone, whether slave or free, for the good **work** he does.
6.21 faithful servant in the Lord's **work,** will give you all the
Phil 1. 5 have helped me in the **work** of the gospel from the very
1. 6 God, who began this good **work** in you, will carry it on
1.16 know that God has given me the **work** of defending the gospel.
1.22 I can do more worthwhile **work,** then I am not sure which
2.12 Keep on **working** with fear and trembling to complete your salvation,
2.13 because God is always at **work** in you to make you willing
2.16 will show that all my effort and **work** have not been wasted.
2.22 son and his father, have **worked** together for the sake of the
2.25 our brother Epaphroditus, who has **worked** and fought by my
2.30 for the sake of the **work** of Christ, in order to give
4. 3 for they have **worked** hard with me to spread the gospel,
Col 1.29 strength which Christ supplies and which is at **work** in me.
2. 1 you how hard I have **worked** for you and for the people
3. 5 earthly desires at **work** in you, such as sexual immorality,
3.23 Whatever you do, **work** at it with all your heart,
3.23 as though you were **working** for the Lord
4. 7 and fellow-servant in the Lord's **work,** will give you all the
4.11 the only Jewish believers who **work** with me for the Kingdom
4.13 personally testify to his hard **work** for you and for the
1 Thes 1. 3 how your love made you **work** so hard, and how your hope
2. 9 Surely you remember, our brothers, how we **worked** and toiled!
2. 9 We **worked** day and night so that we would not be any
2.13 For God is at **work** in you who believe.
3. 2 sent Timothy, our brother who **works** with us for God in
3. 5 Devil had tempted you and all our **work** had been for nothing!
5.12 proper respect to those who **work** among you, who guide and
5.13 the greatest respect and love because of the **work** they do.
2 Thes 1.11 your desire for goodness and complete your **work** of faith.
2. 7 Mysterious Wickedness is already at **work,** but what is going
2.11 the power of error to **work** in them so that they believe
3. 8 Instead, we **worked** and toiled;
3. 8 we kept **working** day and night so as not to be an
3.10 to you, "Whoever refuses to **work** is not allowed to eat."
3.12 to lead orderly lives and **work** to earn their own living.
1 Tim 1.12 Christ Jesus our Lord, who has given me strength for my **work.**
3. 1 eager to be a church leader, he desires an excellent **work.**
3.13 Those helpers who do their **work** well win for themselves
4.10 We struggle and **work** hard, because we have placed our
5.17 The elders who do good **work** as leaders should be
5.17 especially those who **work** hard at preaching and teaching.
6. 2 who benefit from their **work** are believers whom they love.
6.18 to be rich in good **works,** to be generous and ready to
2 Tim 2. 6 who has done the hard **work** should have the first share of

2 Tim 2.15 is not ashamed of his **work,** one who correctly teaches the
4. 5 suffering, do the **work** of a preacher of the Good News,
4.11 bring him with you, because he can help me in the **work.**
Tit 1. 7 leader is in charge of God's **work,** he should be blameless.
Heb 3. 2 chose him to do this **work,**
3. 2 just as Moses was faithful in his **work** in God's house.
4. 3 said this even though his **work** had been finished from the
4. 4 "God rested on the seventh day from all his **work."**
4.10 will rest from his own **work,** just as God rested from his.
6. 1 of turning away from useless **works** and believing in God;
6.10 He will not forget the **work** you did or the love you
7.11 Now, if the **work** of the levitical priests had been perfect,
7.23 because they died and could not continue their **work.**
7.24 on for ever, and his **work** as priest does not pass on
8. 5 The **work** they do as priests is really only a copy and
8. 6 Jesus has been given priestly **work** which is superior to theirs,
13.17 If you obey them, they will do their **work** gladly;
Jas 2.22 His faith and his actions **worked** together;
5. 4 not paid any wages to the men who **work** in your fields.
1 Pet 1.12 prophets that their **work** was not for their own benefit,
5. 2 Do your **work,** not for mere pay, but from a real desire
2 Jn 8 not lose what we have **worked** for, but will receive your
3 Jn 5 so faithful in the **work** you do for your fellow-Christians,
8 people, so that we may share in their **work** for the truth.
Rev 2. 2 know how hard you have **worked** and how patient you have been.
13.18 Whoever is intelligent can **work** out the meaning of the
14.13 enjoy rest from their hard **work,** because the results of

WORKER
[FELLOW-WORKER]

Ex 12.45 No temporary resident or hired **worker** may eat it.
Ruth 2. 2 fields to gather the corn that the harvest **workers** leave.
2. 3 fields and walked behind the **workers,** picking up the corn
2. 4 later Boaz himself arrived from Bethlehem and greeted the **workers.**
2. 7 me to let her follow the **workers** and pick up the corn.
2.14 So she sat with the **workers,** and Boaz passed some roasted
2.15 up corn, Boaz ordered the **workers,** "Let her pick it up even
2.21 up corn with his **workers** until they finish the harvest."
2 Kgs 4.18 his father, who was in the field with the harvest **workers.**
24.16 and one thousand skilled **workers,** including the blacksmiths,
Neh 13.13 in distributing the supplies to their **fellow-workers.**
Job 7. 2 like a **worker** waiting for his pay.
Prov 13. 4 A hard **worker** will get everything he wants.
31.17 She is a hard **worker,** strong and industrious.
Is 58. 3 you pursue your own interests and oppress your **workers.**
Jer 24. 1 leaders of Judah, the craftsmen, and the skilled **workers.)**
Mt 9.37 harvest is large, but there are few **workers** to gather it in.
9.38 that he will send out **workers** to gather in his harvest."
10.10 A **worker** should be given what he needs.
13.30 I will tell the harvest **workers** to pull up the weeds first,
13.39 is the end of the age, and the harvest **workers** are angels.
20. 8 his foreman, 'Call the **workers** and pay them their wages,
Lk 10. 2 "There is a large harvest, but few **workers** to gather it in.
10. 2 that he will send out **workers** to gather in his harvest.
10. 7 they offer you, for a **worker** should be given his pay.
15.17 'All my father's hired **workers** have more than they can eat,
15.19 treat me as one of your hired **workers.'**
Acts 19.24 his business brought a great deal of profit to the **workers.**
19.38 If Demetrius and his **workers** have an accusation against anyone,
Rom 16. 3 Priscilla and Aquila, my **fellow-workers** in the service of Christ Jesus;
16. 9 Greetings also to Urbanus, our **fellow-worker** in Christ's service, and to Stachys,
16.13 to Rufus, that outstanding **worker** in the Lord's service,
16.21 Timothy, my **fellow-worker,** sends you his greetings;
Phil 4. 3 Clement and all my other **fellow-workers,** whose names are in
Col 1. 7 Epaphras, our dear fellow-servant, who is Christ's faithful **worker** on our behalf.
4. 7 Tychicus, who is a faithful **worker** and fellow-servant in the Lord's work,
1 Tim 5.18 to thresh corn" and "A **worker** should be given his pay."
2 Tim 2.15 in God's sight, as a **worker** who is not ashamed of his
Phlm 1 To our friend and **fellow-worker** Philemon, [2]and the church
24 his greetings, [24]and so do my **fellow-workers** Mark,

WORKMAN

Ex 35.10 "All the skilled **workmen** among you are to come and make
Judg 5.26 a tent peg in one hand, a **workman's** hammer in the other;
1 Kgs 5.18 Solomon's and Hiram's **workmen** and men from the city of
2 Kgs 12.14 all used to pay the **workmen** and to buy the materials used
24.14 deported all the skilled **workmen,** including the blacksmiths,
25.11 the city, the remaining skilled **workmen,** and those who had
1 Chr 4.14 Valley of Craftsmen, where all the people were skilled **workmen.**
9. 2 Israelite laymen, priests, Levites, and temple **workmen.**
22.15 You have many **workmen.**
28.21 **Workmen** with every kind of skill are eager to help you, and
2 Chr 2.10 As provisions for your **workmen,** I will send you two
3. 7 On the walls the **workmen** carved designs of winged creatures.
3.10 The king also ordered his **workmen** to make two winged
34.12 All the **workmen** worked hard, and they restored the
34.13 materials and supervising the **workmen** on various jobs,
34.17 Temple and handed it over to the **workmen** and their supervisors."
Ezra 2.43 Clans of temple **workmen** who returned from exile:
2.58 of descendants of the temple **workmen** and of Solomon's
2.70 guards, and the temple **workmen** settled in nearby towns;
7. 6 Levites, temple musicians, temple guards, and **workmen.**
7.24 the priests, Levites, musicians, guards, **workmen,** or anyone
8.17 and his associates, the temple **workmen,** to send us people to
Ezra 8.20 addition there were 220 temple **workmen** whose ancestors had
Neh 3.25 of the city called Ophel, where the temple **workmen** lived.)
3.31 building used by the temple **workmen** and the merchants, which
7.46 Clans of temple **workmen** who returned from exile:
7.60 of descendants of the temple **workmen** and of Solomon's
7.73 the ordinary people, the temple **workmen**—all the people of
10.28 the temple musicians, the temple **workmen,** and all others who
11. 3 priests, the Levites, the temple **workmen,** and the
11.21 The temple **workmen** lived in the part of Jerusalem called
Job 3.17 men stop their evil, and tired **workmen** find rest at last.
Is 19.10 weavers and skilled **workmen** will be broken and depressed.
40.19 not like an idol that **workmen** make, that metalworkers cover
Jer 29. 2 and the skilled **workmen** had been taken into exile.
52.15 the city, the remaining skilled **workmen,** and those who had
Zech 1.20 Then the Lord showed me four **workmen** with hammers.
Rev 18.22 No **workman** in any trade will ever be found in you again;

WORLD
[THIS WORLD]
see also **WORLD ABOVE, WORLD OF THE DEAD, WORLDLY**

Gen 6. 1 had spread all over the **world,** and girls were being born,
6.12 God looked at the **world** and saw that it was evil, for
6.13 because the **world** is full of their violent deeds.
7. 1 the only one in all the **world** who does what is right.
8.22 As long as the **world** exists, there will be a time for
9.13 It will be the sign of my covenant with the **world.**
10. 8 named Nimrod, who became the **world's** first great conqueror.
10.25 during his time the people of the **world** were divided;
11. 1 the people of the whole **world** had only one language and used
19.31 no men in the whole **world** to marry us so that we
41.57 Egypt from all over the **world** to buy corn from Joseph,
42. 6 Egypt, was selling corn to people from all over the **world.**
Ex 9.14 know that there is no one like me in all the **world.**
9.16 you live so that my fame might spread over the whole **world.**
Deut 7.14 No people in the **world** will be as richly blessed as you.
29.24 Then the whole **world** will ask, 'Why did the Lord do this
1 Sam 2. 8 on them he has built the **world.**
2.10 The Lord will judge the whole **world;**
17.46 Then the whole **world** will know that Israel has a God,
2 Sam 7. 9 make you as famous as the greatest leaders in the **world.**
7.23 you did for them have spread your fame throughout the **world.**
1 Kgs 4.34 Kings all over the **world** heard of his wisdom and sent
8.43 all the peoples of the **world** may know you and obey you,
8.60 all the nations of the **world** will know that the Lord alone
10.24 other king, [24]and the whole **world** wanted to come and
18.10 has made a search for you in every country in the **world.**
2 Kgs 19.15 you alone are God, ruling all the kingdoms of the **world.**
19.19 all the nations of the **world** will know that only you, O
1 Chr 1.10 named Nimrod, who became the **world's** first great conqueror.)
1.19 time the people of the **world** were divided, and the other was
16.14 his commands are for all the **world.**
16.23 Sing to the Lord, all the **world!**
17. 8 make you as famous as the greatest leaders in the **world.**
17.21 you did for them spread your fame throughout the **world.**
2 Chr 6.33 all the peoples of the **world** may know you and obey you,
9.22 Solomon was richer and wiser than any other king in the **world.**
16. 9 close watch over the whole **world,** to give strength to those
20. 6 you rule in heaven over all the nations of the **world.**
36.23 me ruler over the whole **world** and has given me the
Ezra 1. 2 me ruler over the whole **world** and has given me the
Job 9.24 God gave the **world** to the wicked.
11.15 Then face the **world** again, firm and courageous.
34.13 Did someone put him in charge of the **world?**
37.12 They do all that God commands, everywhere throughout the **world.**
38. 4 Were you there when I made the **world?**
38. 6 Who laid the corner-stone of the **world?**
38.18 Have you any idea how big the **world** is?
38.21 you're so old and were there when the **world** was made!
39. 3 they will crouch down and bring their young into the **world?**
41.11 No one in all the **world** can do it.
42.15 women in the whole **world** as beautiful as Job's daughters.
Ps 2.10 learn this lesson, you rulers of the **world:**
8. 1 O Lord, our Lord, your greatness is seen in all the **world!**
8. 9 O Lord, our Lord, your greatness is seen in all the **world!**
9. 8 He rules the **world** with righteousness;
19. 4 goes out to all the **world** and is heard to the ends
22.27 From every part of the **world** they will turn to him;
24. 1 The **world** and all that is in it belong to the Lord;
33. 8 Honour him, all peoples of the **world!**
33. 9 When he spoke, the **world** was created;
46. 9 He stops wars all over the **world;**
46.10 I am God, supreme among the nations, supreme over the **world."**
47. 2 he is a great king, ruling over all the **world.**
47. 7 God is king over all the **world;**
48. 2 the city of the great king brings joy to all the **world.**
50.12 you for food, for the **world** and everything in it is mine.
52. 5 he will remove you from the **world** of the living.
58.11 there is indeed a God who judges the **world."**
65. 5 People all over the **world** and across the distant seas trust
65. 8 The whole **world** stands in awe of the great things that you
67. 2 kindness, [2]so that the whole **world** may know your will;
68.32 to God, kingdoms of the **world,** sing praise to the Lord,
72.19 May his glory fill the whole **world.**
76. 8 the **world** was afraid and kept silent, [9]when you rose up
77.18 rolled out, and flashes of lightning lit up the **world;**
82. 5 completely corrupt, and justice has disappeared from the **world.**
82. 8 Come, O God, and rule the **world;**
89.11 you made the **world** and everything in it.
90. 2 or brought the **world** into being, you were eternally God,

Ps 96. 1 Sing to the Lord, all the **world!**
96.13 He will rule the peoples of the **world** with justice and fairness.
97. 4 His lightning lights up the **world;**
98. 9 He will rule the peoples of the **world** with justice and fairness.
100. 1 Sing to the Lord, all the **world!**
105. 7 his commands are for all the **world.**
116. 9 in the presence of the Lord in the **world** of the living.
119.72 gave means more to me than all the money in the **world.**
138. 4 All the kings in the **world** will praise you, Lord, because
Prov 8.23 the very beginning, at the first, before the **world** began.
8.31 happy with the **world** and pleased with the human race.
30.24 are four animals in the **world** that are small, but very, very
Ecc 1. 4 and generations go, but the **world** stays just the same.
1. 9 There is nothing new in the whole **world.**
1.13 and study all the things that are done in this **world.**
1.14 seen everything done in this **world,** and I tell you, it is
2.19 everything my wisdom has earned for me in this **world.**
3. 1 that happens in this **world** happens at the time God chooses.
3.16 also noticed that in this **world** you find wickedness where
4. 1 again at all the injustice that goes on in this **world.**
4. 3 have never seen the injustice that goes on in this **world.**
4.15 people who live in this **world,** and I realized that somewhere
5.13 Here is a terrible thing that I have seen in this **world:**
5.15 We leave this **world** just as we entered it—with nothing.
6. 1 I have noticed that in this **world** a serious injustice is done.
6.12 anyone know what will happen in the **world** after he dies?
8. 9 done in this world, a **world** where some men have power and
8.14 Look at what happens in the **world:**
8.15 during the life that God has given him in this **world.**
8.16 what goes on in the **world,** I realized that you could stay
9. 3 and this is as wrong as anything that happens in this **world.**
9. 4 who is alive in the **world** of the living has some hope;
9. 6 again take part in anything that happens in this **world.**
9. 9 live the useless life that God has given you in this **world.**
9.11 another thing, that in this **world** fast runners do not always
9.13 saw, a good example of how wisdom is regarded in this **world.**
10. 5 I have seen in the **world**—an injustice caused by rulers.
11. 2 kind of bad luck you are going to have in this **world.**
Is 6. 3 His glory fills the **world."**
10.14 The nations of the **world** were like a bird's nest, and I
12. 5 Let the whole **world** hear the news.
14. 7 Now at last the whole **world** enjoys rest and peace, and
14.17 man who destroyed cities and turned the **world** into a desert?
14.26 is my plan for the **world,** and my arm is stretched out
18. 2 smooth-skinned people, who are feared all over the **world.**
18. 7 smooth-skinned people, who are feared all over the **world.**
19.24 and these three nations will be a blessing to all the **world.**
23.17 she will hire herself out to all the kingdoms of the **world.**
24. 4 the whole **world** grows weak;
24.13 This is what will happen in every nation all over the **world.**
24.16 most distant parts of the **world** we will hear songs in praise
24.20 The **world** is weighed down by its sins;
25. 6 all the nations of the **world**—a banquet of the richest food
25. 8 the disgrace his people have suffered throughout the **world.**
37.16 you alone are God, ruling all the kingdoms of the **world.**
37.20 all the nations of the **world** will know that you alone are
38.11 I thought that in this **world** of the living I would never
40.21 Have you not heard how the **world** began?
40.28 he created all the **world.**
42.10 sing his praise, all the **world!**
43. 6 return from distant lands, from every part of the **world.**
45. 6 from one end of the **world** to the other may know that
45.22 "Turn to me now and be saved, people all over the **world!**
49. 6 to the nations— so that all the **world** may be saved."
52.10 he will save his people, and all the **world** will see it.
54. 5 will save you— he is the ruler of all the **world.**
58.14 you honoured all over the **world,** and you will enjoy the land
62. 7 Jerusalem And makes it a city the whole **world** praises.
66.16 all the people of the **world** whom he finds guilty—and many
Jer 3.19 delightful land, the most beautiful land in all the **world.**
10.10 When you are angry, the **world** trembles;
10.12 by his wisdom he created the **world** and stretched out the heavens.
15. 4 all the people of the **world** horrified at them because of
15.10 Why did my mother bring me into the **world?**
24. 9 on them that all the nations of the **world** will be terrified.
26. 6 all the nations of the **world** will use the name of this
27. 5 and strength I created the **world,** mankind, and all the
29.18 all the nations of the **world** will be horrified at what they
33. 9 and every nation in the **world** will fear and tremble when
34.17 make every nation in the **world** horrified at what I do to
46. 8 Egypt said, 'I will rise and cover the **world;**
50.23 Babylonia hammered the whole **world** to pieces, and now
51. 7 like a gold cup in my hand, making the whole **world** drunk.
51.15 by his wisdom he created the **world** and stretched out the heavens.
51.25 mountain that destroys the whole **world,** but I, the Lord, am
51.41 "The city that the whole **world** praised has been captured!
51.49 of people all over the **world,** and now Babylonia will fall
Lam 1. 1 Once honoured by the **world,** she is now like a widow;
2.15 Is this the pride of the **world?"**
3.45 You have made us the refuse heap of the **world.**
Ezek 5. 5 the centre of the **world,** with other countries all round her.
20.23 I vowed that I would scatter them all over the **world.**
27.36 and merchants all over the **world** are terrified, afraid that
29.12 I will make Egypt the most desolate country in the **world.**
30. 7 the most desolate in the **world,** and its cities will be left
30.23 I am going to scatter the Egyptians throughout the **world.**
30.26 I will scatter the Egyptians throughout the **world.**
31. 6 The nations of the **world** rested in its shade.
32. 4 all the birds and animals of the **world** to feed on you.
32. 8 the lights of heaven and plunge your **world** into darkness.
35.14 desolate that the whole **world** will rejoice at your downfall,
Ezek 38.12 and property and live at the crossroads of the **world.**
Dan 4. 1 people of all nations, races, and languages in the **world:**
4.11 reached the sky and could be seen by everyone in the **world.**
4.12 loaded down with fruit—enough for the whole **world** to eat.
4.20 it reached the sky, could be seen by everyone in the **world.**
4.21 and it had enough fruit on it to feed the whole **world.**
4.22 reach the sky, and your power extends over the whole **world.**
4.26 again when you acknowledge that God rules all the **world.**
8.17 The vision has to do with the end of the **world."**
12. 4 and put a seal on it until the end of the **world.**
Amos 9. 5 The whole **world** rises and falls like the River Nile.
Mic 4.13 you will present to me, the Lord of the whole **world."**
Nah 1. 5 the **world** and all its people tremble.
Hab 1. 6 They are marching out across the **world** to conquer other lands.
2. 8 violence against the people of the **world** and its cities.
2.17 violence against the people of the **world** and its cities.
Zeph 2.15 Its people think that their city is the greatest in the **world.**
3.19 their shame to honour, and all the **world** will praise them.
3.20 throughout the **world** and make you prosperous once again."
Hag 2. 8 All the silver and gold of the **world** is mine.
Zech 1.11 have been all over the **world** and have found that
1.11 the whole **world** lies helpless and subdued."
1.19 answered, "They stand for the **world** powers that have
12. 3 All the nations of the **world** will join forces to attack her.
Mal 1.11 People from one end of the **world** to the other honour me.
Mt 4. 8 him all the kingdoms of the **world** in all their greatness.
5.14 "You are like light for the whole **world.**
10.34 not think that I have come to bring peace to the **world.**
13.35 I will tell them things unknown since the creation of the **world."**
13.38 the field is the **world;**
16.26 gain anything if he wins the whole **world** but loses his life?
17.25 Who pays duties or taxes to the kings of **this world?**
18. 7 How terrible for the **world** that there are things that make
24.14 preached through all the **world** for a witness to all mankind;
24.21 ever been, from the beginning of the **world** to this very day.
24.31 his chosen people from one end of the **world** to the other.
25.34 been prepared for you ever since the creation of the **world.**
26.13 is preached all over the **world,** what she has done will be
Mk 4.31 the smallest seed in the **world,** and plants it in the ground.
8.36 gain anything if he wins the whole **world** but loses his life?
9. 3 white—whiter than anyone in the **world** could wash them.
13.19 far worse than any the **world** has ever known from the very
13.19 beginning when God created the **world** until the present time.
13.27 God's chosen people from one end of the **world** to the other.
14. 9 is preached all over the **world,** what she has done will be
16.15 them, "Go throughout the whole **world** and preach the gospel
Lk 4. 5 and showed him in a second all the kingdoms of the **world.**
9.25 if he wins the whole **world** but is himself lost or defeated?
11.50 since the creation of the **world,** [51] from the murder of Abel
12.30 (For the pagans of **this world** are always concerned about
12.51 Do you suppose that I came to bring peace to the **world?**
16. 8 because the people of **this world** are much more shrewd
Jn 1. 1 Before the **world** was created, the Word already existed;
1. 9 light that comes into the **world** and shines on all mankind.
1.10 The Word was in the **world,**
1.10 and though God made the **world** through him,
1.10 yet the **world** did not recognize him.
1.29 the Lamb of God, who takes away the sin of the **world!**
3.12 believe me when I tell you about the things of **this world;**
3.16 For God loved the **world** so much that he gave his only
3.17 send his Son into the **world** to be its judge, but to
3.19 light has come into the **world,** but people love the darkness
4.42 and we know that he really is the Saviour of the **world."**
6.14 "Surely this is the Prophet who was to come into the **world!"**
6.33 he who comes down from heaven and gives life to the **world."**
6.51 is my flesh, which I give so that the **world** may live."
7. 4 doing these things, let the whole **world** know about you!"
7. 7 The **world** cannot hate you, but it hates me, because I keep
8.12 "I am the light of the **world,"** he said.
8.23 Jesus answered, "You belong to **this world** here below,
8.23 You are from **this world,** but I am not from this world.
8.26 truthful, and I tell the **world** only what I have heard from
9. 5 I am in the world, I am the light for the **world."**
9.32 Since the beginning of the **world** nobody has ever heard
9.39 Jesus said, "I came to **this world** to judge,
10.36 for me, the Father chose me and sent me into the **world.**
11. 9 does not stumble, for he sees the light of **this world.**
11.27 Messiah, the Son of God, who was to come into the **world."**
12.19 Look, the whole **world** is following him!"
12.25 hates his own life in **this world** will keep it for life
12.31 Now is the time for **this world** to be judged;
12.31 now the ruler of **this world** will be overthrown.
12.46 I have come into the **world** as light, so that everyone
12.47 I came, not to judge the **world,** but to save it.
13. 1 come for him to leave **this world** and go to the Father.
13. 1 always loved those in the **world** who were his own, and he
14.17 The **world** cannot receive him, because it cannot see him or
14.19 In a little while the **world** will see me no more, but
14.22 that you will reveal yourself to us and not to the **world?"**
14.27 I do not give it as the **world** does.
14.30 you much longer, because the ruler of **this world** is coming.
14.31 power over me, [31] but the **world** must know that I love the
15.18 "If the **world** hates you, just remember that it has
15.19 If you belonged to the **world,**
15.19 then the **world** would love you as its own.
15.19 But I chose you from **this world,** and you do not belong
15.19 that is why the **world** hates you.
16. 8 to the people of the **world** that they are wrong about sin
16.11 because the ruler of **this world** has already been judged.
16.20 you will cry and weep, but the **world** will be glad;
16.21 she is happy that a baby has been born into the **world.**

Jn 16.28 I did come from the Father, and I came into the **world;**
16.28 and now I am leaving the **world** and going to the Father."
16.33 The **world** will make you suffer.
16.33 I have defeated the **world!"**
17. 5 the same glory I had with you before the **world** was made.
17. 6 made you known to those you gave me out of the **world.**
17. 9 do not pray for the **world** but for those you gave me,
17.11 am no longer in the **world,** but they are in the world.
17.13 say these things in the **world** so that they might have my
17.14 them your message, and the **world** hated them, because they
17.14 do not belong to the **world,**
17.14 just as I do not belong to the **world.**
17.15 take them out of the **world,** but I do ask you to
17.16 not belong to the world, they do not belong to the **world.**
17.18 them into the world, just as you sent me into the **world.**
17.21 be one, so that the **world** will believe that you sent me.
17.23 one, in order that the **world** may know that you sent me
17.24 for you loved me before the **world** was made.
17.25 The **world** does not know you, but I know you, and these
18.36 Jesus said, "My kingdom does not belong to **this world;**
18.36 if my kingdom belonged to **this world,** my followers would fight
18.37 born and came into the **world** for this one purpose, to speak
21.25 I suppose that the whole **world** could not hold the books that
Acts 2. 5 Jerusalem, religious men who had come from every country in the **world.**
4.12 in all the **world** there is no one else whom God has
13.47 for the Gentiles, so that all the **world** may be saved.' "
17.24 God, who made the **world** and everything in it, is Lord of
17.31 he will judge the whole **world** with justice by means of a
19.27 worshipped by everyone in Asia and in all the **world!"**
24. 5 the Jews all over the **world** and is a leader of the
Rom 1. 8 of you, because the whole **world** is hearing about your faith.
1.20 Ever since God created the **world,** his invisible qualities,
3. 6 If God is not just, how can he judge the **world?**
3.19 excuses and bring the whole **world** under God's judgement.
4.13 and his descendants that the **world** would belong to him, he
5.12 Sin came into the **world** through one man, and his sin
5.13 There was sin in the **world** before the Law was given;
9.17 show my power and to spread my fame over the whole **world."**
9.28 for the Lord will quickly settle his full account with the **world."**
10.18 "The sound of their voice went out to all the **world;**
11.12 brought rich blessings to the **world,** and their spiritual
12. 2 to the standards of **this world,** but let God transform you
1 Cor 1.20 or the skilful debaters of **this world?**
1.20 God has shown that **this world's** wisdom is foolishness!
1.27 God purposely chose what the **world** considers nonsense in
1.27 and he chose what the **world** considers weak in order to shame
1.28 He chose what the **world** looks down on and despises, and
1.28 in order to destroy what the **world** thinks is important.
2. 6 the wisdom that belongs to **this world**
2. 6 powers that rule **this world**—powers that are losing
2. 7 already chosen for our glory even before the **world** was made.
2. 8 None of the rulers of **this world** knew this wisdom.
2.12 We have not received **this world's** spirit;
3. 1 as though you belonged to **this world,** as children
3. 3 because you still live as the people of **this world** live.
3. 3 prove that you belong to **this world,** living by its standards?
3.18 that he is wise by **this world's** standards, he should become
3.19 For what **this world** considers to be wisdom is nonsense
3.22 **this world,** life and death, the present and the future—
4. 9 as a spectacle for the whole **world** of angels and of mankind.
4.13 We are no more than **this world's** refuse;
5.10 them you would have to get out of the **world** completely.
6. 2 Don't you know that God's people will judge the **world?**
6. 2 you are to judge the **world,** aren't you capable of judging
7.31 For **this world,** as it is now, will not last much longer.
11.32 Lord, so that we shall not be condemned together with the **world.**
14.10 many different languages in the **world,** yet none of them is
15.19 we deserve more pity than anyone else in all the **world.**
2 Cor 1.12 us that our lives in **this world,** and especially our relations
4. 4 been kept in the dark by the evil god of **this world.**
10. 3 that we live in the **world,** but we do not fight from
10. 4 are not the **world's** weapons but God's powerful weapons,
Gal 3.22 says that the whole **world** is under the power of sin;
6.14 world is dead to me, and I am dead to the **world.**
Eph 1. 3 by giving us every spiritual blessing in the heavenly **world.**
1. 4 Even before the **world** was made, God had already chosen us
1.20 and seated him at his right side in the heavenly **world.**
1.21 to all titles of authority in **this world** and in the next.
2. 2 At that time you followed the **world's** evil way;
2. 6 us up with him to rule with him in the heavenly **world.**
2.12 you lived in **this world** without hope and without God.
3.10 and powers in the heavenly **world** might learn of his wisdom
6.12 spiritual forces in the heavenly **world,** the rulers,
Phil 2.15 children, who live in a **world** of corrupt and sinful people.
3.19 and they think only of things that belong to **this world.**
Col 1. 6 and is spreading throughout the **world,** just as it has among
1.23 gospel which has been preached to everybody in the **world.**
2.20 Why, then, do you live as though you belonged to **this world?**
1 Tim 1.15 Christ Jesus came into the **world** to save sinners.
3.16 in throughout the **world,** and was taken up to heaven.
6. 7 What did we bring into the **world?**
6. 7 What can we take out of the **world?**
2 Tim 4.10 in love with this present **world** and has deserted me, going
Tit 2.12 upright, and godly lives in **this world,** [13] as we wait for
Heb 1. 6 his first-born Son into the **world,** he said, "All God's
2. 5 rulers over the new **world to come**—
2. 5 the **world** of which we speak.
4. 3 work had been finished from the time he created the **world.**
9.11 tent, that is, it is not a part of this created **world.**
9.26 to suffer many times ever since the creation of the **world.**
Heb 10. 5 Christ was about to come into the **world,** he said to God:
11. 7 As a result, the **world** was condemned, and Noah received from
11.38 The **world** was not good enough for them!
Jas 1. 1 Greetings to all God's people scattered over the whole **world.**
1.27 and to keep oneself from being corrupted by the **world.**
2. 5 chose the poor people of **this world** to be rich in faith
3. 6 It is a **world** of wrong, occupying its place in our bodies
3.15 it belongs to the **world,** it is unspiritual and demonic.
4. 4 know that to be the **world's** friend means to be God's enemy?
4. 4 Whoever wants to be the **world's** friend makes himself God's enemy.
1 Pet 1.20 before the creation of the **world** and was revealed in these
2.11 to you, my friends, as strangers and refugees in **this world!**
5. 9 fellow-believers in all the **world** are going through the same
2 Pet 1. 4 lust that is in the **world,** and may come to share the
2. 5 did not spare the ancient **world,**
2. 5 but brought the flood on the **world** of godless people;
2.20 the corrupting forces of the **world**
3. 4 still the same as it was since the creation of the **world!"**
3. 6 the water of the flood, that the old **world** was destroyed.
1 Jn 2.15 Do not love the **world** or anything that belongs to the world.
2.15 If you love the **world,** you do not love the Father.
2.16 Everything that belongs to the **world**—what the sinful self desires,
2.16 and everything in **this world** that people are so proud
2.16 it all comes from the **world.**
2.17 The **world** and everything in it that people desire is passing away;
3. 1 This is why the **world** does not know us:
3.13 my brothers, if the people of the **world** hate you.
4. 3 it would come, and now it is here in the **world** already.
4. 4 powerful than the spirit in those who belong to the **world.**
4. 5 speak about matters of the **world,**
4. 5 and the **world** listens to them
4. 5 because they belong to the **world.**
4. 9 his only Son into the **world,** so that we might have life
4.14 the Father sent his Son to be the Saviour of the **world.**
4.17 because our life in **this world** is the same as Christ's.
5. 4 because every child of God is able to defeat the **world.**
5. 4 we win the victory over the **world** by means of our faith.
5. 5 Who can defeat the **world?**
5.19 God even though the whole **world** is under the rule of the
2 Jn 7 gone out all over the **world,** people who do not acknowledge
Rev 1. 5 and who is also the ruler of the kings of the **world.**
3.10 which is coming upon the **world** to test all the people
11.15 power to rule over the **world** belongs now to our Lord
12. 9 called the Devil, or Satan, that deceived the whole **world.**
13. 8 before the creation of the **world** in the book of the living
16.14 all the kings of the **world,** to bring them together for the
17. 2 the people of the **world** became drunk from drinking the wine
17. 5 Babylon, the mother of all the prostitutes and perverts in the **world."**
17. 8 before the creation of the **world** in the book of the living,
18. 3 businessmen of the **world** grew rich from her unrestrained lust."
18.23 most powerful in all the **world,** and with your false magic
18.23 you deceived all the peoples of the **world!"**
20. 8 nations scattered over the whole **world,** that is, Gog and Magog.
21.24 The peoples of the **world** will walk by its light,

WORLD ABOVE
[HEAVENLY WORLD]

Rom 8.39 neither the **world above** nor the world below—
Eph 1. 3 by giving us every spiritual blessing in the **heavenly world.**
1.20 and seated him at his right side in the **heavenly world.**
2. 6 us up with him to rule with him in the **heavenly world.**
3.10 rulers and powers in the **heavenly world** might learn of his
6.12 wicked spiritual forces in the **heavenly world,** the rulers,

WORLD BELOW see WORLD OF THE DEAD

WORLD OF THE DEAD
[UNDERGROUND WORLD]
see also **HADES**

Gen 37.35 go down to the **world of the dead** still mourning for my
Num 16.30 down alive to the **world of the dead,** you will know that
16.33 down alive to the **world of the dead,** with their possessions.
Deut 32.22 It will reach to the **world below** and consume the roots of
1 Sam 2. 6 sends people to the **world of the dead** and brings them back
Job 11. 8 God knows the **world of the dead,** but you do not know
14.13 I wish you would hide me in the **world of the dead;**
17.13 only hope is the **world of the dead,** where I will lie
17.16 with me when I go down to the **world of the dead.**
26. 6 The **world of the dead** lies open to God;
33.22 he is about to go to the **world of the dead.**
33.24 He is not to go down to the **world of the dead.**
33.28 from going to the **world of the dead,** and I am still
36.12 ignorance and cross the stream into the **world of the dead.**
38.17 shown you the gates that guard the dark **world of the dead?**
40.13 bind them in the **world of the dead.**
Ps 6. 5 In the **world of the dead** you are not remembered;
16.10 and you will not abandon me to the **world of the dead.**
28. 1 be among those who go down to the **world of the dead.**
31.17 may they go silently down to the **world of the dead.**
49.14 decay in the **world of the dead** far from their homes.
55.15 may they go down alive into the **world of the dead!**
63. 9 to kill me will go down into the **world of the dead.**
139. 8 lay down in the **world of the dead,** you would be there.
143. 7 be among those who go down to the **world of the dead.**
Prov 2.18 To go there is to approach the **world of the dead.**
5. 5 She will take you down to the **world of the dead;**

Prov 7.27 house, you are on the way to the **world of the dead.**
9.18 have already entered are now deep in the **world of the dead.**
15.11 Not even the **world of the dead** can keep the Lord from
27.20 desires are like the **world of the dead**—there is always room
30.16 the **world of the dead,**
Ecc 9.10 no wisdom in the **world of the dead**—and that is where
Is 5.14 The **world of the dead** is hungry for them, and it opens
7.11 from deep in the **world of the dead** or from high up
14. 9 "The **world of the dead** is getting ready to welcome the
14.11 harps, but now here you are in the **world of the dead.**
14.15 brought down to the deepest part of the **world of the dead.**
28.15 death and reached an agreement with the **world of the dead.**
28.18 your agreement with the **world of the dead** will be cancelled.
38.10 was going to the **world of the dead,** Never to live out
38.18 No one in the **world of the dead** can praise you;
57. 9 send messengers far and wide, even to the **world of the dead.**
59.10 night, as if we were in the dark **world of the dead.**
Ezek 26.20 you down to the **world of the dead** to join the people
26.20 you stay in that **underground world** among eternal ruins,
31.14 to join those who go down to the **world of the dead."**
31.15 tree goes to the **world of the dead,** I will make the
31.16 it down to the **world of the dead,** the noise of its
31.16 who have gone to the **world below** will be pleased at its
31.17 with it to the **world of the dead** to join those that
31.18 go down to the **world of the dead** and join the ungodly
32.18 with the other powerful nations to the **world of the dead.**
32.19 go down to the **world of the dead** and lie there among
32.21 Egyptian side welcome the Egyptians to the **world of the dead.**
32.23 graves are in the deepest parts of the **world of the dead.**
32.24 and they went down, uncircumcised, to the **world of the dead.**
32.27 fully armed to the **world of the dead,** their swords placed
32.29 they lie in the **world of the dead** with the uncircumcised who
32.30 disgrace of those who go down to the **world of the dead.**
Hos 13.14 this people from the **world of the dead** or rescue them from
13.14 Bring on your destruction, **world of the dead!**
Amos 9. 2 way down to the **world of the dead,** I will catch them.
Jon 2. 2 From deep in the **world of the dead** I cried for help,
Acts 2.27 because you will not abandon me in the **world of the dead;**
2.31 he said, 'He was not abandoned in the **world of the dead;**
Rom 8.39 the world above nor the **world below**—there is nothing in all
10. 7 are you to ask, Who will go down into the **world below?"**
Phil 2.10 on earth, and in the **world below** will fall on their knees,
Rev 1.18 I have authority over death and the **world of the dead.**
5. 3 on earth or in the **world below** who could open the scroll
5.13 heaven, on earth, in the **world below,** and in the sea—
20.13 Death and the **world of the dead** also gave up the dead
20.14 Then death and the **world of the dead** were thrown into

WORLD-FAMOUS see FAMOUS

WORLDLY

Lk 16. 9 make friends for yourselves with **worldly** wealth,
16.11 not been faithful in handling **worldly** wealth, how can you be
1 Cor 3. 4 Paul," and another, "I follow Apollos"—aren't you acting like **worldly** people?
7.33 married man concerns himself with **worldly** matters,
7.34 married woman concerns herself with **worldly** matters,
2 Cor 10. 2 harshly with those who say that we act from **worldly** motives.
10. 3 live in the world, but we do not fight from **worldly** motives.
Tit 2.12 give up ungodly living and **worldly** passions,

WORM

Ex 16.20 morning it was full of **worms** and smelt rotten, and Moses was
16.24 it did not spoil or get **worms** in it.
Deut 28.39 or drink wine from them, because **worms** will eat the vines.
Job 7. 5 My body is full of **worms;**
17.14 grave my father, and the **worms** that eat me I will call
21.26 they all are covered with **worms.**
24.20 he is eaten by **worms** and destroyed like a fallen tree.
25. 6 Then what about man, that **worm,** that insect?
Ps 22. 6 I am a **worm,** despised and scorned by everyone!
Is 14.11 a bed of maggots and are covered with a blanket of **worms.'**
66.24 The **worms** that eat them will never die, and the fire that
Jon 4. 7 at God's command, a **worm** attacked the plant, and it died.
Mk 9.48 There 'the **worms** that eat them never die, and the fire
Acts 12.23 He was eaten by **worms** and died.

WORN-OUT see WEAR (2)

WORRY

Gen 21.12 said to Abraham, "Don't be **worried** about the boy and your
32. 7 Jacob was frightened and **worried.**
40. 7 He asked them, "Why do you look so **worried** today?"
41. 8 In the morning he was **worried,** so he sent for all the
43.23 The servant said, "Don't **worry.**
45.20 They are not to **worry** about leaving their possessions behind;
Judg 18. 6 The priest answered, "You have nothing to **worry** about.
Ruth 3.11 Now don't **worry,** Ruth.
1 Sam 9. 5 thinking about the donkeys and start **worrying** about us."
9.20 that were lost three days ago, don't **worry** about them;
10. 2 so that your father isn't **worried** any more about them but
25.35 brought him and said to her, "Go back home and don't **worry.**
1 Kgs 17.13 "Don't **worry,"** Elijah said to her.
20.43 The king went back home to Samaria, **worried** and depressed.
Neh 4.14 saw that the people were **worried,** so I said to them and
Job 5. 2 To **worry** yourself to death with resentment would be a foolish,
30.27 I am torn apart by **worry** and pain;
Ps 25.17 Relieve me of my **worries** and save me from all my troubles.
37. 1 Don't be **worried** on account of the wicked;
37. 7 don't be **worried** about those who prosper or those who
37. 8 Don't give in to **worry** or anger;
55. 2 I am worn out by my **worries.**
77. 4 I am so **worried** that I cannot speak.
94.19 Whenever I am anxious and **worried,** you comfort me and
112. 8 He is not **worried** or afraid;
Prov 3.25 You will not have to **worry** about sudden disasters, such
12.25 **Worry** can rob you of happiness, but kind words will
24.19 Don't let evil people **worry** you;
31.21 She doesn't **worry** when it snows, because her family has warm
Ecc 1.18 The wiser you are, the more **worries** you have;
2.22 You work and **worry** your way through life, and what do
2.23 everything you do brings nothing but **worry** and heartache.
5. 3 The more you **worry,** the more likely you are to have bad
5.12 A rich man, however, has so much that he stays awake **worrying.**
5.17 to live our lives in darkness and grief, **worried,** angry, and
5.20 be happy, he will not **worry** too much about how short life
11.10 Don't let anything **worry** you or cause you pain.
Is 32. 9 an easy life, free from **worries,** listen to what I am saying.
32.11 You have been living an easy life, free from **worries;**
32.18 be free from **worries,** and their homes peaceful and safe.
Jer 17. 8 it has no **worries** when there is no rain;
49.23 of Hamath and Arpad are **worried** and troubled because they
Dan 2. 1 It **worried** him so much that he couldn't sleep, [2] so he sent
2. 3 he said to them, "I'm **worried** about a dream I have had.
10.19 "God loves you, so don't let anything **worry** you or frighten you."
Mt 6.25 tell you not to be **worried** about the food and drink
6.27 Can any of you live a bit longer by **worrying** about it?
6.28 "And why **worry** about clothes?
6.31 "So do not start **worrying:**
6.34 So do not **worry** about tomorrow;
6.34 it will have enough **worries** of its own.
9.36 because they were **worried** and helpless, like sheep without
10.19 you to trial, do not **worry** about what you are going to
13.22 but the **worries** about this life and the love for riches
15.14 "Don't **worry** about them!
22.16 God's will for man, without **worrying** about what people think,
28.14 you are innocent, and you will have nothing to **worry** about."
Mk 4.19 hear the message, [19] but the **worries** about this life,
12.14 you tell the truth, without **worrying** about what people think.
13.11 taken to court, do not **worry** beforehand about what you are
Lk 2.48 Your father and I have been terribly **worried** trying to find you."
8.14 the **worries** and riches and pleasures of this life crowd in
10.41 You are **worried** and troubled over so many things,
12.11 do not be **worried** about how you will defend yourself
12.22 I tell you not to **worry** about the food you need
12.25 Can any of you live a bit longer by **worrying** about it?
12.26 even such a small thing, why **worry** about the other things?
21.14 not to **worry** about how you will defend yourselves,
21.34 and drinking and with the **worries** of this life,
Jn 14. 1 "Do not be **worried** and upset," Jesus told them.
14.27 Do not be **worried** and upset;
Acts 20.10 "Don't **worry,"** he said, "he is still alive!"
1 Cor 7.32 I would like you to be free from **worry.**
2 Cor 2.13 But I was deeply **worried,** because I could not find our
Gal 4.11 I am **worried** about you!
4.20 I am so **worried** about you!
Phil 4. 6 Don't **worry** about anything, but in all your prayers ask God
1 Pet 3.14 Do not be afraid of anyone, and do not **worry.**
5. 7 Leave all your **worries** with him, because he cares for you.

WORSE

Gen 19. 9 Out of our way, or we will treat you **worse** than them."
41.56 The famine grew **worse** and spread over the whole country,
43. 1 The famine in Canaan got **worse,** [2] and when the family of
Ex 10. 6 They will be **worse** than anything your ancestors ever saw.'"
Lev 26.28 again make your punishment seven times **worse** than before.
Num 13.28 Even **worse,** we saw the descendants of the giants there.
Judg 2.19 the old ways and behave **worse** than the previous generation.
1 Sam 14.19 in the Philistine camp got **worse and worse,** so Saul said to
23. 3 it will be much **worse** if we go to Keilah and attack
2 Sam 4.11 How much **worse** it will be for evil men who murder an
1 Kgs 17.17 he got **worse and worse,** and finally he died.
2 Kgs 21.11 things far **worse** than what the Canaanites did;
2 Chr 21.15 disease of the intestines that will grow **worse** day by day."
21.19 two years it grew steadily **worse** until finally the king died
32.16 Assyrian officials said even **worse** things about the Lord
Ps 39. 2 my suffering only grew **worse,** [3] and I was overcome with anxiety.
Is 7.17 royal family, days of trouble **worse** than any that have come
14.29 When one snake dies, a **worse** one comes in its place.
15. 9 God has something even **worse** in store for the people there.
24.16 continue to betray, and their treachery grows **worse and worse.**
Jer 7.24 told them to do, and they became **worse** instead of better.
16.12 But you have done even **worse** than your ancestors.
23.14 But I have seen the prophets in Jerusalem do even **worse:**
Ezek 16.47 little while you were behaving **worse** than they were in
16.52 Your sins are so much **worse** than those of your sisters that
29.12 will lie in ruins, ruins **worse** than those of any other city.
Jon 1.11 The storm was getting **worse** all the time, so the sailors
1.13 But the storm was getting **worse and worse,** and they got nowhere.
Zech 1.15 those nations made the sufferings of my people **worse.**
Mt 10.25 Beelzebul, the members of the family will be called even **worse** names!
12.45 seven other spirits even **worse** than itself, and they come
12.45 that person is in a **worse** state than he was
27.64 This last lie would be even **worse** than the first one."
Mk 5.26 but instead of getting better she got **worse** all the time.

Mk 12.40 Their punishment will be all the **worse!"**
13.19 those days will be far **worse** than any the world has ever
Lk 3.20 Then Herod did an even **worse** thing by putting John in prison.
11.26 brings seven other spirits even **worse** than itself,
11.26 that person is in a **worse** state than he was
12. 4 who kill the body but cannot afterwards do anything **worse.**
13. 2 that they were **worse** sinners than all the other Galileans?
13. 4 that they were **worse** than all the other people living
20.47 Their punishment will be all the **worse!"**
Jn 5.14 so stop sinning or something **worse** may happen to you."
19.11 who handed me over to you is guilty of a **worse** sin."
2 Cor 12.13 How were you treated any **worse** than the other churches,
1 Tim 5. 8 he has denied the faith and is **worse** than an unbeliever.
5.13 but even **worse,** they learn to be gossips and busybodies,
2 Tim 3.13 going from bad to **worse,** deceiving others and being deceived
Heb 10.29 Just think how much **worse** is the punishment he will deserve!
2 Pet 2.20 such people are in a **worse** state at the end than they

WORSHIP

see also **PLACE OF WORSHIP**

WORSHIP (1) (OF GOD)

Gen 4.26 that people began using the Lord's holy name in **worship.**
12. 8 There also he built an altar and **worshipped** the Lord.
13. 4 There he **worshipped** the Lord.
21.33 in Beersheba and **worshipped** the Lord, the Everlasting God.
22. 5 will go over there and **worship,** and then we will come back
24.26 Then the man knelt down and **worshipped** the Lord.
24.48 I knelt down and **worshipped** the Lord.
24.52 Abraham heard this, he bowed down and **worshipped** the Lord.
26.25 Isaac built an altar there and **worshipped** the Lord.
28.22 the place where you are **worshipped,** and I will give you a
31.53 God whom his father Isaac **worshipped,** Jacob solemnly vowed
Ex 3.12 people out of Egypt, you will **worship** me on this mountain.
4.23 my son go, so that he might **worship** me, but you refused.
4.31 were being treated cruelly, they bowed down and **worshipped.**
7.16 his people go, so that they can **worship** him in the desert.
8. 1 Lord says, 'Let my people go, so that they can **worship** me.
8.20 Lord says, 'Let my people go, so that they can **worship** me.
9. 1 says, 'Let my people go, so that they may **worship** me.
9.13 says, 'Let my people go, so that they may **worship** me.
10. 3 Let my people go, so that they may **worship** me.
10. 7 Israelite men go, so that they can **worship** the Lord their God.
10. 8 said to them, "You may go and **worship** the Lord your God.
10.11 the men may go and **worship** the Lord if that is what
10.24 called Moses and said, "You may go and **worship** the Lord;
10.26 select the animals with which to **worship** the Lord our God.
12.16 and again on the seventh day you are to meet for **worship.**
12.27 The Israelites knelt down and **worshipped.**
12.31 go and **worship** the Lord, as you asked.
18.12 with him to eat the sacred meal as an act of **worship.**
19.10 spend today and tomorrow purifying themselves for **worship.**
19.14 the mountain and told the people to get ready for **worship.**
20. 3 **"Worship** no god but me.
20.24 set aside for you to **worship** me, I will come to you
23.15 Never come to **worship** me without bringing an offering.
23.17 all your men must come to **worship** me, the Lord your God.
23.25 If you **worship** me, the Lord your God, I will bless you
24. 1 while you are still some distance away, bow down in **worship.**
34. 8 Moses quickly bowed down to the ground and **worshipped.**
34.23 your men must come to **worship** me, the Lord, the God of
35.21 for use in **worship** and for making the priestly garments.
Lev 9. 5 and the whole community assembled there to **worship** the Lord.
19.30 Keep the Sabbath, and honour the place where I am **worshipped.**
23. 2 when the people of Israel are to gather for **worship.**
23. 3 On that day do not work, but gather for **worship.**
23. 7 days you shall gather for **worship** and do none of your daily
23. 8 you shall again gather for **worship,** but you shall do none of
23.21 that day do none of your daily work, but gather for **worship.**
23.23 rest, and come together for **worship** when the trumpets sound.
23.26 for **worship,** and present a food-offering
23.35 these days come together for **worship** and do none of your
23.36 come together again for **worship** and present a food-offering.
23.36 It is a day for **worship,** and you shall do no work.
23.37 gathering together for **worship** and presenting food-offerings,
26. 2 honour the place where I am **worshipped.**
Num 28.18 you are to gather for **worship,** and no work is to be
28.25 Meet for **worship** on the seventh day and do no work.
28.26 you are to gather for **worship,** and no work is to be
29. 1 you are to gather for **worship,** and no work is to be
29. 7 Gather for **worship** on the tenth day of the seventh month;
29.12 Gather for **worship** on the fifteenth day of the seventh month.
29.35 On the eighth day gather for **worship** and do no work.
Deut 5. 7 **" 'Worship** no god but me.
6.13 Honour the Lord your God, **worship** only him, and make
10.12 **Worship** the Lord and do all that he commands.
10.20 Obey the Lord your God and **worship** only him.
12. 4 "Do not **worship** the Lord your God in the way that these
12. 5 the people are to come into his presence and **worship** him.
12. 8 now you have all been **worshipping** as you please, [9]because
12.11 where he is to be **worshipped,** and there you must bring to
12.31 Do not **worship** the Lord your God in the way they worship
13. 4 **worship** him and be faithful to him.
14.23 place where the Lord your God has chosen to be **worshipped;**
16. 8 the seventh day assemble to **worship** the Lord your God, and
16.16 nation are to come to **worship** the Lord three times a year
26.10 set the basket down in the Lord's presence and **worship** there.
31.11 Israel when they come to **worship** the Lord your God at the
Josh 1. 8 that the book of the Law is always read in your **worship.**
Josh 5.14 on the ground in **worship** and said, "I am your servant,
9.27 work in the place where the Lord has chosen to be **worshipped.**
22.19 land is not fit to **worship** in, come over into the Lord's
22.25 might make our descendants stop **worshipping** the Lord.
22.27 us, that we do indeed **worship** the Lord before his sacred
Judg 2.12 They stopped **worshipping** the Lord, the God of their ancestors,
2.13 They stopped **worshipping** the Lord and served the Baals
7.15 what it meant, he fell to his knees and **worshipped** the Lord.
10. 6 They abandoned the Lord and stopped **worshipping** him.
10.16 So they got rid of their foreign gods and **worshipped** the Lord;
18.31 that the Tent where God was **worshipped** remained at Shiloh.
1 Sam 1. 3 Elkanah went from Ramah to **worship** and offer sacrifices to
1.19 got up early, and after **worshipping** the Lord, they went back
1.28 Then they **worshipped** the Lord there.
7. 3 completely to the Lord and **worship** only him, and he will
7. 4 idols of Baal and Astarte, and **worshipped** only the Lord.
12.10 Rescue us from our enemies, and we will **worship** you!'
15.25 and go back with me, so that I can **worship** the Lord."
15.30 back with me so that I can **worship** the Lord your God."
15.31 So Samuel went back with him, and Saul **worshipped** the Lord.
2 Sam 8.11 dedicated them for use in **worship,** along with the silver and
12.20 Then he went and **worshipped** in the house of the Lord.
15. 8 take me back to Jerusalem, I would **worship** him in Hebron."
1 Kgs 1.47 Then King David bowed in **worship** on his bed [48]and prayed,
5. 3 build a temple for the **worship** of the Lord his God until
5. 5 to build that temple for the **worship** of the Lord my God.
8.16 which a temple should be built where I would be **worshipped.**
8.17 build a temple for the **worship** of the Lord God of Israel,
8.20 built the Temple for the **worship** of the Lord God of Israel.
8.29 night, this place where you have chosen to be **worshipped.**
8.41 your people, and comes to **worship** you and to pray at this
8.43 I have built is the place where you are to be **worshipped.**
9. 3 built as the place where I shall be **worshipped** for ever.
9. 7 I have consecrated as the place where I am to be **worshipped.**
11.36 the city I have chosen as the place where I am **worshipped.**
12.28 "You have been going long enough to Jerusalem to **worship.**
14.21 of Israel as the place where he was to be **worshipped.**
18. 3 (Obadiah was a devout **worshipper** of the Lord, [4]and when
18.12 I have been a devout **worshipper** of the Lord ever since I
18.21 If the Lord is God, **worship** him;
18.32 stones he rebuilt the altar for the **worship** of the Lord.
2 Kgs 10.23 present and that no **worshipper** of the Lord has come in."
12. 9 put in the box all the money given by the **worshippers.**
17.25 settled there, they did not **worship** the Lord, and so he sent
17.28 Bethel, where he taught the people how to **worship** the Lord.
17.32 These people also **worshipped** the Lord and chose from
17.33 So they **worshipped** the Lord,
17.34 They do not **worship** the Lord nor do they obey the laws
17.41 So those people **worshipped** the Lord,
18.22 Judah and Jerusalem to **worship** only at the altar in Jerusalem.
21. 4 that the Lord had said was where he should be **worshipped.**
21. 7 tribes of Israel as the place where I am to be **worshipped.**
23.27 the place I said was where I should be **worshipped."**
1 Chr 6.49 were responsible for all the **worship** in the Most Holy Place
9.28 Other Levites were responsible for the utensils used in **worship.**
15.13 God punished us for not **worshipping** him as we should have done."
16. 4 the Levites to lead the **worship** of the Lord, the God of
16.10 let all who **worship** him rejoice!
16.11 Go to the Lord for help, and **worship** him continually.
16.37 in permanent charge of the **worship** that was held at the
16.39 were in charge of the **worship** of the Lord at the place
18.11 dedicated them for use in **worship,** along with the silver and
21.30 able to go there to **worship** God, because he was afraid of
22.19 Lord and all the other sacred objects used in **worshipping** him."
23.13 to burn incense in the **worship** of the Lord, to serve him,
23.26 Tent of the Lord's presence and all the equipment used in **worship."**
23.28 from Aaron with the temple **worship,** to take care of its
23.31 Levites were assigned the duty of **worshipping** the Lord for all time.
23.32 the priests descended from Aaron, in the temple **worship.**
25. 1 chose the following Levite clans to lead the services of **worship:**
25. 1 persons chosen to lead the **worship,** with the type of service
25. 6 their father's direction, to accompany the temple **worship.**
2 Chr 1. 5 King Solomon and all the people **worshipped** the Lord there.
1. 6 of the Tent the king **worshipped** the Lord by offering
2. 1 where the Lord would be **worshipped,** and also to build a
2. 4 my people and I will **worship** him by burning incense of
5.11 Lord's presence, and they could not continue the service of **worship.**
6. 5 temple where I would be **worshipped,** and I did not choose
6. 6 place where I will be **worshipped,** and you, David, to rule my
6. 7 build a temple for the **worship** of the Lord God of Israel,
6.10 built a temple for the **worship** of the Lord God of Israel.
6.20 is where you will be **worshipped,** so hear me when I face
6.33 this Temple I have built is where you are to be **worshipped.**
7. 3 face downwards on the pavement, **worshipping** God and praising
7.16 it as the place where I will be **worshipped** for ever.
7.20 I have consecrated as the place where I am to be **worshipped.**
11.16 who sincerely wanted to **worship** the Lord, the God of Israel,
12.13 of Israel as the place where he was to be **worshipped.**
15.12 in which they agreed to **worship** the Lord, the God of their
15.13 or female, who did not **worship** him was to be put to
15.15 They took delight in **worshipping** the Lord, and he accepted
20. 9 and stand in front of this Temple where you are **worshipped.**
20.18 and all the people bowed with him and **worshipped** the Lord.
20.33 to the **worship** of the God of their ancestors.
24.18 So the people stopped **worshipping** in the Temple of the Lord,
29.11 incense to him and to lead the people in **worshipping** him."
29.17 sixteenth of the month, preparing the Temple for **worship.**

2 Chr	29.23	and to the other **worshippers,** who laid their hands on them.
	29.28	who was there joined in **worship,** and the singing and the
	29.29	Hezekiah and all the people knelt down and **worshipped** God.
	29.30	So everyone sang with great joy as they knelt and **worshipped** God.
	29.35	And so **worship** in the Temple was begun again.
	30. 8	made holy for ever, and **worship** him so that he will no
	30.19	forgive those who are **worshipping** you with all their heart,
	30.22	Levites for their skill in conducting the **worship** of the Lord.
	31. 2	taking part in the temple **worship,** and giving praise and
	32.12	of Judah and Jerusalem to **worship** and burn incense at one
	33. 4	Lord had said was where he should be **worshipped** for ever.
	33. 7	tribes of Israel as the place where I am to be **worshipped.**
	33.16	altar where the Lord was **worshipped,** and he sacrificed
	33.16	the people of Judah to **worship** the Lord, the God of Israel.
	34. 3	very young, he began to **worship** the God of his ancestor King
	35.16	done that day for the **worship** of the Lord, the keeping of
Ezra	1. 3	the God of Israel, the God who is **worshipped** in Jerusalem.
	3. 5	at which the Lord is **worshipped,** as well as all the
	4. 2	We **worship** the same God you worship, and we have been
	6.12	where he is to be **worshipped** overthrow any king or nation
	6.21	land and who had come to **worship** the Lord God of Israel.
	8.36	gave their support to the people and the temple **worship.**
Neh	1. 9	I have chosen to be **worshipped,** even though you are
	8. 6	They knelt in **worship,** with their faces to the ground.
	9. 3	confessed their sins and **worshipped** the Lord their God.
	9. 5	The following Levites gave a call to **worship:**
	9. 6	The heavenly powers bow down and **worship** you.
	10.33	We will provide for the temple **worship** the following:
	13.14	things that I have done for your Temple and its **worship.**
Job	1. 1	the land of Uz, who **worshipped** God and was faithful to him.
	1. 8	He **worships** me and is careful not to do anything evil."
	1. 9	Satan replied, "Would Job **worship** you if he got nothing
	2. 3	He **worships** me and is careful not to do anything evil.
	4. 6	You **worshipped** God, and your life was blameless;
	33.26	he will **worship** God with joy;
Ps	5. 7	I can **worship** in your holy Temple and bow down to you
	14. 2	see if there are any who are wise, any who **worship** him.
	15. 1	Who may **worship** on Zion, your sacred hill?
	22.23	**Worship** him, you people of Israel!
	22.25	the presence of those who **worship** you I will offer the
	22.27	all races will **worship** him.
	26. 6	that I am innocent and march in **worship** round your altar.
	27. 8	When you said, "Come and **worship** me," I answered, "I
	33. 8	**Worship** the Lord, all the earth!
	42. 2	when can I go and **worship** in your presence?
	44.20	If we had stopped **worshipping** our God and prayed to a
	53. 2	see if there are any who are wise, any who **worship** him.
	55.14	with each other and **worshipped** together in the Temple.
	66. 4	Everyone on earth **worships** you;
	69. 6	bring disgrace to those who **worship** you, O God of Israel!
	69.32	those who **worship** God will be encouraged.
	72. 5	May your people **worship** you as long as the sun shines, as
	74. 7	they desecrated the place where you are **worshipped.**
	79. 6	the nations that do not **worship** you, on the people who do
	89.15	happy are the people who **worship** you with songs, who live in
	95. 6	Come, let us bow down and **worship** him;
	99. 5	**worship** before his throne!
	99. 9	Praise the Lord our God, and **worship** at his sacred hill!
	100. 2	**Worship** the Lord with joy;
	102.22	when nations and kingdoms come together and **worship** the Lord.
	105. 3	let all who **worship** him rejoice.
	105. 4	and **worship** him continually.
	115.11	Trust in the Lord, all you that **worship** him.
	118. 4	Let all who **worship** him say, "His love is eternal."
	132. 7	let us **worship** before his throne."
	135.20	praise him, all you that **worship** him!
Prov	14.31	but kindness shown to the poor is an act of **worship.**
	28. 5	is, but those who **worship** the Lord understand it well.
Is	1.12	you to bring me all this when you come to **worship** me?
	18. 7	They will come to Mount Zion, where the Lord Almighty is **worshipped.**
	19.21	then they will acknowledge and **worship** him, and bring him
	19.23	fro between them, and the two nations will **worship** together.
	23.18	it away, but those who **worship** the Lord will use her money
	27.13	They will come and **worship** the Lord in Jerusalem, on his
	29.13	"These people claim to **worship** me, but their words are meaningless,
	31. 9	spoken—the Lord who is **worshipped** in Jerusalem and whose
	36. 7	people of Judah and Jerusalem to **worship** at one altar only.
	43.22	you did not **worship** me.
	48. 1	the Lord and claim to **worship** the God of Israel— but
	56. 3	say, "The Lord will not let me **worship** with his people."
	57.13	will live in the land and will **worship** me in my Temple."
	58. 2	They **worship** me every day, claiming that they are eager to
	58. 2	just laws and that they take pleasure in **worshipping** me."
	59. 2	sins that separate you from God when you try to **worship** him.
	60.14	All who once despised you will **worship** at your feet.
	65.10	They will **worship** me and will lead their sheep and
	65.13	tell you that those who **worship** and obey me will have plenty
	66.23	every nation will come to **worship** me here in Jerusalem,"
Jer	2.20	you refused to obey me and **worship** me.
	3.17	the Lord,' and all nations will gather there to **worship** me.
	5. 2	Even though you claim to **worship** the Lord, you do not mean
	7. 1	of the Temple where the people of Judah went in to **worship.**
	7.12	where I chose to be **worshipped,** and see what I did to
	10.25	the nations that do not **worship** you and on the people who
	26. 2	people who come from the towns of Judah to **worship** there.
	32.34	the Temple built for my **worship,** and they have defiled it.
	34.15	in my presence, in the Temple where I am **worshipped.**
	44. 3	neither they nor you nor your ancestors ever **worshipped.**
Lam	1. 4	one comes to the Temple now to **worship** on the holy days.
	2. 6	He smashed to pieces the Temple where we **worshipped** him;
	2. 7	They shouted in victory where once we had **worshipped** in joy.
Ezek	7.24	when I let the nations profane the places where you **worship.**
	11.15	They say, 'The exiles are too far away to **worship** the Lord.
	20.40	of Israel, all you people of Israel will **worship** me.
	44.16	Temple, serve at my altar, and conduct the temple **worship.**
	46. 2	There at the gate he must **worship** and then go out again.
	46. 3	also to bow down and **worship** the Lord in front of the
	46. 9	"When the people come to **worship** the Lord at any festival,
	46. 9	south gate after they have **worshipped,** and those who enter
	46.11	and whatever the **worshipper** wants to give with each lamb.
Dan	11.38	other rich gifts to a god his ancestors never **worshipped.**
Hos	5. 3	She has been unfaithful, and her people are unfit to **worship** me."
	7.13	I wanted to save them, but their **worship** of me was false.
	12. 5	the Lord is the name by which he is to be **worshipped.**
Amos	5. 5	Do not go to Beersheba to **worship.**
	7. 9	The places where Isaac's descendants **worship** will be destroyed.
Jon	1. 9	"I **worship** the Lord, the God of heaven, who made land and
Mic	4. 5	own god, but we will **worship** and obey the Lord our God
	6. 6	the Lord, the God of heaven, when I come to **worship** him?
Zeph	1. 5	also destroy those who **worship** me and swear loyalty to me,
	2.11	then every nation will **worship** him, each in its own land.
Hag	1. 8	I will be pleased and will be **worshipped** as I should be.
Zech	5.11	the basket will be placed there to be **worshipped."**
	8.21	another, 'We are going to **worship** the Lord Almighty and pray
	8.22	will come to Jerusalem to **worship** the Lord Almighty, and to
	10.12	they will **worship** and obey me."
	14. 9	everyone will **worship** him as God and know him by the same
	14.16	go there each year to **worship** the Lord Almighty as king, and
	14.17	nation refuses to go and **worship** the Lord Almighty as king,
	14.21	be set apart for use in the **worship** of the Lord Almighty.
Mt	2. 2	came up in the east, and we have come to **worship** him."
	2. 8	let me know, so that I too may go and **worship** him."
	2.11	with his mother Mary, they knelt down and **worshipped** him.
	4.10	**'Worship** the Lord your God and serve only him!' "
	6. 2	hypocrites do in the houses of **worship** and on the streets.
	6. 5	pray in the houses of **worship** and on the street corners,
	14.33	Then the disciples in the boat **worshipped** Jesus.
	15. 9	no use for them to **worship** me, because they teach man-made
	28. 9	came up to him, took hold of his feet, and **worshipped** him.
	28.17	When they saw him, they **worshipped** him,
Mk	7. 7	no use for them to **worship** me, because they teach man-made
Lk	2.36	day and night she **worshipped** God, fasting and praying.
	4. 8	"The scripture says, **'Worship** the Lord your God
	24.52	They **worshipped** him and went back into Jerusalem,
Jn	4.20	"My Samaritan ancestors **worshipped** God on this mountain,
	4.20	Jews say that Jerusalem is the place where we should **worship** God."
	4.21	people will not **worship** the Father either on this mountain
	4.22	You Samaritans do not really know whom you **worship;**
	4.22	we Jews know whom we **worship,** because it is from the Jews
	4.23	people will **worship** the Father as he really is,
	4.23	offering him the true **worship** that he wants.
	4.24	of his Spirit can people **worship** him as he really is."
	12.20	who had gone to Jerusalem to **worship** during the festival.
Acts	7. 7	come out of that country and will **worship** me in this place.'
	8.27	had been to Jerusalem to **worship** God and was going back
	9.14	authority from the chief priests to arrest all who **worship** you."
	9.21	in Jerusalem was killing those who **worship** that man Jesus?
	10. 2	he and his whole family **worshipped** God.
	10.22	is a good man who **worships** God and is highly respected
	10.35	Whoever **worships** him and does what is right is acceptable
	13.16	"Fellow-Israelites and all Gentiles here who **worship** God:
	13.26	descendants of Abraham, and all Gentiles here who **worship** God:
	13.50	Gentile women of high social standing who **worshipped** God.
	16.14	She was a woman who **worshipped** God, and the Lord opened her
	17. 4	leading women and a large group of Greeks who **worshipped** God.
	17.17	and with the Gentiles who **worshipped** God,
	17.23	That which you **worship,** then, even though you do not know it,
	18. 7	house of a Gentile named Titius Justus, who **worshipped** God;
	18.13	trying to persuade people to **worship** God in a way that is
	24.11	than twelve days ago that I went to Jerusalem to **worship.**
	24.14	I **worship** the God of our ancestors by following that Way
	26. 7	people hope to receive, as they **worship** God day and night.
	27.23	I belong and whom I **worship** came to me [24]and said,
Rom	1.23	instead of **worshipping** the immortal God, they worship images
	3.11	no one who is wise or who **worships** God.
	9. 4	they have the true **worship;**
	12. 1	This is the true **worship** that you should offer.
1 Cor	1. 2	all people everywhere who **worship** our Lord Jesus Christ,
	11. 4	God's message in public **worship** with his head covered disgraces Christ.
	11. 5	proclaims God's message in public **worship** with nothing on
	11.13	to pray to God in public **worship** with nothing on her head.
	11.16	nor the churches of God have any other custom in **worship.**
	11.17	your meetings for **worship** actually do more harm than good.
	14.19	But in church **worship** I would rather speak five words that
	14.25	bow down and **worship** God, confessing, "Truly God is here
	14.26	When you meet for **worship,** one person has a hymn, another a
Phil	3. 3	true circumcision, for we **worship** God by means of his Spirit
Heb	1. 6	he said, "All God's angels must **worship** him."
	9. 1	first covenant had rules for **worship**
	9. 1	and a man-made place for **worship** as well.
	9. 9	cannot make the **worshipper's** heart perfect,
	9.21	the Covenant Tent and over all the things used in **worship.**
	10. 2	If the people **worshipping** God had really been purified from their sins,
	11.21	He leaned on the top of his walking-stick and **worshipped** God.
	12.28	Let us be grateful and **worship** God in a way that will
	13.10	in the Jewish place of **worship** have no right to eat any

Rev 4.10 sits on the throne, and **worship** him who lives for ever
5.14 And the elders fell down and **worshipped.**
7.11 in front of the throne and **worshipped** God, [12]saying, "Amen!
11. 1 and count those who are **worshipping** in the temple.
11.16 threw themselves face downwards and **worshipped** God,
14. 7 **Worship** him who made heaven, earth, sea,
15. 4 nations will come and **worship** you, because your just actions
19. 4 living creatures fell down and **worshipped** God,
19.10 **Worship** God!"
22. 3 Lamb will be in the city, and his servants will **worship** him.
22. 9 **Worship** God!"

WORSHIP (2) (OF OTHER GODS)

[IDOL WORSHIP]

Ex 20. 3 **"Worship no god** but me.
20. 5 down to any idol or **worship** it, because I am the Lord
20.23 gods of silver or gold to be **worshipped** in addition to me.
23.24 down to their gods or **worship** them, and do not adopt their
23.33 If you **worship their gods,** it will be a fatal trap for
32. 8 gold and have **worshipped** it and offered sacrifices to it.
32.31 They have made a god out of gold and **worshipped** it.
34.14 "Do not **worship any other god,** because I, the Lord,
34.15 when they **worship their pagan gods** and sacrifice to them,
34.16 to be unfaithful to me and to **worship their pagan gods.**
34.17 "Do not make and **worship gods** of metal.
Lev 18.21 be used in the **worship of the god Molech,** because that would
19. 4 "Do not abandon me and **worship idols;**
19. 4 do not make gods of metal and **worship** them.
20. 2 be used in the **worship of the god Molech** shall be stoned
20. 5 join him in being unfaithful to me and **worshipping Molech.**
26. 1 set up statues, stone pillars, or carved stones to **worship.**
Num 21.29 You **worshippers of Chemosh** are brought to ruin!
25. 2 to sacrificial feasts, where the god of Moab was **worshipped.**
25. 2 The Israelites ate the food and **worshipped the god [3]Baal of Peor.**
25. 5 your tribe who has become a **worshipper of Baal of Peor."**
25.11 refused to tolerate the **worship of any god** but me, and that
Deut 4. 3 He destroyed everyone who **worshipped Baal** there, [4]but those
4.19 Do not be tempted to **worship** and serve what you see in
4.19 God has given these to all other peoples for them to **worship.**
5. 7 " '**Worship no god** but me.
5. 9 down to any idol or **worship** it, for I am the Lord
6.14 Do not **worship other gods,** any of the gods of the
6.15 If you do **worship other gods,** the Lord's anger will come
7. 4 lead your children away from the Lord to **worship other gods.**
7.16 Do not **worship their gods,** for that would be fatal.
8.19 your God or turn to other gods to **worship and serve them.**
11.16 be led away from the Lord to **worship and serve other gods.**
11.28 to worship other gods that you have never **worshipped** before.
12. 2 where the people **worship their gods** on high mountains,
12. 3 that they will never again be **worshipped** at those places.
12. 4 Lord your God in the way that these people **worship their gods.**
12.30 how they **worship their gods,**
12.30 so that you can **worship** in the same way.
12.31 in the way they **worship their gods,**
12.31 for in the **worship of their gods** they do all the
13. 2 worship and serve gods that you have not **worshipped** before.
13. 6 secretly encourage you to **worship other gods,**
13. 6 gods that you and your ancestors have never **worshipped.**
13. 7 may encourage you to **worship the gods** of the people who live
13.13 town to worship gods that you have never **worshipped** before.
16.22 And do not set up any stone pillar for **idol worship;**
17. 3 broken his covenant [3]by **worshipping and serving other gods**
20.18 things that they do in the **worship of their gods.**
27.15 an idol of stone, wood, or metal and secretly **worships** it;
28.14 disobey them in any way, or **worship and serve other gods.**
28.64 neither you nor your ancestors have ever **worshipped** before.
29.18 from the Lord our God to **worship the gods** of other nations.
29.26 worshipped before, gods that the Lord had forbidden them to **worship.**
30.17 are led away to **worship other gods,** [18]you will be
31.16 will abandon me and **worship the pagan gods** of the land they
31.18 because they have done evil and **worshipped other gods.**
31.20 But they will turn away and **worship other gods.**
Josh 23. 7 in taking vows or **worship those gods** or bow down to them.
23.16 if you serve and **worship other gods,** then in his anger he
24. 2 other side of the River Euphrates and **worshipped other gods.**
24.14 your ancestors used to **worship** in Mesopotamia and in Egypt,
24.15 serve, the gods your ancestors **worshipped** in Mesopotamia or
Judg 2. 3 and you will be trapped by the **worship of their gods."**
2.12 and they began to **worship other gods,** the gods of the
2.17 Israel was unfaithful to the Lord and **worshipped other gods.**
2.19 They would serve and **worship other gods,** and refused to give
3. 6 They intermarried with them and **worshipped their gods.**
3. 7 against him and **worshipped the idols** of Baal and Asherah.
6.10 that you should not **worship the gods** of the Amorites, whose
8.27 All the Israelites abandoned God and went there to **worship the idol.**
8.33 Israel were again unfaithful to God and **worshipped the Baals.**
10. 6 against the Lord by **worshipping the Baals** and the Astartes,
10.10 you, for we left you, our God, and **worshipped the Baals."**
10.13 still left me and **worshipped other gods,** so I am not going
18.30 up the idol to be **worshipped,** and Jonathan, the son of
1 Sam 5. 5 of Dagon and all his **worshippers** in Ashdod step over that
8. 8 they have turned away from me and **worshipped other gods;**
12.10 you, Lord, and **worshipped the idols** of Baal and Astarte.
26.19 Lord's land to a country where I can only **worship foreign gods.**
1 Kgs 9. 6 have given you, and **worship other gods,** [7]then I will remove
9. 9 They gave their allegiance to other gods and **worshipped** them.
11. 4 was old they had led him into the **worship of foreign gods.**
11. 5 He **worshipped Astarte** the goddess of Sidon,
1 Kgs 11. 7 a place to **worship Chemosh,** the disgusting god of Moab,
11. 7 and a place to **worship Molech,** the disgusting god of Ammon.
11. 9 commanded him not to **worship foreign gods,** Solomon did not obey
11.33 Solomon has rejected me and has **worshipped foreign gods:**
12.30 the people sinned, going to **worship** in Bethel and in Dan.
14. 9 my anger by making idols and metal images to **worship.**
14.23 They built places of **worship for false gods,** and put up
14.23 and symbols of Asherah to **worship** on the hills and under
16.31 the daughter of King Ethbaal of Sidon, and **worshipped Baal.**
18.18 disobeying the Lord's commands and **worshipping the idols** of Baal.
18.21 but if Baal is God, **worship** him!"
21.26 sins by **worshipping idols,** as the Amorites had done,
22.53 **He worshipped and served Baal,** and like his father before him,
2 Kgs 3. 2 down the image his father had made for the **worship of Baal.**
5.18 to the temple of Rimmon, the god of Syria, and **worship** him.
10.19 prophets of Baal, all his **worshippers,** and all his priests.
10.19 Jehu by which he meant to kill all the **worshippers of Baal.)**
10.20 Then Jehu ordered, "Proclaim a day of **worship** in honour of Baal!"
10.21 All who **worshipped Baal** came;
10.22 to bring the robes out and give them to the **worshippers.**
10.23 "Make sure that only **worshippers of Baal** are present and
10.28 That was how Jehu wiped out the **worship of Baal** in Israel.
10.29 Israel into the sin of **worshipping** the gold bull-calves he
17. 7 They **worshipped other gods,** [8]followed the customs of the
17.12 and disobeyed the Lord's command not to **worship idols.**
17.15 They **worshipped worthless idols** and became worthless themselves,
17.16 Lord their God and made two metal bull-calves to **worship;**
17.16 Asherah, **worshipped the stars,** and served the god Baal.
17.33 Lord, but they also **worshipped their own gods** according to
17.35 "Do not **worship other gods;**
17.41 worshipped the Lord, but they also **worshipped their idols;**
19.37 One day, when he was **worshipping** in the temple of his
21. 3 built altars for the **worship of Baal** and made an image of
21. 3 Manasseh also **worshipped the stars.**
21. 5 of the Temple he built altars for the **worship of the stars.**
21.21 and he **worshipped the idols** that his father had worshipped.
23. 4 objects used in the **worship of Baal,** of the goddess Asherah,
23. 7 there that women wove robes used in the **worship of Asherah.)**
23.11 had dedicated to the **worship of the sun,**
23.11 and he burnt the chariots used in this **worship.**
23.13 of Olives, for the **worship of disgusting idols**—Astarte the
23.24 gods, idols, and all other pagan objects of **worship.**
1 Chr 5.25 and deserted him to **worship the gods** of the nations whom God
2 Chr 7.19 have given you, and **worship other gods,** [20]then I will
7.22 They gave their allegiance to other gods and **worshipped** them.
11.15 places of worship and to **worship demons** and the idols he
17. 3 example of his father's early life and did not **worship Baal.**
19. 3 the goddess Asherah which people **worshipped,** and you have
21.11 even built pagan places of **worship** in the Judaean highlands
24. 7 used many of the sacred objects in the **worship of Baal.)**
24.18 their ancestors, and began to **worship idols** and the images
25.14 set them up, **worshipped** them, and burnt incense to them.
25.15 demanded, "Why have you **worshipped foreign gods** that could
25.20 Amaziah to be defeated, because he had **worshipped the Edomite idols.**
28. 4 At the pagan places of **worship,** on the hills, and under
28.25 he built pagan places of **worship,** where incense was to be
33. 3 built altars for the **worship of Baal,**
33. 3 images of the goddess Asherah, and **worshipped the stars.**
33. 5 of the Temple he built altars for the **worship of the stars.**
33.19 and the idols that he **worshipped**—are all recorded in The
33.22 and he **worshipped the idols** that his father had worshipped.
34. 4 the altars where Baal was **worshipped** and tore down the
34. 5 the pagan priests on the altars where they had **worshipped.**
34. 8 the Temple by ending pagan **worship,** King Josiah sent three
36.14 the nations round them in **worshipping idols,** and so they
Job 31.26 I have never **worshipped the sun** in its brightness or the
Ps 10.16 Those who **worship other gods** will vanish from his land.
16. 4 I will not **worship their gods.**
24. 4 thought, who do not **worship idols** or make false promises.
31. 6 You hate those who **worship false gods,** but I trust in you.
40. 4 do not turn to idols or join those who **worship false gods.**
81. 9 You must never **worship another god.**
97. 7 Everyone who **worships idols** is put to shame;
106.19 They made a gold bull-calf at Sinai and **worshipped that idol;**
106.28 people joined in the **worship of Baal,** and ate sacrifices
106.36 God's people **worshipped idols,** and this caused their destruction.
Is 1.29 that you ever **worshipped trees** and planted sacred gardens.
2. 8 full of idols, and they **worship objects** that they have made
10.10 to punish those kingdoms that **worship idols,** idols more
10.11 to Jerusalem and the images that are **worshipped** there."
17.10 you plant sacred gardens in order to **worship a foreign god.**
21. 9 All the idols they **worshipped** lie shattered on the ground."
37.38 One day when he was **worshipping** in the temple of his god
41.24 those who **worship** you are disgusting!
44. 9 Those who **worship these gods** are blind and ignorant—and they
44.10 It's no good making a metal image to **worship as a god!**
44.11 Everyone who **worships** it will be humiliated.
44.15 with the other part he makes a god and **worships** it.
44.17 makes into an idol, and then he bows down and **worships** it.
46. 1 Bel and Nebo once were **worshipped,** but now they are loaded
46. 6 then they bow down and **worship** it!
57. 5 You **worship the fertility gods** by having sex under those
57. 6 You take smooth stones from there and **worship them as gods.**
57. 9 perfumes and ointments and go to **worship the god Molech.**
57. 9 To find gods to **worship,** you send messengers far and wide,
65.11 Zion, my sacred hill, and **worship Gad** and Meni, the gods of

Is	66. 3	They take pleasure in disgusting ways of **worship.**
	66.17	who purify themselves for pagan **worship,** who go in
Jer	1.16	to other gods, and have made idols and **worshipped** them.
	2. 5	They **worshipped worthless idols** and became worthless themselves.
	2. 8	the prophets spoke in the name of Baal and **worshipped useless idols.**
	2.20	and under every green tree you **worshipped fertility gods.**
	2.23	not defiled yourself, that you have never **worshipped Baal?**
	3. 9	and she committed adultery by **worshipping stones** and trees.
	3.23	not helped at all by our pagan **worship** on the hill-tops.
	3.24	But the **worship of Baal,** the god of shame, has made us
	5. 7	They have abandoned me and have **worshipped gods** that are not real.
	7. 6	Stop **worshipping other gods,** for that will destroy you.
	7. 9	offer sacrifices to Baal, and **worship gods** that you had not
	8. 2	and served, and which they have consulted and **worshipped.**
	8.19	made me angry by **worshipping your idols** and by bowing down
	9.14	been stubborn and have **worshipped the idols** of Baal as their
	11.10	they have **worshipped other gods.**
	13.10	wicked as ever, and have **worshipped and served other gods.**
	16.11	turned away from me and **worshipped and served other gods.**
	17. 2	Your people **worship** at the altars and the symbols that
	22. 9	me, your God, and have **worshipped and served other gods."**
	25. 6	told you not to **worship and serve other gods** and not to
	25. 6	make the Lord angry by **worshipping the idols** you had made.
	35.15	warned you not to **worship and serve other gods,** so that you
	44. 8	you make me angry by **worshipping idols** and by sacrificing to
	48.46	The people who **worshipped Chemosh** have been destroyed, and
	49. 1	they let the people who **worship Molech** take the territory of
	51.44	the nations will not **worship** him any more.
Ezek	6. 3	a sword to destroy the places where people **worship idols.**
	8.10	of the other things which the Israelites were **worshipping.**
	8.12	They are all **worshipping** in a room full of images.
	8.16	bowing low towards the east, **worshipping** the rising sun.
	11.21	I will punish the people who love to **worship filthy, disgusting idols.**
	14. 7	turns away from me and **worships idols,** and then goes to
	16.24	you built places to **worship idols** and practise prostitution.
	16.31	On every street you built places to **worship idols**
	16.39	places where you engage in prostitution and **worship idols.**
	18. 6	He doesn't **worship the idols** of the Israelites or eat the
	18.12	**worships disgusting idols,** [13]and lends money for profit.
	18.15	He doesn't **worship the idols** of the Israelites or eat
	20.16	profaned the Sabbath—they preferred to **worship their idols.**
	20.24	and **worshipped the same idols** their ancestors had served.
	20.32	who live in other countries and **worship trees** and rocks.
	21. 2	Denounce the places where people **worship.**
	22. 3	defiled yourself by **worshipping idols,** your time is coming.
	23. 7	led her to defile herself by **worshipping Assyrian idols.**
	23.49	you for your immorality and your sin of **worshipping idols.**
	33.25	You **worship idols.**
	43. 7	my holy name by **worshipping other gods** or by burying the
	43. 9	Now they must stop **worshipping other gods** and remove the
	44.10	of the people of Israel, deserted me and **worshipped idols.**
	44.12	because they conducted the **worship of idols** for the people
Dan	3. 5	to bow down and **worship the gold statue** that King
	3. 6	does not bow down and **worship** will immediately be thrown
	3. 7	languages bowed down and **worshipped the gold statue** which
	3.10	to bow down and **worship the gold statue,** [11]and that anyone
	3.11	does not bow down and **worship** it is to be thrown into
	3.12	They do not **worship your god** or bow down to the statue
	3.14	that you refuse to **worship my god** and to bow down to
	3.15	all the other instruments, bow down and **worship the statue.**
	3.18	that we will not **worship your god,** and we will not bow
	3.28	rather than bow down and **worship** any god except their own.
	11.39	fortresses, he will use people who **worship a foreign god.**
Hos	2. 8	the silver and gold that she used in the **worship of Baal.**
	4.10	You will **worship the fertility gods,** but still have no children,
	4.15	Don't **worship** at Gilgal or Bethaven, or make promises there
	6.10	my people have defiled themselves by **worshipping idols.**
	8. 5	I hate the gold bull **worshipped** by the people of the city
	8. 6	The gold bull **worshipped** in Samaria will be smashed to pieces!
	9.10	Mount Peor, they began to **worship Baal,** and soon became as
	10. 1	beautiful they made the sacred stone pillars they **worship.**
	10. 8	where the people of Israel **worship idols,** will be destroyed.
	12.11	Yet idols are **worshipped** in Gilead,
	12.11	and those who **worship** them will die.
	13. 1	But the people sinned by **worshipping Baal,** and for this they
	13. 2	by making metal images to **worship—idols** of silver, designed
Amos	2. 8	At every place of **worship** men sleep on clothing that they
	5.26	But now, because you have **worshipped images** of Sakkuth,
Jon	2. 8	Those who **worship worthless idols** have abandoned their loyalty
Mic	4. 5	Each nation **worships** and obeys its own god, but we will worship
	5.13	will you **worship** the things that you yourselves have made.
Hab	1.16	They even **worship** their nets and offer sacrifices to them,
Zeph	1. 4	last trace of the **worship of Baal** there, and no one will
	1. 5	on the roof and **worships the sun,** the moon, and the stars.
	1. 9	I will punish all who **worship** like pagans and who steal
Zech	13. 2	be a prophet and will take away the desire to **worship idols.**
Mal	2.11	Men have married women who **worship foreign gods.**
Mt	4. 9	the Devil said, "if you kneel down and **worship** me."
Lk	4. 7	All this will be yours, then, if you **worship** me."
Acts	7.42	and gave them over to **worship the stars** of heaven,
	7.43	they were idols that you had made to **worship.**
	17.23	at the places where you **worship,** I found an altar on which
	19.27	will be destroyed—the goddess **worshipped** by everyone in Asia
Rom	1.23	they **worship images** made to look like mortal man
	1.25	they **worship** and serve what God has created instead of the
	11. 4	seven thousand men who have not **worshipped the false god Baal."**
1 Cor	5.10	immoral or greedy or are thieves or who **worship idols.**
	5.11	is immoral or greedy or **worships idols** or is a slanderer
	6. 9	immoral or who **worship idols** or are adulterers
	10. 7	nor to **worship idols,** as some of them did.
	10.14	my dear friends, keep away from the **worship of idols.**
	12. 2	led astray in many ways to the **worship of lifeless idols.**
Gal	5.20	in **worship of idols** and witchcraft.
Col	2.18	who insists on false humility and the **worship of angels.**
	2.23	in their forced **worship of angels,** and false humility,
2 Thes	2. 4	so-called god or object of **worship** and will put himself
1 Pet	4. 3	drinking parties, and the disgusting **worship of idols.**
Rev	9.20	They did not stop **worshipping demons,** nor the idols of gold,
	13. 4	Everyone **worshipped the dragon** because he had given his authority
	13. 4	**worshipped the beast** also, saying, "Who is like the beast?
	13. 8	people living on earth will **worship** it, except those whose names
	13.12	who live on it to **worship** the first beast,
	13.15	and put to death all those who would not **worship** it.
	14. 9	in a loud voice, "Whoever **worships the beast** and its image
	14.11	or night for those who **worship the beast** and its image,
	16. 2	the beast and on those who had **worshipped its image.**
	19.10	down at his feet to **worship** him, but he said to me,
	19.20	those who had **worshipped the image** of the beast.)
	20. 4	They had not **worshipped the beast** or its image,
	21. 8	who practise magic, those who **worship idols,** and all liars—
	22. 8	had shown me these things, and I was about to **worship** him.
	22.15	murderers, those who **worship idols** and those who are liars

WORST

Gen	35.17	labour pains were at their **worst,** the midwife said to her,
Ex	9.24	It was the **worst** storm that Egypt had ever known in all
Ruth	1.17	May the Lord's **worst** punishment come upon me if I let
2 Sam	19. 7	That would be the **worst** disaster you have suffered in all
1 Kgs	14.24	**Worst** of all, there were men and women who served as
	18. 2	in Samaria was at its **worst,** [3]so Ahab called in Obadiah,
	18.17	"So there you are—the **worst** troublemaker in Israel!"
2 Kgs	7. 4	the **worst** they can do is kill us, but maybe they will
2 Chr	28.22	his troubles were at their **worst,** that man Ahaz sinned
Job	19.11	he treats me like his **worst** enemy.
Ps	41. 7	to each other about me, they imagine the **worst** about me.
Prov	29.24	A thief's partner is his own **worst** enemy.
Jer	2.33	Even the **worst** of women can learn from you.
Ezek	14.21	"I will send my four **worst** punishments on Jerusalem—war,
Dan	12. 1	troubles, the **worst** since nations first came into existence.
Mt	10.36	a man's **worst** enemies will be the members of his own family.
1 Tim	1.15	I am the **worst** of them, [16]but God was merciful to me
	1.16	in dealing with me, the **worst** of sinners, as an example for
Rev	16.18	this was the **worst** earthquake of all!

WORTH

Gen	23.15	"Sir, land **worth** only four hundred pieces of silver—what
	32.10	I am not **worth** all the kindness and faithfulness that
Judg	8. 2	men of Ephraim did is **worth** more than what my whole clan
2 Sam	18. 3	but you are **worth** ten thousand of us.
Job	25. 6	What is man **worth** in God's eyes?
	28.17	It is **worth** more than gold, Than a gold vase or finest
	28.27	saw wisdom and tested its **worth**— He gave it his approval.
Ps	37.16	a good man owns is **worth** more than the wealth of all
Prov	3.14	it is **worth** more to you than gold.
	23.23	and good sense—these are **worth** paying for, but too valuable
	31.10	She is **worth** far more than jewels!
Is	2.22	What are they **worth?**
	7.23	a thousand vines and each **worth** a thousand pieces of silver,
Zech	11.13	sum they thought I was **worth**—and put them in the temple
Mt	6.25	After all, isn't life **worth** more than food?
	6.25	And isn't the body **worth** more than clothes?
	6.26	Aren't you **worth** much more than birds?
	10.31	you are **worth** much more than many sparrows!
	12.12	And a man is **worth** much more than a sheep!
	17.27	will find a coin **worth** enough for my temple-tax and yours.
Mk	12.42	dropped in two little copper coins, **worth** about a penny.
Lk	12. 7	you are **worth** much more than many sparrows!
	12.24	You are **worth** so much more than birds!
1 Cor	12.23	parts that we think aren't **worth** very much are the ones
Phil	2.22	how he has proved his **worth,**
Heb	11.26	for the Messiah was **worth** far more than all the treasures

WORTHLESS

[NOT WORTH]

Deut	13.13	you may hear [13]that some **worthless** men of your nation have
Judg	9. 4	money he hired a bunch of **worthless** scoundrels to join him.
	11. 3	he attracted a group of **worthless** men, and they went round
1 Sam	1.16	Don't think I am a **worthless** woman.
	10.27	But some **worthless** people said, "How can this fellow do
	15. 9	they destroyed only what was useless or **worthless.**
	30.22	But some mean and **worthless** men who had gone with David said,
2 Sam	20. 1	be in Gilgal a **worthless** character named Sheba son of Bikri,
2 Kgs	17.15	They worshipped **worthless** idols and became worthless themselves,
2 Chr	13. 7	gathered together a group of **worthless** scoundrels, and they
Job	11.11	God knows which men are **worthless;**
	15.16	man is **worthless.**
	30. 1	fathers have always been so **worthless** that I wouldn't let
	30. 8	A **worthless** bunch of nameless nobodies!
	34.18	God condemns kings and rulers when they are **worthless**
Ps	4. 2	will you love what is **worthless** and go after what is false?
	26. 4	I do not keep company with **worthless** people;
	60.11	human help is **worthless.**

Ps 62. 9 great and small alike are **worthless.**
108.12 human help is **worthless.**
118.22 which the builders rejected as **worthless** turned out to be
119.37 Keep me from paying attention to what is **worthless;**
Prov 6.12 **Worthless,** wicked people go around telling lies.
10.20 a wicked man's ideas are **worthless.**
17. 2 gain authority over a master's **worthless** son and receive a
Is 1.22 Jerusalem, you were once like silver, but now you are **worthless;**
3. 5 and **worthless** people will not respect their superiors.
33.11 You make **worthless** plans and everything you do is useless.
44. 9 those who make idols are **worthless,** and the gods they prize
48.10 But I have found that you are **worthless.**
Jer 2. 5 They worshipped **worthless** idols and became worthless themselves.
2.21 You are like a rotten, **worthless** vine.
6.30 They will be called **worthless** dross, because I, the
10. 3 The religion of these people is **worthless.**
10.15 They are **worthless** and should be despised;
14.14 predictions are **worthless** things that they have imagined.
51.18 They are **worthless** and should be despised;
Amos 8. 6 We can sell **worthless** wheat at a high price.
9. 9 them among the nations to remove all who are **worthless.**
Jon 2. 8 who worship **worthless** idols have abandoned their loyalty to you.
Mic 7. 4 the best and most honest of them are as **worthless** as weeds.
Zech 11.15 again act the part of a shepherd, this time a **worthless** one.
11.17 That **worthless** shepherd is doomed!
Mal 1. 7 This is how—by offering **worthless** food on my altar.
1.12 say that my altar is **worthless** and when you offer on it
1.14 the cheat who sacrifices a **worthless** animal to me, when he
Mt 5.13 It has become **worthless,** so it is thrown out and people
5.22 whoever calls his brother a **worthless** fool will be in danger
13.48 go into their buckets, the **worthless** ones are thrown away.
18.32 'You **worthless** slave!'
21.42 which the builders rejected as **worthless** turned out to be
Mk 12.10 which the builders rejected as **worthless** turned out to be
Lk 16.15 of great value by man are **worth nothing** in God's sight.
20.17 which the builders rejected as **worthless** turned out to be
Jn 8.54 "If I were to honour myself, that honour would be **worth nothing.**
Acts 14.15 turn you away from these **worthless** things to the living God,
17. 5 gathered some of the **worthless** loafers from the streets
20.24 But I reckon my own life to be **worth nothing** to me;
Rom 4.14 Law, then man's faith means nothing and God's promise is **worthless.**
1 Cor 3.20 "The Lord knows that the thoughts of the wise are **worthless."**
Eph 4.17 the heathen, whose thoughts are **worthless** [18] and whose minds
5.11 nothing to do with the **worthless** things that people do,
Col 2. 8 by means of the **worthless** deceit of human wisdom,
1 Tim 4. 7 But keep away from those godless legends, which are **not worth** telling.
Tit 3. 9 They are useless and **worthless.**
Heb 6. 8 But if it grows thorns and weeds, it is **worth nothing;**
Jas 1.26 tongue, his religion is **worthless** and he deceives himself.
1 Pet 1.18 set you free from the **worthless** manner of life handed down
2. 4 rejected by man as **worthless** but chosen by God as valuable.
2. 7 which the builders rejected as **worthless** turned out to be

WORTHWHILE

Prov 17. 7 do not tell lies, and fools have nothing **worthwhile** to say.
Jer 15.19 talking nonsense you proclaim a **worthwhile** message, you will
1 Cor 16. 4 If it seems **worth while** for me to go,
16. 9 opportunity here for great and **worthwhile** work,
Phil 1.22 live I can do more **worthwhile** work, then I am not sure

WORTHY
[UNWORTHY]

Deut 22.26 girl, because she has not committed a sin **worthy** of death.
32. 5 But you are unfaithful, **unworthy** to be his people, a
2 Sam 7.18 and prayed, "I am not **worthy** of what you have already done
1 Chr 17.16 and prayed, "I am not **worthy** of what you have already done
Esth 2.18 the whole empire and distributed gifts **worthy** of a king.
Prov 22.29 who is better than most and **worthy** of the company of kings.
Lk 7. 7 neither do I consider myself **worthy** to come to you in person.
20.35 men and women who are **worthy** to rise from death and live
Acts 5.41 because God had considered them **worthy** to suffer disgrace
13.46 do not consider yourselves **worthy** of eternal life, we will leave
1 Cor 7.25 opinion as one who by the Lord's mercy is **worthy** of trust.
1 Thes 2. 4 because he has judged us **worthy** to be entrusted with the
2 Thes 1. 5 a result you will become **worthy** of his Kingdom,
1.11 our God to make you **worthy** of the life he has called
1 Tim 1.12 for considering me **worthy** and appointing me to serve him,
5.17 leaders should be considered **worthy** of receiving double pay,
6. 1 slaves must consider their masters **worthy** of all respect,
Heb 3. 3 Jesus is **worthy** of much greater honour than Moses.
Rev 3. 4 clothed in white, because you are **worthy** to do so.
4.11 You are **worthy** to receive glory, honour, and power.
5. 2 a loud voice, "Who is **worthy** to break the seals and open
5. 4 could be found who was **worthy** to open the scroll or look
5. 9 "You are **worthy** to take the scroll and to break open its
5.12 Lamb who was killed is **worthy** to receive power, wealth, wisdom,

WOUND

Ex 21.25 burn for burn, **wound for wound,** bruise for bruise.
Deut 32.39 and I give life, I **wound** and I heal, and no one
32.42 even the **wounded** and prisoners will die.'
Josh 5. 8 whole nation stayed in the camp until the **wounds** had healed.
Judg 9.40 Many were **wounded,** even at the city gate.
1 Sam 17.52 The Philistines fell **wounded** all along the road
31. 3 and he himself was hit by enemy arrows and badly **wounded.**
2 Sam 1. 9 I have been badly **wounded,** and I'm about to die.'
1.15 struck the Amalekite and mortally **wounded** him, [16] and David
10.18 horsemen, and they **wounded** Shobach, the enemy commander,
1 Kgs 22.34 "I'm **wounded!"**
22.35 The blood from his **wound** ran down and covered the bottom of
2 Kgs 8.28 at Ramoth in Gilead, and Joram was **wounded** in battle.
8.29 Jezreel to recover from his **wounds,** and Ahaziah went there
9.14 gone to recover from the **wounds** which he had received in the
9.27 ordered his men, and they **wounded** him as he drove his
1 Chr 10. 3 Saul, and he was hit by enemy arrows and badly **wounded.**
2 Chr 18.33 "I'm **wounded!"**
22. 5 at Ramoth in Gilead, and Joram was **wounded** in battle.
22. 6 Jezreel to recover from his **wounds,** and Ahaziah went there
24.25 He was severely **wounded,** and when the enemy withdrew,
28.15 enough to eat and drink, and put olive-oil on their **wounds.**
Job 5.18 God bandages the **wounds** he makes;
16.13 at me from every side— arrows that pierce and **wound** me;
16.14 He **wounds** me again and again;
24.12 In the cities the **wounded** and dying cry out, but God
34. 6 I am fatally **wounded,** but I am sinless."
41.26 There is no sword that can **wound** him;
Ps 38. 2 You have **wounded** me with your arrows;
60. 2 now heal its **wounds,** because it is falling apart.
64. 7 But God shoots his arrows at them, and suddenly they are **wounded.**
69.26 they talk about the sufferings of those you have **wounded.**
129. 3 They cut deep **wounds** in my back and made it like a
147. 3 He heals the broken-hearted and bandages their **wounds.**
Prov 3. 8 good medicine, healing your **wounds** and easing your pains.
6.15 them without warning, and they will be fatally **wounded.**
12.18 Thoughtless words can **wound** as deeply as any sword, but
25.20 clothes on a cold day or like rubbing salt in a **wound.**
Is 1. 5 head is already covered with **wounds,** and your heart and mind
1. 6 You are covered with bruises and sores and open **wounds.**
1. 6 Your **wounds** have not been cleaned or bandaged.
28.13 You will be **wounded,** trapped, and taken prisoner.
30.26 Lord bandages and heals the **wounds** he has given his people.
53. 5 of our sins he was **wounded,** beaten because of the evil we
58. 8 the morning sun, and your **wounds** will be quickly healed.
Jer 6. 7 sickness and **wounds** are all I see.
6.14 They act as if my people's **wounds** were only scratches.
8.11 They act as if my people's **wounds** were only scratches.
10.19 Our **wounds** will not heal.
14.17 for my people are deeply **wounded** and are badly hurt.
15.18 Why are my **wounds** incurable?
30.12 "Your **wounds** are incurable, your injuries cannot be healed.
30.17 I will heal your **wounds,** though your enemies say, 'Zion is
37.10 Babylonian army, so that only **wounded** men are left, lying in
51. 4 They will be **wounded** and die in the streets of their cities.
51. 8 Get medicine for its **wounds,** and perhaps it can be healed.
51.52 and the **wounded** will groan throughout the country.
Lam 2.12 though they were **wounded,** And slowly die in their mothers'
Hos 5.13 when Judah saw her own **wounds,** then Israel went to Assyria
5.13 for help, but he could not cure them or heal their **wounds.**
6. 1 he has **wounded** us, but he will bandage our wounds, won't he?
Mic 1. 9 Samaria's **wounds** cannot be healed, and Judah is about to
Nah 3.19 remedy for your injuries, and your **wounds** cannot be healed.
Zech 13. 6 Then if someone asks him, 'What are those **wounds** on your chest?'
Lk 10.34 poured oil and wine on his **wounds** and bandaged them;
20.12 the tenants **wounded** him, too, and threw him out.
Acts 16.33 the jailer took them and washed their **wounds;**
19.16 from his house, **wounded** and with their clothes torn off.
1 Cor 8.12 sinning against your Christian brothers and **wounding** their weak conscience.
1 Pet 2.24 It is by his **wounds** that you have been healed.
Rev 13. 3 to have been fatally wounded, but the **wound** had healed.
13.12 to worship the first beast, whose **wound** had healed.
13.14 the beast that had been **wounded** by the sword and yet lived.

WOVEN see WEAVE

WRAP

Gen 44.30 His life is **wrapped** up with the life of the boy, and
Ex 12.34 baking-pans with unleavened dough, **wrapped** them in clothing,
Num 4.10 They shall **wrap** it and all its equipment in a fine
4.12 used in the Holy Place, **wrap** them in a blue cloth, put
1 Sam 21. 9 it is behind the ephod, **wrapped** in a cloth.
1 Kgs 20.32 **wrapped** sackcloth round their waists and ropes round their necks,
Job 8.17 Their roots **wrap** round the stones and hold fast to every rock.
38. 9 I who covered the sea with clouds and **wrapped** it in darkness.
Prov 30. 4 Or **wrapped** up water in a piece of cloth?
Is 28.20 out on, with a blanket too narrow to **wrap** himself in.
Ezek 5. 3 back a few hairs and **wrap** them in the hem of your
16. 4 washed you or rubbed you with salt or **wrapped** you in cloth.
Dan 4.23 **Wrap** a band of iron and bronze round it, and leave it
Jon 2. 5 covered me completely, and seaweed was **wrapped** round my head.
Mt 27.59 So Joseph took it, **wrapped** it in a new linen sheet,
Mk 15.46 took the body down, **wrapped** it in the sheet, and placed
Lk 2. 7 birth to her first son, **wrapped** him in strips of cloth
2.12 you will find a baby **wrapped** in strips of cloth and lying
23.53 he took the body down, **wrapped** it in a linen sheet,
24.12 he bent down and saw the linen **wrappings** but nothing else.
Jn 11.44 his hands and feet **wrapped** in grave clothes,
19.40 men took Jesus' body and **wrapped** it in linen with the spices
20. 5 saw the linen **wrappings,** but he did not go in.
20. 6 He saw the linen **wrappings** lying there [7] and the cloth which
20. 7 lying with the linen **wrappings** but was rolled up by itself.
21. 7 it was the Lord, he **wrapped** his outer garment round him

Acts 5. 6 The young men came in, **wrapped** up his body, carried him out,
Rev 10. 1 He was **wrapped** in a cloud and had a rainbow round his

WRATH

Job 19.29 the sword that brings God's **wrath** on sin, so that you will
21.20 let them feel the **wrath** of Almighty God.
Jer 21. 5 you with all my might, my anger, my **wrath,** and my fury.

AV WRATH

see also **ANGER, FURY, PUNISH**

Gen 31.36 Then Jacob lost his **temper.**
2 Kgs 5.11 But Naaman left in a **rage,** saying, "I thought that he
Esth 2.21 the king's rooms, became **hostile** to King Xerxes and plotted
Job 5. 2 worry yourself to death with **resentment** would be a foolish,
Ps 69.24 let your **indignation** overtake them.
Prov 11. 4 on the day you face **death,** but honesty can save your life.
12.16 When a fool is **annoyed,** he quickly lets it be known.
14.29 if you have a hot **temper,** you only show how stupid you
15.18 Hot **tempers** cause arguments, but patience brings peace.
19.19 If someone has a hot **temper,** let him take the consequences.
Is 16. 6 We know that they are **arrogant** and conceited, but their boasts
Jer 48.30 I, the Lord, know of their **arrogance.**
Rev 12.12 and he is filled with **rage,** because he knows that he has

WREATH

1 Cor 9.25 in order to be crowned with a **wreath** that will not last;

WRECK

[SHIPWRECKS]

1 Kgs 22.48 but they were **wrecked** at Eziongeber and never sailed.
2 Chr 20.37 And the ships were **wrecked** and never sailed.
Ps 74. 7 They **wrecked** your Temple and set it on fire;
Ezek 19. 7 He **wrecked** forts, he ruined towns.
27.26 you out to sea, An east wind **wrecked** you far from land.
27.27 All, all were lost at sea When your ship was **wrecked.**
27.34 Now you are **wrecked** in the sea;
2 Cor 11.25 I have been in three **shipwrecks,** and once I spent

WRENCH

Ezek 29. 7 pierced their armpits, and made them **wrench** their backs.

WRESTLE

Gen 32.24 a man came and **wrestled** with him until just before daybreak.

WRIGGLE

Is 27. 1 sword to punish Leviathan, that **wriggling,** twisting dragon,

WRING

[WRUNG]

Lev 1.15 present it at the altar, **wring** its neck, and burn its head
Judg 6.38 he squeezed the wool and **wrung** enough dew out of it to
Ezek 6.11 The Sovereign Lord said, **"Wring** your hands!

WRINKLE

Eph 5.27 pure and faultless, without spot or **wrinkle** or any other imperfection.

WRIST

Is 3.19 on their heads, on their necks, [19]and on their **wrists.**
Jer 40. 4 I am taking the chains off your **wrists** and setting you free.

WRISTBANDS

Ezek 13.18 You sew magic **wristbands** for everyone and make magic scarves
13.20 "I hate the **wristbands** that you use in your attempt to

WRITE

[WROTE]

Ex 17.14 the Lord said to Moses, **"Write** an account of this victory,
24. 4 Moses **wrote** down all the Lord's commands.
24. 7 which the Lord's commands were **written,** and read it aloud to
24.12 that I have **written** for the instruction of the people."
25.16 I will give you, on which the commandments are **written.**
31.18 tablets on which God himself had **written** the commandments.
32.15 stone tablets with the commandments **written** on both sides.
32.32 book in which you have **written** the names of your people."
34. 1 first ones, and I will **write** on them the words that were
34.27 The Lord said to Moses, **"Write** these words down,
34.28 He **wrote** on the tablets the words of the covenant—the Ten
38.21 were kept on which the Ten Commandments were **written.**
Num 5.23 Then the priest shall **write** this curse down
5.23 and wash the **writing** off into the bowl of bitter
17. 2 **Write** each man's name on his stick
17. 3 and then **write** Aaron's name on the stick representing
33. 2 command of the Lord, Moses **wrote** down the name of the place
Deut 4.13 the Ten Commandments, which he **wrote** on two stone tablets.
5.22 Then he **wrote** them on two stone tablets and gave them to
6. 9 **Write** them on the door-posts of your houses and on your gates.
9. 9 stone tablets on which was **written** the covenant that the
9.10 tablets on which he had **written** with his own hand what he
Deut 9.11 the two stone tablets on which he had **written** the covenant.
9.15 the two stone tablets on which the covenant was **written.**
10. 2 and I will **write** on those tablets
10. 2 what I **wrote** on the tablets that you broke,
10. 4 Then the Lord **wrote** on those tablets the same words
10. 4 that he had **written** the first time,
11.20 **Write** them on the door-posts of your houses and on your gates.
24. 1 So he **writes** out divorce papers, gives them to her, and
24. 3 want her, so he also **writes** out divorce papers, gives them
27. 3 cover them with plaster, [3]and **write** on them all these laws
27. 8 with plaster **write** clearly every word of God's laws."
28.58 all God's teachings that are **written** in this book and if you
29.20 him, and all the disasters **written** in this book will fall on
29.21 in the covenant that is **written** in this book of the Lord's
29.27 on their land all the disasters **written** in this book.
30.10 all his laws that are **written** in this book of his teachings.
31. 9 So Moses **wrote** down God's Law and gave it to the
31.19 "Now, **write** down this song.
31.22 That same day Moses **wrote** down the song and taught it
31.24 Moses **wrote** God's Law in a book, taking care not to
Josh 1. 8 night, and make sure that you obey everything **written** in it.
8.32 on the stones a copy of the Law which Moses had **written.**
8.34 curses, just as they are **written** in the book of the Law.
10.13 This is **written** in The Book of Jashar.
18. 6 **Write** down a description of these seven divisions and
18. 9 land and set down in **writing** how they divided it into seven
23. 6 and do everything that is **written** in the book of the Law
24.26 Joshua **wrote** these commands in the book of the Law of God.
Judg 8.14 The young man **wrote** down for Gideon the names of the
1 Sam 10.25 of a king, and then **wrote** them in a book, which he
2 Sam 11.14 The next morning David **wrote** a letter to Joab and sent
11.15 He **wrote:**
1 Kgs 2. 3 his laws and commands, as **written** in the Law of Moses, so
21. 8 Then she **wrote** some letters, signed them with Ahab's name,
2 Kgs 10. 1 Jehu **wrote** a letter and sent copies to the rulers of the
10. 6 Jehu **wrote** them another letter:
17.37 always obey the laws and commands that I **wrote** for you.
22.16 and all its people, as **written** in the book that the king
22.18 You listened to what is **written** in the book, [19]and you
23. 3 demands attached to the covenant, as **written** in the book.
23.21 the Lord their God, as **written** in the book of the covenant.
23.24 order to enforce the laws **written** in the book that the High
1 Chr 2.55 following clans of experts in **writing** and copying documents
16.40 in accordance with what was **written** in the Law which the
28.19 contained in the plan **written** according to the instructions
2 Chr 2.11 He **wrote,** "Because the Lord loves his people, he has made
13.22 and what he did, is **written** in The History of Iddo the
29.30 songs of praise that were **written** by David and by Asaph the
32.17 The letter that the emperor **wrote** defied the Lord, the
34.24 its people with the curses **written** in the book that was read
34.26 You listened to what is **written** in the book, [27]and you
34.31 demands attached to the covenant, as **written** in the book.
36.22 and send it out in **writing** to be read aloud everywhere in
Ezra 1. 1 and send it out in **writing** to be read aloud everywhere in
3. 2 according to the instructions **written** in the Law of Moses,
4. 6 Judah and Jerusalem brought **written** charges against them.
4. 7 Tabeel, and their associates **wrote** a letter to the emperor.
4. 7 The letter was **written** in Aramaic and was to be translated
4. 8 the secretary of the province, **wrote** the following letter to
5. 5 action until they could **write** to Darius and receive a reply.
Neh 8.15 according to the instructions **written** in the Law."
9.38 hereby make a solemn **written** agreement, and our leaders,
Esth 1.19 Order it to be **written** into the laws of Persia and Media,
1.22 language and the system of **writing** of that province, saying
2.23 account of this to be **written** down in the official records
3.12 every language and system of **writing** used in the empire and
8. 8 You may, however, **write** to the Jews whatever you wish;
8. 8 and you may **write** it in my name and stamp it with
8. 9 The letters were **written** to each province in its own
8. 9 own language and system of **writing**
8. 9 and to the Jews in their language and system of **writing.**
8.10 Mordecai had the letters **written** in the name of King Xerxes,
9.20 Mordecai had these events **written** down and sent letters
9.25 king, and the king issued **written** orders with the result
9.29 Abihail, along with Mordecai, also **wrote** a letter, putting
9.29 the letter about Purim, which Mordecai had **written** earlier.
9.32 the rules for Purim, was **written** down on a scroll.
Job 19.24 my words in stone and **write** them so that they would last
31.35 opponent brings against me were **written** down so that I could
Ps 45. 1 the pen of a good **writer** my tongue is ready with a
87. 6 The Lord will **write** a list of the peoples and include them
102.18 **Write** down for the coming generation what the Lord has done,
Prov 3. 3 **write** them on your heart.
7. 3 **write** it on your heart.
22.20 I have **written** down thirty sayings for you.
Ecc 12.10 find comforting words, but the words he **wrote** were honest.
12.12 is no end to the **writing** of books, and too much study
Is 8. 1 "Take a large piece of **writing material**
8. 1 and **write** on it in large letters:
28.16 solid cornerstone on which are **written** the words, 'Faith
30. 8 God told me to **write** down in a book what the people
38. 9 After Hezekiah recovered from his illness, he **wrote** this song
49.16 I have **written** your name on the palms of my hands.
65. 6 on their punishment, and their sentence is **written** down.
Jer 17. 1 "People of Judah, your sin is **written** with an iron pen;
17.13 They will disappear like names **written** in the dust, because
29. 1 I **wrote** a letter to the priests, the prophets, the leaders
29. 2 I **wrote** it after King Jehoiachin, his mother,
29.24 In this letter, Shemaiah **wrote** to Zephaniah:
30. 2 **"Write** down in a book everything that I have told you,
31.33 will put my law within them and **write** it on their hearts.

Book	Ref	Context
Jer	36. 2	me, [2]"Get a scroll and **write** on it everything that I have
	36. 2	**Write** everything that I have told you from the time I first
	36. 4	And Baruch **wrote** it all down on a scroll.
	36.17	him, "Tell us, now, how did you come to **write** all this?
	36.18	it to me, and I **wrote** it down in ink on this
	36.28	to take another scroll and **write** on it everything that
	36.29	have asked Jeremiah why he **wrote** that the king of Babylonia
	36.32	Baruch, and he **wrote** down everything that I dictated.
	36.32	He **wrote** everything that had been on the first scroll and
	45. 1	was king of Judah, Baruch **wrote** down what I had dictated to
	51.60	I **wrote** in a book an account of all the destruction that
	51.61	to read aloud to the people everything that is **written** here.
Ezek	2.10	I saw that there was **writing** on both sides—
	2.10	cries of grief were **written** there, and wails and groans.
	9. 2	dressed in linen clothes, carrying something to **write** with.
	24. 2	"Mortal man," he said, **"write** down today's date,
	27.35	their kings are terrified, and fear is **written** on their faces.
	37.16	"take a wooden stick and **write** on it the words, 'The
	37.16	Then take another stick and **write** on it the words, 'The
	43.11	**Write** all this down for them so that they can see how
Dan	1. 4	was to teach them to read and **write** the Babylonian language.
	5. 5	human hand appeared and began **writing** on the plaster wall of
	5. 5	And the king saw the hand as it was **writing.**
	5. 7	"Anyone who can read this **writing** and tell me what it means
	5. 8	of them could read the **writing** or tell the king what it
	5.15	brought in to read this **writing** and tell me what it means,
	5.16	If you can read this **writing** and tell me what it means,
	5.17	Your Majesty what has been **written** and tell you what it means.
	5.24	That is why God has sent the hand to **write** these words.
	5.25	"This is what was **written:**
	6.25	Then King Darius **wrote** to the people of all nations,
	7. 1	I **wrote** the dream down, and this is the record [2]of what
	9.11	us the curses that are **written** in the Law of Moses, your
	10.20	to reveal to you what is **written** in the Book of Truth.
	12. 1	nation whose names are **written** in God's book will be saved.
Hos	8.12	I **write** down countless teachings for the people, but
	14. 9	are wise understand what is **written** here, and may they take
Hab	2. 2	**"Write** down clearly on clay tablets what I reveal to you,
	2. 3	Put it in **writing,** because it is not yet time for it
Zech	5. 3	to me, "On it is **written** the curse that is to go
Mal	3.16	In his presence, there was **written** down in a book a record
Mt	2. 5	"For this is what the prophet **wrote:**
	5.31	his wife must give her a **written** notice of divorce.'
	21.13	to them, "It is **written** in the Scriptures that God said,
	26.56	make what the prophets **wrote** in the Scriptures come true."
	27.37	they put the **written** notice of the accusation against him:
Mk	1. 2	It began as the prophet Isaiah had **written:**
	7. 6	You are hypocrites, just as he **wrote:**
	10. 4	permission for a man to **write** a divorce notice and send his
	10. 5	Jesus said to them, "Moses **wrote** this law for you because
	11.17	"It is **written** in the Scriptures that God said, 'My Temple
	12.19	Jesus and said, [19]"Teacher, Moses **wrote** this law for us:
	12.26	There it is **written** that God said to Moses, 'I am the
Lk	1. 1	have done their best to **write** a report of the things that
	1. 2	They **wrote** what we have been told by those who saw these
	1. 3	it would be good to **write** an orderly account for you.
	1.63	Zechariah asked for a **writing tablet**
	1.63	and **wrote,** "His name is John."
	2.23	the Lord, [23]as it is **written** in the law of the Lord:
	3. 4	As it is **written** in the book of the prophet Isaiah:
	4.17	the place where it is **written,** [18]"The Spirit of the Lord
	10.20	rather be glad because your names are **written** in heaven."
	16. 6	'sit down and **write** fifty.'
	16. 7	**'write** eight hundred.'
	16.16	Law of Moses and the **writings** of the prophets were in effect
	18.31	Jerusalem where everything the prophets **wrote** about the Son
	19.46	saying to them, "It is **written** in the Scriptures that God said,
	20.28	Jesus and said, [28]"Teacher, Moses **wrote** this law for us:
	22.37	me, because what was **written** about me is coming true."
	23.38	Above him were **written** these words:
	24.27	the books of Moses and the **writings** of all the prophets.
	24.44	everything **written** about me in the Law of Moses,
	24.44	the **writings** of the prophets, and the Psalms
	24.46	Scriptures, [46]and said to them, "This is what is **written:**
Jn	1.45	found the one whom Moses **wrote** about in the book of the
	1.45	and whom the prophets also **wrote** about.
	5.46	Moses, you would have believed me, because he **wrote** about me.
	5.47	do not believe what he **wrote,** how can you believe what I
	6.45	The prophets **wrote,** 'Everyone will be taught by God.'
	8. 6	But he bent over and **wrote** on the ground with his finger.
	8. 8	Then he bent over again and **wrote** on the ground.
	8.17	It is **written** in your Law that when two witnesses agree,
	10.34	Jesus answered, "It is **written** in your own Law that God said,
	15.25	happen so that what is **written** in their Law may come true:
	19.19	Pilate **wrote** a notice and had it put on the cross.
	19.19	"Jesus of Nazareth, the King of the Jews," is what he **wrote.**
	19.20	The notice was **written** in Hebrew, Latin, and Greek.
	19.21	said to Pilate, "Do not **write** 'The King of the Jews,' but
	19.22	Pilate answered, "What I have **written** stays written."
	20.30	many other miracles which are not **written** down in this book.
	20.31	But these have been **written** in order that you may
	21.24	who spoke of these things, the one who also **wrote** them down;
	21.25	If they were all **written** down one by one, I suppose that
	21.25	whole world could not hold the books that would be **written.**
Acts	1. 1	In my first book I **wrote** about all the things that Jesus
	1.20	"For it is **written** in the book of Psalms, 'May his
	1.20	It is also **written,** 'May someone else take his place of service.'
	7.42	of heaven, as it is **written** in the book of the prophets:
	13.15	of Moses and from the **writings** of the prophets, the
	13.32	As it is **written** in the second Psalm, 'You are my Son;
	15.20	Instead, we should **write** a letter telling them not to
Acts	15.27	who will tell you in person the same things we are **writing.**
	17.23	I found an altar on which is **written,** 'To an Unknown God'.
	18.27	in Ephesus helped him by **writing** to the believers in Achaia,
	22. 5	I received from them letters **written** to fellow-Jews in Damascus,
	23.25	Then the commander **wrote** a letter that went like this:
	24.14	I also believe in everything **written** in the Law of Moses and
	25.26	But I have nothing definite about him to **write** to the Emperor.
	25.26	after investigating his case, I may have something to **write.**
	28.23	from the Law of Moses and the **writings** of the prophets.
Rom	1. 2	God through his prophets, as **written** in the Holy Scriptures.
	1. 7	And so I **write** to all of you in Rome whom God
	2.15	shows that what the Law commands is **written** in their hearts.
	2.27	Law, even though you have it **written** down and are circumcised;
	2.29	this is the work of God's Spirit, not of the **written** Law.
	4.23	"he was accepted as righteous" were not **written** for him alone.
	4.24	They were **written** also for us who are to be accepted as
	7. 6	the old way of a **written** law, but in the new way
	10. 5	Moses **wrote** this about being put right with God by obeying
	15. 4	Everything **written** in the Scriptures was written to teach us,
	16.22	I, Tertius, the **writer** of this letter, send you Christian greetings.
	16.26	out into the open through the **writings** of the prophets;
1 Cor	4.14	I **write** this to you, not because I want to make you
	5. 9	In the letter that I **wrote** you I told you not to
	7. 1	Now, to deal with the matters you **wrote** about.
	7.25	Now, concerning what you **wrote** about unmarried people:
	8. 1	Now, concerning what you **wrote** about food offered to idols.
	9.10	Of course that was **written** for us.
	9.15	these rights, nor am I **writing** this now in order to claim
	10.11	for others, and they were **written** down as a warning for us.
	12. 1	Now, concerning what you **wrote** about the gifts from the Holy Spirit.
	14.21	In the Scriptures it is **written,** "By means of men
	14.37	realize that what I am **writing** to you is the Lord's command.
	15. 3	that Christ died for our sins, as **written** in the Scriptures;
	15. 4	to life three days later, as **written** in the Scriptures;
	16. 1	Now, concerning what you **wrote** about the money to be
	16.21	With my own hand I **write** this:
2 Cor	1.13	We **write** to you only what you can read and understand.
	2. 3	That is why I **wrote** that letter to you—I did not
	2. 4	I **wrote** to you with a greatly troubled and distressed
	2. 9	I **wrote** you that letter because I wanted to find out how
	3. 2	are the letter we have, **written** on our hearts for everyone
	3. 3	is clear that Christ himself **wrote** this letter and sent it
	3. 3	It is **written,** not with ink but with the Spirit of the
	3. 6	which consists not of a **written** law but of the Spirit.
	3. 6	The **written** law brings death, but the Spirit gives life.
	7. 8	of mine made you sad, I am not sorry I **wrote** it.
	7.12	So, even though I **wrote** that letter, it was not because
	7.12	Instead, I **wrote** it to make plain to you, in God's sight,
	9. 1	no need for me to **write** to you about the help being
	10.11	no difference between what we **write** in our letters when we
	13.10	That is why I **write** this while I am away from you;
Gal	1.20	What I **write** is true.
	3.10	always obey everything that is **written** in the book of the
	6.11	letters I make as I **write** to you now with my own
Eph	3. 3	(I have **written** briefly about this, [4]and if you will read
	3. 4	what I have **written,** you can learn about my understanding
Phil	3. 1	mind repeating what I have **written** before, and you will be
Col	4.18	With my own hand I **write** this:
1 Thes	4. 9	There is no need to **write** to you about love for your
	5. 1	There is no need to **write** to you, brothers, about the
2 Thes	2. 2	prophesying or preaching, or that we **wrote** it in a letter.
	3.17	With my own hand I **write** this:
	3.17	this is how I **write.**
1 Tim	3.14	As I **write** this letter to you, I hope to come and
2 Tim	2.19	and on it are **written** these words:
Tit	1. 4	I **write** to Titus, my true son in the faith that we
Phlm	19	Here, I will **write** this with my own hand:
	21	I am sure, as I **write** this, that you will do what
Heb	8.10	put my laws in their minds and **write** them on their hearts.
	9. 4	the two stone tablets with the commandments **written** on them.
	10. 7	God, just as it is **written** of me in the book of
	10.16	put my laws in their hearts and **write** them on their minds."
	12.23	of God's first-born sons, whose names are **written** in heaven.
	13.22	for this letter I have **written** to you is not very long.
1 Pet	5.12	I **write** you this brief letter with the help of Silas,
2 Pet	3. 1	this is now the second letter I have **written** to you.
	3.15	as our dear brother Paul **wrote** to you, using the wisdom that
	3.16	he says in all his letters when he **writes** on the subject.
1 Jn	1. 1	We **write** to you about the Word of life, which has existed
	1. 4	We **write** this in order that our joy may be complete.
	2. 1	I am **writing** this to you, my children, so that you will
	2. 7	dear friends, this command I am **writing** to you is not new;
	2. 8	the command I am now **writing** to you is new, because its
	2.12	I am **writing** to you, my children, because your sins are
	2.13	I am **writing** to you, fathers, because you know him who
	2.13	I am **writing** to you, young men, because you have defeated
	2.14	I am **writing** to you, my children, because you know the Father.
	2.14	I am **writing** to you, fathers, because you know him who has
	2.14	I am **writing** to you, young men, because you are strong;
	2.21	I am **writing** to you, then, not because you do not know
	2.26	I am **writing** this to you about those who are trying to
	5.13	I am **writing** this to you so that you may know that
2 Jn	5	This is no new command I am **writing** to you;
3 Jn	9	I **wrote** a short letter to the church;
Jude	3	was doing my best to **write** to you about the salvation we
	3	I felt the need of **writing** at once to encourage you to
Rev	1. 3	prophetic message and obey what is **written** in this book!
	1.11	It said, **"Write** down what you see, and send the book to
	1.19	**Write,** then, the things you see, both the things that
	2. 1	"To the angel of the church in Ephesus **write:**

Rev 2. 8 “To the angel of the church in Smyrna **write:**
2.12 “To the angel of the church in Pergamum **write:**
2.17 white stone on which is **written** a new name that no one
2.18 “To the angel of the church in Thyatira **write:**
3. 1 “To the angel of the church in Sardis **write:**
3. 7 “To the angel of the church in Philadelphia **write:**
3.12 I will **write** on him the name of my God and the
3.12 I will also **write** on him my new name.
3.14 “To the angel of the church in Laodicea **write:**
5. 1 it was covered with **writing** on both sides and was sealed
10. 4 As soon as they spoke, I was about to **write.**
10. 4 do not **write** it down!”
13. 8 except those whose names were **written** before the creation of
14. 1 his name and his Father's name **written** on their foreheads.
14.13 Then I heard a voice from heaven saying, “**Write** this:
17. 3 beast that had names insulting to God **written** all over it;
17. 5 On her forehead was **written** a name that has a secret meaning:
17. 8 whose names have not been **written** before the creation of the
19. 9 Then the angel said to me, “**Write** this:
19.12 He had a name **written** on him, but no one except himself
19.16 On his robe and on his thigh was **written** the name:
20.15 did not have his name **written** in the book of the living
21. 5 He also said to me, “**Write** this, because these words are
21.12 On the gates were **written** the names of the twelve tribes of
21.14 twelve foundation-stones, on which were **written** the names of
21.27 Only those whose names are **written** in the Lamb's book of the
22. 4 his face, and his name will be **written** on their foreheads.

WRITHE

Hos 8.10 Soon they will **writhe** in pain, when the emperor of Assyria

WRONG

Gen 20. 5 this with a clear conscience, and I have done no **wrong.**”
20. 9 What **wrong** have I done to you to make you bring this
20.16 everyone will know that you have done no **wrong.**”
41. 9 to the king, “I must confess today that I have done **wrong.**
50.17 the crime your brothers committed when they **wronged** you.'
50.17 Now please forgive us the **wrong** that we, the servants of
Ex 2.13 one who was in the **wrong,** “Why are you beating up a
9.27 in the right, and my people and I are in the **wrong.**
23. 2 the majority when they do **wrong** or when they give evidence
Num 5. 6 the Lord and commits a **wrong** against someone, [7] he must
5. 7 an additional twenty per cent, to the person he has **wronged.**
16.15 I have not **wronged** any of them;
22.34 if you think it is **wrong** for me to go on, I
Deut 1.39 young to know right from **wrong,** will enter the land—the
15.21 But if there is anything **wrong** with the animals, if they
16.19 wise and honest men, and cause them to give **wrong** decisions.
27.18 on anyone who leads a blind man in the **wrong** direction.'
Judg 11.27 No, I have not done you any **wrong.**
11.27 You are doing **wrong** by making war on me.
1 Sam 11. 5 from the field with his oxen, and he asked, “What's **wrong?**
12. 3 If I have done anything **wrong,** accuse me now in the presence
19. 4 Saul and said, “Sir, don't do **wrong** to your servant David.
19. 4 He has never done you any **wrong;**
19. 5 you now want to do **wrong** to an innocent man and kill
20. 1 What **wrong** have I done to your father to make him want
24.11 to kill me, even though I have not done you any **wrong.**
24.12 May the Lord judge which one of us is **wrong!**
24.15 will judge, and he will decide which one of us is **wrong.**
24.17 Then he said to David, “You are right, and I am **wrong.**
24.17 so good to me, while I have done such **wrong** to you!
25.28 Please forgive me, sir, for any **wrong** I have done.
25.39 insulting me and has kept me his servant from doing **wrong.**
26.21 Saul answered, “I have done **wrong.**
29. 8 David answered, “What have I done **wrong,** sir?
2 Sam 7.14 When he does **wrong,** I will punish him as a father punishes
14.13 to him, “Why have you done such a **wrong** to God's people?
19.19 “Your Majesty, please forget the **wrong** I did that day you
21. 3 to make up for the **wrong** that was done to you, so
22.24 I am faultless, that I have kept myself from doing **wrong.**
24.17 I am the one who did **wrong.**
1 Kgs 2.44 know very well all the **wrong** that you did to my father
8.31 a person is accused of **wronging** another and is brought to
11.33 he has done **wrong,** and has not kept my laws and commands
21.20 completely to doing what is **wrong** in the Lord's sight.
21.25 himself so completely to doing **wrong** in the Lord's sight as
2 Kgs 4.41 And then there was nothing **wrong** with it.
5.21 his chariot to meet him, and asked, “Is something **wrong?**”
6.19 Elisha went to them and said, “You are on the **wrong** road;
17.17 completely to doing what is **wrong** in the Lord's sight, and
18.14 “I have done **wrong;**
1 Chr 21.17 David prayed, “O God, I am the one who did **wrong.**
2 Chr 6.22 a person is accused of **wronging** another and is brought to
Ezra 9.13 punishment for our sins and **wrongs,** we know that you, our
Neh 5. 9 Then I said, “What you are doing is **wrong!**
Job 6.30 I am lying— you think I can't tell right from **wrong.**
7.21 Can't you pardon the **wrong** I do?
11.14 Put away evil and **wrong** from your home.
13.23 What **wrongs** have I done?
14.17 you will wipe out all the **wrongs** I have done.
16.18 O Earth, don't hide the **wrongs** done to me!
19. 4 Even if I have done **wrong,** how does that hurt you?
31. 3 He sends disaster and ruin to those who do **wrong.**
32. 3 Job, and this made it appear that God was in the **wrong.**
33. 9 I have done nothing **wrong.**
33.12 But I tell you, Job, you are **wrong.**
34. 6 He asks, “How could I lie and say I am **wrong?**
34.10 Will Almighty God do what is **wrong?**
Job 35. 6 If you do **wrong** many times, does that affect him?
40. 8 to put me in the **wrong** and yourself in the right?
Ps 5. 4 You are not a God who is pleased with **wrongdoing;**
7. 3 my God, if I have **wronged** anyone, if I have betrayed a
9.12 not forget their cry, and he punishes those who **wrong** them.
10.15 punish them for the **wrong** they have done until they do it
14. 3 But they have all gone **wrong;**
15. 3 He does no **wrong** to his friends nor spreads rumours about
17.15 But I will see you, because I have done no **wrong;**
18.23 I am faultless, that I have kept myself from doing **wrong.**
32. 1 Happy are those whose sins are forgiven, whose **wrongs** are pardoned.
32. 2 does not accuse of doing **wrong** and who is free from all
32. 5 I did not conceal my **wrongdoings.**
37. 1 don't be jealous of those who do **wrong.**
58. 3 Evil men go **wrong** all their lives;
59. 3 because of any sin or **wrong** I have done, [4] nor because of
85. 2 have forgiven your people's sins and pardoned all their **wrongs.**
89.32 I will make them suffer for their **wrongs.**
92. 7 the wicked may grow like weeds, those who do **wrong** may prosper;
92.15 the Lord is just, that there is no **wrong** in my protector.
103.10 as we deserve or repay us according to our sins and **wrongs.**
119. 3 They never do **wrong;**
119.29 Keep me from going the **wrong** way, and in your goodness
119.67 me, I used to go **wrong,** but now I obey your word.
119.128 I hate all **wrong** ways.
141. 4 me from wanting to do **wrong** and from joining evil men in
Prov 2.12 protect you [12] and prevent you from doing the **wrong** thing.
2.14 find pleasure in doing **wrong** and who enjoy senseless evil,
3. 7 simply obey the Lord and refuse to do **wrong.**
4.16 Wicked people cannot sleep unless they have done something **wrong.**
10.17 those who will not admit that they are **wrong** are in danger.
10.23 It is foolish to enjoy doing **wrong.**
10.29 The Lord protects honest people, but destroys those who do **wrong.**
11.19 will live, but anyone who insists on doing **wrong** will die.
12. 1 Anyone who loves knowledge wants to be told when he is **wrong.**
13. 1 him, but an arrogant person never admits he is **wrong.**
15.10 If you do what is **wrong,** you will be severely punished;
17. 9 want people to like you, forgive them when they **wrong** you.
17. 9 Remembering **wrongs** can break up a friendship.
19.11 When someone **wrongs** you, it is a great virtue to ignore it.
20.22 Don't take it on yourself to repay a **wrong.**
20.26 out who is doing **wrong,** and will punish him without pity.
24.23 It is **wrong** for a judge to be prejudiced.
25. 8 another witness later proves you **wrong,** what will you do then?
28.21 Prejudice is **wrong.**
28.21 But some judges will do **wrong** to get even the smallest bribe.
28.24 Anyone who thinks it isn't **wrong** to steal from his
30.20 a bath, and says, “But I haven't done anything **wrong!**”
Ecc 5. 1 foolish people do, people who don't know right from **wrong.**
6. 2 It is useless, and it's all **wrong.**
9. 3 alike, and this is as **wrong** as anything that happens in this
10. 2 the right thing and for a fool to do the **wrong** thing.
10. 4 serious **wrongs** may be pardoned if you keep calm.
Is 19.14 a result, Egypt does everything **wrong** and staggers like a
26.10 Even here in a land of righteous people they still do **wrong;**
43.24 you wore me out with the **wrongs** you committed.
59.11 God to save us from oppression and **wrong,** but nothing happens.
59.17 and to punish and avenge the **wrongs** that people suffer.
64. 5 anger we have continued to do **wrong** since ancient times.
65. 2 who stubbornly do what is **wrong** and go their own way.
Jer 2.19 will learn how bitter and **wrong** it is to abandon me, the
8. 6 not one of you has asked, ‘What have I done **wrong?**’
11.17 They have brought this on themselves because they have done **wrong;**
14.10 I will remember the **wrongs** they have done and punish them
23.14 they help people to do **wrong,** so that no one stops doing
31.34 their sins and I will no longer remember their **wrongs.**
38. 9 king, [9] “Your Majesty, what these men have done is **wrong.**
50. 7 against the Lord, and so what we have done is not **wrong.**
Lam 3.59 you know the **wrongs** done against me.
Ezek 16.63 I will forgive all the **wrongs** you have done, but you
29.16 fate will remind Israel how **wrong** it was to rely on them.
33.10 ‘We are burdened with our sins and the **wrongs** we have done.
36.31 your evil conduct and the **wrongs** that you committed, and you
48.11 of the Israelites in doing **wrong,** as the other members of
Dan 6. 4 governors tried to find something **wrong** with the way Daniel
6. 4 Daniel was reliable and did not do anything **wrong** or dishonest.
6.22 and because I have not **wronged** you, Your Majesty.”
9. 5 “We have sinned, we have been evil, we have done **wrong.**
9.15 we have done **wrong.**
Amos 6.12 Yet you have turned justice into poison, and right into **wrong.**
Mic 3. 9 of Israel, you that hate justice and turn right into **wrong.**
7. 9 defend us and right the **wrongs** that have been done to us.
Hab 1. 3 How can you endure to look on such **wrongdoing?**
1.13 evil, and you cannot stand the sight of people doing **wrong.**
Zeph 3. 5 he does what is right and never what is **wrong.**
3. 5 people there keep on doing **wrong** and are not ashamed.
3.13 who survive will do no **wrong** to anyone, tell no lies, nor
Mal 1. 8 to me, do you think there's nothing **wrong** with that?
2. 6 They taught what was right, not what was **wrong.**
2. 8 Your teaching has led many to do **wrong.**
Mt 5.39 do not take revenge on someone who **wrongs** you.
6.12 Forgive us the **wrongs** we have done,
6.12 as we forgive the **wrongs** that others have done to us.
6.14 “If you forgive others the **wrongs** they have done to you,
6.15 then your Father will not forgive the **wrongs** you have done.
12.10 to accuse Jesus of doing **wrong,** so they asked him, “Is it
12.27 What your own followers do proves that you are **wrong!**

Mt 17.17 Jesus answered, "How unbelieving and **wrong** you people are!
22.29 Jesus answered them, "How **wrong** you are!
Mk 3. 2 Some people were there who wanted to accuse Jesus of doing **wrong;**
3. 5 sorry for them, because they were so stubborn and **wrong.**
11.25 Father in heaven will forgive the **wrongs** you have done."
12.24 Jesus answered them, "How **wrong** you are!
12.27 You are completely **wrong!"**
Lk 6. 7 to accuse Jesus of doing **wrong,** so they watched him closely
9.41 Jesus answered, "How unbelieving and **wrong** you people are!
11. 4 Forgive us our sins, for we forgive everyone who does us **wrong.**
11.19 Your own followers prove that you are **wrong!**
11.54 trying to lay traps for him and catch him saying something **wrong.**
23.41 but he has done no **wrong."**
Jn 16. 8 the world that they are **wrong** about sin and about what is
16. 9 They are **wrong** about sin, because they do not believe in me;
16.10 they are **wrong** about what is right, because I am going
16.11 and they are **wrong** about judgement, because the ruler of
18.23 "If I have said anything **wrong,** tell everyone here what it was.
Acts 18.14 of some evil crime or **wrong** that has been committed, it
23. 9 "We cannot find anything **wrong** with this man!
25. 5 with me and accuse the man if he has done anything **wrong."**
25. 8 "I have done nothing **wrong** against the Law of the Jews or
25.10 I have done no **wrong** to the Jews, as you yourself well
Rom 1.27 the punishment they deserve for their **wrongdoing.**
2. 8 and reject what is right, in order to follow what is **wrong;**
3. 5 But what if our doing **wrong** serves to show up more clearly
3. 5 Can we say that God does **wrong** when he punishes us?
3.12 they have all gone **wrong;**
4. 7 "Happy are those whose **wrongs** are forgiven, whose sins are pardoned!
5.20 Law was introduced in order to increase **wrongdoing;**
12.17 someone has done you wrong, do not repay him with a **wrong.**
13.10 If you love someone, you will never do him **wrong;**
14.20 be eaten, but it is **wrong** to eat anything that will cause
1 Cor 6. 7 Would it not be better for you to be **wronged?**
6. 8 Instead, you yourselves **wrong** one another and rob one another,
13. 5 love does not keep a record of **wrongs;**
2 Cor 6.14 How can right and **wrong** be partners?
7. 2 We have **wronged** no one;
7.11 such devotion, such readiness to punish **wrongdoing!**
7.12 of the one who did **wrong** or the one who was wronged.
11. 7 Was that **wrong** of me?
13. 7 that you will do no **wrong**—not in order to show that
Gal 2.11 Antioch, I opposed him in public, because he was clearly **wrong.**
3.19 in order to show what **wrongdoing** is, and it was meant to
4.12 You have not done me any **wrong.**
6. 1 caught in any kind of **wrongdoing,** those of you who are
Phil 1.18 in every way possible, whether from **wrong** or right motives.
Col 3.25 And every **wrongdoer** will be repaid for the wrong things he does,
1 Thes 4. 6 then, no man should do **wrong** to his fellow-Christian or take
5.15 that no one pays back **wrong** for wrong, but at all times
1 Tim 4. 3 people teach that it is **wrong** to marry and to eat certain
6.20 arguments of what some people **wrongly** call "Knowledge."
2 Tim 2.19 he belongs to the Lord must turn away from **wrongdoing."**
Tit 3. 3 For we ourselves were once foolish, disobedient, and **wrong.**
3.11 a person is corrupt, and his sins prove that he is **wrong.**
Phlm 18 he has done you any **wrong** or owes you anything, charge it
Heb 1. 9 You love what is right and hate what is **wrong.**
5.13 without any experience in the matter of right and **wrong.**
8. 7 If there had been nothing **wrong** with the first covenant,
8.12 I will forgive their sins and will no longer remember their **wrongs."**
9.15 sets people free from the **wrongs** they did while the first
Jas 3. 6 It is a world of **wrong,** occupying its place in our bodies
4.16 all such boasting is **wrong.**
5.20 a sinner back from his **wrong** way will save that sinner's
1 Pet 2.20 you endure the beatings you deserve for having done **wrong?**
2 Pet 2.15 would get for doing **wrong** [16] and was rebuked for his sin.
1 Jn 1. 9 forgive us our sins and purify us from all our **wrongdoing.**
3.12 things he himself did were **wrong,** but the things his brother
5.17 All **wrongdoing** is sin, but there is sin which does not

WROUGHT

Ezek 27.18 They exchanged **wrought** iron and spices for your goods.

AV WROUGHT

see also **DO, WORK**

Ex 10. 2 I made fools of the Egyptians when I **performed** the miracles.
39. 6 They **prepared** the carnelians and mounted them in gold settings;
Deut 21. 3 to select a young cow that has never been **used** for work.
Josh 7.15 he owns, for he has **brought** terrible shame on Israel and has
Ruth 2.19 Naomi asked her, "Where did you **gather** all this?
1 Sam 19. 5 killed Goliath, and the Lord **won** a great victory for Israel.
1 Kgs 9.23 the forced **labour** working on Solomon's various building projects.
1 Chr 22. 2 Some of them **prepared** stone blocks for building the Temple.
Ps 31.19 good you are, how securely you **protect** those who trust you.
68.28 God, the power you have **used** on our behalf [29] from your
78.43 them from their enemies [43] and **performed** his mighty acts
Is 26.18 We have **won** no victory for our land;
Ezek 20. 9 not, since that would have **brought** dishonour to my name, for
20.14 not, since that would have **brought** dishonour to my name
20.22 not, since that would have **brought** dishonour to my name
Zeph 2. 3 all you humble people of the land, who **obey** his commands.
Acts 5.12 and wonders were being **performed** among the people by the apostles.
15.12 wonders that God had **performed** through them among the Gentiles.
19.11 God was **performing** unusual miracles through Paul.
Rom 7. 8 sin found its chance to **stir up** all kinds of selfish desires
2 Cor 5. 5 is the one who has **prepared** us for this change,
12.12 I am an apostle were **performed** among you with much patience.
Eph 1.20 strength [20] which he **used** when he raised Christ from death
Rev 19.20 with the false prophet who had **performed** miracles in his presence.

XERXES

Ruler of the Persian Empire, who chose Esther as his wife.

Ezra 4. 6 beginning of the reign of **Xerxes** the emperor, the enemies of
Esth 1. 1 capital city of Susa, King **Xerxes** ruled over 127 provinces,
1.15 to these men, "I, King **Xerxes,** sent my servants to Queen
1.17 They'll say, 'King **Xerxes** commanded Queen Vashti to come to him,
2.12 After that, each girl would be taken in turn to King **Xerxes.**
2.16 So in **Xerxes'** seventh year as king, in the tenth month,
2.16 Esther was brought to King **Xerxes** in the royal palace.
2.21 hostile to King **Xerxes** and plotted to assassinate him.
3. 1 Some time later King **Xerxes** promoted a man named Haman to
3. 7 the twelfth year of King **Xerxes'** rule, in the first month,
3.12 issued in the name of King **Xerxes** and stamped with his ring.
7. 5 Then King **Xerxes** asked Queen Esther, "Who dares to do
8. 1 That same day King **Xerxes** gave Queen Esther all the
8. 7 King **Xerxes** then said to Queen Esther and Mordecai, the
8.10 in the name of King **Xerxes,** and he stamped them with the
10. 1 King **Xerxes** imposed forced labour on the people of the
10. 3 Mordecai the Jew was second in rank only to King **Xerxes** himself.
Dan 9. 1 was the son of **Xerxes,** ruled over the kingdom of Babylonia.

YARD

Neh 8.16 of their houses, in their **yards,** in the temple courtyard,

YEAR

see also **RESTORATION**

Gen 1.14 the time when days, **years,** and religious festivals begin;
5. 3 When Adam was 130 **years old,** he had a son who was
5. 4 After that, Adam lived another 800 **years.**
5. 7 105, he had a son, Enosh, [7] and then lived another 807 **years.**
5.10 90, he had a son, Kenan, [10] and then lived another 815 **years.**
5.13 70, he had a son, Mahalalel, [13] and then lived another 840 **years.**
5.16 65, he had a son, Jared, [16] and then lived another 830 **years.**
5.19 162, he had a son, Enoch, [19] and then lived another 800 **years.**
5.22 in fellowship with God for 300 **years** and had other children.
5.23 He lived to be 365 **years old.**
5.26 187, he had a son, Lamech, [26] and then lived another 782 **years.**
5.30 Lamech lived another 595 **years.**
5.32 After Noah was 500 **years old,** he had three sons, Shem,
6. 3 they will live no longer than a hundred and twenty **years."**
7. 6 Noah was six hundred **years old** when the flood came on the
7.11 When Noah was six hundred **years old,** on the seventeenth
8.13 When Noah was 601 **years old,** on the first day of the
9.28 flood Noah lived for 350 **years** [29] and died at the age of
11.10 Two **years** after the flood, when Shem was 100 years old, he
11.11 he lived another 500 **years** and had other children.
11.12 When Arpachshad was 35 **years old,** he had a son, Shelah;
11.13 he lived another 403 **years** and had other children.
11.14 When Shelah was 30 **years old,** he had a son, Eber;
11.15 he lived another 403 **years** and had other children.
11.16 When Eber was 34 **years old,** he had a son, Peleg;
11.17 he lived another 430 **years** and had other children.
11.18 When Peleg was 30 **years old,** he had a son, Reu;
11.19 he lived another 209 **years** and had other children.
11.20 When Reu was 32 **years old,** he had a son, Serug;
11.21 he lived another 207 **years** and had other children.
11.22 When Serug was 30 **years old,** he had a son, Nahor;
11.23 he lived another 200 **years** and had other children.
11.24 When Nahor was 29 **years old,** he had a son, Terah;
11.25 he lived another 119 **years** and had other children.
11.26 After Terah was 70 **years old,** he became the father of Abram,
12. 4 When Abram was seventy-five **years old,** he started out from Haran,
14. 4 of Chedorlaomer for twelve **years,**
14. 4 but in the thirteenth **year** they rebelled against him.
14. 5 In the fourteenth **year** Chedorlaomer and his allies came
15. 9 ram, each of them three **years old,** and a dove and a
15.13 there and will be treated cruelly for four hundred **years.**
16. 3 (This happened after Abram had lived in Canaan for ten **years.**)
16.16 Abram was eighty-six **years old** at the time.
17. 1 When Abram was ninety-nine **years old,** the Lord appeared to
17.17 a man have a child when he is a hundred **years old?**
17.21 who will be born to Sarah about this time next **year."**
17.24 Abraham was ninety-nine **years old** when he was circumcised,
21. 5 Abraham was a hundred **years old** when Isaac was born.
23. 1 Sarah lived to be a hundred and twenty-seven **years old.**
25.17 Ishmael was a hundred and thirty-seven **years old** when he died.
25.20 Isaac was forty **years old** when he married Rebecca, the
25.26 Isaac was sixty **years old** when they were born.
26.12 in that land, and that **year** he harvested a hundred times as
26.34 When Esau was forty **years old,** he married two Hittite girls,
29.18 said, "I will work seven **years** for you, if you will let
29.20 Jacob worked seven **years** so that he could have Rachel,
29.27 you Rachel, if you will work for me another seven **years."**
29.30 Then he worked for Laban another seven **years.**
31.38 I have been with you now for twenty **years;**
31.41 was like that for the whole twenty **years** I was with you.
31.41 For fourteen **years** I worked to win your two daughters—
31.41 and six **years** for your flocks.
35.28 be a hundred and eighty **years old** [29] and died at a ripe

Book	Ref	Context
Gen	41. 1	After two **years** had passed, the king of Egypt dreamt that
	41.26	seven fat cows are seven **years,**
	41.26	and the seven full ears of corn are also seven **years;**
	41.27	corn scorched by the desert wind are seven **years** of famine.
	41.29	There will be seven **years** of great plenty in all the
	41.30	that, there will be seven **years** of famine,
	41.30	and all the good **years** will be forgotten, because the famine
	41.34	take a fifth of the crops during the seven **years** of plenty.
	41.35	the food during the good **years** that are coming, and give
	41.36	the country during the seven **years** of famine which are going
	41.45	Joseph was thirty **years old** when he began to serve the king
	41.47	During the seven **years** of plenty the land produced abundant
	41.50	Before the **years** of famine came, Joseph had two sons
	41.53	The seven **years** of plenty that the land of Egypt had
	41.54	an end, [54] and the seven **years** of famine began, just as
	45. 6	This is only the second **year** of famine in the land;
	45. 6	there will be five more **years** in which there will be neither
	45.11	There will still be five **years** of famine;
	47. 9	"My life of wandering has lasted a hundred and thirty **years.**
	47. 9	Those **years** have been few and difficult,
	47. 9	unlike the long **years** of my ancestors in their wanderings."
	47.17	That **year** he supplied them with food in exchange for all
	47.18	The following **year** they came to him and said, "We will
	47.28	lived in Egypt for seventeen **years,**
	47.28	until he was a hundred and forty-seven **years old.**
	50.22	he was a hundred and ten **years old** when he died.
Ex	2.23	**Years** later the king of Egypt died, but the Israelites
	6.16	Levi lived 137 **years.**
	6.18	Kohath lived 133 **years.**
	6.20	Amram lived 137 **years.**
	7. 7	Moses was eighty **years old,** and Aaron was eighty-three.
	12. 2	month is to be the first month of the **year** for you.
	12.40	The Israelites had lived in Egypt for 430 **years.**
	12.41	On the day the 430 **years** ended, all the tribes of the
	13. 5	celebrate this festival in the first month of every **year.**
	13.10	Celebrate this festival at the appointed time each **year.**
	16.35	manna for the next forty **years,** until they reached the land
	21. 2	you buy a Hebrew slave, he shall serve you for six **years.**
	21. 2	In the seventh **year** he is to be set free without having
	23.10	"For six **years** sow your field and gather in what it produces.
	23.11	But in the seventh **year** let it rest, and do not harvest
	23.14	"Celebrate three festivals a **year** to honour me.
	23.17	Every **year** at these three festivals all your men must
	23.19	"Each **year** bring to the house of the Lord your God the
	23.29	I will not drive them out within one **year;**
	30.10	Once a **year** Aaron is to perform the ritual for purifying
	30.10	This is to be done every **year** for all time to come.
	30.14	that is, every man twenty **years old** or older, is to pay
	34.23	"Three times a **year** all your men must come to worship me,
	34.26	"Each **year** bring to the house of the Lord the first
	38.26	There were 603,550 men twenty **years old** or older enrolled in
	40.17	first month of the second **year** after they left Egypt, the
Lev	2.12	that you harvest each **year** shall be brought to the Lord,
	14.10	and one female lamb a **year** old that are without any defects,
	16.34	must be performed once a **year** to purify the people of Israel
	19.23	the fruit ritually unclean for the first three **years.**
	19.24	In the fourth **year** all the fruit shall be dedicated as
	19.25	But in the fifth **year** you may eat the fruit.
	25. 2	the Lord by not cultivating the land every seventh **year.**
	25. 3	prune your vineyards, and gather your crops for six **years.**
	25. 4	But the seventh **year** is to be a year of complete rest
	25. 4	for the land, a **year** dedicated to the Lord.
	25. 5	it is a **year** of complete rest for the land.
	25. 6	cultivated during that **year,** it will provide food for you,
	25. 8	Count seven times seven **years,** a total of forty-nine years.
	25.10	you shall set the fiftieth **year** apart and proclaim freedom
	25.10	During this **year** all property that has been sold shall be
	25.12	The whole **year** shall be sacred for you;
	25.13	In this **year** all property that has been sold shall be
	25.15	according to the number of **years** the land can produce crops
	25.16	If there are many **years,** the price shall be higher, but
	25.16	there are only a few **years,** the price shall be lower,
	25.20	to eat during the seventh **year,** when no fields are sown and
	25.21	the land in the sixth **year** so that it will produce enough
	25.21	it will produce enough food for two **years.**
	25.22	your fields in the eighth **year,** you will still be eating
	25.22	you harvested during the sixth **year,** and you will have
	25.22	to eat until the crops you plant that **year** are harvested.
	25.27	will make up for the **years** remaining until the next Year of
	25.28	In that **year** it will be returned to its original owner.
	25.29	it back during the first full **year** from the date of sale.
	25.30	it back within the **year,** he loses the right of repurchase,
	25.50	and they must count the **years** from the time he sold himself
	25.51	according to the number of **years** left, [53] as if he had been
	26.10	they will last for a **year,** and even then you will have
	26.34	the land will enjoy the **years** of complete rest that you
	27. 3	adult male, twenty to sixty **years old:**
	27. 3	—young male, five to twenty **years old:**
	27. 3	3 pieces of silver —male above sixty **years** of age:
	27.18	according to the number of **years** left until the next Year of
	27.23	to the number of **years** until the next Year of Restoration,
Num	1. 1	second month in the second **year** after the people of Israel
	1. 3	of all the men [3] twenty **years old** or older who are fit
	1.18	of all the men twenty **years old** or older were recorded and
	1.20	The men twenty **years old** or older who were fit for
	9. 1	first month of the second **year** after the people of Israel
	9.22	two days, a month, a **year,** or longer, as long as the
	10.11	second month in the second **year** after the people left Egypt,
	13.22	(Hebron was founded seven **years** before Zoan in Egypt.)
	14.29	none of you over twenty **years** of age will enter that land.
	14.33	for forty **years,** suffering for your unfaithfulness,
Num	14.34	for forty years, one **year** for each of the forty days
	18.12	of the first produce which the Israelites give me each **year:**
	20.15	how our ancestors went to Egypt, where we lived many **years.**
	26. 2	Israel, of all men twenty **years old** or older who are fit
	28.14	for the first day of each month throughout the **year.**
	32.11	none of the men twenty **years old** or older who came out
	32.13	in the wilderness for forty **years** until that whole
	33. 3	first month of the **year,** the day after the first Passover.
	33.38	of the fortieth **year** after the Israelites had left Egypt.
Deut	1. 3	month of the fortieth **year** after they had left Egypt,
	2. 7	been with you these forty **years,** and you have had everything
	2.14	This was thirty-eight **years** after we had left Kadesh Barnea.
	8. 2	these past forty **years,** sending hardships to test you,
	8. 4	During these forty **years** your clothes have not worn out,
	11.12	care of this land and watches over it throughout the **year.**
	14.22	a tithe—a tenth of all that your fields produce each **year.**
	14.28	the end of every third **year** bring the tithe of all your
	15. 1	the end of every seventh **year** you are to cancel the debts
	15. 9	just because the **year** when debts are cancelled is near.
	15.12	are to release him after he has served you for six **years.**
	15.12	When the seventh **year** comes, you must let him go free.
	15.18	has served you for six **years** at half the cost of a
	15.20	Each **year** you and your family are to eat them in the
	16.16	the Lord three times a **year** at the one place of worship:
	17.20	he will reign for many **years,** and his descendants will rule
	24. 5	excused from duty for one **year,** so that he can stay at
	26.12	"Every third **year** give the tithe—a tenth of your
	29. 5	For forty **years** the Lord led you through the desert, and
	31. 2	now a hundred and twenty **years old** and am no longer able
	31.10	the end of every seven **years,**
	31.10	when the **year** that debts are cancelled comes round,
	34. 7	Moses was a hundred and twenty **years old** when he died;
Josh	5. 4	during the forty **years** the people spent crossing the desert,
	14. 7	I was forty **years old** when the Lord's servant Moses sent
	14.10	It has been forty-five **years** since the Lord said that to Moses.
	14.10	I am eighty-five **years old** [11] and I'm just as strong today
Judg	3. 8	Mesopotamia conquer them, and he ruled over them for eight **years.**
	3.11	peace in the land for forty **years,** and then Othniel died.
	3.14	The Israelites were subject to Eglon for eighteen **years.**
	3.30	Moab, and there was peace in the land for eighty **years.**
	4. 3	people of Israel with cruelty and violence for twenty **years.**
	5.31	And there was peace in the land for forty **years.**
	6. 1	so he let the people of Midian rule them for seven **years.**
	6.25	bull and another bull seven **years old,** tear down your
	8.28	The land was at peace for forty **years,** until Gideon died.
	9.22	Abimelech ruled Israel for three **years.**
	10. 2	He was Israel's leader for twenty-three **years.**
	10. 3	He led Israel for twenty-two **years.**
	10. 8	For eighteen **years** they oppressed and persecuted all the
	11.26	For three hundred **years** Israel has occupied Heshbon and Aroer,
	11.40	away for four days every **year** to grieve for the daughter of
	12. 7	Jephthah led Israel for six **years.**
	12. 9	Ibzan led Israel for seven **years,** [10] then he died and was
	12.11	After Ibzan, Elon from Zebulun led Israel for ten **years.**
	12.14	Abdon led Israel for eight **years,** [15] then he died and was
	13. 1	Lord again, and he let the Philistines rule them for forty **years.**
	15.20	Samson led Israel for twenty **years** while the Philistines
	16.31	He had been Israel's leader for twenty **years.**
	17.10	ten pieces of silver a **year,** some clothes, and your food."
	21.19	Then they thought, "The **yearly** festival of the Lord at
Ruth	1. 4	About ten **years** later [5] Mahlon and Chilion also died, and
1 Sam	1. 3	Every **year** Elkanah went from Ramah to worship and offer
	1. 7	This went on **year** after year;
	1.21	offer to the Lord the **yearly** sacrifice and the special
	2.19	Each **year** his mother would make a little robe and take
	2.19	she accompanied her husband to offer the **yearly** sacrifice.
	4.15	(Eli was now ninety-eight **years old** and almost completely blind.)
	4.18	He had been a leader in Israel for forty **years.**
	7. 2	Lord stayed in Kiriath Jearim a long time, some twenty **years.**
	7.16	Every **year** he would go round to Bethel, Gilgal, and
2 Sam	2.10	He was forty **years old** when he was made king of Israel,
	2.10	and he ruled for two **years.**
	2.11	he ruled in Hebron over Judah for seven and a half **years.**
	4. 4	son Mephibosheth, who was five **years old** when Saul and
	5. 4	David was thirty **years old** when he became king,
	5. 4	and he ruled for forty **years.**
	5. 5	for seven and a half **years,** and in Jerusalem
	5. 5	over all Israel and Judah for thirty-three **years.**
	7.19	made promises about my descendants in the **years** to come.
	11. 1	at the time of the **year** when kings usually go to war,
	13.23	Two **years** later Absalom was having his sheep sheared
	13.37	Geshur, Talmai son of Ammihud, and stayed there three **years.**
	14.26	to cut it once a **year,** when it grew too long and
	14.28	Absalom lived two **years** in Jerusalem without seeing the king.
	15. 7	After four **years** Absalom said to King David, "Sir, let
	19.32	Barzillai was a very old man, eighty **years old.**
	19.35	I am already eighty **years old,** and nothing gives me
	21. 1	there was a severe famine which lasted for three full **years.**
	24.13	Three **years** of famine in your land or three months of
1 Kgs	2.11	king of Israel for forty **years,** ruling seven years in Hebron
	2.11	and thirty-three **years** in Jerusalem.
	2.39	Three **years** later, however, two of Shimei's slaves ran
	4. 7	each man being responsible for one month out of the **year.**
	5.11	litres of pure olive-oil every **year** to feed his men.
	6. 1	Four hundred and eighty **years** after the people of Israel left
	6. 1	during the fourth **year** of Solomon's reign over Israel,
	6.37	the month of Ziv, in the fourth **year** of Solomon's reign.
	6.38	of Bul, in the eleventh **year** of Solomon's reign, the Temple
	6.38	It had taken Solomon seven **years** to build it.
	7. 1	built a palace for himself, and it took him thirteen **years.**

1 Kgs 9.10 It took Solomon twenty **years** to build the Temple
9.25 Three times a **year** Solomon offered burnt-offerings and
10.14 Every **year** King Solomon received almost twenty-three
10.22 Every three **years** his fleet would return, bringing gold,
10.25 This continued **year** after year.
11.42 He was king in Jerusalem over all Israel for forty **years.**
14.20 Jeroboam ruled as king for twenty-two **years.**
14.21 Solomon's son Rehoboam was forty-one **years old** when he
14.21 and he ruled for seventeen **years** in Jerusalem, the city
14.25 In the fifth **year** of Rehoboam's reign King Shishak of
15. 1 In the eighteenth **year** of the reign of King Jeroboam of Israel,
15. 2 king of Judah, [2]and he ruled for three **years** in Jerusalem.
15. 9 In the twentieth **year** of the reign of King Jeroboam of Israel,
15.10 of Judah, [10]and he ruled for forty-one **years** in Jerusalem.
15.25 In the second **year** of the reign of King Asa of Judah,
15.25 son Nadab became king of Israel, and he ruled for two **years.**
15.28 This happened during the third **year** of the reign of King
15.33 In the third **year** of the reign of King Asa of Judah,
15.33 of all Israel, and he ruled in Tirzah for twenty-four **years.**
16. 8 In the twenty-sixth **year** of the reign of King Asa of Judah,
16. 8 became king of Israel, and he ruled in Tirzah for two **years.**
16.10 This happened in the twenty-seventh **year** of the reign of
16.15 In the twenty-seventh **year** of the reign of King Asa of Judah,
16.23 So in the thirty-first **year** of the reign of King Asa of
16.23 Omri became king of Israel, and he ruled for twelve **years.**
16.23 The first six **years** he ruled in Tirzah, [24]and then he
16.29 In the thirty-eighth **year** of the reign of King Asa of Judah,
16.29 of Israel, and he ruled in Samaria for twenty-two **years.**
17. 1 rain for the next two or three **years** until I say so."
18. 1 some time, in the third **year** of the drought, the Lord said
22. 1 Syria for the next two **years,**
22. 2 but in the third **year** King Jehoshaphat of Judah
22.41 In the fourth **year** of the reign of King Ahab of Israel,
22.42 and he ruled in Jerusalem for twenty-five **years.**
22.51 In the seventeenth **year** of the reign of King Jehoshaphat
22.51 king of Israel, and he ruled in Samaria for two **years.**
2 Kgs 1.17 as king in the second **year** of the reign of Jehoram son
3. 1 In the eighteenth **year** of the reign of King Jehoshaphat of Judah,
3. 1 king of Israel, and he ruled in Samaria for twelve **years.**
3. 4 Moab bred sheep, and every **year** he gave as tribute to the
4.16 her, "By this time next **year** you will be holding a son
4.17 about that time the following **year** she gave birth to a son.
4.18 Some **years** later, at harvest time, the boy went out one
4.42 harvested that **year,** and some freshly-cut ears of corn.
8. 1 which would last for seven **years,** and that she should leave
8. 2 with her family to live in Philistia for the seven **years.**
8. 3 the end of the seven **years,** she returned to Israel and went
8. 6 had produced during the seven **years** she had been away.
8.16 In the fifth **year** of the reign of Joram son of Ahab
8.17 of thirty-two, and he ruled in Jerusalem for eight **years.**
8.25 In the twelfth **year** of the reign of Joram son of Ahab
8.26 age of twenty-two, and he ruled in Jerusalem for one **year.**
9.29 of Judah in the eleventh **year** that Joram son of Ahab was
10.36 Jehu had ruled in Samaria as king of Israel for twenty-eight **years.**
11. 3 For six **years** Jehosheba took care of the boy and kept him
11. 4 But in the seventh **year** Jehoiada the priest sent for the
12. 1 In the seventh **year** of the reign of King Jehu of Israel,
12. 1 king of Judah, and he ruled in Jerusalem for forty **years.**
12. 6 But by the twenty-third **year** of Joash's reign the priests
13. 1 In the twenty-third **year** of the reign of Joash son of
13. 1 king of Israel, and he ruled in Samaria for seventeen **years.**
13.10 In the thirty-seventh **year** of the reign of King Joash of Judah,
13.10 king of Israel, and he ruled in Samaria for sixteen **years.**
13.20 Every **year** bands of Moabites used to invade the land of Israel.
14. 1 In the second **year** of the reign of Jehoash son of Jehoahaz
14. 2 and he ruled in Jerusalem for twenty-nine **years.**
14.17 Amaziah of Judah lived fifteen **years** after the death of King
14.23 In the fifteenth **year** of the reign of Amaziah son of
14.23 king of Israel, and he ruled in Samaria for forty-one **years.**
15. 1 In the twenty-seventh **year** of the reign of King Jeroboam II
15. 2 of sixteen, and he ruled in Jerusalem for fifty-two **years.**
15. 8 In the thirty-eighth **year** of the reign of King Uzziah of Judah,
15.13 In the thirty-ninth **year** of the reign of King Uzziah of Judah,
15.17 In the thirty-ninth **year** of the reign of King Uzziah of Judah,
15.17 king of Israel, and he ruled in Samaria for ten **years.**
15.23 In the fiftieth **year** of the reign of King Uzziah of Judah,
15.23 king of Israel, and he ruled in Samaria for two **years.**
15.27 In the fifty-second **year** of the reign of King Uzziah of Judah,
15.27 king of Israel, and he ruled in Samaria for twenty **years.**
15.30 In the twentieth **year** of the reign of Jotham son of
15.32 In the second **year** of the reign of Pekah son of
15.33 of twenty-five, and he ruled in Jerusalem for sixteen **years.**
16. 1 In the seventeenth **year** of the reign of Pekah son of
16. 2 age of twenty, and he ruled in Jerusalem for sixteen **years.**
17. 1 In the twelfth **year** of the reign of King Ahaz of Judah,
17. 1 king of Israel, and he ruled in Samaria for nine **years.**
17. 3 surrendered to Shalmaneser and paid him tribute every **year.**
17. 4 But one **year** Hoshea sent messengers to So, king of Egypt,
17. 5 In the third **year** of the siege,
17. 6 which was the ninth **year** of the reign of Hoshea, the
18. 1 In the third **year** of the reign of Hoshea son of Elah
18. 2 and he ruled in Jerusalem for twenty-nine **years.**
18. 9 In the fourth **year** of Hezekiah's reign—
18. 9 which was the seventh **year** of King Hoshea's reign over Israel
18.10 In the third **year** of the siege, Samaria fell;
18.10 this was the sixth **year** of Hezekiah's reign,
18.10 and the ninth **year** of Hoshea's reign.
18.13 In the fourteenth **year** of the reign of King Hezekiah,
19.29 This **year** and next you will have only wild grain to eat,
19.29 but the following **year** you will be able to sow
20. 6 I will let you live fifteen **years** longer.
2 Kgs 21. 1 Manasseh was twelve **years old** when he became king of Judah,
21. 1 and he ruled in Jerusalem for fifty-five **years.**
21.19 Amon was twenty-two **years old** when he became king of Judah,
21.19 and he ruled in Jerusalem for two **years.**
22. 1 Josiah was eight **years old** when he became king of Judah,
22. 1 and he ruled in Jerusalem for thirty-one **years.**
22. 3 In the eighteenth **year** of his reign, King Josiah sent the
23.23 at last, in the eighteenth **year** of the reign of Josiah, the
23.31 Joahaz was twenty-three **years old** when he became king of Judah,
23.36 Jehoiakim was twenty-five **years old** when he became king of Judah,
23.36 and he ruled in Jerusalem for eleven **years.**
24. 1 invaded Judah, and for three **years** Jehoiakim was forced to
24. 8 Jehoiachin was eighteen **years old** when he became king of Judah,
24.12 In the eighth **year** of Nebuchadnezzar's reign he took
24.18 Zedekiah was twenty-one **years old** when he became king of Judah,
24.18 and he ruled in Jerusalem for eleven **years.**
25. 1 of the tenth month of the ninth **year** of Zedekiah's reign.
25. 2 and kept it under siege until Zedekiah's eleventh **year.**
25. 3 fourth month of that same **year,** when the famine was so bad
25. 8 of the nineteenth **year** of King Nebuchadnezzar of Babylonia,
25.25 the seventh month of that **year,** Ishmael, the son of
25.27 In the **year** that Evilmerodach became king of Babylonia,
25.27 twelfth month of the thirty-seventh **year** after Jehoiachin
1 Chr 2.21 When Hezron was sixty **years old,** he married Machir's daughter,
3. 4 Hebron during the seven and a half **years** that David ruled there.
3. 4 ruled as king for thirty-three **years,** [5]and many sons were
12.15 the first month of one **year,** the time when the River Jordan
17.17 about my descendants in the **years** to come, and you, Lord
20. 1 at the time of the **year** when kings usually go to war,
21.12 Three **years** of famine?
23.24 Each of his descendants, twenty **years** of age or older, had a
26.31 In the fortieth **year** that David was king, an investigation
27. 1 Each month of the **year** a different group of twenty-four
29.27 David son of Jesse ruled over all Israel [27]for forty **years.**
29.27 He ruled in Hebron for seven **years** and in Jerusalem
2 Chr 3. 2 in the second month of the fourth **year** that he was king.
8. 1 It took Solomon twenty **years** to build the Temple
9.13 Every **year** King Solomon received almost twenty-three thousand
9.21 Every three **years** his fleet would return, bringing gold,
9.24 This continued **year** after year.
9.30 Solomon ruled in Jerusalem over all Israel for forty **years.**
11.17 of Judah, and for three **years** they supported Rehoboam son of
12. 2 In the fifth **year** of Rehoboam's reign their disloyalty to
12.13 He was forty-one **years old** when he became king,
12.13 and he ruled for seventeen **years** in Jerusalem, the city
13. 1 In the eighteenth **year** of the reign of King Jeroboam of Israel,
13. 2 king of Judah, [2]and he ruled for three **years** in Jerusalem.
14. 1 as king, and under Asa the land enjoyed peace for ten **years.**
14. 6 this time, and for several **years** there was no war, because
15.10 in the third month of the fifteenth **year** that Asa was king.
15.19 There was no more war until the thirty-fifth **year** of his reign.
16. 1 In the thirty-sixth **year** of the reign of King Asa of Judah,
16.12 In the thirty-ninth **year** that Asa was king, he was
16.13 Two **years** later he died [14]and was buried in the rock
17. 7 In the third **year** of his reign he sent out the following
18. 2 A number of **years** later Jehoshaphat went to the city of
20.31 and had ruled in Jerusalem for twenty-five **years.**
21. 5 of thirty-two, and he ruled in Jerusalem for eight **years.**
21.19 For almost two **years** it grew steadily worse until
21.20 of thirty-two and had ruled in Jerusalem for eight **years.**
22. 2 age of twenty-two, and he ruled in Jerusalem for one **year.**
22.12 For six **years** he remained there in hiding, while
23. 1 After waiting six **years** Jehoiada the priest decided that
24. 1 the age of seven, and he ruled in Jerusalem for forty **years.**
24.23 When autumn came that **year,** the Syrian army attacked Judah
25. 1 and he ruled in Jerusalem for twenty-nine **years.**
25. 5 This included all men twenty **years** of age or older, 300,000
25.25 Amaziah of Judah outlived King Jehoash of Israel by fifteen **years.**
26. 3 of sixteen, and he ruled in Jerusalem for fifty-two **years.**
27. 1 of twenty-five, and he ruled in Jerusalem for sixteen **years.**
27. 5 to pay him the following tribute each **year** for three years:
27. 8 Jotham was twenty-five **years old** when he became king,
27. 8 and he ruled in Jerusalem for sixteen **years.**
28. 1 age of twenty, and he ruled in Jerusalem for sixteen **years.**
29. 1 and he ruled in Jerusalem for twenty-nine **years.**
29. 3 the first month of the **year** after Hezekiah became king, he
29.19 Ahaz took away during those **years** he was unfaithful to God,
31.16 share to all males thirty **years** of age or older who had
31.17 clans, and the Levites twenty **years** of age or older were
33. 1 Manasseh was twelve **years old** when he became king of Judah,
33. 1 and he ruled in Jerusalem for fifty-five **years.**
33.21 Amon was twenty-two **years old** when he became king of Judah,
33.21 and he ruled in Jerusalem for two **years.**
34. 1 Josiah was eight **years old** when he became king of Judah,
34. 1 and he ruled in Jerusalem for thirty-one **years.**
34. 3 In the eighth **year** that Josiah was king, while he was
34. 3 Four **years** later he began to destroy the pagan places of worship,
34. 8 In the eighteenth **year** of his reign, after he had
35.19 and Jerusalem [19]in the eighteenth **year** of Josiah's reign.
36. 2 Joahaz was twenty-three **years old** when he became king of Judah,
36. 5 Jehoiakim was twenty-five **years old** when he became king of Judah,
36. 5 and he ruled in Jerusalem for eleven **years.**
36. 9 Jehoiachin was eighteen **years old** when he became king of Judah,

2 Chr 36.11 Zedekiah was twenty-one **years old** when he became king of Judah,
36.11 and he ruled in Jerusalem for eleven **years.**
36.21 will lie desolate for seventy **years,** to make up for the
36.22 In the first **year** that Cyrus of Persia was emperor, the
Ezra 1. 1 In the first **year** that Cyrus of Persia was emperor, the
3. 8 the second month of the **year** after they came back to the
3. 8 All the Levites twenty **years** of age or older were put in
4.24 a standstill until the second **year** of the reign of Darius,
5.11 originally built and equipped many **years** ago by a powerful
5.13 Then in the first **year** of the reign of King Cyrus as
6. 3 "In the first **year** of his reign Cyrus the emperor
6.15 month Adar in the sixth **year** of the reign of Darius the
6.19 the fourteenth day of the first month of the following **year.**
7. 1 Many **years** later, when Artaxerxes was emperor of Persia,
7. 6 In the seventh **year** of the reign of Artaxerxes, Ezra set out
Neh 1. 1 in the twentieth **year** that Artaxerxes was emperor of Persia,
5.14 During all the twelve **years** that I was governor
5.14 from the twentieth **year** that Artaxerxes was emperor
5.14 until his thirty-second **year,** neither my relatives nor I ate
9.21 Through forty **years** in the desert you provided all that they
9.30 **Year** after year you patiently warned them.
10.31 Every seventh **year** we will not farm the land, and we will
10.32 Every **year** we will each contribute five grammes of
10.34 Levites, will draw lots each **year** to determine which clans
10.35 take to the Temple each **year** an offering of the first corn
10.37 corn harvested each **year** and our other offerings
12.44 tithes and the first corn and fruit that ripened each **year.**
13. 6 Jerusalem, because in the thirty-second **year** that Artaxerxes
Esth 1. 3 In the third **year** of his reign he gave a banquet for
2.12 for the women lasted a **year**—massages with oil of myrrh for
2.16 So in Xerxes' seventh **year** as king, in the tenth month,
3. 7 In the twelfth **year** of King Xerxes' rule, in the first month,
9.21 and fifteenth days of Adar as holidays every **year.**
9.27 at the proper time each **year** these two days would be
Job 3. 6 that night out of the **year,** and never let it be counted
16.22 My **years** are passing now, and I walk the road of no
36.26 fully know his greatness or count the number of his **years.**
42.16 lived a hundred and forty **years** after this, long enough to
Ps 61. 6 Add many **years** to the king's life;
77. 5 I think of days gone by and remember **years** of long ago.
90. 4 A thousand **years** to you are like one day;
90.10 Seventy **years** is all we have—
90.10 eighty **years,** if we are strong;
90.15 as the sadness you gave us during all our **years** of misery.
95.10 For forty **years** I was disgusted with those people.
Prov 9.11 Wisdom will add **years** to your life.
Ecc 6. 6 never enjoys life, though he may live two thousand **years.**
11. 8 Be grateful for every **year** you live.
12. 1 before those dismal days and **years** come when you will say,
Is 6. 1 In the **year** that King Uzziah died, I saw the Lord.
7. 8 As for Israel, within sixty-five **years** it will be too
14.28 that was proclaimed in the **year** that King Ahaz died.
16.14 "In exactly three **years** Moab's great wealth will disappear.
20. 2 Three **years** earlier the Lord had told Isaiah son of Amoz
20. 3 Isaiah has been going about naked and barefoot for three **years.**
21.16 to me, "In exactly one **year** the greatness of the tribes of
23.15 Tyre will be forgotten for seventy **years,** the lifetime of a king.
23.15 When those **years** are over, Tyre will be like the prostitute
23.17 When the seventy **years** are over, the Lord will let Tyre
29. 1 Let another **year** or two come and go, with its feasts and
32.10 now, but this time next **year** you will be in despair because
36. 1 In the fourteenth **year** that Hezekiah was king of Judah,
37.30 This **year** and next you will have only wild grain to eat,
37.30 but the following **year** you will be able to sow
38. 5 I will let you live fifteen **years** longer.
Jer 1. 2 to Jeremiah in the thirteenth **year** that Josiah son of Amon
1. 3 many times, until the eleventh **year** of the reign of Zedekiah
1. 3 the fifth month of that **year** the people of Jerusalem were
5.24 the spring rains and give you the harvest season each **year.**
25. 1 In the fourth **year** that Jehoiakim son of Josiah was king
25. 1 was the first **year** that Nebuchadnezzar was king of Babylonia.)
25. 3 "For twenty-three **years,**
25. 3 from the thirteenth **year** that Josiah son of Amon was
25.11 nations will serve the king of Babylonia for seventy **years.**
28. 1 That same **year,** in the fifth month
28. 1 of the fourth **year** that Zedekiah was king, Hananiah
28. 3 Within two **years** I will bring back to this place all the
28.11 and he will do this within two **years."**
28.16 Before this **year** is over you will die because you have told
28.17 And Hananiah died in the seventh month of that same **year.**
29.10 Lord says, 'When Babylonia's seventy **years** are over, I will
32. 1 to me in the tenth **year** that Zedekiah was king of Judah,
32. 1 the eighteenth **year** of King Nebuchadnezzar of Babylonia.
32.14 clay jar, so that they may be preserved for **years** to come.
34.14 told them that [14]every seven **years** they were to set free
34.14 any Hebrew slave who had served them for six **years.**
36. 1 In the fourth **year** that Jehoiakim son of Josiah was king
36. 9 month of the fifth **year** that Jehoiakim was king of Judah,
39. 1 month of the ninth **year** that Zedekiah was king of Judah,
39. 2 fourth month of Zedekiah's eleventh **year** as king, the city
41. 1 the seventh month of that **year,** Ishmael, the son of
45. 1 In the fourth **year** that Jehoiakim son of Josiah was king
46. 2 River Euphrates in the fourth **year** that Jehoiakim was king
51.46 Every **year** a different rumour spreads—rumours of violence in
51.59 In the fourth **year** that Zedekiah was king of Judah, Seraiah
52. 1 Zedekiah was twenty-one **years old** when he became king of Judah,
52. 1 and he ruled in Jerusalem for eleven **years.**
52. 4 of the tenth month of the ninth **year** of Zedekiah's reign.
52. 5 and kept it under siege until Zedekiah's eleventh **year.**
Jer 52. 6 fourth month of that same **year,** when the famine was so bad
52.12 of the nineteenth **year** of King Nebuchadnezzar of Babylonia,
52.28 in his seventh **year** as king he carried away 3,023;
52.29 in his eighteenth **year,** 832 from Jerusalem;
52.30 and in his twenty-third **year,** 745—taken away by Nebuzaradan.
52.31 In the **year** that Evilmerodach became king of Babylonia,
52.31 twelfth month of the thirty-seventh **year** after Jehoiachin
Ezek 1. 1 fourth month of the thirtieth **year,** I, Ezekiel the priest,
1. 2 (It was the fifth **year** since King Jehoiachin had been
4. 4 you to one day for each **year** their punishment will last.
4. 6 Judah for forty days—one day for each **year** of their punishment.
8. 1 sixth month of the sixth **year** of our exile, the leaders of
20. 1 day of the fifth month of the seventh **year** of our exile.
24. 1 tenth month of the ninth **year** of our exile, the Lord spoke
26. 1 month of the eleventh **year** of our exile, the Lord spoke to
29. 1 tenth month of the tenth **year** of our exile, the Lord spoke
29.11 For forty **years** nothing will live there.
29.12 For forty **years** the cities of Egypt will lie in ruins, ruins
29.13 Sovereign Lord says, "After forty **years** I will bring the
29.17 first month of the twenty-seventh **year** of our exile, the
30.20 first month of the eleventh **year** of our exile, the Lord
31. 1 third month of the eleventh **year** of our exile, the Lord
32. 1 twelfth month of the twelfth **year** of our exile, the Lord
32.17 first month of the twelfth **year** of our exile, the Lord spoke
33.21 tenth month of the twelfth **year** of our exile, a man who
38. 8 After many **years** I will order him to invade a country
39. 9 and clubs, and will have enough to last for seven **years.**
40. 1 tenth day of the new **year,**
40. 1 which was the twenty-fifth **year** after we had been taken into
40. 1 exile and the fourteenth **year** after Jerusalem was captured.
Dan 1. 1 In the third **year** that Jehoiakim was king of Judah, King
1. 5 After three **years** of this training they were to appear
1.18 At the end of three **years** set by the king, Ashpenaz took
2. 1 In the second **year** that Nebuchadnezzar was king, he had a dream.
4.16 For seven **years** he will not have a human mind, but the
4.23 and let him live there with the animals for seven **years.'**
4.25 For seven **years** you will eat grass like an ox, and sleep
4.32 with wild animals, and eat grass like an ox for seven **years.**
4.34 "When the seven **years** had passed," said the king, "I
5.31 who was then sixty-two **years old,** seized the royal power.
7. 1 In the first **year** that Belshazzar was king of Babylonia, I
7.25 people will be under his power for three and a half **years.**
8. 1 In the third **year** that Belshazzar was king, I saw a second
9. 2 In the first **year** of his reign, I was studying the sacred
9. 2 about the seventy **years** that Jerusalem would be in ruins,
9.24 "Seven times seventy **years** is the length of time God
9.25 God's chosen leader comes, seven times seven **years** will pass.
9.25 stand for seven times sixty-two **years,** but this will be a
9.27 with many people for seven **years,** and when half this time is
10. 1 (In the third **year** that Cyrus was emperor of Persia, a
10. 4 the first month of the **year,** I was standing on the bank
11. 6 After a number of **years** the king of Egypt will make an
11. 8 After several **years** of peace [9]the king of Syria will invade
12. 7 I heard him say, "It will be three and a half **years.**
Joel 2.25 what you lost in the **years** when swarms of locusts ate your
Amos 1. 1 Two **years** before the earthquake, when Uzziah was king of
2.10 through the desert for forty **years,** and gave you the land of
5.25 and offerings during those forty **years** that I led you
Hag 1. 1 During the second **year** that Darius was emperor of Persia,
1.15 the sixth month of the second **year** that Darius was emperor.
2. 1 seventh month of that same **year,** the Lord spoke again
2.10 ninth month of the second **year** that Darius was emperor, the
Zech 1. 1 month of the second **year** that Darius was emperor of Persia,
1. 7 In the second **year** that Darius was emperor, on the
1.12 Jerusalem and the cities of Judah for seventy **years** now.
7. 1 In the fourth **year** that Darius was emperor, on the fourth
7. 3 the fifth month as we have done for so many **years** now?"
7. 5 seventh months during these seventy **years,** it was not in
10. 1 Ask the Lord for rain in the spring of the **year.**
14. 8 It will flow all the **year** round, in the dry season as
14.16 Jerusalem will go there each **year** to worship the Lord
Mt 2.16 its neighbourhood who were two **years old** and younger—this
9.20 from severe bleeding for twelve **years** came up behind Jesus
Mk 5.25 from severe bleeding for twelve **years,** [26]even though she
5.42 (She was twelve **years old.)**
Lk 2.36 been married for only seven **years**
2.36 and was now eighty-four **years old.**
2.41 Every **year** the parents of Jesus went to Jerusalem for
2.42 When Jesus was twelve **years old,** they went to the
3. 1 It was the fifteenth **year** of the rule of the Emperor Tiberius;
3.23 When Jesus began his work, he was about thirty **years old.**
4.25 for three and a half **years** and a severe famine spread
8.42 because his only daughter, who was twelve **years old,**
8.43 who had suffered from severe bleeding for twelve **years;**
12.19 You have all the good things you need for many **years.**
13. 7 his gardener, 'Look, for three **years** I have been coming here
13. 8 But the gardener answered, 'Leave it alone, sir, just one more **year;**
13. 9 Then if the tree bears figs next **year,** so much the better;
13.11 had an evil spirit that had made her ill for eighteen **years;**
13.16 of Abraham whom Satan has kept bound up for eighteen **years;**
15.29 his father, 'Look, all these **years** I have worked for you
Jn 2.20 "It has taken forty-six **years** to build this Temple!"
5. 5 A man was there who had been ill for thirty-eight **years.**
8.57 "You are not even fifty **years old**—and you have seen Abraham?"
11.49 Caiaphas, who was High Priest that **year,** said, "What fools you are!
11.51 he was High Priest that **year,** he was prophesying that Jesus
18.13 He was the father-in-law of Caiaphas, who was High Priest that **year.**

Acts 4.22 of healing had been performed was over forty **years old.**
7. 6 be slaves and will be badly treated for four hundred **years.**
7.23 "When Moses was forty **years old,** he decided to find out
7.30 "After forty **years** had passed, an angel appeared to
7.36 and at the Red Sea and for forty **years** in the desert.
7.42 and sacrificed animals for forty **years** in the desert.
9.33 had not been able to get out of bed for eight **years.**
11.26 Antioch, and for a whole **year** the two met with the people
13.18 and for forty **years** he endured them in the desert.
13.20 All this took about four hundred and fifty **years.**
13.21 the tribe of Benjamin, to be their king for forty **years.**
18.11 Paul stayed there for a **year** and a half, teaching the people
19.10 This went on for two **years,** so that all the people who
20.31 day and night, I taught every one of you for three **years.**
24.10 over this nation for many **years,** and so I am happy to
24.17 away from Jerusalem for several **years,** I went there to take
24.27 After two **years** had passed, Porcius Festus succeeded Felix as governor.
28.30 For two **years** Paul lived in a place he rented for himself,
Rom 4.19 He was then almost one hundred **years old;**
15.23 been wanting for so many **years** to come to see you, [24] I
2 Cor 8.10 is better for you to finish now what you began last **year.**
9. 2 Achaia," I said, "have been ready to help since last **year."**
12. 2 certain Christian man who fourteen **years** ago was snatched up
Gal 1.18 It was three **years** later that I went to Jerusalem to
2. 1 Fourteen **years** later I went back to Jerusalem with Barnabas,
3.17 given four hundred and thirty **years** later, cannot break that
4.10 You pay special attention to certain days, months, seasons, and **years.**
1 Tim 5. 9 the list of widows unless she is over sixty **years** of age.
Heb 3. 9 God, although they had seen what I did for forty **years.**
3.17 With whom was God angry for forty **years?**
4. 7 Many **years** later he spoke of it through David in the
9. 7 into the inner Tent, and he does so only once a **year.**
9.25 the Most Holy Place every **year** with the blood of an animal.
10. 1 The same sacrifices are offered for ever, **year after year.**
10. 3 serve **year after year** to remind people of their sins.
Jas 4.13 where we will stay a **year** and go into business and make
5.17 no rain fell on the land for three and a half **years.**
2 Pet 3. 8 in the Lord's sight between one day and a thousand **years;**
Rev 9.15 of this very month and **year** they had been kept ready to
12.14 for three and a half **years,** safe from the dragon's attack.
20. 2 the Devil, or Satan—and chained him up for a thousand **years.**
20. 3 the nations any more until the thousand **years** were over.
20. 4 to life and ruled as kings with Christ for a thousand **years.**
20. 5 did not come to life until the thousand **years** were over.)
20. 6 Christ, and they will rule with him for a thousand **years.**
20. 7 After the thousand **years** are over, Satan will be let loose
22. 2 which bears fruit twelve times a **year,** once each month;

YEAST

see also **LEAVEN, UNLEAVENED**

Ex 12. 8 eaten with bitter herbs and with bread made without **yeast.**
12.15 not eat any bread made with **yeast—**eat only unleavened bread.
12.15 get rid of all the **yeast** in your houses, for if anyone
12.15 days eats bread made with **yeast,** he shall no longer be
12.18 day, you must not eat any bread made with **yeast.**
12.19 For seven days no **yeast** must be found in your houses,
12.19 foreign, eats bread made with **yeast,** he shall no longer be
13. 7 For seven days you must not eat any bread made with **yeast;**
13. 7 must be no **yeast** or leavened bread anywhere in your land.
23.15 eat any bread made with **yeast** during the seven days of this
23.18 not offer bread made with **yeast** when you sacrifice an animal
29. 2 flour, but no **yeast,** and make some bread with olive-oil,
34.25 not offer bread made with **yeast** when you sacrifice an animal
Lev 2. 4 is bread baked in an oven, it must be made without **yeast.**
2. 5 to be made of flour mixed with olive-oil but without **yeast.**
2.11 which you present to the Lord may be made with **yeast;**
2.11 you must never use **yeast** or honey in food offered to the
6.16 into bread baked without **yeast** and eaten in a holy place,
7.12 to be sacrificed, an offering of bread made without **yeast:**
7.13 In addition, he shall offer loaves of bread baked without **yeast.**
23. 6 for seven days you must not eat any bread made with **yeast.**
23.17 kilogrammes of flour baked with **yeast** and shall be presented
Num 6.15 He shall also offer a basket of bread made without **yeast:**
28.17 which only bread prepared without **yeast** is to be eaten.
Deut 16. 3 When you eat this meal, do not eat bread prepared with **yeast.**
16. 3 to eat bread prepared without **yeast,** as you did when you had
16. 4 one in your land is to have any **yeast** in his house;
16. 8 to eat bread prepared without **yeast,** and on the seventh day
Josh 5.11 roasted grain and bread made without **yeast.**
Judg 6.19 ten kilogrammes of flour to make bread without any **yeast.**
1 Sam 28.24 some flour, prepared it, and baked some bread without **yeast.**
1 Chr 23.29 the wafers made without **yeast,** the baked offerings,
Ezek 45.21 For seven days everyone will eat bread made without **yeast.**
Mt 13.33 A woman takes some **yeast** and mixes it with forty litres of
16. 6 guard against the **yeast** of the Pharisees and Sadducees."
16.11 Guard yourselves from the **yeast** of the Pharisees and Sadducees!"
16.12 to guard themselves from the **yeast** used in bread but from
Mk 8.15 against the yeast of the Pharisees and the **yeast** of Herod."
Lk 12. 1 "Be on guard against the **yeast** of the Pharisees—I mean
13.21 A woman takes some **yeast** and mixes it with forty litres of
1 Cor 5. 6 saying, "A little bit of **yeast** makes the whole batch of
5. 7 You must remove the old **yeast** of sin so that you will
5. 7 batch of dough without any **yeast,** as indeed I know you
5. 8 with bread having the old **yeast** of sin and wickedness, but
5. 8 the bread that has no **yeast,** the bread of purity and truth.
Gal 5. 9 "It takes only a little **yeast** to make the whole batch of

YELL

Judg 7.21 round the camp, and the whole enemy army ran away **yelling.**
Is 31. 4 "No matter how shepherds **yell** and shout, they can't scare

YELLOW

Lev 13.30 the hairs in it are **yellowish** and thin, it is a dreaded
13.32 spread and there are no **yellowish** hairs in it and it does
13.36 If the sore has spread, he need not look for **yellowish** hairs;
Num 11. 7 (Manna was like small seeds, whitish **yellow** in colour.
Rev 9.17 red as fire, blue as sapphire, and **yellow** as sulphur.
21.20 carnelian, the seventh **yellow** quartz, the eighth beryl,

YES

Gen 18.15 **"Yes,** you did," he replied.
20. 6 God replied in the dream, **"Yes,** I know that you did it
22. 1 And Abraham answered, **"Yes,** here I am!"
22. 7 He answered, **"Yes,** my son?"
22.11 He answered, **"Yes,** here I am."
24.58 **"Yes,"** she answered.
27. 1 **"Yes,"** he answered.
27.18 **"Yes,"** he answered.
29. 5 **"Yes,** we do," they answered.
29.14 that had happened, [14] Laban said, **"Yes,** indeed, you are my
31.11 **'Yes,'** I answered.
32.20 You must say, **'Yes,** your servant Jacob is just behind us.' "
37.33 He recognized it and said, **"Yes,** it is his!
42.21 and said to one another, **"Yes,** now we are suffering the
46. 2 **"Yes,** here I am," he answered.
Ex 3. 4 He answered, **"Yes,** here I am."
16. 7 heard your complaints against him—**yes,** against him, because
Deut 9.11 **Yes,** after those forty days and nights the Lord gave me
11. 7 **Yes,** you are the ones who have seen all these great things
Josh 24.22 **"Yes,"** they said, "we are witnesses."
Judg 5. 4 **Yes,** water poured down from the clouds.
5.15 **yes,** Issachar came and Barak too, and they followed him
5.16 **Yes,** the tribe of Reuben was divided;
13.11 **"Yes,"** he answered.
20.22 The Lord answered, **"Yes."**
20.39 **"Yes,** we've beaten them just as we did before."
Ruth 2.22 Naomi said to Ruth, **"Yes,** my daughter, it will be better
4.11 The leaders and the others said, **"Yes,** we are witnesses.
1 Sam 3. 4 He answered, **"Yes,** sir!"
3.16 **"Yes,** sir," answered Samuel.
9.12 **"Yes,** he is," the girls answered.
12. 5 **"Yes,** the Lord is our witness," they answered.
15.24 **"Yes,** I have sinned," Saul replied.
16. 5 **"Yes,"** he answered.
22.15 **Yes,** I consulted God for him, and it wasn't the first time.
23. 2 **"Yes,"** the Lord answered.
26.17 **"Yes,** Your Majesty," David answered.
2 Sam 1. 7 I answered, **'Yes,** sir!'
2. 1 **"Yes,"** the Lord answered.
2.20 **"Yes,"** he answered.
5.19 **"Yes,** attack!"
12.19 **"Yes,** he is," they answered.
12.22 **"Yes,"** David answered, "I did fast and weep while he
15.15 **"Yes,** Your Majesty," they answered.
20.17 **"Yes,** I am," he answered.
1 Kgs 18. 8 **"Yes,** I'm Elijah," he answered.
21.20 **"Yes,** I have," Elijah answered.
2 Kgs 2. 3 **"Yes,** I know," Elisha answered.
2. 5 **"Yes,** I know," Elisha answered.
1 Chr 14.10 The Lord answered, **"Yes,** attack!
Job 5.11 **Yes,** it is God who raises the humble and gives joy to
8.19 **Yes,** that's all the joy evil men have;
9. 1 **Yes,** I've heard all that before.
12. 1 **Yes,** you are the voice of the people.
15.16 **yes,** man is corrupt;
21.10 **Yes,** all their cattle breed and give birth without trouble.
22.23 **Yes,** you must humbly return to God and put an end to
40.12 **Yes,** look at them and bring them down;
Ps 76. 3 enemy, their shields and swords, **yes,** all their weapons.
Prov 2. 3 **Yes,** beg for knowledge;
5.10 **Yes,** strangers will take all your wealth, and what you
24. 5 **yes,** knowledge is more important than strength.
Ecc 2. 9 **Yes,** I was great, greater than anyone else who had ever
6. 2 wealth, honour, and property, **yes,** everything he wants,
7.27 **Yes,** said the Philosopher, I found this out little by
8.10 **Yes,** I have seen wicked men buried and in their graves,
8.12 Oh **yes,** I know what they say:
9. 5 **Yes,** the living know they are going to die, but the dead
Is 1.16 **Yes,** stop doing evil [17] and learn to do right.
3. 8 **Yes,** Jerusalem is doomed!
3.25 The men of the city, **yes,** even the strongest men, will
7.22 **Yes,** the few survivors left in the land will have milk and
7.24 **Yes,** the whole country will be full of briars and thorn-bushes.
8. 9 **Yes,** get ready, but be afraid!
10.23 **Yes,** throughout the whole country the Sovereign Lord
15. 9 **Yes,** there will be a bloody slaughter of everyone left in Moab.
27. 5 **Yes,** let them make peace with me."
40. 8 **Yes,** grass withers and flowers fade, but the word of our
Jer 2.16 **Yes,** the men of Memphis and Tahpanhes have cracked his skull.
3.22 You say, **"Yes,** we are coming to the Lord, because he is
11. 5 I said, **"Yes,** Lord."
28. 4 **Yes,** I will break the power of the king of Babylonia.
29.14 **Yes,** I say, you will find me, and I will restore you
31. 6 **Yes,** the time is coming when watchmen will call out on the
Ezek 6.14 **Yes,** I will stretch out my hand and destroy their country.

Ezek 16. 8 **Yes,** I made a marriage covenant with you, and you became mine."
16.34 **Yes,** you are different."
16.53 **Yes,** I will make you prosperous too.
17.10 **Yes,** it is planted, but will it live and grow?
21.27 **Yes,** I will make the city a ruin.
22.21 **Yes,** I will gather them in Jerusalem, build a fire under them,
23.25 **Yes,** they will take your sons and daughters from you and
30.25 **Yes,** I will weaken him and strengthen the king of Babylonia.
35.15 The mountains of Seir, **yes,** all the land of Edom, will be
Dan 3.24 They answered, **"Yes,** we did, Your Majesty."
6.12 The king replied, **"Yes,** a strict order, a law of the Medes
Hos 1.11 **Yes,** the day of Jezreel will be a great day!
7. 6 **Yes,** they burned like an oven with their plotting.
Joel 1.11 the wheat, the barley, **yes** all the crops are destroyed.
Hag 2.13 The priests answered, **"Yes."**
Mt 5.37 Just say **'Yes'** or 'No'—anything else you say comes from
11. 9 **Yes** indeed, but you saw much more than a prophet.
11.26 **Yes,** Father, this was how you wanted it to happen.
13.51 **"Yes,"** they answered.
21.30 **'Yes,** sir,' he answered, but he did not go.
24. 2 **"Yes,"** he said, "you may well look at all these.
Mk 8.24 man looked up and said, **"Yes,** I can see people, but they
9.23 **"Yes,"** said Jesus, "if you yourself can!
10.29 **"Yes,"** Jesus said to them, "and I tell you that
Lk 7.26 **Yes** indeed, but you saw much more than a prophet.
7.40 **"Yes,** Teacher," he said, "tell me."
10.21 **Yes,** Father, this was how you wanted it to happen.
11.51 **Yes,** I tell you, the people of this time will be punished
18.29 **"Yes,"** Jesus said to them, "and I assure you that
Jn 14.12 will do what I do—**yes,** he will do even greater things,
21.15 **"Yes,** Lord," he answered, "you know that I love you."
21.16 **"Yes,** Lord," he answered, "you know that I love you."
Acts 2.18 **Yes,** even on my servants, both men and women, I will
5. 8 **"Yes,"** she answered, "the full amount."
22.27 **"Yes,"** answered Paul.
Rom 11.19 But you will say, **"Yes,** but the branches were broken
12.14 bless those who persecute you—**yes,** ask him to bless, not to
1 Cor 1.16 (Oh **yes,** I also baptized Stephanas and his family;
2 Cor 1.17 selfish motives, ready to say **"Yes,** yes" and "No, no"
1.18 truth, my promise to you was not a **"Yes"** and a "No."
1.19 is not one who is **"Yes"** and "No."
1.19 On the contrary, he is God's **"Yes"**;
1.20 for it is he who is the **"Yes"** to all God's promises.
Eph 3.19 **Yes,** may you come to know his love—although it can never
Jas 5.12 only "Yes" when you mean **yes,** and "No" when you mean no,
1 Jn 1. 1 **yes,** we have seen it, and our hands have touched it.
2.28 **Yes,** my children, remain in union with him, so that when
Rev 18.24 **yes,** the blood of all those who have been killed on earth.
22.20 He who gives his testimony to all this says, **"Yes**
also Mt 9.28 Jn 11.27 1 Cor 6.12 1 Cor 6.13 Rev 14.13

YESTERDAY

1 Sam 20.27 "Why didn't David come to the meal either **yesterday** or today?"
2 Kgs 9.26 'I saw the murder of Naboth and his sons **yesterday.**
Ps 90. 4 they are like **yesterday,** already gone, like a short hour
Jn 4.52 "It was one o'clock **yesterday** afternoon when the fever left him."
Acts 7.28 to kill me, just as you killed that Egyptian **yesterday?'**
Heb 13. 8 Jesus Christ is the same **yesterday,** today, and for ever.

YIELD

Prov 13.23 Unused fields could **yield** plenty of food for the poor,
Is 5.10 ten hectares of land will **yield** only eight litres of wine.
Ezek 36.30 I will increase the **yield** of your fruit-trees and your fields,
45.13 1/100th of the **yield** of your trees

YOKE

A heavy bar of wood which is fitted over the necks of two oxen to make it possible for them to pull a plough or a cart. The word is used to describe the rules for living that a teacher passes on to his pupils.

1 Sam 6. 7 prepare a new wagon and two cows that have never been **yoked;**
2 Sam 24.22 are their **yokes** and the threshing-boards to use as fuel."
1 Kgs 19.21 and cooked the meat, using the **yoke** as fuel for the fire.
Is 9. 4 For you have broken the **yoke** that burdened them and the
10.27 power of Assyria, and their **yoke** will no longer be a burden
14.25 my people from the Assyrian **yoke** and from the burdens they
58. 6 chains of oppression and the **yoke** of injustice, and let the
Jer 27. 2 me [2] to make myself a **yoke** out of leather straps and wooden
28.10 Then Hananiah took the **yoke** off my neck, broke it in pieces,
28.11 how he will break the **yoke** that King Nebuchadnezzar has put
28.13 able to break a wooden **yoke,**
28.13 but he will replace it with an iron **yoke.**
28.14 he will put an iron **yoke** on all these nations and that
30. 8 comes, I will break the **yoke** that is round their necks and
Hos 10.11 I decided to put a **yoke** on her beautiful neck and to
11. 7 cry out because of the **yoke** that is on them, but no
Mt 11.29 Take my **yoke** and put it on you, and learn from me,
11.30 For the **yoke** I will give you is easy,

YOUNG

Gen 4.23 I have killed a **young** man because he struck me.
8.21 know that from the time he is **young** his thoughts are evil.
9.24 again and learnt what his **youngest** son had done to him,
19. 4 All the men of the city, both **young** and old, were there.
19.35 drunk, and the **younger** daughter had intercourse with him.
19.38 The **younger** daughter also had a son, whom she named Benammi.
Gen 24.13 at the well where the **young** women of the city will be
24.16 She was a very beautiful **young** girl and still a virgin.
24.43 When a **young** woman comes out to get water, I will ask
24.61 Then Rebecca and her **young** women got ready and mounted
25.23 The older will serve the **younger."**
27. 9 and pick out two fat **young** goats, so that I can cook
29.16 the elder was named Leah, and the **younger** Rachel.
29.26 to give the **younger** daughter in marriage before the elder.
30.32 every black lamb and every spotted or speckled **young** goat.
30.39 of the branches, they produced **young** that were streaked,
31. 8 be your wages,' all the flocks produced speckled **young.**
31. 8 shall be your wages,' all the flocks produced striped **young.**
32.13 milk camels with their **young,** forty cows and ten bulls,
33.13 I must think of the sheep and livestock with their **young.**
34.19 his son Shechem, [19] and the **young** man lost no time in doing
37. 2 Joseph, a **young** man of seventeen, took care of the sheep
38.14 As she well knew, Judah's **youngest** son Shelah had now grown up,
38.17 He answered, "I will send you a **young** goat from my flock."
41.12 A **young** Hebrew was there with us, a slave of the captain
42.13 One brother is dead, and the **youngest** is now with our father."
42.15 you will never leave unless your **youngest** brother comes here.
42.20 Then you must bring your **youngest** brother to me.
42.32 brother is dead, and the **youngest** is still in Canaan with
42.34 Bring your **youngest** brother to me.
43.29 said, "So this is your **youngest** brother, the one you told
43.33 in the order of their age from the eldest to the **youngest.**
44. 2 in the top of the **youngest** brother's sack, together with the
44.12 eldest and ending with the **youngest,** and the cup was found
44.20 who is old and a **younger** brother, born to him in his
44.23 again unless your **youngest** brother comes with you.'
44.26 the man's presence unless our **youngest** brother is with us.
44.26 We can go only if our **youngest** brother goes also.'
47.12 rest of his father's family, including the very **youngest.**
48.14 even though he was the **younger,** and his left hand on the
48.19 But his **younger** brother will be greater than he, and his
49.11 He ties his **young** donkey to a grapevine, To the very
Ex 12. 3 must choose either a lamb or a **young** goat for his household.
12.21 choose a lamb or a **young** goat and kill it, so that
19. 4 as an eagle carries her **young** on her wings, and brought you
23.19 "Do not cook a **young** sheep or goat in its mother's milk.
24. 5 Then he sent **young** men, and they burnt sacrifices to the
29. 1 Take one **young** bull and two rams without any defects.
33.11 But the **young** man who was his helper, Joshua son of Nun,
34.26 "Do not cook a **young** sheep or goat in its mother's milk."
Lev 4. 3 people, he shall present a **young** bull without any defects
4.14 the community shall bring a **young** bull as a sin-offering.
8. 2 the anointing oil, the **young** bull for the sin-offering,
8.14 Then Moses brought the **young** bull for the sin-offering,
9. 2 said to Aaron, "Take a **young** bull and a ram without any
9. 8 the altar and killed the **young** bull which was for his own
16. 3 after he has brought a **young** bull for a sin-offering and a
27. 3 —**young** male, five to twenty years old:
27. 3 —**young** female:
Num 7.12 **young** bull, one ram, and a one-year-old lamb, for the burnt-offering;
8. 8 they are to take a **young** bull and the required
11.27 A **young** man ran out to tell Moses what Eldad and Medad
11.28 helper since he was a **young** man, spoke up and said to
28.11 two **young** bulls, one ram, seven one-year-old male lambs, all
28.19 two **young** bulls, one ram, and seven one-year-old male lambs,
28.27 two **young** bulls, one ram, and seven one-year-old male lambs,
29. 2 one **young** bull, one ram, and seven one-year-old male lambs,
29. 8 one **young** bull, one ram, and seven one-year-old male lambs,
29.13 **young** bulls, two rams, and fourteen one-year-old male lambs,
29.17 the second day offer twelve **young** bulls, two rams, and
29.20 the third day offer eleven **young** bulls, two rams, and
29.23 the fourth day offer ten **young** bulls, two rams, and fourteen
29.26 the fifth day offer nine **young** bulls, two rams, and fourteen
29.29 the sixth day offer eight **young** bulls, two rams, and
29.32 the seventh day offer seven **young** bulls, two rams, and
29.36 one **young** bull, one ram, and seven one-year-old male lambs,
30. 3 When a **young** woman still living in her father's house
Deut 1.39 children, who are still too **young** to know right from wrong,
14.21 "Do not cook a **young** sheep or goat in its mother's milk.
21. 3 found are to select a **young** cow that has never been used
22. 6 the eggs or with her **young,** you are not to take the
22. 7 You may take the **young** birds, but you must let the mother
28.50 will be ruthless and show no mercy to anyone, **young** or old.
32. 2 will fall like showers on **young** plants, like gentle rain on
32.11 Like an eagle teaching its **young** to fly, catching them
32.25 **Young** men and young women will die;
33.22 "Dan is a **young** lion;
Josh 6.21 they killed everyone in the city, men and women, **young** and
6.26 Whoever builds the gates will lose his **youngest."**
Judg 1.13 Othniel, the son of Caleb's **younger** brother Kenaz,
3. 9 This was Othniel, the son of Caleb's **younger** brother Kenaz.
6.19 his house and cooked a **young** goat and used ten kilogrammes
8.14 he captured a **young** man from Sukkoth and questioned him.
8.14 The **young** man wrote down for Gideon the names of the
9. 5 But Jotham, Gideon's **youngest** son, hid and was not killed.
9.54 Then he quickly called the **young** man who was carrying
9.54 So the **young** man ran him through, and he died.
11.40 custom in Israel [40] that the **young** women would go away for
13.15 Let us cook a **young** goat for you."
13.19 So Manoah took a **young** goat and some grain, and offered
14. 5 through the vineyards there, he heard a **young** lion roaring.
14. 6 apart with his bare hands, as if it were a **young** goat.
14.10 This was a custom among the **young** men.
14.11 Philistines saw him, they sent thirty **young** men to stay with him.
15. 1 his wife during the wheat harvest and took her a **young** goat.
15. 2 But her **younger** sister is prettier, anyway.

Judg	17. 7	same time there was a **young** Levite who had been living in
	17.11	The **young** Levite agreed to stay with Micah and became
	18. 3	recognized the accent of the **young** Levite, so they went up
	18.15	into Micah's house, where the **young** Levite lived, and asked
	21.12	Jabesh they found four hundred **young** virgins, so they
Ruth	2. 5	Boaz asked the man in charge, "Who is that **young** woman?"
	3.10	have gone looking for a **young** man, either rich or poor, but
	4.12	will give you by this **young** woman make your family like the
1 Sam	1.24	She took Samuel, **young** as he was, to the house of the
	2.31	I will kill all the **young** men in your family and your
	5. 9	in all the people of the city, **young** and old alike.
	7. 9	Samuel killed a **young** lamb and burnt it whole as a
	8. 2	The elder son was named Joel and the **younger** one Abijah;
	10. 3	them will be leading three **young** goats, another one will be
	14. 1	day Jonathan said to the **young** man who carried his weapons,
	14. 6	Jonathan said to the **young** man, "Let's cross over to the
	14. 7	The **young** man answered, "Whatever you want to do, I'm with you."
	14.12	called out to Jonathan and the **young** man, "Come on up here!
	14.12	Jonathan said to the **young** man, "Follow me.
	14.13	pass on his hands and knees, and the **young** man followed him.
	14.13	Philistines and knocked them down, and the **young** man killed them.
	14.14	first slaughter Jonathan and the **young** man killed about
	14.17	found that Jonathan and the **young** man who carried his
	14.49	His elder daughter was named Merab, and the **younger** one Michal.
	16.11	answered, "There is still the **youngest**, but he is out
	16.12	He was a handsome, healthy **young** man, and his eyes sparkled.
	16.20	David to Saul with a **young** goat, a donkey loaded with bread,
	17.14	David was the **youngest** son, and while the three eldest
	17.58	Saul asked him, **"Young** man, whose son are you?"
	20.35	He took a **young** boy with him [36]and said to him, "Run
	25. 5	it, [5]so he sent ten **young** men with orders to go to
	30.17	Except for four hundred **young** men who mounted camels and got away,
	31. 4	said to the **young** man carrying his weapons, "Draw your sword
	31. 4	But the **young** man was too terrified to do it.
	31. 5	The **young** man saw that Saul was dead, so he too threw
	31. 6	that is how Saul, his three sons, and the **young** man died;
2 Sam	1. 2	The next day a **young** man arrived from Saul's camp.
	1.13	David asked the **young** man who had brought him the news,
	2.14	"Let's get some of the **young** men from each side to fight
	9.12	Mephibosheth had a **young** son named Mica.
	14.21	Go and get the **young** man Absalom and bring him back here."
	18. 5	"For my sake don't harm the **young** man Absalom."
	18.12	'For my sake don't harm the **young** man Absalom.'
	18.29	"Is the **young** man Absalom safe?"
	18.32	"Is the **young** man Absalom safe?"
1 Kgs	1. 2	Majesty, let us find a **young** woman to stay with you and
	3. 7	even though I am very **young** and don't know how to rule.
	11.28	Jeroboam was an able **young** man, and when Solomon noticed
	12. 8	and went instead to the **young** men who had grown up with
	12.14	harshly to the people, [14]as the **younger** men had advised.
	14.10	will kill all your male descendants, **young** and old alike.
	16.34	foundation of Jericho, and his **youngest** son Segub when he
	20.14	"The Lord says that the **young** soldiers under the command of
	20.15	the king called out the **young** soldiers who were under the
	20.17	The **young** soldiers advanced first.
	20.19	The **young** soldiers led the attack, followed by the Israelite army,
	21.21	get rid of every male in your family, **young** and old alike.
2 Kgs	3.21	from the oldest to the **youngest**, were called out and
	8.12	their finest **young** men, batter their children to death,
	9. 1	Elisha called one of the **young** prophets and said to him,
	9. 4	So the **young** prophet went to Ramoth, [5]where he found the
	9. 6	them went indoors, and the **young** prophet poured the
	9. 8	get rid of every male in his family, **young** and old alike.
	9.10	After saying this, the **young** prophet left the room and fled.
1 Chr	6.28	Joel, the elder, and Abijah, the **younger.**
	10. 4	said to the **young** man carrying his weapons, "Draw your sword
	10. 4	But the **young** man was too terrified to do it.
	10. 5	The **young** man saw that Saul was dead, so he too threw
	12.23	Relatives of Zadok, an able **young** fighter:
	22. 5	But he is **young** and inexperienced, so I must make
	24.31	one of his **younger** brothers drew lots for their assignments,
	25. 8	lots, whether they were **young** or old, experts or beginners.
	29. 1	God has chosen, but he is still **young** and lacks experience.
2 Chr	10. 8	and went instead to the **young** men who had grown up with
	10.14	harshly to the people, [14]as the **younger** men had advised.
	13. 7	Solomon, who was too **young** and inexperienced to resist them.
	15.13	Anyone, **young** or old, male or female, who did not
	21.17	the king's wives and sons except Ahaziah, his **youngest** son.
	22. 1	killed all King Jehoram's sons except Ahaziah, the **youngest.**
	34. 3	while he was still very **young,** he began to worship the God
	35. 7	sheep, lambs, and **young** goats, and three thousand bulls.
	35. 8	thousand six hundred lambs and **young** goats and three hundred
	35. 9	contributed five thousand lambs and **young** goats and five
	36.17	The king killed the **young** men of Judah, even in the Temple.
	36.17	had no mercy on anyone, **young** or old, man or woman, sick
Ezra	6. 9	**young** bulls, sheep, or lambs to be burnt as offerings to the
Esth	2. 2	"Why don't you make a search to find some beautiful **young** virgins?
	2. 3	to bring all these beautiful **young** girls to your harem here
	3.13	day of Adar, all Jews—**young** and old, women and children—were
Job	13.26	charges against me, even for what I did when I was **young.**
	14. 9	the ground, [9]with water it will sprout like a **young** plant.
	20.11	His body used to be **young** and vigorous, but soon it will
	29. 8	took my place among them, [8]**young** men stepped aside as soon
	30. 1	But men **younger** than I am make fun of me now!
	32. 4	Because Elihu was the **youngest** one there, he had waited
	32. 6	I am **young,** and you are old, so I was afraid to
Job	33.25	His body will grow **young** and strong again;
	36.14	die while they are still **young,** worn out by a life of
	38.39	to eat, and satisfy hungry **young** lions [40]when they hide in
	38.41	wander about hungry, when their **young** cry to me for food?
	39. 2	Do you know how long they carry their **young?**
	39. 3	they will crouch down and bring their **young** into the world?
	39. 4	In the wilds their **young** grow strong;
	39.30	the eagles gather, and the **young** eagles drink the blood.
	42.14	Jemimah, the second Keziah, and the **youngest** Keren Happuch.
Ps	29. 6	like calves and makes Mount Hermon leap like a **young** bull.
	34.11	Come, my **young** friends, and listen to me, and I will
	65.10	the soil with showers and cause the **young** plants to grow.
	71. 5	I have trusted in you since I was **young.**
	71.17	me ever since I was **young,** and I still tell of your
	78.31	killed their strongest men, the best **young** men of Israel.
	78.63	**Young** men were killed in war,
	78.63	and **young** women had no one to marry.
	80.15	that you planted, this **young** vine you made grow so strong!
	84. 3	they keep their **young** near your altars, Lord Almighty, my
	88.15	Ever since I was **young,** I have suffered and been near death;
	102.23	The Lord has made me weak while I am still **young;**
	103. 5	good things, so that I stay **young** and strong like an eagle.
	104.21	The **young** lions roar while they hunt, looking for the
	110. 3	dew of early morning your **young** men will come to you on
	119. 9	How can a **young** man keep his life pure?
	127. 4	man has when he is **young** are like arrows in a soldier's
	128. 3	your sons will be like **young** olive-trees round your table.
	129. 1	your enemies have persecuted you ever since you were **young.**
	129. 2	"Ever since I was **young,** my enemies have persecuted me cruelly,
	144.13	sheep in our fields bear **young** by the tens of thousands.
	147. 9	their food and feeds the **young** ravens when they call.
	148.12	girls and **young** men, old people and children too.
Prov	1. 4	person clever and teach **young** men how to be resourceful.
	5. 9	had, and you will die **young** at the hands of merciless men.
	7. 7	and I saw many inexperienced **young** men, but noticed one
	7.13	threw her arms round the **young** man, kissed him, looked him
	8.32	"Now, **young** men, listen to me.
	19.18	Discipline your children while they are **young** enough to learn.
	28. 7	A **young** man who obeys the law is intelligent.
Ecc	4.13	as well off as a **young** man who is poor but intelligent.
	4.15	among them there is a **young** man who will take the king's
	8.13	and they will die **young,** because they do not obey God."
	11. 9	**Young** people, enjoy your youth.
	11. 9	Be happy while you are still **young.**
	11.10	You aren't going to be **young** very long.
	12. 1	Creator while you are still **young,** before those dismal days
Song	2. 9	My lover is like a gazelle, like a **young** stag.
	6. 8	sixty queens, eighty concubines, **young** women without number!
	6.11	the almond-trees to see the **young** plants in the valley, to
	8. 8	We have a **young** sister, and her breasts are still small.
	8. 8	What will we do for her when a **young** man comes courting?
	8.14	like a gazelle, like a **young** stag on the mountains where
Is	3. 5	**Young** people will not respect their elders, and worthless
	5.17	lambs will eat grass and **young** goats will find pasture.
	7.14	a **young** woman who is pregnant will have a son and will
	7.21	able to save only one **young** cow and two goats, [22]they will
	9.17	not let any of the **young** men escape, and he will not
	11. 6	in peace, and leopards will lie down with **young** goats.
	13.18	With their bows and arrows they will kill the **young** men.
	20. 4	**Young** and old, they will walk barefoot and naked, with their
	31. 5	its nest to protect its **young,** so I, the Lord Almighty, will
	31. 8	run from battle, and their **young** men will be made slaves.
	34. 7	fall like wild oxen and **young** bulls, and the earth will be
	34.15	nests, lay eggs, hatch their **young,** and care for them there.
	40.24	They are like **young** plants, just set out and barely rooted.
	40.30	Even those who are **young** grow weak;
	40.30	**young** men can fall exhausted.
	47.12	you have used them since you were **young.**
	54. 4	forget your unfaithfulness as a **young** wife, and your
	54. 6	Israel, you are like a **young** wife, deserted by her husband
	62. 5	Like a **young** man taking a virgin as his bride, He who
	65.20	Those who live to be a hundred will be considered **young.**
Jer	1. 6	I am too **young."**
	1. 7	say that you are too **young,** but go to the people I
	2. 2	you were when you were **young,** how you loved me when we
	2.32	Does a **young** woman forget her jewellery,
	6.11	in the streets and on the gatherings of the **young** men.
	9.21	in the streets and the **young** men in the market-places.
	11.22	Their **young** men will be killed in war;
	13.14	them like jars against one another, old and **young** alike.
	15. 8	I killed your **young** men in their prime and made their
	18.21	men die of disease and the **young** men be killed in battle.
	31.13	will dance and be happy, and men, **young** and old, will
	31.19	We were ashamed and disgraced, because we sinned when we were **young.'**
	48.15	its finest **young** men have been slaughtered.
	49.26	On that day her **young** men will be killed in the city
	50.30	So its **young** men will be killed in the city streets, and
	51. 3	Do not spare the **young** men!
	51.22	women, to slay old and **young,** to kill boys and girls, [23]to
Lam	1.15	He sent an army to destroy my **young** men.
	1.18	My **young** men and women have been taken away captive.
	2.10	**Young** girls bow their heads to the ground.
	2.21	**Young** and old alike lie dead in the streets,
	2.21	**Young** men and women, killed by enemy
	4. 2	Zion's **young** men were as precious to us as gold, but now
	4. 3	but my people are like ostriches, cruel to their **young.**
	5.13	Our **young** men are forced to grind corn like slaves;
	5.14	the city gate, and the **young** people no longer make music.
Ezek	9. 6	Kill the old men, **young** men, young women, mothers, and

Ezek 16. 7 You grew strong and tall and became a **young** woman.
16.43 treated you when you were **young,** and you have made me angry
16.46 Your **younger** sister, with her villages, is Sodom, in the
16.60 with you when you were **young,** and I will make a covenant
16.61 when you get your elder sister and your **younger** sister back.
17. 5 Then he took a **young** plant from the land of Israel and
20.18 Instead, I warned the **young** people among them:
23. 3 When they were **young,** living in Egypt, they lost their
23. 4 (she represents Samaria), and the **younger** one was named
23. 6 all of them were handsome **young** cavalry officers.
23.12 for the cavalry officers, all those handsome **young** men.
23.23 will gather all those handsome **young** noblemen and officers,
24.21 And the **younger** members of your families who are left in
30.17 The **young** men of the cities of Heliopolis and Bubastis
31. 6 The wild animals bore their **young** in its shelter;
43.19 You will give them a **young** bull to offer as a sacrifice
43.23 finished doing that, take a **young** bull and a young ram, both
46. 6 Festival he will offer a **young** bull, six lambs, and a ram,
Dan 1. 3 among the Israelite exiles some **young** men of the royal
1.10 look as fit as the other **young** men, he may kill me."
1.13 Then compare us with the **young** men who are eating the
1.17 God gave the four **young** men knowledge and skill in
1.18 the king, Ashpenaz took all the **young** men to Nebuchadnezzar.
Hos 2.15 as she did when she was **young,** when she came from Egypt.
10.11 was once like a well-trained **young** cow, ready and willing to
Joel 2.28 men will have dreams, and your **young** men will see visions.
Amos 2.11 to be prophets, and some of your **young** men to be Nazirites.
3. 4 Does a **young** lion growl in his den unless he has caught
4.10 I killed your **young** men in battle and took your horses away.
8.13 On that day even healthy **young** men and women will
Mic 7. 6 mothers, and **young** women quarrel with their mothers-in-law;
Nah 2.11 of lions, the place where **young** lions were fed, where the
Zech 2. 4 other, "Run and tell that **young** man with the measuring-line
9.17 The **young** people will grow strong on its corn and wine.
Mal 2.14 your promise to the wife you married when you were **young.**
Mt 2.16 were two years old and **younger**—this was done in accordance
13. 6 But when the sun came up, it burnt the **young** plants;
19.20 "I have obeyed all these commandments," the **young man** replied.
19.22 When the **young man** heard this, he went away sad, because
Mk 4. 6 Then, when the sun came up, it burnt the **young** plants;
10.20 "ever since I was **young,** I have obeyed all these commandments."
14.51 A certain **young man,** dressed only in a linen cloth, was
15.40 Mary the mother of the **younger** James and of Joseph, and
16. 5 tomb, where they saw a **young man** sitting on the right,
Lk 2.24 pair of doves or two **young** pigeons, as required by the law
7.14 Jesus said, **"Young man!**
15.12 The **younger** one said to him, 'Father, give me my share
15.13 After a few days the **younger** son sold his part of the
18.21 "Ever since I was **young,** I have obeyed all these commandments."
22.26 you must be like the **youngest,** and the leader must be like
Jn 12.15 Here comes your king, riding on a **young** donkey."
21. 5 Then he asked them, **"Young men,** haven't you caught anything?"
21.18 when you were **young,** you used to get ready and go anywhere
Acts 2.17 your **young men** will see visions, and your old men will
5. 6 The **young men** came in, wrapped up his body, carried him out,
5.10 The **young men** came in and saw that she was dead, so
7.58 left their cloaks in the care of a **young man** named Saul.
20. 9 A **young man** named Eutychus was sitting in the window, and
20.12 They took the **young man** home alive and were greatly comforted.
23.17 and said to him, "Take this **young man** to the commander;
23.18 asked me to bring this **young man** to you, because he has
23.22 And he sent the **young man** away.
26. 4 the Jews know how I have lived ever since I was **young.**
Rom 9.11 God said to her, "The elder will serve the **younger."**
Gal 4. 1 while he is **young,** even though he really owns everything.
4. 2 While he is **young,** there are men who take care of him
1 Tim 4.12 on you because you are **young,** but be an example for the
5. 1 Treat the **younger** men as your brothers, [2]the older women as mothers,
5. 2 mothers, and the **younger** women as sisters, with all purity.
5.11 But do not include **younger** widows in the list;
5.14 I would prefer that the **younger** widows get married, have
Tit 2. 4 in order to train the **younger** women to love their husbands
2. 6 In the same way urge the **young men** to be self-controlled.
1 Pet 5. 5 In the same way you **younger** men must submit to the older
1 Jn 2.13 I am writing to you, **young men,** because you have defeated
2.14 I am writing to you, **young men,** because you are strong;

YOUTH

1 Sam 12. 2 I have been your leader from my **youth** until now.
Ps 25. 7 Forgive the sins and errors of my **youth.**
144.12 May our sons in their **youth** be like plants that grow up
Prov 20.29 We admire the strength of **youth** and respect the grey
Ecc 10.16 when its king is a **youth** and its leaders feast all night
11. 9 Young people, enjoy your **youth.**
Lam 3.27 And it is best to learn this patience in our **youth.**
2 Tim 2.22 Avoid the passions of **youth,** and strive for righteousness,

ZADOK (1)

Priest in Jerusalem in David and Solomon's time.

2 Sam 8.17 **Zadok** son of Ahitub and Ahimelech son of Abiathar were priests;
15.24 **Zadok** the priest was there, and with him were the Levites,
15.25 Then the king said to **Zadok,** "Take the Covenant Box
15.27 went on to say to **Zadok,** "Look, take your son Ahimaaz and
15.29 So **Zadok** and Abiathar took the Covenant Box back into
15.35 The priests **Zadok** and Abiathar will be there;
17.15 Then Hushai told the priests **Zadok** and Abiathar what
17.17 Abiathar's son Jonathan and **Zadok's** son Ahimaaz were
18.19 Then Ahimaaz son of **Zadok** said to Joab, "Let me run to
19.11 So he sent the priests **Zadok** and Abiathar to ask the leaders
20.25 **Zadok** and Abiathar were the priests, [26]and Ira from the
1 Kgs 1. 8 But **Zadok** the priest, Benaiah son of Jehoiada, Nathan the prophet,
1.26 not invite me, sir, or **Zadok** the priest, or Benaiah, or
1.32 Then King David sent for **Zadok,** Nathan, and Benaiah.
1.34 the spring of Gihon, [34]where **Zadok** and Nathan are to
1.38 So **Zadok,** Nathan, Benaiah, and the royal bodyguard put
1.39 **Zadok** took the container of olive-oil which he had
1.44 He sent **Zadok,** Nathan, Benaiah, and the royal bodyguard
1.45 on the king's mule, [45]and **Zadok** and Nathan anointed him as
2.35 Joab's place and put **Zadok** the priest in Abiathar's place.
4. 2 Azariah son of **Zadok** [3]The court secretaries:
4. 4 **Zadok** and Abiathar [5]Chief of the district governors:
1 Chr 15.11 David called in the priests **Zadok** and Abiathar and the six Levites,
16.39 **Zadok** the priest and his fellow-priests, however, were
18.16 **Zadok** son of Ahitub and Ahimelech son of Abiathar were priests;
24. 3 was assisted in this by **Zadok,** a descendant of Eleazar, and
24. 6 his officials, the priest **Zadok,** Ahimelech son of Abiathar,
24.31 King David, **Zadok,** Ahimelech, and the heads of families of
27.16 **Aaron** Zadok
29.22 Lord they anointed him as their ruler and **Zadok** as priest.
2 Chr 31.10 High Priest, a descendant of **Zadok,** said to him, "Since the
Ezra 7. 2 son of Shallum, son of **Zadok,** son of Ahitub, [3]son of Amariah,
Ezek 40.46 All the priests are descended from **Zadok;**
43.19 Levi who are descended from **Zadok** are the only ones who are
44.15 Levi who are descended from **Zadok,** however, continued to
48.11 area is to be for the priests who are descendants of **Zadok.**
also 1 Chr 6.8 1 Chr 6.53

ZEAL

2 Sam 21. 2 destroy them because of his **zeal** for the people of Israel
Phil 3. 6 Pharisee, [6]and I was so **zealous** that I persecuted the church.

AV ZEAL

see also **DEVOTE**

Num 25.11 He refused to **tolerate** the worship of any god but me, and
25.13 priests, because he did not **tolerate** any rivals to me and
2 Kgs 19.31 because the Lord is **determined** to make this happen.
Ps 119.139 My **anger** burns in me like a fire, because my enemies
Is 9. 7 The Lord Almighty is **determined** to do all this.
37.32 because the Lord Almighty is **determined** to make this happen.
59.17 clothe himself with the strong **desire** to set things right
63.15 Where is your great **concern** for us?
Ezek 5.13 spoken to you because I am **outraged** at your unfaithfulness.
Acts 22. 3 ancestors and was just as **dedicated** to God as are all of
1 Cor 14.12 Since you are **eager** to have the gifts of the Spirit,
2 Cor 9. 2 Your **eagerness** has stirred up most of them.
Col 4.13 personally testify to his hard **work** for you and for the
Tit 2.14 people who belong to him alone and are **eager** to do good.
Rev 3.19 Be in **earnest,** then, and turn from your sins.

ZEBEDEE

[SONS OF ZEBEDEE]
James and John's father.

Mt 4.21 saw two other brothers, James and John, the **sons of Zebedee.**
4.21 boat with their father **Zebedee,** getting their nets ready.
10. 2 James and his brother John, the **sons of Zebedee;**
20.20 Then the wife of **Zebedee** came to Jesus with her two sons,
26.37 He took with him Peter and the two **sons of Zebedee.**
27.56 Mary the mother of James and Joseph, and the wife of **Zebedee.**
Mk 1.19 saw two other brothers, James and John, the **sons of Zebedee.**
1.20 they left their father **Zebedee** in the boat with the hired
3.17 his brother John, the **sons of Zebedee** (Jesus gave them the
10.35 Then James and John, the **sons of Zebedee,** came to Jesus.
Lk 5.10 of Simon's partners, James and John, the **sons of Zebedee.**
Jn 21. 2 Cana in Galilee), the **sons of Zebedee,** and two other

ZEBULUN

Jacob and Leah's son, the tribe descended from him and its territory in n. Israel.

Gen 30.20 so she named him **Zebulun.**
35.23 Leah were Reuben (Jacob's eldest son), Simeon, Levi, Judah, Issachar, and **Zebulun.**
46.14 **Zebulun** and his sons:
49.13 **"Zebulun** will live beside the sea.
Ex 1. 3 Reuben, Simeon, Levi, Judah, [3]Issachar, **Zebulun,**
Num 10.16 Eliab son of Helon was in command of the tribe of **Zebulun.**
Deut 27.13 Reuben, Gad, Asher, **Zebulun,** Dan, and Naphtali.
33.18 About the tribes of **Zebulun** and Issachar he said:
33.18 "May **Zebulun** be prosperous in their trade on the sea, And
Josh 19.10 made was for the families of the tribe of **Zebulun.**
19.16 of the tribe of **Zebulun** received as their possession.
19.27 border went to Bethdagon, touching **Zebulun** and the Valley of
19.34 from there to Hukkok, touching **Zebulun** on the south, Asher
21. 7 cities from the territories of Reuben, Gad, and **Zebulun.**
21.34 Merari, received from the territory of **Zebulun** four cities:
Judg 1.30 The tribe of **Zebulun** did not drive out the people
4. 6 tribes of Naphtali and **Zebulun** and lead them to Mount Tabor.
4.10 Barak called the tribes of **Zebulun** and Naphtali to Kedesh,
5.14 The commanders came down from Machir, the officers down from **Zebulun.**
5.18 But the people of **Zebulun** and Naphtali risked their
6.35 to the tribes of Asher, **Zebulun,** and Naphtali, and they also
12.11 After Ibzan, Elon from **Zebulun** led Israel for ten years.
12.12 died and was buried at Aijalon in the territory of **Zebulun.**
1 Chr 2. 1 Reuben, Simeon, Levi, Judah, Issachar, **Zebulun,** [2]Dan,

1 Chr 6.63 territories of Reuben, Gad, and **Zebulun** were assigned to the
6.77 In the territory of **Zebulun:**
12.40 **Zebulun,** and Naphtali, people came bringing donkeys,
2 Chr 30.10 north as the tribe of **Zebulun,** but people laughed at them
30.11 tribes of Asher, Manasseh, and **Zebulun** who were willing to
30.18 of Ephraim, Manasseh, Issachar, and **Zebulun** had not
Ps 68.27 followed by the leaders of **Zebulun** and Naphtali.
Is 9. 1 of the tribes of **Zebulun** and Naphtali was once disgraced,
Ezek 48.23 Benjamin Simeon Issachar **Zebulun** Gad
48.30 in the south wall, after Simeon, Issachar, and **Zebulun;**
Mt 4.13 by Lake Galilee, in the territory of **Zebulun** and Naphtali.
4.15 "Land of **Zebulun** and land of Naphtali,
Rev 7. 5 Simeon, Levi, Issachar, **Zebulun,** Joseph, and Benjamin.
also Num 1.5 Num 1.20 Num 2.3 Num 7.12 Num 13.3 Num 26.26
Num 34.19 1 Chr 12.23 1 Chr 27.16

ZECHARIAH (1)
John the Baptist's father.

Lk 1. 5 there was a priest named **Zechariah,** who belonged to the
1. 7 not have any, and she and **Zechariah** were both very old.
1. 8 One day **Zechariah** was doing his work as a priest in the
1.12 When **Zechariah** saw him, he was alarmed and felt afraid.
1.13 But the angel said to him, "Don't be afraid, **Zechariah!**
1.18 **Zechariah** said to the angel, "How shall I know if this
1.21 the people were waiting for **Zechariah** and wondering why he
1.23 of service in the Temple was over, **Zechariah** went back home.
1.40 She went into **Zechariah's** house and greeted Elizabeth.
1.59 and they were going to name him **Zechariah,** after his father.
1.63 **Zechariah** asked for a writing tablet and wrote, "His name is John."
1.64 At that moment **Zechariah** was able to speak again, and he
1.67 John's father **Zechariah** was filled with the Holy Spirit,
3. 2 word of God came to John son of **Zechariah** in the desert.

ZEDEKIAH (1)
Last king of Judah. see also MATTANIAH (1)

2 Kgs 24.17 Mattaniah king of Judah and changed his name to **Zedekiah.**
24.18 **Zedekiah** was twenty-one years old when he became king of Judah,
24.19 King **Zedekiah** sinned against the Lord,
25. 1 **Zedekiah** rebelled against King Nebuchadnezzar of Babylonia,
25. 1 of the tenth month of the ninth year of **Zedekiah's** reign.
25. 2 and kept it under siege until **Zedekiah's** eleventh year.
25. 5 the Babylonian army pursued King **Zedekiah,** captured him in
25. 6 **Zedekiah** was taken to King Nebuchadnezzar, who was in the
25. 7 While **Zedekiah** was looking on, his sons were put to death;
25. 7 Nebuchadnezzar had **Zedekiah's** eyes put out, placed him in chains,
1 Chr 3.15 Johanan, Jehoiakim, **Zedekiah,** and Joahaz.
2 Chr 36.10 Nebuchadnezzar made Jehoiachin's uncle **Zedekiah** king of Judah
36.11 **Zedekiah** was twenty-one years old when he became king of Judah,
36.13 **Zedekiah** rebelled against King Nebuchadnezzar, who had
Jer 1. 3 the eleventh year of the reign of **Zedekiah** son of Josiah.
21. 1 King **Zedekiah** of Judah sent Pashhur son of Malchiah and
21. 4 sent to me [4] to tell **Zedekiah** that the Lord,
21. 4 God of Israel, had said, **"Zedekiah,** I am going to defeat
24. 8 "As for King **Zedekiah** of Judah, the politicians round him,
27. 1 Soon after Josiah's son **Zedekiah** became king of Judah, the
27. 3 ambassadors who had come to Jerusalem to see King **Zedekiah.**
27.12 the same thing to King **Zedekiah** of Judah, "Submit to the
28. 1 fourth year that **Zedekiah** was king, Hananiah son of Azzur,
29. 3 son of Hilkiah, whom King **Zedekiah** of Judah was sending to
32. 1 in the tenth year that **Zedekiah** was king of Judah, which was
32. 3 King **Zedekiah** had imprisoned me there and had accused me
32. 4 Babylonia capture this city, [4] and King **Zedekiah** will not escape.
32. 5 **Zedekiah** will be taken to Babylonia, and he will remain
34. 2 go and say to King **Zedekiah** of Judah, "I, the Lord, will
34. 4 **Zedekiah,** listen to what I say about you.
34. 6 gave this message to King **Zedekiah** in Jerusalem [7] while the
34. 8 King **Zedekiah** and the people of Jerusalem had made an
34.21 will also hand over King **Zedekiah** of Judah and his officials
37. 1 King Nebuchadnezzar of Babylonia made **Zedekiah** son of
37. 2 But neither **Zedekiah** nor his officials nor the people
37. 3 King **Zedekiah** sent Jehucal son of Shelemiah and the priest
37. 7 told me [7] to say to **Zedekiah,** "The Egyptian army is on its
37.17 Later on King **Zedekiah** sent for me, and there in the
37.21 So King **Zedekiah** ordered me to be locked up in the
38. 5 **Zedekiah** answered, "Very well, then, do what you wish with him;
38.14 On another occasion King **Zedekiah** had me brought to him
38.16 So King **Zedekiah** promised me in secret, "I swear by the
38.17 Then I told **Zedekiah** that the Lord Almighty, the God of Israel,
38.24 **Zedekiah** replied, "Don't let anyone know about this conversation,
39. 1 of the ninth year that **Zedekiah** was king of Judah, King
39. 2 of the fourth month of **Zedekiah's** eleventh year as king, the
39. 4 When King **Zedekiah** and all his soldiers saw what was happening,
39. 5 Babylonian army pursued them and captured **Zedekiah** in the plains
39. 6 At Riblah he put **Zedekiah's** sons to death
39. 6 while **Zedekiah** was looking on, and he also
39. 7 After that, he had **Zedekiah's** eyes put out and had him
44.30 as I handed over King **Zedekiah** of Judah to King
49.34 Soon after **Zedekiah** became king of Judah, the Lord
51.59 King **Zedekiah's** personal attendant was Seraiah, the son
51.59 In the fourth year that **Zedekiah** was king of Judah, Seraiah
52. 1 **Zedekiah** was twenty-one years old when he became king of Judah,
52. 2 King **Zedekiah** sinned against the Lord,
52. 3 **Zedekiah** rebelled against King Nebuchadnezzar of Babylonia,
Jer 52. 4 of the tenth month of the ninth year of **Zedekiah's** reign.
52. 5 and kept it under siege until **Zedekiah's** eleventh year.
52. 8 the Babylonian army pursued King **Zedekiah,** captured him in
52. 9 **Zedekiah** was taken to King Nebuchadnezzar, who was in the
52.10 At Riblah he put **Zedekiah's** sons to death
52.10 while **Zedekiah** was looking on
52.11 After that, he had **Zedekiah's** eyes put out and had him
52.11 **Zedekiah** remained in prison in Babylon until the day he died.

ZERAH (1)
Judah's son and the clan descended from him.

Gen 38.30 with the red thread on his arm, and he was named **Zerah.**
46.12 Shelah, Perez, and **Zerah.**
Num 26.19 the clans of Shelah, Perez, **Zerah,** Hezron, and Hamul.
Josh 7. 1 belonged to the clan of **Zerah,** a part of the tribe of
7.17 forward, clan by clan, and the clan of **Zerah** was picked out.
7.17 he brought the clan of **Zerah** forward, family by family, and
22.20 Remember how Achan son of **Zerah** refused to obey the
1 Chr 2. 4 By his daughter-in-law Tamar, Judah had two more sons, Perez and **Zerah.**
2. 6 His brother **Zerah** had five sons:
2. 7 son of Carmi, one of **Zerah's** descendants, brought disaster
9. 4 The descendants of Judah's son **Zerah** had Jeuel as their leader.
27. 2 member of the clan of **Zerah,** a part of the tribe of
27. 2 Netophah (he was a member of the clan of **Zerah**) Eleventh month:
Neh 11.24 Meshezabel, of the clan of **Zerah** and the tribe of Judah,
Mt 1. 2 then Perez and **Zerah** (their mother was Tamar), Hezron, Ram,

ZERUBBABEL
One of the leaders of those who returned from exile (to Jerusalem).

1 Chr 3.19 Pedaiah had two sons, **Zerubbabel** and Shimei.
3.19 **Zerubbabel** was the father of two sons, Meshullam and Hananiah,
Ezra 2. 2 Their leaders were **Zerubbabel,** Joshua, Nehemiah, Seraiah,
3. 2 his fellow-priests, and **Zerubbabel** son of Shealtiel,
3. 8 **Zerubbabel,** Joshua, and the rest of their fellow-countrymen,
4. 2 So they went to see **Zerubbabel** and the heads of the clans
4. 3 **Zerubbabel,** Joshua, and the heads of the clans said to them,
5. 2 When **Zerubbabel** son of Shealtiel and Joshua son of
Neh 7. 7 Their leaders were **Zerubbabel,** Joshua, Nehemiah, Azariah,
12. 1 who returned from exile with **Zerubbabel** son of Shealtiel and
12.47 In the time of **Zerubbabel** and also in the time of Nehemiah,
Hag 1. 1 for the governor of Judah, **Zerubbabel** son of Shealtiel, and
1.12 Then **Zerubbabel** and Joshua and all the people who had
1.14 **Zerubbabel,** the governor of Judah;
2. 2 told Haggai to speak to **Zerubbabel,** the governor of Judah,
2.21 Lord gave Haggai a second message [21] for **Zerubbabel,**
2.23 day I will take you, **Zerubbabel** my servant, and I will
Zech 4. 6 The angel told me to give **Zerubbabel** this message from the Lord:
4. 9 He said, **"Zerubbabel** has laid the foundation of the Temple,
4.10 But they will see **Zerubbabel** continuing to build the Temple,
Mt 1.12 Jehoiachin, Shealtiel, **Zerubbabel,** Abiud, Eliakim, Azor,
Lk 3.27 the son of **Zerubbabel,** the son of Shealtiel,

ZERUIAH
Mother of Abishai, Joab and Asahel.

1 Sam 26. 6 of Joab (their mother was **Zeruiah**), "Which of you two will
2 Sam 2.13 Joab, whose mother was **Zeruiah,** and David's other
2.18 The three sons of **Zeruiah** were there:
3.39 These sons of **Zeruiah** are too violent for me.
8.16 Joab, whose mother was **Zeruiah,** was the commander of the army;
16. 9 Abishai, whose mother was **Zeruiah,** said to the king,
17.25 daughter of Nahash and the sister of Joab's mother **Zeruiah.)**
19.21 Abishai son of **Zeruiah** spoke up:
21.17 But Abishai son of **Zeruiah** came to David's help,
23.18 brother Abishai (their mother was **Zeruiah**) was the leader of
1 Kgs 1. 7 Joab (whose mother was **Zeruiah**) and with Abiathar the priest,
1 Chr 2.16 He also had two daughters, **Zeruiah** and Abigail.
2.16 Jesse's daughter **Zeruiah** had three sons:
11. 6 mother was **Zeruiah,** led the attack and became commander.
18.12 Abishai, whose mother was **Zeruiah,** defeated the
26.28 Saul, by Abner son of Ner, and by Joab son of **Zeruiah.**
27.24 Joab, whose mother was **Zeruiah,** began to take a census,

ZIBA
Saul's servant, later Mephibosheth's.

2 Sam 9. 2 servant of Saul's family named **Ziba,** and he was told to go
9. 2 "Are you **Ziba?"**
9. 3 **Ziba** answered, "There is still one of Jonathan's sons.
9. 4 "At the home of Machir son of Ammiel in Lodebar," **Ziba** answered.
9. 9 Then the king called **Ziba,** Saul's servant, and said, "I
9.10 **(Ziba** had fifteen sons and twenty servants.)
9.11 **Ziba** answered, "I will do everything Your Majesty commands."
9.12 All the members of **Ziba's** family became servants of Mephibosheth.
16. 1 he was suddenly met by **Ziba,** the servant of Mephibosheth,
16. 2 **Ziba** answered, "The donkeys are for Your Majesty's family to ride,
16. 3 "He is staying in Jerusalem," **Ziba** answered, "because he
16. 4 The king said to **Ziba,** "Everything that belonged to Mephibosheth
16. 4 "I am your servant," **Ziba** replied.
19.17 And **Ziba,** the servant of Saul's family, also came with his
19.29 I have decided that you and **Ziba** will share Saul's property."
19.30 "Let **Ziba** have it all," Mephibosheth answered.

AV **ZIF** see **ZIV**

ZIKLAG
Philistine city given to David by the king of Gath.

Josh	15.31	Iim, Ezem, [30]Eltolad, Chesil, Hormah, [31]**Ziklag,**
	19. 5	Eltolad, Bethul, Hormah, [5]**Ziklag,** Beth Marcaboth, Hazar Susah, [6]Beth Lebaoth,
1 Sam	27. 6	gave him the town of **Ziklag,**
	27. 6	and for this reason **Ziklag** has belonged to the kings
	30. 1	Two days later David and his men arrived back at **Ziklag.**
	30. 1	The Amalekites had raided southern Judah and attacked **Ziklag.**
	30.14	territory of the clan of Caleb, and we burnt down **Ziklag."**
	30.26	When David returned to **Ziklag,** he sent part of the loot
2 Sam	1. 1	over the Amalekites and stayed in **Ziklag** for two days.
	4.10	who came to me at **Ziklag** and told me of Saul's death
1 Chr	4.30	Bilhah, Ezem, Tolad, [30]Bethuel, Hormah, **Ziklag,** [31]Beth Marcaboth,
	12. 1	David was living in **Ziklag,** where he had gone to escape
	12.19	to his former master Saul, so they sent him back to **Ziklag.**
Neh	11.28	lived in the city of **Ziklag,** in Meconah and its villages,

ZIMRI (1)
King who reigned briefly over n. Israel.

1 Kgs	16. 9	**Zimri,** one of his officers who was in charge of half the
	16.10	**Zimri** entered the house, assassinated Elah,
	16.11	As soon as **Zimri** became king he killed off all the
	16.12	**Zimri** killed all the family of Baasha.
	16.15	of King Asa of Judah, **Zimri** ruled in Tirzah over Israel for
	16.16	and when they heard that **Zimri** had plotted against the
	16.18	When **Zimri** saw that the city had fallen, he went into
	16.20	Everything else that **Zimri** did, including the account of his conspiracy,
2 Kgs	9.31	As Jehu came through the gate, she called out, "You **Zimri!**

ZIN
Desert area on the Israelites' route to Canaan.

Num	13.21	land from the wilderness of **Zin** in the south all the way
	20. 1	Israel came to the wilderness of **Zin** and camped at Kadesh.
	27.14	of you rebelled against my command in the wilderness of **Zin.**
	27.14	(Meribah is the spring at Kadesh in the wilderness of **Zin.)**
	33.15	Abronah, Eziongeber, the wilderness of **Zin** (that is,
	34. 3	extend from the wilderness of **Zin** along the border of Edom.
	34. 4	and continue on through **Zin** as far south as Kadesh Barnea.
Deut	32.51	Kadesh in the wilderness of **Zin,** you dishonoured me in the
Josh	15. 1	point of the wilderness of **Zin,** at the border of Edom.
	15. 3	went southwards from the Akrabbim Pass and on to **Zin.**

ZION
Originally a name for David's city, later used to refer to hill on which the Temple stood.

2 Sam	5. 7	did capture their fortress of **Zion,** and it became known as
1 Kgs	8. 1	take the Lord's Covenant Box from **Zion,** David's City, to the
2 Kgs	19.31	in Jerusalem and on Mount **Zion** who will survive, because the
1 Chr	11. 5	David captured their fortress of **Zion,** and it became known
2 Chr	5. 2	take the Lord's Covenant Box from **Zion,** David's City, to the
Ps	2. 6	"On **Zion,** my sacred hill," he says, "I have installed my king."
	9.11	Sing praise to the Lord, who rules in **Zion!**
	14. 7	How I pray that victory will come to Israel from **Zion.**
	15. 1	Who may worship on **Zion,** your sacred hill?
	20. 2	you help from his Temple and give you aid from Mount **Zion.**
	43. 3	and bring me back to **Zion,** your sacred hill, and to your
	48. 2	**Zion,** the mountain of God, is high and beautiful;
	48. 4	The kings gathered together and came to attack Mount **Zion.**
	48.11	let the people of **Zion** be glad!
	48.12	People of God, walk round **Zion** and count the towers;
	50. 2	God shines from **Zion,** the city perfect in its beauty.
	51.18	O God, be kind to **Zion** and help her;
	53. 6	How I pray that victory will come to Israel from **Zion.**
	65. 1	us to praise you in **Zion** and keep our promises to you,
	74. 2	Remember Mount **Zion,** where once you lived.
	76. 2	he lives on Mount **Zion.**
	78.68	the tribe of Judah and Mount **Zion,** which he dearly loves.
	84. 5	you, who are eager to make the pilgrimage to Mount **Zion.**
	84. 7	they will see the God of gods on **Zion.**
	87. 5	Of **Zion** it will be said that all nations belong there and
	87. 7	They dance and sing, "In **Zion** is the source of all our
	97. 8	The people of **Zion** are glad, and the cities of Judah
	99. 2	The Lord is mighty in **Zion;**
	102.13	You will rise and take pity on **Zion;**
	102.16	When the Lord rebuilds **Zion,** he will reveal his greatness.
	102.21	name will be proclaimed in **Zion,** and he will be praised in
	110. 2	From **Zion** the Lord will extend your royal power.
	125. 1	the Lord are like Mount **Zion,** which can never be shaken,
	128. 5	May the Lord bless you from **Zion!**
	129. 5	May everyone who hates **Zion** be defeated and driven back.
	132.13	The Lord has chosen **Zion;**
	132.15	I will richly provide **Zion** with all she needs;
	133. 3	like the dew on Mount Hermon, falling on the hills of **Zion.**
	134. 3	May the Lord, who made heaven and earth, bless you from **Zion!**
	135.21	Praise the Lord in **Zion,** in Jerusalem, his home.
	137. 1	there we wept when we remembered **Zion.**
	137. 3	"Sing us a song about **Zion."**
	146.10	Your God, O **Zion,** will reign for all time.
	147.12	Praise your God, O **Zion!**
	149. 2	rejoice, people of **Zion,** because of your king!
Song	3.11	Women of **Zion,** come and see King Solomon.
Is	2. 3	from **Zion** he speaks to his people."
	4. 5	Then over Mount **Zion** and over all who are gathered there,
	8.18	whose throne is on Mount **Zion,** has sent us as living
	10.12	I am doing on Mount **Zion** and in Jerusalem, I will punish
	10.24	his people who live in **Zion,** "Do not be afraid of the
	10.32	their fists at Mount **Zion,** at the city of Jerusalem.
	11. 9	On **Zion,** God's sacred hill, there will be nothing harmful or evil.
	12. 6	Let everyone who lives in **Zion** shout and sing!
	14.32	that the Lord has established **Zion** and that his suffering
	18. 7	come to Mount **Zion,** where the Lord Almighty is worshipped.
	24.23	rule in Jerusalem on Mount **Zion,** and the leaders of the
	25. 6	Here on Mount **Zion** the Lord Almighty will prepare a
	25.10	The Lord will protect Mount **Zion,** but the people of Moab
	28.16	"I am placing in **Zion** a foundation that is firm and strong.
	31. 4	can keep me, the Lord Almighty, from protecting Mount **Zion.**
	33.14	The sinful people of **Zion** are trembling with fright.
	33.20	Look at **Zion,** the city where we celebrate our religious festivals.
	34. 8	Lord will rescue **Zion** and take vengeance on her enemies.
	37.32	in Jerusalem and on Mount **Zion** who will survive, because the
	40. 9	Call out with a loud voice, **Zion;**
	41.27	I, the Lord, was the first to tell **Zion** the news;
	52. 2	Undo the chains that bind you, captive people of **Zion!**
	52. 7	He announces victory and says to **Zion,** "Your God is king!"
	52. 8	see with their own eyes the return of the Lord to **Zion!**
	56. 7	"I will bring you to **Zion,** my sacred hill, give you joy
	60.14	'The City of the Lord,' **'Zion,** the City of Israel's Holy God.'
	61. 3	those who mourn in **Zion** Joy and gladness instead of grief,
	65.11	that forsake me, who ignore **Zion,** my sacred hill, and
	65.25	On **Zion,** my sacred hill, there will be nothing harmful or evil."
	66. 8	**Zion** will not have to suffer long, before the nation is born.
Jer	3.14	from each clan, and I will bring you back to Mount **Zion.**
	4. 6	Point the way to **Zion!**
	6. 2	The city of **Zion** is beautiful, but it will be destroyed;
	8.19	hear my people crying out, "Is the Lord no longer in **Zion?**
	8.19	Is **Zion's** king no longer there?"
	9.19	Listen to the sound of crying in **Zion,**
	14.19	Do you hate the people of **Zion?**
	26.18	**'Zion** will be ploughed like a field, Jerusalem will become a
	30.17	your wounds, though your enemies say, **'Zion** is an outcast;
	31. 6	of Ephraim, 'Let's go up to **Zion,** to the Lord our God.' "
	31.12	sing for joy on Mount **Zion** and be delighted with my gifts
	50. 5	will ask the way to **Zion** and then go in that direction.
	51.35	Let the people of **Zion** say, "May Babylonia be held
Lam	1. 4	The city gates stand empty, and **Zion** is in agony.
	2. 1	The Lord in his anger has covered **Zion** with darkness.
	2. 8	The Lord was determined that the walls of **Zion** should fall;
	4. 2	**Zion's** young men were as precious to us as gold, but now
	4.11	he lit a fire in **Zion** that burnt it to the ground.
	4.22	**Zion** has paid for her sin;
	5.11	Our wives have been raped on Mount **Zion** itself;
	5.18	our tears, [18]because Mount **Zion** lies lonely and deserted,
Joel	2. 1	sound the alarm on **Zion,** God's sacred hill.
	2.15	Blow the trumpet on Mount **Zion;**
	2.23	"Be glad, people of **Zion,** rejoice at what the Lord your
	3.16	The Lord roars from Mount **Zion;**
	3.17	I live on **Zion,** my sacred hill.
	3.20	for ever, and I the Lord, will live on Mount **Zion."**
Amos	1. 2	"The Lord roars from Mount **Zion;**
	6. 1	such an easy life in **Zion** and for you that feel safe
Obad	17	"But on Mount **Zion** some will escape, and it will be a
Mic	3.12	And so, because of you, **Zion** will be ploughed like a field,
	4. 2	from **Zion** he speaks to his people."
	4. 7	rule over them on Mount **Zion** from that time on and for
Zeph	3.16	will say to Jerusalem, "Do not be afraid, city of **Zion!**
Zech	9. 9	Rejoice, rejoice, people of **Zion!**
	9.13	will use the men of **Zion** like a sword, to fight the
Mt	21. 5	"Tell the city of **Zion,** Look, your king is coming to you!
Jn	12.15	as the scripture says, [15]"Do not be afraid, city of **Zion!**
Rom	9.33	"Look, I place in **Zion** a stone that will make people stumble,
	11.26	"The Saviour will come from **Zion** and remove all wickedness
Heb	12.22	you have come to Mount **Zion** and to the city
1 Pet	2. 6	stone, which I am placing as the cornerstone in **Zion;**
Rev	14. 1	Then I looked, and there was the Lamb standing on Mount **Zion;**

ZITHER

Dan	3. 5	trumpets, followed by the playing of oboes, lyres, **zithers,**
	3.15	oboes, lyres, **zithers,** harps, and all the other instruments,

ZIV
Second month of the Hebrew calendar.

1 Kgs	6. 1	month, the month of **Ziv,** Solomon began work on the Temple.
	6.37	second month, the month of **Ziv,** in the fourth year of

ZOBAH
Syrian state conquered by David.

1 Sam	14.47	Ammon, and of Edom, the kings of **Zobah,** and the Philistines.
2 Sam	8. 3	of the Syrian state of **Zobah,** Hadadezer son of Rehob, as
	10. 6	Syrian soldiers from Bethrehob and **Zobah,**
	10.16	Shobach, commander of the army of King Hadadezer of **Zobah.**
	23.24	Igal son of Nathan from **Zobah** Bani from Gad Zelek from Ammon
1 Kgs	11.23	his master, King Hadadezer of **Zobah,** [24]and had become the
1 Chr	11.26	Elnaam Ithmah from Moab Eliel, Obed, and Jaasiel from **Zobah**
	18. 3	of the Syrian state of **Zobah,** near the territory of Hamath,
	19. 6	Upper Mesopotamia and from the Syrian states of Maacah and **Zobah.**
	19.16	Shobach, commander of the army of King Hadadezer of **Zobah.**
2 Chr	8. 3	the territory of Hamath and **Zobah** [4]and fortified the city

ZONES

Is 47.13 stars, who map out the **zones** of the heavens and tell you

ZORAH

[ZORITES]

Town in Dan, Samson's home.

Josh 15.33 in the foothills were Eshtaol, **Zorah,** Ashnah, [34] Zanoah,
19.41 Its area included **Zorah,** Eshtaol, Irshemesh,
Judg 13. 2 time there was a man named Manoah from the town of **Zorah.**
Judg 13.25 him while he was between **Zorah** and Eshtaol in the Camp of
16.31 back and buried him between **Zorah** and Eshtaol in the tomb of
18. 2 them from the towns of **Zorah** and Eshtaol with instructions
18. 8 the five men returned to **Zorah** and Eshtaol, their countrymen
18.11 the tribe of Dan left **Zorah** and Eshtaol, ready for battle.
1 Chr 2.53 people of the cities of **Zorah** and Eshtaol were members of
2.54 Beth Joab, and of the **Zorites,** who were one of the two
4. 2 Ahumai and Lahad, the ancestors of the people who lived in **Zorah.**
2 Chr 11.10 Gath, Mareshah, Ziph, [9] Adoraim, Lachish, Azekah, [10] **Zorah,**
Neh 11.29 its villages, [29] in Enrimmon, in **Zorah,** in Jarmuth, [30] in

NUMERICS

Numbers *ONE to TWELVE* and *HUNDRED, THOUSAND* and *MILLION* appear as words in their appropriate alphabetical position in the main Concordance.

This list is arranged according to the first digit of the number, so all numbers beginning with 1 are followed by those beginning with 2 etc.

1.3

Ex 27. 1 and it is to be **1.3** metres high.
38. 1 and it was **1.3** metres high.
1 Kgs 7.27 was 1.8 metres long, 1.8 metres wide, and **1.3** metres high.
2 Kgs 25.17 with a bronze capital on top, **1.3** metres high.
2 Chr 6.13 It was 2.2 metres square and **1.3** metres high.

1.32

Num 7.84 weighing a total of **1.32** kilogrammes, filled with incense

1.5

Num 7.12 one silver bowl weighing **1.5** kilogrammes and one silver

1.8

1 Kgs 7.19 capitals were shaped like lilies, **1.8** metres tall,
7.27 was **1.8** metres long, 1.8 metres wide, and 1.3 metres high.
7.38 Each basin was **1.8** metres in diameter, and held about 800 litres.

1/100

Ezek 45.13 **1/100th** of the yield of your trees

1/60

Ezek 45.13 **1/60th** of your harvest
45.13 **1/60th** of your harvest

10,000

Lev 26. 8 hundred, and a hundred will be able to defeat **ten thousand.**
Deut 32.30 a thousand defeated by one, and **ten thousand** by only two?
33. 2 **Ten thousand** angels were with him, a flaming fire at his
33.17 His horns are Manasseh's thousands And Ephraim's **ten thousands.**
Judg 1. 4 and they defeated **ten thousand** men at Bezek.
3.29 they killed about **ten thousand** of the best Moabite soldiers;
4. 6 'Take **ten thousand** men from the tribes of Naphtali and
4.10 to Kedesh, and **ten thousand** men followed him.
4.14 So Barak went down from Mount Tabor with his **ten thousand** men.
7. 3 So twenty-two thousand went back, but **ten thousand** stayed.
20.34 **Ten thousand** men, specially chosen out of all Israel,
1 Sam 15. 4 were 200,000 soldiers from Israel and **10,000** from Judah.
18. 7 "Saul has killed thousands, but David **tens of thousands."**
18. 8 "For David they claim **tens of thousands,** but only thousands for me.
21.11 'Saul has killed thousands, but David has killed **tens of thousands.'**
29. 5 'Saul has killed thousands, but David has killed **tens of thousands.' "**
2 Sam 18. 3 but you are worth **ten thousand** of us.
1 Kgs 4.22 litres of fine flour and **ten thousand** litres of meal;
5.14 them into three groups of **10,000** men, and each group spent
2 Kgs 13. 7 fifty horsemen, ten chariots, and **ten thousand** men on foot,
14. 7 Amaziah killed **ten thousand** Edomite soldiers in Salt Valley;
18.14 that Hezekiah should send him **ten thousand** kilogrammes of
24.14 royal princes, and all the leading men, **ten thousand** in all.
2 Chr 25.11 There they fought and killed **ten thousand** Edomite soldiers
25.12 Edomite soldiers [12] and captured another **ten thousand.**
30.24 gave them another thousand bulls and **ten thousand** sheep.
Ezra 7.22 of 3,400 kilogrammes of silver, **10,000** kilogrammes of wheat,
Ps 91. 7 may fall dead beside you, **ten thousand** all round you, but
144.13 sheep in our fields bear young by the **tens of thousands.**
Song 5.10 he is one in **ten thousand.**
Dan 11.41 kill **tens of thousands,** but the countries of Edom,
Mt 25.28 him and give it to the one who has **ten thousand** coins.
Lk 14.31 a king goes out with **ten thousand** men to fight another king
1 Cor 4.15 For even if you have **ten thousand** guardians in your Christian life,

100,000

1 Kgs 20.29 and the Israelites killed a **hundred thousand** Syrians.
2 Kgs 3. 4 to the king of Israel **100,000** lambs,
3. 4 and the wool from **100,000** sheep.
1 Chr 5.21 250,000 sheep, and 2,000 donkeys, and took **100,000** prisoners of war.
2 Chr 25. 6 In addition, he hired **100,000** soldiers from Israel at a

1,017

Ezra 2.36 Harim - **1,017**
Neh 7.39 Harim - **1,017**

105

Gen 5. 6 When Seth was **105,** he had a son, Enosh,

1,052

Ezra 2.36 Immer - **1,052**
Neh 7.39 Immer - **1,052**

110

Gen 50.22 he was a **hundred and ten** years old when he died.
50.26 Joseph died in Egypt at the age of a **hundred and ten.**
Ex 25.10 of acacia-wood, **110** centimetres long, 66 centimetres wide,
25.17 of pure gold, **110** centimetres long and 66 centimetres wide.
37. 1 Covenant Box out of acacia-wood, **110** centimetres long, 66 centimetres wide,
37. 6 of pure gold, **110** centimetres long and 66 centimetres wide.
Num 7.12 one gold dish weighing **110** grammes, full of incense;
Josh 24.29 son of Nun died at the age of a **hundred and ten.**
Judg 2. 8 son of Nun died at the age of a **hundred and ten.**
Ezra 8. 2 the clan of Azgad, with **110** men Eliphelet, Jeuel, and

1,100

Judg 16. 5 Each one of us will give you **eleven hundred** pieces of silver."
17. 2 "When someone stole those **eleven hundred** pieces of silver from you,

1,100,000

1 Chr 21. 5 **1,100,000** in Israel, and 470,000 in Judah.

112

1 Chr 15.10 and from the clan of Uzziel, Amminadab, in charge of **112.**
Ezra 2. 3 Jorah - **112**
Neh 7. 8 Hariph - **112**

1,150

Dan 8.14 answer, "It will continue for **1,150** days, during which

119

Gen 11.25 after that, he lived another **119** years and had other children.

120

Gen 6. 3 they will live no longer than a **hundred and twenty** years."
Deut 31. 2 "I am now a **hundred and twenty** years old and am no
34. 7 Moses was a **hundred and twenty** years old when he died;
1 Chr 15. 5 of Kohath came Uriel, in charge of **120** members of his clan;
2 Chr 5.11 with them were a **hundred and twenty** priests playing trumpets.
Dan 6. 1 decided to appoint a **hundred and twenty** governors to hold
Acts 1.15 the believers, about a **hundred and twenty** in all, and Peter

1,200

2 Chr 12. 3 Jerusalem [3] with an army of **twelve hundred** chariots,

12,000

Num 31. 5 each tribe, a total of **twelve thousand** men ready for battle.
Josh 8.25 of Ai was killed that day—**twelve thousand** men and women.
Judg 21.10 So the assembly sent **twelve thousand** of their bravest
2 Sam 10. 6 from Bethrehob and Zobah, **twelve thousand** men from Tob,
17. 1 to Absalom, "Let me choose **twelve thousand** men, and tonight
1 Kgs 4.26 for his chariot-horses and **twelve thousand** cavalry horses.
10.26 hundred chariots and **twelve thousand** cavalry horses.
2 Chr 1.14 hundred chariots and **twelve thousand** cavalry horses.
9.25 chariots and horses, and had **twelve thousand** cavalry horses.
Rev 7. 5 from the twelve tribes of Israel, [5-8] **twelve thousand** from each

120,000

Judg 8.10 **120,000** soldiers had been killed.
1 Kgs 8.63 He sacrificed 22,000 head of cattle and **120,000** sheep as fellowship-offerings.
1 Chr 12.23 **120,000** men trained to use all kinds of weapons.
2 Chr 7. 5 He sacrificed 22,000 head of cattle and **120,000** sheep as fellowship-offerings.
28. 5 Remaliah, defeat Ahaz and kill **120,000** of the bravest
Jon 4.11 it has more than **120,000** innocent children in it,

122

Ezra 2.21 Michmash - **122**
Neh 7.26 Michmash - **122**

1,222

Ezra 2. 3 Azgad - **1,222**

123

Num 33.38 At the age of **123** he died there on the first day
Ezra 2.21 Bethlehem - **123**
Neh 7.26 Bethel and Ai - **123**

1,247

Ezra 2.36 Pashhur - **1,247**
Neh 7.39 Pashhur - **1,247**

125

Ezek 48.17 on each side there will be an open space **125** metres across.

1,254

Ezra 2. 3 Elam - **1,254**
2.21 The other Elam - **1,254**
Neh 7. 8 Elam - **1,254**
7.26 The other Elam - **1,254**

1,260

Rev 11. 3 they will proclaim God's message during those **1,260** days."
12. 6 where she will be taken care of for **1,260** days

127

Gen 23. 1 Sarah lived to be a **hundred and twenty-seven** years old.
Esth 1. 1 Susa, King Xerxes ruled over **127** provinces, all the way from
8. 9 and officials of all the **127** provinces from India to Sudan.
9.30 were sent to all the **127** provinces of the Persian Empire.

128

Ezra 2.21 Anathoth - **128**
2.40 Temple musicians (descendants of Asaph) - **128**
Neh 7.26 Anathoth - **128**
11.14 There were **128** members of this clan who were outstanding soldiers.

1,290

Dan 12.11 from the time of The Awful Horror, **1,290** days will pass.

13

Gen 6.15 Make it 133 metres long, 22 metres wide, and **13** metres high.
14. 4 years, but in the **thirteenth** year they rebelled against him.
17.25 he was circumcised, [25] and his son Ishmael was **thirteen.**
Ex 26. 8 all the same size, **thirteen** metres long and two metres wide.
36.15 all the same size, **thirteen** metres long and two metres wide.
Num 29.13 **thirteen** young bulls, two rams, and fourteen one-year-old male lambs,
Josh 19. 6 **thirteen** cities, along with the towns round them.
21. 4 **thirteen** cities from the territories of Judah,
21. 6 assigned **thirteen** cities from the territories of Issachar,
21.19 **Thirteen** cities in all, with their pasture lands,
21.33 Gershon received a total of **thirteen** cities
1 Kgs 7. 1 built a palace for himself, and it took him **thirteen** years.
1 Chr 6.60 This made a total of **thirteen** towns for all their families
6.62 were assigned **thirteen** towns in the territories of Issachar,
26.11 In all there were **thirteen** members of Hosah's family who
Esth 3. 7 The **thirteenth** day of the twelfth month, the month of Adar,
3.12 So on the **thirteenth** day of the first month Haman called
3.13 on a single day, the **thirteenth** day of Adar, all Jews—young
8.12 of the Jews, the **thirteenth** of Adar, the twelfth month.
Esth 9. 1 The **thirteenth** day of Adar came, the day on which the
9.17 This was on the **thirteenth** day of Adar.
9.18 slaughtered their enemies on the **thirteenth** and fourteenth
Jer 1. 2 spoke to Jeremiah in the **thirteenth** year that Josiah son of
25. 3 "For twenty-three years, from the **thirteenth** year that
also 1 Chr 24.7 1 Chr 25.9

13.2

1 Kgs 7.23 4.4 metres in diameter, and **13.2** metres in circumference.
2 Chr 4. 2 4.4 metres in diameter, and **13.2** metres in circumference.

13.5

1 Kgs 6. 2 it was 27 metres long, 9 metres wide, and **13.5** metres high.
7. 2 Lebanon was 44 metres long, 22 metres wide, and **13.5** metres high.
7. 6 The Hall of Columns was 22 metres long and **13.5** metres wide.

130

Gen 5. 3 When Adam was **130** years old, he had a son
47. 9 "My life of wandering has lasted a **hundred and thirty** years.
1 Chr 15. 7 from the clan of Gershon, Joel, in charge of **130;**
2 Chr 24.15 reaching the very old age of a **hundred and thirty,** he died.

133

Gen 6.15 Make it **133** metres long, 22 metres wide,
Ex 6.18 Kohath lived **133** years.

1,335

Dan 12.12 Happy are those who remain faithful until **1,335** days are over!

1,365

Num 3.50 Moses obeyed and took [50] the **1,365** pieces of silver

137

Gen 25.17 Ishmael was a **hundred and thirty-seven** years old when he died.
Ex 6.16 Levi lived **137** years.
6.20 Amram lived **137** years.

138

Neh 7.43 Hatita, and Shobai) - **138**

139

Ezra 2.40 Akkub, Hatita, and Shobai) - **139**

14

Gen 14. 5 In the **fourteenth** year Chedorlaomer and his allies came with
31.41 For **fourteen** years I worked to win your two daughters—
46.22 These **fourteen** are the descendants of Jacob by Rachel.
Ex 12. 6 on the evening of the **fourteenth** day of the month,
12.18 From the evening of the **fourteenth** day of the first month
Lev 12. 5 For **fourteen** days after a woman gives birth to a daughter,
23. 5 begins at sunset on the **fourteenth** day of the first month.
Num 9. 2 "On the **fourteenth** day of this month, beginning at sunset,
9. 5 on the evening of the **fourteenth** day of the first month they
9.11 on the evening of the **fourteenth** day of the second month.
28.16 is to be held on the **fourteenth** day of the first month.
29.13 two rams, and **fourteen** one-year-old male lambs,
29.17 two rams, and **fourteen** one-year-old male lambs,
29.20 two rams, and **fourteen** one-year-old male lambs,
29.23 two rams, and **fourteen** one-year-old male lambs,
29.26 two rams, and **fourteen** one-year-old male lambs,
29.29 two rams, and **fourteen** one-year-old male lambs,
29.32 two rams, and **fourteen** one-year-old male lambs,
Josh 5.10 Passover on the evening of the **fourteenth** day of the month.
15.36 **fourteen** cities, along with the towns round them.
18.28 **fourteen** cities, along with the towns round them.
1 Kgs 18.32 trench round it, large enough to hold almost **fourteen** litres
2 Kgs 18.13 In the **fourteenth** year of the reign of King Hezekiah,
1 Chr 25. 4 The **fourteen** sons of Heman:
25. 5 Heman, the king's prophet, these **fourteen** sons and also three
2 Chr 13.21 He had **fourteen** wives and fathered twenty-two sons
30.15 on the **fourteenth** day of the month they killed the lambs
35. 1 the **fourteenth** day of the first month they killed the animals
Ezra 6.19 celebrated Passover on the **fourteenth** day of the first month
Esth 9.15 On the **fourteenth** day of Adar the Jews of Susa got
9.17 On the next day, the **fourteenth,** there was no more killing,
9.18 enemies on the thirteenth and **fourteenth** and then stopped
9.19 in small towns observe the **fourteenth** day of the month of
9.21 to observe the **fourteenth** and fifteenth days of Adar as
Is 36. 1 In the **fourteenth** year that Hezekiah was king of Judah,
Ezek 40. 1 into exile and the **fourteenth** year after Jerusalem was captured.
45.21 "On the **fourteenth** day of the first month you will begin
Mt 1.17 So then, there were **fourteen** generations from Abraham to David,
1.17 and **fourteen** from David to the exile
1.17 and **fourteen** from then to the birth
Acts 27.27 It was the **fourteenth** night, and we were being driven
27.33 "You have been waiting for **fourteen** days now, and all this
2 Cor 12. 2 a certain Christian man who **fourteen** years ago was snatched
Gal 2. 1 **Fourteen** years later I went back to Jerusalem with Barnabas,
also 1 Chr 24.7 1 Chr 25.9

140

Job 42.16 Job lived a **hundred and forty** years after this,
also Neh 7.70

1,400

1 Kgs 10.26 built up a force of **fourteen hundred** chariots and twelve
2 Chr 1.14 built up a force of **fourteen hundred** chariots and twelve

14,000

1 Kgs 9.28 back to Solomon more than **fourteen thousand** kilogrammes of gold.
Job 42.12 Job owned **fourteen thousand** sheep, six thousand camels,

144,000

Rev 7. 4 marked with God's seal on their foreheads was **144,000.**
14. 1 **144,000** people who have his name and his Father's name
14. 3 **144,000** people stood before the throne,

147

Gen 47.28 years, until he was a **hundred and forty-seven** years old.

14,700

Num 16.49 of people who died was **14,700,** not counting those who died

148

Neh 7.43 (descendants of Asaph) - **148**

15

Ex 16. 1 from Elim, and on the **fifteenth** day of the second month
26.26 "Make **fifteen** cross-bars of acacia-wood, five for the
36.31 They made **fifteen** cross-bars of acacia-wood, five for
Lev 23. 6 On the **fifteenth** day the Festival of Unleavened Bread begins,
23.33 of Shelters begins on the **fifteenth** day of the seventh month
23.39 days, beginning on the **fifteenth** day of the seventh month.
27. 3 **15** pieces of silver
Num 28.17 On the **fifteenth** day a religious festival begins
29.12 Gather for worship on the **fifteenth** day of the seventh month.
33. 3 Israel left Egypt on the **fifteenth** day of the first month of
2 Sam 9.10 (Ziba had **fifteen** sons and twenty servants.)
19.17 family, also came with his **fifteen** sons and twenty servants,
1 Kgs 7. 2 three rows of cedar pillars, **fifteen** in each row, with cedar
12.32 religious festival on the **fifteenth** day of the eighth month,
12.33 And on the **fifteenth** day of the eighth month, the day
2 Kgs 14.17 King Amaziah of Judah lived **fifteen** years after the
14.23 In the **fifteenth** year of the reign of Amaziah son of
20. 6 I will let you live **fifteen** years longer.
2 Chr 3.15 made two columns, each one **fifteen** and a half metres tall,
15.10 in the third month of the **fifteenth** year that Asa was king.
25.25 outlived King Jehoash of Israel by **fifteen** years.
Esth 9.18 made the **fifteenth** a holiday, since they had slaughtered
9.18 and then stopped on the **fifteenth.**
9.21 to observe the fourteenth and **fifteenth** days of Adar as
Is 38. 5 I will let you live **fifteen** years longer.
Ezek 32.17 On the **fifteenth** day of the first month of the twelfth
45.25 which begins on the **fifteenth** day of the seventh month,
46.21 courtyard, twenty metres long and **fifteen** metres wide.
Hos 3. 2 So I paid **fifteen** pieces of silver and 150 kilogrammes of
Lk 3. 1 It was the **fifteenth** year of the rule of the Emperor Tiberius;
also 1 Chr 24.7 1 Chr 25.9

150

Gen 7.24 did not start going down for a **hundred and fifty** days.
8. 3 the water gradually went down for a **hundred and fifty** days.
1 Kgs 10.29 for 600 pieces of silver each and horses for **150** each.
1 Chr 8.40 He had a **hundred and fifty** sons and grandsons in all.
2 Chr 1.17 of silver each and horses for a **hundred and fifty** each.
Ezra 8. 2 the clan of Parosh, with **150** men of his clan (there were
Neh 5.17 at my table a **hundred and fifty** of the Jewish people and
Hos 3. 2 pieces of silver and **150** kilogrammes of barley to buy her.

15,000

Judg 8.10 Of the whole army of desert tribesmen, only about **15,000** were left;
2 Chr 8.18 to Solomon more than **fifteen thousand** kilogrammes of gold.

153

Jn 21.11 ashore full of big fish, a **hundred and fifty-three** in all;

153,600

2 Chr 2.17 There were **153,600** resident foreigners.

156

Ezra 2.21 Magbish - **156**

16

Gen 46.18 These **sixteen** are the descendants of Jacob by Zilpah,
Ex 26.25 with their **sixteen** silver bases, two under each frame.
36.30 frames and **sixteen** silver bases, two under each frame.
Josh 15.41 **sixteen** cities, along with the towns round them.
19.22 It included **sixteen** cities along with the towns round them.
1 Sam 27. 7 David lived in Philistia for **sixteen** months.
2 Kgs 13.10 king of Israel, and he ruled in Samaria for **sixteen** years.
14.21 Judah then crowned his **sixteen-year-old** son Uzziah as king.
15. 2 Judah [2]at the age of **sixteen,** and he ruled in Jerusalem for
15.33 of twenty-five, and he ruled in Jerusalem for **sixteen** years.
16. 2 age of twenty, and he ruled in Jerusalem for **sixteen** years.
1 Chr 4.27 Shimei had **sixteen** sons and six daughters, but his
24. 4 of Eleazar were organized into **sixteen** groups, while the
2 Chr 13.21 and fathered twenty-two sons and **sixteen** daughters.
26. 1 people of Judah chose Amaziah's **sixteen-year-old** son Uzziah
26. 3 king at the age of **sixteen,** and he ruled in Jerusalem for
27. 1 of twenty-five, and he ruled in Jerusalem for **sixteen** years.
27. 8 he became king, and he ruled in Jerusalem for **sixteen** years.
28. 1 age of twenty, and he ruled in Jerusalem for **sixteen** years.
29.17 next eight days, until the **sixteenth** of the month, preparing
also 1 Chr 24.7 1 Chr 25.9

160

Ezra 8. 2 the clan of Bani, with **160** men

16,000

Num 31.36 and **16,000** virgins for the soldiers,
31.42 36,000 cattle, 30,500 donkeys, and **16,000** virgins.

162

Gen 5.18 When Jared was **162,** he had a son, Enoch, [19]and then

168

Neh 7.70 Heads of clans **168** kilogrammes of gold
7.70 **168** kilogrammes of gold

17

Gen 7.11 on the **seventeenth** day of the second month all
8. 4 On the **seventeenth** day of the seventh month the boat came
37. 2 Joseph, a young man of **seventeen,** took care of the sheep
47.28 Jacob lived in Egypt for **seventeen** years, until he was
1 Sam 25.18 five roasted sheep, **seventeen** kilogrammes of roasted grain,
1 Kgs 14.21 and he ruled for **seventeen** years in Jerusalem, the city which
22.51 In the **seventeenth** year of the reign of King Jehoshaphat of
2 Kgs 13. 1 king of Israel, and he ruled in Samaria for **seventeen** years.
16. 1 In the **seventeenth** year of the reign of Pekah son of
2 Chr 12.13 king, and he ruled for **seventeen** years in Jerusalem, the city
Jer 32. 9 the price came to **seventeen** pieces of silver.
Ezek 45.24 to be an offering of **seventeen** and a half litres of corn
46. 5 to bring an offering of **seventeen** and a half litres of corn,
46. 7 the offering is to be **seventeen** and a half litres of corn,
46.11 festivals the grain-offering will be **seventeen** and a half litres
also 1 Chr 24.7 1 Chr 25.9

170

1 Chr 29. 7 more than **170** metric tons of gold, over 340 metric tons of

1,700

2 Sam 8. 4 David captured **seventeen hundred** of his horsemen and twenty
1 Chr 26.30 Hebron, Hashabiah and **seventeen hundred** of his relatives,

172

Neh 11.19 Akkub, Talmon, and their relatives, **172** in all.

17,200

1 Chr 7.11 Their descendants included **17,200** men eligible for military service.

175

Gen 25. 7 Abraham died at the ripe old age of a **hundred and seventy-five.**

1,760

1 Chr 9.13 Immer [13]The priests who were heads of families totalled **1,760.**

18

Judg 3.14 The Israelites were subject to Eglon for **eighteen** years.
10. 8 For **eighteen** years they oppressed and persecuted all the
1 Kgs 6.17 in front of the Most Holy Place was **eighteen** metres long.
7.31 from the top of the cart and **18** centimetres down into it.
15. 1 In the **eighteenth** year of the reign of King Jeroboam of Israel,
2 Kgs 3. 1 In the **eighteenth** year of the reign of King Jehoshaphat of Judah,
22. 3 In the **eighteenth** year of his reign, King Josiah sent the
23.23 Now at last, in the **eighteenth** year of the reign of Josiah,
24. 8 Jehoiachin was **eighteen** years old when he became king of Judah,
1 Chr 26. 9 Meshelemiah's family furnished **eighteen** qualified men.
2 Chr 11.21 In all, Rehoboam had **eighteen** wives and sixty concubines,
13. 1 In the **eighteenth** year of the reign of King Jeroboam of Israel,
34. 8 In the **eighteenth** year of his reign, after he had
35.19 and Jerusalem [19]in the **eighteenth** year of Josiah's reign.
36. 9 Jehoiachin was **eighteen** years old when he became king of Judah,

Ezra 8.18 the clan of Mahli, and **eighteen** of his sons and brothers
Is 5.10 eighty litres of seed will produce only **eighteen** litres of corn."
Jer 32. 1 the **eighteenth** year of King Nebuchadnezzar of Babylonia.
52.29 in his **eighteenth** year, 832 from Jerusalem;
Lk 13. 4 What about those **eighteen** people in Siloam who were killed
13.11 had an evil spirit that had made her ill for **eighteen** years;
13.16 whom Satan has kept bound up for **eighteen** years;
also 1 Chr 24.7 1 Chr 25.9

180

Gen 35.28 lived to be a **hundred and eighty** years old [29] and died at
Is 5.10 A **hundred and eighty** litres of seed will produce only

18,000

Judg 20.25 they killed **eighteen thousand** trained Israelite soldiers.
20.44 **Eighteen thousand** of the best Benjaminite soldiers were killed.
2 Sam 8.13 when he returned from killing **eighteen thousand** Edomites in
1 Chr 12.23 **18,000** men chosen to go and make David king;
18.12 Edomites in the Valley of Salt and killed **eighteen thousand**

180,000

1 Kgs 12.21 in Jerusalem, he called together **180,000** of the best
2 Chr 11. 1 he called together a **hundred and eighty thousand** of the best
17.18 Jehozabad with **180,000** men, well-equipped for battle.

182

Gen 5.28 When Lamech was **182,** he had a son, [29] and said, "From

185,000

2 Kgs 19.35 Lord went to the Assyrian camp and killed **185,000** soldiers.
Is 37.36 Lord went to the Assyrian camp and killed **185,000** soldiers.

187

Gen 5.25 When Methuselah was **187,** he had a son, Lamech,

188

Neh 7.26 Bethlehem and Netophah - **188**

19

Josh 19.38 **nineteen** cities, along with the towns round them.
2 Sam 2.30 his men and found that **nineteen** of them were missing, in
2 Kgs 25. 8 of the **nineteenth** year of King Nebuchadnezzar of Babylonia,
Jer 52.12 of the **nineteenth** year of King Nebuchadnezzar of Babylonia,
also 1 Chr 24.7 1 Chr 25.9

2.2

Ex 27. 1 It is to be square, **2.2** metres long and 2.2 metres wide,
27.18 to be 44 metres long, 22 metres wide, and **2.2** metres high.
38. 1 It was square, **2.2** metres long and 2.2 metres wide, and it
1 Kgs 6. 5 three-storied annexe was built, each storey **2.2** metres high.
6. 6 in the lowest storey was **2.2** metres wide, in the middle
6.10 The three-storied annexe, each storey **2.2** metres high,
6.24 had two wings, each wing **2.2** metres long, so that the
7.16 two bronze capitals, each one **2.2** metres tall, to be placed
7.23 tank of bronze, **2.2** metres deep, 4.4 metres in diameter,
2 Chr 3.11 had two wings, each wing **2.2** metres long, which were spread
3.15 Each one had a capital **2.2** metres tall.
4. 2 tank of bronze, **2.2** metres deep, 4.4 metres in diameter,
6.13 It was **2.2** metres square and 1.3 metres high.
Jer 52.21 column was a bronze capital **2.2** metres high, and all round

2.7

1 Kgs 6. 6 in the middle storey **2.7** metres wide,

20

Gen 18.31 Suppose that only **twenty** are found?"
18.31 He said, "I will not destroy the city if I find **twenty."**
31.38 I have been with you now for **twenty** years;
31.41 was like that for the whole **twenty** years I was with you.
32.13 two hundred female goats and **twenty** males,
32.13 two hundred female sheep and **twenty** males,
32.13 **twenty** female donkeys and ten males.
37.28 and sold him for **twenty** pieces of silver to the Ishmaelites,
Ex 16.36 (The standard dry measure then in use equalled **twenty** litres.)
26.18 Make **twenty** frames for the south side
26.20 Make **twenty** frames for the north side of the Tent
27.10 supported by **twenty** bronze posts in twenty bronze bases,
30.14 census, that is, every man **twenty** years old or older, is to
36.23 They made **twenty** frames for the south side
36.25 They made **twenty** frames for the north side of the Tent
38.10 supported by **twenty** bronze posts in twenty bronze bases,
38.26 There were 603,550 men **twenty** years old or older enrolled in
Lev 5.16 to hand over and must pay an additional **twenty** per cent.
6. 4 repay the owner in full, plus an additional **twenty** per cent.
22.14 priest its full value plus an additional **twenty** per cent.
27. 3 adult male, **twenty** to sixty years old:
27. 3 —young male, five to **twenty** years old:
27. 3 **20** pieces of silver
27.13 he must pay the price plus an additional **twenty** per cent.
27.15 he must pay the price plus an additional **twenty** per cent.
Lev 27.16 ten pieces of silver for every **twenty** kilogrammes of barley.
27.19 he must pay the price plus an additional **twenty** per cent.
27.27 at the standard price plus an additional **twenty** per cent.
27.31 pay the standard price plus an additional **twenty** per cent.
Num 1. 3 names of all the men [3] **twenty** years old or older who are
1.18 names of all the men **twenty** years old or older were recorded
1.20 The men **twenty** years old or older who were fit for
5. 7 full repayment, plus an additional **twenty** per cent, to the
10.11 On the **twentieth** day of the second month in the second
11.19 or ten, or even **twenty** days, [20] but for a whole month,
14.29 me, none of you over **twenty** years of age will enter that
26. 2 of Israel, of all men **twenty** years old or older who are
32.11 me, none of the men **twenty** years old or older who came
Judg 4. 3 people of Israel with cruelty and violence for **twenty** years.
8.26 that Gideon received weighed nearly **twenty** kilogrammes, and
11.33 to the area round Minnith, **twenty** cities in all, and as far
15.20 Samson led Israel for **twenty** years
16.31 He had been Israel's leader for **twenty** years.
Ruth 3.15 and he poured out nearly **twenty** kilogrammes of barley and
1 Sam 7. 2 stayed in Kiriath Jearim a long time, some **twenty** years.
14.14 the young man killed about **twenty** men in an area of about
2 Sam 3.20 to David at Hebron with **twenty** men, David gave a feast for
9.10 (Ziba had fifteen sons and **twenty** servants.)
19.17 with his fifteen sons and **twenty** servants, and they arrived
24. 8 So after nine months and **twenty** days they returned to Jerusalem,
1 Kgs 4.23 ten stall-fed cattle, **twenty** pasture-fed cattle,
9.10 It took Solomon **twenty** years to build the Temple and his palace.
9.11 King Solomon gave Hiram **twenty** towns in the region of Galilee.
15. 9 In the **twentieth** year of the reign of King Jeroboam of Israel,
2 Kgs 4.42 from Baal Shalishah, bringing Elisha **twenty** loaves of bread
15.27 king of Israel, and he ruled in Samaria for **twenty** years.
15.30 In the **twentieth** year of the reign of Jotham son of
16. 2 Judah [2] at the age of **twenty,** and he ruled in Jerusalem for
1 Chr 23.24 Each of his descendants, **twenty** years of age or older, had a
23.27 age of **twenty,** [28] and were assigned the following duties:
27.23 were under the age of **twenty,** because of the Lord's promise
2 Chr 3. 8 Over **twenty** metric tons of gold were used to cover the walls
8. 1 It took Solomon **twenty** years to build the Temple and his palace.
25. 5 This included all men **twenty** years of age or older, 300,000
28. 1 king at the age of **twenty,** and he ruled in Jerusalem for
31.17 by clans, and the Levites **twenty** years of age or older were
Ezra 3. 8 All the Levites **twenty** years of age or older were put in
8.19 Jeshaiah of the clan of Merari, with **twenty** of their relatives.
8.26 **20** gold bowls -
10. 9 the three days, on the **twentieth** day of the ninth month, all
Neh 1. 1 month of Kislev in the **twentieth** year that Artaxerxes was
5.14 land of Judah, from the **twentieth** year that Artaxerxes was
Ezek 41. 2 it was **twenty** metres long, and ten metres wide.
45.12 **20** gerahs = 1 shekel
46.21 courtyard, **twenty** metres long and fifteen metres wide.
also 1 Chr 24.7 1 Chr 25.9

200

Gen 11.23 he lived another **200** years and had other children.
32.13 **two hundred** female goats and twenty males,
32.13 **two hundred** female sheep and twenty males,
Num 31.52 weighed nearly **two hundred** kilogrammes.
Judg 17. 4 She took **two hundred** of the pieces of silver and gave them
1 Sam 18.27 David and his men went and killed **two hundred** Philistines.
25.13 of his men, leaving **two hundred** behind with the supplies.
25.18 Abigail quickly collected **two hundred** loaves of bread,
25.18 and **two hundred** cakes of dried figs,
30.10 the other **two hundred** men were too tired to cross the brook
30.21 David went back to the **two hundred** men who had been too
2 Sam 15.11 There were **two hundred** men who at Absalom's invitation
16. 1 couple of donkeys loaded with **two hundred** loaves of bread, a
1 Kgs 7.20 There were **two hundred** pomegranates in two rows round each capital.
10.16 Solomon made **two hundred** large shields, and had each
2 Kgs 6.25 eighty pieces of silver, and **two hundred** grammes of dove's
14.13 Gate to the Corner Gate, a distance of nearly **two hundred** metres.
1 Chr 12.23 **200** leaders, together with the men under their command
15. 8 from the clan of Elizaphan, Shemaiah, in charge of **200;**
2 Chr 9.15 Solomon made **two hundred** large shields, each of which
25.23 Gate to the Corner Gate, a distance of nearly **two hundred** metres.
29.32 bulls, a hundred sheep, and **two hundred** lambs as
Ezra 2.64 Male and female musicians - **200**
6.17 they offered a hundred bulls, **two hundred** sheep, and four
8. 2 clan of Pahath Moab, with **200** men Shecaniah son of Jahaziel,
Song 8.12 coins, and the farmers to **two hundred** as their share;
Ezek 45.13 1 sheep out of every **200** from the meadows of Israel
Hag 2.16 of corn expecting to find **two hundred** kilogrammes, but there
Mk 6.37 us to go and spend **two hundred** silver coins on bread in
Jn 6. 7 it would take more than **two hundred** silver coins to buy
Acts 23.23 his officers and said, "Get **two hundred** soldiers ready to
23.23 with seventy horsemen and **two hundred** spearmen, and be ready to

2,000

Judg 20.45 continued to pursue the rest to Gidom, killing **two thousand.**
1 Sam 13. 2 picked three thousand men, keeping **two thousand** of them with
1 Kgs 5.11 and Solomon provided Hiram with **two thousand** metric tons
2 Kgs 18.23 I will give you **two thousand** horses if you can find that
1 Chr 5.21 50,000 camels, 250,000 sheep, and **2,000** donkeys, and took
2 Chr 2.10 I will send you **two thousand** metric tons of wheat,
2.10 **two thousand** metric tons of barley,
Ezra 7.22 2,000 litres of wine, **2,000** litres of olive-oil,
Job 42.12 sheep, six thousand camels, **two thousand** head of cattle,
Ecc 6. 6 never enjoys life, though he may live **two thousand** years.

Is 36. 8 I will give you **two thousand** horses if you can find that
Mt 25.15 coins, to another he gave **two thousand,** and to another he
25.17 the servant who had received **two thousand** coins
25.17 earned another **two thousand.**
25.22 servant who had been given **two thousand** coins came in
25.22 and said, 'You gave me **two thousand** coins, sir.
25.22 Here are another **two thousand** that I have earned.'
Mk 5.13 The whole herd—about **two thousand** pigs in all—rushed down

20,000

2 Sam 8. 4 of his horsemen and **twenty thousand** of his foot soldiers.
10. 6 their enemy, so they hired **twenty thousand** Syrian soldiers
18. 7 a terrible defeat, with **twenty thousand** men killed that day.
1 Chr 18. 4 seven thousand horsemen, and **twenty thousand** foot soldiers.
Lk 14.31 who comes against him with **twenty thousand** men, he will sit

200,000

1 Sam 15. 4 were **200,000** soldiers from Israel and 10,000 from Judah.
2 Chr 17.16 and third was Amasiah son of Zichri, with **200,000.**
17.17 in command of **200,000** men armed with shields and bows.
28. 8 fellow-countrymen, the Israelite army captured **200,000** women

200,000,000

Rev 9.16 it was **two hundred million.**

20,200

1 Chr 7. 9 families listed **20,200** men eligible for military service.

205

Gen 11.32 Terah died there at the age of **two hundred and five.**

2,056

Ezra 2. 3 Bigvai - **2,056**

2,067

Neh 7. 8 Bigvai - **2,067**

207

Gen 11.21 after that, he lived another **207** years and had other children.

20,800

1 Chr 12.23 **20,800** men famous in their own clans;

209

Gen 11.19 after that, he lived another **209** years and had other children.

21

Ex 12.18 to the evening of the **twenty-first** day, you must not eat any
2 Kgs 24.18 Zedekiah was **twenty-one** years old when he became king of Judah,
2 Chr 36.11 Zedekiah was **twenty-one** years old when he became king of Judah,
Jer 52. 1 Zedekiah was **twenty-one** years old when he became king of Judah,
Dan 10.13 of the kingdom of Persia opposed me for **twenty-one** days.
Hag 2. 1 On the **twenty-first** day of the seventh month of that same year,
also 1 Chr 24.7 1 Chr 25.9

212

1 Chr 9.22 In all, **212** men were chosen as guards for the entrances

2,172

Ezra 2. 3 Parosh - **2,172**
Neh 7. 8 Parosh - **2,172**

218

Ezra 8. 2 the clan of Joab, with **218** men

22

Gen 6.15 Make it 133 metres long, **22** metres wide, and 13 metres high.
Ex 27.12 there are to be curtains **22** metres long, with ten posts and
27.13 the entrance is, the enclosure is also to be **22** metres wide.
27.18 to be 44 metres long, **22** metres wide, and 2.2 metres high.
28.16 folded double, **22** centimetres long and **22** centimetres wide.
38.12 west side there were curtains **22** metres long, with ten posts
38.13 the entrance was, the enclosure was also **22** metres wide.
39. 9 folded double, **22** centimetres long and 22 centimetres wide.
Josh 19.30 **twenty-two** cities, along with the towns round them.
Judg 10. 3 He led Israel for **twenty-two** years.
1 Kgs 7. 2 Lebanon was 44 metres long, **22** metres wide, and 13.5 metres high.
7. 6 The Hall of Columns was **22** metres long and 13.5 metres wide.
7.35 There was a **22** centimetre band round the top of each cart;
14.20 Jeroboam ruled as king for **twenty-two** years.
16.29 of Israel, and he ruled in Samaria for **twenty-two** years.
2 Kgs 8.26 at the age of **twenty-two,** and he ruled in Jerusalem
21.19 Amon was **twenty-two** years old when he became king of Judah,
1 Chr 12.23 **22** leading men;
2 Chr 13.21 He had fourteen wives and fathered **twenty-two** sons and sixteen daughters.
22. 2 king at the age of **twenty-two,** and he ruled in Jerusalem for
33.21 Amon was **twenty-two** years old when he became king of Judah,
Ezra 8.26 silver - **22** metric tons
Esth 5.14 "Why don't you have a gallows built, **twenty-two** metres tall?
7. 9 And it's **twenty-two** metres tall!"
also 1 Chr 24.7 1 Chr 25.9

220

1 Chr 15. 6 from the clan of Merari came Asaiah, in charge of **220;**
Ezra 8.20 In addition there were **220** temple workmen whose

22,000

Num 3.39 Moses enrolled by clans at the command of the Lord, was **22,000.**
Judg 7. 3 So **twenty-two thousand** went back, but ten thousand stayed.
20.21 over they had killed **twenty-two thousand** Israelite soldiers.
2 Sam 8. 5 David attacked it and killed **twenty-two thousand** men.
1 Kgs 8.63 He sacrificed **22,000** head of cattle and 120,000 sheep
1 Chr 18. 5 David attacked it and killed **twenty-two thousand** men.
2 Chr 7. 5 He sacrificed **22,000** head of cattle and 120,000 sheep

22,034

1 Chr 7. 7 descendants included **22,034** men eligible for military service.

22,200

Num 26.14 These clans numbered **22,200** men.

22,273

Num 3.43 the total was **22,273.**

223

Ezra 2. 3 Hashum - **223**
2.21 Bethel and Ai - **223**

2,250

Ezek 48.16 and it will be a square, measuring **2,250** metres on each side.
48.30 of the four walls measures **2,250** metres and has three gates

22,600

1 Chr 7. 2 At the time of King David their descendants numbered **22,600.**

23

Judg 10. 2 He was Israel's leader for **twenty-three** years.
2 Kgs 12. 6 But by the **twenty-third** year of Joash's reign the priests
13. 1 In the **twenty-third** year of the reign of Joash son of
23.31 Joahaz was **twenty-three** years old when he became king of Judah,
1 Chr 2.22 Jair ruled **twenty-three** cities in the territory of Gilead.
2 Chr 7.10 following day, the **twenty-third** day of the seventh month,
36. 2 Joahaz was **twenty-three** years old when he became king of Judah,
Esth 8. 9 This happened on the **twenty-third** day of the third month,
Jer 25. 3 Judah and of Jerusalem, [3] "For **twenty-three** years, from the
52.30 and in his **twenty-third** year, 745—taken away by Nebuzaradan.
also 1 Chr 24.7 1 Chr 25.9

230

Ezek 4.10 You will be allowed **230** grammes of bread a day,

23,000

Num 26.62 The male Levites who were one month old or older numbered **23,000.**
1 Kgs 10.14 year King Solomon received almost **twenty-three thousand**
2 Chr 9.13 King Solomon received almost **twenty-three thousand** kilogrammes of gold,
1 Cor 10. 8 were—and in one day **twenty-three thousand** of them fell dead.

232

1 Kgs 20.15 young soldiers who were under the district commanders, **232**

2,322

Neh 7. 8 Azgad - **2,322**

24

Num 7.84 **twenty-four** bulls, sixty rams, sixty goats,
2 Sam 2.16 so that all **twenty-four** of them fell down dead together.
1 Kgs 15.33 of all Israel, and he ruled in Tirzah for **twenty-four** years.
1 Chr 24. 7 the **twenty-four** family groups were given their assignments:
25. 7 All these **twenty-four** men were experts;
25. 9 according to families into **twenty-four** groups of twelve,
Neh 9. 1 On the **twenty-fourth** day of the same month the people
Dan 10. 4 On the **twenty-fourth** day of the first month of the year,
Hag 1.15 Almighty, their God, [15] on the **twenty-fourth** day of the
2.10 On the **twenty-fourth** day of the ninth month of the
2.18 Today is the **twenty-fourth** day of the ninth month, the

Hag 2.20 On that same day, the **twenty-fourth** of the month, the
Zech 1. 7 Darius was emperor, on the **twenty-fourth** day of the eleventh
2 Cor 11.25 three shipwrecks, and once I spent **twenty-four** hours in the water.
Rev 4. 4 circle round the throne were **twenty-four** other thrones,
4. 4 on which were seated **twenty-four** elders dressed in white
4.10 When they do so, [10] the **twenty-four** elders fall down before the
5. 8 creatures and the **twenty-four** elders fell down before the Lamb.
11.16 Then the **twenty-four** elders who sit on their thrones in front
19. 4 The **twenty-four** elders and the four living creatures fell down
also 1 Chr 24.7 1 Chr 25.9

240

1 Chr 29. 4 finest gold and almost **two hundred and forty** metric tons of

2,400

Rev 21.16 it was **2,400** kilometres long

24,000

Num 25. 9 but it had already killed **twenty-four thousand** people.
1 Chr 23. 4 The king assigned **twenty-four thousand** to administer the work
27. 1 a different group of **twenty-four thousand** men was on duty

242

Neh 11.13 In all, **242** members of this clan were heads of families.

2,425

Ex 38.29 The bronze which was dedicated to the Lord amounted to **2,425** kilogrammes.

245

Ezra 2.64 Mules - **245**
Neh 7.66 Male and female musicians - **245**
7.66 Mules - **245**

25

Num 8.24 Moses, [24] "From the age of **twenty-five** each Levite shall
1 Kgs 22.42 and he ruled in Jerusalem for **twenty-five** years.
2 Kgs 14. 2 Judah [2] at the age of **twenty-five,** and he ruled in Jerusalem
15.33 Judah [33] at the age of **twenty-five,** and he ruled in
18. 2 Judah [2] at the age of **twenty-five,** and he ruled in Jerusalem
23.36 Jehoiakim was **twenty-five** years old when he became king of Judah,
2 Chr 20.31 and had ruled in Jerusalem for **twenty-five** years.
25. 1 king at the age of **twenty-five,** and he ruled in Jerusalem
27. 1 king at the age of **twenty-five,** and he ruled in Jerusalem
27. 8 Jotham was **twenty-five** years old when he became king, and
29. 1 Judah at the age of **twenty-five,** and he ruled in Jerusalem
36. 5 Jehoiakim was **twenty-five** years old when he became king of Judah,
Neh 6.15 was finished on the **twenty-fifth** day of the month of Elul.
Jer 52.31 This happened on the **twenty-fifth** day of the twelfth month
Ezek 8.16 the altar and the passage, were about **twenty-five** men.
11. 1 near the gate I saw **twenty-five** men, including Jaazaniah son
40. 1 new year, which was the **twenty-fifth** year after we had been
40.15 to the far side of the last room was **twenty-five** metres.
40.21 of the gateway was **twenty-five** metres, and the width twelve
40.25 of the gateway was **twenty-five** metres, and the width twelve
40.29 The total length was **twenty-five** metres and the width twelve
40.33 The total length was **twenty-five** metres and the width twelve
40.36 Its total length was **twenty-five** metres and its width twelve
42. 2 This building was fifty metres long and **twenty-five** metres wide.
42. 7 building was solid for **twenty-five** metres, half its length;
42. 7 and there were rooms in the remaining **twenty-five** metres.
43.13 with a rim at the outside edge **twenty-five** centimetres high.
43.17 with a rim at the outside edge **twenty-five** centimetres high.
45. 2 surrounded by an open space **twenty-five** metres wide.

250

Num 16. 1 son of Peleth—and by **250** other Israelites, well-known
16.16 Korah, "Tomorrow you and your **250** followers must come to
16.35 out and burnt up the **250** men who had presented the incense.
26.10 with Korah and his followers when fire destroyed **250** men;
2 Chr 8.10 There were **250** officials in charge of the forced labour
Ezek 42.16 and measured the east side, and it was **250** metres.
42.17 side had the same length, **250** metres, [20] so that the wall
42.20 so that the wall enclosed a square **250** metres on each side.
45. 2 of land for the Temple, **250** metres along each side, entirely

25,000

Judg 20.46 In all, **twenty-five thousand** Benjaminites were killed

250,000

1 Chr 5.21 the enemy 50,000 camels, **250,000** sheep, and 2,000 donkeys,

25,100

Judg 20.35 The Israelites killed **25,100** of the enemy that day, [36] and

26

1 Kgs 16. 8 In the **twenty-sixth** year of the reign of King Asa of Judah,

2,600

2 Chr 26.12 The army was commanded by **2,600** officers.
35. 8 Jehiel—gave the priests **two thousand six hundred** lambs and

26,000

Judg 20.15 They called out **twenty-six thousand** soldiers from their cities
1 Chr 7.40 Asher's descendants included **26,000** men eligible for military service.

2,630

Num 4.34 Gershon **2,630**

27

Gen 8.14 By the **twenty-seventh** day of the second month the earth
1 Kgs 6. 2 Inside it was **27** metres long, 9 metres wide, and 13.5
16.10 This happened in the **twenty-seventh** year of the reign of
16.15 In the **twenty-seventh** year of the reign of King Asa of Judah,
2 Kgs 15. 1 In the **twenty-seventh** year of the reign of King Jeroboam
25.27 This happened on the **twenty-seventh** day of the twelfth month
2 Chr 3. 3 King Solomon built was **twenty-seven** metres long
Ezra 6. 3 The Temple is to be **twenty-seven** metres high and twenty-seven metres wide.
Ezek 29.17 the first month of the **twenty-seventh** year of our exile, the
Dan 3. 1 had a gold statue made, **twenty-seven** metres high and nearly

27.6

Num 7.84 twelve silver basins weighing a total of **27.6** kilogrammes

2,700

1 Chr 26.32 King David chose **two thousand seven hundred** outstanding

27,000

1 Kgs 20.30 where the city walls fell on **twenty-seven thousand** of them.

273

Num 3.46 sons outnumber the Levites by **273,** you must buy back the

2,750

Num 4.34 Kohath **2,750**

276

Acts 27.37 There was a total of **276** of us on board.

28

2 Kgs 10.36 Jehu had ruled in Samaria as king of Israel for **twenty-eight** years.
2 Chr 11.21 and he fathered **twenty-eight** sons and sixty daughters.
Ezra 8. 2 the clan of Bebai, with **28** men

2,800

Ezra 2.69 to 500 kilogrammes of gold, **2,800** kilogrammes of silver, and

280,000

2 Chr 14. 8 and **280,000** men from Benjamin,
17.15 Jehohanan, with **280,000** soldiers,

2,812

Ezra 2. 3 Pahath Moab (descendants of Jeshua and Joab) - **2,812**

2,818

Neh 7. 8 (descendants of Jeshua and Joab) - **2,818**

284

Neh 11.18 In all, **284** Levites lived in the holy city of Jerusalem.

28,600

1 Chr 12.23 **28,600** trained men;

288

1 Chr 25. 7 There were **288** men in all.
25. 9 These **288** men were divided according to families

29

Gen 11.24 When Nahor was **29** years old, he had a son, Terah;
Josh 15.32 **twenty-nine** cities in all, along with the towns round them.
2 Kgs 14. 2 and he ruled in Jerusalem for **twenty-nine** years.
18. 2 and he ruled in Jerusalem for **twenty-nine** years.
2 Chr 25. 1 and he ruled in Jerusalem for **twenty-nine** years.
29. 1 and he ruled in Jerusalem for **twenty-nine** years.
Ezra 1. 9 other bowls **29**

3.1

1 Kgs 6. 6 2.7 metres wide, and in the top storey **3.1** metres wide.

30

Gen 11.14 When Shelah was **30** years old, he had a son, Eber;
11.18 When Peleg was **30** years old, he had a son, Reu;
11.22 When Serug was **30** years old, he had a son, Nahor;
18.30 What if there are only **thirty?"**
18.30 He said, "I will not do it if I find **thirty."**
32.13 sheep and twenty males, **thirty** milk camels with their young,
41.45 Joseph was **thirty** years old when he began to serve the king
Ex 21.32 the owner of the slave **thirty** pieces of silver, and the bull
38.28 With the remaining **30** kilogrammes of silver Bezalel made the rods,
Lev 27. 3 **30** pieces of silver
Num 4. 3 men between the ages of **thirty** and fifty who were qualified
4.23 men between the ages of **thirty** and fifty who were qualified
4.30 men between the ages of **thirty** and fifty who were qualified
4.34 men between the ages of **thirty** and fifty who were qualified
20.29 Aaron had died, and they all mourned for him for **thirty** days.
Deut 34. 8 Israel mourned for him for **thirty** days in the plains of Moab.
Judg 10. 4 He had **thirty** sons who rode thirty donkeys.
10. 4 They had **thirty** cities in the land of Gilead, which are
12. 9 He had **thirty** sons and thirty daughters.
12. 9 and brought **thirty** girls from outside the clan
12.14 He had forty sons and **thirty** grandsons,
14.11 Philistines saw him, they sent **thirty** young men to stay with him.
14.19 to Ashkelon, where he killed **thirty** men, stripped them, and
20.31 They killed about **thirty** Israelites.
20.39 the Benjaminites had already killed the **thirty** Israelites.
1 Sam 9.22 of the table where the guests, about **thirty** in all, were
2 Sam 5. 4 David was **thirty** years old when he became king, and he
23.13 harvest time three of "The **Thirty"** went down to the cave
23.18 was the leader of "The Famous **Thirty."**
23.18 and killed them, and became famous among "The **Thirty."**
23.19 the most famous of "The **Thirty"** and became their leader,
23.22 the brave deeds of Benaiah, who was one of "The **Thirty."**
23.24 Other members of "The **Thirty"** included:
1 Chr 11.15 One day three of the **thirty** leading soldiers went to a
11.20 Joab's brother Abishai was the leader of "The Famous **Thirty."**
11.20 and killed them, and became famous among "The **Thirty."**
11.21 the most famous of "The **Thirty"** and became their leader,
11.24 the brave deeds of Benaiah, who was one of "The **Thirty."**
11.25 He was outstanding among "The **Thirty,"** but not as
11.26 with his own group of **thirty** soldiers) Hanan son of Maacah
12. 3 of the leaders of "The **Thirty"**
12.18 became the commander of "The **Thirty,"** and he called out,
23. 3 took a census of all the male Levites aged **thirty** or older.
27. 2 was the leader of "The **Thirty"** (his son Amizzabad
2 Chr 31.16 a share to all males **thirty** years of age or older who
Ezra 1. 9 gold bowls for offerings **30**
1. 9 small gold bowls **30**
Prov 22.20 I have written down **thirty** sayings for you.
Ezek 1. 1 fourth month of the **thirtieth** year, I, Ezekiel the priest,
40.17 There were **thirty** rooms built against the outer wall, and in
41. 6 rooms were in three storeys, with **thirty** rooms on each floor.
Dan 6. 7 Give orders that for **thirty** days no one be permitted to
6.12 order that for the next **thirty** days anyone who requested
Zech 11.12 So they paid me **thirty** pieces of silver as my wages.
11.13 So I took the **thirty** pieces of silver—the magnificent sum
Mt 13. 8 a hundred grains, others sixty, and others **thirty."**
13.23 some as much as a hundred, others sixty, and others **thirty."**
26.15 They counted out **thirty** silver coins and gave them to him.
27. 3 and took back the **thirty** silver coins to the chief priests
27. 9 "They took the **thirty** silver coins, the amount the people
Mk 4. 8 had **thirty** grains, others sixty, and others a hundred."
4.20 some **thirty,** some sixty, and some a hundred."
Lk 3.23 When Jesus began his work, he was about **thirty** years old.
Jn 19.39 Joseph, taking with him about **thirty** kilogrammes of spices,
Acts 27.28 they did the same and found that it was **thirty** metres deep.

300

Gen 5.22 in fellowship with God for **300** years and had other children.
45.22 clothes, but he gave Benjamin **three hundred** pieces of silver
Judg 7. 6 There were **three hundred** men who scooped up water in their
7. 7 Midianites with the **three hundred** men who lapped the water.
7. 8 the Israelites home, except the **three hundred,** who kept all
7.16 He divided his **three hundred** men into three groups and
8. 4 this time Gideon and his **three hundred** men had come to the
11.26 For **three hundred** years Israel has occupied Heshbon and Aroer,
15. 4 So he went and caught **three hundred** foxes.
2 Sam 23.18 with his spear against **three hundred** men and killed them,
1 Kgs 10.17 He also made **three hundred** smaller shields, overlaying
11. 3 seven hundred princesses and also had **three hundred** concubines.
1 Chr 11.11 fought with his spear against **three hundred** men and killed
11.20 with his spear against **three hundred** men and killed them,
2 Chr 9.16 of beaten gold, [16]and **three hundred** smaller shields,
14. 9 of a million men and **three hundred** chariots and advanced as
35. 8 lambs and young goats and **three hundred** bulls for sacrifices
Ezra 8. 2 the clan of Zattu, with **300** men Ebed son of Jonathan,
Esth 9.15 again and killed **three hundred** more men in the city.
Mk 14. 5 been sold for more than **three hundred** silver coins and the
Jn 12. 5 wasn't this perfume sold for **three hundred** silver coins and
Rev 14.20 the winepress in a flood **three hundred** kilometres long and

3,000

Ex 32.28 The Levites obeyed, and killed about **three thousand** men that day.
Josh 7. 3 Send only about two or **three thousand** men.
7. 4 So about **three thousand** Israelites made the attack, but
Judg 15.11 So **three thousand** men of Judah went to the cave in the
16.27 there, and there were about **three thousand** men and women on
1 Sam 13. 2 2 Saul picked **three thousand** men, keeping two thousand of
24. 2 Saul took **three thousand** of the best soldiers in Israel
25. 2 the owner of **three thousand** sheep and one thousand goats.
26. 2 Saul went at once with **three thousand** of the best soldiers
1 Kgs 4.32 He composed **three thousand** proverbs
20.39 life or else pay a fine of **three thousand** pieces of silver.'
2 Kgs 5.22 like you to give them **three thousand** pieces of silver and
1 Chr 12.23 **3,000** men (most of the people of Benjamin had remained loyal
2 Chr 25.13 Samaria and Beth Horon, killed **three thousand** men, and
29.33 brought six hundred bulls and **three thousand** sheep as
35. 7 sheep, lambs, and young goats, and **three thousand** bulls.
Job 1. 3 and owned seven thousand sheep, **three thousand** camels, one
Acts 2.41 and were baptized, and about **three thousand** people were

30,000

Josh 8. 3 He picked out **thirty thousand** of his best troops and sent
1 Sam 4.10 **thirty thousand** Israelite soldiers were killed.
11. 8 there were 300,000 from Israel and **30,000** from Judah.
13. 5 had **thirty thousand** war chariots, six thousand horsemen,
2 Sam 6. 1 in Israel, a total of **thirty thousand** men, [2]and led them to
1 Kgs 5.13 King Solomon drafted **30,000** men as forced labour
2 Kgs 5. 5 So Naaman set out, taking **thirty thousand** pieces of silver,
2 Chr 35. 7 and flocks **thirty thousand** sheep, lambs, and young goats,

300,000

1 Sam 11. 8 there were **300,000** from Israel and 30,000 from Judah.
2 Chr 14. 8 Asa had an army of **300,000** men from Judah, armed with
17.14 the clans of Judah, and he had **300,000** soldiers under him.
25. 5 all men twenty years of age or older, **300,000** in all.

3,023

Jer 52.28 in his seventh year as king he carried away **3,023;**

30,500

Num 31.36 **30,500** donkeys for the soldiers, of which 61 were the tax
31.42 36,000 cattle, **30,500** donkeys, and 16,000 virgins.

307,500

2 Chr 26.13 Under them were **307,500** soldiers able to fight

31

Josh 12.24 and Tirzah—**thirty-one kings in all**
1 Kgs 16.23 So in the **thirty-first** year of the reign of King Asa of
2 Kgs 22. 1 of Judah, and he ruled in Jerusalem for **thirty-one** years.
2 Chr 34. 1 of Judah, and he ruled in Jerusalem for **thirty-one** years.

318

Gen 14.14 fighting men in his camp, **318** in all, and pursued the four

32

Gen 11.20 When Reu was **32** years old, he had a son, Serug;
Num 31.36 for the soldiers, of which **32** were the tax for the Lord.
1 Kgs 20. 1 his troops, and supported by **thirty-two** other rulers with
20.16 noon, as Benhadad and his **thirty-two** allies were getting
20.24 Now, remove the **thirty-two** rulers from their commands
22.31 of Syria had ordered his **thirty-two** chariot commanders to
2 Kgs 8.17 Judah [17]at the age of **thirty-two,** and he ruled in
2 Chr 21. 5 king at the age of **thirty-two,** and he ruled in Jerusalem for
21.20 king at the age of **thirty-two** and had ruled in Jerusalem for
Neh 5.14 Artaxerxes was emperor until his **thirty-second** year, neither
13. 6 in Jerusalem, because in the **thirty-second** year that

320

Ezra 2.21 Harim - **320**
Neh 7.26 Harim - **320**

3,200

Num 4.34 Merari **3,200**

32,000

Num 31.32 675,000 sheep and goats, 72,000 cattle, 61,000 donkeys, and **32,000** virgins.
1 Chr 19. 7 The **thirty-two thousand** chariots they hired and the army

32,200

Num 1.20 Manasseh **32,200**
also Num 2.18

323

Ezra 2. 3 Bezai - **323**

324

Neh 7. 8 Bezai - **324**

32,500

Num 26.37 These clans numbered **32,500** men.

328

Neh 7. 8 Hashum - **328**

33

Gen 46.15 In all, his descendants by Leah numbered **thirty-three.**
Lev 12. 4 Then it will be **thirty-three** more days before she is
2 Sam 5. 5 Jerusalem over all Israel and Judah for **thirty-three** years.
1 Kgs 2.11 seven years in Hebron and **thirty-three** years in Jerusalem.
1 Chr 3. 4 he ruled as king for **thirty-three** years, [5] and many sons
29.27 He ruled in Hebron for seven years and in Jerusalem for **thirty-three.**

3,300

1 Kgs 5.16 carry it, [16] and he placed **3,300** foremen in charge of them

337,500

Num 31.36 half-share of the soldiers was **337,500** sheep and goats, of
31.42 **337,500** sheep and goats, 36,000 cattle, 30,500 donkeys,

34

Gen 11.16 When Eber was **34** years old, he had a son, Peleg;
Ex 38.27 Tent and for the curtain, **34** kilogrammes for each base.
2 Kgs 23.33 and **thirty-four** kilogrammes of gold as tribute.
1 Chr 20. 2 a gold crown which weighed about **thirty-four** kilogrammes.
2 Chr 36. 3 3,400 kilogrammes of silver and **34** kilogrammes of gold as tribute.

340

1 Chr 29. 7 metric tons of gold, over **340** metric tons of silver,

3,400

Ex 38.27 Of the silver, **3,400** kilogrammes were used to make the
2 Kgs 23.33 Hamath, and made Judah pay **3,400** kilogrammes of silver and
1 Chr 22.14 I have accumulated more than **3,400** metric tons of gold and
29. 7 tons of bronze, and more than **3,400** metric tons of iron.
2 Chr 25. 6 from Israel at a cost of about **3,400** kilogrammes of silver.
27. 5 **3,400** kilogrammes of silver, 1,000 metric tons of wheat, and
36. 3 prisoner and made Judah pay **3,400** kilogrammes of silver and
Ezra 7.22 up to a limit of **3,400** kilogrammes of silver, 10,000
8.26 gold - **3,400** kilogrammes

34,000

2 Kgs 15.19 Israel, and Menahem gave him **thirty-four thousand**
1 Chr 19. 6 their enemy, so they paid **thirty-four thousand** kilogrammes
22.14 tons of gold and over **34,000** metric tons of silver to be

340,000

Esth 3. 9 able to put more than **340,000** kilogrammes of silver into the

3,430

Ex 38.25 census of the community weighed **3,430** kilogrammes,

345

Ezra 2.21 Jericho - **345**
Neh 7.26 Jericho - **345**

35

Gen 11.12 When Arpachshad was **35** years old, he had a son, Shelah;
Ex 25.39 Use **thirty-five** kilogrammes of pure gold to make the
37.24 He used **35** kilogrammes of pure gold to make the
2 Sam 12.30 gold crown which weighed about **thirty-five** kilogrammes and
1 Kgs 22.42 Judah [42] at the age of **thirty-five,** and he ruled in
2 Chr 15.19 There was no more war until the **thirty-fifth** year of his reign.
20.31 Judah at the age of **thirty-five** and had ruled in Jerusalem
Ezek 41.12 a building forty-five metres long and **thirty-five** metres wide;

350

Gen 9.28 the flood Noah lived for **350** years [29] and died at the age

35,400

Num 1.20 Benjamin **35,400**
also Num 2.18

36

Josh 7. 5 some quarries and killed about **thirty-six** of them on the way
2 Chr 16. 1 In the **thirty-sixth** year of the reign of King Asa of Judah,

360

2 Sam 2.31 David's men had killed **360** of Abner's men from the tribe

3,600

2 Chr 2. 2 **three thousand six hundred** men responsible for supervising the work.
2.18 in the mountains, and appointed **3,600** supervisors to make

36,000

Num 31.36 **36,000** cattle for the soldiers, of which 72 were the tax for
31.42 337,500 sheep and goats, **36,000** cattle, 30,500 donkeys,
1 Chr 7. 4 were able to provide **36,000** men for military service.

3,630

Ezra 2.21 Senaah - **3,630**

365

Gen 5.23 He lived to be **365** years old.

37

2 Sam 23.24 There were **thirty-seven** famous soldiers in all.
2 Kgs 13.10 In the **thirty-seventh** year of the reign of King Joash of Judah,
25.27 the twelfth month of the **thirty-seventh** year after
Jer 52.31 the twelfth month of the **thirty-seventh** year after

3,700

1 Chr 12.23 **3,700** men;

37,000

1 Chr 12.23 1,000 leaders, together with **37,000** men armed with shields and spears;

372

Ezra 2. 3 Shephatiah - **372**
Neh 7. 8 Shephatiah - **372**

38

Deut 2.14 This was **thirty-eight** years after we had left Kadesh Barnea.
1 Kgs 16.29 In the **thirty-eighth** year of the reign of King Asa of Judah,
2 Kgs 15. 8 In the **thirty-eighth** year of the reign of King Uzziah of Judah,
Jn 5. 5 A man was there who had been ill for **thirty-eight** years.

38,000

1 Chr 23. 3 The total was **thirty-eight thousand.**

39

2 Kgs 15.13 In the **thirty-ninth** year of the reign of King Uzziah of Judah,
15.17 In the **thirty-ninth** year of the reign of King Uzziah of Judah,
2 Chr 16.12 In the **thirty-ninth** year that Asa was king, he was
2 Cor 11.24 Five times I was given the **thirty-nine** lashes by the Jews;

390

Ezek 4. 4 For **390** days you will stay there and suffer because of their
4. 9 are to eat during the **390** days you are lying on your

392

Ezra 2.58 and of Solomon's servants who returned from exile was **392.**
Neh 7.60 and of Solomon's servants who returned from exile was **392.**

3,930

Neh 7.26 Senaah - **3,930**

4.4

1 Kgs 6.23 and placed in the Most Holy Place, each one **4.4** metres tall.
6.24 the distance from one wing-tip to the other was **4.4** metres.
7.23 of bronze, 2.2 metres deep, **4.4** metres in diameter, and 13.2
2 Chr 4. 2 of bronze, 2.2 metres deep, **4.4** metres in diameter, and 13.2

4.5

1 Kgs 6. 3 The entrance room was **4.5** metres deep and 9 metres wide,

40

Gen 7. 4 rain that will fall for **forty** days and nights, in order to
7.12 and rain fell on the earth for **forty** days and nights.
7.17 The flood continued for **forty** days, and the water became
8. 6 After **forty** days Noah opened a window [7] and sent out a raven.
18.29 "Perhaps there will be only **forty.**"
18.29 He replied, "I will not destroy it if there are **forty.**"
25.20 Isaac was **forty** years old when he married Rebecca,
26.34 When Esau was **forty** years old, he married two Hittite girls,
32.13 milk camels with their young, **forty** cows and ten bulls, twenty
50. 3 It took **forty** days, the normal time for embalming.
Ex 16.35 ate manna for the next **forty** years, until they reached the

Ex 24.18 There he stayed for **forty** days and nights.
26.19 for the south side [19] and **forty** silver bases to go under them,
26.21 the Tent [21] and **forty** silver bases, two under each frame.
34.28 stayed there with the Lord **forty** days and nights, eating
36.24 for the south side [24] and **forty** silver bases to go under them,
36.26 of the Tent [26] and **forty** silver bases, two under each frame.
Num 13.25 After exploring the land for **forty** days, the spies returned
14.33 wander in the wilderness for **forty** years, suffering for your
14.34 consequences of your sin for **forty** years, one year for each
14.34 for each of the **forty** days you spent exploring the land.
32.13 in the wilderness for **forty** years until that whole generation
33.38 fifth month of the **fortieth** year after the Israelites had left
Deut 1. 3 eleventh month of the **fortieth** year after they had left Egypt,
2. 7 has been with you these **forty** years, and you have had
8. 2 through the desert these past **forty** years, sending hardships to
8. 4 During these **forty** years your clothes have not worn out,
9. 9 I stayed there **forty** days and nights and did not eat or
9.11 Yes, after those **forty** days and nights the Lord gave me
9.18 in the Lord's presence for **forty** days and nights and did not
9.25 the Lord's presence those **forty** days and nights, because I knew
10.10 "I stayed on the mountain **forty** days and nights, as I
25. 3 He may be given as many as **forty** lashes, but no more;
29. 5 For **forty** years the Lord led you through the desert, and
Josh 5. 4 during the **forty** years the people spent crossing the desert,
14. 7 I was **forty** years old when the Lord's servant Moses sent
Judg 3.11 peace in the land for **forty** years, and then Othniel died.
5.31 And there was peace in the land for **forty** years.
8.28 The land was at peace for **forty** years, until Gideon died.
12.14 had **forty** sons and thirty grandsons, who rode on seventy donkeys.
13. 1 and he let the Philistines rule them for **forty** years.
1 Sam 4.18 He had been a leader in Israel for **forty** years.
17.16 the Israelites every morning and evening for **forty** days.
2 Sam 2.10 He was **forty** years old when he was made king of Israel,
5. 4 years old when he became king, and he ruled for **forty** years.
1 Kgs 2.11 been king of Israel for **forty** years, ruling seven years in
11.42 He was king in Jerusalem over all Israel for **forty** years.
19. 8 enough strength to walk **forty** days to Sinai, the holy mountain.
2 Kgs 8. 9 So Hazael loaded **forty** camels with all kinds of the finest
12. 1 king of Judah, and he ruled in Jerusalem for **forty** years.
1 Chr 26.31 the **fortieth** year that David was king, an investigation was made
29. 4 almost two hundred and **forty** metric tons of pure silver for
29.27 David son of Jesse ruled over all Israel [27] for **forty** years.
2 Chr 9.30 Solomon ruled in Jerusalem over all Israel for **forty** years.
24. 1 the age of seven, and he ruled in Jerusalem for **forty** years.
Neh 5.15 the people and had demanded **forty** silver coins a day for
9.21 Through **forty** years in the desert you provided all that
Job 42.16 Job lived a hundred and **forty** years after this, long enough
Ps 95.10 For **forty** years I was disgusted with those people.
Ezek 4. 6 the guilt of Judah for **forty** days—one day for each year
29.11 For **forty** years nothing will live there.
29.12 For **forty** years the cities of Egypt will lie in ruins, ruins
29.13 Lord says, "After **forty** years I will bring the Egyptians
Amos 2.10 you through the desert for **forty** years, and gave you the
5.25 sacrifices and offerings during those **forty** years that I led
Jon 3. 4 he proclaimed, "In **forty** days Nineveh will be destroyed!"
Hag 2.16 a hundred litres of wine from a vat, but find only **forty**.
Mt 4. 2 After spending **forty** days and nights without food, Jesus was hungry.
13.33 yeast and mixes it with **forty** litres of flour until the
Mk 1.13 where he stayed **forty** days, being tempted by Satan.
Lk 4. 2 desert, [2] where he was tempted by the Devil for **forty** days.
13.21 yeast and mixes it with **forty** litres of flour until the
Acts 1. 3 For **forty** days after his death he appeared to them many
4.22 of healing had been performed was over **forty** years old.
7.23 "When Moses was **forty** years old, he decided to find out
7.30 "After **forty** years had passed, an angel appeared to
7.36 and at the Red Sea and for **forty** years in the desert.
7.42 and sacrificed animals for **forty** years in the desert.
13.18 his great power, [18] and for **forty** years he endured them in
13.21 the tribe of Benjamin, to be their king for **forty** years.
23.13 There were more than **forty** who planned this together.
23.21 because there are more than **forty** men who will be hiding and
27.28 tied to it and found that the water was **forty** metres deep;
Heb 3. 9 God, although they had seen what I did for **forty** years.
3.17 With whom was God angry for **forty** years?

400

Gen 15.13 slaves there and will be treated cruelly for **four hundred** years.
23.15 "Sir, land worth only **four hundred** pieces of silver—what is
23.16 the hearing of the people—**four hundred** pieces of silver,
32. 6 He has **four hundred** men with him."
33. 1 saw Esau coming with his **four hundred** men, so he divided the
Judg 21.12 people in Jabesh they found **four hundred** young virgins, so they
1 Sam 22. 2 dissatisfied went to him, about **four hundred** men in all, and
25.13 sword and left with about **four hundred** of his men, leaving
30.10 David continued on his way with **four hundred** men;
30.17 **four hundred** young men who mounted camels and got away,
1 Kgs 7.40 chains on each capital The **four hundred** bronze pomegranates,
18.19 prophets of Baal and the **400** prophets of the goddess Asherah
22. 6 called in the prophets, about **four hundred** of them, and asked
2 Chr 4.11 chains on each capital The **four hundred** bronze pomegranates
18. 5 called in the prophets, about **four hundred** of them, and asked
Ezra 6.17 bulls, two hundred sheep, and **four hundred** lambs as sacrifices,
Acts 5.36 to be somebody great, and about **four hundred** men joined him.
7. 6 be slaves and will be badly treated for **four hundred** years.

4,000

1 Sam 4. 2 killed about **four thousand** men on the battlefield.
1 Kgs 9.14 had sent Solomon more than **four thousand** kilogrammes of gold.
10.10 more than **four thousand** kilogrammes of gold
1 Chr 23. 5 **four thousand** to do guard duty,
23. 5 and **four thousand** to praise the Lord,
2 Chr 9. 9 more than **four thousand** kilogrammes of gold
9.25 King Solomon also had **four thousand** stalls for his chariots
Mt 15.38 of men who ate was **four thousand,** not counting the women and
16.10 And what about the seven loaves for the **four thousand** men?
Mk 8. 8 Everybody ate and had enough—there were about **four thousand** people.
8.20 the seven loaves for the **four thousand** people," asked
Acts 21.38 started a revolution and led **four thousand** armed terrorists

40,000

Josh 4.13 presence of the Lord about **forty thousand** men ready for war
Judg 5. 8 Of the **forty thousand** men in Israel, did anyone carry shield
2 Sam 10.18 and **forty thousand** horsemen, and they wounded Shobach,
1 Kgs 4.26 Solomon had **forty thousand** stalls for his chariot-horses
7.26 The tank held about **forty thousand** litres.
1 Chr 12.23 **40,000** men ready for battle;
19.18 Syrian chariot drivers and **forty thousand** foot-soldiers.

400,000

Judg 20. 2 of God's people, and there were **400,000** foot-soldiers.
20.17 the Israelite tribes gathered **400,000** trained soldiers.
1 Kgs 5.11 **four hundred thousand** litres of pure olive-oil
2 Chr 2.10 **four hundred thousand** litres of wine,
2.10 and **four hundred thousand** litres of olive-oil."
13. 3 Abijah raised an army of **400,000** soldiers, and Jeroboam

403

Gen 11.13 after that, he lived another **403** years and had other children.
11.15 after that, he lived another **403** years and had other children.

40,500

Num 1.20 Ephraim **40,500**
26.18 These clans numbered **40,500** men.
also Num 2.18

41

1 Kgs 14.21 Rehoboam was **forty-one** years old when he became king of
15.10 king of Judah, [10] and he ruled for **forty-one** years in Jerusalem.
2 Kgs 14.23 king of Israel, and he ruled in Samaria for **forty-one** years.
2 Chr 12.13 He was **forty-one** years old when he became king, and he ruled

410

Ezra 1. 9 small silver bowls **410**

41,500

Num 1.20 Asher **41,500**
also Num 2.25

42

Num 35. 6 In addition, give them **forty-two** other cities [7] with their
2 Kgs 2.24 out of the woods and tore **forty-two** of the boys to pieces.
10.14 There were **forty-two** people in all, and not one of them was
Ezra 2.21 Azmaveth - **42**
Neh 7.26 Beth Azmaveth - **42**
Rev 11. 2 who will trample on the Holy City for **forty-two** months.
13. 5 God, and it was permitted to have authority for **forty-two** months.

42,000

Judg 12. 6 At that time **forty-two thousand** of the Ephraimites were killed.

42,360

Ezra 2.64 Total number of exiles who returned - **42,360**
Neh 7.66 returned - **42,360**

430

Gen 11.17 after that, he lived another **430** years and had other children.
Ex 12.40 The Israelites had lived in Egypt for **430** years.
12.41 On the day the **430** years ended, all the tribes of the
Gal 3.17 Law, which was given **four hundred and thirty** years later,

435

Ezra 2.64 Camels - **435**
Neh 7.66 Camels - **435**

43,730

Num 26. 7 These clans numbered **43,730** men.

44

Gen 6.16 and leave a space of **44** centimetres between the roof and the
Ex 25.23 88 centimetres long, **44** centimetres wide, and 66 centimetres high.
27. 9 the curtains are to be **44** metres long, [10] supported by
27.18 The enclosure is to be **44** metres long, 22 metres wide,
37.10 88 centimetres long, **44** centimetres wide, and 66 centimetres high.

Ex 38. 9 south side the curtains were **44** metres long, [10]supported
1 Kgs 7. 2 the Forest of Lebanon was **44** metres long, 22 metres wide,

440

Neh 3.13 and repaired the wall for **440** metres, as far as the Rubbish

44,760

1 Chr 5.18 and East Manasseh there were **44,760** soldiers, well-trained

45

Gen 18.28 But perhaps there will be only **forty-five** innocent people
18.28 will not destroy the city if I find **forty-five** innocent people."
Ex 30. 2 It is to be square, **45** centimetres long and 45 centimetres wide,
37.25 It was square, **45** centimetres long and 45 centimetres wide,
Josh 14.10 It has been **forty-five** years since the Lord said that to Moses.
1 Kgs 7.31 It projected upwards **45** centimetres from the top of the cart
Ezek 41.12 Temple there was a building **forty-five** metres long

450

Num 35. 4 outwards from the city walls **450** metres in each direction,
1 Kgs 18.19 Bring along the **450** prophets of Baal and the 400 prophets of
18.22 of the Lord still left, but there are **450** prophets of Baal.
Acts 13.20 All this took about **four hundred and fifty** years.

454

Ezra 2. 3 Adin - **454**

45,400

Num 26.50 These clans numbered **45,400** men.

45,600

Num 26.41 These clans numbered **45,600** men.

45,650

Num 1.20 Gad **45,650**
also Num 2.10

46

Jn 2.20 "It has taken **forty-six** years to build this Temple!"

4,600

1 Chr 12.23 **4,600** men;
Jer 52.30 In all, **4,600** people were taken away.

46,500

Num 1.20 Reuben **46,500**
also Num 2.10

468

Neh 11. 6 descendants of Perez, **468** outstanding men lived in Jerusalem.

470,000

1 Chr 21. 5 1,100,000 in Israel, and **470,000** in Judah.

48

Num 35. 7 cities [7]with their pasture land, making a total of **forty-eight.**
Josh 21.41 Israel possessed, a total of **forty-eight** cities,

480

1 Kgs 6. 1 **Four hundred and eighty** years after the people of Israel left

49

Lev 25. 8 Count seven times seven years, a total of **forty-nine** years.

5.3

1 Kgs 7.15 one 8 metres tall and **5.3** metres in circumference, and
Jer 52.21 each one was 8 metres high and **5.3** metres round.

50

Gen 18.24 If there are **fifty** innocent people in the city, will you
18.24 Won't you spare it in order to save the **fifty?**
18.26 Lord answered, "If I find **fifty** innocent people in Sodom, I
18.28 there will be only forty-five innocent people instead of **fifty.**
Ex 18.21 leaders of thousands, hundreds, **fifties,** and tens.
18.25 He appointed them as leaders of thousands, hundreds, **fifties,**
26. 5 Put **fifty** loops on the first piece of the first set
26. 5 and **fifty** loops matching them on the last
26. 6 Make **fifty** gold hooks with which to join the two sets into
26.10 Put **fifty** loops on the edge of the last piece
26.10 of one set, and **fifty** loops on the edge of the
26.11 Make **fifty** bronze hooks and put them in the loops to
26.13 The extra **fifty** centimetres on each side of the length
36.12 They put **fifty** loops on the first piece of the first set
Ex 36.12 and **fifty** loops matching them on the last
36.13 They made **fifty** gold hooks, with which to join the two
36.17 They put **fifty** loops on the edge of the last piece
36.17 of one set and **fifty** loops on the edge of the
36.18 They made **fifty** bronze hooks to join the two sets, so as
Lev 23.16 On the **fiftieth** day, the day after the seventh Sabbath,
25.10 way you shall set the **fiftieth** year apart and proclaim
27. 3 **50** pieces of silver
Num 4. 3 the ages of thirty and **fifty** who were qualified to work in
4.23 the ages of thirty and **fifty** who were qualified to work in
4.30 the ages of thirty and **fifty** who were qualified to work in
4.34 the ages of thirty and **fifty** who were qualified to work in
8.25 of my presence, [25]and at the age of **fifty** he shall retire.
31.30 take one out of every **fifty** prisoners and the same
31.47 took one out of every **fifty** prisoners and animals, and as
Deut 1.15 some for a hundred, some for **fifty,** and some for ten.
22.29 father the bride price of **fifty** pieces of silver, and she is
Judg 3.16 a double-edged sword nearly **fifty** centimetres long.
1 Sam 8.12 charge of a thousand men, and others in charge of **fifty** men.
2 Sam 15. 1 chariot and horses for himself, and an escort of **fifty** men.
24.24 the threshing-place and the oxen for **fifty** pieces of silver.
1 Kgs 1. 5 chariots, horses, and an escort of **fifty** men.
18. 4 caves in two groups of **fifty,** and provided them with food
18.13 caves, in two groups of **fifty,** and supplied them with food
2 Kgs 1. 9 Then he sent an officer with **fifty** men to get Elijah.
1.11 king sent another officer with **fifty** men, who went up and
1.13 Once more the king sent an officer with **fifty** men.
2. 7 So they went on, [7]and **fifty** of the prophets followed them
2. 7 river, and the **fifty** prophets stood a short distance away.
2.15 The **fifty** prophets from Jericho saw him and said, "The
2.16 and said, "There are **fifty** of us here, all strong men.
2.17 The **fifty** of them went and looked high and low for Elijah
13. 7 no armed forces left except **fifty** horsemen, ten chariots,
15.20 Israel by forcing each one to contribute **fifty** pieces of silver.
15.23 In the **fiftieth** year of the reign of King Uzziah of Judah,
15.25 son of Remaliah, plotted with **fifty** men from Gilead,
Ezra 8. 2 the clan of Adin, with **50** men
Neh 7.70 **50** ceremonial bowls
Ezek 40.12 a low wall **fifty** centimetres high and fifty centimetres thick.
40.19 distance between the two gateways, and it was **fifty** metres.
40.23 between these two gateways, and it was **fifty** metres.
40.27 distance to this second gateway, and it was **fifty** metres.
40.42 They were **fifty** centimetres high,
40.47 measured the inner courtyard, and it was **fifty** metres square.
41.13 the outside of the Temple, and it was **fifty** metres long.
41.13 building to the west, the distance was also **fifty** metres.
41.14 the open space on either side, was also **fifty** metres.
41.15 its corridors on both sides, and it was also **fifty** metres.
42. 2 This building was **fifty** metres long and twenty-five metres wide.
42. 4 passage five metres wide and **fifty** metres long, with
43.13 a gutter **fifty** centimetres deep and fifty centimetres wide,
43.14 set back from the edge **fifty** centimetres all round, and was
43.14 was also set back from the edge **fifty** centimetres all round.
43.17 (The gutter was **fifty** centimetres wide.)
Mk 6.40 down in rows, in groups of a hundred and groups of **fifty.**
Lk 7.41 him five hundred silver coins, and the other owed him **fifty.**
9.14 "Make the people sit down in groups of about **fifty** each."
16. 6 'sit down and write **fifty.'**
Jn 8.57 him, "You are not even **fifty** years old—and you have seen
Rev 16.21 each weighing as much as **fifty** kilogrammes, fell from the

500

Gen 5.32 After Noah was **500** years old, he had three sons, Shem,
11.11 After that, he lived another **500** years and had other children.
Num 31.28 one out of every **five hundred** prisoners and the same
1 Chr 4.42 **Five hundred** other members of the tribe of Simeon went east
2 Chr 35. 9 lambs and young goats and **five hundred** bulls for the Levites
Ezra 2.69 and the total came to **500** kilogrammes of gold, 2,800
Esth 9. 6 Susa, the capital city itself, the Jews killed **five hundred** men.
9.12 Jews have killed **five hundred** men, including Haman's ten sons.
Job 1. 3 one thousand head of cattle, and **five hundred** donkeys.
Ezek 47. 3 the man measured **five hundred** metres downstream to the east
47. 4 he measured another **five hundred** metres, and the water came up
47. 4 Another **five hundred** metres further down, the water was up
47. 5 He measured **five hundred** metres more, and there the stream was
Lk 7.41 "One owed him **five hundred** silver coins, and the other owed
1 Cor 15. 6 appeared to more than **five hundred** of his followers at once,

5,000

Josh 8.12 He took about **five thousand** men and put them in hiding
Judg 20.45 **Five thousand** of them were killed along the road.
1 Kgs 4.22 Solomon needed each day were **five thousand** litres of fine flour
2 Chr 35. 9 and Jozabad—contributed **five thousand** lambs and young goats
Mt 14.21 men who ate was about **five thousand,** not counting the women
16. 9 when I broke the five loaves for the **five thousand** men?
25.15 to one he gave **five thousand** gold coins, to another he gave
25.16 The servant who had received **five thousand** coins went at
25.16 and invested his money and earned another **five thousand.**
25.20 The servant who had received **five thousand** coins came in
25.20 and handed over the other **five thousand.**
25.20 'You gave me **five thousand** coins, sir,' he said.
25.20 Here are another **five thousand** that I have earned.'
Mk 6.44 The number of men who were fed was **five thousand.**
6.52 the real meaning of the feeding of the **five thousand;**
8.19 when I broke the five loaves for the **five thousand** people?
Lk 9.14 (There were about **five thousand** men there.)
Jn 6.10 there were about **five thousand** men.
Acts 4. 4 and the number of men grew to about **five thousand.**

50,000

1 Chr 5.21 They captured from the enemy **50,000** camels, 250,000 sheep,
12.23 **50,000** loyal and reliable men ready to fight, trained to use
Acts 19.19 books, and the total came to **fifty thousand** silver coins.

500,000

2 Sam 24. 9 800,000 in Israel and **500,000** in Judah.

52

2 Kgs 15. 2 of sixteen, and he ruled in Jerusalem for **fifty-two** years.
15.27 In the **fifty-second** year of the reign of King Uzziah of Judah,
2 Chr 26. 3 of sixteen, and he ruled in Jerusalem for **fifty-two** years.
Ezra 2.21 Nebo - **52**
Neh 6.15 After **fifty-two** days of work the entire wall was
7.26 The other Nebo - **52**

52,700

Num 26.34 These clans numbered **52,700** men.

530

Neh 7.70 **530** robes for priests

53,400

Num 1.20 Naphtali **53,400**
26.47 These clans numbered **53,400** men.
also Num 2.25

54

2 Chr 3. 4 of the Temple, nine metres, and was **fifty-four** metres high.

5,400

Ezra 1.11 In all there were **5,400** gold and silver bowls and other

54,400

Num 1.20 Issachar **54,400**
also Num 2.3

55

2 Kgs 21. 1 of Judah, and he ruled in Jerusalem for **fifty-five** years.
2 Chr 33. 1 of Judah, and he ruled in Jerusalem for **fifty-five** years.

550

1 Kgs 9.23 There were **550** officials in charge of the forced labour

56

Ezra 2.21 Netophah - **56**

57

1 Sam 17. 5 weighed about **fifty-seven** kilogrammes and a bronze helmet.

570

2 Chr 3. 9 **570** grammes of gold were used for making nails, and the

57,400

Num 1.20 Zebulun **57,400**
also Num 2.3

59,300

Num 1.20 Simeon **59,300**
also Num 2.10

595

Gen 5.30 Lamech lived another **595** years.

6.6

Ex 27.14 entrance there are to be **6.6** metres of curtains, with three
38.14 of the entrance there were **6.6** metres of curtains, with

60

Gen 25.26 Isaac was **sixty** years old when they were born.
Lev 27. 3 adult male, twenty to **sixty** years old:
27. 3 —male above **sixty** years of age:
27. 3 —female above **sixty**:
Num 7.84 **sixty** rams, sixty goats, sixty one-year-old lambs,
Deut 3. 4 In all we captured **sixty** towns—the whole region of Argob,
Josh 13.30 Bashan, as well as all **sixty** of the villages of Jair in
1 Kgs 4.13 region of Argob in Bashan, **sixty** large towns in all,
2 Kgs 25.19 charge of military records, and **sixty** other important men.
1 Chr 2.21 When Hezron was **sixty** years old, he married Machir's daughter,
2.23 of Geshur and Aram conquered **sixty** towns there, including
2 Chr 11.21 Rehoboam had eighteen wives and **sixty** concubines,
11.21 and he fathered twenty-eight sons and **sixty** daughters.
Ezra 8. 2 the clan of Adonikam, with **60** men (they returned at a later
Song 3. 7 **sixty** soldiers form the bodyguard, the finest soldiers in Israel.
6. 8 Let the king have **sixty** queens, eighty concubines,
Jer 52.25 charge of military records, and **sixty** other important men.
Ezek 45.12 **60** shekels = 1 mina
Mt 13. 8 a hundred grains, others **sixty**, and others thirty."
13.23 some as much as a hundred, others **sixty**, and others thirty."
Mk 4. 8 had thirty grains, others **sixty**, and others a hundred."
4.20 some thirty, some **sixty**, and some a hundred."
1 Tim 5. 9 the list of widows unless she is over **sixty** years of age.
Rev 21.17 the wall, and it was **sixty** metres high,

600

Gen 7. 6 Noah was **six hundred** years old when the flood came on the
7.11 When Noah was **six hundred** years old, on the seventeenth
Ex 14. 7 the **six hundred** finest, commanded by their officers.
Judg 3.31 did so by killing **six hundred** Philistines with an ox-goad.
18.11 So **six hundred** men from the tribe of Dan left Zorah and
18.16 Meanwhile the **six hundred** soldiers from Dan, ready for battle,
18.17 priest stayed at the gate with the **six hundred** armed men.
20.47 But **six hundred** men were able to escape to the open
1 Sam 13.15 Saul inspected his troops, about **six hundred** men.
14. 2 he had about **six hundred** men with him.
23.13 David and his men—about **six hundred** in all—left Keilah at
27. 2 So David and his **six hundred** men went over at once to
30. 9 So David and his **six hundred** men started out, and when
2 Sam 15.18 The **six hundred** soldiers who had followed him from Gath also
1 Kgs 10.29 and chariots, selling chariots for **600** pieces of silver each
1 Chr 21.25 paid Araunah **six hundred** gold coins for the threshing-place.
2 Chr 1.17 and chariots, selling chariots for **six hundred** pieces of
2. 2 three thousand **six hundred** men responsible for supervising
29.33 they also brought **six hundred** bulls and three thousand
35. 8 gave the priests two thousand **six hundred** lambs and young

6,000

1 Sam 13. 5 had thirty thousand war chariots, **six thousand** horsemen, and
1 Kgs 16.24 the hill of Samaria for **six thousand** pieces of silver from a
2 Kgs 5. 5 thousand pieces of silver, **six thousand** pieces of gold,
5.23 "Please take **six thousand** pieces of silver," Naaman replied.
1 Chr 23. 4 the work of the Temple, **six thousand** to keep records and
Job 42.12 Job owned fourteen thousand sheep, **six thousand** camels, two

60,000

2 Chr 4. 5 The tank held about **sixty thousand** litres.
12. 3 army of twelve hundred chariots, **sixty thousand** horsemen,

600,000

Ex 12.37 There were about **six hundred thousand** men, not counting women
Num 11.21 Lord, "Here I am leading **600,000** people, and you say that

601

Gen 8.13 When Noah was **601** years old, on the first day of the

601,730

Num 26.51 The total number of the Israelite men was **601,730.**

603,550

Ex 38.26 There were **603,550** men twenty years old or older enrolled in
Num 2.32 Israel enrolled in the divisions, group by group, was **603,550.**
also Num 1.20

60,500

Num 26.27 These clans numbered **60,500** men.

61

Num 31.36 for the soldiers, of which **61** were the tax for the Lord;

61,000

Num 31.32 72,000 cattle, **61,000** donkeys, and 32,000 virgins.

62

1 Chr 26. 8 a total of **sixty-two** highly qualified men for this work.
Dan 5.31 who was then **sixty-two** years old, seized the royal power.
9.25 will stand for seven times **sixty-two** years, but this will be

620

1 Chr 29. 7 metric tons of silver, almost **620** metric tons of bronze, and

6,200

Num 3.34 males one month old or older that were enrolled was **6,200.**

621

Ezra 2.21 Ramah and Geba - **621**
Neh 7.26 Ramah and Geba - **621**

623

Ezra 2. 3 Bebai - **623**

62,700

Num 1.20 Dan **62,700**
also Num 2.25

628

Neh 7. 8 Bebai - **628**

642

Ezra 2. 3 Bani - **642**
Neh 7.61 There were **642** belonging to the clans of Delaiah,

64,300

Num 26.25 These clans numbered **64,300** men.

64,400

Num 26.43 the clan of Shuham, [43] which numbered **64,400** men.

648

Neh 7. 8 Binnui - **648**

65

Gen 5.15 When Mahalalel was **65**, he had a son, Jared, [16] and then
5.21 When Enoch was **65**, he had a son, Methuselah.
Is 7. 8 As for Israel, within **sixty-five** years it will be too

652

Ezra 2.59 There were **652** belonging to the clans of Delaiah,
Neh 7. 8 Arah - **652**

655

Neh 7. 8 Adin - **655**

66

Gen 46.26 Jacob who went to Egypt was **sixty-six**, not including his sons'
Ex 25.10 **66** centimetres wide, and 66 centimetres high.
25.17 of pure gold, 110 centimetres long and **66** centimetres wide.
25.23 44 centimetres wide, and **66** centimetres high.
26.16 and **66** centimetres wide, [17] with two matching projections,
36.21 **sixty-six** centimetres wide, [22] with two matching projections,
37. 1 **66** centimetres wide, and 66 centimetres high.
37. 6 of pure gold, 110 centimetres long and **66** centimetres wide.
37.10 44 centimetres wide, and **66** centimetres high.
Lev 12. 5 Then it will be **sixty-six** more days before she is ritually
1 Kgs 7.32 The wheels were **66** centimetres high;

666

Ezra 2. 3 Adonikam - **666**
Rev 13.18 Its number is **666.**

667

Neh 7. 8 Adonikam - **667**

67

Neh 7.70 **67** robes for priests

6,720

Ezra 2.64 Donkeys - **6,720**
Neh 7.66 Donkeys - **6,720**

675

Num 31.36 sheep and goats, of which **675** were the tax for the Lord;

675,000

Num 31.32 **675,000** sheep and goats, 72,000 cattle, 61,000 donkeys,

68

1 Chr 16.38 Edom son of Jeduthun and **sixty-eight** men of his clan were to

6,800

1 Chr 12.23 **6,800** well-equipped men, armed with shields and spears;

690

1 Chr 9. 4 There were **690** families of the tribe of Judah who

70

Gen 5.12 When Kenan was **70**, he had a son, Mahalalel, [13] and then
11.26 After Terah was **70** years old, he became the father of Abram,
46.27 bringing to **seventy** the total number of Jacob's family
50. 3 The Egyptians mourned for him **seventy** days.
Ex 1. 5 number of these people directly descended from Jacob was **seventy.**
15.27 Elim, where there were twelve springs and **seventy** palm-trees;
24. 1 Aaron, Nadab, Abihu, and **seventy** of the leaders of Israel;
24. 9 Moses, Aaron, Nadab, Abihu, and **seventy** of the leaders of Israel
Num 11.16 "Assemble **seventy** respected men who are recognized as
11.24 assembled **seventy** of the leaders and placed them round the Tent.
11.25 he had given to Moses and gave it to the **seventy** leaders.
11.26 Two of the **seventy** leaders, Eldad and Medad, had stayed
11.30 Then Moses and the **seventy** leaders of Israel went back to camp.
33. 9 there were twelve springs of water and **seventy** palm-trees there.
Deut 10.22 your ancestors went to Egypt, there were only **seventy** of them.
Judg 1. 7 Adonibezek said, **"Seventy** kings with their thumbs and big toes
8.30 He had **seventy** sons, because he had many wives.
9. 2 To be governed by all **seventy** of Gideon's sons or by just
9. 4 **seventy** pieces of silver from the temple of Baal-of-the-Covenant,
9. 5 single stone he killed his **seventy** brothers, Gideon's sons.
9.18 You killed his sons—**seventy** men on a single stone—and just
9.24 encouraged him to murder Gideon's **seventy** sons,
9.56 against his father in killing his **seventy** brothers.
12.14 forty sons and thirty grandsons, who rode on **seventy** donkeys.
1 Sam 6.19 The Lord killed **seventy** of the men of Beth Shemesh
2 Kgs 10. 1 There were **seventy** descendants of King Ahab living in the city
10. 6 The **seventy** descendants of King Ahab were under the care of
10. 7 leaders of Samaria killed all **seventy** of Ahab's descendants,
2 Chr 29.32 brought **seventy** bulls, a hundred sheep, and two hundred lambs
36.21 land will lie desolate for **seventy** years, to make up for the
Ezra 8. 2 the clan of Elam, with **70** men Zebadiah son of Michael, of
8. 2 date) Uthai and Zaccur, of the clan of Bigvai, with **70** men
8.26 100 silver utensils - **70** kilogrammes
Ps 90.10 **Seventy** years is all we have— eighty years, if we are
Is 23.15 Tyre will be forgotten for **seventy** years, the lifetime of a king.
23.17 When the **seventy** years are over, the Lord will let Tyre
Jer 25.11 nations will serve the king of Babylonia for **seventy** years.
29.10 "The Lord says, 'When Babylonia's **seventy** years are over,
Ezek 8.11 **Seventy** Israelite leaders were there, including Jaazaniah
Dan 9. 2 and thinking about the **seventy** years that Jerusalem would be in
9.24 "Seven times **seventy** years is the length of time God
Zech 1.12 Jerusalem and the cities of Judah for **seventy** years now.
7. 5 and seventh months during these **seventy** years, it was not in
Mt 18.22 seven times," answered Jesus, "but **seventy** times seven,
Acts 23.23 go to Caesarea, together with **seventy** horsemen and two hundred spearmen,

700

Judg 20.15 citizens of Gibeah gathered **seven hundred** specially chosen men
2 Sam 10.18 David and his men killed **seven hundred** Syrian chariot drivers
1 Kgs 11. 3 Solomon married **seven hundred** princesses
2 Kgs 3.26 he took **seven hundred** swordsmen with him
2 Chr 15.11 **seven hundred** head of cattle and seven thousand sheep.

7,000

1 Kgs 19.18 Yet I will leave **seven thousand** people alive in Israel—
20.15 out the Israelite army, a total of **seven thousand** men.
2 Kgs 24.16 the important men to Babylonia, **seven thousand** in all,
1 Chr 18. 4 a thousand of his chariots, **seven thousand** horsemen,
19.18 David and his men killed **seven thousand** Syrian chariot drivers
2 Chr 15.11 seven hundred head of cattle and **seven thousand** sheep.
30.24 contributed a thousand bulls and **seven thousand** sheep
Job 1. 3 and owned **seven thousand** sheep,
Rom 11. 4 "I have kept for myself **seven thousand** men who have not
Rev 11.13 city was destroyed, and **seven thousand** people were killed.

70,000

2 Sam 24.15 of the country to the other **seventy thousand** Israelites died.
1 Kgs 5.15 hill-country quarrying stone, with **70,000** men to carry it,
1 Chr 21.14 on the people of Israel, and **seventy thousand** of them died.
2 Chr 2. 2 He put **seventy thousand** men to work transporting materials,
2.18 He assigned **70,000** of them to transport materials and

7,100

1 Chr 12.23 **7,100** well-trained men;

72

Num 31.36 for the soldiers, of which **72** were the tax for the Lord;
Lk 10. 1 the Lord chose another **seventy-two** men and sent them out two
10.17 The **seventy-two** men came back in great joy.

72,000

Num 31.32 675,000 sheep and goats, **72,000** cattle, 61,000 donkeys,

721

Neh 7.26 Lod, Hadid, and Ono - **721**

725

Ezra 2.21 Lod, Hadid, and Ono - **725**

7,337

Ezra 2.64 Their male and female servants - **7,337**
Neh 7.66 Their male and female servants - **7,337**

736

Ezra 2.64 Horses - **736**
Neh 7.66 Horses - **736**

74

Ezra 2.40 Jeshua and Kadmiel (descendants of Hodaviah) - **74**
Neh 7.43 Hodaviah) - **74**

743

Ezra 2.21 Kiriath Jearim, Chephirah, and Beeroth - **743**
Neh 7.26 and Beeroth - **743**

745

Jer 52.30 and in his twenty-third year, **745**—taken away by Nebuzaradan.

74,600

Num 1.20 Judah **74,600**
also Num 2.3

75

Gen 12. 4 When Abram was **seventy-five** years old, he started out from Haran,
Ex 25.25 Make a rim **75** millimetres wide round it and a gold
37.12 He made a rim **75** millimetres wide round it and put a
1 Kgs 7.26 The sides of the tank were **75** millimetres thick.
2 Chr 4. 5 The sides of the tank were **75** millimetres thick.
Jer 52.21 They were hollow, and the metal was **75** millimetres thick.
Ezek 40.42 and their tops were **seventy-five** centimetres square.
40.43 Ledges **seventy-five** millimetres wide ran round the edge
Acts 7.14 him and the whole family, **seventy-five** people in all, to

7,500

Num 3.22 males one month old or older that were enrolled was **7,500.**

75,000

Esth 9.16 by killing **seventy-five thousand** people who hated them.

760

Ezra 2. 3 Zaccai - **760**
Neh 7. 8 Zaccai - **760**

76,500

Num 26.22 These clans numbered **76,500** men.

77

Gen 4.24 for killing Cain, **Seventy-seven** will be taken if anyone kills
Judg 8.14 for Gideon the names of the **seventy-seven** leading men of Sukkoth.
Ezra 8.35 They offered 12 bulls for all Israel, 96 rams, and **77** lambs;

7,700

2 Chr 17.11 and some Arabs brought him **7,700** sheep and 7,700 goats.

775

Ezra 2. 3 Arah - **775**

777

Gen 5.31 He had other children [31] and died at the age of **777.**

782

Gen 5.26 187, he had a son, Lamech, [26] and then lived another **782** years.

8.4

Ezra 8.26 20 gold bowls - **8.4 kilogrammes**

80

Ex 7. 7 Moses was **eighty** years old, and Aaron was eighty-three.
Judg 3.30 Moab, and there was peace in the land for **eighty** years.
2 Sam 19.32 Barzillai was a very old man, **eighty** years old.
19.35 I am already **eighty** years old, and nothing gives me
2 Kgs 6.25 that a donkey's head cost **eighty** pieces of silver, and two
10.24 He had stationed **eighty** men outside the temple
1 Chr 15. 9 from the clan of Hebron, Eliel, in charge of **80;**
2 Chr 26.17 accompanied by **eighty** strong and courageous priests,
Ezra 8. 2 the clan of Shephatiah, with **80** men
Ps 90.10 years is all we have— **eighty** years, if we are strong;
Song 6. 8 Let the king have sixty queens, **eighty** concubines,
Jer 41. 5 about Gedaliah's murder, [5] **eighty** men arrived from Shechem,

800

Gen 5. 4 After that, Adam lived another **800** years.
5.19 162, he had a son, Enoch, [19] and then lived another **800** years.
Num 7.12 silver basin weighing **800** grammes, by the official standard,
2 Sam 23. 8 fought with his spear against **eight hundred** men and killed
1 Kgs 7.38 basin was 1.8 metres in diameter, and held about **800** litres.
Lk 16. 7 'write **eight hundred.'**

80,000

1 Kgs 5.15 Solomon also had **80,000** men in the hill-country quarrying stone,
2 Chr 2. 2 materials, and **eighty thousand** men to work quarrying stone.
2.18 and **80,000** to cut stones in the mountains,

800,000

2 Sam 24. 9 **800,000** in Israel and 500,000 in Judah.
2 Chr 13. 3 and Jeroboam opposed him with an army of **800,000.**

807

Gen 5. 7 he had a son, Enosh, [7] and then lived another **807** years.

815

Gen 5.10 he had a son, Kenan, [10] and then lived another **815** years.

822

Neh 11.12 In all, **822** members of this clan served in the Temple.

83

Ex 7. 7 Moses was eighty years old, and Aaron was **eighty-three.**

830

Gen 5.16 he had a son, Jared, [16] and then lived another **830** years.

832

Jer 52.29 in his eighteenth year, **832** from Jerusalem;

84

Lk 2.36 married for only seven years and was now **eighty-four** years old.

840

Gen 5.13 he had a son, Mahalalel, [13] and then lived another **840** years.

845

Neh 7. 8 Zattu - **845**

85

Josh 14.10 I am **eighty-five** years old [11] and I'm just as strong today
1 Sam 22.18 On that day he killed **eighty-five** priests who were qualified

86

Gen 16.16 Abram was **eighty-six** years old at the time.

8,600

Num 3.28 males one month old or older that were enrolled was **8,600.**

87,000

1 Chr 7. 5 Issachar listed **87,000** men eligible for military service.

88

Ex 25.23 of acacia-wood, **88** centimetres long, 44 centimetres wide,
37.10 of acacia-wood, **88** centimetres long, 44 centimetres wide,

895

Gen 5.17 He had other children [17] and died at the age of **895.**

90

Gen 5. 9 When Enosh was **90**, he had a son, Kenan,
17.17 Can Sarah have a child at **ninety?"**
Ex 30. 2 45 centimetres wide, and it is to be **90** centimetres high.
37.25 and 45 centimetres wide, and it was **90** centimetres high.

900

Num 35. 5 is a square area measuring **900** metres on each side, with the
Judg 4. 3 Jabin had **nine hundred** iron chariots, and he ruled the
4.13 Tabor, [13] he called out his **nine hundred** iron chariots and

9,000

Ezek 48.35 wall on all four sides of the city is **nine thousand** metres.

905

Gen 5.11 He had other children [11] and died at the age of **905.**

910

Gen 5.14 He had other children [14] and died at the age of **910.**

912

Gen 5. 8 He had other children [8] and died at the age of **912.**

928

Neh 11. 8 In all, **928** Benjaminites lived in Jerusalem.

930

Gen 5. 5 He had other children [5] and died at the age of **930.**

945

Ezra 2. 3 Zattu - **945**

95

Ezra 2. 3 Gibbar - **95**
Neh 7. 8 Gibeon - **95**

950

Gen 9.29 Noah lived for 350 years [29] and died at the age of **950.**

956

1 Chr 9. 9 There were **956** families of this tribe living there.

96

Ezra 8.35 They offered 12 bulls for all Israel, **96** rams, and 77 lambs;
Jer 52.23 hundred pomegranates in all, and **ninety-six** of these were

962

Gen 5.20 He had other children [20] and died at the age of **962.**

969

Gen 5.27 He had other children [27] and died at the age of **969.**

973

Ezra 2.36 Jedaiah (descendants of Jeshua) - **973**
Neh 7.39 Jedaiah (descendants of Jeshua) - **973**

98

1 Sam 4.15 (Eli was now **ninety-eight** years old and almost completely blind.)
Ezra 2. 3 Ater (also called Hezekiah) - **98**
Neh 7. 8 Ater (also called Hezekiah) -**98**

99

Gen 17. 1 When Abram was **ninety-nine** years old, the Lord appeared to
17.24 Abraham was **ninety-nine** years old when he was circumcised,
Mt 18.12 He will leave the other **ninety-nine** grazing on the hillside
18.13 one sheep than over the **ninety-nine** that did not get lost.
Lk 15. 4 He leaves the other **ninety-nine** sheep in the pasture and goes
15. 7 sinner who repents than over **ninety-nine** respectable people who

CONCORDANCE OF BIBLICAL NAMES

Entries in bold capitals are the more common names. Full details are to be found in the main Concordance.

Entries preceded by *AV* are forms of names used in older Bible translations. They are cross-referenced to the GNB form of the name.

People or places who share the same name are distinguished by numbers in brackets following the name.

See also *How to use the Concordance* (page ix).

A

AARON		
Abaddon	Rev	9.11
Abagtha	Esth	1.10
Abana	2 Kgs	5.12
Abarim	Num	21.11
		27.12
		33.41
		33.41
	Deut	32.49
Abda (1)	1 Kgs	4. 6
Abda (2)	Neh	11.17
Abdeel	Jer	36.26
Abdi (1)	1 Chr	6.44
	2 Chr	29.12
Abdi (2)	Ezra	10.26
Abdiel	1 Chr	5.15
Abdon (1)	Judg	12.13
		12.14
Abdon (2) *see also* Achbor (2)		
	2 Chr	34.20
Abdon (3)	Josh	21.30
	1 Chr	6.74
Abdon (4)	1 Chr	8.30
		9.36
Abdon (5)	1 Chr	8.23
ABEDNEGO		
ABEL (1)		
Abel (2)	2 Sam	20.18
Abel Beth Maacah	2 Sam	20.14
	1 Kgs	15.20
	2 Kgs	15.29
	2 Chr	16. 4
Abel Keramim *see also* Atad		
	Judg	11.33
Abel Meholah	Judg	7.22
	1 Kgs	4.12
		19.16
Abel Mizraim	Gen	50.11
AV Abel-Cheramim *see* Abel Keramim		
AV Abel-Maim *see* Abel Beth Maacah		
AV Abel-Shittim *see* Acacia (2)		
AV Abez *see* Ebez		
AV Abi *see* Abijah		
AV Abia *see* Abijah (1)		
AV Abiah *see* Abijah (7)		
Abialbon *see also* Abiel (2)		
	2 Sam	23.24
Abiasaph	Ex	6.24
ABIATHAR		
ABIB		
Abida	Gen	25. 4
	1 Chr	1.33
Abidan	Num	1. 5
		2.18
		7.12
		10.24
Abiel (1)	1 Sam	9. 1
		14.51
Abiel (2) *see also* Abialbon		
	1 Chr	11.26
Abiezer (1)	Josh	17. 2
	Judg	6.11
		6.24
Abiezer (1) (cont.)		
	Judg	6.34
		8.32
	1 Chr	7.18
Abiezer (2)	2 Sam	23.24
	1 Chr	11.26
		27. 2
ABIGAIL (1)		
Abigail (2)	2 Sam	17.25
	1 Chr	2.16
		2.17
AV Abigal *see* Abigail (2)		
Abihail (1)	Num	3.35
Abihail (2)	1 Chr	2.29
Abihail (3)	1 Chr	5.14
		5.14
Abihail (4)	2 Chr	11.18
Abihail (5)	Esth	2.15
		9.29
Abihu	Ex	6.23
		24. 1
		24. 9
		28. 1
	Lev	10. 1
	Num	3. 2
		3. 4
		26.60
		26.61
	1 Chr	6. 3
		24. 1
		24. 2
Abihud	1 Chr	8. 3
ABIJAH (1)		
Abijah (2)	1 Kgs	14. 1
Abijah (3)	1 Chr	24. 7
	Lk	1. 5
Abijah (4)	2 Kgs	18. 2
	2 Chr	29. 1
Abijah (5)	Neh	10. 2
Abijah (6)	Neh	12. 2
		12.12
Abijah (7)	1 Sam	8. 2
	1 Chr	6.28
Abijah (8)	1 Chr	7. 8
AV Abijam *see* Abijah (1)		
Abilene	Lk	3. 1
Abimael	Gen	10.28
	1 Chr	1.22
ABIMELECH (1)		
ABIMELECH (2)		
Abinadab (1)	1 Sam	16. 8
		17.13
	1 Chr	2.13
Abinadab (2)	1 Sam	7. 1
	2 Sam	6. 3
		6. 3
	1 Chr	13. 7
Abinadab (3)	1 Sam	31. 2
	1 Chr	8.33
		9.39
		10. 2
AV Abinadab *see* Benabinadab		
Abinoam	Judg	4. 6
		5. 1
		5.12
ABIRAM (1)		
Abiram (2)	1 Kgs	16.34
Abishag	1 Kgs	1. 3
		1.15
		2.17
		2.21
		2.22
ABISHAI		
Abishua (1)	1 Chr	6. 4
		6.50
	Ezra	7. 5
Abishua (2)	1 Chr	8. 4
Abishur	1 Chr	2.28
		2.29
		2.30
Abital	2 Sam	3. 4
	1 Chr	3. 1
Abitub	1 Chr	8.11
Abiud	Mt	1.12
ABNER		
ABRAHAM		
Abram *see* Abraham		
Abronah	Num	33.15
ABSALOM		
ABSALOM'S MONUMENT		
Acacia (1)	Josh	2. 1
		3. 1
	Mic	6. 5
Acacia (2)	Num	25. 1
		33.41
	Joel	3.18
Acacia (3)	Hos	5. 2
Accad	Gen	10.10
AV Accho *see* Acco		
Acco	Judg	1.31
AV Aceldama *see* Akeldama		
ACHAIA		
Achaicus	1 Cor	16.17
ACHAN		
AV Achar *see* Achan		
AV Achaz *see* Ahaz		
Achbor (1)	Gen	36.31
	1 Chr	1.43
Achbor (2) *see also* Abdon (2)		
	2 Kgs	22.12
		22.14
	Jer	26.22
		36.12
Achim	Mt	1.12
ACHISH (1)		
ACHISH (2)		
AV Achmetha *see* Ecbatana		
AV Achor *see* Trouble Valley		
Achsah	Josh	15.16
		15.17
	Judg	1.12
		1.13
	1 Chr	2.49
Achshaph	Josh	11. 1
		12.20
		19.25
Achzib (1)	Gen	38. 5
	Josh	15.44
	Mic	1.14
Achzib (2)	Josh	19.29
	Judg	1.31
Adadah	Josh	15.22
Adah (1)	Gen	4.19
		4.20
		4.23
Adah (2)	Gen	36. 2
		36. 4
		36.10
		36.16
Adaiah (1)	2 Kgs	22. 1
Adaiah (2)	1 Chr	6.41
Adaiah (3)	1 Chr	8.21
Adaiah (4)	1 Chr	9.10
Adaiah (5)	2 Chr	23. 1
Adaiah (6)	Ezra	10.29
Adaiah (7)	Ezra	10.38
Adaiah (8)	Neh	11. 5
Adaiah (9)	Neh	11.12
Adalia	Esth	9. 7
ADAM (1)		
Adam (2)	Josh	3.16
	Hos	6. 7
Adamah	Josh	19.36
Adaminekeb	Josh	19.33
ADAR		
Adbeel	Gen	25.13
	1 Chr	1.29
Addan	Ezra	2.59
Addar *see also* Ataroth Addar		
Addar (1) *see also* Hazar Addar		
	Josh	15. 3
Addar (2)	1 Chr	8. 3
Addi	Lk	3.28
Addon	Neh	7.61
AV Ader *see* Eder		
Adiel (1)	1 Chr	4.34
Adiel (2)	1 Chr	9.10
Adiel (3)	1 Chr	27.25
Adin (1)	Ezra	2. 3
	Neh	7. 8
Adin (2)	Ezra	8. 2
Adin (3)	Neh	10.14
Adina	1 Chr	11.26
Adithaim	Josh	15.36
Adlai	1 Chr	27.25
Admah	Gen	10.19
		14. 2
		14. 8
	Deut	29.23
	Hos	11. 8
Admatha	Esth	1.14
Admin	Lk	3.33
Adna (1)	Ezra	10.30
Adna (2)	Neh	12.12
Adnah (1)	1 Chr	12.20
Adnah (2)	2 Chr	17.14
Adonibezek	Judg	1. 5
		1. 7
ADONIJAH (1)		
Adonijah (2)	2 Chr	17. 8
Adonijah (3)	Neh	10.14
Adonikam (1)	Ezra	2. 3
	Neh	7. 8
Adonikam (2)	Ezra	8. 2
Adoniram	2 Sam	20.24
	1 Kgs	4. 6
		5.14
		12.18
	2 Chr	10.18
Adonizedek	Josh	10. 1
		10. 3
Adoraim	2 Chr	11. 9
AV Adoram *see* Adoniram		
Adrammelech (1)	2 Kgs	17.31
Adrammelech (2)	2 Kgs	19.37
	Is	37.38
Adramyttium	Acts	27. 2
AV Adria *see* Mediterranean		
Adriel	1 Sam	18.19
	2 Sam	21. 8
ADULLAM		
Adummim	Josh	15. 7
		18.17
Aeneas	Acts	9.33
		9.34
		9.34
Aenon	Jn	3.23

Agabus Acts 11.28
21.10
AGAG
AV Agar *see* Hagar
Agee 2 Sam 23.11
AGRIPPA
Agur Prov 30. 1
AHAB (1)
Ahab (2) Jer 29.21
29.22
Aharah 1 Chr 8. 1
Aharhel 1 Chr 4. 8
Ahasbai 2 Sam 23.24
AV Ahasuerus *see* Xerxes
Ahava Ezra 8.15
8.21
8.31
AHAZ (1)
Ahaz (2) 1 Chr 8.35
8.36
9.41
9.42
AHAZIAH (1)
AHAZIAH (2)
Ahban 1 Chr 2.29
Ahi 1 Chr 5.15
Ahiah Neh 10.14
AV Ahiah *see* Ahijah (1), (2), (6)
Ahiam 2 Sam 23.24
1 Chr 11.26
Ahian 1 Chr 7.19
Ahiezer (1) Num 1. 5
2.25
7.12
10.25
Ahiezer (2) 1 Chr 12. 3
Ahihud (1) Num 34.19
Ahihud (2) 1 Chr 8. 6
AHIJAH (1)
Ahijah (2) 1 Sam 14. 3
14.18
14.18
Ahijah (3) 1 Kgs 4. 3
Ahijah (4) 1 Kgs 15.27
15.33
21.22
Ahijah (5) 1 Chr 2.25
Ahijah (6) 1 Chr 8. 6
Ahijah (7) 1 Chr 11.26
Ahikam 2 Kgs 22.12
22.14
25.22
2 Chr 34.20
Jer 26.24
39.14
40. 5
Ahilud 2 Sam 8.16
20.24
1 Kgs 4. 3
4.12
1 Chr 18.15
AHIMAAZ (1)
Ahimaaz (2) 1 Sam 14.50
Ahimaaz (3)
possibly the same as (1)
1 Kgs 4.15
Ahiman (1) Num 13.22
Josh 15.14
Judg 1.10
Ahiman (2) 1 Chr 9.17
AHIMELECH (1)
Ahimelech (2) 1 Sam 26. 6
Ahimoth 1 Chr 6.25
6.26
Ahinadab 1 Kgs 4.14
Ahinoam (1) 1 Sam 25.43
27. 3
30. 5
2 Sam 2. 2
3. 2
1 Chr 3. 1
Ahinoam (2) 1 Sam 14.50
Ahio (1) 2 Sam 6. 3
6. 4
1 Chr 13. 7
Ahio (2) 1 Chr 8.14
Ahio (3) 1 Chr 8.31
9.37
Ahira Num 1. 5
2.25
7.12
10.27
Ahiram Num 26.38
Ahisamach Ex 31. 6
35.34
38.23
Ahishahar 1 Chr 7.10
Ahishar 1 Kgs 4. 6
AHITHOPHEL
Ahitub (1) 1 Sam 14. 3
Ahitub (2) 1 Sam 22. 9

Ahitub (3) 2 Sam 8.17
1 Chr 6. 7
6.52
18.16
Ezra 7. 2
Ahitub (4) 1 Chr 6.11
Ahitub (5) 1 Chr 9.10
Neh 11.11
Ahlab Judg 1.31
Ahlai (1) 1 Chr 2.31
Ahlai (2) 1 Chr 11.26
Ahoah 1 Chr 8. 4
Ahoh (1)
(perhaps the same as Ahohi.)
2 Sam 23. 9
1 Chr 11.12
Ahoh (2) 2 Sam 23.24
1 Chr 11.26
Ahohi
see also Ahoh
1 Chr 27. 2
AV Aholah *see* Oholah
AV Aholiab *see* Oholiab
AV Aholibah *see* Oholibah
AV Aholibamah *see* Oholibamah
Ahumai 1 Chr 4. 2
Ahuzzam 1 Chr 4. 6
Ahuzzath Gen 26.26
Ahzai Neh 11.13
AI (1)
Ai (2) Is 10.28
Aiah (1) Gen 36.24
1 Chr 1.38
Aiah (2) 2 Sam 3. 7
21. 8
21.10
AV Aiath *see* Ai (2)
AV Aija *see* Ai (1)
Aijalon (1) Josh 10.12
19.42
21.24
Judg 1.35
1 Sam 14.31
1 Chr 6.69
8.13
2 Chr 11.10
28.18
Aijalon (2) Judg 12.12
Ain (1) Num 34.11
Ain (2) Josh 15.32
19. 7
21.16
1 Chr 4.32
AV Ajalon *see* Aijalon (1)
Akan Gen 36.27
Akeldama Acts 1.19
Akkub (1) 1 Chr 3.24
Akkub (2) 1 Chr 9.17
Neh 11.19
12.25
Akkub (3) Ezra 2.40
Neh 7.43
Akkub (4) Ezra 2.43
Akkub (5) Neh 8. 7
Akrabbim Num 34. 4
Josh 15. 3
Judg 1.36
AV Alameth *see* Alemeth (1)
Alemeth (1) 1 Chr 7. 8
Alemeth (2) 1 Chr 8.36
9.42
Alemeth (3)
see also Almon
1 Chr 6.60
Alexander (1) Mk 15.21
Alexander (2) Acts 4. 6
Alexander (3) Acts 19.33
19.33
Alexander (4) 1 Tim 1.20
Alexander (5) 2 Tim 4.14
Alexandria Acts 6. 9
18.24
27. 6
28.11
Allam Melech Josh 19.26
Allon 1 Chr 4.34
AV Allon-Bachuth *see* Oak of Weeping
ALMIGHTY
Almodad Gen 10.26
1 Chr 1.20
Almon
see also Alemeth (3)
Josh 21.18
Almon Diblathaim
see also Beth Diblathaim
Num 33.41
AV Aloth *see* Bealoth
Alphaeus (1) Mk 2.14
Alphaeus (2) Mt 10. 3
Mk 3.18

Alphaeus (2) (cont.)
Lk 6.15
Acts 1.13
Alush Num 33.13
Alvah Gen 36.40
1 Chr 1.51
Alvan Gen 36.23
1 Chr 1.38
Amad Josh 19.26
Amal 1 Chr 7.35
AMALEK
Amam Josh 15.26
Amana Song 4. 8
Amariah (1) 1 Chr 6. 7
6.52
Ezra 7. 3
Amariah (2) 1 Chr 6.11
Amariah (3) 1 Chr 23.19
24.23
Amariah (4) 2 Chr 19.11
Amariah (5) 2 Chr 31.15
Amariah (6) Ezra 10.38
Amariah (7) Neh 10. 2
12. 2
12.12
Amariah (8) Neh 11. 4
Amariah (9) Zeph 1. 1
AMASA (1)
Amasa (2) 2 Chr 28.12
Amasai (1) 1 Chr 6.25
6.35
2 Chr 29.12
Amasai (2) 1 Chr 12.18
Amasai (3) 1 Chr 15.23
Amashsai Neh 11.13
Amasiah 2 Chr 17.16
17.16
Amaw Num 22. 5
AMAZIAH (1)
Amaziah (2) Amos 7.10
7.12
7.17
Amaziah (3) 1 Chr 6.45
Amaziah (4) 1 Chr 4.34
AMEN
Ami
see also Amon
Ezra 2.55
AV Aminadab *see* Amminadab (2)
Amittai 2 Kgs 14.25
Jon 1. 1
Amizzabad 1 Chr 27. 2
Ammah 2 Sam 2.24
AV Ammi *see* God's People
Ammiel (1) Num 13. 3
Ammiel (2) 2 Sam 9. 4
17.27
Ammiel (3) 1 Chr 26. 5
Ammiel (4)
see also Eliam (1)
1 Chr 3. 5
Ammihud (1) Num 1. 5
2.18
7.12
10.22
1 Chr 7.26
Ammihud (2) Num 34.19
Ammihud (3) Num 34.19
Ammihud (4) 2 Sam 13.37
Ammihud (5) 1 Chr 9. 4
Amminadab (1) Ex 6.23
Amminadab (2) Num 1. 5
2. 3
7.12
10.14
Ruth 4.18
1 Chr 2.10
Mt 1. 2
Lk 3.33
Amminadab (3) 1 Chr 6.22
Amminadab (4) 1 Chr 15.10
15.11
Ammishaddai Num 1. 5
2.25
7.12
10.25
AV Ammizabad *see* Amizzabad
AMMON
AMNON (1)
Amnon (2) 1 Chr 4.20
Amok Neh 12. 2
12.12
AMON (1)
Amon (2) 1 Kgs 22.26
2 Chr 18.25
Amon (3) Neh 7.57
Amon (4) Jer 46.25
AMORITES
Amos (1) Amos 1. 1
1. 1
1. 2

Amos (1) (cont.)
Amos 7. 8
7.10
7.12
7.14
8. 1
Amos (2) Lk 3.25
Amoz 2 Kgs 19. 2
20. 1
2 Chr 26.22
32.20
32.32
Is 1. 1
2. 1
13. 1
20. 2
37. 2
38. 1
Amphipolis Acts 17. 1
Ampliatus Rom 16. 8
Amram (1) Ex 6.18
6.20
6.20
Num 3.17
3.27
26.58
26.59
1 Chr 6. 2
6. 3
6.18
23.12
23.13
24.20
26.23
Amram (2) Ezra 10.34
Amraphel Gen 14. 1
Amzi (1) 1 Chr 6.46
Amzi (2) Neh 11.12
Anab Josh 11.21
15.50
Anah (1) Gen 36. 2
36.14
36.18
36.20
36.25
36.25
36.29
Anah (2)
possibly the same as (1).
Gen 36.24
36.24
1 Chr 1.38
1.38
Anaharath Josh 19.19
Anaiah (1) Neh 8. 4
Anaiah (2) Neh 10.14
ANAKIM
Anam Gen 10.13
1 Chr 1.11
Anammelech 2 Kgs 17.31
Anan Neh 10.14
Anani 1 Chr 3.24
Ananiah (1) Neh 3.23
Ananiah (2) Neh 11.32
ANANIAS (1)
ANANIAS (2)
ANANIAS (3)
Anath Judg 3.31
5. 6
Anathoth (1) Josh 21.18
2 Sam 23.24
1 Kgs 2.26
1 Chr 6.60
11.26
12. 3
27. 2
Ezra 2.21
Neh 7.26
11.32
Is 10.30
Jer 1. 1
11.21
11.23
29.27
32. 7
Anathoth (2) 1 Chr 7. 8
Anathoth (3) Neh 10.14
ANDREW
Andronicus Rom 16. 7
Anem 1 Chr 6.73
Aner (1) Gen 14.13
14.24
Aner (2) 1 Chr 6.70
AV Anet(h)othite *see* Anathoth (1)
Aniam 1 Chr 7.19
Anim Josh 15.50
Anna Lk 2.36
Annas Lk 3. 2
Jn 18.13
18.24
Acts 4. 6

Anthothijah 1 Chr 8.24
ANTIOCH IN PISIDIA
ANTIOCH IN SYRIA
Antipas Rev 2.13
Antipatris Acts 23.31
AV Antothite *see* Anathoth (1)
Anub 1 Chr 4. 8
Apelles Rom 16.10
Apharsachites
(Apharsites) *see* Officials
Aphek (1) Josh 12.18
1 Sam 4. 1
29. 1
Aphek (2) 1 Kgs 20.26
20.30
2 Kgs 13.17
Aphek (3) Josh 13. 4
19.30
Judg 1.31
Aphekah Josh 15.53
Aphiah 1 Sam 9. 1
AV Aphik *see* Aphek (3)
AV Aphrah *see* Leaphrah
AV Aphses *see* Hapizzez
Apis Jer 46.15
Apollonia Acts 17. 1
APOLLOS
Apollyon Rev 9.11
Appaim 1 Chr 2.30
2.31
Apphia Phlm 2
AV Appii Forum *see* Market Of Appius
Appius Acts 28.15
AQABA
Aquila Acts 18. 2
18.18
18.19
18.26
Rom 16. 3
1 Cor 16.19
2 Tim 4.19
Ar Num 21.15
21.28
22.36
Deut 2. 9
2.10
2.18
2.29
Is 15. 1
Ara 1 Chr 7.38
ARAB (1)
Arab (2) Josh 15.52
2 Sam 23.24
Arabah
see also Beth Arabah, (Jordan) Valley
Arabah (1) 2 Sam 23.24
Arabah (2) Amos 6.14
Arad (1) 1 Chr 8.15
Arad (2) Num 21. 1
33.40
Josh 12.14
Judg 1.16
Arah (1) 1 Chr 7.39
Arah (2) Ezra 2. 3
Neh 7. 8
Arah (3) Neh 6.18
Aram
see also Ram (2), Syria
Aram (1) Gen 10.22
10.23
1 Chr 1.17
Aram (2) Gen 22.21
Aram (3) 1 Chr 2.23
Aram (4) 1 Chr 7.34
AV Aram-Maacah *see* Maacah
ARAMEAN
Aran Gen 36.28
1 Chr 1.38
Ararat (1) Gen 8. 4
Ararat (2) 2 Kgs 19.37
Is 37.38
Jer 51.27
ARAUNAH
Arba
see also Kiriath Arba, Hebron
Josh 14.15
14.15
15.13
21.11
Arbah
see also Beth Arabah
1 Chr 11.26
AV Arbathite *see* Arabah (1), Arbah
AV Arbite *see* Arab (1)
Archelaus Mt 2.22
AV Archevite *see* Erech
Archippus Col 4.17
Phlm 2

Archite Josh 16. 2
2 Sam 15.32
1 Chr 27.33
Ard (1) Gen 46.21
Ard (2) Num 26.40
Ardon 1 Chr 2.18
Areli Gen 46.16
Num 26.17
AREOPAGUS
Aretas 2 Cor 11.32
Argob Deut 3. 4
3.13
3.14
1 Kgs 4.13
Aridai Esth 9. 7
Aridatha Esth 9. 7
Ariel Ezra 8.16
AV Ariel *see* Jerusalem, (God's) Altar
Arimathea Mt 27.57
Mk 15.42
Lk 23.50
Jn 19.38
Arioch (1) Gen 14. 1
Arioch (2) Dan 2.14
2.15
2.15
2.24
2.25
Arisai Esth 9. 7
Aristarchus Acts 19.29
20. 4
27. 2
Col 4.10
Phlm 24
Aristobulus Rom 16.10
Arkites Gen 10.17
1 Chr 1.15
Armageddon Rev 16.16
AV Armenia *see* Ararat (2)
Armoni 2 Sam 21. 8
Arnan 1 Chr 3.21
Arni Lk 3.33
ARNON
Arod Gen 46.16
Num 26.17
AROER (1)
Aroer (2) Num 32.34
Josh 13.25
2 Sam 24. 5
Aroer (3) 1 Sam 30.28
Arpachshad Gen 10.22
10.24
11.10
11.12
1 Chr 1.17
1.18
1.24
Arpad 2 Kgs 18.34
19.13
Is 10. 9
36.19
37.13
Jer 49.23
Arphaxad Lk 3.36
ARTAXERXES (1)
ARTAXERXES (2)
ARTAXERXES (3)
Artemas Tit 3.12
Artemis Acts 19.24
19.27
19.28
19.34
19.35
Arubboth 1 Kgs 4.10
Arumah Judg 9.31
9.41
Arvad Ezek 27. 8
27.11
Arvadites Gen 10.18
1 Chr 1.16
Arza 1 Kgs 16. 9
ASA (1)
Asa (2) 1 Chr 9.14
ASAHEL (1)
Asahel (2) 2 Chr 17. 8
Asahel (3) 2 Chr 31.13
Asahel (4) Ezra 10.15
AV Asahiah *see* Asaiah (5)
Asaiah (1) 1 Chr 4.34
Asaiah (2) 1 Chr 6.30
Asaiah (3) 1 Chr 9. 4
Asaiah (4) 1 Chr 15. 6
15.11
Asaiah (5) 2 Kgs 22.12
22.14
2 Chr 34.20
ASAPH (1)
Asaph (2) 2 Kgs 18.18
Is 36. 3

Asaph (3)
Perhaps the same as Ebiasaph
1 Chr 26. 1
Asaph (4) Neh 2. 8
Asarel 1 Chr 4.16
Asenath Gen 41.45
41.50
46.20
AV Aser *see* Asher
Ashan Josh 15.42
19. 7
1 Chr 4.32
6.57
Asharelah 1 Chr 25. 2
25. 9
Ashbea *see* Beth Ashbea
Ashbel Gen 46.21
Num 26.38
1 Chr 8. 1
ASHDOD
ASHER (1)
Asher (2) Josh 17. 7
ASHERAH
AV Asherim *see* Asherah
Ashhur 1 Chr 2.24
4. 5
4. 7
Ashima 2 Kgs 17.30
ASHKELON
Ashkenaz (1) Gen 10. 3
1 Chr 1. 6
Ashkenaz (2) Jer 51.27
Ashnah (1) Josh 15.33
Ashnah (2) Josh 15.43
Ashpenaz Dan 1. 3
1. 4
1. 8
1. 9
1.10
1.11
1.18
AV Ashriel *see* Asriel
Ashtaroth (1) Deut 1. 4
Josh 9.10
12. 4
13.12
13.31
Ashtaroth (2)
see also Ashterah
1 Chr 6.71
Ashterah
see also Ashtaroth (2)
1 Chr 11.26
Ashteroth Karnaim
perhaps the same as Ashtaroth (1).
Gen 14. 5
Ashurbanipal Ezra 4.10
Ashvath 1 Chr 7.33
ASIA
Asiel 1 Chr 4.34
AV Askelon *see* Ashkelon
Asnah Ezra 2.43
AV Asnapper *see* Ashurbanipal
Aspatha Esth 9. 7
Asriel (1) Num 26.31
Josh 17. 2
Asriel (2) 1 Chr 7.14
Asshur
see also Assyria
Asshur (1) Gen 10.22
1 Chr 1.17
Asshur (2) Ezek 27.23
Asshurim Gen 25. 3
Assir (1) Ex 6.24
1 Chr 6.22
Assir (2) 1 Chr 6.23
6.37
Assos Acts 20.13
20.14
ASSYRIA
ASTARTE
AV Asuppim *see* Storerooms
Aswan Is 49.12
Ezek 29.10
30. 6
Asyncritus Rom 16.14
Atad Gen 50.10
50.11
AV Atad *see* Abel Mizraim
Atarah 1 Chr 2.26
Ataroth (1) Num 32. 3
32.34
Ataroth (2) Josh 16. 7
Ataroth Addar Josh 16. 2
16. 5
18.13
Ater (1)
see also Hezekiah (2)
Ezra 2. 3
Neh 7. 8

Ater (2) Ezra 2.40
Neh 7.43
Ater (3) Neh 10.14
Athach 1 Sam 30.30
Athaiah Neh 11. 4
ATHALIAH (1)
Athaliah (2) 1 Chr 8.26
Athaliah (3) Ezra 8. 2
Atharim Num 21. 1
Athens Acts 17.15
17.16
17.21
17.22
18. 1
1 Thes 3. 1
Athlai Ezra 10.28
Atroth Beth Joab 1 Chr 2.54
Atroth Shophan Num 32.35
Attai (1) 1 Chr 2.35
2.36
2.36
Attai (2) 1 Chr 12. 9
Attai (3) 2 Chr 11.20
Attalia Acts 14.25
Augustus Lk 2. 1
AV Ava *see* Ivvah
Aven (1)
see also Bethel
Hos 10. 8
Aven (2) Amos 1. 5
AV Aven *see* Heliopolis
Avith Gen 36.31
1 Chr 1.43
Avvim (1) Deut 2.23
Josh 13. 3
Avvim (2) Josh 18.23
Ayyah 1 Chr 7.28
AV Azal *see* (in) Two
Azaliah 2 Kgs 22. 3
2 Chr 34. 8
Azaniah Neh 10. 9
Azarel (1) 1 Chr 12. 3
Azarel (2) 1 Chr 27.16
Azarel (3) Ezra 10.38
Azarel (4) Neh 11.13
Azarel (5) Neh 12.36
Azariah (1) 1 Kgs 4. 2
Azariah (2) 1 Kgs 4. 5
Azariah (3) 1 Chr 2. 8
Azariah (4) 1 Chr 2.38
Azariah (5) 1 Chr 6. 9
Azariah (6) 1 Chr 6.10
Azariah (7) 1 Chr 6.13
9.10
Ezra 7. 1
Azariah (8) 1 Chr 6.36
Azariah (9) 2 Chr 15. 1
15. 8
Azariah (10) 2 Chr 21. 2
Azariah (11) 2 Chr 23. 1
Azariah (12) 2 Chr 23. 1
Azariah (13) 2 Chr 26.17
26.20
Azariah (14) 2 Chr 28.12
Azariah (15) 2 Chr 29.12
Azariah (16) 2 Chr 29.12
Azariah (17) 2 Chr 31.10
31.13
Azariah (18) Ezra 7. 3
Azariah (19) Neh 3.23
3.24
Azariah (20) Neh 7. 7
Azariah (21) Neh 8. 7
Azariah (22) Neh 10. 2
Azariah (23) Neh 12.33
Azariah (24) Jer 42. 1
43. 2
Azariah (25)
see also Abednego
Dan 1. 6
1.19
2.17
AV Azariah *see* Azariahu, Uzziah
Azariahu 2 Chr 21. 2
Azaz 1 Chr 5. 8
Azazel Lev 16. 8
16.10
16.10
16.20
16.26
Azaziah (1) 1 Chr 15.17
Azaziah (2) 1 Chr 27.16
Azaziah (3) 2 Chr 31.13
Azbuk Neh 3.16
Azekah Josh 10.10
10.11
15.35
1 Sam 17. 1
2 Chr 11. 9
Neh 11.30
Jer 34. 7

Azel	1 Chr	8.37
		8.38
		8.39
		9.43
		9.44
AV Azem *see* Ezem		
Azgad (1)	Ezra	2. 3
	Neh	7. 8
Azgad (2)	Ezra	8. 2
Azgad (3)	Neh	10.14
AV Aziel *see* Jaaziel		
Aziza	Ezra	10.27
Azmaveth (1)	2 Sam	23.24
	1 Chr	11.26
Azmaveth (2)	1 Chr	12. 3
Azmaveth (3)	1 Chr	27.25
Azmaveth (4)	1 Chr	8.36
		9.42
Azmaveth (5) *see also* Beth Azmaveth		
	Ezra	2.21
	Neh	12.29
Azmon	Num	34. 4
	Josh	15. 4
Aznoth Tabor	Josh	19.34
Azor	Mt	1.12
Azotus *see also* Ashdod		
	Acts	8.40
Azriel (1)	1 Chr	5.24
Azriel (2)	1 Chr	27.16
Azriel (3)	Jer	36.26
Azrikam (1)	1 Chr	3.23
Azrikam (2)	1 Chr	8.38
		9.44
Azrikam (3)	1 Chr	9.14
	Neh	11.15
Azrikam (4)	2 Chr	28. 7
Azubah (1)	1 Chr	2.18
		2.19
Azubah (2)	1 Kgs	22.42
	2 Chr	20.31
AV Azur *see* Azzur (3)		
AV Azzah *see* Gaza		
Azzan	Num	34.19
Azzur (1)	Neh	10.14
Azzur (2)	Jer	28. 1
Azzur (3)	Ezek	11. 1

B

Baal *see also* Bamoth Baal, Kiriath Baal		
BAAL (1)		
Baal (2)	1 Chr	5. 4
Baal (3)	1 Chr	8.30
		9.36
Baal Hamon	Song	8.11
Baal Hanan (1)	Gen	36.31
	1 Chr	1.43
Baal Hanan (2)	1 Chr	27.25
Baal Hazor *see also* Hazor (2)		
	2 Sam	13.23
Baal Hermon	Judg	3. 3
	1 Chr	5.23
Baal Meon *see also* Beon, Beth Baalmeon, Bethmeon		
	Num	32.38
	1 Chr	5. 8
	Ezek	25. 9
Baal Perazim *see also* Perazim		
	2 Sam	5.20
		5.20
	1 Chr	14.11
		14.11
Baal Shalishah	2 Kgs	4.42
Baal Zephon	Ex	14. 2
		14. 9
	Num	33. 7
AV Baal-Berith *see* Baal-Of-The-Covenant		
BAAL-OF-THE-COVENANT		
Baalah (1) *see also* Kiriath Baal, Kiriath Jearim		
	Josh	15. 9
		15.10
	1 Chr	13. 6
Baalah (2)	Josh	15.11
Baalah (3)	Josh	15.29
Baalah (4)	2 Sam	6. 2
Baalath *see* Bamoth Baal, Kiriath Baal		
	Josh	19.44
	1 Kgs	9.18
	1 Chr	4.33
	2 Chr	8. 6
Baalath Beer *see also* Ramah (5)		
	Josh	19. 8
Baalgad	Josh	11.17
		12. 7
		13. 5
Baalis	Jer	40.14
Baalmeon *see* Beth Baalmeon		
Baaltamar	Judg	20.33
BAALZEBUB		
Baana (1)	1 Kgs	4.12
Baana (2)	1 Kgs	4.16
Baana (3)	Neh	3. 4
Baanah (1)	2 Sam	23.24
	1 Chr	11.26
Baanah (2)	2 Sam	4. 2
		4. 5
		4. 6
		4.12
Baanah (3)	Ezra	2. 2
	Neh	7. 7
		10.14
Baara	1 Chr	8. 8
Baaseiah	1 Chr	6.40
BAASHA		
AV Babel *see* Babylon		
BABYLON		
Baca	Ps	84. 6
AV Bachrite *see* Becher		
Bahurim	2 Sam	3.16
		16. 5
		17.18
		19.16
		23.24
	1 Kgs	2. 8
Bahurum	1 Chr	11.26
Bakbakkar	1 Chr	9.14
Bakbuk	Ezra	2.43
	Neh	7.46
Bakbukiah	Neh	11.17
		12. 9
		12.25
BALAAM		
AV Balac *see* Balak		
Baladan *see also* Merodach Baladan		
	2 Kgs	20.12
	Is	39. 1
Balah	Josh	19. 3
BALAK		
AV Bamah *see* High Places		
Bamoth *see also* Bamoth Baal		
	Num	21.19
		21.20
Bamoth Baal	Num	22.41
	Josh	13.17
Bani *see also* Binnui (5)		
Bani (1)	2 Sam	23.24
Bani (2)	1 Chr	6.46
Bani (3)	1 Chr	9. 4
Bani (4)	Ezra	2. 3
		10.29
Bani (5)	Ezra	10.34
Bani (6)	Neh	3.17
		8. 7
		9. 4
		9. 5
Bani (7)	Neh	9. 4
		10. 9
Bani (8)	Neh	10.14
Bani (9)	Neh	11.22
Bani (10)	Ezra	8. 2
Bar-Jesus	Acts	13. 6
AV Bar-Jona *see* (son of) John (4)		
BARABBAS		
AV Barachel *see* Barakel		
AV Barachiah *see* Berechiah (7)		
AV Barachias *see* Berachiah		
BARAK		
Barakel	Job	32. 2
AV Barhumite *see* Bahurim		
Bariah	1 Chr	3.22
Barkos	Ezra	2.43
	Neh	7.46
BARNABAS		
Barnea *see also* Kadesh (1)		
Barsabbas (1) *see also* Joseph (8), Justus (1)		
	Acts	1.23
Barsabbas (2) *see also* Judas (6)		
	Acts	15.22
Bartholomew	Mt	10. 3
	Mk	3.18
	Lk	6.14
	Acts	1.13
Bartimaeus	Mk	10.46
BARUCH (1)		
Baruch (2)	Neh	3.20
		10. 2
Baruch (3)	Neh	11. 5
Barzillai (1)	2 Sam	17.27
		19.31
		19.32
		19.34
		19.39
	1 Kgs	2. 7
	Ezra	2.61
	Neh	7.63
Barzillai (2)	2 Sam	21. 8
Barzillai (3)	Ezra	2.61
		2.61
	Neh	7.63
		7.63
Basemath (1)	Gen	26.34
Basemath (2)	Gen	36. 3
		36. 4
		36.10
		36.17
Basemath (3)	1 Kgs	4.15
BASHAN		
AV Bashan Havoth Jair *see* (villages of) Jair		
AV Bashemath (Basmath) *see* Basemath		
Basshebeth *see* Josheb Basshebeth		
AV Bath Rabbim *see* (that great) City		
BATHSHEBA		
Bathshua	1 Chr	2. 3
Bavvai	Neh	3.18
Bazlith	Neh	7.46
Bazluth	Ezra	2.43
Bealiah	1 Chr	12. 3
Bealoth	Josh	15.24
	1 Kgs	4.16
BEAUTIFUL GATE		
Bebai (1)	Ezra	2. 3
	Neh	7. 8
Bebai (2)	Ezra	8. 2
		10.28
Bebai (3)	Neh	10.14
Becher (1)	Gen	46.21
	1 Chr	7. 6
		7. 8
Becher (2) *see also* Bered		
	Num	26.35
Becorath	1 Sam	9. 1
Bedad	Gen	36.31
	1 Chr	1.43
Bedan	1 Chr	7.17
Bedeiah	Ezra	10.34
Beeliada	1 Chr	14. 7
BEELZEBUL		
Beer *see also* Baalath Beer, Wells		
Beer (2)	Judg	9.21
AV Beer Lahai Roi *see* (The) Well Of The Living One Who Sees Me		
Beera	1 Chr	7.37
Beerah	1 Chr	5. 4
		5. 4
Beerelim	Is	15. 8
Beeri (1)	Gen	26.34
Beeri (2)	Hos	1. 1
Beeroth	Josh	9.17
		18.25
	2 Sam	4. 2
		4. 2
		23.24
	1 Chr	11.26
	Ezra	2.21
	Neh	7.26
BEERSHEBA		
Beeshterah	Josh	21.27
BEHEMOTH		
Bel	Is	46. 1
	Jer	51.44
Bela (1) *see also* Zoar		
	Gen	14. 2
		14. 8
Bela (2)	Gen	36.31
	1 Chr	1.43
Bela (3)	Gen	46.21
	Num	26.38
		26.40
	1 Chr	7. 6
		7. 7
		8. 1
		8. 3
Bela (4)	1 Chr	5. 8
AV Belial, Son Of *see* Criminal, Godless, Good-For-Nothing, Pervert, Pigheaded, Scoundrel, Worthless		
BELSHAZZAR		
BELTESHAZZAR		
Benabinadab	1 Kgs	4.11
BENAIAH (1)		
Benaiah (2)	2 Sam	23.24
	1 Chr	11.26
		27. 2
Benaiah (3)	1 Chr	4.34
Benaiah (4)	1 Chr	15.17
		15.23
		16. 5
		16. 6
Benaiah (5)	1 Chr	27.34
Benaiah (6)	2 Chr	20.14
Benaiah (7)	2 Chr	31.13
Benaiah (8)	Ezra	10.25
Benaiah (9)	Ezra	10.30
Benaiah (10)	Ezra	10.34
Benaiah (11)	Ezra	10.43
Benaiah (12)	Ezek	11. 1
Benammi	Gen	19.38
Bendeker	1 Kgs	4. 9
Bene Jaakan	Num	33.15
Beneberak	Josh	19.45
Bengeber	1 Kgs	4.13
BENHADAD (1)		
BENHADAD (2)		
BENHADAD (3)		
BENHADAD (4)		
Benhail	2 Chr	17. 7
Benhanan	1 Chr	4.20
Benhesed	1 Kgs	4.10
Benhur	1 Kgs	4. 8
Beninu	Neh	10. 9
BENJAMIN (1)		
Benjamin (2)	1 Chr	7.10
Benjamin (3)	Ezra	10.31
Benjamin (4)	Neh	3.23
Benjamin (5)	Neh	12.33
BENJAMIN GATE		
Benoni *see also* Benjamin (1)		
	Gen	35.18
Benoth *see* Succoth Benoth		
Benzoheth	1 Chr	4.20
Beon *see also* Baal Meon, Beth Baalmeon, Bethmeon		
	Num	32. 3
Beor (1)	Gen	36.31
	1 Chr	1.43
Beor (2)	Num	22. 5
		24. 3
		24.15
		31. 8
	Deut	23. 4
	Josh	13.22
		24. 9
	Mic	6. 5
	2 Pet	2.15
Bera	Gen	14. 2
Beracah (1)	1 Chr	12. 3
Beracah (2)	2 Chr	20.26
		20.26
Berachiah *see also* Berechiah (7)		
	Mt	23.35
Beraiah	1 Chr	8.21
Berea	Acts	17.10
		17.13
		17.14
		17.15
		20. 4
Berechiah (1)	1 Chr	3.20
Berechiah (2)	1 Chr	6.39
		15.17
Berechiah (3)	1 Chr	9.14
Berechiah (4)	1 Chr	15.23
Berechiah (5)	2 Chr	28.12
Berechiah (6)	Neh	3. 4
		3.30
		6.18
Berechiah (7) *see also* Berachiah		
	Zech	1. 1
Bered *see also* Becher (2)		
Bered (1)	Gen	16.14
Bered (2)	1 Chr	7.20
Beri	1 Chr	7.36
Beriah (1)	Gen	46.17
		46.17
	Num	26.44
		26.45
	1 Chr	7.30
		7.31
Beriah (2)	1 Chr	7.23
Beriah (3)	1 Chr	8.13
		8.14
Beriah (4)	1 Chr	23.10
		23.10
AV Berith *see* Baal-Of-The-Covenant		

Bernice Acts 25.13
25.23
26.30
AV Berodach-Baladan *see* Merodach Baladan
Berothah Ezek 47.16
Berothai 2 Sam 8. 8
Besai Ezra 2.43
Neh 7.46
Besodeiah Neh 3. 6
Besor 1 Sam 30. 9
30.21
Betah 2 Sam 8. 8
Beten Josh 19.25
Beth Arabah Josh 15.61
18.22
Beth Ashbea 1 Chr 4.21
Beth Azmaveth Neh 7.26
Beth Baalmeon
see also Baal Meon, Beon, Bethmeon
Josh 13.17
Beth Diblathaim
see also Almon Diblathaim
Jer 48.22
AV Beth Eked *see* Shepherds' Camp
Beth Haccherem Neh 3.14
Jer 6. 1
Beth Haggan 2 Kgs 9.27
Beth Hanan 1 Kgs 4. 9
Beth Haram
see also Beth Haran
Josh 13.27
Beth Haran
see also Beth Haram
Num 32.36
Beth Hoglah Josh 15. 6
18.19
18.21
BETH HORON
Beth Jeshimoth Num 33.41
Josh 12. 3
13.20
Ezek 25. 9
Beth Joab *see* Atroth Beth Joab
Beth Leaphrah Mic 1.10
Beth Lebaoth
see also Lebaoth
Josh 19. 6
Beth Maacah *see* Abel Beth Maacah
Beth Marcaboth Josh 19. 5
1 Chr 4.31
Beth Nimrah
see also Bethnimrah
Num 32.36
Beth Shan Josh 17.11
17.16
Judg 1.27
1 Sam 31.10
31.12
2 Sam 21.12
1 Kgs 4.12
1 Chr 7.29
BETH SHEMESH (1)
Beth Shemesh (2) Josh 19.22
Beth Shemesh (3) Josh 19.38
Beth Shittah Judg 7.22
Beth Tappuah Josh 15.53
Beth Togarmah
see also Togarmah
Ezek 27.14
38. 6
AV Beth-Shean *see* Beth Shan
AV Bethabara *see* Bethany (1)
Bethanath Josh 19.38
Judg 1.33
Bethanoth Josh 15.59
BETHANY (1)
BETHANY (2)
AV Betharam *see* Beth Haram
Betharbel Hos 10.14
Bethaven Josh 7. 2
18.12
1 Sam 13. 5
14.23
Hos 4.15
5. 8
Bethbarah Judg 7.24
7.24
Bethbiri 1 Chr 4.31
Bethcar 1 Sam 7.11
Bethdagon (1) Josh 15.41
Bethdagon (2) Josh 19.27
Betheden 2 Kgs 19.12
Is 37.12
Amos 1. 5
BETHEL (1)
Bethel (2) Zech 7. 2
Bethel (3) Jer 48.13
Bethemek Josh 19.27
Bether Song 2.17

AV Bethesda *see* Bethzatha
Bethezel Mic 1.11
Bethgader 1 Chr 2.51
Bethgamul Jer 48.23
Bethgilgal Neh 12.29
BETHLEHEM (1)
Bethlehem (2) Josh 19.15
Bethmeon
see also Baal Meon, Beon, Beth Baalmeon
Jer 48.23
Bethmillo Judg 9. 6
9.20
9.20
Bethnimrah
see also Beth Nimrah
Josh 13.27
Bethpazzez Josh 19.21
Bethpelet Josh 15.27
Neh 11.26
Bethpeor Deut 3.29
4.45
34. 6
Josh 13.20
Bethphage Mt 21. 1
Mk 11. 1
Lk 19.29
Bethrapha 1 Chr 4.12
Bethrehob Judg 18.27
2 Sam 10. 6
Bethsaida Mt 11.21
Mk 6.45
8.22
Lk 9.10
10.13
Jn 1.44
12.21
Bethuel (1) Gen 22.22
24.15
24.24
24.47
24.50
25.20
28. 2
28. 5
Bethuel (2)
see also Bethul
1 Chr 4.30
Bethul
see also Bethuel (2)
Josh 19. 4
Bethzatha Jn 5. 2
Bethzur (1) Josh 15.58
2 Chr 11. 7
Neh 3.16
Bethzur (2) 1 Chr 2.45
Betonim Josh 13.26
AV Beulah *see* Happily Married
Bezai (1) Ezra 2. 3
Neh 7. 8
Bezai (2) Neh 10.14
BEZALEL (1)
Bezalel (2) Ezra 10.30
Bezek (1) Judg 1. 4
Bezek (2) 1 Sam 11. 8
Bezer (1) Deut 4.43
Josh 20. 8
21.36
1 Chr 6.78
Bezer (2) 1 Chr 7.37
AV Bichri *see* Bikri
Bidkar 2 Kgs 9.25
Bigtha Esth 1.10
Bigthana Esth 2.21
6. 2
Bigvai (1) Ezra 2. 2
Neh 7. 7
Bigvai (2) Ezra 2. 3
Neh 7. 8
Bigvai (3) Ezra 8. 2
Bigvai (4) Neh 10.14
Bikri 2 Sam 20. 1
20.14
20.21
Bildad Job 2.11
8. 1
18. 1
25. 1
26. 4
42. 9
Bileam 1 Chr 6.70
Bilgah (1) 1 Chr 24. 7
Bilgah (2) Neh 12. 2
12.12
Bilgai Neh 10. 2
BILHAH (1)
Bilhah (2) 1 Chr 4.29
Bilhan (1) Gen 36.27
1 Chr 1.38
Bilhan (2) 1 Chr 7.10

Bilshan Ezra 2. 2
Neh 7. 7
Bimhal 1 Chr 7.33
Binea 1 Chr 8.37
9.43
Binnui (1) Ezra 8.33
Binnui (2) Ezra 10.30
Binnui (3) Ezra 10.38
Binnui (4) Neh 3.24
10. 9
Binnui (5) Neh 7. 8
Binnui (6) Neh 12. 8
12.24
Birsha Gen 14. 2
Birzaith 1 Chr 7.31
Bishlam Ezra 4. 7
Bithiah 1 Chr 4.17
AV Bithron *see* (next) Morning
Bithynia Acts 16. 7
1 Pet 1. 1
Biziothiah Josh 15.28
Biztha Esth 1.10
Blastus Acts 12.20
Boanerges Mk 3.17
BOAZ (1)
Boaz (2) 1 Kgs 7.21
2 Chr 3.17
Bocheru 1 Chr 8.38
9.44
Bochim Judg 2. 1
2. 5
Bohan Josh 15. 6
18.17
AV Booz *see* Boaz
Borashan 1 Sam 30.30
AV Boscath *see* Bozkath
AV Bosor *see* Beor
Bozez 1 Sam 14. 4
Bozkath Josh 15.39
2 Kgs 22. 1
Bozrah (1) Gen 36.31
1 Chr 1.43
Is 34. 6
63. 1
Jer 49.13
49.22
Amos 1.12
Bozrah (2) Jer 48.24
BROAD WALL
Bubastis Ezek 30.17
Bukki (1) 1 Chr 6. 5
6.51
Ezra 7. 4
Bukki (2) Num 34.19
Bukkiah 1 Chr 25. 4
25. 9
BUL
Bunah 1 Chr 2.25
Bunni (1) Neh 9. 4
Bunni (2) Neh 10.14
Bunni (3) Neh 11.15
Buz (1) Gen 22.21
Buz (2) 1 Chr 5.14
Buz (3) Job 32. 2
Buz (4) Jer 25.19
Buzi Ezek 1. 1
Byblos 1 Kgs 5.18
Ezek 27. 9

C

Cabbon Josh 15.40
Cabul (1) Josh 19.27
Cabul (2) 1 Kgs 9.13
CAESAREA
CAESAREA PHILIPPI
CAIAPHAS
CAIN
Cainan Lk 3.36
Calah Gen 10.11
10.12
Calcol 1 Kgs 4.31
1 Chr 2. 6
CALEB (1)
Caleb (2) 1 Chr 2. 9
2.18
2.19
2.24
2.42
2.50
2.50
4. 3
Caleb (3) 1 Chr 4.11
Calneh Amos 6. 2
Calno Is 10. 9
AV Calvary *see* Skull
AV Camon *see* Kamon
CAMP OF DAN

Cana Jn 2. 1
2.11
4.46
21. 2
CANAAN
AV Cananaean *see* Patriot, Simon (2)
Canneh Ezek 27.23
CAPERNAUM
AV Caphtor *see* Crete
Cappadocia Acts 2. 9
1 Pet 1. 1
Carchemish 2 Chr 35.20
Is 10. 9
Jer 46. 2
AV Careah *see* Kareah
AV Carite *see* Bodyguard
Carkas Esth 1.10
CARMEL (1)
Carmel (2) Josh 15.55
1 Sam 15.12
25. 2
25. 2
25. 5
25. 7
25.40
27. 3
2 Sam 2. 2
3. 3
23.24
1 Chr 3. 1
11.26
Carmi (1) Josh 7. 1
7.18
1 Chr 2. 7
4. 1
Carmi (2) Gen 46. 9
Ex 6.14
Num 26. 6
1 Chr 5. 3
Carpus 2 Tim 4.13
Carshena Esth 1.14
Casiphia Ezra 8.17
Casluh Gen 10.14
1 Chr 1.12
AV Castor *see* Twin Gods
Cauda Acts 27.16
AV Cedron *see* Kidron
Cenchreae Acts 18.18
Rom 16. 1
Cephas
see also Peter
Jn 1.42
AV Chalcol *see* Calcol
Chaldean Ezra 5.12
Job 1.17
Ezek 23.23
AV Chaldean *see* Babylonian
AV Chanaan *see* Canaan
AV Charashim *see* (Valley of) Craftsmen
AV Charran *see* Haran
CHEBAR
Chedorlaomer Gen 14. 1
14. 4
14. 5
14.17
Chelal Ezra 10.30
AV Chelluh *see* Cheluhi
Chelub 1 Chr 27.25
AV Chelub *see* Caleb (3)
Cheluhi Ezra 10.34
AV Chemarim *see* (pagan) Priests
CHEMOSH
Chenaanah (1) 1 Kgs 22.11
2 Chr 18.10
Chenaanah (2) 1 Chr 7.10
Chenani Neh 9. 4
Chenaniah (1) 1 Chr 15.22
15.27
Chenaniah (2) 1 Chr 26.29
Chepharammoni Josh 18.24
Chephirah Josh 9.17
18.26
Ezra 2.21
Neh 7.26
Cheran Gen 36.25
1 Chr 1.38
Cherethites 1 Sam 30.14
AV Cherethites
see also Bodyguard
Cherith 1 Kgs 17. 3
17. 5
Cherub Ezra 2.59
Neh 7.61
Chesalon
see also (Mount) Jearim
Josh 15.10
Chesed Gen 22.22
Chesil Josh 15.30
Chesulloth Josh 19.18

AV Chezib *see* Achzib (1)
Chidon 1 Chr 13. 9
Chileab 2 Sam 3. 3
Chilion Ruth 1. 1
1. 5
4. 9
Chilmad Ezek 27.23
Chimham (1) 2 Sam 19.37
19.40
Chimham (2) Jer 41.17
Chinnereth
see also Galilee
Josh 19.35
Chios Acts 20.15
Chislon Num 34.19
Chisloth Tabor Josh 19.12
Chitlish Josh 15.40
AV Chittim *see* Cyprus, Romans
AV Chiun *see* Kaiwan
Chloe 1 Cor 1.11
AV Chorashan *see* Borashan
Chorazin Mt 11.21
Lk 10.13
AV Chozeba *see* Cozeba
CHRIST
AV Chub *see* Kub
AV Chun *see* Kun
AV Chusan-Rishathaim *see* Cushan Rishathaim
Chuza Lk 8. 3
CILICIA
AV Cinneroth *see* Chinnereth, Galilee
AV Cis *see* Kish
CITY OF THE SUN
AV Clauda *see* Cauda
Claudia 2 Tim 4.21
Claudius Acts 11.28
18. 2
Clement Phil 4. 3
Cleopas Lk 24.18
AV Cleophas *see* Clopas
Clopas Jn 19.25
Cnidus Acts 27. 7
Colhozeh Neh 3.15
11. 5
Colossae Col 1. 2
Conaniah (1) 2 Chr 31.12
Conaniah (2) 2 Chr 35. 9
AV Coniah *see* Jehoiachin
AV Cononiah *see* Conaniah (1)
AV Coos *see* Cos
AV Core *see* Korah
CORINTH
CORNELIUS
CORNER GATE
Cos Acts 21. 1
Cosam Lk 3.28
Cozbi Num 25.15
25.18
Cozeba 1 Chr 4.22
Crescens 2 Tim 4.10
CRETE
Crispus Acts 18. 8
1 Cor 1.14
Cush
see also Sudan
Cush (1) Gen 10. 6
10. 7
10. 8
1 Chr 1. 8
1. 9
1.10
Cush (2) Gen 2.13
Cushan Hab 3. 7
Cushan Rishathaim Judg 3. 8
Cushi (1) Jer 36.14
Cushi (2) Zeph 1. 1
Cushite Num 12. 1
Cuth 2 Kgs 17.24
17.30
AV Cuthah *see* Cuth
CYPRUS
Cyrene Mt 27.32
Mk 15.21
Lk 23.26
Acts 2.10
6. 9
11.20
13. 1
AV Cyrenius *see* Quirinius
CYRUS

D

AV Dabareh *see* Daberath
Dabbesheth Josh 19.11
Daberath Josh 19.12
21.28
1 Chr 6.72
Dagon Judg 16.23
1 Sam 5. 2
5. 3
5. 5
5. 7
1 Chr 10.10
Dalmanutha Mk 8.10
Dalmatia 2 Tim 4.10
Dalphon Esth 9. 7
Damaris Acts 17.34
DAMASCUS
Dammim *see* Ephes Dammim, Pas Dammim
DAN (1)
DAN (2)
Danel Ezek 14.14
14.20
28. 3
DANIEL (1)
Daniel (2) 1 Chr 3. 1
Daniel (3) Ezra 8. 2
Neh 10. 2
Dannah Josh 15.49
AV Dara *see* Darda
Darda 1 Kgs 4.31
1 Chr 2. 6
DARIUS (1)
DARIUS (2)
DARIUS (3)
Darkon Ezra 2.55
Neh 7.57
DATHAN
DAVID
DEAD SEA
Debir (1)
see also Kiriath Sepher
Josh 10.38
10.39
11.21
12.13
15. 7
15.15
15.49
21.15
Judg 1.11
1 Chr 6.57
Debir (2) Josh 10. 3
DEBORAH (1)
Deborah (2) Gen 35. 8
AV Decapolis *see* Ten Towns
Dedan (1) Gen 10. 7
1 Chr 1. 9
Is 21.13
Jer 25.19
Ezek 25.13
27.20
38.13
Dedan (2) Gen 25. 3
25. 3
1 Chr 1.32
Jer 49. 8
Delaiah (1) 1 Chr 24. 7
Delaiah (2) Jer 36.12
36.25
Delaiah (3) Ezra 2.59
Neh 7.61
Delaiah (4) 1 Chr 3.24
Delaiah (5) Neh 6.10
DELILAH
Demas Col 4.14
2 Tim 4.10
Phlm 24
Demetrius (1) Acts 19.24
19.38
Demetrius (2) 3 Jn 12
Derbe Acts 14. 6
14.20
14.21
16. 1
20. 4
DESERTED WIFE
DESTROYER
Deuel Num 1. 5
2.10
7.12
10.20
AV Diana *see* Artemis
AV Diblah *see* Riblah
Diblaim Hos 1. 3
Diblathaim *see* Almon Diblathaim, Beth Diblathaim
Dibon (1) Num 21.30
32. 3
32.34
Josh 13. 9
13.17
Is 15. 2
15. 9
Dibon (1) (cont.)
Jer 48.18
48.22
Dibon (2)
see also Dimonah
Neh 11.25
Dibon Gad Num 33.41
Dibri Lev 24.10
AV Didymus *see* Twin
Diklah Gen 10.27
1 Chr 1.21
Dilean Josh 15.38
Dimnah Josh 21.35
AV Dimon *see* Dibon
Dimonah
see also Dibon (2)
Josh 15.22
Dinah Gen 30.21
34. 1
34.11
34.13
34.25
34.26
46.15
AV Dinaite *see* Judge(s)
Dinhabah Gen 36.31
1 Chr 1.43
Dionysius Acts 17.34
Diotrephes 3 Jn 9
AV Diphath *see* Riphath
Dishan Gen 36.20
36.28
36.29
1 Chr 1.38
Dishon (1) Gen 36.20
36.29
1 Chr 1.38
Dishon (2) Gen 36.25
1 Chr 1.38
Dizahab Deut 1. 1
Dodai 1 Chr 27. 2
AV Dodanim *see* Rhodes
Dodavahu 2 Chr 20.37
Dodo (1) Judg 10. 1
Dodo (2) 2 Sam 23. 9
1 Chr 11.12
Dodo (3) 2 Sam 23.24
1 Chr 11.26
Doeg 1 Sam 21. 7
22. 9
22.18
22.18
22.22
Dophkah Num 33.12
Dor
see also Hamoth Dor
Josh 11. 2
12.23
17.11
Judg 1.27
1 Kgs 4.11
1 Chr 7.29
Dorcas
see also Tabitha
Acts 9.36
9.39
Dothan Gen 37.17
37.17
2 Kgs 6.13
DRAGON'S FOUNTAIN
Drusilla Acts 24.24
Dumah (1) Gen 25.14
1 Chr 1.30
Dumah (2) Josh 15.52
Dura Dan 3. 1

E

EAST GATE
Ebal (1) Gen 36.23
1 Chr 1.38
Ebal (2) Deut 11.29
27. 4
27.13
Josh 8.30
8.33
Ebal (3) 1 Chr 1.22
Ebed (1) Judg 9.26
9.31
Ebed (2) Ezra 8. 2
Ebedmelech Jer 38. 7
38. 8
38.10
38.11
39.16
Ebenezer
see also Stone Of Help
1 Sam 4. 1
5. 1
Eber (1) Gen 10.24
10.25
11.14
11.16
1 Chr 1.18
1.19
1.25
Lk 3.35
Eber (2) Num 24.24
Eber (3) 1 Chr 5.13
Eber (4) 1 Chr 8.12
Eber (5) 1 Chr 8.22
Eber (6) Neh 12.12
Ebez Josh 19.20
Ebiasaph 1 Chr 6.23
6.37
9.19
Ebron Josh 19.28
AV Ebronah *see* Abronah
Ecbatana Ezra 6. 2
AV Ed *see* Witness
Eden
see also Betheden
EDEN (1)
Eden (2) Ezek 27.23
Eden (3) 2 Chr 31.15
Eden (4) 2 Chr 29.12
Eder (1) Gen 35.21
Eder (2) Josh 15.21
Eder (3) 1 Chr 23.23
24.30
Eder (4) 1 Chr 8.15
EDOM
Edrei Num 21.33
Deut 1. 4
3. 1
3.10
Josh 12. 4
13.12
13.31
19.37
Eglah 2 Sam 3. 5
1 Chr 3. 1
Eglaim Is 15. 8
Eglath Shelishiyah Is 15. 5
Jer 48.34
Eglon (1) Judg 3.12
3.13
3.14
3.15
3.17
3.19
Eglon (2) Josh 10. 3
10. 5
10.23
10.34
10.36
10.37
12.12
15.39
EGYPT
Ehi Gen 46.21
EHUD (1)
Ehud (2) 1 Chr 7.10
8. 6
AV Eked *see* Shepherds' Camp
Eker 1 Chr 2.26
EKRON
El Gen 33.20
AV El-Bethel *see* (God of) Bethel
AV El-Elohe-Israel *see* El
Ela 1 Kgs 4.18
Elah (1) Gen 36.40
1 Chr 1.52
Elah (2) 1 Sam 17. 2
17.19
21. 9
Elah (3) 1 Kgs 16. 6
16. 8
16. 9
16.10
16.13
16.14
Elah (4) 2 Kgs 15.30
17. 1
18. 1
Elah (5) 1 Chr 4.15
4.15
Elah (6) 1 Chr 9. 7
ELAM (1)
Elam (2) 1 Chr 8.24
Elam (3) 1 Chr 26. 3
Elam (4) Ezra 2. 3
Neh 7. 8
Elam (5) Ezra 2.21
Neh 7.26
Elam (6) Ezra 8. 2
Elam (7)
perhaps the same as (6).
Ezra 10. 2
10.26

Elam (8)	Neh	10.14
Elam (9)	Neh	12.42
Elasah (1)	Ezra	10.22
Elasah (2)	Jer	29. 3
Elath	Deut	2. 8
	1 Kgs	9.26
	2 Kgs	14.22
		16. 6
		16. 6
	2 Chr	8.17
		26. 2
Eldaah	Gen	25. 4
	1 Chr	1.33
Eldad	Num	11.26
		11.27
Elead	1 Chr	7.21
Eleadah	1 Chr	7.20
Elealeh	Num	32. 3
		32.37
	Is	15. 4
		16. 9
	Jer	48.34
Eleasah (1)	1 Chr	2.39
Eleasah (2)	1 Chr	8.37
		8.37
		9.43
		9.43
ELEAZAR (1)		
Eleazar (2)	1 Sam	7. 1
Eleazar (3)	2 Sam	23. 9
		23.10
	1 Chr	11.12
Eleazar (4)	1 Chr	23.21
		23.22
		24.28
		24.28
Eleazar (5)	Neh	12.42
Eleazar (6)	Ezra	8.33
Eleazar (7)	Ezra	10.25
Eleazar (8)	Mt	1.12
Eleoenai	1 Chr	7. 8
AV Eleph *see* Haeleph		
Elhanan (1)	2 Sam	21.19
	1 Chr	20. 5
Elhanan (2)	2 Sam	23.24
	1 Chr	11.26
ELI (1)		
Eliab (1)	Num	1. 5
		2. 3
		7.12
		10.16
Eliab (2)	Num	16. 1
		26. 8
	Deut	11. 6
Eliab (3)		
see also Elihu (4)		
	1 Sam	16. 6
		17.13
		17.28
	1 Chr	2.13
	2 Chr	11.18
Eliab (4)		
see also Eliel (7), Elihu (1)		
	1 Chr	6.27
Eliab (5)	1 Chr	12. 9
Eliab (6)	1 Chr	15.17
		16. 5
Eliada (1)	2 Sam	5.16
	1 Chr	3. 8
Eliada (2)	2 Chr	17.17
Eliada (3)	1 Kgs	11.23
AV Eliadah *see* Eliada (3)		
AV Eliah *see* Elijah (2), (4)		
Eliahba	2 Sam	23.24
	1 Chr	11.26
Eliakim (1)	2 Kgs	18.18
		18.26
		18.37
		19. 2
	Is	22.20
		36. 3
		36.11
		36.22
		37. 2
Eliakim (2)		
see also Jehoiakim		
	2 Kgs	23.34
	2 Chr	36. 4
Eliakim (3)	Neh	12.41
Eliakim (4)	Mt	1.12
Eliakim (5)	Lk	3.30
Eliam (1)		
see also Ammiel (4)		
	2 Sam	11. 3
Eliam (2)	2 Sam	23.24
AV Elias *see* Elijah (1)		
Eliasaph (1)	Num	1. 5
		2.10
		7.12
		10.20
Eliasaph (2)	Num	3.24
ELIASHIB (1)		
Eliashib (2)	1 Chr	3.24
Eliashib (3)	1 Chr	24. 7
Eliashib (4)	Ezra	10.24
Eliashib (5)	Ezra	10.27
Eliashib (6)	Ezra	10.34
Eliathah	1 Chr	25. 4
		25. 9
Elidad	Num	34.19
Eliehoenai (1)	1 Chr	26. 3
Eliehoenai (2)	Ezra	8. 2
Eliel (1)	1 Chr	11.26
Eliel (2)	1 Chr	11.26
Eliel (3)	1 Chr	12. 9
Eliel (4)	1 Chr	15. 9
		15.11
Eliel (5)	2 Chr	31.13
Eliel (6)	1 Chr	5.24
Eliel (7)		
see also Eliab (4), Elihu (1)		
	1 Chr	6.34
Eliel (8)	1 Chr	8.20
Eliel (9)	1 Chr	8.22
Elienai	1 Chr	8.20
Eliezer (1)	Gen	15. 2
		15. 4
Eliezer (2)	Ex	18. 3
		18. 4
	1 Chr	23.15
		23.17
		26.25
		26.25
Eliezer (3)	1 Chr	7. 8
Eliezer (4)	1 Chr	15.23
Eliezer (5)	Ezra	10.18
Eliezer (6)	1 Chr	27.16
Eliezer (7)	2 Chr	20.37
Eliezer (8)	Ezra	8.16
		10.23
Eliezer (9)	Ezra	10.31
Eliezer (10)	Lk	3.29
Elihoreph	1 Kgs	4. 3
Elihu (1)		
see also Eliab (4), Eliel (7)		
	1 Sam	1. 1
Elihu (2)	1 Chr	12.20
Elihu (3)	1 Chr	26. 6
Elihu (4)		
see also Eliab (3)		
	1 Chr	27.16
Elihu (5)	Job	32. 2
		32. 2
		32. 4
		32. 6
ELIJAH (1)		
Elijah (2)	1 Chr	8.27
Elijah (3)	Ezra	10.21
Elijah (4)	Ezra	10.26
Elika	2 Sam	23.24
Elim	Ex	15.27
		16. 1
		16. 1
	Num	33. 9
		33.10
Elimelech	Ruth	1. 1
		1. 3
		2. 1
		4. 1
		4. 3
		4. 9
Elioenai		
see also Eleoenai, Eliehoenai		
Elioenai (1)	1 Chr	3.23
		3.24
Elioenai (2)	1 Chr	4.34
Elioenai (3)	Ezra	10.22
Elioenai (4)	Ezra	10.27
Elioenai (5)	Neh	12.41
Eliphal	1 Chr	11.26
Eliphaz (1)	Gen	36. 4
		36.10
		36.15
	1 Chr	1.35
		1.36
Eliphaz (2)	Job	2.11
		4. 1
		15. 1
		22. 1
		42. 7
		42. 9
Eliphelehu	1 Chr	15.17
Eliphelet (1)	2 Sam	5.16
	1 Chr	3. 8
		14. 7
Eliphelet (2)	2 Sam	23.24
Eliphelet (3)	1 Chr	8.39
Eliphelet (4)	Ezra	8. 2
Eliphelet (5)	Ezra	10.33
AV Eliseus *see* Elisha		
ELISHA		
Elishah		
see also Cyprus		
	Gen	10. 4
	1 Chr	1. 7
Elishama (1)	Num	1. 5
		2.18
		7.12
		10.22
	1 Chr	7.26
Elishama (2)	2 Sam	5.16
	1 Chr	3. 8
		14. 7
Elishama (3)	Jer	36.12
		36.20
		36.21
Elishama (4)	2 Kgs	25.25
	Jer	41. 1
Elishama (5)	1 Chr	2.36
		2.41
Elishama (6)	2 Chr	17. 8
Elishaphat	2 Chr	23. 1
Elisheba	Ex	6.23
Elishua	2 Sam	5.15
	1 Chr	3. 6
		14. 5
Eliud	Mt	1.12
ELIZABETH		
Elizaphan (1)		
see also Elzaphan		
	Num	3.30
	1 Chr	15. 8
	2 Chr	29.12
Elizaphan (2)	Num	34.19
Elizur	Num	1. 5
		2.10
		7.12
		10.18
ELKANAH (1)		
Elkanah (2)	1 Chr	6.23
		6.25
		6.36
Elkanah (3)	2 Chr	28. 7
Elkanah (4)	1 Chr	12. 3
Elkanah (5)	1 Chr	9.14
Elkanah (6)	1 Chr	15.23
Elkanah (7)	1 Chr	6.26
		6.35
Elkanah (8)	Ex	6.24
Elkosh	Nah	1. 1
Ellasar	Gen	14. 1
		14. 9
Elmadam	Lk	3.28
Elnaam	1 Chr	11.26
Elnathan (1)	2 Kgs	24. 8
	Jer	26.22
		36.12
		36.25
Elnathan (2)	Ezra	8.16
Elnathan (3)	Ezra	8.16
Elnathan (4)	Ezra	8.16
Elon (1)	Gen	46.14
	Num	26.26
Elon (2)	Gen	26.34
		36. 2
Elon (3)	Judg	12.11
		12.13
Elon (4)	Josh	19.43
	1 Kgs	4. 9
AV Eloth *see* Elath		
Elpaal	1 Chr	8.11
		8.12
		8.17
Elparan	Gen	14. 6
Elpelet	1 Chr	3. 6
		14. 5
Eltekeh	Josh	19.44
		21.23
Eltekon	Josh	15.59
Eltolad	Josh	15.30
		19. 4
ELUL		
Eluzai	1 Chr	12. 3
Elymas	Acts	13. 8
		13.11
Elzabad (1)	1 Chr	12. 9
Elzabad (2)	1 Chr	26. 6
Elzaphan		
see also Elizaphan (1)		
	Ex	6.22
	Lev	10. 4
Emek Keziz	Josh	18.21
Emim	Gen	14. 5
	Deut	2.10
		2.11
AV Emmanuel *see* Immanuel		
Emmaus	Lk	24.13
AV Emmor *see* Hamor		
AV En-Hakkore *see* Hakkore		
Enaim	Gen	38.14
		38.21
Enam	Josh	15.34
Enan		
see also Hazar Enan		
	Num	1. 5
		2.25
		7.12
		10.27
Endor	Josh	17.11
	1 Sam	28. 7
	Ps	83.10
AV Eneas *see* Aeneas		
Eneglaim	Ezek	47.10
Engannim (1)	Josh	15.34
Engannim (2)	Josh	19.21
		21.29
Engedi		
see also Hazazon Tamar		
	Josh	15.62
	1 Sam	23.29
		24. 1
	2 Chr	20. 2
	Song	1.14
	Ezek	47.10
Enhaddah	Josh	19.21
Enhazor	Josh	19.37
Enmishpat		
see also Kadesh (1)		
	Gen	14. 7
ENMITY		
ENOCH (1)		
Enoch (2)	Gen	4.17
		4.18
Enon	Ezek	47.17
		48. 1
Enosh	Gen	4.26
		5. 6
		5. 9
	1 Chr	1. 1
	Lk	3.38
Enrimmon	Neh	11.29
Enrogel	Josh	15. 7
		18.16
	2 Sam	17.17
	1 Kgs	1. 9
Enshemesh	Josh	15. 7
		18.17
Entappuah	Josh	17. 7
Epaenetus	Rom	16. 5
Epaphras	Col	1. 7
		4.12
	Phlm	23
Epaphroditus	Phil	2.25
		4.18
Ephah (2)	Gen	25. 4
	1 Chr	1.33
	Is	60. 6
Ephah (3)	1 Chr	2.47
Ephah (4)	1 Chr	2.46
Ephai	Jer	40. 8
Epher (1)	Gen	25. 4
	1 Chr	1.33
Epher (2)	1 Chr	4.17
Epher (3)	1 Chr	5.24
Ephes Dammim		
see also Pas Dammim		
	1 Sam	17. 1
EPHESUS		
Ephlal	1 Chr	2.37
Ephod (2)	Num	34.19
EPHRAIM (1)		
Ephraim (2)	2 Sam	18. 6
Ephraim (3)	2 Sam	13.23
	Jn	11.54
EPHRAIM GATE		
AV Ephrain *see* Ephron		
Ephrath (1)		
see also Bethlehem (1)		
	Gen	35.16
		35.19
		48. 7
		48. 7
		48. 7
	1 Sam	17.12
	Mic	5. 2
Ephrath (2)		
see also (1)		
	Ruth	1. 1
		4.11
Ephrath (3)	1 Chr	2.19
		2.50
		4. 3
Ephrath (4)		
Perhaps the same as (3)		
	1 Chr	2.24
EPHRON (1)		
Ephron (2)	Josh	15. 9
Ephron (3)	2 Chr	13.19
EPICUREAN		
Er (1)	Gen	38. 3
		38. 6
		38. 7
		38. 8

Er (1) (cont.)		
	Gen	46.12
	Num	26.19
	1 Chr	2. 3
		2. 3
Er (2)	1 Chr	4.21
Er (3)	Lk	3.28
Eran	Num	26.36
Erastus (1)	Rom	16.23
Erastus (2)	Acts	19.22
	2 Tim	4.20
Erech	Gen	10.10
	Ezra	4. 9
Eri	Gen	46.16
	Num	26.16
AV Esaias *see* Isaiah		
Esarhaddon	2 Kgs	19.37
	Ezra	4. 2
	Is	37.38
ESAU		
AV Esek *see* Quarrel		
Eshan	Josh	15.52
Eshbaal		
see also Ishbosheth		
	1 Chr	8.33
		9.39
Eshban	Gen	36.25
	1 Chr	1.38
Eshcol (1)	Gen	14.13
		14.24
Eshcol (2)	Num	13.23
		13.24
		32. 9
	Deut	1.24
Eshek	1 Chr	8.39
AV Eshkalon *see* Ashkelon		
Eshtaol	Josh	15.33
		19.41
	Judg	13.25
		16.31
		18. 2
		18. 8
		18.11
	1 Chr	2.53
Eshtemoa	Josh	15.50
		21.14
	1 Sam	30.28
	1 Chr	4.17
		4.19
		6.57
Eshton	1 Chr	4.11
Esli	Lk	3.25
AV Esrom *see* Hezron		
ESTHER		
Etam (1)	Judg	15. 8
		15.11
Etam (2)	1 Chr	4. 3
		4. 3
Etam (3)	1 Chr	4.32
Etam (4)	2 Chr	11. 6
Etham	Ex	13.20
	Num	33. 6
Ethan (1)	1 Kgs	4.31
Ethan (2)	1 Chr	2. 6
		2. 8
Ethan (3)	1 Chr	6.42
Ethan (4)	1 Chr	6.44
		6.44
		15.17
ETHANIM		
Ethbaal	1 Kgs	16.31
Ether	Josh	15.42
		19. 7
Ethiopia		
see also Cushite, Seba, Sudan		
	Acts	8.27
		8.27
Ethkazin	Josh	19.13
Ethnan	1 Chr	4. 7
Ethni	1 Chr	6.41
Eubulus	2 Tim	4.21
Eunice	2 Tim	1. 5
Euodia	Phil	4. 2
EUPHRATES (1)		
EUPHRATES (2)		
Eutychus	Acts	20. 9
		20. 9
EVE		
Evi	Num	31. 8
	Josh	13.21
Evilmerodach	2 Kgs	25.27
		25.28
	Jer	52.31
		52.32
Ezbai	1 Chr	11.26
Ezbon (1)	Gen	46.16
Ezbon (2)	1 Chr	7. 7
AV Ezekias *see* Hezekiah		
Ezekiel	Ezek	1. 1
		29.21
AV Ezel *see* Pile (of stones)		
Ezem	Josh	15.29
		19. 3
	1 Chr	4.29
Ezer		
see also Romamti Ezer		
Ezer (1)	Gen	36.20
		36.27
		36.29
	1 Chr	1.38
Ezer (2)	1 Chr	4. 3
		4. 3
Ezer (3)	1 Chr	7.21
Ezer (4)	1 Chr	12. 9
Ezer (5)	Neh	3.19
Ezer (6)	Neh	12.42
Eziongeber	Num	33.15
	Deut	2. 8
	1 Kgs	9.26
		22.48
	2 Chr	8.17
		20.36
EZRA (1)		
Ezra (2)	Neh	12. 2
Ezra (3)	Neh	12.12
AV Ezra *see* Ezrah		
Ezrah	1 Chr	4.17
Ezrahite	1 Kgs	4.31
Ezri	1 Chr	27.25

F

AV Fair Havens *see* Safe Harbours		
FELIX		
FESTUS		
FIELD OF BLOOD		
FIELD OF SWORDS		
FISH GATE		
Fortunatus	1 Cor	16.17
FOUNDATION GATE		
FOUNTAIN GATE		

G

GAAL		
Gaash	Josh	24.30
	Judg	2. 9
	2 Sam	23.24
	1 Chr	11.26
AV Gaba *see* Geba		
Gabbai	Neh	11. 8
Gabbatha	Jn	19.13
Gabriel	Dan	8.16
		8.17
		9.21
	Lk	1.19
		1.26
Gad		
see also Dibon Gad		
GAD (1)		
GAD (2)		
Gad (3)	Is	65.11
Gadara	Mt	8.28
AV Gadarene *see* Gerasa		
Gaddah *see* Hazar Gaddah		
Gaddi	Num	13. 3
Gaddiel	Num	13. 3
Gadi	2 Kgs	15.14
		15.17
Gaham	Gen	22.24
Gahar	Ezra	2.43
	Neh	7.46
Gaius (1)	Rom	16.23
	1 Cor	1.14
Gaius (2)	Acts	19.29
Gaius (3)	Acts	20. 4
Gaius (4)	3 Jn	1
Galal (1)	1 Chr	9.14
Galal (2)	1 Chr	9.14
	Neh	11.17
Galatia	Acts	16. 6
		18.23
	1 Cor	16. 1
	Gal	1. 2
		3. 1
	2 Tim	4.10
	1 Pet	1. 1
Galeed		
see also Jegar Sahadutha, Mizpah (4)		
	Gen	31.47
		31.48
GALILEE		
Gallim	1 Sam	25.44
	Is	10.30
Gallio	Acts	18.12
		18.14
		18.17
Gamad	Ezek	27.11
Gamaliel (1)	Num	1. 5
		2.18
		7.12
		10.23
Gamaliel (2)	Acts	5.34
		5.39
		22. 3
Gamul	1 Chr	24. 7
Gareb (1)	2 Sam	23.24
	1 Chr	11.26
Gareb (2)	Jer	31.39
Garm	1 Chr	4.19
AV Gashmu *see* Geshem		
Gatam	Gen	36.10
		36.16
	1 Chr	1.36
GATH		
Gath Hepher	Josh	19.13
	2 Kgs	14.25
Gath Rimmon		
see also Gathrimmon (2)		
	1 Chr	6.69
Gathrimmon (1)	Josh	19.45
Gathrimmon (2)		
see also Gath Rimmon		
	Josh	21.24
Gathrimmon (3)	Josh	21.25
GAZA		
AV Gazathite (Gazite) *see* Gaza		
Gazez (1)	1 Chr	2.46
Gazez (2)	1 Chr	2.46
Gazzam	Ezra	2.43
	Neh	7.46
GEBA		
Gebal	Ps	83. 7
AV Gebal *see* Byblos, Gebalites		
Gebalites	Josh	13. 5
Geber	1 Kgs	4.19
Gebim	Is	10.31
GEDALIAH (1)		
Gedaliah (2)	1 Chr	25. 3
		25. 9
Gedaliah (3)	Ezra	10.18
Gedaliah (4)	Jer	38. 1
Gedaliah (5)	Zeph	1. 1
AV Gedeon *see* Gideon		
Geder	Josh	12.13
	1 Chr	27.25
Gederah (1)	Josh	15.36
	1 Chr	12. 3
Gederah (2)	1 Chr	4.23
Gederoth	Josh	15.41
	2 Chr	28.18
Gederothaim	Josh	15.36
Gedor (1)	Josh	15.58
Gedor (2)		
perhaps the same as (1).		
	1 Chr	12. 3
Gedor (3)	1 Chr	8.31
		9.37
Gedor (4)		
perhaps the same as (1).		
	1 Chr	4. 3
		4.17
GEHAZI		
Geliloth	Josh	18.17
		22.10
		22.11
Gemalli	Num	13. 3
Gemariah (1)	Jer	29. 3
Gemariah (2)	Jer	36.10
		36.11
		36.12
		36.25
Gennesaret	Mt	14.34
	Mk	6.53
	Lk	5. 1
Genubath	1 Kgs	11.20
Gera	Gen	46.21
	Judg	3.15
	2 Sam	16. 5
		19.16
	1 Kgs	2. 8
	1 Chr	8. 3
		8. 5
		8. 6
		8. 6
GERAR		
Gerasa	Mk	5. 1
	Lk	8.26
AV Gergesenes *see* Gerasa		
Gerizim	Deut	11.29
		27.12
	Josh	8.33
	Judg	9. 7
Gershom		
see also Gershon		
Gershom (1)	Ex	2.22
		18. 3
		18. 3
Gershom (1) (cont.)		
	Judg	18.30
	1 Chr	23.15
		23.16
		26.24
		26.25
Gershom (2)	Ezra	8. 2
GERSHON		
Geshan	1 Chr	2.47
Geshem	Neh	2.19
		6. 1
		6. 2
		6. 6
GESHUR (1)		
Geshur (2)	Josh	13. 2
	1 Sam	27. 8
Gether	Gen	10.23
	1 Chr	1.17
Gethsemane	Mt	26.36
	Mk	14.32
Geuel	Num	13. 3
GEZER		
Giah	2 Sam	2.24
Gibbar	Ezra	2. 3
Gibbethon	Josh	19.44
		21.23
	1 Kgs	15.27
		16.15
		16.17
Gibea	1 Chr	2.49
GIBEAH (1)		
Gibeah (2)	Josh	15.57
Gibeah (3)	Josh	24.33
AV Gibeath-Haaraloth *see* Circumcision Hill		
GIBEON		
AV Giblite *see* Gebal		
Giddalti	1 Chr	25. 4
		25. 9
Giddel (1)	Ezra	2.43
	Neh	7.46
Giddel (2)	Ezra	2.55
	Neh	7.57
GIDEON		
Gideoni	Num	1. 5
		2.18
		7.12
		10.24
Gidom	Judg	20.45
Gihon (1)	Gen	2.13
Gihon (2)	1 Kgs	1.33
		1.38
		1.45
	2 Chr	32.30
		33.14
Gilalai	Neh	12.36
Gilboa	1 Sam	28. 4
		31. 1
		31. 8
	2 Sam	1. 6
		1.21
		21.12
	1 Chr	10. 1
		10. 8
GILEAD (1)		
GILEAD (2)		
Gilead (3)	Judg	7. 3
Gilead (4)	Judg	11. 1
Gilead (5)	1 Chr	5.14
GILGAL (1)		
Gilgal (2)	2 Kgs	2. 1
		4.38
Gilgal (3)	Josh	15. 7
Gilgal (4)	Deut	11.30
Gilo	2 Sam	15.12
		23.24
Giloh	Josh	15.51
AV Gilonite *see* Gilo		
Gimzo	2 Chr	28.18
Ginath	1 Kgs	16.21
Ginnethoi	Neh	12. 2
Ginnethon	Neh	10. 2
		12.12
Girgashites	Gen	10.16
		15.21
	Deut	7. 1
	Josh	3.10
		24.11
	1 Chr	1.14
	Neh	9. 8
Girzi	1 Sam	27. 8
Gishpa	Neh	11.21
AV Gittah Hepher *see* Gath Hepher		
Gittaim (1)	2 Sam	4. 3
Gittaim (2)	Neh	11.33
AV Gittite *see* Gath		
Gizon	1 Chr	11.26
Goah	Jer	31.39
Gob	2 Sam	21.18
		21.19
GOG (1)		

Name	Book	Ref
Gog (2)	1 Chr	5. 4
Goiim (1)	Gen	14. 1
		14. 9
Goiim (2)	Josh	12.23
Golan	Deut	4.43
	Josh	20. 8
		21.27
	1 Chr	6.71
Golgotha	Mt	27.33
	Mk	15.22
	Jn	19.17
GOLIATH		
Gomer (1)	Gen	10. 2
		10. 3
	1 Chr	1. 5
		1. 6
Gomer (2)	Ezek	38. 6
Gomer (3)	Hos	1. 3
		1. 6
		1. 8
GOMORRAH		
GOSHEN (1)		
Goshen (2)	Josh	10.41
		11.16
		15.51
Gozan	2 Kgs	17. 6
		18.11
		19.12
	1 Chr	5.26
	Is	37.12
Graves Of Craving *see* Kibroth Hattaavah		
AV Grecia *see* Greece		
GREECE		
GUARD GATE		
Gudgodah	Deut	10. 7
Guni (1)	Gen	46.24
	Num	26.48
	1 Chr	7.13
Guni (2)	1 Chr	5.15
Gur	2 Kgs	9.27
Gurbaal	2 Chr	26. 7

H

Name	Book	Ref
Haahashtari	1 Chr	4. 6
Habaiah	Ezra	2.61
Habakkuk	Hab	1. 1
		3. 1
Habazziniah	Jer	35. 3
Habor	2 Kgs	17. 6
		18.11
	1 Chr	5.26
Hacaliah	Neh	1. 1
		10. 1
Haccherem *see* Beth Haccherem		
Hachilah	1 Sam	23.19
		26. 1
		26. 3
Hachmon	1 Chr	11.11
Hachmoni	1 Chr	27.32
HADAD (1)		
Hadad (2)	Gen	25.15
	1 Chr	1.30
Hadad (3)	Gen	36.31
	1 Chr	1.43
Hadad (4)	Gen	36.31
	1 Chr	1.43
Hadad-Rimmon	Zech	12.11
HADADEZER		
AV Hadar *see* Hadad		
AV Hadarezer *see* Hadadezer		
Hadashah	Josh	15.37
Hadassah		
see also Esther		
	Esth	2. 7
Hadattah *see* Hazor Hadattah		
HADES		
Hadid	Ezra	2.21
	Neh	7.26
		11.34
Hadlai	2 Chr	28.12
Hadoram	Gen	10.27
	1 Chr	1.21
Hadrach	Zech	9. 1
		9. 2
Haeleph	Josh	18.28
Hagab	Ezra	2.43
Hagaba	Neh	7.46
Hagabah	Ezra	2.43
HAGAR		
AV Hagarenes (Hagarite(s)) *see* Hagrite(s)		
HAGGAI		
Haggan *see* Beth Haggan		
Haggi	Gen	46.16
	Num	26.15
Haggiah	1 Chr	6.30

Name	Book	Ref
Haggidgad *see* Hor Haggidgad		
Haggith	2 Sam	3. 4
	1 Kgs	1. 5
		1.11
		2.13
	1 Chr	3. 1
Hagri	1 Chr	11.26
Hagrite	1 Chr	5.10
		5.19
		5.20
		27.25
	Ps	83. 6
Hahiroth *see* Pi Hahiroth		
AV Hai *see* Ai		
Hakkatan	Ezra	8. 2
Hakkore	Judg	15.19
Hakkoz	1 Chr	24. 7
	Ezra	2.61
	Neh	3. 4
		3.21
		7.63
Hakupha	Ezra	2.43
	Neh	7.46
Halah	2 Kgs	17. 6
		18.11
	1 Chr	5.26
Halak	Josh	11.17
		12. 7
Halhul	Josh	15.58
Hali	Josh	19.25
Hallohesh (1)	Neh	3.12
Hallohesh (2)	Neh	10.14
HAM (1)		
Ham (2)	Gen	14. 5
HAMAN		
HAMATH		
AV Hamath-Zobah *see* Hamath, Zobah		
Hamathites	Gen	10.18
	1 Chr	1.16
Hammath	Josh	19.35
AV Hammeah *see* (the) Hundred		
Hammedatha	Esth	3. 1
		3.10
		8. 5
		9. 7
		9.24
AV Hammelech *see* Prince		
Hammolecheth	1 Chr	7.18
Hammon (1)	Josh	19.28
Hammon (2)	1 Chr	6.76
Hammoth Dor	Josh	21.32
Hammuel	1 Chr	4.26
AV Hamon-Gog *see* (Valley of) Gog's (Army)		
AV Hamonah *see* (the) Army		
HAMOR		
Hamran	1 Chr	1.38
Hamul	Gen	46.12
	Num	26.19
	1 Chr	2. 5
Hamutal	2 Kgs	23.31
		24.18
	Jer	52. 1
AV Hanameel *see* Hanamel		
Hanamel	Jer	32. 7
		32. 8
		32. 9
		32.12
Hanan		
see also Baal Hanan, Beth Hanan		
Hanan (1)	1 Chr	8.23
Hanan (2)	1 Chr	8.38
		9.44
Hanan (3)	1 Chr	11.26
Hanan (4)	Ezra	2.43
	Neh	7.46
Hanan (5)	Neh	8. 7
Hanan (6)	Neh	10. 9
		13.13
Hanan (7)	Neh	10.14
Hanan (8)	Neh	10.14
Hanan (9)	Jer	35. 4
AV Hananeel *see* Hananel		
Hananel	Neh	3. 1
		12.39
	Jer	31.38
	Zech	14.10
Hanani (1)	1 Chr	25. 4
		25. 9
Hanani (2)	2 Chr	16. 7
Hanani (3)	1 Kgs	16. 1
	2 Chr	19. 2
		20.34
Hanani (4)	Ezra	10.20
Hanani (5)	Neh	1. 2
		7. 2
Hanani (6)	Neh	12.36
Hananiah (1)	Jer	28. 1
		28. 5

Name	Book	Ref
Hananiah (1) (cont.)		
	Jer	28.10
		28.13
		28.15
		28.17
Hananiah (2)		
see also Shadrach		
	Dan	1. 6
		1.19
		2.17
Hananiah (3)	1 Chr	25. 4
		25. 9
Hananiah (4)	2 Chr	26.11
Hananiah (5)	Jer	36.12
Hananiah (6)	Jer	37.13
Hananiah (7)	1 Chr	8.24
Hananiah (8)	1 Chr	3.19
		3.21
Hananiah (9)	Ezra	10.28
Hananiah (10)	Neh	3. 8
Hananiah (11)	Neh	3.30
Hananiah (12)	Neh	7. 2
		7. 2
Hananiah (13)	Neh	10.14
Hananiah (14)	Neh	12.12
		12.41
Hanes	Is	30. 4
HANNAH		
Hannathon	Josh	19.14
Hanniel (1)	Num	34.19
Hanniel (2)	1 Chr	7.39
Hanoch (1)	Gen	25. 4
	1 Chr	1.33
Hanoch (2)	Gen	46. 9
	Ex	6.14
	Num	26. 5
	1 Chr	5. 3
Hanun (1)	2 Sam	10. 1
		10. 2
		10. 4
	1 Chr	19. 1
		19. 2
		19. 2
		19. 4
		19. 6
Hanun (2)	Neh	3.13
Hanun (3)	Neh	3.30
Hapharaim	Josh	19.19
HAPPILY MARRIED		
Happizzez	1 Chr	24. 7
Happuch *see* Keren Happuch		
Hara	1 Chr	5.26
Haradah	Num	33.15
Haram *see* Beth Haram		
Haran		
see also Beth Haran		
HARAN (1)		
Haran (2)	Gen	11.26
		11.27
		11.27
		11.28
		11.29
		11.31
Haran (3)	1 Chr	23. 9
Haran (4)	1 Chr	2.46
		2.46
Harar	2 Sam	23.11
		23.24
	1 Chr	11.26
Harbel	Num	34.11
Harbona	Esth	1.10
Harbonah	Esth	7. 9
Hareph	1 Chr	2.51
AV Hareth *see* Hereth		
Harhaiah	Neh	3. 8
Harhas	2 Kgs	22.14
	2 Chr	34.22
Harhur	Ezra	2.43
	Neh	7.46
Harim (1)	1 Chr	24. 7
Harim (2)	Ezra	2.21
		10.31
	Neh	3.11
		7.26
Harim (3)	Ezra	2.36
		10.21
	Neh	7.39
		12.12
Harim (4)	Neh	10. 2
Harim (5)	Neh	10.14
Hariph (1)	1 Chr	12. 3
Hariph (2)	Neh	7. 8
Hariph (3)	Neh	10.14
HARMLESS DRAGON		
Harnepher	1 Chr	7.36
Harod	Judg	7. 1
	2 Sam	23.24
	1 Chr	11.26
Haroeh	1 Chr	2.52
AV Harorite *see* (from) Harod		

Name	Book	Ref
Harosheth-Of-The-Gentiles	Judg	4. 2
		4.13
		4.16
Harsha		
see also Tel Harsha		
	Ezra	2.43
	Neh	7.46
AV Harsith *see* Potsherd		
Harum	1 Chr	4. 8
Harumaph	Neh	3.10
Haruz	2 Kgs	21.19
Hasadiah	1 Chr	3.20
Hashabiah (1)	1 Chr	6.45
Hashabiah (2)	1 Chr	9.14
Hashabiah (3)	1 Chr	25. 3
Hashabiah (4)	1 Chr	25. 9
Hashabiah (5)	1 Chr	26.30
Hashabiah (6)	1 Chr	27.16
Hashabiah (7)	2 Chr	35. 9
Hashabiah (8)	Ezra	8.19
Hashabiah (9)	Ezra	8.24
Hashabiah (10)	Neh	3.17
Hashabiah (11)	Neh	10. 9
Hashabiah (12)	Neh	11.15
Hashabiah (13)	Neh	11.22
Hashabiah (14)	Neh	12.12
Hashabiah (15)	Neh	12.24
Hashabnah	Neh	10.14
Hashabneiah (1)	Neh	3.10
Hashabneiah (2)	Neh	9. 5
Hashbaddanah	Neh	8. 4
Hashem	1 Chr	11.26
Hashmonah	Num	33.15
Hashubah	1 Chr	3.20
Hashum (1)	Ezra	2. 3
		10.33
	Neh	7. 8
Hashum (2)	Neh	8. 4
Hashum (3)	Neh	10.14
AV Hasrah *see* Harhas		
Hassenaah	Neh	3. 3
Hassenuah (1)	1 Chr	9. 7
Hassenuah (2)	Neh	11. 9
Hasshub (1)	1 Chr	9.14
	Neh	11.15
Hasshub (2)	Neh	3.11
Hasshub (3)	Neh	3.23
Hasshub (4)	Neh	10.14
Hassophereth	Ezra	2.55
Hasupha	Ezra	2.43
	Neh	7.46
Hathach	Esth	4. 5
		4. 6
		4. 8
		4. 9
Hathath	1 Chr	4.13
Hatipha	Ezra	2.43
	Neh	7.46
Hatita	Ezra	2.40
	Neh	7.43
Hattaavah *see* Kibroth Hattaavah		
Hattil	Ezra	2.55
	Neh	7.57
Hattush (1)	1 Chr	3.22
Hattush (2)	Ezra	8. 2
Hattush (3)	Neh	3.10
Hattush (4)	Neh	10. 2
Hattush (5)	Neh	12. 2
Hauran	Ezek	47.16
		47.18
Havilah (1)	Gen	2.11
Havilah (2)	Gen	10. 7
	1 Chr	1. 9
Havilah (3)	Gen	10.29
	1 Chr	1.23
Havilah (4)	Gen	25.18
	1 Sam	15. 7
AV Havoth Jair *see* (Villages of) Jair		
HAZAEL		
Hazaiah	Neh	11. 5
Hazar Addar		
see also Hezron (2)		
	Num	34. 4
Hazar Enan	Num	34. 9
		34.10
Hazar Gaddah	Josh	15.27
Hazar Shual	Josh	15.28
		19. 3
	1 Chr	4.28
	Neh	11.27
Hazar Susah	Josh	19. 5
AV Hazar-Enan *see* Enon		
AV Hazar-Hatticon *see* Ticon		
Hazarmaveth	Gen	10.26
	1 Chr	1.20
Hazarsusim	1 Chr	4.31
Hazazon Tamar	Gen	14. 7
	2 Chr	20. 2
AV Hazerim *see* (their) Land		

Hazeroth Num 11.35
12.16
33.15
Deut 1. 1
Haziel 1 Chr 23. 9
Hazo Gen 22.22
Hazor
see also Kerioth Hezron
HAZOR (1)
Hazor (2)
see also Baal Hazor
Neh 11.33
Hazor (3) Josh 15.23
Hazor (4) Jer 49.28
49.30
49.33
Hazor (5)
see also Hazor Hadattah
Josh 15.25
Hazor Hadattah
see also Hazor (5)
Josh 15.25
Hazzebaim
see Pochereth Hazzebaim
Hazzelelponi 1 Chr 4. 3
Heber (1) Gen 46.17
Num 26.45
1 Chr 7.31
7.32
Heber (2) Judg 4.11
4.17
4.17
5.24
Heber (3) 1 Chr 4.17
Heber (4) 1 Chr 8.17
HEBRON (1)
Hebron (2) Ex 6.18
Num 3.17
3.27
26.58
1 Chr 6. 2
6.18
15. 9
23.12
23.19
24.23
26.23
26.30
26.31
26.31
Hebron (3) 1 Chr 2.42
2.43
Hegai Esth 2. 3
2. 8
2. 9
2.15
AV Hege *see* Hegai
Helah 1 Chr 4. 5
4. 7
Helam 2 Sam 10.16
10.17
Helbah Judg 1.31
Helbon Ezek 27.18
Heldai (1) 1 Chr 27. 2
Heldai (2) Zech 6.10
6.14
Heleb 2 Sam 23.24
Heled 1 Chr 11.26
Helek Num 26.30
Josh 17. 2
AV Helem *see* Hotham, Heldai
Heleph Josh 19.33
Helez (1) 2 Sam 23.24
1 Chr 11.26
27. 2
Helez (2) 1 Chr 2.39
Heli Lk 3.23
Heliopolis Gen 41.45
46.20
Jer 43.13
Ezek 30.17
Helkai Neh 12.12
Helkath Josh 19.25
21.31
AV Helkath-Hazzurim *see* Field Of Swords
Helon Num 1. 5
2. 3
7.12
10.16
AV Hemam *see* Heman
Heman (1) 1 Kgs 4.31
1 Chr 2. 6
Heman (2) 1 Chr 6.33
6.33
15.17
16.41
16.42
25. 1
25. 4
25. 5

Heman (2) (cont.)
1 Chr 25. 5
25. 6
2 Chr 5.11
29.12
35.15
Heman (3) Gen 36.22
AV Hemath *see* Intermarry
Hemdan Gen 36.25
AV Hen *see* Josiah
Hena 2 Kgs 18.34
19.13
Is 37.13
Henadad Ezra 3. 9
Neh 3.18
3.24
10. 9
AV Henoch *see* Enoch
Hepher
see also Gath Hepher
Hepher (1) Num 26.32
26.33
27. 1
Josh 17. 2
17. 3
Hepher (2) 1 Chr 4. 6
Hepher (3) 1 Chr 11.26
Hepher (4) Josh 12.17
1 Kgs 4.10
Hephzibah
see also (God is) Pleased (with her)
2 Kgs 21. 1
Heres
see also Kir Heres
Heres (1) Judg 1.35
Heres (2) Judg 8.13
Heresh 1 Chr 9.14
Hereth 1 Sam 22. 5
Hermas Rom 16.14
Hermes (1) Acts 14.12
Hermes (2) Rom 16.14
Hermogenes 2 Tim 1.15
HERMON
HEROD (1)
HEROD (2)
HEROD (3)
Herodias Mt 14. 3
14. 4
14. 6
Mk 6.17
6.19
6.21
6.22
Lk 3.19
Herodion Rom 16.11
Hesed *see* Jushab Hesed
Heshaiah Jer 42. 1
HESHBON
Heshmon Josh 15.27
Heth
see also Hittites
Gen 10.15
1 Chr 1.13
Hethlon Ezek 47.15
48. 1
HEZEKIAH (1)
Hezekiah (2)
see also Hizkiah
Ezra 2. 3
Neh 7. 8
10.14
Hezion 1 Kgs 15.18
Hezir (1) 1 Chr 24. 7
Hezir (2) Neh 10.14
AV Hezrai *see* Hezro
Hezro 2 Sam 23.24
1 Chr 11.26
Hezron
see also Kerioth Hezron, Hazor
Hezron (1) Gen 46. 9
Ex 6.14
Num 26. 6
1 Chr 5. 3
Hezron (2)
see also Hazar Addar
Josh 15. 3
Hezron (3) Gen 46.12
Num 26.19
Ruth 4.18
1 Chr 2. 5
2. 9
2.18
2.21
2.24
2.25
4. 1
Mt 1. 2
Lk 3.33
Hiddai 2 Sam 23.24
AV Hiddekel *see* Tigris

Hiel 1 Kgs 16.34
16.34
Hierapolis Col 4.13
Hilen 1 Chr 6.57
HILKIAH (1)
Hilkiah (2) 2 Kgs 18.18
Is 22.20
36. 3
Hilkiah (3) 1 Chr 6.45
Hilkiah (4) 1 Chr 26.11
Hilkiah (5) Neh 8. 4
12. 2
12.12
Hilkiah (6) Jer 1. 1
Hilkiah (7) Jer 29. 3
Hillel Judg 12.13
HINNOM
Hirah Gen 38. 1
38.12
38.20
38.20
HIRAM
HITTITES
HIVITES
Hizki 1 Chr 8.17
Hizkiah 1 Chr 3.23
AV Hizkijah *see* Hezekiah
Hobab Num 10.29
10.30
Judg 4.11
Hobah Gen 14.15
Hobaiah Neh 7.63
Hod 1 Chr 7.37
AV Hodaiah *see* Hodaviah (3)
Hodaviah (1) 1 Chr 5.24
Hodaviah (2) 1 Chr 9. 7
Hodaviah (3) 1 Chr 3.24
Hodaviah (4) Ezra 2.40
Neh 7.43
Hodaviah (5)
(Hebrew Judah)
Ezra 3. 9
Hodesh 1 Chr 8. 8
AV Hodevah *see* Hodaviah (4)
Hodiah (1) 1 Chr 4.19
Hodiah (2) Neh 8. 7
9. 5
10. 9
10. 9
Hodiah (3) Neh 10.14
Hoglah
see also Beth Hoglah
Num 26.33
27. 1
36.10
Josh 17. 3
Hoham Josh 10. 3
Holon (1) Josh 15.51
21.15
Holon (2) Jer 48.21
Homam 1 Chr 1.38
Hophni 1 Sam 1. 3
2.34
4. 4
4.11
4.17
Hophra Jer 44.30
Hor
see also Hor Haggidgad
HOR (1)
Hor (2) Num 34. 7
Hor Haggidgad Num 33.15
Horam Josh 10.33
AV Horeb *see* Sinai
Horem Josh 19.38
Horesh 1 Sam 23.15
23.18
23.19
Hori (1) Gen 36.22
1 Chr 1.38
Hori (2) Num 13. 3
AV Horims *see* Horites
Horite Gen 14. 6
36.20
36.29
Deut 2.12
2.22
Hormah Num 14.45
21. 3
Deut 1.44
Josh 12.14
15.30
19. 4
Judg 1.17
1 Sam 30.30
1 Chr 4.30
Horon *see* Beth Horon
Horonaim 2 Sam 13.34
Is 15. 5
Jer 48. 3

Horonaim (cont.)
Jer 48. 5
48.34
HORSE GATE
Hosah (1) Josh 19.29
Hosah (2) 1 Chr 16.38
26.10
26.11
26.16
Hosea Hos 1. 1
1. 2
1. 2
1. 3
1. 4
1. 6
1. 9
Rom 9.25
Hoshaiah (1) Neh 12.32
Hoshaiah (2) Jer 43. 2
Hoshama 1 Chr 3.18
HOSHEA (1)
Hoshea (2)
see also Joshua (1)
Num 13. 3
13.16
Hoshea (3) 1 Chr 27.16
Hoshea (4) Neh 10.14
Hotham (1) 1 Chr 7.32
7.35
Hotham (2) 1 Chr 11.26
AV Hothan *see* Hotham
Hothir 1 Chr 25. 4
25. 9
AV Hozai *see* Prophet(s)
Hukkok Josh 19.34
Hukok 1 Chr 6.75
Hul Gen 10.23
1 Chr 1.17
Huldah 2 Kgs 22.14
2 Chr 34.22
Humtah Josh 15.54
Hupham Num 26.39
Huppah 1 Chr 24. 7
Huppim Gen 46.21
1 Chr 7.12
7.15
Hur (1) Ex 17.10
17.12
24.14
Hur (2) Ex 31. 2
35.30
38.22
1 Chr 2.19
2.20
2.50
2.50
4. 3
4. 3
2 Chr 1. 5
Hur (3) Num 31. 8
Josh 13.21
Hur (4) 1 Chr 4. 1
Hur (5) Neh 3. 9
Hurai 1 Chr 11.26
HURAM (1)
Huram (2) 1 Chr 8. 5
Huri 1 Chr 5.14
5.14
Hushah 2 Sam 21.18
23.24
1 Chr 4. 3
11.26
20. 4
27. 2
HUSHAI
Husham Gen 36.31
1 Chr 1.43
AV Hushathite *see* Hushah
Hushim (1) Gen 46.23
1 Chr 7.12
Hushim (2) 1 Chr 8. 8
8.11
AV Huz *see* Uz
Huzoth Num 22.39
AV Huzzab *see* Queen
Hymenaeus 1 Tim 1.20
2 Tim 2.17

I

I AM
Ibhar 2 Sam 5.15
1 Chr 3. 6
14. 5
Ibleam Josh 17.11
Judg 1.27
2 Kgs 9.27
15.10
Ibneiah 1 Chr 9. 7

Ibnijah	1 Chr	9. 7
Ibri	1 Chr	24.27
Ibsam	1 Chr	7. 2
Ibzan	Judg	12. 8
		12. 9
		12.11
Ichabod	1 Sam	4.21
		14. 3
Iconium	Acts	13.51
		14. 1
		14.19
		14.21
		16. 2
	2 Tim	3.11
Idalah	Josh	19.15
Idbash	1 Chr	4. 3
Iddo (1)	1 Kgs	4.14
Iddo (2)	1 Chr	6.21
Iddo (3)	1 Chr	27.16
Iddo (4)	2 Chr	9.29
		12.15
		13.22
Iddo (5)	Ezra	5. 1
	Zech	1. 1
Iddo (6)	Ezra	8.17
Iddo (7)	Neh	12. 2
		12.12
Idumea	Mk	3. 8
Iezer	Num	26.30
Igal (1)	Num	13. 3
Igal (2)	2 Sam	23.24
Igal (3)	1 Chr	3.22
Igdaliah	Jer	35. 4
Iim	Josh	15.29
AV Ije-Abarim *see* (ruins of) Abarim		
Ijon	1 Kgs	15.20
	2 Kgs	15.29
	2 Chr	16. 4
Ikkesh	2 Sam	23.24
	1 Chr	11.26
		27. 2
Ilai	1 Chr	11.26
Illyricum	Rom	15.19
Imlah	1 Kgs	22. 8
	2 Chr	18. 7
IMMANUEL		
Immer (1)	1 Chr	9.10
	Ezra	2.36
		10.20
	Neh	7.39
		11.13
Immer (2)	1 Chr	24. 7
Immer (3)	Ezra	2.59
	Neh	7.61
Immer (4)	Neh	3.29
Immer (5)	Jer	20. 1
Imna	1 Chr	7.35
Imnah (1)	Gen	46.17
	Num	26.44
	1 Chr	7.30
Imnah (2)	2 Chr	31.14
AV Imnites *see* Imnah (1)		
Imrah	1 Chr	7.36
Imri (1)	1 Chr	9. 4
Imri (2)	Neh	3. 2
India	Esth	1. 1
		8. 9
Iphdeiah	1 Chr	8.25
Iphtah	Josh	15.43
Iphtahel	Josh	19.14
		19.27
Ir *see* Rehoboth Ir		
AV Ir-Nahash *see* Nahash		
Ira (1)	2 Sam	20.26
Ira (2)	2 Sam	23.24
	1 Chr	11.26
		27. 2
Ira (3)	2 Sam	23.24
	1 Chr	11.26
Irad	Gen	4.18
Iram	Gen	36.40
	1 Chr	1.54
Iri	1 Chr	7. 7
Irijah	Jer	37.13
		37.14
AV Iron *see* Yiron		
Irpeel	Josh	18.27
Irshemesh	Josh	19.41
Iru	1 Chr	4.15
ISAAC		
ISAIAH		
Iscah	Gen	11.29
Iscariot *see* Judas (1)		
AV Ish-Tob *see* Tob		
Ishbah	1 Chr	4.17
		4.17
Ishbak	Gen	25. 2
	1 Chr	1.32
Ishbibenob	2 Sam	21.16
ISHBOSHETH		
Ishi (1)	1 Chr	2.31
Ishi (2)	1 Chr	4.20
Ishi (3)	1 Chr	4.42
Ishi (4)	1 Chr	5.24
Ishma	1 Chr	4. 3
ISHMAEL (1)		
ISHMAEL (2)		
Ishmael (3)	2 Chr	19.11
Ishmael (4)	1 Chr	8.38
		9.44
Ishmael (5)	2 Chr	23. 1
Ishmael (6)	Ezra	10.22
Ishmaiah (1)	1 Chr	12. 3
Ishmaiah (2)	1 Chr	27.16
Ishmerai	1 Chr	8.18
Ishod	1 Chr	7.18
Ishpah	1 Chr	8.16
Ishpan	1 Chr	8.22
Ishvah	Gen	46.17
	1 Chr	7.30
Ishvi (1)	Gen	46.17
	Num	26.44
	1 Chr	7.30
Ishvi (2)	1 Sam	14.49
AV Ishvites *see* Ishvi		
Ismachiah	2 Chr	31.13
ISRAEL (1)		
ISRAEL (2)		
ISSACHAR (1)		
Issachar (2)	1 Chr	26. 5
Isshiah (1)	1 Chr	7. 3
Isshiah (2)	1 Chr	12. 3
Isshiah (3)	1 Chr	23.20
		24.25
Isshiah (4)	1 Chr	24.21
Isshijah	Ezra	10.31
AV Isuah (Ishuah) *see* Ishvah		
AV Isui (Ishui, Ishuai) *see* Ishvi		
Italy	Acts	18. 2
		27. 1
		27. 6
	Heb	13.24
Ithai	1 Chr	11.26
ITHAMAR		
Ithiel	Neh	11. 7
Ithlah	Josh	19.42
Ithmah	1 Chr	11.26
Ithnan	Josh	15.23
AV Ithra *see* Jether		
Ithran (1)	Gen	36.25
	1 Chr	1.38
Ithran (2)	1 Chr	7.37
Ithream	2 Sam	3. 5
	1 Chr	3. 1
Ithrites	1 Chr	2.53
AV Ittah-Kazin *see* Ethkazin		
Ittai (1)	2 Sam	15.19
		15.21
		15.22
		18. 2
		18. 5
		18.12
Ittai (2)	2 Sam	23.24
Iturea	Lk	3. 1
Ivvah	2 Kgs	17.24
		17.31
		18.34
		19.13
	Is	37.13
AV Iye-Abarim *see* (ruins of)Abarim		
AV Iyim *see* Ruin(s)		
Izhar	Ex	6.18
		6.21
	Num	3.17
		3.27
		16. 1
	1 Chr	4. 7
		6. 2
		6.18
		6.38
		23.12
		23.18
		24.22
		26.23
		26.29
		27. 2
Izliah	1 Chr	8.18
Izrahiah	1 Chr	7. 3
		7. 3
AV Izri *see* Zeri		
Izziah	Ezra	10.25

J

Jaakan		
see also Bene Jaakan		
	Deut	10. 6
	1 Chr	1.38
Jaakobah	1 Chr	4.34
Jaalah	Ezra	2.55
	Neh	7.57
AV Jaare-Oregim *see* Jair		
Jaareshiah	1 Chr	8.27
Jaasiel (1)	1 Chr	11.26
Jaasiel (2)	1 Chr	27.16
Jaasu	Ezra	10.34
Jaazaniah (1)	Jer	35. 3
Jaazaniah (2)	Ezek	8.11
Jaazaniah (3)	Ezek	11. 1
Jaaziah	1 Chr	24.26
		24.27
Jaaziel	1 Chr	15.17
Jabal	Gen	4.20
Jabbok	Gen	32.22
	Num	21.24
	Deut	2.37
		3.16
	Josh	12. 2
	Judg	11.13
		11.22
JABESH (1)		
Jabesh (2)	2 Kgs	15.10
		15.13
Jabez (1)	1 Chr	2.55
Jabez (2)	1 Chr	4. 9
		4. 9
		4.10
Jabin (1)	Josh	11. 1
Jabin (2)	Judg	4. 2
		4. 3
		4. 7
		4.17
		4.23
	Ps	83. 9
AV Jabneel (Jabneh) *see* Jamnia		
Jacan	1 Chr	5.13
Jachin (1)	Gen	46.10
	Ex	6.15
	Num	26.12
Jachin (2)	1 Kgs	7.21
	2 Chr	3.17
Jachin (3)	1 Chr	9.10
		24. 7
	Neh	11.10
JACOB (1)		
Jacob (2)	Mt	1.12
Jada	1 Chr	2.28
		2.32
AV Jadau *see* Jaddai		
Jaddai	Ezra	10.43
Jaddua (1)	Neh	10.14
Jaddua (2)	Neh	12.11
		12.22
Jadon	Neh	3. 7
Jael	Judg	4.17
		4.18
		4.21
		4.22
		5. 6
		5.24
Jagur	Josh	15.21
AV Jah *see* Lord		
Jahath (1)	1 Chr	4. 2
Jahath (2)	1 Chr	6.20
		6.43
Jahath (3)	1 Chr	23.10
Jahath (4)	1 Chr	24.22
Jahath (5)	2 Chr	34.12
Jahaz	Num	21.23
	Deut	2.32
	Josh	13.18
		21.36
	Judg	11.20
	Is	15. 4
	Jer	48.34
AV Jahaza *see* Jahaz, Jahzah		
AV Jahaziah *see* Jahzeiah		
Jahaziel (1)	1 Chr	12. 3
Jahaziel (2)	1 Chr	16. 6
Jahaziel (3)	2 Chr	20.14
		20.15
Jahaziel (4)	Ezra	8. 2
Jahdai	1 Chr	2.47
Jahdiel	1 Chr	5.24
Jahdo	1 Chr	5.14
Jahleel	Gen	46.14
	Num	26.26
Jahmai	1 Chr	7. 2
Jahzah	1 Chr	6.78
	Jer	48.21
Jahzeel	Gen	46.24
	Num	26.48
Jahzeiah	Ezra	10.15
Jahzerah	1 Chr	9.10
Jahziel	1 Chr	7.13
JAIR (1)		
Jair (2)	Judg	10. 3
		10. 4
		10. 5
Jair (3)	2 Sam	21.19
	1 Chr	20. 5
Jair (4)	Esth	2. 5
Jair (5)	2 Sam	20.26
Jairus	Mk	5.22
		5.35
		5.38
	Lk	8.41
		8.49
		8.50
Jakeh	Prov	30. 1
Jakim (1)	1 Chr	8.19
Jakim (2)	1 Chr	24. 7
Jalam	Gen	36. 5
		36.14
		36.18
	1 Chr	1.35
Jalon	1 Chr	4.17
Jambres	2 Tim	3. 8
		3. 9
JAMES (1)		
JAMES (2)		
JAMES (3)		
JAMES (4)		
JAMES (5)		
JAMES (6)		
JAMES (7)		
Jamin (1)	Gen	46.10
	Ex	6.15
	Num	26.12
	1 Chr	4.24
Jamin (2)	1 Chr	2.26
Jamin (3)	Neh	8. 7
Jamlech	1 Chr	4.34
Jamnia (1)	Josh	15.11
Jamnia (2)	Josh	19.33
Jamnia (3)	2 Chr	26. 6
Janai	1 Chr	5.12
Janim	Josh	15.53
AV Janna *see* Jannai		
Jannai	Lk	3.24
Jannes	2 Tim	3. 8
		3. 9
Janoah (1)	Josh	16. 6
		16. 7
Janoah (2)	2 Kgs	15.29
AV Janohah *see* Janoah		
AV Janum *see* Janim		
JAPHETH		
Japhia (1)	Josh	10. 3
Japhia (2)	Josh	19.12
Japhia (3)	2 Sam	5.15
	1 Chr	3. 7
		14. 6
Japhlet	1 Chr	7.32
		7.33
AV Japhleti *see* Japhletites		
Japhletites	Josh	16. 3
AV Japho *see* Joppa		
Jarah	1 Chr	9.42
AV Jareb (King) *see* (great)Emperor		
Jared	Gen	5.15
		5.18
	1 Chr	1. 2
		1. 3
	Lk	3.37
Jarha	1 Chr	2.34
Jarib (1)	1 Chr	4.24
Jarib (2)	Ezra	8.16
Jarib (3)	Ezra	10.18
Jarmuth (1)	Josh	10. 3
		10. 5
		10.23
		12.11
		15.35
	Neh	11.29
Jarmuth (2)	Josh	21.29
Jaroah	1 Chr	5.14
Jashar	Josh	10.13
	2 Sam	1.18
Jashen	2 Sam	23.24
Jashobeam (1)	1 Chr	11.11
Jashobeam (2)	1 Chr	12. 3
Jashobeam (3)	1 Chr	27. 2
Jashub		
see also Shear Jashub		
Jashub (1)	Gen	46.13
	Num	26.24
	1 Chr	7. 1
Jashub (2)	Ezra	10.29
AV Jashubi-Lehem *see* (settled in) Bethlehem		
Jason	Acts	17. 5
		17. 6
		17. 7
		17. 9
	Rom	16.21
Jathniel	1 Chr	26. 2
Jattir	Josh	15.48
		21.14
	1 Sam	30.27

Jattir (cont.)
2 Sam 23.24
1 Chr 6.57
11.26
Javan
see also Greece
Gen 10. 2
10. 4
1 Chr 1. 5
1. 7
JAZER
Jaziz 1 Chr 27.25
Jearim
see also Kiriath Jearim
Jearim (1) Josh 15.10
Jearim (2) Ps 132. 6
Jeatherai 1 Chr 6.21
Jeberechiah Is 8. 2
JEBUSITES
AV Jechonias *see* Jehoiachin
Jecoliah 2 Kgs 15. 2
2 Chr 26. 3
AV Jeconiah *see* Jehoiachin
Jedaiah (1) 1 Chr 4.34
Jedaiah (2) Neh 3.10
Jedaiah (3) Zech 6.10
6.14
Jedaiah (4) 1 Chr 9.10
24. 7
Jedaiah (5) Ezra 2.36
Neh 7.39
Jedaiah (6) Neh 11.10
12. 2
12.12
Jedaiah (7) Neh 12. 2
12.12
Jediael (1) 1 Chr 7. 6
7.10
Jediael (2) 1 Chr 11.26
12.20
Jediael (3) 1 Chr 26. 2
Jedidah 2 Kgs 22. 1
Jedidiah
see also Solomon
2 Sam 12.25
JEDUTHUN
AV Jeezer, -ite *see* Iezer
Jegar Sahadutha
see also Galeed, Mizpah (4)
Gen 31.47
Jehallelel (1) 1 Chr 4.16
Jehallelel (2) 2 Chr 29.12
Jehaziel 1 Chr 23.19
24.23
Jehdeiah (1) 1 Chr 24.20
Jehdeiah (2) 1 Chr 27.25
Jehezkel 1 Chr 24. 7
Jehiah 1 Chr 15.23
Jehiel (1) 1 Chr 15.17
16. 5
Jehiel (2) 1 Chr 23. 8
Jehiel (3) 1 Chr 26.21
Jehiel (4) 1 Chr 27.32
Jehiel (5)
Perhaps the same as (2).
1 Chr 29. 8
Jehiel (6) 2 Chr 21. 2
Jehiel (7) 2 Chr 31.13
Jehiel (8) 2 Chr 35. 8
Jehiel (9) Ezra 8. 2
Jehiel (10) Ezra 10. 2
Jehiel (11) Ezra 10.21
Jehiel (12) Ezra 10.26
AV Jehieli *see* Jehiel, Ladan
Jehizkiah 2 Chr 28.12
Jehoaddah 1 Chr 8.36
AV Jehoaddan *see* Jehoaddin
Jehoaddin 2 Kgs 14. 2
2 Chr 25. 1
JEHOAHAZ
JEHOASH
Jehohanan (1) 1 Chr 26. 3
Jehohanan (2) 2 Chr 28.12
Jehohanan (3) Ezra 10. 6
Jehohanan (4) Ezra 10.28
Jehohanan (5) Neh 6.18
Jehohanan (6) Neh 12.12
Jehohanan (7) Neh 12.42
Jehohanan (8) 2 Chr 17.15
Jehohanan (9)
Perhaps the same as (8).
2 Chr 23. 1
JEHOIACHIN
JEHOIADA (1)
JEHOIADA (2)
Jehoiada (3) 1 Chr 27.34
JEHOIAKIM
Jehoiarib 1 Chr 9.10
24. 7
Jehonathan (1) 2 Chr 17. 8
Jehonathan (2) Neh 12.12

JEHORAM (1)
Jehoram (2) 2 Chr 17. 8
AV Jehoshabeath *see* Jehosheba
Jehoshaphat
see also (Valley of) Judgement
JEHOSHAPHAT (1)
Jehoshaphat (2) 2 Sam 8.16
20.24
1 Kgs 4. 3
1 Chr 18.15
Jehoshaphat (3) 1 Kgs 4.17
Jehoshaphat (4) 2 Kgs 9. 2
Jehosheba 2 Kgs 11. 2
11. 3
2 Chr 22.11
AV Jehoshua *see* Joshua
AV Jehovah *see* Lord
AV Jehovah-Jireh *see* (the Lord) Provides
AV Jehovah-Nissi *see* (the Lord is my) Banner
AV Jehovah-Shalom *see* (the Lord is) Peace
Jehozabad (1) 2 Kgs 12.20
2 Chr 24.26
Jehozabad (2) 1 Chr 26. 4
Jehozabad (3) 2 Chr 17.18
Jehozadak 1 Chr 6.14
6.15
Ezra 3. 2
5. 2
10.18
Neh 12.26
Hag 1. 1
Zech 6.11
JEHU (1)
Jehu (2) 1 Kgs 16. 1
16. 7
16.12
2 Chr 19. 2
20.34
Jehu (3) 1 Chr 4.34
Jehu (4) 1 Chr 12. 3
Jehu (5) 1 Chr 2.38
Jehubbah 1 Chr 7.34
Jehucal Jer 37. 3
38. 1
Jehud Josh 19.45
Jehudi Jer 36.14
36.21
36.23
AV Jehudijah *see* (woman from the tribe of) Judah
Jehuel 2 Chr 29.12
AV Jehush *see* Jeush
Jeiel (1) 1 Chr 5. 7
Jeiel (2) 1 Chr 8.29
9.35
Jeiel (3) 1 Chr 11.26
Jeiel (4) 1 Chr 16. 5
Jeiel (5) 2 Chr 26.11
Jeiel (6) 2 Chr 35. 9
Jeiel (7) Ezra 10.43
Jeiel (8) 1 Chr 15.17
16. 5
Jeiel (9)
Perhaps the same as (8).
2 Chr 20.14
Jekabzeel Neh 11.25
Jekameam 1 Chr 23.19
24.23
Jekamiah (1) 1 Chr 2.41
Jekamiah (2) 1 Chr 3.18
Jekuthiel 1 Chr 4.17
Jemimah Job 42.14
Jemuel Gen 46.10
Ex 6.15
JEPHTHAH
AV Jephthai *see* Jephthah
Jephunneh (1) Num 13. 3
14. 6
26.65
32.12
34.19
Deut 1.36
Josh 14. 6
14.13
14.14
15.13
21.12
1 Chr 4.15
6.56
Jephunneh (2) 1 Chr 7.38
Jerah Gen 10.26
1 Chr 1.20
Jerahmeel (1) 1 Sam 27.10
30.29
1 Chr 2. 9
2.25
2.26

Jerahmeel (1) (cont.)
1 Chr 2.33
2.42
Jerahmeel (2) 1 Chr 24.28
Jerahmeel (3) Jer 36.26
Jered 1 Chr 4.17
Jeremai Ezra 10.33
JEREMIAH (1)
Jeremiah (2) 2 Kgs 23.31
24.18
Jer 52. 1
Jeremiah (3) 1 Chr 5.24
Jeremiah (4) 1 Chr 12. 3
Jeremiah (5) 1 Chr 12. 9
Jeremiah (6) 1 Chr 12. 9
Jeremiah (7) Neh 10. 2
Jeremiah (8)
Perhaps the same as (7).
Neh 12. 2
Jeremiah (9)
Perhaps the same as (7).
Neh 12.12
Jeremiah (10)
Perhaps the same as (7).
Neh 12.33
AV Jeremias *see* Jeremiah (1)
Jeremoth (1) 1 Chr 7. 8
Jeremoth (2) 1 Chr 8.14
Jeremoth (3) 1 Chr 23.23
Jeremoth (4) 1 Chr 24.30
Jeremoth (5) 1 Chr 27.16
Jeremoth (6) Ezra 10.26
Jeremoth (7) Ezra 10.27
Jeremoth (8) Ezra 10.29
AV Jeremy *see* Jeremiah (1)
Jeriah 1 Chr 23.19
24.23
26.31
26.32
Jeribai 1 Chr 11.26
JERICHO
Jeriel 1 Chr 7. 2
AV Jerijah *see* Jeriah
Jerimoth (1) 1 Chr 7. 7
Jerimoth (2) 1 Chr 12. 3
Jerimoth (3) 1 Chr 25. 4
Jerimoth (4) 1 Chr 25. 9
Jerimoth (5) 2 Chr 11.18
Jerimoth (6) 2 Chr 31.13
Jerioth 1 Chr 2.18
JEROBOAM (1)
JEROBOAM (2)
Jeroham (1) 1 Sam 1. 1
Jeroham (2) 1 Chr 9. 7
Jeroham (3) 1 Chr 9.10
Jeroham (4) 1 Chr 12. 3
Jeroham (5) 1 Chr 27.16
Jeroham (6) 2 Chr 23. 1
Jeroham (7) Neh 11.12
Jeroham (8) 1 Chr 8.26
Jeroham (9) 1 Chr 6.27
Jeroham (10)
Perhaps the same as (9).
1 Chr 6.34
Jerubbaal
see also Gideon
Judg 6.32
AV Jerubbesheth *see* Gideon
Jeruel 2 Chr 20.16
JERUSALEM
Jerusha 2 Kgs 15.33
Jerushah 2 Chr 27. 1
Jeshaiah (1) 1 Chr 3.21
3.21
Jeshaiah (2) Ezra 8. 2
Jeshaiah (3) Ezra 8.19
Jeshaiah (4) Neh 11. 7
Jeshaiah (5) 1 Chr 25. 3
Jeshaiah (6)
Perhaps the same as (5).
1 Chr 25. 9
Jeshanah
see also Jeshanah Gate
2 Chr 13.19
JESHANAH GATE
AV Jesharelah *see* Asharelah
Jeshebeab 1 Chr 24. 7
Jesher 1 Chr 2.18
Jeshiah 1 Chr 26.25
AV Jeshimon *see* Desert, (Judaean) Wilderness
Jeshimoth *see* Beth Jeshimoth
Jeshishai 1 Chr 5.14
Jeshohaiah 1 Chr 4.34
Jeshua (1) Neh 11.26
Jeshua (2) 1 Chr 24. 7
Jeshua (3)
Perhaps the same as (2).
Ezra 2.36
Neh 7.39
Jeshua (4) 2 Chr 31.15

Jeshua (5) Ezra 8.33
Jeshua (6) Ezra 2. 3
Neh 7. 8
Jeshua (7)
Perhaps the same as (6).
Neh 3.19
Jeshua (8) Ezra 2.40
3. 9
Neh 7.43
Jeshua (9)
Perhaps the same as (8).
Neh 8. 7
9. 4
9. 5
10. 9
12. 8
12.24
AV Jeshua *see* Joshua (2)
AV Jeshurun *see* God's People, Israelite(s)
AV Jesiah *see* Isshiah
Jesimiel 1 Chr 4.34
JESSE
AV Jesui *see* Ishvi
AV Jesuites *see* Ishvites
JESUS
Jesus Barabbas *see* Barabbas
Jether (1) Judg 8.20
Jether (2) 2 Sam 17.25
1 Kgs 2. 5
1 Chr 2.17
Jether (3) 1 Chr 2.32
2.32
Jether (4) 1 Chr 4.17
Jether (5) 1 Chr 7.38
Jetheth Gen 36.40
1 Chr 1.51
AV Jethlah *see* Ithlah
JETHRO
Jetur Gen 25.15
1 Chr 1.31
5.19
Jeuel (1) 1 Chr 9. 4
Jeuel (2) 2 Chr 29.12
Jeuel (3) Ezra 8. 2
Jeush (1) Gen 36. 5
36.14
36.18
1 Chr 1.35
Jeush (2) 1 Chr 7.10
Jeush (3) 1 Chr 8.39
Jeush (4) 1 Chr 23.10
23.10
Jeush (5) 2 Chr 11.19
Jeuz 1 Chr 8.10
JEW
Jezaniah 2 Kgs 25.23
Jer 40. 8
JEZEBEL (1)
JEZEBEL (2)
Jezer Gen 46.24
Num 26.49
1 Chr 7.13
AV Jeziah *see* Izziah
Jeziel 1 Chr 12. 3
AV Jezliah *see* Izliah
AV Jezoar *see* Izhar
Jezrahiah Neh 12.42
JEZREEL (1)
Jezreel (2) Josh 15.56
Jezreel (3) 1 Chr 4. 3
Jezreel (4) Hos 1. 4
AV Jibsam *see* Ibsam
Jidlaph Gen 22.22
AV Jimna(h), -ite *see* Imnah
AV Jiphtah *see* Iphtah
AV Jiphthahel *see* Iphtahel
Joab
see also Atroth Beth Joab
JOAB (1)
Joab (2) 1 Chr 4.14
Joab (3) Ezra 2. 3
8. 2
Joab (4)
Perhaps the same as (3).
Neh 7. 8
Joah (1) 2 Kgs 18.18
18.26
18.37
Is 36. 3
36.11
36.22
Joah (2) 1 Chr 26. 4
Joah (3) 2 Chr 34. 8
Joah (4) 1 Chr 6.21
Joah (5)
Perhaps the same as (4).
2 Chr 29.12
29.12
JOAHAZ (1)
Joahaz (2) 2 Chr 34. 8

AV Joahaz *see* Shallum (1)		
Joanan	Lk	3.27
Joanna	Lk	8. 3
		24.10
JOASH (1)		
Joash (2)	Judg	6.11
		6.29
		6.30
		6.31
		6.32
		7.14
		8.32
		8.32
Joash (3)	1 Kgs	22.26
	2 Chr	18.25
Joash (4)	1 Chr	4.22
Joash (5)	1 Chr	12. 3
AV Joatham *see* Jotham		
JOB (2)		
Job (3)	Ezek	14.14
		14.20
Jobab (1)	Gen	10.29
	1 Chr	1.23
Jobab (2)	Gen	36.31
Jobab (3)	Josh	11. 1
Jobab (4)	1 Chr	8. 8
Jobab (5)	1 Chr	8.18
Jochebed	Ex	6.20
	Num	26.59
Joda	Lk	3.26
Joed	Neh	11. 7
Joel (1)	1 Chr	4.34
Joel (2)	1 Chr	5. 4
		5. 8
Joel (3)	1 Chr	5.12
Joel (4)	1 Chr	7. 3
Joel (5)	1 Chr	11.26
Joel (6)	1 Chr	27.16
Joel (7)	Ezra	10.43
Joel (8)	Neh	11. 9
Joel (9)	Joel	1. 1
	Acts	2.16
Joel (10)	1 Chr	6.36
Joel (11)	2 Chr	29.12
Joel (12)	1 Chr	23. 8
		26.22
Joel (13)		
Perhaps the same as (12).	1 Chr	15. 7
		15.11
Joel (14)		
Perhaps the same as (13) or (15).	1 Chr	15.17
Joel (15)	1 Sam	8. 2
	1 Chr	6.28
		6.33
		6.33
Joelah	1 Chr	12. 3
Joezer	1 Chr	12. 3
Jogbehah	Num	32.35
	Judg	8.11
Jogli	Num	34.19
Joha (1)	1 Chr	8.16
Joha (2)	1 Chr	11.26
Johab	1 Chr	1.43
Johanan (1)	2 Kgs	25.23
	Jer	40. 8
		40.13
		40.15
		41.11
		41.13
		41.15
		41.16
		42. 1
		42. 8
		43. 2
		43. 4
		43. 5
Johanan (2)	1 Chr	3.15
Johanan (3)	1 Chr	3.24
Johanan (4)	1 Chr	6. 9
Johanan (5)	1 Chr	12. 9
Johanan (6)	Ezra	8. 2
Johannan	1 Chr	12. 3
JOHN (1)		
JOHN (2)		
JOHN (3)		
JOHN (4)		
JOHN (5)		
JOHN (6)		
Joiada (1)	Neh	12.10
		12.11
		12.22
		13.28
		13.28
		13.28
Joiada (2)	Neh	3. 6
Joiakim	Neh	12.10
		12.10
		12.12
		12.26
Joiarib (1)	Neh	11. 5
Joiarib (2)	Neh	11.10
		12. 2
		12.12
Joiarib (3)	Ezra	8.16
Jokdeam	Josh	15.56
Jokim	1 Chr	4.22
Jokmeam	1 Kgs	4.12
	1 Chr	6.68
Jokneam	Josh	12.22
		19.11
		21.34
Jokshan	Gen	25. 2
		25. 3
	1 Chr	1.32
		1.32
Joktan	Gen	10.25
		10.26
		10.29
	1 Chr	1.19
		1.20
Joktheel		
see also Sela		
Joktheel (1)	Josh	15.38
Joktheel (2)	2 Kgs	14. 7
Jonadab (1)	2 Kgs	10.15
		10.15
		10.23
		10.24
	Jer	35. 6
		35. 8
		35. 9
		35.14
		35.16
		35.18
		35.19
Jonadab (2)	2 Sam	13. 3
		13. 4
		13. 5
		13.32
		13.35
JONAH		
Jonam	Lk	3.30
JONATHAN (1)		
Jonathan (2)	Judg	18.30
Jonathan (3)	2 Sam	15.27
		15.36
		17.17
		17.20
		17.21
	1 Kgs	1.42
		1.43
Jonathan (4)	2 Sam	23.24
	1 Chr	11.26
Jonathan (5)	1 Chr	2.32
		2.33
Jonathan (6)	1 Chr	27.25
Jonathan (7)	Ezra	8. 2
Jonathan (8)	Ezra	10.15
Jonathan (9)	Neh	12.11
		12.11
		12.22
		12.23
Jonathan (10)	Neh	12.12
Jonathan (11)	Neh	12.33
Jonathan (12)	Jer	37.15
		37.20
Jonathan (13)	2 Sam	21.21
	1 Chr	20. 7
Jonathan (14)	1 Chr	27.32
JOPPA		
Jorah	Ezra	2. 3
Jorai	1 Chr	5.13
JORAM (1)		
Joram (2)	2 Sam	8.10
		8.10
	1 Chr	18.10
		18.10
Joram (3)	1 Chr	26.25
JORDAN		
Jorim	Lk	3.29
Jorkeam	1 Chr	2.44
AV Josaphat *see* Jehoshaphat		
AV Jose *see* Joshua		
Josech	Lk	3.26
AV Josedech *see* Jehozadak		
JOSEPH (1)		
JOSEPH (2)		
JOSEPH (3)		
JOSEPH (4)		
JOSEPH (5)		
JOSEPH (6)		
JOSEPH (7)		
JOSEPH (8)		
JOSEPH (9)		
Joseph (10)	Num	13. 3
Joseph (11)	1 Chr	25. 2
		25. 9
Joseph (12)	Ezra	10.38
Joseph (13)	Neh	12.12
AV Joses *see* Joseph		
Joshah	1 Chr	4.34
Joshaphat (1)	1 Chr	11.26
Joshaphat (2)	1 Chr	15.23
Joshaviah	1 Chr	11.26
Joshbekashah	1 Chr	25. 4
		25. 9
Josheb Basshebeth	2 Sam	23. 8
Joshibiah	1 Chr	4.34
JOSHUA (1)		
JOSHUA (2)		
Joshua (3)	2 Kgs	23. 8
Joshua (4)	1 Sam	6.14
		6.18
Joshua (5)	Lk	3.29
Joshua (6)		
see also Justus (3)		
	Col	4.11
JOSIAH (1)		
Josiah (2)	Zech	6.10
		6.14
AV Josias *see* Josiah		
Josiphiah	Ezra	8. 2
Jotbah	2 Kgs	21.19
Jotbathah	Num	33.15
	Deut	10. 7
JOTHAM (1)		
Jotham (2)	Judg	9. 5
		9. 7
		9.16
		9.21
		9.57
Jotham (3)	1 Chr	2.47
Jozabad (1)	1 Chr	12. 3
Jozabad (2)	1 Chr	12.20
Jozabad (3)	1 Chr	12.20
Jozabad (4)	2 Chr	31.13
Jozabad (5)	2 Chr	35. 9
Jozabad (6)	Ezra	8.33
Jozabad (7)	Ezra	10.22
Jozabad (8)	Ezra	10.23
Jozabad (9)	Neh	8. 7
Jozabad (10)	Neh	11.16
Jozacar	2 Kgs	12.20
AV Jozadak *see* Jehozadak		
Jubal	Gen	4.21
AV Jucal *see* Jehucal		
JUDAEA		
JUDAH (1)		
JUDAH (2)		
Judah (3)	Ezra	10.23
Judah (4)	Neh	11. 9
Judah (5)	Neh	12. 8
Judah (6)	Neh	12.36
Judah (7)	Lk	3.30
JUDAS (1)		
JUDAS (2)		
JUDAS (3)		
JUDAS (4)		
JUDAS (5)		
JUDAS (6)		
Jude	Jude	1
Judith	Gen	26.34
Julia	Rom	16.15
Julius	Acts	27. 1
		27. 3
Junias	Rom	16. 7
AV Jupiter *see* Zeus		
Jushab Hesed	1 Chr	3.20
Justus (1)		
see also Barsabbas (1), Joseph (8)		
	Acts	1.23
Justus (2)	Acts	18. 7
Justus (3)		
see also Joshua (6)		
	Col	4.11
Juttah	Josh	15.55
		21.16

K

Kabzeel	Josh	15.21
	2 Sam	23.20
	1 Chr	11.22
KADESH (1)		
Kadesh (2)	2 Sam	24. 6
Kadesh Meribah		
see also Meribah		
	Ezek	47.19
Kadmiel (1)	Ezra	2.40
	Neh	7.43
Kadmiel (2)	Ezra	3. 9
Kadmiel (3)	Neh	9. 4
		9. 5
		10. 9
		12. 8
		12.24
Kadmonites	Gen	15.19
Kain	Josh	15.57
Kaiwan	Amos	5.26
Kallai	Neh	12.12
Kamon	Judg	10. 5
Kanah (1)	Josh	16. 8
		17. 9
Kanah (2)	Josh	19.28
Kareah	2 Kgs	25.23
	Jer	40. 8
		42. 1
		43. 2
Karka	Josh	15. 3
Karkor	Judg	8.10
Karnaim		
see also Ashteroth Karnaim		
	Amos	6.13
Kartah	Josh	21.34
Kartan	Josh	21.32
Kattath	Josh	19.15
KEDAR		
Kedemah	Gen	25.15
	1 Chr	1.31
Kedemoth (1)	Deut	2.26
Kedemoth (2)	Josh	13.18
		21.37
	1 Chr	6.79
Kedesh (1)	Josh	20. 7
		21.32
	Judg	4. 6
		4. 9
		4.10
		4.11
	2 Kgs	15.29
	1 Chr	6.76
Kedesh (2)		
Perhaps the same as (1).		
	Josh	12.22
		19.37
Kedesh (3)	1 Chr	6.72
Kedesh (4)	Josh	15.23
Kehelathah	Num	33.15
KEILAH		
Kelaiah	Ezra	10.23
Kelita	Ezra	10.23
	Neh	8. 7
		10. 9
AV Kelita *see* Kelaiah		
Kemuel (1)	Gen	22.21
Kemuel (2)	Num	34.19
Kemuel (3)	1 Chr	27.16
Kenan	Gen	5. 9
		5.12
	1 Chr	1. 1
		1. 2
	Lk	3.37
Kenath		
see also Nobah (2)		
	Num	32.42
	1 Chr	2.23
Kenaz (1)	Gen	36.10
		36.40
	1 Chr	1.53
Kenaz (2)		
Perhaps the same as (1).		
	Gen	36.15
	1 Chr	1.36
Kenaz (3)		
Perhaps the same as (1).		
	Josh	15.17
	Judg	1.13
		3. 9
	1 Chr	4.13
		4.15
AV Kenezite *see* Kenizzite		
KENITES		
Kenizzite	Gen	15.19
	Num	32.12
	Josh	14. 6
		14.14
Keramim *see* Abel Keramim		
Keren Happuch	Job	42.14
Kerioth	Jer	48.24
	Amos	2. 2
Kerioth Hezron	Josh	15.25
Keros	Ezra	2.43
	Neh	7.46
Keturah	Gen	25. 1
		25. 4
	1 Chr	1.32
Keziah	Job	42.14
Keziz *see* Emek Keziz		
Kibroth Hattaavah	Num	11.34
		33.15
	Deut	9.22
Kibzaim	Josh	21.22
KIDRON		
Kinah	Josh	15.22
KING'S GATE		
KING'S POOL		
KING'S VALLEY		
Kir (1)	2 Kgs	16. 9
	Is	22. 6

Kir (1) (cont.) Amos 1. 5
9. 7
Kir (2)
see also Kir Heres
Is 15. 1
Kir Heres
see also Kir (2)
2 Kgs 3.25
Is 16. 7
16.11
Jer 48.31
48.36
Kir-Haraseth, Kir-Hareseth *see* Kir Heres
Kiriath Arba
see also Hebron
Judg 1.10
Neh 11.25
Kiriath Baal
see also Baalah (1), Kiriath Jearim
Josh 15.60
18.14
Kiriath Jearim
see also Baalah (1), Kiriath Baal
Josh 9.17
15. 9
15.60
18.14
18.15
18.28
Judg 18.12
1 Sam 6.21
7. 1
7. 2
1 Chr 2.50
2.52
2.53
13. 5
13. 6
2 Chr 1. 4
Ezra 2.21
Neh 7.26
Jer 26.20
Kiriath Sepher
see also Debir
Josh 15.15
15.16
15.49
Judg 1.11
1.12
Kiriathaim (1) 1 Chr 6.76
Kiriathaim (2) Num 32.37
Josh 13.19
Jer 48. 1
48.23
Ezek 25. 9
Kiriathaim (3) Gen 14. 5
AV Kirjath *see* Kiriath Jearim
AV Kirjath-Arim *see* Kiriath Jearim
AV Kirjath-Baal *see* Kiriath Baal
AV Kirjath-Huzoth *see* Huzoth
AV Kirjath-Jearim *see* Kiriath Jearim
AV Kirjath-Sannah *see* Kiriath Sepher
AV Kirjath-Sepher *see* Kiriath Sepher
AV Kirjathaim *see* Kiriathaim
KISH (1)
Kish (2) 1 Chr 23.21
23.22
24.28
24.28
Kish (3) 2 Chr 29.12
Kish (4) Esth 2. 5
Kish (5) 1 Chr 8.30
9.36
Kishi 1 Chr 6.44
Kishion Josh 19.20
21.28
Kishon Judg 4. 7
4.13
5.21
5.21
1 Kgs 18.40
Ps 83. 9
KISLEV
AV Kison *see* Kishon
AV Kithlish *see* Chitlish
Kitron Judg 1.30
AV Kittim *see* Cyprus
AV Kittim *see* Roman(s)
Koa Ezek 23.23
KOHATH
Kolaiah (1) Neh 11. 7
Kolaiah (2) Jer 29.21
KORAH (1)
Korah (2) Gen 36. 5
36.14
Korah (2) (cont.) Gen 36.18
1 Chr 1.35
Korah (3) Gen 36.16
Korah (4) 1 Chr 2.43
Korah (5)
Perhaps the same as (1)
1 Chr 6.22
Kore (1) 1 Chr 9.19
26. 1
Kore (2) 2 Chr 31.14
Koz 1 Chr 4. 8
Kub Ezek 30. 5
AV Kue *see* Cilicia
Kun 1 Chr 18. 8
Kushaiah 1 Chr 15.17

L

Laadah 1 Chr 4.21
LABAN (1)
Laban (2) Deut 1. 1
LACHISH
Ladan (1) 1 Chr 7.26
Ladan (2) 1 Chr 23. 7
23. 8
23. 9
26.21
26.22
Lael Num 3.24
Lahad 1 Chr 4. 2
AV Lahairoi *see* (The) Well of The Living One Who Sees Me
Lahmam Josh 15.40
Lahmi 1 Chr 20. 5
Laish (1)
see also Dan (2)
Josh 19.47
19.47
Judg 18. 7
18. 9
18.14
18.27
18.27
18.29
Laish (2) 1 Sam 25.44
2 Sam 3.15
Laishah Is 10.30
Lakkum Josh 19.33
Lamech (1) Gen 4.18
4.19
4.23
Lamech (2) Gen 5.25
5.28
5.30
1 Chr 1. 3
Lk 3.36
Laodicea Col 2. 1
4.13
4.15
4.16
4.16
Rev 1.11
3.14
Lappidoth Judg 4. 4
Lasea Acts 27. 8
Lasha Gen 10.19
Lasharon Josh 12.18
LAZARUS (1)
LAZARUS (2)
LEAH
Leaphrah *see* Beth Leaphrah
Lebana Neh 7.46
Lebanah Ezra 2.43
LEBANON
Lebaoth
see also Beth Lebaoth
Josh 15.32
Lebonah Judg 21.19
Lecah 1 Chr 4.21
AV Legion *see* Mob
Lehab Gen 10.13
1 Chr 1.11
Lehi
see also Ramath Lehi
Judg 15. 9
15.14
15.19
15.19
2 Sam 23.11
Lemuel Prov 31. 1
31. 4
AV Leshem *see* Laish
Letushim Gen 25. 3
Leummim Gen 25. 3
LEVI (1)
LEVI (2)
LEVI (3)
LEVI (4)
LEVIATHAN
LEVITES
AV Libertines *see* Freedmen
LIBNAH (1)
Libnah (2) Num 33.15
Libnath *see* Shihor Libnath
Libni Ex 6.17
Num 3.17
3.21
26.58
1 Chr 6.17
6.20
6.29
Libya Gen 10. 6
1 Chr 1. 8
2 Chr 12. 3
16. 8
Is 66.19
Jer 46. 9
Ezek 27.10
30. 5
38. 5
Dan 11.43
Nah 3. 9
Acts 2.10
27.17
Likhi 1 Chr 7.19
Linus 2 Tim 4.21
AV Lo-Ammi *see* Not-My-People
AV Lo-Ruhamah *see* Unloved
Lod 1 Chr 8.12
Ezra 2.21
Neh 7.26
11.35
Lodebar Josh 13.26
2 Sam 9. 4
17.27
Amos 6.13
Lois 2 Tim 1. 5
LORD
LORD OUR SALVATION
LORD-IS-HERE
LOT (2)
Lotan Gen 36.20
36.22
36.22
36.29
1 Chr 1.38
1.38
LOVED-BY-THE-LORD
AV Lubim(s) *see* Libya
AV Lucas *see* Luke
AV Lucifer *see* (King of) Babylonia
Lucius (1) Acts 13. 1
Lucius (2) Rom 16.21
Lud Gen 10.22
1 Chr 1.17
AV Lud(im) *see* Lydia (1)
Luhith Is 15. 5
Jer 48. 5
Luke Col 4.14
2 Tim 4.11
Phlm 24
Luz (1)
see also Bethel (1)
Gen 28.19
35. 6
48. 3
Josh 16. 2
18.13
Judg 1.22
Luz (2) Judg 1.26
Lycaonia Acts 14. 6
14.11
Lycia Acts 27. 5
Lydda Acts 9.32
9.35
9.38
9.38
Lydia (1) Gen 10.13
1 Chr 1.11
Is 66.19
Jer 46. 9
Ezek 27.10
30. 5
Lydia (2) Acts 16.14
16.40
Lysanias Lk 3. 1
Lysias Acts 23.26
24.22
Lystra Acts 14. 6
14. 8
14.21
16. 1
16. 2
2 Tim 3.11

M

Maacah
see also Abel Beth Maacah
Maacah (1) Deut 3.14
Josh 12. 5
13.11
13.13
2 Sam 10. 6
10. 8
23.24
2 Kgs 25.23
1 Chr 19. 6
19. 7
Jer 40. 8
Maacah (2) Gen 22.24
Maacah (3) 2 Sam 3. 3
1 Chr 3. 1
Maacah (4) 1 Kgs 2.39
Maacah (5) 1 Kgs 15. 2
15.10
15.13
2 Chr 11.20
11.21
15.16
Maacah (6) 1 Chr 2.48
Maacah (7) 1 Chr 7.15
Maacah (8) 1 Chr 7.16
Maacah (9) 1 Chr 8.29
9.35
Maacah (10) 1 Chr 11.26
Maacah (11) 1 Chr 27.16
Maacath 1 Chr 4.19
AV Maachathite(s) *see* Maacah (1), Maacath
Maadai Ezra 10.34
Maadiah Neh 12. 2
Maai Neh 12.36
AV Maale-Acrabbim *see* Akrabbim (Pass)
Maarath Josh 15.59
Maasai 1 Chr 9.10
Maaseiah (1) 1 Chr 15.17
Maaseiah (2) 2 Chr 23. 1
Maaseiah (3) 2 Chr 26.11
Maaseiah (4) 2 Chr 28. 7
Maaseiah (5) 2 Chr 34. 8
Maaseiah (6) Ezra 10.18
Maaseiah (7) Ezra 10.21
Maaseiah (8) Ezra 10.22
Maaseiah (9) Ezra 10.30
Maaseiah (10) Neh 3.23
Maaseiah (11) Neh 8. 4
Maaseiah (12) Neh 8. 7
Maaseiah (13) Neh 10.14
Maaseiah (14) Neh 11. 5
Maaseiah (15) Neh 11. 7
Maaseiah (16) Neh 12.41
Maaseiah (17) Neh 12.42
Maaseiah (18) Jer 21. 1
29.24
37. 3
Maaseiah (19) Jer 29.21
Maaseiah (20) Jer 35. 4
Maath Lk 3.26
Maaz 1 Chr 2.26
Maaziah (1) 1 Chr 24. 7
Maaziah (2) Neh 10. 2
MACEDONIA
Machbannai 1 Chr 12. 9
Machbenah 1 Chr 2.49
Machi Num 13. 3
MACHIR (1)
Machir (2) 2 Sam 9. 4
17.27
Machnadebai Ezra 10.38
Machpelah Gen 23. 9
23.17
25. 9
49.30
50.13
Madai Gen 10. 2
1 Chr 1. 5
AV Madian *see* Midian
Madmannah (1) Josh 15.31
Madmannah (2) 1 Chr 2.49
Madmen Jer 48. 2
Madmenah Is 10.31
Madon Josh 11. 1
12.19
Magadan Mt 15.39
Magbish Ezra 2.21
AV Magdala *see* Magadan
Magdalene *see* Mary (2)
Magdiel Gen 36.40
1 Chr 1.54
Magog Gen 10. 2
1 Chr 1. 5

Magog (cont.)
Ezek 38. 2
39. 6
Rev 20. 8
AV Magor-Missabib *see* Terror (Everywhere)
Magpiash Neh 10.14
Mahalab Josh 19.29
Mahalaleel Lk 3.37
Mahalalel (1) Gen 5.12
5.15
1 Chr 1. 2
1. 2
Mahalalel (2) Neh 11. 4
Mahalath (1) Gen 28. 9
Mahalath (2) 2 Chr 11.18
Mahanaim Gen 32. 2
Josh 13.26
13.30
21.38
2 Sam 2. 8
2.12
2.29
17.24
17.27
19.32
1 Kgs 2. 8
4.14
1 Chr 6.80
AV Mahaneh-Dan *see* Camp Of Dan
Maharai 2 Sam 23.24
1 Chr 11.26
27. 2
Mahath (1) 1 Chr 6.35
Mahath (2) 2 Chr 29.12
Mahath (3) 2 Chr 31.13
Mahavah 1 Chr 11.26
Mahazioth 1 Chr 25. 4
25. 9
AV Maher-Shalal-Hash-Baz *see* Quick-Loot-Fast-Plunder
Mahlah (1) Num 26.33
27. 1
36.10
Josh 17. 3
Mahlah (2) 1 Chr 7.18
Mahli (1) Ex 6.19
Num 3.17
3.33
26.58
1 Chr 6.19
6.29
23.21
23.21
24.26
24.28
Ezra 8.18
Mahli (2) 1 Chr 6.47
23.23
24.30
Mahlon Ruth 1. 1
1. 5
4. 9
4.10
Mahol 1 Kgs 4.31
Mahseiah Jer 32.12
51.59
Maim *see* Misrephoth Maim
Makaz 1 Kgs 4. 9
Makheloth Num 33.15
Makkedah Josh 10.10
10.16
10.21
10.28
10.28
10.29
12.16
15.41
AV Maktesh *see* (the) Lower (part of the city)
Malachi Mal 1. 1
Malcam 1 Chr 8. 8
Malchiah (1) Jer 21. 1
38. 1
Malchiah (2) Jer 38. 6
Malchiel Gen 46.17
Num 26.45
1 Chr 7.31
7.31
Malchijah (1) 1 Chr 6.40
Malchijah (2) 1 Chr 9.10
Neh 11.12
Malchijah (3) 1 Chr 24. 7
Malchijah (4) Ezra 10.25
Malchijah (5) Ezra 10.25
Malchijah (6) Neh 3.14
Malchijah (7) Neh 3.31
Malchijah (8) Neh 8. 4
Malchijah (9) Neh 10. 2
Malchijah (10) Neh 12.42
Malchijah (11) Ezra 10.31

Malchijah (12)
Perhaps the same as (11).
Neh 3.11
Malchiram 1 Chr 3.18
Malchishua 1 Sam 14.49
31. 2
1 Chr 8.33
9.39
10. 2
Malchus Jn 18.10
AV Maleleel *see* Mahalaleel
Mallothi 1 Chr 25. 4
25. 9
Malluch (1) 1 Chr 6.44
Malluch (2) Ezra 10.29
Malluch (3) Ezra 10.31
Malluch (4) Neh 10. 2
Malluch (5) Neh 10.14
Malluch (6) Neh 12. 2
Malluchi Neh 12.12
Malta Acts 28. 1
Mamre (1) Gen 13.18
18. 1
20. 1
23.17
25. 9
35.27
49.30
50.13
Mamre (2) Gen 14.13
14.13
14.24
Manaen Acts 13. 1
Manahath (1) Gen 36.23
1 Chr 1.38
Manahath (2) 1 Chr 2.54
Manahath (3)
Perhaps the same as (2).
1 Chr 8. 6
MANASSEH (1)
MANASSEH (2)
Manasseh (3) Ezra 10.30
Manasseh (4) Ezra 10.33
AV Manasses *see* Manasseh
MANOAH
Maoch 1 Sam 27. 2
Maon (1) Josh 15.55
1 Sam 23.24
23.25
25. 2
Maon (2) 1 Chr 2.45
Maonites Judg 10.12
Marah (1) Ex 15.23
15.23
Num 33. 8
Marah (2)
see also Naomi
Ruth 1.20
AV Maralah *see* Mareal
Marcaboth *see* Beth Marcaboth
AV Marcus *see* Mark (2)
Marduk Jer 50. 2
Mareal Josh 19.11
Mareshah (1) Josh 15.44
1 Chr 4.21
2 Chr 11. 8
14. 9
14.10
20.37
Mic 1.15
Mareshah (2) 1 Chr 2.42
MARK (2)
MARKET OF APPIUS
Maroth Mic 1.12
AV Mars Hill *see* Areopagus
Marsena Esth 1.14
MARTHA
MARY (1)
MARY (2)
MARY (3)
MARY (4)
MARY (5)
MARY (6)
MARY (7)
AV Mash *see* Meshek
Mashal 1 Chr 6.74
Masrekah Gen 36.31
1 Chr 1.43
Massa Gen 25.14
1 Chr 1.30
Massah
see also Meribah
Ex 17. 7
Deut 6.16
9.22
33. 8
Ps 95. 8
AV Mathusala *see* Methuselah
Matred Gen 36.31
1 Chr 1.43

Matri 1 Sam 10.21
10.21
Mattan (1) 2 Kgs 11.18
2 Chr 23.17
Mattan (2) Jer 38. 1
Mattanah Num 21.18
Mattaniah (1)
see also Zedekiah (1)
2 Kgs 24.17
Mattaniah (2) 1 Chr 9.14
Mattaniah (3) 1 Chr 25. 4
25. 9
Mattaniah (4) Neh 12.33
Mattaniah (5) 2 Chr 20.14
Mattaniah (6) 2 Chr 29.12
Mattaniah (7) Ezra 10.26
Mattaniah (8) Ezra 10.27
Mattaniah (9) Ezra 10.30
Mattaniah (10) Ezra 10.34
Mattaniah (11) Neh 12.25
Mattaniah (12) Neh 13.13
Mattaniah (13) Neh 11.17
11.17
Mattaniah (14) Neh 11.22
Mattaniah (15) Neh 12. 8
Mattatha Lk 3.31
Mattathias (1) Lk 3.25
Mattathias (2) Lk 3.26
Mattattah Ezra 10.33
Mattenai (1) Ezra 10.33
Mattenai (2) Ezra 10.34
Mattenai (3) Neh 12.12
Matthan Mt 1.12
Matthat (1) Lk 3.24
Matthat (2) Lk 3.29
Matthew
see also Levi (4)
Mt 9. 9
9. 9
9.10
10. 3
Mk 3.18
Lk 6.15
Acts 1.13
Matthias Acts 1.23
1.26
Mattithiah (1) 1 Chr 9.31
Mattithiah (2) Ezra 10.43
Mattithiah (3) Neh 8. 4
Mattithiah (4) 1 Chr 15.17
Mattithiah (5)
perhaps the same as (4).
1 Chr 16. 5
Mattithiah (6)
perhaps the same as (4).
1 Chr 25. 3
25. 9
AV Mazzaroth *see* Stars
AV Meah *see* (Tower of the) Hundred
Mearah Josh 13. 4
Mebunnai 2 Sam 23.24
Mecherah 1 Chr 11.26
AV Mecherathite *see* Mecherah
Meconah Neh 11.28
Medad Num 11.26
11.27
Medan Gen 25. 2
1 Chr 1.32
Mede *see* Media
Medeba Num 21.30
Josh 13. 9
13.16
1 Chr 19. 7
Is 15. 2
MEDIA
MEDITERRANEAN
MEGIDDO
AV Megiddon *see* Megiddo
Mehetabel (1) Gen 36.31
1 Chr 1.43
Mehetabel (2) Neh 6.10
Mehida Ezra 2.43
Neh 7.46
Mehir 1 Chr 4.11
4.11
Meholah
see also Abel Meholah
1 Sam 18.19
2 Sam 21. 8
AV Meholathite *see* Meholah
Mehujael Gen 4.18
4.18
Mehuman Esth 1.10
Mejarkon Josh 19.46
Melah *see* Tel Melah
Melatiah Neh 3. 7
Melchi (1) Lk 3.24
Melchi (2) Lk 3.28
AV Melchisedec *see* Melchizedek
MELCHIZEDEK
Melea Lk 3.31

Melech
see also Allam Melech, Nathan Melech
1 Chr 8.35
9.41
AV Melicu *see* Malluchi
AV Melita *see* Malta
AV Melzar *see* Guard
Memphis Is 19.13
Jer 2.16
44. 1
46.14
46.19
Ezek 30.13
Hos 9. 6
Memucan Esth 1.14
1.16
1.21
MEN OF THUNDER
Menahem 2 Kgs 15.14
15.16
15.17
15.19
15.19
15.20
15.21
15.23
Meni Is 65.11
Menna Lk 3.31
Menuhoth 1 Chr 2.52
Meon *see* Baal Meon
AV Meonenim *see* Fortune-Tellers
Meonothai 1 Chr 4.13
4.14
Mephaath Josh 13.18
21.37
1 Chr 6.79
Mephath Jer 48.21
MEPHIBOSHETH (1)
Mephibosheth (2) 2 Sam 21. 8
Merab 1 Sam 14.49
18.17
18.19
2 Sam 21. 8
Meraiah Neh 12.12
Meraioth (1) 1 Chr 6. 6
6.52
Ezra 7. 3
Meraioth (2) 1 Chr 9.10
Neh 11.11
Meraioth (3) Neh 12.12
MERARI
Merathaim Jer 50.21
AV Mercurius *see* Hermes
Mered 1 Chr 4.17
4.17
4.17
Meremoth (1) Ezra 8.33
Neh 3. 4
3.21
10. 2
Meremoth (2) Ezra 10.34
Meremoth (3) Neh 12. 2
Meres Esth 1.14
MERIBAH
Meribbaal
see also Mephibosheth (1)
1 Chr 8.34
9.40
Merodach Baladan 2 Kgs 20.12
Is 39. 1
Merom Josh 11. 5
11. 7
Meron *see* Shimron Meron
Meronoth 1 Chr 27.25
Neh 3. 7
Meroz Judg 5.23
Mesha (1) Gen 10.30
Mesha (2) 2 Kgs 3. 4
3. 5
Mesha (3) 1 Chr 2.42
2.42
Mesha (4) 1 Chr 8. 8
MESHACH
Meshech Gen 10. 2
1 Chr 1. 5
Ps 120. 5
Ezek 27.13
32.26
38. 2
39. 1
Meshek Gen 10.23
1 Chr 1.17
Meshelemiah 1 Chr 9.21
26. 1
26. 9
Meshezabel (1) Neh 3. 4
Meshezabel (2) Neh 10.14
Meshezabel (3) Neh 11.24
Meshillemith 1 Chr 9.10
Meshillemoth (1) 2 Chr 28.12
Meshillemoth (2) Neh 11.13

Meshobab	1 Chr	4.34
Meshullam (1)	2 Kgs	22. 3
Meshullam (2)	1 Chr	3.19
Meshullam (3)	1 Chr	5.13
Meshullam (4)	1 Chr	8.17
Meshullam (5)	1 Chr	9. 7
Meshullam (6)	1 Chr	9. 7
Meshullam (7)	1 Chr	9.10
Meshullam (8)	1 Chr	9.10
	Neh	11.11
Meshullam (9)	2 Chr	34.12
Meshullam (10)	Ezra	8.16
Meshullam (11)	Ezra	10.29
Meshullam (12)	Neh	3. 4
		3.30
		6.18
Meshullam (13)	Neh	3. 6
Meshullam (14)	Neh	10. 2
Meshullam (15)	Neh	10.14
Meshullam (16)	Neh	11. 7
Meshullam (17)	Neh	12.12
Meshullam (18)	Neh	12.25
Meshullam (19)	Neh	12.12
		12.33
Meshullam (20)	Ezra	10.15
Meshullam (21)	Neh	8. 4
Meshullemeth	2 Kgs	21.19
AV Mesobaite *see* Zobah		
MESOPOTAMIA		
AV Metheg-Ammah *see* (their) Control (over the land)		
Methuselah	Gen	5.21
		5.25
	1 Chr	1. 3
		1. 3
	Lk	3.37
Methushael	Gen	4.18
Meunim	Ezra	2.43
	Neh	7.46
Meunites	2 Chr	20. 1
		26. 7
Mezahab	Gen	36.31
	1 Chr	1.43
AV Miamin *see* Mijamin		
Mibhar	1 Chr	11.26
Mibsam (1)	Gen	25.13
	1 Chr	1.29
Mibsam (2)	1 Chr	4.25
Mibzar	Gen	36.40
	1 Chr	1.53
Mica (1) *see also* Micah (3)		
	2 Sam	9.12
Mica (2)	1 Chr	9.14
	Neh	11.17
		11.22
Mica (3)	Neh	10. 9
MICAH (1)		
Micah (2)	Jer	26.18
		26.19
	Mic	1. 1
		1. 1
		1. 8
Micah (3) *see also* Mica (1)		
	1 Chr	8.34
		8.35
		9.40
		9.41
Micah (4)	1 Chr	23.20
		24.24
		24.25
Micah (5)	1 Chr	5. 4
MICAIAH (1)		
Micaiah (2)	Jer	36.11
		36.13
Micaiah (3)	2 Kgs	22.12
	2 Chr	34.20
Micaiah (4)	Neh	12.41
Micaiah (5)	Neh	12.33
Micaiah (6)	2 Chr	13. 2
Micaiah (7)	2 Chr	17. 7
AV Micha *see* Mica		
MICHAEL (1)		
Michael (2)	Num	13. 3
Michael (3)	1 Chr	5.13
Michael (4)	1 Chr	5.14
Michael (5)	1 Chr	6.40
Michael (6)	1 Chr	7. 3
Michael (7)	1 Chr	8.16
Michael (8)	1 Chr	12.20
Michael (9)	1 Chr	27.16
Michael (10)	2 Chr	21. 2
Michael (11)	Ezra	8. 2
MICHAL		
MICHMASH		
Michmethath	Josh	16. 6
		17. 7
Michri	1 Chr	9. 7
Middin	Josh	15.61
MIDDLE GATE		

MIDIAN		
Migdalel	Josh	19.38
Migdalgad	Josh	15.37
Migdol	Ex	14. 2
	Num	33. 7
	Jer	44. 1
		46.14
	Ezek	29.10
		30. 6
Migron	1 Sam	14. 2
	Is	10.28
Mijamin (1)	1 Chr	24. 7
Mijamin (2)	Ezra	10.25
Mijamin (3)	Neh	10. 2
Mijamin (4) *perhaps the same as (3).*		
	Neh	12. 2
Mikloth (1)	1 Chr	8.32
		9.37
Mikloth (2)	1 Chr	27. 2
Mikneiah	1 Chr	15.17
Milalai	Neh	12.36
Milcah (1)	Gen	11.29
		22.20
		22.23
		24.15
		24.24
		24.47
Milcah (2)	Num	26.33
		27. 1
		36.10
	Josh	17. 3
AV Milcom *see* Molech		
Miletus	Acts	20.15
		20.17
	2 Tim	4.20
AV Millo, house of *see* Bethmillo		
AV Millo *see* (where land was) Filled (in)		
Miniamin (1)	2 Chr	31.15
Miniamin (2)	Neh	12.12
		12.41
Minni	Jer	51.27
Minnith	Judg	11.33
MIPHKAD GATE		
MIRIAM (1)		
Miriam (2)	1 Chr	4.17
Mirmah	1 Chr	8.10
AV Misgab *see* (mighty) Fortress		
Mishael (1)	Ex	6.22
	Lev	10. 4
Mishael (2) *see also* Meshach		
	Dan	1. 6
		1.19
		2.17
Mishael (3)	Neh	8. 4
Mishal	Josh	19.26
		21.30
Misham	1 Chr	8.12
Mishma	Gen	25.14
	1 Chr	1.30
		4.25
		4.26
Mishmannah	1 Chr	12. 9
Mishraites	1 Chr	2.53
Mispar	Ezra	2. 2
Mispereth	Neh	7. 7
Misrephoth Maim	Josh	11. 8
		13. 6
Mithan	1 Chr	11.26
Mithkah	Num	33.15
Mithredath (1)	Ezra	1. 8
Mithredath (2)	Ezra	4. 7
Mitylene	Acts	20.14
Mizar	Ps	42. 6
MIZPAH (1)		
Mizpah (2)	Judg	10.17
		11.11
		11.29
		11.34
	Hos	5. 1
Mizpah (3)	Josh	11. 3
		11. 8
Mizpah (4) *see also* Galeed, Jegar Shadutha		
	Gen	31.49
Mizpah (5)	1 Sam	22. 3
Mizpah (6)	Josh	15.38
Mizpeh *see* Ramath Mizpeh		
Mizraim *see* Abel Mizraim		
Mizzah	Gen	36.10
		36.17
	1 Chr	1.37
Mnason	Acts	21.16
MOAB		
Moadiah	Neh	12.12
MOB (1)		
Moladah	Josh	15.26
		19. 2

Moladah (cont.)		
	1 Chr	4.28
	Neh	11.26
MOLECH		
Molid	1 Chr	2.29
AV Morasthite *see* Moresheth		
MORDECAI (1)		
Mordecai (2)	Ezra	2. 2
	Neh	7. 7
Moreh (1)	Gen	12. 6
	Deut	11.30
Moreh (2)	Judg	7. 1
Moresheth	Jer	26.18
	Mic	1. 1
Moresheth Gath	Mic	1.14
Moriah	Gen	22. 2
	2 Chr	3. 1
Moserah	Deut	10. 6
Moseroth	Num	33.15
MOSES		
Moza (1)	1 Chr	2.46
Moza (2)	1 Chr	8.36
		8.37
		9.42
		9.43
Mozah	Josh	18.26
Muppim	Gen	46.21
Mushi	Ex	6.19
	Num	3.17
		3.33
		26.58
	1 Chr	6.19
		6.47
		23.21
		23.23
		24.26
		24.30
Musri	1 Kgs	10.28
	2 Chr	1.16
		9.28
Myra	Acts	27. 5
Mysia	Acts	16. 7
		16. 8

N

Naam	1 Chr	4.15
Naamah (1)	1 Kgs	14.21
	2 Chr	12.13
Naamah (2)	Gen	4.22
Naamah (3)	Josh	15.41
Naamah (4)	Job	2.11
NAAMAN (1)		
Naaman (2)	Gen	46.21
	Num	26.40
	1 Chr	8. 4
		8. 6
AV Naamathite *see* Naamah		
Naarah (1)	Josh	16. 7
Naarah (2)	1 Chr	4. 5
		4. 6
Naarai	1 Chr	11.26
Naaran	1 Chr	7.28
AV Naason *see* Nahshon		
NABAL		
NABOTH		
AV Nachor *see* Nahor		
Nacon	2 Sam	6. 6
NADAB (1)		
Nadab (2)	1 Kgs	14.20
		15.25
		15.27
		15.27
		15.28
		15.31
Nadab (3)	1 Chr	2.28
		2.30
Nadab (4)	1 Chr	8.30
		9.36
Naggai	Lk	3.25
Nahalal	Josh	19.15
		21.35
	Judg	1.30
Nahaliel	Num	21.19
		21.19
AV Nahalol *see* Nahalal		
Naham	1 Chr	4.19
Nahamani	Neh	7. 7
Naharai	2 Sam	23.24
	1 Chr	11.26
NAHASH (1)		
Nahash (2)	2 Sam	17.25
Nahash (3)	1 Chr	4.12
Nahath (1)	Gen	36.10
		36.17
	1 Chr	1.37
Nahath (2)	1 Chr	6.26

Nahath (3)	2 Chr	31.13
Nahbi	Num	13. 3
NAHOR (1)		
Nahor (2)	Gen	11.22
		11.24
	1 Chr	1.26
	Lk	3.34
Nahshon	Ex	6.23
	Num	1. 5
		2. 3
		7.12
		10.14
	Ruth	4.18
	1 Chr	2.10
	Mt	1. 2
	Lk	3.32
Nahum	Nah	1. 1
	Lk	3.25
Nain	Lk	7.11
Naioth	1 Sam	19.18
		19.19
		19.22
		19.23
		20. 1
NAOMI		
Naphish	Gen	25.15
	1 Chr	1.31
		5.19
NAPHTALI		
Naphtuh	Gen	10.13
	1 Chr	1.11
Narcissus	Rom	16.11
Nashim	Num	21.30
NATHAN (1)		
Nathan (2)	2 Sam	5.14
	1 Chr	3. 5
		14. 4
	Lk	3.31
Nathan (3)	2 Sam	23.24
Nathan (4)	Zech	12.12
Nathan (5)	1 Chr	11.26
Nathan (6)	Ezra	8.16
Nathan (7)	Ezra	10.38
Nathan (8)	1 Kgs	4. 5
Nathan (9) *perhaps the same as (8).*		
	1 Kgs	4. 5
Nathan (10) *perhaps the same as (9).*		
	1 Chr	2.36
Nathan Melech	2 Kgs	23.11
Nathanael	Jn	1.45
		1.46
		1.47
		1.48
		1.49
		21. 2
AV Naum *see* Nahum		
NAZARENE		
NAZARETH		
Neah	Josh	19.13
Neapolis	Acts	16.11
Neariah (1)	1 Chr	3.22
		3.23
Neariah (2)	1 Chr	4.42
Nebai	Neh	10.14
Nebaioth	Gen	25.13
		28. 9
		36. 3
	1 Chr	1.29
	Is	60. 7
Neballat	Neh	11.34
Nebat	1 Kgs	11.26
		12. 2
		12.15
		21.22
	2 Kgs	3. 3
		14.24
		15. 9
		15.18
		15.24
		15.28
		17.21
		23.15
	2 Chr	10. 2
		10.15
		13. 6
Nebo *see also* Samgar Nebo		
Nebo (1) *see also* Pisgah		
	Num	33.41
	Deut	32.49
		34. 1
Nebo (2)	Num	32. 3
		32.38
	1 Chr	5. 8
	Is	15. 2
	Jer	48. 1
		48.22

Nebo (3)	Ezra	2.21
		10.43
	Neh	7.26
Nebo (4)	Is	46. 1
NEBUCHADNEZZAR		
AV Nebuchadrezzar *see* Nebuchadnezzar		
Nebushazban	Jer	39.13
NEBUZARADAN		
NECO		
Nedabiah	1 Chr	3.18
Nehelam	Jer	29.24
Nehemiah (1)	Neh	1. 1
		1. 1
		8. 9
		10. 1
		12.26
		12.47
Nehemiah (2)	Neh	3.16
Nehemiah (3)	Ezra	2. 2
	Neh	7. 7
Nehum	Neh	7. 7
Nehushta	2 Kgs	24. 8
Nehushtan	2 Kgs	18. 4
Neiel	Josh	19.27
AV Nekeb *see* Adaminekeb		
Nekoda	Ezra	2.43
		2.59
	Neh	7.46
		7.61
Nemuel (1)	Num	26. 9
Nemuel (2)	Num	26.12
	1 Chr	4.24
Nepheg (1)	Ex	6.21
Nepheg (2)	2 Sam	5.15
	1 Chr	3. 7
		14. 6
AV Nephilim *see* Giant		
Nephisim	Ezra	2.43
AV Nephthalim *see* Naphtali		
Nephtoah	Josh	15. 9
		18.15
Nephushesim	Neh	7.46
Ner (1)	1 Sam	14.50
		14.51
		26. 5
	2 Sam	2. 8
	1 Kgs	2. 5
	1 Chr	26.28
Ner (2)	1 Chr	8.30
		8.33
		9.36
		9.39
Nereus	Rom	16.15
Nergal	2 Kgs	17.30
Nergal Sarezer (1)	Jer	39. 3
Nergal Sarezer (2)	Jer	39. 3
		39.13
Neri	Lk	3.27
Neriah	Jer	32.12
		36. 4
		43. 3
		51.59
Netaim	1 Chr	4.23
Nethanel (1)	Num	1. 5
		2. 3
		7.12
		10.15
Nethanel (2)	1 Chr	2.14
Nethanel (3)	1 Chr	15.23
Nethanel (4)	1 Chr	24. 6
Nethanel (5)	1 Chr	26. 4
Nethanel (6)	2 Chr	17. 7
Nethanel (7)	2 Chr	35. 9
Nethanel (8)	Ezra	10.22
Nethanel (9)	Neh	12.12
Nethanel (10)	Neh	12.36
Nethaniah (1)	2 Kgs	25.23
		25.25
	Jer	40. 8
		41. 1
Nethaniah (2)	2 Chr	17. 8
Nethaniah (3)	Jer	36.14
Nethaniah (4)	1 Chr	25. 2
Nethaniah (5) *perhaps the same as (4).*	1 Chr	25. 9
AV Nethinims *see* (Temple) Workmen		
Netophah	2 Sam	23.24
		23.24
	2 Kgs	25.23
	1 Chr	9.14
		11.26
		11.26
		27. 2
		27. 2
	Ezra	2.21
	Neh	7.26
		12.28
	Jer	40. 8
Netophath	1 Chr	2.54
NEW GATE		
Neziah	Ezra	2.43
	Neh	7.46
Nezib	Josh	15.43
Nibhaz	2 Kgs	17.31
Nibshan	Josh	15.62
Nicanor	Acts	6. 5
Nicodemus	Jn	3. 1
		3. 4
		3. 9
		7.50
		19.39
Nicolaitans	Rev	2. 6
		2.15
AV Nicolas *see* Nicolaus		
Nicolaus	Acts	6. 5
Nicopolis	Tit	3.12
AV Niger *see* (the) Black		
NILE		
Nimrah *see also* Beth Nimrah	Num	32. 3
Nimrim	Is	15. 6
	Jer	48.34
Nimrod	Gen	10. 8
		10. 9
	1 Chr	1.10
	Mic	5. 6
Nimrod *see also* Assyria		
Nimshi	1 Kgs	19.16
	2 Kgs	9. 2
	2 Chr	22. 7
NINEVEH		
NISAN		
Nisroch	2 Kgs	19.37
	Is	37.38
AV No *see* Thebes		
Noadiah	Ezra	8.33
AV Noadiah *see* Nodiah		
NOAH (1)		
Noah (2)	Num	26.33
		27. 1
		36.10
	Josh	17. 3
Nob	1 Sam	21. 1
		22. 9
		22.11
		22.19
	Neh	11.32
	Is	10.32
Nobah (1)	Num	32.42
Nobah (2) *see also* Kenath	Num	32.42
	Judg	8.11
AV Nobai *see* Nebai		
AV Nod *see* Wandering		
Nodab	1 Chr	5.19
Nodiah	Neh	6.14
AV Noe *see* Noah (1)		
Nogah	1 Chr	3. 7
		14. 6
Nohah	1 Chr	8. 2
AV Non *see* Nun		
AV Noph *see* Memphis		
Nophah	Num	21.30
NORTH GATE		
NORTH-EASTER		
NOT-MY-PEOPLE		
NUN		
Nympha	Col	4.15

O

OAK OF WEEPING		
Obadiah (1)	1 Kgs	18. 3
		18. 3
		18. 4
		18. 5
		18. 7
		18. 9
		18.16
Obadiah (2)	1 Chr	3.21
Obadiah (3)	1 Chr	7. 3
Obadiah (4)	1 Chr	9.14
Obadiah (5)	1 Chr	8.38
		9.44
Obadiah (6)	1 Chr	12. 9
Obadiah (7)	1 Chr	27.16
Obadiah (8)	2 Chr	17. 7
Obadiah (9)	2 Chr	34.12
Obadiah (10)	Ezra	8. 2
Obadiah (11) *possibly the same as (10).*	Neh	10. 2
Obadiah (12)	Neh	12.25
Obadiah (13)	Obad	1
Obal	Gen	10.28
Obed (1)	Ruth	4.17
		4.17
		4.18
	1 Chr	2.12
	Mt	1. 2
	Lk	3.32
Obed (2)	1 Chr	2.37
Obed (3)	1 Chr	11.26
Obed (4)	1 Chr	26. 6
Obed (5)	2 Chr	23. 1
OBED EDOM (1)		
OBED EDOM (2)		
Obil	1 Chr	27.25
Oboth	Num	21.10
		33.41
Ochran	Num	1. 5
		2.25
		7.12
		10.26
Oded (1)	2 Chr	15. 1
		15. 8
Oded (2)	2 Chr	28. 9
OG		
Ohad	Gen	46.10
	Ex	6.15
Ohel	1 Chr	3.20
Oholah	Ezek	23. 4
		23. 5
		23.11
		23.36
		23.44
Oholiab	Ex	31. 6
		35.34
		36. 1
		36. 2
		38.23
Oholibah	Ezek	23. 4
		23.11
		23.21
		23.22
		23.36
		23.44
Oholibamah (1)	Gen	36. 2
		36. 5
		36.14
		36.18
		36.25
Oholibamah (2)	Gen	36.40
	1 Chr	1.52
AV Olivet *see* (Mount of) Olive(s)		
Olympas	Rom	16.15
Omar	Gen	36.10
		36.15
	1 Chr	1.36
AV Omega *see* Last (2)		
OMRI (1)		
Omri (2)	1 Chr	7. 8
Omri (3)	1 Chr	9. 4
Omri (4)	1 Chr	27.16
On	Num	16. 1
Onam (1)	Gen	36.23
	1 Chr	1.38
Onam (2)	1 Chr	2.26
		2.28
Onan	Gen	38. 4
		38. 8
		38. 9
		46.12
	Num	26.19
	1 Chr	2. 3
Onesimus	Col	4. 9
	Phlm	10
		15
Onesiphorus	2 Tim	1.16
		4.19
Ono (1)	1 Chr	8.12
	Ezra	2.21
	Neh	7.26
		11.35
Ono (2)	Neh	6. 2
Ophel	2 Chr	27. 3
		33.14
	Neh	3.25
		3.27
		11.21
Ophir (1)	Gen	10.29
	1 Chr	1.23
Ophir (2) *perhaps the same as (1).*	1 Kgs	9.28
		10.11
		22.48
	2 Chr	8.18
		9.10
Ophni	Josh	18.24
Ophrah (1)	Judg	6.11
		6.24
		8.27
		8.32
		9. 5
Ophrah (2)	Josh	18.23
	1 Sam	13.17
Ophrah (3)	1 Chr	4.14
Oreb	Judg	7.25
		8. 3
	Ps	83.11
Oreb Rock	Judg	7.25
	Is	10.26
Oren	1 Chr	2.25
AV Ornan *see* Araunah		
Orpah	Ruth	1. 4
		1.14
AV Osee *see* Hosea		
AV Oshea *see* Hoshea		
AV Osnappar *see* Asnapper		
Othni	1 Chr	26. 6
OTHNIEL		
Ozem (1)	1 Chr	2.15
Ozem (2)	1 Chr	2.25
AV Ozias *see* Uzziah		
Ozni	Num	26.16

P

Paarai	2 Sam	23.24
AV Padan (Aram) *see* Mesopotamia		
Padon	Ezra	2.43
	Neh	7.46
Pagiel	Num	1. 5
		2.25
		7.12
		10.26
Pahath Moab (1)	Ezra	2. 3
		8. 2
		10.30
	Neh	7. 8
Pahath Moab (2)	Neh	3.11
Pahath Moab (3)	Neh	10.14
AV Pai *see* Pau		
Palal	Neh	3.25
AV Palestina, -ine *see* Philistines, Philistia		
Pallu	Gen	46. 9
	Ex	6.14
	Num	26. 5
		26. 8
	1 Chr	5. 3
Palmyra	2 Chr	8. 4
Palti (1)	Num	13. 3
Palti (2)	1 Sam	25.44
Paltiel (1)	Num	34.19
Paltiel (2)	2 Sam	3.15
		3.16
Pamphylia	Acts	2.10
		13.13
		14.24
		15.38
		27. 5
Paneah *see* Zaphenath Paneah		
Paphos	Acts	13. 6
		13.13
Parah	Josh	18.23
PARAN		
AV Parbar *see* Pavilion		
Parmashta	Esth	9. 7
Parmenas	Acts	6. 5
Parnach	Num	34.19
Parosh (1)	Ezra	2. 3
		8. 2
		10.25
	Neh	3.25
		7. 8
Parosh (2)	Neh	10.14
Parshandatha	Esth	9. 7
Parthia	Acts	2. 9
Paruah	1 Kgs	4.17
Parvaim	2 Chr	3. 6
Pas Dammim *see also* Ephes Dammim	1 Chr	11.13
Pasach	1 Chr	7.33
Paseah (1)	1 Chr	4.12
Paseah (2)	Ezra	2.43
	Neh	7.46
Paseah (3)	Neh	3. 6
Pashhur (1)	Jer	20. 1
		20. 3
		20. 3
		20. 6
Pashhur (2)	1 Chr	9.10
	Neh	11.12
	Jer	21. 1
		38. 1
Pashhur (3)	Ezra	2.36
		10.22
	Neh	7.39
Pashhur (4)	Jer	38. 1
Pashhur (5)	Neh	10. 2

Patara	Acts	21. 1
Pathros	Is	11.11
Pathrus	Gen	10.14
	1 Chr	1.12
Patmos	Rev	1. 9
Patrobas	Rom	16.14
Pau	Gen	36.31
	1 Chr	1.43
PAUL		
Paulus *see* Sergius Paulus		
Pedahel	Num	34.19
Pedahzur	Num	1. 5
		2.18
		7.12
		10.23
Pedaiah (1)	2 Kgs	23.36
Pedaiah (2)	1 Chr	3.18
		3.19
Pedaiah (3)	1 Chr	27.16
Pedaiah (4)	Neh	3.25
Pedaiah (5)	Neh	11. 7
Pedaiah (6)	Neh	8. 4
Pedaiah (7)	Neh	13.13
PEKAH		
Pekahiah	2 Kgs	15.22
		15.23
		15.25
		15.25
		15.26
Pekod	Jer	50.21
	Ezek	23.23
Pelaiah (1)	1 Chr	3.24
Pelaiah (2)	Neh	8. 7
		10. 9
Pelaliah	Neh	11.12
Pelatiah (1)	1 Chr	3.21
Pelatiah (2)	1 Chr	4.42
Pelatiah (3)	Neh	10.14
Pelatiah (4)	Ezek	11. 1
		11.13
Peleg	Gen	10.25
		11.16
		11.18
	1 Chr	1.19
		1.25
	Lk	3.35
Pelet (1)	2 Sam	23.24
	1 Chr	11.26
Pelet (2)	1 Chr	2.47
Pelet (3)	1 Chr	12. 3
Peleth (1)	Num	16. 1
Peleth (2)	1 Chr	2.33
Pelon	1 Chr	11.26
		27. 2
Pelusium		
see also Sin (2)		
	Ezek	30.15
		30.16
Peniel		
see also Penuel (1)		
	Gen	32.30
		32.31
Peninnah	1 Sam	1. 2
		1. 2
		1. 4
		1. 6
		1. 7
Penuel (1)		
see also Peniel		
	Judg	8. 8
		8. 8
		8.17
	1 Kgs	12.25
Penuel (2)	1 Chr	4. 3
		4. 3
Penuel (3)	1 Chr	8.25
PEOPLE'S GATE		
PEOR		
Perazim		
see also Baal Perazim		
	Is	28.21
AV Peres *see* Division(s)		
Peresh	1 Chr	7.16
		7.16
PEREZ		
Perez Uzzah	2 Sam	6. 8
	1 Chr	13.11
Perga	Acts	13.13
		13.14
		14.25
Pergamum	Rev	1.11
		2.12
Perida	Neh	7.57
Perizzites	Gen	13. 7
		15.20
		34.30
	Ex	3. 8
		3.17
		23.23
		33. 2
		34.11
Perizzites (cont.)		
	Deut	7. 1
		20.17
	Josh	3.10
		9. 1
		11. 3
		12. 8
		17.15
		24.11
	Judg	1. 4
		3. 5
	1 Kgs	9.20
	2 Chr	8. 7
	Ezra	9. 1
	Neh	9. 8
PERSIA		
Persis	Rom	16.12
Peruda	Ezra	2.55
PETER		
Pethahiah (1)	1 Chr	24. 7
Pethahiah (2)	Ezra	10.23
	Neh	9. 5
Pethahiah (3)	Neh	11.24
Pethor	Num	22. 5
	Deut	23. 4
Pethuel	Joel	1. 1
Peullethai	1 Chr	26. 5
AV Phalec *see* Peleg		
AV Phallu *see* Pallu		
AV Phalti, -iel *see* Palti		
Phanuel	Lk	2.36
PHARAOH		
AV Phares *see* Perez		
Pharpar	2 Kgs	5.12
AV Pharzites *see* Perez		
AV Phebe *see* Phoebe		
AV Phenice *see* Phoenix		
AV Phenicia *see* Phoenicia		
AV Phi-Beseth *see* Bubastis		
Phicol	Gen	21.22
		21.32
		26.26
Philadelphia	Rev	1.11
		3. 7
Philemon	Phlm	1
		4
Philetus	2 Tim	2.17
PHILIP (1)		
PHILIP (2)		
PHILIP (3)		
PHILIP (4)		
Philippi		
see also Caesarea Philippi		
	Acts	16.12
		20. 6
	Phil	1. 1
		4.15
	1 Thes	2. 2
PHILISTIA		
AV Philistim *see* Philistines		
PHILISTINES		
Philologus	Rom	16.15
PHINEHAS (1)		
Phinehas (2)	1 Sam	1. 3
		2.34
		4. 4
		4.11
		4.17
		4.19
		14. 3
Phinehas (3)	Ezra	8.33
Phlegon	Rom	16.14
Phoebe	Rom	16. 1
Phoenicia	Is	23. 6
		23.11
	Obad	20
	Mk	7.26
	Acts	11.19
		15. 3
		21. 2
Phoenix	Acts	27.12
		27.12
Phrygia	Acts	2.10
		16. 6
		18.23
AV Phurah *see* Purah		
AV Phut *see* Libya		
AV Phuvah *see* Puah		
Phygelus	2 Tim	1.15
Pi Hahiroth	Ex	14. 2
		14. 9
	Num	33. 7
		33. 8
AV Pi-Beseth *see* Bubastis		
PILATE		
Pildash	Gen	22.22
Pileser *see* Tiglath Pileser		
Pilha	Neh	10.14
Piltai	Neh	12.12
Pinon	Gen	36.40
	1 Chr	1.52
Piram	Josh	10. 3
Pirathon	Judg	12.13
		12.15
	2 Sam	23.24
	1 Chr	11.26
		27. 2
Pisgah		
see also Nebo (1)		
	Num	21.20
		23.14
	Deut	3.17
		3.27
		4.49
		34. 1
	Josh	12. 3
		13.20
Pishon	Gen	2.11
Pisidia	Acts	13.14
		14.19
		14.21
		14.24
AV Pison *see* Pishon		
Pispa	1 Chr	7.38
Pithom	Ex	1.11
Pithon	1 Chr	8.35
		9.41
Pochereth Hazzebaim	Ezra	2.55
	Neh	7.57
AV Pollux *see* Twin Gods		
Pontius Pilate *see* Pilate		
Pontus	Acts	2. 9
		18. 2
	1 Pet	1. 1
Poratha	Esth	9. 7
Porcius Festus *see* Festus		
Potiphar	Gen	37.36
		39. 1
		39. 4
		39. 6
Potiphera	Gen	41.45
		46.20
POTSHERD GATE		
POTTER'S FIELD		
AV Prisca *see* Priscilla		
Priscilla	Acts	18. 2
		18.18
		18.19
		18.26
	Rom	16. 3
	1 Cor	16.19
	2 Tim	4.19
Prochorus	Acts	6. 5
Ptolemais	Acts	21. 7
AV Pua *see* Puah		
Puah (1)	Gen	46.13
	Num	26.23
	1 Chr	7. 1
Puah (2)	Ex	1.15
Puah (3)	Judg	10. 1
Publius	Acts	28. 7
		28. 8
Pudens	2 Tim	4.21
AV Puhites *see* Puthites		
Pul		
see also Tiglath Pileser, Libya		
	1 Chr	5.26
AV Punites *see* Puah		
Punon	Num	33.41
AV Pur *see* Lot (1)		
Purah	Judg	7.10
		7.11
AV Put *see* Libya		
Puteoli	Acts	28.13
Puthites	1 Chr	2.53
Putiel	Ex	6.25
Pyrrhus	Acts	20. 4

Q

QUARREL		
Quartus	Rom	16.23
QUICK-LOOT-FAST-PLUNDER		
Quirinius	Lk	2. 2

R

Raamah	Gen	10. 7
		10. 7
	1 Chr	1. 9
		1. 9
	Ezek	27.22
Raamiah	Neh	7. 7
AV Raamses *see* Rameses		
AV Rab-Shakeh *see* (Assyrian) Official		
RABBAH (1)		
Rabbah (2)	Josh	15.60
AV Rabbath *see* Rabbah		
Rabbith	Josh	19.20
Racal	1 Sam	30.29
AV Rachab *see* Rahab (3)		
RACHEL		
Raddai	1 Chr	2.14
AV Ragau *see* Reu		
AV Raguel *see* Jethro		
RAHAB (1)		
RAHAB (2)		
Rahab (3)	Mt	1. 2
AV Rahab *see* Egypt		
Raham	1 Chr	2.44
AV Rahel *see* Rachel		
Rakem	1 Chr	7.16
Rakkath	Josh	19.35
Rakkon	Josh	19.46
Ram (2)	Ruth	4.18
	1 Chr	2. 9
		2.10
		2.10
	Mt	1. 2
Ram (3)	1 Chr	2.25
		2.26
Ram (4)	Job	32. 2
RAMAH (1)		
RAMAH (2)		
Ramah (3)	Josh	19.29
Ramah (4)	Josh	19.36
Ramah (5)		
see also Baalath Beer		
	Josh	19. 8
	1 Sam	30.27
Ramath Lehi	Judg	15.17
Ramath Mizpeh	Josh	13.26
AV Ramathaim-Zophim *see* Ramah		
Rameses	Gen	47.11
	Ex	1.11
		12.37
	Num	33. 3
		33. 5
Ramiah	Ezra	10.25
RAMOTH (1)		
Ramoth (2)		
City in Issachar.		
	1 Chr	6.73
Rapha	1 Chr	8. 2
Raphah	1 Chr	8.37
Raphu	Num	13. 3
Reaiah (1)	1 Chr	4. 2
Reaiah (2)	1 Chr	5. 4
Reaiah (3)	Ezra	2.43
	Neh	7.46
Reba	Num	31. 8
	Josh	13.21
REBECCA		
AV Rebekah *see* Rebecca		
Recah	1 Chr	4.12
Rechab (1)	2 Sam	4. 2
		4. 5
		4. 6
		4.12
Rechab (2)	2 Kgs	10.15
		10.23
	Jer	35. 6
		35.19
Rechab (3)		
perhaps the same as (2).		
	Neh	3.14
Rechabite		
see also Rechab (2)		
	1 Chr	2.55
	Jer	35. 2
		35. 3
		35. 5
		35.18
RED SEA		
Reelaiah	Ezra	2. 2
Regem	1 Chr	2.47
Regemmelech	Zech	7. 2
Rehabiah	1 Chr	23.17
		24.21
		26.25
Rehob (1)	Josh	19.28
		19.30
		21.31
	Judg	1.31
	1 Chr	6.75
Rehob (2)	Num	13.21
Rehob (3)	2 Sam	8. 3
Rehob (4)	Neh	10. 9
REHOBOAM		
AV Rehoboth *see* Freedom		
Rehoboth Ir	Gen	10.11
Rehoboth-On-The-River	Gen	36.31
	1 Chr	1.43
Rehum (1)	Ezra	4. 8
		4. 9
		4.17
		4.23

Rehum (2) Ezra 2. 2
Rehum (3) Neh 10.14
Rehum (4) Neh 3.17
Rehum (5) Neh 12. 2
Rei 1 Kgs 1. 8
Rekem (1) Num 31. 8
Josh 13.21
Rekem (2) Josh 18.27
Rekem (3) 1 Chr 2.43
2.44
Remaliah 2 Kgs 15.25
15.27
15.32
16. 1
2 Chr 28. 5
Is 7. 1
Remeth Josh 19.21
AV Remmon-Methoar *see* Rimmon
AV Remphan *see* Rephan
Rephael 1 Chr 26. 6
Rephah 1 Chr 7.25
Rephaiah (1) 1 Chr 3.21
Rephaiah (2) 1 Chr 4.42
Rephaiah (3) 1 Chr 7. 2
Rephaiah (4) 1 Chr 9.43
Rephaiah (5) Neh 3. 9
REPHAIM (1)
Rephaim (2) Josh 15. 8
18.16
2 Sam 5.18
5.22
23.13
1 Chr 11.15
14. 9
Is 17. 5
Rephan Acts 7.43
Rephidim Ex 17. 1
17. 8
19. 1
Num 33.14
33.15
Resen Gen 10.12
Resheph 1 Chr 7.25
Reu Gen 11.18
11.20
1 Chr 1.25
Lk 3.35
REUBEN
Reuel (1) Gen 36. 4
36.10
36.17
1 Chr 1.35
1.37
Reuel (2) 1 Chr 9. 7
Reumah Gen 22.24
Rezeph 2 Kgs 19.12
Is 37.12
Rezin (1) 2 Kgs 15.37
16. 5
16. 9
Is 7. 1
7. 4
7. 8
8. 6
Rezin (2) Ezra 2.43
Neh 7.46
Rezon 1 Kgs 11.23
11.23
11.24
Rhegium Acts 28.13
Rhesa Lk 3.27
Rhoda Acts 12.13
Rhodes Gen 10. 4
1 Chr 1. 7
Ezek 27.15
Acts 21. 1
Ribai 2 Sam 23.24
1 Chr 11.26
Riblah 2 Kgs 23.33
25. 6
25.20
Jer 39. 5
39. 6
52. 9
52.10
52.26
Ezek 6.14
AV Riblah *see* Harbel
Rimmon
see also Gath Rimmon
Rimmon (1) Judg 20.45
20.47
21.13
Rimmon (2) 2 Kgs 5.18
Rimmon (3) 2 Sam 4. 2
Rimmon (4) Josh 19.13
Rimmon (5) Josh 15.32
19. 7
1 Chr 4.32
Rimmon (6) Zech 14.10
Rimmon Perez Num 33.15
Rimmono 1 Chr 6.77
Rinnah 1 Chr 4.20
Riphath Gen 10. 3
1 Chr 1. 6
Rishathaim *see* Cushan Rishathaim
Rissah Num 33.15
Rithmah Num 33.15
Rizia 1 Chr 7.39
Rizpah 2 Sam 3. 7
21. 8
21.10
21.11
AV Roboam *see* Rehoboam
AV Rodanim *see* Rhodes
Rogelim 2 Sam 17.27
19.31
Rohgah 1 Chr 7.34
Romamti Ezer 1 Chr 25. 4
25. 9
Roman *see* Rome
ROME
Rosh Gen 46.21
RUBBISH GATE
Rufus (1) Mk 15.21
Rufus (2) Rom 16.13
AV Ruhamah *see* Loved-By-The-Lord
Rumah 2 Kgs 23.36
RUTH

S

AV Sabaoth *see* Almighty
Sabeans (1) Job 1.15
Sabeans (2) Joel 3. 8
Sabtah Gen 10. 7
1 Chr 1. 9
Sabteca Gen 10. 7
1 Chr 1. 9
Sachar (1) 1 Chr 11.26
Sachar (2) 1 Chr 26. 4
Sachia 1 Chr 8.10
AV Sadoc *see* Zadok
SAFE HARBOURS
Sahadutha *see* Jegar Sahadutha, Galeed
Sahar Ezek 27.18
Sakkuth Amos 5.26
AV Sala(h) *see* Shelah
Salamis Acts 13. 5
AV Salathiel *see* Shealtiel
Salecah Deut 3.10
Josh 12. 5
13.11
1 Chr 5.11
Salem Gen 14.18
Heb 7. 1
7. 2
Salim Jn 3.23
Sallai (1) Neh 12.12
Sallai (2) Neh 11. 8
Sallu (1) 1 Chr 9. 7
Sallu (2) Neh 11. 7
11. 8
Sallu (3) Neh 12. 2
Salma 1 Chr 2.51
2.54
Salmon Ruth 4.18
1 Chr 2.11
Mt 1. 2
Lk 3.32
Salmone Acts 27. 7
Salome Mk 15.40
16. 1
SALT (2)
SALT VALLEY
Salu Num 25.14
SAMARIA
Samgar Nebo Jer 39. 3
Samlah Gen 36.31
1 Chr 1.43
Samos Acts 20.15
Samothrace Acts 16.11
SAMSON
SAMUEL
Sanballat Neh 2.10
2.19
4. 1
4. 7
6. 1
6. 2
6. 5
6.12
6.14
13.28
Sansannah Josh 15.31
Saph 2 Sam 21.18
Sapphira Acts 5. 1
SARAH
AV Sarah *see* Serah
Sarai *see* Sarah
Saraph 1 Chr 4.22
Sardis Obad 20
Rev 1.11
3. 1
3. 4
AV Sarepta *see* Zarephath
Sarezer *see* Nergal Sarezer
Sargon Is 20. 1
Sarid Josh 19.10
19.12
AV Saron *see* Sharon
Sarsechim Jer 39. 3
AV Saruch *see* Serug
SATAN
SAUL
Saul Of Tarsus *see* Paul
Sceva Acts 19.14
Seba Gen 10. 7
1 Chr 1. 9
Ps 72.10
Is 43. 3
45.14
AV Sebam *see* Sibmah
AV Sebat *see* Shebat
Secacah Josh 15.61
Secu 1 Sam 19.22
Secundus Acts 20. 4
Segub (1) 1 Kgs 16.34
Segub (2) 1 Chr 2.21
2.22
Seir Gen 36.20
Judg 5. 4
1 Chr 1.38
Ezek 35.15
Seirah Judg 3.26
Sela
see also Joktheel
Judg 1.36
2 Kgs 14. 7
2 Chr 25.12
Is 16. 1
42.11
AV Sela-Hammahlekoth *see* Separation Hill
Seled 1 Chr 2.30
2.30
Seleucia Acts 13. 4
AV Sem *see* Shem
Semachiah 1 Chr 26. 6
AV Semei *see* Semein
Semein Lk 3.26
Senaah Ezra 2.21
Neh 7.26
Seneh 1 Sam 14. 4
Senir
see also (Mount) Hermon, Sirion
Deut 3. 9
1 Chr 5.23
Song 4. 8
SENNACHERIB
AV Senuah *see* Hassenuah
Seorim 1 Chr 24. 7
SEPARATION HILL
Sephar Gen 10.30
AV Sepharad *see* Sardis
Sepharvaim 2 Kgs 17.24
17.31
18.34
19.13
Is 36.19
37.13
Sepher *see* Kiriath Sepher
Serah
see also Timnath Serah
Gen 46.17
Num 26.46
1 Chr 7.30
Seraiah (1) 2 Sam 8.17
1 Chr 18.16
Seraiah (2) 2 Kgs 25.18
Jer 52.24
Seraiah (3) 1 Chr 4.13
4.14
Seraiah (4) 1 Chr 4.34
Seraiah (5) 1 Chr 6.14
Seraiah (6) Ezra 2. 2
Seraiah (7) Ezra 7. 1
Seraiah (8) Neh 10. 2
Seraiah (9) Jer 36.26
Seraiah (10) 2 Kgs 25.23
Jer 40. 8
Seraiah (11) Jer 51.59
51.59
51.61
51.63
Seraiah (12) Neh 12. 2
12.12
Seraiah (13) Neh 11.11
Sered Gen 46.14
Num 26.26
Sergius Paulus Acts 13. 7
Serug Gen 11.20
11.22
1 Chr 1.26
Lk 3.35
Seth (1) Gen 4.25
4.26
5. 3
5. 6
1 Chr 1. 1
1. 1
Lk 3.38
Seth (2) Num 24.17
Sethur Num 13. 3
AV Seveneh *see* Aswan
AV Shaalabbin *see* Shaalbim
Shaalbim Josh 19.42
Judg 1.35
1 Kgs 4. 9
Shaalbon 2 Sam 23.24
1 Chr 11.26
Shaalim 1 Sam 9. 4
Shaaph (1) 1 Chr 2.47
Shaaph (2) 1 Chr 2.49
Shaaraim (1) Josh 15.36
1 Sam 17.52
Shaaraim (2) 1 Chr 4.31
Shaashgaz Esth 2.14
Shabbethai Ezra 10.15
Neh 8. 7
11.16
AV Shaddai *see* Almighty
SHADRACH
Shagee 1 Chr 11.26
Shaharaim 1 Chr 8. 8
AV Shahazimah *see* Shahazumah
Shahazumah Josh 19.22
AV Shalem *see* Safely
AV Shalim *see* Shaalim
Shalishah
see also Baal Shalishah
1 Sam 9. 4
SHALLECHETH GATE
Shallum (1) 2 Kgs 15.10
15.13
15.14
15.15
Shallum (2) 2 Kgs 22.14
2 Chr 34.22
Shallum (3) 1 Chr 2.40
Shallum (4) 1 Chr 4.25
Shallum (5) 1 Chr 6.12
Ezra 7. 2
Shallum (6) 1 Chr 7.13
Shallum (7) 2 Chr 28.12
Shallum (8) Ezra 10.24
Shallum (9) Ezra 10.38
Shallum (10) Neh 3.12
Shallum (11) Neh 3.15
Shallum (12) Jer 35. 4
Shallum (13) Jer 32. 7
Shallum (14) 1 Chr 9.17
9.17
Shallum (15) Ezra 2.40
Neh 7.43
Shallum (16) 1 Chr 9.19
Shallum (17) 1 Chr 9.31
AV Shallun *see* Shallum (11)
Shalmai Neh 7.46
Shalman Hos 10.14
Shalmaneser 2 Kgs 17. 3
17. 3
17. 4
17. 5
18. 9
Shamgar Judg 3.31
5. 6
Shamhuth 1 Chr 27. 2
Shamir (1) Judg 10. 1
10. 2
Shamir (2) Josh 15.48
Shamir (3) 1 Chr 24.24
Shamlai Ezra 2.43
Shamma (1) 1 Chr 7.37
Shamma (2) 1 Chr 11.26
Shammah (1) 1 Sam 16. 9
17.13
2 Sam 13. 3
13.32
21.21
1 Chr 2.13
20. 7
Shammah (2) Gen 36.10
36.17
1 Chr 1.37
Shammah (3) 2 Sam 23.11
23.12
Shammah (4) 2 Sam 23.24
Shammah (5) 2 Sam 23.24

Shammai (1) 1 Chr 2.28
2.28
2.32
Shammai (2) 1 Chr 2.44
Shammai (3) 1 Chr 4.17
Shammoth 1 Chr 11.26
Shammua (1) 2 Sam 5.14
1 Chr 14. 4
Shammua (2) Num 13. 3
Shammua (3) Neh 11.17
Shammua (4) Neh 12.12
Shamsherai 1 Chr 8.26
Shan *see* Beth Shan
Shapham 1 Chr 5.12
SHAPHAN (1)
Shaphan (2) 2 Kgs 22.12
25.22
Jer 26.24
39.14
40. 5
Shaphan (3) Jer 29. 3
Shaphan (4) Jer 36.10
36.11
36.12
Shaphan (5) Ezek 8.11
Shaphat (1) 1 Kgs 19.16
2 Kgs 3.11
Shaphat (2) Num 13. 3
Shaphat (3) 1 Chr 3.22
Shaphat (4) 1 Chr 5.12
Shaphat (5) 1 Chr 27.25
AV Shapher *see* Shepher
Shaphir Mic 1.11
Sharai Ezra 10.38
Sharar 2 Sam 23.24
Sharezer (1) 2 Kgs 19.37
Is 37.38
Sharezer (2) Zech 7. 2
Sharon (1) 1 Chr 27.25
27.25
Song 2. 1
Is 33. 9
35. 2
65.10
Acts 9.35
Sharon (2) 1 Chr 5.16
Sharuhen Josh 19. 6
Shashai Ezra 10.38
Shashak 1 Chr 8.14
8.22
Shaul (1) Gen 36.31
1 Chr 1.43
Shaul (2) Gen 46.10
Ex 6.15
Num 26.13
1 Chr 4.24
4.25
Shaul (3) 1 Chr 6.24
Shaveh
see also King's Valley
Gen 14.17
AV Shaveh Kiriathaim *see* (Plain of) Kiriathaim
AV Shavsha *see* Seraiah
Sheal Ezra 10.29
Shealtiel 1 Chr 3.17
Ezra 3. 2
5. 2
Neh 12. 1
Hag 1. 1
Mt 1.12
Lk 3.27
Shear Jashub Is 7. 3
Sheariah 1 Chr 8.38
9.44
SHEBA (1)
SHEBA (2)
Sheba (3) Josh 19. 2
Sheba (4) 1 Chr 5.13
AV Shebah *see* Vow
AV Shebam *see* Sibmah
Shebaniah (1) 1 Chr 15.23
Shebaniah (2) Neh 9. 4
9. 5
10. 9
Shebaniah (3) Neh 10. 9
Shebaniah (4) Neh 10. 2
Shebaniah (5) Neh 12.12
AV Shebarim *see* Quarries
SHEBAT
Sheber 1 Chr 2.48
SHEBNA
Shebuel (1) 1 Chr 23.16
24.20
26.24
Shebuel (2) 1 Chr 25. 4
25. 9
Shecaniah (1) 2 Chr 31.15
Shecaniah (2) Ezra 8. 2
Shecaniah (3) Ezra 10. 2
10. 5

Shecaniah (4) Neh 3.29
Shecaniah (5) Neh 6.18
Shecaniah (6) 1 Chr 24. 7
Shecaniah (7) Neh 12. 2
Shecaniah (8) 1 Chr 3.21
3.22
Shecaniah (9) Ezra 8. 2
SHECHEM (1)
SHECHEM (2)
Shechem (3) Num 26.31
Josh 17. 2
1 Chr 7.19
Shedeur Num 1. 5
2.10
7.12
10.18
SHEEP GATE
Sheerah
see also Uzzen Sheerah
1 Chr 7.24
Shehariah 1 Chr 8.26
SHELAH (1)
Shelah (2) Gen 10.24
11.12
11.14
1 Chr 1.18
1.24
Lk 3.35
Shelah (3) Neh 3.15
Shelemiah (1) 1 Chr 26.14
Shelemiah (2) Ezra 10.38
Shelemiah (3) Ezra 10.38
Shelemiah (4) Neh 3.30
Shelemiah (5) Neh 13.13
Shelemiah (6) Jer 36.14
Shelemiah (7) Jer 36.26
Shelemiah (8) Jer 37.13
Shelemiah (9) Jer 37. 3
38. 1
Sheleph Gen 10.26
1 Chr 1.20
Shelesh 1 Chr 7.35
Shelomi Num 34.19
Shelomith (1) Lev 24.10
Shelomith (2) 1 Chr 3.19
Shelomith (3) 1 Chr 23.18
24.22
Shelomith (4) 1 Chr 26.25
26.25
26.26
26.28
Shelomith (5) 2 Chr 11.20
Shelomith (6) Ezra 8. 2
Shelomoth 1 Chr 23. 9
Shelumiel Num 1. 5
2.10
7.12
10.19
34.19
SHEM
Shema (1) Josh 15.26
Shema (2) 1 Chr 2.43
2.44
2.44
Shema (3) 1 Chr 5. 8
Shema (4) 1 Chr 8.13
Shema (5) Neh 8. 4
Shemaah 1 Chr 12. 3
Shemaiah (1) 1 Kgs 12.22
2 Chr 11. 2
12. 5
12. 7
12.15
Shemaiah (2) Jer 29.24
29.24
29.31
29.31
Shemaiah (3) 1 Chr 3.22
Shemaiah (4) 1 Chr 4.34
Shemaiah (5) 1 Chr 5. 4
Shemaiah (6) 1 Chr 9.14
Shemaiah (7) 1 Chr 9.14
Shemaiah (8) 1 Chr 15. 8
15.11
Shemaiah (9) 1 Chr 24. 6
Shemaiah (10) 1 Chr 26. 4
26. 6
Shemaiah (11) 2 Chr 17. 8
Shemaiah (12) 2 Chr 29.12
Shemaiah (13) 2 Chr 31.15
Shemaiah (14) 2 Chr 35. 9
Shemaiah (15) Ezra 8. 2
Shemaiah (16) Ezra 8.16
Shemaiah (17) Ezra 10.21
Shemaiah (18) Ezra 10.31
Shemaiah (19) Neh 3.29
Shemaiah (20) Neh 6.10
6.12
Shemaiah (21) Neh 10. 2
Shemaiah (22) Neh 11.15

Shemaiah (23) Neh 12. 2
12.12
Shemaiah (24) Neh 12.33
Shemaiah (25) Neh 12.33
Shemaiah (26) Neh 12.36
Shemaiah (27) Neh 12.42
Shemaiah (28) Jer 26.20
Shemaiah (29) Jer 36.12
Shemariah (1) 1 Chr 12. 3
Shemariah (2) 2 Chr 11.19
Shemariah (3) Ezra 10.31
Shemariah (4) Ezra 10.38
Shemeber Gen 14. 2
Shemed 1 Chr 8.12
8.12
Shemer (1) 1 Kgs 16.24
16.24
Shemer (2) 1 Chr 6.46
Shemesh *see* Beth Shemesh
Shemida Num 26.32
Josh 17. 2
1 Chr 7.19
Shemiramoth (1) 1 Chr 15.17
16. 5
Shemiramoth (2) 2 Chr 17. 8
Shemuel 1 Chr 7. 2
Shen 1 Sam 7.12
Shenazzar 1 Chr 3.18
Shepham Num 34.10
1 Chr 27.25
Shephatiah (1) 2 Sam 3. 4
1 Chr 3. 1
Shephatiah (2) 1 Chr 9. 7
Shephatiah (3) 1 Chr 12. 3
Shephatiah (4) 1 Chr 27.16
Shephatiah (5) 2 Chr 21. 2
Shephatiah (6) Ezra 2. 3
Neh 7. 8
Shephatiah (7) Neh 11. 4
Shephatiah (8) Jer 38. 1
Shephatiah (9) Ezra 2.55
Neh 7.57
Shephatiah (10) Ezra 8. 2
Shepher Num 33.15
SHEPHERDS' CAMP
Shephi 1 Chr 1.38
Shepho Gen 36.23
Shephupham Num 26.39
Shephuphan 1 Chr 8. 5
Sherebiah Ezra 8.18
8.24
Neh 8. 7
9. 4
9. 5
10. 9
12. 8
12.24
Sheresh 1 Chr 7.16
AV Sheshach *see* Babylon
Sheshai Num 13.22
Josh 15.14
Judg 1.10
Sheshan (1) 1 Chr 2.31
2.31
Sheshan (2) 1 Chr 2.34
Sheshbazzar Ezra 1. 8
1.11
5.14
5.16
AV Sheth *see* Seth
Shethar Esth 1.14
Shethar Bozenai Ezra 5. 3
6. 6
6.13
Sheva 2 Sam 20.25
Shevah 1 Chr 2.49
AV Shibah *see* Shebah
AV Shibmah *see* Sibmah
AV Shicron *see* Shikkeron
Shihor Josh 13. 3
Shihor Libnath Josh 19.26
Shikkeron Josh 15.11
Shilhi 1 Kgs 22.42
2 Chr 20.31
Shilhim Josh 15.32
Shillem Gen 46.24
Num 26.49
Shiloah Is 8. 6
SHILOH
AV Shiloni *see* Shelah
AV Shilonite *see* Shiloh, Shelah
Shilshah 1 Chr 7.37
Shimea (1) 1 Chr 3. 5
Shimea (2) 1 Chr 6.30
Shimea (3) 1 Chr 6.39
Shimeah 1 Chr 8.32
9.38
Shimeath 2 Kgs 12.20
2 Chr 24.26
Shimeathites 1 Chr 2.55
SHIMEI (1)

Shimei (2) Ex 6.17
Num 3.17
3.21
1 Chr 6.17
6.29
23. 7
23. 9
23.10
Zech 12.12
Shimei (3) 1 Kgs 1. 8
Shimei (4) 1 Kgs 4.18
Shimei (5) 1 Chr 3.19
Shimei (6) 1 Chr 4.26
4.27
Shimei (7) 1 Chr 5. 4
Shimei (8) 1 Chr 6.42
Shimei (9) 1 Chr 25. 9
Shimei (10) 1 Chr 27.25
Shimei (11) 2 Chr 29.12
Shimei (12) 2 Chr 31.12
Shimei (13) Ezra 10.23
Shimei (14) Ezra 10.33
Shimei (15) Ezra 10.38
Shimei (16) Esth 2. 5
Shimei (17) 1 Chr 25. 3
Shimei (18) 1 Chr 8.19
Shimeon Ezra 10.31
AV Shimma *see* Shamma
Shimon 1 Chr 4.20
Shimrath 1 Chr 8.21
Shimri (1) 1 Chr 4.34
Shimri (2) 1 Chr 11.26
Shimri (3) 1 Chr 26.10
Shimri (4) 2 Chr 29.12
Shimrith 2 Chr 24.26
Shimron (1) Gen 46.13
Num 26.24
1 Chr 7. 1
Shimron (2)
see also Shimron Meron
Josh 11. 1
19.15
Shimron Meron
see also Shimron (2)
Josh 12.20
Shimshai Ezra 4. 8
4. 9
4.17
4.23
Shinab Gen 14. 2
AV Shinar *see* Babylon
Shion Josh 19.19
Shiphi 1 Chr 4.34
AV Shiphmite *see* Shepham
Shiphrah Ex 1.15
Shiphtan Num 34.19
Shirtai 1 Chr 27.25
Shisha 1 Kgs 4. 3
Shishak 1 Kgs 11.40
14.25
2 Chr 12. 2
12. 5
12. 5
12. 7
12. 8
12. 9
AV Shitrai *see* Shirtai
Shittah *see* Beth Shittah
AV Shittim *see* Acacia
Shiza 1 Chr 11.26
Shoa Ezek 23.23
Shobab (1) 2 Sam 5.14
1 Chr 3. 5
14. 4
Shobab (2) 1 Chr 2.18
Shobach 2 Sam 10.16
10.18
1 Chr 19.16
19.18
Shobai Ezra 2.40
Neh 7.43
Shobal (1) Gen 36.20
36.23
36.29
1 Chr 1.38
Shobal (2) 1 Chr 2.50
2.52
Shobal (3) 1 Chr 4. 1
4. 2
Shobek Neh 10.14
Shobi 2 Sam 17.27
Shoham 1 Chr 24.27
Shomer (1) 2 Kgs 12.20
Shomer (2) 1 Chr 7.32
7.34
AV Shophach *see* Shobach
Shophan *see* Atroth Shophan
Shua (1) Gen 38. 2
Shua (2) 1 Chr 7.32
Shuah (1) Gen 25. 2
1 Chr 1.32

Shuah (2)	Job	2.11
Shual		
see also Hazar Shual		
Shual (1)	1 Sam	13.17
Shual (2)	1 Chr	7.36
AV Shubael *see* Shebuel		
Shuhah	1 Chr	4.11
Shuham	Num	26.42
AV Shuhite *see* Shuah		
Shulam	Song	6.13
Shumathites	1 Chr	2.53
AV Shunammite *see* Shunem		
SHUNEM		
Shuni	Gen	46.16
	Num	26.15
AV Shupham, -ites *see* Shephupham		
Shuppim (1)	1 Chr	7.12
		7.15
Shuppim (2)	1 Chr	26.16
Shur	Gen	16. 7
		20. 1
		25.18
	Ex	15.22
	Num	33. 8
	1 Sam	15. 7
		27. 8
AV Shushan *see* Susa		
AV Shushanchites *see* Susa		
AV Shuthalhites *see* Shuthelah		
Shuthelah (1)	Num	26.35
		26.36
	1 Chr	7.20
		7.21
Shuthelah (2)	1 Chr	7.21
Sia	Neh	7.46
Siaha	Ezra	2.43
Sibbecai	2 Sam	21.18
	1 Chr	11.26
		20. 4
		27. 2
Sibmah	Num	32. 3
		32.38
	Josh	13.19
	Is	16. 8
		16. 9
	Jer	48.32
		48.32
Sibraim	Ezek	47.16
AV Sichem *see* Shechem		
Siddim	Gen	14. 3
		14. 8
SIDON (1)		
Sidon (2)	Gen	10.15
	1 Chr	1.13
SIHON		
AV Sihor *see* Egypt, Nile, Shihor		
SILAS		
Silla	2 Kgs	12.20
AV Siloah *see* Shelah		
Siloam	Lk	13. 4
	Jn	9. 7
		9.11
AV Silvanus *see* Silas		
SIMEON (1)		
SIMEON (2)		
SIMEON (3)		
SIMEON (4)		
SIMON (1)		
SIMON (2)		
SIMON (3)		
SIMON (4)		
SIMON (5)		
SIMON (6)		
SIMON (7)		
SIMON (8)		
SIMON (9)		
Simon Peter *see* Peter		
Sin (2)		
see also Pelusium		
	Ex	16. 1
		17. 1
	Num	33.11
AV Sina *see* Sinai		
SINAI		
AV Sinim *see* Aswan		
Sinites	Gen	10.17
	1 Chr	1.15
AV Sion *see* Sirion, Zion		
Siphmoth	1 Sam	30.28
Sippai	1 Chr	20. 4
Sirah	2 Sam	3.26
Sirion		
see also (Mount) Hermon, Senir		
	Deut	3. 9
		4.48
SISERA (1)		
Sisera (2)	Ezra	2.43
	Neh	7.46
Sismai	1 Chr	2.40
Sithri	Ex	6.22
AV Sitnah *see* Enmity		

SIVAN		
SKULL		
Smyrna	Rev	1.11
		2. 8
So	2 Kgs	17. 4
Soco (1)	2 Chr	11. 7
		28.18
Soco (2)	1 Chr	4.17
Socoh (1)	Josh	15.35
	1 Sam	17. 1
		17. 1
	1 Kgs	4.10
Socoh (2)	Josh	15.48
Sodi	Num	13. 3
SODOM		
AV Sodoma *see* Sodom		
SOLOMON		
SOLOMON'S PORCH		
Sopater	Acts	20. 4
Sophereth	Neh	7.57
Sorek	Judg	16. 4
Sosipater	Rom	16.21
Sosthenes (1)	Acts	18.17
Sosthenes (2)		
perhaps the same as (1).		
	1 Cor	1. 1
Sotai	Ezra	2.55
	Neh	7.57
SPAIN		
Stachys	Rom	16. 9
Stephanas	1 Cor	1.16
		16.15
		16.17
STEPHEN		
STOIC		
STONE OF HELP		
STONE PAVEMENT		
STRAIGHT STREET		
Suah	1 Chr	7.36
Sucathites	1 Chr	2.55
AV Succoth *see* Sukkoth		
Succoth Benoth	2 Kgs	17.30
SUDAN		
Suez		
see also Aqaba		
	Ex	10.19
	Num	33.10
	Is	11.15
AV Sukkiims *see* Sukkite		
Sukkite	2 Chr	12. 3
SUKKOTH (1)		
Sukkoth (2)	Ex	12.37
		13.20
	Num	33. 5
Sukkoth (3)	1 Kgs	7.46
	2 Chr	4.17
Suph	Deut	1. 1
Suphah	Num	21.14
SUR GATE		
SUSA		
Susah *see* Hazar Susah		
AV Susanchites *see* Susa		
Susanna	Lk	8. 3
Susi	Num	13. 3
Sychar	Jn	4. 5
AV Sychem *see* Shechem		
AV Syene *see* Aswan		
Syntyche	Phil	4. 2
Syracuse	Acts	28.12
SYRIA		
AV Syrophoenician *see* Phoenicia (in Syria)		

T

Taanach	Josh	12.21
		17.11
		21.25
	Judg	1.27
		5.19
	1 Kgs	4.12
	1 Chr	7.29
Taanath Shiloh	Josh	16. 6
Tabbaoth	Ezra	2.43
	Neh	7.46
Tabbath	Judg	7.22
Tabeel (1)	Ezra	4. 7
Tabeel (2)	Is	7. 6
Taberah	Num	11. 3
	Deut	9.22
Tabitha		
see also Dorcas		
	Acts	9.36
		9.40
Tabor		
see also Aznoth Tabor, Chisloth Tabor		
Tabor (1)	1 Sam	10. 3
Tabor (2)	Judg	4. 6
		4.12

Tabor (2) (cont.)		
	Judg	4.14
	Ps	89.12
	Jer	46.18
	Hos	5. 1
Tabor (3)	1 Chr	6.77
Tabor (4)	Josh	19.22
Tabor (5)	Judg	8.18
Tabrimmon	1 Kgs	15.18
Tachemon	2 Sam	23. 8
AV Tachmonite *see* Tachemon		
AV Tadmor *see* Palmyra, Tamar		
Tahan	Num	26.35
	1 Chr	7.25
AV Tahapanes *see* Tahpanhes		
Tahash	Gen	22.24
Tahath (1)	Num	33.15
Tahath (2)	1 Chr	6.24
Tahath (3)	1 Chr	6.37
Tahath (4)	1 Chr	7.20
Tahath (5)	1 Chr	7.20
Tahpanhes	Jer	2.16
		43. 7
		44. 1
		46.14
	Ezek	30.18
Tahpenes	1 Kgs	11.19
AV Tahrea *see* Tarea		
AV Tahtim-Hodshi *see* Kadesh (in Hittite territory)		
Talmai (1)	Num	13.22
	Josh	15.14
	Judg	1.10
Talmai (2)	2 Sam	3. 3
		13.37
	1 Chr	3. 1
Talmon (1)	1 Chr	9.17
	Ezra	2.40
	Neh	7.43
Talmon (2)	Neh	11.19
		12.25
AV Tamah *see* Temah		
Tamar		
see also Hazazon Tamar, Engedi		
TAMAR (1)		
Tamar (2)	Gen	38. 6
		38.11
		38.11
		38.13
		38.19
		38.24
	Ruth	4.12
	1 Chr	2. 4
	Mt	1. 2
Tamar (3)	2 Sam	14.27
Tamar (4)	1 Kgs	9.18
	Ezek	47.18
		47.19
		48.28
Tammuz	Ezek	8.14
AV Tanach		
see Taanach		
Tanhumeth	2 Kgs	25.23
	Jer	40. 8
Taphath	1 Kgs	4.11
Tappuah		
see also Beth Tappuah		
Tappuah (1)	1 Chr	2.43
Tappuah (2)	Josh	12.17
		15.34
Tappuah (3)	Josh	16. 8
		17. 8
		17. 8
Tappuah (4)	2 Kgs	15.16
AV Tarah *see* Terah (2)		
Taralah	Josh	18.27
Tarea	1 Chr	8.35
		9.41
AV Tarpelites *see* Officials		
Tarshish		
see also Spain		
Tarshish (1)	1 Chr	7.10
Tarshish (2)	Esth	1.14
Tarsus	Acts	9.11
		9.30
		11.25
		21.39
		22. 3
Tartak	2 Kgs	17.31
AV Tartan *see* Official, Commander-In-Chief		
Tattenai	Ezra	5. 3
		6. 6
		6.13
Tebah	Gen	22.24
Tebaliah	1 Chr	26.11
TEBETH		
AV Tehaphnehes *see* Tahpanhes		
Tehinnah	1 Chr	4.12
		4.12
TEKOA		

Tel Abib	Ezek	3.15
Tel Harsha	Ezra	2.59
	Neh	7.61
Tel Melah	Ezra	2.59
	Neh	7.61
Telah	1 Chr	7.25
AV Telaim *see* Telem		
Telassar	2 Kgs	19.12
	Is	37.12
Telem (1)	Josh	15.24
	1 Sam	15. 4
Telem (2)	Ezra	10.24
Tema (1)	Gen	25.15
	1 Chr	1.30
Tema (2)	Job	6.19
	Is	21.14
	Jer	25.19
Temah	Ezra	2.43
	Neh	7.46
Teman (1)	Gen	36.10
		36.15
		36.40
	1 Chr	1.36
		1.53
Teman (2)	Gen	36.31
	1 Chr	1.43
	Job	2.11
	Jer	49.20
	Ezek	25.13
	Amos	1.12
	Obad	9
AV Temani *see* Teman		
Temeni	1 Chr	4. 6
TEN TOWNS		
Terah (1)	Gen	11.24
		11.26
		11.27
		11.31
		11.32
	Josh	24. 2
	1 Chr	1.26
	Lk	3.34
Terah (2)	Num	33.15
Teresh	Esth	2.21
		6. 2
Tertius	Rom	16.22
Tertullus	Acts	24. 1
		24. 2
Thaddaeus	Mt	10. 3
	Mk	3.18
AV Thamah *see* Temah		
AV Thamar *see* Tamar		
AV Thara *see* Terah		
AV Tharshish *see* Tarshish		
The Lord Is My Banner *see* Banner		
The Lord Provides *see* Provide		
The Place Of The Skull *see* Place (1), Skull		
The Stone Pavement *see* Pavement		
Thebes	Jer	46.25
	Ezek	30.14
		30.15
		30.16
	Nah	3. 8
		3.10
Thebez	Judg	9.50
	2 Sam	11.21
AV Thelasar *see* Telassar		
Theophilus	Lk	1. 1
	Acts	1. 1
THESSALONICA		
Theudas	Acts	5.36
AV Thimnathah *see* Timnah		
THOMAS		
THREE INNS		
AV Three Taverns *see* Three Inns		
Thyatira	Acts	16.14
	Rev	1.11
		2.18
		2.24
Tiberias		
see also (Lake) Galilee		
	Jn	6. 1
		6.23
		21. 1
Tiberius	Lk	3. 1
Tibhath	1 Chr	18. 8
Tibni	1 Kgs	16.21
		16.22
Ticon	Ezek	47.16
Tidal	Gen	14. 1
TIGLATH PILESER		
AV Tiglath-Pilneser *see* Tiglath Pileser		
Tigris	Gen	2.14
	Dan	10. 4
Tikvah (1)	2 Kgs	22.14
	2 Chr	34.22
Tikvah (2)	Ezra	10.15

AV Tikvath *see* Tikvah
Tilon 1 Chr 4.20
Timaeus Mk 10.46
Timna (1) Gen 36.40
1 Chr 1.51
Timna (2) 1 Chr 1.36
Timna (3) Gen 36.22
1 Chr 1.38
Timna (4) Gen 36.10
Timnah (1) Gen 38.12
38.13
38.14
Timnah (2) Josh 15.57
Timnah (3) Josh 15.10
19.43
Judg 14. 1
14. 2
14. 5
15. 6
2 Chr 28.18
Timnath Serah Josh 19.50
24.30
Judg 2. 9
AV Timnath-Heres *see* Timnath Serah
AV Timnite *see* Timnah
Timon Acts 6. 5
AV Timotheus *see* Timothy
TIMOTHY
Tiphsah 1 Kgs 4.24
Tiras Gen 10. 2
1 Chr 1. 5
Tirathites 1 Chr 2.55
Tirhakah 2 Kgs 19. 9
Is 37. 9
Tirhanah 1 Chr 2.48
Tiria 1 Chr 4.16
AV Tirshatha *see* Governor
TIRZAH (1)
Tirzah (2) Num 26.33
27. 1
36.10
Josh 17. 3
Tishbe 1 Kgs 17. 1
21.17
2 Kgs 1. 3
Titius Justus Acts 18. 7
TITUS
Tiz 1 Chr 11.26
Toah 1 Chr 6.34
Tob Judg 11. 3
11. 5
2 Sam 10. 6
10. 8
Tobadonijah 2 Chr 17. 8
TOBIAH (1)
Tobiah (2) Ezra 2.59
Neh 7.61
Tobijah (1) 2 Chr 17. 8
Tobijah (2) Zech 6.10
6.14
Tochen 1 Chr 4.32
Togarmah
see also Beth Togarmah
Gen 10. 3
1 Chr 1. 6
Tohu 1 Sam 1. 1
Toi 2 Sam 8. 9
8.10
1 Chr 18. 9
18.10
AV Tokhath *see* Tikvah
Tola (1) Gen 46.13
Num 26.23
1 Chr 7. 1
7. 2
7. 2
Tola (2) Judg 10. 1
10. 3
Tolad 1 Chr 4.29
Tophel Deut 1. 1
Topheth
see also Hinnom, (Valley of) Slaughter
2 Kgs 23.10
Jer 7.31
7.32
19. 6
19.11
19.12
19.13
19.14
AV Tou *see* Toi
Trachonitis Lk 3. 1
AV Transjordan *see* East (of the Jordan)
TRAVELLERS' VALLEY
Troas Acts 16. 8
16.11
20. 5
20. 6
Troas (cont.)
2 Cor 2.12
2 Tim 4.13
Trophimus Acts 20. 4
21.29
2 Tim 4.20
TROUBLE VALLEY
Tryphaena Rom 16.12
Tryphosa Rom 16.12
Tubal Gen 10. 2
1 Chr 1. 5
Is 66.19
Ezek 27.13
32.26
38. 2
39. 1
Tubal Cain Gen 4.22
4.22
TWIN GODS
Tychicus Acts 20. 4
Eph 6.21
Col 4. 7
2 Tim 4.12
Tit 3.12
Tyrannus Acts 19. 9
TYRE

U

Uel Ezra 10.34
Ulai Dan 8. 2
8.16
Ulam (1) 1 Chr 7.16
7.17
Ulam (2) 1 Chr 8.39
8.40
Ulla 1 Chr 7.39
Ummah Josh 19.30
UNLOVED
Unni 1 Chr 15.17
Unno Neh 12. 9
Uphaz Jer 10. 9
Ur (1) Gen 11.28
11.31
15. 7
Neh 9. 7
Ur (2) 1 Chr 11.26
Urbanus Rom 16. 9
Uri (1) Ex 31. 2
35.30
38.22
1 Chr 2.20
2 Chr 1. 5
Uri (2) 1 Kgs 4.19
Uri (3) Ezra 10.24
URIAH (1)
Uriah (2) 2 Kgs 16.10
16.11
16.15
16.16
Is 8. 2
Uriah (3) Jer 26.20
26.21
26.21
26.22
Uriah (4) Ezra 8.33
Neh 3. 4
3.21
Uriah (5)
perhaps the same as (4).
Neh 8. 4
AV Urias *see* Uriah (1)
Uriel (1) 1 Chr 6.24
15. 5
15.11
Uriel (2) 2 Chr 13. 2
AV Urijah *see* Uriah
Uthai (1) 1 Chr 9. 4
Uthai (2) Ezra 8. 2
Uz (1) Gen 10.23
1 Chr 1.17
Uz (2) Gen 22.21
Uz (3) Gen 36.28
1 Chr 1.38
Uz (4) Job 1. 1
Jer 25.19
Lam 4.21
Uzai Neh 3.25
Uzal Gen 10.27
1 Chr 1.21
Uzza (1) 2 Kgs 21.18
21.26
Uzza (2) 1 Chr 8. 6
Uzza (3) Ezra 2.43
Neh 7.46
Uzzah
see also Perez Uzzah
Uzzah (1) 2 Sam 6. 3
6. 6
Uzzah (1) (cont.)
2 Sam 6. 7
6. 7
6. 8
1 Chr 13. 7
13. 9
13.10
13.11
Uzzah (2) 1 Chr 6.29
Uzzen Sheerah 1 Chr 7.24
Uzzi (1) 1 Chr 6. 5
6.51
Ezra 7. 4
Uzzi (2) Neh 11.22
Uzzi (3) Neh 12.12
12.42
Uzzi (4) 1 Chr 7. 2
7. 3
Uzzi (5) 1 Chr 7. 7
Uzzi (6) 1 Chr 9. 7
Uzzia 1 Chr 11.26
UZZIAH (1)
Uzziah (2) 1 Chr 27.25
Uzziah (3) 1 Chr 6.24
Uzziah (4) Ezra 10.21
Uzziah (5) Neh 11. 4
UZZIEL (1)
Uzziel (2) 1 Chr 25. 4
Uzziel (3) 2 Chr 29.12
Uzziel (4) 1 Chr 4.42
Uzziel (5) Neh 3. 8
Uzziel (6) 1 Chr 25. 9
Uzziel (7) 1 Chr 7. 7

V

AV Vaheb *see* Waheb
Vaizatha Esth 9. 7
AV Vajezatha *see* Vaizatha
VALLEY GATE
Vaniah Ezra 10.34
AV Vashni *see* Joel
VASHTI
Vophsi Num 13. 3

W

Waheb Num 21.14
WANDERING
WATER GATE
WELL OF THE LIVING ONE WHO SEES ME
WELLS
WILD GOAT ROCKS

X

XERXES

Y

Yiron Josh 19.38

Z

AV Zaanaim *see* Zanannim
Zaanan Mic 1.11
Zaanannim Josh 19.33
Zaavan Gen 36.27
1 Chr 1.38
Zabad (1) 1 Chr 2.36
Zabad (2) 1 Chr 7.21
Zabad (3) 1 Chr 11.26
Zabad (4) 2 Chr 24.26
Zabad (5) Ezra 10.27
Zabad (6) Ezra 10.33
Zabad (7) Ezra 10.43
Zabbai (1) Ezra 10.28
Zabbai (2) Neh 3.20
AV Zabbud *see* Zaccur (6)
Zabdi (1) Josh 7. 1
7.17
7.18
7.18
Zabdi (2) 1 Chr 8.19
Zabdi (3) 1 Chr 27.25
Zabdi (4)
see also Zichri (5)
Neh 11.17
Zabdiel (1) 1 Chr 27. 2
Zabdiel (2) Neh 11.14
Zabud 1 Kgs 4. 5
AV Zabulon *see* Zebulun
Zaccai Ezra 2. 3
Neh 7. 8
Zacchaeus Lk 19. 2
19. 5
19. 6
19. 8
Zaccur (1) Num 13. 3
Zaccur (2) 1 Chr 4.26
Zaccur (3) 1 Chr 24.27
Zaccur (4) 1 Chr 25. 2
25. 9
Neh 12.33
Zaccur (5) Neh 10. 9
Zaccur (6) Ezra 8. 2
Zaccur (7) Neh 3. 2
Zaccur (8) Neh 13.13
Zachariah
see also Zechariah (3)
Mt 23.35
AV Zacharias *see* Zechariah
ZADOK (1)
Zadok (2) 1 Chr 6.12
Zadok (3) 1 Chr 9.10
Neh 11.11
Zadok (4) 2 Kgs 15.33
2 Chr 27. 1
Zadok (5) Neh 3. 4
Zadok (6) Neh 3.29
Zadok (7) Neh 10.14
Zadok (8) Neh 13.13
Zadok (9) 1 Chr 12.23
Zadok (10) Mt 1.12
Zaham 2 Chr 11.19
Zair 2 Kgs 8.21
Zalaph Neh 3.30
Zalmon (1) Judg 9.48
Ps 68.14
Zalmon (2) 2 Sam 23.24
Zalmonah Num 33.41
Zalmunna Judg 8. 5
8. 6
8. 7
8.10
8.12
8.15
8.18
8.21
Ps 83.11
Zamzummim Deut 2.20
Zanannim Judg 4.11
Zanoah (1) Josh 15.34
1 Chr 4.17
Neh 3.13
11.30
Zanoah (2) Josh 15.56
Zaphenath Paneah Gen 41.45
Zaphon Josh 13.27
Judg 12. 1
AV Zara(h) *see* Zerah
AV Zareah *see* Zorah
AV Zareathites *see* Zorah
AV Zared *see* Zered
Zarephath 1 Kgs 17. 9
17.10
Obad 20
Lk 4.26
AV Zaretan *see* Zarethan
Zarethan
see also Zeredah (2)
Josh 3.16
Judg 7.22
1 Kgs 4.12
7.46
AV Zartanah *see* Zarethan
AV Zarthan *see* Zarethan
Zattu (1) Ezra 2. 3
8. 2
10.27
Neh 7. 8
Zattu (2) Neh 10.14
Zaza 1 Chr 2.33
Zebadiah (1) 1 Chr 26. 2
Zebadiah (2) 2 Chr 17. 8
Zebadiah (3) 2 Chr 19.11
Zebadiah (4) 1 Chr 8.15
Zebadiah (5) 1 Chr 8.17
Zebadiah (6) 1 Chr 12. 3
Zebadiah (7) 1 Chr 27. 2
Zebadiah (8) Ezra 8. 2
Zebadiah (9) Ezra 10.20
Zebah Judg 8. 5
8. 6
8. 7
8.10
8.12
8.15
8.18
8.21
Ps 83.11

AV Zebaim *see* Pochereth Hazzebaim		
ZEBEDEE		
Zebidah	2 Kgs	23.36
Zebina	Ezra	10.43
Zeboiim	Gen	10.19
		14. 2
		14. 8
	Deut	29.23
	Hos	11. 8
Zeboim (1)	1 Sam	13.18
Zeboim (2)	Neh	11.34
AV Zebudah *see* Zebidah		
Zebul	Judg	9.28
		9.30
		9.36
		9.36
		9.38
		9.41
ZEBULUN		
ZECHARIAH (1)		
Zechariah (2)	2 Kgs	14.29
		15. 8
		15.10
		15.11
Zechariah (3)		
Son of Berachiah (or Jehoiada). Probably the same as (23). see also Zachariah		
	Lk	11.51
Zechariah (4)	Ezra	5. 1
		6.14
	Neh	12.12
	Zech	1. 1
		1. 2
		7. 8
		8. 1
		8.18
Zechariah (5)	2 Kgs	18. 2
	2 Chr	29. 1
Zechariah (6)	Is	8. 2
Zechariah (7)	1 Chr	5. 7
Zechariah (8)		
see also Zecher		
	1 Chr	9.37
Zechariah (9)	1 Chr	27.16
Zechariah (10)	2 Chr	21. 2
Zechariah (11)	2 Chr	17. 7
Zechariah (12)	2 Chr	26. 5
Zechariah (13)	1 Chr	15.17
		16. 5
Zechariah (14)	1 Chr	24.25
Zechariah (15)	1 Chr	9.21
		26. 2
		26.14
Zechariah (16)	1 Chr	26.11
Zechariah (17)	2 Chr	20.14
Zechariah (18)	2 Chr	29.12
Zechariah (19)	2 Chr	34.12
Zechariah (20)	Neh	12.33
Zechariah (21)	1 Chr	15.23
Zechariah (22)	2 Chr	35. 8
Zechariah (23)	2 Chr	24.20
		24.21
		24.21
		24.22
		24.22
		24.22
Zechariah (24)	Neh	11.12
Zechariah (25)	Ezra	8. 2
Zechariah (26)	Ezra	8.16
Zechariah (27)	Neh	8. 4
Zechariah (28)	Ezra	8. 2
Zechariah (29)	Ezra	10.26
Zechariah (30)	Neh	11. 4
Zechariah (31)	Neh	11. 5
Zechariah (32)	Neh	12.41
Zecher		
see also Zechariah (8)		
	1 Chr	8.31
Zedad	Num	34. 8
	Ezek	47.15
ZEDEKIAH (1)		
Zedekiah (2)	1 Kgs	22.11
		22.24
	2 Chr	18.10
		18.23
Zedekiah (3)	Jer	29.21
		29.22
Zedekiah (4)	Jer	36.12
Zedekiah (5)	Neh	10. 1
Zedekiah (6)	1 Chr	3.16
Zeeb	Judg	7.25
		7.25
		8. 3
	Ps	83.11
Zela	Josh	18.28
	2 Sam	21.14
Zelek	2 Sam	23.24
	1 Chr	11.26
Zelophehad	Num	26.33
		27. 1
		27. 7
		36. 2
		36. 4
		36. 6
		36.10
	Josh	17. 3
	1 Chr	7.15
AV Zelotes *see* Patriot, Simon (2)		
Zelzah	1 Sam	10. 2
Zemaraim (1)	Josh	18.22
Zemaraim (2)	2 Chr	13. 4
Zemarites	Gen	10.18
	1 Chr	1.16
Zemirah	1 Chr	7. 8
Zenan	Josh	15.37
Zenas	Tit	3.13
Zephaniah (1)	2 Kgs	25.18
	Jer	21. 1
		29.24
		29.24
		29.29
		37. 3
		52.24
Zephaniah (2)	Zeph	1. 1
		1. 1
Zephaniah (3)	Zech	6.10
Zephaniah (4)	1 Chr	6.36
Zephath	Judg	1.17
Zephathah	2 Chr	14.10
Zephi	1 Chr	1.36
Zepho	Gen	36.10
		36.15
Zephon		
see also Baal Zephon		
	Gen	46.16
	Num	26.15
Zer	Josh	19.35
ZERAH (1)		
Zerah (2)	Gen	36.10
		36.17
	1 Chr	1.37
Zerah (3)	Gen	36.31
	1 Chr	1.43
Zerah (4)	Num	26.13
	1 Chr	4.24
Zerah (5)	1 Chr	6.21
Zerah (6)	1 Chr	6.41
Zerah (7)	2 Chr	14. 9
Zerahiah (1)	1 Chr	6. 6
		6.51
	Ezra	7. 4
Zerahiah (2)	Ezra	8. 2
Zered	Num	21.12
	Deut	2.13
Zeredah (1)		
perhaps the same as (2).		
	1 Kgs	11.26
Zeredah (2)		
see also Zarethan		
	2 Chr	4.17
AV Zererath *see* Zarethan		
Zeresh	Esth	5.10
Zereth	1 Chr	4. 7
Zereth-Shahar	Josh	13.19
Zeri	1 Chr	25. 3
		25. 9
Zeror	1 Sam	9. 1
Zeruah	1 Kgs	11.26
ZERUBBABEL		
ZERUIAH		
Zetham	1 Chr	23. 8
		26.22
Zethan	1 Chr	7.10
Zethar	Esth	1.10
Zeus	Acts	14.12
		14.13
Zia	1 Chr	5.13
ZIBA		
Zibeon	Gen	36. 2
		36.14
		36.20
		36.24
		36.29
	1 Chr	1.38
Zibia	1 Chr	8. 8
Zibiah	2 Kgs	12. 1
	2 Chr	24. 1
Zichri (1)	1 Chr	27.16
Zichri (2)	2 Chr	17.16
Zichri (3)	Ex	6.21
Zichri (4)	1 Chr	26.25
Zichri (5)		
see also Zabdi (4)		
	1 Chr	9.14
Zichri (6)	Neh	12.12
Zichri (7)	1 Chr	8.19
Zichri (8)	1 Chr	8.23
Zichri (9)	1 Chr	8.27
Zichri (10)	Neh	11. 9
Zichri (11)	2 Chr	23. 1
Zichri (12)	2 Chr	28. 7
Ziddim	Josh	19.35
AV Zidkijah *see* Zedekiah (5)		
AV Zidon *see* Sidon		
Ziha	Ezra	2.43
	Neh	7.46
		11.21
ZIKLAG		
Zillah	Gen	4.19
		4.22
		4.23
Zillethai (1)	1 Chr	8.20
Zillethai (2)	1 Chr	12.20
Zilpah	Gen	29.24
		30. 9
		30.10
		30.12
		35.26
		37. 2
		46.18
Zimmah (1)	1 Chr	6.20
Zimmah (2)	1 Chr	6.42
Zimnah	2 Chr	29.12
Zimran	Gen	25. 2
	1 Chr	1.32
ZIMRI (1)		
Zimri (2)	Num	25.14
Zimri (3)	1 Chr	2. 6
Zimri (4)	1 Chr	8.36
		8.36
		9.42
		9.42
Zimri (5)	Jer	25.19
ZIN		
Zina	1 Chr	23.10
ZION		
Zior	Josh	15.54
Ziph (1)	Josh	15.24
Ziph (2)	Josh	15.55
	1 Sam	23.14
		23.15
		23.19
		23.24
		26. 1
Ziph (2) (cont.)		
	1 Sam	26. 2
	2 Chr	11. 8
Ziph (3)	1 Chr	2.42
Ziph (4)	1 Chr	4.16
Ziphah	1 Chr	4.16
AV Ziphion *see* Zephon		
Ziphron	Num	34. 9
Zippor	Num	22. 2
		23.18
	Josh	24. 9
	Judg	11.25
Zipporah	Ex	2.21
		4.25
		18. 2
AV Zithri *see* Sithri		
ZIV		
Ziz	2 Chr	20.16
Ziza (1)	1 Chr	4.34
Ziza (2)	2 Chr	11.20
Zoan	Num	13.22
	Ps	78.12
		78.43
	Is	19.11
		19.13
		30. 4
	Ezek	30.14
Zoar		
see also Bela (1)		
	Gen	13.10
		14. 2
		19.22
		19.23
		19.30
	Deut	34. 3
	Is	15. 5
	Jer	48.34
ZOBAH		
Zobebah	1 Chr	4. 8
Zohar (1)	Gen	23. 8
		25. 9
Zohar (2)	Gen	46.10
	Ex	6.15
AV Zoheleth *see* Snake (Rock)		
Zoheth	1 Chr	4.20
Zophah	1 Chr	7.35
		7.36
Zophai		
see also Zuph (1)		
	1 Chr	6.26
Zophar	Job	2.11
		11. 1
		20. 1
		24.17
		27.12
		42. 9
Zophim	Num	23.14
ZORAH		
Zorites *see* Zorah		
AV Zorobabel *see* Zerubbabel		
Zuar	Num	1. 5
		2. 3
		7.12
		10.15
Zuph (1)		
see also Zophai		
	1 Sam	1. 1
	1 Chr	6.35
Zuph (2)	1 Sam	9. 5
Zur (1)	Num	25.15
		31. 8
	Josh	13.21
Zur (2)	1 Chr	8.30
		9.36
Zuriel	Num	3.35
Zurishaddai	Num	1. 5
		2.10
		7.12
		10.19
Zuzim	Gen	14. 5

THEMATIC INDEX

Words in capitals are theme headings, and grouped below each is a list of words related to that heading.

If the word you look up is not a theme heading, you will be directed to one or more theme headings under which this word appears.

For a full study of a theme, look up in the main Concordance the most appropriate words listed under the theme heading.

The titles of well-known *Bible passages, parables and miracles* with their references are included in this listing.

See also *How to use the Concordance* (page ix).

A

ABANDON
- depart
- desert
- forsake
- leave
- NEGLECT
- turn (from)
- withdraw

Abib *see* MONTH

ABLE
- able-bodied
- authority
- capable
- competent
- DESERVE
- entitled
- fit
- might
- power
- powerful
- privilege
- qualified
- resourceful
- rights
- strong
- suitable
- suited
- talent
- worthy

Able-bodied *see* ABLE
Abnormal *see* USUAL
Aboard *see* SHIP
Abolish *see* DESTROY
Above *see* HEAVEN
Abroad *see* FOREIGN
see TRAVEL

ABSENCE
- depart
- dispel
- disperse
- distant
- DIVIDE
- far
- far-off
- good-bye
- homesick
- leave
- long (way)
- missing
- remove
- scatter
- separate

Abstain *see* LACK
Abundant *see* ENOUGH

ABUSE
- blaspheme
- curse
- INSULT
- misuse
- slander
- swear

Abyss *see* DEVIL
see HELL
Acacia-wood *see* WOOD
Accent *see* SPEAK

ACCEPT
- admit
- adopt
- allow
- approve
- bless
- concession
- conform
- consent
- GOOD
- include
- inherit
- permit
- receive
- tolerate
- voluntary
- volunteer
- welcome
- willing

ACCIDENT
- aimless
- blunder
- ERROR
- happen
- LUCK
- mistake
- unintentional

Accompany *see* FOLLOW

ACCOMPLISH
- achieve
- complete
- effect
- fulfil
- succeed
- triumph

ACCOUNT
- add
- afford
- funds
- MONEY
- PAY
- settle
- TELL

Accumulate *see* COLLECT
Accurate *see* CORRECT
Accuse *see* JUDGEMENT
Ache *see* PAIN
Achieve *see* ACCOMPLISH

ACKNOWLEDGE
- admit
- affirm
- agree
- confess
- confirm
- profess
- testify
- testimony
- uphold

Acquire *see* BELONG
see COLLECT
Acquit *see* FREE
see JUDGEMENT

Act *see* ACTION

ACTION
- act
- activity
- affairs
- affect
- behave
- character
- conduct
- deed
- function
- manner
- principle

Activity *see* ACTION
Adam *see* JESUS
Adar *see* MONTH
Add *see* ACCOUNT
see COUNT
Address *see* COMMUNICATE
see SPEAK
Administer *see* CONTROL
Administrator *see* OFFICIAL
Admire *see* RESPECT
Admit *see* ACCEPT
see ACKNOWLEDGE
Adopt *see* ACCEPT
see FAMILY

ADORN
- armlets
- ARTS
- braided
- carving
- COLOUR
- decorate
- design
- draw
- embroider
- engrave
- eyeshadow
- fancy
- glamour
- hair style
- inlaid
- JEWEL
- mosaic
- necklace
- nose-ring
- ornament
- overlay
- paint
- panel
- relief
- ring
- tattoo

Adult *see* AGE
see FAMILY
Adultery *see* LUST

ADVANCE
- DIRECTION
- forward
- front
- improve
- MOVE
- progress

ADVANTAGE
- benefit
- gain

ADVANTAGE (cont.)
- GOOD
- HELP
- opportunity
- profit
- use

Advertise *see* SHOW
Advice *see* SUGGEST
Adviser *see* OFFICIAL
see SUGGEST
Affairs *see* ACTION
Affect *see* ACTION
Affection *see* LOVE
Affirm *see* ACKNOWLEDGE
Afford *see* ACCOUNT
Afraid *see* FEAR
After (me) *see* FOLLOW
Afterbirth *see* BIRTH
Afternoon *see* TIME
Against *see* DIFFERENT
see ENMITY
see RESIST
Agate *see* JEWEL

AGE
- adult
- aged
- ageless
- ancient
- child
- elder
- grey-haired
- immature
- infant
- manhood
- mature
- old
- ripe
- TIME
- unripe
- young
- youth

Aged *see* AGE
Ageless *see* AGE
Agent *see* REPRESENT
Aggressive *see* VIOLENCE
Agony *see* PAIN
Agree *see* ACKNOWLEDGE
Agreement *see* ALLY
see PROMISE
Aground *see* SHIP
Aid *see* HELP
Aide *see* OFFICIAL
Ailment *see* ILLNESS
Aim *see* DIRECTION
see EFFORT
Aimless *see* ACCIDENT
Air *see* FLY
Alabaster *see* STONE
Alarm *see* FEAR
see VIOLENCE
Alcohol *see* DRINK

ALERT
- arouse
- awake
- careful
- cautious
- sleepless
- wake
- watch

Alien see FOREIGN
Alight see FLY
Alive see LIVE
All-powerful see GOD
All-wise see GOD

ALLEGIANCE
faithful
FOLLOW
footstool
kneel
loyal
obey
subject
tribute

Alley see ROAD
Alliance see ALLY
Allot see GIVE
Allow see ACCEPT
Allowance see EMPLOY

ALLY
agreement
alliance
associate
colleague
pact
partner
treaty

Almighty see GOD
Almond see FOOD
see TREE
Aloes see PERFUME
see SPICES

ALONE
fatherless
independent
individual
isolate
lonely
one
orphan
private
single
unmarried
widow

Aloud see NOISE
see SPEAK
Altar see IDOL
see WORSHIP
Always see CONSTANT

AMAZE
astonished
astound
breathless
breathtaking
marvel
miracle
stunned
surprise
wonder

Ambassador see REPRESENT
Ambition see INTEND
see WANT
Ambush see VIOLENCE
see WAR
Amen see JESUS
see WORSHIP
Amethyst see JEWEL
Amount see COUNT
see MONEY
Amuse see ENTERTAIN
Ancestor see FAMILY
Anchor see SHIP
Ancient see AGE
Angel see COMMUNICATE
see HEAVEN

ANGER
annoy
bad-tempered
cross
displease
frown
fury
indignation
irritate
outrage
quick-tempered
rage
ranting
resent
scowl
snarl
temper

ANGER (cont.)
wrath

Angles see PART
see SHAPE
Anguish see WORRY

ANIMAL
antelope
ants
apes
bat
bear
beast
bees
BIRD
BREED
camel
CATTLE
cobra
creature
cricket
crocodile
cross-breed
cub
deer
dog
domestic
donkey
dragon
ewe
fawn
flea
flock
fly
fox
frog
gazelle
gnat
goat
grasshopper
herd
HORSE
hyena
insect
jackal
kid
lamb
leech
leopard
Leviathan
lice
lion
lizard
locust
maggot
mice
mole
monkey
monster
moth
mule
pet
pig
rabbit
ram
rats
reptile
rock-badger
roebuck
scorpion
serpent
sheep
snail
snake
spider
stag
tail
tame
watchdog
wild
wolf
worm

Ankles see BODY
Annexe see BUILDING
Announce see TELL
Annoy see ANGER
Annual see TIME
Annul see DESTROY

ANNUNCIATION: Lk 1.26f.

Anoint see CHOOSE
Answer see TELL
Antelope see ANIMAL
Ants see ANIMAL
Anxious see WORRY
Apart see CHOOSE
see DIVIDE
Apes see ANIMAL

Apology see REPENT
Apostle see CHURCH
Appeal see ASK
Appear see REVEAL
Appetite see EAT
see WANT
Apple see FRUIT
see TREE
Apply see INTEND
Appoint see CHOOSE

APPRECIATE
approve
attractive
enjoy
favourite
like
popular

Approach see NEAR
Approve see ACCEPT
see APPRECIATE
see GOOD
Apron see CLOTHING
Aramaic see LANGUAGE
Arch see BUILDING
Archer see SOLDIER
Architect see BUILDING
Architecture see BUILDING
Area see PLACE

ARGUE
claim
contradict
convince
debate
DIFFERENT
disagree
discuss
disprove
dispute
persuade
protest
prove
quarrel
refute
SPEAK

Arise see RISE
Arm see ARMOUR
see BODY
see WEAPON
Armlets see ADORN
see JEWEL

ARMOUR
arm
armoury
arsenal
breastplate
helmet
PROTECT
shield
WEAPON

Armour-bearer
see SOLDIER
Armoury see ARMOUR
Armpit see BODY

ARMY
barracks
battalion
bugle
camp
chariot
company
CONQUER
foot-soldier
force
horde
horseman
military
OFFICER
rearguard
regiment
SOLDIER
troops
uniform
unit
WAR
WEAPON

Arouse see ALERT
Arrange see CONTROL
Arrest see CAPTURE
Arrive see NEAR
Arrogant see PRIDE
Arrow see WEAPON
Arsenal see ARMOUR
see WEAPON

Article see CLOTHING
see UTENSIL
Artist see ARTS

ARTS
ADORN
artist
carve
chalk
COMMUNICATE
draw
figure
INSTRUMENT
MUSIC
paint
poetry
WRITE

ASCENSION: Acts 1.6f.

Ash see FIRE
see POWDER

ASHAMED
blush
embarrass
shame

Asher see TRIBE
Asherah see IDOL
Ashore see SHIP

ASK
appeal
beg
consult
demand
favour
inquire
persuade
petition
plead
pray
QUESTION
request
urge
WANT

Asleep see SLEEP
Assassin see CRIMINAL
Assassinate see KILL
Assault see WAR
Assemble see COLLECT
Assembly see GROUP
Assign see GIVE
Assist see HELP
Associate see ALLY
Assume see THINK
Assure see PROMISE
Astonished see AMAZE
Astound see AMAZE
Astray see LOST
see SIN
Astrologer see MAGIC
see PROPHECY
Athlete see EFFORT
see MOVE
see SPEED

ATONEMENT
blood
child of God
cross
FORGIVE
friend
JESUS
reconcile
redeem
right with God
righteous
sacrifice
salvation

Attach see TIE
Attack see VIOLENCE
see WAR
Attempt see EFFORT
Attend see SERVE
Attention see PERCEIVE
Attitude see THINK
Attractive see APPRECIATE
see BEAUTY
Aunt see RELATIVE
Authorities see OFFICIAL
Authority see ABLE
Authorized interpreters
see COMMUNICATE
Avenge see REVENGE
Avoid see ESCAPE
see RESIST
Await see WAIT

Awake *see* ALERT
Aware *see* KNOW
see PERCEIVE
Awe *see* FEAR
Awful *see* BAD
Awful Horror *see* DEFILE
Awnings *see* SHIP
Axe *see* TOOLS
Axle *see* WHEEL

B

Baby *see* BIRTH
Back *see* BODY
Backwards *see* DIRECTION
Bad-tempered
see ANGER

BAD
awful
DEFILE
dismal
evil
horrible
horror
indecent
shameless
SIN
ugly
unjust
unreasonable
unrighteous
wicked
worse
worst
wrong

Bag *see* CONTAINER
see MONEY
Bake *see* COOK
Baking-pan *see* COOK
Balcony *see* BUILDING
Bald *see* HAIR
Ball *see* ENTERTAIN
Balsam *see* SPICES
see TREE
Band *see* GROUP
see TIE
Bandage *see* MEDICINE
Bandit *see* CRIMINAL
see VIOLENCE
Banish *see* EXPEL
Bank *see* MONEY
see WATER
Banner *see* SHOW
Banquet *see* EAT
see ENTERTAIN
Baptize *see* CHURCH
Bar *see* CLOSE
see PIECE
see PREVENT
Barbarians *see* FOREIGN
Barber *see* HAIR

BARE
barefoot
bareheaded
expose
naked
shorn
strip
take off
uncovered
undressed

Barefoot *see* BARE
Bareheaded *see* BARE
Bargain *see* TRADE
Bark *see* NOISE
see TREE
Barley *see* CROP
Barn *see* BUILDING
see CULTIVATE
Barracks *see* ARMY
Barrel *see* CONTAINER

BARREN
childless
desert
desolate
dry
stagnant
sterile
uninhabited
waste
waterless
wilderness
wilt
wither

Barricade *see* WAR
Base *see* PART
Basin *see* CONTAINER

BASIS
cause
effect
grounded
motive
reason

Basket *see* CONTAINER
Bastard *see* FAMILY
Bat *see* ANIMAL
see FLY
Batch *see* PIECE
Bath *see* MEASURE
see WASH
Bathe *see* WASH
Battalion *see* ARMY
Batter *see* VIOLENCE
Battering-ram
see WEAPON
Battle *see* WAR
Battlefield *see* WAR
Bay *see* WATER
Beach *see* WATER
Beak *see* BIRD
Beam *see* BUILDING
Bean *see* VEGETABLES
Bear *see* ANIMAL
see BIRTH
see BURDEN
see CARRY
Beard *see* HAIR
Beast *see* ANIMAL
see DEVIL
Beat *see* HIT
see PUNISH
see VIOLENCE

BEATITUDES: Mt 5.3f. Lk 6.20f.

BEAUTY
attractive
good-looking
handsome
lovely
ugly
pretty

Bed *see* FURNISHINGS
see SLEEP
see WATER
Bedding *see* FURNISHINGS
Bedroom *see* SLEEP
Bedspread *see* FURNISHINGS
Beef *see* CATTLE
see MEAT
Beelzebul *see* DEVIL
Beer *see* DRINK
Bees *see* ANIMAL
Beforehand *see* TIME
Beg *see* ASK
Beget *see* BIRTH
Beggar *see* POOR

BEGIN
create
found
institute
invent
MAKE
origin
source
start

Behalf *see* REPRESENT
Behave *see* ACTION
Beheaded *see* KILL
Being *see* PERSON
Belief *see* FAITH
Believe *see* FAITH
Believer *see* CHURCH
see FAITH
Bell *see* INSTRUMENT
Bellow *see* CATTLE
see NOISE
Belly *see* BODY

BELONG
acquire
claim
gain
goods
obtain
own
possess
property
regain

Belongings *see* MONEY
Beloved *see* LOVE
Below *see* EARTHLY
Belt *see* CLOTHING
Bend *see* SHAPE

BENEDICTUS: Lk 1.68f.

Benefit *see* ADVANTAGE
Benjamin *see* TRIBE
Beryl *see* JEWEL
Besiege *see* WAR
Best *see* GOOD
Bet *see* MONEY

BETRAY
conspire
disloyal
plot
rebel
traitor
treachery
treason
unfaithful
VIOLENCE

Better *see* GOOD
see HEALTHY
Big *see* SIZE
Bind *see* TIE

BIRD
beak
buzzard
chick
chicken
claws
cock
cormorant
crow
dove
eagle
falcon
feathers
FLY
hawk
heron
hoopoe
ibis
nest
ostrich
owl
pelican
perch
pigeon
plumage
poultry
quail
raven
seagull
sparrow
stork
swallow
thrush
vulture
wing

BIRTH
afterbirth
baby
bear
beget
birthday
born
breast
child
childbirth
conceive
FAMILY
first-born
hatch
infant
labour
midwife
miscarriage
mother
new-born
nurse
pregnant
RELATIVE
still-born
umbilical
weaned
wet-nurse
womb

Birthday *see* BIRTH
Biscuit *see* BREAD
Bit *see* HARNESS
see HORSE
Bite *see* EAT

Bitter *see* TASTE
Black *see* COLOUR
see DARK
Blacksmith *see* WORKMAN
Blame *see* COMPLAIN
see SIN
Blameless *see* PURE
Blank *see* IGNORANT
Blanket *see* SLEEP
Blaspheme *see* ABUSE
Blasphemy *see* SIN
Blast *see* NOISE
see WEATHER
Blaze *see* FIRE
Bleat *see* NOISE
Bleed *see* INJURE
Bleeding *see* MEDICINE

BLEMISH
fault
flaw
imperfect
impure
PURE
SIN
spot
wrinkle

Bless *see* ACCEPT
Blind *see* ILLNESS
see SEE
Blinking *see* BRIEF
Block *see* CLOSE
see PIECE
see PREVENT
see STONE
see WOOD
Blockade *see* WAR
Blood *see* VIOLENCE
Bloodshed *see* VIOLENCE
Bloodthirsty *see* VIOLENCE
Bloom *see* PLANT
Blossom *see* PLANT
Blow *see* HIT
Blue *see* COLOUR
Blunder *see* ACCIDENT
Blush *see* ASHAMED
Board *see* SHIP
see WOOD
Boast *see* PRIDE
Boat *see* SHIP
Body *see* DIE

BODY
ankles
arm
armpit
back
belly
bone
bowels
breast
brow
buttocks
cheek
chest
chin
ear
entrails
eye
eye-lash
eyebrow
eyelid
face
finger
flesh
foot
forehead
foreskin
genital
HAIR
hand
head
heart
heel
hip
intestines
jaw
joint
knee
leg
ligaments
limb
lips
lobe
marrow
mouth
muscle
nail
neck
nose

BODY (cont.)
nostrils
ORGANS
palm
penis
rib
scalp
shoulder
sinews
skin
skull
stomach
thigh
throat
thumb
toe
tongue
tooth
waist
wrist

Bodyguard *see* PROTECT
Boil *see* COOK
see ILLNESS
see STIR
Bold *see* COURAGE
Bolt *see* CLOSE
Bonds *see* FASTEN
Bone *see* BODY
see ORGANS
Bonfire *see* FIRE
Book *see* WRITE
Boots *see* CLOTHING

BORDER
boundary
boundary-mark
DIVIDE
edge
fence
frontier
limit
territory

Born *see* BIRTH
Borrow *see* LOAN
see MONEY
Bother *see* WORRY
Bottle *see* CONTAINER
Bottom *see* PART
Bough *see* TREE
Bound *see* NECESSARY
Boundary *see* BORDER
Boundary-mark
see BORDER
Bow *see* WEAPON
Bow (down) *see* WORSHIP
Bowels *see* BODY
see ORGANS
Bowl *see* CONTAINER
Bowmen *see* SOLDIER
Box *see* CONTAINER
see HIT
see MONEY
Boy *see* FAMILY
see PERSON
Brace *see* READY
Bracelet *see* JEWEL
Brag *see* PRIDE
Braided *see* ADORN
Branch *see* TREE
see WOOD
Brass *see* METAL
Brat *see* INSULT
Brave *see* COURAGE
see FEAR

BREAD
biscuit
cake
crust
dough
FOOD
loaf
pastries
unleavened
wafer
yeast

BREAK
burst
crack
crumble
CUT
damage
INJURE
PIECE
POWDER
shatter
smash
snap

BREAK (cont.)
split
tear

Break (bread)
see WORSHIP
Breast *see* BIRTH
see BODY
Breast-piece *see* CLOTHING
Breastplate *see* ARMOUR
Breath *see* LIVE
Breathless *see* AMAZE
Breathtaking *see* AMAZE

BREED
ANIMAL
cross-breed
crouch
hatch
mate
multiply

Breeze *see* WEATHER
Briars *see* PLANT
Bribe *see* PAY
Brick *see* BUILDING
Bride *see* MARRY
Bridegroom *see* MARRY
Bridesmaids *see* MARRY
Bridle *see* HARNESS
see HORSE

BRIEF
blinking
instant
moment
pass
puff
quick
second
short
SIZE
SPEED
sudden
temporary

Bright *see* LIGHT
Brilliance *see* LIGHT
Brim *see* PART
Bristled *see* FEAR
see HAIR
Broad *see* SIZE
Bronze *see* METAL
Brook *see* WATER
Broom *see* TIDY
Broom-tree *see* TREE
Broth *see* FOOD
Brother *see* FELLOWSHIP
see RELATIVE
Brotherly *see* LOVE
Brow *see* BODY
Brown *see* COLOUR
Bruise *see* INJURE
Brush *see* COOK
Brutal *see* VIOLENCE
Bubble *see* STIR
Bucket *see* CONTAINER
Buckle *see* TIE
Bud *see* PLANT
Bugle *see* ARMY
see INSTRUMENT
Build *see* BUILDING
Builder *see* WORKMAN

BUILDING
annexe
arch
architect
architecture
balcony
barn
beam
brick
build
capital
ceiling
cellar
chimney
clay
column
construction
corridor
court
courtyard
dome
door
door-posts
eaves
floor
foundation
gate

BUILDING (cont.)
hall
house
hut
mansion
mortar
palace
passage
pavilion
porch
rafters
rebuild
roof
room
sanctuary
shed
STONE
storey
temple
theatre
threshold
tile
timber
tower
wall
watch-tower
window
WOOD
yard

Bul *see* MONTH
Bull *see* CATTLE
Bull-calf *see* CATTLE
see IDOL
Bullocks *see* CATTLE
Bunch *see* COLLECT
Bundle *see* COLLECT

BURDEN
bear
CARRY
heavy
load
WORRY
yoke

Burglars *see* STEAL
Burn *see* FIRE
see INJURE
Burst *see* BREAK
Bury *see* DIE
Bush *see* PLANT
see TREE
Business *see* TRADE
Businessmen *see* WORKMAN
Busybodies *see* RUMOUR
Butchered *see* KILL
see VIOLENCE
Butt *see* HIT
see PUSH
Butter *see* FOOD
Buttocks *see* BODY
Buy *see* TRADE
Buzzard *see* BIRD
Bystander *see* FOLLOW

C

Cage *see* CAPTURE
Cake *see* BREAD
Calamity *see* DISASTER
Calamus *see* PERFUME
Calf *see* CATTLE
Call *see* NAME
see SPEAK
Calm *see* LEVEL
see QUIET
Camel *see* ANIMAL
Camp *see* ARMY
see DWELL
see PLACE
Campaign *see* WAR
Canal *see* WATER
Cancel *see* END
Cancer *see* ILLNESS
Cane *see* PERFUME
Cap *see* CLOTHING
Capable *see* ABLE
Cape *see* CLOTHING
Capital *see* BUILDING
see PLACE
Captain *see* OFFICER
Captive *see* CAPTURE

CAPTURE
arrest
cage
captive
catch

CAPTURE (cont.)
cell
chains
confined
CONQUER
dungeon
ESCAPE
grab
harpoon
hostage
hunt
irons
jail
kidnap
net
prey
prison
prisoner
seize
snare
TIE
trap

Caravan *see* TRAVEL
Carcass *see* DIE
Care *see* PROTECT
see THOROUGH
see WORRY
Career *see* WORK
Carefree *see* HAPPY
Careful *see* ALERT
Careless *see* NEGLECT
Caress *see* LOVE
Cargo *see* SHIP
see TRADE
Carnelian *see* JEWEL
Carnival *see* VIOLENCE
Carousing *see* DRINK
Carpenter *see* WOOD
see WORKMAN
Carpet *see* FURNISHINGS
Carriage *see* TRAVEL

CARRY
bear
BURDEN
carrying-poles
carrying-rings
support
transport

Carrying-poles
see CARRY
Carrying-rings
see CARRY
Cart *see* TRAVEL
Carve *see* ARTS
Carving *see* ADORN
Case *see* JUDGEMENT
Cash *see* MONEY
Cassia *see* SPICES
Cast *see* CHOOSE
see METAL
Castrate *see* INJURE
Catapult *see* THROW
see WEAPON
Catch *see* CAPTURE

CATTLE
ANIMAL
beef
bellow
bull
bull-calf
bullocks
calf
cow
cud
livestock
moo
ox
pasture
team
veal

Cauldron *see* CONTAINER
Cause *see* BASIS
see CONTROL
Cautious *see* ALERT
Cavalry *see* HORSE
see SOLDIER
Cave *see* COUNTRYSIDE
Caw *see* NOISE
Cease *see* END
Ceaseless *see* CONSTANT
Cedar *see* TREE
see WOOD
Ceiling *see* BUILDING
Celebrate *see* HAPPY
see WORSHIP
Cell *see* CAPTURE

Cellar see BUILDING
Cemetery see DIE
Census see COUNT
see LIST
Centimetre see MEASURE
Centre see PART
Ceremony see WORSHIP

CERTAIN
clear
definite
distinct
sure

Chaff see USELESS
Chains see CAPTURE
Chair see FURNISHINGS
Chalcedony see JEWEL
Chalk see ARTS
Challenge see DEFY
Chance see LUCK
Change see MONEY

CHANGE
distort
exchange
fickle
reform
shifting
transform
turn
unstable

Channel see WATER
Chant see MUSIC
Chaos see DISASTER
Character see ACTION
see PERSON
Charcoal see FIRE
Charge see COMMAND
see CONTROL
see PAY
see WAR
Chariot see ARMY
see TRAVEL
Charity see GIVE
Charm see MAGIC
Charred see FIRE
Chase see FOLLOW
Cheap see MONEY
see USELESS
Cheat see DECEIVE
see VIOLENCE
Check see PREVENT
see SEARCH
Cheek see BODY
Cheeky see INSULT
Cheer see PRAISE
Cheerful see HAPPY
Cheese see FOOD
Cherish see LOVE
Chest see BODY
Chew see EAT
Chick see BIRD
Chicken see BIRD
Chief see STATUS
Child see AGE
see BIRTH
see FAMILY
see PERSON
Child of God see ATONEMENT
Childbirth see BIRTH
Childless see BARREN
Chimney see BUILDING
Chin see BODY
Chip see PIECE
Chirp see SPEAK
Chisel see TOOLS
Choir see MUSIC
Choke see DIE
see KILL
see PREVENT
see SPIT

CHOOSE
anoint
apart
appoint
cast
decide
dice
lot
pick
select
undecided
vote

Chop see CUT
Christ see JESUS
Christian see CHURCH
Chronic see ILLNESS

CHURCH
apostle
baptize
believer
Christian
convert
disciple
doctrine
elder
evangelist
FELLOWSHIP
God's people
Good News
gospel
helper
pastor
preach
proclaim
prophet
teacher
WORSHIP

Churn see STIR
Cinnamon see PERFUME
see SPICES
Circle see SHAPE
Circumcise see JUDAISM
Cistern see CONTAINER
Citizen see DWELL
City see NATION
see PLACE
Claim see ARGUE
see BELONG
see DECEIVE
Clamps see TOOLS
Clan see TRIBE
Clanging see NOISE
Clap see PRAISE
Clash see WAR
Clasp see HOLD
Class see GROUP
Classify see STATUS
Clatter see NOISE
Claws see BIRD
Clay see BUILDING
see STONE
Clean see PURE
see TIDY
see WASH
Clear see CERTAIN
see JUDGEMENT
see READY

CLEVER
crafty
cunning
LEARNING
sensible
shrewd
skilful
skill
wise
wit

Cliff see COUNTRYSIDE
Climb see MOVE
Cling see HOLD
Cloak see CLOTHING
Close see NEAR

CLOSE
bar
block
bolt
door
gate
key
lock
shut

CLOTH
CLOTHING
cotton
embroider
leather
linen
loom
patch
sackcloth
satin
sew
sheet
shuttle
silk
weave
wool

CLOTHING
apron
article
belt

CLOTHING (cont.)
boots
breast-piece
cap
cape
cloak
CLOTH
coat
collar
dress
ephod
garment
gown
handkerchief
hat
headband
hem
naked
pocket
rags
ribbon
robe
sandal
sash
scarf
seam
sew
shirt
shoes
shorts
skirt
sleeves
straps
tassel
trousers
turban
uniform
veil
wear
wristbands

Clothmakers see WORKMAN
Cloud see WEATHER
Club see WEAPON
Cluster see COLLECT
Coal see FIRE
Coarse see ROUGH
Coast see COUNTRYSIDE
Coat see CLOTHING
Cobra see ANIMAL
Cobwebs see DELICATE
Cock see BIRD
Coffin see DIE
Coin see MONEY
Cold see HEAT
see WEATHER
Collapse see FALL
Collar see CLOTHING
Colleague see ALLY

COLLECT
accumulate
acquire
assemble
bunch
bundle
cluster
gather
GROUP
harvest
heap
pile
together

Colony see DWELL

COLOUR
ADORN
black
blue
brown
dappled
dye
golden
green
grey
paint
pale
purple
red
scarlet
speckled
spotted
streaked
stripe
tanned
violet
white
whitewash
yellow

Colt see HORSE
Column see BUILDING
Comb see HAIR
Combat see WAR
Comet see UNIVERSE

COMFORT
content
cosy
ease
LOVE
luxury
REST
soft

Coming see NEW

COMMAND
charge
CONTROL
instruct
LAW
order
TELL

COMMANDMENTS (the Ten): Ex 20.1f. Deut 5.6f.

Commander see OFFICER
see SOLDIER
Commandment
see LAW
Commentary see COMMUNICATE
Commerce see TRADE
Commissioner
see OFFICIAL
Commit see SIN
Common see USUAL
Commotion see DISTURB

COMMUNICATE
address
angel
ARTS
authorized interpreters
commentary
confer
conversation
deliver
dictate
express
LANGUAGE
news
oral translation
parable
phrase
proverb
quote
read
saying
send
sign
SPEAK
speech
state
TELL
tongue
translate
word
WRITE

Community see GROUP
Companion see FOLLOW
Company see ARMY
see GROUP
Compare see STATUS
Compassion see KIND
see LOVE
Competent see ABLE

COMPLAIN
blame
CORRECT
criticize
curse
denounce
grumble
mind
object
PUNISH
rebuke
reprimand
reproach
scold

Complete see ACCOMPLISH
see THOROUGH
Complicated see PROBLEM
Compose see MUSIC
Conceal see HIDE
Conceited see PRIDE

Conceive *see* BIRTH
Concern *see* KIND
see WORRY
Concession *see* ACCEPT
Concubine *see* MARRY
Condemn *see* JUDGEMENT
see SIN
Conduct *see* ACTION
Confer *see* COMMUNICATE
Confess *see* ACKNOWLEDGE
Confidence *see* FAITH
Confined *see* CAPTURE
see PUNISH
Confirm *see* ACKNOWLEDGE
Confiscate *see* PUNISH
Conform *see* ACCEPT
Confuse *see* WORRY
Congratulate *see* PRAISE

CONQUER
ARMY
CAPTURE
CONTROL
crush
defeat
dominate
give up
invade
occupy
oppress
overcome
overpower
overthrow
overwhelm
prize
rule
subdue
subject
submit
surrender
trample
triumph
underfoot
victory
win

Conscience *see* SIN
Conscious *see* KNOW
Consecrate *see* WORSHIP
Consent *see* ACCEPT
Consider *see* LOVE
Considerate *see* KIND
Consist *see* MAKE
Conspire *see* BETRAY

CONSTANT
always
ceaseless
continue
depend
endless
endure
eternal
ever
ever-living
everlasting
firm
fix
immortal
incorruptible
infinite
last
LOVE
perfect
permanent
persevere
persist
rely
repeat
resolute
steady
unbreakable
unbroken
unchanging
undivided
undying
unending
unfailing

Constellation *see* UNIVERSE
Construct *see* MAKE
Construction *see* BUILDING
Consult *see* ASK
Consume *see* EAT
Contact *see* MEET

CONTAINER
bag
barrel
basin
basket

CONTAINER (cont.)
bottle
bowl
box
bucket
cauldron
cistern
cup
dish
firepan
jar
pack
pan
pipes
pot
purse
sack
tank
tray
trough
tub
UTENSIL
vase
vat
vessel
wineskin

Contaminated
see DEFILE
Contempt *see* MOCK
Content *see* COMFORT
see HAPPY
see MAKE
Contest *see* WAR
Continue *see* CONSTANT
Contract *see* PROMISE
Contradict *see* ARGUE
Contrary *see* DIFFERENT
Contribute *see* GIVE

CONTROL
administer
arrange
cause
charge
COMMAND
CONQUER
council
direct
force
govern
impose
manage
NECESSARY
organize
policies
responsible

Conversation *see* COMMUNICATE
Convert *see* CHURCH
see JUDAISM
Convict *see* JUDGEMENT
Convince *see* ARGUE
see FAITH

COOK
bake
baking-pan
boil
brush
FOOD
griddle
kitchen
oven
pan
raw
roast
soup
stew
stove
uncooked

Cool *see* HEAT
Copper *see* METAL
see MONEY
Copy *see* WRITE
Coral *see* JEWEL
Cord *see* TIE
Cormorant *see* BIRD
Corn *see* CROP
Corner *see* PART
Cornfield *see* CROP
Corpse *see* DIE

CORRECT
accurate
COMPLAIN
proper
PUNISH
rebuke
right

CORRECT (cont.)
rightful

Correspondence
see WRITE
Corridor *see* BUILDING
Corrode *see* DECAY
Corrupt *see* DEFILE
see SIN
Cosmic *see* UNIVERSE
Cost *see* PAY
Cosy *see* COMFORT
Cotton *see* CLOTH
Couch *see* FURNISHINGS
Council *see* CONTROL
see GROUP
see JUDAISM
Counsel *see* SUGGEST

COUNT
add
amount
census
majority
many
MEASURE
more
much
number
numerous
quantity
reckon
sum
total

Country *see* NATION
see PLACE

COUNTRYSIDE
cave
cliff
coast
crest
crevice
desert
foothills
highlands
hill
hill-country
island
lowlands
mainland
mound
mount
mountain
peak
plain
plateau
rock
shore
slope
valley
wilderness

Couple *see* TWO

COURAGE
bold
brave
DANGER
dare
FEAR
fearless
hero
morale
nerve
reckless
unafraid

Course *see* ROAD
Court *see* BUILDING
see ENCLOSURE
see JUDGEMENT
see KING
see MARRY
Courtyard *see* BUILDING
see ENCLOSURE
Cousin *see* RELATIVE
Covenant *see* PROMISE
Covenant Box
see WORSHIP
Cover *see* PART
Cow *see* CATTLE
Coward *see* FEAR
Crack *see* BREAK
Crackle *see* NOISE
Craftsman *see* WORKMAN
Crafty *see* CLEVER
Crash *see* NOISE
Crave *see* WANT
Crawl *see* MOVE

Crazy *see* MAD
Cream *see* FOOD
Create *see* BEGIN
see MAKE
Creator *see* GOD
Creature *see* ANIMAL
Credit *see* DESERVE
see PRAISE
Creditors *see* LOAN
Creep *see* MOVE
Crest *see* COUNTRYSIDE
Crevice *see* COUNTRYSIDE
see HOLE
Crew *see* SHIP
Cricket *see* ANIMAL
Crime *see* SIN
see VIOLENCE

CRIMINAL
assassin
bandit
law-breaker
lawless
murderer
outlaw
STEAL
unjust

Cripple *see* INJURE
Crisis *see* DISASTER
Criticize *see* COMPLAIN
Crocodile *see* ANIMAL
Crooked *see* SHAPE
Crop *see* ORGANS

CROP
barley
corn
cornfield
CULTIVATE
ear of corn
farm
field
FOOD
grain
hay
meal
millet
PLANT
produce
sheaf
spelt
straw
stubble
wheat
yield

Cross *see* ANGER
see ATONEMENT
see TRAVEL
Cross-breed *see* ANIMAL
see BREED
Crossroads *see* ROAD
Crouch *see* BREED
Crow *see* BIRD
see NOISE
Crowd *see* GROUP
Crown *see* KING
Crucify *see* KILL
see VIOLENCE

CRUEL
hard
harsh
ill-treat
inconsiderate
merciless
ROUGH
severe
sternly
unkind
VIOLENCE

Crumble *see* BREAK
see DECAY
see POWDER
Crush *see* CONQUER
see VIOLENCE
Crust *see* BREAD
Cry *see* LAMENT
see NOISE
see SPEAK
Crystal *see* GLASS
see JEWEL
Cub *see* ANIMAL
Cucumber *see* VEGETABLES
Cud *see* CATTLE

CULTIVATE
barn
CROP

CULTIVATE (cont.)
farm
fertile
field
granary
grow
harrow
harvest
manure
meadow
orchard
PLANT
plough
prune
reap
seed
soil
sow
thresh
winnowing shovel

Cumin *see* HERBS
Cunning *see* CLEVER
Cup *see* CONTAINER
see DRINK
Cure *see* MEDICINE
Curl *see* SHAPE
Curse *see* ABUSE
see COMPLAIN
Curtain *see* FURNISHINGS
Curve *see* SHAPE
Cushion *see* FURNISHINGS
Custom *see* USUAL
Customer *see* TRADE

CUT
BREAK
chop
DIVIDE
gash
jab
knife
PIECE
pierce
rip
saw
separate
sharp
shear
slash
sliced
trim

Cymbals *see* INSTRUMENT
Cypress *see* TREE

D

Daddy *see* RELATIVE
Daft *see* MAD
Dagger *see* WEAPON
Daily *see* TIME
Dainty *see* DELICATE
Dam *see* WATER
Damage *see* BREAK
Damp *see* WATER
Dan *see* TRIBE
Dance *see* HAPPY

DANGER
COURAGE
FEAR
risk
threat
WORRY

Dappled *see* COLOUR
Dare *see* COURAGE
see DEFY

DARK
black
dim
midnight
night
nightfall
shade
shadow
twilight

Darling *see* LOVE
Dart *see* SPEED
Dash *see* SPEED
Date *see* FRUIT
see TIME
Daughter *see* RELATIVE
Daughter-in-law
see RELATIVE
Dawn *see* LIGHT

Day *see* LIGHT
see TIME
Day of Judgement
see JUDGEMENT
Day of the Lord
see JUDGEMENT
Day-dreaming
see SLEEP
Daybreak *see* LIGHT
Daylight *see* LIGHT
Dazzling *see* LIGHT
Dead *see* DIE
Deadly *see* DIE
Deaf *see* ILLNESS
Deal *see* TRADE
Dear *see* LOVE
Death (from-)
see RISE
Death *see* DIE
see KILL
see VIOLENCE
Debate *see* ARGUE
see SPEAK
Debt *see* MONEY

DECALOGUE: Ex 20.1f. Deut 5.6f.

DECAY
corrode
crumble
DESTROY
DIE
dissolve
dust
END
mildew
moth-eaten
mouldy
perish
rot
rust
shrivel
wear out
wither
worm

DECEIVE
cheat
claim
disguise
dishonest
false
flatter
fraud
hypocrite
illusion
impostor
insincere
legend
lie
made-up
mislead
pretend
trick
unfair
untrue

Decide *see* CHOOSE
Deck *see* SHIP
Declare *see* TELL
Decorate *see* ADORN
Decrease *see* SIZE
Decree *see* LAW
Dedicate *see* WORSHIP
Deed *see* ACTION
Deep *see* SIZE
see WATER
Deer *see* ANIMAL
Defeat *see* CONQUER
see WAR
Defect *see* DEFILE
Defend *see* PROTECT
see RESIST
Defendant *see* JUDGEMENT

DEFILE
Awful Horror
BAD
contaminated
corrupt
defect
degrading
desecrate
DIRT
disgrace
disgusting
dishonour
impurity
irreverence
latrine
obscene

DEFILE (cont.)
pervert
pollute
profane
SIN
spoil
stain
unclean
unholy
violate

Definite *see* CERTAIN
Deformed *see* INJURE

DEFY
challenge
dare
ENMITY

Degrading *see* DEFILE
Delay *see* WAIT
Deliberate *see* INTEND

DELICATE
cobwebs
dainty
fine
flimsy

Delight *see* HAPPY
Deliver *see* COMMUNICATE
see PROTECT
Delusion *see* ERROR
see MAD
Demand *see* ASK
see WANT
Demolish *see* DESTROY
Demon *see* DEVIL
Demonstrate *see* SHOW
Den *see* ENCLOSURE
Denounce *see* COMPLAIN
Dense *see* OVERGROWN

DENY
disown
no
PREVENT
refuse
reluctant
reservation
unwilling

Depart *see* ABANDON
see ABSENCE
Depend *see* CONSTANT
Dependant *see* FAMILY
Deport *see* EXPEL
Deposit *see* MONEY
Depressed *see* WORRY
Deprive *see* POOR
Deputy *see* OFFICIAL
Descendant *see* FAMILY
Describe *see* SHOW
Desecrate *see* DEFILE
Desert *see* ABANDON
see BARREN
see COUNTRYSIDE

DESERVE
ABLE
credit
due
GOOD
worth

Design *see* ADORN
Desire *see* LOVE
see WANT
Desolate *see* BARREN
Despair *see* WORRY
Despise *see* ENMITY
see MOCK
Destiny *see* INTEND

DESTROY
abolish
annul
DECAY
demolish
devastate
DISASTER
END
erase
KILL
moth
perish
ruin
VIOLENCE

Detail *see* THOROUGH

Determine *see* INTEND
see OBSTINATE
Detest *see* ENMITY
Devastate *see* DESTROY
Develop *see* SIZE

DEVIL
abyss
beast
Beelzebul
demon
dragon
enemy
evil
Evil One
goat-demon
HELL
Mob
Satan
serpent
spirit
SUPERNATURAL
tempt
Wicked One

Devotion *see* LOVE
see ZEAL
Devour *see* EAT
Devout *see* WORSHIP
Dew *see* WATER
Diamond *see* JEWEL
Dice *see* CHOOSE
Dictate *see* COMMUNICATE
see SPEAK

DIE
body
bury
carcass
cemetery
choke
coffin
corpse
dead
deadly
death
DECAY
drown
embalm
fatal
funeral
grave
Hades
hang
HELL
KILL
lifeless
mortal
perish
poison
suicide
tomb
VIOLENCE
world below

Diet *see* FOOD

DIFFERENT
against
ARGUE
contrary
disagree
distinguish
DIVIDE
oppose
opposite
separate

Difficult *see* PROBLEM
Dig *see* HOLE
see WORK
Digestion *see* EAT
Dignity *see* RESPECT
Dill *see* HERBS
Dim *see* DARK
see UNSEEN
Dine *see* EAT
Direct *see* CONTROL

DIRECTION
aim
backwards
downstream
east
forward
goal
head
lead
north
north-east
north-west

DIRECTION (cont.)
point
signpost
straight
south
south-east
south-west
TRAVEL
west

DIRT
DEFILE
dung
dust
excrement
filthy
manure
muck
mud
slime

Disabled *see* INJURE
Disagree *see* ARGUE
see DIFFERENT
Disappear *see* UNSEEN
Disappoint *see* HOPELESS

DISASTER
calamity
chaos
crisis
DESTROY
doom
earthquake
flood
landslide
quake
storm

DISCARD
dump
EXPEL
rid
THROW
USELESS

Discharge *see* ILLNESS
Disciple *see* CHURCH
see LEARNING
Discipline *see* PUNISH
Discourage *see* HOPELESS
Discover *see* KNOW
see SEARCH
Discuss *see* ARGUE
see SPEAK
Disease *see* ILLNESS
Disfigured *see* INJURE
Disgrace *see* DEFILE
Disguise *see* DECEIVE
Disgusting *see* DEFILE
see SIN
Dish *see* CONTAINER
see FOOD
Dishonest *see* DECEIVE
Dishonour *see* DEFILE
Disillusioned *see* HOPELESS
Disinfect *see* PURE
Disloyal *see* BETRAY
Dismal *see* BAD
Dismay *see* HOPELESS
see WORRY
Dismiss *see* EXPEL
Dismount *see* HORSE
Disobey *see* SIN
Disorder *see* ILLNESS
Disown *see* DENY
Dispel *see* ABSENCE
Disperse *see* ABSENCE
Display *see* SHOW
Displease *see* ANGER
Disprove *see* ARGUE
Dispute *see* ARGUE
Disqualify *see* PREVENT
Disregard *see* NEGLECT
Disrespect *see* INSULT
Dissatisfy *see* HOPELESS
Dissolve *see* DECAY
Distant *see* ABSENCE
Distinct *see* CERTAIN
Distinguish *see* DIFFERENT
see DIVIDE
see PERCEIVE
Distort *see* CHANGE
Distress *see* WORRY
Distribute *see* GIVE
District *see* PLACE

DISTURB
commotion
overturn
SHAKE

DISTURB (cont.)
shock
STIR
turmoil
upset
upside down
WORRY

Ditch *see* HOLE

DIVIDE
ABSENCE
apart
BORDER
CUT
DIFFERENT
distinguish
fork
intersect
partitioned
PIECE
proportion
separate
SIEVE

Divination *see* MAGIC
see PROPHECY
Divine *see* GOD
Divorce *see* MARRY
Do away with *see* END
Doctor *see* MEDICINE
Doctrine *see* CHURCH
Document *see* WRITE
Dodge *see* ESCAPE
Dog *see* ANIMAL
Dome *see* BUILDING
Domestic *see* ANIMAL
Dominate *see* CONQUER
Dominion *see* KING
Donkey *see* ANIMAL
see HORSE
Doom *see* DISASTER
Door *see* BUILDING
see CLOSE
Door-posts *see* BUILDING
Double *see* TWO
Double-edged *see* TWO

DOUBT
unbelief
unbeliever
uncertain
undecided
wonder

Dough *see* BREAD
Dove *see* BIRD
Downfall *see* FALL
Downhearted *see* HOPELESS
Downstream *see* DIRECTION
Doze *see* SLEEP
Drag *see* PUSH
Dragon *see* ANIMAL
see DEVIL
Drain *see* EMPTY
see FLOW
Draught *see* PUSH
Draw *see* ADORN
see ARTS
see PUSH
Dread *see* FEAR
Dream *see* PROPHECY
see SLEEP
Drench *see* WATER
Dress *see* CLOTHING
Dribble *see* SPIT
Drift *see* TRAVEL

DRINK
alcohol
beer
carousing
cup
drunk
drunkard
lap
liquor
milk
sober
stupor
thirst
WATER
wine
wine-drinkers

Drip *see* FALL
see FLOW
Drive out *see* EXPEL
Drop *see* FALL
see FLOW
Dross *see* USELESS

Drought *see* LACK
see WEATHER
Drown *see* DIE
Drowsy *see* SLEEP
Drug *see* SLEEP
Drum *see* INSTRUMENT
Drunk *see* DRINK
Drunkard *see* DRINK
Dry *see* BARREN
see WEATHER
Due *see* DESERVE
see PAY
see READY
Dull *see* IGNORANT
Dumb *see* ILLNESS
Dump *see* DISCARD
Dung *see* DIRT
Dungeon *see* CAPTURE
Dust *see* DECAY
see DIRT
see POWDER
Duty *see* MONEY
see PAY
see SERVE
Dwarf *see* SIZE

DWELL
camp
citizen
colony
home
household
inn
inhabit
lodging
LIVE
native
occupy
PLACE
quarter
population
spend
stay
reside
settle

Dye *see* COLOUR
Dynasty *see* KING
Dysentery *see* ILLNESS

E

Each other *see* FELLOWSHIP
Eager *see* ZEAL
Eagle *see* BIRD
Ear *see* BODY
Ear of corn *see* CROP
Earn *see* MONEY
Earnest *see* SERIOUS
Earrings *see* JEWEL

EARTHLY
below
material
natural
physical
unspiritual
world
worldly

Earthquake *see* DISASTER
see SHAKE
Earthworks *see* WAR
Ease *see* COMFORT
see REST
East *see* DIRECTION

EASTER: Mt 28 Mk 16 Lk 24 Jn 20

EAT
appetite
banquet
bite
chew
consume
devour
digestion
dine
DRINK
feast
FOOD
gnaw
graze
greedy
hunger
lunch
meal
mouthful
starve

EAT (cont.)
stomach
stuff
supper
swallow
TASTE
tasty

Eaves *see* BUILDING
Ebony *see* WOOD
Echo *see* NOISE
Ecstatic *see* HAPPY
Edge *see* BORDER
see PART
Educate *see* LEARNING
Effect *see* ACCOMPLISH
see BASIS

EFFORT
aim
athlete
attempt
exercise
persevere
practice
resolute
strain
strive
struggle
try
WORK
ZEAL

Egg *see* FOOD
Elder *see* AGE
see CHURCH
Eloquent *see* SPEAK
Elul *see* MONTH
Embalm *see* DIE
Embarrass *see* ASHAMED
Embers *see* FIRE
Embrace *see* HOLD
see LOVE
Embroider *see* ADORN
see CLOTH
Emerald *see* JEWEL
Emperor *see* KING
Empire *see* KING

EMPLOY
allowance
hire
PAY
use
wage
WORK

Empress *see* KING

EMPTY
drain
evaporate
FLOW
gap
HOLE
hollow
LACK
space
spill

ENCLOSURE
court
courtyard
den
fence
hedge
pen
railing
sheepfold
wall

Encourage *see* HELP

END
cancel
cease
DECAY
DESTROY
do away with
final
finish
never again
remove
stop

Endless *see* CONSTANT
Endure *see* CONSTANT
Enemy *see* DEVIL
see ENMITY
Engaged *see* MARRY
Engrave *see* ADORN

Enjoy *see* APPRECIATE
see GOOD
see HAPPY
Enlarge *see* SIZE
Enlist *see* SOLDIER

ENMITY
against
DEFY
despise
detest
enemy
foe
grudge
hate
hostile
look down on
malice
opponent
oppose
reject
resent
resist
rival
spiteful

Enormous *see* SIZE

ENOUGH
abundant
fill
full
left over
plenty
satisfy
spare
sufficient
surplus

Enrol *see* LIST

ENTERTAIN
amuse
ARTS
ball
banquet
feast
festivities
guest
hospitality
host
invite
party
play
spectacle
uninvited
visit

Enthusiasm *see* ZEAL
Entire *see* THOROUGH
Entitled *see* ABLE
Entrails *see* BODY
see ORGANS
Entrust *see* FAITH
Envoy *see* REPRESENT
Envy *see* WANT
Ephah *see* MEASURE
Ephod *see* CLOTHING
Ephraim *see* TRIBE
Epidemic *see* ILLNESS
Epileptic *see* ILLNESS

EPIPHANY: Mt 2.1f.

Equal *see* SAME
Equipment *see* UTENSIL
Equivalent *see* SAME
Erase *see* DESTROY

ERROR
ACCIDENT
delusion
mistake
wrong

Eruption *see* ILLNESS

ESCAPE
avoid
CAPTURE
dodge
flee
FREE
get away
HIDE
refugee
run
runaway

Escort *see* FOLLOW
Esteem *see* RESPECT

Eternal *see* CONSTANT
see GOD
Ethanim *see* MONTH

EUCHARIST: Mt 26.26f. Mk 14.22f. Lk 22.14f. 1 Cor 11.17f.

Eunuch *see* OFFICIAL
Evangelist *see* CHURCH
Evaporate *see* EMPTY
Even *see* LEVEL
Evening *see* TIME
Ever *see* CONSTANT
Ever-living *see* CONSTANT
see GOD
Evergreen *see* TREE
Everlasting *see* CONSTANT
Evidence *see* JUDGEMENT
Evident *see* SHOW
Evil *see* BAD
see DEVIL
see SIN
Evil One *see* DEVIL
Ewe *see* ANIMAL
Exalted *see* WORSHIP
Examine *see* SEARCH
Example *see* SHOW
Excellent *see* GOOD
Exchange *see* CHANGE
Exclude *see* EXPEL
Excrement *see* DIRT
Execute *see* KILL
Exercise *see* EFFORT
Exhausted *see* WEARY
Exile *see* EXPEL
Expect *see* INTEND
see THINK
Expedition *see* WAR

EXPEL
banish
deport
DISCARD
dismiss
drive out
exclude
exile
homeless
outcast
rid
send

Expense *see* MONEY
Expensive *see* PRECIOUS
see WEALTH
Expert *see* LEARNING
Explain *see* SHOW
Export *see* TRADE
Expose *see* BARE
Express *see* COMMUNICATE
Extend *see* SIZE
Exterminate *see* KILL

EXTERNAL
outcast
outdoor
outer
outside
outsider

Extraordinary
see USUAL
Eye *see* BODY
see SEE
Eye-lash *see* BODY
Eyebrow *see* BODY
Eyelid *see* BODY
Eyeshadow *see* ADORN

F

Face *see* BODY
Facet *see* JEWEL
Fade *see* UNSEEN
Fail *see* NEGLECT
Faint *see* SLEEP
see UNSEEN
Fair *see* HONEST

FAITH
belief
believe
believer
confidence
convince
entrust
faithful
hope
trust

Faithful *see* ALLEGIANCE
see FAITH
Falcon *see* BIRD

FALL
collapse
downfall
drip
drop
sink
slip
stagger
stumble
tip
trip
tumble

Fallen *see* SIN
False *see* DECEIVE
see USELESS

FAMILY
adopt
adult
ancestor
bastard
BIRTH
boy
child
dependant
descendant
generation
girl
heir
household
MARRY
orphan
RELATIVE
TRIBE
twin

Famine *see* FOOD
see LACK
Famous *see* STATUS
Fancy *see* ADORN
Far *see* ABSENCE
Far-off *see* ABSENCE
Fare *see* PAY
Farm *see* CROP
see CULTIVATE
Fashioned *see* MAKE
Fast *see* FOOD
see LACK
see SPEED
Fasten *see* TIE
Fat *see* SIZE
Fatal *see* DIE
Father *see* GOD
see RELATIVE
Father-in-law *see* RELATIVE
Fatherless *see* ALONE
Fault *see* BLEMISH
see SIN
Faultless *see* PURE
Favour *see* ASK
Favourite *see* APPRECIATE
Fawn *see* ANIMAL

FEAR
afraid
alarm
awe
brave
bristled
COURAGE
coward
DANGER
dread
fearful
fearless
fright
HOPELESS
horrify
nerve
panic
scare
shrink
terrify
terror
threat
timid
tremble
WORRY

Fearful *see* FEAR
Fearless *see* COURAGE
see FEAR
Feast *see* EAT
see ENTERTAIN
see FOOD
Feathers *see* BIRD

Feed *see* FOOD
Feel *see* PERCEIVE
Feldspar *see* JEWEL
see STONE
Fellow-townsmen
see NATION

FELLOWSHIP
brother
CHURCH
each other
friend
GROUP
LOVE
neighbour
one another
others
sister

Female *see* PERSON
Fence *see* BORDER
see ENCLOSURE
Fertile *see* CULTIVATE
Fervent *see* SERIOUS
see ZEAL
Festival *see* JUDAISM
see WORSHIP
Festivities *see* ENTERTAIN
Fever *see* ILLNESS
Fickle *see* CHANGE
Field *see* CROP
see CULTIVATE
Fierce *see* VIOLENCE
Fig *see* FRUIT
see TREE
Fight *see* VIOLENCE
see WAR
Figure *see* ARTS
see IMAGE
see SHAPE
Fill *see* ENOUGH
Filthy *see* DIRT
Final *see* END
Find *see* SEARCH
Find out *see* KNOW
Fine *see* DELICATE
see JUDGEMENT
see PAY
see PUNISH
Finger *see* BODY
Finish *see* END
Fir *see* TREE

FIRE
ash
blaze
bonfire
burn
charcoal
charred
coal
embers
fire-pot
fire-wood
firepan
fireplace
flame
fuel
furnace
HEAT
kindle
LIGHT
scorch
singe
smoke
smoulder
spark
sulphur

Fire-pot *see* FIRE
Fire-wood *see* FIRE
see WOOD
Firepan *see* CONTAINER
see FIRE
Fireplace *see* FIRE
Firm *see* CONSTANT
First-born *see* BIRTH
Fish *see* FOOD
Fishermen *see* WORKMAN
Fist *see* HIT
Fit *see* ABLE
see ILLNESS
Fix *see* CONSTANT
Flag *see* SHOW
Flame *see* FIRE
see LIGHT
Flash *see* LIGHT
Flat *see* LEVEL
see SHAPE
Flatter *see* DECEIVE
Flavour *see* TASTE

Flaw *see* BLEMISH
Flax *see* PLANT
Flea *see* ANIMAL
Flee *see* ESCAPE
Fleet *see* SHIP
Flesh *see* BODY
Flickering *see* LIGHT
Flimsy *see* DELICATE
Fling *see* THROW
Flint *see* STONE
Flit *see* FLY
Float *see* WATER
Flock *see* ANIMAL
see GROUP
Flog *see* PUNISH
Flood *see* DISASTER
see FLOW
see WATER
Floor *see* BUILDING
Flour *see* FOOD
Flourish *see* LIVE

FLOW
drain
drip
drop
flood
gush
gutter
liquid
pour
run
torrent
WATER

Flower *see* PLANT
Flute *see* INSTRUMENT
Fly *see* ANIMAL

FLY
air
alight
bat
BIRD
flit
hover
MOVE
wing

Foal *see* HORSE
Foam *see* WATER
Fodder *see* FOOD
Foe *see* ENMITY

FOLLOW
accompany
after me
ALLEGIANCE
bystander
chase
companion
escort
go with
guide
imitate
lead
overtake
predecessor
pursue
straggling
succeed

Follower *see* LEARNING
Folly *see* IGNORANT
see MAD
Fond *see* LOVE

FOOD
almond
BREAD
broth
butter
cheese
COOK
cream
CROP
diet
dish
DRINK
EAT
egg
famine
fast
feast
feed
fish
flour
fodder
FRUIT
HERBS
honey

FOOD (cont.)
LACK
manna
MEAT
nourish
nut
olive-oil
pistachio
provisions
salt
sauce
soup
SPICES
stew
TASTE
VEGETABLES
vinegar
yeast

Fool *see* IGNORANT
see MAD
Foot *see* BODY
Foot-soldier *see* ARMY
see SOLDIER
Foothills *see* COUNTRYSIDE
Footstool *see* ALLEGIANCE
Forbid *see* PREVENT
Force *see* ARMY
see CONTROL
see NECESSARY
Forehead *see* BODY

FOREIGN
abroad
alien
barbarians
Gentile
outsider
overseas
strange
stranger

Foreman *see* WORKMAN
Foresee *see* PROPHECY
Foreskin *see* BODY
Forest *see* OVERGROWN
see TREE
Foretell *see* PROPHECY
Forge *see* METAL
Forget *see* NEGLECT

FORGIVE
ATONEMENT
JUDGEMENT
overlook
pardon
reconcile
redeem
relent

Fork *see* DIVIDE
see UTENSIL
Form *see* MAKE
see SHAPE
Former *see* TIME
Formula *see* MAKE
Forsake *see* ABANDON
Fort *see* WAR
Fortify *see* WAR
Fortress *see* WAR
Fortune *see* LUCK
see MONEY
Fortune-teller *see* MAGIC
Forward *see* ADVANCE
see DIRECTION
Found *see* BEGIN
Foundation *see* BUILDING
Foundry *see* METAL
Fountain *see* WATER
Fox *see* ANIMAL
Fractured *see* INJURE
Fragrant *see* PERFUME
see SMELL
Frank *see* HONEST
Frankincense *see* PERFUME
see SPICES
Fraud *see* DECEIVE
Free *see* PAY

FREE
acquit
ESCAPE
freedmen
let go
liberty
ransom
release
untie

Freedmen *see* FREE
Freeze *see* HEAT
Frequent *see* TIME
Fresh *see* NEW
Friend *see* ATONEMENT
see FELLOWSHIP
see LOVE
Friendly *see* KIND
Fright *see* FEAR
Frog *see* ANIMAL
Front *see* ADVANCE
Frontier *see* BORDER
Frost *see* HEAT
see WEATHER
Frown *see* ANGER

FRUIT
apple
date
fig
FOOD
grape
melon
olive
orchard
PLANT
pomegranate
raisins
vine
vineyard
water-melon

Frustrate *see* PREVENT
Fuel *see* FIRE
Fulfil *see* ACCOMPLISH
Full *see* ENOUGH
see THOROUGH
Full-bodied *see* SIZE
Full-grown *see* SIZE
Fun (make-) *see* MOCK
Function *see* ACTION
see WORK
Funds *see* ACCOUNT
Funeral *see* DIE
Furnace *see* FIRE

FURNISHINGS
bed
bedding
bedspread
carpet
chair
couch
curtain
cushion
rug
stool
table

Fury *see* ANGER
Future *see* TIME

G

Gad *see* TRIBE
Gain *see* ADVANTAGE
see BELONG
Galbanum *see* SPICES
Gallop *see* HORSE
see MOVE
Gallows *see* PUNISH
Gamble *see* MONEY
Gang *see* GROUP
Gap *see* EMPTY
Gape *see* SEE
Garden *see* PLANT
Garlic *see* VEGETABLES
Garment *see* CLOTHING
Garnet *see* JEWEL
Gash *see* CUT
Gasp *see* WEARY
Gate *see* BUILDING
see CLOSE
Gate-keeper *see* WORKMAN
Gather *see* COLLECT
Gazed *see* SEE
Gazelle *see* ANIMAL
Gem *see* JEWEL
General *see* OFFICER
see USUAL
Generation *see* FAMILY
Generous *see* GIVE
Genital *see* BODY
see ORGANS
Gentile *see* FOREIGN
see PAGAN
Gentle *see* KIND
Gerah *see* MEASURE
Get away *see* ESCAPE

Get up *see* RISE
Ghost *see* SUPERNATURAL
Giant *see* SIZE
Gift *see* GIVE
Gigantic *see* SIZE
Girl *see* FAMILY
see PERSON

GIVE
allot
assign
charity
contribute
distribute
generous
gift
God-given
grant
hand
LOAN
present
provide
share
supply
undeserved
will

Give up *see* CONQUER
Glad *see* HAPPY
Glamour *see* ADORN
Glance *see* SEE
Glare *see* LIGHT

GLASS
crystal
glaze
mirror
SEE

Glaze *see* GLASS
Gleam *see* LIGHT
Glee *see* MOCK
Glitter *see* LIGHT
Gloat *see* MOCK
Gloom *see* LAMENT
Glorify *see* WORSHIP
Glory *see* PRAISE
Glow *see* LIGHT
Glutton *see* EAT
Gnat *see* ANIMAL
Gnaw *see* EAT
Go *see* TRAVEL
Go with *see* FOLLOW
Go without *see* LACK
Go-between *see* REPRESENT
Goal *see* DIRECTION
Goat *see* ANIMAL
Goat-demon *see* DEVIL

GOD
all-powerful
all-wise
almighty
creator
divine
eternal
ever-living
Father
goddess
HEAVEN
holy
I am
IDOL
KING
Lord
majesty
Most High
sacred
sovereign
SUPERNATURAL

God-given *see* GIVE
God's people *see* CHURCH
see JUDAISM
Goddess *see* GOD
see IDOL
Godly *see* GOOD
Gold *see* METAL
see MONEY
Golden *see* COLOUR
Goldsmith *see* WORKMAN
Gong *see* INSTRUMENT
Gonorrhoea *see* ILLNESS

GOOD
ACCEPT
ADVANTAGE
approve
best
better
DESERVE

GOOD (cont.)
enjoy
excellent
godly
like
magnificent
nice
outstanding
pleasant
please
pleasure
PURE
quality
useful
virtue

Good News see CHURCH
Good-bye see ABSENCE
Good-for-nothing see USELESS
Good-looking see BEAUTY
Goods see BELONG
Goodwill see LOVE
Gore see INJURE
Gospel see CHURCH
see WRITE
Gossip see RUMOUR
Gourd see PLANT
Govern see CONTROL
see KING
Governor see OFFICIAL
Gown see CLOTHING
Grab see CAPTURE
see HOLD
Grace see LOVE
Gracious see KIND
Grain see CROP
Grains of sand see POWDER

GRAMMAR
letter
plural
singular
word
WRITE

Gramme see MEASURE
Granary see CULTIVATE
Grandchildren see RELATIVE
Granddaughter see RELATIVE
Grandfather see RELATIVE
Grandmother see RELATIVE
Grandparents see RELATIVE
Grandson see RELATIVE
Grant see GIVE
Grape see FRUIT
Grapevine see TREE
Grasp see HOLD
Grass see PLANT
Grasshopper see ANIMAL
Grateful see THANK
Grave see DIE
see HOLE
Grave-digger see WORKMAN
Gravel see STONE
Graze see EAT
Great Bear see UNIVERSE
Great-grandchildren see RELATIVE
Great-grandfather see RELATIVE
Greedy see EAT
Greek see LANGUAGE
Green see COLOUR
Greet see MEET
Grey see COLOUR
Grey-haired see AGE
see HAIR
Griddle see COOK
Grief see LAMENT
Grin see MOCK
Grind see POWDER
Grip see HOLD
Groan see PAIN
Grope see SEARCH
Grounded see BASIS

GROUP
assembly
band
CHURCH
class
COLLECT
community
company
council
crowd

GROUP (cont.)
FELLOWSHIP
flock
gang
horde
huddle
join
meeting
member
mob
party
public
regroup
society
unite

Grow see CULTIVATE
see SIZE
Growl see NOISE
Grown-up see SIZE
Grudge see ENMITY
Grumble see COMPLAIN
Guarantee see PROMISE
Guard see PROTECT
see SOLDIER
Guardian see PROTECT
Guest see ENTERTAIN
Guide see FOLLOW
Guilt see SIN
Guilty see JUDGEMENT
Gulf see WATER
Gush see FLOW
Gutter see FLOW

H

Habit see USUAL
Hades see DIE
see HELL
Hail see WEATHER

HAIR
bald
barber
beard
bristled
comb
grey-haired
lock
mane
razor
shave

Hair style see ADORN
Half see PIECE
Half-brother see RELATIVE
Half-sister see RELATIVE
Hall see BUILDING
Hammer see TOOLS
Hand see BODY
see GIVE
Handiwork see WORK
Handkerchief see CLOTHING
Handle see HOLD
see TOOLS
Handsome see BEAUTY
Hang see DIE
see KILL
Happen see ACCIDENT

HAPPY
carefree
celebrate
cheerful
content
dance
delight
ecstatic
enjoy
glad
joy
laugh
merry
overjoyed
pleased
rejoice
smile
thrill

Harbour see SHIP
Hard see CRUEL
see PROBLEM
Hardship see WEARY
Harm see INJURE
Harmony see MUSIC

HARNESS
bit
bridle

HARNESS (cont.)
muzzle
saddle
TIE

Harp see INSTRUMENT
Harpoon see CAPTURE
see WEAPON
Harrow see CULTIVATE
see TOOLS
Harsh see CRUEL
Harvest see COLLECT
see CULTIVATE
Hat see CLOTHING
Hatch see BIRTH
see BREED
Hate see ENMITY
Haunt see SUPERNATURAL
Have to see NECESSARY
Haven see SHIP
Hawk see BIRD
Hay see CROP
Head see BODY
see DIRECTION
Headband see CLOTHING
Heal see MEDICINE

HEALTHY
better
MEDICINE
recover
remedy
restore
sane
senses
sound
well
whole

Heap see COLLECT
Hear see PERCEIVE
Hearsay see RUMOUR
Heart see BODY
see ORGANS
Heartache see LAMENT
Heat see LUST

HEAT
cold
cool
FIRE
freeze
frost
hot
lukewarm
melt
warm

Heathen see PAGAN

HEAVEN
above
angel
GOD
kingdom
sky
SUPERNATURAL
world above

Heavy see BURDEN
Hebrew see JUDAISM
see LANGUAGE
Hedge see ENCLOSURE
see TREE
Heel see BODY
Heir see FAMILY

HELL
abyss
DEVIL
DIE
Hades
pit
SUPERNATURAL
world below

Helmet see ARMOUR

HELP
ADVANTAGE
aid
assist
encourage
guide
inspire
PROTECT
reinforce
SERVE
strengthen
support
sustain

HELP (cont.)
uphold

Helper see CHURCH
Helpless see HOPELESS
Hem see CLOTHING
Henna see SPICES
Herald see TELL

HERBS
cumin
dill
FOOD
mint
PLANT
rue
seasoning herbs

Herd see ANIMAL
Hero see COURAGE
Herod's Party see JUDAISM
Heron see BIRD
Hesitate see WAIT

HIDE
conceal
ESCAPE
hideout
private
secret
UNSEEN

Hideout see HIDE
High places see IDOL
High see SIZE
High Priest see WORSHIP
Highlands see COUNTRYSIDE
Highway see ROAD
Hill see COUNTRYSIDE
Hill-country see COUNTRYSIDE
Hint see SUGGEST
Hip see BODY
Hire see EMPLOY
see LOAN
Hiss see NOISE
History see WRITE

HIT
beat
blow
box
butt
fist
knock
punch
slap
strike

Hitch see TIE
Hoard see KEEP
Hoe see TOOLS
Hold see SHIP

HOLD
clasp
cling
embrace
grab
grasp
grip
handle
hug
KEEP
PREVENT
touch

HOLE
crevice
dig
ditch
EMPTY
grave
hollow
mine
pit
tomb

Hollow see EMPTY
see HOLE
Holy see GOD
see PURE
see WORSHIP
Holy Place see WORSHIP
Home see DWELL
Homeless see EXPEL
Homer see MEASURE
Homesick see ABSENCE
Homicide see KILL
Homosexual see LUST

HONEST
fair
frank
impartial
integrity
just
real
sincere
true
truth
upright

Honey see FOOD
Honour see RESPECT
Hoof see HORSE
Hook see TIE
Hoopoe see BIRD
Hoot see NOISE
Hop see MOVE
Hope see FAITH
see WANT

HOPELESS
disappoint
discourage
disillusioned
dismay
dissatisfy
downhearted
FEAR
helpless
incurable
WEARY

Horde see ARMY
see GROUP
Horizon see UNIVERSE
Horn see INSTRUMENT
Horrible see BAD
Horrify see FEAR
Horror see BAD

HORSE
bit
bridle
cavalry
colt
dismount
donkey
foal
gallop
hoof
horseman
mane
mare
mount
mule
ride
rider
saddle
stallion

Horseman see ARMY
see HORSE
see SOLDIER
Hospitality see ENTERTAIN
Host see ENTERTAIN
Hostage see CAPTURE
Hostile see ENMITY
Hot see FIRE
see HEAT
see WEATHER
Hour see TIME
House see BUILDING
Household see DWELL
see FAMILY
Housewife see MARRY
Hover see FLY
Howl see NOISE
Hub see WHEEL
Huddle see GROUP
Hug see HOLD
see LOVE
Huge see SIZE
Human see PERSON
Humble see POOR
Humiliate see MOCK
Hunchback see INJURE
Hunger see EAT
see LACK
Hunt see CAPTURE
Hurl see THROW
Hurry see SPEED
Hurt see PAIN
Husband see MARRY
see RELATIVE
Hut see BUILDING
Hyena see ANIMAL
Hymn see WORSHIP
Hypocrite see DECEIVE
Hyssop see PLANT

I

I am see GOD
see JESUS
Ibis see BIRD
Ice see WEATHER
Idea see THINK
Identical see SAME
Idle see USELESS

IDOL
altar
Asherah
bull-calf
god
goddess
high places
IMAGE
PAGAN
pillar
shrine
statue
symbol
tree
WORSHIP

IGNORANT
blank
childish
dull
folly
fool
LEARNING
stupid
THINK
unthinking

Ignore see NEGLECT
Ill see ILLNESS
Ill-mannered see INSULT
Ill-treat see CRUEL

ILLNESS
ailment
blind
boil
cancer
chronic
deaf
discharge
disease
disorder
dumb
dysentery
epidemic
epileptic
eruption
fever
fit
gonorrhoea
ill
incurable
infectious
inflammation
MEDICINE
PAIN
paralyse
plague
pus
sea-sick
sick
skin disease
sore
stroke
swell
tumours
unhealthy
vomit

Illusion see DECEIVE
Illustration see IMAGE
see SHOW

IMAGE
figure
IDOL
illustration
model
outline
REPRESENT
SHAPE
symbol

Imagine see THINK
Imitate see FOLLOW
Immature see AGE
see SIZE
Immoral see SIN
Immorality see LUST

Immortal see CONSTANT
Impartial see HONEST
Impatient see WAIT
Impediment see PREVENT
Imperfect see BLEMISH
Imperial see KING
Imply see SUGGEST
Import see TRADE
Important see STATUS
Impose see CONTROL
Impostor see DECEIVE
Impress see RESPECT
Improve see ADVANCE
Impure see BLEMISH
Impurity see DEFILE
Incense see PERFUME
see WORSHIP
Incest see LUST
Incite see STIR
see SUGGEST
Include see ACCEPT
Income see MONEY
Inconsiderate see CRUEL
Incorruptible see CONSTANT
Increase see SIZE
Incurable see HOPELESS
see ILLNESS
Indecent see BAD
Independent see ALONE
Indicate see SHOW
Indignation see ANGER
Individual see ALONE
Indoors see INSIDE
Industrious see WORK
Infant see AGE
see BIRTH
Infectious see ILLNESS
Inferior see STATUS
Infinite see CONSTANT
Inflammation see ILLNESS
Inform see TELL
Information see TELL
Inhabit see DWELL
Inherit see ACCEPT
Iniquity see SIN

INJURE
bleed
break
bruise
burn
castrate
cripple
deformed
disabled
disfigured
fractured
gore
harm
hunchback
lame
limp
mutilated
PAIN
scab
scar
wound

Injustice see JUDGEMENT
Ink see WRITE
Inlaid see ADORN
Inlet see WATER
Inn see DWELL
Inner see INSIDE
Innocent see JUDGEMENT
Inquire see ASK
Insane see MAD
Inscribe see WRITE
Insect see ANIMAL

INSIDE
indoors
inner
interior
inwardly
ORGANS
within

Insight see LEARNING
Insignificant see USELESS
Insincere see DECEIVE
Insist see WANT
Insolent see INSULT
Inspect see SEE
Inspire see HELP
Instant see BRIEF
Instinct see KNOW
Institute see BEGIN
Instruct see COMMAND
see LEARNING

INSTRUMENT
bell
bugle
cymbals
drum
flute
gong
harp
horn
lyre
MUSIC
oboe
rattle
stringed
tambourine
trumpet
zither

INSULT
ABUSE
brat
cheeky
disrespect
ill-mannered
insolent
MOCK
rude

Integrity see HONEST
Intelligent see LEARNING

INTEND
ambition
apply
deliberate
destiny
determine
expect
mean
OBSTINATE
plan
PROMISE
purpose
refer
try
wilful
will

Intently see SERIOUS
Intercourse see MARRY
Interest see LOAN
see MONEY
Interfere see WORRY
Interior see INSIDE
Intermarry see MARRY
Internal organs
see ORGANS
Interpret see LANGUAGE
see SHOW
Interrupt see PREVENT
Intersect see DIVIDE
Intestines see BODY
see ORGANS
Intimate see MARRY
Introduce see MEET
Invade see CONQUER
Invent see BEGIN
see MAKE
Inventory see LIST
Invest see LOAN
Investigate see SEARCH
Investments see MONEY
Invisible see UNSEEN
Invite see ENTERTAIN
Inwardly see INSIDE
Iron see METAL
Irons see CAPTURE
Irreligious see SIN
Irresponsible see NEGLECT
Irreverence see DEFILE
see SIN
Irrigate see WATER
Irritate see ANGER
Island see COUNTRYSIDE
Isolate see ALONE
Israel see JUDAISM
Issachar see TRIBE
Issue see TELL

J

Jab see CUT
Jackal see ANIMAL
Jagged see ROUGH
Jail see CAPTURE
see PUNISH
Jar see CONTAINER
Jasper see JEWEL
Javelin see WEAPON

Jaw see BODY
Jealous see WANT
Jeer see MOCK

JESUS
Adam
Amen
ATONEMENT
Christ
I am
Lamb
Lord
Messiah
save
Saviour
Son of David
Son of God
Son of Man
Word

Jew see JUDAISM

JEWEL
ADORN
agate
amethyst
armlets
beryl
bracelet
carnelian
chalcedony
coral
crystal
diamond
earrings
emerald
facet
feldspar
garnet
gem
jasper
jeweller
mother-of-pearl
necklace
onyx
ornament
pearl
pin
PRECIOUS
quartz
ring
ruby
sapphire
STONE
topaz
turquoise

Jeweller see JEWEL
Jingle see NOISE
Job see WORK
Join see GROUP
see TIE
Joint see BODY
see ORGANS
Joke see MOCK
Jolt see SHAKE
Journey see TRAVEL
Joy see HAPPY
Joyless see LAMENT
Judah see TRIBE

JUDAISM
circumcise
convert
council
festival
God's people
Hebrew
Herod's Party
Israel
Jew
LAW
Passover
Pentecost
Pharisees
Rabbi
Rabboni
Sabbath
Sadducees
teacher of the Law
tradition

Judge see JUDGEMENT
see OFFICIAL

JUDGEMENT
accuse
acquit
case
clear
condemn

JUDGEMENT (cont.)
convict
court
Day of Judgement
Day of the Lord
defendant
evidence
fine
FORGIVE
guilty
injustice
innocent
judge
just
justice
justify
LAW
lawsuit
magistrate
penalty
prejudice
PUNISH
sentence
standard
sue
test
trial
try
verdict

Jump see MOVE
Jungle see OVERGROWN
Junior officers
see OFFICER
Juniper see TREE
Just see HONEST
see JUDGEMENT
Justice see JUDGEMENT
Justify see JUDGEMENT

K

KEEP
hoard
HOLD
maintain
preserve
PREVENT
PROTECT
reserve
save
SELFISH
store

Key see CLOSE
Kick see RESIST
Kid see ANIMAL
Kidnap see CAPTURE
Kidneys see ORGANS

KILL
assassinate
beheaded
butchered
choke
crucify
death
DESTROY
DIE
execute
exterminate
hang
homicide
manslaughter
murder
PUNISH
slaughter
slay
stab
stone
strangled
VIOLENCE

Kilogramme see MEASURE
Kilometre see MEASURE

KIND
compassion
concern
considerate
friendly
gentle
gracious
merciful
mercy
pity
spare

KIND (cont.)
sympathy
tender

Kindle see FIRE

KING
court
crown
dominion
dynasty
emperor
empire
empress
GOD
govern
imperial
kingdom
majesty
Pharaoh
prince
princess
queen
reign
royal
rule
sceptre
sovereign
throne
tyrant

Kingdom see HEAVEN
see KING
Kinsman see RELATIVE
Kislev see MONTH
Kiss see LOVE
Kitchen see COOK
Knee see BODY
Kneel see ALLEGIANCE
see WORSHIP
Knife see CUT
see TOOLS
see WEAPON
Knock see HIT
Knot see TIE

KNOW
aware
conscious
discover
find out
instinct
learn
LEARNING
PERCEIVE
realize
recognize
understand

Knowledge see LEARNING
Kor see MEASURE

L

Labour see BIRTH
see WORK
Labourer see WORKMAN

LACK
abstain
drought
EMPTY
famine
fast
FOOD
go without
hunger
need
POOR
shortage
starve

Lady see PERSON
Lake see WATER
Lamb see ANIMAL
see JESUS
see MEAT
Lame see INJURE

LAMENT
cry
gloom
grief
heartache
joyless
misery
mourn
PAIN
regret

LAMENT (cont.)
remorse
REPENT
sad
sigh
sorrow
sorry
tear
unhappy
wail
weep
whining
WORRY

Lamp see LIGHT
Lamp-stand see LIGHT
Lance see WEAPON
Land see PLACE
Landowner see MASTER
Landslide see DISASTER
Lane see ROAD

LANGUAGE
Aramaic
COMMUNICATE
Greek
Hebrew
interpret
Latin
tongue
translate

Lantern see LIGHT
Lap see DRINK
Large see SIZE
Lash see PUNISH
see TIE
Last see CONSTANT
Late see WAIT
Latest see NEW
Latin see LANGUAGE
Latrine see DEFILE
Laugh see HAPPY
see MOCK
Laurel-tree see TREE

LAW
COMMAND
commandment
decree
JUDAISM
JUDGEMENT
lawgiver
lawyer
legal
ordinance
regulation
statute

Law-breaker see CRIMINAL
Lawgiver see LAW
Lawless see CRIMINAL
Lawsuit see JUDGEMENT
Lawyer see LAW
Lazy see USELESS
Lead see DIRECTION
see FOLLOW
see METAL
Leader see OFFICIAL
see STATUS
Leap see MOVE
Learn see KNOW
see PERCEIVE

LEARNING
CLEVER
disciple
educate
expert
follower
IGNORANT
insight
instruct
intelligent
KNOW
knowledge
lesson
philosopher
pupil
read
scholar
scribe
student
study
teach
train
understand
wisdom
wise
WRITE

Least see SIZE
 see USELESS
Leather see CLOTH
Leave see ABANDON
 see ABSENCE
Leech see ANIMAL
 see SELFISH
Leeks see VEGETABLES
Left over see ENOUGH
Leg see BODY
Legal see LAW
Legend see DECEIVE
Lend see LOAN
 see MONEY
Leopard see ANIMAL
Less see SIZE
Lesson see LEARNING
Let see LOAN
Let go see FREE
Letter see GRAMMAR
 see WRITE

LEVEL
 calm
 even
 flat
 plain
 plateau
 smooth

Leviathan see ANIMAL
Liberty see FREE
Lice see ANIMAL
Lid see PART
Lie see DECEIVE
 see REST
Lieutenant-governors
 see OFFICIAL
Life (to-) see RISE
Lifeless see DIE
Lifetime see TIME
Ligaments see BODY
 see ORGANS

LIGHT
 bright
 brilliance
 day
 daybreak
 daylight
 dawn
 dazzling
 FIRE
 flame
 flash
 flickering
 glare
 gleam
 glitter
 glow
 lamp
 lamp-stand
 lantern
 lightning
 moon
 ray
 reflect
 reveal
 shine
 sparkle
 splendour
 sun
 sunrise
 sunshine
 torch
 wick

Lightning see LIGHT
 see WEATHER
Like see APPRECIATE
 see GOOD
 see LOVE
Likeness see SAME
Lily see PLANT
Limb see BODY
Lime see STONE
Limit see BORDER
Limp see INJURE
Linen see CLOTH
Linen-weavers
 see WORKMAN
Lion see ANIMAL
Lips see BODY
Liquid see FLOW
 see WATER
Liquor see DRINK

LIST
 census
 enrol
 inventory

LIST (cont.)
 record
 register
 roll

Listen see PERCEIVE
Literature see WRITE
Litre see MEASURE
Little see SIZE
Little Bear see UNIVERSE

LIVE
 alive
 breath
 DWELL
 flourish
 outlive
 survive
 thrive

Liver see ORGANS
Livestock see CATTLE
Living see PERSON
Lizard see ANIMAL
Load see BURDEN
Loaf see BREAD
Loafers see USELESS

LOAN
 borrow
 creditors
 GIVE
 hire
 interest
 invest
 lend
 let
 money-lender
 PAY
 rent
 tenant

Lobe see BODY
Local see NEAR
Located see PLACE
Lock see CLOSE
 see HAIR
Locust see ANIMAL
Lodging see DWELL
Log see WOOD
Lonely see ALONE
Long (way) see ABSENCE
Long see SIZE
 see WANT
Look see SEE
Look after see PROTECT
Look down on
 see ENMITY
 see MOCK
Look for see SEARCH
Loom see CLOTH
Loops see TIE
Loot see STEAL
Lord see GOD
 see JESUS
 see MASTER

LORD'S PRAYER: Mt 6.9f. Lk 11.2f.

LORD'S SUPPER: Mt 26.26f. Mk 14.22f.
 Lk 22.14f. 1 Cor 11.17f.

LOST
 astray
 roam
 SEARCH
 stray
 wander

Lot see CHOOSE
 see PROPHECY
Loud see NOISE
 see SPEAK

LOVE
 affection
 beloved
 brotherly
 caress
 cherish
 COMFORT
 compassion
 consider
 CONSTANT
 darling
 dear
 desire
 devotion
 embrace
 FELLOWSHIP
 fond

LOVE (cont.)
 friend
 goodwill
 grace
 hug
 kiss
 like
 lover
 prefer
 sweetheart
 well-liked

Lovely see BEAUTY
Lover see LOVE
 see LUST
Lowlands see COUNTRYSIDE
Lowly see POOR
Loyal see ALLEGIANCE

LUCK
 ACCIDENT
 chance
 fortune
 misfortune
 unlucky

Lukewarm see HEAT
Lulled see SLEEP
Lump see PIECE
Lunch see EAT

LUST
 adultery
 heat
 homosexual
 immorality
 incest
 lover
 orgy
 oversexed
 passion
 pervert
 prostitute
 seduce
 sex
 SIN
 sleep with
 unnatural
 virginity
 whore

Luxury see COMFORT
 see WEALTH
Lyre see INSTRUMENT

M

MAD
 crazy
 daft
 delusion
 folly
 fool
 IGNORANT
 insane
 meaningless
 nonsense
 rave
 senseless
 silly
 stupid
 unstable

Made-up see DECEIVE
Maggot see ANIMAL

MAGIC
 astrologer
 charm
 divination
 fortune-teller
 magician
 medium
 sorcerer
 spell
 SUPERNATURAL
 witchcraft
 wizard

Magician see MAGIC
Magistrate see JUDGEMENT
 see OFFICIAL

MAGNIFICAT: Lk 1.46f.

Magnificent see GOOD
Maid see SERVE
Mainland see COUNTRYSIDE

Maintain see KEEP
Majesty see GOD
 see KING
Majority see COUNT

MAKE
 BEGIN
 consist
 construct
 content
 create
 fashioned
 form
 formula
 invent
 produce

Male see PERSON
Malice see ENMITY
Man see PERSON
Manage see CONTROL
Manasseh see TRIBE
Mandrake see PLANT
 see VEGETABLES
Mane see HAIR
 see HORSE
Manhood see AGE
Mankind see PERSON
Manna see FOOD
Manner see ACTION
Mansion see BUILDING
Manslaughter
 see KILL
Manual see WORK
Manure see CULTIVATE
 see DIRT
Many see COUNT
Marble see STONE
March see MOVE
Mare see HORSE
Marital relations
 see MARRY
Mark see SHOW
Market see TRADE
Marrow see BODY
 see ORGANS

MARRY
 bride
 bridegroom
 bridesmaids
 concubine
 court
 divorce
 engaged
 FAMILY
 housewife
 husband
 intercourse
 intermarry
 intimate
 marital relations
 RELATIVE
 sex
 single
 unmarried
 wedding
 wedlock
 widow
 wife

Marvel see AMAZE
Mason see STONE

MASTER
 landowner
 lord
 mistress
 owner
 SERVE
 sir
 teacher

Mate see BREED
Material see EARTHLY
Mature see AGE
 see SIZE
Meadow see CULTIVATE
Meal see CROP
 see EAT
 see POWDER
Mean see INTEND
 see SELFISH
Meaningless see MAD
 see USELESS

MEASURE
 bath
 centimetre
 COUNT
 ephah

MEASURE (cont.)
gerah
gramme
homer
kilogramme
kilometre
kor
litre
metre
millimetre
mina
quantity
scale
shekel
SIZE
ton
weigh

Measuring-line see SIZE
see TOOLS
Measuring-rod see SIZE
see TOOLS

MEAT
beef
FOOD
lamb
pork
poultry
veal

Meddle see WORRY

MEDICINE
bandage
bleeding
cure
doctor
heal
HEALTHY
ILLNESS
ointment
paste
recover
remedy
sling
well

Meditate see THINK
Medium see MAGIC
Meek see POOR

MEET
contact
greet
introduce
NEAR
salute
touch
visit
welcome

Meeting see GROUP
Melody see MUSIC
Melon see FRUIT
Melt see HEAT
Member see GROUP
Memorial see REMEMBER
Memory see REMEMBER
Menial see SERVE
Mention see TELL
Merchandise see TRADE
Merchant see TRADE
Merciful see KIND
Merciless see CRUEL
Mercy see KIND
Mere see SIZE
see USELESS
Merry see HAPPY
Message see TELL
Messenger see TELL
Messiah see JESUS

METAL
brass
bronze
cast
copper
forge
foundry
gold
iron
lead
mine
ore
sheet
silver
soldering
tin

Metal-worker see WORKMAN
Metre see MEASURE
Mice see ANIMAL
Midday see TIME
Middle see PART
Midnight see DARK
see TIME
Midwife see BIRTH
Might see ABLE
Mildew see DECAY
Military see ARMY
see SOLDIER
Milk see DRINK
Millet see CROP
Millimetre see MEASURE
Millstone see POWDER
see STONE
Mina see MEASURE
Mind see COMPLAIN
see THINK
Mine see HOLE
see METAL
Mint see HERBS
Minute see TIME
Miracle see AMAZE

MIRACLES OF JESUS

(a) general
Mt 4.23-24; Mt 8.16; Mt 9.35;
Mt 12.15; Mt 14.14,35-36;
Mt 15.30-31; Mt 19.2; Mt 21.14;
Mk 1.32-34,39; Mk 3.9-12;
Mk 6.5,53-56; Lk 4.40-41; Lk 5.15;
Lk 6.18-19; Lk 7.21; Lk 9.11;
Jn 2.23; Jn 3.2; Jn 6.2; Jn 12.37;
Jn 20.30; Acts 10.38

(b) driving out demons:
blind and dumb
Mt 12.22;
daughter of woman of Tyre
Mt 15.21-28; Mk 7.24-30;
dumb man
Mt 9.32-33; Lk 11.14;
epileptic boy
Mt 17.14-20; Mk 9.14-21; Lk 9.37-43;
Gerasene men
Mk 5.1-20; Lk 8.26-39;
man in Capernaum
Mk 1.23-28; Lk 4.33-37;
Mary Magdalene
Mk 16.9; Lk 8.2;
men of Gadara
Mt 8.28-34;
woman in synagogue
Lk 13.10-17

(c) other cures:
blind Bartimaeus
Mt 20.29-34; Mk 10.46-52;
Lk 18.35-43;
blind man at Bethsaida
Mk 8.22-26;
man born blind
Jn 9.1-7;
two blind men
Mt 9.27-31;
deaf-mute
Mk 7.31-37;
man with skin-disease
Mt 8.1-4; Mk 1.40-45; Lk 5.12-16;
man with crippled hand
Mt 12.9-14; Mk 3.1-6; Lk 6.6-11;
man with swollen arms and legs
Lk 14.1-6;
officer's servant
Mt 8.5-13; Lk 7.1-10;
paralysed man in Capernaum
Mt 9.1-8; Mk 2.1-12; Lk 5.17-26;
paralysed man in Jerusalem
Jn 5.1-9;
Peter's mother-in-law
Mt 8.14-15; Mk 1.29-31; Lk 4.38-39;
slave of High Priest
Lk 22.50-51;
son of official
Jn 4.46-54;
ten men with skin-disease
Lk 17.11-19;
woman with severe bleeding
Mt 9.20-22; Mk 5.23-34; Lk 8.43-48

(d) raising of dead:
daughter of Jairus
Mt 9.18-26; Mk 5.21-43; Mk 8.40-56;
son of widow of Nain
Lk 7.11-17;
Lazarus
Jn 11.1-44

MIRACLES OF JESUS (cont.)
(e) other miracles:
coin in fish's mouth
Mt 17.24-27;
cursing the fig-tree
Mt 21.19; Mk 11.14,20;
feeding the five thousand
Mt 14.13-21; Mk 6.30-44; Lk 9.10-17;
Jn 6.1-14;
feeding the four thousand
Mt 15.32-39; Mk 8.1-10;
great catch of fish
Lk 5.4-10;
another catch of fish
Jn 21.6-11;
stilling the storm
Mt 8.23-27; Mk 4.35-41; Lk 8.22-25;
walking on the water
Mt 14.22-33; Mk 6.45-52; Jn 6.16-21;
water changed to wine
Jn 2.1-11

MIRACLES OF OTHERS

[OT] of Moses
Ex 4.3-7; Ex 7.10—10.28; Ex 14.21-28;
Ex 15.25; Ex 17.6; Num 16.32;
Num 20.11; Num 21.8-9;
of Joshua
Josh 3; Josh 6; Josh 10.12-14;
of Samuel
1 Sam 12.18;
of Elijah
1 Kgs 17.1,14,22; 1 Kgs 18.38,41-45;
2 Kgs 1.10; 2 Kgs 2.8;
of Elisha
2 Kgs 2.14,21,24; 2 Kgs 3.16-20;
2 Kgs 4.4-7,35,41,43-44;
2Kgs 5.10,14,27; 2 Kgs 6.6,18;
2 Kgs 13.21;
of Isaiah
2 Kgs 20.7,11;
of Daniel
Dan 6.22

[NT] of apostles
Mt 10.1,8; Mk 6.7,13; Lk 9.2,6;
Acts 5.12,16;
of the seventy-two
Lk 10.9,17;
of Philip
Acts 8.6,7,13;
of Peter
Acts 3.6-8; Acts 9.34,40-41;
of Paul
Acts 13.11; Acts 14.9,9,10;
Acts 16.18; Acts 19.11-12;
2 Cor 12.12

Mirror see GLASS
Miscarriage see BIRTH
Misery see LAMENT
Misfortune see LUCK
Mislead see DECEIVE
Missing see ABSENCE
Mist see WEATHER
Mistake see ACCIDENT
see ERROR
Mistress see MASTER
Misuse see ABUSE
Moan see NOISE
Mob see DEVIL
see GROUP

MOCK
contempt
despise
fun (make-)
glee
gloat
grin
humiliate
INSULT
jeer
joke
laugh
look down on
ridicule
scoff
scorn
smirk
sneer
taunt

Model see IMAGE
Moisture see WATER
Mole see ANIMAL
Molest see VIOLENCE
Moment see BRIEF
see TIME

MONEY
ACCOUNT
amount
bag
bank
belongings
bet
borrow
box
cash
change
cheap
coin
copper
debt
deposit
duties
earn
expense
fortune
gamble
gold
income
interest
investments
lend
mortgage
offering box
owe
PAY
penny
POOR
pound
PRECIOUS
profit
purchase
purse
receipt
resources
revenue
riches
silver
sum
TRADE
treasure
treasury
WEALTH

Money-lender see LOAN
Monkey see ANIMAL
Monster see ANIMAL

MONTH
Abib
Adar
Bul
Elul
Ethanim
Kislev
Nisan
Shebat
Sivan
Tebeth
TIME
Ziv

Moo see CATTLE
see NOISE
Moon see LIGHT
see UNIVERSE
Morale see COURAGE
More see COUNT
Morning see TIME
Mortal see DIE
see PERSON
Mortar see BUILDING
Mortgage see MONEY
Mosaic see ADORN
Most High see GOD
Moth see ANIMAL
see DESTROY
Moth-eaten see DECAY
Mother see BIRTH
see RELATIVE
Mother-in-law
see RELATIVE
Mother-of-pearl
see JEWEL
Motion see MOVE
Motive see BASIS
Mould see SHAPE
Mouldy see DECAY
Mound see COUNTRYSIDE
Mount see COUNTRYSIDE
see HORSE
Mountain see COUNTRYSIDE
Mourn see LAMENT
Mouth see BODY
Mouthful see EAT

MOVE
athlete
climb
crawl
creep
FLY
gallop
hop
jump
leap
march
motion
pounce
prowl
race
run
rush
skip
spring
squirm
stagger
step
strutting
swim
trample
TRAVEL
walk
wriggle

Muck *see* DIRT
Mud *see* DIRT
Muffled *see* QUIET
Mulberry tree *see* TREE
Mule *see* ANIMAL
see HORSE
Multiply *see* BREED
Mummy *see* RELATIVE
Murder *see* KILL
see VIOLENCE
Murderer *see* CRIMINAL
Muscle *see* BODY
see ORGANS

MUSIC
ARTS
chant
choir
compose
harmony
INSTRUMENT
melody
musician
note
pitch
psalm
refrain
response
sing
song
stringed
tune

Musician *see* MUSIC
Mustard seed *see* SPICES
Mutilated *see* INJURE
see VIOLENCE
Mutter *see* SPEAK
Muzzle *see* HARNESS
see TIE
Myrrh *see* PERFUME
see SPICES
Myrtle *see* TREE
Mystery *see* QUESTION

N

Nag *see* SPEAK
Nail *see* BODY
see TOOLS
Naked *see* BARE
see CLOTHING

NAME
call
nickname
so-called
summon
title

Nap *see* SLEEP
Naphtali *see* TRIBE
Nard *see* PERFUME
see SPICES
Narrow *see* SHAPE
see SIZE

NATION
city

NATION (cont.)
country
fellow-townsmen
people
race
TRIBE

Native *see* DWELL
Natural *see* EARTHLY
Nazirite *see* PROMISE

NEAR
approach
arrive
close
local
MEET
nearby
neighbouring
presence
reach
surrounding

Nearby *see* NEAR

NECESSARY
bound
CONTROL
force
have to
necessities
need
obligation
ought

Necessities *see* NECESSARY
Neck *see* BODY
Necklace *see* ADORN
see JEWEL
Need *see* LACK
see NECESSARY
see WANT
Needy *see* POOR

NEGLECT
ABANDON
careless
disregard
fail
forget
ignore
irresponsible
overlook
unnoticed

Neigh *see* NOISE
Neighbour *see* FELLOWSHIP
Neighbourhood *see* PLACE
Neighbouring *see* NEAR
Nephew *see* RELATIVE
Nerve *see* COURAGE
see FEAR
Nest *see* BIRD
Net *see* CAPTURE
Never again *see* END

NEW
coming
fresh
latest
new-born
not yet
renew

New-born *see* BIRTH
see NEW
News *see* COMMUNICATE
Nice *see* GOOD
Nickname *see* NAME
Night *see* DARK
see TIME
Nightfall *see* DARK
Nightmare *see* SLEEP
Nisan *see* MONTH
No *see* DENY
Noble *see* OFFICIAL
Nobodies *see* USELESS
Nod *see* SLEEP

NOISE
aloud
bark
bellow
blast
bleat
caw
clanging
clatter
crackle
crash

NOISE (cont.)
crow
cry
echo
growl
hiss
hoot
howl
jingle
loud
moan
moo
neigh
note
rattle
ring
roar
rumble
scream
shout
shrill
snort
sound
uproar
whistle

Nonsense *see* MAD
Noon *see* TIME
Normal *see* USUAL
North *see* DIRECTION
North-easter *see* WEATHER
Nose *see* BODY
Nose-ring *see* ADORN
Nostrils *see* BODY
Not yet *see* NEW
Note *see* MUSIC
see NOISE
see PERCEIVE
Notice *see* PERCEIVE
see SEE
Nourish *see* FOOD
Now *see* TIME
Nowadays *see* TIME
Nuisance *see* WORRY
Number *see* COUNT
Numerous *see* COUNT

NUNC DIMITTIS: Lk 2.29f.

Nurse *see* BIRTH
Nut *see* FOOD

O

O'clock *see* TIME
Oak *see* TREE
Oars *see* SHIP
Oasis *see* WATER
Oath *see* PROMISE
Obey *see* ALLEGIANCE
Object *see* COMPLAIN
Obligation *see* NECESSARY
Oboe *see* INSTRUMENT
Obscene *see* DEFILE
Observe *see* PERCEIVE
see SEE
Obstacle *see* PREVENT

OBSTINATE
determine
INTEND
pigheaded
resist
resolute
resolved
stubborn

Obtain *see* BELONG
Occasion *see* TIME
Occupy *see* CONQUER
see DWELL
Ocean *see* WATER
Odour *see* SMELL
Offering box *see* MONEY

OFFICER
ARMY
captain
commander
general
rank
junior officers
SOLDIER

OFFICIAL
administator
adviser
aide
authorities

OFFICIAL (cont.)
commissioner
deputy
eunuch
governor
judge
leader
lieutenant-governors
magistrate
noble
police
politician
prince
ruler
secretary
staff
statesmen
steward
supervisor
town clerk
treasurer

Officiate *see* WORSHIP
Offspring *see* RELATIVE
Ointment *see* MEDICINE
see PERFUME
Old *see* AGE
Olive *see* FRUIT
see TREE
Olive-oil *see* FOOD
Once *see* TIME
One *see* ALONE
One another *see* FELLOWSHIP
Onions *see* VEGETABLES
Onlookers *see* SEE
Onycha *see* SPICES
Onyx *see* JEWEL
Opinion *see* THINK
Opponent *see* ENMITY
Opportunity *see* ADVANTAGE
Oppose *see* DIFFERENT
see ENMITY
see RESIST
Opposite *see* DIFFERENT
Oppress *see* CONQUER
Oral translation *see* COMMUNICATE
see SPEAK
Orchard *see* CULTIVATE
see FRUIT
Ordain *see* WORSHIP
Order *see* COMMAND
see WANT
Ordinance *see* LAW
Ordinary *see* USUAL
Ore *see* METAL
Organize *see* CONTROL

ORGANS
BODY
bone
bowels
crop
entrails
genital
heart
internal organs
intestines
joint
kidneys
ligaments
liver
marrow
muscle
sinews
stomach
testicles

Orgy *see* LUST
Origin *see* BEGIN
Orion *see* UNIVERSE
Ornament *see* ADORN
see JEWEL
Orphan *see* ALONE
see FAMILY
see POOR
Ostrich *see* BIRD
Others *see* FELLOWSHIP
Ought *see* NECESSARY
Outcast *see* EXPEL
see EXTERNAL
Outdoor *see* EXTERNAL
Outer *see* EXTERNAL
Outlaw *see* CRIMINAL
Outline *see* IMAGE
Outlive *see* LIVE
Outrage *see* ANGER
Outside *see* EXTERNAL
Outsider *see* EXTERNAL
see FOREIGN
Outstanding *see* GOOD

Oven *see* COOK
Overboard *see* SHIP
Overcome *see* CONQUER
Overflow *see* WATER

OVERGROWN
dense
forest
jungle
thick
WOOD

Overhear *see* PERCEIVE
Overjoyed *see* HAPPY
Overlay *see* ADORN
Overlook *see* FORGIVE
see NEGLECT
Overpower *see* CONQUER
Overseas *see* FOREIGN
see TRAVEL
Oversexed *see* LUST
Overtake *see* FOLLOW
Overthrow *see* CONQUER
Overturn *see* DISTURB
Overwhelm *see* CONQUER
Overworked *see* WORK
Owe *see* MONEY
Owl *see* BIRD
Own *see* BELONG
Owner *see* MASTER
Ox *see* CATTLE

P

Pack *see* CONTAINER
Pact *see* ALLY
see PROMISE

PAGAN
Gentile
heathen
IDOL
uncircumcised
ungodly

PAIN
ache
agony
groan
hurt
ILLNESS
INJURE
LAMENT
sore
sting
suffer
torment
torture
WORRY
wound
writhe

Paint *see* ADORN
see ARTS
see COLOUR
Pair *see* TWO
Palace *see* BUILDING
Pale *see* COLOUR
Palm *see* BODY
see TREE

PALM SUNDAY: Mt 21.1f. Mk 11.1f. Lk 19.28f. Jn 12.12f.

Pan *see* CONTAINER
see COOK
Panel *see* ADORN
Panic *see* FEAR
Paper *see* WRITE
Parable *see* COMMUNICATE

PARABLES

(a) reason and use
Mt 13.1-17,34-35; Mk 4.10-12; Lk 8.9-10,16-18

(b) told by Jesus:
children playing
Mt 11.16-19; Lk 7.31-35;
faithful servant
Mt 24.45-51; Lk 12.42-46;
fig-tree
Mt 24.32-33; Mk 13.28-29; Lk 21.29-31;
friend at midnight
Lk 11.5-8;
gold coins
Lk 19.11-27;

PARABLES [NT] (cont.)
Good Samaritan
Lk 10.29-37;
great feast
Lk 14.15-24;
hidden treasure
Mt 13.44;
house owner
Mt 13.51-52;
king going to war
Lk 14.31-32;
lamp under a bowl
Mt 5.15; Mk 4.21; Lk 8.16; Lk 11.33;
lost coin
Lk 15.8-10;
lost sheep
Mt 18.10-14; Lk 15.3-7;
lost son
Lk 15.11-32;
mustard seed
Mt 13.31-32; Mk 4.30-32; Lk 13.18-19;
net
Mt 13.47-50;
new patch
Mt 9.16; Mk 2.21; Lk 5.36;
pearl
Mt 13.45-46;
Pharisee and tax collector
Lk 18.9-14;
places at wedding feast
Lk 14.7-11;
rich fool
Lk 12.16-21;
rich man and Lazarus
Lk 16.19-31;
seed growing
Mk 4.26-29;
servant
Lk 17.7-10;
shrewd manager
Lk 16.1-9;
sower
Mt 13.3-9,18-23; Mk 4.2-9,13-20; Lk 8.5-8,11-15;
ten girls
Mt 25.1-13;
tenants in vineyard
Mt 21.33-46; Mk 12.1-12; Lk 20.9-19;
three servants
Mt 25.14-30;
tower builder
Lk 14.28-30;
two debtors
Lk 7.40-43;
two house builders
Mt 7.24-27; Lk 6.47-49;
two sons
Mt 21.28-32;
unforgiving servant
Mt 18.23-35;
unfruitful fig-tree
Lk 13.6-9;
watchful house owner
Mt 24.42-44; Lk 12.39-40;
watchful servants
Mk 13.33-37; Lk 12.35-38;
wedding feast
Mt 22.1-14;
wedding guests
Mt 9.15; Mk 2.19-20; Lk 5.34-35;
weeds
Mt 13.24-30,36-43;
widow and judge
Lk 18.1-8;
wine and wineskins
Mt 9.17; Mk 2.22; Lk 5.37-38;
workers in vineyard
Mt 20.1-16;
yeast
Mt 13.33; Lk 13.20-21

(c) in [OT]
Judg 9.8-20; 2 Sam 12.1-14; 1 Kgs 20.35-42; 2 Kgs 14.9-10; 2 Chr 25.18-19; Is 5.1-7; Ezek 17.1-10; Ezek 19.1-9; Ezek 23.1-49; Ezek 24.1-14

Paralyse *see* ILLNESS
Parchment *see* WRITE
Pardon *see* FORGIVE
Parent *see* RELATIVE

PART
angles
base
bottom
brim
centre
corner

PART (cont.)
cover
edge
lid
middle
PIECE
side
top

Partitioned *see* DIVIDE
Partner *see* ALLY
Party *see* ENTERTAIN
see GROUP
Pass *see* BRIEF
Passage *see* BUILDING
see WRITE
Passenger *see* TRAVEL
Passion *see* LUST
Passover *see* JUDAISM
Past *see* TIME
Paste *see* MEDICINE
Pastor *see* CHURCH
Pastries *see* BREAD
Pasture *see* CATTLE
Patch *see* CLOTH
Path *see* ROAD
Patient *see* WAIT
Pavement *see* ROAD
Pavilion *see* BUILDING

PAY
ACCOUNT
bribe
charge
cost
due
duty
EMPLOY
fare
fine
free
LOAN
MONEY
price
ransom
refund
repay
REVENGE
revenue
reward
settle
spend
tax
wage

Peace *see* QUIET
Peak *see* COUNTRYSIDE
Pearl *see* JEWEL
Peas *see* VEGETABLES
Peg *see* TOOLS
Pelican *see* BIRD
Pen *see* ENCLOSURE
see WRITE
Penalty *see* JUDGEMENT
Penis *see* BODY
Penny *see* MONEY
Pentecost *see* JUDAISM

PENTECOST: Acts 2.1f.

People *see* NATION

PERCEIVE
attention
aware
distinguish
feel
hear
KNOW
learn
listen
note
notice
observe
overhear
recognize
SEE
sense
SMELL
TASTE
touch

Perch *see* BIRD
Perfect *see* CONSTANT

PERFUME
aloes
calamus
cane
cinnamon
fragrant

PERFUME (cont.)
frankincense
incense
myrrh
nard
ointment
scent
SMELL
SPICES

Period *see* TIME
Perish *see* DECAY
see DESTROY
see DIE
Permanent *see* CONSTANT
Permit *see* ACCEPT
Persecute *see* VIOLENCE
Persevere *see* CONSTANT
see EFFORT
Persist *see* CONSTANT

PERSON
being
boy
character
child
female
girl
human
lady
living
male
man
mankind
mortal
soul
woman

Persuade *see* ARGUE
see ASK
Pervert *see* DEFILE
see LUST
see SIN
Pet *see* ANIMAL
Petal *see* PLANT
Petition *see* ASK
Pharaoh *see* KING
Pharisees *see* JUDAISM
Philosopher *see* LEARNING
Phrase *see* COMMUNICATE
see SPEAK
Physical *see* EARTHLY
Pick *see* CHOOSE

PIECE
bar
batch
block
BREAK
chip
CUT
DIVIDE
half
lump
PART
portion
quarter
section
speck
strip

Pierce *see* CUT
Pig *see* ANIMAL
Pigeon *see* BIRD
Pigheaded *see* OBSTINATE
Pile *see* COLLECT
Pilgrimage *see* WORSHIP
Pillar *see* IDOL
Pillow *see* SLEEP
Pilot *see* SHIP
Pin *see* JEWEL
Pine *see* TREE
see WOOD
Pipes *see* CONTAINER
Pistachio *see* FOOD
Pit *see* HELL
see HOLE
Pitch *see* MUSIC
Pity *see* KIND

PLACE
area
camp
capital
city
country
district
DWELL
land
located
neighbourhood

PLACE (cont.)
plot
province
region
site
territory
town
village

Place of Worship see WORSHIP
Plague see ILLNESS
Plain see COUNTRYSIDE
see LEVEL
see REVEAL
Plan see INTEND
see READY
Plane-tree see TREE
Planet see UNIVERSE

PLANT
bloom
blossom
briars
bud
bush
CROP
CULTIVATE
flax
flower
FRUIT
garden
gourd
grass
HERBS
hyssop
lily
mandrake
petal
pods
reed
rush
sprig
sprout
stalk
thistle
thorn
TREE
vine
weed

Plateau see COUNTRYSIDE
see LEVEL
Play see ENTERTAIN
Plead see ASK
Pleasant see GOOD
Please see GOOD
Pleased see HAPPY
Pleasure see GOOD
Pledge see PROMISE
Pleiades see UNIVERSE
Plenty see ENOUGH
Plot see BETRAY
see PLACE
Plough see CULTIVATE
see TOOLS
Ploughmen see WORKMAN
Plumage see BIRD
Plumb line see TOOLS
Plunder see STEAL
Plural see GRAMMAR
Pocket see CLOTHING
Pods see PLANT
Poet see WRITE
Poetry see ARTS
Point see DIRECTION
see SHOW
Poison see DIE
Pole see UTENSIL
Police see OFFICIAL
Policies see CONTROL
Polished see TIDY
Polite see RESPECT
Politician see OFFICIAL
Pollute see DEFILE
Pomegranate see FRUIT
see TREE
Pomp see PRIDE
Pond see WATER
Pool see WATER

POOR
beggar
deprive
humble
LACK
lowly
meek
MONEY
needy
orphan

POOR (cont.)
poverty
underprivileged
widow

Poplar see TREE
Popular see APPRECIATE
Population see DWELL
Porch see BUILDING
Pork see MEAT
Port see SHIP
see TRAVEL
Portion see PIECE
Position see STATUS
Possess see BELONG
Post see SOLDIER
Pot see CONTAINER
Poultry see BIRD
see MEAT
Pounce see MOVE
Pound see MONEY
Pour see FLOW
Poverty see POOR

POWDER
ash
BREAK
crumble
dust
grains of sand
grind
meal
millstone

Power see ABLE
Powerful see ABLE
Practice see EFFORT

PRAISE
cheer
clap
congratulate
credit
glory
honour
prize
WORSHIP
worthy

Pray see ASK
see WORSHIP
Prayer see WORSHIP
Preach see CHURCH
see TELL

PRECIOUS
expensive
JEWEL
MONEY
priceless
valuables
WEALTH

Predecessor see FOLLOW
Predict see PROPHECY
Prefer see LOVE
Pregnant see BIRTH
Prejudice see JUDGEMENT
Prepare see READY
Presence see NEAR
Present see GIVE
see TIME
Preserve see KEEP
see PROTECT
Pressure see WORRY
Pretend see DECEIVE
Pretty see BEAUTY

PREVENT
bar
block
check
choke
DENY
disqualify
forbid
frustrate
hold
impediment
interrupt
KEEP
obstacle
prohibit
refuse
RESIST
restrain
restrictions
stop
unauthorized
withhold

Prey see CAPTURE
Price see PAY
see TRADE
Priceless see PRECIOUS

PRIDE
arrogant
boast
brag
conceited
pomp
puffed-up
self-satisfied
show off
vain

Priest see WORSHIP
Prince see KING
see OFFICIAL
Princess see KING
Principal see STATUS
Principle see ACTION
Prison see CAPTURE
see PUNISH
Prisoner see CAPTURE
Private see ALONE
see HIDE
Privilege see ABLE
Prize see CONQUER
see PRAISE

PROBLEM
complicated
difficult
hard
QUESTION

Procession see WORSHIP
Proclaim see CHURCH
see TELL
Produce see CROP
see MAKE
Profane see DEFILE
Profess see ACKNOWLEDGE
Profit see ADVANTAGE
see MONEY
see TRADE
Progress see ADVANCE
Prohibit see PREVENT
Prominent see STATUS

PROMISE
agreement
assure
contract
covenant
guarantee
INTEND
Nazirite
oath
pact
pledge
swear
vow

Prompted see SUGGEST
Promptly see SPEED
Pronounce see SPEAK
Proper see CORRECT
Property see BELONG

PROPHECY
astrologer
divination
dream
foresee
foretell
lot
predict
prophet
seer
Thummim
trance
Urim
vision

Prophet see CHURCH
see PROPHECY
Proportion see DIVIDE
Propose see SUGGEST
Prosperity see WEALTH
Prostitute see LUST

PROTECT
ARMOUR
bodyguard
care
defend
deliver
guard
guardian

PROTECT (cont.)
HELP
KEEP
keep safe
look after
preserve
rescue
safe
safe-keeping
save
self-defence
shelter
shepherd
stronghold
tend
unharmed
watchman

Protest see ARGUE
Prove see ARGUE
see REVEAL
Proverb see COMMUNICATE
Provide see GIVE
Province see PLACE
Provisions see FOOD
Prowl see MOVE
Prune see CULTIVATE
Pruning knife see TOOLS
Psalm see MUSIC
see WORSHIP
Public see GROUP
Puff see BRIEF
Puffed-up see PRIDE
Pull see PUSH
Punch see HIT

PUNISH
beat
COMPLAIN
confined
confiscate
CORRECT
discipline
fine
flog
gallows
jail
JUDGEMENT
KILL
lash
prison
REVENGE
spanking
VIOLENCE
whip

Pupil see LEARNING
Purchase see MONEY
see TRADE

PURE
blameless
blemish
clean
disinfect
faultless
GOOD
holy
purify
refine
undefiled
WASH

Purify see PURE
see WASH
Purple see COLOUR
Purpose see INTEND
Purse see CONTAINER
see MONEY
Pursue see FOLLOW
Pus see ILLNESS

PUSH
butt
drag
draught
draw
pull

Puzzled see QUESTION

Q

Quail see BIRD
Quake see SHAKE
Qualified see ABLE
Quality see GOOD
Quantity see COUNT
see MEASURE

Quarrel *see* ARGUE
Quarry *see* STONE
Quarter *see* DWELL
see PIECE
Quartz *see* JEWEL
Queen *see* KING

QUESTION
ASK
mystery
PROBLEM
puzzled
riddle
solve

Quick *see* BRIEF
see SPEED
Quick-tempered
see ANGER

QUIET
calm
muffled
peace
silence
speechless
still
undisturbed
whisper

Quiver *see* SHAKE
Quote *see* COMMUNICATE

R

Rabbi *see* JUDAISM
Rabbit *see* ANIMAL
Rabboni *see* JUDAISM
Race *see* MOVE
see NATION
see SPEED
Raft *see* SHIP
Rafters *see* BUILDING
Rage *see* ANGER
Rags *see* CLOTHING
Raid *see* WAR
Railing *see* ENCLOSURE
Rain *see* WEATHER
Rainbow *see* WEATHER
Raise *see* RISE
Raisins *see* FRUIT
Ram *see* ANIMAL
Rank *see* OFFICER
see STATUS
Ransom *see* FREE
see PAY
Ranting *see* ANGER
Rape *see* VIOLENCE
Rapid *see* SPEED
Rare *see* USUAL
Rats *see* ANIMAL
Rattle *see* INSTRUMENT
see NOISE
Rave *see* MAD
Raven *see* BIRD
Raw *see* COOK
Ray *see* LIGHT
Razor *see* HAIR
Reach *see* NEAR
Read *see* COMMUNICATE
see LEARNING
see WRITE

READY
brace
clear
due
plan
prepare

Real *see* HONEST
Realize *see* KNOW
Reap *see* CULTIVATE
Rearguard *see* ARMY
Reason *see* BASIS
see THINK
Rebel *see* BETRAY
Rebuild *see* BUILDING
Rebuke *see* COMPLAIN
see CORRECT
Recall *see* REMEMBER
Receipt *see* MONEY
Receive *see* ACCEPT
Recite *see* SPEAK
Reckless *see* COURAGE
Reckon *see* COUNT
Recline *see* REST
Recognize *see* KNOW
see PERCEIVE

Recommend *see* SUGGEST
Reconcile *see* ATONEMENT
see FORGIVE
Record *see* LIST
see WRITE
Recover *see* HEALTHY
see MEDICINE
Rectangular *see* SHAPE
Red *see* COLOUR
Redeem *see* ATONEMENT
see FORGIVE
Reduce *see* SIZE
Reed *see* PLANT
Refer *see* INTEND
Refine *see* PURE
Reflect *see* LIGHT
Reform *see* CHANGE
Refrain *see* MUSIC
Refugee *see* ESCAPE
Refund *see* PAY
Refuse *see* DENY
see PREVENT
see USELESS
Refute *see* ARGUE
Regain *see* BELONG
Regard *see* THINK
Regiment *see* ARMY
Region *see* PLACE
Register *see* LIST
Regret *see* LAMENT
see REPENT
Regroup *see* GROUP
Regular *see* TIME
Regulation *see* LAW
Reign *see* KING
Reinforce *see* HELP
Reject *see* ENMITY
Rejoice *see* HAPPY
Relate *see* TELL

RELATIVE
aunt
BIRTH
brother
cousin
daddy
daughter
daughter-in-law
FAMILY
father
father-in-law
grandchildren
granddaughter
grandfather
grandmother
grandparents
grandson
great-grandchildren
great-grandfather
half-brother
half-sister
husband
kinsman
MARRY
mother
mother-in-law
mummy
nephew
offspring
parent
sister
sister-in-law
son
son-in-law
stepmother
stepsister
uncle
wife

Release *see* FREE
Relent *see* FORGIVE
Relief *see* ADORN
Religion *see* WORSHIP
Reluctant *see* DENY
Rely *see* CONSTANT
Remain *see* WAIT
Remedy *see* HEALTHY
see MEDICINE

REMEMBER
memorial
memory
recall
remind
THINK

Remind *see* REMEMBER
see TELL
Remorse *see* LAMENT
Remove *see* ABSENCE
see END

Renew *see* NEW
Rent *see* LOAN
Repay *see* PAY
see REVENGE
Repeat *see* CONSTANT

REPENT
apology
LAMENT
regret
sackcloth
sorrow
sorry

Reply *see* TELL
Report *see* TELL

REPRESENT
agent
ambassador
behalf
envoy
go-between
IMAGE
representative
spokesman

Representative
see REPRESENT
Reprimand *see* COMPLAIN
Reproach *see* COMPLAIN
Reptile *see* ANIMAL
Reputation *see* STATUS
Request *see* ASK
Require *see* WANT
Rescue *see* PROTECT
Resent *see* ANGER
see ENMITY
Reservation *see* DENY
Reserve *see* KEEP
Reservoir *see* WATER
Reside *see* DWELL
Resin *see* SPICES

RESIST
against
avoid
defend
ENMITY
kick
OBSTINATE
oppose
PREVENT

Resolute *see* CONSTANT
see EFFORT
see OBSTINATE
Resolved *see* OBSTINATE
Resourceful *see* ABLE
Resources *see* MONEY

RESPECT
admire
dignity
esteem
honour
impress
polite
reverence

Response *see* MUSIC
Responsible *see* CONTROL

REST
COMFORT
ease
lie
recline
retire
SLEEP

Restore *see* HEALTHY
Restrain *see* PREVENT
Restrictions *see* PREVENT
Resurrection *see* RISE
Retire *see* REST
Reuben *see* TRIBE

REVEAL
appear
LIGHT
plain
prove
SHOW
uncover

REVENGE
avenge
PAY
PUNISH
repay

REVENGE (cont.)
vengeance

Revenue *see* MONEY
see PAY
Reverence *see* RESPECT
see WORSHIP
Revolution *see* WAR
Reward *see* PAY
Rib *see* BODY
Ribbon *see* CLOTHING
Rich *see* WEALTH
Riches *see* MONEY
see WEALTH
Rid *see* DISCARD
see EXPEL
Riddle *see* QUESTION
Ride *see* HORSE
see TRAVEL
Rider *see* HORSE
Ridicule *see* MOCK
Rigging *see* SHIP
Right *see* CORRECT
Right with God
see ATONEMENT
Righteous *see* ATONEMENT
Rightful *see* CORRECT
Rights *see* ABLE
Rim *see* WHEEL
Ring *see* ADORN
see JEWEL
see NOISE
Rinse *see* WASH
Riot *see* VIOLENCE
Rip *see* CUT
Ripe *see* AGE

RISE
arise
death (from-)
get up
life (to-)
raise
resurrection

Risk *see* DANGER
Ritual *see* WORSHIP
Rival *see* ENMITY
River *see* WATER

ROAD
alley
course
crossroads
highway
lane
path
pavement
route
street
track
TRAVEL
way

Roam *see* LOST
see TRAVEL
Roar *see* NOISE
Roast *see* COOK
Rob *see* STEAL
Robe *see* CLOTHING
Rock *see* COUNTRYSIDE
see SHAKE
see STONE
Rock-badger *see* ANIMAL
Rocky *see* ROUGH
Roebuck *see* ANIMAL
Roll *see* LIST
Roof *see* BUILDING
Room *see* BUILDING
Root *see* TREE
Rope *see* TIE
Rot *see* DECAY

ROUGH
course
CRUEL
jagged
rocky
storm

Round *see* SHAPE
Route *see* ROAD
Row *see* SHIP
Royal *see* KING
Rubbish *see* USELESS
Ruby *see* JEWEL
Rudder *see* SHIP
Rude *see* INSULT
Rue *see* HERBS
Rug *see* FURNISHINGS
Ruin *see* DESTROY

Rule *see* CONQUER
see KING
Ruler *see* OFFICIAL
Rumble *see* NOISE

RUMOUR
busybodies
gossip
hearsay
slander
whisper

Run *see* ESCAPE
see FLOW
see MOVE
see SPEED
see TRAVEL
Runaway *see* ESCAPE
Rush *see* MOVE
see PLANT
see SPEED
Rust *see* DECAY
Ruthless *see* VIOLENCE

S

Sabbath *see* JUDAISM
Sack *see* CONTAINER
Sackcloth *see* CLOTH
see REPENT
Sacred *see* GOD
see WORSHIP
Sacrifice *see* ATONEMENT
see WORSHIP
Sad *see* LAMENT
Saddle *see* HARNESS
see HORSE
Sadducees *see* JUDAISM
Safe *see* PROTECT
Safe-keeping *see* PROTECT
Saffron *see* SPICES
Sail *see* SHIP
Sailor *see* SHIP
Salt *see* FOOD
Salty *see* TASTE
Salute *see* MEET
Salvation *see* ATONEMENT

SAME
equal
equivalent
identical
likeness

Sanctuary *see* BUILDING
see WORSHIP
Sandal *see* CLOTHING
Sane *see* HEALTHY
Sapphire *see* JEWEL
Sash *see* CLOTHING
Satan *see* DEVIL
Satin *see* CLOTH
Satisfy *see* ENOUGH
Sauce *see* FOOD
Savage *see* VIOLENCE
Save *see* JESUS
see KEEP
see PROTECT
Saviour *see* JESUS
Saw *see* CUT
see TOOLS
Say *see* SPEAK
Saying *see* COMMUNICATE
see SPEAK
Scab *see* INJURE
Scabbard *see* WEAPON
Scale *see* MEASURE
Scalp *see* BODY
Scar *see* INJURE
Scarce *see* USUAL
Scare *see* FEAR
Scarf *see* CLOTHING
Scarlet *see* COLOUR
Scatter *see* ABSENCE
Scent *see* PERFUME
Sceptre *see* KING
Scholar *see* LEARNING
Scoff *see* MOCK
Scold *see* COMPLAIN
Scorch *see* FIRE
Scorn *see* MOCK
Scorpion *see* ANIMAL
Scowl *see* ANGER
Scream *see* NOISE
see SPEAK
Scribble *see* WRITE
Scribes *see* LEARNING
see WRITE
Scripture *see* WRITE

Scroll *see* WRITE
Scrub *see* WASH
Scum *see* USELESS
Sea *see* SHIP
see WATER
Sea-sick *see* ILLNESS
Seagull *see* BIRD
Seal *see* WRITE
Seam *see* CLOTHING
Seaman *see* SHIP

SEARCH
check
discover
examine
find
grope
investigate
look for
LOST
seek
spy

Season *see* TIME
Seasoning herbs
see HERBS
Second *see* BRIEF
see TIME
see TWO
Secret *see* HIDE
Secretary *see* OFFICIAL
Section *see* PIECE
Secure *see* TIE
Seduce *see* LUST

SEE
blind
eye
gape
gazed
glance
inspect
look
mirror
notice
observe
onlookers
PERCEIVE
sight
spectacle
stare
transparent
visible
vision
watch

Seed *see* CULTIVATE
Seek *see* SEARCH
Seer *see* PROPHECY
Seize *see* CAPTURE
Select *see* CHOOSE
Self-defence *see* PROTECT
Self-satisfied *see* PRIDE

SELFISH
KEEP
leech
mean
stingy

Sell *see* TRADE
Send *see* COMMUNICATE
see EXPEL
Sense *see* PERCEIVE
Senseless *see* MAD
Senses *see* HEALTHY
Sensible *see* CLEVER
Sentence *see* JUDGEMENT
Sentry *see* SOLDIER
Separate *see* ABSENCE
see CUT
see DIFFERENT
see DIVIDE
see SIEVE

SERIOUS
earnest
fervent
intently
sober
solemn

Serpent *see* ANIMAL
see DEVIL
Servant *see* SERVE

SERVE
attend
duty
HELP
maid

SERVE (cont.)
MASTER
menial
servant
service
slave
wait on

Service *see* SERVE
see WORSHIP
Settle *see* ACCOUNT
see DWELL
see PAY
Severe *see* CRUEL
Sew *see* CLOTH
see CLOTHING
Sex *see* LUST
see MARRY
Shade *see* DARK
Shadow *see* DARK

SHAKE
DISTURB
earthquake
jolt
quake
quiver
rock
STIR
tremble

Shame *see* ASHAMED
Shameless *see* BAD

SHAPE
angles
bend
circle
crooked
curl
curve
figure
flat
form
IMAGE
mould
narrow
rectangular
round
square
straight
wide

Share *see* GIVE
Sharp *see* CUT
Shatter *see* BREAK
Shave *see* HAIR
Sheaf *see* CROP
Shear *see* CUT
Sheath *see* WEAPON
Shebat *see* MONTH
Shed *see* BUILDING
see VIOLENCE
Sheep *see* ANIMAL
Sheepfold *see* ENCLOSURE
Sheet *see* CLOTH
see METAL
Shekel *see* MEASURE
Shelter *see* PROTECT
Shepherd *see* PROTECT
Shield *see* ARMOUR
Shifting *see* CHANGE
Shine *see* LIGHT

SHIP
aboard
aground
anchor
ashore
awnings
board
boat
cargo
crew
deck
fleet
harbour
haven
hold
oars
overboard
pilot
port
raft
rigging
row
rudder
sail
sailor
sea
seaman

SHIP (cont.)
shipwreck
sink
steer
TRAVEL
WATER

Shipwreck *see* SHIP
Shirt *see* CLOTHING
Shock *see* DISTURB
Shoes *see* CLOTHING
Shoot *see* WEAPON
Shop *see* TRADE
Shore *see* COUNTRYSIDE
Shorn *see* BARE
Short *see* BRIEF
see SIZE
Shortage *see* LACK
Shorts *see* CLOTHING
Shoulder *see* BODY
Shout *see* NOISE
see SPEAK
Shovel *see* TOOLS

SHOW
advertise
banner
demonstrate
describe
display
evident
example
explain
flag
illustration
indicate
interpret
mark
point
REVEAL
sign
signal
signpost

Show off *see* PRIDE
Shower *see* WEATHER
Shrewd *see* CLEVER
Shrill *see* NOISE
Shrine *see* IDOL
see WORSHIP
Shrink *see* FEAR
Shrivel *see* DECAY
Shut *see* CLOSE
Shuttle *see* CLOTH
Sick *see* ILLNESS
Sickle *see* TOOLS
Side *see* PART
Siege *see* WAR
Siege (-mound)
see WAR
Siege (-tower)
see WAR

SIEVE
DIVIDE
separate
sift
strain
TOOLS

Sift *see* SIEVE
Sigh *see* LAMENT
Sight *see* SEE
Sign *see* COMMUNICATE
see SHOW
see WRITE
Signal *see* SHOW
Signpost *see* DIRECTION
see SHOW
Silence *see* QUIET
Silk *see* CLOTH
Silly *see* MAD
Silver *see* METAL
see MONEY
Silversmith *see* WORKMAN
Simeon *see* TRIBE

SIN
astray
BAD
blame
blasphemy
BLEMISH
commit
condemn
conscience
corrupt
crime
DEFILE
disgusting
disobey

SIN (cont.)
evil
fallen
fault
guilt
immoral
iniquity
irreligious
irreverence
LUST
pervert
tempt
ungodly
unnatural
vice
weakness
wicked
worldly
wrong

Sincere see HONEST
Sinews see BODY
see ORGANS
Sing see MUSIC
Singed see FIRE
Single see ALONE
see MARRY
Singular see GRAMMAR
Sink see FALL
see SHIP
Sir see MASTER
Sister see FELLOWSHIP
see RELATIVE
Sister-in-law see RELATIVE
Site see PLACE
Sivan see MONTH

SIZE
big
brief
broad
decrease
deep
develop
dwarf
enlarge
enormous
extend
fat
full-bodied
full-grown
giant
gigantic
grow
grown-up
high
huge
immature
increase
large
least
less
little
long
mature
MEASURE
measuring-line
measuring-rod
mere
narrow
reduce
short
small
stretch
stunted
tall
tape measure
thick
thin
tiny
ton
tremendous
unit
unripe
vast
weigh
wide
young

Skilful see CLEVER
Skill see CLEVER
Skin see BODY
Skin disease see ILLNESS
Skip see MOVE
Skirt see CLOTHING
Skull see BODY
Sky see HEAVEN
Slander see ABUSE
see RUMOUR
Slap see HIT
Slash see CUT

Slaughter see KILL
Slave see SERVE
Slay see KILL
see VIOLENCE
Sledge hammer
see TOOLS

SLEEP
asleep
bed
bedroom
blanket
day-dreaming
doze
dream
drowsy
drug
faint
lulled
nap
nightmare
nod
pillow
REST
unconscious

Sleep with see LUST
Sleepless see ALERT
Sleeves see CLOTHING
Sliced see CUT
Slime see DIRT
Sling see MEDICINE
see THROW
Slinger see SOLDIER
Slip see FALL
Slope see COUNTRYSIDE
Slow see SPEED
Small see SIZE
Smash see BREAK

SMELL
fragrant
odour
PERCEIVE
PERFUME
stench
stink
sweet-smelling

Smile see HAPPY
Smirk see MOCK
Smoke see FIRE
Smooth see LEVEL
Smoulder see FIRE
Snail see ANIMAL
Snake see ANIMAL
Snap see BREAK
Snare see CAPTURE
Snarl see ANGER
Snatch see STEAL
Sneer see MOCK
Sneeze see SPIT
Snort see NOISE
Snow see WEATHER
Snuffer see UTENSIL
So-called see NAME
Soak see WATER
Soap see WASH
Sober see DRINK
see SERIOUS
Society see GROUP
Soft see COMFORT
Soil see CULTIVATE
Soldering see METAL

SOLDIER
archer
armour-bearer
ARMY
bowmen
cavalry
commander
enlist
foot-soldier
guard
horseman
military
OFFICER
post
sentry
slinger
spearmen
swordsmen
veteran
WAR
warrior
WEAPON

Solemn see SERIOUS
Solve see QUESTION
Son see RELATIVE

Son of David see JESUS
Son of God see JESUS
Son of Man see JESUS
Son-in-law see RELATIVE
Song see MUSIC
Sorcerer see MAGIC
Sore see ILLNESS
see PAIN
Sorrow see LAMENT
see REPENT
Sorry see LAMENT
see REPENT
Soul see PERSON
Sound see HEALTHY
see NOISE
Soup see COOK
see FOOD
Sour see TASTE
Source see BEGIN
South see DIRECTION
Sovereign see GOD
see KING
Sow see CULTIVATE
Space see EMPTY
see UNIVERSE
Spanking see PUNISH
Spare see ENOUGH
see KIND
Spark see FIRE
Sparkle see LIGHT
Sparrow see BIRD

SPEAK
accent
address
aloud
ARGUE
call
chirp
COMMUNICATE
cry
debate
dictate
discuss
eloquent
loud
mutter
nag
oral translation
phrase
pronounce
recite
say
saying
scream
shout
speech
spokesman
spout
talk
TELL
utter
voice
windbags
yell

Spear see WEAPON
Spearmen see SOLIDER
Special see USUAL
Speck see PIECE
Speckled see COLOUR
Spectacle see ENTERTAIN
see SEE
Speech see COMMUNICATE
see SPEAK
Speechless see QUIET

SPEED
athlete
BRIEF
dart
dash
fast
hurry
promptly
quick
race
rapid
run
rush
slow
sudden
swift

Spell see MAGIC
Spelt see CROP
Spend see DWELL
see PAY
Spew see SPIT

SPICES
aloes
balsam
cassia
cinnamon
frankincense
galbanum
henna
mustard seed
myrrh
nard
onycha
PERFUME
resin
saffron
stacte

Spider see ANIMAL
Spill see EMPTY
Spirit see DEVIL
see SUPERNATURAL

SPIT
choke
dribble
sneeze
spew
vomit

Spiteful see ENMITY
Splash see WATER
Splendour see LIGHT
Splinters see WOOD
Split see BREAK
Spoil see DEFILE
Spokes see WHEEL
Spokesman see REPRESENT
see SPEAK
Spot see BLEMISH
Spotted see COLOUR
Spout see SPEAK
Sprig see PLANT
Spring see MOVE
see WATER
Sprinkle see WATER
Sprout see PLANT
Spy see SEARCH
Square see SHAPE
Squirm see MOVE
Stab see KILL
see VIOLENCE
Stacte see SPICES
Staff see OFFICIAL
see WOOD
Stag see ANIMAL
Stagger see FALL
see MOVE
Stagnant see BARREN
Stain see DEFILE
Stalk see PLANT
Stallion see HORSE
Standard see JUDGEMENT
Standing see STATUS
Star see UNIVERSE
Stare see SEE
Start see BEGIN
Starve see EAT
see LACK
State see COMMUNICATE
see TELL
Statesmen see OFFICIAL
Stationed see WAIT
Statue see IDOL
Stature see STATUS

STATUS
chief
classify
compare
famous
important
inferior
leader
position
principal
prominent
rank
reputation
standing
stature
superior
supreme

Statute see LAW
Stay see DWELL
see WAIT
Steady see CONSTANT

STEAL
burglars
CRIMINAL

STEAL (cont.)
loot
plunder
rob
snatch
thief

Steer *see* SHIP
Stench *see* SMELL
Step *see* MOVE
Stepmother *see* RELATIVE
Stepsister *see* RELATIVE
Sterile *see* BARREN
Sternly *see* CRUEL
Stew *see* COOK
see FOOD
Steward *see* OFFICIAL
Stick *see* WOOD
Still *see* QUIET
Still-born *see* BIRTH
Sting *see* PAIN
Stingy *see* SELFISH
Stink *see* SMELL

STIR
boil
bubble
churn
DISTURB
incite
SHAKE

Stomach *see* BODY
see EAT
see ORGANS
Stone *see* KILL
see THROW

STONE
alabaster
block
BUILDING
clay
feldspar
flint
gravel
JEWEL
lime
marble
mason
millstone
quarry
rock

Stool *see* FURNISHINGS
Stop *see* END
see PREVENT
Store *see* KEEP
Storey *see* BUILDING
Stork *see* BIRD
Storm *see* DISASTER
see ROUGH
see WEATHER
Story *see* TELL
Stove *see* COOK
Straggling *see* FOLLOW
Straight *see* DIRECTION
see SHAPE
Strain *see* EFFORT
see SIEVE
Strange *see* FOREIGN
Stranger *see* FOREIGN
Strangled *see* KILL
Strap *see* CLOTHING
see TIE
Straw *see* CROP
Stray *see* LOST
Streaked *see* COLOUR
Stream *see* WATER
Street *see* ROAD
Strengthen *see* HELP
Stretch *see* SIZE
Strike *see* HIT
Stringed *see* INSTRUMENT
see MUSIC
Strip *see* BARE
see PIECE
Stripe *see* COLOUR
Strive *see* EFFORT
Stroke *see* ILLNESS
Strong *see* ABLE
Stronghold *see* PROTECT
Struggle *see* EFFORT
see WORRY
Strutting *see* MOVE
Stubble *see* CROP
Stubborn *see* OBSTINATE
Student *see* LEARNING
Study *see* LEARNING
Stuff *see* EAT
Stumble *see* FALL

Stunned *see* AMAZE
Stunted *see* SIZE
Stupid *see* IGNORANT
see MAD
Stupor *see* DRINK
Subdue *see* CONQUER
Subject *see* ALLEGIANCE
see CONQUER
Submit *see* CONQUER
Succeed *see* ACCOMPLISH
see FOLLOW
Sudden *see* BRIEF
see SPEED
Sue *see* JUDGEMENT
Suffer *see* PAIN
Sufficient *see* ENOUGH

SUGGEST
advice
adviser
counsel
hint
imply
incite
prompted
propose
recommend
STIR
TELL
tempt
urge

Suicide *see* DIE
Suitable *see* ABLE
Suited *see* ABLE
Sulphur *see* FIRE
Sum *see* COUNT
see MONEY
Summon *see* CALL
Sun *see* LIGHT
see UNIVERSE
Sunrise *see* LIGHT
see TIME
Sunset *see* TIME
Sunshine *see* LIGHT
Superior *see* STATUS

SUPERNATURAL
DEVIL
ghost
GOD
haunt
HEAVEN
HELL
MAGIC
spirit

Supervisor *see* OFFICIAL
Supper *see* EAT
see WORSHIP
Supply *see* GIVE
Support *see* CARRY
see HELP
Supreme *see* STATUS
Sure *see* CERTAIN
Surplus *see* ENOUGH
Surprise *see* AMAZE
Surrender *see* CONQUER
Surrounding *see* NEAR
Survive *see* LIVE
Suspect *see* THINK
Suspense *see* WORRY
Sustain *see* HELP
Swallow *see* BIRD
see EAT
Swear *see* ABUSE
see PROMISE
Sweat *see* WEARY
Sweep *see* TIDY
Sweet *see* TASTE
Sweet-smelling
see SMELL
Sweetheart *see* LOVE
Swell *see* ILLNESS
Swift *see* SPEED
Swim *see* MOVE
see WATER
Sword *see* WEAPON
Swordsmen *see* SOLDIER
Sycomore *see* TREE
Symbol *see* IDOL
see IMAGE
Sympathy *see* KIND
Synagogue *see* WORSHIP

T

Table *see* FURNISHINGS
Tablet *see* WRITE
Tail *see* ANIMAL
Take off *see* BARE
Talented *see* ABLE
Talk *see* SPEAK
Tall *see* SIZE
Tamarisk-tree
see TREE
Tambourine *see* INSTRUMENT
Tame *see* ANIMAL
Tangle *see* TIE
Tank *see* CONTAINER
Tanned *see* COLOUR
Tanner *see* WORKMAN
Tape measure
see SIZE
Task *see* WORK
Tassel *see* CLOTHING

TASTE
bitter
EAT
flavour
FOOD
PERCEIVE
salty
sour
sweet

Tasty *see* EAT
Tattoo *see* ADORN
Taunt *see* MOCK
Tax *see* PAY
Teach *see* LEARNING
Teacher *see* CHURCH
see MASTER
Teacher of the Law *see* JUDAISM
Team *see* CATTLE
Tear *see* BREAK
see LAMENT
Tebeth *see* MONTH

TELL
account
announce
answer
COMMAND
COMMUNICATE
declare
herald
inform
information
issue
mention
message
messenger
preach
proclaim
relate
remind
reply
report
SPEAK
state
story
SUGGEST

Temper *see* ANGER
Tempests *see* WEATHER
Temple *see* BUILDING
see WORSHIP
Temporary *see* BRIEF
see TIME
Tempt *see* DEVIL
see SIN
see SUGGEST
Tenant *see* LOAN
Tend *see* PROTECT
Tender *see* KIND
Tent *see* WORSHIP
Terrify *see* FEAR
Territory *see* BORDER
see PLACE
Terror *see* FEAR
Terrorize *see* VIOLENCE
Test *see* JUDGEMENT
Testicles *see* ORGANS
Testify *see* ACKNOWLEDGE
Testimony *see* ACKNOWLEDGE
Text *see* WRITE
Thank-offering
see THANK

THANK
grateful

THANK (cont.)
thank-offering
thanksgiving-offering
ungrateful

Thanksgiving-offering *see* THANK
Theatre *see* BUILDING
Thick *see* OVERGROWN
see SIZE
Thief *see* STEAL
Thigh *see* BODY
Thin *see* SIZE

THINK
assume
attitude
expect
idea
IGNORANT
imagine
meditate
mind
opinion
reason
regard
remember
suspect
thoughtless
unthinking

Thirst *see* DRINK
Thistle *see* PLANT
Thorn *see* PLANT
see TREE

THOROUGH
care
complete
detail
entire
full
whole

Thoughtless *see* THINK
Threat *see* DANGER
see FEAR
Thresh *see* CULTIVATE
Threshold *see* BUILDING
Thrill *see* HAPPY
Thrive *see* LIVE
Throat *see* BODY
Throne *see* KING

THROW
catapult
DISCARD
fling
hurl
sling
stone
toss

Thrush *see* BIRD
Thumb *see* BODY
Thummim *see* PROPHECY
Thunder *see* WEATHER
Tide *see* WATER

TIDY
broom
clean
polished
sweep

TIE
attach
band
bind
bonds
buckle
CAPTURE
cord
fasten
HARNESS
hitch
hook
join
knot
lash
loops
muzzle
rope
secure
strap
tangle

Tile *see* BUILDING
Timber *see* BUILDING
see TREE
see WOOD

TIME
afternoon
AGE
annual
beforehand
daily
date
day
evening
former
frequent
future
hour
lifetime
midday
midnight
minute
moment
MONTH
morning
night
noon
now
nowadays
o'clock
occasion
once
past
period
present
regular
season
second
sunrise
sunset
temporary
today
tomorrow
tonight
twilight
week
year
yesterday

Timid *see* FEAR
Tin *see* METAL
Tiny *see* SIZE
Tip *see* FALL
Tired *see* WEARY
Title *see* NAME
Today *see* TIME
Toe *see* BODY
Together *see* COLLECT
Toil *see* WORK
Tolerate *see* ACCEPT
Tomb *see* DIE
see HOLE
Tomorrow *see* TIME
Ton *see* MEASURE
see SIZE
Tongs *see* TOOLS
Tongue *see* BODY
see COMMUNICATE
see LANGUAGE
Tonight *see* TIME

TOOLS
axe
chisel
clamps
hammer
handle
harrow
hoe
knife
measuring-line
measuring-rod
nail
peg
plough
plumbline
pruning knife
saw
shovel
sickle
sieve
sledge hammer
tongs
UTENSIL

Tooth *see* BODY
Top *see* PART
Topaz *see* JEWEL
Torch *see* LIGHT
Torment *see* PAIN
Torrent *see* FLOW
see WATER
Torture *see* PAIN
Toss *see* THROW
Total *see* COUNT

Touch *see* HOLD
see MEET
see PERCEIVE
Towel *see* WASH
Tower *see* BUILDING
Town *see* PLACE
Town clerk *see* OFFICIAL
Track *see* ROAD

TRADE
bargain
business
buy
cargo
commerce
customer
deal
export
import
market
merchandise
merchant
MONEY
price
profit
purchase
sell
shop
wares
WORK

Traders *see* WORKMAN
Tradition *see* JUDAISM
Traffic *see* TRAVEL
Train *see* LEARNING
Traitor *see* BETRAY
Trample *see* CONQUER
see MOVE
Trance *see* PROPHECY

TRANSFIGURATION: Mt 17.1f. Mk 9.2f. Lk 9.28f.

Transform *see* CHANGE
Translate *see* COMMUNICATE
see LANGUAGE
Transparent *see* SEE
Transport *see* CARRY
see TRAVEL
Trap *see* CAPTURE

TRAVEL
abroad
caravan
carriage
cart
chariot
cross
DIRECTION
drift
go
journey
MOVE
overseas
passenger
port
ride
ROAD
roam
run
SHIP
traffic
transport
trip
voyage
wagon
walk
WHEEL

Tray *see* CONTAINER
Treachery *see* BETRAY
Treason *see* BETRAY
Treasure *see* MONEY
see WEALTH
Treasurer *see* OFFICIAL
Treasury *see* MONEY
Treaty *see* ALLY

TREE
almond
apple
balsam
bark
bough
branch
broom-tree
bush
cedar
cypress
evergreen
fig

TREE (cont.)
fir
forest
grapevine
hedge
IDOL
juniper
laurel-tree
mulberry tree
myrtle
oak
olive
palm
pine
plane-tree
PLANT
pomegranate
poplar
root
sycomore
tamarisk-tree
thorn
timber
vine
willow
WOOD

Tremble *see* FEAR
see SHAKE
Tremendous *see* SIZE
Trench *see* WAR
Trial *see* JUDGEMENT
see WORRY

TRIBE
Asher
Benjamin
clan
Dan
Ephraim
FAMILY
Gad
Issachar
Judah
Manasseh
Naphtali
NATION
Reuben
Simeon
Zebulun

Tribute *see* ALLEGIANCE
Trick *see* DECEIVE
Trim *see* CUT
Trip *see* FALL
see TRAVEL
Triumph *see* ACCOMPLISH
see CONQUER
Troops *see* ARMY
Trouble *see* WORRY
Trough *see* CONTAINER
Trousers *see* CLOTHING
True *see* HONEST
Trumpet *see* INSTRUMENT
Trust *see* FAITH
Truth *see* HONEST
Try *see* EFFORT
see INTEND
see JUDGEMENT
Tub *see* CONTAINER
Tumble *see* FALL
Tumours *see* ILLNESS
Tune *see* MUSIC
Turban *see* CLOTHING
Turmoil *see* DISTURB
see WORRY
Turn (from) *see* ABANDON
Turn *see* CHANGE
Turquoise *see* JEWEL
Twice *see* TWO
Twilight *see* DARK
see TIME
Twin *see* FAMILY

TWO
couple
double
double-edged
pair
second
twice
two-edged

Two-edged *see* TWO
Tyrant *see* KING

U

Ugly *see* BAD
see BEAUTY
Umbilical *see* BIRTH
Unafraid *see* COURAGE
Unauthorized *see* PREVENT
Unbelief *see* DOUBT
Unbeliever *see* DOUBT
Unbreakable *see* CONSTANT
Unbroken *see* CONSTANT
Uncertain *see* DOUBT
Unchanging *see* CONSTANT
Uncircumcised
see PAGAN
Uncle *see* RELATIVE
Unclean *see* DEFILE
Unconscious *see* SLEEP
Uncooked *see* COOK
Uncover *see* REVEAL
Uncovered *see* BARE
Undecided *see* CHOOSE
see DOUBT
Undefiled *see* PURE
Underfoot *see* CONQUER
Underprivileged
see POOR
Understand *see* KNOW
see LEARNING
Undeserved *see* GIVE
Undisturbed *see* QUIET
Undivided *see* CONSTANT
Undressed *see* BARE
Undying *see* CONSTANT
Unending *see* CONSTANT
Unfailing *see* CONSTANT
Unfair *see* DECEIVE
Unfaithful *see* BETRAY
Ungodly *see* PAGAN
see SIN
Ungrateful *see* THANK
Unhappy *see* LAMENT
Unharmed *see* PROTECT
Unhealthy *see* ILLNESS
Unholy *see* DEFILE
Uniform *see* ARMY
see CLOTHING
Unimportant *see* USELESS
Uninhabited *see* BARREN
Unintentional *see* ACCIDENT
Uninvited *see* ENTERTAIN
Unit *see* ARMY
see SIZE
Unite *see* GROUP

UNIVERSE
comet
constellation
cosmic
Great Bear
horizon
Little Bear
moon
Orion
planet
Pleiades
space
star
sun
zones

Unjust *see* BAD
see CRIMINAL
Unkind *see* CRUEL
Unleavened *see* BREAD
Unlucky *see* LUCK
Unmarried *see* ALONE
see MARRY
Unnatural *see* LUST
see SIN
Unnoticed *see* NEGLECT
Unreasonable
see BAD
Unrighteous *see* BAD
Unripe *see* AGE
see SIZE

UNSEEN
dim
disappear
fade
faint
HIDE
invisible
vanish

Unspiritual *see* EARTHLY
Unstable *see* CHANGE
see MAD

Unthinking *see* IGNORANT
see THINK
Untie *see* FREE
Untrue *see* DECEIVE
Unusual *see* USUAL
Unwilling *see* DENY
Uphold *see* ACKNOWLEDGE
see HELP
Upright *see* HONEST
Uproar *see* NOISE
Upset *see* DISTURB
see WORRY
Upside down *see* DISTURB
Urge *see* ASK
see SUGGEST
Urim *see* PROPHECY
Use *see* ADVANTAGE
see EMPLOY
Useful *see* GOOD

USELESS
chaff
cheap
DISCARD
dross
false
good-for-nothing
idle
insignificant
lazy
least
loafers
meaningless
mere
nobodies
refuse
rubbish
scum
unimportant
vain
waste
worthless

USUAL
abnormal
common
custom
extraordinary
general
habit
normal
ordinary
rare
scarce
special
unusual

UTENSIL
article
CONTAINER
equipment
fork
pole
snuffer
TOOLS

Utter *see* SPEAK

V

Vain *see* USELESS
Valley *see* COUNTRYSIDE
Valuables *see* PRECIOUS
Vanish *see* UNSEEN
Vase *see* CONTAINER
Vast *see* SIZE
Vat *see* CONTAINER
Veal *see* CATTLE
see MEAT

VEGETABLES
bean
cucumber
garlic
leeks
mandrake
onions
peas

Veil *see* CLOTHING
Vengeance *see* REVENGE
Verdict *see* JUDGEMENT
Verses *see* WRITE
Vessel *see* CONTAINER
Veteran *see* SOLDIER
Vicious *see* VIOLENCE
Victory *see* CONQUER
Village *see* PLACE

Vine *see* FRUIT
see PLANT
see TREE
Vinegar *see* FOOD
Vineyard *see* FRUIT
Violate *see* DEFILE
see VIOLENCE

VIOLENCE
aggressive
alarm
ambush
attack
bandit
batter
beat
BETRAY
blood
bloodshed
bloodthirsty
butchered
carnival
cheat
crime
crucify
cruel
crush
death
DESTROY
DIE
fierce
fight
KILL
molest
murder
mutilated
persecute
punish
rape
riot
ruthless
savage
shed
slay
stab
terrorize
vicious
violate
WAR
war-loving

Violet *see* COLOUR
Virginity *see* LUST
Virtue *see* GOOD
Visible *see* SEE
Vision *see* PROPHECY
see SEE
Visit *see* ENTERTAIN
see MEET
Voice *see* SPEAK
Voluntary *see* ACCEPT
Volunteer *see* ACCEPT
Vomit *see* ILLNESS
see SPIT
Vote *see* CHOOSE
Vow *see* PROMISE
Vulture *see* BIRD

W

Wade *see* WATER
Wafer *see* BREAD
Wage *see* EMPLOY
see PAY
Wagon *see* TRAVEL
Wail *see* LAMENT
Waist *see* BODY

WAIT
await
delay
hesitate
impatient
late
patient
remain
stationed
stay

Wait on *see* SERVE
Wake *see* ALERT
Walk *see* MOVE
see TRAVEL
Wall *see* BUILDING
see ENCLOSURE
Wander *see* LOST

WANT
ambition

WANT (cont.)
appetite
ASK
crave
demand
desire
envy
hope
insist
jealous
long
need
order
require
wish

WAR
ambush
ARMY
assault
attack
barricade
battle
battlefield
besiege
blockade
campaign
charge
clash
combat
contest
defeat
earthworks
expedition
fight
fort
fortify
fortress
raid
revolution
siege
siege (-mound)
siege (-tower)
SOLDIER
trench
VIOLENCE
WEAPON

War-loving *see* VIOLENCE
Wares *see* TRADE
Warm *see* HEAT
Warrior *see* SOLDIER

WASH
bath
bathe
clean
PURE
purify
rinse
scrubbed
soap
towel
WATER

Waste *see* BARREN
see USELESS
Watch *see* ALERT
see SEE
Watch-tower *see* BUILDING
Watchdog *see* ANIMAL
Watchman *see* PROTECT

WATER
bank
bay
beach
bed
brook
canal
channel
dam
damp
deep
dew
drench
DRINK
float
flood
FLOW
foam
fountain
gulf
inlet
irrigate
lake
liquid
moisture
oasis
ocean
overflow

WATER (cont.)
pond
pool
reservoir
river
sea
SHIP
soak
splash
stream
spring
sprinkle
swim
tide
torrent
wade
WASH
waterfall
watertight
wave
well
wet

Water-melon *see* FRUIT
Waterfall *see* WATER
Waterless *see* BARREN
Watertight *see* WATER
Wave *see* WATER
Way *see* ROAD
Weakness *see* SIN

WEALTH
expensive
luxury
MONEY
PRECIOUS
prosperity
rich
riches
treasure
well-off

Weaned *see* BIRTH

WEAPON
arm
ARMOUR
ARMY
arrow
arsenal
battering-ram
bow
catapult
club
dagger
harpoon
javelin
knife
lance
scabbard
sheath
shoot
SOLDIER
spear
sword
WAR

Wear *see* CLOTHING
Wear out *see* DECAY
see WEARY

WEARY
exhausted
gasp
hardship
HOPELESS
sweat
tired
wear out

WEATHER
blast
breeze
cloud
cold
drought
dry
frost
hail
hot
ice
lightning
mist
north-easter
rain
rainbow
shower
snow
storm
tempests
thunder

WEATHER (cont.)
wet
whirlwind
wind

Weave see CLOTH
Wedding see MARRY
Wedlock see MARRY
Weed see PLANT
Week see TIME
Weep see LAMENT
Weigh see MEASURE
see SIZE
Welcome see ACCEPT
see MEET
Well see HEALTHY
see MEDICINE
see WATER
Well-liked see LOVE
Well-off see WEALTH
West see DIRECTION
Wet see WATER
see WEATHER
Wet-nurse see BIRTH
Wheat see CROP

WHEEL
axle
hub
rim
spokes
TRAVEL

Whining see LAMENT
Whip see PUNISH
Whirlwind see WEATHER
Whisper see QUIET
see RUMOUR
Whistle see NOISE
White see COLOUR
Whitewash see COLOUR
Whole see HEALTHY
see THOROUGH
Whore see LUST
Wick see LIGHT
Wicked see BAD
see SIN
Wicked One see DEVIL
Wide see SHAPE
see SIZE
Widow see ALONE
see MARRY
see POOR
Wife see MARRY
see RELATIVE
Wild see ANIMAL
Wilderness see BARREN
see COUNTRYSIDE
Wilful see INTEND
Will see GIVE
see INTEND
Willing see ACCEPT
Willow see TREE
Wilt see BARREN
Win see CONQUER
Wind see WEATHER
Windbags see SPEAK
Window see BUILDING
Wine see DRINK
Wine-drinkers
see DRINK
Wineskin see CONTAINER
Wing see BIRD
see FLY
Winnowing shovel
see CULTIVATE
Wisdom see LEARNING
Wise see CLEVER
see LEARNING
Wish see WANT
Wit see CLEVER
Witchcraft see MAGIC
Withdraw see ABANDON

Wither see BARREN
see DECAY
Withhold see PREVENT
Within see INSIDE
Wizard see MAGIC
Wolf see ANIMAL
Woman see PERSON
Womb see BIRTH
Wonder see AMAZE
see DOUBT

WOOD
acacia-wood
block
board
branch
BUILDING
carpenter
cedar
ebony
fire-wood
log
OVERGROWN
pine
splinters
staff
stick
timber
TREE

Woodcarver see WORKMAN
Woodmen see WORKMAN
Wool see CLOTH
Word see COMMUNICATE
see GRAMMAR
see JESUS

WORK
career
dig
EFFORT
EMPLOY
function
handiwork
industrious
job
labour
manual
overworked
task
toil
TRADE
WORKMAN

Worker see WORKMAN

WORKMAN
blacksmith
builder
businessmen
carpenter
clothmakers
craftsman
fishermen
foremen
gate-keeper
goldsmith
grave-digger
labourer
linen-weavers
metal-worker
ploughmen
silversmith
tanner
traders
woodcarver
woodmen
WORK
worker

World see EARTHLY
World above see HEAVEN

World below see DIE
see HELL
Worldly see EARTHLY
see SIN
Worm see ANIMAL
see DECAY

WORRY
anguish
anxious
bother
BURDEN
care
concern
confuse
DANGER
depressed
despair
dismay
distress
DISTURB
FEAR
interfere
LAMENT
meddle
nuisance
PAIN
pressure
struggle
suspense
trial
trouble
turmoil
upset

Worse see BAD

WORSHIP
altar
Amen
bow (down)
break (bread)
celebrate
ceremony
consecrate
Covenant Box
dedicate
devout
exalted
festival
glorify
High Priest
holy
Holy Place
hymn
IDOL
incense
kneel
officiate
ordain
pilgrimage
Place of Worship
PRAISE
pray
prayer
priest
procession
psalm
religion
reverence
ritual
sacred
sacrifice
sanctuary
service
shrine
supper
synagogue
temple
tent

Worst see BAD
Worth see DESERVE

Worthless see USELESS
Worthy see ABLE
see PRAISE
Wound see INJURE
see PAIN
Wrath see ANGER
Wriggle see MOVE
Wrinkle see BLEMISH
Wrist see BODY
Wristbands see CLOTHING

WRITE
ARTS
book
COMMUNICATE
copy
correspondence
document
gospel
GRAMMAR
history
ink
inscribe
LEARNING
letter
literature
paper
parchment
passage
pen
poets
read
record
scribble
scribe
scripture
scroll
seal
sign
tablet
text
verses

Writhe see PAIN
Wrong see BAD
see ERROR
see SIN

Y

Yard see BUILDING
Year see TIME
Yeast see BREAD
see FOOD
Yell see SPEAK
Yellow see COLOUR
Yesterday see TIME
Yield see CROP
Yoke see BURDEN
Young see AGE
see SIZE
Youth see AGE

Z

ZEAL
devotion
eager
EFFORT
enthusiasm
fervent

Zebulun see TRIBE
Zither see INSTRUMENT
Ziv see MONTH
Zones see UNIVERSE